CIVIL PROCEDURE

2009

Additional Content Online or on CD

Paragraph numbers in the main text marked with a "+", together with a symbol in the margin, denote content available only on *White Book on Westlaw UK* and the *Civil Procedure CD*.

See page v and the list of content available online and on CD on page xiii for further details.

Published in 2009 by Thomson Reuters (Legal) Limited
(Registered in England & Wales, Company No 1679046.
Registered Office and address for service:
100 Avenue Road, London, NW3 3PF) trading as Sweet & Maxwell.
Table of International and European Legislation and Additional Content Online and On CD Contents typeset by Hobbs the Printers Ltd, Totton, Hampshire. All other typesetting by Sweet & Maxwell electronic publishing system.
Printed by L.E.G.O. S.p.A., Lavis (TN), Italy.
For further information on our products and services, visit
www.sweetandmaxwell.co.uk.

No natural forests were destroyed to make this product; only farmed timber was used and replanted.

British Library Cataloguing in Publication Data
A catalogue record for this book is available from the British Library

ISBN 978-1-84703-823-4

CIVIL PROCEDURE

Volume 1

The Civil Procedure Rules and Practice Directions contained in this volume are up-to-date to April 6, 2009. For further updates, see http://www.sweetandmaxwell.co.uk/whitebook.

Civil Procedure Rules Online and Forms Alerter—Password

To access the White Book Civil Procedure Rules website and to register for the Forms Alerter service you will need to enter the following password:

WB2009

LONDON
SWEET & MAXWELL
2009

ADDITIONAL CONTENT ONLINE AND ON CD

A selection of existing content, together with brand new content, is available only on *White Book on Westlaw UK* and the *Civil Procedure CD*. This process has been started principally with Vol.2. We welcome any feedback—please email *whitebook@sweetandmaxwell.co.uk*

Please refer to the separate Additional Content Online and on CD list on page xiii for a detailed list of this material.

In order to assist navigation and to draw your attention to the relocated material, a symbol is placed in the margin of the main text.

In tandem with the symbol a system of cross-references is used. References to the relocated material are placed at the beginning of statutes or sections to flag that some or all of the content is online or and on CD only. References also appear within statutes or sections where a selection of material has been relocated. The latter alerts readers to relocated paragraph numbers and statutory sections (and relevant commentary).

Paragraph numbers marked with a "+" appear in the tables and index. The "+" denotes electronic content. Similar paragraph numbers appear in the cross-references mentioned above and within the statutory arrangement of sections.

On *White Book on Westlaw UK* and the *Civil Procedure CD*, the "+" paragraph numbers appear in their correct places, with the additional content remaining inline.

CONTENTS

See page xiii for a list of additional content online and on CD.

See page xiii for a list of additional content online and on CD.

See page xiii for a list of additional content online and on CD.

See page xiii for a list of additional content online and on CD.

See page xiii for a list of additional content online and on CD.

ADDITIONAL CONTENT ONLINE AND ON CD

This is a list of content and associated commentary available **only** on **White Book on Westlaw UK** or the **Civil Procedure CD**. This list does not refer to print content (please see the previous print contents on page vii).

We welcome any feedback—please email whitebook@sweetandmaxwell.co.uk.

VOLUME ONE

VOLUME TWO

Section 10—Court Fees

Appendix 1—Courts Directory

PREFACE

The annual demands placed on those who serve as editors for the *White Book* do not abate. In my capacity as Editor-in-Chief, I express my great thanks to the General Editor, to the members of the Senior Editorial Board, and to the many expert editors for all of the work they have done in various ways and, in particular, in preparing and organising material for this 2009 edition.

The principal primary sources published in the *White Book* are the Civil Procedure Rules 1998 and the practice directions supplementing those rules. The publication of the 2009 edition coincides almost exactly with the 10th anniversary of the coming into force of the CPR ("Woolf day" was April 26, 1999). A single volume edition of the *White Book*, containing the CPR and basic commentary thereon, was published in January 1999, and this was followed by a comprehensive two volume edition (containing not only rules of court, but also other material required by judges and practitioners) published in the Spring of 1999. It is interesting to note that seven of the editors involved during late 1998 and early 1999 in the very complicated task of adjusting *White Book* content in the light of the CPR still serve as expert editors for this publication. In this 10th anniversary year, and in the absence of a long-service medal suitable to be pinned upon them, it is appropriate that I should express very great thanks to them.

The work of the editors would come to nought if it were not for the efforts of the members of the publisher's staff charged with the responsibility of editing copy and seeing each edition through to publication. The staff members with whom the General Editor and the expert editors had routine contact during the production of the 2009 edition were David Cobb (Senior Publishing Editor), Emma Wilkin (Senior House Editor), Rebecca Morris (House Editor) and Serahna Cross (Editorial Manager). Special thanks are due to them for the skill and cheerfulness with which they coped with the very great demands made on them.

In the year since the 2008 edition went to press there have been some retirements from the ranks of the expert editors. Master Miller leaves us, having retired from the Masters' bench in September 2008. He was a Master of the Supreme Court (Queen's Bench Division) and Admiralty Registrar. He served as a *White Book* Editor for 16 years. Other departures include Judge David Wilcox, Bryony Young and A.R. Donnelly. We are greatly indebted to them for the service they rendered.

There have been some recruits to the ranks of expert editors. It is my pleasure to welcome Mr Justice Coulson, Deputy Master Roger Eastman, A.D.R. Brown (of the Interim Applications Court), Joan Goulbourn (of the Public Guardianship Office) and Tim Wallis (Solicitor and Mediator).

In the Preface to the 2008 edition of the *White Book* I explained that the publishers had embarked upon a programme for developing the work which affects its structure, its content and style of presentation. In that edition, substantial structural changes were made implementing that programme. In particular, extended commentary sections were added at the end of Vol.2, and access to a greater range of, and more detailed, primary sources were provided by the *White Book* online and CD services. It is encouraging to know that subscribers readily understand the problems posed for the publishers by the inexorable growth in the primary material that has to be included and in the demand for expert commentary. The structural changes are designed to provide a sustainable and flexible means for dealing with these problems. The publishers and editors keep the whole content of the *White Book* Service under continuous review and, for each new edition and for each supplement, consider whether adjustments should be made to the manner in which existing and new material is presented within the Service. In this respect they are very much assisted by comments received from subscribers.

In a number of respects, the 2009 edition builds on the foundations laid in the previous edition. Significant additions, both in the form of substantial new commentary and in the form of primary text have been made. For example, Section 14 in Vol.2 (which deals with ADR) has been further developed by an expert editor recruited to the *White Book* team, in Section 15 (Interim Remedies) an improved sub-section on interim injunctions in patent and other intellectual property claims has been added, and in Section 3F (Personal Injury) the MIB Supplementary Uninsured Drivers Agreement 2008 and the model schedule for periodical payment orders have been included.

During 2008, significant changes to the CPR were made by three statutory instruments; they were the Civil Procedure (Amendment) Rules 2008 (SI 2008/2178), the Civil Procedure (Amendment No.2) Rules 2008 (SI 2008/3085), and the Civil Procedure (Amendment No.3) Rules 2008 (SI 2008/3327). This has required considerable editing of the CPR and supplementing practice directions and the amendment and (where necessary) the addition of commentary text. The impacts of these statutory instruments are outlined below.

The Civil Procedure (Amendment) Rules 2008 were laid before Parliament on August 15 and came into effect on October 1. Their chief effect was the replacement of the whole of CPR Pt 6 (Service of Documents), including the practice directions supplementing that Part. The background to this very important development may be briefly explained. In July 2007, the Ministry of Justice published Consultation Paper 14/07, entitled *Review of Part 6 of the Civil Procedure Rules: Service of Documents*. The consultation was conducted on behalf of the Civil Procedure Rule Committee with the purpose of seeking views on proposals to clarify and improve the rules relating to service of documents within England and Wales, that is to say, the rules within Section I (General Rules about Service) and Section II (Special Provisions about Service of the Claim Form) of Pt 6. The proposals took account of a number of Court of Appeal decisions about the construction of these provisions. In February 2008, a post-consultation paper summarising the responses was published, and in the months following the Rule Committee considered the proposals and the responses thereto.

Since the CPR came into effect, problems relating to the service of claim forms have arisen regularly. Not surprisingly, the bulk of the issues that were raised in the Consultation Paper, though related to service of documents generally, were, as a practical matter, particularly relevant to the service of claim forms. Thus, for example, the Paper sought views on (1) whether, where a claimant knows that the defendant no longer resides at the last known address, he should be required to make reasonable enquiries as to the current address and consider alternative methods of service; (2) whether the time limit for serving the claim form should relate to the period within which the claimant must dispatch the claim form (rather than from when service is effected); and (3) whether there should be a consistent approach to determining the deemed date of service applicable to all methods of service.

A striking feature of the "new" Pt 6 is that provisions as to the service of claim forms within the jurisdiction are clearly separated from those dealing with the service of other documents, with the former being dealt with in Section II and the latter in Section III of the Part. Of the various significant changes in the effects of the claim form service rules that have been made, one that particularly stands out is the change in the manner in which the period of validity of a claim form for service within the jurisdiction is calculated. As it happens, the key provision here is not in Pt 6 but in Pt 7 (How to Start Proceedings—The Claim Form). Formerly, r.7.5 (Service of a claim form) stated the general rule that a claim form "must be served" within four months after the date of issue. As amended, that rule states that it must be dispatched for service within that period.

Up until shortly before its enactment in August 2008, the provisions of the Civil Procedure (Amendment) Rules 2008, insofar as they related to Pt 6, were subject to significant amendments. *White Book* subscribers were kept informed of these developments, and CPR amendments consequential upon them, in the July and September issues of *Civil Procedure News*. A Special Supplement to the 2008 edition of the *White Book*, containing the texts of the "new" Pt 6 and the two practice directions, and commentary thereon, was published in September. In this edition of the *White Book* the Pt 6 commentary has been completely rewritten in the light of the new rules and the Special Supplement commentary has been incorporated.

Amendments and additions to CPR practice directions made necessary by the enactment of the new Pt 6 were made by TSO CPR Update 47. That Update also included some changes to practice directions with a different provenance. The addition of Practice Direction—Automatic Orders Pilot Scheme should be particularly noted. The scheme is restricted to a small number of county courts. It modifies certain CPR provisions in proceedings to which it applies for the purpose of testing new ways for dealing with the automatic striking out of proceedings on the ground of procedural default. The pre-CPR excursion into this territory during the 1990s (through the notorious CCR O.9, r.11) was not a happy one. The goals of the pilot scheme are more modest.

The second of the 2008 statutory instruments amending the CPR, the Civil Procedure (Amendment No.2) Rules 2008 (SI 2008/3085), was rather unusual in that it was made, not by the Civil Procedure Rule Committee, exercising power conferred by the Civil Procedure Act 1997 s.1, but by the Lord Chancellor, exercising powers conferred by the Counter-Terrorism Act 2008 s.72 to make rules of court under s.1 of the 1997 Act (subject to positive resolution of each House of Parliament). This statutory instrument was made on December 2 and inserted Pt 79 in the CPR, with effect from December 4, a wholly new Part containing rules of court regulating "financial restrictions proceedings" under the 2008 Act. These proceedings consist of applications to the High Court by persons affected by "financial restriction decisions" made, not by a lower court or by a tribunal, but by HM Treasury under exceptional powers derived from the 2008 Act and elsewhere, and of any appeal to the Court of Appeal.

One of the striking features of the CPR, as a body of rules of court, is that they deal with the enormously wide range of civil proceedings over which the High Court and the county courts (which have remained as courts of general jurisdiction) have jurisdiction. It is a grave distortion to say that the CPR are concerned simply with "litigation", as "litigation" (which is a term of art) is but one variety of civil proceedings. Many of the varieties of civil proceedings require special rules supplementing, amending or even misapplying the normal rules; the new "financial restrictions proceedings" provide a good example. Section 1(3)(b) of the 1997 Act states that the power to make Civil Procedure Rules should be exercised with a view to securing that "the rules are both simple and simply expressed". The history of English procedure (civil, family and criminal) reveals that in circumstances where, because of an expansion in jurisdiction, modifications have had to be made to the relevant procedural code, frequently the drafting solution adopted has been the easy but crude one of tacking new rules on at the end. Generally, that solution does not result in the conjunction of the new rules with those existing rules that are, as a consequence, supplemented, amended or misapplied, being notable examples of rules that are "both simple and simply expressed".

The third of the 2008 statutory instruments amending the CPR, the Civil Procedure (Amendment No.3) Rules 2008 (SI 2008/3327) was laid before Parliament on January 7, 2009. Among the significant changes made to the CPR by this statutory instrument are amendments to existing provisions having the effect of increasing the financial limit of the fast track procedure from £15,000 to £25,000 for claims issued on or after April 6, 2009 (see rr.16.3, 26.6 and 46.2) and the insertion of new rules making express provision for costs capping orders (rr.44.18 to 44.20). Changes to CPR practice directions reflecting these and the other amendments made by SI 2008/3327, and some other substantial changes to practice directions not triggered by that statutory instrument (e.g. amendments to Practice Direction (Appeals)), were published in TSO CPR Update 49. As these changes to rules and practice directions emerged at a very late stage in the *White Book* production cycle and, indeed, in some respects had not been settled at the time of going to press, the expert commentary accompanying them had to be restricted to the essentials. Where necessary, fuller explanations will be included in Supplement 1.

Significant case law developments coming about after the publication of the 2008 edition and before the Autumn of that year were noted in the commentaries in Supplements 1 and 2 to that edition. The great proportion of cases decided by the Court of Appeal in the second half of 2008, and raising issues related to topics covered in *White Book* commentary, consisted of cases on costs and conditional fee agreements. For example, *Oriakhel v Vickers* [2008] EWCA Civ 748, July 4, 2008, CA, unrep. (non-party costs orders); *Hedrich v Standard Bank Ltd* [2008] EWCA Civ 905, July 30, 2008, CA, unrep. (wasted costs order procedure); *R. (Buglife-The Invertebrate Conservation Trust) v Thurrock Thames Gateway Development Corp* [2008] EWCA Civ 1209, November 4, 2008, CA, unrep. (protective costs orders); *Tankard v John Fredericks Plastics Ltd* [2008] EWCA Civ 1375, December 11, 2008, CA, unrep. (solicitors' interest in CFA); and *C. v W.* [2008] EWCA Civ 1459, December 19, 2008, CA, unrep. (reasonable CFA success fee). A number of other decisions of the court dealt with questions relating to the application of limitation provisions, for example, *Pierce v Doncaster MBC* [2008] EWCA Civ 1416, December 12, 2008, CA, unrep. (constructive knowledge); *Cain v Francis* [2008] EWCA Civ 1451, December 18, 2008, CA, unrep. (prejudice of disapplication to defendant). In *Tombstone Ltd v Raja* [2008] EWCA Civ 1444, December 17, 2008, CA, unrep., the court dealt with the important matter of the relationship between the High Court's inherent jurisdiction and certain powers expressly referred to and provided for in the CPR.

Lord Justice Waller
Vice-President of the Court of Appeal (Civil Division)
Royal Courts of Justice
London
February 2009

SERVICE INFORMATION

The White Book Service 2009

During 2008 we undertook a range of research with subscribers in order to help steer the continuing development of the White Book Service. As in previous years, we received a good response to our annual subscriber survey, which was followed up by a number of face-to-face interviews. Thank you to all who participated. A reminder that we welcome feedback from subscribers throughout the year—please email *whitebook@sweetandmaxwell.co.uk*.

Additional Content Online and on CD

A selection of existing content, together with brand new content, is available only on *White Book on Westlaw UK* and the *Civil Procedure CD*. We have started this process principally with Vol.2. Please refer to the Additional Content Online and on CD on page xiii for a detailed list.

In order to assist navigation and to draw your attention to the relocated material, a symbol is placed in the margin of the text.

In tandem with the symbol, a system of cross-references is used. References to relocated material are placed at the beginning of statutes or sections to flag that some or all of the content is online and on CD only. References also appear within statutes or sections where a selection of material has been relocated. The latter alerts readers to relocated paragraph numbers and statutory sections (and relevant commentary).

Paragraph numbers marked with a "+" symbol appear in the tables and index. The "+" symbol denotes electronic content. Similar paragraph numbers appear in the cross-references mentioned above and within the statutory arrangement of sections.

On *White Book on Westlaw UK* and the *Civil Procedure CD*, the "+" paragraph numbers appear in their correct places, with the additional content online and on CD remaining inline.

Up-to-date to April 6, 2009

Civil Procedure published on April 9, 2009. The Rules and Practice Directions have been updated to include changes introduced by the Civil Procedure (Amendment No.2) Rules 2008 (SI 2008/3085), in force on December 4, 2008 and TSO Update 48, and Civil Procedure (Amendment No.3) Rules 2008 (SI 2008/3327), in force April 6, 2009 and TSO Update 49. Amendments announced after April 6 will be published in the updating supplements in July and December. Notes have been included to indicate the in-force date of changes where necessary.

For further updates see **http://www.sweetandmaxwell.co.uk/whitebook**. You will need to enter your subscriber password: **WB2009**. This site contains the latest Civil Procedure Rules and Practice Directions. Changes which have been introduced since *The White Book* published in April are highlighted in red.

Every effort has been made to ensure that the commentary and case law is as stated at April 6, 2009. *Civil Procedure News* and the two updating supplements will keep you abreast of developments through the subscription year.

Forms

The Forms Volume is no longer automatically included in the White Book Service (for new subscribers). New subscribers may order the Forms Volume separately. However, all subscribers will continue to be updated with the latest forms by way of receiving the Forms Release. We do ask that you keep your Forms Volume from one year to the next and update by way of filing the releases supplied, particularly as we cross-refer from the text of the CPR to forms in the Forms Volume and Forms CD in greater numbers this year. We avoid the duplication of forms in both the main volumes and the Forms Volume. This now includes Practice Direction forms, for which there is a new section in the Forms Volume and Forms CD.

The forms release is nominally published three times a year. In 2009, again in response to customer requests, we will not publish a paper forms release with the two supplements unless the number of new or amended forms released by the MOJ demands it (we will continue to release the Forms CD as normal). You will find a paper forms release released with the main volumes, which is the twenty-second release.

Electronic forms on the Forms and the White Book CDs are available in two formats—RTF/Word and PDF.

As a basic requirement, all 600-odd court forms and notes are available in RTF/Word format, just under 500 are also available as interactive PDFs, while 80 PDFs are able to be edited and saved using Adobe functionality.

Of course, you may wish to sign up to receive our Forms email alerter service. An email notice is sent to you when new court forms are published by the Court Service. You can also download forms from our website: **http://www.sweetandmaxwell.co.uk/whitebook**. You will need to enter the password: **WB2009**.

You may also wish to sign up to receive our email alerter service to notify you of changes to the Civil Procedure Rules as they are introduced by Statutory Instrument and as the changes come into force. This service is also available on ***http://www.sweetandmaxwell.co.uk/whitebook***.

Civil Procedure Forms CD and Adobe forms

Your 2009 subscription includes a CD-ROM containing all the forms provided in the Civil Procedure Forms Volume. We publish these forms as RTF/Word documents and PDFs. In addition, we have converted 80 PDFs of the most commonly used forms to allow edit and save functionality. See the accompanying Quick Reference Card for full details of this new service.

A reminder to register for the Forms Email Alerter Service—go to **http://www.sweetandmaxwell.co.uk/whitebook** to register to receive an email notice when new court forms are published by the Court Service. You can also download the forms from our website. You will need to enter the password: **WB2009**.

If you were a subscriber to the White Book Service in 2008, please remember to retain your *White Book Forms Volume*. This will continue to be updated during the 2009 subscription year. The twenty-second forms release is included with this new edition.

How to use Civil Procedure 2009

As ever, we have endeavoured to ensure that the content of *The White Book* is presented logically. The Civil Procedure Rules are reproduced in bold type to ensure they are easily distinguished from editorial comment and Practice Directions. Notes have been added to provide a full record of the changes to the Civil Procedure Rules. CPR Part numbers have been added to the thumb tabs at the side of each page.

Please refer to your User Guide which walks you through the navigational features and various components of *The White Book Service*, including the new cross-references to the additional content online and on CD.

Volume 1

The Civil Procedure Rules and Practice Directions (including Schs 1 and 2 containing those RSC and CCR still in force) are contained in Vol.1 with the following exceptions:

- *CPR on Specialist lists*—CPR Pts 58–63 (dealing with the Commercial Court, the Mercantile Courts, the Technology and Construction Court, Admiralty Claims and Arbitrations, and Patents and Other Intellectual Property Claims) are set out in Vol.2, Section 2.

- *CPR Pt 49—Specialist proceedings* —the proceedings dealt with under the Practice Direction to Pt 49 (Proceedings under the Companies Acts) are set out in Vol.2, Section 2.

Miscellaneous Practice Directions, Pre-Action Protocols, procedural guides and a guide to time limits are also reproduced in Vol One.

Volume 2

The main elements of Vol.2 are the specialist areas of practice and procedure: the specialist lists dealt with by CPR Pts 58–63 and the specialist proceedings under CPR Pt 49, other specialist proceedings (e.g. Housing and Consumer) and procedural legislation. Volume 2 also includes Litigation and Procedural Topics such as Interim Remedies and Alternative Dispute Resolution.

A quick guide to finding key materials is set out below. See the separate User Guide for further information.

How to find ...

... CPR Rules and Supplementary Practice Directions (Vol.1, Section A)

The Civil Procedure Rules and Practice Directions are contained in Section A, which adopts the following paragraph system.

Part 3, r.1	para. **3.1**
Commentary to Part 3, r.1	para.3.1.**1**, (3.1.**2** etc.)
Practice Direction supplementing Part 3	para. 3**PD**.1
Second Practice Direction supplementing Part 3	para.3**B**PD.1

The paragraph numbers appear at the top outside corner of each page.

... Rules of the Supreme Court, County Court Rules and Supplementary Practice Directions

Section A also contains the re-enacted Rules of the Supreme Court and County Court Rules, with all supplementary Practice Directions. The following paragraph system is used:

RSC Order 52, r.1	para.**sc**52.1
Commentary to RSC Order 52.1	para.sc52.1.**1**, (sc52.1.**2** etc.)
Practice Direction supplementing Order 52	para.sc**pd**52.1
CCR Order 1, r.6	para.**cc**1.6
Commentary to CCR Order 1, r.6	para.cc1.6.**1**

... Miscellaneous Practice Direction (Vol.1, Section B)

Practice Directions which are not supplementary to a rule (e.g. the Practice Direction on Insolvency Proceedings) are contained in Section B, which adopts the following paragraph system.

Practice Direction Insolvency Proceedings, etc.	para.B1-001

... Pre-Action Protocols (Vol.1, Section C)

The Pre-Action Protocols are contained in Section C, which adopts the following paragraph system:

Practice Direction—Protocols	para.C**0**–001
Pre-Action Protocol for Personal Injury Claims	para.C**1**-001

... Chancery Guide

The Chancery Guide Appears in Section 1 of Vol.2 and is numbered para.1-1 onwards.

... Specialist Practice Directions under CPR Parts 58-63 and Specialist Court Guides, Applications under the Companies Act

Specialist Proceedings under CPR Parts 58-63 and Specialist Court Guides Applications under the Companies Act appear in Section 2 of Vol.2 as follows:

CPR 58	Commercial Court
CPR 59	Mercantile Courts
CPR 60	Technology and Construction Courts

CPR 61	Admiralty Claims
CPR 62	Arbitration Claims
CPR 63	Patents and other Intellectual Property Claims
Practice Direction to CPR 49	Applications Under the Companies Act

... Forms
The forms are located in the Civil Procedure Forms Volume and on the Forms CD.

... Litigation and Procedural Topics...
These are located at the end of Vol.2 in Sections 11 to 15.

Service Elements

The White Book Service allows you to choose a customised product to suit your requirements.

Civil Procedure CD and Print Service
Annual subscription includes:
CD (includes all content in Vols 1 and 2 and the Forms Volume and additional research materials)
Civil Procedure 2009 Vol.1
Civil Procedure 2009 Vol.2
Civil Procedure Forms Updates
Civil Procedure Forms Volume (on request to new subscribers)
Two paper supplements
Civil Procedure News (10 issues a year)
Internet-based primary law updating
Forms email Alerter Service
Rules email Alerter Service
Subscription price: £499 plus VAT

Civil Procedure Volumes 1 and 2
Annual subscription includes:
Civil Procedure 2009 Vol.1
Civil Procedure 2009 Vol.2
Civil Procedure Forms CD
Civil Procedure Forms Updates
Civil Procedure Forms Volume (on request to new subscribers)
Two paper supplements
Civil Procedure News (10 issues a year)
Internet-based primary law updating
Forms email Alerter Service
Rules email Alerter Service
Subscription price: £429 plus VAT

Civil Procedure Volume 1
Annual subscription includes:
Civil Procedure 2009 Vol.1
Civil Procedure Forms CD
Civil Procedure Forms Updates
Civil Procedure Forms Volume (on request to new subscribers)

Two paper supplements
Civil Procedure News (10 issues a year)
Internet-based primary law updating
Forms email Alerter Service
Rules email Alerter Service
Subscription price: £329 plus VAT

Premium Online Service

Please contact our Westlaw UK helpdesk for further information on 0800 028 2200.

Customer Services

If you have a query relating to your subscription or you wish to purchase extra copies of Civil Procedure 2009, please call our Customer Services team on:

UK direct customers: 0845 600 9355

UK trade customers: 0845 082 1032

International customers: +44 (0) 1264 388560

Or you can write to:

Customer Services
Sweet & Maxwell
Freepost
PO Box 2000
Andover
SP10 9AH
United Kingdom
Website: *http://www.sweetandmaxwell.co.uk*
Email: *sweetandmaxwell.customer.services@thomson.com*

Comments and feedback

We are always pleased to receive comments and suggestions from customers. Address correspondence to: Publishing Editor, The White Book Service, Sweet & Maxwell, 100 Avenue Road, London, NW3 3PF or email *whitebook@sweetandmaxwell.co.uk*

The White Book Team
April 2009

TABLE OF CASES

Paragraph numbers marked with a "+" can be found online and on CD.

Paragraph numbers marked with a "+" can be found online and on CD.

Paragraph numbers marked with a "+" can be found online and on CD.

Paragraph numbers marked with a "+" can be found online and on CD.

Paragraph numbers marked with a "+" can be found online and on CD.

Paragraph numbers marked with a "+" can be found online and on CD.

Paragraph numbers marked with a "+" can be found online and on CD.

Paragraph numbers marked with a "+" can be found online and on CD.

Paragraph numbers marked with a "+" can be found online and on CD.

Paragraph numbers marked with a "+" can be found online and on CD.

Paragraph numbers marked with a "+" can be found online and on CD.

Paragraph numbers marked with a "+" can be found online and on CD.

Paragraph numbers marked with a "+" can be found online and on CD.

Paragraph numbers marked with a "+" can be found online and on CD.

Paragraph numbers marked with a "+" can be found online and on CD.

Paragraph numbers marked with a "+" can be found online and on CD.

Paragraph numbers marked with a "+" can be found online and on CD.

Paragraph numbers marked with a "+" can be found online and on CD.

Paragraph numbers marked with a "+" can be found online and on CD.

Paragraph numbers marked with a "+" can be found online and on CD.

Paragraph numbers marked with a "+" can be found online and on CD.

Paragraph numbers marked with a "+" can be found online and on CD.

Paragraph numbers marked with a "+" can be found online and on CD.

Paragraph numbers marked with a "+" can be found online and on CD.

Paragraph numbers marked with a "+" can be found online and on CD.

Paragraph numbers marked with a "+" can be found online and on CD.

Paragraph numbers marked with a "+" can be found online and on CD.

Paragraph numbers marked with a "+" can be found online and on CD.

Paragraph numbers marked with a "+" can be found online and on CD.

Paragraph numbers marked with a "+" can be found online and on CD.

Paragraph numbers marked with a "+" can be found online and on CD.

Paragraph numbers marked with a "+" can be found online and on CD.

Paragraph numbers marked with a "+" can be found online and on CD.

Paragraph numbers marked with a "+" can be found online and on CD.

Paragraph numbers marked with a "+" can be found online and on CD.

Berezovsky *v* Forbes Inc (No.1), *sub nom.* Glouchkov v Forbes Inc; Berezovsky v Michaels; Glouchkov v Michaels [2000] 1 W.L.R. 1004; [2000] 2 All E.R. 986; [2001] I.L.Pr. 21; [2000] E.M.L.R. 643; (2000) 97(22) L.S.G. 44; (2000) 150 N.L.J. 741; *The Times*, May 16, 2000; *Independent*, May 18, 2000, HL; affirming [1999] I.L.Pr. 358; [1999] E.M.L.R. 278; *The Times*, November 27, 1998, CA (Civ Div); reversing *Times*, January 19, 1998 . . . . 6.33.14

—— *v* Forbes Inc (No.2) [2001] EWCA Civ 1251; [2001] E.M.L.R. 45 . . . . 53PD.35

Berg *v* IML London Ltd [2002] 1 W.L.R. 3271; [2002] 4 All E.R. 87 . . . . 31.3.40, 9A–48

Berge Sisar, The. *See* Borealis AB (formerly Borealis Petrokemi AB and Statoil Petrokemi AB) v Stargas Ltd (The Berge Sisar)

Bergen, The (No.2), *sub nom.* Bergen, The (No.2) [1997] 2 Lloyd's Rep. 710 . . . . 6.37.20

Berkeley & Young Ltd *v* Stillwell (1940) 57 R.P.C. 291 . . . . 2F–23

Berkeley *v* Secretary of State for the Environment, Transport and the Regions (No.1) [2001] 2 A.C. 603; [2000] 3 W.L.R. 420; [2000] 3 All E.R. 897; [2001] 2 C.M.L.R. 38; [2001] Env. L.R. 16; (2001) 81 P. & C.R. 35; [2000] 3 P.L.R. 111; [2001] J.P.L. 58; [2000] E.G. 86 (C.S.); [2000] N.P.C. 77; *The Times*, July 7, 2000, HL; reversing [1999] 1 C.M.L.R. 945; [1998] Env. L.R. 741; [1998] 3 P.L.R. 39; [1998] P.L.C.R. 97; [1998] N.P.C. 18; *The Times*, March 2, 1998 . . . . 54.1.10

Berkeley Administration Inc *v* McClelland (Estoppel) [1996] I.L.Pr. 772; *The Times*, August 13, 1996 15–29

—— *v* McClelland (Inquiry as to Damages: Striking Out) [1995] I.L.Pr. 201 . . . . 74.10.2, 74.10.17, 5–93+

—— *v* McClelland (Security for Costs) [1990] 2 Q.B. 407; [1990] 2 W.L.R. 1021; [1990] 1 All E.R. 958; [1990] B.C.C. 272; [1990] 2 C.M.L.R. 116; [1991] I.L.Pr. 45; (1990) 87(36) L.S.G. 45; (1990) 140 N.L.J. 289; *The Times*, February 20, 1990; *Independent*, March 16, 1990; *Financial Times*, February 28, 1990, CA (Civ Div); reversing [1990] 1 C.M.L.R. 193; *The Times*, December 12, 1989; *Financial Times*, January 23, 1990 . . . . 7C–247+

—— *v* McClelland (Specific Discovery) [1990] F.S.R. 381 . . . . 31.12.1

Berkeley Hotel Co Ltd *v* Berkeley International (Mayfair) Ltd [1971] F.S.R. 300; [1972] R.P.C. 237 . . . . 15–47.10

Berkoff *v* Burchill [1996] 4 All E.R. 1008; [1997] E.M.L.R. 139; *Times*, August 9, 1996; *Independent*, October 4, 1996 . . . . 53PD.32

Berkshire CC *v* Greenfield, *sub nom.* Greenfield v Berkshire CC (1996) 28 H.L.R. 691; (1997) 73 P. & C.R. 280; [1996] E.G.C.S. 38 . . . . 3A–500

Berliner Bank *v* Karageorgis [1996] 1 Lloyd's Rep. 426; *Times*, November 27, 1995 . . . . 74.10.7

Berliner Bank AG *v* C Czarnikow Sugar Ltd (The Rama), *sub nom.* Rama, The [1996] 2 Lloyd's Rep. 281 . . . . 2D–159

Berliner Industriebank Aktiengesellschaft *v* Jost [1971] 2 Q.B. 463; [1971] 3 W.L.R. 61; [1971] 2 All E.R. 1513; 115 S.J. 505; affirming [1971] 1 Q.B. 278; [1970] 3 W.L.R. 743; [1971] 2 All E.R. 117; 114 S.J. 492 . . . . sc46.2.12

Bermuda International Securities Ltd *v* KPMG [2001] EWCA Civ 269; [2001] C.P. Rep. 73; [2001] C.P.L.R. 252; [2001] Lloyd's Rep. P.N. 392; (2001) 98(15) L.S.G. 33; (2001) 145 S.J.L.B. 70; *The Times*, March 14, 2001, CA (Civ Div) 25.1.28, 48.1.2, C1A–012

Bernard, The [1905] W.N. 73 . . . . 2D–31

Bernard *v* Dudley MBC [2003] EWHC 147 . . . . 44.3.7

—— *v* Enfield LBC [2001] EWCA Civ 1831; [2002] H.L.R. 46; [2001] N.P.C. 178; *Independent*, December 12, 2001 . . . . 3A–1429

Bernina, The. *See* Mills v Armstrong (The Bernina)

Bernstein *v* Bernstein [1893] P. 292 . . . . sc52.5.1

—— *v* Pamson Motors (Golders Green) Ltd [1987] 2 All E.R. 220; [1987] R.T.R. 384; *The Times*, October 25, 1986 . . . . 3H–653

Berny, The. *See* Owners of Cargo Lately Laden on Board the Berny v Owners of the Berny (The Berny)

Berostar, The. *See* Sameiet Stavos (OH Meling Rederi) v Owners of the Berostar

Paragraph numbers marked with a "+" can be found online and on CD.

Paragraph numbers marked with a "+" can be found online and on CD.

Paragraph numbers marked with a "+" can be found online and on CD.

Paragraph numbers marked with a "+" can be found online and on CD.

Paragraph numbers marked with a "+" can be found online and on CD.

Paragraph numbers marked with a "+" can be found online and on CD.

Paragraph numbers marked with a "+" can be found online and on CD.

Paragraph numbers marked with a "+" can be found online and on CD.

Paragraph numbers marked with a "+" can be found online and on CD.

Paragraph numbers marked with a "+" can be found online and on CD.

Paragraph numbers marked with a "+" can be found online and on CD.

Paragraph numbers marked with a "+" can be found online and on CD.

Paragraph numbers marked with a "+" can be found online and on CD.

Paragraph numbers marked with a "+" can be found online and on CD.

Paragraph numbers marked with a "+" can be found online and on CD.

Paragraph numbers marked with a "+" can be found online and on CD.

Paragraph numbers marked with a "+" can be found online and on CD.

Paragraph numbers marked with a "+" can be found online and on CD.

Paragraph numbers marked with a "+" can be found online and on CD.

Paragraph numbers marked with a "+" can be found online and on CD.

Paragraph numbers marked with a "+" can be found online and on CD.

Paragraph numbers marked with a "+" can be found online and on CD.

Paragraph numbers marked with a "+" can be found online and on CD.

Paragraph numbers marked with a "+" can be found online and on CD.

Paragraph numbers marked with a "+" can be found online and on CD.

Paragraph numbers marked with a "+" can be found online and on CD.

Paragraph numbers marked with a "+" can be found online and on CD.

Paragraph numbers marked with a "+" can be found online and on CD.

Paragraph numbers marked with a "+" can be found online and on CD.

Paragraph numbers marked with a "+" can be found online and on CD.

Paragraph numbers marked with a "+" can be found online and on CD.

Paragraph numbers marked with a "+" can be found online and on CD.

Paragraph numbers marked with a "+" can be found online and on CD.

Paragraph numbers marked with a "+" can be found online and on CD.

Paragraph numbers marked with a "+" can be found online and on CD.

Paragraph numbers marked with a "+" can be found online and on CD.

Paragraph numbers marked with a "+" can be found online and on CD.

Paragraph numbers marked with a "+" can be found online and on CD.

Paragraph numbers marked with a "+" can be found online and on CD.

Paragraph numbers marked with a "+" can be found online and on CD.

Paragraph numbers marked with a "+" can be found online and on CD.

Paragraph numbers marked with a "+" can be found online and on CD.

Paragraph numbers marked with a "+" can be found online and on CD.

Paragraph numbers marked with a "+" can be found online and on CD.

Paragraph numbers marked with a "+" can be found online and on CD.

Paragraph numbers marked with a "+" can be found online and on CD.

Paragraph numbers marked with a "+" can be found online and on CD.

Paragraph numbers marked with a "+" can be found online and on CD.

Paragraph numbers marked with a "+" can be found online and on CD.

Paragraph numbers marked with a "+" can be found online and on CD.

Paragraph numbers marked with a "+" can be found online and on CD.

Paragraph numbers marked with a "+" can be found online and on CD.

Paragraph numbers marked with a "+" can be found online and on CD.

Paragraph numbers marked with a "+" can be found online and on CD.

Paragraph numbers marked with a "+" can be found online and on CD.

Paragraph numbers marked with a "+" can be found online and on CD.

Paragraph numbers marked with a "+" can be found online and on CD.

Paragraph numbers marked with a "+" can be found online and on CD.

Paragraph numbers marked with a "+" can be found online and on CD.

Paragraph numbers marked with a "+" can be found online and on CD.

Paragraph numbers marked with a "+" can be found online and on CD.

Paragraph numbers marked with a "+" can be found online and on CD.

Paragraph numbers marked with a "+" can be found online and on CD.

Paragraph numbers marked with a "+" can be found online and on CD.

Paragraph numbers marked with a "+" can be found online and on CD.

Paragraph numbers marked with a "+" can be found online and on CD.

Paragraph numbers marked with a "+" can be found online and on CD.

Paragraph numbers marked with a "+" can be found online and on CD.

Paragraph numbers marked with a "+" can be found online and on CD.

Paragraph numbers marked with a "+" can be found online and on CD.

Paragraph numbers marked with a "+" can be found online and on CD.

Paragraph numbers marked with a "+" can be found online and on CD.

Paragraph numbers marked with a "+" can be found online and on CD.

Paragraph numbers marked with a "+" can be found online and on CD.

Paragraph numbers marked with a "+" can be found online and on CD.

Paragraph numbers marked with a "+" can be found online and on CD.

Paragraph numbers marked with a "+" can be found online and on CD.

Paragraph numbers marked with a "+" can be found online and on CD.

Paragraph numbers marked with a "+" can be found online and on CD.

Paragraph numbers marked with a "+" can be found online and on CD.

Paragraph numbers marked with a "+" can be found online and on CD.

Paragraph numbers marked with a "+" can be found online and on CD.

Paragraph numbers marked with a "+" can be found online and on CD.

Paragraph numbers marked with a "+" can be found online and on CD.

Paragraph numbers marked with a "+" can be found online and on CD.

Paragraph numbers marked with a "+" can be found online and on CD.

Paragraph numbers marked with a "+" can be found online and on CD.

Paragraph numbers marked with a "+" can be found online and on CD.

Paragraph numbers marked with a "+" can be found online and on CD.

Paragraph numbers marked with a "+" can be found online and on CD.

Paragraph numbers marked with a "+" can be found online and on CD.

Paragraph numbers marked with a "+" can be found online and on CD.

Paragraph numbers marked with a "+" can be found online and on CD.

Paragraph numbers marked with a "+" can be found online and on CD.

Paragraph numbers marked with a "+" can be found online and on CD.

Paragraph numbers marked with a "+" can be found online and on CD.

Paragraph numbers marked with a "+" can be found online and on CD.

Paragraph numbers marked with a "+" can be found online and on CD.

Paragraph numbers marked with a "+" can be found online and on CD.

Paragraph numbers marked with a "+" can be found online and on CD.

Paragraph numbers marked with a "+" can be found online and on CD.

Paragraph numbers marked with a "+" can be found online and on CD.

Paragraph numbers marked with a "+" can be found online and on CD.

Paragraph numbers marked with a "+" can be found online and on CD.

Paragraph numbers marked with a "+" can be found online and on CD.

Paragraph numbers marked with a "+" can be found online and on CD.

Paragraph numbers marked with a "+" can be found online and on CD.

Paragraph numbers marked with a "+" can be found online and on CD.

Paragraph numbers marked with a "+" can be found online and on CD.

Paragraph numbers marked with a "+" can be found online and on CD.

Paragraph numbers marked with a "+" can be found online and on CD.

Paragraph numbers marked with a "+" can be found online and on CD.

Paragraph numbers marked with a "+" can be found online and on CD.

Paragraph numbers marked with a "+" can be found online and on CD.

Paragraph numbers marked with a "+" can be found online and on CD.

Paragraph numbers marked with a "+" can be found online and on CD.

Paragraph numbers marked with a "+" can be found online and on CD.

Paragraph numbers marked with a "+" can be found online and on CD.

Paragraph numbers marked with a "+" can be found online and on CD.

Paragraph numbers marked with a "+" can be found online and on CD.

Paragraph numbers marked with a "+" can be found online and on CD.

Paragraph numbers marked with a "+" can be found online and on CD.

Paragraph numbers marked with a "+" can be found online and on CD.

Paragraph numbers marked with a "+" can be found online and on CD.

Paragraph numbers marked with a "+" can be found online and on CD.

Paragraph numbers marked with a "+" can be found online and on CD.

Paragraph numbers marked with a "+" can be found online and on CD.

Paragraph numbers marked with a "+" can be found online and on CD.

Paragraph numbers marked with a "+" can be found online and on CD.

Paragraph numbers marked with a "+" can be found online and on CD.

Paragraph numbers marked with a "+" can be found online and on CD.

Paragraph numbers marked with a "+" can be found online and on CD.

Paragraph numbers marked with a "+" can be found online and on CD.

Paragraph numbers marked with a "+" can be found online and on CD.

Paragraph numbers marked with a "+" can be found online and on CD.

Paragraph numbers marked with a "+" can be found online and on CD.

Paragraph numbers marked with a "+" can be found online and on CD.

Paragraph numbers marked with a "+" can be found online and on CD.

Paragraph numbers marked with a "+" can be found online and on CD.

Paragraph numbers marked with a "+" can be found online and on CD.

Paragraph numbers marked with a "+" can be found online and on CD.

Paragraph numbers marked with a "+" can be found online and on CD.

Paragraph numbers marked with a "+" can be found online and on CD.

Paragraph numbers marked with a "+" can be found online and on CD.

Paragraph numbers marked with a "+" can be found online and on CD.

Paragraph numbers marked with a "+" can be found online and on CD.

Paragraph numbers marked with a "+" can be found online and on CD.

Paragraph numbers marked with a "+" can be found online and on CD.

Paragraph numbers marked with a "+" can be found online and on CD.

Paragraph numbers marked with a "+" can be found online and on CD.

Paragraph numbers marked with a "+" can be found online and on CD.

Paragraph numbers marked with a "+" can be found online and on CD.

Paragraph numbers marked with a "+" can be found online and on CD.

Paragraph numbers marked with a "+" can be found online and on CD.

Paragraph numbers marked with a "+" can be found online and on CD.

Paragraph numbers marked with a "+" can be found online and on CD.

Paragraph numbers marked with a "+" can be found online and on CD.

Paragraph numbers marked with a "+" can be found online and on CD.

Paragraph numbers marked with a "+" can be found online and on CD.

Paragraph numbers marked with a "+" can be found online and on CD.

Paragraph numbers marked with a "+" can be found online and on CD.

Paragraph numbers marked with a "+" can be found online and on CD.

Paragraph numbers marked with a "+" can be found online and on CD.

Paragraph numbers marked with a "+" can be found online and on CD.

Paragraph numbers marked with a "+" can be found online and on CD.

Paragraph numbers marked with a "+" can be found online and on CD.

Paragraph numbers marked with a "+" can be found online and on CD.

Paragraph numbers marked with a "+" can be found online and on CD.

Paragraph numbers marked with a "+" can be found online and on CD.

Paragraph numbers marked with a "+" can be found online and on CD.

Paragraph numbers marked with a "+" can be found online and on CD.

Paragraph numbers marked with a "+" can be found online and on CD.

Paragraph numbers marked with a "+" can be found online and on CD.

Paragraph numbers marked with a "+" can be found online and on CD.

Paragraph numbers marked with a "+" can be found online and on CD.

Paragraph numbers marked with a "+" can be found online and on CD.

Paragraph numbers marked with a "+" can be found online and on CD.

Paragraph numbers marked with a "+" can be found online and on CD.

Paragraph numbers marked with a "+" can be found online and on CD.

Paragraph numbers marked with a "+" can be found online and on CD.

Paragraph numbers marked with a "+" can be found online and on CD.

Paragraph numbers marked with a "+" can be found online and on CD.

Paragraph numbers marked with a "+" can be found online and on CD.

Paragraph numbers marked with a "+" can be found online and on CD.

Paragraph numbers marked with a "+" can be found online and on CD.

Paragraph numbers marked with a "+" can be found online and on CD.

1 All E.R. 351; [2002] 2 Lloyd's Rep. 228; [2002] 1 Lloyd's Rep. 424; *The Times*, January 17, 2002 .... 52.12.3, 1A–71

Practice Direction (Sup Ct: References to the Court of Justice of the European Communities), *sub nom.* Practice Direction (ECJ: References to the ECJ by CA and HC under Art.177) [1999] 1 W.L.R. 260; [1999] 1 Cr. App. R. 452; [1999] 2 C.M.L.R. 799; *The Times*, January 19, 1999 .... 1B–96

Practice Direction (Sup Ct: Tape Recorders in Court) [1981] 1 W.L.R. 1526; [1981] 3 All E.R. 848; (1982) 74 Cr. App. R. 73 .... 3C–22

Practice Direction (Supreme Court Taxing Office: Admiralty: Costs) [1986] 1 W.L.R. 1310; [1986] 3 All E.R. 178 .... 2D–144

Practice Note (CA: Citation of Reports). *See* Practice Direction (CA: Citation of Authority)

Practice Note (CA: Hear by Dates and Listing Windows) (Revised), *sub nom.* Practice Note (CA: Listing Windows) (No.2) [2003] 1 W.L.R. 838; [2003] 2 All E.R. 399; *The Times*, March 14, 2003 .... 52.12.7

Practice Note (CA: Hear by Dates and Listing Windows), *sub nom.* Practice Note (CA: Listing Windows) [2001] 1 W.L.R. 1517; [2001] 3 All E.R. 479; *The Times*, July 25, 2001 .... 52.12.7

Practice Note (CA: Listing Windows) (No.2). *See* Practice Note (CA: Hear by Dates and Listing Windows) (Revised)

Practice Note (CA: Listing Windows). *See* Practice Note (CA: Hear by Dates and Listing Windows)

Practice Note (CA: Skeleton Arguments) [1989] 1 W.L.R. 281; [1989] 1 All E.R. 891 12–55

Practice Note (CAFCASS and National Assembly for Wales: Appointment of Guardians in Private Law Pro [2006] 2 F.L.R. 143 .... 23BPD.8

Practice Note (Court of Appeal: Money Laundering: Discovery of Documents) [1999] 1 W.L.R. 1551 .... 25.1.26

Practice Note (Crown Office List: Uncontested Proceedings) [1997] 2 All E.R. 799 (May 12 .... scpd54.9

Practice Note (Crown Office List: Uncontested Proceedings: Applications outside London: Delay); Practice Direction (QBD: Uncontested Proceedings: Crown Office List: Applications outside London: J. *See* Practice Direction (Crown Office List: Criminal Proceedings)

Practice Note (DC: Habeas Corpus); Cook, Re. *See* Wring, Re

Practice Note (Divisional Court: Extension of Time). *See* Raymond and Reid v Granger (Practice Note)

Practice Note (Fam Div: Incapacitated Adults: Declaratory Proceedings) [2002] 1 W.L.R. 325; [2002] 1 All E.R. 794; [2002] 1 F.L.R. 177; [2002] 1 F.C.R. 479; (2002) 65 B.M.L.R. 72; *The Times*, January 4, 2002 .... 40.0.9—40.0.10, 40.20.2

Practice Note (HC: Civil Litigation: Case Management); Practice Direction (QBD: Pre-trial Checklist: Civil Litigation); Practice Direction (QBD and Ch D: Case Management). *See* Practice Direction (HC: Civil Litigation: Case Management)

Practice Note (QBD: Crown Office List). *See* Practice Direction (Crown Office List: Estimated Length of Hearing)

——. *See* Practice Direction (Crown Office List)

Practice Note (QBD: Crown Office List: Penalties for Late Papers); Practice Direction (QBD: Crown Office List: Time Estimates, Skeleton Arguments and Paginated Bundle. *See* Practice Direction (QBD: Crown Office List: Preparation for Hearings)

Practice Note (citation of cases: restrictions and rules) [2001] 1 W.L.R. 1001 .... 1A–71

Practice Note [1927] W.N. 290 .... 40.6.2

Practice Note: (Fam Div: HIV Testing of Children). *See* President's Direction (Fam Div: HIV Testing of Children)

Practice Statement (Admin Ct: Administration of Justice), *sub nom.* Practice Statement (Admin Ct: Listing and Urgent Cases) [2002] 1 W.L.R. 810; [2002] 1 All E.R. 633; *[2002] A.C.D. 64* 23.0.7, 54.3.5, 54.4.1, 54.6.1, 54.16.1

Practice Statement (Admin Ct: Listing and Urgent Cases). *See* Practice Statement (Admin Ct: Administration of Justice)

Paragraph numbers marked with a "+" can be found online and on CD.

Paragraph numbers marked with a "+" can be found online and on CD.

Paragraph numbers marked with a "+" can be found online and on CD.

Paragraph numbers marked with a "+" can be found online and on CD.

Paragraph numbers marked with a "+" can be found online and on CD.

Paragraph numbers marked with a "+" can be found online and on CD.

Paragraph numbers marked with a "+" can be found online and on CD.

Paragraph numbers marked with a "+" can be found online and on CD.

Paragraph numbers marked with a "+" can be found online and on CD.

Paragraph numbers marked with a "+" can be found online and on CD.

Paragraph numbers marked with a "+" can be found online and on CD.

Paragraph numbers marked with a "+" can be found online and on CD.

Paragraph numbers marked with a "+" can be found online and on CD.

Paragraph numbers marked with a "+" can be found online and on CD.

Paragraph numbers marked with a "+" can be found online and on CD.

Paragraph numbers marked with a "+" can be found online and on CD.

Paragraph numbers marked with a "+" can be found online and on CD.

Paragraph numbers marked with a "+" can be found online and on CD.

Paragraph numbers marked with a "+" can be found online and on CD.

Paragraph numbers marked with a "+" can be found online and on CD.

Paragraph numbers marked with a "+" can be found online and on CD.

Paragraph numbers marked with a "+" can be found online and on CD.

Paragraph numbers marked with a "+" can be found online and on CD.

Paragraph numbers marked with a "+" can be found online and on CD.

Paragraph numbers marked with a "+" can be found online and on CD.

Paragraph numbers marked with a "+" can be found online and on CD.

Paragraph numbers marked with a "+" can be found online and on CD.

Paragraph numbers marked with a "+" can be found online and on CD.

Paragraph numbers marked with a "+" can be found online and on CD.

Paragraph numbers marked with a "+" can be found online and on CD.

Paragraph numbers marked with a "+" can be found online and on CD.

Paragraph numbers marked with a "+" can be found online and on CD.

Paragraph numbers marked with a "+" can be found online and on CD.

Paragraph numbers marked with a "+" can be found online and on CD.

Paragraph numbers marked with a "+" can be found online and on CD.

Paragraph numbers marked with a "+" can be found online and on CD.

Paragraph numbers marked with a "+" can be found online and on CD.

Paragraph numbers marked with a "+" can be found online and on CD.

Paragraph numbers marked with a "+" can be found online and on CD.

Paragraph numbers marked with a "+" can be found online and on CD.

Paragraph numbers marked with a "+" can be found online and on CD.

Paragraph numbers marked with a "+" can be found online and on CD.

Paragraph numbers marked with a "+" can be found online and on CD.

Paragraph numbers marked with a "+" can be found online and on CD.

Paragraph numbers marked with a "+" can be found online and on CD.

Paragraph numbers marked with a "+" can be found online and on CD.

Paragraph numbers marked with a "+" can be found online and on CD.

Paragraph numbers marked with a "+" can be found online and on CD.

Paragraph numbers marked with a "+" can be found online and on CD.

Paragraph numbers marked with a "+" can be found online and on CD.

Paragraph numbers marked with a "+" can be found online and on CD.

Paragraph numbers marked with a "+" can be found online and on CD.

Paragraph numbers marked with a "+" can be found online and on CD.

Paragraph numbers marked with a "+" can be found online and on CD.

Paragraph numbers marked with a "+" can be found online and on CD.

Paragraph numbers marked with a "+" can be found online and on CD.

Paragraph numbers marked with a "+" can be found online and on CD.

Paragraph numbers marked with a "+" can be found online and on CD.

Paragraph numbers marked with a "+" can be found online and on CD.

Paragraph numbers marked with a "+" can be found online and on CD.

Paragraph numbers marked with a "+" can be found online and on CD.

Paragraph numbers marked with a "+" can be found online and on CD.

Paragraph numbers marked with a "+" can be found online and on CD.

Paragraph numbers marked with a "+" can be found online and on CD.

Paragraph numbers marked with a "+" can be found online and on CD.

Paragraph numbers marked with a "+" can be found online and on CD.

Paragraph numbers marked with a "+" can be found online and on CD.

Paragraph numbers marked with a "+" can be found online and on CD.

Paragraph numbers marked with a "+" can be found online and on CD.

Paragraph numbers marked with a "+" can be found online and on CD.

Paragraph numbers marked with a "+" can be found online and on CD.

Paragraph numbers marked with a "+" can be found online and on CD.

Paragraph numbers marked with a "+" can be found online and on CD.

Paragraph numbers marked with a "+" can be found online and on CD.

Paragraph numbers marked with a "+" can be found online and on CD.

Paragraph numbers marked with a "+" can be found online and on CD.

South Glamorgan CC *v* Griffiths (1992) 24 H.L.R. 334; [1992] 2 E.G.L.R. 232; [1992] N.P.C. 13 . . . 3A–500

South Northamptonshire DC *v* Power [1987] 1 W.L.R. 1433; [1987] 3 All E.R. 831; (1988) 20 H.L.R. 133; [1988] Fam. Law 384; (1988) 138 N.L.J. Rep. 19; (1987) 131 S.J. 1514 . . . 3A–402

South Shropshire DC *v* Amos [1986] 1 W.L.R. 1271; [1987] 1 All E.R. 340; [1986] 2 E.G.L.R. 194; (1986) 280 E.G. 635; [1986] R.vR. 235; (1986) 83 L.S.G. 3513; (1986) 136 N.L.J. 800; (1986) 130 S.J. 803 . . . 31.3.40

South Tyneside BC *v* Wickes Building Supplies Ltd [2004] EWHC 2428 . . . 34.3.5

South West Yorkshire Mental Health NHS Trust *v* Bradford Crown Court. *See* R. (South West Yorkshire Mental Health NHS Trust) v Bradford Crown Court

Southco Inc *v* Dzus Fastener Europe Ltd (No.1) [1989] R.P.C. 82 . . . 15–47.12

Southern & District Finance Plc *v* Turner [2003] EWCA Civ 1574; (2003) 147 S.J.L.B. 1362 . . . 3.1.4, 52.10.6, 11–8

Southern and District Finance Plc *v* Barnes [1996] 1 F.C.R. 679 . . . 3H–290, 3H–311

Southwark LBC *v* Afolabi. *See* Afolabi v Southwark LBC

—— *v* Jiminez, *sub nom.* Jiminez v Southwark LBC [2003] EWCA Civ 502; [2003] I.C.R. 1176; [2003] I.R.L.R. 477; (2003) 100(23) L.S.G. 37; (2003) 147 S.J.L.B. 476; *The Times*, May 1, 2003 . . . 9A–48

—— *v* Joseph, March 2000, Legal Action 29 . . . 39.3.2

—— *v* Kofi–Adu [2006] EWCA Civ 281; [2006] H.L.R. 33; [2006] N.P.C. 36; *The Times*, June 1, 2006 . . . 9A–48, 11–5

—— *v* Mills, *sub nom.* Baxter v Camden LBC (No.2); Southwark LBC v Tanner [2001] 1 A.C. 1; [1999] 3 W.L.R. 939; [1999] 4 All E.R. 449; [2000] Env. L.R. 112; (2000) 32 H.L.R. 148; [2000] B.L.G.R. 138; [2000] L. & T.R. 159; [1999] 3 E.G.L.R. 35; [1999] 45 E.G. 179; [1999] E.G. 122 (C.S.); (1999) 96(42) L.S.G. 41; (1999) 96(42) L.S.G. 45; (1999) 149 N.L.J. 1618; (1999) 143 S.J.L.B. 249; [1999] N.P.C. 123; (2000) 79 P. & C.R. D13; *The Times*, October 22, 1999, HL; affirming [2001] Ch. 1; [1999] 2 W.L.R. 409; (1999) 31 H.L.R. 187; [1999] B.L.G.R. 71; (1998) 10 Admin. L.R. 621; [1998] L. & T.R. 251; [1998] 3 E.G.L.R. 46; [1998] 45 E.G. 151; (1998) 162 J.P.N. 945; [1998] E.G. 132 (C.S.); (1998) 95(34) L.S.G. 31; (1998) 142 S.J.L.B. 221; [1998] N.P.C. 126; *The Times*, August 20, 1998; *Independent*, October 2, 1998, CA (Civ Div); reversing [1998] 3 W.L.R. 49; (1998) 10 Admin. L.R. 353; [1998] 2 E.G.L.R. 30; [1998] 22 E.G. 151; (1998) 162 J.P.N. 722; [1998] E.G. 39 (C.S.); (1998) 95(16) L.S.G. 25; (1998) 142 S.J.L.B. 119; [1998] N.P.C. 34; *The Times*, March 11, 1998 . . . 3A–560

—— *v* Sarfo (2000) 32 H.L.R. 602; (1999) 78 P. & C.R. D41, CA (Civ Div) . . . 3A–388

—— *v* St Brice. *See* St Brice v Southwark LBC

—— *v* Tornaritis [1999] 7 C.L.D. 330 . . . 3A–1054

—— *v* Storrie [1997] C.L.Y. 632, December 3, 1997 . . . 15–35

Southwark Water Co *v* Quick (1878) 3 Q.B.D. 315 . . . 31.3.6, 31.3.12

Sowerby *v* Charlton [2005] EWCA Civ 1610; [2006] 1 W.L.R. 568; [2006] C.P. Rep. 16; [2006] P.I.Q.R. P15; (2006) 103(3) L.S.G. 28; *The Times*, January 5, 2006; *Independent*, January 11, 2006, CA (Civ Div); affirming [2005] EWHC 949; [2006] P.I.Q.R. P4 . . . 14.1.8—14.1.9, C2A–005, 12–5

Span Terza, The, *sub nom.* Span Terza, The [1982] 1 Lloyd's Rep. 225 . . . 2D–18

Spanish General Agency Corp *v* Spanish Corp (1891) 63 L.T. 161 . . . 15–2

Spargo *v* North Essex DHA [1997] P.I.Q.R. P235; [1997] 8 Med. L.R. 125; (1997) 37 B.M.L.R. 99; (1997) 94(15) L.S.G. 26; (1997) 141 S.J.L.B. 90; *The Times*, March 21, 1997, CA (Civ Div); reversing [1996] 7 Med. L.R. 219 . . . 8–3

Sparks *v* Harland [1997] 1 W.L.R. 143; *The Times*, August 9, 1996 . . . 9A–18

Special Effects Ltd *v* L'Oreal SA [2007] EWCA Civ 1; [2007] Bus. L.R. 759; [2007] E.T.M.R. 51; [2007] R.P.C. 15; (2007) 151 S.J.L.B. 126; *The Times*, January 24, 2007, CA (Civ Div); reversing [2006] EWHC 481; [2006] R.P.C. 33; (2006) 29(5) I.P.D. 29041; *The Times*, May 1, 2006 . . . 2F–8

Spectravest Inc *v* Aperknit Ltd [1988] F.S.R. 161 . . . sc45.5.5—sc45.5.6, sc52.1.

Paragraph numbers marked with a "+" can be found online and on CD.

Paragraph numbers marked with a "+" can be found online and on CD.

Paragraph numbers marked with a "+" can be found online and on CD.

Paragraph numbers marked with a "+" can be found online and on CD.

Paragraph numbers marked with a "+" can be found online and on CD.

Paragraph numbers marked with a "+" can be found online and on CD.

Paragraph numbers marked with a "+" can be found online and on CD.

Paragraph numbers marked with a "+" can be found online and on CD.

Paragraph numbers marked with a "+" can be found online and on CD.

Paragraph numbers marked with a "+" can be found online and on CD.

Paragraph numbers marked with a "+" can be found online and on CD.

Paragraph numbers marked with a "+" can be found online and on CD.

Paragraph numbers marked with a "+" can be found online and on CD.

Paragraph numbers marked with a "+" can be found online and on CD.

Paragraph numbers marked with a "+" can be found online and on CD.

Paragraph numbers marked with a "+" can be found online and on CD.

Paragraph numbers marked with a "+" can be found online and on CD.

Paragraph numbers marked with a "+" can be found online and on CD.

Paragraph numbers marked with a "+" can be found online and on CD.

Paragraph numbers marked with a "+" can be found online and on CD.

Paragraph numbers marked with a "+" can be found online and on CD.

Paragraph numbers marked with a "+" can be found online and on CD.

Paragraph numbers marked with a "+" can be found online and on CD.

Paragraph numbers marked with a "+" can be found online and on CD.

Paragraph numbers marked with a "+" can be found online and on CD.

Paragraph numbers marked with a "+" can be found online and on CD.

Paragraph numbers marked with a "+" can be found online and on CD.

Paragraph numbers marked with a "+" can be found online and on CD.

Paragraph numbers marked with a "+" can be found online and on CD.

Paragraph numbers marked with a "+" can be found online and on CD.

Paragraph numbers marked with a "+" can be found online and on CD.

Paragraph numbers marked with a "+" can be found online and on CD.

Paragraph numbers marked with a "+" can be found online and on CD.

Paragraph numbers marked with a "+" can be found online and on CD.

Paragraph numbers marked with a "+" can be found online and on CD.

Paragraph numbers marked with a "+" can be found online and on CD.

Paragraph numbers marked with a "+" can be found online and on CD.

TABLE OF STATUTES

[References in bold type are to the paragraph at which that section, or part of that section, is set out in full.]

Paragraph numbers marked with a "+" can be found online and on CD.

Paragraph numbers marked with a "+" can be found online and on CD.

Paragraph numbers marked with a "+" can be found online and on CD.

Paragraph numbers marked with a "+" can be found online and on CD.

Paragraph numbers marked with a "+" can be found online and on CD.

Paragraph numbers marked with a "+" can be found online and on CD.

Paragraph numbers marked with a "+" can be found online and on CD.

Paragraph numbers marked with a "+" can be found online and on CD.

Paragraph numbers marked with a "+" can be found online and on CD.

Paragraph numbers marked with a "+" can be found online and on CD.

Paragraph numbers marked with a "+" can be found online and on CD.

Paragraph numbers marked with a "+" can be found online and on CD.

Paragraph numbers marked with a "+" can be found online and on CD.

Paragraph numbers marked with a "+" can be found online and on CD.

Paragraph numbers marked with a "+" can be found online and on CD.

Paragraph numbers marked with a "+" can be found online and on CD.

Paragraph numbers marked with a "+" can be found online and on CD.

Paragraph numbers marked with a "+" can be found online and on CD.

Paragraph numbers marked with a "+" can be found online and on CD.

Paragraph numbers marked with a "+" can be found online and on CD.

Paragraph numbers marked with a "+" can be found online and on CD.

Paragraph numbers marked with a "+" can be found online and on CD.

Paragraph numbers marked with a "+" can be found online and on CD.

Paragraph numbers marked with a "+" can be found online and on CD.

Paragraph numbers marked with a "+" can be found online and on CD.

Paragraph numbers marked with a "+" can be found online and on CD.

Paragraph numbers marked with a "+" can be found online and on CD.

Paragraph numbers marked with a "+" can be found online and on CD.

Paragraph numbers marked with a "+" can be found online and on CD.

Paragraph numbers marked with a "+" can be found online and on CD.

Paragraph numbers marked with a "+" can be found online and on CD.

Paragraph numbers marked with a "+" can be found online and on CD.

Paragraph numbers marked with a "+" can be found online and on CD.

Paragraph numbers marked with a "+" can be found online and on CD.

Paragraph numbers marked with a "+" can be found online and on CD.

Paragraph numbers marked with a "+" can be found online and on CD.

Paragraph numbers marked with a "+" can be found online and on CD.

Paragraph numbers marked with a "+" can be found online and on CD.

Paragraph numbers marked with a "+" can be found online and on CD.

Paragraph numbers marked with a "+" can be found online and on CD.

Paragraph numbers marked with a "+" can be found online and on CD.

Paragraph numbers marked with a "+" can be found online and on CD.

Paragraph numbers marked with a "+" can be found online and on CD.

Paragraph numbers marked with a "+" can be found online and on CD.

Paragraph numbers marked with a "+" can be found online and on CD.

Paragraph numbers marked with a "+" can be found online and on CD.

Paragraph numbers marked with a "+" can be found online and on CD.

Paragraph numbers marked with a "+" can be found online and on CD.

Paragraph numbers marked with a "+" can be found online and on CD.

Paragraph numbers marked with a "+" can be found online and on CD.

Paragraph numbers marked with a "+" can be found online and on CD.

Paragraph numbers marked with a "+" can be found online and on CD.

Paragraph numbers marked with a "+" can be found online and on CD.

Paragraph numbers marked with a "+" can be found online and on CD.

Paragraph numbers marked with a "+" can be found online and on CD.

Paragraph numbers marked with a "+" can be found online and on CD.

Paragraph numbers marked with a "+" can be found online and on CD.

Paragraph numbers marked with a "+" can be found online and on CD.

Paragraph numbers marked with a "+" can be found online and on CD.

Paragraph numbers marked with a "+" can be found online and on CD.

Paragraph numbers marked with a "+" can be found online and on CD.

Paragraph numbers marked with a "+" can be found online and on CD.

Paragraph numbers marked with a "+" can be found online and on CD.

Paragraph numbers marked with a "+" can be found online and on CD.

Paragraph numbers marked with a "+" can be found online and on CD.

Paragraph numbers marked with a "+" can be found online and on CD.

Paragraph numbers marked with a "+" can be found online and on CD.

Paragraph numbers marked with a "+" can be found online and on CD.

Paragraph numbers marked with a "+" can be found online and on CD.

Paragraph numbers marked with a "+" can be found online and on CD.

Paragraph numbers marked with a "+" can be found online and on CD.

Paragraph numbers marked with a "+" can be found online and on CD.

Paragraph numbers marked with a "+" can be found online and on CD.

Paragraph numbers marked with a "+" can be found online and on CD.

Paragraph numbers marked with a "+" can be found online and on CD.

Paragraph numbers marked with a "+" can be found online and on CD.

Paragraph numbers marked with a "+" can be found online and on CD.

Paragraph numbers marked with a "+" can be found online and on CD.

Paragraph numbers marked with a "+" can be found online and on CD.

Paragraph numbers marked with a "+" can be found online and on CD.

Paragraph numbers marked with a "+" can be found online and on CD.

Paragraph numbers marked with a "+" can be found online and on CD.

Paragraph numbers marked with a "+" can be found online and on CD.

Paragraph numbers marked with a "+" can be found online and on CD.

Paragraph numbers marked with a "+" can be found online and on CD.

Paragraph numbers marked with a "+" can be found online and on CD.

Paragraph numbers marked with a "+" can be found online and on CD.

Paragraph numbers marked with a "+" can be found online and on CD.

Paragraph numbers marked with a "+" can be found online and on CD.

Paragraph numbers marked with a "+" can be found online and on CD.

Paragraph numbers marked with a "+" can be found online and on CD.

Paragraph numbers marked with a "+" can be found online and on CD.

Paragraph numbers marked with a "+" can be found online and on CD.

Paragraph numbers marked with a "+" can be found online and on CD.

Paragraph numbers marked with a "+" can be found online and on CD.

Paragraph numbers marked with a "+" can be found online and on CD.

Paragraph numbers marked with a "+" can be found online and on CD.

Paragraph numbers marked with a "+" can be found online and on CD.

Paragraph numbers marked with a "+" can be found online and on CD.

Paragraph numbers marked with a "+" can be found online and on CD.

Paragraph numbers marked with a "+" can be found online and on CD.

Paragraph numbers marked with a "+" can be found online and on CD.

Paragraph numbers marked with a "+" can be found online and on CD.

Paragraph numbers marked with a "+" can be found online and on CD.

Paragraph numbers marked with a "+" can be found online and on CD.

Paragraph numbers marked with a "+" can be found online and on CD.

Paragraph numbers marked with a "+" can be found online and on CD.

Paragraph numbers marked with a "+" can be found online and on CD.

Paragraph numbers marked with a "+" can be found online and on CD.

Paragraph numbers marked with a "+" can be found online and on CD.

Paragraph numbers marked with a "+" can be found online and on CD.

Paragraph numbers marked with a "+" can be found online and on CD.

Paragraph numbers marked with a "+" can be found online and on CD.

Paragraph numbers marked with a "+" can be found online and on CD.

Paragraph numbers marked with a "+" can be found online and on CD.

Paragraph numbers marked with a "+" can be found online and on CD.

Paragraph numbers marked with a "+" can be found online and on CD.

Paragraph numbers marked with a "+" can be found online and on CD.

Paragraph numbers marked with a "+" can be found online and on CD.

Paragraph numbers marked with a "+" can be found online and on CD.

Paragraph numbers marked with a "+" can be found online and on CD.

Paragraph numbers marked with a "+" can be found online and on CD.

Paragraph numbers marked with a "+" can be found online and on CD.

Paragraph numbers marked with a "+" can be found online and on CD.

Paragraph numbers marked with a "+" can be found online and on CD.

Paragraph numbers marked with a "+" can be found online and on CD.

Paragraph numbers marked with a "+" can be found online and on CD.

Paragraph numbers marked with a "+" can be found online and on CD.

Paragraph numbers marked with a "+" can be found online and on CD.

Paragraph numbers marked with a "+" can be found online and on CD.

Paragraph numbers marked with a "+" can be found online and on CD.

Paragraph numbers marked with a "+" can be found online and on CD.

Paragraph numbers marked with a "+" can be found online and on CD.

Paragraph numbers marked with a "+" can be found online and on CD.

Paragraph numbers marked with a "+" can be found online and on CD.

Paragraph numbers marked with a "+" can be found online and on CD.

Paragraph numbers marked with a "+" can be found online and on CD.

Paragraph numbers marked with a "+" can be found online and on CD.

Paragraph numbers marked with a "+" can be found online and on CD.

Paragraph numbers marked with a "+" can be found online and on CD.

Paragraph numbers marked with a "+" can be found online and on CD.

Paragraph numbers marked with a "+" can be found online and on CD.

Paragraph numbers marked with a "+" can be found online and on CD.

TABLE OF INTERNATIONAL AND EUROPEAN LEGISLATION, TREATIES AND CONVENTIONS

*[**References in bold type** are to the paragraph at which that article is set out in full. All references to material in **Volume 2** are enclosed within square parentheses.]*

Paragraph numbers marked with "+" can be found online and on CD.

Paragraph numbers marked with "+" can be found online and on CD.

Paragraph numbers marked with "+" can be found online and on CD.

Paragraph numbers marked with "+" can be found online and on CD.

Paragraph numbers marked with "+" can be found online and on CD.

Paragraph numbers marked with "+" can be found online and on CD.

CIVIL PROCEDURE RULES

SECTION A

CIVIL PROCEDURE RULES 1998

PART 1

OVERRIDING OBJECTIVE

Contents

1.0.1

Editorial Introduction

Subject to exceptions (notably family proceedings), the Civil Procedure Rules 1998 (CPR) apply to all proceedings in county courts, the High Court, and the Court of Appeal (Civil Division) (see r.2.1 below). Before the CPR came into effect on April 26, 1999, rules governing comparable proceedings, on the one hand (1) in the High Court and the Court of Appeal (Civil Division) (both superior courts) were found in the Rules of the Supreme Court 1965 (RSC) (as amended), and, on the other (2) in the county courts (inferior courts) were found in the County Court Rules 1981 (CCR) (as amended). The CPR constitute a single body of court rules, supplemented in certain respects by practice directions, covering the same procedural matters as those formerly covered by the RSC and the CCR. 1.0.2

The enactment of uniform rules was recommended in the Report of the Review Body on Civil Justice (Cm. 740, 1989) but the necessary work involved in drafting new rules was not immediately put in hand. In March 1994, the Lord Chancellor appointed Lord Woolf to review and make recommendations for the reform of the rules and procedure then current in the civil courts in England and Wales and to prepare uniform rules merging the RSC and CCR and carrying into effect such recommendations. Lord Woolf conducted the "Access to Justice" review over a period of 2¼ years, and the conclusions were set out in two reports, namely the Interim Report (June 1995), and the Final Report (July 1996). A draft, but far from complete, set of uniform rules was annexed to the latter report. After further work, a final draft of the CPR was produced bringing together the RSC and the CCR, and incorporating most of the recommendations made in the "Access to Justice" Reports, but also including significant changes to civil procedure having a different provenance.

For a detailed account of the provenance of, the extent and application of, and the structure of, the CPR, see Vol.2 Sect.12 (CPR: Application, Amendments and Interpretation), subss.A to C and E (paras 12–2 to 12–28 and 12–35).

Necessarily, the CPR contain many provisions having the same effects as provisions found in the RSC and CCR, but they also contain much that is, when compared with the former rules, innovative, including the provisions found in this Part. The principal purpose of the provisions in this Part is to signal a substantial change in the handling of civil cases in the courts (by judges and lawyers) whilst at the same time reinforcing "procedural values" which, although acknowledged before 1998, were not always put into effect.

Amendments to CPR

Amendments to the CPR are made by statutory instrument. For a detailed account, including a complete list of statutory instruments enacted since 1998, their commencement dates and transitional provisions included in them (if any), see Vol.2 Sect.12 (CPR:Application, Amendments and Interpretation), subs.D (para.12–29). 1.0.3

The most recent amending statutory instruments and their commencement dates are:

Civil Jurisdiction and Judgments Regulations 2007 (SI 2007/1655)—July 1, 2007

Civil Procedure (Amendment) Rules 2007 (SI 2007/2204)—October 1, 2007

Civil Procedure (Amendment) Rules 2007 (SI 2007/2204)—October 1, 2007

Civil Procedure (Amendment No.2) Rules 2007 (SI 2007/3543)—March 31, 2008 and April 6, 2008

Civil Procedure (Amendment) Rules 2008 (SI 2008/2178)—October 1 and December 12, 2008, and January 1, 2009

Civil Procedure (Amendment No.2) Rules 2008 (SI 2008/3085)—December 4, 2008

Civil Procedure (Amendment No.3) Rules 2008 (SI 2008/3327)—April 6, 2009

Related sources

1.0.4 • Rule 3.1 (Court's general powers of case management).

The overriding objective

1.1 **1.1—(1) These Rules are a new procedural code with the overriding objective of enabling the court to deal with cases justly.**

(2) Dealing with a case justly includes, so far as is practicable—

(a) ensuring that the parties are on an equal footing;

(b) saving expense;

(c) dealing with the case in ways which are proportionate—

(i) to the amount of money involved;

(ii) to the importance of the case;

(iii) to the complexity of the issues; and

(iv) to the financial position of each party;

(d) ensuring that it is dealt with expeditiously and fairly; and

(e) allotting to it an appropriate share of the court's resources, while taking into account the need to allot resources to other cases.

Application by the court of the overriding objective

1.2 **1.2— The court must seek to give effect to the overriding objective when it—**

(a) exercises any power given to it by the Rules; or

(b) interprets any rule,

subject to rules 76.2 and 79.2.

Duty of the parties

1.3 **1.3 The parties are required to help the court to further the overriding objective.**

Effect of rules 1.1 to 1.3

1.3.1 CPR Pt 1 contains four rules. The Part has no supplementing practice direction. The words "subject to rule 76.2" were inserted in r.1.2 when Pt 76 was added to the CPR by the Civil Procedure (Amendment No.2) Rules 2005 (SI 2005/656), and were amended to read "subject to rules 76.2 and 79.2" by the Civil Procedure (Amendment No.2) Rules 2008 (SI 2008/3085).

Provisions similar to those found in these rules (and in r.1.4) were included in the incomplete draft for a uniform set of rules annexed to the Final Report of Lord Woolf's "Access to Justice" inquiry. These novel provisions were intended to set out the basic principles (a) upon which the new procedural rules were founded, and (b) which should influence civil courts in exercising their numerous discretions under the rules. In the Final Report it was said (at p.274) that, ultimately, the purpose of rules of court "is to guide the court and the litigants towards the just resolution of the case". Rules of court contain detailed directions for the steps which must be taken. The effectiveness of those steps "depends upon the spirit in which they are carried out". That, in turn, "depends on an understanding of the fundamental purpose of the rules and of the underlying system of procedure". The "overriding objective", as stated in r.1.1 and r.1.2, encapsulates that fundamental purpose. The CPR are deliberately not designed expressly to answer every question which could arise. The statement of the overriding objective in those rules "provides a compass to guide courts and litigants and legal advisers as to their general course" (Final Report, p 275). The rules in this Part, which are directed as much to the judges of the courts as to parties and their legal representatives, summarise the policies expounded in the "Access to Justice" Reports and which should inform the operation in practice of the rules of civil procedure as stated in the CPR and related practice directions See further Vol.2 Sect.11 (The Overriding Objective), subs.A (para.11–2).

In addition, by virtue of s.3 of the Human Rights Act 1998 (see para.3D–1) the provisions of the CPR must be read and given effect in a manner which is compatible with the rights and freedoms set out in the European Convention on Human Rights so far as it is possible to do so. If a compatible interpretation is impossible the rules will be ultra vires unless the incompatibility is required by s.1 and Sch.1 of the Civil Procedure Act 1997: see, mutatis mutandis, *General Mediterranean Holdings SA v Patel* [2000] 1 W.L.R. 272, QBD. Further, s.6 of the Human Rights Act 1998 obliges the courts, as public authorities, to act in a manner which is compatible with Convention rights. A court may act incompatibly only if it is required to do so by legislation which is irremediably incompatible with Convention rights; see further Vol.2 Sect.12 (CPR:Application, Amendments and Interpretation), subs.G.14 (para.12–58).

For significance of qualification of r.1.2 by r.76.2 and r.76.9, see commentary on those rules and also Vol.2, Section 11 (Overriding Objective of CPR), subs.B (para.11–3).

For a detailed account of the ways in which (1) the various elements of the overriding objective are implemented in the CPR, (2) the courts in their judgments have made use of these elements when exercising powers given to them by the CPR, and (3) the overriding objective affects the interpretation of particular rules, see Vol.2, Section 12 (CPR: Application, Amendments and Interpretation), subs.G.3 (para.12–45), and Vol.2,Section 11 (The Overriding Objective), subs.A (para.11–2).

Duty of the parties (r.1.3)

The structure of the rules in Pt 1 suggest that the achievement of the overriding **1.3.2**
objective is the duty of the court. The rules are designed to enable "the court" to deal with cases justly (r.1.1), it is "the court" that must seek to give effect to the overriding objective (r.1.2), and it is "the court" that must further that objective by actively managing cases (r.1.4). (Note also r.3.1(2)(m)). No such duty is directly imposed on the parties. However, r.1.3 states that the parties are required "to help the court" to further the overriding objective. For detailed commentary on this rule, including notes on relevant cases, see Vol.2 Sect.11 (The Overriding Objective), subs.E (para.11–14).

Court's resources (r.1.1(2)(e))

Dealing with a case justly includes, so far as is practicable, "allotting to it an ap- **1.3.3**
propriate share of the court's resources, while taking into account the need to allot resources to other cases" (r.1.1(2)(e)). In the years since the CPR came into effect, this element of the overriding objective has assumed increasing importance. The duties imposed on parties and their professional advisers to keep the court informed of developments that may affect the use by the court of its resources are particularly noteworthy. For a detailed account of this and other implications of this element of the overriding objective, see Vol.2 Sect.11 (The Overriding Objective), subs.D.5 (para.11–12).

CPR "a new procedural code"

In CPR r.1.1(1), it is asserted that the CPR "are a new procedural code". This **1.3.4**
concept was not referred to in the penultimate draft of the CPR published in July 1998. The purpose and significance of this very late addition were not immediately clear as it is obvious that the CPR do not constitute a 'code" in any technical sense understood by lawyers, and much of the content of the CPR is far from "new". Experience has shown that the effects of the assertion have been, and continue to be, both good and bad. For detailed explanation, see Vol.2 Sect.12 (CPR: Application, Amendments and Interpretation), subs.G.12 (para.12–56).

Court's duty to manage cases

1.4 **1.4—(1) The court must further the overriding objective by actively managing cases.**

(2) Active case management includes—

(a) encouraging the parties to co-operate with each other in the conduct of the proceedings;

(b) identifying the issues at an early stage;

(c) deciding promptly which issues need full investigation and trial and accordingly disposing summarily of the others;

(d) deciding the order in which issues are to be resolved;

(e) encouraging the parties to use an alternative dispute resolution(GL) procedure if the court considers that appropriate and facilitating the use of such procedure;

(f) helping the parties to settle the whole or part of the case;

(g) fixing timetables or otherwise controlling the progress of the case;

(h) considering whether the likely benefits of taking a particular step justify the cost of taking it;

(i) dealing with as many aspects of the case as it can on the same occasion;

(j) dealing with the case without the parties needing to attend at court;

(k) making use of technology; and

(l) giving directions to ensure that the trial of a case proceeds quickly and efficiently.

Effect of rule

1.4.1 Rule 1.4(1) states that the court's duty to further the overriding objective (rr.1.1 and 1.2) includes the duty actively to manage cases. The concept of "case management" was the single most important recommendation to emerge from the "Access to Justice" Reports. This recommendation was based on the conclusion that the problems in the civil justice system could be remedied if many detailed changes were made to existing practices and procedures and that those changes could only be rendered effective in the context of a "managed system of dispute resolution" (see notes to rr.1.1 to 1.3 above). In the "Access to Justice" Reports, the concept of case management was not defined and it was used in broad and narrow senses depending on the context in which it was applied (for a statement of the objectives of case management in the broad sense, see Interim Report, p.30). To an extent, the inconsistency which resulted is perpetuated in the CPR.

It is perhaps understandable that, having stated in r.1.4(1) that the overriding duty is to be furthered by a case management system, the rules should go on to give some indication as to what is meant by "actively managing cases". Thus r.1.4(2) contains a list of what could be called case management "elements" or "objectives"; it is not exhaustive. The list is not prescriptive. It summarises objectives which are implemented in many and various ways by provisions found throughout the CPR and related practice directions. The list has no logic about it. Further, the matters stated are not at the same level of abstraction; some are quite general, others quite detailed. Rule 1.4(2) does not confer powers on the court. In this respect it may be contrasted with r.3.1(2) which lists the court's "general powers of case management". Those powers are in addition to any other *powers given to the court (including* those derived from the inher*ent jurisdiction)* and include the power "to take any other step or make any or order for the purpose of managing the case and furthering the overriding objective" (r.3.1(2)(m)). The powers listed in r.3.1(2) include powers not generally thought of as being properly described as aspects of the "management" of cases and which have long been part of English civil procedure (e.g. the powers to consolidate proceedings or to direct the separate trial of any issue). Provisions relating to appeals from "case management decisions" are found in Section I of Practice Direction (Appeals) and in para.4.4 such decisions are defined as including decisions made under rule 3.1(2) and decisions about certain other matters (e.g. disclosure).

As is explained below, the provenance for much of what is said in r.1.4(2) is a passage in the Final Report. In that report it was said (p.18) that the principal "essential element" of the recommended case management system is the procedure by which each case is allocated to an appropriate "track" and court (whether High Court or a county court). Detailed provisions relating to this element are found in Pts 26 to 29 and related practice directions. It was said, further, that other essential elements of the recommended case management system include (a) "encouraging and assisting the parties to settle cases or, at least, to agree on particular issues", (b) "identifying at an early stage the key issues which need full trial", (c) "summarily disposing of weak cases and hopeless issues", (d) "fixing and enforcing strict timetables for procedural steps leading to trial and for the trial itself", and (e) "encouraging the use of ADR". Detailed provisions reflecting these elements are found throughout the CPR and cannot be easily summarised.

In the list of case management objectives given in r.1.4(2) no mention is made of the principal essential element but the other essential elements are covered in paras (a) to (c) and (e) to (g). The remaining paragraphs in r.1.4(2) refer to other matters which may be regarded as "elements" of the case management system introduced by the CPR. However, the means by which these elements have been identified and the reasoning behind their inclusion (and the exclusion of other possible elements) is not immediately apparent. The result is that the purpose of r.1.4(2) is rendered obscure. It at least has the advantage of drawing to the attention of parties, lawyers and judges important aspects of the wholesale reforms in civil justice introduced by the CPR. Some Practice Directions speak of r.1.4 as imposing "duties" on the court.

The various aspects of case management as listed in r.1.4(2) are not mutually exclusive and if severally pursued may reach contradictory ends. In a given case, two or more may be relevant to the management of the case and the court may have difficulty in reconciling the weight to be given to each (e.g. *Rotodata Ltd*, Re, August 19, 1999, unrep. (possible conflict between encouraging parties to co-operate and resolving issues speedily)).

The court has power to strike out a statement of case (r.3.4) and power to grant summary judgment (r.24.2). In a given case, the exercise of these powers may, in the circumstances, be Draconian. The Court of Appeal has emphasised that, in discharging its duty actively to manage cases (as provided for in r.1.4 and elsewhere in the CPR) and in the exercise of its discretion, the court may impose sanctions falling short of striking out in appropriate cases (*Biguzzi v Rank Leisure Plc* [1999] 1 W.L.R. 1926, CA; see also *Asiansky Television Plc v Bayer Rosin*, December 14, 2000, unrep. (Steel J.) where the authorities on alternatives to striking out are referred to). Where the court effectively manages a case resort to the exercise of the power to strike out on the ground that a party has failed to comply with a rule, practice direction or court order (r.3.4(2)(c)) is made less likely.

A judge's responsibility in the course of properly managing cases requires him, when exercising his discretion in accordance with the overriding objective (see r.1.1), to consider the effect of his decision on civil proceedings generally; for example, its effect in deterring parties involved in other proceedings from engaging in improper conduct (*Jones v University of Warwick* [2003] EWCA Civ 151; *The Times*, February 7, 2003, CA, per Lord Woolf C.J.).

Controlling progress of case

In the common law world, the expression "case management" is used in various senses. The significance of case management procedures is that they mark a change from the traditional position under which the progress of cases was left largely in the hands of the parties. In its narrow sense, "case management" means the exercise by the court of powers given to it to enable it, and not the parties, to dictate the progress of cases at the pre-trial stage, ensuring that the practices and procedures applicable during that stage are complied with promptly and not abused. Under the CPR, the expression "case management" is used in a much wider sense. The powers given to the court go far beyond those necessary merely to ensure the avoidance of unnecessary delay and include powers to manipulate the application of pre-trial procedures **1.4.2** on a case by case basis, principally in the interest of saving costs and reducing delays. Case management in its narrow sense is encapsulated by r.1.4(2)(g) which states that active case management includes the "controlling" of "the progress of the case" by the court by "fixing timetables or otherwise".

As was the case in the RSC and CCR (and in former practice directions), many provisions in the CPR (and related practice directions) stipulate that particular steps in the proceedings must be taken within time limits. Traditionally, these time limits were not self-enforcing and, on the whole, securing compliance was regarded as a matter for the party disadvantaged or inconvenienced by the delay. The case management Practice Directions issued in 1995 marked a shift towards a court controlled approach to case progress. Under the new scheme, the court is able to monitor the progress of cases from an early stage in the proceedings and compliance with time limits stipulated in rules, practice directions and bespoke orders is not solely a matter for the parties, even where they are in agreement. The power to control case progress "by fixing timetables or otherwise" is a power which complements and supplements the time limits stipulated by rules and practice directions. Rule 28.2(1) states that, when the court allocates a case to the fast track, the court will give directions (dealing with the matters listed in r.28.3) for the management of the case and set a timetable for the steps to be taken between the giving of directions and the trial and r.29.2 has a similar effect in relation to multi-track cases. These are the most obvious of the provisions implementing the power referred to in r.1.4(2)(g). Other opportunities for the court to give case progress directions (of its own initiative if necessary), including directions laying down timetables, arise at various points in the pre-trial process; for example, after determining a summary judgment application (r.24.6(b)), after expiration of a stay to allow for settlement (r.26.4(5)), and after a defence to a Pt 20 claim is filed (r.20.13). Where a party fails to comply with a rule, practice direction or court order, including a rule etc. imposing a time limit, any sanction for that failure has effect unless the party in default applies for and obtains relief from the sanction (r.3.8(1)). Where a party is required to do something within a specified time and a consequence for failing to comply is specified, the time may not be extended by agreement between the parties (r.3.8(2)).

Note also "Dealing simultaneously with as many aspects of case as practicable" below, para.1.4.14. See also paras 23.0.9 and 23.0.13 below.

Trial directions

1.4.3 Active case management includes the court "giving directions to ensure that the trial of a case proceeds quickly and efficiently" (r.1.4(2)(l)). It is important that the time of judges available for the hearing of trials should be used as efficiently as possible. Various provisions in the CPR are designed to ensure that trials are not prolonged. Perhaps the most striking is the provision (formerly found in practice directions) that normally a witness's statement should stand as his evidence in chief (see now r.32.5(2)). Further, in cases allocated to the fast track, the expectation is that the trial will last for no longer than one day (r.26.6(6)). Obviously, the time taken to try a case can be affected by orders made before trial, for example, orders as to the number of expert witnesses, and as to the extent of disclosure of documents. Illustrations of the power of the court to give directions specifically designed to ensure that the trial of a case proceeds not only quickly but also efficiently are found in rr.28.6 and 29.8; these rules deal, respectively, with fast track and multi-track cases, and include power to give any directions for the trial, including a trial timetable. Such timetables are to be set by the court in consultation with the parties (r.39.4). Unless the trial judge otherwise directs, the trial will be conducted in accordance with any order previously made (rr.28.7 and 29.9). In certain specific contexts in the CPR and supplementing directions, express reference is made to the court's power to give directions designed to ensure that the trial of a case proceeds quickly; e.g. Practice Direction (Possession Claims), para.3.3 (court to consider what steps are needed finally to determine "as quickly as reasonably practicable" possession claim where assault and property damage threatened) (see para.55PD.6 below).

Encouraging co-operation between parties

1.4.4 Active case management includes encouraging the parties to co-operate with each other in the conduct of the proceedings (r.1.4(2)(a)). In the Interim Report it was recommended that the court should use its power over costs to encourage co-operative conduct on the part of litigants and to discourage unreasonable conduct, both before and after proceedings have been commenced (p.204, see also Final Report, p.79). These recommendations are brought into effect by rr.44.3 and 44.5 and by other provisions in the CPR. The objective is to make the court's powers as to the award of costs more effective as incentives for responsible party behaviour and more compelling as deterrents against unreasonable behaviour (see further "Cost-benefit of taking particular step" below, para.1.4.10). It may be noted that r.44.3(4) makes particular mention of the extent to which the parties followed any relevant pre-action protocol. The increased powers given to the court to order disclosure of documents or inspection of property before a claim is made (brought about by amendments to the Supreme Court Act 1981 s.33 and the County Courts Act 1984 s.52) have been introduced partly for the purpose of encouraging co-operation between the parties (Interim Report, p.151) (see further notes to rr.25.1 and 25.4). Rule 1.4(2)(a) can be regarded as a pointed illustration of the duty of the parties to help the court further the overriding objective imposed by r.1.3.

Various provisions in the CPR encourage party co-operation once proceedings have been commenced. A good illustration is provided by r.29.4 which states that the court may approve without a hearing proposals agreed by the parties for the management of proceedings on the multi-track and give directions in the terms proposed. Other illustrations include r.15.5 (agreement extending period for filing defence) and r.26.4 (agreement to request stay to allow for settlement of case), and r.35.7 (agreement on single joint expert). The efforts made by the parties to resolve their dispute is a factor to which the court should have regard in deciding the amount of costs (r.44.5(3)(a)). In *Hertsmere Primary Care Trust v Rabindra-Anandh* [2005] EWHC 320 (Ch); *The Times*, April 25, 2005, Lightman J. disapproved of a party's failure to cooperate with his opponents by his declining to respond to their request for him to explain to them the basis upon which he asserted that their offer did not comply with the provisions of Pt 36.

Identification, clarification and ordering of issues

Paragraphs (b) to (d) of r.1.4(2) go together. The court must further the overriding objective by actively managing cases. In a given case, this includes the court doing the following things in relation to the issues: (1) at an early stage in the proceedings, "identifying the issues" (para.(b)); (2) promptly classifying those issues according to whether (a) they "need full investigation and trial" or (b) they may be disposed of summarily (para.(c)); and (3) deciding "the order in which issues are to be resolved" (para.(d)). The provenance of paras (b) to (d) is a passage in the Final Report (pp.14 and 16) in which the matters mentioned therein are said to be "essential elements" of the recommendations made as to case management. These elements are made operational by their incorporation in the provisions of the CPR and related practice directions in various ways. The most obvious examples are the references in r.3.1 (The court's general powers of management) to the jurisdiction of the court to direct a separate trial of any issue and to decide the order in which issues are to be tried (paras (i) and (j) of r.3.1(2)). **1.4.5**

Before the coming into effect of the CPR, from time to time the Court of Appeal warned that the separating out of particular questions within an action to be dealt with as preliminary issues could be counter-productive. It is probably true to say that, since the coming into effect of the CPR, judges have felt under greater pressure than previously to identify and deal with preliminary issues in the hope that that procedural strategy will reduce costs and delays. In any event, the Court of Appeal has continued to warn of the risks involved, especially in complex cases; see *McLoughlin v Grovers* [2002] EWCA Civ 1743; [2002] 2 W.L.R. 1279, CA; *Robinson v St. Helens Metropolitan BC* [2002] EWCA Civ 1099; July 25, 2002, unrep., CA; *Shaker v Al-Bedrawi* [2002] EWCA Civ 1452; October 18, 2002, unrep.,CA. In *McLoughlin v Grovers, ibid.*, it was said (at para.66, per David Steel J.): (1) any order for the trial of a preliminary issue should be made by the court following a case management conference (2) only issues which are decisive or potentially decisive should be identified, (3) such issues (a) should usually be questions of law, (b) should be decided on the basis of a schedule of agreed or assumed facts, and (c) should be triable without significant delay, making full allowance for the implications of a possible appeal. The policy of identifying issues early on and, where appropriate, dealing with them summarily, is exemplified by the procedures found in Pt 14 (Admissions) for dealing with claims for specified amounts of money where defendants admit part of the claim under which judgment without trial may be given on part of a claim, perhaps at a disposal hearing (see Practice Direction (Case Management—Preliminary Stage: Allocation and Re-Allocation), para.12.8). The provenance of Pt 14 does not lie in the Access to Justice Reports but in former CCR O.9.

Early identification of issues

1.4.6 Under the case management system introduced by the CPR and related practice directions, the court is involved in the process of identifying and clarifying the issues between the parties from an early stage in the proceedings. In the years immediately preceding the coming into effect of the CPR, the involvement of the court in the early identification of issues had become a feature of the interlocutory procedure applied in certain types of proceedings.Under the CPR proceedings are started when a claim form is issued. The expression "statements of case" is used to describe what were formerly known as "pleadings". Such statements include "particulars of claim", "defence" and "reply to defence" (see Pt 16). It is important that the parties should state plainly the factual ingredients of their case so that the true nature of the dispute can be identified because, on the basis of the information given in the statement of claim and the defence, the court will allocate the case to an appropriate case management track (Pt 26). For the purpose of clarifying the issues so that the case may be allocated to an appropriate track, the court may require a party to provide further information about his case and may hold an allocation hearing. The court's concern with identifying issues does not cease once a case is allocated to a case management track but, in the interests of encouraging settlement and of minimising the burden on the court at trial, continues throughout the pre-trial process generally. The power of the court to direct, in advance of trial, a discussion between expert witnesses under r.35.12 is designed to assist, not only in the limiting by agreement of the issues for trial, but also in the early identification of the issues between the parties.

Full investigation or summary disposal of issues

1.4.7 According to r.1.4(2)(c), active case management includes deciding promptly which issues need full investigation and trial "and accordingly disposing summarily of the others". In Practice Direction (Case Management—Preliminary Stage: Allocation and Re-Allocation) (see para.26PD.1) it is explained in para.5.2 that the court's powers to make orders for the summary disposal of issues which do not need "full investigation and trial" include the power under r.3.4 to strike out a statement of case, or part of a statement of a case, and the power to give summary judgment where a claimant or defendant has no reasonable prospect of success in accordance with the provisions in Pt 24. The court may use these powers on an application or of its own initiative. The court's general powers of case management as listed in r.3.1(2) includes the power to "exclude an issue from consideration" (see r.3.1(2)(k)). If a judge thinks there is no real prospect of a claim succeeding, then he ought, when exercising his case management powers, to dismiss it summarily (*Pepin v Taylor* [2002] EWCA Civ 1522; October 10, 2002, CA, para.9).

It would seem that r.1.4(2)(c) does not grant the court a discrete power to dispose of issues summarily but merely directs attention to the court's powers of summary disposal as found elsewhere, for example, in rr.3.1(2)(k), 3.4(2) and 24.2. Certainly, a claim arguable on the pleadings needs to be decided and should not be excluded by exercise of the court's powers under r.1.4(2)(c) (or under r.3.1(2)(k)) (*Royal Brompton Hospital NHS Trust v Hammond (No.5)*, [2001] EWCA Civ 550, CA). In a case raising multiple issues, it may be unsatisfactory, given the connections between them, to dispose summarily of some and to allow others to go to trial (*Tawl v Harrods Limited* [2001] EWCA Civ 1695; November 2, 2001, unrep., CA).

The summary disposal of issues may raise questions in relation to the ECHR art.6 right of access to a court: see further para.3.4.1 below.

Order in which issues resolved

1.4.8 The court's general powers of case management as listed in r.3.1(2) includes the power to direct that part of any proceeding be dealt with as separate proceedings and to decide the order in which issues are to be tried (paras (e), (i) and (j)). These powers are familiar. When utilised they have the effect of adjusting the order in which issues are resolved. (As to trial of counterclaim, see r.20.9.) Rule 3.1(2) also states that the court may consolidate proceedings or try two or more claims on the same occasion (paras (g) and (h)). Again, these are familiar powers. They may be used to enable the resolution together of issues which otherwise would be resolved separately.

In *GKR Karate UK Ltd v Yorkshire Post Newspapers Ltd* [2000] 2 All E.R. 931, CA, the court said the judge's decision to determine issues of privilege and malice as preliminary issues at the outset of a libel trial in advance of the issue of justification was fair, sensible and economic and observed that libel cases are especially amenable to active case management for the purpose of ensuring that they were dealt with proportionately, expeditiously and fairly.

In *Worsley v Tambrands Ltd, The Times*, February 11, 2000, CA, the claim was brought under the Consumer Protection Act 1987 ss.2 and 3, and the court held that the judge erred in directing that the issue of the adequacy of packaging warnings should be tried as a preliminary issue, because the evidence on the issues of causation and the adequacy of warnings could not be separated and these issues were inextricably bound together (see *Ashmore v Corporation of Lloyd's* [1992] 1 W.L.R. 446, HL).

Generally, claims are tried by a judge sitting alone but (subject to exceptions) the court should order trial by judge and jury in the circumstances provided for by the Supreme Court Act 1981 s.69 and the County Courts Act 1984 s.66 (see Vol.2, paras 9A–256 and 9A–546). Where appropriate, in the same proceedings the court may in the exercise of powers listed in r.3.1(2) order that certain issued be tried by judge alone and others by judge and jury (*ibid.* s.69(4)); however, where it is clear that some issues could not conveniently be tried with a jury it may be more appropriate for the whole case to be tried by judge alone e.g. where questions of credibility are universally relevant (*Phillips v Commissioner of Police of the Metropolis* [2003] EWCA Civ 382; *The Times*, April 2, 2003, CA).

Helping parties to settle

Active case management includes helping the parties to settle the whole or part of **1.4.9**
the case (r.1.4(2)(f)). Two significant aims of the recommendations made in the "Access to Justice" Reports are (1) that of encouraging the resolution of disputes before they come to litigation, and (2) that of encouraging the settlement of claims commenced (Final Report, p.16). Provisions in the CPR designed to achieve the former aim include those expanding pre-litigation disclosures (r.25.1(1)(i) and (j) and rr.31.16 and 31.17) and those encouraging greater use of alternative dispute resolution procedures (see "Encouraging use of alternative dispute resolution (ADR) procedure" below). Provisions designed to achieve the latter aim include those providing for claimants' offers to settle (Pt 36) and for the summary disposal of issues so as to narrow the dispute. All of these devices are intended to divert cases from the court system or to ensure that those cases which do go through the system are disposed of as rapidly as possible (Final Report, *ibid.*).

Cost-benefits of taking particular step

Active case management includes considering whether the likely benefits of taking a **1.4.10**
particular step justify the cost of taking it (r.1.4(2)(h)). This can be regarded as an aspect of "proportionality" (see "Proportionality", para.1.3.5 above). Virtually all of the recommendations made in the "Access to Justice" Reports and implemented by the CPR are designed to tackle the problem of costs. In the Interim Report it was recommended that the court's discretion as to costs should be exercised so that parties were encouraged to conduct litigation "in a proportionate manner" and to discourage "excess" (see too Final Report, p.80). Rule 44.3 now provides that in exercising its costs discretion the court should consider the conduct of all the parties and this includes taking into account the several matters listed in r.44.3(4) (see too r.43.6). In terms, that paragraph does not repeat r.1.4(2)(h). However, it achieves a similar result by stating that the conduct of a party includes the manner in which he has pursued or defended his case or a particular allegation or issue, and whether it was reasonable for him to raise, pursue or contest a particular allegation or issue. Cases allocated to the small claims track or to the fast track are conducted according to limited procedures. Necessarily, the question whether the benefits of a particular step justified the taking of it is more likely to arise in multi-track cases. All cases on all case management tracks proceed according to a pre-trial timetable. The effect of this discipline alone is likely to discourage parties from attempting to take steps where their likely benefits do not justify the cost of taking it.

Despite the futurity apparent in the terms of r.1.4(2)(h) that provision does not in terms give the court a general power to prevent a party from taking a particular step otherwise open to him (whether it involves making an application to the court or not). However, it seems clear that the court has jurisdiction to dismiss a pre-trial application summarily on the ground that it is not an appropriate application to make because it is likely to add to the costs without any significant benefit to the conduct of the case, and is therefore contrary to the overriding objective (*Norwich Union Linked Life Assurance Ltd v Mercantile Credit Company Ltd* [2003] EWHC 3064 (Ch); December 19, 2003, unrep., (David Richards J.)). The rules as to costs constitute the principal mechanism by which parties are encouraged to conduct litigation in a proportionate manner and by which excess is discouraged and those rules take effect after the event (but, of course, their expected application may modify party conduct prospectively). However, in particular contexts the court does have specific powers clearly aimed at these ends. The best illustrations are found in the powers given to the court in Pt 31 to regulate the disclosure of documents. Further, to an extent, a party can protect himself from demands made on him by his opponent as to disclosure on the grounds that they make expectations of him which are onerous and which are not justified in the circumstances of the case (see rr.31.3(2) and 31.7(3)).

Where the "particular step" taken by a party consists of an application to the court and that application fails the costs of the application would normally be awarded against that party. Where the application was unjustified the court may assess those costs and order them to be paid forthwith.

Encouraging use of alternative dispute resolution (ADR) procedure

1.4.11 The furthering of the overriding objective (of enabling the court to deal with cases justly) by "actively managing cases", includes encouraging the parties to use an alternative dispute resolution (ADR) procedure "if the court considers that appropriate" and facilitating the use of such procedure (r.1.4(2)(e)) (see Interim Report, pp.136 et seq.). For detailed commentary on the effect of this aspect of the overriding objective and provisions found elsewhere in the CPR, and in pre-action protocols and court guides, see Vol.2 Sect.14 (Alternative Dispute Resolution).

Attendance at court

1.4.12 The furthering of the overriding objective (of enabling the court to deal with cases justly) by "actively managing cases", includes "dealing with the case without the parties needing to attend court"(r.1.4(1)(j)). Obviously, it is to the advantage of the court and of the parties and their legal advisers if attendances at court can be minimised. Parties and their legal representatives (and witnesses if any) are expected to attend trials and other hearings relating to the proceedings in which they are involved. However, in the CPR in a variety of circumstances express provision is made permitting the court to deal with certain matters without a hearing, thus accomplishing the objective stated in r.1.4(1)(j); examples are, r.23.8, r.29.4, and r.40.6(6). The court may decide a claim for judicial review without a hearing where all the parties agree (r.54.18). Further, CPR provisions expressly state that certain applications relating to the enforcement of judgments and orders should or may be dealt with without a hearing (e.g. r.70.5(7), r.71.2(4), r.72.4(1) and r.73.4(1)).

Under Pt 55 (Possession Claims), after considering a claim for a possession order and the defence to it, unless satisfied as to certain matters, the court should make the order requested without requiring the attendance of the parties (r.55.17). In paras 10.1 and 10.2 of Practice Direction (Arbitration), supplementing CPR Pt 62, examples are given of decisions that the court is likely to make without a hearing in arbitration claims.

Another way in which parties, representatives and witnesses may be relieved of the requirement to attend court for hearings is where technology is used to enable them to participate from a distance; see "Use of technology" below.

Use of technology

1.4.13 The furthering of the overriding objective (of enabling the court to deal with cases justly) by "actively managing cases", includes "making use of technology" (r.1.4(1)(k)). This particular aspect of active case management is rather different to the other aspects listed in r.1.4(1). Presumably what is intended is that judges and parties and their representatives should take advantage of communication and other technologies to the extent that they are available. For a detailed account of this subject, with illustrations and references to relevant rules, practice directions and cases, see Vol.2 Sect.11 (The Overriding Objective), subs.D.6 (para.11–13).

Dealing simultaneously with as many aspects of case as practicable

See also "Order in which issues resolved" (para.1.4.8 above). **1.4.14**

The furthering of the overriding objective (of enabling the court to deal with cases justly) by "actively managing cases", includes "dealing with as many aspects of the case as is practicable on the same occasion" (r.1.4(1)(i)). During the pre-trial stages of cases the court stands ready to react to the needs of the parties by making necessary orders and directions. Further, under the case management system introduced by the CPR and related practice directions, the court is able to intervene of its own initiative in the pre-trial development and progress of cases. Usually, when the court reacts or intervenes it will be for a particular purpose; for example, to deal with an application made by one party and an application made by his opponent in response. Clearly, costs and delays would be increased and court resources wasted if, in dealing with a case for one purpose (whether by a hearing or otherwise), the court did not deal with other matters which had arisen or were looming and which required or justified the court's attention. Obviously, it is important that rules of court or practice directions should not be drafted in a way which prevents the court from dealing with multiple pre-trial issues on the same occasion. Further, it is important that parties and judges should not be encouraged to deal (perhaps for reasons of their own convenience only) with several "aspects" of a case on successive "occasions" where it would be practicable to deal with them on one "occasion". This aspect of case management is not new. However, it gains new significance now that the court has greater powers than heretofore to intervene in cases of its own initiative. Various provisions in the CPR and supplementing practice directionsillustrate the policy stated in r.1.4(2)(i) in operation. Examples include those rules which state that, when dealing with particular pre-trial matters, the court may, in addition, give directions as to the further progress of the case (see "Controlling progress of case", para.1.4.2 above and "Hearing of application", para.23.0.9 below). An example of the policy in operation is provided by the general rule that an application by a claimant to continue an order for an interim injunction made without notice, and an application by the defendant to discharge the injunction forthwith on the ground of material non-disclosure, should be heard together, see para.25.3.5 below. See further paras 1.4.15, 3.3.2, 23.0.9, 23.0.14, 23.0.15 and 23.8.1.

Final determination and avoidance of multiplicity of proceedings

The Supreme Court Act 1981 s.49(2) provides (in part) that, subject to the provi- **1.4.15**
sions of that Act itself or any other enactment, every court shall so exercise its jurisdiction in every cause or matter before it so as to secure that (a) as far as possible, all matters in dispute between the parties are completely and finally determined, and (b) as far as possible, all multiplicity of legal proceedings with respect to any of those matters is avoided. For an explanation of this provision and its relationship to rules of court, see Vol.2, paras 9A–175 *et seq.* The Court of Appeal has said that, as a general rule of public policy, a claimant has to bring forward his entire case in a single action and, where he has a choice of remedies, elect which remedy to pursue (*De Crittenden v Bayliss (Deceased)* [2005] EWCA Civ 1425; October 13, 2005, unrep.,CA, where it was held that a second action seeking a proprietary remedy in connection with a claim for which damages had been awarded and paid was an abuse of process). Clearly, in furthering the overriding objective by actively managing cases in the manner provided for in r.1.4, and by exercising its general powers of management referred to in r.3.1, a court may, in a variety of ways, seek to ensure that, as far as possible, all matters in dispute are completely and finally determined, and that multiplicity of legal proceedings is avoided. The principle that a multiplicity of proceedings should be avoided underlies a number of the provisions found in the Brussels Convention (see further *Knauf UK GmbH v British Gypsum Ltd* [2001] EWCA Civ 1570; [2002] 1 W.L.R. 907, CA). Further, the doctrine that a cause of action is "merged" in a judgment upon it and ceases to have an independent existence, is underpinned by the principle that a multiplicity of proceedings should be avoided (as well as principles of double jeopardy, and (possibly) of finality of judgment) and can become relevant in various procedural contexts, in particular in applications under CPR Pt 13 to set aside default judgments (*Messer Griesheim GmbH v Goyal* [2006] EWHC 79 (Comm); February 7, 2006, unrep. (Langley J.)).

The established rule (now stated in r.7.3) that a claimant may use a single claim form to start all claims which can be conveniently disposed of in the same proceedings helps to ensure that a multiplicity of proceedings is avoided. In the past, difficulties could arise where a claimant wished to couple with a claim for judicial review, a claim for other forms of relief. In such cases the claimant faced the prospect of having to bring separate claims in different courts for complete relief. However, these problems are now largely avoided by the provisions of CPR Pt 54 (see *R. (Barron) v Surrey County Council* [2002] EWCA Civ 713; May 7, 2002, unrep., CA; *R. (Heather) v Leonard Cheshire Council Foundation* [2002] EWCA Civ 366; [2002] 2 All E.R. 936, CA). The avoidance of a multiplicity of proceedings is also enhanced by the court's powers to strike out proceedings as an abuse of process in circumstances where the issues sought to be raised might have been dealt with in earlier proceedings. The principal authority on this power is now *Johnson v Gore Wood & Co (No.1)* [2002] 2 A.C. 1, HL. (In the Court of Appeal proceedings in this case, Ward L.J. explained that "*Henderson v Henderson* abuse of process" as now understood had become "an increasingly prominent weapon in the arsenal of court control". In *Nikken Kosakusho Works v Nikken Kosakusho (UK) Limited* [2005] EWCA Civ 906, June 29, 2005, unrep., CA, in refusing to allow (because it would in effect involve a second trial) a post-trial pleading amendment designed to save a patent from invalidity, the Court of Appeal said (at para.15) that *Henderson v Henderson* "is fully reinforced by the new rules".) See further para.3.4.3 and Vol.2 para.9A–175 below.

For the avoidance of a multiplicity of interlocutory applications within proceedings, see para.1.4.14 above and paras 3.3.1, 23.0.9, 23.0.14, 23.0.15, 23.8.1 and 25.1.4.

For procedure for avoiding multiplicity of claims under the Landlord and Tenant Act 1954 ss.24(1) and 29(2), see Practice Direction (Landlord and Tenant Claims and Miscellaneous Provisions About Land), para.3.2 (para.56PD.4 below).

Applications for writ of habeas corpus are rare (see CPR Sch.1 RSC Ord.54), but are likely to be repeated if refused. The Administration of Justice Act s.14 (Procedure for application for habeas corpus) provides that, where such an application has been made in respect of any person, no such application shall again be made on the same grounds "unless fresh evidence is adduced in support of the application".

PART 2

APPLICATION AND INTERPRETATION OF THE RULES

Contents 2.0.1

Editorial note

The rules in this Part contain provisions similar to those formerly found in RSC O.1 and O.3 and CCR O.1. The table in r.2.1 was amended by the Civil Procedure (Amendment) Rules 1999 (SI 1999/1008), the Civil Procedure (Amendment No.2) Rules 2003 (SI 2003/1242) and the Civil Procedure (Amendment) Rules 2007 (SI 2007/2204). Rule 2.3(1) was amended by the Civil Procedure (Amendment No.4) Rules 2000 (SI 2000/2092) and the Civil Procedure (Amendment No.5) Rules 2001 (SI 2001/4015). 2.0.2

Part 2 is supplemented by Practice Direction (Court Offices) (see para.2PD.1). Paras 2.1, 3.2 and 3.3 of this Practice Direction deal with court office opening hours and are relevant to r.2.8 (Time); the provenance of these provisions is explained in para.2.8.4 below. Other provisions are not related to any of the rules in Pt 2. Thus, para.1 replaces RSC O.63, r.1 (Distribution of business in the Central Office), para.2.2 replaces RSC O.63, r.3 (Practice Master) and r.3.1 replaces CCR O.2, r.1 (County courts to have offices).

Part 2 is also supplemented by Practice Direction (Allocation of Cases to Levels of Judiciary) (see para.2BPD.1 below); for explanation, see notes following r.2.4 below. This Practice Direction has been amended on a number of occasions since it was first published in March 2000.

Application of the Rules[1]

2.1—(1) Subject to paragraph (2), these Rules apply to all proceedings in— 2.1

(a) county courts;

(b) the High Court; and

(c) the Civil Division of the Court of Appeal.

(2) These Rules do not apply to proceedings of the kinds specified in the first column of the following table (proceedings for which

[1] Amended by the Civil Procedure (Amendment No.2) Rules 2003 (SI 2003/1242), the Civil Procedure (Amendment No.4) Rules 2005 (SI 2005/3515) and the Civil Procedure (Amendment) Rules 2007 (SI 2007/2204).

rules may be made under the enactments specified in the second column) except to the extent that they are applied to those proceedings by another enactment—

	Proceedings	Enactments
1.	**Insolvency proceedings**	**Insolvency Act 1986 ss.411 and 412**[1]
2.	**Non-contentious or common form probate proceedings**	**Supreme Court Act 1981, s.127**[2]
3.	**Proceedings in the High Court when acting as a Prize Court**	**Prize Courts Act 1894, s.3**[3]
4.	**Proceedings before the Court of Protection**	**Mental Capacity Act 2005, s.51**[4]
5.	**Family proceedings**	**Matrimonial and Family Proceedings Act 1984, s.40**[5]
6.	**Adoption proceedings**	**Adoption Act 1976, s.66**[6] **or Adoption and Children Act 2002, s.141(c)**[7]
7.	**Election petitions in the High Court**	**Representation of the People Act 1983, s.182**[8]

General note on application of rules (r.2.1)

2.1.1 The Civil Procedure Rules 1998 (CPR) are made under the Civil Procedure Act 1997 s.1 (see Vol.2, para.9A–738) and, in accordance with that provision, are to govern "the practice and procedure to be followed" in the courts mentioned in para.(1). Accordingly, they are "rules of court" as defined by the Interpretation Act 1978 s.5, Sch.1. In r.1.1(1) they are described as "a new procedural code". Previously, proceedings in county courts were governed by the County Court Rules and in the High Court and Court of Appeal (Civil Division) by the Rules of the Supreme Court (RSC). The CPR constitute a single set of rules replacing the RSC and the CCR. The CPR contain much that is new (implementing recommendations made in the Access to Justice Reports) but also much that is the same as that formerly found in the RSC and the CCR. Most of what is new is found in Pts 1 to 49. The rules found in the Schedules (see Pt 50) incorporate in the CPR rules formerly found in the RSC and CCR (see, respectively, Schs 1 and 2). Parts 1 to 50 came into effect in April 1999. Parts 52 *et seq* were added subsequently. The CPR are divided, not into Orders, but into Parts. A number of the Parts are supplemented by Practice Directions.

In terms, the RSC and CCR have not been repealed. To an extent they remain relevant to civil proceedings in the High Court and the county courts beyond the date when the CPR came into force (see Pt 51 Transitional Arrangements).

Subject to the exceptions mentioned in para.(2) of r.2.1, the CPR apply to "all proceedings" in county courts, the High Court, and the Court of Appeal (Civil Division). Therefore, except where the rules provide otherwise, the "general powers of

1 1986 c.45.
2 1981 c.54.
3 1894 c.39.
4 2005 c.9
5 *1984* c.*42*. Section 40 was amended by the Courts and Legal Services Act 1990 (c.41), Sch.18,, para.50.
6 1976 c.36.
7 2002 c.38.
8 1983 c.2.

management" listed in r.3.1 (the list is not exhaustive) are enjoyed by each and every one of those courts (*Contract Facilities Ltd v Estate of Rees (Application to Strike Out)* [2003] EWCA Civ 1105; July 24, 2003, unrep., CA).

Specialist proceedings

In r.49(1) it is said that the CPR shall apply to "specialist proceedings" subject to the provisions of the relevant practice direction which applies to those proceedings. In this context, "specialist proceedings" means the proceedings listed in r.49(2). In the CPR as originally enacted, several varieties of proceedings were listed in r.49(2). In the years since, most of the practice directions relating to "specialist proceedings" have been incorporated in the CPR as discrete Parts. For explanation, see para.49.0.1 below, and Vol.2 Sect.12 (CPR: Application, Amendments and Interpretation), subss.C.2 and D.2 (paras 12–16 and 12–30.) For distinction between "specialist proceedings" and "special lists", see para.2.3.19 below. **2.1.2**

Proceedings to which CPR do not apply

Proceedings of the type referred to in the first column of the Table in r.2.1(2) may be taken either in the High Court or a county court (sometimes exclusively one or the other) and in the Court of Appeal. Such proceedings may be subject to rules of court made under the enactments referred to in the second column (see further below). **2.1.3**

Paragraph (2) states that the CPR "do not apply to proceedings of the kinds specified in the first column" of the Table, except to the extent that they are applied "by another enactment". This formulation follows that formerly found in RSC O.2, r.2 (*cf.* CCR O.1, r.2).

For detailed commentary on enactments applying the CPR (at least to some extent) to proceedings referred to in r.2.1, viz., insolvency, probate, family, adoption and election petition proceedings, and to proceedings in the Prize Court, the Court of Protection and the Lands Tribunal, see Vol.2 Sect.12 (CPR: Application, Amendments and Interpretation), subs.B.3 (para.12–5).

Proceedings to which CPR apply with necessary modifications

The CPR apply "with necessary modifications" to European order for payment applications, and to claims under the European small claims procedure (see Vol.2 Section 12 (CPR: Application, Amendment and Interpretation), subs.B.3 (para.12–14.1). **2.1.4**

The glossary

2.2—(1) The glossary at the end of these Rules is a guide to the meaning of certain legal expressions used in the Rules, but is not to be taken as giving those expressions any meaning in the Rules which they do not have in the law generally. **2.2**

(2) Subject to paragraph (3), words in these Rules which are included in the glossary are followed by^{GL}.

(3) The words "counterclaim", "damages", "practice form" and "service", which appear frequently in the Rules, are included in the glossary but are not followed by^{GL}.

Note

The Glossary is printed below at G1.1. For commentary on the Glossary as an aid to see Vol.2 Section 12 (CPR: Application, Amendments and Interpretation), subs.G.5 (para.12–47). **2.2.1**

Interpretation[1]

2.3—(1) In these Rules— **2.3**

[1] Amended by the Civil Procedure (Amendment No.4) Rules 2000 (SI 2000/2092), the Civil Procedure (Amendment No.5) Rules 2001 (SI 2001/4015), Civil Procedure (Amendment) Rules 2007 (SI 2007/2204) and the Civil Procedure (Amendment) Rules 2008 (SI 2008/2178).

"child" has the meaning given by rule 21.1(2);

"civil restraint order" means an order restraining a party—

- **(a) from making any further applications in current proceedings (a limited civil restraint order);**
- **(b) from issuing certain claims or making certain applications in specified courts (an extended civil restraint order); or**
- **(c) from issuing any claim or making any application in specified courts (a general civil restraint order).**

"claim for personal injuries" means proceedings in which there is a claim for damages in respect of personal injuries to the claimant or any other person or in respect of a person's death, and "personal injuries" includes any disease and any impairment of a person's physical or mental condition;

"claimant" means a person who makes a claim;

"CCR" is to be interpreted in accordance with Part 50;

"court officer" means a member of the court staff;

"defendant" means a person against whom a claim is made;

"defendant's home court" means—

- **(a) if the claim is proceeding in a county court, the county court for the district in which the defendant resides or carries on business; and**
- **(b) if the claim is proceeding in the High Court, the district registry for the district in which the defendant resides or carries on business or, where there is no such district registry, the Royal Courts of Justice;**

(Rule 6.23 provides for a party to give an address for service.)

"filing", in relation to a document, means delivering it, by post or otherwise, to the court office;

"judge" means, unless the context otherwise requires, a judge, Master or district judge or a person authorised to act as such;

"jurisdiction" means, unless the context requires otherwise, England and Wales and any part of the territorial waters of the United Kingdom adjoining England and Wales;

"legal representative" means a barrister or a solicitor, solicitor's employee or other authorised litigator (as defined in the Courts and Legal Services Act 1990) [1] who has been instructed to act for a party in relation to a claim;

"litigation friend" has the meaning given by Part 21;

"protected party" has the meaning given by rule 21.1(2);

"RSC" is to be interpreted in accordance with Part 50;

"statement of case"—

- **(a) means a claim form, particulars of claim where these are not included in a claim form, defence, Part 20 claim, or reply to defence; and**
- **(b) includes any further information given in relation to them voluntarily or by court order under rule 18.1;**

"statement of value" is to be interpreted in accordance with rule 16.3;

[1] 1990 c.41.

"summary judgment" is to be interpreted in accordance with Part 24.

(2) A reference to a "specialist list" is a reference to a list[GL] that has been designated as such by a rule or practice direction.

(3) Where the context requires, a reference to "the court" means a reference to a particular county court, a district registry, or the Royal Courts of Justice.

Effect of rule

This rule is of general application. Some particular Parts in the CPR have their own "local" interpretation provisions, see further Vol.2 Sect.12 (CPR:Application, Amendments and Interpretation), subs.G.5 (para.12–47). **2.3.1**

Paragraph (1) of this rule contains a list of particular words and expressions used in the CPR for which the draftsman has thought it either necessary or helpful to provide specific meanings. For commentary on these words and expressions, see para.2.3.3 et seq. below.

For commentary on para.(2), see para.2.3.14 below.

Paragraph (3) recognises that rules of court may have to use the expression "the court" in more than one sense; for commentary see para.2.3.11 below and note also commentary following r.2.4 (Power of judge etc to perform functions of court).

For detailed commentary on the construction and interpretation of provisions in the CPR, see Vol.2 Sect.12 (CPR: Application, Amendments and Interpretation), subs.G (para.12–43). That commentary deals with the following matters:

1. The purposive method of interpretation
2. The Access to Justice Reports as aids to interpretation
3. Interpretation to give effect to overriding objective
4. Interpretation Act 1978
5. Meaning of particular words and expressions—Glossary (CPR rr.2.2 and 2.3)
6. Practice directions as aids to interpretation
7. Court Guides
8. Cross-references as aids to interpretation
9. CPR check-lists and judge-made check-lists
10. Case law as aid to construction
11. Doctrine of precedent and restrictions on citation
12. The significance of the CPR as "a new procedural code"
13. Reliance on pre-CPR authorities
14. Human Rights Act 1998 and the CPR
15. European Law and the CPR

Interpretation of Rules—restriction on citation of authorities

When it comes to the citation of previous authorities (in skeleton arguments and legal submissions), whether of binding or persuasive authority, and whether on procedural or substantive issues, *Practice Direction (Citation of Authorities)* [2001] 1 W.L.R. 1001, must be borne in mind. Paras 6.1 and 6.2 of this Practice Direction provide that (1) judgments given on applications attended by one party only, (2) applications for permission to appeal, and (3) decisions given on applications that only decide that the application is arguable, may not in future be cited before any court "unless it clearly indicates that it purports to establish a new principle or to extend the present law". To be citable, decisions rendered after April 9, 2001, must have an *express statement* to that effect. Further, county court cases may not be cited in any court unless (1) cited in order to illustrate the conventional measure of damages in a personal injury case, or (2) cited in a county court in order to demonstrate current authority at that level on an issue in respect of which no decision at a higher level of authority is available. For further information on the effect of these provisions as demonstrated in modern cases, see Vol.2 Sect.12 (CPR: Application, Amendments and Interpretation), subs.G.11(b) (para.12–55). **2.3.2**

Words and expressions defined in r.2.3(1)

"child" —The words "child", "infant" and "minor" have been used to describe a **2.3.3**

person who has not attained the age of 18 years (Family Law Reform Act 1969 ss.1(1) and 1(2). Since the enactment of the Children Act 1989, in the drafting of legislation "child" appears to be the preferred word and is used throughout the CPR (see particularly Pt 21). By the Court Funds (Amendment) Rules 2007 (SI 2007/729), "minor" was changed to "child" throughout the Court Funds Rules 1987.

2.3.4 *"civil restraint order"* —This definition was inserted in r.2.3(1) when r.3.11 (Power of court to make civil restraint orders) and r.23.12 (Dismissal of totally without merit application) were added to the CPR, and rr.3.3, 3.4 and 52.10 were amended, by the Civil Procedure (Amendment No.2) Rules 2004 (SI 2004/2072), with effect from October 1, 2004. These amendments put into rule form the procedure outlined by the Court of Appeal in *Bhamjee v Forsdick (Practice Note)* [2003] EWCA Civ 1113; [2004] 1 W.L.R. 88, CA, and amplified in *Mahajan v Department of Constitutional Affairs* [2004] EWCA Civ 96, June 30, 2004, unrep., CA. See further the commentary to Pt 3.

2.3.5 *"claim for personal injuries"* —Rule 2.3(1) states that, in the CPR, "claim for personal injuries" means proceedings in which there is a claim for damages (1) "in respect of personal injuries" (a) to the claimant or (b) any other person (see further below), or (2) "in respect of a person's death". The expression "personal injuries" is further defined and "includes any disease and any impairment of a person's physical or mental condition" (see further below). These definitions follow those given in RSC O.1, r.4(1). Proceedings raising claims for personal injuries (as defined) form a significant proportion of the courts' caseloads and, for case management purposes, are subject to special rules of practice and procedure in a number of respects.

Claims for personal injuries are referred to at various places in the CPR (see, e.g. r.16.3(3) (statement of value in claim form), r.19.5(4) (addition or substitution of parties after limitation period) and r.26.6(1)(a) and (2) (allocation of claims to small claims track)). As is explained below, some of the CPR provisions making particular reference to personal injury claims exist for the purpose of carrying into effect statutory schemes wherein the nature of such claims is affected by provisions in the primary legislation (with case law glosses) setting up the schemes (e.g. r.41.1 (provisional damages)). Other CPR provisions, though making no reference at all to personal injury claims may be affected in their application to particular circumstances by primary legislation definitions (e.g. r.19.5 (adding or substituting parties after the end of a relevant limitation period)). Yet other CPR provisions are, in this respect, free-standing and have no statutory scheme provenance (e.g. r.16.3 (statement of value of claim to be included in claim form) and r.26.6 (scope of each track)). References to claims for personal injuries are also found in several practice directions supplementing CPR Parts.

A "claim for personal injuries" includes proceedings in which a claim for damages is made in respect of personal injuries, not to the claimant, but to "any other person". This follows the definition given in the Limitation Act 1980 s.11 (special time limit for actions in respect of personal injuries). For an illustration of such a claim, see *Howe v David Brown Tractors (Retail) Ltd* [1991] 4 All E.R. 30, CA, at 42, per Nicholls L.J.

A "claim for personal injuries" includes proceedings in which a claims for damages is made "in respect of a person's death". It would seem that what is meant here is an action under the Fatal Accidents Act 1976 (see Limitation Act 1980 s.12, *cf.* Limitation Act 1963 s.3(2)).

The expression "personal injuries" includes, not only personal injuries in the strict sense, but also "any disease and any impairment of a person's physical or mental condition". In this respect the definition follows important statutory provisions of long-standing (e.g. the Law Reform (Miscellaneous Provisions) Act 1934 s.3 (as amended) (interest on damages), the Law Reform (Personal Injury) Act 1948 ss.2 and 3 (measure of damages), the Supreme Court Act 1981 s.35(5) and s.35A(7), the County Courts Act 1984 s.54(5) and the Limitation Act 1980 s.38(1)).

The Supreme Court Act 1981 s.35A states that, subject to rules of court, in proceedings before the High Court for damages for personal injuries or death which exceed £200, simple interest (at such rate as the court thinks fit or as rules of court may provide) shall be included in any sum for which judgment is given unless the court is satisfied that there are special reasons to the contrary. In s.35A(7) "personal injuries" is defined and, as in r.2.3(1), "includes any disease and any impairment of a person's physical or mental condition" (see Vol.2, para.9A–122).

The Supreme Court Act 1981 s.32A and the County Courts Act 1984 s.51 give the court jurisdiction, in accordance with rules of court, to make orders for provisional damages, "in an action for personal injuries", and it is expressly provided (see s.35(5) and s.51(5)) that in these sections (replicating the definition in r.2.3(1)) "personal injuries" includes "any disease and any impairment of a person's physical or mental condition" (see Vol.2, paras 9A–107 and 9A–497). The rules of court are found in CPR Pt 41. In r.41.1(2)(c), "award of provisional damages" is defined as meaning "an award of damages for personal injuries".

The Supreme Court Act 1981 s.32 and the County Courts Act 1984 s.50 give the court jurisdiction, in accordance with rules of court, to make orders for interim payments (see Vol.2, paras 9A–103 and 9A–494). The rules of court are found in CPR rr.25.6 to 25.9. Until it was amended by the Civil Procedure (Amendment No.4) Rules 2004 (SI 2004/3419), r.25.7 imposed certain special requirements where an interim payment order was made "in a claim for personal injury" That statutory instrument amended r.25.7 in respect of the categories of defendant against whom an interim payment may be made, with the result that special reference to personal injury claims was no longer required.

According to the definition given in r.2.3(1), the claim for damages must be "in respect of" personal injuries. Guidance as to what is meant by this "in respect of" in this context may perhaps be gained from cases on statutory provisions containing this phrase; in particular, the Limitation Act 1980 s.11. Section 2 of the 1980 Act provides that actions founded on tort shall not be brought after the expiration of six years from the date on which the cause of action accrued (or, in the case of a child, from the date of his majority, see s.28). However, s.11 provides that certain actions for damages, including actions where the damages claimed "consist of or include damages in respect of personal injuries to the plaintiff or any other person", are subject to a special time limit of three years from (1) the date on which the cause of action accrued, or (2) the date of knowledge (if later) of the person injured (see Vol.2, para.8–23). Section 38 provides (as does r.2.3(1)) that "personal injuries" includes "any disease and any impairment of a person's physical or mental condition" (see Vol.2, para.8–119). Section 14 defines the date of knowledge. Section 33 gives the court a discretionary power to disapply the three year time limit imposed by s.11. The effect of s.14 and s.33 is to make it possible for the court to order that a claimant should be permitted to continue with a claim for damages "in respect of personal injuries", not only after the three year time limit (imposed by s.11) has expired, but perhaps also after the six year time limit (imposed by s.2) has expired. Not surprisingly, applications by claimants for orders of these types are commonplace and in some cases the defence argument has been that the claimant's claim is not a claim for damages "in respect of personal injuries" and, therefore, the claim is statute barred. This statutory scheme has generated much elaborate case law. Generally, the court's have been sympathetic to claimants with the result that the statutory phrase "in respect of personal injuries" has been given a generous construction. In particular, the phrase "any impairment of a person's ...mental condition" has been interpreted broadly, with the result that claimants have succeeded even in cases where they have not alleged that they suffered a recognisable psychiatric injury (see, e.g. *Phelps v Hillingdon LBC* [2001] 2 A.C. 619, HL, as explained in *Robinson v St. Helens MBC* [2002] EWCA Civ 1099; July 25, 2002, unrep., CA). The question which arises is whether the broad construction given by the courts in the context of the Limitation Act 1980 applies where the phrase arises in other contexts, in particular, those contexts in the CPR where the definition of "claim for personal injuries" given in r.2.3(1) (which includes "impairment of mental condition") applies.Limitation problems can arise where new claims are brought in pending actions. In the circumstances provided for by s.35 of the 1980 Act (see Vol.2, para.8–102+), a new claim apparently brought out of time will not be statute barred. Rules of court supporting s.35 are found in CPR r.17.4 (Amendments to statements of case after the end of the relevant limitation period). This statutory scheme also has generated much elaborate case law (lamented by Robert Walker L.J. in *Smith v Henniker-Major & Co* [2002] EWCA Civ 762; July 22, 2002, CA). On an application under r.17.4, circumstances can arise where the court, for the purposes of fixing the relevant limitation period, is required to investigate the question whether the claimant's claim is a "claim for personal injuries". In that situation, the constructions given by the courts to the 1980 Act provisions referred to above would govern.

Before the CPR came into effect, the Supreme Court Act 1981 s.33 (Powers of High Court exercisable before commencement of action) and s.34 (Power of High Court to order disclosure of documents, inspection of property, etc.), and the comparable provisions in the County Courts Act 1984 (viz., ss.52 and 53), were confined in their applications to proceedings where claims were likely to be made, or were made, "in respect of personal injuries to a person, or in respect of a person's death", and the meaning of a claim "in respect of personal injuries" in the context of those statutory provisions had fallen for authoritative determination in several cases (e.g. *Paterson v Chadwick* [1974] 1 W.L.R. 890). With the coming into effect of the CPR, these statutory provisions, and the rules of court implementing them, were no longer confined to personal injury and wrongful death proceedings, and so courts and practitioners were relieved of the difficulty of determining in these contexts what is meant by "a claim in respect of personal injuries".

2.3.6 *"claimant" "defendant"*—Whereas previously proceedings were started by the court issuing a writ or a summons (or some other form of originating process) under the CPR proceedings are started by the court issuing a "claim" in the prescribed form (Final Report, p.116). A person who makes a claim is referred to in these rules as a "claimant" and the person against whom a claim is made as a "defendant" (see r.7.2). Where a claim form is validly served on one defendant (D1), but service of the claim form on a person named as second defendant (D2) has been set aside, a contribution notice whereby D1 makes a Pt 20 claim against D2 under r.20.6 (Defendant's claim for contribution from co-defendant) is invalid and should be set aside, because D2, not being a person "against whom a claim is made" within r.2.3, is not "another defendant" within r.20.6 (*Knauf UK GmbH v British Gypsum Ltd* [2002] EWHC 739 (Comm); [2002] 2 Lloyd's Rep. 416, David Steel J.). Part 23 contains general rules about applications for court orders. An application is made by an "application notice" against a "respondent". Both of these terms are defined in r.23.1. By necessary implication, an application is made by an "applicant", but that term is not defined in Pt 23.

2.3.7 *"court officer"*—See r.2.5 and notes thereto.

2.3.8 *"defendant's home court"*—The concept of the "home court" was used in the CCR (see CCR O.1, rr.3 and 13) and is carried forward into the CPR with modifications. References to "the defendant's home court" are found in Pt 14 (Admissions) (rr.14.12 and 14.13) and in CCR O.22, r.10 (Variation of payment), a CCR provision which survives in Sch.2 of the CPR. See also r.13.4 (Application to set aside or vary judgment procedure), where the definition of "defendant's home court" is varied slightly (by r.13.4(1A)).

2.3.9 *"filing"*—In the CPR and supplementing practice directions, provisions dealing with the circumstances under which a party or non-party may be permitted or required to deliver documents to the court, whether documents in the form of process (e.g. claim form, applications notices), pleadings (statements of case), evidence, notices or requests etc., are many and various. Many, but by no means all, of the provisions expressly or impliedly permitting or requiring such delivery describe the action by uses of words based on the verb "to file" ("file and serve" is a common formulation). Sometimes the place at which the document is to be delivered is expressly stated, sometimes not. In r.2.3(1) it is stated that, in the CPR, "filing", in relation to a document, means "delivering it by post, or otherwise, to the court office". This definition has the merit of making it unnecessary to include, in CPR provisions requiring or permitting filing, specific references to the fact that the document should be delivered to the court office; although some rules and practice directions have to go to the length of making it clear that filing has to be at the "relevant" or "appropriate" court; e.g. r.47.4(1) (Venue for detailed assessment proceedings), and Practice Direction (Landlord and Tenant Claims and Miscellaneous Provisions About Land), para.13.2 (see para.56PD.30 below), Practice Direction (Appeals), para.15.1 (filing of documents at Civil Appeals Registry) (see para.52PD.51 below). Under CCR O.2, r.4, "filing" was given a different interpretation to that found in r.2.3(1). In the RSC there was no comparable provision, though RSC O.1, r.4(3), which was not brought into the CPR, referred to "lodging", not for the purpose of explaining what "lodging" meant, but for the purpose of explaining that any reference to "acknowledging service of a document" or "giving notice of intention to defend" meant lodging in a court office a document having those effects (see now r.9.2). Practice Direction (Court Documents), para.5.4 states that, where the court orders any document "to be lodged in court" the document must, unless otherwise directed, be deposited in the office of that court (see para.5PD.6 below). The word "lodge" is still used extensively in rules relating to probate proceedings (e.g. r.57.5). CPR r.5.5 paves the way for a practice direction permitting documents, not only "to be filed", but also "to be sent" to the court, by electronic means, suggesting that there is a distinction between delivery by "filing" and delivery by "sending". Provisions in Practice Direction (Electronic Communication and Filing of Documents) (supplementing CPR, r.5.5) enable parties to claims in specified courts to communicate with the court by email and to file certain documents either by email or by accessing an online forms service. It is expressly provided that a document that is required by a rule of practice direction to be filed at court is not filed when it is sent to the judge by email (para.8.9). The hours in which court offices are open to the public are restricted (Practice Direction (Court Offices), para.2.1(2), see para.2PD.3). A document delivered at a court office after closing time on a particular day by posting through the court office letter box is filed on that day (*Van Aken v London Borough of Camden* [2002] EWCA Civ 1724; October 11, 2002, unrep., CA).

Special provisions relating to the filing of an application for a European order for payment, and for other documents in EOP proceedings, are found in Practice Direction—European Order for Payment and European Small Claims Procedures at respectively paras 2.1(2) and 3 (see para.78PD.2 below). Special provisions relating to the filing of a European small claims procedure claim form, and for other documents in ESCP proceedings, are found in the same practice direction at respectively paras 11 and 14 (see para.78PD.11 below).

"statement of value" —A claimant claiming an unspecified amount of money must include on the claim form a certificate, known as a "statement of value", stating that he believes that there is good reason for him to expect to recover amounts falling in particular bands (r.16.3). The purpose of the statement is to facilitate the allocation of the claim to an appropriate case management track. **2.3.10**

"the court" —Rule 2.3(3) states that, where in these rules the context requires, a reference to "the court" means a reference to a particular county court, a district registry, or the Royal Courts of Justice. On the face of it, this seems a curious provision. However, in certain contexts in the CPR it is convenient; see, e.g. r.23.2 (Where to make an application). (It provides good illustration of the difficulties inherent in marrying together rules of court applicable to a superior court with those applicable to inferior courts.) The CPR apply to all proceedings in county courts, in the High Court and in the Civil Division of the Court of Appeal (r.2.1(1)). The High Court is a superior court and, therefore, notionally, there is one High Court and, though it is based at the RCJ in London, its business (and the business of the Court of Appeal) may be conducted at "any place in England and Wales" (Supreme Court Act 1981 ss.57 and 67). The principal registry of the High Court, known as the Central Office of the Supreme Court (Supreme Court Act 1981 s.96) is located at the RCJ in London. (The Central Office was established by the Supreme Court of Judicature (Officers) Act 1879 s.4.) By the Supreme Court Act 1981 s.99, the Lord Chancellor has power by order to direct that there will be a district registry of the High Court at such places and for such county court district as are specified in the order to support the business of the High Court conducted at provincial court centres (see the Civil Courts Order 1983 (SI 1983/713) (as amended) (see Vol.2, Section 11)). **2.3.11**

The county courts, on the other hand, are inferior courts with limited legal jurisdiction and limited territorial jurisdiction, and, therefore, there are many county court districts, each with at least one county court. Over the years, the limits on the legal jurisdiction of county courts have been relaxed and the problems inherent in the territorial limits on jurisdiction have been largely overcome, mainly by rules enabling the easy movement of cases from court to court. The CPR contain rules of court applicable to proceedings both in the High Court and in the county courts. In various contexts it is convenient if the expression "the court" can be taken to mean, not only the county courts (wherever located) and the High Court, but also the High Court either at the RCJ or at a location where a district registry of the High Court is situated (see, particularly, Pt 30 (Transfer)).

"legal representative" —Note also distinction between "a lawyer" and "a lay representative" in Practice Direction (Small Claims Track), para.3.1 (see para.27PD.1). **2.3.12**

"statement of case" —Under the CPR, proceedings are commenced by a "claim form" and not by writ or summons (r.7.2(1)). Further, in the CPR the formal exchanges between parties formerly described as "pleadings" are described as "state- **2.3.13**

ments of case" and include the claimant's "particulars of claim" (formerly statement of claim under the RSC), the defendant's defence and any reply thereto. (It would seem that there may be further statements of case subsequent to a rely to a defence, even though the definition in r.2.3(1) does not extend to this, see r.15.9 and note para.22.1.7 below). As defined in r.2.3(1), "statement of case" includes a "Part 20 claim". One effect of the amendments to CPR Pt 20 made in April 2006, was that the term "Part 20 claim" was replaced with the term "additional claim". As defined, "statement of case" does not include a winding up petition, because the CPR do not generally apply to insolvency proceedings (*Investment Invoice Financing Ltd v Limehouse Board Mills Ltd* [2006] EWCA Civ 9; [2006] 1 W.L.R. 985, CA). The general rule is that the claimant's particulars of claim must be contained in or served with the claim form (r.7.4) but in certain circumstances they may be served separately. It is surprising that "statement of case" is defined as meaning, not only the formal exchanges between parties formerly described as "pleadings", but also as meaning the claim form, whether or not the particulars of claim are contained in it. Although "claim form" is defined as meaning "statement of case", the reverse is not true. When served (see Pt 6), the claim form founds the jurisdiction of the court and, conceptually, is quite distinct from any statement of case. Where leave to serve a claim form out of the jurisdiction is sought, the claimant's cause of action is ascertained from the claim form (*Canadian Union Insurance Co v Catatumbo Compania Aninima de Seguros* April 17, 2000, unrep., Timothy Walker J.). Doubtless, the inclusion of the claim form within the definition of statement of case has the advantage of simplifying the drafting of rules in some respects. However, it can also lead to confusion where in particular rules the expression "statement of case" is used in a context where, traditionally, the distinction between process and pleadings has been meaningful; e.g. r.17.4 (Amendments to statements of case after the end of a relevant limitation period) and r.19.5 (Special provisions about adding or substituting parties after the end of a relevant limitation period) (see *Gregson v Channel Four Television Corp (Amendment of Party Name)* [2000] C.P. Rep. 60, CA). The meaning of "statement of case" in the context of r.5.4C (Supply of documents to non-party from court records) has occasioned some difficulty; see para.5.4C.3 below.

Specialist lists (r.2.3(2))

2.3.14 The Glossary explains that cases are allocated to different "lists" depending on the subject-matter of the proceedings (see Vol.1, Section F below). Such lists are used for administrative purposes and may also have their own procedures and judges. As amended by the Civil Procedure (Amendment No.5) Rules 2001 (SI 2001/4015), r.2.3(2) states that a reference in the CPR to a "specialist list" is a reference to a list that has been designated as such by "a rule or practice direction". As was explained above (see para.2.1.2), when the CPR came into effect several varieties of proceedings were listed in Pt 49 as "specialist proceedings" and the CPR applied to them "subject to the relevant practice direction". "Specialist lists" are to be distinguished from "specialist proceedings". However, some of the practice directions relevant to "specialist proceedings" provided that those proceedings should be handled through "specialist lists". The coincidence of "proceedings" and "lists" is also apparent in various other procedural contexts; e.g. Practice Direction (How to Start Proceedings – The Claim Form), para.3.7 (see para.7PD.2 below). Most of the proceedings originally designated in Pt 49 as "specialist proceedings" now have there own dedicated CPR Parts. Therefore they are no longer subject to Pt 49. More particularly, they are no longer regulated solely by "the relevant practice direction" but are regulated by rules (hence the amendment to r.2.3(2)) referred to above. In some instances, rules in such new Parts state that the proceedings will be assigned to specialist lists. For example, r.58.2 states that the commercial list is a specialist list for claims proceeding in the Commercial Court, r.59.1 states that "Mercantile Court" means a specialist list established either in the Central London County Court and certain designated district registries, and r.60.2(1) states that Technology and Construction Court claims form a specialist list. Rule 63.4 is more precise and states that claims in the Patents Court, and a patents county court, for specialist lists "for the purposes of rule 30.5" (see below). Numerous references to "specialist lists" are found throughout the CPR and related practice directions (e.g. r.13.4(2) (Transfer of application to set aside judgment to defendant's home court), r.16.3(5) (Statement of value in claim form issued in High Court), r.26.2(2) (Automatic transfer) and r.30.5 (Transfer between Divisions and to and from a specialist list)). Note also, r.14.13(3)(e) (No transfer to defendant's home court of application for re-determination of time and rate of payment in admitted money claim where claim started in specialist list).

Clerical and judicial responsibility for public law proceedings rests with the Crown Office. Until October 2, 2000, claims in such proceedings were entered in the Crown Office list and were largely dealt with by Divisional Courts of the Queen's Bench Division. This list was constructed and managed in accordance with a number of practice directions made before the CPR came into effect in April, 1999. In the Report of the Review of the Crown Office List (March 2000) it was recommended that the Crown Office list should be renamed "The Administrative Court". This recommendation was implemented by *Practice Direction (Administrative Court: Establishment)* [2000] 1 W.L.R. 1654. The Crown Office has been renamed as the "Administrative Court Office". A large proportion of the business dealt by the Administrative Court consists of applications for judicial review and is therefore handled in accordance with Pt 53 (Judicial Review) and the practice direction supplementing that Part. Proceedings handled by the Administrative Court (including judicial review applications) do not constitute "specialist proceedings" within the meaning of CPR r.49(2). It was not clear whether the Crown Office list was a "specialist list" within the meaning of r.2.3(2) and the same uncertainty arises in relation to the "Administrative Court List" referred to in Practice Direction (Sch.1, RSC O.54 (Application for Writ of Habeas Corpus)), para.6.1, and elsewhere.

Power of judge, Master or district judge to perform functions of the court

2.4 Where these Rules provide for the court to perform any act then, except where an enactment, rule or practice direction provides otherwise, that act may be performed— 2.4

(a) in relation to proceedings in the High Court, by any judge, Master or district judge of that Court; and

(b) in relation to proceedings in a county court, by any judge or district judge.

Effect of rule

This rule distinguishes High Court proceedings from county court proceedings. 2.4.1
Since the 1990s, especially following the implementation of the Access to Justice reforms and the bringing into effect of the CPR, there has been increasing integration between the operations of the High Court, on the one hand, and the network of county courts, on the other.Nevertheless, the two levels of court remain quite distinct. The High Court is a superior court, the county courts are inferior courts. The Supreme Court Act 1981 s.4(1) states that the High Court "consists of" certain *ex officio* judges and puisne judges. The judges are the Court and the Court is the judges. The judges exercise the jurisdiction of the Court (see Vol.2, para.9A–16+). Generally, the jurisdiction of the Court may be exercised by a single judge sitting alone. The county courts (as they are not superior courts) do not "consist of" judges at all. The County Courts Act 1984 s.1 states that (1) England and Wales shall be divided into districts, (2) a court to be called "a county court" shall be held as provided by the Act for each district, and (3) the jurisdiction and powers of every such court shall be as provided for by legislation. Section 5 of the 1984 Act states that (amongst others) every circuit judge and every recorder shall "by virtue of his office" be capable of sitting as a judge of a county court. Section 6 of the Act states that each appointed district judge must be assigned to one or more districts (see Vol.2, paras 9A–419+ *et seq.*).

Persons who are not judges of the High Court may exercise the jurisdiction of the High Court. The Supreme Court Act 1981 s.9(1) states that at the request of the appropriate authority "a person" who is not a High Court judge may exercise the jurisdiction of the High Court. Such a "person" may be a circuit judge or a recorder (see Vol.2, para.9A–30). The result is that judges who, by virtue of their office, have authority to exercise the jurisdiction of an (inferior) county court may, where requested, have authority to exercise the jurisdiction of the (superior) High Court (colloquially, such judges are said to be "ticketed"). Section 68(1) of the 1981 Act states that provision may be made by rules of court as to cases in which jurisdiction of the High Court may be exercised by such circuit judges or recorders as the Lord Chief Justice may (with the concurrence of the Lord Chancellor) nominate "to deal with official referees, business", that is to say, with Technology and Construction Court business. Rules of court dealing with TCC claims are now found in CPR Pt 60. A TCC judge means any judge authorised to hear TCC claims (see paras 2E–1 and 9A–253). TCC claims may be begun and dealt with in the High Court or in certain county courts. Where a claim is dealt with in the High Court, and by a circuit judge duly nominated, the result is that High Court jurisdiction is being exercised by a person other than a High Court judge. Formerly, para.(c) of s.68(1) of the 1981 Act also stated that provision could be made by rules of court as to cases in which jurisdiction of the High Court could be exercised by masters, registrars, district registrars [i.e. district judges] or other officers of the court. Paragraph (c) was omitted by the Civil Procedure Act 1997, and Sch.1, para.2 of that Act now states that Civil Procedure Rules may provide for the exercise of the jurisdiction of any court within the scope of the rules (which includes the High Court and the county courts) "by officers or other court staff" (Vol.2, para.9A–766).

Circuit judges nominated pursuant to the Supreme Court Act 1981, s.68(1) fall into two categories: "full time" TCC judges and "part time" TCC judges. "Full time" TCC judges spend most of their time dealing with TCC business, although they will do other work when there is no TCC business requiring their immediate attention. "Part time" TCC judges are circuit judges who are only available to sit in the TCC for part of their time. They have substantial responsibilities outside the TCC. (See further *Technology and Construction Court: Statement by the Lord Chief Justice*, [2005] 3 All E.R. 289.)

Practice Direction 54D (Administrative Court (Venue)) contains special provisions for the management and determination of certain classes of claim issued and proceeding in the Administrative Court, including provisions requiring that urgent applications should be dealt with by designated judges (para.54DPD.1 below).

CPR, r.63.4A states that proceedings in the patents county court shall be dealt with by the patents judge but provides that an urgent matter may be dealt with by another nominated judge with appropriate specialist experience.

The arrangements for "ticketing" and "nominating" judges, so that they may deal with cases that normally they would not be able to hear and determine, and for stipulating the limits of the jurisdiction of masters, district judges and other officers of the court, are sufficiently complicated to admit of the real possibility that, in a given case, it may become apparent in retrospect that the judicial officer acting lacked jurisdiction. The question which then arises is: what are the effects of such want of jurisdiction? Logic might compel the conclusion that the proceedings would be void *ab initio* and the result a nullity. However, in *Fawdry & Co v Murfitt* [2002] EWCA Civ 643; [2002] 3 W.L.R. 1354, CA, the Court of Appeal explained that, where a judicial officer acts in his office under a general supposition of his competence to do so, his acts may be upheld though in truth had no legal power. However, in this case the Court did not have to reach a concluded view on the limits of the common law doctrine of de facto authority. See also *Coppard v Customs and Excise Commissioners* [2003] EWCA Civ 511; [2003] Q.B. 1428, CA; *Baldock v Webster* [2004] EWCA Civ 1869.

By virtue of his office, every judge of the Court of Appeal, every judge of the High Court and every Recorder, is capable of sitting as a judge of any county court in the circumstances provided for by the County Courts Act 1984 s.5(3) (see Vol.2, para.9A–419+). There is nothing to prevent a High Court judge with Administrative Court experience from sitting in a county court for the purpose of trying a claim in which the claimant claimed (1) a declaration that a public body had acted incompatibly with his Convention rights, and (2) damages for false imprisonment (*D. v Home Office* [2005] EWCA Civ 38; [2006] 1 W.L.R. 1003, CA (where held that the bringing of such an action in a county court, rather than by way of proceedings under Pt 54, is not an abuse of process)).

Throughout the CPR, references are made to the "court", rather than to a judge or to a particular court (whether the High Court, a county court, or the Court of Appeal) except where it is necessary to do otherwise (e.g. r.29.9 (Powers of "trial judge" in relation to orders previously made), r.30.2 (Transfer between county courts and within the High Court), r.34.13 (High Court's power to order letter of request) and r.43.2(1) (defining "costs judge")). Where the context requires, a reference to "the court" means a reference to a particular county court, a district registry or the Royal Courts of Justice (r.2.3(2)). Rule 2.3 states that "judge" means, unless the context otherwise requires, a judge, Master or district judge or a person authorised to act as such. Rule 2.4 states the general rule that where "the court" may perform any act then that act may be performed, not only by the judges of the court, but also by lesser judicial officers. Rule 2.4 draws a clear distinction between proceedings in the High Court and proceedings in a county court. The rule is confined to circumstances in which these Rules refer to the performance of an "act" by the court. The general principle is that Masters and district judges should have power to act. It should be noted that the rule speaks, not of "any act" that the court may perform, but of "any act" which "these Rules provide for the court to perform". Where the court performs an "act" not provided for by the CPR (e.g. tries a claim) the rule has no application.

The expression "the High Court" or "the court" or "the court or a judge" if used in a statute does not include lesser judicial officers unless jurisdiction is expressly conferred upon them by rules of court.

In various circumstances it is necessary to be clear about the limits of the powers and jurisdiction of Masters and district judges in relation to proceedings in the High Court, and about the limits of the powers and jurisdiction of district judges in relation to proceedings in a county court. Practice Direction (Allocation of Cases to Levels of Judiciary) (see para.2BPD.1 below) conveniently sets out the matters over which masters and district judges do not have jurisdiction or which they may deal with only on certain conditions. The extent of the jurisdiction of district judges is not always free from doubt; see e.g. commentary in paras 56PD.7F.1 and 56PD.7H.3 (level of judge in claims for lease renewal). Elsewhere in the CPR, provisions are found stating clearly for the avoidance of doubt the level of judge to whom certain applications should be made in circumstances where, conceivably, the application could be made either to a judge or to a lesser judge; e.g. Practice Direction (Alternative Procedure for Claims) para.12A.5(supplementing Pt 8); Practice Direction (Enforcement of Judgments in Different Jurisdictions), paras 4.1 to 4.3 (supplementing Pt 74). In some instances it is provided that powers that would otherwise be exercisable exclusively by a High Court judge may be exercised by a designated civil judge (or his deputy); e.g. Practice Direction (Civil Restraint Orders), para.3.1. The Supreme Court Act 1981 s.19(3) states that in the High Court any jurisdiction of the court shall be exercised only by a single judge of that court, except in so far as it is by rules of court made exercisable by a Master, district judge or other officer of the court, or by any other person (note also SCA s.68) (see Vol.2, paras 9A–65 and 9A–253). An example of High Court jurisdiction being made exercisable by a Master or district judge by rules of court is provided by CPR r.67.3(3). The County Courts Act 1984 s.62, states the general rule that, subject to other provisions in the Act and rules of court, the judge of a county is the sole judge in all proceedings and shall determine all questions of fact and law and CCA 1984 s.37(1) states that any jurisdiction and powers conferred by that Act or any other Act on a county court or on the judge of a county court may be exercised by any judge of the court. In former RSC O.1, r.4(2) "the court" was defined as including a judge, a Master or a district judge. The CCR contained no such general provision (but see CCR O.1, r.8).

It should be noted that r.2.4 and the practice direction supplementing it are concerned with the allocation of cases to appropriate levels of judge in proceedings to which the CPR apply. The need to provide for such allocation also arises in proceedings which are not subject to the CPR. In such other jurisdictions, problems can arise in determining the limits of the powers of Masters, registrars and district judges. In *Lynch Hall & Hornby v Thakerar* [2005] EWHC 2752 (Ch); *The Times*, January 9, 2006 (Lewison J.) it was held that a deputy registrar has the jurisdiction to make a third party debt order where the order is made in relation to insolvency proceedings in the High Court.

A significant feature of the English civil justice system is that, in many instances, cases (particularly cases proceeding on the fast track) are not assigned at the point of commencement to a particular judge for handling until ultimate disposal (whether by trial or otherwise) or for the duration of their pre-trial stages. The result is that, in a case that goes to trial or which settles or is discontinued at a late stage, case management hearings and hearings of pre-trial applications and, perhaps, appeals from decisions made at such hearings, may be dealt with by a number of different judges of different standing. The risks of pre-judgment and apparent bias which, as a practical matter, may arise in any system for the allocation of cases to levels of judiciary, can be reduced by this flexibility in the deployment of judge power. Nevertheless, the risks remain, and in cases that are assigned to a particular judge for the duration, are indeed likely to arise. In a given case, despite what the law may actually say about the powers of judges of different levels to deal with particular matters, a judge may have to recuse himself from a particular hearing. In a civil justice system which is heavily orientated towards case management the chances of this being necessary are increased.

See further Vol.2, para.9A–48, and note *Collier v Williams* [2006] EWCA Civ 20; [2006] 1 W.L.R. 1945, CA (where out of court communication between two district judges about issue arising in case said to be unfortunate).

It will be clear from what has been said above that the jurisdiction of the several judicial officers who may sit in the High Court, or in a county court, is not mutually exclusive. Circumstances may arise where a particular hearing in the High Court may be before either a High Court judge or before a lesser judge (a master or a district judge), or in a county court either before a circuit judge or a lesser judge (a recorder or a district judge). A good example is provided by the situation where judgment is given in a money claim and an order is made that the amount to be paid by one party to another is to be decided by the court at a further hearing (e.g. a judgment on liability with damages to be assessed). It may be noted that in circumstances such as these Practice Direction (Case Management—Preliminary Stage: Allocation and Reallocation), para.12.2(2) states that the court may give directions specifying "the level or type of judge" before whom the hearing will take place (see PD 10, para.26 below). Note also *Rosling King v Rothschild Trust* [2002] EWHC 1346 (Ch); May 24, 2002, unrep. (Neuberger J.) (whether outstanding issues should be determined by High Court judge or a costs judge).

It is not possible in a short compass to state the limits of the jurisdiction and powers of Masters and district judges. However, it may be noted that a broad distinction can be drawn between the exercise of any jurisdiction or power conferred on the court by rules of court (1) at the trial or hearing of a claim, and (2) at any other stage of the proceedings (see, e.g. former CCR O.1, r.8). Historically speaking, the exercise of jurisdiction and powers in the first circumstance were reserved to the judge (whether of the High Court or a county court) and in the second, subject to some exceptions, were readily delegated to lesser judicial officers in the form of Masters and district judges (see e.g. former CCR O.1, r.8 and O.13, r.1(6) and RSC O.32, rr.11 and 14). However, in modern times the jurisdiction of lesser judicial officers to hear and determine claims has been established and increased (see, e.g. former CCR O.19, r.5 and O.21, r.5 (note also O.50, r.2) and RSC O.14, r.6(2), O.33, r.2(e), O.36, r.11 and O.37, r.1). Most of the acts which the court may perform in accordance with rules of court are not performed at the trial or hearing of a claim but at other stages of proceedings. Consequently, the circumstances in which such acts cannot be performed by a lesser judicial officer, and must be performed by a judge, can be regarded as exceptional. Such circumstances may be stipulated by statute, by rules of court or by practice directions (e.g. Practice Direction (Case Management–Preliminary Stage, etc.), para.12.10 (Jurisdiction of Masters and District Judges) (see para.26PD.12)). Various provisions restricting the jurisdiction of Masters and district judges in the High Court are found in Practice Direction (Allocation of Cases to Level of Judiciary) (see para.2BPD.1 below), and Practice Direction (Patents and Other Intellectual Property Claims) para.8.1 (see Vol.2, para.2F-90 below). Provisions concerning the respective powers of circuit judges and district judges in county court proceedings are found in Practice Direction (Allocation of Cases to Level of Judiciary), paras 8.1 to 12 (see para.2BPD.8 *et seq.* below); note also para.13 (Distribution of business where both circuit judge and district judge have jurisdiction). As a practical matter, the most important restrictions on the jurisdiction of lesser judges relate to the court's power to grant injunctions (Practice Direction (Allocation of Cases to Levels of Judiciary) paras 2.1 to 2.4 (see para.2BPD.2, below). See further paras 25.0.10 and 25.1.10 below. A civil restraint order is not an injunction. A master or a district judge may make a limited civil restraint order. But the more stringent types of such order should be made only be a designated civil judge or his deputy, or by a judge of the High Court or the Court of Appeal (*Wickramaratna v Cambridge University Chemistry Department* [2004] EWCA Civ 1532; November 2, 2004, unrep. (at para.35); see also *Foenander v Foenander* [2004] EWCA Civ 1675, December 10, 2004, unrep., (Wall L.J.). Practice Direction (Civil Restraint Orders) (see para.3PD.1 below) states that, in certain circumstances, the power to make a CRO may be exercised only by a Court of Appeal judge, a High Court judge, or a designated civil judge (see paras 2.7, 3.1, 4.1 and 4.7), and proceedings must be transferred accordingly (see paras 3.11 and 4.11).

Other provisions dealing with the allocation of cases to levels of judiciary include Practice Direction (Appeals) para.8.13 (appeals and applications for permission to appeal where the lower court is a county court), para.8.14 (appeals, applications for permission to appeal, etc. where the appeal is from a master or district judge of the High Court), para.23.8C (appeal under European Public Limited-Liability Company

Regulations2004 reg.74) (para.52PD.1 below), Practice Direction (Court Documents) para.4.4 (application under r.5.4(7) to restrict persons who may obtain copies of claim form from court records), Practice Direction (Applications Under the Companies Act 1985 and Other Legislation Relating to Companies) para.3B (proceedings under aPDrt.25 and 26 of Council Regulation 2157/2001 of October 8, 2001 on the Statute for a European Company (SE)) and para.14(2) (Applications under the Criminal Justice and Police Act 2001 s.59) (Vol.2, para.2G–7 below) and Practice Direction (Depositions and Court Attendance by Witnesses) para.2.3 (applications to set aside witness summons issued in aid of inferior court or tribunal) (para.34PD.2 below).

Practice Direction (Proceedings Relating to Solicitors) supplements CPR Pt 67. It relates to proceedings under r.67.2, and to certain claims under r.67.3 and the Solicitors Act 1974 Pt II. Rule 67.3 indicates that the circumstances in which a claim for an order under Pt III of the 1974 Act should be brought either in the High Court or in a county court. Paragraph 3.2 of the practice direction states that claims for orders to which the practice direction applies should normally be made to a Master, costs judge or district judge. Only special circumstances will justify making the claim directly to a High Court judge.

When dealing with an application, a Master or district judge may refer to a judge any matter which he thinks should properly be decided by a judge, and the judge may either dispose of the matter or refer it back to the Master or district judge (Practice Direction (Applications) para.1 (see para.23PD.1 below)).

Circumstances may arise where although a Master or district judge as a matter of law has jurisdiction, it would not be appropriate for him to exercise it; see *Sandry v Jones*, *The Times*, August 3, 2000, CA (district judges should not assess damages in substantial dispute). In *Stevens v Leeder* [2004] EWCA Civ 50; *The Times* January 14, 2005, CA, it was said that it was not appropriate for the designated civil judge to have given permission for a county court case proceeding on the multi-track raising an issue whether a transaction should be set aside for undue influence to be allocated to a district judge. The Court said, when requested to exercise his powers under Practice Direction (Allocation of Cases to Levels of Judiciary) para.11.1, a designated civil judge should consider carefully the nature of the case and the skills and experience of the district judge, and should not be influenced by the consideration that there may be compensation to be paid to the parties if a fixed trial date cannot otherwise be complied with.

Rule 2.4 refers to the creation of exceptions to the rule by practice directions, for example, by Practice Direction (Allocation of Cases to Levels of Judiciary) supplementing the rule (see para.2BPD.1 below). For information on the power to make directions, see commentary to the Civil Procedure Act 1997 s.5 (Vol.2 para.9A–752, and Vol.2, Sect.12 (CPR: Application, Amendments and Interpretation), para.12–17). Section 5(6) makes express reference to the making of practice directions that consist of criteria for determining which judges may be allocated to hear particular categories of case.

"district judge of that Court"

Formerly, at court centres out of London where district registries of the High Court are located, the functions of Master were discharged by selected county court registrars each designated as "a district registrar of the High Court". By the Courts and Legal Services Act 1990 s.74, the offices of county court registrar and of district registrar became the office of district judge. Thereafter, the proper designation for a district registrar became "a district judge of the High Court" (Supreme Court Act 1981 s.100, see Vol.2, para.9A–335+). For each district registry of the High Court the Lord Chancellor is required to appoint at least one district judge for a county court district as district judge of the High Court (*ibid.*), hence the distinction between district judges generally and district judges of the High Court. References in any enactment, instrument or other document to a district judge or deputy district judge do not include (a) a district judge (magistrates' courts) or (b) a deputy district judge (magistrates' courts) (Courts Act 2003 s.65(3)). **2.4.2**

Masters

For appointment of Masters of the Queen's Bench and Chancery Divisions of the High Court, see the Supreme Court Act 1981 s.89 (Vol.2, para.9A–303+). Under r.2.4, except where otherwise provided, Masters may perform any act which may be performed by the court "in relation to proceedings in the High Court"; no distinction **2.4.3** is drawn between High Court cases proceeding at the Royal Courts of Justice or in a district registry. The jurisdiction of Masters in relation to proceedings in county courts granted by former RSC 107 is now dealt with under Pt 30 (Transfer) of the CPR. As to special powers of Queen's Bench Masters on certain applications returnable in the month of August, see Practice Direction (Court Sittings), para.3.5 (39BPD.3).

As to designation of certain officers of Court of Appeal as Masters or Deputy Masters for particular circumstances, see para.2.5.3 below.

Performance of "acts...provided for" by CPR

2.4.4 Rule 2.4 speaks of circumstances in which "these Rules provide for the court to perform any act" and provides that generally such acts may be performed by lesser judicial officers. This formula has no exact counterpart in former rules. The former provisions spoke variously of the exercise by lesser judicial officers of power, authority, and jurisdiction, and their transaction of business. Further, they were not always limited to the exercise of power, etc., conferred by the RSC and the CCR. In the CPR, sometimes the source of the court's power to perform particular acts is found within the CPR and sometimes the power has a provenance without (Pt 3 (Court's case management powers) and Pt 25 (Interim remedies) contain illustrations of both categories). It would seem that, whatever the provenance of the court's power to perform an "act" if it is mentioned in the CPR the Rules "provide for" it and, therefore, unless excepted by statute, rule or practice direction, it may be performed by a lesser judicial officer.

Court staff

2.5 **2.5—(1) Where these Rules require or permit the court to perform an act of a formal or administrative character, that act may be performed by a court officer.**

(2) A requirement that a court officer carry out any act at the request of a party is subject to the payment of any fee required by a fees order for the carrying out of that act.

(Rule 3.2 allows a court officer to refer to a judge before taking any step.)

Effect of rule

2.5.1 The CPR may provide for the exercise of the jurisdiction of any court within the scope of the rules by officers or other staff of the court (Civil Procedure Act 1997 s.1; and Sch.1, para.2, see Vol.2, para.9A–766).

Court staff

2.5.2 The rule is headed "Court staff", by which must be meant members of the Court Service. In *Quinland v Governor of Swaleside Prison* [2002] EWCA Civ 174; [2002] 3 W.L.R. 807, CA, Hale L.J. explained (para.41) that, although the Court Service is an agency of the executive branch of government, it exists, in part if not in whole, to facilitate and implement the workings of the judiciary. Her ladyship added there are some of its activities "over which the judiciary and not the executive must have the ultimate control" (e.g. the putting into effect of the orders or directions of the court) as there is little point in having an independent judiciary "if the executive, through the Court Service, is free to pick and choose which of its orders to implement" (see further Vol.2, para.9B–110+).

"act of a formal or administrative character"

2.5.3 A court officer means a member of the court staff (r.2.3(1)). In modern times the trend has been towards devolving to civil servants working in the Court Service, tasks that formerly were thought proper for discharge only by a judge, Master or district judge. Under the former CCR, various functions were to be performed by "the proper officer" by which was meant the district judge or, in relation to any act of a formal or administrative character which was not by statute the responsibility of the district judge, the court manager or any other officer of the court acting on his behalf in accordance with directions given by the Lord Chancellor (O.1, r.3). Further, the chief clerk, court manager (or officer authorised on his behalf) could discharge certain listed functions which were not obviously merely formal or administrative (e.g. the oral examination of debtors in county courts) (*ibid*). Rule 2.5 is confined to acts of a formal or administrative character and is not in terms restricted to such acts as are not by statute the responsibility of the district judge or any other judicial officer. The Civil Procedure Act 1997 s.1 and Sch.1, para.2 provides that rules in the CPR may provide for the exercise "of the jurisdiction of any court within the scope of the rules" by officers or other staff of the court. Thus, for example, r.14.11 provides that, in certain circumstances, a court officer may exercise the powers of the court under r.14.10 to determine the rate of payment where a defendant has admitted a money claim and requested time to pay, and r.40.6 states that, in certain circumstances, a court officer may enter and seal an agreed judgment or order. Further, under Pt 43 court officers may be authorised to exercise certain powers in relation to the assessment of costs (see r.47.3). Note also r.5.2 (court officer directing that document should be prepared by court rather than party). Some practice directions make express reference to the powers of court staff; for example the practice direction referred to in r.75.5 (functions of court officer in relation to enforcement of traffic penalties by a county court), and Practice Direction (Applications under the Companies Act 1985 and the Insurance Companies Act 1982), para.8.1 (applications in the long vacation to the court manager to fix hearings for purpose of sanctioning schemes and reductions) (see Vol.2, para.2G–7). Where decision-making powers are devolved to court officers, generally express provision is made for the review of their decisions by a judge (see e g. r.75.5A).

Rule 3.2 provides that, where in the exercise of the court's case management powers, "a step is taken" by a court officer, the court officer may consult a judge before taking that step, and the step may be taken by the judge instead of by the court officer.

Various provisions refer to the powers of court officers to discharge certain functions (not all merely of a formal or administrative character) in the handling of appeals. For example, Practice Direction (Appeals) para.2A.5 states that. where an applicant attempts to file an appellant's notice and the court to which the appeal is directed does not have jurisdiction to issue the notice, a court officer may notify the applicant in writing that the appeal court does not have jurisdiction in respect of the notice. And r.52.16 provides that a court officer assigned to the Civil Appeals Office of the Court of Appeal who is a barrister or solicitor may exercise the jurisdiction of the Court with the consent of the Master of the Rolls with regard to the matters set out in that rule. When the Head of the Civil Appeals Office acts in a judicial capacity pursuant to r.52.16, he shall be known as Master. Other eligible officers may also be designated by the Master of the Rolls to exercise judicial authority under r.52.16 and shall then be known as Deputy Masters (see Practice Direction (Appeals) para.15.5).

Court documents to be sealed

2.6—(1) The court must seal[GL] **the following documents on issue—** 2.6

- **(a) the claim form; and**
- **(b) any other document which a rule or practice direction requires it to seal.**

(2) The court may place the seal[GL] **on the document—**

- **(a) by hand; or**
- **(b) by printing a facsimile of the seal on the document whether electronically or otherwise.**

(3) A document purporting to bear the court's seal[GL] **shall be *admissible in evidence without* further proof.**

Effect of rule

A seal on a document indicates that it has been issued by the court (see Glossary). 2.6.1
Formerly, the County Courts Act 1984 s.134(1) (now omitted, see "Sealed documents as evidence" below) stated that all summonses issued out of a county court, and all such other documents so issuing as may be prescribed, should be"sealed and stamped" with the seal of the court. Under the RSC, various forms of process were validly issued only when sealed (e.g. RSC O.6 r.7(3) (Issue of writ)). Rule 2.6(1) replaces these and other provisions.

Proceedings are started when the court issues a claim form at the request of the claimant (r.7.2(1)). A claim form must be sealed on issue (r.2.6(1)(a)). The date of issue of a claim form is the date entered on the form by the court (r.7.2(2)).

As to sealing of judgments and orders, see r.40.2(2)(b) and rr.40.2 to 40.6.

As to the signature of documents used in court proceedings, see r.5.3.

As to sealing of copy of claim form where it is to be served through judicial authority of foreign country, etc., see r.6.26(3).

Placing of seal

2.6.2 The court may place the seal in the manner provided by r.2.6(2). Claim forms issued by the Summons Production Centre (r.7.10) may be sealed electronically and means of sealing otherwise than by hand may be more widely used in the future as the courts gain the benefits of information technology.

Sealed documents as evidence

2.6.3 The general rule is that a party wishing to rely on a document must adduce primary evidence of its contents. At common law, by way of exception to the general rule, the contents of most public documents could be proved by copies of various kinds on account of the inconvenience that would have been occasioned by production of the originals. This common law rule is declared in many specific contexts by statutes. Examples include the Supreme Court Act 1981 s.132, which states that any document purporting to be "sealed or stamped" by the Supreme Court shall be received in evidence "in all parts of the United Kingdom without further proof". The County Courts Act 1984 s.134(2) was to similar effect, but limited to "all parts of England and Wales", and has been omitted from that Act by the Civil Procedure (Modification of Enactments) Order 1998 (SI 1998/2940).

Former RSC 38 r.10(2) stated that every document purporting to be sealed with the seal of any office or department of the Supreme Court should be received in evidence without further proof. This sub-rule further stated that any document purporting to be so sealed and to be a copy of a document filed in, or issued out of, that office or department should be deemed to be an office copy of that document without further proof unless the contrary is shown. Rule 2.6(3) follows former RSC 38 r.10(2) and declares that a sealed document is admissible in evidence without further proof in the courts to which the CPR. The effect of the Evidence Act 1845 s.1 is that, when a statute permits a document to be proved by certified or sealed copy, it is unnecessary to prove certification or sealing; the mere production of the copy suffices.

Where it can be shown that the court has affixed a seal to an application for a default judgment, made in circumstances in which rules of court required that the judgment should be entered within a particular time, but the court records contain no record of such judgment having been entered, it may properly be inferred from the sealed application that the judgment was entered in time (*Sullivan v Blanning* [2000] C.P. Rep. 15, CA).

Court's discretion as to where it deals with cases

2.7 **2.7 The court may deal with a case at any place that it considers appropriate.**

Effect of rule

2.7.1 The County Courts Act 1984 s.3(3) stated that county court proceedings (whether heard by a judge or a district judge) or any question arising in proceedings "may be heard or determined at any place either within or without the district". The exercise of this power was subject to the consent of the parties. This provision could be explained in historical terms but in modern times its purpose and scope had become matters for doubt, largely because its original objectives had come to be met by other provisions. The sub-section was omitted by the Civil Procedure Act 1997 s.10 and Sch.2, para.2. However, it would seem that it is revived by r.2.7. In terms, the rule grants the court a wide power as to venue. In contrast to former CCA 1984 s.3(3), the rule makes no mention of the consent of the parties. Further, it is not limited to sittings of county courts but applies to all courts covered by the CPR. However, the need to give effect to the overriding objective stated in r.1.1 may impose some restraint and ensure that, in a given case, the power is not exercised purely for the convenience of the court. It would seem that, formerly, CCA 1984 s.3(3) was used, not for the purpose of moving cases from a court in one county court district to a venue in another district, but for the purpose of enabling the court, with the consent of the parties, to sit at a location within its district which was not a court house. It may be that the intention is that r.2.7 should be interpreted in a similarly restricted manner.

Rule 2.7 states that the court may deal with "a case" at any place that it considers appropriate. This would include holding a hearing of any kind provided for by the CPR (including case management events) and not merely (as provided by CCA 1984 s.3(3)) a hearing for the determination of "any question arising in proceedings". In the case of *In the Matter of Oral Contraceptive Litigation* [2006] EWHC 823, QB; March 31, 2006, unrep., for the purpose of saving costs the hearing of a detailed assessment of costs was held at the offices of a firm of solicitors in a provincial town.

Rule 2.7 is not concerned with the transfer of proceedings between one court and another. Provisions as to transfer are found in Pt 30. It may be noted that r.30.6 states that the court may specify the place (for instance a particular county court) where the trial or some other hearing in any proceedings is to be held and may do so without ordering the proceedings to be transferred (see further Practice Direction (The Fast Track), para.8.1 (28PD.8) and Practice Direction (The Multi-Track), para.10.1 (29PD.10)). It may be noted that Practice Direction (Miscellaneous Provisions Relating to Hearings) para.1.7 (39PD.1) states that the hearing of small claim "in premises other than the court will not be a hearing in public". That rule has a different provenance. Its relationship with r.2.7 is not obvious.

Other provisions deal with "sittings" of the court. A distinction should be drawn between the determination of the question where a court may sit and of the question where it might need, in particular cases, to receive evidence (*Peer International Corporation v Termidor Music Publishers Ltd* [2005] EWHC 1048, Ch; *The Times* June 2, 2005 (Lindsay J.)).

There is some doubt as to whether r.2.7 lies within the rule-making power. The question is unlikely to arise unless an attempt is made to exercise it without the consent of the parties. The rule-making power for the CPR includes power to make rules about any matters which were governed by the former CCR (Civil Procedure Act 1997 s.1 and Sch.1, para.1). As explained above, formerly, the power now granted by r.2.7 was not granted by rule but by the County Courts Act 1984 s.3(3). Section 75 of that Act (now omitted) stated that the rule making power extended to prescribing the circumstances in which proceedings may be transferred from one court to another court (but not to a non-court location).

As to sittings of High Court and Court of Appeal, see Practice Direction (Court Sittings) (para.39BPD.1 below) and Supreme Court Act 1981 s.71 (Vol.2, para.9A–264).

Practice Direction 54D—Administrative Court (Venue) contains special provisions concerning the place in which a claim before the Administrative Court "should be started and administered and the venue at which it will be determined" (see para.54DPD.1 below).

As to the examination of witnesses out of the jurisdiction see CPR r.34.13.

Time

2.8—(1) This rule shows how to calculate any period of time for doing any act which is specified— 2.8

(a) by these Rules;

(b) by a practice direction; or

(c) by a judgment or order of the court.

***(2) A period of time expressed* as a number of days shall be computed as clear days.**

(3) In this rule "clear days" means that in computing the number of days—

(a) the day on which the period begins; and

(b) if the end of the period is defined by reference to an event, the day on which that event occurs are not included.

Examples—

(i) Notice of an application must be served at least 3 days before the hearing.

An application is to be heard on Friday 20 October.
The last date for service is Monday 16 October.

(ii) The court is to fix a date for a hearing.

The hearing must be at least 28 days after the date of notice.
If the court gives notice of the date of the hearing on 1 October, the earliest date for the hearing is 30 October.

(iii) Particulars of claim must be served within 14 days of service of the claim form.

The claim form is served on 2 October.
The last day for service of the particulars of claim is 16 October.

(4) Where the specified period—

(a) is 5 days or less; and

(b) includes—

(i) a Saturday or Sunday; or

(ii) a Bank Holiday, Christmas Day or Good Friday,

that day does not count.

Example—

Notice of an application must be served at least 3 days before the hearing.
An application is to be heard on Monday 20 October.
The last date for service is Tuesday 14 October.

(5) When the period specified—

(a) by these Rules or a practice direction; or

(b) by any judgment or court order,

for doing any act at the court office ends on a day on which the office is closed, that act shall be in time if done on the next day on which the court office is open.

Effect of rule

2.8.1 Circumstances in which periods of time for doing any act are specified or may be specified are many and various. Under a case management system the circumstances in which time limits may be fixed are increased and the attitude of the court to compliance with time limits is more strict than under a system in which case progress is largely controlled by the wishes of parties. Further, the circumstances in which time limits may be varied are restricted and the procedures enabling variation are likely to involve monitoring by the court.

Formerly, any periods of time fixed by the RSC or the CCR or "by any judgment, order or direction" for doing any act were reckoned in accordance with the provisions in, respectively, RSC 3 rr.2 and 4 and CCR 1 r.9. The calculation of periods of time is now dealt with by the provisions in r.2.8. Rule 2.8(1) states that the provisions which follow are to be used for the purpose of calculating any period of time for doing any act which is specified by the CPR, by a practice direction, or by "a judgment or order" of the court. In terms, this does not include times specified by directions other than practice directions but this omission would appear to be an oversight (see rr.2.9(1) and 2.10). Nor does it include procedural time limits fixed by statute (see, e.g. *Aadan v Brent LBC*, *The Times*, December 3, 1999, CA). It seems that the normal consequences of r.2.8 may be varied by practice direction (see, e.g. Practice Direction (Procedure for Detailed Assessment of Costs and Default Provisions) para.8.13 (para.47PD.20)). Depending on the circumstances, an act may have to be done within a specified period, or after or from a specified date or it may have to be done within or not less than a specified period before a specified date. Where expressly so provided, a time limit fixed by a rule may be varied by a practice direction (see, e.g. r.26.3(7)).

When a step has to be taken within a period described as "beginning with" a specified day, then that day is included in the period; but if the period is described as running "from" or "after" a specified day, then that day is not included in the period (*Zoan v Rouamba* [2000] 1 W.L.R. 1509, CA).

In *Anderton v Clwyd CC* [2002] EWCA Civ 933; 152 New L.J. 1125 (2002), CA, the Court of Appeal emphasised that the several time-calculation provisions stated in r.2.8 do not apply whenever there is a reference in the CPR, a practice direction or a court order, to the calculation of a period of time. The rule generally is in restricted terms, as it only applies to the calculation of any period of time "for doing any act" which is so specified (see further para.2.8.3 below).

Number of days as "clear" days

A period of time expressed as a number of days may be calculated in different ways. **2.8.2**
Rule 2.8(2) states that such periods shall be "computed as clear days". In itself, this is not entirely free from ambiguity. Consequently, r.2.8(3) explains that what is meant is that (a) the day on which the period begins shall not be included, and that (b) if the end of the period is defined by reference to an event, the day on which that event occurs is not included either. The explanation is followed by examples. The first and the last are based on, respectively, r.23.7(1)(b) and r.7.4(1)(b). The second relates to those many rules which provide that the court must give parties a minimum period of notice of a hearing (e.g. r.27.4(2)). It should be noted that these provisions are not concerned with periods of time expressed otherwise than as numbers of days, e.g. expressed in weeks (e.g. r.28.6(2)) or months (e.g. r.7.5(2)).

In the past, the language used by draftsmen of rules of court to express periods of time has not been consistent. Clearly, drafting styles have changed from time to time. Many of the rules now found in the CPR are based on former provisions of the RSC and CCR. The unfortunate result is that the old inconsistencies are perpetuated. Thus, for example, where providing that a party must take a particular action before a certain event occurs, rules state variously that he must do so "at least", "no later than", "not less than", or "not more than" a certain number of days before that event. Rules providing that certain actions must be taken after particular events show similar disparities in addition to providing in a number of rules that action should be taken "within" a number of days "of" or "after" an event. In some rules, periods of time are expressed in elaborate terms and this complexity is not always made necessary by the context. If one of the goals of the CPR was to standardise and simplify rules of court they have failed in this respect.

Specified periods of five days or less

Where a period of time is expressed as a number of days and the number does not **2.8.3**
exceed five, it is conceivable that such short period may as a practical matter be further reduced by the fact that it includes days falling on weekends, etc. Consequently, r.2.8(4) provides that in these circumstances such days shall not count. The provision follows former RSC 3 r.1(5) (which applied to periods of seven days or less) and CCR 1 r.9(3) (which applied to periods of three days or less). Provisions in the CPR specifying time periods of seven days are quite common but provisions imposing limits of five days or less are rare: examples are r.23.7(1)(b) and r.24.5(2). In some circumstances, and for obvious reasons, r.2.8(4) is expressly disapplied in relation to particular provisions specifying periods of five days or less. The best known example is r.55.20(3), which states that where any provision in Pt 55 (Possession Claims), Section III (Interim Possession Orders) requires an act to be done within a specified number of hours, r.2.8(4) does not apply. (Former CCR 24 r.8(2) was to the same effect).

Rule 6.7 explains how the "deemed day of service" of a document (including a claim form), served in accordance with the CPR or any relevant practice direction, is to be calculated. Under the CPR, the method of service that may be adopted varies depending on the nature of the document to be served. Some of the calculations in r.6.7 relate to periods of five days or less, and r.2.8(4) is incorporated by reference in r.6.7. However, after some uncertainty, it was held that, as r 2.8(4) is restricted in its effect to the "doing of any act" (see r.2.8(1)) within a specified period of five days or less, it does not apply to any of these calculations. This is because r.6.7 does not specify a period of time for doing any act under the CPR. Rather it sets out the methods of calculating the days on which the event of service of a document (perhaps a claim form) is deemed to happen as a result of doing acts under other rules involving the use of the various available methods for service of the document (*Anderton v Clwyd CC*

[2002] EWCA Civ 933; 152 New L.J. 1125 (2002), CA). (For the purpose of making this clear, the express reference to r.2.8 in r.6.7 was subsequently deleted.)

Specified period ending on day on which court office closed

2.8.4 Rule 2.8(5) states that, where a specified period of time, whether expressed in a number of days or otherwise, for doing an act at the court office ends on day on which the office is closed, that act shall be done in time if done on the next day on which the court office is open. A similar dispensation was given by former RSC O.1, r.4 and CCR O.1, r.9(5). Presumably, this rule applies where the period of time is specified by a direction other than a practice direction (see "Effect of rule", para.2.8.1 above).

The days on which court offices are open, and the hours during which they are open on those days, are stipulated by Practice Direction (Court Offices), para.2.1 (offices of the Supreme Court) and paras 3.2 and 3.3 (county court offices) (see paras 2PD.1 *et seq.*). Formerly, comparable provisions were found in, respectively, RSC O.64, rr.7 and 8 and CCR O.2, rr.2 and 3. A document delivered at a court office after closing time on a particular day by posting through the court office letter box is filed on that day (*Van Aken v London Borough of Camden* [2002] EWCA Civ 1724; October 11, 2002, unrep., CA).

Documents filed at court "treated as filed ... on the next day"

2.8.5 Practice Direction (Communication and Filing of Documents by E-mail) permits parties to claims in specified courts to use email for the purpose of communicating with the court, filing at court specified documents, and making certain applications to a court. It is expressly provided that, if an email is received after 4pm the email will be treated as received, and any documents to the email will be treated as filed, on the next day the court office is open (paras 4.4 and 9.1) (see para.5BPD.4 below). Similarly, in Practice Direction (Court Documents) para.5.3, which states that a party may file a document at court by sending it by facsimile ("fax"), it is expressly provided that, if in these circumstances, the fax is delivered after 4pm it will be treated as filed on the next day the court office is open (see para.5PD.6 below). In Practice Direction (Commercial Court) it is stated that, where the procedure for issuing a claim form in the Admiralty and Commercial Registry when that Registry is closed is used, the claim form is issued "when the fax is received by the Registry" (para.2.3 and App. A para.7, see Vol.2, para.2A–23 below).

Dates for compliance to be calendar dates and to include time of day

2.9 **2.9—(1) Where the court gives a judgment, order or direction which imposes a time limit for doing any act, the last date for compliance must, wherever practicable—**

(a) be expessed as a calendar date; and

(b) include the time of day by which the act must be done.

(2) Where the date by which an act must be done is inserted in any document, the date must, wherever practicable, be expressed as a calendar date.

Effect of rule

2.9.1 It is important that the court, lawyers and parties should be clear as to the final dates for compliance with time limits imposed by judgments, orders or directions for doing particular acts. This is especially true under a case management system. A date expressed as a calendar date is much more satisfactory than one which has to be calculated in relation to another date or the occurrence of a particular event. Rule 2.9 provides that calendar dates should be used wherever practicable. This rule has no counterpart in the former RSC or CCR.

In certain circumstances it may be convenient or necessary to stipulate that an act must be done by a particular time on a particular day. Rule 2.9 states that this should be done wherever practicable, whether or not there is any obvious reason for doing so.

Meaning of "month" in judgments, etc.

2.10 **2.10 Where "month" occurs in any judgment, order, direction or other document, it means a calendar month.**

Effect of rule

Rule 2.10 follows former RSC O.3 r.1. **2.10.1**

In the CPR, examples of periods of time being specified in terms of months are not common. Most are found in the provisions relating to procedures for assessment of costs (see r.46.8, r.46.16(1), r.46.19(2), r.47.10(5)). Other examples include r.7.5(2)(3) (service of a claim form), r.15.11 (claim stayed if not defended or admitted), r.40.8(1) (default judgment against State).

Time limits may be varied by parties

2.11 Unless these Rules or a practice direction provides otherwise or the court orders otherwise, the time specified by a rule or by the court for a person to do any act may be varied by the written agreement of the parties. **2.11**

(Rules 3.8 (sanctions have effect unless defaulting party obtains relief), 28.4 (variation of case management timetable—fast track) and 29.5 (variation of case management timetable—multi-track), provide for time limits that cannot be varied by agreement between the parties).

Effect of rule

Formerly, except where otherwise provided, the period within which a person was required or authorised by rules or by any judgment, order or direction to do any act in any proceedings could be extended or abridged by consent of all the parties or by order of the court on the application of any party (RSC O.3 r.5(1) and CCR O.13 r.4). Former RSC O.3 r.5(2) stated that the period within which a person was required by court rules, or by any order of direction, to serve, file or amend any pleading or other document could be extended by consent given in writing without an order of the court being made for that purpose. Now, the general power of the court to shorten or extend the time for complying with any rule, practice direction or court order is found in r.3.1(2)(a). An express power in the hands of the court to extend time for serving a claim form is found in r.7.6. Under the CPR, the scope for variation of time limits by agreement between parties is curtailed. **2.11.1**

Under r.2.11, variation by agreement between the parties of times specified is limited to the variation of times specified "by a rule or by the court". This phrase would include a time specified in a judgment, direction or order of the court. It does not in terms include a time specified by other means, for example, in a practice direction. However, presumably it could be argued that a time specified by a practice direction is a time specified "by the court". The rule speaks of "a person" being required to do any act; such person may or may not be a party in the proceedings (e.g. an expert witness). In the interests of case management, parties should not be permitted to vary certain time limits without the permission of the court. Rules containing provisions expressly forbidding variation by agreement are referred to in r.2.11.

One example of a situation in which a time limit may be varied by agreement of the parties is provided by r.15.5 which states that the defendant and the claimant may agree that the period for filing a defence specified in r.15.4 shall be extended by up to 28 days; the defendant must notify the court in writing of any such agreement (r.15.5(2)).

One of the circumstances in which a time limit may not be varied by written agreement between parties is where "the court orders otherwise". When the court makes an order, not only may it make it subject to conditions, including conditions as to the time within which acts must be done, but also it may specify the consequence of failure to comply with the order (r.3.1(3)). In this situation the order comes within r.3.8 and, consequently, by operation of r.3.8(2) the time specified may not be varied by written agreement between the parties (see para.2.11.2 below) and the order need not contain an express term to that effect. Where a court order contains a term specifying a period of time for a person to do an act, but specifies no consequence for failure to comply with that or any other term of the order, variation of the specified time period by written agreement between the parties is permitted unless the order contains an express term to the contrary (or unless not permitted by a rule or practice direction).

Practice Direction (The Fast Track), para.4.5 and Practice Direction (The Multi-

Track), para.6.5 state that where the parties take advantage of r.2.11 and vary a time limit, thereby affecting directions previously given by the court, the parties need not file the written agreement (see respectively, paras 28PD.4 and 29PD.6).

Rule 2.11 is incorporated by reference in Sch.1, RSC 45, r.5(1)(a) and r.7(5) (Enforcement of judgment to do or abstain from doing any act). Formerly, these provisions contained no express reference to extension of time by agreement, whether written or otherwise.

In Pt 52 (Appeals), r.52.6 (which replaces CPR Sch.1, RSC 59, r.2C) states that parties may not agree to extend any date or time limit relating to appeals set by rules of court, practice direction, or an order of the appeal court or a lower court. An application to vary the time limit for filing an appeal notice must be made to the appeal court (r.52.6(1)). Presumably, "these Rules" include schedule rules stating time limits (but note CPR r.52.1(4)).

In relation to certain proceedings, the circumstances in which particular time limits may or may not be varied by agreement between the parties are affected by provisions in practice directions (e.g. Practice Direction (Directors Disqualification Proceedings), paras 9.7, 11.7 and 32.5, see para.B1-001 below).

"written agreement"

2.11.2 An agreement between parties varying a time limit must be a written agreement. This matter was examined by the Court of Appeal in *Thomas v Home Office* [2006] EWCA Civ 1355; [2007] 1 W.L.R. 230, October 19, 2006, unrep., CA, where it was held that the operation of r.2.11 is not excluded by r.7.5 (consequently it is opento parties by written agreement to agree an extension of time for the service of a claim form). The court stated that "written agreement of the parties" may include an exchange of letters in which the variation is agreed or an oral agreement which is then confirmed in writing by both parties. Further, where a variation of a time limit is made in writing, any subsequent variation, being a variation to the time limit agreed in the written variation, is a variation of the time limit "specified by a rule" within the meaning of r.2.11, and therefore, to be valid, must itself be in writing.

PRACTICE DIRECTION—COURT OFFICES

This Practice Direction supplements CPR Part 2

Central Office of the High Court at the Royal Courts of Justice

1 The Central Office shall be divided into such departments, and the business performed in the Central Office shall be distributed among the departments in such manner, as is set out in the Queen's Bench Division Guide. **2PD.1**

Business in the Offices of the Supreme Court

2.1(1) The offices of the Supreme Court shall be open on every day of the year except— **2PD.2**

(a) Saturdays and Sundays,

(b) Good Friday and the day after Easter Monday,

(c) Christmas Day and, if that day is a Friday or Saturday, then 28th December,

(d) Bank Holidays in England and Wales under the Banking and Financial Dealings Act 1971, and,

(e) such other days as the Lord Chancellor, with the concurrence of the Lord Chief Justice, the Master of the Rolls, the President of the Family Division and the Vice-Chancellor ("the Heads of Division") may direct.

(2) The hours during which the offices of the Supreme Court at the Royal Courts of Justice and at the Principal Registry of the Family Division at First Avenue House, 42-49 High Holborn, London WC1V 6NP shall be open to the public shall be as follows:

(a) from 10 a.m. to 4.30 p.m.;

(b) such other hours as the Lord Chancellor, with the concurrence of the Heads of Division, may from time to time direct.

(3) Every District Registry shall be open on the days and during the hours that the Lord Chancellor from time to time directs and, in the absence of any such directions, shall be open on the same days and during the same hours as the county court offices of which it forms part are open.

2.2 One of the Masters of the Queen's Bench Division (the "Practice Master") shall be present at the Central Office every day on which the office is open for the purpose of superintending the business performed there and giving any directions which may be required on questions of practice and procedure.

Note—The title of the former Vice-Chancellor is now "The Chancellor of the High Court." **2PD.2.1**

County Courts

3.1 Every County Court shall have an office or, if the Lord Chancellor so directs, two or more offices, situated at such place or places as he may direct, for the transaction of the business of the court. **2PD.3**

3.2(1) Every County Court office, or if a court has two or more offices at least one of those offices, shall be open on every day of the year except—

(a) Saturdays and Sundays,

(b) the day before Good Friday from noon onwards and Good Friday,

(c) the Tuesday after the Spring bank holiday,

(d) Christmas Day and, if that day is a Friday or Saturday, then the 28th December,

(e) bank holidays, and

(f) such other days as the Lord Chancellor may direct.

(2) In this paragraph "bank holiday" means a bank holiday in England and Wales under the Banking and Financial Dealings Act 1971 and "Spring holiday" means the bank holiday on the last Monday in May or any day appointed instead of that day under section 1(2) of that Act.

3.3 Subject to paragraph 3.2(1)(b), the hours during which any court office is open to the public shall be from 10 a.m. to 4 p.m. or such other hours as the Lord Chancellor may from time to time direct.

PRACTICE DIRECTION—ALLOCATION OF CASES TO LEVELS OF JUDICIARY

1.1 Rule 2.4 provides that Judges, Masters and District Judges may exercise any function of the court except where an enactment, rule or practice direction provides otherwise. This Practice Direction sets out the matters over which Masters and District Judges do not have jurisdiction or which they may deal with only on certain conditions. It does not affect jurisdiction conferred by other enactments. Reference should also be made to other relevant Practice Directions (e.g. Part 24, paragraph 3 and Part 26, paragraphs 12.1–10). References to Circuit Judges include Recorders and Assistant Recorders and references to Masters and District Judges include Deputies. **2BPD.1**

1.2 Wherever a Master or District Judge has jurisdiction, he may refer the matter to a Judge instead of dealing with it himself.

The High Court

Injunctions

2.1 Search orders (rule 25.1(1)(h)), freezing orders (rule 25.1(1)(f)), an ancillary order under rule 25.1(1)(g) and orders authorising a person to enter land to recover, inspect or sample property (rule 25.1(1)(d)) may only be made by a Judge. **2BPD.2**

2.2 Except where paragraphs 2.3 and 2.4 apply, injunctions and orders relating to injunctions, including orders for specific performance where these involve an injunction, must be made by a Judge.

2.3 A Master or a District Judge may only make an injunction:

(a) in terms agreed by the parties;

(b) in connection with or ancillary to a charging order;

(c) in connection with or ancillary to an order appointing a receiver by way of equitable execution; or

(d) in proceedings under rule 66.7 (order restraining person from receiving sum due from the Crown).

2.4 A Master or District Judge may make an order varying or discharging an injunction or undertaking given to the court if all parties to the proceedings have consented to the variation or discharge.

Other pre-trial Orders and Interim Remedies

3.1 A Master or District Judge may not make orders or grant interim remedies: **2BPD.3**

(a) relating to the liberty of the subject;

(b) relating to criminal proceedings or matters except procedural applications in appeals to the High Court (including *appeals by case stated*) under any enactment;

(c) relating to a claim for judicial review, except that interim applications in claims for judicial review may be made to a Master of the Queen's Bench Divison.

(d) relating to appeals from Masters or District Judges;

(e) in appeals against costs assessment under Parts 43 to 48, except on an appeal under rule 47.20 against the decision of an authorised court officer;

(f) in applications under section 42 of the Supreme Court Act 1981 by a person subject to a Civil or a Criminal or an All Proceedings Order (vexatious litigant) for permission to start or continue proceedings;

(g) in applications under section 139 of the Mental Health Act 1983 for permission to bring proceedings against a person.

3.2 This Practice Direction is not concerned with family proceedings. It is also not concerned with proceedings in the Family Division except to the extent that such proceedings can be dealt with in the Chancery Division or the Family Division, e.g. proceedings under the Inheritance (Provision for Family and Dependants) Act 1975 or under section 14 of the Trusts of Land and Appointment of Trustees Act 1996. District Judges (including District Judges of the Principal Registry of the Family Division) have jurisdiction to hear such proceedings, subject to any Direction given by the President of the Family Division.

Trials and Assessments of damages

2BPD.4 **4.1** A Master or District Judge may, subject to any Practice Direction, try a case which is treated as being allocated to the multi-track because it is proceeding under Part 8 (see rule 8.9(c)). He may try a case which has been allocated to the multi-track under Part 26 only with the consent of the parties. Restrictions on the trial jurisdiction of Masters and District Judges do not prevent them from hearing applications for summary judgment or, if the parties consent, for the determination of a preliminary issue.

4.2 A Master or a District Judge may assess the damages or sum due to a party under a judgment without limit as to the amount.

Chancery Proceedings

2BPD.5 **5.1** In proceedings in the Chancery Division, a Master or a District Judge may not deal with the following without the consent of the Chancellor:

(a) approving compromises (other than applications under the Inheritance (Provision for Family and Dependants) Act 1975) (i) on behalf of a person under disability where that person's interest in a fund, or if there is no fund, the maximum amount of the claim, exceeds £100,000 and (ii) on behalf of absent, unborn and unascertained persons;

(b) making declarations, except in plain cases;

(c) making final orders under section 1(1) of the Variation of Trusts Act 1958, except for the removal of protective trusts where the interest of the principal beneficiary has not failed or determined;

(d) where the proceedings are brought by a Part 8 claim form, seeking determination of any question of law or as to the construction of a document which is raised by the claim form;

(e) *giving permission* to executors, administrators and trustees to bring or defend proceedings or to continue the prosecution or defence of proceedings, and granting an indemnity for costs out of the trust estate, except in plain cases;

(f) granting an indemnity for costs out of the assets of a company on the application of minority shareholders bringing a derivative action, except in plain cases;
(g) making an order for rectification, except for—
 (i) rectification of the register under the Land Registration Act 1925; or
 (ii) alteration or rectification of the register under the Land Registration Act 2002,

in plain cases;
(h) making orders to vacate entries in the register under the Land Charges Act 1972, except in plain cases;
(i) making final orders on applications under section 19 of the Leasehold Reform Act 1967, section 48 of the Administration of Justice Act 1985 and sections 21 and 25 of the Law of Property Act 1969;
(j) making final orders under the Landlord and Tenant Acts 1927 and 1954, except (i) by consent, and (ii) orders for interim rents under sections 24A to 24D of the 1954 Act;
(k) making orders in proceedings in the Patents Court except (i) by consent, (ii) to extend time, (iii) on applications for permission to serve out of the jurisdiction and (iv) on applications for security for costs.

5.2 A Master or District Judge may only give directions for early trial after consulting the Judge in charge of the relevant list.

5.3 Where a winding-up order has been made against a company, any proceedings against the company by or on behalf of debenture holders may be dealt with, at the Royal Courts of Justice, by a Registrar and, in a District Registry with insolvency jurisdiction, by a District Judge.

Note —The title of the former Vice-Chancellor is now "The Chancellor of the High Court." **2BPD.5.1**

Assignment of Claims to Masters and Transfer between Masters

6.1 The Senior Master, and the Chief Master will make arrangements for proceedings to be assigned to individual Masters. They may vary such arrangements generally or in particular cases, for example, by transferring a case from a Master to whom it had been assigned to another Master. **2BPD.6**

6.2 The fact that a case has been assigned to a particular Master does not prevent another Master from dealing with that case if circumstances require, whether at the request of the assigned Master or otherwise.

Freezing Orders: Cross Examination of Deponents about Assets

7 Where the court has made a freezing order under rule 25.1(f) and has ordered a person to make a witness statement or affidavit about his assets and to be cross-examined on its contents, unless the Judge directs otherwise, the cross-examination will take place before a Master or a District Judge, or if the Master or District Judge directs, before an examiner of the Court. **2BPD.7**

Human Rights

7A A deputy High Court Judge, a Master or District Judge may not try— **2BPD.7A**

(1) a case in a claim made in respect of a judicial act under the Human Rights Act 1998, or

(2) a claim for a declaration of incompatibility in accordance with section 4 of the Human Rights Act 1998.

County Courts

Injunctions, Anti-social Behaviour Orders and Committal

2BPD.8 **8.1** Injunctions which a county court has jurisdiction to make may only be made by a Circuit Judge, except:

(a) where the injunction is to be made in proceedings which a District Judge otherwise has jurisdiction to hear (see paragraph 11.1 below);

(b) where the injunction is sought in a money claim which has not yet been allocated to a track, where the amount claimed does not exceed the fast track financial limit;

(c) in the circumstances provided by paragraph 2.3;

(d) where the injunction is to be made under any of the following provisions—

(i) section 153A, 153B or 153D of the Housing Act 1996; or

(ii) section 3 of the Protection from Harassment Act 1997.

8.1A

A District Judge has jurisdiction to make an order under—

(1) section 1B or 1D of the Crime and Disorder Act 1998 (anti-social behaviour); and

(2) section 26A, 26B or 26C of the Anti-Social Behaviour Act 2003 (parenting orders).

8.2 A District Judge may make orders varying or discharging injunctions in the circumstances provided by paragraph 2.4.

8.3 A District Judge may not make an order committing a person to prison except where an enactment authorises this: see section 23 of the Attachment of Earnings Act 1971, sections 14 and 118 of the County Courts Act 1984, sections 152–157 of the Housing Act 1996, and the relevant rules.

Homelessness Appeals

2BPD.9 **9** A District Judge may not hear appeals under section 204 or section 204A of the Housing Act 1996.

Other pre-trial Orders and Interim Remedies

2BPD.10 **10.1** In addition to the restrictions on jurisdiction mentioned at paragraphs 8.1–3, paragraph 3.1(d) and (e) above applies.

Trials and Assessments of Damages

2BPD.11 **11.1** A District Judge has jurisdiction to hear the following:

(a) any claim which has been allocated to the small claims track or fast track or which is treated as being allocated to the multi-track under rule 8.9(c) and the table at Section B of the Practice Direction to Part 8, except claims:

(i) under Part I of the Landlord and Tenant Act 1927;

(ii) for a new tenancy under section 24 or for the termination of a tenancy under section 29(2) of the Landlord and Tenant Act 1954;

(iii) for an order under section 38 or 40 of the Landlord and Tenant Act 1987;

(iv) under paragraph 26 or 27 of Schedule 11 to or section 27 of the Agricultural Holdings Act 1986;

(v) under section 45(2) of the Matrimonial Causes Act 1973 for a declaration of legitimation by virtue of the Legitimacy Act 1976;

(vi) under section 35, 38 or 40 of the Fair Trading Act 1973; or

(vii) under Part II of the Mental Health Act 1983.

(b) proceedings for the recovery of land proceedings under section 82A(2) of the Housing Act 1985 or section 6A(2) of the Housing Act 1988 (demotion claims) or proceedings in a county court under Chapter 1A of the Housing Act 1996 (demoted tenancies);

(c) the assessment of damages or other sum due to a party under a judgment without any financial limit;

(d) with the permission of the Designated Civil Judge in respect of that case, any other proceedings.

11.2 A case allocated to the small claims track may only be assigned to a Circuit Judge to hear with his consent.

Freezing Orders: Cross Examination of Deponents about Assets

12 To the extent that a county court has power to make a freezing order, paragraph 7 applies as appropriate. **2BPD.12**

Distribution of Business between Circuit Judge and District Judge

13 Where both the Circuit Judge and the District Judge have jurisdiction in respect of any proceedings, the exercise of jurisdiction by the District Judge is subject to any arrangements made by the Designated Civil Judge for the proper distribution of business between Circuit Judges and District Judges. **2BPD.13**

14.1 In District Registries of the High Court and in the county court, the Designated Civil Judge may make arrangements for proceedings to be assigned to individual District Judges. He may vary such arrangements generally or in particular cases. **2BPD.14**

14.2 The fact that a case has been assigned to a particular District Judge does not prevent another District Judge from dealing with the case if the circumstances require.

Human Rights

15 A District Judge may not try a case in which an allegation of indirect discrimination is made against a public authority that would, if the court finds that it occurred, be unlawful under section 19B of the Race Relations Act 1976. **2BPD.15**

PART 3

The Court's Case Management Powers

Contents

Editorial Introduction

3.0.2 This Part provides the court with the powers which it is essential for the court to have in order to undertake active case management. The powers fall into three main categories:

(1) General powers, including notably, power for the court to make orders of its own initiative (rr.3.1, 3.2, 3.3 and 3.10);

(2) Coercive powers (r.3.1(3) and (5), rr.3.4, 3.5 and 3.7);

(3) Power to give relief against sanctions (rr.3.6, 3.8 and 3.9).

Related sources

3.0.3 • Part 24 (summary judgment).

Forms

3.0.4
- **N19** Limited Civil Restraint Order
- **N19A** Extended Civil Restraint Order
- **N19B** General Civil Restraint Order

Practice Directions

3.0.5 Part 3 is supplemented by Practice Direction (Striking Out a Statement of Case): see para.3PD.1 below; Practice Direction (Sanctions for Non-Payment of Fees): see para.3BPD.1 below; Practice Direction (Civil Restraint Orders): see para.3CPD.1; and Practice Direction (Mesothelioma Claims): see para.3DPD.1.

The court's general powers of management[1]

3.1 ***3.1***—**(1) The list of powers in this rule is in addition to any pow-**

[1] Amended by the Civil Procedure (Amendment No.3) Rules 2006 (SI 2006/3435).

ers given to the court by any other rule or practice direction or by any other enactment or any powers it will otherwise have.

(2) Except where these Rules provide otherwise, the court will—

(a) extend or shorten the time for compliance with any rule, practice direction or court order (even if an application for extension is made after the time for compliance has expired);

(b) adjourn or bring forward a hearing;

(c) require a party or a party's legal representative to attend the court;

(d) hold a hearing and receive evidence by telephone or by using any other method of direct oral communication;

(e) direct that part of any proceedings (such as a counterclaim) be dealt with as separate proceedings;

(f) stay[GL] the whole or part of any proceedings or judgment either generally or until a specified date or event;

(g) consolidate proceedings;

(h) try two or more claims on the same occasion;

(i) direct a separate trial of any issue;

(j) decide the order in which issues are to be tried;

(k) exclude an issue from consideration;

(l) dismiss or give judgment on a claim after a decision on a preliminary issue;

(ll) order any party to file and serve an estimate of costs;

(m) take any other step or make any other order for the purpose of managing the case and furthering the overriding objective.

(3) When the court makes an order, it will—

(a) make it subject to conditions, including a condition to pay a sum of money into court; and

(b) specify the consequence of failure to comply with the order or a condition.

(4) Where the court gives directions it will take into account whether or not a party has complied with the Practice Direction (Pre-Action Conduct) and any relevant pre-action protocol[GL].

(5) The court will order a party to pay a sum of money into court if that party has, without good reason, failed to comply with a rule, practice direction or a relevant pre-action protocol.

(6) When exercising its power under paragraph (5) the court must have regard to—

(a) the amount in dispute; and

(b) the costs which the parties have incurred or which they may incur.

(6A) Where a party pays money into court following an order under paragraph (3) or (5), the money shall be security for any sum payable by that party to any other party in the proceedings.

(7) A power of the court under these Rules to make an order includes a power to vary or revoke the order.

Effect of rule

3.1.1 The powers listed in r.3.1(2) enable the court to carry out its duty to *actively* manage cases (r.1.4(1)) so as to further the overriding objective (r.1.1). The list of powers is not exhaustive (see r.3.1(1) and r.3.1(2)(m)).

Extending or shortening time limits

3.1.2 Under r.3.1(2)(a), the court may make an Order extending or shortening the time for compliance with any Rule, Practice Direction or Court Order and may grant such an Order retrospectively, i.e. even after the time limit in question has expired. As to the parties' power to vary time limits by written agreement, see r.2.11 and the commentary thereto.

In *Sayers v Clarke Walker* [2002] EWCA Civ 645; [2002] 1 W.L.R. 3095; [2002] 3 All E.R. 490, CA, the Court of Appeal set out the guidance to be found in the CPR as to the court's exercise of discretion when making orders under r.3.1(2)(a). The rule sets out the court's general powers as to time limits in rules, orders and practice directions. In deciding how to exercise that power the court must take into account the overriding objective in r.1.1. In cases of any complexity the court should also have regard to the matters listed in r.3.9 (relief from sanctions). That rule provides a checklist which it is preferable to use rather than the judge-made checklists which are set out in some previous cases. Rule 3.9 governs the court's approach in other applications under Pt 3 (i.e. applications under rr.3.6 and 3.8). Although, strictly speaking, the inability to take a procedural step because the court will not alter the time limit for it, is not a sanction expressly "imposed" by a rule, order or practice direction, the consequence for an unsuccessful applicant will be exactly the same as if it was. The principles concerning the extension of time for filing originating applications at first instance (including the application of r.3.9) are also applicable where an application is made in the Court of Appeal for an extension of a time limit for filing a notice of appeal (*R. (Awan) v Immigration Appeal Tribunal* [2004] EWCA Civ 922; *The Times*, January 23, 2004, CA).

The decision in *Sayers* (see above) was distinguished in *Robert v Momentum Services Ltd* [2003] EWCA Civ 299, CA; [2003] 1 W.L.R. 1577; [2003] 2 All E.R. 74, in which it was held that it was not necessary to go through the checklist contained in r.3.9 where an application for an extension of time is made before the expiry of the time limit sought to be extended. In such cases the discretion should be exercised having regard to the overriding objective of enabling the court to deal with cases justly, including, so far as practicable, the matters set out in r.1.1(2). In *Robert* it was held that it would rarely be appropriate to dismiss an application for an extension of time on the grounds that the claim is weak unless the court is able to conclude that an application to strike out (under r.3.4), or for summary judgment (under Pt 24), would succeed. To refuse an application for an extension of time without crossing that threshold would be a draconian step and might well infringe a claimant's rights under art.6 of ECHR. It was said that if a defendant wishes to make a challenge on the ground that the claim is weak, then he would be well advised to issue an application to strike out, or for summary judgment, to be heard at the same time as the application for an extension of time. Furthermore, if a defendant does wish to pray in aid the merits of the claim as a reason for refusing an application for an extension of time, then notice should be given to the claimant to enable him to submit evidence directed to that point.

As to extending time limits in consent orders, see *Siebe Gorman & Co Ltd v Pneupac Ltd* [1982] 1 W.L.R. 185; [1982] 1 All E.R. 377, CA; *Ropac Ltd v Inntrepreneur Pub Co* [2001] C.P. Rep 31; [2001] L. & T.R. 10; *Zappia Middle East Construction Co Ltd v Clifford Chance (Extension of Time)* [2001] EWCA Civ 1387; and *Placito v Slater* [2003] EWCA Civ 1863; [2004] 1 W.L.R. 1605, CA. In *Siebe Gorman* the Court of Appeal made the point that when an order is expressed to be made "by consent" it is ambiguous. One meaning is that the words evidence a real contract between the parties (i.e. a contract excluding the jurisdiction of the court to extend time) in which case the court would only interfere with such an order on the same grounds as it would with any other contract. The other meaning is that the words mean "the parties hereto not objecting". In the latter case there is no real contract and the order can be varied by the court in the same circumstances as any other order. In *Ropac*, Neuberger J. held that given the overriding objective under r.1.1, the court had jurisdiction under r.3.1(2)(a) and r.3.9 to extend a time limit even where this was contrary to an agreement between the parties. This was a wider jurisdiction than under the RSC. However, he added that the court should place very great weight on what the parties have agreed and should be slow, save in unusual circumstances, to depart from what the parties have agreed. In *Ferrotex*, the Court of Appeal found it unnecessary to decide whether Neuberger J. was correct as it was satisfied that, although the consent order under consideration was made pursuant to a "real contract", such a conclusion was not decisive because the parties had not expressly or impliedly intended to oust the jurisdiction of the court to extend the time provided for in the order. In *Di Placito v Slater* [2003] EWCA Civ 1863 the Court of Appeal again declined to decide whether or not the court had a wider jurisdiction to extend time under the CPR given that the time limit relied on was contained in an undertaking which the court had jurisdiction to discharge or modify.

Rule 3.1(2)(a) does not empower the court to extend the time for serving a claim form. This is because rule 3.1(2) gives the court powers "except where these Rules provide otherwise" and rule 7.6(3), by its inclusion of the words "only if" does provide otherwise (*Vinos v Marks & Spencer Plc* [2001] 3 All E.R. 784, CA). A claimant cannot circumvent the restrictions in r.7.6(3) by applying under r.3.9 (Relief from Sanctions) or r.3.10 (general power of the Court to rectify matters where there has been an error of procedure) (*Kaur v CTP Coil Ltd* [2001] C.P. Rep. 34; *Elmes v Hygrade Food Products Plc* [2001] EWCA Civ 121). Contrast the regime which applies to particulars of claim: although they must be served "no later than the latest time for serving a claim form" (r.7.4(2)) an extension of time for service may be granted even after that latest time has passed (*Totty v Snowden* [2001] EWCA Civ 1415; [2002] 1 W.L.R. 1384; [2001] 4 All E.R. 577).

The court's general case management powers under r.3.1(2)(a) to extend time periods specified in an Order of the court are not cut down by r.3.8 (sanctions to have effect unless defaulting party obtains relief): a time limit in an order imposing sanctions for delay can be extended even if no application is made under r.3.8 for relief from sanctions (*Keen Phillips (a Firm) v Field* [2006] EWCA Civ 1524; [2007] 1 W.L.R. 686, as to which, see further, para.3.8.1, below).

As to the criteria to be applied on applications under r.52.6 to extend the time for appealing, see para.52.6.2, below and *Smith v Brough* [2005] EWCA Civ 261. Where the time limit prescribed by r.52.4(2)(b) for filing an appellant's notice has expired, the lower court still has jurisdiction to extend time for appealing. However, such extension should be granted only where appropriate in exceptional circumstances. The lower court should not exercise its discretion to grant such an extension if a Notice of Appeal has already been lodged with the Court of Appeal (*Aujla v Sanghera* [2004] EWCA Civ 121; [2004] C.P. Rep.31, CA).

For discussion of the defendant's ECHR art.6(1) right to a fair trial within a reasonable time in the context of an application by a claimant to extend time, see *Woodhouse v Consignia Plc* [2002] EWCA Civ 275 at [43]–[44]; [2002] 1 W.L.R. 2558 and *Price v Price* [2003] EWCA Civ 888 at [34]–[35]; [2003] 3 All E.R. 911. ECHR art.13 requires the state to provide an effective domestic law remedy to allow a claimant to complain about a failure to provide a hearing within a reasonable time: *Kudla v Poland App. 30210/96* (2002) 35 E.H.R.R. 11, October 26, 2000, ECtHR.

Adjourning hearings

In determining whether to grant an adjournment the court must have regard to the overriding objective. Therefore the court should deal with appellant's case in a manner which saves expense, is proportionate to the amount of money involved and allocates to it an appropriate share of the court's resources (*Boyd & Hutchinson (A Firm) v Foenander* [2003] EWCA Civ 1516; October 23, 2003, unrep., CA (court proceeding to hear appeal where appellant made late application for adjournment on basis that it would refuse an adjournment if it concluded that the appeal had no prospect of success, rather than simply putting the point off to a future occasion)). For an example of circumstances in which a trial judge's (1) refusal to grant a defendant an adjournment of a trial, with the result that the trial proceeded in his absence, and (2) his subsequent refusal to set aside that judgment under r.39.3(3), were upheld on appeal, see *National Westminster Bank v Aaronson* [2004] EWHC 618; March 9, 2004, unrep. (Royce J.) (neither decision exceeded the generous ambit within which a reasonable disagreement is possible). **3.1.3**

A refusal to adjourn a hearing pursuant to r.3.1(2)(b) was unsuccessfully challenged in *Daisystar Limited v Woolwich Plc* March 16, 2000, unrep., CA. See also *Lloyds Bank Plc v Dix* 2000 WL 1918520; October 26, 2000, unrep., CA (adjournment would have made no material difference to the outcome of the litigation in view of the weakness of the appellants' case). Where a litigant in person requests an adjournment on the ground of ill-health the court should be slow to refuse, provided that it is his first request and his case has some prospect of success: *Fox v Graham Group Ltd The Times*, August 3, 2001, Neuberger J.; as to the further proceedings in that case, see *Fox v Graham Group Ltd* [2002] EWCA Civ 1124.

Generally, no appeal from the decision of a court may be made without permission. Rule 52.3(2) states that, where an application for permission to appeal may or should be made to the lower court, it is to be made at the hearing at which the decision to be appealed against is made. Notices of Appeal must be filed within the time limits fixed by the rules in relation to the date of the decision of the lower court (see r.52.4). Paragraph 4.3B of Practice Direction (Appeals), supplementing Pt 52, states that, where no application is made for permission to appeal at the hearing at which the decision to be appealed against is made, but a party requests further time to make such application, the court may adjourn the hearing to give that party the opportunity to do so.

Making orders subject to conditions

3.1.4 In order to encourage a party to carry out his duty to help the court to further the overriding objective (r.1.3) an order may be made subject to conditions and may specify the consequence of failure to comply with an order or a condition (r.3.1(3)). The conditions should be expressed clearly and precisely (*Morgans v Needham, The Times*, November 5, 1999, CA). The condition must be one which is capable of being complied with; an impecunious party should not be ordered to pay into court a sum of money which he is unlikely to be able to raise (*M.V. Yorke Motors v Edwards* [1982] 1 W.L.R. 444; [1982] 1 All E.R. 1024, HL; *Chapple v Williams* [1999] C.P.L.R 731; [1999] L.T.L., December 8, CA; *Sweetman v Shepherd, The Times*, March 29, 2000, CA). The court is not required to impose an express sanction for failing to comply with an order or condition. However, when making an order requiring somebody to do something for the first time, the court may be less reluctant than it previously was to impose an express sanction in the event of non-compliance. Even if no express sanction is stated the court may later strike out all or part of a statement of case of a party who fails to comply with the order (see further r.3.4).

In *Price v Price* [2003] EWCA Civ 888; [2003] 3 All E.R. 911 the Court of Appeal encouraged the wider use by the courts of the power to impose conditions upon extensions of time: C had delayed serving particulars of claim for over fifteen months and had failed to supply information to D despite repeated requests for it; the Court of Appeal granted an extension allowing C a further 28 days to serve particulars of claim on condition that no claim was made for compensation other than what might be substantiated by the medical evidence which was available when the claim form was issued. See also *Southern & District Finance Plc v Turner* [2003] EWCA Civ 1574 November 11, 2003, unrep., CA, where the Court of Appeal made observations on the usefulness of the court's power under r.3.1(3) to impose conditions on orders made under r.3.1(2)(a); and *Jones v T Mobile (UK) Ltd* [2003] EWCA Civ 1162; [2003] 3 E.G.L.R. 55; [2004] C.P. Rep. 10 (condition that appellant's costs of hearing should be irrecoverable imposed when granting an extension of time).

If an order against a defendant includes a condition as to the payment of a sum of money into court, the defendant may treat a sum paid into court following that order as a Pt 36 payment (r.3.1(6A) and, for a definition of Pt 36 payments, see r.36.2).

Where a party refuses to comply with an order to pay costs which he has the means to pay the court may make an order debarring him from taking any further part in the proceedings unless, by a date stated in the order, he complies with the previous order (*Days Healthcare UK Ltd v Pihsiang Machinery Manufacturing Co Ltd* [2006] EWHC 1444; [2006] 4 All E.R. 233, QB. An intentional failure to comply with an order made in proceedings the litigant seeks to participate in may also amount to a contempt of court (*Days Healthcare UK Ltd*, above).

Ordering security

3.1.5 If a party has, without good reason, failed to comply with a rule, practice direction or a relevant pre-action protocol, the court may order him to pay a sum of money into court (r.3.1(5)); see *Olatawura v Abiloye* [2002] EWCA Civ 998; [2003] 1 W.L.R. 275; [2002] 4 All E.R. 903, CA. The sum of money will be security for any sum payable by that party to any other party in the proceedings (r.3.1(6A)). An order such as this can be made against a claimant or a defendant. In exercising this power the court must have regard to the amount in dispute and the costs incurred and to be incurred (r.3.1(6)). In the case of claimants, an order under r.3.1(5) significantly broadens the court's powers to order security for costs (as to which, see generally CPR Pt 25, Sect.II). As to defendants and defendants to counterclaims they may be ordered to give security for costs and also for any money remedy claimed against them.

It is to be noted that the circumstances when it would be appropriate to order a party to pay a sum of money into court are limited. In *Olctawura* (above) Simon Brown L.J. suggested that a party only becomes exposed to an adverse order for security under r.3.1(5) once he can be seen either to be regularly flouting proper court procedures or otherwise to be demonstrating a want of good faith—good faith for this purpose consisting of a will to litigate a genuine claim or defence as economically and expeditiously as reasonably possible in accordance with the overriding objective. See also: *CIBC v Mellon Trust Co v Mora Hotel* [2002] EWCA Civ 1688; [2003] 1 All E.R. 564, CA; and *Ali v Hudson* [2003] EWCA Civ 1793; December 11, 2003, unrep., CA.

In *Olatawura* the point was also made that before ordering security for costs in any case (i.e. whether or not under Pt 25) the court should be alert to the risk that by making such an order it may be denying the party concerned the right to access to the court. It was said that whether or not the person concerned has (or can raise) the money will always be a prime consideration, not least since art.6 of the European Convention for the Protection of Human Rights and Fundamental Freedoms 1950 (as set out in Sch.1 to the Human Rights Act 1998) became incorporated into domestic law; see para.22 of the judgment.

In *Ali v Hudson* [2003] EWCA Civ 1793; December 11, 2003, unrep., CA the Court of Appeal set aside an order made which, because of the appellant's delay, stayed an appeal pending the provision of security for the costs of the appeal. In his judgment, with which the other two lords justices agreed, Clark L.J. quoted passages of the judgment of Simon Brown L.J. in *Olawatura v Abiloye* [2002] EWCA Civ 988; [2003] 1 W.L.R. 275 (see above) and stated:

> "Those principles show that the power to order security for costs in a case of this kind should be exercised with great caution. The correct general approach may be summarised as follows: (i) it would only be in an exceptional case (if ever) that a court would order security for costs if the order would stifle a claim or an appeal; (ii) in any event, (a) an order should not ordinarily be made unless the party concerned can be shown to be regularly flouting proper court procedures or otherwise to be demonstrating a want of good faith; good faith being understood to consist (as Simon Brown L.J. put it) of a will to litigate a genuine claim or defence (or appeal) as economically and expeditiously as reasonably possible in accordance with the overriding objective; and (b) an order will not be appropriate in every case where a party has a weak case. The weakness of the party's case will ordinarily be relevant only where he has no real prospect of succeeding."

See also, *Ford v Labrador* [2003] UKPC 41; [2003] 1 W.L.R. 2082 and para.3.4.4, ("Failure to comply with a rule, practice direction or court order") below. In this case an order requiring the appellant to pay costs before proceeding further was set aside as the order impeded the appellant's right of access to the court.

Award of interest on debt or damages as condition

The court's discretion as to the award of interest on debts or damages granted by the Supreme Court Act 1981 s.35A and the County Courts Act 1984 s.69 (see Vol.2, paras 9A–122 and 9A–554), extends to (1) reducing the period for which interest is payable on an award, or (2) altering the rate at which interest is calculated, or both, in the light of the manner in which a party has conducted the litigation. Since the coming into effect of the CPR, the court's powers in this respect have been emphasised for the purpose of demonstrating the range of conditions which the court may attach to a procedural order (r.3.1(3)) and, especially, conditions in the form of procedural sanctions (r.3.8) imposed for the purpose of dealing with delay, whether caused by a claimant or a defendant (see *Biguzzi v Rank Leisure Plc* [1999] 1 W.L.R. 1926, CA; *Baron v Lovell*, *The Times*, September 14, 1999, CA; *Dean v Dean*, November 17, 1999, unrep. (Jacob J.); *Abbahall Ltd v Smee* 2000 WL 442, January 24, 2000, unrep., CA; *Adcock v Cooperative Insurance Society Ltd* [2000] Lloyd's Rep. I.R. 657, CA; *UYB Ltd v British Railways Board*, *The Times*, November 15, 2000, CA). Note also r.36.21(2) (interest consequences for defendant where claimant does better than he proposed in his Pt 36 offer). As to awards of interest generally, see paras 7.0.9 to 7.0.24 below. **3.1.6**

Stay of proceedings

3.1.7 The court has an inherent jurisdiction to stay the whole or any part of the proceedings and this is recited in r.3.1(2)(f). The circumstances in which a stay may be appropriate are many and various and need not be explained here. Note the court's discretion to stay subsequent proceedings until the costs of the first claim have been paid; r.3.4(4) and see para.3.4.8 below. See further Vol.2, paras 9A–176 *et seq.*, and note in particular para.9A–178 ("Stay under the CPR"). For practice where application is made to stay civil proceedings pending the determination of related criminal proceedings, see Practice Direction (Applications), paras 11A.1 *et seq.* (para.23PD.11A below).

In *Zambia v Meer Care & Desai* [2006] EWCA Civ 390; [2006] 1 C.L.C. 436, the court was concerned with a claim brought by the Attorney General of Zambia on behalf of Zambia to recover substantial sums of government money that had been allegedly fraudulently misappropriated by the defendants. The defendants applied for a stay of the proceedings as they were subject to criminal proceedings in Zambia which covered the same ground and under their bail conditions they had to surrender their passports and would be unable to conduct their defence in England. The application was refused and an order was made that the English proceedings be ring-fenced so that none of the evidence adduced or documents disclosed could be used against the defendants in the criminal proceedings. In this way the defendants' right to silence in the criminal proceedings would not be undermined. The criminal proceedings were unlikely to be concluded before mid 2007 and when the appeals process in Zambia would be concluded was not known. The defendants appealed. The Court of Appeal dismissed the appeal holding that the ring-fencing of the English proceedings (including conducting the trial in private) provide appropriate protection for the defendants. The claimant was prepared to give appropriate undertakings and there was no reason to think that the Zambian government would not abide by the order. The Court of Appeal further held that the right to attend trial was not an absolute right. The defendants would know the case against them and would be able to answer that case. It was envisaged that evidence could be given in Zambia and transmitted by videolink and/or given in Zambia before an examiner, preferably the trial judge. The judge would be astute to ensure the defendants were able to give evidence and that lawyers would have time to take instructions. On the facts, there was no risk that the defendants would not receive a fair trial by not being able to be present. It is to be noted, however, that the Court of Appeal made the point that each case turns on its own facts and that there might be cases where it would be appropriate to stay the proceedings until the criminal proceedings were over.

In *Phillips v Symes* [2006] EWHC 1721 (Ch) a stay of proceedings was ordered in an attempt to bring finality to a long standing dispute which had involved a number of hearings, applications and issue trials. The judge stayed the proceedings for two years (to allow the trustees and administrators to negotiate a settlement) after which the parties would be debarred from bringing any further claims. The parties were given permission to apply to extend the two year period provided that they could show why they could not proceed within the deadline. On a subsequent application to vary this order the judge (Peter Smith J.) rejected the submission that the stay was a civil restraint order. He held (unrep., October 16, 2006) that he was not invoking the civil restraint jurisdiction (see r.3.11) but was using the court's extensive case management powers under r.3.1 to ensure that the overriding objective was achieved (for subsequent proceedings, see *Phillips v Symes* [2008] UKHL 1, noted in para.3.10.3).

In *Smith v ADVFN Plc* [2008] EWHC 1797 (QB), the court maintained stays on 37 separate defamation claims brought in relation to postings on an internet bulletin board, where the postings were likely to be found to be fair comment or mere vulgar abuse or to have qualified privilege. Eady J. stated that the court had a wide discretion under r.3.1(2)(f) for imposing or maintaining a stay, and the only reason for lifting a stay was to allow a genuine claim to progress towards trial in order to achieve some legitimate advantage: that is to say, vindication or compensation.

Prospective costs cap orders

3.1.8 In *Griffiths v Solutia (UK) Ltd* [2001] EWCA Civ 736; [2001] 1 Costs L.R. 99; [2002] *P.I.Q.R.* P16 two members of the Court of Appeal commented upon the power to set costs budgets given to arbitrators by s.65 of the Arbitration Act 1996 and expressed the view that the general case management powers set out in CPR Pt 3 should be employed in future to set costs budgets wherever appropriate. Section 65 of the Arbitration Act 1996 (for the text of which, see Vol.2, para.2E–240+) permits arbitrators to limit in advance the amount which can be incurred as costs by the parties to an arbitration. This provision is frequently used and is generally regarded as beneficial in creating "equality of arms" (a rich party cannot blackmail a poorer party by threatening to cause or recover substantial costs) and in promoting proportionality (making sure that the costs are in proportion to the amount or value in dispute). In cases governed by the CPR, the Costs Practice Direction places an obligation on represented parties to file and serve, at certain stages in the proceedings, estimates of the base costs they have incurred and the base costs likely to be incurred (see Costs Practice Direction, paras 6.1 to 6.6, para.43PD.6 below and, for the definition of "base costs", para.2.2, para.43PD.2 below). In 2005, r.3.1(2) was amended to expressly include in the list of powers given to the court, the power to "order any party to file and serve an estimate of costs" (r.3.1(2)(ll)). Such estimates may persuade the judge exercising case management powers to set a cap on the amount of costs which one party may recover from his opponents should he later obtain a costs order in his favour. Such orders (now called "prospective costs cap orders", see *Leigh v Michelin Tyre Plc* [2003] EWCA Civ 1766; [2004] 1 W.L.R 846; [2004] 2 All E.R. 175) can have a significantly beneficial effect in keeping costs within bounds and concentrating minds on keeping costs proportionate throughout the litigation. each order should contain provision for the court to review the cap where it is shown that it has become inappropriate due to circumstances that could not reasonably have been forseen at the time the order was made.

Prospective costs cap orders of the type described above have been made in two cases, both of which were subject to group litigation orders (*A.B. v Leeds Teaching Hospitals NHS Trust* [2003] EWHC 1034, QB, a decision by Gage J., and *Various Ledward Claimants v Kent & Medway Health Authority* [2003] EWHC 2551, QB, a decision of Hallet J. In another case, not involving group litigation, Gage J. set out a three-point test to be adopted.

> "In my judgment the court should only consider making a costs cap order in such cases [i.e. ordinary litigation including clinical negligence cases] where the applicant shows by evidence that there is a real and substantial risk that without such an order costs will be disproportionately or unreasonably incurred; and that this risk may not be managed by conventional case management and a detailed assessment of costs after a trial; and that it is just to make such an order" (*Smart v East Cheshire NHS Trust* [2003] EWHC 2806, QB at [22]; [2004] 1 Costs L.R. 12; and see *Petursson v Hutchison 3G UK Ltd (No.2)* [2005] EWHC 920).

In *Sheppard v Mid Essex Health Authority* [2005] EWHC 1518, QB; [2006] 1 Costs L.R. 8, Hallett J., as she then was, explained one of the main advantages of prospective costs cap orders as she saw them:

> "In my judgment it is far better for the court to attempt to control and budget for costs where appropriate, than to allow costs to be incurred and then have them submitted to detailed assessment … It seems to me that such an approach is entirely in accordance with the spirit and the letter of the CPR."

However, in deciding whether to impose a costs cap, the court should still apply the principles set out by Gage J. in *Smart v East Cheshire NHS Trust* (see above). In *Knight v Beyond Properties Pty Ltd* [2006] EWHC 1242 (Ch); [2007] 1 W.L.R 625; [2007] 1 All E.R 91, Mann J. (refusing to make a costs capping order at an early stage in a passing off action) summarised the position as follows:

> "The present case is one in which there is a CFA with a large mark up, and with no ATE cover. That, by itself, is not enough to justify costs-capping at this stage. Applying Gage J's principles, it is necessary to go further and demonstrate the risk of excessive or extravagant expenditure, and that such expenditure cannot be controlled by case management techniques or post-trial detailed assessments. I do not think that Brooke LJ was intending the jurisdiction to operate without some evidence of such risks, or that if he was that that should apply outside defamation cases, and I have given my reasons for following Gage J's guidelines on the latter point (control)."

In *Leigh v Michelin Tyre Plc* [2003] EWCA Civ 1766; [2004] 1 W.L.R. 846; [2004] 2 All E.R. 175 (a case concerning the relevance of costs estimates in detailed assessment proceedings) the Court of Appeal referred to the possible advantages of prospective costs cap orders but made no decision thereon save to invite the Civil Procedure Rule Committee to reconsider whether any express provision should be made for them in the CPR. In *King v Telegraph Group Ltd (Practice Note)* [2004] EWCA Civ 613; [2005] 1

W.L.R. 2282, it was held that in a defamation case initiated under a conditional fee agreement without "after-the-event" insurance cover (as to which see r.43.2(k)) the court should consider making a costs capping order if there was a danger that, unless a cap was imposed, the freedom of the press would be jeopardised. In such cases a party who has given a notice of funding in respect of an "after-the-event" policy (as to which, see rr.43.2(k) and 44.15) should also disclose to the other parties the amount of cover the policy provides and also the terms of any material exclusions it contains (*Henry v British Broadcasting Corp* [2005] EWHC 2503; [2006] 1 All E.R. 154). In *Willis v Nicolson* [2007] EWCA Civ 199; [2007] P.I.Q.R P22 the Court of Appeal noted some divergence of judicial opinion as to costs capping but declined an invitation to give guidance which would resolve it. Buxton L.J. commented that further guidance should come from the Civil Procedure Rule Committee.

The appropriate time to apply for a costs capping order is at an early stage of the proceedings when the parties and the court can together plan the steps needed to bring the matter to trial, the costs implications of those steps and whether a cap is appropriate; a costs cap should normally be prospective, not retrospective (*Petursson v Hutchison 3G UK Ltd (No.2)* [2005] EWHC 920; *Henry v British Broadcasting Corp* [2005] EWHC 2503; [2006] 1 All E.R. 154). The task of setting a costs cap should normally be undertaken by a costs judge, or a High Court judge sitting with a costs judge (*Henry v British Broadcasting Corp*). In *Tierney v Newsgroup Newspapers Ltd* [2006] EWHC 50, QB important guidance was given as to how the court should minimise the costs and delay which a costs capping exercise may cause:

> "... I would suggest that costs saving techniques should be applied ... using limited written submissions, confined to a short number of pages (as opposed to an extensive "costs draftsman's" approach) and, so far as necessary, with limited oral argument" (McCombe J.).

A prospective costs cap order may also be made in circumstances in which the court is willing to make a "protective costs order" ('PCO')" in favour of the party whose costs are to be capped. In public interest cases in which the applicants are not seeking to establish or protect any private law rights the court may, in its discretion, depart from the "costs follow the event" principle applicable in private civil and family cases by making an order which will limit or extinguish the applicants' liability to pay the opposing parties' costs even if the application fails. An applicant who wishes to obtain the benefit of a PCO without a corresponding restriction upon its own right to recover costs if it wins should expect to be made subject to a capping order which will restrict the opposing party's liability to a reasonably modest amount. The principles upon which PCOs are to be made were considered in depth and somewhat restated by the Court of Appeal in *R. (Corner House Research) v Sec. of State for Trade and Industry* [2005] EWCA Civ 192; [2005] 1 W.L.R. 2600. In that case a PCO was made which included a cost-capping order along the lines suggested by the Court of Appeal in *King v Telegraph Group Ltd (Practice Note)* [2004] EWCA Civ 613; [2005] 1 W.L.R. 2282, CA.

For the procedure to be followed, and for the matters to be taken into account by the court, where a party makes an application for an order limiting the amount of future costs (including disbursements) which a party may recover pursuant to an order for costs subsequently made (a "costs capping order"), see rr.44.18 to 44.20. That procedure does not apply to applications for protective costs orders (r.44.18(3)); see further paras 43.2.1.2, 48.15.7 and 54.6.3 below, and note guidance on principles and procedure (both at first instance and on appeal) given by the Court of Appeal in *R. (Buglife: The Invertebrate Conservation Trust) v. Thurrock Thames Gateway Development Corp* [2008] EWCA Civ 1209, November 4, 2008, CA, unrep.

Court's power to vary or revoke an order (r.3.1(7))

3.1.9 In the RSC and CCR, where particular rules granted the courts powers (as an alternative to a remedy by way of appeal) to make certain procedural orders, further rules were commonly made enabling the courts to vary or revoke any orders made in exercise of those powers. For example, such bespoke rules were made in relation to discovery orders (see RSC O.24, r.17 and CCR O.14, r.12), third party directions and orders (see RSC O.16 r.4(5) and CCR O.12 r.5), and pre-trial evidence orders (see *RSC O.38, r.6* and CCR O.20 r.9). In the CPR there are no such bespoke varying and revoking rules. Instead there is an omnibus provision found in r.3.1(7) which states that "a power of the court under these Rules to make an order includes a power to vary or revoke the order". It may be that that is the sole purpose of r.3.1(7) and that it was introduced in an effort to avoid repetition elsewhere. However, it should be noted that, in terms, r.3.1(7) is not restricted to procedural orders. It should also be noted that the rule refers to "order" and not to "judgment or order", which is the formulation used in other provisions permitting revocation and variation (see further below). In certain contexts, the distinction between "judgment" and "order" is not unimportant (see para.40.1.1 below).

The power to vary or revoke an order given by r.3.1(7) is only exercisable in relation to an order that the court has previously made, and not to an order that is deemed to have been made by operation of the rules (*Lahey v Pirelli Tyres Ltd* [2007] EWCA Civ 91; [2007] 1 W.L.R. 998, CA, approving *Walker Residential Ltd v Davis* [2005] EWHC 3483 (Ch) (Park J.)).

The circumstances in which the court may make orders (procedural or otherwise) are legion. The questions whether, as a matter of law, an order may be varied or revoked, and whether it should be varied or revoked, must be determined in the contexts in which they arise.

The authorities demonstrate that the grounds for setting aside a consent order fall into two categories. First, cases in which it is alleged that there was at the date of the consent order an erroneous basis of fact (e.g. misrepresentations or misunderstandings as to position or assets). Secondly, cases in which there has been a material or unforeseen change in circumstances after the order, so as to undermine or invalidate the basis of the consent order. In cases in the first category the court and the parties would not have made the order if the true state had been known. In cases in the second category, the court and the parties would not have considered the order appropriate, had it been known what was about to happen (*S v S. (Ancillary Relief: Consent Order)* [2002] EWHC 223 (Fam); [2003] Fam. 1 (Bracewell J.); *Raja v Van Hoogstraten* [2005] EWHC 2668 (Ch), November 23, 2005, unrep. (Lightman J.)).

Presumably, r.3.1(7) should not be construed as conferring a power allowing any court at any time "simply to reverse itself if it happens to change its mind" (*SCT Finance Ltd v Bolton* [2002] EWCA Civ 56; [2003] 3 All E.R. 434, CA, at para.58, per Waller L.J.) (whether final certificate made in detailed costs assessment may be set aside where made in Pt 20 proceedings held in absence of ultimate paying party). In *Paragon Finance v Pender* [2003] EWHC 2834 (Ch), Peter Smith J. held that r.3.1(7) gave the court the power to revoke a final possession order. However, it seems that the scope of r.3.1(7) was not fully argued in that case. In *Customs & Excise Commissioners v Anchor Foods Ltd (No 3)* [1999] EWHC 834 (Ch); *The Times*, September 28, 1999, Neuberger J. stated:

> "It seems to me that when the court makes an order, only in the most exceptional circumstances such as those involving fraud or the slip rule, could the court revisit the order even where it is for costs. The court cannot act as an appellate court in respect of its own orders."

In *Lloyd's Investment (Scandinavia) Limited v Ager-Hanssen* [2003] EWHC 1740 (Ch); July 15, 2003, unrep., the claimants entered judgment against the defendant after he had failed to comply with conditions imposed on him by an order setting aside an earlier judgment obtained in default of defence. The defendant applied to vary the terms of the setting aside order. In dismissing the application Patten J. noted that r.3.1(7) is not confined to procedural orders and that no real guidance is found within the rule or elsewhere as to the possible limits of the jurisdiction. Without intending to offer an exhaustive definition of the circumstances in which the power under the rule is exercisable, his lordship said that in his opinion, for the High Court to revisit one of its earlier orders, the applicant must either show some material change of circumstances or that the judge who made the earlier order was misled in some way, whether innocently or otherwise, as to the correct factual position before him. The latter type of case would include, for example, a case of material non-disclosure on an application for an injunction. If all that is sought is a reconsideration of the order on the basis of the same material, then that can only be done in the context of an appeal. Similarly it is not open to a party to the earlier application to seek in effect to re-argue that application by relying on submissions and evidence which were available to him at the time of the earlier hearing, but which, for whatever reason, he or his legal representatives chose not to employ. For an elaboration of the distinction in this context between a material change of circumstances and a judge being misled on the facts, see *Simms v Carr* [2008] EWHC 1030 (Ch), February 7, 2008, unrep. (Morgan J.) at para.45.

A party cannot fight over again a battle which has already been fought unless there are good grounds; see *Chanel Ltd v F.W. Woolworth & Co Ltd* [1981] 1 W.L.R. 485; [1981] 1 All E.R 745, applied in *Leadmill Ltd v Omare* [2002] LTL, April 23. In *Wood-*

house v Consignia plc [2002] EWCA Civ 275; [2002] 1 W.L.R. 2558; [2002] 2 All E.R. 737, it was said that there is a public interest in discouraging a party who makes an unsuccessful interlocutory application from making a subsequent application for the same relief, based on material which was not, but could have been, deployed in support of the first application.

In *Collier v Williams* [2006] EWCA Civ 20, the Court of Appeal stated that the power given by r.3.1(7) cannot be used simply as an equivalent to an appeal against an order with which the applicant is dissatisfied. The Court endorsed the approach adopted in *Lloyds Investment (Scandinavia) v Ager-Hanssen*, op. cit., and said that the circumstances outlined by Patten J. in that case are the only ones in which the power should be exercised. In summarising the position the Court said (para.120) the power should not normally be exercised "unless the applicant is able to place new material before the court, whether in the form of evidence or argument, which was not placed before the court on the earlier occasion". In *Edwards v Golding* [2007] EWCA Civ 416; *The Times* May 22, 2007, CA, the court said the power is exercisable where there is additional material before the court in the form of evidence (or, possibly, argument). In that case the Court held that, for the purpose of correcting a Master's fundamental procedural error in ordering the joinder of a new defendant, the judge had power under r.3.1(7) to revoke the order, rather than requiring the mis-joined party (against whom a default judgment had been obtained) to make an appeal out of time. In *W.L. Gore & Associates GmbH v Geox SpA* [2008] EWHC 462 (Pat), March 5, 2008, unrep. (Lewison J.) an application under r.3.1(7) by the claimants to vary an order to which they had consented was refused, the judge holding that their changed appreciation of the commercial effects of what they had agreed to did not amount to a material change of circumstances.

In *Deg-Deutsche Investitions und Entwicklungsgesellschaft MbH v Koshy* [2004] EWHC 2896 (Ch); [2005] 1 W.L.R. 2434 (Hart J.), it was held that the power of the court under r.3.1(7) is confined to the variation or revocation of an order made by the court in exercise of "a power of the court under these Rules", not any order of a type which might have been made under these Rules; i.e. r.3.1(7) did not permit the variation of orders made under the old RSC. Where the order was made by the court in the exercise of a power derived from elsewhere, then any power to alter that order must also be found elsewhere.

It seems that somewhat laxer principles may apply where the order in question contains an express "liberty to apply". In such cases the court making the order does not lose seisin of the matter: the inclusion of a liberty to apply indicates that it is foreseen that further applications are likely in the course of implementing the decision. However, the liberty does not constitute a "broad licence to avoid appeals" (Lindsay J. in *Russell-Cooke Trust Co v Prentis* [2002] EWHC 1435 (Ch), January 21, 2003, unrep.). In *Russell-Cooke* Lindsay J. decided several questions of broad principle concerning the division of assets between hundreds of investors in a series of investment schemes. Many of the findings of fact he made derived from an accountant's report which incorrectly classified one group of investors. The fact that the judge had proceeded on an incorrect basis was not discovered until after the judgment had been drawn up and perfected. A further order revising the first was made in order to correct the mistake made. The further order did not overturn any of the matters of principle which had been determined; no-one oppposed the making of the further order; had it not been made the trustees would have been put to the delay and expense of an appeal.

Where the order in question is a search order made by the High Court, the rule is that, subject to an exception, a county court may not vary or revoke the order (County Court Remedies Regulations 1991 reg.3(1), see Vol.2, para.9B–78). The exception is that a county court may vary such an order (but may not revoke it) where all the parties are agreed on the terms of the variation (*ibid.* reg.3(4)(b)).

Where a Group Litigation Order (GLO) is in place, a party to a claim entered on the group register after a judgment or order which is binding on him was given or made may not apply for the judgment or order to be set aside, varied or stayed (and may not appeal), but may apply for an order that the judgment or order is not binding on him (r.19.12(3)).

The court has an inherent jurisdiction to vary its own orders to make the meaning and intention of the court clear (Practice Direction (Judgments and Orders), para.4.5, see para.40BPD.4 below).

Some other provisions in the CPR, in addition to r.3.1(7), deal with the varying and revoking of orders, or of judgments or orders (including final orders). Rule 3.1(7) must be read in conjunction with them. The relevant provisions are briefly outlined below.

Rule 23.10(1) and r.23.11(2) both deal with orders made on application notices. The first of these rules states that a person against whom an order was made on an application made without notice may apply to the court to have the order set aside or varied. The second states that, where the applicant or any respondent fails to attend the hearing of an application and the court makes an order at the hearing, the court may, on application or of its own initiative, re-list the application for further consideration.

Rule 3.6 states that, where, after the automatic striking out of a party's statement of case on the ground that he had failed to comply with a court order (e.g. under a conditonal order made on an application for summary judgment), the court gives judgment without trial against him under r.3.5 on a request for judgment, that party may apply to have the judgment set aside. Rule 39.3(3) states that, where a party does not attend a trial and the court gives judgment or makes an order against him, that party may apply for the judgment or order to be set aside (see former RSC O.35, r.2 and CCR O.37, r.2).

Where a defendant fails to file either an acknowledgment of service or a defence, a judgment without trial, known as a default judgment, may be obtained against him by the claimant in the circumstances provided for in CPR Pt 12. Such judgment may be given on the whole or a part of a claim. Rules providing for the setting aside or varying of default judgments are found in Pt 13, in particular r.13.2 and r.13.3. Similarly, r.20.11(5) expressly provides for the setting aside or varying of default judgments entered in certain Pt 20 claims. (Note also Practice Direction (Admiralty) para.7.4 (see Vol.2, para.2D–76), replacing former RSC 75 r.21(9)). Normally (and for obvious reasons) an application to set aside a default judgment will be made by the defendant (i.e. the judgment debtor). In certain circumstances a claimant has a duty to apply to set aside a default judgment in his favour (see r.13.5), and circumstances may arise in which a claimant may wish to make such an application with a view to commencing a fresh action (e.g. *O'Neill v O'Brien*, *The Times*, March 21, 1997, CA, where the application was granted).

Rule 40.9 states that a person "who is not a party but who is directly affected by a judgment or order" may apply to have the judgment or order set aside or varied. See further notes following that rule (paras 40.9.1 and 40.9.3 below).

Rule 41.8 deals with periodical payment orders made in exercise of the court's jurisdiction to award damages for future pecuniary loss in personal injury cases. This jurisdiction is derived from the Damages Act 1996, s.2. Under that statutory scheme, when assessing damages and making an order for periodical payments, the court may in addition provide in that order that it should be a "variable order"; that is to say, that it should be a periodical payments order which, although disposing of the issue of damages, may be altered by the court subsequently in restricted circumstances. The power to make a periodical payments order, whether of the variable variety or not, is not a power to make an order "under these Rules" within the meaning of r.3.1(7). The court's jurisdiction to vary an order in these circumstances is regulated by the 1996 Act and delegated legislation made thereunder (see further para.41.8.6 below).

Rule 44.13(1B) states that where an order for costs is deemed to have been made in the circumstances provided for by r.44.13(1A) any party affected by the order "may apply at any time to vary the order".

Rule 44.18(7) assumes that a party may apply to vary a costs capping order, but in terms restricts the circumstances in which variation may be allowed.

Under Pt 55, Sect.II (Accelerated Possession claims of property let on an assured shorthold tenancy) the court will, in certain circumstances, make an order for possession without requiring the attendance of the parties (r.55.17). In that event, r.55.19 provides that on the application of a party (or of its own motion) the court may set aside or vary the order made.

CPR Sch.2, CCR O.22, r.10 states that, where a judgment or order has been given or made for the payment of money, the judgment creditor (the person "entitled to the benefit of the order") or the judgment debtor (the person "liable to make the payment") may apply in accordance with the provisions of the rule for a variation in the date or rate of payment.

Rule 77.4 is rather unusual. It relates to the Serious Crime Act 2007 which provides for the making of serious crime prevention orders (SCPOs). Sections 17 and 18 provide, respectively, for the variation and discharge of such orders, whether made by the High Court or the Crown Court. Rule 77.4 is concerned merely with the procedure for an application to the High Court to vary or discharge an SCPO made by the Crown Court, stating that it "must be started in accordance with Part 8".

The Charging Orders Act 1979 s.3(5) (see Vol.2, para.9B–1022) and the Council Tax (Administration and Enforcement) Regulations 1992 reg.51(4) provide that the court may at any time, on the application of the debtor, or any person interested in any property to which a charging order relates, or (where the 1992 Regulations apply) of the authority, make an order discharging or varying the order. Rules of court supporting this legislation are found in r.73.9. Under Pt 75 (Traffic Enforcement) orders may be revoked upon the respondent's application by statutory declaration made under the primary legislation to which that Part relates. Express powers to revoke an administration order are found in Sch.2, CCR 39 rr.13A and 14 (see para.cc39.13A below). Practice Direction (Appeals), para.13.1 states that an appeal court may set aside or vary the order of the lower court with consent and without determining the merits of the appeal, if it is satisfied that there are good and sufficient reasons for doing so (see para.52PD.44 below).

In what has been said above attention has focussed on CPR provisions dealing with the court's power to vary or revoke "orders". The case management rules introduced by the CPR place great emphasis on "directions" given by the court, and provision is made for the variation and revocation of directions. As directions may be expressed in the form of orders, there is scope for confusion between provisions directed at, on the one hand, the variation of orders (generally derived from old RSC and CCR rules) and, on the other, at directions (introduced by the CPR). It could be said that two separate regimes for revoking and varying court orders and directions have grown up. For example r.28.4 and r.29.5 deal with the variation of dates fixed for certain events in case management timetables in, respectively, fast track and multi-track cases. Rule 28.4 refers to the variation of dates fixed for the return of a pre-trial check list, and for the trial or the trial period. Rule 29.5 refers to, in addition, the dates fixed for a case management conference and for a pre-trial review. Normally, the events referred to in r.28.4 and r.29.5 will be fixed in orders made by the court and perfected. Consequently, any variation of them will be a variation of a court order. The principal purpose of r.28.4 and r.29.5 is to make it clear that these event dates as expressed in court orders cannot be varied by agreement between the parties.Where a party wishes to vary a date he must apply to the court. Rule 28.4 and r.29.5 are supplemented by, respectively, Practice Direction (The Fast Track), paras 4.1 to 4.5 (see para.28PD.4), and Practice Direction (The Multi-Track), paras 6.1 to 6.5 (see para.29PD.6). These paragraphs state the procedure to be adopted in fast track and multi-track cases (1) where a party is dissatisfied with a direction given by the court, (2) where the parties agree about changes they wish made to the directions given, or (3) where a party wishes to apply to vary a direction. Practice Direction (The Multi-Track), para.3.4 states that the court may give or vary directions at any hearing which may take place on the application of a party or of its own initiative (see para.29PD.3). In terms, the procedures for variations of directions set out in these practice direction paragraphs are not confined in their application to directions of the types stated in r.28.4 and r.29.5 (which refer only to the timetabling of certain events) but seem to apply to any direction given by the court. Their contexts might suggest that their application is confined to, what might be called, "case management directions", but as "case management" is not a term of art in the CPR and frequently is used to include procedural matters going beyond mere timetabling of events (e.g. whether joinder of parties should be permitted).

Rule 28.6(1) and r.29.2(2) states that the court will fix a trial date "as soon as practicable". Rule 29.2(2) is expressly referred to in Practice Direction (The Multi-Track), para.5.4 (see para.29PD.5). Rule 29.4 states that, if (a) the parties agree proposals for the management of the proceedings (including a proposed trial date or period in which the trial is to take place), and (b) the court considers that the proposals are suitable, it may approve them without a hearing and give directions in the terms proposed. Practice Direction (The Multi-Track), para.4.6 encourages parties and their advisers to take advantage of this rule (see para.29PD.4). Applications to "abandon" of "postpone" trial dates (i.e. to revoke or vary directions or orders fixing such dates) are common and are sometimes presented as applications to adjourn or stay proceedings (e.g. *Bass Taverns Ltd v Carford Engineering Ltd* [2002] EWCA Civ 671; April 23, 2002, unrep., CA; *Rosling King v Rothschild Trust* [2002] EWHC 1346 (Ch); May 24, 2002, unrep. (Neuberger J.); *Powell v Pallisers of Hereford Ltd* [2002] EWCA

Civ 959; July 1, 2002, unrep., CA). The general rule is that the court will not allow a failure to comply with case management directions to lead to the postponement of the trial (i.e. will not allow the variation of an order or direction fixing a date for trial) unless the circumstances are exceptional (Practice Direction (The Fast Track), para.5.4, Practice Direction (The Multi-Track), para.7.4 (see paras 28PD.5 and 29PD.7 below).

Consolidating proceedings (r.3.1(2)(g))

Rule 3.1(2)(g) lists amongst the court's general powers of management, the power to "consolidate proceedings". It would appear that this is derived from RSC 4 r.9(1) and CCR O.13 r.9(1), which provided that, in certain circumstances, where (in the case of the RSC) several "causes or matters", or (in the case of the CCR) several "actions or matters" were extant, the court could order (1) that they be consolidated, (2) that they be tried at the same time, (3) that they be tried one after the other, or (4) that any of them be stayed until after the determination of any other of them. These orders were not mutually exclusive. Further, an order for consolidation was not a necessary pre-requisite for an order that several claims be tried together. **3.1.10**

Under the CPR, these powers are retained by the court. Rule 3.1(2)(g) is confined in its effect to the court's power to make an order of the first variety, that is to say an order consolidating proceedings. References to the court's power to make orders of the other varieties formerly provided for in RSC 4 r.9(1) and CCR 13 r.9(1) are found elsewhere in the CPR (e.g. in paras (f), (h) and (i) of r.3.1(2)). Under CPR Pt 19, Sect.III, several sets of proceedings may be managed under a Group Litigation Order (GLO). The GLO procedure was introduced partly for the purpose of making up for perceived deficiencies in the procedure for consolidation of claims where several claims "give rise to common or related issues of fact or law" (r.19.10), especially where a large number of claimants bring separate claims against a single defendant (see para.19.0.10 below). The GLO procedure has not rendered the power to consolidate redundant.

The power of the court to consolidate proceedings was introduced to avoid a multiplicity of proceedings (see para.1.4.15 above) and, thus, to reduce costs and delays (*Martin v Martin* [1897] 1 Q.B. 429, CA). The power was originally designed to protect a defendant from the cost and vexation of having to defend against suits that a plaintiff had chosen to bring against him severally, rather than in the one suit. But it has long-since been the rule that consolidation may be ordered on the application of any party.

Under the CPR, "proceedings" are started when the court issues a claim form at the request of the claimant (r.7.2(1)). Where several proceedings have been started, consolidation may be ordered at any time, whether or not the claim forms have been served (a similar position obtained under the former rules by operation of case law, see *Arab Monetary Fund v Hashim (No.4)* [1992] 1 W.L.R. 1176, CA).

A claimant may use a single claim form to start all claims which can be conveniently disposed of "in the same proceedings" (r.7.3). It is probably accurate to say that consolidation may be permitted where the joinder of claims and the joinder of parties resulting would satisfy the law as to such joinder; but that does not mean that consolidation should be ordered in all such circumstances.

The court must take care to act justly. Conceivably, an application to consolidate may be, quite simply, an application to consolidate one claim brought by A against B with another claim brought by A against B. But the position may be much more complicated than that. The application may be made for the purpose of bringing together numerous claims of different weights and in which the parties are not coincident. Further, the parties (whether on the same or opposite sides of the record) may be far from agreed as to whether consolidation should be effected or to what extent. The court must be alert to the fact that, at bottom, the application may be an attempt by certain parties (resisted by others) to control the conduct of the several proceedings in which they are embroiled.

An application for consolidation should be made as soon as it becomes apparent that it is necessary or desirable to make it (see para.23.0.8 below).

Under the former rules, consolidation of proceedings could be ordered where it appeared to the court (a) that some common question of law or fact arose in both or all of them, (b) that the rights to relief claimed were in respect of or arose out of the same transaction or series of transactions, or (c) that for some other reason it was desirable to make an order for consolidation. These conditions reflected the fact that the main object of the consolidating power was to save costs and time by avoiding a multiplicity of proceedings covering largely the same ground. Rule 3.1(2)(g) contains no such confining conditions. But as the court, in exercising this power, must seek to give effect to the overriding objective (see r.1.1), the conditions stated in the former rules are bound to remain important considerations. The consolidation of proceedings has always been regarded as a flexible concept (*Healy v A. Waddington & Sons Ltd* [1954] 1 W.L.R. 688, CA). The cases decided under the pre-CPR rules of court disclose no principle upon which the discretion to make a consolidating order should be exercised, save the possible principle that it should be confined to cases where several separate claims have been brought which might have been joined in the same originating process (*Horwood v Statesman Publishing Co* (1929) 98 L.J.K.B. 450; *Payne v British Time Recorder Co Ltd* [1921] 2 K.B. 1, CA).

The effect of the consolidation of proceedings is to combine two or more claims so that they will proceed thereafter as one claim. Whether or not the several proceedings are ultimately tried together, this can bring the benefits of avoiding the costs and delays involved in a multiplicity of pleadings, of pre-trial steps taken by the parties, and of interlocutory applications. The achievement of this objective (reflecting the overriding objective) is more likely to be accomplished if the order for consolidation is made early in the proceedings. Where an application is made late in the development of the proceedings to be consolidated the costs involved (e.g. in re-drafting the pleadings) may be sufficiently substantial to tip the scales against an order, especially where the principal advantages sought to be gained by an order (e.g. the admissibility of the evidence in one case in another) could be gained by an order that the two claims should be tried together (r.3.1(2)(h)). Aspects of the overriding objective other than those concerned with cost and delay may also be engaged in the question whether consolidation should be ordered (e.g. ensuring that the parties are on an equal footing and dealing with the case in ways which are proportionate). Upon investigation it may be recognised that the advantages sought to be achieved by an application for consolidation may be achieved by an order under r.3.1(2)(h) for the several claims to be tried on the same occasion (see para.3.1.11 below) and that an order for consolidation is neither desirable nor necessary.

Two claims cannot be consolidated where the claimant in one claim is the defendant in the other, unless one claim can be ordered to stand as a Pt 20 claim in the other.

Consolidation cannot be accomplished simply be agreement between the parties affected. An order of the court is required. The court may exercise its power to consolidate several claims in one claim on application (under Pt 23) or on its own initiative (r.3.3(1)). *Daws v Daily Sketch* [1960] 1 W.L.R. 126, CA, provides authority for the proposition that, as an order for consolidation will not be made without hearing all parties affected, such an order will only be made on the hearing of applications for consolidation made in each of the proceedings to be consolidated. Generally, this creates no difficulty as the question of consolidation will not normally arise unless one party common to each of the claims applies for a consolidation order. Where the court proposes to make an order on its own initiative it must proceed in accordance with the provisions of r.3.3.

Where there are co-claimants in a claim, if they are legally represented they must be jointly represented by the same legal representatives unless it is specially ordered otherwise, or is expressly provided otherwise (e.g. Practice Direction (Probate), para.17 (Separate representation of claimants with conflict of interests)). If separate representation were permitted, many difficult problems could arise, especially at trial (*Lewis v Daily Telegraph (No.2)* [1964] 2 Q.B. 601, CA, at pp.620–621 per Pearson L.J.; see also *Black King Shipping Corporation v Massie* (1984) 134 N.L.J. 887). This rule can cause complications where the effect of the consolidation of several proceedings would be to bring together as co-claimants in the single claim parties represented by different firms of solicitors and counsel. Where consolidation is ordered, usually one firm of solicitors will be given the conduct of the claim on behalf of all claimants thus maintaining the rule of joint representation. Where there are several proceedings brought by different claimants, with different legal representation, in which damages are claimed for personal injuries occasioned in the same accident, it may be possible to consolidate the proceedings up to the point where the issue of liability is decided, giving the conduct of the proceedings up to that point to one claimant's solicitors, and leaving the proceedings separate upon the issues as to the quantum of damages payable to the several claimants (*Healey v A. Waddington & Sons Ltd* [1954] 1 W.L.R. 688, CA). But the better course may be for the court not to order such "partial consolidation", but to order that one claimant's claim should proceed to the trial of liability with the other claimants' claims being stayed pending the outcome, especially where the other claimants are prepared to consent to an order that they should be bound by the decision on liability.

The court may change its mind; consolidated proceedings may be deconsolidated (*Lewis v Daily Telegraph (No.2)* [1964] 2 Q.B. 601, CA); for example, where it emerges that the interests of several claimants are not ad idem and they should be permitted separate legal representation. Where proceedings are consolidated, subsequent developments may make it desirable that the court should order that questions arising in one of the consolidated claims should be tried as preliminary issues (e.g. *Kinstreet Ltd v Balmargo Corporation Ltd* [2000] C.P. Rep. 62, Arden J.).

Trial of two or more claims on the same occasion (r.3.1(2)(h))

Under the former rules, the court could order (in the case of the RSC) that several "causes or matters", or (in the case of the CCR) that several "actions or matters" should be tried (1) at the same time, or (2) one immediately after the other (see RSC 4 r.9(1) and CCR 13 r.9(1)). Although the classification of proceedings according to whether they are "causes", "actions" or "matters" is derived from primary legislation, these expressions find no place in the CPR. Instead the expression "claim" is required to do double duty. Rule 3.1(2)(h) does not expressly state that the court may order that claims arising in separate originating process (i.e. separate claim forms), or some of them, should be tried (1) at the same time, or (2) one immediately after the other before the same forum. Rather it states that they may be tried "on the same occasion". This formulation is broad enough to encompass an order of either variety. An order of the latter variety has the advantage (amongst others) of saving common witnesses the costs of two attendances. As explained above (para.3.1.11), where proceedings are consolidated in exercise of the power referred to in r.3.1(2)(g), the claims arising in the consolidated claim will be tried together, but the court may order that they be tried separately or that certain issues be tried as preliminary issues. **3.1.11**

Court officer's power to refer to a judge

3.2 Where a step is to be taken by a court officer— **3.2**

(a) the court officer may consult a judge before taking that step;

(b) the step may be taken by a judge instead of the court officer.

Effect of rule

"Court officer" means a member of the court staff (r.2.3(1)) Many steps taken by court officers concern the filing of documents, the issue of claim forms and the entry of default judgments. This rule enables court officers to refer to a judge any such document, form or request for judgment which appears to be irregular or inappropriate. In respect of that matter the judge may give directions to the court officer as to the step to be taken, or may take the step himself. In either case the judge may also exercise the court's power to make orders of its own initiative (see r.3.3). **3.2.1**

para.4.2.2 of the Queen's Bench Guide states that any claim form which does not comply with the requirements of r.16.2 or which is garbled or abusive will be referred to a Master and is likely to be struck out (see Vol.2, para.1B–20).

Court's power to make order of its own initiative

***3.3*—(1) *Except where a rule* or some other enactment provides otherwise, the court may exercise its powers on an application or of its own initiative.** **3.3**

(Part 23 sets out the procedure for making an application.)

(2) Where the court proposes to make an order of its own initiative—

(a) it may give any person likely to be affected by the order an opportunity to make representations; and

(b) where it does so it must specify the time by and the manner in which the representations must be made.

(3) Where the court proposes—

(a) to make an order of its own initiative; and

(b) to hold a hearing to decide whether to make the order,

it must give each party likely to be affected by the order at least 3 days' notice of the hearing.

(4) The court may make an order of its own initiative, without hearing the parties or giving them an opportunity to make representations.

(5) Where the court has made an order under paragraph (4)—

(a) a party affected by the order may apply to have it set aside[GL], varied or stayed[GL]; and

(b) the order must contain a statement of the right to make such an application

(6) An application under paragraph (5)(a) must be made—

(a) within such period as may be specified by the court; or

(b) if the court does not specify a period, not more than 7 days after the date on which the order was served on the party making the application.

(7) If the court of its own initiative strikes out a statement of case or dismisses an application (including an application for permission to appeal or for permission to apply for judicial review), and it considers that the claim or application is totally without merit—

(a) the court's order must record that fact; and

(b) the court must at the same time consider whether it is appropriate to make a civil restraint order.

Effect of rule

3.3.1 The court's duty of active case management includes narrowing the issues, controlling the timetable and moving the case forward quickly and efficiently (r.1.4(2)(b), (c), (g) and (l)). By giving him power to make orders on his own initiative, r.3.3 enables the judge to manage cases proactively as well as reactively. The judge has power to:

(1) make a provisional order containing a procedure for representations, e.g. requiring representations to be made orally or in writing and fixing deadlines (r.3.3(2)); or

(2) convene a hearing to decide whether to make a specified order (r.3.3(3)); or

(3) make an order without hearing the parties or giving them an opportunity to make representations (r.3.3(4)). In this instance the parties may later apply to set aside that order (r.3.3(5) and (6)).

Elsewhere in the CPR, the power of the court to act on its own initiative is reinforced in particular contexts; e.g. r.68.2 (reference to European Court of Justice).

Before exercising its powers under r.3.3(4) to make an order without hearing the parties or giving them an opportunity to make representations, the court must be very certain that it has all the material which it needs in order to make such an order fairly and in compliance with the overriding objective (*Shawton Engineering Ltd v DGP International Ltd* [2003] EWCA Civ 1956, December 19, 2003, unrep., CA (appeal against order under r.30.2(4) made on court's own initiative transferring case from provincial city to London allowed).

Sub-rule (7) of r.3.3 was added by the Civil Procedure (Amendment No.2) Rules 2004 (SI 2004/2072). A similar addition was made to r.3.4. These and related amendments put on to a statutory basis the court's jurisdiction, when striking out a statement of case and in other circumstances, to impose orders restraining parties bringing proceedings or making applications that are vexatious in character. For explanation, see para.3.4.10 below.

Rule 23.8 states that, in certain circumstances, the court may deal with an application without a hearing. One of the circumstances is that the court does not consider that a hearing would be appropriate (r.28.3(c)). Paragraph 11.2 of Practice Direction (Applications), supplementing Pt 23 (see para.2PD.12 below) states that, where that particular circumstance applies, the court will treat the application "as if it were proposing to make an order on its own initiative". Accordingly, where the court, acting under r.23.8(c), dispenses with the hearing of an application and deals with it on paper, the provisions of r.3.3 apply, with the result (amongst other things) that a party affected by the order has the right under r.3.3(5) to apply to the court to have it set aside, varied or stayed (rather than being left to the remedy of pursing an appeal); see e.g. *Collier v Williams* [2006] EWCA Civ 20; [2006] 1 W.L.R. 1945; [2006] P.I.Q.R. P18

ECHR art.6(1) provides for a fair and public hearing in the determination of civil rights and obligations: *Stallinger and Kuso v Austria* (1998) 26 E.H.R.R 81, ECtHR; *Helmers v Sweden* (1993) 15 E.H.R.R 285, ECtHR; and *Axen v Germany* (1984) 6 E.H.R.R 195, ECtHR.

Not all orders will be considered determinative of a civil right or obligation such that the requirements of ECHR art.6(1) apply. For consideration of the issue of striking out a statement of case which discloses no reasonable cause of action see para 3.4.1 below. Article 6(1) is not generally considered to apply to interlocutory hearings: see further para.39.2.1.

Where a court has made an order without hearing the parties the existence of a right to apply to the court to set the order aside will probably be sufficient in the majority of cases to ensure compliance with the requirements of ECHR art.6(1).

Where parties have agreed directions and informed the court as to them, the court should not exercise its power to make different directions of its own motion, without notice and without hearing representations from either party, unless the circumstances were exceptional (*Re A Debtor, No.20* SD 1999 [2000] L.T.L. February 8, Ch D).

Application to set aside

In *Collier v Williams* [2006] EWCA Civ 20; [2006] 1 W.L.R 1945; [2006] P.I.Q.R. **3.3.2**
P18, CA, the Court of Appeal said it is good practice to require any application under r.3.3(5) to be made at a hearing rather than on paper. If a judge dismisses an application under r.3.3(5), whether on paper or at a hearing, any further application under r.3.3(5) should usually be struck out as an abuse of process, unless it is based on substantially different material from the earlier application (in which case different considerations will arise) (*ibid.* para.37). See further para.23.0.14 below.

Power to strike out a statement of case

3.4—(1) In this rule and rule 3.5, reference to a statement of case **3.4**
includes reference to part of a statement of case.

(2) The court may strike out[GL] a statement of case if it appears to the court—

- **(a) that the statement of case discloses no reasonable grounds for bringing or defending the claim;**
- **(b) that the statement of case is an abuse of the court's process or is otherwise likely to obstruct the just disposal of the proceedings; or**
- ***(c) that there has been a failure to comply with a rule, practice direction or court order.***

(3) When the court strikes out a statement of case it may make any consequential order it considers appropriate.

(4) Where—

- **(a) the court has struck out a claimant's statement of case;**
- **(b) the claimant has been ordered to pay costs to the defendant; and**

(c) before the claimant pays those costs, he starts another claim against the same defendant, arising out of facts which are the same or substantially the same as those relating to the claim in which the statement of claim was struck out,

the court may, on the application of the defendant, stay[GL] that other claim until the costs of the first claim have been paid.

(5) Paragraph (2) does not limit any other power of the court to strike out[GL] a statement of case.

(6) If the court strikes out a claimant's statement of case and it considers that the claim is totally without merit—

(a) the court's order must record that fact; and

(b) the court must at the same time consider whether it is appropriate to make a civil restraint order.

Effect of rule

3.4.1 "Statement of case" means "a claim form, particulars of claim where these are not included in the claim form, defence, Pt 20 claim, or a reply to a defence; and includes any further information given in relation to them voluntarily or by court order under rule 18.1" see r.2.3(1). "Strike out" is defined in the Glossary as "Striking out means the court ordering written material to be deleted so that it ay no longer be relied upon". This rule enables the court to strike out statements of case in whole or in part and then make consequential orders.

A statement of case may be struck out (in whole or in part) if:

(a) it discloses no reasonable grounds for bringing or defending the claim;

(b) it is an abuse of the court's process or is otherwise likely to obstruct the just disposal of the proceedings; or

(c) there has been a failure to comply with a rule, practice direction or court order.

Generally, an application for an order striking out of a statement of case will be made during the pre-trial stages of proceedings (often together with an application for summary judgment). But the court may exercise the power immediately before trial or even during the course of trial (and may do so whether or not an application was made before trial and adjourned to be dealt with at the trial). Further, the court may act of its own volition (see r.3.3). However, the occasion to exercise the jurisdiction after the start of trial is likely to be very rare (*National Westminster Bank Plc v Rabobank Nederland* [2006] EWHC 2959 (Comm), November 14, 2006, unrep. (Colman J.)).

Grounds (a) and (b) cover statements of case which are unreasonably vague, incoherent, vexatious, scurrilous or obviously ill-founded and other cases which do not amount to a legally recognisable claim or defence. This power can be exercised by a judge acting on his or her own initiative at the stage of issuing a claim (perhaps with a court officer referring the case to the judge under r.3.2) and thus defendants against whom an ill-founded action is sought to be brought will be spared needless expense in having to initiate "strike out" proceedings; see Practice Direction (Striking out a Statement of Case), para.2.1 (para.3PD.2 below).

Ground (c) covers cases where the abuse lies not in the statement of case itself but in the way the claim or defence (as the case may be) has been conducted. The strike-out can be made even where there was nothing in the rule, practice direction or court order breached which specified that this might happen as a consequence of breach. In many circumstances such a strike-out would seem unduly harsh unless the party concerned was warned (possibly in writing by another party) of the risk of his statement of case being struck out if he did not comply with the rule, practice direction or court order in question.

In the case of non-compliance with a rule or practice direction the court may instead order the non-complying party to pay a sum of money into court (see r.3.1(5) and (6)). In the case of non-compliance with a court order the court may instead repeat its order, this time imposing conditions and/or specifying the consequences of failure to comply with the order or condition (r.3.1(3)).

In *Biguzzi v Rank Leisure Plc* [1999] 1 W.L.R. 1926; [1999] 4 All E.R. 934, the Court of Appeal drew attention to several alternatives to a strike out under r.3.4 which may be appropriate to deal with non-compliance with time limits laid down by rules or orders: awarding costs on the indemnity basis payable forthwith, ordering a party to pay money into court and awarding interest at a higher or lower rate.

If the failure to comply with a rule, practice direction or court order has not rendered a fair trial impossible, an order striking out a case even for contumacious breach is likely to be a breach of ECHR art.6 as being a breach of the Respondent's right to a determination of his civil rights and obligations at a fair and public hearing within a reasonable time by an independent tribunal (*Arrow Nominees Inc v Blackledge* [2000] C.P. Rep. 59; [2000] 2 B.C.L.C. 167, Ch D reversed on the facts, *The Times*, July 7, 2000, CA). See also *Swaptronics Ltd, Re, The Times*, August 17, 1998, Ch D. *cf. Canada Trust Co v Stolzenberg (No.2)* [1998] 1 W.L.R. 547, October 14, 1998, unrep., Ch D. To strike out a claim solely on the ground of the claimant's delay where the claim has reasonable prospects of success is unlikely to be considered justifiable under ECHR art.6(1): *Annodeus Ltd v Gibson, The Times*, March 3, 2000, Ch D.

In *Whittaker v Soper* [2001] EWCA Civ 1462, CA, the defendants were ordered to pay money into court which orderwas later varied to executing charges over certain land failing which they would be debarred from defending the claim. The defendants did not fully comply with the order and, at the start of the trial, the claimants applied without notice to strike out the defence. The Court of Appeal held that the defendants should not have been debarred from defending the claim on the day of the trial unless there were no other sanctions available to prevent prejudice to the claimants.

In *Purdy v Cambran* [2000] C.P. Rep 67, CA, the Court of Appeal explained the relevance of the former authorities on striking out for delay in the light of *Biguzzi v Rank Leisure Plc, op cit.* In a number of other cases the court has referred to this matter; see, e.g. *Woodward v Finch* December 8, 1999, unrep., CA; *Chapple v Williams* [1999] C.P.L.R. 731, CA; [1999] L.T.L. December 8; *Williamson v Commissioner of Police for the Metropolis*, December 13, 1999, unrep., CA; and *AXA Insurance Co Ltd v Swire Fraser Ltd (formerly Robert Fraser Insurance Brokers Ltd)* [2001] C.P. Rep 17; [2000] C.P.L.R. 142, CA; *Walsh v Misseldine* [2000] C.P. Rep 74; [2000] C.P.L.R. 201, CA (in which it was said that a difference in approach to striking out maybe justified where liability was not in issue; see para.[100] of the judgment); *Habib Bank Ltd v Jaffer (Gulzar Haider)* [2000] C.P.L.R. 438, CA.

In *Asiansky Television plc v Bayer Rosin* [2001] EWCA Civ 1792, having reviewed the authorities Clarke L.J. stated at para.49:

> "The essential question in every case is: what is the just order to make, having regard to all the circumstances of the case? As May LJ put it [in *Purdy v Cambran* [2000] CP Rep 67 at para 51] it is necessary to concentrate on the intrinsic justice of a particular case in the light of the overriding objective. The cases to which I have referred emphasise the flexible nature of the CPR and the fact that they provide a number of sanctions short of the draconian remedy of striking out the action. It is to my mind important that the Master or Judge exercising his discretion should consider alternative possibilities short of striking out."

Clarke L.J. went on to state that consideration should be given to the question whether striking out the claim or defence would be disproportionate. He also accepted the submission of counsel that only in a case of 'flagrant' abuse would a court be likely to strike out an action where a fair trial was still possible.

In *Raja v Van Hoogstraten* [2006] EWHC 1315 (Ch), Lightman J. struck out a defence and counterclaim on the ground that by murdering an opposing party, who would have been a vital witness in the litigation, the defendant had rendered a fair trial impossible and his conduct amounted to an abuse of process.

While many applications under r.3.4(2) can be made without evidence in support (usually if the statement of case discloses no reasonable grounds for bringing or defending the claim), the applicant should consider whether facts need to be proved and, if so, whether evidence in support should be filed and served; see Practice Direction (Striking Out a Statement of Case), para.5.2 (para.3PD.5 below).

Applications under r.3.4 should be made as soon as possible and before allocation if possible (Practice Direction supplementing r.3.4, para.5.1, see para.3PD.5). If the application is made by the defendant against the claimant's statement of case, the claimant cannot obtain a default judgment until that application is disposed of (r.12.3(3)(a)).

The court may make an order under r.3.4 of its own initiative (r.3.3). The most likely occasion for such an order would be on the filing of a claim form or defence which appears to fall within grounds (a) or (b) above (Practice Direction supplementing r.3.4, paras 2.2 and 3.2, see paras 3PD.2 and 3PD.3). The fact that the court allows such a claim or defence to proceed does not prejudice the right of any other party to apply for an order under r.3.4 (Practice Direction supplementing r.3.4, paras 2.6 and 3.5, see paras 3PD.2 and 3PD.3).

Other provisions in the CPR refer to the court's power to strike out, not (in particular) a statement of case, but (variously) "the claim, "defence" or "any counterclaim", where certain procedural failures occur, and do so in terms that expressly state that the strike out will take effect "without further order of the court". For example, failing to file an allocation questionnaire (Practice Direction (Case Management etc.) para.2.5(1)), or a pre-trial checklist (rr.28.5(3), 29.6(3), Practice Direction (The Fast Track) para.6.5(1)), Practice Direction (The Multi-Track) para.8.3(1)). See also, the rules in this Part dealing with non-payment of fees (rr.3.7, 3.7A and 3.7B).

Statement of case discloses no reasonable grounds for bringing or defending the claim (r.3.4(2)(a))

3.4.2 Paragraph 1.4 of the Practice Direction (Striking Out a Statement of Case), para.3PD.1, gives examples of cases where the court may conclude that particulars of claim disclose no reasonable grounds for bringing the claim: those claims which set out no facts indicating what the claim is about; those claims which are incoherent and make no sense; and those claims which contain a coherent set of facts but those facts even if true, do not disclose any legally recognisable claim against the defendant.

Para 1.6 of the Practice Direction, para.3PD.1, states that a defence may fall within r.4.4(2)(a) where it consists of a bare denial or otherwise sets out no coherent statement of facts, or the facts it sets out, while coherent, would not even if true amount in law to a defence to the claim.

Statements of case which are suitable for striking out on ground (a) include those which raise an unwinnable case where continuance of the proceedings is without any possible benefit to the respondent and would waste resources on both sides (*Harris v Bolt Burdon* [2000] L.T.L., February 2, 2000, CA). A claim or defence may be struck out as not being a valid claim or defence as a matter of law (*Price Meats Ltd v Barclays Bank Plc* [2000] 2 All E.R. (Comm) 346, Ch D). However, it is not appropriate to strike out a claim in an area of developing jurisprudence, since, in such areas, decisions as to novel points of law should be based on actual findings of fact (*Farah v British Airways*, *The Times*, January 26, 2000, CA referring to *Barrett v Enfield BC* [1989] 3 W.L.R. 83, HL; [1999] 3 All E.R. 193). A statement of case is not suitable for striking out if it raises a serious live issue of fact which can only be properly determined by hearing oral evidence (*Bridgeman v McAlpine-Brown* [2000] L.T.L. January 19, CA). An application to strike out should not be granted unless the court is certain that the claim is bound to fail (*Hughes v Colin Richards & Co* [2004] EWCA Civ 266; [2004] P.N.L.R. 35, CA (relevant area of law subject to some uncertainty and developing, and it was highly desirable that the facts should be found so that any further development of the law should be on the basis of actual and not hypothetical facts)).

The ECHR art.6(1) right of access to a court may require caution on the part of courts in exercising the r.3.4(2)(a) power to strike out a statement of case which appears to disclose no reasonable grounds for bringing or defending a claim, particularly where it would be applying the rules in such a way as to exclude an entire category of claims from the courts or confer blanket "immunities" from civil liability on particular groups: *Fayed v United Kingdom* (1994) 18 E.H.R.R 393, para.65, ECtHR. In *Osman v United Kingdom* (2000) 29 E.H.R.R 245, the ECtHR held that the striking out by the Court of Appeal of the applicant's statemnet of claim on the basis that it was contrary to public policy for the police to be under a duty of care in the circumstances of the case was a breach of the art.6(1) right of access to a court. The ECtHR found that the court had proceeded on the basis that the police had a blanket immunity from civil liability in respect of their acts and omissions in the investigation and suppression of crime.

The force of *Osman* was weakened by a subsequent judgment of the ECtHR in *Z v United Kingdom* [2002] 34 E.H.R.R. 3; [2001] 2 F.L.R. 612, ECtHR. The court affirmed that striking out a claim was not inherently contrary to the right of access to a court. It upheld a decision to strike out a claim in negligence on the basis that the strike out resulted not from a blanket immunity but from the application of domestic law principles governing the constituent elements of a cause of action.

English courts have taken the view that art.6(1) does not prevent the striking out of claims in appropriate cases since it applies only to "genuine and serious" disputes about civil rights and obligations, although a claim submitted to a tribunal for determination must be presumed to be genuine and serious unless there are indications to the contrary. See also *Palmer v Tees Health Authority*, *The Times*, July 6, 1999, CA and *Jarvis v Hampshire CC* [1999] 1 W.L.R. 2042, CA (strike out refused on appeal on other grounds, *sub nom. Phelps v Hillingdon LBC* [2000] 3 W.L.R. 776) (*Osman* did not prevent the court exercising its power to strike out in a "clear and obvious" case: see transcipt). In *Kent v Griffiths* [2001] Q.B. 36, CA Lord Woolf stated that:

> "it would be wrong for the *Osman* decision to be taken as a signal that, even when the legal position is clear and an investigation of the facts would provide no assistance, the Courts should be reluctant to dismiss cases which have no real prospect of success. Courts are now encouraged, where an issue or issues can be identified which will resolve or help to resolve litigation, to take that issue or those issues at an early stage of the proceedings so as to achieve expedition and save expense. There is no question of any contravention of art.6 in so doing".

Lord Woolf's comments were endorsed in *Outram v Academy Plastics Limited* [2001] I.C.R. 367, CA.

A statement of case which discloses no reasonable grounds may also be an abuse of the court's process, and, in respect of it, the opposing party may be entitled to summary judgment under Pt 24. Thus, there is no exact dividing line between ground (a) and ground (b) (as to which see para.3.4.3 or between either of them and Pt 24 (as to which see para.3.4.6).

Statement of case is an abuse of the court's process or is otherwise likely to obstruct the just disposal of the proceedings (r.3.4.(2)(b))

Although the term "abuse of the court's process" is not defined in the rules or practice direction, it has been explained in another context as "using that process for a purpose or in a way significantly different from its ordinary and proper use" (*Attorney General v Barker* [2000] 1 F.L.R. 759, DC, per Lord Bingham of Cornhill, Lord Chief Justice). The categories of abuse of process are many and are not closed. The main categories which have been recognised in the case law to date are described in the following paragraphs. The court has power to strike out a prima facie valid claim where there is abuse of process. But there has to be an abuse, and striking out has to be supportive of the overriding objective. It does not follow from this that in all cases of abuse the correct response is to strike out the claim. The striking out of a valid claim should be the last option. If the abuse can be addressed by a less Draconian course, it should be (*Reckitt Benkiser (UK) Ltd v Home Pairfum Ltd* [2004] EWHC 302 (Pat); February 13, 2004, unrep. (Laddie J.) (claimant's application to have defendant's counterclaim in trade mark case struck out, so far as it related to threats, dismissed); see also *Taylor v Nugent Care Society* [2004] EWHC 302 (Pat); [2004] F.S.R. 37 (claimant bringing individual action when group litigation order in place)). **3.4.3**

Vexatious proceedings

The function of the court is to do justice between the parties, not to allow its process to be used as a means of achieving injustice. In an extreme case, a party by his conduct may forfeit his right to take part in a trial. For example, where he demonstrates that he is determined to pursue proceedings with the object of preventing a fair trial (*Arrow Nominees Inc v Blackledge* [2000] 2 B.C.L.C. 167, CA (forgery of documents as part of disclosure process, coupled with perjured evidence)). In such circumstances, his object is inimical to the process which he purports to invoke. It is an abuse to bring vexatious proceedings, i.e. two or more sets of proceedings in respect of the same subject matter which amount to harassment of the defendant in order to make him fight the same battle more than once with the attendant multiplication of costs, time and stress. In this context it is immaterial whether the proceedings are brought concurrently or serially. In addition to striking out the statements of case in such proceedings the court may make a civil restraint order, as to which, see para.3.4.10, below. Whilst it might not be appropriate for the County Court to make such an order in relation to the High Court, there is no difficulty in the High Court making such a order in relation to the County Court if the facts merit it (*Ebert v Birch* [2000] Ch. 484, CA). **3.4.3.1**

There is no abuse if the claimant has sufficient justification for commencing concurrent proceedings (*Merrill Lynch, Pierce Fenner & Smith Inc v Raffa* [2001] C.P. Rep 44, QB; claimant seeking summary judgment in England where concurrent proceeding in Egypt were deferred pending the conclusion of linked criminal proceedings there;

and see further, the commentary to SCA 1981 s.49, Vol.2, paras 9A–183 ("Concurrent civil proceedings") and 9A–185 ("Lis alibi pendens, forum non conveniens and foreign jurisdiction clauses").

Attempts to re-litigate decided issues

3.4.3.2 As a general rule a party should not be allowed to litigate issues which have already been decided by a court of competent jurisdiction. Also, where a matter becomes the subject of litigation, parties to that litigation should bring forward the whole of their cases (*Henderson v Henderson* (1843) 3 Hare 100). However, whether litigation of a decided issue is an abuse depends upon all of the circumstances. It is wrong to hold that simply because a matter could have been raised in earlier proceedings it should have been, so as to render the raising of it in later proceedings necessarily abusive. A broad, merits-based judgment should be adopted, taking account of all the public and private interests involved and all the facts of the case (*Johnson v Gore Wood & Co (No.1)* [2002] 2 A.C. 1, HL: in all the circumstances of that case it was held not to be an abuse for a claimant to commence proceedings seeking remedies in respect of matters which had formed the subject matter of previous proceedings brought by a company which he controlled).

In *Aldi Stores Ltd v WSP Group Plc* [2008] 1 W.L.R. 748; [2008] P.N.L.R 14, the Court of Appeal was concerned with the application of the principles set out in *Johnson v Gore Wood & Co* (above) to an attempt to strike out a claim for abuse of process on the basis that the claim should have been brought in previous litigation in which the defendants were not a party. The Court of Appeal referred with approval to the judgment of Clarke L.J. in *Dexter v Vlieland-Boddy* [2003] EWCA Civ 14, where he summarised the principles to be derived from *Johnson v Gore-Wood* as follows:

- (i) Where A has brought an action against B, a later action against B or C may be struck out where the second action is an abuse of process.
- (ii) A later action against B is much more likely to be held to be an abuse of process than a later action against C.
- (iii) The burden of establishing abuse of process is on B or C or as the case may be.
- (iv) It is wrong to hold that because a matter could have been raised in earlier proceedings it should have been, so as to render the raising of it in later proceedings necessarily abusive.
- (v) The question in every case is whether, applying a broad merits based approach, A's conduct is in all the circumstances an abuse of process.
- (vi) The court will rarely find that the later action is an abuse of process unless the later action involves unjust harassment or oppression of B or C.

Clarke L.J. said (at para.50) that proposition (ii) above:

> "seems to me to be of importance because it is one thing to say that A should bring all his claims against B in one action, whereas it is quite another thing to say that he should bring all his claims against B and C (let alone against B, C, D, E, F and G) in one action. There may be many entirely legitimate reasons for a claimant deciding to bring an action against B first and, only later (and if necessary) against others."

In *Aldi Stores*, the Court of Appeal held that the fact that the defendants to the original action and to the new action were different did not operate as a bar to the finding of abuse but was a powerful factor in the application of the broad merits based judgment. It was also held that no distinction in law between cases where the original action concludes by settlement and where it concludes by judgment. It was further held that that the decision as to whether or not there has been an abuse is not the exercise of a discretion. It was a decision involving the assessment of a large number of factors to which there can only be one correct answer as to whether or not there has been an abuse. On the facts in *Aldi Stores*, the claimant had not behaved in any way that was culpable or improper and this was held to be an important factor even though neither impropriety or culpability is a necessary finding before a claim can be struck out. The claimant's decision not to proceed against the present defendants in the first action was commercially reasonable, forensically legitimate and reasonably *transparent* and the present defendants were being faced with a claim for the first time. The Court of Appeal, allowing the appeal against the order striking out the claim, held that there was no abuse.

Aldi Stores was applied in *Stuart v Goldberg Linde* [2008] EWCA Civ 2; [2008] 1 W.L.R. 823, CA. In that case the claimant had successfully sued the defendant solicitor for breach of a solicitor's undertaking given in anticipation of a contract being concluded between the claimant and the solicitor's client. The claimant then brought a second action against the solicitor alleging inducement of a breach of contract and misrepresentation. The Court of Appeal, allowing the appeal, held on the facts that the second action was not an abuse of process. The majority of the Court of Appeal regarded it as reasonable to proceed with the breach of undertaking claim alone. The issues in the first action were clear, simple and self-contained. The proceedings would have been on a different scale had the inducement or misrepresentation claims been included. Furthermore, the second action was not an abuse of process as the claimant only became aware of the facts of the inducement claim about three months before the trial of the first action and was only aware of all of the facts relating to the misrepresentation claim after trial. The Court of Appeal made four points of general application: [1] if the prospects of success are uncertain but the case is not suitable for summary judgment for either party, it is inappropriate to weigh the prospects of success in the balance in deciding whether it is an abuse of process to bring the claim in later proceedings (the "broad, merits based" approach in *Johnson v Gore Wood* was not a reference to the substantive merits but to the merits relevant to the question whether the claimant should have brought his claim as part of the earlier proceedings); [2] delay, of itself, is not relevant to whether the second claim is an abuse of process; [3] a claimant's failure to use reasonable diligence in finding out facts relevant to whether he had a possible claim might be relevant to the abuse of process issue, but there was no general principle that a potential claimant was under a duty to exercise reasonable diligence to find out the facts relevant to whether he had or might have a claim; and [4] a claimant who keeps a second claim against the defendant up his sleeve while prosecuting the first is at high risk of being held to have abused the court's process. Furthermore, as was stated in Aldi Stores, the proper course is for the claimant to raise the possibility of a second claim with the court so that appropriate case management directions can be given.

See also *Toth v Jarman* [2000] L.T.L. December 21, CA (it was not an abuse to commence proceedings for damages for nervous shock in respect of an accident which had formed the subject matter of a claim under the Fatal Accidents Act 1976 brought by the same claimant). Nor was it an abuse for a party who had been held liable in one action, to bring a subsequent claim for indemnity or contribution in a separate action even though he could have raised such claims in the earlier action (*Sweetman v Shepherd* [2002] C.P. Rep 56; *The Times*, March 29, 2000, CA). In *Perkins v Devoran Joinery Company Ltd* [2006] EWHC 582; [2006] B.L.R. 218, QB, Eady J. held, on appeal, that it was not an abuse of process for the claimants to bring proceedings against the defendant joinery company alleging design defects in windows and doors that it had fitted, even though they had previously brought proceedings alleging defective workmanship only, given that the need to bring the second set of proceedings was attributable largely to the fact that the defendant appeared to have deliberately concealed the defects. Where in fatal accident proceedings a claimant had not given notice to the Motor Insurers' Bureau within the time limit stipulated by the MIB Agreement, and the MIB was not prepared to overlook this, it was not an abuse of process for the claimant to discontinue the proceedings and commence a fresh action in which timely notice was given (*Richardson v Watson* [2006] EWCA Civ 1662; [2007] R.T.R. 21 (disapplying limitation period and allowing fresh action to proceed)).

In *Koshy v Deg-Deutsche* [2008] EWCA Civ 27, it was held that where the claimant had elected to continue with his appeal against a costs order on a limited basis before the Court of Appeal rather than having the issue of non-disclosure remitted for trial, he had accepted that the price of pursuing his appeal was the abandonment of all alternative procedural routes in the event of failure. Accordingly, a second action raising the same issue was an abuse of process. The claimant had had the benefit of legal advice and had the opportunity to have his allegations made the subject of judicial determination. Arden L.J., observed that although the allegations which the claimant raised were serious and important, the justice system was not bound to provide more than one opportunity to run such issues. This was because the court had to strike a fair balance between the interests of the claimant on the one hand and of the other parties and the general interest on the other hand.

The case law above-mentioned concerns attempts to re-litigate issues which have been or should have been litigated in earlier proceedings. Contrast cases in which a judgment creditor brings an action upon a judgment he has obtained as a means of enforcing it. In these circumstances the second action is not, by itself, an abuse of process (*Bennett v Governor & Company of the Bank of Scotland* [2004] EWCA Civ 988; *Kuwait Oil Tanker Co SAK v Al Bader* [2008] EWHC 2432 (Comm)).

Collateral attacks upon earlier decisions

3.4.3.3 A further potential form of abuse of process is where a party mounts an attack on a final decision adverse to him which has been made by a court of competent jurisdiction. In *Hunter v Chief Constable of the West Midlands Police* [1982] A.C. 529 it was said that it was an abuse of process to initiate:

> "proceedings in a court of justice for the purpose of mounting a collateral attack upon a final decision against the intending (claimant) which had been made by another court of competent jurisdiction in previous proceedings in which the intending (claimant) had full opportunity of contesting the decision in the court in which it was made."

However, it was recognised in *Hunter* that it might not be an abuse of process if the claimant could show that he had fresh evidence which entirely changed the previous case and that the further evidence could not by reasonable diligence have been obtained beforehand. (The law relating to res judicata raises similar principles). The cases relevant to this head of abuse, including those following *Hunter*, were reviewed by Sir Andrew Morritt V.-C. in *Secretary of State for Trade and Industry v Bairstow* [2003] EWCA Civ 321; [2004] 1 Ch. 1; [2003] 3 W.L.R 841; [2004] 4 All E.R. 325. It was important to consider (1) the nature and extent of the earlier judgment; (2) the nature and basis of the claim made in the later proceedings; and (3) the grounds relied on to justify the collateral challenge. The principles relevant to this head of abuse were summarised by Sir Andrew Morritt V.-C. He said that a collateral attack on an earlier decision of a court of competent jurisdiction might be, but was not necessarily, an abuse of process; that if the earlier decision was that of a court exercising a civil jurisdiction then it was binding on the parties to that action and their privies in any later civil proceedings; that if the parties to later civil proceedings had not been parties to the earlier action it would only be an abuse of process to challenge that decision if re-litigation of the same issues would be manifestly unfair or would bring the administration of justice into disrepute.

In *Taylor Walton (a firm) v Laing* [2007] EWCA Civ 1146, the claimant, a property developer, sued a firm of solicitors in negligence for having failed to draft two agreements so as to reflect what had been agreed by him with another developer. There had been previous proceedings between the two developers (which largely turned on what or had not been agreed) in which the trial judge heard evidence from the developers and rejected the present claimant's case. There was no appeal against the decision of the trial judge. In the present case, the claimant could only succeed if he was able to establish that the underlying agreements were as he alleged—a contention which had been rejected by the trial judge. The Court of Appeal found that everything submitted to them could have been submitted to the trial judge and could have been the subject of an appeal which was never brought. What was sought to be achieved in the second claim was not the addition of matter which was omitted from the first case, but a re-litigation of the case on the basis of exactly the same material as was or could have been before the trial judge. The Court of Appeal held that the second action involved an impermissible challenge to the facts found by the trial judge and was an abuse of process. The claimant could not establish that his solicitor's drafting of the agreements was negligent without challenging the judge's findings as to credibility and fact. The Court of Appeal contrasted the situation with the more normal professional negligence claim in which the impugned conduct of the lawyer was independent of the factual conclusions of the court—cases where the claimant attempts to demonstrate that the previous conclusion of the court would have been different but for the negligence of the lawyer.

Pointless and wasteful litigation

3.4.3.4 Yet another form of abuse can arise in circumstances where it can be demonstrated that the benefit attainable by the claimant in the action is of such limited value that "the game is not worth the candle" and the costs of the litigation will be out of all proportion to the benefit to be achieved; see *Jameel v Dow Jones and Co* [2005] EWCA Civ 75; [2005] Q.B. 946; [2005] 2 W.L.R. 1614 (see below).

In *Wallis v Valentine* [2002] EWCA Civ 1034; [2003] E.M.L.R. 8, CA, a libel claim which arose out of a lengthy neighbour dispute was struck out as an abuse of process: in all the circumstances any damages recoverable if the claim succeeded would be nominal only and would be wholly disproportionate to the costs of the proceedings. The claim was being brought, not to vindicate a right, but to cause expense, harassment or commercial prejudice beyond that normally encountered in the course of properly conducted litigation.

Jameel v Dow Jones and Co [2005] EWCA Civ 75; [2005] Q.B. 946; [2005] 2 W.L.R. 1614 was another libel claim. It involved limited publication within the jurisdiction and limited damages. The claim was struck out as an abuse of process. Lord Phillips of Worth Matravers M.R. (as he then was) summarised the position as follows at [69]:

> "If the claimant succeeds in this action and is awarded a small amount of damages, it can perhaps be said that he will have achieved vindication for the damage done to his reputation in this country, but both the damage and the vindication will be minimal. The cost of the exercise will have been out of all proportion to what has been achieved. The game will not merely not have been worth the candle, it will not have been worth the wick."

At [54] he said:

> "An abuse of process is of concern not merely to the parties but to the court. It is no longer the role of the court simply to provide a level playing field and to referee whatever game the parties choose to play upon it. The court is concerned to ensure that judicial and court resources are appropriately and proportionately used in accordance with the requirements of justice."

Lord Phillips said at [70]:

> "It would be an abuse of process to continue to commit the resources of the English court, including substantial judge and possibly jury time, to an action where so little is now seen to be at stake. Normally where a small claim is brought, it will be dealt with by a proportionate small claims procedure. Such a course is not available in an action for defamation where, although the claim is small, the issues are complex and subject to special procedure under the CPR."

In *Evans v Secretary of State for the Environment, Transport and the Regions* [2006] EWHC 322, QB, H.H.J. Mackie Q.C. (sitting as a Judge of the High Court) having given summary judgment for the first defendant in respect of various heads of damage, struck out the balance of the claimant's claim as an abuse of process. The second defendant (the MIB) had made an open offer to waive a costs order in its favour and the claimant's remaining heads of damage amounted to less than this offer. The offer was still current at trial. The judge regarded the continuation of the claim as a pointless waste of time, costs and other resources.

Delay

Rule 3.4(2)(b) is not strictly relevant where the complaint is one of delay rather than a complaint as to the form or content of a statement of case (*Western Trust & Savings Ltd v Acland & Lenson (a firm)* [2000] L.T.L. June 19, QB). However, in *Habib Bank Ltd v Jaffer (Gulzar Haider)* [2000] C.P.L.R. 438, CA, a claim was struck out where delays were caused by a claimant acting in wholesale disregard of the norms of conducting serious litigation and doing so with full awareness of the consequences (*cf. Grovit v Doctor* [1997] 1 W.L.R. 640; [1997] 2 All E.R. 417, HL, noted in para.3.4.5 below). **3.4.3.5**

Where a previous claim was struck out on grounds of delay (as to which, see further para.3.4.4 below) the court may strike out at the statement of case in a subsequent action on the same subject matter even though the relevant limitation period has not expired: the claimant's wish to have a "second bite at the cherry" has to be weighed with the overriding objective of the CPR in mind, and in particular, the court's need to allot its limited resources to other cases. However that factor would carry little weight if the second action also raised claims which, for good reasons, were not raised in the previous action (*Securum Finance Ltd v Ashton* [2001] Ch. 291; [2000] 3 W.L.R. 1400, CA). Whenever a claim is struck out for misconduct by the claimant and that claimant commences a second claim in respect of the same subject matter, the court should start with the assumption that some special reason has to be identified to justify the second claim being allowed to proceed; see *Securum Finance* (above).

Other forms of abuse

It is an abuse of process to bring by an ordinary claim proceedings which should normally be brought by judicial review in order to take advantage of the longer limitation period in ordinary claims (*Clark v University of Lincolnshire and Humberside* [2000] 1 W.L.R. 1988, CA, obiter, and see *Carter Commercial Developments v Bedford BC* [2001] 34 E.G.C.S. 99, QB). **3.4.3.6**

In *Stoke on Trent Council v Walley* [2006] EWCA Civ 1137; [2007] 1 W.L.R 352; [2006] 4 All E.R. 1230 the claimant applied under r.3.4(2) to strike out a defence denying liability on the ground that it amounted to a withdrawal of a pre-action admission. In the Court of Appeal it was held that for a claimant to show that the withdrawal of a pre-action admission would amount to an abuse of process, it will usually be necessary to show that the defendant has acted in bad faith. In order to show that the withdrawal was likely to obstruct the just disposal of the case, it would usually be necessary for the claimant to show that he will suffer some prejudice which will affect the fairness of the trial. (As to the withdrawal of admissions made before commencement of proceedings, or of admissions made after commencement of proceedings, see r.14.1A and r.14.1(5), respectively.)

In *Nomura International Plc v Granada Group Ltd* [2008] Bus. L.R.1 (Cooke J.), the judge struck out a claim on the basis that it was an abuse of process for the claimant to issue a claim form in the absence of knowledge of any basis for a claim and the inability to formulate a claim at the time of issue. The claimant had issued the claim form to protect its position on limitation in the context of a potential claim against it by a third party. The judge found that the claimant at the time of issuing its claim form was not in a position to do the minimum necessary to set out the nature of the claim (as required by r.16.2(1)) and was seeking an illegitimate benefit, namely the prevention of further time running under the Limitation Acts for a claim it could not properly identify or plead. Given that the very commencement of proceedings was an abuse of process, the judge held that striking out was the only proper sanction.

In *Ul-Haq v Shah* [2008] EWHC 1896 (QB) Walker J. considered at length the principles to apply in the exercise of the court's power to strike out a genuine claim where the claimant has supported the fraudulent claim made by a fellow litigant (a "phantom passenger" claim in respect of a road accident). After an examination of the judgments in *Arrow Nominees Inc v Blackedge* [2000] C.P. Rep. 59; [2000] 2 B.C.L.C. 167, CA, and subsequent cases, Walker J. adopted and approved the approach taken by HH.J. Phillips in *Ghalib and Ghaffar v Hadfield* January 29, 2004, unrep., CC (Preston)) which was to consider two questions: (1) to what extent had the claimants failed to help the court to further the overriding objective, taking into account the definition of that objective in CPR 1.1; and (2) whether, in the light of the conclusions on (1), to exercise the court's discretion to strike out the statements of case under CPR 3.4 (2). Walker J. upheld the trial judge's conclusion that it was not appropriate to strike out the genuine claims given that the court had been able to resolve the issues fairly at trial and given that the indemnity costs orders made against the claimants had effectively deprived them of their claims in damages.

The word "obstruct" in r.3.4(2)(b) means "impede to a high extent". The court will not strike out a statement of case merely because it raises some irrelevant issues or otherwise generates some untidiness in the pleadings (*Atos Consulting Ltd v Avis Europe Plc* [2005] EWHC 982, TCC). However, the circumstances may warrant the making of an "unless order", i.e. an order directing that a badly drafted statement will be struck out unless, by a stated date, the party at fault provides a clear and concise statement of his case (*Forrester Ketley & Co v Brent* [2004] EWCA Civ 1836) dismissing an appeal against such an order which had been made in respect of a defence and counterclaim set out in eight documents comprising 100 pages).

Failure to comply with a rule, practice direction or court order (r.3.4(2)(c))

3.4.4 Rule 3.4(2)(c) gives the court an unqualified discretion to strike out a claim or defence where a party has failed to comply with a time limit fixed by a rule, practice direction or court order. In *Nomura International Plc v Granada Group Ltd* [2007] EWHC 642 (Comm) (noted in para.3.4.3, above and para.16.2.1, below) a failure to comply with r.16.2 led to the striking out of the claim form; this was held to be the only appropriate sanction because, on the facts, the very commencement of proceedings amounted to an abuse of process. However, in many cases there may be alternatives to a strike out which may be more appropriate: awarding costs on the indemnity basis payable forthwith, ordering a party to pay money into to court and awarding interest at a higher or lower rate (*Biguzzi v Rank Leisure Plc* [1999] 1 W.L.R. 1926, CA).

Where liability is not in issue, it is no longer necessary for the court to make an "all or nothing order" on a strike out application if it would be unjust to do so: instead, the court should take a careful look at all of the relevant circumstances and weigh up carefully the order that it considered it would be just to make on the facts before it: for example, restrictions may be placed upon the claimant's right to claim interest and special damages accruing during the period of delay; the claim could be allowed to proceed to trial on the basis that the judge will assess compensation which would have been payable to the claimant had the trial not suffered delay (*Walsh v Misseldine* [2000] L.T.L. May 18, CA).

The relevant circumstances include any prejudice suffered by other parties but it is no longer necessary to consider prejudice in the way it was considered pre-CPR or to ascribe it to a particular period or periods of delay (*Axa Insurance Co Ltd v Swire Fraser Ltd (formerly Robert Fraser Insurance Brokers Ltd)* [2001] C.P. Rep. 17; [2000] C.P.L.R. 142, CA). "I can see that were delay to have occasioned prejudice short of an inability of the court to be able to provide a fair trial, then there would be, or may be, scope for the use of other forms of sanction. But where the conclusion that is reached is that the prejudice has resulted in an inability of the court to deal fairly with the case, there can only be one answer and one sanction; that is for the [proceedings] to be struck out" (per Latham L.J. in *Purefuture Ltd v Simmons & Simmons*, May 25, 2000, CA). The relevant circumstances may also include the weakness of the claim even if it is not so weak as to have no real prospects of success (*Cohort Construction (UK) Ltd v M Julius Melchior* [2001] C.P. Rep. 23, CA; *cf. Chapple v Williams* [2000] L.T.L. December 8, CA, concerning applications under r.3.9).

The court's power to strike out under r.3.4(2)(c) is not confined to circumstances in which the upshot of the party's failure to comply with a rule, practice direction or order has been serious delay (of the kind that pre-CPR might have led to an application to strike out for want of prosecution), though that is the more usual case. Where the breach of an order is not a gross breach, striking out is likely to be an unjust outcome, especially where it is not suggested that the claim had no prospects of success (*Carlco Ltd v Chief Constable of Dyfed Powys* [2002] EWCA Civ 1754 (claimant failing to give proper disclosure in accordance with a peremptory order)). Where an application is made to strike out a claimant's statement of case, principally because of his non-compliance with court orders, the question whether a fair trial is still possible is not determinative (*Eatwell v Smith & Williamson* [2003] EWHC 2098 (Ch); July 21, 2003, unrep. (Lewison J.)).

The use of an obsolete form was contrary to the practice direction supplementing Pt 7 and brought about several other technical breaches of the rules and practice directions. However, the form used contained all the information which the defendants needed in order to understand the claim being made against them. In those circumstances it was not appropriate to strike out the claim and instead an order was made directing the correction of the defects *Hannigan v Hannigan* [2000] 2 F.C.R. 650, CA, *cf. Cala Homes (South) Ltd v Chichester DC (Time Limits)* [2000] 79 P. & C.R. 430; [2000] C.P. Rep. 28, noted in para.3.10.1, below.

Striking out a statement of case because of a litigant's failure to comply with a court order for the payment of a sum of money which is beyond his means to pay may amount to a breach of the ECHR art.6(1) right of access to a court (*cf. Ford v Labrador* [2003] UKPC 41; [2003] 1 W.L.R. 2082. However, in *Oil & Minerals Development Corp v Sajjad* April 4, 2002, unrep. (Gibbs J.), the defendants were ordered to pay the costs of interlocutory proceedings and failed to comply with an order for payment on account of those costs; holding that there was no possible or credible excuse for that failure, Gibbs J. fixed further dates for payment on terms that, in default the defence would be struck out (see also *Crystal Decisions (UK) Ltd v Vedatech Corp* [2006] EWHC 3500 (Ch), Patten J. noted in para.44.3.15, below).

Striking out sanction effective without need for further order ("unless" orders)

Rule 3.1(3) states that, when the court makes an order, it may (a) make it subject to conditions, and (b) specify the consequence of failure to comply with the order or a condition. This provision and r.3.4(2)(c) (when put together) confirm that the court may make a conditional order in the form of an order stating that, unless by a particular date a party complies with a procedural order made by the court (e.g. a disclosure order, or an order to give security for costs), his statement of claim shall be struck out and his claim dismissed. (The existence of such power is assumed in r.3.5 and r.3.8, see further below.) The consequence (i.e. the striking out and dismissal sanctions) follows automatically upon the party's failure to comply with the condition, without any further order of the court. In Practice Direction (Striking Out a Statement of Case) (supplementing r.3.4) it is stated in para.1.9 (inserted in October 2005) that, where an order (or a rule or a practice direction) states that a statement of case "shall be struck out" or "will be struck out or dismissed", this means that the striking out or dismissal **3.4.4.1** "will be automatic and that no further order of the court will be required" (see para.3PD.1 below). Obviously, the automatic imposing of the striking out and dismissal sanction can have very serious consequences for the defaulting party. In *Marcan Shipping (London) Ltd v Kefalas* [2007] EWCA Civ 463; [2007] 1 W.L.R. 1864; [2007] 3 All E.R. 365, CA, the Court of Appeal stressed that, in making a conditional (or "unless") order containing such sanction, a judge should consider carefully whether that sanction is appropriate in all the circumstances of the case.

Where an unless order has had this effect, the court retains jurisdiction to grant the defaulting party relief (usually in the form of an extension of time for complying) if that party makes an application under r.3.8 (in which event the court will consider all the circumstances, in particular, those listed in r.3.9). (The importance of maintaining the distinction between the effect of the order itself and the exercise of the court's jurisdiction to grant relief was stressed in the *Marcan Shipping* case.)

Further, where an unless order has had this effect, the defaulting party's opponent may obtain judgment by complying with r.3.5. In such event, (a) in the circumstances provided for by r.3.5(2), the party against whom the claim was made may obtain judgment by filing a request for judgment, but (b) otherwise he must make an application in accordance with Pt 23 if he wishes to obtain judgment under r.3.5 (see r.3.5(5)). In the *Marcan Shipping* case the Court of Appeal held that, at the hearing of such an application, (a) the court's function is limited to deciding what order should properly be made to reflect the sanction which has already taken effect, and (b) the operation of the sanction does not lie in the discretion of the court, as it is only if there is an application under r.3.8 by the defaulting party that the court is required to consider whether, in all the circumstances, it is just to make an order granting relief from the sanction automatically imposed.

Inherent jurisdiction to strike out

3.4.5 In addition to the power under r.3.4, the court has an inherent jurisdiction to strike out any documents or strike out, dismiss or stay any proceedings which amount to an abuse of the court's process (as to which, see para.3.4.3 above). This jurisdiction is preserved by r.3.1(1) and r.3.4(5). It duplicates but is not limited to the express powers to strike out which are conferred by r.3.4(2). The undoubted jurisdiction of the court to strike out material in a witness statement which was both scandalous and irrelevant should only be exercised sparingly (*Sandhurst Holdings Ltd v Grosvenor Assets Ltd* [2001] L.T.L., October 25, Ch D).

Where proceedings have been dismissed with costs it is an abuse for an assignee of the claimant to commence or continue fresh proceedings in respect of the same matter without paying the costs previously awarded against the assignor (*Investment Invoice Financing Ltd v Limehouse Board Mills Ltd* [2006] EWCA Civ 9; [2006] 1 W.L.R. 985, CA; and see further, para.3.4.8 below).

The court may strike out vexatious applications in an action and may, in addition, make an order prohibiting further applications being made without the court's permission. However, such powers will now be exercised under r.3.11.

For a claimant to commence or continue litigation with no intention of bringing it to a conclusion can amount to an abuse (*Grovit v Doctor* [1997] 1 W.L.R. 640, HL; *cf. Habib Bank Ltd v Jaffer (Gulzar Haider)* [2000] C.P.L.R. 438, CA, noted in para.3.4.3 above).

The court may strike out a claim where the claimant was guilty of conduct which put the fairness of any trial in jeopardy, or which was such as to render further proceedings unsatisfactory and prevent the court from doing justice (*cf. Arrow Nominees Inc v Blackledge* [2000] C.P. Rep. 59; [2000] 2 B.C.L.C. 167, Ch D reversed on the facts, *The Times*, July 7, 2000, CA)

It is an abuse of process for a defendant to appeal against the refusal of an adjournment in circumstances in which he also has the opportunity to apply under r.39.3(3) (application for a judgment or order to be set aside made by a party who failed to attend the trial): *Tennero Ltd v Arnold* [2006] EWHC 1530, QB.

In *Nolan v Devonport* [2007] 1 W.L.R. 1025, an application to set aside a default judgment was struck out on the ground that the defendant had unreasonably delayed the application until the claimant had commenced proceedings for a charging order by way of enforcement; by not making her set aside application expeditiously the defendant had failed in her duty to help the court to further the overriding objective. In striking out the application HH Judge Grenfell, sitting as a Judge of the High Court, placed reliance upon r.3.1(2)(m) rather than upon the inherent jurisdiction; r.3.1(2)(m) enables the court to make any "order for the purpose of managing the case and furthering the overriding objective".

Overlap with Pt 24 (summary judgment)

The rules give the court two distinct powers which may be used to achieve the summary disposal of issues which do not need full investigation at trial. Rule 3.4 enables the court to strike out the whole or part of a statement of case which discloses no reasonable grounds for bringing or defending a claim (r.3.4(2)(a)), or which is an abuse of the process of the court or otherwise likely to obstruct the just disposal of the proceedings (r.3.4(2)(b)). Rule 24.2 enables the court to give summary judgment against a claimant or defendant where that party has no real prospect of succeeding on his claim or defence. Both those powers may be exercised on an application by a party or on the court's own initiative; see para.1.2 of the Practice Direction (Striking Out a Statement of Case). Many cases fall within both r.3.4 and Pt 24 and it is often appropriate for a party to combine a striking out application with an application for summary judgment. Indeed, the court may treat an application under r.3.4(2)(a) as if it was an application under Pt 24; see, *Taylor v Midland Bank Trust Co Ltd (No.2)* [2002] W.T.L.R 95. 3.4.6

A party may believe he can show without a trial that an opponent's case has no real prospect of success on the facts, or that the case is bound to succeed or fail, as the case may be, because of a point of law (including the construction of a document). In such a case the party concerned may make an application under r.3.4 or Pt 24 (or both) as he thinks appropriate; see para 1.7 Practice Direction (Striking Out a Statement of Case), para.3PD.1.

However, the overlap between r.3.4 and Pt 24 is not complete:

(1) Unlike Pt 24, r.3.4, also applies to cases of non-compliance with a rule, practice direction or court order.
(2) Unlike r.3.4, Pt 24 also applies to the summary disposal of issues including preliminary issues.
(3) There are various procedural requirements in Pt 24 which do not apply to r.3.4.
(4) Unlike Pt 24, r.3.4 applies to all proceeding. Thus, an order akin to summary judgment may be obtained under r.3.4 in proceedings which are excluded from Pt 24 (*Shephard v Wheeler, The Times*, February 15, 2000 noted in para.24.3.1).

In *Independents' Advantage Insurance Co Ltd v Cook*, [2003] EWCA Civ 1103; [2004] P.N.L.R. 3, CA, the Court of Appeal explained the difference between r.3.4 and r.24.2. The court queried whether, on the defendant's (D) application to strike out the claimant's (C) statement of case under r.3.4(2)(a), an application by D for summary judgment under r.24.2(a) should have been joined. On a holding by the court that D had not shown (under r.3.4(2)(a)) that the C's claim disclosed no reasonable grounds it would be impossible to hold (under r.24.2(a)) that C's statement of case disclosed no reasonable grounds. But where the court finds (under r.3.4(2)(a)) that C's statement of case discloses no reasonable grounds, then the court may strike it out (r.3.4(3)) and may enter judgment for D without having recourse to r.24.2(a).

Consequential orders after striking out

If the court has struck out a claim form or defence of its own initiative shortly after that document was filed the court may give directions permitting, for example the filing of an amended document (Practice Direction supplementing r.3.4, paras 2 and 3, see paras 3PD.2 and 3PD.3). 3.4.7

Where an order of strike out has been made the court may enter such judgment for the other party as that party appears entitled to (Practice Direction supplementing r.3.4, para.4.2, see para.3PD.4). Where the strike out relates only to part of a statement of case the court may also give directions for the management of any remaining parts of the proceedings, for example allocating them to a case management track (r.3.1).

Staying subsequent claim until costs paid

Rule 3.4(4) applies where a claimant's statement of case has been struck out, the claimant has been ordered to pay costs to the defendant and before paying those costs he starts another claim against the same defendant arising out of facts which are the 3.4.8

same or substantially the same as those relating to the first claim. In such a case the defendant may apply for a stay of the second claim until the costs of the first claim have been paid. The term "stay" is defined in the Glossary. As to the expression "arising out of facts which are the same or substantially the same" see the commentary to r.17.4 in which similar words are used. As to the circumstances in which a subsequent claim may be struck out as an abuse of the court process, see para.3.4.3 above and *Securum Finance Ltd v Ashton* [2001] Ch. 291; [2000] 3 W.L.R. 1400, CA.

It has been held that a stay of subsequent proceedings until the costs of earlier proceedings have been paid does not, if reasonably imposed, amount to an infringement of ECHR art.6(1) (*Stevens v School of Oriental and African Studies, The Times*, February 2, 2001).

In *Investment Invoice Financing Ltd v Limehouse Board Mills Ltd* [2006] EWCA Civ 9; [2006] 1 W.L.R. 985, CA, C1 presented a winding up petition against D in respect of certain alleged debts which D disputed. The petition was dismissed with costs assessed at £18,000. C1 then commenced new proceedings against D in respect of the same alleged debts which debts it then purported to assign to C2 who was joined as a claimant. C1 was ordered to give security for future costs and for the costs of the winding up and, on C1's failure to comply with that order, C1's claim was struck out with costs assessed at £5,000. The Courtof Appeal upheld an order staying C2's claim until the costs awarded against C1 totalling £23,000 had been paid. The court had an inherent jurisdiction to make such an order which was analogous to an order under r.3.4(4). Even though C2 had not commenced the proceedings it was an abuse for him, as successor in title to C1, to continue the proceedings whilst the costs orders against C1 remained unsatisfied.

As to the orders appropriate for failure to comply with an order to pay costs of interlocutory proceedings see *Oil & Minerals Development Corp v Sajjad* [2002] EWHC 1258, noted in para.3.4.4 above and *Reed v Oury (No.2)* [2002] EWHC 369; *CIBC Mellon Trust Co v Mora Hotel Corp NV* [2002] EWCA Civ 1688; [2003] 1 All E.R. 564 (Ch) noted below.

In *Reed v Oury (No.2)* (above) breach of trust claims were made against the defendant, an accountant who counterclaimed in respect of fees for work done and services provided. Although judgment by consent was entered against the defendant for damages and costs on the claim, no payments were made under that judgment and, some months later, the defendant sought to reactivate his counterclaim. It was held that, having regard to the conduct of the litigation, the weakness of the counterclaim, the cost of having it determined and the likelihood that even if it was successful, he would continue to owe a very large sum to the claimants, the proportionate way of achieving the overriding objective was to stay his counterclaim until he had paid the amount incontestably due from him by way of damages and costs. The decision in *Reed v Oury* was cited with approval in *Ali v Hudson* [2003] EWCA Civ 1793; [2004] CP Rep 15; (noted in para.3.1.5, above).

In *CIBC Mellon Trust Co v Mora Hotel Corp NV* (above), as a result of extremely protracted proceedings in various courts in England and New York, the claimants obtained English freezing orders and default judgments which were recognised by the courts of New York. After a two year delay an application was made, funded by the controlling shareholder of the defendants, to set aside the default judgments. The claimants applied for a stay of that application unless and until certain sums were paid by way of damages and costs. The claimants refused to permit payment of those sums out of assets secured for them by the freezing orders. The Court of Appeal lifted a stay imposed by the lower court which required the payment of £1.5 million in respect of past orders for costs; as a matter of discretion, it was inappropriate to order a stay which retrospectively improved the claimant's position in relation to costs orders where to do so would indirectly compel substantial payments to be made by a non-party who was not otherwise liable to pay those costs.

Vexatious litigants

3.4.9 Paragraphs 7.1 to 7.10 of the practice direction supplementing r.3.4 contains provisions that apply where a "civil proceedings order" or an "all proceedings order", as defined under the Supreme Court Act 1981 s.42(1A), is in force against a person (see *para.3PD.7* below). Those paragraphs are headed "Vexatious litigants". Such orders should be distinguished from civil restraint orders (see para.3.4.10 below, and r.3.11 and commentary following).

The term "vexatious litigant" is used to describe a person who has habitually and persistently and without reasonable ground instituted vexatious proceedings, whether in the High Court or an inferior court, made vexatious applications in such proceedings or instituted vexatious prosecutions. In respect of such a person an order may be made under SCA 1981 s.42 requiring him to obtain the permission of a High Court judge to begin or continue or to make any application in proceedings covered by the order (see Vol.2, para.9A–148). Where a person subject to an order under s.42 wishes to apply for leave to institute or continue, or to make an application in, any civil proceedings he should follow the procedure stated in paras 7.1 to 7.10.

Normally, the civil proceedings which the person subject to the order is prevented from instituting or continuing, or from making an application in, will include claims for judicial review. CPR r.54.4 states that the court's permission to proceed is required in a claim for judicial review. (Applications for such permission are normally dealt with on paper.) Where a person subject to a civil proceedings order wishes to bring a claim for judicial review, he will require the leave of court under s.42. Therefore, in these circumstances, two quite distinct applications for permission are involved; one for leave to institute the proceedings under s.42 made in accordance with Pt 23 (see para.7.10), and the other for permission to proceed with the claim under r.54.4. The applications, though raising distinct issues, may be dealt with together.

It is conceivable that a person's application for leave under s.42 may be, not for permission to institute a judicial review claim, but to be joined as a co-claimant to judicial review proceedings for which there is a concurrent application for permission to proceed under r.54.4 by a competent claimant. In *R. (Ewing) v Office of the Deputy Prime Minister (Practice Note)* [2005] EWCA Civ 1583; [2006] 1 W.L.R. 1260, CA, the Court of Appeal explained how the two applications should be handled in these unusual circumstances (*ibid.* at para.33 *et seq. per* Carnwath L.J.).

Paragraph 7 of the Practice Direction (Striking Out a Statement of Case), see para.3PD.73 (below) sets out what is required to be stated in applications for permission and how such applications may be dealt with. No appeal shall lie from a decision of the High Court refusing permission (s.42(4)).

The provision in para.7.6(3) of the Practice Direction to the effect that an application for leave to institute proceedings may be determined by a High Court judge without an oral hearing, is neither ultra vires nor a violation of the right of access to the Court under art.6 of the European Convention on Human Rights (*R. (Ewing) v Department for Constitutional Affairs* [2006] EWHC 504 (Admin); [2006] 2 All E.R. 993 (Sullivan J.).

Claim "totally without merit"

By the Civil Procedure (Amendment No.2) Rules 2004 (SI 2004/2072) r.3.11, which refers to the court's power of the court to make civil restraint orders (CRO), was added to Pt 3 (see further para.3.11.1 below). A CRO may be one of three varieties, "limited", "extended" or "general". By the same statutory instrument, sub-r.(7) was added to r.3.3, and sub-r.(5) to r.3.4. These additions came into force on October 1, 2004. **3.4.10**

By r.3.4(6), where, in striking out a claimant's case, the court considers that the claim or application is "totally without merit", the court is required "at the same time" to consider whether it is appropriate to make a CRO. In addition, whether or not it makes a CRO, in its order the court must record the fact that it did consider that the claim or application was totally without merit. Obviously, that finding may become relevant on a subsequent occasion. Rule 3.3(7) makes it clear that the court is under similar obligations when, of its own initiative, it strikes out a statement of case or dismisses an application.

In r.3.4(6), the requirement that the court should consider making a CRO is triggered where the court strikes out a statement of case. In r.3.3(7), as amended, it is triggered, not only where the court strikes out a statement of case, but also where it dismisses an application (including an application for permission to appeal or for permission to apply for judicial review). By r.23.12 (Dismissal of totally without merit applications), the requirement (and the duty to record the fact that it was totally without merit) arises where the court dismisses an application, no matter what the purpose of the application was or the relief sought by it (see para.23.12.1 below). See also r.52.10(5)and (6) (duty of appeal court to consider whether it is appropriate to make a CRO).

In *R. (Kumar) v Secretary of State for Constitutional Affairs (Practice Note)* [2006] EWCA Civ 990; [2007] 1 W.L.R 536, CA, it was held that in deciding whether or not to make a civil restraint order a court is entitled to consider whether a judge on an earlier occasion must have rejected an application or dismissed an action as being "totally without" merit—and was not confined to considering orders which had those words on its face. However, if the earlier order does not speak for itself, a rather more detailed examination of the earlier litigation history must be undertaken. The Court of Appeal stressed that if the civil restraint order regime is to operate smoothly, court staff and judges must ensure that if an application or statement of case is regarded as being totally without merit, the court order must record that fact. This would avoid the expense of disinterring and examining the evidence of past litigation.

Judgment without trial after striking out[1]

3.5 **3.5—(1) This rule applies where—**

(a) the court makes an order which includes a term that the statement of case of a party shall be struck out if the party does not comply with the order; and

(b) the party against whom the order was made does not comply with it.

(2) A party may obtain judgment with costs by filing a request for judgment if—

(a) the order referred to in paragraph (1)(a) relates to the whole of a statement of case; and

(b) where the party wishing to obtain judgment is the claimant, the claim is for—

(i) a specified amount of money;

(ii) an amount of money to be decided by the court;

(iii) delivery of goods where the claim form gives the defendant the alternative of paying their value; or

(iv) any combination of these remedies.

(3) Where judgment is obtained under this rule in a case to which paragraph (2)(b)(iii) applies, it will be judgment requiring the defendant to deliver goods, or (if he does not do so) pay the value of the goods as decided by the court (less any payments made).

(4) The request must state that the right to enter judgment has arisen because the court's order has not been complied with.

(5) A party must make an application in accordance with Part 23 if he wishes to obtain judgment under this rule in a case to which paragraph (2) does not apply.

Effect of rule

3.5.1 This rule applies where a striking out occurs automatically because of non-compliance with the terms of a court order, for example an unless order. In such circumstances this rule enables the other party to obtain judgment with costs.

In the cases falling within r.3.5(2) the judgment can be obtained by filing a request stating that the right to enter judgment has arisen because the court's order has not been complied with. In other cases the party entitled to judgment under this rule must make an application in accordance with Pt 23 (General rules about applications for court orders).

Where the court makes an order directly striking out a statement of case it may also

[1] Amended by the Civil Procedure (Amendment) Rules 2000 (SI 2000/221).

make any consequential order it thinks appropriate (r.3.4(3)) including entering such judgment for the other party as that party appears entitled to (Practice Direction supplementing r.3.4, para.4.2, see para.3PD.4). Rule 3.5 does not apply in these circumstances.

In *Marcan Shipping (London) Ltd v Kefalas* [2007] EWCA Civ 643; [2007] 1 W.L.R. 1864; [2007] 3 All E.R. 365, CA, the Court of Appeal stated that, at the hearing of an application made under r.3.5(5), the court's function is limited to deciding what order should properly be made to reflect the striking out sanction which has already taken effect. The Court rejected the submission that, at such a hearing, it was open to the defaulting party to contend that striking out could not be justified unless the breach of the order was so serious as to prevent there being a fair trial (see further para.3.4.4.1 above). It is only if there is an application under r.3.8 by the defaulting party that the court is required to consider whether, in all the circumstances, it is just to make an order granting relief from the sanction automatically imposed.

In *Richardson v Langtree Group Plc* [2004] EWCA Civ 1447; October 14, 2004, unrep., CA, acting on own motion and in the absence of the parties, a district judge ordered that unless the claimant complied with a direction as to disclosure of documents by a particular their "claim will be struck out without further order". The claimants did not comply but the defendant made no attempt to request judgment against the claimant until the start of the trial, by which time disclosure had been made. The Court of Appeal referred to the question whether r.3.5 applied in these circumstances. The defendant's contention that it did not was based on the argument that the district judge's "springing" order was not merely an order which included a term that the claimant's case should be struck out, but an order actually striking out the claim once the date for compliance had passed. The defendant further argued that r.3.5 did not apply because he was not seeking a "judgment with costs". The court managed to dispose of the appeal on other grounds but it doing so doubted the validity of the claimant's arguments as to the application of r.3.5.

Setting aside judgment entered after striking out

3.6—(1) A party against whom the court has entered judgment under rule 3.5 may apply to the court to set the judgment aside. 3.6

(2) An application under paragraph (1) must be made not more than 14 days after the judgment has been served on the party making the application.

(3) If the right to enter judgment had not arisen at the time when judgment was entered, the court must set aside[GL] the judgment.

(4) If the application to set aside[GL] is made for any other reason, rule 3.9 (relief from sanctions) shall apply.

Effect of rule

This rule applies to a judgment entered under r.3.5, i.e. a judgment with costs entered where a statement of case has been struck out automatically as a consequence of non-compliance with the terms of a court order. It does not apply to orders directly striking out a statement of case (for example, a striking out under r.3.4). 3.6.1

The party against whom the judgment under r.3.5 was entered may apply to the court to set the judgment aside (r.3.6(1)). The application must be made promptly within 14 days of service of the judgment on the applicant (r.3.6(2); as to the calculation of time periods under these rules, see r.2.8 and the commentary thereto). If the judgment was entered prematurely, the court must set it aside. In other cases the court has a discretion, to be exercised after considering all the circumstances (r.3.6(4) which refers to r.3.9 (relief from sanctions)).

Where the court has made an order directly striking out a statement of case (for example, an order under r.3.4(2)(c) the party against whom that order was made may apply under r.3.9 for relief from that order.

Sanctions for non-payment of certain fees[1]

3.7 **3.7—(1) This rule applies where—**

(a) an allocation questionnaire or a pre-trial check list (listing questionnaire) is filed without payment of the fee specified by the relevant Fees Order;

(b) the court dispenses with the need for an allocation questionnaire or a pre-trial check list or both;

(c) these Rules do not require an allocation questionnaire or a pre-trial check list to be filed in relation to the claim in question;

(d) the court has made an order giving permission to proceed with a claim for judicial review;or

(e) the fee payable for a hearing specified by the relevant Fees Order is not paid.

(Rule 26.3 provides for the court to dispense with the need for an allocation questionnaire and rules 28.5 and 29.6 provide for the court to dispense with the need for a pre-trial check list).

(Rule 54.12 provides for the service of the order giving permission to proceed with a claim for judicial review).

(2) The court will serve a notice on the claimant requiring payment of the fee specified in the relevant Fees Order if, at the time the fee is due, the claimant has not paid it or made an application for full or part remission.

(3) The notice will specify the date by which the claimant must pay the fee.

(4) If the claimant does not—

(a) pay the fee; or

(b) make an application for full or part remission of the fee,

by the date specified in the notice—

(i) the claim will automatically be struck out without further order of the court; and

(ii) the claimant will be liable for the costs which the defendant has incurred unless the court orders otherwise.

(Rule 44.12 provides for the basis of assessment where a right to costs arises under this rule) and contains provisions about when a costs order is deemed to have been made and applying for an order under section 194(3) of the Legal Services Act 2007.

(5) Where an application for full or part remission of a fee is refused, the court will serve notice on the claimant requiring payment of the fee by the date specified in the notice.

(6) If the claimant does not pay the fee by the date specified in the notice—

[1] Amended by the Civil Procedure (Amendment No.4) Rules 2000 (SI 2000/2092), the Civil Procedure (Amendment) Rules 2002 (SI 2002/2058) and the Civil Procedure (Amendment No.2) Rules 2003 (SI 2003/1242) and the Civil Procedure (Amendment) Rules 2008 (SI 2008/2178).

(a) the claim will automatically be struck out without further order of the court; and

(b) the claimant shall be liable for the costs which the defendant has incurred unless the court orders otherwise.

(7) If—

(a) a claimant applies to have the claim reinstated; and

(b) the court grants relief;

the relief will be conditional on the claimant either paying the fee or filing evidence of full or part remission of the fee within the period specified in paragraph (8).

(8) The period referred to in paragraph (7) is—

(a) if the order granting relief is made at a hearing at which the claimant is present or represented, 2 days from the date of the order;

(b) in any other case, 7 days from the date of service of the order on the claimant.

The relevant fees

This rule makes provisions concerning the fees payable by a claimant on the filing of an allocation questionnaire (as to which, see r.26.3) or a pre-trial checklist (as to which, see r.28.5 (fast track cases) and r.29.6 (multi-track cases)), and in cases in which the rules do not require the filing of an allocation questionnaire or pre-trial checklist (for example, in all proceedings in the commercial list, see r.58.13) and in claims for judicial review after the making of an order giving permission to proceed (as to which, see r.54.12) and in cases in which a fee is payable for a hearing specified in the relevant Fees Order (for example, Fee 10.5 in the Civil Proceedings Fee Order 2004 as amended which levies fees for every day after the first day of the hearing before a judge of the Commercial Court or a judge of the Technology and Construction Court). As to the amounts payable in these circumstances and as to applications for full or part remission, see the Civil Proceedings Fees Order 2004 (SI 2004/3121), as amended (Vol.2, para.10–1). **3.7.1**

Consequences of non-payment

If the claimant fails to pay these fees and does not apply for full or part remission in respect of them, the court will serve a notice on him requiring payment and specifying the date of payment. If the claimant fails to pay the fee or apply for full or part remission by that date: **3.7.2**

(1) the claim will be automatically struck out without any further order of the court, and

(2) the claimant will be liable for the defendant's costs of the claim unless the court otherwise orders.

A similar procedure applies where an application for full or part remission is made but is refused. Where a claim is automatically struck out under this rule the claimant can apply under r.3.9 (relief from sanctions) to have it reinstated on the strict terms set out in r.3.7(7).

If a claim is struck out under this rule the court will send a notice to the defendant stating that the claim has been stuck out and explaining the effect that has upon any *interim injunction* granted (Practice Direction supplementing r.3.7, see para.3BPD.1). The defendant must file this notice if it becomes necessary to commence proceedings for a detailed assessment of costs (see r.44.12 and para.40.4 of the Costs Practice Direction, see 47PD.13).

3.7A—(1) This rule applies where— **3.7A**

(a) a defendant files a counterclaim without—

(i) payment of the fee specified by the relevant Fees Order; or

(ii) making an application for full or part remission of the fee;

(b) the proceedings continue on the counterclaim alone and—

(i) an allocation questionnaire or a pre-trial check list (listing questionnaire) is filed without payment of the fee specified by the relevant Fees Order;

(ii) the court dispenses with the need for an allocation questionnaire or a pre-trial check list or both;

(iii) these Rules do not require an allocation questionnaire or a pre-trial check list to be filed in relation to the claim in question; or

(iv) the fee payable for a hearing specified by the relevant Fees Order is not paid.

(2) The court will serve a notice on the defendant requiring payment of the fee specified in the relevant Fees Order if, at the time the fee is due, the defendant has not paid it or made an application for full or part remission.

(3) The notice will specify the date by which the defendant must pay the fee.

(4) If the defendant does not—

(a) pay the fee; or

(b) make an application for full or part remission of the fee,

by the date specified in the notice, the counterclaim will automatically be struck out without further order of the court.

(5) Where an application for full or part remission of a fee is refused, the court will serve notice on the defendant requiring payment of the fee by the date specified in the notice.

(6) If the defendant does not pay the fee by the date specified in the notice, the counterclaim will automatically be struck out without further order of the court.

(7) If—

(a) the defendant applies to have the counterclaim reinstated; and

(b) the court grants relief,

the relief will be conditional on the defendant either paying the fee or filing evidence of full or partor remission of the fee within the period specified in paragraph (8).

(8) The period referred to in paragraph (7) is—

(a) if the order granting relief is made at a hearing at which the defendant is present or represented, 2 days from the date of the order;

(b) in any other case, 7 days from the date of service of the order on the defendant.

The relevant fees

This rule makes provisions concerning the fees payable by a defendant on the filing of a counterclaim (as to which, see Pt 20). As to the amount payable and as to applications for exemption or remission, see the Civil Proceedings Fees Order 2004 (SI 2004/3121), as amended (Vol.2, para.10–1). 3.7A.1

Consequences of non-payment

If the defendant fails to pay this fee and does not apply for exemption or remission in respect of it, the court will serve a notice on him requiring payment and specifying the date of payment. If the defendant fails to pay the fee or apply for exemption or remission by that date the defence will be automatically struck out without any further order of the court. A similar procedure applies where an application for exemption or remission is made but is refused. Where a defence is automatically struck out under this rule the defendant can apply under r.3.9 (relief from sanctions) to have it reinstated on the strict terms set out in r.3.7A(7). 3.7A.2

Rule 3.7A does not make a defendant whose counterclaim has been struck out liable for the claimant's costs of the counterclaim (contrast the sanctions provided by r.3.7 where a claimant fails to pay certain fees, and the sanctions provided by r.3.7B where a claimant or defendant pays any court fee by a cheque which is subsequently dishonoured).

Sanctions for dishonouring cheque

3.7B—(1) This rule applies where any fee is paid by cheque and that cheque is subsequently dishonoured. 3.7B

(2) The court will serve a notice on the paying party requiring payment of the fee which will specify the date by which the fee must be paid.

(3) If the fee is not paid by the date specified in the notice—

(a) where the fee is payable by the claimant, the claim will automatically be struck out without further order of the court;

(b) where the fee is payable by the defendant, the defence will automatically be struck out without further order of the court,

and the paying party shall be liable for the costs which any other party has incurred unless the court orders otherwise.

(Rule 44.12 provides for the basis of assessment where a right to costs arises under this rule)

(4) If—

(a) the paying party applies to have the claim or defence reinstated; and

(b) the court grants relief,

the relief shall be conditional on that party paying the fee within the period specified in paragraph (5).

(5) The period referred to in paragraph (4) is—

(a) if the order granting relief is made at a hearing at which the paying party is present or represented, 2 days from the date of the order;

(b) in any other case, 7 days from the date of service of the order on the paying party.

(6) For the purposes of this rule, "claimant" includes a Part 20 claimant and "claim form" includes a Part 20 claim.

Effect of rule

3.7B.1 This rule specifies the procedure to be followed where a claimant or defendant pays a court fee by cheque and the cheque is subsequently dishonoured; the court will serve a notice on him requiring payment and specifying the date of payment. (The court is not required to invite the making of an application for exemption or remission in respect of the fee; contrast the provisions of rr.3.7 and 3.7A.) If the paying party is the claimant and the fee is not paid by the date specified in the notice:

(1) the claim will be automatically struck out without any further order of the court, and

(2) the claimant will be liable for the defendant's costs of the claim unless the court otherwise orders.

If the paying party is the defendant and the fee is not paid by the date specified in the notice:

(1) the defence will be automatically struck out without any further order of the court, and

(2) the defendant will be liable for the claimant's costs of the defence unless the court otherwise orders.

A party whose claim or defence has been automatically struck out under this rule can apply under r.3.9 (relief from sanctions) to have it reinstated on the strict terms set out in r.3.7B(4).

Sanctions have effect unless defaulting party obtains relief

3.8 **3.8—(1) Where a party has failed to comply with a rule, practice direction or court order, any sanction for failure to comply imposed by the rule, practice direction or court order has effect unless the party in default applies for and obtains relief from the sanction.**

(Rule 3.9 sets out the circumstances which the court may consider on an application to grant relief from a sanction).

(2) Where the sanction is the payment of costs, the party in default may only obtain relief by appealing against the order for costs.

(3) Where a rule, practice direction or court order—

(a) requires a party to do something within a specified time, and

(b) specifies the consequence of failure to comply,

the time for doing the act in question may not be extended by agreement between the parties.

Effect of rule

3.8.1 This rule confirms the validity of any sanction imposed by a rule, practice direction or court order whilst at the same time providing that the party in default may apply for relief from the sanction. In most cases an application for relief can be made under r.3.9. However, if the sanction is an order for the payment of costs the party in default may obtain relief only by way of appealing against the order for costs (r.3.8(2)).

This rule also removes the right which the parties would otherwise have (r.2.11) to extend by agreement the time for doing an act specified in a rule, practice or court order where the rule, practice direction or court order also specifies the time for doing that act and the consequences of failure to comply (r.3.8(3)).

In *Keen Phillips v Field* [2006] EWCA Civ 1524; [2007] 1 W.L.R. 686, CA, a circuit judge directed that, on an appeal to him by the claimants (C) from a district judge's decision refusing their application for summary judgment, C should file an approved transcript of the district judge's judgment by a particular date and that in default permission to appeal was refused. In the event, because C encountered difficulties not of their own making in securing a transcript, that document was filed one day late. At the hearing of the appeal the defendant (D) took the preliminary point that, in the circumstances, permission to appeal was refused. The judge, acting under r.3.1(2)(a) (and apparently acting on his own initiative under r.3.3(1)) extended the time for filing, and allowed the appeal, granting C summary judgment. On D's appeal to the

Court of Appeal against this decision, the preliminary point was renewed and elaborated with D submitting that, in the absence of any application by C under rr.3.8 and 3.9 for relief from the automatic imposition of the sanction of permission to appeal being refused, the circuit judge had no jurisdiction to extend time under r.3.1(2)(a). The court rejected this submission, but did so in terms that could be construed as suggesting that r.3.1(2)(a) could be used in a manner that by-passed the strictures imposed by r.3.8 and r.3.9 (see paras 18 and 19). In *Marcan Shipping (London) Ltd v Kefalas* [2007] EWCA Civ 463; [2007] 1 W.L.R. 1864, CA, (see para.3.4.4.1 above) the court clarified the matter and explained that the only question for decision in the *Keen Phillips* case was whether a court has jurisdiction to grant relief from sanctions under r.3.8 in the absence of an application by the party in default, and that the significance of that case is the holding that, despite the wording of r.3.8 (which naturally assumes that the party in default will make an application for relief), the court has jurisdiction to act of its own initiative in an appropriate case.

Relief from sanctions

3.9—(1) On an application for relief from any sanction imposed for a failure to comply with any rule, practice direction or court order the court will consider all the circumstances including— 3.9

- **(a) the interests of the administration of justice;**
- **(b) whether the application for relief has been made promptly;**
- **(c) whether the failure to comply was intentional;**
- **(d) whether there is a good explanation for the failure;**
- **(e) the extent to which the party in default has complied with other rules, practice directions, court orders and any relevant preaction protocol[GL];**
- **(f) whether the failure to comply was caused by the party or his legal representative;**
- **(g) whether the trial date or the likely date can still be met if relief is granted;**
- **(h) the effect which the failure to comply had on each party; and**
- **(i) the effect which the granting of relief would have on each party.**

(2) An application for relief must be supported by evidence.

Effect of rule

This rule sets out the court's general discretion to give relief against any sanction imposed for failure to comply with any rule, practice direction or court order. The circumstances listed in r.3.9(1) are routinely referred to in cases where a party applies for an extension of time, having suffered a procedural sanction for his failure to comply with a time limit set by rule, practice direction or order (see para.3.1.2 above). The automatic stay imposed on claims under the transitional arrangements in CPR (see para.51PD.19 below) is a sanction for the purpose of this rule (*Woodhouse v Consignia Plc* [2002] EWCA Civ 275; [2002] 1 W.L.R. 2558; [2002] 2 All E.R. 737, CA). The words "the witness may not be called to give oral evidence unless the court gives permission" in r.32.10 (Consequence of failure to serve witness statement) impose a sanction so that r.3.9(1) fall to be systematically considered (*Priumus Telecommunications Netherlands BV v Pan European Ltd* [2005] EWCA Civ 273). 3.9.1

Rule 3.9(1) lists various circumstances the court must consider. When considering an application for relief it is essential for courts to consider each matter listed in r.3.9(1) systematically in the same way that courts go systematically through the matters listed in s.33 of the Limitation Act 1980 when an application is made under that section (*Bansal v Cheema* [2001] C.P. Rep. 6; *Woodhouse v Consignia Plc* [2002] EWCA Civ 275; [2002] 1 W.L.R. 2558; [2002] 2 All E.R. 737, CA; *R.C. Residuals Ltd v Linton Fuel Oils Ltd* [2002] EWCA Civ 911; [2002] 1 W.L.R. 2782). The list is not exhaustive;

the court must consider "all the circumstances". Thus, when considering whether to grant relief to a defendant, the court is entitled to consider the merits of the defence (*Chapple v Williams* [1999] C.P.L.R. 731. For a good illustration of the circumstances listed in r.3.9(1) being rigorously applied, see *Leckstein v Menon* [2003] EWHC 90, QB; January 30, 2003, unrep. (Eady J.) (application to lift automatic stay imposed under transitional arrangements refused).

It should be noted that r.3.9 comes into play, not merely where a party has failed to comply with any rule etc., but where a sanction is imposed as a result of that failure. No sanction is imposed, for example, where a party fails to comply with r.33.2(4)(a), a provision imposing a time limit for service of notice of intention to rely on hearsay evidence. Consequently, on an application to extend time in this context, neither r.3.8 nor r.3.9 applies (*Cottrell v General Cologne Re UK Ltd* [2004] EWHC 2402 (Comm); October 20, 2004, unrep. (Morison J.)).

In *CIBC Mellon Trust Company v Stolzenberg* [2004] EWCA Civ 827 June 30, 2004, unrep., CA, Arden L.J. analysed carefully the various circumstances listed in r.3.9(1) and reviewed the authorities, particularly those dealing with non-compliance with "unless" orders. A significant feature of the case is that it involved an application under r.3.9 to set aside a judgment (not merely a procedural order) entered in default of compliance with an order of the court. In the context of r.3.9, a finding of intentional failure to comply with a rule is a highly significant and may or may not be decisive, depending on the circumstances of the case (*Bournemouth & Boscombe Athletic Football Club Ltd v Lloyds TSB Bank Plc* [2003] EWCA Civ 1755; December 10, 2003, CA)

As to the relevance of this rule in applications to shorten or extend any time limit fixed by a rule, order or practice direction, see *Sayers v Clarke Walker* [2002] 1 W.L.R. 3095; [2002] 3 All E.R. 490, noted in para.3.1.2 above.

Rule 3.9(2) states that an application for relief against sanctions must be supported by evidence. Such applications are normally made under Pt 23 with a witness statement in support. However, a failure to adduce supporting evidence is an irregularity only which the court has power to waive (see below, r.3.10 (General power of the court to rectify matters where there has been an error of procedure) and the commentary thereto). In *Supperstone v Hurst* [2008] EWHC 735 (Ch) (Floyd J.)) a detailed assessment of the respondent's bill of costs was made by a costs officer. The appellant argued that the respondent had failed to comply with a requirement to give adequate notice of funding in accordance with r.44.3B, the sanction for which is the disallowance of certain costs. The costs officer held that adequate notice had been given and that decision was taken on appeal to a costs judge. In his Respondent's Notice in the appeal, the respondent said that he would apply for relief from sanction if, on the appeal, the costs judge was against him on whether he had given adequate notice. A witness statement was also served indicating that an application for relief from sanction would be made. The costs judge held that there had been non-compliance with r.44.3B but granted the respondent relief against the sanction imposed by that rule. On a further appeal to a High Court judge the grounds of appeal included a ground directed at the fact that there had not been a separate application notice and witness statement in support. Lewison J. refused permission to appeal on that ground. (The subsequent decision of Floyd J. in *Supperstone v Hurst* is noted at para.44.3B.2, below.)

Where failure to comply was caused by the legal representative only

3.9.2 One of the circumstances the court must consider on applications for relief from sanctions is "whether the failure to comply was caused by the party or his legal representative" (r.3.9(1)(f)). Valuable guidance on this part of the rule was given by Peter Gibson L.J. in *Training in Compliance Ltd v Dewse* [2001] C.P. Rep 46 at [66], CA:

> "Of course, if there is evidence put before the court that a party was not consulted and did not give his consent to what the legal representatives had done in his name, the court may have regard to that as a fact, though it does not follow that it would necessarily, or even probably, lead to a limited order against the legal representatives. It seems to me that, in general, the action or inaction of a party's legal representatives must be treated under the Civil Procedure Rules as the action or inaction of the party himself. So far as the other party is concerned, it matters not what input the party has made into what the legal representatives have done or have not done. The other party is affected in the same way; and dealing with a case justly involves dealing with the other party justly. It would not in general be desirable that the time of the court should be taken up in considering seperately the conduct of the legal representatives from that which the party himself must be treated as knowing, or encouraging, or permitting."

However, *Training in Compliance Ltd* (above) did not directly concern r.3.9. In other cases the court has taken into account in favour of the party seeking relief the fact that the fault was one for which his legal representative only was responsible. In one case, the court took into account the detriment the claimant may suffer if the current proceedings are brought to an end and he is left to sue his legal representative instead (*Hansom v E Rex Makin & Co* [2003] EWCA Civ 1801; December 18, 2003, unrep., CA and *Flaxman-Binns v Lincolnshire CC* [2004] EWCA Civ 424; [2004] 1 W.L.R. 2232, CA at para.[41]). In *Short v Birmingham City Council* [2004] EWHC 2112, QB; [2005] H.L.R. 6 (Tugendhat J.), a claimant's application for extension of time for appealing was granted in circumstances where a significant period of the delay was attributable to an unintentional error of law made by his legal advisers. In *Confetti Records v Warner Music (UK) Ltd* [2004] EWCA Civ 1748; November 26, 2003, unrep., CA, a claimant was refused permission to appeal against the dismissal of his application for an extension of time for complying with consent order where one of the relevant factors was his solicitor's mis-understanding of the effect of the interim order for costs. It seems that the Court of Appeal attached particular importance to the fact that it was a consent order.

In *Welsh v Parnianzadeh* [2004] EWCA Civ 1832; [2004] All E.R (D) 170, the Court of Appeal indicated that "a claimant who is reduced to a claim which would perforce be on a percentage basis for loss of a chance against her legal advisers is not only suffering a real loss in the sense of being caused further delay and expense, but is also suffering a real reduction in the value of her claim" (per Mance L.J.) In that case the claim was allowed to proceed and one of the features was that there was no prejudice to the defendant.

General power of the court to rectify matters where there has been an error of procedure

3.10 Where there has been an error of procedure such as a failure to comply with a rule or practice direction— 3.10

(a) the error does not invalidate any step taken in the proceedings unless the court so orders; and

(b) the court may make an order to remedy the error.

Effect of non-compliance

In these rules, as under the previous rules, non-compliance with a rule, or (under these rules) a practice direction, does not nullify the proceedings or any step taken in the proceedings unless the court so orders. Instead the court has power to make an order to remedy the error, i.e. deal with the non-compliance. This power is additional to its power to strike out a statement of case (r.3.4) or order a party to pay a sum of money into court (r.3.1(5)) in cases in which such orders would be appropriate where there is some failure to comply with a rule or practice direction. (The power in r.3.4 also applies on non-compliance with a court order. The power in r.3.1(5) also applies on non-compliance with a pre-action protocol.) 3.10.1

In *Cala Homes (South) Ltd v Chichester DC (Time Limits)* [2000] C.P. Rep. 28; [2000] 79 P. & C.R. 430, an application was made under Pt 8 in the High Court Central Office which should have been made under RSC O.94, r.1 in the High Court Crown Office. On an application to transfer the proceedings to the correct office it was held that, in the absence of a court ruling under r.3.10 that the proceedings had not been started, neither the use of the wrong claim form nor its filing in the wrong office made the application a nullity. Since the forms used fully set out the basis for the grounds of the application in terms that were conceded to be sufficient, the overriding objective was best achieved by transferring the proceedings to the High Court Crown Office.

(In July 2000 the Crown Office was renamed as the Administrative Court: see further para.54.0.4.)

Practice Direction (Committal Applications), para.10 (see para.scpd52.6 below) states that on an application for an order for committal of a person to prison for contemptof court the court may waive any procedural defect "in the commencement or conduct of" the application if satisfied that "no injustice has been cased to the respondent by the defect" (see also *M v P (Contempt of Court: Committal Order); Butler v Butler* [1992] 3 W.L.R. 813, CA (in determining whether to reverse or vary a contempt order on appeal the court should ask itself whether notwithstanding any departure from the proper procedure the alleged contemnor had suffered any injustice)).

Note also r.52.11(3)(b) (power of appeal court to allow appeal where decision of lower court unjust because of serious procedural irregularity).

Remedying procedural errors

3.10.2 An application for an order to remedy an error of procedure may be made by application notice (as to which see r.23.1) or in response to an application to strike out a statement of case under r.3.4. The court may also make the order of its own initiative (r.3.3).

The court has a discretion as to whether to remedy the error and, if so, on what terms including terms as to costs. Alternatively, the court may make a dispensing order waiving the error. In many cases the way in which the discretion is exercised will depend on whether it appears that the other parties have suffered prejudice as a consequence of the error, but the rule gives the court the widest possible discretion and the court can look at all the circumstances. Hence, although prejudice or lack of prejudice to the other party will often be the all important factor in the exercise of discretion, it will not always be so. For a recent case illustration see *Cala Homes (South) Ltd v Chichester DC (Time Limits)* [2000] C.P. Rep. 28; [2000] 79 P. & C.R. 430, noted in para.3.10.1 above; *Hannigan v Hannigan* [2000] 2 F.C.R. 650, CA, noted in para.3.4.4 above; *Fawdry & Co v Murfitt* [2002] EWCA Civ 643; [2002] 3 W.L.R. 1354 (order of transfer for trial in the Technology and Construction Court which, in error, was made without notice to the parties; error waived); *Supperstone v Hurst* [2008] EWHC 735 (Ch)) noted in para.3.9.1, above.

Meaning of "procedural error"

3.10.3 Rule 3.10 gives examples of procedural errors but does not attempt a definition. It has been held that procedural errors are not confined to the two examples given in r.3.10, failures to comply with a rule or practice direction; it can apply to any procedural step taken in error, including a step which was permitted by the rules or practice directions. In *Steele v Mooney* [2005] EWCA Civ 96; [2005] 1 W.L.R. 2819; [2005] 2 All E.R. 256, CA the claimant took a procedural step which was permitted by the rules (an application for an extension of time for service of particulars of claim) but, by mistake, failed to apply also for an extension of time for service of the claim form. The Court of Appeal did not adopt the approach taken by the lower court that this mistake was a drafting error rather than a procedural error. The Court of Appeal held instead that it was an error which was capable of being remedied under r.3.10. This was so even though, at the time relief was sought under r.3.10, an extension of time for service of the claim form was prohibited by r.7.6(3). Whilst the Court of Appeal accepted that r.3.10 cannot be successfully invoked so as to circumvent the prohibition of late applications for extension (as to this, see *Vinos v Marks & Spencer plc* [2001] 3 All E.R. 784, CA) a distinction must be drawn between (a) making an application which contains an error (as occurred in *Steele*) and (b) erroneously not making an application at all (as occurred in *Vinos*).

In *Nelson v Clearsprings (Management) Ltd* [2006] EWCA Civ 1252; [2007] 1 W.L.R. 962, CA, the Court of Appeal said that where (1) a claim form was served by a county court, by posting it by first class post to the address for the defendant as given in the claim form by the claimant, but that address was incorrect, and (2) judgment was given against the defendant at a trial which (because of his lack of notice of the proceedings) he failed to attend, there had been an "error of procedure" which, on the application of the defendant, a court in exercise of its power under para.(b) of r.3.10 (strengthened if necessary by r.3.1(2)(m)) could remedy by an order setting aside the (irregular) judgment (see further paras 39.3.1 and 39.3.7 below).

In *Phillips v Symes* [2008] UKHL 1; [2008] 1 W.L.R.180; [2008] 1 Lloyd's Rep 344, HL, errors were made by court clerks in England and Switzerland, and by the Swiss Post Office, as a result of which one defendant was served without an English translation of the claim form and another defendant did not receive any of the claim form documents posted to it. The House of Lords held that, on these facts, the English court could and should use its power under r.3.10(b) to order that the defendants were to be regarded as properly served; the service upon the defendants, although irregular, was sufficient to give the English courts seisin over the parties' dispute even though, before any order under r.3.10(b) had been made, the defendants had issued proceedings in Switzerland in respect of the same subject matter and between the same parties. The House also held that it had been appropriate for the Court of First Instance to make an order dispensing with service, (as to which, see r.6.9 and the commentary thereto).

Power of the court to make civil restraint orders

3.11 A practice direction may set out— 3.11

(a) the circumstances in which the court has the power to make a civil restraint order against a party to proceedings;

(b) the procedure where a party applies for a civil restraint order against another party; and

(c) the consequences of the court making a civil restraint order.

Civil restraint orders

This rule was added to Pt 3 by the Civil Procedure (Amendment No.2) Rules 2004 (SI 2004/2072) and came into effect on October 1, 2004. The rule puts on to a statutory basis the jurisdiction, based on the court's inherent jurisdiction to prevent abuse of its process, explained by the Court of Appeal in *Bhamjee v Forsdick (Practice Note)* [2003] EWCA Civ 1113; [2004] 1 W.L.R. 88, CA (see also *Mahajan v Department of Constitutional Affairs* [2004] EWCA Civ 946 June 30, 2004, unrep., CA). 3.11.1

This jurisdiction is to be distinguished from the court's jurisdiction derived from the Supreme Court Act 1981 s.42 (see Vol.2 para.9A–148) under which, on the application of the Attorney General, the High Court may make a "civil proceedings order" (or an "all proceedings order") preventing the person against whom it is made from instituting or carrying on proceedings without the leave of the court (see CPR Sch.1, RSC O.94, r.15). In *Attorney General v Perrotti* [2006] EWHC 1002 (Admin), an order under s.42 of the Supreme Court Act 1981 was made in circumstances where extended and general restraint orders had been ineffective.

In r.2.3 (Interpretation) it is stated that "civil restraint order" means an order restraining a party (a) from making any further applications in current proceedings (a "limited civil restraint order"), (b) from issuing any further applications or making certain applications in specified courts (an "extended civil restraint order"), or (c) from issuing any claim or making any application in specified courts (a "general civil restraint order").

Rule 3.4(6) states that, when striking out a statement of case, in certain circumstances the court is required to consider whether it is appropriate to make a CRO (see also r.3.3(7)), and a similar duty is imposed by r.23.12 when the court dismisses an application (see para.3.4.10 (Application "totally without merit") above). The duty also arises where an appeal court refuses an application for permission to appeal, strikes out an appellant's notice, or dismisses an appeal (see r.52.10(5) and (6)).

The practice direction referred to in r.3.11 is Practice Direction (Civil Restraint Orders) (see para.3CPD.1 below). As the rule indicates, the practice direction deals with the circumstances in which the court may make a CRO, whether of the limited, extended or general variety, and of the consequences of the court making an order. In addition, examples of the three varieties of CRO are annexed to the practice direction (respectively, Forms **N19**, **N19A** and **N19B**).

In certain circumstances, a CRO may only be made by a Court of Appeal judge, a High Court judge, or a designated civil judge (see paras 2.7, 3.1, 4.1 and 4.7 of the practice direction), and proceedings must be transferred accordingly (see paras 3.11 and 4.11). A Master has jurisdiction to make a CRO but that jurisdiction does not extend to making an extended CRO (*Wickramaratna v Cambridge University Chemistry Department* [2004] EWCA Civ 1532; November 2, 2004, unrep., CA).

The court may make a CRO on its own initiative. Paragraph 5.1 of the practice direction states that one party to the proceedings may make an application for a CRO against another party. In that event, the application must be made using the Part 23 procedure, unless the court otherwise directs, and the application must specify which type of CRO is sought (para.5.2).

It would seem that Practice Direction (Civil Restraint Orders) is intended to be a self-contained code. The inspiration for its terms is the judgment of the Court of Appeal in *Bhamjee v Forsdick (Practice Note)* [2003] EWCA Civ 1113; [2004] 1 W.L.R. 88, CA. Paragraph 3.1 of the Practice Direction differs from the judgment in the *Bhamjee* case to the extent that it does not stipulate, as a pre-condition for the making of an extended CRO, that all claims and applications made by the party are without merit, although that is relevant to the exercise of discretion (*Thakerar v Lynch Hall & Hornby (Practice Note)* [2005] EWHC 2751 (Ch); [2006] 1 W.L.R. 1511 (Lewison J.)).

In *R. (Kumar) v Secretary of State for Constitutional Affairs* [2006] EWCA Civ 990; [2007] 1 W.L.R. 536, CA, the Court of Appeal stated that it would be a very rare case in which a judge could rely on the court's inherent jurisdiction to make a civil restraint order in an area which appeared to have been comprehensively covered by the rules. Dealing with para.4 of Practice Direction C to Pt 3 (which had been amended as from October 1, 2005) the Court of Appeal said that the new language relating to the power to make general restraint orders is apt to cover a situation in which a litigant adopts:

> "a scattergun approach to litigation on a number of different grievances without necessarily exhibiting such an obsessive approach to a single topic that an extended CRO can appropriately be made against him/her".

The Court of Appeal also said that if the facts are clear and simple enough it might be appropriate for the court to proceed to make a civil restraint order immediately rather than adjourn the application. However, if the history of the previous litigation is complicated an adjournment might be appropriate. (In that case the previous history was complicated by the failure to record on previous orders that the applications or statements of case had been totally without merit; see r.3.3(7); r.3.4(6) and r.3.4(10).)

PRACTICE DIRECTION—STRIKING OUT A STATEMENT OF CASE

This Practice Direction supplements CPR Rule 3.4

1. Introductory

1.1 Rule 1.4(2)(c) includes as an example of active case management the summary disposal of issues which do not need full investigation at trial. **3PD.1**

1.2 The rules give the court two distinct powers which may be used to achieve this. Rule 3.4 enables the court to strike out the whole or part of a statement of case which discloses no reasonable grounds for bringing or defending a claim (rule 3.4(2)(a)), or which is an abuse of the process of the court or otherwise likely to obstruct the just disposal of the proceedings (rule 3.4(2)(b)). Rule 24.2 enables the court to give summary judgment against a claimant or defendant where that party has no real prospect of succeeding on his claim or defence. Both those powers may be exercised on an application by a party or on the court's own initiative.

1.3 This practice direction sets out the procedure a party should follow if he wishes to make an application for an order under rule 3.4.

1.4 The following are examples of cases where the court may conclude that particulars of claim (whether contained in a claim form or filed separately) fall within rule 3.4(2)(a):

(1) those which set out no facts indicating what the claim is about, for example "Money owed £5,000",

(2) those which are incoherent and make no sense,

(3) those which contain a coherent set of facts but those facts, even if true, do not disclose any legally recognisable claim against the defendant.

1.5 A claim may fall within rule 3.4(2)(b) where it is vexatious, scurrilous or obviously ill-founded.

1.6 A defence may fall within rule 3.4(2)(a) where:

(1) it consists of a bare denial or otherwise sets out no coherent statement of facts, or

(2) the facts it sets out, while coherent, would not even if true amount in law to a defence to the claim.

1.7 A party may believe he can show without a trial that an opponent's case has no real prospect of success on the facts, or that the case is bound to succeed or fail, as the case may be, because of a point of law (including the construction of a document). In such a case the party concerned may make an application under rule 3.4 or Part 24 (or both) as he thinks appropriate.

1.8 The examples set out above are intended only as illustrations.

1.9 Where a rule, practice direction or order states "shall be struck out or dismissed" or "will be struck out or dismissed" this means that the striking out or dismissal will be automatic and that no further order of the court is required.

2. Claims which appear to fall within rule 3.4(2)(a) or (b)

2.1 If a court officer is asked to issue a claim form which he believes may fall within rule 3.4(2)(a) or (b) he should issue it, but may then **3PD.2**

consult a judge (under rule 3.2) before returning the claim form to the claimant or taking any other step to serve the defendant. The judge may on his own initiative make an immediate order designed to ensure that the claim is disposed of or (as the case may be) proceeds in a way that accords with the rules.

2.3 The judge may allow the claimant a hearing before deciding whether to make such an order.

2.4 Orders the judge may make include:

(1) an order that the claim be stayed until further order,

(2) an order that the claim form be retained by the court and not served until the stay is lifted,

(3) an order that no application by the claimant to lift the stay be heard unless he files such further documents (for example a witness statement or an amended claim form or particulars of claim) as may be specified in the order.

2.5 Where the judge makes any such order or, subsequently, an order lifting the stay he may give directions about the service on the defendant of the order and any other documents on the court file.

2.6 The fact that a judge allows a claim referred to him by a court officer to proceed does not prejudice the right of any party to apply for any order against the claimant.

3. Defences which appear to fall within rule 3.4(2)(a) or (b)

3PD.3 **3.1** A court officer may similarly consult a judge about any document filed which purports to be a defence and which he believes may fall within rule 3.4(2)(a) or (b).

3.2 If the judge decides that the document falls within rule 3.4(2)(a) or (b) he may on his own initiative make an order striking it out. Where he does so he may extend the time for the defendant to file a proper defence.

3.3 The judge may allow the defendant a hearing before deciding whether to make such an order.

3.4 Alternatively the judge may make an order under rule 18.1 requiring the defendant within a stated time to clarify his defence or to give additional information about it. The order may provide that the defence will be struck out if the defendant does not comply.

3.5 The fact that a judge does not strike out a defence on his own initiative does not prejudice the right of the claimant to apply for any order against the defendant.

4. General Provisions

3PD.4 **4.1** The court may exercise its powers under rule 3.4(2)(a) or (b) on application or on its own initiative at any time.

4.2 Where a judge at a hearing strikes out all or part of a party's statement of case he may enter such judgment for the other party as that party appears entitled to.

5. Applications for orders under rule 3.4(2)

3PD.5 ***5.1*** *Attention is drawn* to Part 23 (General Rules about Applications) and to the practice direction that supplements it. The practice direction requires all applications to be made as soon as possible and before allocation if possible.

5.2 While many applications under rule 3.4(2) can be made without evidence in support, the applicant should consider whether facts need to be proved and, if so, whether evidence in support should be filed and served.

6. Applications for summary judgment

6.1 Applications for summary judgment may be made under Part 24. Attention is drawn to that Part and to the practice direction that supplements it. **3PD.6**

7. Vexatious Litigants

7.1 This Practice Direction applies where a "civil proceedings order" or an "all proceedings order" (as respectively defined under section 42(1A) of the Supreme Court Act 1981) is in force against a person ("the litigant"). **3PD.7**

7.2 An application by the litigant for permission to begin or continue, or to make any application in, any civil proceedings shall be made by application notice issued in the High Court and signed by the litigant.

7.3 The application notice must state:

(1) the title and reference number of the proceedings in which the civil proceedings order or the all proceedings order, as the case may be, was made,

(2) the full name of the litigant and his address,

(3) the order the applicant is seeking, and

(4) briefly, why the applicant is seeking the order.

7.4 The application notice must be filed together with any written evidence on which the litigant relies in support of his application.

7.5 Either in the application notice or in written evidence filed in support of the application, the previous occasions on which the litigant made an application for permission under section 42(1A) of the said Act must be listed.

7.6 The application notice, together with any written evidence, will be placed before a High Court judge who may:

(1) without the attendance of the applicant make an order giving the permission sought;

(2) give directions for further written evidence to be supplied by the litigant before an order is made on the application;

(3) make an order dismissing the application without a hearing; or

(4) give directions for the hearing of the application.

7.7 Directions given under paragraph 7.6(4) may include an order that the application notice be served on the Attorney General and on any person against whom the litigant desires to bring the proceedings for which permission is being sought.

7.8 Any order made under paragraphs 6 or 7 will be served on the litigant at the address given in the application notice. CPR Part 6 will apply.

7.9 A person may apply to set aside the grant of permission if:

(1) the permission allowed the litigant to bring or continue

proceedings against that person or to make any application against him, and

(2) the permission was granted other than at a hearing of which that person was given notice under paragraph 7.

7.10 Any application under paragraph 7.9 must be made in accordance with CPR Part 23.

PRACTICE DIRECTION—SANCTIONS FOR NON-PAYMENT OF FEES

This Practice Direction supplements CPR Rule 3.7

1. If a claim is struck out under rule 3.7, the court will send notice that it has been struck out to the defendant. **3BPD.1**

2. The notice will also explain the effect of rule 25.11. This provides that any interim injunction will cease to have effect 14 days after the date the claim is struck out under rule 3.7. Paragraph (2) provides that if the claimant applies to reinstate the claim before the interim injunction ceases to have effect, the injunction will continue until the hearing of the application unless the court orders otherwise. If the claimant makes such an application, the defendant will be given notice in the ordinary way under rule 23.4. **3BPD.2**

PRACTICE DIRECTION—CIVIL RESTRAINT ORDERS

This Practice Direction supplements CPR Rule 3.11

Introduction

3CPD.1 **1.** This practice direction applies where the court is considering whether to make—

(a) a limited civil restraint order;
(b) an extended civil restraint order; or
(c) a general civil restraint order,

against a party who has issued claims or made applications which are totally without merit.

Rules 3.3(7), 3.4(6) and 23.12 provide that where a statement of case or application is struck out or dismissed and is totally without merit, the court order must specify that fact and the court must consider whether to make a civil restraint order. Rule 52.10(6) makes similar provision where the appeal court refuses an application for permission to appeal, strikes out an appellant's notice or dismisses an appeal.

Limited Civil Restraint Orders

3CPD.2 **2.1** A limited civil restraint order may be made by a judge of any court where a party has made 2 or more applications which are totally without merit.

2.2 Where the court makes a limited civil restraint order, the party against whom the order is made—

(1) will be restrained from making any further applications in the proceedings in which the order is made without first obtaining the permission of a judge identified in the order;
(2) may apply for amendment or discharge of the order provided he has first obtained the permission of a judge identified in the order; and
(3) may apply for permission to appeal the order and if permission is granted, may appeal the order.

2.3 Where a party who is subject to a limited civil restraint order—

(1) makes a further application in the proceedings in which the order is made without first obtaining the permission of a judge identified in the order, such application will automatically be dismissed—
   (a) without the judge having to make any further order; and
   (b) without the need for the other party to respond to it;
(2) repeatedly makes applications for permission pursuant to that order which are totally without merit, the court may direct that if the party makes any further application for permission which is totally without merit, the decision to dismiss the application will be final and there will be no *right of appeal*, unless the judge who refused permission grants permission to appeal.

2.4 A party who is subject to a limited civil restraint order may not make an application for permission under paragraphs 2.2(1) or 2.2(2) without first serving notice of the application on the other party in accordance with paragraph 2.5.

2.5 A notice under paragraph 2.4 must—

(1) set out the nature and grounds of the application; and
(2) provide the other party with at least 7 days within which to respond.

2.6 An application for permission under paragraphs 2.2(1) or 2.2(2)—

(1) must be made in writing;
(2) must include the other party's written response, if any, to the notice served under paragraph 2.4; and
(3) will be determined without a hearing.

2.7 An order under paragraph 2.3(2) may only be made by—

(1) a Court of Appeal judge;
(2) a High Court judge or master; or
(3) a designated civil judge or his appointed deputy.

2.8 Where a party makes an application for permission under paragraphs 2.2(1) or 2.2(2) and permission is refused, any application for permission to appeal—

(1) must be made in writing; and
(2) will be determined without a hearing.

2.9 A limited civil restraint order—

(1) is limited to the particular proceedings in which it is made;
(2) will remain in effect for the duration of the proceedings in which it is made, unless the court otherwise orders; and
(3) must identify the judge or judges to whom an application for permission under paragraphs 2.2(1), 2.2(2) or 2.8 should be made.

Extended Civil Restraint Orders

3.1 An extended civil restraint order may be made by— **3CPD.3**

(1) a judge of the Court of Appeal;
(2) a judge of the High Court; or
(3) a designated civil judge or his appointed deputy in the county court,

where a party has persistently issued claims or made applications which are totally without merit.

3.2 Unless the court otherwise orders, where the court makes an extended civil restraint order, the party against whom the order is made—

(1) will be restrained from issuing claims or making applications in—
    (a) any court if the order has been made by a judge of the Court of Appeal;
    (b) the High Court or any county court if the order has been made by a judge of the High Court; or
    (c) any county court identified in the order if the order has been made by a designated civil judge or his appointed deputy,

concerning any matter involving or relating to or touching upon or leading to the proceedings in which the order is made without first obtaining the permission of a judge identified in the order;

(2) may apply for amendment or discharge of the order provided he has first obtained the permission of a judge identified in the order; and

(3) may apply for permission to appeal the order and if permission is granted, may appeal the order.

3.3 Where a party who is subject to an extended civil restraint order—

(1) issues a claim or makes an application in a court identified in the order concerning any matter involving or relating to or touching upon or leading to the proceedings in which the order is made without first obtaining the permission of a judge identified in the order, the claim or application will automatically be struck out or dismissed—

(a) without the judge having to make any further order; and

(b) without the need for the other party to respond to it;

(2) repeatedly makes applications for permission pursuant to that order which are totally without merit, the court may direct that if the party makes any further application for permission which is totally without merit, the decision to dismiss the application will be final and there will be no right of appeal, unless the judge who refused permission grants permission to appeal.

3.4 A party who is subject to an extended civil restraint order may not make an application for permission under paragraphs 3.2(1) or 3.2(2) without first serving notice of the application on the other party in accordance with paragraph 3.5.

3.5 A notice under paragraph 3.4 must—

(1) set out the nature and grounds of the application; and

(2) provide the other party with at least 7 days within which to respond.

3.6 An application for permission under paragraphs 3.2(1) or 3.2(2)—

(1) must be made in writing;

(2) must include the other party's written response, if any, to the notice served under paragraph 3.4; and

(3) will be determined without a hearing.

3.7 An order under paragraph 3.3(2) may only be made by—

(1) a Court of Appeal judge;

(2) a High Court judge; or

(3) a designated civil judge or his appointed deputy.

3.8 Where a party makes an application for permission under paragraphs 3.2(1) or 3.2(2) and permission is refused, any application for permission to appeal—

(1) must be made in writing; and

(2) will be determined without a hearing.

3.9 An extended civil restraint order—
(1) will be made for a specified period not exceeding 2 years;
(2) must identify the courts in which the party against whom the order is made is restrained from issuing claims or making applications; and
(3) must identify the judge or judges to whom an application for permission under paragraphs 3.2(1), 3.2(2) or 3.8 should be made.

3.10 The court may extend the duration of an extended civil restraint order, if it considers it appropriate to do so, but it must not be extended for a period greater than 2 years on any given occasion.

3.11 If he considers that it would be appropriate to make an extended civil restraint order—
(1) a master or a district judge in a district registry of the High Court must transfer the proceedings to a High Court judge; and
(2) a circuit judge or a district judge in a county court must transfer the proceedings to the designated civil judge.

General Civil Restraint Orders

4.1 A general civil restraint order may be made by— 3CPD.4
(1) a judge of the Court of Appeal;
(2) a judge of the High Court; or
(3) a designated civil judge or his appointed deputy in a county court,

where the party against whom the order is made persists in issuing claims or making applications which are totally without merit, in circumstances where an extended civil restraint order would not be sufficient or appropriate.

4.2 Unless the court otherwise orders, where the court makes a general civil restraint order, the party against whom the order is made—
(1) will be restrained from issuing any claim or making any application in—
(a) any court if the order has been made by a judge of the Court of Appeal;
(b) the High Court or any county court if the order has been made by a judge of the High Court; or
(c) any county court identified in the order if the order has been made by a designated civil judge or his appointed deputy,

without first obtaining the permission of a judge identified *in the order;*
(2) may apply for amendment or discharge of the order provided he has first obtained the permission of a judge identified in the order; and
(3) may apply for permission to appeal the order and if permission is granted, may appeal the order.

4.3 Where a party who is subject to a general civil restraint order—

(1) issues a claim or makes an application in a court identified in the order without first obtaining the permission of a judge identified in the order, the claim or application will automatically be struck out or dismissed—
(a) without the judge having to make any further order; and
(b) without the need for the other party to respond to it;
(2) repeatedly makes applications for permission pursuant to that order which are totally without merit, the court may direct that if the party makes any further application for permission which is totally without merit, the decision to dismiss that application will be final and there will be no right of appeal, unless the judge who refused permission grants permission to appeal.

4.4 A party who is subject to a general civil restraint order may not make an application for permission under paragraphs 4.2(1) or 4.2(2) without first serving notice of the application on the other party in accordance with paragraph 4.5.

4.5 A notice under paragraph 4.4 must—
(1) set out the nature and grounds of the application; and
(2) provide the other party with at least 7 days within which to respond.

4.6 An application for permission under paragraphs 4.2(1) or 4.2(2)—
(1) must be made in writing;
(2) must include the other party's written response, if any, to the notice served under paragraph 4.4; and
(3) will be determined without a hearing.

4.7 An order under paragraph 4.3(2) may only be made by—
(1) a Court of Appeal judge;
(2) a High Court judge; or
(3) a designated civil judge or his appointed deputy.

4.8 Where a party makes an application for permission under paragraphs 4.2(1) or 4.2(2) and permission is refused, any application for permission to appeal—
(1) must be made in writing; and
(2) will be determined without a hearing.

4.9 A general civil restraint order—
(1) will be made for a specified period not exceeding 2 years;
(2) must identify the courts in which the party against whom the order is made is restrained from issuing claims or making applications; and
(3) must identify the judge or judges to whom an application for permission under paragraphs 4.2(1), 4.2(2) or 4.8 should be made.

4.10 The court may extend the duration of a general civil restraint order, if it considers it appropriate to do so, but it must not be extended for a period greater than 2 years on any given occasion.

4.11 If he considers that it would be appropriate to make a general civil restraint order—

(1) a master or a district judge in a district registry of the High Court must transfer the proceedings to a High Court judge; and

(2) a circuit judge or a district judge in a county court must transfer the proceedings to the designated civil judge.

General

5.1 The other party or parties to the proceedings may apply for any civil restraint order. 3CPD.5

5.2 An application under paragraph 5.1 must be made using the Part 23 procedure unless the court otherwise directs and the application must specify which type of civil restraint order is sought.

5.3 Examples of a limited civil restraint order, an extended civil restraint order and a general civil restraint order are annexed to this practice direction. These examples may be modified as appropriate in any particular case.

Editorial note

The following forms which are annexes to this PD can be found in the *Civil Procedure Forms Volume*: 3CPD.6

- **N19**
- **N19A**
- **N19B**

PRACTICE DIRECTION—MESOTHELIOMA CLAIMS

Scope

3DPD.1 **1.** This Practice Direction applies to claims for compensation for mesothelioma.

"Mesothelioma"

3DPD.1.1 Mesothelioma is a highly aggressive cancer. The majority of cases originate in the pleura, but it is sometimes peritoneal or pericardial. It is a rare cancer in persons who have not been exposed to the inhalation of asbestos dust. Characteristically there is a long latency period between the first exposure to asbestos dust and the first clinical signs of mesothelioma, more than30 years in most cases, but intervals of as little as 10 years are found and less in rare cases. There is no upper limit to the latency period. That period is not the same as the period in which the tumour grows, which period is thought to commence on average 10 years before clinical signs of the tumour appear.

All types of asbestos fibres can cause mesothelioma but they differ in potency. Crocidolite (blue asbestos) is thought to be the most potent, then amosite (brown or grey asbestos) and chrysotile (white asbestos) is thought to be the least potent. The cancer may occur after low levels of exposure but the risk of contracting it increases in proportion to the dose received, thought the severity of the cancer does not. Successive periods of exposure each increase the risk that the cancer will occur and consequently, Mesothelioma is characterised as an "indivisible" disease.

The rate of occurrence of mesothelioma in the UK has been characterised as an epidemic. In 2004 the authors of a paper in the British Medical Journal (Treasure et al, *Radical Surgery for Mesothelioma* (January 31, 2004) stated that there were at that time over 1,800 deaths per year in Britain (that is, about 1 in 200 of all deaths in men and 1 in 1,500 in women) and that the number was still increasing. They predicted that the peak of the epidemic was to be expected in 2015 to 2020 when the death rate was likely to be 2,000 a year in the UK.

In May 2002 a special list for asbestos related illness claims was set up at the Royal Courts of Justice (RCJ), supervised by one of the Masters of the Queen's Bench Division. Over the years since then, an efficient practice has been developed in that list to resolve claims for damages for mesothelioma (most of which are made against former employers) quickly and wherever possible, to provide compensation during the lifetime of the victim of exposure either by interim payment or full assessment of damages. Experience in that list has shown that in over 95 per cent of claims, there is no real prospect of success of any defence and that if liability can be eliminated as an issue at an early stage, by pro-active use of the court's case management powers, then almost all claims can be quickly timetabled and managed to settlement of the issue of quantum. Experience has also shown that in many claims in which life expectancy is short and which need to be dealt with expeditiously, where there is some probability of a real prospect of a defence being shown which relates to exposure and breach of duty, the alleged victim's evidence should be taken on deposition and recorded on a DVD and a transcript made available, in case death occurs before any sort of trial can be arranged and the victim's evidence is lost.

In 2007 the Civil Justice Council brought together the Master in charge of the RCJ list and other judges from courts where these claims are issued and representative claimant and defendant lawyers, to establish by consensus a standard method of resolving these claims based on the system in use at the RCJ. This Practice Direction, in force from April 6, 2008 is the result.

The Compensation Act 2006

3DPD.1.2 This Act in ss.16 and 17 establishes two basic principles which modify the law as laid down by the House of Lords in *Barker v Corus (UK) Plc* [2006] UKHL 20 and which apply to all mesothelioma claims:

(1) a person who has exposed a victim in circumstances amounting to a breach of duty, who has consequently contracted mesothelioma, will be liable for all the damage flowing and will not be able to reduce that liability by reference to any other exposure:

(a) by any other person whether it was tortuous or non-tortious or

(b) by the victim, of himself, unless that exposure can found a defence of contributory negligence;

(2) where more than one person has exposed the victim in breach of duty the liability of each such person will be for all the damage and will be joint and several.

Definitions

2. In this Practice Direction— **3DPD.2**

"show cause procedure" means (without prejudice to the court's general case management powers in Part 3 of the CPR) the procedure set out in paragraph 6;

"outline submissions showing cause" means an outline or skeleton argument of the defendant's case within the show cause procedure; and

"standard interim payment" means the standard payment in respect of interim damages, and (if appropriate) interim costs and disbursements as determined from time to time by the Head of Civil Justice. The amount of this payment is currently £50,000.

"show cause procedure"

See the notes to para.6 below. **3DPD.2.1**

"standard interim payment"

The making of a standard interim payment order in the majority of cases avoids the expense of a separate application and prolonged argument over the correct level of payment during CMCs that are usually allocated no more than half an hour of the court's time. The payment also provides early interim payment to living victims in cases in which liability is no longer in issue. The practice at the RCJ is that the standard payment is seldom exceeded though it may be cut back in low value claims where the standard level of payment would far exceed a reasonable proportion of the damages likely to be payable. The figure is currently £47,000 and it is usually determined by the lower level of damages for mesothelioma in the JSB Guide to Damages. In future it will be set by the Head of Civil Justice. **3DPD.2.2**

Starting proceedings

3.1 The claim form and every statement of case must be marked with the title 'Living Mesothelioma Claim' or 'Fatal Mesothelioma Claim' as appropriate. **3DPD.3**

3.2 In order for the court to adopt the show cause procedure in the first case management conference, the claimant must file and serve any witness statements about liability (as are available)—

(1) either—

(a) at the same time as filing and serving the claim form and (where appropriate) the particulars of claim; or

(b) as soon as possible after filing and serving the claim form and (where appropriate) the particulars of claim; and

(2) in any event not less than 7 days before the case management conference.

3.3 Any witness statement about liability must identify as far as is possible—

(1) the alleged victim's employment history and history of exposure to asbestos;

(2) the identity of any employer where exposure to asbestos of the alleged victim is alleged;

(3) details of any self employment in which the alleged victim may have been exposed; and

(4) details of all claims made and payments received under the Pneumoconiosis etc. (Workers' Compensation) Act 1979.

3.4 The claimant must also attach to the claim form—

(1) a work history from H M Revenue and Customs (where available); and

(2) any pre-action letter of claim.

"adopt ... in the first case management conference"

3DPD.3.1 It is a key part of the process of these claims that a CMC is called as early as possible and certainly as soon as possible after a defence has been filed. The court will not wait for all defences to be filed in a multi-defendant claim as in most such claims in relation to mesothelioma there will be defendants who will not respond. Unless it is able to concede liability or has already done so before the first CMC, the defendant may be called on to do so at that conference. Some defendants at that CMC will consent to judgment. Some will not be able to consent, but will not oppose and judgment may then be entered. Others will ask for more time to investigate liability or obtain factual or expert evidence. In many cases, where sufficient time for investigation has passed since the receipt of the pre-action protocol letter, defendants will be unable to produce any (or any relevant) factual evidence of their own and there will be no reason on the face of the claimant's expert medical evidence to allow a defendant to obtain its own such evidence. However, unless judgment is consented to or not opposed, the Court will not normally enter judgment in those circumstances without seeing the claimant's evidence. In some cases the totality of the evidence will be available at the first CMC. The court will decide the matter as far as possible on the material that would be available at a trial and in particular the factual and expert evidence. Hence the requirement here for the claimant to ensure that that evidence is before the court at the first CMC if the show cause procedure is to be invoked at that time. This paragraph of the PD sets out what material should be included where possible. In some cases, where the defendant is an extant company known to have contemporary evidence, the claimant may wish the normal procedure of simultaneous exchange of evidence to be followed and then seek to invoke the show cause procedure at a later stage in the proceedings. In paragraph 2 of the PD it is made clear that the show cause procedure is without prejudice to the court's general case management powers in Pt 3 of the CPR. In urgent living claims where there is disputed evidence the court will often send the claim for an urgent trial of liability as a preliminary issue and order an interim payment to be made if the claimant is successful.

Claimants with severely limited life expectancy

3DPD.4 **4.1** Where the claimant believes that the claim is particularly urgent then on issue of the claim form, the claimant—

(1) may request in writing that the court file is placed immediately before a judge nominated to manage such cases in order to fix a case management conference; and

(2) must explain in writing to the court why the claim is urgent.

4.2 Where the court decides that the claim is urgent (and notwithstanding that a claim has not yet been served or a defence has not yet been filed) it will—

(1) fix the date for the case management conference to take place within a short period of time; and

(2) give directions as to the date by which the claimant must serve the claim form if it has not been served already.

"Claimants with a severely limited life expectancy ... the claim is particularly urgent"

3DPD.4.1 The default trigger of the case management process in mesothelioma claims is the filing of any defence or the making of a default judgment (see para.5 below). In some claims in which the alleged victim is still alive, the prognosis is such that the claim should be case managed by the Court urgently and a date fixed for a CMC without waiting for the time for acknowledgement and defence to expire. This paragraph explains that in such cases the claimant's solicitor may request an urgent CMC when the claim is issued, giving an explanation in writing (which includes email where such communication is accepted by the Court in question) and the file will then be referred to the judge at that stage rather than after any defence has been filed. If the Court accepts that there is urgency, it may fix a CMC and require the claim form to be served, if it has not already been served and set a timetable for acknowledgement and defence or it may simply order a CMC. Experience in the RCJ list has shown that frequently (notwithstanding the terms of the pre-action protocol) little or no investigation of liability has been carried out by defendants before the issue of proceedings and in cases where the alleged victim is still alive and has an uncertain prognosis, urgent case management is not only beneficial but also necessary if the aim of bringing living claims to either a trial an assessment of damages or a trial of liability as a preliminary issue, followed by the standard interim payment, can be achieved within 16 weeks of service of proceedings (see para.7.1 below).

Fixing the case management conference for other claims

5.1 Where paragraph 4 does not apply and— 3DPD.5

(1) a defence is filed by the defendant or one of the defendants (where there is more than one); or

(2) the claimant has obtained a default judgment,

the court file will be referred to a judge nominated to manage such cases and the judge will give directions for the date of the case management conference.

5.2 Claims marked 'Living Mesothelioma Claim' will be given priority when fixing a case management conference.

"where paragraph 4 does not apply"

Paragraph 5 applies (a) to claims by alleged victims who are alive but whose life expectancy is such that the normal period for acknowledgement and defence (as extended by agreement by the parties if appropriate) will be acceptable, and (b) to claims in which the alleged victim has died before proceedings were commenced. Both types of claim are covered by the PD because the methods that can be used for expeditious resolution of mesothelioma claims are the same for both living and fatal claims, the difference being that there is not the same need for an urgent timetable in fatal claims. Nevertheless it has been the aim at the RCJ to dispose of fatal claims, where possible, within six months of service of proceedings. 3DPD.5.1

Living mesothelioma claims given priority when fixing CMC

Paragraph 7.1 of the PD aims for a period of 16 weeks from service of the claim form to a trial (if necessary of liability as a preliminary issue) or assessment of damages in claims where the alleged victim is still alive therefore even in the case of less urgent live claims under this paragraph there will be a need to set a case management conference within weeks in order for this to be achievable. In such cases the normal notice requirement for CMCs will often have to be abridged. Fatal claims lack the urgency of living claims but the aim of the PD to eliminate the issue of liability at an early stage where possible means that as early a CMC date as possible should be set after any defence has been filed. 3DPD.5.2

The show cause procedure

6.1 The show cause procedure is a requirement by the court, of its own initiative and usually on a 'costs in the case' basis, for the defendant to identify the evidence and legal arguments that give the defendant a real prospect of success on any or all issues of liability. The court will use this procedure for the resolution of mesothelioma claims. 3DPD.6

6.2 At the first case management conference, unless there is good reason not to do so, the defendant should be prepared to show cause why—

(1) a judgment on liability should not be entered against the defendant; and

(2) a standard interim payment on account of damages and (if appropriate) costs and disbursements should not be made by the defendant by a specified date.

6.3 At the first case management conference if liability remains in issue the court will normally order that the defendant show cause within a further given period.

6.4 The order requiring the defendant to show cause within a further given period will direct—

(1) that the defendant file and serve on the claimant by a specified date outline submissions showing cause and—

(a) if the outline submissions are not filed and served by a specified date, judgment, for a sum to be determined by the court, will be entered against the defendant without the need for any further order and the defendant will be ordered to make a standard interim payment by a specified date; or

(b) if the outline submissions are filed and served by the specified date, the claim will be listed for a show cause hearing; or

(2) that the defendant show cause at a hearing on a date fixed by the court.

6.5 At the first case management conference the court will—

(1) fix the date or trial window for the determination of damages and give any other case management directions as appropriate where the defendant admits liability or judgment is entered;

(2) fix the date or trial window for the determination of damages and give any other case management directions as appropriate where an order to show cause under paragraph 6.3 has been made (if the defendant subsequently shows cause then the determination date or trial window may be utilised for the trial of any issue); or

(3) in cases in which there is to be a trial on liability, give directions including the date or window for the trial.

6.6 Where the defendant fails to show cause on some issues, the court will normally enter judgment on those issues.

6.7 Where the defendant fails to show cause on all issues, the court will enter judgment for a sum to be determined and will normally order that a standard interim payment be made.

6.8 Where the defendant succeeds in showing cause on some or all issues, the court will order a trial of those issues. The court may also require the issue of quantum or apportionment (as appropriate) to be dealt with at the trial provided that it does not delay the date for the fixing of the trial.

"show cause procedure"

3OPD.6.1 This is defined as a requirement by the court, of its own initiative and usually on a "costs in the case" basis, for the defendant to identify the evidence and legal arguments that give the defendant a real prospect of success on any or all issues of liability. It is the keystone of the procedure for resolving mesothelioma claims and is a court imposed filter, which, applying the summary judgment test, prevents the scarce resources of the court being used for liability trials, where there is no defence to liability that has a real prospect of success. The justification for the court imposing this filter rather that requiring a full blown application under Pt 24 to be initiated by the claimant, is the fact that the RCJ experience has shown that in about 95 per cent of claims there is no such defence and a summary judgment application simply duplicates work and increases costs unnecessarily. The requirement to "show cause" may be imposed at any stage of the interlocutory process and may be imposed on successive occasions, for example, at the first CMC and then at a later "show cause hearing" if the defendant is able to persuade the court to allow more time. The court's order is to show cause not only as to liability but also as to why the usual standard interim payment should not be made.

"The show cause procedure...usually on a costs in the case basis"

This is a summary judgment filter imposed by the court which utilises the documents and evidence prepared in the normal course of the interlocutory process, thus avoiding the need for the preparation of a specific Pt 24 application and supporting evidence. By this method the court ensures that only cases with a real prospect of a defence on any issue go forward to use trial listing resources. In those circumstances the practice at the RCJ has been to order the costs of any "show cause hearings" to be "in the case" whatever the outcome. There is overall fairness in this approach because the procedure is imposed by the court and not by choice of the parties and if a defendant is able to go to trial there is nothing unfair in that defendant loosing the costs of having shown cause if it fails at trial or in gaining them from the claimant if it succeeds at trial. The practice also avoids lengthy argument over costs at show cause hearings which are seldom given more than one hour of the court's time, or at CMCs which are seldom given more than half an hour. **3DPD.6.2**

"unless there is good reason not to do so"

Good reason usually consists of some acceptable reason for allowing a defendant more time to investigate or to obtain and rely on further evidence, either from factual witnesses, forensic engineers or medical witnesses. It will not usually be a good reason to allow more time (or at least to allow more than a week or two) that there has been a failure by the defendant to investigate liability and find witnesses in the period following the pre-action protocol letter. In the case of a company which is extant and trading, it is the responsibility of that company as defendant to investigate (either themselves or through solicitors) and not to leave it to brokers or insurers once they have been traced, sometimes several weeks later. There is nothing unacceptable in trying to trace insurers who can respond to the claim, but not at the expense of urgent investigation of liability. **3DPD.6.3**

"within a further given period" "The order requiring the defendant to show cause"

The RCJ practice is to order **either** (1) that unless the defendant files (this may, in courts which accept it, be done by email) and serves outline submissions by a certain date, judgment on the issue of liability will be entered without need for further order and the standard interim payment will be made within 14 days and if submissions are filed the court will conduct a "show cause hearing" **or** (2) simply, that the defendant will show cause at a hearing the date of which is fixed there and then. The latter course is the one usually taken where it is clear that the defendant is likely to want to show cause. **3DPD.6.4**

"At the first case management conference the court will..."

It is the practice in all mesothelioma claims for the court not only to order an early CMC but also at that first CMC wherever possible to set the date for (and timetable to) an assessment of damages, on the supposition that the defendant will not be, or has not been, able to show cause. If the defendant does show cause that date or one as near to it as possible can be used for a trial though in urgent cases the court will order liability to be tried as a preliminary issue as soon after the successful show cause hearing as possible. **3DPD.6.5**

"Where the defendant fails to show cause"

If this happens at the first CMC or at a later hearing set for showing cause, the court will enter judgment and make the interim payment order. Where the "unless" **3DPD.6.6** form of show cause order has been made, the judgment will normally have been ordered to be entered automatically without need for further order.

"Where the defendant succeeds in showing cause"

3DPD.6.7 What happens at this stage will depend on a number of factors; the urgency of the claim, the delay in obtaining further expert evidence if necessary, etc. In claims by living victims, where there is nothing more to do in relation to liability except have a trial, either because there is only a factual dispute or there is a dispute on the expert opinions but the evidence is ready, then a trial will often be ordered to take place within weeks, so that an interim payment can be made if the claimant succeeds. If quantum can be assessed at that early time as well then the court will order a full trial rather that the trial of a preliminary issue.

Setting the trial date

3DPD.7 **7.1** In Living Mesothelioma Claims the date of the determination of damages or the trial will generally not be more than 16 weeks following service of the claim form.

7.2 In Fatal Mesothelioma Claims the hearing date may be more than 16 weeks following service of the claim form.

"16 weeks following service of the claim form"

3DPD.7.1 This is a reference to either a full trial if that is possible or a trial of liability only followed by an interim payment. Where it is necessary to obtain expert evidence, particularly expert engineering / health and safety evidence, it will not always be possible to have a trial, even of liability only within such a time limit, because of the shortage of experts in this field. However, generally the 16 week timetable for disposal should be the aim and this requires efficient listing of CMCs and trials if it is to be achieved.

Taking evidence by deposition

3DPD.8 **8.1** Any party who for good reason wishes evidence to be taken by deposition may apply to the court at any time for such an order. However, the court will normally expect that such a request is made at a case management conference. The order will include a direction for the recording of such evidence on DVD and for the provision of a transcript. The parties must also be prepared to arrange for the provision of equipment to view the DVD by the court.

(Part 34 contains provisions for evidence to be taken by deposition.)

"who for good reason wishes evidence to be taken by deposition"

3DPD.8.1 At the first CMC where the alleged victim is still alive, the court should always consider making an order that the claimant's evidence be taken on deposition by a certain date or that the claimant's solicitors have permission to have it taken on short notice if the claimant's health deteriorates. The importance of a live victim as a primary source of evidence cannot be over stressed, particularly in cases where the defendant is likely to be able to put forward its own live witnesses at a trial. The live victim is also a valuable source of information for the defendants for them to assess their chances of success on liability and to be able to take an early decision thereon. Many disputes on liability are conceded after evidence is taken on deposition. If there is any likelihood that the claimant might be lost as a source of evidence then that claimant's evidence should be taken as soon as possible so that the defendant can also cross examine as to its case. The invariable practice at the RCJ is to order the evidence to be recorded on a DVD as well as having the usual transcript made available. The DVD medium is readily useable on judicial laptops. This evidence is most likely to be used at a trial after the alleged victim has died or is too ill to attend trial and often when the defendants are able to call witnesses. The deployment of this evidence on DVD "levels the playing field" as much as possible in those circumstances. It is particularly useful to order evidence to be taken on deposition, where possible, after the closing date in the court's order for the production of witness statements although in particularly urgent cases it may be done earlier. If the evidence has been taken and the claimant then dies or is too ill to give further evidence or assistance, it would be unusual for the court to consider allowing the defendants to put in further evidence.

Compliance with pre-action protocols

9.1 In Living Mesothelioma Claims the court may decide not to require strict adherence to Practice Direction (Pre-Action Conduct) and any relevant pre-action protocol. **3DPD.9**

"strict adherence to any relevant pre-action protocol"

Although a specific pre-action protocol for mesothelioma claims is under discussion it is not likely to be promulgated for some time. The protocol that applies to these and other asbestos induced illness claims is the Disease and Illness Protocol in which mesothelioma is specifically mentioned at para.2.5 where it is made clear that in cases where a claimant has mesothelioma the timescales of the protocol may be too long. In claims where the alleged victim is still alive, if it seems that the defendant is not investigating liability after the pre-action protocol letter has been sent, that fact will often justify the immediate issue of proceedings so that the court can set an urgent timetable. **3DPD.9.1**

PART 4

FORMS

Contents

4.0.1

Editorial Introduction

4.0.2 The forms which may be used in conjunction with the CPR are not prescribed by rules (as was formerly the case under the RSC and the CCR). Instead, as r.4(1) states, they are as prescribed by practice direction. The relevant practice direction is Practice Direction (Forms) (see para.4PD.1, below). Prescribed forms cover the whole range of practice and procedure. Where they reflect what rules and practice directions state they should faithfully reflect those provisions. Sometimes difficulties may be encountered where the publication of revised forms falls behind the coming into effect of amendments to provisions they are meant to support. Instances have arisen of forms of orders being found to have improperly restricted the powers of the court (e.g. *Bristol City Council v Hassan* [2006] EWCA Civ 656, May 23, 2006, unrep., CA (use of Form **N28** (Order for possession) where order against secure tenant taking effect but tenant remaining as "tolerated trespasser)).

Civil Procedure Forms Volume

4.0.3 The *Civil Procedure Forms Volume* is provided as part of the *White Book* Service subscription. That Volume contains a comprehensive set of forms for use in the High Court and in the county courts, and includes forms listed in the several tables attached to Practice Direction (Forms) (see para.4PD.1 below). It also reproduces Part 4 in full including Tables 1, 2 and 3. For a fuller explanation of the relationship between the Tables in the practice direction and the forms contained in the *Civil Procedure Forms Volume*, see the Service Information page of the *Forms Volume*.

4.1 **4—(1) The forms set out in a practice direction shall be used in the cases to which they apply.**

(2) A form may be varied by the court or a party if the variation is required by the circumstances of a particular case.

(3) A form must not be varied so as to leave out any information or guidance which the form gives to the recipient.

(4) Where these Rules require a form to be sent by the court or by a party for another party to use, it must be sent without any variation except such as is required by the circumstances of the particular case.

(5) Where the court or a party produces a form shown in a practice direction with the words "Royal Arms", the form must include a replica of the Royal Arms at the head of the first page.

"forms set out in a practice direction"

4.1.1 As is explained in para.1.3 of Practice Direction (Forms), that practice direction contains three tables containing lists of forms. The contents of Table 1 is explained in para.3.1, of Table 2 in paras 4.1 to 4.3, and of Table 3 in paras 5.1 and 5.2.

Use of forms, with or without variation

4.1.2 Subsections (2) to (4) of r.4 are self-explanatory. It should be noted that many CPR provisions make express reference to specific forms, sometimes stating that a form must be used and at other times stating that it may be used. The question whether a form must or may be used is separate from the question whether the form may or may not be varied. Subsection (3) is important as many forms contain quite elaborate guidance for those instigating the use of a certain form and for those to whom it is directed (see Practice Direction (Forms), para.1.2).

Royal Arms

Where a form must include a Royal Arms the same format as is used on the published form need not be used; all that is necessary is that there is a complete Royal Arms. **4.1.3**

PRACTICE DIRECTION—FORMS

This Practice Direction supplements Part 4 of the Civil Procedure Rules

Scope of this practice direction

4PD.1 **1.1** This practice direction lists the forms to be used in civil proceedings on or after 26th April 1999, when the Civil Procedure Rules (CPR) came into force.

1.2 The forms may be modified as the circumstances require, provided that all essential information, especially information or guidance which the form gives to the recipient, is included.

1.3 This practice direction contains 3 tables—

- Table 1 lists forms required by CPR Parts 1–75
- Table 2 lists High Court forms in use before 26th April 1999 which have remained in use on or after that date (see paragraph 4 below)
- Table 3 lists county court forms in use before 26th April 1999 that will remain in use on or after that date (see paragraph 5 below)

1.4 Former prescribed forms are shown as 'No 00'. The former practice forms where they are appropriate for use in either the Chancery or Queen's Bench Division (or where no specific form is available for use in the county court, in that court also) are prefixed 'PF' followed by the number. Where the form is used mainly in the Chancery or Queen's Bench Division, the suffix CH or QB follows the form number.

Other forms

4PD.2 **2.1** Other forms may be authorised by practice directions. For example the forms relating to Part 61 Admiralty claims are authorised by, and annexed to, the Admiralty Claims practice direction.

Table 1

"N" Forms

Contents:

4PD.3 **3.1** This table lists the forms that are referred to and required by Rules or Practice Directions supplementing particular Parts of the CPR. A Practice Direction and its paragraphs are abbreviated by reference to the Part of the CPR which it supplements and the relevant paragraph of the Practice Direction, for example PD34 1.2. For ease of reference, forms required for claims in the Commercial Court, Technology and Construction Court and for Admiralty claims and Arbitration claims, are separately listed.

3.2 There are Court Funds Office forms referred to in Part 37. These are not listed below. They are Form 100 (Request for Lodgment (General)), Form 201 (Request for payment out of money in court to satisfy a Part 36 offer) and Form 202 (Notice of Defendant's consent to payment out of money in court to satisfy a Part 36 offer). It should also be noted that use of Form N242A—Offer to settle—Part 36, referred to in paragraph 1.1 of the Practice Direction supplementing Part 36 and in the table below, is not mandatory.

Note —The forms included in Table 1 are here omitted (as are the forms listed in Table 2 and Table 3). As is explained in para.4.0.3 above, the *Civil Procedure Forms Volume* contains a comprehensive set of forms for use in the High Court and in the county courts, and includes forms listed in the several tables attached to the Practice Direction. **4PD.3.1**

Table 2

Practice Forms

Contents:

4.1 This table lists the Practice Forms that may be used under this Practice Direction. It contains forms that were previously— **4PD.4**

- Prescribed Forms contained in Appendix A to the Rulesof the Supreme Court 1965
- Queen's Bench Masters' Practice Forms
- Chancery Masters' Practice Forms

4.2 Where a rule permits, a party intending to use a witness statement as an alternative to an affidavit should amend any form in this Table to be used in connection with that rule so that "witness statement" replaces "affidavit" wherever it appears in the form.

4.3 The forms in this list are reproduced in an Appendix to the Chancery and Queen's Bench Guides, and in practitioners' text books and on the Court Service website (*www.hmcourts-service.gov.uk*).

Note —The forms included in Table 2 are here omitted. For explanation, see note attached to Table 1 above. **4PD.4.1**

Table 3

Contents:

5.1 This table lists county court forms in use before 26 April 1999 that will have continued to be used on or after that date. **4PD.5**

5.2 Where a rule permits, a party intending to use a witness statement as an alternative to an affidavit should amend any form in this Table to be used in connection with that rule so that "witness statement" replaces "affidavit" wherever it appears in the form.

Note —The forms included in Table 3 are here omitted. For explanation, see note attached to Table 1 above. **4PD.5.1**

PART 5

COURT DOCUMENTS

Contents

5.0.1

Editorial introduction

5.0.2 Rule 5.1 does not really do justice to the range of matters dealt with in this Part. The rules in this Part deal with the preparation of certain court documents (r.5.2), with the signature of documents by mechanical means (r.5.3), with the supply of documents from court records (rr.5.4 to 5.4D), and with the filing and sending of documents by facsimile or other electronic means (r.5.5).

Since the CPR came into force, the provisions relating to the supply of documents from court records have undergone substantial amendment on a number of occasions. Originally there was but one rule (r.5.4). Rule 5.4A was added by the Civil Procedure (Amendment) Rules 2004 (SI 2004/1306), and r.5.5 by the Civil Procedure (Amendment) Rules 2002 (SI 2002/2058). Rule 5.4 was substituted entirely by the Civil Procedure (Amendment No.2) Rules 2004 (SI 2004/2072) and was amended subsequently by the Civil Procedure (Amendment No.3) Rules 2005 (SI 2005/2292). By the Civil Procedure (Amendment) Rules 2006 r.5.4 was divided into three discrete rules; rr.5.4, 5.4B and 5.4C. Rule 5.4A (Supply of court documents to Attorney-General from court records) was not affected by those amendments and remained as it was. Paras (1) and (2) of the former r.5.4 came to constitute the new r.5.4, re-titled as "Register of claims", paras (3) and (4) to constitute paras (1) and (2) of r.5.4B, entitled "Supply of documents to a party from court records", and paras (8) to (10) in r.5.4D (Supply of documents from court records—general). The substance of paras (5) to (7) of former r.5.4 are now found in r.5.4C (Supply of documents to a non-party from court records). The re-arrangement of these provisions in this last-mentioned respect effected some substantial changes to what had gone before. Rule 5.4C was further amended by the Civil Procedure (Amendment No.2 Rules) 2006 (SI 2006/3132).

This Part is supplemented by Practice Direction (Court Documents) (see para.5PD.1 below). This Practice Direction does much more than merely supplement rules in this Part (e.g. it deals with the supply of documents to new parties joined to existing proceedings, and with the filing of documents by facsimile).

Rule 5.5 is supplemented by Practice Direction (Electronic Communication and Filing of Documents) (see para.5BPD.1 below).

Related sources

5.0.3

- Rule 2.6 (Court documents to be sealed)
- Rule 4(5) (Forms including replica of Royal Arms)
- Rule 31.22 (Subsequent use of disclosed documents)

- Rule 32.13 (Availability of witness statements for inspection)
- Rule 39.7 (Impounded documents)
- Rule 76.34 (proceedings under Prevention of Terrorism Act 2005)
- Practice Direction (Possession Claims Online), para.14.2 (Viewing case record)
- Practice Direction (Interim Injunctions), para.9.2 (Injunctions against third parties)
- Practice Direction (Applications for Statutory Review Under Section 103A of the Nationality, Immigration and Asylum Act 2002), paras 3.1 and 3.2
- Practice Direction (Application for a Warrant under the Enterprise Act 2002), para.3.2
- Practice Direction (Reserved Judgments)
- Practice Statement (Supreme Court: Judgments) [1998] 1 W.L.R. 825
- CCR 25 r.8(9) (reissue of warrant where condition upon which warrant was suspended or not complied with) (CPR Sch.2)
- CCR 28 r.11(1) (issue of warrant of committal) (CPR Sch.2)
- Queen's Bench Guide, Vol.2, para.1B–12
- Freedom of Information Act 2000 s.32
- Access to Justice Act 1999 s.20
- Insolvency Rules 1986 r.7.86

Scope of this Part

5.1 This Part contains general provisions about— **5.1**

(a) documents used in court proceedings; and

(b) the obligations of a court officer in relation to those documents.

Effect of Rule

As indicated above (para.5.0.2), the Practice Direction supplementing this Part deals with some important matters concerning the handling of court documents not foreshadowed in rr.5.2 to 5.4. Those matters are outlined in the following paragraphs. **5.1.1**

Form of court documents

Every document prepared by a party for filing or use at court must comply with the provisions in Practice Direction (Court Documents), para.2.2 (see para.5PD.2 below) as to size of paper and width of margins, as to numbering of pages and paragraphs, and as to binding, etc. Further, claim forms, statements of case and other documents drafted by a legal representative must be signed as required by para.2.1. **5.1.2**

Obligations of a court officer—documents filed at court

Rule 5.1(b) indicates that Pt 5 contains general provisions about the obligations of a court officer in relation to documents used in court proceedings. The rules in Pt 5 have little to say about such obligations. More detail is contained in Practice Direction (Court Documents), paras 5.1 and 5.2 where certain of the obligations of court officers arising upon the filing of court documents are stated (see para.5PD.5 below). These include recording on a document the date on which it was filed and, if it was delivered at the court office by post, the time of delivery. Particulars of the date of delivery and the title of the proceedings in which the document is field are to be entered in court records, or the court file, or on the computer kept in the court office for the purpose; see further para.5.2.6 below. As to meaning of "filing", see r.2.3 (Interpretation) and commentary in para.2.3.14.1 above. In *Van Aken v London Borough of Camden* [2002] EWCA Civ 1724; October 11, 2002, unrep., CA, it was said that the duties imposed on court officers by paras 5.1 and 5.2 deal only with matters of internal management in the court office and do not affect the definition of "filing" given in r.2.3(1). Numerous CPR provisions place particular obligations on court officers upon the filing of certain documents; e.g. Practice Direction (Enforcement of Judgments and Orders), para.2.2 (para.70PD.2 below), and Sch.2, CCR 27 r.4(2) (para.cc27.4 below). **5.1.2.1**

Filing document at court by facsimile

Practice Direction (Court Documents), para.5.3 (see para.5PD.6 below) was inserted **5.1.3** in November 1999 and was amplified (by the additions of sub-paras (6) to (11)) in March 2000. With effect from December 2, 2002, sub-para.(2) was amended to provide that a hard copy of document filed by fax must not be sent to the court. In *Van Aken v London Borough of Camden* [2002] EWCA Civ 1724; October 11, 2002, unrep., CA, Ward L.J. doubted the purpose of sub-para.(6). Rule 5.5 (Filing and sending documents), which paves the way for a practice direction making provision for documents to be filed or sent to the court by fax or other electronic means was not added to the CPR until December 2002, see para.5.5.1 below. It is important to note that fax should not be used to send to the court letters or documents of a routine or non–urgent nature and should not be used, except in unavoidable emergency, to deliver a document which attracts a fee, a Pt 36 payment notice, a document relating to a hearing less than two hours ahead, trial bundles, or skeleton arguments.

Other provisions dealing with transmission of documents by fax include Practice Direction (Service), paras 3.1 to 3.4 (see para.6PD.3 below), and Practice Direction (Admiralty), para.17.1 (see Vol.2, para.2D–142). See further para.1.4.13 above. Note also Chancery Guide, para.14.10), and Commercial Court Guide, para.B3.11 (see Vol.2, para.2D–40).

Electronic communication and filing of documents

5.1.4 Rule 5.5(1) states that a practice direction may make provision for documents to be filed or sent to the court by electronic means other than facsimile. This creates scope for the development of practices enabling documents to be filed by email or through dedicated websites. See further commentary following r.5.5 below.

Production of court documents to any court, tribunal or arbitrator

5.1.5 Practice Direction (Court Documents), para.5.5 replaces former RSC 63 r.9 and states the general rule that a document filed, lodged or held in court shall not be taken out of that office without the permission of the court (see para.5PD.7 below). Where the production of such a document is required by any court, tribunal or arbitrator, the detailed procedure stated in para.5.6 of the Practice Direction is to be followed. (These provisions replace the Supreme Court (Production) Rules 1926 (S.R. & O. 1926 No.461).) (In para.5.5 of the Practice Direction, "paragraph 5.5" should read "paragraph 5.6".) It may be noted that para.5.6(4) states that, where court documents are to be sent to another court, or to a tribunal or arbitrator, they should be sent by registered post. In this respect the Practice Direction faithfully replicates the 1926 Rules, made under the Supreme Court Act 1981 s.136. After the coming into force of the Recorded Delivery Service Act 1962 those Rules, insofar as they permitted production by registered post, were to be read as also permitting production by recorded delivery service (see Vol.2, para.9A–379). Presumably, para.5.6(4) is to be read in a similar fashion.

Enrolment of deeds and other documents

5.1.6 Practice Direction (Court Documents), para.6.1(1) (see para.5PD.6 below) states that any deed or document which by virtue of any enactment is required or authorised to be enrolled in the Supreme Court may be enrolled in the Central Office (formerly, this provision was found in RSC 63 r.10). The enrolment of deeds is under the jurisdiction of the Master of the Rolls by virtue of the Supreme Court Act 1981 s.133 (see Vol.2, para.9A–373+). Many statutes have in the past required or expressly permitted enrolments. Of these many have been repealed; under others, enrolments are now obsolete or very rare. Nowadays, deeds for change of name (see para.5.1.7 below) form the bulk of the instruments enrolled. Apart from instruments required or permitted to be enrolled by any enactment, any deed may be enrolled for safe record if desired, but such enrolments are rare. In case of any doubt as to the propriety of any enrolment the Central Office would consult the Master of the Rolls. The matters of practice outlined above are referred to briefly in the Queen's Bench Guide, para.13.5.1 (see Vol.2, para.1B–94). For fees payable for enrolment of deeds, see Enrolment of Deeds (Fees) Regulations 1994 (SI 1994/604) (Vol.2, para.10–31+).

Enrolment of deeds evidencing change of name

5.1.7 *Practice Direction (Court Documents)*, para.6.1(2) (see para.5PD.6 below) draws attention to the Enrolment of Deeds (Change of Name) Regulations 1994 (SI 1994/604) and para.6.3 describes the practice to be followed in any case in which a child's name is to be changed and to which the 1994 Regulations apply. The Regulations themselves are reproduced in the Appendix to this Practice Direction (see para.5PD.9 below).

Documents in Braille

Where a party is blind, there is no procedural rule requiring that documents served on him by the court or by a party should be in Braille, but the court may order that they should be served in that form (*Herskovic v Davenport & Lyons* [2002] EWHC 1855 (Ch); May 29, 2002, unrep. (Lawrence Collins J.), where held that, in the circumstances, there had been no breach of the Human Rights Act 1998 Sch.1 Pt I, art.6, or the Disability Discrimination Act 1995). 5.1.8

Preparation of documents[1]

5.2—(1) Where under these Rules, a document is to be prepared by the court, the document may be prepared by the party whose document it is, unless— 5.2

(a) a court officer otherwise directs; or

(b) it is a document to which—

(i) [Revoked]

(ii) CCR Order 25, rule 8(9) (reissue of warrant where condition upon which warrant was suspended has not been complied with); or

(iii) CCR Order 28, rule 11(1) (issue of warrant of committal), applies.

(2) Nothing in this rule shall require a court officer to accept a document which is illegible, has not been duly authorised, or is unsatisfactory for some other similar reason.

Effect of rule

The CPR cover proceedings in the High Court and proceedings in the county courts. Historically speaking, the two levels of court were meant to operate in quite distinctive ways. In particular, the county courts were meant to be easily accessible to litigants who did not have the benefit of legal representation. Consequently, under the rules of court applicable, it was provided that most documents which had to be prepared for the purpose of proceedings (e.g. a summons) were prepared, not by the parties, but by the court at the request of the parties. In 1991, when the jurisdiction of the county courts was expanded significantly, enabling these courts to deal with many matters formerly falling within the exclusive jurisdiction of the High Court, the CCR were amended to permit parties to prepare court documents. These amendments were contained in CCR 3 r.3 (originating process) and CCR 50 r.4A (documents generally). Rule 5.2 follows the terms of former CCR 50 r.4A. 5.2.1

Excluded documents

Certain county court documents are excluded and may not be prepared by a party (r.5.2(1)(b)). In this respect, r.5.2 follows exactly the terms of former, CCR 50 r.4A(2)(b). The exclusions are contained in certain provisions in the CCR which are included in Sch.2 to the CPR and continue in force. Consequently, documents prepared under those scheduled provisions are documents which "under these Rules" are to be prepared by the court. Formerly, sub-para.(i) of r.5 2(1)(b) referred to CCR 25 r.5(3) (re-issue of enforcement proceedings). Rule 5 was revoked when Pt 70 (General Rules About Enforcement of Judgments and Orders) was inserted in the CPR by the Civil Procedure (Amendment No.4) Rules 2001 (SI 2001/2792) with effect from March 25, 2002. Accordingly, sub-para.(i) was omitted from r.5.2(1)(b) by that statutory instrument. 5.2.2

"document ... unsatisfactory"

A court officer is not required to accept a document "which is illegible, has not been duly authorised, or is unsatisfactory for some other similar reason" (r.5.2(2)). This is an improvement on the wording of former CCR 50 r.4A(2)(a), which was open to the 5.2.3

[1] Amended by the Civil Procedure (Amendment No.4) Rules 2001 (SI 2001/2792).

interpretation that the proper officer could reject a document as being unsatisfactory for reasons not necessarily similar to illegibility or lack of authorisation.

Court officer

5.2.4 A "court officer" is a member of the court staff (r.2.3(1)). Where the CPR require or permit the court to perform an act of a formal or administrative character, that act may be performed by a court officer (r.2.5(1)). Under the former rules, it was the "proper officer" who had power to allow a party to prepare a document.

Court documents to be sealed

5.2.5 Rule 2.6 states that the court must seal on issue claim forms and any other documents which a rule or practice direction requires it to seal. A document purporting to bear the court's seal shall be admissible in evidence without further proof.

Filing of documents at court

5.2.6 Former RSC 63 r.3 (Date of filing to be marked, etc.), r.5 (Deposit of documents) and r.9 (Restriction on removal of documents) are replaced by, respectively, Practice Direction (Court Documents), paras 5.3 and 5.4, para.5.5, and para.5.6 (see para.5PD.5 below). See further para.5.1.2.1 above.

Signature of documents by mechanical means

5.3 **5.3 Where any of these Rules or any practice direction requires a document to be signed, that requirement shall be satisfied if the signature is printed by computer or other mechanical means.**

Effect of rule

5.3.1 This rule is based on CCR 50 r.6A. That provision was introduced into the CCR in 1991 when the Summons Production Centre was established (see CCR 2 Pt II) (there was no comparable provision in the RSC). The wording in r.5.3 is not quite the same. Rule 6A said a requirement that any document should "bear a person's signature" would be satisfied if "that person's name" was printed by computer or other mechanical means.

For Production Centre, see now r.7.10 and note Practice Direction (Court Documents), para.1 (see 5PD.1 below). Practice Direction (Production Centre), para.1.4(4) makes special provision for the signature by mechanical means of statements of truth where a party files with the Production Centre a batch of requests for the issue of claim forms (see 7CPD.1).

As to the sealing of court documents otherwise than by hand, see r.2.6 (Court documents to be sealed).

Note also r.4(5) (Forms including replica of Royal Arms).

The rule refers to any requirement that "a document" be signed. The question what is, and what is not, a "document" for these purposes is not free from doubt. There are many documents which, in accordance with CPR provisions should be signed. They include the following (the list is not exhaustive): acknowledgments of service (r.10.5), statements of truth (verifying statements of case, witness statements, and application notices) (r.22.1), witness statements (r.32.4), written consents of trustees to act (r.33.8), certificates of witness's failure to attend for examination (r.34.10), and draft consent orders (r.40.6(5)). Practice Direction (Court Documents), para.2.1 states that, not only statements of case, but also "other documents drafted by a legal representative", should bear his signature and, if they are drafted by a legal representative as a member or employee of a firm, they should be signed in the name of the firm (see para.5PD.1 below). For meaning of "legal representative", see r.2.3(1).

Register of claims[1]

5.4 **5.4—(1) A court or court office may keep a publicly accessible register of claims which have been issued out of that court or court office.**

[1] Amended by the Civil Procedure (Amendment) Rules 2006 (SI 2006/1689).

(2) Any person who pays the prescribed fee may, during office hours, search any available register of claims.

(The practice direction contains details of available registers).

Effect of rule

As originally enacted in the CPR r.5.4 dealt with the supply of copies of court documents to parties and to non-parties. The rule was substantially amended for the purpose of dealing with that matter until 2006 when, upon rr.5.4B, 5.4C and 5.4D being inserted, paras (3) to (9) of the rule were revoked, leaving paras (1) and (2) as the only surviving provisions in the rule. Those surviving paragraphs had been originally inserted in r.5.4 by the Civil Procedure (Amendment No.2) Rules 2004 (SI 2004/2072) and, as they clearly had nothing to do with the supply of copies of court documents to parties and to non-parties, when paras (3) to (9) were revoked the rule was given the heading "Register of claims", accurately reflecting its function. 5.4.1

This rule does not apply in relation to any proceedings in respect of which a rule or a practice direction makes different provision (r.5.4D(3)).

It is expressly provided in Practice Direction (Application for a Warrant under the Enterprise Act 2002), para.3.2 (see para.B14–001 below) that in an application for a warrant under the Enterprise Act 2002 s.194, r.5.4(2) does not apply and paras 3.3 and 3.4 of that practice direction shall have effect in their place.

Unless the court directs otherwise, the rule does not apply to any proceedings to which the CPR Pt 76 (Prevention of Terrorism Act 2005) applies (r.76.34).

Unless the court otherwise directs, this rule does not apply to any proceedings to which CPR Pt 79 (Financial Restrictions Proceedings Under the Counter-Terrorism Act 2008) applies (r.79.30).

Inspection of register of claims

A court or court office may keep a register of claims. Practice Direction (Court Documents), paras 4.1 and 4.2 explain that registers of claims are kept and are available for inspection at some court offices at the Royal Courts of Justice (see para.5PD.4 below). However, no registers are at present available for inspection in county courts or in District Registries or other offices of the High Court. 5.4.2

A person who pays the prescribed fee may, during office hours, search any available register of claims. The fee for an official certificate of the result of a search of any register held by the court (including, presumably, any register referred to in r.5.4(1)) is as prescribed by the Civil Procedure Fees Order 2004 (SI 2004/3121) art.2, Sch.1 para.9.2. The days and hours during which court offices are open are stated in Practice Direction (Court Offices) (see para.2PD.1 above).

As to searches of court records of insolvency proceedings and of court files of individual cases, see the Insolvency Rules 1986 r r.7.27 to 7.31. Authorities giving guidance on multiple searches of such registers by third parties are *Ex p. Creditnet Ltd* [1996] 1 W.L.R. 1291; *Ex p. Austintel Ltd* [1997] 1 W.L.R. 616, CA; *In re Haines Watts* [2004] EWHC 1970 (Ch); July 22, 2004, unrep.; *Franbar Holdings Ltd v Patel* [2008] EWHC 1534 (Ch), July 2, 2008, unrep.

Supply of documents to Attorney-General from court records

5.4A—(1) The Attorney-General may search for, inspect and take a copy of any documents within a court file for the purpose of preparing an application or considering whether to make an application under section 42 of the Supreme Court Act 1981[1] or section 33 of the Employment Tribunals Act 1996[2] (restriction of vexatious proceedings). 5.4A

(2) The Attorney-General must, when exercising the right under paragraph (1)—

(a) pay any prescribed fee; and

[1] 1981 c.54.
[2] 1996 c.17.

(b) file a written request, which must—

(i) confirm that the request is for the purpose of preparing an application or considering whether to make an application mentioned in paragraph (1); and

(ii) name the person who would be the subject of the application.

Effect of rule

5.4A.1 This rule was inserted in the CPR with effect from June 1, 2004, by the Civil Procedure (Amendment) Rules 2004 (SI 2004/1306).

An application by the Attorney General for an order under s.42 of the 1981 Act or s.33 of the 1996 Act, necessarily involves presenting to the High Court a full account of the legal proceedings alleged to have been taken by the respondent habitually and persistently and without any reasonable ground. This, in turn will involve presenting evidence from court records. Rule 5.4A enables the Attorney General, on the terms mentioned therein, to search for, inspect and take a copy of any documents within a court file for the purpose of making, or considering whether to make, an application under s.42 or s.33. In other circumstances, the Attorney General (perhaps as a party, or as a non party) may take advantage of rr.5.4, 5.4B and 5.4C.

As to the payment of any prescribed fee, see "Prescribed fee" para.5.4D.2 below.

Supply of documents to a party from court records[1]

5.4B **5.4B—(1) A party to proceedings may, unless the court orders otherwise, obtain from the records of the court a copy of any document listed in paragraph 4.2A of the Practice Direction.**

(2) A party to proceedings may, if the court gives permission, obtain from the records of the court a copy of any other document filed by a party or communication between the court and a party or another person.

Effect of rule and practice direction

5.4B.1 This rule was inserted by the Civil Procedure (Amendment) Rules 2006 (SI 2006/1689) (together with rr.5.4C and 5.4D), and came into force on October 2, 2006. In effect, the rule replaced paras (3) and (4) of r.5.4, provisions that had always dealt with the supply of court documents to a party, as distinct from to a non-party (see r.5.4C). (For provenance of the rule in former RSC and CCR provisions, see *Civil Procedure 2004*, Vol.1, para.5.4.1, and earlier editions.) Aspects of the rule are supplemented by Practice Direction (Court Documents) para.4 (see para.5PD.4 below).

Rule 5.4B does not apply in relation to any proceedings in respect of which a rule or practice direction makes different provision; see "Limits to application of r.5.4B" (para.5.4B.6 below).

The distinction between para.(1) and (2) of the rule is that the party does not need the court's permission in order to obtain the documents referred to in para.(1) and may obtain a copy of the document unless the court orders otherwise. The list of documents referred to in Practice Direction (Court Documents), para.4.2A (see para.5PD.4 below) is extensive.

A party wishing to obtain a copy of a document under this rule must pay the prescribed fee and (a) if the court's permission is required, file an application notice in accordance with Pt 23, or (b) if permission is not required, file a written request for the document (r.5.4D(1)).

A party's application for permission to obtain a copy of a document under this rule may be made without notice, but the court may direct that notice should be given to *any person who would be affected* by its decision (r.5.4D(2)). Even if made without notice, the application must be made under Pt 23 and the application notice must identify

[1] Introduced by the Civil Procedure (Amendment) Rules 2006 (SI 2006/1689).

the document or class of document in respect of which permission is sought and the grounds relied on (Practice Direction (Court Documents), para.4.4 (see para.5PD.4 below).

As to the disclosure to litigants in person and McKenzie friends assisting them of confidential court documents and information in family proceedings, see *In re O. (Children) (Hearing in Private: Assistance)* [2005] EWCA Civ 759; [2005] 3 W.L.R. 1191, CA.

"a party to proceedings"

Paragraph 4.5 was added to Practice Direction (Court Documents) by TSO CPR Update 42 (August 2006) and came into effect on October 2, 2006 (see para.5PD.4 below). It states that a person who has been named as a party on a statement of case, irrespective of whether he has been served with that statement of case, is "a party to proceedings" within the meaning of r.5.4B. Circumstances may arise where a person may suspect that a claim form in which he is named as a party has been issued. He may inquire of the court to determine whether or not his suspicions are correct and, if they are, he is a party to proceedings for the purposes of r.5.4B and may obtain copies of documents as permitted by the rule. (It would seem that para.4.5 deals with the problem which arose in *Advanced Specialist Treatment Engineering Ltd v Cleveland Structural Engineering (Hong Kong) Ltd* [2000] 1 W.L.R. 558 (Colman J.).) **5.4B.2**

"records of the court"

In the development of particular proceedings, copies of documents relating to the case may, in accordance with the normal rules and practices as to disclosure of documents, to the preparation and exchange of witness statement etc and with directions given by the court, pass into the hands of persons who are non-parties quite legitimately (perhaps subject to express or implied conditions as to their further use). In those circumstances, the documents do not come from court records. Rules 5.4B (parties) and 5.4C (non-parties) are concerned with the obtaining of copies of documents "from court records", the former by a party applicant and the latter by a non-party applicant. The documents kept in a court office as part of the court's file of particular proceedings include the formal documents issued by the court itself, in particular, forms of process such as claim forms and application notices, and orders. But they include much else besides.The long list of documents in Practice Direction (Court Documents), para.4.2A (see para.5PD.4 below) gives an indication of the wide variety of documents that may be generated in the course of civil proceedings and which conceivably may held in court records. The range of documents referred to in r.5.4C to which a non-party may have access is much more limited. The documents referred to in para.4.2A and r.5.4C should be distinguished from documents in the form of registers etc which a court office may maintain for its own record keeping purposes. In given proceedings, documents may come into existence and be used in the course of proceedings and yet not be filed (e.g. requests for information and replies thereto); or they may be filed and subsequently retrieved by the parties (e.g. bundles of documents) (e.g. *Chan U Seek v Alvis Vehicles Ltd* [2004] EWHC 3092 (Ch); [2005] 1 W.L.R. 2965; sub nom. *In re Guardian Newspapers Ltd* [2005] 3 All E.R. 155). An application for a document which never was in court records, or was and no longer is, would be misconceived. Where an applicant (whether a party or a non-party) seeks a copy of a document used in proceedings, but which formed no part of the record of the court, the jurisdiction of the court to grant such an application is not derived from r.5.4B or r.5.4C, but from the court's inherent jurisdiction. **5.4B.3**

Rules 5.4B and 5.4C (as supplemented by para.4 of Practice Direction (Court Documents)) do not make sense unless they are read as indicating that, save as permitted under the rules, documents on a court file of particular proceedings are not intended to be inspected or copied. That is to say, a court file is not a publicly available register It is a file maintained by the court for the proper conduct of the proceedings. Documents in the file do not become available for inspection or copying save to the extent that access to specified documents or classes of documents is granted, either generally under the rules or by leave of the court in a particular case (*Dobson v Hastings* [1992] Ch 394, Sir Donald Nicholls V.-C).

"listed" and "other" documents

The rule refers to "listed" documents (being documents which a party may obtain without the court's permission) and to "other" documents (being documents which a party may obtain when permission is granted). As originally enacted, the provisions **5.4B.4** now found in this rule stated simply that a party to proceedings could be supplied from the records of the court with a copy of "any document relating to those proceedings (including documents filed before the claim was commenced)". The power of the court to order otherwise was implied. No distinction was drawn between documents that could be obtained without permission and those for which permission was required. Subsequently, the rule became steadily more complicated. Before the rule was brought into its present form by the Civil Procedure (Amendment) Rules 2006 (SI 2006/1689), consolidating what had gone before, the principal amendments were made by the Civil Procedure (Amendment No.2) Rules 2004 (SI 2004/2072) and the Civil Procedure (Amendment No.3) Rules 2005 (SI 2005/2292). The former statutory instrument introduced the distinction between those documents that could be supplied with permission and those without. It was the latter statutory instrument that relegated from rule to practice direction the documents in the first category (the necessary amendment was made by TSO CPR Update 36 (August 2004)).

The listed documents are those referred to Practice Direction (Court Documents), para.4.2A (see para.5PD.4 below). It may be noted that included among the listed documents are a claim form or other statement of case and an acknowledgment of service "together with any documents filed with or attached to or intended ... to be served" with such documents. (This may contrasted with the formulation in r.5.4C(1) relating to documents generally obtainable as of right by non-parties; see para.5.4C.3 below.) The list also includes a judgment or order given or made in public, an application notice (subject to exceptions), any written evidence (subject to exceptions), and an appellant's notice or a respondent's notice. It is conceivable that, in given proceedings, documents falling in this category may include documents filed with the court before the claim to which they relate was commenced (e.g. relating to an order for disclosure of documents before claim made). An application notice relating to an application (1) by a solicitor for an order declaring that he has ceased to be the solicitor acting for a party, or (2) for an order that the identity of a party or witness should not be disclosed, does not fall within the first category of documents as listed in para.4.2A, and therefore copies of such documents may not be supplied to a party to proceedings upon request. Presumably, such a document would be "any other document" within r.5.4B(2) and a copy could be supplied if the court gave permission under that rule.

"judgment or order given or made in public"

5.4B.5 The list of documents referred to in Practice Direction (Court Documents), para.4.2A (see para.5PD.4 below), being documents which a party (unless the court orders otherwise) may obtain without permission under r.5.4B(1) includes "a judgment or order given or made in public (whether made at a hearing or without a hearing". (Such a document may also be obtained by a non-party under r.5.4C (see para.5.4C.5 below).)

Terms of a compromise scheduled to a Tomlin order are not part of the order as such. In *L'Oréal SA v eBay International AG* , July 15, 2008, unrep., a trade mark infringement case, claims made against certain of several defendants jointly were compromised and Tomlin orders were made by the court, subject to a direction that the schedule terms should be separate from the orders and should not be inspected without permission of the court. Subsequently, other defendants in the proceedings applied under r.5.4B for an order permitting them to inspect the schedules, for the purpose of enabling them to consider whether the terms contained therein released them from liability. A Master granted the application, but limited it (in the first instance) to inspection by the applicant's legal advisers.

Where a court sits in private, for example, as permitted by r.39.2(3), the court is entitled to pronounce its judgment in private and is not required to give it in public, especially where it cannot be anonymised or abridged. See further paras 39.2.9 and 40.2.5 below.

Circumstances may arise where part of a judge's judgment must remain confidential to the parties but the rest need not, with only the latter being given in public (e.g. *E.P I. Environmental Technologies Inc v Symphony Plastic Technologies (Practice Note)* [2004] EWHC 2945 (Ch); [2005] 1 W.L.R. 3456; *Madarassay v Nomura International Plc* [2006] *EWHC 748 (QB); April 6, 2006, unrep.* (in giving judgment on application by employers to strike out employee's Employment Tribunal claim and appeal to Employment Appeal Tribunal judge allocating to confidential appendix of his judgment his views on certain live issues)). In *McKennitt v Ash* [2006] EWCA Civ 1714; [2007] 3 W.L.R. 194, CA, where the claimant brought proceedings to restrain by injunction further publication of a book containing personal and private information about her, the trial was heard in private, as a public hearing would have defeated the object of that hearing. The judge delivered an open judgment, in which the objectionable material was described in general terms, but appended a confidential appendix in which the actual enjoined material was fully described. When granting the defendants permission to appeal, the Court of Appeal ordered (1) that the appeal hearing should be in private whenever reference was to be made to any part of the information contained in that appendix, and (2) that there should be "no reporting of any matter withheld from the public in these proceedings".

As to the making available to parties and their legal representatives before handing down of copies of reserved judgments, see *Practice Statement (Supreme Court: Judgments)* [1998] 1 W.L.R. 825 (see para.B5–001 below) and Practice Direction (Reserved Judgments) (supplementing Pt 40) (see para.40EPD.1 below).

Limits to application of r.5.4B

Rule 5.4D(3) states that r.5.4B (parties) and r.5.4C (non-parties) do not apply in relation to any proceedings in respect of which a rule or practice direction makes different provision (r.5.4D(3)). Most (but not all) of the rules and practice directions imposing limits to the providing of copies of documents from court records operate to restrict supply to non-parties. See further "Limits to application of r. 5.4B and r. 5.4C" (para.5.4C.9 below), where other rules and practice directions limiting the application of both r.5.4B and r.5.4C are noted. **5.4B.6**

Supply of documents to party subject to conditions

See "Supply of documents to non-party subject to conditions" para.5.4C.8 below. **5.4B.7**

Supply of documents to new parties

Parties may be removed, added or substituted in existing proceedings either on the court's own initiative or on the application of either an existing party or a person who wishes to become a party (r.19.3 and Practice Direction (Addition and Substitution of Parties), para.1.1, see para.19PD.1 below). Obviously, a party joined to existing proceedings, as well as an original party, may take advantage of r.5.4B, but, for reasons which are immediately explained, he may not have to. **5.4B.8**

Practice Direction (Court Documents), para.3.1 states that, where a party is joined to existing proceedings, the party joined shall be entitled to require "the party joining him" to supply, without charge, copies of all statements of case, written evidence and any documents appended or exhibited to them which have been served in the proceedings by or upon the joining party which relate to any issues between the joining party and the party joined, and copies of all orders made in those proceedings (see para.5PD.3 below). Presumably, "the party joining him" is an existing party (to existing proceedings) who has made a successful application for a party to be joined. The documents should be supplied within 48 hours after a written request for them is received and if they are not application may be made for an order under Pt 23 (*ibid.*).

Where an interim injunction is made (e.g. a freezing order), it is conceivable that a person, other than the applicant or the respondent, who did not attend the hearing at which the order was made may be served with the order (e.g. a person holding assets subject to a freezing order). In these circumstances, para.9 2 of Practice Direction (Interim Injunctions) (see para.25PD.14 below) provides that, where such a person requests a copy of any material read by the judge, including material prepared after the hearing at the direction of the judge or in compliance with the order, or a note of the hearing, the applicant (or his legal representative) must comply promptly with the request, unless the court orders otherwise.

Viewing the case record

Other provisions, apart from r.5.4B, may provide for parties or their representatives to have access to court records. Particular examples are Practice Direction (Money Claim Online), para.15.1 (see para.7EPD.15 below) and Practice Direction (Possession Claims Online), para.14.2 (see para.55BPD.14 below) which make provision for the viewing of case records on court-maintained websites in the proceedings to which they apply. **5.4B.9**

Supply of documents to a non-party from court records[1]

5.4C **5.4C—(1) The general rule is that a person who is not a party to proceedings may obtain from the court records a copy of—**

(a) a statement of case, but not any documents filed with or attached to the statement of case, or intended by the party whose statement it is to be served with it;

(b) a judgment or order given or made in public (whether made at a hearing or without a hearing).

(1A) Where a non-party seeks to obtain a copy of a statement of case filed before 2nd October 2006—

(a) this rule does not apply; and

(b) the rules of court relating to access by a non-party to statements of case in force immediately before 2nd October 2006 apply as if they had not been revoked.

(The rules relating to access by a non-party to statements of case in force immediately before 2nd October 2006 were contained in the former rule 5.4(5) to 5.4(9). The Practice Direction to this Part sets out the relevant provisions as they applied to statements of case.).

(2) A non-party may, if the court gives permission, obtain from the records of the court a copy of any other document filed by a party, or communication between the court and a party or another person.

(3) A non-party may obtain a copy of a statement of case or judgment or order under paragraph (1) only if—

(a) where there is one defendant, the defendant has filed an acknowledgment of service or a defence;

(b) where there is more than one defendant, either—

(i) all the defendants have filed an acknowledgment of service or a defence;

(ii) at least one defendant has filed an acknowledgment of service or a defence, and the court gives permission;

(c) the claim has been listed for a hearing; or

(d) judgment has been entered in the claim.

(4) The court may, on the application of a party or of any person identified in a statement of case—

(a) order that a non-party may not obtain a copy of a statement of case under paragraph (1);

(b) restrict the persons or classes of persons who may obtain a copy of a statement of case;

(c) order that persons or classes of persons may only obtain a copy of a statement of case if it is edited in accordance with the directions of the court; or

(d) make such other order as it thinks fit.

(5) A person wishing to apply for an order under paragraph (4) ***must file an application*** **notice in accordance with Part 23.**

[1] Introduced by the Civil Procedure (Amendment) Rules 2006 (SI 2006/1689) and amended by the Civil Procedure (Amendment No.2) Rules 2006 (SI 2006/3132).

(6) Where the court makes an order under paragraph (4), a non-party who wishes to obtain a copy of the statement of case, or to obtain an unedited copy of the statement of case, may apply on notice to the party or person identified in the statement of case who requested the order, for permission.

Effect of rule and practice direction

When the CPR were drafted, it was necessary to marry together former RSC and CCR provisions regulating the supply of documents from court records to non-parties. The CCR provisions (CCR O.50, r.10) were more restrictive than the RSC provisions (RSC O.63, r.4). (It has been an unhappy marriage and the rules have had to be amended on a number of occasions.) Rule 5.4C was inserted by the Civil Procedure (Amendment) Rules 2006 (SI 2006/1689) (together with rr.5.4B and 5.4D). In effect, the rule replaced paras (5) to (7) of r.5.4, provisions that had always dealt with the supply of court documents to a non-party, as distinct from to a party (see r.5.4B). It was intended that the rule should come into force on October 2, 2006. In the event that did not happen. By the Civil Procedure (Amendment No 2) Rules 2006 (SI 2006/3132) para.(1A) was inserted in r.5.4C and the whole of the rule then came into force on December 18, 2006. The reason for the unexpected delay in bringing the rule into force is found in para.(1A) (see para.5.4C.3 below). In practice, difficulties were encountered in applying the provisions previously found in paras (5) to (7) of r.5.4 (particularly where the non-parties were members of the press) and it was expected that r.5.4C would rectify matters. Aspects of the rule are supplemented by Practice Direction (Court Documents) para.4 (see para.5PD.4 below). **5.4C.1**

In *McKennitt v Ash* [2006] EWCA Civ 1714; [2007] 3 W.L.R. 194, CA, when granting permission to appeal on November 21, 2006, in proceedings where judgment had been given (on December 21, 2005) granting the claimant injunctive relief preventing further publication of a book (see further para.5.4B.5 above), the Court of Appeal ordered: "That no person may obtain a copy of any document disclosed by the parties or of any document before the court or on the court records (including statements of case, witness statements and transcripts of evidence) without the consent of the claimants, or, failing that, the leave of the court, and this shall be until further order of the court".

Rule 5.4C does not apply in relation to any proceedings in respect of which a rule or practice direction makes different provision; see "Limits to application of r.5.4B and r.5.4C" (para.5.4C.9 below).

A person who is "a party to proceedings" is defined (see para.5.4B.2 above); and "a person who is not a party to proceedings" (a "non-party") is anyone else, including a person whose interests in no way are going to be affected by the progress or outcome of the proceedings (e.g. a journalist). In a given case the non-party may be a person with a direct or indirect interest in the events to which the proceedings relate, perhaps even a person who might well have been, or who might well become, a party.

The Attorney General, whether a party to proceedings or not (and therefore in the same position as any other person within r.5.4C), may search for, inspect and take copies of documents contained in court records for the purpose stated in, and in the circumstances provided for by r.5.4A (see para.5.4A.1 above).

A non-party wishing to obtain a copy of a document under this rule must pay the prescribed fee and (a) if the court's permission is required, file an application notice in accordance with Pt 23, or (b) if permission is not required, file a written request for the document (r.5.4D(1)).

There is no absolute rule, and nothing in r.5.4C(5) to suggest, that an application to inspect documents on a court file has to be made whilst a case is still in progress (*Chan U Seek v Alvis Vehicles Ltd [2004] EWHC 3092 (Ch), op. cit.*).

Before proceedings have been concluded, application for permission may be made to the court seised of the proceedings. After proceedings have been concluded, application may still be made to that court, as it is the court amongst whose records the court file relating to the proceedings is kept (*Chan U Seek v Alvis Vehicles Ltd* [2004] EWHC 3092 (Ch); [2005] 1 W.L.R. 2965, Park J., sub nom. *In re Guardian Newspapers Ltd* [2005] 3 All E.R. 155).

A non-party's application for permission to obtain a copy of a document under this rule may be made without notice, but the court may direct that notice should be given to any person who would be affected by its decision (r.5.4D(2)). Even if made without notice, the application must be made under Pt 23 and the application notice must identify the document or class of document in respect of which permission is sought and the grounds relied on (Practice Direction (Court Documents) para.4.3 (see para.5PD.4 below).

An application for an order under r.5.4C(4), that is to say, an application made by a party or a person identified in a statement of case, must be made by filing an application notice in accordance with Pt 23 (r.5.4C(5)). Such application may be made without notice, but the court may direct that notice should be given to any person who would be affected by its decision (r.5.4D(2)). The application must be made to a Master or a district judge, unless the court directs otherwise (Practice Direction (Court Documents), para.4.4 (see para.5PD.4 below).

"court records"

5.4C.2 See "records of the court" para.5.4B.3 above.

"statement of case" filed on or after October 2, 2006

5.4C.3 The provisions from which this rule grew, as originally enacted, were quite simple. They stated that a non-party, without permission, could obtain "a claim form which had been served", and any judgment or order given or made in public (see para.5.4C.5 below). The power of the court to order otherwise was implied. If the court gave permission, "any other document" could be obtained. Subsequently, in the light of practical difficulties that arose, the provisions were made more elaborate. By the Civil Procedure (Amendment No.2) Rules 2004 (SI 2004/2072), the obtaining of those documents that could be obtained without permission was restricted to the "only if" circumstances now found in r.5.4C(3). And, by the same statutory instrument, "any other document" became "any other document filed by a party, or communication between the court and a party or another person" (see now r.5.4C(2)).

Under the CPR, no clear distinction is drawn between originating process and pleadings. It was partly for this reason that difficulties were encountered in determining just precisely which documents a non-party seeking to obtain a claim form was entitled to receive. By the Civil Procedure (Amendment No.3) Rules 2005 (SI 2005/2292), it was made clear that where a non-party obtained a copy of "a claim form" this did not include "any documents filed with or attached to or intended by the claimant to be served with such claim form". The right to obtain (without permission) a copy of a claim form did not carry with it a right to obtain copies of pleadings. (Pleadings fell into "any other document" category, and a non-party had to apply for permission if he wished to obtain copies of them, as in *Cleveland Bridge (UK) Ltd v Multiplex Construction (UK) Ltd* [2005] EWHC 2101 (TCC); August 31, 2005, unrep. (Judge David Wilcox); see para.5.4C.7 below.) That provision was re-enacted in r.5.4C(1)(a), but "statement of case" is there substituted for "claim form". The meaning of "statement of case" is found in r.2.3 (Interpretation) (see para.2.3.13, above) where it is said that it means (amongst other things) a claim form, particulars of claim (where these are not included in a claim form) and defence. The result is that, under r.5.4C(1), a non-party may, without applying for permission, obtain a wider range of pleading documents than previously (being documents that may well continue to evolve as the issues are refined up to the time of trial). However, it is expressly provided in r.5.4C(1A) that, where a non-party seeks to obtain a copy of a statement of case filed before October 2, 2006, the rules of court "relating to access by a non-party to statements of case" before that date apply as if they had not been revoked. That is to say, paras (5) to (9) of r.5.4 as that rule stood before the amendments brought about by the Civil Procedure (Amendment) Rules 2006 (SI 2006/1689) apply in such circumstances. (For convenience, those provisions as they applied to statements of case are set out in the Practice Direction; see para.5PD.4A below.) To this extent, r.5.4C does not operate retrospectively.

Where the claimant commences proceedings in accordance with the provisions of Pt 8 (Alternative Procedure for Claims), the claim form must state the question which the claimant wants the court to decide, or the remedy which the claimant is seeking and the legal basis for the claim to that remedy (r.8.2(b)). Further, r.8.3 provides that if the *defendant wishes to defend*, he must file an acknowledgment of service stating whether he contests the claim and, "if he seeks a different remedy from that set out in the claim form", what that remedy is. There is no reason why a defendant should limit himself to the matters required by r.8.3. He may, instead of simply stating that he contests the claim (a bare denial), set out what his case is; in effect pleading a defence. A question which then may arise is whether the acknowledgment of service is a "statement of case" for the purposes of r.5.4C. The matter becomes more complicated where the judicial review procedure provided for by Section I of CPR Pt.54 is used (either because it must or because it may be). In such circumstances the Pt 8 procedure applies and glosses on the roles played by r.8.2 and by r.8.3 are imposed, respectively, by r.54.6 (Claim form) and r.54.8 (Acknowledgment of service). Amongst other things, r.54.6 states that the claim form "must be accompanied by the documents required by the relevant practice direction", and these include a detailed statement of the claimant's grounds for bringing the claim and a statement of the facts relied on (Practice Direction (Judicial Review) para.5.6). And r.54.8 states that any person "served with the claim form" who wishes to take part in the judicial review must file an acknowledgment of service. Where the person filing the acknowledgment of service intends to contest the claim, he must "set out a summary of his grounds for doing so". Unlike the position where r.8.3 applies, a bare denial will not suffice. Rule 54.14 states that a defendant and any other person served with the claim form who wishes to contest the claim or support it "on additional grounds" must file and serve "detailed grounds" for doing so. In *R. (Corner House Research) v Director of the Serious Fraud Office* [2008] EWHC 246 (Admin), February 4, 2008, unrep., the question which arose was whether, under r.5.4C, a non-party could obtain from court records copies of documents filed in accordance with r.54.8 and r.54.14. Collins J. held that the answer to this question was "yes". His lordship noted that in r.2.3(1) it is stated that in the CPR "statement of case" means "a claim form, particulars of claim where these are not included in the claim form, defence, Pt 20 claim, or reply to defence" and said that "it does not do violence to the language of the rule to take the view that 'defence' includes the judicial review equivalent to a defence". It is always open to a party to include either in the claim form or any acknowledgment of service, a request (giving reasons) that there should not be disclosure of the whole or part of the document unless the court approves (e.g. in a case involving mental health or children or other sensitive matters). See further para.5.4C.6 below.

As noted above, the original provision upon which this rule is based provided that a claim form "which had been served" could be obtained by a non-party. The "only if" provisions now found in r.5.4C(3) impose more sophisticated criteria for establishing, according to the stage the proceedings have reached, whether a non-party may (without first obtaining the court's permission) obtain a copy of a statement of case.

The phrase "and the court gives permission" in para (b)(ii) of r.5.4C(3) may be noted, as it may impose on the non-party an additional hurdle to be overcome before a copy of a statement of case (or judgment or order) may be obtained. In proceedings where there is more than one defendant all of them have filed an acknowledgment of service or a defence then a non-party may, without first obtaining the permission of the court, may obtain a copy of a statement of case (or judgment or order). If at least one defendant has filed an acknowledgment of service or a defence, then the non-party may obtain a copy of a statement of case (or judgment or order) provided the court gives permission. An application for such permission must be made on notice under Pt 23 (r.5.4D(3)) and the provisions of Practice Direction (Court Documents), para.4.3 apply.

Where, in accordance with r.5.4C, without permission a non-party is entitled to a copy of a statement of case, on the application under r.5.4C(4) of a party or any person identified in a statement of case, the court may grant relief as provided for in that sub-rule (see para.5.4C.6 below).

The provisions in r.5.4C dealing with the supply of copies of claim forms do not apply in relation to any proceedings in respect of which a rule or practice direction makes different provision; see "Limits to application of r.5.4B and r.5.4C" (para.5.4C.9 below).

"statement of case" ("claim form") filed before October 2, 2006

Paragraph (1A) of r.5.4C states that "this rule" (presumably that means the whole of r.5.4C and not the "general rule" stated in para.(1)) does not apply where a non-party seeks to obtain a copy of a statement of case filed before October 2, 2006. Instead the rules as to the obtaining by a non-party of a copy of a claim form apply, specifically paras (4) to (9) of r.5.4 as that rule stood before the amendments brought about by the Civil Procedure (Amendment) Rules 2006 (SI 2006/1689) came into effect, continue to apply (see para.5.4C.3 above). For ease of reference, those rules (with appropriate re-casting) as they applied to statements of case before October 2, 2006, are set out in **5.4C.4** para.4A of Practice Direction (Court Documents), inserted by TSO CPR Update 43 (see para.5PD.4A below). Paragraph 4A also incorporates paras r.4.3 and 4.4 of the Practice Direction as they applied in these circumstances. In the CPR "statement of case" means a claim form and other documents (r.2.3(1)). A non-party, without permission, may obtain a copy of a claim form filed before October 2, 2006, but requires permission if he is to obtain copies of such other documents. Paragraphs (4) to (9) of r.5.4 as preserved do not apply in relation to any proceedings in respect of which a rule or a practice direction makes different provision; see further "Limits to application of r.5.4B and r.5.4C" (para.5.4C.9 below).

"judgment or order given or made in public"

5.4C.5 It has long-since been the case that in English civil procedure "judgments" are "given" and "orders" are "made". The word "judgment" and the word "order" are terms of art (see para.40.1.1 below).

Paragraph (1)(b) of r.5.4C(1) states the general rule that a non-party may obtain a copy of "a judgment or order given or made in public (whether made at a hearing or without a hearing)". Where a court sits in private, for example, as permitted by r.39.2(3), the court is entitled to pronounce its judgment in private and is not required to give it in public, especially where it cannot be anonymised or abridged. Among the justifications that may be given for this is that copies of a judgment given in private may be provided to a non-party in accordance with r.5.4C. In this respect, para.(1)(b) of the rule makes express that which had to be implied under the former r.5.4 (see *In re Trusts of X Charity* [2003] EWHC 1462; June 24, 2003, unrep. (Sir Andrew Morritt V.-C.) (holding that such a judgment was "any other document" within the meaning of former r.5.4(5)(b)). See further para.5.4B.5 above.

The obtaining by a non-party of a copy of a judgment or order under r.5.4C(1) is subject to the "only if" circumstances stated in r.5.4C(3). However, most of those circumstances are apt to the situation where a non-party seeks to obtain, not a judgment or order, but a statement of case (see para.5.4C.3 above).

Where a hearing takes place in public, members of the public may obtain a transcript of any judgment given or a copy of any order made, subject to payment of the appropriate fee (Practice Direction (Miscellaneous Provisions Relating to Hearings) para.1.11 (see para.39.PD.1 below)).

As to the making available of copies of handed down judgments to persons other than the parties, see *Practice Statement (Supreme Court: Judgments)* [1998] 1 W.L.R. 825 (see para.B5–001 below) and Practice Direction (Reserved Judgments) (supplementing Pt 40) (see para.40EPD.1 below).

Application in opposition by party or person identified

5.4C.6 Rule 5.4C(1) states the general rule that a non-party may without permission obtain from court records a copy of a statement of case (filed on or after October 2, 2006) and of a judgment or order. Until the amendments made by the Civil Procedure (Amendment) Rules 2006 (SI 2006/1689) came into effect, the relevant rule stated that this was so unless the court ordered otherwise. Instead r.5.4C(4) now provides that the court may, on the application of a party or of any person identified in a statement of case order that a non-party may not obtain a copy of a statement of case under r.5.4C(1). Where a non-party seeks a copy of claim form filed before October 2, 2006, a party or a person identified in the claim may apply for similar relief under the rules of court specifically preserved by r.5.4C(1A) (see para.5.4C.5 above).

This rule is based on the assumption that there may be circumstances where for good reason a party or a person named in a statement of case might object to a non-party obtaining a copy of a statement of case at all, or at least to the obtaining of such copy immediately, or unconditionally. The rule provides that a party or such person may apply for relief. Paragraph (5) of the rule, r.5.4D(2), and Practice Direction (Court Documents), para.4.4 (see para.5PD.4 below) deal with matters of practice in relation to such application.

As explained above (para.5.4C.3), in *R. (Corner House) v Director of the Serious Fraud Office* [2008] EWHC 246 (Admin), February 4, 2008, unrep., where it was held that, in *a judicial review claim, under r.5.4C* a non-party could obtain from court records copies of documents filed in accordance with r.54.8 (acknowledgment of service) and r.54.14 (response), Collins J. explained that a party may include in a claim form or acknowledgment of service a request that the document (or part of it) should not be disclosed unless the court approves. A specific application (for which payment of a court fee would have to be made) would not be necessary, as "it suffices if, at the same time as the acknowledgment of service, there is served a document requesting it and giving reason for requesting any embargo upon disclosure without a court order" (op cit. para.28).

Paragraph (6) is a provision inserted in the CPR for the first time in 2006 (to which, it may be noted, r.5.4D(2) does not apply). It is unusual provision, but its purpose is clear enough from its own terms.

Permission to obtain "any other document"

An application by a non-party under r.5.4C(2) for permission to obtain a copy of "any other document" (meaning a document other than those referred to in r.5.4C(1)), or communication between the court and a party or another person, even if made without notice, must be made under Pt 23 (Practice Direction (Court Documents), para.4.3 (see para.5PD.4 below)). **5.4C.7**

Before the CPR came into effect, the distinction between those specified High Court documents that a non-party might obtain as of right and "any other document" which could be obtained only with the permission of the court was based on a discernible principle. It was that documents in the latter category were all interlocutory in character and, in the event, may or may not be used or affect the justice of the case when the proceedings surfaced in open court. Given the changes that have occurred in civil procedure and practice in modern times, particularly as applied to pre-trial matters, that is not a principle that can easily be applied nowadays.

The range of documents in the "any other" category that might be held in court records in addition to those to which a non-party may have access as of right in accordance with r.5.4C(1) is very wide. It includes documents described in r.5.4C(1) as "any documents filed with or attached to the statement of case, or intended by the party whose statement it is to be served with it". Not surprisingly therefore Practice Direction (Court Documents), para.4.3, *op. cit.* states that a non-party's application for permission under r.5.4C(2) "must identify the documents or class of documents in respect of which permission is sought and the grounds relied on'. This requirement was inserted following *Dian AO v David Frankel Mead* [2004] EWHC 2662; [2005] 1 W.L.R. 2951 (Moore Bick J.) (non-party not entitled to ask for permission to search the whole of a court file relating to particular proceedings, but must identify with some precision the documents or class of documents copies of which he wishes to obtain). A non-party's opportunity to obtain a copy of "any other document" does not entitle him to trawl through the whole of the court's file of particular proceedings.

The provisions in r.5.4C(2) dealing with the supply to a non-party of a copy of "any other document" do not apply in relation to any proceedings in respect of which a rule or practice direction makes different provision; see "Limits to application of r. 5.4B and r. 5.4C" (para.5.4C.9 below). It may be noted that r.32.13 makes different provision to the extent that it states that an "other document" in the form of a witness statement which stands in evidence in chief is open to inspection during the course of trial unless the court otherwise directs.

Rule 5.4C(2) gives the court a discretion to be exercised in accordance with the overriding objective (r.1(2)). The discretion is to be exercised after taking account all the circumstances, including the applicant's reasons and, where the documents relate to proceedings that have been concluded, whether the documents sought were read as part of the decision making process (*Dian AO v David Frankel Mead*, *op. cit.*). The authorities proceed on the basis that the court should lean in favour of giving permission for those documents which are in the public domain either, because they have been read in public or should be treated as having been read in public (*Mansell v. Acton* [2005] EWHC 3048 (Ch); December 1, 2005, unrep. (Judge Weeks Q.C.)).

In *Glidepath BV v Thompson* [2005] EWHC 818 (Colman J.), a case decided before the enactment of r.5.4C, a claim was brought by a company and its shareholders (C) against the company's management team (D), alleging secret profits etc. The claim was stayed under the Arbitration Act 1996 s.9 pending arbitration. In part, the claimants' allegations arose out of a transaction involving the transfer of part of the business of one company (X) to another. In separate legal proceedings, a former employee (O) of X made claims against X, in part arising out of that transaction. In the claim of C against D, O applied under the relevant rule in Pt 5 as it then stood for permission to inspect the particulars of claim, the notices of applications and respective orders made and granted before C's claim was stayed, and any witness statements filed with the court in those proceedings. The judge held (1) that O was (what would now be termed) "a non-party" within (what is now) r.5.4C, and was a stranger to the arbitration and to the s.9 application, and (2) that in the absence of the consent of C and D, the court's discretion should be exercised by reference to the principle of confidentiality attaching to arbitral proceedings. (It may be noted that, since the enactment of r.5.4C, a person in O's position would not require permission to inspect the particulars of claim.)

Supply of documents to non-party subject to conditions

5.4C.8 Rule 3.1(3) states the general rule that, when the court makes an order, it may make it subject to conditions. Where the supply of a document, whether to a party or a non-party, is subject to the court's permission, in granting permission the court may, either under r.3.1(3) or its inherent jurisdiction, impose conditions. Rule 31.22 (Subsequent use of disclosed documents) expressly restricts the use that a party may make of documents disclosed to him in accordance with the normal rules as to disclosure of documents contained in Pt 31. That rule is based on principles that might also apply when the question of imposing conditions where documents are supplied to a party or to a non-party arise under r.5.4B and r.5.4C. The relationship between the court's power (1) to supply documents from court records to non parties under (what is now) r.5.4C, and (2) to restrict access to documents disclosed in the course of proceedings under r.31.22, was referred to in *Lilly Icos Ltd v Pfizer Ltd (No.2)* [2002] EWCA Civ 2; [2002] 1 W.L.R. 2253, CA (commercially sensitive documents disclosed in the course of patent revocation proceedings). Where the circumstances are (1) that a non-party is seeking the supply of a statement of case or a judgment or order, and (2) a party or a person identified in a statement of case makes an application in opposition under para.(4) of r.5.4C, then the court may have to turn its attention to the question whether such supply should be made subject any of conditions of the type referred to in that paragraph (see further para.5.4C.6).

In English vaccine damage litigation (which did not come to trial), claimants (C) relied on expert's reports referring to data compiled in tests conducted on specimens provided by C and others. Subsequently, in analogous American litigation brought against US government (X), other claimants relied on the same test results. X's application to the English court under r.5.4C(2) for permission to obtain from court records copies of the expert's reports (opposed by C, but not by D) was granted, subject to the condition that they were sufficiently anonymised so that no question of any infringement of the Data Protection Act 1998 arose (*Sayers v Smithkline Beecham Ltd* [2007] EWHC 1346 (QB), June 6, 2007, unrep. (Keith J.)).

Limits to application of r.5.4B and r.5.4C

5.4C.9 Rule 5.4D(3) states that r.5.4C does not apply (and r.5.4B does not apply) in relation to any proceedings in respect of which a rule or practice direction makes different provision. Examples of different provision being made by rule or practice direction for the supply of copies of documents from court records are set out immediately below. Some of these different provisions apply to parties and non-parties alike, some to non-parties only, some expressly refer to rr.5.4B and 5.4C and some do not, and some have the effect of imposing greater restriction on the supply of documents than do r.5.4B and 5.4C, and some less. In a given case, whether or not any of them would have the effect of making different provision to that which would be made by the normal application of r.5.4C (or of r.5.4B) would of course depend on the context and circumstances.

Rule 32.13 states that a witness statement which stands as evidence in chief is open to inspection during the course of the trial unless the court otherwise directs.

Section III of CPR Pt 54 contains rules relating to applications for statutory review under s.103A of the Nationality, Immigration and Asylum Act 2002. Rule 54.34 contains special provisions dealing with the service of orders made in such proceedings. Section III is supplemented by Practice Direction (Applications for Statutory Review Under s.103A of the Nationality, Immigration and Asylum Act 2002). Paragraph 3.1 of that practice direction states that, where, in accordance with r.54.34(2), the court sends a copy of its order to the Secretary of State on an application under s.103A of the 2002 Act, then r.5.4(3)(b) and r.5.4(5)(a)(ii) are modified as provided in para.3.2 *(see para.54BPD.3 below)*. Presumably, the reference in para.3.1 to r.5.4(3)(b) should now be read as a reference to subpara.(j) of para.4.2A of Practice Direction (Court Documents) (see para.5PD.4 below), and the reference to r.5.4(5)(a)(ii) should now be read as a reference to r.5.4C(1)(b).

CPR r.57.5 (Lodging of testamentary documents and filing of evidence about testamentary documents) states that, except with the permission of the court, a party shall not be allowed to inspect the testamentary documents or written evidence lodged or filed by any other party until he himself has lodged his testamentary documents and filed his evidence (r.57.5(5)) (see para.57.5 below).

In Practice Direction (Commercial Court), supplementing CPR Pt 58, para.2.2 states that, when the Admiralty and Commercial Registry is closed, a claim form for a claim in the Commercial Court may be issued by fax if the procedure set out in Appendix A to this practice direction is followed. The procedure requires the issuing solicitor to fax certain documents to the Registry and, when the Registry is next open for business, to attend and file and deliver certain documents. Paragraph 6 of Appendix A states that any person served with a claim form issued under this procedure may, without paying a fee, inspect and take copies of the documents so faxed and delivered (see Vol.2, para.2A–37). These provisions apply to Admiralty claims; see Practice Direction (Admiralty Claims) para.1.1 (Vol.2, para.2D–85).

In para.5.1 of Practice Direction (Arbitration) (supplementing CPR Pt 62) it is stated that an arbitration claim form may only be inspected (either by a party or a non-party) with the permission of the court (see Vol.2, para.2E–50). It may be noted that no distinction is drawn here between a claim form that has been (a) issued and served, and (b) issued and not served.

CPR r.76.34 states that, unless the court orders otherwise, r.5.4C and r.5.4B do not apply to any to any proceedings to which Pt 76 (Proceedings Under the Prevention of Terrorism Act 2005) applies.

CPR r.79.30 states that, unless the court directs otherwise, r.5.4B and r.5.4C do not apply to any proceedings to which Pt 79 (Financial Restrictions Proceedings Under the Counter-Terrorism Act 2008) applies or to any document relating to such proceedings.

It is expressly provided in Practice Direction (Application for a Warrant under the Enterprise Act 2002) para.3.2 (see para.B14–001, below) that, in an application for a warrant under the Enterprise Act 2002 s.194, r.5.4C does not apply (and r.5.4B does not apply) and paras 3.3 and 3.4 of that practice direction shall have effect instead.

Statutory provisions may also in effect disapply r.5.4C (or r.5.4B) or, at least, override its normal effects in some important respect. The Access to Justice Act 1999 s.20 refers to information furnished to the Legal Services Commission, or to any court, tribunal or other person or body, on whom functions are imposed or conferred by Pt I of that Act, and in connection with the case of any individual seeking or receiving services funded by the LSC. Such information shall not be disclosed except as permitted by that section. Conceivably, such information may find its way on to court records.

Rule 5.4B and 5.4C, and the other rules and practice direction making different provision, in their various ways permit the inspection and copying of documents held in court records. They are not concerned with the releasing from the custody of the court of original documents. Rule 39.7 states that documents impounded by the court must not be released from the custody of the court except as provided by that rule.

As part of the CPR rr.5.4B and 5.4C are restricted in their application to proceedings to which the CPR apply (see r.2.1). Therefore, for example, they do not apply to insolvency proceedings. For the purposes of those proceedings the Insolvency Rules 1986 make separate provision for the inspection by non-parties of documents held in court records (see *Mansell v Acton* [2005] EWHC 3048 (Ch); December 1, 2005, unrep. (Judge Weeks Q.C.), explaining the different considerations that apply under those rules).

Open justice—availability of documents to non-parties

The general rule is that court hearings should be in public (r.39.2). Increasingly, in making their decisions in cases coming before them, judges rely on papers prepared by the parties and not read out in open court (including disclosed documents, witness statements and skeleton arguments). Such documents may be among the types of documents referred to in Practice Direction (Court Documents), para.4.2A, in r.5.4B or r.5.4C, but they need not be. They may or may not be documents correctly described as documents "filed by a party". If not, they are not documents to which a non-party may have access, even with permission under r.5.4C. The courts have recognised that it is necessary to give the public access to documents that contain material that has been placed before the judge, but not read out in open court as would once have been the case. The two most obvious categories of document are statements of witnesses who are called to give evidence at trial and the skeleton arguments of advocates. By r.32.13 a witness statement which stands as evidence in chief is open to inspection by a non-party during the course of trial unless the court otherwise directs. **5.4C.10**

This modern practice raises new questions as to the extent to which, either by recourse to r.5.4C or by other means, non parties should be given access to such documents in the hands of the parties (copies of which may or may not be in the hands of the court) (*GIO Personal Investment Services Ltd v Liverpool and London Steamship Protection & Indemnity Association Ltd* [1999] 1 W.L.R. 984, CA). (It also raises questions as to the extent to which parties may make collateral use of such documents; see r.31.22 and note *SmithKline Beecham Biologicals SA v Connaught Laboratories Inc (Disclosure of Documents)* [1999] 4 All E.R. 498, CA). It has been said that these questions have to be resolved in the light of the policy of the law that, so far as possible, litigation should be conducted under public gaze and under the critical scrutiny of all who wished to report legal proceedings (*R. v Secretary of the Central Office of the Employment Tribunals (England and Wales) Ex p. Public Concern* [2000] I.R.L.R. 658 (Jackson J.)). The general tenor of the authorities is to favour disclosure to the public of materials which in proceedings in open court entered into the public domain (though perhaps not actually read out in court). There should be as few impediments as possible to the reporting of cases, not only by specialist law reporters, but also by the national and local press. Members of the public should not lose the ability to know the contents of a witness's evidence which would have been given orally under earlier practices (*Chan U Seek v Alvis Vehicles Ltd* [2004] EWHC 3092 (Ch), *op. cit.*, Park J. It has been said that the starting point is the basic principle that practices adopted by the courts and parties to ensure the efficient resolution of litigation should not be allowed adversely to affect the ability of the public to know what was happening in the course of proceedings (*Barings Plc v Coopers & Lybrand* [2000] 1 W.L.R. 2353, CA (whether transcripts of investigation interviews read by judge in disqualification proceedings had been made "available to the public" within the Banking Act 1987 s.82. and therefore were no longer protected from disclosure).

In *Law Debenture Trust Corp (Channel Islands) Ltd v Lexington Insurance Co (Application for Disclosure)* [2003] EWHC 2297; [2003] All E.R. (D) 165 (Oct), Colman J. said (granting the application of a non party in part) (1) the purpose of the inherent jurisdiction to grant a non party access to written skeletons or submissions is to ensure open justice, (2) where a court is invited to exercise the jurisdiction it is essential for the court to investigate what part those documents played in the trial, (3) from the commencement of trial, written submissions play an active role in facilitating the conduct of the trial, (4) the policy of openness requires that non parties should be given access to those documents in the course of hearing before judgment, (5) there is no logical objection to an order to this effect being made where a case is settled in the course of trial. (The particular issue arising in this case was whether it would be unfair to a defendant to permit information in their written submissions relating to unpleaded allegations against them to be exposed to a non-party.)

Freedom of Information Act 2000

5.4C.11 Section 32 of the Freedom of Information Act 2000 states that information held by a public authority is "exempt information"if it is held only by virtue of being contained in (a) any document filed with, or otherwise placed in the custody of, a court for the purposes of proceedings in a particular cause or matter, (b) any document served upon, or by, a public authority for the purposes of proceedings in a particular cause or matter, or (c) any document created by (i) a court, or (ii) a member of the administrative staff of a court, for the purposes of proceedings in a particular cause or matter. This exemption is an absolute one (see s.2(3) of the 2000 Act). It seems that the explanation for this exemption is that rules of court, in particular the provisions in r.5.4C, already provide a comprehensive code governing the disclosure of court documents, and documents served in the course of proceedings, and that the 2000 Act should leave those provisions untouched. By the Freedom of Information (Removal and Relaxation of Statutory Prohibitions on Disclosure of Information) Order 2004 (SI 2004/3363), the Access to Justice Act 1999 s.20 (see para.5.4C.9 above) was amended so as to provide that the restriction on disclosure of information relating to the providing of funded legal services by the LSC furnished to courts does not prevent disclosure after the end of a restricted period of 100 years.

Supply of documents to a party from court records — general[1]

5.4D—(1) A person wishing to obtain a copy of a document under rule 5.4B or rule 5.4C must pay any prescribed fee and— 5.4D

(a) if the court's permission is required, file an application notice in accordance with Part 23; or

(b) if permission is not required, file a written request for the document.

(2) An application for an order under rule 5.4C(4) or for permission to obtain a copy of a document under rule 5.4B or rule 5.4C (except an application for permission under rule 5.4C(6)) may be made without notice, but the court may direct notice to be given to any person who would be affected by its decision.

(3) Rules 5.4, 5.4B and 5.4C do not apply in relation to any proceedings in respect of which a rule or practice direction makes different provision.

Effect of rule

This rule was inserted by the Civil Procedure (Amendment) Rules 2006 (SI 2006/1689) (together with rr.5.4B and 5.4C), and came into force on October 2, 2006. In effect, the rule replaced paras (8) to (10) of r.5.4. The terms of this rule supplement rr.5.4, 5.4B and 5.4C. See respectively the commentary following those rules. 5.4D.1

Prescribed fee

Fees for the supply of copy documents are prescribed by the Civil Proceedings Fees Order 2004 (SI 2004/3121) art.2, Sch.1, paras 4.1 to 4.3 (see Vol.2 para.10–12). The normal rules as the exemption, reduction, remission or refund of fees apply to these fees (*ibid.* art.4). 5.4D.2

Filing and sending documents[2]

5.5—(1) A practice direction may make provision for documents to be filed or sent to the court by— 5.5

(a) facsimile; or

(b) other electronic means.

(2) Any such practice direction may—

(a) provide that only particular categories of documents may be filed or sent to the court by such means;

(b) provide that particular provisions only apply in specific courts; and

(c) specify the requirements that must be fulfilled for any document filed or sent to the court by such means.

Filing by electronic means

This rule was added to the CPR by the Civil Procedure (Amendment) Rules 2002 (SI 2002/2058) r.4, and came into effect December 2, 2002. Various provisions in the CPR and supplementing directions deal with the filing of documents by fax; see paras 1.4.13 and 5.1.3 above. *Practice Direction (Electronic* Communication and Filing of Documents) supplements r.5.5 (see para.5PD.1 below) and provides for communication with the court by electronic means other than facsimile, principally by email and through dedicated websites. Practice Direction (Appeals), para.15.1A provides for filing by email of an appeal notice or application notice in the Civil Division of the Court of Appeal. 5.5.1

[1] Introduced by the Civil Procedure (Amendment) Rules 2006 (SI 2006/1689).
[2] Introduced by the Civil Procedure (Amendment) Rules 2002 (SI 2002/2058).

PRACTICE DIRECTION—COURT DOCUMENTS

This Practice Direction supplements CPR Part 5

Signature of Documents by mechanical means

5PD.1 **1** Where, under rule 5.3, a replica signature is printed electronically or by other mechanical means on any document, the name of the person whose signature is printed must also be printed so that the person may be identified. This paragraph does not apply to claim forms issued through the Claims Production Centre.

Form of Documents

5PD.2 **2.1** Statements of case and other documents drafted by a legal representative should bear his/her signature and if they are drafted by a legal representative as a member or employee of a firm they should be signed in the name of the firm.

2.2 Every document prepared by a party for filing or use at the Court must—

(1) Unless the nature of the document renders it impracticable, be on A4 paper of durable quality having a margin, not less than 3.5 centimetres wide,

(2) be fully legible and should normally be typed,

(3) where possible be bound securely in a manner which would not hamper filing or otherwise each page should be endorsed with the case number,

(4) have the pages numbered consecutively,

(5) be divided into numbered paragraphs,

(6) have all numbers, including dates, expressed as figures, and

(7) give in the margin the reference of every document mentioned that has already been filed.

2.3 A document which is a copy produced by a colour photostat machine or other similar device may be filed at the court office provided that the coloured date seal of the Court is not reproduced on the copy.

Supply of Documents to New Parties

5PD.3 **3.1** Where a party is joined to existing proceedings, the party joined shall be entitled to require the party joining him to supply, without charge, copies of all statements of case, written evidence and any documents appended or exhibited to them which have been served in the proceedings by or upon the joining party which relate to any issues between the joining party and the party joined, and copies of all orders made in those proceedings. The documents must be supplied within 48 hours after a written request for them is received.

3.2 If the party joined is not supplied with copies of the documents requested under paragraph 3.1 within 48 hours, he may apply under Part 23 for an order that they be supplied.

3.3 The party by whom a copy is supplied under paragraph 3.1 or, if he is acting by a solicitor, his solicitor, shall be responsible for it being a true copy.

Supply of documents from court records

5PD.4 **4.1** Registers of claims which have been issued are available for inspection at the following offices of the High Court at the Royal Courts of Justice:

(1) the Central Office of the Queen's Bench Division;

(2) Chancery Chambers;

(3) the Admiralty and Commercial Court Registry;

4.2 No registers of claims are at present available for inspection in county courts or in District Registries or other offices of the High Court.

4.2A A party to proceedings may, unless the court orders otherwise, obtain from the records of the court a copy of—

(a) a certificate of suitability of a litigation friend;

(b) a notice of funding;

(c) a claim form or other statement of case together with any documents filed with or attached to or intended by the claimant to be served with such claim form;

(d) an acknowledgement of service together with any documents filed with or attached to or intended by the party acknowledging service to be served with such acknowledgement of service;

(e) a certificate of service, other than a certificate of service of an application notice or order in relation to a type of application mentioned in sub-paragraph (h)(i) or (ii);

(f) a notice of non-service;

(g) an allocation questionnaire;

(h) an application notice, other than in relation to—

(i) an application by a solicitor for an order declaring that he has ceased to be the solicitor acting for a party; or

(ii) an application for an order that the identity of a party or witness should not be disclosed;

(i) any written evidence filed in relation to an application, other than a type of application mentioned in sub-paragraph (h)(i) or (ii);

(j) a judgment or order given or made in public (whether made at a hearing or without a hearing);

(k) a statement of costs;

(l) a list of documents;

(m) a notice of payment into court;

(n) a notice of discontinuance;

(o) a notice of change of solicitor; or

(p) an appellant's or respondent's notice of appeal.

4.3 An application under rule 5.4B(2), 5.4C(2) or 5.4C(3)(b)(ii) for permission to obtain a copy of a document, even if made without notice, must be made under CPR Part 23 and the application notice must identify the document or class of document in respect of which permission is sought and the grounds relied upon.

4.4 An application under rule 5.4C(4) by a party or a person identified in a claim form must be made—

(1) under CPR Part 23; and

(2) to a Master or district judge, unless the court directs otherwise.

4.5 Rule 5.4B allows a person who is a party to proceedings to obtain copies of documents from court records. A person is a party to proceedings who has been named as a party on a statement of case irrespective of whether they have been served with that statement of case.

Supply of documents from court records – statements of case filed before 2nd October 2006

5PD.4A **4A.1** Rule 5.4C(1A) provides that the rules of court relating to access by a non-party to statements of case in force immediately before 2nd October 2006 apply to statements of case filed before that date as if they had not been revoked. For ease of reference, those rules are set out in the following paragraphs as they applied to statements of case, along with the relevant supplementary provisions previously contained in this practice direction.

4A.2 A person who is not a party to proceedings may—

(1) unless the court orders otherwise, obtain from the records of the court a copy of a claim form, but not any documents filed with or attached to or intended by the claimant to be served with such claim form, subject to paragraph 4A.3 and to any order of the court under paragraph 4A.4; and

(2) if the court gives permission, obtain from the records of the court a copy of any other statement of case.

4A.3 A person may obtain a copy of a claim form under paragraph 4A.2(1) only if—

(1) where there is one defendant, the defendant has filed an acknowledgment of service or a defence;

(2) where there is more than one defendant, either—

(a) all the defendants have filed an acknowledgment of service or a defence;

(b) at least one defendant has filed an acknowledgment of service or a defence, and the court gives permission;

(3) the claim has been listed for a hearing; or

(4) judgment has been entered in the claim.

4A.4 The court may, on the application of a party or any person identified in the claim form—

(1) restrict the persons or classes of persons who may obtain a copy of the claim form;

(2) order that persons or classes of persons may only obtain a copy of the claim form if it is edited in accordance with the directions of the court; or

(3) make such other order as it thinks fit.

4A.5 A person wishing to obtain a copy of a document under paragraph 4A.2 must pay any prescribed fee and—

(a) if the court's permission is required, file an application notice in accordance with Part 23; or

(b) if permission is not required, file a written request for the document.

4A.6 An application for permission to obtain a copy of a statement of case, or for an order under paragraph 4A.4, may be made without notice, but the court may direct notice to be given to any person who would be affected by its decision.

4A.7 An application under paragraph 4A.3(2)(b) for permission to obtain a copy of a claim form must be made under Part 23.

4A.8 An application notice under paragraph 4A.2(2) or paragraph 4A.3(2)(b) must identify the document or class of document in respect of which permission is sought and the grounds relied upon.

4A.9 An application under paragraph 4A.4 by a party or a person identified in a claim form must be made—

(a) under Part 23; and

(b) to a Master or district judge, unless the court directs otherwise.

Documents for Filing at Court

5.1 The date on which a document was filed at court must be recorded on the document. This may be done by a seal or a receipt stamp. **5PD.5**

5.2 Particulars of the date of delivery at a court office of any document for filing and the title of the proceedings in which the document is filed shall be entered in court records, on the court file or on a computer kept in the court office for the purpose. Except where a document has been delivered at the court office through the post, the time of delivery should also be recorded.

5.3 Filing by Facsimile **5PD.6**

(1) Subject to paragraph (6) below, a party may file a document at court by sending it by facsimile ("fax").

(2) Where a party files a document by fax, he must not send a hard copy in addition.

(3) A party filing a document by fax should be aware that the document is not filed at court until it is delivered by the court's fax machine, whatever time it is shown to have been transmitted from the party's machine.

(4) The time of delivery of the faxed document will be recorded on it in accordance with paragraph 5.2.

(5) It remains the responsibility of the party to ensure that the document is delivered to the court in time.

(6) If a fax is delivered after 4p.m. it will be treated as filed on the next day the court office is open.

(7) If a fax relates to a hearing, the date and time of the hearing should be prominently displayed.

(8) Fax should not be used to send letters or documents of a routine or non-urgent nature.

(9) Fax should not be used, except in an unavoidable emergency, to deliver:

(a) a document which attracts a fee

(b) omitted

(c) a document relating to a hearing less than two hours ahead

(d) trial bundles or skeleton arguments

(10) Where (9)(a) or (b) applies, the fax should give an explana-

tion for the emergency and include an undertaking that the fee or money has been dispatched that day by post or will be paid at the court office counter the following business day.

(11) Where courts have several fax machines, each allocated to an individual section, fax messages should only be sent to the machine of the section for which the message is intended.

5.4 Where the Court orders any document to be lodged in Court, the document must, unless otherwise directed, be deposited in the office of that Court.

5PD.7 **5.5** A document filed, lodged or held in any court office shall not be taken out of that office without the permission of the Court unless the document is to be sent to the office of another court (for example under CPR Part 30 (Transfer)), except in accordance with CPR rule 39.7 (impounded documents) or in accordance with paragraph 5.6 below.

5.6(1) Where a document filed, lodged or held in a court office is required to be produced to any Court, Tribunal or arbitrator, the document may be produced by sending it by registered post (together with a Certificate as in paragraph 5.6(8)(b)) to the Court, Tribunal or arbitrator in accordance with the provisions of this paragraph.

(2) Any Court, Tribunal or arbitrator or any party requiring any document filed, lodged or held in any court office to be produced must apply to that court office by sending a completed request (as in paragraph 5.6(8)(a)), stamped with the prescribed fee.

(3) On receipt of the request the court officer will submit the same to a Master in the Royal Courts of Justice or to a District Judge elsewhere, who may direct that the request be complied with. Before giving a direction the Master or District Judge may require to be satisfied that the request is made in good faith and that the document is required to be produced for the reasons stated. The Master or District Judge giving the direction may also direct that, before the document is sent, an official copy of it is made and filed in the court office at the expense of the party requiring the document to be produced.

(4) On the direction of the Master or District Judge the court officer shall send the document by registered post addressed to the Court, Tribunal or arbitrator, with:

(a) an envelope stamped and addressed for use in returning the document to the court office from which it was sent;

(b) a Certificate as in paragraph 5.6(8)(b);

(c) a covering letter describing the document, stating at whose request and for what purpose it is sent, referring to this paragraph of the Practice Direction and containing a request that the document be returned to the court office from which it was sent in the enclosed envelope as soon as the Court or Tribunal no longer requires it.

(5) It shall be the duty of the Court, Tribunal or arbitrator to

whom the document was sent to keep it in safe custody, and to return it by registered post to the court office from which it was sent, as soon as the Court, Tribunal or arbitrator no longer requires it.

(6) In each court office a record shall be kept of each document sent and the date on which it was sent and the Court, Tribunal or arbitrator to whom it was sent and the date of its return. It shall be the duty of the court officer who has signed the certificate referred to in para.5.6(8)(b) below to ensure that the document is returned within a reasonable time and to make inquiries and report to the Master or District Judge who has given the direction under paragraph (3) above if the document is not returned, so that steps may be taken to secure its return.

(7) Notwithstanding the preceding paragraphs, the Master or District Judge may direct a court officer to attend the Court, Tribunal or arbitrator for the purpose of producing the document.

(a) I, of , an officer of the Court/Tribunal at /an arbitrator of /the Claimant/Defendant/Solicitor for the Claimant/Defendant *[describing the Applicant so as to show that he is a proper person to make the request]* in the case of v. [19No.]

REQUEST that the following document [or documents] be produced to the Court/Tribunal/arbitrator on the day of 19 [and following days] and I request that the said document [or documents] be sent by registered post to the proper officer of the Court/Tribunal/arbitrator for production to that Court/Tribunal/arbitrator on that day.

(Signed).

Dated the day of 1999/2 .

(b) I, A.B. an officer of the Court of certify that the document sent herewith for production to the Court/Tribunal/arbitrator on the day of 1999/2 in the case of v. and marked "A.B." is the document requested on the day of 1999/2 and I FURTHER CERTIFY that the said document has been filed in and is produced from the custody of the Court.

(Signed)

Dated the day of 1999/2 .

Enrolment of Deeds and other Documents

6.1(1) Any deed or document which by virtue of any enactment is required or authorised to be enrolled in the Supreme Court may be enrolled in the Central Office of the High Court. **5PD.8**

(2) Attention is drawn to the Enrolment of Deeds (Change of

Name) Regulations 1994 which are reproduced in the Appendix to this Practice Direction.

6.2 The following paragraph of the Practice Direction describes the practice to be followed in any case in which a child's name is to be changed and to which the 1994 Regulations apply.

6.3(1) Where a person has by any order of the High Court, County Court or Family Proceedings Court been given parental responsibility for a child and applies to the Central Office, Filing Department, for the enrolment of a Deed Poll to change the surname (family name) of a child who is under the age of 18 years (unless a child who is or has been married or has formed a civil partnership), the application must be supported by the production of the consent in writing of every other person having parental responsibility.

(2) In the absence of that consent, the application will be adjourned generally unless and until permission is given in the proceedings, in which the said order was made, to change the surname of the child and the permission is produced to the Central Office.

(3) Where an application is made to the Central Office by a person who has not been given parental responsibility for a child by any order of the High Court, County Court or Family Proceedings Court for the enrolment of a Deed Poll to change the surname of the child who is under the age of 18 years (unless the child is or has been married or has formed a civil partnership), permission of the Court to enrol the Deed will be granted if the consent in writing of every person having parental responsibility is produced or if the person (or, if more than one, persons) having parental responsibility is dead or overseas or despite the exercise of reasonable diligence it has not been possible to find him or her for other good reason.

(4) In cases of doubt the Senior Master or, in his absence, the Practice Master will refer the matter to the Master of the Rolls.

(5) In the absence of any of the conditions specified above the Senior Master or the Master of the Rolls, as the case may be, may refer the matter to the Official Solicitor for investigation and report.

Appendix

Regulations made by the Master of the Rolls, Sir Thomas Bingham M.R. on March 3, 1994 (SI 1994/604) under s.133(1) of the Supreme Court Act 1981

5PD.9 **1**(1) These regulations may be cited as the Enrolment of Deeds (Change of Name) Regulations 1994 and shall come into force on April 1, 1994.

(2) These Regulations shall govern the enrolment in the Central Office of the Supreme Court of deeds evidencing change of name (referred to in these Regulations as "deeds poll").

2(1) A person seeking to enrol a deed poll ("the applicant") must be a Commonwealth citizen as defined by section 37(1) of the British Nationality Act 1981.

(2) If the applicant is a British citizen, a British Dependent Territories citizen or a British Overseas citizen, he must be described as such in the deed poll, which must also specify the section of the British Nationality Act under which the relevant citizenship was acquired.

(3) In any other case, the applicant must be described as a Commonwealth citizen.

(4) The applicant must be described in the deed poll as single, married, widowed, divorced, a civil partner or former civil partner and, if a former civil partner, whether the civil partnership ended on death or dissolution.

3(1) As proof of the citizenship named in the deed poll, the applicant must produce:
(a) a certificate of birth; or
(b) a certificate of citizenship by registration or naturalisation or otherwise; or
(c) some other document evidencing such citizenship.

(2) In addition to the documents set out in paragraph (1), an applicant who is married or a civil partner must:
(a) produce his certificate of marriage or civil partnership certificate; and
(b) show that the notice of his intention to apply for the enrolment of the deed poll had been given to his spouse or civil partner by delivery or by post to his spouse's or civil partner's last known address; and
(c) show that he has obtained the consent of his spouse or civil partner to the proposed change of name or that there is good reason why such consent should be dispensed with.

4(1) The deed poll and the documents referred to in regulation 3 must be exhibited to a statutory declaration by a Commonwealth citizen who is a householder in the United Kingdom and who must declare that he is such in the statutory declaration.

(2) The statutory declaration must state the period, which should ordinarily not be less than 10 years, during which the householder has known the applicant and must identify the applicant as the person referred to in the documents exhibited to the statutory declaration.

(3) Where the period mentioned in paragraph (2) is stated to be less than 10 years, the Master of the Rolls may in his absolute discretion decide whether to permit the deed poll to be enrolled and may require the applicant to provide more information before so deciding.

5 If the applicant is resident outside the United Kingdom, he must provide evidence that such residence is not intended to be permanent and the applicant may be required to produce a certificate by a solicitor as to the nature and probable duration of such residence.

6 The applicant must sign the deed poll in both his old and new names.

7 Upon enrolment the deed poll shall be advertised in the London Gazette by the clerk in charge for the time being of the Filing and Record Department at the Central Office of the Supreme Court.

8(1) Subject to the following provisions of this regulation, these Regulations shall apply in relation to a deed poll evidencing the change of name of a child as if the child were the applicant.

(2) Paragraphs (3) to (8) shall not apply to a child who has attained the age of 16, and is or has been married or a civil partner.

(3) If the child is under the age of 16, the deed poll must be executed by a person having parental responsibility for him.

(4) If the child has attained the age of 16, the deed poll must, except in the case of a person mentioned in paragraph (2), be executed by a person having parental responsibility for the child and be endorsed with the child's consent signed in both his old and new names and duly witnessed.

(5) The application for enrolment must be supported:

(a) by a witness statement showing that the change of name is for the benefit of the child, and—

(i) that the application is submitted by all persons having parental responsibility for the child; or

(ii) that it is submitted by one person having parental responsibility for the child with the consent of every other person; or

(iii) that it is submitted by one person having parental responsibility for the child without the consent of every other such person, or by some other person whose name and capacity are given, for reasons set out in the affidavit; and

(b) by such other evidence, if any, as the Master of the Rolls may require in the particular circumstances of the case.

(6) Regulation 4(2) shall not apply but the statutory declaration mentioned in regulation 4(1) shall state how long the householder has known the deponent under paragraph (5)(a) and the child respectively.

(7) Regulation 6 shall not apply to a child who has not attained the age of 16.

(8) In this regulation "parental responsibility" has the meaning given in section 3 of the Children Act 1989.

9 The Enrolment of Deeds (Change of Name) Regulations 1983 and the Enrolment of Deeds (Change of Name) (Amendment) Regulations1990 are hereby revoked.

PRACTICE DIRECTION—ELECTRONIC COMMUNICATION AND FILING OF DOCUMENTS

This Practice Direction supplements CPR rule 5.5.

General

1.1 Section I of this practice direction provides for parties to claims in specified courts to— **5BPD.1**

(1) communicate with the court by e-mail; and

(2) file specified documents by e-mail.

1.2 Section II of this practice direction provides for parties to claims in specified courts to file specified documents electronically via an online forms service.

1.3 Section III of this practice direction contains general provisions which apply to both Section I and Section II.

1.4 This practice direction does not allow—

(1) communication with the court or the filing of documents by e-mail; or

(2) use of the online forms service,

in proceedings to which the Civil Procedure Rules do not apply.

Section I—Communication and Filing of Documents by E-mail

Interpretation

2.1 For the purposes of this Section— **5BPD.2**

(1) a specified court is a court or court office which has published an e-mail address for the filing of documents on the Court Service website *www.hmcourts-service.gov.uk* ("the Court Service website"); and

(2) a specified document is a document listed on the Court Service website as a document that may be sent to or filed in that court by e-mail.

Communications and documents which may be sent by e-mail

3.1 Subject to paragraph 3.2, a party to a claim in a specified court may send a specified document to the court by e-mail. **5BPD.3**

3.2 Subject to paragraph 3.2A, a party must not use e-mail to take any step in a claim for which a fee is payable.

3.2A A party may make an application using e-mail in the Preston Combined Court, where he is permitted to do so by PREMA (Preston E-mail Application Service) User Guide and Protocols.

3.3 Subject to paragraph 3.3A and paragraph 15.1A of the Practice Direction which supplements Part 52, if—

(a) a fee is payable on the filing of a particular document; and

(b) *a party purports to file that document by e-mail,*

the court shall treat the document as not having been filed.

3.3A A party may file by email an application notice in the Preston Combined Court where permitted to do so by PREMA (Preston E-mail Application Service) User Guide and Protocols.

(Paragraph 15.1A of the Practice Direction which supplements CPR Part 52 provides for filing by email an appeal notice or application notice in proceedings in the Court of Appeal, Civil Division.)

(Rules 6.3(1)(d) and 6.20(1)(d) permit service by e-mail in accordance with the relevant practice direction. Rule 6.23(6) and paragraph 4 of Practice Direction A supplementing Part 6 set out the circumstances in which a party may serve a document by e-mail.)

Technical specifications of e-mail

5BPD.4 **4.1** The e-mail message must contain the name, telephone number and e-mail address of the sender and should be in plain text or rich text format rather than HTML.

4.2 Correspondence and documents may be sent as either text in the body of the e-mail, or as attachments, except as mentioned in paragraph 4.3.

4.3 Documents required to be in a practice form must be sent in that form as attachments.

4.4 Court forms may be downloaded from the Court Service website.

4.5 Attachments must be sent in a format supported by the software used by the specified court to which it is sent. The format or formats which may be used in sending attachments to a particular specified court are listed on the Court Service website.

4.6 An attachment which is sent to a specified court in a format not listed on the Court Service website as appropriate for that court will be treated as not having been received by the court.

4.7 The length of attachments and total size of e-mail must not exceed the maximum which a particular specified court has indicated that it can accept. This information is listed on the Court Service website.

4.8 Where proceedings have been commenced, the subject line of the e-mail must contain the following information—

(1) the case number;
(2) the parties' names (abbreviated if necessary); and
(3) the date and time of any hearing to which the e-mail relates.

Section II—Online Forms Service

Scope and interpretation

5BPD.5 **5.1** Reference to an online forms service is reference to a service available at *www.hmcourts-service.gov.uk* ("the forms website"). The forms website contains certain documents which a user may complete online and then submit electronically to a specified court.

5.2 For the purposes of this Section—

(1) a specified court is a court or court office listed on the Court Service website as able to receive documents filed electronically via the online forms service; and
(2) a specified document is a document which is available for completion on the forms website.

(Paragraph 15.1B of the Practice Direction which supplements CPR Part 52 provides for certain notices to be filed electronically at the Court of Appeal, Civil Division using the online forms service on the Court of Appeal, Civil Division website)

Filing of documents online

5BPD.6 **6.1** A party to a claim in a specified court may send a specified document to the court using the online forms service.

6.2 A party may use the online forms service to take a step in a claim for which a fee is payable. The fee must be paid, using the facilities available at the online forms service, before the application, or other document attracting a fee, is forwarded to the specified court.

6.3 The online forms service will assist the user in completing a document accurately but the user is responsible for ensuring that the rules and practice directions relating to the document have been complied with. Transmission by the service does not guarantee that the document will be accepted by the specified court.

Section III—General Provisions

Interpretation

7 In this Section— **5BPD.7**

(1) filing or sending a document 'electronically', means filing or sending it in accordance with Section I or Section II; and

(2) a reference to 'transmission' means, unless the context otherwise requires—

(a) in relation to Section I, the e-mail sent by the party to the court; and

(b) in relation to Section II, the electronic transmission of the form by the online forms service to the court.

Provisions relating to the filing of documents electronically

8.1 Where a party files a document electronically, he must not send a hard copy of that document to the court. **5BPD.8**

8.2 A document is not filed until the transmission is received by the court, whatever time it is shown to have been sent.

8.3 The time of receipt of a transmission will be recorded electronically on the transmission as it is received.

8.4 If a transmission is received after 4pm—

(1) the transmission will be treated as received; and

(2) any document attached to the transmission will be treated as filed,

on the next day the court office is open.

8.5 A party—

(1) sending an e-mail in accordance with Section I; or

(2) using the online forms service in accordance with Section II,

is responsible for ensuring that the transmission or any document attached to it is filed within any relevant time limits.

8.6 The court will normally reply by e-mail where—

(1) the response is to a message transmitted electronically; and

(2) the sender has provided an e-mail address.

8.7 Parties are advised not to transmit electronically any correspondence or documents of a confidential or sensitive nature, as security cannot be guaranteed.

8.8 If a document transmitted electronically requires urgent attention, the sender should contact the court by telephone.

8.9 A document that is required by a rule or practice direction to be filed at court is not filed when it is sent to the judge by e-mail.

Statement of truth in documents filed electronically

5BPD.9 9 Where a party wishes to file a document containing a statement of truth electronically, that party should retain the document containing the original signature and file with the court a version of the document satisfying one of the following requirements—

(1) the name of the person who has signed the statement of truth is typed underneath the statement;

(2) the person who has signed the statement of truth has applied a facsimile of his signature to the statement in the document by mechanical means; or

(3) the document that is filed is a scanned version of the document containing the original signature to the statement of truth.

Guidance notes to Communication and Filing by E-mail Practice Direction

5BPD.10 Practice Direction (Communication and Filing of Documents by E-mail) was revised with effect from October 6, 2003, and in January 2004 was substituted entirely with effect from May 1, 2004. It permits parties in a case to communicate and file certain documents at specified courts by email.

Filing by email is limited to courts which have received the appropriate technology to operate email. As at the beginning of 2004, the specified courts are the Commercial Court and the following county courts: Preston, Walsall, Leicester, Basildon, Coventry.

The "E-mail Court User Guidance" is available on a website maintained by the Court Service. The address is:

http://www.hmcourts-service.gov.uk/infoabout/email_guidance/index.htm [Accessed July 3, 2007].

This Guidance consists of two documents, one for those wishing to use the services available at one or other of the specified county courts and a separate set of guidelines for those wishing to use the services of the Commercial Court (see further para.5BPD.8).

The document containing guidance relating to the specified county courts lists the email accounts maintained for each court, with links to information on the following matters: (1) What you can file by email, (2) What you cannot file by email, (3) Form and content of emails, (4) Where to send your email, (5) What the court will do with your email, (6) Points to remember.

Forms for filing by email

5BPD.11 Below is a list of forms that will be accepted by a specified county court if filed by email in accordance with the Practice Direction. There are other types of work that are accepted by email. For a list of work accepted by a particular court and more information, see the guidance document referred to in para.5BPD.6, above.

- **N9** Response Pack
- **N9B** Defence and counterclaim (specified amount)
- **N9C** Admission (unspecified amount, non-money and return of goods claims)
- **N150** Allocation questionnaire
- **N170** Listing questionnaire
- **N215** Certificate of service
- **N225** Request for judgment and reply to admission (specified amount)
- **N226** Notice of admission (unspecified amount)
- **N227** Request for judgment by default (amount to be decided by the court)
- **N228** Notice of admission - Return of goods (hire purchase or conditional sale)
- **N236** Notice of defence that amount claimed has been paid
- ***N243A*** *Notice of acceptance* and request for payment (Part 36)
- **N265** List of documents: standard disclosure
- **N279** Notice of discontinuance
- **N293A** Combined certificate of judgment and request for writ of fieri facias or writ of possession

- **N294** Claimant's application for a variation order (without hearing)
- **N434** Notice of change of solicitor

Commercial Court

For guidance as to Commercial Court, see annotations to CPR Pt 58 (Vol.2, Section 2A). **5BPD.12**

PART 6

SERVICE OF DOCUMENTS

Contents

6.0.1

I. Scope of this Part and Interpretation

II. Service of the Claim Form in the Jurisdiction

III. Service of Documents other than the Claim Form in the United Kingdom

IV. Service of the Claim Form and other Documents out of the Jurisdiction

V. Service Of Documents from Foreign Courts or Tribunals

Editorial introduction

6.0.2 Rules 5 and 6 and Sch.1 of the Civil Procedure (Amendment) Rules 2008 (SI 2008/2178), enacted in August 2008, substituted a new CPR Pt 6 (Service of Documents) for the existing Part, and a new r.7.5 (Service of a claim form). In addition, the statutory instrument made consequential amendments to numerous individual CPR provisions. By TSO CPR Update 47, the two practice directions supplementing Pt 6 were also replaced.

The statutory instrument and TSO CPR Update 47 amended in numerous respects other provisions in the CPR quite apart from those in Pt 6.

These changes came into effect on October 1, 2008.

In July 2007, the Ministry of Justice published Consultation Paper 14/07, entitled Review of Part 6 of the Civil Procedure Rules: Service of Documents. The consultation was conducted on behalf of the Civil Procedure Rule Committee with the purpose of seeking views on proposals to clarify and improve the rules relating to service of documents within England and Wales. The proposals took account of a number of Court of Appeal decisions about the construction of these provisions. In February 2008, a post-consultation paper summarising the responses was published. In the months following the Rule Committee considered the proposals and the responses thereto and came to decisions.

Before the CPR came into effect, rules as to the service of documents (including originating process) were found principally in RSC Ords 10, 11 and 65, and in CCR O.7. Particular service rules were also found scattered throughout the RSC, for example in O.80 (service on persons under disability) and O.81 (service on partners). In structure, and in many respects in detail, CCR O.7 provided the model for CPR Pt 6 as originally enacted. However, by the amendments introduced in October 2008, the structure of the Part was changed significantly and the CCR model was abandoned in an important respect. Whereas previously Sections I and II of the Part consisted of, respectively, general rules about service of all forms of documents and a few special rules about service of claim forms in the jurisdiction in particular, under the new structure detailed rules about all aspects of the service of claim forms in the jurisdiction come first, in Section II (Service of the Claim Form in the Jurisdiction), and are followed by detailed rules about service of other documents in the United Kingdom, in Section III (Service of Documents other than the Claim Form in the United Kingdom). As re-enacted, these Sections effected some important changes in the law. The separating out of rules about the service of claim forms from rules about service of other documents reflects the structure of the former RSC.

As amended with effect from October 1, 2008, Section IV (Service of the Claim Form and Other Documents out of the Jurisdiction) and Section V (Service of Documents from Foreign Courts and Tribunals) replace former Section III (Special Provisions about Service out of the Jurisdiction) and Section IV (Service of Foreign Process). As re-enacted, the rules in these Sections in effect remain the same as previously (subject to a few exceptions) but they have been tidied up considerably.

Practice Directions

6.0.3 This Part is supplemented by two practice directions, Practice Direction A—Service Within the United Kingdom (see para.6APD.1 below), and Practice Direction B—Service Out of the Jurisdiction (see para.6BPD.1), referred to in the text of the rules, respectively, as "Practice Direction A" and "Practice Direction B". Both practice directions were published in TSO CPR Update 47. The former replaced Practice Direction (Service) and the latter Practice Direction (Service Out of the Jurisdiction).

Related sources

6.0.4
- CPR r.55.6 (Service of claims against trespassers)
- CPR r.55.23 (Service of claim form for interim possession order
- Companies Act 1985 ss.694A, 695 and 725
- *Companies Act 2006 s.1139*

Forms

6.0.5
- **N215** Certificate of service (see the Civil Procedure Forms section of the *Civil Procedure Forms Volume*)

- **N217** Order for substituted service (see the Civil Procedure Forms section of the *Civil Procedure Forms Volume*)
- **N251** Notice of funding of case or claim (see the Civil Procedure Forms section of the *Civil Procedure Forms Volume*)
- **N510** Service out of the jurisdiction (see the Civil Frocedure Forms section of the *Civil Procedure Forms Volume*)

I. Scope of this Part and Interpretation

Part 6 rules about service apply generally[1]

6.1 This Part applies to the service of documents, except where— **6.1**

(a) another Part, any other enactment or a practice direction makes different provision; or

(b) the court orders otherwise.

(Other Parts, for example, Part 54 (Judicial Review) and Part 55 (Possession Claims) contain specific provisions about service.)

Effect of rule (r.6.1)

6.1.1 This rule is in similar terms to r.6.1 as it stood before Pt 6 was replaced on October 1, 2008. Other Parts and practice directions in the CPR making significantly different provision to that made in Pt 6 include Pt 54 (Judicial Review and Statutory Review) and Pt 55 (Possession Claims) and the practice directions supplementing those Parts.

In *Godwin v Swindon BC* [2001] EWCA Civ 641; [2002] 1 W.L.R. 997, CA, it was held that the court could not dispense with service under r.6.1(b) (or under what is now r.6.16) where such a dispensation would constitute a retrospective extension of time for service specifically forbidden by r.7.6(3) (see further commentary following r.6.16).

Methods of service—general[2]

6.2—(a) "bank holiday" means a bank holiday under the Banking and Financial Dealings Act 1971 in the part of the United Kingdom where service is to take place; **6.2**

(b) "business day" means any day except Saturday, Sunday, a bank holiday, Good Friday or Christmas Day;

(c) "claim" includes petition and any application made before action or to commence proceedings and "claim form", "claimant" and "defendant" are to be construed accordingly;

(d) "solicitor" includes authorised litigators within the meaning of the Courts and Legal Services Act 1990.

Effect of rule (r.6.2)

6.2.1 This rule brings together definitions particularly relevant in the texts of the rules in Pt 6 generally, especially in Sections II and III. Dedicated provisions containing definitions for recurring expressions in Sections IV and V of Pt 6 are found in, respectively, r.6.31 and r.6.49.

Jurisdiction

6.2.2 Throughout Pt 6, the distinction between service of claim forms and of other documents within the jurisdiction and without the jurisdiction is important. In CPR r.2.3(1) it is stated that in theCPR generally "jurisdiction" means, unless the context requires otherwise, England and Wales and any part of the territorial waters of the United Kingdom adjoining England and Wales.

---

[1] Added by the Civil Procedure (Amendment) Rules 2008 (SI 2008/2178).
[2] Added by the Civil Procedure (Amendment) Rules 2008 (SI 2008/2178).

"claim" "claim form"

6.2.3 The meaning of "claim form" in this context is important, as it is the distinction between claim forms (as defined) and other documents relating to the proceedings that distinguishes Section II from Section III, both of which are concerned with the service of documents "in the jurisdiction". Before October 1, 2008, the expressions "claim" and "claim form" had, for the purposes of service out of the jurisdiction, the meanings ascribed to them by paras (h) and (i) of r.6.18. (As to the meaning of "claim form" in Section IV, see commentary following r.6.30 below.)

Rule 7.2(1) states that proceedings are started when the court issues a claim form. According to para.(c) of r.6.2, for the purposes of Pt 6, "claim form" includes, in addition, a petition and any application made before action (e.g. for an order for disclosure of documents before a claim has been made) or to commence proceedings. The definition of "claim form" does not include an application notice, except in those circumstances where it is the appropriate process for the making of an application before action. The general rule is that particulars of claim must be contained in or served with the claim form (r.7.4(1)). Where the general rule does not apply, and the particulars of claim are contained in a separate document and are not served with the claim form, that document is not "a claim form" for the purposes of Pt 6.

"bank holiday" "business day"

6.2.4 In combination, these definitions have the same effects as those previously offered in para.(3) of former r.6.7 (Deemed service). The definition of "bank holiday" acknowledges that service of a document (in certain circumstances) may be effected in Scotland or Northern Ireland, rather than in England and Wales, in which event any differences in the bank holiday arrangements between the several jurisdictions may have to be taken into account. In fact, in Pt 6, the only provision in which "bank holiday" is referred to is r.6.2(b).

II. Service of the Claim Form in the Jurisdiction

Methods of service[1]

6.3 **6.3—(1) A claim form may be served by any of the following methods—**

> **(a) personal service in accordance with rule 6.5;**
>
> **(b) first class post, document exchange or other service which provides for delivery on the next business day, in accordance with Practice Direction A supplementing this Part;**
>
> **(c) leaving it at a place specified in rule 6.7, 6.8, 6.9 or 6.10;**
>
> **(d) fax or other means of electronic communication in accordance with Practice Direction A supplementing this Part; or**
>
> **(e) any method authorised by the court under rule 6.15.**

(2) A company may be served—

> **(a) by any method permitted under this Part; or**
>
> **(b) by any of the methods of service set out in the Companies Act 1985 or the Companies Act 2006.**

(3) A limited liability partnership may be served—

> **(a) by any method permitted under this Part; or**
>
> ***(b) by any of the methods of service set out in section 725 of the Companies Act 1985.***

[1] Added by the Civil Procedure (Amendment) Rules 2008 (SI 2008/2178).

Effect of rule (r.6.3)

This rule and the following rules in Section II of Pt 6 (rr.6.4 to 6.19) are concerned with the service of claim forms within the jurisdiction. Provisions about methods of service of claim forms out of the jurisdiction are found in Section IV (especiallyrr.6.40 to 6.42). **6.3.1**

With effect from October 1, 2008, r.6.3 replaced former r.6.2, insofar as it applied to such service. As to the meaning of "claim form" for these purposes, see commentary following r.6.2 above.

For methods for service within the jurisdiction of documents other than claim forms (as defined in r.6.2(c)), see r.6.20 below.

Rule 6.6(1) states that the claim form must be served within the jurisdiction except where r.6.11 (Service by a contractually agreed method) applies, or as provided by Section IV of this Part.

The CPR do not define what is meant by service other than by prescribing how it may be done (*Asia Pacific (HK) Ltd v Hanjin Shipping Co Ltd* [2005] EWHC 2443 (Comm), November 7, 2005, unrep. (Christopher Clarke J.) at para.20). In the *Access to Justice—Final Report* (July 1996) it was said (in relation to the service of documents generally, if not of service of claim forms in particular) that, before any procedural step which depends on proper service of a document can take place, "the court would have to be satisfied that the method used either had put the recipient in a position to ascertain its contents or was reasonably likely to enable him to do so within any relevant time period" (Ch.12, para.25). (The phrase "put . . . in position" takes account of the situation where the recipient "deliberately avoids informing himself".) The several methods of service are designed to achieve that objective. (In this vein, r.6.15(2) speaks of steps taken "to bring the claim form to the attention of the defendant".)

As a practical matter, the law as to the service of originating process provides answers to five questions: by whom? on whom? when? where? and how? In a given case, depending on the circumstances, the answer to one or other of these questions may admit of multiple, alternative or cumulative answers; e.g., the answer to "by whom?" may be by the court, by the claimant or by his agent (see r.6.5(4)), and the answer to "on whom?" may be not only the defendant but on others as well (see Sch.1, RSC O.115, r.7). The expression "method of service" is a term of art of long standing in English law and is primarily concerned with the question of "how?". However, the definition of a particular "method" (in order to be comprehensible and to differentiate it from other methods) may also touch upon the question of "where?". Questions of "how?" demand answers in the form of active, transitive verbs (leaving with, posting to, delivering at, transmitting to, etc.). Such words appear, expressly or impliedly, in the various methods of service listed in this rule. They are brought out more clearly generally in r.7.5 (Service of a claim form) and, in relation to personal service particularly, in r.6.5.

It might be expected that, in a set of rules designed to act as a comprehensive (if not complete) code, the five questions would be dealt with in a logical order. However, that is not the way that Section II of Pt 6 runs. It begins with the last question first.

Once upon a time, personal service was the dominant method. Over time, other methods were permitted (but were tightly controlled) and were listed in rules of court. Those rules are the ancestors of r.6.3.

For an explanation as to why it is that methods of service cannot be at large and have to be restricted by law to certain prescribed methods, see *Access to Justice—Final Report* (July 1996) Ch.12, para.20.

In a given case, the questions that are likely to cause the most anxiety for the moving party are "on whom?", "when?", and "where?". Answers to those questions require reference to other provisions. (The question "by whom?" is not unimportant and, in relation to the method of personal service, is given a comprehensive answer by r.6.5(4).)

Practice direction provisions supplementing r.6.3(1)

Paragraph (b) of r.6.3(1) is supplemented by paras 2.1 and 3.1 of Practice Direction A (Service Within the United Kingdom), and para.(d) by para.4; see para.6APD.2 below. (In effect, these provisions replace those found in the practice direction that supplemented the provisions replaced by r.6.3.) **6.3.2**

"first class post" or "other service" (r.6.3(1)(b))

6.3.3 Initially, service by post was confined to service by Royal Mail first class post. In April 6, 2006, the rule was expanded to include other Royal Mail services (apart from first class post) providing for delivery "on the next working day". (Previously, it had been held that service by Royal Mail "special delivery" (guaranteed for the next day) was the same as first class post for these purposes (*Petford v Shaw* [2002] C.L.Y. 478).) The Royal Mail's postal service monopoly ended in 2006. The rule now permits in addition, as a service method, service by a non-Royal Mail providers of services providing for delivery "on the next business day". Paragraph 3.1 of Practice Direction A (Service Within the United Kingdom) indicates how service is effected by such "other service" (para.3.1 also applies to service by post and by DX) (see para.6APD.3 below).

"business day" (r.6.3(1)(b))

6.3.4 See definition in r.6.2(b) above.

"electronic communication" (r.6.3(1)(d))

6.3.5 Paragraph (d) of r.6.3(1) is supplemented by Practice Direction A (Service Within the United Kingdom) paras 4.1 to 4.3 (see para.6APD.4 below). Those provisions also supplement para.(d) of r.6.20(1). As some of those provisions are more likely to be of practical relevance where the document to be served is a document other than a claim form, they are more fully dealt with in the commentary following r.6.20 (Methods of service of documents other than the claim form). See "Service of claim form by electronic method" para.6.20.4 below.

Service on a company (r.6.3(2))

6.3.6 Paragraph (2) of r.6.3 states that a claim form may be served in the jurisdiction on a company by any method of service permitted by Pt 6 (see para.6.3.10 below) (including personal service, see r.6.5(3)(b)) or by any of the methods of service set out in the Companies Act 1985 or the Companies Act 2006 (see para.6.3.7 below).

Methods of service on company permitted by Companies Acts

6.3.7 Provisions in the 1985 Act relevant to the service of claim forms on companies ares.725 (service on registered company) (see para.6.3.8 below) and s.694A and s.695 (service on overseas company) (see para.6.3.9 below). These provisions will be replaced by s.1139 of the 2006 Act when that section is brought into force.

6.3.8 *Registered company*—Section 725(1) (s.1139(1) of the 2006 Act) states that a document may be served on a company in England and Wales "by leaving it at, or sending it by post to, the company's registered office". Section 725(2) and (3) (s.1139(4) of the 2006 Act) state that, where a company registered in Scotland or Northern Ireland carries on business in England and Wales, the process of any court in England may be served on the company by leaving it at, or sending it by post to, the company's principal place of business in England and Wales, addressed to the manager or other head officer in England and Wales of the Company. Where court process is so served, the person issuing out the process must send a copy of it by post to the company's registered office.

This statutory provision is to be read in the light of the Interpretation Act 1978 s.7, which states that service "by post" is "deemed to be effected by properly addressing, prepaying, and posting a letter containing the document". Thus "post" in this context is wide enough to include both ordinary and registered post (cf. r.6.3(1)(b)). Therefore a company is properly served with a document (including a claim form) which is sent by registered post to its registered office (*T.O. Supplies (London) Ltd v Jerry Creighton Ltd* [1952] 1 K.B. 42).

Section 725(1) is not, in terms, expressed to relate only to service of court process (cf. s.725(2)). Further, there is nothing in it to suggest that it applies only to service on a company that is a party to legal proceedings. Accordingly, if a company is held out as authorised to accept service of process on behalf of a defendant (e.g. under r.6.11), that service can be effected in accordance with s.725(1) (*Amerada Hess v C W Rome* January 19, 2000, unrep. (Colman J.)).

In *Cranfield v Bridgegrove Ltd* [2003] EWCA Civ 656; [2003] 1 W.L.R. 2441, CA, the Court of Appeal explained (at paras 83 to 85) that service of the claim form on a defendant company, either by leaving it at, or by sending it by post to, the company's registered office in accordance with s.725(1), or in accordance with one of the methods of service permitted byr.6.3(1), are true alternative service routes available to the claimant. Various consequences followed from this. For example, (1) if a defendant company or the company's solicitors act in accordance with r.6.7, a claimant may choose whether to follow the s.725(1) route or serve at the business address of the solicitors; and (2) if a defendant company has not given an address for service, a claimant may choose whether to follow the s.725(1) or the r.6.9 route for service. It is possible for the parties to make a binding contract whereby the claimant agrees to serve the claim form by the r.6.3(1) route rather than under s.725(1) or vice versa (see r.6.11), in which event the respective routes cease to be true alternatives.

The court gave the following three examples of differences between the two service routes: (1) service under s.725(1) may be by second class post, whereas r.6.3(1)(b) provides for service by first class post; (2) service under s.725(1) is deemed to have been effected at the time at which the letter would be delivered "in the ordinary course of post" (Interpretation Act s.7) unless the contrary is proved, whereas r.6.14 provides that, where service is by first class post, the document is irrefutably deemed to have been served on the second business day after completion of the relevant step under r.7.5(1); and (3) service under s.725(1) must be by leaving the document at, or posting it to, the registered office, whereas r.6.3(1) provides for a variety of permitted methods of service.

Overseas company—Section 694A and s.695 of the 1985 Act constitute two parallel and very similar sets of provisions for service on overseas companies (companies incorporated outside the United Kingdom). (The two are brought together in s.1139(2) of the 2006 Act.) Section 694A provides for service on a company incorporated in a state within the European Union and having a branch within the United Kingdom, and s.695 provides for service on an overseas company establishing a place of business in the United Kingdom. Both statutory schemes impose a duty on the companies to which they apply to deliver to the Registrar of Companies for registration (and to keep up-to-date) a return containing specified particulars, including information concerning persons within the jurisdiction authorised to accept service and the addresses of those persons. In addition, both schemes provide for circumstances in which a company does not comply with those requirements. In effect, these statutory schemes (amongst other things) provide claimants having claims against foreign companies ab initio with the means for service of court process within the jurisdiction, free from the inconvenience of seeking out those companies in their places of incorporation. For an explanation of the origins and purposes of s.695, see *Rome v Punjab National Bank (No.2)* [1989] 1 W.L.R. 1211, CA, and for the purpose of the later enactment of s.694A, see *Sea Assets Ltd v P T Garuda Indonesia* [2000] 4 All E.R. 371, CA, at p.372 per Longmore L.J. **6.3.9**

Section 695(1) states that service is sufficiently made if the process is addressed to any person whose name has been delivered to the Registrar and is "left at or sent by post to the address which has been so delivered". Section 695(2) states that (a) where an overseas company makes default in delivering to the Registrar the name and address of a person resident in the United Kingdom who is authorised to accept on behalf of the company service of process or notices, or (b) if at any time all the persons whose names and addresses have been so delivered are dead or have ceased so to reside, or refuse to accept service on the company's behalf, or for any reason cannot be served, a document may be served on the company by leaving it at, or sending it by post to, any place of business established by the company in the United Kingdom.

In *Rome v Punjab National Bank (No.2)*, op cit, it was held that, where service of originating process was effected in accordance with s.695(1) it was sufficiently served, notwithstanding (1) that the company had ceased to carry on business in the UK, (2) that the persons registered as authorised to accept service were no longer resident there, and (3) that those facts had been notified to the Registrar. Note also, *Employers Liability Assurance Corp Ltd v Sedgwick Collins & Co Ltd* [1927] A.C. 95, HL, (service on person authorised valid, notwithstanding that he had done his best to have his name removed from the register); *Emil Rind v Anglo-Prague Credit Bank,* February 21, 1940, unrep. (Tucker J.) (authorised person has no standing to apply to have service set aside).

Methods of service on company permitted by Pt 6

A company may be served by any method permitted under Pt 6 as an alternative to those set out in the statutory provisions in the Companies Acts referred to above. There is some overlap between the statutory and rule provisions. Service under Pt 6 will usually be simpler and cheaper than service under the legislation. **6.3.10**

Express provision for personal service of a claim form on a company or other corporation is made by r.6.5(3)(b).

Express rule provisions concerning the place at which a company may be served are found in r.6.9 (Service of the claim form where the defendant does not give an address for service etc). Where that rule applies, and service on a company is to be effected under it, the company should be served at the place listed in the table in r.6.9(2). It may be noted that r.6.9(2) is broader than s.694A of the 1985 Act in that it is not confined to service of a claim form "in respect of the carrying on of the business of a branch". It is not necessary for the claimant to establish any link between the process and the business being conducted at that place; it is sufficient if the claim is at least partly in respect of that business (*Saab v Saudi American Bank* [1999] 1 W.L.R. 1861, CA). Section 694A is not mandatory (*Sea Assets Ltd v P T Garuda Indonesia*, op cit).

It seems that, where an overseas company has complied with the statutory provisions and registered an address for service (see para.6.3.9 above), that does not amount to the giving of an address for service in particular proceedings within r.6.8.

Limited liability partnerships (r.6.3(3))

6.3.11 The Limited Liability Partnership Act 2000 came into effect on April 6, 2001, and created a new form of legal person, the limited liability partnership (LLP). The Companies Act 1985 s.725, which provides for service of documents on companies by leaving the document at or posting it to an authorised place, is among the provisions in that Act applied to LLPs by Regulations made under the 2000 Act (see SI 2001/1090). Previously, express provision for LLPs was not made in this rule.

Service on defendant in Scotland or Northern Ireland

6.3.12 Section IV contains rules dealing with the service of claim forms out of the jurisdiction. In that section, r.6.40(2) states that, where a claimant serves a claim form on a defendant in Scotland or Northern Ireland it must be served by a method permitted by Section II, that is to say, by a method referred to in r.6.3, *et seq*. (In such circumstances, the references to "jurisdiction" in Section II (viz. in rr.6.6, 6.7, 6.8, 6.11 and 6.12) are modified accordingly.) See further commentary following r.6.40.

For service on companies registered in Scotland or Northern Ireland carrying on business in England and Wales, see para.6.3.8 above, and note para.6.40.4 below.

Service "for information only"

6.3.13 Circumstances may arise where it is practical and convenient for both claimant and defendant for the claimant, having issued a claim form, to send to the defendant a copy of it, not "by way of service", but "for information only". Generally, as it is a copy of the claim form that is sent to the defendant, and not the issued form that may in due course be served on the defendant by way of one of the methods of service permitted (other than by an electronic method), no question arises of such service being valid service, whatever the intention of the parties. In *Asia Pacific (HK) Ltd v Hanjin Shipping Co Ltd* [2005] EWHC 2443 (Comm), November 7, 2008, unrep. (Christopher Clarke J.) the question which arose was whether service "by way of service" could be implied in circumstances where it was arguable that it was "for information only". The intriguing feature of this case was that the method of service adopted by the claimants had been service by fax, so the fact that the claim form received by the defendants was not a form issued by the court, but a copy of it, would not in itself affect the validity of service. The judge concluded that, when a claim form is delivered to the recipient in a manner provided for by therules it is served unless it is made clear by the person delivering the form by such a method he is not in fact serving it. The judge rejected the submission that the faxed claim form should have been accompanied by a letter stating that it was sent "by way of service". See further para.6.20.4 below.

Who is to serve the claim form[1]

6.4 **6.4—(1) The court will serve the claim form except where—**

(a) a rule or practice direction provides that the claimant must serve it;

(b) the claimant notifies the court that the claimant wishes to serve it; or

[1] Added by the Civil Procedure (Amendment) Rules 2008 (SI 2008/2178).

(c) the court orders or directs otherwise.

(2) Where the court is to serve the claim form, it is for the court to decide which method of service is to be used.

(3) Where the court is to serve the claim form, the claimant must, in addition to filing a copy for the court, provide a copy for each defendant to be served.

(4) Where the court has sent—

(a) a notification of outcome of postal service to the claimant in accordance with rule 6.18; or

(b) a notification of non-service by a bailiff in accordance with rule 6.19,

the court will not try to serve the claim form again.

Effect of rule (r.6.4)

This rule is in similar terms to r.6.3 as it stood before Pt 6 was replaced on October 1, 2008, insofar as it applied to the service of claim forms. (Insofar as it applied to other documents, r.6.3 was replaced by r.6.21.) **6.4.1**

The general rule is that claim forms are served by the court. Where it applies it is for the court to decide which method of service (see r.6.3) is to be used. Normally the court will serve by first class post; see Practice Direction A (Service Within the United Kingdom) para.8.1 (para.6APD.8 below). Where the claim form is to be served on a solicitor (r.6.7), service may be through a document exchange Where the court serves a claim form it will also serve a copy of any notice of funding (Form N251 Notice of funding of case or claim ((see the Civil Procedure Forms section of the Civil Procedure Forms Volume)) that has been filed if it was filed as the same time as the claim form and copies of it were provided for service (*ibid* para.8.2) The court will not do the photocopying. (Failure to notify the other party of a funding arrangement may mean that all or part of a success fee or insurance premium will not be recoverable.)

Where the court serves a claim form, the court will send to the claimant a notice which will include the date on which the claim form is deemed served under r.6.14 (see r.6.17(1)).

When the court has served the claim form by post and it is returned to the court, the court must send notification to the claimant (r.6.18). In such event, the court will not try to serve the claim form again (r.6.4(4)).

Personal service[1]

6.5—(1) Where required by another Part, any other enactment, a practice direction or a court order, a claim form must be served personally. **6.5**

(2) In other cases, a claim form may be served personally except—

(a) where rule 6.7 applies; or

(b) in any proceedings against the Crown.

(Part 54 contains provisions about judicial review claims and Part 66 contains provisions about Crown proceedings.)

(3) A claim form is served personally on—

(a) *an individual* by leaving it with that individual;

(b) a company or other corporation by leaving it with a person holding a senior position within the company or corporation; or

(c) a partnership (where partners are being sued in the name of their firm) by leaving it with—

[1] Added by the Civil Procedure (Amendment) Rules 2008 (SI 2008/2178).

(i) a partner; or

(ii) a person who, at the time of service, has the control or management of the partnership business at its principal place of business.

(Practice Direction A supplementing this Part sets out the meaning of "senior position".)

Effect of rule (r.6.5)

6.5.1 With effect from October 1, 2008, this rule replaced former r.6.4, insofar as it applied to the service of claim forms within the jurisdiction. For personal service within the jurisdiction of documents other than claim forms (as defined in r.6.2(c)), see r.6.22 below. (Rule 6.22 incorporates by reference certain provisions in r.6.5.)

Personal service is one of the "methods of service" for the service of claim forms listed in r.6.3(1). In the CPR, the most important of the provisions requiring service by the method of personal service are those relating to the commencement by claim form of committal proceedings; see Sch.1, RSC O.52, rr.3 and 4 (both of which expressly empower the court to dispense with service), and Sch.2, CCR O.29, r.1, and note commentaries following those rules.

Service on a solicitor

6.5.2 Except where personal service is required by another Part, any other enactment, a practice direction or court order, a claim form may not be served on a defendant personally where, by virtue of r.6.7, it should be served on the defendant's solicitor. See further commentary following r.6.7 below.

Proceedings against the Crown

6.5.3 See further r.6.10 (Service of the claim form in proceedings against the Crown) and commentary following that rule.

Personal service on company—"person holding a senior position"

6.5.4 Practice Direction A (Service Within the United Kingdom) para.6.2 explains what is meant by "a person holding a senior position" (see para.6APD.6 below). Whether or not a person upon whom service is effected does hold such a position is a matter to be determined on the evidence (*Lakah Group v Al Jazeera Satellite Channel* [2003] EWHC 1231, March 26, 2003, unrep. (Gray J.)). Before the CPR came into effect, what is now stated in para.6.2 was in part stated in RSC O.65, r.3(1) and in *Kuwait Airways Corp v Iraqi Airways Co* [1995] 1 W.L.R. 1147, HL, it was held that an employee of a foreign body corporate carrying on business in England, who was in England and was in charge of its business there, fell within the description of "other similar officer" in that rule.

"principal place of business"

6.5.5 See also, r.6.9(2).

Where to serve the claim form—general provisions[1]

6.6 **6.6—(1) The claim form must be served within the jurisdiction except where rule 6.11 applies or as provided by Section IV of this Part.**

(2) The claimant must include in the claim form an address at which the defendant may be served. That address must include a full postcode, unless the court orders otherwise.

(Paragraph 2.4 of the practice direction supplementing Part 16 contains provisions about postcodes.)

(3) Paragraph (2) does not apply where an order made by the

[1] Added by the Civil Procedure (Amendment) Rules 2008 (SI 2008/2178).

court under rule 6.15 (service by an alternative method or at an alternative place) specifies the place or method of service of the claim form.

Effect of rule (r.6.6)

This rule is concerned with, what is called elsewhere (e.g. in r.6.9(2)), "place of service". The expression "general provisions" reflects the fact that the rules immediately following (rr.6.7 to 6.13) contain particular provisions answering, not only the question "where?", but also the question "on whom?" a claim form should be served. 6.6.1

In terms, para.(2) is similar to r.6.13 as it stood before the substitution of Pt 6 on October 1, 2008.

Rule 6.11 is concerned with the service of the claim form by a contractually agreed method (a method that may involve service at a place outside the jurisdiction) (see further commentary following that rule).

Section IV is concerned with service of the claim form (and other documents in proceedings) out of the jurisdiction, including on parties in Scotland or Northern Ireland (as to which, see further commentary following r.6.3).

Rule 6.15 refers to the court's power to authorise service of a claim form "at a place not otherwise permitted by this Part" where there is "a good reason" to do so.

Address for service to be included in claim form (r.6.6(2))

The drafting of the claim form is the responsibility of the claimant, and it is the claimant who must ensure (in compliance with r.6.6(2)) that the address at which the defendant may be served is included in it. In those cases where the claim form is to be served by the court the sense of this requirement is obvious. (In this respect the provision is traceable to former r.6.13.) In those cases where it is to be served by the claimant it has practical utility (e.g. by ensuring congruence between the claim form and the certificate of service filed by the claimant). 6.6.2

Before a claim form is issued against him, no individual or corporate defendant is required to offer up for the convenience of the claimant or the court an address at which he may be served. Of course, he may do so and defendants very often do. He may, under r.6.8, give an address within the jurisdiction "for the purpose of being served with the proceedings", or he may, under r.6.7, give the address of a solicitor at which he "may be served with the claim form", or he may, under r.6.11, have agreed by contract to a particular method and place of service (note also r.6.10 (standing arrangements for service on Crown)). Where a defendant does not cooperate with the claimant in this manner, then in accordance with r.6.9, the claim form must be served at "the place" shown in the table in that rule. Where r.6.7 or r.6.9 applies (neither will apply where personal service is mandatory) the address for service included in the claim form should be the address of the solicitor or the address of "the place" as the case may be, as it is at those places at which service must be effected otherwise there will be mis-service. Where r.6.8 applies, service at the address given is not mandatory, but as a practical matter, that is the address at which the claimant will intend the claim form to be served and therefore will be the address included in it in compliance with r.6.6(2).

The address at which the defendant may be served included in the claim form must include a full postcode unless the court orders otherwise. The sign post following para.(2) of r.6.6 draws attention to Practice Direction (Statements of Case) (16PD) para.2.4 (see para.16PD.2 below) wherein it is noted that postcode information may be obtained from *http://www.royalmail.com* [Accessed November 18, 2008], or the Royal Mail Address Management Guide. Paragraph 2.3 of 16PD states that, where the defendant is an individual the claimant should (if he is able to do so) include in the claim form "an address at which the defendant resides or carries on business" and further states that this requirement applies "even though the defendant's solicitors have agreed to accept service on the defendant's behalf" (*ibid*). This facilitates the identification of the "defendant's home court" (see r.2.3(1) and para.2.3.8). Note also para.2.5 of 16PD.

Service of the claim form on a solicitor[1]

6.7 **6.7 Subject to rule 6.5(1), where—**

(a) the defendant has given in writing the business address within the jurisdiction of a solicitor as an address at which the defendant may be served with the claim form; or

(b) a solicitor acting for the defendant has notified the claimant in writing that the solicitor is instructed by the defendant to accept service of the claim form on behalf of the defendant at a business address within the jurisdiction,

the claim form must be served at the business address of that solicitor. ("Solicitor" has the extended meaning set out in rule 6.2(d).)

Effect of rule (r.6.7)

6.7.1 In terms, this rule is similar to para.(2) of r.6.4 as it stood before the substitution of Pt 6 on October 1, 2008, insofar as it affected service of claim forms, but the conditions stated in paras (a) and (b) are drawn differently. As drafted, r.6.7 deals with certain problems exposed by Court of Appeal cases decided before that date (in particular, in *Collier v Williams* [2006] EWCA Civ 20; [2006] 1 W.L.R. 1945, CA).

As to service on a party's solicitor of documents in proceedings (other than claim forms, as defined in r.6.2(c)), see r.6.23 (Address for service).

Leaving a claim form at the business address of a solicitor where one or other of the conditions stated in this rule is satisfied is one of the methods of service permitted by r.6.3.

Presumably "has given in writing" a solicitor's address for service (in r.6.7(a)) means has given to a particular claimant. Where a solicitor gives written notice (under r.6.7(b)) that he is instructed to accept service, that notice will only take effect if it is directed to "the claimant". In *Firstdale Ltd v Quinton* [2004] EWHC 1926 (Comm), August 8, 2004, unrep. (Colman J.), a case decided under the former (less precise) rules, it was held that an indication by a defendant's solicitor that he was authorised to accept service of proceedings by a particular claimant, could not ordinarily be taken to have indicated his authority to accept service of a claim form arising from the same dispute but from a different claimant (an assignee). Service on the defendant (rather than on the solicitor) was, therefore, valid service.

The rule is expressed in mandatory terms, subject to any requirement of personal service on the defendant (r.6.5(1)). In the (rare) circumstances where personal service of the claim form on the defendant is mandatory, r.6.7 yields. In the (usual) circumstances where personal service of the claim form on the defendant is but one of the methods of service that may be used, then r.6.7 has its full effect. In those circumstances, service on the defendant instead of on the solicitor is not valid service (*Nanglegan v Royal Free Hampstead NHS Trust* [2001] EWCA Civ 127; [2002] 1 W.L.R. 1043, CA). Paragraph (2)(a) of r.6.5 (Personal service) expressly states that, where a claim form may (rather than must) be served personally it may not be so served where r.6.7 applies. For obvious reasons, in that event r.6.9 (Service of the claim form where the defendant does not give an address for service) does not apply, and this is expressly stated in para.(1)(b) of r.6.9.

If the circumstances are (1) that the defendant is a company which may be served by a method of service set out in the Companies Act 1985 or the Companies Act 2006 (see r.6.3(2)), (2) that before any service is effected, one or other of the conditions in r.6.7 is satisfied, and (3) that service is effected, not on the solicitors, but on the company by one of the statutory methods, the service is good service (*Cranfield v Bridgegrove Ltd* [2003] EWCA Civ 656; [2003] 1 W.L.R. 2441, CA). Rule 6.3(2) makes it clear that a defendant company can be served under either "any method permitted under this Part" or by any of the statutory methods. Service on a solicitor where *required under* r.6.7 because the conditions therein have been met is a method "permitted under this Part", but it is nevertheless an alternative method to service

[1] Added by the Civil Procedure (Amendment) Rules 2008 (SI 2008/2178).

under the statutory provisions (see paras 6.3.7 *et seq.* above). The same reasoning applies where the defendant is an LLP (see r.6.3(3)).

It would seem thatr.6.7 and r.6.8 are mutually exclusive. Under r.6.8 a defendant can give any address, subject to this: if he gives the address in writing it cannot be a solicitor's business address (because in that event r.6.7 applies). It follows that, where a defendant in writing gives a solicitor's address for service that is an address given under r.6.7 and not under r.6.8, and that is so (1) even though the defendant had not instructed the solicitors to accept service on his behalf, and (2) even though the defendant had instructed the solicitors but they had not informed the claimant accordingly (cf. former 6.4(2)). Where a defendant in writing gives a solicitor's business address as his address for service, r.6.7 applies even though the solicitors had neither received nor accepted instructions (but, presumably, the effect of service on the solicitors in those events would not place the solicitors "on the record"; see further below). As a practical matter of course, in most cases the defendant's wish to be served in accordance with r.6.7 will be conveyed to the claimant by the solicitors as provided for by r.6.7(b).

Where the address for service of a party is the business address of his solicitor, the solicitor is considered to be "on the record" and will remain so. One consequence of the general rule that personal service on a party is disallowed where that party has a solicitor, is that a solicitor "on the record" cannot refuse service. If the solicitor finds himself without instructions and cannot continue to act he must promptly apply for an order declaring that he has ceased to be the solicitor acting for a party (see r.42.3). Until this is done the solicitor will be considered to be acting for that party (r.42.1) and service must be effected upon him. As a practical matter, this consequence is more important where the document to be served is not a claim form, but is another document in proceedings; that is to say, in circumstances where r.6.23, and not r.6.5 and r.6.7, applies.

In this context, "solicitor" includes other authorised litigators (see r.6.2(d)).

Service of the claim form where the defendant gives an address at which the defendant may be served[1]

6.8 Subject to rule 6.5(1) and 6.7— 6.8

(a) the defendant may be served with the claim form at an address within the jurisdiction which the defendant has given for the purpose of being served with the proceedings; or

(b) in any claim by a tenant against a landlord, the claim form may be served at an address given by the landlord under section 48 of the Landlord and Tenant Act 1987.

Effect of rule (r.6.8)

6.8.1 Rule 6.5(1) states that a claim form must be served personally on the defendant in those (rare) circumstances where this is required by a Part of the CPR other than Pt 6, or by any other enactment, a practice direction or court order. Rule 6.7 deals with the circumstances in which the claim form must be served at the business address of the defendant's solicitor.

Leaving a claim form "at a place specified in rule 6.8" is one of the methods for the service of claim forms permitted by r.6.3. However, r.6.8 makes no mention of "place" but speaks of "address". Presumably what is meant is the "address" of a "place". See further, r.6.6(2) and commentary following (address "at which the defendant may be served" *to be included in claim form*).

In this context, an address "within the jurisdiction" given by the defendant for the purpose of his being served with the proceedings means an address within England and Wales (see r.2.3). (For address for service of a party in Scotland or Northern Ireland in cases of service out of the jurisdiction, see r.6.40 and commentary following that rule.)

Rule 6.8 can be seen as replacing (with effect from October 1, 2008) former r.6.5

[1] Added by the Civil Procedure (Amendment) Rules 2008 (SI 2008/2178).

(Address for service), to the extent that that provision could be said to apply to the providing by a defendant of an address for service on him of a claim form (other than his solicitor's address). For provisions as to service at an address given by a party to proceedings at which that party (whether claimant or defendant) may be served with documents in proceedings other than a claim form (as defined in r.6.2(c)), see r.6.23 (Address for service).

Where an overseas company has complied with the statutory provisions and registered an address for service (see para.6.3.9 above), that does not amount to the giving of an address for service in particular proceedings within r.6.8. This is because service under s.694A and s.695 of the Companies Act 1985 (s.1139(2) of the Companies Act 2006) is an alternative to any form of service under Pt 6.

Landlord and Tenant Act 1987 s.48

6.8.2 Paragraph (b) of this rule was a new provision when introduced with effect from October 1, 2008. Subsection (1) of s.48 (Notification by landlord of address for service of notices) states that a landlord of premises to which Pt VI of the Act applies shall by notice furnish the tenant with an address in England and Wales at which notices (including notices in proceedings) may be served on him by the tenant; see Vol.2 at para.3A–718+.

Service of the claim form where the defendant does not give an address at which the defendant may be served[1]

6.9 **6.9—(1) This rule applies where—**

(a) rule 6.5(1) (personal service);

(b) rule 6.7 (service of claim form on solicitor); and

(c) rule 6.8 (defendant gives address at which the defendant may be served),

do not apply and the claimant does not wish to effect personal service under rule 6.5(2).

(2) Subject to paragraphs (3) to (6), the claim form must be served on the defendant at the place shown in the following table.

Nature of defendant to be served	*Place of service*
1. Individual	**Usual or last known residence.**
2. Individual being sued in the name of a business	**Usual or last known residence of the individual; or principal or last known place of business.**
3. Individual being sued in the business name of a partnership	**Usual or last known residence of the individual; or principal or last known place of business of the partnership.**
4. Limited liability partnership	**Principal office of the partnership; or any place of business of the partnership within the jurisdiction which has a real connection with the claim.**

[1] Added by the Civil Procedure (Amendment) Rules 2008 (SI 2008/2178).

5. Corporation (other than a company) incorporated in England and Wales	**Principal office of the corporation; or any place within the jurisdiction where the corporation carries on its activities and which has a real connection with the claim.**
6. Company registered in England and Wales	**Principal office of the company; or any place of business of the company within the jurisdiction which has a real connection with the claim.**
7. Any other company or corporation	**Any place within the jurisdiction where the corporation carries on its activities; or any place of business of the company within the jurisdiction.**

(3) Where a claimant has reason to believe that the address of the defendant referred to in entries 1, 2 or 3 in the table in paragraph (2) is an address at which the defendant no longer resides or carries on business, the claimant must take reasonable steps to ascertain the address of the defendant's current residence or place of business ("current address").

(4) Where, having taken the reasonable steps required by paragraph (3), the claimant—

(a) ascertains the defendant's current address, the claim form must be served at that address; or

(b) is unable to ascertain the defendant's current address, the claimant must consider whether there is—

(i) an alternative place where; or

(ii) an alternative method by which,

service may be effected.

(5) If, under paragraph (4)(b), there is such a place where or a method by which service may be effected, the claimant must make an application under rule 6.15.

(6) Where paragraph (3) applies, the claimant may serve on the defendant's usual or last known address in accordance with the table in paragraph (2) where the claimant—

(a) cannot ascertain the defendant's current residence or place of business; and

(b) cannot ascertain an alternative place or an alternative method under paragraph (4)(b).

Effect of rule (r.6.9)

Rule 6.9 is primarily concerned with the matter of ascertaining the proper place at which service of the claim form on the defendant is to be effected in those circumstances where the defendant has not given the claimant an address for service on which he may safely rely. (Before the rule came into effect on October 1, 2008, provisions similar to those now found in para.(1) of this rule appeared in former r.6.5; the provisions in paras (3) to (6) of the rule were new.) **6.9.1**

Where the method of service adopted is personal service (either because it must be or may be adopted) the question of "place of service" is not crucial to effectiveness (hence the exclusion of mandatory or discretionary personal service in r.6.9(1)); the defendant may be served wherever he is found within the jurisdiction.

In addition, for obvious reasons, the question of place of service is foreclosed where the position is that service must be effected on the defendant's solicitors at their business address (hence the exclusion in r.6.9(1)(b)), or where the defendant has given an address at which he may be served (hence the exclusion in r.6.9(1)(c)). (Further the question does not arise where service is to be effected by fax or other means of electronic communication, where the defendant has given an "electronic identification" to which the claim form may be transmitted.)

Service "method" and "place" of service

6.9.2 Rule 6.3(1) states that a claim form may be served by any one of several listed "methods" (including the methods falling within the exclusions in para.(1) of this rule). Among them (and not falling within the exclusions) is that of "leaving it at" a place specified in r.6.9 (r.6.3(1)(c)). So it can be said that, for the purposes of Section II of Pt 6, "leaving it at a place specified in r.6.9" is a discrete "method" of service. The interesting feature of this particular method of service is that it is customised according to the "nature" of the defendant to be served; "place" is determined by "nature". Further by paras (2) and (3) of r.6.3, the "leaving it at a place specified by r.6.9" method of service is made applicable where the "nature" of the defendant is that of a company or a limited liability partnership.

Another "method" of service permitted by r.6.3 to which the nature/place scheme in r.6.9 is relevant is the method of service by first class post, document exchange or other service etc (r.6.3(1)(b)). By definition, such method requires that the claim form be sent to a particular place of service. (It is assumed here that para.(c) of r.6.3(1) is not to be taken literally and that "leaving it at a place specified" includes posting to such a place.)

Thus, where the exclusions stated in para.(1) of r.6.9 apply, para.(2) of this rule comes to the aid of the claimant and provides a place at which the claim form should be left or to which it should be sent.

Service "place" and "address" thereof

6.9.3 The table in para.(2) of r.6.9 describes "place" of service in various ways; viz., "residence", "place of business", "principal office", and "place where corporation carries on activities". In some instances, qualifications are added: thus, for example, "usual or last known" residence, and "principal or last known" place of business or place of business having "a real connection with the claim". Obviously, such places have "addresses", but no mention is made of this in the table. However, in paras (3) to (6) references are made to the defendant's "address". Further, in those paragraphs (but not in the table), for purposes explained below, references are made to the defendant's "current residence" and "current place of business".

Claimant's knowledge of individual defendant's residence or place of business

6.9.4 This rule proceeds on the assumption that the claimant has knowledge of the "place" at which the claim form may be left or to which it may be posted. If the claimant (for example) wishes to serve the claim form on an individual defendant, and he has no knowledge of the defendant's "usual" or "last known" residence, the rule does not avail him.

Where, in accordance with para.(2) of r.6.9, a claimant serves a claim form on an individual defendant, it will normally be the case that the claimant will know, or at least believe, that the address at which it is left or to which it is posted, is the address of the defendant's usual or last known residence or principal or last known place of business (as the case may be). In those circumstances, provided the claim form is dispatched for service within the time limits fixed by r.7.5, the normal consequences of good service then follow. The service cannot be impugned by the defendant's showing that, nevertheless, the claim form did not come to his knowledge. Whether any judgment or order regularly obtained by the claimant following such service should be set aside on the ground of the defendant's lack of such knowledge is a different matter; see further r.13.2 (setting aside default judgment) and r.39.3 (setting aside judgment or order obtained in party's absence) and commentaries thereon.

In practice, difficulties can arise where the claimant's knowledge in this respect turns out to be inaccurate, with the result that the claim form is left at or posted to a place that is not the defendant's "usual" or "last known" residence, or not the "principal" or "last known" place of his business or of the partnership to which he belongs. These difficulties are of long standing, not only in relation to the service of originating process, but in relation to the service of documents generally. Former r.6.5 was drafted with the intention of overcoming known difficulties in the pre-CPR document service rules (*Akram v Adam* [2004] EWCA Civ 1601; [2005] 1 W.L.R. 2762, CA) but was not wholly successful in that endeavour.

The question of whether the claim form was served at the defendant's "usual", or "last known" residence or the "principal" or "last known" place of his business, is separate from the question of whether the claim form came to his notice (actually or constructively). Modern cases raising the first question include: *Marshall v Maggs* [2006] EWCA Civ 20; [2006] 1 W.L.R. 1945, CA (service not effected where claim form posted to an address at which, contrary to the claimant's belief, the defendant had never resided); *O'Hara v McDougal* [2005] EWCA Civ 1623, November 22, 2005, unrep., CA (service not effected where claim form served at an address that was not the defendant's place of business); *Lexi Holdings Plc v Luqman*, October 22, 2007, unrep. (service not effected at defendant's residence where, at time during which defendant serving substantial term in prison, claim form served at residence occupied by defendant beforehand).

Paragraph (3) of r.6.9 seeks to deal with a particular difficulty that may arise, that is to say, with the situation where the claimant has "reason to believe" that the defendant no longer resides at, or carries on business at, "the address of the defendant referred to in entries 1, 2 or 3 in the table in paragraph (2)". On the face of it, this is a rather odd provision, given that there is no mention in the table of the "address" of a defendant. However, it is tolerably clear that what is meant is that para.(3) is engaged where (a) the claimant knows or believes that the defendant's last known residence or his last known place of business is (say) X, but (b) the claimant has reason to believe that X is not the place at which the defendant now resides or carries on business.

In these circumstances, para.(3) requires the claimant "to take reasonable steps" to discover the address of the defendant's "current residence or place of business" and, having taken such steps, then to proceed in accordance with paras (4) and (5) (see further below). It is important to notice that para.(6) allows that, if the process outlined in paras (3) to (5) proves unfruitful, service at the defendant's usual or last known address in accordance with the table in para.(2) will be good service, despite the fact that the claimant had "reason to believe" that the defendant no longer resides or carries on business there.

Before the provisions in paras (3) to (6) of r.6.9 came into effect, there was some authority for the proposition that (at least in certain circumstances) a claimant was required to make reasonable inquiries as to the defendant's "current" place of residence or of business, before purporting to effect service at the defendant's "last known" residence or place of business (see *Cranfield v Bridgegrove Ltd* [2003] EWCA Civ 656; [2003] 1 W.L.R. 2441, CA; *Collier v Williams* [2006] EWCA Civ 20; [2006] 1 W.L.R. 1945, CA, and cases referred to therein). The new provisions make it clear that that duty arises only where the claimant has "reason to believe" the matters referred to in para.(3).

Duty to take "reasonable steps" to ascertain current address and consequences thereof

The expression "reasonable steps" is not embellished by the rule, or by any provision in practice directions supplementing this Part. **6.9.5**

Conceivably, in a given case, although the claimant believed (because he had reason to do so) that the defendant no longer resided or carried on business at a particular address (i.e. place), he may be wrong about that, and this may be revealed by his taking of reasonable steps to ascertain the defendant's current address.

Paragraph (4)(b) of the rule proceeds on the assumption that the reasonable steps taken by the claimant have not yielded a current address for the defendant. In those circumstances, the claimant "must consider" whether there is an "alternative place" (that is to say, a place other than the places referred to in the table following para.(2)) where service may be effected, and if there is such a place, must make an application to the court for an order under r.6.15 (Service of claim form by an alternative method or at an alternative place). Paragraph (4)(b) further provides that the claimant must consider whether there is "an alternative method" by which service may be effected, and if there is must make an application under r.6.15. The point here is that (as was explained above) not all of the permitted methods of service listed in r.6.3 are available when r.6.9(2) is relied on. Under r.6.15 the court has power to authorise service by a method "not otherwise permitted by this Part". (See further commentary following r.6.15.)

The effect of para.(6) of r.6.9 is clear enough (but "ascertain . . . an alternative method" is ugly). The effect of the provision (which in a given case could be harsh) points up the importance of the duties imposed on the claimant by paras (4) and (5) of the rule.

Defendant out of jurisdiction at time of service

6.9.6 Where an individual defendant does not give an address for service and service is effected on him by an appropriate method at a place for service as stipulated in r.6.9, it is conceivable that the defendant may be out of the jurisdiction at the time of service. It is a common law principle that a defendant may be served with originating process within the jurisdiction only if he is present in the jurisdiction at the time of service or deemed service. In *City & Country Properties Ltd v Kamali* [2006] EWCA Civ 1879; [2007] 1 W.L.R. 1219, CA, the Court of Appeal (1) explained that, before the CPR came into effect, the court had held that that principle did not apply to provisions in the CCR as to postal service, and (2) held that, as the CPR service rules (including the postal service provisions therein) are modelled, not on the former RSC, but on the former CCR provisions, they also have the effect of displacing the common law principle. Accordingly, postal service at the defendant's place of business, though effected at a time when he was out of the jurisdiction, was good service.

Service of the claim form in proceedings against the Crown[1]

6.10 **6.10 In proceedings against the Crown—**

(a) service on the Attorney General must be effected on the Treasury Solicitor; and

(b) service on a government department must be effected on the solicitor acting for that department.

(The practice direction supplementing Part 66 gives the list published under section 17 of the Crown Proceedings Act 1947 of the solicitors acting in civil proceedings (as defined in that Act) for the different government departments on whom service is to be effected, and of their addresses.)

Effect of rule (r.6.10)

6.10.1 In civil proceedings against the Crown, the claim form must be served in accordance with this rule (Practice Direction—Crown Proceedings para.2.1, see para.66PD.2 below).

In terms, this rule is similar to r.6.5(8) as it stood before the substitution of Pt 6 on October 1, 2008. The former rule applied to service of documents in civil proceedings (as defined) generally, and therefore took effect both in proceedings by the Crown as well as against. Rule 6.10 is confined to the service of claim forms on the Crown in proceedings against the Crown. The effect of the rule is not confined to "civil" proceedings (see further below).

Rule 6.5(2) states that a claim form may not be served personally "in any proceedings against the Crown". To compensate for this restriction, other arrangements are made for the service of claim forms on the Crown. (In any proceedings by or against the Crown, other documents must not be served personally in the Crown; see r.6.22(2)(b).)

Rule 6.10 follows statutory provisions found in the Crown Proceedings Act 1947, *the effects of which* have been extended by rules to service on the Crown of claim forms for claims for judicial review.

[1] Added by the Civil Procedure (Amendment) Rules 2008 (SI 2008/2178).

Service of claim form on Crown in civil proceedings

The Crown Proceedings Act 1947 s.18 (Service of documents) states that all documents required to be served on the Crown for the purposes of or in connection with any "civil proceedings" by or against the Crown shall, if those proceedings are by or against an authorised Government department, be served on the solicitor for that department or the person, if any, acting for the purposes of this Act as solicitor for that department. If there is no such solicitor and no person so acting, or if the proceedings are brought by or against the Attorney-General, the documents are to be served on the Treasury Solicitor (see Vol.2 para.9B–1130+below). (This section was enacted at a time when the principal means of service was personal service and came to be seen as a provision stating that documents to be served on the Crown cannot be served personally.) **6.10.2**

For the purpose of facilitating the operation of subs.(1) of s.18 of the 1947 Act (Parties in proceedings) provides that the Minister of the Civil Service shall prepare, publish and maintain a list: (a) specifying the several Government departments which are "authorised" departments for the purposes of the Act; and (b) specifying the name and address for service of the person who is the solicitor for each department (see Vol.2 para.9B–1134+). For convenience, this list is annexed to the practice direction supplementing CPR Pt 66 (Crown Proceedings) (para.66PD.4 below).

Subsection (3) of s.18 states that civil proceedings against the Crown shall be instituted against the appropriate authorised Government department. If none is appropriate or if the person instituting proceedings has any reasonable doubt as to which (if any) is, proceedings should be instituted against the Attorney-General (bringing into play s.18(4)).

These provisions apply to service of all documents required to be served on the Crown, and therefore include originating process in the form of claim forms. (It could be said that, in effect, the Crown is placed in a similar position to a putative defendant who has given the business address of his solicitor as an address at which he may be served with the claim form; see r.6.7.)

It should be noted that this statutory scheme for enabling and facilitating service on the Crown by providing for service on solicitors for authorised Government department does not apply to all civil proceedings to which the CPR applies. For the purposes of the scheme, "civil proceedings" by the Crown or against the Crown within s.17 is to be interpreted as defined in the 1947 Act. In this context, "civil proceedings against the Crown" (that is to say, proceedings in which questions as to the appropriate practice for the service of claim forms may arise) means the civil proceedings described in s.23(2) of the Act, but excluding the proceedings described in s.23(3) and subject to the definition of "civil proceedings" in s.38(2) (see Vol.2 paras 9B–1145+and 9B–1167+). One effect of these provisions is to exclude from the operation of the scheme for service of documents civil proceedings in the form of claims against the Crown for judicial review (as to which, see immediately below).

Service of claim form on Crown in judicial review claims

For the reasons explained in the commentary immediately above, the predecessor to r.6.5 expressly provided that personal service could not be effected on the Crown in "civil proceedings" as defined in the Crown Proceedings Act 1947. By providing that personal service of claim form cannot be effected in "any proceedings" against the Crown, r.6.5(2)(b) reflects the fact that this restriction extends to judicial review claims. By amendments brought into effect on October 1, 2008, the statutory scheme for service of documents on the solicitor for the appropriate authorised Government department, designed to compensate for the restriction, but In terms, limited to civil proceedings as defined in the 1947 Act, is extended to judicial review claims. This change is reflected in para.6.2 of Practice Direction (Judicial Review) (see para.54PD.5, below). **6.10.3**

Service of the claim form by contractually agreed method[1]

6.11—(1) Where— **6.11**

(a) a contract contains a term providing that, in the event of a claim being started in relation to the contract, the claim form may be served by a method or at a place specified in the contract; and

[1] Added by the Civil Procedure (Amendment) Rules 2008 (SI 2008/2178).

(b) a claim solely in respect of that contract is started, the claim form may, subject to paragraph (2), be served on the defendant by the method or at the place specified in the contract.

(2) Where in accordance with the contract the claim form is to be served out of the jurisdiction, it may be served—

(a) if permission to serve it out of the jurisdiction has been granted under rule 6.36; or

(b) without permission under rule 6.32 or 6.33.

Effect of rule (r.6.11)

6.11.1 In terms, this rule is similar to r.6.15 as it stood before the substitution of Pt 6 on October 1, 2008.

The rule acknowledges that it is conceivable that a party may issue a claim form, starting a claim in respect of a contract over which the court has jurisdiction, in circumstances where the contract itself contains a term stipulating that, in such an event, the claim form may be served by a particular method or at a particular place specified therein. Historically speaking, the rule was introduced into High Court practice at a time when the only permitted methods of service were personal service or service by leaving the originating process at the defendant's residence. The rule enabled parties by contract to agree a wider range of service methods (most of which are now expressly permitted by the rules), including service at a place outside the jurisdiction, not only in cases where, normally, the court's leave would be required before such service could be effected, but also in cases where such service was not permitted (whether with or without leave). In Pt 6, rules relating to the service of claim forms in the jurisdiction are contained in Section II (the Section within which r.6.11 is placed), and rules for service out of the jurisdiction are contained in Section IV. As, in a given case, r.6.11 can have the effect of authorising service out of the jurisdiction (possibly its most important practical effect nowadays), it has to be drafted In terms, that bridge Sections II and IV of this Part and it has to be treated as an exception to r.6.6(1).

The rule makes it clear that service of a claim form pursuant to a provision in a contract is good service where the English court has jurisdiction to try the claim whether jurisdiction is conferred by a term in the contract or vests or is assumed by the court apart from such contract.

Therule covers service pursuant to a contract within the jurisdiction as well as out of the jurisdiction. However, permission to serve out of the jurisdiction is required under r.6.36, unless permission is not required by virtue of r.6.36, 6.32 or 6.33.

In *Society of Lloyds v Tropp*, where the defendant was a US citizen who objected to service on a UK based agent for Lloyds names, a judge held that service on the underwriting agency appointed by contract to accept service of English proceedings in respect of names domiciled abroad was valid service ([2004] EWHC 33 (Comm), January 20, 2004 (Gross J.)), and the defendant was refused permission to appeal ([2006] EWCA Civ 88, April 11, 2006, unrep.).

"jurisdiction"

6.11.2 For the purposes of the CPR generally, and therefore for all Sections of Pt 6, unless the context requires otherwise, "jurisdiction" means England and Wales (see r.2.3).

Service of the claim form relating to a contract on an agent of a principal who is out of the jurisdiction[1]

6.12 **6.12—(1) The court may, on application, permit a claim form relating to a contract to be served on the defendant's agent where—**

(a) the defendant is out of the jurisdiction;

(b) the contract to which the claim relates was entered into *within* the jurisdiction with or through the defendant's agent; and

[1] Added by the Civil Procedure (Amendment) Rules 2008 (SI 2008/2178).

(c) at the time of the application either the agent's authority has not been terminated or the agent is still in business relations with the defendant.

(2) An application under this rule—

(a) must be supported by evidence setting out—

(i) details of the contract and that it was entered into within the jurisdiction or through an agent who is within the jurisdiction;

(ii) that the principal for whom the agent is acting was, at the time the contract was entered into and is at the time of the application, out of the jurisdiction; and

(iii) why service out of the jurisdiction cannot be effected; and

(b) may be made without notice.

(3) An order under this rule must state the period within which the defendant must respond to the particulars of claim.

(4) Where the court makes an order under this rule—

(a) a copy of the application notice and the order must be served with the claim form on the agent; and

(b) unless the court orders otherwise, the claimant must send to the defendant a copy of the application notice, the order and the claim form.

(5) This rule does not exclude the court's power under rule 6.15 (service by an alternative method or at an alternative place).

Effect of rule (r.6.12)

In terms, this rule is similar to r.6.16 as it stood before the substitution of Pt 6 on October 1, 2008. The rule has been substantially re-arranged. A practice direction provision which supplemented the former rule has been brought into the text of the rule, as para.(2). **6.12.1**

The significance of the rule is that it provides an exception to the general rule that service must be effected on a defendant in the jurisdiction. It enables service to be effected on a principal residing and carrying on business out of the jurisdiction but who has entered into a contract by or through an agent residing or carrying on business within the jurisdiction. The effect of the rule is to enable the claimant to serve the agent without having to obtain an order for service on the principal out of the jurisdiction under r.6.36. Permission must first be obtained under this rule and the order authorising service must state the period within which the defendant must respond to the particulars of claim. It should be noted that the response is required to the particulars of claim not the claim form (see Pt 7). In addition to effecting service on the agent the claimant must also send to the defendant copies of the order under r.6.16 and the claim form.

In proceedings in the Commercial Court and in Mercantile Courts, the time period provided by r.6.12(3) for responding to the particulars of claim (see Pt 9) applies after service of the claim form (see rr.58.6(3) and 59.5(3)).

Service of the claim form on children and protected parties[1]

6.13—(1) Where the defendant is a child who is not also a protected party, the claim form must be served on— **6.13**

(a) one of the child's parents or guardians; or

[1] Added by the Civil Procedure (Amendment) Rules 2008 (SI 2008/2178).

(b) if there is no parent or guardian, an adult with whom the child resides or in whose care the child is.

(2) Where the defendant is a protected party, the claim form must be served on—

(a) one of the following persons with authority in relation to the protected party as—

(i) the attorney under a registered enduring power of attorney;

(ii) the donee of a lasting power of attorney; or

(iii) the deputy appointed by the Court of Protection; or

(b) if there is no such person, an adult with whom the protected party resides or in whose care the protected party is.

(3) Any reference in this Section to a defendant or a party to be served includes the person to be served with the claim form on behalf of a child or protected party under paragraph (1) or (2).

(4) The court may make an order permitting a claim form to be served on a child or protected party, or on a person other than the person specified in paragraph (1) or (2).

(5) An application for an order under paragraph (4) may be made without notice.

(6) The court may order that, although a claim form has been sent or given to someone other than the person specified in paragraph (1) or (2), it is to be treated as if it had been properly served.

(7) This rule does not apply where the court has made an order under rule 21.2(3) allowing a child to conduct proceedings without a litigation friend.

(Part 21 contains rules about the appointment of a litigation friend and "child" and "protected party" have the same meaning as in rule 21.1.)

Effect of rule (r.6.13)

6.13.1 "Child" and "protected party" have the meanings given them by r.21.1(2) (see r.2.3(1)). CPR Pt 21 contains special provisions which apply in proceedings involving children and protected parties. A protected party must, and a child generally must, have a litigation friend to conduct proceedings on his or her behalf (r.21.2). The term "Persons under Disability" is no longer in use.

In terms, this rule is similar to r.6.6 as it stood before the substitution of Pt 6 on October 1, 2008, insofar as it applied to the service of claim forms.

Paragraph (3) states expressly what was formerly implied under the old rule. Paragraph (4) is interesting. It is derived from former RSC O.80, r.16(3), a provision that gave the court a similar power which could be exercised, not only (as para.(3) provides) retrospectively, but also prospectively. Under the CPR r.6.15 provides the basis for the exercise of the court's power prospectively. In either event, a copy of the order should be served on the person on whom the claim form has been served or is to be served.

For service on children and protected parties of documents other than claim forms (as defined in r.6.2(c)), see r.6.25 (wherein reference is made to r.21.8 (service of application for an order appointing a litigation friend)).

Deemed service[1]

6.14 A claim form served in accordance with this Part is deemed to be served on the second business day after completion of the relevant step under rule 7.5(1). **6.14**

Effect of rule (r.6.14)

This rule provides for the fixing of the deemed day of service of a claim form (as defined in r.6.2(c)) within the jurisdiction. A separate rule provides for fixing such days for other documents in proceedings (see r.6.26). The two rules replace, with amendments, a single rule (former r.6.7), a provision that created some difficulty. **6.14.1**

In a given case, the day on which service was actually effected on the defendant may not be the same day as the day on which, by operation of this rule, service was deemed to have been effected. The deemed day is a construction. Such construction is justified by the need to provide certainty. In the interests of certainty, a deemed day is not rebuttable by evidence of actual receipt of the claim form by the defendant on a day before or after the deemed day (*Godwin v Swindon BC* [2001] EWCA Civ 641; [2002] 1 W.L.R. 997, CA; *Anderton v Clwyd CC (No.2)* [2002] EWCA Civ 933; [2002] 1 W.L.R. 3174, CA).

In any given proceedings, it is for various reasons important that there should be no room for doubt as to the day on which (and therefore the date on which) service of originating process is deemed effected. Within the CPR, the time limits for the taking of certain procedural steps are calculated by reference to the day on which service is deemed to have been effected (e.g. r.10.3 (The period for filing an acknowledgment of service)).

A deemed day is fixed for all methods by which service of a claim form may be effected within the jurisdiction, including personal service (see below).

The deemed day is calculated from the "completion of the relevant step" (leaving with, posting, delivering to, etc.) under r.7.5(1). Rule 7.5(1) (which incorporates by reference r.6.5) stipulates, depending on the particular method of service chosen, the "step" that the claimant must "complete" where the claim form is to be served within the jurisdiction. For further explanation, see "relevant step under rule 7.5(1)" below.

This arrangement marks a significant change from the effect which r.7.5 had before October 1, 2008. The principal objective of the change was to reduce the instances in which the deemed day of service provisions had the effect of rendering service of claim forms out of time, with the result that, for the purpose of doing justice in individual cases, other provisions in the CPR that might conceivably be called in aid to rescue the claimant's claim, for example r.3.10 (court's power to rectify error of procedure), and r.6.16 (power of court to dispense with service), were pressed into uses for which they were not designed. (A similar policy objective underlies the provision now found in r.6.15(2); see para.6.15.5 below.)

In effect, r.6.14 provides that the time between the completion of the relevant step and the deemed day should be the same for all methods of service (the second business day after completion of the relevant step), thereby removing distinctions that existed under the previous rule between "day after" and "second day after". Further, no matter what method of service is used, the deemed day will be a business day.

In this context, "business day" means any day except Saturday, Sunday, a bank holiday, Good Friday or Christmas Day (r.6.2).

Deemed day of personal service

Under the former rule (r.6.7), a claim form served personally was served on the day on which personal service was effected. No "deemed day" provision applied to that method of service. However, if it was served personally after 5pm on a business day or at any time on a non-business day, it was "treated as being served" on the next business day. Underr.6.14, where service is effected by personal service the claim form is deemed to be served, not on the day on which is has been left with the appropriate person, but on the second business day after that day. Therefore, if a party was required to effect personal service not later than (say) February 6 and on that day (at any time) he left the claim form with the person to be served, it would be deemed to be served on the second business day after that day. **6.14.2**

[1] Added by the Civil Procedure (Amendment) Rules 2008 (SI 2008/2178).

"relevant step under rule 7.5(1)"

6.14.3 Rule 7.5(1) is referred to in r.6.14. That rule states that where the claim form is to be served within the jurisdiction, the claimant must "complete the step required" before midnight on the calendar day four months after the date of issue of the claim form. (As a result of an amendment to r.56.3, the four month limit now applies to claim forms for new tenancies of the variety referred to in that rule.) (For extension of time for serving a claim form, see r.7.6).

A table following r.7.5(1) stipulates the "step" required to be completed, according to the method of service employed (as permitted by r.6.3). That table, for convenience set out immediately below, states as follows:

Method of service	*Step required*
First class post, document exchange or other service which provides for delivery on the next business day	Posting, leaving with, delivering to or collection by the relevant service provider
Delivery of the document to or leaving it at the relevant place	Delivering to or leaving the document at the relevant place
Personal service under rule 6.5	Completing the relevant step required by rule 6.5(3)
Fax	Completing the transmission of the fax
Other electronic method	Sending the email or other electronic transmission

The step required by r.6.5(3), in the case of personal service on an individual, is that of "leaving it with that individual"; the steps required in the case of such service on a company or a partnership are also stipulated in that provision.

It is important to notice that the question whether there has been compliance with the time limit fixed by r.7.5 for service of a claim form within the jurisdiction is determined, not by inquiring as to whether the deemed day for service fell within the period, or whether personal service was effected within it (as was the case before October 1, 2008), but by asking whether the "step required" was "completed" within the period. Consequently, the problems encountered under the former rule, and dealt with by the Court of Appeal in cases such as *Godwin v Swindon BC* [2001] EWCA Civ 1478; [2002] 1 W.L.R. 997, CA, and *Anderton v Clwyd CC (No.2)* [2002] EWCA Civ 933; [2002] 1 W.L.R. 3174, CA, are avoided.

Rule 7.5(2) states that, where the claim form is to be served out of the jurisdiction, it must be served in accordance with Section IV of Pt 6 within six months of the date of issue. The new deemed service regime explained in the above commentary does not apply to service of claim forms out of the jurisdiction. If challenged, the claimant has to show that service was effected within the foreign jurisdiction within the six months allowed.

Before October 1, 2008, for certain methods of service, the time of day before which a document, including a claim form, was dispatched for service could be critical to the calculation of the deemed day of service (e.g. a document transmitted by fax after 4pm on a business day was not deemed to have been served on that day but on the next business day) (*Anderton v Clwyd CC (No.2)* [2002] EWCA Civ 933; [2002] 1 W.L.R. 3174, CA, at para.82). From October 1, 2008, onwards such "time of day" provisions do not apply to the calculation of the deemed day for service of claim forms, but they remain relevant to the calculation of the deemed day of service of other documents; see r.6.26 and commentary following that rule.

For further information on the effects of r.7.5, see commentary following that rule.

"served in accordance with this Part"

6.14.4 The deemed service day provisions as implemented by this rule apply where the claim form is served "in accordance with this Part". Where a claim form is served on a defendant company by sending it by post to the company's registered office as permitted by the Companies Act 1985 s.725(1) (re-enacted as the Companies Act 2006 s.1139(1)) it would seem that it is not "served in accordance with this Part"; see para.6.3.8 above (and note also para.6.3.11). Consequently, in such circumstances the *claim form is not* deemed (by operation of r.6.14 and r.7.5(1)) to have been served on the second business day after posting, but is deemed to be effected at the time at which it would be delivered in the ordinary course of post (provided it was properly addressed pre-paid and posted to the proper address) (see the Interpretation Act 1978 s.7).

Transition to new deemed day rules

In combination, r.6.14 and r.7.5(1) alter the previous law as to the fixing of the deemed day for service of a claim form. By providing that the deemed day is fixed in relation to the day on which the claim form was dispatched for service, r.7.5, the new rules reduce the likelihood that in a given case the deemed day will be a day falling after the day on which the period for service fixed by r.7.5 has expired. The new rules are not subject to transitional provisions. (For an explanation of their effect where the period for service fixed by r.7.5 expires on September 30 or October 1, 2008, see the Preface to the Special Supplement to the 2008 Edition for CPR Part 6 ("When do the new dispatching for service rules apply?"), published in Autumn 2008.) 6.14.5

Service of the claim form by an alternative method or at an alternative place[1]

6.15—(1) Where it appears to the court that there is a good reason to authorise service by a method or at a place not otherwise permitted by this Part, the court may make an order permitting service by an alternative method or at an alternative place. 6.15

(2) On an application under this rule, the court may order that steps already taken to bring the claim form to the attention of the defendant by an alternative method or at an alternative place is good service.

(3) An application for an order under this rule—
- **(a) must be supported by evidence; and**
- **(b) may be made without notice.**

(4) An order under this rule must specify—
- **(a) the method or place of service;**
- **(b) the date on which the claim form is deemed served; and**
- **(c) the period for—**
  - **(i) filing an acknowledgment of service;**
  - **(ii) filing an admission; or**
  - **(iii) filing a defence.**

Effect of rule (r.6.15)

In combination, this rule and r.6.27 replaced r.6.8 as it stood before October 1, 2008. 6.15.1

A claim form may be served by any of the methods listed in r.6.3(1), and "by any method authorised by the court under rule 6.15" (r.6.3(1)(e)).

Rules of court permitting substituted service were first introduced when virtually the only prescribed method for service of originating process on an individual was personal service and were designed to assist claimants where defendants were deliberately evading service. The introduction of methods of service other than personal service (especially service by post) reduced the need for reliance on these rules.

The expression "service by an alternative method" in this rule reflects the use in r.6.3 of the expression "methods of service" to describe the various ways in which service of originating service may be effected validly. The rule provides for service, not only "by an alternative method", but also "at an alternative place". This reflects the fact that some particular methods of service permit of a choice of places at which service may be effected.

An application for an order under r.6.15(1) may be made either before or after the claimant has attempted service by a method permitted by Pt 6, as there is nothing in the rule restricting the exercise of the court's powers to the latter circumstance.

[1] Added by the Civil Procedure (Amendment) Rules 2008 (SI 2008/2178).

What is (or is not) a method of service "not otherwise permitted by this Part" will depend upon the circumstances of the case. In making an order authorising service by an alternative method, the court is not restricted to making a choice from among the various methods provided for by r.6.3.

In *Access to Justice—Final Report (July 1996)* it was stated that a party who chose an alternative method must be able to satisfy the court that "(a) the person intended to be served was able to ascertain the contents of the document, or (b) it is likely that he was able to do so" (Ch.12, para.25).

RSC O.65, r.4 and CCR O.7, r.8, provided for the "substituted service" of documents, including documents in the form of originating process, where it appeared to the court that it was "impracticable for any reason" to serve the document in the manner prescribed by the rules; such service to be effected by taking "such steps" as the court might direct "to bring the document to the notice of the person to be served".

These provisions are replaced in the CPR by the single, and much simpler, rule expressed in para.(1) of r.6.15 (before October 1, 2008, it was in r.6.8(1)). The absence of any reference in the simpler rule to the prescribed method of service being "impracticable" has been regarded as giving the court a discretion broader than that given by the former rules (*Marconi Communications International Ltd v PT Pan Indonesia Bank Ltd TBK* [2004] EWHC 129 (Comm); [2004] 1 Lloyd's Rep. 594 (David Steel J.); *Knauf UK GmbH v British Gypsum Ltd* [2001] EWCA Civ 1570; [2002] 1 W.L.R. 907, CA), opening up the possibility that applications that would have failed under the old rules (e.g. *Paragon Group Ltd v Burell* [1991] Ch. 498, CA (agreement sued on stipulating time limit for bringing claim not rendering prescribed service method impracticable)) would not necessarily fail under r.6.15.

In terms, r.6.15(1), being free of any reference to "steps" directed to bringing the document to the notice of the person to be served, gives support to the Court of Appeal's decision in the *Abbey National plc v Frost* [1999] 1 W.L.R. 1080, CA, a case decided very shortly before the CPR came into effect and in which the Court examined the history of RSC O.65, r.4 and the authorities relevant to it, including the authorities on the substituted service of originating process on insurers (or on the MIB) instead of on tortfeasors in personal injury claims (culminating in *Clarke v Vedel* [1979] R.T.R. 26, CA). In this case it was argued that, where service in the prescribed manner was impracticable, substituted service of a writ could not be ordered where the defendant's whereabouts were unknown and there was no likelihood that the writ would reach him or come to his knowledge. The court held that no absolute bar to that effect was imposed by para.(3) of RSC O.65, r.4 (a provision not replicated in r.6.15). (See further, *Lennon v Tunstall*, May 27, 1999, unrep. (Judge Peter Baker Q.C.).)

Rule 6.15 falls within Section II of Pt 6, and is therefore concerned with the court's power to permit service by an alternative method where the method (or methods) available to the claimant under the rules provide for service of the claim form (as defined in r.6.2(c)) within the jurisdiction. Section III of Pt 6, is concerned with the service of documents other than the claim form within the jurisdiction, and service of such documents by an alternative method is provided for by r.6.27 by stating simply that r.6.15 applies to them as it applies to a claim form. As to alternative methods of service in cases of service abroad of domestic process, see para.6.15.7 below.

Paragraph 3.6 of Practice Direction (Admiralty Claims) stipulates the ways in which a claim form in rem may be served and provides that the court may direct an alternative method of service under r.6.15 "provided that the property against which the claim is brought or part of it is within the jurisdiction of the court" (see Vol.2 para.2D–92).

Paragraph 11 of Practice Direction (Insolvency Proceedings) deals with substituted service of statutory demands and petitions (see Vol.2 para.3E–11).

Practice and supporting evidence

6.15.2 An application for an alternative method service order for the service of a claim form may be made without notice and must be supported by evidence (r.6.15(3)). The supporting evidence must deal with the matters referred to and explained (with examples) in para.9 of Practice Direction A (Service Within the United Kingdom) (see *para.6APD.9 below*).

"good reason to authorise"

6.15.3 An alternative service order is an exceptional order. Once satisfied that there is a good reason to make an order the court must decide whether in the exercising of discretion it ought to make the order. At both stages it is of critical importance that the court has in mind the overriding objective (*Albon v Naza Motor Trading SDN BHD* [2007] EWHC 327 (Ch), March 9, 2007, unrep. (Lightman J.)).

In *Knauf UK GmbH v British Gypsum Ltd* [2001] EWCA Civ 1570; [2002] 1 W.L.R. 907, CA, a German company (C) issued a claim form for claim against another German company (D1) and against a British company (D2). C applied for an alternative method of service order permitting, as an alternative to serving the claim form on D1 out of the jurisdiction under the Hague Convention or the 1928 UK and Germany Convention (processes likely to take up to three months and which would otherwise be the prescribed methods of service), service within the jurisdiction on D1's London solicitors. The application was made principally for the purpose of ensuring that the English court would be "first seised" within the meaning of art.21 of the Brussels Convention and would therefore have priority over any proceedings that might be brought by D1 against C in Germany before C had managed to effect service on D1 in Germany. The Court of Appeal held that the application should be refused. There cannot be "good reason" for ordering service in England by an alternative method on a foreign defendant when such an order subverts, and is designed to subvert, in the absence of any difficulty about service, the principles on which service and jurisdiction are regulated by agreement between the UK and its Convention partners. An interesting feature of this case is that the court did not base its decision on C's inability to show that service by a prescribed means was "impracticable" (which under the pre-CPR rule might have provided D with a complete answer).

Claimant unable to ascertain defendant's current address (r.6.9(4)(b))

Where disputes arise as to whether or not service of a claim form has been properly **6.15.4** effected as prescribed by the rules, it is likely to be in a case to which r.6.9 applies; that is to say, where r.6.5 (Personal service) and r.6.7 (Service of claim form on a solicitor) do not apply and the defendant has not given an address for service (r.6.8). In particular, it is likely to be a case where the defendant is an individual and (as the rules prescribe) the claim form must be served on him at his "usual or last known address" or "principal or last known place of business" (either by post or by leaving it there). Where the claimant "has reason to believe" that such address is an address at which the defendant no longer resides or carries on business, paras (3) to (6) of r.6.9 come into play with the result that the claimant may be required to make an application for an order under r.6.15 permitting service by an alternative method or at an alternative place (see further commentary following r.6.9). It would seem that, if a claimant does not make such an application when he should have done so, nevertheless he might still apply under r.6.15(2) for an order to the effect that such service as he did effect was valid.

Retrospective operation—"steps already taken"

Paragraph (2) of r.6.15 is designed to remedy what were thought to be defects in **6.15.5** the law as it stood before October 1, 2008. The point is illustrated by *Elmes v Hygrade Food Products plc* [2001] EWCA Civ 121; January 24, 2001, unrep., CA. In that case a claimant making a personal injury claim, instead of serving the claim form on the defendant, served it on the defendant's insurers. The Court of Appeal rejected the claimant's submission (made after the time for service had expired) that the court had power to order retrospectively that the erroneous method of service already adopted by the claimant should be allowed to stand as service by an alternative method permitted by the court. (See also *Maggs v Marshall* [2005] EWHC 200 (QB), January 25, 2005, unrep. (Gray J.).) Paragraph (2) states that the court may order that "steps already taken to bring the claim form to the attention of the defendant by an alternative method or at an alternative place" is good service. The particular significance of this provision is that it may enable a claimant to escape the serious consequences that would normally ensue where there has been mis-service and, not only has the period for service of the claim form fixed by r.7.5 has run, but also the relevant limitation period has expired.

The question as to whether there is good reason to authorise service by an alternative method or at an alternative place is distinct from the question as to whether an alternative service order should take effect retrospectively.

Application of r.6.15 to service of other documents in proceedings

In terms, r.6.15 is confined to the service of claim forms (as defined in r.6.2(c)). Ser- **6.15.6** vice by an alternative method or at an alternative place of other documents in proceedings is provided for by r.6.27. That rule simply incorporates r.6.15 by reference.

It may be noted that by these means, a claimant who failed to serve particulars of claim by a method provided for by this Part may apply for an alternative service order. In the well known case of *Nanglegan v Royal Free Hampstead N.H.S. Trust* [2001] EWCA Civ 127; [2002] 1 W.L.R. 1043, CA, the Court of Appeal held that a court did not have power to order retrospectively that the claimant's mis-service of his particulars of claim (in the form of service by post on the defendant instead of on his nominated solicitor) should stand as permitted alternative service. It is now clear that the combined effect of r.6.27 and 6.15 gives the court such power.

Service abroad of domestic process

6.15.7 Section IV of Pt 6 contains provisions dealing with the service of the claim form and other documents out of the jurisdiction. That Section contains no provision dealing with service "by an alternative method" of a claim form or any other document. This omission raises the question whether the court has power to order service by an alternative method where a claim form or other document is to be served out of the jurisdiction. Under the pre-CPR rules, and before the Civil Procedure (Amendment) Rules 2000 (SI 2000/221) came into effect, it was clear that the court's power to order substituted or alternative service extended to such documents. However, after SI 2000/221 came into effect, the CPR provision for alternative service, then r.6.8, was not expressly incorporated in the rules applying to service out of the jurisdiction, then found in Section III of Pt 6. However, in *Knauf UK GmbH v British Gypsum Ltd* [2001] EWCA Civ 1570; [2002] 1 W.L.R. 907, CA, the judge at first instance stated that the effect of r.6.1 (as it then stood) was to incorporate r.6.8 by reference in Section III ([2002] EWHC 739 (Comm); [2002] 2 Lloyd's Rep. 416, at para.28), and the Court of Appeal (obiter) agreed (*op cit* at para.38). As a result of the changes made to Pt 6 and taking effect on October 1, 2008, it is doubtful whether the construction adopted in this case is now sustainable. Some other means will have to be found for providing a basis for the court's jurisdiction to order service by an alternative method of documents to which Section IV of this Part applies.

Power of court to dispense with service of the claim form[1]

6.16 **6.16—(1) The court may dispense with service of a claim form in exceptional circumstances.**

(2) An application for an order to dispense with service may be made at any time and—

(a) must be supported by evidence; and

(b) may be made without notice.

Effect of rule (r.6.16)

6.16.1 This rule gives the court power on application to dispense with service of a claim form. The application may be made without notice, but must be supported by evidence (in the form of a witness statement or affidavit). (Before the CPR came into effect, although the court had power to dispense with the service of a petition for a matrimonial cause, it had no power under rules of court to dispense with the service of other forms of originating process.)

This rule is similar to r.6.9 as it stood before the substitution of Pt 6 on October 1, 2008. That rule gave the court an unrestricted discretionary power to dispense with service "of a document", and in *Anderton v Clwyd CC (No.2)* [2002] EWCA Civ 933; [2002] 1 W.L.R. 3174, CA, the Court of Appeal held that it applied to the service of a document in the form of a claim form. In terms, r.6.16 applies to dispensing with the service of claim forms (as defined in r.6.2(c)), and of claim forms only. For the power to dispense with service of other documents, see r.6.28 below.

A principal objective of the changes made (with effect from October 1, 2008) to the rules dealing with the manner in which the deemed day of service is fixed for the service of claim forms (r.6.14 and r.7.5(1)) was to reduce the instances of applications to

---

[1] Added by the Civil Procedure (Amendment) Rules 2008 (SI 2008/2178).

the court by claimants who were disadvantaged by the fact that such rules had rendered service of their claim forms out of time, and who were driven to relying on the court's power to dispense with service for relief (see further para.6.16.3 below). The advantage given to claimants by those changes (albeit claimants who leave service to the last minute) is balanced by the fact that applications to dispense with service under r.6.16 should be granted only in exceptional circumstances.

Prospective service dispensing orders

A significant feature of the rule as it is now formulated is that the "in exceptional circumstances" test applies, not only to retrospective exercises of the power, but also to prospective exercises of the power. **6.16.2**

The vast majority of applications, in which it will be appropriate to make an order to dispense with service, will be for prospective orders sought and granted before the end of the period for service of the claim form.

Retrospective service dispensing orders

Under the CPR, applications by claimants for extensions of the period of validity for service of claim forms (as fixed by r.7.5) are subject to stricter control than under the former rules (see r.7.6 and commentary thereon). This has drawn attention to the question whether the court, in circumstances where it would not extend time for service after the period for validity for service had expired, may nevertheless exercise its power to dispense with service. **6.16.3**

In *Godwin v Swindon BC* [2001] EWCA Civ 1478; [2002] 1 W.L.R. 997, CA, the Court of Appeal held that the discretionary power to dispense with service under the former rule (i.e. r.6.9) should not be used as a means of circumventing and rendering nugatory the statutory limitation provisions and to do what is forbidden by the clear provisions of r.7.6(3). The court should only dispense with service where there is a possibility of effective service, which is capable of being dispensed with. There was no such possibility of effective service where the time for service of the claim form had already expired.

In *Anderton v Clwyd CC (No.2)*, op cit, the court concluded that the former rule was sufficiently widely worded to entitle the court to dispense retrospectively with service of the claim form in an appropriate case. The court acknowledged that, as a general rule, applications made for retrospective orders to dispense with service will be caught by the reasoning in the *Godwin* case, but held that there may be exceptional cases in which it is appropriate to dispense with service without undermining the principle in that the court's power to dispense with service should not be used to circumvent the restrictions on granting extensions of time for service as laid down in r.7.6(3) and thereby validate late service of the claim form.

In the *Anderton* case, the court held that this rule as it stood before October 1, 2008, gave the court power to dispense with service of a claim form after the period in which it remained valid for service (in accordance with r.7.5), as well as before; that is to say, the power could be exercised retrospectively as well as prospectively. But the court further held that it is only exercisable retrospectively in exceptional circumstances. The court drew a distinction between an application (1) for a retrospective dispensing order made by a claimant who has not even attempted to serve a claim form in time by one of the methods permitted, and (2) for a dispensing order made by a claimant, who has in fact already made an ineffective attempt in time to serve a claim form by one of the methods permitted. In the first instance the claimant still needs to serve the claim form in order to comply with the rules and to bring it to the attention of the defendant; that case is clearly caught by the *Godwin* case principles as an attempt to circumvent the limitations in r.7.6(3) on the grant of extensions of time for service of the claim form. In the second instance (subsequently referred to in reported cases as a "Category 2 case") the claimant's case is not that he needs to obtain permission to serve the defendant out of time in accordance with the rules, but rather that he should be excused altogether from the need to prove service of the claim form in accordance with the rules.

In some of the reported cases illustrating a Category 2 case in the context of the dispensing with service rule as it stood before October 1, 2008, the claimant's attempt in time to serve the claim form was ineffective because the method of service adopted did not accord with the methods stipulated by Pt 6 (the "simple mis-service cases"). In other cases the facts were that, although the period of validity expired after the claim form actually had been received by the defendant, the period had expired before the deemed day of service as fixed by the rules (so-called "deemed late service cases"). In *Kuenyehia v International Hospitals Group Ltd* [2006] EWCA Civ 21; *The Times* February 17, 2006, CA, the Court of Appeal reviewed the authorities on both varieties of Category 2 case (including *Wilkey v British Broadcasting Corp* [2002] EWCA Civ 1561; [2003] 1 W.L.R. 1, CA, and *Cranfield v Bridgegrove Ltd* [2003] EWCA Civ 656; [2003] 1 W.L.R. 2441, CA) and stated that the principles to be derived (and applicable to each variety) are: (1) it requires an exceptional case before the court will exercise its powers to dispense with service where the time limit for service of the claim form in r.7.5 has expired before service was effected in accordance with Pt 6, (2) the power is unlikely to be exercised save where the claimant has either made an ineffective attempt to serve by one of the methods permitted by (what is now) r.6.3, or has served in time in a manner which involved a minor departure from one of those permitted methods of service, (3) it is not possible to give an exhaustive guide to the circumstances in which it would be right to dispense with service of a claim form.

Before October 1, 2008, some of the "simple mis-service cases" variety of Category 2 case were cases in which mis-service had come about as a result of the claimant's non-compliance with the detailed provisions in (what is now) r.6.9(2) (service of claim form where defendant does not give an address for service). It is important to note that, with effect from that date, innovative provisions in paras (3) to (6) of r.6.9 impose duties on claimants to take steps in certain circumstances to ascertain the defendant's current address. It could be argued that, where a claimant did not discharge those duties when he ought, it would be difficult for him to submit subsequently that the circumstances were exceptional and service should be dispensed with under r.6.16.

In *Olafsson v Gissurarson (No.2)* [2008] EWCA Civ 152; [2008] 1 W.L.R. 2016, CA, where the claimant made an ineffective attempt within the relevant time limits to serve a claim form out of the jurisdiction by a method allowed by the service rules, the Court of Appeal held (1) the court's power to dispense with service retrospectively under (what is now) r.6.16 should be limited to truly exceptional cases, (2) there is no reason why the general principles identified in the domestic law cases on that rule should not be applied to the exercise of the court's discretion to dispense with service, whether the purported service is invalid in England or elsewhere (see further commentary following r.6.43).

It should be noted that the changes made to r.7.5 (with effect from October 1, 2008) are designed (at least in part) to deal with the problems caused by the so-called "deemed late service cases" variety of Category 2 case, and to make it unnecessary for the court to consider in such cases whether the court's power under r.6.16 should be invoked. Under r.7.5 (as amended), a claim form is served within the period of validity provided it is dispatched for service within the period. The fact that the deemed day (see r.6.14) falls after the period has expired does not render the service ineffective (and therefore the claimant is not forced to make an application for a dispensing order for the purpose of maintaining his claim).

Notice and certificate of service relating to the claim form[1]

6.17 **6.17—(1) Where the court serves a claim form, the court will send to the claimant a notice which will include the date on which the claim form is deemed served under rule 6.14.**

(2) Where the claimant serves the claim form, the claimant—

(a) must file a certificate of service within 21 days of service of the particulars of claim, unless all the defendants to the proceedings have filed acknowledgments of service within that time; and

(b) may not obtain judgment in default under Part 12 unless a certificate of service has been filed.

(3) The certificate of service must state—

(a) where rule 6.7, 6.8, 6.9 or 6.10 applies, the category of

[1] Added by the Civil Procedure (Amendment) Rules 2008 (SI 2008/2178).

address at which the claimant believes the claim form has been served; and

(b) the details set out in the following table.

Method of service	Place of service
1. Personal service	Date of personal service.
2. First class post, document exchange or other service which provides for delivery on the next business day	Date of posting, or leaving with, delivering to or collection by the relevant service provider.
3. Delivery of document to or leaving it at a permitted place	Date when the document was delivered to or left at the permitted place.
4. Fax	Date of completion of the transmission.
5. Other electronic method	Date of sending the e-mail or other electronic transmission.
6. Alternative method or place	As required by the court.

Effect of rule (r.6.17)

This rule replaced (with amendments) provisions formerly found in two separate rules (r.6.10, which applied to certificates of service generally, and r.6.14, which applied to certificates of service of claim forms particularly, and also to court notices). **6.17.1**

Paragraph (2)(a) of this rule is expressly disapplied by r.55.8(6) in proceedings to which r.55.8 applies (hearing of certain possession claims).

For certificates relating to service within the jurisdiction of documents other than claim forms (as defined in r.6.2(c)), see r.6.29.

Notice by court

Generally, a claim form is served in the jurisdiction, not by the claimant, but by the court (r.6.4). Clearly it is essential that the court should notify the claimant, not only that service has been effected, but also when, so that the claimant can calculate the relevant date for the taking of the next step (which may be, for example, the entry of judgment in default). That is provided for by r.6.17(1). **6.17.2**

However, when the court staff fail to complete the endorsement on the court file confirming service of the claim form on the defendant by post, there is no presumption that service has been effected, if the claimant provides evidence to the contrary (*Patel v Smeaton* October 24, 2000, unrep., CA).

Certificate of service

For form of certificate of service of a claim form in the jurisdiction, see Form N215 Certificate of service (see the Civil Procedure Forms section of the Civil Procedure Forms Volume). **6.17.3**

The matters referred to in para.(3) of r.6.17 must be dealt with in the certificate.

A certificate of service is included amongst the documents that must be verified by a *statement of truth (r.22.1(1)(f)). It has been the position* since June 30, 2004, that a certificate of service is no longer required to state expressly that the claim form served has not been returned undelivered.

The details required by r.6.17(3) appear to assume that service of the claim form has been effected by, as r.6.3(2) states, "any method permitted under this Part". Where, in the case of a registered company defendant or LLP defendant, the method of service is not by any such method but "by leaving it at or by sending it by post to" a place as permitted by the Companies Act 1985 s.725(1) (Companies Act 2006 s.1139(1)), the requirement imposed by r.6.17(2) still arises, and the details given in the certificate should be adjusted accordingly.

Time limit for filing certificate of service

6.17.4 With effect from October 1, 2008, para.(2)(a) of r.6.17 had the effect of extending the time for filing from (as stated in former r.6.14(2)) "within 7 days of service of the claim form" to "within 21 days of service of the particulars of claim". Further, it also had the effect of providing that a claimant is not required to file a certificate of service under para.(2)(a) where an acknowledgment of service has been filed (as in that circumstance, a certificate would be either unnecessary or otiose). CPR r.10.3(1) states that, as a general rule, the period for filing an acknowledgment of service is, (a) where the defendant is served with a claim form which states that the particulars of claim are to follow, 14 days after service of the particulars of claim and, (b) in any other case, 14 days after service of the claim form.

Where a defendant does not file an acknowledgment of service within the periods stipulated by r.10.3(1) the claimant has a further week in which to file a certificate of service. Rule 7.4(3) states that, where a claimant serves particulars of claim separately from the claim form (as provided by r.7.4(1)(b)), the claimant must within seven days of service file a copy of the particulars. As a consequence of para.(2) of r.6.17, the further requirement in r.7.4(3) to the effect that the claimant should file with the particulars a certificate of service has been excised from that provision.

Documents to be filed by claimant with certificate of service

6.17.5 Where, pursuant to r.6.17(2), the claimant files a certificate of service, the claimant is not required to file, and should not file, with the certificate a further copy of the claim form. The claimant is not required to file, and should not file, with the certificate the particulars of claim (where not included in the claim form) or any document attached to the particulars of claim where that document has already been filed with the court; see Practice Direction A (Service Within the United Kingdom) para.7.1 (para.6APD.7 below). (Where particulars of claim are served separately from the claim form, a copy of them should be filed with the court within seven days of service on the defendant; see r.7.4(3).)

Notification of outcome of postal service by the court[1]

6.18 **6.18—(1) Where—**

(a) the court serves the claim form by post; and

(b) the claim form is returned to the court,

the court will send notification to the claimant that the claim form has been returned.

(1) The claim form will be deemed to be served unless the address for the defendant on the claim form is not the relevant address for the purpose of rules 6.7 to 6.10.

Effect of rule (r.6.18)

6.18.1 Paragraph (1) of this rule replaces r.6.11 as it stood before October 1, 2008, insofar as it applied to the service of claim forms.

Where the court has sent the claimant a notice under r.6.18(1), the court will not try to serve the claim form again (r.6.4(4)(a)).

Paragraph (2) is important (it did not appear in former r.6.11). Presumably it is intended that that paragraph takes effect in the circumstances referred to in para.(1). The claim form may be served either by the court or by the claimant (r.6.4(1)). Where it is served by the court the method of service will be service by first class post.

A claimant must include in the claim form an address for service (r.6.6(2)). That address must be that of the defendant's solicitor (where r.6.7 applies), or may be an address given by the defendant as an address at which he may be served (r.6.8), or if the defendant has not given such an address, an address derived from the terms of r.6.9. In proceedings against the Crown the address must be as derived from r.6.10. The claim form may be served either by the court or by the claimant (r.6.4(1)). Where it is served by the court the method of service will be service by first class post at the address as given by the claimant in the claim form (an address derived in accordance

[1] Added by the Civil Procedure (Amendment) Rules 2008 (SI 2008/2178).

with rr.6.7 to 6.10). The effect of para.(2) of r.6.18 is to provide that, in these circumstances, the claim form will be deemed to be served, despite the fact that it is returned to the court, unless the address on the claim form is not "the relevant address" for the purposes of rr.6.7 to 6.10.

Receipt of a notice under r.6.18(1) (or r.6.19) should prompt the serving party to consider what further action should be taken (e.g. whether to attempt personal service, to check the address, to apply for an extension of time for service under r.7.6, or (relying on r.6.18(2)), after the appropriate interval, to apply for judgment in default of an acknowledgement of service or defence).

Notice of non-service by bailiff[1]

6.19 Where— 6.19

(a) the court bailiff is to serve a claim form; and

(b) the bailiff is unable to serve it on the defendant,

the court will send notification to the claimant.

Effect of rule (r.6.19)

This rule replaced r.6.11A as it stood before the substitution of Pt 6 on October 1, 2008, and is, in terms, limited to notice of non-service of claim forms (as defined in r.6.2(c)). 6.19.1

Where the court has sent the claimant a notice under r.6.19, the court will not try to serve the claim form again (r.6.4(4)(b)).

Service of Documents other than the Claim Form in the United Kingdom

Methods of service[2]

6.20—(1) A document may be served by any of the following methods— 6.20

(a) personal service, in accordance with rule 6.22;

(b) first class post, document exchange or other service which provides for delivery on the next business day, in accordance with Practice Direction A supplementing this Part;

(c) leaving it at a place specified in rule 6.23;

(d) fax or other means of electronic communication in accordance with Practice Direction A supplementing this Part; or

(e) any method authorised by the court under rule 6.27.

(2) A company may be served—

(a) by any method permitted under this Part; or

(b) by any of the methods of service set out in the Companies Act 1985 or the Companies Act 2006.

(3) A limited liability partnership may be served—

(a) by any method permitted under this Part; or

(b) by any of the methods of service set out in section 725 of the Companies Act 1985.

1 Added by the Civil Procedure (Amendment) Rules 2008 (SI 2008/2178).
2 Added by the Civil Procedure (Amendment) Rules 2008 (SI 2008/2178).

Effect of rule (r.6.20)

6.20.1 As the heading to Section III indicates, the rules in this Section are confined to the service of documents "other than the claim form". Necessarily, the range of documents to which this rule, and the other rules in Section III of Pt 6, might apply is wide.

Rule 6.20 plays the same role for service in the jurisdiction of documents other than claim forms (as defined in r.6.2(c)) as r.6.3 plays for the service of claim forms. (Before October 1, 2008, r.6.2 (Methods of service—general) did duty for all documents, subject to some express provisions for service of claim forms. In effect, that rule is replaced by r.6.3 and r.6.20.)

The rule applies generally to the service of non-claim form documents in cases where the claim form is served within the jurisdiction. In many CPR provisions particular methods of service for such documents are stipulated; often in provisions stating that the document may be served by personal service or by a particular method alternative thereto (see further commentary on r.6.22).

The heading to Section III refers to service "in the United Kingdom", whereas the heading to Section II refers to service "in the jurisdiction" (by which is meant England and Wales). The explanation for the difference lies in the fact that, in proceedings where (in accordance with the provisions of Section II) the claim form is served on a defendant in the jurisdiction, other documents in the proceedings may be served on parties at an address in England and Wales, in Scotland, or in Northern Ireland.

Provisions about methods of service for service of non-claim form documents out of the jurisdiction in proceedings where the claim form is served out of the jurisdiction, including in Scotland or Northern Ireland, are found in Section IV (especially in rr.6.40 to 6.42).

For the definition of "business day", see. r.6.2.

In civil proceedings by or against the Crown documents in the proceedings required to be served on the Crown must be served in accordance with this rule (Practice Direction—Crown Proceedings para.2.1, see para.66PD.2 below).

"first class post, document exchange or other service" (r.6.20(1)(b))

6.20.2 Paragraph (b) of r.6.20(1) is supplemented by Practice Direction A (Service Within the United Kingdom) paras 2 and 3 (see para.6APD.2 below).

For further information on this method of service, see the commentary on r.6.3(1)(b) above.

"electronic communication" (r.6.20(1)(d))

6.20.3 Paragraph (d) of r.6.20(1) is supplemented by Practice Direction A (Service Within the United Kingdom) paras 4.1 to 4.3 (as is para.(d) of r.6.3(1)); see para.6APD.4 below). For obvious reasons, para.4.1 is expressed as subject to paras (5) and (6) of r.6.23 (Address for service)).

Paragraph 4.1 is slightly different to the provision it replaced. The explanation is as follows. The former provision was para.3.1 of Practice Direction (Service). That paragraph stated that, as a condition for use of methods of service involving "electronic means" (in the circumstances in which they are permitted by the Rules), the party to be served or his "legal representative" must have "indicated in writing to the party serving" his willingness to accept service by the method. Such indication could be given expressly, but para.3.1(2)(b) stated that it would be implied where the party to be served set out in a statement of case or a response to a claim filed with the court a fax number, an email address or an electronic identification. Further, para.3.1(2)(a) stated that an indication of willingness to accept service by fax, but not by email or other electronic method, would be implied from the fact that a fax number is set out on the writing paper of the "legal representative" of the party who is to be served. Paragraph 4.1. is different in two respects. First, throughout the provision "legal representative" is replaced by "solicitor", by which is meant the solicitor "acting for" the party to be served (presumably retained by and acting for the party in the proceedings in which the document is to be served and not in related proceedings, see *Hart Investments Ltd v Fidler* [2006] EWHC 2857 (TCC); [2007] B.L.R. 30). Secondly, the restriction (by para.3.1(2)(b)) of para.3.1(2)(a) to service by fax has been removed and its effect extended to an email address set out on the solicitor's writing paper, but only where it is expressly stated there that it may be used for service. As to deemed willingness to accept service by fax, see further para.6.23.2 below.

Paragraph 4.2 states that, where a party intends to serve a document by electronic means (other than by fax) he must first request from the intended recipient the information referred to in that paragraph (specification of format, etc.).

Paragraph 4.3 states that, where a document is served by electronic means, the party serving the document need not in addition send a hard copy. But, unless there has been acknowledgement of receipt of the electronic version, sending a hard copy is prudent.

Service of claim form by electronic method (r.6.3(1)(b))

Service by electronic means is a method of service permitted by the rules, not only for the service of documents in proceedings other than the claim form (as r.6.20(1)(d) states), but also for the service within the jurisdiction of a claim form (see r.6.3(1)(b)). Necessarily, a claim form received by a defendant when it is served by an electronic method is not a document issued by the court (as in the case of personal service or service by first class post) but a copy of it (*Cranfield v Bridgegrove* [2003] EWCA Civ 256; [2003] 1 W.L.R. 2441, CA, at para.87; see further para.6.3.13 above). Much of what is contained in paras 4.1 and 4.2 of Practice Direction A is clearly directed at the service of "other documents". As there are traps for the unwary in the provisions for service by electronic means and scope for misunderstandings arising between putative parties, and as mis-service of a claim form can have serious consequences (not associated with the mis-service of other documents), claimants should scrutinise those paragraphs carefully before adopting this method of service for service of a claim form. In *Kuenyehia v International Hospitals Group Ltd* [2006] EWCA Civ 21; *The Times* February 17, 2006, CA, it was held that the failure of the claimant's solicitor to obtain from the defendant the required written consent before attempting to effect service of the claim form by fax rendered the service invalid and rejected the submission that, in the circumstances, the court should exercise its power under (what is now) r.6.16 to dispense with service. Particular care should be taken in noting the differences between what may be taken as a sufficient indication in writing of a willingness to accept service given by, on the one hand, the defendant, and on the other, the defendant's solicitor (in those circumstances where the solicitor is authorised to accept service). For example, it should be noted that a putative defendant's inclusion in their business letterhead of a fax number is not an indication in writing of their willingness to accept service of a claim form by that electronic method (*Molins Plc v GD SpA* [2000] 1 W.L.R. 1741, CA). **6.20.4**

For deemed day of service of claim form, where served by fax or by other electronic method, see r.6.14 and r.7.5(1).

Service on company or limited liability partnership (r.6.20(2) and (3))

See commentary on r.6.3(2) and (3) above. **6.20.5**

Service on party in Scotland or Northern Ireland

Section IV contains rules dealing with the service of documents in proceedings where the claim form is served out of the jurisdiction. In that Section, r.6.40(2) states that, where a party serves a document in proceedings on a party in Scotland or Northern Ireland it must be served by a method permitted by Section III, that is to say, by a method referred to in r.6.20 *et seq*. See further commentary following r.6.40. **6.20.6**

Who is to serve[1]

6.21—(1) A party to proceedings will serve a document which that party has prepared except where— **6.21**

(a) a rule or practice direction provides that the court will serve the document; or

(b) the court orders otherwise.

(2) The court will serve **a document which it has prepared except where—**

(a) a rule or practice direction provides that a party must serve the document;

(b) the party on whose behalf the document is to be served notifies the court that the party wishes to serve it; or

[1] Added by the Civil Procedure (Amendment) Rules 2008 (SI 2008/2178).

(c) the court orders otherwise.

(3) Where the court is to serve a document, it is for the court to decide which method of service is to be used.

(4) Where the court is to serve a document prepared by a party, that party must provide a copy for the court and for each party to be served.

Effect of rule (r.6.21)

6.21.1 This rule plays the same role for service in the jurisdiction of documents other than claim forms (as defined in r.6.2(c)) as r.6.4 plays for the service of claim forms. (Before October 1, 2008, r.6.3 (Who is to serve) did duty for all documents, subject to some express provisions for service of claim forms. In effect, that rule is replaced by r.6.4 and r.6.21.)

The rule starts with the assumption that was implied in the rule that it replaces; that is to say, that (subject to exceptions) a party who has prepared a non-claim form document will serve it.

Where the court serves a document to which this rule applies, the method will normally be service by first class post; see Practice Direction A (Service Within the United Kingdom) para.8.1 (see para.6APD.8 below). Where the court delivers a defence to a claimant or notifies a claimant that a defendant has filed an acknowledgment of service, the court will also deliver a copy of any notice of funding (Form N251) that has been filed if it was filed as the same time as the defence or acknowledgment of service and copies of it were provided for service (*ibid.* para.8.2) The court will not do the photocopying. (Failure to notify the other party of a funding arrangement may mean that all or part of a success fee or insurance premium will not be recoverable.)

Where a document to which this rule applies served by the court is returned, the court is not required by the rule to send notification to any party affected (cf.r.6.18).

See further, commentary following r.6.4 above.

Personal service[1]

6.22 **6.22—(1) Where required by another Part, any other enactment, a practice direction or a court order, a document must be served personally.**

(2) In other cases, a document may be served personally except—

(a) where the party to be served has given an address for service under rule 6.23(2)(a); or

(b) in any proceedings by or against the Crown.

(3) A document may be served personally as if the document were a claim form in accordance with rule 6.5(3).

Effect of rule (r.6.22)

6.22.1 This rule replaces former r.6.4, insofar as it applied to the service of documents other than claim forms within the jurisdiction. For personal service within the jurisdiction of claim forms, see r.6.5 above. For commentary on certain matters common to both rules, see commentary on r.6.5, above.

The mandatory exceptions stipulated in para.(2) accord with those in r.6.5.

Personal service is one of the "methods of service" for the service of documents (other than claim forms) listed in r.6.20(1). Examples of provisions in the CPR requiring service by the method of personal service of such documents are: r.71.3, Sch.1 RSC O.45, r.7, O.46, r.5, and Sch.2 CCR O.29, r.1 (each of these provisions is expressed as subject to the court's power to dispense with service); note also r.65.3 (service of applications for housing injunctions), Practice Direction (Interim Injunc-

[1] Added by the Civil Procedure (Amendment) Rules 2008 (SI 2008/2178).

tions) para.7.4 (service of search orders) (see para.25PD.7 below). As to personal service of judgment summonses, see Sch.2, CCR O.27, rr.2 and 4.

Numerous provisions in the CPR state that particular documents may be served personally or by some other stipulated method. Examples are: r.62.18(7), Sch.1 RSC O.115, r.17.

Address for service[1]

6.23—(1) A party to proceedings must give an address at which that party may be served with documents relating to those proceedings. The address must include a full postcode unless the court orders otherwise. (Paragraph 2.4 of the practice direction supplementing Part 16 contains provisions about postcodes.) 6.23

(2) A party's address for service must be—

(a) the business address within the United Kingdom of a solicitor acting for the party to be served; or

(b) where there is no solicitor acting for the party to be served, an address within the United Kingdom at which the party resides or carries on business.

(3) Where there is no solicitor acting for the party to be served and the party does not have an address within the United Kingdom at which that party resides or carries on business, the party must give an address for service within the United Kingdom.

(Part 42 contains provisions about change of solicitor. Rule 42.1 provides that where a party gives the business address of a solicitor as that party's address for service, that solicitor will be considered to be acting for the party until the provisions of Part 42 are complied with.)

(4) Any document to be served in proceedings must be sent or transmitted to, or left at, the party's address for service under paragraph (2) or (3) unless it is to be served personally or the court orders otherwise.

(5) Where, in accordance with Practice Direction A supplementing this Part, a party indicates or is deemed to have indicated that they will accept service by fax, the fax number given by that party must be at the address for service.

(6) Where a party indicates in accordance with the Practice Direction A supplementing this Part that they will accept service by electronic means other than fax, the e-mail address or electronic identification given by that party will be deemed to be at the address for service.

(7) In proceedings by or against the Crown, service of any document in the proceedings on the Crown must be effected in the same manner prescribed in rule 6.10 as if the document were a claim form.

(8) This rule does not apply where an order made by the court under rule 6.27 (service by an alternative method or at an alternative place) specifies where a document may be served.

[1] Added by the Civil Procedure (Amendment) Rules 2008 (SI 2008/2178).

Effect of rule (r.6.23)

6.23.1 Much of former r.6.5, insofar as its provisions were relevant to parties' addresses for service of documents other than claim forms, is re-enacted in this rule. A notable difference is that, whereas in the previous rule an address for service provided by a party had to be a residential or business address "within the jurisdiction", para.(2) of this rule enables a party to give such an address "within the United Kingdom" (cf. r.6.8). (This relieves defendants in Scotland and Northern Ireland from the need to find an address within the jurisdiction as a post box.) Further, para.(3) requires a party to give such an address in the circumstances stated in that provision.

Paragraph (6) of former r.6.5 anticipated that a party might fail to provide an address for service of documents and explained how service should be effected in that circumstance. In relation to the service of claim forms, that provision is in effect replicated in r.6.9(2), but it is not replicated in r.6.23.

Cases may arise in which a party (often an unrepresented party) does not adequately comply with r.6.23(1), or does not notify changes of address (as required by r.6.24), or, in any event, in the course of pre-trial proceedings persistently asserts (either rightly or wrongly) that he has not received documents required to be served on him by the court or by other parties (e.g. applications notices, notices of hearings, copies of orders, amended pleadings, witness statements etc). In *E Group Ltd v Bay Baker* [2008] EWHC 2349 (TCC); September 18, 2008, unrep., for the purpose of preventing further delays and the increase of the claimant's costs, the court ordered that an address provided by the defendant at a particular hearing should stand forthwith as the defendant's proper address for service (such address not to be disclosed to a third party without an order of the court).

For address for service within the jurisdiction of claim forms (as defined in r.6.2(c)), as distinct from other documents provided for by this rule, see r.6.8.

Address for service where service by means of electronic communication

6.23.2 Another notable difference between this rule and former r.6.5 is the express provision made in paras (5) and (6) for the service of documents by the method of service permitted by para.(1)(d) of r.6.20, that is to say, "by fax or by other means of electronic communication". Generally, an "address" for service is understood as an identification of a "place" for service, being premises of some kind having a physical location (a party's residence, place of business, or his solicitor's place of business). It is an "address" for service, and not a "place" for service, that a party is enjoined by r.6.23(1) to supply. There is no inherent difficulty in regarding the giving of a "fax number" or an "electronic identification" as being sufficient to satisfy the requirement imposed on a party by r.6.23(1) of giving an "address" at which he may be served, unless it is assumed that "address" means the address of a "place" for service. Paras (5) and (6) appear to be based on that assumption; they anticipate practical difficulties and provide solutions. The fax number must be "at the address for service" and the electronic identification will be deemed to be so.

Paragraphs (5) and (6) are supplemented by para.4 of Practice Direction A (Service Within the United Kingdom) (see para.6APD.4 below). See further commentary following r.6.20 (especially para.6.20.3).

Change of address for service[1]

6.24 **6.24 Where the address for service of a party changes, that party must give notice in writing of the change as soon as it has taken place to the court and every other party.**

Effect of rule (r.6.24)

6.24.1 In terms, this rule is similar to para.7 of Practice Direction (Service), as it stood before October 1, 2008. It is conceivable that the address for service given by a party may be that of the party's legal representative. In that circumstance, the party's duty to give notice extends to giving notice of any change of address of the legal representative.

[1] Added by the Civil Procedure (Amendment) Rules 2008 (SI 2008/2178).

Service on children and protected parties[1]

6.25—(1) An application for an order appointing a litigation friend where a child or protected party has no litigation friend must be served in accordance with rule 21.8(1) and (2). 6.25

(2) Any other document which would otherwise be served on a child or a protected party must be served on the litigation friend conducting the proceedings on behalf of the child or protected party.

(3) The court may make an order permitting a document to be served on the child or protected party or on some person other than the person specified in rule 21.8 or paragraph (2).

(4) An application for an order under paragraph (3) may be made without notice.

(5) The court may order that, although a document has been sent or given to someone other than the person specified in rule 21.8 or paragraph (2), the document is to be treated as if it had been properly served.

(6) This rule does not apply where the court has made an order under rule 21.2(3) allowing a child to conduct proceedings without a litigation friend.

Effect of rule (r.6.25)

This rule replaces former r.6.6(1) as it applied to the service of documents in proceedings other than claim forms. (Insofar as that provision applied to service of claim forms, it has been replaced by r.6.13.) 6.25.1

CPR Pt 21 contains special provisions which apply in proceedings involving children (a person under 18) and protected parties (a party, or intended party, who lacks capacity to conduct the proceedings); in particular, rules providing for the appointment of a litigation friend. Paragraphs (1) and (2) of r.21.8 deal with the service of application notices for the appointment of litigation friends by court order. Where such an application is made before proceedings are commenced it could perhaps be argued that the notice is, by definition, a claim form (see r.6.2(c)), and that service thereof is governed, not by the provisions of Section III of Pt 6, but by those in Section II. However, it seems that that is not intended and, as a practical matter, nothing turns on the distinction.

Deemed service[2]

6.26 A document, other than a claim form, served in accordance with these Rules or any relevant practice direction is deemed to be served on the day shown in the following table— 6.26

Method of service	*Deemed date of service*
1. First class post (or other service which provides for delivery on the next business day)	**The second day after it was posted, left with, delivered to or collected by the relevant service provider provided that day is a business day; or if not, the next business day after that day.**

[1] Added by the Civil Procedure (Amendment) Rules 2008 (SI 2008/2178).
[2] Added by the Civil Procedure (Amendment) Rules 2008 (SI 2008/2178).

2. Document exchange	**The second day after it was left with, delivered to or collected by the relevant service provider provided that day is a business day; or if not, the next business day after that day.**
3. Delivering the document to or leaving it at a permitted address	**If it is delivered to or left at the permitted address on a business day before 4.30p.m., on that day; or in any other case, on the next business day after that day.**
4. Fax	**If the transmission of the fax is completed on a business day before 4.30p.m., on that day; or in any other case, on the next business day after the day on which it was transmitted.**
5. Other electronic method	**If the e-mail or other electronic transmission is sent on a business day before 4.30p.m., on that day; or in any other case, on the next business day after the day on which it was sent.**
6. Personal service	**If the document is served personally before 4.30p.m. on a business day, on that day; or in any other case, on the next business day after that day.**

Effect of rule (r.6.26)

6.26.1 In Pt 6, as it existed before October 1, 2008, provisions giving the deemed "day of service" for each of six methods of service were found in r.6.7. That rule applied to all documents, including claim forms.

This rule deals with deemed service of documents other than claim forms (as defined in r.6.2(c)). Rule 6.14 deals with deemed service of claim forms. (Rule 6.14 is a much simpler provision than this rule, as it is able to incorporate by reference the "relevant steps" in new r.7.5(1).)

In the former rule there was a table showing "Method of Service", listing in one column (but not numbering) five methods of service, and indicating in another column the means by which the deemed "day of service" for each was to be calculated, and personal service was dealt with in narrative form in para.(2). In r.6.26, the calculations of the deemed day of service for all six methods of service are dealt with in tabular form. (The description of each method reflects paras (a) to (d) of r.6.20(1)). (Though the text of r.6.26 speaks of "the day" on which a document is deemed to be served, the column heading in the table speaks of "date"; it is submitted that "day" is to be preferred to "date".) As the signpost at the end of the rule indicates, worked examples showing how the day of deemed service is to be calculated are set out in Practice Direction A (Service Within the United Kingdom) para.10 (see para.6APD.10 below).

For definition of "business day", see. r.6.2.

When contrasted with its predecessor, there are two significant features of this rule. First, it provides that the deemed day of service should always be, whatever the method of service adopted, a business day. Secondly, it provides a uniform method for calculating the deemed day in cases where service is by fax or by another electronic method. The result is that unjustifiable anomalies in the calculation of the deemed day are removed.

In relation to four of the methods of service (nos. 3 to 6 in the table) for documents to which this rule applies, the time of "before 4.30 pm" on a business day may be critical to the calculation of the deemed day of service. Before October 1, 2008, "before 4 pm", or in the case of personal service, "before 5.00 pm", could be critical to the calculation of the deemed day of service for claim forms. Since that date, the rules applicable to the calculation of the deemed day of service for claim forms (r.6.14 and r.7.5(1)) do not, in relation to any particular method of service, turn on the time of day before which the "step required" to dispatch the claim form for service was completed.

In *Moulai v Deputy Public Prosecutor, Creteil* [2008] EWHC 1024 (Admin); [2008] 1 W.L.R. 2460, DC, a Divisional Court held that, in the circumstances of the case and notwithstanding (what is now) r.6.26, an appellant's notice required to be served on the CPS in an extradition appeal should be deemed to be served on the day on which it was transmitted (see further para.6.28.1 below).

For further commentary, relevant both to this rule and to r.6.14 (Deemed service of claim form), see commentary following r.6.14.

Service by an alternative method or at an alternative place[1]

6.27 Rule 6.15 applies to any document in the proceedings as it applies to a claim form and reference to the defendant in that rule is modified accordingly. 6.27

Effect of rule (r.6.27)

In combination, this rule and r.6.15 and r.6.26 replace r.6.8 as it stood before October 1, 2008. 6.27.1

In Section II of Pt 6, r.6.15 contains provisions dealing with the service of the claim form (as defined by r.6.2(c)) by an alternative method of service or at an alternative place. In that rule, alternative means alternative to the methods and places stipulated or permitted directly or indirectly by other provisions in Section II. Rules dealing with methods of service and places for service of documents in proceedings, that is to say, documents other than claim forms, are found elsewhere in Section III of Pt 6. By the device of incorporating r.6.15 by reference, this rule gives the court power to order the service of such documents by an alternative method or at alternative place to those otherwise permitted where it appears to the court that there is "good reason" to do so. The power thus incorporated includes the power to order that steps already taken by a method of service not permitted by the rules to bring a document (e.g. particulars of claim where they are not contained in and served with the claim form) to the attention of the other party is good service.

An application for an alternative method service order may be made without notice and must be supported by evidence (r.6.15(3)). The supporting evidence must deal with the matters referred to and explained (with examples) in para.9 of Practice Direction A (Service Within the United Kingdom) (see para.6APD.9 below).

See further commentary following r.6.15 (Service of the claim form by an alternative method or at an alternative place).

Power to dispense with service[2]

6.28—(1) The court may dispense with service of any document which is to be served in the proceedings. 6.28

(2) An application for an order to dispense with service must be supported by evidence and may be made without notice.

[1] Added by the Civil Procedure (Amendment) Rules 2008 (SI 2008/2178).
[2] Added by the Civil Procedure (Amendment) Rules 2008 (SI 2008/2178).

Effect of rule (r.6.28)

6.28.1 In terms, this rule is similar to r.6.9 as it stood before the substitution of Pt 6 on October 1, 2008, insofar as it applied to the service documents other than claim forms. For the power to dispense with service of claim forms, see r.6.16 above.

The rule gives the court an unfettered discretion, whereas under r.6.16 the power to dispense with service of a claim form (whether prospectively or retrospectively) may be granted "in exceptional circumstances".

In practice the power granted by the rule is useful for dispensing with the re-service of a document; for example, where a document is attached to an application to amend which is successful, service of the amended document may be dispensed with.

See further commentary on r.6.16.

Paragraph 22.6A(3)(d) of Practice Directions (Appeals) requires an appellant in an appeal under the Extradition Act 2003 to serve on the CPS within a specified time a copy of the appellant's notice filed in the court (see para.52PD.120, below). In *Moulai v Deputy Public Prosecutor, Creteil* [2008] EWHC 1024 (Admin); [2008] 1 W.L.R. 2460, DC, the effect of (what is now) r.6.26 was to render the appellant's attempt to effect such service by fax out of time. A Divisional Court held that, in the circumstances of the case, the court had power (1) under r.3.1(2)(a) (court's general power to extend time for compliance with any rule or practice direction) to rule that, notwithstanding r.6.26, the notice was deemed served on the day on which it was transmitted, or, alternatively, (2) to grant the appellant relief under r.3.10 (general power to rectify matters where there has been an error of procedure), or under (what is now) r.6.28 (power to dispense with service). cf., *Mucelli v Government of Albania* [2007] EWHC 2632 (Admin); [2008] 1 W.L.R. 2438, DC.

Certificate of service[1]

6.29 **6.29 Where a rule, practice direction or court order requires a certificate of service, the certificate must state the details required by the following table—**

Method of service	*Details to be certified*
1. Personal service	**Date and time of personal service.**
2. First class post, document exchange or other service which provides for delivery on the next business day	**Date of posting, or leaving with, delivering to or collection by the relevant service provider.**
3. Delivery of document to or leaving it at a permitted place	**Date and time of when the document was delivered to or left at the permitted place.**
4. Fax	**Date and time of completion of the transmission.**
5. Other electronic method	**Date and time of sending e-mail or other electronic transmission.**
6. Alternative method or place permitted by the court	**As required by the court.**

Effect of rule (r.6.29)

6.29.1 This rule replaces r.6.10 as it stood before the substitution of Pt 6 on October 1, 2008, insofar as it applied to certificates of service of documents other than claim forms.

Express CPR provisions requiring certificates of service of documents other than

[1] Added by the Civil Procedure (Amendment) Rules 2008 (SI 2008/2178).

claim forms are rare. One example is r.55.8(6), which requires the production at the hearing of certain possession proceedings of a certificate of service of a document in the form particulars of claim (such document not being a claim form *within Section II* of Pt 6).

Rule 22.1(1)(f) and Practice Direction (Statements of Truth) para.1.1(6) state that a certificate of service must be verified by a statement of truth (see para.22PD.1 below).

For certificates of service of claim forms, see r.6.17 above.

IV. Service of the Claim Form and other Documents out of the Jurisdiction

Scope of this Section[1]

6.30—(1) This Section contains rules about— 6.30

(a) service of the claim form and other documents out of the jurisdiction;

(b) when the permission of the court is required and how to obtain that permission; and

(c) the procedure for service.

("Jurisdiction" is defined in rule 2.3(1).)

Editorial introduction

Service is a procedural mechanism which is normally a precondition to the exercise of jurisdiction. Service does not create jurisdiction, but except for limited situations, such as where applications are made without notice before proceedings are started, the court's jurisdiction cannot be exercised against an individual unless either he has been served or the court has dispensed with service. In this context the expression "jurisdiction" relates to the subject matter of the proceedings whether with regard to the nature of the claim or the person against whom the claim is brought. The courts also have a general jurisdiction to decide whether they have jurisdiction to try any case or part of a case having regard to the subject matter of the claim, the nature of the defendant and whether adequate procedural steps have been taken against the defendant in question to make him a party to the proceedings (*Canada Trust Co v Stolzenberg* [1997] 1 W.L.R. 1582, CA; [1997] 4 All E.R. 983, CA). In appropriate circumstances the courts also have a discretion to decide whether to exercise jurisdiction where there is a more suitable jurisdiction for the trial of a case. 6.30.1

"service of the claim form"

The bulk of the provisions in this Section are concerned with the service of claim forms and not of "other documents". This was true also of the Section in Pt 6 now replaced by this Section. The former Section contained a definition provision (r.6.18) in which it was stated that "claim" included petition and application, and "claim form" included petition and application notice. The interpretation provision in Section IV (see r.6.31) below contains no such definitions. Insofar as it is necessary in this Section to determine what is meant by "claim form" it is necessary to refer to r.6.2 (Interpretation) for such guidance as may be gleaned from there. Paragraph (c) of that rule states that "claim" includes petition and any application made before action or to commence proceedings, and "claim form" is to be construed accordingly. 6.30.2

Service within the jurisdiction

The general rule is that persons within the jurisdiction can be served whatever their domicile. However, that general default position is hedged about with major qualifications as follows. First, it may be that the court will decline jurisdiction because the case is more suitably dealt with in a foreign court. Secondly, the English court may be obliged to decline jurisdiction because proceedings here would be inconsistent with the obligations of the United Kingdom under the Brussels or Lugano Conventions, or under the Judgments Regulation. Thirdly, there may be restrictions on service under 6.30.3

[1] Added by the Civil Procedure (Amendment) Rules 2008 (SI 2008/2178).

other enactments such as the Crown Proceedings Act 1947 (see further commentary following r.6.10) or the Diplomatic Immunities and Privileges Act 1964.

Service outside the territorial jurisdiction

6.30.4 Except for actions in rem, the ability to exercise civil jurisdiction in this country is founded upon the concept of personal service. The rigour of the concept has been modified both in respect of corporations and natural persons situated within the jurisdiction by provisions such as the ability to serve by post, but the position remains that where a defendant is outside the jurisdiction he can only be made a party to proceedings within the jurisdiction either by service or where service has been expressly dispensed with. Since the Common Law Procedure Act 1852, statutory powers have been used to limit situations in which service may be made upon persons who are out of the jurisdiction, subject to permission being given by the court. The grant of permission is discretionary. The Civil Jurisdiction and Judgments Act 1982, as amended, enables service of proceedings without the permission of the court in a wide variety of civil and commercial matters where the Brussels and Lugano Conventions apply. As from March 1, 2002, the Brussels Convention has been largely superseded in relation to proceedings between persons domiciled in Member States of the European Union by the Judgments Regulation (see further below).

Service under the Brussels and Lugano Conventions and the Judgments Regulation

6.30.5 The Brussels Convention on jurisdiction and the enforcement of judgments in civil and commercial matters was concluded on September 27, 1968. It is published in the Official Journal at O.J. C189, 28.07.1990 and created a new regime for service of proceedings amongst signatory states. The rules of the Brussels Convention were extended to the States belonging to the European Free Trade Association ("EFTA") by the Lugano Convention, signed on September 16, 1988. The Brussels Convention was extended successively to all the new Member States of the European Union and, most recently, by the Accession Convention of November 29, 1996 to Austria, Finland and Sweden (O.J. C15, 15.01.1997). A consolidated version of the Convention was published in 1998 (O.J. C27, 26.01.1998). Work on revision of the Brussels and Lugano Conventions led to political agreement in the Council in May 1999. There followed a proposal for a Regulation in the light of the coming into force of the Amsterdam Treaty and inclusion of judicial cooperation in civil matters within the Community framework. Accordingly, by Council Regulation (EC) 44/2001 ("the Judgments Regulation", see Vol.2 Section 5) the Brussels Convention was superseded. For a period, Denmark was no subject to this Regulation but it came to be applied in that jurisdiction by an agreement between the European Union and Demark made on October 19, 2005. The Judgments Regulation has direct effect in Member States of the European Union (aside from Denmark) and that effect is recognised in Civil Jurisdiction and Judgments Order 2001 (SI 2001/3929) which makes consequential amendments to the Civil Jurisdiction and Judgments Act 1982. For the most part, the jurisdictional rules in the Judgments Regulation reflect the rules in the Brussels and Lugano Conventions, and judicial interpretation of the latter will remain relevant where the Regulation applies. The Lugano Convention continues to apply. A summary of the central jurisdictional regime in the Judgments Regulation, the Brussels and the Lugano Conventions is provided below at paras 6.33.6 *et seq.*

Service in Scotland or Northern Ireland

6.30.6 The United Kingdom includes in addition to that of England and Wales, two other legal systems. They are those of Scotland and Northern Ireland. In certain circumstances, a claim form may be served on a defendant in either of those jurisdictions. The matter is mainly regulated by a modified version of the Judgments Regulation set out in Sch.4 to the Civil Jurisdiction and Judgments Act 1982, see para.5.7. The general rule is that persons domiciled in a part of the United Kingdom shall be sued in the courts of that part. However, a person domiciled in a part of the United Kingdom may be sued in the courts of another part insofar as that is permitted by the modified Judgments Regulation. By agreement, parties may confer jurisdiction on the courts of a particular part (r.12 cf Sch.4). The result is that cases can arise under this Convention where a claimant can bring proceedings in the High Court by serving his claim form on a defendant in Scotland or Northern Ireland. In these circumstances, the jurisdiction of the High Court is not based on service of the claim form on the defendant within the jurisdiction or on the extended jurisdiction rules provided by r.6.36.

Service in Scotland and Northern Ireland will be effective service and no permission of the court to make such service is required. This state of affairs is acknowledged by r.6.32. However where the Act does not apply, permission to serve out of the jurisdiction will be required.

Schedule 4 of the Civil Jurisdiction and Judgments Act 1982 was amended by Sch.2, paras 3 and 4 of the Civil Jurisdiction and Judgments Order 2001 broadly to bring those provisions into line with the equivalent provisions of the Judgments Regulation. Sch.2, paras 6 and 7 of the Civil Jurisdiction and Judgments Order 2001 made similar amendments to Sch.8 to the Act, which contains provisions on jurisdiction in Scotland.

Summary of service regimes for service out of the jurisdiction

The rules of service out of the jurisdiction can be divided into two categories—where permission of the court is required and where permission is not required. **6.30.7**

The situations where permission is not required are:

(1) Cases where the court has jurisdiction under the Judgments Regulation or the Brussels or Lugano Conventions (r.6.33(1)(2)).

(2) Similar cases where the defendant is domiciled in Scotland or Northern Ireland (r.6.32).

(3) Cases where the court has been given jurisdiction by statute to entertain a claim notwithstanding that the defendant is not within the jurisdiction (r.6.33(3)).

Permission is required where:

The case is outside (1) to (3) above, a jurisdictional gateway exists under r.6.36 and a court in England or Wales can be shown to be the most appropriate forum for the resolution of the dispute.

Related Sources

- Civil Jurisdiction and Judgments Act 1982 (see Vol.2 para.5–7) **6.30.8**
- Judgments Regulation (EC) No.44/2001 (see Vol.2 para.5–249)
- Civil Jurisdiction and Judgments Order 2001 (see Vol.2 para.5–200)
- Practice Direction B—Service out of the Jurisdiction (see para.6BPD.1)
- Practice Direction—Admiralty Claims (see Vol.2 para.2D–85)
- Practice Direction—Arbitration (see Vol.2 para.2E–46)
- Service Regulation (EC) No.1393/2007 (see Vol.2 para.5–22)
- The Admiralty and Commercial Court Guide (see Vol.2 para.2A–39)

Interpretation[1]

6.31 For the purposes of this Section— **6.31**

(a) "the Hague Convention" means the Convention on the service abroad of judicial and extrajudicial documents in civil or commercial matters signed at the Hague on 15 November 1965;

(b) "the 1982 Act" means the Civil Jurisdiction and Judgments Act 1982;

(c) "Civil Procedure Convention" means the Brussels and Lugano Conventions (as defined in section 1(1) of the 1982 Act) and any other Convention (including the Hague Convention) entered into by the United Kingdom regarding service out of the jurisdiction;

(d) "the Judgments Regulation" means Council Regulation (EC) No.44/2001 of 22 December 2000 on jurisdiction and the recognition and enforcement of judgments in civil and commercial matters, as amended from time to time and as applied by the Agreement made on 19 October 2005 between the European Community

[1] Added by the Civil Procedure (Amendment) Rules 2008 (SI 2008/2178).

and the Kingdom of Denmark on jurisdiction and the recognition and enforcement of judgments in civil and commercial matters;

(e) "the Service Regulation" means Regulation (EC) No.1393/2007 of the European Parliament and of the Council of 13 November 2007 on the service in the Member States of judicial and extrajudicial documents in civil or commercial matters (service of documents), and repealing Council Regulation (EC) No.1348/2000, as amended from time to time and as applied by the Agreement made on 19 October 2005 between the European Community and the Kingdom of Denmark on the service of judicial and extrajudicial documents in civil and commercial matters;

(f) "Commonwealth State" means a state listed in Schedule 3 to the British Nationality Act 1981;

(g) "Contracting State" has the meaning given by section 1(3) of the 1982 Act;

(h) "Convention territory" means the territory or territories of any Contracting State to which the Brussels or Lugano Conventions (as defined in section 1(1) of the 1982 Act) apply; and

(i) "domicile" is to be determined—

(i) in relation to a Convention territory, in accordance with sections 41 to 46 of the 1982 Act; and

(ii) in relation to a Member State, in accordance with the Judgments Regulation and paragraphs 9 to 12 of Schedule 1 to the Civil Jurisdiction and Judgments Order 2001.

Service of the claim form where the permission of the court is not required—Scotland and Northern Ireland[1]

6.32 **6.32—(1) The claimant may serve the claim form on a defendant in Scotland or Northern Ireland where each claim made against the defendant to be served and included in the claim form is a claim which the court has power to determine under the 1982 Act and—**

(a) no proceedings between the parties concerning the same claim are pending in the courts of any other part of the United Kingdom; and

(b) (i) the defendant is domiciled in the United Kingdom;

(ii) the proceedings are within paragraph 11 of Schedule 4 to the 1982 Act; or

(iii) the defendant is a party to an agreement conferring jurisdiction, within paragraph 12 of Schedule 4 to the 1982 Act.

(2) The claimant may serve the claim form on a defendant in Scotland or Northern Ireland where each claim made against the defendant to be served and included in the claim form is a claim which the court has power to determine under any enactment other *than the 1982* Act notwithstanding that—

[1] Added by the Civil Procedure (Amendment) Rules 2008 (SI 2008/2178).

(a) the person against whom the claim is made is not within the jurisdiction; or

(b) the facts giving rise to the claim did not occur within the jurisdiction.

Effect of rule (r.6.32)

6.32.1 See commentary following r.6.33.

Service of the claim form where the permission of the court is not required—out of the United Kingdom[1]

6.33—(1) The claimant may serve the claim form on a defendant out of the United Kingdom where each claim made against the defendant to be served and included in the claim form is a claim which the court has power to determine under the 1982 Act and— 6.33

(a) no proceedings between the parties concerning the same claim are pending in the courts of any other part of the United Kingdom or any other Convention territory; and

(b) (i) the defendant is domiciled in the United Kingdom or in any Convention territory;

(ii) the proceedings are within article 16 of Schedule 1 or article 16 of Schedule 3C to the 1982 Act; or

(iii) the defendant is a party to an agreement conferring jurisdiction, within article 17 of Schedule 1 or article 17 of Schedule 3C to the 1982 Act.

(2) The claimant may serve the claim form on a defendant out of the United Kingdom where each claim made against the defendant to be served and included in the claim form is a claim which the court has power to determine under the Judgments Regulation and—

(a) no proceedings between the parties concerning the same claim are pending in the courts of any other part of the United Kingdom or any other Member State; and

(i) the defendant is domiciled in the United Kingdom or in any Member State;

(ii) the proceedings are within article 22 of the Judgments Regulation; or

(iii) the defendant is a party to an agreement conferring jurisdiction, within article 23 of the Judgments Regulation.

(3) The claimant may serve the claim form on a defendant out *of the United Kingdom* where each claim made against the defendant to be served and included in the claim form is a claim which the court has power to determine other than under the 1982 Act or the Judgments Regulation, notwithstanding that—

(a) the person against whom the claim is made is not within the jurisdiction; or

[1] Added by the Civil Procedure (Amendment) Rules 2008 (SI 2008/2178).

(b) the facts giving rise to the claim did not occur within the jurisdiction.

Effect of rules (rr.6.32 and 6.33)

6.33.1 The general rule is that a claim form cannot be served on a defendant out of the jurisdiction; that is to say, out of England and Wales (r.2.3(1)). The circumstances stated in r.6.32 and r.6.33 provide for exceptions. Where the circumstances stated in r.6.32 apply, the claimant may serve the claim form on a defendant in Scotland or Northern Ireland. Where the circumstances stated in r.6.33 apply, the claimant may serve the claim form on a defendant out of the United Kingdom. (Before October 1, 2008, the provisions in these rules were found in a single rule, r.6.19.)

Where the claimant intends to serve a claim form on a defendant under r.6.32 or r.6.33, the notice referred to in r.6.34 must be filed and served.

The Civil Jurisdiction and Judgments Act 1982 and the Brussels and Lugano Conventions

6.33.2 The Brussels Convention was entered into by the Member States of the European Community. It regulates jurisdiction and the recognition and enforcement of judgments in civil and commercial matters. The Brussels Convention was incorporated into domestic law by the Civil Jurisdiction and Judgments Act 1982 ("the 1982 Act").

The Lugano Convention was entered into by the Member States of the European Free Trade Association and is closely modelled on the Brussels Convention. It was incorporated into domestic law by the Civil Jurisdiction and Judgments Act 1991.

Service without the need for permission (r.6.33)

6.33.3 *Rule 6.33(1)*—Rule 6.33(1) states that a claim form may be served out of the jurisdiction on a defendant without the permission of the court provided that each claim against that defendant is a claim which by virtue of the Civil Jurisdiction and Judgments Act 1982 the court has power to hear and determine. A claimant may take advantage of this rule and serve the defendant out of the jurisdiction without first obtaining the court's permission provided the conditions stated in r.6.33(1) are satisfied. Under the 1982 Act, jurisdiction arising under various Conventions is conferred on the English courts.

The conditions stated in r.6.33(1) are:

(i) no proceedings between the parties concerning the same cause of action are pending in the courts of any other part of the United Kingdom or of any other Convention territory; and

(ii) either the defendant is domiciled in any part of the United Kingdom or in any other Convention territory, or the proceedings begun by the claim form are proceedings to which art.16 of Sch.1, 3C of the 1982 Act or para.11 of Sch.4 to that Act refers, or the defendant is a party to an agreement conferring jurisdiction to which art.17 of Sch.1, 3C to the 1982 Act or para.12 of Sch.4 to that Act refers.

For definition of "Convention territory", see r.6.31(h).

6.33.4 *Rule 6.33(2)*—Rule 6.33(2) states that a claim may be served out of the jurisdiction on a defendant without the permission of the court provided that each claim against that defendant is a claim which by virtue of the Judgments Regulation the court has the power to determine. A claimant may take advantage of this rule and serve the defendant out of the jurisdiction without first obtaining the permission of the court provided the conditions set out in r.6.33(2) are satisfied. The Judgments Regulation is directly applicable in the United Kingdom and, subject to certain conditions, confers jurisdiction on the English courts.

The conditions stated in r.6.33(2) are:

(i) no proceedings between the parties concerning the same claim are pending in the courts of any other part of the United Kingdom or any other Regulation State; and

(ii) either the defendant is domiciled in any part of the United Kingdom or in any other Regulation State, or the proceedings begun by the claim form are proceedings to which art.22 refers, or the defendant is a party to an agreement conferring jurisdiction to which art.23 of the Judgments Regulation refers.

"Member State" means every Member State of the EC.

Rule 6.33(3)—Rule 6.33(3) states that a claim form may be served out of the jurisdiction on a defendant without the permission of the court provided that each claim against the defendant is a claim which the court is empowered to hear by any other enactment (as to which see paras (1) and (2) of r.6.33) notwithstanding that the defendant is abroad and the relevant conduct occurred overseas. In the case of *In re Harrods (Buenos Aires) Ltd* [1992] Ch. 72, CA, the background to this rule was explained and it was said (at p.116 per Dillon L.J.) that, to be within what is now r.6.33(3) an enactment must, if it does not use the precise wording of the rule, at least indicate on its face that it is expressly contemplating proceedings against persons who are not within the jurisdiction of the court or where the wrongful act, neglect or default giving rise to the claim did not take place within the jurisdiction. (In the *Harrods* case it was held that RSC O.11, r.1(2)(b) (now r.6.33(3)) did not permit the service out of the jurisdiction without leave, of a petition under the Companies Act 1985 s.459). **6.33.5**

It should be noted that where the claim form makes several claims against the defendant, each claim must fall within these categories. It is conceivable that a claim form may make claims against two (or more) defendants out of the jurisdiction and that the claim or claims made against one defendant will all fall within the categories mentioned above, with the result that permissions to serve the claim form on him will not be required, but that the claim or claims made against the other defendant will not all fall within the categories, with the result that permissions to serve the claim form on him will be required.

The Civil Jurisdiction and Judgment Acts 1982 and 1991 and the Judgments Regulation

Introduction—As was explained above (para.6.30.5) the Judgments Regulation came into force on March 1, 2002 and is directly effective in all Member States except Denmark. The necessary changes to the Civil Jurisdiction and Judgments Act 1982 were made by the Civil Jurisdiction and Judgments Order 2001 (SI 2001/3929). **6.33.6**

References below will be generally given to articles in the Judgments Regulation, with corresponding references to articles in the Brussels Convention in parentheses.

The text of the Judgments Regulation and of the Civil Jurisdiction and Judgments Order 2001 (SI 2001/3929) is at Vol.2, Section 5. The Regulation itself is directly applicable in Member States. Consequential statutory amendments may be found in the Civil Jurisdiction and Judgments Act 1982 (Amendment) Order 2000 (SI 2000/1824). For full details see the current edition of the International Litigation Procedure Reports.

For detailed commentaries on the rules see the leading textbooks, e.g. Dicey, Morris and Collins, *The Conflict of Laws*, 14th edn (London: Sweet & Maxwell, 2006) and A. Briggs and P. Rees, *Civil Jurisdiction and Judgments*, 4th edn (Informa Finance, 2005).

The discussion relates primarily to the Brussels Convention, but much of the relevant jurisprudence relates equally to the Judgments Regulation and the Lugano Convention. The Lugano Convention is closely modelled on the 1968 Brussels Convention. However, the Lugano Convention was entered into between the members of the European Free Trade Association while the Brussels Convention was entered into by the members of the European Union.

The Court of Justice of the European Communities ("the Court of Justice") has jurisdiction to give rulings on the interpretation of the Brussels Convention under the 1971 Protocol to the Brussels Convention (Sch.2 to the 1982 Act), but not in the case of the Lugano Convention. However, Protocol No.2 to the Lugano Convention makes any ruling on the Brussels Convention by the Court of Justice highly relevant to any decision as to the interpretation of the corresponding provisions of the Lugano Convention: *Agnew v Lansforsakringsbolagens AB* [2001] 1 A.C. 223, HL.

The Judgments Regulation and the Conventions regulate jurisdiction issues in litigation between parties domiciled in Regulation and Contracting States. They do so at the price of rigidity (*Airbus Industrie G.I.E. v Patel* [1999] 1 A.C. 119, HL), and where they operate, they preclude a common law analysis of which forum is the most appropriate and convenient to deal with a particular case.

Where jurisdiction in this country is justifiable under the Judgments Regulation or Conventions, it is not necessary to obtain permission to serve proceedings outside the jurisdiction. In these circumstances, the jurisdiction of the High Court under the Regulation or Conventions is not based on service of the claim form on the defendant within the jurisdiction or on the extended jurisdiction rules provided by r.6.36. Service elsewhere within the Community in accordance with the Service Regulation will be effective service and no permission of the court to make such service is required. This is acknowledged by r.6.33.

The object of the Regulation and the Conventions is not to unify the rules of substantive law and of procedure of different Regulation and Convention States, but to determine which courts have jurisdiction in disputes relating to civil and commercial matters in relations between Regulation and Convention States and to facilitate the enforcement of judgments (see *Shevill v Presse Alliance* [1996] A.C. 959, HL).

6.33.7 *Interpretation*—The 1982 Act authorises references to reports of official commentators to assist interpretation of the Brussels and Lugano Conventions; see ss.3 and 3B.

The jurisprudence of the Court of Justice distinguishes between those concepts in the Brussels Convention which have an autonomous or independent meaning, irrespective of their content in the law of any particular national system, and those which require the national court to give content to the Convention concept in accordance with its domestic law; *Canada Trust Co v Stolzenberg* [2002] 1 A.C. 1, HL.

On the need for homogeneity of interpretation of particular concepts, see *R. v Secretary of State for the Home Department, Ex p. Adan* [2001] 2 A.C. 477, HL, and *Martin Peters Bauunternehmung GmbH v Zuid Nederlandse Aannemers Vereniging (34/82)* [1983] E.C.R. 987.

6.33.8 *Scope*—The Judgments Regulation and Conventions regulate jurisdiction in civil and commercial matters between parties domiciled in Regulation and Contracting States. For this purpose "civil and commercial matters" has a generic Regulation and Convention meaning. It has been held to cover, among other things, forfeiture proceedings in relation to unauthorised use of trademarks and false trade descriptions; *R. v Crown Court at Harrow, Ex p. UNIC Centre SARL* [2000] 1 W.L.R. 2112.

6.33.9 *Burden and standard of proof*—The burden is upon the claimant to satisfy the court that it is seised of the case, but where a court is so seised and a defendant seeks a stay to give effect to an exclusive jurisdiction clause in respect of a non-Convention or non-Regulation state, the burden is probably on him (*Konkola Copper Mines Plc v Caromin* [2006] EWCA Civ 5; [2006] 1 Lloyd's Rep. 410, CA). The standard of proof is that of a good arguable case (*Canada Trust v Stolzenberg (No.2)* [1998] 1 W.L.R. 547, CA and *Konkola Copper Mines Plc v Caromin*, op cit). As to the meaning of a good arguable case, see *Bols Distilleries BV v Superior Yacht Services Ltd* [2006] UKPC 45; [2007] 1 W.L.R. 12; [2007] 1 All E.R. (Comm) 461; [2007] 1 Lloyd's Rep. 683; *WPP Holdings Italy Srl v Benatti* [2007] EWCA Civ 263; [2007] 1 W.L.R. 2316; [2007] 2 All E.R. (Comm) 525; [2008] 1 Lloyd's Rep. 396.

6.33.10 *The basic jurisdictional regime*—The basic rule is that persons domiciled in a Regulation or Contracting State should, whatever their nationality, be sued in the courts of that State. However, a person domiciled in a Regulation or Contracting State may be sued in the courts of another Regulation or Contracting State insofar as that is permitted by the Judgments Regulation and Conventions (see art.2 of the Judgments Regulation and art.2 of the Brussels Convention).

For a situation in which the defendant company has no real business either to administer or to operate on the date on which proceedings are issued; see *Ministry of Defence and Support of the Armed Forces for Iran v Faz Aviation* [2007] EWHC 1042 (Comm); [2008] 1 All E.R. (Comm) 372; [2007] I.L.Pr. 42. A very wealthy person with numerous houses and business interests in various parts of the world is not necessarily domiciled within the jurisdiction for the purposes of s.41 of the Civil Jurisdiction and Judgments Act 1982 or the Judgments Regulations because he owns two substantial homes in England; *High Tech International AG v Deripaska* [2006] EWHC 3276 (QBD); [2007] E.M.L.R. 15; *Chervey v Deripaska* [2007] EWHC 965 (Comm); [2007] 2 All E.R. (Comm) 785; [2007] I.L.Pr. 49.

Where the claimant has founded jurisdiction on art.2 of the Brussels Convention on the basis of one of the defendants' domicile in a Contracting State, that state cannot decline jurisdiction on forum conveniens grounds in favour of the courts of a non-contracting state, where the other defendants are not domiciled in a Contracting State; see *Owusu v Jackson* (C281/02) [2005] Q.B. 801, ECJ.

It remains to be seen whether the domicile of both parties in Contracting States may make a difference, where one of them attempts to sue the other in a non-Contracting State.

The House of Lords has referred to the European Court of Justice the question whether it was consistent with the Judgment Regulation for a court of a Member State to make an order to restrain a person from commencing or continuing proceedings in another Member State on the ground that such proceedings were in breach of an arbitration agreement; *The Front Comor* [2007] UKHL 4; [2007] 1 All E.R. (Comm) 794; [2007] I.L.Pr. 20, HL.

Article 57(2)(a) of the Brussels Convention is to be interpreted as meaning that the court of a Contracting State in which a defendant domiciled in another Contracting State is sued can derive its jurisdiction from a specialised convention to which the first State is a party as well and which contains specific rules on jurisdiction, even where the defendant, in due course of the proceedings has submitted the pleas on the merits; *Nurnberger Allgemeine Versicherungs AG v Portbridge Transport International BV (C148/03)* [2005] 1 Lloyd's Rep. 592, ECJ.

Where the claimant is not domiciled in a Contracting State, he is nevertheless subject to the Judgments Regulation or Conventions as appropriate if he seeks to sue a defendant domiciled in a Regulation or Contracting State different from the Defendant's state of domicile; *Universal General Insurance Co (UGIC) v Group Josi Reinsurance Co SA* (C412/98) [2000] E.C.R. I-5925; [2001] Q.B. 68, ECJ. It was there held that the application of the jurisdictional rules of the Convention generally depends on whether the defendant has its seat or domicile in a Contracting State, and it is only in the exceptional cases expressly provided for in the Conventions that the claimant's domicile is material. Accordingly, the Judgments Regulation and the Conventions can in principle apply to a dispute between a defendant domiciled in a contracting state and a claimant domiciled in a non-Regulation or non-Contracting State.

The English court has jurisdiction over a claim for costs against a non-party domiciled in another Regulation or Contracting State in the context of the English proceedings to which the costs relate; *National Justice Compania Naviera SA v Prudential Assurance Co Ltd (The Ikarian Reefer) (No.2)* [2000] 1 W.L.R. 603; [2000] 1 All E.R. 37; [2000] 1 Lloyd's Rep. 129, CA.

Actions against foreign States—The Judgments Regulation does not preclude reliance upon state immunity even where the relevant act is motivated by malice. In most cases where state immunity is invoked it would be a waste of time fully to review all the facts of the case with a view to deciding the issue of proportionality in connection with the right to a fair trial; *Grovit v De Nederlandsche Bank* [2005] EWHC 2944 (QB); [2006] 1 W.L.R. 3323; [2006]1 Lloyds Rep. 636; [2006] 1 All E.R. (Comm) 397 (confirmed on appeal [2007] EWCA Civ 953; [2008] 1 W.L.R. 51; [2008] 1 All E.R. (Comm) 106; [2008] I.L.Pr. 19). **6.33.11**

Special provisions on jurisdiction—"Special provisions" on jurisdiction allowing derogation from the default jurisdiction of the defendant's home state appear in arts 5 and 6 of the Judgments Regulation (arts 5 and 6 of the Brussels Convention). Due to them being derogations, they are to be construed restrictively; *Kalfelis v Bankhaus Schroder Munchmeyer Hengst & Co* (189/87) [1988] E.C.R. 5565, ECJ, at para.19; *Kleinwort Benson Ltd v Glasgow City Council* [1999] 1 A.C. 153, HL. In applying the *Kalfelis* test to art.6(1) of the Judgments Regulation, a broad common sense approach is to be adopted; *FKI Engineering Ltd v Dewind Holdings* [2007] EWHC 72 (Comm); [2007] I.L.Pr. 17; however, see below. **6.33.12**

Article 6(1) of the Judgments Regulation cannot be interpreted in such a way as to make its application dependant on the effects of domestic rules, therefore it can be relied upon where an action is brought in a member state against a defendant who is domiciled there and a co-defendant domiciled in another member state where, under a provision of the state in which the action is brought, the action is regarded as inadmissible from the time it was brought in relation to the first defendant; *Reisch Montage Attorney General* v Kiesel Baumaschinen Handels GmbH (C-103/05) [2007] I.L.Pr. 10, ECJ.

Article 6(1) of the Judgments Regulation does not include a requirement that the action brought against the different defendants have identical legal bases. For decisions to be regarded as contradictory the divergence must arise in the context of the same situation of law and fact; *Freeport Plc v Anderson* (C-98/06) [2008] Q.B. 634; [2007] I.L.Pr. 58.

Alternative or contingent claims are commonplace in domestic litigation and art.6(1) of the Judgments Regulation is not to be given so restricted a meaning as to exclude them; *FKI Engineering Ltd v Dewind Holdings Ltd* [2008] EWCA Civ 316; [2008] I.L.Pr. 33.

Where it is expedient to hear claims together under art.6(1) there is no further need to establish separately that the claims are not brought with the sole object of ousting the jurisdiction of the courts of the Member State where one of the defendants is domiciled. See *Freeport Plc v Anderson*, above.

Article 6(1) of the Brussels Convention does not apply in European patent infringement proceedings involving a number of companies established in various contracting states, where those companies, which belong to the same group, may have acted in an identical or similar manner in accordance with a common policy elaborated by one of them; *Roche Nederland BV v Primus and Goldenberg* (C-539/03) [2007] I.L.Pr. 9. If a patentee possessing a bundle of European patent applications wished to enforce them, it has to do so on a state by state basis; *SanDisk Corp v Koninklijke Philips Electronics NV* [2007] EWHC 332 (Ch); [2007] I.L.Pr. 22 (Pumfrey J.). See also para.6.19.18 below.

6.33.13 *Matters relating to a contract*—By art.5(1)(a) of the Judgments Regulation (art.5(1) of the Brussels Convention), in matters relating to a contract, a person domiciled in a Regulation State may be sued in the courts of the place of performance of the obligation in question.

Where an English court was first seised of proceedings served on the defendant bank, which was domiciled in England, there was no jurisdiction to order a stay in favour of proceedings in Switzerland on the grounds of forum non conveniens; both England and Switzerland being subject to the Lugano Convention, although articles of the Convention gave the claimants a right, at their discretion, to litigate in Switzerland. The discretion is not that of the court. The situation is no different in the case of a bank with overseas branches; *Mahme Trust v Lloyds TSB Bank Plc* [2004] EWHC 1931; [2004] I.L.Pr. 43.

The relevant obligation for this purpose is the obligation on which the claim is based; *Ets. A. de Bloos S.P.R.L. v Société en commandite par actions Bouyer* (14/76) [1976] E.C.R. 1497; *Custom Made Commercial Ltd v Stawa Metallbau GmbH* (C-288/92) [1994] E.C.R. 2913; *Royal & Sun Alliance Insurance Plc v MK Digital FZE (Cyprus Ltd)* [2006] EWCA Civ 629; [2007] I.L.Pr. 3; [2006] 2 Lloyd's Rep. 110. A payment obligation may well be the obligation in question on this basis even though conditions of payment are to be satisfied elsewhere; *Chailease Finance Corp v Credit Agricole Indosuez* [2000] 1 Lloyd's Rep. 348, CA. Where a number of obligations are in issue, it is the principal obligation which determines jurisdiction; see *Royal & Sun Alliance* case above.

Where relations between parties are characterised by the absence of obligations freely assumed by one party towards another on the occasion of negotiations with a view to the formation of a contract and by a possible breach of rules of law, an action founded on the pre-contractual liability of the defendant is a matter relating to tort, delict or quasi-delict within art.5(3) of the Brussels Convention and not within art.5(1). See *Case Fonderie Officine Meccaniche Tacconi SpA v Heinrich Wagner Sinto Maschinenfabrik GmbH (HWS)* (C-334/00), September 17, 2002, unrep.

A finding that a legal action was not contractual in nature for the purposes of art.13.1 of the Brussels Convention does not prevent that action relating to a contract for the purposes of art.13(3); *In re Jurisdiction in a Claim Based on a Prize Draw Notification* [2007] I.L.Pr. 15.

In determining the relevant obligation, evidence of a course of dealing, for example the place where payments are made, may assist; *Deutsche Ruckversicherung AG v La Fondaria Assicurazioni SpA* [2001] 2 Lloyd's Rep. 621 (Steel J.).

"Obligation in question" does not include a quasi-contractual obligation to make restitution, as to which the default position applies under art.2; *Kleinwort Benson Ltd v Glasgow City Council* [1999] 1 A.C. 153, HL.

On the other hand, the obligation in question could be the obligation to make full disclosure on placement of reinsurance in London; *Agnew v Lansforsakringsbolagens AB* [2001] 1 A.C. 223; [2000] Lloyd's Rep 317; [2000] 1 All E.R. 737, HL.

The place of performance of the obligation in question is determined by the law governing the contract; *GIE Groupe Concorde* v Master of the Vessel Suhadiwarno Panjan (C-440/97) [1999] E.C.R. I-6307. This may accordingly involve issues under the Rome Convention; *Raiffeisen Zentralbank Osterreich Aktiengesellschaft v National Bank of Greece SA* [1999] 1 Lloyd's Rep. 408; *Chailease Finance Corporation v Credit Agricole Indosuez* [2000] 1 Lloyd's Rep. 348, CA; *Definitely Maybe (Touring) Ltd v Marek Lieberberg Konzertagentur GmbH* [2001] 1 W.L.R. 1745 (Morison J.).

An English court does not have jurisdiction under art.5(1) of the Judgments Regulation where a guarantor of general average has the right to make payment outside the jurisdiction; *Mora Shipping Inc of Monrovia v AXA Corporate Solutions Assurance SA* [2005] EWCA Civ 1069; [2006] I.L.Pr. 10, CA.

In *Kenburn Waste Management Ltd v Bergmann* [2002] EWCA Civ 98, the Court of Appeal determined that in proceedings concerning a negative obligation made by a German resident to refrain from communicating with individuals or companies in the United Kingdom, the proper law of the obligation in question was English law and the place of performance of that obligation was the United Kingdom. However, where an obligation not to do something has no geographical limit and no specific place for performance can be identified, it is art.2 which governs the position; *Besix SA v Wasserreinigungsbau Alfred Kretzschmar GmbH & Co KG (Wabag)* (C256/00) [2003] 1 W.L.R. 1113.

Where a warranty is given as to existing rights in intellectual property that are transferred in London, there can be a good arguable case that London is the place of performance of the warranty for the purposes of art.5(1) of the Lugano Convention; *Crucial Music Corp v Klondyke Management AG* [2007] EWHC 1782 (Ch); [2008] 1 All E.R. (Comm) 642; [2007] I.L.Pr. 54.

As a matter of English law the place for performance of a carrier's obligation to use due diligence to make the ship seaworthy is the load port; The "Sea Maas" [1999] 2 Lloyd's Rep. 281.

Generally, determination of the place of performance will involve weighing factors in each direction; *Viskase Ltd v Paul Kiefel GmbH* [1999] 3 All E.R. 362 (this was a claim by the English purchaser of machines to be supplied by the German defendant with delivery in Germany. The English claimant sued for damages on the basis that the machines were not fit for their purpose. It was held by the Court of Appeal that the obligations of manufacture and supply in question, which formed the basis of the claimant's damages claim, were to be performed in Germany. Accordingly, the English court did not have jurisdiction under art.5(1)). *MBM Fabri-Clad Ltd v Eisen-und-Huttenwerke Thale AG* [2000] C.L.C. 373; [2000] I.L.Pr. 505, CA was a damages claim by the English purchaser of rain panels for GCHQ which the German Defendant had agreed to supply in England. It was held by the Court of Appeal that the obligation in question on which the claim for damages was based was the obligation to deliver in England. Accordingly, the English Courts had jurisdiction.

Article 5(1)(b) of the Judgments Regulation expressly provides that the place of performance of the obligation in question shall be in the case of:

(i) the sale of goods, the place in a Regulation State where, under the contract, the goods were delivered or should have been delivered; and

(ii) the provision of services, the place in a Regulation State where, under the contract, the services were provided or should have been provided.

Where there are several places of delivery of goods, "place of delivery" for the purposes of art.5(1)(b) of the Judgments Convention has to be understood as the place with the closest linking factor between the contract and the court with jurisdiction which would, as a general rule, be at the place of the principal delivery. If a principal place of delivery cannot be determined the claimant may sue in the court for the place of delivery of its choice; *Color Drack GmbH v Lexx International Vertriebs GmbH* (C-386/05) [2007] I.L.Pr. 35; [2008] 1All E.R. (Comm) 169.

In the case of documentary sales where the place of destination differs from the place of contractual delivery, it is appropriate to interpret art.5(1)(b) as referring to the place where delivery is due under the contract; *Scottish & Newcastle International Ltd v Othon Ghalanos Ltd* [2008] UKHL 11; [2008] I.L.Pr. 30, HL.

Where, under the terms of the Judgments Regulation, an entity could bring proceedings within the jurisdiction to assert a contractual obligation, it is open to the entity against which the assertion could be made to seek within the jurisdiction a declaration to the contrary effect, even where the existence of a contract is denied; *Equitas v Wave City Shipping* [2005] EWHC 923 (Comm); [2005] 2 All E.R. (Comm) 301.

Matters relating to tort, delict or quasi-delict

By art.5(3) of the Judgments Regulation (art.5(3) of the Brussels Convention), in matters relating to tort, delict or quasi-delict, a person domiciled in a Regulation State may be sued in the courts for the place where the harmful event occurred. As to the exercise of the discretion; see *Mahme Trust v Lloyds TSB Bank Plc*, at para.6.33.13 above. **6.33.14**

For the purposes of art.5(3) of the Judgments Regulation "tort, delict or quasi-delict" has an autonomous meaning, and covers actions which seek to establish the liability of a defendant and which are not related to a contract within the meaning of art.5(1); *Mazur Media Ltd v Mazur Media GmbH* [2004] EWHC 1566 (Ch); [2004] 1 W.L.R. 2966.

A preventive action brought by a consumer protection organisation for the purpose of preventing a trader from using terms considered to be unfair in contracts with private individuals is a matter relating to tort, delict or quasi-delict within the meaning of art.5(3) of the Convention; *Verein für Konsumenteninformation v Karl Heinz Henkel* (C-167/00), October 1, 2002, unrep.

The location of the harmful event can be both the place where loss is sustained and the place where the event occurs which precipitates loss; see *Handelskwekerij GJ Bier BV v Mines de Potasse d'Alsace SA (C-2176)* [1976] E.C.R. 1735, where French mines caused pollution of the Rhine damaging Bier's horticulture business in Holland. See also *Kronhoffer v Maier* (C-168/02) [2005] 1 Lloyd's Rep 284; [2004] All E.R. (EC) 939, and *Sunderland Marine Mutual Insurance Co Ltd v Wiseman* [2007] EWHC 1460 (Comm); [2007] 2 Lloyd's Rep. 308. In a case of negligent mis-statement, it is likely to be the place where the statement is made; see *Domicrest Ltd v Swiss Bank Corp* [1999] Q.B. 548 and *Sunderland Marine Mutual Insurance Co Ltd v Wiseman* [2007] EWHC 1460 (Comm); [2007] 2 Lloyd's Rep. 308. See also *London Helicopters Ltd v Heliportugal LDA-INAC* [2006] EWHC 108; [2006] 1 All E.R. (Comm) 595; [2006] I.L.Pr. 28 for a consideration of the place where damage occurred and that of the harmful event giving rise to the damage. Where a claim for damage to goods is made by the consignee against the actual carrier with whom he does not have a contract, the claim is within art.5(3) rather than art.5(1). The place where the harmful event occurred in such a case will be taken as the place where the cargo is to be discharged; see *Reunion Europeenne SA v Spliethoffs Bevrachtingskantoor BV (C5197)* [2000] Q.B. 690.

Where a defendant procures the payment of money by a third party from a foreign bank account into his own account in England, and thereafter uses that money for his own purposes in England, a harmful act within the meaning of art.5(3) has occurred in England; see *Cronos Containers NV v Palatin* [2002] EWHC 2819 (Comm); [2003] 2 Lloyd's Rep 489. See Bank of Tokyo-Mitsubishi Ltd v Baskan Gida Sanayi Ve Pazarlama AS [2004] EWHC 945 (Ch); [2004] I.L.Pr. 26 for the place of loss where banks within the jurisdiction are victims of a conspiracy in which a letter of credit is drawn outside the jurisdiction.

Where an agreement is made pursuant to a misrepresentation that procures a greater price for the assets acquired than would otherwise have been the case, the place of the making of the agreement is that where a harmful event has occurred for the purposes of art.5(3) of the Lugano Convention; *Crucial Music Corp v Klondyke Management AD* [2007] EWHC 1782; [2007] I.L.Pr. 54.

The term "harmful event" is an autonomous Regulation and Convention concept, not to be determined by reference to national law. In *Henderson v Jaouen* [2002] EWCA Civ 75, CA; [2002] 1 W.L.R. 2971; [2002] I.L.Pr. 32, the issue was whether, where a French civil court had awarded damages to a party injured in a traffic accident with the right to return to court to seek a further award, that party could issue proceedings in the English courts on the basis that the "harmful event", namely the deterioration of his condition, had occurred in England. The Court of Appeal held that the "harmful event" was the original tort which had occurred in France and that "aggravation" was not a fresh tort but a worsening of the condition arising directly from the original tort. The English court had no jurisdiction.

In a libel case there may be a number of different places where harm occurs depending on the range of publication, and the English courts will not regard the tort as actionable only in the jurisdiction of primary publication; *Lukowiak v Unidad Editorial SA (No.1)* [2001] E.M.L.R. 46; *Shevill v Presse Alliance SA* [1996] A.C. 959, HL. Moreover this jurisdiction is not to be declined on the ground of forum non conveniens; *Berezovsky v Michaels* [2000] 1 W.L.R 1004, HL.

A party may seek a negative declaration within the same jurisdiction as positive relief can be sought under art.5(3) of the Judgments Regulation; see *Equitas v Wave City Shipping* [2005] EWHC 923 (Comm); [2005] 2 All E.R. (Comm) 301. A claim under the Civil Liability (Contribution) Act 1978 falls within the European concept of "matters relating to tort, delict or quasi-delict" and therefore falls within art.5(3) of the Regulation; *Hewden Tower Cranes Ltd v Wolffkran GmbH* [2007] EWHC 857 (TCC); [2007] 2 Lloyd's Rep. 138; [2007] I.L.Pr. 43.

6.33.15 *Claims for restitution*—In *Kleinwort Benson v Glasgow City Council* [1999] 1 A.C. 153; [1997] 4 All E.R. 641, HL, one of the cases arising from local authority swap transactions, Lord Goff said, at p.172, that a claim for restitution such as was made in that case could not be brought within art.5(3), "if only because a claim based on unjust enrichment does not, apart from exceptional circumstances, presuppose either a harmful event or a threatened wrong".

However this analysis has been distinguished in constructive trust cases because a claim based on a constructive trust does presuppose a harmful event, constituted either by a breach of fiduciary duty or alternatively dishonest assistance in it; see *Casio Computer Co Ltd v Sayo (No.3)* [2001] EWCA Civ 661, CA, and *Dexter Ltd v Harley The Times*, April 2, 2001. See also *Cronos Containers NV v Palatin* [2002] EWHC 2819 (Comm). Where an act of dishonest assistance has been undertaken in this jurisdiction, art.5(3) jurisdiction is not to be displaced on the basis of subtle causation arguments to the effect that by the time of the relevant act of assistance, the claimant's loss had already been sustained; *Casio Computer Co Ltd v Sayo (No.3)*, op cit per Tuckey L.J. at paras 13 to16, and per Pill L.J. at para.50.

Activities of a branch or agency

By art.5(5) of the Judgments Regulation (art.5(5) of the Brussels Convention), as regards a dispute arising out of the operations of a branch, agency or other establishment, a person domiciled in a Member State may be sued in the courts for the place in which the branch, agency or other establishment is situated. In tort, as well as in contract, all that is necessary to establish jurisdiction under art.5(5) is such nexus between the operations of the branch and the dispute as renders it natural to describe the dispute as one which has arisen out of the operations of the branch; *Anton Durbeck GmbH v Den Norske Bank ASA* [2003] EWCA Civ 147; [2003] Q.B. 1160, CA. **6.33.16**

Trusts

By art.5(6) of the Judgments Regulation a person domiciled in a Member State may, in another Member State, be sued as settler, trustee or beneficiary of a trust, created as provided in the article, in the courts of the Member State in which the trust is domiciled. Prima facie, the system of law with which a trust has its closest and most real connection is the governing system of law, not the geographical location nor the jurisdiction with which it has its closet and most real connection; *Gomez v Gomez-Monche Vives* [2008] EWHC 29 (Ch); [2008] 3 W.L.R. 309; [2008] 1 All E.R. (Comm) 273. **6.33.17**

The natural meaning of the words used in art.5(6) requires the court to ask whether the claim is brought against the defendant in his or her capacity as a beneficiary, rather than someone not beneficially entitled to moneys received, and the article should be construed restrictively since it is a derogation from the basic principle of domicile in the Judgments Regulation; see *Gomez v Gomez-Monche Vives*, above.

For the purposes of art.5(6) the donee of a fiduciary power should not necessarily be equated with a trustee; *Gomez v Gomez-Monche Vives*, above.

Co-defendants

Article 6 of the Judgments Regulation (art.6 of the Brussels Convention) provides: **6.33.18**

"A person domiciled in a Contracting State may also be sued

(1) where he is one of a number of defendants, in the courts for the place where any one of them is domiciled;

(2) as a third party in an action on a warranty or guarantee or in any third-party proceedings, in the court seized of the original proceedings, unless these were instituted solely with the object of removing him from the jurisdiction of the court which would be competent in his case.

(3) on a counterclaim arising from the same contract or facts on which the original claim was based, in the court in which the original claim is pending."

The relevant date under art.6(1) for determining whether the English court has jurisdiction over a prospective co-defendant is the date when the claim form is issued; see *Petrotrade Inc v Smith* [1999] 1 W.L.R. 457.

Where the existence of proceedings against one defendant in England is the basis for service of proceedings on other defendants in other Contracting States under art.6, the claimant must show a good arguable case that the defendant sued in England was domiciled in England when the claim form was issued. It is not necessary that the proceedings should at that stage have been served; *Canada Trust Co v Stolzenberg (No.2)* [2002] 1 A.C. 1, HL.

For the test as to whether proceedings are sufficiently related to justify service on a third party under art.6(1), see para.6.19.10 above and the discussion of Priority of Jurisdiction, below.

Article 6(2) does not impose any obligation on the court to accede to a request to join a third party; see *Kongress Agentur Hagen GmbH v Zeehcghe BV* [1990] E.C.R.

I-1845. It must be established that it is appropriate to override the third party's right to be sued in the country of his domicile; see *Kinnear v Falcon.lms NV* [1996] 1 W.L.R. 920; *Knauf UK GmbH v British Gypsum Ltd* [2002] 2 Lloyd's Rep. 416, CA.

Article 6(2) will not prevail over a contrary jurisdiction agreement between the defendant and a third party which binds them to another jurisdiction under art.17; *Hough v P&O Containers Ltd* [1999] Q.B. 834.

Article 6(2) allows a claim for costs against a defendant domiciled in another Contracting State who has supported, or is the alter ego of, the losing party in litigation in England; *National Justice Compania Naviera SA v Prudential Assurance Co Ltd (The Ikarian Reefer) (No.2)* [2000] 1 W.L.R. 603; [2000] 1 All E.R. 37; [2000] 1 Lloyd's Rep. 129, CA.

The power to bring a counterclaim under art.6(3) where the original claim is pending does not allow an insurer to join insureds other than in their state of domicile, having regard to the special provisions on insurance in art.11 *et seq.*; *Jordan Grand Prix Ltd v Baltic Insurance Group* [1999] 2 A.C. 127; [1999] 2 W.L.R. 134; [1999] Lloyd's Rep. IR 93; [1999] 1 All E.R. 289, HL.

Article 6(1) of the Judgments Regulation is wide enough to encompass defendants and claims in more than one action; *Masri v Consolidated Contractors Int (UK) Ltd* [2005] EWCA Civ 1436; [2006] 1 W.L.R. 830; [2006] 1 Lloyd's Rep. 391, CA. Article 6(1) of the Judgments Regulation can be relied upon where an action is brought in a Member State against a defendant who is domiciled there and a co-defendant domiciled on another Member State where, under a provision of the State in which the action is brought, it is regarded as inadmissible from the time that it had been brought in relation to the first defendant; *Reisch Montage AG v Kiesel Baumaschinen Handels GmbH* (Case C-103/05) [2007] I.L.Pr. 10.

For a consideration of the circumstances in which a Pt 20 claim for relief under s.1(1) of the Civil Liability (Contribution) Act 1978 can fall within art.6(2) of the Judgments Regulation; see *Barton v Golden Sun Holidays Ltd v Avlida Hotel Ltd* [2007] 151 S.J.L.B. 1128; [2007] I.L.Pr. 57.

Priority of jurisdiction

6.33.19 Articles 27, 28 and 29 of the Judgments Regulation (Articles 21, 22 and 23 of the Brussels Convention) address priority between courts in different Contracting States in which connected proceedings are brought.

Where courts of different Regulation or Contracting States potentially have coextensive jurisdiction, the solution is generally to accord precedence to the court first seised. For an interpretation given by the Court of Justice of the meaning of "first seised" in art.21 of the Brussels Convention; see *Zelger v Salinitri (No.2)* [1984] E.C.R. 2397, paras 14–16; see also *Tavoulareas v Tsavliris (The Atlas Pride)* [2004] EWCA Civ 48; [2004] 1 Lloyd's Rep. 445.

Unless service is dispensed with under r.6.16, Convention proceedings only become definitively pending in England upon service; see *Dresser UK Ltd v Falcongate Freight Management Ltd (The Duke of Yare)* [1992] Q.B. 502, CA and *Neste Chemicals S.A. v D.K. Line S.A.* [1994] 3 All E.R. 180; *Molins Plc v GD SpA* [2000] 1 W.L.R. 1741, CA; but note *Canada Trust Co v Stolzenberg (No.2)* [2002] 1 A.C. 1, HL; *Phillips v Nussberger* [2008] UKHL 1; [2008] 1 W.L.R. 180; [2008] 1 Lloyd's Rep. 344; [2008] I.L.Pr. 21, HL. Article 30 of the Judgments Regulation provides that a court is deemed seised when the document instituting the proceedings is received by the court, or, if it requires service before lodging with the court, when it is received by the agency responsible for service, provided that the claimant then gets on with service or lodging as appropriate. Accordingly, in relation to parties in Regulation States, the English court will presumably be seised on issue of a claim form, although it is necessary to get on with service.

Where English proceedings were issued and served by a claimant in England, but meanwhile, with the leave of an Italian judge, Italian proceedings were faxed to the claimant, the English action was first commenced. The Italian proceedings, though pending earlier under Italian law, would not prevail, because service by fax was not legitimate service without prior agreement of the claimant to receive process by fax; *Molins Plc v GD SpA [2000]* 1 W.L.R. 1741; [2000] 2 Lloyd's Rep. 234, CA.

For a consideration of the meaning of "first seised" in the context of English and Finnish proceedings, see *Carnoustie Universal SA v International Transport Workers Federation* [2002] EWHC 1624 (Comm); [2003] I.L.Pr. 7.

"Served" in art.34(2) of the Judgment Regulation bears the same meaning as it bears in art.30 of that Regulation and in the Service Regulation (EC) 1348/2000 and so a person has not been "served" with proceedings for the purposes of art.34(2) merely by virtue of having been notified of them at a time and in a way which enabled him to defend the proceedings if he wished to do so; *Tavoulareas v Tsavliris (No.2)* [2006] EWCA Civ 1772; [2007] 1 W.L.R. 1573; [2007] 2 All E.R. (Comm) 356. However, since art.30 of the Judgements Regulation is concerned with seising, not services, it is not relevant to the article whether service governed by art.30(3) is valid service under the Service Regulation; *WPP Holdings Italy Srl v Benatti* [2007] EWCA Civ 263; [2007] 1 W.L.R. 2316; [2007] 2 All E.R. (Comm) 525; [2008] 1 Lloyd's Rep. 396.

Negative declarations—It should be noted that Convention jurisprudence does not preclude the establishment of prior jurisdiction by way of an early claim for a negative declaration. That device is an accepted device in virtually all of the Member States which are parties to the Convention as is clear from the opinion of Advocate General Tesauro in *"The Tatry"* (C-406/92) [1994] E.C.R. I-5439: **6.33.20**

> "23. It should also be borne in mind that the bringing of proceedings to obtain a negative finding, which is generally allowed under the various national procedural laws and is entirely legitimate in every respect is an appropriate way of dealing with genuine needs on the part of the person who brings them. For example, he may have an interest, where the other party is temporizing, in securing a prompt judicial determination if doubts exist or objections are raised of the rights obligations or responsibilities deriving from a given contractual relationship..."

The Court of Justice has said that it makes no difference for the purposes of arts 21 and 22 of the Brussels Convention (arts 27 and28 of the Judgments Regulation) whether the first claim is framed in positive or negative terms (*ibid*). However, as a matter of English domestic law, a negative declaration can only be sought in England if a declaration is properly sought by domestic standards, which requires, in effect, that it would serve a useful purpose; see *Messier-Dowty Ltd v Sabena SA* [2000] 1 W.L.R. 2040, CA.

Same parties—As to the "same parties" requirement under art.27 of the Judgments Regulation (art.21 of the Brussels Convention), it has been held by the Court of Justice that the hull insurer would not be regarded as the same party as the shipowner (where the insurer had brought proceedings for contribution from cargo and the shipowner had brought proceedings elsewhere for limitation) unless it was established that the interests of those parties, the insurer and its insured, were identical and indissociable; *Drouot Assurances SA v Consolidated Metallurgical Industries (CMI Industrial Sites)* (C-351/96) [1998] E.C.R. I-3075; [1999] Q.B. 497; [1999] 2 W.L.R. 163. **6.33.21**

Two legal entities such as an assignor and an assignee can have a sufficient identity of interest in the subject matter of proceedings so as to be regarded as the same party for the purposes of art.27 of the Judgments Regulation; *Kolden Holdings v Rodette Commerce Ltd* [2008] EWCA Civ 10; [2008] 1 Lloyd's Rep. 197; [2008] 2 All E.R. (Comm) 289; [2008] I.L.Pr. 20, CA.

Same cause of action—As to the "same cause of action" requirement, it has been held by the Court of Appeal that a straightforward civil claim for money was different from a tracing claim into assets based on breach of fiduciary duty for the purpose of art.21 of the Brussels Convention (art.27 of the Judgments Regulation). The court also considered that it would be inappropriate to defer to the jurisdiction of another Contracting State where the competing civil claim was tacked on to criminal proceedings in another Contracting State which made art.22 of the Brussels Convention (art.28 of the Judgments Regulation) inappropriate; *Haji-Ioannou v Frangos* [1999] 2 Lloyd's Rep. 337, CA. **6.33.22**

For the approach to cases where positive relief is sought in one jurisdiction and negative relief in another and the definition of "cause of action" for the purposes of art.27; see *JP Morgan Europe Ltd v Primacom AG* [2005] EWHC 508 (Comm); [2005] 2 Lloyd's Rep. 665.

The Brussels Convention is to be interpreted as precluding the grant of an injunction whereby a court of a Contracting State prohibits a party to proceedings pending before it from commencing or continuing legal proceedings before a court of another Contracting State, even where that party is acting in bad faith with a view to frustrating the existing proceedings; *Turner v Grovit* (C159/02) [2005] 1 A.C. 101; [2004] All E.R. (EC) 485; [2004] 1 Lloyd's Rep. 216.

Degree to which proceedings must be "related"—arts 6(1) and 28 of the Judgments Regulation (arts 6(1) and 22 of the Brussels Convention) have the common objective of allowing consolidation where related proceedings in different Contracting or Regula- **6.33.23** tion States would create a risk of irreconcilable judgments; Kalfelis v Bankhaus Schroder Munchmeyer Hengst & Co [1988] E.C.R. 5565, at paras 11 to 13. See also the exposition of the *Kalfelis* test in *Gascoine v Pyrah* [1994] I.L.Pr. 82, CA.

The assessment of the risk of irreconcilability is broadly the same under arts 6(1) and 22 of the Brussels Convention (arts 6(1) and 28 of the Judgments Regulation), and relevant risk extends to findings of law as well as fact; see *Casio Computer Co Ltd v Sayo* [2001] EWCA Civ 661; [2001] I.L.Pr. 43, per Tuckey L.J. The test is to be applied pragmatically. According to Lord Saville in *Sarrio SA v Kuwait Investment Authority* [1999] 1 A.C. 32, HL, at page 41:

"there should be a broad common sense approach to the question whether the actions in question are related, bearing in mind the objective of the article, applying the simple wide test set out in Article 22 and refraining from an oversophisticated analysis of the matter."

For a further consideration of the relevant criteria, see *Bank of Tokyo-Mitsubishi Ltd v Baskan Gida Sanayi Ve Pazarlama AS* [2004] EWHC 945; [2004] I.L.Pr. 26; and *Research in Motion UK Ltd v Visto Corporation* [2008] 2 All E.R. (Comm) 560, CA.

On this basis, passing-off proceedings in England did not give way to earlier proceedings in Germany for infringement of a German trade mark registration where the defendant in the German proceedings was a mere licensee of the English claimant; *Mecklermedia Corp v D.C. Congress GmbH* [1998] Ch. 40. Where Dutch proceedings were issued against insurers seeking a declaration of non-liability and the assured subsequently issued proceedings seeking compensation from the claimants in the Dutch proceedings in respect of the same incident, although the parties and issues in the two actions were not identical they were related for the purposes of art.28 of the Judgments Regulation and the English court declined the jurisdiction in the light of the arguments in favour of the Dutch courts; *Sony Computer Entertainment Ltd v RH Freight Services Ltd* [2007] EWHC 302 (Comm); [2007] I.L.Pr. 21.

A particular difficulty has been created as regards the question of whether parallel tort and contract claims against different defendants are sufficiently related for combination under art.6(1) because of dicta of the Court of Justice in *Réunion Européenne S.A. v Spliethoff's Bevrachttingskantoor B.V.* [2000] Q.B. 690, ECJ, in relation to the *Kalfelis* case.

In *Kalfelis* the Court of Justice held that a court with special jurisdiction under art.5(3) over the tort part of an action would not thereby have jurisdiction to try other non-tort parts of the action, unless there was an alternative basis for jurisdiction under art.6(1).

In *Réunion Européenne* French consignees of a shipment of peaches sued in France the Australian issuers of the bill of lading under which the goods were carried (a contract claim) and the Dutch carriers and master of the ship in which they were carried (tort claims). In the course of its reasoning the Court of Justice observed at para.50 that two claims in one action for compensation, directed against different defendants and based in one instance on contractual liability and in the other on liability in tort or delict, could not be regarded as connected. In *Casio Computer Co Ltd v Sayo* [2001] EWCA Civ 661; [2001] I.L.Pr. 43, Tuckey L.J. said that there is nothing in the *Réunion Européenne* case which cuts down, qualifies or explains what was said in *Kalfelis*. However, in *Watson v First Choice Holidays and Flights Limited* [2001] EWCA Civ 972; [2001] 2 Lloyd's Rep 339, the Court of Appeal considered that para.50 of the *Réunion Européenne* ruling was clear in saying that parallel contract and tort claims could not be regarded as connected for purposes of art.6(1). It accordingly referred to the Court of Justice the question whether its statement at para.50 of the *Réunion Européenne* judgment was intended to have that effect. It could be that the analysis of Tuckey L.J. in Casio (apparently not cited in Watson) provides a cogent basis for considering joinder under art.6(1) pending clarification by the Court of Justice.

For further discussion of the matter see para.6.33.12 above.

6.33.24 *Counterclaims*—Article 6(3) of the Judgment Regulation (art.6(3) of the Brussels Convention) provides that a person domiciled in a Contracting State may also be sued on a counterclaim arising from the same contract or facts on which the original claim was based, in the court in which the original claim is pending. This situation does not cover a Pt 20 claim against a claimant by a party, nor a defendant in the proceedings, in respect of discrete groups of facts that enjoy a common background; *Dollfus Mieget Compagnie v CDW International Ltd* [2004] I.L.Pr. 12.

6.33.25 *Exclusive jurisdiction in relation to particular subject matter*—Article 22 of the Judgments Regulation (art.16 of the Brussels Convention) provides for exclusive jurisdiction in relation to certain matters regardless of the domicile of the parties. It covers proceedings concerning rights in rem, or tenancies of immovable property (as in *Dansommer A/S v Gotz* (C8/98) [2001] 1 W.L.R. 1069) where exclusive jurisdiction belongs to the Contracting State in which the property is situated. Thus an English court did not have jurisdiction to order the sale of Portuguese land on the application of an English Trustee in bankruptcy; *Ashurst v Pollard* [2001] Ch. 595, CA. A TOLATA claim is not an action in rem for the purposes of art.22 of the Judgments Regulation; *Prazic v Prazic* [2006] EWCA Civ 497; [2007] I.L.Pr. 31.

However, the scope of exclusive jurisdiction is not to be construed more broadly than is necessary to give effect to their policy of allowing local courts to deal with the complexities of local law. In particular, financing arrangements related to land transactions will not necessarily be caught; *Jarrett v Barclays Bank Plc* [1999] Q.B. 1, CA.

However, art.16(2) of the Lugano Convention which, for practical purposes, is in the same terms as art.22 of the Judgments Regulation, is to be construed in a non-restrictive sense and, where applicable, a court with exclusive jurisdiction will take precedence over a first seised court with non-exclusive jurisdiction; *Speed Investments Limited v Formula One Holdings Limited* [2004] EWCA Civ 1512; [2005] 1 W.L.R. 1936; [2005] I.L.Pr. 5.

For a consideration of the relationship between art.16(4) of the Brussels Convention providing for exclusive jurisdiction in matters and art.26 of the Brussels Convention providing for the enforcement of judgments of other Contracting States; see *Prudential Assurance Co Ltd v Prudential Insurance Co of America* [2003] EWCA Civ 327; [2003] 1 W.L.R. 2295, CA.

A claimant cannot rely upon art.17 of the Brussels Convention to establish exclusive jurisdiction arising from a term of contract to which it asserts that it is not a party. The agreement must be clearly and precisely demonstrated by looking at all the circumstances; *Andromeda Marine SA v O W Bunker & Trading A/S (The Mana)* [2006] EWHC 777 (Comm); [2006] 2 Lloyd's Rep. 319.

Jurisdiction agreements—Generally, the Judgments Regulation and Conventions defer **6.33.26**
to an express choice of jurisdiction by the parties to an agreement, though the restrictions on the efficacy of agreements which are inconsistent with the special regimes for policyholders and consumers below should be noted. A jurisdiction agreement will preclude joinder of claims under art.6 where it stipulates a different jurisdiction; *Hough v P&O Containers Ltd* [1999] Q.B. 834. The agreement must be "either in writing or evidenced in writing or, in international trade or commerce, in a form which accords with practices in that trade or commerce of which the parties are or ought to have been aware." It has to be clearly and precisely demonstrated that the parties actually agreed to every clause conferring jurisdiction. The purpose of art.23(1) is to neutralise the effect of jurisdiction clauses that might pass unnoticed in contracts; *Bols Distilleries BV v Superior Yacht Services Ltd* [2006] UKPC 45; [2007] 1 W.L.R. 12; [2007] 1 Lloyd's Rep. 683; [2007] All E.R. (Comm) 461.

Where an exclusive jurisdiction clause appears in a contract in a dispute where another contract contains a conflicting clause, the dispute does not fall within art.23 of the Judgments Regulation, *UBS v HSH Nordbank* [2008] EWHC 1529 (Comm); [2008] 2 Lloyd's Rep. 500; [2008] I.L.Pr. 46; see also *ACP Capital Ltd v IFR Capital plc* [2008] EWHC 1627 (Comm); [2008] I.L.Pr. 47.

The question as to whether a party is bound by a jurisdiction clause is governed by the law of the Regulation rather than by that of a Member State and a third party will not be bound by such a clause; *Knorr-Bremse Systems v Haldex Brake Products* [2008] EWHC 156 (Pat); [2008] 2 All E.R. (Comm) 448; [2008] I.L.Pr. 26.

General words of incorporation in a reinsurance contract are not sufficient to incorporate a jurisdiction clause in the underlying insurance contract; *AIG Europe SA v QBE International Insurance Ltd* [2001] 2 Lloyds Rep. 268.

On the other hand, in relation to a contract concluded orally in international trade or commerce, an agreement conferring jurisdiction is validly concluded under art.17 of the Brussels Convention (art.23 of the Judgments Regulation) if one party to the contract did not react to a commercial letter of confirmation sent to it by the other party or repeatedly paid invoices without objection, where those documents contained a pre-printed reference to the courts having jurisdiction, provided that such conduct was consistent with a practice in force in the field of international trade or commerce in which the parties operated and the parties were or ought to have been aware of that practice; *Mainschiffahrts v Les Gravières S.a.r.l.* (C106/95) [1997] E.C.R. I-947; [1997] Q.B. 731. A jurisdiction clause in a bill of lading is an effective agreement under art.17 of the Brussels Convention between the parties to the bill of lading contract, and the English court can restrain by means of an anti-suit injunction earlier proceedings brought in breach of such a clause in another Contracting State; *OT Africa Line Ltd v Hijazy (The Kribi)* [2001] 1 Lloyd's Rep. 76. Printed clauses on the back of an order may be incorporated in this way; *Lafi Office and International Business SL v Meriden Animal Health Ltd* [2000] 2 Lloyd's Rep. 51, but see *Insured Financial Structures Ltd v Elektrocieplownia Tychy SA* [2003] EWCA Civ 110; [2003] Q.B. 1260, CA, to the effect that the language of art.17(1) of the Lugano Convention has to be given effect in a manner that takes into account the intentions of the parties.

However, in the absence of a relevant practice, there will be no jurisdiction agreement compliant with art.17 of the Brussels Convention (art.23 of the Judgments Regulation) where acceptance of the clause is not manifest in writing; *Lafarge Plasterboard v Fritz Peters & Co KG* [2000] 2 Lloyd's Rep. 689. Where an offer is contained in a faxed quotation that expressly states that it is "according to the offeror's general terms and conditions" and those terms contain an exclusive jurisdiction clause, a signed purchase order accepting the quotation may constitute a contract constituting an agreement within art.23 of the Judgments Regulation; *7E Communications v Vertex Anntennentechnik GmbH* [2007] EWCA Civ 140; [2007] 1 W.L.R. 2175; [2007] 2 All E.R. (Comm) 798; [2007] 2 Lloyd's Rep. 411.

The effect of art.17 of the Brussels Convention can be to elevate even an agreement on the non-exclusive jurisdiction of a Contracting State to exclusive jurisdiction; *Lafi Office and International Business SL v Meriden Animal Health Ltd*, op cit, but see *Insured Financial Structures Ltd v Elektrocieplownia Tychy SA*, op cit, to the effect that the language of art.17(1) of the Lugano Convention has to be given effect in a manner that takes into account the intentions of the parties.

It is difficult to see how a jurisdiction or arbitration clause obtained by duress could encompass a challenge to the clause based on duress; *Carnoustie Universal SA v International Transport Workers Federation* [2002] EWHC 1624; [2003] I.L.Pr. 17.

Where a court is seised of jurisdiction under art.21 of the Brussels Convention, it is that court which must decide whether it lacks jurisdiction by reason of a jurisdiction agreement; *Erich Gasser GmbH v Misat Srl* (C116/02) [2005] 1 Q.B. 1; [2004] 1 Lloyd's Rep. 222; [2004] I.L.Pr. 7.

The standard of proof required when a defendant seeks to rely on a foreign jurisdiction agreement in a case where, apart from the alleged agreement, the English court would have jurisdiction under the Judgments Regulation is that of a good arguable case; *Bank of Tokyo-Mitsubishi Ltd v Baskan Gida Sanayi Ve Pazarlama AS* [2004] EWHC 945; [2004] I.L.Pr. 26. As to the burden of proof and the meaning of good arguable case, see *Konkola Copper Mines Plc v Caromin* [2006] EWCA Civ 5; [2006] I.L.Pr. 46; [2006] 1 Lloyd's Rep. 410, *Bols Distilleries BV v Superior Yacht Services Ltd* [2006] UKPC 45; [2007] 1 W.L.R. 12; [2007] 1 Lloyd's Rep. 683; [2007] 1 All E.R. (Comm) 461; *WPP Holdings Italy Srl v Benatti* [2007] EWCA Civ 263; [2007] 1 W.L.R. 2316; [2007] 2 All E.R. (Comm) 525; [2008] 1 Lloyd's Rep. 396; *Deutsche Bank AG v Asia Pacific Broadband Wireless Communications Inc* [2008] EWHC 918 (Comm); [2008] 2 Lloyd's Rep. 177.

In determining whether a forum clause was "an agreement conferring jurisdiction" within the ambit of art.23 of the Judgments Regulation, the court had to treat those words as an independent concept and not simply as referring to the national law of one or other of the Member States concerned; albeit that the starting point was to consider the meaning of the relevant clause under the proper law of the contract; *British Sugar Plc v Fratelli Babbini di Lionello Babbini & Co SAS* [2004] EWHC 2560; [2005] 1 Lloyd's Rep 332; [2005] 1 All E.R. (Comm) 55.

Special jurisdiction regimes

6.33.27 *Insurance*—The special insurance regime of the Judgments Regulation and Conventions does not apply to reinsurance; *Universal General Insurance Co (UGIC) v Group Josi Reinsurance Co SA* (C412/98) [2001] Q.B. 68; *Agnew v Lansforsakringsbolagens AB* [2001] 1 A.C. 223,HL; [2000] Lloyd's Rep. IR 317; [2000] 1 All E.R. 737. Accordingly, in *Agnew*, a claim to set aside a reinsurance contract for material misrepresentation and non-disclosure was not a matter relating to insurance within Section 3 but rather a matter "relating to a contract" within art.5. The obligation in question was the pre-obligation to make a proper presentation of the risk.

Broadly, the effect of the insurance regime is to give a policy holder a wide choice of courts but to confine the insurer to the court of the policy-holder's domicile. The provisions of the section cannot be departed from by agreement unless that agreement complies with the stringent conditions of art.13 of the Judgments Regulation (art.12 of the Brussels Convention). Moreover the special insurance regime binds insurers wherever domiciled in relation to litigation involving a policyholder in a Contracting State; *Jordan Grand Prix Ltd v Baltic Insurance Group* [1999] 2 A.C. 127, HL. The reference in art.11(2) of the Judgments Regulation to art.9(1)(b) of the Regulation is to be interpreted as meaning that the injured party can bring an action directly before the courts of the place in a Member State where that injured party is domiciled, provided that such direct action is permitted and the insurer is domiciled in a Member State, *Odenbreit v FBTO Schadeverzekeringen NV* (Case C-463/06), [2008] 2 All E.R. (Comm) 733.

A jurisdiction clause conforming with art.12(3) of the Brussels Convention cannot be relied on against a beneficiary under that contract who has not expressly subscribed to that clause and is domiciled in a Contracting State other than that of the policyholder and the insurer; *Societe Financiere Industrielle du Peloux v AXA Belgium* (C-112/03) [2006] Q.B. 251; [2005] 2 All E.R. (Comm) 419; [2005] I.L.Pr. 32.

Third-party proceedings between insurers based on multiple insurance are not subject to the provisions of s.3 of art.11 of the Brussels Convention; *Groupement d'Interet Economique (GIE) Reunion Europeenne v Zurich España* (C-77/04) [2005] I.L.Pr. 33.

Consumer contracts—A special jurisdiction regime covers consumer contracts which, in broad terms, are contracts for the provision of goods or services (excluding transport) to a person operating outside his trade or profession, where the contract involves the provision of credit, or where the contract resulted from a specific invitation addressed to the consumer in his state of domicile, or from advertising in his state of domicile, causing the consumer to take the steps necessary to conclude the contract in that state. **6.33.28**

Articles 15 to 17 of the Judgments Regulation (arts 13 to 15 of the Brussels Convention) lay down special rules for consumer contracts which are similar to those in respect of insurance contracts and policyholders. Consumers for this purpose are persons dealing outside their trade or profession, and relevant contracts include credit agreements and contracts for the supply of goods and services.

A person who concludes a contract relating to goods which are in part within and in part outside his trade or profession can only rely on the special rule if the trade or professional purpose is negligible in the overall context of the supply and, where that person has acted in such a way as to lead the supplier reasonably to believe that the person was acting for business purposes, he cannot rely upon the special rule; *Gruber v Bay Wa AG* (C464/01) [2006] Q.B. 204, ECJ.

A consumer can sue a supplier in the Regulation where either of them is domiciled (art.16 of the Judgments Regulation and art.14 of the Brussels Convention) which is deemed to include, in relation to the supplier, a Regulation where the supplier has a branch, agency or establishment whose operations have given rise to the dispute. The consumer can only be sued in the Regulation where he is domiciled.

The Court of Justice has interpreted art.13(3) of the Brussels Convention (art.15(3) of the Judgments Regulation) in proceedings where an Austrian national consumer domiciled in Vienna sought an order against a mail-order company established in Germany requiring that mail-order company to pay him a financial benefit. In *Gabriel Schlank and Schick GmbH* (C-96/00) [2002] ECR I-6367, ECJ, the court held that where a company had sent the consumer in person a letter likely to create the impression that a prize would be awarded to him on the condition that he ordered goods to a specified amount, and where that consumer actually placed an order in the State of his domicile without, however, obtaining payment of that financial benefit, judicial proceedings brought by the consumer against the company are contractual within the nature contemplated by art.13(3) of the Brussels Convention (art.15(3) of the Judgments Regulation). In *Engler v Janus Versand GmbH* (C-27/02) [2005] 1 I.L.Pr.8 the Court of Justice held that a claim fell within art.5(1) and art.13(1) of the Brussels Convention where a private individual was sent a letter addressed to her personally stating that she had won a prize without the imposition of any condition in respect of goods sold by the company offering the prize, cf. In *re Jurisdiction in a Claim Based on a Prize Draw Notification* [2007] I.L.Pr. 15.

The *Gabriel* case was considered by the Court of Appeal in *Rayner v Davies* [2002] EWCA Civ 1880; [2003] I.L.Pr. 15, where it held that for a consumer contract to come within art.13(3) of the Brussels Convention it is the seller who must have invited the business and that a faxed offer from a defendant surveyor to a claimant purchaser regarding the terms of a survey was not the sort of specific invitation which art.13(3) contemplated on the grounds, inter alia, that there had not been advertising or positive conduct on the part of the surveyor preceding the contract and that, in this case, it was the claimant purchaser who had invited the surveyor to do business.

6.33.29 *Employment contracts*—The provisions in art.5(1) of the Brussels Convention dealing with special jurisdiction in matters relating to individual contracts of employment appear in an amended form at Section 5 (arts 18 to 21) of the Judgments Regulation, which reflects the established jurisprudence of the Court of Justice in this field.

Article 19 of the Judgments Regulation preserves the position in art.5(1) of the Brussels Convention. An employer may be sued in the courts of the Member State where he is domiciled, or in another Member State (a) in the courts for the place where the employee habitually carries out his work or in the courts for the last place where he did so, or (b) if the employee does not or did not habitually carry out his work in any one country, in the courts for the place where the business which engaged the employee is or was situated.

In *G. Pugliese v Finmeccanica SpA* (C437/00) [2003] I.L.Pr.21, the Court of Justice held that in a dispute between an employee and a first employer, the place where the employee performs his obligations to a second employer can be regarded as the place where he habitually carries out his work when the first employer, with respect to whom the employee's contractual obligations are suspended, has, at the time of the conclusion of the second contract of employment, an interest in the performance of the service by the employee to the second employer in a place decided on by the latter.

Further, by art.18(2) of the Judgments Regulation, where an employee enters into an individual contract of employment with an employer who is not domiciled in a Member State but has a branch, agency or other establishment in one of the Member States, the employer shall, in disputes arising out of the operations of the branch, agency or establishment, be deemed to be domiciled in that Member State. Article 20(1) of the Judgments Regulation provides that an employer may bring proceedings only in the courts of the Member State in which the employee is domiciled.

A member of a group of companies that does not directly employ the relevant employee may be treated as an employer for the purposes of Section 5 of the Judgments Regulation; *Samengo-Turner v J & H Marsh &McLennon (Services) Ltd* [2007] EWCA Civ 723; [2007] 2 All E.R. (Comm) 813; [2007] I.L.Pr. 52.

Interim Measures

6.33.30 Article 31 of the Judgments Regulation (art.24 of the Brussels Convention) allows the courts of a Regulation State which does not qualify for the exercise of substantive jurisdiction under the jurisdictional rules above nevertheless to exercise jurisdiction for the limited purpose of imposing protective measures.

However, the measures must be of a provisional nature and there must be some territorial connection between the relief sought and the territorial jurisdiction of the state of the courts to which the application is made; *Van Uden B.V. v K.G. Deco-Line* [1999] Q.B. 1225, ECJ.

The English courts may nevertheless grant worldwide freezing orders against a defendant who is resident and domiciled in England, notwithstanding that the courts of another Contracting State have substantive jurisdiction, and that those courts do not have power to give such relief; *Crédit Suisse Trust S.A. v Cuoghi* [1998] Q.B. 818, CA.

Service in Scotland or Northern Ireland without permission

6.33.31 The Civil Jurisdiction and Judgments Act 1982 was not only intended to render the Brussels Convention applicable in the United Kingdom but also by Sch.4 provided for the allocation of civil jurisdiction between the three separate jurisdictions within the United Kingdom. These provisions are now modelled on the Judgments Regulation and by s.16(3) in determining any question as to the meaning of any provision in Sch.4:

"regard shall be had to any relevant principles laid down by the European Court in connection with title II of the 1968 Convention or Chapter II of the Regulation and to any relevant decision of that court as to the meaning or effect of any provisions of that Title or that Chapter."

Where in a case where there was a question on the interpretation and inter-relations between arts 5(1) and 5(3) and, depending upon the answer, whether the English or

Scottish courts had jurisdiction and the question had been referred to the European Court of Justice by the Court of Appeal, the European Court held that the interpretation of Sch.4 was a matter for the United Kingdom national courts and that it did not have any jurisdiction to rule on the matter; *Kleinwort Benson Ltd v City of Glasgow City Council* (C-346/93) [1996] Q.B. 57, ECJ.

In all cases that fall within art.5 of Sch.4, jurisdiction will depend on the terms of the article and service must be effected, if permitted, without permission. In cases covered by r.6.36 which fall outside the Judgments Regulation or the Conventions it may still be possible to obtain permission to serve in Scotland or Northern Ireland applying the principles set out in the notes.

A court has the power to stay an English libel action on the grounds of forum non conveniens where an action based on the same libel is proceeding in Scotland (*Cumming v Scottish Daily Mail*, *The Times*, June 8, 1995; [1995] E.M.L.R. 538). In this case Drake J. declined to follow an earlier decision of his in *Foxen v Scotsman Publications The Times*, February 17, 1994; [1995] E.M.L.R. 145.

This case should be contrasted with the Convention cases of *S & W Berisford Plc v New Hampshire Insurance Co* [1990] 2 Q.B. 631, and *Arkwright Mutual Insurance Co v Bryanston Insurance Co Ltd* [1990] 2 Q.B. 649, in both of which there was only one set of proceedings and it should also be noted that art.21 of the Convention (giving jurisdiction to the court first seised.) is not included in Sch.4.

Schedule 4 of the Civil Jurisdiction and Judgments Act 1982 has been amended by Sch.2, paras 3 and 4 of the Civil Jurisdiction and Judgments Order 2001 broadly to bring those provisions into line with the equivalent provisions of the Judgments Regulation. Schedule 2, paras 6 and 7 of the Civil Jurisdiction and Judgments Order 2001 makes similar amendments to Sch.8 to the Act, which contains provisions on jurisdiction in Scotland.

Notice of statement of grounds where the permission of the court is not required for service[1]

6.34—(1) Where the claimant intends to serve a claim form on a defendant under rule 6.32 or r.6.33, the claimant must— 6.34

(a) file with the claim form a notice containing a statement of the grounds on which the claimant is entitled to serve the claim form out of the jurisdiction; and

(b) serve a copy of that notice with the claim form.

(2) Where the claimant fails to file with the claim form a copy of the notice referred to in paragraph (1)(a), the claim form may only be served—

(a) once the claimant files the notice; or

(b) if the court gives permission.

Effect of rule (r.6.34)

This rule amended and replaced (with effect from October 1, 2008) former r.6.19(3). 6.34.1
That rule stated that where a claim form is to be served out of the jurisdiction under, what is now r.6.32 or r.6.23, "it must contain a statement of the grounds on which the claimant is entitled to serve it out of the jurisdiction". Under r.6.34, as supplemented by Practice Direction B (Service Out of the Jurisdiction) para.2.1, the function of former provision is to be fulfilled by a new practice form (see further below), to be filed by the claimant when claim form is issued and served with the claim form. Paragraph (2) of r.6.34 is a new provision. The former rule made no express provision for the consequences of a failure to endorse the claim form with the requisite statement of grounds. However, in *Trustor AB v Barclays Bank Plc*, *The Times* November 22, 2000 (Rimer J.) it was held that the claimant's failure to comply with that rule did not necessarily render service invalid. The judge concluded that, although non-compliance was not trifling, it did not justify the court in saying that there had been no service at

[1] Added by the Civil Procedure (Amendment) Rules 2008 (SI 2008/2178).

all; it was at most an irregularity and, since there had been no prejudice, the claim form had been validly served (see also *Harris Calnan Construction Co. Ltd. v Ridgewood (Kensington) Ltd.* [2007] EWHC 2738 (TCC), November 15, 2007, unrep. (Coulson J.)).

Practice form—statement of grounds

6.34.2 Practice Direction B (Service Out of the Jurisdiction) para.2.1 states that, where r.6.34 applies, the claimant must file practice form N510 Service out of the Jurisdiction (see the Civil Procedure Forms section of the *Civil Procedure Forms Volume*) when filing the claim form (see para.6BPD.2 below).

Period for responding to the claim form where permission was not required for service[1]

6.35 **6.35—(1) This rule sets out the period for—**

(a) filing an acknowledgment of service;

(b) filing an admission; or

(c) filing a defence,

where a claim form has been served out of the jurisdiction under rule 6.32 or 6.33.

(2) Where the claimant serves on a defendant in Scotland or Northern Ireland under rule 6.32, the period—

(a) for filing an acknowledgment of service or admission is 21 days after service of the particulars of claim; or

(b) for filing a defence is—

(i) 21 days after service of the particulars of claim; or

(ii) where the defendant files an acknowledgment of service, 35 days after service of the particulars of claim.

(Part 7 provides that particulars of claim must be contained in or served with the claim form or served separately on the defendant within 14 days after service of the claim form.)

(3) Where the claimant serves the claim form on a defendant in a Convention territory within Europe or a Member State under rule 6.33, the period —

(a) for filing an acknowledgment of service or admission, is 21 days after service of the particulars of claim; or

(b) for filing a defence is—

(i) 21 days after service of the particulars of claim; or

(ii) where the defendant files an acknowledgment of service, 35 days after service of the particulars of claim.

(4) Where the claimant serves the claim form on a defendant in a Convention territory outside Europe under rule 6.33, the period—

(a) for filing an acknowledgment of service or admission, is 31 days after service of the particulars of claim; or

(b) for filing a defence is—

[1] Added by the Civil Procedure (Amendment) Rules 2008 (SI 2008/2178).

(i) **31 days after service of the particulars of claim; or**

(ii) **where the defendant files an acknowledgment of service, 45 days after service of the particulars of claim.**

(5) Where the claimant serves the claim form under rule 6.33 in a country not referred to in paragraph (3) or (4), the period for responding to the claim form is set out in Practice Direction B supplementing this Part.

Effect of rule (r.6.35)

This rule replaces two rules. One (former r.6.22) dealt with the periods within which a defendant served out of the jurisdiction should file an acknowledgment of service or should file or serve an admission, and the other (former r.6.23) with the period within which he should file a defence. **6.35.1**

When particulars of claim are served on a defendant, the defendant may (a) file or serve an admission in accordance with Pt 14, (b) file a defence in accordance with Pt 15 (or do both, if he admits only part of the claim), or (c) file an acknowledgment of service in accordance with Pt 10 (r.9.2).

The periods (a) for returning an admission or for filing it under rr.14.5, 14.6 or 14.7, (b) for filing a defence, and (c) for filing an acknowledgment of service, are fixed, respectively, by r.14.2, r.15.4 and r.10.3. (In proceedings in the Commercial Court and in Mercantile Courts, provisions in Pts 14, 15 and 10 take effect subject to certain modifications made by rules in Pts 58 and 59, one of which is that an acknowledgment of service should be filed in all contested cases.)

Rule 6.35 modifies the effect of the time period provisions in r.14.2, r.15.4 and r.10.3 in the circumstances in which the rule applies. The rule is an improvement on the two rules it replaces in that it brings out more clearly the distinction between service on a defendant (a) in Scotland or Northern Ireland, (b) in a Member State or a Convention Territory within Europe, and (c) in a country not referred to in (a) or (b) ("elsewhere"). Where a claimant serves the claim form on a defendant elsewhere, the period for responding is now determined in accordance with para.6 of Practice Direction B (Service Out of the Jurisdiction) (see para.6BPD.6 below).

Rule 6.35 extends the periods for the filing of the documents referred to beyond those that would normally apply. This is done in recognition of the fact that it is reasonable to give a defendant served out of the jurisdiction, including those in Scotland and Northern Ireland (who now may be served by "domestic" methods of service, see r.6.40(2)), extra time in which to comply.

In proceedings in the Commercial Court and in Mercantile Courts, the time periods provided by r.6.35 apply "after service of the claim form" (see rr.58.6(3) and 59.5(3)).

Rule 6.35 (in relation to the period for filing a defence where the claim form is served out of the jurisdiction) applies to claims in the commercial list and to mercantile claims, except that if the particulars of claim are served after the defendant has filed an acknowledgment of service the period for filing a defence is 28 days from service of the particulars of claim (see rr.58.10(2) and 59.9(2)).

"after service"

In this rule, and in para.6 of Practice Direction B, the response periods are fixed as a certain number of days "after service". Where a document is served within the jurisdiction, it is deemed served on a day as calculated in accordance with r.6.14 and r.6.26. Where a document is served out of the jurisdiction, those deeming provisions do not apply. **6.35.2**

Service of the claim form where the permission of the court is required[1]

6.36 In any proceedings to which rule 6.32 or 6.33 does not ap- **6.36**

[1] Added by the Civil Procedure (Amendment) Rules 2008 (SI 2008/2178).

ply, the claimant may serve a claim form out of the jurisdiction with the permission of the court if any of the grounds set out in paragraph 3.1 of Practice Direction B supplementing this Part apply.

Effect of rule (r.6.36)

6.36.1 See commentary following r.6.37.

Application for permission to serve the claim form out of the jurisdiction[1]

6.37 **6.37—(1) An application for permission under rule 6.36 must set out—**

(a) which ground in paragraph 3.1 of Practice Direction B supplementing this Part is relied on;

(b) that the claimant believes that the claim has a reasonable prospect of success; and

(c) the defendant's address or, if not known, in what place the defendant is, or is likely, to be found.

(2) Where the application is made in respect of a claim referred to in paragraph 3.1(3) of Practice Direction B supplementing this Part, the application must also state the grounds on which the claimant believes that there is between the claimant and the defendant a real issue which it is reasonable for the court to try.

(3) The court will not give permission unless satisfied that England and Wales is the proper place in which to bring the claim.

(4) In particular, where—

(a) the application is for permission to serve a claim form in Scotland or Northern Ireland; and

(b) it appears to the court that the claimant may also be entitled to a remedy in Scotland or Northern Ireland,

the court, in deciding whether to give permission, will—

(i) compare the cost and convenience of proceeding there or in the jurisdiction; and

(ii) (where relevant) have regard to the powers and jurisdiction of the Sheriff court in Scotland or the county courts or courts of summary jurisdiction in Northern Ireland.

(5) Where the court gives permission to serve a claim form out of the jurisdiction—

(a) it will specify the periods within which the defendant may—

(i) file an acknowledgment of service;

(ii) file or serve an admission;

(iii) file a defence; or

(iv) file any other response or document required by a rule in another Part, any other enactment or a practice direction; and

[1] Added by the Civil Procedure (Amendment) Rules 2008 (SI 2008/2178).

(b) it may—

(i) give directions about the method of service; and

(ii) give permission for other documents in the proceedings to be served out of the jurisdiction.

(The periods referred to in paragraphs (5)(a)(i), (ii) and (iii) are those specified in the Table in Practice Direction B supplementing this Part.)

Service "out of the jurisdiction" (rr.6.36 and 6.37)

Rule 6.36 states that, in any proceedings to which rule 6.32 or 6.33 does not apply, the claimant may serve a claim form out of the jurisdiction with the permission of the court if any of "the grounds" set out in para.3.1 of Practice Direction B supplementing this Part apply (see para.6BPD.1 below). Before October 1, 2008, those grounds were stated in a rule in Pt 6 (r.6.20) (and before the CPR came into effect, they were stated in RSC O.11, r.1(1)). **6.37.1**

The matters that the court should or may take into account in determining whether permission to serve out of the jurisdiction should be granted in the circumstances provided for by rr.6.36 and 6.37 are many and various and go beyond a mere consideration of the question whether the claimant's claim falls within one of the several grounds stated in para.3.1 of 6BPD. These matters include, for example, the questions as to whether England is the forum conveniens, whether the parties have agreed that a particular court should have jurisdiction (jurisdiction clauses), and whether, in any event, the proceedings should be stayed. In what follows, commentary on such matters precedes commentary on the several grounds in para.3.1 (as to which, see para.6.37.25 *et seq.* below).

The expression "jurisdiction" in this context denotes the area of the territorial jurisdictions of the High Court and the county courts, as the case may be.

The application for permission

Practice in obtaining permission (r.6.37)—Applications for permission to serve out are made under Pt 23. In an appropriate case, permission may be granted retrospectively (*Comminos v Prudential Assurance Co Ltd* [2000] 1 W.L.R. 603, CA, also reported as *National Justice Compania Naviera SA v Prudential Assurance Company Limited (The Ikarian Reefer) (No.2)* [2000] 1 W.L.R. 603; [2002] 1 All E.R. 37; [2000] 1 Lloyd's Rep. 129, CA). **6.37.2**

Time Limits—On an application for permission to serve a claim form out of the jurisdiction more than four months after the issue of a claim form marked "not for service out of the jurisdiction", the discretion exercisable by the court is governed by the special provisions in Section IV of Pt 6, and the discretion is not restricted by any express or implied requirement or condition that the application is to be made within four months of the issue of the claim form or that different criteria apply depending on whether the application is made before or after four months from the issue of the claim form; *Anderton v Clwyd CC (No.2)* [2002] EWCA Civ 933; [2002] 1 W.L.R. 3174, followed in *S T Shipping & Transport Inc v Vyzantio Shipping Ltd (The Byzantio)* [2004] EWHC 3067 (Comm); [2005] 1 Lloyd's Rep. 531. **6.37.3**

QBD—The application is made without notice to a Master. The documents should be left in the Master's Secretary's Department (Room E16) and collected when the Master's decision has been placed upon it. Applications in the Commercial Court are similarly made, without notice, to a judge of that court. **6.37.4**

Applications may also be made to a relevant Mercantile Judge or to a district registrar.

Chancery Division—The relevant documents should be delivered to the Masters' Appointments Clerk in Room TM7.09. In a clear case the Master himself gives permission (Memo. of the Chancery Judges, March 30, 1955). Otherwise the Master refers to the judge who, if satisfied, gives permission which is indorsed on the claim form. **6.37.5**

Paragraph 4.1 of Practice Direction B (see para.6BPD.1 below) gives details of the documents that the claimant should file for service on the other parties out of the jurisdiction (see further commentary following r.6.43).

The written evidence—The written evidence may be given by any person with knowledge of the facts but it is more usually made by the claimant's solicitor upon knowl- **6.37.6** edge, information and belief. The altered requirement of r.6.37(1)(b) should be noted. There is no practical difference between the new requirement and that of CPR Sch.1, O.11, r.4(1)(b). The contents of the written evidence are set out in r 6.37 but the following points should be borne in mind:

(a) The evidence should be sufficiently full to show that the claimant has established his right to permission to the standards of proof that govern the different elements of the application.

(b) The evidence must make clear which sub rule of para.3.1 of 6BPD is relied on.

(c) The evidence must set out sufficient facts to show that England and Wales constitute the forum conveniens.

(d) The evidence must be frank. If any material fact is omitted this would itself justify the court in discharging the order, even though the party might be in a position to apply again (*The Hagen* [1908] P.189 at 201, CA; *The Hai Hing* [2000] 1 Lloyd's Rep. 300). Whilst an applicant must disclose anything which casts doubt upon his case, it is unreasonable to expect him to anticipate all the arguments or points which might be raised against his case (*Electric Furnace Co v Selas Corp of America* [1987] R.P.C. 23); for a rather more robust approach, see *MRG (Japan) Ltd v Engelhard Metals Japan Ltd* [2003] EWHC 3418; [2004] 1 Lloyd's Rep. 731.

(e) All relevant information must be referred to in the relevant statement or affidavit. The court will not be expected to make an untutored examination of exhibits (*ABCI v Banque Franco-Tunisienne* [1996] 1 Lloyd's Rep. 485).

The provisions of Section IV of Pt 6 apply to the service out of the jurisdiction, not only of claim forms (as defined), but also of other documents served in proceedings. Consequently, the same practice (as outlined above) is, with any necessary modifications, applied where an application is made for permission to serve any other document in the proceedings out of the jurisdiction (see r.6.38).

In *MRG (Japan) Ltd v Engelhard Metals Japan Ltd* [2003] EWHC 3418; [2004] 1 Lloyd's Rep. 731, Toulson J. held that the duty to make full disclosure is confined to disclosure of all that is relevant to considering the criteria relevant to permission to serve out of the jurisdiction and does not include an obligation to set out matters that would go no further than showing that the defendant had or might have arguable grounds for disputing the validity of contracts relied upon to found jurisdictions. Practitioners would do well to err on the side of caution.

The matters to be taken into consideration by the court in exercising its discretion to grant permission to serve out of the jurisdiction and the standard of proof to be applied are the subject of the decision by the House of Lords in *Seaconsar Far East Ltd v Bank Markazi Jomhouri Islam Iran* [1994] 1 A.C. 438; [1993] 4 All E.R. 456, HL. There is no presumption in favour of granting permission in a case falling within para.3.1(3) of 6BPD but as the forum is already chosen the only questions that may remain are (1) is the foreign defendant (or Pt 20 defendant) a necessary or proper party and (2) is it right to bring him here as a party (*The Eras Eil Actions* [1992] 2 All E.R. 82; [1992] 1 Lloyd's Rep. 570, CA).

Application for permission under r.6.36 to serve in Scotland or Northern Ireland

6.37.7 *Effect of rule 6.37(4)*—This is often misunderstood. It is not an additional ground for giving permission to serve out of the jurisdiction; it is an additional obstacle that the applicant has to surmount (see *Williams v Cartwright* [1895] 1 Q.B. 142, CA, at p.146 per Lord Esher M.R.). Since the coming into effect of the Civil Jurisdiction and Judgments Act 1982, generally service of a claim form in Scotland or Northern Ireland may be made without permission under r.6.32 (see para.6.33.31 above). In the rare circumstances where permission is required r.6.37(4) applies.

6.37.8 *"Comparative cost and convenience"*—The cost and convenience of all parties to the action, not of the claimant alone, is relevant (*Williams v Cartwright*, op cit, at pp.147 and 149; *Kinahan v Kinahan*, (1890) 45 Ch D 78; *Washburn & Moen etc Co v Cunard S.S. Co*, (1889) 5 T.L.R. 592; *Logan v Bank of Scotland (No.2)* [1906] 1 K.B. 141, CA, at p.147; for other early authorities, see White Book 2008 Vol.1 para.6.21.8). The early cases show that the chief considerations of convenience are the obvious ones of the residence of the parties and witnesses, the inconvenience of double litigation and the fact of one of the courts having already acquired seisin of the case, the situation of documents for convenience of disclosure, the probability of despatch or delay, and the enforcement of the remedy sought in the action. Those cases were decided at a time when the differences between the considerations that the court had to take into account in this context, and where defendants were resident in other countries, were more marked than they subsequently became.

Admiralty actions

Subject to the application of the Judgments Regulation, the Admiralty practice is to be found in Appendix 15 to the Admiralty and Commercial Court Guide (see Vol.2 para.2A–39), and appears not to differ from the practice in the Commercial Court. **6.37.9**

Adding in the claim form or particulars of claim, a cause of action other than that for which permission was given to serve

This is not permissible where the added cause of action is not one of those in respect of which there is power to serve out of the jurisdiction (*Waterhouse v Reid* [1938] 1 K.B. 743, CA). Subject to this, the rules as to the amendment of claim forms and particulars of claim apply in regard to claim forms for service out of the jurisdiction as in other actions (*Holland v Leslie* [1894] 2 Q.B. 346, at p.450, CA; *Dickson v Law* [1895] 2 Ch.62; *N. v Kwik Hoo Tong etc v J. Finlay & Co* [1927] A.C. 604; see *Indigo Co v Ogilvy* [1891] 2 Ch.31, CA). These authorities concern whether amendments should be allowed with permission after the unamended claim form has been served. The situation is different where the claimant seeks permission to amend a claim form after permission has been given to serve out of the jurisdiction, but before service has been effected. In such a case the claimant may not serve under the original permission but must return to the court to seek permission to serve the claim form in its amended form (*Trafalgar Tours Ltd v Henry* [1990] 2 Lloyd's Rep. 298, CA). **6.37.10**

Where there is some basis upon which a defendant can resist the grant of permission to serve out of the jurisdiction, the principles preventing the addition of a new cause of action revealed in respect of RSC O.11 continue to have effect under the CPR; *E D & F Man Sugar v Lendoudis* [2007] EWHC 2268 (Comm); [2008] 1 All E.R. (Comm) 359.

There is nothing in CPR Pt 11 which expressly excludes power to make amendments while there is a jurisdictional challenge under Pt 11; no such implied limitation exists; and there is no incongruity in recognising that the court might by its rules or by permission allow ancillary amendments to statements of case which do not introduce a new cause of action (*Grupo Torras SA v Al-Sabah (No.1)* [1995] 1 Lloyd's Rep. 374).

Counterclaim

Permission is not needed to serve a counterclaim on a foreign claimant; by suing in England he submits to the jurisdiction in regard to any counterclaim (*Derby & Co v Larsson* [1976] 1 W.L.R. 202, at p.205; [1976] All E.R. 401, at p.414, HL). **6.37.11**

Service of claim form

See the subsequent rules of this Part. **6.37.12**

Application to set aside the order or service

See the notes to Pt 11. **6.37.13**

Appeal

Appeal from the refusal of the Master to give permission to serve the claim form lies from the Master to the Judge, and from him permission is required for any appeal to the Court of Appeal (see r.52.3). **6.37.14**

Principles upon which permission to serve outside the jurisdiction is granted

The principles upon which permission to serve outside the jurisdiction is granted are set out in r.6.36 and para.3.1 of 6BPD and r.6.37, as explained in the case law. The two most important authorities are *Seaconsar Far East Ltd v Bank Markazi Jomhouri Islam Iran* [1994] 1 A.C. 438; [1993] 4 All E.R. 456, HL, and *Spiliada Maritime Corp v Consulex Ltd, sub nom. The Spiliada* [1987] A.C. 460; [1986] 3 All E.R. 843, HL. Although the wording of r.6.36 and para.3.1 of 6BPD and r.6.37 differs from that of CPR Sch.1, O.11, rr.1(1) and 4, the principles remain the same. For a general summary, see *ABCI v Banque Franco-Tunisienne* [2002] EWHC 567; [2002] 1 Lloyd's Rep. 805, and in the Court of Appeal [2003] EWCA Civ 205; [2003] 2 Lloyd's Rep. 146, CA; also *Albon v Naza Motor Trading Sdn Bhd* [2007] EWHC 9 (Ch); [2007] 1 W.L.R. 2489; [2007] 2 All E.R. 719; [2007] 1 Lloyd's Rep. 297. Further authorities and consideration of the principles may be found in Dicey, Morris and Collins, *The Conflict of Laws*, 14th edn (London: Sweet & Maxwell, 2006), Rule 24 and commentary thereon. The principles can be summarised as follows. **6.37.15**

(1) Rule 6.36 and para.3.1 of 6BPD

The applicant must show that each claim made by him has the attributes set out in at least one of the sub-paragraphs listed under para.3.1 of 6BPD; each such sub-paragraph being read, generally speaking, disjunctively (*Matthews v Kuwait Bechtel Corp* [1959] 2 Q.B. 57).

The burden is upon the applicant to show in respect of each claim that he has a good arguable case that it falls within a relevant sub-paragraph of para.3.1 of 6BPD (*Seaconsar v Bank Markazi*, above).

Although the test is always the same, its application is flexible having regard to whether the question will be revisited by the court (e.g. breach of contract within the jurisdiction) or will only be decided once (e.g. domicile) (see *Canada Trust Co v Stolzenberg (No.2)* [1998] 1 W.L.R. 54; [1998] 1 All E.R. 318, CA, and [2002] 1 A.C. 1, HL.). As to burden and standard of proof, see para.6.33.9 above.

Where a cause or causes of action are expressly mentioned in the claim form and the particulars of claim if they accompany the form, the court must decide the application upon any cause of action so mentioned. The claimant will not be allowed to rely upon an alternative cause of action which he seeks to spell out of the facts pleaded, if such cause of action has not been so mentioned (*Metall und Rohstoff A.G. v Donaldson Lufkin & Jenrette Inc* [1990] 1 Q.B. 391, CA; *DSQ Property Co Ltd v Lotus Cars Ltd The Times*, June 28, 1990, CA). Where the cause of action has not been mentioned a more flexible approach may be adopted; *Schiffahrtsgesellschaft Detlev Von Appen GmbH v Voest Alpine Intertrading GmbH* [1997] 2 Lloyd's Rep. 279, CA. See also *ABCI v Banque Franco-Tunisienne*, above.

(2) The Merits

The applicant must show a serious issue to be tried in respect of each cause or cause of action in respect of which he asks for permission (*Seaconsar v Bank Markazi*, above). Serious issue to be tried has been equated to the prospects of success needed successfully to resist an application for a Pt 24 order (*De Molestina v Ponton* [2002] 1 Lloyd's Rep. 271; *Swiss Reinsurance Co Ltd v United India Insurance Co* [2003] EWHC 741, March 28, 2003, unrep.).

The test is the same as a "reasonable prospect of success" (*BAS Capital Funding Corp v Medfinco Ltd* [2003] EWHC 1798; [2004] 1 Lloyd's Rep. 652). Where extremely serious allegations are made, the proof to establish that there is a serious issue to be tried must be commensurate to the seriousness of the alteration; *Ashton Investments Ltd v Rusal* [2006] EWHC 2545 (Comm); [2007] 1 Lloyd's Rep. 311.

(3) Discretion

The court has a general discretion to decide whether or not the case is a proper one for service out of the jurisdiction. In particular it must consider the question of forum conveniens namely, in which forum the case could most suitably be tried for the interests of all the parties and for the ends of justice (*The Spiliada*, above). Part 1 governs the exercise of the discretion.

(4) Forum Conveniens

Subject to the differences set out below, the criteria that govern the application of the principle of forum conveniens where permission is sought to serve out of the jurisdiction are the same as those that govern the application of the principle of forum non conveniens where a stay is sought in respect of proceedings started within the jurisdiction. Those criteria are set out in *The Spiliada*, above:

(i) The burden is upon the claimant to persuade the court that England is clearly the appropriate forum for the trial of the action.

(ii) The appropriate forum is that forum where the case may most suitably be tried for the interests of all the parties and the ends of justice.

(iii) One must consider first what is the "natural forum"; namely that with which the action has the most real and substantial connection. Connecting factors will include not only factors concerning convenience and expense (such as the availability of witnesses), but also factors such as the law governing the relevant transaction and the places where the parties reside and respectively carry on business.

(iv) In considering where the case can be tried most "suitably for the interests of all the parties and for the ends of justice" ordinary English procedural advantages such as a power to award interest, are normally irrelevant as are more generous English limitation periods where the claimant has failed to act prudently in respect of a shorter limitation period elsewhere.

(v) If the court concludes at that stage that there is another forum which is apparently as suitable or more suitable than England, it will normally refuse permission unless there are circumstances by reason of which justice requires that permission should nevertheless be granted. In this inquiry the court will consider all the circumstances of the case, including circumstances which go beyond those taken into account when considering connecting factors with other jurisdictions. One such factor can be the fact, if established objectively by cogent evidence, that the claimant will not obtain justice in the foreign jurisdiction. Other factors include the absence of legal aid or the ability to obtain contribution in the foreign jurisdiction.

(vi) Where a party seeks to establish the existence of a matter that will assist him in persuading the court to exercise its discretion in his favour, the evidential burden in respect of that matter will rest upon the party asserting it.

Criteria governing the grant of a stay of proceedings started within the jurisdiction on the grounds of forum non conveniens

In the great majority of cases the criteria that govern the stay on the grounds of forum non conveniens of proceedings started within the jurisdiction are the converse of those set out in respect of the forum conveniens element of permission to serve out of the jurisdiction; subject to the fact that where a defendant is served as of right within the jurisdiction it would appear that the court will place more weight in favour of the claimant where he has the benefit of a limitation period within the jurisdiction that would be lost in competing forum (*Spiliada Maritime Corp v Cansulex Ltd (The Spiliada)* [1987] A.C. 460, HL, at p.484; [1986] 3 All E.R. 843 at pp.860 and 861). However the power to stay proceedings is part of the general powers of management of the court and in exceptional circumstances may be exercised to stay proceedings where the interests of justice so require even where the matter does not come within Spiliada (*Reichhold Norway ASA v Goldman Sachs* [2000] 1 W.L.R. 173, CA; [1999] 2 Lloyd's Rep. 567, CA). The court has an interest in deciding in which order related proceedings should be tried. There has to be very strong reasons for ordering a stay, but the risk of inconsistent decisions is capable of amounting to a very strong reason (*Curtis v Lockheed Martin UK Holdings* [2008] EWHC 260 (Comm), February 20, 2008, unrep. (Teare J.)). **6.37.16**

Relevant factors

For a recent consideration of the appropriate factors to be reviewed, see *Limit (No.3) Ltd v PDV Insurance Co Ltd* [2005] EWCA Civ 383; [2005] 2 All E.R. (Comm) 347. **6.37.17**

Subject to the principles governing agreement as to jurisdiction, special considerations apply where proceedings are already on foot in another jurisdiction (see *The Hagen* [1908] P. 189, at p.202, and *GAF Corp v Amahen Products Inc* [1975] 1 Lloyd's Rep. 601, CA). The fact that foreign proceedings have been under way for a substantial time, have involved the parties in substantial costs and are ready for trial, will be a strong factor in favour of the grant of a stay of English proceedings (*Cleveland Museum of Art v Capricorn Art International SA* [1990] B.C.L.C 546; [1990] 2 Lloyd's Rep 166). A claimant who initiates proceedings against the same defendant in two separate jurisdictions in respect of the same subject matter is required to elect which set of proceedings he wishes to pursue, and, if he elects to pursue the proceedings abroad, the English action will be dismissed, not merely stayed (*Australian Commercial Research and Development Ltd v ANZ McCaughan Merchant Bank Ltd* [1989] 3 All E.R. 65, see also *In re Harrods (Buenos Aires) Ltd (No.2)* [1992] Ch. 72, CA).

Where a claimant who has sued the defendant in a foreign jurisdiction and has abandoned those proceedings so as to sue in England the defendant (whose domicile and place of business is in England), the claimant should not be permitted to apply to the English court to stay the English proceedings so that he may revive the proceedings in the foreign jurisdiction. In such circumstances the English court will not only refuse the claimant a stay of his own proceedings but following the reasoning in *Société Nationale Industrielle Aerospatiale v Lee Jui Jak (SNIA)* [1987] A.C. 871, PC, grant the defendant an injunction restraining the foreign proceedings as it would be oppressive to force the defendant to fight the case in two jurisdictions (*Advanced Portfolio Technologies Inc v Ainsworth* [1996] C.L.C. 360). In the *SNIA* case, the Privy Council held that the court would not restrain proceedings in a jurisdiction other than the forum conveniens unless it could be shown that such proceedings were oppressive or vexatious.

Where a stay of an action for breach of contract is sought on the grounds of forum non conveniens, the proper law of the contract has to be identified. It would not be conducive to justice to require a claimant with an arguable claim under what the En- **6.37.18** glish court is likely to hold to be the proper law to litigate in another jurisdiction where his claim will be summarily rejected; in such circumstances the application to stay the English action will be dismissed (*Banco Atlantico SA v The British Bank of the Middle East* [1990] 2 Lloyd's Rep. 504, CA).

The court may refuse to stay proceedings on the grounds of forum non conveniens, even if satisfied that a foreign country is a more appropriate forum than England, if the party opposing the stay has been convicted and sentenced in his absence to a term of imprisonment in that country (*Purcell v Khayat, The Times*, November 23, 1987, CA). Where adequate protective conditions can be imposed, English proceedings will not necessarily be stayed because of criminal proceedings in another jurisdiction (*Zambia v Meer Care & Desai* [2006] EWCA Civ 390; [2006] 1 C.L.C. 436, CA).

In deciding whether the appropriate forum for trying an action is England or a specified foreign forum, the court may take into account the different rules as to costs in that forum and in England; where costs in the foreign forum do not follow the event, and where the damages awarded to a successful claimant will effectively be diminished by such costs, the court may properly conclude that justice will not be done, and that, not withstanding that the foreign forum is otherwise appropriate, the forum should be England (*Roneleigh Ltd v MII Exports Inc* [1989] 1 W.L.R. 619, CA). Furthermore if it can be shown that in the foreign forum, costs are not awarded on a realistic basis, or if there is substantial evidence indicating that trial in the foreign forum may be delayed for many years, the court may refuse to stay the English proceedings (*The Vishva Ajay* [1989] 2 Lloyd's Rep. 558).

For assessment of factors in granting a stay of proceedings in England in respect of a major commercial dispute where the alternative forum has little experience of handling such disputes; see *Ceskoslovenska Obchodni Banka AS v Nomura International Plc* [2003] I.L.Pr. 20.

In a case of internet libel the court's discretion in ascertaining the most appropriate forum will tend to be more open textured than otherwise; *Lewis v King* [2004] EWCA Civ 1329; [2005] I.L.Pr.16 (a case concerned with permission to serve out of the jurisdiction).

The court has no discretion to stay proceedings on the ground of forum non conveniens or lis alibi pendens if the proceedings fall within the Judgments Regulation or Conventions embodied in the Civil Jurisdiction and Judgments Act 1982 (*S & W Berisford Plc v New Hampshire Insurance Co* [1990] 2 Q.B. 631; [1990] 2 All E.R. 321; *Arkwright Mutual Insurance Co v Bryanston Insurance Co Ltd* [1990] 2 Q.B. 649; [1990] 2 All E.R. 335). There is an authority to the effect that where an exclusive jurisdiction clause confers jurisdiction on a non-contracting state, a court can order a stay of proceedings on the ground of forum non conveniens in favour of a non contracting state notwithstanding a defendant being domiciled in a contracting state (*Ace Insurance SA-NV v Zurich Insurance Co* [2001] EWCA Civ 173; [2001] 1 Lloyd's Rep. 618, CA); but this is unlikely to have survived *Owusu v Jackson* (C-281/02) [2005] Q.B. 801, ECJ.

Notwithstanding s.33(1)(b) of the Legal Aid Act 1988 which provides that the receipts of legal aid "shall not affect ... the principles on which the discretion of any court or tribunal is normally exercised" the court may take into account the fact that a claimant is legally aided in considering whether to stay proceedings on the grounds of forum conveniens. So, where a defendant had made out a prima facie case that the action had the closest connection with the foreign jurisdiction, the fact that legal aid was available in this country but not in the foreign jurisdiction was the decisive consideration which influenced the majority of the House of Lords in overruling the Court of Appeal which had granted a stay (*Connelly v RTZ Corp Plc* [1998] A.C. 854, HL.). The question of funding was also decisive against the granting of a stay in *Lubbe v Cape Plc* [2000] 1 W.L.R. 1545; [2000] 4 All E.R. 268, HL.

The principles on which the doctrine of forum conveniens rest leave no room for considerations of public interest or public policy which cannot be related to the private interests of any of the parties or the ends of justice in the case before the court (see the *Lubbe* case, above).

Jurisdiction clauses

6.37.19 *Special considerations* also apply where the parties have agreed that a particular court shall have jurisdiction over the dispute. When considering whether choice of law or jurisdiction clauses have been incorporated from one contract into another clear words of incorporation are required (*Dornoch v Mauritius Union Assurance Co Ltd* [2006] EWCA Civ 389; [2006] 2 All E.R. (Comm) 385, CA). The only distinction in principle between an exclusive and a non-exclusive jurisdiction clause is that under the former a defendant has a contractual right to require litigation in the agreed forum; while in each case the defendant can raise no contractual objection if the claimant litigates in the designated forum. In such an event the court will ordinarily enforce the agreement, if asked, and, if the chosen court is foreign, will refuse permission to serve proceedings out of the jurisdiction under r.6.36 and para.3.1 of 6BPD (*Mackender v Feldia A.G.* [1967] 2 Q.B. 590; [1966] 3 All E.R. 847, CA; *Mercury Communications Ltd v Communication Telesystems International* [1999] 2 All E.R. (Comm) 33; *In re Jogia* [1988] 1 W.L.R. 484; [1988] 2 All E.R. 328; *Antec International Ltd v BiosafetyUse Inc* [2006] EWHC 47 (Comm), January 27, 2006, unrep.; *Konkola Copper Mines plc v Coromin Ltd (No.2)* [2006] EWHC 1093; [2006] I.L.Pr. 46; [2006] 2 Lloyd's Rep. 446). Very strong grounds are required to override a choice of English jurisdiction (*BAS Capital Funding Corp v Medfinco Ltd* [2003] EWHC 1798; [2004] 1 Lloyd's Rep. 652). Where there is an effective jurisdiction clause the possibility of a multiplicity of proceedings will not necessarily prevent it being given effect (*Mercury Communications Ltd v Communication Telesystems International*, op cit; *Sinochem International Oil (London) Co Ltd v Mobile Sales and Supply Corp* [2000] 1 Lloyd's Rep. 670). However, see *Donohue v Armco Inc* [2001] UKHL 64; [2002] 1 Lloyd's Rep. 425; [2002] 1 All E.R. 97 (Comm), HL. Legislation permitting proceedings in the courts of a state in the face of an exclusive jurisdiction clause in favour of the High Court in London does not provide an exceptional circumstance and such proceedings would potentially be subject to an anti-suit injunction; *O.T. Africa Line Ltd v Magic Sportswear Corp* [2005] EWCA Civ 710; [2005] 2 Lloyd's Rep. 170, CA; *Horne Linie GmbH & Co v Panamerican Formas E Impresos SA (The Hornbay)* [2006] EWHC 373; [2006] 2 Lloyd's Rep. 44 (Morison J.). Where a jurisdiction clause in a contract of insurance gave a right to sue the state of Nebraska and provided for English law (described as "UK law") to apply, the English court declined to exercise jurisdiction albeit that the Nebraska court was likely to decide that the choice of English law should be declared invalid; *Catlin Syndicate Ltd v Adams Land & Cattle Co* [2006] EWHC 2065 (Comm); [2006] 2 C.L.C. 425 (Cooke J.).

The risk of inconsistent decisions in different jurisdictions is one that will be regarded as having been in the contemplation of the parties when agreeing an exclusive jurisdiction clause (*Konkola Copper Mines Plc v Coromin Ltd* [2006] EWHC 1093 (Comm); [2006] 2 Lloyd's Rep. 446).

The court retains a discretion under r.6.36 when allowing service out of the jurisdiction not to give effect to a foreign jurisdiction clause. At lowest, strong cause has to be shown to override a foreign jurisdiction clause (*Aratra Potato Co Ltd v Egyptian Navigation Co (The El Amria)* [1981] 2 Lloyd's Rep. 119, CA; *UBS A.G. v Omni Holding A.G.* [2000] 1 W.L.R. 916; *Sinochem International Oil (London) Co Ltd v Mobile Sales and Supply Corp*, op cit). The discretion might still be exercised in a claimant's favour even where the claimant has allowed his claim to become time-barred in the chosen jurisdiction provided he has acted reasonably in so doing (*Citi-March Ltd v Neptune Orient* [1996] 2 All E.R. 545 (Colman J.)).

Where a time bar point may not be waived by a defendant in a foreign jurisdiction, a court may refuse to stay proceedings that would otherwise be stayed where the claimants had acted reasonably in commencing proceedings in England (*Baghlaf Al Zafer Factory Co BR for Industry Ltd v Pakistan National Shipping Co (No.2)* [2000] 1 Lloyd's Rep. 1, CA).

A non-exclusive jurisdiction clause raises a strong prima facie case that such jurisdiction is forum conveniens (*E.D. & F. Man Ship Ltd v Kvaerner Gibraltar Ltd (The Rothnie)* [1996] 2 Lloyd's Rep. 206 (Creswell J.)).

The logic of such clauses has been taken to its contractual conclusion in the cases of *British Aerospace Plc v Dee Howard Co* [1993] 1 Lloyd's Rep. 368; *Mercury Communications Ltd v Communication Telesystems International*, op cit, and *JP Morgan Securities Asia Private Ltd v Malaysian Newsprint Industries Sdn Bhd* [2001] 2 Lloyd's Rep. 41. In some cases the fact that the clause was non-exclusive might make it easier to displace the strong presumption in favour of giving effect to them, (*BP Plc v AON Ltd (No.1)* [2005] EWHC 2554; [2006] 1 Lloyd's Rep. 549) particularly where more than one jurisdiction was chosen and one feature that may be highly relevant is where there are already proceedings in a foreign country which involve overlapping issues, especially if they have been commenced by a party which subsequently seeks to sue in England (see *BAS Capital Funding Corp*, above).

Where the application of the principle of forum non conveniens involves a jurisdiction clause, there is no obvious logic in applying the itemised factors employed in

Mackender v Feldia AG [1967] 2 Q.B. 590; [1966] 3 All E.R. 847, CA; see *British Aerospace*, op cit, and *Mercury Communications Ltd*, op cit. This is particularly so where the clause concerns a neutral forum (*Attock Cement Co Ltd v Romanian Bank for Foreign Trade* [1989] 1 Lloyd's Rep. 572, CA, at p.582, and *JP Morgan Securities Asia Private Ltd*, op cit) and even more so where the chosen jurisdiction is the "home" court of one of the parties; *Beazley v Horizon Offshore Contractors Inc* [2004] EWHC 2555 (Comm); [2005] I.L.Pr. 11.

If, however, the legal and political systems of the foreign country have changed since the contract was made, different considerations may apply, both as a matter of construction and of discretion (*Carvalho v Hull Blyth (Angola) Ltd* [1979] 1 W.L.R. 1228; [1979] 3 All E.R. 280, CA).

Where it was held that claims in tort fell outside an exclusive jurisdiction clause which provided for proceedings to be brought in Cyprus and that a ship owner employer had its only visible place of business in England, the jurisdiction clause was not given effect in respect of other causes of action that fell within it (*Domansa v Derin Shipping and Trading Co Inc* [2001] 1 Lloyd's Rep. 362). For the effect of duress on a jurisdiction clause, see *Carnoustie Universal SA v International Transport Workers Federation* [2002] EWHC 1624 (Comm) [2003] I.L.Pr. 7 (Richard Siberry Q.C). In a case of internet libel the court's discretion in ascertaining the most appropriate forum will tend to be more open textured than otherwise; *Lewis v King* [2004] EWCA Civ 1329; [2005] I.L.Pr.16. CA.

The jurisdiction to stay proceedings by reason of foreign jurisdiction clauses in respect of non-Contracting and non-Member States is unaffected by *Owuso v Jackson (C-281/02)* [2005] Q.B. 801, ECJ.; see *Konkola Copper Mines Plc v Caromin* [2006] EWCA Civ 5; [2006] 1 Lloyd's Rep. 410, CA, which also indicates the proper approach to burden and standard of proof in such cases.

6.37.20 The more important of the reported cases in which the *Spiliada* principles have been considered are as follows:

Applied

E.I. Du Pont de Nemours & Co v Agnew [1987] 2 Lloyd's Rep. 585, CA

Mitsubishi Corp v Alfafouzos [1988] 1 Lloyd's Rep. 191

de Dampierre v de Dampierre [1988] A.C. 92, HL

Virgo Steamship Co SA v Skaarup Shipping Corp [1988] 1 Lloyd's Rep. 352

Roneleigh Ltd v MII Exports Inc [1989] 1 W.L.R. 619, CA

Irish Shipping Ltd v Commercial Union Assurance Co Plc (The Irish Rowan) [1991] 2 Q.B. 206, CA

Cleveland Museum of Art v Capricorn Art International S.A. [1990] 2 Lloyd's Rep. 166

Marc Rich & Co AG v Societa Italiana Impianti PA (The Atlantic Emperor) (No.1) [1989] 1 Lloyd's Rep. 548, CA

Marc Rich & Co AG v Societa Italiana Impianti PA (C-190/89) [1992] 1 Lloyd's Rep. 342, ECJ

In re Harrods (Buenos Aires) Ltd [1992] Ch. 72, CA

The Varna (No.2) [1994] 2 Lloyd's Rep. 41

Bank of Credit and Commerce Hong Kong Ltd v Sonali Bank [1995] 1 Lloyd's Rep. 227

Connelly v R.T.Z. Corp Plc [1996] Q.B. 361, HL

Mohammed v Bank of Kuwait and the Middle East K.S.C. [1996] 1 W.L.R. 1483, CA

Citi-March Ltd v Neptune Orient Lines Ltd [1996] 1 W.L.R. 1367

The Bergen (No.2) [1997] 2 Lloyd's Rep. 710

Chadha v Dow Jones & Co Inc, The Times, May 18, 1999, CA

Lubbe v Cape Plc [2000] 1 W.L.R. 1545, CA

Navigators Insurance Co v Atlantic Methanol Production Co LLC [2003] EWHC 1706 (Comm) [2004] Lloyd's Rep. I.R. 418

6.37.21 *Considered*

Saipem S.p.A. v Dredging VO2 B.V. [1988] 2 Lloyd's Rep. 361, CA

Meadows Indemnity Co Ltd v Insurance Corp of Ireland Plc [1989] 1 Lloyd's Rep. 181

British Aerospace Plc v Dee Howard Co [1993] 1 Lloyd's Rep. 368

Egon Oldendorff v Liberia Corp [1995] 2 Lloyd's Rep. 64

Butler v Butler [1998] 1 W.L.R. 1208, CA

Reichhold Norway ASA v Goldman Sachs International [2000] 1 W.L.R. 173, CA

Limit (No.3) Ltd v PDV Insurance Co [2005] EWCA Civ 383; [2005] 2 All E.R. (Comm) 347, CA

Discretion and delay

Inordinate delay in seeking permission to serve the claim form may be a ground for refusing permission (*Schothorst and Schuitema v Franz Dauter GmbH (The Nimrod)* [1973] 2 Lloyd's Rep. 91 (two-and-a-half years' delay between issuing writ and seeking permission to serve, during which the limitation period expired)). Further, it would be appropriate only in very limited circumstances to allow service out the jurisdiction where to do so would enable a claimant to escape the consequences of his delay (*National Bank of Greece SA v Outhwaite* [2001] C.P. Rep. 69). **6.37.22**

Restraint of foreign proceedings

1. In considering whether an injunction should be granted to restrain a claimant beginning or pursuing an action in another jurisdiction the court does not proceed on the same principles as those applied when granting a stay of proceedings on the grounds of forum non conveniens. **6.37.23**

First, the jurisdiction is to be exercised when the "ends of justice" require it.

Secondly, where the court decides to grant an injunction restraining proceedings in a foreign court, its order is directed not against the foreign court but against the parties so proceeding or threatening to proceed.

Thirdly, it follows that an injunction will only be issued restraining a party who is amenable to the jurisdiction of the court, against whom an injunction will be an effective remedy. In general, comity requires that the English courts have a sufficient interest in, or connection with, the disputed proceedings in order to grant an anti-suit injunction.

Fourthly, since such an order indirectly effects the foreign court, the jurisdiction is one which must be exercised with caution.

In a case where a remedy for a particular wrong is available both in the English court and in a foreign court, the English court will, generally speaking, only restrain the claimant from pursuing proceedings in the foreign court if such pursuit would be vexatious or oppressive. This presupposes that, as a general rule, the English court must conclude that it provides the natural forum for the trial of the actions; and further, since the court is concerned with the ends of justice, that account must be taken not only of injustice to the defendant if the claimant is allowed to pursue the foreign proceedings, but also of injustice to the claimant if he is not allowed to do so. So the court will not grant an injunction if, by doing so, it will deprive the claimant of advantages in the foreign forum of which it would be unjust to deprive him. That problem can often be overcome by appropriate undertakings given by the defendant, or by granting an injunction upon appropriate terms; just as, in cases of stay of proceedings, the parallel problem of advantages to the claimant in the domestic forum which are prima facie, inappropriate, can likewise often be solved by granting a stay upon terms.

See *Société Nationale Industrielle Aerospatiale v Lee Jui Jak (SNIA)* [1987] A C. 871, PC; *Schiffahrtsgesellschaft Detlev Von Appen GmbH v Voest Alpine Intertrading GmbH* [1997] 2 Lloyd's Rep. 279, CA; *Airbus Industrie G.I.E. v Patel* [1999] 1 A.C. 119, HL; *Donohue v Armco Inc* [2001] UKHL 64; [2002] 1 Lloyd's Rep. 425; [2002] 1 All E.R. 97 (Comm), HL; *American International Speciality Lines v Abbot Laboratories* [2002] EWHC 2714 (Comm); [2003] 1 Lloyd's Rep. 267; *General Star International Indemnity Ltd v Stirling Cooke Brown Reinsurance Brokers Ltd* [2003] EWHC 3 (Comm) [2003] I.L.Pr. 19 (injunctions where parallel proceedings in New York steeped in English attributes). Where foreign proceedings are properly commenced abroad by a party that is subsequently a defendant in proceedings within the jurisdiction brought by the defendant on the foreign proceedings and those proceedings have no unconscionable vexatious or oppressive aspect, they will not be restrained by an anti-suit injunction. This is particularly so where the foreign proceedings have been fully contested over an appreciable period. However, where such a defendant seeks such a stay of English proceedings, an anti-suit injunction may be granted to protect the proceedings seeking the stay; *Albon v Naza Motor Trading (No.4)* [2008] EWCA Civ 1124; [2008] 1 Lloyd's Rep. 1, CA. The presence of a non-exclusive jurisdiction clause might lighten the burden of an applicant in establishing vexatious or oppressive conduct but will not be construed as giving primacy to the English courts in any conflict arising from the prospect of virtually simultaneous trials in parallel proceedings; *Royal Bank of Canada v Cooperatieve Centrale Raiffeisen-Boerenleenbank BA* [2004] EWCA Civ 7; [2004] 1 Lloyd's Rep. 471, CA Where proceedings are properly brought and continued in England and the defendant in the English proceedings brings proceedings in another jurisdiction in order to prevent proceedings in England and it is not unjust to prevent the continuation of those proceedings, an anti-suit injunction restraining the foreign proceedings may be granted (*Cadre SA v Astra Asigurari SA* [2005] EWHC 2626 (Comm); [2006] 1 Lloyd's Rep. 560). An anti-suit injunction may be granted in respect of foreign proceedings where an English court post judgment has a strong legitimate interest in protecting its proceedings and it would be vexatious to pursue proceedings elsewhere; *Trafigura Beheer BV v Kookmin Bank Co (No.2)* [2006] EWHC 1921 (Comm); [2007] 1 Lloyd's Rep 669. See also *Masri v Consolidated Contractors International Co* [2008] EWCA Civ 625; [2008] 2 Lloyd's Rep. 301, CA.

A collateral attack on a binding judgment or award is just as capable of amounting to oppressive conduct as proceedings pre-dating the award or judgment. In appropriate cases summary declaratory relief rather than injunctive relief is sufficient to produce a just result; see *Noble Assurance Co v Gerling-Konzern General Insurance Co* [2007] EWHC 253 (Comm); [2007] 1 C.L.C. 85.

Enforcement of patent rights can only be considered abusive if the patent is obviously not infringed or is invalid, and, in either case, the patentee either knows or believes that to be the case; *Sandisk Corp v Koninklijke Philips Electronics NV* [2007] EWHC 332; [2007] I.L.Pr. 22 (a Judgments Regulation case).

It is not for an English court to restrain a party in proceedings before it from suing in another jurisdiction on the ground of the English court's own perception as to the fairness or unfairness of the proceedings in the other jurisdiction, where the country in which the party seeks to sue is not itself bound by the European Convention on Human Rights 1950; *Al-Bassam v Al-Bassam* [2004] EWCA Civ 857; [2004] W.T.L.R. 757, CA

The Brussels Convention is to be interpreted as precluding the grant of an injunction whereby a court of a Contracting State prohibits a party to proceedings pending before it from commencing or continuing legal proceedings before a court of another Contracting State, even where that party is acting in bad faith with a view to frustrating the existing proceedings; *Turner v Grovit* (C159/02) [2005] 1 A.C. 101, ECJ.

Where an anti-suit injunction has been granted in respect of proceedings of which a non-Contracting and non-Regulation state is first seised, the subsequent accession of that state to the EU will not, of itself, render the injunction ineffective, even where the substantive proceedings in the English court are stayed pursuant to art.66 of the Judgment Regulation; *Advent Capital Plc v G N Ellinas Imports-Exports Ltd* [2005] EWHC 1242 (Comm) [2005] 2 Lloyd's Rep, (Colman J.).

Where a party is properly before the court, an application for an anti-suit injunction on the ground of unconscionable conduct is not a separate claim requiring its own basis of jurisdiction, and, in such a case, the right to apply exists regardless of whether the respondent is domiciled in a Convention or Regulation state, *Masri v Consolidated Contractors International Co* [2008] EWCA Civ 625; [2008] 2 Lloyd's Rep. 301, CA.

In the exceptional case of a claim being purely vexatious in the true sense, it may be sufficient for the grant of an injunction that the English court is a natural forum for the claim (*Shell International Petroleum Co Ltd v Coral Oil Co Ltd (No.2)* [1999] 2 Lloyd's Rep. 606).

2. The English court has a discretionary power to restrain by injunction a breach of contract and that power can be used to restrain foreign proceedings where, for example, there is an agreement to arbitrate the dispute (*Toepfer v Société Cargill* [1998] 1 Lloyd's Rep. 379, CA; *Shell International Petroleum Co Ltd v Coral Oil Co Ltd* [1999] 1 Lloyd's Rep. 72; *Youell v Kara Mara Shipping Co Ltd* [2000] 2 Lloyd's Rep. 102; *American International Speciality Lines v Abbott Laboratories* [2002] EWHC 2714 (Comm); [2003] 1 Lloyd's Rep. 267). In *Donohue v Armco Inc* [2001] UKHL 64; [2002] 1 Lloyd's Rep. 425; [2002] 1 All E.R. 97 (Comm), HL, the House of Lords found that the need to dispose of issues common to parties not all of whom were bound by an exclusive jurisdiction clause provided the necessary strong reasons not to apply the clauses. As to the difficulty of starting proceedings in this jurisdiction simply to prevent proceedings abroad where there is no enabling contractual provision; see *Amoco (UK) Exploration Co v British American Offshore Ltd* [1999] 2 All E.R. (Comm) 201. (See also para.6.37.19 above.) Where a legitimate claim for security in another jurisdiction is also used to defeat a jurisdictional agreement, an anti-suit injunction may be granted to restrain the impermissible conduct both against the party to the agreement and a party "calling the shots"; *Kallang Shipping SA v AXA Assurances Senegal* [2006] EWHC 2825 (Comm); [2007] 1 Lloyd's Rep. 160. Where the law of a State gives a third party a direct right of action against an insurer, an arbitration clause governing relations be-

tween the insurer and the assured will probably not afford the insurer grounds for an anti-suit injunction against the third party; *Markel International Co Ltd v Craft* [2006] EWHC 3150 (Comm); [2007] Lloyd's Rep. I.R. 403 (the choice of seat of an arbitration is the choice of forum for remedies seeking to attack the award; *C v D* [2007] EWCA Civ 1282; [2008] 1 Lloyd's Rep. 239; [2008] 1 All E.R. (Comm) 1001).

For the relationship between the Supreme Court Act 1981 s.37 and the Arbitration Act 1996 s.44, see *Starlight Shipping Co v Tai Ping Insurance Co Ltd (The Alexandros T)* [2007] EWHC 1893 (Comm); [2008] 1 All E.R. (Comm) 593.

The discretion under a jurisdiction clause to grant an anti-suit injunction in respect of proceedings in a non-Contracting and non-Member State is unaffected by *Owusu v Jackson* (C-281/02) [2005] Q.B. 801, ECJ; see *Konkola Copper Mines Plc v Coromin* [2006] EWCA Civ 5; [2006] 1 Lloyd's Rep. 410, CA. Where the Judgments Regulation requires a matter to be litigated within this jurisdiction and an exclusive jurisdiction clause provides for litigation in a non-Member State, proceedings in the non-Member State may be restrained; *Samengo-Turner v J & H Marsh & McLennan (Services) Ltd* [2007] EWCA Civ 723; [2007] 2 All E.R. (Comm) 813, CA.

See *Sabah Shipyard (Pakistan) Ltd v Pakistan* [2002] EWCA Civ 1643; [2003] 2 Lloyd's Rep. 571, CA, at para.6.37.24 below, for anti-suit injunction against State.

The longer the delay in making applications for an anti-suit injunction, the more likely it is that there will be good reason to refuse it, but there is not culpable delay where it is caused by a party taking appropriate steps to challenge the jurisdiction in a foreign forum (*Advent Capital Plc v GN Ellinas Importers-Exporters Ltd* [2003] EWHC 3330 (Comm); [2004] I.L.Pr. 23 (Morison J.).

Actions against foreign states

The State Immunity Act 1978 came into force on November 22, 1978. It gives statutory force to the doctrine of restrictive immunity, by which the immunity of a foreign state from action is not absolute but is restricted to acts of a governmental nature, jure imperii, and not of a commercial nature jure gestionis. The conflict between the theories of absolute and restrictive immunity is explained in the judgment of Lord Denning M.R. in *Trendtex Trading v Central Bank of Nigeria* [1977] Q.B. 529, CA. See also *Kuwait Airways Corp v Iraqi Airways Co* [1995] 1 W.L.R. 1147, HL. **6.37.24**

Under the Act, activities which could equally well be performed by a trading corporation or private individual will not generally enjoy immunity from the jurisdiction of the UK courts merely because they are carried on by a state or by a "separate entity" under the control of a state and on its behalf. The Act is complex and presents many problems.

The practitioner should note:

(i) The Act restricts immunity; it does not directly confer jurisdiction. If, in order to institute proceedings, it is necessary to serve the claim form or other process outside the jurisdiction, permission must be obtained under r.6.36 or r.6.38.

(ii) Although the circumstances which will restrict immunity will, in most cases, bring the case within one of the headings of para.3.1 of 6BPD; the Act and para.3.1 do not precisely correspond. An application for permission under Section IV of Pt 6 must show distinctly; (a) why the prospective defendant is not absolutely immune from suit; (b) under which heading of para.3.1 of 6BPD the action falls

(iii) The consideration that it is undesirable to subject to the jurisdiction of the English courts a foreigner who owes no allegiance here, applies with peculiar force to a suit against a foreign state. Dubious or borderline applications ought not to be made and it should be made clearly to appear that the case is a proper one for the English courts.

(iv) It will also be relevant to consider whether a judgment of the English court is likely to be effective. For the service of process against a foreign state see s.12 of the Act.

In *Sabah Shipyard (Pakistan) Ltd v Pakistan* [2002] EWCA Civ 1643; [2003] 2 Lloyd's Rep. 571, CA, the court granted an anti-suit injunction against the government of Pakistan where it had waived its sovereign immunity, when giving a collateral guarantee which contained an English jurisdiction clause. A waiver of state immunity in a contract will not necessarily amount to a submission to the jurisdiction under s.2 of the State Immunity Act 1978; *Svenska Petroleum v Lithuania (No.2)*. [2005] EWHC 2437 (Comm); [2006] 1 All E.R. (Comm) 730.

For the purposes of s.3 of the State Immunity Act 1978 the words "proceedings relating to a commercial transaction" should be given a narrow construction, see *Svenska Petroleum*, above.

The immunity from legal process conferred by the Specialised Agencies of the United Nations (Immunities and Privileges) Order (SI 1974/1260) and Specialised Agencies of the United Nations (Immunities and Privileges of UNESCO) Order (SI 2001/2560) does not violate art.6(1) of the European Convention for the Protection of Human Rights and Fundamental Freedoms 1950; *Entico v UNESCO* [2008] EWHC 531 (Comm); [2008] 1 Lloyd's Rep. 673; [2008] 2 All E.R. (Comm) 97.

Where acts of torture are concerned, a state and its servants, so acting, are entitled to claim immunity against suit ratione personae in an English court under s.1(1) of the State Immunity Act 1978;*Jones v Ministry of Interior of the Kingdom of Saudi Arabia* [2006] UKHL 26; [2007] 1 A.C. 270; [2007] 1 All E.R. 113, HL. A claim in respect of sovereign acts is not justiciable where those responsible for such acts seek to recover losses said to have arisen from such acts and said to have been caused by those who occasioned those acts; *Mbasogo v Logo Ltd* [2006] EWCA Civ 1370; [2007] Q.B. 846, CA

In most cases where state immunity is invoked it would be a waste of time fully to review all the facts of the case with a view to deciding the issue of proportionality in connection with the right to a fair trial; *Grovit v De Nederlandsche Bank* [2005] EWHC 2944 (QB); [2006] 1 W.L.R. 3323; [2006] 1 All E.R. (Comm) 397 (confirmed on appeal [2007] EWCA Civ 953; [2008] 1 W.L.R. 51; [2008] 1 All E.R. (Comm) 106; [2008] I.L.Pr. 19, CA).

Grounds on which service out permissible with court's permission (r.6.37(1))

6.37.25 An application for permission to serve the claim form out of the jurisdiction must set out which ground in para.3.1 of Practice Direction B (see 6BPD.3below) is relied on. The following paragraphs (to para.6.37.55) contain commentary on the several grounds.

Paragraph 3.1(1) to (5) of 6BPD: General grounds and interim remedies

6.37.26 *Paragraph 3.1(1) of 6BPD: "domiciled within the jurisdiction"*—A claim form may be served out of the jurisdiction with the permission of the court if "a claim is made for a remedy" against a person domiciled within the jurisdiction. In this context, by virtue of r.6.31(i) "domicile" is to be determined in accordance, not with the common law, but with the Civil Jurisdiction and Judgments Act 1982 ss.41 to 46.

6.37.27 *Paragraph 3.1(2) of 6BPD: Injunction*—A claim form may be served out of the jurisdiction with the permission of the court if an injunction is sought. (Formerly, RSC O.11, r.1(1)(b) stated that the injunction had to be sought "in the action begun by the writ"; now it would seem to be a matter of necessary inference that the injunction must be sought in the claim form.) The discretion to grant permission under this provision will not be exercised unless: (i) an injunction is a genuine part of the substantive relief sought and has not been claimed merely to bring the case within the rule (*Rosler v Hilbery* [1925] 1 Ch. 250, CA, at p.261 *et seq.*), and (ii) there is a reasonable prospect of an injunction (itself a discretionary remedy) being granted (*Watson v Daily Record* [1907] 1 K.B. 853, CA). The injunction must be an order against the defendant to do or refrain from doing an act within the jurisdiction and the provision will not ground an attempt to restrain foreign proceedings (*Amoco (UK) Exploration Co v British American Offshore Ltd* [1999] 2 All E.R. (Comm) 201).

6.37.28 *Paragraph 3.1(3) of 6BPD: "necessary or proper party" where a claim is made against someone on whom the claim form has been or will be served*—A significant aspect of this provision is that it may be invoked even where service has not yet occurred on the original defendant.

Where a claim is brought against a person duly served with the claim form either within or out of the jurisdiction, the court may grant permission for the claim form to be served on another person, being a person out of the jurisdiction, where that other person is "a necessary or proper party" to the claim. Indeed, such permission may be given even before the first person has been duly served. All this is provided for in paras 3.1(3) and 3.1(4) of 6BPD (3) and (4). By these means, persons who could be joined as parties under Pt 19, or in relation to whom an additional claim could be made under Pt 20, may be served if the court permits. Before the CPR came into effect, the claimant applying for such permission was required to support his application with an affidavit stating the grounds for his belief that there was between him and the first person a "real issue" which he "may reasonably ask the court to try" (see RSC O.11, rr.1(c) and 4(1)(d) and O.16, r.3(4)). The justification for this requirement was the need for a safeguard against a specious claim against the first person being used as a device to found jurisdiction to serve another person out of the jurisdiction. When RSC O.11 was removed from CPR Sch.1 and replaced by rules inserted in CPR Pt 6, this requirement was re-enacted in part (in former r.6.21(2)), but in terms it does not appear in r.6.37.

The proceedings against the original defendant must have been brought bona fide and not merely to provide a basis upon which to make an application under this rule for service on a person out of the jurisdiction (*Witted v Galbraith* [1893] 1 Q.B. 577; *Deutsche National Bank v Paul* [1898] 1 Ch. 283; *Bloomfield v Serenyi* [1945] 2 All E.R. 646, CA; *Derby & Co Ltd v Larsson* [1976] 1 W.L.R. 202, HL). It is to be presumed that the same principle will apply where service has not yet occurred. However, such proceedings, though bona fide, are not properly brought against the original defendant where the law is plain or the facts are uncontradicted and it is clear that the claimant could not succeed against the defendant (*Tyne Improvement Commissioners v Armement Anversois SA (The Brabo)* [1949] A.C. 326, HL; *Multinational Gas and Petrochemical Co v Multinational Gas and Petrochemical Services Ltd* [1983] 2 All E.R. 563, CA; *The Berge Sisar* [2001] 1 Lloyd's Rep. 663, HL). As a safeguard against a specious claim against the original defendant being used as a device to found jurisdiction to serve another party outside the jurisdiction, r.6.37(2) requires that the written evidence supporting the application for permission must state that there is a real issue between the claimant and the original defendant, which the claimant may reasonably ask the court to try.

"necessary or proper party"—The terms are alternative. Generally, a person who may be joined in proceedings in accordance with the rules as to joinder of parties is a "proper" party (*Massey v Heynes* [1881] 21 Q.B.D. 330, CA). **6.27.29**

The court's power to permit service out of the jurisdiction under para.3.1(3) of 6BPD is no less wide than the court' power to add or substitute a party under r.19.2(2) (*United Film Distribution Ltd v Chabria, The Times*, April 5, 2001, CA).

A person may be a proper party when the liability of several persons whether cumulative or alternative depends upon one investigation (*Massey v Heynes* [1881] 21 Q.B.D. 330, CA; *Petroleo Brasiliero SA v Mellitus Shipping Inc (The Baltic Flame)* [2001] EWCA Civ 418; [2001] 2 Lloyd's Rep. 203, CA, and *Carvill America Inc v Camperdown UK Ltd* [2005] EWCA Civ 645; [2005] 2 Lloyd's Rep 457, CA). For the joinder of a party being necessary for justice to be done, see *Electric Furance Co v Selas Corp of America* [1987] R.P.C. 23. Where the proposed joinder would confer no real additional advantage on the claimant, e.g. where the proposed defendant outside the jurisdiction has merely induced the tort of the internal defendant and the total damages will not be increased by the joinder, permission may not be given; but where the claimant has a cause of action for damages against two possible defendants, and where it may be valuable to have the ability to choose against which of them to enforce judgment, or, a fortiori, where the relief claimed is an account of profits, permission will be granted (*ibid.*). A person out of the jurisdiction not shown to be arguably liable is not a "proper party", and permission under para.3.1(3) of 6BPD should not be granted merely for the purpose of making him a party to proceedings to enable the claimant to obtain disclosure of documents from him (see *Unilever Plc v Chefaro Proprietaries Ltd* [1994] F.S.R. 135, CA, where the question arose in the context of the Brussels Convention, art.6).

A court may refuse permission where the claimant and proposed defendant are parties to an exclusive foreign jurisdiction clause; *Konkola Copper Mines Plc v Caromin* [2006] EWHC 1093 (Comm); [2006] I.L.Pr. 46; [2006] 2 Lloyd's Rep. 446.

Disclosure—Where relevant documents in a case between domestic parties are in the possession of the overseas holding company of one of them, it is not a good arguable case against the overseas holding company under para.3.1(3) of 6BPD if the only purpose of joining the overseas company to the proceedings is to obtain disclosure. The same principles would apply to prevent joinder of a party for that purpose under the Brussels Convention (art.6) (*Unilever plc v Chefaro Proprietaries Ltd* [1994] F.S.R. 135, CA). **6.37.30**

Counterclaims and other additional claims—Permission is not needed to serve a Pt 20 claim in the form of a counterclaim on a foreign claimant because, by suing in England, he submits to the jurisdiction in regard to any counterclaim (*Derby & Co v Larsson* [1976] 1 W.L.R. 202, HL, at p.205). **6.37.31**

Where the law of another available jurisdiction allows no remedy of contribution, that fact may decide a court to exercise its discretion in favour of permission to serve out of the jurisdiction under rr.6.36 and 6.37 (*Petroleo Brasiliero SA v Mellitus Shipping Inc (The Baltic Flame)* [2001] EWCA Civ 418; [2001] 2 Lloyd's Rep. 203, CA).

For application for permission to bring counterclaim or other additional claim against a party out of the jurisdiction other than the claimant, see para.6.37.22 below.

6.37.32 *Paragraph 3.1(4) of 6BPD: "necessary or proper party" where a claim is an additional claim under Pt 20*—Paragraph 3.1(4) replaced, but in slightly amended terms, para.(3A) of r.6.20. Paragraph (3A) was inserted in r.6.20 in 2000 (after certain problems had been exposed in decided cases) and stated that a claim form may be served out of the jurisdiction with the permission of the court if "a claim is a Part 20 claim and the person to be served is a necessary or proper party to the claim against the Part 20 claimant". Sub-paragraph (4) of para.3.1 now states that the claimant may serve a claim form out of the jurisdiction with the permission of the court where "a claim is an additional claim under Part 20 and the person to be served is a necessary or proper party *to the claim* or additional claim" (emphasis added). The purpose of the phrase emphasised is not obvious. (In the CPR, "additional claim" means "any claim other than the claim by the claimant against the defendant" (r.20.2(2)(a).)

Permission is not needed to serve a Pt 20 claim in the form of a counterclaim on a foreign claimant because, by suing in England, he submits to the jurisdiction in regard to any counterclaim (*Derby & Co v Larsson* [1976] 1 W.L.R. 202, HL, at p.205).

Where the law of another available jurisdiction allows no remedy of contribution, that fact may decide a court to exercise its discretion in favour of permission to serve out of the jurisdiction under rr.6.36 and 6.37 (*Petroleo Brasiliero SA v Mellitus Shipping Inc (The Baltic Flame)* [2001] EWCA Civ 418; [2001] 2 Lloyd's Rep. 203, CA).

6.37.33 *Paragraph 3.1(5) of 6BPD: claim made for an interim remedy under s.25(1) of the 1982 Act*—Where there are no substantive proceedings, following the full implementation of s.25 of the Civil Jurisdiction and Judgments Act 1982 and the introduction (in 1997) of (what is now) para.3.1(5) of 6BPD (formerly RSC O.11, r.8A) applications may now be made with permission for interim remedies in support of overseas proceedings. In the Commercial Court applications for relief are made under CPR Pt 8; elsewhere they are made under Pt 23.

Paragraph 3.1(6) of 6BPD: Claims in relation to contracts

6.37.34 *Paragraph 3.1(6) of 6BPD: claim made in respect of a contract*—This wide provision is subject to one or other of the conditions stated in sub-paras (a) to (d) (see paras 6.37.36 to 6.37.39 below). For other claims in relation to contracts, see paras 6.37.41 and 6.37.42 below).

6.37.35 *"a contract"*—The connecting thread is the existence of a contract. In order to bring a claim within the scope of para.3.1(6) the claimant must show that there is a good arguable case that there exists a contract between himself and the defendant and that there is a good arguable case that the claim is made in respect of that contract. The wording is new and it remains to be shown how central must be the role of the contract in the claim in order to found jurisdiction.

For a case of an implied contract, see *Bowling v Cox* [1926] A.C. 751, PC.

The wording of para.3.1(6) is deliberately wider than the provision in RSC O.11 and requires only that the claim relates to or is connected with the contract. A restitutionary claim can fall within para.3.1(6); *Albon v Naza Motor Trading* [2007] EWHC 9 (Ch); [2007] 1 W.L.R. 2489; [2007] 2 All E.R. 719; [2007] 1 Lloyd's Rep. 297.

An action on an award is an action on the contract contained in the submission to arbitration, but the award itself may also, it seems, be treated as the contract, in that it contains an implied agreement to perform it (*Bremer Oeltransport v Drewry* [1933] 1 K.B. 753, CA and cases there cited). An action on a judgment is also an action on the implied contract, contained in the judgment, to perform it (*Grant v Easton* (1883) 13 Q.B.D. 302, CA).

An action for a declaration that a contract has been discharged by frustration or repudiation or otherwise is one brought in respect of the contract and is within this sub-rule (*BP Exploration (Libya) Ltd v Hunt* [1976] 1 W.L.R. 788; [1976] 1 Lloyd's Rep. 471; [1976] 3 All E.R. 879, CA).

A *claim for negative declaratory relief* can fall within para.3.1(6) (*HIB Ltd v Guardian Insurance Co Inc* [1997] 1 Lloyd's Rep. 412), but para.3.1(8) makes specific provision for a negative declaration. Where a claimant seeks a negative declaration in England and the defendant commences proceedings in an alternative forum, it is necessary to consider whether the application in England serves a useful purpose and, if so, if it is proper to grant permission to serve out of the jurisdiction notwithstanding the undesirability of concurrent proceedings (*Ark Therapeutics Plc v True North Capital Ltd* [2005] EWHC 1585; [2006] 1 All E.R. (Comm) 138).

Paragraphs 3.1(6) and 3.1(7) are unlikely to extend to cover a claim against a company director based upon his appointment as director without a specific contract of employment (*New Therapeutics Ltd v Katz* [1991] Ch. 226; [1991] 2 All E.R. 151).

If a claimant has a remedy in contract or tort upon the same facts, he can choose his remedy and, if choosing tort, may seek permission to serve out of the jurisdiction under para.3.1(9) (*Matthews v Kuwait Bechtel Corp* [1959] 2 Q.B. 57, CA).

Made within the jurisdiction (para.3.1(6)(a) of 6BPD)—The jurisdiction is the territorial jurisdiction (see r.2.3(1)). **6.37.36**

Where a contract is concluded by cable or letter passing between one country and another, prima facie the contract is made where the offer is accepted, by posting the letter or dispatching the cable of acceptance or sending off the goods ordered (per du Parcq J., in chambers, June 22, 1934, unrep.; following *Cowan v O'Conner* (1888) 20 Q.B.D. 640). On the other hand, in the case of telex or telephone communications, the contract is made at the place where the offeror receives the notification of the acceptance by the offeree (*Entores v Miles Far East Corp* [1955] 2 Q.B. 327, CA). By parity of reasoning communication by facsimile and email is governed by the principles set out in *Entores v Miles Far East Corp*.

A quasi-contract or other similar obligation comes within the meaning of "contract" in this rule, and in such a case the word "made" in this rule should be read as "arising" (*Rousou's (A Bankrupt) Trustee v Rousou* [1955] 3 All E.R. 486, affirming [1955] 1 W.L.R. 545).

If a contract which was made within the jurisdiction is subsequently amended by an agreement made outside the jurisdiction, it seems that the amended contract will still be taken as made within the jurisdiction unless the amendment has the effect of substituting a new agreement (*BP Exploration (Libya) Ltd v Hunt* [1976] 1 W.L.R. 788; [1976] 1Lloyd's Rep. 471; [1976] 3 All E.R. 879).

Made through an agent, etc. (para.3.1(6)(b) of 6BPD)—"Contract made by or through an agent trading or residing within the jurisdiction, and "through" denotes the case of a contract negotiated by an agent in this country but concluded by the principal abroad (*National Mortgage Co v Gosselin* (1922) 38 T.L.R. 832, CA). See also CPR r.6.12(1)(b) (formerly RSC O.10, r.2(1)(a)); and *The Metamorphosis* [1953] 1 W.L.R. 543; [1953] 1 All E.R. 723. **6.37.37**

Paragraph 3.1(6)(b) applies where the principal of the agent in question is the defendant, and not where the principal is the claimant (*Union International Insurance Co Ltd v Jubilee Insurance Co Ltd* [1991] 1 All E.R. 740).

Governed by English law (para.3.1(6)(c) of 6BPD)—For the rules for ascertaining which is the law of the contract, see Dicey, Morris and Collins, *The Conflict of Laws*, 14th edn (London: Sweet & Maxwell, 2006), Chs 28 *et seq*. See also the Rome Convention as applied by the Contracts (Applicable Law) Act 1990 which came into force on April 1, 1991. Typical cases of contracts governed by English law are where the contract provides for arbitration in England and enforcement of an award in England (*N.V. Kwik Hoo Tong, etc. v J. Finlay & Co* [1927] A.C. 604) or that disputes shall be determined by the English courts or contains a clause such as the "follow London" clause in an insurance contract, showing an intention that claims should be negotiated and settled by Lloyd's underwriters in London (*Armadora Occidental SA v Horace Mann Insurance Co* [1977] 1 W.L.R. 1098; [1978] 1 All E.R. 407, CA). But in the absence of express agreement as to the proper law, no one factor is necessarily decisive. The ultimate test both at common law and under the Convention (art.4(1)) appears to be: what is the system of law with which the transaction has the closest and most real connection? (*Compagnie Tunisienne de Navigation SA v Compagnie d'Armement Maritime SA* [1971] A.C. 572; [1970] 3 All E.R. 71 HL); *Coast Lines v Hudig & Veder Chartering NV* [1972] 2 Q.B. 34; [1972] 1 All E.R. 451, CA, per Lord Denning M.R.; *Schiffahrtsgesellschaft Detlev Von Appen GmbH v Voest Alpine Intertrading GmbH* [1997] 2 Lloyd's Rep. 279, CA; *American Motorist Insurance Co v Cellstar Corp* [2003] EWCA Civ 206; [2003] I.L.Pr. 22.) See in respect of art.4(2), *Ennstone Building Products Ltd v Stanger Ltd* [2002] EWCA Civ 916; [2002] 1 W.L.R. 3059, CA; *Apple Corps Ltd v Apple Computer Inc* [2004] EWHC 768 (Ch) [2004] I.L.Pr 34; and *Iran Continental Shell Oil Co v IRI International Corp* [2002] EWCA Civ 1024; [2004] C.L.C. 696, CA, where the contract made is performed through a branch. Where letters of credit are concerned, the correct approach for the purposes of identifying the governing law is to look at how the contract **6.37.38** was intended to operate at the time that it was made and it is desirable that the same system of law should govern the co-existing contracts between (a) the issuing bank and the beneficiary, (b) the confirming bank and the beneficiary, and (c) the issuing bank and the confirming bank. In such situations the presumption under art.4(2) of the Rome Convention is likely to be displaced by art.4(5); *Marconi Communications International Ltd v PT Pan Indonesia Bank TBK* [2005] EWCA Civ 422; [2007] 2 Lloyd's Rep. 72; [2005] 2 All E.R. (Comm) 325. Where a contract is entered into in the course of the trade or profession of the party who has to effect the performance which is characteristic of the contract, the presumption is that the contract is most closely connected with the country in which the principal place of business of that party is situated; *Albon v Naza Motor Trading Sdn Bhd* [2007] EWHC 9 (Ch); [2007] 1 W.L.R. 2489; [2007] 2 All E.R. 719; [2007] 1 Lloyd's Rep. 297.

At common law the proper law of a contract must be either English law or the law of another country. The English courts will not apply any other system of law (such as Shia Sharia law) to a contract; *Musawi v RE International (UK) Ltd* [2007] EWHC 2981 (Ch) [2008] 1 Lloyd's Rep. 326 (David Richards J.).

Where parties have had a course of dealing in a market where their contracts have contained a number of express terms including one that the governing law is English, when they enter a new market under a contract that is silent on the governing law and other terms, the court may infer that the parties intended to contract on the same terms, including the governing law, unless such terms were inapplicable in the new market or clearly and indisputably inconsistent with its practice; *Banque Paribas v Cargill International S.A.* [1992] 1 Lloyd's Rep. 96 (Webster J.), affirmed CA [1992] 2 Lloyd's Rep. 19, CA.

For a discussion of the proper law of a contract of agency for a foreign principal, see *Mauroux v Soc. Com. Pereira, etc.* [1972] 1 W.L.R. 962; [1972] 2 All E.R. 1085, not following Dicey, Morris and Collins.

To imply a choice of law that choice must either have been intended or be so obvious that the parties would regard it as such; see *American Motorist Insurance Co*, above.

Article 3.3 of the Rome Convention provides an exception to the freedom of parties to choose the applicable law where that choice is designed to circumvent the mandatory rules of the country which is alone concerned with the transaction. In applying the article, the relevant elements are not those laid down by the mandatory rules of the law of the country in question; *Caterpillar Financial Services Corp v SNC Passion* [2004] EWHC 569 (Comm); [2004] 2 Lloyd's Rep. 99.

Where an international contract is expressly made subject to English law in a manner of which those interested in the contract must be deemed to have had notice, the contract may be determined by the law of the contract on the assumption that it is valid despite local law providing to the contrary (*Horne Linie GmbH & Co v Panamerican Formas E Impresos SA (The Hornbay)* [2006] EWHC 373; [2006] 2 Lloyd's Rep. 44 (Morison J.)).

Where an insurance policy was expressly governed by English law but the centre of gravity of the litigation was Texas and there was no persuasive reason to litigate elsewhere, permission to serve proceedings out of the jurisdiction for a declaration of non-liability was set aside; *Navigators Insurance Co v Atlantic Methanol Production Co LLC* [2003] EWHC 1706 (Comm); [2004] Lloyd's Rep. I.R. 418.

A claim for an anti-suit injunction in connection with a contract governed by English law may fall within the ambit of r.6.20(5); *Albon v Naza Motor Trading (No.4)* [2007] EWHC 1879 (Ch); [2007] 2 Lloyd's Rep. 420.

6.37.39 *Jurisdiction (para.3.1(6)(d) of 6BPD)*—Although of more significance in the context of applications under CPR Pt 11, and anti-suit injunctions, it may be noted that effect will normally be given jurisdiction clauses both in the context of protecting litigation within the jurisdiction; *Aratra Potato Co Ltd v Egyptian Navigation Co (The El Amria)* [1981] 2 Lloyd's Rep. 119, CA; *Sinochem International Oil (London) Co Ltd v Mobile Sales and Supply Corp* [2000] 1 Lloyd's Rep. 670 and agreements to litigate elsewhere (*Ingosstrakh Ltd v Latvian Shipping Co* [2000] I.L.Pr. 164, *CA Donohue v Armco Inc* [2001] UKHL 64; [2002] 1 Lloyd's Rep. 425; [2002] 1 All E.R. 97 (Comm), HL, is an example of the non-application of an English jurisdiction clause.

6.37.40 *"Contract or tort?"*—The grounds stated in para.3.1 of 6BPD include "claims in relation contract" and also "claims in tort". If, upon the same facts, a claimant has a remedy in contract or tort, he can choose whether to seek permission for service out of the jurisdiction either on the ground that his claim is relation contract or on the ground that it is in tort (*Matthews v Kuwait Bechtel Corp* [1959] 2 Q.B. 57, CA).

Paragraph 3.1(7) of 6BPD: Breach within the jurisdiction of a contract wherever made

A good arguable case of breach of contract must be made out (*Seaconsar Far East Ltd v Bank Markazi Jomhouri Islam Iran* [1994] 1 A.C. 438; [1993] 4 All E.R. 456, HL). Where no place of payment is provided by the terms of the contract (including such as are to be implied from the course of dealing between the parties) it is the duty of the debtor to seek out his creditor at his residence or place of business, and therefore a failure to pay money due to a claimant who resides or carries on business within the jurisdiction falls within this sub-rule (*Robey v Snaefell Co* (1887) 20 Q.B.D. 152; *The Eider* [1893] P.119, CA; *Thompson v Palmer* [1893] 2 Q.B. 80, CA; *Chas. Duval & Co v Gans* [1904] 2 K.B. 685; *Drexel v Drexel* [1916] 1 Ch. 251; *Bremer Oeltransport v Drewry* [1933] 1 K.B. 753, CA). As to a breach of contract to deliver goods, see *Nathan v Seitz* (1888) 4 T.L.R. 570; Wancke v Wingren (1889) 58 L.J.Q.B. 519; *Crozier, Stephens & Co v Auerbach* [1908] 2 K.B. 161, CA; *Johnson v Taylor* [1920] A.C. 144, HL). On the other hand, if there is no obligation which has to be performed within the jurisdiction, no breach can be committed within the jurisdiction within this sub-paragraph (*Cuban Atlantic Sugar Sales Corp v Compania de Vapores, etc.* [1960] 1 Q.B. 187; [1960] 1 All E.R. 141, CA). Where a contract is made by a defendant in country A to employ the claimant as his representative in country B, and the defendant wrongfully dismisses the claimant by a letter posted in country A, the breach takes place there (*Holland v Bennett* [1902] 1 K.B. 867; *Martin v Stout* [1925] A.C. 359, PC), and if by a letter posted in country B, the breach takes place there (*Mutzenbacher v La Aseguradora Espanola* [1906] 1 K.B. 254; *Oppenheimer v Rosenthal* [1937] 1 All E.R. 23). **6.37.41**

There is no doubt that the wording is intended to cover the case of *Johnson v Taylor* [1920] A.C. 144, HL, where it was decided, under the previous form of the subparagraph, that where there was a breach of contract abroad to ship goods c.i.f. England, and a breach of contract within the jurisdiction to deliver shipping documents to the buyer, leave would not be given in respect of the latter breach of contract to serve the writ out of the jurisdiction.

Paragraph 3.1(8) of 6BPD: Claim made for a declaration that no contract exists

This provision applies where, if the contract was found to exist, it would comply with the conditions set out in para.3.1(6) of 6BPD. **6.37.42**

Paragraph 3.1(9) of 6BPD: Claims in tort

Under para.3.1(9) the claimant must show that his claim is founded on a tort, and either (a) damage has been sustained within the jurisdiction or (b) damage has resulted from an act committed within the jurisdiction. Under requirement (a) it is enough that some significant damage has been sustained in England. Requirement (b) obliges the court to look at the tort alleged in a common sense way, and to ask whether damage has resulted from substantial and efficacious acts committed within the jurisdiction, regardless of whether or not such acts have been committed elsewhere (*Metall und Rohstoff AG v Donaldson Lufkin & Jenrette Inc* [1990] 1 Q.B. 391, CA). For the purposes of (b) in the context of negligent or fraudulent misstatement, the place where the where the harmful event giving rise to the damage has occurred is where the misstatement was made rather than where it was received (*Newsat Holdings Ltd v Zani* [2006] EWHC 342; [2006] 1 Lloyd's Rep. 707). See *London Helicopters Ltd v Heliportugal LDA-INAC* [2006] EWHC 108; [2006] 1 All E.R. (Comm) 595; [2006] 1 All E.R. (Comm) 595; [2006] I.L.Pr. 28 for the position under art.5.3 of the Regulation where a certificate said to have been issued negligently in Portugal was alleged to have caused damage in England. *Metall und Rohstoff* is authority for the phrase "the damage" (in para.3.1(9)) meaning some significant damage. See *Morin v Bonhams & Brooks Ltd* [2003] EWCA Civ 1802; [2004] 1 Lloyd's Rep. 702, CA, for the proper approach to para.3.1(9) and the irrelevance of other provisions and authorities. "Damage" should be given its natural and ordinary meanings, namely harm which has been sustained by the claimant whether physical or economic; *Booth v Phillips* [2004] EWHC 1437 (Comm); [2004] 1 W.L.R. 3292; *SA Cooley v TR Ramsey* [2008] EWHC 129 (QB); [2008] I.L.Pr. 27 (permission to serve in Australia in respect of a motorcycle accident there resulting in consequential damage in England). **6.37.43**

In deciding whether a tort has been committed in this or another country, the court should look back over the events constituting the tort and ask where in substance the cause of action arises. In answering that question the court must apply English law. If the court finds that the tort has in substance been committed in this country, the fact that some of the relevant events have happened abroad is irrelevant, as is the law of the foreign country where such events may have happened. If, on the other hand, the tort has in substance been committed in a foreign country, the court must apply the rule in *Boys v Chaplin* [1971] A.C. 356; [1969] 2 All E.R. 1085, HL, as developed by *Red Sea Insurance Co Ltd v Bouygues S.A.* [1995] 1 A.C. 190, PC; [1994] 3 All E.R. 749, PC, in respect of torts committed before the coming into force of Pt III of the Private International Law (Miscellaneous Provisions) Act 1995 on May 1, 1996. Torts committed after that date are governed by Pt III of the Act. Where an English court applies s.9(2) of the Private International Law (Miscellaneous Provisions) Act 1995 the exercise should not only be by reference to English legal concepts and classifications but by taking a broad "internationalist" view of legal concepts; *Trafigura Beheer BV v Kookmin Bank Co* [2006] EWHC 1450 (Comm); [2006] 2 Lloyd's Rep. 455.

Where an attack emanating from another jurisdiction is directed at a computer server in London which is where hacking occurs, "significant damage" occurs in England and such damage occurs from acts committed within the jurisdiction where the hacking occurred and access to the server was achieved; *Ashton Investments Ltd v Rusal* [2006] EWHC 2545 (Comm); [2007] 1 Lloyd's Rep. 311.

Infringement of copyright is not tortious but only a breach of statutory rights; acts done outside the U.K. are not unlawful by the Act; nor, not being tortious, do they fall within the rule. See further Dicey, Morris and Collins, *The Conflict of Laws*, 14th edn (London: Sweet & Maxwell, 2006). Accordingly service out of the jurisdiction will be set aside (*Def Lepp Music v Stuart-Browne* [1986] R.P.C. 273).

The decision in *PSM International v Specialised Fastener Products (Southern) Ltd* [1993] F.S.R. 113 (where *Def Lepp Music* was not cited) must be taken to be wrong on this point, unless it can be argued that infringement of copyright can be a tort for one purpose but not for another.

6.37.44 *Libel*—An alleged libel published in more than one country could give rise to a cause of action in each country in which the victim was known and in which he claimed to have suffered injury. A multi-jurisdictional libel should not be treated as giving rise to a single cause of action in respect of which the court had to ascertain where the global cause of action arose. The principles applied in the Convention case of *Shevill v Presse Alliance* [1996] A.C. 959, HL, followed in a non-convention case therefore allowing Russian nationals with a demonstrated connection with this country to sue in England the publisher of an American magazine with a circulation in England; *Berezovsky v Michaels* [2001] I.L.Pr. 21, HL.

Paragraph 3.1(10) of 6BPD: Judgment or award

6.37.45 The presence of assets within the jurisdiction does not in itself give the English courts jurisdiction over a person outside the jurisdiction. Accordingly, previously, a foreign judgment could not be enforced against English assets in cases not falling within the provisions for the reciprocal enforcement of judgments legislation unless the debtor could be served in England or was "domiciled or ordinarily resident within the jurisdiction". Now the foreign judgment or award is itself a sufficient ground for the grant of permission. The presence of assets within the jurisdiction is not a precondition to the exercise of the jurisdiction; *Tasarruff Mevduati Sigorta Fonu v Demirel* [2007] EWCA Civ 799; [2007] 1 W.L.R. 2508; [2007] 2 Lloyd's Rep. 440, CA. An interim order freezing assets in pending litigation in a foreign jurisdiction is not a judgment within the meaning of this paragraph (*Mercedes-Benz A.G. v Leiduck* [1995] 2 All E.R. 929, PC).

Paragraph 3.1(11) of 6BPD: claims about property within the jurisdiction

6.37.46 This wide and new provision is no longer confined to land and the old cases are redundant. Confidential information contained in digital form on a server constitutes property within para.3.1(11); *Ashton Investments Ltd v Rusal* [2006] EWHC 2545 (Comm); [2007] 1 Lloyd's Rep. 311.

Paragraphs 3.1(12) to 3.1(16) of 6BPD: Claims about trusts etc

6.37.47 It is not necessary that the trust property should be within the jurisdiction; an absconding trustee will not now be able to rely on his success in removing the assets. If he is in a Regulation or Convention State the English courts will probably have jurisdiction under art.5(6) of the Regulation or Convention, read with s.45 of the 1982 Act. Even though the question of legal entitlement to a European patent application by a non resident cannot (by virtue of the Patents Act 1977 s.82) be tried by an English court, the question whether the patent is held in trust by a non-resident for an English resident is not within the scope of *ibid.* s.82(3) and can be dealt with by an English court (*Kakkar v Szelke* [1988] F.S.R. 97).

Paragraph 3.1(13) of 6BPD: Administration of the estate of a person who died domiciled within the jurisdiction—Despite the provisions under r.6.31(i) that domicile is to be determined in accordance with ss.41 to 46 of the 1982 Act, it may be that the context requires the word to be used in its habitual sense. The exercise of the general discretion will probably have this effect. **6.37.48**

Paragraph 3.1(14) of 6BPD: Probate proceedings—Formerly, this paragraph said that service out of the jurisdiction was permissible with the leave of the court where the claim was brought "in a probate action within the meaning of Order 76" (see also former CCR O.8, r.2(1)(k) where O.41 was referred to) and "probate action" was defined accordingly in RSC O.1, r.4(1)). Initially, contentious probate proceedings constituted one of the "specialist Proceedings" referred to in CPR Pt 49. By r.49(1) the CPR were applied to such proceedings subject to the provisions of the relevant practice direction. The relevant practice direction was Practice Direction—Contentious Probate Proceedings (replacing RSC O.76 and CCR O.41). Probate proceedings are now dealt with in accordance with CPR Pt 57 and "probate claim" is defined in r.57.1(2)(a). **6.37.49**

Paragraph 3.1(15) of 6BPD: Constructive Trustee—See next paragraph. **6.37.50**

Paragraph 3.1(16) of 6BPD: claim for restitution—This provision may owe more to the "etc" of the title under which it appears. Restitution covers a wide variety of matters that do not involve trusts. For the meaning of "constructive trust" for the purposes of para.3.1(15) of 6BPD and discussion of the meaning of "restitution" for those of para.3.1(16) of 6BPD; see *Nabb Brothers Ltd v Lloyds International (Guernsey) Ltd* [2005] EWHC 405 (Ch); [2005] I.L.Pr. 37. **6.37.51**

Paragraph 3.1(17) of 6BPD: Duties and taxes

This paragraph is worded as it is for technical reasons and in order to avoid having to list a number of statutes. **6.37.52**

Paragraph 3.1(18) of 6BPD: Claim for a costs order under section 51 of the Supreme Court Act 1981

This provision was introduced to cure the omission identified in *National Justice Compania Naviera SA v Prudential Assurance Co Ltd (The Ikarian Reefer) (No.2)* [2000] 1 W.L.R. 603; [2000] 1 All E.R. 37; [2000] 1 Lloyd's Rep. 129, CA. **6.37.53**

Paragraph 3.1(19) of 6BPD: Admiralty claims

When Pt 61 (Admiralty Claims) was inserted in the CPR by Civil Procedure (Amendment No.5) Rules 2001 (SI 2001/4015) and former RSC O.75 revoked, what is now para.3.1(19) of 6BPD was inserted in Pt 6 (as r.6.20(17A)). In relation to limitation claims, see r.61.11(5) and commentary thereon. **6.37.54**

See also para.6.37.9 above.

Paragraph 3.1(20) of 6BPD: Claims under various enactments

With effect form October 1, 2008, this provision replaced former r.6.20(18). That rule provided that a claim form could be served out of the jurisdiction with the court's permission if the claim was made "under an enactment specified in the relevant Practice Direction". Accordingly, such enactments were specified in para.5.2 of the practice direction that supplemented former r.6.20(18). Paragraph 3.1(20) is in different terms to the former rule and contains no list of specified enactments. It expressly refers to (as para.5.2 did) Council Directive of 15 March 1976 No.76/308/EEC, but otherwise states simply that a claim form may be served out of the jurisdiction with the court's permission if the claim is made under an enactment which allows proceedings to be brought and those proceedings are not covered by any of the other grounds referred to in para.3.1. **6.37.55**

Service of documents other than the claim form—permission[1]

6.38 **6.38—(1) Unless paragraph (2) or (3) applies, where the permission of the court is required for the claimant to serve the claim form out of the jurisdiction, the claimant must obtain permission to serve any other document in the proceedings out of the jurisdiction.**

(2) Where—

(a) the court gives permission for a claim form to be served on a defendant out of the jurisdiction; and

(b) the claim form states that particulars of claim are to follow, the permission of the court is not required to serve the particulars of claim.

(3) The permission of the court is not required if a party has given an address for service in Scotland or Northern Ireland.

Effect of rule (r.6.38)

6.38.1 Paragraphs (1) and (2) of this rule replace paras (2) and (3) of former r.6.30, insofar as those provisions apply to documents other than claim forms.

"any other document"

6.38.2 The rule applies to any document other than a claim form. Under Pt 6, "claim" includes an application made before action (as well as a claim made "to commence proceedings"), and "claim form" is "to be construed accordingly" (see r.6.2(c)). Consequently, by definition a claim form includes an application notice issued before action and is not a document falling within r.6.38.

There is power to serve an application notice under r.6.38(1) in order to join a person (B) as a party to proceedings on the basis of para.3.1(3) of 6BPD where a receiving order is sought in aid of a judgment against a defendant (A) who is resident abroad and it is anticipated that the receiver will seek to enforce an obligation that B is said to owe A (*C Inc Plc v L* [2001] 2 All E.R. (Comm) 446, Aikens J.).

Particulars of claim

6.38.3 Practice Direction (How to Start Proceedings—The Claim Form) para.6.2 states that, if the particulars of claim are not included in, or have not been served with, the claim form (r.7.4), the claim form must contain a statement that the particulars of claim will follow (see para.7PD.6 below).

Address for service in Scotland or Northern Ireland

6.38.4 Where a party serves a document other than a claim form on a party in Scotland or Northern Ireland it must be served by a method permitted by Section III of Pt 6 (r.6.40(2)). In Section III, r.6.23(1) states that a party to proceedings must give an address at which that party may be served with documents relating to those proceedings. That address must be within the United Kingdom (r.6.23(2) and (3)). See further commentary following r.6.40.

Service of application notice on a non-party to the proceedings[2]

6.39 **6.39—(1) Where an application notice is to be served out of the jurisdiction on a person who is not a party to the proceedings rules 6.35 and 6.37(5)(a)(i), (ii) and (iii) do not apply.**

(1) Where an application is served out of the jurisdiction on a person who is not a party to the proceedings, that person may make an application to the court under Part 11 as if that person were a defendant, but rule 11(2) does not apply.

(Part 11 contains provisions about disputing the court's *jurisdiction.*)

[1] Added by the Civil Procedure (Amendment) Rules 2008 (SI 2008/2178).
[2] Added by the Civil Procedure (Amendment) Rules 2008 (SI 2008/2178).

Effect of rule (r.6.39)

With effect from October 1, 2008, this rule replaced para.(1) of former r.6.30. The provision has been slightly amended, for purposes of clarification. 6.39.1

It expressly provides for a Pt 11 challenge to the jurisdiction in respect of an application notice. The rule does not provide that r.6.32, r.6.33 and r.6.36 do not apply. Therefore where service of originating process is made under the Service Regulation, that should be followed for service of other documents, e.g. application notices, orders. Under r.6.38(1) the requirements of r.6.36 and para.3.1 of 6BPD with regard to claim forms are expressly preserved in relation to other documents.

Provisions disapplied

The rules disapplied by para.(1) are provisions (1) that set out the periods for filing an acknowledgment of service, filing or serving an admission, or filing a defence, where permission to serve the claim form out of the jurisdiction either (a) was not required (and the claim form has been served) (r.6.35), or (b) was required and has been granted (r.6.37(5)), and (2) which might otherwise apply. Paragraph (2) of r.11, disapplied by para.(2) of this rule, states that a defendant who wishes to dispute the court's jurisdiction, or to argue that the court should not exercise its jurisdiction, must first file an acknowledgment of service. 6.39.2

Application notice

The rule applies where an application notice is served or is to be served. It does not apply where the application notice is for pre-action relief, as in Pt 6 such a notice is, by definition, a claim form (see. r.6.2(c)) to which the service rules in Section IV for the service of claim forms apply. 6.39.3

Methods of service—general provisions[1]

6.40—(1) This rule contains general provisions about the method of service of a claim form or other document on a party out of the jurisdiction. 6.40

(2) Where a party serves any document on a party in Scotland or Northern Ireland, it must be served by a method permitted by Section II (and references to "jurisdiction" in that Section are modified accordingly) or Section III of this Part and rule 6.23(4) applies.

(3) Where the claimant wishes to serve a claim form or any other document on a defendant out of the United Kingdom, it may be served—

(a) by any method provided for by—

(i) rule 6.41 (service in accordance with the Service Regulation);

(ii) rule 6.42 (service through foreign governments, judicial authorities and British Consular authorities); or

(iii) rule 6.44 (service of claim form or other document on a State);

(b) by any method permitted by a Civil Procedure Convention; or

(c) by any other method permitted by the law of the country in which it is to be served.

(4) Nothing in paragraph (3) or in any court order authorises or requires any person to do anything which is contrary to the law of the country where the claim form or other document is to be served.

(A list of the countries with whom the United Kingdom has

[1] Added by the Civil Procedure (Amendment) Rules 2008 (SI 2008/2178).

entered into a Civil Procedure Convention, and a link to the relevant Convention, may be found on the Foreign and Commonwealth Office website at— http://www.fco.gov.uk/en/about-the-fco/publications/treaties/ lists-treaties/bilateral-civil-procedure.)

Effect of rule (r.6.40)

6.40.1 With effect from October 1, 2008, paras (3) and (4) of this rule replaced paras (1) and (2) of former r.6.24. Former r.6.24 was restricted in its effect to the service out of the jurisdiction of claim forms. Rule 6.40 applies to claim forms (as defined in r.6.2(c)) or any other document in proceedings. Paragraph (2) did not form part of former r.6.24 (see further "Service on a party in Scotland or Northern Ireland" below).

Service regulation

6.40.2 For explanation, see para.(e) of r.6.31 (Interpretation) above.

Civil Procedure Convention

6.40.3 For explanation, see para.(c) of r.6.31 (Interpretation) above.

Service on a party in Scotland or Northern Ireland

6.40.4 A claimant may serve a claim form out of the jurisdiction on a defendant in Scotland or Northern Ireland without the permission of the court in the circumstances provided for in r.6.32. Where a claimant serves a defendant under r.6.32, the periods within which the defendant should file an acknowledgment of service, an admission and a defence are longer than those that would apply when a defendant was served within the jurisdiction (see r.6.35).

The methods of service permitted by Section II are methods relating to the service of claim forms (as defined in r.6.2(c)) in the jurisdiction, and the methods of service permitted by Section III are methods relating to service of documents other than claim forms, again in the jurisdiction.

Note also, service on a company registered in Scotland or Northern Ireland and carrying on business in the jurisdiction by a method of service, not permitted by Pt 6, but by statute; see r.6.3(2) and commentary thereon.

Paragraph (2) of this rule states that these methods of service are permitted for service of the documents to which they relate on a party not in the jurisdiction but in Scotland or Northern Ireland. Indeed, not only may they be used, they must be used. This marks a significant change in the rules. Heretofore, the general rule that service out of the jurisdiction must be effected in accordance with the law of the receiving country or a relevant international treaty applied to service of documents in those jurisdictions.

The fact that Scotland and Northern Ireland, though separate legal systems, are parts of the same State (the United Kingdom) makes a departure from the general rule, not only possible, but (on grounds of convenience for parties to proceedings) desirable. Service of a document (whether claim form or other document in proceedings) out of England and Wales on a party in Scotland or Northern Ireland must be effected by any of the methods of service permitted by Section II or Section III, including personal service. The particular significance of this is that the English personal service rules apply, even though the comparable Scottish and Northern Irish rules (by limiting the persons by whom such service may be effected) are more restrictive.

Rule 6.23 (Address for service) applies to documents to be served in proceedings other than the claim form and para.(4) of that rule (referred to in r.6.40(2)) states that such document must be sent or transmitted to, or left at, the party's address for service, under paras (2) or (3) of the rule, unless it is to be served personally or the court orders otherwise. Under para.(2) or (3) the address for service which a party is required to give under r.6.23 may be in Scotland or Northern Ireland (see further commentary following r.6.23).

Presumably, where service is to be effected on a party in Scotland or Northern Ireland under r.6.40(2), the "deemed day" of service provisions in r.6.14 and r.6.26 apply. This would seem to follow from the terms of r.6.40(2), wherein it is stated that service should be "by a method permitted" by Section II or Section III (though, strictly speaking, the determination of deemed day is a consequence of, and not a method of, service), and from the phrases "in accordance with this Part" (in r.6.14) and "in accordance with these Rules" (in r.6.26).

Service on a defendant out of the United Kingdom (r.6.40(3) and (4))

By virtue of r.6.40(4) no order of the English court can be taken to authorise or direct the doing of anything contrary to the law of the state where service is to be effected. Thus where service of a claim form is purportedly made in a foreign country by a private person instructed by the claimant, and where the law of that country stipulates that service should be through official channels, the English court will not, except in a very strong and unusual case, exercise discretion to allow the purported service to stand (*Ferrarini S.p.A. v Magnol Shipping Co Inc (The Sky One)* [1988] 1 Lloyd's Rep. 238, CA). **6.40.5**

Service by registered post on a defendant in France, although a valid method of service under French law, is not a valid method under CPR r.6.14, but it would appear that the general rules—as to service in Pt I of CPR 6 (including r.6.14)—do apply to service of "out of the jurisdiction" under Section III, where that service accords with the law of the foreign country; *Burns-Anderson Independent Network plc v Wheeler* [2005] EWHC 575 (QB); [2005] 1 Lloyd's Rep. 580, at para.25.

Also in *Arros Invest Ltd v Nishanov* [2004] EWHC 576; [2004] I.L.Pr. 22, Lawrence Collins J. accepted that (what is now) r.6.40(3)(c) "has to be applied with a reasonable degree of flexibility when applied to foreign systems of law", but concluded in that case that where the defendant had not received actual notice, the onus was on the claimant to show that the method of service adopted was adequate and in accordance with the local rules.

The function of CPR r.6.40(3) is to prevent service by a method forbidden by the law of the place of service; *Shiblaq v Sadikoglu* [2004] EWHC 1890 (Comm); [2003] All E.R. (D) 428 (Comm). It is implicit in CPR r.6.40(4) that the court may permit any alternative method of service abroad so long as it does not contravene the law of the country where service is to be effected; *Habib Bank Ltd v Central Bank of Sudan* [2006] EWHC 1767 (Comm); [2007] 1 W.L.R. 470; [2007] 1 All E.R. (Comm) 53; [2006] 2 Lloyd's Rep. 412.

Parties are free to agree an ad hoc mode of service outside the methods set in the CPR; *McCulloch v Bank of Nova Scotia* [2006] EWHC 790 (Ch); [2006] 2 All E.R. (Comm) 714.

Service on foreign companies abroad—Service must not contravene the law of the country where the service is to be effected. If, however, the company has established a branch or a place of business in England, no question need arise of service out of the jurisdiction (see commentary following r.6.3). **6.40.6**

In *Habib Bank Ltd v Central Bank of Sudan* [2006] EWHC 1767 (Comm); [2007] 1 W.L.R. 470; [2007] 1 All E.R. (Comm) 53; [2006] 2 Lloyd's Rep. 412, where the defendant was the national bank of Sudan, the court held that CPR r.6.40(3) did not require service abroad "by any method ... permitted by the law of the country in which it was to be served". On the contrary, it was implicit in CPR r.6.40(4) that the court could permit any alternative method of service so long as it did not contravene the law of the country where service was to be effected. It followed in the instant case that the order made permitting service was valid.

Service on foreign firms

Part 6 applies to partners, or an individual, carrying on a business under a firm name within the jurisdiction. A firm that trades only abroad presents difficulties: if such a firm has no legal existence apart from its individual members, those members ought to be named and served (*Von Hellfeld v Rechnityer* [1914] 1 Ch. 748 at 755). It is, however, difficult to ascertain the legal status of foreign firms, particularly in continental countries, where there are bodies of a status not found in England. As a working rule it is often fairly safe to sue a firm in the style in which it enjoys legal rights and liabilities in its country of domicile. **6.40.7**

Service on a foreign state

See s.12 of the State Immunity Act 1978 and r.6.44. **6.40.8**

Hague Convention

Printed HMSO, Cmnd. 3986 (1969). This Convention came into effect on February 10, 1969, after ratification by three States (art.27). It provides (inter alia) that each contracting state shall designate a Central Authority to receive requests for service coming from other contracting states and execute them. Documents for service must be lodged with the Masters' Secretary's Foreign Process Office, Room E10, Royal **6.40.9**

Courts of Justice, Strand, London WC2A 2LL, for onward transmission. The contracting states are at liberty to impose restrictions under certain articles of the Convention and information as to these can be obtained from the above-named Department. This multilateral Convention does not invalidate the bilateral Conventions already in force and listed in the websites referred to at the end of r.6.40.

Argentina
Belarus
Belgium
Bulgaria
Canada
China
China, Hong Kong Special Administrative Region only
China, Macau Special Administrative Region only
Cyprus
Czech Republic
Denmark
Egypt
Estonia
Finland
France
Germany
Greece
Ireland
Israel
Italy
Japan
Republic of Korea
Latvia
Lithuania
Luxembourg
Netherlands
Norway
Poland
Portugal
Russian Federation
Slovakia
Slovenia
Spain
Sri Lanka
Sweden
Switzerland
Turkey
United Kingdom

Service abroad without permission

6.40.10 Rule 6.40(3) applies to a claim form which it is proposed to serve out of the jurisdiction without the permission of the court.

The Hague Convention permits the sending of "judicial documents by postal channels directly to persons abroad" provided "the state of destination does not object" to such method of service (see arts 10 and 19). Provided therefore that service by post is permitted by and effected in accordance with the law of the country in which service is effected, there is nothing in the Hague Convention or in the Brussels Convention which cuts down the scope of this permission (*Noirhomme v Walklate* [1992] 1 Lloyd's Rep. 427).

Service under Hague Convention, Brussels and Lugano Conventions and Judgments Regulation

6.40.11 Article 27(2) of the Brussels Convention (art.34(2) of the Judgments Regulation) denies recognition to a judgment given in default if the defendant "was not duly served with the document which instituted the proceedings in sufficient time for him to arrange his defence". In *Minalmet GmbH* v Brandeis Ltd (C-123/91) [1993] I.L.Pr. 132, the European Court of Justice held that lack of due service precluded the enforcement of a default judgment even though the defendant had become aware of it and had taken no steps to set aside the judgment. The steps taken in the action were as follows:

(1) English proceedings sent under art.5(a) of the Hague Convention to the Amtsgericht which certified that service had been duly effected;

(2) Default judgment entered in the High Court;

(3) Enforcement of the judgment authorised by the Landgericht;

(4) The defendant appealed this order to the Oberlandesgericht which dismissed the appeal;

(5) The defendant further appealed this order to the Bundesgerichthof which decided that service did not accord with the provisions of German Civil Law (lex loci executionis) but that the defendants had become aware of the judgment and had taken no steps to set it aside in England (lex loci decisionis) and referred the question of whether the default judgment should nevertheless be recognised to the European Court.

A certificate of due service sent from a foreign authority under the Hague Convention to the court issuing a claim form cannot of itself validate an invalid form of service where service did not in fact comply with the rules of service in the state of destination (*Postal Service Abroad, Re* [1995] I.L.Pr. 523 (Bundesgerichthof)).

Note that the wording of art.34.2 of the Judgments Regulation is slightly different to art.27(2) of the Brussels Convention, the word "duly" being omitted from "duly served". The European Court has interpreted the wording of art.27(2) favourably to the rights of defendants; *Klomps v Michel* [1981] E.C.R.1593; [1982] C.M.L.R. 773, ECJ.

These cases underline problems that may face the holder of a default judgment and should be borne in mind when choosing to use the exceptional jurisdiction under art.5 rather than proceeding under art.2.

In *Scania Finance France SA v Rockinger Spezialfabrik fur Anhangerkupplungen GmbH & Co* (C522/03) [2005] E.C.R. I-8639; [2005] All E.R. (D.) 146 (Oct); [2006] I.L.Pr. 1, the ECJ (1st Chamber) held that art.27 of the Brussels Convention and the first paragraph of art.IV of the Protocol annexed to the Convention had to be interpreted as meaning that, where a relevant international convention was applicable between the state in which the judgment was given and the state in which recognition was sought, the question whether the document instituting the proceedings was duly served had to be determined in the light of the provisions of that convention, without prejudice to the use of direct transmissions between public officers, where the state in which recognition was sought had not officially objected, in accordance with the second paragraph of art.IV of the Protocol.

Service in accordance with the Service Regulation[1]

6.41—(1) This rule applies where the claimant wishes to serve the claim form or other document in accordance with the Service Regulation. 6.41

(2) The claimant must file—

(a) the claim form or other document;

(b) any translation; and

(c) any other documents required by the Service Regulation.

(3) When the claimant files the documents referred to in paragraph (2), the court officer will—

(a) seal ([GL]) the copy of the claim form; and

(b) forward the documents to the Senior Master.

[1] Added by the Civil Procedure (Amendment) Rules 2008 (SI 2008/2178).

(4) Rule 6.47 does not apply to this rule.

(The Service Regulation is annexed to Practice Direction B supplementing this Part.)

(Article 20(1) of the Service Regulation provides that the Regulation prevails over other provisions contained in any other agreement or arrangement concluded by Member States.)

Effect of rule (r.6.41)

6.41.1 With effect from October 1, 2008, this rule replaced former r.6.26A. Rule 6.47 (disapplied by para.(4)) in certain circumstances (which otherwise might apply) prevents a claimant from taking further steps against a defendant served with a claim form out of the jurisdiction until the defendant files written evidence showing that such service has been duly effected.

Service Regulation

6.41.2 In this rule (and in other provisions in Section IV of Pt 6) "Service Regulation" means Regulation (EC) No.1393/2007 of the European Parliament and of the Council of 13 November 2007, which came into force on 13th November 2008. This Regulation applies in Denmark as well as other EU States as a result of Denmark's declaration to that effect. For further explanation, see para.(e) of r.6.31 (Interpretation) above.

As the first signpost at the end of r.6.41 indicates, the Service Regulation is annexed to the new version of Practice Direction B (Service Out of the Jurisdiction). The previous Service Regulation was also annexed to the old version of this practice direction; see the White Book 2008, Vol.1 at para.6BPD.14 and Vol.2, para.5–222.

The most frequently used method of service under the Regulation which must be provided and accepted by all States is, pursuant to art.4, transmission between transmitting and receiving agencies established by a State under art.2. This will usually be between the Judicial Authorities or Ministries of Justice of one State and another. The Transmitting and Receiving Agency for England and Wales is The Senior Master (For the attention of the Foreign Process Section (Room E10) Royal Courts of Justice Strand London WC2A 2LL).

There are certain other methods provided for. All are equally valid under the Regulation. Under art.12, Member States are free, in exceptional circumstances, to use consular or diplomatic channels to forward judicial documents for the purpose of service, to agencies of another Member State which are designated pursuant to arts 2 or 3 of the Regulation. This provision, would haveto be invoked in England and Wales through the Senior Master who, in an appropriate case, would forward the papers to the Foreign and Commonwealth Office.

Under art.13 Member States are free to effect service of judicial documents on persons residing in another Member State, without application of any compulsion, directly through its diplomatic or consular agents but a Member State may make it known that it is opposed to such service within its territory unless the documents are to be served on nationals of the Member State in which the documents originate. The United Kingdom does not intend to oppose the exercise in its territory of the right conferred by art.13(1).

Under art.14, Member States are free to effect service of judicial documents directly by postal services on persons residing in another Member State by registered letter with acknowledgement of receipt or equivalent. In England and Wales service under art.14 is done by the Senior Master of the Queen's Bench Division through the Foreign Process Section. The procedure is that the papers for service should be taken or sent to the Section as if to be served under art.4 with an envelope for the Section's use. The papers will be sealed with the Court Seal in the normal way and sealed in the envelope. The solicitors effecting service will then be asked to sign an undertaking to post the same and obtain a receipt of posting in the name and address of the Foreign Process Section so that evidence of delivery will be returned from the state in which service is effected to the Section and to return the receipt to the Section to hold.

Under art.15 any person interested in a judicial proceeding may effect service of judicial documents directly through the judicial officers, officials or other competent persons of the Member State addressed, where such direct service is permitted under the law of that Member State. England and Wales has indicated that it will not be effecting service under this provision.

The Central Body in England and Wales for this Regulation is the Senior Master of the Queen's Bench Division who will supply information to the transmitting agencies; seek solutions to any difficulties which may arise during transmission of documents for service and forward, in exceptional cases, at the request of a transmitting agency, a request for service to the competent receiving agency.

Service through foreign governments, judicial authorities and British Consular authorities[1]

6.42—(1) Where the claimant wishes to serve a claim form or any other document on a defendant in any country which is a party to a Civil Procedure Convention providing for service in that country, it may be served— 6.42

(a) through the authority designated under the Hague Convention (where relevant) in respect of that country; or

(b) if the law of that country permits—

(i) through the judicial authorities of that country, or

(ii) through a British Consular authority in that country (subject to any provisions of the applicable convention about the nationality of persons who may be served by such a method).

(2) Where the claimant wishes to serve a claim form or any other document on a defendant in any country with respect to which there is no Civil Procedure Convention providing for service in that country, the claim form or other document may be served, if the law of that country so permits—

(a) through the government of that country, where that government is willing to serve it; or

(b) through a British Consular authority in that country.

(3) Where the claimant wishes to serve the claim form or other document in—

(a) any Commonwealth State which is not a party to the Hague Convention;

(b) the Isle of Man or the Channel Islands; or

(c) any British overseas territory,c

the methods of service permitted by paragraphs (1)(b) and (2) are not available and the claimant or the claimant's agent must effect service direct, unless Practice Direction B supplementing this Part provides otherwise.

(A list of British overseas territories is reproduced in paragraph 5.2 of *Practice* Direction B supplementing this Part.)

Effect of rule (r.6.42)

With effect from October 1, 2008, this rule replaced former r.6.25, but has been adjusted to take account of the new provision made in para.(2) of r.6.40 for service of documents in Scotland and Northern Ireland. It applies to the service of "other documents" as well as to claim forms. 6.42.1

[1] Added by the Civil Procedure (Amendment) Rules 2008 (SI 2008/2178).

Hague Convention

6.42.2 For explanation, see para.(a) of r.6.31 (Interpretation) above.

Civil Procedure Convention

6.42.3 For explanation, see para.(c) of r.6.31 (Interpretation) above.

Commonwealth State

6.42.4 For explanation, see para.(f) of r.6.31 (Definitions) above. Paragraph (3) of r.6.42 does not apply where, in the case of a Commonwealth State, the judicial authorities have required service to be in accordance with r.6.42(1)(b)(i) (see Practice Direction B (Service Out of the Jurisdiction) para.5.1).

British overseas territory

6.42.5 For the purposes of para.(3)(c) of r.6.42, the territories are as listed in para.5.2 of Practice Direction B (Service Out of the Jurisdiction); see para.6BPD.5 below.

Procedure where service is to be through foreign governments, judicial authorities and British Consular authorities[1]

6.43 **6.43—(1) This rule applies where the claimant wishes to serve a claim form or any other document under rule 6.42(1) or 6.42(2).**

(2) Where this rule applies, the claimant must file—

(a) a request for service of the claim form or other document specifying one or more of the methods in rule 6.42(1) or 6.42(2);

(b) a copy of the claim form or other document;

(c) any other documents or copies of documents required by Practice Direction B supplementing this Part; and

(d) any translation required under rule 6.45.

(3) Where the claimant files the documents specified in paragraph (2), the court officer will—

(a) seal (GL) the copy of the claim form or other document; and

(b) forward the documents to the Senior Master.

(4) The Senior Master will send documents forwarded under this rule—

(a) where the claim form or other document is being served through the authority designated under the Hague Convention, to that authority; or

(b) in any other case, to the Foreign and Commonwealth Office with a request that it arranges for the claim form or other document to be served.

(5) An official certificate which—

(a) states that the method requested under paragraph (2)(a) has been performed and the date of such performance;

(b) states, where more than one method is requested under paragraph (2)(a), which method was used; and

(c) is made by—

(i) a British Consular authority in the country where the method requested under paragraph (2)(a) was performed;

[1] Added by the Civil Procedure (Amendment) Rules 2008 (SI 2008/2178).

(ii) the government or judicial authorities in that country; or

(iii) the authority designated in respect of that country under the Hague Convention,

is evidence of the facts stated in the certificate.

(6) A document purporting to be an official certificate under paragraph (5) is to be treated as such a certificate, unless it is proved not to be.

Effect of rule (r.6.43)

With effect from October 1, 2008, this rule replaced former r.6.26. When contrasted with the former rule it is more prescriptive in certain respects (especially in para.(5)), but generally has the same effects. It applies to the service of "other documents" as well as to claim forms. **6.43.1**

The claimant must provide copies of the documents referred to in para.(2)(c) of the rule for each party to be served out of the jurisdiction (Practice Direction B (Service Out of the Jurisdiction) para.4.1; note also para.4.2).

Where it is common ground that the defendant has not received actual notice of the proceedings, the onus is on the claimant to show that the method of service adopted was adequate and in compliance with the local rules; *Arros Invest Ltd v Rafik Nishanov* [2004] EWHC 576; [2004] I.L.Pr. 22.

In *Chare v Fairclough* [2003] EWHC 180, January 20, 2003, unrep. (Treacy J.), it was held that where service was effected through the Foreign and Commonwealth Office under CPR r.6.43, service was not effected by the court but by the claimant through the medium of the Foreign and Commonwealth Office. Therefore, cases where service was effected pursuant to CPR r.6.43 fell within CPR r.7.6(3)(b), not r.7.6(3)(a), and the onus was on the claimant to show that he had taken all reasonable steps to effect service.

Note that in the case of *Olafsson v Gissurarson* [2008] EWCA Civ 152; [2008] 1 All E.R. (Comm) 1106, the Court of Appeal upheld the judge's decision ([2006] EWHC 3162 (QB); [2007] 1 Lloyd's Rep. 184), that this was a truly exceptional case in which service could be dispensed with retrospectively. Although service had been effected through British Consular authorities in Iceland, as a signatory to the Lugano Convention, based on a request for service made under CPR r.6.43 and there was no dispute that the defendant had received the papers, the Consular Officer serving the papers had failed to obtain from the defendant a signed receipt for the papers being served. The failure to obtain the receipt rendered service ineffective under Icelandic law. The Consular Authority provided a certificate of personal service on the basis of which interlocutory judgment was entered. While the court had sympathy in this case with the claimant's solicitors who believed that the process had been validly served, the Master of the Rolls expressed the view that "the experience of this case should lead claimant's solicitors in the future to ensure that the service is in fact valid by the relevant law". It would seem therefore that solicitors requesting service through the Senior Master and the FCO should satisfy themselves as to what is proper service under the law of the country in which it is to be effected and ensure that the FCO are requested to serve in a specific manner accordingly. It should be borne in mind that, as per the decision of Treacy J. in *Chare v Fairclough* [2003] EWHC 180 (QB), January 20, 2003, unrep, service through the Senior Master and the FCO is service by the claimant and not service by the court.

Service of claim form or other document on a State[1]

***6.44*—*(1)* This rule applies where a claimant wishes to serve the claim form or other document on a State.** **6.44**

(2) In this rule, "State" has the meaning given by section 14 of the State Immunity Act 1978.

(3) The claimant must file in the Central Office of the Royal Courts of Justice—

[1] Added by the Civil Procedure (Amendment) Rules 2008 (SI 2008/2178).

(a) (a) a request for service to be arranged by the Foreign and Commonwealth Office;

(b) a copy of the claim form or other document; and

(c) any translation required under rule 6.45.

(4) The Senior Master will send the documents filed under this rule to the Foreign and Commonwealth Office with a request that it arranges for them to be served.

(5) An official certificate by the Foreign and Commonwealth Office stating that a claim form has been duly served on a specified date in accordance with a request made under this rule is evidence of that fact.

(6) A document purporting to be such a certificate is to be treated as such a certificate, unless it is proved not to be.

(7) Where—

(a) section 12(6) of the State Immunity Act 1978 applies; and

(b) the State has agreed to a method of service other than through the Foreign and Commonwealth Office,

the claim form or other document may be served either by the method agreed or in accordance with this rule.

(Section 12(6) of the State Immunity Act 1978 provides that section 12(1) enables the service of a claim form or other document in a manner to which the State has agreed.)

Section 12(1)

6.44.1 Except where there is agreement to the contrary under s.12(6) of the Act, the requirements are mandatory and good service cannot be made without adhering to them (*Kuwait Airways Corp v Iraqi Airways Co (No.2)* [1995] 1 W.L.R. 1147; [1995] 3 All E.R. 694, HL).

Translation of claim form or other document[1]

6.45 **6.45—(1) Except where paragraph (4) or (5) applies, every copy of the claim form or other document filed under rule 6.43 (service through foreign governments, judicial authorities etc.) or 6.44 (service of claim form or other document on a State) must be accompanied by a translation of the claim form or other document.**

(2) The translation must be—

(a) in the official language of the country in which it is to be served; or

(b) if there is more than one official language of that country, in any official language which is appropriate to the place in the country where the claim form or other document is to be served.

(c)

(3) Every translation filed under this rule must be accompanied by a statement by the person making it that it is a correct translation, and the statement *must include that* person's name, address *and qualifications* for making the translation.

---

[1] Added by the Civil Procedure (Amendment) Rules 2008 (SI 2008/2178).

(4) The claimant is not required to file a translation of a claim form or other document filed under rule 6.43 (service through foreign governments, judicial authorities etc.) where the claim form or other document is to be served—

(a) in a country of which English is an official language; or

(b) on a British citizen (within the meaning of the British Nationality Act 1981),

unless a Civil Procedure Convention requires a translation.

(5) The claimant is not required to file a translation of a claim form or other document filed under rule 6.44 (service of claim form or other document on a State) where English is an official language of the State in which the claim form or other document is to be served.

(The Service Regulation contains provisions about the translation of documents.)

Undertaking to be responsible for expenses[1]

6.46 Every request for service filed under rule 6.43 (service through foreign governments, judicial authorities etc.) or rule 6.44 (service of claim form or other document on a State) must contain an undertaking by the person making the request— **6.46**

(a) to be responsible for all expenses incurred by the Foreign and Commonwealth Office or foreign judicial authority; and

(b) to pay those expenses to the Foreign and Commonwealth Office or foreign judicial authority on being informed of the amount.

Proof of service before obtaining judgment[2]

6.47 Where— **6.47**

(a) a hearing is fixed when the claim form is issued;

(b) the claim form is served on a defendant out of the jurisdiction; and

(c) that defendant does not appear at the hearing, the claimant may not obtain judgment against the defendant until the claimant files written evidence that the claim form has been duly served in accordance with this Part.

V. Service of Documents from Foreign Courts or Tribunals

Scope of this Section[3]

6.48 This Section— **6.48**

(a) applies to the service in England and Wales of any document in connection with civil or commercial proceedings in a foreign court or tribunal; but

(b) does not apply where the Service Regulation (which has the same meaning as rule 6.31(e)) applies.

[1] Added by the Civil Procedure (Amendment) Rules 2008 (SI 2008/2178).
[2] Added by the Civil Procedure (Amendment) Rules 2008 (SI 2008/2178).
[3] Added by the Civil Procedure (Amendment) Rules 2008 (SI 2008/2178).

Effect of rule (r.6.48)

6.48.1 This rule introduces Section V. That Section replaces Section IV of Pt 6 as it stood before the substitution of the whole of that Part with effect from October 1, 2008. The language of the several rules (rr.6.49 to 6.52) in this Section have been re-phrased in a number of respects. In terms, the Section now applies to service in England and Wales of "any document" (rather than "any court process") in connection with civil or commercial proceedings in a foreign court or tribunal.

For further commentary, see para.6.52.1 below.

Interpretation[1]

6.49 **6.49 In this Section—**

(a) "convention country" means a country in relation to which there is a Civil Procedure Convention (which has the same meaning as in rule 6.31(c));

(b) "foreign court or tribunal" means a court or tribunal in a country outside of the United Kingdom; and

(c) "process server" means—

(i) a process server appointed by the Lord Chancellor to serve documents to which this Section applies, or

(ii) the process server's agent.

Request for service[2]

6.50 **6.50 The Senior Master will serve a document to which this Section applies upon receipt of—**

(a) a written request for service—

(i) where the foreign court or tribunal is in a convention country, from a consular or other authority of that country; or

(ii) from the Secretary of State for Foreign and Commonwealth Affairs, with a recommendation that service should be effected;

(b) a translation of that request into English;

(c) two copies of the document to be served; and

(d) unless the foreign court or tribunal certifies that the person to be served understands the language of the document, two copies of a translation of it into English.

Request for service[3]

6.51 **6.51 The Senior Master will determine the method of service.**

After service[4]

6.52 **6.52—(1) Where service of a document has been effected by a process server, the process server must—**

(a) send to the Senior Master a copy of the document, and

(i) proof of service; or

[1] Added by the Civil Procedure (Amendment) Rules 2008 (SI 2008/2178).
[2] Added by the Civil Procedure (Amendment) Rules 2008 (SI 2008/2178).
[3] Added by the Civil Procedure (Amendment) Rules 2008 (SI 2008/2178).
[4] Added by the Civil Procedure (Amendment) Rules 2008 (SI 2008/2178).

(ii) a statement why the document could not be served; and

(b) if the Senior Master directs, specify the costs incurred in serving or attempting to serve the document.

(2) The Senior Master will send to the person who requested service—

(a) a certificate, sealed with the seal of the Supreme Court for use out of the jurisdiction, stating—

(i) when and how the document was served or the reason why it has not been served; and

(ii) where appropriate, an amount certified by a costs judge to be the costs of serving or attempting to serve the document; and

(b) a copy of the document.

Effect of Section V

6.52.1 Although Pts 6.32 to 6.35 set out the procedure for service of judicial documents through the courts, parties are still able to effect service as set out in art.10 of the Hague Convention, which states:

"Provided the State of destination does not object, the present Convention shall not interfere with—

(a) the freedom to send judicial documents, by postal channels, directly to persons abroad,

(b) the freedom of judicial officers, officials or other competent persons of the State of origin to effect service of judicial documents directly through the judicial officials or other competent persons of the State of destination,

(c) the freedom of any person interested in a judicial proceeding to effect service of judicial documents directly through the judicial officials or other competent persons of the State of destination."

In art.10 "other competent persons of the State of destination" in the case of service in England and Wales is regarded by The Senior Master as meaning Solicitors of the Supreme Court. The Central Authority Section for the UK on the HCCH website contains the following statements in that respect:

"Extract from a letter dated 11 September 1980 addressed by the Foreign and Commonwealth Office of the Permanent Bureau:

'(...) Thank you for your letter of 31 July in which you ask for assistance in the interpretation of the declaration made by the United Kingdom on 17 November 1967 in relation to Article 10(c) of the Convention. I am happy to confirm that our declaration does not preclude any person in another Contracting State who is interested in a judicial proceeding (including his lawyer) from effecting service in the United Kingdom "directly" through a competent person other than a judicial officer or official, e.g., a solicitor. (...)' Conclusion and Recommendation No 58 of the 2003 Special Commission (SC): "The 2003 SC noted that the UK confirmed its position expressed at the Special Commission meeting of 1989, indicating its preference for the use of direct service through English solicitors on residents of England and Wales."

PRACTICE DIRECTION A—SERVICE WITHIN THE UNITED KINGDOM

This Practice Direction supplements CPR Part 6

Scope of this Practice Direction

6APD.1 **1.1** This Practice Direction supplements—

(1) Section II (service of the claim form in the jurisdiction) of Part 6;

(2) Section III (service of documents other than the claim form in the United Kingdom) of Part 6; and

(3) rule 6.40 in relation to the method of service on a party in Scotland or Northern Ireland.

(Practice Direction B supplementing Part 6 contains provisions relevant to service on a party in Scotland or Northern Ireland, including provisions about service out of the jurisdiction where permission is and is not required and the period for responding to an application notice.)

When service may be by document exchange

6APD.2 **2.1** Service by document exchange (DX) may take place only where—

(1) the address at which the party is to be served includes a numbered box at a DX, or

(2) the writing paper of the party who is to be served or of the solicitor acting for that party sets out a DX box number, and

(3) the party or the solicitor acting for that party has not indicated in writing that they are unwilling to accept service by DX.

How service is effected by post, an alternative service provider or DX

6APD.3 **3.1** Service by post, DX or other service which provides for delivery on the next business day is effected by—

(1) placing the document in a post box;

(2) leaving the document with or delivering the document to the relevant service provider; or

(3) having the document collected by the relevant service provider.

Service by fax or other electronic means

6APD.4 **4.1** Subject to the provisions of rule 6.23(5) and (6), where a document is to be served by fax or other electronic means—

(1) the party who is to be served or the solicitor acting for that party must previously have indicated in writing to the party serving—

(a) that the party to be served or the solicitor is willing to accept service by fax or other electronic means; and

(b) the fax number, e-mail address or other electronic identification to which it must be sent; and

(2) the following are to be taken as sufficient written indications for the purposes of paragraph 4.1(1)—

(a) a fax number set out on the writing paper of the solicitor acting for the party to be served;
(b) an e-mail address set out on the writing paper of the solicitor acting for the party to be served but only where it is stated that the e-mail address may be used for service; or
(c) a fax number, e-mail address or electronic identification set out on a statement of case or a response to a claim filed with the court.

4.2 Where a party intends to serve a document by electronic means (other than by fax) that party must first ask the party who is to be served whether there are any limitations to the recipient's agreement to accept service by such means (for example, the format in which documents are to be sent and the maximum size of attachments that may be received).

4.3 Where a document is served by electronic means, the party serving the document need not in addition send or deliver a hard copy.

Service on members of the Regular Forces and United States Air Force

5.1 The provisions that apply to service on members of the regular forces (within the meaning of the Armed Forces Act 2006) and members of the United States Air Force are annexed to this practice direction. **6APD.5**

Personal service on a company or other corporation

6.1 Personal service on a registered company or corporation in accordance with rule 6.5(3) is effected by leaving a document with a person holding a senior position. **6APD.6**

6.2 Each of the following persons is a person holding a senior position—

(1) in respect of a registered company or corporation, a director, the treasurer, the secretary of the company or corporation, the chief executive, a manager or other officer of the company or corporation; and
(2) in respect of a corporation which is not a registered company, in addition to any of the persons set out in sub-paragraph (1), the mayor, the chairman, the president, a town clerk or similar officer of the corporation.

Certificate of service where claimant serves the claim form

7.1 Where, pursuant to rule 6.17(2), the claimant files a certificate of service, the claimant is not required to and should not file— **6APD.7**

(1) *a further copy of the* claim form with the certificate of service; and
(2) a further copy of—
(a) the particulars of claim (where not included in the claim form); or
(b) any document attached to the particulars of claim,
with the certificate of service where that document has already been filed with the court.

(Rule 7.4 requires the claimant to file a copy of the particulars of claim (where served separately from the claim form) within 7 days of service on the defendant.)

Service by the court

6APD.8 **8.1** Where the court serves a document in accordance with rule 6.4 or 6.21(2), the method will normally be first class post.

8.2 Where the court serves a claim form, delivers a defence to a claimant or notifies a claimant that the defendant has filed an acknowledgment of service, the court will also serve or deliver a copy of any notice of funding that has been filed, if—

(1) it was filed at the same time as the claim form, defence or acknowledgment of service, and

(2) copies of it were provided for service.

(Rule 44.15 deals with the provision of information about funding arrangements.)

Application for an order for service by an alternative method or at an alternative place

6APD.9 **9.1** Where an application for an order under rule 6.15 is made before the document is served, the application must be supported by evidence stating—

(1) the reason why an order is sought;

(2) what alternative method or place is proposed, and

(3) why the applicant believes that the document is likely to reach the person to be served by the method or at the place proposed.

9.2 Where the application for an order is made after the applicant has taken steps to bring the document to the attention of the person to be served by an alternative method or at an alternative place, the application must be supported by evidence stating—

(1) the reason why the order is sought;

(2) what alternative method or alternative place was used;

(3) when the alternative method or place was used; and

(4) why the applicant believes that the document is likely to have reached the person to be served by the alternative method or at the alternative place.

9.3 Examples—

(1) an application to serve by posting or delivering to an address of a person who knows the other party must be supported by evidence that if posted or delivered to that address, the document is likely to be brought to the attention of the other party;

(2) an application to serve by sending a SMS text message or leaving a voicemail message at a particular telephone number saying where the document is must be accompanied *by evidence that* the person serving the document has taken, or will take, appropriate steps to ensure that the party being served is using that telephone number and is likely to receive the message; and

(3) an application to serve by e-mail to a company (where paragraph 4.1 does not apply) must be supported by evidence that the e-mail address to which the document will be sent is one which is likely to come to the attention of a person holding a senior position in that company.

Deemed service of a document other than a claim form

10.1 Rule 6.26 contains provisions about deemed service of a document other than a claim form. Examples of how deemed service is calculated are set out below. 6APD.10

10.2 Example 1
Where the document is posted (by first class post) on a Monday (a business day), the day of deemed service is the following Wednesday (a business day).

10.3 Example 2
Where the document is left in a numbered box at the DX on a Friday (a business day), the day of deemed service is the following Monday (a business day).

10.4 Example 3
Where the document is sent by fax on a Saturday and the transmission of that fax is completed by 4.30p.m. on that day, the day of deemed service is the following Monday (a business day).

10.5 Example 4
Where the document is served personally before 4.30p.m. on a Sunday, the day of deemed service is the next day (Monday, a business day).

10.6 Example 5
Where the document is delivered to a permitted address after 4.30p.m. on the Thursday (a business day) before Good Friday, the day of deemed service is the following Tuesday (a business day) as the Monday is a bank holiday

10.7 Example 6
Where the document is posted (by first class post) on a bank holiday Monday, the day of deemed service is the following Wednesday (a business day).

ANNEX

Service on Members of the Regular Forces

1. The following information is for litigants and legal representatives who wish to serve legal documents in civil proceedings in the courts of England and Wales on parties to the proceedings who are (or who, at the material time, were) members of the regular forces (as defined in the Armed Forces Act 2006). 6APD.11
2. The proceedings may take place in the county court or the High Court, and the documents to be served may be claim forms, interim application notices and pre-action application

notices. Proceedings for divorce or maintenance and proceedings in the Family Courts generally are subject to special rules as to service which are explained in a practice direction issued by the Senior District Judge of the Principal Registry on 26 June 1979.

3. In this Annex, the person wishing to effect service is referred to as the 'claimant' and the member of the regular forces to be served is referred to as 'the member'; the expression 'overseas' means outside the United Kingdom.

Enquiries as to address

6APD.12 4. As a first step, the claimant's legal representative will need to find out where the member is serving, if this is not already known. For this purpose the claimant's legal representative should write to the appropriate officer of the Ministry of Defence as specified in paragraph 10 below.

5. The letter of enquiry should in every case show that the writer is a legal representative and that the enquiry is made solely with a view to the service of legal documents in civil proceedings.

6. In all cases the letter must give the full name, service number, rank or rate, and Ship, Arm or Trade, Regiment or Corps and Unit or as much of this information as is available. Failure to quote the service number and the rank or rate may result either in failure to identify the member or in considerable delay.

7. The letter must contain an undertaking by the legal representative that, if the address is given, it will be used solely for the purpose of issuing and serving documents in the proceedings and that so far as is possible the legal representative will disclose the address only to the court and not to the claimant or to any other person or body. A legal representative in the service of a public authority or private company must undertake that the address will be used solely for the purpose of issuing and serving documents in the proceedings and that the address will not be disclosed so far as is possible to any other part of the legal representative's employing organisation or to any other person but only to the court. Normally on receipt of the required information and undertaking the appropriate office will give the service address.

8. If the legal representative does not give the undertaking, the only information that will be given is whether the member is at that time serving in England or Wales, Scotland, Northern Ireland or overseas.

9. It should be noted that a member's address which ends with a British Forces Post Office address and reference (BFPO) will nearly always indicate that the member is serving *overseas*.

10. The letter of enquiry should be addressed as follows—

(a) Royal Navy and Royal Marine Officers, Ratings and Other Ranks—

Director Naval Personnel
Fleet Headquarters
MP 3.1
Leach Building
Whale Island
Portsmouth
Hampshire
PO2 8BY

(b) Army Officers and other Ranks—

Army Personnel Centre
Disclosures 1
MP 520
Kentigern House
65 Brown Street
Glasgow
G2 8EX

(c) Royal Air Force Officers and Other Ranks—

Manning 22E
RAF Disclosures
Room 221B
Trenchard Hall
RAF Cranwell
Sleaford
Lincolnshire
NG34 8HB

Assistance in serving documents on members

11. Once the claimant's legal representative has ascertained the member's address, the legal representative may use that address as the address for service by post, in cases where this method of service is allowed by the Civil Procedure Rules. There are, however, some situations in which service of the proceedings, whether in the High Court or in the county court, must be effected personally; in these cases an appointment will have to be sought, through the Commanding Officer of the Unit, Establishment or Ship concerned, for the purpose of effecting service. The procedure for obtaining an appointment is described below, and it applies whether personal service is to be effected by the claimant's legal representative or the legal representative's agent or by a court bailiff, or, in the case of proceedings served overseas (with the leave of the court) through the British Consul or the foreign judicial authority. **6APD.13**

12. The procedure for obtaining an appointment to effect personal service is by application to the Commanding Officer of the Unit, Establishment or Ship in which the member is serving. The Commanding Officer may grant permission for the document server to enter the Unit, Establishment or Ship but if this is not appropriate the Commanding Officer may offer arrangements for the member to attend at a place in the vicinity of the Unit, Establishment or Ship in order

that the member may be served. If suitable arrangements cannot be made the legal representative will have evidence that personal service is impracticable, which may be useful in an application for service by an alternative method or at an alternative place.

General

6APD.14 13. Subject to the procedure outlined in paragraphs 11 and 12, there are no special arrangements to assist in the service of legal documents when a member is outside the United Kingdom. The appropriate office will, however, give an approximate date when the member is likely to return to the United Kingdom.

14. It sometimes happens that a member has left the regular forces by the time an enquiry as to address is made. If the claimant's legal representative confirms that the proceedings result from an occurrence when the member was in the regular forces and the legal representative gives the undertaking referred to in paragraph 7, the last known private address after discharge will normally be provided. In no other case, however, will the Ministry of Defence, disclose the private address of a member of the regular forces.

Service on Members of United States Air Force

6APD.15 15. In addition to the information contained in the memorandum of 26 July 1979, and after some doubts having been expressed as to the correct procedure to be followed by persons having civil claims against members of the United States Air Force in England and Wales, the Lord Chancellor's Office (as it was then) issued the following notes for guidance with the approval of the appropriate United States authorities.

16. Instructions have been issued by the United States authorities to the commanding officers of all their units in England and Wales that every facility is to be given for the service of documents in civil proceedings on members of the United States Air Force. The proper course to be followed by a creditor or other person having a claim against a member of the United States Air Force is for that person to communicate with the commanding officer or, where the unit concerned has a legal officer, with the legal officer of the defendant's unit requesting the provision of facilities for the service of documents on the defendant. It is not possible for the United States authorities to act as arbitrators when a civil claim is made against a member of their forces. It is, therefore, essential that the claim should either be admitted by the defendant or judgment should be obtained on it, whether in the High Court or a county court. If a claim has *been admitted* or judgment has been obtained and the claimant has failed to obtain satisfaction within a reasonable period, the claimant's proper course is then to write to: Office of the Staff Judge Advocate, Headquarters, Third Air

Force, R.A.F. Mildenhall, Suffolk, enclosing a copy of the defendant's written admission of the claim or, as the case may be, a copy of the judgment. Steps will then be taken by the Staff Judge Advocate to ensure that the matter is brought to the defendant's attention with a view to prompt satisfaction of the claim.

PRACTICE DIRECTION B—SERVICE OUT OF THE JURISDICTION

This Practice Direction supplements CPR Part 6

Scope of this Practice Direction

6BPD.1 **1.1** This Practice Direction supplements Section IV (service of the claim form and other documents out of the jurisdiction) of Part 6. (Practice Direction A supplementing Part 6 contains relevant provisions supplementing rule 6.40 in relation to the method of service on a party in Scotland or Northern Ireland.)

Service out of the jurisdiction where permission of the court is not required

6BPD.2 **2.1** Where rule 6.34 applies, the claimant must file practice form N510 when filing the claim form.

Service out of the jurisdiction where permission of the court is not required

6BPD.3 **3.1** The claimant may serve a claim form out of the jurisdiction with the permission of the court under rule 6.36 where—

General grounds

(1) A claim is made for a remedy against a person domiciled within the jurisdiction.

(2) A claim is made for an injunction (GL) ordering the defendant to do or refrain from doing an act within the jurisdiction.

(3) A claim is made against a person ("the defendant") on whom the claim form has been or will be served (otherwise than in reliance on this paragraph) and—
  (a) there is between the claimant and the defendant a real issue which it is reasonable for the court to try; and
  (b) the claimant wishes to serve the claim form on another person who is a necessary or proper party to that claim.

(4) A claim is an additional claim under Part 20 and the person to be served is a necessary or proper party to the claim or additional claim.

Claims for interim remedies

(5) A claim is made for an interim remedy under section 25(1) of the Civil Jurisdiction and Judgments Act 1982.

Claims in relation to contracts

(6) A claim is made in respect of a contract where the contract—
  (a) was made within the jurisdiction;
  (b) was made by or through an agent trading or residing within the jurisdiction;
  (c) is governed by English law; or
  (d) contains a term to the effect that the court shall have jurisdiction to determine any claim in respect of the contract.

(7) A claim is made in respect of a breach of contract committed within the jurisdiction.

(8) A claim is made for a declaration that no contract exists where, if the contract was found to exist, it would comply with the conditions set out in paragraph (6).

Claims in tort

(9) A claim is made in tort where—
(a) damage was sustained within the jurisdiction; or
(b) the damage sustained resulted from an act committed within the jurisdiction.

Enforcement

(10) A claim is made to enforce any judgment or arbitral award.

Claims about property within the jurisdiction

(11) The whole subject matter of a claim relates to property located within the jurisdiction.

Claims about trusts etc.

(12) A claim is made for any remedy which might be obtained in proceedings to execute the trusts of a written instrument where—
(a) the trusts ought to be executed according to English law; and
(b) the person on whom the claim form is to be served is a trustee of the trusts.

(13) A claim is made for any remedy which might be obtained in proceedings for the administration of the estate of a person who died domiciled within the jurisdiction.

(14) A probate claim or a claim for the rectification of a will.

(15) A claim is made for a remedy against the defendant as constructive trustee where the defendant's alleged liability arises out of acts committed within the jurisdiction.

(16) A claim is made for restitution where the defendant's alleged liability arises out of acts committed within the jurisdiction.

Claims by HM Revenue and Customs

(17) A claim is made by the Commissioners for H.M. Revenue and Customs relating to duties or taxes against a defendant not domiciled in Scotland or Northern Ireland.

Claim for costs order in favour of or against third parties

(18) A claim is made by a party to proceedings for an order that the court exercise its power under section 51 of the Supreme Court Act 1981 to make a costs order in favour of or against a person who is not a party to those proceedings.

(Rule 48.2 sets out the procedure where the court is considering whether to exercise its discretion to make a costs order in favour of or against a non-party.)

(19) A claim is—
(a) in the nature of salvage and any part of the services took place within the jurisdiction; or

(b) to enforce a claim under section 153, 154, 175 or 176A of the Merchant Shipping Act 1995.

Claims under various enactments

(20) A claim is made—

(a) under an enactment which allows proceedings to be brought and those proceedings are not covered by any of the other grounds referred to in this paragraph; or

(b) under the Directive of the Council of the European Communities dated 15 March 1976 No.76/308/EEC, where service is to be effected in a Member State of the European Union.

Documents to be filed under rule 6.43(2)(c)

6BPD.4 **4.1** The claimant must provide the following documents for each party to be served out of the jurisdiction—

(1) a copy of the particulars of claim if not already contained in or served with the claim form;

(2) a duplicate of the claim form, of the particulars of claim (if not already contained in or served with the claim form) and of any documents accompanying the claim form;

(3) forms for responding to the claim; and

(4) any translation required under rule 6.45 in duplicate.

4.2 Some countries require legalisation of the document to be served and some require a formal letter of request which must be signed by the Senior Master. Any queries on this should be addressed to the Foreign Process Section (Room E02) at the Royal Courts of Justice.

Service in a Commonwealth State or British overseas territory

6BPD.5 **5.1** The judicial authorities of certain Commonwealth States which are not a party to the Hague Convention require service to be in accordance with rule 6.42(1)(b)(i) and not 6.42(3). A list of such countries can be obtained from the Foreign Process Section (Room E02) at the Royal Courts of Justice.

5.2 The list of British overseas territories is contained in Schedule 6 to the British Nationality Act 1981. For ease of reference, these are—

(a) Anguilla;
(b) Bermuda;
(c) British Antarctic Territory;
(d) British Indian Ocean Territory;
(e) British Virgin Islands;
(f) Cayman Islands
(g) Falkland Islands;
(h) Gibraltar;
(i) Montserrat;
(j) Pitcairn, Henderson, Ducie and Oeno;
(k) St. Helena and Dependencies;
(l) South Georgia and the South Sandwich Islands;

(m) Sovereign Base Areas of Akrotiri and Dhekelia; and
(n) Turks and Caicos Islands.

Period for responding to a claim form

6.1 Where rule 6.35(5) applies, the periods within which the defendant must— **6BPD.6**

(1) file an acknowledgment of service;
(2) file or serve an admission; or
(3) file a defence,

will be calculated in accordance with paragraph 6.3, 6.4 or 6.5.

6.2 Where the court grants permission to serve a claim form out of the jurisdiction the court will determine in accordance with paragraph 6.3, 6.4 or 6.5 the periods within which the defendant must—

(1) file an acknowledgment of service;
(2) file or serve an admission; or
(3) file a defence.

(Rule 6.37(5)(a) provides that when giving permission to serve a claim form out of the jurisdiction the court will specify the period within which the defendant may respond to the claim form.)

6.3 The period for filing an acknowledgment of service under Part 10 or for filing or serving an admission under Part 14 is the number of days listed in the Table after service of the particulars of claim.

6.4 The period for filing a defence under Part 15 is—

(1) the number of days listed in the Table after service of the particulars of claim; or
(2) where the defendant has filed an acknowledgment of service, the number of days listed in the Table plus an additional 14 days after the service of the particulars of claim.

6.5 Under the State Immunity Act 1978, where a State is served, the period permitted under paragraphs 6.3 and 6.4 for filing an acknowledgment of service or defence or for filing or serving an admission does not begin to run until 2 months after the date on which the State is served.

6.6 Where particulars of claim are served out of the jurisdiction any statement as to the period for responding to the claim contained in any of the forms required by rule 7.8 to accompany the particulars of claim must specify the period prescribed under rule 6.35 or by the order permitting service out of the jurisdiction under rule 6.37(5).

Period for responding to an application notice

7.1 Where an application notice or order is served out of the jurisdiction, the period for responding is 7 days less than the number of days listed in the Table. **6BPD.7**

will be calculated in accordance with paragraph 6.3, 6.4 or 6.5.

7.2 Further information

Further information concerning service out of the jurisdiction can be obtained from the Foreign Process Section, Room E02, Royal Courts of Justice, Strand, London WC2A 2LL (telephone 020 7947 6691).

Table

6BPD.8

Place or country	Number of days
Afghanistan	23
Albania	25
Algeria	22
Andorra	21
Angola	22
Anguilla	31
Antigua and Barbuda	23
Antilles (Netherlands)	31
Argentina	22
Armenia	21
Ascension Island	31
Australia	25
Austria	21
Azerbaijan	22
Azores	23
Bahamas	22
Bahrain	22
Balearic Islands	21
Bangladesh	23
Barbados	23
Belarus	21
Belgium	21
Belize	23
Benin	25
Bermuda	31
Bhutan	28
Bolivia	23
Bosnia and Herzegovina	21
Botswana	23
Brazil	22
British Virgin Islands	31
Brunei	25
Bulgaria	23
Burkina Faso	23
Burma	23
Burundi	22
Cambodia	28
Cameroon	22
Canada	22
Canary Islands	22
Cape Verde	25
Caroline Islands	31

Cayman Islands	31
Central African Republic	25
Chad	25
Chile	22
China	24
China (Hong Kong)	31
China (Macau)	31
China (Taiwan)	23
China (Tibet)	34
Christmas Island	27
Cocos (Keeling) Islands	41
Colombia	22
Comoros	23
Congo (formerly Congo Brazzaville or French Congo)	25
Congo (Democratic Republic)	25
Corsica	21
Costa Rica	23
Croatia	21
Cuba	24
Cyprus	31
Czech Republic	21
Denmark	21
Djibouti	22
Dominica	23
Dominican Republic	23
East Timor	25
Ecuador	22
Egypt	22
El Salvador	25
Equatorial Guinea	23
Eritrea	22
Estonia	21
Ethiopia	22
Falkland Islands and Dependencies	31
Faroe Islands	31
Fiji	23
Finland	24
France	24
French Guyana	31
French Polynesia	31

French West Indies	31
Gabon	25
Gambia	22
Georgia	21
Germany	21
Ghana	22
Gibraltar	31
Greece	21
Greenland	31
Grenada	24
Guatemala	24
Guernsey	21
Guinea	22
Guinea-Bissau	22
Guyana	22
Haiti	23
Holland (Netherlands)	21
Honduras	24
Hungary	22
Iceland	22
India	23
Indonesia	22
Iran	22
Iraq	22
Ireland (Republic of)	21
Ireland (Northern)	21
Isle of Man	21
Israel	22
Italy	21
Ivory Coast	22
Jamaica	22
Japan	23
Jersey	21
Jordan	23
Kazakhstan	221
Kenya	22
Kiribati	23
Korea (North)	28
Korea (South)	24
Kosovo	21
Kuwait	22
Kyrgyzstan	21
Laos	30
Latvia	21

Lebanon	22
Lesotho	23
Liberia	22
Libya	21
Liechtenstein	21
Lithuania	21
Luxembourg	21
Macedonia	21
Madagascar	23
Madeira	31
Malawi	23
Malaysia	24
Maldives	26
Mali	25
Malta	21
Mariana Islands	26
Marshall Islands	32
Mauritania	23
Mauritius	22
Mexico	23
Micronesia	23
Moldova	21
Monaco	21
Mongolia	24
Montenegro	21
Montserrat	31
Morocco	22
Mozambique	23
Namibia	23
Nauru	36
Nepal	23
Netherlands	21
Nevis	24
New Caledonia	31
New Zealand	26
New Zealand Island Territories	50
Nicaragua	24
Niger (Republic of)	25
Nigeria	22
Norfolk Island	31
Norway	21
Oman (Sultanate of)	22
Pakistan	23

Palau	23
Panama	26
Papua New Guinea	26
Paraguay	22
Peru	22
Philippines	23
Pitcairn, Henderson, Ducie and Oeno Islands	31
Poland	21
Portugal	21
Portuguese Timor	31
Puerto Rico	23
Qatar	23
Reunion	31
Romania	22
Russia	21
Rwanda	23
Sabah	23
St. Helena	31
St. Kitts and Nevis	24
St. Lucia	24
St. Pierre and Miquelon	31
St. Vincent and the Grenadines	24
Samoa (U.S.A. Territory) (See also Western Samoa)	30
San Marino	21
Sao Tome and Principe	25
Sarawak	28
Saudi Arabia	24
Scotland	21
Senegal	22
Serbia	21
Seychelles	22
Sierra Leone	22
Singapore	22
Slovakia	21
Slovenia	21
Society Islands (French Polynesia)	31
Solomon Islands	29
Somalia	22
South Africa	22
South Georgia (Falkland Island Dependencies)	31

South Orkneys	21
South Shetlands	21
Spain	21
Spanish Territories of North Africa	31
Sri Lanka	23
Sudan	22
Surinam	22
Swaziland	22
Sweden	21
Switzerland	21
Syria	23
Tajikistan	21
Tanzania	22
Thailand	23
Togo	22
Tonga	30
Trinidad and Tobago	23
Tristan Da Cunha	31
Tunisia	22
Turkey	21
Turkmenistan	21
Turks & Caicos Islands	31
Tuvalu	23
Uganda	22
Ukraine	21
United Arab Emirates	22
United States of America	22
Uruguay	22
Uzbekistan	21
Vanuatu	29
Vatican City State	21
Venezuela	22
Vietnam	28
Virgin Islands - U.S.A	24
Wake Island	25
Western Samoa	34
Yemen (Republic of)	30
Zaire	25
Zambia	23
Zimbabwe	22

Annex—Service Regulation (Rule 6.41)

Note —The Service Regulation is printed in Vol.2, para.5–222. **6BPD.9**

PART 7

How to Start Proceedings—The Claim Form

Contents

7.0.1

Editorial Introduction

7.0.2 The rules in Pt 7 should be read together with the rules in Pts 6, 9, 10, 11, 15 and 16 and the pre-action protocols. To overcome the perceived weakness in the former system of pleadings the system is simplified. The new code of rules in Pt 7 *et seq.* is much simpler and shorter than that previously found in RSC O.5 to 9.

Proceedings are commenced by a claimant making a claim. A defendant may respond by filing a defence; a claimant may file a reply to a defendant's defence. The "claim", "defence" and "reply" are no longer described generically as "pleadings" but as "statements of case" (see r.2.3(1)).

Statements of case should enable the court and the parties to identify and define the real issues in dispute. In particular they should enable the court to allocate the case to the appropriate track, to give appropriate case management directions, to direct trial of specific issues, to direct summary trial of specific issues and to limit matters which will eventually need to be tried.

The former rules of court as to pleadings were a mixture of general and specific requirements. Some of the specific provisions dealt with issues which the courts had had to resolve from case to case over the years. However, there were many more such points which were not explicitly covered by the rules. Many of these points were reflections of an over-technical approach which should not survive in a case-management system under which "statements of case" ("pleadings") are subject to judicial scrutiny. For this reason, the new provisions are fairly short. Detailed provisions are limited to those situations where more general provisions cannot guide the parties as to what they should put in their statements of case.

Note also r.3.4 (Court's power to strike out a statement of case) and r.18.1 (Court's power to obtain further information).

In the majority of cases the claimant will issue a "claim form" to commence legal proceedings. The claim form is the main (but not the only) form of originating process under the CPR. See also r.25.4 (application for an interim remedy where there is no related claim) which requires an application under Pt 23, and, in particular, Pt 8—Alternative Procedure for Claims. Although basically sound, it is nonetheless an oversimplification to say that claims which would have been brought by writ (High Court) or summons (county court) should now be brought by claim form under Pt 7 and claims which would bave been brought by originating summons (High Court) or originating application (county court) should now be brought under the alternative procedure of Pt 8. Claims for return of goods still are fixed-date actions 7BPD.1. Rule 44.12A introduced a new Pt 8 claim for costs only proceedings where the substantive claim has been settled pre-action. Note that Pt 8 can only effectively be used "by consent". If the paying party disputes any entitlement or agreement to costs, the substantive claim must still be issued under Pt 7. It is worth verifying, therefore, that a case is not one which could or should be commenced under Pt 8 before issuing a claim form pursuant to Pt 7. The original intention of having just one simple and straightforward way to commence any case in any court has not materialised.

Nevertheless, for the majority of claims, the "claim form" issued pursuant to Pt 7 is the appropriate originating process.

The Pt 7 Practice Direction, para.4.1 requires the title of the proceedings on the claim form and statements of case to state, inter alia, the full name of each party. From October 2005 this paragraph carries a footnote referring to the Pt 16 Practice Direction, para.2.67, which sets out what constitutes the full name for an individual, a partnership and a company. This guidance should be followed carefully as incorrect titles and descriptions of parties frequently cause problems at later stages.

Pre-action protocols

Before issuing a claim form it is necessary to consider Practice Direction—Protocols, see para.C1–001 and any applicable protocol. Litigation should no longer be regarded as the first or main method of resolving disputes. Lord Woolf in his final "Access to Justice" Report recommended the development of pre-action protocols "to build on and increase the benefits of early but well informed settlement which genuinely satisfy both parties to dispute". The CPR enable the court to take into account compliance or non-compliance with pre-action protocols (rr.3.1(4) and 5. 3.9(e), 44.3(5)(a)). Both prospective claimants and prospective defendants should comply with the substance of an approved protocol. Paragraph 4.1 of the Practice Direction—Protocols (see para.C1–003) states "In cases not covered by any approved protocol, the court will expect the parties, in accordance with the overriding objective and the matters referred to in CPR r.1.1(2)(a), (b) and and (c), to act reasonably in exchanging information and documents relevant to the claim and generally in trying to avoid the necessity for the start of proceedings." Thus, for all cases, the pre-action protocols indicate the sort of behaviour now expected of lawyers and potential litigants. **7.0.3**

Interest in personal injury cases—when does it start to run?

The new procedural code did not, of itself, change the law on interest: see s.35A of the SCA 1981 and s.69 of the CCA 1984. Nevertheless, there is one important matter which still invites re-consideration by the courts. **7.0.4**

Interest on general damages for pain and suffering and loss of amenities has been awarded from the date of service of the writ (now a claim form) until the date of trial (*Wright v B.R.B.* [1983] 2 A.C. 773, HL, approving *Birkett v Hayes* [1982] 1 W.L.R. 816, CA). It is submitted that this rule is inconsistent with the philosophy and tenor of the CPR. Claimants are now expected to attempt to settle the dispute without proceedings and comply with pre-action protocols (see para.7.0.3 above) whereas awarding interest from the date of *service* of a claim form pulls in the opposite direction by encouraging early issue and service of proceedings. This inconsistency has still not been addressed. However, as the rate of interest is 2 per cent (the Court of Appeal has declined to depart from this guideline rate: *L (A Patient) v Chief Constable of Staffordshire*, [2000] P.I.Q.R. Q349) the sum involved will usually be small. See further paras 7.0.9 *et seq.*

Human Rights

Paragraph 2.10 to PD 7 contains a prompt with regard to claims under the Human Rights Act 1998.The normal rules apply as to venue and how to start proceedings (under Pts 7, 8, or 54 (Judicial Review)) with the one exception that a claim for damages in respect of a judicial act should be started in the High Court (see r.7.11). Claim forms **N1** and **N205** were amended to include a question on whether the claim includes an issue under the Human Rights Act. **7.0.5**

Related sources

7.0.6
- Part 1 (Overriding Objective)
- Rule 3.4 (Power to strike out statement of case)
- Rule 6 (Service)
- Part 8 (Alternative Procedure for Claims)
- Part 9 (Responding to Particulars of Claim—General)
- Part 10 (Acknowledgment of Service)
- Part 11 (Disputing the Court's Jurisdiction)
- Part 15 (Defence and Reply)
- Part 16 (Statements of Case)
- Part 17 (Amendments to Statements of Case)
- Part 18 (Further Information)
- Part 19 (Parties and Group Litigation)
- Part 20 (Counterclaims and other additional claims)
- Rule 21.10 (Compromise etc. by or on behalf of child or patient)
- Part 23 (General Rules about Applications for Court Orders)
- Rule 25.4 (Application for an interim remedy where there is no related claim)
- Part 44 (Costs)
- RSC O.17 (Interpleader)—re-enacted in Sch.1, CPR
- CCR O. 33 (Interpleader)—re-enacted in Sch.2, CPR

Forms

7.0.7
- **N1** Part 7 Claim Form

Practice Directions

7.0.8 Five practice directions supplement this Part. The first (How to Start Proceedings—The Claim Form) contains provisions of general application, replacing certain former RSC and CCR provisions (especially CCR O.6). Three other practice directions (dealing with Consumer Credit Act procedure, the Production Centre, and claims for the recovery of duties) supplement particular rules for the purposes expressly stated in those rules, see r.7.9 (Fixed date and other claims) and r.7.10 (Production Centre for claims). The relevance of the fifth practice direction to Pt 7 is that it provides for a scheme enabling claimants to start certain types of county court claims by requesting by electronic means the issue of claim forms (this practice direction also provides for the filing of certain other documents by such means).

Claim for interest—history and basic law

7.0.9 At common law interest on a debt was not recoverable in the absence of a contract, express or implied (see *London, Chatham and Dover Ry Co v South Eastern Ry Co* [1893] A.C. 429 at 434 *et seq.*). It was not allowed on damages but, under the law merchant interest was allowed in respect of dishonoured bills of exchange and in certain other cases (*ibid.*). It was also allowed in the Admiralty Court on damages arising out of a collision at sea where the claimant had suffered prejudice by delay in meeting his claim.

Under its equitable jurisdiction the court had, and still has, power to award interest as ancillary relief in respect of equitable remedies such as specific performance, rescission or the taking of an account. Under this jurisdiction, interest may be ordered to be paid where money has been obtained and retained by fraud (*Johnson v R.* [1904] A.C. 817), or where money has been withheld or misapplied by an executor, trustee or anyone else in a fiduciary position and, in such case, the court has an inherent power to order the payment of interest at whatever rate is equitable in the circumstances and may direct that such interest be compounded at appropriate intervals (*Wallersteiner v Moir (No.2)* [1975] Q.B. 373, CA).

The jurisdiction of the court to award compound interest (other than where it could be claimed by contract or usage) could not be extended and the power of the court to make such an award was confined to the equitable jurisdiction to award compound interest against a trustee or other person owing fiduciary duties who was *personally* accountable and had made use of the claimant's monies (*Westdeutsche Landesbank Girozentrale v Islington LBC* [1996] 2 All E.R. 961).

The complications and contradictions of the common law and law merchant are now largely matters of history. The Law Reform (Miscellaneous Provisions) Act 1934 gave general power to a court of record to award interest in proceedings for the recovery of a debt or damages. These provisions were replaced by s.35A of SCA 1981 and s.69 of CCA 1984. Section 35A(1) provides:

> "Subject to rules of court, in proceedings (whenever instituted) before the High Court for the recovery of a debt or damages there may be included in any sum for which judgment is given simple interest, at such rate as the court thinks fit or as rules of court may provide, on all or any part of the debt or damages in respect of which judgment is given, or payment is made before judgment, for all or any part of the period between the date when the cause of action arose and—
> (a) in the case of any sum paid before judgment, the date of the payment; and
> (b) in the case of the sum for which judgment is given, the date of the judgment."

The expression "judgment is given" used in this section clearly includes an "order is made" (see Pt 40).

In consequence, the law as to interest is as follows.

All claims for interest must be pleaded

If a claimant is seeking interest he must provide in his particulars of claim the detailed information stated in r.16.4(2) (see further para.16.4.2), but, in *Greer v Alstons Engineering Sales & Services Ltd* [2003] UKPC 46 it was held that the power to award interest is exercisable whether or not there is a claim for interest in the claim form/ statement of case. **7.0.10**

Interest on debts

(a) Interest by contract —Interest pursuant to contract may be claimed and awarded as a specific sum. **7.0.11**

(b) Bills of exchange —By the Bills of Exchange Act 1882 s.57 interest on a dishonoured bill may be recovered from the date of dishonour until judgment or sooner payment as liquidated damages. The court may, by s.57(3) withhold interest if justice requires it. These provisions are not affected by the SCA 1981 (see s.35A(8)).

(c) Special statutory provisions —Several statutes provide that interest may be recovered on debts or other liquidated demands; e.g. the Taxes Management Act 1970 ss.86–92 (interest on overdue taxes); Solicitors (Non Contentious Business) Remuneration Order 1994 art.5(1); (interest on unpaid bill for non-contentious work); Late Payment of Commercial Debts (Interest) Act 1998 fully in force from August 7, 2002—it provides for a higher rate of interest than the court will normally have discretion to allow.

Any claim under statute for interest must specify the particular statutory provision relied on; "Interest pursuant to statute" is insufficient.

(d) Interest under s.35A(1) —This section gives a general power to the court to award interest upon both debt and damages. In theory the interest is in the discretion of the court and must be awarded at a trial or assessment. but there is an important exception. A default judgment on a claim for a specified amount of money may include interest to the date of judgment subject to the provisions of r.12.6.

(e) Compound interest —The practice whereby banks charge customers compound interest has become recognised as a usage of bankers, and as such is implied into a contract between banker and customer; a bank's right to charge compound interest does not cease upon its demand for repayment of the sums outstanding on the customer's account, but continues until all such sums are paid or until judgment is given on the bank's claim (*National Bank of Greece SA v Pinios Shipping Co (No.1) The Maira* [1990] 1 A.C. 638; [1990] 1 All E.R. 78, HL).

Interest under the equitable jurisdiction

The jurisdiction, referred to in para.7.0.9 is unchanged. **7.0.12**

Interest on damages

Section 35A of the SCA 1981 and s.69 of the CCA 1984 give the court general **7.0.13** power to award interest on damages in its discretion; by s.35A(2) the discretion must be exercised in favour of a claimant who recovers damages exceeding £200 for personal injuries or death "unless the court is satisfied that there are special reasons to the contrary". For the principles and practice see para.7.0.22. When damages are limited by the Warsaw-Hague Convention applied by the Carriage by Air Act 1961 Sch.1, the total award of damages and interest must not exceed this Convention limit (*Swiss Bank Corp v Brink's-M.A.T. Ltd* [1986] Q.B. 853; [1986] 3 W.L.R. 12).

Personal injury claims are in a special category (para.7.0.22). Interest will not be awarded on non-economic loss where the cause of action is fraudulent misrepresentation (*Saunders v Edwards* [1987] 1 W.L.R. 1116; [1987] 2 All E.R. 651, CA), or on general damages for wrongful arrest and false imprisonment (*Holatham v Commr of Police for the Metropolis*, *Independent*, November 26, 1987, CA).

Interest in r.36.21 offers to settle

7.0.14 "Interest" within the meaning of r.36.21, which empowers the court to award interest at 10 per cent over base rate as a "sanction", against a party who has failed to accept a reasonable offer to settle, is not the same as "interest" within the meaning of s.35A of the Supreme Court Act 1981: *All in One Design & Build Limited v Motcomb Estates Ltd* (2000) 144 S.J.L.B. 219. For a more detailed discussion on interest in relation to offers to settle see the notes to Pt 36.

Principles upon which interest is awarded—discretion

7.0.15 If a claimant is entitled to interest by statute or statutory instrument or by contract, the claimant is entitled to interest as of right (unless in a contract case he falls foul of the provisions of the Consumer Credit Act 1974 as to exorbitant interest in consumer contracts (ss.137–40)).

In other cases a degree of discretion is involved, which may be as to whether interest is awarded at all, as to the rate of interest or as to the period for which it should run. In claims for interest under the Bills of Exchange Act 1882 s.57, or upon damages for personal injuries under s.35A(2) of the SCA 1981, the onus is on the defendant to show that interest should not be awarded; in other cases the onus is upon the claimant to obtain an award; the rate and period are, generally, discretionary.

As Lord Diplock has pointed out in *Wright v British Railways Board* [1983] 2 A.C. 773; [1983] 2 All E.R. 698, binding rules cannot be laid down as to how a discretion is to be exercised; however, as a matter of convenience the courts have, from time to time, issued "guidelines" (and amended them) which are often followed in practice; there are a number of reported cases as to how the discretion has been exercised. A summary of the general considerations which arise is given in para.7.0.16 and a more detailed account of the practice in relation to damages for personal injuries is given in para.7.0.22.

When the court is minded to exercise discretion as to the period or amount of interest, the parties should be given an opportunity to be heard. *Amonoo v Grant Seifert Grower* [2001] EWCA Civ 150; January 26, 2001, CA.

As to (1) reducing the period for which interest is payable on an award, or (2) altering the rate at which interest is calculated, or both, as a procedural sanction, see para.3.1.5.

General considerations

7.0.16 The overriding principle is that interest should be awarded to the claimant not as compensation for the damage done but for being kept out of money which ought to have been paid to him (per Lord Herschell L.C. in *London, Chatham and Dover Ry Co v South Eastern Ry Co* [1893] A.C. 429 at 437). This principle is more easily applied to a debt or a particular expense which the defendant ought to have made good, than to unascertained damages in relation to which it is difficult to say when the money *ought* to have been paid; the approach of the courts has been pragmatic.

The chief points that have arisen are as follows.

Rates of interest

7.0.17 *A number of different rates have been applied:*

(a) *The commercial rate*—or rate which the claimant would have had to pay to borrow the money. The personal circumstances of the claimant are relevant; there is a discussion in the judgment of Forbes J. in *Tate and Lyle Food and Distribu-*

tion v GLC [1982] 1 W.L.R. 149; [1981] 3 All E.R. 716, which suggests that a claimant of high standing should receive somewhat less than the ordinary run of claimant and vice versa, but that the abatement or increase should be moderate. See also para.(h) below.

The commercial rate is commonly used in commercial cases, including claims on bills of exchange. Generally the Commercial Court will award interest at base rate plus one per cent. This, however, is no more than a presumption which can be displaced by evidence showing that such a rate will be unfair to one party or the other (*Shearson Lehman Hutton Inc v Maclaine Watson & Co Ltd (No.2)* [1990] 3 All E.R. 723). In *Claymore Services Ltd v Nautilus Properties Ltd* [2007] EWHC 805 (TCC) Jackson J. considered the question of the rate of interest in detail (see paras 61 to 82) and concluded that, on the facts, the appropriate rate was two per cent above the base rate.

(b) *The investment rate*—at which the claimant could have invested the money. This is the basis of the practice in personal injury cases (see para.7.0.22).

(c) *The "true" interest rate*—disregarding that element in the market rates of interest attributable to "inflation" (i.e. the depreciation in the value of the currency). This rate is reflected in the yield on index-linked government stock. This rate is used if damages are assessed as at the date of trial in depreciated currency; the claimant might be over-compensated if he were awarded interest from the accrual of the cause of action at market rates; see *Wright v British Railways Board* [1983] 2 A.C. 773; [1983] 2 All E.R. 698 for a fuller explanation.

(d) *The "wilful default" rate*—In its equitable jurisdiction (para.7.0.9) the court may award a high rate to ensure that no profit is made from a breach of a fiduciary duty.

(e) *Foreign interest rates*—If judgment is given in a foreign currency, interest is usually taken at the rate at which that currency could be borrowed in the country in which the debt should have been paid. That rate must be proved by evidence (*Miliangos v George Frank (Textiles) Ltd (No.2)* [1977] Q.B. 489).

(f) *Special account rate*—The special account (formerly the short term investment account) is fixed by statutory instrument from time to time. It is not generally a rate used to award interest on debt or damages but has a limited use in personal injury claims pursuant to the *Jefford v Gee* [1970] 2 Q.B. 130 guidelines discussed at para.7.0.22.The rates of interest on special account are as follows:

From January 1, 1980, 15 per cent.
From January 1, 1981, 12½ per cent.
From December 1, 1981, 15 per cent.
From March 1, 1982, 14 per cent.
From July 1, 1982, 13 per cent.
From April 1, 1983, 12½ per cent.
From April 1, 1984, 12 per cent.
From August 1, 1986, 11½ per cent.
From January 1, 1987, 12¼ per cent.
From April 1, 1987, 11¾ per cent.
From November 1, 1987, 11¼ per cent.
From December 1, 1987, 11 per cent.
From May 1, 1988, 9½ per cent.
From August 1, 1988, 11 per cent.
From November 1, 1988, 12¼ per cent.
From January 1, 1989, 13 per cent.
From November 1, 1989, 14¼ per cent.
From April 1, 1991, 12 per cent.
From October 1, 1991, 10¼ per cent.
From February 1, 1993, 8 per cent.
From August 1, 1999, 7 per cent.
From February 1, 2002 6 per cent

(g) *The "Judgment Debt" rate*—Once judgment has been obtained the judgment itself attracts interest. All High Court judgments carry interest pursuant to s.17 of the Judgments Act 1838, and county court judgments over £5000.00 carry interest pursuant to the County Court (Interest on Judgment Debts) Order

1991 (SI 1991/1184). This aspect of interest is quite distinct from interest awarded on the debt or damages as part of the judgment itself and is considered in detail in the commentary to Pt 40; see para.40.8.1 *et seq*.

The "judgment debt" rate is 8 per cent and has been since April 1, 1993 (see para.40.8.3).

The judgment debt rate has a limited role when the court awards interest on the debt when giving judgment. The rate has been used because it is readily ascertainable, changes infrequently, is easily applied and avoids the need for many hearings (the costs of which would be disproportionate and would often be more than the interest) which would otherwise be required. Thus, where interest is pleaded as required by r.16.4 a default judgment on a claim for a specified amount of money may include interest to the date of judgment if "the rate is no higher than the rate of interest payable on judgment debts at the date when the claim form was issued" (see r.12.6).

What if the debt is disputed? Generally the judgment debt rate will still be used where judgment is given following a trial of a claim on the small claims track or where judgment is given on a successful application for summary judgment under Pt 24. Thus the judgment debt rate is frequently applied in cases dealt with by Masters and district judges.

However, as a general rule, the judgment debt rate is not the correct rate to be awarded after a trial. In *Reed Executive plc v Reed Business Information Ltd* [2004] EWCA Civ 887; [2004] 4 All E.R. 942 CA, Jacob L.J. said that the judgment debt rate is an artificial rate that must be imposed as provided for by legislation but he saw no reason for it to be imposed except in those cases where it must be (this passage of the judgment is not included in the report of the case at [2004] 1 W.L.R. 3026).

In *Pinnock v Wilkins & Sons The Times*, January 29, 1990, the claimant suffered injuries in a road traffic accident and recovered damages from solicitors for mishandling his litigation. The trial judge awarded interest at judgment debt rate on the basis that, but for solicitors' negligence, he would have obtained a judgment carrying interest at that rate. The Court of Appeal upheld the award.

In *Watts v Morrow* [1991] 1 W.L.R. 1421 claimants recovered damages against a surveyor for a negligent survey report. The Court of Appeal declined to interfere with the judge's award of interest at the judgment debt rate though Bingham L.J. (at p.1446) had reservations about the use of that rate in that case. Neither is a commercial case. In *Claymore Services Ltd v Nautilus Properties Ltd* [2007] EWHC 805 (TCC) Jackson J. held (at para.68) that the judgment debt rate "is not normally an appropriate rate of interest to award in the context of a dispute between two businesses".

(h) *Base rate*—There are many commercial cases where the court has awarded interest at a stated per cent above base rate (*Tate and Lyle Food and Distribution Ltd v Greater London Council* [1982] 1 W.L.R. 149; [1981] 3 All E.R. 716, 1 per cent above; *Claymore Services Ltd v Nautilus Properties Ltd* [2007] EWHC 805 (TCC), 2 per cent above; *Javra v Ahmed* [2002] EWCA Civ 210, 3 per cent above). Much turns on the status of the successful party and the rate at which they would have been able to borrow commercially.

The base rate is set by the Bank of England and can change frequently. However, the Bank's website at *http://www.bankofengland.co.uk* [Accessed November 19, 2007] records all rates (including its predecessors such as "minimum lending rate" and "bank rate") since 1694 so all relevant rates are readily ascertainable.

Rates for the last 10 years are:

Thursday, February 5, 2009—1.00
Thursday, January 8, 2009—1.50
Thursday, December 4, 2008—2.00
Thursday, November 6, 2008—3.00
Wednesday, October 8, 2008—4.50
Thursday, April 10, 2008—5.00
Thursday, February 7, 2008—5.25
Thursday, December 6, 2007—5.50

Thursday, July 5, 2007—5.75
Thursday, May 10, 2007—5.50
Thursday, January 11, 2007—5.25
Thursday, November 9, 2006—5.00
Thursday, August 3, 2006 —4.75
Thursday, August 4, 2005—4.50
Thursday, August 5, 2004—4.75
Thursday, June 10, 2004—4.50
Thursday, May 6, 2004—4.25
Thursday, February 5, 2004—4.00
Thursday, November 6, 2003—3.75
Thursday, July 10, 2003—3.50
Thursday, February 6, 2003—3.75
Thursday, November 8, 2001—4.00
Thursday, October 4, 2001—4.50
Tuesday, September 18, 2001—4.75
Thursday, August 1, 2001—5.00
Thursday, May 10, 2001—5.25
Thursday, April 5, 2001—5.50
Thursday, February 8, 2001—5.75
Thursday, February 10, 2000—6.00
Thursday, January 13, 2000—5.75

Period for which interest is awarded

The following is the normal practice as to the dates *from* which interest is awarded: **7.0.18**

(a) *Debts*—from the date upon which the money should have been paid. If a loan was made in circumstances where the borrower was led to believe that no interest would be charged, the date taken is often that upon which repayment was asked for.

(b) *Economic loss*—from the date of the loss, if this can be identified. If the loss cannot be quantified until judgment, the court has a discretion to award interest from the date upon which the cause of action arose or any proper later date (*BP Exploration Co (Libya) Ltd v Hunt* [1982] 2 W.L.R. 253; [1982] 1 All E.R. 925, HL).

(c) *Non-economic loss*—e.g. damages for personal injuries. The date most usually taken has been the date of service of the writ/claim form but this date may no longer be the most appropriate: see para.7.0.4. In some cases, e.g. libel, it is not usual to award interest.

(d) *Quantum meruit*—The leading case is *Claymore Services Ltd v Nautilus Properties Ltd* [2007] EWHC 805(TCC) where Jackson J. held that interest should start to run when the contractor has furnished his final account and the building owner has had a reasonable opportunity to assess it.

The date to which interest is awarded is ordinarily the date of the judgment or sooner payment. The judgment debt itself carries interest at the prescribed rate (see para.7.0.17(g) above). However, if, as is usually the case in claims for debt or damages, the rights of the parties merge in the judgment, any contractual right to higher interest ceases (*Re Sneyd Ex p. Fewings* [1883] 25 Ch.D. 338). Merger does not apply where there is an independent covenant; thus it is possible for the parties to agree by such a covenant that any judgment shall carry interest at a particular rate, and an action on such a covenant may be brought; there is no machinery, however, enabling this right to future interest to be embodied in the judgment itself. And merger does not apply to a security as distinct to a contract, nor can it override a statutory provision prescribing a rate to be payable until actual payment (*Economic Life Assurance Society v Usborne* [1902] A.C. 147; *Ealing LBC v El Isaac* [1980] 1 W.L.R. 932; [1980] 2 All E.R. 348). The latter case is sometimes misunderstood; it did not, generally, challenge the doctrine of merger, but successfully sought to get over the anomaly that, as county court judgments did not then carry interest; the defendant would, thus, have paid much less than he should unless the statute prevailed. The same result can be simply obtained by making payment of interest a term of a stay of execution. (County court judgments over £5,000 do now carry interest).

The considerable authority on the question as to the date from which interest should run and the rate of interest was reviewed in *Kuwait Airways Corp v Kuwait Insurance Co* [2000] Lloyd's Rep. I.R. 678 (Langley J.); see also *Westminster City Council v Porter* [2002] EWHC 1589 (Ch); July 16, 2002, unrep. (Hart J.).

Date of judgment

7.0.19 Interest cannot be awarded on the same sum in respect of the same period under both the Supreme Court Act 1981 s.35A (or the County Courts Act 1984 s.69) and the Judgments Act 1838 s.17. Interest on damages may be awarded under s.35A(1)(b) of the 1981 Act until "date of the judgment". Under s.17.1 of the 1838 Act interest on a High Court judgment runs "from such time as may be prescribed by rules of court". CPR r. 40.8(1) says that interest shall run from the date when judgment is given, except where a rule or Practice Direction provides differently, or the court decides otherwise. Rule 40.8(2) states that the court may order that interest shall run from an earlier date. When judgment is entered on liability with damages to be assessed, the House of Lords held in *Thomas v Bunn* [1991] 1 A.C. 362; [1991] 1 All E.R. 193 that interest on the judgment is payable from the date when the damages are assessed, not from the date when judgment on liability was given.

Delay and merits

7.0.20 It should be remembered that the award of interest under s.35A of the SCA 1981 is discretionary, and it may not be awarded if the court thinks that it would be unjust to do so (e.g. if it has been difficult to tell whether anything is payable (*Business Computers Ltd v Anglo-African Leasing Ltd* [1977] 1 W.L.R. 578; [1977] 2 All E.R. 74); if the claimant has been guilty of great delay (see *Birkett v Hayes* [1982] 1 W.L.R. 816; [1982] 2 All E.R. 710 and para.7.0.22). After reviewing the authorities on delay, Jackson J. in *Claymore Services Ltd v Nautilus Properties Ltd* [2007] EWHC 805 (TCC) derived three propositions (see para.55):

(1) Where a claimant has delayed unreasonably in commencing or prosecuting proceedings, the court may exercise its discretion either to disallow interest for a period or to reduce that rate of interest.

(2) The court must take a realistic view of delay. Litigation is an unwelcome distraction. Delay is unreasonable only when, after the allowance for the circumstances, the claimant neglected to pursue the claim for a significant period.

(3) If a disallowance or reduction is made, the court should bear in mind that the defendant has had the use of the money during the delay.

Practice

7.0.21 Interest must be specifically claimed in the particulars of claim (see r.16.4). Particulars of claim must be served in every case (see r.7.4). A claim for interest in any case should therefore be pleaded in accordance with r.16.4(2).

Exercise of power to award interest on damages for personal injuries

7.0.22 The principles to be applied when awarding interest on damages for personal injuries or death have been fully stated by the Court of Appeal in *Jefford v Gee* [1970] 2 Q.B. 130, which have been substantially modified by the Court of Appeal itself in *Birkett v Hayes* [1982] 1 W.L.R. 816; [1982] 2 All E.R. 710 in relation to general damages for pain and suffering and loss of amenities. They may be summarised as follows:

(1) Section 35A(2) (like the superseded s.22 of the AJA 1969, which had amended s.3 of the Act of 1934) has not altered the principles which the court should apply in awarding interest, but it does *oblige* the court to apply those principles.

(2) The governing principle is that interest should be awarded to the claimant, not as compensation for the damage done, but for being kept out of money which ought to have been paid to him (see per Lord Herschell L.C. in *London, Chatham and Dover Ry Co v South Eastern Ry Co* [1893] A.C. 429 at 437).

(3) In order to carry out its obligation to award interest under s.35A(2), the court will normally have to "itemise" the damages in personal injury actions (other than actions under the Fatal Accidents Act and under the Law Reform (Miscellaneous Provisions) Act 1934) into three categories, i.e. to find and state explicitly the amount of its award of damages under each of the following three heads of damages, namely:

(a) special damages, i.e. the actual pecuniary loss suffered by the claimant up to the date of trial;

(b) damages for loss of future earnings and loss of earning capacity; and
(c) damages for pain and suffering and loss of amenities.

(4) The rate of interest to be awarded on the special damages should be a realistic rate and should normally be based on the "appropriate" rate, e.g. the *average* rate of interest allowed on money in court placed on Special Account over the period for which the interest is awarded: see para.7.0.17(f).

(5) *On special damages*, the interest should be dealt with on broad lines without entering into minute attention to detail. Frequently interest is awarded on the total sum of the special damages from the date of the accident until the date of trial at *half* the appropriate rate of interest, including cases where the special damage ceases to accrue, or stops and re-starts before the date of the trial (*Dexter v Courtaulds Ltd* [1984] 1 W.L.R. 372; [1984] 1 All E.R. 70, CA). On occasions the court will award interest at the full rate but for a specific period (*Prokop v DHSS* [1985] C.L.Y. 1037). Special circumstances, however, may require the court to depart from the ordinary principle, and, where the claimant intends to rely on such circumstances, he should say so in his particulars of claim, and set out the relevant facts (*ibid.*).

(6) *On damages for loss of future earnings or earning capacity*, no interest should be awarded, because the claimant will not have been kept out of his money but on the contrary will have received it in advance. By analogy, interest will not be awarded on the amount of damages awarded in respect of loss of earning capacity (*Clarke v Rotaz Aircraft Equipment Ltd* [1975] 1 W.L.R. 1570; [1975] 3 All E.R. 794). See also *Joyce v Yeomans* [1981] 1 W.L.R. 549; [1981] 2 All E.R. 21, CA.

(7) *On general damages for pain and suffering and loss of amenities*, interest has been awarded at the rate of about 2 per cent per annum from the date of the service of the writ until the date of trial (*Wright v British Railways Board* [1983] 2 A.C. 773; [1983] 2 All E.R. 698, HL, approving *Birkett v Hayes* [1982] 1 W.L.R. 816; [1982] 2 All E.R. 710, CA, applying *Pickett v British Rail Engineering Ltd* [1980] A.C. 136 and dictum of Lord Denning M.R. in *Cookson v Knowles* [1977] Q.B. 913, at 921, and modifying *Jefford v Gee* [1970] 2 Q.B. at 130, CA). In *L (A Patient) v Chief Constable of Staffordshire*, [2000] P.I.Q.R. Q349, CA, it was argued unsuccessfully, that in the light of *Wells v Wells* [1999] 1 A.C. 345, HL, the rate of interest for damages of this variety should be whatever rate the Lord Chancellor might from time to time prescribe under the Damages Act 1996 s.1. Consider whether a new "start date" is required, see further para.7.0.4.

(8) In exceptional cases, such as when one party or the other has been guilty of gross delay, the court may increase or diminish the award of interest or alter the period for which it is allowed; see *Birkett v Hayes* [1982] 1 W.L.R. 816; [1982] 2 All E.R. 710, CA. *Walsh v Misseldine* [2000] C.P. Rep. 74, CA was a personal injury claim which had previously been struck out twice, and had twice been reinstated. On a third application to strike out, the Court of Appeal decided this would not be in the interests of justice as the defendant had admitted liability, and had caused serious injuries to the claimant, but the court then declined to award the claimant interest on damages beyond the date when the case should have been determined but for the delay.

(9) Interest should be computed and awarded as a gross sum without any deduction of tax.

(10) The judgment should state the rate of interest and the amount on which interest is awarded and the period for which it is awarded.

(11) In personal injury claims, the claimant is entitled to interest on the gross damages, rather than the net amount after deduction of relevant social security benefits—*Wisely v John Fulton (Plumbers) Ltd* [2000] UKHL 24; [2000] 1 W.L.R. 820, HL. See further commentary on the Supreme Court Act 1981 s.35A, at Vol.2 para.9A–124 below.

How interest is awarded

(a) If there is a trial, (including an assessment of damages by a master or district judge), all questions of interest are dealt with at the trial. **7.0.23**

(b) If there is a default judgment for a debt or specified sum: (i) if the interest is specified, interest is included in the default judgment see r.12.6; (ii) if the interest is discretionary, final judgment is entered for the principal sum together with judgment for interest to be assessed by the court; see rr.12.4 *et seq*. The assessment will be by the master/district judge.

(c) If judgment is given under Pt 24 or by an order striking out the defence for some good cause, the court may at the same time award interest.

Evidence

7.0.24 The court does not require proof of special account or Judgments Act rates. Other rates should be proven, e.g. by witness statement or, in very simple cases, a letter from a bank. Current and previous base rates are readily ascertainable (see para.7.0.17(h)).

Where to start proceedings

7.1 **7.1 Restrictions on where proceedings may be started are set out in the relevant practice direction.**

Practice Direction

7.1.1 See paras 7PD.1 *et seq.*; in particular, para.2 of the Practice Direction, especially paragraph 2.10 with regard to claims under the Human Rights Act 1998 (for which also see Editorial Introduction 7.0.2 and r.7.11 below).

How to start proceedings[1]

7.2 **7.2—(1) Proceedings are started when the court issues a claim form at the request of the claimant.**

(2) A claim form is issued on the date entered on the form by the court.

(A person who seeks a remedy from the court before proceedings are started or in relation to proceedings which are taking place, or will take place, in another jurisdiction must make an application under Part 23).

(Part 16 sets out what the claim form must include).

(The costs practice direction sets out the information about a funding arrangement to be provided with the claim form where the claimant intends to seek to recover an additional liability).

("Funding arrangements" and "additional liability" are defined in rule 43.2).

(Part 78 provides procedures for European orders for payment and for the European small claims procedure.)

7.2A **7.2AThe practice direction supplementing this Part makes provision for procedures to be followed when claims are brought by or against a partnership within the jurisdiction.[2]**

Effect of rule

7.2.1 This rule is at the heart of the CPR reforms. It introduces the "claim form"—a single form of originating process for all claims in the High Court and county court. (The concept is diluted somewhat by Pt 8—Alternative Procedure for Claims which is akin to the originating summons/originating application procedure and is for use only in appropriate cases as provided by r.8.1).

The plethora of originating process previously available in the High Court (writ, originating summons, originating motion and petition) and in the county court (summons, originating application, petition and notice of appeal) were all abolished and replaced by the "claim form".

In 2001 a scheme was introduced for the issue of money claims electronically on line through the Court Service website (*http://www.courtservice.gov.uk* [Accessed January 9, 2009]) (see the Practice Direction). The claim must be for less than £100,000 (excluding interest and costs), the Pt 7 procedure must be used, neither the claimant nor the

---

[1] Amended by the Civil Procedure (Amendment No.3) Rules 2000 (SI 2000/1317) and the Civil Procedure (Amendment) Rules 2008 (SI 2008/2178).

[2] Introduced by the Civil Procedure (Amendment) Rules 2006 (SI 2006/1689).

defendant must be a child or a patient, the claimant must not be fees exempt or publicly funded, and the defendant must not be the Crown. Also particulars of claim must be shorter than 1080 characters, including spaces. The claim is printed, issued and served by the Northampton Court in the usual way. The defendant can acknowledge/admit/defend in all the usual ways and also by email to the Court Service (courtservice@gsi.gov.uk). Defended claims are transferred to the defendant's county court. Judgments can be entered on line in undefended claims and in default and the claimant can check the position electronically without having to telephone—probably the most popular innovation. Note that Moneyclaimsonline has been made permanent. (In October 2006 a similar online scheme was introduced for possession claims of residential property for rent arrears—See Pt 55.)

In a number of cases decided since the implementation of the CPR, the courts have taken a liberal approach to "technical errors" made by a party, which did not cause any real prejudice to the other party, including issuing a claim on the wrong form. In *Hannigan v Hannigan* [2000] 2 F.C.R. 650, CA said it was disproportionate, and unjust (under r.1.1 the overriding objective) to strike out a claim made on the wrong form when the defendant had been given all the information required to understand what the claimant was seeking.

Salford City Council v Garner [2004] EWCA Civ 364 decided that the power of the court to decide a claim was brought when the claim form was received in the court office, rather than when it was issued (see the Practice Direction para.5.1) only applies when a limitation date under the Limitation Acts is imminent, and not in other situations (here a one year time limit from the date of an introductory tenancy to issue possession proceedings). *St Helens MBC v Barnes* [2006] EWCA Civ 1372 confirmed the *Salford* decision, and held that a claim was brought when a claimant's request to issue a claim form was delivered to the correct court office during opening hours (in the instant case the claim form was so delivered but was not issued until four days later because of industrial action at the court). Prudent claimants will ensure that the court records the date of receipt of the claim form. (See also the Pt 7 Practice Direction, para.5.)

Claim Form

The expression "statement of case" (which, broadly, has replaced the term "pleadings") includes a claim form (r.2.3(1)). **7.2.2**

Part 23

General Rules about applications for court orders. Part 23 is referred to in the note in brackets immediately after r.7.2. The "application notice" referred to in r.23.1 is a further dilution of the principle that all claims are made by one simple claim form in the sense that Pt 23 applies where an application is made before a claim has been started (r.23.2(4)) or in relation to proceedings which are taking place in another jurisdiction. **7.2.3**

Prescribed Forms

See Practice Direction at paras 7PD.1 *et seq.*; and the list of forms at para.48PD.15. **7.2.4**

Right to use one claim form to start two or more claims

7.3 A claimant may use a single claim form to start all claims which can be conveniently disposed of in the same proceedings. **7.3**

Starting two or more claims

In the simplest case, in a single claim form one claimant (C) brings one claim against one defendant (D). The more complicated situations are these (or some mixture of them); in a single claim form— **7.3.1**

(1) C brings two (or more) claims against D

(2) C brings a claim (or claims) against D1 and D2

(3) C1 and C2 bring a claim (or claims) against D (or against D1 and D2)

(4) C1 brings a claim against D1 and C2 brings a claim against D2

Traditionally, by a mixture of procedural and substantive rules applying various tests the law has regulated the circumstances in which parties and claims may be joined in the same originating process. The assumption has been that, for a variety of reasons, there should be limits. On the whole, constraints on party joinder have been more severe than constraints on claims joinder. Further, with some exceptions, the joinder rules have been permissive and not mandatory. However, a party who failed to join a claim when he might have done so may run the risk that, on limitation grounds or on *res judicata* or issue estoppel grounds, he will be prevented from pursuing it subsequently on separate originating process. Obviously, the parameters of a claim are not fixed by rules regulating the joinder of claims and parties in originating process but may be expanded or contracted subsequently by amendment (see particularly Pt 19 (Addition and substitution of parties) and Pt 17 (Amendments to statements of case)).

Over the years, the trend has been towards liberalising the rules restraining joinder and encouraging the joinder in the same proceedings of all claims and interested parties. This has had the advantages of (1) avoiding a multiplicity of proceedings (and attendant costs and delays), and (2) minimising the risk that claims might be defeated on technical grounds. The liberalising trend is continued by r.7.3. (The Civil Procedure Act 1997 s.1(3) states that the rule-making power shall be exercised "with a view to securing that the civil justice system is accessible fair and efficient". Joinder provisions can be regarded as being consistent with that policy.)

Multiple claims against the same defendant

7.3.2 Former RSC 15 r.1(1) and CCR 5 r.1 stated that, with the leave of the court, a plaintiff could in one action claim relief against the same defendant in respect of more than one cause of action and, in certain circumstances (concerning the capacities of the parties), without the leave of the court relief for more than one cause of action could be claimed in the one action. These provisions were subject to the court's power to order separate trials or to make such other order as may be expedient where it appeared to the court that the joinder of the causes of action "may embarrass or delay the trial or is otherwise inconvenient".

Rule 7.3 provides that a claimant may use a single claim form "to start all claims which can be conveniently disposed of in the same proceedings". Under this rule the joinder in the one claim form of several claims against a defendant does not require the permission of the court and does not depend on the capacities in which the parties sue or are sued. However, the claimant's freedom to include more than one claim is limited by the test of convenience.

As noted above, the former rules contained an express provision stating that the court had power to order separate trials where several "causes of action" were joined in one action. The CPR contain no such express provision as to "claims". However, r.3.1(2)(i) states that the court may direct a separate trial "of any issue".

Claims involving multiple claimants or defendants

7.3.3 Former RSC 15 r.4(1) and CCR 5 r.1 stated that, with the leave of the court, two or more persons could be joined together in one action as plaintiffs or as defendants and, in certain circumstances (concerning the relationship between the issues raised in the several claims and the rights to relief claimed), they could be joined without the leave of the court. These provisions were subject to the court's power to order separate trials or to make such other order as may be expedient where it appeared to the court that the joinder of the causes of action "may embarrass or delay the trial or is otherwise inconvenient" (RSC 15 r.5(1), CCR 5 r.3).

Rule 19.1 states that any number of claimants or defendants "may be joined as parties to the claim". Under r.7.3 the joinder in the one claim form of two or more persons as claimants or as defendants does not require the permission of the court and does not depend on the relationship between the issues raised in the several claims and the rights to relief claimed. However, the joinder of parties is limited by the test of convenience.

Joinder of persons jointly entitled to a remedy

7.3.4 Rule 19.2 (which is derived from RSC 15 r.4(2)) provides that where a claimant *seeks a remedy to which some other* person is jointly entitled with him, all persons jointly entitled to the remedy must be parties unless the court otherwise orders. (See further Pt 19 and commentary thereon.) The procedure for adding parties is in r.19.3. If a jointly entitled person does not agree to be a claimant, he must be made a defendant unless the court orders otherwise (r.19.2(2)).

"Claims which can be conveniently disposed of in the same proceedings" (the convenience test)

The test for joinder in r.7.3 is merely whether the several claims "can be conveniently disposed of in the same proceedings". In terms neither the rule nor its related practice direction provides any further test. **7.3.5**

Many matters may be relevant to the question whether two or more claims "can be conveniently disposed of in the same proceedings". It may be inconvenient to attempt to try the claims together. In this event, there is no need to impugn the validity of the initial joinder of the claims in the one claim form; instead reliance may be placed on the court's powers to order separate trials to mitigate the inconvenience (see r.3.1(2)(e) and (i)). It may also be inconvenient to attempt to handle two or more claims together throughout all or part of the pre-trial process. If the expression "disposed of" is given a broad meaning and is not confined to those steps in the procedural process which will (e.g. a trial) or may (e.g. an application for summary judgment) result in the disposal of the claim, but is interpreted as including the pre-trial process generally, additional inconvenience concerns may arise. However, even in these circumstances, having regard to the "overriding objective" in Pt 1, the court's case management powers should be adequate and it is unlikely that there should be need to impugn the validity of the initial joinder of the claims in the one claim form.

Addition and substitution of parties, representative parties and group litigation

See Pt 19. **7.3.6**

Causes of Action, Counterclaims and Parties (O.15)

RSC 15 rr.6A to 17 (excluding rr.8 to 10) were re-enacted in CPR Sch.1, RSC 15 and CCR O.5, rr.5 to 14 (excluding r.11) were re-enacted in CPR Sch.2, CCR 5. By the Civil Procedure (Amendment) Rules 2000 (SI 2000/221), most of these rules were replaced by provisions now found in CPR Pt 19 (Parties and Group Litigation). **7.3.7**

Particulars of claim[1]

7.4—(1) Particulars of claim must— **7.4**

(a) be contained in or served with the claim form; or

(b) subject to paragraph (2) be served on the defendant by the claimant within 14 days after service of the claim form.

(2) Particulars of claim must be served on the defendant no later than the latest time for serving a claim form.

(Rule 7.5 sets out the latest time for serving a claim form).

(3) Where the claimant serves particulars of claim separately from the claim form in accordance with paragraph (1)(b), the claimant must, within 7 days of service on the defendant, file a copy of the particulars except where—

(a) paragraph 5.2(4) of the Practice Direction (Production Centre) supplementing Part 7 applies; or

(b) paragraph 6.4 of the Practice Direction (Money Claim Online) supplementing Part 7 applies.

(Part 16 sets out what the particulars of claim must include).

(Part 22 requires a particulars of claim to be verified by a statement of truth).

Effect of rule

It is important to distinguish between what the claim form must contain and what the particulars of claim must contain. Part 7 deals with the claim form; Pt 16 with the particulars of claim. Broadly, the claim form has replaced the High Court writ and Particulars of Claim have replaced the former Statement of Claim. County court pro- **7.4.1**

[1] Amended by the Civil Procedure (Amendment) Rules 2008 (SI 2008/2178).

cedure is now the same. In effect, the CPR have here merged High Court and county court Practice by adopting the old county court jargon of the CCR and applying it to the High Court procedure of the RSC to create the current CPR.

Particulars of claim

7.4.2 Rule 7.4 provides for three possible ways of dealing with the Particulars of Claim:

(i) C may include his particulars of claim on the claim form itself (r.7.4(1)(a)).

(ii) C may prepare his particulars of claim as a separate document and serve them with the claim form (r.7.4(1)(a)).

(iii) C may prepare his particulars of claim as a separate document and serve them later (r.7.4(1)(b) and r.7.4(3)).

The first option is likely to be used where particulars of claim are short and can be stated in a few lines: typically a straightforward debt claim (where previously a "specially indorsed writ" would have been used).

Options (ii) and (iii) reflect the old "generally indorsed writ". Given the importance of pre-action preparation (and, in particular, the importance of complying with pre-action protocols) option (ii) is more common and preferred to option (iii). Option (iii) can be used where the claim form has to be issued quickly, for example for limitation purposes.

The two practice directions referred to in r.7.4(3) contain special provisions as to the separate serving and filing of particulars of claim that apply where the claimant uses the services (both administered by the county court at Northampton) provided by those practice directions for commencing proceedings (see paras 7CPD.1 and 7EPD.1 below). Where the case is not transferred by the administering court to another county court, the claimant is not required to comply with r.7.4(3) unless ordered to do so.

Service of particulars of claim

7.4.3 Rule 7.4(2) is often overlooked. If the claim form is served close to the end of the four month period specified in Rule 7.5(2) the particulars must be served with it, or at least within 14 days of service of the claim form. The court may agree an extension of time—see para.7.6.8—but this is not automatic.

Service of particulars of claim 11 days after the service of the claim form by a litigant in person who had misunderstood the rules, on the last day for service of the claim form under r.7.5(2), could provide grounds for the exercise of discretion under r.3.9 not to apply the sanction of striking out the claim (*Bournemouth & Boscombe Athletic Football Club Ltd v Lloyds TSB Bank Plc* [2003] EWCA Civ 1755).

7.5 Service of a claim form[1]

7.5—(1) Where the claim form is served within the jurisdiction, the claimant must complete the step required by the following table in relation to the particular method of service chosen, before 12.00 midnight on the calendar day four months after the date of issue of the claim form.

Method of service	*Step required*
First class post, document exchange or other service which provides for delivery on the next business day	**Posting, leaving with, delivering to or collection by the relevant service provider**
Delivery of the document to or leaving it at the relevant place	**Delivering to or leaving the document at the relevant place**
Personal service under rule 6.5	**Completing the relevant step required by rule 6.5(3)**

[1] Amended by the Civil Procedure (Amendment) Rules 2008 (SI 2008/2178).

Fax	**Completing the transmission of the fax**
Other electronic method	**Sending the e-mail or other electronic transmission**

(2) Where the claim form is to be served out of the jurisdiction, the claim form must be served in accordance with Section IV of Part 6 within 6 months of the date of issue.

Effect of rule

This rule has been substantially changed with effect from October 1, 2008. The previous rule provided that a claim form had to be served within four months of issue or within six months if service was out of the jurisdiction. The thrust of the new rule is to require the claimant to "complete the step required" before 12 midnight on the calendar day four months after the date of issue of the claim form, rather than to achieve service in that time. As a result of an amendment to r.56.3 the four month limit now applies to claims for new tenancies referred to in that rule. **7.5.1**

For service outside the jurisdiction the claim form must still be served within the six months, i.e. the requirement remains as it was before October 1, 2008.

The table below the rule sets out the "step" required to be "completed" according to the method of service used (as permitted by r.6.3). For personal service on an individual the step is that of leaving it with that individual, for delivery or leaving at the relevant place the step is just to do that. For the various means of postal service, including DX, the step is posting, leaving with, delivery to, or collection by the relevant postal service provider, i.e. in effect dispatching the claim form. For fax the step is completing the transmission, and for email it is sending the email. It is important to note that compliance with r.7.5 is now determined by asking whether the required step was completed within the four month period not by asking whether the deemed day for service fell within that period (as was the case before October 1, 2008).

The Pt 6 deemed service provisions have also been changed from October 1, 2008. Under the old rules claimants had to factor into their plans for service the different deemed service provisions for the various methods of service in the then r.6.7, and the case-law in relation to service on non-business days. That caused many problems, much satellite litigation and failures in service. The new deemed service rule, r.6.14, simply provides that a claim form is deemed to be served on the second business day after completion of the relevant step under r.7.5(1). That provision applies to *all methods* of service including personal service, service by delivering to or leaving at an address, post, DX, fax or email.

In the new regime, therefore, it should be easier for claimants to comply with the service rules because there is one regime for all methods of service and the claimant only needs to complete the relevant step i.e. dispatch the claim form within four months of issue.

However, solicitors representing claimants will need to keep records of when the claim form was dispatched, as this might be challenged. That should not be a problem for personal service and service by delivering as process servers will give them a written report, or for service by fax or email as an electronic record is created which needs only to be printed and filed. Solicitors must check that the date and time setting on their fax and email is accurate.

Service by post or other means of next day delivery or by DX will require the solicitor to set up a record of the date and time of dispatch, particularly if the dispatch is carried out late in the day. For instance if the claim form is put in the post box at 11.30pm, and there is no collection until 7am the next day, the envelope will be stamped on the collection day and actual service may not be effected until the third day after the dispatch. If the four months from issue for service expires on the dispatch day, and actual service is three days later, not the deemed two days, the defendant may seek to challenge whether valid service was effected under the rules.

Before October 1, 2008, for certain methods of service, the time of day before which a claim form was dispatched for service could be critical to the calculation of the deemed day of service (e.g. a document transmitted by fax after 4pm on a business day was not deemed to have been served on that day but on the next business day: *Anderton v Clwyd CC (No.2)* [2002] EWCA Civ 933; [2002] 1 W.L.R. 3174, CA, at para.82). From October 1, 2008 onwards, such "time of day" provisions do not apply to the calculation of the deemed day for service of claim forms provided that the claimant can prove that the relevant step was completed before midnight.

If a claim form gives an address for service within the jurisdiction, the court can nonetheless give permission, outside the four month period, for service out of the jurisdiction under r.7.5(3), but will gave regard to the requirement that the claimant has acted promptly and has taken all reasonable steps under r.7.6(3): *National Bank of Greece SA v Outhwaite* [2001] C.P. Rep. 69.

In *Corus UK Ltd v Erewash BC* [2006] EWCA Civ 1175 the claimant issued Pt 8 proceedings to challenge the defendant's local plan for which an application had to be made by September 20, 2005 in accordance with s.287 of the Town and Country Planning Act 1990. The claim was issued on September 20 but not served until September 23. The claimant applied to extend time to serve the claim form. The first instance judge and the Court of Appeal decided that CPR rr.7.5 and 6 were not engaged because this was a Pt 8 claim and the Pt 8 PD provides only that a claim form must be served not less than 21 days before the hearing, that it was open to the court to exercise the discretion in CPR r.3.1(2)(a) to extend time for service as making an application in accordance with s.287 meant issuing the claim.

7.6 **Extension of time for serving a claim form**[1]

7.6—(1) The claimant may apply for an order extending the period for compliance with rule 7.5.

(2) The general rule is that an application to extend the time for compliance with rule 7.5 must be made—

(a) within the period specified by rule 7.5; or

(b) where an order has been made under this rule, within the period for service specified by that order.

(3) If the claimant applies for an order to extend the time for compliance after the end of the period specified by rule 7.5 or by an order made under this rule, the court may make such an order only if—

(a) the court has failed to serve the claim form; or

(b) the claimant has taken all reasonable steps to comply with rule 7.5 but has been unable to do so; and

(c) in either case, the claimant has acted promptly in making the application.

(4) An application for an order extending the time for compliance with rule 7.5 —

(a) must be supported by evidence; and

(b) may be made without notice.

Effect of rule

7.6.1 The general rule since October 1, 2008 is that the relevant step to serve the claim form within the jurisdiction must be completed within the four months for service allowed by r.7.5. For service outside the jurisdiction the claim form as previously must be served within six months. If it is not so served, an application to extend its validity should be made within that same initial period (r.7.6(2)(a)). If no such application is made, an order is required under r.7.6(3) and the court can only make the order if the three requirements of r.7.6(3) are met. In *Marshall v Maggs* reported under *Collier v Williams [2006] EWCA Civ 20 the Court* of Appeal confirmed that an application to extend time is made when the application is issued not when it is decided or heard.

[1] Amended by Civil Procedure (Amendment) Rules 2008 (SI 2008/2178).

Applications under 7.6(2)

In *Marshall v Maggs* reported under *Collier v Williams* [2006] EWCA Civ 20 the Court of Appeal held that the court can allow an application to extend time prospectively under r.7.6(2) without being satisfied that the claimant has taken all reasonable steps to comply with r.7.5 as is required in a retrospective application under r.7.6(3) but the court should still follow the guidance set out in *Hashtroodi v Hancock* [2004] EWCA Civ 652 (see Supported by evidence, para.7.6.2 below). And in *Leeson v Marsden* and in *Glass v Surrendram* also reported under *Collier v Williams* [2006] EWCA Civ 20 the Court of Appeal held that in neither case had the claimant's application under r.7.6(2) provided good reasons for an extension of time to serve the claim form (in *Leeson* the reason given was that one of the two defendants had not replied to the letter of claim, and in *Glass* the reasons were that an accountant's report with regard to quantum had arrived late, and Counsel's drafting of the particulars of claim had been delayed) even if these might have been sufficient reasons for granting an extension of time to serve the particulars of claim. **7.6.2**

In *Hoddinott, Hoddinott and R.G. Hoddinott Ltd v Persimmon Homes (Wessex) Ltd* [2007] EWCA Civ 1203 it was held that the applicant had not been entitled to an extension of time to serve the claim form, granted at first instance on an ex parte application, when the only reason advanced was that an expert's report concerning the costs of reinstatement work was not ready, because the applicant should have served the claim form and asked for an extension to serve the particulars of claim (if that could not be agreed). Nonetheless, the District Judge was wrong to have set aside the order granting the extension, because the respondent had been sent a copy of the claim form for information and had not disputed the court's jurisdiction within 14 days of acknowledging service so was deemed to have accepted that the court had jurisdiction to try the claim. The claim was not time-barred so if it was struck out for ineffective service the applicant could issue fresh proceedings.

Applications under 7.6(3)

In *Cranfield v Bridgegrove Ltd* [2003] EWCA Civ 656 the Court of Appeal decided that r.7.6(3) includes cases where the court has not even tried to serve the claim form through neglect. However, most of the cases have turned on the interpretation of "reasonable steps" by the claimant (to effect service) in r.7.6 (3)(b). In *Vinos v Marks & Spencer Plc* [2001] 3 All E.R. 784, the defendant had admitted liability and had made an interim payment but the claimant's solicitors offered no good reason for serving the claim form a week out of time. *Kaur v CTP Coil Ltd* [2001] C.P. Rep. 34, CA was decided similarly. The Court of Appeal overturned the first instance decision to extend time retrospectively, when the claimant's argument that there were difficulties in preparing the schedule of special damage in time had been accepted. **7.6.3**

In *Nanglegan v Royal Free Hampstead NHS Trust, The Times*, February 14, 2001; [2001] EWCA Civ 127, CA the claimant served the claim form on the defendant when solicitors had been nominated. The claimant realised the mistake and could have faxed the claim form to the defendant's solicitors within the four month period for service. In *Elmes v Hygrade Food Products Plc* [2001] EWCA Civ 121 the claimant faxed the claim form to the defendant's insurers on the last day of the four month period.

In none of these cases was the claimant given permission to proceed.

In *Chaudri v Post Office* April 26, 2001, unrep. the claim form was sent to the defendant by DX. The defendant was not a member of the DX. An application to extend time for service retrospectively was refused.

Chare v Fairclough [2003] EWHC 180 decided that lodging the claim form with the Queen's Bench Masters for onward transmission to consular services to arrange service out of the jurisdiction did not fall within CPR r.7.6(3)(a) as the court was not serving the claim form, only acting as a conduit. The claimant's solicitor therefore, should check within the 6 month period from issue of the claim form whether service has been effected, and if not apply prospectively for an extension of time. A retrospective application would be considered under CPR r.7.6(3)(b) and the application would have had to be made promptly—it was not in this case.

Mersey Docks Property Holdings v Kilgour [2004] EWHC 1638 decided that reasonable steps must be taken to locate a defendant before serving at his last known address (see notes to new r.6.9 Service of the Claim Form, where the defendant does not give an address at which the defendant may be served.

Steele v Mooney [2005] EWCA Civ 96 decided that an application to correct an error made in an application to extend time (that was made before the end of the four months specified in CPR 7.5) that had referred only to the particulars of claim and not the claim form (when the application had been granted for good reasons) did not preclude the making of an order under CPR r.3.10 (to correct errors of procedure) and did not circumvent the prohibition in CPR r.7.6(3) to apply for an extension after the end of the four month period.

Drury v BBC & Carnegie [2007] EWCA Civ 497 decided that in determining whether a claimant has taken "all reasonable steps to serve the claim form" the court is limited to taking into account steps taken during the 4 month period allowed by r.7.5, and steps taken after that time are irrelevant, and a claimant who leaves his effort to effect proper service on a defendant whose address he does not have, until the day before the expiry of the 4 month period, did not comply with the rule.

Retrospective approval of steps taken to serve the claim form and dispensing with service

7.6.4 See also notes to r.6.15 and r.6.16.

Under new r.6.15(2) the court may order that steps already taken to bring the claim form to the attention of the defendant by an alternative method of service or at an alternative method of service or at an alternative place thos those specified in Pt 6, amount to good service. This rule is designed to remedy difficulties with the law before October 1, 2008. The change may enable a claimant to escape the serious consequences of mis-service (but not non-service), especially where the four or six months for service has run and the limitation period has also expired. For instance the court would now have discretion to decide that service had been effected where the claim form had been served in time but on the wrong person (as in *Nanglegan v Royal Free Hampstead NHS Trust* and in *Elmes v Hygrade Food Products Ltd op cit.*—see applications under r.7.6(3) above).

Under new r.6.16 the court also has the power to dispense with service. Before October 1, 2008 there was a similar rule, r.6.9, but the new rule specifies that the power should be exercised only in exceptional circumstances, and stipulates (as the previous rule did not) at r.6.16(2), that an application may be made at any time without notice and that it must be supported by evidence.

In cases decided under the old r.6.9, the Court of Appeal decided that the power to dispense with service should not generally be applied where the claimant had not served the claim form at all within the time required under the old rules (four months including allowing for deemed service) but might be applied exceptionally where the defendant received the claim form in time but service was otherwise defective under the old rules. It seems likely that the same principles may apply after October 1, 2008.

Supported by evidence

7.6.5 It always was the better practice when applying to extend or re-new a writ under RSC 6 r.8(2) or to extend or renew a summons under CCR 7 r.20(2) to do so by application supported by affidavit although an affidavit was not a strict requirement of either rule. Rule 7.6(4) clarifies the former procedure and requires an application to be "supported by evidence". Although this rule requires "evidence" it is clearly the better practice for that evidence to be reduced to writing in the form of a witness statement or affidavit. The written evidence is placed on the court file and provides a permanent record of the evidence on which the court relied.

The rules do not prescribe the evidence that is required (but see PD7 para.8.2). The Court of Appeal has decided that for an extension to be granted the claimant must put forward a valid reason. In *Hashtroodi v Hancock* [2004] EWCA Civ 652 the claimant applied ex parte for an extension of time of three weeks to serve the claim form one day before the expiry of the claim form. The extension was granted. The claim form was apparently put in the DX within the three weeks but never arrived. The Master decided to allow the claim to continue. The Court of Appeal said that the power to extend time prospectively must be exercised in accordance with the overriding objective which means a valid reason must be advanced in the application; no reason was advanced in this case—the delay was due to the solicitor's incompetence and the extension should not have been granted.

Lease Logic Ltd v Flavia Enterprises [2005] EWCA Civ 477 confirmed that an extension of time for service of the claim form should be for no longer than is necessary.

Made without notice

7.6.6 *Mason v First Leisure Corp Plc* [2003] EWHC 1814 (QB) decided that it would be disproportionate to set aside service of a claim form when an extension of time had been granted ex parte and there was no prejudice to the defendant as a preaction protocol letter of claim had been sent when the extension of time was granted.

In *Uphill v BRB Ltd* [2005] EWCA Civ 60 an extension of time for service was obtained without notice and without providing a reason. Service was effected on BRB's solicitors within the extended time. Although this was contrary to the Court of Appeal authority in *Hashtroodi v Hancock* (see notes to para.7.6.2 above) permission for a second appeal was refused because BRB had failed to draw that authority to the judge's attention and the point had already been decided. *Lease Logic Ltd v Flavia Enterprises* [2005] EWCA Civ 477 confirmed that an order for an extension of time for service of the claim form made without notice cannot safely be relied upon by the party who obtains it because the court may order, at a subsequent on notice hearing, that the order has no validity. This is what happened in *Dickins v Solicitors Indemnity Fund Ltd* [2005] EWHC 2754, Ch D—the defendants successfully applied to set aside the order because there was no justification for the seven day extension granted by the Deputy Master.

Parties agreeing to extend time

Parties can agree to extend time for service of the claim form as this is not one of the steps excluded under CPR 2.11, and as CPR 7.5 does not expressly preclude such agreement. However, in *Thomas v Home Office* [2006] EWCA Civ 1355; [2007] 1 W.L.R. 230, CA, the Court of Appeal held that the agreement must be to a specific date and must be in writing in a document or exchange of documents by the parties (which could be by email) specifically intended to record or confirm that agreement, and that a letter from one party only, or internal file notes, or a letter addressed to a third party (here an expert) did not comply with the "in writing" provisions of CPR 2.11. **7.6.7**

Extension of time for serving particulars of claim

The particulars of claim need not be indorsed on the claim form but can be in a separate document served subsequently (r.7.4). Having served the claim form the parties can agree in writing to extend the period for service of the particulars of claim (see r.2.11). **7.6.8**

The court's power to extend time for service of the claim form is clearly circumscribed (see note to r.7.6.1), but there is more flexibility with regard to service of the particulars of claim—the rationale being that the claim form may be the defendant's first notification of the dispute, and his first opportunity to investigate, while the particulars of claim are the details (*Austin v Newcastle Chronicle & Journal Ltd* [2001] EWCA Civ 834; *Totty v Snowden* [2001] EWCA Civ 1415; [2002] 1 W.L.R. 1384; *Hewitt v Wirral NHS Trust*). In *Price v Price (t/a Poppyland Headware)* [2003] EWCA Civ 888; [2003] 3 All E.R. 911 the Court of Appeal disapproved of the claimant's solicitors not applying for an extension of time to serve the particulars of claim until 15 months after service of the claim form, but allowed an appeal to permit a 28 day extension to serve, in the interests of justice, on condition that no claim was made for special or general damages other than what might have been substantiated at the date when the claim form was issued. Service of particulars of claim 11 days after the service of the claim form by a litigant in person who had misunderstood the rules, on the last day for service of the claim form under r.7.5(2), could provide grounds for the exercise of discretion under r.3.9 not to apply the sanctin of striking out the claim (*Bournemouth & Boscombe Athletic Football Club Ltd v Lloyds TSB Bank plc* [2003] EWCA Civ 1755).

Application by defendant for service of claim form

7.7—(1) Where a claim form has been issued against a defendant, but has not yet been served on him, the defendant may serve a notice on the claimant requiring him to serve the claim form or discontinue the claim within a period specified in the notice. **7.7**

(2) The period specified in a notice served under paragraph (1) must be at least 14 days after service of the notice.

(3) If the claimant fails to comply with the notice, the court may, on the application of the defendant—

(a) dismiss the claim; or

(b) make any other order it thinks just.

Effect of rule

7.7.1 Once a claim form has been issued it may, depending on the circumstances, be served on the defendant by the claimant or by the court (see r.6.3). In either event, it must be served within the time limits imposed by r.7.5 unless extended under r.7.6. Circumstances may arise in which it is in the interests of the defendant, against whom a claim form has been issued but not yet served, to compel service by the claimant so that he can respond to the claim form in accordance with r.9.2. Before 1979, when the process of "acknowledgment of service" was substituted for the time honoured process of "entry of appearance", it was possible for a defendant to appear to a writ even though it had not been served upon him by the so-called "appearance gratis". After 1979 it was held that the "appearance gratis" did not survive the abolition of "entry of appearance"; there was no such thing as "acknowledgment of service gratis" (*Abu Dhabi Helicopters v Aeradio Plc* [1986] 1 W.L.R. 312, CA). As a result, in 1987 the RSC were amended by the addition of RSC 12 r.8A from which the current r.7.7 is derived. The usefulness of the provision can be questioned and its practical application is expected to be rare. The provision was more useful in the days when writs were valid for 12 months and readily extended for further periods. There was no equivalent provision in the CCR (though the county court, prior to the CPR, never had "acknowledgment of service").

Under r.7.7, where the claimant issues a claim form but delays serving it, the defendant may by notice require the claimant to serve the claim form or discontinue the action within a period of at least 14 days after service of the notice. Where the claimant complies by serving the claim form the defendant must acknowledge service within the time limit for so doing (see r.8.3).

Form for defence, etc., must be served with particulars of claim

7.8 **7.8—(1) When particulars of claim are served on a defendant, whether they are contained in the claim form, served with it or served subsequently, they must be accompanied by—**

(a) a form for defending the claim;

(b) a form for admitting the claim; and

(c) a form for acknowledging service.

(2) Where the claimant is using the procedure set out in Part 8 (alternative procedurefor claims)—

(a) paragraph (1) does not apply; and

(b) a form for acknowledging service must accompany the claim form.

Effect of rule

7.8.1 The High Court has always had a system for acknowledging service of originating process. In 1979 the "acknowledgment of service" replaced "entry of appearance" and this procedure is retained in the CPR.

In contrast, the county courts never had an acknowledgment of service. This stage was omitted. The common procedure of the CPR now brings county courts into line with the High Court on this aspect of procedure.

However, it is important to note that the acknowledgment of service is served with the "particulars of claim". The defendant is required to acknowledge service of the particulars of claim, not the claim form. As r.7.8(1) repeats (see also r.7.4) the particulars of claim can be contained in the claim form, served with the claim form or served separately and subsequently.

Rule 7.8 requires not only service of "a form for acknowledging service" but also "a form for defending the claim" and "a form for admitting the claim". This aspect of procedure is new to the High Court but reflects established county court practice and is derived from CCR 9. The new forms are based on well established county court forms.

If a claimant elects to serve the claim form and particulars of claim (rather than allowing the court to do so) but fails to enclose the "response pack" for the defendant, this is a technical error which does not justify a strike out—see *Hannigan v Hannigan* [2000] 2 F.C.R. 650, CA.

Prescribed forms

See Practice Direction at paras 7PD.1 *et seq.* and the *Civil Procedure Forms Volume*. **7.8.2**

Fixed date and other claims

7.9 A practice direction— **7.9**

(a) may set out the circumstances in which the court may give a fixed date for a hearing when it issues a claim;

(b) may list claims in respect of which there is a specific claim form for use and set out the claim form in question; and

(c) may disapply or modify these Rules as appropriate in relation to the claims referred to in paragraphs (a) and (b).

Fixed date actions

Prior to 1981 all county court actions were classified as "default actions" or "ordinary actions". Since 1981 all actions excluded from the definition of "default action" in CCR O.3, r.2 were classified as "fixed date actions". **7.9.1**

There are some types of claim which, by their nature, require a court trial but do not require an extensive, or any, pre-trial procedure. The most common examples are mortgage possession actions, rent possession actions, and actions for the return of goods. These—and some other—claims have long had special forms of county court summons each specifically for the type of fixed date claim.

The Practice Direction which supplements r.7.9 relates only to claims under the Consumer Credit Act 1974. Claims by mortgages and landlords seeking recovery of property are now covered by Pts 55 and 56.

Practice Directions

See paras 7PD.1 and 8PD.1. **7.9.2**

Production Centre for claims

7.10—(1) There shall be a Production Centre for the issue of claim forms and other related matters. **7.10**

(2) The relevant practice direction makes provision for—

(a) which claimants may use the Production Centre;

(b) the type of claims which the Production Centre may issue;

(c) the functions which are to be discharged by the Production Centre;

(d) the place where the Production Centre is to be located; and

(e) other related matters.

(3) The relevant practice direction may disapply or modify these Rules as appropriate in relation to claims issued by the Production Centre.

Production Centre

In 1989, a "Summons Production Centre" was established by the Lord Chancellor, under powers then given by CCR O.2, r.7, for the purpose of enabling county courts to deal more efficiently with the "bulk issue" by utility companies, credit card companies and the like, of summonses for the collection of money owed. **7.10.1**

Practice Direction

7.10.2 Practice Direction—Production Centre supplements r.7.10 (see para.7CPD.1 below). Initially, this practice direction followed provisions formerly found in Pt II of CCR O.2. Subsequently, it underwent minor amendments and by TSO CPR Update 49 it was replaced entirely with effect from April 6, 2009. The practice direction modifies the effects of certain CPR provisions. For example, para.1.4(4) enables a claimant to attach a single statement of truth to a batch of claim forms, and para.5.2 (a provision first introduced by the 2009 amendments) makes special arrangements for the situation where a claimant wishes to serve particulars of claim separately from the claim forms to which they relate (modifying r.7.4).

Human Rights[1]

7.11 **7.11—(1) A claim under section 7(1) of the Human Rights Act 1998[2] in respect of a judicial act may be brought only in the High Court.**

(2) Any other claim under section 7(1)(a) of that Act may be brought in any court.

Electronic issue of claims[3]

7.12 **7.12—(1) A practice direction may make provision for a claimant to start a claim by requesting the issue of a claim form electronically.**

(2) The practice direction may, in particular—

(a) specify—

(i) the types of claim which may be issued electronically; and

(ii) the conditions which a claim must meet before it may be issued electronically;

(b) specify—

(i) the court where the claim will be issued; and

(ii) the circumstances in which the claim will be transferred to another court;

(c) provide for the filing of other documents electronically where a claim has been started electronically;

(d) specify the requirements that must be fulfilled for any document filed electronically; and

(e) provide how a fee payable on the filing of any document is to be paid where that document is filed electronically.

(3) The practice direction may disapply or modify these Rules as appropriate in relation to claims started electronically.

---

1 Introduced by the Civil Procedure (Amendment No.4) Rules 2000 (SI 2000/2092).
2 1998 c.42.
3 Introduced by the Civil Procedure (Amendment No.5) Rules 2003 (SI 2003/3361).

PRACTICE DIRECTION—HOW TO START PROCEEDINGS—THE CLAIM FORM

This Practice Direction supplements CPR Part 7

General

1. Subject to the following provisions of this practice direction, proceedings which both the High Court and the county courts have jurisdiction to deal with may be started in the High Court or in a county court. **7PD.1**

Where to start proceedings

2.1 Proceedings (whether for damages or for a specified sum) may not be started in the High Court unless the value of the claim is more than £25,000. **7PD.2**

2.2 Proceedings which include a claim for damages in respect of personal injuries must not be started in the High Court unless the value of the claim is £50,000 or more (paragraph 9 of the High Court and County Courts Jurisdiction Order 1991 (S.I. 1991 No. 724 as amended) describes how the value of a claim is to be determined).

2.3 A claim must be issued in the High Court or a county court if an enactment so requires.

2.4 Subject to paragraphs 2.1 and 2.2 above, a claim should be started in the High Court if by reason of—

(1) the financial value of the claim and the amount in dispute, and/or

(2) the complexity of the facts, legal issues, remedies or procedures involved, and/or

(3) the importance of the outcome of the claim to the public in general,

the claimant believes that the claim ought to be dealt with by a High Court judge.

(CPR Part 30 and the practice direction supplementing Part 30 contain provisions relating to the transfer to the county court of proceedings started in the High Court and vice-versa).

2.5 A claim relating to Chancery business (which includes any of the matters specified in paragraph 1 of Schedule 1 to the Supreme Court Act 1981) may, subject to any enactment, rule or practice direction, be dealt with in the High Court or in a county court. The claim form should, if issued in the High Court, be marked in the top right hand corner "Chancery Division" and, if issued in the county court, be marked "Chancery Business".

(For the equity jurisdiction of county courts, see County Courts Act 1984 s.23).

2.6 A claim relating to any of the matters specified in subparagraphs (a) and (b) of paragraph 2 of Schedule 1 to the Supreme Court Act 1981 must be dealt with in the High Court and will be assigned to the Queen's Bench Division.

2.7 Practice directions applying to particular types of proceedings, or to proceedings in particular courts, will contain provisions relating to the commencement and conduct of those proceedings.

2.8 A claim in the High Court for which a jury trial is directed will, if not already being dealt with in the Queen's Bench Division, be transferred to that Division.

2.9 The following proceedings may not be started in a county court unless the parties have agreed otherwise in writing:

(1) a claim for damages or other remedy for libel or slander, and

(2) a claim in which the title to any toll, fair, market or franchise is in question.

2.10(1) The normal rules apply in deciding in which court and specialist list a claim that includes issues under the Human Rights Act 1998 should be started. They also apply in deciding which procedure to use to start the claim; this Part or CPR Part 8 or CPR Part 54 (judicial review).

(2) The exception is a claim for damages in respect of a judicial act, which should be commenced in the High Court. If the claim is made in a notice of appeal then it will be dealt with according to the normal rules governing where that appeal is heard.

(A county court cannot make a declaration of incompatibility in accordance with section 4 of the Human Rights Act 1998. Legislation may direct that such a claim is to be brought before a specified tribunal).

The claim form

7PD.3 **3.1** A claimant must use practice form **N1** or practice form **N208** (the Part 8 claim form) to start a claim (but see paragraphs 3.2 and 3.4 below).

3.2 Rule 7.9 deals with fixed date claims and rule 7.10 deals with the Production Centre for the issue of claims; there are separate practice directions supplementing rules 7.9 and 7.10.

3.3 If a claimant wishes the claim to proceed under Part 8, or if the claim is required to proceed under Part 8, the claim form should so state. Otherwise the claim will proceed under Part 7. Note that in respect of claims in specialist proceedings (listed in CPR Part 49) and claims brought under the RSC or CCR set out in the Schedule to the CPR (see CPR Part 50) the CPR will apply only to the extent that they are not inconsistent with the rules and practice directions that expressly apply to those claims.

3.4 Other practice directions may require special practice forms to be used to commence particular types of proceedings, or proceedings in particular courts.

3.5 Where a claim form to be served out of the jurisdiction is one which the court has power to deal with—

(a) under the Civil Jurisdiction and Judgments Act 1982; and

(b) the Judgments Regulation (which has the same meaning as in rule 6.31(d)),

the claim form must, pursuant to rule 6.34, be filed and served with the notice referred to in that rule and paragraph 2.1 of Practice Direction B supplementing Part 6.

3.6 If a claim for damages or for an unspecified sum is started in the High Court, the claim form must:

(1) state that the claimant expects to recover more than £25,000 (or £50,000 or more if the claim is for personal injuries); or
(2) state that some enactment provides that the claim may only be commenced in the High Court and specify that enactment; or
(3) state that the claim is to be in one of the specialist High Court lists (see CPR Parts 49 and 58–62) and specify that list.

3.7 If the contents of a claim form commencing specialist proceedings comply with the requirements of the specialist list in question the claim form will also satisfy paragraph 3.6 above.

3.8 If a claim for damages for personal injuries is started in the county court, the claim form must state whether or not the claimant expects to recover more than £1,000 in respect of pain, suffering and loss of amenity.

3.9 If a claim for housing disrepair which includes a claim for an order requiring repairs or other work to be carried out by the landlord is started in the county court, the claim form must state:

(1) whether or not the cost of the repairs or other work is estimated to be more than £1,000, and
(2) whether or not the claimant expects to recover more than £1,000 in respect of any claim for damages.[1]

If either of the amounts mentioned in (1) and (2) is more than £1,000, the small claims track will not be the normal track for that claim.

(Section 19 of the Costs Practice Direction supplementing Parts 43 to 48 contains details of the information required to be filed with a claim form to comply with rule 44.15 (providing information about funding arrangements)).

Title of proceedings

4.1 The claim form and every other statement of case, must be headed with the title of the proceedings. The title should state: **7PD.4**

(1) the number of proceedings,
(2) the court or Division in which they are proceeding,
(3) the full name of each party,
(4) each party's status in the proceedings (i.e. claimant/defendant).

(Paragraph 2.6 of the Practice Direction to Part 16 sets out what is meant by a full name in respect of each type of claimant.)

4.2 Where there is more than one claimant and/or more than one defendant, the parties should be described in the title as follows:

(1) AB
(2) CD
(3) EF Claimants
and
(4) GH

[1] See rules 16.3(4) and 26.6.

(5) IJ
(6) KL Defendants

Start of proceedings

7PD.5 **5.1** Proceedings are started when the court issues a claim form at the request of the claimant[1] (see rule 7.2) but where the claim form as issued was received in the court office on a date earlier than the date on which it was issued by the court, the claim is "brought" for the purposes of the Limitation Act 1980 and any other relevant statute on that earlier date.

5.2 The date on which the claim form was received by the court will be recorded by a date stamp either on the claim form held on the court file or on the letter that accompanied the claim form when it was received by the court.

5.3 An enquiry as to the date on which the claim form was received by the court should be directed to a court officer.

5.4 Parties proposing to start a claim which is approaching the expiry of the limitation period should recognise the potential importance of establishing the date the claim form was received by the court and should themselves make arrangements to record the date.

5.5 Where it is sought to start proceedings against the estate of a deceased defendant where probate or letters of administration have not been granted, the claimant should issue the claim against "the personal representatives of A.B. deceased". The claimant should then, before the expiry of the period for service of the claim form, apply to the court for the appointment of a person to represent the estate of the deceased.

Claims by and against partnerships within the jurisdiction

7PD.5A **5A.1** Paragraphs 5A and 5B apply to claims that are brought by or against two or more persons who—

(1) were partners; and
(2) carried on that partnership business within the jurisdiction,

at the time when the cause of action accrued.

5A.2 For the purposes of this paragraph, 'partners' includes persons claiming to be entitled as partners and persons alleged to be partners.

5A.3 Where that partnership has a name, unless it is inappropriate to do so, claims must be brought in or against the name under which that partnership carried on business at the time the cause of action accrued.

Partnership membership statements

7PD.5B **5B.1** In this paragraph a 'partnership membership statement' is a written statement of the names and last known places of residence of all the persons who were partners in the partnership at the time when the cause of action accrued, being the date specified for this purpose in accordance with paragraph 5B.3.

[1] See rule 7.2.

5B.2 If the partners are requested to provide a copy of a partnership membership statement by any party to a claim, the partners must do so within 14 days of receipt of the request.

5B.3 In that request the party seeking a copy of a partnership membership statement must specify the date when the relevant cause of action accrued.

(Signing of the acknowledgment of service in the case of a partnership is dealt with in paragraph 4.4 of the Practice Direction supplementing Part 10)

Persons carrying on business in another name

5C.1 This paragraph applies where— **7PD.5C**

(1) a claim is brought against an individual;
(2) that individual carries on a business within the jurisdiction (even if not personally within the jurisdiction); and
(3) that business is carried on in a name other than that individual's own name ("the business name").

5C.2 The claim may be brought against the business name as if it were the name of a partnership.

Particulars of claim

6.1 Where the claimant does not include the particulars of claim in the claim form, they may be served separately: **7PD.6**

(1) either at the same time as the claim form, or
(2) within 14 days after service of the claim form provided that the service of the particulars of claim is within 4 months after the date of issue of the claim form [1] (or 6 months where the claim form is to be served out of the jurisdiction [2]).

6.2 If the particulars of claim are not included in or have not been served with the claim form, the claim form must contain a statement that particulars of claim will follow.[3]

(These paragraphs do not apply where the Part 8 procedure is being used. For information on matters to be included in the claim form or the particulars of claim, see Part 16 (statements of case) and the practice direction which supplements it.)

Statement of truth

7.1 Part 22 requires the claim form and, where they are not included in the claim form, the particulars of claim, to be verified by a statement of truth. **7PD.7**

7.2 The form of the statement of truth is as follows:

"[I believe][the claimant believes] that the facts stated in [this claim form] [these particulars of claim] are true."

7.3 Attention is drawn to rule 32.14 which sets out the consequences of verifying a statement of case containing a false statement without an honest belief in its truth.

Extension of time

8.1 An application under rule 7.6 (for an extension of time for **7PD.8**

[1] See rules 7.4(2) and 7.5(1).
[2] See rule 7.5(2).
[3] See rule 16.2(2).

serving a claim form under rule 7.6(1)) must be made in accordance with Part 23 and supported by evidence.

8.2 The evidence should state:

(1) all the circumstances relied on,

(2) the date of issue of the claim,

(3) the expiry date of any rule 7.6 extension, and

(4) a full explanation as to why the claim has not been served.

(For information regarding (1) written evidence see Part 32 and the practice direction which supplements it and (2) service of the claim form see Part 6 and the practice direction which supplements it).

Notes on Practice Direction supplementing CPR Pt 7 (see PD 1 para.7 et seq.)

7PD.9 **2.4** Not all cases over the financial limits specified by paras 2.1 and 2.2 will be suitable for trial in the High Court and some will be transferred elsewhere. The guidelines in this paragraph will assist the court in this exercise.

2.6 This refers to writs of *habeas corpus* and claims for judicial review.

3.3 A large number of procedures under the RSC and CCR are preserved in the Schedules to the CPR and the old rules with some modification continue to apply. These proceedings include in the High Court:

• Interpleader Proceedings	O.17
• Committal	O.52
• Criminal Proceedings	O.79
• Various statutory proceedings	O.93
• Applications under Local Government Finance Act 1982 Pt III	O.98
• Summary Proceedings for Possession	O.113
• Criminal Confiscation Orders	O.115

5A–C These paragraphs were added in October 2006 when O.81 Partnerships was revoked from Sch.1, to give effect to rr.1, 2 and 9 of that Order.

5A The name of the firm. This must be the name at the time the cause of action accrued, not the name at the date of the proceedings. If the firm has been dissolved before proceedings are issued the claim can still be made against the former partners in the name of the dissolved firm.

5B Partnership membership statements. This provision enables the other party to obtain information on the partners that may be necessary for security for costs or enforcement. The old rule specifically gave the court the power to order the provision of the statement. Presumably if the partnership fails to provide the statement in accordance with a request under the PD the party could make an application under Pt 23 seeking an order for compliance.

5C Persons carrying on business in another name. This provision enables proceedings to be brought against a business even if the name of the individual or company who carry on that business is not known, providing the trading name is known.

PRACTICE DIRECTION—CONSUMER CREDIT ACT 2006—UNFAIR RELATIONSHIPS

This Practice Direction supplements CPR rule 7.9

1.1 In this practice direction "the Act" means the Consumer Credit Act 1974, a section referred to by number means the section with that number in the Act, and expressions which are defined in the Act have the same meaning in this practice direction as they have in the Act. **7BPD.1**

1.2 "Consumer Credit Act procedure" means the procedure set out in this practice direction.

When to use the Consumer Credit Act procedure

2.1 A claimant must use the Consumer Credit Act procedure where he makes a claim under a provision of the Act to which paragraph 3 of this practice direction applies. **7BPD.2**

2.2 Where a claimant is using the Consumer Credit Act procedure the CPR are modified to the extent that they are inconsistent with the procedure set out in this practice direction.

2.3 The court may at any stage order the claim to continue as if the claimant had not used the Consumer Credit Act procedure, and if it does so the court may give any directions it considers appropriate.

2.4 This practice direction also sets out matters which must be included in the particulars of claim in certain types of claim, and restrictions on where certain types of claim may be started.

The provisions of the Act

3.1 Subject to paragraph 3.2 and 3.3 this practice direction applies to claims made under the following provisions of the Act: **7BPD.3**

(1) section 141 (claim by the creditor to enforce regulated agreement relating to goods, etc.);

(2) section 129 (claim by debtor or hirer for a time order);

(3) section 90 (creditor's claim for an order for recovery of protected goods);

(4) section 92(1) (creditor's or owner's claim to enter premises to take possession of goods);

(5) section 140B(2)(a) (debtor's or surety's application for an order relating to an unfair relationship);

(6) creditor's or owner's claim for a court order to enforce a regulated agreement relating to goods or money where the court order is required by—

(a) section 65(1) (improperly executed agreement),

(b) section 86(2) (death of debtor or hirer where agreement is partly secured or unsecured),

(c) section 111(2) (default notice, etc. not served on surety),

(d) section 124(1) or (2) (taking of a negotiable instrument in breach of terms of section 123), or

(e) section 105(7)(a) or (b) (security not expressed in writing, or improperly executed).

3.2 This practice direction does not apply to any claim made under the provisions listed in paragraph 3.1 above if that claim relates to the recovery of land.

3.3 This practice direction also does not apply to a claim made by the creditor under section 141 of the Act to enforce a regulated agreement where the agreement relates only to money. Such a claim must be started by the issue of a Part 7 claim form.

Restrictions on where to start some Consumer Credit Act claims

7BPD.4 **4.1** Where the claim includes a claim to recover goods to which a regulated hire purchase agreement or conditional sale agreement relates, it may only be started in the county court for the district in which the debtor, or one of the debtors:

(1) resides or carries on business; or

(2) resided or carried on business at the date when the defendant last made a payment under the agreement.

4.2 In any other claim to recover goods, the claim may only be started in the court for the district:

(1) in which the defendant, or one of the defendants, resides or carries on business; or

(2) in which the goods are situated.

4.3 A claim of a debtor or hirer for an order under section 129(1)(b) or 129(1)(ba).of the Act (a time order) may only be started in the court where the claimant resides or carries on business.

(Costs rule 45.1(2)(b) allows the claimant to recover fixed costs in certain circumstances where such a claim is made).

(Paragraph 7 sets out the matters the claimant must include in his particulars of claim where he is using the Consumer Credit Act procedure).

The Consumer Credit Act procedure

7BPD.5 **5.1** In the types of claim to which paragraph 3 applies the court will fix a hearing date on the issue of the claim form.

5.2 The particulars of claim must be served with the claim form.

5.3 Where a claimant is using the Consumer Credit Act procedure, the defendant to the claim is not required to:

(1) serve an acknowledgment of service; or

(2) file a defence, although he may choose to do so.

5.4 Where a defendant intends to defend a claim, his defence should be filed within 14 days of service of the particulars of claim. If the defendant fails to file a defence within this period, but later relies on it, the court may take such a failure into account as a factor when deciding what order to make about costs.

5.5 Part 12 (default judgment) does not apply where the claimant is using the Consumer Credit Act procedure.

5.6 Each party must be given at least 28 days' notice of the hearing date.

5.7 Where the claimant serves the claim form, he must serve notice of the hearing date at the same time, unless the hearing date is specified in the claim form.

Powers of the court at the hearing

7BPD.6 **6.1** On the hearing date the court may dispose of the claim.

6.2 If the court does not dispose of the claim on the hearing date:

(1) if the defendant has filed a defence, the court will:
- (a) allocate the claim to a track and give directions about the management of the case, or
- (b) give directions to enable it to allocate the claim to a track,

(2) if the defendant has not filed a defence, the court may make any order or give any direction it considers appropriate.

6.3 Rule 26.5(3) to (5) and rules 26.6 to 26.10 apply to the allocation of a claim under paragraph 6.2.

Matters which must be included in the particulars of claim

7.1 Where the Consumer Credit Act procedure is used, the claimant must state in his particulars of claim that the claim is a Consumer Credit Act claim. **7BPD.7**

7.2 A claimant making a claim for the delivery of goods to enforce a hire purchase agreement or conditional sale agreement which is:

(1) a regulated agreement for the recovery of goods, and

(2) let to a person other than a company or other corporation, must also state (in this order) in his particulars of claim:
- (a) the date of the agreement,
- (b) the parties to the agreement,
- (c) the number or other identification of the agreement (with enough information to allow the debtor to identify the agreement),
- (d) where the claimant was not one of the original parties to the agreement, the means by which the rights and duties of the creditor passed to him,
- (e) the place where the agreement was signed by the defendant (if known),
- (f) the goods claimed,
- (g) the total price of the goods,
- (h) the paid up sum,
- (i) the unpaid balance of the total price,
- (j) whether a default notice or a notice under section 76(1) or section 88(1) of the Act has been served on the defendant, and, if it has, the date and the method of service,
- (k) the date on which the right to demand delivery of the goods accrued,
- (l) the amount (if any) claimed as an alternative to the delivery of goods, and
- (m) *the amount (if any)* claimed in addition to:
  - (i) the delivery of the goods, or
  - (ii) any claim under subparagraph (l) above with the grounds of each such claim.

7.3 A claimant who is a debtor or hirer making a claim for an order under section 129(1)(b) or 129(1)(ba) of the Act (a time order) must state (in the following order) in the particulars of claim:

(1) the date of the agreement,

(2) the parties to the agreement,
(3) the number or other means of identifying the agreement,
(4) details of any sureties,
(5) if the defendant is not one of the original parties to the agreement then the name of the original party to the agreement,
(6) the names and addresses of the persons intended to be served with the claim form,
(7) the place where the claimant signed the agreement,
(8) details of the notice served by the creditor or owner giving rise to the claim for the time order,
(9) the total unpaid balance the claimant admits is due under the agreement, and—
   (a) the amount of any arrears (if known), and
   (b) the amount and frequency of the payments specified in the agreement,
(10) the claimant's proposals for payments of any arrears and of future instalments together with details of his means,
(11) where the claim relates to a breach of the agreement other than for the payment of money the claimant's proposals for remedying it.

7.3A A claimant who is a debtor or hirer making a claim for an order under section 129(1)(ba) of the Act must attach to the particulars of claim a copy of the notice served on the creditor or owner under section 129A(1)(a) of the Act.

7.4(1) This paragraph applies where a claimant is required to obtain a court order to enforce a regulated agreement by:
   (a) section 65(1) (improperly-executed agreement),
   (b) section 105(7)(a) or (b) (security not expressed in writing, or improperly-executed),
   (c) section 111(2) (default notice, etc., not served on surety),
   (d) section 124(1) or (2) (taking of a negotiable instrument in breach of terms of section 123); or
   (e) section 86(2) of the Act (death of debtor or hirer where agreement is partly secured or unsecured).
(2) The claimant must state in his particulars of claim what the circumstances are that require him to obtain a court order for enforcement.

Admission of certain claims for recovery of goods under regulated agreements

7BPD.8 **8.1** In a claim to recover goods to which section 90(1)[1] applies:
(1) the defendant may admit the claim, and

[1] Section 90(1) provides that: "At any time when—(a) the debtor is in breach of a regulated hire-purchase or a regulated conditional sale agreement relating to goods, and (b) the debtor has paid to the creditor one-third or more of the total price of the goods, and (c) the property in the goods remains in the creditor, the creditor is not entitled to recover possession of the goods from the debtor except on an order of the court."

(2) offer terms on which a return order should be suspended under section 135(1)(b).

8.2 He may do so by filing a request in practice form **N9C**.

8.3 He should do so within the period for making an admission specified in rule 14.2(b). If the defendant fails to file his request within this period, and later makes such a request, the court may take the failure into account as a factor when deciding what order to make about costs.

8.4 On receipt of the admission, the court will serve a copy on the claimant.

8.5 The claimant may obtain judgment by filing a request in practice form **N228**.

8.6 On receipt of the request for judgment, the court will enter judgment in the terms of the defendant's admission and offer and for costs.

8.7 If:

(1) the claimant does not accept the defendant's admission and offer, and

(2) the defendant does not appear on the hearing date fixed when the claim form was issued,

the court may treat the defendant's admission and offer as evidence of the facts stated in it for the purposes of sections 129(2)(a)[1] and 135(2).[2]

Additional requirements about parties to the proceedings

9.1 The court may dispense with the requirement in section 141(5) (all parties to a regulated agreement and any surety to be parties to any proceedings) in any claim relating to the regulated agreement, if: **7BPD.9**

(1) the claim form has not been served on the debtor or the surety, and

(2) the claimant either before or at the hearing makes an application (which may be made without notice) for the court to make such an order.

9.2 In a claim relating to a regulated agreement where—

(1) the claimant was not one of the original parties to the agreement, and

(2) the former creditor's rights and duties under the agreement have passed to him by—

(a) operation of law, or

(b) assignment,

the requirement of section 141(5) (all parties to a regulated agree-

[1] Section 129(2) provides that—"A time order shall provide for one or both of the following, as the court considers just—(a) the payment by the debtor or hirer or any surety of any sum owed under a regulated agreement or a security by such instalments, payable at such times, as the court, having regard to the means of the debtor or hirer and any surety, considers reasonable; (b) the remedying by the debtor or hirer of any breach of a regulated agreement (other than non-payment of money) within such period as the court may specify."

[2] Section 135(2) provides that—"The court shall not suspend the operation of a term [in an order relating to a regulated agreement] requiring the delivery up of goods by any person unless satisfied that the goods are in his possession or control."

ment and any surety to be parties to any proceedings) does not apply to the former creditor, unless the court otherwise orders.

9.3 Where a claimant who is a creditor or owner makes a claim for a court order under section 86(2) (death of debtor or hirer where agreement is partly secured or unsecured) the personal representatives of the deceased debtor or hirer must be parties to the proceedings in which the order is sought, unless no grant of representation has been made to the estate.

9.4 Where no grant of representation has been made to the estate of the deceased debtor or hirer, the claimant must make an application in accordance with Part 23 for directions about which persons (if any) are to be made parties to the claim as being affected or likely to be affected by the enforcement of the agreement.

9.5 The claimant's application under paragraph 9.4:

(a) may be made without notice, and

(b) should be made before the claim form is issued.

Notice to be given to re-open a consumer credit agreement

7BPD.10 **10.1** Paragraph 10.2 applies where

(1) a debtor or any surety intends to seek an order relating to an unfair relationship between a creditor and that debtor, arising out of a credit agreement (taken together with any related agreement);

(2) a claim relating to that agreement or any related agreement has already begun; and,

(3) section 140B(2)(b) or section 140B(2)(c) applies.

10.2 The debtor or surety must serve written notice of service on the court and every other party to the claim within 14 days of the service of the claim form.

10.3 A debtor or surety (as the case may be) who serves a notice under paragraph 10.2 will be treated as having filed a defence for the purposes of the Consumer Credit Act procedure.

Editorial note

7BPD.10.1 By TSO CPR Update 44, paras 3.1(5), 10.1 and 10.2 of this Practice Direction were amended as a consequence of amendments made to the Consumer Credit Act 1974 by the Consumer Credit Act 2006, having the effect of replacing provisions on extortionate credit bargains (ss.137 to 140) with new provisions about unfair relationships (ss.140A to 140D). By TSO CPR Update 49, the Practice Direction was further amended, with effect from April 6, 2009, by the deletion of para.10.2A and a consequential amended was made to para.10.3 accordingly. (This deletion reflected a transitional provision permitting the continued application of s.139 to agreements made before April 6, 2007 for a period of one year.) For text and commentary on the 1974 Act (as amended), see Vol.2, Section 3H.

PRACTICE DIRECTION—PRODUCTION CENTRE

This Practice Direction supplements CPR rule 7.10

General

1.1 In this Practice Direction: 7CPD.1

"the Centre" means the Production Centre;

"Centre user" means a person who is for the time being permitted to start a claim through the Centre, and includes a legal representative acting for such a person;

"officer" means the court officer in charge of the Centre or another officer of the Centre acting on the former's behalf;

"national creditor code" means the number or reference allotted to a Centre user by the officer;

"Code of Practice" means any code of practice which may at any time be issued by Her Majesty's Courts Service relating to the discharge by the Centre of its functions and the way in which a Centre user is to conduct business with the Centre; and

"data" means any information which is required to be given to the court or which is to be contained in any document to be sent to the court or to any party.

1.2 For any purpose connected with the exercise of its functions, the Centre will be treated as part of the office of the court whose name appears on the claim form to which the functions relate, or in whose name the claim form is requested to be issued, and the officer will be treated as an officer of that court.

1.3(1) The functions of the Centre include the provision of a facility which, through the use of information technology, enables a Centre user to have claim forms issued and served, whether or not those claim forms are to be treated as issued in the Northampton County Court or in another county court.

(2) If a Centre user files claim forms in the name of Northampton County Court, the functions of the Centre also include—

(a) the handling of defences and admissions;

(b) the entry of judgment in default, on admission, on acceptance, or on determination;

(c) the registration of judgments;

(d) the issue of warrants of execution;

(e) where the defendant is an individual, the transfer to the defendant's home court of any case that is to continue following the filing of a defence or where a hearing is required before judgment; or, where the defendant is not an individual, the transfer to the court for the area of the claimant's, or where legally represented, the claimant's legal representative's address; and

(f) the transfer to the defendant's home court of any case for the questioning of the defendant pursuant to an order for information under Part 71 or where enforcement of a judgment (other than by warrant of execution, charging order or third party debt order) is to follow.

1.4(1) Where the officer is to take any step, any rule or practice direction which requires a document to be filed before such step is taken will be treated as complied with if the data which that document would contain are delivered to the Centre in computer readable form in accordance with the Code of Practice.

(2) Data relating to more than one case may be included in a single document or delivery of data.

(3) Rules 6.4(3) and 6.21(4) (copies of documents to be served by the court) do not apply to any document which is to be produced by electronic means from data supplied by a Centre user.

(4) The practice direction supplementing Part 22 (statements of truth) is modified as follows—

(a) a single statement of truth may accompany each batch of requests to issue claim forms and may be in electronic form;

(b) the form of such a statement must be: "I believe that the facts stated in the attached claim forms are true."; and

(c) the signature of the appropriate person (as to which see paragraph 3 of the practice direction supplementing Part 22) may be in electronic form.

Claims which may not be issued through the Centre

7CPD.2 **2.1** The Centre will not issue any claim form which is to be issued in the

2.2 The Centre will only issue a claim form if the claim is for a specified sum of money less than £100,000.

2.3 The Centre will not issue any of the following types of claim—

(1) a claim against more than two defendants;

(2) a claim against two defendants where a different sum is claimed against each of them;

(3) a claim against the Crown;

(4) a claim for an amount in a foreign currency;

(5) a claim where either party is known to be a child or protected party within Part 21;

(6) a claim where the claimant is a legally assisted person within the meaning of the Legal Aid Act 1988;

(7) a claim where the defendant's address for service as it appears on the claim form is not in England and Wales;

(8) a claim which is to be issued under Part 8.

Centre users

7CPD.3 **3.1** Only a Centre user may start or conduct claims through the Centre.

3.2 The officer may permit any person to be a Centre user.

3.3 The officer may withdraw the permission for any person to be a Centre user.

3.4 A Centre user must comply with the provisions of the Code of Practice in dealing with the Centre.

3.5 The officer will allot a national creditor code to each Centre user.

The Code of Practice

4.1 The Code of Practice will contain provisions designed to ensure that the Centre can discharge its functions efficiently, and it may in particular provide for— **7CPD.4**

(1) the forms of magnetic media that may be used;
(2) the circumstances in which data may or must be supplied in magnetic form;
(3) the circumstances in which data may or must be supplied in a document and the form that such a document must take;
(4) how often data may be supplied;
(5) the numbering of cases and data relating to cases;
(6) data to be given to the Centre by the Centre user about cases which have been settled or paid or are otherwise not proceeding; and
(7) accounting arrangements and the method of payment of fees.

4.2 Her Majesty's Courts Service may change the Code of Practice from time to time.

Other modifications to the Civil Procedure Rules

Powers of the officer to make orders

5.1 The officer may make the following orders— **7CPD.5**

(1) an order to set aside a default judgment where, after that judgment has been entered, the claim form is returned by the Post Office as undelivered;
(2) an order to set aside a judgment on application by a Centre user;
(3) an order to transfer a case to another county court for enforcement or for a judgment debtor to attend court for questioning pursuant to an order for information under CPR Part 71.

Filing separate particulars of claim

5.2(1) Subject to the sub-paragraphs below, the claimant may serve and file particulars of claim separately from the claim form but the claimant must in the claim form— **7CPD.6**

(a) state that the particulars of claim will follow; and
(b) include a brief summary of the claim.

(2) Where the claimant serves the particulars of claim separately from the claim form pursuant to sub-paragraph (1), the claimant must—

(a) serve the particulars of claim in accordance with rule 7.4(1)(b); and

(b) file a certificate of service in form N215 at the Centre within 14 days of service of the particulars of claim on the defendant.

(3) The claimant must file the particulars of claim at the court to which the proceedings are transferred under paragraph 1.3(2)(e) within 7 days of service of the notice of transfer.

(4) Where the proceedings are not transferred under paragraph 1.3(2)(e) and remain at the Centre, the claimant is not required to file the particulars of claim unless ordered to do so.

Procedure on the filing of a defence

7CPD.7 **5.3**(1) This paragraph applies where a Centre user has started a claim in the Northampton County Court and the defendant has filed a defence to the claim or to part of the claim.

(2) On the filing of the defence the officer will serve a notice on the Centre user requiring the Centre user to state within 28 days whether the claim is to proceed.

(3) If the Centre user does not notify the officer within the time specified in the notice that the claim is to proceed, the claim will be stayed, and the officer will notify the parties accordingly.

(4) The proceedings will not be transferred as provided by paragraph 1.3(2)(e) until the Centre user notifies the officer that the claim is to continue.

Note on Practice Direction—Production Centre

7CPD.7.1 With effect from April 6, 2009, this Practice Direction was substituted in its entirety by TSO CPR Update 49. Most of the changes made consisted of necessary updating. Significant additions were the insertion of provisions enabling a claimant to file separate particulars of claim and requiring the claimant to file a certificate of service in such circumstances (see para.5.2).

Paragraph 1.4(4) of the Practice Direction permits a claimant to attach a single signed statement of truth to a batch of claim forms. There is no requirement for the Production centre to transfer the signature to the individual forms for service. In *FHG Publications v Tee-Hillman* [2001] C.L.Y. 662 this confused a litigant in person and the court commented on this omission from the Practice Direction.

PRACTICE DIRECTION—CLAIMS FOR THE RECOVERY OF TAXES AND DUTIES

This Practice Direction supplements CPR rule 7.9

Scope

1.1 This practice direction applies to claims by HM Revenue and Customs for the recovery of— **7DPD.1**

(a) Income Tax,
(b) Corporation Tax,
(c) Capital Gains Tax,
(d) Interest, penalties and surcharges on Income Tax, Corporation Tax or Capital Gains Tax which by virtue of section 69 of the Taxes Management Act 1970 are to be treated as if they are taxes due and payable,
(e) National Insurance Contributions and interest, penalties and surcharges thereon,
(f) student loan repayments deducted by and recoverable from an employer under Part IV of the Education (Student Loans) (Repayment) Regulations 2000 (S.I. 2000/944),
(g) Value added tax and interest and surcharges thereon,
(h) Insurance premium tax and interest and penalties thereon,
(i) Stamp duty land tax and interest and penalties thereon,
(j) the following environmental taxes—
 (i) landfill tax and interest and penalties thereon,
 (ii) aggregates levy and interest and penalties thereon, and
 (iii) climate change levy and interest and penalties thereon,
(k) the following duties of customs and excise—
 (i) amusement machine licence duty and penalties thereon,
 (ii) air passenger duty and interest and penalties thereon,
 (iii) beer duty and penalties thereon,
 (iv) bingo duty and penalties thereon,
 (v) cider and perry duty,
 (vi) excise and spirits duty,
 (vii) excise wine duty,
 (viii) gaming duty and penalties thereon,
 (ix) general betting duty,
 (x) lottery duty and penalties thereon,
 (xi) REDS (registered excise dealers and shippers) duty,
 (xii) road fuel duty and penalties thereon,
 (xiii) tobacco duty, and
 (xiv) wine and made-wine duty.

Procedure

2.1 If a defence is filed, the court will fix a date for the hearing. **7DPD.2**

2.2 Part 26 (Case management—preliminary stage) apart from CPR rule 26.2 (automatic transfer) does not apply to claims to which this practice direction applies.

At the hearing

3.1 On the hearing date the court may dispose of the claim. **7DPD.3**

(Section 25A(1) and (2) of the Commissioners for Revenue and Customs Act 2005 ("the 2005 Act") provides that a certificate of an officer of Revenue and Customs that, to the best of that officer's knowledge and belief, a sum payable to the Commissioners under or by virtue of an enactment or by virtue of a contract settlement (within the meaning of section 25(6) of the 2005 Act) has not been paid, is sufficient evidence that the sum mentioned in the certificate is unpaid.)

3.2 But exceptionally, if the court does not dispose of the claim on the hearing date it may give case management directions, which may, if the defendant has filed a defence, include allocating the case.

PRACTICE DIRECTION—MONEY CLAIM ONLINE

General

1.1 This practice direction provides for a scheme in which, in the circumstances set out in this practice direction, a request for a claim form to be issued and other specified documents may be filed electronically ("Money Claim Online"). **7EPD.1**

1.2 This practice direction enables claimants—

(1) to start certain types of county court claims by requesting the issue of a claim form electronically via Her Majesty's Courts Service website; and

(2) where a claim has been started electronically—

(a) to file electronically a request for—

(i) judgment in default;

(ii) judgment on acceptance of an admission of the whole of the amount claimed; or

(iii) the issue of a warrant of execution; and

(b) to view an electronic record of the progress of the claim.

1.3 This practice direction also enables defendants—

(1) to file electronically—

(a) an acknowledgment of service;

(b) a part admission;

(c) a defence; or

(d) a counterclaim (if filed together with a defence), and

(2) to view an electronic record of the progress of the claim.

1.4 Claims started using Money Claim Online will be issued by Northampton County Court and will proceed in that court unless they are transferred to another court. The address for filing any document, application or request (other than one which is filed electronically in accordance with this practice direction) is Northampton County Court, St Katharine's House, 21–27 St Katharine's Street, Northampton, NN1 2LH, DX 702885 Northampton 7, fax no. 0845 6015889.

Security

2. Her Majesty's Courts Service will take such measures as it thinks fit to ensure the security of steps taken or information stored electronically. These may include requiring users of Money Claim Online— **7EPD.2**

(1) to enter a customer identification and password;

(2) to provide personal information for identification purposes; and

(3) to comply with any other security measures,

before taking any of the steps mentioned in paragraph 1.2 or 1.3.

Fees

3.1 Where this practice direction provides for a fee to be paid electronically, it may be paid by— **7EPD.3**

(1) credit card;

(2) debit card; or

(3) any other method which Her Majesty's Courts Service may permit.

3.2 A step may only be taken using Money Claim Online on payment of the prescribed fee. The Civil Proceedings Fees Order 2008 provides that a party may, in certain circumstances, be entitled to a remission or part remission of a fee prescribed by that Order. Her Majesty's Courts Service website contains guidance as to when this entitlement might arise.

3.3 A claimant who wishes to apply for a remission or part remission of fees must not use Money Claim Online and must file the claim form at a court office.

Types of claims which may be started using Money Claim Online

7EPD.4 **4.** A claim may be started using Money Claim Online if it meets all the following conditions—

(1) the only remedy claimed is a specified amount of money—
  (a) less than £100,000 (excluding any interest or costs claimed); and
  (b) in sterling;
(2) the procedure under Part 7 is used;
(3) the claimant is not—
  (a) a child or protected party; or
  (b) funded by the Legal Services Commission;
(4) the claim is against—
  (a) a single defendant; or
  (b) two defendants, if the claim is for a single amount against each of them;
(5) the defendant is not—
  (a) the Crown; or
  (b) a person known to be a child or protected party; and
(6) the defendant's address for service is within England and Wales.

("Protected party" has the same meaning as in rule 21.1(2).)

Starting a claim

7EPD.5 **5.1** A claimant may request the issue of a claim form by—

(1) completing and sending an online claim form; and
(2) electronically paying the appropriate issue fee, at *www.hmcourts-service.gov.uk/onlineservices/mcol*.

5.2 Detailed particulars of claim must either be—

(1) included in the online claim form but must be limited in size to not more than 1080 characters (including spaces); or
(2) served and filed by the claimant separately from the claim form in accordance with paragraph 6 but the claimant must—
  (a) state that detailed particulars of claim will follow; and
  (b) include a brief summary of the claim,

in the online claim form in the section headed "particulars of claim".

5.3 When an online claim form is received by the Money Claim Online website, an acknowledgment of receipt will automatically be sent to the claimant. The acknowledgment of receipt does not constitute a notice that the claim form has been issued.

5.4 When the court issues a claim form following the submission of an online claim form, the claim is 'brought' for the purposes of the Limitation Act 1980 and any other enactment on the date on which the online claim form is received by the court's computer system. The court will keep a record, by electronic or other means, of when online claim forms are received.

5.5 When the court issues a claim form, it will—

(1) serve a printed version of the claim form on the defendant; and

(2) send the claimant notice of issue.

5.6 The claim form will have printed on it a unique customer identification number or a password by which the defendant may access details of the claim on Her Majesty's Courts Service website.

5.8 The claim form will be deemed to be served on the fifth day after the claim was issued irrespective of whether that day is a business day or not. "Business day" has the same meaning as in rule 6.2(b).

Particulars of claim and certificate of service

6.1 Where the particulars of claim are served by the claimant separately from the claim form pursuant to paragraph 5.2(2), the claimant must— **7EPD.6**

(1) serve the particulars of claim in accordance with rule 7.4(1)(b); and

(2) file a certificate of service in form N215 at Northampton County Court within 14 days of service of the particulars of claim on the defendant.

6.2 The certificate of service may be filed at the court by sending form N215 by e-mail to mcolaos@hmcourts-service.gsi.gov.uk. However, the subject line to the e-mail must contain the claim number.

6.3 The claimant must file the particulars of claim at the court to which the proceedings are transferred under paragraph 12.1 or 12.2 within 7 days of service of the notice of transfer by the court.

6.4 Where the proceedings are not transferred under paragraph 12.1 or 12.2 and remain at Northampton County Court, the claimant is not required to file the particulars of claim at that court unless ordered to do so.

Online response

7.1 A defendant wishing to file— **7EPD.7**

(1) *an acknowledgment* of service of the claim form under Part 10;

(2) a part admission under rule 14.5;

(3) a defence under Part 15; or

(4) a counterclaim (to be filed together with a defence),

may, instead of filing a written form, do so by completing and sending the relevant online form at *www.hmcourts-service.gov.uk/onlineservices/mcol*.

7.2 Where a defendant files an online form—

(1) a hard copy must not be sent in addition;

(2) the form is not filed until it is received by the court, whatever time it is shown to have been sent;

(3) an online form received after 4 p.m. will be treated as filed on the next day the court office is open; and

(4) where a time limit applies, it remains the responsibility of the defendant to ensure that the online form is filed in time.

Counterclaim

7EPD.8 **8** Where a counterclaim is filed using an online form, any fee payable must be paid to the court to which the claim is transferred under paragraph 12.1 or 12.2.

Statement of truth

7EPD.9 **9.1** Part 22 requires any statement of case to be verified by a statement of truth. This applies to all online forms.

9.2 The statement of truth in an online statement of case must be in the form—

"[I believe][The claimant believes] that the facts stated in this claim form are true."; or

"[I believe][The defendant believes] that the facts stated in this defence are true.",

as appropriate.

9.3 Attention is drawn to—

(1) paragraph 3 of the practice direction supplementing Part 22, which provides who may sign a statement of truth; and

(2) rule 32.14, which sets out the consequences of making, or causing to be made, a false statement in a document verified by a statement of truth, without an honest belief in its truth.

Signature

7EPD.10 **10.1** Any provision of the CPR which requires a document to be signed by any person is satisfied by that person entering their name on an online form.

Request for judgment or issue of warrant

7EPD.11 **11.1** If, in a claim started using Money Claim Online—

(1) the claimant wishes to apply for judgment in default in accordance with Part 12; or

(2) the defendant has filed or served an admission of the whole of the claim in accordance with rule 14.4,

the claimant may request judgment to be entered in default or on the admission (as the case may be) by completing and sending an online request form at *www.hmcourts-service.gov.uk/onlineservices/mcol*.

11.2 Where—

(1) judgment has been entered following a request under paragraph 11.1; and

(2) the claimant is entitled to the issue of a warrant of execution without requiring the permission of the court,

the claimant may request the issue of a warrant of execution by—

(a) completing and sending an online request form; and

(b) electronically paying the appropriate fee,
at *www.hmcourts-service.gov.uk/onlineservices/mcol*.

(Order 26 of the County Court Rules ("CCR") contains rules about warrants of execution. Among other matters, CCR Order 26 rule 1 contains restrictions on when a warrant of execution may be issued if the court has made an order for payment of a sum of money by instalments, and CCR Order 26 rule 5 sets out certain circumstances in which a warrant of execution may not be issued without the permission of the court.)

11.3 A request under paragraph 11.1 or 11.2 will be treated as being filed—

(1) on the day the court receives the request, if it receives it before 9a.m. on a working day (which is any day on which the court is open); and

(2) otherwise, on the next working day after the court receives the request.

Transfer of claim

12.1 Where the defendant is an individual and Northampton County Court is not their home court, the court will transfer the claim to the defendant's home court— **7EPD.12**

(1) under rule 13.4, if the defendant applies to set aside or vary judgment;

(2) under rule 14.12, if there is to be a hearing for a judge to determine the time and rate of payment;

(3) under rule 26.2, if a defence is filed to all or part of the claim; or

(4) if either party makes an application which cannot be dealt with without a hearing.

12.2 Where the defendant is not an individual, if—

(1) the claimant's address for service on the claim form is not within the district of Northampton County Court; and

(2) one of the events mentioned in paragraph 12.1 arises,

the court will transfer the claim to the county court for the district in which the claimant's address for service on the claim form is situated.

Viewing the case record

13.1 A facility will be provided for parties or their legal representatives to view an electronic record of the status of claims started using Money Claim Online. **7EPD.13**

13.2 The record of each claim will be reviewed and, if necessary, updated at least once each day until the claim is transferred from Northampton County Court.

Note on Practice Direction—Money Claim Online

With effect from April 6, 2009, this Practice Direction was substituted in its entirety by TSO CPR Update 49. Most of the changes made consisted of necessary updating. Significant additions were the insertion of provisions enabling a claimant to file separate particulars of claim and requiring the claimant to file a certificate of service in such circumstances (see para.6). **7EPD.13.1**

PART 8

ALTERNATIVE PROCEDURE FOR CLAIMS

Contents

8.0.1

Editorial introduction

8.0.2 The rules in this Part deal with the alternative procedure for claims.

The main difference between the general procedure and the Pt 8 procedure is that a defence is not required (Pt 15), default judgment (Pt 12) is not available and the claim is treated as allocated to the multi-track (Rule 8.9(c)).

The rules in this Part should be read together with the general rules. The general rules apply subject to express contrary provisions. Reference should be made to r.8.9.

Accordingly, the rules relating to striking out (Pt 3), addition and substitution of parties (Pt 19) and summary judgment (Pt 24) apply. Part 50 contains as schedules to the rules former rules of Court which are re-enacted without substantial changes. Pt 8, will be generally suitable for use in situations where previously proceedings were commenced by originating summons. Examples would be declarations as to construction of documents and questions of law and administration of estates.

The Pt 8 procedure replaces, in a simplified form, the former High Court originating summons procedure in RSC O.7 and O.28. Rule 8.1 and para.3.1 of the Pt 8 Practice Direction (see para.8PD.1) provides for the types of claim in which the Pt 8 procedure may be followed. These are claims for the court's decision on a question which is unlikely to involve a substantial dispute of fact or where a rule or practice direction requires or permits the use of alternative procedure, e.g. claims under the Inheritance (Provision for Family and Dependants) Act 1975 (CPR r.57.16(1)). Part 8 claims will normally be heard and disposed of on written evidence.

The wording "unlikely to involve substantial dispute of fact" is similar to the former O.5, r.4(2)(b) of the RSC. Contentious claims involving substantial factual dispute were not suitable under the former procedure and nor will they usually be under the Pt 8 procedure.

In essence, the Pt 8 procedure, is in general terms designed for the determination of relevant claims without elaborate pleadings. If the procedure is misused, the defendant can object and equally the court of its own motion, and as part of its function to manage claims, will order the claim to proceed under the general procedure and allocate a track and give appropriate directions.

Modifications to Pt 8 procedure apply in the Commercial Court and reference should be made to the Admiralty and Commercial Courts Guide, Part B4.

The following provisions in Pt 8 do not apply to an application under Pt 79 (Financial Restrictions Proceedings Under the Counter-Terrorism Act 2008): rr.8.1(3), 8.2A, 8.4, 8.5, 8.6 and 8.8.

Appeals

It is to be noted that there is a distinction between Pt 8 claims which are treated as allocated to the multi-track (r.8.9(c)) and those where the Court has specifically allocated. The distinction is of significance when determining the destination of appeals in Pt 8 claims under Pt 52. Reference must be made to Pt 52 and the PD to Pt 52 and in particular to Table 1 of the PD to Pt 52. If the claim is not specifically allocated any appeal from a final judgment in a Pt 8 claim other than given by a High Court judge will not lie to the Court of Appeal. **8.0.3**

Part 8 Practice Direction

A new Pt 8 Practice Direction, replacing the two earlier Practice Directions, came into force on April 6, 2007 and is in three sections. Section A sets out in paras 4–8 general provisions dealing with issuing the claim and responding to it. Paragraph 3.1 refers to the types of claim where the Pt 8 procedure may be used. Paragraph 3.2 refers to the claims and applications listed in Section B where the Pt 8 procedure must be followed and para.3.3. makes it clear that Pt 8 must also be used where any Act, rule or practice direction provides that a claim or application shall be brought by originating summons, originating motion or originating application. **8.0.4**

In Section B, para.9.4 explains that, for applications that may or must be brought in the High Court, where no other rule or practice direction assigns the application to a Division of the Court, the table specifies "the Division to which the application is assigned". This is misleading because in some instances it is indicated that a particular type of claim or application is assigned, not to a Division or to a Divisional Court of a Division, but to a court within a Division (e.g. the Administrative Court). In using the table, care should be taken in distinguishing between the forum to which a Pt 8 claim or application will be assigned, and the place at which the claim form should be issued.

Landlord and Tenant Claims

These claims must be commenced using a Pt 8 claim form (para.2.1 of Practice Direction 56, as qualified by para.2A of the Practice Direction). Possession Claims must be commenced using the claim form specified in para.1.5 of the Practice Direction to Pt 55 and reference made to Table 1 to CPR Pt 4. **8.0.4.1**

Section B lists claims and applications where the Pt 8 procedure must be followed and these are set-out in tabular form.

Section C identifies a number of applications under various Acts and sets out specific procedural provisions for them. Here the Pt 8 procedure applies, subject to such modifications. In substance the procedures under the various Acts remain largely unaltered.

A new para.9.4 to PD 8 was introduced with effect from October 1, 2007 by CPR Update 45. It specifies in a table the divisions of the High Court to which listed applications are assigned.

Managing the Claim

All Pt 8 claims are treated as allocated to the multi-track. Accordingly, there is no allocation questionnaire in Pt 8 claims. The court may give directions immediately after the procedural judge reviews the court file in an appropriate case and the Practice Direction at para.6.1 (see para.8PD.1) gives examples. If the court does not fix a hearing date when the claim is issued and give directions immediately then it will do so "as soon as practicable" after the defendant has acknowledged service or the time for acknowledgment of service has expired. In practice it is unlikely that in any substantial Pt 8 case the court will be able to give effective directions until that stage of the proceedings. The court can order a directions hearing (case management conference) if appropriate. *The multi track* rules in para.29 apply to Pt 8. **8.0.5**

Related sources

8.0.6

- CPR r.79.5 (Modification of Part 8)
- Practice Direction (Alternative Procedure for Claims)
- **N208** Part 8 claim form
- **N208A** Part 8 notes for claimants
- **N208C** Part 8 notes for defendant
- **N212** Part 8 notice of issue
- Part 8 acknowledgment of service (**N210**)

- Costs—Only Part 8 Claim (**N210A**)
- Chancery Guide (General Commentary) (see paras 2.13–2.20; Vol.2, para.1A–9)
- Queen's Bench Guide (paras 6.7–6.8; Vol.2, paras 1B–36 and 1B–37)
- Admiralty and Commercial Courts Guide (Part B4) (see Vol.2, para.2A–47)

Types of claim in which Part 8 procedure may be followed[1]

8.1 **8.1—(1) The Part 8 procedure is the procedure set out in this Part.**

(2) A claimant may use the Part 8 procedure where—

(a) he seeks the court's decision on a question which is unlikely to involve a substantial dispute of fact; or

(b) paragraph (6) applies.

(3) The court may at any stage order the claim to continue as if the claimant had not used the Part 8 procedure and, if it does so, the court may give any directions it considers appropriate.

(4) Paragraph (2) does not apply if a practice direction provides that the Part 8 procedure may not be used in relation to the type of claim in question.

(5) Where the claimant uses the Part 8 procedure he may not obtain default judgment under Part 12.

(6) A rule or practice direction may, in relation to a specified type of proceedings—

(a) require or permit the use of the Part 8 procedure; and

(b) disapply or modify any of the rules set out in this Part as they apply to those proceedings.

(Rule 8.9 provides for other modifications to the general rules where the Part 8 is being used).

(Part 78 provides procedures for European orders for payment and for the European small claims procedure.)

Types of claim in which Part 8 procedure may or must be followed

8.1.1 Rule 8.1 specifies the types of claim for which the alternative procedure may be followed.

Rule 8.1(2)(a) provides that the procedure may be used where a claimant seeks the court's decision on a question which is unlikely to involve a substantial dispute of fact, for example a declaration as to construction of a document or a question of law.

Rule 8.1(2)(b) is important as setting out the authority of the practice direction by providing that such direction can require or permit the use of the Pt 8 procedure and further by r.8.1(6)(b) by providing that the practice direction may disapply or modify any Pt 8 rule. This is given effect in, for example, Section C of PD 8.

Rule 8.1(3) permits the court to order a claim to continue as if the Pt 8 procedure had not been used, for example in a case where a Pt 8 claim has been issued in the erroneous belief that there would be no substantial dispute of fact. In such a case the court will order that the claim continues as a Pt 7 claim, allocate to track and give directions.

The other types of claim for which the Pt 8 procedure is expressly permissible are set out in para.3.1 of the Practice Direction.

If there is a common theme in the types of Pt 8 claims and applications set out in the *Practice Direction at para.1.4*, it is that they are likely to be capable of disposal without there being substantial disputes of fact.

---

[1] Amended by Civil Procedure (Amendment) Rules 2008 (SI 2008/2178).

If any substantial dispute of fact is anticipated then the Pt 8 procedure should, unless otherwise specified in Sections B and C of the PD, not be used.The court will assess the suitability of the procedure at the stage it gives directions. This is particularly recognised in paras 3.4 and 3.5 of the Practice Direction which underlines the court's function in managing Pt 8 claims.

An application to vary or discharge a stop notice under CPR r.73.21 should be by Pt 8 claim.

See also under Editorial introduction.

Contents of the claim form[1]

8.2 Where the claimant uses the Part 8 procedure the claim form must state— 8.2

(a) that this Part applies;

(b) (i) the question which the claimant wants the court to decide; or

(ii) the remedy which the claimant is seeking and the legal basis for the claim to that remedy;

(c) if the claim is being made under an enactment, what that enactment is;

(d) if the claimant is claiming in a representative capacity, what that capacity is; and

(e) if the defendant is sued in a representative capacity, what that capacity is.

(Part 22 provides for the claim form to be verified by a statement of truth).

(Rule 7.5 provides for service of the claim form).

(The costs practice direction sets out the information about a funding arrangement to be provided with the claim form where the claimant intends to seek to recover an additional liability).)

("Funding arrangement" and "additional liability" are defined in rule 43.2).

Contents of the Claim Form

Claims to which Pt 8 apply are commenced by the issue of a Pt 8 claim form (**N208**). 8.2.1

The claim form should, in general, not contain the same amount of detail as a Pt 7 claim form on statement of case for other claims and should set out in summary form only the facts and the question or issue the claimant wants the court to decide or the remedy that is sought, as the case may be.

Paragraph 4.2 of the Practice Direction provides that the claim form must be in practice form **N208**. The claim form must state that Pt 8 applies. The burden is put upon the claimant that the claim is suitable for Pt 8 procedure.

The claim form contains guidance notes on the completion of the form and the description and details of parties, for example minors, companies and unincorporated associations. If, in error, a claiment uses an incorrect claim form the Court will not strike out the claim but will make an order rectifying the position. *Hannigan v Hannigan* [2000] 2 F.C.R. 650.

Issue of claim form without naming defendants[2]

8.2A—(1) A practice direction may set out circumstances in 8.2A

[1] Amended by the Civil Procedure (Amendment No.3) Rules 2000 (SI 2000/1317).

[2] Introduced by the Civil Procedure (Amendment) Rules 2000 (SI 2000/221), and amended by the Civil Procedure (Amendment) Rules 2001 (SI 2001/256).

which a claim form may be issued under this Part without naming a defendant.

(2) The practice direction may set out those cases in which an application for permission must be made by application notice before the claim form is issued.

(3) The application notice for permission—

(a) need not be served on any other person; and

(b) must be accompanied by a copy of the claim form that the applicant proposes to issue.

(4) Where the court gives permission it will give directions about the future management of the claim.

No Party to be served

8.2A.1 Rule 8.2A (inserted by SI 2000/221 and amended by SI 2001/256) accommodates a previous gap in Pt 8 procedure for cases in which it is wished to issue a claim without naming a defendant, e.g. where there is no person to be served such as applications for payment or transfers of monies in court. Permission is requested from the court before the claim form is issued and this is by application notice accompanied by a copy of the claim form to be issued. Rule 8.2A envisages the court giving directions as to the management of the claim if permission is given. The application should be accompanied by draft directions for consideration by the Master or district judge.

Part 8 Claims and estates of deceased Lloyd's names

8.2A.2 Personal representatives who wish to apply to the court for permission to distribute the estates of deceased Lloyd's names are not required to make a separate application pursuant to rule 8.2A and can proceed to issue a Pt 8 Claim Form.

Acknowledgment of service[1]

8.3 **8.3—(1) The defendant must—**

(a) file an acknowledgment of service in the relevant practice form not more than 14 days after service of the claim form; and

(b) serve the acknowledgment of service on the claimant and any other party.

(2) The acknowledgment of service must state—

(a) whether the defendant contests the claim; and

(b) if the defendant seeks a different remedy from that set out in the claim form, what that remedy is.

(3) The following rules of Part 10 (acknowledgment of service) apply—

(a) rule 10.3(2) (exceptions to the period for filing an acknowledgment of service); and

(b) rule 10.5 (contents of acknowledgment of service).[2]

(The costs practice direction sets out the information about a funding arrangement to be provided with the acknowledgment of service where the defendant intends to seek to recover an additional liability).

---

[1] Amended by the Civil Procedure (Amendment No.3) Rules 2000 (SI 2000/1317), and the Civil Procedure (Amendment No.5) Rules 2001 (SI 2001/4015).

[2] Paragraph (4) deleted by the Civil Procedure (Amendment No.5) Rules 2001 (SI 2001/4015) (L.32).

("Funding arrangement" and "additional liability" are defined in rule 43.2).

Rule 8.3

8.3.1 An acknowledgment of service in Form **N210** should be verified by a statement of truth; see r.22.1(1)(e) and para.1.1(4) of the PD to Pt 22. Particular attention should be paid to section E of Form **N210**. A defendant who objects to use of the Pt 8 procedure should state this in his acknowledgment of service (PD 8 para.5.3).

Consequence of not filing an acknowledgment of service

8.4—(1) This rule applies where— 8.4

(a) the defendant has failed to file an acknowledgment of service; and

(b) the time period for doing so has expired.

(2) The defendant may attend the hearing of the claim but may not take part in the hearing unless the court gives permission.

Responding to claim

8.4.1 The combined effect of r.8.3 and para.7.3 of the Practice Direction is that if a defendant wishes to *respond* to a Pt 8 claim he must acknowledge service within 14 days of service of the claim form using Form **N210** and this involves filing and servingan acknowledgement of service.

It is at this stage that, in practice, a defendant must either respond to the claim, for example if a different remedy to the remedy claimed is sought he should set this out with particulars, *or* seek to dispute the court's jurisdiction (a directions hearing will then be appointed) *or* object to the use of the Pt 8 procedure, for example, on the ground that a substantial dispute of fact needs to be considered by the court in the particular claim (again a directions hearing will be appointed).

Directions already given

8.4.2 If the court has already given directions, a copy of the court order will be served on the defendant with the claim form. In that case the defendant must not only file and serve his acknowledgment of service but also comply with the directions. If a defendant wishes to seek to vary any directions already given he should, in most cases, ask for a variation at a directions hearing and state the variation sought in his written evidence accompanying his acknowledgment of service.

Agreed Directions

8.4.3 It is sensible practice for the parties to seek to agree directions and submit them to the court immediately after the time limited for filing an acknowledgment by the defendant. CPR r.29.4 applies to Pt 8 claims and the guidance in the Practice Direction supplementing CPR Pt 29 encourages the parties to agree suitable directions. At the latest the parties will be expected to have tried to agree directions by the time of any case management conference and produced a draft order for consideration by the court.

Filing and serving witness statements

8.5—(1) The claimant must file any written evidence on which he intends to rely when he files his claim form. 8.5

(2) The claimant's evidence must be served on the defendant with the claim form.

(3) A defendant who wishes to rely on written evidence must file it when he files his acknowledgment of service.

(4) If he does so, he must also, at the same time, serve a copy of his evidence on the other parties.

(5) The claimant may, within 14 days of service of the defendant's evidence on him, file further written evidence in reply.

(6) If he does so, he must also, within the same time limit, serve a copy of his evidence on the other parties.

(7) The claimant may rely on the matters set out in his claim form as evidence under this rule if the claim form is verified by a statement of truth.

Filing and serving written evidence

8.5.1 *Claimant's evidence* —Rule 8.5 is important as providing that if the claimant wishes to file any written evidence this must be filed and served with the claim form unless the evidence is contained on the claim form itself and is supported by a statement of truth.

8.5.2 *Defendant's evidence* —Similarly, the defendant must file his evidence with his acknowledgment of service and serve it on all parties. Rule 8.5(4) gives 14 days in which the claimant can serve evidence in reply. The former originating summons procedure allowed 28 days after receipt of the claimant's evidence and 14 days may prove short for a defendant. Paragraph 7.4 of the practice direction provides that any party may apply for an extension of time to serve and file evidence and para.7.4 makes provision for the parties agreeing between themselves an extension of time for serving and filing evidence under r.8.5(3) or 8.5(5). Paragraph 7.5 imposes time limits to such agreement and makes clear that any agreement extending time is to be filed with the court by the defendant with his acknowledgment of service. This is consistent with the court managing the case. Attention is drawn to section E in Form **N210**. This section must be completed in order to assist the court in managing the claim.

Evidence for the purposes of Pt 8 is in the form of an affidavit or a witness statement, subject to the court's power to admit oral evidence.

8.5.3 *Timings* —Timings are important and are set out in this part. In summary the claimant must be ready to serve all his evidence with his claim form. The defendant then has 14 days from service on him to file his acknowledgment of service and any evidence in reply to be filed by the claimant must be within 14 days of service of the acknowledgment of service by the defendant. Attention is drawn to the provisions of para.7.5 of the Pt 8 Practice Direction concerning the limits on agreements to extend time. A defendant who does not intend to file evidence should expressly notify the court of that in the acknowledgment of service.

Evidence—general

8.6 **8.6—(1) No written evidence may be relied on at the hearing of the claim unless—**

(a) it has been served in accordance with rule 8.5; or

(b) the court gives permission.

(2) The court may require or permit a party to give oral evidence at the hearing.

(3) The court may give directions requiring the attendance for cross-examination[GL] of a witness who has given written evidence.

(Rule 32.1 contains a general power for the court to control evidence).

Evidence

8.6.1 Rule 8.6 governs the position in relation to evidence in Pt 8 claims. Generally, the position is that no written evidence may be filed unless it has been served in accordance with the rules or the court gives permission.

Rule 8.6(2) gives the court power to authorise a party to adduce oral evidence at the hearing and r.8.6(3) gives to the court power to make an order requiring the attendance of a person who has given written evidence to attend for cross examination.

In practice, it is unlikely that the court will permit oral evidence unless it has been foreshadowed in earlier written evidence. Equally, if it becomes apparent that the claim is one that is going to involve substantial cross examination involving disputed matters of fact, it is likely that the court will take the view that the case is not suitable for the Pt 8 procedure and will give directions accordingly including allocation to a track.

Part 20 claims

8.7 Where the Part 8 procedure is used, Part 20 (counterclaims additional and other claims) applies except that a party may not make a Part 20 claim (as defined by rule 20.2) without the court's permission. 8.7

Procedure where defendant objects to use of the Part 8 procedure

8.8—(1) Where the defendant believes that the Part 8 procedure should not be used because— 8.8

(a) there is a substantial dispute of fact; and

(b) the use of the Part 8 procedure is not required or permitted by a rule or practice direction,

he must state his reasons when he files his acknowledgment of service.

(Rule 8.5 requires a defendant who wishes to rely on written evidence to file it when he files his acknowledgment of service).

(2) When the court receives the acknowledgment of service and any written evidence it will give directions as to the future management of the case.

(Rule 8.1(3) allows the court to make an order that the claim continue as if the claimant had not used the Part 8 procedure).

Procedure where defendant objects to use Part 8 procedure

This provision is set out in r.8.8. An objection will be considered by the court. Even if no objection is taken by a defendant in section D of Form **N210** (Acknowledgment of Service) the court officer may bring to the attention of the Master or District Judge any case where he considers that the procedure is being used inappropriately. 8.8.1

In practice, the judge will consider the appropriateness or otherwise of the use of the alternative procedure when the claim comes before him either initially or at the directions hearing. A person who uses the Pt 8 procedure inappropriately, e.g. knowing that there are significant issues of fact, and incurs a defendant in costs will be likely to be the subject to an order for summary assessment of costs. By comparison, if it becomes apparent after the filing of the defendant's acknowledgment of service that the claim is not suitable for Pt 8, the parties should act co-operatively and submit an appropriate consent order to the Master or district judge pursuant to r.8.1(3) together with suggested Pt 7 trial directions.

In an appropriate case the court may order that the Pt 8 claim form stands as particulars of claim, direct the filing of a defence and give Pt 7 trial directions including a direction for disclosure and witness statements.

Modifications to the general rules

8.9 Where the Part 8 procedure is followed— 8.9

(a) provision is made in this Part for the matters which must be stated in the claim form and the defendant is not required to file a defence and therefore—

(i) Part 16 (statements of case) does not apply;

(ii) Part 15 (defence) does not apply;

(iii) any time limit in these Rules which prevents the

parties from taking a step before a defence is filed does not apply;

(iv) the requirement under rule 7.8 to serve on the defendant a form for defending the claim does not apply;

(b) the claimant may not obtain judgment by request on an admission and therefore—

(i) rules 14.4 to 14.7 do not apply;

(ii) the requirement under rule 7.8 to serve on the defendant a form for admitting the claim does not apply; and

(c) the claim shall be treated as allocated to the multi-track and therefore Part 26 does not apply.

PRACTICE DIRECTION—ALTERNATIVE PROCEDURE FOR CLAIMS

This Practice Direction supplements CPR Part 8 and Schedule 1 and Schedule 2 to the CPR

Terminology

1.1 In this Practice Direction, "Schedule rules" means provisions contained in the Schedules to the CPR, which were previously contained in the Rules of the Supreme Court (1965) or the County Court Rules (1981). **8PD.1**

Application of this Practice Direction

2.1 Section A contains general provisions about claims and applications to which Part 8 applies. Section B comprises a table listing claims, petitions and applications under various enactments which must be made under Part 8. Section C contains certain additions and modifications to the Part 8 procedure that apply to the particular claims and applications identified. **8PD.2**

2.2 Some of the claims and applications listed in the table in Section B are dealt with in the Schedule Rules in the CPR. The table in Section B contains cross-reference to the relevant Schedule Rules.

Section A

General Provisions Applicable to Part 8 Claims

Types of claim in which the Part 8 procedure may be used

3.1 The types of claim for which the Part 8 procedure may be used include— **8PD.3**

(1) a claim by or against a child or protected party, as defined in rule 21.1(2), which has been settled before the commencement of proceedings and the sole purpose of the claim is to obtain the approval of the court to the settlement; or

(2) a claim for provisional damages which has been settled before the commencement of proceedings and the sole purpose of the claim is to obtain a consent judgment.

3.2(1) The Part 8 procedure must be used for those claims, petitions and applications listed in the table in Section B.

(2) Where a claim is listed in the table in Section B and is identified as a claim to which particular provisions of Section C apply, the Part 8 procedure shall apply subject to the additions and modifications set out in the relevant paragraphs in Section C.

3.3 The Part 8 procedure must also be used for any claim or application in relation to which an Act, rule or practice direction provides that the claim or application is brought by originating summons, originating motion or originating application.

3.4 Where it appears to a court officer that a claimant is using the Part 8 procedure inappropriately, he may refer the claim to a judge for the judge to consider the point.

3.5 The court may at any stage order the claim to continue as if the claimant had not used the Part 8 procedure and, if it does so, the court will allocate the claim to a track and give such directions as it considers appropriate.

Issuing the claim

8PD.4 **4.1** Part 7 and the practice direction which supplements it contain a number of rules and directions applicable to all claims, including those to which Part 8 applies. Those rules and directions should be applied where appropriate.

4.2 Where a claimant uses the Part 8 procedure, the claim form (practice form N208) should be used and must state the matters set out in rule 8.2 and, if rule 8.1(6) applies, must comply with the requirements of the rule or practice direction in question. In particular, the claim form must state that Part 8 applies; a Part 8 claim form means a claim form which so states. (The Costs Practice Direction supplementing Parts 43 to 48 contains details of the information required to be filed with a claim form to comply with rule 44.15 (providing information about funding arrangements).)

Responding to the claim

8PD.5 **5.1** The provisions of Part 15 (defence and reply) do not apply where the claim form is a Part 8 claim form.

5.2 Where a defendant who wishes to respond to a Part 8 claim form is required to file an acknowledgment of service, that acknowledgment of service should be in practice form N210.

5.3 Where a defendant objects to the use of the Part 8 procedure, and his statement of reasons includes matters of evidence, the acknowledgment of service must be verified by a statement of truth.

Managing the claim

8PD.6 **6.1** The court may give directions immediately a Part 8 claim form is issued either on the application of a party or on its own initiative. The directions may include fixing a hearing date where—

(1) there is no dispute, such as in child and protected party settlements; or

(2) where there may be a dispute, but a hearing date could conveniently be given.

6.2 Where the court does not fix a hearing date when the claim form is issued, it will give directions for the disposal of the claim as soon as practicable after the defendant has acknowledged service of the claim form or, as the case may be, after the period for acknowledging service has expired.

6.3 Certain applications may not require a hearing.

6.4 The court may convene a directions hearing before giving directions.

Evidence

8PD.7 **7.1** A claimant must file the written evidence on which he relies when his Part 8 claim form is issued (unless the evidence is contained in the claim form itself).

7.2 Evidence will normally be in the form of a witness statement or an affidavit but a claimant may rely on the matters set out in his claim form provided that it has been verified by a statement of truth.

(For information about (1) statements of truth see Part 22 and the practice direction that supplements it, and (2) written evidence see Part 32 and the practice direction that supplements it.)

7.3 A defendant wishing to rely on written evidence, must file it with his acknowledgment of service.

7.4 A party may apply to the court for an extension of time to serve and file evidence under rule 8.5 or for permission to serve and file additional evidence under rule 8.6(1).

(For information about applications see Part 23 and the practice direction that supplements it.)

7.5(1) The parties may, subject to the following provisions, agree in writing on an extension of time for serving and filing evidence under rule 8.5(3) or rule 8.5(5).

(2) An agreement extending time for a defendant to file evidence under rule 8.5(3)—

(a) must be filed by the defendant at the same time as he files his acknowledgement of service; and

(b) must not extend time by more than 14 days after the defendant files his acknowledgement of service.

(3) An agreement extending time for a claimant to file evidence in reply under rule 8.5(5) must not extend time to more than 28 days after service of the defendant's evidence on the claimant.

Hearing

8.1 The court may on the hearing date— **8PD.8**

(1) proceed to hear the case and dispose of the claim;

(2) give case management directions.

8.2 Case management directions may include the specific allocation of a case to a track.

8.3 CPR rules 26.5(3) to (5) and rules 26.6 to 26.10 apply to the allocation of a claim under paragraph 8.2.

Section B

Claims and Applications that Must be Made under Part 8

9.1 The claimant must use the Part 8 procedure if the claim is listed in the table below. **8PD.9**

9.2 Section C of this Practice Direction contains special provisions modifying the Part 8 procedure, and where it does so, those provisions should be followed. The table below refers to the relevant paragraph of Section C where it applies.

9.3 Some of the claims and applications listed in the table below are dealt with in the Schedule Rules, and those rules modify the Part 8 procedure. A cross-reference to the relevant Schedule Rule is contained in the table below.

9.4 For applications that may or must be brought in the High Court, where no other rule or practice direction assigns the application to a Division of the court, the table specifies the Division to which the application is assigned.

Type of Claim or Application	Paragraph of Section C	Division	Schedule Rule
Application under section 14 of the Bills of Sale Act 1878 (Rectification of register)	Paragraph 10A	Queen's Bench Central Office	
Application under section 15 of the Bills of Sale Act 1878 (Entry of satisfaction)	Paragraph 11	Queen's Bench Central Office	
Application under section 16 of the Bills of Sale Act 1878 (Search of the bills of sale register)	Paragraph 11A	Queen's Bench Central Office	
Application under the proviso to section 7 of the Bills of Sale Act (1878) Amendment Act 1882 (Restraining removal on sale of goods seized)		Queen's Bench Central Office	
Application under the Public Trustee Act 1906 (free-standing proceedings)	Paragraph 12	Chancery	
Application under section 7 of the Deeds of Arrangement Act 1914 (Rectification of register)	Paragraph 12A	Queen's Bench Central Office	
Proceedings under the Trustee Act 1925		Chancery	
Application under section 7 of the Deeds of Arrangement Act 1914 (Rectification of Register)		Chancery	
Applications under section 2(3) of the Public Order Act 1936	Paragraph 13	Chancery	
Proceedings under jurisdiction conferred by section 1 of the Railway and Canal Commission (Abolition) Act 1949	Paragraph 14	Chancery	
Administration of Justice Act 1960 (Applications under the Act)		Divisional Court	RSC 0.109 r.1(3)
Administration of Justice Act 1960 (Appeals under section *13 of the Act)*		Divisional Court	RSC 0.109, r.2(4)

Proceedings under section 14 of the Commons Registration Act 1965		Chancery	
Application under the Mines (Working Facilities and Support) Act 1966	Paragraph 15	Chancery	
Proceedings under section 21 or 25 of the Law of Property Act 1969		Chancery	
Local Government Act 1972 (claims under section 92—proceedings for disqualification)		Queen's Bench Central Office	
Application under article 10 of the Mortgaging of Aircraft Order 1972 (Rectification of register)	Paragraph 15A	Chancery	
Application to register an assignment of book debts (section 344 of the Insolvency Act 1986)	Paragraph 15B	Queen's Bench Central Office	
Proceedings under the Control of Misleading Advertisements Regulations 1988		Chancery	
Application under section 42 of the Supreme Court Act 1981	Paragraph 16	Administrative Court	
Proceedings in the High Court under Representation of the People Acts	Paragraph 17A	Queen's Bench Central Office	
Applications under Part II of the Mental Health Act 1983	Paragraph 18	Administrative Court	
Applications under section 13 of the Coroners Act 1988	Paragraph 19	Administrative Court	
Application for an injunction to prevent environmental harm under section 187B or 214A of the Town and Country Planning Act 1990; section 44A of the Planning (Listed Buildings and Conservation Areas) Act 1990; or section 26AA of the Planning (Hazardous Substances) Act 1990	Paragraph 20	Queen's Bench	

Confiscation and Forfeiture in Connection with Criminal Proceedings (I. Drug Trafficking Act 1994 and Criminal Justice (International Co-operation) Act 1990—Application for a confiscation Order)		Queen's Bench	RSC O.115, r.2B(1)
Confiscation and Forfeiture in Connection with Criminal Proceedings (I. Drug Trafficking Act 1994 and Criminal Justice (International Co-operation) Act 1990—Application for a restraint order or charging order)		Queen's Bench	RSC O.115, r.3(1)
Confiscation and Forfeiture in connection with criminal proceedings (I. Drug Trafficking Act 1994 and Criminal Justice (International Co-operation) Act 1990—Realisation of property)		Queen's Bench	RSC O.115, r.7(1)
Criminal Procedure and Investigations Act 1996 (Application under section 54(3)).		Queen's Bench	RSC O.116, r.5(1)
Confiscation and Forfeiture in Connection with Criminal Proceedings (III. Terrorism Act 2000—Application for a restraint order)		Queen's Bench	RSC O.115, r.26(1)
Proceedings under the Financial Services and Markets Act 2000)	Paragraph 21	Chancery	
Application for an injunction under s.21 or s.26 of the Energy Act 2008	Paragraph 20	Queen's Bench	
Interpleader (Mode of application)		Chancery or Queen's Bench	RSC O.17, r.3(1)
Criminal proceedings (estreat of recognizances)		Queen's Bench	RSC O.79, r.8(2)
Criminal Proceedings (Bail)		Queen's Bench	RSC O.79, r.9(2)

Application under an enactment giving the High Court jurisdiction to quash or prohibit any order, scheme, certificate or plan, any amendment or approval of a plan, any decision of a Minister or government department or any action on the part of a Minister or government department	Paragraph 22	Administrative Court	

SECTION C SPECIAL PROVISIONS

10.1 The following special provisions apply to the applications indicated. 8PD.10

Applications under section 14 of the Bills of Sale Act 1878

10A.1 This paragraph applies to an application under section 14 of the Bills of Sale Act 1878 for an order to rectify an omission or mis-statement in relation to the registration, or renewal of the registration, of a bill of sale—

(1) by inserting in the register the true name, residence or occupation of a person; or

(2) by extending the time for registration of the bill of sale or an affidavit of its renewal.

10A.2 The application must be made—

(1) by claim form under Part 8; or

(2) by witness statement.

10A.3 Where the application is made by witness statement—

(1) Part 23 applies to the application;

(2) the witness statement constitutes the application notice under that Part;

(3) the witness statement does not need to be served on any other person; and

(4) the application will normally be dealt with without a hearing.

10A.4 The application must set out—

(1) the particulars of the bill of sale and of the omission or mis-statement; and

(2) the grounds on which the application is made.

10A.5 The application must be made to a Master of the Queen's Bench Division and accompanied by payment of the prescribed fee.

Applications under Section 15 of the Bills of Sale Act 1878

11.1 This paragraph applies where an application is made under section 15 of the Bills of Sale Act 1878 for an order that a memorandum of satisfaction be written on a registered copy of a bill of sale. 8PD.11

11.2 If the person entitled to the benefit of the bill of sale has not consented to the satisfaction, the claim form—

(1) must be served on that person; and

(2) must be supported by evidence that the debt (if any) for which the bill of sale was made has been satisfied or discharged.

11.3 If the person entitled to the benefit of the bill of sale has consented to the satisfaction, the application may be made by—

(1) claim form under Part 8; or

(2) witness statement.

11.4 Where paragraph 11.3 applies and the application is made by Part 8 claim form, the claim form—

(1) must contain details of the consent;

(2) must be supported by a witness statement by a person who witnessed the consent verifying the signature on it; and

(3) must not be served on any person other than the person entitled to the benefit of the bill of sale.

11.5 Where paragraph 11.3 applies and the application is made by witness statement—

(1) Part 23 will apply to the application;

(2) the witness statement will constitute the application notice under that Part;

(3) the witness statement does not need to be served on any other person; and

(4) the application will normally be dealt with without a hearing.

Applications under section 16 of the Bills of Sale Act 1878

11A.1 This paragraph applies to an application under section 16 of the Bills of Sale Act 1878 for a search of the bills of sale register and for a certificate of the results of the search.

11A.2 The application must be made—

(1) by claim form under Part 8; or

(2) by written request.

11A.3 The application must give sufficient information to enable the relevant bill of sale to be identified.

11A.4 The application must be made to a Master of the Queen's Bench Division and accompanied by payment of the prescribed fee.

Application under the Public Trustee Act 1906

8PD.12 **12.1** An application under the Public Trustee Act 1906 must be made—

(1) where no proceedings have been issued, by a Part 8 claim;

(2) in existing proceedings, by a Part 23 application.

12.2 Without prejudice to sections 10(2) and 13(7) of the Public Trustee Act 1906, the jurisdiction of the High Court under the Act is exercised by a single judge of the Chancery Division sitting in private.

Applications under section 7 of the Deeds of Arrangement Act 1914

12A.1 This paragraph applies to an application under section 7 of the Deeds of Arrangement Act 1914 for an order to rectify an omission or mis-statement in relation to the registration of a deed of arrangement—

(1) by inserting in the register the true name, residence or description of a person; or

(2) by extending the time for registration.

12A.2 The application must be made—

(1) by claim form under Part 8; or

(2) by witness statement.

12A.3 Where the application is made by witness statement

(1) Part 23 applies to the application;

(2) the witness statement constitutes the application notice under that Part;

(3) the witness statement does not need to be served on any other person; and

(4) the application will normally be dealt with without a hearing.

12A.4 The application must set out—

(1) the particulars of the deed of arrangement and of the omission or mis-statement; and

(2) the grounds on which the application is made.

12A.5 The application must be made to a Master of the Queen's Bench Division and accompanied by payment of the prescribed fee.

Application under section 2(3) of the Public Order Act 1936

13.1 The Attorney General may determine the persons who should be made defendants to an application under section 2(3) of the Public Order Act 1936. **8PD.13**

13.2 If the court directs an inquiry under section 2(3), it may appoint the Official Solicitor to represent any interests it considers are not sufficiently represented and ought to be represented.

Proceedings under section 1 of the Railway and Canal Commission (Abolition) Act 1949

14.1 Paragraphs 15.3 to 15.14 apply, with appropriate modifications, to proceedings in which jurisdiction has been conferred on the High Court by section 1 of the Railway and Canal Commission (Abolition) Act 1949, except to the extent that— **8PD.14**

(1) an Act;

(2) a rule;

(3) a practice direction,

provides otherwise.

Application under the Mines (Working Facilities and Support) Act 1966

15.1 In this paragraph— **8PD.15**

(1) 'the Act' means the Mines (Working Facilities and Support) Act 1966;

(2) 'the applicant' means the person who has applied for the grant of a right under the Act.

15.2 This paragraph applies where the Secretary of State refers an application to the High Court under any provision of the Act.

15.3 The Secretary of State must—

(1) file a reference signed by him or a person authorised to sign on his behalf in the Chancery Division of the High Court;

(2) file, along with the reference, any documents and plans

deposited with him by the applicant in support of his application; and

(3) within 3 days of filing the reference, give notice to the applicant that the reference has been filed.

15.4 Within 10 days of receiving the notice referred to in paragraph 15.3(3), the applicant must issue a claim form.

15.5 The claim form—

(1) must identify the application under the Act and the remedy sought; and

(2) need not be served on any other party.

15.6 Within 7 days of the claim form being issued, the applicant must

(1) apply for the claim to be listed for a hearing before a Master; and

(2) give notice of the hearing date to the Secretary of State.

15.7 The applicant must, not less than 2 days before the date fixed for a hearing, file at court—

(1) a witness statement in support of the claim, giving details of all persons known to the applicant to be interested in, or affected by, the application; and

(2) a draft of any proposed advertisement or notice of the application.

15.8 At the hearing, the Master will—

(1) fix a date by which any notice of objection under paragraph 15.9 must be filed;

(2) fix a date for a further hearing of the claim; and

(3) give directions about—

(a) any advertisement that is to be inserted or notice of the application and hearing date that is to be given; and

(b) what persons are to be served with a copy of the application or any other document in the proceedings.

15.9 Any person who wishes to oppose the application must, within the time fixed by the court under paragraph 15.8, serve notice of objection on the applicant, stating

(a) his name and address;

(b) the name and address of his solicitor, if any;

(c) the grounds of his objection;

(d) any alternative method for effecting the objects of the application that he alleges may be used; and

(e) the facts on which he relies.

15.10 Any document that is required to be served on the person who has given notice of objection ('the objector') may be served by posting it to the following address—

(1) where the notice of objection gives the name and address of a solicitor, to the solicitor;

(2) in any other case, to the objector at the address stated in the notice of objection.

15.11 The objector may appear, or be represented at any further hearing, and may take such part in the proceedings as the court allows.

15.12 The applicant must, not less than two days before the date set for the further hearing, file at court-

(1) any notices of objection served on him;

(2) a list of objectors, together with—

(a) their names and addresses;

(b) the names and addresses of their solicitors, if any; and

(c) a summary of their respective grounds of objection.

15.13 If the objector does not appear, or is not represented, at the further hearing—

(1) his notice of objection will have no effect; and

(2) he will not be entitled to take any further part in the proceedings unless the court orders otherwise.

15.14 At the further hearing, the court will—

(1) give directions about the future conduct of the claim, including—

(a) any further information the applicant is required to give in relation to any of the grounds or facts relied on in support of the application;

(b) any further information the objector is required to give in relation to any of the grounds or facts relied on in opposition to the application;

(c) whether the applicant may serve a reply to any notice of objection;

(d) whether any particular fact should be proved by a witness statement;

(e) whether any statements of case or points of claim or defence are to be served; and

(2) adjourn the claim for hearing before a judge.

Applications under article 10 of the Mortgaging of Aircraft Order 1972

15A.1 This paragraph applies to an application under article 10 of the Mortgaging of Aircraft Order 1972 for an order to amend the Register of Aircraft Mortgages.

15A.2 The application must be made by claim form under Part 8.

15A.3 Every person (other than the claimant) who appears in the register as mortgagor or mortgagee of the aircraft concerned must be made a defendant to the claim.

15A.4 A copy of the claim form must be sent to the Civil Aviation Authority.

15A.5 The application will be assigned to the Chancery Division.

15A.6 The Civil Aviation Authority is entitled to be heard in the proceedings.

Applications under section 344 of the Insolvency Act 1986 for registration of assignments of book debts

15B.1 This paragraph applies to an application under section 344 of the Insolvency Act 1986 to register an assignment of book debts.

15B.2 The application must be made—

(1) by claim form under Part 8; or

(2) by witness statement.

15B.3 The application must be made to a Master of the Queen's Bench Division and accompanied by payment of the prescribed fee.

15B.4 Where the application is made by witness statement—

(1) Part 23 applies to the application;

(2) the witness statement constitutes the application notice under that Part;

(3) the witness statement does not need to be served on any other person; and

(4) the application will normally be dealt with without a hearing.

15B.5 The application—

(1) must have exhibited to it a true copy of the assignment and of every schedule to it;

(2) must set out the particulars of the assignment and the parties to it; and

(3) must verify the date and time of the execution of the assignment, and its execution in the presence of a witness.

15B.6 Upon the court being satisfied, the documents so exhibited will be filed and the particulars of the assignment and of the parties to it entered in the register.

Application under Section 42 of the Supreme Court Act 1981

8PD.16 **16.1** An application under section 42 of the Supreme Court Act 1981 is heard and determined by a Divisional Court.

16.2 The claim form must be filed at the Administrative Court and—

(1) be accompanied by a witness statement in support; and

(2) be served on the person against whom the order is sought.

Application for detailed assessment of a returning officer's account

8PD.17 **17.1** An application by the Secretary of State under section 30 of the Representation of the People Act 1983 for the detailed assessment of a returning officer's account must be made by claim form.

17.2 When it issues the claim form, the court will fix a date for the hearing of the detailed assessment to be dealt with if the application is granted.

17.3 The returning officer may, on the application, apply to the court to examine any claim made against him in respect of matters charged in the account.

17.4 To make an application under paragraph 17.3, the returning officer must file an application within 7 days of being served with a copy of the application for detailed assessment.

17.5 When an application is filed under paragraph 17.3, the court will—

(a) fix a date for the hearing;

(b) give notice of the hearing date to the returning officer; and

(c) serve a copy of the application and notice of hearing on the claimant.

17.6 The examination and detailed assessment may take place on the same day, provided that the examination is determined before the detailed assessment is concluded.

17.7 The district judge may hear and determine—

(a) an application for detailed assessment;
(b) any application under paragraph 17.3.

17.8 The court will serve a copy of the order made in the application on—

(a) the Secretary of State;
(b) the returning officer; and
(c) in an application under paragraph 17.3, the claimant.

Other proceedings under the Representation of the People Acts

17A.1(1) This paragraph applies to proceedings under the Representation of the People Acts (other than proceedings under section 30 of the Representation of the People Act 1983).

(2) The jurisdiction of the High Court under those Acts in matters relating to Parliamentary and local government elections will be exercised by the Divisional Court except that—

(a) any jurisdiction, under a provision of any of those Acts, exercisable by a single judge will be exercised by a single judge;
(b) any jurisdiction, under any such provision, exercisable by a Master will be exercised by a Master; and
(c) where the court's jurisdiction in matters relating to Parliamentary elections is exercisable by a single judge, that jurisdiction in matters relating to local government elections is also exercisable by a single judge.

Application under Mental Health Act 1983

18.1 In this paragraph— 8PD.18

(1) a section referred to by a number refers to the section so numbered in the Mental Health Act 1983 and 'Part II' means Part II of that Act;
(2) 'hospital manager' means the manager of a hospital as defined in section 145(1) of the Act; and
(3) 'place of residence' means, in relation to a patient who is receiving treatment as an in-patient in a hospital or other institution, that hospital or institution.

18.2 The claim form must be filed—

(1) in the court for the district in which the patient's place of residence is situated; or
(2) in the case of an application under section 30, in the court that made the order under section 29 which the application seeks to discharge or vary.

18.3 *Where an application* is made under section 29 for an order that the functions of the nearest relative of the patient are to be exercisable by some other person—

(1) the nearest relative must be made a respondent, unless
(a) the application is made on the grounds that the patient has no nearest relative or that it is not reasonably practicable to ascertain whether he has a nearest relative; or

(b) the court orders otherwise; and

(2) the court may order that any other person shall be made a respondent.

18.4 Subject to paragraph 18.5, the court may accept as evidence of the facts relied upon in support of the application, any report made—

(1) by a medical practitioner; or

(2) by any of the following acting in the course of their official duties—

(a) a probation officer;

(b) an officer of a local authority;

(c) an officer of a voluntary body exercising statutory functions on behalf of a local authority; or

(d) an officer of a hospital manager.

18.5 The respondent must be informed of the substance of any part of the report dealing with his fitness or conduct that the court considers to be material to the determination of the claim.

18.6 An application under Part II shall be heard in private unless the court orders otherwise.

18.7 The judge may, for the purpose of determining the application, interview the patient. The interview may take place in the presence of, or separately from, the parties. The interview may be conducted elsewhere than at the court. Alternatively, the judge may direct the district judge to interview the patient and report to the judge in writing.

Applications under section 13 of the Coroners Act 1988

8PD.19 **19.1** An application under section 13 of the Coroners Act 1988 is heard and determined by a Divisional Court.

19.2 The application must, unless made by the Attorney General, be accompanied by the Attorney General's fiat.

19.3 The claim form must—

(1) state the grounds for the application;

(2) be filed at the Administrative Court; and

(3) be served upon all persons directly affected by the application within six weeks of the grant of the Attorney General's fiat.

Application for injunction to prevent environmental harm or unlicensed activities

8PD.20 **20.1** This paragraph relates to applications under—

(1) section 187B or 214A of the Town and Country Planning Act 1990;

(2) section 44A of the Planning (Listed Buildings and Conservation Areas) Act 1990;

(3) section 26AA of the Planning (Hazardous Substances) Act *1990; or*

(4) section 12 or 26 of the Energy Act 2008.

20.2 An injunction may be granted under those sections against a person whose identity is unknown to the applicant.

20.3 In this paragraph, an injunction refers to an injunction under one of those sections and 'the defendant' is the person against whom the injunction is sought.

20.4 In the claim form, the applicant must describe the defendant by reference to—

(1) a photograph;

(2) a thing belonging to or in the possession of the defendant; or

(3) any other evidence.

20.5 The description of the defendant under paragraph 20.4 must be sufficiently clear to enable the defendant to be served with the proceedings.

(The court has power under Part 6 to dispense with service or make an order permitting service by an alternative method or at an alternative place).

20.6 The application must be accompanied by a witness statement. The witness statement must state—

(1) that the applicant was unable to ascertain the defendant's identity within the time reasonably available to him;

(2) the steps taken by him to ascertain the defendant's identity;

(3) the means by which the defendant has been described in the claim form; and

(4) that the description is the best the applicant is able to provide.

20.7 When the court issues the claim form it will—

(1) fix a date for the hearing; and

(2) prepare a notice of the hearing date for each party.

20.8 The claim form must be served not less than 21 days before the hearing date.

20.9 Where the claimant serves the claim form, he must serve notice of the hearing date at the same time, unless the hearing date is specified in the claim form.

(CPR rules 3.1(2) (a) and (b) provide for the court to extend or shorten the time for compliance with any rule or practice direction, and to adjourn or bring forward a hearing.)

20.10 The court may on the hearing date—

(1) proceed to hear the case and dispose of the claim; or

(2) give case management directions.

Proceedings under the Financial Services and Markets Act 2000

21.1 This paragraph applies to proceedings in the High Court under the Financial Services and Markets Act 2000. **8PD.21**

21.2 Proceedings in the High Court under the Act (other than applications for a mandatory order) and actions for damages for breach of a statutory duty imposed by the Act shall be assigned to the Chancery Division.

21.3 Such proceedings and actions must be begun by claim form (except for applications by petition by the Financial Services Authority under section 367 of the Act).

21.4 The Financial Services Authority may make representations to the court where there is a question about the meaning of any rule or other instrument made by, or with the approval or consent of, the Financial Services Authority.

Application to quash certain orders, schemes, etc

8PD.22 **22.1** This paragraph applies where the High Court has jurisdiction under any enactment, on the application of any person to quash or prohibit any—

(a) order, scheme, certificate or plan of;
(b) amendment or approval of a plan of;
(c) decision of;
(d) action on the part of,

a Minister or government department.

22.2 The jurisdiction shall be exercisable by a single judge of the Queen's Bench Division.

22.3 The claim form must be filed at the Administrative Court and served within the time limited by the relevant enactment for making the application. Practice Direction 54D (Administrative Court (Venue)) applies to applications under this paragraph.

22.4 Subject to paragraph 22.6, the claim form must be served on the appropriate Minister or government department and on the person indicated in the following table.

If the application relates to— (i) a compulsory purchase order made by an authority other than the appropriate Minister or government department; or (ii) a clearance order under the Housing Act 1985	The authority that made the order.
If the application relates to a scheme or order— (i) to which Section 2 of the Highways Act 1980 applies; and (ii) which was made by an authority other than the Secretary of State	The authority that made the scheme or order.
If the application relates to a structure plan, local plan or other development plan within the meaning of the *Town and Country Planning Act 1990*	The local planning authority who prepared the plan.

If the application relates to any decision or order, or any action on the part of a Minister of the Crown to which— (i) section 21 of the Land Compensation Act 1961; or (ii) section 288 of the Town and Country Planning Act 1990, applies	(a) The authority directly concerned with such decision, order or action; or (b) if that authority is the applicant, on every person who would, if he were aggrieved by the decision, order or action, be entitled to apply to the High Court under section 21 of the Land Compensation Act or section 288 of the Town and Country Planning Act, as the case may be.
If the application relates to a scheme to which Schedule 32 of the Local Government, Planning and Land Act 1980 applies	The body which adopted the scheme.

22.5 In paragraph 22.4, 'the appropriate Minister or government department' means the Minister of the Crown or government department—

(1) by whom the order, scheme, certificate, plan, amendment, approval or decision in question was or may be made, authorised, confirmed, approved or given;

(2) on whose part the action in question was or may be taken.

22.6 Where the application relates to an order made under the Road Traffic Regulation Act 1984, the claim form must be served

(1) if the order was made by a Minister of the Crown, on that Minister;

(2) if the order was made by a local authority with the consent, or following a direction, of a Minister of the Crown, on that authority and also on that Minister;

(3) in any other case, on the local authority by whom the order was made.

22.7 Evidence at the hearing of an application under this paragraph is by witness statement.

22.8 The applicant must—

(1) file a witness statement in support of the application in the Administrative Court within 14 days after service of the claim form; and

(2) serve a copy of the witness statement and of any exhibit on the respondent at the time of filing.

22.9 The respondent must—

(1) file any witness statement in opposition to the application in the Administrative Court within 21 days after service on him of the applicant's witness statement; and

(2) serve a copy of his witness statement and of any exhibit on the applicant at the time of filing.

22.10 A party must, when filing a witness statement, file a further copy of the witness statement, including exhibits, for the use of the court.

22.11 Unless the court otherwise orders, the application will not be heard earlier than 14 days after the time for filing a witness statement by the respondent has expired.

PART 9

RESPONDING TO PARTICULARS OF CLAIM—GENERAL

Contents 9.0.1

Editorial introduction

The two rules in this very short Part are general and do no more than foreshadow procedures found in five other Parts of the CPR. They are Pt 10 (Acknowledgment of Service), Pt 11 (Disputing the Court's Jurisdiction), Pt 12 (Default Judgment), Pt 14 (Admissions) and Pt 15 (Defence and Reply). Which one these five other Parts becomes relevant to the particular case depends on the choices made by the defendant. 9.0.2

There has always been a default procedure in the High Courts and county courts. Default judgment is now governed by Pt 12 and, broadly speaking, if the defendant chooses to ignore the proceedings, the claimant can obtain judgment in default.

Essentially, the procedure for responding to the service of process under the CPR is based on the former RSC but incorporates some features previously found only in the CCR.

The rules contained in Pt 7 (How to start proceedings—The Claim Form) have the effect of injecting a degree of urgency into the civil process. The rules designed for the purpose of dictating how a defendant should respond to a claim form keep up the momentum. The various routes which the defendant may take, and which are briefly outlined in this Part, are foreshadowed in r.7.8 which states that when particulars of claim are served on a defendant they must be served with a form for defending the claim, a form for admitting the claim and a form for acknowledging service. (See further, Pt 7 and commentary thereon).

Related sources 9.0.3

- Part 7 (How to Start Proceedings—the claim form)
- Part 8 (Alternative Procedure for Claims)
- Part 10 (Acknowledgment of Service)
- Part 11 (Disputing the Court's Jurisdiction)
- Part 12 (Default Judgment)
- Part 14 (Admissions)
- Part 15 (Defence and Reply)

Forms

None—but see generally Part 4. 9.0.4

Scope of this Part

9.1—(1) This Part sets out how a defendant may respond to particulars of claim. 9.1

(2) Where the defendant receives a claim form which states that particulars of claim are to follow, he need not respond to the claim until the particulars of claim have been served on him.

"Claim form"

The claim form is the form of originating process (see Pt 7). Note that Pt 9 does *not* require a response to the claim form as such. The defendant must respond to the "particulars of claim". The particulars of claim can be indorsed on the claim form, contained in a separate document served with the claim form or separately later. Rule 9.1(2) applies where the particulars of claim are served separately: the defendant need not respond to the claim form but must respond to the particulars of claim. 9.1.1

Irregular default judgment

9.1.2 Unfortunately, r.9.1(2) is still not as widely known as it should be. A claimant who has not served Particulars of Claim is in error in entering judgment because the defendant has not acknowledged the claim form. The defendant would have an unanswerable application to set aside such a default judgment (with costs) under r.13.2.

Defence, admission or acknowledgment of service

9.2 **9.2 When particulars of claim are served on a defendant, the defendant may—**

(a) file or serve an admission in accordance with Part 14;

(b) file a defence in accordance with Part 15,

(or do both, if he admits only part of the claim); or

(c) file an acknowledgment of service in accordance with Part 10.

(Paragraph 10.6 of the Practice Direction to Part 16 contains provision about the content of the admission, defence or acknowledgment of service).

Effect of rule

9.2.1 If the defendant admits the claim he must, as r.9.2(a) provides, file *or* serve an admission in accordance with Pt 14. Note the use of the word "or". Thus the defendant can either file the admission with the court or serve it on the claimant: he is not required to do both. See further, Pt 14 and commentary thereon. The defendant should also make an appropriate admission where part of the claim is admitted.

If the defendant wishes to defend (in whole or in part) he has a choice: he can file a defence within 14 days (see r.15.4 and Pt 15 generally) or he can acknowledge service within 14 days (see r.10.3 and Pt 10 generally). If the defendant adopts the latter course and files an acknowledgment of service he must serve his defence later: the period is 28 days after service of the particulars of claim (see r.15.4(1)(b)).

Consequences of not responding

9.2.2 If the defendant does none of the things required by r.9.2 the claimant can proceed to obtain a default judgment (see Pt 12).

Electronic communication and filing of documents

9.2.3 For special provisions dealing with the filing by electronic means, in particular circumstances, of documents to which Pt 9 applies, see Practice Direction—Electronic Communication and Filing of Documents (para.5BPD.1 above), Practice Direction—Production Centre (para.7CPD.1 above), and Practice Direction—Money Claim Online (para.7EPD.1 above).

Commercial Court

9.2.4 It is always necessary to file an acknowledgement of service in the Commercial Court: r.58.6(1).

Service Abroad

9.2.5 Where the claim form is served out of the jurisdiction, see r.6.21(4) and r.6.22.

PART 10

ACKNOWLEDGMENT OF SERVICE

Contents

Editorial introduction

All procedural codes have to have a machinery for requiring a defendant to respond to service of process and signal his intentions. However, the defendant is not required to acknowledge the claim form as such. Rather, the defendant has to acknowledge the "particulars of claim" (which can be on the claim form, served separately either with the claim form or subsequently). Secondly, the defendant can choose to omit the acknowledgment of service stage altogether by filing an admission in accordance with Pt 14 or a defence in accordance with Pt 15 (see r.9.2). 10.0.2

Related sources

- Part 10 is supplemented by a Practice Direction (Acknowledgment of Service): see para.10PD.1. 10.0.3
- Rule 6.5 (Address for Service)
- Rule 9.2 (Defence, admission or acknowledgment of service)
- Part 11 (Disputing the Court's Jurisdiction)
- Part 12 (Default Judgment)
- Rule 12.2 (Claims in which default judgment may be obtained)
- Part 14 (Admissions)
- Part 15 (Defence)
- Part 24 (Summary Judgment) (note in particular r.24.4—claimant may not apply for summary judgment until defendant has filed acknowledgment of service or defence)
- Rule 25.2(2)(c) (defendant may not apply for interim remedy until he has filed an acknowledgment of service)

Forms

For form of Acknowledgment of Service see Practice Direction at para.10PD.2 and list of forms at para.48PD.15. 10.0.4

Acknowledgment of service

10.1—(1) This Part deals with the procedure for filing an acknowledgment of service. 10.1

(2) Where the claimant uses the procedure set out in Part 8 (*alternative procedure for claims*) this Part applies subject to the modifications set out in rule 8.3.

(3) A defendant may file an acknowledgment of service if—

(a) he is unable to file a defence within the period specified in rule 15.4; or

(b) he wishes to dispute the court's jurisdiction.

(Part 11 sets out the procedure for disputing the court's jurisdiction).

"Filing"

10.1.1 Means delivering, by post or otherwise, to the court office. The defendant delivers the acknowledgment of service to the court office; the court office notifies the claimant (see r.10.4). Rule 5PD.6 (5.3(1)) provides that a document may be filed at court by fax.

"a form for acknowledging service"

10.1.2 See r.7.8(c): the form must be served by the claimant with the particulars of claim. See also the list of forms at para.48PD.15.

"alternative procedure for claims"

10.1.3 The "alternative procedure" is governed by Pt 8. In such cases Pt 10 applies subject to the modifications in r.8.3.

"defendant ... unable to file a defence within the period specified"

10.1.4 A defendant must respond to service of the particulars of claim in accordance with r.9.2. One of the three choices given to the defendant by r.9.2 is to "file an acknowledgment of service in accordance with Part 10". Rule 10.1(3)(a) by the use of the words "unable to file a defence within the period specified in r.15.4" clearly implies that a defendant who is able to file a defence within the period specified should do so (in which case no acknowledgment of service is required). The period for filing a defence is 14 days after service of the particulars of claim or 28 days after service of the particulars of claim if the defendant files an acknowledgment of service within 14 days after service of the particulars of claim (see rr.15.4 and 10.3). Thus, a defendant who does acknowledge service has twice as long to file a defence as a defendant who chooses to file a defence without first filing an acknowledgment. The CPR contain no incentives to encourage a defendant to file a defence within the shorter period rather than the acknowledgment of service. However, a defendant who is merely playing for time and who has no defence can be immediately subjected to an application for summary judgment under Pt 24 as soon as he has filed an acknowledgment of service (see r.24.4 and Pt 24 generally). If a claimant applies for summary judgment against a defendant who has not yet filed a defence that defendant need not do so before the hearing of the application (r.24.4(2)). This is significant in that the court cannot proceed to allocate a case to a track in accordance with Pt 26 (Case Management—Preliminary Stage) so that if the claimant obtains summary judgment the case concludes without having ever become subject to the costs limitations of the small-claims track or the fast-track. (Costs would be governed by Pt 45).

Summary judgment

10.1.5 See above note and Pt 24.

Default judgment

10.1.6 See Pt 12. Basically, a claimant has the opportunity to obtain a default judgment at two distinct stages. First, if the defendant does not file an acknowledgment of service or otherwise respond in accordance with r.9.2. Secondly, if the defendant does file an acknowledgment of service but then fails to file a defence within the specified period.

"dispute the court's jurisdiction"

10.1.7 This important topic is in Pt 11. A defendant who wishes to dispute the jurisdiction of the court does not submit to the jurisdiction and thereby lose the opportunity to do so merely by acknowledging service (contrast if he served a defence). Indeed, as r.10.1(3) makes clear, a defendant who does wish to dispute jurisdiction must file an acknowledgment of service. He then proceeds in accordance with Pt 11.

Consequence of not filing an acknowledgment of service

10.2 **10.2 If—**

(a) a defendant fails to file an acknowledgment of service within the period specified in rule 10.3; and

(b) *does not within* that period file a defence in accordance with Part 15 or serve or file an admission in accordance with Part 14,

the claimant may obtain default judgment if Part 12 allows it.

"default judgment"

See note under r.10.1 and Pt 12 generally. If the defendant does not file an acknowledgment of service within the specified period or otherwise respond as mentioned in r.10.2(b), a default judgment is the usual consequence. However, there is nothing to prevent a defendant filing a late acknowledgment of service if the claimant has not entered a default judgment in the interim. It is also apparent that the court has power to extend the time for filing an acknowledgement of service after the time provided for in the Rules has expired (*ESR Insurance Services Ltd v Clemons* [2008] EWHC 2023 (Comm). 10.2.1

The period for filing an acknowledgment of service[1]

10.3—(1) The general rule is that the period for filing an acknowledgment of service is— 10.3

- **(a) where the defendant is served with a claim form which states that particulars of claim are to follow, 14 days after service of the particulars of claim; and**
- **(b) in any other case, 14 days after service of the claim form.**

(2) The general rule is subject to the following rules—

- **(a) rule 6.35 (which specifies how the period for filing an acknowledgment of service is calculated where the claim form is served out of the jurisdiction under rule 6.32 or 6.33);**
- **(b) rule 6.12(3) (which requires the court to specify the period for responding to the particulars of claim when it makes an order under that rule); and**
- **(c) rule 6.37(5) (which requires the court to specify the period within which the defendant may file an acknowledgment of service calculated by reference to Practice Direction B supplementing Part 6 when it makes an order giving permission to serve a claim form out of the jurisdiction.**

"general rule"

The particulars of claim can be indorsed on the claim form, or contained in a separate document served with or subsequently to the claim form. As the general rule in r.10.3 makes clear, therefore, the defendant is required to acknowledge service of the particulars of claim. He is not required to respond to service of the claim form if it states that the particulars of claim are to follow (see r.10.3(1)(a) and compare r.10.3(1)(b)). 10.3.1

CPR Pt 6

Acknowledgment of service of, and filing a defence to, process out of the jurisdiction is governed by CPR rr.6.35 and 6.36(5). The effect of the rule is considered in the note to r.6.35. 10.3.2

"Rule 6.12"

This rule is entitled "Service of claim form relating to a contract on an agent of a principal who is out of the jurisdiction". It is, in the cases to which it applies, an 10.3.3

---

[1] Amended by the Civil Procedure (Amendment No.2) Rules 2000 (SI 2000/940), Civil Procedure (Amendment No.3) Rules 2005 (SI 2005/2292), Civil Procedure (Amendment) Rules 2006 (SI 2006/1689) (L.6) and the Civil Procedure (Amendment) Rules 2008 (SI 2008/2178).

alternative to serving the overseas principal. See the rule and commentary therein, especially r.6.16(4).

Notice to claimant that defendant has filed an acknowledgment of service

10.4 **10.4 On receipt of an acknowledgment of service, the court must notify the claimant in writing.**

Effect of rule

10.4.1 The responsibility for telling the claimant that the defendant has acknowledged service is placed on the court. The court's duty arises "on receipt of an acknowledgment of service". It is the defendant's duty to file the acknowledgment. "Filing" is defined in r.2.3 and means "delivering it, by post or otherwise, to the court office". When sent by post, the date of filing is the date on which it is received by the office (and not the date of posting or a fixed number of days after that). A defendant who sends an acknowledgment by post is unlikely to be able to call in aid the provisions of s.7 of the Interpretation Act 1978 as this refers to "service" of documents and not to "filing". The risk of loss or delay in the post lies entirely upon the defendant using this mode of acknowledging service. The duty of the court arises "on receipt".

Contents of acknowledgment of service[1]

10.5 **10.5 An acknowledgment of service must—**

(a) be signed by the defendant or his legal representative; and

(b) include the defendant's address for service.

(Rule 6.23 provides that an address for service must be within the jurisdiction.)

(Rule 19.8A modifies this Part where a notice of claim is served under that rule to bind a person not a party to the claim).

Form of acknowledgment

10.5.1 See para.C9–001.

"must ... be signed by the defendant or his legal representative"

10.5.2 See further the Practice Direction at para.10PD.4. Rule 10.5(a) is clear and mandatory. The acknowledgment of service can be signed by the defendant being sued or his "legal representative" (a term defined in r.2.3—"a barrister or a solicitor, solicitor's employee or other authorised litigator (as defined in the Courts and Legal Services Act1990")). Thus it is *not* a compliance with r.10.5(a) if the form is signed by, e.g. the defendant's accountant, estate agent, debt collector, probation officer or anyone else not within the definition.

A form of acknowledgment purporting to be signed otherwise than in accordance with r.10.5(a) is irregular and should not be accepted by the court. The court should return it and insist upon compliance with the rule.

Claim against partnership

10.5.2.1 The amendment to the Practice Direction at para.4.4 makes new provisions for the signing of the Acknowledgment of Service where the claim is made against a partnership (Civil Procedure (Amendment) Rules 2006 (SI 2006/1689)—came into force October 2, 2006).

"must ... include the defendant's address for service"

10.5.3 The note in brackets immediately after r.10.5 is a reminder that an address for service must be within the United Kingdom. See generally r.6.23. Where a solicitor is act-

[1] Amended by the Civil Procedure (Amendment) Rules 2001 (SI 2001/256).

ing for the defendant, the address for service will be the business address of the solicitor.

Formal requirements

Rule 10.5 clearly states the only two mandatory formal requirements of an acknowledgment of service. As noted above, the court must insist on strict compliance and return a purported acknowledgment which does not comply with the rule. See further the Practice Direction at para.10PD.1. Thus, for example, if a defendant does not include an address for service within the United Kingdom (see 10.5.3) the court will not accept the acknowledgement. **10.5.4**

If the court is forced to return a purported acknowledgment which is irregular, the claimant can enter a default judgment upon expiry of the specified period (see r.10.2) if no valid acknowledgment is received by the court before then.

PRACTICE DIRECTION—ACKNOWLEDGMENT OF SERVICE

This Practice Direction supplements CPR Part 10

Responding to the claim

10PD.1 **1.1** Part 9 sets out how a defendant may respond to a claim.

1.2 Part 10 sets out the provisions for acknowledging service (but see rule 8.3 for information about acknowledging service of a claim under the Part 8 procedure).

The Form of Acknowledgment of Service

10PD.2 **2.** A defendant who wishes to acknowledge service of a claim should do so by using form **N9**.

Address for Service

10PD.3 **3.1** The defendant must include in the acknowledgment of service an address for the service of documents.[1]

3.2 Where the defendant is represented by a legal representative [2] and the legal representative has signed the acknowledgment of service form, the address must be the legal representative's business address; otherwise the address for service that is given should be as set out in rule 6.23.

Signing the Acknowledgment of Service

10PD.4 **4.1** An acknowledgment of service must be signed by the defendant or by his legal representative.

4.2 Where the defendant is a company or other corporation, a person holding a senior position in the company or corporation may sign the acknowledgment of service on the defendant's behalf, but must state the position he holds.

4.3 Each of the following persons is a person holding a senior position:

(1) in respect of a registered company or corporation, a director, the treasurer, secretary, chief executive, manager or other officer of the company or corporation, and

(2) in respect of a corporation which is not a registered company, in addition to those persons set out in (1), the mayor, chairman, president, town clerk or similar officer of the corporation.

4.4 Where a claim is brought against a partnership—

(1) service must be acknowledged in the name of the partnership on behalf of all persons who were partners at the time when the cause of action accrued; and

(2) the acknowledgment of service may be signed by any of those partners, or by any person authorised by any of those partners to sign it.

4.5 Children and protected parties may acknowledge service only by their litigation friend or his legal representative unless the court otherwise orders.[3]

---

[1] See rule 6.23.

[2] See rule 2.3 for the definition of legal representative.

[3] See Part 21.

General

5.1 The defendant's name should be set out in full on the acknowledgment of service. **10PD.5**

5.2 Where the defendant's name has been incorrectly set out in the claim form, it should be correctly set out on the acknowledgment of service followed by the words "described as" and the incorrect name.

5.3 If two or more defendants to a claim acknowledge service of a claim through the same legal representative at the same time, only one acknowledgment of service need be used.

5.4 An acknowledgment of service may be amended or withdrawn only with the permission of the court.

5.5 An application for permission under paragraph 5.4 must be made in accordance with Part 23 and supported by evidence.

(Paragraph 8.2 of Practice Direction A supplementing Part 6 contains provisions about service by the court on the claimant of any notice of funding filed with an acknowledgment of service.)

PART 11

DISPUTING THE COURT'S JURISDICTION

Contents

Editorial introduction

11.0.2 Part 11 is short and simple, containing just one rule prescribing the procedure for disputing the court's jurisdiction. Though short, it is eminently sensible to have this important topic in this readily identifiable rule rather than tucked away in a rule primarily dealing with a different matter altogether, as was formerly the case.

Part 11 is derived from RSC O.12, r.8.

Practice Direction

11.0.3 This Part is not supplemented by a Practice Direction.

Procedure for disputing the court's jurisdiction[1]

11.1 **11—(1) A defendant who wishes to—**

(a) dispute the court's jurisdiction to try the claim; or

(b) argue that the court should not exercise its jurisdiction,

may apply to the court for an order declaring that it has no such jurisdiction or should not exercise any jurisdiction which it may have.

(2) A defendant who wishes to make such an application must first file an acknowledgment of service in accordance with Part 10.

(3) A defendant who files an acknowledgment of service does not, by doing so, lose any right that he may have to dispute the court's jurisdiction.

(4) An application under this rule must—

(a) be made within 14 days after filing an acknowledgment of service; and

(b) be supported by evidence.

(5) If the defendant—

(a) files an acknowledgment of service; and

(b) does not make such an application within the period for specified in paragraph (4),

he is to be treated as having accepted that the court has jurisdiction to try the claim.

(6) An order containing a declaration that the court has no jurisdiction or will not exercise its jurisdiction may also make further provision including—

(a) setting aside the claim form;

(b) setting aside service of the claim form;

(c) discharging any order made before the claim was commenced or before the claim form was served; and

(d) staying[GL] the proceedings.

---

[1] Amended by Civil Procedure (Amendment No.5) Rules 2001 (SI 2001/4015).

(7) If on an application under this rule the court does not make a declaration—

(a) the acknowledgment of service shall cease to have effect;

(b) the defendant may file a further acknowledgment of service within 14 days or such other period as the court may direct; and

(c) the court shall give directions as to the filing and service of the defence in a claim under Part 7 or the filing of evidence in a claim under Part 8 in the event that a further acknowledgment of service is filed.

(8) If the defendant files a further acknowledgment of service in accordance with paragraph (7)(b) he shall be treated as having accepted that the court has jurisdiction to try the claim.

(9) If a defendant makes an application under this rule, he must file and serve his written evidence in support with the application notice, but he need not before the hearing of the application file—

(a) in a Part 7 claim, a defence; or

(b) in a Part 8 claim, any other written evidence.

Effect of Part 11

Although most obviously of relevance to service out of the jurisdiction and applications to stay proceedings with an extraterritorial element, the procedure is available in all cases where the court's jurisdiction is challenged or its exercise opposed, and where a defendant has filed an acknowledgment of service but not made an application under r.11(1) within 10 days he will be treated as having accepted the courts jurisdiction to try the claim even if he has made an application to set aside an extension of time for service of a calim form before filign an acknowledgment of source: *Hoddinott v Persimmon Homes (Wessex) Ltd* [2007] EWCA Civ 1203; [2008] 1 W.L.R. 806. This includes the taking of jurisdictional points in public law proceedings: *Shah v Immigration Appeal Tribunal* [2004] EWCA Civ 1665; *The Times*, December 9, 2004. Where a jurisdiction clause specifies a specific place for proceedings, the term operates to the exclusion of other places within the jurisdiction, *Snookes v Jani-King (GB) Ltd* [2006] EWHC 289 (QB); [2006] I.L.Pr. 19. The High Court has a universal and unrestricted jurisdiction to decide the existence and limits of its own jurisdiction (*Canada Trust Co v Stolzenberg* [1997] 1 W.L.R. 1582; [1997] 4 All E.R. 983, CA). **11.1.1**

A defendant does not submit to the jurisdiction of the court by reason only of having acknowledged service of the proceedings for the purpose of disputing the court's jurisdiction to try the claim or by arguing that the court should not exercise its jurisdiction (e.g. on the grounds that the dispute should be submitted to arbitration). There is no submission to the jurisdiction in the time for challenge provided under r.11(4) unless the conduct is wholly unequivocal. Therefore there is no submission where the purpose of appearance is to challenge a freezing order (*SMAY Investments Ltd v Sachdev* [2003] EWHC 474 (Ch); [2003] 1 W.L.R. 1973)

However it is inconsistent with an intention to challenge the jurisdiction that a defendant should seek an extension of time for his defence, advance a defence on the merits in reliance of a purported settlement and threaten to strike out the claim if the claimant refuses to discontinue it, *Global Multimedia International Ltd v ARA Media Services [2006] EWHC 3107(Ch)*; [2007] 1 All E.R. (Comm) 1160. The rule is strict: the application must be promptly made and be supported by evidence (r.11(4)). There is, however, power to extend time for compliance: see *Sawyer v Atari Interactive Inc* [2005] EWHC 2351 (Ch); [2006] I.L.Pr. 8, paras 42–48. A request by a defendant for an extension of time for service of a defence cannot be construed as also being a request for an extension of time for making an application to contest the jurisdiction. A request for an extension of time for service of a defence is capable of amounting to a submission to the jurisdiction. Where waiver by conduct is asserted the question is whether a reasonable person in the shoes of the claimant would have understood the defendant's conduct as waiving any irregularity as to service. Furthermore, r.11(5) carries with it a presumption of waiver, *Hoddinott v Persimmon Homes (Wessex) Ltd, The Times*, December 28, 2007. A defendant cannot rely upon r.3.4 to avoid the Part II regime: *Burns-Anderson Independent Network Plc v Wheeler* [2005] EWHC 575. If the application is successful the court will grant a declaration (see r.11(6)); if the application is not successful the acknowledgment of service ceases to have effect but the defendant may file a further acknowledgment which does then amount to a submission to the jurisdiction (see r.11(7) and (8)). Not every issue of jurisdiction has to be disposed of at this stage and the court may postpone a question of jurisdiction to a later stage where it is convenient to do so; as for instance, where the justiciability of an issue may be disputed (*Kuwait Airways Corp v Iraqi Airways Co* [1995] 1 W.L.R. 1147; [1995] 3 All E.R. 694, HL). Although not expressly stated in Part 11, the relief granted by the court may relate to only part of the case (*Kuwait Airways Corp* above).

Applications are governed by Pt 23 and will normally be decided on the written evidence of the parties, although the court does have power to allow cross-examination of a signatory of written evidence, to order disclosure and further information (*Bank of Credit and Commerce International SA v Al Kaylain* [1999] I. L.Pr. 278, Ch D). Where the challenge is against service out of the jurisdiction the general burden of proof is upon the claimant to establish the necessary elements of his case (*Canada Trust Co v Stolzenberg (No.2)* [1998] 1 W.L.R. 547, CA and *Bols Distilleries BV v Superior Yacht Services Ltd* [2006] UKPC 45; [2007] 1 W.L.R. 12; [2007] 1 Lloyd's Rep. 683; [2007] All E.R. (Comm) 461). The relevant elements are set out in the notes to r.6.17 and the rules following it. Where a defendant seeks the stay of proceedings brought as of right within the jurisdiction, the general burden of proof is upon him to make his case, except to the extent that a claimant alleges that there is a special aspect of his case that takes it outside the general principles (*Spiliada Maritime Corp v Cansulex Ltd* [1987] A.C. 460; [1986] 3 All E.R. 843, see also *Konkola Copper Mines Plc v Coromin* [2006] EWCA Civ 5; [2006] I.L.Pr. 46; [2006] 1 Lloyd's Rep. 410). Where a claimant has served a defendant pursuant to permission obtained without notice, the claimant will be under the normal obligation fully to inform the court of all relevant circumstances and will be liable to have his permission set aside where there has been a breach of that duty and if the situation warrants it. For the differing approaches in a variety of circumstances, see *Albon v Naza Motor Trading* [2007] EWHC 9 (Ch); [2007] 1W.L.R. 2489; [2007] 1 Lloyd's Rep. 297.

The court has power to waive irregularities in compliance with rr.6.20 and 6.21 for "good reason" (*Golden Ocean Assurance and World Mariner Shipping SA v Martin (The Goldean Mariner)* [1990] 2 Lloyd's Rep. 215, CA; *Kuwait Oil Tanker SAR v Al Bader* [1991] 1 W.L.R. 1410, CA; and *Youell v Kara Mara Shipping Co Ltd* [2000] 2 Lloyd's Rep. 102). The exercise of discretion might involve a grant of retrospective permission (*National Justice Compania Naviera SA v Prudential Assurance Co Ltd (The Ikarian Reefer) (No.2)* [2000] 1 W.L.R. 603, 616, CA; [2002] 1 All E.R. 37, 49). Compliance with CPR r.6.19(1)(A) in relation to one cause of action among several should not have the effect that service of the proceedings is necessarily set aside. Such an omission can be cured by use of CPR r.3.10: *Bank of Tokyo-Mitsubishi Ltd v Baskan Gida Sanayi Ve Pazarlama AS* [2004] EWHC 945; [2004] I.L.Pr. 26. Failure to serve a claim form in a Contracting State or one to which the Judgments Regulation applies does not invalidate the proceedings unless successfully relied upon in a challenge to the jurisdiction. In exceptional cases the court has power to dispense with service under CPR r.6.9: *Phillips v Nussberger* [2008] UKHL 1; [2008] 1 W.L.R. 180; [2008] 1 Lloyd's Rep. 344; [2008] I.L.Pr. 21; *Olafsson v Gissurarson* [2006] EWHC 3162 (QB); [2007] 1 Lloyd's Rep. 182.

The erroneus omission of an English language claim form from an otherwise regular package of documents can be remedied under CPR r.3.10(b) in order to establish priority of seisin under the Lugano Convention.

Service under the Judgments Regulation can be effective where a claim form does not include a statement of the ground on which there is entitlement to serve out of the jurisdiction: *Harris Calnan Construction Co Ltd v Ridgewood* [2007] EWHC 2738 (TCC); [2008] I.L.Pr. 13.

Service of an untranslated document in a state to which the Service Regulation applies is not a nullity and the initial date of service will operate to the benefit of the claimant albeit that time may begin to run against the addressee only when the translation is served. It is for the national court to deal with the immediate consequences of failure to serve a translation: *Leffler v Berlin Chemie AG (C-445/03)* [2006] I.L.Pr. 6.

The view has been expressed that where the assertion of extra-territorial jurisdiction is concerned, it being important to ensure compliance with the rules, irregularities should be cured only in exceptional cases. The existence of overlapping proceedings in a foreign jurisdiction between the same or related parties (whether pending or prospective) is likely to be a particularly relevant matter which in normal circumstances must be disclosed: *Ophthalmic Innovations International (United Kingdom) Limited v Ophthalmic Innovations International Incorporated (A Company Incorporated in Delaware USA)* [2004] EWHC 2948 (Ch); [2005] I.L.Pr. 10. CPR r.3.10 should not be used retrospectively to cure a method of service which was defective under the law of the state where service was effected: *Olafsson v Gissurarson* above.

Where a default judgment has been obtained in circumstances suggestive of a claimant's failure to take common sense steps to alert a foreign defendant of proceedingswhich circumstances had lulled that defendant into thinking would not be pursued, these factors are relevant to a decision to set aside the judgment although service stands: *The Byzantio* [2004] EWHC 3067 (Comm); [2005] 1 Lloyd's Rep. 531.

When permission to serve out of the jurisdiction has been properly given, it cannot be discharged simply because circumstances have changed, unless further evidence throws a new light on what should have been a relevant consideration at the time that permission was granted (*I.S.C. Technologies v Guerin* [1992] 2 Lloyd's Rep. 430).

Rule 6.30 provides for a challenge to the jurisdiction under Pt 11 in respect of an application notice.

Where jurisdiction under the Conventions or the Judgments Regulation is challenged, it is sufficient for the Claimant to demonstrate a good arguable case that the English Courts have jurisdiction on some basis under the relevant Convention or the Judgments Regulation see *Canada Trust Co v Stolzenberg* [1998] 1 W.L.R. 547 at p.555G and *Konkola Copper Mines Plc v Coromin* above.

Where a defendant challenges the jurisdiction under Pt 11 and the claimant makes an application for summary judgment under Pt 24; although the court has power to hear the claimant's application before or concurrently with the jurisdictional challenge, the power will be exercised only in rare cases: *Speed Investments Ltd v Formula One Holdings Ltd* [2004] EWHC 1772 (Ch); [2005] 1 W.L.R. 1233.

PART 12

DEFAULT JUDGMENT

Contents

Editorial introduction

12.0.2 A default judgment is a judgment without trial and is obtained by procuring an administrative act rather than by judicial decision. A defendant who fails to file an acknowledgment of service or a defence or, having filed an acknowledgment of service then fails to file a defence, is liable to have a default judgment entered against him save in those specific cases where it is prohibited. If the claim is for a specified sum the claimant can usually enter judgment for a sum of money and no judicial decision is required. However, where the claim is for an unspecified sum the judgment is final as to liability but there will need to be a trial to decide the quantum of damages.

Related sources

12.0.3
- Practice Direction (Default Judgment), para.12PD.1
- Part 13 (Setting Aside or Varying Default Judgment)
- Part 24 (Summary Judgment)
- Practice Direction supplementing Part 26—Allocation and Case Management of Assessment of Damages and Allied Proceedings—para.26PD.1

Forms

12.0.4
- **N10** Notice that acknowledgment of service has been filed
- **N205A** Request for judgment (part of notice of issue (specified amount))
- **N205B** Request for judgment (part of notice of issue (specified amount))
- **N225** Request for judgment and reply to admission (specified amount)
- **N227** Request for judgment by default (amount to be decided by the court)
- **N254** Request for a default costs certificate (Practice Direction supplementing Pt 47, para.3.3)

Meaning of "default judgment"

12.1 **12.1 In these Rules, "default judgment" means judgment without trial where a defendant—**

(a) has failed to file an acknowledgment of service; or

(b) has failed to file a defence.

(Part 10 contains provisions about filing an acknowledgment of service and Part 15 contains provisions about filing a defence).

Scope of provision

Rule 12.1 lays down the only two situations where a default judgment can be obtained. The period for filing an acknowledgment of service is prescribed by r.10.3 (14 days after service of the claim form or service of the particulars of claim if later). The period for filing a defence is prescribed by r.15.4 (14 days after service of the particulars of claim or 28 days if the defendant has first filed an acknowledgment of service under Pt 10). If the defendant fails to do either of these things the claimant may, subject to the rules in Pt 12, enter a default judgment. 12.1.1

Claims in which default judgment may not be obtained

12.2 A claimant may not obtain a default judgment— 12.2

(a) on a claim for delivery of goods subject to an agreement regulated by the Consumer Credit Act 1974[1];

(b) where he uses the procedure set out in Part 8 (alternative procedure for claims); or

(c) in any other case where a practice direction provides that the claimant may not obtain default judgment.

Scope of provision

There is a risk of being misled by the brevity of r.12.2. See also r.12.3 (conditions to be satisfied), and r.12.10 which deals with cases where default judgment can be obtained only on application. 12.2.1

This rule prohibits obtaining default judgment on a claim for delivery of goods subject to an agreement regulated by the Consumer Credit Act (such a claim would in any event be a "fixed date claim"—see r.7.9); in cases where the claim was begun not by a claim form pursuant to Pt 7 but by the alternative procedure for claims governed by Pt 8; and in any other case pursuant to a practice direction. The Practice Direction's provisions are set out below and extend to mortgage claims and those subject to Pt 49. (See para.1.2 of the Practice Direction (at para.12PD.1) and the examples given in para.1.3.) Part 55.7(4) provides that Pt 12 does not apply to possession claims.

Conditions to be satisfied[2]

12.3—(1) The claimant may obtain judgment in default of an acknowledgment of service only if— 12.3

(a) the defendant has not filed an acknowledgment of service or a defence to the claim (or any part of the claim); and

(b) the relevant time for doing so has expired;

(2) Judgment in default of defence may be obtained only—

(a) where an acknowledgment of service has been filed but a defence has not been filed;

(b) in a counterclaim made under rule 20.4, where a defence has not been filed,

and, in either case, the relevant time limit for doing so has expired.

(Rule 20.4 makes general provision for a defendant's counter-

[1] 1974 c.39.

[2] Amended by the Civil Procedure (Amendment) Rules 2000 (SI 2000/221), the Civil Procedure (Amendment No.2) Rules 2001 (SI 2001/1388) and the Civil Procedure (Amendment) Rules 2008 (SI 2008/2178).

claim against a claimant, and rule 20.4(3) provides that Part 10 (acknowledgment of service) does not apply to a counterclaim made under that rule).

(3) The claimant may not obtain a default judgment if—

(a) the defendant has applied—

(i) to have the claimant's statement of case struck out under rule 3.4; or

(ii) for summary judgment under Part 24,

and, in either case, that application has not been disposed of;

(b) the defendant has satisfied the whole claim (including any claim for costs) on which the claimant is seeking judgment; or

(c) (i) the claimant is seeking judgment on a claim for money; and

(ii) the defendant has filed or served on the claimant an admission under rule 14.4 or 14.7 (admission of liability to pay all of the money claimed) together with a request for time to pay.

(Part 14 sets out the procedure where a defendant admits a money claim and asks for time to pay).

(Rule 6.17 provides that, where the claim form is served by the claimant, the claimant may not obtain default judgment unless a certificate of service has been filed.)";

(Article 19(1) of the Service Regulation (which has the same meaning as in rule 6.31(e)) applies in relation to judgment in default where the claim form is served in accordance with that Regulation.)

"judgment in default of an acknowledgment of service"

12.3.1 Acknowledgment of service is governed by Pt 10. The time for acknowledging service is prescribed by r.10.3 (14 days from service of the claim form or from service of the particulars of claim if later). Subject to the provisions of Pt 12 (see, in particular, r.12.4, r.12.8, r.12.10 and r.12.11), if the defendant fails to file an acknowledgment of service the claimant can enter default judgment. Under r.12.3(1) this is known as "judgment in default of an acknowledgment of service".

The procedure is now the same in the county courts as in the High Court.

Setting aside a default judgment

12.3.2 Where no solicitor is acting for the defendant and he has not given an address for service, service of the claim form must be at his usual or last known residence (see Pt 6.9(2)). Where a claim form so served is not received by the defendant, then unless he can comply with Pt 13.3(1) and can satisfy the court that he has applied promptly to set aside the judgment and that the defence has a real prospect of success or that there is some other compelling reason why a trial should be conducted, the judgment should not be set aside: per Brooke L.J. in *Akram v Adan* [2004] EWCA Civ 1601 at para.43; but see also *Godwin v Swindon BC* [2001] EWCA Civ 1478 per May L.J. at para.49. It is therefore essential that a Claimant can demonstrate full compliance with the conditions in Pt 12.3 before a default judgment can be entered.

"judgment in default of defence"

12.3.3 Judgment in default of defence has long been available but under the CPR the defendant must have filed an acknowledgment of service but then failed to field a defence within the time limit prescribed by r.15.4 (28 days from service of the particulars of claim).

"summary judgment"

Summary judgment has also long been available and is now governed by Pt 24. For the purposes of Pt 12, r.3 it is necessary to note one fundamental distinction between Pt 24 and the former rules, namely that it is now possible for a defendant as well as a claimant to apply for summary judgment. Hence r.12.3(3)(a), which prevents a claimant obtaining a default judgment where the defendant has applied for summary judgment. Summary judgment is obtained by judicial decision only upon application: if the defendant makes such an application it effectively stays the claim pending the disposal thereof. See further Pt 24 and the commentary thereon. **12.3.4**

"satisfied the whole claim (including any claim for costs)"

Rule 12.3(3)(b) is self-explanatory. If the defendant has paid the claim and costs there is now nothing to enter judgment for. For the position where the defendant has paid the claim but not the costs, see r.12.9—procedure for obtaining default judgment for costs only. **12.3.5**

"admission ... together with a request from time to pay"

Admitting a claim and requesting time to pay is now of general application under the CPR. In the High Court and in the county court, when served with the claim form the defendant will also be served with "a form for admitting the claim" in accordance with r.7.8(1). The defendant uses that form to make an admission in accordance with Pt 14 (see rr.14.4 and 14.7). Where such an admission is filed the claimant cannot obtain a default judgment. He can instead obtain judgment on the admission: see rr.14.10, 14.11 and 14.12. **12.3.6**

"certificate of service"

Proof that an opponent has been served is often important and is of particular importance when it is proposed to take a step because the other party is in default. The normal method of proof of service is by a certificate of service. Usually the claim form is served by the court but where it has been served by the claimant he must file a certificate of service. By r.6.17 the claimant cannot obtain a default judgment unless he has done so. **12.3.7**

Procedure for obtaining default judgment[1]

12.4—(1) Subject to paragraph (2), a claimant may obtain a default judgment by filing a request in the relevant practice form where the claim is for— **12.4**

(a) a specified amount of money;

(b) an amount of money to be decided by the court;

(c) delivery of goods where the claim form gives the defendant the alternative of paying their value; or

(d) any combination of these remedies.

(2) The claimant must make an application in accordance with Part 23 if he wishes to obtain a default judgment—

(a) on a claim which consists of or includes a claim for any other remedy; or

(b) where rule 12.9 or rule 12.10 so provides,

and where the defendant is an individual, the claimant must provide the defendant's date of birth (if known) in Part C of the application notice.

(3) Where a claimant—

(a) claims any other remedy in his claim form in addition to those specified in paragraph (1); but

(b) abandons that claim in his request for judgment,

[1] Amended by the Civil Procedure (Amendment) Rules 2008 (SI 2008/2178).

he may still obtain a default judgment by filing a request under paragraph (1).

(4) In civil proceedings against the Crown, as defined in rule 66.1(2), a request for a default judgment must be considered by a Master or district judge, who must in particular be satisfied that the claim form and particulars of claim have been properly served on the Crown in accordance with section 18 of the Crown Proceedings Act 1947 and rule 6.10).

"request in the relevant practice form"

12.4.1 See Forms **N205A** and **N227**. There is a different prescribed form for each of the cases described in r.12.4(1).

Scope of r.12.4(1)

12.4.2 In the types of case described—and most claims issued do fit one of these descriptions—the claimant obtains a default judgment simply by filing a request in the relevant practice form. "Request" is the name of the form now used.

"a specified amount of money"

12.4.3 The former term "liquidated sum" is replaced by "specified amount of money". Default judgment can be entered for the specified sum, plus interest pursuant to r.12.6, plus fixed costs pursuant to r.45.4. However, it is important to note that "a specified sum of money" is wider than the old term "liquidated sum". Clearly it covers a case where the claim is for a debt. However, it appears that "a specified amount of money" covers any case where the claimant puts a figure on the amount of his claim whether it is debt, damages or any other sum. If the claimant chooses to put a value on his claim in a specified sum, the claimant can request a default judgment in that sum (plus interest if claimed: see r.12.6) and fixed costs (see r.45.4). The term "specified amount of money" is used not only in r.12.4 but throughout the CPR, see, e.g. r.26.2 on automatic transfer. Claiming a specified amount of money will cause the rules for automatic transfer to the defendant's home court to apply if the claim is defended. This change in practice accords with the system in Commonwealth countries where the law is based on Roman-Dutch principles.

One example, where the new rule is proving useful in practice, is a claim for the cost of repairs arising out of a road traffic accident where no personal injury ensued. Claiming the cost of the repairs and any ancillary claim such as hire-car charges as "a specified sum of money" enables a claimant to obtain a default judgment for that sum thus avoiding a "disposal hearing" held in accordance with the Practice Direction supplementing Pt 26, para.12.8. It is the better practice to claim a specified sum in such cases.

"an amount of money to be decided by the court"

12.4.4 In a claim which is not for "a specified amount of money" (see above) the amount has to be decided by the court. Default judgment is obtained by filing a request in Form **N205B** or **N227**. The judgment is final on the issue of liability but the sum to be paid still has to be decided by the court. Directions for assessing the damages will be given when judgment is entered, see r.12.7(2)(a) and, if necessary, the case will be allocated to the appropriate track. (See generally, Pt 26 and in particular, para.26, PD12.3).

A judgment in default is conclusive on liability but damages still have to be proved and a defendant can raise any issue which is not inconsistent with the judgment. (*Lunnun v Singh (Hajar), The Times*, July [1999] C.P.L.R. 587.). See also para.12.7.5, disposal hearings.

"delivery of goods where the claim form gives the defendant the alternative of paying their value"

12.4.5 These words are in r.12.4(1)(c). Default judgment in such a case is obtained by a request in Form **N205A**; if the claim form does not give the alternative mentioned an application is required in accordance with r.12.4(2). Note that in neither case can default judgment be obtained if the goods are subject to an agreement regulated by the Consumer Credit Act 1974 (r.12.2(a)). Consequently the main value of the rule in practice is in claims in the tort of conversion.

Scope of r.12.4(2)

Rule 12.4 distinguishes between those cases where a default judgment is obtained by filing a request and those where an application is required. If the case does not fall within r.12.4(1) then an application in accordance with Pt 23 is required in order to obtain a default judgment under r.12.4(2). Also an application is required if r.12.9(1)(b) (default judgment for costs only where costs are not fixed) or r.12.10 applies. **12.4.6**

Scope of r.12.4(3)

Only claims within r.12.4(1) are susceptible to default judgment by request. If an additional remedy is claimed, the claimant can obtain default judgment if that remedy is abandoned in the request for default judgment. It has long been the practice to allow this. **12.4.7**

Defendant's date of birth

From April 6, 2006 when the last sentence in r.12.4(2) comes into force, the claimant will be required to provide the defendant's date of birth when he applies under Pt 23 for a default judgment, if he knows it. This could be of particular relevance to any direction the court might give as to service of the application or subsequent enforcement. **12.4.8**

Nature of judgment where default judgment obtained by filing a request

12.5—(1) Where the claim is for a specified sum of money, the claimant may specify in a request filed under rule 12.4(1)— **12.5**

(a) the date by which the whole of the judgment debt is to be paid; or

(b) the times and rate at which it is to be paid by instalments.

(2) Except where paragraph (4) applies, a default judgment on a claim for a specified amount of money obtained on the filing of a request, will be judgment for the amount of the claim (less any payments made) and costs—

(a) to be paid by the date or at the rate specified in the request for judgment; or

(b) if none is specified, immediately.

(Interest may be included in a default judgment obtained by filing a request if the conditions set out in Rule 12.6 are satisfied.)

(Rule 45.4 provides for fixed costs on the entry of a default judgment.)

(3) Where the claim is for an unspecified amount of money a default judgment obtained on the filing of a request will be for an amount to be decided by the court and costs.

(4) Where the claim is for delivery of goods and the claim form gives the defendant the alternative of paying their value, a default judgment obtained on the filing of a request will be judgment *requiring the defendant to*—

(a) deliver the goods or (if he does not do so) pay the value of the goods as decided by the court (less any payments made); and

(b) pay costs.

(Rule 12.7 sets out the procedure for deciding the amount of a judgment or the value of the goods.)

(5) The claimant's right to enter judgment requiring the defen-

dant to deliver goods is subject to rule 40.14 (judgment in favour of certain part owners relating to the detention of goods).

Scope of provision

12.5.1 Rule 12.5 deals with the nature of the default judgment and is self-explanatory. When entering a default judgment the claimant can enter judgment for payment "immediately" (replacing the former term "forthwith"), on a specified date or by instalments, the amount and frequency of which will be decided by the claimant.

A judgment pursuant to r.12.5(3) was formerly known as "interlocutory judgment for damages to be assessed" but the modern rule used the expression judgment "for an amount to be decided by the court".

Interest

12.6 **12.6—(1) A default judgment on a claim for a specified amount of money obtained on the filing of a request may include the amount of interest claimed to the date of judgment if—**

- **(a) the particulars of claim include the details required by rule 16.4;**
- **(b) where interest is claimed under section 35A of the Supreme Court Act 1981[1] or section 69 of the County Courts Act 1984,[2] the rate is no higher than the rate of interest payable on judgment debts at the date when the claim form was issued; and**
- **(c) the claimant's request for judgment includes a calculation of the interest claimed for the period from the date up to which interest was stated to be calculated in the claim form to the date of the request for judgment.**

(2) In any case where paragraph (1) does not apply, judgment will be for an amount of interest to be decided by the court.

(Rule 12.7 sets out the procedure for deciding the amount of interest.)

Effect of rule

12.6.1 Rule 12.6 was derived from CCR O.9, r.8, but effected no change in practice for claiming interest. The rule is self-explanatory. A default judgment can include interest provided it has been claimed (see r.16.4) at a rate no higher than judgment debt rate and is calculated by r.12.6(1)(c).

Rate of interest payment on judgment debts

12.6.2 The rate is 8 per cent and has been since April 1993 (Judgment Debts (Rate of Interest) Order 1993 (SI 1993/564)).

Procedure for deciding an amount or value

12.7 **12.7—(1) This rule applies where the claimant obtains a default judgment on the filing of a request under rule 12.4(1) and judgment is for—**

- **(a) an amount of money to be decided by the court;**
- **(b) the value of goods to be decided by the court; or**
- **(c) an amount of interest to be decided by the court.**

---

[1] 1981 c.54. Section 35A was inserted by the Administration of Justice Act 1982 (c.53) s.15(1), Sch.1, Pt I.

[2] 1984 c.28. Section 69 was amended by the Courts and Legal Services Act 1990 (c.41) Sch.18, para.46.

(2) Where the court enters judgment it will—

(a) give any directions it considers appropriate; and

(b) if it considers it appropriate, allocate the case.

Scope of provision

Judgments entered pursuant to r.12.4(1) may be final both as to liability and the amount of the judgment (judgment for "a specified amount of money": see r.12.4(1)(a)) or final only as to liability leaving a further issue to be decided by the court. The latter is governed by r.12.7. The rule is helpfully straightforward. Judgment will be obtained by filing a request in Form **N227**. **12.7.1**

Directions

Rule 12.7(2)(a) enables the court to give "any directions it considers appropriate". It is good practice for solicitors, when obtaining a default judgment which will be followed by a hearing, to suggest appropriate directions in the form of a draft order. Directions will have to deal with disclosure, exchange of witness statements, expert evidence, the need for allocation and/or a case management conference, a suggested timetable for the subsequent hearing and any other matters relevant to the particular case (see further para.12.7.6, Disposal hearings and para.12.7.7, Allocation). **12.7.2**

Judgment for an amount to be decided by the court

This expression, in r.12.7, has replaced the former term "interlocutory judgment". **12.7.3**

Assessment of Damages

See now "disposal hearings". **12.7.4**

Disposal hearings

This term is used in the Practice Direction which supplements Pt 26 see PD26 paras 12.1(1) and 12.4. The term "disposal" is now described in para 12.4(1) as a hearing which will not normally last longer than 30 minutes and at which the court will not normally hear oral evidence. **12.7.5**

Although not a requirement of either the rule or the Practice Direction, it is helpful to give the court all appropriate information so that directions can be given without a hearing and the case can then proceed straight to a disposal hearing where damages can be assessed. If such information is not provided the court is unlikely to be able to give meaningful directions and may have to convene a disposal hearing to do so. The default judgment is final on the issue of liability but the "default" process plays no part in deciding the amount to be paid. This aspect of the case has to be proved (see *Lunnun v Singh (Hajar)*, *The Times*, [1999] C.P.L.R. 587 referred to above at para.12.4.4).

Allocation

It is not always necessary to allocate to a track and the case can proceed to a disposal hearing without allocation. However allocation to track is now considered to be better practice and the court will allocate the case "if it considers it appropriate" (r.12.7(2)(b)). Allocation is governed by Pt 26 and its supplementary Practice Direction. **12.7.6**

If the value of the claim is such that it would, if defended, be allocated to the small claims track, the court "will normally allocate it to the track ..." see the Practice Direction supplementing Pt 26, para.12.8 at para.26PD.12, thus keeping the case within the very limited costs regime which applies to cases on the small claims track. If the value of the claim is within the normal fast track limits (£5000 – £15000) and will be heard within a day, the court may allocate the claim to the fast track and so bring the fast track fixed trial costs into operation (see r.46.1(2)(c) and r.46.2).

Claim against more than one defendant

12.8—(1) A claimant may obtain a default judgment on request under this Part on a claim for money or a claim for delivery of goods against one of two or more defendants, and proceed with his claim against the other defendants. **12.8**

(2) Where a claimant applies for a default judgment against one of two or more defendants—

(a) if the claim can be dealt with separately from the claim against the other defendants—

(i) the court may enter a default judgment against that defendant; and

(ii) the claimant may continue the proceedings against the other defendants;

(b) if the claim cannot be dealt with separately from the claim against the other defendants—

(i) the court will not enter default judgment against that defendant; and

(ii) the court must deal with the application at the same time as it disposes of the claim against the other defendants.

(3) A claimant may not enforce against one of two or more defendants any judgment obtained under this Part for possession of land or for delivery of goods unless—

(a) he has obtained a judgment for possession or delivery (whether or not obtained under this Part) against all the defendants to the claim; or

(b) the court gives permission.

Effect of rule

12.8.1 r.12.8 helpfully gathers in one rule the practice on default judgment where the claim is against more than one defendant. In the case of joint liability, the position is covered by s.3 of the Civil Liability Contribution Act 1978 which abolishes the common law doctrine that judgment against one defendant discharges the liability of the other. Where there is several liability, the common law continues to apply to unliquidated demands: see *Blyth v Fladgate* [1891] 1 Ch. 337. Where the claim is brought in the alternative against two defendants, the Court of Appeal has held in *Pendleton & Pendleton v A.C. Westwater & Swingwear Ltd* [2001] EWCA Civ 1841 that "if the doctrine of election threatens to work injustice, it must be applied rigorously, with great care and as narrowly as may be consistent with legal principle" per Laws L.J. In *Yates v Elaby t/a United Property Management & Moss*, Nov 17, 2003, unrep., Mitting J. held that where a claim was brought in the alternative, the court not only has the power under CPR r.12.8(2)(b) not to enter default judgment against one defendant but has the duty not to do so. There seems to be no reason why the court could not debar that defendant from defending the claim so as to ensure that a late defence is not filed which might result in a new order for directions and an adjournment of the hearing.

Procedure for obtaining a default judgment for costs only

12.9 **12.9—(1) Where a claimant wishes to obtain a default judgment for costs only—**

(a) if the claim is for fixed costs, he may obtain it by filing a request in the relevant practice form;

(b) if the claim is for any other type of costs, he must make an application in accordance with Part 23.

(2) Where an application is made under this rule for costs only, judgment shall be for an amount to be decided by the court.

(Part 45 sets out when a claimant is entitled to fixed costs).

Effect of rule

12.9.1 It is common for a defendant who does not dispute liability for, say, a debt to pay the debt on being served with the claim form but to refuse to pay the costs typically because he was "going to pay anyway" or because he alleges that the proceedings were issued prematurely. A claimant who is content with payment of the debt and is prepared to write-off the costs incurred need do no more. A claimant who wishes to obtain a default judgment for costs only can do so pursuant to r.12.9. The judgment, if granted, will be "for an amount to be decided by the court". The use of this phrase invokes the procedure for deciding an amount in r.12.7.

Default judgment obtained by making an application[1]

12.10 The claimant must make an application in accordance with Part 23 where— 12.10

(a) the claim is—

(i) a claim against a child or protected party; or

(ii) a claim in tort by one spouse or civil partner against the other.

(b) the claimant wishes to obtain a default judgment where the defendant has failed to file an acknowledgment of service—

(i) against a defendant who has been served with the claim out of the jurisdiction under rule 6.32(1), 6.33(1) or 6.33(2) (service where permission of the court is not required under the Civil Jurisdiction and Judgments Act 1982) [2];

(ii) against a defendant domiciled in Scotland or Northern Ireland or in any other Convention territory or Regulation State;

(iii) against a State;

(iv) against a diplomatic agent who enjoys immunity from civil jurisdiction by virtue of the Diplomatic Privileges Act 1964 [3]; or

(v) against persons or organisations who enjoy immunity from civil jurisdiction pursuant to the provisions of the International Organisations Acts 1968 and 1981.[4]

Effect of rule

12.10.1 "Child" is defined in r.21.1(2) and is the expression which has replaced the old terms "infant" or "minor". "Protected Party" is defined in CPR r.21.1(2)(d) as a party, or an intended party, who lacks capacity to conduct the proceedings. This amendment takes effect on October 1, 2007 on the implementation of the Civil Procedure (Amendment) Rules 2007 (SI 2007/2204). These amendments are the result of the Mental Capacity Act 2005. Civil partner is now included pursuant to the Civil Partnership Act 2004 which came into force on December 5, 2005.

It has never been possible to obtain a default judgment by administrative act against either a child or a protected party, see also Pt 21—Children and Protected Parties. The court will have to consider where a defendant who is a child or protected party *needs a "litigation friend". The court will not* grant a default judgment even on an application in accordance with Pt 23 until this has been done.

---

[1] Amended by the Civil Procedure (Amendment No.2) Rules 2000 (SI 2000/940), the Civil Procedure (Amendment No.5) Rules 2001 (SI 2001/4015), Civil Procedure (Amendment) Rules 2007 (SI 2007/2204) and the Civil Procedure (Amendment) Rules 2008 (SI 2008/2178).

[2] 1982 c.27

[3] 1964 c.81.

[4] 1968 c.48; 1981 c.9.

Apart from children and protected parties, all other situations in r.12.10 are governed by specific statutory provisions. A claim in tort by one spouse against another was governed by the Law Reform (Husband and Wife) Act 1962 which obliged a court to consider a stay of proceedings between husband and wife in an action in tort. However, paragraph 4 of the Civil Procedure (Modification of Enactments) Order 1998 (SI 1998/2940) has abrogated this rule so the purpose of r.12.10(a)(ii) is not clear unless it be to protect a spouse from a malicious action. The several situations in r.12.10(b) are governed by the statutes mentioned in the rule: hence the need for an application under Pt 23 before the claimant can obtain judgment.

Rule 12.10 needs to be read in conjunction with r.12.11 and Civil Procedure (Amendment No.3) Rules 2005 in force October 1, 2005.

Supplementary provisions where applications for default judgment are made[1]

12.11 **12.11—(1) Where the claimant makes an application for a default judgment, judgment shall be such judgment as it appears to the court that the claimant is entitled to on his statement of case.**

(2) Any evidence relied on by the claimant in support of his application need not be served on a party who has failed to file an acknowledgment of service.

(3) An application for a default judgment on a claim against a child or protected party or a claim in tort between spouses or civil partners must be supported by evidence.

(4) An application for a default judgment may be made without notice if—

(a) the claim under the Civil Jurisdiction and Judgments Act 1982 or the Judgments Regulation, was served in accordance with rules 6.32(1), r.6.33(1) or r.6.33(2) as appropriate;

(b) the defendant has failed to file an acknowledgment of service; and

(c) notice does not need to be given under any other provision of these Rules.

(5) Where an application is made against a State for a default judgment where the defendant has failed to file an acknowledgment of service—

(a) the application may be made without notice, but the court hearing the application may direct that a copy of the application notice be served on the State;

(b) if the court—

(i) grants the application; or

(ii) directs that a copy of the application notice be served on the State,

the judgment or application notice (and the evidence in support) may be served out of the jurisdiction without any further order;

---

[1] Amended by the Civil Procedure (Amendment No.2) Rules 2000 (SI 2000/940), Civil Procedure (Amendment No.5) Rules 2001 (SI 2001/4015), Civil Jurisdiction and Judgments Regulations 2007 (SI 2007/1655), Civil Procedure (Amendment) Rules 2007 (SI 2007/2204) and the Civil Procedure (Amendment) Rules 2008 (SI 2008/2178).

(c) where paragraph (5)(b) permits a judgment or an application notice to be served out of the jurisdiction, the procedure for serving the judgment or the application notice is the same as for serving a claim form under Section III of Part 6 except where an alternative method of service has been agreed under section 12(6) of the State Immunity Act 1978.[1]

(Rule 23.1 defines "application notice".)

(6) For the purposes of this rule and rule 12.10—

(a) "domicile" is to be determined—

(i) in relation to a Convention territory, in accordance with sections 41 to 46 of the Civil Jurisdiction and Judgments Act 1982;

(ii) in relation to a Member State, in accordance with the Judgments Regulation and paragraphs 9 to 12 of Schedule 1 to the Civil Jurisdiction and Judgments Order 2001;

(b) "Convention territory" means the territory or territories of any Contracting State, as defined by section 1(3) of the Civil Jurisdiction and Judgments Act 1982, to which the Brussels Conventions or Lugano Convention apply;

(c) "State" has the meaning given by section 14 of the State Immunity Act 1978;

(d) "Diplomatic agent" has the meaning given by Article 1(e) of Schedule 1 to the Diplomatic Privileges Act 1964; and

(e) "the Judgments Regulation" means Council Regulation (EC) No. 44/2001 of 22nd December 2000 on jurisdiction and the recognition and enforcement of judgments in civil and commercial matters, as amended from time to time and as applied by the Agreement made on 19th October 2005 between the European Community and the Kingdom of Denmark on jurisdiction and the recognition and enforcement of judgments in civil and commercial matters.

Scope of provision

Rules 12.11(1) and 12.11(2) are of general application and are self-explanatory. **12.11.1**

Rule 12.11(3) supplements r.12.10(a): see commentary thereon. Rules 12.11(4), 12.11(5) and 12.11(6) supplement r.12.10(b).

Rules 12.11(6)(e) and (f) have been amended with effect from July 1, 2007 on the implementation of the Civil Jurisdiction and Judgment Regulations 2007 (SI 2007/1655) which in effect extend the provisions of the Civil Jurisdiction and Judgments Act 1982 *to Denmark*.

[1] 1978 c.33.

PRACTICE DIRECTION—DEFAULT JUDGMENT

12PD.1 *This Practice Direction supplements CPR Part 12*

Default judgment

1.1 A default judgment is judgment without a trial where a defendant has failed to file either:

(1) an acknowledgment of service, or
(2) a defence.

For this purpose a defence includes any document purporting to be a defence.

(See Part 10 and the practice direction which supplements it for information about the acknowledgment of service, and Parts 15 and 16 and the practice directions which supplement them for information about the defence and what it should contain.)

1.2 A claimant may not obtain a default judgment under Part 12 (notwithstanding that no acknowledgment of service or defence has been filed) if:

(1) the procedure set out in Part 8 (Alternative Procedure for Claims) is being used, or
(2) the claim is for delivery of goods subject to an agreement regulated by the Consumer Credit Act 1974, or

1.3 Other rules and practice directions provide that default judgments under Part 12 cannot be obtained in particular proceedings. Examples are:

(1) admiralty proceedings;
(2) arbitration proceedings;
(3) contentious probate proceedings;
(4) claims for provisional damages;
(5) possession claims.

Obtaining default judgment

12PD.2 **2.1** Rules 12.4(1) and 12.9(1) describe the claims in respect of which a default judgment may be obtained by filing a request in the appropriate practice form.

2.2 A default judgment on:

(1) the claims referred to in rules 12.9(1)(b) and 12.10, and
(2) claims other than those described in rule 12.4(1),

can only be obtained if an application for default judgment is made and cannot be obtained by filing a request.

2.3 The following are some of the types of claim which require an application for a default judgment:

(1) against children and protected parties[1],
(2) for costs (other than fixed costs) only[2],
(3) by one spouse or civil partner against the other[3] on a claim in tort[4],

[1] See rule 12.10(a)(i).
[2] See rule 12.9(b).
[3] See rule 12.10(a)(ii).
[4] Tort may be defined as an act or a failure to do an act which causes harm or dam-

(4) for delivery up of goods where the defendant will not be allowed the alternative of paying their value; and
(5) omitted;
(6) against persons or organisations who enjoy immunity from civil jurisdiction under the provisions of the International Organisations Acts 1968 and 1981.

Default judgment by request

3.1 Requests for default judgment: **12PD.3**
(1) in respect of a claim for a specified amount of money or for the delivery of goods where the defendant will be given the alternative of paying a specified sum representing their value, or for fixed costs only, must be in Form **N205A** or **N225**, and
(2) in respect of a claim where an amount of money (including an amount representing the value of goods) is to be decided by the court, must be in Form **N205B** or **N227**.

3.2 The forms require the claimant to provide the date of birth (if known) of the defendant where the defendant is an individual.

Evidence

4.1 Both on a request and on an application for default judgment **12PD.4** the court must be satisfied that:
(1) the particulars of claim have been served on the defendant (a certificate of service on the court file will be sufficient evidence),
(2) either the defendant has not filed an acknowledgment of service or has not filed a defence and that in either case the relevant period for doing so has expired,
(3) the defendant has not satisfied the claim, and
(4) the defendant has not returned an admission to the claimant under rule 14.4 or filed an admission with the court under rule 14.6.

4.2 On an application against a child or protected party[1]:
(1) a litigation friend[2] to act on behalf of the child or protected party must be appointed by the court before judgment can be obtained, and
(2) the claimant must satisfy the court by evidence that he is entitled to the judgment claimed.

4.3 On an application where the defendant was served with the claim either:
(1) *outside* the jurisdiction[3] without leave under the Civil Jurisdiction and Judgments Act 1982, or the Judgments Regulation, or

---

age to another person and which gives the other person a right to claim compensation without having to rely on a contract with the person who caused the harm or damage.

[1] As defined in rule 21.1(2).

[2] As defined in the practice direction which supplements Part 21.

[3] As defined in rule 2.3.

(2) within the jurisdiction but when domiciled [1] in Scotland or Northern Ireland or in any other Convention territory,[2] or Member State

and the defendant has not acknowledged service, the evidence must establish that:

(a) the claim is one that the court has power to hear and decide,

(b) no other court has exclusive jurisdiction under the Act or Judgments Regulation to hear and decide the claim, and

(c) the claim has been properly served in accordance with Article 20 of Schedule 1 or 3C to the Act, paragraph 15 of Schedule 4 to the Act, or Article 26 of the Judgments Regulation.

4.4 On an application against a State[3] the evidence must:

(1) set out the grounds of the application,

(2) establish the facts proving that the State is excepted from the immunity conferred by section 1 of the State Immunity Act 1978,

(3) establish that the claim was sent through the Foreign and Commonwealth Office to the Ministry of Foreign Affairs of the State or, where the State has agreed to another form of service, that the claim was served in the manner agreed; and

(4) establish that the time for acknowledging service, (which is extended to two months by section 12(2) of the Act when the claim is sent through the Foreign and Commonwealth Office to the Ministry of Foreign Affairs of the State) has expired.

(See rule 40.8 for when default judgment against a State takes effect.)

4.5 Evidence in support of an application referred to in paragraphs 4.3 and 4.4 above must be by affidavit.

4.6 On an application for judgment for delivery up of goods where the defendant will not be given the alternative of paying their value, the evidence must identify the goods and state where the claimant believes the goods to be situated and why their specific delivery up is sought.

12PD.4.1 *Note* — Regulation State now means a Member State: see reg.2(3) of the Civil Jurisdiction and Judgment Regulations 2007 (SI 2007/1655).

General

12PD.5 **5.1** On all applications to which this practice direction applies, other than those referred to in paragraphs 4.3 and 4.4 above,[4] notice should be given in accordance with Part 23.

5.2 Where default judgment is given on a claim for a sum of money

[1] As determined in accordance with the provisions of ss.41 to 46 of the Civil Jurisdiction and Judgments Act 1982.

[2] Means the territory of a Contracting State as defined in s.1(3) of the Civil Jurisdiction and Judgments Act 1982.

[3] As defined in s.14 of the State Immunity Act 1978.

[4] See rule 12.11(4) and (5).

expressed in a foreign currency, the judgment should be for the amount of the foreign currency with the addition of "or the Sterling equivalent at the time of payment".

PART 13

SETTING ASIDE OR VARYING DEFAULT JUDGMENT

Contents

Editorial introduction

13.0.2 A default judgment is invariably obtained by an administrative act (see Pt 12). This puts default judgments in a different category from summary judgment (see Pt 24) or a judgment following a trial. These latter judgments cannot be "set aside"; but they maybe reviewed on appeal. In contrast a default judgment will not usually have been subject to judicial scrutiny and there is no provision to apply for leave to appeal. Hence the need for a procedure to apply to set aside or vary a default judgment.

Part 13 is limited in scope to the setting aside (or varying) of a default judgment. Part 13 has not effected any changes in practice under the old rules.

Related sources

13.0.3

- Part 12 (Default Judgment)
- Part 23 (General Rules for Applications)
- Rule 39.3(3) (Setting aside on application of party who failed to attend)
- Rule 40.9 (Application to set aside by a person who is not a party but who is directly affected by judgment)
- See CCR O.22, r.10 (Varying the rate at which a judgment debt is paid)

Forms

13.0.4 None are currently prescribed. See list of forms at para.48PD.15.

Practice Direction

13.0.5 Part 13 is not supplemented by a practice direction.

Scope of this Part

13.1 **13.1 The rules in this Part set out the procedure for setting aside or varying judgment entered under Part 12 (default judgment).**

(CCR Order 22, r.10 sets out the procedure for varying the rate at which a judgment debt must be paid.)

Effect of rule

13.1.1 Part 13 is not a comprehensive code for setting aside judgments generally but is confined to the setting aside of a default judgment which has been obtained pursuant to Pt 12.

CCR O.22, r.10 is re-enacted in Sch.2 to the CPR. It deals with an application to vary the rate at which a judgment debt must be paid on the application of either the judgment creditor or the judgment debtor.

Cases where the court must set aside judgment entered under Part 12

13.2 **13.2 The court must set aside[GL] a judgment entered under Part 12 if judgment was wrongly entered because—**

(a) in the case of a judgment in default of an acknowledgment of service, any of the conditions in rule 12.3(1) and 12.3(3) was not satisfied;

(b) in the case of a judgment in default of a defence, any of the conditions in rule 12.3(2) and 12.3(3) was not satisfied; or

(c) the whole of the claim was satisfied before judgment was entered.

Effect of rule

Rule 13.2 refers to judgment being "wrongly entered", i.e. the judgment is irregular. **13.2.1** The court must set aside the wrongly entered judgment in the three situations specified in the rule

A default judgment must be set aside irrespective of the defendant's lack of prospects of success if the claim has not been served (*Credit Agricole Indosuez v Unicof Ltd* [2003] EWHC 77 (Comm); [2003] All E.R., and *Shiblaq v Sadikoglu (Application to Set Aside) (No.2)* [2004] EWHC 1890 (Jul) (Comm.) ("In the absence of proof of valid service, a claimant was not entitled to judgment in default under CPR 12.3")). But see *Akram v Adam* [2004] EWCA Civ 1601; *The Times*, December 29, 2004: as long as service is effected in accordance with the CPR, it is not a contravention of Art 6 ECHR if the defendant never in fact received the proceedings.

Judgment set aside on grounds of invalid service

The case of *Olafsson v Gissurarson* [2006] EWHC 3162 (QB); [2007] 1 Lloyd's Rep. **13.2.2** 182 involved an application to set aside judgment relying on a failure to serve in accordance with the law of Iceland, the country of service. The case was unusual for a number of reasons. Service had been made by the British Consular authorities in Iceland, and there was no dispute that the defendant had received the proceedings. The claimant's solicitors kept the defendant fully informed of the progress of the action (in libel), but the defendant chose to take no part in the process. The action progressed to trial, culminating in an assessment of damages and a permanent injunction.

Six months after the assessment of damages the defendant applied to set aside the judgment under CPR r.13.2(a), because the Consul had failed to obtain from the defendant a signed receipt on an appropriate court form of the papers being served, and this rendered service ineffective under Icelandic law. At the same hearing the claimant applied under CPR r.3.10 for relief in respect of the invalid service. Although the Master granted the claimant's application, holding that the irregularity in service ought properly to be cured by the application of CPR r.3.10, that decision was overturned on appeal by Mackay J. The judge relied a decision of the Court of Appeal, *Phillips v Nussberger* [2006] EWCA Civ 654; [2006] 1 W.L.R. 2598, CA, (which was not before the Master) where Neuberger L.J. took the view, obiter, that a claimant could not rely on CPR r.3.10 to correct a defect in service. Mackay J. held that the claimant could not rely on CPR r.3.10 in this case to remedy the failed attempt at service, and the defendant was entitled to have the judgment set aside. However, he acceded to the claimant's application for an order under Pt 6.9 dispensing with service of the claim form, with the effect of retrospectively validating service. (There was an unsuccessful appeal by the defendant against the order made under Pt 6.9 reported at [2008] EWCA Civ 152.)

Note also *Fairmays (A Firm) v Palmer* [2006] EWHC 96 (Ch): it is not open to a court, in the light of the provisions of CPR r.6.5(1), to conclude that proceedings issued for service within the jurisdiction can properly be served when, at the time of deemed service the defendant was physically out of the jurisdiction. Accordingly judgment entered in default was set aside under CPR r.13.2 because judgment had been wrongly entered.

Note that in *City & Country Properties Ltd v Kamali* [2006] EWCA Civ 1879; [2007 1 W.L.R. 1219, CA, the Court of Appeal held that, where proceedings have been issued for service within the jurisdiction, there is no requirement for the defendant to be within the jurisdiction at the time of service for service to be effective. In reaching this conclusion, the Court of Appeal disapproved the statement made by Lawrence Collins J. in *Chellaram v Chellaram (No.2)* [2002] 3 All E.R. 17 (at para.47) that:

> "it has always been, and remains, a fundamental rule of English procedure and jurisdiction that a defendant may be served with originating process within the jurisdiction only if he is present in the jurisdiction at the time of service or deemed service".

May L.J. held that this was "intrinsically" incorrect, and also wrong in that it failed to follow the Court of Appeal decision in *Rolph v Zolan* [1993] 1 W.L.R. 1305, CA, which, if not strictly binding, was "indistinguishably applicable". This decision casts doubt on whether *Fairmays* (which followed *Chellaram*)was correctly decided.

Cases where the court may set aside or vary judgment entered under Part 12[1]

13.3 **13.3—(1) In any other case, the court may set aside^{GL} or vary a judgment entered under Part 12 if—**

(a) the defendant has a real prospect of successfully defending the claim; or

(b) it appears to the court that there is some other good reason why—

(i) the judgment should be set aside or varied; or

(ii) the defendant should be allowed to defend the claim.

(2) In considering whether to set aside^{GL} or vary a judgment entered under Part 12, the matters to which the court must have regard include whether the person seeking to set aside the judgment made an application to do so promptly.

(Rule 3.1(3) provides that the court may attach conditions when it makes an order).

(Article 19(4) of the Service Regulation (which has the same meaning as in rule 6.31(e)) applies to applications to appeal a judgment in default when the time limit for appealing has expired.)

Effect of rule

13.3.1 Rule 13.3 deals with the setting aside of a regular judgment (contrast r.13.2—cases where the court must set aside).

The use of the word "may" shows that the court has a discretion but act in accordance with Pt 1 (the Overriding Objectives).

The defendant applying to set aside the judgment must come within r.13.3(1)(a) or (b). It is not enough to show an "arguable" defence; the defendant must show that he has "a real prospect of successfully defending the claim". It is essentially the same test as applied to summary judgment applications under Pt 24. This test is more fully covered in para.24.2.3; see also *Swain v Hillman* [2001] 1 All E.R. 91, CA.

In *ED&F Man Liquid Products Ltd v Patel* [2003] EWCA Civ 472; [2003] All E.R. (D)75; [2003] C.P.Rep. 51, Potter L.J. explained the distinction between the tests: "..the only significant difference between the provisions of CPR 24.2 and 13.3(1), is that under the former the overall burden of proof rests upon the claimant to establish that there are grounds for his belief that the respondent has no real prospect of success whereas, under the latter, the burden rests upon the defendant to satisfy the court that there is good reason why a judgment regularly obtained should be set aside. That being so, although generally the burden of proof is in practice of only marginal importance in relation to the assessment of evidence, it seems almost inevitable that, in particular cases, a defendant applying under CPR 13.3(1) may encounter a court less receptive to applying the test in his favour than if he were a defendant advancing a *timely round of resistance* to summary judgment under CPR 24.2".

---

[1] Amended by the Civil Procedure (Amendment No.2) Rules 2001 (SI 2001/1388) and the Civil Procedure (Amendment) Rules 2008 (SI 2008/2178).

The discretionary power to set aside is unconditional. The purpose of the power is to avoid injustice. The major consideration on an application to set aside is whether the defendant has shown a real prospect of successfully defending the claim or some other goodreason why judgment should be set aside or he should be allowed to defend the claim. The defendant is seeking to deprive the claimant of a regular judgment which the claimant has validly obtained in accordance with Pt 12: this is not something which the court will do lightly.

Judgment not set aside although court considered entered without jurisdiction in exceptional case: *Continuity Promotions Ltd v O'Connor's Nenagh Shopping Centre Ltd* [2005] EWHC 3462.

Rule 13.3(1)(b) "some other good reason"

See the judge's comments about the claimant's solicitors' "unnecessarily aggressive conduct" in *Hart Investments Ltd v Fidler* [2006] EWHC 2857, TCC; [2006] 2 All E.R. (D.) 232 Nov. **13.3.2**

Rule 13.3(2)—need to act promptly

Rule 13.3(2) gives added emphasis to the need to act promptly in seeking to set aside. Indeed the need to comply with time-limits and generally to act promptly is a feature of the CPR. In applying to set aside the court has always considered delay and the reasons for it (*Evans v Bartlam* [1937] A.C. 473). But see also *Manolakaki v Constantinides* [2003] EWHC 401; [2003] All E.R. (D) 95: even if the application was not made 'promptly' within the meaning of the Rule, if the defendant made it in sufficient time for it to be just that judgment should be set aside it should be set aside; provided the test set out in r.13.3(1)(a) was met. **13.3.3**

Other cases where delay was considered are:

Strachan v Gleaner [2005] UKPC 33; [2005] 1 W.L.R. 3204; [2005] All E.R. (D.) 358 (Jul): the fact that damages had been assessed and a final judgment entered did not deprive the court of jurisdiction to set aside a default judgment, but it was highly relevant to the question of discretion. It was an aspect of, but separate from, the question of delay. It could not safely be assumed in every case that any prejudice to the claimant could be met by putting the defendant on terms to pay the costs thrown away by the assessment hearing. There could be no rigid ruleeither way; it depended on the facts of the particular case.

Hussain v Birmingham City Council [2005] EWCA Civ 1570; 149 Sol Jo LB 1487; [2005] All E.R. (D.) 353 (Nov): defendants and Pt 20 defendants issued applications to set aside default judgments in the main action and the Pt 20 claim only a week before trial. The Court of Appeal allowed the defendant's appeal from the judge's order refusing to set the judgments aside. It was held, *inter alia*, that a judge's discretionary power was not to be exercised to punish a party for incompetence, but to further the overriding objective.

Nolanv Devonport [2006] EWHC 2025 (QB), unrep.: a debtor who did nothing until the creditor sought to enforce the judgment, then applied to set aside, was refused permission to set aside, it being held that the debtor's conduct amounted to an abuse of process.

An application to set aside must be supported by evidence (see r.13.4(3)). If a defendant has not acted promptly he would be well advised to address the reason for this in his witness statement or affidavit having regard to r.13.3(2).

In *Harrison v Hockey* [2007] All E.R. (D.) 336 (Mar), Mann J. refused the defendant's application to set aside judgment after a trial in his absence on the basis of his inability to attend the hearing. It was held that four and half months was too great a delay in making the application.

In *Khan v Edgbaston Holdings [2007]* EWHC 2444 (QB), H.H. Judge Coulson Q.C., sitting as a Deputy Judge of the High Court, cited a passage by Simon Brown L.J. in *Regency Rolls v Murat Carnall* [2000] EWCA Civ 379, at para.45, in the context of considering the meaning of the word "promptly" within CPR 39, as providing "the clearest exposition" of what is required by "promptly" whether contained in CPR Pt 13 or 39. In *Regency Rolls* Simon Brown L.J. held that 30 days was too long a delay before making the application. H.H. Judge Coulson held in *Khan* that the defendant had not acted promptly, which he described as being "with all reasonable celerity in the circumstances".

H.H. Judge Coulson in *Khan* also referred to the decision in *Hart Investments v Fidler*

[2006] EWHC 2857, (see Note at 13.3.2 above) where the judge concluded that a delay of 59 days in making an application under CPR Pt 13 was "very much at the outer limit of what could possibly be acceptable" and that in the context of a case where the applicant was not legally represented, the certificate of service recorded the wrong date and the application was premature, the conduct of the respondent's solicitors was criticised as "unnecessarily aggressive", the default judgment was only one of a number of procedural aspects of the case and the default judgment against the second defendant in the main proceedings would not bring finality in the proceedings as a whole.

Application to set aside judgment by a non party

13.3.4 In *Humber Work Boats Ltd v Owners of the Selby Paradigm* [2004] EWHC 1804 permission was granted to a non party, X, insurers of the defendant, to be joined as a second defendant under Pt 19.2, and to set aside the default judgment against the defendant under Pt 13.3(1) or Pt 61.9(5). It was held that the default judgment was not a bar to the joinder of X and the question was whether D or X had a defence that had a real prospect of success. In *Latif v Imaan Inc* [2007] EWHC 3179 (Ch) a third party was permitted to be joined to proceedings for the purpose of applying to set aside a default judgment, pursuant to Pt 40.9. (see Note at 40.9.5). Under r.40.9 a person who is not a party but who is "directly affected" by a judgment or order may apply to have it set aside. It would seem that this rule applies to default judgments; see further para.40.9.1 below. Under r.40.9 a person who is not a party but who is "directly affected" by a judgment or order may apply to have it set aside. It would seem that this rule applies to default judgments; see further para.40.9.1 below.

Application to set aside or vary judgment—procedure[1]

13.4 **13.4—(1) Where—**

(a) the claim is for a specified amount of money;

(b) the judgment was obtained in a court which is not the defendant's home court;

(c) the claim has not been transferred to another defendant's home court under rule 14.12 (admission—determination of rate of payment by judge) or rule 26.2 (automatic transfer); and

(d) the defendant is an individual;

the court will transfer an application by a defendant under this Part to set aside[GL] or vary judgment to the defendant's home court.

(2) Paragraph (1) does not apply where the claim was commenced in a specialist list.

(3) An application under rule 13.3 (cases where the court may set aside[GL] or vary judgment) must be supported by evidence.

Effect of rule

13.4.1 Rule 13.4(1) is derived from CCR O.37, r.4(2), but is modified. Automatic transfer to the defendant's home court (defined in r.2.3) now occurs only if the four specified conditions in the rule are satisfied (see r.26.2). The phrase "a specified amount of money" is wider than the old expression "liquidated sum" and includes any claim where the claimant has put a specific figure on his claim rather than claim damages. Automatic transfer now only occurs where the defendant "is an individual" not, for example, where the defendant is a company or partnership sued as a firm.

There is no automatic transfer where the claim was commenced in a specialist list.

Rule 13.4(3) does not expressly require a witness statement but does require the application to be "supported by evidence". The filing and service of a witness statement to support the application is undoubtedly the better practice. In a clear case the ser-

[1] Amended by the Civil Procedure (Amendment No.4) Rules 2000 (SI 2000 No.2092).

vice of the witness statement may induce the claimant not to oppose the application. Even where the claimant does wish to oppose, the service of the witness statement gives time for the claimant to consider his position and file and serve a witness statement in reply.

Claimant's duty to apply to set aside judgment

13.5 [...] 13.5

Abandoned claim restored where default judgment set aside

13.6 Where— 13.6

(a) the claimant claimed a remedy in addition to one specified in rule 12.4(1) (claims in respect of which the claimant may obtain default judgment by filing a request);

(b) the claimant abandoned his claim for that remedy in order to obtain default judgment on request in accordance with 12.4(3); and

(c) the default judgment is set aside[GL] under this Part,

the abandoned claim is restored when the default judgment is set aside.

Effect of rule

13.6.1 Default judgment is not available on the filing of a request in all cases: only the claims specified in r.12.4(1). Claimants will sometimes claim remedies where it is not possible to enter judgment in default on request but a claimant is entitled, if he so chooses, to abandon the claim for that remedy and enter judgment for the remainder of the claim: see r.12.4(3). If a claimant does this but his default judgment is subsequently set aside; the abandoned claim is automatically restored pursuant to r.13.6 when the default judgment is set aside.

PART 14

ADMISSIONS

Contents

14.0.1

Editorial Introduction

14.0.2 Part 14 now covers three separate situations. First, "formal admissions" (typically an admission made in a defence), secondly, pre-action admissions made after April 6, 2007 and after receipt of a letter of claim under one of the three pre-action protocols listed in 14PD1.1(2) or, if made before a letter of claim is received, is stated to be made under Pt 14 and thirdly a debtor's admission of a debt (usually accompanied by an offer to pay by instalments) on a form provided by the court and served with with the claim form. In the first case the appropriate judgment can be obtained by an application to the court under r.14.4; in the second case judgment can be obtained on the pre-action admission by an application made under r.23. In both instances the application will be heard by a District Judge or, if in the High Court in London, by a Master. In the third case there is usually no judicial input and judgment is obtained administratively.

Related sources

14.0.3

- Practice Direction (Admissions), see para.14PD.1
- Rule 7.8 (Form for defence [and admitting the claim] to be served with claim form)
- *Part* 15 (Defence and Counterclaim)
- Part 24 (Summary Judgment)
- Part 23 (General Rules About Applications for Court Orders)
- Part 16 (Statements of Case)

Forms

- **N9A** Admission (specified amount) 14.0.4
- **N9C** Admission (unspecified amount and non-money claims)
- **N225** Request for judgment and reply to admission (specified amount)
- **N225A** Notice of part admission (specified amount)
- **N226** Notice of admission (unspecified amount)
- **N228** Notice of admission (return of goods)

Admissions made after commencement of proceedings[1]

14.1—(1) A party may admit the truth of the whole or any part of another party's case. 14.1

(2) He may do this by giving notice in writing (such as in a statement of case or by letter).

(3) Where the only remedy which the claimant is seeking is the payment of money, the defendant may also make an admission in accordance with—

- **(a) rule 14.4 (admission of whole claim for specified amount of money);**
- **(b) rule 14.5 (admission of part of claim for specified amount of money);**
- **(c) rule 14.6 (admission of liability to pay whole of claim for unspecified amount of money); or**
- **(d) rule 14.7 (admission of liability to pay claim for unspecified amount of money where defendant offers a sum in satisfaction of the claim).**

(4) Where the defendant makes an admission as mentioned in paragraph (3), the claimant has a right to enter judgment except where—

- **(a) the defendant is a child or protected party; or**
- **(b) the claimant is a child or protected party and the admission is made under rule 14.5 or 14.7.**

(Rule 21.10 provides that, where a claim is made by or on behalf of a child or protected party or against a child or protected party, no settlement, compromise or payment shall be valid, so far as it relates to that person's claim, without the approval of the court.)

(5) The permission of the court is required to amend or withdraw an admission.

(Rule 3.1(3) provides that the court may attach conditions when it makes an order.)

Admissions made before commencement of proceedings[2]

14.1A—(1) A person may, by giving notice in writing, admit the truth of the whole or any part of another party's case before commencement of proceedings (a 'pre-action admission'). 14.1A

***(2)* Paragraphs (3) to (5) of this rule apply to a pre-action admission made in the types of proceedings listed at paragraph 1.1(2) of the Practice Direction to this Part if one of the following conditions is met—**

---

[1] Amended by the Civil Procedure (Amendment No.3) Rules 2006 (SI 2006/3435) and the Civil Procedure (Amendment) Rules 2007 (SI 2007/2204).

[2] Introduced by Civil Procedure (Amendment No.3) Rules 2006 (SI 2006/3435).

(a) it is made after the party making it has received a letter before claim in accordance with the Practice Direction (Pre-Action Conduct) or any relevant pre-action protocol; or

(b) it is made before such letter before claim has been received, but it is stated to be made under Part 14.

(3) A person may, by giving notice in writing, withdraw a pre-action admission—

(a) before commencement of proceedings, if the person to whom the admission was made agrees;

(b) after commencement of proceedings, if all parties to the proceedings consent or with the permission of the court.

(4) After commencement of proceedings—

(a) any party may apply for judgment on the pre-action admission; and

(b) the party who made the pre-action admission may apply to withdraw it.

(5) An application to withdraw a pre-action admission or to enter judgment on such an admission—

(a) must be made in accordance with Part 23;

(b) may be made as a cross-application.

Formal admission

14.1.1 In various ways, for the purposes of reducing costs and delay and of narrowing the issues in dispute, the CPR encourage parties, where appropriate, to make admissions of fact and to concede claims (or parts of a claim) and not to contest the incontestable throughout the pre-trial process.

"notice in writing"

14.1.2 Rule 14.1(2) does not require an admission to be in any particular form, merely that it be "in writing". If it is not in writing it may still be admissible in evidence but it is not a formal admission for the purposes of Pt 14.

"statement of case"

14.1.3 This is a new phrase (defined in r.2.3(1)) which has replaced the former term "pleadings" and is not to be confused with "statement of claim" (a term which has now been replaced by "particulars of claim").

A defendant who wishes to admit the whole or part of the claim should do so in his defence. See further r.16.5.

"admissions of fact"

14.1.4 An admission may be express or implied but must be clear (*Ellis v Allen* [1914] 1 Ch. 904 at 909; *Ash v Hutchinson & Co. (Publishers) Ltd* [1936] Ch. 489 at 503; *Technistudy v Kelland* [1976] 1 W.L.R. 1042; *Murphy v Culhane* [1977] Q.B. 94). Where the defendant admits a document but does not admit that its terms are fully or correctly pleaded, the claimant may obtain judgment if the document, on production, clearly establishes the claim (*Barnard v Wieland* (1882) 30 W.R. 947; but see *Rutter v Tregent* (1879) 12 Ch.D. 758 and *Smith v Davies* (1884) 28 Ch.D. 650).

An admission in a defence in one action has been held not to be binding in other proceedings between the same parties on a different issue (*Re Walters* (1889) 61 L.T. 872).

Judgment on admission

14.1.5 See r.14.3. Where an admission is made pursuant to r.14.1(1)(2) an application to the court for judgment is necessary. This contrasts with the claimant's right to enter judgment under r.14.1(4) whereby judgment is obtained administratively without judicial involvement.

"claimant ... seeking ... the payment of money"

Rule 14.1(3) sets out the four situations where the defendant can make an admission on the relevant practice form. See further the four specific rules referred to. Usually, an admission under any of these rules will be accompanied by a request for time to pay (see r.14.9). If the defendant makes an offer to pay by instalments which the claimant accepts, judgment can be entered accordingly. If the claimant rejects the offer, rr.14.10 *et seq.* provide for determination of the rate of payment. **14.1.6**

"claimant has a right to enter judgment"

The claimant's right to enter judgment on an admission pursuant to r.14.1(3) is subject only to the usual requirement, pursuant to r.21.10, where the defendant is a child or protected party or the claimant is a child or protected party and the admission is under r.14.5 or r.14.7 (but note, not if the admission is under r.14.4 or r.14.6). In these cases, involving a child or protected party, an application to the court is necessary. (See Pt 21— Children and Protected Parties, and Pt 23—General Rules about applications for court orders.) Otherwise—i.e. in the vast majority of cases—the claimant has a right to enter judgment. Judgment is obtained merely by completing the appropriate court form (the CPR retain the CCR term "request": see rr.14.4(3), 14.5(6), 14.6(4) and 14.7(5)). Judgment is entered administratively by a member of the court staff without any judicial input. **14.1.7**

"amend or withdraw an admission"

The court did not historically permit the withdrawal of an admission consciously made but by mistake without the imposition of conditions (see *Hollis v Burton* [1892] 3 Ch.D. 226). In other cases decided before the implementation of the CPR in April 1999, the Court of Appeal e.g. in *Gale v Superdrug Stores Plc* [1996] 1 W.L.R. 1089, had accepted that a party needed the permission of the court to withdraw an admission, whether it had been made before or after the commencement of the proceedings. The court had held that the provisions of RSC O.27, r.3 (which contained the previous provisions concerning admissions) were sufficiently wide so as to include admissions made both before and after the issue of proceedings. The issue raised in many of the authorities was the test which a court should apply in the exercise of its discretion to grant or refuse permission to withdraw an admission. CPR r.14.1(5) now contains a clear provision that the court may allow a party to withdraw an admission. This had only been considered at first instance until December 21, 2005 when the Court of Appeal handed down its decision in *Sowerby v Charlton* [2005] EWCA Civ 1610 in which Brooke L.J. held that r.14.1(5) does not apply to pre action admissions and indicated that the authorities decided under RSC Order 27 should now be approached with caution, particularly the decision of the majority in *Gale v Superdrug Stores Ltd*. On the particular facts of the case, the judgment was not set aside. He also held that when the court is determining whether to grant or refuse permission to withdraw an admission, the decision of Sumner J. in *Braybrook v Basildon & Thurrock University NHS Trust*, October 7, 2004 (Lawtel) contained valuable guidance at para.45 where it was held that: **14.1.8**

> "45. From these cases and the CPR I draw the following principles:
>
> 1. In exercising its discretion the court will consider all the circumstances of the case and seek to give effect to the overriding objective.
> 2. Amongst the matters to be considered will be:
>   (a) the reasons and justification for the application which must be made in good faith;
>   (b) the balance of prejudice to the parties;
>   (c) whether any party has been the author of any prejudice they may suffer;
>   (d) the prospects of success of any issue arising from the withdrawal of an admission;
>   (e) the public interest, in avoiding where possible satellite litigation, disproportionate use of court resources and the impact of any strategic manoeuvring.
> 3. The nearer any application is to a final hearing the less chance of suc-

cess it will have even if the party making the application can establish clear prejudice. This may be decisive if the application is shortly before the hearing."

The issue of what reliance can be placed on pre-action admissions has been considered by the Court of Appeal again in *Stoke on Trent City Council v John Whalley* [2006] EWCA Civ 1137; [2007] 1 W.L.R. 352. This appeal was brought after the publication of the decision in *Sowerby*. Smith L.J. held that *Sowerby* was binding on the court and that the appropriate way in which to challenge a pre-action admission which the defendant had sought to withdraw was by application under r.3.4(2) to strike out the defence or part of it as an abuse of the process of the court or otherwise likely to obstruct the just disposal of the case. Smith L.J. held that (a) a claimant would usually have to show the defendant had acted in bad faith in order to establish that the withdrawal of an admission would amount to an abuse of the process of the court; or(b) a claimant would usually need to show he would suffer some prejudice which would affect the fairness of the trial if he argues that the withdrawal of a pre-action admission is likely to obstruct the just disposal of the case. Brooke L.J. added that the issues highlighted in *Sowerby* and in this case warrant the early attention of the Civil Justice Council and he suggested that the position of a pre-action admission in a multi track case under the Pre Action Protocol should be reconsidered.

The practical effect of these decisions will be curtailed by the addition of Pt 14.1A which came into force on April 6, 2007. In other cases which are likely to be allocated to the multi track when issued and which are not covered by the pre-action protocols for personal injury, clinical disputes or disease and illness, it remains to be seen whether parties will be able to rely on any pre-action admissions with confidence, save in the clearest of cases. In such cases, claimants may well decide that they are obliged to continue to prepare a case on liability, even where an admission is made until proceedings are issued and a defence filed. It may be difficult for defendants to object to these costs and the result may be an overall increase in costs, which would be unfortunate.

An attempt to avoid the consequences of the decisions in *Sowerby* and *Stoke* was made in Sheffield County Court in the unreported decision of *Telling v OCS Group Ltd* (April 7, 2008) in which the circuit judge held that where the defendant's loss adjusters withdrew an unequivocal admission made to the claimant's solicitors, there had been a valid compromise in that the claimant's solicitors had given up the best opportunity to investigate the circumstances in which their client's husband met his death in return for the admission of liability. Accordingly he held there was a valid and binding agreement and summary judgment for damages to be assessed was entered. It remains to be seen whether this approach will find favour with the Court of Appeal but it would seem unlikely. On the basis of the present law as set out in *Sowerby*, it could be viewed as negligent for solicitors to stop all investigations into an accident on the basis of the defendant's admission which he could later withdraw without even requiring permission of the court.

Pre-action admissions made after April 6, 2007

14.1.9 The new rule was implemented to overcome the effect of the decision of the Court of Appeal in *Sowerby v Charlton* [2005] EWCA Civ 1610. It is not retrospective and does not apply to any pre-action admissions made before April 6, 2007. The existing law therefore continues to apply to such admissions and any application to challenge them would have to be made in accordance with guidance given by Smith L.J. in *Stoke on Trent City Council v John Whalley* [2006] EWCA Civ 1137; [2007] 1 W.L.R. 352.. This rule only applies to pre-action admissions made in cases within the three pre action protocols set out in 14PD1.1(2), which are those relating to personal injury, clinical disputes and disease and illness claims. In particular it does not apply to any other contractual dispute. The practical effect of this new rule is to be welcomed as it gives a claimant confidence that he can rely on a pre-action admission made under it in the knowledge that it can only be withdrawn either with his consent or with the permission of the court. This should result in claimants deciding there is no need to continue to investigate and gather evidence in relation to the issue of liability in the vast major*ity of such cases.*

14 PD7.2 sets out a non exhaustive list of matters the court must take into account when considering an application for permission to withdraw a pre-action admission. The list of such matters bears a resemblance to those set out in Pt 3.9 which the court must consider when hearing an application for relief from sanctions. It remains to be

seen whether the courts will decide whether the judge must deal with each of the matters in a judgment, as has been held to be the position on applications under r.3.9 (see *Bansal v Cheema* [2001] C.P. Rep. 6). Practitioners would be well advised to ensure that the evidence in support of any such application for permission to withdraw such a pre-action admission deals with each of these matters in the Practice Direction in turn.

In *White v Greensand Homes Ltd* [2007] EWCA Civ 643 the Court of Appeal considered the principles to be applied on an application for permission to withdraw an admission made in compliance with a Pre-Action Protocol and later repeated in a defence (where CPR r.14.1A did not apply). The defendant applied for permission to amend its defence by withdrawing its admission in circumstances where one limitation period had expired after the pre-action admission was made but before the claim was issued but a second limitation period in respect of a negligence claim had not. It considered the guidance given by Smith L.J. in *Stoke on Trent City Council v John Whalley* [2006] EWCA Civ 1137; [2007] 1 W.L.R. 352 that it would usually be necessary to show the defendant had acted in bad faith and that the claimant had to show that the withdrawal of a pre-action admission was likely to obstruct the just disposal of the case in that he would suffer some prejudice which would affect the fairness of the trial. Chadwick L.J. held in *White* that when the pre-action admission had not been repeated in a statement of case, the question for the court to decide is whether to allow it to be withdrawn in the pleaded case would be an abuse of the process or a course likely to obstruct the just disposal of the proceedings.

Period for making an admission[1]

14.2—(1) The period for returning an admission under rule 14.4 or for filing it under rules 14.5, 14.6 or 14.7 is— **14.2**

(a) where the defendant is served with a claim form which states that particulars of claim will follow, 14 days after service of the particulars; and

(b) in any other case, 14 days after service of the claim form.

(2) Paragraph (1) is subject to the following rules—

(a) rule 6.35 (which specifies how the period for filing or returning an admission is calculated where the claim form is served out of the jurisdiction under rule 6.32 or 6.33); and

(b) rule 6.12(3) (which requires the court to specify the period for responding to the particulars of claim when it makes an order under that rule).

(3) A defendant may return an admission under rule 14.4 or file it under rules 14.5, 14.6 or 14.7 after the end of the period for returning or filing it specified in paragraph (1) if the claimant has not obtained default judgment under Part 12.

(4) If he does so, this Part shall apply as if he had made the admission within that period.

Effect of rule

Rule 14.2 has no application to an admission made in a statement of case pursuant to r.14.1(1) and (2), but is confined to the four situations in r.14.1(3) re-stated in r.14.2(1). It is therefore concerned with four situations where the claimant seeks the payment of money as the only remedy, i.e. admission of whole claim for a specified amount of money (r.14.4); admission of part of claim for specified amount of money (r.14.5); admission of liability to pay whole of claim for unspecified amount of money **14.2.1**

[1] Amended by the Civil Procedure (Amendment No.2) Rules 2000 (SI 2000/940) and the Civil Procedure (Amendment) Rules 2008 (SI 2008/2178).

(r.14.6) and admission of liability to pay claim for unspecified amount of money where defendant offers a sum in satisfaction (r.14.7). The effect of r.14.2(1) is to give the defendant 14 days from service of the particulars of claim to return the admission. These may be endorsed on the claim form or contained in a separate document served with or after the claim form; if endorsed on the claim form, r.14.2(1)(b) applies and the defendant has 14 days from service of the claim form to return the admission. Where the claimant has elected to serve particulars of claim separately but subsequently to the claim form, r.14.2(1)(a) applies and the defendant has 14 days after service of the particulars.

Service out of jurisdiction

14.2.2 This is now governed by CPR Pt 6.30—6.47.

Rule 6.12

14.2.3 This rule (service of claim form on agent of principal who is overseas) provides a procedure whereby an agent within the jurisdiction can be served instead of serving the principal under the provisions of Pt 6, rr.17–31. Rule 6.16(4) requires the court to specify the period for responding to the particulars of claim. An agent's address is not a place of business established in Great Britain for a foreign company for the purpose of service by post of a claim form (*Rakusens Ltd v Baser Ambalaj Plastik Sanayi Ticaret AS* [2001] EWCA Civ 1820, CA).

"default judgment"

14.2.4 Where a defendant fails to respond to service of the particulars of claim as required by the rules, the claimant can enter a default judgment (see further Pt 12). If, however, the claimant is slow to seek judgment and in the interim the defendant files a late admission the admission is treated as if it were in time (r.14.2(3) and (4)).

Admission by notice in writing—application for judgment

14.3 **14.3—(1) Where a party makes an admission under rule 14.1(2) (admission by notice in writing), any other party may apply for judgment on the admission.**

(2) Judgment shall be such judgment as it appears to the court that the applicant is entitled to on the admission.

"admission by notice in writing"

14.3.1 This is a new phrase not found in the former RSC or CCR and is the only formal requirement of the rule. It is clearly envisaged that no particular form is required so long as the admission is in writing: it could be in a statement of case (typically, the defence), by letter or in any written form so long as it is clear.

Effect of rule

14.3.2 By admitting a fact a party can save costs by obviating the need to call evidence to prove that fact. Where a party has made an admission of fact, r.14.3 enables the court to give his opponent such judgment that he is entitled to without waiting for the determination of any other questions between the parties. If the relief claimed is an injunction in a case which would expect to be allocated to the multi track, application should be made to the judge. Otherwise where the case would expect to be allocated to the small claims track or to the fast track, application can be made to the District Judge. In other cases application should normally be to the District Judge or Master as appropriate.

"any other party"

14.3.3 Either claimant or defendant can apply. It was held in *Re Wright, Kirke v North* [1895] 2 Ch. 747 that one only of several plaintiffs could not apply. There is no reason why application could not be made against one of several defendants.

Admission of liability

14.3.4 If the defendant in a damages action admits the claim, the claimant can obtain judgment for "an amount to be decided by the court" (one reason for doing so is to enable the claimant to obtain an order for an interim payment: see r.25.7(1)(b) and Pt 25 generally). The court giving judgment will give case-management directions for the assessment of damages.

For the claimant to obtain judgment in a negligence action the defendant must have admitted both that he was negligent and that the claimant thereby suffered damage: an admission of the negligence only is not sufficient (*Blundell v Rimmer* [1971] 1 W.L.R. 123; [1971] 1 All E.R. 1072, approved in *Rankine v Garton Sons & Co* [1979] 2 All E.R. 1185 and *Parrott v Jackson*, [1996] P.I.Q.R. P394; (1996) 93(22) L.S.G. 26; *The Times* February 14, 1996, CA). The reason is that an admission of negligence without an admission that the claimant suffered injury thereby is not an admission of liability. The claimant, therefore, cannot obtain judgment on an application under r.14.3 but may be able to obtain, in an appropriate case, summary judgment under Pt 24 (see *Dummer v Brown* [1953] 1 Q.B. 710; [1953] 1 All E.R. 1158 and Pt 24 generally).

As where a judgment in default is entered, a judgment entered on an admission for an amount to be decided by the court does not preclude the defendant from raising an issue as to any particular head of loss or damage provided that to do so is not inconsistent with the judgment. See also para.12.4.4.

Claim and counterclaim

Where a defendant admits a claim but pleads a counterclaim the usual practice has been to grant judgment on terms. For example, there may be judgment on the claim with a stay of execution pending trial of the counterclaim (if not already done, the court will give case-management directions for the trial of the counterclaim). Alternatively, the defendant could be required to pay money into court pending trial of the counterclaim. **14.3.5**

"may apply for judgment"

Unless the defendant consents to a judgment being entered (in which case a consent judgment can be obtained in accordance with r.40.6) the claimant will have to make an application to the court. See, generally, Pt 23. **14.3.6**

Admission of whole of claim for specified amount of money

14.4—(1) This rule applies where— **14.4**

(a) the only remedy which the claimant is seeking is the payment of a specified amount of money; and

(b) the defendant admits the whole of the claim.

(2) The defendant may admit the claim by returning to the claimant an admission in the relevant practice form.

(3) The claimant may obtain judgment by filing a request in the relevant practice form and, if he does so—

(a) if the defendant has not requested time to pay, the procedure in paragraphs (4) to (6) will apply;

(b) if the defendant has requested time to pay, the procedure in rule 14.9 will apply.

(4) The claimant may specify in his request for judgment—

(a) the date by which the whole of the judgment debt is to be paid; or

(b) the times and rate at which it is to be paid by instalments.

(5) On receipt of the request for judgment the court will enter judgment.

(6) Judgment will be for the amount of the claim (less any payments made) and costs—

(a) to be paid by the date or at the rate specified in the request for judgment; or

(b) if none is specified, immediately.

(Rule 14.14 deals with the circumstances in which judgment under this rule may include interest.)

Scope of provision

14.4.1 As the title to the rule, reinforced by r.14.4(1), makes clear, this rule only applies where the claimant has sued for a specified sum and the defendant admits the claim in full.

"specified amount of money"

14.4.2 This term, found in r.14.4(1)(a) and in many other rules in the CPR, is the term which has replaced the former term "liquidated sum". It is not a synonym for the old term, however, and is wider. Clearly, it covers a case where the claim is for a debt (which, in practice, will be the most common use of r.14.4). However, "specified amount of money" is wide enough to cover any case where the claimant has put a figure on the amount of his claim, e.g. a claim for damages arising out of a road traffic accident where the claimant has not claimed "damages" but a "specified amount of money" such as the repair bill. In this case, or indeed any other where the claimant claims a "specified amount of money" if the defendant admits not only the claim but also the specified sum he can make an admission and r.14.4 applies.

"an admission in the relevant practice form"

14.4.3 The relevant form is served on the defendant with the particulars of claim: see r.7.8. Rule 14.4(2) requires the defendant to send the admission "to the claimant", not to the court.

"claimant may obtain judgment"

14.4.4 Rule 14.4(3), (4), (5) and (6) are clearly drafted and are self-explanatory. If the defendant has not requested time to pay, r.14.4(4) to (6) apply. The claimant has the choice of requesting judgment payable immediately, payable on a specified date or payable by instalments, the frequency and size of which is determined by the claimant.

If, as is more usual, the defendant is making an offer to pay by instalments and the claimant is accepting that offer, r.14.9 applies (if the claimant is *not* accepting the instalments offered, r.14.10 applies).

Note that under r.14.4(6) if the claimant fails to request payment by instalments or on a specified date, the judgment will be payable immediately. This rule only applies where the defendant is not requesting time to pay.

Interest

14.4.5 Judgment can include interest: see r.14.14.

Costs

14.4.6 Judgment will include fixed costs: see further Pt 45.

Admission of part of a claim for a specified amount of money

14.5 **14.5—(1) This rule applies where—**

(a) the only remedy which the claimant is seeking is the payment of a specified amount of money; and

(b) the defendant admits part of the claim.

(2) The defendant may admit part of the claim by filing an admission in the relevant practice form.

(3) On receipt of the admission, the court will serve a notice on the claimant requiring him to return the notice stating that—

(a) he accepts the amount admitted in satisfaction of the claim;

(b) he does not accept the amount admitted by the defendant and wishes the proceedings to continue; or

(c) if the defendant has requested time to pay, he accepts the amount admitted in satisfaction of the claim, but not the defendant's proposals as to payment.

(4) The claimant must—

(a) file the notice; and

(b) serve a copy on the defendant,

within 14 days after it is served on him.

(5) If the claimant does not file the notice within 14 days after it is served on him, the claim is stayed[GL] until he files the notice.

(6) If the claimant accepts the amount admitted in satisfaction of the claim, he may obtain judgment by filing a request in the relevant practice form and, if he does so—

(a) if the defendant has not requested time to pay, the procedure in paragraphs (7) to (9) will apply;

(b) if the defendant has requested time to pay, the procedure in rule 14.9 will apply.

(7) The claimant may specify in his request for judgment—

(a) the date by which the whole of the judgment debt is to be paid; or

(b) the time and rate at which it is to be paid by instalments.

(8) On receipt of the request for judgment, the court will enter judgment.

(9) Judgment will be for the amount admitted (less any payments made) and costs—

(a) to be paid by the date or at the rate specified in the request for judgment; or

(b) if none is specified, immediately.

(If the claimant files notice under paragraph (3) that he wishes the proceedings to continue, the procedure which then follows is set out in Part 26.)

Scope of provision

Rule 14.5(1) clearly sets out the limited situation to which r.14.5 applies, i.e. only where the claimant seeks a specified sum of money and the defendant admits part of the claim. **14.5.1**

"specified amount of money"

This term is wider than the former term "liquidated sum". See paras 14.4.2 and 12.8.4. **14.5.2**

"relevant practice form"

The form is served on the defendant with the particulars of claim: see r.7.8. Rule 14.5(2) requires the defendant to file the admission with the court (*cf.* an admission under r.14.4 which the defendant must send "to the claimant". This unnecessary distinction will surely lead to confusion). **14.5.3**

"filing an admission"

The defendant by filing an admission, albeit of part of the claim, prevents the claimant entering a default judgment. **14.5.4**

"the court will serve a notice"

The defendant, by filing an admission of part of the claim has notified the court, but not the claimant. It is therefore the court's task to notify the claimant of the partial admission. The claimant must return the notice, in accordance with r.14.5(3) stating **14.5.5** his response to the partial admission. The three options open to the claimant are clearly set out in that rule. The claimant has 14 days to respond (r.14.5(4)) and if he does not do so the action is stayed (r.14.5(5)).

Acceptance of partial admission

14.5.6 If the claimant accepts the partial admission note that it is not sufficient to merely return the notice in accordance with r.14.5(3) and (4). He must also file "a request in the relevant practice form" in accordance with r.14.5(6) in order to obtain judgment. The relevant form is **N225A**.

Request for time to pay

14.5.7 See rr.14.9 and 14.10.

Non-acceptance of partial admission

14.5.8 The claimant can refuse the partial admission and continue his claim for the whole sum. He must file the notice of part admission sent to him by the court pursuant to r.14.5(3) and (4). The court will then proceed to allocate the case to the appropriate track and give case management directions (see further, Pt 26); see Form **N225A**.

Rule 14.5(6), (7), (8) and (9)

14.5.9 Rule 14.5(6) is a necessary modification of r.14.4(3). Rule 14.5(7), (8) and (9) are in identical terms to r.14.4(4), (5) and (6).

Interest

14.5.10 See r.14.14 and commentary thereon. That rule, surprisingly, does not apply and r.14.5 contains no provision for including interest.

Costs

14.5.11 See Pt 45—fixed costs.

Admission of liability to pay whole of claim for unspecified amount of money

14.6 **14.6—(1) This rule applies where—**

(a) the only remedy which the claimant is seeking is the payment of money;

(b) the amount of the claim is not specified; and

(c) the defendant admits liability but does not offer to pay a specified amount of money in satisfaction of the claim.

(2) The defendant may admit the claim by filing an admission in the relevant practice form.

(3) On receipt of the admission, the court will serve a copy on the claimant.

(4) The claimant may obtain judgment by filing a request in the relevant practice form.

(5) If the claimant does not file a request for judgment within 14 days after service of the admission on him, the claim is stayed[GL] until he files the request.

(6) On receipt of the request for judgment the court will enter judgment.

(7) Judgment will be for an amount to be decided by the court ***and costs.***

Scope of provision

14.6.1 Rule 14.6 is clear and self-explanatory. It applies only where the claimant sues to recover an "unspecified amount of money", the defendant does not dispute liability to pay and the court's task is therefore limited to deciding the amount to be paid and costs.

"relevant practice form"

A form to admit the claim must be served on the defendant with the particulars of claim: see r.7.8. **14.6.2**

"filing an admission"

The rule requires the defendant to file the admission with the court and the court to serve a copy on the claimant. **14.6.3**

"filing a request"

The claimant, on receipt of a copy of the admission from the court, can request judgment on the relevant practice form which he does by ticking Box C on Form **N226** (the form of Notice of Admission sent to him by the court). He should do so within 14 days (r.14.6(4), (5) and (6)) and r.14.8(1)). **14.6.4**

Judgment

As provided by r.14.6(7), judgment is for "an amount to be decided by the court". The court will give case-management directions including allocating the case to the relevant track if it is necessary. **14.6.5**

Disposal hearing

Paragraph 12.2 of the Practice Direction which supplements Pt 26 (26PD.12) enables the court to order a disposal hearing. At a disposal hearing the court "may give directions or decide the amount payable" (see para.12.8 at 26PD.12). See further, para.12.7.6. **14.6.6**

Admission of liability to pay claim for unspecified amount of money where defendant offers a sum in satisfaction of the claim

14.7—(1) This rule applies where— **14.7**

(a) the only remedy which the claimant is seeking is the payment of money;

(b) the amount of the claim is not specified; and

(c) the defendant—

(i) admits liability; and

(ii) offers to pay a specified amount of money in satisfaction of the claim.

(2) The defendant may admit the claim by filing an admission in the relevant practice form.

(3) On receipt of the admission, the court will serve a notice on the claimant requiring him to return the notice stating whether or not he accepts the amount in satisfaction of the claim.

(4) If the claimant does not file the notice within 14 days after it is served on him, the claim is stayed[GL] until he files the notice.

(5) If the claimant accepts the offer he may obtain judgment by *filing a request in the relevant* practice form and if he does so—

(a) if the defendant has not requested time to pay, the procedure in paragraphs (6) to (8) will apply;

(b) if the defendant has requested time to pay, the procedure in rule 14.9 will apply.

(6) The claimant may specify in his request for judgment—

(a) the date by which the whole of the judgment debt is to be paid; or

(b) the times and rate at which it is to be paid by instalments.

(7) On receipt of the request for judgment, the court will enter judgment.

(8) Judgment will be for the amount offered by the defendant (less any payments made) and costs—

(a) to be paid on the date or at the rate specified in the request for judgment; or

(b) if none is specified, immediately.

(9) If the claimant does not accept the amount offered by the defendant, he may obtain judgment by filing a request in the relevant practice form.

(10) Judgment under paragraph (9) will be for an amount to be decided by the court and costs.

Scope of provision

14.7.1 Rule 14.7 is the longest rule in Pt 14 and the least used in practice. The rule only applies if the three conditions in r.14.7(1) apply. The rule then goes on to provide for all possible permutations that can arise if r.14.7(1) is satisfied: hence the length of the rule. However, the rule is clearly drafted and self-explanatory. All forms referred to are available from the court; and can be found in the *Civil Procedure Forms Volume*; see in particular Form **N226**.

Allocation of claims in relation to outstanding matters

14.8 **14.8—(1) Where the court enters judgment under rule 14.6 or 14.7 for an amount to be decided by the court it will—**

(a) give any directions it considers appropriate; and

(b) if it considers it appropriate, allocate the case.

Scope of provision

14.8.1 Rule 14.6 applies where the claim is for an "unspecified amount of money" and the defendant admits liability. One of the permutations which can arise under r.14.7 is a judgment for an amount to be decided by the court. In either case, the court's only task is to decide the amount to be paid by the defendant. Rule 14.8 requires the court to give necessary directions for that issue to be tried. Directions for trial of the issue of damages will always be necessary and appropriate. In particular the court will have to consider the need for disclosure, exchange of witness statements and permission for either party to call expert evidence or rely on an expert's report. (See generally, Pt 31—Disclosure and Inspection of Documents; Pt 32—Evidence and Pt 35—Experts and Assessors.) Clearly the giving of directions is important. As r.14.8(b) recognises it may not always be appropriate to allocate the case to a specific track. Allocation could be important, however, as it can have costs consequences. For the scope of each track see r.26.6. A case will only be allocated to the fast-track if within the financial limits (see r.26.6(4)) and if it can be concluded in one day. There will be costs limitations if the case is allocated to the small-claims track (see r.27.14). Although the court can allocate a case to a higher track than its "normal track" it cannot allocate a case to a lower track than its normal track unless all parties consent (r.26.7(3)). See generally Pt 26, and, in particular, at para.26PD.12—Allocation and Case Management of Assessment of Damages and Allied Proceedings. Cases within the financial limits of the small-claims track are usually allocated to that track (the Court considering it "appropriate" pursuant to r.14.8(1)(b)) so as to keep the costs within the very limited costs regime of *that track*.

Request for time to pay

14.9 **14.9—(1) A defendant who makes an admission under rules 14.4,**

14.5 or 14.7 (admission relating to a claim for a specified amount of money or offering to pay a specified amount of money) may make a request for time to pay.

(2) A request for time to pay is a proposal about the date of payment or a proposal to pay by instalments at the times and rate specified in the request.

(3) The defendant's request for time to pay must be served or filed (as the case may be) with his admission.

(4) If the claimant accepts the defendant's request, he may obtain judgment by filing a request in the relevant practice form.

(5) On receipt of the request for judgment, the court will enter judgment.

(6) Judgment will be—

(a) where rule 14.4 applies, for the amount of the claim (less any payments made) and costs;

(b) where rule 14.5 applies, for the amount admitted (less any payments made) and costs; or

(c) where rule 14.7 applies, for the amount offered by the defendant (less any payments made) and costs; and

(in all cases) will be for payment at the time and rate specified in the defendant's request for time to pay.

(Rule 14.10 sets out the procedure to be followed if the claimant does not accept the defendant's request for time to pay.)

"request for time to pay"

A request by the defendant for time to pay an admitted claim is a very common occurrence in practice. Rule 14.9 applies to three distinct situations which all have the common feature of a defendant's request for time to pay, namely under r.14.4 admission of whole of claim for a specified amount of money; under r.14.5 admission of part of claim for a specified amount of money which the claimant is accepting in full settlement of the claim; under r.14.7 admission of liability in a claim for an unspecified amount of money where the defendant also offers a sum in satisfaction of the claim which the claimant is accepting. A "request for time to pay" is defined in r.14.9(2). **14.9.1**

Scope of provision

Rule 14.9 applies to the three situations specified in r.14.9(1) (see commentary above) where the defendant has made a request for time to pay and the claimant is agreeing to that request (if he is not agreeing to it see r.14.10). The rule enables judgment to be obtained administratively without the need for a hearing or any judicial input. **14.9.2**

"request for time to pay must be served or filed ..."

An admission under r.14.4 must be served on the claimant (r.14.4(2)). An admission under r.14.5 or r.14.7 must be filed with the court (rr.14.5(2) and 14.7(2)). In all cases the request for time to pay must accompany the admission: it will be on the relevant practice form which will have been served on the defendant with the particulars of claim (r.7.8). **14.9.3**

Determination of rate of payment

14.10—(1) This rule applies where the defendant makes a request for time to pay under rule 14.9. **14.10**

(2) If the claimant does not accept the defendant's proposals for payment, he must file a notice in the relevant practice form.

(3) Where the defendant's admission was served direct on the

claimant, a copy of the admission and the request for time to pay must be filed with the claimant's notice.

(4) When the court receives the claimant's notice, it will enter judgment for the amount admitted (less any payments made) to be paid at the time and rate of payment determined by the court.

"request for time to pay under rule 14.9"

14.10.1 Rule 14.9 applies to three distinct situations where the defendant has requested time to pay an admitted sum. See r.14.9 and commentary thereon. Essentially, r.14.9 applies where the claimant is agreeing to the request for time to pay in the terms offered by the defendant and r.14.10 applies where the claimant is not so agreeing.

"request for time to pay"

14.10.2 This phrase is defined in r.14.9(2).

"admission ... served ... on the claimant"

14.10.3 An admission under r.14.4 (admission of whole claim for a specified amount of money) should be served on the claimant (r.14.4(2)). The claimant must file it with the court pursuant to r.14.10(3) when he is giving notice of non-acceptance of the defendant's proposals for payment pursuant to r.14.10(2).

"relevant practice form"

14.10.4 All such forms can be obtained from the court office. Usually, however, it is merely a question of ticking the appropriate reply box on the form of notice served by the court: see, e.g. Forms **N225A** and **N226**.

"time and rate of payment determined by the court"

14.10.5 In most cases this is done by a court officer, not a judge (see r.14.11). The court officer works to prescribed guidelines. For the right to have the payment rate redetermined by a judge see r.14.13. For variation of orders to pay by instalments see Sch.2, CCR O.22, r.10 and 14PD.6.

Determination of rate of payment by court officer

14.11 **14.11—(1) A court officer may exercise the powers of the court under rule 14.10(4) where the amount outstanding (including costs) is not more than £50,000.**

(2) Where a court officer is to determine the time and rate of payment, he must do so without a hearing.

Scope of provision

14.11.1 Rule 14.10 applies where the defendant has requested time to pay an admitted sum but the claimant does not agree to the defendant's request for time to pay in the terms offered. The only issue for determination by the court is the time and rate of payment to be made by the defendant. Rule 14.10(4) requires the court to enter judgment for the amount admitted "to be paid at the time and rate of payment determined by the court". Rule 14.11 entrusts this task to a court officer (not a judge) where the amount outstanding is not more than £50,000. This is a paper exercise: no hearing is involved. The court officer works to prescribed guidelines and has regard to the statement of means filed by the defendant with the admission. For the right to have the court officer's decision redetermined by a judge see r.14.13.

"including costs"

14.11.2 The £50,000 limit in r.14.11(1) expressly includes costs. Costs will be fixed costs (see *Pt 45). The rule does* not mention interest. However, it is submitted that interest too must be included within the £50,000 limit for the purposes of this rule. The rule refers to "the amount outstanding" (not, e.g. the amount claimed or amount admitted) and interest added to the claim pursuant to r.14.14 is just as much part of the "amount outstanding" as the sum claimed.

Variation

Variation of an order is governed by Sch.2, CCR O.22, r.10 and by PD 14 para.6.1. **14.11.3**

Determination of rate of payment by judge

14.12—(1) Where a judge is to determine the time and rate of payment, he may do so without a hearing. **14.12**

(2) Where a judge is to determine the time and rate of payment at a hearing, the proceedings must be transferred automatically to the defendant's home court if—

- **(a) the only claim is for a specified amount of money;**
- **(b) the defendant is an individual;**
- **(c) the claim has not been transferred to another defendant's home court under rule 13.4 (application to set aside[GL] or vary default judgment—procedure) or rule 26.2 (automatic transfer);**
- **(d) the claim was not started in the defendant's home court; and**
- **(e) the claim was not started in a specialist list.**

(Rule 2.3 explains which court is a defendant's home court.)

(3) If there is to be a hearing to determine the time and rate of payment, the court must give each party at least 7 days' notice of the hearing.

Scope of provision

In most cases determination of the rate of payment is by a court officer and not a judge (see r.14.11). There are two distinct situations where determination is by a judge: first, where the amount outstanding is more than £50,000 (see r.14.11(1)) and, secondly, where the court officer is unable to make a determination in accordance with the prescribed guidelines (typically where the information provided by the defendant is inadequate or his income, having regard to necessary outgoings, is a "negative income" so that apparently the defendant has no means to pay the admitted sum). **14.12.1**

"without a hearing"

Wherever possible the judge will determine the time and rate of payment as a paper exercise without the need for the expense and inevitable delay of a court hearing. It is a judicial exercise: there are no prescribed guidelines. For the right to seek a re-determination at a hearing see r.14.13 and commentary thereon. **14.12.2**

With a hearing

Where the judge is not able to make a determination as a paper exercise, or considers it inappropriate to do so, the court will give each party at least 7 days notice of the hearing (r.14.12(3)) so that each can attend to make representations and/or provide further evidence. Rule 14.12(2) provides that the case is to be transferred to another court if the five specified conditions are all met. The transfer is to the "defendant's home court", a term defined in Pt 2.3. **14.12.3**

Right of re-determination

14.13—(1) Where— **14.13**

- **(a) a court officer has determined the time and rate of payment under rule 14.11; or**
- **(b) a judge has determined the time and rate of payment under rule 14.12 without a hearing,**

either party may apply for the decision to be re-determined by a judge.

(2) An application for re-determination must be made within 14 days after service of the determination on the applicant.

(3) Where an application for re-determination is made, the proceedings must be transferred to the defendant's home court if—

(a) the only claim (apart from a claim for interest or costs) is for a specified amount of money;

(b) the defendant is an individual;

(c) the claim has not been transferred to another defendant's home court under rule 13.4 (application to set aside[GL] or vary default judgment—procedure) or rule 26.2 (automatic transfer);

(d) the claim was not started in the defendant's home court; and

(e) the claim was not started in a specialist list.

(Rule 2.3 explains which court is a defendant's home court.)

Scope of provision

14.13.1 Where the claimant has not accepted the defendant's proposal for payment determination of the time and rate of payment is carried out by the court and in the vast majority of cases this is done as a paper exercise without a court hearing. Most determinations are by a court officer under r.14.11 but a significant number are by a judge under r.14.12.

Where the time and rate of payment have been determined as a paper exercise (whether by court officer or judge) either party can apply for re-determination at a hearing by a judge pursuant to r.14.13(1).

Rule 14.13 does not apply to a determination by a judge at a hearing pursuant to r.14.12(2). In such a case a dissatisfied party must accept the decision or appeal. For variation of an order see Sch.2, CCR O.22, r.10 and PD 14 para.6.1.

"within 14 days"

14.13.2 Rule 14.13(2) prescribes a 14 day time period in which to seek a re-determination.

"defendant's home court"

14.13.3 This term is defined in r.2.3. If the case is not already proceeding there and if the five conditions set out in r.14.13(3) are met, the proceedings will be transferred to that court for the re-determination to take place there. This is so whether it is the claimant or defendant who seeks re-determination and is something the claimant should have in mind as he may find he has to travel to the "defendant's home court" for the re-determination.

Evidence of means

14.13.4 The initial determination will be based on the statement of means filed by the defendant with the admission. A claimant is entitled to adduce evidence that the means are greater than stated. Indeed if the claimant is unable to do so he should consider carefully whether it is worth seeking a re-determination. Where the defendant is an individual there is little the court can do where the means are plainly inadequate to justify a higher order and a claimant's plea that "it will take eight years to pay the debt at that rate" is, of itself, likely to be insufficient to justify a higher order. On the other hand, if the defendant is a trader,it is not usual to allow time for payment. A trader ought to be able to pay business debts as and when due.

Interest

14.14 **14.14—(1) Judgment under rule 14.4 (admission of whole of claim for specified amount of money) shall include the amount of interest claimed to the date of judgment if—**

(a) the particulars of claim include the details required by rule 16.4;

(b) where interest is claimed under section 35A of the Supreme Court Act 1981[1] or section 69 of the County Courts Act 1984,[2] the rate is no higher than the rate of interest payable on judgment debts at the date when the claim form was issued; and

(c) the claimant's request for judgment includes a calculation of the interest claimed for the period from the date up to which interest was stated to be calculated in the claim form to the date of the request for judgment.

(2) In any case where judgment is entered under rule 14.4 and the conditions in paragraph (1) are not satisfied judgment shall be for an amount of interest to be decided by the court.

(3) Where judgment is entered for an amount of interest to be decided by the court, the court will give directions for the management of the case.

Scope of provision

Rule 14.14(1) sets out the requirements for interest to be included in a judgment based on an admission. The law on interest in s.35A of the Supreme Court Act 1981 and s.69 of the County Courts Act 1984 remains unaffected by the new procedural code introduced by the CPR. Under SCA 1981 s.35A and CCA 1984 s.69 the court has power to award interest in all cases. Whether interest should be awarded, and if so, at what rate and for what period, are all at the discretion of the court. However, the court invariably does award interest nowadays. The rate of interest payable on judgment debts, for the sake of uniformity and simplicity, has been the rate adopted by rules of court for many purposes including default judgments and judgment on admissions. **14.14.1**

Rate of interest

See para.12.6.2. The relevant rate is the judgment debt rate (currently, still 8 per cent). **14.14.2**

"details required by rule 16.4"

See this rule, in particular r.16.4(2) and commentary thereon, which clearly sets out the necessary detail to be included in a statement of case when claiming interest. **14.14.3**

"Judgment under rule 14.4"

Somewhat surprisingly r.14.14 applies only to judgment on admission under r.14.4. It does not apply to judgment on admission under either r.14.5 or r.14.7. Clearly it is not necessary for r.14.14 to apply to judgment under r.14.6 (where, in any event, there will be a hearing to assess damages so that interest can be considered then) but it is odd that r.14.14 is confined to judgments under r.14.4. For the sake of simplicity and consistency and to avoid hearings purely to determine the issue of interest, it is submitted that r.14.14 should be amended to extend it to judgments under rr.14.5 and 14.7 subject, of course, to the existing reasonable requirements set out in paragraphs (a), (b) and (c) in r.14.14(1). **14.14.4**

"conditions in paragraph (1) are not satisfied"

Rule 14.14(1) is strict in its requirements and judgment on admission cannot include *interest unless they are met. A hearing is necessary.* Rule 14.14(2) also only applies to judgments under r.14.4 and not those under rr.14.5 or 14.7. **14.14.5**

---

[1] 1981 c.54. Section 35A was inserted by the Administration of Justice Act 1982 (c.53) s.15(1), Sch.1, Pt I.

[2] 1984 c.28. Section 69 was amended by the Courts and Legal Services Act 1990 (c.41) s.125(3), Sch.18, para.46.

PRACTICE DIRECTION—ADMISSIONS

14PD.1 *This Practice Direction supplements CPR Part 14*

Admissions generally

1.1(1) Rules 14.1, 14.1A and 14.2 deal with the manner in which a defendant may make an admission of a claim or part of a claim.

(2) Rule 14.1A makes provision about admissions made before commencement of a claim. It applies only to admissions made after 6th April 2007, and only in proceedings to which one of the following pre-action protocols apply—

(a) the pre-action protocol for personal injury claims;

(b) the pre-action protocol for the resolution of clinical disputes; or

(c) the pre-action protocol for disease and illness claims.

(The pre-action protocol for personal injury claims states that it is primarily designed for certain types of personal injury claim with a value of less than £15,000. But, paragraph 2.2 of the protocol indicates that it generally applies to all claims which include a claim for personal injury.)

1.2 Rules 14.3, 14.4, 14.5, 14.6 and 14.7 set out how judgment may be obtained on a written admission.

Forms

14PD.2 **2.1** When particulars of claim are served on a defendant the forms for responding to the claim that will accompany them will include a form[1] for making an admission.

2.2 If the defendant is requesting time to pay he should complete as fully as possible the statement of means contained in the admission form, or otherwise give in writing the same details of his means as could have been given in the admission form.

Returning or filing the admission

14PD.3 **3.1** If the defendant wishes to make an admission in respect of the whole of a claim for a specified amount of money, the admission form or other written notice of the admission should be completed and returned to the claimant within 14 days of service of the particulars of claim.[2]

3.2 If the defendant wishes to make an admission in respect of a part of a claim for a specified amount of money, or in respect of a claim for an unspecified amount of money, the admission form or other written notice of admission should be completed and filed with the court within 14 days of service of the particulars of claim.[3]

3.3 The defendant may also file a defence under rule 15.2.

Request for time to pay

14PD.4 **4.1** A defendant who makes an admission in respect of a claim for a specified sum of money or offers to pay a sum of money in respect

[1] Practice forms **N9A** (specified amount) or **N9C** (unspecified amount).
[2] Rules 14.2 and 14.4.
[3] Rules 14.2 14.5, 14.6 and 14.7.

of a claim for an unspecified sum may, in the admission form, make a request for time to pay.[1]

4.2 If the claimant accepts the defendant's request, he may obtain judgment by filing a request for judgment contained in Form **N225A**[2]; the court will then enter judgment for payment at the time and rate specified in the defendant's request.[3]

4.3 If the claimant does not accept the request for time to pay, he should file notice to that effect by completing Form **N225A**; the court will then enter judgment for the amount of the admission (less any payments made) at a time and rate of payment decided by the court (see rule 14.10).

Determining the rate of payment

5.1 In deciding the time and rate of payment the court will take into account: **14PD.5**

(1) the defendant's statement of means set out in the admission form or in any other written notice of the admission filed,

(2) the claimant's objections to the defendant's request set out in the claimant's notice,[4] and

(3) any other relevant factors.

5.2 The time and rate of payment may be decided:

(1) by a judge with or without a hearing, or

(2) by a court officer without a hearing provided that—

(a) the only claim is for a specified sum of money, and

(b) the amount outstanding is not more than £50,000 (including costs).

5.3 Where a decision has been made without a hearing whether by a court officer or by a judge, either party may apply for the decision to be re-determined by a judge.[5]

5.4 If the decision was made by a court officer the re-determination may take place without a hearing, unless a hearing is requested in the application notice.

5.5 If the decision was made by a judge the re-determination must be made at a hearing unless the parties otherwise agree.

5.6 Rule 14.13(2) describes how to apply for a re–determination.

Varying the rate of payment

6.1 Either party may, on account of a change in circumstances since the date of the decision (or re-determination as the case may be) apply to vary the time and rate of payment of instalments still remaining unpaid. **14PD.6**

6.2 An application to vary under paragraph 6.1 above should be made in accordance with Part 23.

Withdrawing an admission

7.1 An admission made under Part 14 may be withdrawn with the court's permission. **14PD.7**

---

[1] Rule 14.9.
[2] Rule 14.9(4).
[3] Rule 14.9(5) and (6).
[4] Practice form **N225A**.
[5] Rule 14.13(1).

7.2 In deciding whether to give permission for an admission to be withdrawn, the court will have regard to all the circumstances of the case, including—

(a) the grounds upon which the applicant seeks to withdraw the admission including whether or not new evidence has come to light which was not available at the time the admission was made;

(b) the conduct of the parties, including any conduct which led the party making the admission to do so;

(c) the prejudice that may be caused to any person if the admission is withdrawn;

(d) the prejudice that may be caused to any person if the application is refused;

(e) the stage in the proceedings at which the application to withdraw is made, in particular in relation to the date or period fixed for trial;

(f) the prospects of success (if the admission is withdrawn) of the claim or part of the claim in relation to which the offer was made; and

(g) the interests of the administration of justice.

PART 15

Defence and Reply

Contents

15.0.1

Editorial Introduction

15.0.2 The rules in this part deal with some of the statements of case subsequent to particulars of claim. The term "statement of case" means "a claim form, particulars of claim where these are not included in a claim form, defence, Pt 20 claim, or reply to defence" (r.2.3(1)).

The defendant is not required to respond to service of the claim form as such but must respond to service of the particulars of claim.

The defendant does not have to file an acknowledgment of service as a prerequisite to filing a defence but can omit the acknowledgment stage and file a defence within 14 days of service of the particulars of claim. However, a defendant can file an acknowledgment of service in which case a defence must be filec within 28 days of service of the particulars of claim.

The claimant can file a reply to the defence. For further details of the basic procedure outlined above see the Parts of the CPR referred to in "Related Sources" below.

Related sources

15.0.3

- Practice Direction (Defence and Reply), see para.15PD.1, below
- Part 7 (How to Start Proceedings—the Claim Form)
- Part 8 (Alternative Procedure for Claims)
- Part 9 (Responding to Particulars of Claim—General)
- Part 10 (Acknowledgment of Service)
- Part 12 (Default Judgment)
- Part 16 (Statements of Case)
- Part 17 (Amendments to Statements of Case)
- *Part 20 (Counterclaims and Oth*er Additional Claims)
- Part 22 (Statements of Truth)

Practice Direction

15.0.4 Part 15 is supplemented by a Practice Direction: see para.15PD.1.

Part not to apply where claimant uses the Part 8 procedure

15.1 **15.1 This Part does not apply where the claimant uses the procedure set out in Part 8 (alternative procedure for claims).**

"alternative procedure for claims"

15.1.1 The alternative procedure for claims (see Pt 8 and commentary thereon) is akin to the procedure commenced under the previous rules by originating summons or originating application. Where the Pt 8 procedure is used the defendant is not required to file a defence, but is required to file and serve an acknowledgment of service (r.8.3).

Filing a defence

15.2 **15.2 A defendant who wishes to defend all or part of a claim must file a defence.**

(Part 14 contains further provisions which apply where the defendant admits a claim.)

"must file a defence"

15.2.1 "Filing" is defined in r.2.3 and simply means delivering it (by post or otherwise) to the court office. Rule 15.2 is based on established practice in county courts. Hitherto, in the High Court, a defendant did not file, but merely served, his defence. The change in High Court practice effected by r.15.2 means, of course, that the High Court must now keep a file for every defended case. Clearly this is necessary for effective case-management.

Service of defence

15.2.2 See r.15.6.

Contents of defence

15.2.3 See r.16.5. Note also Pt 22—Statements of Truth.

Consequence of not filing a defence

15.3 **15.3 If a defendant fails to file a defence, the claimant may obtain default judgment if Part 12 allows it.**

"default judgment"

15.3.1 See Pt 12 and commentary thereon.

The period for filing a defence[1]

15.4 **15.4—(1) The general rule is that the period for filing a defence is—**

(a) 14 days after service of the particulars of claim; or

(b) if the defendant files an acknowledgment of service under Part 10, 28 days after service of the particulars of claim.

(Rule 7.4 provides for the particulars of claim to be contained in or served with the claim form or served within 14 days of service of the claim form.)

(2) The general rule is subject to the following rules—

(a) rule 6.35 (which specifies how the period for filing a defence is calculated where the claim form is served out of the jurisdiction under rule 6.32 or r.6.33);

(b) rule 11 (which provides that, where the defendant makes an application disputing the court's jurisdiction the defendant need not file a defence before the hear-*ing*);

---

[1] Amended by the Civil Procedure (Amendment No.2) Rules 2000 (SI 2000/940) and the Civil Procedure (Amendment) Rules 2008 (SI 2008/2178).

(c) rule 24.4(2) (which provides that, if the claimant applies for summary judgment before the defendant has filed a defence, the defendant need not file a defence before the summary judgment hearing); and

(d) rule 6.12(3) (which requires the court to specify the period for responding to the particulars of claims when it makes an order under that rule).

Effect of rule

The period for filing a defence runs from service of the particulars of claim, a document which may be endorsed on the claim form or served with, or subsequently to, the claim form (for time limit see r.7.4). The period for filing a defence is 14 days after service of the particulars of claim or 28 days after service of the particulars of claim if the defendant files an acknowledgment under Pt 10. Rule 2.8 sets out how to calculate any period of time under the CPR. A defendant who first files an acknowledgment of service has twice as long to file a defence as one who does not. However, as r.10.1(3)(a) states, a defendant may file an acknowledgment of service if "he is unable to file a defence within the period specified in rule 15.4". The reference in r.10.1(3)(a) to r.15.4 is clearly intended to be a reference to r.15.4(1)(a). Having regard to the detail now required in a defence (see r.16.5) in anything but the most straightforward of cases, 14 days from service of particulars of claim is likely to be too short leading to most defendants first acknowledging service so as to obtain a total of 28 days for filing a defence. See r.15.5 for extending the period for the defence. **15.4.1**

In four exceptional cases, listed in r.15.4(2) a longer period for filing a defence is specified by another rule:

(1) where the claim form has been served out of the jurisdiction (as to the time for filing a defence in such a case see CPR r.6.23;

(2) where a defendant applies to the court for an order declaring that it has no jurisdiction to try the claim or should not exercise any jurisdiction which it may have (as to the time for filing a defence in such a case see r.11(9), see above para.11.1);

(3) where, before the defence is filed, the claimant applies for summary judgment on the whole of the claim or on a particular issue (as to the time for filing a defence in such a case see r.24.4(2); an application for summary judgment made by a defendant does not extend the period for filing the defence but does prevent the claimant obtaining judgment in default until the application has been disposed of (see r.12 3(3));

(4) where the court makes an order for service of a claim form on an agent of a principal who is overseas (as to the time for filing a defence in such a case see r.6.16(4)).

A longer period for filing a defence is also allowed in certain intellectual property claims (rr.63.6 and 63.9 set out in Vol.2, paras 2F–26 and 2F–61).

Filing of a late defence

Is the court's permission required for the filing of a late defence? In *Coll v Tattum*, *The Times*, December 3, 2001 Neuberger J. stated that the rules were unclear on this point but that the general principle was that a party wishing to do something outside the prescribed time limit ought to obtain the consent of the other parties or the permission of the court. In contrast to Pt 15, Pt 14, which deals with admissions contains specific rules (rr.14.2(3) and (4)) expressly dealing with filing of a late admission. Provided the claimant has not already obtained a default judgment the admission is effective and treated as if it were in time. There is no equivalent provision in Pt 15 dealing with filing of a late defence. Nevertheless, it is submitted that the onus is on the claimant to act promptly if he wishes to obtain a default judgment. In practice, if the time for filing a defence has expired but the claimant has taken no step to obtain default judgment and the defendant then files a late defence, the court office will accept the defence, file it and proceed as usual so that the claimant will not now be able to obtain default judgment. Note also, r.15.11 which provides for an automatic stay in certain circumstances. If no defence has been filed and the claim has been stayed pursuant to r.15.11, the defendant would need to apply under r.15.11(2) to lift the stay before filing a defence. The reality is that the court office will accept a late defence unless the claim has been stayed. **15.4.2**

Agreement extending the period for filing a defence

15.5—(1) The defendant and the claimant may agree that the pe- **15.5**

riod for filing a defence specified in rule 15.4 shall be extended by up to 28 days.

(2) Where the defendant and the claimant agree to extend the period for filing a defence, the defendant must notify the court in writing.

"period for filing a defence ... shall be extended by up to 28 days"

15.5.1 One aim of the CPR is to set a tight but realistic timetable and insist on compliance with it. There is, in general, limited scope for the parties to extend time periods by consent (see, e.g. rr.2.11, 28.4 and 29.5). The court cannot allocate the case to its appropriate track, nor proceed to give case-management directions and timetable the case, until the defence is filed and then allocation questionnaires filed (see Pt 26). There is therefore some urgency in requiring the defence to be filed.

Rule 15.5(1) allows the claimant and defendant to agree that the period for filing a defence be extended "by up to 28 days". Although the agreement need not be in writing the defendant must give written notice of it to the court.

Extension beyond 28 days

15.5.2 Rule 15.5 is silent as to the position if the parties wish to extend the period beyond 28 days. It is submitted that the parties cannot agree an extension beyond 28 days and that the onus is on the defendant to apply to the court for an order extending time for filing a defence beyond 28 days. Whether or not the application is made by consent of all parties, the court may deal with it without a hearing (see r.23.8 and the commentary thereto). If the application is opposed, the court's decision whether or not to grant more time will depend on the circumstances of the case and, in particular, whether the claimant has complied with any relevant Pre-Action Protocol (see paras C1–001 *et seq.*). If the claimant has not, the court will certainly be more sympathetic to the defendant's application and may penalise the claimant in costs.

Holding defence

15.5.3 A defendant cannot legitimately obtain more time for preparing his defence by filing the so-called "holding defence" such as "I deny this debt: full defence to follow". Such a defence does not comply with Pt 16 (contents of defence). A defence which consists of a bare denial may be struck out under r.3.4 (see Practice Direction supplementing r.3.4, para.1.6, see above para.3PD.1). Indeed on the filing of such a defence a court officer may refer it to a judge and the court may strike it out on its own initiative (see rr.3.2 and 3.3).

Filing of a late defence

15.5.4 See commentary to r.15.4 under this heading.

"defendant must notify the court in writing"

15.5.5 Once the time limit for filing a defence has expired the claimant can enter a default judgment under Pt 12. It is therefore in the defendant's interest—and r.15.5(2) so provides—for the defendant to notify the court of any extension of time agreed under r.15.5(1).

Automatic stay

15.5.6 Note the provisions of r.15.11 imposing an automatic stay after 6 months inactivity.

Service of copy of defence[1]

15.6 **15.6 A copy of the defence must be served on every other party.**

(Part 16 sets out what a defence must contain.)

(The costs practice direction sets out the information about a *funding* arrangement to be provided with the defence where the defendant intends to seek to recover an additional liability.)

[1] Amended by Civil Procedure (Amendment No.3) Rules 2000 (SI 2000/1317).

("Funding arrangement" and "additional liability" are defined in rule 43.2).

"a copy of the defence must be served"

Rule 15.6 is disappointingly vague about who should serve a copy of the defence. Nor is it followed by any helpful cross-reference. The forms themselves refer only to the filing of a defence (see response pack, **N9** *et seq.* and *cf.* r.9.2). The former practice under the RSC was for the defendant to serve the defence (RSC O.18, r.2). However, unlike CPR, r.15.2, there was no requirement to file the defence. The former practice under the CCR was for the defendant to file the defence and for the court to serve a copy of it on the plaintiff (CCR O.9, r.2(6) and (7)). Who then is to serve a copy of the defence under r.15.6? The rule does not expressly require the court to serve it but it will do so in practice provided that the defendant sends the necessary copy to the court. The court will then serve it pursuant to r.6.3(3). It is not for the court to make an extra copy for service so if the defendant does not provide a copy for service the court may assume that the defendant has done so direct. It is therefore suggested that defendants should either serve copies direct and, on filing the defence, inform the court that they have done so or, on filing the defence, supply sufficient copies for the court to serve pursuant to r.6.3(3). The court will then serve form **N152** on all parties enclosing with it a copy of the defence and an allocation questionnaire. 15.6.1

Making a counterclaim

15.7 Part 20 applies to a defendant who wishes to make a counterclaim. 15.7

"counterclaim"

This term is defined in the glossary (see Section F below). A defendant may make a counterclaim against a claimant by filing particulars of the counterclaim (r.20.4). Practice directions state that "the defence and counterclaim should normally form one document with the counterclaim following on from the defence". (Practice Direction supplementing Pt 15, para.3.1 (see para.15PD.3) and Practice Direction supplementing Pt 20, para.6.1 (see para.20PD.6).) 15.7.1

Defence to counterclaim

A counterclaim is treated for certain purposes as if it were a claim (r.20.3). Thus, a claimant served with a counterclaim must file a defence in accordance with r.15.4 or risk judgment in default if Pt 12 allows it (r.15.3). If the claimant also wishes to serve a reply, see para.15.8.3, below. 15.7.2

Time for defence to a counterclaim

Unless the court otherwise orders, the period for filing a defence to counterclaim is normally 14 days after receipt of the counterclaim (see r.15.4(1)(a)). However, if this date is earlier than the date for filing a reply the court will normally order that the defence to counterclaim must be filed by the same date as the reply (para.3.2A of the Practice Direction Supplementing Pt 15; see para.15PD.3). 15.7.3

Reply to defence

15.8 If a claimant files a reply to the defence, he must— 15.8

(a) file his reply when he files his allocation questionnaire; and

(b) serve his reply on the other parties at the same time as he files it.

(Rule 26.3(6) requires the parties to file allocation questionnaires and specifies the period for doing so).

(Part 22 requires a reply to be verified by a statement of truth).

"If a claimant files a reply"

15.8.1 Rule 15.8 makes clear that a reply is optional. A claimant need not serve a reply unless he wishes to allege facts in answer to the defence which were not included in his claim. See further as to the contents of a reply r.16.7 and the commentary thereto.

Time for reply

15.8.2 The claimant must file a reply "when he files his allocation questionnaire". The allocation questionnaire is served by the court pursuant to r.26.3. It states on it the date by which it is to be returned which will be "at least 14 days after the date when it is deemed to be served" (r.26.3(6)).

Rule 15.8(b)—unlike r.15.6—expressly states who is to serve the reply, i.e. the claimant not the court.

Serving a reply and defence to counterclaim

15.8.3 Practice Directions state that "the reply and defence to counterclaim should normally form one document with the defence to counterclaim following on from the reply" (Practice Direction supplementing Pt 15, para.3.2, (see para.15PD.3) and Practice Direction supplementing Pt 20, para.6.2, (see para.20PD.6)). However, the rules fix different time limits for defences to counterclaims and replies (see paras 15.7.3 and 15.8.2). The Practice Direction supplementing Pt 15 provides that, where the time limit for the defence to counterclaim is shorter than the time limit for the reply, the court will normally order that the defence to counterclaim must be filed by the same date as the reply. It also provides that, if no such order is made, the reply and defence to counterclaim may form separate documents (see para.3.2A of the Practice Direction Supplementing Pt 15, para.15PD.3).

Reply served by defendant

15.8.4 A counterclaim is treated for certain purposes as if it were a claim (r.20.3). Thus, in receipt of defence to counterclaim the defendant may serve a reply if he wishes to allege facts in answer to the defence to counterclaim which were not included in his counterclaim. See further as to the contents of a reply, r.16.7 and the commentary thereto.

Reply in specialist proceedings

15.8.5 Various rules govern certain specialist proceedings in which the allocation stage is dispensed with. The rules applicable to these cases specify a time limit of 21 days from service of the defence (rr.58.10 (Commercial Court), r.59.7 (Mercantile Courts), r.60.5 (Technology and Construction Court Claims), r.61.1(3) (Admiralty Claims), r.62.1(3) (Arbitration Claims) and r.63.6 (Patents and Other Intellectual Property Claims).

No statement of case after a reply to be filed without court's permission

15.9 **15.9 A party may not file or serve any statement of case after a reply without the permission of the court.**

Effect of rule

15.9.1 No party has a right to file or serve a statement of case subsequent to a reply. This rule acknowledges that the court may permit such a step but such permission will be appropriate only in the most exceptional circumstances. Instead of permitting further statements of case, the court is more likely to permit amendments to earlier statements of case.

For a case illustration under the previous rules in which parties were permitted to serve pleading subsequent to a reply see *Tito v Waddell (No.2)* [1977] Ch. 106; [1977] 3 All E.R. 129.

Claimant's notice where defence is that money claimed has been paid

15.10 **15.10—(1) Where—**

(a) the only claim (apart from a claim for costs and interest) is for a specified amount of money; and

(b) the defendant states in his defence that he has paid to the claimant the amount claimed,

the court will send notice to the claimant requiring him to state in writing whether he wishes the proceedings to continue.

(2) When the claimant responds, he must serve a copy of his response on the defendant.

(3) If the claimant fails to respond under this rule within 28 days after service of the court's notice on him the claim shall be stayed[GL].

(4) Where a claim is stayed under this rule any party may apply for the stay[GL] to be lifted.

(If the claimant files notice under this rule that he wishes the proceedings to continue, the procedure which then follows is set out in Part 26.)

Effect of rule

The rule is intended to provide a simple procedure where the defendant has in fact paid the debt before receiving the claim form. When the court receives a "states paid" defence it sends a notice to the claimant which, in effect, asks the claimant whether the defence is correct. The claimant must respond within 28 days and the claim is stayed if he does not do so. Whatever his response, the claimant must serve a copy on the defendant. If the claimant does not wish to continue that is the end of the case. If the claimant does wish to continue (because he does not agree that the debt has been paid or because, for example, he still wishes to recover interest and costs) the court will proceed to allocate the case to the appropriate track and give directions pursuant to Pt 26. **15.10.1**

"specified sum of money"

In respect of all money claims, whether debt or damages, the claimant may if he wishes, put a precise figure on the amount of his claim: see further para.12.4.3 above. **15.10.2**

Claim stayed if it is not defended or admitted

15.11—(1) Where— **15.11**

(a) at least 6 months have expired since the end of the period for filing a defence specified in rule 15.4;

(b) no defendant has served or filed an admission or filed a defence or counterclaim; and

(c) the claimant has not entered or applied for judgment under Part 12 (default judgment), or Part 24 (summary judgment),

the claim shall be stayed[GL].

(2) Where a claim is stayed[GL] under this rule any party may apply for the stay to be lifted.

Effect of rule

This rule imposes an automatic stay after 6 months if the defendant fails to file an admission, defence or counterclaim and the claimant has not sought default judgment or summary judgment. Any party can apply for the stay to be lifted. **15.11.1**

PRACTICE DIRECTION—DEFENCE AND REPLY

This Practice Direction supplements CPR Part 15

Defending the claim

15PD.1 **1.1** The provisions of Part 15 do not apply to claims in respect of which the Part 8 procedure is being used.

1.2 In relation to specialist proceedings (see CPR Part 49) in respect of which special provisions for defence and reply are made by the rules and practice directions applicable to those claims, the provisions of Part 15 apply only to the extent that they are not inconsistent with those rules and practice directions.

1.3 Form **N9B** (specified amount) or **N9D** (unspecified amount or non-money claims) may be used for the purpose of defence and is included in the response pack served on the defendant with the particulars of claim.

1.4 Attention is drawn to rule 15.3 which sets out a possible consequence of not filing a defence. (Part 16 (statements of case) and the practice direction which supplements it contain rules and directions about the contents of a defence). (The Costs Practice Direction supplementing Parts 43 to 48 contains details of the information required to be filed with a defence to comply with rule 44.15 (providing information about funding arrangements)).

Statement of Truth

15PD.2 **2.1** Part 22 requires a defence to be verified by a statement of truth.

2.2 The form of the statement of truth is as follows:

"[I believe] [the defendant believes] that the facts stated in this defence are true."

2.3 Attention is drawn to rule 32.14 which sets out the consequences of verifying a statement of case containing a false statement without an honest belief in its truth. (For information about statements of truth see Part 22 and the practice direction which supplements it).

General

15PD.3 **3.1** Where a defendant to a claim serves a counterclaim under Part 20, the defence and counterclaim should normally form one document with the counterclaim following on from the defence.

3.2 Where a claimant serves a reply and a defence to counterclaim, the reply and defence to counterclaim should normally form one document with the defence to counterclaim following on from the reply.

3.2A Rule 15.8(a) provides that a claimant must file any reply with his allocation questionnaire. Where the date by which he must file his allocation questionnaire is later than the date by which he must file his defence to counterclaim (because the time for filing the allocation questionnaire under rule 26.3(6) is more than 14 days after the date on which it is deemed to be served), the court will normally order that the defence to counterclaim must be filed by the same date as the reply. Where the court does not make such an order the reply and defence to counterclaim may form separate documents.

3.3 Where a claim has been stayed under rules 15.10(3) or 15.11(1) any party may apply for the stay to be lifted.[1]

3.4 The application should be made in accordance with Part 23 and should give the reason for the applicant's delay in proceeding with or responding to the claim.

(Paragraph 8.2 of Practice Direction A supplementing Part 6 contains provisions about service by the court on the claimant of any notice of funding filed with a defence.)

[1] Rules 15.10(4) and 15.11(2).

PART 16

Statements of Case

Contents

Editorial introduction

16.0.2 The rules in this part deal with the contents of "statements of case", a term which means "a claim form, particulars of claim where these are not included in the claim form, defence, Pt 20 claim or a reply to a defence" (r.2.3(1)). Parts 7, 15 and 20 deal with the filing and serving of these documents and Pt 12 deals with the consequences of failing to file a defence or defence to counterclaim.

The main differences between the previous rules and these rules are:

(1) Statements of case must be verified by a statement of truth.

(2) A defence must provide a comprehensive response to the particulars of claim; a simple denial of an allegation will not suffice.

(3) The defence of tender before action (which has been renamed "tender before claim") is available in response to claims for damages as well as debts.

Part 16 and the Practice Direction supplementing it offers little guidance on drafting statements of case and contain no precedents or specimens. Various specimen forms of particulars of claim and defence have been prescribed for use in possession claims: the parties to such claims are required to use the appropriate forms (Practice Direction supplementing Pt 55, para.1.5, see para.55PD.1. Useful guidance on drafting statements of case is set out in App. 1 of the Chancery Guide (see Vol.2, para.1–202, para.5.6 of the Queen's Bench Guide (see Vol.2, para.1B–28) and App.4 of the Commercial Court Guide (see Vol.2, para.2A–160). Further guidance and precedents may also be found in text books and other works (for example Jackson and Powell, *Professional Liability Precedents*, Sweet and Maxwell, looseleaf).

In *McPhilemy v Times Newspapers Ltd* [1999] 3 All E.R. 775, Lord Woolf M.R. gave the following guidance as to the purpose and importance of statements of case. Statements of case are required to mark out the parameters of the case that is being advanced by each party. It is important that they identify the issues and the extent of the dispute between the parties. They should state concisely the general nature of each party's case. The need for extensive detail and particulars has been reduced by the requirement that witness statements must be exchanged. In the majority of proceedings, identification of the documents upon which a party relies, together with copies of the party's witness statements, will make the detail of the nature of the case the other side has to meet obvious. This reduces the need for particulars in order to avoid being taken by surprise.

Related sources

16.0.3

- Part 7 (How to start proceedings—the claim form)
- Part 15 (Defence and reply)
- Part 20 (Counterclaims and other additional claims)
- Part 22 (Statements of truth)

- Part 53 (Defamation claims)
- Chancery Guide (See para.1–1)
- Commercial Court Guide (See para.2A–39)

Part not to apply where claimant uses Part 8 procedure

16.1 This Part does not apply where the claimant uses the procedure set out in Part 8 (alternative procedure for claims). 16.1

Part 8 procedure

Part 8 provides an alternative procedure for claims which largely reproduces the procedure applicable to cases commenced under the previous rules by originating summons or originating application. Rule 8.2 deals with the contents of the claim form for use in cases under the alternative procedure and there is no requirement for particulars of claim, defences or replies in such cases. 16.1.1

Counterclaims and other additional claims

Part 16 applies to counterclaims, third party proceedings and other similar claims governed by Pt 20. All such claims fall within the definition of the term "statement of case" (r.2.3). The person on whom such a claim is served must file a defence (see r.15.2 and r.15.6). Subsequently, a reply may be served (r.15.8). 16.1.2

Specialist proceedings

Parts 49, 58, 59, 60, 61, 62 and 63 and the Practice Directions supplementing them deal with various types of specialist proceedings and make some special provisions for statements of case in such proceedings. Part 16 and the Practice Direction supplementing it apply to specialist proceedings only to the extent that they are not inconsistent with the rules and practice directions applicable to them (see para.1.2 of the Practice Direction supplementing Pt 16). 16.1.3

Contents of the claim form[1]

16.2—(1) The claim form must— 16.2

(a) contain a concise statement of the nature of the claim;

(b) specify the remedy which the claimant seeks;

(c) where the claimant is making a claim for money, contain a statement of value in accordance with rule 16.3;

(cc) where the claimant's only claim is for a specified sum, contain a statement of the interest accrued on that sum; and

(d) contain such other matters as may be set out in a practice direction.

(1A) In civil proceedings against the Crown, as defined in rule 66.1(2), the claim form must also contain—

(a) the names of the government departments and officers of the Crown concerned; and

(b) brief details** **of the circumstances in which it is alleged that the liability of the Crown arose.

(2) If the particulars of claim specified in rule 16.4 are not contained in, or are not served with the claim form, the claimant must state on the claim form that the particulars of claim will follow.

[1] Amended by Civil Procedure (Amendment No.3) Rules 2000 (SI 2000/1317) and Civil Procedure (Amendment No.4) Rules 2005 (SI 2005/3515).

(3) If the claimant is claiming in a representative capacity, the claim form must state what that capacity is.

(4) If the defendant is sued in a representative capacity, the claim form must state what that capacity is.

(5) The court may grant any remedy to which the claimant is entitled even if that remedy is not specified in the claim form.

(Part 22 requires a claim form to be verified by a statement of truth.)

(The costs practice direction sets out the information about a funding arrangement to be provided with the statement of case where the defendant intends to seek to recover an additional liability.)

("Funding arrangement" and "additional liability" are defined in rule 43.2.)

"a concise statement of the nature of the claim"

16.2.1 This phrase is derived from the description of an indorsement on a writ under the previous rules. Such indorsements, formerly called general indorsements, will often provide useful precedents.

The claim form should identify the tort, breach of contract or other civil wrong complained of. In *Nomura International Plc v Granada Group Ltd* [2007] EWHC 642 (Comm) C obtained the issue of a claim form which was in general terms in order to cover any claim C may have against D if C was subsequently sued by X: C had not decided which claim to pursue against D but commenced proceedings merely to protect its position on limitation; the claim form was struck out as an abuse of process.

"specify the remedy which the claimant seeks"

16.2.2 In respect of money claims (whether debt or damages) the claimant may, if he wishes, put a precise figure on the amount of his claim. If he does so the claimant, even a claimant in a personal injury claim, may later obtain a default judgment for that sum, plus costs and interest, if the defendant does not respond (see Pt 12 and the commentary thereto and in particular para.12.4.3). Another consequence of specifying the amount claimed in a damages claim is that, if no other remedies are claimed and if the defendant responds, the rules for automatic transfer to the defendant's home court will apply (see r.26.2).

The court may grant any remedy to which the claimant is entitled even if that remedy is not specified in the claim form (r.16.2(5)).

"a statement of value in accordance with rule 16.3"

16.2.3 See the commentary to r.16.3.

"such other matters as may be set out in a practice direction"

16.2.4 Examples are the indorsement which is required in certain cases where a claim is to be served out of the jurisdiction (see Practice Direction supplementing Pt 7, para.3.5, (para.7PD.3)) and the statement which is required where a claim is for a sum of money expressed in a foreign currency (see Practice Direction supplementing Pt 16 para.11.1, (para.16PD.11)). The Practice Direction supplementing Pt 56 (56PD.1) sets out details which must be included in claim forms in the Landlord and Tenant claims governed by Pt 56 (see paras 5.2, 8.2, 9.2 and 11.2).

Paragraph 2 of the Practice Direction supplementing Pt 16 states that the claim form must include an address at which the claimant resides or carries on business (even where the claimant's address for service is a solicitor's address; para.2(2)). Where the defendant is an individual the claimant should (if he is able to do so) include in the claim form an address at which the defendant resides or carries on business; this is so even where the defendant's solicitors have agreed to accept service on the defendant's behalf (para.2.3). The addresses above referred to must include the postcode, unless the court otherwise orders (para.2.4). Failure to give the full address including post-code will not delay issue of the claim form but will delay service. The issued claim form will be retained by the court and the court will inform the claimant that the it will not be served until the claimant supplies a full address or until the court has dispensed with the requirement to do so (para.2.5). The heading of the claim form must include the full name of each party (see para.2.6, which gives guidance as to what comprises a party's full name).

Paragraph 3.1 of the Practice Direction (Mesothelioma Claims) (see para.3DPD.3, above) provides that, in any claim for compensation for mesothelioma, the claim form and every statement of case must be marked with the title "Living Mesothelioma Claim" or "Fatal Mesothelioma Claim" as appropriate. Paragraph 5.2 of that Practice Direction (see para.3DPD.5, above) states that claims marked "Living Mesothelioma Claim" will be given priority when fixing a case management conference.

Civil proceedings against the Crown

The term "civil proceedings against the Crown" is defined in r.66.1(2)(c). In such proceedings r.16.2(1A) provides that the claim form should state the names of the government departments and officers of the Crown concerned and should include a statement of the circumstances in which the Crown's liability is alleged to have arisen. The rule does not specify the consequences of failure to comply with these requirements (but see r.3.10, "General power of the court to rectify matters where there has been an error of procedure"). Contrast the effect of non-compliance here with the former rules which permitted the Crown to postpone the taking of any procedural step in the claim until the missing information was supplied (RSC O.77, r.10 now repealed, a provision which derived from s.35(2)(b) of the Crown Proceedings Act 1947, a provision which was removed by the Civil Procedure (Modification of the Crown Proceedings Act 1947) Order 2005 (SI 2005/2712)). **16.2.5**

Particulars of claim

As to the content of the particulars of claim, see r.16.4 and the commentary thereto. The particulars of claim must be contained in or served with the claim form or served within 14 days after service of the claim form, or within the time allowed for service of the claim form, if less (r.7.4). Where the particulars of claim are served separately the claim form must state that the particulars of claim will follow (r.16.2(2) and see further, para.3.2 of the Practice Direction supplementing Pt 16 (para.16PD.3)) and when served, a copy must be filed together with a certificate of service (r.7.4(3)). **16.2.6**

The Practice Direction supplementing Pt 16 states that, if practicable, the particulars of claim should be set out in the claim form (see para.3.1). The time limits for filing an acknowledgment of service and a defence both run from the date of service of the particulars of claim, not the claim form (see r.10.3 and r.15.4 respectively). It therefore follows that a claimant cannot obtain a default judgment before serving his particulars of claim (see r.12.3).

"a representative capacity"

If the claimant is claiming in, or the defendant is being sued in, a representative capacity, the claim form must state what that capacity is (r.16.2(3) and (4)). As to representative proceedings generally see rr.19.6 to 19.9. **16.2.7**

Statement of truth

A claim form must be verified by a statement of truth (r.22.1) in the following form "[I believe] [the claimant believes] that the facts stated in this claim form are true" (para.6.2 of the Practice Direction supplementing Pt 7 (see para.7PD.6)). If the statement of truth is contained in a separate document, it should specify the date on which the claim form was issued (para.2.3 of the Practice Direction supplementing Pt 22 (see para.22PD.2)). **16.2.8**

The statement of truth must be signed by the claimant or his legal representative (para.3.1 of the Practice Direction supplementing Pt 22, para.3.1; and the subsequent paras also make provision for signing where the claimant is a child, a patient or a company or other corporation and where the claim form is issued on behalf of a partnership).

A claim form verified by a statement of truth may be used as evidence by the claimant at any hearing other than the trial (r.32.6).

As to the significance of a statement of truth signed by a legal representative, see para.3.8 of the Practice Direction supplementing Pt 22 (see para.22PD.3). As to the consequence of verifying a claim form containing a false statement without an honest behalf in its truth, see r.32.14.

The purpose of the statement of truth is to eliminate claims in which a party has no honest belief and to discourage the pleading of cases unsupported by evidence which are put forward in the hope that something might turn up on disclosure or at the trial (*Clarke v Marlborough Fine Art (London) Ltd (Amendments)* [2002] 1 W.L.R. 1731, Ch D, *per* Patten J. and, see further, *Binks v Securicor Omega Express Ltd* [2003] EWCA Civ 993; [2003] 1 W.L.R. 2557, CA, noted in para.16.4.6, below).

The court may strike out a claim form which is not verified by a statement of truth (r.22.2(2)).

Supply of documents from court records

16.2.9 Rule 5.4, as amended in October 2004, sets out the circumstances in which members of the public may be entitled (on payment of any prescribed fee) to obtain copies of statements of case from court records. As a general rule, copies of a claim form can be obtained once an acknowledgment of service or defence has been filed or the claim is listed for a hearing, or judgment has been entered. Other documents filed by parties cannot be obtained by non-parties unless the court gives permission.

Providing information about a funding arrangement

16.2.10 In certain circumstances a party may be entitled to recover from another party certain success fees and sums in respect of insurance cover if he has entered into a relevant "funding arrangement" (defined in r.43.2) and if he has filed or served on the other party a valid notice of funding (see generally rr.44.3B, 44.15 and the commentary thereto: for the form of notice see Form **N251**). A claimant who has entered into a funding arrangement before starting the proceedings must file the notice when he issues the claim form and must serve the notice with the claim form or, if the court is to serve the claim form, file sufficient copies of the notice for service by the court. A claimant who enters into a funding arrangement on or after starting the proceedings must file and serve notice within seven days of entering the funding arrangement (Costs Practice Direction, para.19.2, see 44PD.13).

Statement of value to be included in the claim form

16.3 **16.3—(1) This rule applies where the claimant is making a claim for money.**

(2) The claimant must, in the claim form, state—

(a) the amount of money claimed;

(b) that the claimant expects to recover—

(i) not more than £5,000;

(ii) more than £5,000 but not more than £25,000; or

(iii) more than £25,000; or

(c) that the claimant cannot say how much is likely to be recovered.

(3) In a claim for personal injuries, the claimant must also state in the claim form whether the amount which the claimant expects to recover as general damages for pain, suffering and loss of amenity is—

(a) not more than £1,000; or

(b) more than £1,000.

(4) In a claim which includes a claim by a tenant of residential premises against a landlord where the tenant is seeking an order requiring the landlord to carry out repairs or other work to the premises, the claimant must also state in the claim form—

***(a)* whether the estimated costs of those repairs or other work is—**

(i) not more than £1,000; or

(ii) more than £1,000; and

(b) whether the value of any other claim for damages is—

(i) not more than £1,000; or

(ii) more than £1,000.

(5) If the claim form is to be issued in the High Court it must, where this rule applies—

(a) state that the claimant expects to recover more than £25,000;

(b) state that some other enactment provides that the claim may be commenced only in the High Court and specify that enactment;

(c) if the claim is a claim for personal injuries state that the claimant expects to recover £50,000 or more; or

(d) state that the claim is to be in one of the specialist High Court lists and state which list.

(6) When calculating how much the claimant expects to recover, the claimant must disregard any possibility—

(a) that the court may make an award of—

(i) interest;

(ii) costs;

(b) that the court may make a finding of contributory negligence;

(c) that the defendant may make a counterclaim or that the defence may include a set-off; or

(d) that the defendant may be liable to pay an amount of money which the court awards to the claimant to the Secretary of State for Social Security under section 6 of the Social Security (Recovery of Benefits) Act 1997.[1]

(7) The statement of value in the claim form does not limit the power of the court to give judgment for the amount which it finds the claimant is entitled to.

Effect of rule

This rule was amended, with effect from April 6, 2009, by the Civil Procedure (Amendment No.3) Rules 2008 (SI 2008/3327) r.6, reflecting the amendment, also made by that statutory instrument, to r.26.6 which amendment had the effect of increasing the financial limit of the fast track case management procedure from £15,000 to £25,000 for proceedings issued on or after that date. **16.3.1**

A statement of value must be included in the claim form if the claimant is making a claim for money. The statement may prevent the claim form being issued in the High Court (see r.16.3(5) and the Practice Direction supplementing Pt 7, paras 2.1 to 2.9 (see para.7PD.2)). The statement will be considered by the court before the case is allocated to a case management track (see Pt 26 and the commentary thereto). The statement of value does not limit the amount the court may later award (r.15.3(7)). As to meaning of "a claim for personal injuries", see r.2.3(1) above and para.2.3.11.

Matters to be disregarded in calculation of value

Rule 16.3(6) states that in calculating how much he expects to recover the claimant **16.3.2**
must disregard the following matters:

(1) claims for interest

(2) claims for costs

(3) any defence of contributory negligence which may be raised against him

[1] 1997 c.27.

(4) any set off or counterclaim which may be made against him
(5) the value of any state benefits received which the defendant may be liable to pay under the Social Security (Recovery of Benefits) Act 1997.

Money claim expressed in a foreign currency

16.3.3 Where a claim is for a sum of money expressed in a foreign currency the claim form must expressly state a variety of matters including the Sterling equivalent of the sum at the date of the claim and the source of the exchange rate relied on to calculate the Sterling equivalent (para.9.1 of the Practice Direction supplementing Pt 16 (see para.16PD.9)).

Contents of the particulars of claim

16.4 **16.4—(1) Particulars of claim must include—**

(a) a concise statement of the facts on which the claimant relies;

(b) if the claimant is seeking interest, a statement to that effect and the details set out in paragraph (2);

(c) if the claimant is seeking aggravated damages[GL] or exemplary damages[GL], a statement to that effect and his grounds for claiming them;

(d) if the claimant is seeking provisional damages, a statement to that effect and his grounds for claiming them; and

(e) such other matters as may be set out in a practice direction.

(2) If the claimant is seeking interest he must—

(a) state whether he is doing so—

(i) under the terms of a contract;

(ii) under an enactment and if so which; or

(iii) on some other basis and if so what that basis is; and

(b) if the claim is for a specified amount of money, state—

(i) the percentage rate at which interest is claimed;

(ii) the date from which it is claimed;

(iii) the date to which it is calculated, which must not be later than the date on which the claim form is issued;

(iv) the total amount of interest claimed to the date of calculation; and

(v) the daily rate at which interest accrues after that date.

(Part 22 requires particulars of claim to be verified by a statement of truth.)

"concise statement of facts"

16.4.1 The primary function of the particulars of claim is to state concisely the facts on which the claimant relies (*cf.* the claim form which should contain a concise statement *of the nature of the* claim, see r.16.2(1)(a)). The claimant should state all the facts necessary for the purpose of formulating a complete cause of action. A claimant may also:

(1) refer in his particulars of claim to any point of law on which his claim is based;
(2) give in his particulars of claim the name of any witness whom he proposes to call; and

(3) attach to or serve with the particulars of claim a copy of any document which he considers is necessary to his claim (including any expert's report to be filed in accordance with Pt 35) (para.14.3 of the Practice Direction supplementing Pt 16, para.16PD.14).

"if the claimant is seeking interest"

16.4.2 If the claimant is seeking interest, the particulars of claim must contain a statement to that effect and details as to the basis on which the right to interest is said to arise. If the interest is claimed in respect of a specified amount of money the particulars of claim must also include various details such as the percentage rate at which interest is claimed (r.16.4(1)(b) and (2)).

On claims for interest, see further notes in paras 7.0.9 to 7.0.24 above.

"aggravated damages ... exemplary damages ... provisional damages"

16.4.3 The terms "aggravated damages" and "exemplary damages" are defined in the Glossary (see Section F below). If these remedies are claimed the claimant must include in his particulars of claim a statement to that effect specifying the grounds relied on. Rule 41.5 makes similar provision for particulars of claim in which the claimant states that he considers that periodical payments or a lump sum is the more appropriate form for all or any part of any damages claimed. If such a statement is made the particulars of claim must also state relevant particulars of the circumstances which are relied on in support of it. As to provisional damages and periodical payments generally, see Pt 41 and the commentary thereto.

"such other matters as may be set out in a practice direction"

16.4.4 Paragraphs 4 to 7 of the Practice Direction supplementing Pt 16 set out lengthy details of matters which must be included in the particulars of claim in the following types of claim:

(1) Personal injury claims
(2) Fatal accident claims
(3) Recovery of land claims
(4) Hire purchase

As to statements of case in mesothelioma claims, see paragraph 3.1 of the Practice Direction (Mesothelioma Claims) (see para.3DPD.3, above).

As to statements of case in defamation claims, see the Practice Direction supplementing Pt 53, para.53PD.1.

Paragraph 8 of the Practice Direction supplementing Pt 16 sets out other matters to be included in particulars of claim in the following circumstances:

(1) where a claim is made for an injunction or declaration in respect of or relating to any land or the possession, occupation, use or enjoyment of any land;
(2) where a claim is brought to enforce a right to recover possession of goods;
(3) where a claim is based upon a written agreement;
(4) where a claim is based upon an oral agreement;
(5) where a claim is based upon an agreement by conduct;
(6) where a claim relating to a Consumer Credit Agreement is issued in the High Court.

Paragraph 9.1 of the Practice Direction supplementing Pt 16 (see para.16PD.9) states certain matters which must be specifically set out in the particulars of claim if the claimant wishes to rely on evidence under s.11 or 12 of the Civil Evidence Act 1968.

Paragraph 9.2 of the Practice Direction supplementing Pt 16 requires the claimant to specifically set out the following matters in his particulars of claim where he wishes to rely on them in support of his claim:

(1) any allegation of fraud:
(2) the fact of any illegality;
(3) details of any misrepresentation;
(4) details of all breaches of trust;
(5) notice or knowledge of a fact;
(6) details of unsoundness of mind or undue influence;
(7) details of wilful default; and
(8) any facts relating to mitigation of loss or damage.

Paragraph 15.4 of the Practice Direction supplementing Pt 16 (see para.16PD.14) sets out the matters to be included in a statement of case by a party who wishes to rely on a finding of the Office of Fair Trading as provided by s.58 of the Competition Act.

As to further matters which are specifically required to be set out, see para.3.8 of the Practice Direction supplementing Pt 16 (16PD.3) (see "Particulars of claim served separately from the claim form" below), the Practice Direction supplementing r.7.9 (Consumer Credit Act claims) at para.7BPD.1 and the Practice Directions supplementing Pt 49 (Specialist Procedures), Pt 53 (Defamation claims), Pt 55 (Possession claims), Pt 58 (Commercial Court) and Pt 59 (Mercantile Courts).

If the particulars of claim exceed 25 pages (excluding schedules) an appropriate short summary must also be filed and served (para.1.4 of the Practice Direction supplementing Pt 16, para.16PD.1, below).

Particulars of claim served separately from the claim form

16.4.5 The Practice Direction supplementing Pt 16, para.3.1, states that if practicable, the particulars of claim should be set out in the claim form (see para.16PD.3). If not so set out they should be served separately with the claim form or alternatively within 14 days after service of the claim form or within four months from the date of issue of the claim form (six months where the claim form is to be served out of the jurisdiction) whichever is the earlier (para.3.20). An extension of time for service may be granted (under r.3.1(2)(a) even after the initial period for service has elapsed (*Totty v Snowden* [2001] 4 All E.R. 577).

Where particulars of claim are not contained in or served with the claim form, the claimant must, within seven days of service of the particulars on the defendant, file a copy of them together with a certificate of service (r.7.4(3)).

Particulars of claim served separately from the claim form must be verified by a statement of truth (see "Statement of truth" below) and must contain details as to the court in which the claim is proceeding, the claim number, the title of the proceedings and the claimant's address for service (para.3.8 of the Practice Direction supplementing Pt 16 (see para.16PD.3)).

Serving particulars of claim separately from the claim form may prevent members of the public inspecting and taking copies of them: see further "supply of documents from court records" under r.16.2 above.

Statement of truth

16.4.6 Particulars of claim which are not included in the claim form must be verified by a statement of truth (r.22.1) in the following form "[I believe] [the claimant believes] that the facts stated in these particulars of claim are true" (para.3.4 of the Practice Direction supplementing Pt 16 (see para.16PD.3)). If the statement of truth is contained in a separate document it should specify the date on which the particulars of claim were issued (para.2.3 of the Practice Direction supplementing Pt 22 (see para.22PD.2)).

The statement of truth must be signed by the claimant or his legal representative (para.3.1 of the Practice Direction supplementing Pt 22 (see para.22PD.3); para.3.1 and the subsequent paras also make provision for signing where the claimant is a child, a patient or a company or other corporation and where the particulars of claim are issued on behalf of a partnership).

Particulars of claim verified by a statement of truth may be used as evidence by the claimant at any hearing other than the trial (r.32.6).

As to the significance of a statement of truth signed by a legal representative, see para.3.8 of the Practice Direction supplementing Pt 22. As to the consequences of verifying particulars of claim containing a false statement of fact without an honest belief in its truth, see r.32.14.

The purpose of the statement of truth is to eliminate claims in which a party has no honest belief and to discourage the pleading of cases unsupported by evidence which are put forward in the hope that something might turn up on disclosure or at the trial (*Clarke v Marlborough Fine Art (London) Ltd (Amendments)* [2002] EWHC 11, *per* Patten, J., para.21). However, a claimant may assert alternative factual possibilities provided that he makes this clear. If the alternatives are clearly pleaded as such the claimant is entitled to give a statement of truth asserting an honest belief that either set of facts is true (*Clarke*, above, para.30). In *Binks v Securicor Omega Express Ltd* [2003] EWCA Civ 993; [2003] 1 W.L.R. 2557, CA, Maurice Kay J. stated, "I do not consider it objectionable in principle for a claimant to advance an alternative case based on material put forward by his opponent. In such circumstances it may be possible for him to append a statement of truth, suitably drafted, making it clear that while his primary case is not an assertion of the truth of his opponent's account, if the court finds that to be the truth, he will seek to rely upon it as an alternative basis for liability."

The court may strike out particulars of claim which are not verified by a statement of truth (r.22.2(2)).

Contents of defence[1]

16.5—(1) In his defence, the defendant must state— 16.5

(a) which of the allegations in the particulars of claim he denies;

(b) which allegations he is unable to admit or deny, but which he requires the claimant to prove; and

(c) which allegations he admits.

(2) Where the defendant denies an allegation—

(a) he must state his reasons for doing so; and

(b) if he intends to put forward a different version of events from that given by the claimant, he must state his own version.

(3) A defendant who—

(a) fails to deal with an allegation; but

(b) has set out in his defence the nature of his case in relation to the issue to which that allegation is relevant;

shall be taken to require that allegation to be proved.

(4) Where the claim includes a money claim, a defendant shall be taken to require that any allegation relating to the amount of money claimed be proved unless he expressly admits the allegation.

(5) Subject to paragraphs (3) and (4), a defendant who fails to deal with an allegation shall be taken to admit that allegation.

(6) If the defendant disputes the claimant's statement of value under rule 16.3 he must—

(a) state why he disputes it; and

(b) if he is able, give his own statement of the value of the claim.

(7) If the defendant is defending in a representative capacity, he must state what that capacity is.

(8) If the defendant has not filed an acknowledgment of service under Part 10, the defendant he must give an address for service.

(Part 22 requires a defence to be verified by a statement of truth).

(Rule 6.23 provides that an address for service must be within the United Kingdom).

Contents of defence

16.5.1

The defence must:

(1) provide a comprehensive response to the particulars of claim;
(2) state any representative capacity in which the defendant is defending;
(3) include any other matters required by a practice direction;
(4) unless an acknowledgment of service has been filed, give an address for service.

The defence may also refer to any point of law on which it is based, or name any witnesses whom the defendant proposes to call or have attached to it or served with it

[1] Amended by the Civil Procedure (Amendment) Rules 2008 (SI 2008/2178).

a copy of any document considered essential to it (para.16.3 of the practice direction supplementing Pt 16 (see para.16PD.3)). There are also some specific requirements as to points of law and documents (see "Other matters required by a practice direction" below).

The defence must be verified by a statement of truth (see "Statement of truth" below).

Comprehensive response to the particulars of claim

16.5.2 In respect of each allegation in the particulars of claim there should be an admission, a denial or a requirement for proof (r.16.5(1)). Denials must be explicit; the defendants must state his reasons for denying the allegation and, if he intends to put forward a different version of events from that given by the claimant, he must state his own version (r.16.5(2)). Similarly, if he disputes the statement of value included in the claim form he must state why he disputes it and, if he is able, must give his own statement of the value of the claim (r.16.5(3)).

Defending in a representative capacity

16.5.3 If the defendant is defending in a representative capacity, he must state what that capacity is (r.16.5(7)). As to the term "representative capacity" see further the commentary to r.16.2 under the heading "a representative capacity" (para.16.2.6).

Other matters required by a practice direction

16.5.4 Paragraph 10 of the Practice Direction supplementing Pt 16 (see para.16PD.10) requires a defendant who is an individual to give certain further information: an address including postcode at which the defendant resides or carries on business (unless the claim form already states such an address which is correct). A full address must be given, even where the defendant has specified an address for service (as to which, see para.16.5.5, below) which is not an address at which he resides or carries on business. A defendant to a claim or counterclaim who is an individual must also state his date of birth (if known) in the acknowledgment of service, admission, defence, defence to counterclaim, reply or other response (para.10.7).

Paragraphs 12 and 13 of the Practice Direction supplementing Pt 16 (see paras 16PD.12 *et seq.*) set out various matters (including in some cases an obligation to deal with points of law or annex documents) which must be dealt with in the defence in the following circumstances:

(1) where the claim is for personal injuries;

(2) where the defendant relies on a limitation period as a defence.

As to various matters which must be dealt with in the defence to a defamation claim, see the Practice Direction supplementing Pt 53 (defamation claims).

Paragraph 14 of the Practice Direction supplementing Pt 16 (see para.16PD.15) sets out the matters to be included in a statement of case by a party who wishes to rely on a finding of the Office of Fair Trading as provided by s.58 of the Competition Act 1998.

If the defence exceeds 25 pages (excluding schedules) an appropriate short summary must also be filed and served (para.1.4 of the Practice Direction supplementing Pt 16, para.16PD.1, below).

Give an address for service

16.5.5 If the defendant has not filed an acknowledgment of service under Pt 10 he must give an address for service (r.16.5(8)). As to addresses for service see r.6.5 and the commentary thereto (para.6.5.3).

Defence of tender

16.5.6 The expression "defence of tender" is defined in the Glossary. The defence may be raised in response to any money claim, whether or not a specified amount is claimed. Where the defendant wishes to rely on this defence he must make a payment into court of the amount he says was tendered (r.37.3).

Filing a defence and counterclaim

16.5.7 A defendant who wishes to defend must file a defence (r.15.2) and a copy of it must be served on every other party (r.15.6). A defendant may make a counterclaim against a claimant by filing particulars of the counterclaim (r.20.4). Practice Directions state that "the defence and counterclaim should normally form one document with the counterclaim following on from the defence" (Practice Direction supplementing Pt 15, para.3.1 (see para.15PD.3) and Practice Direction supplementing Pt 20, para.6.1 (see para.20PD.6)).

If the statement of case exceeds 25 pages (excluding schedules) an appropriate short summary must also be filed and served (para.1.4 of the Practice Direction supplementing Pt 16, para.16PD.1, below).

Consequences of not dealing with an allegation

In two cases allegations in the particulars of claim which are not expressly dealt with in the defence will be treated as allegations which the claimant is required to prove: **16.5.8**

(1) where the allegations are inconsistent with the nature of the case set out in the defence (this appears to be the effect of r.16.5(3)); and

(2) in money claims allegations relating to the amount of money claimed (r.16.5(4)).

Save in those two cases a defendant who fails to deal with an allegation shall be taken to admit that allegation (r.16.5(5)).

Statement of truth

A defence must be verified by a statement of truth (r.22.1) in the following form "[I believe] [the defendant believes] that the facts stated in the defence are true" (para.11.2 of the Practice Direction supplementing Pt 16). If the statement of truth is contained in a separate document it should specify the date on which it was served and the name of the party on whom it was served (para.2.3 of the Practice Direction supplementing Pt 22 (see para.22PD.2)). **16.5.9**

The statement of truth must be signed by the defendant or his legal representative (para.3.1 of the Practice Direction supplementing Pt 22; para.3.1 and the subsequent paras also make provision for signing where the defendant is a child, a patient or a company or other corporation and where the defence is served on behalf of a partnership).

A defence verified by a statement of truth may be used as evidence by the defendant at any hearing other than the trial (r.32.6).

As to the significance of a statement of truth signed by a legal representative, see para.3.8 of the Practice Direction supplementing Pt 22 (para.22PD.3). As to the consequence of verifying a defence containing a false statement of fact without an honest belief in its truth, see r.32.14.

The purpose of the statement of truth is to eliminate claims in which a party has no honest belief and to discourage the pleading of cases unsupported by evidence which are put forward in the hope that something might turn up on disclosure or at the trial (*Clarke v Marlborough Fine Art (London) Ltd (Amendments)* [2002] 1 W.L.R. 1731, *per* Patten J.). For the procedure to follow if a defendant wishes to deny allegations made by the claimant but also wishes to advance an alternative defence based on those allegations, see *Binks v Securicor Omega Express Ltd* [2003] EWCA Civ 993; [2003] 1 W.L.R. 2557, CA, noted in para.16.4.6, above.

The court may strike out a defence which is not verified by a statement of truth (r.22.2(2)).

Providing information about a funding arrangement

In certain circumstances a party may be entitled to recover from another party certain success fees and sums in respect of insurance cover if he has entered into a relevant "funding arrangement" (defined in r.43.2) and if he has filed or served on the other party a valid notice of funding (see generally rr.44.3B, 44 15 and the commentary thereto: for the form of notice see Form **N251**). **16.5.10**

A defendant who has entered into a funding arrangement before filing any document must file the notice with his first document (whether it is an acknowledgment of service, a defence or a specification to set aside a default judgment) and must serve the notice with his first document or, if the court is to serve the first document, must file sufficient copies of the notice for service by the lower court. A defendant who enters into a funding arrangement on or after filing his first document must file and serve the notice of funding within seven days of entering into the funding arrangement (Costs Practice Direction, para.19.2, see 44PD.13).

Defence of set-off

16.6 **16.6 Where a defendant—**

(a) contends he is entitled to money from the claimant; and

(b) relies on this as a defence to the whole or part of the claim, the contention may be included in the defence and set off against the claim, whether or not it is also a Part 20 claim.

Effect of rule

16.6.1 This rule makes wide provisions for monetary cross-claims "to be included in the defence and set-off against the claim" whether or not the cross-claim is a claim in debt or is inter-related with the claimant's claim. The previous High Court rules contained a provision (RSC O.18, r.17) which was almost identical to this rule. However, when that provision was in force there was established case law to the effect that the question whether or not a cross-claim amounted to a set-off was a "matter of law" and did not depend upon the form in which it was pleaded. ("The question as to what is a set off is to be determined as a matter of law and is not in any way governed by the language used by the parties in their pleadings" (*per* Morris L.J. in *Hanak v Green* [1958] 2 Q.B. 9 at 26 and see SCA 1981 s.49(2)(a)). That "matter of law" was both complex and restrictive and from time to time attracted judicial criticism (see for example *Axel Johnson Petroleum AB v MG Mineral Group AG* [1992] 1 W.L.R. 270, CA). It is possible that the court will take the opportunity which the wide words of r.16.6 allows to define "set-offs" differently in future. Even if the widest possible definition was given, the court would still be able to summarily dispose of issues raised by the claimant's claim which do not need full investigation and trial. In all such cases the defendant's position would have to be protected by an order delaying enforcement of judgment on the claim until after the trial of any cross-claim (see r.24.2, and the commentary thereto and r.24.6 under "Judgment on the claim or on an issue therein").

Reply to defence

16.7 **16.7—(1) A claimant who does not file a reply to the defence shall not be taken to admit the matters raised in the defence.**

(2) A claimant who—

(a) files a reply to a defence; but

(b) fails to deal with a matter raised in the defence,

shall be taken to require that matter to be proved.

(Part 22 requires a reply to be verified by a statement of truth.)

Where reply necessary

16.7.1 A reply is optional (see r.15.8). A claimant need not serve a reply unless he wishes to allege facts in answer to the defence which were not included in his claim.

No implied admission of the defence

16.7.2 Unless the claimant makes an express admission, the defendant will be required to prove facts raised in his defence whether the claimant files a reply (r.16.7(2)) or does not file a reply (r.16.7(1)).

Reply must not contradict the claim

16.7.3 A reply must not contradict or be inconsistent with the claim; for example it must not bring in a new claim. If the claimant wishes to depart from the case set out in his claim he should seek to amend that claim rather than serve a reply (see generally para.10.2 of the Practice Direction supplementing Pt 16 (para.16PD.10)).

Serving a reply and defence to counterclaim

16.7.4 A claimant who wishes to rely on a reply must file it and serve copies on the other parties (r.15.8). A claimant who wishes to defend a counterclaim must file a defence and a copy of it must be served on every other party (see r.15.2, r.15.6 and r.20.2).

Practice Directions provide that "the reply and defence to counterclaim should normally form one document with the defence to counterclaim following on from the reply" (Practice Direction supplementing Pt 15, para.3.2 (see para.15PD.3) and Practice Direction supplementing Pt 20, para.6.2 (see para.20PD.6)). However they may be served as separate documents if the time limit for serving the defence to counterclaim is shorter than the time limit for the reply. (See further para.3.2A of the Practice Direction supplementing Pt 15, para.15PD.3 and para.15.8.3 above.

If the statement of case exceeds 25 pages (excluding schedules) an appropriate short summary must also be filed and served (para.1.4 of the Practice Direction supplementing Pt 16, para.16PD.1 below).

Statement of truth

A reply must be verified by a statement of truth (r.22.1) in the following form "[I believe] [the claimant believes] that the facts stated in this reply are true" (para.2.1 of the Practice Direction supplementing Pt 22 (see para.22PD.2)). If the statement of truth is contained in a separate document it should specify the date on which it was served and the name of the party on whom it was served (para.2.3). **16.7.5**

The statement of truth must be signed by the claimant or his legal representative (para.3.1 of the Practice Direction supplementing Pt 22; para.3.1 and the subsequent paras also make provision for signing where the claimant is a child, a patient, or a company or other corporation and where the reply is served on behalf of a partnership.

A reply verified by a statement of truth may be used as evidence by the claimant at any hearing other than the trial (r.32.6).

As to the significance of a statement of truth signed by a legal representative, see para.3.8 of the Practice Direction supplementing Pt 22. As to the consequences of verifying a reply containing a false statement of fact without an honest belief in its truth, see r.32.14.

The purpose of the statement of truth is to eliminate claims in which a party has no honest belief and to discourage the pleading of cases unsupported by evidence which are put forward in the hope that something might turn up on disclosure or at the trial (*Clarke v Marlborough Fine Art (London) Ltd (Amendments)* [2002] 1 W.L.R. 1731, *per* Patten J.).

The court may strike out a reply which is not verified by a statement of truth (r.22.2(2)).

Statements of case subsequent to a reply

No party may file or serve a statement of case after thereply without the court's permission (r.15.9). **16.7.6**

Court's power to dispense with statements of case

16.8 If a claim form has been— **16.8**

(a) issued in accordance with rule 7.2; and

(b) served in accordance with rule 7.5,

the court may make an order that the claim will continue without any other statement of case.

Effect of rule

This rule gives the court express power to make an order which dispenses with all statements of case other than the claim form. The power is first exercisable once the claim form has been issued and served. On making the order the court may give further directions as to case management including perhaps the allocation of the claim to a particular case management track. **16.8.1**

A claim in which there are no statements of case other than the claim form is analogous to the alternative procedure for claims (Pt 8). Where that procedure is followed the claim is treated as allocated to the multi-track (r.8.9(c)).

PRACTICE DIRECTION—STATEMENTS OF CASE

This Practice Direction supplements CPR Part 16

General

16PD.1 **1.1** The provisions of Part 16 do not apply to claims in respect of which the Part 8 procedure is being used.

1.2 Where special provisions about statements of case are made by the rules and practice directions applying to particular types of proceedings, the provisions of Part 16 and of this practice direction apply only to the extent that they are not inconsistent with those rules and practice directions.

1.3 Examples of types of proceedings with special provisions about statements of case include—

(1) defamation claims (Part 53);

(2) possession claims (Part 55); and

(3) probate claims (Part 57).

1.4 If exceptionally a statement of case exceeds 25 pages (excluding schedules) an appropriate short summary must also be filed and served.

The claim form

16PD.2 **2.1** Rule 16.2 refers to matters which the claim form must contain. Where the claim is for money, the claim form must also contain the statement of value referred to in rule 16.3.

2.2 The claim form must include an address at which the claimant resides or carries on business. This paragraph applies even though the claimant's address for service is the business address of his solicitor.

2.3 Where the defendant is an individual, the claimant should (if he is able to do so) include in the claim form an address at which the defendant resides or carries on business. This paragraph applies even though the defendant's solicitors have agreed to accept service on the defendant's behalf.

2.4 Any address which is provided for the purpose of these provisions must include a postcode, unless the court orders otherwise. Postcode information may be obtained from *www.royalmail.com* or the Royal Mail Address Management Guide.

2.5 If the claim form does not show a full address, including postcode, at which the claimant(s) and defendant(s) reside or carry on business, the claim form will be issued but will be retained by the court and will not be served until the claimant has supplied a full address, including postcode, or the court has dispensed with the requirement to do so. The court will notify the claimant.

2.6 The claim form must be headed with the title of the proceedings, including the full name of each party. The full name means, in each case where it is known:

(a) in the case of an individual, his full unabbreviated name *and title* by which he is known;

(b) in the case of an individual carrying on business in a name other than his own name, the full unabbreviated name of the individual, together with the title by which he is known, and the full trading name (for example, John Smith 'trading as' or 'T/as' 'JS Autos');

(c) in the case of a partnership (other than a limited liability partnership (LLP))—

(i) where partners are being sued in the name of the partnership, the full name by which the partnership is known, together with the words "(A Firm)"; or

(ii) where partners are being sued as individuals, the full unabbreviated name of each partner and the title by which he is known;

(d) in the case of a company or limited liability partnership registered in England and Wales, the full registered name, including suffix (plc, limited, LLP, etc), if any;

(e) in the case of any other company or corporation, the full name by which it is known, including suffix where appropriate.

(For information about how and where a claim may be started see Part 7 and the practice direction which supplements it.)

Particulars of claim

3.1 If practicable, the particulars of claim should be set out in the claim form. **16PD.3**

3.2 Where the claimant does not include the particulars of claim in the claim form, particulars of claim may be served separately:

(1) either at the same time as the claim form, or

(2) within 14 days after service of the claim form [1] provided that the service of the particulars of claim is not later than 4 months from the date of issue of the claim form [2] (or 6 months where the claim form is to be served out of the jurisdiction [3]).

3.3 If the particulars of claim are not included in or have not been served with the claim form, the claim form must also contain a statement that particulars of claim will follow[4].

3.4 Particulars of claim which are not included in the claim form must be verified by a statement of truth, the form of which is as follows:

"[I believe] [the claimant believes] that the facts stated in these particulars of claim are true."

3.5 Attention is drawn to rule 32.14 which sets out the consequences of verifying a statement of case containing a false statement without an honest belief in its truth.

3.6 The full particulars of claim must include:

(1) the matters set out in rule 16.4, and

(2) where appropriate, the matters set out in practice directions relating to specific types of claims.

---

[1] See r.7.4(1)(b).
[2] See r.7.4(1)(b).
[3] See r.7.5(2).
[4] See r.16.2(2).

3.7 Attention is drawn to the provisions of rule 16.4(2) in respect of a claim for interest.

3.8 Particulars of claim served separately from the claim form must also contain:

(1) the name of the court in which the claim is proceeding,
(2) the claim number,
(3) the title of the proceedings, and
(4) the claimant's address for service.

Matters which must be included in the particulars of claim in certain types of claim

Personal injury claims

16PD.4 **4.1** The particulars of claim must contain:

(1) the claimant's date of birth, and
(2) brief details of the claimant's personal injuries.

4.2 The claimant must attach to his particulars of claim a schedule of details of any past and future expenses and losses which he claims.

4.3 Where the claimant is relying on the evidence of a medical practitioner the claimant must attach to or serve with his particulars of claim a report from a medical practitioner about the personal injuries which he alleges in his claim.

4.4 In a provisional damages claim the claimant must state in his particulars of claim:

(1) that he is seeking an award of provisional damages under either section 32A of the Supreme Court Act 1981 or section 51 of the County Courts Act 1984,
(2) that there is a chance that at some future time the claimant will develop some serious disease or suffer some serious deterioration in his physical or mental condition, and
(3) specify the disease or type of deterioration in respect of which an application may be made at a future date.

(Part 41 and the practice direction which supplements it contain information about awards for provisional damages.)

Fatal accident claims

16PD.5 **5.1** In a fatal accident claim the claimant must state in his particulars of claim:

(1) that it is brought under the Fatal Accidents Act 1976,
(2) the dependants on whose behalf the claim is made,
(3) the date of birth of each dependant, and
(4) details of the nature of the dependency claim.

5.2 A fatal accident claim may include a claim for damages for bereavement.

5.3 In a fatal accident claim the claimant may also bring a claim under the Law Reform (Miscellaneous Provisions) Act 1934 on behalf of the estate of the deceased.

(For information on apportionment under the Law Reform (Miscellaneous Provisions) Act 1934 and the Fatal Accidents Act 1976 or between dependants see Part 37 and the practice direction which supplements it.)

Hire purchase claims

6.1 Where the claim is for the delivery of goods let under a hire-purchase agreement or conditional sale agreement to a person other than a company or other corporation, the claimant must state in the particulars of claim: **16PD.6**

(1) the date of the agreement,
(2) the parties to the agreement,
(3) the number or other identification of the agreement,
(4) where the claimant was not one of the original parties to the agreement, the means by which the rights and duties of the creditor passed to him,
(5) whether the agreement is a regulated agreement, and if it is not a regulated agreement, the reason why,
(6) the place where the agreement was signed by the defendant,
(7) the goods claimed,
(8) the total price of the goods,
(9) the paid-up sum,
(10) the unpaid balance of the total price,
(11) whether a default notice or a notice under section 76(1) or 98(1) of the Consumer Credit Act 1974 has been served on the defendant, and if it has, the date and method of service,
(12) the date when the right to demand delivery of the goods accrued,
(13) the amount (if any) claimed as an alternative to the delivery of goods, and
(14) the amount (if any) claimed in addition to—
    (a) the delivery of the goods, or
    (b) any claim under (13) above,
    with the grounds of each claim.

(If the agreement is a regulated agreement the procedure set out in the practice direction relating to consumer credit act claims (which supplements Part 7) should be used.)

6.2 Where the claim is not for the delivery of goods, the claimant must state in his particulars of claim:

(1) the matters set out in paragraph 6.1(1) to (6) above,
(2) the goods let under the agreement,
(3) the amount of the total price,
(4) the paid-up sum,
(5) the amount (if any) claimed as being due and unpaid in respect of any instalment or instalments of the total price, and
(6) the nature and amount of any other claim and how it arises.

Other matters to be included in particulars of claim

7.1 Where a claim is made for an injunction or declaration in respect of or relating to any land or the possession, occupation, use or enjoyment of any land the particulars of claim must: **16PD.7**

(1) state whether or not the injunction or declaration relates to residential premises, and

(2) identify the land (by reference to a plan where necessary).

7.2 Where a claim is brought to enforce a right to recover possession of goods the particulars of claim must contain a statement showing the value of the goods.

7.3 Where a claim is based upon a written agreement:

(1) a copy of the contract or documents constituting the agreement should be attached to or served with the particulars of claim and the original(s) should be available at the hearing, and

(2) any general conditions of sale incorporated in the contract should also be attached (but where the contract is or the documents constituting the agreement are bulky this practice direction is complied with by attaching or serving only the relevant parts of the contract or documents).

7.4 Where a claim is based upon an oral agreement, the particulars of claim should set out the contractual words used and state by whom, to whom, when and where they were spoken.

7.5 Where a claim is based upon an agreement by conduct, the particulars of claim must specify the conduct relied on and state by whom, when and where the acts constituting the conduct were done.

7.6 In a claim issued in the High Court relating to a Consumer Credit Agreement, the particulars of claim must contain a statement that the action is not one to which section 141 of the Consumer Credit Act 1974 applies.

Matters which must be specifically set out in the particulars of claim if relied on

16PD.8 **8.1** A claimant who wishes to rely on evidence:

(1) under section 11 of the Civil Evidence Act 1968 of a conviction of an offence, or

(2) under section 12 of the above-mentioned Act of a finding or adjudication of adultery or paternity,

must include in his particulars of claim a statement to that effect and give the following details:

(1) the type of conviction, finding or adjudication and its date,

(2) the court or Court-Martial which made the conviction, finding or adjudication, and

(3) the issue in the claim to which it relates.

8.2 The claimant must specifically set out the following matters in his particulars of claim where he wishes to rely on them in support of his claim:

(1) any allegation of fraud,

(2) the fact of any illegality,

(3) details of any misrepresentation,

(4) details of all breaches of trust,

(5) notice or knowledge of a fact,

(6) details of unsoundness of mind or undue influence,

(7) details of wilful default, and

(8) any facts relating to mitigation of loss or damage.

General

9.1 Where a claim is for a sum of money expressed in a foreign currency it must expressly state: 16PD.9

(1) that the claim is for payment in a specified foreign currency,
(2) why it is for payment in that currency,
(3) the Sterling equivalent of the sum at the date of the claim, and
(4) the source of the exchange rate relied on to calculate the Sterling equivalent.

9.2 A subsequent statement of case must not contradict or be inconsistent with an earlier one; for example a reply to a defence must not bring in a new claim. Where new matters have come to light the appropriate course may be to seek the court's permission to amend the statement of case.

9.3 In clinical negligence claims, the words "clinical negligence" should be inserted at the top of every statement of case.

The defence

General

10.1 Rule 16.5 deals with the contents of the defence. 16PD.10

10.2 A defendant should deal with every allegation in accordance with rule 16.5(1) and (2).

10.3 Rule 16.5(3), (4) and (5) sets out the consequences of not dealing with an allegation.

10.4 Where the defendant is an individual, and the claim form does not contain an address at which he resides or carries on business, or contains an incorrect address, the defendant must provide such an address in the defence.

10.5 Where the defendant's address for service is not where he resides or carries on business, he must still provide the address required by paragraph 10.4.

10.6 Any address which is provided for the purpose of these provisions must include a postcode, unless the court orders otherwise. Postcode information may be obtained from *www.royalmail.com* or the Royal Mail Address Management Guide.

10.7 Where a defendant to a claim or counterclaim is an individual, he must provide his date of birth (if known) in the acknowledgment of service, admission, defence, defence and counterclaim, reply or other response.

Statement of truth

11.1 *Part 22 requires a defence* to be verified by a statement of truth. 16PD.11

11.2 The form of the statement of truth is as follows:

"[I believe] [the defendant believes] that the facts stated in the defence are true."

11.3 Attention is drawn to rule 32.14 which sets out the consequences of verifying a statement of case containing a false statement without an honest belief in its truth.

Matters which must be included in the defence

Personal injury claims

16PD.12 **12.1** Where the claim is for personal injuries and the claimant has attached a medical report in respect of his alleged injuries, the defendant should:

(1) state in his defence whether he—
  (a) agrees,
  (b) disputes, or
  (c) neither agrees nor disputes but has no knowledge of,
  the matters contained in the medical report,

(2) where he disputes any part of the medical report, give in his defence his reasons for doing so, and

(3) where he has obtained his own medical report on which he intends to rely, attach it to his defence.

12.2 Where the claim is for personal injuries and the claimant has included a schedule of past and future expenses and losses, the defendant should include in or attach to his defence a counter-schedule stating:

(1) which of those items he—
  (a) agrees,
  (b) disputes, or
  (c) neither agrees nor disputes but has no knowledge of, and

(2) where any items are disputed, supplying alternative figures where appropriate.

Other matters

16PD.13 **13.1** The defendant must give details of the expiry of any relevant limitation period relied on.

13.2 Rule 37.3 and paragraph 2 of the practice direction which supplements Part 37 contains information about a defence of tender.

13.3 A party may:

(1) refer in his statement of case to any point of law on which his claim or defence, as the case may be, is based,

(2) give in his statement of case the name of any witness he proposes to call, and

(3) attach to or serve with this statement of case a copy of any document which he considers is necessary to his claim or defence, as the case may be (including any expert's report to be filed in accordance with Part 35).

(The Costs Practice Direction supplementing Parts 43 to 48 contains details of the information required to be filed with certain statements of case to comply with rule 44.15 (providing information about funding arrangements).)

Competition Act 1998

16PD.14 **14** A party who wishes to rely on a finding of the Office of Fair Trading as provided by section 58 of the Competition Act 1998 must include in his statement of case a statement to that effect and identify the Office's finding on which he seeks to rely.

Human Rights

15.1 A party who seeks to rely on any provision of or right arising under the Human Rights Act 1998 or seeks a remedy available under that Act— **16PD.15**

(1) must state that fact in his statement of case; and

(2) must in his statement of case—

(a) give precise details of the Convention right which it is alleged has been infringed and details of the alleged infringement;

(b) specify the relief sought;

(c) state if the relief sought includes—

(i) a declaration of incompatibility in accordance with section 4 of that Act, or

(ii) damages in respect of a judicial act to which section 9(3) of that Act applies;

(d) where the relief sought includes a declaration of incompatibility in accordance with section 4 of that Act, give precise details of the legislative provision alleged to be incompatible and details of the alleged incompatibility;

(e) where the claim is founded on a finding of unlawfulness by another court or tribunal, give details of the finding; and

(f) where the claim is founded on a judicial act which is alleged to have infringed a Convention right of the party as provided by section 9 of the Human Rights Act 1998, the judicial act complained of and the court or tribunal which is alleged to have made it.

(The practice direction to Part 19 provides for notice to be given and parties joined in the circumstances referred to in (c), (d) and (f).)

15.2 A party who seeks to amend his statement of case to include the matters referred to in paragraph 15.1 must, unless the court orders otherwise, do so as soon as possible.

(Part 17 provides for the amendment of a statement of case.)

PART 17

AMENDMENTS TO STATEMENTS OF CASE

Contents

17.0.1

Editorial Introduction

17.0.2 The rules in this Part deal with amendments to "statements of case", a term which means "a claim form, particulars of claim where these are not included in the claim form, defence, Part 20 claim or a reply to a defence" (r.2.3(1)).

Related sources

17.0.3
- Practice Direction (Amendments to Statements of Case) (see para.17PD.1)
- Part 19 (Addition and substitution of parties)
- Part 23 (General rules about applications for court orders)

Amendments to statements of case[1]

17.1 **17.1—(1) A party may amend his statement of case at any time before it has been served on any other party.**

(2) If his statement case has been served, a party may amend it only—

(a) with the written consent of all the other parties; or

(b) with the permission of the court

(3) If a statement of case has been served, an application to amend it by removing, adding or substituting a party must be made in accordance with rule 19.4.

(Part 22 requires amendments to a statement of case to be verified by a statement of truth unless the court orders otherwise.)

Effect of rule

17.1.1 A party who has served his statement of case must obtain the permission of the court if he later wishes to amend it so as to remove, add or substitute a party (r.17.1(3) which applies r.19.4) or if he later wishes to amend it so as to withdraw an admission it contains relating to another party's case (r.14.1, and see the Practice Direction supplementing Pt 14, para.7.2). In other respects a statement of case which has been served can be amended if:

(1) all other parties give written consent, or

(2) the court gives permission.

Accordingly, the right to amend without consent or permission arises only in respect of statements of case which are filed but not served.

---

[1] Amended by the Civil Procedure (Amendment) Rules 2000 (SI 2000/221).

Practice on amendment

A party amending his statement of case is not required to retain the superseded text in the amended document unless the court directs him to do so. If the superseded text is included it should be shown either: **17.1.2**

(1) struck through in the appropriate colour: new text should be inserted or underlined in the same colour (see Practice Direction supplementing Pt 17, para.2.3 (para.17PD.2): the order of colours is, as previously, red, green, violet and then yellow),

(2) printed in monochrome document in a different type-face from the new text: the document must include a numerical code defining the different typefaces (see Practice Direction supplementing Pt 17, para.2.2 (see para.17PD.2). As to the practice in the Commercial Court (which is substantially different) see para.17.8 of the Practice Direction supplementing Pt 58 (para.58PD.18 below) and para.C5 of the Commercial Court Guide (Vol.2, para.2A–60).

A statement of case amended without permission must be endorsed as follows "Amended [Particulars of Claim *or as may be*] under CPR [17.1(1)(c) or (2)(a)] dated ..." and should be filed as well as served.

A statement of case amended by order must be endorsed as follows "Amended [Particulars of Claim *or as may be*] by Order of [Master ...] [District Judge ... *or as may be*] dated ..." and should be filed within 14 days of the date of the order or within such other period as the court may direct (Practice Direction supplementing Pt 17, paras 1.3 and 2.1 (see paras 17PD.1 and 17PD.2)).

Where a statement of case is amended, the amendments must be verified by a statement of truth unless the court otherwise orders (r.22.1(2) and Practice Direction supplementing Pt 17, para.1.4; see paras 17PD.1 and 22.1.8 below). The purpose of the statement of truth is to eliminate claims in which a party has no honest belief and to discourage the pleadings of cases unsupported by evidence which are put forward in the hope that something might turn up on disclosure as at the trial (*Clarke v Marlborough Fine Art (London) Ltd* [2002] 1 W.L.R. 1731 at 1746A. The court may strike out a statement of case which is not verified by a statement of truth (r.22.2).

In several cases a party has been permitted to advance an alternative case based on material put forward by his opponent which was inconsistent with the case he had already pleaded: *Goode v Martin* [2001] EWCA Civ 1899; [2001] 3 All E.R 562 (see para.17.4.2, below); *Kelly v Chief Constable of South Yorkshire (No.1)* [2001] EWCA Civ 1632 (see para.17.3.8, below) and *Binks v Securicor Omega Express Ltd* [2003] EWCA Civ 993; [2003] 1 W.L.R. 2557, CA (see para.16.4.6, above). In *Binks* it was suggested that, where appropriate, the court might dispense with verification by statement of truth; alternatively the amending party might be able to give a suitably qualified statement of truth (see further, para.16.4.6, above).

Power of court to disallow amendments made without permission

17.2—(1) If a party has amended his statement of case where permission of the court was not required, the court may disallow the amendment. **17.2**

(2) A party may apply to the court for an order under paragraph (1) within 14 days of service of a copy of the amended statement of case on him.

Effect of rule

An application under this rule is appropriate if the amendment challenged is one which, if permission to amend it had been necessary, that permission would not have been granted. The clearest examples of such amendments are those which are scurrilous, vexatious or shown to be dishonest. In such cases an application might also be made under r.3.4 (Power to strike out a statement of case) or Pt 24 (summary judgment). **17.2.1**

If an amendment is irregular, i.e. made without permission where permission was necessary, a party wishing to challenge it should apply under r.3.4 (Power to strike out a statement of case).

Time limit for application

A party wishing to apply under r.17.2 should do so within 14 days of service of a copy of the amended statement of case (r.17.2(2)). **17.2.2**

Amendments to the statements of case with the permission of the court

17.3 **17.3—(1) Where the court gives permission for a party to amend his statement of case, it may give directions as to—**

(a) amendments to be made to any other statement of case; and

(b) service of any amended statement of case

(2) The power of the court to give permission under this rule is subject to—

(a) rule 19.1 (change of parties—general);

(b) rule 19.4 (special provisions about adding or substituting parties after the end of a relevant limitation period[GL]); and

(c) rule 17.4 (amendments of statement of case after the end of a relevant limitation period).

When permission needed

17.3.1 A party who has served his statement of case must obtain the permission of the court if he later wishes to amend it so as to remove, add or substitute a party (r.17.1(3) which applies r.19.4) or if he later wishes to amend it so as to withdraw an admission it contains relating to another party's case (r.14.1, and see the Practice Direction supplementing Pt 14, para.7.2). In other respects a statement of case which has been served can be amended without the permission of the court if all other parties give written consent.

As from May 2000, r.17.3(2) requires amendment to take account of the amendments to Pt 19; what was r.19.1 is now r.19.2 and what was r.19.4 is now r.19.5.

For limits on the court's power to allow amendments after the end of a relevant limitation period, see r.17.4.

Procedure on application

17.3.2 On an application under r.17.3 a copy of the statement of case should be filed with the application notice (as to which, see r.23.6 and the Practice Direction supplementing Pt 23, para.2.1 (para.23PD.2)). If the application is made at an early stage of the proceedings it may be appropriate to request the court to deal with it without a hearing (r.23.8 and see the Practice Direction supplementing Pt 23, para.2.1).

If the court gives permission to amend it may give directions as to consequential amendments to other statements of case and as to the service of the amended statement of case (r.17.3(1)). Unless the court otherwise orders the applicant should file the amended statement of case within 14 days of the order and must serve a copy of the order and the amended statement of case on every other party to the proceedings (Practice Direction supplementing Pt 17, paras 1.3 and 1.5 (see para.17PD.1)).

Practice on amendment

17.3.3 See this heading under r.17.1.

Effect of amendment

17.3.4 Under the previous rules, an amendment duly made, with or without leave, took effect, not from the date when the amendment was made, but from the date of the original document which it amended. This rule applied to every successive amendment of whatever nature and at whatever stage the amendment was made. Thus, when an amendment was made to the writ, the amendment dated back to the date of the original issue of the writ and the action continued as if the amendment had been inserted from the beginning: "the writ as amended becomes the origin of the action, and the claim thereon endorsed is substituted for the claim originally endorsed" (*per* Collins M.R. in *Sneade v Wotherton, etc.* [1904] 1 K.B. 295 at 297). Similarly in the pleadings: "once pleadings are amended, what stood before amendment is no longer material before the court and no longer defines the issues to be tried" (*per* Hodson L.J. in *Warner v Sampson* [1959] 1 Q.B. 297 at 321). The fact that a pleading had been amended could sometimes affect the orders for costs which the court would make at trial: "As a general rule, where a plaintiff makes a late amendment, as here, which substantially alters the case the defendant has to meet and without which the action will fail, the defendant is entitled to the costs of the action down to the date of the amendment" (*per* Stuart-Smith L.J. in *Beoco Ltd v Alfa Laval Co Ltd* [1995] Q.B. 137). In *Gold v Mincoff Science & Gold* [2004] EWHC 2036, Ch, the claimant made an amendment at trial (in reply to a limitation defence, which reply the defendants had anticipated some months earlier when making offers to settle): had the amendment been made earlier, the claimant would have been awarded 85 per cent of his costs; because of the real possibility that the late amendment had prejudiced the defendants, Neuberger J. awarded the claimant only 62.5 per cent of his costs up to the date of the amendment and 85 per cent thereafter.

The making of an amendment on the basis of which the amending party ultimately succeeds at trial may affect the costs consequences which flow from a Pt 36 offer made before the amendment. In *Norwegian Cruise Line Ltd v Thompson Holidays Ltd*, December 15, 2000, unrep., Ch D, the claimant made such an amendment some five weeks after making a Pt 36 offer and, some three weeks later made another Pt 36 offer. Because of the amendment the defendant lost at trial and failed to beat the first Pt 36 offer. It was held appropriate to allow the defendant a notional period in which to reconsider its case following the amendment. In all the circumstances the claimant was awarded costs on the standard basis up to a date four weeks after the second Pt 36 offer with costs on the indemnity basis and additional interest thereafter.

A claim allocated to the fast track may remain on that track even though the court has permitted the claimant to amend the claim so as to claim damages for an amount in excess of that fixed by para.(4) of r.26.6 (Scope of each track). It does not follow that such a case must inevitably be reallocated to the multi track (*Maguire v Molin* [2002] EWCA Civ 1083; [2003] 1 W.L.R. 644).

General principles for grant of permission to amend

Except in cases to which r.17.4 applies (i.e. cases in which a limitation period has expired), the provisions as to amendment of statements of case in Pt 17 give no indication as to the principles which the court should apply in determining whether an amendment may be made and whether, in the exercise of the court's discretion, it should be permitted (*Thurrock BC v Secretary of State for the Environment, Transport and the Regions (No.1)*, [2001] C.P. Rep. 55, CA). **17.3.5**

A dictum of Peter Gibson L.J. (see below) in *Cobbold v Greenwich LBC* August 9, 1999, unrep., CA, has been relied upon in many cases, both at first instance and on appeal (e.g. *Sumitomo Corp v Credit Lyonnais Rouse Ltd* [2003] EWHC 833, (Comm), April 8, 2003, unrep. (Cooke J.); *Law Debenture Trust Corporation (Channel Islands) Ltd, The v Lexington Insurance Co* [2001] EWCA Civ 1673, November 11, 2002, unrep., CA; *Cluley v RL Dix Heating* [2003] EWCA Civ 1595, October 31, 2003, unrep. CA; *Daniels v Thompson* [2004] EWCA Civ 307, March 18, 2004, unrep., CA). In the *Cobbold* case, the facts were that on August 5, 1999, a county court judge refused a housing authority's application to amend their defence in a repair action brought against them by a tenant and due to be tried on August 10. On August 9, a two-judge court of the Court of Appeal gave the defendants permission to appeal and granted the appeal. The Court said that the judge had erred in, amongst other things, coming to the conclusion that the defendants would suffer no prejudice were the amendment not allowed. In allowing the appeal Peter Gibson L.J. said (with Sedley L.J. concurring):

> "The overriding objective (of the CPR) is that the court should deal with cases justly. That includes, so far as is practicable, ensuring that each case is dealt with not only expeditiously but also fairly. Amendments in general ought to be allowed so that the real dispute between the parties can be adjudicated upon provided that any prejudice to the other party caused by the amendment can be compensated for in costs, and the public interest in the administration of justice is not significantly harmed".

In some subsequent cases this dictum has not been stated accurately. In particular, it has been stated in terms that elide with it the Court's comment, directed at their disagreement with the judge on the matter of prejudice to the defendants (and coming shortly after the passage quoted above), to the effect that "there is always prejudice when a party is not allowed to put forward his real case, provided it is properly arguable" (e.g. *Bowerbank v Amos* [2003] EWCA Civ 1161, July 31, 2003, unrep., CA). This elision has had the unfortunate effect of lending weight to the erroneous argument that, where there is prejudice to a party seeking an amendment, it should be allowed, when the true position is that the existence and weight of such prejudice is just one the factors to be taken into account.

In considering whether to permit amendments withdrawing an admission previously made in a statement of case the court must have regard to r.14.1 and the practice under that rule (as to which, see para.14.1.8, above, and see *White v Greensand Homes Ltd* [2007] EWCA Civ 643). *Lenton v Abrahams* [2003] EWHC 1104, QB, concerned a Fatal Accidents Act claim brought by the second claimant arising out of a road accident in which both drivers were killed; D admitted duty and breach of duty but did not admit that the second claimant had been a dependent of the other deceased driver "G". After the claimants had disposed of the car in which G had been travelling, D applied to amend the defence to allege that G had negligently contributed to her own death by failing to wear a seatbelt; the Master's decision refusing permission to amend was upheld on appeal. *Cluley v R.L. Dix Heating (A Firm)* [2003] EWCA Civ 1595 concerned a contractual claim in respect of plumbing works carried out at a dwelling house built for the claimants; in their defence the defendants admitted the existence of a contract between them and the claimants; later they obtained permission to amend to deny any such contract; by that stage it was too late for the claimants to take proceedings against the main contractor or the architect; the Court of Appeal struck out the amendment.

Although amendments take effect from the date of the original document which it amended (see para.17.3.4 above) there is no absolute rule of law or practice which precludes an amendment to rely on a cause of action which accrued only after the date of the original claim in circumstances where (but for the amendment) the claim could fail (*Maridive & Oil Services SAE v CNA Insurance Co (Europe) Ltd* [2002] EWCA Civ 369. In *British Credit Trust Holdings v UK Insurance Ltd* [2003] EWHC 2404 (Comm), C was permitted to amend the particulars of claim in an insurance dispute in order to seek declaratory relief in respect of insurance claims arising after the proceedings had started.

In *Finlan v Eyton Morris Winfield (a firm)* [2007] EWHC 914 (Ch); [2007] 4 All ER 143, a claimant sought to amend his Particulars of Claim to allege a deed of assignment to him of the causes of action which were the subject matter of the action. This was permitted even though the assignment post-dated the issue of the claim form so that, at the time of issue of the claim form, the claimant had not had title to sue upon those causes of action.

Need to show some prospects of success

17.3.6 An application for permission to amend a defence was refused when it was clear that the proposed amendment had no prospect of success (Oil & Minerals Development Corp v *Sajjad* [2002] EWHC 1258, QBD). The test to be supplied was the same as that in Pt 24 (Summary judgment); permission to amend was granted where the proposed amendments were arguable (*Flexitallic Group Inc v T & N Ltd* December 19, 2001, unrep., QBD).

Given the purpose of the statement of truth verifying an amendment (see para.17.1.2 above) a party will not be permitted to raise by amendment an allegation which is unsupported by any evidence and is therefore pure speculation or invention (*Clarke v Marlborough Fine Art (London) Ltd* [2002] EWHC 11).

A claimant should not be granted permission to amend his claim in order to raise a claim which is not maintainable in established law; the possibility that the House of Lords may develop or change the law was not sufficient to afford the claimant a real prospect of success at trial; the duty of the court is to apply the law as it stands (*Mandrake Holdings Ltd v Countrywide Assured Group Plc* [2005] EWHC 311, Ch, refusing permission to amend so as to add what was held to be a claim for damages for late payment of damages: a decision which was upheld by the Court of Appeal, [2005] EWCA Civ 638.).

Late amendments

17.3.7 An important factor for the court to consider when permission to amend is sought close to the trial date is whether the amendment will put the parties on an unequal footing or will place or add an excessive burden to the respondent's task of preparing for trial so as to jeopardise the trial date or so as to inevitably cause a postponement of the trial. In the following cases permission to make such an amendment was refused: *Woods v Chaleff* [1999] EWCA Civ 1522; [1999] C.L.Y. 500; *Morris v Bank of America National Trust and Savings Association (Amendment of Claim)* [2002] EWCA Civ 425, January 1, 2002 CLD. In the following cases permission to amend at or just before trial was granted: *Cobbold v Greenwich LBC* [1999] EWCA Civ 2074; August 9, 1999, unrep., CA; *Willis v Quality Heating Services* [2000] L.T.L., March 24, CA; *Electronic Data Systems Ltd v National Air Traffic Services* [2002] EWCA Civ 13, CA.

In *Cook v News Group Newspapers Ltd* [2002] EWHC 1070 (QB) the defendants sought permission to make amendments some five months before the date the trial would begin: permission was given only on matters which went to the central allegations of the defence; permission was refused for matters which were minor or peripheral.

In *National Westminster Bank Plc v Rabobank Nederland* [2006] EWHC 2959 (Comm) the trial court, which had already allowed amendments to be made to a counterclaim, was invited by the claimants to exercise its discretion of its own volition to strike out part of the new claim raised on the ground that it disclosed no reasonable cause of action (see further r.3.3(1) and r.3.4(2)(a)). Refusing that invitation, Colman J. stated that the circumstances in which such a course of action would be appropriate must be rare. The position was analogous to the hearing of a submission of no case to answer, as to which, see further para.32.1.6.

Amendment after evidence heard at trial

At the trial of a claim for assault, battery and false imprisonment, both sides called evidence as to the circumstances of the claimant's arrest and removal to a police station. The claimant then sought permission to amend her claim in order to allege that she had been assaulted an an earlier stage of her journey to the police station: such permission should have been granted (*Kelly v Chief Constable of South Yorkshire (No.1)* [2001] EWCA Civ 1632. **17.3.8**

One week before trial the claimant raised allegations of negligence which were different from the allegations in her particulars of claim. At the trial both sides called evidence on the case pleaded and on the new case. Before the defence evidence was concluded the claimant's counsel produced a note which the judge treated as amendment to the particulars of claim which included the new case. The claimant succeeded on the new case. In those circumstances the amendment to the claim did not amount to an unfair advantage to the claimant. The defendant had been able to make submissions as to it and it was not shown that the defendant would have called further evidence had it been able to see the note in advance (*Hall v Bolton MBC* [2001] EWCA Civ 1717, CA).

The court does have power to permit an amendment which is sought after judgment has been given but before an order recording that judgment has been drawn up and sealed. However, before permitting such an amendment the court must first decide whether there are exceptional circumstances or strong reasons for taking the unusual course of reopening the earlier decision (*Stewart v Engel (Permission to Amend)* [2000] 1 W.L.R. 2268, CA). "It is clearly not satisfactory for the (claimant) to be allowed to wait to see the outcome of the defendants' application (for summary judgment) and then, if the judge decides in the defendants' favour, to apply for an amendment. There must be some satisfactory reason for failure to apply for the amendment at the proper time. The proper time is either before the defendants' application is heard or during the hearing of the application" (*per* Roch L.J. in *Stewart v Engel (Permission to Amend)* [2000] 1 W.L.R. 2268, CA).

Amendment to include an original set-off or counterclaim which, if raised in separate proceedings, would be statute-barred

Under s.35(3) of the Limitation Act 1980, a claim is an original set-off or counterclaim for the purposes of s.35(3) if it is a claim made by way if set-off or (as the case may be) by way of counterclaim by a party who has not previously made any claim in the action. Under s.35(1) and (2) of the Limitation Act 1980, an original set-off or counterclaim is deemed, for the purposes of the Limitation Act, to be a separate action commenced on the same date as the original action in which it is raised. In *JFS (UK) Ltd v Dwr Cymru Cyf (No.1)* [1999] 1 W.L.R. 231, CA, it was held that "claim" in s.35(3) means "claim for relief" and therefore does not encompass any positive averment made in a defence. Thus, the court had jurisdiction to grant permission to a defendant to add a counterclaim to his defence which had not previously contained a counterclaim even though the counterclaim, if raised in separate proceedings would have been statute-barred. Although the court would consider the staleness of the counterclaim when deciding whether to grant permission, such staleness was not an insuperable objection to the grant of permission. **17.3.9**

Costs of amendments

17.3.10 Applicants who obtain permission to amend are often ordered to pay the other parties' "costs of and caused by" the application (as to the meaning of such an order, see the Costs Practice Direction, para.8.5 (44PD.2). However, parties ought to consent to amendments they cannot reasonably oppose because, if they do not, they may be penalised in costs. In *La Chemise Lacoste SA v Sketchers USA Ltd* [2006] EWHC Civ 3642 (Ch).C sought D's consent to amendments to the particulars of claim; when D made half-hearted attempts to resist by making proposals to deal with the matter in another way.C successfully applied for permission to amend and was awarded the costs of the application against D.

Amendments to statements of case after the end of a relevant limitation period[1]

17.4 **17.4—(1) This rule applies where—**

(a) a party applies to amend his statement of case in one of the ways mentioned in this rule; and

(b) a period of limitation has expired under—

(i) the Limitation Act 1980[2]; or

(ii) the Foreign Limitation Periods Act 1984[3] or;

(iii) any other enactment which allows such an amendment, or under which such an amendment is allowed.

(2) The court may allow an amendment whose effect will be to add or substitute a new claim, but only if the new claim arises out of the same facts or substantially the same facts as a claim in respect of which the party applying for permission has already claimed a remedy in the proceedings.

(3) The court may allow an amendment to correct a mistake as to the name of a party, but only where the mistake was genuine and not one which would cause reasonable doubt as to the identity of the party in question.

(4) The court may allow an amendment to alter the capacity in which a party claims if the new capacity is one which that party had when the proceedings started or has since acquired.

(Rule 19.5 specifies the circumstances in which the court may allow a new party to be added or substituted after the end of a relevant limitation period[GL]).

Effect of rule

17.4.1 The term "limitation period" is defined in the Glossary. This rule limits the court's power to allow amendments after a relevant limitation period has expired unless the application is to amend in one of the following ways:

(1) Adding or substituting a new claim arising out of the same facts or substantially the same facts as an existing claim;

(2) Correcting a mistake as to the name of a party;

(3) Altering a capacity in which a party claims.

These three occasions for amendments derive mainly from s.35 of the Limitation Act 1980 and therefore case law on the previous High Court rule (RSC O.20, r.5) which was similar to r.17.4, may still be applicable and is summarised below.

---

[1] Amended by the Civil Procedure (Amendment) Rules 2001 (SI 2001/256).
[2] 1980 c.58.
[3] 1984 c.16.

Mistakes as to the name of a party can be classified as mistakes as to the identity of a party named the correction of which requires the substitution of a party. These cases fall within rule 19.5 (special provisions about adding or substituting parties after the end of a relevant limitation period).

Power to amend after expiry of limitation period

This rule deals with the making of amendments even though the current limitation period has expired in the particular circumstances specified in the three classes of cases mentioned in paras (2), (3) and (4) and must be read closely with and subject to the provisions of s.35 of the Limitation Act 1980 (see Vol.2, para.8–102+ and r.19.5). **17.4.2**

Under s.35(2) of the Limitation Act 1980, which deals with new claims in pending actions, a "new claim" includes any claim involving the addition or substitution of a new cause of action or the addition or substitution of a new party and any such new claim is deemed to be a separate action and to have been commenced on the same date as the original action (s.35(1)(b)). The Act is imperative in its terms that the Court must not allow such a new claim to be made in the course of any action after the expiry of any time limit under the Act which would affect a new action brought to enforce that claim, except as provided by s.33 of the Act which provides a discretionary power to extend the time-limits in respect of actions for damages for personal injuries or death or as provided by rules of the Court.

Where it is reasonably arguable that the relevant limitation period has expired before an amendment is made, the onus is on the applicant to show that the amendment falls within the provisions of rr.17.4 or 19.5. A new claim under s.35(3) is not made until the statement of case is actually amended, which, by definition, cannot be earlier than the date upon which permission to make specific amendments is given. Unless the case falls within one of the exceptions, such permission cannot be given after the relevant limitation period has expired. It is immaterial that the limitation period had not expired on the date the application to amend was made (*Welsh Development Agency v Redpath Dorman Long Ltd* [1994] 1 W.L.R. 1409; [1994] 4 All E.R. 10, CA) or on the date upon which the court adjourned a hearing on the basis that the specific amendments sought would be revised and brought back to court later for approval (*Bajwa v Furini* [2004] EWCA Civ 412).

Where it does appear reasonably arguable that the defendant has a limitation defence in respect of a new claim, the court should not permit the claimant to raise that new claim by amendment since to do so could defeat the arguable defence, i.e., the amendment would take effect from the date of the original document amended (see para.17.3.4 above). Instead the claimant should be left to bring fresh proceedings on the new claim (*Goode v Martin* [2001] 3 All E.R. 562), reversed on other grounds, [2001] EWCA Civ 1899; [2002] 1 All E.R. 620.

Under r.17.4, the power to amend extends to a time limit which applies to the proceedings in question by virtue of the Foreign Limitation Periods Act 1984, i.e. any English proceedings in which the law of a foreign country falls, in accordance with the applicable rules of private international law, to be taken into account in the determination of any matter, since for the purposes of such proceedings, the law of that foreign country relating to limitation will apply in respect of that matter (*ibid.*, s.1).

Under r.17.4(1)(b)(iii) the power to amend extends to time limits under "any other enactment which allows such an amendment or under which such an amendment is allowed". This curious phrase also appears in r.19.5(1)(c) and its meaning was considered and explained in *Parsons v George* [2004] 1 W.L.R. 3264, CA at paras 34 to 37.

For the cases specified in paras (2), (3) and (4) of this rule, see, "Adding or substituting new cause of action", "Correcting name of party", and "Altering capacity of party" below.

Amendments to allow new claims

Rules of Court for allowing new claims can be made only if the conditions specified by the Limitation Act 1980 are satisfied (s.35(4)). This provision seems to emphasise that the principle underlying the provisions of s.35 and the rules made thereunder is restrictive. **17.4.3**

In relation to a claim involving a new cause of action r.17.4(2) follows the requirement of s.35(5)(a), which provides as follows:

"(a) in the case of a claim involving a new cause of action, if the new cause of action arises out of the same facts or substantially the same facts as are already in issue on any claim previously made in the original action."

In relation to a claim involving a new party, r.19.5 follows the requirement of s.35(5)(b) which provides as follows:

"(b) in the case of a claim involving a new party, if the addition or substitution of the new party is necessary for the determination of the original action."

and the requirement of s.35(6) of the Act which provides that such addition or substitution will not be regarded as necessary unless either:

"(a) the new party is substituted for a party whose name was given in any claim made in the original action in mistake for the new party's name; or

(b) any claim already made in the original action cannot be maintained by or against an existing party unless the new party is joined or substituted as plaintiff or defendant in that action."

The decision in *Gregson v Channel Four Television Corporation* [2000] C.P. Rep. 60; [2000] EWCA Civ 214; July 11, 2000, CA shows that r.17.4(3) does not derive from s.35 of the Act and that, if an amendment does not require the addition or substitution of any party it is not necessary to travel on to r.19.5 (see further para.17.4.1 above).

So far as the capacities in which a party may sue are concerned, r.17.4(4) follows the provisions of s.35(3).

Adding or substituting new cause of action (r.17.4(2))

17.4.4 In *Hoescht UK Ltd v Inland Revenue Commissioners* [2003] EWHC 1002 (Ch); [2004] S.T.C. 412, Park J. referred to subsection (1) to (5) of the Limitation Act 1980 and to CPR r.17.4(2) and said (at paras. 22 and 23) the effect of these provisions could be summarised as follows. Where an amendment to a claimant's pleading is proposed outside the limitation period, the first question is whether the amendment would involve the addition or substitution of a new cause of action to or for the cause or causes of action already pleaded (see s.35(5)(a)). If it would not, the court has a discretion to allow the amendment. If the amendment would add or substitute a new cause of action, another question has to be asked: would the new cause of action arise out of the same facts or a substantially the same facts as those out of which a cause of action which has already been pleaded arises? If it would not, the court may not allow the amendment. Put another way, an amendment for which permission may not be given is one of which the following three propositions are true: (1) the amendment is sought to be made outside the limitation period, (2) the amendment involves the addition of a new cause of action, and (3) the new cause of action does not arise out of the same facts or substantially the same facts as a cause of action already pleaded. As to meaning of "cause of action" and "new claim" in this context, see *Aldi Stores Ltd v Holmes Buildings Plc* [2003] EWCA Civ 1882, December 1, 2003, unrep., CA.

Amending a claim form to specify a cause of action not previously mentioned therein does not raise a new cause of action if the amendment is made simply to resolve an obvious inconsistency between the claim form and the particulars of claim served with it. In deciding whether the amendment raises a new cause of action the court should consider the proposed amendment in the context of the statements of case as a whole, not just the claim form by itself. In *Evans v CIG Mon Cymru* (2008) P.I.Q.R. P17, the claimant had considered bringing a claim in respect of an accident at work and also workplace bullying but subsequently decided not to pursue the bullying claim. The particulars of claim sought remedies for an accident at work but, owing to a clerical error, the claim form sought remedies only for "abuse at work". After the expiry of the relevant limitation period the defendant applied for an order striking out the particulars of claim on the ground that they were irrelevant to the claim form and the claimant applied for permission to amend the claim form so as to substitute the words "an accident at work" for the words "abuse at work". The Court of Appeal held that the amendment should be allowed and that the particulars of claim should not be struck out.

The Court has power to grant or allow an amendment after the expiry of any relevant period of limitation notwithstanding that the effect of the amendment will be to add or substitute a new cause of action provided that the new cause of action arises out of the same facts or substantially the same facts as a cause of action in respect of which relief has already been claimed in the proceedings by the party applying for permission to make the amendment (r.17.4(2). There is a wealth of case law on this topic, some of which is summarised below (for further pre-CPR authorities see earlier editions of the *White Book*).

An amendment which relies on the same facts but alleges a novation of a contract as between the claimant, the defendant and the other original contracting party may be allowed after the expiry of the period of limitation (*Chatsworth Investments Ltd v Cussins (Contractors) Ltd* [1969] 1 W.L.R. 1; [1969] 1 All E.R. 143, CA).

An allegation of negligence against an architect in the *design* of a building arises out of the same or substantially the same facts as an allegation of negligence against him in the *supervision* of the building and will be allowed after the expiry of the current period of limitation, even though it may thereby be adding a new cause of action (*Brickfield Properties Ltd v Newton* [1971] 1 W.L.R. 862; [1971] 3 All E.R. 328, CA). But in an action for breach of a written contract to modify a ship's engines and fuel system, in the face of a defence that the alleged breach was not covered by the written term, the Court of Appeal dismissed an appeal to allow the plaintiff to amend to add an allegation of breach of a duty of care in the design of and the carrying out of the modifications either in contract or in tort, but allowed an appeal and gave leave to amend to add an allegation of breach of an implied contractual term that the modifications would be reasonably fit for their purpose. The Court held that all these allegations were new causes of action, but only in respect of the last was it satisfied that there was little or no prejudice to the defendant and that it was just to do so (*The "Casper Trader"* [1991] 2 Lloyd's Rep. 237).

So also, an allegation of negligence in respect of the *design* of drawings and specification may be added to a claim for negligence in respect of building works not in accordance with the drawings and specifications (*Circle Thirty Three Housing Trust v Fairview Estates (Housing)* 8 Con. L.R. 1, CA). But see *Balfour Beatty Construction v Parsons Brown and Newton* (1991) 7 Const.L.J. 205, CA.

In *Hydrocarbons Great Britain Ltd v Cammell Laird Shipbuilders and Automotive Products Ltd (t/a Ap Precision Hydraulics) and Redman Bro* (1991) 58 B.L.R. 123, H.H. Judge Forbes Q.C. held that a proposed amendment to allege a claim for negligent misstatement was not within the language of the unamended statement of claim which pleaded negligence in act, that accordingly the proposed amendment was in respect of a new cause of action, that it did not arise out of the same or substantially the same facts as the cause of action pleaded and thus there was no jurisdiction pursuant to s.35 of the Limitation Act 1980 to allow the amendment.

There is power under rule 17.4(2) to give permission to amend a statement of case after the limitation has expired in order to add or substitute a new cause of action arising out of the same facts as those already pleaded but which in fact disclosed no sustainable cause of action (*Sion v Hampstead Health Authority*, *The Times*, June 10, 1994, CA).

An amendment to add a new allegation of intentional wrongdoing by pleading fraud where previously mere negligence had been alleged constituted the introduction of a new cause of action and would not be allowed after the expiry of any relevant limitation period since the new cause of action did not arise out of the same facts or substantially the same facts as a cause of action in respect of which relief had already been claimed in the action. Nor was it possible to circumvent the effect under this subrule of the expiry of a period of limitation in respect of a common law claim by seeking to invoke a concurrent equitable jurisdiction where the claims in equity were not different causes of action but merely equitable counterparts of the claims at common law: see *Paragon Finance Plc v Thakerar & Co* [1999] 1 All E.R. 400, CA.

Where the claim was based on a breach of duty whether arising from contract or in tort, the question whether an amendment raised a new cause of action required comparison with the unamended claim to determine (a) whether a different duty was alleged; (b) whether the breaches alleged differed substantially and, where appropriate, (c) the nature and extent of the damage of which complaint was made; see *Darlington Building Societyv O'Rourke, James Scourfield & McCarthy (a Firm)*, The Times, November 20, 1998, CA.

In *Lloyd's Bank Plc v Rogers* [1999] 3 E.G.L.R. 83, mortgage possession proceedings were commenced in 1992. No money claim was made. In 1998, after expiry of the relevant limitation period the claimant obtained permission to amend the claim to add a money claim. That permission was upheld on appeal to the Court of Appeal on the basis that a claim for a new remedy did not amount to claim for a new cause of action (*per* Auld L.J.) or because the facts relied on in support of the money claim were undoubtedly the same, or substantially the same, as the facts relied on in support of the possession claim (*per* Auld and Evans L.JJ.).

In *Senior v Pearson & Ward* [2001] EWCA Civ 229, CA, the claimants sued their former solicitors alleging actions without or in disregard of instructions and were given permission to amend claiming failure to advise: the new claim was different from the original claims but arose out of the same facts or substantially the same facts as the original claims.

In *Goode v Martin* [2001] EWCA Civ 1899; [2002] 1 W.L.R. 1828, CA, r.17.4 and s.35(5) of the 1980 Act were construed in the light of the Human Rights Act 1998 and it was held that para.(2) of r.17.4 should be read as providing that the same or substantially similar facts upon which a new claim may be based should be facts "as are already in issue" on a claim in respect of which the party applying for permission has already claimed a remedy in the proceedings. If the rule is expanded in this way, a claimant may be permitted to amend his statement of case to add a new claim arising, not out of facts that he had pleaded, but out of facts put in issue by the defence.

Where there is a single defendant the facts already in issue in a claim, being (as r.17.4(2) states) a claim "in respect of which the party applying for permission has already claimed a remedy in the proceedings", will be facts arising in the pleadings of the two parties. But suppose there are two defendants (D1 and D2) to the claimant's (C) action. If D2 pleads facts by way of defence to C's claim, can C adopt those facts as the basis of a new claim against D1? In *Charles Church Developments Limited v Stent Foundations Limited* ; [2006] EWHC 3158 (TCC) *The Times*, January 4, 2007 (Jackson J.), where it was common ground that (following *Goode v Martin*) the extended version of r.17.4(2) should be applied, the judge gave an affirmative answer to this question, holding that, in a case where there are several defendants, the effect of s.35(5)(a) and r.17.4(2) together is to give the court a discretionary power, after expiry of the relevant limitation period, to allow a claimant to plead a new cause of action based upon substantially the same facts as have been put in issue by the defence of any defendant.

Section 35 restricts new claims, i.e. causes of action; it does not restrict amendments which merely raise new instances or particulars of causes of action already raised. In *Savings & Investment Bank Ltd (In Liquidation) v Fincken*, [2003] EWCA Civ 1630, CA, which was a claim for breach of warranty and fraudulent misrepresentation and in which the limitation period had expired, the claimant was permitted to amend the claim to raise new allegations concerning failure to disclose material assets including expensive firearms and ownership of firearms; the Court of Appeal held that the new allegations did not amount to new causes of action.

In a claim for compensation for overpayment of certain taxes it was held that claims for the overpayment of certain other taxes amounted to a new cause of action which was not the same or substantially the same as the existing causes raised (*Hoechst UK Ltd v Inland Revenue Commissioners* [2003] EWHC 1002).

In a counterclaim for damages for negligent professional advice, new allegations relating to periods earlier than those already pleaded amounted to a new cause of action which, the Court of Appeal held, was the same or substantially the same as the causes already pleaded and, therefore, permission to amend was given (*Chantrey Vellacott v Convergence Group Plc* [2005] EWCA Civ 290).

Correcting name of party (r.17.4(3))

17.4.5 An amendment to correct the name of a party may be allowed, even if made after the expiry of any relevant period of limitation provided the Court is satisfied that the mistake sought to be corrected was a genuine mistake and was not misleading, or such as to cause any reasonable doubt as to the identity of the person intending to sue or to be sued; *Gregson v Channel Four Television Corp (Amendment of Party Name)* [2000] C.P. Rep. 60.

An amendment to correct the name of a party may be allowed, even after a final default judgment has been entered, e.g. to substitute the correct name of the defendant for the incorrect name in which he was sued where it is plain that the mistake was genuine and that the defendant knew that the plaintiff intended to sue him as the person against whom the claim was being made (*Singh v Atombrook Ltd* [1989] 1 W.L.R. 810; [1989] 1 All E.R. 385, CA; distinguishing *Davies v Elsby Bros. Ltd* [1961] 1 W.L.R. 170; [1960] 3 All E.R. 672).

The transposition of the names of the parties in the claim form, e.g. that of the defendants as the claimants and that of the claimants as the defendants does not render the claim form a nullity but it is an irregularity, and if it is made by a genuine mistake and is not misleading, permission to amend may be given, even after the expiry of the current period of limitation (*Teltscher Brothers Ltd v London & India Dock Investments Ltd* [1989] 1 W.L.R. 770).

The word "mistake" in r.17.4(3) should not be narrowly construed to mean error without fault (*per* Russell L.J. in *Mitchell v Harris Engineering Co* [1967] 2 Q.B. 703, CA).

Where an action is mistakenly commenced in the name of a claimant company which had ceased to exist as a result of a merger, the Court has power, to correct the name of the claimant company, since the mistake had gone to the name rather than the identity of the claimant, and such amendment would relate back to the date of commencement of proceedings so that there never was a non-existent claimant (*Sardinia Sulcis, The* [1991] 1 Lloyd's Rep. 201, CA. After explaining the previous case law on this point Lloyd L.J. stated:

> "In all these cases it was possible to identify the intending plaintiff or intended defendant by reference to a description which was more or less specific to the particular case. Thus if, in the case of an intended defendant, the plaintiff gets the right description but the wrong name, there is unlikely to be any doubt as to the identity of the person intended to be sued. But if he gets the wrong description, it will be other wise."

This has become known as "the test in the *Sardinia Sulcis*".

Rules 17.4 and 19.5 both deal with mistakes as to the name of a party intending to sue or be sued. Both are to be construed as the CPR equivalent to RSC Ord 20, r.5 and so should be read together. The statutory authority for them, so far as they involve issues of limitation, is s.35 of the Limitation Act 1980. A major difficulty with these rules is that r.19.5, unlike r.17.4(3) and RSC Ord 20, r.5, does not specify that the mistake must not be such as to cause any reasonable doubt as to the party intending to sue or be sued. This difficulty explains in part the wealth of recent Court of Appeal authorities propounding inconsistent accounts of the principles to be applied. It is hoped that the latest authority, *Adelson v Associated Newspapers Ltd* [2007] EWCA Civ 701; [2007] 4 All E.R. 330, has clarified the law, has provided a definitive account of the principles to be applied and has put to rest the maelstrom stirred up by some of the earlier cases. Mistakes as to the name of a party divide into two categories: errors of identification (e.g. "X" erroneously identified as the proper party instead of "Y"); and errors of nomenclature, i.e. errors merely as to the name of the intended party (e.g. proper party identified but erroneously called "X" instead of "Y"); see *Adelson*, para.[29]. The mistake envisaged by rr.17.4 and 19.5 is one of nomenclature, not of identification; see *Adelson*, para.[33]. In the simplest cases the error will be merely as to a part of the name (e.g., John Jones incorrectly sued as Kevin Jones). However, the problem cases are those in which the claimant knows only the attributes of the person he wishes to sue (e.g. his landlord, his employer or the manufacturer of an object) but has no personal knowledge of the identity of that person. The guidance given in *Adelson* is that, where such a claimant has made inquiries, has been incorrectly informed that a named third party has those attributes and has commenced an action naming that third party as defendant but describing in his statement of case the attributes of the person intended to be sued, his mistake is likely to be classified as an error of nomenclature and therefore remediable (if the court thinks it just to allow the amendment) even where the relevant limitation period has expired; see *Adelson*, paras [30] and [56] in which the test applied in the *Sardinia Sulcis* (see above) was cited with approval. A mistake as to the correct defendant may result in the correct defendant being unaware of the claim until after the relevant limitation period has expired; in such a case the court may well exercise its discretion to disallow the amendment; see *Adelson*, para.[57].

Altering capacity of party (r.17.4(4))

"Capacity" is used in the sense of legal competence or status to bring or defend a claim. A change of capacity is an alteration from a personal capacity to a representative capacity, or an alteration from a representative capacity to another representative capacity or to a personal capacity (*Haq v Singh* [2001] 1 W.L.R. 1594, CA). **17.4.6**

An amendment to alter the capacity in which a party sues may be allowed under r.17.4(4) if the new capacity is one which that party had at the commencement of the proceedings or has since acquired. This will allow a party to amend the capacity in which he or she sues as executor or executrix after the grant of probate, since this would relate back to the date of death (see *Stebbings v Holst & Co* [1953] 1 W.L.R. 603; [1953] 1 All E.R. 925; *Bowler v John Mowlem & Co Ltd* [1954] 1 W.L.R. 1445; [1954] 3 All E.R. 556, CA) but it will also allow a party to amend the capacity in which he or she sues as administrator or administratrix after the grant of administration even though this may take place after the issue of the claim.

PRACTICE DIRECTION—AMENDMENTS TO STATEMENTS OF CASE

This Practice Direction supplements CPR Part 17

A party applying for an amendment will usually be responsible for the costs of and arising from the amendment. **17PD.1**

Applications to amend where the permission of the court is required

1.1 The application may be dealt with at a hearing or, if rule 23.8 applies, without a hearing.

1.2 When making an application to amend a statement of case, the applicant should file with the court;

(1) the application notice, and

(2) a copy of the statement of case with the proposed amendments.

1.3 Where permission to amend has been given, the applicant should within 14 days of the date of the order, or within such other period as the court may direct, file with the court the amended statement of case.

1.4 If the substance of the statement of case is changed by reason of the amendment, the statement of case should be re-verified by a statement of truth.[1]

1.5 A copy of the order and the amended statement of case should be served on every party to the proceedings, unless the court orders otherwise.

General

2.1 The amended statement of case and the court copy of it should be endorsed as follows: **17PD.2**

(1) where the court's permission was required:

"Amended [Particulars of Claim *or as may be*] by Order of [Master . . . .] [District Judge *or as may be*] dated ...."

(2) Where the court's permission was not required:

"Amended [Particulars of Claim *or as may be*] under CPR [rule 17.1(1) or (2)(a)] dated ...."

2.2 The statement of case in its amended form need not show the original text. However, where the court thinks it desirable for both the original text and the amendments to be shown, the court may direct that the amendments should be shown either:

(1) by coloured amendments, either manuscript or computer generated, or

(2) by use of a numerical code in a monochrome computer generated document.

2.3 Where colour is used, the text to be deleted should be struck through in colour and any text replacing it should be inserted or underlined in the same colour.

2.4 The order of colours to be used for successive amendments is: (1) red, (2) green, (3) violet and (4) yellow.

---

[1] See Part 22 for information about the statement of truth.

(For information about changes to parties see Part 19 and the practice direction which supplements it).

PART 18

Further Information

Contents

18.0.1

Editorial Introduction

Rule 2.3(1) states that "statement of case" means a claim form, particulars of claim where these are not included in a claim form, defence, Pt 20 claim, or reply to defence; and includes any further information given in relation to them voluntarily or by court order under CPR, r.18.1. (These documents were formerly known as pleadings). A major objective of case management under the CPR is to ensure that statements of case do indeed set out the parties' case and define the dispute between them. The rules as to the contents of statements of case have been made simpler and they are now subject to "judicial scrutiny" at an early stage. As part of its responsibility for managing cases, the court will ensure that the parties plainly state the factual ingredients of their case so that the true nature and scope of the dispute can be identified. The particulars of claim and defence are considered by the procedural judge after the defence is filed and, if the issues cannot be readily identified from statements of case, directions are given to rectify this. **18.0.2**

It is to be noted that a party may provide further information on a voluntary basis on his own initiative, or following a request by anotherparty, or under a court order. The court may make an order under this Part on its own initiative or on an application by a party.

In various circumstances, special provisions as to the contents of statements of case applicable in various circumstances may require a party in his pleadings to give to his opponent information that otherwise he might be required to provide to the opponent under the terms of Pt 18. For example, the Crown Proceedings Act 1947 s.35 states that provision shall be made by rules of court for securing that where any civil proceedings are brought against the Crown in accordance with the 1947 Act the claimant "shall provide the Crown with information as to the circumstances in which it is alleged that the liability of the Crown has arisen and as to the departments and officers of the Crown concerned" Since October 1, 2005, such rules of court have been found in CPR r.16.2(1A).

Part 18 is concerned with the providing by parties of information for the purpose of clarifying matters in dispute in the proceedings. (Such clarification operates for the benefit of the parties and for the court.) The object and function of Pt 18 should be distinguished from three other circumstances in which, for other purposes, the parties may or must provide the court with information. First, where a party responds to an allocation questionnaire served on him by the court under Pt 26, he may take advantage of Practice Direction (Case Management – Preliminary Stage), para.2.2 and give the court "extra information" relevant to the allocation of the case to an appropriate case management track or to case management. Secondly, when the court has considered the statements of case and allocation questionnaire responses filed, before making a decision about allocation, it may serve on the parties an "order for further information" in Form **N156**; see CPR r.26.5(3) and PD 26 para.2.2 requiring them to provide information about particular matters relevant to allocation. Thirdly, where a party has access to information which is not reasonably available to the other party, the court may direct the former party to provide the latter with that information (CPR r.35.9). The expression "further information" is used in some other contexts within the CPR where no confusion with Pt 18 is at all likely (e.g. CPR r.75.10 (further information to be provided on application for enforcement of traffic penalty), Practice Direction (Costs) para.43.4 (further information relating to bill for detailed assessment hearing)).

Under r.25.1(1)(g) the court may grant an order directing a party to provide information about the location of relevant property or assets or to provide information about relevant property or assets which are or may be the subject of an application for a freezing injunction (see para.25.1.28 below).

Sch.1, RSC O.17 (Interpleader), r.10 expressly states that the provisions of Pt 18 shall, with necessary modifications, apply in relation to an interpleader issue as they apply in relation to other proceedings (see para.sc17.10 below).

An order under Pt 18 for a party to give additional information may not be made against a respondent to a committal application (Practice Direction (Committal Applications) para.6; see para.scpd52.6 below). CPR r.53.3 states that, in a defamation claim, unless the court orders otherwise, a party will not be required to provide further information about the identity of the defendant's sources of information.

Part 18 does not apply to small claims: CPR r.27.2(1)(f).

In cases allocated to the fast track, directions as to requests for further information will normally be included in the Standard Directions; see Practice Direction (The Fast Track) Appendix (see paras 28PD.10 and 28PD.15). As to such directions in multi-track cases, see Practice Direction (The Multi-Track), para.4.8 (see para.29PD.4).

Related sources

18.0.3
- Part 22 (Statements of truth)
- Part 23 General rules about applications for court orders)
- Rule 27.2(3) (Extent to which other Parts apply to small claims)
- Rule 26.5(3) (Information about case for case allocation purposes)
- Rule 35.9 (Power of court to direct a party to provide information)
- Rule 53.3 (Sources of information in defamation claims)
- Rule 66.2 (Application of Civil Procedure Rules in Crown Proceedings)
- Sch.1, RSC O.17 (Interpleader), r.10 (Disclosure) (see para.sc17.10)
- Practice Direction (Further Information) (see para.18PD.1)
- Practice Direction (Applications) (see para.23PD.1)
- Practice Direction (Committal Applications), para.6 (see para.scpd52.63)
- Practice Direction (Patents, Etc.), para.11.2(1) (see Vol.2, para.2F–108)
- Queen's Bench Guide, para.7.7 (see Vol.2, para.1B–47)
- Chancery Guide, para.3.10 (see Vol.2, para.1A–12)
- Admiralty and Commercial Courts Guide, Sect.D15 (see Vol.2, para.2A–75)
- Practice Direction to Part 47—Costs Practice Direction para.35.7

Forms

18.0.4
- **N244** Application notice
- **PF56** Request for further information or clarification with provision for response
- **PF57** Application for further information or clarification
- **PF58** Order for further information or clarification

Practice Direction

18.0.5 Part 18 is supplemented by Practice Direction (Further Information), see para.18PD.1 below.

Obtaining further information[1]

18.1 **18.1—(1) The court may at any time order a party to—**

(a) clarify any matter which is in dispute in the proceedings; or

(b) give additional information in relation to any such matter,

whether or not the matter is contained or referred to in a statement of case.

(2) Paragraph (1) is subject to any rule of law to the contrary.

[1] Amended by the Civil Procedure (Amendment) Rules 2000 (SI 2000/221).

(3) Where the court makes an order under paragraph (1), the party against whom it is made must—

(a) file his response; and

(b) serve it on the other parties

within the time specified by the court.

(Part 22 requires a response to be verified by a statement of truth).

(Part 53 (defamation) restricts requirements for providing further information about sources of information in defamation claims).

History of rule

Amended by the Civil Procedure (Amendment) Rules 2000 (SI 2000/221). **18.1.1**

Effect of rule

Rule 18.1(1) states that the court may order a party to clarify or give additional information in relation to any matter which is "in dispute in the proceedings". In most instances whether or not a matter is "in dispute" will be apparent only from a reading of the parties' statements of case and, therefore, the disputed matter will be "contained or referred to in, a statement of case". However, in terms r.18.1 gives the court power to order a party to clarify, or give additional information in relation to, any disputed matter even though the matter is not contained or referred to in a statement of case (e.g. in a notice verified by a statement of truth). Requests which do not relate to a matter which is contained or referred to in a statement of case are akin to interrogatories under the old civil procedure rules. A preliminary request for further information or clarification should be concise and strictly confined "to matters which are reasonably necessary and proportionate" to enable the party seeking clarification or information "to prepare his own case or to understand the case he has to meet" (Practice Direction (Further Information), para.1.2, see para.18PD.1 below). In *King v Telegraph Group Ltd* [2004] EWCA Civ 613; [2005] 1 W.L.R. 2282, Brooke L.J. observed that the emphasis is on strictly what is necessary and proportionate and to the avoidance of disproportionate expense. **18.1.2**

The purpose of the court's power in this respect is to ensure that the parties have all the information they need to deal efficiently and justly with the matters which are in dispute between them. The wording of the rule should be interpreted reasonably liberally. The "matter" upon which clarification or additional information is sought, though described as a matter "in dispute", need not be one on which there is a live disagreement between the parties, since on very many occasions parties are required to furnish information precisely for the purpose of discovering whether there is such disagreement (*Harcourt v Griffin* [2007] EWHC 1500 (QB); [2007] P.I.Q.R Q9 (Irwin J.), granting claimant's application in substantial personal injury claim where liability had been admitted for information from defendants about the nature and extent of their insurance cover). Irwin J. expressed the view that disclosure of information of this kind should only be ordered where it can be demonstrated that there is some real basis for concern that a realistic award may not be satisfied. The exercise of such jurisdiction will be approached with caution.

In a case where a defendant's liability, if any, is believed by the claimant to be covered by an insurance policy, the claimant's view of the merit of pursuing the claim is likely to be coloured by the nature and extent of such cover. In *West London Pipeline & Storage Ltd v Total UK Ltd* [2008] EWHC 1296 (Comm), June 9, 2008, unrep. (David Steel J.) the claimant's submission in a contribution claim that, on case management grounds, the court had power under r.18.1 to order the defendant to give additional information about their insurance arrangements (even though no dispute as to insurance arose in the proceedings) was rejected. The judge was not persuaded that the provisions of the CPR, however liberally interpreted, have led to a significant change in law and practice in this respect. Details of insurance are a private matter between an insurer and an insured, production of which would encourage speculative "deep pocket" litigation.

Where, in a claim brought against the Crown, a claimant is required by r.16.2(1A) in his claim form to provide the Crown with information as to the circumstances in which it is alleged that liability has arisen and as to the department and officers concerned, the Crown might rely on Pt 18 for the purpose of obtaining clarification from the claimant where the information provided was inadequate.

In *McPhilemy v Times Newspapers Ltd (Re-Amendment: Justification)* [1999] 3 All E.R. 775, Lord Wolf M.R. said that the need for extensive pleadings including particulars should be reduced by the requirement that witness statements are now exchanged and that in the majority of proceedings the identification of the documents upon which a party relies, together with copies of that party's witness statements, will make the detail of the nature of the case the other side has to meet obvious. However, although sometimes a witness statement can supplement a pleaded case by putting flesh on the bones, and that is often a preferable course to ordering further information, a Claimant cannot proceed with a defective pleading and then serve an extensive witness statement leaving it for the Defendant to find his way through it "without a map or compass"; see *Delos Ltd v CAE Electronics Ltd*, February 21, 2001, unrep. (Eady J.).

Requests for further information will not be allowed if they go solely to cross-examination as to credit; see *Thorpe v Chief Constable of Greater Manchester* [1989] 1 W.L.R. 665; [1989] 2 All E.R. 827, CA. Requests for further information which are merely "fishing" will not be allowed. These are requests for information in which a party is trying to see if he can find a case, either of complaint or defence, of which he knows nothing or which is not yet pleaded; see *Hennessy v Wright (No.2)* (1890) 24 Q.B.D. 445, CA. Similarly, a request for further information in order to obtain evidence for use in subsequent proceedings, such as a response which might provide an acknowledgment under s.29 of the Limitation Act 1980 and enable the Claimant to circumvent a limitation defence in a fresh action, will not be allowed; see *Lovell v Lovell* [1970] 1 W.L.R. 1451; [1970] 3 All E.R. 721, CA. In fact, these are all instances where the request is not reasonably necessary to enable a party to prepare his own case or to understand the case he has to meet.

The court may exercise its powers under this rule at any time. However, in *Watson v Ian Snipe & Co* [2002] EWCA Civ 293, the Court of Appeal stated that in principle, a request for further information implies that further information may exist. Such an application should, therefore, be made before there is an application for summary judgment unless that application for summary judgment is already justified. The Court of Appeal observed that combining an application for further information and an application for summary judgment was likely to result in a procedural muddle.

It is said in r.18.1(2) that the power to require a party to give further information in accordance with r.18.1(1) is "subject to any rule or law to the contrary". This makes it clear that the power cannot be used to order the disclosure of information which, as a matter of law, cannot be compelled (e.g. on grounds of privilege).

Rule 18.1 is of general application. In particular circumstances, a party seeking further information may be able to rely on other legislative provisions. For example, in proceedings to which the Third Parties (Rights Against Insurers) Act 1930 applies, the duty imposed on insurers by s.2 of that Act to give information to third parties may have the required effect of eliciting the information sought (e.g. *In re OT Computers Limited* [2004] EWCA Civ 653; [2004] Ch. 317, CA (court ordering defendant to give pre-issue disclosure of insurance details)).

Paragraph 35.7 of the Costs Practice Direction (CPR PD 47) allows a paying party, when the receiving party claims an additional liability, to request information about other methods of financing that were available to the receiving part, under Pt 18, using the procedure set out in CPR PD 18.

Small claims

18.1.2.1 Rule 27.2(1)(f) states that, generally, Pt 18 does not apply to claims proceeding on the small claims track. However, as a result of an amendment to that provision made by the Civil Procedure (Amendment No.3) Rules 2005 (SI 2005/2292), r.27(2)(3) provides that in such proceedings the court "of its own initiative" may order a party to provide further information "if it considers it appropriate to do so". Presumably, in these circumstances the requirements imposed on the court by r.3.3 (Court's power to make order of its own initiative) do not apply (see further para.18.1.4 below).

Application by party

18.1.3 A party may apply for an order under r.18.1. Rule 18.1 is supplemented by Practice Direction (Further Information) (see para.18PD.1) in which, amongst other things, the practice for making an application for an order for clarification or further information and the position as to costs is explained. The Practice Direction states (in para.1.1) that, before making an application to the court, the party seeking clarification or information should first serve on the party from whom it is sought a written request and gives detailed guidance as to the form in which this should be done. Subject to the provisions of Practice Direction (Service) paras 3.1 to 3.3 (service by fax) (see para.6PD.3 above), this request should be served by email if reasonably practicable (para.1.7). In Queen's Bench proceedings parties may use form **PF56** for a combined request and reply, if they so wish (Queen's Bench Guide, para.7.7.1, see Vol.2, para.1B–47).

The provisions in Pt 23 (General rules about applications for court orders) apply to an application under r.18.1.

An application should set out or have attached to it the material referred to in Practice Direction (Further Information), para.5 (see para.18PD.5 below).

Order on court's own initiative

The court may exercise its powers under this rule on an application or of its own **18.1.4** initiative (r.3.3(1)). Where acting on its own initiative the provisions of r.3.3 apply.

The court has a duty to actively manage cases (r.1.4) and this duty includes, amongst other things, identifying the issues at an early stage, and deciding promptly which issues need full investigation and trial and accordingly disposing summarily of the others (so-called "rolling adjudication") (r.1.4(2)(b)(c)). If the court has recourse to r.18.1 on its own initiative it is likely to be for the purpose of enabling it to discharge this aspect of its case management duties.

Court's discretion

When considering whether to make an order the court must have regard (a) to the **18.1.5** likely benefit which will result if the information is given; and (b) to the likely cost of giving it; and (c) to whether the financial resources of the party against whom the order is sought are likely to be sufficient to enable that party to comply with such an order. These considerations, though not stated in r.18.1, are consistent with the "overriding objective" stated in r.1.1, and which the court is obliged to give effect to when exercising any power given to it by the CPR. For example of specific reference to r.1.1 in ruling on an application for further information under r.18.1, see *Toussaint v Mattis* [2001] C.P. Rep. 61, CA (whether party should be required to give information as to identity of intermediary where anonymity guaranteed). See also *Harcourt v Griffin* [2007] EWHC 1500 (QB); [2007] P.I.Q.R Q9 (Irwin J.), referred to in para.18.1.2 above.

In patent infringement cases it has not been the standard practice to order parties to give particulars of the construction which they propose to put on the patent claim. However, in *Novartis AG v Johnson & Johnson Medical Ltd* [2008] EWHC 293 (Pat), Floyd J. ordered the claimant to answer certain requests for further information relating to its proposed construction of certain terms at trial in order to ensure that the defendant's clinical trials were conducted on the correct basis. The judge found that it was not satisfactory to allow the claimant to identify only at the stage of experts reports the characteristics for testing. By the time of the experts' reports, experts ought to be in possession of all the material necessary.

Form of Order

For form of order in Queen's Bench proceedings, see **PF58** (Order for clarification **18.1.6** or further information).

Response to order

Where the court makes an order under r.18.1(1) the party against whom it is made **18.1.7** must (a) file his response, and (b) serve it on the other parties within the time specified by the court. For form and content of response, see Practice Direction (Further Information), para.2 and 4 (see para.18PD.2 below). The general grounds of privilege applicable to giving disclosure of documents may also apply to requests for, and orders for, further information under Pt 18. Note also Civil Evidence Act 1968 s.14 (Privilege against self-incrimination), see Vol.2, para.9B–1042.

A response is filed if it is delivered by post or otherwise to the court office (r.2.3(1)). As to service, see Pt 6.

Verification of response by statement of truth

18.1.8 It is expressly provided by r.22.1(1)(b) that a response complying with an order of the court under r.18.1 to provide further information must be verified by a statement of truth (see para.22.1.9 below).

Consequences of failure to respond

18.1.9 When the court makes an order it may make it subject to conditions, and specify the consequences of failure to comply with the order (r.3.1(3)). Where a party has failed to comply with a court order made under r.18.1, any sanction for failure to comply with the order imposed by the order has effect unless the party in default applies for and obtains relief from the sanction (r.3.9(1)). The court may strike out a statement of case or part of a statement of case, if it appears to the court that there has been a failure to comply with a court order (r.3.4(2)(c)). Presumably, a failure to provide information may be treated as conduct relevant to the question of costs (see r.44.3(4)).

Under the law as it existed before the CPR came into effect, the issue whether or not a party's response to an order for further particulars was adequate could arise. The issue could be crucial where the failure to comply with the order was striking out. It was said that the extent and quality of the party's breach must be taken into account in considering whether and to what extent the sanction of barring him from advancing a claim or defence should be imposed (*QPS Consultants Ltd v Kruger Tissue (Manufacturing) Ltd* [1999] B.L.R. 366, CA). In that case it was also said that an order for further and better particulars (whether or not in Unless form) is not to be regarded as breached merely because one or more of the replies is insufficient. If the answers could reasonably have been thought complete and sufficient, then the correct view is that they require only expansion or elucidation for which a further order for particulars should be sought and made. The same issue may arise in relation to a response to an order for further information under r.18.1.

Further information given voluntarily or by court order is included within the definition of "statement of case." Under CPR r.18.1, the court may order a party to clarify or give additional information in relation to any matter arising in the further information.

Practice Direction

18.1.10 Rule 18.1 is supplemented by Practice Direction (Further Information) (see para.18PD.1) in which various matters of practice relating to written requests and applications for clarification or further information are dealt with.

Restriction on the use of further information

18.2 **18.2 The court may direct that information provided by a party to another party (whether given voluntarily or following an order made under rule 18.1) must not be used for any purpose except for that of the proceedings in which it is given.**

Effect of rule

18.2.1 When the court makes an order it may make it subject to conditions (r.3.1(3)). This rule specifically provides that, where the court makes an order under r.18.1 ordering a party to give further information, it may direct that the information provided must not be used for any purpose "except for that of the proceedings in which it is given". Consequently, for example, the information could not be used in other proceedings. Whether or not it will be appropriate for the court to give a direction restricting use will depend on the nature of the further information which the party is ordered to provide. If it is in the nature of, what used to be called, further and better particulars of pleading, then no restriction should be imposed.

The meaning of the phrase "proceedings in which it is given" may require consideration. It may be appropriate to limit the use that may be made of "further information" to proceedings within the proceedings, as it were. For example, it may be appropriate to limit use to proceedings for an interim remedy thereby prohibiting use at trial.

Other provisions in the CPR impose restrictions on the use that may be made by one party of information provided by another (possibly under compulsion). For example, r.31.22 states that, subject to exceptions, a party to whom a document has been disclosed may use the document "only for the purpose of the proceedings in which it is disclosed". Further, r.34.12 states that, subject to exceptions, where the court orders a party to be examined about his or any other assets for the purpose of any hearing except the trial, the deposition may be used "only for the purpose of the proceedings in which the order was made". Also, r.32.12 states that, subject to exceptions, a witness statement may be used "only for the purpose of the proceedings in which it is served". Rule 35.9 states that where a party has access to information which is not reasonably available to the other party, the court may direct the party who has access to the information to (a) prepare and file a document recording the information, and (b) to serve a copy of that document on the other party.

PRACTICE DIRECTION—FURTHER INFORMATION

This Practice Direction supplements CPR Part 18
Attention is also drawn to Part 22 (Statements of Truth).

Preliminary Request for Further Information or Clarification

18PD.1 **1.1** Before making an application to the court for an order under Part 18, the party seeking clarification or information (the first party) should first serve on the party from whom it is sought (the second party) a written request for that clarification or information (a Request) stating a date by which the response to the Request should be served. The date must allow the second party a reasonable time to respond.

1.2 A Request should be concise and strictly confined to matters which are reasonably necessary and proportionate to enable the first party to prepare his own case or to understand the case he has to meet.

1.3 Requests must be made as far as possible in a single comprehensive document and not piecemeal.

1.4 A Request may be made by letter if the text of the Request is brief and the reply is likely to be brief; otherwise the Request should be made in a separate document.

1.5 If a Request is made in a letter, the letter should, in order to distinguish it from any other that might routinely be written in the course of a case,

(1) state that it contains a Request made under Part 18, and
(2) deal with no matters other than the Request.

1.6(1) A Request (whether made by letter or in a separate document) must—

(a) be headed with the name of the court and the title and number of the claim,
(b) in its heading state that it is a Request made under Part 18, identify the first party and the second party and state the date on which it is made,
(c) set out in a separate numbered paragraph each request for information or clarification,
(d) where a Request relates to a document, identify that document and (if relevant) the paragraph or words to which it relates,
(e) state the date by which the first party expects a response to the Request.

(2) (a) A Request which is not in the form of a letter may, if convenient, be prepared in such a way that the response may be given on the same document.
(b) To do this the numbered paragraphs of the Request should appear on the left hand half of each sheet so that the paragraphs of the response may then appear on the *right.*
(c) Where a Request is prepared in this form an extra copy should be served for the use of the second party.

1.7 Subject to the provisions of rule 6.23(5) and (6) and paragraphs

4.1 to 4.3 of Practice Direction A supplementing Part 6, a request should be served by email if reasonably practicable.

CPR 18

Responding to a Request

2.1 A response to a Request must be in writing, dated and signed by the second party or his legal representative. **18PD.2**

2.2(1) Where the Request is made in a letter the second party may give his response in a letter or in a formal reply.

(2) Such a letter should identify itself as a response to the Request and deal with no other matters than the response.

2.3(1) Unless the Request is in the format described in paragraph 1.6(2) and the second party uses the document supplied for the purpose, a response must:

(a) be headed with the name of the court and the title and number of the claim,

(b) in its heading identify itself as a response to that Request,

(c) repeat the text of each separate paragraph of the Request and set out under each paragraph the response to it,

(d) refer to and have attached to it a copy of any document not already in the possession of the first party which forms part of the response.

(2) A second or supplementary response to a Request must identify itself as such in its heading.

2.4 The second party must when he serves his response on the first party serve on every other party and file with the court a copy of the Request and of his response.

Statements of Truth

3. Attention is drawn to Part 22 and to the definition of a statement of case in Part 2 of the rules; a response should be verified by a statement of truth. **18PD.3**

General Matters

4.1(1) If the second party objects to complying with the Request or part of it or is unable to do so at all or within the time stated in the Request he must inform the first party promptly and in any event within that time. **18PD.4**

(2) He may do so in a letter or in a separate document (a formal response), but in either case he must give reasons and, where relevant, give a date by which he expects to be able to comply.

***4.2**(1) There is no need for a second party to apply to the court if* he objects to a Request or is unable to comply with it at all or within the stated time. He need only comply with paragraph 4.1(1) above.

(2) Where a second party considers that a Request can only be complied with at disproportionate expense and objects to comply for that reason he should say so in his reply and explain briefly why he has taken that view.

Applications for Orders under Part 18

18PD.5 **5.1** Attention is drawn to Part 23 (Applications) and to the Practice Direction which supplements that Part.

5.2 An application notice for an order under Part 18 should set out or have attached to it the text of the order sought and in particular should specify the matter or matters in respect of which the clarification or information is sought.

5.3(1) If a Request under paragraph 1 for the information or clarification has not been made, the application notice should, in addition, explain why not.

(2) If a Request for clarification or information has been made, the application notice or the evidence in support should describe the response, if any.

5.4 Both the first party and the second party should consider whether evidence in support of or in opposition to the application is required.

5.5(1) Where the second party has made no response to a Request served on him, the first party need not serve the application notice on the second party, and the court may deal with the application without a hearing.

(2) Sub-pararaph (1) above only applies if at least 14 days have passed since the Request was served and the time stated in it for a response has expired.

5.6 Unless paragraph 5.5 applies the application notice must be served on the second party and on all other parties to the claim.

5.7 An order made under Part 18 must be served on all parties to the claim.

5.8 Costs:

(1) Attention is drawn to the Costs Practice Direction and in particular the court's power to make a summary assessment of costs.

(2) Attention is also drawn to rule 44.13(1) which provides that the general rule is that if an order does not mention costs no party is entitled to costs relating to that order.

PART 19

Parties and Group Litigation

CPR 19

Contents

19.0.1

Editorial introduction

19.0.2 This Part is divided into three sections: I. Addition and Substitution of Parties (rr.19.2 to 19.5), II. Representative Parties (rr.19.6 to 19.9F) and III. Group Litigation (rr.19.10 to 19.15).

The rules in the first section provide simple rules for the addition and substitution of parties which give the judge a wide discretion which is exercisable if it is "desirable". Particular rules apply after the expiry of a limitation period (r.19.5).

Related sources

19.0.3
- Practice Direction to Pt 19 (see para.19PD.1)
- Part 1 (Overriding objective)
- Part 3 (The court's case management powers)
- Limitation Act 1980 (Vol.2, Section 8, para.8–1)
- Foreign Limitation Periods Act 1984
- Merchant Shipping Act 1995
- Part 17, especially r.17.4 (other changes after the end of a limitation period)
- Practice Direction to Pt 17 (Amendments) (see para.17PD.1)
- Part 23 (applications)
- Companies Act 2006 ss.260 to 264 inclusive (Vol.2 Section 2G)

Parties—general[1]

19.1 **19.1 Any number of claimants or defendants may be joined as parties to a claim.**

I. Addition and Substitution of Parties

Changes of parties—general[2]

19.2 **19.2—(1) This rule applies where a party is to be added or substituted except where the case falls within rule 19.5 (special provisions about changing parties after the end of a relevant limitation period^GL^).**

(2) The court may order a person to be added as a new party if—

(a) it is desirable to add the new party so that the court can resolve all the matters in dispute in the proceedings; or

(b) there is an issue involving the new party and an existing party which is connected to the matters in dispute in the proceedings, and it is desirable to add the new party so that the court can resolve that issue.

(3) The court may order any person to cease to be a party if it is not desirable for that person to be a party to the proceedings.

(4) The court may order a new party to be substituted for an existing one if—

(a) the existing party's interest or liability has passed to the new party; and

[1] Amended by the Civil Procedure (Amendment) Rules 2000 (SI 2000/221).
[2] Amended by the Civil Procedure (Amendment) Rules 2000 (SI 2000/221).

(b) it is desirable to substitute the new party so that the court can resolve the matters in dispute in the proceedings.

"court" (r.19.2)

The power may be exercised by a circuit judge or district judge in a county court or by a judge, master or district judge in the High Court—r.2.4. It may be exercised on application or on the court's own initiative. See Practice Direction, para.1.1 and r.3.3. An application may be dealt with without a hearing where all the parties are in agreement (r.1.4(2)(j) and Practice Direction 1.2). **19.2.1**

Contrast the position under Pt 17 where an amendment can be made to correct the name of a party by consent subject to the overall jurisdiction of the court to disallow amendment.

"The court may order" (r.19.2)

The substitution can be made without permission if the claim form has not been served; but see para.19.4.1 for notes on the application which can be made if permission is required. **19.2.2**

Relationship of rule 19.2 with the courts case management powers

In the case of *R. (Johnson) v Secretary of State for Health* [2006] EWHC 288 the Administrative court at first instance considered whether to permit a representative of a charity to pursue a claim in substitution for the original claimant where the original claimant had died. Having determined that the proposed new claimant to be substituted had not had the original claim "passed" to him and that it was not "desirable" for him to be substituted the court went on to consider its general case management powers under CPR r.3.1. (2)(m). On analysis the court accepted that it had a theoretical power to substitute a claimant under its general case management powers but on the facts of this particular case did not do so and stated that there would have to be 'very cogent factors ' for relying on its long stop case management powers to make the substitution sought. **19.2.3**

"connected issues" (r.19.2(2)(b))

See *Umm Qarn Management Co Ltd v (1) Valerie Ann Bunting (2) Esteem Bloodstock Ltd* [2001] 1 C.P.L.R. 20, CA as an example of a case where the Court of Appeal refused to allow joinder of a claimant on finding that the case advanced by the existing parties did not raise any issues in relation to the proposed new party. **19.2.4**

Substitution of parties after judgment

The court has the power to substitute parties after judgment should the overriding objective require such an order. *Humber Boats Ltd v Owners of the Selby Paradigm* [2004] EWHC 1804; [2004] 2 Lloyds Rep. 714; [2005] C.L. Y 310. **19.2.5**

"order any person to cease to be a party" (r.19.2(3))

When the court makes an order for the removal of a party, the claimant must file (see r.2.3) with the court an amended claim form (Pt 7) and particulars of claim and serve a copy of the order on every party to the proceedings and on any other person affected by the order (Practice Direction para.4). **19.2.6**

Copies

Practice Direction supplementing Pt 5, para.3.1 provides that new parties joined to existing proceedings are entitled to require the party joining them to supply, without charge, copies of all statements of case, written evidence and any other documents appended or exhibited to them which have been served. Such copies should be supplied within 48 hours of any request. If this is not done, the new party may apply for an order. **19.2.7**

Costs

Part 19 does not include any specific provisions dealing with costs of adding or substituting parties. See CPR Pts 43 to 48, especially r.44.3. The practice is to allow amendments, including the addition and substitution of parties, as this enables that all questions in issue are determined in one set of proceedings (r.19.2(2)(a)) provided the **19.2.8** other parties are safeguarded in costs. Upon giving an order to substitute or add a party the court generally makes an order for costs against the party seeking the change.

Death of a party

19.2.9 On the death of a sole claimant after an action brought in a case where the cause of action survives, the executor or administrator may obtain an order to carry on the proocedings. In the case where one of several claimants in a joint action which survives to the remaining claimants, they may continue the action without adding the personal representative of the deceased.

If a sole defendant dies and the cause of action is one that survives, the claimant may obtain an order to continue the proceedings as against the executor or administrator, or the executor or administrator may himself apply to be substituted. Until the executor or adminitrator has been added, the action cannot be continued.

Provisions applicable where two or more persons are jointly entitled to a remedy[1]

19.3 **19.3—(1) Where a claimant claims a remedy to which some other person is jointly entitled with him, all persons jointly entitled to the remedy must be parties unless the court orders otherwise.**

(2) If any person does not agree to be a claimant, he must be made a defendant, unless the court orders otherwise.

(3) This rule does not apply in probate proceedings.

"claimant" (rr.19.3 and 19.4)

19.3.1 See r.2.3.

Probate proceedings

19.3.2 See Practice Direction supplementing Pt 49, especially paras 2.6 and 2.7.

Addition or substitution of Defendant

19.3.3 The CPR apply to a new defendant who has been added or substituted as they do to any other defendant—see in particular Pt 9 (Responding to Particulars of Claim), Pt 10 (Acknowledgment of Service), Pt 11 (Disputing the Court's Jurisdiction) and Pt 15 (Defence and Reply).

A new defendant does not become a party to the proceedings until the amended claim form has been served (see Pt 6) on him— Practice Direction, para.3.4. Practice Direction, para.3.3, see para.19PD.1 deals with the making of directions when making an order adding or substituting a defendant.

See also para.3.4.3 and in particular the decision in *Securum Finance Ltd v Ashton* [2001] Ch 291, CA where a claimant was denied the chance to have a "second bite of the cherry" for starting a fresh action even though the limitation period had not expired: Applied in *Ann Kent (as executrix of Mabel Mary Chapper Deceased) v (1) M & L Management & Legal Ltd (2) Joseph Graham Chapper* [2005] EWHC 2546 (Ch) LTL 28/11/2005 where a defendant was not re-joined to a claim under CPR r.19.2 where it was not possible for him to receive a fair trial.

Transfer of interest or liability

19.3.4 See Practice Direction, para.5, see para.19PD.5.

Procedure for adding and substituting parties[2]

19.4 **19.4—(1) The court's permission is required to remove, add or substitute a party, unless the claim form has not been served.**

(2) An application for permission under paragraph (1) may be *made by—*

[1] Amended by the Civil Procedure (Amendment) Rules 2000 (SI 2000/221).
[2] Amended by the Civil Procedure (Amendment) Rules 2000 (SI 2000/221).

(a) an existing party; or

(b) a person who wishes to become a party.

(3) An application for an order under rule 19.2(4) (substitution of a new party where existing party's interest or liability has passed)—

(a) may be made without notice; and

(b) must be supported by evidence.

(4) Nobody may be added or substituted as a claimant unless—

(a) he has given his consent in writing; and

(b) that consent has been filed with the court.

(4A) The Commissioners for HM Revenue and Customs may be added as a party to proceedings only if they consent in writing.

(5) An order for the removal, addition or substitution of a party must be served on—

(a) all parties to the proceedings; and

(b) any other person affected by the order.

(6) When the court makes an order for the removal, addition or substitution of a party, it may give consequential directions about—

(a) filing and serving the claim form on any new defendant;

(b) serving relevant documents on the new party; and

(c) the management of the proceedings.

"The courts permission is required"

CPR r.19.4 provides that addition, substitution or removal of a party can take place without permission of the court before service of the claim form. If additions or substitutions are by agreement or are not contentious they may be made by application without a hearing—r.23.8 and Practice Direction supplementing Pt 19, para.1.2. All applications should be supported by evidence—either in the form of a completed Part C to Form **N244** or in a separate witness statement (Practice Direction supplementing Pt 19, para.1.3). Where the applicant is not already a party, the application notice must include his or her address for service (Practice Direction supplementing Pt 23, para.2.1(4)). The court should deal with as many aspects of the case as it can on the same occasion (CPR r.1.4(i)) the court may consider giving case management directions on joining a new party. On the other hand, the interests of justice may require that the new party have the opportunity of making representations before directions are given (see generally CPR Pt 3). **19.4.1**

"evidence" (r.19.4)

See Practice Direction, para.1.3 (see para.19PD.1), Pt 32 and the Practice Direction to Pt 32 (see para.32PD.1). In *Allergan Inc v Sauflon Pharmaceuticals Ltd* [2000] All E.R. (D.) 106, Ch D, Pumfrey J. refused an application to join a party as a second defendant where the claimant failed to plead a good arguable case. **19.4.2**

"filed" (r.19.4(4))

See r.2.3. **19.4.3**

"Nobody may be added or substituted as a claimant unless...he has given his consent in writing" (r.19.4(4))

Where an application is made to add or substitute a new party as claimant, the party applying must file (see r.2.3) the application notice, the proposed amended claim form and the signed, written consent of the new claimant (see Practice Direction, para.2.1 (see para.19PD.1)). **19.4.4**

"serving" (r.19.4(6))

See Pt 6. **19.4.5**

Human Rights

19.4A **19.4A Section 4 of the Human Rights Act 1998**

(1) The court may not make a declaration of incompatibility in accordance with section 4 of the Human Rights Act 1998 unless 21 days' notice, or such other period as the court directs, has been given to the Crown.

(2) Where notice has been given to the Crown a Minister, or other person permitted by that Act, shall be joined as a party on giving notice to the court.

(Only courts specified in section 4 of the Human Rights Act 1998 can make a declaration of incompatibility).

Section 9 of the Human Rights Act 1998

(3) Where a claim is made under that Act for damages in respect of a judicial act—

(a) that claim must be set out in the statement of case or the appeal notice; and

(b) notice must be given to the Crown.

(4) Where paragraph (3) applies and the appropriate person has not applied to be joined as a party within 21 days, or such other period as the court directs, after the notice is served, the court may join the appropriate person as a party.

(A practice direction makes provision for these notices).

Effect of rule

19.4A.1 This rule was inserted by the Civil Procedure (Amendment No.4) Rules 2000 (SI 2000/2092). The rule is supplemented by Practice Direction (Addition and Substitution of Parties) para.6.1 *et seq.* (see para.19PD.6 below).

Giving notice to the Crown

19.4A.2 Paragraph 6.4 of Practice Direction (Addition and Substitution of Parties), one of the practice directions supplementing Pt 19, states that the notice given under this rule must be served on the person named in the list published under s.17 of the Crown Proceedings Act 1947. Section 17 states that the Minister for the Civil Service shall publish a list specifying the several Government departments which are authorised for the purposes of that Act and the names and addresses of the person who is, or who is acting as, solicitor for such Departments. The list is issued by the Cabinet Office and is superseded from time to time. As is mentioned in para.6.4(1), the list is annexed to the practice direction (see para.19PD.7, below). From time to time, the version of the list annexed to the offical version of the Practice Direction as published by HMSO is not always the latest version. There is a link to the latest version of the list on the homepage of the Treasury Solicitor's Department website (i.e. *www.tsol.gov.uk*). Click on the links for "serving proceedings".

Special provisions about adding or substituting parties after the end of a relevant limitation period[1]

19.5 **19.5—(1) This rule applies to a change of parties after the end of a period of limitation under—**

(a) the Limitation Act 1980[2];

[1] Amended by the Civil Procedure (Amendment) Rules 2000 (SI 2000/221), and Civil Procedure (Amendment) Rules 2001 (SI 2001/256).

[2] 1980 c.58.

(b) the Foreign Limitation Periods Act 1984[1]; or

(c) any other enactment which allows such a change, or under which such a change is allowed.

(2) The court may add or substitute a party only if—

(a) the relevant limitation period[GL] was current when the proceedings were started; and

(b) the addition or substitution is necessary.

(3) The addition or substitution of a party is necessary only if the court is satisfied that—

(a) the new party is to be substituted for a party who was named in the claim form in mistake for the new party;

(b) the claim cannot properly be carried on by or against the original party unless the new party is added or substituted as claimant or defendant; or

(c) the original party has died or had a bankruptcy order made against him and his interest or liability has passed to the new party.

(4) In addition, in a claim for personal injuries the court may add or substitute a party where it directs that—

(a)

(i) section 11 (special time limit for claims for personal injuries); or

(ii) section 12 (special time limit for claims under fatal accidents legislation), of the Limitation Act 1980 shall not apply to the claim by or against the new party; or

(b) the issue of whether those sections apply shall be determined at trial.

(Rule 17.4 deals with other changes after the end of a relevant limitation period[GL]).

Effect of rule

It is conceivable that, after civil proceedings have been started by the issue of a claim form, and before those proceedings have been concluded, one of the parties or a third party may wish to start a new claim in those pending proceedings. Such a new claim may involve either (a) the addition or substitution of a new cause of action, or (b) the addition or substitution of a new party, or possibly both. **19.5.1**

Commencement date for new claims —Procedural law has to deal with the question: in these circumstances, when is the new claim commenced? Two answers have been offered: (1) at the date when the new claim is started (the "date of amendment" theory), and (2) the date when the original claim was commenced (the "reference back" theory).

If the first answer is correct, then one of the consequences is that the question whether any limitation period relevant to the new claim has run is answered by asking: had time run before the (later) date on which the new claim was brought? On the other hand, if the second answer is correct, the answer is: had time run before the (earlier) date on which the original claim was brought? Obviously, as a practical matter, parties are more likely to find their new claims barred by limitation if the first answer is correct. Where a relevant limitation period for a party's new claim expires after the original claim was commenced but before the new claim was commenced, the reference back theory comes to the rescue of the party.

[1] 1984 c.16.

Limitation Act 1980 s.35 —The Limitation Act 1980 s.35 (New claims in pending actions: rules of court) seeks to resolve the matter, at least for the purposes of new claims that are subject to limitation periods imposed by that Act (see Vol.2 para.8–102+ and commentary following). Section 35(1)(b) states that new claims are deemed to have been commenced on the same (earlier) date as the original action (i.e. the reference back theory prevails). There is a qualification to this. If the new claim is made "in or by way of third party proceedings" the claim is deemed to have been commenced on the (later) date on which they are in fact commenced (i.e. the date of amendment theory prevails). (Section 35(2) elaborates on what is meant by "new claim" and "third party proceedings" in this context.)

Conditions under which new claim may be allowed —If that were all that s.35 said, the conclusion would be that, for new claims deemed to have been commenced on the same (earlier) date as the original action, the date for determining whether or not a limitation defence may be successfully pleaded is the (earlier) date on which the original claim was commenced. That is to say, as a result of the deeming provision in s.35(1)(b), in circumstances where a relevant limitation period expired after the original claim was commenced, a plea of limitation could not be raised in defence of the new claim (whether it involved a new cause of action, or a new party, or both).

But that is not all that the section says. Section 35(3) states that, although new claims are deemed to have been commenced on the same date as the original action, the court shall not, except in certain circumstances, allow such new claims to be made in the course of any action "after the expiry of any time limit under the Act which would affect a new action to enforce that claim". (The circumstances in which s.33 of the Act apply are also excepted; see further para.19.5.9). Subsection (4) states that rules of court may provide for allowing a new claim to be made "but only if the conditions specified in sub-section (5) below are satisfied and subject to any further restrictions the rules may impose". The conditions foreshadowed there have the effect of restricting the circumstances in which parties commencing new claims may enjoy the boon that the reference back theory gives. The policy consideration underlying this part of the legislation seems to be that any limitation advantage that may accrue to a party by virtue of the reference back theory should be subject to limits.

Now, what are the conditions under which the court may allow a new claim to be brought in these circumstances, thereby enabling a party to deflect a limitation defence?

If the new claim is *a claim including a new cause of action*, the condition is that the new cause of action "arises out of the same facts or substantially the same facts as are already in issue on any claim previously made in the original action" (s.35(5)(b)). The rules of court dealing with this condition (as authorised by s.35(4)) are now found in CPR r.17.4 (Amendment to statements of case after the end of a relevant limitation period) (see para.17.4.1 *et seq.* above). That rule replaces former RSC O.20. r.5.

If the new claim is *a claim involving a new party*, the condition is that the addition or substitution of the new party "is necessary for the determination of the original action" (s.35(5)(b)). The addition or substitution of a new party shall not be regarded as necessary unless either (a) the new party is substituted for a party whose name was given in any claim made in the original action in mistake for the new party's name, or (b) any claim already made in the original action cannot be maintained by or against an existing party unless the new party is joined or substituted as plaintiff or defendant in that action" (s.35(6)). The rules of court dealing with this condition (as authorised by s.35(4)) are now found in CPR r.19.5 (Special provisions about adding or substituting parties after the end of a relevant limitation period). It is that rule with which this commentary paragraph and those immediately following are concerned.

A convenient test is to ask whether the identity of the claimant could be changed without significantly altering the claim (*Roger James Weston* v (1) John Gribben & (2) Foreign and Commonwealth Office [2006] EWCA Civ 1425 CA).

It may be noted that, whereas under the CPR rules as to the commencement of a new claim (a) being a claim involving a new cause of action, and (b) being a new claim including a new party, are kept quite distinct, with the former being in Pt 17 (Amendment, etc.) and the latter in Pt 19 (Parties, etc.), that was not so under the former RSC.

When does r.19.5 apply (r.19.5(1))?

19.5.2 *Limitation Act 1980 s.35* —Rule 19.5 is one of two rules (the other is r.17.4) which carry into effect the Limitation Act 1980 s.35. Therefore it applies when "any new claim is made in the course of any action" (s.35(1)), and for these purposes "a new claim" means any claim involving the addition or substitution of a new party (s.35(2)(b)). The substitution or addition of a new party "in the course of any action" need not involve the making a "new claim". If it does not, r.19.5 does not apply, and the question then whether a change of parties should be permitted is governed by r.19.2. For example, to substitute a defendant who has taken over a claim by assignment.

Sub-rule (1) is not very helpful. It says that r.19.5 applies to a change of parties "after the end of a period of limitation". It does not make clear whether the period of limitation referred to is one relating to the "new claim" (involving the addition or substitution of a new party), or to (to what s.35 calls) the "original action". Recourse to s.35 indicates that the rules are meant to provide for circumstances in which a "new claim" (adding or substituting a new party) may "be made in the course of any action after the expiry of any time limit under this Act which would affect a new action to enforce that claim". It is clear that "that claim" means the "new claim" (involving the substitution or addition of a new party) and not the "original action". Needless to say, the original action must be properly constituted. It will not be properly constituted if, for example, the claimant in the original action was not merely the wrong or a misdescribed claimant, but a non-existent legal person (*International Bulk Shipping and Services Ltd v Minerals and Metals Trading Corp of India* [1996] 1 All E.R. 1017, CA).

The Foreign Limitation Periods Act 1984 provides for any law relating to the limitation of actions to be treated, for the purpose of cases in which effect is given to foreign law (or to determinations by foreign courts), as a matter of substance rather than (as in English law) as a matter of procedure. Section 1(3) of that Act states that, where an English court applies a foreign law relating to limitation, English law shall determine whether, and the time at which, proceedings have been commenced in respect of an matter; further, s.35 of the 1980 Act shall apply in relation to time limits applicable by virtue of the foreign law as it applies in relation to time limits under that Act.

"any other enactment" —The Limitation Act 1980 s.35 (as extended by the 1984 Act) makes provision for a "new claim" to be "made in the course of any action" after the "expiry of any time limit" imposed by the Act and which would "affect a new action to enforce that claim". Such "new claim" includes any claim "involving the addition or substitution of a new party". Thus it could be said, as is said in r.19.5, that the section allows a "change of parties" after the "end of a period of limitation".

Rule 19.5 recognises that there may be other statutory provisions, apart from s.35, that "allow such a change". Thus r.19.5(1)(c) states that the rules contained in r.19.5 should apply where application is made to make a new claim involving the addition or substitution of a new party after the expiry of a period of limitation as permitted by any such other statutory provisions. By this device, the listing in r.19.5(1) of each individual statutory provision of this type is avoided. The Town and Country Planning Act 1990 s.288 (which imposes a time limit on the bringing of High Court proceedings questioning certain decisions made under the Act) is not an enactment imposing a period of limitation for these purposes (*Eco-Energy (GB) Limited v First Secretary of State* [2004] EWCA Civ 1566, November 9, 2004, CA).

It is important to note that r.19.5(1)(c) extends the operation of r.19.5, not only to enactments that "allow such a change" of parties as that allowed by s.35, but also to enactments "under which such a change is allowed". On the face of it, the addition here of the phrase "under which such a change is allowed" may seem tautologous. But the addition does have purpose. The explanation is as follows.

There are many statutory provisions that impose time limits on the commencement of certain types of claim. Some of these provisions are not normally thought of as limitation statutes properly so-called, because usually the time limit can be extended by order of the court and sometimes by agreement between the parties. Nevertheless, they do impose procedural bars. But they differ from s.35 in that they do not expressly provide for a "change of parties" in the sense that they do not provide for "new claim" to be made "involving the addition or substitution of a new party" after the time limit has expired.

However, it may be argued that, although these statutory provisions do not expressly provide for a new claim to be made involving the addition or substitution of a new party, they do not prohibit it either. If it can be said that the enactment is one which, whilst not expressly providing for change of parties after time has run, is nevertheless one "under which such a change is allowed", then the provisions of r.19.5 apply. This argument was accepted by the Court of Appeal in *Parsons v George* [2004] EWCA Civ 912; [2004] 1 W.L.R. 3264, CA, where the enactment involved imposed a time limit for the bringing of claims for the renewal of business leases (the provision has since been amended and no longer contains such a time limit).

Whether this reasoning should apply to any particular statutory provision imposing a procedural time limit has to be decided in the light of the express terms of the provision and its context. It would seem that it is intended that the reasoning would apply to the Merchant Shipping Act 1995 s.190 (time limit for proceedings against owners or ship) (see Vol.2 para.2D–253) as that section was listed in r.19.5(1) before the rule was amended by SI 2000/221. And it would apply in circumstances where the time limit on bringing claims imposed by art.26 of the Convention on the Contract for the International Carriage of Goods by Road, incorporated in English law by the Carriage of Goods by Road Act 1965, takes effect (*International Distillers and Vinters Ltd v JF Hillebrand (UK) Ltd, The Times*, January 25, 2000). The advantage of the generic definition in r.19.5(1)(c) is that avoids overburdening the rule by including and keeping up-to-date a comprehensive list of enactments imposing limitation periods.

"relevant limitation period ... current" (r.19.5(2)(a))

19.5.3 In this respect, r.19.5(2)(a) re-enacts the first part of former RSC O.15, r.6(5)(a) without significant change. In this context, the "relevant limitation period" is the period relevant to the "new claim" (involving the substitution or addition of a new party). The court may add or substitute a party only if that period was current "when the proceedings were started"; that is to say, where the "relevant limitation period" had not expired when the "original action" was commenced.

A "relevant limitation period" includes any time limit under the legislation referred to in r.19.5(1) (see para.19.5.2 above). Obviously, it includes the limits described in s.35(3) of the Limitation Act 1980 as "any time limit under this Act"; it has been held that such a limit includes the 10 year limitation period imposed by s.11A(3) of that Act as inserted by the Consumer Protection Act 1987 (*Horne-Roberts v SmithKline Beecham Plc* [2001] EWCA Civ 2006; [2001] EWCA Civ 2006, CA).

"the addition or substitution is necessary" (r.19.5(2)(b) and r.19.5(3))

19.5.4 In this respect, r.19.5(2)(b) re-enacts the second part of former RSC O.15, r.6(5)(a) without significant change. Rule 19.5(3) replaces former RSC O.15, r.6(6) but in simpler and less prescriptive terms. The rule carries into effect the Limitation Act 1980 s.35(6) which states (but which r.19.5(2)(b) fails to state) that the addition or substitution of a new party is necessary "for the determination of the original action". Rule 19.5(3) states that the addition or substitution of a new party is necessary only if the court is satisfied as to the matters listed in that rule (see further below). In this respect, the rule implements the Limitation Act 1980 s.35(6). It is clear from s.35(4) that rules of court may impose further restrictions on the circumstances in which a new claim involving a new party may be added after the expiry of the limitation period, but cannot relax the statutory requirements in s.35(6) (*Merrett v Babb* [2001] EWCA Civ 214; [2001] Q.B. 1174, CA at para.53 per May L.J).

In *Roberts v Gill & Co* [2008] EWCA Civ 803; *The Times* August 18, 2008, CA, an individual had commenced proceedings, within the limitation period, in a personal capacity against solicitors for breach of duty of care owed to him as beneficiary of his deceased mother's estate. Subsequently, he applied for permission to continue those proceedings in a representative capacity under a derivative claim on behalf of the estate. The court held that, where a court grants such an application the personal representative or administrator has to be joined as a party to those proceedings. If (as in this case) the application is made after the limitation period had expired, r.19.5 applies.

"party ... named in mistake for the new party" (r.19.5(3)(a) and s.35(6)(a))

19.5.5 One of the three conditions (for others, see paras 19.5.7 and 19.5.9 below) which will be sufficient to satisfy the court that it is necessary that a new claim involving the *addition or substitution* of a new party should be allowed is that "the new party is to be substituted for a party who was named in the claim form in mistake for the new party" (r.19.5(3)(a)). In this respect, the rule implements the Limitation Act 1980 s.35(6)(a). It is interesting to note, that both the rule and the sub-section speak of a new party being "substituted" and not being "added or substituted".

Neither r.19.5(3)(a) nor s.35.6(a) elaborate on what is meant by "mistake" in this context (*cf.* r.17.4(3)). In English law, where a defendant successfully raises a plea of limitation, the claimant's cause of action is not extinguished but a procedural bar is placed upon it; it has a Draconian effect on the claimant's claim. The policies underlying the plea include fairness to the defendant and finality. Where the plea has the effect of defeating a meritorious claim a sense of injustice is likely to arise, and is perhaps bound to arise where the claimant by his own mistake played a critical part in the success of the plea (all the more so where the mistake was genuine and caused no prejudice to the proper defendant). The case law on mistake in this context, both pre- and post-CPR is extensive; see para.19.5.7 below.

Relationship between r.19.5(3)(a) and r.17.4(3) mistakes

Rule 17.4(3) applies where the intended party was named in the claim form but there was a genuine mistake as to the name of the party and no one was misled; the mistake is a mere mistake as to a name such as causes no reasonable doubt as to the identity of the party in question. **19.5.6**

By contrast, a mistake to which r.19.5(3)(a) applies is a more fundamental mistake which can only be cured if a new party is substituted; this rule applies where the application is to substitute a new party for a party who was named in the claim form in mistake for the new party (*Gregson v Channel Four Television Corp* [2000] C.P. Rep. 60, at paras 18 and 29 per May L.J. and Peter Gibson L.J.). The important point is that r.19.5(3)(a) is engaged where the mistake can only be rectified by the making of a new claim involving, not simply the addition or substitution of a new cause of action, but involving the addition or substitution of a new party (see subss. (1)(b), (2)(b) and (3) of s.35 of the 1980 Act). An application to bring a new claim involving the addition or substitution of a new cause of action, but not involving the addition or substitution of a new party (see subss. (1)(b) and (2)(a) of s.35 of the 1980 Act) does not engage any aspect of r.19.5, but is dealt with under whichever one or other of the sub-rules of r.17.4 as is appropriate.

Cases on mistake (r.19.5(3)(a))

Much of the case law relating to r.19.5 involves applications for the substitution of a new party for a party named in the claim form (either as claimant, but more usually as defendant) on the ground that the latter party was named by mistake. Both before and after the CPR came into effect, the courts have often had difficulty in dealing with these applications. Pre-CPR cases had to take into account the elaboration of s.35.6(a) offered by RSC O.20, r.5(3) (see para.19.5.5 above) and the cases thereon. As drafted, r.19.5(3)(a) gives the courts the opportunity to go back to s.35.6(a) in its pure form. In interpreting r.15.5(3)(a), a court is usually really interpreting s.35(6)(a). CPR r.1.2 states that, when exercising any power given to it by the rules, or interpreting any rule, the court must seek to give effect to the overriding objective (see r.1.1). It seems clear that, in some cases arising since the CPR came into effect, courts have approached r.19.5(3)(a) with the overriding objective very much in mind and have done so even in circumstances where the reality is that they are not interpreting the rule but the statutory provision which it recites. It has been said that there are no grounds for supposing that r.19.5 intended to change the rules so as to deny the court the jurisdiction it enjoyed before the CPR came into effect (*Parsons v George* [2004] EWCA Civ 912; [2004] 1 W.L.R. 3264, CA at para.29, per Dyson L.J.). **19.5.7**

Wherever issues of mistake arise in the law (whether e.g. in contract, tort or crime) the law flounders; the area of procedural law under discussion here provides no exception.

Where a claimant (C) pursues a claim against a legal person (X) named Smith (or Smith & Co) but addressed by C in his claim form as Jones (or Jones & Co), C has made a mistake, not as to the legal person as against whom he is proceeding, but as to X's name. Where, on the other hand, C pursues a claim against a legal person (X) named Smith and correctly addressed as such by C, when his claim ought to have been against legal person (Y) named Jones, C has made a mistake not as to name but as to the legal person against whom he wishes to proceed. In either event, for a period at least, C's mistake may have been shared by X.

In the former event, the correction of X's name involves no change in the legal person as against whom C is intending to proceed; in the latter event it does. In the latter event, at one extreme X and Y may be complete strangers to one another or, at the other extreme, may be related; for example, where Y is a holding company of X, or where X was a company bought by Y (another company) some time after the cause of action arose but before the claim form was issued, and in circumstances where a cause of action or liability was not assigned or transferred.

Over the years (and both before and after the CPR came into effect), in the voluminous case law on s.35 of the 1980 Act and the related rules of court the scenarios outlined above and variations on them have arisen. The short question is: what type of mistake is covered by s.35(6)(a) as implemented by r.19.5(3)(a)? The question has vexed the courts for many years.

In recent years, the Court of Appeal has made brave attempts to clarify and simplify the application of r.19.5(3)(a) area of the law, whilst remaining faithful to previous authority (including decisions of the House of Lords) on the former rules and s.35(6)(a) insofar as it may be regarded as still binding since the CPR came into effect. (For a full coverage of the authorities, see the commentary following s.35 in Vol.2, para.8–86.)

The leading case is *Horne-Roberts v SmithKline Beecham plc* [2001] EWCA Civ 2006, CA; [2002] 1 W.L.R. 1662 in which the court applied the approach adopted in *Sardinia Sulcis* [1991] 1 Lloyd's Rep. 201, CA.

The approach adopted in *Horne-Roberts* has recently been applied by the Court of Appeal in the case of *Adelson v Associated Newspapers Ltd* [2007] EWCA Civ 701; *The Times* July 18 2007; which was a libel case and concerned the substitution of two new claimants. This decision has considerable bearing on the correct approach to be adopted by a court in deciding what type of mistake qualifies for the relief of r.19.5(3)(a); the court considered the history of the rules and their relevance. The provisions of s.35 of the Limitation Act 1980 and of CPR 17.4(3) and CPR 19.5(3) cover the same ground as Order 20 r.5. In the leading judgment in *Morgan Est (Scotland) Ltd v Hanson Concrete Productions Ltd* [2005] EWCA Civ 134; [2005] 1 W.L.R. 2557, CA Jacob L.J. had observed, albeit obiter, that the 1980 Act had the intention of liberalising the position from that under the Limitation Act 1939. This observation was not correct and the reasoning in *Morgan Est* should not be followed. Perhaps the clearest summary of the object of the 1980 Act is to be found in *Yorkshire Regional Health Authority v Fairclough Building Ltd* [1996] 1 All E.R. 519 at p.527 which is quoted in the *Adelson* judgment and is not repeated here. The first known decision on Order 20 r.5 which considered the concept of 'misnomer'is the case of *Mitchell v Harris Engineering* [1967] 2 Q.B. 703, subsequently expanded upon in *Sardinia Sulcis*. The 'working test' suggested in *Weston v Gribben* in as much as it extends the Sardinia Sulcis test should not be relied on.

The points to be derived from *The Sardinia Sulcis* [1991] 1 Lloyd's Rep. 201, CA are these:

(1) r.19.5(3)(a) (and s.35(6)) allows more than the mere correction of the name of a party as it is, after all, a provision that allows the substitution of a new party for the original named party;

(2) in one sense, a claimant always intends to sue the person who is liable for the wrong that he has suffered; but the test cannot be that he has made a mistake which may be corrected where he sues another person, otherwise leave to substitute would always be granted;

(3) so there must be a test that includes, but is broader than, mere correction of name but narrower than substitution of the person intended to be sued for the person actually sued

(4) the test is: is it possible to identify the intended defendant "by reference to a description more or less specific to the particular case"?; if it is, it is a mistake of the type covered by s.35(6)(a) as implemented by r.19.5(3)(a).

(5) thus, if the claimant gets the right description but the wrong name for his intended defendant, there is unlikely to be any doubt as to the identity of the person intended to be sued; but if he gets the wrong description, it will be otherwise

(6) this test might allow the substitution of a new defendant, unconnected with the original defendant and unaware of the claim until after the expiry of a relevant limitation period; but any potential injustice can be avoided by the exercise of the court's discretion under s.35.

The Court of Appeal applied this test in *Parsons v George* [2004] EWCA Civ 912; [2004] 1 W.L.R. 3264, CA (where the pre- and post-CPR authorities are extensively reviewed and explained by Dyson L.J. at paras 8 to 20) and in *Kesslar v Moore & Tibbits (A Firm)* [2004] EWCA Civ 1551, (where it was noted that a striking feature of the test is that it permits, subject to the court's discretion, the substitution of a completely new defendant who had no connection with the party originally impleaded). In the latter case it was said that the approach proposed by the Court in *Parsons v George* (where the *Horne-Roberts* case was followed) involved no infringement of art.6 of the Convention.

Neither the pre-CPR or post-CPR cases suggest that there is a particular list of factors that the court should take into account in determining whether the substitution of a new party is necessary because that party is to be substituted for a party who (as r.19.5(3(a) says) was named in the claim form in mistake for the new party. In *Parsons v George*, *op cit.*, the court was so satisfied, having found that the mistake was clear and unintentional and the identity of the party was obvious from the description in the statement of case.

Cases in which, though a party was mis-named, his identity was made clear by reference to a description which is specific to the particular case, and which therefore may be regarded as examples of the application of the test stated by the Court of Appeal in the *Horne-Roberts* case are:

- *Mitchell v Harris Engineering Co* [1967] 2 Q.B. 703, CA (claimant's employers)
- *Rodriguez v Parker* [1967] 1 Q.B. 116 (driver of a particular car)
- *Evans Construction Co Ltd v Charrington & Co Ltd* [1983] Q.B. 810, CA (competent landlord)
- *Thistle Hotels Ltd v Sir Robert McAlpine & Sons Ltd*, *The Times*, April 11, 1989, CA (proprietor of an hotel)
- *The Sardinia Sulcis*, [1991] 1 Lloyd's Rep. 201 (merger of companies)
- *Crook v Aaron Dale Construction and Roofing Ltd* [1997] P.I.Q.R P36, CA (claimant's employer)
- *Horne-Roberts v Smithkline Beecham Plc* [2001] EWCA Civ 2006; [2002] 1 W.L.R. 1662, CA (manufacturers of a specifically identified batch of vaccine)
- *Declan O'Byrne (claimant) v Aventis Pasteur MSD Ltd (defendant) & Aventis Pasteur SA (Proposed Defendant)* [2006] EWHC 2562, QB (substituting the manufacturers of a vaccine where the distributors had been sued in error). But see also the same parties under appeal at [2008] 3 C.M.L.R. 10 HL, September 2008, the hearing of the appeal adjourned pending clarification of a form of words by ECJ
- *Parsons v George* [2004] EWCA Civ 912; [2004] 1 W.L.R 3264, CA (competent landlord)
- *Kesslar v Moore & Tibbits (A Firm)* [2004] EWCA Civ 1551 (professional advisers)

"claim cannot properly be carried on" (r.19.5(3)(b) and s.35(6)(b))

The second of the three conditions (for other two, see para.19.5.5 and 19.5.7 above, **19.5.8** and para.19.5.9 below) which will be sufficient to satisfy the court that it is necessary that a new claim involving the addition or substitution of a new party should be allowed is that the claim cannot properly be carried on by or against the original party unless the new party is added or substituted as claimant or defendant (r.19.5(3)(b)). In this respect, the rule implements the Limitation Act 1980 s.35(6)(b). It is interesting to note, that both the rule and the sub-section speak of a new party being "joined or substituted" and not simply being "substituted".

Rule 19.5(3)(b) and s.35.6(b) state this condition in slightly different terms. Section 35.6(b) states that the addition or substitution of a new party may be regarded as necessary where the court is satisfied that "any claim already made in the original action cannot be maintained by or against an existing party unless the new party is joined or substituted as plaintiff or defendant in that action". Rule 19.5(3)(b) seeks to implement this provision by stating the court must be satisfied that "the claim cannot properly be carried on by or against the original party unless the new party is added or substituted as claimant or defendant". Both s.35.6(b) and r.19.5(3)(b) are less prescriptive than former RSC provision that carried out the function now carried out by the rule (see RSC O.15, r.6(6)). What is lost in r.19.5(3)(b) (but is found in s.35.6(b)) is that it is the "original action" which the court must be satisfied cannot "properly be carried on" or "cannot be maintained" unless the new party is joined. It has been held that "cannot properly be carried on" in r.19.5(3)(b) is to be taken as meaning the same as "cannot be maintained" in s.35(6)(b) (*Merrett v Babb* [2001] EWCA Civ 214; [2001] Q.B. 1174, CA).

For a modern example of the addition of a new party being permitted on the basis of r.19.5(3)(c), see *Merrett v Babb*, [2001] EWCA Civ 214; [2001] Q.B. 1174, CA (addition of new party as claimant in professional negligence action to whom defendant owed duty of care jointly with original claimant bringing claim for entire loss).

Death or bankruptcy (r.19.5(3)(c))

19.5.9 The third of the three conditions (for others, see para.19.5.5 and 19.5.8 above) which will be sufficient to satisfy the court that it is necessary that a new claim involving the addition or substitution of a new party should be allowed is that the original party has died or had a bankruptcy order made against him and his interest or liability has passed to the new party. This condition is not based on s.35(6) of the 1980 Act. It did not figure in the former rules enacted in the light of that section but its effect was secured by other rules of court.

Where a party to a claim dies or becomes bankrupt, but the cause of action survives, the claim does not abate by reason of the death or bankruptcy. Where, in these circumstances, the interest or liability of any party to proceedings (now deceased or bankrupt) is assigned or transmitted to or devolves upon another person, the court may make an order that that other person be made a party to the proceedings. Normally, the making of such substitution will not involve the making of a new claim within the meaning of s.35 after the limitation period has expired and therefore recourse to that section or to r.19.5 will not be required. However, r.19.5(3)(c) seems to envisage circumstances where such recourse will be required and makes allowance for it accordingly.

"claim for personal injuries" (r.19.5(4))

19.5.10 *Discretionary exclusion of time limit under s.33 (r.19.5(4)(a))* —As mentioned above (para.19.5.1), s.35(3) of the 1980 Act states that the general rule that the court shall not allow a new claim (as defined in s.35(1)(b), and excluding an original set-off or counterclaim) to be made in the course of any action "after the expiry of any time limit under this Act which would affect a new action to enforce that claim". And, as explained above (paras 19.5.4, to 19.5.8), there are exceptions to this general rule found in s.35 and provided for in para.(2) and (3) of r.19.5.

Another exception to the general rule is made by s.35(3) itself and is carried forward in r.19.5(4)(a) (replacing former RSC O.15, r.6(5)). It is an exception made necessary by the fact that the special limitation periods for personal injury and fatal accident claims stated in ss.11 and 12 of the 1980 Act are significantly different from the normal type of limitation enactment in that the court may order that they should be disapplied under s.33 and the limitation period extended to a date fixed by the court.

Such an order may have the effect of allowing a new claim involving the substitution or addition of a new party in circumstances where the general rule is infringed. Section 35(3), as implemented by r.19.5(4)(a), make it clear that an exception to the general rule is made in these circumstances.

Determination of s.33 application at trial (r.19.5(4)(b)) —The question whether, in a personal injury or fatal accident case, the limitation period imposed by s.11 of s.12 of the 1980 Act should be disapplied by order made under s.33, and such period extended to a date fixed by the court, can be exceedingly difficult to determine where it turns on seriously disputed issues of law and fact. In the interest of case management, the court may decide that the question whether an order should be made under s.33 would best be determined at trial and make a direction accordingly. Obviously, where the making of such an order would have the effect of allowing a new claim involving the substitution or addition of a new party it would be unsatisfactory if the addition or substitution could not be made until trial. Accordingly, para.(b) of r.19.5(4) makes it clear the change of party can be made at the time when the direction is made.

A new party may not be joined to a defamation action where the limitation period had expired even if the order allowing the joinder contained the caveat that the joinder was without prejudice to any limitation defence as the court did not have jurisdiction at the time of making the order to add the new party: *Edwards v Golding* [2006] EWHC 1684, QB, July 12, 2006 (Tugendhat J.).

Exercise of discretion under r.19.5

In the commentary on r.19.5 set out above it is explained that where the rule applies (see r.19.5(1)) the court may add or substitute a party only if (a) the relevant limitation period was current when the proceedings were started, and (b) the addition or substitution is necessary (r.19.5(2)). If the court finds these two conditions satisfied there remains the question whether, in the exercise of the court's discretion, the addition or substitution of the new party should be allowed. That discretion should be exercised in accordance with the overriding objective, including the cost and delay elements contained therein, and should take into account all relevant circumstances, including prejudice to the parties, and whether a fair trial of the issues in the new claim (involving the new party) is possible. **19.5.11**

Lloyd L.J. suggested that in considering whether to allow a new party to be substituted for an existing party under r.19.5 "...a convenient working test would be to ask whether you can change the identity of the parties without significantly changing the claim." *Weston v Gribben* [2006] EWCA Civ 1425, November 2, 2006, CA.

Special rules about parties in claims for wrongful interference with goods[1]

19.5A—(1) A claimant in a claim for wrongful interference with goods must, in the particulars of the claim, state the name and address of every person who, to his knowledge, has or claims an interest in the goods and who is not a party to the claim. **19.5A**

(2) A defendant to a claim for wrongful interference with goods may apply for a direction that another person be made a party to the claim to establish whether the other person—

(a) has a better right to the goods than the claimant; or

(b) has a claim which might render the defendant doubly liable under section 7 of the Torts (Interference with Goods) Act 1977.

(3) Where the person referred to in paragraph (2) fails to attend the hearing of the application, or comply with any directions, the court may order that he is deprived of any claim against the defendant in respect of the goods.

(Rule 3.1(3) provides that the court may make an order subject to conditions).

(4) The application notice must be served on all parties and on the person referred to in paragraph (2).

Effect of rule

This rule was inserted by the Civil Procedure (Amendment) Rules 2001 (SI 2001/256) and in effect reinstates former RSC O.15, r.10A. **19.5A.1**

II. Representative Parties

Editorial introduction

The rules in this section of Pt 19 of the CPR were inserted by the Civil Procedure (Amendment) Rules 2000 (SI 2000/221) r.9 and Sch.2. They replace the provisions dealing with representative parties in RSC O.15 (Causes of action, counterclaims and parties) and CCR O.5 (Causes of action and parties) as re-enacted in Schs 1 and 2 of the CPR. **19.6.0**

The residual provisions of RSC O.15 were revoked in December 2002 (SI 2002/2058).

[1] Introduced by the Civil Procedure (Amendment) Rules 2001 (SI 2001/256).

Rule 19.9 was amended by, and the rules following it in this section of Pt 19 were inserted by, the Civil Procedure (Amendment) Rules 2007 (SI 2007/2204); see further para.19.9F.1 below.

Representative parties with same interest[1]

19.6 **19.6—(1) Where more than one person has the same interest in a claim—**

(a) the claim may be begun; or

(b) the court may order that the claim be continued,

by or against one or more of the persons who have the same interest as representatives of any other persons who have that interest.

(2) The court may direct that a person may not act as a representative.

(3) Any party may apply to the court for an order under paragraph (2).

(4) Unless the court otherwise directs any judgment or order given in a claim in which a party is acting as a representative under this rule—

(a) is binding on all persons represented in the claim; but

(b) may only be enforced by or against a person who is not a party to the claim with the permission of the court.

(5) This rule does not apply to a claim to which rule 19.7 applies.

19.6.1 *Note*—This rule was inserted in the CPR by the Civil Procedure (Amendment) Rules 2000 (SI 2000/221) r.9 and Sch.2, and replaced (in much simpler terms) RSC and CCR provisions formerly found in Schs 1 and 2 of the CPR, specifically RSC O.15, r.12 and CCR O.5, r.5.

Effect of rule

19.6.2 Put broadly, r.19.6 provides for legal persons to be represented in civil proceedings by other legal persons. (As to representation of an unincorporated association by one or more of its members, see *Artistic Upholstery Ltd v Art Forma (Furniture) Ltd, The Times*, September 21, 1999, which decided that one or more members of an unincorporated association could act for the association in a representative capacity.) Rule 19.7 provides for the representation in particular proceedings of interested persons who cannot be ascertained. Rule 19.6 does not apply to a claim to which r.19.7 applies (r.19.6(5)). Note also r.19.9 (Derivative claims) which covers a variety of claims, some of which would otherwise fall to be dealt with under r.19.6.

The phrase "the same interest" in a claim must be interpreted to give effect to the overriding objective. Specifically it should be interpreted in a way that makes the representative proceedings machinery available in cases where its use would save expense and enable a matter to be dealt with expeditiously; per Andrew Smith J. in *National Bank of Greece SA v Outhwaite* [2001] C.P. Rep. 69 when allowing one Lloyds syndicate to stand as a representative for a number of 1991 Lloyds syndicates.

Conceivably, a claim may be brought by several legal persons as claimants, or may be brought against several legal persons as defendants, or both. (There is no limit to the number of claimants or defendants who may be joined as parties to a claim (*r.19.1*).) In these circumstances, the law provides that, where they have the same interest, some of the several claimants or some of the several defendants, as the case

[1] Amended by the Civil Procedure (Amendment) Rules 2000 (SI 2000/221).

may be, may be represented in the proceedings by one or more of their co-claimants or co-defendants.

Indeed, the law goes further than that in two respects. First, it provides that one or more claimants, or one or more defendants, may bring or defend a claim representing others who are not parties to the claim, but who have the same interest in the claim as those representing them. Secondly, the law provides that a person who is not a party may be appointed to represent some or all of the parties (whether claimants or defendants) with the same interest, in which event the person appointed should be made a party to the proceedings. (Obviously, the fact that several parties are co-claimants or co-defendants does not necessarily mean that they will have the same interest in the claim.)

Traditionally, proceedings in which several legal persons, whether parties or not, were represented in the manner explained above were known as "representative proceedings". This expression is not used in the CPR but, as it is a convenient one, remains in use.

It should be noted that, where there are multiple claimants or multiple defendants, or both, the common or related claims of issues or fact or law raised by the proceedings make it desirable for the court to make a Group Litigation Order (GLO) under r.19.11 to facilitate the progress of the claim. Similarly, the common or related claims of issues or fact or law raised in representative proceedings make it desirable for the court to make a GLO. The provisions in the CPR as to GLOs were introduced in May 2000 and were designed to deal with problems encountered in the handling of representative proceedings under the former rules replaced by r.19.6. Representative proceedings were not a frequent occurrence under the previous rules of court.

Rule 19.6 may be traced to the practice of the Court of Chancery requiring the presence of all parties interested in the matter or suit to try to end the dispute. In cases where "where one multitude of persons are interested in a right, and another multitude of persons are interested in contesting that right, and the right is a general right", for reasons of convenience the practice was relaxed by selecting some individuals "from each multitude" to represent the rest, "so that the right might be finally decided as between all parties in a suit so constituted" (*Commissioners of Sewers v Gellatly* (1876) 3 Ch.D. 610, at 615 per Jessel M.R.). In given circumstances, the practice has the potential to avoid a multiplicity of proceedings and in this respect is consistent with the Supreme Court Act 1981 s.49(2) (see Vol.2, para.9A–168).

"more than one person has the same interest"

A claim begun as representative proceedings (on either or both sides of the record) **19.6.3**
may be continued as constituted unless the court orders otherwise. The starting point is whether the procedure which the parties wish to adopt is within the rule. If it is, the subsidiary question whether the court should exercise its discretion to order otherwise arises.

Since *Duke of Bedford v Ellis* [1901] A.C. 1, HL, the interpretation and application of the requirement that those represented should have "the same interest" has become increasingly liberal. The relevant authorities have been canvassed at length by the courts in a number of modern cases, e.g. *John v Rees* [1970] Ch. 345; *Prudential Assurance Co Ltd v Newman Industries Ltd* [1981] Ch. 229; *Irish Shipping Ltd v Commercial Union Assurance Co Plc* [1991] 2 Q.B. 206, CA. These and other English authorities were thoroughly and illuminatingly examined by the High Court of Australia and the Supreme Court of New South Wales in *Carnie v Esanda Finance Corporation Ltd* (1995) 182 C.L.R. 398 and (1992) 29 N.S.W.L.R. 382.

Modern cases can be seen to anticipate CPR Pt 1, the overriding objective, by introducing concepts similar to proportionality and ensuring that cases are dealt with expeditiously and fairly (CPR r.1.1(2)(c) and (d)) It is suggested that r.19.6 is designed to allow representative proceedings to be treated, not as a rigid matter of principle, but as a flexible tool of convenience in the administration of justice, and should be applied, not in any strict or rigorous sense, but according to its wide and permissive scope (the dictum of Megarry J. to this effect in *John v Rees* [1970] Ch. 345 at 369–370, has been repeated with approval in many subsequent cases).

In *British Airways Pension Schemes, Re* [2000] Pens. L.R. 311, the court allowed representative defendants, in an action concerning the proposed merger of pension funds, to be separately legally represented on request although there was no apparent conflict of interest. The court also decided it was reasonable to make a pre-emptive costs order in favour of a representative beneficiary joined as a defendant.

In a given case, whether representative proceedings should be continued as constituted may depend on whether a GLO is appropriate (see r.19.11) and, if so, on the manner in which such an order is to be tailored.

Binding character of judgment in representative proceedings

19.6.4 Rule 19.6(4) states that, unless the court otherwise directs, any judgment or order given in a claim in which a party is acting as a representative under this rule is binding "on all persons represented in the claim" (see former RSC O.15, r.12(3) and CCR O.5, r.5(5)).

Conceivably, one or more of the "persons represented in the claim" may not be a party to the claim. A judgment or order in the claim is binding on them in the same way as it is binding on represented person who are parties in the claim, the reason for this being that they were "present by representation" (*Commissioners of Sewers v Gellatly* (1876) 3 Ch.D. 610 at 615 per Jessel M.R.; *Re Calgary & Medicine Hat Land Co Ltd* [1908] 2 Ch. 652, CA, at 659; *Markt & Co Ltd v Knight Steamship Co Ltd* [1910] 2 K.B. 1021, CA, at 1039; *Barker v Allanson* [1937] 1 K.B. 463, CA, at 475). However, it may only be enforced against them with the permission of the court (r.19.6(4)(b)).

A person who is represented in a claim, but who is not a party, may enforce any judgment or order given in the claim, but requires the permission of the court in order to do so (r.19.6(4)(b)); and this is so where enforcement is sought against another party (whether represented or not) or against a person who is represented in the claim but is not a party (*cf.* former RSC O.15, r.12(3) and CCR O.5, r.5(5)).

In *David Roy Howells and James Kelly v Dominion Insurance Company Limited* [2005] EWHC 552, QB the background to this rule was considered and it was confirmed that individual members of a club do not have to authorise the litigation for a judgment to be enforceable against them. On the question of enforcement, permission would be granted only on a case by case basis having regard to whatever special circumstances may be shown to exist, if any, in relation to each of them.

Representation of interested persons who cannot be ascertained etc.[1]

19.7 **19.7—(1) This rule applies to claims about—**

(a) the estate of a deceased person;

(b) property subject to a trust; or

(c) the meaning of a document, including a statute.

(2) The court may make an order appointing a person to represent any other person or persons in the claim where the person or persons to be represented—

(a) are unborn;

(b) cannot be found;

(c) cannot easily be ascertained; or

(d) are a class of persons who have the same interest in a claim and—

(i) one or more members of that class are within sub-paragraphs (a), (b) or (c); or

(ii) to appoint a representative would further the overriding objective.

(3) An application for an order under paragraph (2)—

(a) may be made by—

(i) any person who seeks to be appointed under the order; or

(ii) any party to the claim; and

[1] Amended by the Civil Procedure (Amendment) Rules 2000 (SI 2000/221).

(b) may be made at any time before or after the claim has started.

(4) An application notice for an order under paragraph (2) must be served on—

(a) all parties to the claim, if the claim has started;

(b) the person sought to be appointed, if that person is not the applicant or a party to the claim; and

(c) any other person as directed by the court.

(5) The court's approval is required to settle a claim in which a party is acting as a representative under this rule.

(6) The court may approve a settlement where it is satisfied that the settlement is for the benefit of all the represented persons.

(7) Unless the court otherwise directs, any judgment or order given in a claim in which a party is acting as a representative under this rule—

(a) is binding on all persons represented in the claim; but

(b) may only be enforced by or against a person who is not a party to the claim with the permission of the court.

Note —This rule was inserted in the CPR by the Civil Procedure (Amendment) Rules 2000 (SI 2000/221) r.9 and Sch.2, and replaced (in much simpler terms) RSC and CCR provisions formerly found in Schs 1 and 2 of the CPR, specifically RSC O.15, r.13 (Representation of interested persons who cannot be ascertained, etc.) and CCR O.5, r.6 (Representation of person or class). **19.7.1**

Effect of rule

Paragraphs (3) and (4) of r.19.7 deal with the making of an application to the court for a representation order appointing a person to represent a person or class of persons in the proceedings specified in para.(1). Paragraphs (5) and (6) deal with the sanction of a compromise by the court in such proceedings so as to bind interested or affected but absent persons. The conditions which have to be fulfilled before a representation order can be made are stated in para.(2). Paragraph (7) regulates the enforcement of judgments and orders against persons represented. **19.7.2**

Rule 19.6 (Representative parties with same interest) does not apply to a claim to which r.19.7 applies (r.19.6(5)).

Persons who may be represented

Rule 19.7(1) and (2) replace, in revised form Sch.1, RSC O.15, r.13(1) and (2) and Sch.2, CCR O.5, r.6(1). The provisions so replaced were rather dense. **19.7.3**

Rule 19.7(1) and (2) state that, in a claim which concerns (1) the estate of a deceased person, or (2) property subject to a trust, or (3) the meaning of a document, including a statute, the court may make an order appointing a person (a) to represent another person, or (b) to represent members of a class of persons, interested in the claim. Persons so represented may be born or unborn.

Former RSC O.15, r.13(1) and (2) and CCR O.5, r.6(1) envisaged the appointment of a person (or persons) to represent (1) any person (including an unborn person) or (2) class, who is or may be interested in or affected by the proceedings. The court could make an appointment (1) where it was expedient to do so, and (2) one or more of certain conditions were satisfied. Those conditions were that the person, the class, or some member of the class (a) could not be ascertained or readily ascertained, or (b) though ascertained, could not be found. The court could also make an appointment (1) where it was expedient to do so, and (2) the person, the class, or some member of the class could be ascertained and found, and (3) it appeared to the court expedient to exercise the appointing power for the purposes of saving expense (regard being had to all the circumstances, including the amount at stake and the degree of difficulty of the point to be determined).

In r.19.7(2), the circumstances in which a representation order may be made differ slightly from those provided in the old rules but this may not have been intended. If that is right, under r.19.7 a representative may be appointed in the circumstances stated above subject to this: when considering whether it is "expedient" to make an appointment the court should consider whether the making of an appointment would further "the overriding objective" stated in r.1.1. In r.19.7(2), this is expressly referred to in cases where an appointment may be made of a person to represent a class, but as the overriding objective is to apply whenever the court exercises any power given to it by the CPR (r.1.2) it is obvious that it must also be taken into account where an appointment may be made of a person to represent a person.

Rule 19.7(2) states that the court may appoint a person to represent "any other person or persons in the claim" (an ambiguous phrase) but does not in terms require that the person or persons to be represented should have any interest in the claim. The rule does say that, where a person is appointed to represent a class of persons, the persons in the class should have "the same interest in the claim". The former rules were more detailed in this respect and said that a person could be appointed to represent (1) any person (including an unborn person) or (2) class, "who is or may be interested in or affected by the proceedings". Former RSC O.15, r.13(1) went further and said that where the question was whether a person or class had an interest in the proceedings, that interest may be any present interest, or any future, contingent or unascertained interest. The former rules were more detailed in this respect and said that a person could be appointed to represent (1) any person (including an unborn person) or (2) class "who is or may be interested in or affected by the proceedings". Former RSC O.15, r.13(1) went further and said that, where the question was whether a person or class had an interest in the proceedings, that interest may be any present, or any future, contingent or unascertained interest.

Application for an order

19.7.4 For general rules about application for court orders made by application notice, see Pt 23. Rule 19.7(4) makes special provision for the service of copies of the application notice; see also r.23.45(1) and r.23.7. But the rule does not specify who must serve the notice—the applicant, or the court. As Pt 23 provides that the court generally will serve an application notice, parties making an application under this rule would be well advised to confirm whether or not the court is effecting service to avoid confusion.

Court's approval of settlement of claim affecting represented person

19.7.5 Rule 19.7(5) and (6) replace, in part, RSC O.15, r.13(4) and CCR O.5, r.6(3).

Where an order has been made for the representation of persons interested in a claim and the claim is settled, the court's approval of the settlement is required (r.19.7(5)). The court may approve a settlement where it is satisfied that the settlement is for the benefit of all the represented persons (r.19.7(6)). Difficulties may arise where, at the time approval is sought, (1) the persons represented remain unascertained, or remain ascertained but not found, or (2) the persons represented dissent from the compromise.

Where proceedings between a single claimant and a single defendant, the latter of whom cannot be found, raise issues of disputed fact, it is not appropriate to order that a third party, such as the Official Solicitor, should be appointed to represent the missing defendant with a view to the approval of a compromise binding on the latter (*Cotton v Official Solicitor* [1989] C.L.Y. 3045).

The former rules expressly provided that, in approving a compromise, the court could further order that the compromise should be binding on "absent persons". The former rules also expressly provided that an order binding "absent persons" to a compromise could be set aside where it was subsequently shown that the compromise order had been obtained by fraud or non-disclosure of material facts (thus making it unnecessary for "absent persons" to commence an action to overturn the order).

For the sanction by the court of a compromise where a claim is made (a) by or on behalf of a child or patient, or (b) against a child or patient, see r.21.10.

Judgment or order binding on person represented

19.7.6 Rule 19.7(7) is in the same terms as r.19.6(4). Although no similar provision appeared in the former rules, r.19.7(7) makes no change in the law.

Representation of beneficiaries by trustees etc.[1]

19.7A—(1) A claim may be brought by or against trustees, executors or administrators in that capacity without adding as parties any persons who have a beneficial interest in the trust or estate ("the beneficiaries"). 19.7A

(2) Any judgment or order given or made in the claim is binding on the beneficiaries unless the court orders otherwise in the same or other proceedings.

Recent amendment (r.19.7A)

This rule was inserted by the Civil Procedure (Amendment) Rules 2001 (SI 2001/2056) and replaces Sch.1, RSC O.15 r.14 which was revoked and came into effect on December 2, 2002. This rule is designed to maintain the effect of CPR Sch.1, RSC O.44, r.2. 19.7A.1

Postal Services Act 2000 (c.26)[2]

19.7B—(1) An application under section 92 of the Postal Services Act 2000 for permission to bring proceedings in the name of the sender or addressee of a postal packet or his personal representative is made in accordance with Part 8. 19.7B

(2) A copy of the application notice must be served on the universal service provider and on the person in whose name the applicant seeks to bring the proceedings.

Death[3]

19.8—(1) Where a person who had an interest in a claim has died and that person has no personal representative the court may order— 19.8

(a) the claim to proceed in the absence of a person representing the estate of the deceased; or

(b) a person to be appointed to represent the estate of the deceased.

(2) Where a defendant against whom a claim could have been brought has died and—

(a) grant of probate or administration has been made, the claim must be brought against the persons who are the personal representatives of the deceased;

(b) a grant of probate or administration has not been made—

(i) the claim must be brought against "the estate of" the deceased; and[4]

(ii) the claimant must apply to the court for an order *appointing a person to* represent the estate of the deceased in the claim.

(3) A claim shall be treated as having been brought against "the

---

[1] Introduced by the Civil Procedure (Amendment) Rules 2002 (SI 2002/2058).
[2] Introduced by SI 2005/2292.
[3] Amended by the Civil Procedure (Amendment) Rules 2000 (SI 2000/221).
[4] For procedure relating to deceased uninsured drivers see the notes that appear below.

estate of" the deceased in accordance with paragraph (2)(b)(i) where—

(a) the claim is brought against the "personal representatives" of the deceased but a grant of probate or administration has not been made; or

(b) the person against whom the claim was brought was dead when the claim was started.

(4) Before making an order under this rule, the court may direct notice of the application to be given to any other person with an interest in the claim.

(5) Where an order has been made under paragraphs (1) or (2)(b)(ii) any judgment or order made or given in the claim is binding on the estate of the deceased.

Effect of rule

19.8.1 In *Berti v Steele Raymond* [2001] EWCA Civ 2079, November 16, 2001, CA, unrep., the Court of Appeal stated that it is apparent from this rule as a whole "that it gives the court quite wide powers to dispense with the need for a formal grant of probate or letters of administration after the death of a party". The rule "seems to recognise that, especially with relatively small claims, the need for a formal grant may be disproportionate and cause unnecessary delay and expense". It is often unnecessary to take out a grant of probate (a) in the case of a low-value estate—generally worth less than £5,000 and not including land property or shares or (b) where everything passes to the surviving spouse/civil partner because it was held in joint names. It would be unfortunate if the fact that the deceased had a claim or a defence to a claim made it necessary to take out a grant merely for the estate to have locus in the claim.

Person with interest in a claim (r. 19.8(1))

19.8.2 Sub-rule (1) is the part of the rule under which an order to appoint can be made. It refers neutrally to "a person" and does not distinguish between claimants, defendants or other parties. The phrase "that person has no personal representative" means in effect "has no personal representative because a grant has not been obtained", or there would be no point in having a provision to appoint or dispense. The rule does not deal with the effect of an appointment. An appointment under this part of the rule of a person to represent the estate for the purposes of the claim will have the effect of giving the opposing party a good discharge in respect of the estate by dealing with the court appointed representative. The position as between the estate and the person appointed to represent under this rule would no doubt be regulated by the normal principles of the law of trusts since the person appointed would presumably be classed as a trustee for the estate. Any default by the appointee would then be a matter between the estate and the appointee.

A potential claimant might be said to have an interest in a claim even before it is commenced. When it is commenced, if the potential claimant has died the claim must be brought by the personal representatives of the deceased if they have a grant. In such circumstances the claimant's capacity must be properly stated (see Practice Direction—How to Start Proceedings—The Claim Form, para 5). However, if no grant has been obtained in respect of the estate or if the obtaining of it would be unnecessary or cause delay before proceedings could be commenced then they could be commenced by the estate by obtaining an order to appoint a person under this sub-rule to represent the estate for the purposes of the action. It should be noted that the rule does not have the same effect as a grant and is not a way of obtaining the equivalent of a grant. It is purely a way of appointing someone to represent the estate of a deceased so that an action can be commenced on behalf of that estate and in cases under the Fatal Accidents Act 1976, so that the estate can bring the claim on behalf of any dependants in the normal way or so that a deceased defendant's estate may be represented.

Before making an order under r.19.8(1), the court may direct that notice be given to any other person interested in the claim (r.19.8(4)). But where an order has been made, any judgment or order made or given in the claim is binding on the estate of the deceased (r.19.8(5)).

Death of defendant (r.19.8(2) and (3))

Sub-rule (2), together with sub-rule (3), applies to a potential defendant before the claim is brought. It makes it clear that where there has been a grant the claim must be brought against those with the benefit of that grant—the personal representatives—but where there is no grant it must be brought against the estate of the deceased and an application must be made under r.19.8(1)(b) for someone to be appointed to represent that estate. 19.8.3

Where the claim is brought against a person and unknown to the claimant, the person is already dead (r.19.8(3)(b)), the claim is treated as having been brought against the estate and once the true position is discovered there must be an application under r.19.8(1)(b) unless there has already been grant by that time. The same applies where the claim is started against personal representatives but it turns out that there has been no grant.

Power to make judgments binding on non-parties[1]

19.8A—(1) This rule applies to any claim relating to— 19.8A

(a) the estate of a deceased person;

(b) property subject to a trust; or

(c) the sale of any property.

(2) The court may at any time direct that notice of—

(a) the claim; or

(b) any judgment or order given in the claim,

be served on any person who is not a party but who is or may be affected by it.

(3) An application under this rule—

(a) may be made without notice; and

(b) must be supported by written evidence which includes the reasons why the person to be served should be bound by the judgement in the claim.

(4) Unless the court orders otherwise—

(a) a notice of a claim or of a judgment or order under this rule must be—

(i) in the form required by the practice direction;

(ii) issued by the court; and

(iii) accompanied by a form of acknowledgment of service with any necessary modifications;

(b) a notice of a claim must also be accompanied by—

(i) a copy of the claim form; and

(ii) such other statements of case, witness statements or affidavits as the court may direct; and

(c) a notice of a judgment or order must also be accompanied by a copy of the judgment or order.

(5) If a person served with notice of a claim files an acknowledgment of service of the notice within 14 days he will become a party to the claim.

(6) If a person served with notice of a claim does not acknowledge service of the notice he will be bound by any judgment given in the claim as if he were a party.

[1] Introduced by the Civil Procedure (Amendment) Rules 2001 (SI 2001/256) and Civil Procedure (Amendment) Rules 2002 (SI 2002/2058).

(7) If, after service of a notice of a claim on a person, the claim form is amended so as substantially to alter the relief claimed, the court may direct that a judgment shall not bind that person unless a further notice, together with a copy of the amended claim form, is served on him.

(8) Any person served with a notice of a judgment or order under this rule—

(a) shall be bound by the judgment or order as if he had been a party to the claim; but

(b) may, provided he acknowledges service—

(i) within 28 days after the notice is served on him, apply to the court to set aside or vary the judgment or order; and

(ii) take part in any proceedings relating to the judgment or order.

(9) The following rules of Part 10 (acknowledgment of service) apply—

(a) rule 10.4; and

(b) rule 10.5, subject to the modification that references to the defendant are to be read as references to the person served with the notice.

(10) A notice under this rule is issued on the date entered on the notice by the court.

History and effect of this rule

19.8A.1 This rule was inserted by the Civil Procedure (Amendment) Rules 2001 (SI 2001/2056) and replaces the previous r.19.8A which came into effect in March 2001. The current rule came into effect on December 2, 2002. Sch.1, RSC O.44 r.2 has been revoked.

This rule now applies to both the High Court and county court. The new rule covers claims relating to the sale of any property. The documents to be served with the claim are as specified by the rule plus any additional documents as ordered by the court; attention is drawn to para.3.2 of the accompanying practice direction.

Procedure where claims are brought against the estate of a deceased driver who is uninsured

19.8A.2 The following procedure was agreed between the Official Solicitor and the Motor Insurers Bureau and approved by the Senior Master on March 11, 2003:

Procedure agreed between the Official Solicitor and the Motor Insurers Bureau

1. This procedure applies to damages claims brought against the estate of a deceased driver, where no grant of probate or administration of the estate of the deceased has been obtained, and the claimant contends that the Motor Insurers Bureau is interested under its uninsured drivers agreement.
2. Immediately following the issue of a claim form pursuant to CPR 19.8(2)(b)(i), brought against "the estate of" the deceased, the claimant should write to the MIB enclosing a copy of the issued claim form and enquiring if the MIB is willing to be appointed to represent the estate of the deceased in the claim pursuant to CPR 19.8(2)(b)(ii).
3. If the MIB replies agreeing to accept such appointment, their letter to that effect should be produced to the court in support of an application to give effect to that agreement.
4. *In certain circum*stances the MIB may feel unable to accept such appointment, in which case the Official Solicitor should be approached. He will usually be willing to accept appointment in such circumstances, subject to payment of his proper costs. His involvement will usually be limited to the acceptance of service only and he will not take any subsequent part in the proceedings.

Derivative Claims—how started[1]

19.9—(1) This rule— 19.9

(a) applies to a derivative claim (where a company, other body corporate or trade union is alleged to be entitled to claim a remedy, and a claim is made by a member of it for it to be given that remedy), whether under Chapter 1 of Part 11 of the Companies Act 2006 [2] or otherwise; but

(b) does not apply to a claim made pursuant to an order under section 996 of that Act.

(2) A derivative claim must be started by a claim form.

(3) The company, body corporate or trade union for the benefit of which a remedy is sought must be made a defendant to the claim.

(4) After the issue of the claim form, the claimant must not take any further step in the proceedings without the permission of the court, other than—

(a) a step permitted or required by rule 19.9A or 19.9C; or

(b) making an urgent application for interim relief.

Derivative claims

19.9

By the Civil Procedure (Amendment) Rules 2007 (SI 2007/2204), with effect from October 1, 2007, r.19.9 was amended and new rules 19.9A to 19.9F were inserted as a result of new procedures for derivative claims under the Companies Act 2006. These rules contain provisions dealing with derivative claims brought by members of a company, a body corporate, or a trade union.

In *Roberts v Gill & Co* [2008] EWCA Civ 803; *The Times* August 18, 2008, CA, the Court of Appeal explained (at para.28 per Arden L.J.) that derivative claims may be brought in other circumstances, for example, by a beneficiary suing to enforce the cause of action vested in a trust of which he is a beneficiary, or by a beneficiary under a will suing to enforce a cause of action vested in the estate.

The requirement in r.19.9(3) to the effect that company, body corporate or trade union must be made a defendant to the claim does not mean that it need to take an active part in the proceedings. Because the claimant is the driving force in the claim, it will only be a nominal defendant (*ibid* at para 29).

Although the CPR contains no provision that requires it, where a derivative claim is brought by the beneficiary of an estate, at some stage in the proceedings the personal representative should be joined as a defendant (*ibid* at para.33).

Derivative claims under Chapter 1 of Part 11 of the Companies Act 2006—application for permission[3]

19.9A—(1) In this rule— 19.9A

"the Act" means the Companies Act 2006;

"derivative claim" means a derivative claim under Chapter 1 of Part 11 of the Act;

"permission application" means an application referred to in *section 261(1), 262(2) or 264(2)* of the Act;

"the company" means the company for the benefit of which the derivative claim is brought.

---

[1] Introduced by the Civil Procedure (Amendment) Rules 2000 (SI 2000/221) and amended by the Civil Procedure (Amendment) Rules 2007 (SI 2007/2204) and the Civil Procedure (Amendment) Rules 2008 (SI 2008/2178).

[2] 2006 c.46.

[3] Amended by the Civil Procedure (Amendment) Rules 2008 (SI 2008/2178).

(2) When the claim form for a derivative claim is issued, the claimant must file—

(a) an application notice under Part 23 for permission to continue the claim; and

(b) the written evidence on which the claimant relies in support of the permission application.

(3) The claimant must not make the company a respondent to the permission application.

(4) Subject to paragraph (7), the claimant must notify the company of the claim and permission application by sending to the company as soon as reasonably practicable after the claim form is issued—

(a) a notice in the form set out in the practice direction supplementing this rule, and to which is attached a copy of the provisions of the Act required by that form;

(b) copies of the claim form and the particulars of claim;

(c) the application notice; and

(d) a copy of the evidence filed by the claimant in support of the permission application.

(5) The claimant may send the notice and documents required by paragraph (4) to the company by any method permitted by Part 6 as if the notice and documents were being served on the company.

(6) The claimant must file a witness statement confirming that the claimant has notified the company in accordance with paragraph (4).

(7) Where notifying the company of the permission application would be likely to frustrate some party of the remedy sought, the court may, on application by the claimant, order that the company need not be notified for such period after the issue of the claim form as the court directs.

(8) An application under paragraph (7) may be made without notice.

(9) Where the court dismisses the claimant's permission application without a hearing, the court will notify the claimant and (unless the court orders otherwise) the company of that decision.

(10) The claimant may ask for an oral hearing to reconsider the decision to dismiss the permission application, but the claimant—

(a) must make the request to the court in writing within seven days of being notified of the decision; and

(b) must notify the company in writing, as soon as reasonably practicable, of that request unless the court orders otherwise.

(11) Where the court dismisses the permission application at a hearing pursuant to paragraph (10), it will notify the claimant and the company of its decision.

(12) Where the court does not dismiss the application under *section 261(2)* of the Act, the court will—

(a) order that the company and any other appropriate party must be made respondents to the permission application; and

(b) give directions for the service on the company and any other appropriate party of the application notice and the claim form.

Derivative claims under Chapter 1 of Part 11 of the Companies Act 2006—members of companies taking over claims by companies or other members

19.9B—(1) This rule applies to proceedings under section 262(1) or 264(1) of the Companies Act 2006. 19.9B

(2) The application for permission must be made by an application notice in accordance with Part 23.

(3) Rule 19.9A (except for paragraphs (1), (2) and (4)(b) of that rule, and paragraph (12)(b) so far as it applies to the claim form) applies to an application under this rule and references to the claimant in rule 19.9A are to be read as references to the person who seeks to take over the claim.

Derivative claims—other bodies corporate and trade unions[1]

19.9C—(1) This rule sets out the procedure where— 19.9C

(a) either—

(i) a body corporate to which Chapter 1 of Part 11 of the Companies Act 2006 does not apply; or

(ii) a trade union,

is alleged to be entitled to a remedy; and

(b) either—

(i) a claim is made by a member for it to be given that remedy; or

(ii) a member of the body corporate or trade union seeks to take over a claim already started, by the body corporate or trade union or one or more of its members, for it to be given that remedy.

is alleged to be entitled to a remedy; and

(2) The member who starts, or seeks to take over, the claim must apply to the court for permission to continue the claim.

(3) The application for permission must be made by an application notice in accordance with Part 23.

(4) The procedure for applications in relation to companies under section 261, 262 or 264 (as the case requires) of the Companies Act 2006 applies to the permission application as if the body corporate or trade union were a company.

(5) Rules 19.9A (except for paragraph (1) of that rule) and 19.9B *apply to the permission* application as if the body corporate or trade union were a company.

Derivative claims arising in the course of other proceedings[2]

19.9D If a derivative claim (except such a claim in pursuance of 19.9D

[1] Amended by the Civil Procedure (Amendment) Rules 2008 (SI 2008/2178).
[2] Amended by the Civil Procedure (Amendment) Rules 2008 (SI 2008/2178).

an order under section 996) arises in the course of other proceedings—

(a) in the case of a derivative claim under Chapter 1 of Part 11 of that Act, rule 19.9A or 19.9B applies, as the case requires; and

(b) in any other case, rule 19.9C applies.

Derivative claims – costs

19.9E **19.9E The court may order the company, body corporate or trade union for the benefit of which a derivative claim is brought to indemnify the claimant against liability for costs incurred in the permission application or in the derivative claim or both.**

Derivative claims—discontinuance and settlement[1]

19.9F **19.9F Where the court has given permission to continue a derivative claim, the court may order that the claim may not be discontinued, settled or compromised without the permission of the court.**

Statutory background

19.9F.1 Chapter 1 of Pt 11 of the Companies Act 2006 (The Act), ss.260 to 264, contains a modernised legislative framework for derivative claims in England, Wales and Northern Ireland: the relevant sections are in Vol.2, Section 2G. The associated amendment to the Civil Procedure Rules creates a procedure by which the claimant who brings a derivative claim must apply to the court for permission to continue such a claim. The Act sets out the criteria by which the court is bound in deciding whether to grant permission (s.263). The new rule does not apply to claims brought under s.994 (proceedings for protection of members against unfair prejudice). Derivative claims commenced in Scotland are dealt with under ss.265 to 269 and are not considered here.

The necessary rule changes were accomplished by the Civil Procedure (Amendment) Rules 2007 (SI 2007/2204) and came into effect on October 1, 2007. By that statutory instrument r.19.9 (Derivative claims) was substituted by seven new rules (r.19.9 and rr.19.9A to 19.9F). Subsequently, with effect from April 6, 2008, by the Civil Procedure (Amendment No.2) Rules 2007 (SI 2007/3543) minor amendments were made correcting references to statutory provisions in rr.19.9(1)(b), 19.9A(1) and 19.9D, and the drafting of r.19.9F (Derivative claims—discontinuance and settlement) was improved so as to include compromise. As enacted by SI 2007/2204, para.(5) of r.19.9C (Derivative claims by other bodies and trade unions), which disapplies certain provisions in r.19.9A, was cast in similar terms to para.(3) of r.19.9B (Members of companies taking over claims). Corrections were made to para.(5) of r.19.9C by (SI 2007/3543) to include the incorporation therein by reference of the provisions of r.19.9B, including para.(3) thereof (in turn incorporating by reference certain provisions in r.19.9A). Practice Direction (Group Litigation) (see para.19CPD.1 below) supplements the rules as substituted by SI 2007/2204.

Derivative claims and proceedings by members

19.9F.2 Section 170 of the Act sets out the general duties owed by the directors to the company—these duties are owed to the company alone and not to individual members, employees or pressure groups. The company can bring a claim against a director or former director in three main ways; by action commenced by the board of directors, by action of the liquidator or administrator following the commencement of formal insolvency proceedings or by what is termed a "derivative claim" brought by one or more members to enforce a right vested in the company.

The rule in *Foss v Harbottle* (1843) 2 Hare 461 has for many years now precluded

[1] Amended by the Civil Procedure (Amendment) Rules 2008 (SI 2008/2178).

the court from interfering with the management of a company "at the instance of a minority of its members who are dissatisfied with the conduct of the company's affairs by the majority or the board of the directors". This rule was subject to a number of well-litigated exceptions broadly revolving around whether the action taken was a "fraud on the minority". The *Foss* rule and its common law derivatives ultimately set out a narrow set of circumstances under which a derivative claim could be brought namely the nature of the wrong committed by the directors (especially if it was ratifiable), whether the alleged wrong doers had control of the general meeting and whether the majority of the non involved shareholders favoured the litigation.

The old case law is now replaced by the statutory framework of Pt 11 of the Act. The revised statutory framework, of which the new r.19.9 is an essential component, has been introduced in response to recommendations of the Law Commission (Shareholder remedies, Cm 3769(1997) which recommended adopting a wider approach than the *Foss* rules and that a wider discretion should be vested in the court as to whether to allow a derivative action to proceed. The new framework implements the recommendation that there should be a "new derivative procedure with more modern, flexible and accessible criteria for determining whether a shareholder can pursue an action" (shareholders remedies, para.6.15). Consequently, the new r.19.9 requires the derivative claimant to apply for permission to continue, the court must apply the statutory framework in exercising its discretion.

It would appear that the line of authorities associated with "Foss" may continue to be relevant where the shareholder seeks to enforce a right vested in himself rather than the company— s.265(6)(a) defines a derivative claim as one where the cause of action is "vested in the company".

Derivatives claims: definition and scope

Section 260 provides a new and exclusive statutory definition of a derivative claim namely; "proceedings in England and Wales or Northern Ireland by a member of a company in respect of a cause of action vested in the company and seeking relief on behalf of the company": s.260(1). Proceedings for protection of members against unfair prejudice are considered under s.994 of the Act. **19.9F.3**

The wrongs of the directors covered by the procedure are limited to negligence, default and breach of duty of trust: s.260(3). The term "director" includes former director and shadow director treated as a director: s.260(5) It should be noted that derivative claims can now be brought in respect of breaches not previously permitted under the restrictive 'Foss' rules—it does not encompass all wrongs that a director could conceivably commit but does encompass the general duties set out under Ch.2 of Pt 10 of the Act.

Derivative claims may be commenced by current members only but can apply to acts committed before the claimant became a member: s.260(3).

Section 261 of the 2006 Act (Application for permission to continue a derivative claim) states:

"(1) A member of a company who brings a derivative claim under this Chapter must apply to the court for permission (in Northern Ireland, leave) to continue it.

(2) If it appears to the court that the application and the evidence filed by the applicant in support of it do not disclose a prima facie case for giving permission (or leave), the court—

(a) must dismiss the application, and
(b) may make any consequential order it considers appropriate.

(3) If the application is not dismissed under subsection (2), the court—

(a) may give directions as to the evidence to be provided by the company, and
(b) may adjourn the proceedings to enable the evidence to be obtained.

(4) On hearing the application, the court may—

(a) give permission (or leave) to continue the claim on such terms as it thinks fit,
(b) refuse permission (or leave) and dismiss the claim, or
(c) adjourn the proceedings on the application and give such directions as it thinks fit."

Section 261 sets out the options available to the court. The court may dismiss, allow the claim to proceed or adjourn. The menu of options is comprehensive and allows the court to exercise its discretion to impose conditions and give directions.The Overriding Objective, and the courts general case management powers (Pt 3) will apply, including for example the power to make a Civil Restraint Order; r.3.11. The courts powers include the power to require the company to indemnify the claimant against the costs incurred in the claim on the ground that the claim is brought for the benefit of the company; r.19.9F. The court has no option but to dismiss if the application plus the evidence in support does not disclose a prima facie case for giving permission to proceed. The statutory criteria by which the court exercises its discretion is set out in s.263. Note that the court may consider the evidence in three stages namely on the claimants evidence alone, secondly on the claimants evidence plus evidence produced by the company and thirdly with the defendants evidence in addition.

Section 263 of the 2006 Act (Whether permission to be given) states:

"(1) The following provisions have effect where a member of a company applies for permission (in Northern Ireland, leave) under section 261 or 262.

(2) Permission (or leave) must be refused if the court is satisfied—

(a) that a person acting in accordance with section 172 (duty to promote the success of the company) would not seek to continue the claim, or

(b) where the cause of action arises from an act or omission that is yet to occur, that the act or omission has been authorised by the company, or

(c) where the cause of action arises from an act or omission that has already occurred, that the act or omission—

(i) was authorised by the company before it occurred, or

(ii) has been ratified by the company since it occurred.

(3) In considering whether to give permission (or leave) the court must take into account, in particular—

(a) whether the member is acting in good faith in seeking to continue the claim;

(b) the importance that a person acting in accordance with section 172 (duty to promote the success of the company) would attach to continuing it;

(c) where the cause of action results from an act or omission that is yet to occur, whether the act or omission could be, and in the circumstances would be likely to be—

(i) authorised by the company before it occurs, or

(ii) ratified by the company after it occurs;

(d) where the cause of action arises from an act or omission that has already occurred, whether the act or omission could be, and in the circumstances would be likely to be, ratified by the company;

(e) whether the company has decided not to pursue the claim;

(f) whether the act or omission in respect of which the claim is brought gives rise to a cause of action that the member could pursue in his own right rather than on behalf of the company.

(4) In considering whether to give permission (or leave) the court shall have particular regard to any evidence before it as to the views of members of the company who have no personal interest, direct or indirect, in the matter.

(5) The Secretary of State may by regulations—

(a) amend subsection (2) so as to alter or add to the circumstances in which permission (or leave) is to be refused;

(b) amend subsection (3) so as to alter or add to the matters that the court is required to take into account in considering whether to give permission (or leave).

(6) Before making any such regulations the Secretary of State shall consult such persons as he considers appropriate.

(7) Regulations under this section are subject to affirmative resolution procedure."

Section 263 sets out the way in which the court will exercise its discretion. The court must refuse permission if any of the factors set out in s.263(2) are present. Section 263(3) is a six item checklist to which the court must have regard. In addition the court must have separate and particular regard to the views of the members who have no personal interest: see *Smith v Croft (No.2)* [1988] Ch. 114.

Section 264 makes provision where a member seeks permission to take over a derivative claim already commenced by another member. Section 262 deals with a situation where a company itself has instituted a claim which could be a derivative claim and provides that the court may allow an individual to take over that claim, for example if the company has failed to pursue the claim diligently.

Claim form and application for permission to continue

The application must be commenced by claim form and accompanied with a separate application under Pt 23 for permission to continue the claim. Applications by members under Pt 30 of the Act; s.994 (protection of members against unfair prejudice) are made by petition to the court. The company must not be made a respondent to the permission application (r.19.9A(3)). Part 23 sets out general rules about applications for court orders. An application may be made for an order that the company need not be notified of the application on the grounds that 'the permission application would be likely to frustrate some part of the remedy sought" (r.19.9A(7)); such an application can be made without notice. **19.9F.4**

Disposal of the application for permission to continue

This can be dealt with as a paperwork exercise without a hearing and if dismissed by this procedure the claimant has the right to apply for an oral hearing. This procedure is resonant of the power of an appeal court to dismiss an appeal on paper. The company and the claimant will be notified of the courts decision but the court may make an order not to notify the company of a decision to dismiss on paper (r.19.9A(9) and (10)). **19.9F.5**

Exercise of the court's discretion

The court will have regard to the statutory checklist in s.263 (discussed above). **19.9F.6**

Indemnity for costs

The court may order the company, body corporate or trade union for the benefit of which a derivative claim is brought, to indemnify the claimant against liability for costs incurred in the permission application or in the derivative claim or both (r.19.9F) This power was previously specified in the old r.19.7; termed a "Wallersteiner and Moir" order: [1975] 1 All E.R. 849. Under the old rules it was incumbent on the claimant to establish that such an order was genuinely needed (*Smith v Croft (No.1)* [1986] 1 W.L.R. 580, CA) and such an order was refused where the judge considered that a claimant would in any event have a right to a lien and an indemnity out of the assets recovered (*Mumbray v Lapper and Berkley Square London Ltd* [2005] EWHC 1152). **19.9F.7**

Discontinuance and settlement

Where the court has given permission to continue a derivative claim the court may order that the claim may not be discontinued or settled without the permission of the court (r.19.9F). **19.9F.8**

III. Group Litigation

Editorial introduction

This section of Pt 19 (rr.19.10 to 19.15) was added to the CPR by the Civil Procedure (Amendment) Rules 2000 (SI 2000/221) r.9 and came into force on May 2, 2000. **19.9F.9**

The Final Access to Justice Report (July 1996) in Chapter 17 recommended that experience had shown (1) that there were definite limits to the weight representative actions (O.15, r.4) (now CPR r.19.6) could bear, (2) that consolidation (O.15, r.4) (now CPR r.19.2) deals with situations where actions have already been commenced, and it is better that multi-party litigation be dealt with on a collective basis before then, and (3) that joinder is not satisfactory where the interests of claimants differ. It addition it was said that the existing procedures were difficult to use and had proved disproportionately costly.

It was recommended that new procedures dedicated to multi-party claims should be introduced with the following objectives:

(a) provide access to justice where large numbers of people have been affected by another's conduct, but individual loss is so small that it makes an individual action economically unviable;

(b) provide expeditious, effective and proportionate methods of resolving cases, where individual damages are large enough to justify individual action but where the number of claimants and the nature of the issues involved mean that the cases cannot be managed satisfactorily in accordance with normal procedure;

(c) achieve a balance between the normal rights of claimants and defendants, to pursue and defend cases individually, and the interests of a group of parties to litigate the action as a whole in an effective manner.

Examples of circumstances in which the handling of claims involving multiple parties giving rise to common or related issues of fact or law may be assisted by a dedicated procedure include the following:

(1) personal injury claims, arising from, e.g. (a) sudden disaster, (b) industrial disease or accident, (c) medical investigation or treatment, or (d) taking of medicines, or (e) use of defective products;

(2) financial loss, arising from, e.g. (a) mishandling of investments, (b) publishing misleading information, or (c) fraud on minority shareholders (derivative actions);

(3) damage to property, arising from, e.g. (a) landlord's failure to repair properties with multiple tenants, (b) nuisance or diminution of value of business or residential premises arising from a common cause.

Following the decisions of the House of the Lords in *Connelly v RTZ Corp Plc (No.2)* [1998] A.C. 584 and *Lubbe v Cape Plc* [2000] 1 W.L.R. 1545, it is now clear that proceedings, including group actions, can be brought in this jurisdiction against UK-based parent companies of multinational corporations, arising from the actions of their subsidiaries in other jurisdictions, on *forum conveniens* grounds, but only when the claimants could be denied justice in their own jurisdiction because of the non–availability of funding (legal aid or contingency), legal representation and expert advice and established court procedures for group litigation. The impact of the House of Lord's decision in *Lubbe* is likely to mean that more group actions involving UK based multinational corporations will be brought in the courts of England and Wales.

Rules 19.10 to 19.15 of this section of Pt 19 are designed to achieve the objectives stated in the Final Report. The rules are supplemented by a Practice Direction. The new Group Litigation Order rule and practice direction cannot be treated as a complete guide to the appropriate court procedures for conducting group actions as some provisions affecting group litigation appear elsewhere in the CPR, e.g. the power to vary or revoke an order, CPR r.3.1(7).

The rules establish a framework for the case management of "claims which give rise to common or related issues of fact or law" (r.19.10). They are intended to provide flexibility for the court to deal with the particular problems created by these cases.

This rule and practice direction are silent on issues in relation to costs. CPR Costs r.48.6A provides a basic framework for costs where the court has made a Group Litigation Order and in particular provides that:

> any order for costs against group litigants imposes several (rather than joint) liability for an equal proportion of the common costs unless the court orders otherwise (r.48.6(A)(3)).
>
> Where a group litigant is the paying party he/she will be liable for:
>
> a. any costs he/she is ordered to pay to the receiving party
> b. the individual costs of his/her claim
> c. an equal proportion, together with other group litigant, of the common costs (r.48.6(A)(4)); and
>
> individual litigants can be ordered to pay their share of any common costs incurred before he/she joined the group action, but not after he/she has left the action (e.g. when his/her individual case has been settled) (Rule 48.6(A)(6) and (7)).

This only deals partly with the difficult issue of the liability of individuals in a group action group who do not succeed with their individual claim, particularly where the group was at least partly successful in the generic issues. The notes to r.48.6A summarise the relevant case-law, prior to Pt 19 coming into force. The possibility of individuals becoming liable for a significant proportion of the receiving party's costs, especially where the group action succeeds, at least in part, could deter applications for otherwise sound Group Litigation Orders. Another costs issue which frequently causes difficulties in group actions is also not addressed in either Pt 19 or the costs rules. This is the liability of the paying party for the administration and co-ordination costs of the lead solicitors (or steering committee) of the receiving party, although this should be dealt with early in any group litigation through case management.

Afrika v Cape Plc [2001] EWCA Civ 2017 CA is an important decision on cost sharing in group litigation: the Court of Appeal decided that determining the costs payable by those claimants who leave the litigation before its conclusion should be left until at least the outcome of the common issues part of the proceedings has been determined, because to order individual claimants to pay a share of the common costs as they discontinue could be unfair to those claimants who discontinue when they decide they have "no reasonable prospects of success" in their particular claim, and give an "inappropriate advantage to the defendants".

In *BCCI SA v Ali (Assessment of Costs)* [2000] 2 Costs L.R. 243, all five test claims (out of 369 claims) failed. The court made no order as to *inter partes* costs but, despite findings of dishonesty by some of the test claimants, ordered that the claimants' costs should be shared equally between all 369 claimants, as there had been an understanding to that effect, although no costs sharing order had been made earlier in the action.

Griffiths v Solutia UK Ltd [2001] EWCA Civ 736, CA was a group action by the residents of an area arising from a chemical leak from industrial premises nearby. Damages were agreed at £90,000. The claimant's costs were £210,000. The Court of Appeal dismissed the defendant's appeal against the instruction of London solicitors but nonetheless said the costs were "ludicrous" and that, in future courts needed to exercise greater case management control to limit costs.

In actions involving several parties with closely related claims, in which a Group Litigation Order has not been made, the decision in *Bairstow v Queens Moat Houses Plc (Assessment of Costs)* [2001] C.P. Rep. 59, L.T.L., June 15, 2000 QBD may provide an indication of the court's likely approach. Separate actions by several claimants against several defendants were not consolidated, but were tried together and were dismissed. The claimants were ordered to pay the defendants' costs on an indemnity basis, and the first claimant was ordered to pay the second defendant's costs on the standard basis. Some of the costs incurred by the defendants were common to all four actions, otherswere specific to each claim. On summary assessment it was held that as the claimants had supported each other's false claims, the court should exercise its discretion to make a joint and several liability order against the claimants for the defendants' common costs, despite the claimants' contention that each should pay only the costs of his own action, and no more than 25 per cent of the common costs.

The rules attempt to create a structure in which the often inherently conflicting interests of parties in a group of parties with similar interests may be balanced.

In brief outline the rules provide that where claims which give rise to common or related issues of fact or law emerge (r.19.10) the court has power to make a Group Litigation Order (GLO) enabling the court to manage the claims covered by the order in a co-ordinated way (r.19.11). The GLO will contain directions about the establishment of a "group register" on which the claims to be managed under the GLO will be entered and will specify the court ("the management court") which will manage the claims on the register (r.19.11(2)). Judgments, orders and directions of the court will be binding on all claims within the GLO (r.19.12(1)). The court's case management powers enable it to deal with generic issues, for example, by selecting particular claims as test claims (rr.19.13(b) and 19.15).

For assignment of pre-trial applications in group or multi-party claims to designated judges, see Practice Direction (Allocation of Cases to Levels of Judiciary), paras 6.1 to 6.3 (see para.2BPD.6).

Lord Woolf in *Boake Allen Limited v Revenue and Customs Commissioners* [2007] UKHL 25; [2007] 1 W.L.R. 1386 made several observations on the GLO regime and as to the need for and detail to be contained in individual Claim Forms as well as the approach to be taken to amendment:

> "30. In view of the outcome of this appeal in accordance with the opinion of Lord Hoffmann, the decision of the Court of Appeal as to the amendment is of no practical significance to the parties. However, my concern is as to its possible effect on future practice in relation to GLOs. GLOs can involve hundreds or thousands of different parties. In such a situation any step which each of the many parties has to take can cumulatively so effect the total costs, as to make them disproportionate both to the means of the parties to the action and the issues at stake. For this reason it is important that such steps generate the least possible costs.
>
> 31. This may not appear to be such a problem in this case, as the actions are being brought against a government department over very substantial sums of money. However, where this is avoidable, having one rule for one set of litigants

who have ample means and a different rule for litigants of lesser means, cannot be justified. All litigants are entitled to be protected from incurring unnecessary costs. This is the objective of the GLO regime. Primarily, it seeks to achieve its objective, so far as this is possible, by reducing the number of steps litigants, who have a common interest, have to take individually to establish their rights and instead enables them to be taken collectively as part of a GLO Group. This means that irrespective of the number of individuals in the group each procedural step in the actions need only be taken once. This is of benefit not only to members of the group, but also those against whom proceedings are brought. In a system such as ours based on cost shifting this is of benefit to all parties to the proceedings.

32. Before a GLO can be made it is necessary for each individual potential member who wishes to join the GLO to make an individual claim under CPR Part 7 or Part 8. This in conjunction with the application to register enables the court to determine whether the respective litigants qualify to be a member of the GLO. It also prevents time continuing to run for purposes of limitation of actions. Nonetheless the claim once made will usually almost immediately be of only limited historic interest because what matters is the application to register and the register of the GLO on which all proceedings subject to the GLO are registered. The purpose of a GLO is then 'to provide for the case management of claims which give rise to common or related issues of fact or law.' [Lord Woolf then cites further provisions in CPR r.9.13 and 19.12].

33. In considering the leave to amend issue the Court of Appeal do not appear to have had submissions addressed to them as to the significance of the proceedings being the subject of a GLO. No doubt it was as a result of this, that they failed to consider the question of whether an amendment was necessary and if so whether permission could be given in the context of the GLO. In the context of a GLO, a claim form need be no more than the simplest of documents. It needs to be read together with the application to register and the register bearing in mind its place in the GLO process and the need to limit pre-registration costs so far as this is possible. In this case the suggested deficiency in the claim forms are that they did not sufficiently identify the basis for the Revenue being under an obligation to repay the tax paid assuming this should not have been claimed by the Revenue. This is an area of the law the parameters of which are still evolving. In my judgment it would be wholly inconsistent with the objective of the GLO to require the nature of the remedy claimed to be spelled out in detail in the claim forms of the taxpayers. The Revenue knew perfectly well the basis of the claims once the issues had been defined for the purpose of the GLO. For each of the parties to have to spell out details of the manner in which they would advance their claim at the outset would have caused substantial extra costs to be incurred in researching the law. Cumulatively this would have been grossly wasteful. The decision of the Court [of] Appeal should not be treated as requiring a claim to set out more than an outline of the claim. Furthermore for limitation purposes in the case of a GLO the individual claims should be construed in conjunction with the applications for the claims to be registered and, from the time of registration, the register."

Cited with approval by Henderson J. in *Europcar UK Ltd v Revenue and Customs Commissioners* [2008] EWHC 1363 (Ch).

Definition[1]

19.10 **19.10 A Group Litigation Order ("GLO") means an order made under rule 19.11 to provide for the case management of claims which give rise to common or related issues of fact or law (the "GLO issues").**

Note

19.10.1 *The inclusion* of the words "common or related issues" is significant: the interests of the individuals do not have to be the "same" as in Representative Proceedings.

[1] Amended by the Civil Procedure (Amendment) Rules 2000 (SI 2000/221).

Group Litigation Order[1]

19.11—(1) The court may make a GLO where there are or are likely to be a number of claims giving rise to the GLO issues. (The practice direction provides the procedure for applying for a GLO.) 19.11

(2) A GLO must—

(a) contain directions about the establishment of a register (the "group register") on which the claims managed under the GLO will be entered;

(b) specify the GLO issues which will identify the claims to be managed as a group under the GLO; and

(c) specify the court (the "management court") which will manage the claims on the group register.

(3) A GLO may—

(a) in relation to claims which raise one or more of the GLO issues—

(i) direct their transfer to the management court;

(ii) order their stay[GL] until further order; and

(iii) direct their entry on the group register;

(b) direct that from a specified date claims which raise one or more of the GLO issues should be started in the management court and entered on the group register; and

(c) give directions for publicising the GLO.

Comment

Rule 19.11(1) does not specify a minimum number of claims for a Group Litigation Order to be made, or who may apply for such an order. Either the claimants or a defendant may apply, or the court may make an order of its own initiative. Paragraphs 3.3 to 3.7 of the practice direction (see below) specify that applications should be made to the Senior Master or Chief Chancery Master, (or to a senior judge of the specialist lists) in the RCJ, to the Presiding Judge on Circuit, or to the Designated Civil Judge in the county court. But before an order can be made, the approval is necessary of the President (in the Queen's Bench Division and on Circuit), the Chancellor (in the Chancery Division), or the Head of Civil Justice (in the county court). This may be sought before or after the hearing of the application for the Group Litigation Order. This is an unusual provision, signalling the importance for the courts of effective case management, including by the senior judiciary. 19.11.1

PF19 should be used with appropriate adaptions. Parties are invited to submit to the Senior Master, Room E115 or the Chief Chancery Master in advance of the hearing their own draft order, to enable a check to be made on whether the necessary ingredients have been included. In the Chancery Division parties are advised to contact the Chancery Lawyer, Ms Vicky Bell (Room TM 5.06, Thomas More Building, Royal Courts of Justice, Strand, London, WC2A 2LL, tel. 020 7947 6080) at the earliest opportunity if they are contemplating making an application to the Chief Master for a GLO.

The Group Litigation Order register will usually be maintained by the solicitors acting for one of the parties (frequently the claimants' solicitors). In the Chancery Division the register may alternatively be maintained by the lead solicitors but kept by the court or it may be kept and maintained by the court (the distinction is relevant to the rules for inspecting the register under 19BPD 6.6). As the rule and practice direction do not provide guidance on whether, when, by whom, and how, any specific criteria might be drawn up and applied to control entry to the register, otherwise clear parameters for the scope of the action should be set in the Group Litigation Order, (or

[1] Amended by the Civil Procedure (Amendment) Rules 2000 (SI 2000/221).

the first case management directions), otherwise a situation could arise whereby individuals entered onto the register but later are held not to "qualify". The practice direction (at para.6.4) does provide for parties to apply to the court in respect of a dispute about entry to the register.

An amendment to the Practice Direction (PD B para.6.1A) now makes it clear that individual claimants must issue their own claim form (and pay the issue fee) before their claim can be entered on a group register.

The requirement to define GLO issues might help the parties and the court to make decisions on a number of pertinent matters, including criteria for entry on to the register, and cut-off dates for entry, but the detail of the issues between the parties is not likely to emerge until later in the litigation.

Rule 19.11(3)(c) and the practice direction (para.11) cover publicising a Group Litigation Order. The intention is to enable the court to order the solicitors for the group to "advertise" the making of the order and any cut–off dates for joining the register (see r.19.3) to minimise the risk of individuals trying to start their own separate proceedings at a later date. But neither the rule nor the practice direction give guidance on the form of any publicity, or on who might be ordered to pay the costs of placing the appropriate advertisements.

In the Queen's Bench Division the Senior Master arranges for details of GLOs to be published on the court service website (*www.hmcourts-service.gov.uk/cms/150.htm*) and in various reports as appropriate, and in the Chancery Division the Chief Chancery Master makes similar arrangements.

The practice direction requires the Law Society to be notified of any Group Litigation Order made.

Effect of the GLO[1]

19.12 **19.12—(1) Where a judgment or order is given or made in a claim on the group register in relation to one or more GLO issues—**

(a) that judgment or order is binding on the parties to all other claims that are on the group register at the time the judgment is given or the order is made unless the court orders otherwise; and

(b) the court may give directions as to the extent to which that judgment or order is binding on the parties to any claim which is subsequently entered on the group register.

(2) Unless paragraph (3) applies, any party who is adversely affected by a judgment or order which is binding on him may seek permission to appeal the order.

(3) A party to a claim which was entered on the group register after a judgment or order which is binding on him was given or made may not—

(a) apply for the judgment or order to be set aside[GL], varied or stayed[GL]; or

(b) appeal the judgment or order,

but may apply to the court for an order that the judgment or order is not binding on him.

(4) Unless the court orders otherwise, disclosure of any document relating to the GLO issues by a party to a claim on the group register is disclosure of that document to all parties to claims—

(a) on the group register; and

[1] Amended by the Civil Procedure (Amendment) Rules 2000 (SI 2000/221).

(b) **which are subsequently entered on the group register.**

Case management[1]

19.13 Directions given by the management court may include directions— 19.13

(a) **varying the GLO issues;**

(b) **providing for one or more claims on the group register to proceed as test claims;**

(c) **appointing the solicitor of one or more parties to be the lead solicitor for the claimants or defendants;**

(d) **specifying the details to be included in a statement of case in order to show that the criteria for entry of the claim on the group register have been met;**

(e) **specifying a date after which no claim may be added to the group register unless the court gives permission; and**

(f) **for the entry of any particular claim which meets one or more of the GLO issues on the group register.**

(Part 3 contains general provisions about the case management powers of the court).

Comment

The practice direction clarifies that case management will usually be carried out by one judge throughout the life of the case, assisted as necessary by a Master and/or a Costs Judge. It also specifies that most group actions will be allocated to the multi-track, because of their complexity. 19.13.1

The courts, in the absence of a specific rule of court, in the 1980s and 1990s, developed *ad hoc* procedures for managing group litigation. These frequently included: early identification of generic issues, selection of appropriate representative test or lead cases, and preparation of a master pleading (statement of case).

This approach under CPR continues, but does not resolve the question of whether and when individual particulars of claim may be required. The rule and the practice direction (at para.14.4) do indicate that a schedule of information on individual claims, or questionnaires, may be ordered instead of individual statements of case. This latter approach will usually be welcomed by claimants on the ground that carrying out detailed work at an early stage on all the individual cases could negate many of the cost benefit advantages of a group action. Defendants, on the other hand, have in the past argued, sometimes successfully, that they and the court must have sufficient particulars of each individual claim to be able to investigate the action as a whole, and particularly to be able to challenge the prospects of success of the action, or at least individual cases.

19.13(c) The appointment of lead solicitors is invariably necessary: the rule is intended to be a reserve power as the court will only rarely become involved in appointment of solicitors (see also Pt 42).

19.13(e) Cut-off dates only limit entry to the group litigation They have no bearing on limitation and do not preclude an individual from seeking the court's permission to join the group at a later date or to issue separate proceedings (subject to the overriding objective and proportionality).

Removal from the register[2]

19.14—(1) A party to a claim entered on the group register may 19.14

[1] Amended by the Civil Procedure (Amendment) Rules 2000 (SI 2000/221).
[2] Amended by the Civil Procedure (Amendment) Rules 2000 (SI 2000/221).

apply to the management court for the claim to be removed from the register.

(2) If the management court orders the claim to be removed from the register it may give directions about the future management of the claim.

Test claims[1]

19.15 **19.15—(1) Where a direction has been given for a claim on the group register to proceed as a test claim and that claim is settled, the management court may order that another claim on the group register be substituted as the test claim.**

(2) Where an order is made under paragraph (1), any order made in the test claim before the date of substitution is binding on the substituted claim unless the court orders otherwise.

Comment

19.15.1 Test claim is not defined, or referred to in the CPR Glossary and neither the rule nor the practice direction provide any guidance on when and how test cases might be selected. In fact group litigation can be case managed in a number of different ways, including division of the group into subgroups, identification of generic or common issues, use of a master pleading, trial of preliminary issues, and some investigation of a sample or all individual claims, as well as the test case approach. By only referring to test cases the rule implies that this is the preferred option.

The rule and practice direction do not offer any guidance on, or suggest procedures for, dealing with settlements, although some of the problems specific to group litigation include: (a) what should happen when an "acceptable" offer to settle a lead or test case is made (beyond giving the court the discretion to order that another case might be substituted), and (b) what the court might do when a "global" offer to settle the entire action is made, without the offeree specifying how the sum might be divided between the individual recipients—this can lead to disputes between the claimants, which are far from easy for their legal representatives to resolve. The introduction of Pt 36 offers to settle may further highlight this latter problem.

[1] Amended by the Civil Procedure (Amendment) Rules 2000 (SI 2000/221).

PRACTICE DIRECTION—ADDITION AND SUBSTITUTION OF PARTIES

This Practice Direction supplements CPR Part 19 **19PD.1**

A party applying for an amendment will usually be responsible for the costs of and arising from the amendment.

Changes of parties

General

1.1 Parties may be removed, added or substituted in existing proceedings either on the court's own initiative or on the application of either an existing party or a person who wishes to become a party.

1.2 The application may be dealt with without a hearing where all the existing parties and the proposed new party are in agreement.

1.3 The application to add or substitute a new party should be supported by evidence setting out the proposed new party's interest in or connection with the claim.

1.4 The application notice should be filed in accordance with rule 23.3 and, unless the application is made under rule 19.2(4)[1], be served in accordance with rule 23.4.

1.5 An order giving permission to amend will, unless the court orders otherwise, be drawn up. It will be served by the court unless the parties wish to serve it or the court orders them to do so.

Addition or substitution of claimant

2.1 Where an application is made to the court to add or to substitute a new party to the proceedings as claimant, the party applying must file: **19PD.2**

(1) the application notice,

(2) the proposed amended claim form and particulars of claim, and

(3) the signed, written consent of the new claimant to be so added or substituted.

2.2 Where the court makes an order adding or substituting a party as claimant but the signed, written consent of the new claimant has not been filed:

(1) the order, and

(2) the addition or substitution of the new party as claimant,

will not take effect until the signed, written consent of the new claimant is filed.

2.3 Where the court has made an order adding or substituting a new claimant, the court may direct:

(1) a copy of the order to be served on every party to the proceedings and any other person affected by the order,

(2) copies of the statements of case and of documents referred to in any statement of case to be served on the new party,

(3) the party who made the application to file within 14 days an amended claim form and particulars of claim.

---

[1] See rule 19.4(3)(a).

Addition or substitution of defendant

19PD.3 **3.1** The Civil Procedure Rules apply to a new defendant who has been added or substituted as they apply to any other defendant (see in particular the provisions of Parts 9, 10, 11 and 15).

3.2 Where the court has made an order adding or substituting a defendant whether on its own initiative or on an application, the court may direct:

(1) the claimant to file with the court within 14 days (or as ordered) an amended claim form and particulars of claim for the court file,

(2) a copy of the order to be served on all parties to the proceedings and any other person affected by it,

(3) the amended claim form and particulars of claim, forms for admitting, defending and acknowledging the claim and copies of the statements of case and any other documents referred to in any statement of case to be served on the new defendant,

(4) unless the court orders otherwise, the amended claim form and particulars of claim to be served on any other defendants.

3.3 A new defendant does not become a party to the proceedings until the amended claim form has been served on him.[1]

Removal of party

19PD.4 **4.** Where the court makes an order for the removal of a party from the proceedings:

(1) the claimant must file with the court an amended claim form and particulars of claim, and

(2) a copy of the order must be served on every party to the proceedings and on any other person affected by the order.

Transfer of interest or liability

19PD.5 **5.1** Where the interest or liability of an existing party has passed to some other person, application should be made to the court to add or substitute that person.[2]

5.2 The application must be supported by evidence showing the stage the proceedings have reached and what change has occurred to cause the transfer of interest or liability. (For information about making amendments generally, see the practice direction supplementing Part 17).

Human Rights, Joining The Crown

19PD.6 Section 4 of the Human Rights Act 1998

6.1 Where a party has included in his statement of case—

(1) a claim for a declaration of incompatibility in accordance with section 4 of the Human Rights Act 1998, or

(2) an issue for the court to decide which may lead to the court considering making a declaration,

---

[1] *Kettleman v Hansel Properties Ltd* (1987) A.C. 189, HL.
[2] See rule 19.2(4).

then the court may at any time consider whether notice should be given to the Crown as required by that Act and give directions for the content and service of the notice. The rule allows a period of 21 days before the court will make the declaration but the court may vary this period of time.

6.2 The court will normally consider the issues and give the directions referred to in paragraph 6.1 at the case management conference.

6.3 Where a party amends his statement of case to include any matter referred to in paragraph 6.1, then the court will consider whether notice should be given to the Crown and give directions for the content and service of the notice.

(The practice direction to CPR Part 16 requires a party to include issues under the Human Rights Act 1998 in his statement of case).

6.4(1) The notice given under rule 19.4A must be served on the person named in the list published under section 17 of the Crown Proceedings Act 1947.

(The list, made by the Minister for the Civil Service, is annexed to the Practice Direction to Part 66).

(2) The notice will be in the form directed by the court but will normally include the directions given by the court and all the statements of case in the claim. The notice will also be served on all the parties.

(3) The court may require the parties to assist in the preparation of the notice.

(4) In the circumstances described in the The National Assembly for Wales (Transfer of Functions) (No.2) Order 2000 the notice must also be served on the National Assembly for Wales.

(Section 5(3) of the Human Rights Act 1998 provides that the Crown may give notice that it intends to become a party at any stage in the proceedings once notice has been given).

6.5 Unless the court orders otherwise, the Minister or other person permitted by the Human Rights Act 1998 to be joined as a party must, if he wishes to be joined, give notice of his intention to be joined as a party to the court and every other party. Where the Minister has nominated a person to be joined as a party the notice must be accompanied by the written nomination.

(Section 5(2)(a) of the Human Rights Act 1998 permits a person nominated by a Minister of the Crown to be joined as a party. The nomination may be signed on behalf of the Minister).

6.6 Section 9 of the Human Rights Act 1998

(1) The procedure in paragraphs 6.1 to 6.5 also applies where a claim is made under sections 7(1)(a) and 9(3) of the Human Rights Act 1998 for damages in respect of a judicial act.

(2) Notice must be given to the Lord Chancellor and should be served on the Treasury Solicitor on his behalf, except where the judicial act is of a Court Martial when the appropriate person is the Secretary of State for Defence and the notice must be served on the Treasury Solicitor on his behalf.

(3) The notice will also give details of the judicial act, which is the subject of the claim for damages, and of the court or tribunal that made it.

(Section 9(4) of the Human Rights Act 1998 provides that no award of damages may be made against the Crown as provided for in section 9(3) unless the appropriate person is joined in the proceedings. The appropriate person is the Minister responsible for the court concerned or a person or department nominated by him (section 9(5) of the Act)).

PRACTICE DIRECTION—GROUP LITIGATION

This Practice Direction supplements Section III of CPR Part 19

Section III was added to Pt 19 of the CPR by the Civil Procedure (Amendment) Rules 2000. Section III consists of rr.19.10 to 19.15 and is titled "Group Litigation". The rules establish a framework for the case management of "claims which give rise to common or related issues of fact or law" (r.19.10). These rules are supplemented by this practice direction. **19BPD.1**

Introduction

1. This practice direction deals with group litigation where the multiple parties are claimants. Section III of Part 19 (group litigation orders) also applies where the multiple parties are defendants. The court will give such directions in such a case as are appropriate. **19BPD.2**

Preliminary steps

2.1 Before applying for a Group Litigation Order ("GLO") the solicitor acting for the proposed applicant should consult the Law Society's Multi Party Action Information Service in order to obtain information about other cases giving rise to the proposed GLO issues. **19BPD.3**

Application for a GLO

A list of all GLO's is kept in the office of the Senior Master (Room E115) and appears on the Court Service website (*http://www.hmcourts-service.gov.uk*). **19BPD.3.1**

2.2 It will often be convenient for the claimants' solicitors to form a Solicitors' Group and to choose one of their number to take the lead in applying for the GLO and in litigating the GLO issues. The lead solicitor's role and relationship with the other members of the Solicitors' Group should be carefully defined in writing and will be subject to any directions given by the court under CPR 19.13(c). **19BPD.4**

"directions ... under CPR 19.13(c)"

This provision states directions given by the management court may include directions appointing the solicitor of one or more parties to be the lead solicitor for the claimants or defendants. **19BPD.4.1**

2.3 In considering whether to apply for a GLO, the applicant should consider whether any other order would be more appropriate. In particular he should consider whether, in the circumstances of the case, it would be more appropriate for— **19BPD.5**

(1) the claims to be consolidated; or
(2) the rules in Section II of Part 19 (representative parties) to be used.

"other order ... more appropriate"

As to the consolidation of claims, see CPR r.3.1(2)(g). Rules relevant in this context are: r.19.6 (Representative parties with same interest), r.19.7 (Representation of interested persons who cannot be ascertained), and r.19.9 (Derivative claims). **19BPD.5.1**

Application for a GLO

3.1 An application for a GLO must be made in accordance with CPR Part 23, may be made at any time before or after any relevant claims have been issued and may be made either by a claimant or by a defendant. **19BPD.6**

19BPD.6.1 *Note* —The court may make a GLO where there are or are likely to be a number of claims giving rise to the GLO issues (r.19.11). There is no specified minimum number of individual claims to found an application for a GLO. Paragraph 3.1 and following paragraphs of this practice direction provides the procedure for applying for a GLO. An application notice must state (a) what order the applicant is seeking; and (b) briefly, why the applicant is seeking the order (r.23.6). As to service of application notice, see r.23.7. The information referred to in para.3.2 below should be included in the application notice or in written evidence filed in support.

19BPD.7 **3.2** The following information should be included in the application notice or in written evidence filed in support of the application:

(1) a summary of the nature of the litigation;
(2) the number and nature of claims already issued;
(3) the number of parties likely to be involved;
(4) the common issues of fact or law (the "GLO issues") that are likely to arise in the litigation; and
(5) whether there are any matters that distinguish smaller groups of claims within the wider group.

3.3 A GLO may not be made—

(1) in the Queen's Bench Division, without the consent of the Lord Chief Justice,
(2) in the Chancery Division, without the consent of the Vice–Chancellor, or
(3) in a county court, without the consent of the Head of Civil Justice.

3.4 The court to which the application for a GLO is made will, if minded to make the GLO, send to the Lord Chief Justice, the Vice-Chancellor, or the Head of Civil Justice, as appropriate—

(1) a copy of the application notice,
(2) a copy of any relevant written evidence, and
(3) a written statement as to why a GLO is considered to be desirable.

These steps may be taken either before or after a hearing of the application.

19BPD.7.1 *Note* — The consent now required under 3.3(1) is that of the President of the QBD and not the Lord Chief Justice.

The title of the former Vice-Chancellor is now the "Chancellor of the High Court".

High Court in London

19BPD.8 **3.5** The application for the GLO should be made to the Senior Master in the Queen's Bench Division or the Chief Chancery Master in the Chancery Division. For claims that are proceeding or are likely to proceed in a specialist list, the application should be made to the senior judge of that list.

19BPD.8.1 *Note* —A practice form for GLO's appears in the *Civil Procedure Forms Volume* as ***PF19****. This form can be* adapted to suit particular circumstances.

High Court outside London

19BPD.9 **3.6** Outside London, the application should be made to a Presiding Judge or a Chancery Supervising Judge of the Circuit in which the District Registry which has issued the application notice is situated.

County courts

3.7 The application should be made to the Designated Civil Judge for the area in which the county court which has issued the application notice is situated. **19BPD.10**

3.8 The applicant for a GLO should request the relevant court to refer the application notice to the judge by whom the application will be heard as soon as possible after the application notice has been issued. This is to enable the judge to consider whether to follow the practice set out in paragraph 3.4 above prior to the hearing of the application.

3.9 The directions under paragraphs 3.5, 3.6 and 3.7 above do not prevent the judges referred to from making arrangements for other judges to hear applications for GLOs when they themselves are unavailable.

Court where application for GLO should be made

The general rule is that a Pt 23 application must be made to the court "where the claim was started" (r.23.2). Paragraphs 3.3 to 3.9 stipulate the particular judicial officer to whom an application for a GLO should be made. **19BPD.10.1**

GLO made by court of its own initiative

4. Subject to obtaining the appropriate consent referred to in paragraph 3.3 and the procedure set out in paragraph 3.4, the court may make a GLO of its own initiative. **19BPD.11**

(CPR 3.3 deals with the procedure that applies when a court proposes to make an order of its own initiative.)

The GLO

5. CPR 19.11(2) and (3) set out rules relating to the contents of GLOs. **19BPD.12**

The Group Register

6.1 Once a GLO has been made a Group Register will be established on which will be entered such details as the court may direct of the cases which are to be subject to the GLO. **19BPD.13**

6.1A A claim must be issued before it can be entered on a Group Register.

"a Group Register will be established"

Among the directions that must be included in a GLO are directions "about the establishment of a register (the 'group register') on which the claims managed under the GLO will be entered" (r.19.11(2)(a)). Such details about the claims covered by the GLO as may be directed by the court are to be entered in the Group Register and may be inspected as provided by para.6.6 below. A GLO must specify the court which will manage the claims on the Group Register; this court is known as "the management court" (r.19.11(2)(c)). In paras 6.1 to 6.6 references to "the court" means the management court so specified (para.6.7). As to the appointment of a "managing judge", see para.8 below. **19BPD.13.1**

6.2 An application for details of a case to be entered on a Group Register may be made by any party to the case. **19BPD.14**

6.3 An order for details of the case to be entered on the Group Register will not be made unless the case gives rise to at least one of the GLO issues.

(CPR 19.10 defines GLO issues.)

6.4 The court, if it is not satisfied that a case can be conveniently case managed with the other cases on the Group Register, or if it is satisfied that the entry of the case on the Group Register would adversely affect the case management of the other cases, may refuse to allow details of the case to be entered on the Group Register, or order their removal from the Register if already entered, although the case gives rise to one or more of the Group issues.

6.5 The Group Register will normally be maintained by and kept at the court but the court may direct this to be done by the solicitor for one of the parties to a case entered on the Register.

6.6(1) Rules 5.4 (Register of Claims), 5.4B (Supply of documents from court records – a party) and 5.4C (supply of documents from court records – a non-party) apply where the register is maintained by the court. A party to a claim on the group register may request documents relating to any other claim on the group register in accordance with rule 5.4 as if he were a party to those proceedings.

(2) Where the register is maintained by a solicitor, any person may inspect the Group Register during normal business hours and upon giving reasonable notice to the solicitor; the solicitor may charge a fee not exceeding the fee prescribed for a search at the court office.

6.7 In this paragraph, "the court" means the management court specified in the GLO.

Allocation to track

19BPD.15 **7.** Once a GLO has been made and unless the management court directs otherwise:

(1) every claim in a case entered on the Group Register will be automatically allocated, or re-allocated (as the case may be), to the multi-track;

(2) any case management directions that have already been given in any such case otherwise than by the management court will be set aside; and

(3) any hearing date already fixed otherwise than for the purposes of the group litigation will be vacated.

Automatic allocation to multi-track

19BPD.15.1 The general rules as to the procedure for allocation of cases to a track are found in Pt 26. It might be expected that, in accordance with those rules, cases entered on a Group Register following the making of a GLO would be allocated to the multi-track in the light of the criteria stated in r.26.8. Paragraph 7 provides for the automatic allocation of such cases. In effect, the rules in Pt 26 are overridden by para.7. (The confusion between "claim" and "case", apparent in Pt 26, is evident in para.7.)

Managing judge

19BPD.16 **8.** A judge ("the managing judge") will be appointed for the purpose of the GLO as soon as possible. He will assume overall responsibility for the management of the claims and will generally hear the GLO issues. A Master or a District Judge may be appointed to deal with procedural matters, which he will do in accordance with any directions given by the managing judge. A costs judge may be appointed and may be invited to attend case management hearings.

Appointment of judges

The process for the appointment of a managing judge and a Master or district judge is not immediately clear from para.8. For particular case management powers of the managing judge, see r.19.13 and paras 12.1 *et seq.* below. **19BPD.16.1**

Claims to be started in management court

9.1 The management court may order that as from a specified date all claims that raise one or more of the GLO issues shall be started in the management court. **19BPD.17**

9.2 Failure to comply with an order made under paragraph 9.1 will not invalidate the commencement of the claim but the claim should be transferred to the management court and details entered on the Group Register as soon as possible. Any party to the claim may apply to the management court for an order under CPR 19.14 removing the case from the Register or, as the case may be, for an order that details of the case be not entered on the Register.

Adding subsequent cases

Once a GLO has been made covering a number of claims, other claims commenced subsequently may be added to the Group Register and become subject to the GLO. As to "cut-off" dates, see para.13 below. As enacted, r.19.14(1) does not make sense. Paragraph 9.2 gives clues as to what was meant. **19BPD.17.1**

Transfer

10. Where the management court is a county court and a claim raising one or more of the GLO issues is proceeding in the High Court, an order transferring the case to the management court and directing the details of the case to be entered on the Group Register can only be made in the High Court. **19BPD.18**

Transfer from High Court to a county court

For general rules as to transfer of a claim from the High Court to a county court, see CPR Pt 30. Rule 19.11(3)(a)(i) states that a GLO may, in relation to claims which raise one or more GLO issues, direct their transfer to the management court. Paragraph 10 makes it clear that, where the managing court is a county court, the managing judge cannot order the transfer to the management court of a pending High Court case raising one or more of the GLO issues. It would seem that para.10 covers, not only a case commenced in the High Court after the GLO has been made, but also cases pending in the High Court at the time of the making of the GLO. **19BPD.18.1**

Publicising the GLO

11. After a GLO has been made, a copy of the GLO should be supplied— **19BPD.19**

(1) to the Law Society, 113 Chancery Lane, London WC2A 1PL; and

(2) to the Senior Master, Queen's Bench Division, Royal Courts of Justice, Strand, London WC2A 2LL.

Notifying the Law Society

Where a GLO is made, it is important that legal representatives of parties who have claims which may raise one or more of the GLO issues should be aware of the GLO and any directions made. The requirement that the Law Society should be notified, **19BPD.19.1** ensures that the Society's Multi Party Action Information Service is kept advised but similar information can also be obtained from either the Office of the Senior Master (Room E115) or from the Court Service website (*www.hmcourts-service.gov.uk*).

Case management

19BPD.20 **12.1** The management court may give case management directions at the time the GLO is made or subsequently. Directions given at a case management hearing will generally be binding on all claims that are subsequently entered on the Group Register (see CPR 19.12(1)).

12.2 Any application to vary the terms of the GLO must be made to the management court.

12.3 The management court may direct that one or more of the claims are to proceed as test claims.

12.4 The management court may give directions about how the costs of resolving common issues or the costs of claims proceeding as test claims are to be borne or shared as between the claimants on the Group Register.

Binding directions

19BPD.20.1 Paragraph 12.1 provides that, generally, "case management directions" will be binding on all claims subject to the GLO. The reference here to r.19.12(1) is puzzling. That provision states that, generally, "judgments and orders" made in a claim on the Group Register in relation to one or more GLO issues will be binding on the parties to all other claims on the Group Register.

Costs

19BPD.20.2 See further, CPR Pt 48, in particular r.48.6A, and para.16.2 below.

Cut-off dates

19BPD.21 **13.** The management court may specify a date after which no claim may be added to the Group Register unless the court gives permission. An early cut-off date may be appropriate in the case of "instant disasters" (such as transport accidents). In the case of consumer claims, and particularly pharmaceutical claims, it may be necessary to delay the ordering of a cut-off date.

Statements of case

19BPD.22 **14.1** The management court may direct that the GLO claimants serve "Group Particulars of Claim" which set out the various claims of all the claimants on the Group Register at the time the particulars are filed. Such particulars of claim will usually contain—

(1) general allegations relating to all claims; and

(2) a schedule containing entries relating to each individual claim specifying which of the general allegations are relied on and any specific facts relevant to the claimant.

14.2 The directions given under paragraph 14.1 should include directions as to whether the Group Particulars should be verified by a statement or statements of truth and, if so, by whom.

14.3 The specific facts relating to each claimant on the Group Register may be obtained by the use of a questionnaire. Where this is proposed, the management court should be asked to approve the questionnaire. The management court may direct that the questionnaires completed by individual claimants take the place of the schedule referred to in paragraph 14.1(2).

14.4 The management court may also give directions about the form that particulars of claim relating to claims which are to be entered on the Group Register should take.

Particulars of claim

As to particulars of claim generally, see CPR r.16.4 and Practice Direction (Statements of Case) supplementing Pt 16. If multiple claims made subject to a particular GLO are to be handled effectively and efficiently it is important that the issues, particularly the common issues, be accurately identified and clearly and accurately defined. In this context, the effective judicial scrutiny of pleadings (statements of case and particulars of claim), making full use of the provisions in paras 14.1 to 14.4, plays a crucial role. A schedule of information on individual claims, or questionnaires, will often be more cost effective than requiring each individual group litigants to prepare his/her own particulars of claim. **19BPD.22.1**

The trial

15.1 The management court may give directions— **19BPD.23**

(1) for the trial of common issues; and

(2) for the trial of individual issues.

15.2 Common issues and test claims will normally be tried at the management court. Individual issues may be directed to be tried at other courts whose locality is convenient for the parties.

"common ... and individual issues"

CPR r.3.1(2) states that the court may direct a separate trial of an issue or decide the order in which issues are to be tried. Paragraph 15.1 makes it clear (if it was necessary) that the management court may give such directions in relation to issues arising, not in a single claim, but in several claims subject to a GLO. In r.19.10, "GLO issues" are "common or related issues of fact or law" arising in several claims. **19BPD.23.1**

Costs

16.1 CPR 48 contains rules about costs where a GLO has been made. **19BPD.24**

16.2 Where the court has made an order about costs in relation to any application or hearing which involved both—

(1) one or more of the GLO issues; and

(2) an issue or issues relevant only to individual claims;

and the court has not directed the proportion of the costs that is to relate to common costs and the proportion that is to relate to individual costs in accordance with rule 48.6A(5), the costs judge will make a decision as to the relevant proportions at or before the commencement of the detailed assessment of costs.

"rules about costs"

For comments see the editorial introduction to the Group Litigation Order rule and the notes to rule 48.6(A)(5). **19BPD.24.1**

In *BCCI SA v Ali (Assessment of Costs)* [2000] 2 Costs L.R. 243 all five test claims (out of 369 claims) failed. The court made no order as to *inter partes* costs but, despite findings of dishonesty by some of the test claimants, ordered that the claimants' costs should be shared equally between all 369 claimants, as there had been an understanding to that effect, although no costs sharing had been made earlier in the action.

PRACTICE DIRECTION—DERIVATIVE CLAIMS

This Practice Direction supplements CPR Part 19

Application of this Practice Direction

19CPD.1 **1.** This practice direction—

(a) applies to—

(i) derivative claims, whether under Chapter 1 of Part 11 of the Companies Act 2006 or otherwise; and

(ii) applications for permission to continue or take over such claims; but

(b) does not apply to claims in pursuance of an order under section 996 of that Act.

Claim form

19CPD.2 **2.**(1) A claim form must be headed "Derivative claim".

(2) If the claimant seeks an order that the defendant company or other body concerned indemnify the claimant against liability for costs incurred in the permission application or the claim, this should be stated in the permission application or claim form or both, as the case requires.

Application for Order Delaying Notice

19CPD.3 **3.** If the applicant seeks an order under rule 19.9A(7) delaying notice to the defendant company or other body concerned, the applicant must also—

(a) state in the application notice the reasons for the application; and

(b) file with it any written evidence in support of the application.

Form to be Sent to Defendant Company or Other Body

19CPD.4 **4.** The form required by rule 19.9A(4)(a) to be sent to the defendant company or other body is set out at the end of this practice direction. There are separate versions of the form for claims involving a company, and claims involving a body corporate of another kind or a trade union.

Early Intervention by the Company

19CPD.5 **5.** The decision whether the claimant's evidence discloses a prima facie case will normally be made without submissions from or (in the case of an oral hearing to reconsider such a decision reached pursuant to rule 19.9A(9)) attendance by the company. If without invitation from the court the company volunteers a submission or attendance, the company will not normally be allowed any costs of that submission or attendance. (Sections 261, 262 and 264 of the Companies Act 2006 contain provisions about disclosing a prima facie case in applications to continue a derivative claim.)

Hearing of Applications etc.

19CPD.6 **6.**(1) Where a permission application to which this practice direction applies is made in the High Court it will be assigned to the Chancery Division and decided by a High Court judge.

(2) Where such an application is made in a county court it will be decided by a circuit judge.

Discontinuance of Derivative Claim

7. As a condition of granting permission to continue or take over a derivative claim, the court may order that the claim is not to be discontinued, settled or compromised without the court's permission. Such a condition may be appropriate where any future proposal to discontinue or settle might not come to the attention of members who might have an interest in taking over the claim. **19CPD.7**

Transitional Provisions

8.(1) From 1st October 2007 new rules came into force about procedures for derivative claims. The new rules are set out in CPR rules 19.9 to 19.9F. **19CPD.8**

(2) The rules of court in force immediately before 1st October 2007 apply to derivative claims begun before 1st October 2007. These (former CPR rule 19.9) are set out below:

Derivative Claims **19CPD.9**

(1) This rule applies where a company, other incorporated body or trade union is alleged to be entitled to claim a remedy and a claim is made by one or more members of the company, body or trade union for it to be given that remedy (a "derivative claim").

(2) The company, body or trade union for whose benefit a remedy is sought must be a defendant to the claim.

(3) After the claim form has been issued the claimant must apply to the court for permission to continue the claim and may not take any other step in the proceedings except—

(a) as provided by paragraph (5); or
(b) where the court gives permission.

(4) An application in accordance with paragraph (3) must be supported by written evidence.

(5) The—

(a) claim form;
(b) application notice; and
(c) written evidence in support of the application,

must be served on the defendant within the period within which the claim form must be served and, in any event, at least 14 days before the court is to deal with the application.

(6) If the court gives the claimant permission to continue the claim, the time within which the defence must be filed is 14 days after the date on which the permission is given or such period as the court may specify.

(7) The court may order the company, body or trade union to indemnify the claimant against any liability in respect of costs incurred in the claim.

The forms **19CPD.10**

For claims involving a company:

Companies Act 2006, section 261 *or* 262 *or* 264

Civil Procedure Rules 1998, rule 19.9A(4)(a)

Notice in relation to derivative claim

To [name of company etc] ("the company") in relation to a claim by

[claimant]

Attached to this notice are:

- a copy of the claim form to which this notice relates;
- an application under rule 19.9A of the Civil Procedure Rules 1998 for permission to continue the claim; and

- copies of the evidence to be relied on by the claimant in obtaining permission to continue the claim.

The claim is a derivative claim. The claimant must obtain the permission of the court under section 261 of the Companies Act 2006 to continue the claim. A brief summary of the procedure follows.

The court will make its initial decision on the basis of the evidence filed by the claimant (copies are attached to this notice) and at present the company does not need to acknowledge service, file a defence or become involved in any other way. Initially the court may make its decision on the documents only, without a hearing; if it dismisses the application, the claimant may request reconsideration of that decision at a hearing but even at that hearing no additional evidence will be taken into account. If the court considers that the evidence filed by the claimant does not disclose a prima facie case, it must dismiss the application. It may then make consequential orders. If it does not dismiss the application at that stage, the court will adjourn the application to allow the company to obtain and file evidence and be heard on the application, and will make any necessary orders.

The court will notify the company of the outcome of each stage of the process.

The factors that the court must take into account are set out in section 263 of the Act. A copy of sections 263(1) to (4) of the Act is attached.

19CPD.11 *For claims involving a body corporate that is not a company, or a trade union:*
Civil Procedure Rules 1998, rule 19.9A(4)(a)

Notice in relation to derivative claim

To [name of body corporate etc] ("the corporation") [or as appropriate] in relation to a claim by

[claimant]

Attached to this notice are:

- a copy of the claim form to which this notice relates;
- an application under rule 19.9A of the Civil Procedure Rules 1998 for permission to continue the claim; and
- copies of the evidence to be relied on by the claimant in obtaining permission to continue the claim.

The claim is a derivative claim. Under the Civil Procedure Rules 1998, the claimant must obtain the permission of the court to continue the claim. A brief summary of the procedure follows.

The court will make its initial decision on the basis of the evidence filed by the claimant (copies are attached to this notice) and at present the [corporation] does not need to acknowledge service, file a defence or become involved in any other way. Initially the court may make its decision on the documents only, without a hearing; if it dismisses the application, the claimant may request reconsideration of that decision at a hearing but even at that hearing no additional evidence will be taken into account. If the court considers that the evidence filed by the claimant does not disclose a prima facie case, it will dismiss the application. It may then make consequential orders. If it does not dismiss the application at that stage, the court will adjourn the application to allow the corporation to obtain and file evidence and be heard on the application, and will make any necessary orders.

The court will notify the company of the outcome of each stage of the process.

PART 20

Counterclaims and Other Additional Claims

CPR 20

Contents 20.0.1

Editorial introduction

In a simple case, a claimant will bring a claim against a defendant. But the proceedings may be a little more complicated than that. For example, the claimant may make more than one claim against the defendant in the same proceedings. Also, in the same proceedings there may be more than one claimant and perhaps more than one defendant. Party joinder, and claim joinder rules deal with these situations. However, since the late part of the nineteenth century, rules of court have allowed even greater complexity than this, in particular (in the interests of saving costs and reducing delays) they have enabled the court to deal, in the one set of proceedings, not only with the claim (or claims) that the claimant (or claimants) make against the defendant or (defendants) and the defences thereto, but with additional claims not falling within those categories. 20.0.2

The best-known and most obvious is the additional claim in the form of a claim made against the claimant by the defendant. Historically speaking, such a claim has been known as (copying American procedural terminology) a counterclaim. Clearly, it is not difficult to envisage circumstances where, because of the relationship between the allegations made, it would be sensible to enable a defendant to bring a counterclaim against the claimant rather than to require the defendant to bring fresh proceedings with himself as claimant and the claimant as defendant. The simplest form of counterclaim is the defendant's claim against the claimant. A more complicated form is where the counterclaim is brought, not only against the defendant but also against another party (not previously a party to the proceedings) as a co-defendant to the counterclaim. (These two forms are encapsulated in the CPR Glossary where a counterclaim is defined as "a claim brought by a defendant in response to the claimant's claim which is included in the same proceedings as the claimant's claim"; see Section F below.)

Another example of an additional claim procedure is the procedure that caters for the situation where, in response to the claimant's claim, the defendant (whilst perhaps admitting liability in whole or in part) in effect points his finger at a third party alleging that he is obliged to indemnify him for any liability to the claimant, or to contribute to the satisfaction of any judgment. Again, it is not difficult to envisage circumstances in which it would be sensible to enable him to bring such a claim in the proceedings which he is defending, rather than to require him to commence separate proceedings.

Where an additional claim is made, it is not uncommon for proceedings to develop to the point where the real issues that have to be determined by the court lie not in the claimant's claim against the defendant, but in the additional claim.

Under the CPR, additional claim provisions similar to those found scattered in the former RSC and CCR were brought together in Pt 20. As originally enacted, the rules in this Part endeavoured to improve upon the former rules in some respects, most notably by modernising terminology. The rules introduced the omnibus term "Part 20 claim" covering a variety of additional claims. Early on in the life of the CPR, the Civil Procedure Rules Committee became aware of the fact that the terminology in Pt 20 was causing confusion. In October 2003, the perceived weaknesses in Pt 20 and proposals for remedying them were explained in DCA Consultation Paper CPL 11/03 ("Additional Civil Claims—Changes to Part 20 of the Civil Procedure Rules"). As a result, a new Pt 20 was substituted in the CPR by the Civil Procedure (Amendment No.4) Rules 2005 (SI 2005/3515) and came into effect on April 6, 2006.

The Practice Direction which supplements Pt 20 provides an clear and helpful support to the rules about additional claims including guidance on the practical steps to be followed for the conduct of Pt 20 claims.

As indicated above Pt 20 applies to counterclaims plus claims by a defendant for a contribution, an indemnity or any other remedy against any other person, whether or not that person is already a party. The purpose of Pt 20 is to enable such claims to be managed in the "most convenient and effective manner" (r.20.1) Although these claims have shared features, care must be taken to ensure that the relevant rules are applied depending on the nature of the Pt 20 claim. It is good practice to make a Pt 20 claim at or before the filing of a defence when permission will not be required in most cases; note that permission is always required to issue a counterclaim against a party other than the claimant (r.20.5(1)).

Permission is required to start some types of additional claim and in some circumstances; see rr.20.4(2)(b), 20.5(1), 20.6(2)(ii) and 20.7(3)(b) and in every case when the case is proceeding under the Pt 8 procedure (see r.8.7). An additional claim is made when the court issues an additional claim form (r.20.7(2)) namely form **N211** but this form is not required when starting a counterclaim which usually runs on from the defence (PD 20 para.6.1) or when making a claim for contribution or indemnity (r.20.7(1)). A form for acknowledgment is not provided where the additional claim is a counterclaim.

Failure to file a defence to an additional claim (other than a counterclaim) does not usually have the consequence of the claimant being able to request judgment in default but the party against whom the additional claim is made is deemed to admit the claim (see r.20.11(2)). The default procedure (Pt 12) applies to counterclaims. Rule 20.11 sets out the special procedure relating to default judgment on an additional claim other than a counterclaim or indemnity notice.

The Civil Procedure (Amendment No.4) Rules 2005 which came into force on April 6, 2006 revised Pt 20, changing the term "Part 20 claim" to "additional claim". The Practice Direction concerning the naming of additional parties has been overhauled and the previously clumsy description of Pt 20 parties has been replaced by "third", "fourth" etc parties.

Related sources

20.0.3
- Practice Direction to Part 20 (see para.20PD.1)
- Parts 1, 9, 10, 11 and 15
- Parts 2.3, 22.1, 26.8
- RSC O.77, r.6 and CCR O.42, r.9 (restrictions on Pt 20 claims where the Crown is claimant).
- Civil Liability (Contribution) Act 1978 s.1

Forms

20.0.4
- **N9B** Defence/counterclaim (specified amount)
- **N9D** Defence/counterclaim (unspecified amount and non-money claim)

- **N211** Part 20 claim form
- **N211A** Part 20 notes for claimant
- **N211C** Part 20 notes for defendant
- **N212** Part 20 notice of issue
- **N213** Part 20 acknowledgment of service

Purpose of this part[1]

20.1 The purpose of this Part is to enable counterclaims and other additional claims to be managed in the most convenient and effective manner. **20.1**

"most convenient and effective manner" (r.20.1)

See too r.1.1 (Overriding objective). **20.1.1**

Scope and interpretation[2]

20.2—(1) This Part applies to— **20.2**

(a) a counterclaim by a defendant against the claimant or against the claimant and some other person;

(b) an additional claim by a defendant against any person (whether or not already a party) for contribution[GL] or indemnity[GL] or some other remedy; and

(c) where an additional claim has been made against a person who is not already a party, any additional claim made by that person against any other person (whether or not already a party).

(2) In these Rules—

(a) "additional claim" means any claim other than the claim by the claimant against the defendant; and

(b) unless the context requires otherwise, references to a claimant or defendant include a party bringing or defending an additional claim.

Fee

On the filing of a counterclaim the same fee is payable as if the relief or remedy sought were the subject matter of separate proceedings. **20.2.1**

Application of these Rules to additional claims[3]

20.3—(1) An additional claim shall be treated as if it were a claim for the purposes of these Rules, except as provided by this Part. **20.3**

(2) The following rules do not apply to additional claims—

(a) rules 7.5 and 7.6 (time within which a claim form may be served);

(b) rule 16.3(5) (statement of value where claim to be issued in the High Court); and

(c) Part 26 (case management—preliminary stage).

(3) Part 12 (default judgment) applies to a counterclaim but not to other additional claims.

---

[1] Amended by the Civil Procedure (Amendment No.4) Rules 2005 (SI 2005/3515).
[2] Amended by the Civil Procedure (Amendment No.4) Rules 2005 (SI 2005/3515).
[3] Amended by the Civil Procedure (Amendment) Rules 2000 (SI 2000/221) and the Civil Procedure (Amendment No.4) Rules 2005 (SI 2005/3515).

(4) Part 14 (admissions) applies to a counterclaim, but only—

(a) rules 14.1(1) and 14.1(2) (which provide that a party may admit the truth of another party's case in writing); and

(b) rule 14.3 (admission by notice in writing—application for judgment),

apply to other additional claims.

(Rule 12.3(2) sets out how to obtain judgment in default of defence for a counterclaim against the claimant, and rule 20.11 makes special provision for default judgment for some additional claims).

Relevance of pre-action protocols to additional claims

20.3.1 A party expecting to make an additional claim is not relieved of the obligation to comply with a relevant approved pre action protocol: to permit otherwise would result in unfair commercial advantage or threats of litigation without any real substance: *Daejan Investments Limited v The Park West Club Limited and Buxton Associates (Pt 20 Defendant)* [2004] C.I.L.L. 2084.

"An additional claim shall be treated as if it were a claim for the purposes of these rules" (r.20.3(1))

20.3.2 See too Practice Direction, para.3 (see para.20PD.1)). Note Pt 9 (Responding to Particulars of Claim), Pt 11 (Disputing The Court's Jurisdiction) and Pt 15 (Defence and Reply). For example, a person served with a Pt 20 claim must file a defence in accordance with r.15.2. A Pt 20 defendant reisident out of the jurisdiction can be required to give security for costs *Roto Packing v Latest Technologies* [2004] EWHC 2451 Ch D. However there are exceptions—for example, rr.7.5 and 7.6 (time within which a claim form may be served), r.16.3(5) (statement of value) and Pt 26 (case management—preliminary stage do not apply. A Pt 20 claim must be accompanied by a statement of truth. The fact that the Pt 20 claim stands on its own means that, for example there is no automatic right to a stay of execution on the claim if there is an outstanding counterclaim; whether or not there will be a stay of execution will depend on the circumstances of a particular case (see *Isovel Contracts Ltd v ABB Building Technologies Ltd*, [2002] 1 B.C.L.C. 390) as an example of a case where a stay was not granted.

Default judgment

20.3.3 Part 12 (default judgment) applies to a counterclaim but not to other additional claims. See r.20.11 on the circumstances where the failure to acknowledge or defend an additional claim results in the claim being deemed to be admitted.

Defendant's counterclaim against the claimant[1]

20.4 **20.4—(1) A defendant may make a counterclaim against a claimant by filing particulars of the counterclaim.**

(2) A defendant may make a counterclaim against a claimant—

(a) without the court's permission if he files it with his defence; or

(b) at any other time with the court's permission.

(Part 15 makes provision for a defence to a claim and applies to a defence to a counterclaim by virtue of rule 20.3).

(3) Part 10 (acknowledgment of service) does not apply to a claimant who wishes to defend a counterclaim.

[1] Amended by the Civil Procedure (Amendment No.4) Rules 2005 (SI 2005/3515).

Time for making a counterclaim against claimant

The normal time for making a additional claim is the same time as the defence, but permission may be given at other times—see below. 20.4.1

Permission (rr.20.4(2)(b), 20.5(1) and 20.7(3)(b))

A counterclaim against a claimant may be made without the court's permission if it is filed with the defence (r.20.4(2)(a)). Similarly, a defendant may claim a contribution or indemnity against another defendant without the permission of the court (r.20.6). However, the court's permission is needed if a defendant wants to make a counterclaim against the claimant at any other time (r.20.4(2)(b)), where a defendant wishes to counterclaim against someone other than the claimant (r.20.5(1)) or where he seeks to make any other claim after filing his defence (r.20.7(3)(b)). Permission is also needed to make an additional claim where the Part 8 procedure is used (see CPR r.8.7). Applications under rr.20.5(1) and 20.7(3)(b) may be made without notice (rr.20.5(2) and 20.7(5)—see too r.23.9). 20.4.2

An application for permission must be supported by evidence (see Pt 32 and the Practice Direction to Pt 32 (see para.32PD.1)) stating the stage that the action has reached, the nature of the additional claim, a summary of facts and the name and address of the additional claim defendant (Practice Direction, para.2.1 (see para.20PD.2)). Where there has been delay an explanation should be given. Where possible the applicant should provide a time table of the action to date (Practice Direction, paras 2.2 and 2.3 (see para.20PD.2)).

If permission is given, directions as to service should be given at the same time (r.20.8(3)).

In *Rahman v Sterling Credit Ltd* [2001] 1 W.L.R. 496; July 7. 2000, CA, the Court of Appeal held that where a judgment remained unsatisfied the action was not at an end and the court could grant permission to file a counterclaim.

"court" (rr.20.4(2)(b), 20.5(1) and 20.7(3)(b))

The power may be exercised by a judge or district judge in a county court or by a judge, Master or district judge in the High Court—(r.2.4). It may be exercised on application or on the court's own initiative. See Practice Direction 1.1 (para.20PD.1). An application for permission may be dealt with without a hearing where all the parties are in agreement (r.1.4(2)(j)). 20.4.3

Form of counterclaim and titles of proceedings where there are Pt 20 claims

See Practice Direction, paras 6.1–7.5 (para.20PD.6). 20.4.4

Statement of truth

The contents of an additional claim should be verified by a statement of truth ("[I believe] [the [additional claimant] believes] that the facts stated in this statement of case are true.") (see Practice Direction, para.4.1 (para.20PD.4). Pt 22 and r.32.14). 20.4.5

Counterclaim against a person other than the claimant[1]

20.5—(1) A defendant who wishes to counterclaim against a person other than the claimant must apply to the court for an order that that person be added as an additional party. 20.5

(2) An application for an order under paragraph (1) may be made without notice unless the court directs otherwise.

(3) Where the court makes an order under paragraph (1), it will *give directions as to the management of the case.*

Counterclaim against a person other than the claimant

An application to add a person as a defendant to a counterclaim should be accompanied by a copy of the proposed counterclaim. It must be supported by evidence stating the stage which the action has reached, the nature of the additional claim, a summary of facts upon which it is based and the name and address of the additional 20.5.1

[1] Amended by the Civil Procedure (Amendment No.4) Rules 2005 (SI 2005/3515).

party. If there has been delay, an explanation must be given. Where possible the applicant should provide a timetable of the action to date. (See Practice Direction supplementing Pt 20, paras 2.1 to 2.4). Such an application may be made without notice unless the court directs otherwise (r.20.5(2)). See too CPR Pt 19.

Allocation questionnaire

20.5.2 If a party intends to make an additional claim, or to apply to add another party, this should be stated on the allocation questionnaire (see the Practice Direction supplementing Pt 26, para.2.2(3)(b)).

Must apply to the court for an order

20.5.3 The decision in *Lloyd's Bank Plc v Ellicott* [2002] EWCA Civ 1333, CA is a useful reminder and cross reference to r.3.10 (general power of the court to rectify matters where there has been an error of procedure). Where a judge gives permission to start an additional claim and this is not recorded on the face of the order this is a procedural error which can be rectified and should not be treated as a breach so heinous so as to justify striking out the Pt 20 claim.

Defendant's additional claim for contribution or indemnity from another party[1]

20.6 **20.6—(1) A defendant who has filed an acknowledgment of service or a defence may make an additional claim for contribution^{GL} or indemnity^{GL} against a person who is already a party to the proceedings by—**

(a) filing a notice containing a statement of the nature and grounds of his additional claim; and

(b) serving the notice on that party.

(2) A defendant may file and serve a notice under this rule—

(a) without the court's permission, if he files and serves it—

(i) with his defence; or

(ii) if his additional claim for contribution^{GL} or indemnity^{GL} is against a party added to the claim later, within 28 days after that party files his defence; or

(b) at any other time with the court's permission.

Procedure for making any other additional claim[2]

20.7 **20.7—(1) This rule applies to any additional claim except—**

(a) a counterclaim only against an existing party; and

(b) a claim for contribution^{GL} or indemnity^{GL} made in accordance with rule 20.6.

(2) An additional claim is made when the court issues the appropriate claim form.

(Rule 7.2(2) provides that a claim form is issued on the date entered on the form by the court)[3]

(3) A defendant may make an additional claim—

---

[1] Amended by the Civil Procedure (Amendment No.5) Rules 2001 (SI 2001/4015) and the Civil Procedure (Amendment No.4) Rules 2005 (SI 2005/3515).

[2] Amended by the Civil Procedure (Amendment No.4) Rules 2005 (SI 2005/3515).

[3] Introduced by the Civil Procedure (Amendment No.4) Rules 2003 (SI 2003/2113).

(a) without the court's permission if the additional claim is issued before or at the same time as he files his defence;

(b) at any other time with the court's permission.

(Rule 15.4 sets out the period for filing a defence).

(4) Particulars of an additional claim must be contained in or served with the additional claim.

(5) An application for permission to make an additional claim may be made without notice, unless the court directs otherwise.

Claim form

Part 4(1) and the accompanying Practice Direction sets out the forms which, subject to variations dictated by the circumstances of a particular case, must be used in cases where they apply. The Form **N211** is similar to the usual claim form but is a buff colour and has extra space to include the names of the additional parties. The effect of r.20.7 is that Form **N211** does not have to be used where the additional claim is a counterclaim or where it is a claim for a contribution or indemnity made in accordance with r.20.6. If the additional claim is a counterclaim, the defence and counterclaim should normally be in one document—see PD 20 para.6.1. **20.7.1**

Application without notice

An application may be made without a hearing being listed—see CPR r.20.7(5) and r.23.8. However, all applications should be supported by evidence—either in the form of a completed Pt C to Form **N244** or in a separate witness statement. Evidence should include details about the stage that the action has reached, the nature of the claim to be made, a summary of facts and the name and address of the proposed Pt 20 defendant (Practice Direction supplementing Pt 20, para.2.1. See too Practice Direction supplementing Pt 32). If there has been delay, an explanation should be given (Practice Direction supplementing Pt 20, para.2.2). **20.7.2**

Titles of proceedings where there are additional claims

The terms "third", "fourth" etc party were reintroduced by the Civil Procedure (Amendment No.4) Rules replacing the previous clumsy nomenclature. The phrase "Part 20 claim" will continue to appear on a number of court forms and these references should be construed as being to additional claims. **20.7.3**

Service of claim form[1]

20.8—(1) Where an additional claim may be made without the court's permission, any claim form must— **20.8**

(a) in the case of a counterclaim against an additionalparty only, be served on every other party when a copy of the defence is served;

(b) in the case of any other additional claim, be served on the person against whom it is made within 14 days after the date on which the additional claim is issued by the court.

(2) Paragraph (1) does not apply to a claim for contribution^GL^ or indemnity^GL^ made in accordance with rule 20.6.

(3) Where the court gives permission to make an additional claim it will at the same time give directions as to its service.

Service of an additional claim form (r.20.8)

See also Pt 6 and, for documents which must accompany it where service is upon a **20.8.1**

[1] Amended by the Civil Procedure (Amendment No.4) Rules 2003 (SI 2003/2113) and the Civil Procedure (Amendment No.4) Rules 2005 (SI 2005/3515).

non-party, r.20.12. Defendants to counterclaims should file admissions or defences within 14 days from service, or 28 days if an acknowledgment of service is filed—see r.15.4.

Where an additional claim is to be served out of the jurisdiction permission to issue is needed in cases where CPR r.6.20(3A) applies namely in circumstances where CPR r.6.19 does not apply. The effect of these rules means that permission is not needed to issue Pt 20 proceedings where CPR r.6.19 applies and the additional claim is issued with the defence and the additional party is within the European Union.

Matters relevant to question of whether an additional claim should be separate from the claim[1]

20.9 **20.9—(1) This rule applies where the court is considering whether to—**

(a) permit an additional claim to be made;

(b) dismiss an additional claim; or

(c) require an additional claim to be dealt with separately from the claim by the claimant against the defendant.

(Rule 3.1(2)(e) and (j) deal respectively with the court's power to order that part of proceedings be dealt with as separate proceedings and to decide the order in which issues are to be tried).

(2) The matters to which the court may have regard include—

(a) the connection between the additional claim and the claim made by the claimant against the defendant;

(b) whether the additional claimant is seeking substantially the same remedy which some other party is claiming from him;

(c) whether the additional claimant wants the court to decide any question connected with the subject-matter of the proceedings—

(i) not only between existing parties but also between existing parties and a person not already a party; or

(ii) against an existing party not only in a capacity in which he is already a party but also in some further capacity.

Case management of additional claims

20.9.1 The matters relevant to whether the additional claim should be dealt with separately or together with the claim are self-explanatory. In proper cases, where the cases are managed separately, they can be heard separately and allocated to different tracks. See para.20.13.2.

Effect of service of an additional claim[2]

20.10 **20.10—(1) A person on whom an additional claim is served becomes a party to the proceedings if he is not a party already.**

(2) When an additional claim is served on an existing party for the purpose of requiring the court to decide a question against that party in a further capacity, that party also becomes a party in the further capacity specified in the additional claim.

[1] Amended by the Civil Procedure (Amendment No.4) Rules 2005 (SI 2005/3515).
[2] Amended by the Civil Procedure (Amendment No.4) Rules 2005 (SI 2005/3515).

Special provisions relating to default judgment on an additional claim other than a counterclaim or a contribution or indemnity notice[1]

20.11—(1) This rule applies if— **20.11**

(a) the additional claim is not—

(i) a counterclaim; or

(ii) a claim by a defendant for contribution[GL] or indemnity[GL] against another defendant under rule 20.6; and

(b) the party against whom an additional claim is made fails to file an acknowledgment of service or defence in respect of the additional claim.

(2) The party against whom the additional claim is made—

(a) is deemed to admit the additional claim, and is bound by any judgment or decision in the main proceedings in so far as it is relevant to any matter arising in the additional claim;

(b) subject to paragraph (3), if default judgment under Part 12 is given against the additional claimant, the additional claimant may obtain judgment in respect of the additional claim by filing a request in the relevant practice form.

(3) An additional claimant may not enter judgment under paragraph (2)(b) without the court's permission if—

(a) he has not satisfied the default judgment which has been given against him; or

(b) he wishes to obtain judgment for any remedy other than a contribution[GL] or indemnity[GL].

(4) An application for the court's permission under paragraph (3) may be made without notice unless the court directs otherwise.

(5) The court may at any time set aside[GL] or vary a judgment entered under paragraph (2)(b).

Procedural steps on service of an additional claim form on a non-party[2]

20.12—(1) Where an additional claim form is served on a person who is not already a party it must be accompanied by— **20.12**

(a) a form for defending the claim;

(b) a form for admitting the claim;

(c) a form for acknowledging service; and

(d) a copy of—

(i) every statement of case which has already been served in the proceedings; and

(ii) such other documents as the court may direct.

(2) A copy of the additional claim form must be served on every existing party.

[1] Amended by the Civil Procedure (Amendment No.4) Rules 2005 (SI 2005/3515).
[2] Amended by the Civil Procedure (Amendment No.4) Rules 2005 (SI 2005/3515).

"form for defending the claim" (r.20.12(1)(a))

20.12.1 Forms **N9B** and **N9D**.

"form for admitting the claim" (r.20.12(1)(b))

20.12.2 Forms **N9A** and **N9C**.

"form for acknowledging service" (r.20.12(1)(c))

20.12.3 Form **N213**.

Supply of documents to new parties

20.12.4 Where a party is joined to existing proceedings, the party joined is entitled to require the person joining him to supply, without charge, copies of all statements of case, written evidence and any documents appended or exhibited to them. They should be supplied within 48 hours after reciept of any written request (see the Practice Direction supplementing Pt 5, para.3).

Case management where a defence to an additional claim is filed[1]

20.13 **20.13—(1) Where a defence is filed to an additional claim the court must consider the future conduct of the proceedings and give appropriate directions.**

(2) In giving directions under paragraph (1) the court must ensure that, so far as practicable, the original claim and all additional claims are managed together.

(Part 66 contains provisions about counterclaims and other Part 20 claims in relation to proceedings by or against the Crown.)

Case management where there a defence to an additional claim is filed (r.20.13(1))

20.13.1 See also Practice Direction, paras 5.1 to 5.4 and Pts 1, 28 and 29.

Case management and allocation to track

20.13.2 Rule 20.9 sets out the matters relevant to the question of whether an additional claim should be separate from the main claim. Where an additional party files a defence, other than a counterclaim, the court will arrange a hearing to consider case management of the additional claim (PD 20 para.5.1). The court may make case management orders either before or after any judgment in the claim has been entered by the claimant against the defendant (PD 20 para.5.4). Pt 26 (case management—preliminary stage) does not apply to Pt 20 claims (r.20.(2)(c)). The court's duty to manage a case (r.1.4(2)(i)) and the courts general powers of case management—especially r.3.1(2)(e) and (f) are not excluded. The size of a counterclaim is taken into account when determining track but the numerical value is not determinative and a claim may, for example, be allocated to the small claims track where the counterclaim exceeds £5,000. (*Berridge v Bayliss*, November 23, 1999, CA, LTL 23/11/99).

The Crown

20.13.3 Rule 66.4 covers the situation where a party wishes to raise a counterclaim against Crown or where the Crown wishes to avail itself of any set off or counterclaim.

[1] Amended by the Civil Procedure (Amendment No.4) Rules 2005 (SI 2005/3515) and the Civil Procedure (Amendment) Rules 2008 (SI 2008/2178).

PRACTICE DIRECTION—COUNTERCLAIMS AND OTHER ADDITIONALCLAIMS

This Practice Direction supplements CPR Part 20 **20PD.1**

An additional claim is any claim other than the claim by the claimant against the defendant.

Claims under this Part were formerly known as "Part 20 claims". As a result of the amendments to Part 20, introduced by Civil Procedure (Amendment No.4) Rules 2005, they are now called "additional claims".

However, they are described as "Part 20 claims" on a number of court forms. For the present, some of those forms will continue to refer to Part 20 claims. These references should be construed as being additional claims under this Part. Any reference to a Part 20 claimant or a Part 20 defendant means a claimant or defendant in an additional claim under this Part.

Cases where court's permission to make an additional claim is required

1.1 Rules 20.4(2)(b), 20.5(1) and 20.7(3)(b) set out the circumstances in which the court's permission will be needed for making an additional claim.

1.2 Where an application is made for permission to make an additional claim the application notice should be filed together with a copy of the proposed additional claim.

Applications for permission to issue an additional claim

2.1 An application for permission to make an additional claim must be supported by evidence stating: **20PD.2**

(1) the stage which the proceedings have reached,
(2) the nature of the additional claim to be made or details of the question or issue which needs to be decided,
(3) a summary of the facts on which the additional claim is based, and
(4) the name and address of any proposed additional party.

(For further information regarding evidence see the practice direction which supplements Part 32).

2.2 Where delay has been a factor contributing to the need to apply for permission to make an additional claim an explanation of the delay should be given in evidence.

2.3 Where possible the applicant should provide a timetable of the proceedings to date.

2.4 Rules 20.5(2) and 20.7(5) allow applications to be made to the court without notice unless the court directs otherwise.

General

3. The Civil Procedure Rules apply generally to additional claims as if they were claims. Parties should be aware that the provisions relating to failure to respond to a claim will apply. **20PD.3**

Statement of Truth

4.1 The contents of an additional claim should be verified by a **20PD.4**

statement of truth. Part 22 requires a statement of case to be verified by a statement of truth.

4.2 The form of the statement of truth should be as required by paragraph 2.1 of the practice direction supplementing Part 22.

4.3 Attention is drawn to rule 32.14 which sets out the consequences of verifying a statement of case containing a false statement without an honest belief in its truth.

Case management where there is a defence to an additional claim

20PD.5 **5.1** Where the defendant to an additional claim files a defence, other than to a counterclaim, the court will arrange a hearing to consider case management of the additional claim. This will normally be at the same time as a case management hearing for the original claim and any other additional claims.

5.2 The court will give notice of the hearing to each party likely to be affected by any order made at the hearing.

5.3 At the hearing the court may:

(1) treat the hearing as a summary judgment hearing,

(2) order that the additional claim be dismissed,

(3) give directions about the way any claim, question or issue set out in or arising from the additional claim should be dealt with,

(4) give directions as to the part, if any, the additional defendant will take at the trial of the claim,

(5) give directions about the extent to which the additional defendant is to be bound by any judgment or decision to be made in the claim.

5.4 The court may make any of the orders in 5.3(1) to (5) either before or after any judgment in the claim has been entered by the claimant against the defendant.

Form of counterclaim

20PD.6 **6.1** Where a defendant to a claim serves a counterclaim, the defence and counterclaim should normally form one document with the counterclaim following on from the defence.

6.2 Where a claimant serves a reply and a defence to counterclaim, the reply and the defence to counterclaim should normally form one document with the defence to counterclaim following on from the reply.

Titles of proceedings where there are additional claims

20PD.7 **7.1** Paragraph 4 of the practice direction supplementing Part 7 contains directions regarding the title to proceedings.

7.2 Where there are additional claims which add parties, the title to the proceedings should comprise a list of all parties describing each by giving them a single identification. Subject to paragraph 7.11, this identification should be used throughout.

7.3 Claimants and defendants in the original claim should always be referred to as such in the title to the proceedings, even if they subsequently acquire an additional procedural status.

7.4 Additional parties should be referred to in the title to the proceedings in accordance with the order in which they are joined to the proceedings, for example "Third Party" or "Fourth Party", whatever their actual procedural status.

Examples:

(a) If the defendant makes an additional claim against a single additional party, the additional party should be referred to in the title as "Third Party".

(b) If the defendant makes separate additional claims against two additional parties, the additional parties should be referred to in the title as "Third Party" and "Fourth Party".

(c) If the defendant makes a counterclaim against the claimant and an additional party, the claimant should remain as "Claimant" and the additional party should be referred to in the title as "Third Party".

(d) If the Third Party in example (b) makes an additional claim against a further additional party, that additional party should be referred to in the title as "Fifth Party".

7.5 If an additional claim is brought against more than one party jointly, they should be referred to in the title to the proceedings as, for example, "First Named Third Party" and "Second Named Third Party".

7.6 In group litigation, the court should give directions about the designation of parties.

7.7 All parties should co-operate to ensure that two parties each making additional claims do not attribute the same nominal status to more than one party.

7.8 In proceedings with numerous parties, the court will if necessary give directions as to the preparation and updating of a list of parties giving their roles in the claim and each additional claim.

7.9 If an additional party ceases to be a party to the proceedings, for example because the claim against that party is discontinued or dismissed, all other additional parties should retain their existing nominal status.

7.10 In proceedings where there are additional parties, the description of all statements of case or other similar documents should clearly identify the nature of the document with reference to each relevant party.

Examples:

(e) In example (a), the defendant's additional claim should be headed "Defendant's Additional Claim against Third Party" and the Third Party's defence to it should be headed "Third Party's Defence to Defendant's Additional Claim".

(f) In example (c), the defendant's counterclaim should be headed "Defendant's Counterclaim against Claimant and Third Party" and the Third Party's defence to it should be headed "Third Party's defence to Defendant's Counterclaim".

7.11 In proceedings where there are Fourth or subsequent parties, additional parties should be referred to in the text of statements of case or other similar documents by name, suitably abbreviated if appropriate. If parties have similar names, suitable distinguishing abbreviations should be used.

PART 21

Children and Protected Parties

Contents

Editorial introduction

21.0.2 *The Mental Capacity Act 2005* —The Mental Capacity Act 2005 ("the 2005 Act") came fully into force on October 1, 2007. The Act makes major changes to the law with the object of protecting and empowering those who lack capacity. The Act replaces Pt 7 of the Mental Health Act 1983 and the whole of the Enduring Power of Attorney Act 1985. A new superior court of record known as the Court of Protection is created as well as the new statutory office of Public Guardian. The new Court of Protection has its own procedures and judges; see the Court of Protection Rules 2007 (SI 2007/1744), Vol.2, 6B–96. It has the power to make declarations, decisions and orders affecting people who lack capacity and make decisions for or appoint deputies to make decisions on behalf of people lacking capacity; see the Court of Protection Rules 2007 (SI 2007/1744); Vol.2, para.6B–96. It has a comprehensive jurisdiction over the health, welfare and financial affairs of people who lack capacity. The old Court of Protection, which had a narrower jurisdiction, is abolished.

The powers under the 2005 Act generally only arise where the person lacking capacity is 16 or over; see s.2(5) of the 2005 Act. However, powers in relation to property (including the conduct of legal proceedings; see s.18(1)(k) of the 2005 Act) may be exercised in relation to a younger person if the Court of Protection considers it likely that the person will still lack capacity when he reaches 18; see s.18(3) of the 2005 Act. Section 18(3) of the 2005 Act enables the Court of Protection to take a long term view, for example where a child has been awarded substantial damages and there is no prospect of the child ever gaining the capacity to manage that money.

The Civil Procedure (Amendment) Rules 2007 (SI 2007/2204), which came into *force on* October 1, 2007, substitutes a new Pt 21 and in this way substantial amendments are made to the Part. There is a new Practice Direction supplementing Pt 21. These amendments give effect to the 2005 Act. The amendments serve to reduce repetition between the Rules and the Practice Direction and to ensure that the language used is clear. That said, the structure and object of Pt 21 remain the same.

The term "Patient" has gone and in its place one has the "protected party" and "protected beneficiary".

The protected party —As with the former "patient", a protected party must have a litigation friend to conduct proceedings on his behalf: r.21.2(1). **21.0.3**

Rule 21.1(2)(d) defines a "protected party" as a party, or an intended party, who lacks capacity to conduct the proceedings. A "protected beneficiary" is defined as a protected party who lacks capacity to manage and control any money recovered by him or on his behalf or for his benefit in the proceedings; r.21.1(2)(e). The protected beneficiary features in r.21.11 which deals with the control of money recovered on behalf of a protected party.

Rule 21.1(2)(c) adopts the meaning of "lacks capacity" as contained in the 2005 Act. Section 2(1) of the 2005 Act states that for the purposes of that Act, a person lacks capacity in relation to a matter if at the material time he is unable to make a decision for himself in relation to the matter because of an impairment of, or a disturbance in the functioning of, the mind or brain. It does not matter that the disturbance is permanent or temporary; s.2(2) of the 2005 Act. It is to be noted that the inability to make a decision about the conduct of proceedings is not, by itself, sufficient to make a person a protected party. The inability to make a decision must be caused by an impairment of, or a disturbance in the functioning of the mind or brain. This is known as a "diagnostic test" and could cover a range of problems such as psychiatric illness, learning disability, dementia, and brain damage.

It is to be noted that a child may be a protected party.

Section 1 of the 2005 Act sets out five key principles for the purposes of the Act: (1) a person must be assumed to have capacity unless it is established that he lacks capacity; (2) a person is not to be treated as unable to make a decision unless all practicable steps to help him do so have been taken without success; (3) a person must not be treated as unable to make a decision merely because he makes an unwise decision; (4) an act done, or decision made, under the Act for or on behalf of a person who lacks capacity must be done, or made in his best interests; (5) before the act is done, or the decision is made, regard must be had to whether the purpose for which it is needed can be as effectively achieved in a way that is less restrictive of the person's rights and freedom of action.

The assumption of capacity can only be overridden if the person concerned is assessed as lacking the mental capacity to make a particular decision for himself at the relevant time. The formula to be used in making that assessment is set out in s.3 of the 2005 Act (see below). A person may have capacity in relation to some matters but not others. In the context of Pt 21 the question is whether the person lacks capacity to conduct proceedings. If such capacity is lacking, the person is a "protected party".

Section 3 of the 2005 Act states:

Inability to make decisions

"**3.**—(1) For the purposes of section 2, a person is unable to make a decision for himself if he is unable—

(a) to understand the information relevant to the decision,

(b) to retain that information,

(c) to use or weigh that information as part of the process of making the decision, or

(d) to communicate his decision (whether by talking, using sign language or any other means).

(2) A person is not to be regarded as unable to understand the information relevant to a decision if he is able to understand an explanation of it given to him in a way that is appropriate to his circumstances (using simple language, visual aids or any other means).

(3) The fact that a person is able to retain the information relevant to a decision for a short period only does not prevent him from being regarded as able to make the decision.

(4) The information relevant to a decision includes information about the reasonably foreseeable consequences of—

(a) deciding one way or another, or

(b) failing to make the decision."

In legal proceedings the burden of proof is on the person who asserts that capacity is lacking. If there is any doubt as to whether a person lacks capacity, this is to be decided on the balance of probabilities; see s.2(4) of the 2005 Act.

For the approach under the Mental Health Act 1983 and the former Part; see *Masterman-Lister v Brutton & Co* [2002] EWCA Civ 1889; [2003] 1 W.L.R. 1511; [2003] 3 All. E.R. 162. The Court of Appeal also said that as a matter of practice the court should at the first convenient opportunity, investigate the question of capacity whenever there is any reason to suspect that it may be absent (e.g. significant head injury); and that means that, even where the issue does not seem to be contentious, a Master or district judge who is responsible for case management will almost certainly require the assistance of a medical report before being able to be satisfied that incapacity exists. These observations remain good. See *Saulle v Nouvet* [2007] EWHC 2902 (QB), in which it was held that under the new Pt 21 the court was obliged to adopt the statutory definition of capacity set out in s.2(1) of the 2005 Act. The case also serves as an illustration of the court having to decide the question of a claimant's capacity with neither the claimant nor the defendant positively asserting that capacity was lacking.

21.0.4 *The litigation friend*—As with the former "patient", a protected party must have a litigation friend to conduct proceedings on his behalf: r.21.2(1). A child must have a litigation friend to conduct proceedings on his behalf unless the court makes an order under r.21.2(3). A child is a person under 18: r.21.1(2)(a). As the title to r.21.2 makes clear, the litigation friend is required in proceedings by or against the child or protected party.

21.0.5 *Judgments and settlements*— Rules 21.2 to 21.9 of this Part are concerned with the matters outlined above. Rule 21.10 deals with the approval by the court of settlements of claims on behalf of children and protected parties.

A number of provisions in other Parts of the CPR and Practice Directions have to be borne in mind where a child or protected party is a party to proceedings. For example, r.14.1(4) restricts the right of a claimant to enter judgment on an admission made by a defendant where a party is a child or protected party. Further, under r.12.10 a default judgment cannot be obtained against a child or protected party except on an application to the court supported by evidence: r.12.11(3). It may be noted that the Practice Direction supplementing Pt.12 (Default Judgment) the Pt.12 Practice Direction states that a litigation friend must be appointed by the court (see r.21.6) before the claimant can obtain default judgment in these circumstances (Practice Direction (Obtaining Default Judgment) para.4.2).

Related sources

21.0.6

- Practice Direction (Children and Protected Parties), see para.21PD.1
- Part 8 (Alternative procedure for claims)
- Part 23 (General rules about applications for court orders)
- Rule 6.6 (Service of documents on children and protected parties)
- Rule 14.1(4) (Entering judgment on admission where party child or protected party)
- Rules 12.10 and 12.11 (Application for default judgment in claim against child or protected party)
- Rule 22.1(5)(6) (Statement of truth by litigation friend)
- Rule 39.2(3)(d) (Hearings in private to protect interests of child or protected party)
- Rule 48.5 (Costs where money is payable by or to a child or protected party)
- Vol.2, Section 6B (Court of Protection), paras 6B–1 *et seq.*
- Practice Direction (Obtaining Default Judgment), see para.12PD.1
- Practice Direction (Statement of Truth), para.3.1, see para.22PD.3
- Court of Protection Rules, see Vol.2, paras 6B–96 *et seq.*

Forms

21.0.7

- **N235** Certificate of suitability for litigation friend
- **N292** Court of Protection Form
- Court Funds Office **Form 200** and **Form 320**

Scope of this Part[1]

21.1—(1) This Part— 21.1

(a) contains special provisions which apply in proceedings involving children and protected parties;

(b) sets out how a person becomes a litigation friend.; and

(c) does not apply to proceedings under Part 75 where one of the parties to the proceedings is a child.

(2) In this Part—

(a) 'the 2005 Act' means the Mental Capacity Act 2005;

(b) 'child' means a person under 18;

(c) 'lacks capacity' means lacks capacity within the meaning of the 2005 Act;

(d) 'protected party' means a party, or an intended party, who lacks capacity to conduct the proceedings;

(e) 'protected beneficiary' means a protected party who lacks capacity to manage and control any money recovered by him or on his behalf or for his benefit in the proceedings.

(Rules 6.13 and 6.25 contains provisions about the service of documents on children and protected parties.)

(Rule 48.5 deals with costs where money is payable by or to a child or protected party.)

Note

See the Editorial introduction above. 21.1.1

Requirement for litigation friend in proceedings by or against children and protected parties[2]

21.2—(1) A protected party must have a litigation friend to conduct proceedings on his behalf. 21.2

(2) A child must have a litigation friend to conduct proceedings on his behalf unless the court makes an order under paragraph (3).

(3) The court may make an order permitting a child to conduct proceedings without a litigation friend.

(4) An application for an order under paragraph (3)—

(a) may be made by the child;

(b) if the child already has a litigation friend, must be made on notice to the litigation friend; and

(c) if the child has no litigation friend, may be made without notice.

(5) Where—

(a) the court has made an order under paragraph (3); and

(b) it subsequently appears to the court that it is desirable for a litigation friend to conduct the proceedings on behalf of the child,

the court may appoint a person to be the child's litigation friend.

[1] Introduced by the Civil Procedure (Amendment) Rules 2007 (SI 2007/2204) and amended by the Civil Procedure (Amendment) Rules 2008 (SI 2008/2178).

[2] Introduced by the Civil Procedure (Amendment) Rules 2007 (SI 2007/2204).

Effect of rule

21.2.1 A protected party must have a litigation friend to conduct proceedings on his behalf. Normally, a child should have a litigation friend but the court may make an order permitting him to conduct the proceedings himself, even if the child already has a litigation friend.

Any step taken before a child or protected party has a litigation friend, shall be of no effect, unless the court otherwise orders (r.21.3(4)): see further notes following r.21.3.

The meaning of conduct proceedings on his behalf is not elaborated in the rules but doubtless would include doing anything which in the ordinary conduct of any proceedings is required or authorised by a provision of the CPR to be done by a party to the proceedings. The duty of a litigation friend is no longer expressly defined as it was in the former Practice Direction supplementing this Part. However, the duty must be to fairly and competently conduct proceedings: see r.21.4(3)(a).

There is no requirement that a litigation friend must act by a solicitor in High Court proceedings.

The Official Solicitor will act on behalf of a child or protected party where there is no-one else able and willing to do so; see para.21.5.1.

Rule 3.1(2)(c) states that the court may require a party or a party's legal representative to attend court. Presumably, this extends to a litigation friend and his legal representative.

The requirement that a protected party have a litigation friend is unlikely to breach art.6(1): Cases 27436/95 and 28406/95 *Stewart-Brady v UK* (1997) 24 E.H.R.R. CD 38, ECtHR. See also *Ashingdane v UK* (1985) 7 E.H.H.R 528, ECtHR (statutory requirement for patient to obtain permission before commencing proceedings not an undue interference with art.6(1) right of access to a court).

The requirement that a child have a litigation friend save where the court orders otherwise is similarly unlikely to breach ECHR art.6(1): Case A/18 *Golder v UK* (1970-80) 1 E.H.H.R. 524, para.39, ECtHR. Note that in its report in Case 26494/95 *JT v UK* [2000] 1 F.L.R. 909, adopted on May 20, 1998, the EComHR held unanimously that the absence of any possibility for a patient to change her nearest relative on the ground of concerns about the identity of that person was a disproportionate interference with her rights under ECHR art.8.

Stage of proceedings at which a litigation friend becomes necessary[1]

21.3 **21.3—(1) This rule does not apply where the court has made an order under rule 21.2(3).**

(2) A person may not, without the permission of the court—

(a) make an application against a child or protected party before proceedings have started; or

(b) take any step in proceedings except—

(i) issuing and serving a claim form; or

(ii) applying for the appointment of a litigation friend under rule 21.6,

until the child or protected party has a litigation friend.

(3) If during proceedings a party lacks capacity to continue to conduct proceedings, no party may take any further step in the proceedings without the permission of the court until the protected party has a litigation friend.

(4) Any step taken before a child or protected party has a litigation friend has no effect unless the court orders otherwise.

[1] Introduced by the Civil Procedure (Amendment) Rules 2007 (SI 2007/2204).

Effect of rule

A claimant may issue and serve a claim form against a child or protected party who does not have a litigation friend; however, unless r.21.2(3) applies, he may take no further step in the proceedings without the permission of the court until a litigation friend has been appointed apart from applying to have an appointment made (should that be necessary). A step taken before a child or protected party has a litigation friend shall be of no effect, unless the court otherwise orders: r.21.3(4). **21.3.1**

Rule 21.3(4) allows the court to regularise the position retrospectively. Provided everyone has acted in good faith and there has been no manifest disadvantage to the party subsequently found to have been a protected party at the relevant time it is most unlikely that the court would refuse to regularise the position: see *Masterman-Lister v Brutton & Co* [2002] EWCA Civ 1889; [2003] 1 W.L.R. 1511; [2003] 3 All. E.R. 162, para.31. In that case the Court of Appeal observed that to do otherwise would be unjust and contrary to the overriding objective of the Civil Procedure Rules, "but in any given case the ultimate decision must depend on the particular facts. In the context of litigation Rules as to capacity are designed to ensure that claimants and defendants who would otherwise be at a disadvantage are properly protected, and in some cases that parties to litigation are not pestered by other parties who should be to some extent restrained. However finality in litigation is also important, and the Rules as to capacity are not designed to provide a vehicle for re-opening litigation which having apparently been properly conducted (whatever the wisdom of the individual decisions in relation to it) has for long been understood to be at an end."

Rule 21.3(2) is concerned with the situation where it is the defendant who is the child or protected party. It provides the necessary protection for the defendant child or protected party.

Generally, an additional claim is to be treated as if it were a claim for the purposes of the CPR, r.20(3)(1). Consequently, r.21.3 applies where an additional claim is brought against a child or protected party, for example, a counterclaim or a claim for an indemnity.

Party becoming a protected party during proceedings

Under r.21.3(3) where, after any proceedings have been begun, a party to the proceedings (whether as claimant, defendant or as a party in some other capacity) becomes a protected party, no party (including the party becoming a protected party) may take any step in the proceedings until the protected party has a litigation friend. However, pending the appointment of a litigation friend, further steps in the proceedings may be taken with the permission of the court. In these circumstances it is likely that the litigation friend will be appointed by the court upon an application being made by another party under r.21.6. **21.3.2**

It may be noted that r.3.10 states that, where there has been an error of procedure, such as a failure to comply with a rule or practice direction, the error does not invalidate any step taken in the proceedings unless the court so orders, and the court may make an order to remedy the error. This rule is of general application but should be read as subject to r.21.3(4).

Who may be a litigation friend without a court order[1]

21.4—(1) This rule does not apply if the court has appointed a person to be a litigation friend. **21.4**

(2) A deputy appointed by the Court of Protection under the 2005 Act with power to conduct proceedings on the protected party's behalf is entitled to be the litigation friend of the protected party in any proceedings to which his power extends.

(3) If nobody has been appointed by the court or, in the case of a protected party, has been appointed as a deputy as set out in paragraph (2), a person may act as a litigation friend if he—

(a) can fairly and competently conduct proceedings on behalf of the child or protected party;

[1] Introduced by the Civil Procedure (Amendment) Rules 2007 (SI 2007/2204).

(b) has no interest adverse to that of the child or protected party; and

(c) where the child or protected party is a claimant, undertakes to pay any costs which the child or protected party may be ordered to pay in relation to the proceedings, subject to any right he may have to be repaid from the assets of the child or protected party.

How a person becomes a litigation friend without a court order[1]

21.5 **21.5—(1) If the court has not appointed a litigation friend, a person who wishes to act as a litigation friend must follow the procedure set out in this rule.**

(2) A deputy appointed by the Court of Protection under the 2005 Act with power to conduct proceedings on the protected party's behalf must file an official copy^(GL) of the order of the Court of Protection which confers his power to act either—

(a) where the deputy is to act as a litigation friend for a claimant, at the time the claim is made; or

(b) where the deputy is to act as a litigation friend for a defendant, at the time when he first takes a step in the proceedings on behalf of the defendant.

(3) Any other person must file a certificate of suitability stating that he satisfies the conditions specified in rule 21.4(3) either—

(a) where the person is to act as a litigation friend for a claimant, at the time when the claim is made; or

(b) where the person is to act as a litigation friend for a defendant, at the time when he first takes a step in the proceedings on behalf of the defendant.

(4) The litigation friend must—

(a) serve the certificate of suitability on every person on whom, in accordance with rule 6.13 (service on a parent, guardian etc.), the claim form should be served; and

(b) file a certificate of service when filing the certificate of suitability.

(Rules 6.17 and 6.29 set out the details to be contained in a certificate of service.)

Effect of rules 21.4 and 21.5

21.5.1 For practice relevant to appointment of a litigation friend without order, see Practice Direction (Children and Protected Parties), para.2.

Neither of these rules applies if the court has already appointed a litigation friend or if the court has made an order under r.21.2(3) permitting a child to conduct proceedings without a litigation friend.

A litigation friend may be appointed by order of the court and in some instances a court order is necessary: see r.21.6. Rule 21.5 shows how a person may become a litigation friend (of either a claimant or a defendant) without a court order. Obviously, limits must be placed on the persons who may become a litigation friend without court order: r.21.4 imposes the necessary controls.

[1] Introduced by the Civil Procedure (Amendment) Rules 2007 (SI 2007/2204) and amended by the Civil Procedure (Amendment) Rules 2008 (SI 2008/2178).

The Mental Capacity Act 2005 provides for a system of deputies appointed by the Court of Protection; see ss.16, 19 and 20 of the 2005 Act. This replaces the system of receivership under the Mental Health Act 1983. A deputy may be enabled to make decisions on welfare, healthcare and financial matters as authorised by the Court of Protection. That court will decide the extent of the powers to be conferred on the deputy; s.16(5) of the 2005 Act. The power may extend to the conduct of legal proceedings on behalf of the person lacking capacity; see s.18(1)(k) of the 2005 Act. Those appointed as receivers before the 2005 Act came into force retain their powers concerning property and affairs and are to be treated as deputies; see s.66 of the 2005 Act.

A deputy appointed by the Court of Protection under the 2005 Act with power to conduct proceedings on the protected party's behalf is entitled to be the litigation friend of the protected party in any proceedings to which his power extends: r.21.4(2). Such a deputy is not required to file a certificate of suitability but must file an official copy of the order of the Court of Protection which confers his power to act; see r.21.5(2). Any other person wishing to act as litigation friend must file a certificate of suitability stating that he satisfies the conditions specified in r.21.4(3): see r.21.5(3) and para.2.2 of the Practice Direction.

It is to be noted that in cases involving a protected party it is not necessary to seek the appointment of a deputy to act a as litigation friend. Rule 21.4(3) allows any person to act as a litigation friend so long as that person satisfies the requirements of that rule. Indeed, the appointment of a deputy at the outset of litigation may often be premature and unnecessary. The Court of Protection will only appoint a deputy where an application is made to it for such an appointment and where there are assets to be administered or likely to be administered. In many cases there may be no such assets; e.g., judicial review proceedings and possession claims. The Official Solicitor will act on behalf of the protected party if there is no-one else able and willing to do so.

The certificate of suitability is in Practice Form **N235**. The certificate must be verified by a statement of truth and, in the case of a protected party, must state the grounds of belief that the person is a protected party and, if his belief is based upon medical opinion, attach any relevant documents to the certificate. Where the child or protected party is a claimant, the certificate must contain an undertaking to pay any costs which the child or protected party may be ordered to pay, subject to any right which he may have to be repaid from the assets of the child or the protected party; see r.21.4(3)(c) and para 2.2(e) of the Practice Direction. A deputy, not being required to file a certificate of suitability, gives no such undertaking. For termination of the costs liability see r.21.9(6).

As to costs where money is payable by or to a child or protected party; see r.48.5 and notes under r.21.10.

The proposed litigation friend must file and serve the certificate of suitability; see r.21.5(3) and (4) and file a certificate of service when he files the certificate of suitability. In the case of a protected party, there is no obligation to serve any medical report or relevant documentation with the certificate of suitability although such must be filed; see para 2.4 of the Practice Direction.

The court may, by order, direct that a person who wishes to act as a litigation friend and who follows the procedure stated in r.21.5 may not so act: r.21.7(1).

Rules 21.4 and 21.5 do not apply if the court has appointed a person to be a litigation friend. A court order is required to appoint a new litigation friend in substitution for an existing one: see r.21.7(1)(c).

Certificate of suitability

For form, see certificate of suitability of litigation friend: **N235**. **21.5.2**

How a person becomes a litigation friend by court order[1]

21.6—(1) The court may make an order appointing a litigation friend. **21.6**

(2) An application for an order appointing a litigation friend may be made by—

[1] Introduced by the Civil Procedure (Amendment) Rules 2007 (SI 2007/2204).

(a) a person who wishes to be the litigation friend; or

(b) a party.

(3) Where—

(a) a person makes a claim against a child or protected party;

(b) the child or protected party has no litigation friend;

(c) the court has not made an order under rule 21.2(3) (order that a child can conduct proceedings without a litigation friend); and

(d) either—

(i) someone who is not entitled to be a litigation friend files a defence; or

(ii) the claimant wishes to take some step in the proceedings,

the claimant must apply to the court for an order appointing a litigation friend for the child or protected party.

(4) An application for an order appointing a litigation friend must be supported by evidence.

(5) The court may not appoint a litigation friend under this rule unless it is satisfied that the person to be appointed satisfies the conditions in rule 21.4(3).

Effect of rule

21.6.1 This rule deals with how a person becomes a litigation friend by court order. In certain circumstances a person may act as a litigation friend without a court order so appointing him (see rr.21.4 and 21.5). Further, the court may make an order permitting a child to conduct proceedings without a litigation friend: r.21.2(3).

Rule 21.6(1) states the general proposition that the court may make an order appointing a litigation friend. An application of a court order may be made by (a) a person who wishes to be the litigation friend, or (b) a party: r.21(2). Rule 21.6(3) states the circumstances in which a party who is a claimant must make an application to the court for an order appointing a litigation friend for the child or protected party. Generally, a Pt.20 claim is to be treated as if it were a claim for the purposes of the CPR; r.20.3(1). Consequently, r.21.6(3) applies where a Pt.20 claim is brought against a child or protected party.

Rule 3.1(7) states that where the court has a power under the CPR to make an order (for example, the power to make an order appointing a litigation friend under r.21.6), that power includes a power to vary or revoke the order. For specific power to change a litigation friend and to prevent a person acting as a litigation friend, see r.21.7 below.

As nothing in r.21.6 provides otherwise, the court may exercise its powers under this rule of its own initiative (r.3.3(1)) but, in terms, the rule envisages the powers being exercised on application by the persons referred to in r.21.6(2).

Where the proposed protected party and the litigation friend both consent to the appointment of the latter, where there is adequate evidence to support the application and where there is no evidence suggesting that the application is anything but a bona fide one, the court should make the order sought: *Folks v Faizey* [2006] EWCA Civ 381; [2006] C.P. Rep 30.

The application

21.6.2 For practice relevant to appointment of a litigation friend by court order, see *Practice Direction (*Children and Protected Parties), para.3.

An application for an order appointing a litigation friend must be supported by evidence: r.21.6(4). The evidence in support must satisfy the court that the proposed litigation friend: (1) consents to act; (2) can fairly and competently conduct proceedings on behalf of the child or protected party; (3) has no interest adverse to that of the child or protected party, and (4) where the child or protected party is a claimant, undertakes to pay any costs which the child or protected party may be ordered to pay in relation to the proceedings, subject to any right he may have to be repaid from the assets of the child or protected party; see para.3.3 of the Practice Direction.

Where it is sought to appoint the Official Solicitor as the litigation friend, provision must be made for payment of his charges: para.3.4 of the Practice Direction.

For rules as to applications for court orders, see Pt.23 (General rules about applications for court orders) and note r.32.6 (Evidence in proceedings other than trial). The application notice must state what order is sought and state why it is sought (r.23.5).

The application must be served on every person on whom, in accordance with r.6.6, the claim form must be served. Where the application under r.21.6 is in respect of a protected party, the application must also be served on the protected party unless the court orders otherwise; see r.21.8(1) and (2). The implication is that the application must state, not only that a litigation friend should be appointed, but also propose that a particular person should be appointed. The court may appoint the person proposed or any other person: r.21.8(4).

Where, in the course of proceedings, a party wishes to relinquish his conduct of them and an application is made under r.21.6 for an order appointing a litigation friend to conduct the proceedings on his behalf, thought will need to be given to whether the other party should be served with a copy of the application notice. As the other party is not the person against whom the order is sought the court will need to consider, in the light of the facts of each case, whether there is any need to direct service on him. Although r.21.6(4) requires evidence in support of any application for an order appointing a litigation friend that does not mean that the other party to the litigation is entitled to put in evidence disputing the basis of such an order: see *Folks v Faizey* [2006] EWCA Civ 381; [2006] C.P. Rep. 30.

Court's power to change litigation friend and to prevent person acting as litigation friend[1]

21.7—(1) The court may— 21.7

(a) direct that a person may not act as a litigation friend;

(b) terminate a litigation friend's appointment; or

(c) appoint a new litigation friend in substitution for an existing one.

(2) An application for an order under paragraph (1) must be supported by evidence.

(3) The court may not appoint a litigation friend under this rule unless it is satisfied that the person to be appointed satisfies the conditions in rule 21.4(3).

Effect of rule

This rule deals with the court's power to change a litigation friend and to prevent a person acting as a litigation friend. The power is not restricted to circumstances in which a litigation friend has been appointed by court order, but extends also to circumstances in which he has become a litigation friend without a court order. The rule may apply, for example, where the litigation friend no longer wishes to act as such, or where the court finds it necessary to intervene because the litigation friend is unable to fairly and competently conduct the proceedings on behalf of the child or protected party. If a solicitor is acting for child or protected party, it is thought that he would be under an obligation to inform the court of any concern that the litigation friend was not acting properly. 21.7.1

The general rule is that, once a person has become a litigation friend (whether by court order or otherwise) his position may not be usurped by another. However, the court may make an order (a) directing that he may not act as a litigation friend, (b) terminating his appointment, (c) appointing a new litigation friend in substitution for him.

[1] Introduced by the Civil Procedure (Amendment) Rules 2007 (SI 2007/2204).

The court may exercise its powers under this rule of its own initiative: r.3.3(1).

The application

21.7.2 An application for an order under r.21.7 must be supported by evidence: r.21.7(2). In so far as the application the appointment of a new litigation friend, the evidence will have to satisfy para.3.3 of the Practice Direction; (see the note above under r.21.6).

(If the court is dissatisfied with the actions of a litigation friend it is not obvious who should provide the evidence in support of an application under r.21.7.)

The application must be served on every person on whom, in accordance with r.6.6, the claim form must be served: r,21.8(1). The application must also be served on: (a) the person who is the litigation friend, or who is purporting to act as the litigation friend, when the application is made; and (b) the person who it is proposed should be the litigation friend, if he is not the applicant: see r.21.8(3). The court may appoint the person proposed or any other person who satisfies the conditions specified in r.21.4(3).

Appointment of litigation friend by court order—supplementary[1]

21.8 **21.8—(1) An application for an order under rule 21.6 or 21.7 must be served on every person on whom, in accordance with rule 6.13 (service on parent, guardian etc.), the claim form must be served.**

(2) Where an application for an order under rule 21.6 is in respect of a protected party, the application must also be served on the protected party unless the court orders otherwise.

(3) An application for an order under rule 21.7 must also be served on—

- **(a) the person who is the litigation friend, or who is purporting to act as the litigation friend, when the application is made; and**
- **(b) the person who it is proposed should be the litigation friend, if he is not the applicant.**

(4) On an application for an order under rule 21.6 or 21.7, the court may appoint the person proposed or any other person who satisfies the conditions specified in rule 21.4(3).

Effect of rule

21.8.1 The provisions in this rule supplement two previous rules. See notes following rr.21.6 and 21.7.

Procedure where appointment of litigation friend ceases[2]

21.9 **21.9—(1) When a child who is not a protected party reaches the age of 18, the litigation friend's appointment ceases.**

(2) Where a protected party regains or acquires capacity to conduct the proceedings, the litigation friend's appointment continues until it is ended by court order.

(3) An application for an order under paragraph (2) may be made by—

- **(a) the former protected party;**
- **(b) the litigation friend; or**

[1] Introduced by the Civil Procedure (Amendment) Rules 2007 (SI 2007/2204) and amended by the Civil Procedure (Amendment) Rules 2008 (SI 2008/2178).

[2] Introduced by the Civil Procedure (Amendment) Rules 2007 (SI 2007/2204).

(c) a party.

(4) The child or protected party in respect of whom the appointment to act has ceased must serve notice on the other parties—

(a) stating that the appointment of his litigation friend to act has ceased;

(b) giving his address for service; and

(c) stating whether or not he intends to carry on the proceedings.

(5) If the child or protected party does not serve the notice required by paragraph (4) within 28 days after the day on which the appointment of the litigation friend ceases the court may, on application, strike out(GL) any claim brought by or defence raised by the child or protected party.

(6) The liability of a litigation friend for costs continues until—

(a) the person in respect of whom his appointment to act has ceased serves the notice referred to in paragraph (4); or

(b) the litigation friend serves notice on the parties that his appointment to act has ceased.

Effect of rule

For relevant practice, see Practice Direction (Children and Protected Parties), para.4. **21.9.1**

A protected party must have a litigation friend to conduct proceedings on his behalf and so must a child unless the court makes an order permitting a child to conduct proceedings without a litigation friend; see r.21.2. This rule deals with the situation when the requirement for a litigation friend has come to an end.

In terms, this rule speaks of an appointment as litigation friend ceasing. Strictly speaking, a person who became a litigation friend otherwise than by court order was not appointed as such. However, the rule applies whether the litigation friend has been acting under a court order or otherwise.

When a child who is not a protected party reaches the age of 18, the litigation friend's appointment ceases: r.21.9(1). This is automatic and no court order is required. The child must serve on the other parties to the proceedings and file with the court a notice: stating that he has reached full age; stating that his litigation friend's appointment has ceased, giving an address for service, and stating whether or not he intends to carry on with or continue to defend the proceedings: see r.21.9(4) and para.4.2 of the Practice Direction. Whether or not a child having reached full age serves a notice, a litigation friend may, at any time after the child has reached full age, serve a notice on the other parties that his appointment has ceased; para.4.4 of the Practice Direction.

In contrast to the child reaching the age of 18, where a protected party regains or acquires capacity to conduct the proceedings, the litigation friend's appointment continues until it is ended by court order: r.21.9(2). The provisions of Pt 23 (General rules about applications for court orders) apply; see, generally, the notes following r.21.6.

Paragraph 4.5 of the Practice Direction states that where a protected party regains or acquires capacity to conduct the proceedings, an application under r.21.9(3) must be made for an order under r.21.9(2) that the litigation friend's appointment has ceased. Although, an application for an order under para.(2) may be made by: the former protected party; the litigation friend; or a party (see r.21.9(3)), in practice in most cases the obligation to apply will lie with the litigation friend. The application must be supported by evidence, namely: a medical report or other suitably qualified expert's report indicating that the protected party has regained or acquired capacity to conduct the proceedings; a copy of any relevant order or declaration of the Court of Protection, and, if the application is made by the protected party, a statement whether or not he intends to carry on with or continue to defend the proceedings; see para.4.6 of the Practice Direction.

An order under r.21.9(2) must be served on the other parties to the proceedings. The former protected party must file with the court a notice: stating that his litigation friend's appointment has ceased; giving an address for service, and stating whether or not he intends to carry on with or continue to defend the proceedings; see r.21.9(4) and para.4.7 of the Practice Direction.

Rule 21.9(5) exposes the child or protected party who does not serve the notice required by r.21.9(4) to an application for an order striking out his claim or his defence.

The liability of the former litigation friend for costs ceases as provided by r.21.9(6). Thus, after the child has reached full age, the litigation friend may have an incentive to serve to serve notice that his appointment to act has ceased; see para.4.4 of the Practice Direction.

Compromise, etc. by or on behalf of child or protected party[1]

21.10 **21.10—(1) Where a claim is made—**

(a) by or on behalf of a child or protected party; or

(b) against a child or protected party,

no settlement, compromise or payment (including any voluntary interim payment) and no acceptance of money paid into court shall be valid, so far as it relates to the claim by, on behalf of or against the child or protected party, without the approval of the court.

(2) Where—

(a) before proceedings in which a claim is made by or on behalf of, or against, a child or protected party (whether alone or with any other person) are begun, an agreement is reached for the settlement of the claim; and

(b) the sole purpose of proceedings is to obtain the approval of the court to a settlement or compromise of the claim,

the claim must—

(i) be made using the procedure set out in Part 8 (alternative procedure for claims); and

(ii) include a request to the court for approval of the settlement or compromise.

(3) In proceedings to which Section II of Part 45 applies, the court will not make an order for detailed assessment of the costs payable to the child or protected party but will assess the costs in the manner set out in that Section.

(Rule 48.5 contains provisions about costs where money is payable to a child or protected party.)

Introduction

21.10.1 For relevant practice, see Practice Direction (Children and Protected Parties), paras 5 and 6.

It is to be noted that the rule is not confined to proceedings in which money is claimed and it applies, not only where a claim is made by or on behalf of a child or protected party, but also where it is made against a child or protected party.

Part 21 as substituted by the Civil Procedure (Amendment) Rules 2007 (SI 2007/2204) makes it clear that r.21.10(1) extends to voluntary interim payments; see also *para.1.2* of the Practice Direction supplementing Pt.25. This point is sometimes overlooked by practitioners.

---

[1] Introduced by the Civil Procedure (Amendment) Rules 2007 (SI 2007/2204).

Rules 21.10 and 21.11 and the Practice Direction provide a comprehensive code the objects of which are:

(a) To protect the interests of children and protected parties. This may involve protecting the child from any lack of skill or experience of their legal advisers which might lead to a settlement of a money claim for far less than it is worth; see: *Black v Yates* [1992] QB 526; 4 All E.R. 722. (claim by child dependants for compensation greater than amount awarded by a foreign court).

(b) To provide means by which a defendant may obtain a valid discharge from a child or protected party's claim. At common law a contract of compromise out of court does not bind such a claimant unless it can be proved to have been for his benefit. No prudent defendant would wish to take a risk on this point. A judgment in proceedings or an order approving a settlement of proceedings under r.10 does bind the claimant child or protected party and gives the defendant a discharge.

(c) To make sure that money recovered by or on behalf of a child or protected party is properly looked after and wisely applied. Rule 21.11 provides for the control of money recovered.

(d) To ensure that the interests of all dependants entitled to a possible share in the settlement are properly defined and protected; see para.7 of the Practice Direction. A judgment on or settlement in respect of a claim under the Fatal Accidents Act 1976 must be apportioned between the persons by or on whose behalf the claim has been brought; para.7.1 of the Practice Direction. As r.41.3A and Practice Form **N292** (Order on settlement on behalf of child or protected party) makes clear, there must also be an apportionment in relation to any claim under the Law Reform (Miscellaneous Provisions) Act 1934. Where a claim is brought on behalf of a dependent child or children, any settlement (including an agreement on a sum to be apportioned to a dependent child under the Fatal Accidents Act 1976) must be approved by the court; para.7.2 of the Practice Direction.

It is to be noted that r.48.5, which contains provisions about costs where money is payable to a child or protected party, gives further protection to such parties. The effect of the rule is that the court must order detailed assessment of the costs by a child or protected party to his solicitor, and must also carry out an assessment of the costs payable to the child or protected party in the proceedings, unless a default costs certificate has been issued in respect of those costs. Where costs are recovered from a paying party on behalf of a child or protected party, solicitors frequently waive any further claim for costs, in which case there is no need for a detailed assessment of the solicitor and client costs. Section 51 of the Costs Practice Direction sets out the circumstances in which detailed assessment need not be ordered; see r.48.5.1.

Effect of rule

The approval of the court is required whenever the compromise etc on behalf of the child or protected party is reached: r.21.10(1). **21.10.2**

Where compromise, etc. is reached before proceedings and the sole purpose of the proceedings is to obtain the approval of the court, the claim must be made using the procedure set out in Pt.8 and must include a request to the court for approval of the settlement or compromise: r.21.10(2). In addition, para.5 of the Practice Direction sets out the further information and material which must be provided to the court within the claim. The object is to ensure that the court has a comprehensive view of the case both in respect of liability and quantum and to ensure that the proposed compromise is appropriate. A draft consent order in Practice Form **N292** must be provided (para.5.1(1)) as must the litigation friend's approval of the proposed settlement of compromise (para.5.1(4)) and a copy of any financial advice relating the proposed settlement.

Where in any personal injury case a claim for damages for future pecuniary loss is settled, the court must be satisfied that the parties have considered whether the damages should wholly or partly take the form of periodical payments. Where the settlement includes provision for periodical payments, the claim must set out the terms of the settlement or compromise; or have attached to it a draft consent order, which must satisfy the requirements of rr.41.8 and 41.9 as appropriate; see paras 5.3–5.5.

Paragraph 5.2 of the Practice Direction states that an opinion on the merits of the settlement or compromise given by counsel or solicitor acting for the child or protected party must, except in very clear cases, be obtained. A copy of the opinion and unless the instructions on which it was given are sufficiently set out in it, a copy of the instructions, must be supplied to the court. The opinion is not disclosed to the opposing party.

Paragraph 6 of the Practice Direction deals with the position where the compromise is reached after proceedings have been commenced. An application must be made to for the court's approval of the agreement; see para.6.1. See Pt.23 (General Rules about Applications for Court Orders). The information and material required to be placed before the court under para.6 of the Practice Direction is less than under para.5. This can only be on the basis that it is assumed that the court would have much of the necessary material before it given that proceedings are already underway. It is submitted that if a compromise, etc. is reached after proceedings have commenced, paras 5 and 6 are best read together to ensure that the court has all the material necessary to make an informed judgment.

Paragraph 6 of the Practice Direction appears to be limited to the compromise of personal injury cases. However, r.21.10 extends to any type of case.

Applications for the approval of a settlement or compromise, except at the trial, will normally be heard by a Master or a district judge in proceedings involving a child; and a Master, designated civil judge or his nominee in proceedings involving a protected party; see paras 5.6 and 6.5 of the Practice Direction. On the basis that the word "normally" inparas 5.6 and 6.5 is intended to mean that the application for approval is usually heard by Master or district judge as opposed to a judge, the new Practice Direction has limited the jurisdiction of the district judge in relation to protected parties. It is to be noted that a child may be a protected party, in which case the district judge will not have jurisdiction.

Where the approval of a compromise etc on behalf of a protected party is sought under r.21.10, the decision whether or not to approve it is for the court to which the application is made. However, the court will have regard to any view expressed by the Court of Protection.

Note that where the litigation friend's expenses are not of a type which would be recoverable as costs on an assessment of costs between the parties, the litigation friend may make a claim for expenses under r.21.12(1) to the Master or district judge at the approval hearing. The Master or district judge may adjourn the matter to the costs judge; see para.11.1(2) of the Practice Direction.

For information about provisional damages and periodical payments under the Damages Act 1996 see; Pt.41 and the Practice Directions supplementing that Part.

Control of money recovered by or on behalf of child or protected party[1]

21.11 **21.11—(1) Where in any proceedings—**

(a) money is recovered by or on behalf of or for the benefit of a child or protected party; or

(b) money paid into court is accepted by or on behalf of a child or protected party,

the money will be dealt with in accordance with directions given by the court under this rule and not otherwise.

(2) Directions given under this rule may provide that the money shall be wholly or partly paid into court and invested or otherwise dealt with.

(3) Where money is recovered by or on behalf of a protected party or money paid into court is accepted by or on behalf of a protected party, before giving directions in accordance with this rule, the court will first consider whether the protected party is a protected beneficiary.

[1] Introduced by the Civil Procedure (Amendment) Rules 2007 (SI 2007/2204).

Effect of rule

For relevant practice and further information, see Practice Direction (Children and Protected Parties), paras 8 to 10. **21.11.1**

A "protected beneficiary" means a protected party who lacks capacity to manage and control any money recovered by him or on his behalf or for his benefit in the proceedings: r.21.1(e). The distinction in the rule between protected party and protected beneficiary underlines the point made in the 2005 Act that a person may lack capacity in some matters but not others.

Where a child also lacks capacity to manage and control any money recovered by him or on his behalf in the proceedings, and is likely to remain so on reaching full age, his fund should be administered as a protected beneficiary's fund; para.8.3 of the Practice Direction.

Investment on behalf of a child

Paragraph 9 of the Practice direction deals with the investment of damages on behalf of a child. **21.11.2**

Note that in relation to investment on behalf of a child, the CFO Form **320** which must be used (see para.9.1 of the Practice Direction) must be signed by the Litigation Friend and he must confirm that he is aware that if there are more than 5 years to majority and £5,000 or more to invest, part of the fund may be invested in Unit trusts or similar investment vehicles.

Paragraph 9.3 of the Practice Direction deals with the situation where the award for payment of damages for a child is made at trial. There has been a tendency by some practitioners to overlook making the application to the Master or district judge for further investment directions as directed by the trial judge. The object of Paragraph 9.3 in the new Practice Direction is to ensure that the Litigation Friend or practitioners do indeed make the application for further investment directions. The trial judge may direct that the application for further investment directions be fixed for a date within 28 days from the date of the trial.

If the money to be invested is very small the court may order it to be paid direct to the litigation friend to be put into a building society account (or similar) for the child's use; para.9.7 of the Practice Direction.

Discretionary and bare trusts for children

If the money is invested in court, it must be paid out to the child on application when he reaches full age; see paras 9.8 and 13.2 of the Practice Direction. It is often of great concern to litigation friends (usually parents) that their children should suddenly come into substantial funds on reaching the age of 18. However, the court has no choice but to release funds in court to the child on his reaching his majority. Accordingly, it has become more common for litigation friends to propose that the child's fund be paid into a trust to avoid this happening. Furthermore, trusts can confer fiscal advantages. **21.11.3**

If the fund is paid into a bare trust, the child is entitled to call for the fund to be paid out to him on his majority but the child would have the option to leave the fund in the trust. Indeed, upon reaching his majority, the child may elect to become a trustee and so be involved in the management of the fund while retaining the fiscal and state benefits advantages which the trust may confer. If the fund is in court, the court can only release the fund into a bare trust as the child is already absolutely entitled to the fund. Similarly, if the court has *already* given a judgment for a specific sum, that sum may only be held under a bare trust. The court has no power under r.21.11 to order or impose a discretionary trust on such monies. The court's powers are restricted to facilitating a bare trust which is essentially administrative in nature. However, the court may approve the establishment of a discretionary trust (which would permit the retention of the capital sum beyond the child's majority) provided that it does so *before* it gives judgment for the damages. This will require the co-operation of the defendant. An appropriate form of order might be:

> "The claimant may accept the sum of £x, such sum to be held, as agreed by the parties, on a discretionary trust as set out in Schedule A to this order, in full and final settlement of the claim."

In Fatal Accident cases, where apportionment between dependants is obligatory (see para.21.10.1 above); the apportioned sums belong to the dependants absolutely and cannot be made the subject of a discretionary trust.

Whether a bare trust or discretionary trust is proposed, the court would have to approve the terms of the trust deed and will almost invariably require that that one of the trustees is a professional trustee to ensure that the fund is properly supervised. In cases involving substantial sums the court will also wish to see that professional financial advice has been taken to ensure that there is an investment strategy in place which is in the child's best interests.

Investment on behalf of a protected beneficiary

21.11.4 Paragraph 10 of the Practice Direction deals with investment on behalf of a protected beneficiary.

The court (as opposed to the Court of Protection) will not invest the fund of a protected beneficiary unless it is under £30,000 in which case para.10.2(2) of the Practice Direction provides that it may be retained in court and invested in the same way as the fund of a child.

Paragraph 10.2(1) of the Practice Direction deals with the position where the sum to be administered for the benefit of the protected beneficiary is £30,000 or more. In this situation, the terms of the Practice Direction have been changed to accommodate changes brought about by the Mental Capacity Act 2005. Paragraph 10.2(1) provides that unless a person with authority as: (a) the attorney under a registered enduring power of attorney; (b) the donee of a lasting power of attorney; or (c) the deputy appointed by the Court of Protection, to administer or manage the protected beneficiary's financial affairs has been appointed, the order approving the settlement will contain a direction to the litigation friend to apply to the Court of Protection for the appointment of a deputy, after which the fund will be dealt with as directed by the Court of Protection.

The Mental Capacity Act 2005 allows a person to appoint an attorney to act on their behalf if they should lose capacity in the future (Lasting Powers of Attorney); see ss.9–14 of the 2005 Act. Such a power of attorney gives the attorney authority to make decisions about the donor's property and affairs and health and welfare. Before it can be used a lasting power of attorney must be registered with the Office of the Public Guardian. Enduring Powers of Attorney which existed before the 2005 Act came into force, can be registered after its coming into force but it will no longer be possible to create an enduring power of attorney. The need for registration of the enduring power of attorney and the lasting power of attorney is to be noted.

As to the deputy appointed by the Court of Protection, see the notes to rr.21.4 and 21.5.

Payments out of funds in court

21.11.5 See Paragraph 13 of the Practice Direction. Although the para.13.1 deals with the fund of a child, applications for payment out or to vary an investment strategy may be made in the same way where the fund is of a protected beneficiary held under para.10.2(2) of the Practice Direction.

Expenses incurred by a litigation friend[1]

21.12 **21.12—(1) In proceedings to which rule 21.11 applies, a litigation friend who incurs expenses on behalf of a child or protected party in any proceedings is entitled on application to recover the amount paid or payable out of any money recovered or paid into court to the extent that it—**

(a) has been reasonably incurred; and

(b) is reasonable in amount.

(2) Expenses may include all or part of—

(a) an insurance premium, as defined by rule 43.2(1)(m); or

(b) interest on a loan taken out to pay an insurance premium or other recoverable disbursement.

[1] Introduced by the Civil Procedure (Amendment) Rules 2007 (SI 2007/2204).

(3) No application may be made under the rule for expenses that—

(a) are of a type that may be recoverable on an assessment of costs payable by or out of money belonging to a child or protected party; but

(b) are disallowed in whole or in part on such an assessment.

(Expenses which are also 'costs' as defined in rule 43.2(1)(a) are dealt with under rule 48.5(2).)

(4) In deciding whether the expenses were reasonably incurred and reasonable in amount, the court will have regard to all the circumstances of the case including the factors set out in rule 44.5(3).

(5) When the court is considering the factors to be taken into account in assessing the reasonableness of the expenses, it will have regard to the facts and circumstances as they reasonably appeared to the litigation friend or to the child's or protected party's legal representative when the expense was incurred.

(6) Where the claim is settled or compromised, or judgment is given, on terms that an amount not exceeding £5,000 is paid to the child or protected party, the total amount the litigation friend may recover under paragraph (1) must not exceed 25% of the sum so agreed or awarded, unless the court directs otherwise. Such total amount must not exceed 50% of the sum so agreed or awarded.

Note

See para.11 of the Practice Direction. **21.12.1**

Appointment of guardian of child's estate[1]

21.13—(1) The court may appoint the Official Solicitor to be a guardian of a child's estate where— **21.13**

(a) money is paid into court on behalf of the child in accordance with directions given under rule 21.11 (control of money received by a child or protected party);

(b) the Criminal Injuries Compensation Authority notifies the court that it has made or intends to make an award to the child;

(c) a court or tribunal outside England and Wales notifies the court that it has ordered or intends to order that money be paid to the child;

(d) the child is absolutely entitled to the proceeds of a pension fund; or

(e) in any other case, such an appointment seems desirable to the court.

(2) The court may not appoint the Official Solicitor under this rule unless—

(a) the persons with parental responsibility (within the

[1] Introduced by the Civil Procedure (Amendment) Rules 2007 (SI 2007/2204).

meaning of section 3 of the Children Act 1989 [1]) agree; or

(b) the court considers that their agreement can be dispensed with.

(3) The Official Solicitor's appointment may continue only until the child reaches 18.

[1] 1989 c.41.

PRACTICE DIRECTION—CHILDREN AND PATIENTS

This Practice Direction supplements CPR Part 21

General

1.1 In proceedings where one of the parties is a protected party, the protected party should be referred to in the title to the proceedings as 'A.B. (a protected party by C.D. his litigation friend)'. **21PD.1**

1.2 In proceedings where one of the parties is a child, where—

(1) the child has a litigation friend, the child should be referred to in the title to the proceedings as 'A.B. (a child by C.D. his litigation friend)'; or

(2) the child is conducting the proceedings on his own behalf, the child should be referred to in the title as 'A.B. (a child)'.

1.3 A settlement of a claim by a child includes an agreement on a sum to be apportioned to a dependent child under the Fatal Accidents Act 1976 [1].

The litigation friend

2.1 A person may become a litigation friend: **21PD.2**

(a) without a court order under the provisions of rule 21.5, or

(b) by a court order under rule 21.6.

2.2 A person who wishes to become a litigation friend without a court order pursuant to rule 21.5(3) must file a certificate of suitability in Practice Form N235—

(a) stating that he consents to act,

(b) stating that he knows or believes that the [claimant] [defendant] [is a child][lacks capacity to conduct the proceedings],

(c) in the case of a protected party, stating the grounds of his belief and, if his belief is based upon medical opinion or the opinion of another suitably qualified expert, attaching any relevant document to the certificate,

(d) stating that he can fairly and competently conduct proceedings on behalf of the child or protected party and has no interest adverse to that of the child or protected party, and

(e) where the child or protected party is a claimant, undertaking to pay any costs which the child or protected party may be ordered to pay in relation to the proceedings, subject to any right he may have to be repaid from the assets of the child or protected party.

2.3 The certificate of suitability must be verified by a statement of truth. (Part 22 contains provisions about statements of truth.)

2.4 The litigation friend is not required to serve the document referred to in paragraph 2.2(c) when he serves a certificate of suitability on the person to be served under rule 21.5(4)(a).

Application for a court order appointing a litigation friend

3.1 Rule 21.6 sets out who may apply for an order appointing a litigation friend. **21PD.3**

---

[1] 1976 c.30.

3.2 An application must be made in accordance with Part 23 and must be supported by evidence.

3.3 The evidence in support must satisfy the court that the proposed litigation friend—

(1) consents to act,

(2) can fairly and competently conduct proceedings on behalf of the child or protected party,

(3) has no interest adverse to that of the child or protected party, and

(4) where the child or protected party is a claimant, undertakes to pay any costs which the child or protected party may be ordered to pay in relation to the proceedings, subject to any right he may have to be repaid from the assets of the child or protected party.

3.4 Where it is sought to appoint the Official Solicitor as the litigation friend, provision must be made for payment of his charges.

Procedure where the need for a litigation friend has come to an end

21PD.4 **4.1** Rule 21.9 deals with the situation where the need for a litigation friend comes to an end during the proceedings because either—

(1) a child who is not also a protected party reaches the age of 18 (full age) during the proceedings, or

(2) a protected party regains or acquires capacity to conduct the proceedings.

4.2 A child on reaching full age must serve on the other parties to the proceedings and file with the court a notice

(1) stating that he has reached full age,

(2) stating that his litigation friend's appointment has ceased,

(3) giving an address for service, and

(4) stating whether or not he intends to carry on with or continue to defend the proceedings.

4.3 If the notice states that the child intends to carry on with or continue to defend the proceedings he must subsequently be described in the proceedings as 'A.B. (formerly a child but now of full age)'.

4.4 Whether or not a child having reached full age serves a notice in accordance with rule 21.9(4) and paragraph 4.2 above, a litigation friend may at any time after the child has reached full age serve a notice on the other parties that his appointment has ceased.

4.5 Where a protected party regains or acquires capacity to conduct the proceedings, an application under rule 21.9(3) must be made for an order under rule 21.9(2) that the litigation friend's appointment has ceased.

4.6 The application must be supported by the following evidence—

(1) a medical report or other suitably qualified expert's report indicating that the protected party has regained or acquired *capacity* to conduct the proceedings,

(2) a copy of any relevant order or declaration of the Court of Protection, and

(3) if the application is made by the protected party, a state-

ment whether or not he intends to carry on with or continue to defend the proceedings.

4.7 An order under rule 21.9(2) must be served on the other parties to the proceedings. The protected party must file with the court a notice:

(1) stating that his litigation friend's appointment has ceased,
(2) giving an address for service, and
(3) stating whether or not he intends to carry on with or continue to defend the proceedings.

Settlement or compromise by or on behalf of a child or protected party before the issueof proceedings

5.1 Where a claim by or on behalf of a child or protected party has been dealt with by agreement before the issue of proceedings and only the approval of the court to the agreement is sought, the claim must, in addition to containing the details of the claim and satisfying the requirements of rule 21.10(2), include the following— **21PD.5**

(1) subject to paragraph 5.3, the terms of the settlement or compromise or have attached to it a draft consent order in Practice Form N292;
(2) details of whether and to what extent the defendant admits liability;
(3) the age and occupation (if any) of the child or protected party;
(4) the litigation friend's approval of the proposed settlement or compromise,
(5) a copy of any financial advice relating to the proposed settlement; and
(6) in a personal injury case arising from an accident—
   (a) details of the circumstances of the accident,
   (b) any medical reports,
   (c) where appropriate, a schedule of any past and future expenses and losses claimed and any other relevant information relating to the personal injury as set out in the practice direction which supplements Part 16 (statements of case), and
   (d) where considerations of liability are raised—
      (i) any evidence or reports in any criminal proceedings or in an inquest, and
      (ii) details of any prosecution brought.

5.2(1) An opinion on the merits of the settlement or compromise given by counsel or solicitor acting for the child or protected party must, except in very clear cases, be obtained.

(2) A copy of the opinion and, unless the instructions on which it was given are sufficiently set out in it, a copy of the instructions, must be supplied to the court.

5.3 Where in any personal injury case a claim for damages for future pecuniary loss is settled, the provisions in paragraphs 5.4 and 5.5 must in addition be complied with.

5.4 The court must be satisfied that the parties have considered whether the damages should wholly or partly take the form of periodical payments.

5.5 Where the settlement includes provision for periodical payments, the claim must—

(1) set out the terms of the settlement or compromise; or

(2) have attached to it a draft consent order,

which must satisfy the requirements of rules 41.8 and 41.9 as appropriate.

5.6 Applications for the approval of a settlement or compromise will normally be heard by—

(1) a Master or a district judge in proceedings involving a child; and

(2) a Master, designated civil judge or his nominee in proceedings involving a protected party.

(For information about provisional damages claims see Part 41 and the practice direction which supplements it.)

Settlement or compromise by or on behalf of a child or protected party after proceedings have been issued

21PD.6 **6.1** Where in any personal injury case a claim for damages for future pecuniary loss, by or on behalf of a child or protected party, is dealt with by agreement after proceedings have been issued, an application must be made for the court's approval of the agreement.

6.2 The court must be satisfied that the parties have considered whether the damages should wholly or partly take the form of periodical payments.

6.3 Where the settlement includes provision for periodical payments, an application under paragraph 6.1 must—

(1) set out the terms of the settlement or compromise; or

(2) have attached to it a draft consent order,

which must satisfy the requirements of rules 41.8 and 41.9 as appropriate.

6.4 The court must be supplied with—

(1) an opinion on the merits of the settlement or compromise given by counsel or solicitor acting for the child or protected party, except in very clear cases; and

(2) a copy of any financial advice.

6.5 Applications for the approval of a settlement or compromise, except at the trial, will normally be heard by—

(1) a Master or a district judge in proceedings involving a child; and

(2) a Master, designated civil judge or his nominee in proceedings involving a protected party.

Apportionment under the Fatal Accidents Act 1976

21PD.7 **7.1** A judgment on or settlement in respect of a claim under the *Fatal Accidents Act 1976* must be apportioned between the persons by or on whose behalf the claim has been brought.

7.2 Where a claim is brought on behalf of a dependent child or children, any settlement (including an agreement on a sum to be apportioned to a dependent child under the Fatal Accidents Act 1976) must be approved by the court.

7.3 The money apportioned to any dependent child must be invested on the child's behalf in accordance with rules 21.10 and 21.11 and paragraphs 8 and 9 below.

7.4 In order to approve an apportionment of money to a dependent child, the court will require the following information:

(1) the matters set out in paragraphs 5.1(2) and (3), and

(2) in respect of the deceased—

(a) where death was caused by an accident, the matters set out in paragraphs 5.1(6)(a), (b) and (c), and

(b) his future loss of earnings, and

(3) the extent and nature of the dependency.

Control of money recovered by or on behalf of a child or protected party

8.1 When giving directions under rule 21.11, the court— **21PD.8**

(1) may direct the money to be paid into court for investment,

(2) may direct that certain sums be paid direct to the child or protected beneficiary, his litigation friend or his legal representative for the immediate benefit of the child or protected beneficiary or for expenses incurred on his behalf, and

(3) may direct that the application in respect of the investment of the money be transferred to a local district registry.

8.2 The court will consider the general aims to be achieved for the money in court (the fund) by investment and will give directions as to the type of investment.

8.3 Where a child also lacks capacity to manage and control any money recovered by him or on his behalf in the proceedings, and is likely to remain so on reaching full age, his fund should be administered as a protected beneficiary's fund.

8.4 Where a child or protected beneficiary is in receipt of publicly funded legal services the fund will be subject to a first charge under section 10 of the Access to Justice Act 1999 [1] (statutory charge) and an order for the investment of money on the child's or protected beneficiary's behalf must contain a direction to that effect.

Investment on behalf of a child

9.1 At the hearing of an application for the approval of a settlement or compromise the litigation friend or his legal representative must provide, in addition to the information required by paragraphs 5 and 6— **21PD.9**

(1) a *CFO form* 320 (initial application for investment of damages) for completion by the judge hearing the application; and

(2) any evidence or information which the litigation friend wishes the court to consider in relation to the investment of the award for damages.

[1] 1999 c.22.

9.2 Following the hearing in paragraph 9.1, the court will forward to the Court Funds Office a request for investment decision (form 212) and the Public Trustee's investment managers will make the appropriate investment.

9.3 Where an award for damages for a child is made at trial, unless paragraph 9.7 applies, the trial judge will

(1) direct the money to be paid into court and placed into the special investment account until further investment directions have been given by the court;

(2) direct the litigation friend to make an application to a Master or district judge for further investment directions; and

(3) give such other directions as the trial judge thinks fit, including a direction that the hearing of the application for further investment directions will be fixed for a date within 28 days from the date of the trial.

9.4 The application under paragraph 9.3(2) must be made by filing with the court—

(1) a completed CFO form 320; and

(2) any evidence or information which the litigation friend wishes the court to consider in relation to the investment of the award for damages.

9.5 The application must be sent in proceedings in the Royal Courts of Justice to the Masters' Support Unit (Room E16) at the Royal Courts of Justice.

9.6 If the application required by paragraph 9.3(2) is not made to the court, the money paid into court in accordance with paragraph 9.3(1) will remain in the special investment account subject to any further order of the court or paragraph 9.8.

9.7 If the money to be invested is very small the court may order it to be paid direct to the litigation friend to be put into a building society account (or similar) for the child's use.

9.8 If the money is invested in court, it must be paid out to the child on application when he reaches full age.

Investment on behalf of a protected beneficiary

21PD.10 **10.1** The Court of Protection has jurisdiction to make decisions in the best interests of a protected beneficiary. Fees may be charged for the administration of funds and these must be provided for in any settlement.

10.2 Where the sum to be administered for the benefit of the protected beneficiary is—

(1) £30,000 or more, unless a person with authority as

(a) the attorney under a registered enduring power of attorney;

(b) the donee of a lasting power of attorney; or

(c) the deputy appointed by the Court of Protection, to *administer* or manage the protected beneficiary's financial affairs has been appointed, the order approving the settlement will contain a direction to the litigation friend to apply to the Court of Protection for the appointment of a deputy, after which the fund will be dealt with as directed by the Court of Protection; or

(2) under £30,000, it may be retained in court and invested in the same way as the fund of a child.

10.3 A form of order transferring the fund to the Court of Protection is set out in practice form N292.

10.4 In order for the Court Funds Office to release a fund which is subject to the statutory charge, the litigation friend or his legal representative or the person with authority referred to in paragraph 10.2(1) must provide the appropriate regional office of the Legal Services Commission with an undertaking in respect of a sum to cover their costs, following which the regional office will advise the Court Funds Office in writing of that sum, enabling them to transfer the balance to the Court of Protection on receipt of a CFO form 200 payment schedule authorised by the court.

10.5 The CFO form 200 should be completed and presented to the court where the settlement or trial took place for authorisation, subject to paragraphs 10.6 and 10.7.

10.6 Where the settlement took place in the Royal Courts of Justice the CFO form 200 must be completed and presented for authorisation—

(1) on behalf of a child, in the Masters' Support Unit, Room E105, and

(2) on behalf of a protected beneficiary, in the Judgment and Orders Section in the Action Department, Room E17.

10.7 Where the trial took place in the Royal Courts of Justice, the CFO form 200 is completed and authorised by the court officer.

Expenses incurred by a litigation friend

11.1 A litigation friend may make a claim for expenses under rule 21.12(1) **21PD.11**

(1) where the court has ordered an assessment of costs under rule 48.5(2), at the detailed assessment hearing;

(2) where the litigation friend's expenses are not of a type which would be recoverable as costs on an assessment of costs between the parties, to the Master or district judge at the hearing to approve the settlement or compromise under Part 21 (the Master or district judge may adjourn the matter to the costs judge); or

(3) where an assessment of costs under Part 48.5(2) is not required, and no approval under Part 21 is necessary, by a Part 23 application supported by a witness statement to a costs judge or district judge as appropriate.

11.2 *In all circumstances*, the litigation friend must support a claim for expenses by filing a witness statement setting out—

(1) the nature and amount of the expense; and

(2) the reason the expense was incurred.

Guardian's accounts

12.1 Paragraph 8 of the practice direction supplementing Part 40 (Judgments and Orders) deals with the approval of the accounts of a guardian of assets of a child. **21PD.12**

Payment out of funds in court

21PD.13 **13.1** Applications to a Master or district judge—

(1) for payment out of money from the fund for the benefit of the child, or

(2) to vary an investment strategy,

may be dealt with without a hearing unless the court directs otherwise.

13.2 When the child reaches full age—

(1) where his fund in court is a sum of money, it will be paid out to him on application; or

(2) where his fund is in the form of investments other than money (for example shares or unit trusts), the investments will on application be—

(a) sold and the proceeds of sale paid out to him; or

(b) transferred into his name.

13.3 Where the fund is administered by the Court of Protection, any payment out of money from that fund must be in accordance with any decision or order of the Court of Protection.

13.4 If an application is required for the payment out of money from a fund administered by the Court of Protection, that application must be made to the Court of Protection.

(For further information on payments out of court, see the practice direction supplementing Part 37.)

PART 22

STATEMENTS OF TRUTH

CPR 22

Contents

Editorial introduction

Originally, r.22.1 stated that any statement of case (formerly "pleadings"), a response complying with an order under r.18.1 to provide further information, and any witness statement must be verified by a statement of truth. Subsequently, other particular documents were added to the list. Certain other documents, not mentioned in r.22.1, also may or must be verified by a statements of truth (e.g. an notice of application) (see further notes following r.22.1). Pt 22 is supplemented by Practice Direction (Statements of Truth) (see 22PD.1). This Practice Direction is modified by the Practice Direction supplementing r.7.10. Some other practice directions also refer to statements of truth. 22.0.2

In certain circumstances, a false statement made in a document verified by statement of truth may lead to a liability for contempt of court (see further notes following r.22.1).

The justification for the requirement that a witness statement should be verified is obvious; it provides some guarantee that the statement is made with an honest belief as to the accuracy of its contents. There are two justifications for the requirement that a statement of case should be verified. First, if a party is required to certify his belief in the accuracy and truth of the matters put forward the statement of case is less likely to include assertions that are speculative and fanciful and designed to obfuscate (Interim Report at p.161). Secondly, in certain circumstances, a statement of case may be relied on as evidence. If it is to be used as such it is right that the facts asserted in it should be verified. The same can be said of facts asserted in a notice of application.

To an extent, the pleader's scope for prevarication and obfuscation, and for pleading alternative positions that may come perilously close to flat contradictions, is restricted by the verification requirement in r.22.1. The rule falls short of requiring the claimant to verify his statement of case by affidavit.

Rules 22.2 and 22.3 explain the consequences which may follow from a failure to verify any statement of case or witness statement and r.22.4 sets out the court's power to require a document to be verified.

Related sources

22.0.3

- Practice Direction (Statements of Truth) (see para.22PD.1)
- Rule 5.3 (Signature on documents by mechanical means)
- Rule 8.2 (contents of claim form where Pt 8 procedure used)
- Rule 16.2(1) (Contents of claim form)
- Rule 16.5 (Contents of defence)
- Rule 16.7 (Reply to defence)
- Rule 31.10(6) (Duty to disclose certification)
- Rule 31.23 (False disclosure statements)
- Rule 32.8 (Form of witness statement)
- Rule 32.14 (False statements)
- Rule 54.30 (Application to extend time limit)
- Rule 66.3 (Action on behalf of the Crown)
- Part 17 (Amendments to statements of case)
- Part 18 (Further information)

- Part 20 (Counterclaims, etc.)
- Part 21 (Children and patients)
- Practice Direction (How to Start Proceedings), para.7 (see para.7PD.7)
- Practice Direction (Statements of Case), para.11 (see para.16PD.11)
- Practice Direction (Defence and Reply), para.2 (see para.15PD.2)
- Practice Direction (Counterclaims and Other Part 20 Claims), para.4.1 (see para.20PD.4)
- Practice Direction (Further Information), para.3 (see para.18PD.3)
- Practice Direction (Experts and Assessors) (see para.35PD.1)
- Practice Direction (Judgments and Orders) (see para.40BPD.1)
- Practice Direction (Appeals), para.5.23 (see para.52PD.27)
- Practice Direction (Admiralty), para.4.2(3) (see Vol.2, para.2D–95)
- Practice Direction (Court Documents), para.1 (Signature of documents by mechanical means) (see para.5PD.1)
- Practice Direction (Electronic Communication and Filing of Documents), para.9 (Statement of truth in documents filed electronically) (see para.5BPD.9)
- Practice Direction (Production Centre), para.1.4(4) (Modification of Pt 22) (see para.7CPD.1)
- Practice Direction (Money Claim Online), paras 9 and 10 (Statement of truth and signature) (see paras 7EPD.11 and 7EPD.12)
- Practice Direction (Possession Claims Online), paras 8 and 9 (Statement of truth and signature) (see paras 55BPD.8 and 55BPD.9)

Documents to be verified by a statement of truth

22.1 **22.1—(1) The following documents must be verified by a statement of truth—**

(a) a statement of case;

(b) a response complying with an order under rule 18.1 to provide further information;

(c) a witness statement;

(d) an acknowledgment of service in a claim begun by way of the Part 8 procedure;

(e) a certificate stating the reasons for bringing a possession claim or a landlord and tenant claim in the High Court in accordance with rules 55.3(2) and 56.2(2);

(f) a certificate of service; and

(g) any other document where a rule or practice direction requires.

(2) Where a statement of case is amended, the amendments must be verified by a statement of truth unless the court orders otherwise.

(Part 17 provides for amendments to statements of case).

(3) If an applicant wishes to rely on matters set out in his application notice as evidence, the application notice must be verified by a statement of truth.

(4) Subject to paragraph (5), a statement of truth is a statement that—

(a) the party putting forward the document;

(b) in the case of a witness statement, the maker of the witness statement; or

(c) in the case of a certificate of service, the person who signs the certificate,

believes the facts stated in the document are true.

(5) If a party is conducting proceedings with a litigation friend, the statement of truth in—

(a) a statement of case;

(b) a response; or

(c) an application notice,

is a statement that the litigation friend believes the facts stated in the document being verified are true.

(6) The statement of truth must be signed by—

(a) in the case of a statement of case, a response or an application—

(i) the party or litigation friend; or

(ii) the legal representative on behalf of the party or litigation friend; and

(b) in the case of a witness statement, the maker of the statement.

(7) A statement of truth which is not contained in the document which it verifies, must clearly identify that document.

(8) A statement of truth in a statement of case may be made by—

(a) a person who is not a party; or

(b) by two parties jointly,

where this is permitted by a relevant practice direction.

Effect of rule

Whether or not rules of court require it, the court has a general power to order that a document should be verified by a witness statement or affidavit (r.32.1(1)(c)). Rule 22.1 states that, without any order being made by the court, certain documents should be verified by "a statement of truth". **22.1.1**

Documents required to be verified by a statement of truth are listed in r.22.1(1) but, as is acknowledged there, the list is not exhaustive. Paragraph 1.1 of Practice Direction (Statements of Truth), the practice direction supplementing this Part, repeats the list of documents given in r.22.1(1) and states that some other documents also should be verified (paras 1.2 to 1.4) (see para.22PD.1 below).

In some other parts of the CPR provisions are found repeating what is said in r.22.1(1) and in paras 1.1 to 1.4 of the practice direction. For example, the requirement that an expert's report should be verified is found, not only in para.1.3 of the practice direction supplementing Pt 22, but also in Practice Direction (Experts and Assessors) para.2.3 (see para.35PD.2) below. Practitioners have to be alert to the fact that where this duplication occurs the several provisions have to be read together if the detailed requirements (e.g. as to the form of the statement of truth) concerning the particular document are to be fully understood.

It cannot be assumed that each and every document that should be verified by a statement of truth is referred to either in r.22.1(1) or in the practice direction supplementing Pt 22. Rules and practice directions outwith Pt 22 may require verification (see r.22.1(f)). For example, Practice Direction (Appeals) states that, where an application is made under CPR,r.6.9 by an appellant for an order dispensing with the requirement for service on a respondent of the notice of appeal, the application notice should be verified by a statement of truth (para.52PD.30 below). Further, some other provisions, whilst not requiring verification by a statement of truth, may permit it as an alternative to verification by other means. For example, Practice Direction (Accounts, Inquiries etc.) para.3.3 permits such verification of a notice of objections to an account being taken by the court (para.40PD.3 below).

Provisions requiring the verification of particular documents by statements of truth are also found in rules and practice directions not forming part of the CPR. For example, Practice Direction (Insolvency Proceedings) paras 16A.5, 16A.9, 16A.21 and 16A.26 (Vol.2, para.3E–1 below).

The verification of a document by a statement of truth should be distinguished from the certification of matters contained in a document or of circumstances surrounding the creation of a document. CPR provisions requiring certification include r.31.10 (Procedure for standard disclosure) which provides that a list of documents provided by a party must include a "disclosure statement" (see also Practice Direction (Disclosure and Inspection), para.4.1 and Annex, paras 31PD.1 and 31PD.9 below). Amongst other things, that statement must certify that the party understands the duty to disclose documents.

Where a document, which would otherwise "have to be verified by a statement of truth, is prepared in a form which includes a jurat for the content to be verified by an affidavit, then a statement of truth is not required in addition (Practice Direction (Statement of Truth), para.1.6 (see para.22PD.1 below).

In the case of documents required to be verified by r.22.1, the statement of truth is made by the person (or persons, see r.22.1(8)) referred to in r.22.1(6) as appropriate and is to the effect that he believes that the facts stated are true (r.22.1(4)). If the statement of truth is not contained in the document which it verifies, it must clearly identify that document (r.22.1(7)) in the manner provided by Practice Direction (Statement of Truth), para.2.3 (see 22PD.2).

For appropriate form of statement of truth, see para.22.1.16 "Form of Statement of Truth" below; and para.22.1.17 "Statement of truth in document filed by e-mail".

Rule 5.3 states that, where it is required that "a document" should be signed, the signature may be "printed by computer or other mechanical means". It would seem that this does not apply to statements of truth because a statement of truth is not "a document" but a statement in a document.

In Practice Direction (Money Claim Online), one of the practice directions supplementing CPR Pt 7, it is provided that certain types of county court claim may be started by requesting the issue of claim forms electronically through the Court Service website. For obvious reasons, special provision is made for the verification of claim forms and defences filed by e-mail under this pilot scheme. Paragraph 8.3 states that r.22.1(6) is satisfied if the person verifying the document types his name underneath the statement of truth.

Paragraphs (d) and (e) were added by the Civil Procedure (Amendment No.3) Rules 2001 (SI 2001/1769) rr.3 and 4 with effect, respectively from May 31, 2001 and October 15, 2001 (when Pts 55 and 56 also came into effect). Paragraph (f) was added by the Civil Procedure (Amendment No.5) Rules 2001 (SI 2001/4015). Paragraph (g) was added by the Civil Procedure (Amendment No.4) Rules 2004 (SI 2004/3419).

Statement of case

22.1.2 A "statement of case" is one of the documents which, under the provisions of this Part, "must be verified by a statement of truth" (r.22.1(1)). In Admiralty proceedings, a claim form in limitation proceedings must be accompanied by a declaration and sworn as an affidavit (Practice Direction (Admiralty) para.9.1 (see Vol.2, para.2D–92). (For former law as to signing of pleadings, see RSC O.18, r.6(5) and CCR O.50, r.6A). A "statement of truth" is a statement that "the party putting forward the document" believes the facts stated in the document are true (r.22.1(4)).

The purpose of requiring statements of case (or amendments thereof) to be verified by statements of truth is to eliminate claims in which a party has no honest belief and to discourage the pleading of cases unsupported by evidence which were put forward in the hope that something might turn up on disclosure or at trial (*Clarke v Marlborough Fine Art (London) Ltd*, *The Times*, December 4, 2001 (Patten J.)) (see also para.22.0.2 above). One consequence of the fact that, since the coming into effect of the CPR, statements of case must be verified by a statement of truth is that the court's traditional reluctance to grant declarations of invalidity in patent claims without a full investigation of the facts is less strong (*Lever Faberge Ltd v Colgate-Palmolive Ltd* [2005] EWHC 2655 (Pat), November 10, 2005, unrep. (Lewison J.)).

The statement of truth verifying a statement of case must be signed by either the party or the legal representative on behalf of the party (r.22.1(6)). In either event, it is the party, and not the legal representative, who is "putting forward the document". Where a party is conducting proceedings with a litigation friend (see Pt 21 (Children and Patients), the statement of truth is a statement that the litigation friend believes the facts stated are true (r.22.1(5)(a)) and must be signed by him or his legal representative (r.22.1(6)(a)). However, the purpose and effect of r.22.1(1)(a) is not to exclude the possibility of pleading inconsistent factual alternatives in all cases. The provision does not prevent a party from submitting or amending a pleading which includes an allegation which he is not putting forward as the truth, provided there is an evidential basis for it, and it would not be consistent with the overriding objective to permit that rule to relieve a defendant of liability in a personal injuries claim where his own evidence establishes a cause of action against him (*Binks v Securicor Omega Express Ltd* [2003] EWCA Civ 993; July 16, 2003, unrep., CA, see also *Kelly v Chief Constable of South Yorkshire Police* [2001] EWCA Civ 1632).

A "statement of case" is one or other of the following documents (see r.2.3(1)): (1) a claim form, including a claim form used under the Pt 8 procedure, (2) particulars of claim where these are not included in a claim form, (3) a defence, (4) a Part 20 claim; or (5) a reply to defence. (A statement of case, also includes "further information" given in relation to any of these documents, see further below).

Note Practice Direction (How to Start Proceedings), para.7 (see para.7PD.7) and Practice Direction (Statements of Case), para.11 (see para.16PD.11).

Schedule of expenses and losses

By an addition made to the practice direction supplementing this Part in September 2003, and coming into effect on December 8, 2003, it was provided (in para.1.4(3)) that a document in the form of a schedule or counter-schedule of expenses and losses in a personal injury claim, and any amendments to such a schedule or counter-schedule, whether or not they are contained in a statement of case, must be verified by a statement of truth (see para.22PD.1 below). **22.1.2.1**

Claim form

Rule 16.2(1) states that the claim form must contain: (a) a concise statement of the nature of the claim; (b) specify the remedy which the claimant seeks; (c) where the claimant is making a claim for money, containing a statement of value in accordance with r.16.3; and (d) contain such other matters as may be set out in a practice direction. Particulars of claim must be contained in or served with the claim form (r.7.4(1), but in certain circumstances may be served subsequently (r.7.4(2)). Rule 16.4 states that the particulars of claim must include, amongst other things, "a concise statement of the facts on which the claimant relies". As a practical matter, the signficance of the particulars being verified by a statement of truth is confined to this "concise statement of the facts" in the particulars of claim, whether contained in the claim form or served separately. **22.1.3**

Rule 8.5 states that, under the alternative procedure for claims set out in Pt 8, a claimant must file any "written evidence" on which he intends to rely when he files his claim form. A claimant may rely on the matters set out in his claim form as evidence under that rule if the claim form is verified by a statement of truth (r.8.5(7)). Where the Pt 8 procedure is being used, the claim form must state the matters set out in r.8.2.

Defence

Rule 16.5 states that, in his defence, a defendant must state: (a) which of the allegations in the particulars of claim he denies; (b) which allegations he is unable to admit or deny, but which he requires the claimant to prove; and (c) which allegations he admits; further, (d) where he denies an allegation he must state his reasons for doing so and, (e) if he intends to put forward a different version of events from that given by the claimant, he must state his own version. As a practical matter, the significance of the defence being verified by a statement of truth is confined to the defendant's own "version of events". **22.1.4**

Note Practice Direction (Defence and Reply), para.2 (see para.15PD.2).

Part 20 claim

A Pt 20 claim is defined in r.20.2(1) and includes a counterclaim, a claim against a third party and similar claims. By r.20.2(1), a Pt 20 claim, generally, is to be started as if it were a claim. This provision, together with the inclusion of Pt 20 claims in the definition of a "statement of case" (r.2.3(2)), makes it clear that any statement of case generated under Pt 20 must be verified. **22.1.5**

See further Practice Direction (Counterclaims and Other Part 20 Claims), para.4.1 (see para.20PD.4).

Reply

Should a claimant file a reply to defence (r.15.8), the reply should be verified. **22.1.6**

Statement of case subsequent to reply

22.1.7 With the permission of the court, a party may serve a statement of case after a reply (r.15.9). Such further statement of case does not fall within the definition of "statement of case" given in r.2.3(1) and this omission may create doubts as to whether a further statement is included among the documents which must be verified by a statement of truth by virtue of r.22.1(1). It would be surprising if it were not. In any event, the court, in giving permission for a further statement to be served, could direct that it should be verified.

In applications for statutory review under the Nationality, Immigration and Asylum Act 2002 s.103A, for certain purposes applicants may be represented by persons permitted by statute to provide immigration advice or immigration services. Such a representative shall be regarded as the applicant's legal representative for the purposes of r.22.1 (see r.54.28A(3)).

Verification of amendments to statement of case

22.1.8 A statement of case may be amended as provided by the rules in Pt 17 (Amendments to statements of case). In certain circumstances the permission of the court is required. Obviously, as a party's statement of case has to be verified by a statement of truth any amendment thereto must also be verified (r.22.1(2)). However, the court may order otherwise and is likely to do so in cases where amendment cannot be made without the court's permission and the amendment does not involve any allegations of fact by the party. It may be appropriate for the court to order otherwise for the purpose of enabling a claimant to amend his statement of case to put forward an alternative case which arguably makes a claim in his favour and is not a case which he is able to say is true, but is derived from his opponent's documents, pleadings or evidence (*Binks v Securicor Omega Express Ltd* [2003] EWCA Civ 993; July 16, 2003, unrep., CA, (insofar as Practice Direction (Amendments to Statements of Case) para.1.4 is inconsistent with r.22.1(2), the rule is to be preferred)).

Any "further information" of statement of case to be verified

22.1.9 A "statement of case" includes, not only (1) a claim form, including a claim form used under the Pt 8 procedure, (2) particulars of claim where these are not included in a claim form, (3) a defence, (4) a Pt 20 claim, (5) a reply to defence, but also any "further information" given in relation to them voluntarily or by court order under r.18.1 (r.2.3(1)). Rule 18.1 states that the court may at any time order a party to (a) clarify any matter which is in dispute in the proceedings, or (b) give additional information in relation to any such matter, whether or not the matter is contained or referred to in a statement of case. It is clear from the terms of r.22.1(1)(b) that where a party provides further information in relation to his statement of case by way of a response to a court order under r.18.1 it must be verified by a statement of truth (see further para.18.1.8 above). This proposition is repeated in Practice Direction (Statement of Truth), para.1.1(2). But neither the rule nor the Practice Direction requires a voluntary response to be so verified. By indirect (but not wholly successful) means, Practice Direction (Further Information), para.3 attempts to deal with this apparent gap (see para.18PD.3 above). Clearly, the intention is that voluntary responses should be verified by statements of truth. As to the question whether a voluntary response to a preliminary request for further information in relation to a matter not contained or referred to in a statement of case must be verified by a statement of truth, see para.18.1.8 above.

Verified statement of case as evidence

22.1.10 At hearings other than trial, a party (whether claimant or defendant) may in support of his application, rely on matters set out in his statement of case if it is verified by a statement of truth (r.32.6(2)(a)); an example is provided by r.25.6(5) (application for interim payment).

Rule 8.5 states that, under the alternative procedure for claims set out in Pt 8, a claimant must file any "written evidence" on which he intends to rely when he files his claim form. The claimant may rely on matters set out in his claim form as evidence *under r.8.5 if the claim form is verified* by a statement of truth (r.8.5(7)).

Witness statement

22.1.11 A witness statement is a written statement signed by a person which contains the evidence, and only that evidence which that person would be allowed to give orally (r.32.4(1)). (For form of witness statement, see r.32.8). Rule 22.1(1) states that a witness statement is a document which must be verified by a statement of truth. The statement of truth must state that the maker of the statement "believes the facts stated in the document are true" (r.22.1(4)(b)) and it must be signed by the maker of the statement (r.22.1(6)(b)). (For former law, see RSC O.38, r.2A(4) and CCR O.20, r.12A(4)).

By definition, a written statement signed by a witness, though not verified by a statement of truth, is a witness statement. It would seem therefore that a requirement to serve a witness statement is satisfied if a statement that is signed but not verified is served.

A witness statement is a form of written evidence (see para.32.2.3 below). Some provisions require that "written evidence" should be verified by a statement of truth (e.g. Practice Direction (Appeals) para.25.4 (evidence supporting application for permission to reopen a final determination on an appeal; see para.52PD.126 below)). An application to extend time for making an application under the Nationality, Immigration and Asylum Act 2002 s.103A(1) should be made in the application notice and the grounds on which it is contended that the notice could not reasonably practicably have been filed within time must be supported by written evidence supported by a statement of truth (r.54.30).

In certain circumstances, a "witness summary" may be permitted in lieu of a "witness statement" (r.32.9). Because of the limited nature of these circumstances, there is no requirement for a witness summary to be verified.

Certificate of reasons for bringing claim in High Court

The general rule is that possession claims, including possession claims against trespassers, and claims by tenants seeking relief from forfeiture, must be started in a county court. Rules of court relating to these claims are found in Sect.I of CPR Pt 55. It is also the general rule that landlord and tenant claims should be started in a county court. Rules of court relating to landlord and tenant claims are found in Sect.I of CPR Pt 56. However, in certain circumstances claims falling in these categories may be started in the High Court. Rule 55.3(2) and r.56.2(2) provide that, where a claimant believes that such circumstances exist and wishes to bring his claim in the High Court, he must file with his claim form a certificate stating his reasons accordingly. These rules specifically provide that the certificate should be "verified by a statement of truth in accordance with rule 21.1(1)" and that requirement is repeated in r.22.1(1)(e), a provision inserted in r.22.1(1) when Parts 55 and 56 were added to the CPR by the Civil Procedure (Amendment) Rules 2001 (SI 2001/256). The objective is to ensure that possession claims etc. and landlord and tenant claims are not started in the High Court on the basis of mere assertion. Of course, a claim started in the High Court, and certified as explained above, may subsequently be transferred to a county court in accordance with the normal rules as to the transfer of proceedings from one court to another. Verified certification does not make the jurisdiction of the High Court exclusive, and transfer to a county court is not confined to those cases where the circumstances certified by the claimant turn out not to be wholly true. **22.1.12**

Acknowledgment of service in Part 8 claim

Sub-paragraph (d) in r.22.1(1) was added by the Civil Procedure (Amendment No.3) Rules 2001 (SI 2001/1769) and came into effect on May 31, 2001. Part 10 deals with the procedure for filing an acknowledgment of service. It is provided there that an acknowledgment of service must be signed (r.10.5(a)), but there is no requirement that it should be verified by a statement of truth. Where the claimant uses the procedure set out in Pt 8 (alternative procedure for claims) the provisions of Pt 10 apply subject to the modifications set out in r.8.3 (see r.10.1(2)). Sub-paragraph (d) of r.22.1(1) adds a further modification. The explanation for this lies in the fact that the acknowledgment of service plays a different role in claims proceeding under the Pt 8 procedure than it does in other proceedings. **22.1.13**

Note also r.54.8 (acknowledgment of service in judicial review proceedings).

Certificate of Service

Sub-paragraph (e) in r.22.1(1) was added by the Civil Procedure (Amendment No.4) Rules 2004 (SI 2004/3419) and came into effect on April 1, 2005. This provision states that a certificate of service is a document that must be verified by a statement of truth. Previously, such a requirement was found in the practice direction supplement- **22.1.13A** ing Pt 22. Rule 22.1(4) was also amended by this statutory instrument for the purpose of providing that, in the case of a certificate of service, a statement of truth is a statement that the person who signs such certificate believes the facts stated in it are true. Usually, where a party is represented by a solicitor, it will be the solicitor, and not the party, who effects the service of any document on the party's behalf. Before r.22.1(4) was amended, in these circumstances a solicitor lodging a certificate of service signed the attached statement of truth, not in a personal capacity (as the person who had direct knowledge of the facts as to service), but on behalf of the client. The amendment enables the solicitor to sign in a personal capacity.

Application notice

22.1.14 An application notice is a written document in which the applicant states his intention to seek a court order (r.23.1), for example, an order for an interim remedy. An application notice must state (a) what order the applicant is seeking, and (b) briefly, why the applicant is seeking the order (r.23.6). At the hearing of the application the applicant may in support of his application rely on matters set out in his statement of case, provided it is verified by a statement of truth (r.32.6(2)(a)). If an applicant wishes to rely on matters set out in his application notice, the application notice must be verified by a statement of truth (r.22.1(3) and r.32.6(2)(b)), otherwise the notice need not be verified unless it is expressly provided that reasons given in the notice should be verified (e.g. by Practice Direction (Appeals) para.5.23, see para.52PD.33 below).Verification is by the party (r.22.1(4)(a)) and the statement of truth must be signed by him or by his legal representative (r.22.1(6)(a)). Where a party is conducting proceedings with a litigation friend (see Pt 21 (Children and Patients), verification is by the litigation friend and the statement of truth is signed by him or by his legal representative (r.22.1(5)(c) and r.22.1(6)(a)).

Expert's report

22.1.15 An expert's report must comply with the requirements set out in the relevant practice direction (r.35.10(1)). Practice Direction (Experts and Assessors), para.2.3 states that an expert's report must be verified by a statement of truth and para.2.4 indicate the form such verification should take (see 35PD.2).

Special provision is made in the Practice Direction supplementing Pt 22 for the situation where a document is to be verified by a person who is unable to read or sign the document. The document should be signed by an authorised person who must complete a certificate in the form annexed to the Practice Direction supplementing Pt 22 (*ibid.*, paras 3A.1 to 3A.4). Before these provisions were introduced in 2006, comparable provisions, but limited in their application to witness statements, were found in Practice Direction (Evidence) (supplementing Pt 32).

Documents in costs proceedings

22.1.15.1 By operation of Pt 22, certain documents used in costs proceedings (as in other proceedings) have to be verified by statements of truth. In addition, by operation of provisions found in Practice Direction (Costs) (supplementing CPR Pts 43 to 48), other documents also have to be verified. For example, in para.22.1 it is expressly provided that a "statement of resources" should be verified by a statement of truth (see para.44PD.16).

In para.1.5 of this practice direction (see para.43PD.1 below) it is stated that Pt 22 will apply to any document "which is required by these Directions to be signed by a party or his legal representative" and will apply "as if the document in question was a statement of truth." It seems that there is a typographical error here and it has been argued that what is meant is that Pt 22 applies to such documents as if the document in question "was a statement of case". If that is correct, the various documents required by particular provisions in this Practice Direction to be signed by a party or his legal representative should be verified by a statement of truth. Provisions in the practice direction requiring documents to be so signed include: para.13.5(3) (statement of costs) (Form **N260**) (see para.44PD.7 below), para.35.3(4) (points of dispute) (Precedent G) (see para.47PD.8 below), para.37.1(1) (request for default costs certificate) *(Form **N254**) (see para.47PD.10* below), para.39.1(3) (optional reply) (see para.47PD.12 below), paras 40.2(j), 43.3(h) and 44.3(a) (statement accompanying request for detailed assessment hearing) (see paras 47PD.13, 47PD.16 and 47PD.17 below), and para.56.10(g) (statement accompanying request for detailed assessment hearing date) (see para.48PD.7 below).

Form of statement of truth

The form of statement of truth verifying a statement of case should be as stated in Practice Direction (Statements of Truth), para.2.1 (see 22PD.2); see also Practice Direction (How to Start Proceedings—The Claim Form), para.7 (see 7PD.7), Practice Direction (Statements of Case), para.13 (see 13PD.5), Practice Direction (Defence and Reply), para.2 (see 15PD.1), and Practice Direction (Counterclaim and Other Pt 20 Claims), para.4.1 (see 20PD.1). **22.1.16**

In certain circumstances, claim forms may be issued through the Production Centre. Practice Direction (Production Centre) (see 7CPD.1) modifies the Practice Direction (Statements of Truth) *op. cit.* in a manner which facilitates the preparation of statements of truth where a party files with the Centre a batch of requests for the issue of claim forms (*ibid.* para.1.4(4)).

Where a county court money claim is started under the 'Money Claim Online" pilot scheme, the form of statement of truth appropriate for claim and defence are as stated in para.8.2 of Practice Direction (Money Claim Online) (one of the practice directions supplementing CPR Pt 7). See further para.21.1.17 "Statement of truth in document filed by e-mail" below.

The form of statement of truth verifying an application notice, a response to a further information order, or a notice of objections should be as stated in Practice Direction (Statements of Truth), para.2.1 (see 22PD.1); see also Practice Direction (Further Information), para.3 (see 18PD.2) and Practice Direction (Accounts, Inquiries, etc.), para.3.3 (40PD.3).

For form of statement of truth verifying a witness statement, see Practice Direction (Written Evidence), para.20 (32PD.20).

For form of statement of truth verifying expert's report, see para.22.1.15 "Expert's report" above.

Who may sign the statement of truth

In the case of documents referred to in r.22.1, the statement of truth is to be signed by the persons referred to in r.22.1(5) to (7). The matter is amplified in Practice Direction (Statements of Truth), paras 3.1 *et seq.* (see 22PD.1) where the appropriate person to verify a notice of objections to an account is also explained. In practice the identification of the appropriate person to sign a statement of truth can often present difficulties. In August 1999, in an attempt to deal with this problem in relation to documents other than witness statements, para.3.11 was added to the Practice Direction (see para.22PD.3 below). This paragraph gives guidance as to persons who would be appropriate signatories on behalf of trusts and companies and where parties act through insurers or legal representatives (including "in-house" legal representatives). The Practice Direction contains important provisions concerning the conclusions which the court may draw where a legal representative signs a statement of truth on behalf of the party (*ibid.* paras 3.7 and 3.8). **22.1.17**

Special provision is made in the Practice Direction for cases in which the party verifying a document by a statement of truth is a company or a partnership (*ibid.* paras 3.4 to 3.6). In the case of a company or corporation verification is to be by "a person holding a senior position" and, in effect, this is a person who could swear an affidavit. For meaning of "senior position" in this context, see para.6.2 of Practice Direction A, supplementing CPR Pt 6 (Service of Documents).

Where the legal representative of a party serves a document and, upon lodging the document, completes it by verifying the certificate of service, he verifies it not on the basis that he is his party's representative, but in his personal capacity as the person who has first-hand knowledge of service being effected.

Where, in proceedings by or against the Crown, and other civil proceedings to which the Crown is a party, by reason of a rule, practice direction or court order the Crown is permitted or required to verify a document by a statement of truth, that function shall be performed by an appropriate officer acting on behalf of the Crown (r.66.3(1)(c)). The court may, if necessary, nominate an appropriate officer (r.66.3(2)).

False statements

In certain circumstances, a false statement made in a document verified by statement of truth may lead to a liability for contempt of court. Provisions to this effect are found, not in this Part, but in r.32.14. Proceedings for contempt of court may be brought against a party if he makes, or causes to be made, a false statement in a docu- **22.1.18** ment verified by a statement of truth. This applies, not only to the documents referred to in r.22.1, but also to other documents which may or must be verified by a statement of truth.

See also r.31.23 (Proceedings for contempt against person making false disclosure statement).

Practice Direction (Statements of Truth), para.5 (see para.22PD.5 below) draws attention to r.32.14 and to Practice Direction (Written Evidence), paras 28.1 to 28.4 (see para.32PD.28 below) (where the practice for contempt proceedings under rr.31.23 and 32.14 is stated). In *Carlco Ltd v Chief Constable of Dyfed Powys* [2002] EWCA Civ 1754, it was held that a claimant company's failure to comply with these requirements in relation to a witness statement did not, together with other considerations, constitute a gross breach of a peremptory order sufficient to justify striking out the claim.

Statement of truth in documents filed and applications made by electronic means

22.1.19 Where a document is filed or sent to the court by electronic means other than facsimile, as permitted by a practice direction made under r.5.5, and the document is verified by a statement of truth, the practice direction will contain special provisions indicating how the signature requirements of r.22.1(6) shall be satisfied; e.g. Practice Direction (Money Claim Online), paras 11 and 12 (Statement of truth and signature) (see paras 7EPD.11 and 7EPD.12), and Practice Direction (Electronic Communication and Filing of Documents), para.9 (Statement of truth in documents filed electronically) (see para.5BPD.9). Other practice directions now making special provision for the making of statements of truth in documents filed by electronic means, or forms completed on court websites, include Practice Direction (Possession Claims Online), paras 8 and 9 (Statement of truth and signature) (see paras 55BPD.8 and 55BPD.9). Note also Practice Direction (Court Documents), para.1 (Signature of documents by mechanical means) (see para.5PD.1) and Practice Direction (Production Centre), para.1.4(4) (Modification of Pt 22) (see para.7CPD.1).

Failure to verify a statement of case

22.2 **22.2—(1) If a party fails to verify his statement of case by a statement of truth—**

(a) the statement of case shall remain effective unless struck out; but

(b) the party may not rely on the statement of case as evidence of any of the matters set out in it.

(2) The court may strike out[GL] a statement of case which is not verified by a statement of truth.

(3) Any party may apply for an order under paragraph (2).

Effect of rule

22.2.1 See notes following r.22.3.

Failure to verify a witness statement

22.3 **22.3 If the maker of a witness statement fails to verify the witness statement by a statement of truth the court may direct that it shall not be admissible as evidence.**

Effect of rules 22.2 and 22.3

22.3.1 Statements of case (and amendments thereto) and witness statements should be verified by a statement of truth (r.22.1(1)(2)). Rules 22.2 and 22.3 deal with the consequences that may follow if they are not verified. A notice of application should be verified if a party wants to rely on it as evidence in those circumstances where the contents of a notice can be relied on as evidence. Rules 22.2 and 22.3 are not concerned with the consequences that may follow if a notice of application is not verified (see notes following r.22.1).

Failure to verify a statement of case

See Practice Direction (Statements of Truth), para.4 (see para.22PD.2) (Consequences of failure to verify). **22.3.2**

The rule is that a statement of case must be verified by a statement of truth (r.22.1(1)). Rule 22.1(a) makes it clear that if a statement of case is not verified it is not a nullity. The lack of verification is an irregularity which may be cured (r.3.10). Under r.3.4(2)(c) the court may strike out a statement of case (or part of a statement of case) on the ground that there has been a failure to comply with a rule and by implication this would include a failure to comply with r.22.1. The implication is made specific by r.22.1(2) which states that the court may strike out a statement of case on the additional ground that it is not verified by a statement of truth, and any party may apply for a striking out order on this ground (r.22.2(3)). Any party may apply for an order that, unless within such a period as the court may specify the statement of case is verified by service of a statement of truth, the statement of case will be struck out (Practice Direction (Statements of Case), para.4.2 (see para.22PD.4 below).

Conceptually, a claim form issued by a party is distinct from (what were formerly called) his pleadings. However, it cannot be assumed that a claim form (as distinct, for example, from a party's particulars of claim) could not be struck out under r.22.2(2) because r.2.3(1) states that, in the CPR, the expression "statement of case" includes a claim form and is no confined to pleadings. It is perhaps unlikely that a court would strike out a claim form or a statement of case for failure to comply with r.22.2(2) if the document was verified but not properly verified; see, e.g. *Protea Leasing Ltd v Royal Air Cambodge Co Ltd, March* 7, 2000, unrep. (Timothy Walker J.) (claimant company's statement of case verified by person who was general counsel for a foreign company and who held a power of attorney from claimant where claimant a shell Manx company fronting for the foreign company). Much would depend upon the circumstances in which the question whether the document should be struck out arose and on whether striking out would be appropriate in the light of the overriding objective stated in r.1.1.

In certain circumstances, a party may rely on matters set out in a statement of case as evidence (see r.32.6(2) and r.8.5(7)). However, where a statement of case remains unverified the party may not rely on it as evidence of any matters set out in it (r.22.2(1)(b)) (for unverified witness statements as evidence, see below).

For costs consequences of failure to verify statement of case, see Practice Direction (Statement of Truth), para.4.3 (see para.22PD.4 below).

In certain circumstances, a party may rely on matters set out in an application notice where the notice is verified by statement of truth (see notes following r.22.1).

Failure to verify a witness statement

A witness statement must at least be signed by the maker (r.32.4), must comply with the requirements of the relevant practice direction (r.32.8), and must be verified by a statement of truth (r.22.1(1)). The general rule is that evidence at hearings other than at trial is to be by witness statement (r.32.6(1)). In certain circumstances, witness statements may also be used as evidence at trial (r.32.5). Rule 22.3 provides that a witness statement which is not verified by a statement of truth, signed by the maker of the statement, may be rendered inadmissible as evidence if the court so directs. The lack of verification does not render it *ipso facto* inadmissible (*cf.* unverified statement of case, *supra*). **22.3.3**

Power of the court to require a document to be verified

22.4—(1) The court may order a person who has failed to verify a document in accordance with rule 22.1 to verify the document. **22.4**

(2) Any party may apply for an order under paragraph (1).

Effect of rule

The documents referred to in r.22.1 are statements of case and witness statements. In terms, this rule does not give the court power to require verification of an application notice. **22.4.1**

PRACTICE DIRECTION—STATEMENTS OF TRUTH

This Practice Direction supplements CPR Part 22

Documents to be verified by a statement of truth

22PD.1 **1.1** Rule 22.1(1) sets out the documents which must be verified by a statement of truth. The documents include:

(1) a statement of case,

(2) a response complying with an order under rule 18.1 to provide further information,

(3) a witness statement,

(4) an acknowledgment of service in a claim begun by the Part 8 procedure,

(5) a certificate stating the reasons for bringing a possession claim or a landlord and tenant claim in the High Court in accordance with rules 55.3(2) and 56.2(2),

(6) a certificate of service.

1.2 If an applicant wishes to rely on matters set out in his application notice as evidence, the application notice must be verified by a statement of truth.[1]

1.3 An expert's report should also be verified by a statement of truth. For the form of the statement of truth verifying an expert's report (which differs from that set out below) see the practice direction which supplements Part 35.

1.4 In addition, the following documents must be verified by a statement of truth:

(1) an application notice for—

(a) a third party debt order (rule 72.3),

(b) a hardship payment order (rule 72.7), or

(c) a charging order (rule 73.3);

(2) a notice of objections to an account being taken by the court, unless verified by an affidavit or witness statement;

(3) a schedule or counter-schedule of expenses and losses in a personal injury claim, and any amendments to such a schedule or counter-schedule, whether or not they are contained in a statement of case.

1.5 The statement of truth may be contained in the document it verifies or it may be in a separate document served subsequently, in which case it must identify the document to which it relates.

1.6 Where the form to be used includes a jurat for the content to be verified by an affidavit then a statement of truth is not required in addition.

Form of the statement of truth

22PD.2 **2.1** The form of the statement of truth verifying a statement of case, a response, an application notice or a notice of objections should be as follows:

"[I believe] [the (*claimant or as may be*) believes] that the facts stated in this [*name document being verified*] are true."

[1] See r.22.1(3).

2.2 The form of the statement of truth verifying a witness statement should be as follows:

"I believe that the facts stated in this witness statement are true."

2.3 Where the statement of truth is contained in a separate document, the document containing the statement of truth must be headed with the title of the proceedings and the claim number. The document being verified should be identified in the statement of truth as follows:

(1) claim form: "the claim form issued on [*date*]",
(2) particulars of claim: "the particulars of claim issued on [*date*]",
(3) statement of case: "the [*defence or as may be*] served on the [*name of party*] on [*date*]",
(4) application notice: "the application notice issued on [*date*] for [*set out the remedy sought*]",
(5) witness statement: "the witness statement filed on [*date*] or served on [*party*] on [*date*]".

Who may sign the statement of truth

3.1 In a statement of case, a response or an application notice, the statement of truth must be signed by: **22PD.3**

(1) the party or his litigation friend,[1] or
(2) the legal representative[2] of the party or litigation friend.

3.2 A statement of truth verifying a witness statement must be signed by the witness.

3.3 A statement of truth verifying a notice of objections to an account must be signed by the objecting party or his legal representative.

3.4 Where a document is to be verified on behalf of a company or other corporation, subject to paragraph 3.7 below, the statement of truth must be signed by a person holding a senior position [3] in the company or corporation. That person must state the office or position held.

3.5 Each of the following persons is a person holding a senior position:

(1) in respect of a registered company or corporation, a director, the treasurer, secretary, chief executive, manager or other officer of the company or corporation, and
(2) in respect of a corporation which is not a registered company, in addition to those persons set out in (1), the mayor, chairman, president or town clerk or other similar officer of the corporation.

3.6 Where the document is to be verified on behalf of a partnership, those who may sign the statement of truth are;

(1) any of the partners, or

[1] See Pt 21 (Children and Protected Parties).
[2] See r.2.3 for the definition of legal representative.
[3] Paragraph 6.2 of Practice Direction A supplementing Part 6 sets out the meaning of "senior position".

(2) a person having the control or management of the partnership business.

3.6A An insurer or the Motor Insurers' Bureau may sign a statement of truth in a statement of case on behalf of a party where the insurer or the Motor Insurers' Bureau has a financial interest in the result of proceedings brought wholly or partially by or against that party.

3.6B If insurers are conducting proceedings on behalf of many claimants or defendants a statement of truth in a statement of case may be signed by a senior person responsible for the case at a lead insurer, but –

(1) the person signing must specify the capacity in which he signs;

(2) the statement of truth must be a statement that the lead insurer believes that the facts stated in the document are true; and

(3) the court may order that a statement of truth also be signed by one or more of the parties.

3.7 Where a party is legally represented, the legal representative may sign the statement of truth on his behalf. The statement signed by the legal representative will refer to the client's belief, not his own. In signing he must state the capacity in which he signs and the name of his firm where appropriate.

3.8 Where a legal representative has signed a statement of truth, his signature will be taken by the court as his statement:

(1) that the client on whose behalf he has signed had authorised him to do so,

(2) that before signing he had explained to the client that in signing the statement of truth he would be confirming the client's belief that the facts stated in the document were true, and

(3) that before signing he had informed the client of the possible consequences to the client if it should subsequently appear that the client did not have an honest belief in the truth of those facts (see rule 32.14).

3.9 The individual who signs a statement of truth must print his full name clearly beneath his signature.

3.10 A legal representative who signs a statement of truth must sign in his own name and not that of his firm or employer.

3.11 The following are examples of the possible application of this practice direction describing who may sign a statement of truth verifying statements in documents other than a witness statement. These are only examples and not an indication of how a court might apply the practice direction to a specific situation.

Managing Agent

An agent who manages property or investments for the party cannot sign a statement of truth. It must be signed by the party or by the legal representative of the party.

Trusts

Where some or all of the trustees comprise a single party one, some or all of the trustees comprising the party may sign a statement of truth. The legal representative of the trustees may sign it.

Insurers and the Motor Insurers' Bureau

If an insurer has a financial interest in a claim involving its insured then, if the insured is the party, the insurer may sign a statement of truth in a statement of case for the insured party. Paragraphs 3.4 and 3.5 apply to the insurer if it is a company. The claims manager employed by the insurer responsible for handling the insurance claim or managing the staff handling the claim may sign the statement of truth for the insurer (see next example). The position for the Motor Insurers' Bureau is similar.

Companies

Paragraphs 3.4 and 3.5 apply. The word manager will be construed in the context of the phrase "a person holding a senior position" which it is used to define. The court will consider the size of the company and the size and nature of the claim. It would expect the manager signing the statement of truth to have personal knowledge of the content of the document or to be responsible for managing those who have that knowledge of the content. A small company may not have a manager, apart from the directors, who holds a senior position. A large company will have many such managers. In a larger company with specialist claims, insurance or legal departments the statement may be signed by the manager of such a department if he or she is responsible for handling the claim or managing the staff handling it.

In-house legal representatives

Legal representative is defined in rule 2.3(1). A legal representative employed by a party may sign a statement of truth. However a person who is not a solicitor, barrister or other authorised litigator, but who is employed by the company and is managed by such a person, is not employed by that person and so cannot sign a statement of truth. (This is unlike the employee of a solicitor in private practice who would come within the definition of legal representative.) However such a person may be a manager and able to sign the statement on behalf of the company in that capacity.

Inability of persons to read or sign documents to be verified by a statement of truth

3A.1 Where a document containing a statement of truth is to be signed by a person who is unable to read or sign the document, it must contain a *certificate made by an* authorised person. **22PD.3A**

3A.2 An authorised person is a person able to administer oaths and take affidavits but need not be independent of the parties or their representatives.

3A.3 The authorised person must certify:

(1) that the document has been read to the person signing it;

(2) that that person appeared to understand it and approved its content as accurate;

(3) that the declaration of truth has been read to that person;
(4) that that person appeared to understand the declaration and the consequences of making a false declaration; and
(5) that that person signed or made his mark in the presence of the authorised person.

3A.4 The form of the certificate is set out at Annex 1 to this Practice Direction.

Consequences of failure to verify

22PD.4 **4.1** If a statement of case is not verified by a statement of truth, the statement of case will remain effective unless it is struck out,[1] but a party may not rely on the contents of a statement of case as evidence until it has been verified by a statement of truth.

4.2 Any party may apply to the court for an order that unless within such period as the court may specify the statement of case is verified by the service of a statement of truth, the statement of case will be struck out.

4.3 The usual order for the costs of an application referred to in paragraph 4.2 will be that the costs be paid by the party who had failed to verify in any event and forthwith.

Penalty

22PD.5 **5.** Attention is drawn to rule 32.14 which sets out the consequences of verifying a statement of case containing a false statement without an honest belief in its truth, and to the procedures set out in paragraph 28 of the practice direction supplementing Part 32.

Annex

22PD.6 Certificate to be used where a person is unable to read or sign a document to be verified by a statement of truth

I certify that I [*name and address of authorised person*] have read over the contents of this document and the declaration of truth to the person signing the document [*if there are exhibits, add* "and explained the nature and effect of the exhibits referred to in it"] who appeared to understand (a) the document and approved its content as accurate and (b) the declaration of truth and the consequences of making a false declaration, and made his mark in my presence.

[1] See r.22.2(1).

PART 23

General Rules about Applications for Court Orders

Contents

Editorial introduction

Part 23 is the successor to former RSC O.32 (Applications and proceedings in chambers) and CCR O.13 (Applications and orders in the course of proceedings), especially rr.1 and 3. Rule 23.12 was added to this Part by the Civil Procedure (Amendment No.2) Rules 2004 (SI 2004/2072), and came into effect on October 1, 2004. **23.0.2**

Part 23 contains general provisions relating to applications. They are supplemented by Practice Direction (Applications) (see para.23PD.1 below). (It should be noted that that Practice Direction also contains directions concerning consent orders supplemental to Pt 40 (Judgments and Orders) (specifically r.40.6) and directions relating to applications for the stay of civil proceedings pending the determination of related criminal proceedings (see Vol.2, paras 9A–178 and 9A–184)). In certain proceedings, it may be necessary to read the provisions of Pt 23 and supplementing Practice Directions in conjunction with other provisions in the CPR, for example, provisions relating to "specialist proceedings" and claims proceeding in "specialist lists" (see para.23.0.5 below), and also with the appropriate court guide (see further para.23.0.11 below). Where a particular application is to be made in accordance with Pt 23 it should be made on an "application notice". Application should be made to the appropriate court as explained in r.23.2. Rule 23.6 indicates what the notice should include. Other rules are concerned with the filing (r.23.3) and service of the application notice (rr.23.4, 23.7 and 23.9). The court may proceed with the hearing of an application in the absence of a party (r.23.11) and, in certain circumstances, the court may deal with an application without a hearing (r.23.8).

By *TSO CPR Update 42, Pt 23* was further supplemented by Practice Direction (Applications Under Particular Statutes) with effect from October 2, 2006. This practice direction deals with matters formerly dealt with by CPR Sch.1 RSC O.93, r.1 (Notice of petition under s.55 of the National Debt Act 1870), RSC O.112 (Applications for use of scientific tests in determining parentage) and CCR O.47, r.5 (Family Law Reform Act 1969). Those provisions were revoked by the Civil Procedure (Amendment) Rules 2006 r.12.

An applicant may make an application without filing an application notice if this is permitted by a rule or practice direction or if the court dispenses with the requirement for an application notice (r.23.3(2)) (see paras 23.0.7, 23.3.2 and 23.4.1 below).

An application notice is not necessary where an application for a court order may be made orally.

Where an application should be made with notice to the respondent it must be served on the respondent. Where an application may be made without notice to the respondent it need not be served.

The circumstances in which an application for a court order (a) may be made orally rather than by application notice or (b) should be made with notice or may be made without notice may vary depending upon the nature of the court order sought. Consequently, reference may have to be made, not only to the rules in Pt 23 and to the terms of the supplementing practice direction (see Practice Direction (Applications) para.23PD.1 below) but also to provisions specifically relating to the court order sought (see r.23.3(2) and r.23.4(2)).

The provisions in Pt 23 are, as it were, "default provisions" which generally apply to applications for court orders but which are subject to any express provisions which may apply to applications for specific court orders (see further below).

Under the CPR procedures, defended cases proceed under directions issued by the court and should be constantly subject to court control at case management hearings such as case management conferences, allocation hearings, listing hearings, or pre-trial reviews (as well as by other means). In a given case, matters that otherwise might have to be raised by application notice may be dealt with at a case management hearing.

It should be noted that r.3.3(1) states that the court may exercise its powers, not only "on an application" (e.g. in accordance with Pt 23), but also of its own initiative, except where a rule (e.g. r.42.8) or some other enactment provides otherwise.

When does Part 23 apply?

23.0.3 In civil procedure, "application" is not a term of art. The circumstances in which a person may make an application to the court for "a court order" are many and various. Further, the legal basis upon which such an application is made may be statute, case law, rules of court or practice direction. An "application" should be distinguished from a "request" (see, e.g. r.3.5 (request for judgment without trial after striking out)).

The provisions of Pt 23 do not apply to applications to the High Court relating to derogating control orders made under s.2 of CPR Pt 76 (Proceedings under the Prevention of Terrorism Act 2005) (see r.76.3(2)).

As a practical matter, many applications are made in the course of proceedings already on foot, having been started (usually) by claim form (r.7.2(1)). However, in certain circumstances, proceedings in court may be originated by an application. Whether an application is made in the course of proceedings or is an originating application, the provisions of Pt 23 may apply. Depending on the nature of the relief sought, an application may be dealt with by a judge or by a Master or a district judge.

Some rules draw a distinction between (1) an application made at trial and (2) an application made at any other time in the course of the proceedings, and stipulate that an application of the latter variety (but not the former) should be made in accordance with Pt 23 (or in some other special way); e.g. Practice Direction (Committal Applications), paras 2.2 and 2.3.

In some circumstances, CPR rules provide that a particular application may be made either before or after proceedings have been commenced and, in the former event, the application is made by claim form and, in the latter event, is made in accordance with Pt 23 (e.g. r.73.12(2), (application for stop order)). However, in some other circumstances, an application made before proceedings have been commenced is made, not by claim form, but in accordance with Pt 23 (e.g. r.25.4 (application for interim remedy where there is no related claim) and r.31.16 (disclosure before proceedings start)). A person who seeks a remedy from the court before proceedings are started, or in relation to proceedings which are taking place, or will take place, in another jurisdiction must make an application under Pt 23 (r.23.7(2)).

In some instances, in the "core" CPR rules or in Practice Directions supplementing those rules it is expressly provided that, if an application is to be made to the court, it should be made "in accordance with Pt 23"; e.g. r.12.4 (procedure for obtaining *default judgment), Practice Direction* (Transfer), paras 5.1 and 6.2 (see paras 30PD.5 and 30PD.6), Practice Direction (Group Litigation), para.3.1 (see para.19BPD.6), Practice Direction (Change of Solicitor), para.4.2 (see para.42PD.4 below), Practice Direction (Costs) paras 10.1 and 53.3 (see paras 44PD.4 and 48PD.4 below), r.44.19 (Application for costs capping order), Practice Direction (Transitional Arrangements), para.14 (see para.51PD.14 below), Practice Direction (Pt 53 Claims–Defamation), para.3.2 (see para.53PD.12) and Practice Direction (Arbitration), para.11.1 (application for variation of time). Similarly, such express references are found in some "schedule" rules (viz., former RSC and CCR rules); e.g. Sch.2, CCR O.39, r.12 (application by creditor under County Courts Act 1984 s.112(4) to present bankruptcy petition). By Practice Direction (Directors Disqualification Proceedings), para.24.1, Pt 23 is applied with modifications to applications to which that practice direction relates (note also *ibid.* para.17.1), see para.B1 below. Practice Direction (Appeals) para.1.1 (one of the general provisions about appeals) states that, where a party to an appeal makes an application whether in an appeal notice or by Pt 23 application notice, "the provisions of Part 23 will apply" (see para.52PD.42 below). Where wholly new rules are introduced into the CPR for the purpose of providing rules of court to support innovations, generally in any provisions as to applications that may be made under those rules the requirement that they should be made in accordance with Pt 23 is spelt out, especially where the court's jurisdiction may be invoked by other means (e.g. by filing of relevant practice form) for related purposes (e.g. CPR Pt 74, Sect.V (European Enforcement Orders). European order for payment applications (see CPR Pt 78 Sect.I) are primarily governed by the EOP Regulation. Where that Regulation is silent, the CPR "apply with necessary modifications" (Practice Direction—European Order for Payment, etc. para.1.1). Rule 78.8 (Review in exceptional cases) expressly provides that an application to which that rule applies "must be made in accordance with Part 23".

In other instances, it is merely implied that the application should be made in accordance with Pt 23; sometimes the implication is strong (e.g. r.3.5(4) (judgment without trial after striking out of part of statement of case) and r.24.4 (summary judgment procedure)), but on other times it is weak (e.g. Practice Direction (Allocation and Re-Allocation), para.11.1 (application for case track re-allocation), r.27.11 (application to set aside small claims judgment), r.28.4 (variation of fast-track case management timetable), and Practice Direction (The Fast Track), para.4.3, see para.28PD.4). In r.7.6 (extension of time for serving a claim form) the implication is weak but is made strong by the practice direction supplementing that rule (Practice Direction (The Claim Form), para.8.1, see para.7PD.8); see also r.24.4 (procedure for summary judgment) and Practice Direction (The Summary Disposal of Claims), para.2 (procedure for making an application) (see para.24PD.2). Some CPR provisions in effect contain a short code outwith Pt 23 indicating the practice to be followed in making particular applications, e.g. r.70.5(8) and Practice Direction (Enforcement of Judgments and Orders) paras 5.1 and 5.2 (application to register decision of VAT tribunal for enforcement to be made in writing).

Where former RSC and CCR have been replaced by new Parts and supplemented by practice directions, usually the role of the Pt 23 provisions has been clarified. A good example is provided by Practice Direction (Enforcement of Judgments in Different Jurisdictions), para.4.4, wherein the circumstances in which applications under Pt 74 must be made in accordance with the provisions of Pt 23 are clearly listed.

An application for an extension of a stay of proceedings directed under r.26.4 to allow for settlement of a case may be made by letter (Practice Direction (Case Management—Preliminary Stage: Allocation and Re-allocation), para.3.1, see para.26PD.3). A letter will also suffice as an application notice where a party applies under r.40.12 for the correction of an accidental slip or omission in a judgment or order (Practice Direction (Judgments and Orders), para.4.2, see para.40BPD.4 below); and where a person seeks to intervene in judicial review proceedings under r.54.17 (Practice Direction (Judicial Review), para.13.3, see para.54PD.13 below); see further para.23.3.2 below).

Where it is proposed to make an application to the court for a court order, whether in the course of proceedings or not, care has to be taken in inquiring whether the application should be made in accordance with Pt 23 (and, therefore, by way of application notice) or by some other means. Further, if Pt 23 does apply, care has to be taken to inquire as to the extent to which the provisions of that Part and of the Practice Direction which supplements it must be varied in the light of rules specifically enacted in relation to the particular application which is to be made or practice direction provisions supplementing such specific rules. These specific rules are likely to deal with such matters as the grounds upon which the application is made, the time when it may be made, the service of the application notice, and the nature and extent of the evidence required in support, and may be quite elaborate.

As a result of the Civil Procedure (Amendment No.2) Rules 2004, with effect from October 1, 2004, the Practice Direction to Pt 37 is amended in relation to payments into court under certain enactments so that the requirement to file an application notice is replaced with the requirement to file a witness statement or affidavit.

Application under "schedule" rules

23.0.4 Many of the former RSC and CCR rules re-enacted in the Schedules to the CPR (the "schedule" rules) (see Pt 50) provide for the making of applications to the court (see further para.50.1.7). Some but by no means all of these provisions expressly incorporate Pt 23.

Application in specialist proceedings

23.0.5 The CPR, including Pt 23, apply to the "specialist proceedings" listed in r.49(2) subject to the provisions of the relevant practice direction which applies to those proceedings. Consequently, Pt 23 must be read in the light of any provisions as to applications which may be made in those practice directions. When the CPR were brought into force in April 1999, seven varieties of proceeding were identified as "specialist proceedings" and dealt with as such within the CPR. In the period since, most of them have been brought into the main body of the CPR and dealt with in dedicated Parts each with its own supplementing practice direction (see further para.49.0.1 below). Since October 1, 2007, when the Civil Procedure (Amendment) Rules 2007 (SI 2007/2204) came into effect, the specialist proceedings referred to in r.49 are proceedings under, (a) Companies Act 1985, (b) Companies Act 1989, (c) Companies Act 2006, and (d) other legislation relating to companies, and the relevant practice directions applying to those proceedings are Practice Direction—Applications under the Companies Acts and Related Legislation (see Vol.2 Sect.2G), and Practice Direction—Order Under Section 127 Insolvency Act 1986 (see Vol.2 Sect.2G). The first of these practice directions refers to the making of applications in various circumstances, but in doing so makes not express reference to Pt 23.

It should be noted that in the CPR Parts that now deal with proceedings formerly designated in r.49 as "specialist proceedings", and in the practice directions supplementing those Parts, there are to be found provisions relevant to the making of applications for court orders (often dealing with matters of evidence, see para.23.6.2 below), some of which may (either expressly or impliedly) amplify, modify or even disapply provisions in Pt 23 and the practice direction supplementing that Part. Thus, for example, the effect of para.1.3 of Practice Direction (Commercial Court) is to modify the effect of paras 1 and 2.3 to 2.6 of Practice Direction (Applications) in relation to applications to the Commercial Court. (Note also "Court Guides and general rules about applications", para.23.0.13 below.)

The basic procedure—applications with notice (rr.23.3, 23.4, 23.6 and 23.7)

23.0.6 An application notice must state (a) what order the applicant is seeking, and (b) briefly, why the applicant is seeking the order (r.23.6). Generally, the applicant must:

(1) file an application notice (r.23.3(1)) with the appropriate court (r.23.2);
(2) upon receiving from the court a time and date for the hearing, serve a copy of the application notice on each respondent (r.23.4(1)) as soon as practicable (r.23.7(1)(a), but see following paragraph) and, in any event, at least 3 days before the court is to deal with the application (except where another time limit is specified) (r.23.7(1)(b));
(3) serve with the application notice a copy of (a) any written evidence in support (if it has not already been served) and (b) any draft order attached to the notice (r.23.7(3) and (5)).

It may be noted that r.23.7(1)(a) states that the applicant must serve the notice of application "as soon as practicable after it is filed" whereas para.4.1 of Practice Direction (Applications) (see para.23PD.4 below) says, more realistically, it must be served "as soon as practicable after it is has been issued". An application notice is "issued" when it has been so processed by the court.

Where service of the application notice is to be made by the court, rather than by the applicant, r.23.7(2) applies.

For form of application, see r.23.6 below and notes following.

Applications without notice

23.0.7 An application may be made without serving a copy of the application notice if this is permitted by (a) a rule, (b) a practice direction, or (c) a court order (r.23.4(2)). An example of such permission is provided by r.25.3, which states that the court may grant an interim remedy on an application made without notice if it appears to the court that there are good reasons for not giving notice. Other circumstances in which an application may be made without service of application notice are (a) where the court permits, (b) where the parties consent, (c) where there is "exceptional urgency" and (d) where the overriding objective (r.1.1) is best furthered by doing so; see Practice Direction (Applications), para.3 (see para.23PD.3 below). See also notes following r.23.3 and r.23.4 below. The general rule that the applicant must file the application notice applies to applications made without notice (r.23.3(1)).

The provisions of r.23.9 apply where the court has disposed of an application which it permitted to be made without service of a copy of the application notice. A person served, in accordance with r.23.9, with an order made on an application but on whom a copy of the application notice was not served may apply to the court for the order to be set aside or varied (r.23.10).

For guidance as to practice where applications have to be made (whether with or without notice) in circumstances of exceptional urgency, see Queen's Bench Guide, paras 7.12.9 et seq., (Vol.2, para.1B–52), Chancery Guide, para.5.28 (Vol.2, para.1A–42), *Practice Statement (Administrative Court: Listing and Urgent Cases)* [2002] 1 W.L.R. 810, Section 6 and Annex B, and Practice Direction 54D (Administrative Court (Venue)) para.4 (see para.54DPD.1 below). Note also Practice Direction (Third Party Debt Orders), para.5.4 (application without notice to judgment creditor for hardship payment order made in case of exceptional urgency by judgment debtor subject to interim third party debt order).

Time when application should be made

23.0.8 Every application should be made as soon as it becomes apparent that it is necessary or desirable to make it. Wherever possible, applications should be made so that they can be considered at any other hearing for which a date has already been fixed or for which a date is about to be fixed (particularly where case management conferences, allocation hearings, listing hearings, or pre-trial reviews have been fixed); see Practice Direction (Applications), paras 2.7 and 2.8 (see para.23PD.2 below). This is consistent with the court's duty to manage cases as stated in r.1.4(2)(j)).

Hearing of application

23.0.9 Normally, where an application for a court order is made in accordance with Pt 23, it will be dealt with at a hearing. However, the court may deal with the application without a hearing in the circumstances stated in r.23.8.

Where the court holds a hearing for the purposes of dealing with an application made in the course of proceedings the parties must anticipate that the court may wish to review the conduct of the case as a whole and give any necessary case management directions. Consequently, at such a hearing the parties should be ready to assist the court in doing so and to answer questions the court may ask for this purpose; Practice Direction (Applications), para.2.9 (see para.23PD.2 below). See further para.1.4.14 above and para.23.0.14 below.

Except in the most simple application, the applicant should bring to any hearing a draft of the order sought; see further Practice Direction (Applications), para.6.1 (see para.23PD.6 below).

The judge should keep a note of the proceedings on the application; Practice Direction (Applications), para.8 (see para.23PD.8 below).

As to the disposal of an application without a hearing, see notes following r.23.6 and r.23.8 below.

The disposal of an application, or part of an application, by a "telephone hearing" is provided for by Practice Direction (General Rules about Applications for Court Orders), paras 6.1 *et seq.* (see para.23PD.6 below). Note also Practice Direction (Interim Injunctions), para.4.5 (urgent applications by telephone) (see para.25CPD.4 below).

Hearing of application "in public" or "in private"

23.0.10 Part 23 is the successor to provisions formerly found in RSC O.32 and CCR O.13.

The hearing of applications to which the provisions of Pt 23 apply may be heard either in chambers or in court. The "core" CPR make no reference to "chambers". However, they do draw a distinction between hearings "in private" and hearings "in public". References to "chambers" in RSC and CCR provisions re-enacted in Schs 1 and 2 (the "schedule" rules) have been amended accordingly (see, e.g. RSC O.52, r.6 (provisions as to committal hearings) and Practice Direction (Committal Applications), para.9). The general rule is that, wherever held, hearings will be in public and this includes hearings of Pt 23 applications (r.39.2(1)). But there are exceptions (see r.39.2(3) and they are amplified in Practice Direction (Miscellaneous Provisions Relating to Hearings), para.1.5 (para.39PD.1 below)). For example, the hearing may be in private (a) if publicity would defeat the object of the application, (b) the application involves confidential information and publicity would damage that confidentiality, or (c) the application was made without notice and it would be unjust to any respondent for there to be a public hearing; see further r.39.2 and notes following. In a claim brought under the Race Relations Act 1976 s.57(1) the court has special powers to exclude a claimant (and certain others) from all or part of the proceedings (see CPR r.39.8). In relation to arbitration claims, r.62.10 suspends the general rule and provides that such claims may be heard either in public or in private.

The power to make rules enabling the court to sit in private is not derived wholly from the general rule making power (see e.g. Rent Act 1977 s.143, Housing Act 1985, s.111(2) and Housing Act 1996, s.138(5)). For a detailed account of the development of the law relating to the circumstances in which the court may sit in private, see *Department of Economic Policy and Development of the City of Moscow v Bankers Trust Co* [2004] EWCA Civ 314; [2004] 3 W.L.R. 533, CA.

All of the circumstances in which, contrary to the general rule, the court may or must sit in private (or at least in the first instance must do so) when hearing an application cannot be stated shortly. The matter is not exhausted by r.39.2 and the practice direction supplementing that rule (e.g. Practice Direction (Directors Disqualification Proceedings) para.13.4 (hearings under Carecraft procedure to be in private unless court otherwise orders).

For hearing in private of applications for interim remedies, and of applications for interim payments, see respectively, paras 25.3.4 and 25.9.1 below.

Where an application is heard in private, the court's judgment may be delivered in open court. Alternatively, the judgment may be handed down in private with the judge giving permission for it to be reported (e.g. *DE v Surrey CC* [2006] EWHC 3459 (Fam), December 29, 2006, unrep. (Munby J.)). See further para.39.2.9 below.

Court cause lists will usually indicate if an advocate is to be robed or not robed. Advocates do not robe to appear before Masters or District Judges.

For the approach taken by the ECtHR under ECHR art.6(1) to the issue of private hearings see further para.39.2.1 below.

The court's general powers of case management include the power to hold a hearing and receive evidence by telephone or by using any other method of direct oral communication (except where the rules provide otherwise) (r.3.1(2)(d)). The court may order that an application or part of an application should be dealt with by a "telephone hearing"; for practice, see Practice Direction (Applications), paras 6.1 *et seq.* (see para.23PD.6 below) and note Chancery Guide, Ch. 12, para.12.16 (see Vol.2 para.1A–118). An applicant seeking an order to this effect should indicate accordingly on his application notice (*ibid.* paras 2.3.3 and 6.1A). This power is particularly useful in relation to the hearing of certain Pt 23 applications where it is not necessary for the hearing to be held in public.

Practice Direction (Pilot Scheme for Telephone Hearings) published in May 2003, and made under r.51.2 (see para.23BPD.1 below) provides for a telephone hearings pilot scheme to operate at selected courts, Bedford County Court and Luton County Court to February 27, 2004.

All paper procedures

23.0.10.1 In *Bhamjee v Forsdick* [2003] EWCA Civ 1113; [2004] 1 W.L.R. 88, CA, the Court of Appeal stated that one of the ways in which a court may legitimately regulate its processes is by prescribing a procedure "to be conducted entirely in writing". This was said in the context of procedures designed to protect the court's processes from abuse (whether initiated by the application of a party or on the court's initiative (r.3.3)). However, as the Court noted, in *Taylor v Lawrence* [2002] EWCA Civ 90; [2003] Q.B. 528; [2002] 3 W.L.R. 640; [2002] 2 All E.R. 353, CA, the Court created a new procedure for those seeking to reopen a decision of the Court in an exceptional case, and provided that it should be an all paper procedure even though it is not principally designed to protect the court's processes from abuse (though it may have that virtue in a particular case). Subsequently, r.52.17 was inserted in the CPR and this rule was supplemented by the addition of Section IV to Practice Direction (Appeals) (paras 25.1 to 25.7). It is provided that an application for permission to reopen a final determination of an appeal, and any written statement supporting or opposing it will be considered on paper by a by a single judge and will be allowed to proceed only if the judge so directs. In those circumstances where a court is permitted to deal with a particular matter "without a hearing", in effect the hearing is "on paper" (e.g. Practice Direction (Appeals) para.4.11), but this is not the same thing as permitting a procedure "to be conducted entirely in writing".

See further r.23.8 (Applications which may be dealt with without a hearing) and commentary following.

Costs on application

Note Practice Direction (Applications), paras 13.1 and 13.2 (see para.23PD.3 below) **23.0.11**
and the further sources referred to there. The objective for assessing costs summarily and having them paid promptly is to ensure that applications in the course of proceedings are not made unless necessary and that orders made on such applications are effective (and that further applications are not required for the purpose of securing compliance).

The general rule is that the court will make a summary assessment at the conclusion of any application hearing which has lasted less than one day (Practice Direction (General Rules about Costs), para.13.2, see 44PD.7). The court may order that costs summarily assessed should be paid by some specified date or by instalments. If no such orders is made the costs will be payable within 14 days (r.44.8).

Appeal to judge from order made by Master or district judge on application notice

As a result of amendments made to the CPR by the Civil Procedure (Amendment) **23.0.12**
Rules 2000, provisions relating to appeals are found in Pt 52 and supplementing practice directions. Amongst other things, these provisions replaced schedule rules RSC O.58, r.1(1) and CCR O.13, r.1(10) (appeals to judge).

Court Guides and general rules about applications

The provisions of Pt 23 and the practice directions supplementing the Part are **23.0.13**
referred to, either expressly or by implication, in the Court Guides relating to the Chancery Division, the Queen's Bench Division, the Admiralty and Commercial Courts, the Patents Court and the Technology and Construction Court. Those Guides are listed in para.23.0.17 below, and the sections in which they deal with applications are indicated there in relation to each. Usually, the Court Guides attempt to summarise the ways in which the provisions in Pt 23 and the practice direction supplementing that Part are modified where applications are made in the specialist jurisdiction concerned and also indicate additional points of practice. The Court Guides are not sources of law. Consequently, on the law and practice as to applications (as well as in other procedural contexts) their provisions do not supersede CPR provisions, but in matters not covered by the CPR (or other sources of law) the Guides should be carefully observed (see *Practice Statement (Admiralty and Commercial Courts: Procedure)*, *The Times*, April 2, 2002).

Successive applications for same relief

In relation to cases proceeding on the fast track or on the multi-track it is provided **23.0.14**
by, respectively, r.28.7 and r.29.9, that unless the trial judge otherwise directs, the trial will be conducted in accordance with any order previously made. In a well-run case management system, matters that have to be decided before trial should remain settled once decided. Otherwise parties are likely to be tempted into making last-minute applications to overturn or amend pre-trial directions and orders made at a time when, according to the case management system, they ought to have been made in order to ensure that the case was developed in an orderly manner fair to all parties. Further, once pre-trial directions and orders are made the parties should be entitled to expect that the matters to which they relate are settled and may plan accordingly. This was recognised in the Access to Justice Final Report (July 1996) where it was said that if the fast track, in particular, is to work "it will be necessary for the rules to make it clear that it will not normally be acceptable to overturn earlier procedural decisions unless there has been a material and unforeseeable change of circumstances and it would not be possible to deal with the case fairly without doing so" (*ibid* Ch.6, para.15). If this is the intention, it has to be said that it is not made clear in the CPR. In

themselves, r.28.7 and r.29.9 do nothing to discourage parties from making applications to the procedural judge in attempts to cause the court to re-consider previous procedural directions or orders. It is true that, where the application may be subject to the discipline (such as it is) of the r.3.9 criteria, attempts to overturn previous procedural decisions may be restricted. But this will not cover all cases of "repeat" applications. As a practical matter much may depend on whether the earlier decision is purely a procedural decision or something more substantial, such as a decision on an important interim remedy.

The rule in *Henderson v Henderson* [1843-60] All E.R. Rep. 378 provides that, in the absence of special circumstances, parties should bring their whole case before the court so that all aspects of it may be decided (subject to appeal) once and for all. The policy that underlies that rule is based on the considerations that litigation should not drag on for ever, and that a defendant should not be oppressed by successive suits when one would do. There is also the need for the court to allot its limited resources to other cases. These considerations are relevant, not only where attempts are made to re-litigate matters previously subject to judgment, but also where a party, having made an unsuccessful interlocutory application, makes a subsequent application for the same relief, based on material which was not, but could have been, deployed in support of the first application. However, the Court of Appeal has said "although the policy that underpins the rule in *Henderson v Henderson* has relevance as regards successive pre-trial applications for the same relief, it should be applied less strictly than in relation to a final decision of the court, at any rate where the earlier pre-trial application has been dismissed" (*Woodhouse v Consignia Plc* [2002] EWCA Civ 275; [2002] 1 W.L.R. 2558, CA, at [55] per Brooke L.J.). The overriding objective of dealing with cases justly (CPR r.1.1(2)) may demand that the second application should succeed. In such a case, the failure to deploy the new material at the time of the first application could properly and proportionately be reflected by suitable orders for costs, and (if appropriate) interest (*Woodhouse v Consignia Plc, op cit.* at [57]). Whether a second application for an interim remedy should be entertained where a first has been refused is a matter of discretion (*Laemthong International Lines Co Ltd v Artis* [2004] EWHC 2226, (Comm), October 7, 2004, unrep. (Colman J.). The court's general jurisdiction referred to in r.3.1(7) to vary or revoke an order should not be exercised for the purpose of enabling a party to re-argue an application, relying on submissions and evidence which were available to him at the time of the earlier hearing (*Lloyds Investment (Scandinavia) v Ager-Hanssen*, [2003] EWHC 1740 (Ch), July 15, 2003, unrep.). The court's jurisdiction under that provision should not normally be exercised unless the applicant is able to place new material before the court, whether in the form of evidence or argument, which was not placed before the court on the earlier occasion (*Collier v Williams* [2006] EWCA Civ 20; [2006] 1 W.L.R. 194., CA). See further para.3.1.9 above. In *Experience Hendrix LLC v Purple Haze Records Ltd* [2005] EWCA Civ 1091; August 3, 2005, unrep., CA, a single lord justice ordered that, unless the appellant in a pending appeal paid an interim costs order made against him in favour of the respondent, his appeal should stand dismissed. A further application to another single lord justice to have that order stayed or set aside was dismissed, not on the merits, but simply on the basis that the appellant should not be permitted to re-argue the application. It is expressly provided that a claimant may make more than one application for an interim payment (r.25.6(2); note also para.25.6.7 below). The Admiralty and Commercial Courts Guide states that successive applications can be made by a defendant for orders for security for costs against a claimant (r.25.12) where the circumstances warrant; where a claimant wishes to seek to preclude any further application for such an order it is incumbent on him to make that clear (*ibid.* App.16, para.2, see Vol.2, para.2A–182).

In *Enron (Thrace) Exploration and Production B.V. v Clapp* [2005] EWHC 401 (Comm); March 22, 2005, unrep., the claimant company entered judgment in default under CPR Pt 12 in proceedings against individuals controlling another company to recover payments under a joint venture agreement. After the claimants had taken steps to enforce their judgment abroad, on the defendants' application under CPR r.13.3 to set the default judgment aside, the judge held that they had no realistic prospect of defending the claim save on certain issues of quantum. Accordingly it was ordered that the default judgment should be varied so that, instead of having judgment on the whole of their money claim, the claimants should have judgment in a particular sum but judgment for the balance should be set aside. An order to this effect was drawn up. Subsequently, the defendants served a defence and counterclaim which differed significantly from the draft pleadings produced to the judge and raising for the first time allegations of misrepresentation. In response to the claimants' application to strike out those allegations, the defendants applied (1) for permission further to amend their pleadings, and (2) for an order setting aside the default judgment for the particular sum. In relation to the second aspect of the application the defendants relied on CPR r.13.3(1)(a) and argued that there is nothing in the CPR to prevent a party from making a second application to set aside a default judgment. Aikens J. rejected this submission, holding that the court had no jurisdiction to entertain the application, and if it did it would not be appropriate in the circumstances of this case to exercise it. His lordship said that *Atwood v Chichester* (1878) L.R. 3 Q.B. 722, is not sound authority for the proposition that the court has a general discretionary power to hear a second application to set aside a default judgment.

Before the CPR came into effect there was authority for the proposition that a second application for the transfer of proceedings from one level of court to another would be an abuse of process unless there had been a material change of circumstances (see Vol.2, para.9A–477).

In an extreme case, the court may call upon its powers to impose a civil restraint order or even to commit for contempt to restrain a party from wasting the time of the court staff and disturbing the orderly conduct of court processes in a completely obsessive pursuit of his own litigation, taking it forward by one unmeritorious application after another (*Attorney General v Ebert* [2001] EWHC Admin 695; [2002] 2 All E.R. 789, DC, para.35). See further "Successive applications for interim remedy", para.25.1.4 below. Further, in an appropriate case the court may impose a civil restraint order for the purpose of enabling the court to deal quickly and cheaply with persistent hopeless applications made by a person displaying vexatious behaviour (see *Sandeman Coprimar SA v Transitos y Transportes Integrales SL* [2003] EWCA Civ 113; *The Times*, July 31, 2003, CA) and see r.3.11 and Practice Direction 3C (Civil Restraint Orders); and see r.23.12.

Avoidance of multiplicity of applications

Costs may be increased and case management target dates may be missed if several applications are made to the court where one should have sufficed. In various ways, efforts are made to avoid pre-trial multiple applications. For example, Practice Direction (Applications), para.2.9 provides that parties should anticipate that at any hearing the court may wish to review the conduct of the case as a whole and give any case management directions (see para.23PD.2 below), and Practice Direction (Directors Disqualification Proceedings), para.33.4 states that in applications under the Company Directors Disqualification Act 1986, s.8A the parties should take all such steps as they respectively can to avoid successive directions hearings. See further paras 1.4.14 and 23.0.9 above. **23.0.15**

Where a multiplicity of applications is unavoidable (e.g. where several parties apply for various pre-trial procedural orders), costs and delays can be reduced if the court exercises its power to hear them together. However, circumstances may arise where two (or more) applications should be heard sequentially, and perhaps only in a particular order (see e.g. *Speed Investments Ltd v Formula One Holdings Ltd* [2004] EWHC 1772 (Ch); [2005] 1 W.L.R. 1233, (Lewison J.) (claimant's summary judgment application not to be heard before defendant's challenge to jurisdiction application)).

Applications and the overriding objective

If a court considers that a pre-trial application made by a party in a case will delay resolution of the case or add to costs or take up court time, with no proportionate benefit to the conduct of the case, the court is fully justified in refusing to consider it; whether this is an appropriate course in any case will depend on the particular circumstances of that case (e.g. *Norwich Union Linked Life Assurance Ltd v Mercantile Credit Company Ltd* [2003] EWHC 3064, (Ch); December 19, 2003, unrep., David Richards J. (Master summarily dismissing claimant's application to strike out particular defence allegations and for summary judgment on them on ground that it was contrary to the overriding objective)). **23.0.16**

Related sources

- Practice Direction (Allocation of Cases to Levels of Judiciary) (see para.2PD.1 above) **23.0.17**
- Practice Direction (Applications) (see para.23PD.1 below)
- Practice Direction (Interim Injunctions), paras 2 and 3 (see 25PD.3 below)
- Rule 3.3 (Court's power to make order of its own initiative)

- Rule 22.1 (Documents to be verified by a statement of truth)
- Rule 32.6 (Evidence in proceedings other than at trial)
- Rule 39.2 (General rule—hearing to be in public)
- Part 12 (Default judgment)
- Part 25 (Interim remedies)
- Part 30 (Transfer of proceedings)
- Queen's Bench Guide para.7.12 (Vol.2, para.1B–52)
- Chancery Guide Chaps 5 & 7 (Vol.2, paras 1A–27 and 1A–60)
- Patents Court Guide
- Admiralty and Commercial Courts Guide, Section F (Vol.2, para.2A–85)
- Technology and Construction Court Guide (2nd edn, 2005), Section 6 (Vol.2, para.2C–37)

Forms

23.0.18

- Practice Direction (Forms), Table 1
- **N244** (Application Notice). In the RCJ, PF244 may be used
- **N244A** (Notice of hearing of application)

Forms relevant to particular applications made in accordance with Pt 23 are also found in Tables 2 and 3 of this Practice Direction; e.g. **PF3** (application for an extension of time for serving a claim form (r.7.6(1)).

Meaning of "application notice" and "respondent"

23.1 **23.1 In this Part—**

"application notice" means a document in which the applicant states his intention to seek a court order; and

"respondent" means

(a) **the person against whom the order is sought; and**

(b) **such other person as the court may direct.**

Where to make an application

23.2 **23.2—(1) The general rule is that an application must be made to the court where the claim was started.**

(2) If a claim has been transferred to another court since it was started, an application must be made to the court to which the claim has been transferred.

(3) If the parties have been notified of a fixed date for the trial, an application must be made to the court where the trial is to take place.

(4) If an application is made before a claim has been started, it must be made to the court where it is likely that the claim to which the application relates will be started unless there is good reason to make the application to a different court.

(5) If an application is made after proceedings to enforce judgment have begun, it must be made to any court which is dealing with the enforcement of the judgment unless any rule or practice direction provides otherwise.

Effect of rule

23.2.1 In r.23.2, references to "the court" do not mean, simply, the High Court or a county court (or the Court of Appeal). Rule 2.2(3) states that where the context requires, a reference in the CPR to "the court" means a reference to a particular county court, a district registry, or the Royal Courts of Justice. Rule 23.2 is concerned with where an application should be made, and it would seem that the context suggests that "the court" should bear the meaning indicated by r.2.2(3). Rule 23.2 assumes that a "claim" has an exclusive court locus.Some other CPR provisions stipulate that certain applications must be brought "in the proceedings" to which they relate, and do not assume that the "proceedings" have a court locus (though as a practical matter they will); e.g. Practice Direction (Committal Applications), para.2.2 (see para.scpd52.2 below).

Proceedings may be transferred between county courts, between the High Court and the county courts, and within the High Court in accordance with the provisions of Pt 30 and, in certain circumstances, proceedings may be transferred automatically (see r.26.2). An application to set aside a transfer order is made in accordance with Pt 23 (Practice Direction (Transfer), para.6.2, see para.30PD.1 below).

Proceedings arising on an application may be transferred from one court to another in accordance with r.30.2(1). A county court may order proceedings before that court, or any part of them (such as an application made in the proceedings), to be transferred to another county court. An application for an order to transfer such proceedings must be made to the court where the claim in which the application arises is proceeding and, presumably, should be made in accordance with Pt 23.

A practice direction may stipulate where an application should be made; e.g. Practice Direction (Interim Injunctions), para.8.5 (see para.25PD.13 below) (explained in *Elvee Ltd v Taylor* [2001] EWCA Civ 1943; *The Times*, December 18, 2001, CA). Note also Practice Direction (Commercial Court), para.1.2 (see Vol.2 para.2A–22); Practice Direction (Technology and Construction Court Claims), para.7.1 (see Vol.2, para.2C–25); Practice Direction 54D (Administrative Court (Venue)) paras 4 and 5 (see para.54DPD.1 below)

Applications in Queen's Bench Division

Applications for remedies which a Master has jurisdiction to grant should ordinarily be made to a Master. At the RCJ an application notice for hearing by a Master should be issued in the Masters' Support Unit Room E16 and for hearing by a judge should be issued in the Listing Office Room WG5 (Queen's Bench Guide, para.7.12.2, see Vol.2, para.1B–52). For information about the types of applications which may be dealt with by Masters and judges, see Practice Direction (Allocation of Cases to Levels of Judiciary) (para.2BPD.1) and Queen's Bench Guide, para.7.12.3. **23.2.2**

Pre-claim applications

Rule 25.2 states that an order for an interim remedy may be made at any time, including (a) before proceedings are started, and (b) after judgment has been given. This is reflected in paras (4) and (5) of r.23.2. In fact, the circumstances in which applications may be made to the court before a claim has been started are quite limited. Applications for search orders and freezing injunctions may be made on the basis that proceedings will be commenced forthwith. Further, in certain circumstances, applications may be made for orders that may well have the effect of making the starting of proceedings unnecessary; for example, applications for orders requiring a prospective party to disclose documents, or for permission to inspect property that may become the subject-matter of subsequent proceedings. Pre-claim applications should be made under the Pt 23 procedure and, as is stressed in Practice Direction (Applications), para.5 (see para.23PD.5 below), must be made to the court where it is likely that the claim to which the application relates will be started "unless there is good reason to make the application to a different court" (r.23.2(4)). **23.2.3**

For particular provisions relating to pre-claim applications made in the specialist jurisdictions, see Practice Direction (Commercial Court), para.3.1 (Applications before proceedings are issued) (see Vol.2, para.2A–24), Practice Direction (Mercantile Courts), para.3.1 (Applications before proceedings are issued) (see Vol.2, para.2B–16), Practice Direction (Technology and Construction Court Claims), para.4.1 (see Vol.2, para.2C–20).

Application notice to be filed

23.3—(1) The general rule is that an applicant must file an application notice. **23.3**

(2) An applicant may make an application without filing an application notice if—

(a) this is permitted by a rule or practice direction; or

(b) the court dispenses with the requirement for an application notice.

Effect of rule

23.3.1 See further "Editorial Introduction" above.

On receipt of an application notice containing a request for a hearing, the court will notify the applicant of the time and date for the hearing of the application; see Practice Direction (Applications), para.2.2 (see para.23PD.2 below) unless the applicant chooses to serve the notice himself. For practice where hearing not requested, see r.23.8 below and notes following.

Court dispensing with application notice requirement

23.3.2 Practice Direction (Applications), para.3 states the circumstances in which an application may be made without serving an application notice (see para.23PD.3 below). They include the circumstance where the court permits the application to be made without notice. Thus, for example, where the parties are before the court, the judge may permit one party to make an oral application without having given notice to the other party before the hearing, even though the other party does not consent to this course (e.g. *Connolly v Harrington* May 17, 2002, unrep. (Judge Chapman) (on claimant's oral application made at summary judgment hearing master referring invoices for detailed assessment by costs judge). Another circumstance in which (according to para.3) the court may dispense with notice is where "the overriding objective is best furthered by doing so". Rule 1.4(1)(i) states that the furthering of the overriding objective (of enabling the court to deal with cases justly) by "actively managing cases", includes "dealing with as many aspects of the case as is practicable on the same occasion" (see paras 1.4.14 and 23.0.15 above). In a given case, the duty of ensuring that several aspects of the case are dealt with on the same occasion (thereby avoiding separate hearings) may underpin a judge's decision to dispense with notice requirements.

An example of a practice direction permitting an application to be made without filing an application notice is provided by Practice Direction (Judicial Review), para.13.3 which states that an application under r.54.17 by a person to intervene in judicial review proceedings should be made by letter. See further para.23.0.3 above.

In certain circumstances the court may permit a party to make an application in writing (e.g. by letter); see *Miller v Allied Sainif (UK) Ltd, The Times*, October 31, 2000; *Reliance National Insurance Co v Ropner Insurance Services Ltd* [2001] 1 Lloyd's Rep. 477, CA. Indeed, the court may require a party so to do, see *Ebert v Birch* [2000] Ch. 484 (Neuberger J.), where the claimant was made subject to a *Grepe v Loam* order and required henceforth to make applications, not on application notice, but in writing (thereby saving respondent trustees time and money). Note also that, where a party applies for the correction of an accidental slip or omission in a judgment or order, the application notice may be an informal document, such as a letter (Practice Direction (Judgments and Orders), para.4.2, see para.40BPD.4 below). An application notice is not necessary where an application may be made orally in the course of a hearing. In rare circumstances an application must be in made, not by application notice, but in writing; e.g. Practice Direction (Enforcement of Judgments and Orders), para.5.1 (application to register decision of VAT tribunal for enforcement) (see para.70PD.5 below).

Notice of an application

23.4 **23.4—(1) The general rule is that a copy of the application notice must be served on each respondent.**

(2) An application may be made without serving a copy of the application notice if this is permitted by—

(a) a rule;

(b) a practice direction; or

(c) a court order.

(Rule 23.7 deals with service of a copy of the application notice).

Effect of rule

In a case where an application is made against one party only, and there are other parties to the proceedings, only the party against whom the order is sought should be addressed in the notice of application. It is prudent practice to send a copy to other parties stating, in the covering letter, that it is sent for information only and that if other parties attend they do so at their own risk as to costs. 23.4.1

The circumstances in which application may be made to the court without notice first being given to the respondent by service of the application notice upon him are set out in Practice Direction (Applications), para.3 (see 23PD.3) and they include "exceptional urgency" and the furthering of the "overriding objective"; see further paras 23.0.7 and 23.3.2 above. Commonly, applications for certain interim remedies (see Pt 25) are made without notice. Rule 25.3 states that an application for a court order in the form of an order for an interim remedy may be made without notice "if it appears to the court that there are good reasons for not giving notice". If the applicant makes an application without giving notice, the evidence in support of the application must state the reasons why notice was not given. Under the former rules, provision for application without notice was made in relation to some but not all interim remedies dealt with in RSC O.29. Now, in terms, applications for an interim remedy may be without notice if there appear to the court to be good reasons for dispensing with notice. However, mandatory requirements as to notice are retained by r.25.5 in relation to the interim remedies specifically referred to in that rule (inspection of property before claim or against non-party).

Various CPR provisions stipulate that certain applications (usually with a foreign element) may be made without notice; e.g. r.34.17(b) (application for order for evidence to be obtained for proceedings in other jurisdiction), r.74.3(2) (application for registration of foreign judgment), r.74.25(2) (application for registration of order suspending enforcement of registered Community judgment), r.74.26(2) (application for registration and enforcement of Euratom inspection order where the matter is urgent).

Where the court has dealt with an application made without notice, service of a copy of the application notice and any evidence in support is generally required in accordance with r.23.9 below.

For practice where party does not have time to serve a notice of an application and wishes to make an oral application at a hearing already fixed, see notes following r.23.7 below.

"copy must be served on each respondent"

In this context, "respondent" means (a) the person against whom the order is sought, and (b) such other person as the court may direct (r.23.1). In terms, the general rule stated in r.23.4(1) does not direct service on every person who is a party to the litigation (*Re Creehouse Ltd* [1983] 1 W.L.R. 77; [1982] 3 All E.R. 659, CA (service of application by solicitor to remove his name from the record, see now r.42.3)). 23.4.2

See further r.23.7 (Service of a copy of an application notice) below.

Where, in the course of proceedings, a party wishes to relinquish his conduct of them and an application is made under r.21.6 for an order appointing a litigation friend to conduct the proceedings on his behalf, thought will need to be given to whether the other party should be served with a copy of the application notice. As the other party is not "the person against whom the order is sought" the court will need to consider, in the light of the facts of each case, whether there is any need to direct service upon him (*Folks v Faizey* [2006] EWCA Civ 381; April 6, 2006, unrep., CA).

Time when an application is made

23.5 Where an application must be made within a specified time, it is so made if the application notice is received by the court within that time. 23.5

Effect of rule

Usually, if an application is to be made it will have to be made within a particular time limit fixed by rule, practice direction or court order, otherwise an extension of time will have to be sought. The interesting feature of r.23.5 is that it provides that an application is made when the application notice is received by the court, and not when it is issued or when it is served on the respondent. As to calculation of time generally, 23.5.1

see r.2.8. In calculating the specified time within which a particular application must be made, it is necessary to be clear about the point from which time runs; for example, whether from the date of a previous order, or event, or (as in the case of r.52.4(2)(b)) from the date of the decision of the court (see *Sayers v Clarke Walker* [2002] EWCA Civ 645; [2002] 1 W.L.R. 3095; [2002] 3 All E.R. 490, CA).

What an application notice must include

23.6 **23.6 An application notice must state—**

(a) what order the applicant is seeking;

(b) briefly, why the applicant is seeking the order.

(Part 22 requires an application notice to be verified by a statement of truth if the applicant wishes to rely on matters set out in his application notice as evidence.)

Effect of rule

23.6.1 An application notice must, in addition to the matters set out in r.23.6, be signed, contain a request that the application be dealt with either by a hearing or without a hearing and include the other information listed in Practice Direction (Applications), para.2.1 (see para.23PD.1 below). If the application is to be made to a judge, the application notice should so state (*ibid.* para.2.6)). It is prudent to attach a draft order in the terms sought to this notice.

Grounds for the application should be stated "briefly", but they must also be adequate and, in particular, must be stated in a manner that complies with any special provisions relating to the application made.

Practice Direction (Applications), para.2.1 indicates that Practice Form **N244** may be used. For applications to be dealt with at the Royal Courts of Justice, parties may prefer to use form **PF244**.

Evidence on an application

23.6.2 In many instances, the subject matter of an application will be apparent on the formal procedural documents, that is to say, on the claim form, the statements of case and the application notice, and all of the material requiring consideration by the court will be contained therein, apart from such additions as may be found in the legal submissions of the parties. But also in many instances, the moving party will be required to establish matters of fact if he is to be entitled to the relief he seeks, or the respondent party will be expected to establish facts which may ground his arguments in opposition. Therefore, on proceedings begun by application notice, evidence will be required, especially where matters of fact are contested. A hearing of an application is a hearing "other than a trial" within r.32.6 and, therefore, the general rule is that evidence is to be by witness statement (rather than by affidavit) unless the court, a practice direction or any other enactment requires otherwise (r.32.6(1)). A party may, in support of his application, rely on the matters set out in (a) his statement of case, or (b) his application notice, if the statement of case or application notice is verified by a statement of truth (r.32.6). See further r.22.1(3) and notes following.

For filing and service of evidence on applications for court orders, see Practice Direction (Applications), paras 9.1 *et seq* (see paras 23PD.9 *et seq.* below). Various rules and practice directions stipulate particular requirements for certain types of application. Where there is no specific requirement to provide evidence it should be borne in mind that, as a practical matter, the court will often need to be satisfied by evidence of the facts that are relied on in support of or for opposing the application (*ibid.*). Practice directions making express provision for evidence on applications include Practice Direction (Commercial Court), para.13.1 (Evidence for applications) (see Vol.2, para.2A–34), Practice Direction (Mercantile Courts), para.9.1 (Evidence for applications) (see Vol.2, para.2B–16), Practice Direction (Arbitration), para.9.1 (Applications under sections 32 and 45 of the 1996 Act) (see Vol.2, para.2E–50).

Service of a copy of an application notice

23.7 **23.7—(1) A copy of the application notice—**

(a) must be served as soon as practicable after it is filed; and

(b) except where another time limit is specified in these Rules or a practice direction, must in any event be served at least 3 days before the court is to deal with the application.

(2) If a copy of the application notice is to be served by the court, the applicant must, when he files the application notice, file a copy of any written evidence in support.

(3) When a copy of an application notice is served it must be accompanied by—

(a) a copy of any witness statement in support; and

(b) a copy of any draft order which the applicant has attached to his application.

(4) If—

(a) an application notice is served; but

(b) the period of notice is shorter than the period required by these Rules or a practice direction,

the court may direct that, in the circumstances of the case, sufficient notice has been given, and hear the application.

(5) This rule does not require written evidence—

(a) to be filed if it has already been filed; or

(b) to be served on a party on whom it has already been served.

(Part 6 contains the general rules about service of documents including who must serve a copy of the application notice.)

Effect of rule

The general rule is that the applicant must serve the application notice on each respondent (r.23.4(1)) as soon as practicable after filing (r.23.7(1)(a)) (but see para.23.0.6 above where Practice Direction (Applications), para.4.1 is noted, see 23PD.4) and, in any event, at least three days before the court is to deal with the application (except where another time limit is specified) (r.23.7(1)(b)). Practice Direction (Applications), para.4.2 supplements these provisions and states that, where an application notice should be served but there is not sufficient time to do so, informal notification of the application should be given unless the circumstances of the application require secrecy (see para.23PD.4 below). **23.7.1**

Rules may require that an applicant making an application should give the respondent a particular period of notice. For example, CPR r.24.4(3) states that a respondent to an application for summary judgment should be given at least 14 days' notice of the date fixed for the hearing. Where the required period of notice has not been given, the court has power under r.23.7(4), in the circumstances stated in that provision, to direct that sufficient notice has been given. This power is in addition to the general power which the court has to shorten a time period (see r.3.1(2)(a)) (*Phillips v Avena* [2005] EWHC 3333, Ch; November 10, 2005 (Sir Francis Ferris)).Where a date for a hearing has been fixed (e.g. a case management conference or a pre-trial review) and a party wishes to make an application for a court order at that hearing, but does not have sufficient time to serve an application notice in accordance with r.23.7, he should inform the other party and the court (if possible in writing) as soon as he can of the nature of the application and the reason for it and should then make the application orally at the hearing; Practice Direction (Applications), para.2.10 (see para.23PD.2 below).

Specific provisions found elsewhere in the CPR or in supplementing practice directions, may in relation to applications for particular orders augment r.23.7 (e.g. r.19.7(4) (application for representative order), or even (by making comprehensive alternative arrangements for service) expressly disapply the rule (e.g. Practice Direction (Possession Claims) para.10.8 (see para.55PD.14).

For general rules as to service of documents and court processes, see CPR Pt 6.

Service out of jurisdiction

23.7.2 The provisions of CPR Pt 6 Sect.IV apply to the service of application notices out of the jurisdiction.

Applications which may be dealt with without a hearing

23.8 **23.8 The court may deal with an application without a hearing if—**

(a) the parties agree as to the terms of the order sought;

(b) the parties agree that the court should dispose of the application without a hearing, or

(c) the court does not consider that a hearing would be appropriate.

Effect of rule

23.8.1 The court must further the overriding objective (see r.1.1) by actively managing cases (r.1.4(1)) and this includes dealing with "the case" without the parties needing to attend at the court (r.1.4(2)(j)). The courts have given notice that they will always consider whether it might be possible to deal with certain applications on paper without a hearing (see, e.g. para.5 of Practice Statement (Trust Proceedings: Prospective Costs Orders) [2001] 1 W.L.R. 1082). The effect of r.23.8 is reinforced in certain practice directions supplementing particular CPR Parts. For example, Practice Direction (Judicial Review), para.13.1 states that, where all parties consent, the court may deal with an application under r.54.17 (permission to intervene) without a hearing; and Practice Direction (Striking out a Statement of Case) para.7.6(3) states that in certain circumstances an order dismissing an application made by a vexatious litigant may be made without a hearing.

For the determination without a hearing of an application for permission to proceed with a judicial review claim, see CPR, r.59.10 and Practice Direction (Judicial Review) para.8.4).

When laying down the procedure to be followed in circumstances where doubts have arisen as to the proper procedure, the Court of Appeal has been alert to the advantages that may flow from the court being able to deal with an application on the papers rather than at a hearing (e.g. *Bristol City Council v Hassan* [2006] EWCA Civ 656, May 23, 2006, unrep., CA (fixing date for termination of secure tenant's tenancy where conditional order made previously)).

Except where a rule or some other enactment provides otherwise the court may exercise its powers on an application or of its own initiative (r.3.3(1)). Subject to certain conditions, the court may make an order of its own initiative without hearing the parties or giving them an opportunity to make representations (r.3.3(4)).

An application notice must include either a request for a hearing or a request that the application be dealt with without a hearing; see Practice Direction (Applications), para.2.1(5) (see para.23PD.2 below). Where the request is for the application to be dealt with without a hearing, the practice stated in Practice Direction (Applications), paras 2.3 to 2.6 is to be followed by the court (see para.23PD.2).

Other CPR rules or supplementing practice direction provisions may make other arrangements for the determination of applications without a hearing, and in doing so may in terms disapply r.23.8 or practice directions provisions supplementing that rule (e.g. Practice Direction (Possession Claims) para.10.8 (see para.55PD.14), disapplying paras 2.3 to 2.5 of Practice Direction (Applications)).

Where applications are considered without a hearing in the circumstances provided for by rr.23.8(b) and 23.8(c) the directions in Practice Direction (Applications), para.11.1 and 11.2 apply respectively (see para.23PD.11 below).

Where r.23.8(b) applies the parties should so inform the court in writing and each should confirm that all evidence and other material on which he relies has been *disclosed to the other parties* to the application. Where r.23.8(c) applies the court will treat the application as if it were proposing to make an order on its own initiative. The effect of para.11.2 here is to bring into play r.3.3 (Court's power to make order of its own initiative). The particular significance of this that, where the court makes an order on an application, having dealt with it without a hearing on the basis of r.23.8(c), the right to apply to the court to have the order set aside, varied or stayed conferred by r.3.3(5) accrues to a party affected by the order. The fact that this consequence necessarily accrues is a matter that the court should consider in determining whether a particular application (whether made with or without notice, and whatever the wishes of the applicant) should be determined without a hearing (see further para.3.3.2 above).

On receipt of a without notice application with a request for the matter to be disposed of on paper, the court should consider whether it is appropriate to dispose of the matter without a hearing. In *Collier v. Williams* [2006] EWCA Civ 20; [2006] 1 W.L.R. 1945, CA, the Court of Appeal said (para.38) there is a danger in dealing with important applications on paper, in particular applications without notice for extensions of time for service of claim forms under r.7.6 in circumstances where the outcome is potentially of critical importance. (See further commentary following r.7.6.)

Service of application where application made without notice

23.9—(1) This rule applies where the court has disposed of an application which it permitted to be made without service of a copy of the application notice. 23.9

(2) Where the court makes an order, whether granting or dismissing the application, a copy of the application notice and any evidence in support must, unless the court orders otherwise, be served with the order on any party or other person—

(a) against whom the order was made; and

(b) against whom the order was sought.

(3) The order must contain a statement of the right to make an application to set aside[GL] or vary the order under rule 23.10.

Application to set aside or vary order made without notice[1]

23.10—(1) A person who was not served with a copy of the application notice before an order was made under rule 23.9, may apply to have the order set aside[GL] or varied. 23.10

(2) An application under this rule must be made within 7 days after the date on which the order was served on the person making the application.

History of rule

Amended by the Civil Procedure (Amendment) Rules 2000 (SI 2000/221). 23.10.1

Effect of rules 23.9 and 23.10

The title to r.23.9 is misleading as it does not accurately encapsulate the scope of the rule. Paragraph (1) of r.23.10 was substituted by the Civil Procedure (Amendment) Rules 2000 for the purpose of dealing with a problem explained in *Civil Procedure*, 2nd edn, para.23.10.0. 23.10.2

Where the court makes an order on an application made without notice, the applicant must serve on the respondent the material referred to in r.23.9(2). A respondent not served with a copy of the application notice may apply to have the order set aside or varied (r.23.10(1)). Frequently, if not almost invariably, in practice applications made under certain provisions will be made in the absence of the party affected. Such provisions may draw attention to r.23.10 expressly (e.g. Practice Direction (Depositions and Court Attendance by Witnesses), paras 5.6 and 6.6, see paras 34PD.5 and 34PD.6 below).

In *Tombstone Limited v Raja* [2008] EWCA Civ 1444, December 17, 2008, CA, unrep., the Court of Appeal stated (1) that rr.23.9 and 23.10 must be read together, (2) that applications for setting aside orders made without notice are governed by r.23.10, and

[1] Amended by the Civil Procedure (Amendment) Rules 2000 (SI 2000/221).

(3) that although, in terms, r.23.9 assumes that the order made by the court was made on an application supported by an application notice, r.23.10 gives a respondent a right to have the order set aside even where it was not so supported (e.g. where the application was made on an oral application).

Under r.23.10(2) an application to set aside or vary an order made without notice must be made within seven days of service of the order. The order must contain a statement of the respondent's right to make an application under r.23.10 to set aside or vary the order (r.23.9(3)). The court may extend the seven day time limit under r.3.1(2)(a), in particular when r.23.9(2) and (3) are not complied with; see *Sarayiah v Suren* [2004] EWHC 1981 (QB); September 9, 2004, unrep.(Tugendhat J.).

When a defendant wishes to dispute jurisdiction, and intends to apply to set aside orders made without notice for extension of the validity of the claim form and for service and for permission to serve out of the jurisdiction, he is required to proceed according to the procedure stated in CPR r.11 and, in that event, the seven day time limit fixed by r.23.10(2) for applying to set aside orders made on applications without notice does not apply *(BUA International v Hai Hing Shipping Co Ltd (The "Hai Hing")* [2000] 1 Lloyd's Rep. 300 per Rix J.); *Hoddinott v Persimmon Homes (Wessex) Ltd* [2007] EWCA Civ 1203, November 21, 2007, CA, unrep.

A claimant who, on an application made without notice, gets an extension of time for service of his claim form does so at his peril and should know that it may be set aside by a defendant's application under r.23.10 (*Hoddinott v Persimmon Homes (Wessex) Ltd*, op cit, at para.50).

In *Dadourian Group International Inc v Simms (Practice Note)* [2006] EWCA Civ 399; [2006] 1 W.L.R. 2499, CA, an order releasing the claimants from an undertaking not to seek to enforce a freezing order abroad was made in the circumstances described in r.23.9(1). The order did not contain any term releasing the claimants from the obligations imposed by r.23.9(2) and they did not comply with those obligations until enforcement proceedings in the foreign jurisdiction were commenced. Further, the order did not contain the statement required by r.23.9(3). In dismissing the respondent's application to restrain the foreign proceedings the judge said that, although it is not open to parties to flout CPR provisions, the court must retain a sense of proportion in deciding what should be the consequences of a failure to comply with rules. In the circumstances, the claimants' breaches of r.23.9 were technical and did not justify setting aside the permission to enforce abroad or the freezing order itself ([2005] EWHC 268 (Ch); [2005] 2 All E.R. 651 (Laddie J.)). In dismissing the respondent's appeal (made principally on the ground that there was insufficient evidence to show that he had any assets in the foreign jurisdiction), the Court of Appeal said that the requirements of service stated in r.23.9(2) ought to be complied with promptly and that the claimants clearly ought to have sought an order under that provision deferring service (see further, para.25.1.27 below). The claimants' failure to obtain such an order could not be condoned, but in the circumstances it was not causative to a material extent of the respondent's incurring of costs in the foreign proceedings (*ibid.*, para.68).

Part 6 contains rules as to who is to serve, etc.

Part 40.4 deals with the service of orders.

Rules 23.9 and 23.10 do not apply in committal proceedings; Practice Direction (Committal Proceedings), para.2.4(5) (see para.scpd52.2 below).

Rule 23.10 does not apply to applications under Sect.IV of Practice Direction (Possession Claims) Sect.IV (Orders fixing a date for possession).

Power of the court to proceed in the absence of a party

23.11 **23.11—(1) Where the applicant or any respondent fails to attend the hearing of an application, the court may proceed in his absence.**

(2) Where—

(a) the applicant or any respondent fails to attend the hearing of an application; and

***(b) the court* makes an order at the hearing,**

the court may, on application or of its own initiative, relist the application.

(Part 40 deals with service of orders.)

Effect of rule

This rule deals with two related matters; first, the power of the court to proceed with the hearing of an application for a court order in the absence of a party to the application and, secondly, the power of the court to re-consider any court order made at such hearing. As enacted, the cross-reference to Pt 40 appears to have slipped and should have been inserted at the end of r.23.10. **23.11.1**

"the court may proceed in his absence" (r.23.11(1))

Rule 23.11(1) follows former RSC O.32, r.5(1) and former CCR O.13, r.1(5). Those provisions said that the court could proceed in the absence of any party "if, having regard to the nature of the application", the court thought it "expedient to do so". These words no longer appear but their effect is more than adequately retained by the fact that the court must seek to give effect to the overriding objective when exercising the power to proceed in a party's absence given by r.23.11(1) (see rr.1.1 and 1.2). Former RSC O.32, r.5(2) stated that, before proceeding with the first or any resumed hearing of a summons in the absence of any party, the court "may require to be satisfied that the summons or, as the case may be, notice of the time appointed for the resumed hearing was duly served on that party". It was held that this provision did not empower the court to dispense with service (*Westminster City Council v Government of Iran* [1986] 1 W.L.R. 979). **23.11.2**

The court should be very careful before proceeding with the hearing of an application in the absence of a litigant in person, especially where the litigant for the first time had asked for an adjournment of the hearing but had been refused it. In these circumstances, the court should only proceed in the absence of the litigant where it is satisfied either (a) that it was right to grant the applicant the relief he sought, or (b) that the application was plainly hopeless (*Fox v Graham Group Ltd*, *The Times*, August 3, 2001 (Neuberger J.)).

As to court's power to proceed with a trial in the absence of party, see r.39.2.

As to adjourning hearings, see para.3.1.3 above.

"the court may re-list the application"

The Court has an unfettered discretion to re-list the application. In *Riverpath Properties Ltd v Brammall The Times*, February 16, 2000 Mr Justice Neuberger held that court had power under r.23.11 to set aside an order even after it had been perfected and said that the concept of re-listing an application, referred to in r.23.11(2)(b), effectively meant that the court could rehear the application in full and make such order as it thought appropriate. However, he added that it was unlikely that the court would its exercise its jurisdiction where it was satisfied that there was no real prospect of it changing its original order. Furthermore, there could be circumstances where the order had been acted on in such a way as to make it more unjust to set aside the order than to refuse to do so. **23.11.3**

Clearly, what is meant by "re-list the application" is "re-hear the application". It should be noted that an application may be re-listed on application or on the court's own initiative (*cf.* r.3.3).

The power to re-list the application is in addition to any other powers of the court with regard to the order (e.g. to set aside, vary, discharge or suspend the order) (Practice Direction (Applications), para.12.2, see para.23PD.12 below).

In certain circumstances default judgments are to be obtained by application under Pt 23 (see Editorial Introduction at para.23.0.2 above). As to setting aside and varying default judgments, see Pt 13.

As to setting aside order for summary judgment made against a respondent who did not appear, see Practice Direction (Summary Judgment), para.8.1 (see para.24PD.8 below). See further "Setting aside order for summary judgment', para.24.6.8 below.

Dismissal of totally without merit applications

23.12 If the court dismisses an application (including an application for permission to appeal or for permission to apply for judicial review) and it considers that the application is totally without merit— **23.12**

(a) the court's order must record that fact; and

(b) the court must at the same time consider whether it is appropriate to make a civil restraint order.

Effect of rule

23.12.1 This rule was inserted in Pt 23 by the Civil Procedure (Amendment No.2) Rules 2004 (SI 2004/2072) and came into effect on October 1, 2004, together with r.3.11 (Civil restraint orders). The words in parentheses were added by the Civil Procedure (Amendment No.3) Rules 2005 (SI 2005/2292). Under r.23.11, if the court considers that an application is "totally without merit" it is required to act as the rule requires. Other provisions to similar effect are r.3.3(6), r.3.4(7), and r.52.10(5) and (6). See further para.3.4.10 above.

Rule 3.11 is supplemented by Practice Direction (Civil Restraint Orders) (para.3CPD.1). A civil restraint order (CRO) may be one of three varieties; in ascending order of seriousness they are "limited", "extended" or "general". Examples of the orders which may be made for each variety are annexed to the practice direction. The practice direction deals with the circumstances in which the court has the power to make a civil restraint order; for example, it is provided that a limited CRO may be made where a party has made two or more applications which are totally without merit. It also states that, in certain circumstances, the power to make a CRO may be exercised only by a Court of Appeal judge, a High Court judge, or a designated civil judge (see paras 2.7, 3.1, 4.1 and 4.7), and proceedings must be transferred accordingly (see paras. 3.11 and 4.11). A Master has jurisdiction to make a CRO but that jurisdiction does not extend to making an extended CRO (*Wickramaratna v Cambridge University Chemistry Department* [2004] EWCA Civ 1532, CA, November 2, 2004, unrep.).

The court may make a CRO on its own initiative. Paragraph 5.1 of the practice direction states that one party to the proceedings may make an application for a CRO against another party. In that event, the application must be made using the Pt 23 procedure, unless the court otherwise directs, and the application must specify which type of CRO is sought (para.5.2).

For further information, see the commentary following r.3.11.

Application "totally without merit"

23.12.2 In r.3.4 (Power to strike out a statement of case) it is provided that, if the court strikes out a claimant's statement of case, and it considers that the claim is totally without merit, the court's order must record that fact, and the court must at the same time consider whether it is appropriate to make a civil restraint order (r.3.4(6)). The court has the same responsibilities where, of its own initiative, in these circumstances it strikes out a statement of case or dismisses an application (r.3.3(7)). (It may be noted that, whereas r.3.3(7) refers to the striking out of "a statement of case", r.3.4(6) refers to the striking out of "a claimant's statement of case"). An appeal court also has these responsibilities where it refuses an application for permission to appeal, strikes out an appellant's notice, or dismisses an appeal, and it considers the application, the notice of the appeal to be totally without merit (r.52.10(5) and (6)).

Rule 23.12 applies to applications generally and is not confined to applications under r.3.4 or those referred to in r.52.10. Practice Direction (Civil Restraint Orders), which supplements r.3.11, applies where the court is considering whether to make a civil restraint order, and should be read together with r.23.12 (and with r.3.4 and r.52.10).

It is important that there should be an effective way of ensuring that orders made by courts, either to the effect that an application or action has been dismissed as being totally devoid of merit, or that a civil restraint order has been made, are made widely known to other judges and courts who may be concerned with the same litigant (*Mahajan v Department of Constitutional Affairs* [2004] EWCA Civ 96, CA, June 30, 2004, unrep. at para.46, per Brooke L.J.).

Amongst other things, r.23.12 and the similar provisions referred to above are designed to prevent court resources from being wasted. Thus, they may be seen as an example of the carrying into effect of the policy referred to in the overriding objective (r.1.1) of allotting to each case an appropriate share of the court's resources, while taking into account the need to allot resources to other cases (see para.1.3.7). They also help further the policy of avoiding a multiplicity of proceedings (see para.1.4.15).

PRACTICE DIRECTION—APPLICATIONS

This Practice Direction supplements CPR Part 23

Reference to a judge

1. A Master or district judge may refer to a judge any matter which he thinks should properly be decided by a judge, and the judge may either dispose of the matter or refer it back to the Master or district judge. **23PD.1**

Application notices

2.1 An application notice must, in addition to the matters set out in rule 23.6, be signed and include: **23PD.2**

(1) the title of the claim,
(2) the reference number of the claim,
(3) the full name of the applicant,
(4) where the applicant is not already a party, his address for service, including a postcode. Postcode information may be obtained from *www.royalmail.com* or the Royal Mail Address Management Guide,[1] and
(5) either a request for a hearing or a request that the application be dealt with without a hearing.

(Practice Form **N244** may be used.)

2.2 On receipt of an application notice containing a request for a hearing the court will notify the applicant of the time and date for the hearing of the application.

2.3 On receipt of an application notice containing a request that the application be dealt with without a hearing, the application notice will be sent to a Master or district judge so that he may decide whether the application is suitable for consideration without a hearing.

2.4 Where the Master or district judge agrees that the application is suitable for consideration without a hearing, the court will so inform the applicant and the respondent and may give directions for the filing of evidence. (Rules 23.9 and 23.10 enable a party to apply for an order made without a hearing to be set aside or varied.)

2.5 Where the Master or district judge does not agree that the application is suitable for consideration without a hearing, the court will notify the applicant and the respondent of the time, date and place for the hearing of the application and may at the same time give directions as to the filing of evidence.

2.6 If the application is intended to be made to a judge, the application notice should so state. In that case, paragraphs 2.3, 2.4 and 2.5 will apply as though references to the Master or district judge were references to a judge.

2.7 Every application should be made as soon as it becomes apparent that it is necessary or desirable to make it.

2.8 Applications should wherever possible be made so that they can be considered at any other hearing for which a date has already been fixed or for which a date is about to be fixed. This is particularly

[1] This amendment came into force on April 6, 2006.

so in relation to case management conferences, allocation and listing hearings and pre-trial reviews fixed by the court.

2.9 The parties must anticipate that at any hearing the court may wish to review the conduct of the case as a whole and give any necessary case management directions. They should be ready to assist the court in doing so and to answer questions the court may ask for this purpose.

2.10 Where a date for a hearing has been fixed and a party wishes to make an application at that hearing but he does not have sufficient time to serve an application notice he should inform the other party and the court (if possible in writing) as soon as he can of the nature of the application and the reason for it. He should then make the application orally at the hearing.

Applications without service of application notice

23PD.3 **3.** An application may be made without serving an application notice only:

(1) where there is exceptional urgency,
(2) where the overriding objective is best furthered by doing so,
(3) by consent of all parties,
(4) with the permission of the court,
(5) where paragraph 2.10 above applies, or
(6) where a court order, rule or practice direction permits.

Giving notice of an application

23PD.4 **4.1** Unless the court otherwise directs or paragraph 3 of this practice direction applies the application notice must be served as soon as practicable after it has been issued and, if there is to be a hearing, at least 3 clear days before the hearing date (rule 23.7(1)(b)).

4.2 Where an application notice should be served but there is not sufficient time to do so, informal notification of the application should be given unless the circumstances of the application require secrecy.

Pre-action applications

23PD.5 **5.** All applications made before a claim is commenced should be made under Part 23 of the Civil Procedure Rules. Attention is drawn in particular to rule 23.2(4).

Telephone hearings

6.1 Interpretation

23PD.6 In this paragraph—

(a) 'designated legal representative' means the applicant's legal representative (if any), or the legal representative of such other party as the court directs to arrange the telephone hearing; and
(b) 'telephone conference enabled court' means—
  (i) a district registry of the High Court; or
  (ii) a county court,

in which telephone conferencing facilities are available.

6.2 When a hearing is to be conducted by telephone

Subject to paragraph 6.3, at a telephone conference enabled court the following hearings will be conducted by telephone unless the court otherwise orders—

(a) allocation hearings;

(b) listing hearings; and

(c) interim applications, case management conferences and pre-trial reviews with a time estimate of no more than one hour.

6.3 Paragraph 6.2 does not apply where—

(a) the hearing is of an application made without notice to the other party;

(b) all the parties are unrepresented; or

(c) more than four parties wish to make representations at the hearing (for this purpose where two or more parties are represented by the same person, they are to be treated as one party).

6.4 A request for a direction that a hearing under paragraph 6.2 should not be conducted by telephone—

(a) must be made at least 7 days before the hearing or such shorter time as the court may permit; and

(b) may be made by letter,

and the court shall determine such request without requiring the attendance of the parties.

6.5 The court may order that an application, or part of an application, to which paragraph 6.2 does not apply be dealt with by a telephone hearing. The court may make such order—

(a) of its own initiative; or

(b) at the request of the parties.

6.6 The applicant should indicate on his application notice if he seeks a court order under paragraph 6.5. Where he has not done so but nevertheless wishes to seek an order, the request should be made as early as possible.

6.7 An order under paragraph 6.5 will not normally be made unless every party entitled to be given notice of the application and to be heard at the hearing has consented to the order.

6.8 If the court makes an order under paragraph 6.5 it will give any directions necessary for the telephone hearing.

6.9 Conduct of the telephone hearing

No party, or representative of a party, to an application being heard by telephone may attend the judge in person while the application is being heard unless every other party to the application has agreed that he may do so.

6.10 If an application is to be heard by telephone the following directions will apply, subject to any direction to the contrary—

(1) The designated legal representative is responsible for arranging the telephone conference for precisely the time fixed by the court. The telecommunications provider used must be one on the approved panel of service providers (see Her Majesty's Courts Service website at www.hmcourts-service.gov.uk).

(2) The designated legal representative must tell the operator the telephone numbers of all those participating in the conference call and the sequence in which they are to be called.

(3) It is the responsibility of the designated legal representative to ascertain from all the other parties whether they have instructed counsel and, if so, the identity of counsel, and whether the legal representative and counsel will be on the same or different telephone numbers.

(4) The sequence in which they are to be called will be—

(a) the designated legal representative and (if on a different number) his counsel;

(b) the legal representative (and counsel) for all other parties; and

(c) the judge.

(5) Each speaker is to remain on the line after being called by the operator setting up the conference call. The call shall be connected at least ten minutes before the time fixed for the hearing.

(6) When the judge has been connected the designated legal representative (or his counsel) will introduce the parties in the usual way.

(7) If the use of a "speakerphone" by any party causes the judge or any other party any difficulty in hearing what is said the judge may require that party to use a hand held telephone.

(8) The telephone charges debited to the account of the party initiating the conference call will be treated as part of the costs of the application.

6.11 Documents

The designated legal representative must file and serve a case summary and draft order no later than 4pm on the last working day before the hearing—

(a) if the claim has been allocated to the multi-track; and

(b) in any other case, if the court so directs.

6.12 Where a party seeks to rely on any other document at the hearing, he must file and serve the document no later than 4 p.m. on the last working day before the hearing.

Video conferencing

23PD.7 **7.** Where the parties to a matter wish to use video conferencing facilities, and those facilities are available in the relevant court, they should apply to the Master or district judge for directions.

(Paragraph 29 and Annex 3 of Practice Direction 32 provide guidance on the use of video conferencing in the civil courts)

Note of proceedings

23PD.8 *8. The procedural judge* should keep, either by way of a note or a tape recording, brief details of all proceedings before him, including the dates of the proceedings and a short statement of the decision taken at each hearing.

Evidence

9.1 The requirement for evidence in certain types of applications is set out in some of the rules and practice directions. Where there is no specific requirement to provide evidence it should be borne in mind that, as a practical matter, the court will often need to be satisfied by evidence of the facts that are relied on in support of or for opposing the application. **23PD.9**

9.2 The court may give directions for the filing of evidence in support of or opposing a particular application. The court may also give directions for the filing of evidence in relation to any hearing that it fixes on its own initiative. The directions may specify the form that evidence is to take and when it is to be served.

9.3 Where it is intended to rely on evidence which is not contained in the application itself, the evidence, if it has not already been served, should be served with the application.

9.4 Where a respondent to an application wishes to rely on evidence which has not yet been served he should serve it as soon as possible and in any event in accordance with any directions the court may have given.

9.5 If it is necessary for the applicant to serve any evidence in reply it should be served as soon as possible and in any event in accordance with any directions the court may have given.

9.6 Evidence must be filed with the court as well as served on the parties. Exhibits should not be filed unless the court otherwise directs.

9.7 The contents of an application notice may be used as evidence (otherwise than at trial) provided the contents have been verified by a statement of truth.[1]

Consent orders

10.1 Rule 40.6 sets out the circumstances where an agreed judgment or order may be entered and sealed. **23PD.10**

10.2 Where all parties affected by an order have written to the court consenting to the making of the order a draft of which has been filed with the court, the court will treat the draft as having been signed in accordance with rule 40.6(7).

10.3 Where a consent order must be made by a judge (i.e. rule 40.6(2) does not apply) the order must be drawn so that the judge's name and judicial title can be inserted.

10.4 The parties to an application for a consent order must ensure that they provide the court with any material it needs to be satisfied that it is appropriate to make the order. Subject to any rule or practice direction a letter will generally be acceptable for this purpose.

10.5 Where a judgment or order has been agreed in respect of an application or claim where a hearing date has been fixed, the parties must inform the court immediately. (Note that parties are reminded that under rules 28.4 and 29.5 the case management timetable cannot be varied by written agreement of the parties.)

Other applications considered without a hearing

11.1 Where rule 23.8(b) applies the parties should so inform the **23PD.11**

---

[1] See Pt 22.

court in writing and each should confirm that all evidence and other material on which he relies has been disclosed to the other parties to the application.

11.2 Where rule 23.8(c) applies the court will treat the application as if it were proposing to make an order on its own initiative.

Applications to stay claim where related criminal proceedings

23PD.11A **11A.1** An application for the stay of civil proceedings pending the determination of related criminal proceedings may be made by any party to the civil proceedings or by the prosecutor or any defendant in the criminal proceedings.

11A.2 Every party to the civil proceedings must, unless he is the applicant, be made a respondent to the application.

11A.3 The evidence in support of the application must contain an estimate of the expected duration of the stay and must identify the respects in which the continuance of the civil proceedings may prejudice the criminal trial.

11A.4 In order to make an application under paragraph 11A.1, it is not necessary for the prosecutor or defendant in the criminal proceedings to be joined as a party to the civil proceedings.

Miscellaneous

23PD.12 **12.1** Except in the most simple application the applicant should bring to any hearing a draft of the order sought. If the case is proceeding in the Royal Courts of Justice and the order is unusually long or complex it should also be supplied on disk for use by the court office.

12.2 Where rule 23.11 applies, the power to re-list the application in rule 23.11(2) is in addition to any other powers of the court with regard to the order (for example to set aside, vary, discharge or suspend the order).

Costs

23PD.13 **13.1** Attention is drawn to the costs practice direction and, in particular, to the court's power to make a summary assessment of costs.

13.2 Attention is also drawn to rule 44.13(i) which provides that if an order makes no mention of costs, none are payable in respect of the proceedings to which it relates.

Notes on Practice Direction supplementing CPR Pt 23 (see para.23PD.1)

23PD.14 Several comments may be made on this Practice Direction.

(1) It embodies the former practice found in RSC O.32, r.12 (QBD) and r.14(3) (Ch.D) and in CCR O.13, r.2 (county courts). However, references to a judge are less likely to be made under the CPR except where there is another application pending before that judge and it would be prudent for the outstanding application to be dealt with at the same time, or where an application is likely to affect an early date for trial.

(2) Paragraph 2.9 recommends that all relevant documents must be brought to the hearing and the person attending should be familiar with the solicitor's file.

(3) *Paragraph* 7 *commends* the use of modern means of communication, such as telephone conferences and video hearings. Telephone conferences or hearings can be arranged with the Master's consent. In the Q.B.D. video hearings can be arranged with the Master's consent through the Masters' Support unit (MSU) in Room E16 at the Royal Courts of Justice and Room E110 is used for

these hearings. On request the MSU will provide the protocol for this project. Video hearings before the Senior Master should be arranged direct with him when a hearing in his room is sought. Most major trial centres have video conference suites or courts. Court 36 is so at the R.C.J. and enquiries for its use should be made to the MSU.

(4) The keeping of a note of hearings is commended by para.7. This is now common practice as formerly prescribed by RSC O.32, r.22. A record of oral evidence is obligatory and this may take the form of a written note or a tape recording of the evidence.

PRACTICE DIRECTION—APPLICATIONS UNDER PARTICULAR STATUTES

This Practice Direction supplements CPR Part 23

Applications under Part III of the Family Law Reform Act 1969 for use of scientific tests to determine parentage

23BPD.1 **1.1** In this section—

(1) 'the Act' means the Family Law Reform Act 1969;

(2) 'direction' means a direction under section 20(1) of the Act made in any proceedings in which a person's parentage falls to be determined;

(3) 'responsible adult' means—

(a) in relation to a person under 16 to whom sub-paragraph (b) does not apply, the person having care and control of him;

(b) in relation to a person who lacks capacity (within the meaning of the Mental Capacity Act 2005) to give his consent to tests—

(i) a person having power under that Act to give consent on his behalf; or

(ii) if there is no such person, the person with whom he resides or in whose care he is.

(4) 'samples' means bodily samples within the meaning of section 25 of the Act; and

(5) 'tests' means scientific tests within the meaning of section 25 of the Act.

1.2 Where an application is made for a direction in respect of a person who either—

(a) under 16; or

(b) lacks capacity (within the meaning of the Mental Capacity Act 2005) to give his consent to the tests,

the application notice must state the name and address of the responsible adult.

1.3 Unless the court orders otherwise—

(1) the court will serve a copy of the application notice on every party to the proceedings other than the applicant; and

(2) the applicant must serve a copy of the application notice personally on any other person who would be directed to give samples and, where paragraph 1.2 applies, on the responsible adult.

1.4 Unless the court orders otherwise, where the court gives a direction—

(1) the court will serve a copy of the direction on every party to the proceedings;

(2) the applicant must serve a copy of the direction personally on any other person directed to give samples and, where *paragraph* 1.2 applies, on the responsible adult; and

(3) further consideration of the proceedings shall be adjourned until the court receives a report of the tests carried out or samples taken.

1.5 When the court receives the report of the tests carried out or samples taken, the court officer shall send a copy of the report to—

(1) every party to the proceedings;
(2) the responsible adult where paragraph 1.2 applies; and
(3) every other person directed to give samples.

Applications in proceedings under section 55 of the National Debt Act 1870

2.1 Where a claim is brought under section 55 of the National Debt Act 1870, the claimant must apply to the court for directions about giving notice of the claim. **23BPD.2**

2.2 The court may—

(a) direct that notice of the proceedings shall be given by advertisement or by such other method as appropriate; or
(b) dispense with notice.

Scientific tests to determine parentage

The Family Law Reform Act 1969 s.20 (as amended by the Family Law Reform Act 1987 s.23) confers on the court the power in any civil proceedings in which the parentage of any person falls to be determined, on the application of a party or of its on motion, to give a direction for the use of "scientific tests" to ascertain whether such tests show that a party to the proceedings is or is not the father or mother of that person. By "scientific tests" is meant tests made with the object of ascertaining "the inheritable characteristics of bodily fluids or bodily tissue". In order to ensure that useful scientific tests may be undertaken s.20 also provides that the court may direct the taking of "bodily samples" (by which is meant a sample of bodily fluid or bodily tissue) from all or any of the following; namely, the person whose parentage is to be determined, any party who is alleged to be the father or mother of that person, and any other party to the proceedings. The object of this legislative scheme is to enable scientific tests in the form of blood tests and DNA testing to be undertaken. It should be noted that the 1969 Act does not prohibit the obtaining of bodily sample evidence by agreement between the parties involved and without a direction of the court. Very frequently the parties do so agree with the result that the detailed arrangements explained in para.23BPD.5 below are dispensed with. **23BPD.3**

Section 22 gives the Secretary of State power to provide by Regulations for the manner of giving effect to directions under s.20. Those Regulations are the Blood Tests (Evidence of Paternity) Regulations 1971 (SI 1971/1861) (see Vol.2, para.9B–1263). They contain detailed provisions relating to the taking and testing of samples. Schedule 1 of the Regulations contains two forms; they are a Direction Form (which is issued by the court) and a Report by Tester.

Paragraphs 1.2 to 1.4 of the Practice Direction contain provisions relating to an application for a direction made under s.20, and para 1.5 refers to the duties of the court officer when the court receives a test report.

Under the Family Law Act 1986 s.56, any person domiciled or habitually resident in the jurisdiction may apply to the court for a declaration that he or she is the legitimate child of his or her parents. Rules of court relating to such applications are found in the Family Proceedings Rules 1991 r.3.13. The court's power to order scientific tests to determine parentage may be exercised in proceedings for a declaration under s.56.

Where in civil proceedings parentage is an issue, the parties may agree to the taking of samples and the providing of scientific evidence without a direction from the court under s.20 of the 1969 Act.

If an application under s.20 of the 1969 Act made to a district judge is opposed, the district judge should adjourn the matter to a judge (*R. v. R.* [1973] 1 W.L.R. 1115).

Form of direction for taking of samples

In the case of *Re H (Paternity:Blood Test)* [1996] 2 F.L.R. 65, CA, Ward L.J. proposed the following form of words for the direction: **23BPD.4**

It is directed pursuant to s.20(1) of the Family Law Reform Act 1969:

(a) that blood tests (including DNA tests) be used to ascertain whether such tests show that [Mr. A] is or is not excluded from being the father of [child B] born on [ ]; and

(b) that for that purpose (blood) samples be taken on or before [ ] from the following persons: [Mr. A] [Mrs. X, mother of child B] and [child B]; and

(c) that the person appearing to the court to have the care and control of [child B], who is under the age of 16, [or is suffering from a mental disorder within the meaning of the Mental Health Act 1983 and is incapable of understanding the nature and purpose of bodily samples] is [Mrs. X];

(d) that such tests be carried out by [Mr CD of].

See also the prescribed form at Vol.2, para.9B–1276+

Arrangements for tests

23BPD.5 The arrangements for tests which should be made where the court gives a direction for scientific tests are as stated in *Practice Direction (Blood Tests: Paternity)* [1972] 1 W.L.R. 353. That practice direction remains in force subject to the amendments made to the primary legislation since 1972 and to any other direction of the court. The practice direction states thatwhere a direction for scientific tests is given in the Family Division or in a divorce county court, the arrangements for taking of sample and testing will be made by the solicitor for the party on whose application the direction was given. The Practice Note further states that, where the application is proceeding in the Principal Registry, on receipt of a copy of the court's direction the solicitor should apply to the Registry for the necessary number of copies of the Direction Form. A form is required in respect of each person to be tested. He should, in consultation with the solicitors for the other parties, get in touch with a tester and a sampler and make arrangements for the taking and the testing of the samples. The solicitor should then complete Pts I and II of a Direction Form in respect of each person to be tested and attend with the forms before a district judge by whom the direction was given, or if it was not given by a district judge before the district judge for the day. If the district judge is satisfied with the arrangements he will sign the forms and return them to the solicitor with a copy of the Notes for the Guidance of Samplers.

For list of authorised testers, see para.23BPD.9 below.

For detailed procedure to be followed by solicitors and testers, see para.23BPD.10 *et seq* below.

H.I.V. tests—children

23BPD.6 In *Practice Note (HIV Testing of Children)* [2003] 1 F.L.R. 1299, the President of the Family Division gave revised directions for the procedure to be followed where applications are made to a court to permit the testing of a child for the presence of Human Immunodeficiency Virus (HIV) (replacing guidance given in the case of *Re HIV Tests (Note)* [1994] 2 F.L.R. 116). The directions note that such an application is likely to arise only rarely (para.2) and point out that, where all those with parental responsibility agree to the testing, and it is not opposed by the child (see further below), no reference to the court is necessary, unless the testing is for the preparation of expert evidence (para.3.1). In cases where an application is "a necessary step" it should be made to the appropriate county court and only to the High Court if proceedings concerning the child are pending there or the application is made for an order under the inherent jurisdiction of the High Court (para.2). If there are proceedings concerning the child pending in a family proceedings court, the application should be transferred to county court level for determination; the proceedings may then be remitted to the family proceedings court following the hearing of the application in the county court (para.2.1). An application made to, or transferred to, a county court should be determined by a judge or district judge nominated (at least) for private law children cases. An application made to the High Court may be determined by a district judge of the High Court unless the application is made for an order under the inherent jurisdiction, in which case the application should be made directly to a High Court judge (para.2.2).

The directions also deal with the situation where a child of sufficient understanding to make an informed decision opposes the testing. In such circumstances, reference to the court is necessary (para.3). If there are no pending proceedings, the application should be made under the inherent jurisdiction of the High Court and notice of the application should be given to the Legal Services and Special Casework department of the Children and Family Court Advisory and Support Service (CAFCASS Legal Services) (*ibid.*). Another category of case in which CAFCASS Legal Services should be given notice is where a decision about testing is urgently required and the parents may not be legally represented.

Principles on which court should act

In the case of *Re H (Paternity: Blood Test)* [1996] 2 F.L.R. 65, CA, Ward L.J. stated the following propositions: **23BPD.7**

(i) a parent's refusal to comply with a direction was not determinative of the issue of whether or not a direction should be made;

(ii) the welfare of the child is a relevant but not paramount factor in deciding whether or not to make a direction; the interests of other persons may also be involved (see also *S v S, W v Official Solicitor* [1972] A.C. 24; [1972] 3 All E.R. 107, HL);

(iii) the outcome of the proceedings in which the direction is sought is not a factor in deciding whether to make a direction: the paternity question was a free-standing application entitled to its own considerations;

(iv) a child's welfare generally demands that it know the truth about his or her parentage.

The court can now direct taking a sample from a person below the age of 16, when the person having care and control does not consent (see s.21(3)(b), reversing the effect of *Re O and J (Paternity: Blood Tests)* [2000] 1 F.L.R. 418), but otherwise the court cannot order the taking of samples without a person's consent. The court may consider the guidance in *Gillick v West Norfolk and Wisbech Area HA* [1986] A.C. 112, HL when dealing with the child's wishes or refusal to submit to taking samples.

The court had a duty to determine what inference should be drawn from the refusal to submit to a direction for bodily sample. A forensic inference is the proper inference (*Re G (Parentage: Blood Sample)*, sub nom. *Re G (A Minor) (Paternity: Blood Tests)* [1997] 1 F.L.R. 360, Ward L.J., CA).

In general DNA testing is in the child's best interest where doubts as to paternity are in the public domain. Under art.8 of the Human Rights Act 1998 the child has a right to know its true parentage and any interference with the rights of other parties due to the telling was proportionate to the legitimate aim of giving the child full knowledge as to its parentage: *Re T (Paternity: Ordering Blood Tests)* sub nom.*Re T (A Child) (DNA Tells: Paternity)* [2001] 2 F.L.R. 1190, Bodey J., Fam. Div.

Separate representation

The court has power, if it thinks that separate representation of the child is desirable, to appoint a guardian ad litem to take part in the proceedings on the child's behalf under the Family Proceedings Rules 1991 r.9.5. This enables the guardian to be heard on the question of whether or not bodily samples should be directed, or on the consequences of a finding. Normally now the guardian will be an officer of CAFCASS rather than the Official Solicitor. In cases where the FPR do not apply, the court may consider the appointment of the Official Solicitor as litigation friend for the child. See *President's Direction* (Representation of Children in Family Proceedings Rules 1991 r.9.5), [2004] 1 F.L.R. 1188, and *CAFCASS and the National Assembly for Wales Practice Note (Appointment of Guardians in Private Law Proceedings)* [2006] 2 F.L.R. 143. **23BPD.8**

List of testers

A list of bodies currently accredited by the Department of Constitutional Affairs (as from July 10, 2006) is set out below. This list is available on *http://www.dca.gov.uk/family/accredited-list.pdf* [Accessed April 2, 2007] and should include updates. The statutory provisions do not apply where parties submit DNA evidence by agreement and without any direction being given under the Family Law Reform Act 1969 s.20, and in such cases it is not essential for such tests to be carried out by a laboratory accredited by the Department of Constitutional Affairs. **23BPD.9**

NAME & CONTACT DETAILS	
Anglia DNA Services Ltd Norwich Research Park Colney Lane Norwich NR4 7UH	**Tel no:** 08454 565365 **Fax no:** 01603 450945 **E-mail:** office@angliadna.co.uk **Web-site:** http://www.angliadna.co.uk
Crucial Genetics University Department of Neurology Southern General Hospital Glasgow G51 4TF	**Tel no:** 0870 88 88 088 **Fax no:** 0870 8 88 089 **E-mail:** info@crucialgenetics.com **Web-site:** http://www.crucialgenetics.com
LGC Diagnostics Department LGC Building Queens Road Teddington Middlesex TW11 0NJ	**Tel no:** 020 8943 8400 **Fax no:** 020 8943 8401 **E-mail:** diagnostics@lgc.co.uk **Web-site:** http://www.lgc.co.uk/paternity
Orchid Cellmark Ltd Blacklands Way Abingdon Business Park Abingdon Oxon OX14 1YX	**Tel no:** 01235 528609 **Fax no:** 01235 528141 **E-mail:** info@cellmark.co.uk **Web-site:** http://www.cellmark.co.uk
The Forensic Science Service Ltd New Business Division Sales and Operation Planning Office Trident Court 2920 Solihull Parkway Birmingham Business Park Birmingham B37 7YN	**Tel no:** 0845 120 7272 **Fax no:** 0121 770 9289 **E-mail:** nbdsalesoffice@fss.pnn.police.uk **Web-site:** http:// www.paternity.forensic.gov.uk

Detailed procedure

23BPD.10 On receipt of a copy of the court's direction the solicitor should apply for the necessary number of copies of the prescribed Direction Form to be supplied by the court. One is required for each person to be tested.

The solicitor for the party obtaining the direction should agree with the solicitors for the other parties as to the tester and inform him that a direction for bodily samples has been made in a particular type of proceedings, stating the number of subjects covered by the direction and the area in which they live. The tester should be asked when it will be convenient for him to receive the samples and to suggest the name (or names) of the sampler(s) who could appropriately take the samples. (Any registered medical practitioner may act as a sampler.)

If the parties are unable to agree as to the arrangements the solicitor for the applicant should refer the matter back to the court.

When the arrangements have been made, the solicitor should complete Pts I and II of a Direction Form in respect of each subject and attend before the District Judge by whom the direction was given, or otherwise before the District Judge for the day. The District Judge, if satisfied with the arrangements, will sign Pt I of each form and return the forms to the solicitor together with a copy of the Notes for the Guidance of Samplers.

The solicitor should then affix to Pt III of each Direction Form the photograph required by reg.6(2) (the requirements of reg.2(1) as to type of photograph being noted) except in those cases in which no photograph is required. Application should where necessary be made to the solicitors for the other parties for photographs of the subjects they represent. The solicitor should send the Direction Forms with the Notes for Guidance to the nominated sampler and make arrangements with him as to the attendance of the subjects. A subject who is under 16 or who is a patient must be accompanied by a person of full age who will identify him to the sampler (reg.4). Where, in the case of a patient, no photograph can be obtained, the Direction Form should be accompanied by a medical certificate stating that the subject is suffering from a mental disorder and that a photograph of him cannot, or should not, be taken (reg.6(2)).

Regulations 5 and 6 set out the procedure to be followed by the sampler: the main features are explained in the Notes for Guidance. The solicitor should inform the sampler immediately if any subject cannot attend as arranged.

The sampler has a discretion to alter the arrangements for sampling if those originally made are for any reason unsatisfactory. If there is reason to think that a subject may ultimately refuse to give a sample the solicitor should advise the sampler of this possibility so that samples are not taken from other subjects to no purpose. It is particularly desirable that a sample should not be taken from a child unless it will be used for tests. It should therefore be arranged, if practicable, for the child's sample to be the last to be taken.

If the sampler does not take a sample from any subject he should state on the Direction Form the reason for this, and any reason given by the subject, or the person having his care and control, for any failure to attend.

Where a Direction Form is returned to the court by a sampler (or a tester) and is not accompanied by a Report, a copy of the Direction Form must be sent by the court to each party to the proceedings.

Report by tester

On completion of the tests the tester will send to the court a Report in the prescribed form together with the associated Direction Form (reg.10). A copy of the Report must be sent by the court to every party to the proceedings and to every other person from whom the direction of the court involved the taking of samples. The report on the bodily samples often disposes of the issue or dispute. If no guardian has been appointed of the minor the order for bodily samples will contain a direction that the proceedings be restored for further directions by the District Judge when the report has been filed. If the dispute remains a live one or if there are aspects of the case making it desirable the District Judge will appoint a guardian and make any further directions which seem to be desirable. **23BPD.11**

Section 20(4) of the Act enables the court to give leave for any party to obtain a supplementary report from the tester. There is also provision for a party to call the tester as a witness subject to notice being given to the other parties within 14 days of receipt of the Report (s.20(5)).

Failure to take a necessary step

Section 23 of the 1969 Act sets out the consequences of the failure of any person to take any step required of him for the purpose of giving effect to the direction. Such steps include, inter alia, supplying information as to the persons having care and control of a subject who is under 16 or a patient, supplying a photograph or medical certificate in lieu thereof, and consenting to the taking of a sample either from himself or from a person in his care and control. **23BPD.12**

Blood Tests (Evidence of Paternity) Regulations 1971

For the Blood Tests (Evidence of Paternity) Regulations 1971 as amended by the Blood Tests (Evidence of Paternity) (Amendment) Regulations 2001 (SI 2001/773) see Vol.2, paras 9B–1263 *et seq.* **23BPD.13**

PART 24

Summary Judgment

Contents

24.0.1

Editorial introduction

24.0.2 The rules in this Part provide a procedure by which the court may carry out part of its duty of active case management, the summary disposal of issues which do not need full investigation and trial (r.1.4(2)(c)). The issues disposed of may arise in claims (including claims under the alternative procedure for claims), counterclaims, third party proceedings or similar proceedings.

The rules in this Part permit summary disposal in three types of cases which under the previous High Court rules were dealt with by separate provisions; summary judgment (RSC O.14), summary disposal of a case on a point of law (RSC O.14A) and striking out pleadings (RSC O.18 r.19).

Part 24 also permits the court to summarily dispose of cases and issues in three additional types of case:

(1) allowing summary judgment against a claimant where, on all the facts, the claim has no reasonable prospect of success;
(2) allowing summary disposal of preliminary issues where the court is satisfied that those issues do not need full investigation and trial; and
(3) allowing the court to fix summary judgment hearings of its own initiative.

There is a substantial overlap between Pt 24 and r.3.4 (Power to strike out a statement of case). As with Pt 24 the court's powers under r.3.4 may be exercised on the application of a party or on the court's own initiative. Rule 3.4(2)(a) and (b) cover the strike out of claims or defences which are unreasonably vague, incoherent, vexatious, scurrilous or obviously ill-founded and other cases which do not amount to a legally recognisable claim or defence. For a more detailed discussion of the extent to which r.3.4 overlaps with Pt 24 see the commentary to r.3.4.

Related sources

24.0.3

- Rule 3.3 (Court's power to make order of its own initiative).
- Rule 3.4 (Power to strike out a statement of case).
- Practice Direction (General Rules About Applications for Court Orders) (see para.23PD.1 above)
- Practice Direction (Summary Judgment) (see para.24PD.1 below)
- Practice Direction (Case Management-Preliminary Stage) (see para.26PD.1 below)
- Queen's Bench Guide, para.6.11 (see Vol.2, para.1B–39)

Forms

24.0.4

- ***N244*** Application notice
- **No. 44** Judgment underPt 24
- **No. 48** Judgment after decision of preliminary issue
- **PF11** Application for Pt 24 judgment (whole claim)

- **PF12** Application for Pt 24 judgment (one or some of several claims)
- **PF13** Order under Pt 24 (No.1)
- **PF14** Order under Pt 24 (No.2)
- **PF15** Order under Pt 24 (for assessment of solicitor's bill of costs) (Pt 48)

Scope of this Part[1]

24.1 This Part sets out a procedure by which the court may decide a claim or a particular issue without a trial. 24.1

(Part 53 makes special provision about summary disposal of defamation claims in accordance with the Defamation Act 1996).

"a claim or a particular issue"

These words are not defined in the rules. The word "claim" when used as a noun in other rules usually refers to the whole of a case in question (see, for example, r.8.1 and r.26.2). However, in some rules the word is used to refer to separate causes of action raised in the case in question (see, for example, r.7.3). On the assumption that the usual meaning of "claim" applies in Pt 24, an application for summary judgment which relates to only one of several causes of action raised in a case could be characterised as an application concerning "a particular issue". In case law under the previous rules the word "issue" was defined as "a disputed point of fact or law relied on by way of claim or defence" (*Koiso Finance Establishment Anstalt v John Wedge* February 15, 1994, unrep., CA, Transcript No.94/387). 24.1.1

The word "issue" is also apt to refer to any preliminary issue, i.e. a disputed point upon which a claim or defence depends in part; for example, in a negligence claim the issue of carelessness if determined separately from the issues of causation and quantum. If a party applies for summary judgment on a preliminary issue and is unsuccessful the court will make an order as to that issue which is adverse to the case of the applicant, unless it appears to the court that the preliminary issue needs full investigation and trial.

Defamation claims

Rule 53.2 provides for applications for summary disposal under ss.8 and 9 of the Defamation Act 1996. Rule 53.2 applies Pt 24 with variations. The Defamation Act 1996 permits the court to give summary judgment in any defamation claim: it may dismiss the claimant's claim if it appears to the court that it has no realistic prospect of success and there is no reason why it should be tried (s.8(2)); it may give judgment for the claimant and grant him summary relief (as defined in s.9) if it appears to the court that there is no defence to the claim which has a realistic prospect of success, and that there is no other reason why the claim should be tried (s.8(3)). 24.1.2

Grounds for summary judgment[2]

24.2 The court may give summary judgment against a claimant or defendant on the whole of a claim or on a particular issue if— 24.2

(a) it considers that—

(i) that claimant has no real prospect of succeeding on the claim or issue; or

(ii) that defendant has no real prospect of successfully defending the claim or issue; and

(b) there is no other compelling reason why the case or issue should be disposed of at a trial.

(Rule 3.4 makes provision for the court to strike out[GL] a statement of case or part of a statement of case if it appears that it discloses no reasonable grounds for bringing or defending a claim).

---

[1] Amended by the Civil Procedure (Amendment) Rules 2000 (SI 2000/221).
[2] Amended by the Civil Procedure (Amendment No.3) Rules 2000 (SI 2000/1317).

Effect of rule

24.2.1 The provisions of r.24.2 are supplemented by Practice Direction (The Summary Disposal of Claims) (see para.24PD.1 below).

The rule is badly drafted. Insofar as it provides for summary judgment against a defendant the rule is derived in part from former RSC O.14, r.1(1), which stated the circumstances in which the court could grant summary judgment to a plaintiff.

Rule 24.2 states that summary judgment may be granted "on the whole of a claim or a particular issue in it" if two circumstances are satisfied: first, if the court considers that the party has no real prospect of (as the case may be) succeeding or successfully defending on "the claim or issue", and secondly, there is no other compelling reason why the "case or issue" should be disposed of at a trial (see r.24.2(b)). (The phrase "no other compelling reason" was substituted for "no other reason" by an amendment made in 2000, see further below.) These two requirements, connected by the conjunction "and", do not hang together; the first provides the basis for granting an application for summary judgment (see further para.24.2.3 below), and the second provides a basis for refusing it (see para.24.2.4 below). The court's conclusion that the defendant has no real prospect of successfully defending the claim or issue cannot by any stretch of the imagination be considered to be a "reason" why the case or issue should be disposed of at a trial to which any "other reason" (compelling or otherwise) for so doing might be added.

This problem did not arise under the old rules. Former RSC O.14 r.3(1) stated that the court should refuse an applicaton for summary judgment against a defendant (1) where the defendant satisfied the court that there was an issue which ought to be tried, or (2) where "there ought for some other reason to be a trial". In this provision the "other reason" requirement made perfect sense and was amplified in case law. It appears that the survival in CPR r.24.2(b) of the "other reason" for a trial requirement derived from RSC O.14 r.3(1) is explained on the ground that those responsible for drafting and promulgating the CPR feared that by leaving it out of r.24.2 something important might be lost. That is perhaps understandable. However, it is unfortunate that the rule should have been left in such an unsatisfactory state.

It was perhaps inevitable that in applications for summary judgment under the CPR, whether against a defendant or against a claimant (and whether on an application or on the court's own initiative), the stricter approach evidenced by the "no real prospect of success" requirement introduced in r.24.2(a) would draw attention to the "other reason" requirement stated in r.24.2(b), and that attempts would be made to use the latter for the purpose of weakening the former. For the purpose of discouraging this, r.24.2(b) was amended (as indicated above) by the Civil Procedure (Amendment No.3) Rules 2000, so that "no other compelling reason" was substituted for "no other reason". (Presumably, in r.24.2(b) "case or issue" should read "claim or issue".)

"on the whole of a claim or on a particular issue"

24.2.2 See the commentary to r.24.1.

"no real prospect of succeeding/successfully defending"

24.2.3 In order to defeat the application for summary judgment it is sufficient for the respondent to show some "prospect", i.e. some chance of success. That prospect must be "real", i.e. the court will disregard prospects which are false, fanciful or imaginary. The inclusion of the word "real" means that the respondent has to have a case which is better than merely arguable (*International Finance Corp v Utexafrica Sprl* [2001] C.L.C. 1361 and *ED&F Man Liquid Products Ltd v Patel* [2003] EWCA Civ 472). The respondent is not required to show that his case will probably succeed at trial. A case may be held to have a "real prospect" of success even if it is improbable. However, in such a case the court is likely to make a conditional order (as to which, see the commentary to r.24.6).

The hearing of an application for summary judgment is not a summary trial. The court at the summary judgment application will consider the merits of the respondent's case only to the extent necessary to determine whether it has sufficient merit to proceed to trial. The proper disposal of an issue under Pt 24 does not involve the court conducting a mini-trial (per Lord Woolf M.R. in *Swain v Hillman* [2001] 1 All E.R. 91. How the court decides whether a defence is real without conducting a mini-trial has led to a series of unsatisfactory cases now hopefully concluded by the clear statements of authority in *Three Rivers DC v Bank of England (No.3)* [2001] 2 All E.R. 513, HL (a summary judgment application; see especially, the speech of Lord Hope of Craighead at paras 94 and 95) and *ED&F Man Liquid Products Ltd v Patel* [2003] EWCA Civ 472 (a set aside application; see especially paras 9, 10, 11, 52 and 53 in the judgment of Potter L.J.). At a trial, the criterion to be applied by the court is probability: victory goes to the party whose case is the more probable (taking into account the burden of proof). This is not true of a summary judgment application. "The criterion which the judge has to apply under CPR Pt 24 is not one of probability; it is absence of reality." (Lord Hobhouse of Woodborough in *Three Rivers DC v Bank of England (No.3)* [2001] 2 All E.R. 513).

Where a summary judgment application gives rise to a short point of law or construction, the court should decide that point if it has before it all the evidence necessary for a proper determination and it is satisfied that the parties have had an adequate opportunity to address the point in argument. The court should not allow a case to go forward to trial simply because there is a possibility of some further evidence arising (*ICI Chemicals & Polymers Ltd v TTE Training Ltd* [2007] EWCA Civ 725: "if the respondent's case is bad in law, he will in truth have no real prospect of succeeding on his claim or successfully defending the claim against him, as the case may be. Similarly, if the applicant's case is bad in law, the sooner that is determined, the better" (per Moore-Bick L.J.)). Conversely, an application for summary judgment is not appropriate to resolve a complex question of law and fact, the determination of which necessitates a trial of the issue having regard to all of the evidence (*Apvodedo NV v Collins* [2008] EWHC 775 (Ch)). An additional problem arises when a point of law is taken on an appeal against an award of summary judgment which was not argued in the lower court: a determination of the point by the appeal court would deprive the losing party of an opportunity to bring a first appeal on that point. In a suitable case this problem might be solved by the appeal court allowing the appeal against the award of summary judgment and then immediately rehearing the summary judgment application again, thereby making a first instance decision on the matter (see per MacDuff J. in *Carter v Freeman Group Plc* [2008] EWHC 1572 (QB)).

In practice it is often more difficult to apply the "no real prospect of success" test on an application for summary judgment than it is to try the case in its entirety. The decision-maker at trial will usually have a better grasp of the case as a whole, because of the added benefits of hearing the evidence tested, of receiving more developed submissions and of having more time in which to digest and reflect on the materials (see the judgment of Mummery L.J. in *The Bolton Pharmaceutical Company 100 Ltd v Doncaster Pharmaceuticals Group Ltd* [2006] EWCA Civ 661).

In *Beiersdorf AG v Ramlort Ltd* [2004] EWHC 117, Ch D, the claimants sought injunctions and damages in respect of alleged trademark infringements. The defendants denied liability saying they had letters of consent from the claimant. The claimant submitted that those letters were forged and sought summary judgment. It was held that the matter should go to trial and not be disposed of summarily. The question whether the alleged letters of consent were genuine should be determined after disclosure and cross-examination in the ordinary way.

The disposal of a claim or part of a claim by way of summary judgment may raise issues in relation to the ECHR art.6 right of access to a court: see, by way of analogy, para.3.4.1 above (on the court's power to strike out all or part of a statement of case pursuant to r.3.4(2)).

"no other compelling reason [for] a trial"

In July 2000, r.24.2(b) was amended by the Civil Procedure (Amendment No.3) Rules 2000 to include the word "compelling". Although the inclusion adds clarity to the ambit of summary judgment it does not appear to alter it in substance. Pre-CPR, the following circumstances were held to afford "some other reason for trial": where the claimant's case appears to be "devious and crafty" and not "plain and straightforward" (*Miles v Bull* [1969] 1 Q.B. 258; [1968] 3 All E.R. 632); where the defendant is an executor or administrator who can raise facts by reference to the existence or absence of letters, accounts or such like of the deceased which make it reasonable to require full investigation (*Harrison v Bottenheim* [1878] 26 W.R. 362) where the claimant's case tended to show that he had acted harshly and unconscionably and it is thought desirable that if he were to get judgment at all it should be in the full light of publicity (per Cairns L.J. in *Bank für Gemeinwirtschaft Aktiengesellschaft v City of London Garages* [1971] 1 W.L.R. 149 at 158; [1971] 1 All E.R. 541 at 548). 24.2.4

The previous rule did not apply to proceedings which included a claim by the plaintiff for libel, slander, malicious prosecution or false imprisonment. Cases such as these are not expressly excluded from the current rule. However, in such cases the respondent may have a right to trial by jury (see SCA 1981 s.69 and CCA 1984 s.66; see Vol.2, paras 9A–256 and 9A–546, respectively). This right is not a matter of mere procedure and therefore the CPR cannot and does not override it (*Safeway Stores Plc v Tate* [2001] Q.B. 1120; [2001] 4 All E.R. 193, CA). Although summary judgment may be appropriate on issues of law, these statutory provisions entitle a respondent to have material issues of fact decided by a jury. In *Safeway*, the claim never reached trial by jury: the Court of Appeal declined to anticipate the possibility that the verdict of a jury might be perverse and such that it could be reversed on appeal. Contrast *Alexander v Arts Council* [2001] 1 W.L.R. 1840, CA, a libel claim that did proceed to trial by jury. In *Alexander* the grant of summary judgment made by the trial judge in favour of the defendant was upheld by the Court of Appeal; the claimant's case depended upon a finding that publications had been made maliciously and the evidence in support of the claim, taken at its highest, was such that a jury properly directed could not properly find in favour of the claimant. Summary judgment in such circumstances "was not, as was suggested in *Safeway v Tate*, speculating that the jury *might* reach a perverse decision; rather that the only jury decision capable of supporting the case in question would be bound to be set aside on appeal" (per May L.J at para.38).

It has been said that the decisions in *Safeway* and *Alexander* draw attention to the important distinction in defamation cases between the function of the judge and that of the jury (*Branson v Bower (No.2)* [2002] Q.B. 737 per Eady J. at para.12 and see further, para.16).

The fact that the claim on which summary judgment is sought involves serious allegations of bad faith against a party is not by itself a compelling reason for a trial. Findings of bad faith can be reached in a summary judgment application if, in the circumstances of the case, such issues can be determined without a trial (*Wrexham Association Football Club Ltd v Crucialmove Ltd* [2006] EWCA Civ 237).

Burdens of proof

24.2.5 In *ED&F Man Liquid Products Ltd v Patel* [2003] EWCA Civ 472; [2003] EWCA Civ 472, it was said that under r.24.2 the overall burden of proof rests on the applicant to establish that there are grounds to believe that the respondent has no real prospect of success and that there is no other reason for a trial. The existence of this burden is indicated by para.2(3) of the Practice Direction supplementing Pt 24; the applicant must (a) identify concisely any point of law or provision in a document on which he relies, and/or (b) state that the application is made because the applicant believes that on the evidence the respondent has no real prospect of succeeding on the claim or issue or (as the case may be) of successfully defending the claim or issue to which the application relates, and in either case state that the applicant knows of no other reason why the disposal of the claim or issue should await trial. The essential ingredient is the applicant's belief that the respondent has no real prospect of success and that there is no other reason for a trial.

If the applicant for summary judgment adduces credible evidence in support of his application, the respondent becomes subject to an evidential burden of proving some real prospect of success or some other reason for a trial. The standard of proof required of the respondent is not high. It suffices merely to rebut the applicant's statement of belief. The language of r.24.2 ("no real prospect ... no other reason ...") indicates that, in determining the question, the court must apply a negative test. The respondent's case must carry some degree of conviction: the court is not required to accept without question any assertion he makes *Britannia Building Society v Prangley* June 12, 2000, unrep., Ch D; for pre-CPR authorities on this point see *National Westminster Bank Plc v Daniel* [1993] I W.L.R. 1453; [1994] 1 All E.R. 156 and the cases cited therein. However, the proper disposal of an issue under Pt 24 does not involve the judge in conducting a mini-trial (*Swain v Hillman* [2001] 1 All E.R. 91). Therefore, the Court hearing a Pt 24 application should be wary of trying issues of fact on evidence where the facts are apparently credible and are to be set against the facts being advanced by the other side. Choosing between them is the function of the trial judge, not the judge on an interim application, unless there is some inherent improbability in what is being asserted or some extraneous evidence which would contradict it (*Fashion Gossip Ltd v Esprit Telecoms UK Ltd* [2000] EWCA Civ 235, CA; *cf. Day v RAC Motoring Services Ltd* [1999] 1 All E.R. 1007, per Ward L.J. at 1013 propounding the adoption of a negative test on applications to set aside default judgments). When deciding whether the respondent has some real prospect of success the court should not apply the standard which would be applicable at the trial, namely the balance of probabilities on the evidence presented; on an application for summary judgment the court should also consider the evidence that could reasonably be expected to be available at trial (*Royal Brompton Hospital NHS Trust v Hammond (No.5)*, [2001] EWCA Civ 550, CA).

Effect of a set off or counterclaim

As to the meaning of the term "set off" see r.16.6 and the commentary thereto. As to the meaning of the term "counterclaim" see the Glossary and r.20.2 and the commentary thereto. **24.2.6**

The question which arises here is whether a defendant can rely upon a set off or counterclaim as a "reason why the claim should be dealt with at trial" and thereby defeat a claim for summary judgment. The case law under the previous rules on this point was not coherent. Often the court refused to give summary judgment in such cases or granted summary judgment subject to a stay on enforcement pending trial of a counterclaim (see *Morgan & Son Ltd v S Martin Johnson & Co* [1949] 1 K.B. 107, CA; *Hanak v Green* [1958] 2 Q.B. 9; *United Overseas Ltd v Peter Robinson Ltd*, March 26, 1991, CA, Transcript no.91/0297). In some exceptional cases the claimant obtained summary judgment which was enforceable immediately even though the defendant intended to raise a counterclaim (see "No set off in action on dishonoured bill or cheque" below).

It is possible that, under the new rules, the court may grant summary judgment more frequently than hitherto and may impose a delay on enforcement more frequently than hitherto. Such an approach would appear to be in harmony with the overriding objective to ensure that cases are dealt with "expeditiously and fairly" (r.1.1(2)(d))) and with the court's duty to actively manage cases by "deciding promptly which issues need full investigation and trial and accordingly disposing summarily of the others" (r.1.4(2)(c)).

If a claim is otherwise suitable for summary disposal, the court may prefer to deal with a defence of set off by entering summary judgment on the claim expressing that judgment to be subject to the determination of the defendant's cross claim or until further order, and stating that the summary judgment would not be enforceable until determination of the cross claim or until a further order was made. See further "Judgment on the claim or an issue therein" under r.24.6, para.24.6.3.

No set off in action on dishonoured bill or cheque

Under the previous rules a wholly different practice prevailed concerning the setting up of a defence of set off in proceedings on a dishonoured bill of exchange, or cheque or promissory note. In such proceedings, save in exceptional circumstances or upon strong grounds (per Stephen J. in *Newman v Lever* [1887] 4 T.L.R. 91) the defendant was not allowed to set up a set off or counterclaim for damages for breach of some other contract or the commission of a tort, and the plaintiff was entitled to judgment for the amount of his claim without a stay of execution (*Brown Shipley & Co Ltd v Alicia Hosiery Ltd* [1966] 1 Lloyd's Rep. 668, CA; *James Lamont & Co Ltd v Hylands Ltd* [1950] 1 K.B. 585, CA; *Montebianco Industrie Tessili SpA v Carlyle Mills (London) Ltd* [1981] 1 Lloyd's Rep. 509, CA (summary judgment on dishonoured bill without a stay pending determination of counterclaim for defective goods)). This practice applied whether the counterclaim was connected with or arose out of or was independent of the contract in respect of which the bill, cheque or note was given, and whether or not the proceedings were between the immediate parties to the bill (*Anglo-Italian Bank v Wells & Davies* [1878] 38 L.T. 197, CA). The principle is that a bill, cheque or note is given and taken in payment as so much cash, and not as merely given a right of action for the creditor to litigate a counterclaim (see *Jackson v Murphy* [1887] 4 T.L.R. 92). **24.2.7**

"We have repeatedly said in this court that a bill of exchange or a promissory note is to be treated as cash. It is to be honoured unless there is some good reason to the contrary" (see per Lord Denning M.R. in *Fielding & Platt Ltd v Selim Najjar* [1969] 1 W.L.R. 357 at 361; [1969] 2 All E.R. 150 at 152, CA).

In an action on a dishonoured bill of exchange by one of the immediate parties to the bill against the other, a claim for an unspecified amount of damages under a contract for the sale of goods did not afford a defence, nor was it available as a set off or counterclaim, nor did it afford a ground for a stay of execution (*Nova (Jersey) Knit Ltd v Kammgarn Spinnerei GmbH* [1977] 1 W.L.R. 713; [1977] 2 All E.R. 463, HL). "[A seller] may demand payment in cash; but if the buyer cannot provide this at once, he may agree to take bills of exchange payable at future dates. These are taken as equivalent to deferred instalments of cash. Unless they are to be treated as unconditionally payable instruments ... which the seller can negotiate for cash, the seller might just as well give credit. And it is for this reason that English law ... does not allow cross claims, or defences, except such limited defences as those based on fraud, invalidity, or failure of consideration, to be made." (per Lord Wilberforce at 721). In *Esso Petroleum Co Ltd v Milton* [1997] 1 W.L.R. 938; [1997] 2 All E.R. 593, CA the special rule precluding a defence of set off was applied to direct debit mandates which were treated as equivalent to cheques.

Types of proceedings in which summary judgment is available[1]

24.3 **24.3—(1) The court may give summary judgment against a claimant in any type of proceedings.**

(2) The court may give summary judgment against a defendant in any type of proceedings except—

(a) proceedings for possession of residential premises against—

(i) a mortgagor; or

(ii) a tenant or a person holding over after the end of his tenancy whose occupancy is protected within the meaning of the Rent Act 1977[2] or the Housing Act 1988[3] and;

(b) proceedings for an admiralty claim in rem.

"any type of proceedings"

24.3.1 A valid application for summary judgment can be made in any type of proceedings except those mentioned in r.24.3(2)(a) (applications against a defendant in certain types of proceedings for possession of residential premises) and those mentioned in r.24.3(2)(b) (applications against a defendant in proceedings for an admiralty claim in rem). It is important to note that there are no restrictions on applications for summary judgment against claimants and r.24.3(2)(a) does not restrict applications for summary judgment for possession against any tenant of residential premises, only those tenants whose occupancy is protected within the meaning of the Rent Act 1977 or the Housing Act 1988. Moreover, in any cases which do fall within the exceptions mentioned in r.24.3(2)(a) or (b), an order akin to summary judgment may be obtained against the defendant under r.3.4. In *Shephard v Wheeler* [2000] W.T.L.R. 1175 an application for summary judgment under Pt 24 was made by a claimant in contentious probate proceedings; summary judgment not being available in such proceedings at that time the court treated the application as an application to strike out the defence under r.3.4 and granted that application.

Rule 53.2(3) provides a further exception to Pt 24: an application for summary judgment under Pt 24 may not be made if (a) an application has been made for summary disposal under ss.8 and 9 of the Defamation Act 1996 and that application has not been disposed of; or, (b) summary relief under s.9 has been granted on an application for summary disposal under the Defamation Act 1996. Under RSC O.77 there was a general prohibition on summary judgment against the Crown. This is now modified into a deferral of the earliest date upon which a summary judgment application can be made against the Crown (r.24.4(1A)).

The new rules do not repeat the provisions contained in the old rules which excluded applications for summary judgment in proceedings which included a claim by the plaintiff for libel, slander, malicious prosecution or false imprisonment (former RSC O.14, r.1(2) and CCR O.9, r.14(1)(c)). However in these cases, the defendant may have a right to trial by jury and the CPR cannot and does not override that right (see *Safeway Stores Plc v Tate* [2001] Q.B. 1120, CA and see para.24.2.4 above).

---

[1] Amended by the Civil Procedure (Amendment No.3) Rules 2000 (SI 2000/1317), and the Civil Procedure (Amendment No.4) Rules 2000 (SI 2000/2092).

[2] 1997 c.42.

[3] 1988 c.50.

The new rules do not repeat the provision contained in the old rules which excluded applications for summary judgment in proceedings automatically referred for determination as small claims (former CCR O.9, r.14(1)(a)). Therefore, an application for summary judgment may be made in a claim allocated to the small claims track (however, see further "Ideal time for application", para.24.4.1 below).

Where it is appropriate, the court may treat an application to strike out under r.3.4(2)(a), or an appeal from a refusal to strike out under that provision, as if it was were an application for summary judgment under r.24.2 (*Taylor v Midland Bank Trust Co Ltd (No.2)* [2002] W.T.L.R. 95, July 21, 1999, unrep., CA; *S v Gloucestershire CC* [2000] 3 All E.R. 346, CA, at p.372 per May L.J.).

Pre-CPR, on a claim for an unspecified amount of damages ("unliquidated damages") the court had no power to give summary judgment for an indefinable part of those damages even where it was certain that some substantial sum was due (*Associated Bulk Carriers Limited v Koch Shipping Inc* [1978] 2 All E.R. 254, CA). Instead, the proper course was for the claimant to apply for summary judgment for damages to be assessed and then to seek an interim payment of damages. The two applications could conveniently be made and dealt with together. It is likely that the same principles apply today (*Sinclair Investment Holdings SA v Cushnie* [2006] EWHC 219 (Ch); as to interim payments see para.25.7.27 below).

Accounts and inquiries

Paragraph 6 is limited to claims brought by claim form but see further "Counterclaims, third party proceedings and other similar claims" below. **24.3.2**

Specific performance

Paragraph 7 of the Practice Direction supplementing Pt 24 (see para.24PD.7) **24.3.3** provides for summary judgment applications in respect of the remedy of specific performance and similar remedies in cases in which in the High Court were formerly governed by RSC O.86, rr.1 and 2. The paragraph modifies the provisions otherwise applicable as to the earliest time for application, the documentation to be served with the application notice and the time for service of that documentation (see further "Earliest time for applications in certain specific performance cases", "Evidence in support of the application" and "Timetable for Evidence", under r.24.4).

Paragraph 7 is limited to claims brought by claim form but see further "Counterclaims, third party proceedings and other similar claims" below.

Counterclaims, third party proceedings and other similar claims

Counterclaims, third party proceedings and other similar claims are referred to col- **24.3.4** lectively in these rules as "Pt 20 claims" (see r.20.2). Part 24 applies to Pt 20 claims as if they were claims (see r.20.3).

Alternative procedure for claims

Part 8 provides an alternative procedure for claims which largely reproduces the **24.3.5** procedure applicable to cases commenced under the previous rules by originating summons or by originating application. There is no restriction on applications under Pt 24 in cases in which the claimant uses the Pt 8 procedure. However, that procedure is itself intended to provide a simple and expeditious means of determining cases.

Procedure[1]

24.4—(1) A claimant may not apply for summary judgment until **24.4** **the defendant against whom the application is made has filed—**

(a) an acknowledgment of service; or

(b) a defence,

unless—

(i) the court gives permission; or

(ii) a practice direction provides otherwise.

[1] Amended by the Civil Procedure (Amendment) Rules 2000 (SI 2000/221).

(Rule 10.3 sets out the period for filing an acknowledgment of service and rule 15.4 the period for filing a defence).

(1A) In civil proceedings against the Crown, as defined in rule 66.1(2), a claimant may not apply for summary judgment until after expiry of the period for filing a defence specified in rule 15.4.

(2) If a claimant applies for summary judgment before a defendant against whom the application is made has filed a defence, that defendant need not file a defence before the hearing.

(3) Where a summary judgment hearing is fixed, the respondent (or the parties where the hearing is fixed of the court's own initiative) must be given at least 14 days' notice of—

(a) the date fixed for the hearing; and

(b) the issues which it is proposed that the court will decide at the hearing.

(4) A practice direction may provide for a different period of notice to be given.

(Part 23 contains the general rules about how to make an application).

(Rule 3.3 applies where the court exercises its powers on its own initiative).

Ideal time for application

24.4.1 A party intending to apply for summary judgment should do so before or when filing his Allocation Questionnaire. If he does so, the court will not usually allocate the claim to a track before the hearing of the application. Where a party files an Allocation Questionnaire stating that he intends to apply for summary judgment but has not done so, the case will usually be listed for an Allocation Hearing. The application for summary judgment may be heard at that Allocation Hearing if the application notice has been issued and served in sufficient time (see generally the Practice Direction supplementing Pt 26, para.5.2 (at para.26PD.1 below) and, as to Allocation Questionnaires and Allocation Hearings, rr.26.3 and 26.5, respectively).

The question whether summary judgment should be granted may be raised at trial (e.g. *Evans v James* [1999] EWCA Civ 1759 (judgment for the claimant) and *Alexander v Arts Council of Wales* [2001] EWCA Civ 514 (judgment for the defendant). As to the interrelationship between summary judgment and submissions of no case to answer see *Benham Ltd v Kythira Investments Ltd* [2003] EWCA Civ 1794.

Effect on time for service of defence

24.4.2 If a claimant applies for summary judgment before a defendant against whom the application is made has filed a defence, that defendant need not file a defence before the hearing (r.24.4(2)).

If a defendant applies for summary judgment the claimant cannot obtain a default judgment before that application has been disposed of (r.12.3(3)).

Earliest time for application: general rules

24.4.3 Unless a practice direction provides otherwise a claimant cannot validly apply for summary judgment until:

(1) the defendant against whom the application is made has filed an acknowledgment of service (as to which, see Pt 10); or

(2) the defendant against whom the application is made has filed a defence (as to which, see Pt 15); or

(3) the court gives permission (r.24.4(1)); for a case example see *Phillips v Avena [2005] EWHC 3333* (Ch)).

Rule 24.4(1A) modifies the position in civil proceedings against the Crown; a claimant cannot apply for summary judgment against the Crown until the expiry of the period for filing a defence even if the Crown files an acknowledgment of service or a defence before then.

The time limits for filing an acknowledgment of service and a defence both run from the date of service of the claimant's particulars of claim (see rr.10.3 and 15.4, respectively). It therefore follows that a claimant cannot validly apply for summary judgment before serving his particulars of claim unless the court gives permission under (3) above.

If, after service of the particulars of claim, no acknowledgment of service or defence is filed the claimant should, before seeking the court's permission under (3) above, consider whether he can obtain a default judgment (as to which see Pt 12).

A defendant can apply for summary judgment in his favour on the claimant's claim at any time after the proceedings have been commenced. There is no requirement for him to file an acknowledgment of service or a defence before doing so.

The rules make no special provision as to the earliest time for applications in respect of counterclaims, third party proceedings or other additional claims (as to which, see Pt 20). Presumably the earliest time to apply in such claims is after the counterclaim or other additional claim has been served (see r.20.10).

Earliest time for application in certain specific performance cases

In specific performance cases and similar cases which fall within the limits of para.7 of the Practice Direction supplementing Pt 24 (see para.24PD.7 below), a claimant may apply for summary judgment at any time after the claim form has been served, whether or not the defendant has acknowledged service of the claim form, whether or not the time for acknowledging service has expired and whether or not any particulars of claim have been served. **24.4.4**

Earliest time for application in defamation claims

Applications for summary disposal under s.8 of the Defamation Act 1996 may be made by either party at any time after the service of particulars of claim, whether or not the defendant has acknowledged service of the claim form or has served the defence and whether or not the time for acknowledging service has expired (Practice Direction Supplementing Pt 53, para.5.2 (see para.53PD.3 below). **24.4.5**

Earliest time for application where Part 8 procedure used

The earliest time for an application for summary judgment by a claimant who has used the alternative procedure for claims set out in Pt 8 differs from the general rules set out above because: **24.4.6**

(1) the claimant is not required to file particulars of claim (see r.8.9);
(2) the defendant is not required to file a defence (see r.8.9); and
(3) if the defendant fails to acknowledge service of the claim form the claimant cannot obtain a default judgment (r.12.2(b)).

Therefore, a claimant seeking summary judgment where the Pt 8 procedure has been used must either await the filing of an acknowledgment of service or seek the court's permission to apply (see r.24.4(1)).

Hearings concerning summary judgment fixed of the court's own initiative

Part of the court's duty of active case management is the summary disposal of issues which do not need full investigation and trial (r.1.4(2)(c)). Its case management powers include power to make orders, including orders under Pt 24 of its own initiative (see generally r.3.3). **24.4.7**

Paragraph 5.4 of the Practice Direction supplementing Pt 26 (see para.26PD.5 below) makes specific provision for cases in which the court wishes to consider whether, before allocating a case to a track, whether any claim or issue in that case should be summarily disposed of. In such cases, the court will fix a hearing and give the parties notice of the issues which it is proposed that the court will decide or, alternatively, the court will make an order directing a party to take the steps described in the order within a stated time and specifying the consequences of not taking those steps.

Minimum period of notice of hearing

The minimum period of notice to be given to the respondent (or to the parties where the hearing is fixed of the court's own initiative) is 14 days (r.24.4(3)). For precise details as to the calculation of that time period see r.2.8 and the commentary thereto. **24.4.8**

In certain specific performance cases the minimum period of notice of the application and evidence is only 4 days before the hearing (see Practice Direction supplementing Pt 24, para.7.3, para.24PD.7 below).

Contents of an application notice

24.4.9 An applicant may use Practice Form **N244** suitably completed so as to:

(1) comply with the formal requirements set out in para.2.1 of the Practice Direction supplementing Pt 23 (see para.23PD.2 below),

(2) state that it is an application for summary judgment made under Pt 24 (para.2(2) of the Practice Direction supplementing Pt 24 at para.24PD.2 below)),

(3) state what order the applicant is seeking and, briefly, why he is seeking that order (see r.23.6),

(4) identify the written evidence on which the applicant relies, unless no evidence is relied on or the application notice itself contains all such evidence (see para.2(4) of the Practice Direction supplementing Pt 24 (at para.24PD.2 below)), and

(5) draw the attention of the respondent to r.24.5(1) (see para.2(5) of the Practice Direction supplementing Pt 24 (at para.24PD.2 below)). The Practice Direction supplementing Pt 4 (see 4PD.2) lists two forms of application; **PF11** (for Pt 24 judgment, whole claim) and **PF12** (for Pt 24 judgment, one or some of several claims).

If the application is intended to be made to a Judge other than a Master or District Judge the application notice should so state (para.2.6 of the Practice Direction supplementing Pt 23 at para.23PD.2 below). The hearing of a summary judgment application will normally take place before a Master or District Judge but:

(a) the Master or District Judge may direct that the application be heard by a High Court Judge (if the case is in the High Court) or a Circuit Judge (if the case is in a county court) (see para.3 of the Practice Direction supplementing Pt 24 at para.24PD.3 below);

(b) the jurisdiction of Masters and District Judges to grant injunctions is limited.

In specific performance cases and similar cases which fall within the limits of para.7 of the Practice Direction supplementing Pt 24 (see para.24PD.7 below), the application notice must have attached to it the text of the order sought by the claimant (see para.7.2).

Evidence in support of the application

24.4.10 An applicant cannot rely upon oral evidence unless the court so permits (r.32.6). Instead he may rely upon written evidence set out in his claim form, statement of case, or application notice or in a witness statement. Each item of written evidence relied on must contain a statement of truth (as to which, see further the Practice Direction supplementing Pt 22 (see para.22PD.1) and the Practice Direction supplementing Pt 8, para.5.2 (see para.8PD.5). An applicant may also rely upon affidavit evidence if he so wishes. However, if he does so, he may not recover any additional costs thereby incurred unless the court orders otherwise (r.32.15 and as to affidavits generally, r.32.16, r.32.17 and the Practice Direction which supplements Pt 32 at para.32PD.1 below).

Evidence relied on which is not set out in the application notice itself must be served with the application notice (unless already served) and must also be filed (Practice Direction supplementing Pt 23, paras 9.3 and 9.6, respectively (see para.23PD.9 below)).

Paragraph 2(3) of the Practice Direction supplementing Pt 24 (see para.24PD.2 below) provides that the application notice or the evidence contained or referred to in it or served with it must:

(a) identify concisely any point of law or provision in a document on which the applicant relies; and/or

(b) state that it is made because the applicant believes that on the evidence the respondent has no real prospect of succeeding on the claim or issue or (as the case may be) of successfully defending the claim or issue to which the application relates,

and in either case must state that the applicant knows of no other reason why the disposal of the claim or issue should await trial.

Effect of non-compliance with the requirements of rules and practice directions

The court has general power to rectify matters where there has been an error of procedure such as defects or omissions in the documents supporting an application or a failure to serve documents within the time limits applicable (see r.3.10 and the commentary thereto). **24.4.11**

Evidence for the purposes of a summary judgment hearing

24.5—(1) If the respondent to an application for summary judgment wishes to rely on written evidence at the hearing, he must— **24.5**

(a) file the witness evidence; and

(b) serve copies on every other party to the application,

at least 7 days before the summary judgment hearing.

(2) If the applicant wishes to rely on a witness statement in reply, he must—

(a) file the written evidence; and

(b) serve a copy on the respondent,

at least 3 days before the summary judgment hearing.

(3) Where a summary judgment hearing is fixed by the court of its own initiative—

(a) any party who wishes to rely on written evidence at the hearing must—

(i) file the written evidence; and

(ii) unless the court orders otherwise, serve copies on every other party to the proceedings,

at least 7 days before the date of the hearing;

(b) any party who wishes to rely on written evidence at the hearing in reply to any other party's written evidence must—

(i) file the written evidence in reply; and

(ii) unless the court orders otherwise serve copies on every other party to the proceedings,

at least 3 days before the date of the hearing.

(4) This rule does not require written evidence—

(a) to be filed if it has already been filed; or

(b) to be served on a party on whom it has already been served.

Evidence in support of the application

See the annotation under this heading in the commentary to r.24.4. **24.5.1**

Evidence in response and further evidence in reply

Given the burdens of proof in summary judgment applications (see "Burdens of proof" under r.24.2), the evidence in response to an application should contain: **24.5.2**

(1) if the respondent is the defendant, evidence of facts justifying any reason relied on showing why the claim or issue should be dealt with at trial;

(2) if the respondent is the claimant, evidence of facts showing a case which, if unanswered, would entitle him to judgment on the relevant claim or issue.

If the respondent files and serves written evidence the applicant may, if he wishes, rely on written evidence in reply. There is no requirement for evidence in reply to be identified in the application notice (Practice Direction supplementing Pt 24, para.2(4) at para.24PD.2 below).

No party can rely upon oral evidence unless the court so permits (r.32.6). Instead, a party may rely on written evidence set out in his statement of case (if any) or in a witness statement. Each item of written evidence relied on must contain a statement of truth (as to which, see further Pt 22 and the Practice Direction supplementing it at para.22PD.1). A party may also rely upon affidavit evidence if he so wishes. However, if he does so he may not recover any additional costs thereby incurred unless the court orders otherwise (r.32.15 and, as to affidavits generally, see rr.32.16, 32.17 and the Practice Direction which supplements Pt 32 at para.32PD.1 below).

Timetable for serving evidence

24.5.3 Unless the summary judgment hearing was fixed by the court of its own initiative:

(1) The evidence in support of the application must either be contained in the application notice itself or must be served with the application notice (unless already served) (Practice Direction supplementing Pt 23, para.9.3 (see para.23PD.9). The evidence in support must also be filed (Practice Direction supplementing Pt 23, para.9.6 (see para.23PD.9)).
(2) Evidence in response to the application must be filed and served on every other party to the application at least seven days before the hearing (r.24.5(1)).
(3) Evidence in reply must be filed and served on the respondent at least three days before the hearing (r.24.5(2)).

Where a summary judgment hearing is fixed by the court of its own initiative:

(1) Any party who wishes to rely on written evidence at the hearing must file and serve it on every other party to the proceedings at least seven days before the date of the hearing (r.24.5(3)(a)).
(2) Any party who wishes to rely on written evidence at the hearing in reply to any other party's written evidence must file and (unless the court otherwise orders) serve it on every other party to the proceedings at least three days before the date of the hearing (r.24.5(3)(b)).

In specific performance cases and similar cases which fall within the limits of para.7 of the Practice Direction supplementing Pt 24 (see para.24PD.7 below), the claimant must file and serve on every other party to the application any written evidence he wishes to rely on at least four days before the hearing and r.24.5 does not apply (para.7.3).

As to the effect of late service of evidence and other failures to comply with the requirements of the rules or Practice Directions, see r.3.10 and the commentary thereto.

Court's powers when it determines a summary judgment application

24.6 **24.6 When the court determines a summary judgment application it may—**

(a) give directions as to the filing and service of a defence;
(b) give further directions about the management of the case.

(Rule 3.1(3) provides that the court may attach conditions when it makes an order.)

The court's approach

24.6.1 The court's approach to the question whether or not to grant summary judgment is described in para.24.2.4 above.

Orders which the court may make

24.6.2 The orders which the court may make on an application under Pt 24 include:

(a) judgment on the claim or on an issue therein;
(b) the striking out or dismissal of the claim;
(c) the dismissal of the application;
(d) a conditional order; and
(e) an order dealing with costs.

(See paras 5 and 9 of the Practice Direction supplementing Pt 24 (paras 24PD.5 and 24PD.9 below); a marginal note to para.5 states that the court will not follow its former practice of granting leave to a defendant to defend a claim, whether conditionally or unconditionally.)

Judgment on the claim or on an issue therein

The judgment given may be the grant of remedies sought, an order for damages to be assessed or an order amounting to declaratory relief finally determining a preliminary issue in the proceedings in favour of the claimant or defendant (see further, the commentary to r.24.1). **24.6.3**

In some cases the court will give judgment with a stay of enforcement. Where the claimant has succeeded on his claim but the defendant has shown a plausible counterclaim of a value which equals or exceeds the claim the court may stay enforcement on the claim until after the trial of the counterclaim. Under the previous rules the circumstances in which the court would make such an order were limited. Counterclaims amounting to set-offs would often prevent the entry of summary judgment in the first place. Under the new rules the court may make an order disposing of the issues raised by the claimant by giving summary judgment on his claim subject to the determination of the defendant's cross claim (see further "Effect of a set-off or counterclaim" under r.24.2).

On a claim by a solicitor against his former client for non-payment of costs, the court may, if there is no real prospect of defending the claim, give summary judgment for a sum to be determined by means of a detailed assessment under Pts 47 and 48. For the form of order see **PF15** listed in the Practice Direction supplementing Pt 4. Such an order can be made even if the former client has lost the opportunity to apply for a detailed assessment of the solicitor's bill under Pt III of the Solicitors Act 1974 (*Thomas Watts & Co v Smith* [1998] 2 Costs L.R. 59, March 16, 1998, unrep., CA; *Turner & Co v Palomo SA* [2000] 1 W.L.R. 37). If, in addition to challenging items in the bill, the defendant also counterclaims for negligence, an order in Form **PF15** can be made with a stay of proceedings after the detailed assessment pending the determination of the counterclaim.

The striking out or dismissal of the claim

This order will be made in favour of the defendant if the court is satisfied that the claimant's claim is unwinnable. **24.6.4**

The dismissal of the application

This order will be made if the court is not satisfied that the respondent's case has no real prospect of success or if the court is not satisfied that there is no other reason why the case or issue should be disposed of at a trial. **24.6.5**

A conditional order

This order will be made if it appears to the court that, in respect of some claim or defence or issue, it is possible that that claim, defence or issue may succeed but it is improbable that it will do so (see para.4.3 of the Practice Direction supplementing Pt 24 at para.24PD.1 below). **24.6.6**

Paragraph 5.2 of the Practice Direction supplementing Pt 24 (see para.24PD.1 below) defines a conditional order as an order which requires a party:

(a) to pay a sum of money into court; or
(b) to take a specified step in relation to his claim or defence as the case may be, and which provides that that party's claim will be dismissed or his statement of case will be struck out if he does not comply.

The condition must be one which is capable of being complied with; an impecunious party should not be ordered to pay into court a sum of money which he is unlikely to be able to raise (*Chapple v Williams* (1999) L.T.L., December 8, 1999, CA). However a conditional order may be made against a company which has no assets and which has ceased trading if there is evidence that it is able to raise funds when needed (*Foot & Bowden v Anglo Europe Corp Ltd*, February 17, 2000, unrep., CA).

As a general rule the court should not order the payment of a sum which may be beyond the respondent's means to pay in the absence of any evidence of the respondent's means unless it is satisfied that the respondent has been given appropriate prior notice of such an order: the notice may be given informally by letter sent by the applicant to the effect that, if summary judgment is not granted, the applicant will be seeking a conditional order along the lines set out in the letter; such notice may enable the respondent to prepare a witness statement as to means for production at the stage of proceedings when the court says it intends to make a conditional order (*Anglo Eastern Trust Ltd v Kermanshahchi* [2002] EWCA Civ 198 noted in *Civil Procedure News*, Issue 04/02.

In *Olatawura v Abiloye* [2002] EWCA Civ 998; [2003] 1 W.L.R. 275, Simon Brown L.J. gave guidance as to the court's approach to the making of conditional orders requiring a party advancing an improbable case to give security for his opponent's costs. If, as a condition of pursuing an unpromising defence, it was appropriate to secure the claim, why not also secure the claimant's costs? And, if that, why was it not at least as appropriate to require someone advancing an unpromosing claim to secure the defendant's costs? Conditional orders such as these could be made without giving the person concerned at least three days advance notice (as to which, see *Anglo Eastern Trust Ltd*, above).

In *Homebase Ltd v LSS Services Ltd* [2004] EWHC 3182, Ch. C alleged that D owed him fees for D's occupation of certain premises as a licensee. By witness statement, D alleged that no such fees were payable because of an oral agreement to that effect which had been expressly made by C and D. C denied that any such agreement had been made and sought summary judgment. Peter Smith J. held that, although the evidence relied on by D was not incredible, sufficient doubts as to it had been raised to justify the making of a conditional order requiring D to pay into court the whole sum claimed by C.

An order dealing with costs

24.6.7 The court may make an order for costs, for example, an order for fixed costs (as to which see Pt 45) or an order for costs, to be assessed by way of summary assessment or detailed assessment (as to which, see Pt 43).

Fixed costs may be applicable where the only claim in the proceedings is a claim for a specified sum of money or a claim to which the Practice Direction supplementing r.7.9 applies (Consumer Credit Act claims) and where, in either case, the value of the claim exceeds £25. In all cases the court has power to allow costs other than fixed costs.

Where the court makes an order on an application under Pt 24 which does not mention costs, no party is entitled to costs relating to that order (r.44.13(1)).

Where a claimant makes a Pt 36 offer which is not accepted by the defendant and the claimant recovers more as a result of summary judgment, the court may take the Pt 36 offer into account in deciding what order to make as to costs and interest. Although in these circumstances r.36.21 does not apply (since it applies only "at trial") the court nevertheless has a general jurisdiction to make such orders and r.36.21 provides guidance as to how that jurisdiction should be exercised (*Petrotrade Inc v Texaco Ltd* [2002] 1 W.L.R. 947; [2001] 4 All E.R. 853, CA).

Setting aside order for summary judgment

24.6.8 The orders the court may make on an application for summary judgment include: (1) judgment on the claim, (2) the striking out or dismissal of the claim, (3) the dismissal of the application, (4) a conditional order (Practice Direction (The Summary Disposal of Claims), para.5.1; see para.24PD.5 below). Where the applicant or any respondent to an application for summary judgment fails to attend the hearing of the application, the court may proceed in his absence. Where, in the absence of the applicant or any respondent, an order is made at the hearing, r.23.11 would appear to have the effect of enabling the court on the application of the absent party (or of its own initiative) to re-list the application for further consideration. But if, at the hearing of the application, the court gives summary judgment against the absent party, the question which then arises is whether that party may apply to the court to have the judgment set aside or varied. Under the former summary judgment rules contained in the RSC (and applied in county courts by operation of CCR O.9, r.14(5)), it was expressly provided that any judgment given against a party who did not appear at the hearing of an application for summary judgment could be set aside or varied by the court on such terms as it thought just (RSC O.14, r.11, see also RSC O.86, r.7). The purpose of this rule was to reverse the effect of the decision of the Court of Appeal in *Spira v Spira* [1939] 3 All E.R. 924, CA, and to remove the anomaly that, although every other judgment (including a judgment at trial) given in the absence of a defendant could be set aside (at least in certain circumstances), a summary judgment could *not, though it could* be made the subject of an appeal. CPR Pt 24 contains no such express provision and the omission is not made good by CPR r.39.3(3), as it is confined to the setting aside of a judgment given at trial in the absence of a party (see further para.39.3.8 below). Further, the matter is not dealt with by r.23.11, which is confined to orders made on applications (including, as suggested above, orders made on summary judgment applications other than summary judgment, e.g. conditional orders.) However, it seems to be readily assumed that the position is retrieved by Practice Direction (Summary Disposal of Claims), para.8.1 which states that, if an order for summary judgment under Pt 24 is made against a respondent who does not appear at the hearing of the application, the respondent may apply "for the order to be set aside or varied" (see para.24PD.8 below). In this context "order" includes judgment on the claim (*ibid.*, para.5.1(1)). On the hearing of an application the court "may make such order as it thinks just" (*ibid.*, para.8.2). It is not always easy to tell whether particular paragraphs in practice directions supplementing CPR rules are attempting (1) merely to narrate what the rules they are supplementing say, or (2) to put an authoritative gloss on those rules. If para.8.1 does make good the omission from Pt 24 of an express rule dealing with the setting aside of summary judgment, given at a hearing from which the judgment debtor was absent, the second of these alternatives must be accepted in this instance. Generally, CPR provisions dealing with the relief which a party may seek when judgments are made at a hearing from which he was absent, but which he ought to have attended, stipulate that relief should not be granted unless certain conditions are met (e.g. r.3.6 (see further below) and r.39.3(5)). Presumably, when determining under para.8.2 whether it would be just to set aside or vary summary judgment, the court will impose similar conditions.

See further paras 39.3.8 and 40.9.2.

Case management

Where the court dismisses the application or makes an order that does not completely dispose of the claim, the court will give case management directions as to the future conduct of the case (para.10 of the Practice Direction supplementing Pt 24 (see para.24PD.10 below)). **24.6.9**

Special provision is made for a case in which an order is made for an amount of damages or interest to be decided by the court or for the taking of an account or the making of an inquiry as to any sum due or any similar order (other than certain orders for the assessment of costs). In order to deal with such cases para.12 of the Practice Direction supplementing Pt 26 (see para.26PD.12 below) provides (amongst other things) that the court may:

(a) give directions for the assessment;
(b) make the assessment immediately (if the claimant's evidence for that assessment has been served on the defendant at least 3 days in advance of the hearing);
(c) allocate the claim to the small claims track (if the financial value of the claim is within the scope of that track).

PRACTICE DIRECTION—THE SUMMARY DISPOSAL OF CLAIMS

This Practice Direction supplements CPR Part 24

1. Applications for summary judgment under Part 24

24PD.1 **1.1** Attention is drawn to Part 24 itself and to:

Part 3, in particular rule 3.1(3) and (5),
Part 22,
Part 23, in particular rule 23.6,
Part 32, in particular rule 32.6(2).

1.2 In this paragraph, where the context so admits, the word "claim" includes:

(1) a part of a claim, and
(2) an issue on which the claim in whole or part depends.

1.3 An application for summary judgment under rule 24.2 may be based on:

(1) a point of law (including a question of construction of a document),
(2) the evidence which can reasonably be expected to be available at trial or the lack of it, or
(3) a combination of these.

1.4 Rule 24.4(1) deals with the stage in the proceedings at which an application under Part 24 can be made (but see paragraph 7.1 below).

2. Procedure for making an application

24PD.2 **2**(1) Attention is drawn to rules 24.4(3) and 23.6.

(2) The application notice must include a statement that it is an application for summary judgment made under Part 24.

(3) The application notice or the evidence contained or referred to in it or served with it must—

(a) identify concisely any point of law or provision in a document on which the applicant relies, and/or
(b) state that it is made because the applicant believes that on the evidence the respondent has no real prospect of succeeding on the claim or issue or (as the case may be) of successfully defending the claim or issue to which the application relates,

and in either case state that the applicant knows of no other reason why the disposal of the claim or issue should await trial.

(4) Unless the application notice itself contains all the evidence (if any) on which the applicant relies, the application notice should identify the written evidence on which the applicant relies. This does not affect the applicant's right to file further evidence under rule 24.5(2).

(5) The application notice should draw the attention of the respondent to rule 24.5(1).

(6) Where the claimant has failed to comply with Practice Direction (Pre-Action Conduct) or any relevant pre-action protocol, an action for summary judgment will not normally be entertained before the defence has been filed or, alternatively, the time for doing so has expired.

3. The hearing

3(1) The hearing of the application will normally take place before a Master or a district judge. 24PD.3

(2) The Master or district judge may direct that the application be heard by a High Court Judge (if the case is in the High Court) or a circuit judge (if the case is in a county court).

4. The court's approach

4 Where it appears to the court possible that a claim or defence may succeed but improbable that it will do so, the court may make a conditional order, as described below. 24PD.4

5. Orders the court may make

5.1 The orders the court may make on an application under Part 24 include: 24PD.5

(1) judgment on the claim,
(2) the striking out or dismissal of the claim,
(3) the dismissal of the application,
(4) a conditional order.

5.2 A conditional order is an order which requires a party:

(1) to pay a sum of money into court, or
(2) to take a specified step in relation to his claim or defence, as the case may be, and provides that that party's claim will be dismissed or his statement of case will be struck out if he does not comply.

(Note—the court will not follow its former practice of granting leave to a defendant to defend a claim, whether conditionally or unconditionally.)

6. Accounts and inquiries

6 If a remedy sought by a claimant in his claim form includes, or necessarily involves, taking an account or making an inquiry, an application can be made under Part 24 by any party to the proceedings for an order directing any necessary accounts or inquiries to be taken or made. 24PD.6

(The Accounts practice direction supplementing Part 40 contains further provisions as to orders for accounts and inquiries.)

7. Specific performance

7.1 (1) If a remedy sought by a claimant in his claim form includes a claim— 24PD.7

(a) for specific performance of an agreement (whether in *writing or not*) for the sale, purchase, exchange, mortgage or charge of any property, or for the grant or assignment of a lease or tenancy of any property, with or without an alternative claim for damages, or
(b) for rescission of such an agreement, or
(c) for the forfeiture or return of any deposit made under such an agreement,

the claimant may apply under Part 24 for judgment.

(2) The claimant may do so at any time after the claim form has been served, whether or not the defendant has acknowledged service of the claim form, whether or not the time for acknowledging service has expired and whether or not any particulars of claim have been served.

7.2 The application notice by which an application under paragraph 7.1 is made must have attached to it the text of the order sought by the claimant.

7.3 The application notice and a copy of every affidavit or witness statement in support and of any exhibit referred to therein must be served on the defendant not less than 4 days before the hearing of the application.

(Note—the 4 days replaces for these applications the 14 days specified in rule 24.4(3). Rule 24.5 cannot therefore, apply.)

(This paragraph replaces RSC Order 86, rules 1 and 2 but applies to county court proceedings as well as to High Court proceedings.)

8. Setting aside order for summary judgment

24PD.8 **8.1** If an order for summary judgment is made against a respondent who does not appear at the hearing of the application, the respondent may apply for the order to be set aside or varied (see also rule 23.11).

8.2 On the hearing of an application under paragraph 8.1 the court may make such order as it thinks just.

9. Costs

24PD.9 **9.1** Attention is drawn to Part 45 (Fixed Costs).

9.2 Attention is drawn to the Costs Practice Direction and in particular to the court's power to make a summary assessment of costs.

9.3 Attention is also drawn to rule 44.13(1) which provides that if an order does not mention costs no party is entitled to costs relating to that order.

10. Case management

24PD.10 **10** Where the court dismisses the application or makes an order that does not completely dispose of the claim, the court will give case management directions as to the future conduct of the case.

PART 25

INTERIM REMEDIES AND SECURITY FOR COSTS

Contents

25.0.1

Editorial introduction (Section I: Interim Remedies)

The rules in the first section of this Part deal with two matters formerly treated quite separately: (1) the granting of orders for interim remedies (including interim injunctions) and (2) the granting of orders for interim payments. General rules about applications for court orders, including orders for interim remedies and interim payments, are found in Pt 23. Detailed procedures applicable on applications for interim remedies and interim payments are found in this Part. **25.0.2**

Rule 27.2(1)(a) states that Pt 25 does not apply to small claims "except as it relates to interim injunctions".

Editorial introduction (Section II: Security for Costs)

This section which was added by the Civil Procedure (Amendment) Rules 2000 (SI 2000/221) came into force on May 2, 2000. It does not apply to small claims, see r.27.2(1)(a). Rules 25.12 and 25.13 largely replace the previous rules, RSC O.23. Rule 25.15 (security for costs of an appeal) replaces the former RSC O.59, r.10(5), but applies to all appeals, not just appeals to the Court of Appeal. Rule 25.14 (security for costs other than from the claimant) is new. It remedies certain inadequacies in the former rules which were highlighted in two cases, *Eurocross Sales Ltd v Cornhill Insurance plc* [1995] 1 W.L.R. 1517; [1995] 4 All E.R. 950, CA and *Abraham v Thompson* [1997] 4 All E.R. 362, CA. As to the purpose and effect of an order for security for costs, see below para.25.12.2. The provisions of Sect.II of Pt 25 are applied with modifications to certain proceedings under Pt 74 (Enforcement of Judgments in Different Jurisdictions) **25.0.3** (see r.74.5). By the Civil Procedure (Amendment No.2) Rules 2002 (SI 2002/3219) r.3, with effect from April 2003, para.(2)(a) of r.25.13 was amended. This provision deals with the conditions to be satisfied where the court makes an order for security for costs where the claimant is resident out of the jurisdiction and not in a Convention State and the amendment ensures that the rule complies with the decision of the Court of Appeal in *De Beer v Kanaar & Co (No.1)* [2001] EWCA Civ 1318, CA.

Practice Directions

25.0.4 The provisions of this Part are supplemented by two practice directions: Practice Direction (Interim Injunctions) relates to some of the orders for interim remedies listed in r.25.1(1) and contains examples of a freezing injunction and a search order (see para.25PD.1), and Practice Direction (Interim Payments) relates to r.25.6 (see para.25BPD.1). With effect from December 2, 2002, a third practice direction, Practice Direction (Accounts and Inquiries) was deleted as a consequence of the insertion in the CPR of Pt 69 (Court's Power to Appoint a Receiver) and the coming into effect of a practice direction supplementing that Part.

Forms

25.0.5 See further para.25.1.9 (Form of order for interim injunction) below.

- **N244** Application notice or in the RCJ, **PF244** may be used.

The following county court forms in use before the CPR came into effect on April 26, 1999, continue in use (see Practice Direction (Forms) Tables 1 and 3):

- **N16A** (General form of application for injunction)
- **N361** (Notice of application for relief in pending action)

Forms for orders for freezing injunctions (formerly *Mareva* injunctions) both domestic and worldwide, and for search orders (formerly *Anton Piller* orders), previously found in *Practice Direction (Mareva Injunctions and Anton Piller Orders: Forms)* [1996] 1 W.L.R. 1522, are replaced by forms annexed to the Practice Direction supplementing this Part and referred to above.

See also Admiralty and Commercial Court Guide Appendix 5 (forms of freezing injunction and search order) (see Vol.2, para.2A–162 below).

The following Queen's Bench Master Practice Forms are relevant to section II (security for costs): See Practice Direction supplementing Pt 4, para.4PD.1.

- **PF43** Application for security for costs
- **PF44** Order for security for costs

Court Guides and interim remedies procedure

25.0.6 It was noted above that where applications are made in accordance with the Pt 23 procedure in proceedings in the Commercial Court, and in proceedings in the Chancery Division of the High Court, the provisions of Pt 23 and the practice directions supplementing that Part must be read in conjunction with, respectively, the Queen's Bench Guide, para.7.13 (Vol.2, para.1B–53), the Admiralty and Commercial Court Guide, Section F (Vol.2, para.2A–85), and the Chancery Guide, Chap.5 (Vol. 2, para.1A–27), and the practice directions referred to there. Generally, these Guides repeat, in narrative form, provisions found in Pt 25 and the practice directions supplementing that Part. However, in some respects, the modifications to Pt 23 practice made by these Guides are significant.

As is explained below (para.25.2.1), when an application is made for an interim remedy, the provisions of Pt 23 and the practice directions supplementing that Part are subject to the provisions of Pt 25 and supplementing practice directions. It should also be noted that the Court Guides referred to above deal specifically with applications for certain kinds of interim remedies, in particular, interim injunctions, freezing injunctions and search orders; see the Queen's Bench Guide, para.7.13 (Vol.2, para.1B–53), the Admiralty and Commercial Court Guide, Section F, paras F15 *et seq.* (Vol.2, para.2A–99) and the Chancery Guide Chap.5, para.5.18, see (Vol.2, para.1A–34).

For guidance on practice and listing of interim applications before Masters and judges in the Queen's Bench Division at the RCJ, see Queen's Bench Guide Sections 6 and 9 (Vol.2 paras 1B–29 and 1B–60).

Interim remedies in support of arbitral proceedings

25.0.7 The Arbitration Act 1996 s.44(1) states that, unless otherwise agreed by the parties, the court has for the purposes of and in relation to arbitral proceedings the same power of making orders about certain matters as it has for the purposes of and in relation to legal proceedings (see Vol.2, para.2E–193). The matters referred to are listed in s.44(2) and to an extent coincide with the interim remedies listed in CPR r.25.1(1). Paragraph 8.1 of Practice Direction (Arbitration), supplementing CPR Pt 62, states that an application for an interim remedy under s.44 must be made, not by application notice, but in an arbitration claim form (see Vol.2, para.2E–50).

Powers of Masters and district judges in relation to interim remedies

Masters and district judges may exercise any function of the High Court except where an enactment, rule or practice direction provides otherwise (r.2.4). The circumstances in which Masters and district judges may exercise the jurisdiction of the High Court in relation to the interim remedies listed in r.25.1(1) is restricted by Practice Direction (Allocation of Cases to Levels of Judiciary), paras 2.1 *et seq.* (see para.2BPD.1 above). **25.0.8**

District judges may exercise any function of the county courts except where an enactment, rule or practice direction provides otherwise (r.2.4). The jurisdiction of the county courts to grant the interim remedies listed in r.25.1(1) is not as great as that enjoyed by the High Court (see para.25.1.2 below). The circumstances in which district judges may exercise that limited jurisdiction is restricted by Practice Direction (Allocation of Cases to Levels of Judiciary), paras 2.1 *et seq.* (see para.2BPD.1 above).

Note also Practice Direction (Interim Injunctions), paras 1.1 to 1.4 (see para.25PD.1 below).

Written evidence in applications for interim remedies

Evidence at a hearing other than the trial should normally be given by witness statement. However, affidavits must be used as evidence, not only where sworn evidence is required by an enactment, statutory instrument, rule, order or practice direction, but also in any application for a search order, a freezing injunction, or an order requiring an occupier to permit another to enter his land (Practice Direction (Written Evidence), para.1.4, see para.32PD.1 below). **25.0.9**

I. Interim Remedies

Orders for interim remedies[1]

25.1—(1) The court may grant the following interim remedies— **25.1**

(a) an interim injunction[GL];

(b) an interim declaration;

(c) an order—

(i) for the detention, custody or preservation of relevant property;

(ii) for the inspection of relevant property;

(iii) for the taking of a sample of relevant property;

(iv) for the carrying out of an experiment on or with relevant property;

(v) for the sale of relevant property which is of a perishable nature or which for any other good reason *it is* desirable to sell quickly; and

(vi) for the payment of income from relevant property until a claim is decided;

(d) an order authorising a person to enter any land or

[1] Amended by the Civil Procedure (Amendment) Rules 2000 (SI 2000/221), the Civil Procedure (Amendment) Rules 2002 (SI 2002/2058) and the Civil Procedure (Amendment No.4) Rules 2005 (SI 2005/3515).

building in the possession of a party to the proceedings for the purposes of carrying out an order under sub-paragraph (c);

(e) an order under section 4 of the Torts (Interference with Goods) Act 1977[1] to deliver up goods;

(f) an order (referred to as a "freezing injunction[GL]")—

(i) restraining a party from removing from the jurisdiction assets located there; or

(ii) restraining a party from dealing with any assets whether located within the jurisdiction or not;

(g) an order directing a party to provide information about the location of relevant property or assets or to provide information about relevant property or assets which are or may be the subject of an application for a freezing injunction[GL].

(h) an order (referred to as a "search order") under section 7 of the Civil Procedure Act 1997[2] (order requiring a party to admit another party to premises for the purpose of preserving evidence, etc.);

(i) an order under section 33 of the Supreme Court Act 1981 or section 52 of the County Courts Act 1984 (order for disclosure of documents or inspection of property before a claim has been made);

(j) an order under section 34 of the Supreme Court Act 1981 or section 53 of the County Courts Act 1984 (order in certain proceedings for disclosure of documents or inspection of property against a non-party);

(k) an order (referred to as an order for interim payment) under rule 25.6 for payment by a defendant on account of any damages, debt or other sum (except costs) which the court may hold the defendant liable to pay;

(l) an order for a specified fund to be paid into court or otherwise secured, where there is a dispute over a party's right to the fund;

(m) an order permitting a party seeking to recover personal property to pay money into court pending the outcome of the proceedings and directing that, if he does so, the property shall be given up to him;

(n) an order directing a party to prepare and file accounts relating to the dispute;

(o) an order directing any account to be taken or inquiry to be made by the court; and

(p) an order under Article 9 of Council Directive (EC) 2004/48 on the enforcement of intellectual property rights (order in intellectual property proceedings making the continuation of an alleged infringement subject to the lodging of guarantees).

---

[1] 1977 c.32; s.4 was amended by the Supreme Court Act 1981 (c.54), s.152(1), Sch.5; by the County Courts Act 1984 (c.28), s.148(1), Sch. 2, Pt V, para.64 and by SI 1980/397 (N13).

[2] 1997 c.12.

(Rule 34.2 provides for the court to issue a witness summons requiring a witness to produce documents to the court at the hearing or on such date as the court may direct).

(2) In paragraph (1)(c) and (g), "relevant property" means property (including land) which is the subject of a claim or as to which any question may arise on a claim.

(3) The fact that a particular kind of interim remedy is not listed in paragraph (1) does not affect any power that the court may have to grant that remedy.

(4) The court may grant an interim remedy whether or not there has been a claim for a final remedy of that kind.

Effect of rule

In r.25.1(1) an attempt is made to list all of the interim remedies for which a party may wish to apply (including some available before proceedings are commenced) and which the court, in the exercise of discretion, may be prepared to grant. It is possible that the list is not exhaustive. Consequently, r.25.1(3) states that the fact that a particular kind of interim remedy is not listed in para.(1) does not affect any power that the court may have to grant that remedy. Sub-paragraph (o) was added to r.25.1(1) by the Civil Procedure (Amendment) Rules 2002 (SI 2002/2058) (see further para.25.1.38 below). Sub-paragraph (o) was added to r.25.1(1) by the Civil Procedure (Amendment No.4) Rules 2005 (SI 2005/3515). In certain circumstances, some of the remedies listed in r.25.1, and described as "interim", may be granted after final judgment (r.25.2(1)(b)). Thus the power to grant "a freezing injunction" after judgment is preserved. **25.1.1**

Formerly, rules of court relating to many of the remedies listed in r.25.1 were found in RSC O.29. In that Order, a distinction was drawn between those interim remedies for which the sources of the court's jurisdiction were the rules of court themselves; e.g. r.3 (Power to order samples to be taken, etc.) and those for which the sources were found in common law rules or statute; e.g. r.1 (Application for injunction) (see now, respectively, r.25.1(1)(c)(iii) and r.25.1(1)(a) in this Part). Rules dealing with interim remedies falling within the former category stated in terms that "the court may grant" the remedy (or contained words to similar effect) whereas rules dealing with interim remedies falling in the latter category acknowledged that the jurisdiction was derived from outside the RSC and stated simply that "application may be made". No such distinction is drawn in r.25.1. The rule states that "the court may grant" the remedies listed therein. It is unfortunate that the distinction has disappeared in the CPR but no harm is done so long as it is remembered that the source of the court's jurisdiction to grant many of the interim remedies listed is not to be found in r.25.1; e.g. the source of the court's jurisdiction to grant an interim injunction (r.25.1(1)(a)) is the Supreme Court Act 1981 s.37 (see Vol.2, para.9A–128).

Where, by application to the court, remedies may be granted before final order, that is to say, as interim remedies, various procedural issues concerning the handling of such applications and the conditions in which relief may be granted arise. Those that are not dealt with in Pt 23 (General rules about applications for court orders), or not dealt with completely in that Part, are dealt with in r.25.1 and following rules. Some interim remedies were developed as purely interim remedies and not as interim versions of final remedies.

Depending on the remedy sought, the grant of interim remedies pursuant to r.25.1 may raise issues under ECHR art.8 (the right to respect for private life) or under ECHR Protocol 1, art.1 (the right to peaceful enjoyment of possessions). See, by analogy, in relation to Article 8, *Cantabrica Coach Holdings Ltd v Vehicle Inspectorate*, *The Times*, April 13, 2000, DC. In the majority of cases, however, any interference is likely to be considered justified as necessary "for the protection of the rights and freedoms of others" (Article 8(2)), or as "in the public interest" (Protocol 1, Article 1). Nevertheless, the court must have regard to the principles of proportionality or fair balance inherent in these articles when deciding whether the aim in view can be achieved by means which are less restrictive of Convention rights. The grant of freezing injunctions and search orders is considered in more detail in paras 25.1.27 and 25.1.29 below.

Jurisdiction of county courts to grant interim relief

25.1.2 The County Courts Act 1984 s.38 (as amended in 1990) (see Vol.2, para.9A–468+) provides that, generally, in any proceedings in a county court the court may make any order (final or interlocutory and absolute or conditional) which could be made by the High Court if the proceedings were in the High Court (see also *Burris v Azadani* [1995] 1 W.L.R. 1372, CA). The circumstances in which county courts may grant relief in the form of freezing injunctions and search orders (see, respectively paras 25.1.23 and 25.1.25 below) are restricted by the County Court Remedies Regulations 1991 made under s.38(3)(b) of the 1984 Act (see Vol.2, para.9B–77). However, to compensate for this, art.3 of the High Court and County Courts Jurisdiction Order 1991 provides that the High Court shall have jurisdiction to hear an application for an injunction made in the course of or in anticipation of proceedings in a county court where a county court may not, by virtue of regulations under s.38(3)(b) or otherwise, grant an injunction (see Vol.2, para.9B–933).

Interim remedies and the overriding objective

25.1.3 The court must seek to give effect to the overriding objective stated in r.1.1 when it "exercises any power given to it by the Rules" or when it "interprets the meaning of any rule" (r.1.2). Further, the court is required to further the overriding objective by actively managing cases (r.1.4), and this includes considering "whether the likely benefits of taking a particular step justify the cost of taking it". So far as is practicable, the court must deal with cases so as to save expense, to ensure that they are dealt with expeditiously as well as fairly, and in a manner which is proportionate to what is at stake, etc. It is not immediately clear how these duties relate to the granting of interim remedies (as distinct from the procedures by which the remedies may be sought and granted). The sources of the court's jurisdiction to grant the more important of the interim remedies lie outside the CPR. When considering whether to grant such remedies the court is not merely exercising a "power given to it by the Rules" or deciding whether "a particular step" should be taken. Further, the power to grant interim remedies is not listed among the court's "general powers of management" (see r.3.1), which are to be exercised in a manner which further the overriding objective, unless it is caught by r.3.1(2)(m) (court's power to "take any other step or make any other order for the purpose of managing the case and furthering the overriding objective"). Nevertheless, it seems clear that the intention is that the various elements in the overriding objective should be applied to the granting of interim remedies. The interim remedies are discretionary and the discretion is exercised judicially within a framework of case law. In the past, many factors now formally adopted by the rules in Pt 1 as elements of the overriding objective have routinely influenced the exercise of the discretion and will continue to do so. Both before the coming into effect of the CPR and after, the courts have from time to time expressed concern about (1) the making of unnecessary applications for interim remedies, (2) the making of repeat applications where there has been no material change in the relevant circumstances, (3) the incidence of appeals where an interim remedy is made or refused, (4) the costs and delays involved in making such applications, and (5) the waste of court resources caused thereby. In a variety of ways, the case management scheme under the CPR seeks to ensure that control is exercised (either directly by the court, or indirectly by rules and directions) in a manner that reduces the impact of these mischiefs and ensures that "interlocutory warfare" between the parties does not overwhelm the proceedings. Nevertheless the concerns remain. It is obvious that the CPR has not provided a complete cure though the new procedures have had some successes (notably, in largely stamping out applications for striking out for want of prosecution). In attacking these problems the Court of Appeal has called in aid the overriding objective, in particular, the objective of dealing with the case in ways which are proportionate to the amount of money involved, the importance of the case, the complexity of the issues, and the financial position of each party. A good example is provided by *A v B (A Company)* [2002] EWCA Civ 337; [2002] 2 All E.R. 545, CA, where the Court set down guidelines for the handling of applications for interim injunctions restraining publication in breach of confidence cases designed to ensure that such applications are *dealt with expeditiously* and in a proportionate manner.

Successive applications for interim remedy

25.1.4 There is a public interest in discouraging a party who makes an unsuccessful application for interim relief from making a subsequent application for the same relief, based on material which was not, but could have been, deployed in support of the first application (*Woodhouse v Consignia Plc* [2002] EWCA Civ 275 March 7, 2002, CA at [55] per Brooke L.J.). It is expressly provided that a claimant may make more than one application for an interim payment (r.25.6(2); note also para.25.6.7 below). See further "Successive applications for same relief", para.23.0.14 above.

Inherent jurisdiction

It is expressly provided that the fact that a particular kind of interim remedy is not listed in r.25.1(1) does not affect any power that the court may have to grant that remedy (r.25.1(3)). This provision was inserted principally for the purpose of making it clear that the court's inherent jurisdiction is not limited by r.25.1 but it also has the effect of ensuring that it does not cast doubt on the powers derived from statute (e.g. the power to appoint a receiver derived from the Supreme Court Act 1981 s.37(1)). The expression "interim remedy" is not a term of art and doubts may arise as to whether or not a particular power of the court is properly described as such. **25.1.5**

The High Court has an inherent jurisdiction to make an order for the purpose of preventing abuse of its procedures. This jurisdiction is a fertile source for procedural development. For example, in *Ebert v Birch* [2000] Ch. 484, CA, it was held that the High Court has jurisdiction to make an order (which may, perhaps, properly be described as an order for an "interim remedy") restraining a person from initiating civil proceedings without the permission of the court where those proceedings would be vexatious (an "extended *Grepe v Loam* order"). And in *Attorney General v Ebert* [2001] EWHC Admin 695; [2002] 2 All E.R. 789, DC, it was said that the CPR serves to bolster principle that, in the exercise of its inherent jurisdiction, the court has power to restrain litigants from wasting the time of court staff and disturbing the orderly conduct of court processes in a completely obsessive conduct of their own litigation. The jurisdiction may be exercised where proceedings against the respondent for a civil proceedings order under the Supreme Court Act 1981 s.42 are pending. In *Bhamjee v Forsdick (Practice Note)* [2003] EWCA Civ 1113; [2004] 1 W.L.R. 88, CA, the Court of Appeal referred to the relevant authorities and restated the principle that every court has power to protect its processes from abuse. The Court emphasised that element of the overriding objective that speaks of the need to ensure that, in dealing with a case justly, so far as practicable the case is allotted an appropriate share of the court's resources whilst taking into account the need to allot resources to other cases (see r.1.1(2)(e)). In this case, the Court re-classified "traditional" and "extended" *Grepe v Loam* orders as, respectively, "civil restraint" and "extended civil restraint" orders, and explained the practice and procedure to be followed where a court is minded to make such orders, whether on the application of a party or of its own initiative. See also, *Mahajan v Department of Constitutional Affairs* [2004] EWCA Civ 946, June 30, 2004, CA, unrep. Towards the end of 2004, this aspect of the Court's inherent jurisdiction was put into rule form by the addition to the CPR of r.3.11 (Power of the court to make civil restraint order).

The inherent jurisdiction of the court to stay the whole or part of any proceedings (recited in r.3.2(f)) may perhaps in certain circumstances be regarded as an interim remedy (see Vol.2, para.9A–178 ("Stay under the CPR")).

Interim remedies in cases of doubtful jurisdiction or invalidity

The Civil Jurisdiction and Judgments Act 1982 s.24(1)(a) (see Vol.2, para.5–24) states that the power of any court in England and Wales to grant "interim relief" pending trial, or pending the determination of an appeal, shall extend to a case where the issue to be tried, or which is the subject of the appeal, relates to the jurisdiction of the court to entertain the proceedings (e.g. where there is a question whether the court has jurisdiction under the Brussels Convention) or to entertain the application for the interim relief itself (note also s.24(1)(b)). As defined by s.25(7), in this context "interim relief" would appear to include all of the forms of relief listed as "interim remedies" in r.25.1(1). **25.1.6**

See also, para.25.4.2 "Interim remedy order in support of foreign proceedings" below.

Where, in a claim brought challenging provisions in UK Regulations implementing EU Directives, a question is referred to the ECJ, the court may make an interim order suspending the operation of the provisions in the UK Regulations pending final determination of the reference. For an explanation of the basis of the jurisdiction, see *R. (Abna Ltd) v Secretary of State for Health* [2003] EWHC 2420 (Admin), October 6, 2003, unrep. (Davis J.), and note para.54.3.7 "Interim relief to give effect to European Union law" below.

Interim remedies in judicial review

25.1.7 Rules for applications for judicial review are found in CPR Pt 54, supplemented by Practice Direction (Judicial Review). Pt 54 replaced RSC O.53. Rule 3(10) of that Order stated that, where permission to apply for judicial review was granted, then, depending on the relief sought, the court may could at any time grant in the proceedings "interim remedies in accordance with CPR Pt 25". No such express provision appears in Pt 54 because none is necessary. Rule 54.6 states that an applicant for judicial review must state in his claim form any remedy he is claiming, including any interim remedy, and a cross-reference in r.54.6(c) draws attention to Pt 25.

Interim powers to preserve assets in civil recovery proceedings

25.1.7.1 Provisions in Pt 5 of the Proceeds of Crime Act 2002 enable the High Court to make "a property freezing order". Further, that statute gives the High Court power to make "an interim receiving order" providing for the detention, custody or preservation of assets and the appointment of a receiver. These interim remedies are similar in some respects to remedies referred to in r.25.1 (*Director of Assets Recovery Agency v Creaven* [2005] EWHC 2726 (Admin); [2006] 1 W.L.R. 622 (Stanley Burnton J.)). Practice and procedure provisions dealing specifically with them are found in Practice Direction (Civil Recovery Proceedings); see para.3K–1 below.

Interim remedy not limited by claim form (r.25.1(4))

25.1.8 Interim remedies are of two broad varieties (but some are a mixture). First there are those which are temporary versions of final remedies. In the interests of fairness and justice they are granted pending trial; e.g. a claimant issues a claim for an injunction and is granted a temporary injunction to the same or similar effect. Secondly, there are those which are purely interlocutory; e.g. an order permitting one party to inspect relevant property in the possession of another party. The effect of r.25.1(4) is to make clear that a party may apply for an interim remedy falling in the first category even though he has made no claim in his claim form for a final remedy of that kind. The rule follows former rule RSC O.29, r.1(1) but is cast in broader terms (see also former CCR O.13, r.6(1)).

Interim injunction (r.25.1(1)(a))

25.1.9 *Introduction*—Paragraph (1)(a) of r.25.1 refers to the court's jurisdiction to make an order granting an applicant an interim injunction. The Glossary attached to the CPR (see para.G1.1 below) explains that an injunction is "a court order prohibiting a person from doing something or requiring a person to do something".

For extended commentary on interim injunctions, see Vol.2, Sect.15 Interim Remedies para.15–2

An injunction granted by judicial decision at trial after the claimant has established the existence of his right in law and the fact that the defendant has infringed it or is about to do so may be described as a *perpetual injunction*. An order other than a final judgment, whether such order be made before judgment or not, may properly be described as an interlocutory order. Under the CPR, "interim" is preferred to "interlocutory". Consequently, an injunction granted by interlocutory order as so defined is an *interim injunction*.

A claim form must specify the remedy the claimant seeks (r.16.2) and therefore should include any claim for an injunction as a final order. However, an application for the grant of an interim injunction may be made by any party, whether or not a claim for an injunction was included in that party's claim form or Part 20 claim (e.g. counterclaim), as the case may be (r.25.1(4)). Where the defendant is the applicant the relief sought need not necessarily arise in respect of the claimant's claim. An interim injunction may be in terms which would not be appropriate, or given the nature of the parties' allegations, possible, at the final trial (*Fresh Fruit Wales Ltd v Halbert The Times, January 29, 1991, CA*).

In a claim in which a party (D) is acting as a representative party under r.19.6, an interim injunction granted against D is binding on all persons represented in the claim, but may only be enforced against a person who is not a party to the claim with the permission of the court (r.19.6(4)). Such an injunction may not include a term enabling the applicant to enforce the injunction against unidentified persons represented by D without first obtaining such permission (*Smithkline Beecham Plc v Avery* [2007] EWHC 948 (QB), April 27, 2007, unrep. (Teare J.)).

Where an interim injunction is sought on a without notice application (see para.23.4.1 above) with incomplete evidence it is a basic requirement that there has to be a real urgency for the injunction, particularly where an early effective hearing date is available (*Mayne Pharma (USA) Inc v Teva UK Ltd (Interim Applications: Costs)* [2004] EWHC 2934December 3, 2004, unrep. (application refused in patent claim where no threat and damage requiring immediate intervention of court)).

Subject to certain limits, an interim injunction may be granted at any time (r.25.2) (see further paras 25.2.3 *et seq.* below).

For "freezing injunctions" (formerly *Mareva* injunctions) see para.25.1.25 below.

As to the granting of an injunction on an application for judicial review, see para.25.1.7 "Interim remedies in judicial review" above.

As to applicant's duty to make full and frank disclosure when applying without notice for interim injunction, see para.25.3.5 "Applicant's duties where application made without notice to respondent" below.

Jurisdiction—The Supreme Court Act 1981 s.37 (see Vol.2, para.9A–128) states that the High Court may by order, whether interlocutory or final, grant an injunction in all cases in which it appears to the court to be just and convenient to do so (s.37(1)). Any such order may be made either unconditionally or on such terms and conditions as the court thinks just (s.37(2)). Where the court has in personam jurisdiction over the person against whom an injunction whether interlocutory or final, is sought the court has jurisdiction to grant it (*Fourie v Le Roux* [2007] UKHL 1; [2007] 1 W.L.R. 320, HL, per Lord Scott at para.25). Generally, there is no jurisdiction to grant an interim injunction against the Crown (Crown Proceedings Act 1947 s.21); but see para.25.1.17. **25.1.10**

The County Courts Act 1984 s.38 (see Vol.2, para.9A–468+) provides that, generally, in any proceedings in a county court the court may make any order (final or interlocutory and absolute or conditional) which could be made by the High Court if the proceedings were in the High Court (see also *Burris v Azadani* [1995] 1 W.L.R. 1372, CA). Regulations made under s.38 impose certain restrictions on the jurisdiction of county courts in this respect. Where the jurisdiction of a county court to grant injunctions is restricted, the circumstances may be such as to enable a party to invoke the jurisdiction of the High Court under the High Court and County Courts Jurisdiction Order 1991 art.3 to grant injunctions incidental to and in support of county court proceedings; see para.25.1.2 above, and paras 25.1.27 and 25.1.29 below.

See also Civil Jurisdiction and Judgments Act 1982 s.25 (see Vol.2, para.5–27) explained in para.25.4.2 "Interim remedy order in support of foreign proceedings" below.

In the High Court, in certain circumstances, interim injunctions may be granted by Masters or district judges. Similarly, in county courts, in certain circumstances, interim injunctions may be granted by district judges. For conditions under which Masters and district judges may exercise jurisdiction in relation to interim injunctions, see "Powers of Masters and district judges in relation to interim remedies", para.25.0.10 above, and note Practice Direction (Interim Injunctions), paras 1.1 to 1.4 (see para.25PD.1 below) (where, misleadingly, interim and final injunctions are not distinguished). Paragraph 1.2(1) of that Practice Direction refers to the powers of masters and district judges in High Court proceedings to grant injunctions ancillary or incidental to charging orders or orders for the appointment of receivers by way of equitable execution. Such powers were granted by Schedule rules (RSC O.50 r.9 and O.51, r.2) until they were omitted from CPR Sch.1.

Paragraphs 2.3 and 2.4 of Practice Direction (Allocation of Cases to Levels of Judiciary) (see para.2BPD.2 above) recite various circumstances in which a Master or a district judge may "make an injunction" and para.2.2 states that, otherwise, injunctions and orders "relating to injunctions" must be made by a judge. In *Richmond v Burch* [2006] EWHC 921 (Ch); [2007] 1 All E.R. 658, an interim injunction was made final upon judgment by default of acknowledgment of service being granted to the claimant, but subsequently, on the application of the defendant, the judgment was set aside by order of a Master and the final injunction continued as an interim injunction. On appeal to a judge by the claimant (where, in the event, the injunction was continued by order of the judge) it was held that the Master by his order had either discharged the injunction or varied it, and in either event had made an order "relating to" an injunction within the meaning of para.2.2 and therefore had acted without jurisdiction.

25.1.11 *Principles and guidelines to be applied* —For information on the principles and guidelines to be applied in applications for interim injunctions generally and in particular proceedings, see the extended commentary in Vol.2, Sect.15 Interim Remedies para.15–2

25.1.12 *Practice* —See also "Relationship between Pt 23 and rr.25.2 to 25.5", (para.25.2.1 below) and "Court Guides and interim remedies procedure", para.25.0.6 above.

In Queen's Bench proceedings at the RCJ, an application notice for an interim injunction should be filed in the Listing Office, Room WG5 (Queen's Bench Guide para.7.13.2, see Vol.2, para.1B–53).

An application for an interim injunction is made on an application notice in accordance with the provisions of Pt 23 (General rules about applications for court orders) (see para.23.0.1). The practice and procedure to be followed is as stated in the rules of that Part and the provisions of the practice direction supplementing that part (see 23PD.1) as complemented and modified by rules in Pt 25. Despite its title, this last-mentioned Practice Direction is concerned, not merely with applications for interim injunctions (r.25.1(1)(a)), but also with applications for "freezing injunctions" (r.25.1(1)(f)) and "search orders" (r.25.1(1)(g)) (see further, respectively, paras 25.1.20 and 25.1.22 below). Indeed, in terms, the Practice Direction appears to regard "freezing injunctions" and "search orders" as forms of interim injunction.

For practice where an application is made in the High Court in accordance with Pt 23 for a freezing injunction in support of county court proceedings, see para.25.1.27 below.

When the provisions (1) of Pt 23 and the practice direction supplementing that Part and (2) of Pt 25 and the practice direction supplementing that Part are put side by side, it is not easy to discern to what extent the former are complemented and modified by the latter where applications for interim injunctions are made. Some of the Pt 23 provisions are unaffected by the Pt 25 provisions; e.g. r.23.2 (where to make an application). A degree of repetition is apparent; e.g. the several provisions relating to the service of an application notice (r.23.7(1) and PD 25 para.2.2, but note that the former speaks of filing and the latter of issuing) and to the providing of a draft order (r.23.7(3)(b), PD 23 para.2.1 and PD 25 para.2.4). Rule 23.6 and PD 23 para.2.1 (what an application notice must include) are modified very slightly by PD 25 para.2.1.

The principal modifications and additions to the Pt 23 provisions made by the Pt 25 provisions, in so far as they relate to the applications for interim injunctions (and for freezing injunctions and search orders), are (1) those concerning applications made without notice to the respondent, and made either before or after the issue of a claim form, and (2) those concerning evidence in support of applications. An application may be made without notice if it appears to the court that there are good reasons for not giving notice (r.25.3(1)). Except in cases where secrecy is essential, the applicant should take steps to notify the respondent informally of the application (PD 25 para.4.3(3)). It follows from r.25.2(2)(b) that an application should not made before a claim has been made unless (i) the matter is urgent, or (ii) it is otherwise necessary to do so in the interests of justice (and the same obtains in a case where the respondent has been given notice).

The significant modifications and additions made by Pt 25 provisions relating to evidence in support of applications for interim injunctions (and for freezing injunctions and search orders) include provisions relating to the filing and serving of evidence (see PD 25 paras 2.2 and 2.3). Further, it is provided that an application must be supported by evidence unless the court orders otherwise (r.25.3(2)). Where an application is made without notice to the respondent, the evidence must set out why notice was not given (PD 25 para.3.4). In certain circumstances the evidence should be in affidavit form (PD 25 paras 3.1 and 3.2). The evidence must set out the facts on which the applicant relies for the claim being made against the respondent, including all material facts of which the court should be made aware (PD 25 para.3.3) (see further "Applicant's duties where application made without notice to respondent" para.25.3.5 below).

It seems that, under the CPR, an action may be properly constituted, even though a defendant is not named, but merely described, in the claim form. It follows from this that an interim injunction may be granted against a defendant joined in proceedings by description (*Bloomsbury Publishing Group Ltd v News Group Newspapers Ltd* [2003] EWHC 1205 (Ch); [2003] 1 W.L.R. 1633 (Sir Andrew Morritt V.-C.); distinguishing *Friern Barnet UDC v Adams* [1927] 2 Ch. 25, CA). See also *Hampshire Waste Services Ltd v Persons Unknown* [2003] EWHC 1738, (Ch), July 8, 2003, unrep. (Sir Andrew Morritt V-C), *South Cambridgeshire District Council v Persons Unknown* [2004] EWCA Civ 1280; *The Times* November 11, 2004, CA. As to applications for injunctions against persons unknown under the Town and Country Planning Act 1990, see CPR Sch.2 CCR O. 49, r.7 (para.cc49.7.1 below).

Form of order for interim injunction —For forms for orders for "freezing injunctions" and "search orders", see paras 25PD.13*et seq.*; note also Commercial Court Guide Appendix 5 (Vol.2, para.2A–162). **25.1.13**

The following county court forms in use before the CPR came into effect on April 26, 1999, continue in use (see Practice Direction (Forms), Table 3):

- **N16** General form of injunction
- **N16(1)** General form of injunction (formal parts only)
- **N138** Injunction orders

Standard forms for the following orders were annexed to Practice Direction (Interim Injunctions: Forms) [1996] 1 W.L.R. 1551 and were for use in the Chancery Division and the Queen's Bench Division:

(1) injunctions before the issue of a writ of summons,
(2) order for injunction,
(3) order containing undertaking instead of injunction,
(4) adjournment of application for an injunction,
(5) application for an injunction treated as trial of the action.

This Practice Direction further provided that all such orders made in the Chancery motions court or by the Queen's Bench interim applications judge should, in the absence of good reason to the contrary, follow these forms. Where possible a draft should be provided and a word-processing disk containing the draft should also be made available to the court (for technical details, see para.4 of the Practice Direction). These forms were not re-furbished in time for the commencement of the CPR in April 1999. However, it was made known that these and other forms were being re-drafted for use in the Chancery Division and the Queen's Bench Division and in the county courts, and that, for the time being, the old forms should be used, adapted as necessary.

Discontinuance of claim —Although, generally, a claimant may discontinue all or part of a claim at any time, he must obtain the permission of the court if he wishes to discontinue all or part of a claim in relation to which the court has granted an interim injunction or any party has given an undertaking to the court (r.38.2(2)). **25.1.14**

Interim declaration (r.25.1(1)(b))

It is clear that the court has jurisdiction to grant a declaration as a final remedy at trial, including at the trial of a preliminary issue. It is also clear that in interlocutory proceedings the court may grant a declaration as a final remedy. Further, in judicial review proceedings a declaration may be granted as provided by the Supreme Court Act 1981 s.31 and the Crown Proceedings Act 1947 s.21 provides that, in proceedings against the Crown, in certain circumstances the court shall not grant relief by way of injunction or specific performance but shall in lieu thereof "make an order declaratory of the rights of the parties". **25.1.15**

The circumstances in which the court will grant a declaration as a final remedy cannot be explained shortly. However, it may be noted that CPR r.40.20 states that the court may make "binding declarations" and may do so "whether or not any other remedy is claimed". This rule was first inserted in the CPR by the Civil Procedure (Amendment) Rules 2001 (SI 2001/256) and replaced CPR Sch.1, RSC O.15, r.16. The rule was first introduced in 1883 as a remedial provision for the purpose of ensuring that the court could make "binding declarations of right" even in circumstances where no consequential relief was or could be claimed. Originally, the court's power in this respect was restricted to declaratory judgments as to existing private rights (see *Guaranty Trust Co of New York v Hannay & Co* [1915] 2 K.B. 536, CA), but in modern times the power has been expanded (especially in the field of judicial review). Consequently, whereas RSC O.15, r.16 referred to "binding declarations of right", r.40.20 speaks simply of "binding declarations".

It might be expected that the jurisdiction to grant a declaration as a final remedy would carry with it jurisdiction to grant a declaration as an interim remedy, preserving the status quo (e.g. as to rights over property) in a matter which is to be decided after further hearing in the final judgment of the court. However, in *Riverside Mental Health NHS Trust v Fox* [1994] 1 F.L.R. 614, CA, the Court of Appeal said it was clear from the authorities that interim declaratory relief was "a creature unknown to English law" (see also *Newport Association Football Club Ltd v Football Association of Wales Ltd* [1995] 2 All E.R. 87). In 1994, the Law Commission made recommendations as to the forms of interim relief available in public law proceedings (Administrative Law: Judicial Review and Statutory Appeals (Law Com No.226)). The Commission recommended that the courts should have power to grant interim declarations (as well as interim injunctions and stays of proceedings before courts and tribunals) in proceedings by way of judicial review (*ibid.* paras 6.18 *et seq.*). CPR r.25.1(1)(b), which states simply that the court may grant an interim remedy in the form of an interim declaration, carries that recommendation into effect, but does not in terms confine the court's jurisdiction in this respect to public law proceedings.

As a practical matter, in most instances an interim injunction will achieve the same objective as an interim declaration (e.g. *R. v Secretary of State for Transport, Ex p. Factortame Ltd (No.2)* [1991] 1 A.C. 603, HL (interim injunction in effect declaring Act of Parliament ineffective pending reference to ECJ)). Rule 25.1(1)(b) may prove to be of greatest importance in those cases where the court cannot grant an interim injunction (e.g. where the Crown Proceedings Act 1947 s.21 applies). In any event, the particular problems that arise where a declaration is sought as a final remedy (e.g. whether there is a real question and whether the applicant has standing) will also apply where a declaration is sought as an interim remedy.

In *Bank of Scotland v A. Ltd* [2001] EWCA Civ 52; [2001] 1 W.L.R. 751, CA, it was explained that the court's power to grant interim declarations may prove useful where a financial institution, cooperating with law enforcement authorities in circumstances where "tipping off" legislation may apply (e.g. where money laundering is suspected), was concerned that it should not be affected adversely unnecessarily by the existence of the police powers.

As to whether declarations, whether interlocutory or final, may be granted by consent, and as to the court's jurisdiction to grant a declaration as a final (rather than as an interim) remedy in interlocutory proceedings, see notes following r.40.20.

As to interim declarations in judicial review proceedings, see para.54.3.4 below.

Orders in relation to relevant property (r.25.1(1)(c))

25.1.16 The court (this would normally be a Master or district judge; see r.2.4) may grant as interim remedies a number of different orders relating to "relevant property". (For other orders as to property, see r.25.1(1)(g), (i) and (j).) In r.25.1(1)(c), relevant property means "property (including land) which is the subject of a claim or as to which any question may arise on a claim" (r.25.1(2)).

25.1.17 *Detention, custody or preservation of relevant property (r.25.1(1)(c)(i))* —The court may grant an interim remedy in the form of an order for the detention, custody or preservation of relevant property (r.25.1(1)(c)(i)). For former rules, see RSC O.29, r.2(1) and CCR O.13, r.7(1)(b) (part).

25.1.18 *Inspection of relevant property (r.25.1(1)(c)(ii))* —The court may grant an interim remedy in the form of an order for the inspection of relevant property (r.25.1(1)(c)(ii)). For former rules, see RSC O.29, r.2(1) and CCR O.13, r.7(1)(b) (part). It may be noted that, under former RSC O.29, r.2(1), inspection could be ordered of property "in the possession of a party" only. No such limitation was imposed by former CCR O.13, r.25.1(2) and no such limitation is now imposed by CPR r.25.1(2). One circumstance in which an order may be made under this provision is where a party wishes to introduce evidence in the form of a plan, photograph or model (r.33.6).

25.1.19 *Taking of a sample of relevant property (r.25.1(1)(c)(iii))* —The court may grant an interim remedy in the form of an order for the taking of a sample of relevant property (r.25.1(c)(iii)). For former rules, see RSC O.29, r.3(1) (part) and CCR O.13, r.7(1)(e) (part).

Carrying out of an experiment on or with relevant property (r.25.1(1)(c)(iv))—The court may grant an interim remedy in the form of an order for the carrying out of an experiment on or with relevant property (r.25.1(1)(c)(iv)). For former rules, see RSC O.29, r.3(1) (part) and CCR O.13, r.7(1)(e) (part). **25.1.20**

Sale of property where desirable to sell quickly (r.25.1(1)(c)(v))—The court may grant an interim remedy in the form of an order for the sale of relevant property which is of a perishable nature or which for any other good reason it is desirable to sell quickly (r.25.1(1)(c)(v)). "Relevant property" in this context includes land (r.25.1(2)). Former RSC O.29, r.4(1) dealt with the sale of property other than land (including any interest in, or right over, land); see also former CCR O.13, r.7(f). Former RSC O.31, r.1 dealt with sales of land. **25.1.21**

Payment of income until a claim is decided (r.25.1(1)(c)(vi))—The court may grant an interim remedy in the form of an order for the payment of income from relevant property until a claim is decided (r.25.1(1)(c)(vi)). This is based on former RSC O.29, r.8 (Allowance of income of property *pendente lite*). That rule stated that, where any real or personal property formed the subject-matter of any proceedings, and the court was satisfied that it would be more than sufficient to answer all the claims thereon for which provision ought to be made in the proceedings, "the Court could at any time allow the whole or part of the income of the property to be paid, during such period as it may direct, to any or all of the parties who have an interest therein or may direct that any part of the personal property be transferred or delivered to any or all of such parties". For examples of "good reasons", see *On Demand Information plc v Michael Gerson (Finance) plc* [2002] UKHL 13; [2003] 1 A.C. 368, HL; *Bank of Scotland v Neath Port Talbot County BC* [2006] EWHC Civ 2276 (Ch), August 11, 2006, unrep (David Richards J.). In considering the balance of disadvantage for the purposes of deciding whether to order a sale the court should consider prejudice in relation to the assets in question, and may take into account any collateral considerations, but the weight to be given to the latter will depend on the circumstances of the individual case. Satisfying the court that there is good reason for an order for sale is no more than the threshold issue; it is only then that the question arises as to whether the discretion to order the sale should be exercised (*Bank of Scotland v Neath Port Talbot County BC* op cit.). **25.1.22**

Order authorising entry on land for carrying out interim remedy orders as to relevant property (r.25.1(1)(d))

Where the court grants an interim remedy in the form of any of the orders listed in r.25.1(1)(c) the court (this would normally be at the same judicial level as that granting the primary interim remedy) may grant a further interim remedy in the form of an order authorising a person to enter any land or building in the possession of a party to the proceedings for the purposes of carrying out the first order (r.25.1(d)). This accords with former rules found in RSC O.29, rr.2 and 3 and made applicable in county court proceedings under CCR O.13, r.7. However, the former RSC O.29, r.4, which dealt with the sale of perishable property, etc., other than land, did not permit the making of a supplementary order authorising the entry on any land in the possession of a party for the purpose of enabling the order for sale to be carried out. Of course, r.4(1) did not include sales of land but r.25.1(1)(c)(v) does. **25.1.23**

An order granting an interim remedy of this type may be made only by a judge (Practice Direction (Allocation of Cases to Levels of Judiciary), para.2.1, see para.2BPD.1 above).

Order for delivery up of goods under Torts (Interference with Goods) Act 1977, section 4 (r.25.1(1)(e))

The court may grant an interim remedy in the form of an order under s.4 of the Torts (Interference with Goods) Act 1977 to deliver up goods (r.25.1(1)(e)). According to the statute an application for an interim remedy of this type may be made either before or after a claim is started. Rule 25.1(e) is based on former RSC O.29, r.2A and CCR O.13, r.7(1)(d). In terms, r.2A did not permit applications before proceedings were commenced but now no such limitation is imposed. Section 4(2) of the 1977 Act states that, in proceedings for wrongful interference, the court shall have power to make an order "providing for the delivery up of goods which are or may become the subject-matter of subsequent proceedings". Former RSC O.29, r.2A was broader than the statute and said that an application under s.4 of the 1977 Act could be made for **25.1.24** the delivery up of any goods which are the subject-matter of the cause or matter "or as to which any question may arise therein" (former CCR O.13, r.7(1)(d) was to the same effect). Rule 25.1(1)(e) contains no definition of goods.

Freezing injunction (Mareva injunction) (r.25.1(1)(f))

25.1.25 The court may grant an interim remedy in the form of an injunction (i) restraining a party from removing from the jurisdiction assets located there, or (ii) restraining a party from dealing with any assets whether located within the jurisdiction or not (r.25.1(1)(f)). Before the CPR came into effect, such a remedy was described as a "Mareva" injunction. In r.25.1(1)(f) and r.25.1(1)(g) it is described as a "freezing" injunction. An order granting such an injunctive remedy would properly be described as a "freezing" order. In modern legal parlance the expressions "freezing order" and "freezing injunction" tend to be used indiscriminately.

Practice Direction (Interim Injunctions), supplements Pt 25 (see para.25PD.13 below), and contains provisions dealing with applications for interim injunctions generally and for freezing injunctions in particular. (This Practice Direction replaced *Practice Direction (Mareva Injunctions and Anton Piller Orders)* [1994] 1 W.L.R. 1233.)

The commentary following outlines the bases for the court's jurisdiction to make orders for freezing injunctions and concentrates on matters of practice and procedure. For more detailed commentary on freezing orders, see Vol.2, Sect.15, Interim Remedies, subs.B para.15–54.

25.1.25.1 *Jurisdiction—generally* —In a claim in which the claimant seeks to recover his property, the court has jurisdiction to order an interim injunction restraining the disposal of property over which the claimant has a proprietary claim. Such an injunction was not properly called a "Mareva injunction". A freezing injunction goes further and enables the court to grant the claimant an interim injunction restraining the defendant from disposing of, or even merely dealing with, his assets, being assets over which the claimant asserts no proprietary claim but which after judgment may be granted to satisfy a money judgment. (Frequently, one injunction will achieve both objectives.)

An order granting an interim remedy of this type may be made only by a judge (Practice Direction (Allocation of Cases to Levels of Judiciary), para.2.1, see para.2BPD.1 above). In a case in the High Court, Masters and district judges have the power to grant injunctions (1) by consent, (2) in connection with charging orders and appointments of receivers, (3) in aid of execution of judgments (Practice Direction (Interim Injunctions), para.1.2, see para.25BPD.1 below).

25.1.25.2 *Jurisdiction—county courts* —The power of county courts to make orders for freezing injunctions is restricted by the County Court Remedies Regulations 1991 (see Vol.2, para.9B–77) made under the County Courts Act 1984 s.38 (as amended in 1990) (ibid. Vol.2, para.9A–468+). The general rule is that a county court may not grant a freezing injunction. But there are exemptions. Further, the High Court has jurisdiction to grant freezing injunctions incidental to and in support of county court proceedings. For an explanation of the exemptions and of the High Court's support jurisdiction, see Vol.2, Sect.15 Interim Remedies subs.B para.15–59.

25.1.25.3 *Making an application* —An application for a freezing injunction is made on an application notice in accordance with the provisions of Pt 23 (General rules about applications for court orders) as modified by the provisions of Practice Direction (Interim Injunctions) (see para.25PD.3 below). The modifications are substantial. Note also "Court Guides and interim remedies procedure", para.25.0.6 above.

Generally, and for obvious reasons, in the first instance an application for a freezing injunction is likely to be made without notice and before a claim form has been issued. Further, the application may be an urgent application. In suitable circumstances, an order might be granted and served on a respondent before substantive proceedings had been instituted, though the judge should pay careful attention to the substantive relief that was or would be sought. An order made on a without notice application should include directions about the institution of proceedings by the applicant for *substantive relief.*

The general rule is that court hearings, including hearings of applications for interim remedies, are to be in public (r.39.2(1)), but in particular proceedings a hearing, or any part of it, may be in private "if publicity would defeat the object of the hearing" or "if it involves confidential information" (r.39.2((3)(a) and (b)). Frequently, hearings relating to applications for freezing injunctions will fall into these exceptional categories.

When granted, the order is of immediate effect and it does not depend for its activation on the institution of proceedings for substantive relief. If proceedings for substantive relief are not instituted the order may lapse in accordance with it own terms or, on application by the respondent, may be discharged (*Fourie v Le Roux* [2007] UKHL 1; [2007] 1 W.L.R. 320, HL, per Lord Scott at paras 32, 33 and 37).

See further, Practice Direction (Interim Injunctions) para.2 (Making an application) and para.4 (Urgent applications and applications without notice) (see paras 25PD.2 and 25PD.4 below).

Applicant's duties —As to applicant's duty to make full and frank disclosure when applying without notice for interim injunction and other duties, see para.25.3.5, "Applicant's duties where application made without notice to respondent" below. **25.1.25.4**

Applicants for "without notice" relief generally, and for freezing injunctions in particular, are under a duty to provide full notes of the hearing with all expedition to any party that would be affected by the relief sought (*Interoute Telecommunications (UK) Ltd v Fashion Gossip Ltd, The Times*, November 10, 1999 (Lightman J.)). Where a freezing order is granted, the duty to provide the respondent with a full note arises whether or not the respondent asks for it (*Thane Investments Ltd v Tomlinson, The Times*, December 10, 2002 (Neuberger J.)). If a freezing order is sought immediately after judgment against a respondent who was not a party to the proceedings, particular care should be taken by the applicant to ensure that the respondent is fully informed of the facts and contentions which gave rise to the order (*Flightwise Travel Service Ltd v Gill* [2003] EWHC 3082 (Ch); *The Times*, December 5, 2003 (Neuberger J.)). For practice in family proceedings in this respect, see *W v H (Family Division: Without Notice Orders)* [2001] 1 All E.R. 300; *S (A Child) (Family Division: Without Notice Orders)* [2001] 1 W.L.R. 211, and *Kelly v BBC* [2001] 1 All E.R. 323. See further para.25.3.5 below.

As to applicant's duties where freezing injunction affects a third party, see Practice Direction (Interim Injunctions) para.9 (para.25PD.9 below).

Evidence —Applications for freezing injunctions must be supported by written evidence in the form of affidavit (Practice Direction (Interim Injunctions), para.3.1, see para.25PD.3 below). As to whether the affidavit in support or in reply should be the affidavit of the party or the party's solicitor, see "Contents of witness statements", para.32.4.5 below. But it is not a requirement in every case that an application must be supported by a sworn statement, because it is easy to imagine circumstances where the balance of justice would plainly require an injunction to be granted before the applicant had had an opportunity to prepare a sworn statement. However, in such a case it is important that the court should require the applicant to confirm in the form of a sworn statement all the evidence on which he relied (*Flightwise Travel Service Ltd v Gill* [2003] EWHC 3082 (Ch); *The Times*, December 5, 2003 (Neuberger J.)). **25.1.25.5**

The claimant should depose to objective facts from which it may be inferred that the defendant is likely to move assets or dissipate them; unsupported statements or expressions of fear have little weight (*O'Regan v Iambic Productions* (1989) 139 N.L.J. 1378 (1998) (Sir Peter Pain); *Rosen v Rose* [2003] EWHC 309 (QB); January 27, 2003, unrep. (Fulford J.)). Great care should be taken in the presentation of evidence to the court so that the court can see, not only whether the applicant has a good arguable case, but also whether there is a real risk of dissipation of assets. A freezing order should not be granted unless the applicant has established an appropriately strong case showing, amongst other things, that the respondent owns the assets concerned or has some interest in them. It is for the applicant to make out his case. An order should not be granted simply because the respondent cannot show any immediate and obvious prejudice (*Flightwise Travel Service Ltd v Gill* [2003] EWHC 3082 (Ch); *The Times*, December 5, 2003 (Neuberger J.)). Where the respondent is alleged to have been dishonest, the court should scrutinise with care whether what is alleged in this respect in itself really justifies the inference that he is likely to dissipate assets unless restricted (*Thane Investments Ltd v Tomlinson* [2003] EWCA Civ 1272; July 29, 2003, CA, unrep.). The source of the assets to be frozen, whether legitimate or not, is relevant to the exercise of the discretion to grant an order (*Dakers v Phipps* [2005] EWHC 3391 (Ch), December 1, 2005, unrep. (Judge Hawksworth Q.C.)). Where an application is made without notice to the respondent, the evidence must state why notice was not given (Practice Direction (Interim Injunctions) para.3.4, see para.25PD.3 below). It is essential that the respondent is entitled to a proper opportunity to present his case at the with notice hearing. He therefore has to be supplied with all the evidence on which the applicant is going to rely (*Flightwise Travel Service Ltd v Gill* [2003] EWHC 3082 (Ch); *The Times*, December 5, 2003 (Neuberger J.)).

Where an applicant for a freezing order in his evidence deploys evidence of discussions between the parties covered by without prejudice privilege, it may be unjust to prevent the respondent from deploying the same evidence in an attempt to defeat the applicant's case against him a trial (*Somatra Ltd v Sinclair Roche & Temperley* [2001] 1 W.L.R. 2453, CA).

Information obtained from a prosecuting authority by a party to civil proceedings is admissible in proceedings for a freezing injunction and a disclosure order, although it has been acquired by the authority as a result of letters of request under the Criminal Justice International Cooperation Act 1990 s.3(7), as the restrictions in that Act on the use of material obtained in response to a letter of request apply only to use in criminal investigations and proceedings (*BOC Ltd v Barlow* [2001] EWCA Civ 854; *The Times*, July 10, 2001, CA).

25.1.25.6 *Terms of example of order to restrain disposal of assets* —An example of an order for a freezing injunction is annexed to Practice Direction (Interim Injunctions), supplementing Pt 25 (see para.25PD.13 below). Before March 2002, the Practice Direction contained two examples, one suitable for freezing assets within England and Wales and the other for freezing assets worldwide. The single example now given may be adapted for either purpose. Further, the example may be modified as appropriate in any case. It is expressly provided that the court may, if it considers it appropriate, require the applicant's solicitors, as well as the applicant, to give undertakings (ibid. paras 6.1 and 6.2).

The clauses in the example reflect the case law as it has developed since the 1970s and provide judges and practitioners with a useful guide to the matters that have to be dealt with on an application for such an order. Before the current example was introduced, the freezing injunctions annexed to Practice Direction (Mareva Injunctions and Anton Piller Orders) [1994] 1 W.L.R. 1233 (see also [1996] 1 W.L.R. 1552) were described as "standard forms" and it was required that they should be used "save to the extent that the judge hearing a particular application considers there is good reason for adopting a different form". The change of status from "standard form" to "example" acknowledges the fact that, although it is desirable that a consistent approach should in general be adopted in relation to the forms and carrying out of freezing injunctions, it is important that they should be carefully tailored to meet the circumstances of each case. However, the terms of a freezing injunction are not at large and an injunction obtained without notice and omitting important terms may be set aside (*Bank of Scotland v A Ltd* [2000] Lloyd's Rep. Bank. 271; [2001] C.P. Rep. 14, Laddie J.).

The example contains clauses stating that the terms in the order prohibiting the respondent from dealing etc. with his assets do not prohibit him from spending stipulated sums on living expenses or on legal advice and representation. It has been held that these clauses in combination do not prohibit the respondent from borrowing money to meet living and legal expenses, even though the result is that the amounts then spent on these matters exceed the sums stipulated (or, in relation to legal expenses, a reasonable amount) (*Cantor Index Ltd v Lister*, November 22, 2001, unrep. (Neuberger J.). Further, the clause not prohibiting expenditure "on legal advice and representation may permit such expenditure in relation to legal matters unconnected with the proceedings in which the freezing injunction is granted (ibid.).

Also, the example envisages that notice of the order should be given to third parties handling the respondent's assets (e.g. accountants, lawyers, banks). By this device, where money is passed by a guilty respondent to a third party, the applicant is afforded protection without implicating the third party (who may also turn out to be guilty, but who at the time of application cannot be shown in any way to be or have been guilty). Otherwise the third party itself would have to be joined as a defendant to the claim and made subject to a freezing order in its own name. Such third parties *should not be made* defendants unnecessarily. The reason why a bank is sometimes joined as a defendant is that the claimant wishes to have information about money in accounts of the defendant held at the bank (*Mirchandani v Bannerjee*, December 19, 2000, unrep. (Neuberger J.)).

The example refers to assets held by a defendant as "his assets". Where, in relation to the assets sought to be frozen, the defendant is as a bare trustee and has no beneficial interest in them, they are not "his assets" in this sense and therefore do not come within the scope of a freezing injunction made in the standard form; orders made in a more specific terms might cover bank accounts in which a defendant had no beneficial interest but which were in his name and under his control (*Federal Bank of the Middle East v Hadkinson* [2000] 1 W.L.R. 1695; [2000] 2 All E.R. 395, CA).

Term requiring respondent to provide information about assets —Normally, an interim order in the form of a freezing injunction will contain an order requiring the defendant to provide information about his assets (see r.25.1(1)(g)). Paragraph 9 of the example of a freezing injunction annexed to Practice Direction (Interim Injunctions) is an order to that effect, and it includes a passage notifying the respondent of his privilege not to incriminate himself (see para.25PD.10 below). (As to such privilege, see commentary in CPR Pt 31.) **25.1.25.7**

Commencement and duration of order —A freezing injunction takes effect at the very moment it is pronounced, even though the order has not been drawn up and even though it has not been served on the defendant (*Z Ltd v A–Z and AA–LL* [1982] 1 Q.B. 558 at 572, CA, per Lord Denning M.R.). **25.1.25.8**

The example of an order for a freezing injunction annexed to Practice Direction (Interim Injunctions), supplementing Pt 25, contains standard terms as to the duration of an order. They provide that the injunction will remain in force up to and including a return day when the application shall come back to the court for further hearing. This will be appropriate where the injunction is granted ex parte. The injunction should be granted for a few days until the defendant can be served and the bank or other third party can be given notice by telephoning or telex if necessary (*Z Ltd v A–Z and AA–LL* [1982] 1 Q.B. 558, CA; sub nom. *Z Ltd v A* [1982] 1 All E.R. 556, CA). The date should be the earliest practicable return date. In the alternative, following an inter partes hearing, it may be provided that the injunction will remain in force until judgment in the action. Both alternatives are subject to the contingency that the injunction may be varied or discharged beforehand by a further order of the court. In addition, the specimen order annexed to the Practice Direction contains terms stating that the injunction should cease to have effect (1) if the claimant does not, within a particular date, provide a guarantee to support his undertakings to the court, or (2) if the defendant provides security in the manner stipulated in the injunction.

Where a claimant obtained judgment by consent and, subsequently the Master refused the claimant's application for a third party debt (garnishee) order, but ordered that certain of the respondent's monies should be paid into court, it was held at first instance that the freezing injunction did not come to an end either (a) when judgment was obtained, or (b) when the money was paid into court (*Cantor Index Ltd v Lister*, November 22, 2001, unrep. (Neuberger J.); see also *Halvanon Insurance Co Ltd v Central Reinsurance Corp* [1988] 1 W.L.R. 1122 (Hobhouse J.)).

A party who obtains the grant of a freezing injunction should promptly apply to the court for the discharge of the injunction if the time comes when it is no longer needed; the injunction ought not to be maintained against an individual any longer than is strictly necessary (*Detect Sea Enterprises Ltd v O'Connor*, October 14, 1997 (unrep.), Sir Richard Scott, V.-C.).

It has been said that post-judgment worldwide freezing injunctions should be of limited duration and the judgment creditor should be encouraged to proceed with proper methods of execution (*Republic of Haiti v Duvalier* [1990] 1 Q.B. 202; [1989] 1 All E.R. 454 at 465, CA, per Staughton L.J.).

Note also r.25.11 (Interim injunction to cease after 14 days if claim struck out).

Varying or revoking order —The court may vary or revoke a freezing injunction (r.3.1(7)) and a person who is not a party but who is directly affected by such injunction may apply to have it set aside or varied (r.40.9). Paragraph 13 of the example of a freezing order annexed to Practice Direction (Interim Injunctions) is directed expressly at anyone served with or notified of an order and indicates how such a person should proceed should he wish to apply to the court for the order to be varied or discharged (see para.25PFD.10 below). A person who disobeys a freezing injunction may be dealt with by contempt proceedings (Practice Direction (Judgments and Orders), para.9.1, see para.40BPD.9 below). A party's contempt is not a complete bar to an application for a variation of the terms of a freezing injunction; in such circumstances, the court **25.1.25.9** should exercise its discretion in the best interests of justice (*Federal Bank of the Middle East v Hadkinson*, *The Times*, December 7, 1999 (Arden J.)).

Conduct of claim after grant of freezing injunction

25.1.25.10 A freezing injunction is an adjunct to a claim and not a substitute for the relief to be obtained at the trial. Therefore a claimant applying for and granted such injunction should press on quickly with his action. It as an abuse of process for a litigant to obtain a freezing injunction and then not to prosecute the action; a litigant is under a duty either to proceed with his claim or to apply, on his own motion, to have the injunction discharged (*Town and Country Building Society v Daisystar Ltd*, *The Times*, October 16, 1989, 139 New L.J. 1563 (1989), CA; *Comdel Commodities Ltd v Siporex Trade SA* [1997] 1 Lloyd's Rep. 424, CA; *Lloyds Bowmaker Ltd v Britannia Arrow Holdings Plc* [1988] 1 W.L.R. 1337; [1988] 3 All E.R. 178, CA).

25.1.25.11 *Communications with the court*—At the end of the clauses of the body of the example of a freezing order annexed to Practice Direction (Interim Injunctions) there is a section headed "Communications with the court" in which practitioners and persons affected are given useful information about contact room numbers and telephone numbers where the order is made at the Royal Courts of Justice. It should be noted that these details may be amended from time to time and there may be some considerable delay before the version of the order as annexed to the Practice Direction (and as published elsewhere) is updated accordingly. As a result of amendments made to these details in October 2006, where the order is made in the Queen's Bench Division, communications should be sent to Room WG08 and the telephone number is 020 7947 6010, and where the order is made in the Commercial Court communications should be sent to Room EB09.

Order to provide information about property or assets (r.25.1(1)(g))

25.1.26 The court may grant an interim remedy in the form of an order directing a party to provide information about the location of relevant property or assets or to provide information about relevant property or assets which are or may be the subject of an application for a freezing injunction (r.25.1(1)(g)). This interim remedy complements that stated in r.25.1(1)(f) and in terms is restricted to "freezing injunctions" as defined there. An interlocutory injunction, even when seeking preservation of relevant property only, may not have such an order attached unless such a power could be invoked under r.25.1(3).

The jurisdiction to grant an order ancillary to an order preventing a party from removing or otherwise dealing with assets by requiring the party to make disclosures applies both in cases where the claimant makes a proprietary claim over the assets and where he does not. The jurisdiction was recognised in RSC O.29, r.1A (Cross-examination on assets disclosure affidavit) but, otherwise the RSC made no specific reference to the jurisdiction. (Order 29, r.1A contained rules as to the conduct of the cross-examination of a defendant on his disclosure affidavit. Comparable provisions are now found in rr.32.6 and 32.7.)

An order may be made under this provision before normal disclosure under Pt 31. An order may be made, not only where the property or assets are, but also where they "may be", the subject of an application for a freezing injunction. In the latter event, there must be some credible evidence and grounds upon which to base the application for an order, and an applicant may not use the rule as a fishing expedition to find out whether he had such grounds (*Parker v C.S. Structured Credit Fund Ltd* [2003] EWHC 391 (Ch); [2003] 1 W.L.R. 1680 (Mr Gabriel Moss Q.C.)). A reasonable possibility (not necessarily amounting to a likelihood on the balance of probabilities), based on credible evidence, should be sufficient to satisfy the jurisdictional requirement. Once the court is so satisfied it has to decide whether, in the exercise of discretion, it was just and convenient in all the circumstances to make the order sought (*Lichter & Schwarz v Rubin*, [2008] EWHC 450 (Ch), *The Times* April 18, 2008 (Henderson J.)).

In preparing an affidavit in response to a disclosure order accompanying freezing injunction a defendant is under a duty, not only to give a truthful answer, but also to *take reasonable steps to investigate* its truth (*Bird v Hadkinson*, *The Times*, April 7, 1999 (Neuberger J.)).

Normally, a freezing order cannot properly be policed and rendered effective unless the respondent party against whom it is made complies with the terms of the accompanying disclosure order. Where a respondent makes an application to set aside a freezing order (or makes an appeal for the same purpose), the freezing order remains in effect in the meantime; further, the respondent is not entitled to a stay of the disclosure order pending the determination of the application (or the appeal) (*Motorola Credit Corporation v Uzan* [2002] EWCA Civ 989; *The Times*, July 10, 2002, CA; *Federal Republic of Nigeria v Union Bank of Nigeria*, October 18, 2001, unrep. (Laddie J.)).

In certain circumstances, a party may refuse to provide information on grounds of privilege, see *Den Norske Bank ASA v Antonatos* [1999] Q.B. 271; see further Pt 31.

In r.25.1(1)(g), relevant property means "property which is the subject of a claim or as to which any question may arise on a claim" and includes land (r.25.1(2)).

As to power of court to make against third party order ancillary to interim order against party requiring the third party (e.g. the party's bank) to make disclosures, etc., e.g. Bankers Trust order (*Bankers Trust Co v Shapira* [1980] 1 W.L.R. 1274; [1980] 3 All E.R. 353, CA or *Norwich Pharmacal* order (*Norwich Pharmacal Co v Customs and Excise Commissioners* [1974] A.C. 133, HL)), see Pt 31.

As to practice to be followed where third party had reported information regarding money laundering and is restrained by "tipping-off" provisions of relevant legislation from disclosing information applicant for freezing injunction, see *C v S (Money Laundering: Discovery of Documents)* [1999] 1 W.L.R. 1551, and see further notes to Pt 31.

Search order (Anton Piller order) (r.25.1(1)(h))

Paragraph (h) of r.25.1(1) recites that the court may grant an interim remedy in the form of an order requiring a party to admit another party to premises "for the purpose of preserving evidence, etc." Such an order, formerly known as an Anton Piller order, is now referred to in that provision as a "search order". **25.1.27**

Practice Direction (Interim Injunctions), supplements Pt 25 (see para.25PD.13 below), and contains provisions dealing with applications for interim injunctions generally and for search orders in particular. (This Practice Direction replaced Practice Direction (Mareva Injunctions and Anton Piller Orders) [1994] 1 W.L.R. 1233.)

A person who disobeys a search order may be dealt with by contempt proceedings (Practice Direction (Judgments and Orders), para.9.1, see para.40BPD.9). However, where the defendant is in technical breach of a complex search order, in circumstances where the breach is trivial and non-blameworthy, an application to commit him may be dismissed with costs on the ground that it is a disproportionate response to the breach (*Adam Phones Ltd v Goldschmidt* [1999] 4 All E.R. 486).

The commentary following outlines the bases for the court's jurisdiction to grant search orders and concentrates on matters of practice and procedure. For more detailed commentary on search orders, see Vol.2, Sect.15 Interim Remedies subs.C para.15–89.

Jurisdiction—generally —The jurisdiction of the High Court to grant a search order was put on a statutory basis by the Civil Procedure Act 1997 s.7 (see Vol.2, para.9A–756). **25.1.27.1**

An order granting an interim remedy of this type may be made only by a judge (Practice Direction (Allocation of Cases to Levels of Judiciary), para.2.1, see para.2BPD.1 above). Applications in intellectual property cases should be made in the Chancery Division (Practice Direction (Interim Injunctions), para.8.5, see para.25PD.13 below); see further *Elvee Ltd v Taylor* [2001] EWCA Civ 1943; *The Times*, December 18, 2001, CA (failure to draw this to attention of judge may amount to material non-disclosure).

Jurisdiction—county courts —In any proceedings in a county court the court may make an order which could be made by the High Court if the proceedings were in the High Court (County Courts Act 1984 s.38 (see Vol.2, para.9A–468+). However, the power of county courts to grant search orders is restricted by the County Court Remedies Regulations 1991 (see Vol.2, para.9B–77) made under s.38 (as amended in 1990). The general rule is that a county court may not grant a search order. Exemption from this restriction is enjoyed by a nominated circuit judge sitting in a patents county court and by a High Court judge sitting as judge for any county court district (ibid., reg.3(2)). A county court may not vary or revoke a search order granted by the High Court but may vary (but may not revoke) such an order where all the parties are agreed on the terms of the variation (reg.3(1) and (4)(b)). **25.1.27.2**

Terms of example of search order —An example of a search order is annexed to **25.1.27.3**

Practice Direction (Interim Injunctions), supplementing Pt 25 (see para.25PD.13 below). Paragraph 7.11 of the practice direction provides that this example may be modified as appropriate.

25.1.27.4 *Communications with the court* —At the end of the clauses of the body of the example of a search order annexed to Practice Direction (Interim Injunctions) there is a section headed "Communications with the court" in which practitioners and persons affected are given useful information about contact room numbers and telephone numbers where the order is made at the Royal Courts of Justice. A similar section is included in the example of a freezing order attached to that practice direction. For further information, relevant to both search orders and freezing orders, see para.25.1.25.11 above.

25.1.27.5 *Making an application* —An application for a search order is made on an application notice in accordance with the provisions of Pt 23 (General rules about applications for court orders) as modified by the provisions of Practice Direction (Interim Injunctions) (see 25PD.3 below). The modifications are substantial. This Practice Direction replaces Practice Direction (Mareva Injunctions and Anton Piller Orders) [1994] 1 W.L.R. 1233. Note also "Court Guides and interim remedies procedure", para.25.0.6 above.

Generally, and for obvious reasons, in the first instance applications for search orders are made without notice.

The general rule is that court hearings, including hearings of applications for interim remedies, are to be in public (r.39.2(1)), but in particular proceedings a hearing, or any part of it, may be in private "if publicity would defeat the object of the hearing" (r.39.2((3)(a)). Invariably, hearings relating to initial without notice applications for search orders will fall into this exceptional category.

25.1.27.6 *Evidence* —Applications for search orders must be supported by written evidence in the form of affidavit (Practice Direction (Interim Injunctions), para.3.1, see para.25PD.3 below). As to whether the affidavit in support or in reply should be the affidavit of the party or the party's solicitor, see "Contents of witness statements", para.32.4.5.

25.1.27.7 *Varying or revoking order* —The court may vary or revoke a search order (r.3.1(7)) and a person who is not a party but who is directly affected by such order may apply to have it set aside or varied (r.40.9). ECHR art.6(1) does not necessarily require the court to vary a freezing order to enable a party to pay for his defence (*Re Kingsley Healthcare Limited*, September 25, 2001, unrep. (Ch D)).

Where a search and seizure order is made upon an application which materially departs from the requirements of the Practice Direction (Interim Injunctions) and the recommended form of order, the order may be set aside: *Gadget Shop Ltd v Bug.Com Ltd*, *The Times*, June 28, 2000 (Rimer J.) (see further, "Applicant's duties where application made without notice to respondent", para.25.3.5 below).

Order for disclosure before claim made of documents by prospective party (r.25.1(1)(i))

25.1.28 The court may grant an interim remedy in the form of an order under the Supreme Court Act 1981 s.33(2) or the County Courts Act 1984 s.52(2) (r.25.1(1)(i)). These subsections deal with disclosure of documents before proceedings are commenced by "a person who appears to the court to be likely to be a party to the proceedings". For disclosure orders made after proceedings are commenced against "non-parties" (or "third parties"), see s.34(2) of the 1981 Act and s.53(2) of the 1984 Act and CPR r.25.1(1)(j) as explained in para.25.1.33 below.

In the Final Report (pp.127–128) it was recommended that s.33(2) and s.52(2) should be amended so that the power to order discovery (i.e. disclosure) before claim made was not restricted to situations in which personal injury and wrongful death proceedings were in prospect. Accordingly, these subsections were amended by the Civil Procedure (Modification of Enactments) Order 1998 (SI 1998/2940) art.5 (see Vol.2, paras 9A–110 and 9A–500). (The further recommendation that, where a personal injury or wrongful death action is in prospect, the court should have power under these subsections to make a disclosure order against a person who is not likely to be a party, was not implemented.) In *Burrells Wharf Freeholds Ltd v Galliard Homes Ltd* [2000] C.P. Rep. 4, the submission that art.5 was ultra vires was rejected.

In their amended form s.33(2) of the 1981 Act and s.53(2) of the 1984 Act state that, on the application of a person who appears to the court to be likely to be a party to any subsequent proceedings, the court shall have power (in such circumstances as may be specified in the rules) to order a person who appears to the court to be likely to be a party to the proceedings and to be likely to have or to have had in his possession, custody or power any documents which are relevant to an issue arising or likely to arise out of that claim to disclose whether those documents are in his possession, custody or power. Further, the court may order that person to produce such of those documents as are in his possession, custody or power to the applicant or, on such conditions as may be specified in the order (i) to the applicant's legal advisers, or (ii) to the applicant's legal advisers and any medical or other professional adviser of the applicant, or (iii) if the applicant has no legal adviser, to any medical or other professional adviser of the applicant.

Rules of court supporting s.33(2) of the 1981 Act and s.52(2) of the 1984 Act are to be found in rr.25.2 *et seq.*, and also in r.31.16. Note in particular r.25.4(b) and para.25.4.3 "Interim remedy order for disclosure, inspection, etc., before a claim started" and para.25.2.2 "Disclosure of documents by interim remedy order".

Application should be made under Pt 23 (r.25.4) and be supported by evidence (r.31.16(2)). As to the circumstances in which an order may be made and the terms of the order, see r.31.16(3) to (5).

Rule 31.16(3) states (amongst other things) that the court may make an order only where (a) the respondent is likely to be a party to subsequent proceedings, and (b) the applicant is likely to be a party to those proceedings. The applicant and respondent may agree that these conditions are satisfied (as in *Bermuda International Securities Ltd v K.P.M.G.* [2001] EWCA Civ 268; *The Times*, March 15, 2001, CA). Where they are not, the words of the rule should be given their ordinary meaning (*Burrells Wharf Freeholds Ltd v Galliard Homes Ltd* [2000] C.P. Rep. 4 (Dyson J.)). If there is anything approaching a real issue between the parties, and the parties show by their attitude that they intend to fight it (and to do so perhaps even regardless of the merits), then the court is likely to find paras (a) and (b) of r.31.16(3) satisfied (*Medisys Plc v Arthur Anderson*, October 26, 2001, unrep. (Cooke J.)). It would not be desirable to order disclosure in relation to a claim which was demurrable or doomed to failure, not because the parties were not likely to be parties to proceedings within the meaning of paras (a) and (b) or r.31.16(3), but because other criteria in that sub-rule would not then be met (*ibid.*)

In *Arsenal Football Club Plc v Elite Sports Distribution Ltd* [2002] EWHC 3057 (Mr Geoffrey Vos Q.C.), in dismissing the defendant's application to strike out the claimant's statement of case under r.3.4, the judge noted that the circumstances were that the claimants might have taken advantage of r.25.1(1)(j) and r.31.16 before proceedings were commenced but did not do so, and ordered that the defendants should give specific disclosure under r.31.12 and be at liberty after such disclosure to re-apply under r.3.4.

The regulation of disclosure of documents by prospective parties is not confined to the statutory provisions and rules of court referred to above. Pre-action protocols (see Practice Direction (Protocols), para.C1–001 below) routinely provide for the disclosure of documents before claims are started by prospective parties (see *Bermuda International Securities Ltd v KPMG* [2001] EWCA Civ 269; *The Times*, March 14, 2001, CA).

Disclosure of documents in advance of the commencement of proceedings in effect may be required under other provisions apart from those explained above. For example, in circumstances to which the Third Parties (Rights Against Insurers) Act 1930 applies, in a given case the duty imposed on insurers by s.2 of that Act to give information to third parties may have the effect of requiring the insurers to disclose documents in advance of the commencement of proceedings (*In re O.T. Computers Limited* [2004] EWCA Civ 653; [2004] Ch. 317, CA).

Order to inspect, etc., and to take samples, etc., of property before claim made (*r.25.1(1)(i)*)

The court may grant an interim remedy in the form of an order under the Supreme Court Act 1981 s.33(1) or the County Courts Act 1984 s.52(1) (r.25.1(1)(i)). **25.1.29**

These subsections state that on the application of any person the court has power to make an order providing for (a) the inspection, photographing, preservation, custody and detention of property which appears to the court to be property *which may become the subject-matter of subsequent proceedings in the court*, or as to which any question may arise in any such proceedings, and (b) the taking of samples of any such property and the carrying out of any experiment on or with any such property (see Vol.2, paras 9A–110 and 9A–500).

In effect, these subsections enable the court to make orders similar to those referred to in r.25.1(1)(c)(i) to (iv). The significant feature of the subsections is that they specifically empower the court to make such order before proceedings are commenced. It may be noted that r.25.2(1)(a) states that an order for an interim remedy, including the remedies referred to in paras (i) to (iv) of r.25.1(1)(c), may be made before proceedings are started (that is to say, before the court issues a claim form).

Rules of court supporting s.33(1) of SCA 1981 and s.52(1) of CCA 1984 are to be found in rr.25.2 *et seq.* and notes following those rules.

Order to inspect, etc., and to take samples, etc., of non-party's property after claim made (r.25.1(1)(j))

25.1.30 The court may grant an interim remedy in the form of an order under the Supreme Court Act 1981 s.34(3) or the County Courts Act 1984 s.53(3) (r.25.1(1)(j)).

These subsections state that in any proceedings on the application of a party the court has power to make an order providing for (a) the inspection, photographing, preservation, custody and detention of property which appears to the court to be property *which is not the property of, or in the possession of any party to the proceedings* but which is the subject-matter of the proceedings or as to which any question may arises in the proceedings, and (b) the taking of samples of any such property and the carrying out of any experiment on or with any such property (see Vol.2, paras 9A–115 and 9A–506). Previously these subsections applied only to proceedings in which a claim was made in respect of personal injuries, or in respect of a person's death. This restriction was removed by the Civil Procedure (Modifications of Enactments) Order 1998 (SI 1998/2940).

In effect, these subsections enable the court to make orders similar to those referred to in r.25.1(1)(c)(i) to (iv). The significant feature of the subsections is that they specifically empower the court to make such orders after proceedings are commenced against persons who are not parties to the proceedings.

Rules of court supporting s.34(3) of the SCA 1981 and s.53(3) of the CCA 1984 are to be found in rr.25.2 *et seq.* and notes following those rules.

Order for disclosure of documents by non-party after claim (r.25.1(1)(j))

25.1.31 The court may grant an interim remedy in the form of an order under the Supreme Court Act 1981 s.34(2) or the County Courts Act 1984 s.53(2) (r.25.1(1)(j)). These subsections deal with disclosure of documents after proceedings are commenced by a person who is not a party to the proceedings (i.e. a "non-party" or "third party"). For disclosure orders against prospective parties (as distinct from non-parties) before proceedings are commenced, see s.33(2) of the 1981 Act and s.52(2) of the 1984 Act and CPR r.25.1.1(i) as explained in para.25.1.30 above.

In the Final Report (pp.127–128) it was recommended that the court should have power to make disclosure orders (1) before proceedings for personal injury and wrongful death were commenced against persons who were not likely to be parties to the proceedings and (2) after proceedings of any variety had been commenced against persons who were not parties to the proceedings. The latter, but not the former, of these recommendations was accepted. Accordingly, s.34(2) of the 1981 Act and s.53(2) of the 1984 Act were amended by the Civil Procedure (Modification of Enactments) Order 1998 (SI 1998/2940) art.5 (see Vol.2, paras 9A–115 and 9A–506).

In their amended form, these subsections state that, on the application of a party to any proceedings (not only, as previously, proceedings in which a claim is made in respect of personal injuries or death), the court shall (in such circumstances as may be specified in the rules) have power to make a disclosure order against a person who is not a party to the proceeedings and who appears to the court to be likely to have in his possession, custody or power any documents "which are relevant to an issue arising, out of the said claim". (The expression "said claim" referred back to s.34(1) and s.53(1), but both of these subsections are now repealed.) Further, the court may order that person to produce such of those documents as are in his possession, custody or power to the applicant or, on such conditions as may be specified in the order (i) to the applicant's legal advisers, or (ii) to the applicant's legal advisers and any medical or other professional adviser of the applicant, or (iii) if the applicant has no legal adviser, to any medical or other professional adviser of the applicant.

Rules of court supporting s.34(2) of the SCA 1981 and s.53(2) of the CCA 1984 are to be found in rr.25.2 *et seq.* and commentary following those rules. Note in particular r.25.4(b) and para.25.4.3 "Interim remedy order for disclosure, inspection etc. before a claim started" and para.25.2.2 "Disclosure of documents by interim remedy order".

Application should be made under Pt 23 (r.25.4) and be supported by evidence (r.31.17(2)). As to the circumstances in which an order may be made and the terms of the order, see r.31.17(3) to (5). The leading authority on the operation of r.31.17 is *Three Rivers District Council v Bank of England (No.4)* [2002] EWCA Civ 1182; [2002] 4 All E.R. 881, CA.

Interim payment order (r.25.1(1)(k))

The court (normally a Master or district judge) may grant an interim remedy in the form of an order (referred to as an order for interim payment) under r.25.6 for payment by a defendant on account of any damages, debt or other sum (except costs) which the court may hold the defendant liable to pay (r.25.1(1)(k)). **25.1.32**

See the commentary to r.25.6 to r.25.9 below.

Order for securing of specified fund (r.25.1(1)(l))

The court (normally a Master or district judge) may grant an interim remedy in the form of an order for a specified fund to be paid into court or otherwise secured, where there is a dispute over a party's right to the fund (r.25.1(1)(l)). This is based on former RSC O.29, r.2(3); see also CCR O.13, r.7(1)(c). **25.1.33**

The question of what is meant by "a specified fund" in this context was considered in *Myers v Design Inc (International) Ltd* [2003] EWHC 103 (Ch); [2003] 1 All E.R. 1168, where a claimant suing for the repayment of a loan, instead of applying for an interim remedy in the form of a freezing order, sought an order under this provision requiring the alleged debt to be paid into court. Lightman J. refused the application on the ground that, whatever may have been the position previously, at the time when the application was made there was no "fund" in the defendant's hands and no dispute as to a party's proprietary right or entitlement to or interest in a fund; any debt owed by the defendant to the claimant was a chose in action vested in the claimant.

Order for recovery of personal property subject to lien, etc. (r.25.1(1)(m))

The court (normally a Master or district judge) may grant an interim remedy in the form of an order permitting a party seeking to recover personal property to pay money into court pending the outcome of the proceedings and directing that, if he does so, the property shall be given up to him (r.25.1(1)(m)). This is based on former RSC O.29, r.6 (Recovery of personal property subject to lien, etc.) but is rather cryptic by comparison. Rule 6 stated as follows: "Where the plaintiff, or the defendant by way of counterclaim, claims the recovery of specific property (other than land) and the party from whom recovery is sought does not dispute the title of the party making the claim but claims to be entitled to retain the property by virtue of a lien or otherwise as security for any sum of money, the Court, at any time after the claim to be so entitled appears from the pleadings (if any) or by affidavit or otherwise to its satisfaction, may order that the party seeking to recover the property be at liberty to pay into court, to abide the event of the action, the amount of money in respect of which the security is claimed and such further sum (if any) for interest and costs as the Court may direct and that, upon such payment being made, the property claimed be given up to the party claiming it." However, as in practice doubtless, the former sensible inhibitions will continue to apply the abbreviation will make little difference; this rule seems clear enough. **25.1.34**

It would seem that the purpose of the form of interim remedy stated in r.25.1(1)(m) is to alleviate difficulties caused by the exercise of possessory liens in general. It does not affect the jurisdiction of the court to grant relief in equity against the exercise of a solicitor's lien (see *Ismail v Richards Butler* [1996] Q.B. 711, where the authorities are examined). In *Paragon Finance Plc v Rosling King*, May 26, 2000, unrep (Hart J.), an order sought by a client against his solicitor for delivery up of documents subject to lien was refused.

Order directing a party to prepare and file accounts (r.25.1(1)(n))

The court may grant an interim remedy in the form of an order directing a party to prepare and file accounts relating to the dispute (r.25.1(1)(n)), e.g. where a mortgagor applies for an order that an account of the mortgagee's costs be taken. This power should be distinguished from the power of the court to grant an interim remedy in the form of an order directing an account to be taken or an inquiry to be made by the court (r.25.1(1)(o)) (see para.25.1.38 below). **25.1.35**

Order directing account or inquiry (r.25.1(1)(o))

Sub-paragraph (o) of r.25.1(1) states that the court may grant an interim remedy in **25.1.36** the form of an order directing any account to be taken or inquiry to be made by the court. Historically speaking, inquiries before a master were an important feature of the old Chancery procedure. Accounts, in effect, are a specialised form of inquiry. Sub-paragraph (o) was added to the CPR by the Civil Procedure (Amendment) Rules 2002 (SI 2002/2058) with effect from December 2, 2002. Although this power was not expressly listed in r.25.1(1) previously, it was always clear that the court could order an interim remedy of this type. Former RSC O.43 r.1 stated that, in proceedings where a party made a claim for an account, or made a claim which necessarily involved taking an account, he could apply for an order "that an account be taken". Former RSC O.43 r.2(1) said that in any action the court could at any stage "direct any necessary account or inquiries to be taken or made". See also former CCR O.13 r.7(1)(h), which spoke of "the taking or making of any necessary accounts or inquiries". The court may grant an interim remedy of this type on its own initiative, subject to the terms of r.3.3.

Until December 2, 2002, the practice formerly stated in RSC O.43 r.2(2), to the effect that every direction for an account to be taken or an inquiry to be made "shall be numbered in the order so that, as far as possible, each distinct account and inquiry is given its own number", was continued by a practice direction supplementing Pt 25; i.e. Practice Direction (Accounts and Inquiries), para.3. With effect from that date that practice direction was deleted (see para.25.0.6 above), but presumably the practice formerly stated in para.3 continues.

The power of the court formerly found in former RSC O.43, r.1 (see above) to order summarily that an account be taken in cases where a party made a claim for an account, or made a claim which necessarily involved taking an account, was quite distinct from the power of the court to grant such remedy on the claimant's application for summary judgment under former RSC O.14. Summary judgment is now dealt with by the provisions of Pt 24. The Practice Direction supplementing that Part provides that, if a remedy sought by a claimant in his claim form, includes, or necessarily involves, taking an account or making an inquiry, "an application can be made under Part 24" by any party to the proceedings for an order directing any necessary accounts or inquiries to be taken (Practice Direction (The Summary Disposal of Claims), para.6; see para.24PD.6).

Subject to important exceptions, generally an order for an interim remedy, including an order for an account or inquiry, may be made at any time, including after judgment (see r.25.2). However, it should be noted that provisions as to the court's power to order any account to be taken or any inquiry to be made under a judgment or order (i.e. not at the interlocutory stage) are found in Practice Direction (Accounts, Inquiries Etc.), supplementing Pt 40 (see paras 40PD.2 *et seq.* below). That practice direction contains provisions formerly found in RSC O.43 (Accounts and Inquiries). Provisions relating to accounts and inquiries formerly found in CPR Sch.1, RSC O.44 (Proceedings Under Judgments and Order: Chancery Division) were taken into the Pt 40 practice direction by amendments taking effect on December 2, 2002 (*ibid.* paras 9 *et seq.*).

Continuation of infringement subject to guarantees in intellectual property cases

25.1.37 Sub-paragraph (p) of r.25.1(1) states that the court may grant an interim remedy in the form of an order under art.9 of Council Directive 2004/48. The purpose of this Directive is to harmonise the measures, procedures and remedies under the law of member States in relation to intellectual property rights. It deals with such matters as the parties entitled to bring proceedings, evidence and its preservation, interim and final remedies including injunctions and damages. The implementation of the Directive in UK jurisdictions has necessitated various amendments to existing statutory provisions (see Intellectual Property (Enforcement, etc.) Regulations 2006 (SI 2006/1028)). Sub-paragraph (o) was added to r.25.1(1) by the Civil Procedure (Amendment No.4) Rules 2005 (SI 2005/3515) and came into effect on April 6, 2006.

Article 9 carries the heading "Provisional and precautionary measures" and has a number of elements to it. Most of them are catered for by provisions found elsewhere in Pt 25, and also by provisions found in Pt 23 (notably rr.23.6, 23.9 and 23.10). *Amongst other things,* art.9 requires Member States to ensure that, at the request of an applicant, judicial authorities may issue against the alleged infringer an interlocutory injunction intended to forbid, on a provisional basis (and subject where appropriate to a recurring penalty payment where provided for by national law), the continuation of the alleged infringements of that right, or "to make such continuation subject to the lodging of guarantees intended to ensure the compensation of the rightholder". This last-mentioned aspect of art.9 appears to require that the court should have the power to order security for damages against an alleged infringer whilst permitting the infringement to continue. It is clear that the court has a discretion to award damages in lieu of an injunction, but it will not normally exercise this discretion to sanction future infringements. It would seem that sub-para.(p) was added to r.25.1(1) for the purpose of making it clear that the court has jurisdiction to make an interim order permitting the continuation of alleged infringement subject to the lodging of guarantees. Article 9 expressly states that where an interim remedy is granted before proceedings have been commenced, the procedural law of Member States shall ensure that upon the request of the defendant such remedy shall be revoked or cease to have effect if the applicant does not institute within a reasonable period proceedings leading to a decision on the merits (see further para.25.2.6 below).

Time when an order for an interim remedy may be made[1]

25.2—(1) An order for an interim remedy may be made at any time, including— 25.2

(a) before proceedings are started; and

(b) after judgment has been given.

(Rule 7.2 provides that proceedings are started when the court issues a claim form).

(2) However—

(a) paragraph (1) is subject to any rule, practice direction or other enactment which provides otherwise;

(b) the court may grant an interim remedy before a claim has been made only if—

(i) the matter is urgent; or

(ii) it is otherwise necessary to do so in the interests of justice; and

(c) unless the court otherwise orders, a defendant may not apply for any of the orders listed in rule 25.1(1) before he has filed either an acknowledgement of service or a defence.

(Part 10 provides for filing an acknowledgment of service and Part 15 for filing a defence).

(3) Where it grants an interim remedy before a claim has been commenced, the court should give directions requiring a claim to be commenced.

(4) In particular, the court need not direct that a claim be commenced where the application is made under section 33 of the Supreme Court Act 1981 or section 52 of the County Courts Act 1984 (order for disclosure, inspection, etc., before commencement of a claim).

Relationship between Pt 23 and rr.25.2 to 25.5

Under the CPR, application for court orders, including orders for interim remedies, are to be made in accordance with the general rules found in Pt 23. Further, they apply when an application is made for an interim remedy before a claim is made (see r.25.4 and notes following). Provisions in Pt 23 provide, generally, that an applicant must file an application notice (r.23.3(1)), that the notice must state (a) what order the 25.2.1

[1] Amended by the Civil Procedure (Amendment) Rules 2000 (SI 2000/221) and the Civil Procedure (Amendment No.4) Rules 2005 (SI 2005/3515).

applicant is seeking, and (b) briefly, why the applicant is seeking the order (r.23.6). (Note also the rules as to service and notice, rr.23.4 and 23.9, and as to where applications should be made, r.23.2.) In relation to applications for certain interim remedies, the provisions of Parts other than Pts 23 and 25 are important. For example, rr.31.16 and 31.17 apply to applications for orders for disclosure of documents before proceedings are started and against non-parties (r.25.1(i) and (j)). In some instances, such provisions significantly alter or enhance provisions found in Pts 23 and 25 (and their supplementing Practice Directions) which would otherwise apply unalloyed, but in other instances they do little more than repeat them.

Rule 25.2 and r.25.3 apply where an application for an interim remedy is made. Particular rules as to certain interim remedies are found in rr.25.4 and 25.5. All of these provisions have to be read against the background of the rules found in Pt 23. An application for an interim payment order is an application for an interim remedy (r.25.1(k)). In terms, rr.25.2 and 25.3 would apply to an application for an interim payment order. However, particular rules for such an application are found in rr.25.6 to 25.9 and, presumably, those provisions would prevail in the event of any inconsistency between them and rr.25.2 and 25.3.

Disclosure of documents by interim remedy order

25.2.2 The court may grant an interim remedy order in the form of an order requiring the disclosure of documents before a claim has been made by a prospective party or by a "non-party" (under the Supreme Court Act 1981 s.33(2), or the County Courts Act 1984 s.52(2)), or for an order requiring disclosure by a non-party after a claim has been made (under, respectively, s.34(2) and s.53(2) of these Acts). Detailed provisions for such applications are found in Pt 31 (Disclosure and inspection of documents) (see rr.31.16 and 31.17). Note also r.25.4(1)(b) and r.25.4(2). The advantages of a *Norwich Pharmacal Co v Customs and Excise Commissioners* [1974] A.C. 133, HL, order (identifying the proper defendant to an action) may now, it seems, be obtained by an application in an action without the need to join the proposed information provider or bring separate proceedings for this purpose.

Effect of r.25.2

25.2.3 Generally speaking, an interim remedy is a remedy applied for and granted in the intervening period between the commencement of the proceedings and final judgment or order, and having effect for the duration of that period and no longer. However, in some instances it may be possible for a party to apply for, and appropriate for the court to grant, before proceedings are started or after judgment has been given, one or other of the remedies listed as "interim remedies" in r.25.1(1). Whether or not any one of those remedies may be applied for and granted before proceedings are started or after judgment has been given depends primarily on the law relating to the jurisdiction of the court to grant the remedy. Rule 25.2(1) should not be interpreted as meaning that, subject only to the constraints imposed by r.25.2(2), the court has jurisdiction to grant all of the interim remedies listed in r.25.1(1) at any time. This is acknowledged by r.25.2(2)(a) which states that r.25.2(1) is "subject to any rule, practice direction or other enactment which provides otherwise". (It may be noted that r.23.5 states that, where an application must be made within a specified time, it is so made if the application notice is received by the court within that time).

It would appear that r.25.2(1) is derived from former RSC O.29, r.1(1) which stated that an application for the grant of an injunction could be made "before or after the trial of the cause or matter" (see also CCR O.13, r.6(1)). It is not clear whether any significance should be attached to the fact that in r.25.2(1) the expression "before proceedings are started" is used whereas r.25.2(2) uses the expression "before a claim has been made".

An application made before a claim is commenced should be made under Pt 23 (Practice Direction (Applications), para.5, see para.23PD.5) and, generally, should be made to the court where it is likely that the claim to which it relates will be started (r.23.2(4)).

Practice Direction (Mercantile Courts), paras 3.2 and 3.3 apply where it is proposed to make an application to the court for an interim remedy before the making of a mercantile claim in a mercantile court or a county court business list (see Vol.2, para.2B–16).

Interim remedy granted before claim made—urgency and the interests of justice (r.25.2(2)(b))

The general rule is that an order for an interim remedy may be made at any time; but the court may grant an interim remedy before a claim has been made only if (i) the matter is urgent, or (ii) it is otherwise necessary to do so in the interests of justice (r.25.2(2)(b)). **25.2.4**

Some interim remedies have been designed specifically for use before a claim has been made (*cf.* "before proceedings are started" in r.25.2(1)(a)). A good example is an interim remedy in the form of an order under the Supreme Court Act 1981 s.33(1) or the County Courts Act 1984 s.52(1) (Order to inspect, etc., and to take samples, etc., of property before claim made) (see r.25.1(1)(i)). Former rules of court did not suggest that orders granting such remedies could only be made on a showing that the matter was "urgent". It may be said that they could not be granted unless "necessary to do so in the interests of justice". To that extent the former practice and r.25.2(2)(b) are in accord.

Strictly speaking, timing and urgency are quite separate matters (and both are separate from the question whether application should be made on notice or not). However, it is not surprising that, at least in relation to some interim remedies, they should be mixed. Circumstances can arise when it is in the interests of justice that a person should be able to obtain an order for an interim remedy before beginning his claim, even though that remedy is not specifically designed for use before a claim has been made. Thus, former RSC O.29, r.1(3) stated that a plaintiff could make an application for an injunction before the issue of originating process provided the case was "one of urgency" (see also CCR O.13, r.6(4)–(6)). (By analogy, the same rule was applied, not only to *Mareva* injunctions, but also to *Anton Piller* orders.) Similarly, former RSC O.29, r.2A (see also CCR O.13, r.7(1)(d)) stated that an application could be made for an order under the Torts (Interference with Goods) Act 1977 s.4 for the delivery up of goods before issue of originating process on grounds of urgency (see now r.25.1(1)(e)).

Previously, under the rules urgency was not an essential condition for the granting of other forms of interim relief. Rule 25.2(2)(b)(i) re-enacts former RSC O.29, r.1(3). However, as stated therein, the urgency rule does not have quite the same effect as previously. It is both broader and narrower in its applications. Rule 25.2(2)(b) says that the court may grant any interim remedy before claim (including an interim remedy in the form of an interim injunction) only if (i) the matter is urgent, or (ii) it is otherwise necessary to do so in the interests of justice. In terms, a finding of urgency is no longer essential for the granting of an interim injunction. Further, other forms of interim relief can be denied on the ground that they are not urgent. However, it is doubtful whether any change in the former practice is intended. It could be argued that no harm would be done if the urgency rule were deleted entirely from r 25.2(2)(b). Clearly, there are some interim remedies that ought not to be granted before a claim has been made unless they are urgent. If they are urgent it is in the interests of justice that they should be granted.

No application by defendant before acknowledgment of service or defence (r.25.2(2)(c))

Rule 25.2(1) states the general rule that an order for an interim remedy may be made at any time. However, r.25.2(2)(c) states that a defendant may not apply for any of the orders listed in rule 25.1(1) before he has responded to the claim by filing either an acknowledgment of service or a defence. This rule has a limited application because most of the interim remedies are remedies available to the claimant. Rule 25.2(2)(c) follows former RSC O.29, r.2 (Detention, preservation, etc., of subject-matter of cause or matter), a rule which was incorporated by reference into other rules relating to interim remedies available to defendants (namely, RSC O.29, r.3 (Power to order samples to be taken, etc.), and RSC O.29, r.4 (Sale of perishable property, etc.)). Should a defendant wish to apply for an interim injunction he will be subject to r.25.2(2)(c). However, it will be easy to obtain leave so as to disapply the operation of the rule where the defendant can show a sufficiently strong case for obtaining relief. Although r.25.2(2)(c) speaks of "orders" listed in r.25.1(1) it seems clear that what is intended is that, generally, a defendant should not be able to apply for any of the interim remedies listed there, whether described as "orders" or not, before he has filed either an acknowledgment of service or a defence. **25.2.5**

Directions requiring claim to be commenced (r.25.2(3) and (4))

Former RSC O.29, r.1(3) stated that, where an interim injunction was granted **25.2.6** before originating process was issued it "may be granted on terms providing for the issue of the writ or summons and such other terms, if any, as the court thinks fit" (see also CCR O.13, r.6(4)(b)). (By analogy, the same rule was applied, not only to *Mareva* injunctions, but also to *Anton Piller* orders.) The rule was incorporated by reference in former RSC O.29, r.2A (Delivery up of goods under s.4 of Torts (Interference with Goods) Act 1977) (see also CCR O.13, r.7(1)(d)) (see now r.25.1(1)(e)).

Former RSC O.29, r.1(3) forms the basis of r.25.2(3) and, in terms, is made applicable to all interim remedies that may be granted before claim made. Where an application is made before a claim is made for an interim remedy in the form of an interim injunction, r.25.2(3) is supplemented by Practice Direction (Interim Injunctions), para.4.4 (see 25PD.4). In the penultimate draft of r.25.2(3) it was stated that "the court must give" directions requiring a claim to be commenced and r.25.2(4) created obvious exceptions. However, in the form in which it was enacted in 1998, the provision (perhaps surprisingly) was made permissive, stating that the court "may give" directions, thereby rendering r.25.2(4) merely illustrative. This remained the position until r.25.2(3) was strengthened by the Civil Procedure (Amendment No.4) Rules 2005 (SI 2005/3515) (with effect from April 6, 2006) so as to state that "the court should give" such directions. This brings the rule into line with other provisions. For example, para.4.4 of Practice Direction (Interim Injunctions) states that, where applications are made before the issue of the claim form, either the applicant must undertake to issue a claim form immediately or the court will give directions for the commencement of the claim. And para.5.1 states that an order for an injunction, unless the court orders otherwise, must contain, if made before the issue of a claim form, an undertaking to issue and pay the appropriate fee on the same or next working day, or directions for the commencement of the claim. In the example of a freezing injunction annexed to the Practice Direction, the undertakings given to the court by the applicant include an undertaking to issue and serve the claim form "as soon as practicable". The pretext for a re-examination of r.25.2(3), leading to its amendment in this respect, was the bringing into effect of Council Directive 2004/48 on the enforcement of intellectual property rights. As is explained above (see para.25.1.37) art.9 of that Directive stipulates that certain interim remedies should be available in proceedings for the enforcement of intellectual property rights but, if granted before proceedings have been commenced, should cease to have effect if the applicant does not institute within a reasonable period proceedings leading to a decision on the merits.

How to apply for an interim remedy[1]

25.3 **25.3—(1) The court may grant an interim remedy on an application made without notice if it appears to the court that there are good reasons for not giving notice.**

(2) An application for an interim remedy must be supported by evidence, unless the court orders otherwise.

(3) If the applicant makes an application without giving notice, the evidence in support of the application must state the reasons why notice has not been given.

(Part 3 lists general powers of the court).

(Part 23 contains general rules about making an application).

Effect of rule

25.3.1 Note commentary at para.25.2.1—"Relationship between Pt 23 and rr.25.2 to 25.5" following r.25.2 (Time when an order for an interim remedy may be made).

This rule modifies and amplifies provisions found in Pt 23 (General rules about applications for court orders) in two respects. The general rule is that an application for a court order must be made to the court where the claim was started (or is likely to be started) (r.23.2), it must generally be made by filing an application notice (r.23.3(1)), and the notice must state (a) what order the applicant is seeking, and (b) briefly, why the applicant is seeking the order (r.23.6). The two modifications made in the rule relate to notice and evidence.

[1] Amended by the Civil Procedure (Amendment) Rules 2000 (SI 2000/221).

(For special rules as to notice and evidence on applications for interim remedy order for disclosure of documents, see rr.31.16 and 31.17, and note "Disclosure of documents by interim remedy order" at para.25.2.2.)

Notice

The general rule is that a copy of an application notice for a court order must be served on each respondent (r.23.4(1)) but application may be made without serving a copy of the application notice where this is permitted by rule, practice direction or court order (r.23.4(3)); for other circumstances in which applications may be made without notice, see Practice Direction (Applications), para.3 (para.23PD.3 above) and para.23.0.7 "Applications without notice". **25.3.2**

Such an exception to the general rule is found in r.25.3. An application for a court order in the form of an order for an interim remedy may be made without notice "if it appears to the court that there are good reasons for not giving notice" (r.25.3(1)) (i.e. serving a copy of the notice of application under Pt 23). If the applicant makes an application without giving notice (i.e. without serving a copy of the notice of application under Pt 23), the evidence in support of the application (see further below) must state the reasons why notice was not given (r.25.3(3)).

Under the former rules, provision for application without notice was made in relation to some but not all interim remedies dealt with in RSC O.29. Now, in terms, applications for any interim remedy may be made without notice if it appears to the court that there are good reasons for dispensing with notice. However, mandatory requirements as to notice are retained by r.25.5 in relation to the interim remedies specifically referred to in that rule.

In Practice Direction (Interim Injunctions), paras 4.1 to 4.5 appear under the heading "urgent applications and applications without notice" (see 25PD.4). It is not immediately clear what these paragraphs intend. They distinguish applications made before a claim form is issued and after a claim form is issued. It would seem that they are meant to apply to applications for interim remedies in the form of interim injunctions, freezing injunctions and search orders and that they apply where (1) the application is urgent, and (2) notice is not to be given, either (a) because the urgency makes this impossible or (b) because there are other reasons which justify dispensing with notice (see Practice Direction (Applications), para.3, see para.23PD.3). Paragraph 4.5 states the practice where, because of extreme urgency, the application for an interim injunction, freezing injunction or search order has to be made by telephone.

See also para.25.2.4 (Interim remedy granted before claim made—urgency and the interests of justice) above.

Where an interim application needs to be dealt with urgently in a case in the list of a mercantile court or in the business list of an authorised county court and a mercantile judge of the court in question is not available, the application may be dealt with by another judge, including a district judge (Practice Direction (Mercantile Courts and Business Lists), para.1.3).

Evidence

An application for an interim remedy must be supported by evidence unless the court orders otherwise (r.25.3(2)). **25.3.3**

Rule 32.6(1) states that the general rule is that evidence "at hearings other than the trial" (e.g. proceedings for an interim remedy before or after trial) is to be by witness statement (rather than by affidavit) unless the court, a practice direction or any other enactment requires otherwise.

However, at such hearings a party may, if he wishes, in support of his application rely solely on the matters set out in (a) his statement of case, or (b) his application, *provided that the statement* of case or application is verified by a statement of truth (r.22.1(1) and (3) and r.32.6(2)). (A "statement of truth" is a statement that the party putting forward the document believes the facts stated in the document are true (r.22.1(4)). (See Pt 22 for provisions regarding statement of truth.) Proceedings for contempt of court may be brought against a party if he makes or causes to be made a false statement in an application verified by a statement of truth without an honest belief in its truth (r.32.14(1)).)

Special requirements as to evidence are imposed by r.25.5 in relation to the interim remedies specifically referred to in that rule.

For particular requirements as to evidence on applications for interim injunctions, freezing injunctions and search orders, see Practice Direction (Interim Injunctions), para.3 (para.25PD.3).

For commentary on whether written evidence may be by applicant's solicitor rather than by applicant, see "Preparation and content of witness statements", para.32.4.5 below.

Interim remedy order hearings in private

25.3.4 Rule 39.2(1) states that the general rule is that a hearing (including a hearing other than a trial) is to be in public. However, a hearing, or any part of it, may be in private in the circumstances listed in r.39.2(3); see commentary following r.39.2 below. Exceptional circumstances which may be particularly apposite to the hearing of an application for an order for an interim remedy are: that publicity would defeat the object of the hearing; that it is a hearing on an application without notice and it would be unjust to any respondent for there to be a public hearing; that the hearing involves confidential information (including information relating to personal financial matters) and publicity would damage that confidentiality. In certain circumstances, the important thing is that what transpires at a hearing for an interim order, whether held in public or in private, should not be revealed, either by publicity or otherwise, at least for the time being (e.g. *Bank of Scotland v A. Ltd* [2001] EWCA Civ 52; [2001] 1 W.L.R. 751, CA (application by financial institution where money laundering suspected)). That objective may be achieved by the court's sitting in private, but that cannot be assured. The court has an inherent power to order that information should not be disclosed and certain rules of court are to similar effect (see r.25.9; this imposes a restriction on disclosure of an interim payment). See also "Hearing of application "in public" or "in private"", para.23.0.10 above.

Where an application for an interim remedy is made by way of an arbitration claim, the question whether the court should sit in public or in private is governed, not by Pt 39, but by r.62.10 (see Vol.2, para.2E–18).

Applicant's duties where application made without notice to respondent

25.3.5 As a matter of principle no order should be made in civil proceedings without notice to the other side unless there is a very good reason for departing from the general rule that notice must be given (e.g. where to give notice might itself defeat the ends of justice). To grant an interim remedy in the form of an injunction without notice "is to grant an exceptional remedy" (*Moat Housing Group-South Ltd v Harris* [2005] EWCA Civ 287; [2006] Q.B. 606, CA, at paras 63 and 71).

It is well-established that an applicant who applies for an interim remedy without notice to the respondent is under a duty to investigate the facts and fairly to present the evidence on which he relies. (This duty is obliquely referred to in Practice Direction (Interim Injunctions), para.3.3, but in terms which are misleading and not confined to applications without notice.) The applicant must disclose fully to the court all matters relevant to the application, including all matters, whether of fact or of law, which are, or may be, adverse to it (Chancery Guide para.5.16, see Vol.2, para.1–33). In *Memory Corporation Plc v Sidhu* [2000] 1 W.L.R. 1443, CA, Mummery L.J. said (at p.1459) it is a "high duty" and requires the applicant to make full, fair and accurate disclosure of material information to the court and to draw the court's attention "to significant factual, legal and procedural aspects of the case". See also *Fitzgerald v Williams* [1996] Q.B. 657, CA, at p.667 per Sir Thomas Bingham M.R.

The duty has always been important. The emergence and development of freezing injunctions and search orders as forms of interlocutory relief has given the courts occasion to re-affirm it. Most of the modern case law arises out of applications for relief of this kind, but the principles relating to the duty are fundamental to the proper functioning of the court's process on any application without notice (*Ghafoor v Cliff (Practice Note)* [2006] EWHC 825, Ch; [2006] 1 W.L.R. 3020 (David Richards J.)). The principles were reviewed by Ralph Gibson L.J. in *Brink's MAT Ltd v Elcombe* [1988] 1 W.L.R. 1350 at 1356, CA. In *Marc Rich & Co Holding GmbH v Krasner* [1999] C.L.Y. 487, the Court of Appeal said the duty was clearly described on the basis of the principal authorities by Bingham J. in *Siporex Trade SA v Comdel Commodities* [1986] 2 Lloyd's Rep. 428 at 437. (1) The applicant must show the utmost good faith and disclose his case fully and fairly. (2) He must, for the protection and information of the defendant, in the evidence in support of the application summarise his case and the evidence on which it is based. (3) He must identify the crucial points for and against the application, and not rely on general statements and the mere exhibiting of numerous documents. (4) He must investigate the nature of the claim asserted and the facts relied on before applying and must identify any likely defences. (5) He must disclose all facts which reasonably could or would be taken into account by the judge in deciding whether to grant the application. It is the particular duty of the advocate to see that the correct legal procedures and forms are used; that a written skeleton argument and a properly drafted order are prepared by him personally and lodged with the court before the oral hearing; and that at the hearing the court's attention is drawn by him to unusual features of the evidence adduced, to the applicable law, and to the formalities and procedures to be observed (*Memory Corporation Plc v Sidhu* [2000] 1 W.L.R. 1443, CA per Mummery L.J., above). The duty is not restricted to matters of fact, and no clear distinction between non-disclosure of facts for which the litigant has to bear responsibility and breaches of the advocate's duty to the court can be maintained as these duties often overlap (*Memory Corporation v Sidhu (No.2)* [2000] 1 W.L.R. 1443, CA). Overseas lawyers, seeking world-wide asset freezing orders in English courts should note that practitioners within the jurisdiction carry a heavy responsibility to the court and should not be encouraged to make ill-prepared applications (*Lewis v Eliades (No.1)* [2002] EWHC 335, McCombe J.). For application of these principles in the Family Division, see *W v H (Family Division: Without Notice Orders)* [2001] 1 All E.R. 300, and *Re S (A Child) (Family Division: Without Notice Orders)* [2001] 1 W.L.R. 211.

In an interim injunction case, if the duty of full and fair disclosure is not observed, the court may discharge the injunction. It is no excuse for an applicant to say that he was not aware of the importance of the matters he omitted to state. Further, where the duty is not observed, the court may discharge the injunction even if after full inquiry the view is taken that the order made was just and convenient and would probably have been made even if there had been full disclosure. This last proposition was authoritatively restated by Scrutton L.J. in *R. v Kensington Income Tax Commissioners Ex p. de Polignac* [1917] 1 K.B. 486, CA (at 514) (the authorities were reviewed by Jacob J. in *OMV Supply &Trading AG v Clarke* [1999] C.L.Y. 435, January 14, 1999, unrep.). This rule has a two-fold purpose. It deprives the wrongdoer of an advantage improperly obtained. Further, it serves as a deterrent to ensure that persons who make applications without notice realise that they have this duty and the consequences (which may include a liability in costs) if they fail (see *Brink's-MAT Ltd v Elcombe* [1988] 1 W.L.R. 1350. In deciding what should be the consequences of any breach of duty it is necessary for the court to take account of all the relevant circumstances, including the gravity of the breach, the excuse or explanation offered, and the severity and duration of the prejudice occasioned to the defendant, including whether the consequences of the breach were remediable and had been remedied; above all, the court has to bear in mind the overriding objective and the need for proportionality (see r.1.1) (*Memory Corporation v Sidhu (No.2)* [2000] 1 W.L.R. 1443, CA). (For recent examples of injunctions being discharged on grounds of material non-disclosures, see *CMI Centres for Medical Innovation GmbH v Phytopharm Plc* [1999] F.S.R. 235 (Laddie J.); *Gulf Interstate Oil Corporation v Ant Trade & Transport Ltd of Malta (The "Giovanna")* [1999] 1 Lloyd's Rep. 867 (Rix J.); *Nordic Siltumtehnika Ltd v Keenoil Ltd*, 21 July, 1999, unrep.(Eady J.); *Dora v Simper* [2000] 2 B.C.L.C. 561 (Buckley J.); *ICFI Corporate Securities Fund Plc v International Corp for Finance & Investments* [1999] C.L.Y. 490 (Timothy Walker J.); *Czarnikow-Rionda Sugar Trading Inc v Standard Bank London Ltd* [1999] 2 Lloyd's Rep. 187 (Rix J.); *Bank of Scotland v A Ltd* [2000] Lloyd's Rep. Bank. 271; [2001] C.P. Rep. 14 (Laddie J.); *R. (Lawer) v Restormel BC* [2007] EWHC 2299 (Admin), October 12, 2007, unrep. (Munby J.); *National Landlords Association v Stimpson* [2008] EWHC 2340 (QB), July 31, 2008, unrep. (Judge Seymour Q.C.) *Kulkarni v Milton Keynes Hospital NHS Trust* [2008] EWHC 1861 (QB), August 1, 2008, unrep. (Penry-Davey J.)).

However discharge of the order is not automatic on any non-disclosure being established of any fact known to the applicant which is found by the court to have been material. In these circumstances, the court has a discretion whether or not to discharge and a discretion whether or not to grant fresh injunctive relief (*Dubai Bank v Galadari* [1990] 1 Lloyd's Rep. 120, CA at 127, per Dillon L.J.; *Kuwait Oil Tanker Co v Al Bader*, November 27, 1995, unrep., CA, per Hobhouse L.J.). It should be remembered that the borderline between material facts and non-material facts may be a somewhat uncertain one, particularly in heavy commercial cases. Further, by their very nature, applications without notice usually necessitate the dealing with and taking of instructions and the preparation of the requisite drafts in some haste (*Brink's-MAT Ltd v Elcombe, op. cit.*, at 1359 per Slade L.J.).

In modern cases judges have been critical of a growing tendency among litigants against whom interim injunctions had been granted "to allege non-material disclosure on rather slender grounds" (*Brink's-MAT Ltd v Elcombe*, *op. cit.*, at 1359, above per Slade L.J.) and to seek discharge "on the grounds of the most trifling errors" (*World-com International v Home Communications Ltd*, September 16, 1998, unrep., per Timothy Walker J.). Litigants who behave in this manner are likely to encounter the criticism that, whatever their means and the means of their opponents, they are not entitled to conduct proceedings in a disproportionate manner, and to find that judges are astute to prevent this happening. Further, circumstances can arise in which the conflict of evidence on an alleged issue of non-disclosure is of marginal relevance, or that the issue itself is going to be a contested issue in the trial and is best resolved there (*A v B (A Company)* [2002] EWCA Civ 337; [2002] 2 All E.R. 545, CA, paras 35 and 37).

The courts have expressed concern that applications to set aside freezing injunctions based on allegations of material non-disclosure should not turn into substantial "satellite litigation". Issues of non-disclosure or abuse of process in relation to a freezing order ought to be capable of being dealt with quite concisely. Generally, it is inappropriate to seek to set aside a freezing order for non-disclosure where proof of non-disclosure depends on proof of facts which are themselves in issue in the action, unless the facts are truly so plain that they can be readily and summarily established, otherwise the application to set aside the freezing order is liable to become a form of preliminary trial in which the judge is asked to make findings (albeit provisionally) on issues which should be more properly reserved for the trial itself (*Crown Resources A.G. v Vinogradsky*, June 15, 2001, unrep. (Toulson J.)).

Where serious and culpable non-disclosure sufficient to result in the court discharging an interim injunction granted without notice has been exposed and established, the question whether a fresh injunction should be granted is likely to arise. In these circumstances the judge has a balancing task to perform. On the one hand, if justice requires that a fresh injunction should be granted to protect the applicant from harm that might befall him, it might be thought unjust to refuse it on the ground of non-disclosure ("this judge made rule cannot be allowed itself to become an instrument of injustice") *Brink's-MAT Ltd v Elcombe*, *op. cit.*, at p.1358, per Balcombe L.J.). On the other hand, the courts must uphold and enforce the duty of disclosure as a deterrent to others, otherwise the policy which has been adopted by the courts in this field would be undermined (*Dubai Bank v Galadari* [1990] 1 Lloyd's Rep. 120, CA, at p.134 per Staughton L.J.; see also *Behbehani v Salem (Note)* [1989] 1 W.L.R. 723, CA, at p.734 per Woolf L.J.).

Practice Direction (Interim Injunctions), para.5.1(2) (see paras 25PD.5 below) provides than any order for an injunction, unless the court orders otherwise, must contain, if made without notice to any other party, an undertaking by the applicant to the court to serve on the respondent as soon as practicable the application notice, the evidence in support, and any order made. The single example of a freezing injunction annexed to Practice Direction (Injunctions) (see paras 25PD.13 *et seq.* below) contains forms of undertakings to be given to the court by the applicant. The applicant is required, amongst other things, as soon as practicable (a) to issue and serve on the respondent a claim form in the form of the draft produced to the court, (b) cause an affidavit to be sworn and filed substantially in the terms of the draft affidavit produced to the court or, as the case may be, confirming the substance of what was said to the court by the applicant's counsel or solicitors, (c) serve on the respondent (i) copies of the evidence and other documents provided to the court on the making of the application and (ii) an application notice for continuation of the order.

The responsibilities so imposed on an applicant in relation to evidence reflect the general principle (now underpinned by ECHR art.6 and subject to narrow exceptions, e.g. *Murjani (A Bankrupt), Re* [1996] 1 W.L.R. 1498) that applications for interim injunctions have to be decided solely on the basis of evidence which is known to both parties and it is not right for an applicant to give a judge information in an *Ex p.* application which cannot at a later stage be revealed to a party affected by the result of the application (*WEA Records Ltd v Visions Channel 4 Ltd* [1983] 1 W.L.R. 721, CA; *Pamplin v Express Newspapers Ltd* [1985] 1 W.L.R. 689).

Applicants without notice for relief are under a duty to provide full notes of the hearing with all expedition to any party that would be affected by the relief sought; a failure to do so may result in an award of indemnity costs in favour of the party affected (*Interoute Telecommunications (UK) Ltd v Fashion Gossip Ltd*, *The Times*, November 10, 1999 (Lightman J.)). The allegations made against the respondent should be comprehensively set out in a witness statement which should be served as soon as practicable on the respondent. Counsel and solicitors have responsibility for taking full notes of what was said at the hearing and they should not expect that a transcript of the hearing would be available or would suffice if it were (*Cipres Gas Injection Ltd v Melea Ltd*, [2005] EWHC 3180 (Pat) (setting aside interim injunction made without notice restraining threats against witnesses)). Where a freezing order is granted, the duty to provide the respondent with a full note arises whether or not the respondent asks for it (*Thane Investments Ltd v Tomlinson* [2003] EWCA Civ 1272 (Neuberger J.)). For practice in family proceedings in this respect, see *W v H (Family Division: Without Notice Orders)* [2001] 1 All E.R. 300, *In re S (A Child) (Family Division: Without Notice Orders)* [2001] 1 W.L.R. 211; and *Kelly v BBC* [2001] 1 All E.R. 323.

Frequently, interim orders made without notice to the respondent (especially interim injunctions) will be for a limited period and will have to be continued by further order. Where an application to continue an interim injunction is met by an application to discharge the injunction forthwith on the ground of material non-disclosure, normally the two applications will be heard together (consistent with the court's duty under r.1.4(2)(i) to deal with "as many aspects of the case as it can on the same occasion"). But the balance of prejudice and particular facts and circumstances may dictate a different approach (e.g. where the allegations of non-disclosure are serious, and where the applications raise quite distinct issues) (*Network Multimedia Television Ltd v Jobserve Ltd, The Times*, January 25, 2001 (Neuberger J.)).

Application for an interim remedy where there is no related claim[1]

25.4—(1) This rule applies where a party wishes to apply for an interim remedy but— 25.4

(a) the remedy is sought in relation to proceedings which are taking place, or will take place, outside the jurisdiction; or

(b) the application is made under section 33 of the Supreme Court Act 1981 or section 52 of the County Courts Act 1984 (order for disclosure, inspection, etc., before commencement) before a claim has been commenced.

(2) An application under this rule must be made in accordance with the general rules about applications contained in Part 23.

(The following provisions are also relevant—

Rule 25.5 (inspection of property before commencement or against a non-party)

Rule 31.16 (orders for disclosure of documents before proceedings start)

Rule 31.17 (orders for disclosure of documents against a person not a party).)

Effect of rule

An application for an interim remedy order may be made in circumstances "where there is no related claim". Two circumstances are identified in paras (a) and (b) of r.25.4(1). Where either of those circumstances exists "an application under this rule" must be made in accordance with the general rules about applications for court orders contained in Pt 23. The general rules in Pt 23 proceed on the assumption that a claim has been commenced or will be commenced (as did former CCR O.13 (Applications and orders in the course of proceedings)). This rule makes it clear that those rules apply when an application for an interim remedy is made before a claim is made in the two circumstances stated in paras (a) and (b) of r.25.4(1). The particular significance of this is that these remedies are to be applied for by notice of application without the prior issue of a claim form. 25.4.1

[1] Amended by the Civil Procedure (Amendment) Rules 2000 (SI 2000/221).

Interim remedy order in support of foreign proceedings (r.25.4(1)(a))

25.4.2 The Civil Jurisdiction and Judgments Act 1982 s.25 (see Vol.2, para.5–27) enables the High Court to grant "interim relief" in cases proceeding in courts other than the courts of England and Wales. (For further commentary on s.25, see Vol.2, Sect.15 Interim Remedies subs.A.1 para.15–5.) In such circumstances, an order is sought "where there is no related claim" in the sense that there is no claim made over which the English court has jurisdiction. The court's permission is required for service out of jurisdiction of process seeking such relief (see r.6.36 and para.6.37.33 above). As to the meaning of foreign "proceedings" in s.25(1) of the 1982 Act, see *Fourie v Le Roux*, [2005] EWCA Civ 204, *The Times* April 25, 2005, C.A., affirming [2004] EWHC 2260; *The Times* October 8, 2004, (Ch D), (Mr. John Jarvis Q.C.).

As defined by s.25(7), in this context "interim relief" would appear to include all of the forms of relief listed as "interim remedies" in r.25.1(1), including "freezing injunctions" (*cf. Mercedes-Benz AG v Leiduck* [1996] A.C. 284, PC). Initially, s.25 was confined to cases proceeding in courts in jurisdictions within other constituent parts of the UK and within the EC., but was subsequently extended, notably by the Civil Jurisdiction and Judgments Act 1982 (Interim Relief) Order 1997 (SI 1997/302) (see Vol.2, para.5–161). For general principles to be applied by a court when granting a freezing injunction under s.25, see *Ryan v Friction Dynamics Ltd* [2001] C.P. Rep. 75 (Neuberger J.).

Section 25(2) of the 1982 Act states that, on an application for interim relief under this jurisdiction, the court may refuse to grant relief if in the opinion of the court, the fact that the court has no jurisdiction apart from s.25 in relation to the subject-matter of the proceedings in question "makes it inexpedient for the court to grant it" (on this aspect of s.25, see *Credit Suisse Fides Trust SA v Cuoghi* [1997] 3 W.L.R. 871, CA; [1997] 3 All E.R. 724, CA, and *Refco Inc v Eastern Trading Co* [1999] 1 Lloyd's Rep. 159, CA). No criterion or guideline is provided by s.25(2) as to the test to be applied by the court in considering whether it is expedient to grant an order, but the authorities show that there are certain particular considerations which the court should bear in mind. These considerations are explained by the Court of Appeal in *Motorola Credit Corp v Uzan (No.2)* [2003] EWCA Civ 752; [2004] 1 W.L.R. 113, CA.

Where a foreign judgment has been registered in England for enforcement, the court does not have jurisdiction under art.47(1) of the Judgments Regulation (44/2001) to grant a worldwide freezing order in support (*Banco Nacional de Comerico Exterior SNC v Empresa de Telecommunicaciones de Cuba SA* [2007] EWCA Civ 662, July 4, 2007, CA, unrep. (court further holding that in the circumstances it was not expedient to make such order under s.25)).

Rule 25.2(3) states that, where the court grants an interim remedy before a claim has been commenced, "it must give directions requiring a claim to be commenced". In terms this rule applies where the court grants an interim remedy in support of foreign proceedings yet to be commenced (perhaps on the undertaking recited in the order that proceedings will be commenced in the foreign jurisdiction).

A claimant applying for relief under s.25 must use the Pt 8 claim form and follow the Pt 8 procedure (see para.8BPD.1 above). It is likely that the applicant will wish to serve this claim form on the respondent out of the jurisdiction and in accordance with CPR r.6.36 will require the permission of the court to effect such service. Application for permission is made by application notice and the Pt 23 procedure should be followed subject to the express terms of r.6.37 (*cf.* former RSC O.11, r.8A).

See further para.6.33.30 above.

Interim remedy order for disclosure, inspection etc. before claim commenced (r.25.4(1)(b))

25.4.3 Some interim remedy orders may be sought before a claim has been issued. In this circumstance, an order is sought "where there is no related claim" in the sense that, as yet, no claim has been made. An interim remedy may be applied for before proceedings are started (r.25.2(1)(a)). Two particular interim remedies orders are referred to in r.25.4(1)(b). They are (1) an order to inspect, etc., and to take samples, etc., of property before claim made under the Supreme Court Act 1981 s.33(1) or the County Courts Act 1984 s.52(1) and (2) an order for disclosure before claim made of documents by a prospective party under s.33(2) or s.52(2) of those Acts respectively (see r.25.1(1)(i)). The distinguishing feature of these two remedies is that they cannot be granted after the claim has been started (but other remedies are available having that effect). Rule 25.4(1)(b) states that, where an application is made for one or other of these interim remedies, the general rules in Pt 23 apply. Thus the remedies are sought by an application. The provisions in rr.25.2 to 25.5 are also relevant to such applications (see para.25.2.1 "Relationship between Pt 23 and rr.25.2 to 25.5" and note r.31.16). For obvious reasons, where the court grants the interim remedy applied for it is not required to give directions "requiring a claim to be commenced" (see r.25.2(3) and (4)).

Inspection of property before commencement or against a non-party[1]

25.5—(1) This rule applies where a person makes an application under— 25.5

(a) section 33(1) of the Supreme Court Act 1981 or section 52(1) of the County Courts Act 1984 (inspection, etc., of property before commencement);

(b) section 34(3) of the Supreme Court Act 1981 or section 53(3) of the County Courts Act 1984 (inspection, etc., of property against a non-party).

(2) The evidence in support of such an application must show, if practicable by reference to any statement of case prepared in relation to the proceedings or anticipated proceedings, that the property—

(a) is or may become the subject matter of such proceedings; or

(b) is relevant to the issues that will arise in relation to such proceedings.

(3) A copy of the application notice and a copy of the evidence in support must be served on—

(a) the person against whom the order is sought; and

(b) in relation to an application under section 34(3) of the Supreme Court Act 1981 or section 53(3) of the County Courts Act 1984, every party to the proceedings other than the applicant.

Effect of rule

General rules as to the giving of notice of applications for court orders and for the providing of evidence on such applications are found in Pt 23. The effect of these rules on applications for court orders in the form of interim remedies is modified by r.25.3 and it is further modified by this rule in relation to applications for the particular remedies mentioned in r.25.5(1). They are: an order to inspect etc. and to take samples, etc., of property before claim made (s.33(1) of SCA 1981 or s.52(1) of CCA 1984), and (2) an order to inspect etc. and to take samples etc. of non-party's property after claim made (s.34(3) or s.53(3)). The provisions in this rule are based on former RSC O.29, r.7A and CCR O.13, r.7(3)(4). 25.5.1

The making of the orders referred to in r.25.5(1) may raise issues under ECHR art.8 or ECHR Protocol 1, art.1. The court may require more by way of justification under either Article where orders are sought against a non-party.

Interim payments—general procedure[2]

25.6—(1) The claimant may not apply for an order for an interim payment before the end of the period for filing an acknowledgement of service applicable to the defendant against whom the application is made. 25.6

[1] Amended by the Civil Procedure (Amendment) Rules 2000 (SI 2000/221).
[2] Amended by the Civil Procedure (Amendment) Rules 2000 (SI 2000/221).

(Rule 10.3 sets out the period for filing an acknowledgement of service.)

(Rule 25.1(1)(k) defines an interim payment.)

(2) The claimant may make more than one application for an order for an interim payment.

(3) A copy of an application notice for an order for an interim payment must—

- **(a) be served at least 14 days before the hearing of the application; and**
- **(b) be supported by evidence.**

(4) If the respondent to an application for an order for an interim payment wishes to rely on written evidence at the hearing, he must—

- **(a) file the written evidence; and**
- **(b) serve copies on every other party to the application,**

at least 7 days before the hearing of the application.

(5) If the applicant wishes to rely on written evidence in reply, he must—

- **(a) file the written evidence; and**
- **(b) serve a copy on the respondent,**

at least 3 days before the hearing of the application.

(6) This rule does not require written evidence—

- **(a) to be filed if it has already been filed; or**
- **(b) to be served on a party on whom it has already been served.**

(7) The court may order an interim payment in one sum or in instalments.

(Part 23 contains general rules about applications.)

Effect of rule

25.6.1 For extended commentary on interim payments, see Vol.2, Sect.15 Interim Remedies, subs.D, para.15–94.

The statutory bases for rules of court as to interim payments are the Supreme Court Act 1981 s.32 and the County Courts Act 1984 s.50 (see Vol.2, paras 9A–103 and 9A–494).

The interim payment rules do not apply to cases on the small claims track (r.27.2(1)(a)).

Contrary to what is said in this rule, "interim payment" is not defined by r.25.1(1)(k). That paragraph merely repeats part of the definition of interim payment given by the Supreme Court Act 1981 s.32(5) and leaves out the final phrase "to or for the benefit of another party to the proceedings" (cf. RSC O.29, r.9), a part of the definition that was crucial to the decision in*Securities and Investments Board v Scandex Capital Management A/S* [1998] 1 W.L.R. 712; [1998] 1 All E.R. 514, CA.

Under the Civil Legal Aid (General) Regulations 1989 reg.94(a) interim payments were expressly exempted from the statutory charge, but see now Community Legal Service (Financial) Regulations 2000 reg.44.

Until April 1, 2005, it was expressly provided in r.41.3(6) that rules in Pt 25 about the making of interim payments should apply when, following the making of an order for an award for provisional damages under r.41.2, an application was made for further damages under r.41.3 (see para.41.3.3 below).

Application for an order for interim payment

25.6.2 Rule 25.6 has to be read in conjunction with Pt 23 (see also notes following r.25.3 (How to apply for an interim remedy)) and with the provisions of Practice Direction

(Interim Payments), one of the Practice Directions supplementing Pt 25 (see para.25BPD.1 below).

In Queen's Bench proceedings at the RCJ, the application notices for an interim payment should be filed in the Masters' Support Unit, Room E16 (Queen's Bench Guide para.7.13.6, see Vol.2, para.1B–53).

Time of application

Every application, whether made for an interim remedy or for some other purpose, should be made as soon as it becomes apparent that it is necessary or desirable to make it (Practice Direction (Applications), para.2.7; see para.23PD.1). The general rule is that, subject to any limiting provisions, an application for an interim remedy may be made at any time r.25.2(1) and r.25.6(1) states that the claimant may not apply for an order for an interim payment before the end of the period for filing an acknowledgment of service applicable to the defendant against whom the application is made. It is not necessary to wait until all defendants have been served. Rule 25.6(1) is copied from former RSC O.29, r.10(1) and fails to take account of the fact that, under the CPR, the function of the acknowledgment of service is changed. The period within which a defendant should file an acknowledgment of service, if he is going to do so (taking advantage of r.10.1(3)), is calculated in accordance with r.10.3. Where the Pt 8 procedure is being used, r.8.3 applies. (A claimant may not apply for summary judgment until the defendant has filed an acknowledgment of service or defence; r.24.4.) **25.6.3**

Evidence

As to evidence in applications for interim orders generally, note, in addition to r.25.6(4)(5), rr.22.1(3), and r.32.6. **25.6.4**

As to the service and filing of evidence, see, in addition to r.25(3) to (6), Practice Direction (Applications), paras 9.1 to 9.7 (see para.23PD.2).

The application notice must be supported by evidence (r.25.6(3)). The evidence should be by witness statement (r.32.6(1)), but may be by affidavit, subject to r.32.15(2). The claimant may, in support of his application, rely on the matters set out in his statement of case or his application notice, if they are verified by a statement of truth (rr.25.6(3) and 32.6(2)). The evidence should deal with the matters listed in Practice Direction (Interim Payments), para.2 (see para.25BPD.1).

Prerequisite orders

No special preliminary orders require to be obtained if the application for interim payment for damages or some other sum of money is based on an admission of liability (r.25.7(1)(a)), or on the likelihood of recovery of a substantial sum of money (r.25.7(1)(c)) or a sum of money in a possession case (r.25.7(1)(d)). If it is desired to apply on the ground that the claimant has obtained judgment for damages to be assessed or a sum of money to be assessed (r.25.7(1)(b)), the claimant must obtain the judgment or order before the hearing. It is possible to do this at the same appointment but immediately before the hearing. Thus, in the one application the claimant may apply for (1) summary judgment, and (2) interim payment of part of that judgment, ahead of the assessment of damages. **25.6.5**

Payment by instalments (r.25.6(7))

See former RSC O.29, r.13(3)(4). **25.6.6**

The court may order an interim payment in one sum or in instalments (r.25.6). Where an interim payment is to be paid in instalments, the order should set out the matters listed in Practice Direction (Interim Payments), para.3 (see para.25BPD.3). Former RSC O.29, r.13(4) stated that, where a payment is ordered in respect of the defendant's use and occupation of land under, what is now, r.25.7(1)(d), the order may provide for periodical payments to be made "during the pendency of the action". It would seem that, although "periodical payments" are not the same as "instalments", they too are now covered by r.25.6.

"claimant may make more than one application"

Rule 25.6(2) states that a claimant may make more than one application for an order for interim payment. This would appear to be based on former RSC O.29, r.10(5) which stated, rather more particularly, that, notwithstanding the making or refusal of an order for an interim payment, a second or subsequent application "may be made upon cause shown". Obviously, where there are several defendants it may prove to be **25.6.7** necessary for the claimant to make more than one application. But successive applications should not be made against the same defendant unless the circumstances have changed materially; for instance because of unexpected delay in bringing the case to trial, underestimation of the plaintiff's needs, or some special expense. The witness statement in support of the further application should bring the story up to date but the court file should be bespoken if it is necessary for the judge to see any previous statement.

Hearing of application

25.6.8 Applications for interim payments are heard by a Master or a district judge. The Senior Master has expressed the view that the assigned Master who heard an application for an interim payment which may result in a substantial award of damages (albeit of an interim nature) should not, as a general practice, hear the final assessment.

Interim payments—conditions to be satisfied and matters to be taken into account[1]

25.7 **25.7—(1) The court may only make an order for an interim payment where any of the following conditions are satisfied—**

(a) the defendant against whom the order is sought has admitted liability to pay damages or some other sum of money to the claimant;

(b) the claimant has obtained judgment against that defendant for damages to be assessed or for a sum of money (other than costs) to be assessed;

(c) it is satisfied that, if the claim went to trial, the claimant would obtain judgment for a substantial amount of money (other than costs) against the defendant from whom he is seeking an order for an interim payment whether or not that defendant is the only defendant or one of a number of defendants to the claim;

(d) the following conditions are satisfied—

(i) the claimant is seeking an order for possession of land (whether or not any other order is also sought); and

(ii) the court is satisfied that, if the case went to trial, the defendant would be held liable (even if the claim for possession fails) to pay the claimant a sum of money for the defendant's occupation and use of the land while the claim for possession was pending;

(e) in a claim in which there are two or more defendants and the order is sought against any one or more of those defendants, the following conditions are satisfied—

(i) the court is satisfied that, if the claim went to trial, the claimant would obtain judgment for a substantial amount of money (other than costs) against at least one of the defendants (but the court cannot determine which); and

(ii) all the defendants are either—

[1] Amended by the Civil Procedure (Amendment) Rules 2000 (SI 2000/221) and the Civil Procedure (Amendment No.4) Rules 2004 (SI 2004/3419).

(a) a defendant that is insured in respect of the claim;

(b) a defendant whose liability will be met by an insurer under section 151 of the Road Traffic Act 1988 or an insurer acting under the Motor Insurers Bureau Agreement, or the Motor Insurers Bureau where it is acting itself; or

(c) a defendant that is a public body.

(2) [...]

(3) [...]

(4) The court must not order an interim payment of more than a reasonable proportion of the likely amount of the final judgment.

(5) The court must take into account—

(a) contributory negligence; and

(b) any relevant set-off or counterclaim.

Effect of rule

The jurisdiction to order an interim payment is an exception to the general principle that a defendant has a right not to be held liable to pay until liability has been established by a final judgment and is subject to the strict restrictions stated in r.25.7. The court may make an order for an interim payment in the several circumstances listed in r.25.7(1), but not otherwise. With effect from April 1, 2005, para.(1) of r.25.7 was amended for the purpose of revising the categories of defendant against whom an interim payment order may be made. **25.7.1**

For an elaboration of the points made immediately above, and for further information on the several circumstances in which an order for an interim payment may be made (judgment obtained, liability admitted, judgment predicted, personal injuries claims, and grounds for contesting payment), and on the exercise of the court's discretion in this context, see Vol.2, Sect.15 Interim Remedies, subs D, paras 15–94 to 15–126.

Powers of court where it has made an order for interim payment[1]

25.8—(1) Where a defendant has been ordered to make an interim payment, or has in fact made an interim payment (whether voluntarily or under an order), the court may make an order to adjust the interim payment. **25.8**

(2) The court may in particular—

(a) order all or part of the interim payment to be repaid;

(b) vary or discharge the order for the interim payment;

(c) order a defendant to reimburse, either wholly or partly, another defendant who has made an interim payment.

(3) The court may make an order under paragraph (2)(c) only if—

(a) *the defendant to* be reimbursed made the interim payment in relation to a claim in respect of which he has made a claim against the other defendant for a contribution[GL], indemnity[GL] or other remedy; and

(b) where the claim or part to which the interim payment relates has not been discontinued or disposed of, the

[1] Amended by the Civil Procedure (Amendment) Rules 2000 (SI 2000/221).

circumstances are such that the court could make an order for interim payment under rule 25.7.

(4) The court may make an order under this rule without an application by any party if it makes the order when it disposes of the claim or any part of it.

(5) Where—

(a) a defendant has made an interim payment; and

(b) the amount of the payment is more than his total liability under the final judgment or order,

the court may award him interest on the overpaid amount from the date when he made the interim payment.

Effect of rule

25.8.1 Most of the provisions in this rule are traceable to former RSC O.29, r.17, a rule which had a title which did not adequately reflect its contents. Rule 25.8 goes beyond the former rule in that it contains specific provisions as to interest. The rule provides for the adjustment of interim payment orders in the light of subsequent events, particularly, final judgment or discontinuance.

For extended commentary on matters that may arise where, upon final judgment or order, consideration has to be given to the adjustment of an order for an interim payment, including any adjustment between co-defendants, see Vol.2, Sect.15 Interim Remedies, subs.D, paras 15–122 to 15–126.

Discharge, variation, repayment

25.8.2 The court has wide powers to discharge or vary an interim payment order, including the power to order any money paid repaid. Further, in certain circumstances the court may order a defendant to reimburse, either wholly or partly, another defendant who has made an interim payment (r.25.8(3)). The court may adjust an order that has been made but not yet paid.

The court may make an order under this rule without an application by any party if it makes the order when it disposes of the claim or any part of it (r.25.8(4)) by final judgment or grant of leave to discontinue. Otherwise an application for the relief permitted under this rule may be made by any party at any time.

Interest

25.8.3 Former RSC O.29, r.17 contained no specific provisions as to interest; the matter was dealt with by case law. It is clear that, where, following final judgment or order, the court orders that part of the interim payment should be repaid to the defendant, the court may award him interest on the overpaid amount from the date when he made the interim payment (r.25.8(5)); that is to say, when his "total liability" is less than the interim payment. Presumably, where a defendant is found not liable at all he would be entitled to interest on the full amount of the interim payment. The court may award interest on an interim payment made voluntarily as well as under an order of the court.

Payment into court and interim payment

25.8.4 CPR Pt 36 contains provisions relating to offers to settle. That Part was substituted by the Civil Procedure (Amendment No.3) Rules 2006 (SI 2006/3435) and the new provisions came into effect on April 6, 2007 (subject to transitional provisions affecting offers made before that date). Rule 36.6(2)(d) stated (re-enacting former RSC O.29, r.16) that where, after making an interim payment a defendant offered to settle a money claim by paying a sum into court under Pt 36, the notice of payment should *state that the defendant* had taken into account the interim payment. Before Pt 36 was substituted that Part made provision for offers in the form of payments into court. But, in Pt 36 as substituted, offers made under that Part are no longer made in that form. Consequently, Pt 36 no longer contains any provision comparable to that previously found in r.36.6(2)(d).

Adjustment on final judgment or order or on dicontinuance

Final judgment —Where an action proceeds to trial either on the issue of liability or of damages or both after the defendant or one of two or more defendants has made an interim payment whether voluntarily or pursuant, to order, the court may, before the final judgment or order is given or made, make such adjustments with respect to the interim payment as may be necessary, for the purpose of giving effect to its determination of that defendant's liability. Such adjustments may become necessary (a) as between the plaintiff and that defendant, and (b) as between that defendant and any co-defendant of his (r.25.8(2)(b) and (c)). **25.8.5**

As between the claimant and the defendant, the first and obvious adjustment that needs to be made is that the amount of the interim payment should be deducted from the amount of the total award of damages, and subject to any further adjustment with regard to the interest on the damages (see para.25.8.3) judgment should be entered for the plaintiff only for the difference between these two amounts. The form of the judgment should recite the amount of the final judgment or the assessment of the damages and should further recite the order for interim payment and payment made thereunder or the amount paid voluntarily. The judgment or order should then provide for entry of judgment and payment of the balance (see Practice Direction (Interim Payments), paras 5.2 and 5.3 (para.25BPD.5) and, to same effect, Practice Direction (Judgments and Orders), paras 6.1 and 6.2 are to same effect (para.40BPD.6)).

Where the claimant has invested interim payments received from the defendant and earned interest, that accrued interest should not be deducted from the sum allowed for interest in the final determination of *quantum* (*Parry v North West Surrey Health Authority*, *The Times*, January 5, 2000).

In the unlikely event that the amount of the interim payment should exceed the amount of the final award for damages, debt or other sum, the court will order the claimant to repay the difference to the defendant who made the payment (see r.25.8(2)(c)). In addition, the court may award the defendant interest on the overpaid amount in accordance with r.25.8(5) (putting into legislative form *Mercers Co v New Hampshire Insurance Co* [1991] 1 W.L.R. 1173; [1991] 4 All E.R. 542). For form of judgment in this event, see Practice Direction (Interim Payments), paras 6.3 and 6.4 (para.25BPD.5 below) and, to same effect, Practice Direction (Judgments and Orders), paras 5.4 and 5.5 (see para.40BPD.6 below).

Discontinuance —The court's power to adjust an interim payment may also be exercised where the court grants leave to the claimant to discontinue his action or to withdraw the claim in respect of which the interim payment was made. Rule 38.2(2)(b) states that where the claimant has received an interim payment, whether voluntarily or pursuant to order, in relation to the whole or part of his claim he may discontinue that claim or that part of it only if (1) the defendant who has made the payment consents in writing, or (2) the court gives permission. It should be noted that leave to discontinue is required when the claimant "has received an interim payment", and not where such payment has been ordered but not paid, and leave may be dispensed with where the "defendant who has made the payment" consents, and the consent of all other parties is not required. In these two respects, r.38.2(2)(b) differs from former RSC O.21, r.2(2A). Presumably, "has received an interim payment" includes having received any instalment where the interim payment was to be paid by instalments. **25.8.6**

Adjustment between co-defendants

As between the defendant who makes the interim payment and his co-defendants, the court may order any defendant to pay the whole or part of the interim payment to the defendant who made it. **25.8.7**

The effect of r.25.8 in this context is as follows. Where (1) a defendant has been ordered to make an interim payment, or has in fact made an interim payment (either voluntarily or under an order), and (2) he made that payment in relation to a claim or part of a claim in respect of which he has made a claim against the co-defendant for a contribution, indemnity or other relief (former RSC O.29, r.17 added here "relating to or connected with the plaintiff's claim"), then (3) the court may order the co-defendant to reimburse him either wholly or partly. Obviously, such an order is likely to be made on or after final judgment or discontinuance of the claim or the part of the claim to which the interim payment related. However, subject to r.25.8(3)(b), such order for reimbursement may be made at an earlier stage in the proceedings.

Restriction on disclosure of an interim payment[1]

25.9 **25.9 The fact that a defendant has made an interim payment, whether voluntarily or by court order, shall not be disclosed to the trial judge until all questions of liability and the amount of money to be awarded have been decided unless the defendant agrees.**

Effect of rule

25.9.1 This provision is derived from RSC O.29, r.15, which was applied to county court proceedings by CCR O.13, r.12.

Under the former rule, two things could not be disclosed by pleadings or otherwise: (1) the fact that an order for interim payment had been made, and (2) the fact that an interim payment had been made (either voluntarily or by court order). In terms, r.25.9 is confined to the latter.

Under the former rule, the disclosure prohibited was disclosure "to the Court at the trial, or hearing, of any question or issue as to liability or damages". Under r.25.9 disclosure "to the trial judge" is prohibited. Under the case management system introduced by the CPR, cases on the multi-track are managed by "teams of judges" (Interim Report p.66 and Final Report p.91) and the court is encouraged (in appropriate cases) to resolve issues that have been identified at the pre-trial stage by "rolling adjudication" instead of leaving all issues alive until trial (Interim Report p.50 and Final Report p.63). Under this system, the chances of the prohibited disclosures being made inadvertently are enhanced.

Formerly, the chances of prohibited disclosures being made by any person, whether advertently or inadvertently, were restricted by the fact that most orders were made in chambers and therefore in private. However, following recent developments in the law, the general rule now is that, subject to exceptions, the hearing of applications is to be in public (r.39.2).

By way of exception, disclosures may be made if the party that has made the interim payment agrees. In terms, the former rule provided a further exception to the effect that disclosure could be made if the court so directed.

Although, almost invariably, applications for interim payments will be held in chambers that does not mean that they will be held in private (see r.39.2 and Practice Direction (Miscellaneous Provisions Relating to Hearings), para.1.5 (para.39PD.1)). This creates a risk that the fact that the defendant has made an interim payment may come to the attention of the judge. Circumstances may arise in which a judge would be entitled to make public his reasons for granting an interim payment order for a large amount (*British & Commonwealth Holdings Plc v Quadrex Holdings Inc* [1989] Q.B. 842; [1989] 3 All E.R. 492, CA).

Where a Master or district judge makes an order for an interim payment at the same time as any other order, the order for the interim payment should be sealed as a separate order. This order must not be included in the trial bundle.

Obviously, once the court has decided all questions of liability, and the amount of money to be awarded, the fact that an order for interim payment has been made, what its amount was, the date it was paid and by which of two or more defendants, and all other relevant facts, should be communicated to the court immediately, and before the judgment is perfected by entry, so as to enable the court to make any necessary adjustments under r.25.8, including interest, and to deal with the question of costs.

Interim injunction to cease if claim is stayed[2]

25.10 **25.10 If—**

- **(a) the court has granted an interim injunction[GL] other than a freezing injunction; and**
- **(b) the claim is stayed[GL] other than by agreement between the parties,**

[1] Amended by the Civil Procedure (Amendment) Rules 2000 (SI 2000/221).
[2] Amended by the Civil Procedure (Amendment) Rules 2000 (SI 2000/221), and the Civil Procedure (Amendment No.5) Rules 2001 (SI 2001/4015).

the interim injunction[GL] shall be set aside[GL] unless the court orders that it should continue to have effect even though the claim is stayed.

Effect of rule

An interim injunction (see r.25.1(1)(a)) is granted on the assumption that the claim will be actively pursued. It should not be continued for longer than is necessary. This rule provides that an interim injunction "shall be set aside" where a claim is stayed (other than by agreement between the parties) unless the court orders otherwise. It would seem that what is intended is that, where the court orders the stay of a claim, it should turn its attention to the question whether any interim injunction should be continued and, on its own initiative, should set it aside if it should not be continued. (For explanation of "stay", see Glossary.) In terms, the rule is confined to an interim remedy in the form of an interim injunction and does not extend to other forms of interim remedy as listed in r.25.1(1). For the purpose of making it clear that the rule does not extend to freezing injunctions, the words "other than a freezing injunction" were added to para.(a) by the Civil Procedure (Amendment No.5) Rules 2001 (SI 2001/4015). A party who obtains an interim remedy in the form of a freezing injunction should promptly apply to the court for its discharge if the time comes when it is no longer needed (*Detect Sea Enterprises Ltd v O'Connor*, October 14, 1997, unrep., per Sir Richard Scott V.-C.). Circumstances may arise in which a claimant, after securing an interim injunction, may feel that that remedy is adequate for the purpose of protecting his interests and may be tempted, with the consent of the defendants (either express or implied), to take no further steps in the action, apart from occasional applications to continue the injunction, unless the behaviour of the defendant forces him to do so. Under the case management provisions of the CPR, claimants cannot proceed in this way. An application to continue an interim injunction, if granted, should be accompanied by directions for the further progress of the case (*Heathrow Airport Ltd v Gross*, January 13, 1999, unrep. (Burton J.)). 25.10.1

A claimant needs permission from the court if he wishes to discontinue all or part of a claim in relation to which the court has granted an interim injunction (r.38.2(2)(a)(i)).

Interim injunction to cease after 14 days if claim struck out[1]

25.11—(1) If— 25.11

(a) the court has granted an interim injunction[GL]; and

(b) the claim is struck out under rule 3.7 (sanctions for non-payment of certain fees),

the interim injunction shall cease to have effect 14 days after the date that the claim is struck out unless paragraph (2) applies.

(2) If the claimant applies to reinstate the claim before the interim injunction ceases to have effect under paragraph (1), the injunction shall continue until the hearing of the application unless the court orders otherwise.

Effect of rule

This rule provides for the special situation where an interim injunction is in place, whether in favour of the claimant or the defendant, but the claim is struck out automatically (not merely stayed) for non-payment of certain court fees by the claimant under r.3.7(4)(b)(i). The rule provides that, in that event, after a period the interim injunction will cease to have effect. Where, within the period, a claimant applies under r.3.9 for re-instatement of his claim (see para.3.7.2) by operation of the rule that interim injunction remains in effect beyond the period until the hearing of the application. If, at the hearing, the claim is not re-instated, the interim injunction lapses; if the claim is re-instated the interim injunction (whether in favour of the claimant or the defendant) will not continue unless the court orders that it should. 25.11.1

[1] Amended by the Civil Procedure (Amendment) Rules 2000 (SI 2000/221).

Practice Direction (Sanctions for Non-payment of Fees) supplements r.3.7 and states that, if a claim is struck out under that rule, the court will send a notice to the defendant explaining the effect of r.25.11 (see para.3BPD.1 above).

II. Security for costs

Security for Costs[1]

25.12 **25.12—(1) A defendant to any claim may apply under this Section of this Part for security for his costs of the proceedings. (Part 3 provides for the court to order payment of sums into court in other circumstances. Rule 20.3 provides for this Section of this Part to apply to Part 20 claims).**

(2) An application for security for costs must be supported by written evidence.

(3) Where the court makes an order for security for costs, it will—

(a) determine the amount of security; and

(b) direct—

(i) the manner in which; and

(ii) the time within which

the security must be given.

Editorial Introduction, Related sources and Forms

25.12.1 See paras 25.0.3, 25.0.5 and 25.0.7 respectively.

Security for costs

25.12.2 The purpose of an order for security for costs is to protect a party in whose favour it is made against the risk of being unable to enforce any costs order he may later obtain. The order, if complied with, will provide the party in whose favour it is made with a fund normally held by the court against which he can enforce any award of costs he may later obtain.

In CPR r.3.1 (The court's general powers of case management) it is stated that, in certain circumstances (see paras (3) and (5) of the rule), the court may order a party to pay a sum of money into court. Money paid into court in such circumstances shall be security for "any sum payable" by that party to any other party in the proceedings (r.3.1(6A)). Presumably, "any sum payable" would include a sum payable under an order for costs. Therefore, the exercise by the court of its powers under r.3.1(3) and (5) may in effect amount to an order for security for costs (see para.3.1.5 above).

Security for costs may also be ordered as a result of an application for summary judgment where the party against whom the application is made (whether claimant or defendant) is advancing a case which is improbable (*Olatawura v Abiloye* [2002] EWCA Civ 998; [2003] 1 W.L.R. 275, noted in para.24.6.6 above).

Who can apply for security for costs

25.12.3 Rule 25.12 provides for applications by a "defendant to any claim", as to the meaning of which, see para.25.12.4. A marginal note to the rule confirms that it also covers application by persons served with "Part 20 Claims", i.e. counterclaims and other additional claims. Thus, a claimant may apply for security for costs of a counterclaim against the defendant who brought that counterclaim and, similarly, a third party may apply for security for costs of the third party proceedings against the defendant who commenced those proceedings. However, save under r.3.1(5) or r.25.15, a third party cannot obtain an order for security for costs against the claimant whose claim lies solely against the defendant.

Rule 25.15 provides for applications for security for costs by a respondent to an ap-

[1] Amended by the Civil Procedure (Amendment) Rules 2000 (SI 2000/221).

peal and by the appellant in respect of a cross-appeal, i.e. an appeal brought by the respondent.

Rule 3.1.(5) provides for applications for security for costs against any party, whether claimant, defendant, thirdly party or respondent to an appeal, who fails to comply with a rule, Practice Direction or a relevant Pre-action Protocol.

"A defendant to any claim may apply"

Rule 2.3(1) defines "defendant" as a person against whom a claim is made. The word "claim" is not defined. When used as a noun in other rules it usually refers to the whole of the case in question (see, for example, r.8.1 and r.26.2) or to a separate cause of action raised in proceedings (see, for example, r.7.3). It therefore appears that, under r.25.12, as under the pre-CPR provision (RSC O.23) a claimant is not entitled to apply for security for costs solely in respect of some interim application initiated by the defendant, for example an application under Pt 17 to amend his defence or under Pt 18 for further information as to the Particulars of Claim (for a case authority on the pre-CPR provision, see *B (Infants), Re* [1965] 1 W.L.R. 946; [1965] 2 All E.R. 651 (Note)). **25.12.4**

An order for security for costs can be made in favour of a claimant in respect of a counterclaim brought against him if the counterclaim raises issues which go beyond the defence of his claim (*Thistle Hotels Ltd v Gamma Four Ltd* [2004] EWHC 322; [2004] 2 B.C.L.C. 174). Pre-CPR it was held that, whilst a claimant facing a counterclaim which was wholly distinct from his claim might be entitled to security for his costs of defending it, no such security would be ordered in respect of a counterclaim arising out of the same matter or transaction as the claim (*Neck v Taylor* [1893] 1 Q.B. 560; "...the Court... will in that case consider whether the counter-claim is not in substance put forward as a defence to the claim, whatever form in point of strict law and of pleading it may take..." (Lord Esher M.R.). Indeed, the existence of a linked claim and counterclaim has also been held to disentitle the defendant from an order for security for the costs of defending the claim (*BJ Crabtree (Insulation) v GPT Communications Systems* 59 B.L.R. 43, CA, see further, para.25.13.1 below).

How to apply

The provisions in Pt 23 (General Rules about Applications for Court Orders) apply to an application under this Rule. For a form of application notice see **PF43** (see Practice Direction supplementing Pt 4). The application notice should state which of the grounds in r.25.13 applies and, if the Order is sought under an enactment, should state the enactment authorising the Court to make the Order. **25.12.5**

Rule 25.12(2) states that the application must be supported by written evidence. That evidence should relate to the grounds for seeking security which are specified and the amount of security sought. Ideally it should also give details of the costs already incurred by the applicant and should estimate the likely figure for costs in the future. It is convenient to set out the details of costs substantially in the form of an Estimate of Costs (Costs Precedent H; see para.48PD.10).

The written evidence relied on may be set out in the applicant's Statement of Case, or application notice, or in a witness statement. Each item of written evidence relied on must contain a Statement of Truth as to which see further the Practice Directions supplementing Pt 22, see para.22PD.1, and the Practice Direction supplementing Pt 8, para.5.2, see para.8PD.5. An applicant may also rely on affidavit evidence if he so wishes. However, if he does so, he may not recover any additional costs thereby incurred unless the Court orders otherwise (r.32.15 and as to affidavits generally, r.32.16, r.32.17 and the Practice Direction which supplements Pt 32 at para.32PD.1 below.)

Evidence relied on which is not set out in the application notice itself must be served with the application notice (unless already served) and must also be filed (Practice Direction supplementing Pt 23, para.9.3 and 9.6 respectively; see para.23PD.1). Where more than one ground is raised, the application and evidence should make clear which points of evidence are relied on in support of each ground (see further, *Somerset-Leeke v Kay Trustees (Security for Costs)* [2003] EWHC 1243; [2004] 2 All E.R. 406, (Ch) at paras 4 and 5).

If the application is intended to be made to a judge other than a Master or district judge, the application notice should so state (para.2.6 of the Practice Direction supplementing Pt 23 at para.23PD.2). The hearing of the application will normally take place before a Master or district judge. Applications under s.726(1) of the

Companies Act 1985 are, in the first instance, listed by the Court as hearings in private under r.39.2(3)(c) (Practice Direction supplementing Pt 39, para.1.5(8), see para.39PD.1; as to the Companies Act 1985 s.726(1)).

Proof of one or more grounds for seeking security does not by itself ensure that an Order will be made. The Court has the widest possible discretion whether to award a security and, if so, in what amount; see further r.25.13 and the commentary thereto.

Where, in the Royal Courts of Justice, security for costs is sought for a sum exceeding £500,000 and the correct evaluation of that amount is disputed, the parties should consider whether it would be advantagous for the judge or Master hearing the application to sit with a Costs Judge as an informal assessor (*cf.* the Commercial Court Guide, Appendix 16, para.7; see para.2A–186).

Ideal time for applying

25.12.6 Although an application for an Order for security for costs may be made at any stage of the proceedings, it should be made promptly as soon as the facts justifying the Order are known. Delay in making the application is one of the circumstances to which the court will have regard when exercising its discretion to order security. The court may refuse to order security if the delay has deprived the claimant of time to collect the security, if it has led the claimant to act to his detriment, or may cause him hardship in the future conduct of the action. In other circumstances delay may deprive the applicant for security for some or all of the costs already incurred in the proceedings, security being given for future costs only.

Where time permits a written demand for security should be made to the Respondent's solicitor.

Amount of security

25.12.7 The amount of security awarded is in the discretion of the court, which will fix such sums as it thinks just, having regard to all the circumstances of the case (r.25.13(1)(a)). In some cases the amount of security may be limited to the extra burden or risk involved in seeking to enforce orders for costs subsequently obtained (see further, para.25.13.5). In other cases the amount of security may relate to the total costs likely to be incurred in opposing the claim or appeal but it is not always the practice to order security on a full indemnity basis. If security is sought, as it often is, at an early stage in the proceedings, the court will fix the amount having regard to the costs already incurred and the costs likely to be incurred in the future. At that stage one of the factors for the court to consider is the possibility that the proceedings may soon settle. In such a situation it may will be sensible to make an arbitrary discount of the costs estimated as likely future costs, but there is no hard and fast rule. Each case has to be decided on its own circumstances, and it may not always be appropriate to make such a discount. For a pre-CPR authority on this point, see *Procon (Great Britain) Ltd v Provincial Building Co Ltd* [1984] 1 W.R.L.R. 557, [1984] 2 All E.R. 368, CA.

The amount of security allowed often takes into account costs incurred in complying with a pre-action protocol. However, as to the costs of a failed mediation incurred pre-action, see *Lobster Group Ltd v Heidelberg Graphic Equipment Ltd* [2008] EWHC 413 (TCC).

Frequently the court will seek to estimate the likely costs up to a particular stage in the proceedings, e.g. the listing stage. As to the making of subsequent applications, see para.25.12.11.

In determining the amount of security, the court must take into account the amount which the respondent is likely to be able to raise. The court should not normally make continuation of his claim dependent upon a condition which it is impossible for him to fulfil (see further para.3.1.3 above). An impairment of his right of access to the courts which is disproportionate to the need to protect other parties is likely to be a breach of Article 6(1) E.C.H.R. (see further para.3.1.4 above). On the other hand, where a respondent opposes the making of an Order for security or seeks to limit the amount of security by reason of his own impecuniosity, the onus is upon him to put proper and sufficient evidence before the court, and in doing so, he should make full and frank disclosure (*M.V. Yorke Motors (a firm) v Edwards* [1982] 1 W.L.R. 444; [1982] 1 All E.R. 1204, HL). If he gives an incomplete or misleading account of his resources, the court may, in exercising its discretion, set an amount which represents the court's best estimate of what he can afford (*Al-Koronky v Time-Life Entertainment Group Ltd* [2006] EWCA Civ 1123; and see *Kuenyehia v International Hospitals Group Ltd* [2007] EWCA Civ 274; see also, paras 25.13.1 and 25.13.13).

The requirement to have regard to all the circumstances of the case (r.25.13(1)(a)) will often prevent the applicant obtaining complete security. For examples of the many circumstances which the court may have to take into account, see the commentary to r.25.13.

Manner and time within which security must be given

Rule 25.12(3)(b) requires a court which makes an Order for security for costs to direct the manner in which and the time within which security must be given. For a form of Order see **PF44** (see Practice Directions supplementing Pt 4) the body of which is as follows: **25.12.8**

It is ordered that:

1. The Claimant gives Security for the Defendant's costs [of the Claim] [until *(specify stage in the claim)*] in the sum of £... [by paying the sum of £... into the Court Funds Office] by *(date)* [(by lodging with the Defendant's solicitors a bankers draft *(describe form of bankers draft)*] [in the following manner *(describe)*].
2. [All further proceedings be stayed until Security is given].
3. [Unless Security is given as ordered,
   (a) the Claim is struck out without further order, and
   (b) on production by the Defendant of evidence of default, there be judgment for the Defendant without further Order with costs of the claim to be the subject of a detailed assessment].
4. The costs of this application are [summarily assessed in the sum of £...] [to be the subject of a detailed assessment] and to be paid by *(party)*.

DATED

In *Radu v Houston* [2006] EWCA Civ 1575 Waller L.J. doubted whether it was appropriate to make an order in that case in the unless form (see PF44, para.3 above). An Order for security is intended to give a claimant a choice as to whether he puts up security and continues with his action or withdraws his claim. That choice is meant to be a proper choice. An order to raise a large sum of money should not be made subject to the "unless" sanction until the claimant has been given a real opportunity to find the money. Waller L.J. considered it preferable to adopt instead the practice of the Commercial Court (as to which, see para.25.12.10 below). If an unless order is made, the period for complying with it should be generous. "The making of an order for security is not intended to be a weapon by which a defendant can obtain a speedy summary judgment without a trial."

The directions as to the manner and time within which security must be given which are most frequently used are an Order for a specified sum to be paid into court by a specified date. Money paid into court on such terms should not be looked upon as property recovered or preserved, so as to enable the court to give the solicitor of the paying party a charging order upon it for the amount of his costs (*Wadsworth, Re* (1885) 29 Ch D 517). Nor do such monies in court secure any judgments subsequently obtained against the paying party in other actions (*Crescent Oil & Shipping Services Ltd v Importang UEE* October 20, 1999, unrep.). It is not possible to obtain a third party debt order in respect of money in court. However, r.72.10 provides a procedure which may lead to an order similar to a third party debt order.

Alternative modes of giving security which may be ordered include payment to the applicant's solicitors to hold for the paying party subject to the Order of Security (as to which, see Form **PF44** which is set out above), security by a bank guarantee (as to which see *Rosengrens Ltd v Safe Deposit Centres Ltd* [1984] 1 W.L.R. 1334; [1984] 3 All E.R. 198; *Gulf Azov Shipping Co Ltd v Idisi* [2001] EWCA Civ 505, CA) and security by undertaking to pay costs (as to which see *Hawkins Hill Co v Want* (1893) 69 L.T. 297). Security by way of a charge over real property is not commonly ordered since if the real property is valuable there should be no difficulty in providing security by way of a bank guarantee or some other alternative which would be simpler to enforce if necessary (*AP (UK) Ltd v West Midlands Fire and Civil Defence Authority* [2001] EWCA Civ 1917; [2001] L.T.L., November 16, CA).

In *Belco Trading Ltd v Kordo* [2008] EWCA Civ 205, an order for security was made specifying sums to be paid into court, or provided by an acceptable bank guarantee, or in the form of an after the event insurance policy subject to a proviso that the policy taken out would give the defendants "equal or better security" than would be afforded to them by a payment into court or bank guarantee: the claimant's appeal against the proviso was dismissed.

Procedure on payment of security into court

25.12.9 In a county court the money may be paid by post or otherwise into the Court Office and the proper officer shall give a receipt for it (Court Fund Rules 1987 r.19, see Vol.2, para.6A–66). In the High Court, Chancery Division, the paying party must prepare a lodgement schedule in **Form 101** signed by a Master or District Judge which is then presented with the money to the Court Funds Office either directly or via a District Registry (Court Fund Rules 1987 rr.14 and 16; see Vol.2, paras 6A–44 and 6A–59. In the High Court, Queen's Bench Division, a request for lodgement in **Form 100** should be prepared and delivered, together with the money and a sealed copy of the Order to the Court Funds Office, either directly or via a District Registry (and Court Funds Rules 1987 rr.15 and 16; see Vol.2, paras 6A–52 and 6A–59. The forms relating to Court Funds are reproduced in the *Civil Procedure Forms Volume*).

Default in giving security

25.12.10 Paragraph 3 of Form **PF44** (the text of which is set out in para.25.12.8 above) makes provision for default; the claim is struck out and, on production of evidence of default, judgment can be entered for the defendant with costs of the claim to be the subject of a detailed assessment. If the Order made does not contain such provision, a party alleging default could apply under r.3.4(2)(c) for an Order striking out the opponent's Statement of Case and for consequential orders (as to which see para.3.4.3 above).

Orders for security in the Commercial Court do not usually provide for the claim to be struck out without further order. Instead the other party is given liberty to apply to the court in the event of default. This enables the court to put the paying party to his election and then if appropriate to dismiss the claim.

Subsequent applications for security

25.12.11 Where a previous application was unsuccessful or resulted in an Order for security now said to be insufficient, the applicant may re-apply if he can prove some significant and relevant change of circumstances (*Kristjansson v R. Verney & Co Ltd* (1998) CA (Civ. Div.) Transcript No.1154/1998). The court has a discretion to make such an order even where the previous order was made by consent, or where the security was provided by agreement without an order (*Republic of Kazakhstan v Istil Group Inc* [2005] EWCA Civ 1468; [2006] 1 W.L.R. 596). A relevant change of circumstance may be easily shown if the previous Order described the security as being in respect of costs up to a specified stage in the proceedings and that stage had now been reached (see Form **PF44**, the text of which is set out in para.25.12.8 above).

Alternatively the original Order may provide for separate payments at successive stages in the proceedings.

In *Vedatech Corp v Crystal Decisions (UK) Ltd (formerly Seagate Software IMG Ltd) (Appeal against Security for Costs)* [2002] EWCA Civ 356, CA, an application for further security was made some two months before a trial which was listed for 20 days. An order made just three weeks before that trial which dismissed the claim unless £200,000 was paid was reversed on appeal as oppressive in all the circumstances.

Rules 12 and 13 are wide enough to permit applications against a claimant for security for the costs of proceedings at first instance to be provided pending an appeal brought by the defendant even though the defendant will not be entitled to such costs unless the appeal is successful (*Dar International FEF Co v Aon Ltd* [2003] EWCA Civ 1833; compare *Stabilad Ltd v Stephens & Carter Ltd (No.1)* [1999] 1 W.L.R. 1201, noted in para.25.12.13, below). In *Dar International FEF Cov. Aon Ltd* the defendant obtained an order for security for costs pre-trial. Judgment was given against the defendant and the security (which took the form of a bank guarantee) expired a short time later. The trial judge refused to order reinstatement of the security pending the defendant's appeal. The Court of Appeal held that, although it had jurisdiction to make the order sought, in the circumstances, it was not appropriate to do so in this case.

Return of security

25.12.12 A party ordered to give security for costs cannot seek to have that Order varied or set aside merely by producing fresh evidence about his affairs at the date of the Order. If, however, he can show a material change of circumstances since the date of the Order, he may apply for variation or discharge of the Order. Whether such an application will be allowed depends on the circumstances and is a matter of discretion to be exercised by the Court (*Gordano Building Contractors v Burgess* [1988] 1 W.L.R. 890,

CA). Under the previous Rules a party against to whom an Order for security had been made on account of his residence out of the jurisdiction (see now r.25.13(2)(a)) was allowed to get the Order discharged at his own expense on coming to reside within the jurisdiction if his return from abroad was bona fide and permanent (*Parkinson v Myer Wolff & Manley*, April 23, 1985, unrep., CA). It is likely that similar principles will be applied today. However, a change of address with a view to evading obligations to give security may by itself justify an application for security under r.25.13(2)(d) (*Aoun v Bahri* [2002] EWHC 29 (Comm); [2002] 3 All E.R. 182).

Where a payment into Court was made by an associate of the paying party solely for the purpose of securing the opponent's costs, if the payment was no longer required for that purpose, the Court had power to order its repayment to the associate (*Crescent Oil & Shipping Services Ltd v Importang UEE* October 20, 1999, unrep.).

Similarly, where money paid into court as security was financed by a loan on terms creating a resulting trust in favour of the lender if the money is no longer required as security the court, on receiving notice of the trust, will give effect to it and will not make orders which could defeat it (*R. v Common Professional Examination Board Ex p. Mealing-McCleod*, *The Times*, May 2, 2000, CA).

Payment out of court

Court Funds Rules 1987 rr.8, 9, 40 and 50 enable payments out of court to be made when the court subsequently makes the order for costs for which security was given. The party entitled to the payment out may prepare a payment schedule in **Form 200** to be signed by a Master or District Judge and to be submitted to the appropriate Court Office for authentication together with evidence of the amount of costs agreed or a final costs certificate, as the case may be. The payment schedule and other documentation will be sent to the Court Funds Office by the appropriate Court Office, never by the parties or their solicitors. Although r.8 requires preparation of a payment schedule by a party, in the County Court the payment schedules are usually prepared by the proper officer of the court. **25.12.13**

Where the party ordered to give security later succeeds at trial, the primary rule is that he should not be deprived of the fruits of the action pending appeal. However, if the unsuccessful party brings an appeal against the order made at trial, an order staying payment out of court pending the outcome of that appeal is within the legitimate scope of the jurisdictional basis on which an order for security is made (*Stabilad Ltd v Stephens & Carter Ltd* [1999] 1 W.L.R. 1201; [1998] 4 All E.R 129, CA). The court has a discretion whether to order a stay and the exercise of that discretion must always take account of the particular circumstances of the particular case. The fact that the successful party cannot fund the appeal out of its own resources and cannot obtain further funds from any one else will often be a weighty factor against the grant of a stay. Whether or not the stay is granted the successful party may still seek the assessment and recovery of any costs awarded to him, unless of course that assessment of costs is also stayed.

Conditions to be satisfied[1]

25.13—(1) The court may make an order for security for costs under rule 25.12 if— **25.13**

(a) it is satisfied, having regard to all the circumstances of the case, that it is just to make such an order; and

(b) (i) one or more of the conditions in paragraph (2) applies, or

(ii) an enactment permits the court to require security for costs.

[1] Amended by the Civil Procedure (Amendment) Rules 2000 (SI 2000/221), the Civil Procedure (Amendment No.5) Rules 2001 (SI 2001/4015) and the Civil Procedure (Amendment No.2) Rules 2002 (SI 2002/3219).

(2) The conditions are—

(a) the claimant is—

(i) resident out of the jurisdiction; but

(ii) not resident in a Brussels Contracting State, a Lugano Contracting State or a Regulation State, as defined in section 1(3) of the Civil Jurisdiction and Judgments Act 1982;

(b) [omitted]

(c) the claimant is a company or other body (whether incorporated inside or outside Great Britain) and there is reason to believe that it will be unable to pay the defendant's costs if ordered to do so;

(d) the claimant has changed his address since the claim was commenced with a view to evading the consequences of the litigation;

(e) the claimant failed to give his address in the claim form, or gave an incorrect address in that form;

(f) the claimant is acting as a nominal claimant, other than as a representative claimant under Part 19, and there is reason to believe that he will be unable to pay the defendant's costs if ordered to do so;

(g) the claimant has taken steps in relation to his assets that would make it difficult to enforce an order for costs against him.

(Rule 3.4 allows the court to strike out a statement of case and Part 24 for it to give summary judgment).

Discretionary power to order security for costs

25.13.1 There are two pre-requisites for an Order for security for costs. A party entitled to obtain such an Order (see paras 25.12.3 and 25.12.4) must satisfy the Court that:

(i) having regard to all the circumstances of the case, it is just to make an Order; and

(ii) one or more of the conditions in r.25.13(2) applies, or an enactment permits the Court to require security for costs.

Thus, security cannot be ordered solely because, e.g. one or more of the conditions in r.25.13(2) applies, but only if having regard to all the circumstances of the case, the court is satisfied that it is just to make the Order. A circumstance of increasing importance today is the ability of the respondent to comply with any Order made. A requirement to raise funds which he is unable to raise may amount to a breach of ECHR art.6(1). This circumstance is considered more fully in para.25.12.7. For other circumstances which the court might take into account whether to order security for costs, see per Lord Denning M.R. in *Sir Lindsay Parkinson & Co v Triplan Ltd* [1973] Q.B. 609. See "Companies Act 1985 s.726", para.25.13.12. Another matter for consideration is the likelihood of the respondent's claim succeeding. The purpose of security for costs is to prevent injustice to the applicant but there is also a need to avoid injustice to a respondent who has a meritorious claim who would be prevented from pursuing it if required to provide security for costs. Although it is important to try to avoid a situation in which the merits have to be considered, the overall result requires that the Order should be just (*Fernhill Mining Ltd v Kier Construction Ltd* [2000] L.T.L., January 27, 2000). An application for security for costs should not be made the occasion for a detailed examination of the merits of the case. Parties should not attempt to go into the merits of the case unless it can be clearly demonstrated one way or another that there is a high degree of probability of success or failure. See *Porzelack KG v Porzelack (UK) Ltd* [1987] 1 All E.R. 1074; *Kufaan Publishing Ltd v Al-Warrak Publishing Ltd*, March 1, 2000, unrep., CA. However, a claimant will not be required to provide security for costs where, at the time of the application, the claim appears highly likely to succeed (*Keary Developments Ltd v Tarmac Construction Ltd* [1995] 3 All

E.R. 534, 540, CA; *Al-Koronky v Time Life Entertainment Group Ltd* [2006] EWCA Civ 1123).

In considering an application for security for costs against a claimant, the court must take into account the claimant's prospects of success, admissions by the defendant, open offers and payments into court; but a defendant should not be adversely affected in seeking security merely because he has attempted to reach a settlement. Evidence of negotiations conducted "without prejudice" should not be admitted without his consent (*Simaan Contracting Co v Pilkington Glass Ltd (No.2)* [1988] 2 W.L.R. 761; [1987] 1 All E.R. 345; *Kristjansson v R. Verney & Co Ltd*, 1998, unrep., CA).

A claimant who has satisfactory legal expenses insurance may be able to resist an order for security for costs on the ground that his insurance cover gives the defendant sufficient protection (*Al-Koronky v Time Life Entertainment Group Ltd* [2006] EWCA Civ 1123; however, in that case, the appeal against an order for security was dismissed; the terms of the policy permitted the insurers to avoid any liability for costs which was consequent upon their not having been told the truth. As the claim was for defamation in respect of which the defendants were relying upon a defence of justification, the outcome of the case depended entirely upon which side was telling the truth). See, further, *Belco Trading Ltd v Kordo* [2008] EWCA Civ 205, noted in para.25.12.8, above.

Where a claim and counterclaim both raise the same issues the court should consider whether in all the circumstances to exercise its discretion so as to refuse the defendant any security for his costs of defending the claim; if both claim and counterclaim are going to be litigated anyway, ordering security which was not paid may serve no purpose other than to hamper the claimant's conduct of the case and to give the counterclaiming defendant the right to begin (*BJ Crabtree (Insulation) v GPT Communications Systems* 59 B.L.R. 43, CA).

As to the effect of delay in applying for security on the exercise of discretion, see "Ideal time for application", para.25.12.6.

On the question whether an order for security for costs may infringe a party's right to a fair trial under ECHR art.6(1), see para.3.1.5 above and para.25.13.4 below. A claimant who alleges that an order for security will stifle the claim must adduce satisfactory evidence that he does not have the means to provide security and that he cannot obtain appropriate assistance to do so from any third party, such as a relative or friend, who might reasonably be expected to provide such assistance if they could (*Al-Koronky v Time Life Entertainment Group Ltd* [2005] EWHC 1688). On the question whether an order for security of costs may infinge the prohibition of discrimination set out in ECHR art.14, para.25.13.6 below and *Vedatech Corp v Crystal Decisions (UK) Ltd (formerly Seagate Software IMG Ltd) (Appeal against Security for Costs)* [2002] EWCA Civ 356.

"Resident out of the jurisdiction"

The words quoted form part of ground (a) set out in r.25.13.(2). "Jurisdiction" is defined in r.2.3(1). The burden of proof is on the applicant to show that the respondent is resident out of the jurisdiction. The question is one of fact and of degree. **25.13.2**

As originally drafted ground (a) (and ground (b)) referred to "ordinary residence" rather than "residence". It appears unlikely that this change was intended to change the scope of ground (a).

In *R. v Barnet LBC Ex p. Shah (Nilish)* [1983] 2 A.C. 309; [1983] 2 A.C. 309, HL, it was held that, in the context of the Education Act, the term "ordinarily resident" should be construed according to its ordinary and natural meaning, and that a person is ordinarily resident in a place if he habitually and normally resides lawfully in such place from choice and for a settled purpose, apart from temporary or occasional absences, even if his permanent residence or "real home" is elsewhere. The relevant dicta in *Levene v I.R.C.; Inland Revenue Commissioners v Lysaght* [1928] A.C. 234; and *R. v Barnet LBC Ex p. Shah (Nilish)* [1983] 2 A.C. 309 were applied by the Court of Appeal to an application for security for costs under the previous Rules, RSC O.23, r.1 in *Parkinson v Myer Wolff & Manley* April 23, 1985, unrep., CA. A person who makes a provisional decision to go and live abroad is not "ordinarily resident" out of the jurisdiction, at any rate so long as he has not left the country (*Appah v Monseu* [1967] 1 W.L.R. 893; [1967] 2 All E.R. 583).

To find whether a claimant corporation was ordinarily resident out of the jurisdiction, the Court has to locate its central management and control (*Little Olympian Each Ways Ltd, Re* [1995] 1 W.L.R. 560; [1994] 4 All E.R. 561).

The Brussels Convention and the Lugano Convention

25.13.3 These Conventions are part of UK law pursuant to the Civil Jurisdiction and Judgments Act 1991. The countries currently governed by the Conventions are the Member States of the European Community (EC) and the European Free Trade Area (EFTA), i.e. Austria, Belgium, Denmark, Finland, France, Germany, Greece, Ireland, Iceland, Italy, Luxembourg, Netherlands, Norway, Poland, Portugal, Spain, Sweden, Switzerland and the United Kingdom. Under the Conventions, the United Kingdom is itself divided into three constituent parts for certain purposes; England and Wales, Scotland and Northern Ireland.

All of the countries listed above are the Contracting States referred to in r.25.13(2)(a). As to the distinction between Brussels Contracting State and Regulation State, see Vol.2, para.5–9. The Brussels Convention has been superseded by EC Regulation No.44/2001 ("the Regulation"). However, Denmark has not ratified the Regulation and so remains subject to the Brussels Convention.

Human Rights Act

25.13.4 An order to pay sums ordered by way of security for costs which a litigant lacks the means to pay may amount to a breach of the ECHR art.6(1) right of access to a court: *Ait-Mouhoub v France,* Reports of Judgments and Decisions, 1998–VIII, p.3214, ECtHR. See also *Federal Bank of the Middle East v Hadkinson, The Times,* December 7, 1999, CA (see transcript), *JR and WA v United Kingdom* 14551/89, December 4, 1989, unrep., EComHR, *Grepne v United Kingdom* 17070/90, October 1, 1990, unrep., EComHR, and *X v Sweden* 7973/77 , February 28, 1979, EComHR. See, *mutatis mutandis*, *Kreuz v Poland* 28249/95 June 19, 2001, ECtHR, 1st section (excessive court fees unduly restricted right of access to court).

Claimants resident in an EU or EFTA Contracting State

25.13.5 The text of r.25.13(2)(a) as originally drafted (see earlier editions of this work) was unusually difficult and obscure. The current text derives from the Court of Appeal decision in *De Beer v Kanaar & Co (No.1)* [2001] EWCA Civ 1318 which solved the problems by construing the rule in a purposive manner in its historical context. The provision was originally introduced in order to eliminate any covert discrimination against nationals of states which were signatories to the Brussels Convention (see *Chequepoint SARL v McClelland* [1997] Q.B. 51 and the cases cited therein). It was therefore held that security for costs could be ordered against a claimant who was ordinarily resident in the USA, even though he was a Dutch national who had assets in Switzerland.

As presently drafted, ground (a) prevents the making of orders for costs against persons resident within the jurisdiction or resident within any other Convention state even if they also have one or more residences elsewhere in the world (*Tatnall v Longley Central London County Court, H.H.J. Hallgarten Q.C.*, October 15, 2003, unrep., noted in *New Law Journal*, November 14, 2003, p.1710; and see *Somerset-Leeke v Kay Trustees* [2003] EWHC 1243; [2004] 2 All E.R. 406, (Ch) at para.1). As originally drafted ground (a) (and ground (b)) permitted the making of orders for costs against persons resident within the jurisdiction if they had two or more residences and none of the other residences were within a Convention state (i.e. within any EU or EFTA state other than the UK); see, for example, *Leyvand v Barasch, The Times*, March 23, 2000 (claimant resident in England and Israel). In most cases however, this point was of academic interest only because such a claimant's connection with this country usually led the court to refuse to order security on discretionary grounds.

No discrimination against claimants resident in other States

25.13.6 An order for security for costs cannot be made against a person or body ordinarily resident in England or in a country to which the Brussels convention or the Lugano Convention applies (r.25.13(2)(a)(ii)). Thus, in comparison with persons and bodies ordinarily resident elsewhere in the world, a sharp distinction is drawn. In *Nasser v United Bank of Kuwait* [2002] 1 W.L.R. 1868; [2002] 1 All E.R. 401, CA, the question whether the distinction has the potential of being discriminatory within ECHR art.14 was considered. It was held that where ground (a) (but no other ground) is established, the court should not exercise its discretion to order security for costs unless it does so on grounds relating to obstacles to or the burden of enforcement of a subsequent order for costs in the context of the particular foreign claimant or country concerned. It is discriminatory and wrong to take into account the impecuniosity of an individual foreign claimant.

"In so far as impecuniosity may have a continuing relevance it is not on the ground that the claimant lacks apparent means to satisfy any judgment but on the ground (where this applies) that the effect of the impecuniosity would be either (i) to preclude or hinder or add to the burden of enforcement abroad against such assets as do exist abroad or (ii) as a practical matter, to make it more likely that the claimant would take advantage of any available opportunity to avoid or hinder such enforcement abroad" (per Mance L.J., para.62).

In *Nasser* a reasonable estimate of the applicant's likely costs up to the end of the proceedings in question was £10,000. However, there was no obstacle to or difficulty about the enforcement of an order for costs other than impecuniosity. Therefore, it was appropriate to limit the amount of security to the amount needed to protect the applicant from the extra burden in terms of costs and delay which was likely to be involved in seeking to enforce an order for costs in the country in which the claimant resided (the USA). The costs of enforcement likely to be incurred in excess of the costs of equivalent steps taken in England or in another Convention country were assessed at £5,000 and that was the sum ordered as security.

If there is no obstacle to or difficulty about enforcement against a claimant who has substantial assets, the court should have regard to any possible increased costs in the country in which the claimant's assets are located, rather than the country in which the claimant resides (*Aims Asset Management SDN BHD v Kazakhstan Investment Fund Ltd* May 22, 2002, unrep., (Ch)). However, it is wrong to deduce from that case the proposition that any non-Brussels/Lugano resident must indicate assets in his place of residence (or within Brussels/Lugano) in order to prevent security being ordered (*Somerset-Leeke v Kay Trustees* [2003] EWHC 1243; [2004] 2 All E.R. 406 (Ch) at para.10).

In *De Beer v Kanaar & Co (No.1)* [2001] EWCA Civ 1318, CA (as to which, see further, para.25.13.5 above) a reasonable estimate of the applicant's costs up to the end of the proceedings in question was £130,000. There was evidence that the claimant had sufficient assets out of which he could pay such costs not only in Switzerland but also in the USA. However, the court was satisfied that (i) there was a lack of probity on the part of the claimant in these proceedings, (ii) the claimant's assets in Switzerland were assets which could easily be moved, and (iii) there was a risk that an order for costs against him would be difficult or even impossible to enforce in the USA. In all the circumstances, the amount of security which it was appropriate to award was £130,000.

No formal evidence is required in order to prove the obstacles or difficulties of enforcement which may arise. Whilst there must be a proper basis for considering that such problems exist, the court will take note of obvious realities (*Thistle Hotels Ltd v Gamma Four Ltd* [2004] EWHC 322).

In *Texuna International Ltd v Cairn Energy Ltd* [2004] EWHC 1102 the court estimated the additional costs of enforcement in that case at £50,000 if enforcement took place in Hong Kong and also allowed a further £50,000 to cover the risk that enforcement would become more complex or that enforcement proceedings might have to be brought in another country; the claimant was ordered to provide security in the sum of £100,000.

Other International Conventions affecting security for costs

The following Conventions expressly forbid any requirement of security for costs, namely, Carriage of Goods by Rail (Berne) 1952 art.55(4); Carriage of Passengers by Rail (Berne) 1961 art.56(4); Carriage of Goods by Road (Geneva) 1956 art.31(5); Carriage of Passengers by Road Convention art.41(6). It should be noted, however, that these Conventions although ratified, have not yet been brought into force in England. **25.13.7**

International carriage by rail is now governed by the Convention Concerning International Carriage by Rail Act 1980 (Cmd. 8335) given force of law in the UK by International Transport Conventions Act 1983 and brought into force in 1985 by SI 1985/612.

The following Conventions impliedly exclude requests for security for costs by non-discrimination clauses, i.e. Third Party Liability in the Field of Nuclear Energy (Paris) 1960 art.14(a) as amended by the additional Protocol of 1964; Civil Liability for Nuclear Damage (Vienna) 1963 art.13; Convention for Liability in Nuclear Ships (Brussels) 1962 art.12(3) (not yet ratified).

On the other hand the Warsaw Convention on Carriage by Air 1929, art.28, impliedly permits a requirement of Security for costs by providing that the procedure is to be governed by the *lex fori*.

Conventions with the following countries contain Articles relevant to Security for costs:

Czechoslovakia *	Cmd. 2637 (1926)
Czechoslovakia (supplementary) *	Cmd. 4980 (1935) art.3
Hungary	Cmd. 5190 (1936) art.12
Iraq	Cmd. 5369 (1937) art.12
Israel	Cmd. 3513 (1968) art.13
Turkey	Cmd. 4318 (1933) art.12
Yugoslavia*	Cmd. 5542 (1937) art.12

It would appear that the provisions of these Conventions do not involve any departure from the Rules and practices of the High Court or County Court. Further information regarding these Conventions can be obtained from the Foreign Process Section, Room E10, Royal Courts of Justice, Strand, London WC2A 2LL.

*It must be remembered that these states have subsequently been split into separate states and not all of these conventions may still apply.

Condition (a): individual or company resident abroad

25.13.8 Security for costs may be ordered against an individual who does not, or a company which does not, reside within the jurisdiction and does not reside within any other EU or EFTA State (see above, paras 25.13.2, 25.13.3 and 25.13.5). Condition (a) refers to a "claimant" as to which see above paras 25.12.3 and 25.12.4.

The Isle of Man and the Channel Islands are outside the jurisdiction and are not Member States of the European Community. Accordingly, security for costs may be ordered under condition (a) against a claimant resident in the Isle of Man (*Greenwich Ltd v National Westminster Bank Plc* [1999] 2 Lloyd's Rep. 308).

Security for costs is not ordered under Condition (a) as a matter of course; the power is discretionary (see para.25.13.1 above). For further commentary on individuals and companies resident abroad, see below "Foreign and English co-claimants", para.25.13.10, and "Foreign claimants with property in England", para.25.13.11.

Condition (b): (repealed)

25.13.9 As originally drafted paras (a) and (b) of r.25.13(2) dealt separately with individuals and companies. As from April 2003 the sub-rule has been amended so that para.(a) now applies to both individuals and companies and, accordingly, para.(b) has been omitted.

Foreign and English co-claimants

25.13.10 Where some claimants are resident out of the jurisdiction, but others are not, the court has jurisdiction to order security for costs if, having grant to all the circumstances of the case, the court thinks it just to do so. In deciding whether to order security, the court should take into account the likely prospect that, if the claim fails, an order for costs will be made which will be fully enforceable against the claimants within the jurisdiction. Another factor for consideration is whether any of the claimants has funds within the jurisdiction which are sufficient to meet any liability for costs (*Slazengers Ltd v Seaspeed Ferries Ltd; The Seaspeed Dora* [1988] 1 W.L.R. 221; [1987] 2 All E.R. 90, CA). Security may well be ordered if the English claimant is impecunious and is not a genuine claimant, but was joined merely in the hope of defeating any application for security for costs (*Jones v Gurney* [1913] W.N. 72).

Foreign claimants with property in England

25.13.11 The court, in exercising its discretion may consider whether the claimant has assets within the jurisdiction and also the fixity or permanence of those assets. The court will not infer the existence of a real risk that assets within this country will be dissipated or shipped abroad to avoid their being available to satisfy a judgment for costs unless there is reason to question the probity of the claimant. If there is reason to question the claimants probity, the character of his property within the jurisdiction is relevant in assessing the risk; the risk will be greater if the property is cash or is immediately realisable or transportable (per Lightman J. in *Leyvand v Barasch, The Times*, March 23, *2000*).

Where the subject matter of proceedings for breach of warranty was a Greek statue, it had been alleged that the statue was spurious, application was made that the claimant should give security for costs. The court had already made an order that the statue which was deposited within the jurisdiction, should not be removed without the consent of the defendants or an order of the court. It was held that as in the event of the claimant being unsuccessful in the proceedings, the value of the statue must be more than any order for costs that could be made against him, there ought to be no Order for Security (*Kevorkian v Burney* [1937] 4 All E.R. 468). A fortiori where the statue, the subject matter of the dispute, is said to be by Michelangelo (*De Bry v Fitzgerald* [1990] 1 W.L.R. 552; [1990] 1 All E.R. 560, CA).

Where a claimant seeks security for costs of a counterclaim brought by a defendant resident abroad, the court is likely to refuse to order security if the claimant has already obtained a freezing injunction against the defendant for a sum likley to exceed the amount of the costs of the counterclaim (*Hitachi Shipbuilding & Engineering Co Ltd v Viafel Compania Navieran SA* [1981] 2 Lloyd's Rep. 498, CA).

Condition (c): insolvent or impecunious company

Security for costs may be ordered against a company or other body (whether English or foreign) where there is reason to believe that it will be unable to pay the applicant's costs if ordered to do so. However, security is not ordered as of course against such companies: the court's power is discretionary, to be exercised having regard to all the circumstances of the case (see above para.25.13.1). Rule 25.13(2)(c) refers to a company which is a claimant. As to this, see further paras 25.12.3 and 25.12.4 above. **25.13.12**

An applicant for security for costs relying on Condition (c) must show that the company would not (as opposed to may not) be able to meet its debts when an Order for Costs was made against it. This question has to be answered at the time of the application although the Court can take into account evidence of what is to be expected in the future before any Order would be made. *Unisoft Group (No.2), Re* [1993] B.C.L.C. 532, construing similar words in s.726(1) of the Companies Act 1985. A company with assets with a value exceeding its debts will nevertheless be unable to meet its debts if those assets are illiquid. Thus, a net asset balance is not determinative of the question whether a company can pay a costs liability when it falls due. That issue involves consideration of the nature and liquidity of the assets (*Thistle Hotels Ltd v Gamma Four Ltd* [2004] EWHC 322, (Ch); *Longstaff International Ltd v Baker & McKenzie* [2004] EWHC 1852; [2004] 1 W.L.R. 2917, (Ch)).

In order to establish ground (c) the applicant must show "there is reason to believe that it [i.e. the claimant company] will be unable to pay the defendant's costs if ordered to do so". The opening words "there is reason to believe" have the effect of watering down the obligation which follows, i.e., the obligation to prove the company's inability to pay costs if ordered to do so. The defendant does not have to show on a balance of probabilities that the claimant company "will be unable to pay" etc: the defendant may well be able to show that there is reason to believe that the company will not be able to pay even if the company can adduce substantial evidence to the contrary (see generally *Jirehouse Capital v Beller* [2008] EWCA Civ 908).

A liquidator or receiver bringing proceedings in the name of an insolvent company is not under any duty to ensure that the company has sufficient funds to pay any costs awarded to the defendant. The defendant's primary method of protection here is an application for security for costs against the company. A defendant who fails to make such an application will not normally be entitled to an order for costs payable by the liquidator or receiver personally (*Mills v Birchall* [2008] EWCA Civ 385).

To a large extent r.25.13(2)(e) duplicates s.726(1) of the Companies Act 1985 (see below para.25.13.13). That section applies to companies incorporated in England or Scotland which are limited companies within the meaning of the Companies Act 1985. Rule 25.13(2)(c) also covers two other types of companies which are not covered by s.726(1): companies incorporated outside England and Scotland and companies incorporated in England and Scotland which are not limited companies within the meaning of the Companies Act 1985 (see generally *Jirehouse Capital v Beller* [2008] EWCA Civ 908). As from October 1, 2009, s.726(1) of the Companies Act 1985 is to be repealed and not replaced (the Companies Act 2006 (Commencement No.8, Transitional Provisions and Savings) Order 2008 (SI 2008/2860).

Neither r.25.13(2)(c) nor s.726(1) (see below, para.25.13.13) make any provision for applications for security for costs against an unincorporated association.

Particular discretionary factors where condition (c) relied on

Section 726(1) of the Companies Act 1985 provides as follows: **25.13.13**

"Where in England and Wales a limited company is plaintiff in an action or other legal proceeding, the Court having jurisdiction in the matter may, if it appears by credible testimony that there is reason to believe that the company will be unable to pay the Defendant's costs if successful in his defence, require sufficient security to be given for those costs, and may stay all proceedings until the security is given".

"Sufficient security" within the above section ought not to be either illusory or oppressive (*Dominion Brewery v Foster* (1897) 77 L.T. 507). It should be for the probable amount of costs likely to be incurred by the applicant but the Court must have regard to all the circumstances of the case.

The Court has a discretion under s.726(1) of the Companies Act 1985, just as under r.25.13 whether to order security for costs having regard to all the circumstances of the case. Among the circumstances which the court might take into account are the following:

(1) Whether the claimant's claim is bona fide and not a sham;
(2) Whether the claimant has a reasonably good prospect of success;
(3) Whether there is an admission by the defendants in their defence or elsewhere that money is due;
(4) Whether there is a substantial payment into court or an "open offer" of a substantial amount;
(5) Whether the application for security was being used oppressively, e.g. so as to stifle a genuine claim;
(6) Whether the claimant's want of means has been brought about by any conduct by the defendant, such as delay in payment or in doing their part of any work;
(7) Whether the application for security is made at a late stage of the proceedings.

Sir Lindsay Parkinson & Co v Triplan Ltd [1973] Q.B. 609, CA, per Lord Denning M.R.

The court may order a claimant company in liquidation to give security for costs, even though it is one of two or more claimants, especially where there is comparatively small overlap between its own claims and those of the other claimants (*John Bishop (Caterers) Ltd v National Union Bank Ltd* [1973] 1 All E.R. 707). In the case of a limited company s.726(1) applies to all companies irrespective of whether or not it happens to be suing as a Claimant with a natural person as co-claimant, and the inability of the Claimant company to pay the Defendant's costs is a substantial factor in the Court's decision whether to order security for costs; and while the court must not allow s.726(1) to be used as an instrument of oppression it must equally not allow an impecunious company to put unfair pressure on a prosperous company (*Pearson v Naydler* [1977] 1 W.L.R. 899; [1977] 3 All E.R. 531).

Where an order for security for costs against a claimant company might result in oppression in that the claimant company would be forced to abandon a claim which has a reasonable prospect of success, the court is entitled to refuse to make that order, notwithstanding that the claimant company, if unsuccessful, will be unable to pay the defendant's costs. (*Aquila Design (GRB) Products Ltd v Cornhill Insurance Plc* [1988] B.C.L.C. 134, CA). In this respect it is sufficient for the claimant to show that there is a probability that will be unable to pursue the action if the order is granted; it need not show with certainty that it will be unable to do so (*Trident International Freight Services Ltd v Manchester Ship Canal Co* [1990] B.C.L.C. 263, CA). Before the court refuses to order security on the ground that it would unfairly stifle a valid claim, the court must be satisfied that, in all the circumstances, it is probable that the claim would be stifled (*Keary Developments Ltd v Tarmac Construction Ltd* [1995] 3 All E.R. 534, CA). In considering this issue the court should consider, not only whether the claimant company can provide security out of its own resources to continue the litigation, but also whether it can raise the amount needed from outside sources, for example, its directors, shareholders or other backers or interested persons (including creditors) (*ibid.*). In all but the most unusual cases, the burden lies on the claimant company to show that, apart from the question whether the company's own means are sufficient to meet an order for security, there will be no prospect of funds being available and forthcoming from any outside source (*Kufaan Publishing Ltd v Al-Warrack Bookshop Ltd*, March 1, 2000, unrep., CA). In *Brimko Holdings Ltd v Eastman Kodak Company* [2004] EWHC 1343, the claimant successfully demonstrated that an order for security in the amount sought by the defendant would stifle its claim. Instead, the court made an order for security in a sum slightly larger than the sum which the claimant had volunteered to provide.

When considering the claimant's prospects of success, it is important to try to avoid a situation in which the merits have to be considered in detail (*Fernhill Mining Ltd v Kier Construction Ltd* [2000] C.P. Rep. 69).

Proving insolvency or impecuniosity

An applicant for security for costs who relies upon r.25.13(2)(c) or upon s.726(1) of the Companies Act 1985 has to show that the company would not (as opposed to may not) be able to meet its debts when an order for costs is made against it. This question has to be answered at the time of the application though the Court may take into account evidence of what is expected in the future before any order will be made (*Unisoft Group (No.2), Re* [1993] B.C.L.C. 532). The insolvency or impecuniosity may not be disputed. Alternatively, the fact that a company is in liquidation is prima facie evidence and that it is unable to pay the costs, unless evidence to the contrary is given (*Northampton Coal, Iron & Waggon Co v Midland Maggon Co* [1878] 7 Ch.D. 500, CA; *Pure Spirit Co vFowler* (1890) L.R. 25 Q.B.D. 235: *Smith v UIC Insurance Co Ltd* [2001] B.C.C. 11). Apart from such a case the application for security must be supported by evidence which credibly and reasonably shows the inability of the company to pay the costs of the successful defendant. Often, insolvency is established by means of expert evidence of accounts. In an appropriate case, the Court will appoint a single expert to provide such evidence; *Guinle v Kirreh*; *Kinstreet Ltd v Balmargo Corporation Ltd* [2000] C.P. Rep. 62, August 3, 1999, unrep., Ch D. **25.13.14**

Condition (d): change of address

Rule 25.13.2(d) empowers the court to order security for costs against a party who has changed his address since the claim was commenced with a view to evading the consequences of the litigation. The court's power is discretionary; it must be satisfied, having regard to all the circumstances of the case, that it is just to make the Order. Rule 25.13(2)(d) refers to a claimant as to the meaning of which see above paras 25.12.3 and 25.12.4. **25.13.15**

In *Aoun v Bahri* [2002] EWHC 29 (Comm); [2002] 3 All E.R. 182 it was held obiter that "the consequences of the litigation"could include providing security for costs as well as the payment of costs at the end of the litigation: accordingly, a decision to take up residence in the UK which was motivated by a desire to avoid giving security might, if acted upon, provide justification for an application relying on ground (d).

Condition (e): witholding the correct address

Rule 25.13.2(d) empowers the court to order security for costs against a claimant who failed to give his address in the claim form, or gave an incorrect address in that form. The court's power to order security is discretionary; it must be satisfied, having regard to all the circumstances of the case, that it is just to make such an order. Rule 25.13(2)(e) refers a claimant and a claim form. Claimants may include a defendant who brings a Part 20 Claim (see above paras 25.12.3 and 25.12.4). Rule 20.8 (Service of a Part 20 Claim Form) refers to a counterclaim and a third Party Notice as a "Part 20 Claim Form". **25.13.16**

Condition (f): nominal claimant

Rule 25.13(2)(f) enables the court to order security for costs against a claimant who is acting as a nominal claimant other than as a representative claimant under Pt 19, and there is reason to believe that he will be unable to pay the defendant's costs if ordered to do so. As to "nominal" some pre-CPR case examples of the meaning of this term are given below. Condition (f) refers to a "claimant" who is unable to pay the "defendant's costs". As to the use of this ground against a defendant in respect of a Pt 20 Claim, see above paras 25.12.3 and 25.12.4. Condition (f) does not apply to a representative claimant under Pt 19, which see especially, r.19.6 (representative parties with same interest), r.19.7 representation of interested persons who cannot be ascertained etc., r.19.8 (Death) and r.19.9 (Derivative Claims). The exception does not cover a litigation friend (formerly next friend) of a child or patient as to which see (Pt 21). However, as a matter of discretion, it seems unlikely that a litigation friend will be ordered to give security unless, perhaps, one or more of the other conditions in r.25.13(2) applies to him. **25.13.17**

A trustee in bankruptcy suing as such is not a nominal claimant (*Cowell v Taylor* (1885) 31 Ch.D. 34). However, a trustee in bankruptcy who elects to continue a claim in the County Court commenced by the bankrupt may be ordered to give security under County Court Act 1984 s.49 (see Vol.2, para.9A–492, and see r.25.13(1)(b)(ii)). A claimant who has assigned the benefit of an action may be a nominal claimant (*Semler v Murphy* [1968] Ch. 183). So an insolvent claimant who assigned to a trustee for the benefit of his creditors or his estate, and covenants to prosecute the action is merely a nominal claimant (*Lloyd v Hathern Station Brick Co* [1901] 85 L.T. 158). If the assignment was made with a view to avoiding the possibility of a costs order being made against the creditors, and if the creditors have contributed or agreed to contribute to the claimant's costs, an order for security for costs may also be made against the creditors: see r.25.14.

A bankrupt to whom the trustee in bankruptcy has assigned the right to claim damages for negligence against his former accountants, who undertook to receive only 65 per cent or the net proceeds of the action and to pay to the trustee the remaining 35 per cent was held to be not a "nominal" claimant against whom an order for costs will be made and in any event as a matter of discretion on the grounds that negligence by the defendants had itself led or contributed to the bankruptcy, it was held manifestly unjust to order the claimant to give security for costs (*Ramsey v Hartley* [1977] 1 W.L.R. 686; [1977] 2 All E.R. 673, CA).

Under condition (f) the applicant is not required to prove that the respondent is insolvent or impecunious; it is sufficient to show there is reason to believe that he will be unable to pay the applicant's costs if ordered to do so. However, in exercising its discretion towards the costs, the Court must have regard to all the circumstances of the case. Unless insolvency or impecuniosity is proved (as to which see above para.25.13.14) the Court may not be satisfied that it is just to make the order. As to the discretionary nature of the Court's power to order security for costs, see further para.25.13.1.

Condition (g): taking steps as to assets which hinder enforcement

25.13.18 Under r.25.13(2)(g) security for costs may be ordered against a claimant who has taken steps in relation to his assets that would make it difficult to enforce an order for costs against him. Although Condition (g) refers to a "claimant" it may also apply to defendants in respect of a Pt 20 Claim (see above paras 25.12.3 and 25.12.4).

The purpose of condition (g) is to prevent injustice to a defendant where the assets available to enforce any order for costs he obtains have been or are being put beyond the reach of enforcement. The steps taken may be the dissipation of assets, their transfer overseas or into the names of third parties, or their transfer or removal to places unknown to the defendant. The defendant is not required to show that the steps were taken with the specific intention of defeating enforcement (*Aoun v Bahri* [2002] EWHC 29 (Comm); [2002] 3 All E.R. 182) or that those steps were taken during the litigation or in contemplation of it (*Harris v Wallis*, [2006] EWHC 630 (Ch); *The Times*, May 12, 2006). If all or most of the claimant's assets are put beyond the defendant's reach, the injustice to the defendant if no security is given may be just as great as it would be if the claimant himself had transferred overseas or disappeared. That said, the proof a specific intent to stultify future orders for costs will generally increase the likelihood that an order for security will be made. The principles to be applied are, in some respects, analogous to the principles governing applications for freezing injunctions (as to which see above para.25.1.23) save that, in Condition (g) the applicant must also prove the taking of steps in relation to assets which will hinder enforcement (*Chandler v Brown* [2001] C.P. Rep. 103). The applicant may seek to prove a specific intent to stultify future orders for costs in a variety of ways, e.g. evidence of dishonest behaviour by the claimant, unreliability in the past, evasiveness in these proceedings and statements of intent by the claimant.

As to the discretionary nature of the court's power to order security for costs, see para.25.13.1.

Enactments permitting security for costs

25.13.19 The court may make an order for security for costs if it is satisfied, having regard to all the circumstances of the case, that it is just to do so and "an enactment permits the court to require security for costs" (r.25.13(1)(b)(ii)). As to such an enactment see *above, para.25.13.13* (Companies Act 1985 s.726(1)); (security for costs where claimant is an impecunious limited company) and para.25.13.17 (County Courts Act 1984 s.49 (security for costs where claimant's trustee in bankruptcy elects to continue the claim)).

Under s.70(6) of the Arbitration Act 1996 the High Court has power to order security for the costs of any application under s.67 of the Act (challenging the award;

substantive jurisdiction), s.68 of the Act (challenging the award; serious irregularity) or s.69 of the Act (appeal on point of law). As to the jurisdiction of the High Court and county court under the sections see s.105 of the Act and the High Court and County Courts (Allocation of Arbitration Proceedings) Order 1996, Vol.2, para.2E–375. Section 70(6) expressly prohibits exercise of the power to order security on the ground that the applicant or the appellant is a foreign individual or corporation. On an application for security in respect of an application under s.67 of the Act, the relevant factors include the availability of assets for the satisfaction of any order for costs and the fact that the applicant under s.67 had already lost the arbitration and was effectively having a second bite at the same cherry; the first factor mentioned is significantly more important than the second, *Azov Shipping Co v Baltic Shipping Co* [1999] 2 Lloyd's Rep. 39.

Other circumstances in which security for costs may be ordered

The discretions and conditions set out in r.25.13 relate to applications for security for costs under r.25.12. There are also several other rules and provisions under which security for costs may be ordered; r.3.1(2)(f) (power to stay proceedings either generally or until a specified date or event); r.3.1(5) (sanction for failure to comply with a rule, practice direction or relevant pre-action protocol), Practice direction supplementing Pt 24, paras 4 and 5 (a conditional order on a summary judgment application where the Court considers that the respondent's case may succeed but it is improbable that it will do so) r.25.14 (security for costs other than from the claimant) and r.25.15 (security for costs of an appeal). **25.13.20**

Arbitration proceedings

Unless otherwise agreed by the parties, an arbitral tribunal has power to order a claimant to provide a security for the costs of the arbitration (Arbitration Act 1996 s.38(3); Vol.2, para.2B–18D). The subsection expressly prohibits the exercise of this power on the ground that the claimant is a foreign individual or corporation. The power of an arbitral tribunal to order security for costs was new in 1996. Under the Arbitration Act 1950 the High Court had power to order security for costs of arbitrations (Arbitration Act 1950 s.12(6)). **25.13.21**

As to the making of orders for security for costs in applications to the Court under ss.67, 68 or 69 of the Arbitration Act 1996, see para.25.13.19 above.

Security for costs other than from the claimant[1]

25.14—(1) The defendant may seek an order against someone other than the claimant, and the court may make an order for security for costs against that person if— **25.14**

(a) it is satisfied, having regard to all the circumstances of the case, that it is just to make such an order; and

(b) one or more of the conditions in paragraph (2) applies.

(2) The conditions are that the person—

(a) has assigned the right to the claim to the claimant with a view to avoiding the possibility of a costs order being made against him; or

(b) has contributed or agreed to contribute to the claimant's costs in return for a share of any money or property which the claimant may recover in the proceedings; and

is a person against whom a costs order may be made.

(Rule 48.2 makes provision for costs orders against non-parties).

[1] Amended by the Civil Procedure (Amendment) Rules 2000 (SI 2000/221).

Scope of this rule

25.14.1 The subject matter of this rule is new. It supplies the *lacunae* in the previous rules which were identified in *Eurocross Sales Ltd v Cornhill Insurance Plc* [1995] 1 W.L.R. 1517; [1995] 4 All E.R. 950, CA and *Abraham v Thompson* [1997] 4 All E.R. 362, CA.This rule enables the defendant to obtain an order for security for costs against someone other than the claimant if:

(1) having regard to all the circumstances of the case it is just to make such an order (see para.25.13.1); and
(2) either or both of the following conditions applies;
(a) the respondent to the application has assigned the right to the claim to the claimant with a view to avoiding the possibility of a costs order being made against him (see below para.25.14.2);
(b) the respondent to the application has contributed or agreed to contribute to the claimant's costs in return for a share of any money or property which the claimant may recover in the proceedings (see below para.25.14.3); and
(3) the respondent to the application is a person against whom a costs order may be made (see below para.25.14.5).

Rule 25.14 does not spell out the consequences if a person ordered to give security under this rule fails to do so. An order under this rule should not provide for the claim to be struck out if the order is not complied with since to do so would terminate the current claimant's claim. It would be wrong to impose upon a new claimant an obligation as to security for costs which could not otherwise be imposed upon him under other rules of court (*Investment Invoice Financing Ltd v Limehouse Board Mills Ltd* [2006] EWCA Civ 9; [2006] 1 W.L.R. 985; however, in that case the current claimant's claim was stayed until the payment of 2 adverse orders for costs which had been made against his predecessor in title; see further, para.3.4.8 above).

In many cases claims are assigned to new persons only because of the supervening impecuniosity of the original claimants and not with a view to avoiding any order for costs. In such cases an order under r.25.14 would not seem to be appropriate.

For a recent case illustration (in which it seems no application was made under r.25.14 expressly) see *Compagnie Noga d'Importation et Exportation SA v Australia and New Zealand Banking Group Ltd* [2004] EWHC 2601, (Comm), especially para.130 thereof.

Although r.25.14 refers to applications by a defendant against the person other than the claimant, applications can also be made by claimants and other persons in respect of a Pt 20 Claim (see paras 25.12.3 and 25.12.4).

Condition (a): Assignment so as to avoid costs liability

25.14.2 For this condition to apply it must be shown that the assignment was made with the specific intent of avoiding costs liabilities (see para.25.13.15). For pre-CPR cases in which assignments of causes of action were made see *Eurocross Sales Ltd v Cornhill Insurance Plc* [1995] 1 W.L.R. 1517; [1995] 4 All E.R. 950, CA and *John Ridley Construction Bucks Ltd v C. (a firm)* January 30, 1998, unrep., CA; in neither of those cases was there a finding that the assignment had been made with intent to avoid costs liabilities.

Condition (b): Financing claimant's costs in return for a share of any fruits of proceedings

25.14.3 For this condition to apply, it must be shown that the respondent to the application has made some contribution to the claimant's costs and/or has agreed to make such a contribution and has done so in return for a share of any recoveries the claimant may make in the proceedings. An agreement to fund litigation on such terms may well be champertous and, as such, may amount to an abuse of the process of the court. If so, the defendant may, as an alternative to an application for security for costs, apply for a stay of a proceedings. The court may grant such a stay if there are grounds to believe that the proceedings are being conducted by the claimants or by the funder in bad faith; the mere fact that the proceedings are being financed by a third party with no interest in the outcome, other than in relation to the prospects of repayment, may not be of itself sufficient abuse to justify a stay (*Faryab v Smyth (Stay of Appeal: Champerty)* [1998] C.L.Y. 411 and see also *Stocznia Gdanska SA v Latreefers Inc* [2000] C.P.L.R. 65, *CA)*.

"A person against whom a costs order may be made"

25.14.4 The court's power to award costs is contained in SCA 1981 s.51(1) which is expressed in terms wide enough to permit costs being ordered to be paid by persons who are not parties to the proceedings (*Aiden Shipping CoLtd v Interbulk Ltd: the Vimerion* [1986] A.C. 965; [1986] 2 All E.R. 409). Rule 48.2 (costs orders in favour or against non parties) provides that, where the court is considering whether to make a costs order against a person who is not a party to the proceedings that person must be added as a party to the proceedings for purposes of costs only and must be given a reasonable opportunity to attend a hearing at which the court will consider the matter further (for certain exceptional cases, see r.48.2(2)).

The application for security

If the person against whom security is sought is not already a party to the proceedings, an application must be made joining them as a party (r.48.2). For the procedure to follow see r.19.3 and the commentary thereto. It would seem that an order for security under this rule is unlikely to contain provision for dismissal of the claim in the case of default. In other respects the procedure on an application for security under this rule is as set out in paras 25.12.7 to 25.12.12. **25.14.5**

Disclosure in aid of applications under r.25.14

The court has an implied power to order a claimant to disclose to the defendant the name and address of a third party funder of the claim where such funding is admitted or proved. The court also has an implied power to order the claimant to disclose whether or not that third party funder falls within sub-para.(2) of r.25.14 (*Reeves v Sprecher* [2007] EWHC 3226 (Ch), Rattee J., relying upon a dictum of Ackner L.J. in *AJ Bekhor v Bilton* [1981] Q.B. 923 at 942, cited by Potter L.J. in *Abraham v Thompson* [1997] 4 All E.R. 362: "where the power exists to grant the remedy, there must also be inherent in that power the power to make ancillary orders to make that remedy effective"). In *Reeves*, the defendants also applied for an order compelling the claimant to disclose the terms of an admitted funding agreement. This application was held to be premature unless and until the funder under that agreement had been made a party. At that stage the funder would be able to make representations to the court on the question whether disclosure of the terms of the agreement ought to be ordered. It was not necessary to see the funding agreement in order to commence an application under r.25.14 in respect of it. **25.14.6**

Security for costs of an appeal[1]

25.15—(1) The court may order security for costs of an appeal against— **25.15**

(a) an appellant;

(b) a respondent who also appeals,

on the same grounds as it may order security for costs against a claimant under this Part.

(2) The court may also make an order under paragraph (1) where the appellant, or the respondent who also appeals, is a limited company and there is reason to believe it will be unable to pay the costs of the other parties to the appeal should its appeal be unsuccessful.

Scope of this rule

The rule replaces former RSC O.59, r.10(5). Rule 10(5) stated that the Court of Appeal "may, in special circumstances, order that such security shall be given for the costs of an appeal as may be just". Various categories of "special circumstances" were developed by case law (see S.C.P. 1999, Vol.1, paras 59.10.32 *et seq.*). The classes were not regarded as closed. Further, it was established that, if one of the special circumstances was made out, the Court had a residual discretion to refuse an order where the appellant contended that security should not be awarded because it would prevent him from pursuing his appeal. In significant respects, the rules as to security for costs operated more severely against appellants on appeals than against plaintiffs in first **25.15.1**

[1] Amended by the Civil Procedure (Amendment) Rules 2000 (SI 2000/221).

instance proceedings. (It could be argued that this is justified on the ground that a respondent to an appeal deserves additional protection because of the fact that he has already won in the court below). In the Report of the Review of the Court of Appeal (Civil Division) (the Bowman Review) published in September 1997, it was said that this more stringent approach operated unfairly against appellants of limited means and it was recommended that the approach to security for costs in appellateproceedings should broadly accord with that employed at first instance. Consequently, in r.25.15 the grounds for security are the same as those set out in r.25.13, i.e.:

(1) the court must be satisfied having regard to all the circumstances of the case that it is just to make an order (as to which, see below para.25.15.2); and
(2) one or more of seven specified conditions applies or an enactment permits the court to require security for costs (as to which see para.25.15.3).

Rule 25.15 makes no provision for security for costs applications to an appeal court during the period before any necessary permission to appeal has been obtained. The need for security during such periods may be considerable, e.g. in cases in which an application for permission has been adjourned to an oral hearing with the appeal to follow immediately if permission is granted. In *Great Future International Ltd v Sealand Housing Corpn.* [2003] EWCA Civ 682 it was held that this apparent gap in the CPR was in fact supplied by the general case management powers set out in Pt 3. In *Great Future International Ltd* an order was made staying the application for permission to appeal, and if permission was granted the appeal itself, unless by a specified date the intending appellant paid into court the sum of £1 million previously ordered to be paid in respect of costs in the lower court plus £80,000 as security for the respondents' costs in the Court of Appeal (as to further proceedings in this case, see [2003] EWCA Civ 1175).

Discretionary power to order security for costs

25.15.2 For a commentary upon the discretionary nature of the court's power to order security for costs, see above para.25.13.1. Security is unlikely to be ordered where the liberty of the subject is in question (*Hood Barrs v Heriot* [1896] 2 Q.B. 375, CA, applied in *Gulf Azov Shipping Co Ltd v Chief Idisi (Security for Costs)*, December 19, 2000, unrep., CA). The correct approach is to have in mind whether it is appropriate for an appellant to pursue an appeal without the risk of paying the other side's costs if he were unsuccessful; it does not follow that, because permission to appeal has been granted, security for costs should not be ordered because the appeal has merit (*Federal Bank of the Middle East Ltd v Hadkinson, The Times*, December 7, 1999, CA; see also *Nasser v United Bank of Kuwait* [2001] EWCA Civ 556; [2002] 1 All E.R. 401, CA, and para.25.13.6).

The making of such an order may interfere with an appellant's ECHR art.6(1) right of access to a court: see further para.3.1.5 above. The court should not order security for the costs of an appeal if to do so would stifle the appeal. However, if grounds for security for costs appear to have been established, it is for the appellant to satisfy the court, by evidence, that the effect of ordering security will be to stifle the appeal; also, when deciding the matter, it is relevant to consider the possibility that third parties might provide financial support (*Hammond Suddard Solicitors v Agrichem International Holdings Ltd (Stay of Proceedings)* [2001] EWCA Civ 2065, December 18, 2001, unrep., CA).

Same grounds as for security against a claimant

25.15.3 Commentary upon the seven grounds specified in r.25.13(2) are set out above in paras 25.13.7 to 25.13.18. Rule 25.15(2) does not appear to add anything to ground (c) which it partially duplicates.

The application for security

25.15.4 The application may be made either in the respondent's notice or, subsequently, by a separate application notice. In other respects the procedure is substantially as set out in paras 25.12.6 to 25.12.12, above.

Other circumstances in which security for costs of an appeal may be ordered

25.15.5 In addition to an order under r.25.15, an appellant and a respondent who appeals may be put on terms requiring security for the costs of that appeal under various other rules: r.3.1(5) (sanction for failure to comply with a rule or practice direction), r.52.3(7) (conditions upon which permission to appeal is granted); r.52.9(1)(c) (an order of the appeal court imposing or varying conditions upon which an appeal may be brought).

Human Rights Act

For discussion of the human rights implications of orders for security for costs see generally paras 25.13.4 and 25.13.6 above. An order that an applicant provide security for the costs of an appeal is less likely to be held to breach ECHR art.6(1) than an order for security for costs at first instance: *Tolstoy Miloslavsky v United Kingdom* (A/323) [1996] E.M.L.R. 152, ECtHR. **25.15.6**

PRACTICE DIRECTION—INTERIM INJUNCTIONS

This Practice Direction supplements CPR Part 25

Jurisdiction

25PD.1 **1.1** High Court Judges and any other Judge duly authorised may grant "search orders"[1] and "freezing injunctions".[2]

1.2 In a case in the High Court, Masters and district judges have the power to grant injunctions:

(1) by consent,

(2) in connection with charging orders and appointments of receivers,

(3) in aid of execution of judgments.

1.3 In any other case any judge who has jurisdiction to conduct the trial of the action has the power to grant an injunction in that action.

1.4 A Master or district judge has the power to vary or discharge an injunction granted by any Judge with the consent of all the parties.

Making an application

25PD.2 **2.1** The application notice must state;

(1) the order sought, and

(2) the date, time and place of the hearing.

2.2 The application notice and evidence in support must be served as soon as practicable after issue and in any event not less than 3 days before the court is due to hear the application.[3]

2.3 Where the court is to serve, sufficient copies of the application notice and evidence in support for the court and for each respondent should be filed for issue and service.

2.4 Whenever possible a draft of the order sought should be filed with the application notice and a disk containing the draft should also be available to the court in a format compatible with the word processing software used by the court. This will enable the court officer to arrange for any amendments to be incorporated and for the speedy preparation and sealing of the order.

Evidence

25PD.3 **3.1** Applications for search orders and freezing injunctions must be supported by affidavit evidence.

3.2 Applications for other interim injunctions must be supported by evidence set out in either:

(1) a witness statement, or

(2) a statement of case provided that it is verified by a statement of truth,[4] or

(3) the application provided that it is verified by a statement of truth,

unless the court, an Act, a rule or a practice direction requires evidence by affidavit.

---

[1] r. 25.1(1)(h).
[2] r. 25.1(1)(f).
[3] r.23.7(1) and (2) and see r.23.7(4) (short service).
[4] See Pt 22.

3.3 The evidence must set out the facts on which the applicant relies for the claim being made against the respondent, including all material facts of which the court should be made aware.

3.4 Where an application is made without notice to the respondent, the evidence must also set out why notice was not given.

(See Part 32 and the practice direction that supplements it for information about evidence.)

Urgent applications and applications without notice

4.1 Where in a claim for personal injuries there is an application for an interim payment of damages— 25PD.4

(1) which is other than by consent;

(2) which either—

(i) falls under the heads of damage set out in column 1 of Schedule 2 to the Social Security (Recovery of Benefits) Act 1997 ("the 1997 Act") in respect of recoverable benefits received by the claimant set out in column 2 of that Schedule; or

(ii) includes damages in respect of a disease for which a lump sum payment within the definition in section 1A(2) of the 1997 Act has been, or is likely to be made; and

(3) where the defendant is liable to pay a recoverable amount (as defined in rule 36.15(1)(c)) to the Secretary of State,

the defendant should obtain from the Secretary of State a certificate (as defined in rule 36.15(1)(e)).

4.2 These applications are normally dealt with at a court hearing but cases of extreme urgency may be dealt with by telephone.

4.3 Applications dealt with at a court hearing after issue of a claim form:

(1) the application notice, evidence in support and a draft order (as in 2.4 above) should be filed with the court two hours before the hearing wherever possible,

(2) if an application is made before the application notice has been issued, a draft order (as in 2.4 above) should be provided at the hearing, and the application notice and evidence in support must be filed with the court on the same or next working day or as ordered by the court, and

(3) except in cases where secrecy is essential, the applicant should take steps to notify the respondent informally of the application.

4.4 Applications made before the issue of a claim form:

(1) in addition to the provisions set out at 4.3 above, unless the court orders otherwise, either the applicant must undertake to the court to issue a claim form immediately or the court will give directions for the commencement of the claim,[1]

(2) where possible the claim form should be served with the order for the injunction,

(3) an order made before the issue of a claim form should state

[1] r.25.2(3).

in the title after the names of the applicant and respondent "the Claimant and Defendant in an Intended Action".

4.5 Applications made by telephone:

(1) where it is not possible to arrange a hearing, application can be made between 10.00am and 5.00pm weekdays by telephoning the Royal Courts of Justice on 020 7947 6000 and asking to be put in contact with a High Court Judge of the appropriate Division available to deal with an emergency application in a High Court matter. The appropriate district registry may also be contacted by telephone. In county court proceedings, the appropriate county court should be contacted,

(2) where an application is made outside those hours the applicant should either—

(a) telephone the Royal Courts of Justice on 020 7947 6000 where he will be put in contact with the clerk to the appropriate duty judge in the High Court (or the appropriate area Circuit Judge where known), or

(b) the Urgent Court Business Officer of the appropriate Circuit who will contact the local duty judge,

(3) where the facility is available it is likely that the judge will require a draft order to be faxed to him,

(4) the application notice and evidence in support must be filed with the court on the same or next working day or as ordered, together with two copies of the order for sealing,

(5) injunctions will be heard by telephone only where the applicant is acting by counsel or solicitors.

Orders for injunctions

25PD.5 **5.1** Any order for an injunction, unless the court orders otherwise, must contain:

(1) an undertaking by the applicant to the court to pay any damages which the respondent sustains which the court considers the applicant should pay.

(2) if made without notice to any other party, an undertaking by the applicant to the court to serve on the respondent the application notice, evidence in support and any order made as soon as practicable,

(3) if made without notice to any other party, a return date for a further hearing at which the other party can be present,

(4) if made before filing the application notice, an undertaking to file and pay the appropriate fee on the same or next working day, and

(5) if made before issue of a claim form—

(a) an undertaking to issue and pay the appropriate fee on the same or next working day, or

(b) *directions* for the commencement of the claim.

5.1A When the court makes an order for an injunction, it should consider whether to require an undertaking by the applicant to pay any damages sustained by a person other than the respondent, including another party to the proceedings or any other person who may suffer loss as a consequence of the order.

5.2 An order for an injunction made in the presence of all parties to be bound by it or made at a hearing of which they have had notice, may state that it is effective until trial or further order.

5.3 Any order for an injunction must set out clearly what the respondent must do or not do.

Freezing Injunctions

Orders to restrain disposal of assets worldwide and within England and Wales

6.1 An example of a Freezing Injunction is annexed to this practice direction. **25PD.6**

6.2 This example may be modified as appropriate in any particular case. In particular, the court may, if it considers it appropriate, require the applicant's solicitors, as well as the applicant, to give undertakings.

Search Orders

7.1 The following provisions apply to search orders in addition to those listed above. **25PD.7**

The Supervising Solicitor

7.2 The Supervising Solicitor must be experienced in the operation of search orders. A Supervising Solicitor may be contacted either through the Law Society or, for the London area, through the London Solicitors Litigation Association.

Evidence:

7.3(1) the affidavit must state the name, firm and its address, and experience of the Supervising Solicitor, also the address of the premises and whether it is a private or business address, and

(2) the affidavit must disclose very fully the reason the order is sought, including the probability that relevant material would disappear if the order were not made.

Service:

7.4(1) the order must be served personally by the Supervising Solicitor, unless the court otherwise orders, and must be accompanied by the evidence in support and any documents capable of being copied,

(2) *confidential exhibits* need not be served but they must be made available for inspection by the respondent in the presence of the applicant's solicitors while the order is carried out and afterwards be retained by the respondent's solicitors on their undertaking not to permit the respondent—

(a) to see them or copies of them except in their presence, and

(b) to make or take away any note or record of them,

(3) the Supervising Solicitor may be accompanied only by the persons mentioned in the order,

(4) the Supervising Solicitor must explain the terms and effect of the order to the respondent in everyday language and advise him—

(a) of his right to take legal advice and to apply to vary or discharge the order; and

(b) that he may be entitled to avail himself of—

(i) legal professional privilege; and

(ii) the privilege against self-incrimination.

(5) where the Supervising Solicitor is a man and the respondent is likely to be an unaccompanied woman, at least one other person named in the order must be a woman and must accompany the Supervising Solicitor, and

(6) the order may only be served between 9.30am and 5.30pm Monday to Friday unless the court otherwise orders.

Search and custody of materials:

7.5(1) no material shall be removed unless clearly covered by the terms of the order,

(2) the premises must not be searched and no items shall be removed from them except in the presence of the respondent or a person who appears to be a responsible employee of the respondent,

(3) where copies of documents are sought, the documents should be retained for no more than 2 days before return to the owner,

(4) where material in dispute is removed pending trial, the applicant's solicitors should place it in the custody of the respondent's solicitors on their undertaking to retain it in safekeeping and to produce it to the court when required,

(5) in appropriate cases the applicant should insure the material retained in the repondent's solicitors' custody,

(6) the Supervising Solicitor must make a list of all material removed from the premises and supply a copy of the list to the respondent,

(7) no material shall be removed from the premises until the respondent has had reasonable time to check the list,

(8) if any of the listed items exists only in computer readable form, the respondent must immediately give the applicant's solicitors effective access to the computers, with all necessary passwords, to enable them to be searched, and cause the listed items to be printed out,

(9) the applicant must take all reasonable steps to ensure that no damage is done to any computer or data,

(10) the applicant and his representatives may not themselves search the respondent's computers unless they have sufficient expertise to do so without damaging the respondent's system,

(11) the Supervising Solicitor shall provide a report on the carrying out of the order to the applicant's solicitors.

(12) as soon as the report is received the applicant's solicitors shall—
   (a) serve a copy of it on the respondent, and
   (b) file a copy of it with the court, and

(13) where the Supervising Solicitor is satisfied that full compliance with paragraph 7.5(7) and (8) above is impracticable, he may permit the search to proceed and items to be removed without compliance with the impracticable requirements.

General

7.6 The Supervising Solicitor must not be an employee or member of the applicant's firm of solicitors.

7.7 If the court orders that the order need not be served by the Supervising Solicitor, the reason for so ordering must be set out in the order.

7.8 The search order must not be carried out at the same time as a police search warrant.

7.9 There is no privilege against self incrimination in:

(1) Intellectual Property cases in respect of a "related offence" or for the recovery of a "related penalty" as defined in section 72 Supreme Court Act 1981;

(2) proceedings for the recovery or administration of any property, for the execution of a trust or for an account of any property or dealings with property, in relation to—
   (a) an offence under the Theft Act 1968 (see section 31 of the Theft Act 1968 [1]); or
   (b) an offence under the Fraud Act 2006 (see section 13 of the Fraud Act 2006[2]) or a related offence within the meaning given by section 13(4) of that Act—that is, conspiracy to defraud or any other offence involving any form of fraudulent conduct or purpose; or

(3) proceedings in which a court is hearing an application for an order under Part IV or Part V of the Children Act 1989 (see section 98 Children Act 1989).

However, the privilege may still be claimed in relation to material or information required to be disclosed by an order, as regards potential criminal proceedings outside those statutory provisions.

7.10 Applications in intellectual property cases should be made in the Chancery Division.

7.11 An example of a Search Order is annexed to this Practice Direction. This example may be modified as appropriate in any particular case.

Delivery-Up orders

8.1 The following provisions apply to orders, other than search orders, for delivery up or preservation of evidence or property where **25PD.8**

[1] 1968 c.60.
[2] 2006 c.35.

it is likely that such an order will be executed at the premises of the respondent or a third party.

8.2 In such cases the court shall consider whether to include in the order for the benefit or protection of the parties similar provisions to those specified above in relation to injunctions and search orders.

Injunctions against third parties

25PD.9 **9.1** The following provisions apply to orders which will affect a person other than the applicant or respondent, who:

(1) did not attend the hearing at which the order was made; and

(2) is served with the order.

9.2 Where such a person served with the order requests—

(1) a copy of any materials read by the judge, including material prepared after the hearing at the direction of the judge or in compliance with the order; or

(2) a note of the hearing,

the applicant, or his legal representative, must comply promptly with the request, unless the court orders otherwise.

Editorial note

25PD.10 The following forms which are annexed to this PD can be found in the *Civil Procedure Forms Volume*:

- **Freezing Injunction**
- **Search Order**

PRACTICE DIRECTION—INTERIM PAYMENTS

This Practice Direction supplements CPR Part 25 **25BPD.1**

General

1.1 Rule 25.7 sets out the conditions to be satisfied and matters to be taken into account before the court will make an order for an interim payment.

1.2 The permission of the court must be obtained before making a voluntary interim payment in respect of a claim by a child or protected party.

('Child' and 'protected party' have the same meaning as in rule 21.1(2).)

Evidence

2.1 An application for an interim payment of damages must be supported by evidence dealing with the following: **25BPD.2**

(1) the sum of money sought by way of an interim payment,
(2) the items or matters in respect of which the interim payment is sought,
(3) the sum of money for which final judgment is likely to be given,
(4) the reasons for believing that the conditions set out in rule 25.7 are satsified,
(5) any other relevant matters,
(6) in claims for personal injuries, details of special damages and past and future loss, and
(7) in a claim under the Fatal Accidents Act 1976, details of the person(s) on whose behalf the claim is made and the nature of the claim.

2.2 Any documents in support of the application should be exhibited, including, in personal injuries claims, the medical report(s).

2.3 If a respondent to an application for an interim payment wishes to rely on written evidence at the hearing he must comply with the provisions of rule 25.6(4).

2.4 If the applicant wishes to rely on written evidence in reply he must comply with the provisions of rule 25.6(5).

Interim Payment Where Account To Be Taken

2A.1 This section of this practice direction applies if a party seeks an interim payment under rule 25.7(b) where the court has ordered an account to be taken. **25BPD.2A**

2A.2 If the evidence on the application for interim payment shows that the account is bound to result in a payment to the applicant the court will, before making an order for interim payment, order that the liable party pay to the applicant "the amount shown by the account to be due".

Instalments

3. Where an interim payment is to be paid in instalments the order should set out: **25BPD.3**

(1) the total amount of the payment,
(2) the amount of each instalment,
(3) the number of instalments and the date on which each is to be paid, and
(4) to whom the payment should be made.

Compensation Recovery Payments

25BPD.4 **4.1** Where in a claim for personal injuries there is an application for an interim payment of damages—
(1) which is other than by consent;
(2) which either—
(i) falls under the heads of damage set out in column 1 of Schedule 2 to the Social Security (Recovery of Benefits) Act 1997 ("the 1997 Act") in respect of recoverable benefits received by the claimant set out in column 2 of that Schedule; or
(ii) includes damages in respect of a disease for which a lump sum payment within the definition in section 1A(2) of the 1997 Act has been, or is likely to be made; and
(3) where the defendant is liable to pay a recoverable amount (as defined in rule 36.15(1)(c)) to the Secretary of State,

the defendant should obtain from the Secretary of State a certificate (as defined in rule 36.15(1)(e)).

4.2 A copy of the certificate must be filed at the hearing of the application for an interim payment.

4.3 The order will set out the deductible amount (as defined in rule 36.15(1)(d)).

4.4 The payment made to the claimant will be the net amount but the interim payment for the purposes of paragraph 5 below will be the gross amount.

Adjustment of Final Judgment Figure

25BPD.5 **5.1** In this paragraph "judgment" means:
(1) any order to pay a sum of money,
(2) a final award of damages,
(3) an assessment of damages.

5.2 In a final judgment where an interim payment has previously been made which is less than the total amount awarded by the judge, the order should set out in a preamble:
(1) the total amount awarded by the judge, and
(2) the amounts and dates of the interim payment(s).

5.3 The total amount awarded by the judge should then be reduced by the total amount of any interim payments, and an order made for entry of judgment and payment of the balance.

5.4 In a final judgment where an interim payment has previously been made which is more than the total amount awarded by the judge, the order should set out in a preamble:
(1) the total amount awarded by the judge, and
(2) the amounts and dates of the interim payment(s).

5.5 An order should then be made for repayment, reimbursement, variation or discharge under rule 25.8(2) and for interest on an overpayment under rule 25.8(5).

5.6 A practice direction supplementing Part 40 provides further information concerning adjustment of the final judgment sum.

PART 26

Case Management—Preliminary Stage

Contents

Editorial introduction

26.0.2 The preliminary stage of case management is mainly concerned with the allocation of a defended claim to the appropriate track. There is no "automatic" allocation; each case requires a judicial decision. However, the general rule for allocation is in r.26.7. Note in particular that the court will not allocate a claim to a "lower" track unless all the parties consent (r.26.7(3)).

The court will allocate a defended claim to one of three tracks: the small claims track, the fast track or the multi-track. These tracks are dealt with, respectively, in Pts 27, 28 and 29 and each of those Parts contains rules about case management and conduct of the claim following allocation. The aim is to ensure that each case is dealt with proportionately to its size and complexity.

Rule 26.6 sets out the normal scope of each track. The court will normally send an "allocation questionnaire" to each party on the filing of a defence. The claim will be allocated when the questionnaires have been filed or when the period for filing has expired (see r.26.5). The court will normally deal with allocation on the basis of the information provided but can, if necessary, hold an "allocation hearing" (r.26.5(4)).

Allocation to the correct track is the main, but not the only, function at this preliminary stage of case management. The court will also consider striking out a statement of case (see r.3.4), summary judgment (see r.24.4) and whether to give case management directions pursuant to Pts 27, 28 or 29 as appropriate.

Related sources

26.0.3

- Practice Direction—Case Management—Preliminary Stage: Allocation and Re-Allocation—para.26PD.1
- Part 1 (The Overriding Objective)
- Part 2, r.3(1) (Definition of defendant's home court)
- Part 3 (The Court's Case Management Powers)
- Part 24 (Summary Judgment)
- Part 27 (The Small Claims Track)
- Part 28 (The Fast Track)
- Part 29 (The Multi-Track)
- Part 30 (Transfer)
- Part 31 (Disclosure and Inspection of Documents)
- Part 32 (Evidence)

Forms

- **N150** Allocation questionnaire 26.0.4
- **N151** Allocation questionnaire (amount to be decided by court)
- **N151A** Master/DJ's directions on allocation
- **N152** Notice that [defence] [counterclaim] has been filed (Pt 26, PD para.2.5)
- **N153** Notice of allocation or listing hearing
- **N154** Notice of allocation to fast track
- **N155** Notice of allocation to multi-track
- **N156** Order for further information (for allocation) (Pt 26, PD para.4.2(2))
- **N157** Notice of allocation to small claims track
- **N158** Notice of allocation to small claims track (preliminary hearing)
- **N159** Notice of allocation to small claims track (no hearing)
- **N160** Notice of allocation to small claims track (with parties' consent)

Practice Direction

Part 26 is supplemented by a Practice Direction. See para.26PD.1. 26.0.5

Scope of this Part

26.1—(1) This Part provides for— 26.1

(a) the automatic transfer of some defended cases between courts; and

(b) the allocation of defended cases to case management tracks.

(2) There are three tracks—

(a) the small claims track;

(b) the fast track; and

(c) the multi-track.

(Rule 26.6 sets out the normal scope of each track. Part 27 makes provision for the small claims track. Part 28 makes provision for the fast track. Part 29 makes provision for the multi-track.)

Effect of rule

The automatic transfer provisions of r.26.1(1) and r.26.2 are a modified version of CCR O.1, r.13 (which had no direct equivalent in the RSC). Transfer on application of a party is governed by Pt 30. 26.1.1

Rule 26.1(2) creates the three tracks which are a fundamental feature of the rules. Each track is also governed by its own Part and practice direction.

Note also CPR r.8.9(c) which provides that initially Pt 8 claims are allocated to multi-track.

The small claims track

See too Practice Direction to Pt 26, para.8. 26.1.2

The fast track

See too Practice Direction to Pt 26, para.9. 26.1.3

The multi track

See too Practice Direction to Pt 26, para.10. 26.1.4

Automatic transfer

26.2—(1) This rule applies to proceedings where— 26.2

(a) the claim is for a specified amount of money;

(b) the claim was commenced in a court which is not the defendant's home court;

(c) the claim has not been transferred to another defendant's home court under rule 13.4 (application to set aside[GL] or vary default judgment—procedure) or rule 14.12 (admission—determination of rate of payment by judge); and

(d) the defendant is an individual.

(2) This rule does not apply where the claim was commenced in a specialist list[GL].

(3) Where this rule applies, the court will transfer the proceedings to the defendant's home court when a defence is filed, unless paragraph (4) applies.

(Rule 2.3 defines "defendant's home court".)

(4) Where the claimant notifies the court under rule 15.10 and rule 14.5 that he wishes the proceedings to continue, the court will transfer the proceedings to the defendant's home court when it receives that notification from the claimant.

(Rule 15.10 deals with a claimant's notice where the defence is that money claimed has been paid.)

(Rule 14.5 sets out the procedure where the defendant admits part of a claim for a specified amount of money.)

(5) Where—

(a) the claim is against two or more defendants with different home courts; and

(b) the defendant whose defence is filed first is an individual,

proceedings are to be transferred under this rule to the home court of that defendant.

(6) The time when a claim is automatically transferred under this rule may be varied by a practice direction in respect of claims issued by the Production Centre.

(Rule 7.10 makes provision for the Production Centre.)

Effect of rule

26.2.1 It has always been a feature of the county court system that justice should be "local". This is now of general application. However, "local" means local to the defendant rather than the claimant. Automatic transfer applies only when the defendant is an "individual" (r.26.2(1)(d)) not, for example, a limited company.

This rule deals sensibly with automatic transfer as a preliminary case management issue. It is a self-contained code for automatic transfer and gathers in one place rules previously scattered through the CCR (CCR O.1, r.13; CCR O.9, r.2(8); CCR O.22, r.10(4); CCR O.37, r.4(2)). Any application by either party to transfer to a more convenient court must be made to the defendant's home court after automatic transfer there. Transfer on the application of a party is governed by Pt 30. "Defendant's home court" is defined by CPR r.2.3(1). Where a defendant is represented by solicitors, the address is treated as the business address of the solicitor (see CPR r.6.5(5)). If there is more than one defendant, transfer is to the home court of the first to file a defence (CPR r.26.2(5)).

Note too CPR r.30.2 which deals with transfer where proceedings have been begun in the wrong court.

Specialist list

26.2.2 See Pt 49.

Allocation questionnaire[1]

26.3—(1) When a defendant files a defence the court will serve an allocation questionnaire on each party unless— 26.3

(a) rule 15.10 or rule 14.5 applies; or

(b) the court dispenses with the need for a questionnaire.

(2) Where there are two or more defendants and at least one of them files a defence, the court will serve the allocation questionnaire under paragraph (1)—

(a) when all the defendants have filed a defence; or

(b) when the period for the filing of the last defence has expired,

whichever is the sooner.

(Rule 15.4 specifies the period for filing a defence.)

(3) Where proceedings are automatically transferred to the defendant's home court under rule 26.2, the court in which the proceedings have been commenced will serve an allocation questionnaire before the proceedings are transferred.

(4) Where—

(a) rule 15.10 or rule 14.5 applies; and

(b) the proceedings are not automatically transferred to the defendant's home court under rule 26.2,

the court will serve an allocation questionnaire on each party when the claimant files a notice indicating that he wishes the proceedings to continue.

(5) The court may, on the application of the claimant, serve an allocation questionnaire earlier than it would otherwise serve it under this rule.

(6) Each party must file the completed allocation questionnaire no later than the date specified in it, which shall be at least 14 days after the date when it is deemed to be served on the party in question.

(6A) The date for filing the completed allocation questionnaire may not be varied by agreement between the parties.[2]

(7) The time when the court serves an allocation questionnaire under this rule may be varied by a practice direction in respect of claims issued by the Production Centre.

(Rule 7.10 makes provision for the Production Centre.)

(Rule 6.7 specifies when a document is deemed to be served.)

Effect of rule

Allocation of defended cases to the appropriate track is a crucial preliminary case management issue. Allocation is not automatic; an "allocation questionnaire" is sent by the court to each party. *Parties are required to file (not serve)* the allocation questionnaire; the court should serve a copy of the other party's allocation questionnaire with the allocation decision under r.26.9. As courts sometimes fail to do this, it is good practice for solicitors to serve copies of completed allocation questionnaires on other parties. 26.3.1

[1] Amended by the Civil Procedure (Amendment No.5) Rules 2001 (SI 2001/4015).

[2] Inserted by the Civil Procedure (Amendment No.5) Rules 2001 SI 2001/4015, in force March 25, 2002.

If no party files an allocation questionnaire, the court should automatically order that unless an allocation questionnaire is filed within seven days from the date service of the order, the claim, defence and any counterclaim will be struck out without any further order of the court (PD 26 para.2.5—see too PD 3, para.1.9). The Practice Direction which supplements Pt 26 (see para 26PD.1) encourages consultation and exchange of information between the parties. Note that the allocation questionnaire procedure only applies to defended claims. See too CPR r.14.5 and r.15.10 which deal with part admissions and defendants who contend that the amount claimed has been paid. In such circumstances the claimant should be sent a notice asking whether or not s/he intends to proceed (Forms **N225A** and **N236**) rather than an allocation questionnaire. See Practice Direction to Pt 26, para.12. If judgment for damages to be assessed is entered, the court may then direct that allocation questionnaires be sent out—see Practice Direction to Pt 26, para.12.2(b).

Allocation Questionnaire

26.3.2 See Form **N150**. The court should send copies of completed allocation questionnaires to other parties on allocation—see r.26.9(2).

Each party must file the completed questionnaire no later than the date specified

26.3.3 For the court's powers and approach if any party fails to return an allocation questionnaire, see r.26.5(5) and PD to Pt 26, paras 2.5 and 6.6.

On filing an allocation questionnaire, a fee of £200 is payable if the case is on the fast or multi track, but only £35 where the case is on the small claims track and the claim exceeds £1,500 (the Civil Proceedings Fees Order 2008 (SI 2008/1053) (L.5)). The fee is payable by the claimant, except where the action is proceeding on a counterclaim alone, when it is payable by the defendant. Note that there is now no fee if the amount claimed is £1,500 or less. If a claimant fails to pay the fee, the court may send out a notice requiring payment (Form **N173**). If after receipt of the notice the claimant does not pay the fee or make an application for exemption, the claim shall be struck out and the claimant shall be liable for the costs of the defendant (r.3.7).

Parties cannot vary the date for filing allocation questionnaires without the permission of the court (CPR r.26.3(6A)) as inserted by the Civil Procedure (Amendment No.5) Rules 2001 (SI 2001/4015).

Estimate of costs

26.3.4 Note that para.6.4(1) to the Costs Practice Direction requires parties to file estimates of costs already incurred and likely to be incurred with completed allocation questionnaires except in cases within the limits of the small claims track. There is no need to include any reference to a success fee (see PD 26, para.2.1). See too question I to Form **N150**.

The court dispenses with the need for a questionnaire

26.3.5 See e.g. Practice Direction to Pt 26, para.2.4(1) and CPR r.3.1(2)(m). If a hearing occurs prior to allocation, the court may at that hearing allocate to track and dispense with allocation questionnaires—see Practice Direction to Pt 26, para.2.4.

Pre-Action Protocols

26.3.6 When completing allocation questionnaires parties must state whether a pre-action protocol applies and, if there has been less than complete compliance with it, give an explanation. This should be taken into account when case management directions are given and may be relevant to the question of costs. (See Practice Direction to Pre-Action Potocols, paras 2.1 and 2.3, see para.C1–001.)

Summary judgment

26.3.7 When completing allocation questionnaires parties should state whether they intend to apply for summary judgment or make any other application. (See question D.)

Agree case management directions

26.3.8 When consulting each other about allocation questionnaires, parties should attempt to agree case management directions and invite the court to make them (Practice Direction to Pt 26, para.2.3(2)). See too r.1.4(2)(a).

Extension of time for filing allocation questionnaires

The Civil Procedure (Amendment No.5) Rules 2001 amended CPR r.26.3 to provide that the date for filing allocation questionnaires cannot be extended by the agreement of the parties. **26.3.9**

Stay to allow for settlement of the case

26.4—(1) A party may, when filing the completed allocation questionnaire, make a written request for the proceedings to be stayed[GL] while the parties try to settle the case by alternative dispute resolution[GL] or other means. **26.4**

(2) Where—

(a) all parties request a stay[GL] under paragraph (1); or

(b) the court, of its own initiative, considers that such a stay would be appropriate,

the court will direct that the proceedings, either in whole or in part, be stayed for one month, or for such specified period as it considers appropriate.

(3) The court may extend the stay[GL] until such date or for such specified period as it considers appropriate.

(4) Where the court stays[GL] the proceedings under this rule, the claimant must tell the court if a settlement is reached.

(5) If the claimant does not tell the court by the end of the period of the stay[GL] that a settlement has been reached, the court will give such directions as to the management of the case as it considers appropriate.

Effect of rule

See Practice Direction to Pt 26, para.3. The rules aim to encourage parties to settle disputes without judicial decisions if possible (see, e.g. r.1.4(2)(f)). Rule 26.4 is an example of this. Stay is, in effect, automatic under r.26.4(2). A stay for settlement can now be ordered for more than a month. Where all parties request a stay, or the court of its own initiative considers that a stay would be appropriate, the court should direct that the proceedings, either in whole or in part, be stayed for one month, or for such specified period as the court considers appropriate. Any stay must be seen in the context of case management: it is not possible for a case to "go to sleep" or evade case management. The onus is on the claimant to tell the court if a settlement is reached (r.26.4(4)) and if he does not do so the court will give directions under r.26.4(5). If an action is stayed, any interim injunction is automatically set aside unless the court orders that it should continue—see r.25.10. Note too CPR r.56.3(4)(a) (stays for a period of three months in applications for renewal of business tenancies under Landlord and Tenant Act 1954 Part II). **26.4.1**

For the purposes of the automatic orders pilot scheme operating in proceedings in certain county courts since October 1, 2008, r.26.4 and related provisions in the first of the practice directions supplementing this Part are modified (see Practice Direction—Automatic Orders Pilot Scheme, para.51BPD.1 below). (Modifications are also made to provisions in Pt 28.)

Allocation

26.5—(1) The court will allocate the claim to a track— **26.5**

(a) when every defendant has filed an allocation questionnaire, or

(b) when the period for filing the allocation questionnaires has expired,

whichever is the sooner, unless it has—

(i) stayed[GL] the proceedings under rule 26.4; or

(ii) dispensed with the need for allocation questionnaires.

(Rules 12.7 and 14.8 provide for the court to allocate a claim to a track where the claimant obtains default judgment on request or judgment on admission for an amount to be decided by the court.)

(2) If the court has stayed[GL] the proceedings under rule 26.4, it will allocate the claim to a track at the end of the period of the stay.

(3) Before deciding the track to which to allocate proceedings or deciding whether to give directions for an allocation hearing to be fixed, the court may order a party to provide further information about his case.

(4) The court may hold an allocation hearing if it thinks it is necessary.

(5) If a party fails to file an allocation questionnaire, the court may give any direction it considers appropriate.

Effect of rule

26.5.1 Allocation will be by the Master or district judge on the filing of the allocation questionnaires or when time for filing them has expired. It is envisaged that most cases will be allocated on the basis of the "statements of case" (pleadings) and the information given in the questionnaires. However, there is provision in r.26.5(3) for the court to order a party to provide further information (see Form **N156** and PD to Pt 26, paras 2.2 and 4.2). If necessary the court will hold an "allocation hearing" (r.26.5(4)) which would be held within a matter of a few days. An allocation hearing would be necessary, for example, if the court were minded to seek the consent of the parties under r.26.7(3) to allocation to the fast track of a claim which is financially within the multi-track. Generally, however, allocation will be on paper by the court and allocation hearings are rare.

Allocation hearing

26.5.2 See Practice Direction to Pt 26, para.6. A court will only hold an allocation hearing on its own initiative if it considers it necessary to do so. A legal representative who attends an allocation hearing should be the person responsible for the case or must be familiar with it and must have sufficient authority to deal with any issues likely to arise. At least seven days notice of such a hearing should be given (see Practice Direction to Pt 26, para.6.2(1)).

Appeals

26.5.3 Practice Direction to Pt 26, para.11 provides that a party who is dissatisfied about allocation should appeal if the order was made at a hearing at which s/he was present or represented, but should apply to the court to re-allocate if s/he was not present on the allocation decision.

Scope of each track

26.6 **26.6—(1) The small claims track is the normal track for—**

(a) any claim for personal injuries where—

(i) the value of the claim is not more than £5,000; and

(ii) the value of any claim for damages for personal injuries is not more than £1,000;

***(b)* any claim which includes a claim by a tenant of residential premises against a landlord where—**

(i) the tenant is seeking an order requiring the landlord to carry out repairs or other work to the

premises (whether or not the tenant is also seeking some other remedy);

(ii) the cost of the repairs or other work to the premises is estimated to be not more than £1,000; and

(iii) the value of any other claim for damages is not more than £1,000.

(Rule 2.3 defines "claim for personal injuries" as proceedings in which there is a claim for damages in respect of personal injuries to the claimant or any other person or in respect of a person's death.)

(2) For the purposes of paragraph (1) "damages for personal injuries" means damages claimed as compensation for pain, suffering and loss of amenity and does not include any other damages which are claimed.

(3) Subject to paragraph (1), the small claims track is the normal track for any claim which has a value of not more than £5,000.

(Rule 26.7(4) provides that the court will not allocate to the small claims track certain claims in respect of harassment or unlawful eviction.)

(4) Subject to paragraph (5), the fast track is the normal track for any claim—

(a) for which the small claims track is not the normal track; and

(b) which has a value—

(i) for proceedings issued on or after 6th April 2009, of not more than £25,000; and

(ii) for proceedings issued before 6th April 2009, of not more than £15,000.

(5) The fast track is the normal track for the claims referred to in paragraph (4) only if the court considers that—

(a) the trial is likely to last for no longer than one day; and

(b) oral expert evidence at trial will be limited to—

(i) one expert per party in relation to any expert field; and

(ii) expert evidence in two expert fields.

(6) The multi-track is the normal track for any claim for which the small claims track or the fast track is not the normal track.

Effect of rule

This rule was amended by the Civil Procedure (Amendment No.3) Rules 2008 (SI 2008/3327) r.7. The principal effect of that amendment was to increase the financial limit of the fast track case management procedure from £15,000 to £25,000 for proceedings issued on or after April 6, 2009. **26.6.1**

The three tracks, which are the essence of the CPR, are defined by r.26.6. The rule starts at the bottom by defining the small claims track (generally, claims valued at not more than £5,000 and personal injury claims valued at not more than £1,000: see r.26.6(1)), then the fast track (claims not on the small claims track valued, for proceedings issued before April 6, 2009, at not more than £15,000, or for proceedings issued on or after that date, at not more than £25,000: see r.26.6(4)) and finally the multi-track (any claim not on the small claims track or the fast track: see r.26.6(6)).

Personal injuries

26.6.2 Note the definition of "claim for personal injuries" in r.2.3 and the restrictive meaning given to "damages for personal injuries" in r.26.6(2) ("damages claimed as compensation for pain, suffering and loss of amenity..."). For example, a claim for £4,000 for loss of earnings and other losses plus a claim for £800 for damages for pain and suffering is a claim which would be allocated to the small claims track (see r.26.6(1)(a)).

Claim by a tenant of residential premises

26.6.3 If proceedings include a claim requiring the landlord to carry out works or other repairs, the claim form must state whether the cost of repairs is estimated to be more than £1,000 and whether or not the claimant expects to recover more than £1,000 in respect of any claim for damages (CPR r.16.3(4) and Practice Direction to Pt 7, para.3.9).

Irrespective of their value, harassment and unlawful eviction claims must be allocated either to the fast track or multi-track. (See r.26.7(4) and the note to CPR r.27.1(2).)

The position relating to disrepair cases is less straightforward. If there is simply an action for damages for breach of repairing obligations, with no claim for an order requiring works to be carried out, the case will be allocated to the small claims track unless

(1) the financial value of the claim is £5,000 or more, *or*

(2) the financial value of any claim for personal injuries is £1,000 or more (see CPR r.26.6(1)(a)(ii), *or*

(3) there are abnormal circumstances.

A claim will be allocated to the fast track if the claim has a value, for proceedings issued on or after April 6, 2009, of not more that £25,000 and, for proceedings issued before that date, of not more that £15,000. It will be allocated to the multi-track if the value exceeds those limits. A claim for damages for disrepair (without a claim for specific performance) may be allocated to the fast track if there are abnormal factors, e.g. the likely complexity of the facts, law or evidence, the number of parties, the amount of oral evidence or the importance to persons who are not parties to the proceedings. (See CPR r.26.8 which sets out matters relevant to allocation to track and which states that it is for the court to assess the financial value of a claim.)

If there is a claim for both damages and an order for works to be carried out, the case will *not* be allocated to the small claims track if *either* the cost of works *or* the damages claim is more than £1,000. In such circumstances the case will be allocated to the fast track, unless the financial value of the claim is more than the value fixed by r.26.6(4)(b). Claims for both damages and an order for works to be carried out will only be allocated to the small claims track if the cost of work is less than £1,000 *and* the claim for damages is less than £1,000. This interpretation is borne out by Practice Direction to Pt 7, para.3.9 (see above) and the note to CPR r.27.1(2).

For the Pre-Action Protocol for Housing Disrepair Cases, see C10–001.

26.6.4 *Other landlord and tenant disputes*—The Practice Direction to Pt 26 para.8.1(2)(c) states that "most disputes between a landlord and a tenant other than those for possession" are suitable for the small claims track. This does not however apply to cases "involving a disputed allegation of dishonesty" (Practice Direction to Pt 26, para.8.1(2)(d)), or to possession proceedings (see below).

There is a particular form of Standard Directions for use in small claims track cases where tenants are suing for the return of deposits or where landlords are suing for damage caused by tenants—see Practice Direction to Pt 27, Appendix A, Form D.

Small claims track

26.6.5 Allocation to the small claims track has replaced "reference to arbitration" under former CCR O.19. Subject to r.26.6(1) the small claims track is the normal track for any claim which has a financial value of not more than £5,000. Unlike the fast track there is no envisaged maximum length of trial (compare r.26.6(5)(a)). This is unlikely to matter in practice. Claims allocated to the small claims track are generally given time estimates of between one and three hours.

See also Pt 27 and its related Practice Direction (see para.27PD.1).

Fast track

Basically, the fast track is the normal track for claims valued between £5,000 and (subject to r.26.6(4)) £25,000. The fast track is undoubtedly one of the main innovations of the CPR. See also Pt 28 and its related Practice Direction. Part 26 6(5) is silent as to what will happen when it appears that the trial will last longer than one day and/or extensive expert evidence is required. The court could allocate the case to the multi-track. However, before doing this the court will consider whether it is more appropriate to order a split trial so that, for example, the issue of liability is tried first—although such a course may be disproportionate and uneconomic (*DHL Air Ltd v Wells* [2003] EWCA Civ 1743; *The Times*, November 14, 2003, CA). Experience has shown that the reforms introduced by the Civil Procedure Rules (and in particular the provisions allowing witness statements to stand as evidence in chief) mean that many trials which would previously have lasted for more than a day can now be heard in five hours. **26.6.6**

Note the limitation on expert evidence in r.26.6(5).

Multi-track

The multi-track is the normal track for any claim not allocated to the small claims track or the fast track. See also Pt 29 and its related Practice Direction (para.29PD.1). **26.6.7**

Claims on the small claims or fast track will be in a county court. Claims on the multi-track will be in either a county court or the High Court. Apart from cases in a "specialist list", this makes no difference: the main purpose of the CPR is to repeal and replace both the RSC and CCR with a common code.

However, in general cases with an estimated value of less than £50,000 are heard in county courts. Note Practice Direction to Pt 29, para.2 which provides that such cases issued in the High Court will generally be transferred to a county court unless they are required by an enactment to be tried in the High Court, fall within a specialist list (see CPR Pt 49) or come within Practice Direction to Pt 29, para.2.6 (*viz.* claims involving professional negligence, Fatal Accident Act, fraud or undue influence, defamation, malicious prosecution or false imprisonment, claims against the police and contentious probate claims).

General rule for allocation[1]

26.7—(1) In considering whether to allocate a claim to the normal track for that claim under rule 26.6, the court will have regard to the matters mentioned in rule 26.8(1). **26.7**

(2) The court will allocate a claim which has no financial value to the track which it considers most suitable having regard to the matters mentioned in rule 26.8(1).

(3) The court will not allocate proceedings to a track if the financial value of the claim assessed by the court under rule 26.8, exceeds the limit for that track unless all the parties consent to the allocation of the claim to that track.

(4) The court will not allocate a claim to the small claims track, if it includes a claim by a tenant of residential premises against his landlord for a remedy in respect of harassment or unlawful eviction.

Effect of rule

This short "general rule for allocation" is self-explanatory. Note that r.26.7(3) prevents the court allocating a claim to a lower track (i.e. multi-track claim to the fast track or fast track claim to the small claims track) unless all parties consent. If the court felt that a simple multi-track case ought to be on the fast track no doubt parties would be invited to consent. If one party refused consent, although the court could not then proceed to allocate to the fast track, it could give a timetable and directions of the sort that would be given in a fast track case. **26.7.1**

Matters relevant to allocation to a track

26.8—(1) When deciding the track for a claim, the matters to which the court shall have regard include— **26.8**

[1] Amended by the Civil Procedure (Amendment) Rules 2000 (SI 2000/221).

(a) the financial value, if any, of the claim;
(b) the nature of the remedy sought;
(c) the likely complexity of the facts, law or evidence;
(d) the number of parties or likely parties;
(e) the value of any counterclaim or other Part 20 claim and the complexity of any matters relating to it;
(f) the amount of oral evidence which may be required;
(g) the importance of the claim to persons who are not parties to the proceedings;
(h) the views expressed by the parties; and
(i) the circumstances of the parties.

(2) It is for the court to assess the financial value of a claim and in doing so it will disregard—
(a) any amount not in dispute;
(b) any claim for interest;
(c) costs; and
(d) any contributory negligence.

(3) Where—
(a) two or more claimants have started a claim against the same defendant using the same claim form; and
(b) each claimant has a claim against the defendant separate from the other claimants,

the court will consider the claim of each claimant separately when it assesses financial value under paragraph (1).

Matters relevant to allocation

26.8.1 See too Practice Direction to Pt 26, para.7. Note that additional matters which are relevant to allocation are contained in CPR, r.55.9 (possession claims) and r.65.19 (demotion claims).

Length of trial

26.8.2 Note that in addition to the factors set out in r.26.8, when deciding whether or not to allocate to fast track, the court should take into account the limits likely to be placed on disclosure, the extent to which expert evidence may be necessary and whether the trial is likely to last more than five hours, although the likely length of trial is not necessarily conclusive—see r.26.6(5) and Practice Direction to Pt 26, para.9.1.

Claims with no monetary value

26.8.3 See r.26.7(2). A claim which has no financial value should be allocated to the most suitable track.

Effect of rule

26.8.4 It is for the court to allocate a case to the relevant track. The rule does not expressly require the court to have regard to "all the circumstances" but the use of the word "include" in r.26.8(1) before the nine specific matters (a) to (i) shows that the matters mentioned are not exhaustive.

In the majority of cases the appropriate track will be obvious and largely determined by the financial value of the claim. In all cases the "allocation questionnaire" must be appropriately and fully completed (see Form **N149** or **N150**) to enable the court to perform correctly the essential case management task of allocation.

Under CPR r.26.8(1)(a) the court should have regard to "the financial value, if any, of the claim" when allocating to track, but the court has no power to increase the value of the claim or to include items of claim which the claimant has chosen not to include. It is no part of the judicial function to force a claimant to claim more than he wishes in order to maximise court fees (*Khiaban v Beard* [2003] EWCA Civ 358; [2003] 1 W.L.R. 1626).

In *Kearsley v Klarefield* [2005] EWCA Civ 1510; [2006] 2 All E.R. 303 the defendant claimed that the driver in a low value personal injury case was fabricating his injuries. The claim, which had been previously allocated to the fast track, was re-allocated to the multi-track. The Court of Appeal dismissed an appeal. By the very nature of the issues raised by the defence, expert witnesses would have to be called to give oral evidence if justice was to be done. Although it was a low value claim, it was not disproportionate to allocate it to the multi-track. See too *Casey v Cartwright* [2006] EWCA Civ 1280; *The Times*, October 10, 2006.

The value of any counterclaim or other Part 20 Claim

When allocating to track the court will not generally aggregate claims, but will take into account the largest when determining the financial value (PD 26, para.7.7). **26.8.5**

Notice of allocation

26.9—(1) When it has allocated a claim to a track, the court will serve notice of allocation on every party. **26.9**

(2) When the court serves notice of allocation on a party, it will also serve—

(a) a copy of the allocation questionnaires filed by the other parties; and

(b) a copy of any further information provided by another party about his case (whether by order or not).

(Rule 26.5 provides that the court may, before allocating proceedings, order a party to provide further information about his case).

Effect of rule

The rule requires the court to serve "notice of allocation" as soon as it has allocated the case. It serves with the notice a copy of the allocation questionnaires filed by other parties (hence r.26.3(6) requires a party merely to file, not file and serve, his allocation questionnaire). See Forms **N153** to **N160**. **26.9.1**

Appeals against allocation decisions made at a hearing are likely to be very rare and r.26.9 makes no reference to them. See CPR Pt 52.

Re-allocation

26.10 The court may subsequently re-allocate a claim to a different track. **26.10**

Re-allocation

See too Practice Direction to Pt 26, para.11. If a claim initially allocated to the small claims track is re-allocated to a different track, the limitations on costs cease to apply from that date (see r.27.15). **26.10.1**

A claim does not cease to be allocated to the fast track simply because its financial limit is increased beyond the limit imposed by r.26.6(4). Judges have an unfettered discretion whether or not to re-allocate. There should however be a good reason to re-allocate. On re-allocation the criteria in CPR r.26.8(1) are relevant—but other factors may have to be taken into account as well. Relevant factors to consider are the amount by which the value of the claim exceeds the normal limit and the category of judge chosen to try the case. If the amount by which the claim exceeds the limit imposed by r.26.6(4) is small, the claim should not be re-allocated if it would cause substantial disruption to the progress of litigation. Where the excess is substantial, there should usually be a re-allocation, even if that means delay to the completion of the litigation. (*Maguire v Molin* [2002] EWCA Civ 1083; [2002] 4 All E.R. 325.)

Assessment of damages

See too Practice Direction to Pt 26, para.12. **26.10.2**

Effect of rule

26.10.3 This short rule provides for re-allocation. It seems that it is not possible to allocate different parts of a claim to different tracks simultaneously. However, sequential allocation is possible. Thus, for example, a very large claim where the issue of liability is not complex and could be tried within a day, could (with consent: see r.26.7(3)) be allocated to the fast track for trial on liability. If the claimant succeeds the case could be re-allocated to the multi-track under r.26.10.

Trial with a Jury[1]

26.11 **26.11 An application for a claim to be tried with a jury must be made within 28 days of service of the defence.**

(Section 69 of the Supreme Court Act 1981[2] and section 66 of the County Courts Act 1984[3] specify when a claim may be tried with a jury).

Supreme Court Act 1981 s.69

26.11.1 See Vol.2, para.9A–256.

County Courts Act 1984 s.66

26.11.2 See Vol.2, para.9A–546.

---

[1] Introduced by the Civil Procedure (Amendment No.4) Rules 2000 (SI 2000/2092).
[2] 1981 c.54.
[3] 1984 c.28 amended by the Housing (Consequential Provisions) Act 1985 (c.71) Sch.2, para.57(2) and the Housing Act 1988 (c.50) Sch.17, para.35(1).

PRACTICE DIRECTION—CASE MANAGEMENT—PRELIMINARY STAGE: ALLOCATION AND RE-ALLOCATION

This Practice Direction supplements CPR Part 26

1. Reminders of Important Rule Provisions other than Parts 26–29

1. Attention is drawn in particular to the following provisions of the Civil Procedure Rules: **26PD.1**

Part 1	The Overriding Objective (defined in Rule 1.1). The duty of the court to further that objective by actively managing cases (set out in Rule 1.4). The requirement that the parties help the court to further that objective (set out in Rule 1.3).
Part 3	The court's case management powers (which may be exercised on application or on its own initiative) and the sanctions which it may impose.
Part 24	The court's power to grant summary judgment.
Parts 32–35	Evidence, especially the court's power to control evidence.

Attention is also drawn to the practice directions which supplement those Parts and Parts 27–29, and to those which relate to the various specialist jurisdictions.

2. The Allocation Questionnaire

2.1 Form

(1) The allocation questionnaire referred to in Part 26 will be in Form **N149** or Form **N150**. **26PD.2**

(a) Attention is drawn to Section 6 of the Costs Practice Direction supplementing Parts 43 to 48, which requires an estimate of costs to be filed and served when an allocation questionnaire is filed by a party to a claim which is outside the limits of the small claims track.

(b) A party will comply with that obligation if the costs estimate he files and serves states the figures for the base costs, incurred and to be incurred, which he expects, if he is successful, to recover from the other party. The estimate should show an itemised breakdown of how it is calculated, showing separately the amounts included for profit costs, disbursements and VAT. It should be substantially in the form illustrated in Precedent H in the schedule to the Costs Practice Direction.

(2) (Paragraph 2.2 of the Costs Practice Direction defines "Base costs".)

(c) Any party who has entered into a funding arrangement need not reveal the amount of any additional liability.

(CPR, rule 43.2 defines "funding arrangement" and "additional liability".)

(d) No later than when he files the estimate the solicitor acting for that party must deliver a copy to his client.

2.2 Provision of Extra Information

(1) This paragraph sets out what a party should do when he files his allocation questionnaire if he wishes to give the court information about matters which he believes may affect its decision about allocation or case management.

(2) The general rule is that the court will not take such information into account unless the document containing it either:

(a) confirms that all parties have agreed that the information is correct and that it should be put before the court, or

(b) confirms that the party who has sent the document to the court has delivered a copy to all the other parties.

(3) The following are examples of information which will be likely to help the court:

(a) a party's intention to apply for summary judgment or some other order that may dispose of the case or reduce the amount in dispute or the number of issues remaining to be decided,

(b) a party's intention to issue a Part 20 claim or to add another party,

(c) the steps the parties have taken in the preparation of evidence (in particular expert evidence), the steps they intend to take and whether those steps are to be taken in co-operation with any other party,

(d) the directions the party believes will be appropriate to be given for the management of the case,

(e) about any particular facts that may affect the timetable the court will set,

(f) any facts which may make it desirable for the court to fix an allocation hearing or a hearing at which case management directions will be given.

2.3 Consultation

(1) The parties should consult one another and co-operate in completing the allocation questionnaires and giving other information to the court.

(2) They should try to agree the case management directions which they will invite the court to make. Further details appear in the practice directions which supplement Parts 28 and 29.

(3) The process of consultation must not delay the filing of the allocation questionnaires.

2.4 Hearings Before Allocation

Where a court hearing takes place (for example on an application for an interim injunction or for summary judgment under Part 24) before the claim is allocated to a track, the court may at that hearing:

(1) *dispense with* the need for the parties to file allocation questionnaires, treat the hearing as an allocation hearing, make an order for allocation and give directions for case management, or

(2) fix a date for allocation questionnaires to be filed and give other directions.

2.5 Consequences of Failure to File an Allocation Questionnaire

(1) If no party files an allocation questionnaire within the time specified by Form N152, the court will order that unless an allocation questionnaire is filed within 7 days from service of that order, the claim, defence and any counterclaim will be struck out without further order of the court.

(2) Where a party files an allocation questionnaire but another party does not, the file will be referred to a judge for his directions and the court may:

(a) allocate the claim to a track if it considers that it has enough information to do so, or

(b) order that an allocation hearing is listed and that all or any parties must attend.

3. Stay to Allow for Settlement of the Case

3.1 Procedure for the parties to apply to extend the stay

(a) The court will generally accept a letter from any party or from the solicitor for any party as an application to extend the stay under Rule 26.4. **26PD.3**

(b) The letter should—

(i) confirm that the application is made with the agreement of all parties, and

(ii) explain the steps being taken and identify any mediator or expert assisting with the process.

(a) An order extending the stay must be made by a judge.

(b) The extension will generally be for no more than 4 weeks unless clear reasons are given to justify a longer time.

(3) More than one extension of the stay may be granted.

3.2 Position at the end of the stay if no settlement is reached

(1) At the end of the stay the file will be referred to a judge for his directions.

(2) He will consider whether to allocate the claim to a track and what other directions to give, and may require any party to give further information or fix an allocation hearing.

3.3 Any party may apply for a stay to be lifted.

3.4 Position where settlement is reached during a stay

Where the whole of the proceedings are settled during a stay, the taking of any of the following steps will be treated as an application *for the stay to be lifted:*

(1) an application for a consent order (in any form) to give effect to the settlement,

(2) an application for the approval of a settlement where a party is a person under a disability,

(3) giving notice of acceptance of money paid into court in satisfaction of the claim or applying for money in court to be paid out.

4. Allocation, Re-Allocation and Case Management

4.1 The court's general approach

26PD.4 The Civil Procedure Rules lay down the overriding objective, the powers and duties of the court and the factors to which it must have regard in exercising them. The court will expect to exercise its powers as far as possible in co-operation with the parties and their legal representatives so as to deal with the case justly in accordance with that objective.

4.2 Allocation to track

(1) In most cases the court will expect to have enough information from the statements of case and allocation questionnaires to be able to allocate the claim to a track and to give case management directions.

(2) If the court does not have enough information to allocate the claim it will generally make an order under rule 26.5(3) requiring one or more parties to provide further information within 14 days.

(3) Where there has been no allocation hearing the notice of allocation will be in Forms **N154** (fast track), **N155** (multi-track) or **N157–N160** (small claims).

(a) The general rule is that the court will give brief reasons for its allocation decision, and these will be set out in the notice of allocation.

(b) The general rule does not apply where all the allocation questionnaires which have been filed have expressed the wish for the claim to be allocated to the track to which the court has allocated it.

(5) Paragraph 6 of this practice direction deals with allocation hearings and Paragraph 7 deals with allocation principles.

(6) Paragraph 11 of this practice direction deals with re-allocation.

4.3 The practice directions supplementing Parts 27, 28 and 29 contain further information about the giving of case management directions at the allocation stage.

5. Summary Judgment or Other Early Termination

26PD.5 **5.1** Part of the court's duty of active case management is the summary disposal of issues which do not need full investigation and trial (rule 1.4(2)(c)).

5.2 The court's powers to make orders to dispose of issues in that way include:

(a) under rule 3.4, striking out a statement of case, or part of a statement of case, and

(b) under Part 24, giving summary judgment where a claimant or a defendant has no reasonable prospect of success.

The court may use these powers on an application or on its own initiative. The practice direction "Summary Disposal of Claims" contains further information.

5.3(1) A party intending to make such an application should do so before or when filing his allocation questionnaire.

(2) Where a party makes an application for such an order before a claim has been allocated to a track the court will not normally allocate the claim before the hearing of the application.

(3) Where a party files an allocation questionnaire stating that he intends to make such an application but has not done so, the judge will usually direct that an allocation hearing is listed.

(4) The application may be heard at that allocation hearing if the application notice has been issued and served in sufficient time.

5.4(1) This paragraph applies where the court proposes to make such an order of its own initiative.

(2) The court will not allocate the claim to a track but instead it will either:

(a) fix a hearing, giving the parties at least 14 days' notice of the date of the hearing and of the issues which it is proposed that the court will decide, or

(b) make an order directing a party to take the steps described in the order within a stated time and specifying the consequence of not taking those steps.

5.5 Where the court decides at the hearing of an application or a hearing fixed under paragraph 5.4(2)(a) that the claim (or part of the claim) is to continue it may:

(1) treat that hearing as an allocation hearing, allocate the claim and give case management directions, or

(2) give other directions.

6. Allocation Hearings

6.1 General Principle

The court will only hold an allocation hearing on its own initiative if it considers that it is necessary to do so. **26PD.6**

6.2 Procedure

Where the court orders an allocation hearing to take place:

(1) it will give the parties at least 7 days' notice of the hearing in Form **N153**, and

(2) Form **N153** will give a brief explanation of the decision to order the hearing.

6.3 Power to treat another hearing as an allocation hearing

Where the court may treat another hearing as an allocation hearing it does not need to give notice to any party that it proposes to do so.

6.4 The notice of allocation after an allocation hearing will be in Forms **N154, N155** or **N157**.

6.5 Representation

A legal representative who attends an allocation hearing should, if possible, be the person responsible for the case and must in any event be familiar with the case, be able to provide the court with the information it is likely to need to take its decisions about allocation and case management, and have sufficient authority to deal with any issues that are likely to arise.

6.6 Sanctions

(1) This paragraph sets out the sanctions that the court will usually impose for default in connection with the allocation procedure, but the court may make a different order.

(a) Where an allocation hearing takes place because a party has failed to file an allocation questionnaire or to provide further information which the court has ordered, the court will usually order that party to pay on the indemnity basis the costs of any other party who has attended the hearing, summarily assess the amount of those costs, and order them to be paid forthwith or within a stated period.

(b) The court may order that if the party does not pay those costs within the time stated his statement of case will be struck out.

(3) Where a party whose default has led to a fixing of an allocation hearing is still in default and does not attend the hearing the court will usually make an order specifying the steps he is required to take and providing that unless he takes them within a stated time his statement of case will be struck out.

7. Allocation Principles

7.1 Rules 26.6, 26.7 and 26.8

26PD.7 (1) Rule 26.6 sets out the scope of each track,

(2) Rule 26.7 states the general rule for allocation, and

(3) Rule 26.8 sets out the matters relevant to allocation to a track.

7.2 Objective of this paragraph

The object of this paragraph is to explain what will be the court's general approach to some of the matters set out in rule 26.8.

7.3 "the financial value of the claim"

(1) Rule 26.8(2) provides that it is for the court to assess the financial value of a claim.

(2) Where the court believes that the amount the claimant is seeking exceeds what he may reasonably be expected to recover it may make an order under rule 26.5(3) directing the claimant to justify the amount.

7.4 "any amount not in dispute"

In deciding, for the purposes of rule 26.8(2), whether an amount is in dispute the court will apply the following general principles:

(1) Any amount for which the defendant does not admit liability is in dispute,

(2) Any sum in respect of an item forming part of the claim for which judgment has been entered (for example a summary judgment) is not in dispute,

(3) Any specific sum claimed as a distinct item and which the defendant admits he is liable to pay is not in dispute,

(4) Any sum offered by the defendant which has been accepted by the claimant in satisfaction of any item which forms a distinct part of the claim is not in dispute.

It follows from these provisions that if, in relation to a claim the value of which is above the small claims track limit of £5,000, the defendant makes, before allocation, an admission that reduces the amount in dispute to a figure below £5,000 (see CPR Part 14), the normal track for the claim will be the small claims track. As to recovery of pre-allocation costs, the claimant can, before allocation, apply for judgment with costs on the amount of the claim that has been admitted (see CPR, rule 14.3 but see also paragraph 15.1(3) of the Costs Practice Direction supplementing Parts 43 to 48 under which the court has a discretion to allow pre-allocation costs).

7.5 "the views expressed by the parties"

The court will treat these views as an important factor, but the allocation decision is one for the court, to be taken in the light of all the circumstances, and the court will not be bound by any agreement or common view of the parties.

7.6 "the circumstances of the parties"

See paragraph 8.

7.7 "the value of any counterclaim or other Part 20 claim"

Where the case involves more than one money claim (for example where there is a Part 20 claim or there is more than one claimant each making separate claims) the court will not generally aggregate the claims. Instead it will generally regard the largest of them as determining the financial value of the claims.

8. The Small Claims Track—Allocation and Case Management

8.1 Allocation

(a) The small claims track is intended to provide a proportionate procedure by which most straightforward claims with a financial value of not more than £5,000 can be decided, without the need for substantial pre-hearing preparation and the formalities of a traditional trial, and without incurring large legal costs. (Rule 26.6 provides for a lower financial value in certain types of case) **26PD.8**

(b) The procedure laid down in Part 27 for the preparation of the case and the conduct of the hearing are designed to make it possible for a litigant to conduct his own case without legal representation if he wishes.

(c) Cases generally suitable for the small claims track will include consumer disputes, accident claims, disputes about the ownership of goods and most disputes between a landlord and tenant other than opposed claims under Part 56, disputed claims for possession under Part 55 and demotion claims whether in the alternative to possession claims or under Part 65.

(d) A case involving a disputed allegation of dishonesty will not usually be suitable for the small claims track.

(2) Rule 26.7(3) and rule 27.14(5)

(a) These rules allow the parties to consent to the allocation to the small claims track of a claim the value of which is above the limits mentioned in rule 26.6(2) and, in that event, the rules make provision about costs.

(b) The court will not allocate such a claim to the small claims track, notwithstanding that the parties have consented to the allocation, unless it is satisfied that it is suitable for that track.

(c) The court will not normally allow more than one day for the hearing of such a claim.

(d) The court will give case management directions to ensure that the case is dealt with in as short a time as possible. These may include directions of a kind that are not usually given in small claim cases, for example, for Scott Schedules.

8.2 Case management

(1) Directions for case management of claims allocated to the small claims track will generally be given by the court on allocation.

(2) Rule 27.4 contains further provisions about directions and the practice direction supplementing Part 27 sets out the standard directions which the court will usually give.

9. The Fast Track

9.1 Allocation

26PD.9 (1) Where the court is to decide whether to allocate to the fast track or the multi-track a claim for which the normal track is the fast track, it will allocate the claim to the fast track unless it believes that it cannot be dealt with justly on that track.

(2) The court will, in particular, take into account the limits likely to be placed on disclosure, the extent to which expert evidence may be necessary and whether the trial is likely to last more than a day.

(a) When it is considering the likely length of the trial the court will regard a day as being a period of 5 hours, and will consider whether that is likely to be sufficient time for the case to be heard.

(b) The court will also take into account the case management directions (including the fixing of a trial timetable) that are likely to be given and the court's powers to control evidence and to limit cross-examination.

(c) The possibility that a trial might last longer than one day is not necessarily a conclusive reason for the court to allocate or to re-allocate a claim to the multi-track.

(d) A claim may be allocated to the fast track or ordered to remain on that track although there is to be a split trial.

(e) Where the case involves a counterclaim or other Part 20 claim that will be tried with the claim and as a result the trial will last more than a day, the court may not allocate it to the fast track.

9.2 Case management

(1) Directions for the case management of claims which have been allocated to the fast track will be given at the allocation stage or at the listing stage (in either case with or without a hearing) or at both, and if necessary at other times. The trial judge may, at or before the trial, give directions for its conduct.

(2) The practice direction supplementing Part 28 contains further provisions and contains standard directions which the court may give.

10. The Multi-Track

10.1 Paragraph 10.2 does not apply— **26PD.10**

(1) a claim for possesson of land in the county court or a demotion claim whether in the alternative to a possession claim or under Part 65;

(2) any claim which is being dealt with at the Royal Courts of Justice.

10.2 Venue for allocation and case management

(1) The case management of a claim which is allocated to the multi-track will normally be dealt with at a Civil Trial Centre.

(2) In the case of a claim to which any of Parts 49 or 58–62 apply, case management must be dealt with at a Civil Trial Centre. Sub-paragraphs (4) to (10) do not apply to such a claim. The claim will be allocated to the multi-track irrespective of its value, and must be transferred to a Civil Trial Centre for allocation and case management if not already there.

(3) Where a claim is issued in or automatically transferred to a Civil Trial Centre it will be allocated and managed at that court.

(4) The following *sub-paragraphs* apply to a claim which is issued in or automatically transferred to a court which is not a Civil Trial Centre. Such a court is referred to as a "feeder court".

(5) Where a judge sitting at a feeder court decides, on the basis of the allocation questionnaires and any other documents filed by the parties, that the claim should be dealt with on the multi-track he will normally make an order:

(a) allocating the claim to that track,
(b) giving case management directions, and
(c) transferring the claim to a Civil Trial Centre.

(6) If he decides that an allocation hearing or some pre-allocation hearing is to take place (for example to strike out a statement of case under Part 3 of the Rules) that hearing will take place at the feeder court.

(7) If, before allocation, a hearing takes place at a feeder court and in exercising his powers under paragraph 2.4(1) above the judge allocates the claim to the multi-track, he will also normally make an order transferring the claim to a Civil Trial Centre.

(8) A judge sitting at a feeder court may, rather than making an allocation order himself, transfer the claim to a Civil Trial Centre for the decision about allocation to be taken there.

(9) When, following an order for transfer, the file is received at the Civil Trial Centre, a judge sitting at that Centre will consider it and give any further directions that appear necessary or desirable.

(10) Where there is reason to believe that more than one case management conference may be needed and the parties or their legal advisers are located inconveniently far from the Civil Trial Centre, a judge sitting at a feeder court may, with the agreement of the Designated Civil Judge and notwithstanding the allocation of the case to the multi-track, decide that in the particular circumstances of the case it should not be transferred to a Civil Trial Centre, but should be case managed for the time being at the feeder court.

(11) A Designated Civil Judge may at any time make an order transferring a claim from a feeder court to a Civil Trial Centre and he may do so irrespective of the track, if any, to which it has been allocated. He may also permit a feeder court to keep for trial a claim or (subject to review from time to time) a category of claims. Any such permission should take into account the ability of the feeder court in relation to the Civil Trial Centre to provide suitable and effective trial within an appropriate trial period.

(12) No order will be made by a feeder court fixing a date for a hearing at a Civil Trial Centre unless that date has been given or confirmed by a judge or listing officer of that Centre.

10.3 Case management

Part 29 of the Rules and the practice direction supplementing that Part set out the procedure to be adopted.

11. Re-Allocation of Claims and the Variation of Directions

26PD.11 *11.1(1) Where* a party is dissatisfied with an order made allocating the claim to a track he may appeal or apply to the court to re-allocate the claim.

(2) He should appeal if the order was made at a hearing at

which he was present or represented, or of which he was given due notice.

(3) In any other case he should apply to the court to re-allocate the claim.

11.2 Where there has been a change in the circumstances since an order was made allocating the claim to a track the court may re-allocate the claim. It may do so on application or on its own initiative.

The practice directions supplementing Parts 28 and 29 contain provisions about the variation of case management directions.

12. Determining the amount to be paid under a judgment or order

12.1 Scope

26PD.12

(1) In the following paragraphs—

(a) a "relevant order" means a judgment or order of the court which requires the amount of money to be paid by one party to another to be decided by the court; and

(b) a "disposal hearing" means a hearing in accordance with paragraph 12.4.

(2) A relevant order may have been obtained:

(a) by a judgment in default under Part 12;

(b) by a judgment on an admission under Part 14;

(c) on the striking out of a statement of case under Part 3;

(d) on a summary judgment application under Part 24;

(e) on the determination of a preliminary issue or on a trial as to liability; or

(f) at trial.

(3) A relevant order includes any order for the amount of a debt, damages or interest to be decided by the court (including an order for the taking of an account or the making of an inquiry as to any sum due, and any similar order), but does not include an order for the assessment of costs.

12.2 Directions

(1) When the court makes a relevant order it will give directions, which may include—

(a) listing the claim for a disposal hearing;

(b) allocating or re-allocating the claim (but see paragraph 12.3);

(c) directing the parties to file allocation questionnaires by a specified date; and

(d) *staying the claim* while the parties try to settle the case by alternative dispute resolution or other means.

(2) Directions may specify the level or type of judge before whom a hearing or a further hearing will take place and the nature and purpose of that hearing.

(3) Where the parties apply for a relevant order by consent, they should if possible file with their draft consent order agreed directions for the court's approval.

12.3 Allocation

(1) If, when the court makes a relevant order—
(a) the claim has not previously been allocated to a track; and
(b) the financial value of the claim (determined in accordance with Part 26) is such that the claim would, if defended be allocated to the small claims track,

the court will normally allocate it to that track.

(2) Where paragraph (1)(b) does not apply, the court will not normally allocate the claim to a track (other than the small claims track) unless—
(a) the amount payable appears to be genuinely disputed on substantial grounds; or
(b) the dispute is not suitable to be dealt with at a disposal hearing.

12.4 Disposal hearings

(1) A disposal hearing is a hearing—
(a) which will not normally last longer than 30 minutes, and
(b) at which the court will not normally hear oral evidence.

(2) At a disposal hearing the court may—
(a) decide the amount payable under or in consequence of the relevant order and give judgment for that amount; or
(b) give directions as to the future conduct of the proceedings.

(3) If the claim has been allocated to the small claims track, or the court decides at the disposal hearing to allocate it to that track, the court may treat the disposal hearing as a final hearing in accordance with Part 27.

(4) Rule 32.6 applies to evidence at a disposal hearing unless the court directs otherwise.

(5) Except where the claim has been allocated to the small claims track, the court will not exercise its power under sub-paragraph (2)(a) unless any written evidence on which the claimant relies has been served on the defendant at least 3 days before the disposal hearing.

12.5 Costs

(1) Attention is drawn to—
(a) the costs practice direction and in particular to the court's power to make a summary assessment of costs;
(b) rule 44.13(1) which provides that if an order makes no mention of costs, none are payable in respect of the proceedings to which it relates; and
(c) rule 27.14 (special rules about costs in cases allocated to the small claims track).

(2) *Part 46 (fast track* trial costs) will not apply to a case dealt with at a disposal hearing whatever the financial value of the claim. So the costs of a disposal hearing will be in the discretion of the court.

12.6 Jurisdiction of Masters and district judges

Unless the court otherwise directs, a Master or a district judge may decide the amount payable under a relevant order irrespective of the financial value of the claim and of the track to which the claim may have been allocated.

PRACTICE DIRECTION—PILOT SCHEME FOR MEDIATION IN CENTRAL LONDON COUNTY COURT

This Practice Direction supplements CPR Part 26

General

26BPD.1 **1.1** This practice direction provides for a pilot scheme to operate from 1st April 2004 to 31st March 2005 in relation to claims in the Central London County Court.

1.2 This practice direction enables the Central London County Court to—

(1) require the parties to certain types of claims either to attend a mediation appointment or to give reasons for objecting to doing so; and

(2) stay the claim until such an appointment takes place.

1.3 Cases in which a notice of referral to mediation has been served under paragraph 3.1 prior to 31st March 2005 shall remain subject to this practice direction until either—

(1) a mediation appointment has taken place; or

(2) any stay of execution imposed under paragraph 5 has expired or been lifted by the court,

whichever shall be the sooner.

Types of claims to which this practice direction applies

26BPD.2 **2** This practice direction applies to a claim if it meets all the following conditions—

(1) the small claims track is not the normal track for the claim;

(2) no party to the claim is—

(a) a child or protected party; or

(b) exempt from payment of court fees; and

(3) the court has not granted an interim injunction in the proceedings.

('Child' and 'protected party' have the same meaning as in rule 21.1(2).)

Service of mediation notice

26BPD.3 **3.1** The court may, when it serves the allocation questionnaire under rule 26.3, serve a notice of referral to mediation on each party—

(1) notifying them that the claim is to be referred to mediation; and

(2) requiring them, within 14 days after service of the notice on them, to file and serve a reply to the notice in which they must—

(a) state whether they agree or object to mediation;

(b) specify any dates within three months of the date of filing the response on which they would not be able to attend a mediation appointment; and

(c) if they object to mediation, set out their reasons for doing so.

3.2 The cases where a notice of referral to mediation is served on the parties will be chosen at random from those that meet the criteria set out in paragraph 2.

3.3 A party who receives a notice of referral to mediation need not complete and file an allocation questionnaire unless or until directed to do so by the court.

Objection to mediation

4.1 If one or more of the parties states in his reply that he objects to mediation, the case will be referred to a district judge who may— **26BPD.4**

(1) direct the case to be listed for a hearing of the objections to mediation;

(2) direct that a mediation appointment should proceed;

(3) order the parties to file and serve completed allocation questionnaires; or

(4) give such directions as to the management of the case as he considers appropriate.

4.2 If a party does not file a reply within the time specified in the notice of referral to mediation, the court and all other parties may proceed as if that party has no objection to the use of mediation in the case.

Mediation appointment

5.1 If no party objects to mediation, or the court directs that mediation should proceed, the court will direct that the proceedings be stayed for an initial period of two months. **26BPD.5**

5.2 In accordance with the existing Central London County Court Mediation Scheme, the court will fix a date, time and place for the mediation appointment and notify the parties accordingly once all the parties have paid the mediator's charges.

5.3 When the court fixes a mediation appointment it will if necessary extend the stay of proceedings until the date of the appointment.

Mediator's charges

6.1 A mediator's charge is payable by each party who is to attend a mediation appointment. The court will notify each party of the amount of the charge and request payment of that amount in the notice of referral to mediation. **26BPD.6**

6.2 A party must pay the mediator's charge to the court within 14 days of being requested to do so or such other period as the court may direct. Any request for further time in which to pay the mediator's charge may be made by letter.

6.3 If any party fails to pay the mediator's charge the court will refer the case to a district judge for directions.

Unsuccessful mediation

7. If the mediation does not proceed or does not fully resolve the dispute, the mediator will notify the court and the court will— **26BPD.7**

(1) either—

(a) allocate the claim to a track; or

(b) order the parties to file and serve completed allocation questionnaires (if not already filed); and

(2) give such directions for the further management of the case as it considers appropriate.

PART 27

THE SMALL CLAIMS TRACK

Contents 27.0.1

Editorial introduction

The small claims track is a proportionate method of dealing with straightforward cases of limited financial value. The current rules applicable to small claims have their roots in the "arbitration" procedures which existed prior to the introduction of the Civil Procedure Rules. In the past decade the rules applicable to small claims have become increasingly integrated into the procedures relevant to all claims but the essential elements of a simplified procedure up to and including the final hearing plus restrictions on orders for costs remain. Cases allocated to the small claims track are often conducted by litigants in person who are supported in understanding the basic court procedures by leaflets available at county courts or on line by accessing the Court Service website. 27.0.2

The small claims track is created by r.26.1(2), issues concerning allocation are dealt with in Pt 26 and appeals are governed by Pt 52. Part 27 contains the special rules relating to the small claims track, which limit costs recoverable and simplify the steps needed to prepare a disputed case for a hearing and make the hearing itself a less formal affair than for cases allocated to the fast track and multi-track. Paragraph 3 of the Practice Direction which accompanies Pt 27 makes special provision for parties to be assisted at small claims hearings by Lay Representatives. Some of the Civil Procedure Rules are excluded from cases which have been allocated to the small claims track (see para.27.2). Small claims are, however, integrated into the Civil Procedure Rules; the rules concerning the issue of the claim, statements of case, default, admissions and summary judgment and appeals all apply to small claims cases.

The small claims track is exclusive to the county court, hearings of small claims cases are almost invariably conducted by District Judges. A case allocated to the small claims track may only be assigned to a circuit judge to hear with his consent (Practice Direction – Allocation of cases to Levels of Judiciary, PD 2 para.11.2). References to procedural and trial judges in this commentary are to the District Judge and references to the trial are to the "hearing". There is no separate "small claims court" which is a misnomer.

Features of the small claims track

(i) Cases destined for the small claims track are commenced in the county court using the same forms and procedures as cases of higher financial value. 27.0.3

(ii) Many small claims cases are conducted by litigants without the assistance of legal advice but there is no restriction on the use of legally qualified representatives (see also para.27.8.2).

(iii) Costs recoverable under the small claims track are restricted (see r.27.14) and usually do not include the costs of a legal representative to prepare the case or appear at a hearing. The successful party may, however be awarded some of these costs if the other side has behaved unreasonably (r.27.14(2)(d)) plus the court may take into account a party's rejection of an offer to settle when considering what amounts to unreasonable behaviour.

(iv) The trial is relatively informal and the strict rules of evidence do not apply (see para.27.8); the trial is generally described as a "hearing".

(v) Form **N149** is the allocation questionnaire tailored for cases likely to be allocated to the small claims track.

(vi) Every case is considered by a district judge at the allocation stage; there is no 'automatic' referral. The district judge may use the standard directions suggested by the Practice Direction to Pt 27 or make specially tailored directions including requiring a party to clarify their case.

(vii) The parties may, subject to the approval of the District Judge, agree to use the small claims track even though the case falls outside the usual scope of the small claims track; if this option is chosen then the costs regime applicable to the small claims track applies unless the parties agree otherwise (r.26.14(5)).

(viii) In most cases there is no preliminary hearing but the District Judge may order a preliminary hearing if necessary (r.27.6).

(ix) Either party may apply for summary judgment under Pt 24; and if the hearing takes place before allocation the successful party may be awarded costs (but see para.27.2.1 as to the usefulness of Pt 24 in small claims matters).

(x) Use of expert evidence on the small claims track is limited and permission must always be obtained in advance (see para.27.5).

(xi) Part 27 permits a party to submit its case in writing instead of appearing at the hearing; 7 days notice must be given under r.27.9 to the court and to the other side.

(xii) If the case is dealt with as a paper exercise or where a party has not attended having previously given notice under r.27.9 then the District Judge will prepare a note of reasons for the decision and send a copy to each party (see para.27.9.1).

(xiii) The small claims hearings are in public, albeit usually in the relatively informal setting of the District Judges room (see para.27.8.1). District Judges often adopt an interventionist approach at the hearing which is less structured than a fast track or multi-track trial.

(xiv) Part 27 provides a procedure for a final hearing to be dealt with purely as a paper exercise (but see para.27.2.1 as to the usefulness of this procedure).

(xv) The parties at the hearing may be represented by a lay representative who need not be legally qualified (see para.27.10.1 and the Practice Direction which appears at the end of the rule).

(xvi) Whereas in the past the right to appeal against a small claims track decision was limited, the right to appeal is now consistent with appeals against other judicial decisions—but see para.20.7.4 for more detail.

(xvii) The documentation required to commence an appeal against a decision on the small claims track is simplified (see para.27.0.4).

(xviii) There is a special provision allowing a party who does not attend a hearing for "good reason" to apply to have the decision set aside (r.27.11).

(xix) The court fees payable for small claims cases are lower than those in cases of higher financial value. The commencement fees payable on claims of under £5,000 in value are on a sliding scale but an allocation fee is payable in cases of value £1500 and more; there is no listing questionnaire and hence no fee payable on listing.

(xx) Although there is no fee payable on filing of the pre trial checklist the claimant does have to pay a hearing fee which is on a sliding scale depending on the amount in dispute. This fee is repayable in whole or in part if the hearing date is vacated more than 14 days before the final hearing; the hearing fee was introduced by the Civil Proceedings Fees (Amendment) (No.2) Order 2007 (SI 2007/2176) effective on October1, 2007)

(xxi) The Legal Services Commission has no power to issue a certificate of public funding for a case which is, or is likely to be, referred to the small claims track (para.5.4.6 of the General Funding Criteria) although a person may get limited legal assistance under the Help at Court Scheme offered by solicitors with a contract with the Legal Services Commission. (See also para.27.8.2).

Appeals

A party needs permission to appeal (r.52.3) which can be sought by request at the hearing or afterwards by application when the request is incorporated in the appeal documentation. There is a reduced court fee for an appeal against a decision on the small claims track and the documents required to launch the appeal are simplified; the appellant must complete a Form **N164** which must set out the reasons for the appeal. The application must be supported by a sealed copy of the order being appealed plus any order giving permission to appeal (PD 52 para.5.8). In practice, the Circuit Judge considering an appeal is likely to require that a suitable record of the reasons be produced—usually in the form of a transcript of the court recording of the District Judge's judgment (PD 52 para.5.8D). The appellant may, in addition, provide to the court further documents including witness statements and a skeleton argument (PD 52 para.5.8B). The rules relevant to small claims costs as set in r.27.14 also apply to appeals with effect from October 2, 2006. An appellant in poor financial circumstances may seek an order from a District Judge or the appeal Judge for a transcript of the judgment a public expense; this may be allowed if the Judge considers that the there are reasonable grounds for appeal (PD 52 para.5.17). **27.0.4**

European small claims procedure

From 2009 the European small claims procedure will operate in cross border litigation in civil and commercial matters where the claim does not exceed €2000. It will be available in all EU member states except Denmark. The litigation procedures are simplified and will provide a straightforward procedure for judgment to be enforced in a different jurisdiction. The procedure has been incorporated into the Civil Procedure Rules as a new Pt 78. **27.0.5**

Mediation in small claims cases

Many county courts now promote mediation as an alternative to litigation and some courts have local schemes which are especially tailored to meet the needs of claims allocated to the small claims track. The schemes offer a voluntary, non binding and private service with a neutral mediator who assists the parties to reach a settlement. These schemes can be attractive to both litigants in person and to commercial litigants but generally cost fees in addition to the court fees already paid. In many areas the mediation route offers a faster resolution than waiting for a small claims hearing, but if the process fails the parties must then revert to the court process for a binding decision. Failure to engage in mediation in a small claims case may attract an adverse order for costs—see para.27.14.4. **27.0.6**

Related sources

27.0.7

- Practice Direction—Small Claims Track (see para.27PD.1)
- Part 26 (Case Management—The Preliminary Stage)
- Part 44 (Costs)—in particular r.44.5 and r.44.9
- Part 52 (Appeals)
- County Court Fees Order 1999 (as amended)
- Lay Representatives (Rights of Audience) Order 1999 (SI 1999/1225)
- Part 78 European Order for Payment and European Small Claims Procedures

Forms

27.0.8

- **N157** Notice of Allocation to the Small Claims Track
- **N158** Notice of Allocation to the Small Claims Track (preliminary hearing)
- ***N159*** *Notice of Allocation to* the Small Claims Track (no hearing)
- **N160** Notice of Allocation to the Small Claims Track (with parties consent)

Part 27 Practice Direction

Attention is drawn to the detailed practice direction which accompanies this part (see para.27PD.1). **27.0.9**

Scope of this Part

27.1—(1) This Part— **27.1**

(a) sets out the special procedure for dealing with claims which have been allocated to the small claims track under Part 26; and

(b) limits the amount of costs that can be recovered in respect of a claim which has been allocated to the small claims track.

(Rule 27.14 deals with costs on the small claims track.)

(2) A claim being dealt with under this Part is called a small claim.

(Rule 26.6 provides for the scope of the small claims track. A claim for a remedy for harassment or unlawful eviction relating, in either case, to residential premises shall not be allocated to the small claims track whatever the financial value of the claim. Otherwise, the small claims track will be the normal track for—

- **any claim which has a financial value of not more than £5,000 subject to the special provisions about claims for personal injuries and housing disrepair claims;**
- **any claim for personal injuries which has a financial value of not more than £5,000 where the claim for damages for personal injuries is not more than £1,000; and**
- **any claim which includes a claim by a tenant of residential premises against his landlord for repairs or other work to the premises where the estimated cost of the repairs or other work is not more than £1,000 and the financial value of any other claim for damages is not more than £1,000.)**

Effect of rule

27.1.1 The words in brackets in this rule are a cross reference to the detailed provisions concerning the criteria for allocation (Pt 26 and its accompanying Practice Direction).

The small claims track is the normal track for cases:

- With a financial value of not more than £5000.
- In personal injury cases where claim for personal injuries is not more than £1000.
- Where the claim includes a claim by a tenant against his landlord only if the cost of repairs is not more than £1000.

The value of a counterclaim is relevant when determining the track but the fact that a counterclaim is in excess of £5,000 does not automatically disqualify the case from the small claims track; r.26.8(1)(a) and r.26.8(1)(e) and see also *Berridge v Bayliss*, November 23, 1999, unrep., LTL 23/11/99.

CPR, PD 26 para.8 contains further guidance on the cases suitable for the small claims track describing them as "straightforward claims" which embraces consumer disputes, accident claims and disputes about ownership of goods. The apparent complexity of a case and the importance of the matter to persons who are not parties to the proceedings are also relevant in determining the track, (r.26.8(1)(c) and r.26.8(1)(g)) but this does not mean that the small claims track is not suitable for a wide range of cases, even those involving import questions of law and fact; *Afzal v Ford Motor Co Ltd* [1994] 4 All E.R. 720 was decided prior to the introduction of the Civil Procedure Rules but in determining that accidents at work were suitable for the then arbitration procedure the Court of Appeal set the tone for the scope of the pre CPR arbitration procedure and this approach has continued to inform the allocation jurisdiction exercised by the judiciary. It is not justified to order the wholesale transfer of a category of cases involving complex arguments of law and statutory interpretation[1] merely to enable the claimants to have access to the remedy of an interim payment or to expose the parties to the possibility of an adverse costs order, but individual cases may be transferred for these reasons (*per* Lord Tuckey in *Clark v Ardington Electrical Services* [2002] EWCA Civ 510; [2004] 1 A.C. 1067; [2003] 3 W.L.R. 1571; [2004] 1 All E.R. 277.

There is no restriction on the final remedies available in the small claims track (r.27.3); for example cases which may require an injunction order, e.g. boundary disputes may be determined on the small claims track.

Disposal hearings

Where judgment has been entered for an amount to be decided by the court, and the case falls within the scope of the small claims track, it is usual for the case to be allocated to the small claims track. This provides the parties with the protection of the costs limitation of the small claims track (PD 26 para.12.8(2)). In the absence of allocation to the small claims track for disposal costs remain at the discretion of the trial judge: *Panchal v Maguire (Costs)* [2006] 1 C.L. 59. **27.1.2**

Possession claims

Case management of possession claims are governed by r.55. The court will only allocate such claims to the small claims track if all the parties agree (r.55.9(2); and where possession claims are allocated to the small claims track the claim is treated, for the purposes of costs, as if it were on the fast track, albeit the trial costs are in the discretion of the court and shall not exceed the amount that would be recoverable under r.46.2 if the value of the claim were up to £3,000 (r.55.9(3)). **27.1.3**

Personal injury claims

The small claims procedure can be used for personal injury claims including claims arising from accidents at work, *Afzal v Ford Motor Co Ltd* (1994) 4 All E.R. 720. However, if the personal injury aspect of the claim exceeds £1000 the case will not qualify for the small claims track (r.26.6(1)(a)(i)). Damages for personal injuries means sums claimed as compensation for pain, suffering and loss of amenity and does not include any other damages which are claimed (r.26.6(2)). As to meaning of "a claim for personal injuries" generally in the CPR, see r.2.3(1) above and para.2.3.11. **27.1.4**

Claims by a tenant against a landlord for repairs

Cases of housing disrepair where either the cost of the repair or the damages for non repair are expected to be above £1000 do not qualify for the small claims track (r.27.1(2)). **27.1.5**

Claims for harassment and unlawful eviction

Are not allocated to the small claims track (r.26.7(4)). **27.1.6**

Extent to which other Parts apply[2]

27.2—(1) The following Parts of these Rules do not apply to small claims— **27.2**

(a) Part 25 (interim remedies) except as it relates to interim injunctions[GL];

(b) Part 31 (disclosure and inspection);

(c) Part 32 (evidence) except rule 32.1 (power of court to control evidence);

(d) Part 33 (miscellaneous rules about evidence);

(e) Part 35 (experts and assessors) except rules 35.1 (duty to restrict expert evidence), 35.3 (experts—overriding

[1] In this instance the category cases referred to are the so-called "credit hire cases" which have generally been heard in first instance on the small claims track.

[2] Amended by the Civil Procedure (Amendment) Rules 2000 (SI 2000/221) and the Civil Procedure (Amendment No.3) Rules 2006 (SI 2006/3435).

duty to the court), 35.7 (court's power to direct that evidence is to be given by single joint expert) and 35.8 (instructions to a single joint expert);

(f) Subject to paragraph (3), Part 18 (further information);

(g) Part 36 (offers to settle); and

(h) Part 39 (hearings) except rule 39.2 (general rule—hearing to be in public).

(2) The other Parts of these Rules apply to small claims except to the extent that a rule limits such application.

(3) The court of its own initiative may order a party to provide further information if it considers it appropriate to do so.

Effect of rule

27.2.1 The effect of this rule, combined with the other parts of Pt 27, is to simplify the steps needed to prepare and hear a small claims case and to curtail the type of procedural application which may be made before the final hearing. The overriding objective of the CPR is to deal with cases justly which includes ensuring that cases are dealt with expeditiously and fairly (r.1.1(2)(d)). Rule 27.2 furthers the overriding objective by excluding some of the more elaborate features of the adversarial system.

Given the limits on costs in the small claims track, the restriction on payments into court and offers to settle (Pt 36) is self evident, but does not prevent a party from making without prejudice offers and attempting to settle the claim before the final hearing. The remedy of an interim payment is not available on the small claims track.

The disclosure rules are replaced by the standard direction to send copies of relevant documents to the other side before the hearing (r.27.3(i)) thus no list of documents, disclosure statement or formal inspection is required. The standard directions issued by the court require the parties to bring their original documents to the hearing

The use of experts on the small claims track is limited by r.27.5 and r.35.1 (duty to restrict expert evidence).

There can be no formal requests under Pt 18 for information but the District Judge may give directions, usually at the allocation stage, for either party to clarify their case (r.27.2(3) and Practice direction 2.3).

The final hearing are in public but otherwise Pt 39, which covers miscellaneous rules about hearings, is excluded; the conduct of the small claims hearing and the effect of a party not attending the final hearing is governed by rr.27.8 to 27.11 (inclusive). There is special provision allowing unqualified lay representatives to assist parties at the hearing (see para.27.8.2).

Rule 24 (summary judgment) is not excluded but is not used often. The effect of Pt 27 overall is to offer the parties a relatively swift and straightforward route to a final decision and as such an application of summary judgment does not have the same attraction as for cases allocated to the fast track and multi-track. Further, where the amount of the claim is limited, having to pay an additional fee for a summary judgment application is a disincentive against making the application. If a party submits an application for summary judgment before allocation to the small claims track he may, if successful and subject to the courts overall discretion on costs and issues of proportionality, be awarded costs. (see para.27.14.2).

The court may give further or special directions at any stage including at a preliminary hearing (r.27.4(1)(b) and r.27.6(5)(c)). Individual cases may be transferred to the fast track if special orders e.g. for an interim payment, are required *per* Lord Tuckey in *Clark v Ardington Electrical Services (Appeal against order for Disclosure)* [2001] EWCA Civ 585; [2004] 1 A.C. 1067; [2003] 3 W.L.R. 1571; [2004] 1 All E.R. 277.

Court's power to grant a final remedy

27.3 **27.3 The court may grant any final remedy in relation to a small claim which it could grant if the proceedings were on the fast track or the multi-track.**

Scope of provision

Rule 27.3 makes it clear that no party is disadvantaged as to final remedy by having the claim allocated to the small claims track. The court has the same powers as in other cases and can grant whichever final remedy is appropriate, e.g. damages, injunction, specific performance, rectification, etc. But note that the court is restricted by r.27.2 with respect to interim remedies, not including interim injunctions, and security for costs. **27.3.1**

Preparation for the hearing

27.4—(1) After allocation the court will— **27.4**

(a) give standard directions and fix a date for the final hearing;

(b) give special directions and fix a date for the final hearing;

(c) give special directions and direct that the court will consider what further directions are to be given no later than 28 days after the date the special directions were given;

(d) fix a date for preliminary hearing under rule 27.6; or

(e) give notice that it proposes to deal with the claim without a hearing under rule 27.10 and invite the parties to notify the court by a specified date if they agree the proposal.

(2) The court will—

(a) give parties at least 21 days' notice of the date fixed for the final hearing, unless the parties agree to accept less notice; and

(b) inform them of the amount of time allowed for the final hearing.

(3) In this rule—

(a) "standard directions" means—

(i) a direction that each party shall, at least 14 days before the date fixed for the final hearing, file and serve on every other party copies of all documents (including any expert's report) on which he intends to rely at the hearing; and

(ii) any other standard directions set out in the relevant practice direction; and

(b) "special directions" means directions given in addition to or instead of the standard directions.

Effect of rule

This rule simplifies and standardises the steps to prepare a small claims case for hearing and is a key feature of the small claims track. **27.4.1**

"standard directions"

The appendix to the Practice Direction which accompanies this part sets out the standard directions which apply including directions for use in road traffic accidents, a variety of contractual claims, disputes between landlords and tenants and holiday and wedding claims plus suggested special directions (see paras 27PD.9–27PD.14). The standard directions highlight that the parties should seek to negotiate a settlement, if possible and the fact that parties need permission in advance before instructing an expert. The list of directions in this rule and the Practice Direction is not however exclusive and the District Judge may give special directions in addition (see r.27.7). All **27.4.2** directions for trial are given at the allocation stage or at a preliminary hearing — there is no listing questionnaire.

"Preliminary hearing"

27.4.3 See para.27.6.

"Hearing under Rule 27.10"

27.4.4 The court may deal with the case without a hearing but only if all parties agree (see para.27.10).

"Time allowed for the hearing"

27.4.5 The time allowed is based on the nature of the case and information provided to the parties in the allocation questionnaires including number of witnesses and the number of documents to be used at the hearing. It is essential that the parties inform the court at once if the time allowed by the District Judge appears inadequate for the case; if the case is not completed in the time allowed the matter will go part heard and it could be several weeks before the matter can be re-listed for completion. Although there is no upper limit on the time allowed for the hearing of a small claims case the court will not normally allow more than one day for the hearing (PD 26 para.8.1(2)(c)).

Experts

27.5 **27.5 No expert may give evidence, whether written or oral, at a hearing without the permission of the court.**

(Rule 27.14(3)(d) provides for the payment of an expert's fees.)

Experts in small claims cases

27.5.1 Expert evidence shall be restricted to that which is reasonably required to resolve the proceedings (r.35.1). The court's permission to use an expert must be obtained in advance. Much of Pt 35 (experts and assessors) is excluded from cases allocated to the small claims track but note that the overriding duty of the expert is to the court, the duty to restrict expert evidence, plus the courts power to direct that evidence is given by a single joint expert and to give directions about that evidence are preserved. The effect of excluding much of Pt 35 is that the courts can adopt a flexible approach to the use of such experts that are necessary. An expert's report can be relatively informal, and need not, for example, cite the expert's qualifications in detail; this flexibility allows the parties to use 'local' experts who although unable to produce polished reports can still produce straightforward advice to assist the court. The use of experts is considerably curtailed by the limit on costs imposed by r.27.14(3)(d) which limits the amount of costs recoverable by the successful party for the cost of an expert to the amount specified by PD 27 para.7.3(2), namely £200 for each expert.

Preliminary hearing

27.6 **27.6—(1) The court may hold a preliminary hearing for the consideration of the claim, but only—**

(a) where—

(i) it considers that special directions, as defined in rule 27.4, are needed to ensure a fair hearing; and

(ii) it appears necessary for a party to attend at court to ensure that he understands what he must do to comply with the special directions; or

(b) to enable it to dispose of the claim on the basis that one or other of the parties has no real prospect of success at a final hearing; or

(c) to enable it to strike out[GL] a statement of case or part of a statement of case on the basis that the statement of

case, or the part to be struck out, discloses no reasonable grounds for bringing or defending the claim.

(2) When considering whether or not to hold a preliminary hearing, the court must have regard to the desirability of limiting the expense to the parties of attending court.

(3) Where the court decides to hold a preliminary hearing, it will give the parties at least 14 days' notice of the date of the hearing.

(4) The court may treat the preliminary hearing as the final hearing of the claim if all the parties agree.

(5) At or after the preliminary hearing the court will—

(a) fix the date of the final hearing (if it has not been fixed already) and give the parties at least 21 days' notice of the date fixed unless the parties agree to accept less notice;

(b) inform them of the amount of time allowed for the final hearing; and

(c) give any appropriate directions.

Effect of rule

The expectation is that small claims cases will go direct to a final hearing with no intervening hearing. A preliminary hearing is not routine and bearing in mind the desirability of limiting expense (r.27.6(2)) are held only in a minority of cases. The usual form of notification for a preliminary hearing (Form **N158**) will explain to the parties why they are required to attend the hearing which may be to consider special directions which the District Judge would prefer to explain to the parties personally or to consider if a case should be struck out as having no real prospect of success at the final hearing. Preliminary hearings are used, for example, if the parties propose to use experts at the hearing as the District Judge may wish to offer guidance on how to make the best use of an expert and how to arrange for a single joint expert to be appointed. The preliminary hearing will not be treated as a final hearing unless all parties agree (r.27.6(1)(b)). **27.6.1**

Power of court to add to, vary or revoke directions

27.7 The court may add to, vary or revoke directions. **27.7**

Effect of rule

Rules 27.4 to 27.6 are not the exclusive list of directions which can be given to cases allocated to the small claims track. See para.27.4.2 and the appendix to the Practice Direction which accompanies Pt 27. **27.7.1**

Conduct of the hearing

27.8—(1) The court may adopt any method of proceeding at a hearing that it considers to be fair. **27.8**

(2) Hearings will be informal.

(3) The strict rules of *evidence* do not apply.

(4) The court need not take evidence on oath.

(5) The court may limit cross-examination[GL].

(6) The court must give reasons for its decision.

Effect of rule

This rule is supplemented by Paras 4 and 5 of the Practice Direction which accompanies Pt 27. The majority of Pt 39 (Miscellaneous Provisions Relating to Hear- **27.8.1** ings) is excluded from cases allocated to the small claims track (r.27.2(1)(h)) so the effect of this rule is to give the small claims hearing its own rules of conduct. Note that r.39.2 (hearing to be in public) is not excluded which is a departure from the previous arbitration hearings which were usually in private. The hearing of any civil trial in private is inconsistent with art.6 of the European Convention on Human Rights (right to a fair and public hearing) *Scarth v United Kingdom (33745/96)* (1998) 26 E.H.R.R. CD154.

Small claims hearings are relatively informal (r.27.8(2)). The rooms used by District Judges for the hearings may take the appearance of a formal court room with the judge separated from the parties by a barrier or may take the format of all parties sitting on the same level or literally "round a table". The exact format of the hearing depends on the facilities at an individual court, the preferences of the District Judge and the circumstances of the particular case. In practice, it is unusual for observers who are not connected with a case to attend a small claims hearing. The Court of Appeal previously condoned procedure at an arbitration hearing which was "brisk and effective" (*Starmer v Bradbury, The Times*, April 11, 1994); the conduct of a small claims hearings may seem brusque to those more familiar with the pace of a formal trial. Rule 27.8(3) (the strict rules of evidence do not apply) gives the District Judge flexibility to allow, for example, a liberal interpretation of the hearsay rules. This is proportionate for the hearing of cases of limited financial value but it should be noted that the relaxation of the rules of evidence is in the discretion of the District Judge who will place appropriate, possibly limited, weight on the evidence of witnesses who do not attend a hearing to be questioned about their evidence. There is, in addition, special provision under r.27.9(1)(a) which allows a party to notify the court and the other side at least seven days in advance of a hearing that they will not attend the hearing but wish the court to take into account written evidence. It is usual for the District Judge not to require that evidence is given on oath (r.27.8(5)) but evidence on oath may be required. The District Judge may limit cross examination (r.27.8(6)) and often will ask the parties and their witnesses questions direct. The hearing will be recorded (27PD.5). The judgment may be as simple and as brief as the nature of the case allows (PD 27 para.5.5(1)) and may be given at the hearing or later in writing. Written reasons will be provided where one of the parties has given notice in advance that they will not attend under r.27.9 or the case is conducted without a hearing under r.27.10 (PD 27 para.5.6).

Representation at the small claims hearing

27.8.2 Parties in small claims cases may represent themselves, instruct a solicitor or barrister or use a 'lay representative' which is unique to small claims cases (para.3 of the Practice Direction which accompanies Pt 27). The right to use a lay representative applies at all stages of the small claims case up to judgment, but not on appeal. The usual rule is that the Lay Representative may not exercise the right of audience where his client does not attend the hearing. However the court may hear a lay representative even in circumstances excluded by the order (PD 27 para.3.2).[1]

Failure to attend the hearing

27.8.3 Unless a party has given notice in advance under r.29.9(1) if they fail to attend the hearing they risk their case being struck out under r.27.9(4). If a party has "good reason" not to attend and a "reasonable prospect of success at a hearing" they may apply for an adverse decision made in their absence to be set aside under r.27.11.

Non-attendance of parties at a final hearing

27.9 **27.9—(1) If a party who does not attend a final hearing—**

(a) has given written notice to the court and the other party at least 7 days before the hearing date that he will not attend;

(b) has served on the other party at least 7 days before the hearing date any other documents which he has filed with the court; and

[1] Lay Representatives (Rights of Audience) Order 1999 (SI 1999/1225).

(c) has, in his written notice, requested the court to decide the claim in his absence and has confirmed his compliance with paragraphs (a) and (b) above,

the court will take into account that party's statement of case and any other documents he has filed and served when it decides the claim.

(2) If a claimant does not—

(a) attend the hearing; and

(b) give the notice referred to in paragraph (1),

the court may strike out[GL] the claim.

(3) If—

(a) a defendant does not—

(i) attend the hearing; or

(ii) give the notice referred to in paragraph (1); and

(b) the claimant either—

(i) does attend the hearing; or

(ii) gives the notice referred to in paragraph (1),

the court may decide the claim on the basis of the evidence of the claimant alone.

(4) If neither party attends or gives the notice referred to in paragraph (1), the court may strike out[GL] the claim and any defence and counterclaim.

Effect of rule

Parties may require the District Judge to consider written evidence in their absence. Notice must be given to the court and the other party in writing seven days before the hearing. The party must also send any additional documents filed to the other side plus confirm to the court that this has been done. **27.9.1**

If a party gives notice under r.27.9(1) and does not attend the hearing the District Judge will prepare a written note of the reasons for the decision and send a copy to each party (PD 27 para.5.6).

Unless a party has given notice in advance under r.29.9(1) if they fail to attend the hearing they risk having their case struck out under r.27.9(4). If a party has "good reason" not to attend and a "reasonable prospect of success at a hearing" they may apply for an adverse decision made in their absence to be set aside under r.27.11.

Disposal without a hearing

27.10 The court may, if all parties agree, deal with the claim without a hearing. **27.10**

Effect of rule

This procedure is rarely used. The parties may, subject to the approval of the District Judge, elect to have their case decided purely as a paperwork exercise; the right to a hearing under ECHR art.6(1) can be waived, so long as the waiver is *unequivocal*. The District Judge cannot impose this method of disposal on the parties but may invite them to agree to the case being dealt with in this way. Where the District Judge decides a case using r.27.10 he will prepare a note of his reasons and send a copy to each party (PD 27 para 5.6). **27.10.1**

Setting judgment aside and re-hearing

27.11—(1) A party— **27.11**

(a) who was neither present nor represented at the hearing of the claim; and

(b) who has not given written notice to the court under rule 27.9(1), may apply for an order that a judgment under this Part shall be set aside[GL] and the claim re-heard.

(2) A party who applies for an order setting aside a judgment under this rule must make the application not more than 14 days after the day on which notice of the judgment was served on him.

(3) The court may grant an application under paragraph (2) only if the applicant—

(a) had a good reason for not attending or being represented at the hearing or giving written notice to the court under rule 27.9(1); and

(b) has a reasonable prospect of success at the hearing.

(4) If a judgment is set aside[GL]—

(a) the court must fix a new hearing for the claim; and

(b) the hearing may take place immediately after the hearing of the application to set the judgment aside and may be dealt with by the judge who set aside[GL] the judgment.

(5) A party may not apply to set aside[GL] a judgment under this rule if the court dealt with the claim without a hearing under rule 27.10.

(Rules 27.12 and 27.13 are revoked.)

Effect of rule

27.11.1 Rule 27.11 gives a limited right to apply to have a judgment set aside and the case re-heard. The right to so apply is not available to a party who attended the hearing, was represented at the hearing, who gave notice under r.27.9(1) or who agreed to the case being dealt with without a hearing under r.27.10.

"neither present nor represented"

27.11.2 The special provisions about representation at the small claims hearing are found in para.3 of the Practice Direction which accompanies Pt 27 (see also para.27.8.2).

"good reason for not attending"

27.11.3 The court will probably require evidence of the "good reason", e.g. medical certificate.

"a reasonable prospect of success"

27.11.4 The applicant must show that he has "a reasonable prospect of success". This term is new in the context of setting aside a small claims judgment but is a familiar term in the context of setting aside a default judgment. See *Alpine Bulk Transport Co Inc v Saudi Eagle Shipping Co Inc*; *The Saudi Eagle* [1986] 2 Lloyd's Rep. 221 and commentary to Pt 13, at para.13.3.1.

Deliberate absence

27.11.5 In *Shocked v Goldschmidt* [1998] 1 All E.R. 372 the Court of Appeal held that a party who deliberately chooses to be absent from a hearing is not entitled to a rehearing even if the party has a good claim or defence. Clearly such a party, even if able to comply with r.27.11(3)(b), could not comply with r.27.11(3)(a).

Rule 27.12 and Rule 27.13 (right to appeal and procedures for making an appeal)

27.12 These rules were revoked with effect from October 2000; the rules about appeals in small claims cases are now consistent with the rules about appeals in cases allocated to the fast track and multi-track — see para.27.0.4.

[THE NEXT PARAGRAPH IS 27.14.]

Costs on the small claims track[1]

27.14—(1) This rule applies to any case which has been allocated to the small claims track unless paragraph (5) applies. 27.14

(Rules 44.9 and 44.11 make provision in relation to orders for costs made before a claim has been allocated to the small claims track)

(2) The court may not order a party to pay a sum to another party in respect of that other party's costs, fees and expenses, including those relating to an appeal, except—

(a) the fixed costs attributable to issuing the claim which—

(i) are payable under Part 45; or

(ii) would be payable under Part 45 if that Part applied to the claim.

(b) in proceedings which included a claim for an injunction or an order for specific performance a sum not exceeding the amount specified in the relevant practice direction for legal advice and assistance relating to that claim;

(c) any court fees paid by that other party;

(d) expenses which a party or witness has reasonably incurred in travelling to and from a hearing or in staying away from home for the purposes of attending a hearing;

(e) a sum not exceeding the amount specified in the relevant practice direction for any loss of earnings or loss of leave by a party or witness due to attending a hearing or to staying away from home for the purpose of attending a hearing;

(f) a sum not exceeding the amount specified in the relevant practice direction for an expert's fees; and

(g) such further costs as the court may assess by the summary procedure and order to be paid by a party who has behaved unreasonably.

(3) A party's rejection of an offer in settlement will not of itself constitute unreasonable behaviour under paragraph (2)(g) but the court may take it into consideration when it is applying the unreasonableness test.

(4) The limits on costs imposed by this rule also apply to any fee or reward for acting on behalf of a party to the proceedings charged by a person exercising a right of audience by virtue of an order under section 11 of the Courts and Legal Services Act 1990 (a lay representative).

(5) Where—

(a) the financial value of a claim exceeds the limit for the small claims track; but

[1] Amended by the Civil Procedure (Amendment) Rules 1999 (SI 1999/1008), the Civil Procedure (Amendment No.4) Rules 2000 (SI 2000/2092), the Civil Procedure (Amendment) Rules 2006 (SI 2006/1689) and the Civil Procedure (Amendment No.3) Rules 2006 (SI 2006/3435).

(b) the claim has been allocated to the small claims track in accordance with rule 26.7(3),

the small claims track costs provisions will apply unless the parties agree that the fast track costs provisions are to apply.

(6) Where the parties agree that the fast track costs provisions are to apply, the claim and any appeal will be treated for the purposes of costs as if it were proceeding on the fast track except that trial costs will be in the discretion of the court and will not exceed the amount set out for the value of the claim in rule 46.2 (amount of fast track trial costs).

Effect of rule

27.14.1 This rule must be read in conjunction with para.7 of the Practice Direction which accompanies Pt 27. The costs recoverable in a small claims case are restricted but this is not a true 'no costs' rule. The award for costs and expenses in a small claims case fall into two categories; the award which is made in routine cases and those awarded where a party has behaved unreasonably (r.27.14(2)(d)). The award for costs is subject to the courts general discretion on costs which is exercised with regard to r.44.3 and as applied in the case of *Shah v Oliver* [2005] 10 C.L. 42, p.462, para.20.13.3. Failure to comply with directions may, for example, result in a successful party being deprived of even routine costs (see para.27.14(2) for what amounts to routine cost); see *Damhar v Arriva London Ltd October* [2007] C.L. 37; in which case the successful defendant who had not complied with a direction to serve the statement of a witness in advance of a hearing and subsequently relied on the evidence of that witness at the hearing was deprived of routine costs.

Rule 26.7(3), referred to in para.(5) of r.27.14 allows parties to consent to a claim being allocated to a case management track where the financial value of the claim exceeds the limit for that track.

Routine award for costs

27.14.2 Fixed solicitors costs (r.27.14 (2)(a)) attributable to issuing a claim may be put on the claim form in accordance with the sliding scale in table 1 to Pt 45. The terms of this rule do not provide for the routine award of fixed costs to a successful Pt 20 claimant: *Hibbert v Bates CC* [2002] 3 C.L. 57.

Court fees (r.27.14(3)(a)) include the issue fee and an allocation fee, if paid (no allocation fee is payable on claims under £1,500).

Expenses of a party or a witness (r.27.14(3)(a)) includes the cost of travelling to and from a hearing and overnight expenses. There is no upper limit on the sum recoverable and this is a point which parties may wish to bear in mind when considering the most convenient venue for a hearing (r.30.3) as travelling costs may add a significant sum to a claim of otherwise limited financial value for the purpose of attending a hearing.

Loss of earnings or loss of holiday or the cost of staying away from home (r.27.14(3)(b)) is limited to £50 per person (PD 27 para.7.3(1)).

Expert Fees (r.27.14(3)(d)) are limited to £200 for each expert (PD 27 para.7.3(2)) But note that the court must give permission in advance if an expert is to be used (see para.27.5.1).

Solicitors costs (Injunction claims only) (r.27.14(2)(b)) are limited to £260 (PD 27 para.7.2). This provision was first introduced under the former arbitration procedure to assist litigants claiming injunctions for repairs against landlords and rarely applies today as in any such case where the repairs are likely to cost £1000 or more is now allocated to the fast track (r.26.6(1)(b)(ii)). The provision to claim solicitors costs in injunction cases is not limited to housing disrepair cases.

Where a case does not qualify for the small claims track because the amount of the claim exceeds the usual financial limits but the parties agree that the case should be dealt with on the small claims track (sometimes called 'voluntary' referral to the small claims track) then the usual position is that the costs limits applicable to costs on the small claims track will apply; if the parties want fast track costs to apply, then a specific agreement must be made (r.27.14 (5)); This is a reversal of the position before October

2005[1] where fast track costs automatically applied where a case was voluntarily referred to the small claims track

Costs incurred before allocation: Where a case is allocated to the small claims track the small claims limitation on costs applies to work done before allocation but the allocation does not affect any order for costs made prior to allocation (r.44.11(1) and (2) and see also PD 44 para.15.1(2)). Before a claim is allocated to the small claims track the court is not restricted by the special rules which apply to the track (PD 44 para.15.1(1)).

Infant approval hearings are treated as allocated to the multi-track and the costs assessed accordingly even if the amount of the award might otherwise have justified an allocation to the Small claims track *W (A Child) v Robinson* [2002] 4 C.L. 50.

Possession claims

Where the parties consent for the case to be allocated to the small claims track, fast track costs apply (see para.27.1.3 and r.55.9(3)). **27.14.3**

Costs where a party has behaved unreasonably (r.27.14(2)(d))

There is no specific definition of unreasonable behaviour in the rules and little authority on the subject. It was thought by the Court of Appeal in *Afzal v Ford Motor Co Ltd* (1994) 4 All E.R. 720 it would be unreasonable to pursue a case which was both speculative and unsupportable and in *Martin v Sherwood*, June 9, 1995, unrep., the Court of Appeal said that the fabrication of an untruthful defence might be unreasonable. Cases are reported in Current Law on decisions taken by District Judges and they give a flavour of the type of behaviour which might attract an adverse costs order under this rule: these include; a party in a road traffic case which had rejected a settlement prior to the issue of proceedings which was manifestly to its advantage and had failed to make a clear and objective assessment of its own case acted unreasonably and was held to be liable to pay costs *Clohessy v Homes* [2004] C.L.Y. 418; persisting with a claim when information has been provided which makes it clear that the result of a case is a foregone conclusion: *Performing Right Society Ltd v Fioravant* [2006] 1 C.L. 62; *Hilton v ST1 Ltd* [2006] 3 C.L. 48; failing to serve comprehensible and concise particulars of claim and failing to remedy procedural defects when ordered to do so by the District Judge (*Hayes v Airtour Holidays Ltd (costs) CC* [2001] C.L.Y. 512); failing to give an appropriate defence to the claim or to make any payment despite the sum involved not being large and the case for claimant being clearly set out: *Performing Rights Society v Thompson* [2007] C.L. 38; stating in a defence that a key document exists and then failing to produce that document at the final hearing (*Snow v Frice CC* [2003] C.L.Y. 379); unreasonably contesting liability to a very late stage before giving up (*Mahmood v Watson CC* [2001] C.L.Y. 531; *Gillies v Goulding CC* [2003] C.L.Y. 376) but contrast *Lockley v LEA CC* [2001] C.L. September 71 where it was not unreasonable conduct to settle a case at a late stage after the service of evidence following the standard directions 14 days before the hearing; giving evidence at the hearing which contradicted the signed witness statement which was served prior to the hearing (*Owen v Burnham CC* [2001] C.L.Y. 534)—this was a credit hire case; making successive offers to settle up to the full claim close to the hearing amounting to "drip feeding" combined with failure to comply with the courts direction leading the other solicitors to believe that the defendant had no intention of defending the matter (*Fox v Murray CC* [2000] C.L.Y. 448). In a case where a defendant faced claims from a former employee the claimant embarked on a course of behaviour which included hugely exaggerating his claim, changing address without notifying the court, and unreasonably requesting an adjournment at the last moment. This case is exceptional and resulted in an award for costs assessed at £4,324. See *McPherson v Footlockers Ltd* [2008] C.L.Y. 41. **27.14.4**

In *Rennie v SpA Contractors Electrical* [2006] 1 C.L. 58, a losing party failed in his argument that unreasonable conduct is restricted to matters of procedure.

The court can take into account any offer of settlement when considering unreasonable behaviour; a party's rejection of an offer in settlement will not of itself constitute unreasonable behaviour. The court has power under r.36.2(5) to order Pt 36 costs consequences in a small claim even though Pt 36 does not generally apply to small claims (r.27.2(1)(f)).

See also *Reed Employment plc v M Gaze & Co Ltd* [2007] C.L. 34 where failure to

[1] Introduced by the Civil Procedure (Amendment No.3) Rules 2005).

engage with mediation was successfully relied on in an application for costs under r.27.14(2).

Summary assessment of costs for unreasonable behaviour

27.14.5 Where a party has behaved unreasonably there will be a summary assessment of costs (r.27.14(2)(d)).

Claim reallocated from the small claims track to another track

27.15 **27.15 Where a claim is allocated to the small claims track and subsequently reallocated to another track, rule 27.14 (costs on the small claims track) will cease to apply after the claim has been reallocated, and the fast track or multi-track costs rules will apply from the date of reallocation.**

Costs when a small claims case leaves the small claims track

27.15.1 This rule provides that where a District Judge reallocates a small claims case to another track that the costs incurred to date are subject to the small claims rules and the costs incurred thereafter are subject to the rules applicable to the other track. This is in effect a repeat of the costs r.44.11.

Case Management Directions

27PD.0.1 The allocation stage is crucial for case management because this is usually the only time that a District Judge sees the file before the final hearing. The District Judge may require clarification of the case at allocation stage. The Practice Direction contains lists of information and documentation that the court usually needs in particular types of cases (Appendix A). The District Judge will give straightforward directions for the disclosure of information, including documents and witness statements in advance of the hearing. Standard directions (Appendix B) draw attention to the rules which prevent a party calling expert evidence unless they have obtained permission in advance and encourage the parties to negotiate a settlement. The standard forms of wording contained in the Practice direction are not exclusive and the District Judge may give suitable directions tailored to each case, including use of special directions (Appendix C).

PRACTICE DIRECTION—SMALL CLAIMS TRACK

This Practice Direction supplements CPR Part 27

1. Judges

1. The functions of the court described in Part 27 which are to be carried out by a judge will generally be carried out by a district judge but may be carried out by a Circuit Judge. **27PD.1**

2. Case Management Directions

2.1 Rule 27.4 explains how directions will be given, and rule 27.6 contains provisions about the holding of a preliminary hearing and the court's powers at such a hearing. **27PD.2**

2.2 Appendix A sets out details of the case that the court usually needs in the type of case described. Appendix B sets out the Standard Directions that the court may give. Appendix C sets out Special Directions that the court may give.

2.3 Before allocating the claim to the Small Claims Track and giving directions for a hearing the court may require a party to give further information about that party's case.

2.4 A party may ask the court to give particular directions about the conduct of the case.

2.5 In deciding whether to make an order for exchange of witness statements the court will have regard to the following—

(a) whether either or both the parties are represented;

(b) the amount in dispute in the proceedings;

(c) the nature of the matters in dispute;

(d) whether the need for any party to clarify his case can better be dealt with by an order under paragraph 2.3;

(e) the need for the parties to have access to justice without undue formality, cost or delay.

3. Representation at a Hearing

3.1 In this paragraph: **27PD.3**

(1) a lawyer means a barrister, a solicitor or a legal executive employed by a solicitor, and

(2) a lay representative means any other person.

3.2(1) A party may present his own case at a hearing or a lawyer or lay representative may present it for him.

(2) The Lay Representatives (Right of Audience) Order 1999 provides that a lay representative may not exercise any right of audience:—

(a) where his client does not attend the hearing;

(b) at any stage after judgment; or

(c) on any appeal brought against any decision made by the district judge in the proceedings.

(3) However the court, exercising its general discretion to hear anybody, may hear a lay representative even in circumstances excluded by the Order.

(4) Any of its officers or employees may represent a corporate party.

4. Small Claim Hearing

27PD.4 **4.1**(1) The general rule is that a small claim hearing will be in public.

(2) The judge may decide to hold it in private if:

(a) the parties agree, or

(b) a ground mentioned in rule 39.2(3) applies.

(3) A hearing or part of a hearing which takes place other than at the court, for example at the home or business premises of a party, will not be in public.

4.2 A hearing that takes place at the court will generally be in the judge's room but it may take place in a courtroom.

4.3 Rule 27.8 allows the court to adopt any method of proceeding that it considers to be fair and to limit cross-examination. The judge may in particular:

(1) ask questions of any witness himself before allowing any other person to do so,

(2) ask questions of all or any of the witnesses himself before allowing any other person to ask questions of any witnesses,

(3) refuse to allow cross-examination of any witness until all the witnesses have given evidence in chief,

(4) limit cross-examination of a witness to a fixed time or to a particular subject or issue, or both.

5. Recording Evidence and the Giving of Reasons

27PD.5 **5.1** A hearing that takes place at the court will be tape recorded by the court. A party may obtain a transcript of such a recording on payment of the proper transcriber's charges.

5.2 Attention is drawn to section 9 of the Contempt of Court Act 1981 (which deals with the unauthorised use of tape recorders in court) and to the Practice Direction ([1981] 1 W.L.R. 1526) which relates to it.

5.3(1) The judge may give reasons for his judgment as briefly and simply as the nature of the case allows.

(2) He will normally do so orally at the hearing, but he may give them later at a hearing either orally or in writing.

5.4 Where the judge decides the case without a hearing under rule 27.10 or a party who has given notice under rule 27.9(1) does not attend the hearing, the judge will prepare a note of his reasons and the court will send a copy to each party.

5.5 Nothing in this practice direction affects the duty of a judge at the request of a party to make a note of the matters referred to in section 80 of the County Courts Act 1984.

6. Non-attendance of a Party at a Hearing

27PD.6 **6.1** Attention is drawn to rule 27.9 (which enables a party to give notice that he will not attend a final hearing and sets out the effect of his giving such notice and of not doing so), and to paragraph 3 above.

6.2 Nothing in those provisions affects the general power of the court to adjourn a hearing, for example where a party who wishes to attend a hearing on the date fixed cannot do so for a good reason.

7. Costs

7.1 Attention is drawn to rule 27.14 which contains provisions about the costs which may be ordered to be paid by one party to another. **27PD.7**

7.2 The amount which a party may be ordered to pay under rule 27.14(2)(b) (for legal advice and assistance in claims including an injunction or specific performance) is a sum not exceeding £260.

7.3 The amounts which a party may be ordered to pay under rule 27.14(3)(c) (loss of earnings) and (d) (experts' fees) are:

(1) for the loss of earnings or loss of leave of each party or witness due to attending a hearing or staying away from home for the purpose of attending a hearing, a sum not exceeding £50 per day for each person, and

(2) for expert's fees, a sum not exceeding £200 for each expert.

(As to recovery of pre-allocation costs in a case in which an admission by the defendant has reduced the amount in dispute to a figure below £5,000, reference should be made to paragraph 7.4 of the Practice Direction supplementing CPR Part 26 and to paragraph 5.1(3) of the Costs Directions relating to CPR Part 44.)

8. Appeals

8.1 Part 52 deals with appeals and attention is drawn to that Part and the accompanying practice direction. **27PD.8**

8A An appellant's notice in small claims must be filed and served in Form N164.

8.2 Where the court dealt with the claim to which the appellant is a party:

(1) under rule 27.10 without a hearing; or

(2) in his absence because he gave notice under rule 27.9 requesting the court to decide the claim in his absence,

an application for permission to appeal must be made to the appeal court.

8.3 Where an appeal is allowed the appeal court will, if possible, dispose of the case at the same time without referring the claim to the lower court or ordering a new hearing. It may do so without hearing further evidence.

Appeals **27PD.8.1**

See para.27.0.4.

APPENDIX A

INFORMATION AND DOCUMENTATION THE COURT USUALLY NEEDS IN PARTICULAR TYPES OF CASE **27PD.9**

ROAD ACCIDENT CASES (where the information or documentation is available)

- witness statements (including statements from the parties themselves);
- invoices and estimates for repairs;
- agreements and invoices for any car hire costs;
- the Police accident report;

- sketch plan which should wherever possible be agreed;
- photographs of the scene of the accident and of the damage.

BUILDING DISPUTES, REPAIRS, GOODS SOLD AND SIMILAR CONTRACTUAL CLAIMS (where the information or documentation is available)

- any written contract;
- photographs;
- any plans;
- a list of works complained of;
- a list of any outstanding works;
- any relevant estimate, invoice or receipt including any relating to repairs to each of the defects;
- invoices for work done or goods supplied;
- estimates for work to be completed;
- a valuation of work done to date.

LANDLORD AND TENANT CLAIMS (where the information or documentation is available)

- a calculation of the amount of any rent alleged to be owing, showing amounts received;
- details of breaches of an agreement which are said to justify withholding any deposit itemised showing how the total is made up and with invoices and estimates to support them.

BREACH OF DUTY CASES (negligence, deficient professional services and the like)

Details of the following:

- what it is said by the claimant was done negligently by the defendant;
- why it is said that the negligence is the fault of the defendant;
- what damage is said to have been caused;
- what injury or losses have been suffered and how any (and each) sum claimed has been calculated;
- the response of the defendant to each of the above.

APPENDIX B

27PD.10 **STANDARD DIRECTIONS**

(For use where the district judge specifies no other directions)

THE COURT DIRECTS:

Each party must deliver to every other party and to the court office copies of all documents on which he intends to rely at the hearing no later than [........] [14 days before the hearing]. (These should include the letter making the claim and the reply.)

The original documents must be brought to the hearing.

[Notice of hearing date and time allowed.]

The parties are encouraged to contact each other with a view to trying to settle the case or narrow the issues. However the court must be informed immediately if the case is settled by agreement before the hearing date.

No party may rely at the hearing on any report from an expert unless express permission has been granted by the court beforehand. Anyone wishing to rely on an expert must write to the court immediately on receipt of this Order and seek permission, giving an explanation why the assistance of an expert is necessary.

NOTE: Failure to comply with the directions may result in the case being adjourned and in the party at fault having to pay costs. The parties are encouraged always to try to settle the case by negotiating with each other. The court must be informed immediately if the case is settled before the hearing.

APPENDIX C

SPECIAL DIRECTIONS 27PD.11

The .... must clarify his case.

He must do this by delivering to the court office and to the .... no later than ....

[a list of ....]

[details of ....]

The .... must allow the .... to inspect by appointment within ... days of receiving a request to do so.

The hearing will not take place at the court but at ....

The ....must bring to court at the hearing the ....

Signed statements setting out the evidence of all witnesses on whom each party intends to rely must be prepared and copies included in the documents mentioned in paragraph 1. This includes the evidence of the parties themselves and of any other witness, whether or not he is going to come to court to give evidence.

The court may decide not to take into account a document [or video] or the evidence of a witness if these directions have not been complied with.

If he does not [do so] [...] his [Claim][Defence] [and Counterclaim] will be struck out and (specify consequence).

It appears to the court that expert evidence is necessary on the issue of... and that that evidence should be given by a single expert to be instructed by the parties jointly. If the parties cannot agree about who to choose and what arrangements to make about paying his fee, either party MUST apply to the court for further directions. The evidence is to be given in the form of a written report. Either party may ask the expert questions and must then send copies of the questions and replies to the other party and to the court. Oral expert evidence may be allowed in exceptional circumstances but only after a *further order of the court.* Attention is drawn to the limit of £200 on expert's fees that may be recovered.

If either party intends to show a video as evidence he must—

(a) contact the court at once to make arrangements for him to do so, because the court may not have the necessary equipment, and

(b) provide the other party with a copy of the video or the opportunity to see it at least.......... days before the hearing.

PART 28

THE FAST TRACK

Contents

Editorial introduction

28.0.2 The "fast track" is an innovation of the CPR. One of the unintended consequences of the reforms effected by the CCR 1981 (accentuated by the High Court and County Courts Jurisdiction Order 1991 which further increased the jurisdiction of county courts) was to make litigation in the county courts ever more complex and expensive. Trial in a county court was not simpler and not necessarily cheaper than trial in the High Court. To some extent this problem was ameliorated by a "small claim" regime (see now Pt 27) but this served to highlight the high cost of cases just above the small claims limit. For many years it had been obvious that the county court needed a new procedure rather more detailed than the "small claims" procedure but rather less detailed than the full procedural code necessitated by more complex cases. The "fast track" has been designed to meet that need. Cases on the fast track have more pre-trial stages than cases on the small claims track (compare Pts 27 and 28) but less than most cases on the multi-track (compare Pts 28 and 29).

The fast track is intended as a limited procedure designed to take straightforward cases to trial within a short but reasonable timescale. Rule 26.6 provides that the fast track is the normal case management track for any claim for which the small claims track is not the normal track and which has a value, for proceedings issued on or after April 6, 2009, of not more than £25,000 and, for proceedings issued before that date, of not more than £15,000. It should be noted that para.(1) of r.26.6 has the effect of excluding from the small claims track, and allocating to the fast track instead, certain personal injury claims and certain claims by tenants against landlords that would otherwise be allocated to the former track.Thus a personal injury case is allocated to the fast track if the financial value of the general damages claim exceeds £1000 (rather that £5000), as is a claim by a tenant of residential premises against his landlord for damages for disrepair/injunction where the value exceeds £1000. (Note also r.26.7(4) (excluding certain tenants' claims in respect of harassment and unlawful eviction).)

Initially district judges and circuit judges have concurrent jurisdiction to hear trials of cases on the fast track. (Practice Direction—Allocation of cases to levels of judiciary: 2BPD.1.)

Related sources

28.0.3
- Practice Direction (The Fast Track), para.28PD.1
- Part 3 (The Courts Case Management Powers)
- Part 26 (Case Management—Preliminary Stage)
- Part 31 (Disclosure and Inspection of Documents)
- Part 32 (Evidence)
- Part 35 (Experts and Assessors)
- Part 39 (Miscellaneous Provisions Relating to Hearings)
- Part 43 (Scope of Costs Rules and Definitions)
- Part 44 (General Rules about Costs)
- Part 46 (Fast Track Trial Costs)

Forms

- **N154** Notice of allocation to the fast track 28.0.4
- **N170** Listing Questionnaire (Pre-trial checklist)

Scope of this Part

28.1 This Part contains general provisions about management of cases allocated to the fast track and applies only to cases allocated to that track. 28.1

(Part 27 sets out the procedure for claims allocated to the small claims track).

(Part 29 sets out the procedure for claims allocated to the multi-track).

Effect of rule

There is no "automatic allocation" to a track. Cases are allocated by the judge upon receipt of the "allocation questionnaire" (see rr.26.3 and 26.5). See r.26.6 for the scope of each of the three tracks and in particular r.26.6(4) for the scope of the fast track. 28.1.1

General provisions

28.2—(1) When it allocates a case to the fast track, the court will give directions for the management of the case and set a timetable for the steps to be taken between the giving of the directions and the trial. 28.2

(2) When it gives directions, the court will—

(a) fix the trial date; or

(b) fix a period, not exceeding 3 weeks, within which the trial is to take place.

(3) The trial date or trial period will be specified in the notice of allocation.

(4) The standard period between the giving of directions and the trial will be not more than 30 weeks.

(5) The court's power to award trial costs is limited in accordance with Part 46.

"the court will give directions for the management of the case ..."

It is of the essence of the fast track that pre-trial preparation should be the minimum necessary for the particular case (see further the "overriding objective" in Pt 1). 28.2.1

Pre-action protocols

The pre-action protocols have a significant role in the new regime enacted by the CPR. Nowhere is this role more significant than in the context of fast track cases. As a general rule parties will have to comply with the pre-action protocol relevant to the case. The courts will expect this and will use the case management powers (see Pt 3) to ensure that no party can take advantage of another, by non-compliance with the spirit of the pre-action protocols. In practice, both parties will have to undertake significant preparation of a case before proceedings are issued in anticipation of the court setting a strict timetable on allocation of the case and insisting that it be complied with. As to variation of the case management timetable see r.28.4, but note in particular that parties cannot agree any variation which would delay the trial. 28.2.2

There are now nine pre-action protocols (set out at paras C2–001 et seq.). However, the spirit of the protocols applies to all cases. Paragraphs 4.2–4.10 of the Practice Direction—Protocols came into force on April 1, 2003 and impose specific obligations on the proposed parties (see Practice Directions—Protocols—see C2–001 at para.4).

"the court will fix the trial date or fix a period ... within which the trial is to take place"

28.2.3 In practice it is more likely that the court will fix a "trial window" of one, two or three weeks rather than give a fixed trial date. However some courts do now fix a trial date when giving case management directions. If that is not the practice of the particular court, it can be asked to fix a trial date at the allocation stage if there is a particular reason why it should do so. Early fixing of the trial date or "trial window"—and insisting upon it—is of the essence of the fast-track.

Since October 1, 2007, in addition to the court fee payable on filing of the pre trial checklist, a new hearing fee of £500 is payable for cases allocated to the fast track (see the Civil Proceedings (Amendment)(No.2) Order 2007 (SI 2007/2176).

"not more than 30 weeks"

28.2.4 The aim of this rule is clear. All fast track cases should be compromised or tried within a period of 30 weeks from the giving of directions.

Split trial

28.2.5 One consequence of the fast track regime has been an increase in the number of cases where liability is ordered to be tried separately from and before the issue of quantum. The power to order a split trial is found in r.3.1(2)(i). If the claimant fails on liability a significant costs saving is invariably achieved and the case is concluded at a much earlier stage. If the claimant succeeds on liability it is more probable than not that quantum will be agreed without a further hearing. Often, due to non-availability of experts, it will not be possible to fix a trial date within the 30 week period and ordering a trial on liability only is one way to overcome this difficulty. Furthermore, a case is allocated to the fast track only if the trial is likely to last for no longer than one day and oral expert evidence is limited to one expert per party in relation to any expert field and expert evidence in two fields only (see r.26.6(5)). By narrowing the issue for trial the court will be able to allocate to the fast-track a case that might otherwise have had to be allocated to the multi-track. It must be anticipated that, where a case is within the financial limits of the fast-track, the court will make every effort to allocate it to the fast-track.

"trial costs"

28.2.6 One of Lord Woolf's "Access to Justice" recommendations which has not yet been enacted in the CPR is a recommendation for a fixed costs regime for fast-track cases. There is a fixed costs regime only for the trial itself: see generally Pt 46—Fast track trial costs and the table set out in r.46.2 which has been amended by the Civil Procedure (Amendment) Rules 2007 (SI 2007/2204) in relation to fast track trial which commence on or after October 1, 2007..

Directions

28.3 **28.3—(1) The matters to be dealt with by directions under rule 28.2(1) include—**

(a) disclosure of documents;

(b) service of witness statements; and

(c) expert evidence.

(2) If the court decides not to direct standard disclosure, it may—

(a) direct that no disclosure take place; or

(b) specify the documents or the classes of documents which the parties must disclose.

(Rule 31.6 explains what is meant by standard disclosure.)

(Rule 26.6(5) deals with limitations in relation to expert evidence and the likely length of trial in fast track cases.)

Scope of provision

28.3.1 In a fast-track case, when giving directions the only matters which need to be addressed are the fixing of the trial date or "trial window" and the three matters mentioned in r.28.3(1): disclosure, witness statements, expert evidence. Parties will have to undertake more pre-issue preparation than was formerly the case (see above commentary on "Pre-action protocols" and "Split trial" at paras 28.2.2 and 28.2.5 respectively). Disclosure will be "standard disclosure" (see r.31.6) or less. Exchange of witness statements will always be ordered. If either party is relying on expert evidence (note the limitations in r.26.6(5) and see generally Pt 35) the court will have to give directions as to service of experts reports. Permission is always required to adduce expert evidence (r.35.4(1)). Usually a single joint expert will be directed as this is a proportionate and cost effective way to proceed and so in accordance with the overriding objective. The court will bear in mind that normally trial of a fast-track case "is likely to last for no longer than one day" (see r.26.6(5)).

Cases exceeding fast track value limit

A case which is valued at over £25,000 is normally allocated to the multi-track. The court cannot allocate it to the fast track "unless all the parties consent to the allocation ..." (see r.26.7(3)). However, directions on the multi-track are specific to the case and therefore, for example, if the case only just exceeds £25,000 and the court considers the case otherwise suitable for the fast track the court could give directions in a multi-track case which are identical to the directions it could have given had it been on the fast track. The only practical difference would then be that the fast-track fixed trial costs (see r.46.2) would not apply. Even so, where a trial "has lasted not more than one day" the trial judge will still summarily assess the costs (see para.44PD.7). **28.3.2**

If a late application to amend is made which, if granted, would take the value of the claim above £25,000, the case does not have to be reallocated as the court has an unfettered discretion under CPR r.26.10. The amount by which the financial value of a claim exceeded the normal limit for a track as a result of an amendment was highly relevant. A District Judge could allow an amendment and continue with a claim on the fast track (see *Maguire v Molin* [2002] EWCA Civ 1083; [2003] 1 W.L.R. 644; [2002] 4 All E.R. 32).

Split trial

See above commentary to r.28.2 at para.28.2.5. **28.3.3**

Agreed directions

Parties are encouraged to agree directions. It is good practice to include with the allocation questionnaires when it is filed a draft of the agreed directions, or those sought if they are not agreed. Specimen directions are set out in the Practice Direction to Pt 28 at para.28PD.1. There should not normally be any need for a case management conference in a case allocated to the fast track. **28.3.4**

Expert Evidence

Rule 26.6(5) provides that the fast track is the normal track for claims for which the small claims track is not the normal track and which have a financial value of not more than £25,000 only if the court considers that the trial is likely to last no longer than one day with oral expert evidence limited to one expert per party in relation to any expert field and expert evidence in two expert fields. Thus that rule envisages a maximum of four experts giving oral evidence. However, r.35.5 clearly envisages expert evidence being in writing: "if a claim is on the fast track, the court will not direct an expert to attend a hearing unless it is necessary to do so in the interests of justice". See further the directions on expert evidence in the Standard Directions included in the Practice Direction which supplements Pt 28 at para.28PD.13. **28.3.5**

The court's general approach is:

(i) to limit expert evidence to that which is essential (r.35.4);

(ii) to limit oral expert evidence and exclude it altogether whenever possible by relying on a written report complying with Pt 35 (r.35.5).

In furtherance of this approach the court will make full use of its powers to ensure compliance with pre-action protocols, to direct evidence by a single joint expert (r.35.7) and to limit a party to putting written questions to an expert (r.35.6) rather than calling another.

Variation of case management timetable[1]

28.4 **28.4—(1) A party must apply to the court if he wishes to vary the date which the court has fixed for—**

(a) the return of a pre-trial check list under rule 28.5;

(b) the trial; or

(c) the trial period.

(2) Any date set by the court or these Rules for doing any act may not be varied by the parties if the variation would make it necessary to vary any of the dates mentioned in paragraph (1).

(Rule 2.11 allows the parties to vary a date by written agreement except where the rules provide otherwise or the court orders otherwise.)

Effect of rule

28.4.1 A case management timetable, once set, should be complied with. The aim of the rules is to set a realistic timetable which all must then honour. However, minor variations (e.g. extending by a few days time for exchange of witness statements) can be agreed by the parties without troubling the court: see r.2.11 and note that any such agreement must be in writing. However, the trial date (or "trial window" if the trial date is not yet fixed: see r.28.2 above) is immutable. Accordingly so is the date for return of the pre-trial checklist.

These dates cannot be varied by agreement and a party who wishes to vary any of the dates listed in r.28.4(1) must apply to the court. (See Pt 23 for general rules regarding applications.) It must be anticipated that the court will not be pre-disposed to delaying the trial and very cogent arguments and reasons will be required in order to achieve it. "Litigants and lawyers must be in no doubt that the court will regard the postponement of a trial as an order of last resort. The court may exercise its power to require a party as well as his legal representative to attend court at a hearing where such an order is to be sought"—per para.5.4 (6) of PD 28. In the unlikely event of the court granting an adjournment costs sanctions must be anticipated.

Amendment (r.28.4)

28.4.2 By the Civil Procedure (Amendment) Rules 2002 (SI 2002/2058), r.8, "pre-trial check list" is substituted for "listing questionnaire" in para.(a) of r.28.4(1). This amendment, which is a consequence of the substitution of r.28.5 (see para.28.5.1 below), came into effect on December 2, 2002.

28.5 **Pre-trial checklist (listing questionnaire)**[2]

28.5—(1) **The court will send the parties a pre-trial check list (listing questionnaire) for completion and return by the date specified in the notice of allocation unless it considers that the claim can proceed to trial without the need for a pre-trial check list.**

(2) The date specified for filing a pre-trial check list will not be more than 8 weeks before the trial date or the beginning of the trial period.

(3) If no party files the completed pre-trial checklist by the date specified, the court will order that unless a completed pre-trial checklist is filed within 7 days from service of that order, the claim, defence and any counterclaim will be struck out without further order of the court.

(4) If—

[1] Amended by the Civil Procedure (Amendment) Rules 2002 (SI 2002/2058).
[2] Amended by the Civil Procedure (Amendment) Rules 2002 (SI 2002/2058).

(a) a party files a completed pre-trial checklist but another party does not;

(b) a party has failed to give all the information requested by the pre-trial checklist; or

(c) the court considers that a hearing is necessary to enable it to decide what directions to give in order to complete preparation of the case for trial,

the court may give such directions as it thinks appropriate.

Effect of rule

The court will have fixed a trial date or (more likely) a "trial window" of one, two or three weeks when it gave directions upon allocation (see r.28.2). The trial date or end of the trial window will be not more than 30 weeks from the directions. The court needs to make final listing arrangements (especially where a fixed date has not yet been given) as the period draws to a close. Further, it is anticipated that a significant proportion of cases will have been settled during the trial preparation period and will not now require a trial (settlement rate of fast-track cases is very high). Rule 28.5 therefore requires the court to send out a "pre-trial check list". This will be done about 10 weeks before the trial date or beginning of the trial window. The precise date for the return of the pre-trial check list is specified in the notice of allocation and that date "will not be more than 8 weeks before the trial date or beginning of the trial window". **28.5.1**

In effect the rules envisage directions being given in two stages. The first and the main stage is upon allocation. However, listing provides a second and final opportunity to deal with further directions. This is essentially "fine tuning".

It is essential for all parties to return the pre-trial check list by the specified date. If a party returns a pre-trial checklist without giving all requested information, the court may give directions requiring that party to provide the information or may order a pre trial review when the party in default may be ordered to pay the costs

For the purposes of the automatic orders pilot scheme operating in proceedings in certain county courts since October 1, 2008, r.28.5 is modified (see Practice Direction—Automatic Orders Pilot Scheme, para.51BPD.1 below). (Certain provisions in Pt 26 are also modified; see para.28.4.1 above.)

Amendment (r.28.5)

By the Civil Procedure (Amendment) Rules 2002 (SI 2002/2058) r.9, the "listing questionnaire" provided for by r.28.5 is renamed the "pre-trial checklist" to reflect more accurately the purpose of the document (see also amendment to r.29.6), and by r.8 various consequential amendments are made to r.28.4 and r.28.6 (and to r.44.15) to provide for this. These amendments came into effect on December 2, 2002. **28.5.2**

No Pre-trial checklist

As from October 1, 2005, if no pre-trial checklist is filed, the court will strike out the claim/defence and counterclaim unless the pre-trial checklist is filed within seven days of the debarring order which the court will make. This will occur automatically on the expiry of the seven days andno further order will be required, The result will be that a party in default of this will need to apply for relief from sanctions under r.3.9 if he wishes the claim/defence and counterclaim to be reinstated. Any such application must be supported by evidence (see r.3.9(2)) and should deal not only with the matters set out in that rule but should also explain why the pre trial checklist was not filed by the original date it was due and why the debarring order was not complied with. **28.5.3**

Fixing or confirming the trial date and giving directions[1]

28.6—(1) As soon as practicable after the date specified for filing a completed pre-trial check list the court will— **28.6**

(a) fix the date for the trial (or, if it has already done so, confirm that date);

[1] Amended by the Civil Procedure (Amendment) Rules 2002 (SI 2002/2058).

(b) give any directions for the trial, including a trial timetable, which it considers appropriate; and

(c) specify any further steps that need to be taken before trial.

(2) The court will give the parties at least 3 weeks' notice of the date of the trial unless, in exceptional circumstances, the court directs that shorter notice will be given.

"pre-trial checklist"

28.6.1 See r.28.5.

By the Civil Procedure (Amendment) Rules 2002 (SI 2002/2058) r.9, the "listing questionnaire" provided for by r.28.5 is renamed the "pre-trial checklist" with effect from December 2, 2002. By r.8, as from that date, "'pre-trial check list'" will be substituted for listing questionnaire" in r.28.6(1) (see further para.28.5.2 above).

"fix the date for trial"

28.6.2 Although the court has the option of fixing a trial date at the allocation stage it is more likely that the court will have fixed a trial window of one, two or three weeks, ending not more than 30 weeks ahead. Accordingly all parties and witnesses will have knowledge of the approximate trial date. Upon the filing of a completed pre-trial check list the court will now fix the precise trial date and give the parties at least 3 weeks' notice of it (in exceptional circumstances, shorter notice: see r.28.6(2)).

"directions for the trial"

28.6.3 As noted in the commentary to r.28.5 (see para.28.5.1), the "listing stage" provides a second and final opportunity for the court to give directions. It is envisaged that in the majority of cases the only further directions required will be for the trial timetable.

"trial timetable"

28.6.4 Rule 26.6(5) provides that the fast track is the normal track for cases within its financial limit ("not more than £25,000") "only if the court considers that the trial is likely to last for no longer than one day". The Practice Direction supplementing Pt 28 states that "one day" means five hours (i.e. 10.30am to 4.30pm or thereabouts). It has always been envisaged that, for fast-track cases, in addition to the case-management rules, some firm judicial control of the trial itself will be required. Parties—and especially advocates—need to know in advance how much time has been allocated to the case. Accordingly a trial timetable is necessary and will be given at the listing stage. Rule 26.6(1) requires the court to give a trial timetable. See also Pt 39 and in particular note that r.39.4 provides that when the court sets a timetable for trial it will do so in consultation with the parties. The Practice Direction supplementing Pt 28 (see para.28PD.1) contains the format for a trial timetable.

Specimen Trial Timetable for trial of a case allocated to the Fast Track

28.6.5 Neither r.28.6 nor the Practice Direction supplementing Pt 28 contains a specimen timetable although r.28.6(1)(b) requires the court to give one. A typical timetable is as follows:-

Claimant's opening		10 min
Defendant's opening		10 min
Cross-examination of Claimant's witnesses	1 hr	15 min
Re-examination		15 min
Cross-examination of Defendant's witness	1 hr	15 min
Re-examination		15 min
Defendant's submissions		20 min
Claimant's submissions		20 min
Judge's "thinking time" and judgment		30 min
Costs and consequential orders		30 min

5 hr	00 mins

This timetable makes no provision for evidence in chief as witness statements stand as evidence in chief (r.32.5) and expert evidence is generally given in the form of a written report (r.35.5). The trial judge will have pre-read the papers. It has not been traditional for the defendant to be given an opening speech. However, because of the limited way in which evidence is now given most judges prefer to give the defendant this opportunity to add to the claimants' opening so that the judge is satisfied that he has all the issues to be decided in mind before the rest of the trial proceeds.

A period of five hours is the maximum for a trial on the fast-track: not all cases will require as long as this and the timetable will be varied accordingly.

A fast-track trial concludes with a summary assessment of costs (see para.48PD.5).

Conduct of trial

28.7 Unless the trial judge otherwise directs, the trial will be conducted in accordance with any order previously made. 28.7

Effect of rule

In fast-track cases a "trial timetable" may have been given at the allocation stage or, more usually, it is directed at the listing stage (see r.28.6). Many other rules have consequences for the conduct of the trial (e.g. an order under r.35.4 giving—or refusing—permission to a party to call an expert witness). **28.7.1**

If a party is dissatisfied with a direction the proper course is to appeal, not wait until the trial in the hope that the trial judge will take a different view.

The general rule is that "the trial will be conducted in accordance with any order previously made". Rule 28.7 does enable the trial judge to "otherwise direct". The trial judge is likely to do that only in non-controversial circumstances. Time is limited at a fast-track trial and the trial judge is most unlikely to allow part of it to be used up by what is, in effect, an application to vary or appeal directions previously given. Nevertheless the principle remains that the trial judge is in charge of his/her own court and in an exceptional appropriate case has power to depart from an order previously made.

Trial bundle

See r.39.5. Directions as to what the trial bundle should contain will be given at allocation or listing. See further the Practice Direction supplementing Pt 28 at para.28PD.1.The trial bundle should be limited to those documents/statements/reports actually required at trial. The bundle should begin with an index and a case summary detailing the issues to be decided by the court. **28.7.2**

PRACTICE DIRECTION—THE FAST TRACK

This Practice Direction supplements CPR Part 28

1. General

28PD.1 **1.1** Attention is drawn in particular to the following Parts of the Civil Procedure Rules:

Part 1	The overriding objective
Part 3	The court's case management powers
Part 26	Case management—preliminary stage
Part 31	Disclosure and inspection of documents
Parts 32–34	Evidence
Part 35	Experts and assessors

and to the practice directions which relate to those Parts.

1.2 Attention is also drawn to:

Rule 26.6(5)—which makes provision about limitations on expert evidence and the length of trial in fast track cases.

Part 46—Fast Track Trial Costs.

Rule 19.4A and the practice direction supplementing it on joining the Crown in certain cases raising Convention rights issues.

2. Case Management

28PD.2 **2.1** Case management of cases allocated to the fast track will generally be by directions given at two stages in the case:

(1) at allocation to the track, and

(2) on the filing of pre-trial check lists (listing questionnaires).

2.2 The court will seek whenever possible to give directions at those stages only and to do so without the need for a hearing to take place. It will expect to do so with the co-operation of the parties.

2.3 The court will however hold a hearing to give directions whenever it appears necessary or desirable to do so, and where this happens because of the default of a party or his legal representative it will usually impose a sanction.

2.4 The court may give directions at any hearing on the application of a party or on its own initiative.

2.5 When any hearing has been fixed it is the duty of the parties to consider what directions the court should be asked to give and to make any application that may be appropriate to be dealt with at that hearing.

2.6 When the court fixes a hearing to give directions it will give the parties at least 3 days notice of the hearing.

2.7 Appendix A contains forms of directions. When making an order the court will as far as possible base its order on those forms. Agreed directions which the parties file and invite the court to make should also be based on those forms.

2.8 Where a party needs to apply for a direction of a kind not included in the case management timetable which has been set (for example to amend his statement of case or for further information to be given by another party) he must do so as soon as possible so as to minimise the need to change that timetable.

2.9 Courts will make arrangements to ensure that applications and other hearings are listed promptly to avoid delay in the conduct of cases.

3. Directions on Allocation

3.1 Attention is drawn to the court's duty under rule 28.2(2) to set a case management timetable and to fix a trial date or a trial period, and to the matters which are to be dealt with by directions under rule 28.3(1) **28PD.3**

3.2 The court will seek to tailor its directions to the needs of the case and the steps of which it is aware that the parties have already taken to prepare the case. In particular it will have regard to the extent to which Practice Direction (Pre-Action Conduct) or any practice direction (pre-action conduct) protocol has or (as the case may be) has not been complied with.

3.3 At this stage the court's first concern will be to ensure that the issues between the parties be identified and that the necessary evidence is prepared and disclosed.

3.4 The court may have regard to any document filed by a party with his allocation questionnaire containing further information provided that the document states either that its contents have been agreed with every other party or that it has been served on every other party and when it was served.

3.5 If:

(1) the parties have filed agreed directions for the management of the case, and

(2) the court considers that the proposals are suitable,

it may approve them and give directions in the terms proposed.

3.6(1) To obtain the court's approval the agreed directions must:

(a) set out a timetable by reference to calendar dates for the taking of steps for the preparation of the case,

(b) include a date or a period (the trial period) when it is proposed that the trial will take place,

(c) include provision about disclosure of documents, and

(d) include provision about both factual and expert evidence.

(2) The latest proposed date for the trial or the end of the trial period must be not later than 30 weeks from the date the directions order is made.

(3) The trial period must not be longer than 3 weeks.

(4) The provision in (1)(c) above may:

(a) limit disclosure to standard disclosure between all parties or to less than that, and/or

(b) direct that disclosure will take place by the supply of *copy documents* without a list, but it must in that case either direct that the parties must serve a disclosure statement with the copies or record that they have agreed to disclose in that way without such a statement.

(5) The provision in (1)(d) may be to the effect that no expert evidence is required.

3.7 Directions agreed by the parties should also where appropriate contain provisions about:

(1) the filing of any reply or amended statement of case that may be required,
(2) dates for the service of requests for further information under the practice direction supplementing Part 18 and questions to experts under rule 35.6 and when they are to be dealt with,
(3) the disclosure of evidence,
(4) the use of a single joint expert, or in cases where the use of a single expert has not been agreed the exchange and agreement of expert evidence (including whether exchange is to be simultaneous or sequential) and without prejudice discussions of the experts.

3.8 If the court does not approve the agreed directions filed by the parties but decides that it will give directions on its own initiative without a hearing, it will take them into account in deciding what directions to give.

3.9 Where the court is to give directions on its own initiative and it is not aware of any steps taken by the parties other than the service of statements of case, its general approach will be:

(1) to give directions for the filing and service of any further information required to clarify either party's case,
(2) to direct standard disclosure between the parties,
(3) to direct the disclosure of witness statements by way of simultaneous exchange,
(4) to give directions for a single joint expert unless there is good reason not to do so,
(5) in cases where directions for a single expert are not given:
 (a) to direct disclosure of experts' reports by way of simultaneous exchange, and
 (b) if experts' reports are not agreed, to direct a discussion between the experts for the purpose set out in rule 35.12(1) and the preparation of a report under rule 35.12(3).

3.10(1) If it appears to the court that the claim is one which will be allocated to the fast track but that it cannot properly give directions on its own initiative or approve agreed directions that have been filed, the court may either:
 (a) allocate the claim to the fast track, fix a trial date or trial period and direct that a case management hearing is to be listed and give directions at that hearing, or
 (b) direct that an allocation hearing is to be listed and give directions at that hearing.

(2) In either case the hearing will be listed as promptly as possible.

3.11 Where the court is proposing on its own initiative to make an order under rule 35.15 (which gives the court power to appoint an *assessor), the court* must, unless the parties have consented in writing to the order, list a directions hearing.

3.12 The table set out below contains a typical timetable the court may give for the preparation of the case.

Disclosure	4 weeks
Exchange of witness statements	10 weeks
Exchange of experts' reports	14 weeks
Sending of pre-trial check lists (listing questionnaires) by the court	20 weeks
Filing of completed pre-trial check lists	22 weeks
Hearing	30 weeks

These periods will run from the date of the nctice of allocation.

3.13(1) Where it considers that some or all cf the steps in that timetable are not necessary the court may omit them and direct an earlier trial.

(2) This mayhappen where the court is informed that Practice Direction (Pre-Action Conduct) or any pre-action protocol has been complied with or that steps which it would otherwise order to be taken have already been taken.

(3) It may also happen where an application (for example for summary judgment or for an injunction) has been heard before allocation and little or no further preparation is required. In such a case the court may dispense with the need for a pre-trial check list.

4. Variation of Directions

4.1 This paragraph deals with the procedure to be adopted: **28PD.4**

(1) where a party is dissatisfied with a direction given by the court,

(2) where the parties agree about changes they wish made to the directions given, or

(3) where a party wishes to apply to vary a direction.

4.2(1) It is essential that any party who wishes to have a direction varied takes steps to do so as soon as possible.

(2) The court will assume for the purposes of any later application that a party who did not appeal and who made no application to vary within 14 days of service of the order containing the directions was content that they were correct in the circumstances then existing.

4.3(1) Where a party is dissatisfied with a direction given or other order made by the court he may appeal or apply to the court for it to reconsider its decision.

(2) He should appeal if the direction was given or the order was made at a hearing at which he was present or represented, or of which he had due notice.

(3) *In any other case he should* apply to the court to reconsider its decision.

(4) If an application is made for the court to reconsider its decision:

(a) it will usually be heard by the judge who gave the directions or another judge of the same level,

(b) the court will give all parties at least 3 days' notice of the hearing, and

(c) the court may confirm its decision or make a different order.

4.4 Where there has been a change in the circumstances since the order was made the court may set aside or vary any direction it has given. It may do so on application or on its own initiative.

4.5 Where the parties agree about changes to be made to the directions given:

(1) If rule 2.11 (variation by agreement of a date set by the court for doing any act other than those stated in the note to that rule) or rule 31.5, 31.10(8) or 31.13 (agreements about disclosure) applied the parties need not file the written agreement.

(a) In any other case the parties must apply for an order by consent.

(b) The parties must file a draft of the order sought and an agreed statement of the reasons why the variation is sought.

(c) The court may make an order in the agreed terms or in other terms without a hearing, but it may direct that a hearing is to be listed.

5. Failure to Comply with Case Management Directions

28PD.5 **5.1** Where a party has failed to comply with a direction given by the court any other party may apply for an order to enforce compliance or for a sanction to be imposed or both of these.

5.2 The party entitled to apply for such an order must do so without delay but should first warn the other party of his intention to do so.

5.3 The court may take any such delay into account when it decides whether to make an order imposing a sanction or whether to grant relief from a sanction imposed by the rules or any practice direction.

5.4(1) The court will not allow a failure to comply with directions to lead to the postponement of the trial unless the circumstances of the case are exceptional.

(2) If it is practicable to do so the court will exercise its powers in a manner that enables the case to come on for trial on the date or within the period previously set.

(3) In particular the court will assess what steps each party should take to prepare the case for trial, direct that those steps are taken in the shortest possible time and impose a sanction for non-compliance. Such a sanction may, for example, deprive a party of the right to raise or contest an issue or to rely on evidence to which the direction relates.

(4) Where it appears that one or more issues are or can be made ready for trial at the time fixed while others cannot, the court may direct that the trial will proceed on the issues which are or will then be ready, and order that no costs will be allowed for any later trial of the remaining issues or that those costs will be paid by the party in default.

(5) Where the court has no option but to postpone the trial it will do so for the shortest possible time and will give direc-

tions for the taking of the necessary steps in the meantime as rapidly as possible.

(6) Litigants and lawyers must be in no doubt that the court will regard the postponement of a trial as an order of last resort. The court may exercise its power to require a party as well as his legal representative to attend court at a hearing where such an order is to be sought.

6. Pre-trial check lists (listing questionnaires)

6.1(1) The pre-trial check list (listing questionnaire) will be in form **N170**. **28PD.6**

(2) Unless it has dispensed with pre-trial check lists, the court will send Forms **N170** and **N171** (Notice of date for return of the pre-trial check list) to each party no later than 2 weeks before the date specified in the notice of allocation or in any later direction of the court for the return of the completed check lists.

(3) When all the pre-trial check lists have been filed or when the time for filing them has expired and where a party has filed a pre-trial checklist but another party has not done so, the file will be placed before a judge for his directions.

(4) Although the Rules do not require the parties to exchange copies of the check lists before they are filed they are encouraged to do so to avoid the court being given conflicting or incomplete information.

Attention is drawn to the Costs Practice Direction, Section 6, which requires a costs estimate to be filed and served at the same time as the pre-trial check list is filed.

6.2 Attention is drawn to rule 28.6(1) (which sets out the court's duty at the pre-trial check list stage) and to rule 28.5(4) (which sets out circumstances in which the court may decide to hold a hearing).

6.3 Where the judge decides to hold a hearing under rule 28.5(4) the court will fix a date which is as early as possible and the parties will be given at least 3 days' notice of the date.

The notice of a such a hearing will be in Form **N153**.

6.4 The court's general approach will be as set out in the following paragraphs. The court may however decide to make other orders, and in particular the court will take into account the steps, if any, which the parties have taken to prepare the case for trial.

6.5(1) Where no party files a pre-trial checklist the court will order that unless a completed pre-trial checklist is filed within 7 days from service of that order, the claim, defence and any counterclaim will be struck out without further order of the court.

(2) Where a party files a pre-trial check list but another party does not do so, the court normally will give directions. These will usually fix or confirm the trial date and provide for steps to be taken to prepare the case for trial.

7. Directions the Court will Give on Listing

7.1 Directions the court must give: **28PD.7**

(1) The court must confirm or fix the trial date, specify the place of trial and give a time estimate. The trial date must be fixed and the case listed on the footing that the hearing will end on the same calendar day as that on which it commenced.

(2) The court will serve a notice of hearing on the parties at least 3 weeks before the hearing unless they agree to accept shorter notice or the court authorises shorter service under rule 28.6(2), and

(3) The notice of hearing will be in Form **N172**.

7.2 Other directions:

(1) The parties should seek to agree directions and may file the proposed order. The court may make an order in those terms or it may make a different order.

(2) Agreed directions should include provision about:
(a) evidence,
(b) a trial timetable and time estimate,
(c) the preparation of a trial bundle,
(d) any other matter needed to prepare the case for trial.

(3) The court will include such of these provisions as are appropriate in any order that it may make, whether or not the parties have filed agreed directions.
(a) A direction giving permission to use expert evidence will say whether it gives permission for oral evidence or reports or both and will name the experts concerned.
(b) The court will not make a direction giving permission for an expert to give oral evidence unless it believes it is necessary in the interests of justice to do so.
(c) Where no "without prejudice" meeting or other discussion between experts has taken place the court may grant that permission conditionally on such a discussion taking place and a report being filed before the trial.

7.3 The principles set out in paragraph 4 of this practice direction about the variation of directions apply also to directions given at this stage.

8. The Trial

28PD.8 **8.1** The trial will normally take place at the court where the case is being managed, but it may be at another court if it is appropriate having regard to the needs of the parties and the availability of court resources.

8.2 The judge will generally have read the papers in the trial bundle and may dispense with an opening address.

8.3 The judge may confirm or vary any timetable given previously, or if none has been given set his own.

8.4 Attention is drawn to the provisions in Part 32 and the following parts of the Rules about evidence, and in particular—

(1) to rule 32.1 (court's power to control evidence and to restrict cross-examination), and

(2) to rule 32.5(2) (witness statements to stand as evidence in chief).

8.5 At the conclusion of the trial the judge will normally summarily assess the costs of the claim in accordance with rule 44.7 and Part 46 (fast track trial costs). Attention is drawn to the steps the practice directions about costs requires the parties to take.

8.6 Where a trial is not finished on the day for which it is listed the judge will normally sit on the next court day to complete it.

Appendix

Fast Track Standard Directions

Further Statements of Case

The must file a and serve a copy on no later than . **28PD.9**

Requests for Further Information

Any request for clarification or further information based on another party's statement of case shall be served no later than . [Any such request shall be dealt with no later than]. **28PD.10**

Disclosure of Documents

[No disclosure of documents is required] [[Each party] [The] shall give [to the] [to every other party] standard disclosure of documents [relating to] by serving copies together with a disclosure statement no later than] [Disclosure shall take place as follows: [Each party shall give standard discovery to every other party by list] [Disclosure is limited to [standard] [disclosure by the to the] [of documents relating to damage] [the following documents] [The latest for delivery of the lists is] [The latest date for service of any request to inspect or for a copy of a document is]] **28PD.11**

Witnesses of Fact

Each party shall serve on every other party the witness statements of all witnesses of fact on whom he intends to rely. There shall be simultaneous exchange of such statements no later than . **28PD.12**

Expert Evidence

[No expert evidence being necessary, no party has permission to call or rely on expert evidence]. [On it appearing to the court that expert evidence is necessary on the issue of [ ] and that that evidence should be given by the report of a single expert instructed jointly by the parties, the shall not later than inform the court whether or not such an expert has been instructed]. [The expert evidence on the issue of shall be limited to a *single expert* *jointly instructed* by the parties. If the parties cannot agree by who that expert is to be and about the payment of his fees either party may apply for further directions. Unless the parties agree in writing or the court orders otherwise, the fees and expenses of such an expert shall be paid to him [by the parties equally] [ ] and be limited to £ . [The report of the expert shall be filed at the court no later than]. [No party shall be entitled to recover by way of costs from any other party **28PD.13** more than £ for the fees or expenses of an expert]. The parties shall exchange reports setting out the substance of any expert evidence on which they intend to rely. [The exchange shall take place simultaneously no later than]. [The shall serve his report(s) no later than the and the shall serve his reports no later than the]. [The exchange of reports relating to [causation] [ ] shall take place simultaneously no later than . The shall serve his report(s) relating to [damage] [ ] no later than and the shall serve his reports relating to it no later than].

Reports shall be agreed if possible no later than [days after service] [ ]. [If the reports are not agreed within that time there shall be a without prejudice discussion between the relevant experts no later than to identify the issues between them and to reach agreement if possible. The experts shall prepare for the court a statement of the issues on which they agree and on which they disagree with a summary of their reasons, and that statement shall be filed with the court [no later than] [with] [no later than the date for filing] [the pre-trial check list]. [Each party has permission to use [ ] as expert witness(es) to give [oral] evidence [in the form of a report] at the trial in the field of provided that the substance of the evidence to be given has been disclosed as above and has not been agreed]. [Each party has permission to use in evidence experts' report(s) [and the court will consider when the claim is listed for trial whether expert oral evidence will be allowed].]

Questions to Experts

28PD.14 The time for service on another party of any question addressed to an expert instructed by that party is not later than days after service of that expert's report. Any such question shall be answered within days of service.

Requests for Information etc.

28PD.15 Each party shall serve any request for clarification or further information based on any document disclosed or statement served by another party no later than days after disclosure or service. Any such request shall be dealt with within days of service.

Documents to be filed with pre-trial check lists

28PD.16 The parties must file with their listing questionnaires copies of [their experts' reports] [witness statements] [replies to requests for further information].

Dates for filing pre-trial check lists and the Trial

28PD.17 Each party must file a completed pre-trial check list no later than . The trial of this case will take place [on] [on a date to be fixed between and].

Directions following filing of pre-trial check list

Expert Evidence

The parties have permission to rely at the trial on expert evidence as follows: 28PD.18

The claimant:	Oral evidence—
	Written evidence—
The defendant:	Oral evidence—
	Written evidence—

Trial Timetable

The time allowed for the trial is . [The timetable for the trial may be agreed by the parties, subject to the approval of the trial judge]. [The timetable for the trial (subject to the approval of the trial judge) will be that]. [The evidence in chief for each party will be contained in witness statements and reports, the time allowed for cross-examination by the defendant is limited to and the time allowed for cross-examination by the claimant is limited to]. [The time allowed for the claimant's evidence is . The time allowed for the defendant's evidence is]. The time allowed for the submissions on behalf of each party is . The remainder of the time allowed for the trial (being) is reserved for the judge to consider and give the judgment and to deal with costs].

Trial Bundle Etc.

The claimant shall lodge an indexed bundle of documents contained in a ring binder and with each page clearly numbered at the court not more than 7 days and not less than 3 days before the start of the trial. [A case summary (which should not exceed 250 words) outlining the matters still in issue, and referring where appropriate to the relevant documents shall be included in the bundle for the assistance of the judge in reading the papers before the trial]. [The parties shall seek to agree the contents of the trial bundle and the case summary].

Settlement

Each party must inform the court immediately if the claim is settled whether or not it is then possible to file a draft consent order to give effect to their agreement.

PART 29

THE MULTI-TRACK

29.0.1 **Contents**

Editorial introduction

29.0.2 The rules in this Part set out the procedure to be followed from allocation to trial in multi-track cases. In the period between these stages the court will actively manage each case, running it according to a timetable set by the court and from time to time adjusted if necessary. The parties and their legal representatives are expected to co-operate with each other in the conduct of the proceedings so as to facilitate the court in giving directions suitably tailored to the needs of the case. Where appropriate, the court may give directions requiring the parties to consider ADR (as to which, see further, para.1.4.11, above). A standard form direction relating to ADR is set out in para.4.10(9) of the Practice Direction supplementing Pt 29 (see 29PD.4, below).

Related sources

29.0.3
- Pt 3 (The court's case management powers)
- Pt 26 (Case management—preliminary stage)
- Pt 32 (Evidence)
- Pt 35 (Experts and assessors)
- Chancery Guide, chapters 6 and 8 (see Vol.2, paras 1A–46 and 1A–78)
- Queen's Bench Guide, ss.6, 7, 8 and 9

Forms

29.0.4
- **N155** (Notice of allocation to the multi-track)
- **N170** (Listing questionnaire)
- **N171** (Notice of date for return of listing questionnaire)
- **N172** (Notice of trial date)
- **PF49** (Request to parties to state convenient dates for hearing)
- **PF50** (Application for directions) (Pt 29)
- **PF52** (Draft orders for directions of multi track cases)
- **PF53** (Order for trial of an issue)
- **PF74** (Order for trial by Master)
- **PF168** (Order to transfer claim to county court (County Courts Act 1984))

Scope of this Part

29.1 **29.1 This Part contains general provisions about management of cases allocated to the multi-track and applies only to cases allocated to that track.**

(Part 27 sets out the procedure for claims allocated to the small claims track.)

(Part 28 sets out the procedure for claims allocated to the fast track.)

The multi-track

The multi-track is one of the three management tracks to which a case may be allocated. The other two tracks are the small claims track and the fast track. As to the scope of each track, see r.26.6. Cases allocated to the multi-track includes cases with a financial value exceeding the limit for the fast track (i.e. exceeding £25,000) and also cases with a lower financial value if the court considers that the trial is likely to last longer than one day or that the oral expert evidence at the trial will not be limited to one expert per party in not more than two expert fields. 29.1.1

All claims concerned by way of the alternative procedure for claims are treated as allocated to the multi-track (r.8.9(c)). The Practice Direction supplementing Pt 29, para.3.2 (see para.29PD.3 below) states that the hallmarks of the multi-track are:

(1) the ability of the court to deal with cases of widely differing values and complexity; and

(2) the flexibility given to the court in the way it will manage a case in a way appropriate to its particular needs.

Case management[1]

29.2—(1) When it allocates a case to the multi-track, the court will— 29.2

(a) give directions for the management of the case and set a timetable for the steps to be taken between the giving of directions and the trial; or

(b) fix—

(i) a case management conference; or

(ii) a pre-trial review,

or both, and give such other directions relating to the management of the case as it sees fit.

(2) The court will fix the trial date or the period in which the trial is to take place as soon as practicable.

(3) When the court fixes the trial date or the trial period under paragraph (2), it will—

(a) give notice to the parties of the date or period; and

(b) specify the date by which the parties must file a pre-trial check list.

Management on allocation

Rule 29.2(1) sets out the ways in which the court may give case management directions at the time of allocation: 29.2.1

(1) by setting out comprehensive directions immediately on allocation; and

(2) by fixing a case management conference, a pre-trial review, or both (as to these, see r.29.3).

It should not be thought that every case on the multi-track will go straight to a case management conference. It is envisaged that, in many cases, the court will be able to give comprehensive directions whether on its own initiative (as to which, see r.3.3) or as agreed by the parties and approved by the court (as to which, see r.29.4).

Paragraphs 4.1 to 4.13 to the Practice Direction supplementing Pt 29 (see para.29PD.4 below) set out in detail the approach the court will take to giving directions on allocation and the steps the parties should take.

---

[1] Amended by the Civil Procedure (Amendment) Rules 2002 (SI 2002/2058).

Controlling the timetable

29.2.2 Rule 29.2(2) states that the court will fix the trial date or trial period "as soon as practicable". This major innovation in general civil procedure comprises a key element in furthering the overriding objective, i.e. ensuring that cases are dealt with expeditiously (see r.1.1(1) and (2)(d)). When fixing a trial date or hearing an appeal against a fixture already made, the court should strive to balance the availability of witnesses and advocates, the court timetable, and the principle that justice should not unreasonably be delayed (*Collins v Gordon* [2008] EWCA Civ 110).

A party who considers that a case management conference should be held before any directions are given should complete question J in the allocation questionnaire requesting an appointment, giving reasons justifying the request and supplying a realistic time estimate for the appointment with a list of any dates or times which are inconvenient. In the Chancery Division of the High Court so much is provided for in para.3.6 of the Chancery Guide (see Vol.2, para.1–11, below). In the Queen's Bench Division of the High Court Form **PF49** (Request to parties to state convenient dates for hearing) will be sent to the parties together with the allocation questionnaire so that, in the event of the Master requiring a case management conference, he can fix the hearing having regard as far as possible to the parties' convenience.

If it is appropriate to do so the court will order an early trial on a fixed date (and consequently dispense with the need for pre-trial checklists; see further on this, r.29.6(1)). In other cases the court may set a timetable by reference to calendar dates for the taking of steps for the preparation of the case and, if practicable, specifying the period in which the trial will take place (see Practice Direction supplementing Pt 29, para.4.10 (at para.29PD.4 below)).

Active case management means that the court will manage the case at the speed and on the dates which the court thinks appropriate. Once started the court will be reluctant to let the case slow down except to facilitate the parties to reach settlement.

> "Litigants and lawyers must be left in no doubt that [where a party fails to comply with a case management direction] the court will regard the postponement of a trial as an order of last resort"

(Practice Direction supplementing Pt 29, para.7.4(6) (see para.29PD.7 below)). However, not all applications to postpone a trial date amount to a failure on the part of the applicant to comply with a case management direction (see *Collins v Gordon* [2008] EWCA Civ 110, noted above).

Controlling costs

29.2.3 In *Griffiths v Solutia (UK) Ltd*, April 26, 2001, unrep., CA, Mance L.J. expressed the hope that "judges conducting cases will make full use of their powers under the Practice Direction about costs to obtain estimates of costs and to exercise their powers in respect of costs and case management to keep costs within the bounds of the proportionate in accordance with the overriding objective." In *Leigh v Michelin Tyre Plc* [2003] EWCA Civ 1766 the Court of Appeal stated as follows: "[16] Costs estimates are an important part of the machinery of case management. At the first case management conference, the court will have the parties' statements of case, and will therefore be aware of the issues in the case. The allocation questionnaires will inform the court how many witnesses, and in particular how many expert witnesses, each party wishes to call at the hearing. The parties' costs estimates are part of the material that is placed before the court at this early stage of the litigation to enable it to form a view as to what measures it should take in order to manage and control the case in the interests of what is reasonable and proportionate." See further "Prospective costs cap orders" at para.3.1.8 above.

Jurisdiction of Masters and District Judges

29.2.4 Case management will generally be dealt with by a Master (cases proceeding in London) or a District Judge (cases proceeding in a District Registry of the High Court and cases proceeding in a county court). However, a Master or District Judge may consult and seek directions of a judge of a higher level about any aspect of case management (Practice Direction supplementing Pt 29, para.3.10 (see para.29PD.3 below)). A Master or District Judge may refer to a judge any application which he thinks should properly be decided by a judge (Practice Direction supplementing Pt 23, para.1 (see para.23PD.1)).

Case management in the Royal Courts of Justice and elsewhere

29.2.5 A claim with an estimated value of less than £50,000 which is commenced in the

Central Office of the Royal Courts of Justice will normally be transferred to a county court unless:

(1) it is required by an enactment to be tried in the High Court,
(2) it falls within Pt 49 (specialist proceedings), or
(3) it falls within one of the following categories or is otherwise within the criteria of article 7(5) of the High Court and County Courts Jurisdiction Order 1991:
(a) professional negligence claims;
(b) Fatal Accident Act claims;
(c) fraud or undue influence;
(d) defamation claims;
(e) claims for malicious prosecution; or
(f) claims against the police.

(See Practice Direction supplementing Pt 29, paras 2.1 and 2.2 (para.29PD.2 below)). The decision to transfer should be made as soon as possible. However, if an application is made under r.3.4 (striking out) or under Pt 24 (Summary judgment) or under Pt 25 (Interim remedies) that application will usually be dealt with before a decision to transfer is taken (paras 2.4 and 2.5).

The provisions summarised above (likelihood of transfer of cases to a county court if suitable) apply only to claims issued in the Central Office of the Royal Courts of Justice. Therefore, they do not apply to claims issued in Chancery Chambers in London.

Unless and until an order of transfer is made the case management of a claim which is proceeding at the Royal Courts of Justice will be undertaken there (Practice Direction supplementing Pt 29, para.3.1 (see para.29PD.3 below)).

The case management of any other claim which has been allocated to the multi-track will normally be undertaken at a Civil Trial Centre (para.3.2; for a list of Civil Trial Centres see Vol.2, Section 11). In some cases this will necessitate transfer to a Civil Trial Centre (as to which, see Practice Direction supplementing Pt 26, para.10.2 (para.26PD.10)).

Listing arrangements in the Royal Courts of Justice

The Royal Courts of Justice suffer unique problems in terms of fixing trial dates **29.2.6** because of the number of Judges and Masters involved, the absence of a fully integrated IT support system, and the obligations of judges to go on circuit. To meet these problems guidance as to the fixing of trial dates and windows in multi-track cases in the Chancery and Queen's Bench Divisions (excluding the Admiralty and Commercial Court and the Technology and Construction Court) is given in the Chancery Guide, Ch.6 and in the Queen's Bench guide, para.8.4. Instead of fixing the trial date or window the Master may direct that the trial shall not begin earlier than a specified date (calculated to provide enough time for the parties to complete any necessary preparations for trial) and/or direct that the trial date be within a specified period. Where either direction is given the Master will order the parties to attend before the listing officer within a specified number of days in order to fix a date of trial. The obligation to take out an appointment with the listing officer falls upon the claimant. If no appointment is made the listing officer will appoint a date for a listing hearing and give notice of the date to all parties. Further details as to the listing hearing and details of an appeal against a decision made by the listing officer are also given.

In June 2005 simple cases commenced in the Central Office which had trial estimates not exceeding 3 days could be given trial dates enabling them to be heard within 20 weeks of allocation (see further, *Counsel*, August 2005, p.22).

Pre-trial checklists (r. 29.2(3))

By the Civil Procedure (Amendment) Rules 2002 (SI 2002/2058) the "listing **29.2.7** questionnaire" provided for by r.29.6 was renamed the "pre-trial checklist" with effect from December 2, 2002.

Case management conference and pre-trial review

29.3—(1) The court may fix— **29.3**

(a) a case management conference; or

(b) a pre-trial review, at any time after the claim has been allocated.

(2) If a party has a legal representative, a representative—

(a) familiar with the case; and

(b) with sufficient authority to deal with any issues that are likely to arise,

must attend case management conferences and pre-trial reviews.

(Rule 3.1(2)(c) provides that the court may require a party to attend the court.)

The case management conference

29.3.1 The date of the first case management conference will often be stated in Form **N155** (Notice of allocation to the multi-track). Paragraphs 5.1 and 5.3 of the Practice Direction supplementing Pt 29 (see para.29PD.5 below) explain the court's approach to a case management conference and set out the topics the court is likely to consider at it. Paragraphs 5.6 to 5.8 describe the steps the parties should take in preparation for the conference. These include the preparation of a case summary, a document which should not normally be more than 500 words in length which may be prepared by the claimant and agreed with the other parties if possible. Especially in the first few years of the new rules, a direction for the preparation of a case summary may be made at the time the claim is allocated to the multi-track.

The first case management conference in a claim is likely to be allotted up to one hour of court time. The parties should endeavour to agree the necessary directions for trial in advance of the case management conference using **PF52** as a guide.

The court will give the parties at least three days' notice of the hearing (para.3.7). Where a party wishes to obtain an order not routinely made at a case management conference and believes that his application will be opposed, he should issue and serve the application in time for it to be heard at the case management conference. If this is likely to require the conference to last longer than the court time already allotted, the applicant should inform the court so that a new appointment can be made. Failure to apply promptly or to inform the court of the need for extra time may result in a costs sanction (para.5.8).

Rule 29.3(2) indicates the personal involvement and seniority of the representative who should attend the case management conference on behalf of a represented party. (*cf.* para.7.2.6 of the Queen's Bench Guide which requires the attendance of the advocates instructed or expected to be instructed to appear at the trial, at any hearing at which case management directions are likely to be given). If non-compliance with this sub-rule leads to an adjournment the court will expect to make a wasted costs order (para.5.2(3); as to wasted costs orders see r.48.7). In some cases it may be appropriate for the represented party to attend also (see para.5.6(2)). In some cases it may be appropriate for the case management conference to be conducted by way of a telephone conference or a video conference (as to these, see further the Practice Direction supplementing Pt 23, paras 6 and 7 (paras 23PD.6 and 23PD.7)).

Directions as to expert evidence

29.3.2 Several topics concerning expert evidence are likely to be considered at a case management conference (Practice Direction supplementing Pt 29, paras 4.10 and 4.11, see paras 29PD.4 *et seq.* below).

(1) Directions for a single joint expert on any appropriate issue unless there is good reason to the contrary.

(2) Otherwise, simultaneous exchange of each side's reports.

(3) Directions for a discussion between experts and for the preparation by them of a statement of agreed issues and disputed issues.

(4) Directions for sequential exchange of reports where appropriate.

The court will not at this stage give permission to use expert evidence unless it can identify each expert by name or field in its order and say whether his evidence is to be given orally or by the use of his report (para.5.5(1)).

Failure to comply with case management directions

29.3.3 A party who fails to keep to the timetable fixed by the court is in real jeopardy of orders imposing severe sanctions upon him, including:

(1) the payment of a sum of money into court (r.3.1(5) and (6));

(2) the striking out of the whole or part of his statement of case plus judgment against him accordingly (r.3.4(2) and (3));

(3) a short extension of time specifying the consequence of non-compliance, e.g. depriving him of the right to raise or contest an issue or rely on evidence to which the direction relates (Practice Direction supplementing Pt 29, para.7(3); and

(4) where a trial can proceed as to some issues only, an order disallowing any costs in respect of any later trial of the remaining issues (para.7(4)).

Paragraph 7(2) of the Practice Direction supplementing Pt 29 (see para.29PD.7 below) states that a party who is entitled to apply for a sanction against another party is required to do so without delay but should first warn the party in default of his intention so to apply.

Pre-trial review

See the commentary to r.29.7. 29.3.4

Steps taken by the parties

29.4 If— 29.4

(a) the parties agree proposals for the management of the proceedings (including a proposed trial date or period in which the trial is to take place); and

(b) the court considers that the proposals are suitable;

it may approve them without a hearing and give directions in the terms proposed.

Effect of rule

If the parties agree proposals for the management of the case they should so notify the court. If the court considers them suitable, much time and expense will be saved. Even if the court does not consider them suitable, some time and expense may be saved because the court will take the agreed proposals into account in deciding what directions are appropriate. 29.4.1

Guidance as to the approach the parties should take is given in the Practice Direction supplementing Pt 29, paras 4.6 to 4.10 (see para.29PD.4 below).

This rule provides a practical demonstration of one of the biggest cultural changes made by the new rules. Parties are expected to co-operate with each other in the conduct of the proceedings. Co-operation of this sort is something the court must encourage in order to further the overriding objective (see r.1.4(2)(a)). The parties are expected to help the court to further the overriding objective (r.1.3). Parties who take reasonable steps to co-operate will be rewarded in costs if they later obtain an order for costs (see r.44.3(4)(a)). Parties who persist in the old combative style of litigation can expect to be penalised in costs whether or not their case succeeds at trial.

In the High Court, parties in the QBD will be sent copies of **PF52** to assist them to prepare the necessary directions for trial which they should endeavour to agree.

Variation of case management timetable[1]

29.5—(1) A party must apply to the court if he wishes to vary the date which the court has fixed for— 29.5

(a) a case management conference;

(b) a pre-trial review;

(c) the return of a pre-trial check list under rule 29.6;

(d) the trial; or

(e) the trial period.

(2) Any date set by the court or these Rules for doing any act

[1] Amended by the Civil Procedure (Amendment) Rules 2002 (SI 2002/2058).

may not be varied by the parties if the variation would make it necessary to vary any of the dates mentioned in paragraph (1).

(Rule 2.11 allows the parties to vary a date by written agreement except where the rules provide otherwise or the court orders otherwise.)

Effect of rule

29.5.1 This rule clearly indicates the extent to which the court controls the timetable of the proceedings (see further "Controlling the timetable" under r.29.2).

Paragraphs 6.1 to 6.5 of the Practice Direction supplementing Pt 29 (see para.29PD.6 below) deal generally with the procedure to be adopted in order to obtain any variation in the directions given. The first method of variation mentioned is an appeal (as to which see Pt 50). Alternatively, a party can reapply to the court which gave the direction requesting it to reconsider it if:

(1) there has been a change of circumstances since the order was made; and/or

(2) all parties agree about the changes they wish to make to the directions given.

Pre-trial checklist (listing questionnaire)[1]

29.6 **29.6—(1) The court will send the parties a pre-trial check list (listing questionnaire) for completion and return by the date specified in directions given under rule 29.2(3) unless it considers that the claim can proceed to trial without the need for a pre-trial check list.**

(2) Each party must file the completed pre-trial check list by the date specified by the court.

(3) If no party files the completed pre-trial checklist by the date specified, the court will order that unless a completed pre-trial checklist is filed within 7 days from service of that order, the claim, defence and any counterclaim will be struck out without further order of the court.

(4) If—

(a) a party files a completed pre-trial checklist but another party does not;

(b) a party has failed to give all the information requested by the pre-trial checklist; or

(c) the court considers that a hearing is necessary to enable it to decide what directions to give in order to complete preparation of the case for trial,

the court may give such directions as it thinks appropriate.

Form and purpose of the pre-trial checklist

29.6.1 By the Civil Procedure (Amendment) Rules 2002 (SI 2002/2058) the "listing questionnaire" provided for by this rule was renamed the "pre-trial checklist" with effect from December 2, 2002 so as to more accurately indicate its purpose. For the form of the checklist, see form **N170**. It has two purposes. The first is to check that the case management directions previously given have been complied with (and if not to give the court an opportunity to give further directions, see "Failure to comply with case management directions" under r.29.3). Secondly, it will lead to a firm date for trial being given (r.29.8). Completion and return of the pre-trial checklist on time is, therefore, essential. Failure to do so will lead to a listing hearing, the cost of which will *be borne by the party* in default (r.29.6(3)). Whether or not the defaulting party attends that hearing, the court will normally fix or confirm the trial date and make other

[1] Amended by the Civil Procedure (Amendment) Rules 2002 (SI 2002/2058).

orders about the steps to be taken to prepare the case for trial (Practice Direction supplementing Pt 29, para.8.3(2) (see 29PD.8 below)). If no party files a pre-trial checklist the court will normally make a conditional order striking out the proceedings unless a pre-trial checklist is filed by any party within three days of service of the order (para.8.3(1)).

In the RCJ, the parties will be required shortly after the case management conference, to seek an appointment with the Clerk of the Lists for the fixing of a date for trial.

Timetable for pre-trial checklists

Unless this stage of the proceedings has been dispensed with the court will, at the earliest opportunity practicable, specify the date upon which the parties must file completed checklists (Practice Direction supplementing Pt 29, para.8.1(2) (see para.29PD.8 below)). That date will be a date at least eight weeks before the trial date or the start of the trial period (para.8.1(3)). The court will send copies of the checklist to the parties at least 14 days before the date for filing the completed checklists (para.8.1(4)). Parties are encouraged (but not required) to exchange copies of the checklists before filing so as to avoid the court being given conflicting or incomplete information (para.8.1(5)). **29.6.2**

On listing, the court will also give any necessary directions concerning expert evidence, a trial timetable and time estimate, the preparation of a trial bundle and similar directions (para.9.2).

If some but not all parties file a completed pre-trial checklist by the date specified, the court file will be referred to the Master or District Judge for directions (r.29.6(4)). If no party files a completed pre-trial checklist by the date specified the court will make an "Unless Order" i.e. an order striking out the claim, defence and any counterclaim unless a completed pre-trial checklist is filed by a date specified in the order (r.29.6(3)). Any party's non-compliance with that order will thereby bring his claim, defence or counterclaim to an end.

For cases proceeding to trial in the RCJ, a Practice Note issued by the Clerk of the Lists (see para.29PD.11, below) explains that pre-trial checklists will not be dispensed with save in exceptional circumstances. In most cases in the RCJ the Listing Office will send the pre-trial checklists to the parties at least 11 weeks before the trial date. Failure to return completed pre-trial checklists (to the Listing Office) at least 8 weeks before the trial date may result in the claim being listed for further directions.

Filing costs estimates

The Costs Practice Direction requires parties to file with the pre-trial checklist an estimate of their costs incurred and to be incurred in the proceedings (see para.43PD.6). In most cases this will be the second such estimate parties will file (the first having been filed with the allocation checklist). Such estimates may also be required at other stages if the court so directs. The estimate should be substantially in the form illustrated in Costs Precedent H (see paras 43PD.6 and 48PD.10) As to the use of estimates filed by either party at a subsequent assessment of a party's costs, see Costs Practice Direction, para.6.6 (see para.43PD.6). As to the use of estimates as a means of controlling costs, see paras 3.1.8 and 29.2.3. **29.6.3**

Pre-trial checklist (listing questionnaire)

A notice issued by the Chancery and Queen's Bench Divisions regarding Pre-trial checklists (listing questionnaire) can be found at para.29PD.11. **29.6.4**

Pre-trial review[1]

29.7 If, on receipt of the parties' pre-trial check lists,the court decides— **29.7**

(a) to hold a pre-trial review; or

(b) to cancel a pre-trial review which has already been fixed,

---

[1] Amended by the Civil Procedure (Amendment) Rules 2002 (SI 2002/2058).

it will serve notice of its decision at least 7 days before the date fixed for the hearing or, as the case may be, the cancelled hearing.

Pre-trial review

29.7.1 On receipt of the completed pre-trial checklist the court will again consider whether to hold a pre-trial review or, if one has already been fixed, whether to cancel it. Pre-trial reviews will not be held in every case. However, they are likely to be held in all cases in which the trial is estimated to last more than 10 days.

If practicable the pre-trial review will be conducted by the judge before whom the case will be listed for trial. Similarly, the trial advocates should attend as should the parties or someone authorised to settle the action (see r.29.3 and the commentary thereto).

The purpose of the pre-trial review is to provide a further opportunity for settlement before the full trial costs are incurred and, where settlement is not possible, to prepare an agenda for trial.

The judge will check that the case management directions previously given have been complied with and will explore the extent to which evidence can be agreed. The agenda for trial to be finalised at the hearing will normally comprise a list of issues to be tried and a timetable for the trial. The timetable will break down the trial into stages, allotting time at each stage to each party. Such a timetable will give the judge firm control over the progress of the trial and may focus the advocates' minds on the best method of using time.

Setting a trial timetable and fixing or confirming the trial date or week[1]

29.8 **29.8 As soon as practicable after—**

(a) each party has filed a completed pre-trial check list;

(b) the court has held a listing hearing under rule 29.6(3); or

(c) the court has held a pre-trial review under rule 29.7,

the court will—

(i) set a timetable for the trial unless a timetable has already been fixed, or the court considers that it would be inappropriate to do so;

(ii) fix the date for the trial or the week within which the trial is to begin (or, if it has already done so, confirm that date); and

(iii) notify the parties of the trial timetable (where one is fixed under this rule) and the date ortrial period.

Effect of rule

29.8.1 Once the checklist stage is complete and the pre-trial review (if appropriate) has been held the court will notify the parties of the firm date for trial and of any trial timetable which has been fixed (see further, the commentary to r.29.7).

Conduct of trial

29.9 **29.9 Unless the trial judge otherwise directs, the trial will be conducted in accordance with any order previously made.**

---

[1] Amended by the Civil Procedure (Amendment) Rules 2002 (SI 2002/2058).

Effect of rule

This rule confirms that, despite the timetable (if any) and directions previously given, the trial judge has full power to conduct the trial in the manner he considers best to enable him to deal with the case justly. Paragraphs 10.1 to 10.6 of the Practice Direction supplementing Pt 29 (see para.29PD.10 below) make various provisions about the trial of multi-track cases and draw attention to r.32.1 (court's power to control evidence and to restrict cross-examination) and r.32.5(2) (Statements and reports to stand as evidence in chief). Further guidance as to the conduct of the trial is given in Ch.8 of the Chancery Guide and in s.9 of the Queen's Bench Guide. **29.9.1**

PRACTICE DIRECTION—THE MULTI-TRACK

This Practice Direction supplements CPR Part 29

1. General

29PD.1 **1.1** Attention is drawn in particular to the following Parts of the Civil Procedure Rules:

Part 1	The Overriding Objective
Part 3	The Court's Case Management Powers
Part 26	Case Management—Preliminary Stage
Part 31	Disclosure and Inspection of Documents
Parts 32–34	Evidence
Part 35	Experts and Assessors

and to the Practice Directions which relate to those Parts.

2. Case Management in the Royal Courts of Justice

29PD.2 **2.1** This part of the Practice Direction applies to claims begun by claim form issued in the Central Office or Chancery Chambers in the Royal Courts of Justice.

2.2 A claim with an estimated value of less than £50,000 will generally, unless—

(a) it is required by an enactment to be tried in the High Court,

(b) it falls within a specialist list, or

(c) it falls within one of the categories specified in 2.6 below or is otherwise within the criteria of article 7(5) of the High Court and County Courts Jurisdiction Order 1991,

be transferred to a county court.

2.3 Paragraph 2.2 is without prejudice to the power of the court in accordance with Part 30 to transfer to a county court a claim with an estimated value that exceeds £50,000.

2.4 The decision to transfer may be made at any stage in the proceedings but should, subject to paragraph 2.5, be made as soon as possible and in any event not later than the date for the filing of pre-trial check lists (listing questionnaires).

2.5 If an application is made under rule 3.4 (striking out) or under Part 24 (summary judgment) or under Part 25 (interim remedies), it will usually be convenient for the application to be dealt with before a decision to transfer is taken.

2.6 Each party should state in his allocation questionnaire whether he considers the claim should be managed and tried at the Royal Courts of Justice and, if so, why. Claims suitable for trial in the Royal Courts of Justice include—

(1) professional negligence claims;

(2) Fatal Accidents Act claims;

(3) fraud or undue influence claims;

(4) defamation claims;

(5) claims for malicious prosecution or false imprisonment;

(6) claims against the police;

(7) contentious probate claims.

Such claims may fall within the criteria of article 7(5) of the High Court and County Courts Jurisdiction Order 1991.

2.7 Attention is drawn to the practice direction on transfer (Part 30).

3. Case Management—General Provisions

3.1(1) Case management of a claim which is proceeding at the Royal Courts of Justice will be undertaken there. 29PD.3

(a) Case management of any other claim which has been allocated to the multi-track will normally be undertaken at a Civil Trial Centre.

(b) The practice direction supplementing Part 26 provides for what will happen in the case of a claim which is issued in or transferred to a court which is not a Civil Trial Centre.

3.2 The hallmarks of the multi-track are:

(1) the ability of the court to deal with cases of widely differing values and complexity, and

(2) the flexibility given to the court in the way it will manage a case in a way appropriate to its particular needs.

3.3(1) On allocating a claim to the multi-track the court may give directions without a hearing, including fixing a trial date or a period in which the trial will take place,

(2) Alternatively, whether or not it fixes a trial date or period, it may either—

(a) give directions for certain steps to be taken and fix a date for a case management conference or a pre-trial review to take place after they have been taken, or

(b) fix a date for a case management conference.

(3) Attention is drawn to rule 29.2(2) which requires the court to fix a trial date or period as soon as practicable.

3.4 The court may give or vary directions at any hearing which may take place on the application of a party or of its own initiative.

3.5 When any hearing has been fixed it is the duty of the parties to consider what directions the court should be asked to give and to make any application that may be appropriate to be dealt with then.

3.6 The court will hold a hearing to give directions whenever it appears necessary or desirable to do so, and where this happens because of the default of a party or his legal representative it will usually impose a sanction.

3.7 When the court fixes a hearing to give directions it will give the parties at least 3 days' notice of the hearing unless rule 29.7 applies (7 days' notice to be given in the case of a pre-trial review).

3.8 Where a party needs to apply for a direction of a kind not included in the case management timetable which has been set (for example to amend his statement of case or for further information to be given by another party) he must do so as soon as possible so as to minimise the need to change that timetable.

3.9 Courts will make arrangements to ensure that applications and other hearings are listed promptly to avoid delay in the conduct of cases.

3.10(1) Case management will generally be dealt with by:

(a) a Master in cases proceeding in the Royal Courts of Justice,

(b) a district judge in cases proceeding in a District Registry of the High Court, and

(c) a district judge or a Circuit Judge in cases proceeding in a county court.

(2) A Master or a district judge may consult and seek the directions of a judge of a higher level about any aspect of case management.

(3) A member of the court staff who is dealing with the listing of a hearing may seek the directions of any judge about any aspect of that listing.

3A. Case Management—consideration of periodical payments

29PD.3A **3A** Attention is drawn to Practice Direction 41B supplementing Part 41 and in particular to the direction that in a personal injury claim the court should consider and indicate to the parties as soon as practicable whether periodical payments or a lump sum is likely to be the more appropriate form for all or part of an award of damages for future pecuniary loss.

29PD.3A.1 *Note* —Amended by Civil Procedure (Amendment No.3) Rules 2004 (SI 2004/3129) which came into force April 1, 2005 (SI 2005/910).

4. Directions on Allocation

29PD.4 **4.1** Attention is drawn to the court's duties under rule 29.2.

4.2 The court will seek to tailor its directions to the needs of the case and the steps which the parties have already taken to prepare the case of which it is aware. In particular it will have regard to the extent to which Practice Direction (Pre-Action Conduct) or any pre-action protocol has or (as the case may be) has not been complied with.

4.3 At this stage the court's first concern will be to ensure that the issues between the parties are identified and that the necessary evidence is prepared and disclosed.

4.4 The court may have regard to any document filed by a party with his allocation questionnaire containing further information provided that the document states either that its contents has been agreed with every other party or that it has been served on every other party, and when it was served.

4.5 On the allocation of a claim to the multi-track the court will consider whether it is desirable or necessary to hold a case management conference straight away, or whether it is appropriate instead to give directions on its own initiative.

4.6 The parties and their advisers are encouraged to try to agree directions and to take advantage of rule 29.4 which provides that if:

(1) the parties agree proposals for the management of the proceedings (including a proposed trial date or period in *which the* trial is to take place); and

(2) the court considers that the proposals are suitable,

it may approve them without a hearing and give directions in the terms proposed.

4.7(1) To obtain the court's approval the agreed directions must—

(a) set out a timetable by reference to calendar dates for the taking of steps for the preparation of the case,

(b) include a date or a period (the trial period) when it is proposed that the trial will take place,

(c) include provision about disclosure of documents, and

(d) include provision about both factual and expert evidence.

(2) The court will scrutinise the timetable carefully and in particular will be concerned to see that any proposed date or period for the trial and (if provided for) for a case management conference is no later than is reasonably necessary.

(3) The provision in (1)(c) above may—

(a) limit disclosure to standard disclosure or less than that, and/or

(b) direct that disclosure will take place by the supply of copy documents without a list, but it must in that case say either that the parties must serve a disclosure statement with the copies or that they have agreed to disclose in that way without such a statement.

(4) The provision in (1)(d) about expert evidence may be to the effect that none is required.

4.8 Directions agreed by the parties should also where appropriate contain provisions about:

(1) the filing of any reply or amended statement of case that may be required,

(2) dates for the service of requests for further information under the practice direction supplementing Part 18 and of questions to experts under rule 35.6 and by when they are to be dealt with,

(3) the disclosure of evidence,

(4) the use of a single joint expert, or in cases where it is not agreed, the exchange of expert evidence (including whether exchange is to be simultaneous or sequential) and without prejudice discussions between experts.

4.9 If the court does not approve the agreed directions filed by the parties but decides that it will give directions of its own initiative without fixing a case management conference, it will take them into account in deciding what directions to give.

4.10 Where the court is to give directions on its own intiative without holding a case management conference and it is not aware of any steps taken by the parties other than the exchange of statements of case, its general approach will be:

(1) to give directions for the filing and service of any further information required to clarify either party's case,

(2) to direct standard disclosure between the parties,

(3) to direct the disclosure of witness statements by way of simultaneous exchange,

(4) to give directions for a single joint expert on any appropriate issue unless there is a good reason not to do so.

(5) unless paragraph 4.11 (below) applies, to direct disclosure of experts' reports by way of simultaneous exchange on those issues where a single joint expert is not directed,

(6) if experts' reports are not agreed, to direct a discussion between experts for the purpose set out in rule 35.12(1) and the preparation of a statement under rule 35.12(3),

(7) to list a case management conference to take place after the date for compliance with those directions,

(8) to specify a trial period; and

(9) in such cases as the court thinks appropriate, the court may give directions requiring the parties to consider ADR. Such directions may be, for example, in the following terms:

"The parties shall by [date] consider whether the case is capable of resolution by ADR. If any party considers that the case is unsuitable for resolution by ADR, that party shall be prepared to justify that decision at the conclusion of the trial, should the judge consider that such means of resolution were appropriate, when he is considering the appropriate costs order to make.

The party considering the case unsuitable for ADR shall, not less than 28 days before the commencement of the trial, file with the court a witness statement without prejudice save as to costs, giving reasons upon which they rely for saying that the case was unsuitable."

4.11 If it appears that expert evidence will be required both on issues of liability and on the amount of damages, the court may direct that the exchange of those reports that relate to liability will be exchanged simultaneously but that those relating to the amount of damages will be exchanged sequentially.

4.12(1) If it appears to the court that it cannot properly give directions on its own initiative and no agreed directions have been filed which it can approve, the court will direct a case management conference to be listed.

(2) The conference will be listed as promptly as possible.

4.13 Where the court is proposing on its own initiative to make an order under rule 35.7 (which gives the court power to direct that evidence on a particular issue is to be given by a single expert) or under rule 35.15 (which gives the court power to appoint an assessor), the court must, unless the parties have consented in writing to the order, list a case management conference.

5. Case Management Conferences

29PD.5 **5.1** The court will at any case management conference:

(1) review the steps which the parties have taken in the preparation of the case, and in particular their compliance with any directions that the court may have given,

(2) decide and give directions about the steps which are to be taken to secure the progress of the claim in accordance with *the overriding* objective, and

(3) ensure as far as it can that all agreements that can be reached between the parties about the matters in issue and the conduct of the claim are made and recorded.

5.2(1) Rule 29.3(2) provides that where a party has a legal representative, a representative familiar with the case and with sufficient authority to deal with any issues that are likely to arise must attend case management conferences and pre-trial reviews.

(2) That person should be someone who is personally involved in the conduct of the case, and who has the authority and information to deal with any matter which may reasonably be expected to be dealt with at such a hearing, including the fixing of the timetable, the identification of issues and matters of evidence.

(3) Where the inadequacy of the person attending or of his instructions leads to the adjournment of a hearing, the court will expect to make a wasted costs order.

5.3 The topics the court will consider at a case management conference are likely to include:

(1) whether the claimant has made clear the claim he is bringing, in particular the amount he is claiming, so that the other party can understand the case he has to meet,

(2) whether any amendments are required to the claim, a statement of case or any other document,

(3) what disclosure of documents, if any, is necessary,

(4) what expert evidence is reasonably required in accordance with rule 35.1 and how and when that evidence should be obtained and disclosed,

(5) what factual evidence should be disclosed,

(6) what arrangements should be made about the giving of clarification or further information and the putting of questions to experts, and

(7) whether it will be just and will save costs to order a split trial or the trial of one or more preliminary issues.

5.4 In all cases the court will set a timetable for the steps it decides are necessary to be taken. These steps may include the holding of a case management conference or a pre-trial review, and the court will be alert to perform its duty to fix a trial date or period as soon as it can.

5.5(1) The court will not at this stage give permission to use expert evidence unless it can identify each expert by name or field in its order and say whether his evidence is to be given orally or by the use of his report.

(2) A party who obtains expert evidence before obtaining a direction about it does so at his own risk as to costs, except *where he obtained the* evidence in compliance with a pre-action protocol.

5.6 To assist the court, the parties and their legal advisers should:

(1) ensure that all documents that the court is likely to ask to see (including witness statements and experts' reports) are brought to the hearing,

(2) consider whether the parties should attend,

(3) consider whether a case summary will be useful, and

(4) consider what orders each wishes to be made and give notice of them to the other parties.

5.7(1) A case summary:

(a) should be designed to assist the court to understand and deal with the questions before it,

(b) should set out a brief chronology of the claim, the issues of fact which are agreed or in dispute and the evidence needed to decide them,

(c) should not normally exceed 500 words in length, and

(d) should be prepared by the claimant and agreed with the other parties if possible.

5.8(1) Where a party wishes to obtain an order not routinely made at a case management conference and believes that his application will be opposed, he should issue and serve the application in time for it to be heard at the case management conference.

(2) If the time allowed for the case management conference is likely to be insufficient for the application to be heard he should inform the court at once so that a fresh date can be fixed.

(3) A costs sanction may be imposed on a party who fails to comply with sub-paragraph (1) or (2).

5.9 At a case management conference the court may also consider whether the case ought to be tried by a High Court Judge or by a judge who specialises in that type of claim and how that question will be decided. In that case the claim may need to be transferred to another court.

6. Variation of Directions

29PD.6 **6.1** This paragraph deals with the procedure to be adopted:

(1) where a party is dissatisfied with a direction given by the court,

(2) where the parties have agreed about changes they wish made to the directions given, or

(3) where a party wishes to apply to vary a direction.

6.2(1) It is essential that any party who wishes to have a direction varied takes steps to do so as soon as possible.

(2) The court will assume for the purposes of any later application that a party who did not appeal, and who made no application to vary within 14 days of service of the order containing the directions, was content that they were correct in the circumstances then existing.

6.3(1) Where a party is dissatisfied with a direction given or other order made by the court he may appeal or apply to the court for it to reconsider its decision.

(2) Unless paragraph 6.4 applies, a party should appeal if the *direction* was given or the order was made at a hearing at which he was present, or of which he had due notice.

(3) In any other case he should apply to the court to reconsider its decision.

(4) If an application is made for the court to reconsider its decision:
(a) it will usually be heard by the judge who gave the directions or another judge of the same level,
(b) the court will give all parties at least 3 days' notice of the hearing, and
(c) the court may confirm its directions or make a different order.

6.4 Where there has been a change in the circumstances since the order was made the court may set aside or vary a direction it has given. It may do so on application or on its own initiative.

6.5 Where the parties agree about changes they wish made to the directions given:

(1) If rule 2.11 (variation by agreement of a date set by the court for doing any act other than those stated in the note to that rule) or rule 31.5, 31.10(8) or 31.13 (agreements about disclosure) applies the parties need not file the written agreement.
(a) In any other case the parties must apply for an order by consent.
(b) The parties must file a draft of the order sought and an agreed statement of the reasons why the variation is sought.
(c) The court may make an order in the agreed terms or in other terms without a hearing, but it may direct that a hearing is to be listed.

7. Failure to Comply with Case Management Directions

7.1 Where a party fails to comply with a direction given by the court any other party may apply for an order that he must do so or for a sanction to be imposed or both of these. **29PD.7**

7.2 The party entitled to apply for such an order must do so without delay but should first warn the other party of his intention to do so.

7.3 The court may take any such delay into account when it decides whether to make an order imposing a sanction or to grant relief from a sanction imposed by the rules or any other practice direction.

7.4(1) The court will not allow a failure to comply with directions to lead to the postponement of the trial unless the circumstances are exceptional.

(2) If it is practical to do so the court will exercise its powers in a manner that enables the case to come on for trial on the date or within the period previously set.

(3) In particular the court will assess what steps each party should take to prepare the case for trial, direct that those steps are taken in the shortest possible time and impose a sanction for non-compliance. Such a sanction may, for example, deprive a party of the right to raise or contest an issue or to rely on evidence to which the direction relates.

(4) Where it appears that one or more issues are or can be made ready for trial at the time fixed while otherscannot,

the court may direct that the trial will proceed on the issues which are then ready, and direct that no costs will be allowed for any later trial of the remaining issues or that those costs will be paid by the party in default.

(5) Where the court has no option but to postpone the trial it will do so for the shortest possible time and will give directions for the taking of the necessary steps in the meantime as rapidly as possible.

(6) Litigants and lawyers must be in no doubt that the court will regard the postponement of a trial as an order of last resort. Where it appears inevitable the court may exercise its power to require a party as well as his legal representative to attend court at the hearing where such an order is to be sought.

(7) The court will not postpone any other hearing without a very good reason, and for that purpose the failure of a party to comply on time with directions previously given will not be treated as a good reason.

Pre-trial check lists (listing questionnaires)

29PD.8 **8.1**(1) The pre-trial check list (listing questionnaire) will be in Form **N170**.

(2) Unless it dispenses with pre-trial check lists and orders an early trial on a fixed date, the court will specify the date for filing completed pre-trial check lists when it fixes the trial date or trial period under rule 29.2(2).

(3) The date for filing the completed pre-trial check lists will be not later than 8 weeks before the trial date or the start of the trial period.

(4) The court will serve the pre-trial check lists on the parties at least 14 days before that date.

(5) Although the rules do not require the parties to exchange copies of the check lists before they are filed they are encouraged to do so to avoid the court being given conflicting or incomplete information.

(6) The file will be placed before a judge for his directions when all the check lists have been filed or when the time for filing them has expired and where a party has filed a checklist but another party has not done so.

8.2 The court's general approach will be as set out in the following paragraphs. The court may however decide to make other orders, and in particular the court will take into account the steps, if any, of which it is aware which the parties have taken to prepare the case for trial.

8.3(1) Where no party files a pre-trial checklist the court will order that unless a completed pre-trial checklist is filed within 7 days from service of that order, the claim, defence and any *counterclaim* will be struck out without further order of the court.

(2) Where a party files a pre-trial check list but another party (the defaulting party) does not do so, the court will fix a

hearing under rule 29.6(4). Whether or not the defaulting party attends the hearing, the court will normally fix or confirm the trial date and make other orders about the steps to be taken to prepare the case for trial.

8.4 Where the court decides to hold a hearing under rule 29.6(4) the court will fix a date which is as early as possible and the parties will be given at least 3 days' notice of the date.

8.5 Where the court decides to hold a pre-trial review (whether or not this is in addition to a hearing under rule 29.6(4)) the court will give the parties at least 7 days' notice of the date.

9. Directions the court will give on Listing

9.1 Directions the court must give. **29PD.9**

The court must fix the trial date or week, give a time estimate and fix the place of trial.

9.2 Other directions

(1) The parties should seek to agree directions and may file an agreed order. The court may make an order in those terms or it may make a different order.

(2) Agreed directions should include provision about:
- (a) evidence especially expert evidence,
- (b) a trial timetable and time estimate,
- (c) the preparation of a trial bundle,
- (d) any other matter needed to prepare the case for trial.

(3) The court will include such of these provisions as are appropriate in any order that it may make, whether or not the parties have filed agreed directions.

(4) Unless a direction doing so has been given before, a direction giving permission to use expert evidence will say whether it gives permission to use oral evidence or reports or both and will name the experts concerned.

9.3 The principles set out in paragraph 6 of this Practice Direction about variation of directions applies equally to directions given at this stage.

10. The Trial

10.1 The trial will normally take place at a Civil Trial Centre but it **29PD.10**
may be at another court if it is appropriate having regard to the needs of the parties and the availability of court resources.

10.2 The judge will generally have read the papers in the trial bundle and may dispense with an opening address.

10.3 The judge may confirm or vary any timetable given previously, or if none has been given set his own.

10.4 Attention is drawn to the provisions in Part 32 and the following parts of the Rules about evidence, and in particular:

(1) to rule 32.1 (court's power to control evidence and to restrict cross-examination), and

(2) to rule 32.5(2) statements and reports to stand as evidence in chief.

10.5 In an appropriate case the judge may summarily assess costs in accordance with rule 44.7. Attention is drawn to the practice directions about costs and the steps the parties are required to take.

10.6 Once the trial of a multi-track claim has begun, the judge will normally sit on consecutive court days until it has been concluded.

PART 30

TRANSFER

Contents 30.0.1

Editorial introduction

This Part contains rules relating to transfer: (i) between county courts; (ii) within the High Court; and (iii) from county court to High Court. County Courts Act 1984 s.40 deals with transfer from High Court to county court—see para.30.2.9. Paragraph (2) was added to r.30.1 by the Civil Procedure (Amendment No.4) Rules 2003 and came into effect on October 6, 2003. Rule 30.8, which was added to this Part by the Civil Procedure (Amendment No.5) Rules 2003 with effect from May 1, 2004, disapplies r.30.2 and r.30.3 in certain circumstances. 30.0.2

Related sources

- Practice Direction to Pt 30 (see para.30PD.1) 30.0.3
- Supreme Court Act 1981 ss.61 to 65 and Sch.1 (Vol.2, Section 9A, paras 9A–229 to 9A–242)
- County Courts Act 1984 ss.40 to 45 (Vol.2, Section 9A, paras 9A–472 *et seq.*
- High Court and County Court Jurisdiction Order 1991 (SI 1991/724) (Vol.2, Section 9B, paras 9B–928 to 9B–953)
- Insolvency Rules 1986 r.7.15
- CPR r.26.2 (automatic transfer to defendant's home court (see r.2.3) when defence filed in claim for specified amount of money), r.13.4 (automatic transfer to defendant's home court when application to set aside) and r.14.12 (automatic transfer to defendant's home court when admission—determination of rate of payment by judge)
- CCR O.25, r.2 (transfer of proceedings for enforcement) (see para.cc30.10)
- Practice Direction to Part 29, para.2 (criteria for transfer of multi track cases from High Court to county court) (see para.29PD.1)
- CPR Part 72 (third party debt orders) and para.72PD.4
- CPR r.54.20 (Judicial review transfer)
- Practice Direction 54D (Administrative Court (Venue)) (para.54DPD.1)

Scope of this Part

30.1—(1) This Part deals with the transfer of proceedings between county courts, between the High Court and the county courts and within the High Court. 30.1

(2) The practice direction may make provision about the transfer of proceedings between the court and a tribunal.

(Rule 26.2 provides for automatic transfer in certain cases.)

Transfer between county courts and within the High Court

30.2 **30.2—(1) A county court may order proceedings before that court, or any part of them (such as a counterclaim or an application made in the proceedings), to be transferred to another county court if it is satisfied that—**

(a) an order should be made having regard to the criteria in rule 30.3; or

(b) proceedings for—

(i) the detailed assessment of costs; or

(ii) the enforcement of a judgment or order,

could be more conveniently or fairly taken in that other county court.

(2) If proceedings have been started in the wrong county court, a judge of the county court may order that the proceedings—

(a) be transferred to the county court in which they ought to have been started;

(b) continue in the county court in which they have been started; or

(c) be struck out.

(3) An application for an order under paragraph (1) or (2) must be made to the county court where the claim is proceeding.

(4) The High Court may, having regard to the criteria in rule 30.3, order proceedings in the Royal Courts of Justice or a district registry, or any part of such proceedings (such as a counterclaim or an application made in the proceedings) to be transferred—

(a) from the Royal Courts of Justice to a district registry; or

(b) from a district registry to the Royal Courts of Justice or to another district registry.

(5) A district registry may order proceedings before it for the detailed assessment of costs to be transferred to another district registry if it is satisfied that the proceedings could be more conveniently or fairly taken in that other district registry.

(6) An application for an order under paragraph (4) or (5) must, if the claim is proceeding in a district registry, be made to that registry.

(7) Where some enactment, other than these rules, requires proceedings to be started in a particular county court, neither paragraphs (1) nor (2) give the court power to order proceedings to be transferred to a county court which is not the court in which they should have been started or to order them to continue in the wrong court.

(8) Probate proceedings may only be transferred under paragraph (4) to Chancery Division at the Royal Courts of Justice or to one of the Chancery district registries.

"a county court" (r.30.2(1))

30.2.1 The power may be exercised by a judge or district judge—CPR r.2.4.

"counterclaim" (r.30.2(1))

30.2.2 See Pt 20.

"application" (r.30.2(1), 2(3), 5 and 6)

See Pt 23. 30.2.3

"detailed assessment of costs" (r.30.2(1)(b) and 2(5))

See Pt 47. 30.2.4

"enforcement" (r.30.2(1)(b))

See CPR Parts 70– 73. 30.2.5

"more conveniently and fairly" (r.30.2(1)(b))

This is the same phrase as was used in the former CCR O 16, r.1. If an application is made by one party for transfer, the burden lies upon that party to show that transfer should take place. For the criteria for transfer see r.30.3(2). 30.2.6

Note that the power to transfer may be exercised by judges of their own initiative (r.3.3).

"If proceedings have been commenced in the wrong court ..." (r.30.2(2))

See r.7.1 and the Practice Direction to Pt 7 and Pt 8, especially paras B6 and B7. Rule 30.2(2) replaces CCR O.16, r.2. This rule will always be answer to an objection raised on appeal that proceedings have been commenced in the wrong court—see *R. v Judge Lailey Ex p. Koffman* [1932] 1 K.B. 568 at 577, CA, and *Thomas Allen Ltd v Hagger (No.3)* (1931) 24 B.W.C.C. 513, CA. 30.2.7

Although r.30.2(c) gives the court power to strike out an action commenced in the wrong court, in view of the overriding objective (r.1.1(1) and (2)(b)) the power to strike out is only likely to be exercised in extreme cases. It is more likely that the court will treat issue in the wrong court in breach of a rule or practice direction as an error of procedure which does not invalidate the issue of proceedings (CPR r.3.10). See too *Gwynedd CC v Grunshaw* [2000] 1 W.L.R. 494, CA and *Cala Homes (South) Ltd v Chichester DC (Time Limits)* [2000] C.P. Rep. 28, QBD.

"the county court where the claim is proceeding" (r.30.2(3))

See too r.23.2(1) to (3). 30.2.8

"The High Court may ..." (r.30.2(4))

For the criteria for transfer see r.30.3(2). Note that r.30.2 does not provide for transfer from the High Court to the county court and vice versa—jurisdiction to make such transfers is given by County Courts Act 1984 s.40, as amended (Vol.2, Section 9A, para.9A–472). The jurisdiction may be exercised by any judge, Master or district judge—see r.2.4. 30.2.9

For special provisions concerning the transfer of certain claims pending in the Administrative Court from the RCJ to a district registry (or vice versa) or from one district registry to another, including provisions as to criteria for such transfer, see Practice Direction 54D (Administrative Court (Venue)) (para.54DPD.1 below).

Case management of multi track cases

The norm is for county court cases which are allocated to the multi track to be transferred to the nearest trial centre for case management. 30.2.10

Criteria for a transfer order[1]

30.3—(1) Paragraph (2) sets out the matters to which the court must have regard when considering whether to make an order under— 30.3

> **(a) *section 40(2), 41(1) or 42(2) of the County Courts Act* 1984[2] (transfer between the High Court and a county court);**

[1] Amended by the Civil Procedure (Amendment No.4) Rules 2000 (SI 2000/2092).

[2] 1984 c.28. Section 40 was substituted by s.2(1) of the Courts and Legal Services Act 1990 (c.41). Section 41 was amended by the Matrimonial and Family Proceedings Act 1984 (c.42) Sch.1, para.31 and by s.2(2) of the Courts and Legal Services Act 1990. Section 42 was substituted by s.2(3) of the Courts and Legal Services Act 1990.

(b) rule 30.2(1) (transfer between county courts); or

(c) rule 30.2(4) (transfer between the Royal Courts of Justice and the district registries).

(2) The matters to which the court must have regard include—

(a) the financial value of the claim and the amount in dispute, if different;

(b) whether it would be more convenient or fair for hearings (including the trial) to be held in some other court;

(c) the availability of a judge specialising in the type of claim in question;

(d) whether the facts, legal issues, remedies or procedures involved are simple or complex;

(e) the importance of the outcome of the claim to the public in general;

(f) the facilities available at the court where the claim is being dealt with and whether they may be inadequate because of any disabilities of a party or potential witness;

(g) whether the making of a declaration of incompatibilty under section 4 of the Human Rights Act 1998 has arisen or may arise;

(h) in the case of civil proceedings by or against the Crown, as defined in rule 66.1(2), the location of the relevant government department or officers of the Crown and, where appropriate, any relevant public interest that the matter should be tried in London.

"transfer between the High Court and a county court" (r.30.3(1)(a))

30.3.1 See High Court and County Court Jurisdiction Order 1991 (SI 1991/724) (Vol.2, Section 9B, paras 9B–928 to 9B–953). If proceedings are commenced in the High Court when they should have been commenced in a county court, the High Court must transfer to a county court, but if the person bringing the proceedings knew, or ought to have known, that they should have been brought in the county court, there is a residual jurisdiction to strike out—see *Restick v Crickmore* [1994] 1 W.L.R. 420, CA. However, in view of the overriding objective (r.1.1(1) and (2)(b)) the power to strike out is only likely to be exercised in extreme cases.

See too Practice Direction to Pt 29, para.2 which provides that cases with an estimated value of less than £50,000 issued in the High Court will generally be transferred to a county court unless they are required by an enactment to be tried in the High Court, fall within a specialist list (see CPR Pt 49) or come with Practice Direction to Pt 29, para.2.6 (*viz.* claims involving professional negligence, Fatal Accident Act, fraud or undue influence, defamation, malicious prosecution or false imprisonment, claims against the police and contentious probate claims).

The High Court's power of transfer to a county court under County Courts Act 1984 s.40(2) is not limited to cases which would otherwise be within the county court's jurisdiction (*National Westminster Bank v King* [2008] EWHC 280 (Ch); *The Times*, April 14, 2008 —transfer of proceedings to enforce a charging order where it appears that the value exceeded the county court's £30,000 limit for such cases).

"The matters to which the court must have regard include ..." (r.30.3(2))

30.3.2 The list is not exhaustive. In addition regard should be had to r.1.1 (The overriding objective) and r.1.4 (Court's duty to manage cases). Note that the r.30.3 criteria do *not apply to a transfer under r.30.2(1)(b).*

"the financial value" (r.30.3(2)(a))

30.3.3 See High Court and County Court Jurisdiction Order 1991 (SI 1991/724) (Vol.2, Section 9B, paras 9B–928 to 9B–953) and Pt 29 (The Multi-Track). See too r.16.3.

"the availability of a judge specialising" (r.30.3(2)(c))

Practitioners should ensure that they are aware not only of county courts with specialist lists (see r.2.3(2)) but also of individual judges with specialist knowledge. **30.3.4**

"Transfer between Divisions and to and from a specialist list" (r.30.5)

This rule replaces RSC O.4, r.3. As to transfer within High Court of claims pending in the Administrative Court, see para.30.2.9 above. **30.3.5**

"the place" (r.30.6)

Note that the venue of hearings is not limited to court buildings—see r 2.7. **30.3.6**

"child or patient" (r.30.7)

See r.21.1(2). **30.3.7**

Certiorari or prohibition (r.30.8)

See CPR Pt 54. Permission to apply for judicial review is normally obtained without notice being given—see CPR Pt 54. As to certiorari or prohibition, see too County Courts Act 1984 ss.83 and 84, Vol.2, paras 9A–580 to 9A–581. **30.3.8**

The date of transfer

See the Practice Direction. Transfer takes effect from the date that the order is made. **30.3.9**

Notice of Transfer

The court making the transfer should send notice of the transfer to the receiving court and to all parties. **30.3.10**

Appeals against transfer

See the Practice Direction supplementing PD 30 para.5 which sets out the appropriate court in which to make an appeal depending on where and by when the order of transfer was made (para.30PD.5), and CPR Pt 52. See too County Courts Act 1984 s.40(5) (Vol.2, Section 9A, para.9A–472). **30.3.11**

Applications to set aside transfers

See the Practice Direction, para.6, and rr.3.3(5) and 23.10. Applications to set aside should be made to the court where the order for transfer was made. **30.3.12**

Transfer from county court to High Court

See County Courts Act 1984 s.42 at 9A–482. It is essential that judges in county courts and District Registries transferring cases to the High Court express precisely in their orders the destination for the particular claim, otherwise delay and expense may result. Orders should, for example, provide for transfer to The Registry of the Queen's Bench Division – Central Office; Chancery Chambers; the Companies Court; or the Bankruptcy Court of the High Court at the Royal Courts of Justice. **30.3.13**

Procedure

30.4—(1) Where the court orders proceedings to be transferred, the court from which they are to be transferred must give notice of the transfer to all the parties. **30.4**

(2) An order made before the transfer of the proceedings shall not be affected by the order to transfer.

Transfer between Divisions and to and from a specialist list[1]

30.5—(1) The High Court may order proceedings in any Division of the High Court to be transferred to another Division. **30.5**

[1] Amended by the Civil Procedure (Amendment No.4) Rules 2005 (SI 2005/3515).

(2) A judge dealing with claims in a specialist list may order proceedings to be transferred to or from that list.

(3) An application for the transfer of proceedings to or from a specialist list must be made to a judge dealing with claims in that list.

Specialist list

30.5.1 See r.49 and *Lumbermens Mutual Casualty Company v Bovis Lend Lease Ltd* [2004] EWHC 1614 (Comm); 154 New L.J. 1107 (2004) (Colman J.), noted at Civil Procedure News Issue 08/04 October 25, 2004.

For the guidelines which determine whether or not an application to transfer an action from a county court to the Technology and Construction Court would be successful, see *Brynley Collins v Raymond J Drumgold* [2008] EWHC 584 (TCC); March 12, 2008 (viz. Is it a dispute which is, or arises out of, or has a connection with, one of the types of claim identified in PD 60, para.2.1? Does the financial value of that claim and/or its complexity mean that, in accordance with the overriding objective, the case should be transferred to the TCC? Do questions of convenience to the parties have any effect on that decision?). See too *Neath Port Tablot CBC v Currie* [2008] EWHC 1508 (TCC); June 16, 2008 noted at *Civil Procedure News* 8/08 September 2008 (balance of convenience and fairness favoured the continuance of proceedings in the Technology and Construction Court at Bristol District Registry rather than being transferred to London).

Power to specify place where hearings are to be held

30.6 **30.6 The court may specify the place (for instance, a particular county court) where the trial or some other hearing in any proceedings is to be held and may do so without ordering the proceedings to be transferred.**

(Practice Direction 54D (Administrative Court (Venue)) contains provisions about where hearings may be held in proceedings in the Administrative Court.)

Transfer of control of money in court[1]

30.7 **30.7 The court may order that control of any money held by it under rule 21.11 (control of money recovered by or on behalf of a child or protected party) be transferred to another court if that court would be more convenient.**

Transfer of competition law claims

30.8 **30.8—(1) This rule applies if, in any proceedings in the Queen's Bench Division (other than proceedings in the Commercial or Admiralty Courts), a district registry of the High Court or a county court, a party's statement of case raises an issue relating to the application of—**

(a) Article 81 or Article 82 of the Treaty establishing the European Community; or

(b) Chapter I or II of Part I of the Competition Act 1998.[2]

(2) Rules 30.2 and 30.3 do not apply.

(3) The court must transfer the proceedings to the Chancery *Division of the* High Court at the Royal Courts of Justice.

[1] Amended by the Civil Procedure (Amendment) Rules 2007 (SI 2007/2204).
[2] 1998 c.41.

(4) If any such proceedings which have been commenced in the Queen's Bench Division or a Mercantile Court fall within the scope of rule 58.1(2), any party to those proceedings may apply for the transfer of the proceedings to the Commercial Court, in accordance with rule 58.4(2) and rule 30.5(3). If the application is refused, the proceedings must be transferred to the Chancery Division of the High Court at the Royal Courts of Justice.

Effect of rule

Rule 30.8 was inserted in the CPR by the Civil Procedure (Amendment No.5) Rules 2003 (SI 2003/3361) and came into effect on May 1, 2004. For reasons that will become clear in what is said immediately below, the rule suspends the operation of the normal rules as to transfer of proceedings in proceedings where an issue relating to the application of art.81 or art.82 of the EU Treaty arise. **30.8.1**

The Competition Act 1998 (c.41) replaced the Restrictive Practice Courts Act 1976, the Restrictive Trade Practices Act 1976, the Resale Prices Act 1976 and the Restrictive Trade Practices Act 1977. The Act made new provision about competition and the abuse of a dominant position in the market, and conferred powers in relation to investigations conducted in connection with (what are now) art.81 or 82 of the treaty establishing the European Community.

Provisions in Chapter I of the Act prohibit certain agreements preventing, restricting or distorting certain agreements. Chapter II contains provisions about the abuse of dominant position. These Chapters in the Act reflect, respectively, art.81 and art.82 of the EU Treaty.

Article 15 and art.16 of Council Regulation (EC) 1/2003 of December 16, 2002 on the implementation of rules of competition laid down in Articles 81 and 82 of the Treaty, contain provisions affecting the handling of claims to which r.30.8 refers. These articles are set out below. Their terms are reflected in Practice Direction (Competition Law—Claims Relating to the Application of Arts 81 and 82 of the EC Treaty), which contains provisions dealing with venue, notice of proceedings, case management, avoidance of conflict with Commission decisions, and judgments (see para.B12–001 below).

Article 15

Cooperation with national courts

1. In proceedings for the application of Art.81 or Art.82 of the Treaty, courts of the Member States may ask the Commission to transmit to them information in its possession or its opinion on questions concerning the application of the Community competition rules.

2. Member States shall forward to the Commission a copy of any written judgment of national courts deciding on the application of Art.81 or Art.82 of the Treaty. Such copy shall be forwarded without delay after full written judgment is notified to the parties.

3. Competition authorities of Member States, acting on their own initiative, may submit written observations to the national courts of their member states on issues relating to the application of Art.81 or Art.82 of the Treaty. With the permission of the court in question, they may also submit oral observations to the national courts of the Members States. Where the coherent application of Art.81 or Art.82 of the Treaty so requires, the Commission, acting on its own initiative, may submit written observations to courts of the Member States. With the permission of the court in question, it may also make oral observations.

For the purpose of the preparation of their observations only, the competition authorities of the member states and the Commission may request the relevant court of the Member State to transmit or ensure the transmission to them of any documents necessary for the assessment of the case.

4. This Article is without prejudice to wider powers to make observations before courts conferred on competition authorities of the Member States under the law of their Member state.

Article 16

Uniform application of Community competition law

1. When national courts rule on agreements, decisions or practices under Art.81 or Art.82 of the Treaty which are already the subject of Commission decision, they cannot take decisions running counter to the decision adopted by the Commission. They must also avoid giving decisions which would conflict with a decision contemplated by the Commission in proceedings it has initiated. To that effect, the national court may assess whether it is necessary to stay proceedings. This obligation is without prejudice to the rights and obligations under Art.234 of the Treaty.

2. When competition authorities of the Member States rule on agreements, decisions or practices under Art.81 or Art.82 of the Treaty which are already the subject of a Commission decision, they cannot take decisions which would run counter to the decision adopted by the Commission.

PRACTICE DIRECTION—TRANSFER

This Practice Direction supplements CPR Part 30

Value of a case and transfer

1. In addition to the criteria set out in Rule 30.3(2) attention is drawn to the financial limits set out in the High Court and County Courts Jurisdiction Order 1991, as amended. **30PD.1**

2. Attention is also drawn to paragraph 2 of the Practice Direction on Part 29 (the multi-track). **30PD.2**

Date of Transfer

3. Where the court orders proceedings to be transferred, the order will take effect from the date it is made by the court. **30PD.3**

Procedure on Transfer

4.1 Where an order for transfer has been made the transferring court will immediately send notice of the transfer to the receiving court. The notice will contain: **30PD.4**

(1) the name of the case, and

(2) the number of the case.

4.2 At the same time as the transferring court notifies the receiving court it will also notify the parties of the transfer under rule 30.4(1).

Procedure for an appeal against order of transfer

5.1 Where a district judge orders proceedings to be transferred and both the transferring and receiving courts are county courts, any appeal against that order should be made in the receiving court. **30PD.5**

5.2 The receiving court may, if it is more convenient for the parties, remit the appeal to the transferring court to be dealt with there.

Applications to set aside

6.1 Where a party may apply to set aside an order for transfer (e.g. under rule 23.10) the application should be made to the court which made the order. **30PD.6**

6.2 Such application should be made in accordance with Part 23 of the Rules and the practice direction which supplements it.

Transfer on the Criterion in Rule 30.3(2)(g)

7 A transfer should only be made on the basis of the criterion in rule 30.3(2)(g) where there is a real prospect that a declaration of incompatibility will be made. **30PD.7**

Enterprise Act 2002

8.1 In this paragraph— **30PD.8**

(1) "the 1998 Act" means the Competition Act 1998;

(2) "the 2002 Act" means the Enterprise Act 2002; and

(3) "the CAT" means the Competition Appeal Tribunal.

8.2 Rules 30.1, 30.4 and 30.5 and paragraphs 3 and 6 apply.

Transfer From the High Court or a County Court to the Competition Appeal Tribunal Under Section 16(4) of the Enterprise Act 2002

8.3 The High Court or a county court may pursuant to section 16(4) of the 2002 Act, on its own initiative or on application by the **30PD.9**

claimant or defendant, order the transfer of any part of the proceedings before it, which relates to a claim to which section 47A of the 1998 Act applies, to the CAT.

8.4 When considering whether to make an order under paragraph 8.3 the court shall take into account whether—

(1) there is a similar claim under section 47A of the 1998 Act based on the same infringement currently before the CAT;

(2) the CAT has previously made a decision on a similar claim under section 47A of the 1998 Act based on the same infringement; or

(3) the CAT has developed considerable expertise by previously dealing with a significant number of cases arising from the same or similar infringements.

8.5 Where the court orders a transfer under paragraph 8.3 it will immediately—

(1) send to the CAT—

(a) a notice of the transfer containing the name of the case; and

(b) all papers relating to the case; and

(2) notify the parties of the transfer.

8.6 An appeal against a transfer order made under paragraph 8.3 must be brought in the court which made the transfer order.

Transfer From the Competition Appeal Tribunal to the High Court Under Section 16(5) of the Enterprise Act 2002

30PD.10 **8.7** Where the CAT pursuant to section 16(5) of the 2002 Act directs transfer of a claim made in proceedings under section 47A of the 1998 Act to the High Court, the claim should be transferred to the Chancery Division of the High Court at the Royal Courts of Justice.

8.8 As soon as a claim has been transferred under paragraph 8.7, the High Court must—

(1) allocate a case number; and

(2) list the case for a case management hearing before a judge.

8.9 A party to a claim which has been transferred under paragraph 8.7 may apply to transfer it to the Commercial Court if it otherwise falls within the scope of rule 58.2(1), in accordance with the procedure set out in rules 58.4(2) and 30.5(3).

PART 31

Disclosure and Inspection of Documents

Contents

31.0.1

Duty of court and parties to further overriding objective —The case management powers of the court give the court the responsibility and the means for ensuring that disclosure is limited to what is really necessary in individual cases. Accordingly, the procedure for the "automatic" dicscovery of non-specified documents without order is abolished. In r.1.1(1) it is stated that the overriding objective of the Civil Procedure Rules is "to enable the court to deal with cases justly" and this duty is elaborated in r.1.1(3). The court must apply the Rules to further this objective (r.1.1(2)) and parties must help the court in this endeavour (r.1.2). Ultimate responsibility for the regulation of the disclosure process in accordance with the rules in Pt 31, and in a manner consistent with the furtherance of the overriding objective, rests with the court. The parties have a responsibility only to seek discovery when it is justifiable to do so and to co-operate in giving discovery in response to a reasonable request. Particularly for the purposes of minimising costs they should adopt a co-operative, constructive and sensible approach which the court must encourage, supporting it when necessary by appropriate orders for costs. **31.0.2**

The primacy of the necessity principle —The overriding principle is that disclosure should be restricted to what is necessary in the individual case. **31.0.3**

A distinction is drawn between disclosure in cases proceeding on the multi-track and cases proceeding on the fast track. The assumption is that, normally, the scope of disclosure which will be necessary to ensure that cases proceeding in the fast track are disposed of in accordance with the overriding objective stated in r.1.1 will be quite limited, whereas the scope of disclosure necessary for cases proceeding in the multi-track will be more or less limited, and may amount to "full" disclosure. This distinction is mirrored by a two-fold classification of documents that distinguishes between (1) standard disclosure (see r.31.6), and (2) extra disclosure. Put shortly, in fast track cases, disclosure should normally be confined to documents on which a party relies or which to a material extent undermine his case or support another party's case ("standard disclosure") and in multi-track cases standard disclosure should be the first stage, the extent and timing of "extra disclosure" being determined by the procedural judge (see further "The duty to disclose", para.31.0.4 below).

31.0.4 *The duty to disclose* —"Disclosure" is defined as "stating that a document exists or has existed" (r.31.2). There is no provision under the rules for automatic disclosure. The duty to disclose will arise if and when and to the extent that the court orders disclosure. This will generally be at the first case management hearing or upon an application by a party, but parties are reminded that consistent with the parties' duty to help the court further the overriding objective of the rules the parties can proceed with disclosure and inspection on a consensual basis, albeit subject to review by the Court. Part 31 applies to all claims except claims on the small claims track (see r.31.1(2)). A failure by a "public authority" (within the meaning of s.6(3) of the Human Rights Act 1998) to disclose, or to permit disclosure of, documents relevant to the issues in the case which would assist a party to establish its case may constitute a denial of the ECHR art.6(1) right to a fair hearing, although before seeking to rely on art.6(1) a party may be required to apply for specific disclosure (under r.31.12): *McGinley and Egan v United Kingdom* (1999) 27 E.H.R.R. 1, ECtHR. The ECHR art.8 right to respect for private life may also be relevant in this context: *Roche v United Kingdom* [2006] 42 EHRR 30, ECtHR.

There is a right to inspect a disclosed document save where it is no longer in the control of the disclosing party, or that party has a right to withhold inspection or it would be disproportionate to the issues in the case to permit inspection (see r.31.3).

Central to the rules on disclosure is the concept of standard disclosure. This is defined in terms of:

(a) documents upon which a party relies;
(b) documents which adversely affect his own case, or adversely affect another party's case or which support another party's case; and
(c) documents of which disclosure is required by a relevant practice direction (see r.31.6).

The rules also require that only a reasonable search be made in respect of the documents referred to under (b) and (c) above (see r.31.7) and specify factors relevant to the reasonableness of a search. Such rules on disclosure define and delimit the extent and nature of disclosure and are intended to avoid excesses of effort, resources and costs in relation to disclosure and consequent inspection. They replace the *Peruvian Guano* test which should be discarded.

There is provision for specific disclosure and inspection (see r.31.12). It is considered that the concept of "proportionality" is implicit in the granting of an order for specific disclosure or inspection.

Under the rules there is power in the court to dispense with or limit standard disclosure and the parties may do likewise by agreement (see r.31.5(2) and (3)). However, in many cases disclosure and inspection will still form a fundamental part of the litigation process assisting an evaluation and if called for determination of the respective parties' contentions.

Disclosure may now be obtained:

(a) Between parties to proceedings (see this Part);
(b) Where an Act permits disclosure before proceedings (see r.31.16). Such is permitted by s.33 of the SCA 1981 and s.52 of the CCA 1984 between likely parties to subsequent proceedings in all types of claim. The former restriction to personal injuries claims was removed by The Civil Procedure (Modification of Enactments) Order 1998 (SI 1998/2940) paras 5 and 6;
(c) Where an Act permits disclosure against a non-party during proceedings (see r.31.17). Such is permitted by s.34 of the SCA 1981 and s.53 of the CCA 1984

in all types of claim. The former restriction to personal injuries claim was removed by SI 1998/2940 mentioned under (b) above;

(d) In certain other well-established situations such as under the principles of the *Norwich Pharmacal* case, *Anton Piller* and *Mareva* cases and see r.31.18. and the commentary thereunder.

Part 31 is to be read in conjunction with the Civil Procedure Practice Direction supplementing Pt 31 Disclosure and Inspection: see paras 31PD.1 *et seq.*

Disclosure means stating that a document exists or has existed (r.31.2). There is a right to inspect a disclosed document save where it is no longer in the control (see r.31.8) of the party, that party has a right to withhold it (see further r.31.19) or it would be disproportionate to the issues in the case to permit inspection (r.31.3). The meaning of a document and of a copy is set out in r.31.4 in terms wide enough to embrace modern forms of electronic recording.

Unless the court otherwise orders, disclosure means "standard disclosure" (r.31.5). This may be dispensed with or limited by the court and the parties may do likewise by agreement (r.31.5(2) and (3)). By r.31.6 standard disclosure is defined in terms of:

(a) the documents on which a party relies;
(b) documents which:
(i) adversely affect his own case;
(ii) adversely affect another party's case;
(iii) support another party's case.
(c) documents a party is required to disclose by a relevant practice direction.

As to the documents referred to under (b) and (c) above, r.31.7 requires a reasonable search to be made and where the absence of search is asserted and justified on the basis of unreasonableness that a statement to such effect appear in the disclosure statement.

There is no requirement to disclose more than one copy of a document unless a copy contains a modification obliteration or other marking or feature upon which a party intends to rely or which falls within (b) above (r.31.9).

Standard disclosure is by list in the relevant practice direction form (Form **N265**): see r.31.10. The documents must be identified in "a convenient order and manner and, as concisely as possible". The list must state those documents in respect of which a right to withhold from inspection is claimed and those documents which are no longer in the disclosing party's control and what has happened to the same. The list must include a disclosure statement (see r.31.10(5), (6) and (7)).

The duty to disclose continues throughout the proceedings (r.31.11).

Rule 31.12 provides for specific disclosure and inspection to be ordered. Such may include an order to carry out a search to an extent specified in the order.

Under r.31.13 disclosure and/or inspection may be ordered to take place in stages.

Inspection of documents referred to in a statement of case, a witness statement, a witness summary, an affidavit or an experts' report (subject to the court's powers not to order disclosure of documents of instruction where substance thereof is accurately and completely stated in the report (see r.35.10(4)) is provided by r.31.14.

The formalities of inspection are contained in r.31.15.

Rule 31.16 deals with disclosure sought pursuant to any Act which provides for disclosure before proceedings as is permitted under s.33 of the SCA 1981 and s.52 of the CCA 1984. The respondent must be likely to be a party to subsequent proceedings and who would have to disclose the documents therein as part of his duty to make standard disclosure therein.

Disclosure against a non-party during the proceedings where an Act permits such disclosure as under s.34 of the SCA 1981 and s.53 of the CCA 1984 is provided by r.31.17.

Rule 31.18 expressly states that r.31.16 and r.31.17 do not limit any other power the court may have to order disclosure before proceedings have started or against a non party to proceeedings.

A person may apply without notice for an order to withhold disclosure of a document on the basis that disclosure would damage the public interest: see r.31.19(1). Unless the court otherwise orders an order made under this provision must not be served on any other person, nor be open to inspection by any person r.31.19(2). This rule also deals with a claim of a right to withhold inspection of a document. The claim must be asserted together with the grounds relied upon in the party's list of documents or, if there is no list, to the person wishing to inspect. An application can be made to the court to challenge such a claim (see r.31.19(5), (6) and (7)).

Rule 31.20 provides that where a party inadvertently allows a privileged document to be inspected, the inspecting party may only make use of it or its contents with court permission.

A party in breach of the duty to disclose or allow inspection of a document will not be allowed to rely upon such document unless the court allows: see r.31.21 This rule is far less draconian than the former RSC O.24, r.16.

Rule 31.22 concerns the subsequent use of disclosed documents. This is allowed only where the document has been read to or by the court or referred to a hearing in public unless the court restricts or prohibits the use of such a document, where the court gives permission and where the disclosing party and the person to whom the document belongs agree.

Related sources

31.0.5
- Practice Direction (Disclosure and Inspection) (see para.31PD.1)
- Supreme Court Act 1981 ss.33 and 34 (Vol.2, paras 9A–110 to 9A–115)
- County Courts Act 1984 ss.52 and 53 (Vol.2, paras 9A–500 to 9A–506)
- The Civil Procedure (Modification of Enactments) Order 1998 (SI 1998/2940)
- Part 23 Applications for Court Orders
- Part 35, r.35.10(4) Restrictions on disclosure of instructions to expert
- The Chancery Guide, Section A, Chapter 4 (Disclosure of Documents and Expert Evidence) (see Vol.2, paras 4.1 to 4.5)
- The Admiralty and Commercial Courts Guide, Section E (see Vol.2, Section 2A–39)

Forms

31.0.6
- **N265** List of Documents
- Pt 31, PD Annex Disclosure Statement (see r.31.10)
- Practice Direction (Disclosure and Inspection) Annex: Disclosure Statement, para.31PD.8

Scope of this Part

31.1 **31.1—(1) This Part sets out rules about the disclosure and inspection of documents.**

(2) This Part applies to all claims except a claim on the small claims track.

"document"

31.1.1 "Document" has an extended meaning: see r.31.4 and para.31.4.1 below.

"applies to all claims"

31.1.2 Part 31 does not apply to any proceedings to which Pt 76 (Prevention of Terrorism Act 2005) applies, or to any proceedings to which Pt 79 (Financial Restrictions Proceedings Under the Counter-Terrorism Act 2008) applies (see, respectively, r.76.26(1) and r.79.22(1)).

Meaning of disclosure

31.2 **31.2 A party discloses a document by stating that the document exists or has existed.**

"document"

31.2.1 "Document" has an extended meaning: see r.31.4 and para.31.4.1 below.

"stating that the document exists"

31.2.2 "Disclosure" only means stating that a document exists or has existed. In *Smithkline Beecham plc v Generics (UK) Ltd* [2003] EWCA Civ 1109; [2004] 1 W.L.R. 1479, Aldous

L.J. for the Court of Appeal held at [29] that: "No distinction is sought to be drawn between documents obtained from third parties and no limitation is placed on the way that the statement is made. In my view a reference by a party to a document in a witness statement is a statement that the document exists."

Fast track

For claims on the fast track, the Court may direct less than "standard" disclosure: see CPR Pt 28, Practice Direction, para.3.6(l)(c) and (4). **31.2.3**

Right of inspection of a disclosed document

31.3—(1) A party to whom a document has been disclosed has a right to inspect that document except where— **31.3**

(a) the document is no longer in the control of the party who disclosed it;

(b) the party disclosing the document has a right or a duty to withhold inspection of it; or

(c) paragraph (2) applies.

(Rule 31.8 sets out when a document is in the control of a party.)

(Rule 31.19 sets out the procedure for claiming a right or duty to withhold inspection.)

(2) Where a party considers that it would be disproportionate to the issues in the case to permit inspection of documents within a category or class of document disclosed under rule 31.6(b)—

(a) he is not required to permit inspection of documents within that category or class; but

(b) he must state in his disclosure statement that inspection of those documents will not be permitted on the grounds that to do so would be disproportionate.

(Rule 31.6 provides for standard disclosure.)

(Rule 31.10 makes provision for a disclosure statement.)

(Rule 31.12 provides for a party to apply for an order for specific inspection of documents.)

"... control of the party who disclosed it"

The concept of control is defined in r.31.8(2) below. **31.3.1**

"... right or duty to withhold inspection of it"

For instance: **31.3.2**

(a) Legal professional privilege:

(i) Communications privileged although no litigation was contemplated (legal advice privilege).

(ii) Communications privileged only when litigation is contemplated or pending (litigation privilege).

See paras 31.3.5 to 31.3.19 inclusive below. See too the consequences of fraud or illegality (paras 31.3.22 below) and of waiver/loss of privilege (paras 31.3.27 to 31.3.29 *inclusive below*).

Documents tending to criminate or expose to a penalty. See para.31.3.31 below.

Documents privileged on the ground that inspection would be injurious to the public interest. See paras 31.3.32 to 31.3.33 inclusive below.

Other grounds of privilege such as without prejudice communications: see para.31.3.42 below.

Procedure for claiming a right or duty to withhold inspection

See under r.36.19 below. **31.3.3**

"Disproportionate"

31.3.4 The parties should bear in mind the overriding principle of proportionality (see r.1.1(2)(c)) and the matters set out in r.31.7(2) below, and see Pt 31, PD 2.

Legal professional privilege

31.3.5 It is necessary to divide into two classes the documents that are protected on this ground, namely (a) those that are privileged whether or not litigation was contemplated or pending (legal advice privilege), and (b) those that are only privileged if litigation was contemplated or pending when they were made or came into existence (litigation privilege). Where legal professional privilege exists and is not waived or abrogated, it is paramount and absolute and not subject to the balancing exercise of weighing competing public interests against each other as in the field of public interest immunity; see *R. v Derby Magistrates' Court Ex p. B* [1996] A.C. 487; [1995] 4 All E.R. 526, HL. In this case Lord Taylor C.J. said:

> "The principle which runs through all these cases, and many other cases which were cited, is that a man must be able to consult his lawyer in confidence, since otherwise he might hold back half the truth. The client must be sure that what he tells his lawyers in confidence will never be revealed without his consent. Legal professional privilege is thus much more than an ordinary rule of evidence, limited in its application to the facts of a particular case. It is a fundamental condition on which the administration of justice as a whole rests. ... Nobody doubts that legal professional privilege could be modified, or even abrogated, by statute, subject always to the objection that legal professional privilege is a fundamental human right protected by the European Convention for the Protection of Human Rights and Fundamental Freedoms, as to which we did not hear any argument ... (But) whatever inroads may have been made by Parliament in other areas, legal professional privilege is a field which Parliament has so far left untouched."

In *R. (on the application of Morgan Grenfell & Co Ltd) v Special Commissioner of Income Tax* [2002] UKHL 21; [2003] 1 A.C. 563; [2002] 3 All E.R. 1, HL, the House of Lords held that on its true construction s.20(1) of the Taxes Management Act 1970 did not by necessary implication abrogate legal professional privilege so as to authorise an inspector of taxes to issue a notice requiring a taxpayer to disclose material subject to legal professional privilege.

This privilege cannot be derogated from, e.g. by requirements of CPR r.48.7(3); see *General Mediterranean Holdings v Patel* [2000] 1 W.L.R. 272; [1999] 3 All E.R. 673.

Disclosure of this type of privileged document for a limited purpose does not without more constitute a general waiver or loss of privilege; see *B v Auckland District Law Society* [2003] UKPC 38; [2003] 2 A.C. 736; [2004] 4 All. E.R. 269.

For the position under the ECHR, see *Silver v United Kingdom* (1983) 5 E.H.R.R. 347, ECtHR; *Campbell v United Kingdom* (1993) 15 E.H.R.R. 137, ECtHR; and *General Meditterranean Holdings v Patel* [2000] 1 W.L.R. 272, QB.

(a) Communications privileged although no litigation was contemplated or pending—"legal advice privilege"

Solicitor and client

31.3.6 Letters and other communications passing between a party, or his predecessors in title, and his, or their solicitors are privileged from production, provided they are, and are sworn or statemented to be, confidential, and written to, or by, the solicitor in his professional capacity, and for the purpose of getting legal advice or assistance for the client (*O'Shea v Wood* [1891] P. 286, CA; *Gardner v Irvin* (1878) 4 Ex.D. 49 at 53, CA; *Kennedy v Lyell* (1883) 23 Ch.D. 387 at 404, CA; *Wheeler v Le Marchant* (1881) 17 Ch.D. 675 at 682, CA; *cf. More v Weaver* [1928] 2 K.B. 520; *Minter v Priest* (1930) 46 T.L.R. 301, HL; *Re Duncan, (decd.), Garfield v Fay* [1968] P. 306; [1968] 2 W.L.R. 1479—foreign legal advisers); but not otherwise (*ibid., Original Hartlepool Collieries v Moon* (1874) 30 L.T. 193 at 585; *Moseley v Victoria Co* (1886) 55 L.T. 482).

Although originally confined to advice about litigation, legal professional privilege has long been extended to non-litigious business. The test is whether the communication or other document is made confidentially for the purposes of legal advice. Those purposes have to be construed broadly. Privilege obviously attaches to a document conveying legal advice from solicitor to client and to a specific request from the client for such advice. It does not follow, however, that all other communications between solicitor and client lack privilege. Where information is passed by the solicitor or client to the other as part of a process aimed at keeping both informed, so that advice may be sought and given, privilege will attach. The scope of legal advice privilege is not as extensive as litigation privilege (see below at para.31.3.12 *et seq*). Legal advice privilege extends to advice given as to what should or should not be prudently and sensibly done in a "relevant legal context" and is not confined to advice concerning legal rights and obligations; *Three Rivers DC v Governor and Company of the Bank of England (No.6)* [2004] UKHL 48 [2005] 1 A.C. 610; [2004] 3 W.L.R. 1274; [2005] 4 All E.R. 948, HL. Accordingly, advice on presentation of the Bank's case to the Bingham Inquiry where it was possible that criticism of the Bank's conduct might be expressed in the Report and where the Bank in seeking the advice was seeking in confidence the assistance of the lawyer's legal skills was held protected by the privilege. The House of Lords declined to pronounce in this case upon the criteria govening whether communications between lawyers and employees for their client should be treated as communications between lawyers and client, stating that until such fell for decision in a case before it, the guiding precedent on the issue would continue to be the judgment of the Court of Appeal in the *Three Rivers (No.5)* [2003] EWCA Civ 474; [2003] Q.B. 1556; [2003] 3 W.L.R. 667 CA, that such communications like communication between the lawyers and third parties are not within the privilege.

The reasons for this privilege are fully stated by Lord Brougham in *Greenough v Gaskell* (1833) 1 My. &K. 98; by Lord Cottenham in *Reid v Langlois* (1849) 1 Mac. & G. 627; by Jessel M.R. in *Anderson v Bank of British Columbia* (1875-76) L.R. 2 Ch. D. 644 at 649; by Cotton L.J. in *Southwark Water Co v Quick* (1878) 3 Q.B.D. 315 at 321, and by Stirling J. in *Ainsworth v Wilding* [1900] 2 Ch. 315 at 321; see *Bray* at 350 and more recently by Lord Taylor C.J. in *R. v Derby Magistrates Court* (see above). It precludes an action for libel in respect of statements contained in such communications (*More v Weaver* [1928] 2 K.B. 520, CA; but in *Minter v Priest* [1930] AC 558; (1930) 46 T.L.R. 301, HL, the question whether the privilege was absolute or qualified was expressly reserved).

This privilege extends to documents otherwise within it, although they contain statements of fact as to matters in the public domain, such as statements as to proceedings in private in the presence of the other party (*Ainsworth v Wilding*). It extends to bills of costs relating to litigation actual or in contemplation (*Chant v Brown* (1852) 9 Ha. 790; *Turton v Barber* (1874) 17 L.R. Eq. 329) but it does not extend to a communication which took place in the presence of the opposite party, or with the opposite party (but see *Feuerheerd v LGO Co*) or which are wholly in the public domain (*Ainsworth v Wilding*). The privilege is not affected by the fact that the action in which disclosure is sought is founded on a policy insuring the claimant against damages and costs incurred in an claim to which the disclosure relates (*Daily Express (1908) Ltd v Mountain* (1916) 32 T.L.R. 592, CA).

The privilege extends to information which the solicitor receives in a professional capacity from a third party and which he conveys to his client (*Re Sarah C. Getty Trust, Getty v Getty* [1985] 3 W.L.R. 302; [1985] 2 All E.R. 809).

The principle that a client should be able to obtain legal advice in confidence requires that, where professional privilege applies to lawyer-client communications, internally circulated documents or parts of documents revealing such communications are also privileged, whatever the purpose, other than fraud, for which such documents are brought into existence (*Bank of Nova Scotia v Hellenic Mutual War Risk Assn. (Bermuda) Ltd (The Good Luck)* [1992] 1 A.C. 233; [1991] 2 W.L.R. 1279; [1991] 3 All E.R. 1; [1991] 2 Lloyd's Rep. 191; *Independent*, October 31, 1988, HL), noted at [1992] 2 Lloyd's Rep. 540).

Third party as medium of communications

So confidential letters or communications between a party and his solicitor, in his professional capacity, made through a clerk or agent employed by the solicitor (*Wheeler v Le Marchant* (1881) L.R. 17 Ch. D. 675 at 682, CA) or, and by the client in order to convey information to or from the solicitor (*Reid v Langlois* (1849) 1 Mac. & G. 627; *Hooper v Gumm* (1862) 2 Johns. & H. 602; *MacFarlan v Rolt* (1872) L.R. 14 Eq. 580; *Anderson v Bank of British Columbia* (1875-76) L.R. 2 Ch. D. 644 at 649; *Wheeler v Le Marchant* (1881) 17 Ch.D. 675 at 682, 684) are privileged. **31.3.7**

Solicitors and partners as professional agents

31.3.8 So, too, letters and communications between a solicitor and his partner (*Mostyn v West Mostyn Coal Co* (1876) 34 L.T. 531), or professional agent (*Hughes v Biddulph* (1827) 4 Russ. 190; *Bolton v Liverpool Corp* (1833) 1 My. & K. 88 at 96; *Catt v Tourle* (1870) 23 L.T. 485 at 486; *Goodall v Little* (1851) 1 Sim.(N.S.) 155; *Macfarlan v Rolt* (1872) L.R. 14 Eq. 580) are equally privileged. This does not apply to correspondence between the solicitors for opposite parties (*Gore v Harris* (1851) 21 L.J.Ch.10).

Legal advisers in the service of a party

31.3.9 The same privilege attaches to communications with a solicitor in the whole-time service of a party (e.g. a solicitor to a government department or a commercial enterprise) as to communications with a solicitor practising independently, provided that such communication relates to legal as distinct from administrative matters (*Alfred Crompton Amusement Machines Ltd v Commrs. of Customs and Excise (No.2)* [1974] A.C. 405; [1973] 2 All E.R. 1169, HL). An applicant has no right to inspect communications between in-house lawyers where there is an application for judicial review pending, as such documents are subject to legal professional privilege once litigation has started (*R. v Law Society Ex p. Rosen, Independent*, February 19, 1990). In-house lawyers cannot claim legal professional privilege in respect of investigations by the European Commission; see joined cases T–125/03 and T–253/03 *Akzo Nobel Chemicals Ltd and Akros Chemicals Ltd v Commission* [2008] All E.R. (EC) 1; [2008] Bus L.R. 348. See too further *Turco and Kingdom of Sweden v Council of the European Union, Joined Cases C-39/05P and C-52/05P, The Times*, July 4, 2008, cases regarding public access to European Parliament, Council and Commission documents and art.4(2) of Regulation (EC) No.1049/ 2001.

Counsel

31.3.10 Instructions and briefs to counsel and cases for counsel's opinion and counsel's opinions thereon, and counsel's drafts and notes, are privileged (*Mostyn v West Mostyn Coal and Iron Co*; *Bristol Corp v Cox* (1884) 26 Ch.D. 678; *Curtis v Beaney* [1911] P. 181; *Lowden v Blakey* (1889) 23 Q.B.D. 332, draft advertisements settled by counsel; *Pearse v Pearse* (1846) 1 De G. & S. 12; *Bolton v Liverpool Corp* (1833) 1 My. & K. 88, 93; *Manser v Dix* (1855) 1 K. & J. 451; *In the Estate of Copper* (1911) 27 T.L.R. 462; *Vigneron-Dahl Ltd v Pettit* [1925] W.N. 177, drafts of documents in support of application for consent of Attorney General.) but the indorsement on a brief of the result of the trial or the order made is not (*Walsham v Stainton* (1863) 2 H. & M. 1; *Nicholl v Jones* (1865) 2 H. & M. 588).

Note

31.3.10.1 All the above are privileged, although no litigation was pending or contemplated at the time when the communication took place (*Minet v Morgan* (1873) L.R. 8 Ch. 361; *O'Shea v Wood* [1891] P. 286 at 289, 290; *Mostyn v West Mostyn Coal and Iron Co* (1876) 34 L.T. 531; *Wheeler v Le Marchant* (1881) L.R. 17 Ch. D. 675 at 682; *Turton v Barber* (1874) L.R. 17 Eq. 329; *Lowden v Blakey* (1889) 23 Q.B.D. 332; *Collins v London General Omnibus Co* (1893) 68 L.T. 831; *Greenough v Gaskell* (1833) 1 My. & K. 98 at 102).

Patent and trade mark agents

31.3.11 By virtue of the provisions of s.280 of the Copyright, Designs and Patents Act 1988, communications between a client and his patent agent relating to the protection of any invention, design, technical information or trade mark or any matter involving passing off are privileged in the same way as such communications would be protected if they were between the client and his solicitor. Similarly, by virtue of s.87 of the Trade Marks Act 1994, communications between a client and his trade mark agent in relation to the protection of any design or trade mark or as to any matter involving passing off are also privileged.

(b) Communications privileged only when litigation was contemplated or pending—"litigation privilege"

Solicitors and non-professional agent or third party

31.3.12 Communications between a solicitor and a non-professional agent or a third party, directly, or through an agent (*Anderson v Bank of British Columbia* (1875-76) L.R. 2 Ch. D. 644 at 650) which come into existence after litigation is contemplated or commenced and made with a view to such litigation, either for the purpose of obtaining or giving advice in regard to it, or of obtaining or collecting evidence to be used in it, or obtaining information which may lead to the obtaining of such evidence, are privileged (*Anderson v Bank of British Columbia* (1875-76) L.R. 2 Ch. D. 644 at 649; *Wheeler v Le Marchant* (1881) L.R. 17 Ch. D. 675 at 681, CA; *Steele v Stewart* (1843) 13 Sim. 533, affirmed (1843) 1 Ph. 471; *Walsham v Stainton* (1863) 2 H. & M. 1; *Simpson v Brown* (1864) 33 Beav. 482; *Wilson v Northampton Rail* (1872) 14 L.R. Eq. 477; *Re Duncan (dec'd), Garfield v Fay* [1968] P. 306 [1968] 2 All E.R. 395—litigation in a foreign Court). Except in the case where the non-professional agent is acting merely as the medium of communication between the solicitor and his client (*ibid.*, at 681, and see *Reid v Langlois* and cases cited) such communications between a solicitor and a non-professional agent are not privileged, unless made with a view to litigation contemplated or existing (*Wheeler v Le Marchant* (1881) 17 Ch.D. 675 at 682, CA). This applies to information such as a surveyor's report obtained by a solicitor with a view to giving his client legal advice, and such information is not privileged unless obtained with a view to contemplated or existing litigation (*ibid.*, per Brett L.J. at 683). As to the extent of this principle, see per Cotton L.J. *Kennedy v Lyell* (1883) 23 Ch.D. 387 at 407; per Stirling J. *Learoyd v Halifax Banking Co* [1893] 1 Ch. 686 at 691; per Denman J. *Louden v Blakey* (1889) 23 Q.B.D. 332 at 334; per Lindley M.R. *Calcraft v Guest* [1898] 1 Q.B. 759 at 762. It is not open to a licensee to claim the privilege to which his licensor is entitled if the licensor is not a party to the claim and has not claimed privilege (*Reeves Bros. Inc v Lewis Reed & Co Ltd* [1971] R.P.C. 355, refusing to extend the basis of the reasoning in *Calcraft v Guest*).

Documents obtained by a solicitor with a view to enabling him to prosecute or defend a claim, or give advice with reference to existing or contemplated litigation, are privileged (*Learoyd v Halifax Banking Co* [1893] 1 Ch. 686 at 690; *cf.*, *North Australian Co v Goldsborough* [1893] 2 Ch. 381); so are documents which come into existence merely as materials for the brief (*Southwark Water Co v Quick* (1878) 3 Q.B.D. 315 at 320; *The Palermo* (1883) 9 P.D. 6); but this does not extend to copies of unprivileged documents, such as letters, although obtained by the solicitor (*Chadwick v Bowman* (1886) 16 Q.B.D. 561. See *Lyell v Kennedy* (1883) 23 Ch.D. 387). When depositions of the crew of the R. in regard to a collision with the P. were taken by the Receiver of Wrecks, and in a claim arising out of the collision the Board of Trade refused to give copies of the depositions to the owners of the P., it was held that copies of the depositions obtained for the purpose of the claim by the solicitors to the owners of the R. were privileged (*The Palermo* (1883) L.R. 9 P.D. 6).

Documents which come into existence for some purpose other than to instruct a lawyer or to form part of his brief are not privileged, and do not subsequently become privileged simply because they are sent to a lawyer as part of his instructions. Privilege cannot be claimed in respect of a copy of an affidavit taken for the purposes of legal advice when the original affidavit is not privileged (*Dubai Bank Ltd v Galadari* [1989] 3 All E.R. 769, CA, not following *R. v Board of Inland Revenue Ex p. Goldberg* [1989] Q.B. 267; [1988] 3 All E.R. 248).

Documents prepared confidentially after a dispute has arisen between the claimant and the defendant, and for the purpose of obtaining information, evidence or legal advice with reference to litigation existing or contemplated between the parties to a claim, are privileged (per Cotton L.J. *Wheeler v Le Marchant* (1881) L.R. 17 Ch.D. 675 at 685). So where an examination under s.27 of the B.A. 1883 was held with a view to enable the solicitor of the trustee to advise him whether a claim should be brought, the transcript of notes of the proceedings at the examination was held to be privileged (*Learoyd v Halifax Joint Stock Banking Co* (1893)). So where during a claim, anonymous letters relating to the matters in dispute were sent to the claimant, to her solicitor, and to her counsel, the two latter were held privileged, but not the letter to the claimant (*Holloway, Re* (1887) L.R. 12 P.D. 167, CA).

Client and non-professional agent or third party

The general principle is that documents embodying communications with (including reports to or from) a non-professional servant, agent or third party are privileged if, and only if, coming into existence for the purpose of obtaining legal advice in existing or anticipated proceedings (see the cases summarised in the judgment of Havers J. in *Seabrook v British Transport Commission* [1959] 1 W.L.R. 509; [1959] 2 All E.R. 15). **31.3.13**

The application of this test is easy enough in straightforward cases; privilege will clearly extend to communications for such purposes made to a solicitor through an agent, and to information obtained from a third party at the request of a solicitor to enable him to enforce or resist a claim by legal proceedings. Difficulties arise, however, (a) in determining the status of documents coming into existence for more than one purpose, and (b) in deciding at what stage it can fairly be said any such purpose is obtaining advice in anticipated litigation, as contrasted with obtaining information as to an occurrence which may lead to litigation.

As to (a) a document which is produced or brought into existence where the *dominant* purpose of its author, or of the person or authority under whose direction (whether particular or general) it is produced or brought into existence, is the use of the document or its contents in order to obtain legal advice, or to conduct or aid in the conduct of litigation in reasonable prospect at the time of its production, is privileged and excluded from inspection (*Waugh v British Railways Board* [1980] A.C. 521; [1979] 2 All E.R. 1169; HL).

The dominant purpose of a document does not necessarily fall to be ascertained by reference to the intention of its actual composer (*Guinness Peat Properties Ltd v Fitzroy Robinson Partnership* [1987] 1 W.L.R. 1027; [1987] 2 All E.R. 716, CA). The person or authority under whose direction a document is produced or brought into existence is in many cases the employer of the author; in such cases reference must be made to the intentions of the employer rather than to the intention of the author alone (*Waugh v British Railways Board* (above); *McAvan v London Transport Executive* [1982] CA Transcript 498). In other cases a document may be brought into existence at the direction of insurers (either as a condition of the insurance policy of a party to the claim or otherwise). In such cases reference must be made to the intention of the insurers. Where the dominant purpose of the insurers in procuring the document is its submission to legal advisers for advice on whether the claim should be paid or resisted, e.g. because fraud is suspected (*Re Highgrade Traders Ltd* [1984] B.C.L.C. 151, CA), or because the claim is in a complicated area of indemnity involving large sums of money (*Guinness Peat Properties Ltd v Fitzroy Robinson Partnership* [1987] 1 W.L.R. 1027; [1987] 2 All E.R. 716, CA), the document will be held to be privileged. Such privilege can be claimed by a party to a claim notwithstanding that it is the insurers rather than that party who seek to use the document to obtain legal advice (*Guinness Peat Properties Ltd v Fitzroy Robinson Partnership* (above)). The document will not be held to be privileged, however, where the insurance claim is simple and straightforward, and where the dominant purpose of the insurers in procuring the document is the assessment of the quantum of the claim rather than obtaining of legal advice on liability.

As to (b) the question, which is often closely connected with that raised in (a), is whether it is sufficient that the documents were made against the more or less likely contingency of it becoming necessary to obtain legal advice to make or resist a claim by litigation, or whether there must be an actual, present intention to obtain such advice at the time that the documents are made. In answer to this question the Court of Appeal has held that, if litigation is reasonably in prospect, documents brought into existence for the purpose of enabling solicitors to advise whether a claim shall be made or resisted are protected by privilege, whether or not a decision to instruct solicitors has been made at the time the documents are brought into being, subject only to establishing that such purpose is the dominant purpose of their creation (*Re Highgrade Traders Ltd* [1984] B.C.L.C. 151, CA; *Guinness Peat Properties Ltd v Fitzroy Robinson Partnership* [1987] 1 W.L.R. 1027; [1987] 2 All E.R. 716, CA).

It must always be remembered that the time at which the dominant purpose of the author of a document, or of the person or authority under whose direction it is made, is to be judged, is the time when the document is brought into being. Such judgment ought not to be coloured by the subsequent use of the document or the subsequent intentions of the author, or of the person or authority under whose direction it is made, about how the document may best be used. Thus in *Jones v Great Central Railway Co* [1910] A.C. 4, HL, the dominant purpose of the making of a report by a trade union member to his trade union was, at the time the document was made, to allow the trade union to consider whether or not it should give financial assistance to the member to enable him to bring proceedings against his employer for wrongful dismissal. In *Alfred Crompton Amusement Machines Ltd v Commrs. of Customs and Excise (No.2) [1974] A.C. 405*; [1973] 2 All E.R. 1169, HL, the dominant purpose of the commissioners in procuring certain documents from the third parties was, at the time the documents were brought into being, the valuation of the appellants' goods for purchase tax. In neither case were the documents held to be privileged, notwithstanding that in both cases litigation was reasonably in prospect at the time the documents were brought into being and that in both cases the documents were subsequently used to obtain legal advice and to conduct the litigation.

Accident reports to employers or insurers may fall on either side of the line. In several cases such reports have been held to be privileged on the grounds that, at the time they were made or procured, the dominant purpose of those who made or procured them was the obtaining of legal advice whether to resist a claim for damages (*Ogden v London Electric Ry. Co* (1933) 49 T.L.R. 542; *Westminster Airways v Kuwait Oil Co* [1951] 1 K.B. 134; *Seabrook v British Transport Commission* [1959] 1 W.L.R. 509; [1959] 2 All E.R. 15). On the other hand, an accident report, the preparation of which is required by National Health Service circulars is not subject to legal professional privilege where the dominant purpose of its preparation is not submission to solicitors in anticipation of litigation, even although one of the purposes of such reports, mentioned in the circulars, is use by solicitors if litigation should be commenced in respect of the accident (*Lask v Gloucester Health Authority* [1991] 2 Med LR, 379, CA). Thus where the dominant purpose in the preparation of an accident report is the avoidance of similar accidents in the future, the report will not be privileged, even although a subsidiary purpose in its preparation is its use in the conduct of anticipated litigation.

Where a document produced under a statutory duty (e.g. s.7(3) of the Company Directors Disqualification Act 1986) did not threaten the inviolability of communication between a party and his lawyer, that party could not claim legal professional privilege for it by asserting that the document's dominant purpose was for use in litigation; see *Secretary of State for Trade and Industry v Baker* [1998] Ch. 356; [1998] 2 W.L.R. 667; [1998] 1 All E.R. 673. The court stated that there was no general privilege that attached to documents brought into existence for the purposes of litigation independent of the need to keep inviolate communications between client and legal adviser. If documents for which professional privilege was sought did not relate in some fashion to communications between client and legal adviser, there was no element of public interest that could override the ordinary rights of disclosure and inspection.

(c) Legal Professional Privilege generally

Pre-existing documents or copies of or extracts therefrom

Documents do not become privileged by the mere fact that they have at some time been submitted to a solicitor (*Graham v Bogle* [1924] 1 Ir.R. 68); and copies, obtained by a party from third persons, of unprivileged documents which he had lost, do not necessarily become privileged (*Chadwick v Bowman* (1886) 16 Q.B.D. 561). Thus legal professional privilege does not extend to cover an original document, even if obtained by a party to litigation or his legal adviser for purposes of the litigation, if the document has not come into existence for the purposes of the litigation, but is already in existence before the litigation is contemplated or commenced. A pre-existing document not entitled to privilege does not become privileged merely because it is handed to a solicitor for the purposes of litigation (*Ventouris v Mountain (The Italia Express) (No.1)* [1991] 1 W.L.R. 607, CA). But original or copy documents obtained or prepared by the party for the purpose of obtaining his solicitor's advice in view of pending or anticipated litigation, or by his solicitor for the purposes of pending or anticipated litigation, are privileged (*The Palermo* (1883) L.R. 9 P.D. 6; *Kennedy v Lyell* (1883) 23 Ch.D. 387; *Pearce v Foster* (1885) L.R. 15 Q.B.D. 114; *Watson v Cammell Laird & Co Ltd* [1959] 1 W.L.R. 702; [1959] 2 All E.R. 757). However the notion that there may be a privileged copy of an un-privileged document is now discounted; *Lubrizol v Esso Petroleum Co (No.4)* [1993] F.S.R. 64. Legal professional privilege does not attach to documents which are in the possession of both parties unless the documents would tend to indicate either the advice that might be sought or the advice that was given (*ibid.*, at 70). 31.3.14

Where a solicitor copies or assembles a selection of unprivileged third party documents such selection will be privileged if its production would afford a clue to the advice being tendered, *Lyell v Kennedy* (1884) 27 Ch.D. 1. The same principle does not extend to a selection from client's own unprivileged documents but if production of such selection is sought it is a matter for the court's discretion whether to order production, *Sumitomo Corporation v Credit Lyonnais Rouse Ltd* [2001] EWCA Civ 1152; [2002] 1 W.L.R. 479; [2002] 4 All E.R. 68; [2001] 2 Lloyd's Rep. 517, CA. Further, there is no reason in principle why in the context of legal privilege translations should not be treated in the same way as copies. Neither the process of copying nor the process of translation involves the addition or subtraction of any privilege not enjoyed by the original (*ibid.*).

Confidential documents

31.3.15 No communication made by or on behalf of the opposite party can be confidential; per Cotton L.J. *Kennedy v Lyell* (1883) 23 Ch.D. 387 at 405; *Ainsworth v Wilding* [1900] 2 Ch.321. In *Feuerheerd v LGO. Co* [1918] 2 K.B. 565, however (where the above cases were not cited and the point apparently not even raised) the CA is reported to have held that a statement made and signed by the claimant, and obtained from her by the defendants' claims inspector for the purpose of being laid before the defendants' solicitor was privileged. It is submitted that this decision is wrong, and that *Tobakin v Dublin Southern Trams Co* [1905] 2 I.R. 58, which the CA refused to follow, was right. The previous sentence was cited with approval by the Court of Appeal in Northern Ireland (see *McKay v McKay* [1988] 12 N.I.J.B. 78 at 92–93).

Other legal advisers

31.3.16 The above principles are not confined to solicitors, but extend to confidential communications with any legal adviser, as for instance, a Scots (*Wheeler v Le Marchant* (1881) 17 Ch.D. 675 at 679; *Lawrence v Campbell* (1859) 4 Drew. 485) or French (*MacFarlan v Rolt* (1872) 14 L.R. Eq. 580) or Dutch (*Bunbury v Bunbury* (1839) 2 Beav. 173) legal adviser.

Co-plaintiffs or co-defendants

31.3.17 Communications between co-claimants (*Hutt v Haileybury College* (1888) 4 T.L.R. 277, CA) or co-defendants (*Hamilton v Nott* (1873) L.R. 16 Eq. 112; *Jenkyns v Bushby* (1866) 2 L.R. Eq. 547; *Betts v Menzies* (1857) 26 L.J. Ch. 528; *Goodall v Little* (1851) 1 Sim.(N.S.) 155) stand on the same footing as communications with non-professional agents, and are only privileged under the same circumstances. But where one of several trustees is a solicitor, communications between him and his co-trustees which would be privileged if he were not a co-trustee, are privileged (*Re Whitworth* [1919] 1 Ch.320, CA; affirmed, *sub nom.O'Rourke v Darbishire* [1920] A.C. 581, HL).

Common interest legal privilege

31.3.18 A privilege in aid of anticipated litigation in which several persons have a common interest although all such persons have not been made parties to the claim; see *Buttes Gas and Oil Co v Hammer (No.3)* [1981] 1 Q.B. 223 at 243, 267. Such common interest did not come to an end simply because a dispute arises as to who should conduct the proceedings but documents brought into existence in respect of such dispute did not attract common interest legal privilege though they might attract some other form of privilege; see *Leif Hoegh &Co A/S v Petrolsea Inc (The World Era) (No.2)* [1993] 1 Lloyd's Rep. 363. See too *Formica Ltd v Export Credits Guarantee Department* [1995] 1 Lloyd's Rep. 692; held that where a guarantor of losses incurred by a company had been contractually entitled to view documents which had come into existence in the company's pursuit of its potential losses, the guarantor was entitled to specific discovery of the documents as the guarantor had a common interest with the company in the recovery of the company's debts.

Other advisers

31.3.19 Communications between a party and his medical adviser (*Wheeler v Le Marchant* (1881) 17 Ch.D. 675 at 681) or his spiritual adviser (*ibid.*) or a non-professional friend or adviser (*ibid. Smith v Daniel* (1874) 18 L.R. Eq. 649) are not privileged although of the most confidential kind (*ibid.*); nor are communications with a pursuivant of the Herald's College (*Slade v Tucker* (1880) 14 Ch.D. 824). For position in relation to patent and trade mark agents, see para.31.3.11 above.

Reports prepared by bank accountants in course of investigating problem loans were not protected as (a) such were not communications between bank and its legal advisers and (b) were not documents produced in contemplation of litigation (*Price Waterhouse v BCCI Holdings (Luxembourg) SA* [1992] B.C.L.C. 583).

Where proceedings had been conducted initially by a party receiving advice from a firm of personnel consultants, that advice was not privileged from discovery as it was not covered by legal professional privilege (*New Victoria Hospital v Ryan* [1993] I.C.R. 201, EAT).

The public interest in making confidential documents relating to an alleged fraud of an international bank available to parties to private foreign litigation directed towards exposing such fraud outweighed the public interest in preserving the confidentiality in those documents, *Pharaon v Bank of Credit and Commerce International SA*, Price Waterhouse intervening, (application for permission to comply with a *subpoena* to produce documents) [1998] 4 All E.R. 455.

Subsequent litigation

The general principle is, that a document once privileged is always privileged (*Calcraft v Guest* [1898] 1 Q.B. 759, per Lindley M.R. at 761; *Goldstone v Williams Deacon & Co* [1899] 1 Ch. 47 at 52) and the privilege applies both in the existing or contemplated and any other litigation (*ibid.*; *Pearce v Foster* (1885) 15 Q.B.D. 114; *Bullock v Corrie* [1878] 3 Q.B.D. 356; *Curtis v Beaney* [1911] P. 181). If documents for which privilege can be claimed are brought into existence for the purpose of a claim which ultimately is not proceeded with, the privilege does not cease, but can be claimed in a subsequent claim other than that for which they were originally brought into existence (*Pearce v Foster* (1885) and see *Ainsworth v Wilding* [1900] 2 Ch. 315); and "the mere fact that documents used in a previous litigation are held and have not been destroyed, does not amount to waiver of the privilege" (*Calcraft v Guest* [1898] 1 Q.B. 759). But the privilege can be claimed only by a party to the original litigation or his successor in title (*Reeves Bros. Inc v Lewis Reed & Co Ltd* [1971] F.S.R. 17); a licensing arrangement with such a party is not equivalent to a succession in title (*ibid.*). 31.3.20

If the privilege which prevailed in the original claim is properly claimed in a subsequent claim by the person originally entitled to it, or his successor, there is no additional requirement that the subsequent claim should be between the same parties or involve the same subject-matter; provided there is sufficient connection for the document to be relevant, the party entitled to privilege is able to assert it in the subsequent claim (*The Aegis Blaze* [1986] 1 Lloyd's Rep. 203; (1986) 130 S.J. 15, CA). The same rule prevails even where the original and subsequent claim are in different jurisdictions. A litigant's privilege arising in proceedings in a foreign court is an answer to a claim in subsequent proceedings in England for production of a document the subject of such privilege (*Minnesota Mining & Manufacturing Co v Rennicks (UK) Ltd (No.1)* [1991] F.S.R. 97). Nor does the use of the documents in the foreign proceedings constitute a waiver of the privilege where the documents were called into existence for the purpose of such litigation and remained the subject of a protective order or rule: *ibid.*

A document adduced or evidence given by a party in a private arbitration, however, is not privileged from disclosure in subsequent litigation between such party and others who are not parties to the arbitration (*Shearson Lehman Hutton Inc v Maclaine Watson & Co Ltd (No.3)* [1988] 1 W.L.R. 946; [1989] 1 All E.R. 1056). But see restriction on use without permission in Hassneh Insurance case, para.31.22.1 below.

Documents in the public domain

Documents which are in the public domain are not privileged (*Nicholl v Jones* (1865) 2 Hem. & M. 588; *Goldstone v Williams Deacon & Co* [1899] 1 Ch. 47 at 52). This applies to shorthand or other notes of proceedings in open Court (*ibid.*, *Re Worswick* (1888) 38 Ch.D. 370; *Lambert v Home* [1914] 3 K.B. 86, CA, overruling *Nordon v Defries* (1882) Q.B.D. 508) or in a private hearing (*Ainsworth v Wilding* [1900] 2 Ch. 315) or before an arbitrator (*Rawstone v Preston Corp* (1885) 30 Ch.D. 116) and to the indorsements on counsel's brief of the result of the trial or the order of the Court (*Nicholl v Jones*) or depositions filed in the course of a claim (*Goldstone v Williams Deacon & Co* [1899] 1 Ch. 47) or office copies thereof (*ibid.*). But this does not apply to privileged documents merely because they are exhibited to depositions which are entered and read in an order of compromise (*ibid.*). Nor does it apply to a collection of copies or extracts of public records or documents made by a solicitor for the purposes of a defence, or the result of his research and skill (*Kennedy v Lyell* (1883) 23 Ch.D. 387, CA; see *Lambert v Home* [1914] 3 K.B. 86 at 90, 92) and see Bray, p.490). 31.3.21

Fraud or illegality

This professional privilege does not extend to cases where the document came into existence as a step in a criminal or illegal proceeding, as, e.g. if a solicitor is consulted on how to do an illegal act (*Bullivant v Attorney General of Victoria* [1901] A.C. 196 at 201, per Lord Halsbury and at 206, per Lord Lindley; see also *R. v Cox and Railton* 31.3.22

(1884) L.R. 14 Q.B.D. 153). In a claim against ex-employees for conspiracy to injure, breach of the duty of fidelity and breach of confidence, disclosure was ordered of documents passing between the defendants and their solicitors relating to the setting up of the companies within which the defendants proposed to operate (*Gamlen Chemical Co (UK) Ltd v Rochem Ltd* [1983] R.P.C.1.). But privilege is not lost if the purpose of the document was to ask, or give, advice as to how (lawfully) "to keep out of an Act of Parliament" (*Bullivant v Attorney.General for Victoria*, above, at 207) or to warn against the results of contemplated acts (*Butler v Board of Trade* [1971] Ch. 680; [1970] 3 All E.R. 593). To bring a case within this exception there must be a definite charge of fraud or illegality and a prima facie case must be made out (*O'Rourke v Darbishire* [1919] 1 Ch. 320, HL at 336, 349, CA; affirmed [1920] A.C. 581; [1920] A.C. 581, HL). The Court will be slow to displace the privilege and would not do so on mere suspicion as opposed to the establishment of a prima facie case of fraud or illegality (*Royscott Spa Leasing Ltd v Lovett* [1995] B.C.C. 502). Notwithstanding that the word "fraud" has not been used in the statement of case, privilege can be displaced if the facts alleged enable the Court to recognise fraud (*Gamlen* case, above). It is immaterial whether the solicitor is party to the alleged fraud or not (*Williams v Quebrada Railway, Land & Copper Co* [1895] 2 Ch. 751). Where communications which would otherwise be within the protection of legal professional privilege have been made in furtherance of a fraudulent design, a party is not entitled to assert legal professional privilege as a ground for refusing to disclose such communications in circumstances where the party seeking disclosure is able to establish a strong prima facie case of fraud; the court, however, will be very slow to deprive a party of the important protection of legal professional privilege on an interlocutory application, and will judge each case on its facts, striking a balance between the important considerations on which legal professional privilege is founded and the gravity of the charge of fraud that is made (*Derby & Co Ltd v Weldon (No.7)* [1990] 1 W.L.R. 1156; [1990] 3 All E.R. 161). See also *Nationwide Anglia Building Society v Various Solicitors (No.1), The Times*, February 5, 1998.

Fraud is here used in a relatively wide sense. It embraces the effecting of iniquity. Advice sought for the purpose of effecting iniquity is not privileged. Thus in *Barclays Bank Plc v Eustace* [1995] 1 W.L.R. 1238; [1995] 4 All E.R. 511, CA, court held that where on a prima facie view the client was seeking to enter into transactions at an under value the purpose of which was to prejudice the bank, such purpose was sufficiently iniquitous for public policy to require removal of legal professional privilege from communications between client and solicitor in relation to setting up such transactions.

The existence or absence of privilege cannot be affected by whether the fraud concerns an earlier transaction or the conduct of the proceedings in which disclosure is sought. See too *Dubai Aluminium Co Ltd v Al Alawi* [1999] 1 W.L.R. 1964; [1999] 1 All E.R. 703 where there was found a strong prima facie case of criminal or fraudulent conduct in the obtaining of information relating to the defendent's accounts during a *Mareva* process and the court held that documents generated by or reporting on such conduct fell outside the legitimate area of legal professional privilege. Disclosure at an interlocutory stage, however, based on prima facie evidence of fraud in the conduct of the proceedings, carries a far greater risk of injustice to the party against whom disclosure is sought than disclosure in relation to earlier transactions. The risk of injustice to such party if he is compelled to disclose what he has told his solicitors to enable them to defend him against allegations of fraud, together with the damage to the public interest which would be caused by requiring the disclosure of such confidences, outweighs the risk of the other party being deprived of the information (*Chandler v Church* (1987) 137 N.L.J. 451).

It is not the law that legal professional privilege is defeated whenever there is a fraud. A fraudulent party should not be protected by privilege, but the victim of fraud should not lose the privilege in respect of his innocent correspondence through the fraud of another (*Banque Keyser Ullmann SA v Skandia (UK) Insurance Co (No.1)* [1986] 1 Lloyd's Rep. 336, CA).

In order to determine whether a communication between a solicitor and his client is not privileged because its purpose is the furtherance of crime, the Court is entitled to look at the document in question without requiring the party who objects to the claim for privilege to prove by evidence outside the document that it came into existence for that purpose (*R. v Cox* (1884) 14 Q.B.D. 153; *R. v Governor of Pentonville Prison Ex p. Osman (No.1)* [1989] 3 All E.R. 701. Communications in furtherance of fraud are not protected by legal professional privilege regardless of whether the claimant's case is founded on that particular fraud. Where a defendant, having committed a fraud, subsequently attempts to further the fraud through the deception of his solicitor, the relevant communication between the defendant and his solicitor is deprived of the element of professional confidence and privilege in respect thereof is displaced (*Dubai Bank Ltd v Galadari (No.6), The Times*, October 14, 1992).

In determining whether the privilege is lost because of fraud the court should not resolve issues under trial, but should act upon freestanding and independent evidence, see *Regina (Hallinan Blackburn Gittings & Nott (a firm) v Middlesex Guildhall Crown Court* [2004] EWHC 2726; [2005] 1 W.L.R. 766, DC.

In *Kuwait Airways Corporation v Iraqi Airways Company (No.6)* [2005] EWCA Civ 286; [2005] 1 W.L.R. 2734, the Court of Appeal, at para.42, summarised the position as:

> "(1) the fraud exception can apply where there is a claim to litigation privilege as much as where there is a claim to legal advice privilege;
> (2) nevertheless it can only be used in cases in which the issue of fraud is one of the issues in the action where there is a strong (I would myself use the words 'very strong') prima facie case of fraud as there was in *Dubai Aluminium Co Ltd v Al-Alawi* and there was not in *Chandler v Church*;
> (3) where the issue of fraud is not one of the issues in the action, a prima facie case of fraud may be enough as in *Hallinan*."

Trustee and cestui que trust

31.3.23 Privilege cannot be claimed by a trustee against his *cestui que* trust (*Re Mason* (1883) 22 Ch.D. 609; *Wynne v Humberston* (1858) 27 Beav. 421; *Devaynes v Robinson* (1855) 20 Beav. 42; *Postlethwaite, Re, Re Rickman, Postlethwaite v Rickman* (1887) 35 Ch.D. 722); nor against persons in an analogous position (*Gouraud v Edison Co* (1888) 57 L.J.Ch.498; *cf. Bristol Corp v Cox* (1884) 26 Ch.D. 678 at 683. See also *Re Whitworth* [1919] 1 Ch. 320 affirmed [1920] A.C. 581 (solicitor trustee)).

Proprietary right

31.3.24 The privilege would not cover documents in which the party seeking disclosure has a proprietary right, but he must establish the existence of the right (*Re Whitworth* above).

Company and shareholder

31.3.25 See *Woodhouse & Co Ltd v Woodhouse* (1914) 30 T.L.R. 559

Parties employing same solicitor

31.3.26 Where two parties employ the same solicitor in the course of, for example, a conveyancing transaction, communications between either of them and the solicitor in his joint capacity have to be disclosed in favour of the other; where one of the parties is subsequently adjudicated bankrupt the other party cannot assert legal professional privilege as a ground for refusing to disclose such communications to the trustee in bankruptcy, who is to be treated for such purpose as being in the same position as the bankrupt and not as a third party (*Re Konigsberg (a bankrupt) Ex p. The Trustee v Konigsberg* [1989] 3 All E.R. 289).

Waiver or loss of privilege

31.3.27 The privilege is in all cases the privilege of the client and not of the solicitor or legal adviser (*Anderson v Bank of British Columbia* (1875-76) L.R. 2 Ch. D. 644 at 649; *Procter v Smiles* (1886) 55 L.J.Q.B. 467 at 527, 528, CA) and may be waived by the client (*Calcraft v Guest* [1898] 1 Q.B. 759 at 761, CA) but not by the solicitor or legal adviser (*Procter v Smiles* (1886) 55 L.J. Q.B. 467 at 102). But it is not waived by reason of the documents being put to the defendant in examination before an examiner and exhibited to his depositions, or by being put before a judge in a private hearing in order that he may decide whether a compromise of the claim is a proper one (*Goldstone v Williams Deacon & Co* [1899] 1 Ch. 47). Nor is it waived merely by referring to the documents in a statement of case (*Roberts v Oppenheim* (1884) 26 Ch.D. 724, CA) or in an affidavit (*Infields Ltd v Rosen & Son* [1938] 3 All E.R. 591, CA). Waiver as to some of several documents does not involve a waiver as to the others (*Kennedy v Lyell* (1883) 23 Ch.D. 387, CA). If part of a document is put in evidence, or read to the Court, privilege will be waived for the whole document, unless the remaining part deals with an entirely different subject-matter (*Great Atlantic Insurance Co v Home Insurance Co* [1981] 1 W.L.R. 529; [1981] 2 All E.R. 485, CA). Similarly, if part of a letter is disclosed, the disclosing party is deemed to be waiving privilege in relation to the whole letter, unless it can be shown that the other parts of the letter are so distinct as to amount to different documents (*Pozzi v Eli Lilley & Co, The Times*, December 3, 1986). Likewise disclosure of part of contents of a report waives privilege as to the whole, *Chandris Lines v Wilson & Horton Ltd* [1981] N.Z.L.R. 600. See also *Bank of Nova Scotia v Hellenic Mutual War Risks Assn. (Bermuda) Ltd (The Good Luck)*, [1992] 1 A.C. 233. The rule that the reading in open court of part of a privileged document resulted in waiver of privilege in the whole does not apply where the non-waiving party had already seen the whole document (*Def American Inc v Phonogram Ltd, The Times*, August 16, 1994).

The waiver of privilege implicit in a joint retainer extends to (a) all communications made by, e.g. an insured to the solicitors down to such time as an actual conflict of interest emerges and (b) to all communications made by the insured to those solicitors after notification by the solicitors to the insured of such conflict and the lapse of such further time as the insured reasonably requires to decide whether to instruct separate solicitors; see *TSB Bank Plc v Robert Irving & Burns (a firm) (Colonia Baltica Insurance Ltd, Third Party)* [2000] 2 All E.R. 826, CA.

By CPR, r.35.10(3) an expert's report must state the substance of all material instructions, whether written or oral, on the basis of which the report was written. Sub-section (4) of r.35.10 provides that the "instructions referred to in paragraph (3) shall not be privileged against disclosure but the court will not, in relation to those instructions—

(a) order disclosure of any specific document; or

(b) permit any questioning in court, other than by the party who instructed the expert,

unless it is satisfied that there are reasonable grounds to consider the statement of instructions given under paragraph (3) to be inaccurate or incomplete."

But the use of a document for the purpose of cross-examination does not itself make it part of the evidence so as to entitle the other party to investigate other privileged documents on all the topics mentioned in it; the use of a document for cross-examination waives privilege for the transaction actually described in the document but not for matters merely mentioned in it (*General Accident Fire & Life Assurance Corp Ltd v Tanter, The Zephyr* [1984] 1 W.L.R. 100; [1984] 1 All E.R. 35).

The mere fact that a party may have waived the professional privilege which exists between solicitor and client does not result in the waiver of the further privilege which protects documents brought into existence for the purpose of litigation, pending or contemplated; consequently the opposite party is entitled to the discovery of documents relating to the matters as to which professional privilege has been waived up to the date that litigation was contemplated but not thereafter (*George Doland Ltd v Blackburn Robson Coates & Co* [1972] 1 W.L.R. 1338; [1972] 3 All E.R. 959).

Where legal professional privilege was waived in respect of advice given in relation to one transaction fairness did not require as a necessary consequence the waiver to extend to all advice given relating to the dispute: see *Fulham Leisure Holdings Ltd v Nicholson Graham & Jones (a firm)* [2006] EWHC 158 (Ch); [2006] 2 All E.R. 599, Ch D in which the Court identified the relevant process to be followed as:

"(i) One should first identify the transaction in respect of which the disclosure has been made.

(ii) That transaction might be identifiable simply from the nature of the disclosure made; for example, advice given by counsel on a single occasion.

(iii) However, it might be apparent from that material, or from other available material, that the transaction was wider than that which was immediately apparent. If it did, then the whole of the wider transaction had to be disclosed.

(iv) When that had been done, further disclosure would be necessary if that was necessary in order to avoid unfairness or misunderstanding of what had been disclosed."

The institution of civil proceedings against a solicitor by his client constituted an implied waiver of professional privilege in relation to all relevant documents concerned with the suit to the extent necessary to enable the court to adjudicate the dispute fully and fairly. Where an issue was one of causation of loss and the defendants alleged that the claimants would have gone ahead with the transaction involved irrespectively of the advice received and sought to establish such by reference to earlier transactions in which they had acted for the claimants, the claimants' implied waiver extended to the documents in the other transactions (*Lillicrap v Nalder & Son (a firm)* [1993] 1 W.L.R. 94; [1993] 1 All E.R. 724, CA). Such a waiver is limited. Thus where a client brought proceedings against his former solicitors for negligence in handling a commercial transaction between the client and a third party, the client's waiver of legal privilege implied from his bringing the proceedings did not extend to confidential communications between himself and different solicitors instructed to pursue and settle his claim against the third party; see *Paragon Finance Plc v Freshfields (a firm)* [1999] 1 W.L.R. 1183, CA.

A reference in an affidavit to a legal document or to a conversation with solicitors does not amount to a waiver of legal professional privilege in respect of the communication (*Tate & Lyle International Ltd v Government Trading Corp* (1984) 87 L.S.Gaz. 3341, CA).

The mere service of a witness statement under an order of the court does not waive privilege in connected documents. There is no waiver unless and until statement is deployed in court (*Balkanbank v Taher, The Times*, February 19, 1994). Contrast *Clough v Tameside and Glossop Health Authority* [1998] 1 W.L.R. 1478; [1998] 2 All E.R. 971.

Where a party deploys material in court on an interlocutory application, privilege that can otherwise be claimed in relation to that and associated material will be treated as waived altogether, with the result that the party cannot then assert privilege for the same material at the subsequent trial. Where, however, the party merely refers in interlocutory proceedings to the fact that he has obtained legal advice, and states the effect of that advice without disclosing the substance of it or the extent of the instructions given to the legal adviser, he does not thereby waive the right to claim privilege at the trial in respect of the legal advice itself (*Derby & Co Ltd v Weldon (No.10)* [1991] 1 W.L.R. 660; [1991] 2 All E.R. 908). Affidavit evidence in without notice proceedings exhibiting opinions from counsel and solicitors was not in the public domain and neither party to the claim waived any rights they had to assert against third parties a claim for privilege in respect of such documents; see *Leif Hoegh & Co A/S v Petrolsea Inc (The World Era) (No.2)* [1993] 1 Lloyd's Rep. 363. The question whether, if privilege has been waived in relation to part of a document or evidence by production of a tape recording or transcript of part of a conversation, fairness requires that the other party should be entitled to adduce in evidence the whole of the document or evidence of the whole of the conversation to ensure that the court is not misled by seeing or hearing part out of context, is a question that can only be answered by the judge after he has read the whole of the document or transcript or heard the tape recording in full (*ibid.*). Although the fact that a party may have waived the privilege which protects documents brought into existence for the purpose of litigation does not automatically result in a waiver of the privilege for the same documents which exists between solicitor and client, the court will not sever the two privileges in circumstances where both the privileges attach to a single communication, and say that one has been waived but the other not (*ibid.*).

There is a statutory requirement for a claimant for costs to disclose privileged documents to the Court on taxation, and, when this is done, part of the privilege attaching to such documents is temporarily relaxed. The taxing officer, however, has a duty to be fair to both parties and to ensure that privilege is maintained as far as possible without preventing the other party from having an opportunity to challenge the taxation. In rare circumstances the taxing officer may have to disclose privileged documents in order to strike an appropriate balance, but any disclosure will only be for the purposes of the taxation; the privilege can subsequently be reasserted (*Goldman v Hesper* [1988] 1 W.L.R. 1238; [1988] 3 All E.R. 197, CA; see also *Hobbs v Hobbs* [1960] P. 112; [1959] 3 All E.R. 827, and *Pamplin v Express Newspapers Ltd* [1985] 2 All E.R. 185). Though a costs judge can require production of privileged documents he cannot order such production. Where it is necessary and proportionate the receiving party should be put to the election of waiving privilege and relying thereon or of deciding not to rely thereon, *South Coast Shipping Co Ltd v Havant BC* [2002] 3 All E.R. 779. In *Dickinson v Rushmer (Costs)* [2002] 1 Costs L.R. 128, it was held that it was contrary to natural justice to refuse a paying party access to documents upon which the costs judge had based his decision.

Where documents which are clearly privileged when made are disclosed by a party to the police in accordance with his public duty to assist in a criminal investigation, and where such disclosure is for the limited purpose of such investigation and any subsequent criminal trial, no waiver of privilege in relation to civil proceedings is made or implied. It is contrary to public policy that assistance with a criminal investigation should lead to loss of legal professional privilege in a civil action (*British Coal Corp v Dennis Rye (No.2)* [1988] 3 All E.R. 816, CA).

Privileged documents mistakenly disclosed could generally be used by the receiving party on the basis that they were no longer the subject of legal professional privilege where it was not obvious to a reasonable solicitor that a mistake had been made, subject always to the court's powers of case management; see *Al Fayed v Commissioner of Police of the Metropolis* [2002] EWCA Civ 780; [2002] All E.R.(D) 450; *The Times*, June 17, 2002, CA.

In *ISTIL Group Inc v Zahoor* [2003] EWHC 165 (Ch); [2003] 2 All E.R. 252 (a case involving disclosure by a witness/potential witness of litigation privilege communications) the Court stated at para.74:

> "...First, it is clear that the jurisdiction to restrain the use of privileged documents is based on the equitable jurisdiction to restrain breach of confidence...Second, after a privileged document has been seen by the opposing party, the court may intervene by way of injunction in exercise of the equitable jurisdiction if the circumstances warrant such intervention on equitable grounds. Third, if the party in whose hands the document has come (or his solicitor) either (a) has procured inspection of the document by fraud or (b) on inspection, realises that he has been permitted to see the document only by reason of an obvious mistake, the court has the power to intervene by the grant of an injunction in exercise of the equitable jurisdiction. Fourth, in such cases the court should ordinarily intervene, unless the case is one where the injunction can properly be refused on the general principles affecting the grant of a discretionary remedy, e.g. on the ground of delay."

In this case, the Court found that it was appropriate to balance the public interest in supporting legal professional privilege against public interest in the due administration of justice. See too para.89–94 of the judgment for general propositions of the relevant law and present position.

In Children Act 1989 and wardship matters where the interests of the child were paramount, the legal professional privilege attaching to medical reports yielded to such overriding principle (*Essex CC v R.* [1994] 2 W.L.R. 407 and noted at [1994] Fam. 167; *Oxfordshire CC v M* [1994] Fam. 151; [1994] 2 W.L.R. 393; [1994] 2 All E.R. 269).

Legal privilege may also give way to a contractual obligation to disclose (*Brown v G.R.E.* [1994] 2 Lloyd's Rep. 325, CA). See too *Goshawk Dedicated Ltd v Tyser & Co* [2006] EWCA Civ 54; [2006] 1 All E.R. (Comm) 501; [2006] 1 Lloyd's Rep. 566, CA: held:

> "that in the Lloyd's market there has at all relevant times been a term to be implied in the insurance contracts between underwriters and insureds to this effect: that placing and claims documents which have been previously shown to underwriters, and premium accounting documents which are necessary to the operation of the contract, where retained by the insureds' Lloyd's brokers, should be available to underwriters in case of reasonable necessity. Availability includes the right to take copies."

In *Director General of Fair Trading v Reid*, December 20, 1994, Buckley J., Restrictive Practices Court, held that civil contempt proceedings should be approached more by analogy with the criminal than the civil practice and ordered discovery of prior drafts of witness statements just as a criminal prosecutor would have to in order to comply with his duty to disclose unused material.

Death of client

31.3.28 Privilege is not lost by reason of the death of the client (*Bullivant v Attorney General of Victoria*, above).

Successor in title to party

31.3.29 Legal professional privilege of a party to a claim enures for the benefit of the successor in title to that party, at any rate, where the relevant interest subsists (*Cresent Farm (Sidcup) Sports Ltd v Sterling Offices Ltd* [1972] Ch. 553, [1971] 3 All E.R. 1192; applying *Minet v Morgan (1873)* L.R. 8 Ch. App. 361; *Schneider v Leigh* [1955] 2 Q.B. 195, CA, and doubting *Greenlaw v King* (1838) 1 Beav. 137).

Secondary evidence or copies of privileged document

31.3.30 Secondary evidence as to the contents of a privileged document is admissible as against the party resisting its production (*Calcraft v Guest* [1898] 1 Q.B. 759, CA). Thus if a party has an opportunity of taking or getting a copy of such a document he can use it as secondary evidence (*ibid.*), though use of an improperly acquired document will be restrained.

If, however, he has possession of such a copy document but has not yet used it in his litigation, the mere fact that he intends so to use it in the future is no answer to a claim against him by the person in whom the privilege is vested for delivery up of the copy, or to restrain him from disclosing or making use of its contents (*Goddard v Nationwide Building Society* [1987] Q.B. 670; [1986] 3 W.L.R. 734; [1986] 3 All E.R. 264, CA). Moreover, public policy requires that a litigant should not be permitted to make use of a copy of a privileged document as evidence, where he has obtained it by stealth or a trick, or by otherwise acting improperly (*I.T.C. Film Distributors Ltd v Video Exchange Ltd* [1982] Ch. 431; [1982] 2 All E.R. 241).

Where counsel's papers are accidentally sent to the other side an injunction may be granted against a stranger who has innocently come by confidential information to which he is not entitled, but so as to be capable of being policed the order should be directed towards outward acts rather than inwards thoughts, though without sanctioning deliberate covert action (*English and American Insurance Co Ltd v Herbert Smith* [1988] F.S.R. 232). See too *Ablitt v Mills & Reeve (a firm), The Times*, October 25, 1995; injunction granted restraining the first defendants, solicitors to the seond defendant, from continuing to act on the second defendants' behalf in the main claim in addition to the undertaking they had given not to make use of information gained from files mistakenly sent to them. It does not follow, however, that an injunction will be granted in every case following the unauthorised disclosure of a privileged and confidential document to prevent its future use. The Court must exercise discretion by balancing the legitimate interests of the party to whom the document belongs in seeking to keep its contents suppressed and the legitimate interests of the other party in seeking to make use of it. In carrying out such a balancing exercise, the circumstances in which the document comes into the hands of the latter party, the issues in the claim, the relevance of the document and whether it would in one way or another have to be disclosed, together with the nature of the privilege, are all matters which have to be taken into account (*Webster v James Chapman & Co* [1989] 3 All E.R. 939).

In general, however, and except where it is too late to restore the status quo, the law will not encourage parties to litigation or their solicitors to take advantage of obvious mistakes made in the course of the process of disclosure; where a party seeks to take advantage of an obvious mistake made by his opponent, copies of privileged documents of the other party which may have come into the possession of the party seeking such advantage, or his solicitors, will be ordered to be handed back to the other party, and an injunction will be granted restraining the party seeking such advantage from using information contained in or derived from the documents (*Derby & Co Ltd v Weldon (No.8)* [1991] 1 W.L.R. 73; [1990] 3 All E.R. 762, CA). See too *Breeze (Disclosure) v John Stacey & Sons Ltd* (2000) C.P. Rep. 77, CA to effect that the former rules applicable to cases of inadvertent disclosure of privileged documents had not been affected by the introduction of the present new rules.

Documents tending to incriminate or expose to a penalty

Section 13 of the Fraud Act 2006 abrogated the privilege against self-incrimination in respect of proceedings relating to property (widely defined in s.13(3) q.v. The Act came into force on January 15, 2007. Section 13 is retrospective in effect in the sense that in future proceedings it applies to events before the Act came into force as well as after. See too *Kensington International v The Republic of Congo* [2007] EWHC 1632 (Comm); [2007] 2 Lloyd's Rep. 382 and on appeal [2007] EWCA Civ 1128; [2008] 1 W.L.R. 1144; [2008] 1 Lloyd's Rep. 161. **31.3.31**

In *C Plc v P* [2007] EWCA Civ 493; [2008] Ch.1; [2007] 3 W.L.R. 437; [2007] 3 All E.R. 1034, CA (a case concerning the seizure under a search order of material in respect of which psi was asserted generally), the court held by a majority that at common law and even before the enactment of the Human Rights Act 1998 the privilege against self-incrimination did not extend to documents and things which had an existence independant of the will of the person relying on the privilege and regardless of whether civil or criminal proceedings were involved. Accordingly there was no privilege in the instance case since the material existed independently of the will of the party asserting the privilege even though obtained as a result of executing the compulsory powers/provisions of the search order. Leave to appeal to HL given December 13, 2007; [2008] 1 W.L.R. 153.

In considering the following commentary regarding matters pre-October 2, 2000 the possible effect of the Human Rights Act 1998 should be kept in mind. See further below at para.31.3.32.

A party is not compelled to give disclosure which will tend to incriminate or expose to proceedings for a penalty him or his spouse under the law of any part of the UK (Civil Evidence Act 1968 s.14). It is sufficient if he claims that he believes that the disclosure "will," "would," "may," or "might," tend to incriminate him or so expose him: the difference in phraseology is immaterial, provided the risk is apparent to the court (*Lamb v Munster* (1882) 10 Q.B.D. 110; *Triplex Safety Glass Co Ltd v Lancegaye Safety Glass (1934) Ltd* [1939] 2 K.B. 395, CA; *Spokes v Grosvenor Hotel Co* [1897] 2 Q.B. 124, CA; *National Association of Operative Plasterers v Smithies* [1906] A.C. 434; *Waterhouse v Barker* [1924] 2 K.B. 759; *Sitwell v Sun Engraving Co* [1937] 4 All E.R. 366, CA). In *Den Norske Bank ASA v Antonatos* [1999] Q.B. 271, CA, where this head of privilege was asserted in the context of cross-examination, it was held that the ambit of the privilege is not confined simply to the risk of prosecution but that a witness was entitled to claim the privilege against self-incrimination not merely on the ground that an answer might increase the risk of prosecution, but in respect of any piece of information or evidence on which a prosecuting authority might wish to rely upon in establishing guilt or in determining whether to prosecute, and that the court should uphold the privilege even if he was acting from mixed motives or mala fide as a result of not fully appreciating the risk. The risk of exposure must be real; see *Renworth Ltd v Stephansen* [1996] 3 All E.R. 244, CA, a case where in addition to the protection of s.31 of the Theft Act 1968, the chances of a charge separate and distinct from a Theft Act Offence was remote and the claim to privilege failed.

Proceedings for civil contempt are proceedings for the "recovery of a penalty" within s.14(1) of the Civil Evidence Act 1968 in respect of which there is a privilege against self-incrimination. For the purposes of civil proceedings pertaining to infringement of intellectual property or passing off, such privilege has been withdrawn by s.72 of the Supreme Court Act 1981; see *Cobra Golf Inc v Rata (No.2)* [1998] Ch. 109; 1997 2 W.L.R. 629; [1998] Ch. 109; *Further in Memory Corporation v Sidhu* [2000] Ch 645; [2000] 1 All E.R. 434 (ChD) it was held that the privilege against self-incrimination was available in the proceedings for cross-examination of the defendant in respect of the risk of contempt proceedings in the action.

Claims to withold from inspection on this ground can be made in the party's list see CPR r.31.10(4)(a) and by the procedure set out in rr.31.19(3) *et seq.*

The privilege no longer extends to a liability to penal proceedings abroad (Civil Evidence Act 1968 s.14) but for the purposes of this section liability to a penalty under EEC legislation forming part of the law of the U.K. by virtue of the European Communities Act 1972 is a penalty under the law of the U.K., and privilege may be claimed. It does not extend to a penalty which is no longer recoverable, nor an offence which has been pardoned (see, e.g. *Attorney General v Cunard Co* (1877) 4 T.L.R. 177). Some statutes provide that the liability to criminal prosecution shall afford no objection to discovery in civil suits (*Ramsden v Brearley* (1875) 33 L.T. 322; *Lefroy v Burnside* (1879) 41 L.T. 199) and by s.14(3) of the Civil Evidence Act 1968, this equally applies to such liability of a spouse.

Where a claim to privilege against self-incrimination is made in a case involving allegations of breaches of the Rome Treaty, the Court may order a stay (subject to appropriate conditions) pending investigation by the Commission (*British Leyland Motor Corp v Wyatt* [1979] F.S.R. 583).

By the SCA 1981 s.72, the privilege against compliance with orders for disclosure or the answering of questions on the grounds that compliance might involve penalties or criminal proceedings relating to infringement of industrial property rights, has been withdrawn. The section is not limited to a case where criminal proceedings have not yet been commenced (*Charles of the Ritz Group Ltd v Jory* [1986] F.S.R. 14).

Privilege under this heading will prevail unless the person claiming it can be adequately protected by some other means. In *A.T. & T. Istel Ltd v Tully* [1993] A.C. 45; [1992] 3 W.L.R. 344; [1992] 3 All E.R. 523, the House of Lords stated that although the privilege against self-incrimination existed and could only be removed or altered by Parliament, there was no reason to allow a defendant in civil proceedings to rely upon it thus depriving the claimant of his rights where the defendant's own protection was adequately covered by other means. In this case the C.P.S. had stated by letter that the order for disclosure in its terms restricted them to utilising material already collected or independently gathered and para.33 of the original order of

Buckley J. prohibited use of material so disclosed in the prosecution of either defendant and accordingly compliance with the order for disclosure would not create any real danger for the defendants of prejudice in criminal proceedings. See too *United Norwest Co-operatives Ltd v Johnstone*, *The Times*, February 24, 1994, CA. In civil proceedings under the Drug Trafficking Act 1980, however, where disclosure is sought by the prosecutor in related criminal proceedings, an undertaking by the prosecutor not to use information obtained on disclosure in or in connection with criminal proceedings against the defendant may adequately protect the defendant, and accordingly disclosure may be ordered notwithstanding the plea of privilege (*Re A Defendant, Independent*, April 2, 1987).

The privilege against self-incrimination may be overridden where Parliament has expressly or by necessary implication, so provided (see *R. v Harz; R. v Power* [1967] 1 A.C. 760 (demand for information under the former s.24(6) of the Purchase Tax Act 1963); applied in *Bank of England v Riley* [1992] Ch. 475; [1992] 2 W.L.R. 840, CA (demand for information under s.42 of the Banking Act 1987)).

The survival of the privilege in proceedings under the Terrorism Act 2000 and related terrorism legislation is unclear. In *Malik v Manchester Crown Court* [2008] EWHC 1362 (Admin) the Court held that the privilege had not been ousted by the Terrorism Act 2000 (at [73]), but did not approve the view that the privilege held a decisive sway against disclosure in terrorism proceedings, instead viewing it only as an "important relevant factor" when considering whether to require disclosure in respect of pre-existing documents.

Disclosure to police authority of a report obtained voluntarily and filed without objection did not infringe privilege against self-incrimination; see *Re L (Minors) (Police Investigation: Privilege)* [1995] 1 F.L.R. 999, CA (affirmed by the House of Lords) [1997] A.C. 16; [1996] 2 W.L.R. 395; [1996] 2 All E.R. 78, HL(E). However, the fact that in non-adversarial proceedings like *Re L (minors) (Police Investigation: Privilege)* privilege did not arise in respect of an expert's report based on papers disclosed in those proceedings, the duty of disclosure in such proceedings did not override the right of a party to such proceedings to claim legal professional privilege arising in or in connection with other proceedings and once established to refuse disclosure of material covered by that privilege. Such privilege was absolute provided the party asserting it had a continuing interest to assert it. Accordingly, for legal professional privilege attached both to communications between a father and his solicitor in criminal proceedings and to direct and indirect communications between father and medical experts instructed for the same purpose, see *S. CC v B* [2000] 3 W.L.R. 53.

Human Rights Act 1998

This Act makes the European Convention on Human Rights part of English Law. **31.3.32**
Of particular application for present purposes is art.6 of the Convention which guarantees a fair hearing, the right to remain silent and not to incriminate oneself. This provision came into force on October 2, 2000. In the context of abrogation by statute, Courts will have to consider to what extent statutes which abrogate the privilege against self-incrimination are consistent with art.6, particularly statutes which provide no safeguards or restraints upon the use of material obtained as a result of the abrogation. Regard should be had to the following cases: *Orkem v Commission of the European Communities* Case C374/87 [1989] E.C.R. 3283; *Saunders v United Kingdom (19187/91)* [1997] B.C.C. 872; *Brown (Gary John) v Gallacher* 2002 S.L.T. 756; 2002 S.C.C.R. 415; [2003] R.T.R. 17 and *R. v Hertfordshire CC Ex p. Green Environmental Industries* [2000] A.C. 412; [2000] 1 All E.R. 773, HL (E). See too *Allan v UK* (2003) 36 EHRR 12.

Documents privileged on the ground that production would be injurious to the *public interest*

A special procedure for asserting this head of privilege is provided by CPR r.31.19(1) **31.3.33**
(see below). This provides for an application to be made to the Court without notice. Such privilege may also be claimed in the same way as other heads of privilege see rr.31.19(3) *et seq*.

The law defining this ground of privilege or, more properly, immunity from production and the conditions of its exercise are mainly to be found in the decisions of the House of Lords in *Burmah Oil Co Ltd v Governor and Co of the Bank of England* [1980] A.C. 1090; [1979] 3 All E.R. 700 and *Conway v Rimmer* [1968] A.C. 910; [1968] 1 All E.R. 874. This privilege does not depend on the objection of a party; the rule is one on which a Judge should if necessary insist, even though no objection is taken. The test is not whether the documents are "State documents" or marked "confidential" or whether their production might invoke public discussion or criticism of a government department, or the attendance of officials needed elsewhere, but whether production would be injurious to the public interest—or, in other words, whether the withholding of the documents is necessary for the proper functioning of the public service. The public interest in concealment should be balanced against the public interest that the administration of justice should not be frustrated. The applicable principles are comprehensively re-stated in *Evans v Chief Constable of Surrey* [1989] 2 All E.R. 594, and are also usefully and succinctly summarised in *Barrett v Ministry of Defence* [1995] 1 W.L.R. 1217. See further *R. v Bromell, Re Coventry Evening Newspapers Ltd* [1993] Q.B. 278; [1992] 3 W.L.R. 916, [1993] 1 All E.R. 86, CA—held, re-affirming the requirement to balance the two public interests referred to in the text above, that it would be repugnant to justice to withhold documents which appeared to point to corruption on part of named police officers in a libel claim brought by those officers who had already recovered substantial libel damages from other sections of the media. The requirement of a "fair trial" under Article 6 of the Convention on Human Rights is now relevant to this balancing exercise.

For the application of these principles, see:

- *Alfred Crompton Amusement Machines v Commissioners of Customs and Excise* [1974] A.C. 405; [1973] 2 All E.R. 1169, HL (information obtained confidentially by the Crown for the valuing of goods for tax purposes; not protected);
- *R. v Lewes Justices Ex p. the Gaming Board of Great Britain* [1973] A.C. 388; [1972] 2 All E.R. 1057, HL, affirming D.C. (confidential inquiries by the Gaming Board from the police as to applicants for certificates of consent; protected);
- *Norwich Pharmacal Co v Customs and Excise Commrs.* [1974] A.C. 133; [1973] 2 All E.R. 943 (names of persons likely to have violated the claimant's patent rights not protected);
- *D. v N.S.P.C.C.* [1978] A.C. 171; [1977] 1 All E.R. 589, HL (information as to ill treatment of children given to a charitable body having statutory authority to bring proceedings protected, though the body was not an organ of the government);
- *Re M. (A Minor) The Times*, December 29, 1989, CA (local authority social work records);
- *Lonrho Ltd v Shell Petroleum Ltd* [1980] 1 W.L.R. 627, HL (material furnished in confidence to an inspector inquiring into breaches of sanctions-protected);
- *Arias v Metropolitan Police Commr.* (1984) 128 S.J. 784; CA (documents of finance corporation seized by police investigating offences involving fraud);
- *Hasselblad (G.B.) Ltd v Orbinson* [1985] Q.B. 475; [1985] 1 All E.R. 173, CA (public interest requires that a letter written to the European Community Commission, in the course of proceedings begun by the Commission against the claimant alleging breach of art.85 of the EEC Treaty, could not be used as the basis of a libel claim);
- *Continental Reinsurance Corp (UK) Ltd v Pine Top Insurance Ltd* [1986] 1 Lloyd's Rep. 8, CA (documents brought into being in circumstances of confidentiality protected);
- *R. v Bournemouth Justices, Ex p. Grey* [1986] 150 J.P., 392; [1987] 1 F.L.R. 36 (records of adoption agency, containing admission of paternity by the putative father not protected);
- *Re M (Minors) (Confidential Documents)* [1987] F.L.R. 46 (probation service records, protected unless disclosure requried in the public interest);
- *Barrett v Ministry of Defence, Independent*, January 23, 1989 (report of Ministry of Defence Board to Inquiry into death of airman);
- *Bookbinder v Tebbit (No.2)* [1992] 1 W.L.R. 217 (information obtained during investigations carried out by Audit Commission into local authority spending protected);
- *Gill and Goodwin v Chief Constable of Lancashire, Guardian*, October 27, 1992, (Police Public-Order Manual protected but disclosure could be ordered if otherwise impossible to present case);

- *Re Barlow Clowes Gilt Managers Ltd* [1992] Ch. 208 (transcripts of interviews conducted on behalf of joint liquidators in compulsory winding up prima facie protected. Court also applied *Marcel v Commissioner of Police for the Metropolis* [1992] 2 W.L.R. 50, CA, in directing liquidators not to make voluntary disclosure of transcripts but to restore application (made originally by liquidators for directions in respect of disclosure to Companies Court) in the Crown Court to set aside witness summonses on ground of public interest immunity). In any event there should be no disclosure without notice to witnesses concerned; see *Soden v Burns; R. v Secretary of State for Trade and Industry Ex p. Soden* [1996] 1 W.L.R. 1512;
- *DPP v Morrow, Independent*, April 13, 1993, documents maintained in an abortion clinic relating to abortions carried out under the Abortion Act 1967 protected;
- *Lonhro Plc v Fayed (No.4)* [1994] Q.B. 775; [1994] 2 W.L.R. 209; [1994] 1 All E.R. 870 CA, documents which related to a person's tax affairs and which came into existence with specific reference to his tax liability did not attract public interest immunity where they were held by the taxpayer and he refused consent to their disclosure;
- *Kelly v Commissioner of Police of the Metropolis, The Times*, August 20, 1997, (Forms MG3A, 6, 6A, 6D, 6E and 20 of the forms sent to the Crown Prosecution Service by police forces following an investigation into a suspected criminal offence covered by class public interest immunity).

Woolgar v Chief Constable of Sussex [2000] 1 W.L.R. 25; [2000] 1 W.L.R. 25, CA—disclosure permitted to U.K.C.C. of interview of claimant under caution with police at police station. Case also contains a review of principles and procedure to be adopted.

The confidentiality of the records of a local education authority is insufficient ground for protection from disclosure (*Thompson v Inner London Education Authority* (1977) 74 L.S.G. 66). The Court would not protect information from disclosure just because it was "exempt information" within s.100 of the Local Government Act 1972, but the information could be protected if the necessary elements of breach of confidence could nevertheless be made out (*West Midlands Police Authority v Walsall MBC, Independent*, February 26, 1992).

In *R. v Chief Constable of West Midlands Police Ex p. Wiley; R. v Chief Constable of Nottinghamshire Police Ex p. Sunderland* [1995] 1 A.C. 274; [1994] 3 All E.R. 420, the House of Lords held that there was no general public interest immunity in respect of documents coming into existence during an investigation into a complaint against the police under Pt IX of the Police and Criminal Evidence Act 1984 though there might be reasons why because of the contents of a particular document it would be appropriate to extend such immunity to that document. The House of Lords also sought to discourage the use of collateral proceedings rather than the proceedings in which the document/s were relevant to determine the status of the document/s. *Neilson v Laugharne* [1981] QB 736 case and the cases in which it was subsequently applied should therefore be regarded as wrongly decided. *Quaere* to what extent class immunity in other areas as opposed to individual document immunity is still available. *Quaere* too effect of art.6 of Convention on Human Rights on continued class immunity protection.

See too *Kaufmann v Credit Lyonnais Bank, The Times*, February 1, 1995; no class immunity for confidential bank report sent to SFA (the regulatory body of which the bank was a member) unless it could be clearly demonstrated there was a need to withhold such information from investors. In *Taylor v Chief Constable of Greater Manchester* [1995] 1 W.L.R. 447; [1995] 2 All E.R. 420, CA, the Court of Appeal held that reports prepared by investigating officers on the conduct of proceedings under Pt IX of the Police and Criminal Evidence Act 1984 formed a class which was entitled to public interest immunity and that their disclosure would only be ordered where the public interest in production outweighed that in preserving their confidentiality.

Alfred Crompton Amusement Machines Ltd v Commissioners of Customs and Excise (No.2) [1974] A.C. 405; [1973] 2 All E.R. 1169, HL, prevents the conclusion that confidential information obtained by public authorities from the citizen under compulsion remains inviolate and incommunicable to anyone. See too *Wakefield v Channel Four Television Corporation* [2006] EWHC 3289 (QB); [2007] 94 BMLR 1 ; (balancing exercise between competing policy considerations). Moreover, the police may produce documents in their hands to the court for use in civil proceedings in obedience to an order to produce documents to the court if the owner of the documents could have been required to produce them under such an order if they had still been in his possession (*Marcel v Commissioner of Police* [1992] 2 W.L.R. 50, CA). See too *Preston BC v McGrath, The Times*, February 18, 1999, CA.

Although public interest immunity cannot be waived, it may evaporate if those involved in the giving and receiving of the information concerned consent to its disclosure; in deciding whether the administration of justice should prevail over public interest immunity, the fact that partial disclosure has already eroded the immunity is a relevant consideration (*Multi Guarantee Co v Cavalier Insurance Co Ltd, The Times*, June 24, 1986).

The objection on ground of public interest immunity may be made either on an application for disclosure under this Order—as when inspection is asked of documents referred to in a party's list of documents—or at the trial when, by witness summons or other means, the production of the documents is called for. Where the objection is taken before trial, the decision to object should be taken by the Minister who is the political head of the department, and he should have seen and considered their contents and himself have formed the view that it would be contrary to the public interest to produce them—either because of their actual contents or because of the class of documents to which they belong. And if the objection is that they belong to a class of documents which it would be contrary to the public interest to produce, the class to which they belong must be specified (*Re Grosvenor Hotel, London* [1964] Ch. 464; [1964] 1 All E.R. 92, CA; *Merricks v Nott-Bower* [1965] 1 Q.B. 57; [1964] 1 All E.R. 717). But the decision remains that of the Judge, and if, in spite of the Minister's affidavit, in the view of the Court the objection was not taken bona fide, or there are no reasonable grounds for apprehending danger to the public interest, the Court has a residual power to override the objection. It is generally best that the Judge should see the documents before ordering production, and if he thinks that the Minister's reasons for refusing production are not clearly expressed he will have to see them before ordering production. He can see them without their being shown to the parties and the Minister has a right to appeal before they are produced. However although a court was obliged to be vigilant to see that a claim of public interest immunity was raised only in appropriate circumstances where an appropriate certificate signed by a Secretary of State claiming immunity from disclosure of material on the ground of national security was before the court, the court should not exercise its right to inspect that material (*Balfour v Foreign and Commonwealth Office* [1994] 1 W.L.R. 681; [1994] 2 All E.R. 588, CA).

The objection should be made by affidavit or certified statement of the political head. But where it is not convenient or practicable for the Minister to act, either because he is ill or out of reach or because the effective head of the department is a permanent official, it would be reasonable for the permanent head to take the objection, as, e.g. the Chairman of the Board of Customs and Excise (*Alfred Crompton Amusement Machines v Commissioners of Customs, etc.* [1971] 2 All E.R. 843, per Eveleigh J.). There is, however, no rule of law or practice that precludes the claim being raised in other ways. Thus, where there was clear authority to support the assertion that class immunity applied, it was sufficient for the claim to be raised by a responsible official within the organisation involved; see *O'Sullivan v Commissioner of Police of the Metropolis, The Times*, July 3, 1995, a case concerning Form 151 the initial report sent by police to Crown Prosecution Service following an investigation into a suspected criminal offence where claim made by barrister employed in commissioner's solicitor's department. If the objection to production arises at the trial, it may in the first instance be conveyed to the Court by an official of the department, producing a certificate signed by the Minister, stating what is necessary. If the Court is not satisfied, it can request the Minister's personal attendance (see, on the question whether the Minister can be cross-examined, *Re Grosvenor Hotel* [1964] Ch. 464, CA). The same principles apply to the exclusion of oral as of documentary evidence (*Duncan v Cammell Laird & Co* [1942] A.C. 624 and cases there cited). So, a witness may not look at those documents to refresh his memory and then give oral evidence (*Gain v Gain* [1961] 1 W.L.R. 1469; [1962] 1 All E.R. 63). Once a Court has decided that documents are covered by this privilege, that position continues though they have passed into the possession of another person (*Auten v Rayner (No.2)* [1960] 1 Q.B. 669; [1958] 3 All E.R. 566). The contents of a certificate given by a Secretary of State are evidence in the claim and may be challenged by other parties. Even where such a certificate leads to a consent order whereby other parties agree not to challenge the certificate (i.e. that the documents to which it refers should not be disclosed); it does not prevent them from denying the contents (*Sethia v Stern, The Times*, November 4, 1987, CA).

See further, as to the circumstances in which the objection to disclosure should and will be taken, *Ellis v Home Office* [1953] 2 Q.B. 135, CA.

In *Bennett v Commissioner of Police for the Metropolis* [1995] 1 W.L.R. 488; [1995] 2 All E.R. 1 it was held that it is at least arguable that the Secretary of State concerned is under a duty to consider, before objecting to disclosure, whether the public interest in non-disclosure is outweighed by the public interest in the documents being available in the interests of the administration of justice.

See too *Kuijer v Council of the European Union (T188/98)* [2000] E.C.R. II-1959 where claim to public interest was vitiated by Council's failure to indicate that it had given proper consideration to each of the documents involved individually.

Discovery against the Crown

At the time of the decision of *Duncan v Cammell Laird & Co* [1942] A.C. 624 disclosure **31.3.34** could not be ordered against the Crown. Now, however, by s.28(1) of the Crown Proceedings Act 1947, the Crown, when a party to civil proceedings, may be required to make disclosure of documents or give further information, subject to Crown privilege, and the principles in regard to that privilege and its exercise are the same as in a claim to which the Crown is not a party. See CPR Pt 66.

(d) Other grounds of privilege

Documents relating solely to the case of the party giving discovery

This ground of privilege was abolished by s.16(2) of the Civil Evidence Act 1968. **31.3.35**

Confidential communications

A litigant is not entitled to claim privilege for documents and information merely **31.3.36** because they were supplied to him in confidence by a third party (*Alfred Crompton Amusement Machines Ltd v Commrs. of Customs and Excise (No.2)*, reversing, on this point, the Court of Appeal); but the confidentiality of the communication may be relevant to other heads of privilege, e.g. public interest (*ibid.*). See also *Norwich Pharmacal Co v Commrs. of Customs and Excise* [1974] A.C. 133 and *Science Research Council v Nassé* [1980] A.C. 1028; [1979] 3 All E.R. 673, HL).

A party may be able to resist the disclosure of confidential information relating to a third party where the disclosure would involve a breach of the third party's ECHR art.8 right to respect for private life: *MS v Sweden* (1999) 28 E.H.R.R. 313, ECtHR and *R. v Local Authority in the Midlands and A Police Authority in the Midlands Ex p. LM*, September 6, 1999, unrep., QBD. Disclosure may be justified under art.8(2): *ibid.*, and *R. v Secretary of State for the Home Department Ex p. Kingdom of Belgium* and *R. v Secretary of State for the Home Department Ex p. Amnesty International*, February 15, 2000, unrep., DC.

A party may also be able to resist disclosure of confidential relating to another party where it is necessary for the protection of third party sources (*Gaskin v United Kingdom* (1990) 12 E.H.R.R. 36, ECtHR) or for the protection of that party's mental or physical health (*R. v Mid Glamorgan Family Health Services Ex p. Martin* [1995] 1 W.L.R. 110, CA). For the position regarding disclosure of journalistic sources and ECHR art.10 (freedom of expression) see *Goodwin v United Kingdom* (1996) 22 E.H.R.R. 123, ECtHR; see also *Malik v Manchester Crown Court* [2008] EWHC 1362 (Admin) (journalistic reporting involving matters covered by the Terrorist Act 2000).

The ECHR art.6(1) right to a fair trial may also be relevant in this context: see further para.39.1.2 below.

Technical secrets

Where a party claims secrecy in relevant material (e.g. a defendant in a patent in- **31.3.37** fringement claim asserts that his process is secret) the governing principle is that the Court should order a controlled measure of disclosure to select individuals upon terms ensuring that there should be neither use nor further disclosure of the confidential information to the prejudice of the party concerned and yet so that the other party may have full free disclosure as is consistent with adequate protection of the trade secrets concerned. There is no form of universal order, nor is it the case that at later stages in a claim wider disclosure cannot be ordered. In each case the Court must decide what measure of disclosure is appropriate, to whom it should be made and upon what terms (*Warner-Lambert Co v Glaxo Laboratories Ltd* [1975] R.P.C. 354, CA). See also

Centri-Spray Corp v Cera International Ltd [1979] F.S.R. 175, where disclosure to independent expert of secret drawings is unlikely to be useful, controlled disclosure to the plaintiff's employees may be permitted subject to express undertakings to keep the disclosed material confidential). See further *Format Communications MFG Ltd v ITT (United Kingdom) Ltd* [1983] F.S.R. 473, CA, disclosure and inspection of secret computer source code ordered, subject to suitable safeguards and notwithstanding claimant's offer of inspection by independent expert.

In *Atari Inc v Philips Electronics and Associated Industries Ltd* [1988] F.S.R. 416, disclosure of the claimants' secret computer source code was ordered without limitation on the terms of disclosure upon the defendants and their expert giving strict undertakings as to confidentiality.

Admiralty

31.3.38 A report made by a master to his owners for which privilege is claimed should be identified in the appropriate part of the list of documents and privilege there claimed. Such a document is not one which can be considered covered by the words "letters sent by the claimant (defendant) to his agents or solicitors for the purposes of the claim" (Direction of the Admiralty Registrar, March 8, 1955).

Disclosed documents

31.3.39 Once a document such as a witness statement has been disclosed (by being exchanged or otherwise) no question of privilege can arise but only one of admissibility, and such statements once disclosed can be used as the basis for an application for disclosure (*Black & Decker Inc v Flymo Ltd* [1991] 3 All E.R. 158; [1991] F.S.R. 93).

Without prejudice communications

31.3.40 The "without prejudice" rule governs the admissibility of evidence and is founded upon the public policy of encouraging litigants to settle their differences rather than litigate them to a finish (*Cutts v Head* [1984] Ch. 290; [1984] 1 All E.R. 597, CA). The rule applies to exclude all negotiations genuinely aimed at a settlement, whether oral or in writing, from being given in evidence. The purpose of the rule is to protect a litigant from being embarrassed by any admission made purely in an attempt to achieve a settlement. There must be a dispute which is under settlement discussion and not merely the seeking of a concession as to payment of an undisputed debt sought by a debtor: *Bradford & Bingley Plc v Rashid* [2006] UKHL 37; [2006] 4 All E.R. 705, HL, a case concerning an acknowledgment within s.29(5) of the Limitation Act 1980."Without prejudice" material will be admissible if the issue is whether or not negotiations resulted in an agreed settlement (*Walker v Wilsher* (1889) 23 Q.B.D. 335), but in relation to any other issue an admission made in order to achieve a compromise should not be held against the maker of the admission or received in evidence; moreover an admission made to reach a settlement with a party is not admissible in proceedings between the maker of the admission and a different party, even if such proceedings are within the same litigation (*Rush & Tompkins Ltd v Greater London Council* [1989] A.C. 1280; [1988] 3 W.L.R. 939; [1988] 3 All E.R. 737, HL). The right to disclosure and production of documents does not necessarily depend upon the admissibility of documents in evidence (*O'Rourke v Darbishire* [1920] A.C. 581, HL), but the general public policy that applies to protect genuine negotiations from being admissible in evidence is also extended by the Courts to protect those negotiations from being discloseable to third parties (*Rush & Tompkins Ltd v Greater London Council* (above)). Any discussions between the parties for the purpose of resolving the dispute between them are not admissible, even if the words "without prejudice" or their equivalent are not expressly used (*Chocoladefabriken Lindt & Sprungli AG v Nestle Co Ltd* [1978] R.P.C. 287). It follows that documents containing such material are themselves privileged from production. This head of privilege is not confined to admissions but applies to all bona fide without prejudice statements which touch upon the strengths or weaknesses of the parties' cases or which placed a valuation on a party's rights forming a part of the attempt to compromise the litigation; see *Unilever v Procter & Gamble* [1999] 1 W.L.R. 1630; [1999] 2 All E.R. 691 affirmed, [2000] 1 W.L.R. 2436; [2001] 1 All E.R. 783, CA *and see Instance v Denny Bros Printing Ltd*, *The Times*, February 28, 2000.

The rule in *Walker v Wilsher* (see above) was re-affirmed by the Court of Appeal in a taxation of costs context in *Reed Executive Plc v Reed Business Information Ltd* [2004] EWCA Civ 887; [2004] 1 W.L.R. 3026; [2004] 4 All E.R. 942, CA, even though such "may (indeed does) mean that in some cases the Court when it comes to the question of costs cannot decide whether one side or the other was unreasonable in refusing mediation" (para.34).

The privilege can be asserted in respect of evidence of a pre-litigation dispute and notwithstanding that proceedings had not been threatened so long as there is sufficient proximity to the litigation. In such respects proximity is one of the subject matters of the dispute rather than how long before the threat or the commencement of the litigation it was discussed in negotiations; see *Barnetson v Framlington Group Ltd* [2007] EWCA Civ 502; [2007] 3 All E.R. 1054, CA.

The without prejudice rule is not absolute and resort may be had to the without prejudice material for a variety of reasons when the justice of the case requires it, always giving due weight to the purpose of the rule itself; see *Rush & Tompkins Ltd v Greater London Council* (see above) at 1300. See too *Gnitrow Ltd v Cape Plc* [2000] 1 W.L.R. 2327; [2000] 3 All E.R. 763 CA, where subject to conditions on use and timing of disclosure to the trial court, it was held that where a claimant has settled for a fixed sum a specific claim against him and sought only an indemnity or contribution with respect to that sum, he could not invoke the privilege attaching to without prejudice negotiating to deny disclosure to the defendant in the contribution proceedings of the terms of a settlement between the claimant's insurers and a third party in respect of apportionment of that liability. But see *UYB Ltd v British Railways Board The Times*, November 15, 2000 in which the Court of Appeal held that the trial judge had not been wrong to hold a without prejudice draft report inadmissible to challenge a claim made at trial.

Without prejudice correspondence before settlement of a claim for damages by first named claimant against his former employers not privileged in claimant's subsequent claim for negligence against solicitors who had advised the claimant before his former employer had dismissed him where the statement of case in the subsequent claim asserted that the settlement was an attempt to mitigate loss caused by the negligence and the defendants did not seek to show that admissions made in the course of such correspondence were true. The claimants had put their own conduct in issue and had thereby waived any privilege in such correspondence (*Muller v Linsley & Mortimer*, *The Times*, December 8, 1994; [1996] P.N.L.R. 74, CA). In *Somatra Ltd v Sinclair Roche & Temperley* [2000] 1 Lloyd's Rep. 311 it was held that while it was clear that legal privilege could be waived unilaterally, without prejudice privilege was effectively a joint privilege and could not be waived by one party alone. On appeal [2000] 1 W.L.R. 2453; [2000] 2 Lloyd's Rep. 673 the Court of Appeal held allowing the appeal in part, that a party to litigation was not entitled to rely upon the contents of without prejudice discussions with another party in order to advance its case at trial unless subsequent conduct by the other party entitled it so to do; that, both as a matter of implied contract and public policy, where, in support of its case on the merits of an action, a party deployed material which formed part of without prejudice communications, the other party should be entitled to refer to the contents of the same communications at trial in order to advance its own case on the merits; and that, accordingly, the solicitors were not entitled at trial to rely on the without prejudice nature of the discussions since they had themselves relied on those discussions to support the merits of their case when applying for the *Mareva* injunction.

If one party to negotiations on a without prejudice basis wishes to change the basis thenceforth to an open one, the burden is on that party to bring the change to the attention of the other party and to establish on an objective basis that the recipient would have realised that a change in the basis of negotiation was being made (see *Cheddar Valley Engineering Ltd v Chaddlewood Homes Ltd* [1992] 1 W.L.R. 820)

Conversely the heading "without prejudice" does not conclusively or automatically render privileged a document so marked. If privilege is claimed, but challenged, the Court has to examine the document in question and determine its nature (*South Shropshire DC v Amos [1986] 1 W.L.R. 1271; [1987] 1 All* E.R. 340, CA). The rule which confers privilege on "without prejudice" communications is not limited to documents which constitute offers; privilege may also attach to "without prejudice" documents written in the opening stages of negotiations (*ibid.*).

A letter, stated by a party to be written without prejudice, which amounts not to an offer to negotiate, but merely to an assertion of that party's rights, or an attempt to argue that his case is well founded, is not privileged (*Buckinghamshire CC v Moran* [1989] 2 All E.R. 225, CA).

Transcripts of tape recordings of conversations between the parties, made by one party without the knowledge of the other, where there is a bona fide and reasonably tenable charge of crime or fraud, and where there is a prima facie case that the communications in question are made in preparation for, or in furtherance or as part of it, are not covered by "without prejudice" privilege (*Hawick Jersey International Ltd v Caplan*, *The Times*, March 11, 1988). But an unambiguous admission of impropriety during a conversation is required to render admissible in evidence a tape recording of a negotiation aimed at settling the dispute (*Alizadeh v Nikbin*, *The Times*, March 19, 1993, CA). See further *Forster v Friedland*, November 10, 1992, CA Transcript 92/1052.

The test for loss of without prejudice protection from admissibility is one of unambiguous impropriety and a very clear case of abuse of a privileged occasion, not whether there was a serious and substantial risk of perjury; see *Berry Trade Ltd v Moussavi (No.3)* [2003] EWCA Civ 715; *The Times*, June 3, 2003, CA. In *Savings & Investments Bank Ltd v Fincken* [2003] EWCA Civ 1630; [2004] 1 W.L.R. 667; [2004] 1 All E.R. 1125, CA, it was held that the unambiguous impropriety exception is confined to instances where it is established that the privelege is itself being abused.

A note made by a claimant's solicitor of a telephone conversation between him and the defendant's solicitor, which merely records the substance of the conversation and contains nothing in the nature of a communication to the claimant, is not a document privileged from disclosure as between claimant and defendant even if the subject matter of the conversation is "without prejudice"; hence, where such a note has been properly disclosed by the claimant, the defendant is not entitled, on the principle that waiver of a privileged document requires the release from privilege of all material relevant to the matter as to which professional privilege has been waived (for which see para.31.3.27 above), to disclosure of all memoranda passing between the claimant and his solicitor relating to the conversation, because there has been no waiver of a privileged document (*Parry v News Group Newspapers Ltd* (1990) 140 N.L.J. 1719, CA).

Where a judge sees privileged or inadmissable material does not raise issues of partiality or bias but if rescusation is sought the judge should consider subjectively whether he is disabled from fairly continuing with the case and objectively whether viewed from the standpoint of a fair minded and informed observer there was a real possibility or a real danger of there being seen to be an unfair trial. Further, in a case where privilege over without prejudice material has not been waived, neither side should unilaterally or orally without notice refer to the contents of such communication without first ascertaining the views of the other side to such intended disclosure and notifying the Court of its intended course and seeking the Courts views on whether and how the matter should be adduced, *Berg v IML London Ltd* [2002] 1 W.L.R. 3271.

A letter containing an offer to settle may be written as an open letter and used by the party writing it during the trial, providing it has relevance and does not form part of continuing without prejudice negotiations (*Dixons Stores Group Ltd v Thames Television Plc* [1993] 1 All E.R. 349).

When a solicitor writes "threats" letters on behalf of a client, he has no confidence or legal professional privilege therein, whatever the position as regards his client himself. If such a "threats" letter is inaccurate the solicitor has a duty to put that right, though there may be difficulties when the solicitor has ceased to act for that client or when questions arise as to whether he should write such a correcting letter of his own accord (*CHC Software Care Ltd v Hopkins and Wood* [1993] F.S.R. 241).

Meaning of document

31.4 **31.4 In this Part—**

"document" means anything in which information of any description is recorded; and

"copy", in relation to a document, means anything onto which information recorded in the document has been copied, by whatever means and whether directly or indirectly.

"Document"

31.4.1 *This follows* the definition used in many statutes, e.g. the Police and Criminal Evidence Act 1984 s.118(1); the Criminal Justice Act 1988 s.23(1) (now repealed); the Civil Evidence Act 1995 s.13; and the Criminal Justice Act 2003 s.134(1).

While the word in non-legal usage is commonly associated with information recorded only on paper, the true meaning of the word is far wider. As was pointed out by Walton J. in *Grant v Southwestern and County Properties Ltd* [1975] Ch. 185 at 190E "the derivation of the word is from the Latin 'documentum': it is something which instructs or provides information".

Examples of objects which would be "documents" for the purpose of r.31.4 include audio recordings (*Grant v Southwestern and County Properties Ltd* (ibid.) at 193G and 198B); film (*Senior v Holdsworth* [1976] Q.B. 23 at 36B–D; the apparent indication to the contrary in *Glyn v Western Feature Film Co* [1916] 85 L.J. Ch. 261 at 262–3 does not represent modern law); video-tape (*Garcin v Amerindo Investment Advisors Ltd* [1991] 4 All E.R. 655 at 656g); plans (e.g. *Hayes v Brown* [1920] 1 K.B. 250 at 252) inscriptions on a wall (*Ruscoe v Grounsell* (1903) 20 T.L.R. 5); computer files, so long as there is information capable of being retrieved (*Derby & Co Ltd v Weldon (No.9)* [1991] 1 W.L.R. 652 at 657–8); the hard disk of a computer (*Alliance & Leicester Building Society v Ghahremani* [1992] R.V.R. 198 at 199); computer databases (*Marlton v Tectronix UK Holdings* [2003] EWHC 383 (Ch); [2003] Info. T.L.R. 258; computer software (*Format Communications v I.T.T. (UK) Ltd* [1983] F.S.R. 473). Old cases holding that labels are not documents such as *Burrell v North* (1847) 2 C. & K. 680; 175 E.R. 284 do not represent the modern law.

The fact that an instrument is needed to retrieve, decipher, translate or decode the information does not prevent an object containing information from being a document: *Grant v Southwestern and County Properties Ltd* [1975] Ch. 185 at 191 and 197; *Victor Chandler International Ltd v Commissioners of Customs and Excise* [2000] 1 W.L.R. 1296 at 1302; compare Lord Denning M.R.'s dissent in *Senior v Holdsworth* (ibid.) at 32D. In the Canadian case of *Prism Hospital Software Ltd v Hospital Medical Research Institute* [1992] 2 W.W.R. 157 at 160 (Brit. Colum. Sup Ct) files of information recovered from computer disks by use of specialist software were held to be "documents contained on magnetic media" for the purposes of the relevant Evidence Act. The same result would probably be reached under r.31.4. See para.31.6.5 below for the disclosure of electronic data.

However there must be some information contained for the thing to be a "document". A blank piece of paper may not be a "document": *Hill v The King* [1945] K.B. 329 at 334. Similarly see *Re Alderton and Barry's Application* (1941) 59 R.P.C. 56 at 60 (unused and empty workers' time sheet).

It is questionable whether information which is displayed without being recorded, such that there is no lasting record, is within the definition of a "document". In the criminal case of *Darby v DPP* (1995) 159 J.P. 533 at 538 the visual reading appearing on the screen of a speed camera and not able to be reproduced or have an independent existence was nonetheless assumed to be a 'document'. And in *Chandler International Ltd v Commissioners of Customs and Excise* [2000] 1 W.L.R. 1296 at 1302 the central editing system which produced teletext advertisements was described as a document, though with little consideration of the issue.

"Copy"

This definition is the same as that in the Civil Evidence Act 1995 s.13. For a detailed analysis of different types of copy documents (e.g. examined copies, office copies, certified copies etc.) see *Phipson on Evidence*, 16th edn (2005), pp.1197–1200. By the Civil Evidence Act 1995 s.8, where a statement contained in a document is admissible as evidence in civil proceedings, it may be proved by the production of that document or a copy of that document or of the material part of it, authenticated in such manner as the court may approve, whether or not that document is still in existence; and it is immaterial for this purpose how many removes there are between a copy and the original. As to disclosure of copies see para.31.9 below. **31.4.2**

Note that the undertaking in r.31.22 applies to disclosed copies.

Disclosure limited to standard disclosure

31.5—(1) An order to give disclosure is an order to give standard disclosure unless the court directs otherwise. **31.5**

(2) The court may dispense with or limit standard disclosure.

(3) The parties may agree in writing to dispense with or to limit standard disclosure.

(The court may make an order requiring standard disclosure

under rule 28.3 which deals with directions in relation to cases on the fast track and under rule 29.2 which deals with case management in relation to cases on the multi-track.)

Order for disclosure required

31.5.1 CPR Pt 31 has no provision for disclosure without court order, and so disclosure is not automatic. "Standard disclosure" is the amount of disclosure required where an order is made for "disclosure", with no more detailed specification of the extent of disclosure required. The meaning and scope of standard disclosure is set out in r.31.6 (see below).

Stage at which disclosure occurs

31.5.2 Normally disclosure is ordered at the first case management hearing, after the defence is filed and on the allocation of the case to a track, but prior to service of witness statements: CPR, r.26.3. In *Parker v C S Structured Credit Fund Ltd* [2003] EWHC 391; [2003] 1 W.L.R. 1680 (Ch) the court declined to bring forward disclosure ahead of the normal stage in litigation in which it occurs.

There are important reasons why disclosure takes place before and not after service of witness statements, and the fact that it is feared that a witness may tailor his or her witness statement in the light and to take account of documents disclosed should rarely if ever be a sufficient reason for postponing disclosure of documents until after service of the statements: *Watford Petroleum Ltd v Interoil Trading SA* [2003] EWCA Civ 1417, at [40–42]; see also [29–34], CA.

Standard disclosure in particular classes of case

31.5.3 *Small and fast track claims*—For claims on the small track, Pt 31 does not apply: CPR rr.27.2 (1)(b), 31.1 (2). In such cases the Court will give directions as to disclosure: CPR r.27.4(l)(a)–(c). For claims on the fast track, the Court may direct less than "standard" disclosure: CPR, Pt 28, Practice Direction, para.3.6(l)(c), (4).

Judicial review—Disclosure is not required in judicial review unless the court orders otherwise: Practice Direction to Pt 54, para.12.1. In practice disclosure is not normally given, and parties simply produce the documents they consider relevant, and do so when they file the claim or summary or detailed grounds of defence. The procedure for judicial review claims is such that the Defendant is only required to file the evidence upon which it relies after (and if) permission to apply for judicial review has been granted. Though where the proportionality of a decision or action is in issue, it may be appropriate to require disclosure of documents referred to, and courts should take a flexible and non-prescriptive approach to disclosure in judicial review claims: *Tweed v Parades Commission for Northern Ireland* [2006] UKHL 53; [2007] 1 A.C. 650; [2007] 2 W.L.R. 1 at [32], 38–39.

While there is no general duty of disclosure in judicial review proceedings, there is a very high duty on public authority defendants to assist the court with full and accurate explanations of all the facts relevant to the issue the court must decide (*R. (Quark Fishing Ltd) v. Secretary of State for Foreign and Commonwealth Affairs)* [2002] EWCA Civ 1409 at [50], CA. The expectation that public bodies will act with candour in explaining their actions and disclosing relevant documents was described by Sir John Donaldson M.R. in *R v Lancashire County Council, Ex. p. Huddleston* [1986] 2 All E.R. 941, CA as a "duty to make full and fair disclosure" (at p.945). Claimants are also under a duty to make full and frank disclosure and inform the court of all material facts known to them (*R. (Tshikangu) v London Borough of Newham* [2001] EWHC 92 (Admin) at [23]).

Patent—In patent actions where the validity of the patent is in issue certain documents are omitted from the scope of standard disclosure. See Pt 63, Practice Direction—Patents Etc., para.5.1.

Limiting standard disclosure

31.5.4 The court is more willing to exercise discretion to limit disclosure under the CPR than it was under the RSC. In particular the court may now be more willing to exercise discretion to refuse or limit disclosure on the basis that the disclosure sought would be unduly expensive, inconvenient or troublesome in comparison to the potential forensic benefits to be gained.

The following factors may be relevant in deciding whether it is appropriate to limit standard disclosure:

(1) The amount of documentation may be considerable, given the complexity of the dispute and the underlying contract or contracts, and the process of giving standard disclosure may consequently be disproportionate to the issues and sums in dispute.
(2) The parties may have many of the documents in common from their previous dealings so that disclosure is not necessary or desirable.
(3) The parties may have provided informal disclosure and inspection of the majority of these documents, for example when complying with the pre-action Protocol.
(4) The cost of providing standard disclosure may be disproportionate.

These factors are taken from the Technology and Construction Court Guide, 2nd edn (2005, revised with effect from October 1, 2007), para.11.2.1. However they may potentially apply in any form of proceedings under the CPR.

Agreements in writing

An agreement limiting standard disclosure may do so for example by reference to documents already disclosed following pre-action disclosure under CPR, r.31.16 or in complying with a pre-action protocol. The agreement may limit disclosure to specified categories of documents. An agreement may be entered limiting standard disclosure even after an order for standard disclosure has been made. The Practice Direction provides that where this is done such written agreement should be lodged with the Court: CPR Pt 31, Practice Direction, para.1.4. **31.5.5**

Foreign sovereign or state

Once disclosure has been ordered a foreign sovereign or state suing in this country must give disclosure (*South African Co v Compagnie Franco-Belge* [1898] 1 Ch. 190; *USA v Wagner* (1867) 2 Ch. 582) and the Court will stay proceedings until the claimant has named a proper person to give disclosure (*Costa Rica Republic v Erlanger* (1875) 1 Ch.D. 171; *Peru (Republic) v Weguelin* (1875) 20 L.R. Eq. 140). **31.5.6**

Standard disclosure—what documents are to be disclosed

31.6 Standard disclosure requires a party to disclose only— **31.6**

(a) the documents on which he relies; and

(b) the documents which—

(i) adversely affect his own case;

(ii) adversely affect another party's case; or

(iii) support another party's case; and

(c) the documents which he is required to disclose by a relevant practice direction.

"the documents on which he relies"

There is no definition of "rely" or "reliance". It probably means those documents which are to be used in court, including in use for cross-examination. **31.6.1**

"adversely affect"; "support"

There are no definitions of "adversely affect" or "support". In determining the issues in a party's case the statements of case are an essential reference point: *Harrods Ltd v Times Newspaper Ltd* [2006] EWCA Civ 294; [2006] All E.R. (D) 302 (Feb) at [12]. A document which of itself does not "adversely affect" a case, but which may provide *lines of inquiry leading to other information* having a negative effect, is not covered by this provision. Adverse effect is normally primarily assessed by reference to the material allegations in the statements of case. However there is nothing in the CPR to restrict the concept in this manner, and a document casting doubt on the credibility of a party whose own evidence was important could be seen as one "adversely affecting" that party's case: *Hedrich v Standard Bank London Ltd* [2008] EWCA Civ 905. Parties probably do not need to give disclosure of documents relating to non-material allegations in pleadings, i.e. those which even if substantiated would not affect the result. The confidentiality of a particular document does not of itself justify non-disclosure: see *Science Research Council v Nasse* [1980] A.C. 1028 and 31.3.36 above. Masking irrel- **31.6.2** evant parts of a document by way of redaction is in principle possible under r.31.6 but care must be taken, as the deletion of parts that are relevant could give rise to a specific disclosure order under r.31.12: *Tullett Prebon Group Ltd v Davis* [2007] EWHC 2739.

Documents relating to other incidents or transactions, other than the one directly the subject of the dispute, may be relevant as supporting or adversely affecting another party's case: e.g. *Nyckeln Finance Co Ltd v Edward Symmons & Partners* [1996] P.N.L.R. 245 at 250, CA; *Board v Thomas Hedley & Co* [1951] 2 All E.R. 431 at 432, CA (though the latter case was decided under the RSC "train of enquiry" limb). But a court may refuse to require disclosure of 'similar fact' evidence of other claims for negligence against the same defendant made by other people in respect of other matters: *Thorpe v Chief Constable of Greater Manchester* [1989] 1 W.L.R. 665 at 670 and 674, CA. Even where such material is relevant, the court can limit the disclosure required.

In the RSC case of *Thorpe v Chief Constable of Greater Manchester* [1989] 1 W.L.R. 665, CA discovery was not ordered for material which was sought solely for cross-examination of a witness as to credit; such material not being admissible in evidence. There is no practical reason why a different approach should be taken under the CPR, as compared with the RSC, on this point. However the decision in Thorpe is questionable to the extent that disclosure (as with RSC discovery) extends beyond material admissible in evidence: see para.31.6.6 below.

Categories of documents

31.6.3 Documents may be divided into the following four categories:

(1) The *parties' own documents*: these are documents which a party relies upon in support of his contentions in the proceedings.

(2) *Adverse documents*: these are documents which to a material extent adversely affect a party's own case or support another party's case.

(3) *The relevant documents*: these are documents which are relevant to the issues in the proceedings, but which do not fall into categories 1 or 2 because they do not obviously support or undermine either side's case. They are part of the "story" or background. The category includes documents which, though relevant, may not be necessary for the fair disposal of the case.

(4) *Train of inquiry documents*: these are documents which may lead to a train of inquiry enabling a party to advance his own case or damage that of his opponent (as referred to by Brett L.J. *Compagnie Financiere et Commerciale du Pacifique v Peruvian Guano Co* (1882) L.R. 11 Q.B.D. 55, CA.

Rule 31.6 provides that "standard" disclosure is limited to documents falling within categories 1 and 2.

Whether a document falls into sub-paras (a) or (b) of r.31.6 is to be judged against the statements of case and not by reference to matters raised elsewhere, including in witness statements: *Paddick v Associated Newspapers Ltd* [2003] EWHC 2991 (QB); [2003] All E.R. (D) 179 (Dec) at [11]. If documents are specified in a practice direction then they must be disclosed, whether or not they are relied on, or adversely affect or support any party's case, e.g. Practice Direction—Protocols, the Personal Injury Protocol Annex B, and the Clinical Negligence Protocol.

Disclosure in particular types of cases and circumstances

31.6.4 Documents relevant to quantum are normally disclosable, at least where quantum is in issue, e.g. *Dunn v British Coal Corporation* [1993] I.C.R. 591, CA (in an injury claim where quantum in issue, all medical records relevant to loss of future earnings had to be disclosed, not just those relating to the injury, the subject of the litigation: see also *OCS Group Ltd v Wells* [2008] EWHC 919 (QB); *Hendry v Taylor* [2008] Rep L.R. 38.). In split trials, where quantum of damages is only determined if liability is established, there is no need to disclose documents relevant purely to quantum, and this should only be ordered if and when liability is determined: *Baldock v Addison* [1995] 1 W.L.R. 158, Ch.

Documents relating to the insurance position of a party are not normally relevant and so not disclosable, e.g. *Cox v Bankside Members Agency Ltd* [1995] 2 Lloyd's Rep. 437; [1995] C.L.C. 671. However there may be unusual situations where the insurance position of a party is relevant, e.g. where a party relies on the Unfair Contract Terms Act 1977 and an issue arises as to the availability of insurance or the terms on which it was available: *Flamar Interocean Ltd v Denmac Ltd* [1990] 1 Lloyd's Rep. 434 at 440.

As to disclosure of copies, see r.31.9 below.

Disclosure of electronic data

The disclosure obligation extends to "documents", which are defined in CPR r.31.4 to mean "anything in which information of any description is recorded". This extends to electronic documents, including email and other electronic communications, word processed documents and databases: see the Practice Direction to Pt 31, para.2A.1; as to databases see *Derby & Co Ltd v Weldon (No.9)* [1991] 2 All E.R. 901 at 905–907; *Marlton v Tectronix UK Holdings* [2003] EWHC 383 (Ch.); [2003] Info. T.L.R. 258. It includes both documents readily accessible from computer systems and other electronic devices and media, as well as material stored on servers and back-up systems and electronic documents which have been apparently deleted, but a record of which will often remain on the computer system. **31.6.5**

Failure to deliver up computers and deliberate deletion of files from a computer in contravention of a search order may amount to a contempt of court leading to committal: *LTE Scientific Limited v Thomas* [2005] EWHC 7 (QB) ("deletion of the files, which lies at the heart of the case against him, is a serious criminal contempt").

Both the CPR and the Admiralty and Commercial Courts Guide state that parties should discuss issues that arise regarding searches for and preservation of electronic documents prior to the first case management conference, and in cases of difficulty or disagreement, refer the matter to a judge for directions: Practice Direction to Pt 31, para.2A.2; Admiralty & Commercial Courts Guide (7th edn 2006) para.E3.11 (b).

"Deletion" of computer files may only remove the link to the file directory; the information may remain recorded within the computer disk and potentially recoverable until overwritten. In the Canadian case of *Prism Hospital Software Ltd v Hospital Medical Research Institute* [1992] 2 W.W.R. 157, Brit. Colum. Sup Ct, a party had disclosed computer hard disks and allowed inspection by examination of the physical disks themselves. Inspection was carried out by the principal of the inspecting party, who was very knowledgeable about computers. By application of a software programme, the inspecting party was able to recover information from previously "deleted" material. The information recovered was admitted. The facts that knowledge of computers was required to recover the files and then to read them by means of a computer programme did not mean that the evidence concerning the recovered files was expert opinion.

For the factors relevant in deciding the reasonableness of a search for electronic documents, see para.31.7.4 below.

For a detailed analysis of the practice regarding disclosure of electronic data, see Matthews and Malek, *Disclosure*, 3rd edn (2007), Ch.7.

Disclosure and admissibility

It is important to note that disclosure of documents and admissibility of evidence are two distinct concepts. It is not a ground for refusing disclosure that the document would not be admissible in evidence, and so the existence of potentially inadmissible documents should still be disclosed. See e.g. *O'Rourke v Derbyshire* [1920] A.C. 581 at 624, 630–631 (relating to the pre-CPR position). **31.6.6**

Duty of search

31.7—(1) When giving standard disclosure, a party is required to make a reasonable search for documents falling within rule 31.6(b) or (c). **31.7**

***(2) The factors* relevant in deciding the reasonableness of a search include the following—**

- **(a) the number of documents involved;**
- **(b) the nature and complexity of the proceedings;**
- **(c) the ease and expense of retrieval of any particular document; and**
- **(d) the significance of any document which is likely to be located during the search.**

(3) Where a party has not searched for a category or class of document on the grounds that to do so would be unreasonable, he must state this in his disclosure statement and identify the category or class of document.

(Rule 31.10 makes provision for a disclosure statement.)

"a reasonable search"

31.7.1 See further Practice Direction (Disclosure and Inspection), para.2 (para.31PD.1 below).

Rule 31.7(1) states that, when giving standard disclosure, a party is required to make a "reasonable search" for documents. The person making a disclosure statement is required to set out the extent of the search that has been made to locate documents which he is required to disclose (see r.31.10(6)(a) below). Where it is necessary for the court to determine whether a party under a duty disclose has or has not undertaken a "reasonable search" the factors listed in r.31.7(2) come into play. These factors reflect some of the particular objectives stated in r.1.1(2) (the overriding objective).

While in the first instance assessing what in the circumstances amounts to a reasonable search is a matter for the solicitor, ultimately the task of deciding what is required is given to the Court by the wording of the Rules. The Court's role is not limited to a review of the solicitor's decision making process: *Digicel (St Lucia) Ltd* v Cable & Wireless Plc [2008] EWHC 2522, (Ch), [2008] WL 4698881.

The overriding principle of proportionality is relevant in determining the extent of the search. The Pt 31 Practice Direction notes that it may be reasonable to decide not to search for documents coming into existence before some particular date, or to limit the search of documents to some particular place or places or to documents of a particular category: Practice Direction, Disclosure and Inspection, paras 2 and 2A(4).

Conducting searches in a company or other organisation

31.7.2 In a company or other organisation a number of people may have knowledge of relevant documents. Lord Woolf, in his final report (Access to Justice: Final Report (1996), Chapter 12, para.4.1) recommended that the organisation nominate a supervising officer responsible for identifying individuals who were likely to recollect relevant documents.

"... state this in his disclosure statement ..."

31.7.3 As to this requirement in r.31.7(3), for cases in the Commercial Court a party taking this step must indicate this in the case management information sheet: Admiralty and Commercial Courts Guide, 7th edn (2006), para.E3.2.

Extent of search for electronic data

31.7.4 One of the factors in deciding the reasonableness of a search is the ease and expense of retrieval of any particular document. Guidance as to the assessment of this factor is contained in the Practice Direction to Pt 31, para.2A.4(c); also see the Admiralty and Commercial Courts Guide, 7th edn (2006), para.E3.11(d).

It may be reasonable to search some or all of the parties' electronic storage systems. In some circumstances it may be reasonable to search for electronic documents by means of keyword searches (agreed as far as possible between the parties), even where a full review of each and every document would be unreasonable: Practice Direction to Pt 31, para.2A.5; Admiralty and Commercial Courts Guide, 7th edn (2006) para.E3.11(e); *Digicel (St Lucia) Ltd v Cable & Wireless Plc* [2008] EWHC 2522 (Ch).

The potentially great volume of electronic documents means that issues of the scope and reasonableness of the search need careful consideration. Disclosure of electronic documents may be circumscribed to ensure the disclosure obligation is not too burdensome, e.g. see *Hands v Morrison Construction Services Ltd* [2006] EWHC 2018 (Ch.); [2006] All E.R. (D) 186 (Jun).

The standard disclosure statement has been amended to emphasise the importance of searching for electronically recorded information as part of the disclosure process.

Duty of disclosure limited to documents which are or have been in a party's control

31.8 **31.8—(1) A party's duty to disclose documents is limited to documents which are or have been in his control.**

(2) For this purpose a party has or has had a document in his control if—

(a) it is or was in his physical possession;

(b) he has or has had a right to possession of it; or

(c) he has or has had a right to inspect or take copies of it.

"physical possession"

This equates to the concept of "custody" under the former RSC, and RSC cases concerning that concept may be instructive. **31.8.1**

"right to possession"

This concept covers the situation where a party's documents are in the hands of a servant or agent. It does not apply to the agent's own working papers which belong to him: cf. *Chantrey Martin v Martin* [1953] 2 Q.B. 286, CA; *R. v Mid-Glamorgan Family Health Services, exp. Martin* [1995] 1 W.L.R. 110, CA. Under the revised RSC the term 'possession' included this right to possession: *B. v B.* [1978] Fam. 181 at 186. **31.8.2**

The position of documents which are subject to joint rights to possession is uncertain. Under the RSC such documents were disclosable (*Alfred Crompton Amusement Machines Ltd v Commissioners of Customs & Excise (No.2)* [1974] A.C. 405 at 429). The same should apply under the CPR.

There is nothing in the CPR to limit disclosure to cases where the physical possession is lawful. Even a thief would have to give disclosure of stolen documents if these are relevant to the issues before the court.

"right to inspect or take copies"

This may be a similar concept to that which existed under the former RSC covering documents within a party's "power", so cases concerning that RSC category may be useful; note the manner in which the RSC concept of documents under a party's "power" was described in *Lonrho Ltd v Shell Petroleum Ltd* [1980] 1 W.L.R. 627 at 635. Documents in the possession of subsidiary companies were not in the "power" of the parent companies for the purposes of the RSC. Where there is no presently enforceable legal right to obtain the documents without a third party's consent, then the documents may be outside this concept; for example where there is no enforceable legal right to obtain the documents of a subsidiary company without their consent: see *Lonrho v Shell* (ibid). Documents in the possession and control of a non-party may fall with a party's "control" if there is a prior or current practice of that party having access and inspection rights to the non-party's documents: *Schlumberger Holdings Limited v Electromagnetic Geoservices* [2008] EWHC 56 (Pat) or other "situation in which the separate identity of the company can effectively be ignored" per Patten J. at [39] *Thunder Air Ltd v Hilmarsson* [2008] EWHC 355 (Ch), [2008] WL 678143. **31.8.3**

Sources of the right to inspect or take copies

A right of inspection of documents may arise from contract, in which case the relevant documents would be disclosable. However this is unlikely to be the case where the contract provides that the documents be kept confidential: *Unilever plc v Gillette (UK) Ltd* [1988] R.P.C. 416. The right may arise from various other sources, e.g. a principal's right to see the agent's records; a company director's right to see certain company documents; a partner's similar right in relation to partnership documents; a beneficiary's right to see trust documents or documents relating to a deceased estate. **31.8.4**

Disclosure of copies

31.9—(1) A party need not disclose more than one copy of a document. **31.9**

(2) A copy of a document that contains a modification, obliteration or other marking or feature—

(a) on which a party intends to rely; or

(b) which adversely affects his own case or another party's case or supportsanother party's case;

shall be treated as a separate document.

(Rule 31.4 sets out the meaning of a copy of a document.)

"Copy"; "Document"

31.9.1 See r.31.4 and commentary for explanation of these terms.

An exact copy of a disclosable document is not disclosable: CPR r.31.9(1). However it is disclosable if it contains any modification, obliteration or other marking or feature on which a party intends to rely, or if it supports or adversely affects a party's case: CPR r.31.9(2). This is different from the position under the former RSC: cf. *Dubai Bunk Ltd v Galadari (No.7)* [1992] 1 W.L.R. 106, Ch.

As to whether copies are privileged see 31.3.14 above.

Procedure for standard disclosure

31.10 **31.10—(1) The procedure for standard disclosure is as follows.**

(2) Each party must make, and serve on every other party, a list of documents in the relevant practice form.

(3) The list must identify the documents in a convenient order and manner and as concisely as possible.

(4) The list must indicate—

(a) those documents in respect of which the party claims a right or duty to withhold inspection; and

(b)

(i) those documents which are no longer in the party's control; and

(ii) what has happened to those documents.

(Rule 31.19(3) and (4) require a statement in the list of documents relating to any documents inspection of which a person claims he has a right or duty to withhold.)

(5) The list must include a disclosure statement.

(6) A disclosure statement is a statement made by the party disclosing the documents—

(a) setting out the extent of the search that has been made to locate documents which he is required to disclose;

(b) certifying that he understands the duty to disclose documents; and

(c) certifying that to the best of his knowledge he has carried out that duty.

(7) Where the party making the disclosure statement is a company, firm, association or other organisation, the statement must also—

(a) identify the person making the statement; and

(b) explain why he is considered an appropriate person to make the statement.

(8) The parties may agree in writing—

(a) to disclose documents without making a list; and

(b) ***to disclose documents*** **without the disclosing party making a disclosure statement.**

(9) A disclosure statement may be made by a person who is not a party where this is permitted by a relevant practice direction.

"... a list of documents in the relevant practice form"

The form is **N265**. The list must inter alia identify documents in respect of which privilege is claimed and state those documents which are no longer in the control of the disclosing party and what has happened to such documents (r.31.10(4)). Where privilege is claimed, the grounds on which it is claimed must be stated: see Practice Direction supplementing Pt 31, para.4.5. **31.10.1**

The list of documents is divided into three classes: (1) documents still in the party's control, where inspection is not objected to; (2) documents still in the party's control, where inspection is objected to; and (3) documents no longer in the party's control.

The list does not need to follow the wording in N265 precisely, but Form N265 must be substantively followed: CPR, Pt 4, Practice Direction, para.1.2.

"... in the convenient order and manner and as concisely as possible"

By Practice Direction supplementing Pt 31, para.3.2 (see para.31PD.3) it is provided: **31.10.2**

> "In order to comply with rule 31.10(3) it will normally be necessary to list the documents in date order, to number them consecutively and to give each a concise description (e.g. letter to defendant). Where there is a large number of documents all falling into a particular category the disclosing party may list those documents as a category rather than individually, e.g. 50 bank statements relating to account number ______ at ______ Bank, ______ 19__ to ______ 19__; or, 35 letters passing between ______ and ______ between ______ 19__ and ______ 19__."

Note that descriptions which follow the above form of date, addressor and addressee may not provide any indication of the content of the documents from such description; but it is not the purpose of the disclosure list to do so.

Disclosure by listing documents, or even by categories, may be inconvenient where there are a very large number of documents. In such cases it may be appropriate to list by files or boxes instead of documents or categories. The parties may agree this between themselves, or the court may order it. While it is common or general practice not to insist on individual itemisation of documents in such circumstances, parties can have no expectation that this will always be the case, and a court may in an appropriate case insist on individual itemisation of documents: *Punjab National Bank v Jain* [2004] EWCA Civ 589, CA at [22].

While the Practice Direction to Pt 31 (para.3.2) recommends listing the documents in date order, in some cases the order in which documents appeared in a file may itself be of relevance. If there is a chance this may be the case, then either the file should not be re-ordered, or if it is to be re-ordered, then a copy should be taken of the file in its original order beforehand: Admiralty and Commercial Courts Guide, 7th edn (2006), para.E3.5.

Description-Privileged Documents

So far as describing documents is concerned there is a difference between documents for which privilege from production is claimed and other documents. As regards privileged documents the description is not for the purpose of enabling the other party to learn the contents of the document or to test the truth of the plea of privilege. Nor is it for the purpose of causing the party giving disclosure to furnish evidence against himself (*Gardner v Irvin* (1878) L.R. 4 Ex.D. 49 at 53, CA). It is not required that the dates of the documents should be specified nor the names of the makers (*ibid.*). "Correspondence between the (defendant) and his solicitors for the purpose of obtaining legal advice" is sufficient (*ibid.*). **31.10.3**

This is the long-established and widespread practice of the profession. While it could be argued that it is not in accordance with the strict terms of the requirement in the CPR to identify documents in the list, any stricter interpretation of the requirement to list such documents would risk abrogating the privilege in a manner that does not seem to have been intended by the CPR. See further Hollander, *Documentary Evidence*, 9th edn (2006), p.253.

Where privilege is claimed for professional communications of a confidential character obtained for the purpose of getting legal advice, the claim for privilege is to be treated as itself a sufficient description of the communications, irrespective of the scale of disclosure or the complexity of the issues involved, and consequently the party seeking disclosure is not entitled to satisfy himself by means of fuller description of the communications for which privilege is claimed that it is not claimed for documents outside its proper scope; moreover the court will not order the party claiming privilege to disclose all communications with his legal advisers, or to provide fuller particulars of such communications, even where it has been shown in relation to one transaction that the advice was sought in furtherance of a fraudulent design, since to order such disclosure would be contrary to the public policy on which legal professional privilege is founded (*Derby & Co Ltd v Weldon (No.7)* [1990] 1 W.L.R. 1156; [1990] 3 All E.R. 161).

Where other objections to inspection are claimed there is a similar practice as to that used for privileged documents, i.e. the category of objection is listed, but the individual documents usually are not. Again this common practice is maintained notwithstanding that the effect is to not actually disclose the existence of the individual documents.

"... the party claims a right or duty to withhold inspection"

31.10.4 See commentary "... right or duty to withhold inspection" and "Procedure for claiming a right or duty to withhold inspection" at paras 31.3.2 and 31.3.3 above.

Disclosure statement

31.10.5 The form is set out in Practice Direction (Disclosure and Inspection) Annex, para.31PD.8.

The disclosure statement is designed to bring home to each party his disclosure responsibilities, and is not a mere technicality: *Arrow Trading v Edwardian Group Ltd* [2004] EWHC 1319; [2004] B.C.C. 955; [2005] 1 B.C.L.C. 696 (Ch) (Comm Ct) at [45]. Where a party has not searched for a category or class of document on the grounds that to do so would be unreasonable, he must state this in his disclosure statement and identify the category or class of document: CPR, r.31.7; Practice Direction to Pt 31, para.2. A party's lawyers should ensure that the person making the disclosure statement understands the duty of disclosure: Practice Direction to Pt 31, para.4.4. Where there are several defendants, each must sign the statement: *Arrow Trading v Edwardian Group Ltd* (ibid) at [40]–[45].

The standard disclosure statement has been amended to emphasise the importance of searching for electronically recorded information as part of the disclosure process.

Obligations of solicitors in respect of disclosure and of production by their clients

31.10.6 It is necessary for solicitors to take positive steps to ensure that their clients appreciate at an early stage of the litigation, promptly after the claim form is issued, not only the duties of disclosure and inspection which will arise if disclosure is agreed or ordered by the court, but also the importance of not destroying documents which might possibly have to be disclosed (per Megarry J. in *Rockwell Machine Tool Co Ltd v E.P. Barrus (Concessionaires) Ltd* [1968] 2 All E.R. 98 (Note)). Moreover it is not enough simply to give instructions that documents be preserved. Steps should be taken to ensure that documents are preserved (*Infabrics Ltd v Jaytex Ltd* [1985] F.S.R. 75 where, because a defendant had not preserved documents affecting the quantum of damage, the maxim *omnia praesummuntur contra spoliatorem* was applied against him).

"It cannot be too clearly understood that solicitors owe a duty to the court, as officers of the court, carefully to go through the documents disclosed by their client to make sure, as far as possible, that no relevant documents have been omitted from their clients' [list]", per Salmon J. (as he then was) in *Woods v Martins Bank Ltd* [1959] 1 Q.B. 55 at 60.

See too comments on the duty to notify court and/or to withdraw in the event of a client not complying with proper advice in respect of disclosure in *Myers v Elman* [1940] A.C. 282 at 293–4, 300–301 and 322–323.

See also para.31.11—Duty of disclosure continues during proceedings.

Consequences of failure to disclose documents or permit inspection

31.10.7 See r.31.21 below.

Company, firm, association or other organisation

31.10.8 A disclosure statement made by a shareholder, purportedly on behalf of himself and other defendants, is unlikely to be sufficient: *Arrow Trading v Edwardian Group Ltd* (ibid.) at [44]. It is not sufficient to have a disclosure statement signed by an authorised officer of another company on the basis that that other company is itself the company secretary of the disclosing party: *Carlco Ltd v Chief Constable of Dyfed-Powys Police* [2002] EWCA Civ 1754 at [9–10] and [22], CA.

"... an appropriate person to make the statement ..."

Any person who can be regarded as authorised to search, and has responsibility for the search, would probably be regarded as "an appropriate person to make the statement": cf. Admiralty and Commercial Courts Guide, 7th edn (2006), para.E3.10. A party's lawyer may be an appropriate person in many situations. **31.10.9**

Agreement in writing

The ability conferred by r.31.10(8) to reach a written agreement as to a simplified form of disclosure may be particularly useful where there are very few documents to disclose. Any written agreement must be lodged with the Court: Practice Direction to Pt 31, para.1.4. **31.10.10**

Disclosure statement made by non-party

An insurer or the Motor Insurers' Bureau having a financial interest in proceedings brought by or against a party may sign a disclosure statement on behalf of that other party: Practice Direction to Pt 31, para.4.7. **31.10.11**

Departing from the standard procedure

The standard procedure may be varied by court order, for example, to dispense with the list and to simply have service of copies of all disclosable documents: Practice Direction to Pt 28, para.3.6(4)(b). The standard procedure may also be varied by written agreement: see para.31.10.10 above. **31.10.12**

Duty of disclosure continues during proceedings

31.11—(1) Any duty of disclosure continues until the proceedings are concluded. **31.11**

(2) If documents to which that duty extends come to a party's notice at any time during the proceedings, he must immediately notify every other party.

Supplemental list

If documents falling within a party's duty to give standard disclosure come to a party's notice after service of his list of documents, a supplemental list must be prepared and served. An obvious example is where a claimant who is claiming damages for prospective loss of earnings, obtains new lucrative employment during the course of the case, this fact must be communicated to the defendant and further disclosure must be made. **31.11.1**

The Admiralty and Commercial Courts Guide, 7th edn (2006), para.E2.2 also requires that a supplemental list be served. If the additional material is very small in number, then the sensible course may be for the parties to agree that the extra disclosure simply take the form of listing the documents in a letter.

Documents are not presently disclosable if they may only be coming into a party's control in the future, but are not yet in that party's control: *Lonrho Ltd v Shell Petroleum Co Ltd* [1980] 1 W.L.R. 627 at 635, HL (decided under the RSC). The disclosure obligation does not extend to an obligation to create documents to record information. However a court may exercise power under r.35.9 to direct a party having access to information not reasonably available to the other party to "prepare and file a document recording the information".

In *Vernon v Bosley (No.2)* [1999] Q.B. 18; [1997] 1 All E.R. 614 it was held that where a document was disclosed to a party after he had closed his case, or the evidence as a whole was concluded, he should apply to the court to reopen the case in the light of the disclosure if the document was of real significance and there was otherwise a risk of injustice.

Specific disclosure or inspection

31.12—(1) The court may make an order for specific disclosure or specific inspection. **31.12**

(2) An order for specific disclosure is an order that a party must do one or more of the following things—

(a) disclose documents or classes of documents specified in the order;

(b) carry out a search to the extent stated in the order;

(c) disclose any documents located as a result of that search.

(3) An order for specific inspection is an order that a party permit inspection of a document referred to in rule 31.3(2).

(Rule 31.3(2) allows a party to state in his disclosure statement that he will not permit inspection of a document on the grounds that it would be disproportionate to do so.)

Application for specific disclosure or inspection

31.12.1 The application should be made in accordance with Pt 23. The application should state what order is sought and must be supported by evidence: see r.31.12(2) and Practice Direction supplementing Pt 31, para.5.2.

The application should set out the documents or classes of documents for which disclosure or inspection is sought, or the extent of the search sought. If a class of documents is specified, the class should be carefully defined so it is limited to what is relevant and proportionate, and so the disclosing party is in no doubt as to the scope of his obligation: *City of Gotha v Sotheby's* [1998] 1 W.L.R. 114 at 123H, CA; *Berkeley Administration v McClelland* [1990] F.S.R. 381 at 382. It may also be appropriate to explain why it is reasonable and appropriate for that disclosure or search to be done. The former RSC contained a requirement that the evidence state the source and grounds for believing the document exists. While this is not an express requirement under the CPR, it will be good practice in appropriate cases.

Timing of application

31.12.1.1 An application under this Rule may be made at any stage of the proceedings, and particularly at times when the court is likely to be giving directions in any event, such as allocation, case management conference, with the listing questionnaire, or at the pre-trial review. In Multi-Track cases and in the Commercial Court, applications are usually dealt with at a case management conference: see the Admiralty and Commercial Courts Guide, 7th edn (2006), para.E2.1. In contrast the Queen's Bench Guide para.7.8.5 states that this is not a matter that would be routinely dealt with at the case management conference; a separate application for specific disclosure should be made in accordance with Pt 23. The lateness of an application may undermine its claim that the documents are in fact necessary for the forthcoming proceedings: *Harris v Society of Lloyd's* [2008] EWHC 1433 (Comm) (application for disclosure om eve of hearing of case). In Fast Track cases the appropriate time to apply for specific disclosure may be on allocation to the track and on filing of listing questionnaires, which is when case management takes place: CPR Pt 28, Practice Direction, The Fast Track, para.2.1.

The court may make an order for specific disclosure or specific inspection

31.12.2 The court will take into account all the circumstances of the case and in particular the overriding objective in Pt 1 (see Practice Direction supplementing Pt 31, para.5.4 (para.31PD.5) and the concept of proportionality).

The rationale for the discretion to order specific disclosure is that the overriding objective obliges the parties to give access to those documents which will assist the other's case: *Commissioners of Inland Revenue v Exeter City AFC Ltd* [2004] B.C.C. 519. The court has a discretion as to whether it makes the order. It may make an order at any time, regardless of whether standard disclosure has already occurred; and it may make orders for specific disclosure against a claimant before the service of the defence where it would assist the defendant to plead a full defence rather than an initial bare denial: *Dayman v Canyon Holdings Ltd*, Ch.D Judge Mackie Q.C., January 11, 2006, reported only on Lawtel LTL Doc. No.AC9501271.

The court will need to satisfy itself as to the relevance of the documents sought, and that they are or have been in the party's control, or at least that there is a prima facie case that these requirements will be met. The relevance of documents is analysed by reference to the pleadings, and the factual issues in dispute on the pleadings: *Harrods Ltd v The Times Newspaper Ltd* [2006] EWCA Civ 294; [2006] All E.R. (D) 302 (Feb) at [12]. Where a claim is likely to turn on particular documents there is a stronger case for an order to be made: *Chantrey Vellacott v Convergence Group plc* February 6, 2006, Ch.D Rimer J., reported only on Lawtel LTL Doc. No.AC9100857 (in that case particular emails and draft documents).

The power to order disclosure for the purpose of interlocutory proceedings should be exercised sparingly and then only for such documents as can be shown to be necessary for the just disposal of the application, *Harris v The Society of Lloyd's* [2008] EWHC 1433 (Comm); July 1, 2008 unrep. para.10 applying to the CPR rule, the former RSC approach propounded in *Rome v Punjab National Bank* [1989] 2 All E.R.136.

In determining whether disclosure should be ordered, the court must balance the ECHR art.6(1) right of to a fair hearing for the party seeking disclosure with the other party's art.8 right to respect for private life: *Nayler v Beard* [2001] EWCA Civ 1201.

Small Claims Track cases

In Small Claims Track cases, if a party wants further disclosure beyond that obtained pursuant to the standard Small Claims Track direction requiring parties to disclose copies of documents upon which they intend to rely at the hearing, then he should make an application for special directions, which may be heard and determined at a preliminary hearing: CPR r.27.6. Such an application is not made under r.31.12, as Pt 31 does not apply to Small Claims Track cases. **31.12.3**

Disclosure in stages

31.13 The parties may agree in writing, or the court may direct, that disclosure or inspection or both shall take place in stages. **31.13**

Disclosure in stages

This may be done, for example, where there is a split trial of a particular issue or issues. Where a split trial had been ordered so that the issue of liability was to be determined separately from the issue of quantum. discovery on the issue of quantum would not normally be ordered, and only special circumstances going beyond a plaintiff's or defendant's interest in learning the amount in issue for the purpose of making informed decisions on whether to negotiate a compromise or to proceed with the action or defence would justify making such an order: *Baldock v Addison* [1995] 1 W.L.R. 158; [1995] 3 All E.R. 437; [1994] F.S.R. 665. Compare *Kapur v JW Francis & Co (No.1)*, *The Times*, March 4, 1998. **31.13.1**

In *Buchanan-Michaelson v Rubinstein* [1965] Ch.258; [1965] 1 W.L.R. 390, CA disclosure relating to amounts claimed to be due under an alleged contract was not necessary at that stage as the contract itself was disputed (and described by Harman L.J. as "extremely shadowy"), and that issue was to be determined. A court may in appropriate circumstances make an order for disclosure and inspection at the same time: *Punjab National Bank v Jain* [2004] EWCA Civ 589 at [24], CA.

Documents referred to in statements of case etc.[1]

31.14—(1) A party may inspect a document mentioned in— **31.14**

(a) a statement of case;

(b) a witness statement;

***(c) a witness* summary; or**

(d) an affidavit

(e) [Revoked]

(2) Subject to rule 35.10(4), a party may apply for an order for inspection of any document mentioned in an expert's report which has not already been disclosed in the proceedings.

[1] Amended by the Civil Procedure (Amendment No.5) Rules 2001 (SI. 2001/4015).

(Rule 35.10(4) makes provision in relation to instructions referred to in an expert's report.)

Right to inspect

31.14.1 The right to inspect here arises simply by virtue of the document having been mentioned in one of the documents in r.31.14(1), irrespective of whether or not a List of Documents has been served, and irrespective of whether pleadings are closed. See the RSC authority of *Quilter v Heatly* (1883) 23 Ch. D. 42, CA. The same result would probably be reached under CPR r.31.14. Under the RSC, once a party established that a document was mentioned in a pleading etc., the onus then fell to the other party to show good cause why he should not produce it: see *Quilter v Heatly* (ibid) at 51. Again, the same should apply under the CPR. The same general rights to withhold inspection (see 31.3 and 31.19) apply under this provision, *Expandable Ltd v Rubin* [2008] EWCA Civ 59; [2008] 1 W.L.R. 1099, CA.

"... document mentioned ..."

31.14.2 The wording in the RSC was whether a "reference is made" to the document. The CPR wording probably requires a specific identification of the actual document. The mere mention of a transaction which must have used a particular document is unlikely to suffice; the document itself needs to be mentioned. Even under the RSC reference to a particular transaction was unlikely to constitute "reference" to the documents evidencing that transaction: *Dubai Bank Ltd v Galadari (No.2)* [1990] 1 W.L.R. 731 at [738–739]. A party may seek to obtain a specific reference to the document sufficient to lead to a right of inspection by making a request for further information. In *Expandable Ltd v Rubin* cited above, the Court of Appeal held that the change in terminology between RSC 24.10 ("reference is made") and the present CPR 31.14 ("mentioned in") had not resulted in any change of substance and reaffirmed that the test was that of direct allusion, i.e. a direct or specific reference (*Dubai Bank v Galadari No.2* [1990] 1 W.L.R. 731). Reliance is not a requisite but may be relevant to any issue of waiver. Reference by inference is indirect and insufficient.

In one case it has been held that quoting from a document without identifying the document as the source of the quote did not amount to the mentioning of the document sufficient to lead to a right of inspection: *Rigg v Associated Newspapers* [2003] EWHC 710 (QB); [2004] E.M.L.R. 4. This is a narrow construction of r.31.14(1).

"... a statement of case ..."

31.14.3 "Statement of case" includes a claim form, particulars of claim, defence, Pt 20 claim, reply to defence, and further information given voluntarily or by court order.

"... an affidavit ..."

31.14.4 This includes an affidavit sworn and served on an opposing party though not filed in court (*Re Fenner and Lord* [1897] Q.B. 667, CA); an exhibit to an affidavit (cf. *Re Hinchcliffe* [1895] 1 Ch. 117 at 120, CA); and possibly also affidavits sworn by a third party (*Dubai Bank Ltd v Galadari (No.2) The Times*, December 11, 1989; also [1990] 1 W.L.R. 731 at [736–737]).

Privileged documents mentioned in statements of case

31.14.5 Mere reference to a privileged document in a statement of case may not of itself lead to the implied waiver of the privilege, but reference to the extent of reliance on the privileged document is likely to do so: see the RSC case of *Buttes Gas & Oil Co v Hammer (No.3)* [1981] Q.B. 223; at 246, 252 and 268, CA; reversed by the House of Lords on different grounds: [1982] A.C. 888. This approach is likely to have survived the transition from the RSC to the CPR, r.31.14: see *Lucas v Barking, Havering and Redbridge Hospitals NHS Trust* [2003] EWCA Civ 1102; [2004] 1 W.L.R. 220, CA at [23–26] and [44]. In *Buttes Gas & Oil* the judges would have allowed a party to avoid waiver by amending their pleading to remove reliance on the privileged document. If a party goes beyond reference and discloses the contents of the privileged document, then there is likely to be an implied waiver of the privilege in any event.

Privileged documents mentioned in witness statements

31.14.6 As with statements of case, mere reference to a privileged document in a witness statement may not of itself lead to the implied waiver of the privilege, but waiver will occur where a party is "deploying" the material in court. See *Great Atlantic Insurance Co v Home Insurance Co* [1981] 1 W.L.R. 529 at 538, CA; *Derby & Co Ltd v Weldon (No.10)* [1991] 2 All E.R. 908, Ch. The important issue is whether there is reliance on the contents of the document, rather than its actual existence and effect: e.g. *Burkle Holdings Ltd v Laing (No.2)* [2005] EHWC 2022 (TCC) at [62].

Documents mentioned in expert's report—"subject to rule 35.10(4)..."

CPR, r.31.14(2) provides for an application for inspection of any document mentioned in an expert's report. Before making such an application the party should request inspection of the document informally, and inspection should be provided by agreement unless the request is unreasonable: CPR Pt 31, Practice Direction, para.7.1. If there are a great many documents referred to in the report then the party against whom the application is made may seek to resist an order on the grounds that it is not necessary for the just disposal of the proceedings; that it would be disproportionate to require them to copy or collate all of the documents; and/or that the other party can reasonably obtain the documents from another source: see CPR Pt 31, Practice Direction, para.7.2. CPR r.31.14(2) provides for an application for inspection of any document mentioned in an expert's report. **31.14.7**

For the interplay of r.31.14(2) and r.35.10(4) generally, for the wide interpretation of the concept of "instruction" in order to achieve openness and for the requirement of a factual basis in support of any belief that the instructions given were incomplete, see *Lucas v Barking, Havering and Redbridge Hospitals NHS Trust* [2003] EWCA Civ 1102; [2003] 4 All E.R. 720, CA. See further *Jackson v Marley Davenport Ltd* [2004] EWCA Civ 1225; [2004] 1 W.L.R. 2926, CA, the litigation privilege of an expert's earlier reports not intended to be relied upon at trial is not overriden by the provisions of CPR 35 (e.g. 35.5, 35.10 and 35.13).

Inspection and copying of documents

31.15 Where a party has a right to inspect a document— **31.15**

(a) that party must give the party who disclosed the document written notice of his wish to inspect it;

(b) the party who disclosed the document must permit inspection not more than 7 days after the date on which he received the notice; and

(c) that party may request a copy of the document and, if he also undertakes to pay reasonable copying costs, the party who disclosed the document must supply him with a copy not more than 7 days after the date on which he received the request.

(Rules 31.3 and 31.14 deal with the right of a party to inspect a document.)

"... the party ..."

Inspection usually entails both the actual party and its lawyers seeing the documents. In exceptional cases, where good reason is shown (e.g. in intellectual property cases), the court may impose conditions on the inspection, for example only allowing a party's lawyers to see the documents. As to disclosure by third parties to legal or medical advisers only, see para.31.17.1 below. **31.15.1**

"...right to inspect..."

A right to inspect may arise by any of the following means: (a) by r.31.3, where the document has been disclosed (including by voluntary disclosure), if the document is in the disclosing party's control, there is no right to withhold inspection, and it is not disproportionate to permit inspection; (b) by r.31.14(1), the document being mentioned in a statement of case, witness statement, witness summary or affidavit; (c) by r.31.14(2) the right to inspect also arises where an order for inspection has been made. Inspection extends to examining electronic, audio or visual recordings or other documents with appropriate equipment; see further at para.31.15.8. **31.15.2**

Place of inspection

31.15.3 There is no rule governing where inspection is to take place. The CPR leaves the matter to the parties to sort out between themselves.

In the case of an action proceeding in the Central Office, the appropriate place is the office of the solicitor or agent in London; but if circumstances warrant, the production may be ordered elsewhere, or partly in London and partly elsewhere (*Prestney v Corporation of Colchester* (1883) 24 Ch.D. 376, CA) and even abroad (*Whyte & Co v Ahrens & Co* (1884) 50 L.T. 344). It should never be necessary to bring to the Court a dispute as to the appropriate place of inspection, but the Court has a complete discretion in the matter, e.g. if one party claims the other party is only offering inspection at an unreasonable place or time. It may still order that the documents be deposited in Court to be inspected there in accordance with the old Chancery practice (*Leslie v Cave* [1886] W.N. 162). Otherwise, the usual and proper place for inspection is the office of his solicitors, or in the case of bankers' books or other books of account or books in constant use for the purpose of any trade or business their usual place of custody. The Court has the power to determine the process by which, and the form in which, the parties' documents should be supplied to each other (e.g. whether by CD-ROM or by hard copy): *Grupo Torras SA v Al-Sabah* July 8, 1997, Ch. D. Mance J., reported in [1997] C.L.C. 1553; [1998] Masons C.L.R. Rep. 90; (1997) 94 (30) L.S.G. 28.

Timing of inspection

31.15.4 The general rule is that inspection must be permitted within seven days of receipt of the notice stating that the party wishes to inspect documents: r.31.15(b). This general rule can be varied by court order. A court may in appropriate circumstances order that disclosure and inspection take place at the same time: *Punjab National Bank v Jain* [2004] EWCA Civ 589, CA at [24].

Copying of documents

31.15.5 There is no requirement (as there was under the RSC) that the document need be capable of being copied by photographic or other process. Inspection may be given, for example, by supply of a CD-ROM. The RSC had expressly provided that if a party failed to supply a copy, an application to the court could be made (RSC O.24, r.11A(3)). This is still the case under the CPR, despite the fact that this provision is not replicated in the CPR. The copying of disclosed documents does not infringe copyright: Copyright, Designs and Patents Act 1988 s.45.

"... reasonable copying costs ..."

31.15.6 If a party has already had scanned the documents for their own purposes, they may not be able to charge the scanning costs to a party they are then providing those scanned documents to pursuant to the duty to facilitate inspection. It may be that all that can be charged are the costs of copying and supplying the compact discs: *Grupo Torras S.A. v Al-Sabah* [1997] C.L.C. 1553; [1998] Masons C.L.R. Rep. 90; (1997) 94 (30) L.S.G. 28, July 8, 1997, Ch.D., Mance J.

Documents requiring transcription or translation

31.15.7 A disclosing party is not obliged to provide translations of documents disclosed, where those documents contain material in a foreign language: *Bayer A.G. v Harris Pharmaceuticals Ltd* [1991] F.S.R. 170, Ch (though translations already in existence may be in a different position; as to these, see *Sumitomo v Credit Lyonnais Rouse* [2001] EWCA Civ 1152; [2002] 1 W.L.R. 479, CA).

In a similar vein, where a recording of poor quality is disclosed, it is submitted that the disclosing party should not be obliged to provide a transcription. This point was argued but not decided in *Paddick v Associated Newspapers Ltd* [2003] EWHC 2991 (QB); [2003] All E.R. (D) 179 (Dec) at [23–291]; Tugendhat J. stating at [28] that the issue of translation of documents in a foreign language with which *Bayer v Harris* (above) was concerned "seems to me to be rather different".

The matter of a document's transcription or translation is for the parties to determine between themselves, or for the court to rule on in exercise of its general discretion and powers of case management.

Inspection of electronic documents

31.15.8 As a computer database may contain confidential or privileged material it may not be appropriate to fulfil the obligation to allow inspection by simply giving a party access to the database. See *Derby & Co Ltd v Weldon (No.9)* [1991] 2 All E.R. 901 at 906g–907e for a discussion of the problems associated with granting access to a computer database as a means of facilitating inspection.

If all of the relevant material can simply be printed out, then that may overcome many of the difficulties. In some cases there may be further relevant information within the "document" (i.e. the computer file) that is not apparent from the printout, e.g. date the file was created, who edited it and when, and hidden database fields.

In other cases it will be more appropriate to provide inspection by the provision of the material in electronic form, e.g. a CD-ROM. For example if there is a large amount of material or where printouts will not contain relevant data for reasons given above. The court does have power to order inspection of an electronic database. However that may raise the problems noted at the start of this paragraph.

Disclosure before proceedings start

31.16—(1) This rule applies where an application is made to the court under any Act for disclosure before proceedings have started.[1] 31.16

(2) The application must be supported by evidence.

(3) The court may make an order under this rule only where—

(a) the respondent is likely to be a party to subsequent proceedings;

(b) the applicant is also likely to be a party to those proceedings;

(c) if proceedings had started, the respondent's duty by way of standard disclosure, set out in rule 31.6, would extend to the documents or classes of documents of which the applicant seeks disclosure; and

(d) disclosure before proceedings have started is desirable in order to—

(i) dispose fairly of the anticipated proceedings;

(ii) assist the dispute to be resolved without proceedings; or

(iii) save costs.

(4) An order under this rule must—

(a) specify the documents or the classes of documents which the respondent must disclose; and

(b) require him, when making disclosure, to specify any of those documents—

(i) which are no longer in his control; or

(ii) in respect of which he claims a right or duty to withhold inspection.

(5) Such an order may—

(a) require the respondent to indicate what has happened to any documents which are no longer in his control; and

(b) specify the time and place for disclosure and inspection.

---

[1] An application for disclosure before proceedings have started is permitted under s.33 of the Supreme Court Act 1981 (c.54) or s.52 of the County Courts Act 1984 (c.28).

"... under any Act for disclosure before proceedings have started"

31.16.1 See further, "Order for disclosure before claim made of documents by prospective party", para.25.1.30.

For instance under the Supreme Court Act 1981 s.33 and the County Courts Act 1984 s.52. See too under para.31.0.6 above. In *Burrells Wharf Freeholds Ltd v Galliard Homes Ltd* [1999] 33 E.G. 82, the Court rejected the submission that art.5 of the Civil Procedure (Modification of Enactments) Order 1998 which removed the former restriction to personal injuries cases, was ultra vires.

Section 33(2) of the Supreme Court Act 1981 (which is to be renamed the "Senior Courts Act 1981" on the coming into force of the Constitutional Reform Act 2005) provides that the High Court has power in preliminary proceedings to order a potential defendant to subsequent proceedings to disclose documents which he is likely to have or to have had in his possession, custody or power, relevant to an issue arising or likely to arise out of that claim.

"The application must be supported by evidence"

31.16.2 The application should be made in accordance with Pt 23. The contents of an application notice may be used as evidence provided those contents have been verified by a statement of truth under Pt 22; see PD to Part 23—Application, para.9.7. Otherwise the evidence in support will usually be in writing. Supporting evidence can be in the form of an affidavit but the additional costs of making it may not be allowed unless the court orders otherwise.

Scope of documents covered by pre-action disclosure

31.16.3 Section 33(2) of the Supreme Court Act 1981 applies to documents in a party's "possession, custody or power", which was the terminology applicable under the former RSC discovery rules: see the former RSC O.24, rr.1(1), 2(1), 3(1), 7(1). This is different to the scope of standard disclosure under the CPR, which uses a test of "control" as set out in r.31.8. Rule 31.16(3)(c) states that the scope of disclosure under this Rule is limited to those documents which would fall within the standard disclosure obligation in CPR r.31.6. However r.31.16 does not explicitly incorporate the r.31.8 "control" test for pre-action disclosure. Given that such disclosure would be made pursuant to the Supreme Court Act 1981 s.33(2), the scope of such disclosure must be that of the "possession, custody or power" test rather than the CPR r.31.8 "control" test.

However it is doubtful what difference there is between the tests in any event. "Possession" in s.33(2) accords with "right to possession" in CPR r.31.8(2)(b). "Custody" in s.33(2) accords with "physical possession" in CPR r.31.8(2)(a). "Power" broadly accords with "right to inspect or take copies" in CPR r.31.8(2)(c), though the CPR concept may be broader: see Matthews and Malek, *Disclosure*, 3rd edn (2007), para.5.53.

For the meaning of the terms "possession", "custody" and "power" under the RSC, see: *B v B* [1978] Fam. 181, HC at [186]. Also as to "power" see *Lonrho v Shell Petroleum Ltd* [1980] 1 W.L.R. 627, HL at [635].

Rule 31.16(3)(a), (b) and (d)

31.16.4 For the purposes of r.31.16(3)(a) and (b) the respondent/applicant is "likely to be a party to subsequent proceedings" where it is established that he may well be a party if subsequent proceedings are issued. There is no additional requirement to establish that the initiation of proceedings is itself likely, *Black v Sumitomo Corp* [2001] EWCA Civ 1819; [2003] 3 All E.R. 643; [2002] 1 W.L.R. 1562, CA at [71–72]. The documents or classes of documents sought should be carefully circumscribed, and the application limited to what is strictly necessary: *Snowstar Shipping Co Ltd v Graig Shipping plc* [2003] EWHC 1367 (Comm); [2003] All E.R. (D) 174 (Jun) at [35]. Attempting to obtain pre-action disclosure of documents that would not in due course be subject to standard disclosure by simply calling for classes or categories of documents in which some documents would be disclosable is not permissible: *Hutchison 3G UK Ltd v O2 (UK) Ltd* [2008] EWHC 55 (Comm). It is, further, inappropriate to require a respondent to identify which of its documents are within the scope of standard disclosure. All the documents within a class or category sought under r.31.16 must be within standard disclosure and cannot encompass categories of documents that might prove to be relevant only as "background". An applicant must show that it is more probable than not that the documents are within the scope of standard disclosure should an action commence: *Hutchison 3G UK Ltd v O2 (UK) Ltd* [2008] EWHC 55 (Comm). This Rule may apply as against a foreign corporation which has submitted to the jurisdiction, and to documents held outside the jurisdiction; see *Mitsui & Co Ltd v Nexen Petroleum UK Ltd*

[2005] EWHC 625 (Ch); [2005] 3 All E.R. 511 at [32], Ch. Also note the Council Regulation (EC) No.12061/2001 of May 28, 2001 on co-operation between the courts of the Member States in the taking of evidence in civil or commercial matters.

Whether disclosure is "desirable"within r.31.16(3)(d) involves a two stage process comprising a jurisdictional and and a discretionary aspect. Each such aspect must be addressed though the former may often merge into the latter. In *Black v Sumitomo* (*ibid.*) Rix L.J. stated at para.[81]:

> "... for jurisdictional purposes the court is only permitted to consider the granting of pre-action disclosure where there is a real prospect in principle of such an order being fair to the parties if litigation is commenced, or of assisting the parties to avoid litigation, or of saving costs in any event. If there is such a real prospect, then the court should go on to consider the question of discretion, which has to be considered on all the facts and not merely in principle but in detail."

The jurisdictional threshold has been described as being low: *Mitsui & Co Ltd v Nexen Petroleum UK Ltd* [2005] EWHC 625 (Ch), [2005] 3 All E.R. 511 at [27], per Lightman J. Relevant to the satisfaction of the jurisdictional test under (d) is the extent of the pre-action discovery demanded. An order that in principle is justified under (a) (b) and (c) may still fall foul of (d) by being too wide, necessitating a narrower focus before the court will order disclosure: *Hays Specialist Recruitment (Holdings) Ltd v Ions* [2008] EWHC 745; [2008] All E.R. (D.) 216.

Pre-action disclosure of medical records in personal injury claims, though typically satisfying CPR r.13.16(3)(a), (b) and (c), may not be "desirable" for the purposes enumerated in (d) and thus not be obtainable by other parties in pre-action disclosure: *OCS Group Ltd v Wells* [2008] EWHC 919 (QB); [2008] P.I.Q.R. P18 at [28]. The court in *OCS* preferred the Court of Appeal's view in *Bennett v Compass Group UK & Ireland Ltd* [2002] EWCA Civ 642 as to medical records to that in *Black v Sumitomo Corp* [2001] EWCA Civ 1819; [2002] 1 W.L.R. 1562; [2002] 1 Lloyd's Rep. 693.

Consideration of the relative positions of the parties as regards their possession of documents important to the matter appears particularly relevant in deciding whether disclosure is "desirable": *Birse Construction Limited v HLC Engenharia E Gestao de Projectos SA* [2006] EWHC 1258 (TCC) at [45]–[47]. If an applicant for pre-action disclosure already possesses sufficient material to plead a claim, it is less likely to be "desirable" to order such disclosure: *First Gulf Bank v Wachovia Bank National Association* [2005] EWHC 2827 (Comm). Costs may be saved by obviating by pre-action disclosure the need to amend at a later stage in proceedings: *ibid* at para.85. See too *Hands v Morrison Construction Services Ltd* [2006] EWHC 2018, Ch, unrep.

Relevance of merits of thefuture claim

In *Rose v Lynx Express Ltd* [2004] EWCA Civ 447 [2004] 1 B.C.L.C. 455, the Court of **31.16.5**
Appeal held:

> "courts should be hesitant, in the context of an application for pre-action disclosure, about embarking upon any determination of substantive issues in the case. In our view it will normally be sufficient to found an application under CPR r.31.16(3) for the substantive claim pursued in the proceedings to be properly arguable and to have a real prospect of success, and it will normally be appropriate to approach the conditions in CPR r.31.16(3) on that basis."

The applicant must show at least a prima facie case of entitlement to substantive relief: *Mars UK Ltd v Waitrose* [2004] EWHC 2264 (Ch); [2004] All E.R. (D) 136 (Jul), Ch at [5] and [10] (there the Court refused to make an order as a prima facie case had not been shown). In *Jay v Wilder Coe* [2003] EWHC 1786 (QB); [2003] All E.R. (D) 526 (Jul) at [19] the court was willing to grant an order despite reservations that there may be substance to complaints that the application was merely speculative; though the judge held that he would not have struck out the claim if it had been presented at that point. However the merits of the future claim should be relevant to the assessment to be conducted under r.31.16(3)(d); this appears to be the analysis in *Snowstar Shipping Co Ltd v Graig Shipping plc* [2003] EWHC 1367 (Comm); [2003] All E.R. (D) 174 (Jun) at [33].

Orders for disclosure against a person not a party

31.17—(1) This rule applies where an application is made to the **31.17**

court under any Act for disclosure by a person who is not a party to the proceedings.[1]

(2) The application must be supported by evidence.

(3) The court may make an order under this rule only where—

(a) the documents of which disclosure is sought are likely to support the case of the applicant or adversely affect the case of one of the other parties to the proceedings; and

(b) disclosure is necessary in order to dispose fairly of the claim or to save costs.

(4) An order under this rule must—

(a) specify the documents or the classes of documents which the respondent must disclose; and

(b) require the respondent, when making disclosure, to specify any of those documents—

(i) which are no longer in his control; or

(ii) in respect of which he claims a right or duty to withhold inspection.

(5) Such an order may—

(a) require the respondent to indicate what has happened to any documents which are no longer in his control; and

(b) specify the time and place for disclosure and inspection.

"... under any Act for disclosure by a person who is not a party to the proceedings"

31.17.1 The main such powers are the Supreme Court Act 1981 (to be renamed the "Senior Courts Act 1981" on the coming into force of the Constitutional Reform Act 2005) s.34 and the County Courts Act 1984 s.53. Other statutory powers are contained in the Bankers Books Evidence Act 1879, and the Evidence (Proceedings in other Jurisdictions) Act 1975. For detailed commentary on these latter two statutes see Matthews and Malek, *Disclosure*, 3rd edn (2007), pp.257–270. For the taking of evidence in other European countries see the Council Regulation (EC) No.12061/2001 of May 28, 2001 on co-operation between the courts of the Member States in the taking of evidence in civil or commercial matters.

The making of this type of order may engage ECHR art.8, although depending on the scope of the order, any interference may be justified under ECHR art.8(2) as necessary "for the protection of the rights and freedoms of others". For the position regarding disclosure of journalistic sources and ECHR art.10 (freedom of expression) see *Goodwin v United Kingdom* (1996) 22 E.H.R.R. 123, ECtHR.

Before requiring a non–party who had no access to the pleadings or to such evidence as there might be to disclose a class of documents the court had to be satisfied (i) that there were documents falling within the specified classes, and (ii) that those documents were — not might be — documents whose disclosure would support the case of the applicant or adversely affect the case of another party to the proceedings, *Re Howglen Ltd* [2001] 1 All E.R. 376. See further paras 25.1.30, 25.2.2 and 25.4.5 above.

In *Frankson v Secretary of State for the Home Department* [2003] EWCA Civ 655; [2003] 1 W.L.R. 1952, CA (an action by a prisoner against the Home Department for an alleged assault by a prison officer), disclosure by police of prison officer's statement under caution to police investigating assault ordered on grounds that the public interest in protecting the confidentiality of the statement was outweighed in the circum-

[1] An application for disclosure against a person who is not a party to proceedings is permitted under s.34 of the Supreme Court Act 1981 or s.53 of the County Courts Act 1984.

stances of the particular case and subject to stringent conditions on the extent and nature of the disclosure by the public interest of ensuring as far as possible a fair civil trial.

The court can order that disclosure be made only to legal and/or medical advisers: Supreme Court Act 1981 s.34(2)(b); County Courts Act 1984 s.53(2)(b); *Hipwood v Gloucester Health Authority* [1995] I.C.R. 999 (disclosure to both legal and medical advisers), or on the giving of certain undertakings restricting their future disclosure and use, e.g. *Church of Scientology v DHSS* [1979] 1 W.L.R. 723, CA, where it was alleged that the Church may use the disclosed documents to harass and intimidate its critics.

"The application must be supported by evidence"

The application is made under Pt 23. See too para.31.16.2, above. **31.17.2**

Rule 31.17(3)(a)

For the purposes of this provision documents "are likely to support the case..." if they "may well" do so as opposed to "more probable than not"; see *Three Rivers DC v Bank of England (No.4)* [2002] EWCA Civ 1182; [2003] 1 W.L.R. 210; [2002] 4 All E.R. 881, CA. (See similarly *Black v Sumitomo Corp* [2001] EWCA Civ 1819 under para.31.16.4 above.) **31.17.3**

This is narrower than the test in s.34(2), which provides for disclosure of all documents relevant to an issue.

Where a party seeks disclosure of a class of documents, the relevant test must be met for each of the documents to be disclosed. The party seeking the order must show that all the documents fall within r.31.17(3). The Court should not leave it to the non-party to determine which documents to disclose in this manner.

Rule 31.17(3)(b) "... disclosure is necessary in order to fairly dispose of the claim or to save costs."

The court has a wide discretion as to this issue. Disclosure is restricted to those cases where it is necessary for one or both of the reasons stated. This is unlikely to be the case where the documents are available from another source. Disclosure may add to costs rather than save them. **31.17.4**

Ordering disclosure against non-parties is the exception rather than the rule (*Frankson v Home Office* [2003] EWCA Civ 655; [2003] 1 W.L.R. 1952 at [10]) and the jurisdiction should be exercised with caution (*Re Howglen Ltd* [2001] 1 All E.R. 376, Ch at [382h]).

Rule 31.17(5)(b)

The Rule states that an order may specify the time and place for disclosure. This is something of a misnomer, as disclosure is merely stating that the documents exists: r.31.2. It may be that the meaning intended was "production and inspection". **31.17.5**

Costs of the application

The respondent's costs of the application are normally paid by the applicant: CPR r.48.1(2). The court may make a different order, for example if a respondent unreasonably opposed the application or unreasonably refused to comply with a pre-action protocol: CPR r.48.1(3). In an appropriate case the costs of the application could be ordered to be borne by a party whose failure to disclose documents has led to the need for a third-party disclosure application which should have been unnecessary. **31.17.6**

Rules not to limit other powers of the court to order disclosure

31.18 Rules 31.16 and 31.17 do not limit any other power which *the court may have to order—* **31.18**

(a) disclosure before proceedings have started; and

(b) disclosure against a person who is not a party to proceedings.

"... do not limit any other power which the court may have, etc ..."

Other powers of the court include the *Norwich Pharmacal* principle and claim for disclosure and production, Anton Piller and Mareva relief (q.v.) and disclosure in aid of execution of judgment under CPR Pt 71. **31.18.1**

Disclosing identity of wrongdoer (*Norwich Pharmacal* principle)

31.18.2 Rule 31.18 merely preserves the *Norwich Pharmacal* jurisdiction and does not modify it: *Mitsui & Co Ltd v Nexen Petroleum UK Ltd* [2005] EWHC 625 (Ch); [2005] 3 All E.R. 511, Ch.D. at [36]. A person innocently caught up in the wrongdoing of another so that he is more than a mere witness can be compelled to disclose the identity of the wrongdoer so that proceedings may be brought against the proper defendant: *Norwich Pharmacal v Customs and Excise Commissioners* [1974] A.C. 133; [1973] 2 All E.R. 943, HL per Lord Reid at p.175. Also see, e.g., *P. v T. Ltd* [1997] 1 W.L.R. 1309 at 1315–1319; [1997] 4 All E.R. 200, Ch.

Appropriateness of claim for disclosure and production

31.18.3 This form of claim will be unnecessary where the Court's powers to order disclosure and production against a non-party during proceedings under s.34 of the Supreme Court Act 1981 and s.53 of the County Courts Act 1984 can be invoked but will retain its usefulness where such powers cannot be invoked.

While such applications are most commonly brought for the purpose of obtaining disclosure of the identity of a person, they can still be made for the disclosure of documents and other information.

Requirements for relief

31.18.4 In *Mitsui & Co Ltd v Nexen Petroleum UK Ltd* [2005] EWHC 625 (Ch); [2005] 3 All E.R. 511, Ch.D. at [21] the court summarised the pre-requisites of Norwich Pharmacal relief as:

"(i) a wrong must have been carried out, or arguably carried out, by an ultimate wrongdoer; (ii) there must be the need for an order to enable action to be brought against the ultimate wrongdoer; and (iii) the person against whom the order is sought must: (a) be mixed up in so as to have facilitated the wrongdoing; and (b) be able or likely to be able to provide the information necessary to enable the ultimate wrongdoer to be sued."

Nature of wrongs covered

31.18.5 The first requirement of the Norwich Pharmacal jurisdiction is that a wrong must have been carried out, or believed to be carried out. *Norwich Pharmacal* concerned an alleged tort, but the principle is not limited to torts: *Ashworth Hospital Authority v MGN Ltd* [2001] 1 W.L.R. 515; [2001] 1 All E.R. 991, CA (affirmed by the House of Lords in [2002] UKHL 29; [2002] 1 W.L.R. 2033). The jurisdiction is one of general application, existing in equity wherever the person against whom disclosure was ordered had got "mixed up" in wrongful conduct which infringed a claimant's legal rights, whether civil or criminal. e.g. breach of confidence or contract (as in *Ashworth Hospital* (above)); breach of confidence or copyright (*British Steel Corporation v Granada Television Ltd* [1981] A.C. 1096, HL); breach of contract only (*Carlton Film Distributors Ltd v VCI Plc* [2003] EWHC 616; [2003] F.S.R. 47, Ch); tracing action for money had and received or in deceit and/or conspiracy to defraud (*Bankers Trust v Shapira* [1980] 1 W.L.R. 1274, CA). The applicant does not need to prove the wrong, but must at least show some reasonable basis for claiming that a wrong has been committed.

Need for order to assert rights against wrongdoer

31.18.6 The second requirement of the Norwich Pharmacal jurisdiction is that it must be necessary for an order to enable a party to assert rights against the ultimate wrongdoer, or at least that it is just and convenient in the interests of justice to make the order sought (there is little difference of substance between these two formulations: *President of the State of Equatorial Guinea v Royal Bank of Scotland International* [2006] UKPC 7; [2006] 3 L.R.C. 676, PC at [16].

It is not a requirement that the applicant will be bringing court proceedings. The procedure is available where an applicant "desires to obtain redress against the wrongdoer—or to protect himself against further wrongdoing" (*British Steel v Granada* (ibid.) at 1127, 1132 and 1200); *Ashworth Hospital Authority v MGN Ltd* [2002] UKHL 29; [2002] 1 W.L.R. 2033, HL at [41–49], also [19] (where the claimant intended to dismiss the relevant employee). The jurisdiction can be used in an action for the preservation of assets the subject of a proprietary claim: *Arab Monetary Fund v Hashim (No.5)* [1992] 2 All E.R. 911, Ch.

Norwich Pharmacal relief is a remedy of last resort and should not be available where the information required could be obtained in some other way, for instance under

CPR r.31.16: *Mitsui & Co Ltd v Nexen Petroleum UK Ltd* (ibid.) at [24]. If the applicant already knows the identity of the wrongdoer and has sufficient information to commence an action, a Norwich Pharmacal order may be unnecessary, and so refused: *Nikitin v Butler LLP* [2007] EWHC 173 (Q.B.).

Where the matter is one of disclosure of a journalist's source and the Contempt of Court Act 1981 s.10 is invoked, then in the absence of evidence of an intention to sue the wrongdoer it may not be regarded as necessary in the interests of justice to have his name disclosed; the test under s.10 being "necessity" not expediency or desirability: *Handmade v Express Newspapers* [1986] F.S.R. 463, Ch. If there are facts which will require investigation at trial to determine the application of the Contempt of Court Act 1981 s.10, then it may not be proper to make a Norwich Pharmacal order on a pre-trial application (ibid. at 471).

In *P. v T Ltd* [1997] 1 W.L.R. 1309 the court granted an order to enable the claimant to use the fruits of disclosure to bring proceedings against a third party even though it could not be ascertained whether the third party had committed a tort against the claimant without the information sought, and could not identify the appropriate cause of action (specifically approved on this point by Lord Woolf in *Ashworth Hospital Authority v MGN* (ibid.) at [57]). *CHC Software Care v Hopkins & Wood* [1993] F.S.R. 241 concerned actions for slander of title, malicious falsehood and trade libel. Disclosure was ordered against the defendant solicitors of the names and addresses of the persons to whom allegedly false and damaging letters had been sent together with the text thereof for the purpose of the applicant writing to them to set the record straight, and so protecting itself against the damaging consequences of the allegedly tortuous act. The documents sought were also relevant to the issues pleaded in the claim.

In *Roberts v Jump Knitwear Ltd* [1981] F.S.R. 527, Ch, a copyright infringement action, the court declined to order disclosure of customers' names as until those persons had notice of the claim they were not wrongdoers.

Requirement of connection to wrong-doing

The person against whom the order is sought must be mixed up in the wrongdoing. A claim solely for disclosure and production does not lie against a defendant who is not himself a wrongdoer and has no connection with the wrongdoing, i.e. has neither committed nor facilitated the committal of the wrongdoing (*Norwich Pharmacal* [1974] A.C. 133, HL at 175, 188, 197, 203 and 204; *Ricci v Chow* [1987] 1 W.L.R. 1658; [1987] 3 All E.R. 534, CA). **31.18.7**

Defences

Applying the privilege against self-incrimination, a party has a defence to disclosure of the identity of a wrongdoer where that disclosure would tend to incriminate the disclosing party. In such a case it must be the disclosure of the identity of another person which causes the risk; compare *British Steel v Granada* (ibid.), where this was not the case. **31.18.8**

Section 10 of the Contempt of Court Act 1981 may provide a defence, unless disclosure is "necessary" in the interests of national security, the interests of justice, or for the prevention of disorder or crime. As to the scope of these terms, see *X Ltd v Morgan-Grampian (Publishers) Ltd* [1991] 1 A.C. 1, HL; *Re an Inquiry under the Company Securities (Insider Dealing) Act 1985* [1988] A.C. 660, HL; *Ashworth Hospital Authority v MGN Ltd* [2001] 1 W.L.R. 515, CA at 533–537.

A claim for disclosure and production alone, like the making of an order under the Bankers' Books Evidence Act 1879, requires the exercise of the Crown's Sovereign authority to assist in the administration of justice, and therefore the Court will not, save in exceptional circumstances, impose on a foreigner, in particular a foreign bank, who or which is not a party to the principal proceedings, any requirement to produce documents which are outside the jurisdiction and which concern business transacted outside the jurisdiction (*MacKinnon v Donaldson Lufkin & Jenrette Securities Corp* [1986] Ch. 482, Ch).

Residual discretion and human rights

Norwich Pharmacal orders are equitable remedies, so the court retains a discretion as to whether to make the order. The court may balance the interests in confidentiality and privacy against the interests in disclosure. **31.18.9**

The making of a Norwich Pharmacal order may engage ECHR art.8, although, depending on the scope of the order, any interference may be justified under ECHR art.8(2) as necessary "for the protection of the rights and freedoms of others".

The order must not lead to an infringement of ECHR art.10. In order to guard against such an infringement the jurisdiction must only be exercised when it is proportionate to do so. See further *Ashworth Hospital Authority v MGN Ltd* (ibid.), HL; *Mersey Care NHS Trust v Ackroyd* (ibid.), where the Court held that there was not a pressing social need which would justify requiring the journalist to be ordered to reveal his source of information.

Disclosure by way of interim relief and quia timet injunction

31.18.10 Disclosure of the identities of infringers and other wrongdoers may also be obtained by an interim order in proceedings for other relief in relation to the same subject-matter (*RCA Corp v Reddingtons Rare Records* [1974] 1 W.L.R. 1445, Ch, where disclosure was sought in an injunction to restrain infringement of copyright; [1975] 1 All E.R. 38; *Loose v Williamson* [1978] 1 W.L.R. 639; [1978] 3 All E.R. 89, Ch, where disclosure was sought in an action for a declaration as to rights).

Where a party is properly sued as defendant to a claim for a quia timet injunction restraining him from publishing information imparted to him in breach of confidence, he is amenable to the full scope of the court's wide power to order disclosure between parties, the fact that the claimant's primary purpose in seeking disclosure and production is to identify the source of the information does not inhibit or restrict the court's power to order such for the purposes of the quia timet litigation (*X Ltd v Morgan Grampian (Publishers) Ltd* [1991] 1 A.C. 1, HL at p.39).

Procedure for bringing a Norwich Pharmacal application

31.18.11 The application may be brought under either Pt 7 or Pt 8 (in the *Norwich Pharmacal* case itself the application was brought by originating summons rather than by writ). It can, exceptionally, be granted without notice (e.g. *Bankers Trust Co v Shapira* [1980] 1 W.L.R. 1274, CA). A Norwich Pharmacal order may also be made during an existing action.

The claimant seeking the name of the wrongdoer will have to pay a blameless defendant's expenses in providing the information. If the defendant has any doubts then he may properly require the matter to be submitted to the court before supplying the information and the claimant will nevertheless be obliged to pay the costs of these proceedings (ibid.). Note that in the Norwich Pharmacal litigation itself the costs of that litigation were recovered as damages in the subsequent substantive patent infringement action, on the basis that the infringer could or ought to have foreseen that steps by way of investigation and disclosure were likely to result from his wrong (*Morton Norwich Products Inc v Intercen Ltd (No.2)* [1981] F.S.R. 337, HC).

Claim to withhold inspection or disclosure of a document

31.19 **31.19—(1) A person may apply, without notice, for an order permitting him to withhold disclosure of a document on the ground that disclosure would damage the public interest.**

(2) Unless the court orders otherwise, an order of the court under paragraph (1)—

(a) must not be served on any other person; and

(b) must not be open to inspection by any person.

(3) A person who wishes to claim that he has a right or a duty to withhold inspection of a document, or part of a document must state in writing—

(a) that he has such a right or duty; and

(b) the grounds on which he claims that right or duty.

(4) The statement referred to in paragraph (3) must be made—

(a) in the list in which the document is disclosed; or

(b) if there is no list, to the person wishing to inspect the document.

(5) A party may apply to the court to decide whether a claim made under paragraph (3) should be upheld.

(6) For the purpose of deciding an application under paragraph (1) (application to withhold disclosure) or paragraph (3) (claim to withhold inspection) the court may—

(a) require the person seeking to withhold disclosure or inspection of a document to produce that document to the court; and

(b) invite any person, whether or not a party, to make representations.

(7) An application under paragraph (1) or paragraph (5) must be supported by evidence.

(8) This Part does not affect any rule of law which permits or requires a document to be withheld from disclosure or inspection on the ground that its disclosure or inspection would damage the public interest.

"...would damage the public interest..." and "...a right or duty to withhold inspection..."

See note on public interest and other examples of a right or duty to withhold inspection under r.31.3 above. The application in respect of a public interest claim can be for an order permitting the withholding of disclosure. The other approach envisaged under this rule is a claim to withhold inspection. This claim can be challenged by application to the court. **31.19.1**

"May apply to the court to decide... "

The court's approach to an application under r.31.19(5) was considered in *West London Pipeline and Storage Ltd v Total UK Ltd* [2008] EWHC 1729. An affidavit of documents is difficult to go behind. Where a court is reasonably certain that the affidavit does not make out a satisfactory case for withholding a document, it may order inspection; order another affidavit to deal with the elements of the first that rendered it unsatisfactory; inspect the documents itself; or order cross-examination of a party under r.32.7. Inspection by the court is a solution of last resort; further, there is strong authority against ordering cross-examination on an affidavit of documents. For the principles relevant to a claim for public interest immunity see *Phipson on Evidence*, 19th edn (2005), Ch.25. **31.19.1.1**

The mere mention of a document within CPR r.31.14 does not entail the automatic and absolute loss of any privilege in the document; see *Expandable Ltd v Rubin* [2008] EWCA Civ 59 and commentary at para.31.14.2, above.

An application under paragraph (1) or paragraph (5) must be supported by evidence

See commentary at para.31.16.2 above. Rule 23.4(2) allows the making of an application under Pt 23 without notice as is envisaged in respect of a claim based on damage to the public interest under para.(1). **31.19.2**

"...require the person... to produce that document to the court"

Ordinarily the court would not order inspection unless there is credible evidence that the lawyers have misunderstood their own duty or are not to be trusted and where there is no reasonably practical alternative: *National Westminster Bank Plc v Rabobank Nederland* [2006] EWHC 2332 (Comm) at [60]; see also the five-step approach followed in *Atos v Avis* [2007] EWHC 323 (TCC) at [37]. **31.19.3**

Inherent jurisdiction of court

The court has inherent jurisdiction to take precautions against the possibility that disclosure and inspection may be abused, or cause unjustifiable hardship and may, to that end, impose restrictions upon inspection or permit it subject to undertakings. (*Church of Scientology v D.H.S.S.* [1979] 1 W.L.R. 723); for an example of undertakings against discloure of material obtained on discovery see *Halcon International Inc v Shell* **31.19.4**

Transport & Trading Co [1979] R.P.C. 97, CA (permission to make use of material obtained on disclosure for some purpose other than the claim refused).

Restriction on use of a privileged document inspection of which has been inadvertently allowed

31.20 **31.20 Where a party inadvertently allows a privileged[GL] document to be inspected, the party who has inspected the document may use it or its contents only with the permission of the court.**

Note

31.20.1 For the principles relevant to inadvertent disclosure of privileged documents and loss of confidentiality see para.31.3.27.

This rule represented a significant departure from previous practice. However the Court of Appeal has stated that the previous principles continue to apply: *Al-Fayed v Commissioner of Police of the Metropolis* [2002] EWCA Civ 780; *The Times*, June 17, 2002, CA. In that case Clarke L.J. at [16] stated that the relevant principles were as follows:

> "(i) A party giving inspection of documents must decide before doing so what privileged documents he wishes to allow the other party to see and what he does not (ii) Although the privilege is that of the client and not the solicitor, a party clothes his solicitor with ostensible authority (if not implied or express authority) to waive privilege in respect of relevant documents . . (iii) A solicitor considering documents made available by the other party to litigation owes no duty of care to that party and is in general entitled to assume that any privilege which might otherwise have been claimed for such documents has been waived (iv) In these circumstances, where a party has given inspection of documents, including privileged documents which he has allowed the other party to inspect by mistake, it will in general be too late for him to claim privilege in order to attempt to correct the mistake by obtaining injunctive relief. (v) However, the court has jurisdiction to intervene to prevent the use of documents made available for inspection by mistake where justice requires, as for example in the case of inspection procured by fraud (vi) In the absence of fraud, all will depend upon the circumstances, but the court may grant an injunction if the documents have been made available for inspection as a result of an obvious mistake (vii) A mistake is likely to be held to be obvious and an injunction granted where the documents are received by a solicitor and (a) the solicitor appreciates that a mistake has been made before making some use of the documents; or (b) it would be obvious to a reasonable solicitor in his position that a mistake has been made; and, in either case, there are no other circumstances which would make it unjust or inequitable to grant relief (viii) Where a solicitor gives detailed consideration to the question whether the documents have been made available for inspection by mistake and honestly concludes that they have not, that fact will be a relevant (and in many cases an important) pointer to the conclusion that it would not be obvious to the reasonable solicitor that a mistake had been made, but is not conclusive; the decision remains a matter for the court (ix) In both the cases identified in (vii) (a) and (b) above there are many circumstances in which it may nevertheless be held to be inequitable or unjust to grant relief, but all will depend upon the particular circumstances (x) Since the court is exercising an equitable jurisdiction, there are no rigid rules."

Where there has been inadvertent disclosure to an opponent's lawyers, the court may make an order preventing the lawyers from disclosing the information to their client. This may be inappropriate where the ongoing litigation is criminal rather than civil; see, e.g., *R v G* [2004] EWCA Crim 1368; [2004] 1 W.L.R. 2932, CA.

Consequence of failure to disclose documents or permit inspection

31.21 **31.21 A party may not rely on any document which he fails to disclose or in respect of which he fails to permit inspection unless *the court gives permission.***

Subsequent use of disclosed documents

31.22 **31.22—(1) A party to whom a document has been disclosed may**

use the document only for the purpose of the proceedings in which it is disclosed, except where—

(a) the document has been read to or by the court, or referred to, at a hearing which has been held in public;

(b) the court gives permission; or

(c) the party who disclosed the document and the person to whom the document belongs agree.

(2) The court may make an order restricting or prohibiting the use of a document which has been disclosed, even where the document has been read to or by the court, or referred to, at a hearing which has been held in public.

(3) An application for such an order may be made—

(a) by a party; or

(b) by any person to whom the document belongs.

Subsequent use of disclosed documents

This rule now specifies clear exceptions to the general rule that a document disclosed in the proceedings may only be used for the purpose of the proceedings in which it is disclosed. It avoids concepts of implied or express undertakings. The rule is the statutory enactment so far as civil court proceedings are concerned of the common-law implied undertaking not to use documents disclosed in the course of civil court proceedings save for the purpose of the proceedings in which disclosed without court permission or the consent of the document owner. The rule is concise and avoids the intricacies of the concepts of implied and express undertakings. **31.22.1**

Documents read by the judge out of court before the hearing on which the judge based his decision and to which he made compendious reference in his judgment were documents referred to at a hearing held in public; see *SmithKline Beecham Biologicals SA v Connaught Laboratories Inc* [1999] 4 All E.R. 498, CA (a case under the former RSC O.24, r.14A). Cases involving representation by the same lawyers in concurrent related proceedings give rise to specific issues. In a case where exceptionally sensitive documents are to be disclosed to certain external legal advisers only and not to the parties generally, the Court of Appeal decided in *British Sky Broadcasting Group plc v Virgin Media Communications Ltd (formerly NTL Communications Ltd,* [2008] EWCA Civ 612; All E.R. (D.) 57 that it is is consistent with r.31.22(1) for the same lawyers viewing the sensitive documents under one proceedings to represent their clients in other concurrent and related proceedings. In any case, r.31.22(1)(c) always leaves open the court's explicit power to permit such documents to be used for the purposes of other proceedings.

As regards arbitration proceedings it has been held that an implied undertaking not to use disclosed documents for purposes other than the arbitration in which they are disclosed arises in respect of documents disclosed during arbitration proceedings (*Hassneh Insurance Co of Israel v Steuart J. Mew* [1993] 2 Lloyd's Rep. 243). The qualification to such implied undertaking namely that an award and reasons might be disclosed as of right if it was reasonably necessary for one party to disclose them for the purpose of the establishment of that party's rights against a third party either in order to found a defence or as the basis for a cause of action (see *Hassneh* above) was further considered in *Insurance Company v Lloyd's Syndicate* [1995] 1 Lloyd's Rep. 272, where the court held that "reasonably necessary" covered only the case where the right in question could not be enforced or protected unless the award and reasons are disclosed to a stranger to the arbitration. The making of the award must be a necessary element in the establishment of the party's legal rights aganst the stranger. See too in relation to the implied undertaking *Ali Shipping Corp v Shipyard Trogir* [1999] 1 W.L.R. 314, CA.

See too *John Forster Emmott v Michael Wilson & Partners Limited* [2008] EWCA Civ 184; [2008] 1 Lloyd's Rep. 6116 for a review of the paramountcy in arbitration of privacy and of the associated obligation of confidentiality. At para.107 the exceptions were expressed as follows:

"In my judgment the content of the obligation may depend on the context in which it arises and on the nature of the information or documents at issue. The limits of that obligation are still in the process of development on a case-by-case basis. On the authorities as they now stand, the principal cases in which disclosure will be permissible are these: the first is where there is consent, express or implied; second, where there is an order, or leave of the court (but that does not mean that the court has a general discretion to lift the obligation of confidentiality); third, where it is reasonably necessary for the protection of the legitimate interests of an arbitrating party; fourth, where the interests of justice require disclosure, and also (perhaps) where the public interest requires disclosure."

The case also questioned whether as between the parties to an arbitration the appropriate forum was the arbitrator rather than the court in such matters.

As regards documents disclosed during criminal proceedings the position is mainly governed by s.17 of the Criminal Procedure and Investigations Act 1996 (*q.v.*) which imposes a restriction similar to that contained in the rule above mentioned upon the use of documents disclosed by the prosecution to the defence pursuant to the provisions of the 1996 Act. Criminal sanctions for infringement are provided by s.18 of the 1996 Act. Section 17 is designed to restrict the use of material disclosed to the defence pursuant to the provisions of the 1996 Act but which was unused.

For documents sourced from criminal proceedings otherwise than under the 1996 Act the position at common law is not so clear. Despite *Mahon v Rahn (No.1)* [1998] Q.B. 424; [1997] 3 All E.R. 687 in which a Court of Appeal held that there was no implied undertaking restricting the use of such documents to the proceedings in which they were disclosed analogous to the undertaking which existed in civil proceedings, it is considered that it is open to argue that such an implied undertaking of general applicability to documents disclosed in criminal proceedings exists since in *Taylor v Director of the Serious Fraud Office* [1999] 2 AC 177; [1998] 4 All E.R. 801, HL(E), the case of *Mahon v Rahn* was disapproved of, the House of Lords holding in particular in the case that in order to ensure that the privacy and confidentiality of those who made, and those who were mentioned in, statements contained in unused material which had come into existence as a result of a criminal investigation were not invaded more than was absolutely necessary for the purposes of justice, compliance by the prosecution with its obligation to disclose all such material to the defence generated an implied undertaking not to use the material for any purpose other than the conduct of the defence; and that, accordingly, documents disclosed to solicitors for one of the accused could not be used for the purposes of the claim for defamation by the claimants. The court further held that the absolute immunity from suit which applied to judges, advocates and witnesses in respect of statements made in court extended also to out of court statements which could fairly be said to be part of the process of investigating a crime or a possible crime with a view to a prosecution; and that, accordingly, the statements made in the letter and the file note were subject to absolute immunity from suit in respect of a claim for defamation. There is no similar undertaking upon the prosecution who are able to disclose unused material to a third party where the interests of justice would be served thereby: *Preston BC v McGrath*, *The Times*, May 19, 2000, CA.

At the conclusion of a case the Court will not order one party to return to another photocopies of documents obtained on disclosure, where the party who has obtained the copies has paid photocopying charges and where the title to the paper on which the copies are made is thereby vested in him, and where there is no real cause to believe that he will disregard the obligation not to use the copies for any purpose outside the case (*Brue Ltd v Solly*, *The Times*, February 9, 1988).

Documents disclosed during the process of taxation fall within this provision; see *Bourns Inc v Raychem Corp (No.3)* [1999] 1 All E.R. 908 (a pre-CPR case); affirmed [1999] 3 All E.R. 154, CA.

Permission has been granted to use material obtained on disclosure under the *Anton Piller* jurisdiction to bring proceedings against other parties shown by that material to be involved in misuse of the claimant's name or commercial property (*Sony Corp v Anand*; *Seiko Time Ltd v Domicrest (Fancy Goods) Ltd* [1981] F.S.R. 398).

In *Omar v Omar* [1995] 1 W.L.R. 1428; [1995] 3 All E.R. 571 it was held that the documents disclosed, or to be disclosed, by the bank could be used by the claimant both at the trial of the claim and in foreign proceedings aimed at following and tracing the shares, and to establish ultimate liability in those foreign proceedings; that the use of the documents for a personal claim, being within the broad purpose of the original disclosure, was an entirely legitimate purpose, so that leave to amend the claimant's claim and to use the documents in relation to *Mareva* relief would be granted. In *Miller v Scorey* [1996] 1 W.L.R. 1122; [1996] 3 All E.R. 18, the court held *per curiam* that while it may be that the court has jurisdiction to grant retrospective leave to use disclosed documents for a purpose outside the claim in which they were disclosed, the circumstances in which it would be proper to exercise it would be rare. In this case leave was refused as such would have constituted a de facto validation of the issue of the proceedings obviating the need to issue fresh proceedings, thereby depriving the defendants of a limitation defence and permitting the claimants to take unfair advantage of their own wrong.

In *A v A (Ancillary relief); B v B (Ancillary Relief)* [2000] 1 F.L.R. 701, (such proceedings are generally held in private) it was held inter alia that—

(1) In the absence of any statutory rule prohibiting or restricting disclosure, there is no absolute duty of confidence and a court has discretion to authorise or order disclosure of confidential material where to do so was in the public interest;

(2) In civil proceedings, where there is an implied undertaking that material disclosed by the parties will be used only for the purposes of the proceedings, the court can release or modify that undertaking if to do so would be in the public interest;

(3) There is a strong public interest that all tax, and revenue penalties due, should be paid and that evaders of tax should be convicted and sentenced. Taxpayers, in the interest of the public, have a duty to inform the Revenue as to their affairs.

In *Marlwood Commercial Inc v Kozeny* [2004] EWCA Civ 798; [2005] 1 W.L.R. 104; [2004] 3 All E.R. 648, CA (a case concerning the use sought in connection with a foreign criminal investigation of documents brought within the jurisdiction by a foreign defendent under compulsion of the rules relating to English jurisdiction and disclosure) the Court of Appeal held:

> [52] In such circumstances, (q.v.), and in the absence of any other factors argued to constitute some injustice, it seems to us again that the public interest in the investigation or prosecution of a specific offence of serious or complex fraud should take precedence over the merely general concern of the courts to control the collateral use of compulsary disclosed documents

Documents of a confidential nature, read out in camera in English proceedings may nevertheless be ordered to be available in proceedings before the E.C. Commission: *Apple Corps. Ltd v Apple Computer Inc* [1992] F.S.R. 389; [1992] 1 C.M.L.R. 969.

In *Bank of Crete SA v Koskotas (No.2)* [1992] 1 W.L.R. 919 [1993] 1 All E.R. 748, it was held that the Court should not prevent a party to claim disclosing documents to another person pursuant to a legal obligation in a foreign jurisdiction.

In *Attorney General for Gibraltar v May* [1999] 1 W.L.R. 998, CA it was held that although the Attorney General was bound by an implied undertaking not to use in criminal proceedings against the defendant taking place in Gibraltar the contents of an affidavit sworn by the defendant under a court order ancillary to an application for a *Mareva* injunction to freeze the defendant's assets, the court would exercise is discretion to release the Attorney General from the implied undertaking.

A claim based on a misused document will, ordinarily, be dismissed as an abuse of the process of the Court (*Riddick v Thames Board Mills Ltd* [1977] Q.B. 881; [1977] 3 All E.R. 677, CA). See also *Home Office v Harman* [1983] 1 A.C. 280; [1982] 1 All E.R. 532, HL; and *Wilden Pump Engineering Co v Fusfeld* [1985] F.S.R. 581.

For considerations material to an order maintaining confidentiality after the trial has finished, see *Lilly Icos v Pfiza Ltd (No.2)* [2002] EWCA Civ 2; [2002] 1 W.L.R. 2253; [2002] All E.R. 842, CA. See too *SmithKline Beecham Plc v Generics (UK) Ltd; BASF AG v SmithKline Beecham Plc* [2003] EWCA Civ 1109; [2004] 1 W.L.R. 1479; [2003] 4 All E.R. 1302 CA; restriction in one case did not prevent authorisation of use in another case in appropriate circumstances.

False disclosure statements

31.23—(1) Proceedings for contempt of court may be brought against a person if he makes, or causes to be made, a false disclosure statement, without an honest belief in its truth. **31.23**

(2) Proceedings under this rule may be brought only—

(a) by the Attorney General; or

(b) with the permission of the court.

Proceedings for Contempt

31.23.1 This rule was added by the The Civil Procedure (Amendment) Rules 2000 (SI 2000/221) r.16. Compare former RSC O.24, r.16(2) and former CCR O.14, r.10(2). For "disclosure statement" see r.31.10(5) to (9). See also CPR r.32.14 (false statements).

"with the permission of the Court"

31.23.2 The powers conferred by r.31.23 are wide enough to allow them to be exercised at any point in the proceedings, including at an interlocutory stage: *Prest v Marc Rich & Co* [2006] EWHC 927 at [25]. However this will often be undesirable because of the potential unfairness of examining witnesses of one side without the full deployment of the opponent's evidence: *Lonrho v Fayed* June 14, 1993, unrep., CA per Stuart-Smith L.J., noted in *Prest* at [20]–[25].

PRACTICE DIRECTION—DISCLOSURE AND INSPECTION

This Practice Direction supplements CPR Part 31

General

1.1 The normal order for disclosure will be an order that the parties give standard disclosure. **31PD.1**

1.2 In order to give standard disclosure the disclosing party must make a reasonable search for documents falling within the paragraphs of rule 31.6.

1.3 Having made the search the disclosing party must (unless rule 31.10(8) applies) make a list of the documents of whose existence the party is aware that fall within those paragraphs and which are or have been in the party's control (see rule 31.8).

1.4 The obligations imposed by an order for standard disclosure may be dispensed with or limited either by the court or by written agreement between the parties. Any such written agreement should be lodged with the court.

The Search

2. The extent of the search which must be made will depend upon the circumstances of the case including, in particular, the factors referred to in rule 31.7(2). The parties should bear in mind the overriding principle of proportionality (see rule 1.1(2)(c)). It may, for example, be reasonable to decide not to search for documents coming into existence before some particular date, or to limit the search to documents in some particular place or places, or to documents falling into particular categories. **31PD.2**

Electronic Disclosure

2A.1 Rule 31.4 contains a broad definition of a document. This extends to electronic documents, including e-mail and other electronic communications, word processed documents and databases. In addition to documents that are readily accessible from computer systems and other electronic devices and media, the definition covers those documents that are stored on servers and back-up systems and electronic documents that have been "deleted". It also extends to additional information stored and associated with electronic documents known as metadata. **31PD.2A**

2A.2 The parties should, prior to the first Case Management Conference, discuss any issues that may arise regarding searches for and the preservation of electronic documents. This may involve the parties providing information about the categories of electronic documents within their control, the computer systems, electronic devices and media on which any relevant documents may be held, the storage systems maintained by the parties and their document retention policies. In the case of difficulty or disagreement, the matter should be referred to a judge for directions at the earliest practical date, if possible at the first Case Management Conference.

2A.3 The parties should co-operate at an early stage as to the format in which electronic copy documents are to be provided on inspection. In the case of difficulty or disagreement, the matter should be referred to a Judge for directions at the earliest practical date, if possible at the first Case Management Conference.

2A.4 The existence of electronic documents impacts upon the extent of the reasonable search required by Rule 31.7 for the purposes of standard disclosure. The factors that may be relevant in deciding the reasonableness of a search for electronic documents include (but are not limited to) the following:—

(a) The number of documents involved.

(b) The nature and complexity of the proceedings.

(c) The ease and expense of retrieval of any particular document. This includes:

(i) The accessibility of electronic documents or data including e-mail communications on computer systems, servers, back-up systems and other electronic devices or media that may contain such documents taking into account alterations or developments in hardware or software systems used by the disclosing party and/or available to enable access to such documents.

(ii) The location of relevant electronic documents, data, computer systems, servers, back-up systems and other electronic devices or media that may contain such documents.

(iii) The likelihood of locating relevant data.

(iv) The cost of recovering any electronic documents.

(v) The cost of disclosing and providing inspection of any relevant electronic documents.

(vi) The likelihood that electronic documents will be materially altered in the course of recovery, disclosure or inspection.

(d) The significance of any document which is likely to be located during the search.

2A.5 It may be reasonable to search some or all of the parties' electronic storage systems. In some circumstances, it may be reasonable to search for electronic documents by means of keyword searches (agreed as far as possible between the parties) even where a full review of each and every document would be unreasonable. There may be other forms of electronic search that may be appropriate in particular circumstances.

The List

31PD.3 **3.1** The list should be in practice form **N265**.

3.2 In order to comply with rule 31.10(3) it will normally be necessary to list the documents in date order, to number them consecutively and to give each a concise description (e.g. letter, claimant to defendant). Where there is a large number of documents all falling into a particular category the disclosing party may list those documents as a category rather than individually, e.g. 50 bank statements relating to account number ______ at ______ Bank, ______ 20 ______ to ______ 20 ______; or, 35 letters *passing between* ______ and ______ between ______ 20 ______ and ______ 20 ______.

3.3 The obligations imposed by an order for disclosure will continue until the proceedings come to an end. If, after a list of documents has been prepared and served, the existence of further documents to which the order applies comes to the attention of the disclosing party, the party must prepare and serve a supplemental list.

Disclosure Statement

4.1 A list of documents must (unless rule 31.10.(8)(b) applies) contain a disclosure statement complying with rule 31.10. The form of disclosure statement is set out in the Annex to this practice direction. **31PD.4**

4.2 The disclosure statement should:

(1) expressly state that the disclosing party believes the extent of the search to have been reasonable in all the circumstances, and

(2) in setting out the extent of the search (see rule 31.10(6)) draw attention to any particular limitations on the extent of the search which were adopted for proportionality reasons and give the reasons why the limitations were adopted, e.g. the difficulty or expense that a search not subject to those limitations would have entailed or the marginal relevance of categories of documents omitted from the search.

4.3 Where rule 31.10(7) applies, the details given in the disclosure statement about the person making the statement must include his name and address and the office or position he holds in the disclosing party or the basis upon which he makes the statement on behalf of the party.

4.4 If the disclosing party has a legal representative acting for him, the legal representative must endeavour to ensure that the person making the disclosure statement (whether the disclosing party or, in a case to which rule 31.10(7) applies, some other person) understands the duty of disclosure under Part 31.

4.5 If the disclosing party wishes to claim that he has a right or duty to withhold a document, or part of a document, in his list of documents from inspection (see rule 31.19(3)), he must state in writing:

(1) that he has such a right or duty, and

(2) the grounds on which he claims that right or duty.

4.6 The statement referred to in paragraph 4.5 above should normally be included in the disclosure statement and must indicate the document, or part of a document, to which the claim relates.

4.7 An insurer or the Motor Insurers' Bureau may sign a disclosure statement on behalf of a party where the insurer or the Motor Insurers' Bureau has a financial interest in the result of proceedings brought wholly or partially by or against that party. Rule 31.10(7) and paragraph 4.3 above shall apply to the insurer or the Motor Insurers' Bureau making such a statement.

Specific Disclosure

5.1 If a party believes that the disclosure of documents given by a disclosing party is inadequate he may make an application for an order for specific disclosure (see rule 31.12). **31PD.5**

5.2 The application notice must specify the order that the applicant intends to ask the court to make and must be supported by evidence (see rule 31.12(2) which describes the orders the court may make).

5.3 The grounds on which the order is sought may be set out in the application notice itself but if not there set out must be set out in evidence filed in support of the application.

5.4 In deciding whether or not to make an order for specific disclosure the court will take into account all the circumstances of the case and, in particular, the overriding objective described in Part 1. But if the court concludes that the party from whom specific disclosure is sought has failed adequately to comply with the obligations imposed by an order for disclosure (whether by failing to make a sufficient search for documents or otherwise) the court will usually make such order as is necessary to ensure that those obligations are properly complied with.

5.5 An order for specific disclosure may in an appropriate case direct a party to —

(1) carry out a search for any documents which it is reasonable to suppose may contain information which may —
  (a) enable the party applying for disclosure either to advance his own case or to damage that of the party giving disclosure; or
  (b) lead to a train of enquiry which has either of those consequences; and

(2) disclose any documents found as a result of that search.

Claims to withhold disclosure or inspection of a document

31PD.6 **6.1** A claim to withhold inspection of a document, or part of a document, disclosed in a list of documents does not require an application to the court. Where such a claim has been made, a party who wishes to challenge it must apply to the court (see rule 31.19(5)).

6.2 Rule 31.19(1) and (6) provide a procedure enabling a party to apply for an order permitting disclosure of the existence of a document to be withheld.

Inspection of documents mentioned in expert's report (rule 31.14(2))

31PD.7 **7.1** If a party wishes to inspect documents referred to in the expert report of another party, before issuing an application he should request inspection of the documents informally, and inspection should be provided by agreement unless the request is unreasonable.

7.2 Where an expert report refers to a large number or volume of documents and it would be burdensome to copy or collate them, the court will only order inspection of such documents if it is satisfied that it is necessary for the just disposal of the proceedings and the party cannot reasonably obtain the documents from another source.

False Disclosure Statement

31PD.8 *8. Attention is drawn* to rule 31.23 which sets out the consequences of making a false disclosure statement without an honest belief in its truth, and to the procedures set out in paragraphs 28.1 – 28.3 of the practice direction supplementing Part 32.

Annex

Disclosure statement

I, the above named claimant [or defendant] [if party making disclosure is a company, firm or other organisation identify here who the person making the disclosure statement is and why he is the appropriate person to make it] state that I have carried out a reasonable and proportionate search to locate all the documents which I am required to disclose under the order made by the court on day of . I did not search: **31PD.9**

(1) for documents predating ,
(2) for documents located elsewhere than ,
(3) for documents in categories other than .
(4) for electronic documents

I carried out a search for electronic documents contained on or created by the following:
[list what was searched and extent of search]

I did not search for the following:
(1) documents created before________________,
(2) documents contained on or created by the Claimant's/Defendant's PCs/portable data storage media/databases/servers/back-up tapes/off-site storage/mobile phones/laptops/notebooks/handheld devices/PDA devices (delete as appropriate),
(3) documents contained on or created by the Claimant's/Defendant's mail files/document files/calendar files/spreadsheet files/graphic and presentation files/web-based applications (delete as appropriate),
(4) documents other than by reference to the following keyword(s)/concepts____________________(delete if your search was not confined to specific keywords or concepts).

I certify that I understand the duty of disclosure and to the best of my knowledge I have carried out that duty. I certify that the list above is a complete list of all documents which are or have been in my control and which I am obliged under the said order to disclose.

PART 32

EVIDENCE

Contents

Editorial introduction

32.0.2 This Part contains provisions formerly found in the RSC and CCR modified in some respects for the purpose of implementing particular recommendations made in the Access to Justice Reports. The provenance of many of the rules may be traced to RSC O.38 and O.41 and CCR O.20, Pt II.

The power to make rules of court relating to evidence is derived from various sources (e.g. Courts and Legal Services Act 1990 s.5 (witness statements), Civil Evidence Act 1995 s.12 (hearsay evidence)). In the Civil Procedure Act 1997, the extent of the power to make Civil Procedure Rules is stated as including the power to "modify the rules of evidence as they apply to proceedings in any court within the scope of the rules" (s.1(2) and Sch.1, para.4) (see Vol.2, paras 9A–738 and 9A–765). Neither the Supreme Court Act 1981 s.85 nor the County Courts Act 1984 s.75 contained such a broad rule-making power. The law of evidence covers a wide diversity of topics and is based on a large corpus of case law and legislation. It is to be expected that the fullest range of the rules of evidence will apply to proceedings in courts, as distinct from other tribunals (Cross & Tapper, *Evidence* (9th edn, 2001), p.5). But even in judicial proceedings there are important variations in the precise mixture of rules of evidence which apply (1) to different types of jurisdiction (whether civil, criminal or family, or whether common law, equity or statutory), (2) to different types of court (whether superior (High Court) or inferior (county courts)), and (3) at different stages of the *proceedings* (whether pre-commencement, interlocutory, disposal hearing, trial or appeal) (*ibid.*). Traditionally, rules of court have been confined to a narrow aspect of the law of evidence and have concentrated on matters falling on the border between rules of evidence and rules of procedure (the best example being rules relating to the manner in which evidence may be given). Further, they have provided very good illustrations of the ways in which the "mixture of rules" may be varied at "different stages in the proceedings". But the lines that divide these two bodies of legal rules (evidence and procedure) and which separate them from substantive legal rules are not clear cut. The question as to the extent to which power to make court rules relating to practice and procedure permits the making of rules on evidentiary matters has been much debated (even in the days when rule-making was the province of judges and judges alone). Generally, the suggestion that, what could be called, the substantive law of evidence could be altered by court rules has been resisted. The rule-making power now given by s.1(2) and Sch.1, para.4 of the 1997 Act changes the position significantly (see Vol.2, Sect.12 (CPR: Application, Amendments and Interpretation) paras 12–3 and 12–38. However, most of the rules found in Pt 32, whilst altering the law in some important respects, are confined to matters traditionally thought to be the legitimate concern of rule-making authorities.

The provisions of Pt 32 are supplemented by Practice Direction (Written Evidence) (para.32PD.1 below). As would be expected, given its title, this practice direction contains detailed provisions about written evidence in the form of witness statements and affidavits and exhibits thereto, but it also contains provisions about agreed bundles of documents for hearings, and video-conferencing.

Pt 32 does not apply to any proceedings to which Pt 76 (Prevention of Terrorism Act 2005) applies, or to any proceedings to which Pt 79 (Financial Restrictions Proceedings Under the Counter-Terrorism Act 2008) applies (see, respectively, r.76.26(1) and r.79.22(1)).

Related sources

- Practice Direction (Written Evidence) (see para.32PD.1 below) 32.0.3
- Interim Report, pp.175–180
- Final Report, pp.128–130
- Courts and Legal Services Act 1990 s.5 (witness statements) (see Vol.2, para.9B–104)
- Civil Evidence Act 1995 (admissible hearsay) (see Vol.2, para.9B–1068)
- Part 8 (Alternative procedure for claims), rr.8.5 (Filing and serving witness statements) and 8.6 (Evidence—general)
- Part 22 (Statements of truth)
- Part 33 (Miscellaneous rules about evidence)
- Part 34 (Depositions and court attendance by witnesses)
- Part 35 (Experts and assessors)
- Chancery Guide, Chap. 8 (Vol.2, para.1A–78)
- Admiralty and Commercial Courts Guide, Sect.F, para.7.1, and Sect.H (Vol.2, paras. 2A–91 and 2A–103)
- Technology and Construction Court Guide (October 2, 2005), Sect.12 (Vol.2, para.2C–111)
- Queen's Bench Guide, para.7.10 (Vol.2, para.1B–50)
- Rule 76.26 (Modification of the general rules of evidence and disclosure)

Forms

- **N20** Witness Summons. 32.0.4
- **N21** Order for examination of deponent (before hearing).

Power of court to control evidence

32.1—(1) The court may control the evidence by giving directions as to— 32.1

(a) the issues on which it requires evidence;

(b) the nature of the evidence which it requires to decide those issues; and

(c) the way in which the evidence is to be placed before the court.

(2) The court may use its power under this rule to exclude evidence that would otherwise be admissible.

(3) The court may limit cross-examination[GL].

Effect of rule

32.1.1 Under the CPR and related Practice Directions the court has extensive powers to manage cases and these powers may be used flexibly. The nature of case management may vary, depending on whether a case is allocated to the fast track or is proceeding on the multi-track, and, in the latter event, on whether the case is straightforward or less simple (Final Report, pp.60–61). Rule 32.1 applies to cases proceeding on the small claims track but the other rules in Pt 32 do not apply to such cases (r.27.2(1)(c)). Directions may be given at any time and may include directions as to evidence. Checklists and other documents to be filed by the parties to assist case management are designed in part to alert the court to the possibility that directions as to evidence may be helpful (Final Report, p.61). The provisions of Pt 32 do not apply to proceedings to which Pt 76 (Proceedings under the Prevention of Terrorism Act 2005) (see r.76.26(1)). Special rules as to evidence in proceedings under that Part are found in r.76.26 and elsewhere in that Part.

The general power to "control the evidence" is a far-reaching one to which some of the rules which follow in this Part are subject.

This rule does not exhaust the court's powers to restrict evidence (either to fact or opinion) and to regulate the manner in which it is given. Numerous other provisions in the CPR and supplementing practice directions have the effect of restricting evidence in particular circumstances; e.g. CPR, r.35.4 (Court's power to restrict expert evidence), Practice Direction (Patents, Etc.), para.12.1 (Restrictions on admission of evidence) (see Vol.2, para.2F–13). At the hearing of a claim in which the Pt 8 procedure is followed (Alternative Procedure for Claims) the basic rule is that the evidence will be in written form, but r.8.6(2) provides that the court may "require or permit" a party to give oral evidence at the hearing. Note also r.52.11(2), which provides that, unless it orders otherwise, an appeal court will not receive (a) oral evidence, or (b) evidence which was not before the court below. Many CPR provisions, whilst not in terms restricting the evidence that may be given, focus attention on the evidence that should be given by stipulating, in relation to particular claims and applications, the relevant evidence; e.g. r.74.4 (evidence in support of application for registration of judgment), Practice Direction (Possession Claims), paras 5.1 *et seq.* (see para.55PD.8 below). Provisions lying outside the CPR and relating to particular types of claim can be very prescriptive as to the evidence required to support allegations and can attract the exercise by the court of its power to excise passages from witness statements; e.g. *Secretary of State for Trade and Industry v Swann* [2003] EWHC 1780 (Ch); *The Times*, August 18, 2003 (Laddie J.) (whether evidence against defendant in directors disqualification proceedings supported the gravity of the allegations).

Where a party contends, on the basis of one of the well-known exclusionary rules of evidence, that certain evidence may not be given, for example where a communication is said to be privileged, the source of the court's power to exclude the evidence is not found in r.32.1. However, in such circumstances it is not uncommon for applicants to base their applications on the rule (e.g. *G.E. Capital Commercial Finance Ltd v Sutton* [2003] EWHC 1648 (QB); July 4, 2003, unrep. (McCombe J.)).

In exercising its powers of case management, the court may make rulings which are complemented by directions under r.32.1 controlling the evidence. For example, if a claimant in a loss of earnings claim fails to comply with an order to serve an updated schedule of loss by a particular date, the court may order that the trial of the claim should be restricted to the existing schedule of loss and direct that the evidence should be limited to evidence in support thereof (*Stockman v Payne* February 17, 2000, unrep., Buckley J.; see also *Walsh v Misseldine* February 29, 2000, unrep., CA).

For obvious reasons, the power of the court to "control evidence" is likely to be seen as a power to restrict admissible evidence (principally in the interests of saving costs and reducing delays), rather than as a power to receive evidence in circumstances where, before the CPR came into effect, evidence could not be received, or was not normally received. The extent to which evidence (e.g. in the form of verified statements of case or application notices) may be considered in applications to strike out under r.3.4(2)(a) (no reasonable grounds for bringing or defending claim) or to grant summary judgment under r.24.2 (no real prospect of success) was referred to by May L.J. in *S. v Gloucestershire County Council* [2000] 3 All E.R. 346, CA; see also *E.D. & F. Man Liquid Products Ltd v Patel* [2003] EWCA Civ 472; *The Times*, April 18, 2003, CA; *Marsh v Chief Constable of Lancashire* [2003] EWCA Civ 284; March 6, 2003, unrep., CA.

In *Jones v University of Warwick* [2003] EWCA Civ 151; [2003] 1 W.L.R. 954, CA, the question arose whether the court had exercised its discretion correctly under r.32.1 (power of court to control evidence) in a personal injury case in directing that video evidence covertly obtained by the defendant's insurers through the trespass of their agents should not be excluded on the ground that the claimant's rights under art.8(1) of the Convention (right to respect for private and family life) were infringed. The Court of Appeal rejected the argument that, unless it was necessary for the defendants to take the action they did, in the circumstances of this case the evidence must inevitably be held inadmissible. The Court held that the conduct of the defendants was not so outrageous that the defence should be struck out. However, it was important to make clear that their conduct was improper and not justified. Accordingly, the defendants should be penalised in costs.

Exclusionary rules and Convention rights

In certain circumstances, evidence though relevant may, as a matter of law, be inadmissible. For example, under the "without prejudice" rule, negotiations between parties, whether oral or written, aimed at settling legal proceedings between them are excluded from being given in evidence (see para.31.3.40 above). The operation of exclusionary rules may have to yield to Convention rights and this may have consequences for the court's general power to control evidence referred to in r.32.1. The rule has two justifications. First, the public policy of encouraging parties to negotiate and settle their disputes out of court, and secondly, an implied agreement arising out of what is commonly understood to be the consequences of offering or agreeing to negotiate without prejudice. In some cases both of these justifications are present; in others, only one or the other (*Muller v Linsley & Mortimer* [1996] P.N.L.R. 74, CA, per Hoffmann L.J., explaining *Cutts v Head* [1984] Ch. 290, CA). The dual policy basis justifies the exclusion of without prejudice communications not only from trial proceedings but also from post-trial proceedings (e.g. as to costs liabilities). Exceptionally, evidence of statements made in without prejudice discussions may be admitted where there is unambiguous impropriety and a very clear case of abuse of a privileged occasion (*Berry Trade Ltd v Moussavi (No.3)* [2002] EWCA Civ 715; *The Times*, June 3, 2003, CA (Court commenting on need to avoid risk of "satellite litigation" emerging where factual disputes relevant to the operation of this exception arising). In *Prudential Assurance Co Ltd v Prudential Insurance Co of America* [2003] EWCA Civ 327; [2003] 1 W.L.R. 2295, CA, it was held by the Vice-Chancellor at first instance that the right to freedom of expression guaranteed by art.10 of the Convention is engaged by the "without prejudice" rule, with the result that this exclusionary rule should be applied with restraint and only in cases to which the public interests underlying it are plainly applicable ([2002] EWHC 2809 (Ch); *The Times*, January 2, 2003). However, the Court of Appeal concluded that no issue of public policy arose in this case and in disposing of the appeal expressed no opinion on the Vice-Chancellor's holding as to the applicability of art.10 to the rule ([2003] EWCA Civ 1154; July 31, 2003, CA, at para.29 per Chadwick L.J.). **32.1.1.1**

Under ECHR art.6(1), it is generally for national courts to determine the admissibility of the evidence before them and assess its relevance, subject to the overriding duty to ensure that the proceedings as a whole are fair: *Mantovanelli v France* (1997) 24 E.H.R.R. 370, ECtHR; *Schenk v Switzerland (A/140)* (1991) 13 E.H.R.R. 242, ECtHR; applied in *Miailhe v France (No.2)* (1997) 23 E.H.R.R. 491, ECtHR. See also *Vernon v United Kingdom* (2000) 29 E.H.R.R. CD 264. It is normally for national courts to decide, in particular, whether it is necessary or advisable to be heard (*X v Austria* (C–5362/72), 42 CD 145) although in an individual case the principle of "equality of arms" may require that a particular witness is heard: *Dombo Beheer BV v Netherlands (A/274-A)* (1994) 18 E.H.R.R. 213, ECtHR. The court should exercise care before refusing to look at documents which one party wishes it to consider: *De Haes v Belgium (19983/92)* (1998) 25 E.H.R.R. 1, ECtHR.

Directions as to issues on which evidence required

Courts decide issues of fact on the basis of evidence. Where no evidence is forthcoming, issues have to be determined in accordance with rules as to the incidence of the burden of proof. It may be necessary for the court to determine issues in the light of evidence available, not only at a trial, but also at the pre-trial stage. The powers given by r.32.1(a) may be exercised at any time in relation to any hearing but is likely to be principally used in preparing for trial. The basic proposition stated in this rule would **32.1.2** appear to be that the court can direct that, in preparing for the determination of a particular issue at a particular time, it requires evidence on certain issues only and not on others (or at least no evidence yet or no further evidence on others). Doubtless, the circumstances in which the court would choose to do that are many and various and cannot be stated in a short compass. Having decided that particular issues require determination (whether at trial or other hearing), and having excluded others from consideration (perhaps only temporarily), the court can then further stipulate the nature of the evidence to be given and the way in which the evidence is to be placed before the court. It should be noted that, in terms, r.32.1 is not restricted to evidence as to fact. The court's power to control evidence extends to directing that the evidence of witnesses primarily relevant to a Pt 20 claim could be heard at the trial of the main claim in circumstances where for good reason the main claim is being tried before the Pt 20 claim and the parties to the latter claim are adopting a united front against the claimant (*Powell v Pallisers of Hereford Ltd* [2002] EWCA Civ 959; July 1, 2002, unrep., CA).

At the trial of issues ordered to be tried as preliminary issues, it is for the judge to determine the extent of the evidence to be admitted, exercising his powers under r.32.1 (*G.K.R. Karate (UK) Ltd v Yorkshire Post Newspapers Ltd* [2000] 1 W.L.R. 2571; [2000] 2 All E.R. 931, CA (issues of privilege and malice tried as preliminary issues in defamation claim)).

The close relationship between the identification by the court of issues to be determined, and rulings by the court as to the evidence to be received in relation to those issues, is well illustrated by *Burstein v Times Newspapers Ltd* [2001] 1 W.L.R. 579, CA (where the question was whether evidence of the claimant's conduct (as distinct from evidence of his general reputation) was admissible in support of a plea of mitigation of damages in a libel claim).

The court must further the overriding objective (r.1.1) by actively managing cases (r.1.4(1)) and must give effect to it when exercising any power under the CPR (r.1.2(a)). Active management includes "identifying the issues at an early stage" (r.1.4(2)(b)). The court's case management powers include the power to direct a separate trial of any issue, to decide the order in which issues are to be tried, and to exclude an issue from consideration (r.3.1(2)(i), (j), (k)). In certain circumstances, the court may determine cases without an oral hearing (see rr.1.4(2)(j) and 23.8) (Final Report, p.68). The court is encouraged (in appropriate cases proceeding on the multi-track particularly) to resolve issues that have been identified at the pre-trial stage by "rolling adjudication" instead of leaving all issues alive until trial (Interim Report, p.50 and Final Report, p.63). The discharge of all of these powers is facilitated by the specific power given to the court by r.32.1.

Under the CPR, the admissibility of evidence as to credit is very much a question for the court to be determined in the light of the central issues and facts of the case, the nature of the evidence sought to be adduced, and the reasons advanced for and against admissibility (*Anglo Eastern Trust Ltd v Kermanshahchi* [2002] EWHC 1702 (Ch); July 5, 2002, unrep. (Neuberger J.)).

As to court's power to strike out passages in witness statement served by a party, see para.32.4.20 below.

Nature of the evidence

32.1.3 It should be noted that, under the CPR, evidence may consist, not only of the *viva voce* testimony of witnesses, or their witness statements and affidavits, but also of the statements of case and notices of application (which are to be verified by a "statement of truth").

Exclusion of evidence otherwise admissible (r.32.1(2))

32.1.4 No attempt need be made in this commentary to explain the scope of, and the effect of, exclusionary rules of evidence in civil proceedings. Necessarily, the effect of some particular rules is important in certain procedural contexts; e.g. the "without prejudice" rule in relation to disclosure of documents (see para.31.3.4 above).

Hitherto, the extent to which a judge in civil proceedings (whether sitting with a jury or not) has a discretion to exclude evidence which is relevant and admissible has not been entirely clear (see *Cross and Tapper on Evidence* (9th ed., 1999), p.195). Certainly, a court has no general power to exclude relevant and admissible evidence. Where a court exercises its power under r.32.1(1)(a) and directs that evidence should be given on particular issues only and not on others (having perhaps excluded the other issues in exercise of the power given by r.3.1(2)(k)) the effect of the direction will be (almost inevitably) to exclude admissible evidence. Further, the same result may ensue when the court gives a direction under r.32.1(1)(b) limiting the evidence to be given on a particular issue to evidence of a particular "nature". Rule 32.1(2) rightly assumes that the court has no general power to exclude admissible evidence but provides that the court may exercise its powers under r.32.1(1) even though the effect of doing so will be the exclusion of admissible evidence.

The common law rule to the effect that hearsay evidence was inadmissible was subject to various exceptions developed by case law and, as a result of the enactment of various statutory provisions, the rule has been abrogated almost entirely in civil proceedings. The Civil Evidence Act 1995 s.1(1) states that evidence is not to be excluded in civil proceedings on the ground that it is hearsay. However, under s.4(1) it is for the court to decide "the weight (if any)" to be given to hearsay evidence. That formulation focuses the court's attention on the question of weight in the individual circumstances of the evidence and the case. (A non-exhaustive list of factors for the court's consideration is set out in s.4(2).) The scheme of the Act clearly contemplates that the court may decide to attach no weight at all to particular hearsay evidence. In that event, where it is just to do so, the same result is achieved as if the evidence had been inadmissible or excluded on some other basis. It has been said that, in view of the court's duty under s.4 to consider and decide the weight, if any, to attach to proffered hearsay evidence, there is no need to exclude it under the court's general power to control evidence granted by r.32.1, and may be inappropriate to do so (*Daltel Europe Limited v Makki*, [2005] EWHC 749 (Ch), May 3, 2005, unrep. (David Richards J.) (hearsay evidence adduced in application to commit defendants for breach of court orders)).

In terms, there is no express limitation on the exercise by a trial judge of the power under r.32.1(2) to exclude admissible evidence, however it must be exercised in accordance with the overriding objective of dealing with cases justly (*Grobbelaar v Sun Newspapers Ltd, The Times* August 12, 1999, CA; *O'Brien v Chief Constable of South Wales* [2005] UKHL 26; [2005] 2 A.C. 534, H.L.).

Although the court has power to exclude admissible evidence as part of its case management role and to achieve a fair hearing, it would be a strong thing for a court to use this power for the purpose of excluding secondary evidence of a document where to do so would in effect exclude a party's claim (*Post Office Counters Ltd v Mahida* [2003] EWCA Civ 1583; *The Times*, October 31, 2003, CA (where held that claimant's failure to take care of original document and unfairness of the process generally affected the weight to be given to the secondary evidence to a degree where it failed to prove the precise amount of the debt claimed)).

Although the identifying and confining of the issues to be determined (see para.32.1.2 above) may be regarded as examples of the exercise by the court of its "case management" powers (see para.1.4.1 above), generally speaking, questions as to whether otherwise admissible evidence should be excluded will raise issues properly characterised as questions of law. However, even questions of law of this type may turn on factors that would be regarded nowadays as case management considerations (e.g. the question whether evidence of reputation should be admitted on the issue of reduction of libel damages; see *Burstein v Times Newspapers Ltd* [2001] 1 W.L.R. 579, CA, at p.597 per May L.J.). Whether a ruling as to admissibility of evidence should be characterised as a ruling on a question of law or as a case management decision may be important in determining how any appeal against the ruling should be handled (see CPR Pt 52 below *seriatim*).

The court may be called upon to use this provision to exclude evidence, otherwise admissible at common law, which has arguably been obtained in breach of an ECHR right: *Official Receiver v Stern* [2000] 1 W.L.R. 2230, CA; *Schenk v Switzerland (A/140) (1991) 13 E.H.R.R. 242, ECtHR*; *Khan v United Kingdom, The Times*, May 23, 2000, ECtHR; *Choudhary v United Kingdom (40084/98)*, May 4, 1999, unrep. There is no rule under the ECHR requiring the exclusion of such evidence. The court must act in such a way as to ensure that the proceedings as a whole are fair.

Video evidence

A party wishing to adduce film or video evidence to attack an opponent's case is subject to all the rules as to disclosure and inspection of documents contained in Pt 31. In the interests of case management, and in discharge of the duty arising under r.1.3, the party should raise the matter with the procedural judge at the first practicable op- **32.1.4.1** portunity (see also para.2.7). In exercise of his powers to control evidence at trial (r.32.1) it may be appropriate for a judge to give directions requiring a party to give notice in advance of those parts of the video footage relied on (*Rall v Hume* [2001] EWCA Civ 146; [2001] 3 All E.R. 248, CA). In a personal injuries case, where video evidence is available which, according to the defendant, undermines the case of the claimant to an extent that it would substantially reduce the award of damages, it will usually be in the overall interests of justice to require that the proponent should be permitted to cross-examine the claimant and his expert advisers upon it (*ibid*). See also *Jones v University of Warwick* [2003] EWCA Civ 151; [2003] 1 W.L.R. 954, CA.

Limiting evidence in-chief and cross-examination

32.1.5 The examination of witnesses involves their being examined in-chief, cross-examined, and (possibly) re-examined. Rule 1.2 requires the court to give effect to the overriding objective of dealing with cases justly, and r.1.4 requires the court actively to manage the case in order to further the overriding objective. An important element of case management is the exercise of the court's power, stated in r.32.1(1), to "control the evidence" by giving directions of the type listed in that provision. On its face, the rule does not give the court any direct power to limit evidence in-chief, but r.32.1(3) states expressly that the court may limit cross-examination and the manner in which the court may do this is not restricted to giving directions of the type referred to in r.32.1(1).

The question whether cross-examination should be limited is a different question from whether, in the exercise of the court's discretion, cross-examination should be permitted at all; a question that may arise, for example, where permission is sought on an interlocutory application to cross-examine a witness on his written evidence.

Conceivably, cross-examination may be limited in two ways. First, the court may limit the issues to be explored on cross-examination (e.g. *Watson v Chief Constable of Cleveland* [2001] EWCA Civ 1547; October 12, 2001, unrep., CA (restrictions on cross-examination of claimant as to credit in jury trial)). The power to control evidence referred to in r.32.1(1) would provide authority for this. Secondly, the court may limit the trial time to be devoted to cross-examination of a particular witness (e.g. *Hayes v Transco Plc* [2003] EWCA Civ 1261; September 17, 2003, unrep., CA; *Three Rivers DC v Bank of England* [2005] EWCA Civ 889, July 14, 2005, unrep., CA). See further Chancery Guide, paras 8.3 and 8.15 (see Vol.2, paras 1A–79 and 1A–82).

The Court of Appeal will only interfere with a judge's decision to limit cross-examination if the decision is outside the acceptable range of decisions at which a judge can legitimately arrive (*Watson v Chief Constable of Cleveland Police*, *op cit.*, *Hayes v Transco Plc*, *op cit.*).

In *Hayes v Transco Plc*, *op cit.*, in allowing the defendants' appeal, the Court of Appeal held that the trial judge's rulings (1) restricting the time available for the conclusion of the defendants' cross-examination of the claimant, and (2) refusing the defendants' application to adduce in evidence a supplementary witness statement of one of their witnesses (containing matter relevant to that cross-examination), in the circumstances were wrong in principle and amounted to a serious procedural irregularity.

In *Three Rivers DC v Bank of England* [2005] EWCA Civ 889, July 14, 2005, unrep., CA, in a trial lasting many months, the judge ordered that a cross-examination of one of the defendants' witnesses, estimated to last twelve weeks should be limited to seven weeks. The circumstances were that, if the length of the cross-examination was not limited, the cross-examination would be interrupted by a break of six months (allowing for the Long Vacation and time for the witness's anticipated medical treatment). The Court of Appeal dismissed the claimants' appeal against this ruling, rejecting submissions that it was based solely on the new event of the witness's medical condition and that the judge was not entitled to depart from the professional judgment of counsel as to the time required for cross-examination.

A report prepared by a joint expert should be the evidence in the case on the issues covered and generally there should be no need for the report to be amplified or tested by cross-examination at trial (*Peet v Mid-Kent Healthcare Trust* [2001] EWCA Civ 1703; [2001] 1 W.L.R. 210, CA); see further para.35.7.1 below.

A refusal to allow cross-examination of a particular witness altogether may be considered compatible with ECHR art.6(1) where the court is of the view that this cross-examination would not assist it: *X v Austria*, (5362/72), 42 CD 145. It has been suggested that the ECHR art.6(1) right to a fair trial may, in certain circumstances, require an appellate authority to permit cross-examination of members of the tribunal or court hearing the case at first instance: *Malhotra v Price Waterhouse*, July 29, 1999, unrep., EAT.

In terms, r.32.1(3) is confined to the limitation by the court of cross-examination. It should be noted that the powers of the court to confine issues for determination and to control evidence (r.32.1) may be exercised for the purpose of limiting the duration of examination in-chief (whether the evidence is to be given orally or in written form). In *Burstein v Times Newspapers Ltd* [2001] 1 W.L.R. 579, CA, where the question was whether the defence should be permitted to introduce evidence of the claimant's conduct (as distinct from evidence of his general reputation) in support of a plea of mitigation of damages in a libel claim, May L.J. said it is in accordance with the overriding objective that the evidence should be properly confined "both in its subject matter and its duration" to that which was directly relevant to the publication of the alleged libel. (The court also has power to limit the duration of legal submissions, including submissions about evidence. See *Attorney General v Scriven* February 4, 2000, unrep., CA, where Simon Brown L.J. said: "The courts are not required to listen to litigants, whether represented or not, for as long as they like. It is for the court to control its own process and it is well-entitled to bring arguments to a close when it concludes that its process is being abused and that nothing of value will be lost by ending it".)

As a practical matter, the principal circumstance where the court is likely to consider exercising its powers to limit evidence in-chief is that where a party makes an application (either before or in the course of trial) to strike out parts of a witness statement served by his opponent. Such an application might be made, for example, on the grounds of irrelevance and disproportionality. See further para.32.4.21 below.

In certain circumstances, the court may impose restrictions on the use that a cross-examiner may make of evidence elicited in cross-examination; for example, where an order is made for cross-examination of a defendant on his disclosure statement made in compliance with a freezing injunction (*Motorola Credit Corporation v Uzan* [2002] EWHC 2187 (Comm); October 18, 2002, unrep. (David Steel J.) (undertaking not to use any material obtained for the purpose of bringing contempt proceedings against defendant)).

Practice Direction (Appeals), para.4.4 states that, where an application is made for permission to appeal from "a case management decision", the court dealing with the application may take into account the matters referred to in para.4.5, including (for example) whether it would be more convenient to determine the issue at or after the trial. It may be noted that, although a judge's ruling limiting or not limiting cross-examination (whether made before or during trial) is not included among the decisions described as "case management decisions" for these purposes, the matters referred to in para.4.5 would appear to be apposite in this context. (The *Three Rivers* case was unusual in that the appeal was taken in the course of trial.)

Although it has become fashionable to emphasise the power of the court, in the interests of reducing costs and delays and of husbanding court resources, to restrict cross-examination of witnesses, it is important that cross-examination be allowed to play its proper role. In modern times the appeal courts have been concerned to stress that judges should give adequate reasons for their decisions and, where there is a conflict of evidence (whether as to fact or as to expert opinion), should explain why they preferred the evidence of one witness to another. This has led to a new awareness of the (so-called) rule in *Browne v Dunn* (1894) R. 67, HL, and its implications. One proposition derived from this case is that, where a party contends that the evidence of his opponent's witness should be disbelieved on particular matters, the witness should be cross-examined on them by that party. A failure to put a point to a witness on cross-examination should usually disentitle the point to be taken against the witness in a closing speech. The rule is directed at advocates, rather than at judges, but witnesses may be dealt with unfairly, and judges may be led astray in their fact-finding (e.g. by concluding that certain evidence was uncontradicted when it might well have been, or by disbelieving witnesses on matters on which they were not challenged) if advocates ignore the rule, either through ignorance or by sharp practice. This aspect of the rule in *Browne v Dunn* has achieved a new significance since it has become the practice to allow the statements of witnesses to stand as evidence in chief. Recent cases on this matter (not all of them expressly referring to the rule in terms) include *Markem Corporation v Zipher Limited* [2005] EWCA Civ 267; [2005] R.P.C. 761, CA; *E.P.I. Environmental Technologies Inc v Symphony Plastic Technologies Plc (Practice Note)* [2004]

EWHC 2945 (Ch); [2005] 1 W.L.R. 3456 (Peter Smith J.). In the Chancery Guide, para.8.15 it is stated (on the basis of a dictum in the case of *In re Yarn Spinners* [1959] 1 All E.R. 299) that a party cross-examining is not necessarily obliged to put his case to each witness, even if they deal with the same point (Vol.2, para.1–76).

Submission of no case to answer

32.1.6 See also para.1.3.2 above.

Since the coming into effect of the CPR, the circumstances in which a trial judge should entertain a defendant's submission to dismiss the claimant's action at the close of the claimant's evidence (a submission of no case to answer) and the manner in which such submission should be handled have been thrown into doubt by a series of first instance and appellate decisions. (Cases arose in which submissions were treated by trial judges as if they were, in effect, applications by defendants to strike out a claimant's claim or for summary judgment made, not pre-trial, but in the course of trial.) In several cases, most recently, in *Graham v Chorley BC* [2006] EWCA Civ 92, February 21, 2006, unrep., CA, the Court of Appeal has sought to remove the uncertainty and has held that the law remains as stated in *Alexander v Rayson* [1936] 1 K.B. 169, CA, and *Laurie v Raglan Building Co* [1942] 1 K.B. 152, CA. (It should be remembered that these early cases were decided well before it became necessary for parties to exchange witness statements in advance of trial, and therefore well before trial judges routinely had advance notice of what witnesses were likely to say at the trial of actions.) Thus, as is explained below, the general rule is that a judge should not entertain a submission unless the defendant elects (whatever the outcome of the submission) to call no evidence. Only in exceptional circumstances should the judge deal with a submission without requiring the defendant to elect to call no evidence. Further, in such exceptional circumstances, in ruling on a submission the test that the judge should apply to the claimant's claim is not a "balance of probabilities" test, but the less onerous "prima facie case to answer" test explained by the Court in *Benham Ltd v Kythira Investments Ltd* [2003] EWCA Civ 1794, and endorsed by the Court in *Graham v Chorley Borough Council* , *op cit.* (see further below). The application of the less onerous test makes it possible for a claimant to successfully resist a submission in circumstances where his case is weak and unlikely to succeed without assistance from evidence elicited during the presentation of the defence case or from adverse inferences drawn from the defendant's failure to adduce evidence (either at all, or in relation to certain contested issues). A fuller explanation of the authorities is given in the paragraphs immediately following.

At the end of a claimant's case a defendant may submit that there is no case to answer. If the submission succeeds judgment may be given for the defendant without requiring him to present his case. The submission may be made on grounds of law, fact or mixed fact and law. Nowadays, if the pre-trial case management procedures have worked as they should, in a given case the most likely basis for a submission is that unexpected weaknesses have emerged in the presentation of the claimant's case at trial, in particular weaknesses in the claimant's evidence (which falls to be fully tested for the first time at trial).

The traditional submission of no case to answer test is whether realistically there is no basis upon which a jury could, properly directed, find in favour of the claimant on the evidence that he had adduced. As most civil cases are now tried without a jury, the question is, in effect, "whether there was no such case for the judge to put to himself, wearing his jury hat" (*Bentley v Jones Harris & Co* [2001] EWCA Civ 1724, November 2, 2001, unrep., CA, at para.[64] per Burton J.). In *Benham Ltd v Kythira Investments Ltd* [2003] EWCA Civ 1794; 154 New L.J. 21 (2004), CA, Simon Brown L.J. said the test is whether or not, on the evidence adduced by the claimant, the claimant has "a real prospect of success", but conceded that what is meant by that test in this context (as distinct from the summary judgment context (r.24.2)) is not as clear as it might be. His lordship explained (para.39) that where the defendant's witnesses clearly have material evidence to give on the critical issue in the action the test whether the claimant has "a real prospect of success" may be re-formulated as "have the claimants advanced a prima facie case to answer, a scintilla of evidence in support of the inference for which they contend, sufficient to call for an explanation from the defendant?" His lordship added that the fact that the claimant's case may be a weak case and unlikely to succeed unless assisted, rather than contradicted, by defendant's evidence, or by adverse inferences to be drawn from the defendant's not calling any evidence, would not allow it to be dismissed on a no case submission.

For observations on the similarities between a submission of no case to answer and an application made in the course of trial to strike out a claim under r 3.4, see *National Westminster Bank plc. v. Rabobank Nederland* [2006] EWHC 2959 (Comm); November 14, 2006, unrep. (Colman J.).

The procedure reflects the fact that a trial is an adversarial dispute resolution process in which "he who alleges must prove"; indeed the procedure has no logical place in civil procedure except on that basis. The traditional justification for the existence of the procedure is that it can have the advantage of saving the litigants (both claimant and defendant) expense, time and trouble, to which nowadays might be added the advantage of husbanding court resources. (These are all matters now reflected in the overriding objective stated in r.1.1 but the court is not obliged by r.1.2 to give effect to r.1.1 in this context because the CPR is silent on the procedure and in dealing with a submission of no case to answer the court is not exercising any power given to it under the CPR or interpreting any rule).

As a condition to listening to a submission of no case to answer a judge is required to put the defendant to his election whether or not to call evidence. The general, rule is that the judge should not permit a defendant to make such a submission unless he elects to rely on the submission alone and, whatever the outcome of the submission, he will call no evidence of his own. This general rule may be traced to *Alexander v Rayson* [1936] 1 K.B. 169, CA. It has to be said that, both before and after the coming into effect of the CPR, judicial opinions on the application of the general rule and exceptions to it have not always been in accord, but it is doubtful whether the practical effects of these differences have been significant. It should be noted that, where a defendant making a submission of no case is put to his election and in answer elects to call no evidence the issue for the judge is not whether there was any real or reasonable prospect that the claimant's case might be made out or any case fit to go before a jury or judge of fact. Rather, it is the straightforward issue, arising in any trial after all the evidence has been called, whether or not the claimant has established his case by the evidence called on the balance of probabilities (*Miller v Cawley* [2002] EWCA Civ 1100; July 30, 2002, unrep., CA, at para.11 per Mance L.J.). It is this consideration that lead Simon Brown L.J. to say in *Benham Ltd v Kythira Investments Ltd* (*op cit.*, para.23) that it is meaningless to refer to a submission of no case to answer except on the basis that the defendant has not been put to his election, that is to say, except in those cases where the general rule is suspended.

In *Boyce v Wyatt Engineering* [2001] EWCA Civ 692; *The Times*, June 14, 2001, CA, the Court of Appeal said that, despite the objects of CPR, r.3.4 (power to strike out a statement of case) and r.24.2 (summary judgment) there are very good reasons for the general rule and that the jurisdiction to suspend it should be exercised with considerable caution (see also *Lloyd v John Lewis Partnership* [2001] EWCA Civ 1529; October 9, 2001, unrep., CA). In *Benham Ltd v Kythira Investments Ltd, op cit.*, the point was put more forcefully by the Court of Appeal when it stated that rarely, if ever, should a judge trying a civil action without a jury entertain a defendant's submission of no case to answer without requiring the defendant to elect not to call evidence. If a defendant is not put to his election there is a risk that, if the claim is dismissed and there follows a successful appeal, a re-trial could result leading to greater delay and more expense. On the other hand, in *Bentley v Jones Harris & Co, op cit.*, Latham L.J., whilst also referring to the desirability of reducing delay and saving expense, said (*obiter*) at para.[75]: "If a judge concludes at the end of a claimant's evidence, whether on the application of the defendant or of his own motion, that the claimant has no real prospect of success or, in other words, is bound to fail, on his assessment of the evidence before him at that stage, he is in my view entitled to give judgment for the defendant, in the same way as if there had been an application at an earlier stage in the proceedings for summary judgment under CPR, r.24.2".

As Mance L.J. explained in the Boyce case (at para.[4]), where a defendant is put to his election in a case tried by a judge sitting alone, that is the end of the matter as regards evidence. The judge will not hear any further evidence which might give cause to reconsider findings made on the basis of the claimant's case alone. The case either falls or succeeds, even on appeal. But where no such election is called for, the judge is required to make up his mind as to facts on the basis of one side's case, and then, if he is against the defendant, to hear further evidence and to retain and apply an open mind in relation to all the facts at the end of the trial. That is an inherently difficult exercise.

One of the more obvious cases for the exercise of the jurisdiction to suspend the general rule is the one in which the judge is entitled to conclude that nothing in the defendant's evidence could affect the view he had taken adverse to the claimant's case. This was recognised by the Court of Appeal in the *Boyce v Wyatt Engineering, op cit.*, and was illustrated by the facts in *Bentley v Jones Harris & Co, op cit.*, and *Karia v I.C.S.(Management) Services Ltd* [2001] EWCA Civ 1025; June 21, 2001, unrep., CA.

If guidance is sought on the jurisdiction to suspend the general rule it is perhaps difficult to improve upon the dictum of Branson J. in *Muller and Co v Ebbw Vale Steel Iron and Coal Co Ltd* [1936] 2 All E.R. 1363. His lordship said (at p.1365) it is for the judge to decide "whether, in the particular case before him, and having regard to all the circumstances of it, it is likely to save the litigants before him expense and time and trouble to deal with the case by way of ruling upon the submission without putting any terms upon counsel upon either side, or whether it is better to say: 'In this case I think it would be desirable that before I rule I should hear the whole of the evidence'."

It may be noted that the general rule was established at a time in which the powers of the court to determine a case at an early stage were not as great as they became, both before and after the CPR came into effect, and when the pre-trial exchange of witness statements was not required. Perhaps it is inevitable that it will be argued that the powers that a court has to determine a case at an early stage should be carried over into the trial and should influence the exercise of the jurisdiction to give judgment on a submission of no case to answer. However, it is submitted that trial and pre-trial procedures should not be confused. Trial procedures (in which the submission of no case procedure has its place) and pre-trial procedures (in which striking out and summary judgment procedures have their place, and where evidence is not tested) have different functions and objectives. Under the CPR case management regime, a case that is tried is a case that the court has decided should be tried and is a case in which pre-trial procedures are exhausted having played their role. At trial, what the court may or may not have done pre-trial is irrelevant. It is submitted that the submission of no case to answer procedure should be allowed to stand on its own feet.

Post-CPR first instance decisions on the operation of the general rule decided before the decision of the Court of Appeal in *Boyce v Wyatt Engineering, op cit.*, are: *Mullan v Birmingham City Council, The Times* July 29, 1999; *Worsley v Tambrands Ltd* December 3, 1999, unrep.; *Landare Investments Ltd v Welsh Development Agency,* November 25, 1999, unrep.

In *Miller v Cawley* [2002] EWCA Civ 1100; July 30, 2002, CA, the Court of Appeal noted that it has been suggested that it is open to a judge, at the close of a claimant's case, and without requiring any election by the defendant to call no evidence, to determine whether or not the claimant has on his own evidence made out his case on a balance of probabilities. Mance L.J. doubted (at para.9) whether this is right, not only for the reasons given in the well-known case of *Alexander v Rayson* [1936] 1 K.B. 169, CA, but also for those given in *Royal Brompton Hospital NHS Trust v Hammond (No.5)* [2001] EWCA Civ 550, unrep., CA.

In defamation cases, in the course of trial by judge and jury issues of law for determination by the judge may arise and result in particular issues being withdrawn from the jury. The determination of those issues may turn on disputed questions of fact. It is not for the judge to evaluate the evidence and to reach his own conclusions on those disputed questions.But it is open to the judge, on ruling on the issue of law, and determining whether in the light of that ruling, particular issues should be withdrawn from the jury, "to come to the conclusion that the evidence on the disputed questions of fact, taken at its highest, is such that a jury properly directed could not properly reach a necessary factual decision" (*Alexander v Arts Council for Wales* [2001] EWCA Civ 514; [2001] 1 W.L.R. 1840, CA; *Spencer v Sillitoe* [2002] EWCA Civ 1579; October 22, 2002, unrep., CA). In a given defamation case, the judge's ruling on a question of law in the light of the evidence taken at its highest may not simply result in a particular issue being withdrawn from the jury, but it may have the inevitable result of judgment being given in favour of one party or the other. In other words, it may have the same effect as a successful submission of no case to answer.If the judge was required to rule on the issue of law after the evidence for the claimant had been heard, but before the evidence for the defence had been received, the analogy with the submission of no case to answer procedure is complete.

Similar fact evidence

32.1.7 The power "to exclude evidence that would otherwise be admissible" (r.32.1(2)) may be seen as one of several powers given to the courts under the CPR that have the effect of confining civil proceedings within practicable limits. Historically speaking, one of the grounds upon which the rule that similar fact evidence is generally inadmissible has been justified is that it has the merit of preventing the court from being lead off into the investigation of collateral issues and away from the principal issues to be determined with consequent aggravation of costs and delays.

The question of the extent to which, by way of exception, similar fact evidence may be admitted in civil trials has been considered in numerous cases. Many of the principal authorities were decided when the modern "cards on the table" approach to civil litigation was still in its infancy and before the case management system introduced by the CPR came into effect. A significant number of the cases in which questions as to the circumstances in which similar fact evidence should be admitted have been cases of claims made against the police tried by judge and jury.

The leading case is *O'Brien v Chief Constable of South Wales Police* [2005] UKHL 26; [2005] 2 A.C. 534, HL, where the House of Lords said (1) in civil proceedings (a) the test for admissibility of similar fact evidence is whether the evidence is relevant, as being potentially probative of an issue in the case, and (b) there is no need to insist on the additional requirements for admissibility of such evidence that apply to criminal cases; however (2) a judge managing a civil case should keep well I mind (a) the policy considerations found in the Criminal Justice Act 2003 ss.101 to 106, and (b) the need to deal with the case in a way which was proportionate to what was involved, in a manner which was expeditious and fair. In dismissing the defendant's appeal in this case, the House of Lords adopted reasoning that was similar to, but which differed in some respects from, that used by the Court of Appeal; see [2003] EWCA Civ 1085; [2004] C.P. Rep. 5, CA. (Between them the speech of Lord Phillips M.R. in the House of Lords and the judgment of Brooke L.J. in the Court of Appeal contain an exhaustive review of the authorities on similar fact evidence in civil cases.) Following the *O'Brien* case, in *J.P. Morgan Chase Bank v Springwell Navigation Corporation* [2005] EWCA Civ 1602, December 20, 2005, unrep., CA, the Court of Appeal explained that there is a two-stage test. First it has to be asked: is the proposed evidence potentially probative of one or more issues in the current litigation? If it is, it is legally admissible. Then it has to be asked, secondly: are there good grounds why a court should decline to admit it in the exercise of its case management powers?

Matters relevant to this exercise of discretion include the need to weigh the potential probative value of evidence against its potential for causing unfair prejudice, and the need to consider the burden which its admission would lay on the resisting party. In addition, the court should consider the risk that the admission of similar fact evidence will distort the trial and distract the attention of the decision-maker (whether jury or judge alone) by expecting him to focus attention on, and to pursue thoroughly, issues collateral to the issue to be decided. Where this occurs, the burdens placed, not only on the decision-maker, but also on the parties and on the courts, with attendant increases in costs and delays, can be significant. In the *O'Brien* case, Lord Phillips M.R. said, when considering whether to permit evidence, or permit cross-examination, on matters that are collateral to the central issues "the judge will have regard to the need for proportionality and expedition" (*op. cit.*, para.56). His lordship endorsed earlier authority stating that, in order to entitle a party to give or elicit such evidence he must satisfy the court (1) that the collateral fact which he proposes to prove will, when established, be capable of affording a reasonable presumption or inference as to the matter in dispute, and (2) will not raise a difficult or doubtful controversy of precisely the same kind as that which the court must determine (*ibid.*, para.45).

Evidence of witnesses—general rule

32.2—(1) The general rule is that any fact which needs to be proved by the evidence of witnesses is to be proved— **32.2**

(a) at trial, by their oral evidence given in public; and

(b) at any other hearing, by their evidence in writing.

(2) This is subject—

(a) to any provision to the contrary contained in these Rules or elsewhere; or

(b) to any order of the court.

Proof by oral evidence at trial

32.2.1 Rule 32.2 draws two broad distinctions; one between a hearing in the form of a "trial" and "any other hearing", and the other between "oral evidence" and "evidence in writing" and states the very broad general rule that evidence at a trial should be oral evidence and evidence at any other hearing should be evidence in writing. Another distinction, which is now less clear than it once was, is worth noting. Historically speaking, it was possible to draw quite a clear distinction between documents containing evidence in writing (e.g. affidavits, answers to interrogatories), on the one hand, and formal procedural documents (e.g. forms of originating process, pleadings) on the other. However, in modern times the distinction has become blurred by procedural reforms encouraging or requiring the inclusion of written evidence in formal procedural documents and this trend has been carried forward by various CPR provisions, in particular, those permitting statements of case verified by a statement of truth to be used as evidence.

Traditionally, English law has placed greatest weight on evidence given by witnesses in open court on oath or affirmation under examination by the parties. Rule 32.2(1)(a) follows the former RSC O.38, r.1 and former CCR O.20, r.4 and restates the general principle in relation to the most important part of the civil process, the trial. The rule applies only to evidence as to matters of fact. Before the CPR came into effect, in certain proceedings specially provided for by rules of court, the general rule was reversed and trial evidence was not given by the oral evidence of witnesses but by their written evidence in the form of affidavit (e.g. in matters coming before the Chancery Division on originating summons or motion), with provision for the cross-examination of deponents if need be. Under the CPR, this remains the case. In claims where the Pt 8 procedure is followed, evidence at trial will normally be in the form of a witness statement or affidavit (Practice Direction (Alternative Procedure for Claims), para.5.2 (see para.8PD.5 above)).

In the former rules, a distinction was drawn between evidence given by witnesses *viva voce* and by other means, principally by affidavit (but also by witness statements). In r.32.2, the distinction drawn is between oral evidence and "evidence in writing". The rule that evidence at trial should be given *viva voce* is a "general rule". The court has power to order otherwise (as it did heretofore, see, e.g. RSC O.38, r.2(1) and CCR O.20, r.6). (Former RSC O.38, r.1 was confined to actions commenced by writ and did not apply to proceedings coming before the court on originating summons or motion, see RSC O.8, r.2(3)).

The general rule that, at trial, facts are to be proved by oral evidence is subject to any provision to the contrary contained in the CPR or elsewhere (r.32.2(2)(a)). Rule 32.5 states that if a party wishes to rely at trial on the statement of a witness the general rules are that he must (1) call the witness to give oral evidence, or (2) put in the statement as hearsay evidence, and, in the former event, the witness statement shall stand as evidence in chief. Although the general rule is that at trial facts should be proved by the oral evidence of witnesses, in many ways and in various contexts, CPR provisions encourage the giving of evidence in writing (through statements of case and witness statements) both at trial hearings and at other hearings where claims may be disposed of upon proof of particular facts (see r.32.5 and r.32.6).

Where written evidence may be, or should be, relied on at a hearing, whether a trial or any other hearing, in specific contexts CPR provisions often stipulate particular requirements which must be satisfied. For example, in claims proceeding under the Pt 8 alternative procedure for claims, the requirements as to filing and service of witness statements set out in r.8.5 must be satisfied before the evidence may be relied on at a hearing of the claim, and at hearings in judicial review proceedings regard must be had to the conditions flowing from r.54.16(2).

For the practice of permitting a party to supplement a pleaded case by a witness statement (as an alterative to requiring the party to provide further information under Pt 18), see *McPhilemy v Times Newspapers* [1999] 3 All E.R. 775, CA, and *Delos Ltd v C.A.E. Electronics Ltd*, February 21, 2001, unrep. (Eady J.).

A statement of case may be used as evidence in an interim application provided it is verified by a statement of truth. For form of statement of truth in this context, see *Practice Direction (Written Evidence)*, para.26.2 (see para.32PD.26 below).

It is expressly provided that, where the Pt 8 procedure is used (Alternative procedure for claims), the court may require or permit a party to give oral evidence at the hearing of the claim, and may give directions requiring the attendance for cross-examination of a witness who has given written evidence (r.8.6(2) & (3)). Further, at the hearing of such a claim, no written evidence may be relied on unless (a) it has been served in accordance with rule 8.5, or (b) the court gives permission (r.8.6(1)).

In certain circumstances (e.g. where it is necessary in the interests of justice), trials and other hearings may be heard (at least in part), not in public, but in private (see r.39.2). Conceivably, the nature of the evidence to be given may justify a court's decision to exercise its discretion to sit in private. Where a court rules that public interest immunity attaches to particular evidence, that evidence is excluded as a matter of law, and the court has no discretion (derived from r.32.1 or any other source) to admit it on terms that it be heard in private (*Powell v Chief Constable of North Wales*, *The Times*, February 11, 2000, CA).

As to the examination of a witness giving oral evidence by video conferencing link, see paras 19 to 21 of Annex 3 (Video Conferencing Guidance) to Practice Direction (Written Evidence) (para.32PD.31 below) and note r.32.3.

Unless it orders otherwise, an appeal court will not receive oral evidence (r.52.11(2)(a)).

Oral evidence in judicial review proceedings

Former RSC O.53 (Applications for Judicial Review) incorporated by reference former RSC O.38, r.2(3), thereby providing for the cross-examination of witnesses in judicial review proceedings where permitted by the court. Order 53 was superseded by CPR Pt 54 but no such express provision is made therein. Judicial review proceedings, though subject to the detailed provisions of Pt 54, are brought under the Pt 8 alternative procedure for claims and are therefore subject to r.8.6 (Evidence-general), except insofar as that rule is disapplied in such proceedings by r.54.16(1). Since the amendment of r.54.16(1) by the Civil Procedure (Amendment) Rules 2002 (SI 2002/2058), r.21) it has been clear, if it was not so before (see *R. (G) v Ealing LBC (No.2)* [2002] EWHC 250 (Admin) (Munby J.)), that in judicial review proceedings the court may require or permit a party to give oral evidence at the hearing (r.8.6(2)). The court may give directions requiring the attendance for cross-examination of a witness who has given written evidence (r.8.6(3)). See further commentary following r.54.16 below. As to cross-examination of witnesses in judicial review proceedings, see *R. (Wilkinson) v Broadmoor Special Hospital* [2002] EWCA Civ 1545; [2002] 1 W.L.R. 419, CA; *R. (N) v M* [2002] EWCA Civ 1789; [2003] 1 W.L.R. 562, CA, and note para.54.16.2 below. **32.2.2**

Proof by evidence in writing at any other hearing

Rule 32(1)(b) states that, as a general rule, any fact which needs to be proved by the evidence of witnesses at a hearing other than the trial is to be proved by their evidence in writing. Former rules permitting evidence by affidavit were not confined to evidence tending to prove facts (e.g. RSC O.38, r.2 and CCR O.20, rr.5 and 6). Rule 32(1)(b) should be read with r.32.6 which states, as a further general rule, that evidence at "hearings other than the trial" is to be by witness statement (but may be given by affidavit, see r.32.15(1) and (2), and, in some circumstances, reliance may be placed on a statement of case or notice of application). (Rule 32.6 is not confined to evidence as to facts.) **32.2.3**

The general rules stated in paras (a) and (b) of r.32.2 are subject to "any order of the court" (see r.32.1(1)). This restates in rather broader terms previous court rules (e.g. RSC O.38, r.3 and CCR O.20, r.6). The general rules are also subject "to any provision to the contrary contained in these Rules or elsewhere". Previous court rules were made subject to special rules and to provisions made in or under other enactments.

Examples of specific powers in the hands of the court to order otherwise are found in r.57.10(2) (trial on written evidence of undefended probate claim), Practice Direction (Miscellaneous Provisions Relating to Hearings) para.1.15 (hearing of possession claim in private) (see para.39PD.1).

Where the court in certain circumstances has given a judgment or made an order requiring an amount of money, to be decided by the court, to be paid by one party to another, it may list the claim for a "disposal hearing". Such a hearing is not a trial and, therefore, in accordance with r.32.2(1)(b), any fact which needs to be proved by the evidence of a witness is to be proved by their evidence in writing, subject to any provision to the contrary found elsewhere. It may be noted that Practice Direction (Case Management-Preliminary Stage: Allocation and Re-allocation), para.12.4 states that the court may direct that r.32.6 should not apply at a disposal hearing whilst warning that the court will not normally hear oral evidence at such a hearing.

In a variety of circumstances (far too many to itemise), particular rules and practice directions stipulate that certain types of application must be accompanied by written evidence. Further, such provisions (particularly where they support statutory schemes) may stipulate (sometimes in considerable detail) matters to which the written evidence should be directed (e.g. CPR, r.54.30 (evidence for application to extend time limit), r.65.25 (evidence for anti-social behaviour orders)). When making any application, practitioners must take care to consult the relevant rules and practice directions in order to ensure that the written evidence complies in these respects.

In possession proceedings under Pt 55, the court will fix a date for a hearing when it issues the claim form (r.55.5(1)), and in certain circumstances the court may decide the claim at that hearing on the basis of facts proved by evidence in writing (r.55.8(3)).

For provisions as to written evidence in committal applications, see Practice Direction (Committal Applications), paras 3.1 to 3.4 (see 52PD.3), and for Interim Injunctions, see Practice Direction (Interim Injunctions), paras 3.1 to 3.4 (see 25PD.3).

For further information as to form of written evidence (affidavits or witness summaries), see (in addition to notes following rr.32.4 and 32.8 below), Practice Direction (Written Evidence) (see para.32PD.1 below).

Documents in agreed bundles as evidence of their contents

32.2.4 The general rule is that, where a bundle of documents for use at any hearing has been agreed, the documents contained therein shall be admissible at that hearing as evidence of their contents (see Practice Direction (Written Evidence), paras 27.1 and 27.2). The court may give directions requiring the parties to use their best endeavours to agree a bundle of documents. See further, the relevant passages in Court Guides.

Late application to rely on evidence of proposed witness

32.2.5 In the usual case, case management directions will stipulate what evidence is to be called (r.32.1) and the parties by exchange of witness statements (r.32.4) will reveal which witnesses (both expert and lay) they propose to call and the nature of their evidence. The court may entertain subsequent applications for permission to call further witnesses, either during the pre-trial stage or even in the course of trial. The principle that an appeal court is reluctant to interfere with the rulings of a trial judge is likely to be engaged where there is an appeal against a judge's exercise of discretion to grant or refuse a party's application made in the course of trial for permission to call further witnesses (see e.g. *British Sugar Plc v Cegelec Ltd* [2004] EWCA Civ 1450, CA, October 7, 2004, unrep. (judge's refusal to grant defendant's application upheld where further witness's evidence not directed at new theory put forward by claimants or based on facts emerging at last moment).

In *Choudhury v Ahmed* [2005] EWCA Civ, July 27, 2005, unrep., CA, a witness statement made by one of several claimants (and in effect made on behalf of all of them) was exchanged and that claimant gave evidence at trial. After the evidence for claimants and the defendant had been given, counsel for the claimants applied for permission to call another of the claimants to testify. The judge refused the application. The Court of Appeal upheld his ruling, partly on the ground that, at the outset, the claimants had made a tactical decision not to call the further witness and had had, during the presentation of their case, ample time to reconsider that decision in the light of the way in which the case was developing. In the circumstances, the ruling was a proper exercise of discretion.

Evidence by video link or other means

32.3 **32.3 The court may allow a witness to give evidence through a video link or by other means.**

Effect of rule

32.3.1 This rule is consistent with r.1.4(2)(k) which states that, in furthering the overriding objective stated in r.1.1, the court may make use of appropriate technology. The use of video links was approved under earlier rules. The court may allow a witness to give evidence either through a video link "or by other means"; presumably this means other forms of communications technology (instances have arisen of evidence being given from abroad by satellite TV link). Guidance on the use of video conferencing (VCF) in the civil courts is set out in Annex 3 to Practice Direction (Written Evidence) (see para.32PD.31 below). (Annex 3 was added to the practice direction by HMSO CPR Update 27, February 2002.) The guidance is also printed as Appendix 14 to the Admiralty and Commercial Courts Guide (see Vol.2, para.2A–172).

See further Chancery Guide, Ch.14, para.14.14 (see Vol.2, para.1A–136), Admiralty and Commercial Courts Guide, Sect.H3 (see Vol.2, para.2A–105), Technology and Construction Court Guide (2nd October 2005), Sect.4, para.4.6 (see Vol.2, para.2C–63).

Where an oral hearing is held on an application for a European order for payment, or on an application under art.8 of the ESCP Regulation, it may take place by video conference; Practice Direction—European Order for Payment and European Small Claims Procedures paras 6.2 and 17.2 (see para.78PD.6 and 78PD.17 below).

In the VCF Guidance it is noted that, although the giving of evidence by witnesses by VCF can yield considerable savings in time and costs, inevitably it is not as ideal as having the witnesses physically present in court. Therefore, the convenience of VCF "should not be allowed to dictate its use". Paragraph 2 of the Guidance states:

> "A judgment must be made in every case in which the use of VCF is being considered not only as to whether it will achieve an overall cost saving but also as to whether its use will be likely to be beneficial to the efficient, fair and economic disposal of the litigation. In particular, it needs to be recognised that the degree of control a court can exercise over a witness at the remote site is or may be more limited than it can exercise over a witness physically before it" (see para.32PD.33 below).

In *Rowland v Bock* [2002] EWHC 692 (QB); [2002] 4 All E.R. 370 (Newman J.), a case decided at first instance before the VCF Guidance was published, it was said that the discretion in r.32.3 is in terms unfettered, and is to be exercised in accordance with the considerations of cost, time and convenience relevant to the overriding objective and the need to ensure, so far as is practicable, that the parties are on an equal footing (see rr.1.1 and 1.4). Its exercise is not limited to circumstances in which witnesses, for reasons of pressing need or illness, cannot attend; but a witness's refusal to attend which could be characterised as an abuse, or contemptuous, or an attempt to obtain a collateral advantage, would weigh against an applicant (*ibid.*). In *Polanski v Condé Nast Publications Ltd* [2005] UKHL 10, [2005] 1 W.L.R. 637, HL, the claimant was resident in France and the judge made a VCF order to enable him to give his trial evidence by video link from that country. The claimant's sole reason for applying for the order was that he was not prepared to come to England for fear that he would be arrested and extradited to the USA for sentencing for an offence to which he had pleaded guilty in 1977. The Court of Appeal allowed the defendant's appeal ([2003] EWCA Civ 1573, [2004] 1 W.L.R. 387, CA), but the House of Lords allowed the claimant's further appeal. The House said (1) the administration of justice is not brought into disrepute where a fugitive from justice (a) brings a claim in England, and (b) is allowed the procedural facility of a VCF order, (2) as a general rule, the unwillingness of a such a claimant to come to England is a valid, and could be a sufficient, reason for making a VCF order, (3) the judge was entitled and right to exercise his discretion as he did and his order should be restored. See also, *Bank of Credit and Commerce International S.A. v Rahim* November 11, 2005, unrep. (Lewison J.) (witness permitted to give oral evidence via video link from sub-continent, because his ill health and fear of possible arrest in UK, as well as inconvenience and expense of bringing him from abroad, outweighed disbenefits that defendant would suffer).

The question whether a witness may be permitted to give evidence from a foreign country by a video link may be affected by the law of that country. Instances have arisen in which a party, having obtained the permission of the English court under r.32.3 for evidence to be given by these means by a witness situated in a foreign country, has been prevented from doing so by the law of that country. This problem is referred to in para.4 of Annex 3.

Requirement to serve witness statements for use at trial

32.4—(1) A witness statement is a written statement signed by a person which contains the evidence which that person would be allowed to give orally. 32.4

(2) The court will order a party to serve on the other parties any witness statement of the oral evidence which the party serving the

statement intends to rely on in relation to any issues of fact to be decided at the trial.

(3) The court may give directions as to—

(a) the order in which witness statements are to be served; and

(b) whether or not the witness statements are to be filed.

Effect of rule

32.4.1 This rule builds on the general power of the court to give directions controlling evidence stated in r.32.1. The statutory basis for rules as to service of non-expert witness statements is the Courts and Legal Services Act 1990 s.5. (See Vol.2, para.9B–104).

For requirement to serve written evidence before hearing in proceedings brought under the Pt 8 procedure (Alternative procedure for claims), see r.8.6; and for such requirement in judicial review proceedings, see r.54.16.

Formerly, rules of court as to the service before trial (by one party on another) of the "written statements of oral evidence which the party intends to adduce on any issues of facts to be decided at the trial" were found in RSC O.38, r.2A (Exchange of witness statements) and in CCR O.20, r.12A.

Rule 32.4 requires the court (as did its predecessors) to direct any party at any stage of the proceedings to serve witness statements.

Evidence of experts

32.4.2 See Pt 35 (Experts and Assessors).

Witness "statements" and witness "summaries"

32.4.3 The CPR draw a clearer distinction than heretofore between witness "statements" and witness "summaries" (see rr.32.8 and 32.9). This is a response to perceived weaknesses in the former exchange of witness statements procedure explained in the Interim Report, p.176 *et seq.* (see also Final Report, pp.128 *et seq.*). In particular, witness statements had ceased to be an authentic account of the evidence which the witness could give and had become "an elaborate, costly branch of legal drafting" (Final Report, p.129). This was partly because of practitioners' fears that judges would not permit the witness to give any oral evidence at the trial which was not contained in the witness statement (*King v Telegraph Group Ltd* [2004] EWCA Civ 613; [2005] 1 W.L.R. 2282, CA, at para.69 per Brooke L.J.).

A witness "statement" is, in effect, a full proof of evidence. However, the court may order that initially a witness statement should be limited to certain issues (see r.32.1). It could be said, therefore, that a distinction can be drawn between "full" and "limited" witness statements.

A witness "summary", on the other hand, merely identifies the witness and indicates the issues with which his evidence will deal; see r.32.9(3) below. (Under the former RSC O.38, r.2A(5) and CCR O.20, r.12A(5) a witness summary could be exchanged instead of a witness statement.) In the Interim Report it was recommended (p.43) that in cases proceeding on the fast track oral evidence of witnesses as to fact would be limited, supplemented as necessary by written submissions and written evidence. It was said that, for this purpose, witness summaries would suffice (see also p.178). However, in the Final Report (p.38) it was said that the evidence of witnesses in fast track cases should be handled, not by way of witness summaries, but by way of "brief" witness statements.

Form of witness statement

32.4.4 Witness statements are to be in the form stipulated by r.32.8. They must be signed (r.32.4(1)) and verified by a "statement of truth" (r.22.1(1)); see further notes following r.32.8.

For form of witness summaries, see r.32.9. See further, Final Report, p.130.

Preparation and content of witness statements

32.4.5 A witness statement (or an affidavit) should be in the witness's own words and should be restricted to matters to which the witness himself could readily speak if cross-examined on it (*Alex Lawrie Factors Ltd v Morgan*, *The Times*, August 18, 1999;

CA). In the Final Report, it was said (at p.130) that witness statements should, so far as possible, be in the witness's own words, should not discuss legal propositions, and should not comment on documents. In the Chancery Guide it is said that the guideline that a witness statement should be in the witness's own words "applies unless the perception or recollection of the witness of the events in question is not in issue" (*ibid.* App.9, para.1, see Vol.2, para.1A–233). In the Queen's Bench Guide it is said that the issues covered by a witness statement should consist only of the issues on which the party serving the witness statement wishes that witness to give evidence in-chief, and should not include commentary on the trial bundle or other matters which may arise during trial (*ibid.* para.7.10.4, see Vol.2, para.1B–50). Most of these points are summarised in Practice Direction (Written Evidence) para.18.1 where it is stated that a witness statement must, if practicable, be in intended witness' own words and should be expressed in the first person. The statement must indicate (1) which of the statements in it are made from the witness' own knowledge and which are matters of information or belief, and (2) the source of any matters of information or belief (see para.32PD.18 below).

Whilst it can sometimes be the case that witness statements are drafted by solicitors, they will always endeavour to speak to the witnesses first and put down their evidence in their own words (*Assi v Dina Foods Limited* [2005] EWHC 1099 (QB), May 20, 2005, unrep. (Judge Coulson Q.C.) (whether claimant's role in preparation of co-claimant's witness statement an abuse of process)).

It is improper to put pressure of any kind on a witness to give anything other than his own account of the matters with which his witness statement deals. It is also improper to serve a witness statement which is know to be false or which it is known the maker does not in all respects actually believe to be true (see further, Admiralty and Commercial Courts Guide, Sect.H, para.H1.2 (see Vol.2, para.2A–108), Chancery Guide, Appx.9, para.1 (see Vol.2, para.1A–233), Queen's Bench Guide, para.7.10.4 (see Vol.2 para.1B–50)).

Rule 32.4(1) provides that a witness statement should contain admissible evidence only. Where a party receiving a witness statement contends that it contains inadmissible evidence (e.g. material covered by legal privilege) he may apply to the court for an order that it be re-served with the offending evidence excised (e.g. as in *Barnetson v. Framlington Group Ltd* [2007] EWCA Civ 502; [2007] 1 W.L.R. 2443, CA; [2007] 3 All E.R. 1054, CA.). A lay witness who uses his own words is likely to stray beyond what is admissible into inadmissible evidence (e.g. from fact to opinion) and may lapse into argument. It is advisable that, when being invited to use their own words, such witnesses should be advised as to what the proper scope of a witness statement is (*Rock (Nominees) Ltd v RCO Holdings Plc* [2003] EWHC 80 (Ch); January 20, 2003, unrep., Hart J. (refusing application to order withdrawal of witness statement containing inadmissible material)).

The following points should be noted: (1) it is important that the court should be able to assume that witness statements were properly prepared, (2) it cannot be too strongly emphasised that a witness statement should be in the words which the witness wanted to use and not the words which the person taking the statement would like him to use, (3) where a witness statement is prepared by a legal representative the statement must, so far as practicable, be in the witness's own words, (4) normally, witness statements should be taken by solicitors where they are instructed, (5) where this is not practicable, solicitors are under a duty to ensure that statements are taken by persons who can be relied upon to exercise the same standards as should apply if the statements were taken by the solicitors themselves (*Aquarius Financial Enterprises Inc v Lloyd's Underwriters (The Delphine)* [2001] 2 Lloyd's Rep. 542 (Toulson J.)). See further para.32.8.1 below.

Various rules and practice directions stipulate particular requirements as to the form and content of witness statements for certain applications. One example is r.55.22 (form of defendant's witness statement on application for interim possession order).

In civil proceedings by or against the Crown, and other civil proceedings to which the Crown is a party, where by reason of a rule, practice direction or court order the Crown is permitted or required to make a witness statement, that function shall be performed by an appropriate officer acting on behalf of the Crown (CPR, r.66.3). The court may if necessary nominate an appropriate officer.

It is not uncommon for the evidence of parties to applications to be in the form of affidavits sworn by their representative solicitors. Where affidavit evidence is required urgently the provision of evidence in his way may be necessary for practical reasons. Further, where the evidence given by affidavit takes the form of the exhibiting of documents and comment on them, or where the facts are uncontentious, generally there is no objection to a solicitor's affidavit. However, on an application where affidavit evidence is necessary (e.g. on an application for the grant, continuation or discharge of a freezing injunction) the facts are contentious, and evidence is to be given on matters that are within the personal knowledge of a party to the proceedings, the correct practice is for the affidavit to be sworn by the party personally and not by his solicitor (*Bracken Partners Ltd v Gutteridge*, December 17, 2001, unrep. (Stanley Burton J.)). The court may take into account the unexplained reluctance of a party to swear an affidavit (*ibid.*).

For further guidance as to form and content of witness statements, see Chancery Guide, para.8.10 and Appx. 9 (see Vol.2, paras 1A–81 and 1A–233), Admiralty and Commercial Courts Guide, paras F7 and H1 (see Vol.2, paras 2A–91 and 2A–103) and Queen's Bench Guide, para.7.10 (see Vol.2, para.1B–50). See also Technology and Construction Court Guide (2nd October 2005), Sect.12, para.12.1 (see Vol.2 para.2C–111).

As to court's power to strike out passages in witness statement served by a party, see para.32.4.20 below.

Hearsay evidence in witness statements

32.4.6 With the coming into effect of the Civil Evidence Act 1995, hearsay evidence became generally admissible in civil proceedings, thus relieving lawyers of the task of editing witness statements to remove hearsay. Under s.2(1) of the 1995 Act, a party proposing to adduce hearsay evidence in civil proceedings is obliged to give notice of his intention to do so in accordance with the rules of court found in Pt 33. Where the hearsay evidence is to be given by a witness called to give oral evidence, notice is given by serving the witness's witness statement as directed by the court. Where the intention is not to call the witness and the evidence is contained in a witness statement, again notice is given by serving the witness statement as directed (r.33.2). See further para.32.8.2 below.

Court's directions

32.4.7 When a case is allocated to the fast track the court will give directions under r.28.3 and it is specifically provided in the rules that the matters dealt with will include the service of witness statements (r.28.3(1)(b)); see Appendix to Practice Direction (The Fast Track) (see 28PD.9). When a case is allocated to the multi-track the court will give directions for the management of the case under r.29.2(1) and it is obvious that this would include directions as to witness statements (see also r.32.4(2)); see Practice Direction (The Multi-track), para.4.7(1)(d) (see 29PD.4). It is the intention that, normally, in fast track cases directions will be confined to the service of witness summaries, at least in the first instance.

The court may direct that parties should exchange witness statements simultaneously or sequentially; *cf.* RSC O.38, r.2A(4)(c) and CCR O.20, r.12A(4)(c).

Circumstances in which service of witness statements ordered

32.4.8 In terms, r.32.4 does not stipulate the circumstances in which, and the time at which, the court should order the service of witness statements. It simply says the court should so order. The power is not limited to particular proceedings or to the evidence of the witnesses of particular parties within proceedings. Orders to serve witness statements will be given in accordance with the court's case management powers as stated elsewhere in the CPR and in accordance with relevant Practice Directions. (The pre-action protocols should have the effect of encouraging the exchange of certain witness statements before proceedings are started.)

The powers given by this rule should be exercised in a manner which furthers the overriding objective (r.1.1) including the objective of ensuring that cases are dealt with "expeditiously and fairly" (former RSC O.38, r.2A(1) imposed a similar requirement).

A party ordered to serve a witness statement may apply to serve a witness summary *instead (r.32.9(1))*.

Time limits

32.4.9 Rule 32.4 does not stipulate a period within which witness statements should be served. However, it is to be expected that time limits may be imposed by practice directions and orders made in individual cases (see too r.32.9(4) (Witness summaries to be served within period within which witness statement would have to be served)). A time limit imposed may be altered by the court in the exercise of its general discretion to extend or shorten time limits (see r.3.1(2)(a)). Where a party (C) serves his witness statements after the time limit has expired, and his opposing party (D) objects to this and puts C to the expense of applying to the court for an extension of time, D may be ordered to pay C's costs of the application where the court finds that it would be entirely inappropriate and disproportionate to refuse to admit the evidence (e.g. *I.N. Newman Ltd v Adlem* [2004] EWCA Civ 1492 November 11, 2004, unrep., CA (Jacob L.J.) (C not exchanging witness statements in time because they wanted disclosure of documents)).

Service of witness statement

The witness statement is to be served by the party on such other parties as the order may stipulate. A witness statement is a "document" within Pt 6 (Service of Documents) and the provisions in Section I of that Part will apply to such service except where a practice direction makes a different provision or the court orders otherwise. Where a witness chooses to give evidence by affidavit instead of a witness statement, the rules relating to service of a witness statement apply to the affidavit (r.32.15(3)). **32.4.10**

For rules as to filing and service of witness statements for use at hearing "other than at trial", see r.23.7(2)(3).

In a number of procedural contexts, special rules obtain as to the service of witness statements, e.g. r.24.5 (Evidence for the purposes of a summary judgment hearing).

Order in which witness statements are to be served

Former RSC O.38 r.2A(4)(c) and CCR O.20, r.12A(4)(c) stated that, where witness statements were to be served by more than one party, they were to be "exchanged simultaneously". However, the court could direct otherwise. Now it is stated in r.32.4(3)(a) that the court may give directions as to the order in which witness statements are to be served. In the past it was thought that sequential exchange of statements of lay witnesses should be ordered only in exceptional cases. (In *Rayment v Ministry of Defence*, *The Times*, July 6, 1998, a Master's order in a medical negligence case requiring that parties' expert's reports as to liability should be exchanged simultaneously but those as to quantum should be exchanged sequentially was upheld.) Under the system of case management now being introduced, circumstances in which sequential exchange is appropriate may arise with greater frequency. **32.4.11**

Filing of witness statements

The court may give directions as to whether or not the witness statements are to be filed. In a number of procedural contexts, special rules requiring the filing of witness statements apply, e.g. r.24.5 (Evidence for the purposes of a summary judgment hearing); see further Practice Direction (Written Evidence), para.23 (see para.32PD.23, below). **32.4.12**

Alteration of witness statement

As is explained in SCP 1999, Vol.1, para.38/2A/9, a witness statement was a "document" which could be amended under former RSC O.20, r.8(1). The former provision is not reproduced in the CPR. Nevertheless, presumably the court retains power to amend a witness statement in circumstances similar to those stated in former r.8(1). As to practice relating to alteration of witness statements, see Practice Direction (Written Evidence), para.22 (see para.32PD.22 below). **32.4.13**

Supplementary witness statements

Although there is no express provision to this effect, the court has power to direct that a further written statement of a witness be served supplementary to that already served. See further para.32.5.2 "Amplification of evidence" below. **32.4.14**

Costs for preparation of witness statements

The costs allowed for witness statements (and summaries) should reflect the fact that they are not intended to be elaborate documents (Interim Report, pp.179–180). This is reinforced by the rule that where an affidavit is used where a witness statement would suffice there may be a costs penalty (r.32.15(2)). The court should make it clear that it is not prepared to tolerate extravagance in the preparation of witness statements (Interim Report, *ibid*.). **32.4.15**

Consequences of failure to serve witness statement

32.4.16 See r.32.10.

Written evidence in claim under Pt 8 procedure

32.4.17 If the claimant is intending to use the Pt 8 procedure (Alternative procedure for claims), he must when filing his claim form also file any "written evidence" on which he intends to rely (r.8.5(1)) and the claimant's evidence must be served on the defendant with the claim form (r.8.5(2)). Thereafter, in the Pt 8 procedure r.8.5(3) to (6) deals with the filing and serving of written evidence by the defendant and, if appropriate, by the claimant in reply.

Defects in written statements

32.4.18 Where a written statement or an exhibit to a witness statement is defective, in the sense that it does not conform with the provisions of Pt 32 or the supplementary practice direction, the consequences referred to in Practice Direction (Written Evidence), paras 25.1 and 25.2, follow (see para.32PD.25 below).

References to written evidence in practice forms

32.4.19 The High Court and county court forms in use before April 26, 1999, and remaining in use after that date are listed, respectively, in Practice Direction (Forms), Tables 2 and 3 (see 4PD.2). Where a rule permits, a party intending to use a witness statement as an alternative to an affidavit should amend any form in Table 2 or 3 to be used in connection with that rule so that "witness statement" replaces "affidavit" wherever it appears in the form (*ibid.* paras 4.3 and 5.2).

Application by party to amend opponent's witness statement

32.4.20 Generally, the evidence of a party's witness cannot be received at trial unless the witness's witness statement has been served (see r.32.4). Further, generally, a witness statement will stand as a witness's evidence in-chief (see r.32.5). Similar rules apply where the witness is an expert (see Pt 35 below). Consequently, where a party wishes to object to part of the evidence of one of his opponent's evidence being received at trial (e.g. on the ground that it is irrelevant, or, though relevant, nevertheless should be excluded), that objection may take the form of a pre-trial application (under r.32.1) to have the evidence to which objection is taken struck from that witness's witness statement; as in *Akhtar v Khushi* [2002] EWHC 673; February 18, 2002, unrep. (Mr Bernard Livesey Q.C.), see also *Anglo Eastern Trust Ltd v Kermanshahchi* [2002] EWHC 1702 (Ch); July 5, 2002, unrep. (Neuberger J.). However, such an application would be premature if made before the issues between the parties had crystallised.

Application to strike out witness statement

32.4.21 A party's awareness of the court's wide powers to control evidence may encourage him to apply to the court for an order striking out part of, or the whole of, a witness statement served on him by his opponent. Such an application might be made, for example, on the ground that the material sought to be struck out is irrelevant or would unnecessarily lengthen the proceedings, or is disproportionate (as well as, of course, on the ground that its disclosure would be in breach of a privilege enjoyed by the party). Where an application is made during trial, the judge is well-placed to determine whether particular passages in a witness statement have real value or are irrelevant and/or disproportionate. A judge asked to approach such questions at the interlocutory stage is at a disadvantage and should only strike out profferred evidence if it is quite plain that, no matter how the proceedings may look at trial, the evidence will never appear to be either relevant or, if relevant, will never be sufficiently helpful to make it right to allow the party in question to adduce it (*Wilkinson v West Coast Capital* [2005] EWHC 1606 (Ch), July 22, 2005, unrep. (Mann J.)). The court must be on its guard to ensure that costs and delays are not increased by ill-conceived applications to strike out witness statements (*ibid*).

Use at trial of witness statements which have been served

32.5 ***32.5—(1) If—***

(a) a party has served a witness statement; and

(b) he wishes to rely at trial on the evidence of the witness who made the statement,

he must call the witness to give oral evidence unless the court orders otherwise or he puts in the statement as hearsay evidence.

(Part 33 contains provisions about hearsay evidence.)

(2) Where a witness is called to give oral evidence under paragraph (1), his witness statement shall stand as his evidence in chief[GL] unless the court orders otherwise.

(3) A witness giving oral evidence at trial may with the permission of the court—

(a) amplify his witness statement; and

(b) give evidence in relation to new matters which have arisen since the witness statement was served on the other parties.

(4) The court will give permission under paragraph (3) only if it considers that there is good reason not to confine the evidence of the witness to the contents of his witness statement.

(5) If a party who has served a witness statement does not—

(a) call the witness to give evidence at trial; or

(b) put the witness statement in as hearsay evidence, any other party may put the witness statement in as hearsay evidence.

"witness statement ... as ... evidence in chief" (r.32.5(2))

This sub-rule builds on r.32.1(c) (court's power to give directions as to way in which evidence is to be placed before the court). Parties are required to serve their witness statements on other parties in advance of trial (for the purposes of promoting settlement and avoiding surprise). Further, in the event of the witness being called at trial, his witness statement should normally stand as his evidence-in-chief (for the purpose of reducing trial time). Formerly, the latter practice was stated in *Practice Direction (Case Management)* [1995] 1 W.L.R. 262, para.3; it is now put in rule form (former RSC O.38, r.2A(7) and CCR O.20, r.12A(7) gave the court power to direct that a witness's statement or part of it should stand as evidence-in-chief). The court retains a discretion and may order that the witness's evidence or part of it should be given *viva voce* (*Cole v Kivells, The Times*, May 2, 1997, CA (conflict of evidence on crucial issue); see also *Anonima Petroli Italiana SpA and Neste Oy v Marlucidez Armadora SA (The Filiatra Legacy)* [1991] 2 Lloyd's Rep. 337, CA). 32.5.1

Amplification of evidence (r.32.5(3) and (4))

Former RSC O.38, r.2A(7) and CCR O.20, r.12A(7) restricted the evidence which could be adduced from a party other than that disclosed in his witness statement. Paragraphs (3) and (4) adopt and implement generally the Chancery approach to what was called "supplementary examination in chief". For explanation, see Interim Report, pp.177–178. Obvious circumstances in which a witness may wish to amplify his witness statement and give evidence as to new matters are where events occur, or matters are discovered, after his statement was served, or where a response to matters dealt with in a witness statement of another party's witness is required. 32.5.2

If amplification of witness statements at trial is too strictly limited there is a risk that statements will become over-elaborate and that costs of the preparation will be accordingly increased. If, on the other hand, amplification is too readily allowed there is a risk that statements will fail to deal with important issues. Where a party's witness is allowed to amplify, prejudice to the opponent should not be regarded routinely as remediable simply by an order for costs. A late, unjustified change of tack may be regarded as an injustice to the opponent which, in the light of the overriding objective (r.1.1) should not be permitted (Final Report, p.129).

See also *Mander v Evans* [2001] 1 W.L.R. 2378 (Ferris J.) (judge not willing to allow party to elaborate in evidence-in-chief on witness statement to remedy deficiencies, but agreeing to try question of law involved as a preliminary issue, thereby not putting party to trouble and expense of preparing supplemental witness statement).

In the Admiralty and Commercial Courts Guide it is said that a "supplemental witness statement" should normally be served where the witness proposes materially to add to, alter, correct or retract from what is in his original witness statement (*ibid.* Section H, para.H1.6, see Vol.2, para.2A–103). Permission will be required for the service of a supplemental witness statement. The guidance formerly given in the Chancery Guide as to supplemental witness statements has been deleted.

In some particular procedural contexts, quite prescriptive requirements concerning the filing and exchange of written evidence are to be found, together with provisions expressly permitting the filing of a further witness statement (or affidavit) supplementing previous statements; e.g. Practice Direction (Appeals) para.22.6C(8) (Applications for permission to appeal under the Town and Country Planning Act 1990 s.289) (see para.52 PD.121.1, below).

Witness not called

32.5.3 The general rule under r.32.2(1)(a) is that any fact which needs to be proved by the evidence of witnesses is to be proved at trial, by their oral evidence given in public.

Where a party serves a witness statement of one of his witnesses and wishes to rely on it, he must call the witness to give oral evidence, unless the court orders otherwise, or put the statement in as a hearsay statement in accordance with the Pt 33 procedure. (See "Hearsay evidence in witness statements" in notes following r.32.4.)

The significance of the phrase "unless the court orders otherwise" in r.32.5(1) is not immediately apparent. In early drafts of the CPR, what is now r.32.5 was subject to a further rule dealing specifically with witness statements as evidence where the witness is not called and the meaning of the phrase was clear.

Rule 32.5(5) states that if the party does not wish to have the benefit of the evidence by either calling the witness to give evidence at trial or by putting in the witness statement as hearsay any other party may put in the witness statement as hearsay evidence. The effect of this provision is to overcome the difficulty encountered in *Husbands v Commissioners of Police for the Metropolis*, July 7, 1994, unrep., CA (see *Sandry v Jones*, *The Times*, August 3, 2000 (Creswell J.)). In terms, r.32.5(5) makes permissive what former RSC O.38, r. 2A(6) prevented, but this change in the law did not change the basic rules of the law of evidence. The "other party" is not entitled to put the witness statement in evidence; the court retains a discretion (*McPhilemy v The Times Newspapers Ltd (No.2)* [2000] 1 W.L.R. 1732, CA (claimant not allowed to put in evidence witness statement served by defendant conflicting substantially with claimant's case for purpose of inviting jury in libel trial to conclude that the statement was knowingly fabricated)).

Where a party (C) has served on an opponent (D) a witness statement made by another person (X), but does not call X or put in his witness statement as hearsay evidence, and (as r.32.5(5) permits) B puts it in as hearsay evidence, C may then apply for the court's permission to have X called as a witness for cross-examination on the statement provided to him. In these circumstances the terms of r.33.4 are triggered and C does not fall foul of the rule that prevents a party from cross-examining his own witness (*Douglas v Hello! Ltd* [2003] EWCA Civ 332; [2003] C.P Rep. 42).

Witness statements and statements of case

32.5.4 Historically speaking, the distinction between pleadings and evidence is well understood. The rule that, in advance of trial, parties should exchange witness statements is a modern rule. One of the consequences of its development is that the role of pleadings (now statements of case) has been affected. Whereas previously, parties made and defended their cases through statements of claim and defences (etc), nowadays in effect pleadings can be significantly elaborated by the pre-trial exchange of witness statements and supplementary witness statements. In the pre-trial development of a case, it is not at all unusual for what is not relevant at one stage to appear to be relevant at a later stage, and especially is that likely to be true where experts dealing with technical matters are involved and their reports are exchanged. In these circumstances the court may require the parties to improve their pleadings, so that the trial judge is not faced with the task of searching through witness statements in order to discover the real issues between the parties (*Stephen Hill Partnership v Supaglazing Limited* 2002 WL 31599542, October 16, 2002, unrep. (Lindsay J.)). However, the mere fact that an issue can be said to be raised from witness statements or documents served by one party does not lead to any general presumption in favour of permitting the amendment of statements of case to include such issues. Parties must be alert to the possibility that the process of assembling witness statements, relevant documents and other material may lead to new issues of fact or law being identified. If a party concludes that such issues should be raised then in general the appropriate course would be for him without delay to formulate a proposal to amend his statement of case. Something less formal may be appropriate where the new issue is truly minor, or for other good reason, but a party who proceeds with less formality runs the risk that problems may later emerge (*EDO Technology Ltd v Hills* [2006] EWHC 598 (QB); [2006] All E.R. (D.) 338 (Mar) (Walker J.)).

Evidence in proceedings other than at trial[1]

32.6—(1) Subject to paragraph (2), the general rule is that evidence at hearings other than the trial is to be by witness statement unless the court, a practice direction or any other enactment requires otherwise. **32.6**

(2) At hearings other than the trial, a party may rely on the matters set out in—

(a) his statement of case; or

(b) his application, notice if the statement of case or application notice is verified by a statement of truth.

History of rule

By Civil Procedure (Amendment) Rules 2000 (SI 2000/221) r.17, in r.32.6(2) the words "a party may rely" were substituted for "a party may, in support of his application, rely". The previous wording was unintentionally restrictive. At hearings other than trial a party may wish to rely on matters set out in his statement of case or his application notice for purposes other than supporting an application. **32.6.1**

Effect of rule

This rule should be read with r.32.2(1)(b) which states the general rule that any fact which needs to be proved by the evidence of witnesses is to be proved, at any hearing other than the trial, by their evidence in writing. Rule 32.6(1) adds to this by stating that, as a general rule, evidence in writing in hearings other than the trial should be in the form of witness statements. A statement of case (e.g. a claim form, or a defence) carries a statement of truth and constitutes "evidence in writing". Presumably, in proceedings other than at trial, a party may rely on his statement of case or just the application in support of his application in addition to any witness statements. In any event, r.32.6 provides that he may rely solely on his statement of case (provided it is verified by a statement of truth). Rule 32.6 is expressly referred to elsewhere, e.g. in Practice Direction (Case Management-Preliminary Stage: Allocation and Re-allocation), para.12.4(4) (r.32.6 applies to evidence at a disposal hearing unless the court otherwise directs). In various contexts throughout the CPR, where evidence may be given in writing, there are provisions specifically enabling (indeed, sometimes specifically encouraging) the giving of such evidence in written forms other than witness statements, and permitting the court to proceed on the basis of the evidence; e.g. r.55.8 (first hearing of possession claim) and Practice Direction (Possession Claims), para.5.1 (see para.55PD.8 below). **32.6.2**

For claims under the Pt 8 procedure (Alternative procedure for claims), see also r.8.5(7) which reflects r.32.6 by stating that a Pt 8 claimant may rely on matters set out in his claim form as evidence if the claim form is verified by a statement of truth.

Note Pt 22 (Statement of truth).

Note "Proof by evidence in writing at any other hearing", following r.32.2.

Note "Written evidence in claim under Pt 8 procedure", following r.32.4.

"enactment requires otherwise"

Under many different enactments, applications may be made to the court giving rise to proceedings which are not trials. The provisions in r.32.6 are subject to any provisions as to evidence in such enactments. **32.6.3**

---

[1] Amended by the Civil Procedure (Amendment) Rules 2000 (SI 2000/221).

Order for cross-examination

32.7 **32.7—(1) Where, at a hearing other than the trial, evidence is given in writing, any party may apply to the court for permission to cross-examine the person giving the evidence.**

(2) If the court gives permission under paragraph (1) but the person in question does not attend as required by the order, his evidence may not be used unless the court gives permission.

Effect of rule

32.7.1 Evidence in writing may consist of matters set out in a statement of case, an affidavit, a witness statement, a witness summary, or an application notice. In some instances the evidence either may be or must necessarily be the evidence of a party.

This rule follows former CCR O.20, r.5, which applied to proceedings "in chambers", was confined to evidence by affidavit, and had the same effect as former RSC O.38, r.2(3)). Rule 32.7 is restricted to a hearing "other than a trial". The interesting thing about the rule (and its predecessors) is that it states that the court may permit evidence to be given in writing at a hearing other than a trial even though (1) the court has made an order requiring the person who made the written evidence to attend for cross-examination, and (2) in the event, that person does not attend as ordered. The court may direct that evidence should be given at trial in the form of written evidence and may further direct whether the maker should attend for cross-examination (see former RSC O.38, r.2(2) and CCR O.20, r.6). Where written evidence is given at trial, the question whether the maker should be required to attend for cross-examination may be governed by r.33.4, but that rule is silent as to what should happen if the court gives permission for cross-examination and the person does not then attend as required. Where a witness is cross-examined, whether at a trial or at a hearing other than a trial, the court may limit the cross-examination (r.32.1(3)).

Under the Pt 8 procedure (Alternative procedure for claims), directions may be given for the attendance for cross-examination of a witness who has given written evidence (r.8.6(3)).

In *Phillips v Symes* [2003] EWCA Civ 1769; December 5, 2003, CA, the Court of Appeal stated that, where someone has purported to comply with either undertakings or orders to make disclosure by affidavit, it must be doubted whether it is right to place the deponent in the position that, unless he is prepared to be cross-examined on his affidavits, they count for nothing at all (para.51). On the other hand, without cross-examination, the court is entitled to attach little weight to them (see *Comet Products (UK) Ltd v Hawkex Plastics Ltd* [1971] 2 Q.B. 67, CA). In *Phillips v Symes*, after judgment the defendant made affidavits in purported compliance with undertakings given following his committal for contempt and the claimants successfully applied for an order that he be cross-examined on those affidavits. In the ensuing proceedings the claimants made fresh allegations of contempt and, as a result, it became clear that the application for cross-examination was no longer limited to whether the defendant had complied with his undertakings but was to be directed to his evidence generally in the case. On the defendant's appeal against the directions given by the judge as to his cross-examination the Court of Appeal said that the court's concentration should be on considering whether the evidence given by the defendant now provided the information required to be given by the undertakings and there were dangers involved in permitting a more wide-ranging cross-examination. The Court concluded (para.65) that the judge's view that general cross-examination could be "blended" with consideration whether the defendant was complying with his undertakings was wrong and allowed the appeal to this extent, directing that the defendant's cross-examination be limited accordingly.

Form of witness statement

32.8 **32.8 A witness statement must comply with the requirements set out in the relevant practice direction.**

(Part 22 requires a witness statement to be verified by a statement of truth.)

Effect of rule

Practice Direction (Written Evidence), paras 17 to 22 and Annex 2 contain provisions dealing with the form of witness statements and their verification by statements of truth (see paras 32PD.17 *et seq.*). The requirements as to form, etc., formerly found in RSC O.38, r.2A(4) and CCR O.20, r.12A(4) are not repeated in r.32.8; instead such matters are now dealt with by Practice Direction. 32.8.1

A witness statement must be verified by a statement of truth (r.22.1(1)(b) and r.32.4(1)) stating that the maker of the statement believes the facts stated in the document are true (r.22.1(4)). (See Pt 22 further for provisions regarding the statement of truth.) This requirement follows from RSC O.38, r.2A(4)(a). If the witness statement is not verified by a statement of truth the court may direct that it shall not be admissible as evidence (r.22.3).

The Practice Direction supplementing Pt 32 used to contain provisions dealing with the situation where a witness statement was to be verified by a person who was unable to read or sign the document. Those provisions were omitted when in 2006 comparable provisions, applicable to all documents requiring verification, were inserted in Practice Direction (Statements of Truth) (supplementing Pt 22).

Solicitors and witnesses alike have an obligation to take the greatest care to ensure that statements contain the truth (*ZYX Music GmbH v King* [1995] 3 All E.R. 1). Proceedings for contempt of court may be brought against a witness who makes a false statement without an honest belief in its truth (r.32.14(2)). See further para.32 4.5 above.

Distinguishing witness's own knowledge from belief

Witness statements should be confined to evidence that the person making it would be allowed to give orally (see r.32.4) and, as hearsay evidence is generally admissible in civil proceedings (see para.32.4.6 above), may include such evidence. Thus, in a witness statement a witness is able to refer to matters beyond his direct knowledge or observation. The Civil Evidence Act 1995 s.2 states, as provided for by rules of court, that a party proposing to adduce hearsay evidence (a) must give notice to the other party or parties and (b) should provide particulars sufficient to enable them "to deal with any matters arising from its being hearsay". The matter of giving notice is dealt with by r.33.2 and r.33.3 (see notes following those rules below). The matter of providing details is dealt with by para.18.2 of Practice Direction (Written Evidence) which states that a witness statement must draw attention to any hearsay evidence included by indicating (1) which of the statements in it are made from the witness's own knowledge and which are matters of information or belief, and (2) the source for any matters of information or belief (see para.32PD.18 below). Paragraph 18.2 is not concerned with evidence of primary fact. It is simply a procedural provision requiring the deponent to identify the source of any hearsay evidence. It does not require that that attribution should be based only on admissible evidence (*Clarke v Marlborough Fine Art (London) Ltd (Amendments)*, [2002] 1 W.L.R. 1731 (Patten J.)). See further, para.33.2.4 below. 32.8.2

Witness summaries

32.9—(1) A party who— 32.9

(a) is required to serve a witness statement for use at trial; but

(b) is unable to obtain one, may apply, without notice, for permission to serve a witness summary instead.

(2) A witness summary is a summary of—

(a) the evidence, if known, which would otherwise be included in a witness statement; or

(b) if the evidence is not known, the matters about which the party serving the witness summary proposes to question the witness.

(3) Unless the court orders otherwise, a witness summary must include the name and address of the intended witness.

(4) Unless the court orders otherwise, a witness summary must be served within the period in which a witness statement would have had to be served.

(5) Where a party serves a witness summary, so far as practicable, rules 32.4 (requirement to serve witness statement for use at trial), 32.5(3) (amplifying witness statements), and 32.8 (form of witness statement) shall apply to the summary.

Effect of rule

32.9.1 For distinction between "witness statements" and "witness summaries" see "Witness statements" and "witness summaries" following r.32.4 above.

Under former RSC O.38 r.2A(5) and CCR O.20, r.12A(5), where a party was unable to obtain a witness statement from an intended witness he could apply to the court for a direction permitting him to exchange a witness summary instead. Similar provision is now made in r.32.9. Under the CPR, service of witness summaries may be directed by the court in a broader range of circumstances. The contents of a witness summary should accord with this rule. Otherwise, the rules applicable to witness statements apply to witness summaries as far as may be. However, a witness summary does not include a certificate by its maker as to truth. The court may order that the witness summary should not include the witness's name and address.

Consequence of failure to serve witness statement or summary

32.10 **32.10 If a witness statement or a witness summary for use at trial is not served in respect of an intended witness within the time specified by the court, then the witness may not be called to give oral evidence unless the court gives permission.**

Effect of rule

32.10.1 This rule indicates the consequences that may follow where a witness statement or summary for use at trial is not served. As to consequences of failure to serve written evidence in a claim under the Pt 8 procedure (Alternative procedure for claim), see r.8.6. Presumably, where a party fails to serve a written statement for a hearing other than a trial the court could refuse to admit it if directions for exchange had been given.

"witness may not be called ... unless the court gives permission"

32.10.2 Former RSC O.38, r.2A(10) provided that, where a party failed to comply with a direction for the exchange of witness statements, the sanction was that he would "not be entitled to adduce evidence to which the direction related" without the leave of the court (see also former CCR O.20, r.12A(10)). The same rule was expressly applied in actions proceeding under automatic directions (former RSC O.25, r.8(2), but no express provision was made in the former CCR O.17, r.11(3)(b)).

Whereas the former sanction was that the party would "not be entitled to adduce evidence to which the direction related", in r.32.10 the sanction is that the witness "may not be called to give oral evidence". The latter formulation is broader than the former and this may be significant.

Previously, the nature of the factors to be taken into account by the court in the exercise of its discretion to dis-apply the sanction was the subject of case law (e.g. *Beachley Property Ltd v Edgar, The Times*, July 18, 1996, CA, and *BV Tapijtfabriek van den Brink v Shierson* May 12, 1997, unrep., CA,). Presumably, the rule stated in r.32.10 will be regarded as a "sanction" within r.3.8 (Sanctions having effect unless defaulting party obtains relief) and, therefore, the factors to be taken into account by the court in determining whether to permit a witness to give oral evidence despite the failure to serve a witness statement should include those listed in r.3.9 (Relief from sanctions). In *Bansal v Cheema*, March 2, 2000, unrep., CA, the parties conceded that this was the position and the Court proceeded on the assumption that the concession was correctly made. However, where before trial a party requests the court to exercise its powers under r.3.1(2)(a) to extend the time for serving his witness statements it could be argued that r.3.9 does not apply because at that stage the sanction imposed by r.32.10 has not had "effect" within the meaning of r.3.8.

Where a witness statement is served by a party after the time specified for service has expired it will be unjust to exclude the party from adducing the evidence at trial save in very rare circumstances, e.g. where there had been deliberate flouting of court orders, or inexcusable delay such that the only way the court could fairly entertain the evidence would be by adjourning the trial (*Mealey Horgan Plc v Horgan*, [1999] S.T.C. 711).

Where a party fails to disclose a report of an expert within the time specified by the court, the court may order, on the ground that there should be no further delay, that the party should not be allowed to call that expert at trial where the trial could be conducted justly on the basis of the other evidence available (*Baron v Lovell*, *The Times*, September 14, 1999, CA). Unless the trial judge otherwise directs, the trial will be conducted in accordance with that order (rr.28.7 and 29.9).

"within the time specified by the court"

See "Time limits" in note following r.32.4. **32.10.3**

Cross-examination on a witness statement

32.11 Where a witness is called to give evidence at trial, he may be cross-examined on his witness statement, whether or not the statement or any part of it was referred to during the witness's evidence in chief[GL]. **32.11**

Effect of rule

Under the previous rules, the effect of the service of a witness statement was a matter for some doubt, and some doubts remain. Former RSC O.38, r.2A(6) and CCR O.20, r.12A(6) stated the general proposition that, "where the party serving a statement... does not call the witness to whose evidence it relates, no other party may put the statement in evidence at the trial". A witness statement does not become evidence by service. It becomes evidence by being adopted by the witness in the witness box as his evidence in chief. **32.11.1**

Where a witness is called to give evidence, his witness statement shall stand as his evidence in chief, unless the court orders otherwise (r.32.5(2)). Normally, therefore, it would follow that a witness could be cross-examined on his witness statement as a matter of course. This rule provides that where the witness's statement (or part of it) does not stand as his evidence in chief he may be cross-examined on it (or on that part of it). In the former rules, this rule was stated as an exception to the general proposition mentioned above (RSC O.38, r.2A(7)(c) and CCR O.20, r.12A(7)(c)).

This rule is remedial. It gives an answer to a very specific question. It is not concerned with the circumstances in which it may or may not be appropriate for the court to exercise its discretion to permit the cross-examination of a person on his witness statement at proceedings other than a trial. The restriction of this rule to the circumstance where a witness is called at trial admits of no inference that a witness may not be cross-examined on his statement at other hearings.

Use of witness statements for other purposes

32.12—(1) Except as provided by this rule, a witness statement may be used only for the purpose of the proceedings in which it is served. **32.12**

(2) Paragraph (1) does not apply if and to the extent that—

(a) the witness gives consent in writing to some other use of it;

***(b) the court gives permission* for some other use; or**

(c) the witness statement has been put in evidence at a hearing held in public.

Effect of rule

This rule follows from RSC O.38, r.2A(11) and CCR O.20, r.12A(11). The procedure for requiring parties to serve witness statements has the principal effect of alerting each party to what their opponent's witnesses are going to say at trial, in the event of there being a trial. (This has the advantages of promoting settlements and avoiding **32.12.1** unfair surprise at trial.) If there is a trial and the evidence contained in a particular witness's statement is given in court, the evidence is in the public domain and certain legal consequences follow from that (e.g. any privilege is waived). However, if the case is settled without trial, or if there is a trial but the witness is not called (or his statement adduced in evidence under the hearsay provisions) the general rule is that no other party may make use of that statement subsequently. The difficulty which arises is whether a party upon whom a witness statement has been served may make any use of it before trial (or settlement), during the interlocutory stages of the proceedings. Rule 32.12(1) says a witness statement "may be used only for the purpose of the proceedings in which it is served". The exceptions in (a) and (b) of paras r.32.2 are obvious enough and follow the former rules. Paragraph (c) is new and may go some way towards clarifying problems that have arisen in the past as to the status of witness statements before they are deployed at trial (see further, r.39.2 (General rule—hearing to be in public)). Some of the relevant authorities were discussed in the context of r.31.22 (subsequent use of disclosed documents) in *Cassidy v Hawcroft*, July 27, 2000, unrep., CA (in defamation proceedings claimant entitled to production of letter by third party referred to in affidavit sworn for purposes of applicant for interim remedy in previous proceedings in which claimant and deponent (but not third party) were parties). Note also *Chase v News Group Newspapers Ltd* [2002] EWHC 1101 May 29, 2002, unrep., Eady J. (in defamation proceedings against defendant newspaper, claimant granted permission to use affidavit of his employer filed in successful application for interim injunction made earlier by employer (and in which employer claimed no privilege) to restrain further publication by defendants). It has been held that, where an expert is to be called, being a witness who had prepared a report for use in earlier proceedings, this rule does not prevent the court from ordering disclosure of that report (*L'Oréal v Bellure NV* [2006] EWHC 1503 (Ch), May 24, 2006, unrep. (Peter Smith J.) (disclosure ordered because it was relevant as it went to issue whether the expert's opinion should be accepted on the evidence he would adduce at trial)). In *Zambia v Meer Care & Desai* [2006] EWCA Civ 390; March 7, 2006, unrep., CA, an application was made to stay English civil proceedings pending the determination of foreign criminal proceedings in which some of the same parties were involved. In refusing a stay the judge made various orders to protect the position of those parties, including an order directing that witness statements used in the civil proceedings (and documents disclosed) should not be used in any foreign proceedings without the permission of the court ([2005] EWHC 2102, Ch). The refusal of a stay was upheld by the Court of Appeal.

Availability of witness statements for inspection[1]

32.13 **32.13—(1) A witness statement which stands as evidence in chief[GL] is open to inspection during the course of the trial unless the court otherwise directs.**

(2) Any person may ask for a direction that a witness statement is not open to inspection.

(3) The court will not make a direction under paragraph (2) unless it is satisfied that a witness statement should not be open to inspection because of—

(a) the interests of justice;

(b) the public interest;

(c) the nature of any expert medical evidence in the statement;

(d) the nature of any confidential information (including information relating to personal financial matters) in the statement; or

(e) the need to protect the interests of any child or *protected* party.

[1] Amended by the Civil Procedure (Amendment) Rules 2001 (SI 2001/256) and the Civil Procedure (Amendment) Rules 2007 (SI 2007/2204).

(4) The court may exclude from inspection words or passages in the statement.

Effect of rule

By Civil Procedure (Amendment) Rules 2001 (SI 2001/256), r.12, with effect from March 26, 2001, in r.32.13(1) the words "during the course of the trial unless the court otherwise directs" were substituted for "unless the court otherwise directs during the course of the trial" (see further below). In para.(3)(e), "protected party" was substituted for "patient" by the Civil Procedure (Amendment) Rules 2007 (SI 2007/2204) with effect from October 1, 2007, to reflect the change in nomenclature brought about by the Mental Capacity Act 2005. **32.13.1**

There is a general presumption that the business of the courts is to be done in public unless this is likely to lead to a denial of justice. In the Report of the Review Body on Civil Justice, Cm. 394 (1988) greater use of witness statements was recommended. The Review Body recognised that this recommendation, together with other proposed changes, would lead to less evidence being given orally and in open court with the result that evidence would be "less open to public scrutiny". Consequently, the Review Body further recommended that in cases where written evidence is relied on in court but is not read out public access should be provided for a period after the conclusion of the case (*ibid.* para.298). This recommendation was carried into effect by provisions formerly found in RSC O.38, r.2A(12) to (16) and CCR O.20, r.12A(12) to (16) and supporting Practice Directions. The former rules are recast and in some respects altered in r.32.13. Under the former rules, the presumption was that witness statements standing as evidence in chief were not open to inspection by members of the public. However, a person (e.g. a media representative) could request that such a witness statement be opened to inspection. In these circumstances, the judge could direct that the statement be certified as open to inspection. The request had to be made "during the course of the trial" but the period during which the statement was open to inspection as certified could extend beyond the end of the trial. Under r.32.13 the presumption is reversed. Witness statements standing as evidence in chief are open to inspection, unless the court (in the light of the criteria stated in r.32.13(3)) otherwise directs (e.g. *American Home Products Corporation v Novartis Pharmaceuticals (UK) Ltd* [2001] EWCA Civ 165; [2001] F.S.R. 41, CA (court ordering that exhibits to affidavit filed in application in patent claim should be kept confidential)). Further, as a result of amendments made by the Civil Procedure (Amendment) Rules 2001 (SI 2001/256), in terms r.32.13 limits the period during which such statements are open to inspection to "during the course of the trial". Presumably, on the application of an interested person, the court would have the power to direct that statements should be open to inspection beyond the end of the trial.

In *GIO Personal Investment Services Ltd v Liverpool and London Steamship Protection and Indemnity Association Ltd* [1999] 1 W.L.R. 984, CA, it was held that a person who was not a party to a case which had been tried, but who was a party in related proceedings, was not entitled to inspect documents referred to in the witness statements or the documents on the judge's reading list, but was entitled to inspect and make copies of the written opening submissions or skeleton arguments to which reference was made by the judge at the trial.

For inspection by parties or by any other person of documents from the records of the court generally see r.5.4.

For certification by court officer of material excluded from inspection under r.32.13(2) or r.32.13(4), see Practice Direction (Written Evidence), para.24.1 (see para.32PD.24 below).

False statements

32.14—(1) Proceedings for contempt of court may be brought against a person if he makes, or causes to be made, a false statement in a document verified by a statement of truth without an honest belief in its truth. **32.14**

(Part 22 makes provision for a statement of truth.)

(2) Proceedings under this rule may be brought only—

(a) by the Attorney General; or

(b) with the permission of the court.

Effect of rule

32.14.1 When the CPR were devised, with provision being made for the verification of statements by a statement of truth, which is not made on oath, it was necessary to consider what should be the sanction for non-compliance. A criminal offence could have been created, but it was not. Instead recourse was had to the established concept of contempt, which is not the subject of a prosecution or a trial before a jury, but rather of either proceedings within an existing action or separate proceedings before a Divisional Court brought by a Pt 8 claim form (*Daltel Europe Ltd v Makki* [2006] EWCA Civ 94; [2006] 1 W.L.R. 2704, CA, para.45) (see further para.32.14.2 below).

Rule 32.14 makes no substantial change to the law of contempt. Proceedings under the rule involve allegations of interference with the course of justice, which is a public, not a private, wrong, and therefore cannot be brought without permission. (See *Malgar Ltd v R.E. Leach (Engineering) Ltd* [2000] F.S.R. 393 (Sir Richard Scott V.–C.) and Practice Direction (Written Evidence), para.27.4 (see para.32PD.7 below).) Various documents may or must be verified by a statement of truth (see Pt 22 and notes thereto). Generally, the person who is required to complete the statement of truth is the person making or putting forward the document. However, in certain circumstances, verification may be given by a party's legal representative or by a litigation friend (former "next friend" or guardian *ad litem*).

Where a declaration provided by the claimant under art.7(3) of the European Order for Payment Regulations contains any deliberate false statement, r.32.14 applies as if the EOP application form A were verified by a statement of truth (CPR r.78.3).

Pleadings are now called "statements of case" (r.2.3(1)) and include the claim form, the particulars of claim, the defence, the reply and any Pt 18 response. Statements of case are to carry "statements of truth" (see r.22.1) signed by the parties (or their litigation friend) or their legal representatives to the effect that it is believed that the facts stated in the document being verified are true. In certain circumstances, statements of case may stand as evidence in the course of the proceedings (see, e.g. r.32.6(2)(a)). Further, an application notice for a court order made under Pt 23 may contain a statement, by the applicant or his legal representative, that the applicant believes any facts stated in the application are true (r.22.1(3)). If the application contains a statement of truth, the applicant may rely on the matters set out in the application in support of his application (r.32.6(2)(b)). Furthermore, as was explained above, r.22.1(1)(b) states that the maker of a witness statement must certify that he believes the statements of fact in it are true.

This rule provides that proceedings for contempt of court may be brought against a person who makes or causes to be made a false statement without an honest belief in its truth in a document verified by a statement of truth. Rule 22.1(6) provides that in the case of documents in the form of a statement of case, an application notice, or a response complying with an order under r.18.1 to provide further information, the statement of truth may be signed by a legal representative "on behalf of the party". Where a legal representative signs the statement of truth and it turns out that the document to which it relates contains a false statement a question may arise as to whether the legal representative may be exposed to liability for contempt under r.32.14. (Drafts of r.32.14 said that proceedings for contempt of court could be brought against "a party" who made or caused to be made a false statement in a document in relation to which a legal representative was permitted by the rules to sign the statement of truth on his behalf. In the final version it is said that proceedings may be brought against "a person" who makes or causes to be made a false statement). Where a legal representative has signed a statement of truth on his client's behalf his signature will be taken by the court as his statement that before signing he had informed the client of the possible consequences to the client if it should subsequently appear that the client did not have an honest belief in the truth of those facts (Practice Directions (Statement of Truth), para.3.8.3, see para.22PD.3 above.

The principles to be applied on application to commit under r.32.14 were outlined by the Vice-Chancellor in *Malgar Ltd v R.E. Leach (Engineering) Ltd* [2000] F.S.R. 393 (where it was held that, in all circumstances, the application was disproportionate). The principles were applied in *Sony Computer Entertainment Inc v Ball* [2004] EWHC 1984, (Ch), August 10, 2004, unrep. (Blackburne J.) (penalty of £2,000 imposed on defendant making false statements in defence). The penalty imposed under r.32.14 on a party making false statements in pleadings should reflect the fact that he attempts to interfere with the course of justice and commits a public wrong. If the signing of a statement of truth is to be more than an empty gesture there must be teeth in the sanction imposed (*ibid*).

In the case of a witness statement, the statement of truth must be signed by the maker of the statement. Conceivably, a legal representative who caused the maker of a witness statement to make a false statement in the witness statement could be liable.

The persons who may or must sign the statement of truth are stipulated by the rules, and by Practice Direction (Statements of Truth), para.3.1 (see 22PD.2) and Practice Direction (Experts and Assessors), para.1.3 (see 35PD.1). Presumably, where a false statement is made in a document verified by a statement of truth signed by a person who (in the event) was not permitted by the rules to sign, contempt liability under r.32.14 does not arise.

The contempt consists, not of the breach of a court order or of an undertaking to the court, but in the making of a false statement in a document verified by a statement of truth. It would seem that the maximum penalty is as stated in the Contempt of Court Act 1981 s.14(1) (a fixed term not exceeding on any occasion two years) (see Vol.2, para.3C–38). If proceedings are to be brought by a person other than the Attorney General, the permission of the court is required. When considering whether to grant permission where, in an application under r.32.14 made before trial, allegations are made to the effect that false statements were made in statements of cases and witness statements, the court should be alert to the risk of encouraging substantial satellite litigation which may significantly hinder the efficient and economical disposal of the substantive claim. In general, the proper time for determining the truth or falsity of statements is at trial, when all the relevant issues of fact are before the court and the statements can be considered against the totality of the evidence (*Daltel Europe Limited v Makki*, [2005] EWHC 749 (Ch), May 3, 2005, unrep. (David Richards J.)).

Practice where false statement alleged

As to bringing of proceedings for contempt, see Sch.1, RSC O.52 (paras sc52.0.1 *et* **32.14.2**
seq. below), and Sch.1, CCR O.29 (paras cc29.1 *et seq.* below). Note also Practice Direction (Committal Applications) (paras scpd52.1 *et seq.* below).

Rule 32.14 does not create a new category of contempt of court. It simply provides a procedure for dealing with an allegation of a particular type of contempt falling within the general category of contempt comprising actions which interfere with the administration of justice (*Malgar Ltd v R.E. Leach (Engineering) Ltd*, [2000] F.S.R. 393). It follows that the contempt to which r.32.14 applies is a criminal, not a civil, contempt (a distinction that still remains important for certain purposes). Though the contempt of court which a party may be found to have committed in proceedings brought against him pursuant to r.32.14 is properly characterised as a criminal contempt, the proceedings themselves are civil proceedings; and, because the proceedings are civil, the provisions of the Civil Evidence Act 1995 concerning the admissibility of hearsay evidence in civil proceedings apply (*Daltel Europe Ltd v Makki* [2006] EWCA Civ 94; [2006] 1 W.L.R. 2704, CA). Article 6 of the Convention applies to such proceedings but the reception of hearsay evidence is not precluded by the terms of that Article (*ibid.*). The procedure for appeals in civil cases would apply to an appeal from an order made under r.32.14 (*ibid.*).

The court's powers under r.32.14 (and under r.31.23) may be exercised at any stage in the proceedings, and are not restricted to cases where the falsity of the disclosure or other statement has been proved after a trial of the action. However, it is highly undesirable, not only for there to be satellite litigation, but also for one side's witnesses alone to be cross-examined at an interlocutory stage, without the full deployment of the other party's evidence and without the judge who hears the contempt application having available to him the full documentary and witness evidence in the case (*Prest v Marc Rich & Co Investment A.G.* [2006] EWHC 927 (Comm), March 3, 2006, unrep. (Gloster J.), adjourning to trial judge adjudication of defendant's alleged contempt in falsely verifying disclosure statement). The rule that an affidavit of disclosure is conclusive at the interlocutory stage does not operate as a bar to the exercise of the court's powers under r.32.14 (and under r.31.23) at that stage (*ibid.*).

Practice Direction (Written Evidence), para.27.1 (see para.32PD.27 below) states that, where a party alleges that a statement of truth is false (see r.32.14), or that a disclosure statement is false, (see r.31.23), the party shall refer that allegation to the court dealing with the claim in which the statement of truth or disclosure statement has been made. Upon such reference, the court may (a) exercise any of its powers under the rules, (b) initiate steps to consider if there is a contempt of court, and, where there is, to punish it, or (c) direct the party making the allegation to refer the matter to the Attorney General with a request to him to consider whether he wishes to bring proceedings for contempt of court. The supporting practice is stated in paras 27.2 and 27.3 of this Practice Direction. A person applying to commence contempt proceedings should consider whether the incident complained of does amount to contempt of court and whether such proceedings would further the overriding objective stated in r.1.1 (para.27.4). Paragraphs 27.1 to 27.4 were added to the Practice Direction in January 2001, and came into effect on February 12, 2001.

Affidavit evidence

32.15 **32.15—(1) Evidence must be given by affidavit[GL], instead of or in addition to a witness statement if this is required by the court, a provision contained in any other rule, a practice direction or any other enactment.**

(2) Nothing in these Rules prevents a witness giving evidence by affidavit[GL], at a hearing other than the trial, if he chooses to do so in a case where paragraph (1) does not apply, but the party putting forward the affidavit[GL] may not recover the additional cost of making it from any other party unless the court orders otherwise.

Effect of rule

32.15.1 An affidavit is defined in the Glossary as "a written, sworn statement of evidence". When affidavits are used as evidence in legal proceedings they are a form of "evidence in writing" within r.32.2. In accordance with the general rule stated in r.32.2, evidence at trial should be oral evidence but evidence in any other hearing (e.g. an interlocutory application) should be evidence in writing (e.g. an affidavit). But the general rule is subject to important exceptions and in certain types of proceedings (particularly proceedings in the Chancery Division of the High Court) the rule is that trial evidence should be in affidavit or witness statement form (see para.32.2.1).

When the CPR came into effect the expectation was that there would be greater reliance on evidence in writing other than affidavits and that the circumstances in which parties are obliged to prepare and file affidavits in the course of civil proceedings would be reduced. Where possible, evidence in writing should be given in witness statement form. Although the voluntary use of affidavit evidence is permitted at hearings other than the trial the potential costs penalty is explicit (r.32.15(2)). However, affidavits may be required by order of the court or by Practice Direction, *e.g* Practice Direction (Admiralty), para.9.1 (limitation claim form). Further, affidavits should be used where any enactments relating specifically to the proceedings in hand require them to be used. See further Practice Direction (Written Evidence), paras 1.4 *et seq.* (see para.32PD.1, below but note that none of the rules of court referred to in footnote 6 to that Practice Direction as illustrations of circumstances in which, by operation of rules, written evidence must be in affidavit form does in fact now require an affidavit). The court may give a direction that the evidence shall be given by affidavit of its own initiative or on the application of a party (*ibid.*, para.1.6).

In the years since the CPR came into effect, when the opportunity has arisen, legislative provisions lying outside theCPR have been amended for the purpose of substituting for a requirement that evidence should be in affidavit form a provision that it should or may be in written statement form (e.g. para.8(5) of the Enrolment of Deeds (Change of Name) Regulations 1994, annexed to Practice Direction (Court Documents), supplementing CPR Pt 5).

Practice Direction (Forms) para.4.2 states that, where a rule permits, a party intending to use a witness statement as an alternative to an affidavit should amend any form in Table 2 (Practice Forms) of that practice direction to be used in connection with that rule so that "witness statement" replaces "affidavit" wherever it appears in the form.

Former RSC O.41 contained detailed rules as to affidavits and these were adopted with modifications in county court proceedings by CCR O.20, r.10. Much of what used to be expressed in rule form is now reduced to practice directions.

Service of affidavit

Where appropriate the procedures relating to witness statements apply to affidavits used in lieu of witness statements. In particular, the rules as to the service of witness statements contained in r.32.4 apply where evidence is to be given by affidavit instead of by witness statement. See "Service of witness statement" in notes following r.32.4. In a number of procedural contexts, special rules obtain as to the service of witness statements where particular applications are made, e.g. r.24.5 (Evidence for the purposes of a summary judgment hearing). By operation of r.32.15(3), such special rules apply to the service of affidavits where a witness chooses to give evidence by affidavit instead of a witness statement. **32.15.2**

Filing of affidavit

Formerly, provisions as to the filing of affidavits were found in RSC O.41, r.9 and CCR O.20, r.10(2) and elsewhere. Under the CPR, the court may give directions as to whether or not affidavits are to be filed (r.32.4(3)(b)). For practice as to filing of affidavits, see Practice Direction (Written Evidence), para.10 (see para.32PD 10 below). **32.15.3**

Content of affidavits

See also "Content of witness statements", para.32.4.5 above. **32.15.4**

An affidavit must, if practicable, be in the deponent's own words and should be expressed in the first person (Practice Direction (Written Evidence), para.4.1). Further, an affidavit must indicate (1) which of the statements in it (a) are made from the deponent's own knowledge and which (b) are matters of information or belief, and (2) the source for any matters of information or belief (*ibid.* para.4.2) (see also para.32.8.2 above). Statements which are matters of information or belief if tendered as evidence of the matters stated, are likely to be hearsay. Former RSC O.41 r.5 stated that an affidavit could contain only such facts as the deponent was able of his own knowledge to prove, but if sworn for use in interlocutory proceedings could contain statements of information or belief (with the sources and grounds thereof). No such distinction is drawn in the CPR. By operation of the Civil Evidence Act 1995 s.1(1), in civil proceedings a statement shall not be excluded from evidence on the ground that it is hearsay (see Vol.2, para.9B–1071). Consequently, whether an affidavit is being tendered for a trial hearing or for any other hearing, hearsay statements need not be excised from it. Compliance with para.4.2 should ensure that any hearsay statement within the affidavit will be identified within the body of it. In certain circumstances, a party proposing to rely at a trial on hearsay evidence given in oral evidence or in evidence in writing must give all other parties notice of his intention to this effect (see rr.33 2 and 33.3 below).

Form of affidavit

32.16 An affidavit[GL] must comply with the requirements set out in the relevant practice direction. **32.16**

Effect of rule

Previously, provisions as to the form of affidavits were contained in RSC O.45, r.1 and CCR O.29, r.10. For form and swearing of affidavits, see further Practice Direction (Written Evidence), paras 2 *et seq.* and Annex 1 (see paras 32PD.2 and 32PD.27, below). **32.16.1**

Defects in affidavits

Where an affidavit or an exhibit to an affidavit is defective, in the sense that it does not conform with the provisions of Pt 32 or the supplementary practice direction, the consequences referred to in Practice Direction (Written Evidence), paras 25.1 and 25.2 follow (see para.32PD.25 below). **32.16.2**

Alterations to affidavits

For practice, see Practice Direction (Written Evidence), para.8 (see para.32PD.8 below). **32.16.3**

Exhibits to affidavits

See Practice Direction (Written Evidence), para.11.1 (para.32PD.11 below) and note Admiralty and Commercial Courts Guide, para.F7.2 (see Vol.2, para.2A–91) (relaxing rule that originals of exhibited documents must be available in court). **32.16.4**

Affidavit made outside the jurisdiction

32.17 **32.17 A person may make an affidavit[GL] outside the jurisdiction in accordance with—**

(a) this Part; or

(b) the law of the place where he makes the affidavit[GL].

Effect of rule

32.17.1 The former rules as to the swearing of affidavits outside the jurisdiction contained in RSC O.41, r.12 and elsewhere were unnecessarily complicated. In a given case, ascertaining the place where the affidavit was made should not prove too difficult; where it is necessary to do so, ascertaining whether an affidavit conforms with the law of the place where made may require proof of the relevant foreign law.

Notice to admit facts

32.18 **32.18—(1) A party may serve notice on another party requiring him to admit the facts, or the part of the case of the serving party, specified in the notice.**

(2) A notice to admit facts must be served no later than 21 days before the trial.

(3) Where the other party makes any admission in response to the notice the admission may be used against him only—

(a) in the proceedings in which the notice to admit is served; and

(b) by the party who served the notice.

(4) The court may allow a party to amend or withdraw any admission made by him on such terms as it thinks just.

Effect of rule

32.18.1 Formerly, notices to admit facts were dealt with in RSC O.27, r.2 and CCR O.20, r.2. Under the former rules the time limits for service differed; it is now fixed at 21 days.

Costs where failure to admit facts

32.18.2 Provisions as to the costs implications for a party who failed to admit facts where he ought to have done were found in RSC O.62, r.6(7) and CCR O.20, r.2(2). See now CPR r.44.3 (Court's discretion and circumstances to be taken into account when exercising discretion as to costs) and r.44.4. (Factors to be taken into account in deciding the amount of costs).

Notice to admit or produce documents

32.19 **32.19—(1) A party shall be deemed to admit the authenticity of a document disclosed to him under Part 31 (disclosure and inspection of documents) unless he serves notice that he wishes the document to be proved at trial.**

(2) A notice to prove a document must be served—

(a) by the latest date for serving witness statements; or

(b) within 7 days of disclosure of the document,

whichever is later.

Effect of rule

32.19.1 The former rules as to notices to admit documents were RSC O.27, r.5 and CCR O.20, r.3. Formerly, these rules also dealt with notices requiring production of documents at trial. Rule 32.19 is confined to notices to admit the authenticity of documents, and so the heading to the rule is misleading.

This rule differs from its predecessors in that now a party will be deemed to admit the authenticity of documents disclosed to him unless he serves notice that he wishes the document to be proved at trial. (It is not incumbent on the disclosing party to seek an admission of authenticity).

Notarial acts and instruments

32.20 A notarial act or instrument may be received in evidence without further proof as duly authenticated in accordance with the requirements of law unless the contrary is proved. **32.20**

Effect of rule

This rule was inserted by the Civil Procedure (Amendment No.3) Rules 2005 and came into effect on October 1, 2005. English civil procedure has to interact with procedures used by foreign legal systems, where the common law does not prevail and where attitudes towards proof of the authenticity of documents differ. (The giving effect (by amendment to CPR, Pt 74) of Council Regulation (EC) 805/2004, creating a European Enforcement Order for uncontested claims is a recent example.) The rebuttable presumption relating to notarial acts and instruments generally, introduced by this rule facilitates proof in various procedural contexts, particularly those with a foreign dimension. **32.20.1**

PRACTICE DIRECTION—WRITTEN EVIDENCE

This Practice Direction supplements CPR Part 32

Evidence in General

32PD.1 **1.1** Rule 32.2 sets out how evidence is to be given and facts are to be proved.

1.2 Evidence at a hearing other than the trial should normally be given by witness statement[1] (see paragraph 17 onwards). However a witness may give evidence by affidavit if he wishes to do so[2] (and see paragraph 1.4 below).

1.3 Statements of case (see paragraph 26 onwards) and application notices[3] may also be used as evidence provided that their contents have been verified by a statement of truth.[4]

(For information regarding evidence by deposition see Part 34 and the practice direction which supplements it.)

1.4 Affidavits must be used as evidence in the following instances:

(1) where sworn evidence is required by an enactment,[5] rule,[6] order or practice direction,

(2) in any application for a search order, a freezing injunction, or an order requiring an occupier to permit another to enter his land, and

(3) in any application for an order against anyone for alleged contempt of court.

1.5 If a party believes that sworn evidence is required by a court in another jurisdiction for any purpose connected with the proceedings, he may apply to the court for a direction that evidence shall be given only by affidavit on any pre-trial applications.

1.6 The court may give a direction under rule 32.15 that evidence shall be given by affidavit instead of or in addition to a witness statement or statement of case:

(1) on its own initiative, or

(2) after any party has applied to the court for such a direction.

1.7 An affidavit, where referred to in the Civil Procedure Rules or a practice direction, also means an affirmation unless the context requires otherwise.

Affidavits

Deponent

32PD.2 **2.** A deponent is a person who gives evidence by affidavit or affirmation.

Heading

32PD.3 **3.1** The affidavit should be headed with the title of the proceedings

---

[1] See r.32.6(1).
[2] See r.32.15(2).
[3] See Pt 23 for information about making an application.
[4] *r.32.6(2) and see Pt 22 for information* about the statement of truth.
[5] See, e.g. s.3(5)(a) of the Protection from Harassment Act 1997.
[6] See, e.g. RSC O.115, rr.2B, 14 and others (Confiscation and Forfeiture in Connection with Criminal Proceedings) and RSC O.110, r.1(3) (Environmental Control Proceedings—injunctions "in rem" against unknown Defendant).

(see paragraph 4 of the practice direction supplementing Part 7 and paragraph 7 of the practice direction supplementing Part 20); where the proceedings are between several parties with the same status it is sufficient to identify the parties as follows:

	Number:
A.B. (and others)	Claimants/Applicants
C.D. (and others)	Defendants/ Respondents
	(as appropriate)

3.2 At the top right hand corner of the first page (and on the back-sheet) there should be clearly written:

(1) the party on whose behalf it is made,
(2) the initials and surname of the deponent,
(3) the number of the affidavit in relation to that deponent,
(4) the identifying initials and number of each exhibit referred to, and
(5) the date sworn.

Body of Affidavit

4.1 The affidavit must, if practicable, be in the deponent's own words, the affidavit should be expressed in the first person and the deponent should: **32PD.4**

(1) commence "I (*full name*) of (*address*) state on oath ...",
(2) if giving evidence in his professional, business or other occupational capacity, give the address at which he works in (1) above, the position he holds and the name of his firm or employer,
(3) give his occupation or, if he has none, his description, and
(4) state if he is a party to the proceedings or employed by a party to the proceedings, if it be the case.

4.2 An affidavit must indicate:

(1) which of the statements in it are made from the deponent's own knowledge and which are matters of information or belief, and
(2) the source for any matters of information or belief.

4.3 Where a deponent:

(1) refers to an exhibit or exhibits, he should state "there is now shown to me marked "..." the (*description of exhibit*)", and
(2) makes more than one affidavit (to which there are exhibits) in the same proceedings, the numbering of the exhibits should run consecutively throughout and not start again with each affidavit.

Jurat

5.1 The jurat of an affidavit is a statement set out at the end of the document which authenticates the affidavit. **32PD.5**

5.2 It must:

(1) be signed by all deponents,
(2) be completed and signed by the person before whom the af-

fidavit was sworn whose name and qualification must be printed beneath his signature,
(3) contain the full address of the person before whom the affidavit was sworn, and
(4) follow immediately on from the text and not be put on a separate page.

Format of Affidavits

32PD.6 **6.1** An affidavit should:
(1) be produced on durable quality A4 paper with a 3.5 cm margin,
(2) be fully legible and should normally be typed on one side of the paper only,
(3) where possible, be bound securely in a manner which would not hamper filing, or otherwise each page should be endorsed with the case number and should bear the initials of the deponent and of the person before whom it was sworn,
(4) have the pages numbered consecutively as a separate document (or as one of several documents contained in a file),
(5) be divided into numbered paragraphs,
(6) have all numbers, including dates, expressed in figures, and
(7) give the reference to any document or documents mentioned either in the margin or in bold text in the body of the affidavit.

6.2 It is usually convenient for an affidavit to follow the chronological sequence of events or matters dealt with; each paragraph of an affidavit should as far as possible be confined to a distinct portion of the subject.

Inability of Deponent to read or sign Affidavit

32PD.7 **7.1** Where an affidavit is sworn by a person who is unable to read or sign it, the person before whom the affidavit is sworn must certify in the jurat that:
(1) he read the affidavit to the deponent,
(2) the deponent appeared to understand it, and
(3) the deponent signed or made his mark, in his presence.

7.2 If that certificate is not included in the jurat, the affidavit may not be used in evidence unless the court is satisfied that it was read to the deponent and that he appeared to understand it. Two versions of the form of jurat with the certificate are set out at Annex 1 to this practice direction.

Alterations to Affidavits

32PD.8 **8.1** Any alteration to an affidavit must be initialled by both the deponent and the person before whom the affidavit was sworn.

8.2 An affidavit which contains an alteration that has not been initialled may be filed or used in evidence only with the permission of the court.

Who may administer oaths and take Affidavits

32PD.9 **9.1** Only the following may administer oaths and take affidavits:

(1) Commissioners for Oaths,[1]
(2) practising solicitors,[2]
(3) other persons specified by statute,[3]
(4) certain officials of the Supreme Court,[4]
(5) a circuit judge or district judge,[5]
(6) any justice of the peace,[6] and
(7) certain officials of any county court appointed by the judge of that court for the purpose.[7]

9.2 An affidavit must be sworn before a person independent of the parties or their representatives.

Filing of Affidavits

10.1 If the court directs that an affidavit is to be filed,[8] it must be filed in the court or Division, or Office or Registry of the court or Division where the action in which it was or is to be used, is proceeding or will proceed. **32PD.10**

10.2 Where an affidavit is in a foreign language:

(1) the party wishing to rely on it—
  (a) must have it translated, and
  (b) must file the foreign language affidavit with the court, and
(2) the translator must make and file with the court an affidavit verifying the translation and exhibiting both the translation and a copy of the foreign language affidavit.

Exhibits

Manner of Exhibiting Documents

11.1 A document used in conjunction with an affidavit should be: **32PD.11**

(1) produced to and verified by the deponent, and remain separate from the affidavit, and
(2) identified by a declaration of the person before whom the affidavit was sworn.

11.2 The declaration should be headed with the name of the proceedings in the same way as the affidavit.

11.3 The first page of each exhibit should be marked:

(1) as in paragraph 3.2 above, and
(2) with the exhibit mark referred to in the affidavit.

Letters

12.1 Copies of individual letters should be collected together and **32PD.12**

[1] Commissioner for Oaths Act 1889 and 1891.
[2] S.81 of the Solicitors Act 1974.
[3] S.65 of the Administration of Justice Act 1985; s.113 of the Courts and Legal Services Act 1990 and the Commissioners for Oaths (Prescribed Bodies) Regulations 1994 and 1995.
[4] S.2 of the Commissioners for Oaths Act 1889.
[5] S.58 of the County Courts Act 1984.
[6] S.58 as above.
[7] S.58 as above.
[8] rr.32.1(3) and 32.4(3)(b).

exhibited in a bundle or bundles. They should be arranged in chronological order with the earliest at the top, and firmly secured.

12.2 When a bundle of correspondence is exhibited, the exhibit should have a front page attached stating that the bundle consists of original letters and copies. They should be arranged and secured as above and numbered consecutively.

Other documents

32PD.13 **13.1** Photocopies instead of original documents may be exhibited provided the originals are made available for inspection by the other parties before the hearing and by the judge at the hearing.

13.2 Court documents must not be exhibited (official copies of such documents prove themselves).

13.3 Where an exhibit contains more than one document, a front page should be attached setting out a list of the documents contained in the exhibit; the list should contain the dates of the documents.

Exhibits other than documents

32PD.14 **14.1** Items other than documents should be clearly marked with an exhibit number or letter in such a manner that the mark cannot become detached from the exhibit.

14.2 Small items may be placed in a container and the container appropriately marked.

General provisions

32PD.15 **15.1** Where an exhibit contains more than one document:

(1) the bundle should not be stapled but should be securely fastened in a way that does not hinder the reading of the documents, and

(2) the pages should be numbered consecutively at bottom centre.

15.2 Every page of an exhibit should be clearly legible; typed copies of illegible documents should be included, paginated with "a" numbers.

15.3 Where affidavits and exhibits have become numerous, they should be put into separate bundles and the pages numbered consecutively throughout.

15.4 Where on account of their bulk the service of exhibits or copies of exhibits on the other parties would be difficult or impracticable, the directions of the court should be sought as to arrangements for bringing the exhibits to the attention of the other parties and as to their custody pending trial.

Affirmations

32PD.16 **16.** All provisions in this or any other practice direction relating to affidavits apply to affirmations with the following exceptions:

(1) the deponent should commence "I (*name*) of (*address*) do solemnly and sincerely affirm ...", and

(2) in the Jurat the word "sworn" is replaced by the word "affirmed".

Witness Statements

Heading

32PD.17 **17.1** The witness statement should be headed with the title of the proceedings (see paragraph 4 of the practice direction supplementing Part 7 and paragraph 7 of the practice direction supplementing Part 20); where the proceedings are between several parties with the same status it is sufficient to identify the parties as follows:

	Number:
A.B. (and others)	Claimants/Applicants
C.D. (and others)	Defendants/Respondents (as appropriate)

17.2 At the top right hand corner of the first page there should be clearly written:

(1) the party on whose behalf it is made,
(2) the initials and surname of the witness,
(3) the number of the statement in relation to that witness,
(4) the identifying initials and number of each exhibit referred to, and
(5) the date the statement was made.

Body of Witness Statement

18.1 The witness statement must, if practicable, be in the intended witness's own words, the statement should be expressed in the first person and should also state: **32PD.18**

(1) the full name of the witness,
(2) his place of residence or, if he is making the statement in his professional, business or other occupational capacity, the address at which he works, the position he holds and the name of his firm or employer,
(3) his occupation, or if he has none, his description, and
(4) the fact that he is a party to the proceedings or is the employee of such a party if it be the case.

18.2 A witness statement must indicate:

(1) which of the statements in it are made from the witness's own knowledge and which are matters of information or belief, and
(2) the source for any matters of information or belief.

18.3 An exhibit used in conjunction with a witness statement should be verified and identified by the witness and remain separate from the witness statement.

18.4 Where a witness refers to an exhibit or exhibits, he should state "I refer to the (*description of exhibit*) marked "..." ".

18.5 The provisions of paragraphs 11.3 to 15.4 (exhibits) apply similarly to witness statements as they do to affidavits.

18.6 Where a witness makes more than one witness statement to which there are exhibits, in the same proceedings, the numbering of the exhibits should run consecutively throughout and not start again with each witness statement.

Format of Witness Statement

19.1 A witness statement should: **32PD.19**

(1) be produced on durable quality A4 paper with a 3.5 cm margin,

(2) be fully legible and should normally be typed on one side of the paper only,
(3) where possible, be bound securely in a manner which would not hamper filing, or otherwise each page should be endorsed with the case number and should bear the initials of the witness,
(4) have the pages numbered consecutively as a separate statement (or as one of several statements contained in a file),
(5) be divided into numbered paragraphs,
(6) have all numbers, including dates, expressed in figures, and
(7) give the reference to any document or documents mentioned either in the margin or in bold text in the body of the statement.

19.2 It is usually convenient for a witness statement to follow the chronological sequence of the events or matters dealt with, each paragraph of a witness statement should as far as possible be confined to a distinct portion of the subject.

Statement of Truth

32PD.20 **20.1** A witness statement is the equivalent of the oral evidence which that witness would, if called, give in evidence; it must include a statement by the intended witness that he believes the facts in it are true.[1]

20.2 To verify a witness statement the statement of truth is as follows:

> "I believe that the facts stated in this witness statement are true."

20.3 Attention is drawn to rule 32.14 which sets out the consequences of verifying a witness statement containing a false statement without an honest belief in its truth. (Paragraph 3A of the practice direction to Part 22 sets out the procedure to be followed where the person who should sign a document which is verified by a statement of truth is unable to read or sign the document.)

[THE NEXT PARAGRAPH IS 32PD.22.]

Alterations to Witness Statements

32PD.22 **22.1** Any alteration to a witness statement must be initialled by the person making the statement or by the authorised person where appropriate (see paragraph 21).

22.2 A witness statement which contains an alteration that has not been initialled may be used in evidence only with the permission of the court.

Filing of Witness Statements

32PD.23 **23.1** If the court directs that a witness statement is to be filed,[2] it must be filed in the court or Division, or Office or Registry of the court or Division where the action in which it was or is to be used, is *proceeding or will proceed*.

[1] See Pt 22 for information about the statement of truth.
[2] r.32.4(3)(b).

23.2 Where the court has directed that a witness statement in a foreign language is to be filed:

(1) the party wishing to rely on it must—
  (a) have it translated, and
  (b) file the foreign language witness statement with the court, and

(2) the translator must make and file with the court an affidavit verifying the translation and exhibiting both the translation and a copy of the foreign language witness statement.

Certificate of court officer

24.1 Where the court has ordered that a witness statement is not to be open to inspection by the public[1] or that words or passages in the statement are not to be open to inspection[2] the court officer will so certify on the statement and make any deletions directed by the court under rule 32.13(4). **32PD.24**

Defects in affidavits, witness statements and exhibits

25.1 Where: **32PD.25**

(1) an affidavit,
(2) a witness statement, or
(3) an exhibit to either an affidavit or a witness statement,

does not comply with Part 32 or this practice direction in relation to its form, the court may refuse to admit it as evidence and may refuse to allow the costs arising from its preparation.

25.2 Permission to file a defective affidavit or witness statement or to use a defective exhibit may be obtained from a judge[3] in the court where the case is proceeding.

Statements of Case

26.1 A statement of case may be used as evidence in an interim application provided it is verified by a statement of truth.[4] **32PD.26**

26.2 To verify a statement of case the statement of truth should be set out as follows:

"[I believe] [the *(party on whose behalf the statement of case is being signed)* believes] that the facts stated in the statement of case are true."

26.3 Attention is drawn to rule 32.14 which sets out the consequences of verifying a witness statement containing a false statement without an honest belief in its truth.

(For information regarding statements of truth see Part 22 and the practice direction which supplements it.)

(Practice directions supplementing Parts 7, 9 and 17 provide further information concerning statements of case.)

Agreed bundles for hearings

27.1 The court may give directions requiring the parties to use **32PD.27**

[1] r.32.13(2).
[2] r.32.13(4).
[3] r.2.3(1); definition of judge.
[4] See r.32.6(2)(a).

their best endeavours to agree a bundle or bundles of documents for use at any hearing.

27.2 All documents contained in bundles which have been agreed for use at a hearing shall be admissible at that hearing as evidence of their contents, unless—

(a) the court orders otherwise; or

(b) a party gives written notice of objection to the admissibility of particular documents.

Penalty

32PD.28 **28.1**(1) Where a party alleges that a statement of truth or a disclosure statement is false the party shall refer that allegation to the court dealing with the claim in which the statement of truth or disclosure statement has been made.

(2) The court may—

(a) exercise any of its powers under the rules;

(b) initiate steps to consider if there is a contempt of court and, where there is, to punish it;

(The practice direction to RSC Order 52 (Schedule 1) and CCR Order 29 (Schedule 2) makes provision where committal to prison is a possibility if contempt is proved)

(c) direct the party making the allegation to refer the matter to the Attorney General with a request to him to consider whether he wishes to bring proceedings for contempt of court.

28.2(1) An application to the Attorney General should be made to his chambers at 9 Buckingham Gate London SW1E 6JP in writing. The Attorney General will initially require a copy of the order recording the direction of the judge referring the matter to him and information which—

(a) identifies the statement said to be false; and

(b) explains—

(i) why it is false, and

(ii) why the maker knew it to be false at the time he made it; and

(c) explains why contempt proceedings would be appropriate in the light of the overriding objective in Part 1 of the Civil Procedure Rules.

(2) The practice of the Attorney General is to prefer an application that comes from the court, and so has received preliminary consideration by a judge, to one made direct to him by a party to the claim in which the alleged contempt occurred without prior consideration by the court. An application to the Attorney General is not a way of appealing against, or reviewing, the decision of the judge.

28.3 Where a party makes an application to the court for permission for that party to commence proceedings for contempt of court, it must be supported by written evidence containing the information specified in paragraph 28.2(1) and the result of the application to the Attorney General made by the applicant.

28.4 The rules do not change the law of contempt or introduce new categories of contempt. A person applying to commence such proceedings should consider whether the incident complained of does amount to contempt of court and whether such proceedings would further the overriding objective in Part 1 of the Civil Procedure Rules.

Video conferencing

29.1 Guidance on the use of video conferencing in the civil courts is set out at Annex 3 to this practice direction. **32PD.29**

A list of the sites which are available for video conferencing can be found on Her Majesty's Courts Service website at *www.hmcourts-service.gov.uk*.

Annex 1

Certificate to be used where a deponent to an affidavit is unable to read or sign it

Sworn at ... this ... day of ... Before me, I having first read over the contents of this affidavit to the deponent [*if there are exhibits, add* "and explained the nature and effect of the exhibits referred to in it"] who appeared to understand it and approved its content as accurate, and made his mark on the affidavit in my presence. *Or*, (after, *Before me*) the witness to the mark of the deponent having been first sworn that he had read over etc. (*as above*) and that he saw him make his mark on the affidavit. (*Witness must sign*). **32PD.30**

Certificate to be used where a deponent to an affirmation is unable to read or sign it

Affirmed at ... this ... day of ... Before me, I having first read over the contents of this affirmation to the deponent [*if there are exhibits, add* "and explained the nature and effect of the exhibits referred to in it"] who appeared to understand it and approved its content as accurate, and made his mark on the affirmation in my presence. *Or*, (after, *Before me*) the witness to the mark of the deponent having been first sworn that he had read over etc. (*as above*) and that he saw him make his mark on the affirmation. (*Witness must sign*). **32PD.31**

Annex 2

[Omitted]

[THE NEXT PARAGRAPH IS 32PD.33.]

Annex 3

Video Conferencing Guidance

This guidance is for the use of video conferencing (VCF) in civil proceedings. It is in part based, with permission, upon the protocol of the Federal Court of Australia. It is intended to provide a guide to all persons involved in the use of VCF, although it does not attempt to cover all the practical questions which might arise. **32PD.33**

Video conferencing generally

1. The guidance covers the use of VCF equipment both (a) in a courtroom, whether via equipment which is permanently placed there or via a mobile unit, and (b) in a separate studio or conference room. In either case, the location at which the judge sits is referred to as the "local site". The other site or sites to and from which transmission is made are referred to as "the remote site" and in any particular case any such site may be another courtroom. The guidance applies to cases where VCF is used for the taking of evidence and also to its use for other parts of any legal proceedings (for example, interim applications, case management conferences, pre-trial reviews).

2. VCF may be a convenient way of dealing with any part of proceedings: it can involve considerable savings in time and cost. Its use for the taking of evidence from overseas witnesses will, in particular, be likely to achieve a material saving of costs, and such savings may also be achieved by its use for taking domestic evidence. It is, however, inevitably not as ideal as having the witness physically present in court. Its convenience should not therefore be allowed to dictate its use. A judgment must be made in every case in which the use of VCF is being considered not only as to whether it will achieve an overall cost saving but as to whether its use will be likely to be beneficial to the efficient, fair and economic disposal of the litigation. In particular, it needs to be recognised that the degree of control a court can exercise over a witness at the remote site is or may be more limited than it can exercise over a witness physically before it.

3. When used for the taking of evidence, the objective should be to make the VCF session as close as possible to the usual practice in a trial court where evidence is taken in open court. To gain the maximum benefit, several differences have to be taken into account. Some matters, which are taken for granted when evidence is taken in the conventional way, take on a different dimension when it is taken by VCF: for example, the administration of the oath, ensuring that the witness understands who is at the local site and what their various roles are, the raising of any objections to the evidence and the use of documents.

4. It should not be presumed that all foreign governments are willing to allow their nationals or others within their jurisdiction to be examined before a court in England or Wales by means of VCF. If there is any doubt about this, enquiries should be directed to the Foreign and Commonwealth Office (International Legal Matters Unit, Consular Division) with a view to ensuring that the country from which the evidence is to be taken raises no objection to it at diplomatic level. The party who is directed to be responsible for arranging the VCF (see paragraph 8 below) will be required to make all necessary inquiries about this well in advance of the VCF and must be able to inform the court what those inquiries were and of their outcome.

5. Time zone differences need to be considered when a witness abroad is to be examined in England or Wales by VCF. The convenience of the witness, the parties, their representatives and the court must all be taken into account. The cost of the use of a commercial studio is usually greater outside normal business hours.

6. Those involved with VCF need to be aware that, even with the most advanced systems currently available, there are the briefest of delays between the receipt of the picture and that of the accompanying sound. If due allowance is not made for this, there will be a tendency to "speak over" the witness, whose voice will continue to be heard for a millisecond or so after he or she appears on the screen to have finished speaking.

7. With current technology, picture quality is good, but not as good as a television picture. The quality of the picture is enhanced if those appearing on VCF monitors keep their movements to a minimum.

Preliminary arrangements

8. The court's permission is required for any part of any proceedings to be dealt with by means of VCF. Before seeking a direction, the applicant should notify the listing officer, diary manager or other appropriate court officer of the intention to seek it, and should enquire as to the availability of court VCF equipment for the day or days of the proposed VCF. The application for a direction should be made to the Master, District Judge or Judge, as may be appropriate. If all parties consent to a direction, permission can be sought by letter, fax or e-mail, although the court may still require an oral hearing. All parties are entitled to be heard on whether or not such a direction should be given and as to its terms. If a witness at a remote site is to give evidence by an interpreter, consideration should be given at this stage as to whether the interpreter should be at the local site or the remote site. If a VCF direction is given, arrangements for the transmission will then need to be made. The court will ordinarily direct that the party seeking permission to use VCF is to be responsible for this. That party is hereafter referred to as "the VCF arranging party".

9. Subject to any order to the contrary, all costs of the transmission, including the costs of hiring equipment and technical personnel to operate it, will initially be the responsibility of, and must be met by, the VCF arranging party. All reasonable efforts should be made to keep the transmission to a minimum and so keep the costs down. All such costs will be considered to be part of the costs of the proceedings and the court will determine at such subsequent time as is convenient or appropriate who, as between the parties, should be responsible for them and (if appropriate) in what proportions.

10. The local site will, if practicable, be a courtroom but it may instead be an appropriate studio or conference room. The VCF arranging party must contact the listing officer, diary manager or other appropriate officer of the court which made the VCF direction and make arrangements for the VCF transmission. Details of the remote site, and of the equipment to be used both at the local site (if not being supplied by the court) and the remote site (including the number of ISDN lines and connection speed), together with all necessary contact names and telephone numbers, will have to be provided to the listing officer, diary manager or other court officer. The court will need to be satisfied that any equipment provided by the parties for use at the local site and also that at the remote site is of sufficient quality for a satisfactory transmission. The VCF arranging party must ensure that an appropriate person will be present at the local site to supervise the operation of the VCF throughout the transmission in order to deal with any technical problems. That party must also arrange for a technical assistant to be similarly present at the remote site for like purposes.

11. It is recommended that the judge, practitioners and witness should arrive at their respective VCF sites about 20 minutes prior to the scheduled commencement of the transmission.

12. If the local site is not a courtroom, but a conference room or studio, the judge will need to determine who is to sit where. The VCF arranging party must take care to ensure that the number of microphones is adequate for the speakers and that the panning of the camera for the practitioners' table encompasses all legal representatives so that the viewer can see everyone seated there.

13. The proceedings, wherever they may take place, form part of a trial to which the public is entitled to have access (unless the court has determined that they should be heard in private). If the local site is to be a studio or conference room, the VCF arranging party must ensure that it provides sufficient accommodation to enable a reasonable number of members of the public to attend.

14. In cases where the local site is a studio or conference room, the VCF arranging party should make arrangements, if practicable, for the royal coat of arms to be placed above the judge's seat.

15. In cases in which the VCF is to be used for the taking of evidence, the VCF arranging party must arrange for recording equipment to be provided by the court which made the VCF direction so that the evidence can be recorded. An associate will normally be present to operate the recording equipment when the local site is a courtroom. The VCF arranging party should take steps to ensure that an associate is present to do likewise when it is a studio or conference room. The equipment should be set up and tested before the VCF transmission. It will often be a valuable safeguard for the VCF arranging party also to arrange for the provision of recording equipment at the remote site. This will provide a useful back-up if there is any reduction in sound quality during the transmission. A direction from the court for the making of such a back-up recording must, however, be obtained first. This is because the proceedings are court proceedings and, save as directed by the court, no other recording of them must be made. The court will direct what is to happen to the back-up recording.

16. Some countries may require that any oath or affirmation to be taken by a witness accord with local custom rather than the usual form of oath or affirmation used in England and Wales. The VCF arranging party must make all appropriate prior inquiries and put in place all arrangements necessary to enable the oath or affirmation to be taken in accordance with any local custom. That party must be in a position to inform the court what those inquiries were, what their outcome was and what arrangements have been made. If the oath or affirmation can be administered in the manner normal in England and Wales, the VCF arranging party must arrange in advance to *have the appropriate holy book* at the remote site. The associate will normally administer the oath.

17. Consideration will need to be given in advance to the documents to which the witness is likely to be referred. The parties should

endeavour to agree on this. It will usually be most convenient for a bundle of *the copy documents* to be prepared in advance, which the VCF arranging party should then send to the remote site.

18. Additional documents are sometimes quite properly introduced during the course of a witness's evidence. To cater for this, the VCF arranging party should ensure that equipment is available to enable documents to be transmitted between sites during the course of the VCF transmission. Consideration should be given to whether to use a document camera. If it is decided to use one, arrangements for its use will need to be established in advance. The panel operator will need to know the number and size of documents or objects if their images are to be sent by document camera. In many cases, a simpler and sufficient alternative will be to ensure that there are fax transmission and reception facilities at the participating sites.

The hearing

19. The procedure for conducting the transmission will be determined by the judge. He will determine who is to control the cameras. In cases where the VCF is being used for an application in the course of the proceedings, the judge will ordinarily not enter the local site until both sites are on line. Similarly, at the conclusion of the hearing, he will ordinarily leave the local site while both sites are still on line. The following paragraphs apply primarily to cases where the VCF is being used for the taking of the evidence of a witness at a remote site. In all cases, the judge will need to decide whether court dress is appropriate when using VCF facilities. It might be appropriate when transmitting from courtroom to courtroom. It might not be when a commercial facility is being used.

20. At the beginning of the transmission, the judge will probably wish to introduce himself and the advocates to the witness. He will probably want to know who is at the remote site and will invite the witness to introduce himself and anyone else who is with him. He may wish to give directions as to the seating arrangements at the remote site so that those present are visible at the local site during the taking of the evidence. He will probably wish to explain to the witness the method of taking the oath or of affirming, the manner in which the evidence will be taken, and who will be conducting the examination and cross-examination. He will probably also wish to inform the witness of the matters referred to in paragraphs 6 and 7 above (co-ordination of picture with sound, and picture quality).

21. The examination of the witness at the remote site should follow as closely as possible the practice adopted when a witness is in the courtroom. During examination, cross-examination and re-examination, the witness must be able to see the legal representative asking the question and also any other person (whether another legal representative or the judge) making any statements in regard to the witness's evidence. It will in practice be most convenient if everyone remains seated throughout the transmission.

PART 33

Miscellaneous Rules About Evidence

Contents

33.0.1

Editorial introduction

33.0.2 The rules in this Part replace with modifications those formerly found in RSC O.38, rr.5, 7, 11 and rr.20 to 23, and in CCR O.20, rr.14 to 17 and r.25. Rules 33.1 to 33.5 deal with the adducing of hearsay evidence and are supplemented by Practice Direction (Civil Evidence Act 1995) (see para.33PD.1 below). The remaining four rules deal with matters which, though not unimportant, may be regarded as "miscellaneous", and the same may be said of the other practice direction supplementing this Part, that is Practice Direction—Land Registration Act (see para.33BPD.1 below).

The law as to hearsay in civil proceedings was reformed by the Civil Evidence Act 1995. This Act implemented proposals made by the Law Commission (see "The Hearsay Rule in Civil Proceedings" Law Com. No.216, Cm 2321, 1993). As a result of this reform, rules of court in the RSC and the CCR as to the adducing of hearsay were substantially simplified.

The rules in this Part do not apply to cases allocated to the small claims track (r.27.2(1)(d)).

The provisions of Pt 33 do not apply to proceedings to which Pt 76 (Proceedings under the Prevention of Terrorism Act 2005) applies (see r.76.26(1)). Special rules as to evidence in proceedings under that Part are found in r.76.26 and elsewhere in that Part.

The provisions of Pt 33 do not apply to proceedings to which Pt 79 (Financial Restrictions Proceedings Under the Counter-Terrorism Act 2008) applies. Special rules as to evidence in proceedings under that Part are found in r.79.22 and elsewhere in that Part.

The Civil Evidence Act 1995 s.1(1) states that, in civil proceedings, evidence shall not be excluded on the ground that it is "hearsay" in the sense that hearsay is defined in s.1(2) of the Act. Subsequent sections in the Act constitute a legislative scheme stipulating the circumstances in which, and the conditions under which, hearsay evidence may be received in evidence. This scheme is complemented by the rules of court found in this Part. The power to make rules of court given by the Civil Procedure Act 1997 s.1(2) and Sch.1 includes the power to make "such provision as may be necessary or expedient for carrying into effect" the provisions of the 1995 Act. Further, the rule-making power in the 1997 Act includes the power to "modify the rules of evidence as they apply to proceedings in any court within scope of the rules" (s.1(2) and Sch.1, see Vol.2, paras 9A–738 and 9A–765).

The legislative scheme laid down by the 1995 Act and the rules in this Part apply in relation to hearsay evidence made admissible by the 1995 Act. The scheme does not apply to hearsay evidence made admissible otherwise, notwithstanding that it may also be admissible under the Act (s.1(4)).

Rules of court consequential upon the 1995 Act were introduced in the RSC and CCR in 1996. It was held that the 1995 Act applies to cases begun on or after January 31, 1997 (*Bairstow v Queens Moat Houses Plc* [1998] 1 All E.R. 343, CA) and that the previous law, including the rules of court in effect before 1996, continued to govern cases begun before that date. Subsequently, s.16 of the 1995 Act was amended (see Vol.2, para.9B–1086) so as to enable the Act and CPR provisions related to it to apply to cases begun before January 31, 1997. In December 1999, Practice Direction (Civil Evidence Act 1995) para.3 was amended for the purpose of making it clear that the provisions of the 1995 Act do not apply to claims commenced before January 31, 1997 if, before April 26, 1999, directions were given or orders were made as to the evidence to be given at the trial or hearing (see para.33PD.3 below).

Related sources

- Civil Evidence Act 1995 (see Vol.2, para.9B–1068) **33.0.3**
- Rule 27.2(1)(d) (Part 33 not to apply to small claims)
- Part 6 (Service of documents)
- Part 32 (Evidence)
- Part 34 (Depositions and court attendance by witnesses)
- Rule 76.26 (Modification of the general rules of evidence and disclosure)

Introductory

33.1 In this Part— **33.1**

(a) "hearsay" means a statement made otherwise than by a person while giving oral evidence in proceedings which is tendered as evidence of the matters stated; and

(b) references to hearsay include hearsay of whatever degree.

Definition of "hearsay"

This rule repeats the definition of "hearsay" given in the Civil Evidence Act 1995 s.1(2) (see Vol.2, para.9B–1071). Under the Civil Evidence Act 1968, the precursor to the 1995 Act, a distinction was drawn between "first-hand" and "second-hand" (or "multiple") hearsay and the circumstances in which hearsay of the latter variety was admissible were more limited than the former. Under the 1995 Act and the rules in this Part, "hearsay" includes hearsay "of whatever degree" and therefore includes hearsay of both varieties. (Whether hearsay evidence is "first-hand" or "second-hand" may effect the weight to be given to it, see s.4 of the 1995 Act). **33.1.1**

Notice of intention to rely on hearsay evidence

33.2—(1) Where a party intends to rely on hearsay evidence at trial and either— **33.2**

(a) that evidence is to be given by a witness giving oral evidence; or

(b) that evidence is contained in a witness statement of a person who is not being called to give oral evidence;

that party complies with section 2(1)(a) of the Civil Evidence Act 1995 serving a witness statement on the other parties in accordance with the court's order.

(2) Where paragraph 1(b) applies, the party intending to rely on the hearsay evidence must, when he serves the witness statement—

(a) inform the other parties that the witness is not being called to give oral evidence; and

(b) give the reason why the witness will not be called.

(3) In all other cases where a party intends to rely on hearsay evidence at trial, that party complies with section 2(1)(a) of the

Civil Evidence Act 1995 by serving a notice on the other parties which—

(a) identifies the hearsay evidence; and

(b) states that the party serving the notice proposes to rely on the hearsay evidence at trial; and

(c) give the reason why the witness will not be called.

(4) The party proposing to rely on the hearsay evidence must—

(a) serve the notice no later than the latest date for serving witness statements; and

(b) if the hearsay evidence is to be in a document, supply a copy to any party who requests him to do so.

Effect of rule

33.2.1 See former RSC O.38, r.21 and CCR O.20, r.15.

The Civil Evidence Act 1995 s.2(1)(a) states that a party proposing to adduce hearsay evidence "in civil proceedings" must notify any other party of that fact. The duty to give notice may be excluded by agreement of the parties and may be waived by the person to whom notice is required to be given (s.2(3)).

Section 2(2)(a) states that provision may be made by rules of court as to the manner in which (including the time within which) the duty to give notice is to be complied with. The provisions in r.33.2 are in exercise of that power and are largely self-explanatory.

Section 2(2)(a) also states that provision may be made by rules of court specifying classes of proceedings or evidence in relation to which the duty to give notice does not apply. The provisions in r.33.3 were made in exercise of this power. By that rule civil proceedings in the form of trials are not excluded.

Under former RSC O.38 r.20(3), a party proposing to adduce hearsay at (1) "the trial or hearing of a cause or matter", (2) "the trial or hearing of an issue or question arising in a cause or matter", or (3) "a reference, inquiry and assessment of damages", was required to give a hearsay notice. Former CCR O.20 r.14(3) was to the same effect, except that the third element was rendered as "a reference under s.65 of the Act (Power of judge to refer to district judge or referee)". Rule 33.2, is not as elaborate as the former rules. It states, simply, that notice has to be given where it is proposed to adduce hearsay evidence "at trial". Presumably, it is not intended that the requirement to give notice should be restricted to the first of the three circumstances provided for by the former rules. (Under the CPR, Pt 33 does not apply to cases allocated to the small claims track (see r.27.2(1)(d)) but, of course, such an allocation under the CPR is no longer a reference under s.65 of the County Courts Act 1984 and, in any event, s.65 had, and continues to have, a much wider effect (see Vol.2, para.9A–543)).

Giving notice

33.2.2 Rule 33.2(1) deals with the situation where the hearsay evidence is to be given by a witness called to give oral evidence or in a witness statement of a person who is not being called. (It may be noticed that r.33.2(1)(b) is confined to evidence in writing in the form of witness statements and does not embrace affidavits.) In both events, notice is given by serving the witness statement (no separate notice of hearsay is required) and, in the latter event, by, in addition, informing the other parties that the witness will not be called. The witness statements are to be served on the other parties "in accordance with the court's order" (see r.32.4). In terms, there is no duty on the party required to give notice to identify the hearsay, or to indicate the part of the witness statement in which the hearsay is set out; however, where it is not proposed to call the witness, there is a requirement to say why (see former RSC O.38, r.21(1) and CCR O.20, r.15(1)). Further, a witness statement must draw attention to any statements of information or belief, as distinct from statements made from the witness's own knowledge, and to this extent should draw attention to hearsay statements (see further para.33.2.4 *below*).

Rule 33.2(3) deals with "all other cases". In these cases the party required to give notice must, in doing so, identify the hearsay and state that he proposes to rely on the hearsay evidence at trial. He must give such notice to all other parties and, if the evidence is to be in a document, supply a copy to any party who requests him to do so (r.33.2(4)(b)). (As to proof of statements contained in documents, see Civil Evidence Act 1995 s.8, Vol.2, para.9B–1078.)

Whether the case falls under r.33.2(1) or r.33.2(3) notice must be served no later than the latest date for serving witness statements. That date will be fixed by court order. The court has a general discretion to extend time for giving notice under r.33.2 (see r.3.1(2)(a)).

For guidance as to how parties should proceed where a party on whom a witness statement is served objects to the relevance or admissibility of evidence contained therein, see Chancery Guide, Appx 4, para.4 (Vol.2, para.1A–210).

Failure to give notice of hearsay

A failure to give notice in accordance with s.2 of the 1995 Act and rules of court made thereunder (specifically r.33.2) does not affect the admissibility of the evidence but may be taken into account by the court (a) in considering "the exercise of its powers with respect to the course of proceedings and costs", and (b) as a matter affecting the weight to be given to the evidence in accordance with s.4 (s.2(4)). In the Civil Evidence Act 1968, there was no provision comparable to s.2(1)(b). However, s.8(3)(a) of the 1968 Act expressly conferred upon the court a residual discretion if it thought just to do so to admit a hearsay statement in evidence notwithstanding the failure to comply with the notice requirements prevailing before 1969. The policy of that section was implemented by RSC O.38 r.29 (revoked in 1996). Under the old law, as under the new, the extent to which the circumstances of the failure to give notice affect the weight to be given to the evidence is a matter of degree. The very broad discretion given to the court by CPR r.32.1 to control evidence can be used to exclude admissible hearsay evidence for any appropriate reason, including for failures to comply with procedural requirements. However, it must be remembered that such exclusion would be a procedural "sanction" bringing r.3.8 and r.3.9 and the case law surrounding those provisions into play. Where a party fails to give notice of his intention to rely on hearsay evidence within the time limit imposed by r.33.2(4)(a), r.3.8 and r.3.9 do not apply because no sanction for such failure is provided for by the rule. But in considering whether to grant an application to extend the time limit, r.3.9 sets out all the factors which the court would wish to have regard (*Cottrell v General Cologne Re UK Limited* [2004] EWHC 2402 (Comm), October 20, 2004, unrep. (Morison J.)); see further para.33.4.1 below. Although s.2(4) of the 1995 Act provides that failure to comply with rules of court "does not affect the admissibility" of hearsay evidence, the court has a discretion to refuse to admit hearsay evidence where there is a failure to comply with the time limit in r.33.2(4)(a) (*ibid.*). **33.2.3**

Particulars of hearsay evidence

The Civil Evidence Act 1995 s.2(1)(b) states that, in addition to giving notice, a party proposing to adduce hearsay evidence must give to other parties on request "such particulars of or relating to the evidence as is reasonable and practicable in the circumstances for the purpose of enabling them to deal with matters arising from its being hearsay". Section 2(2)(b) states that provision may be made by rules of court as to the manner in which the duty to give particulars is to be complied with. It may be noted that r.33.2 does not deal expressly with the duty to give particulars upon request. Doubtless, in the ordinary case, if the party proposing to adduce hearsay evidence at trial gives notice in the manner stipulated by the rule, then, not only will that party have complied with the duty to give notice, but also he will have provided particulars to satisfy any request that may be forthcoming from any other party. (Historically speaking, the duty to provide particulars on request predates the mandatory disclosure of witness statements.) But, that will not always be so; where it is not the party upon whom notice of hearsay is served may rely on s.2(1)(b) of the 1995 Act. However, para.18.2 of Practice Direction (Written Evidence) states that a witness statement must draw attention to any hearsay evidence included by indicating (1) which of the statements in it are made from the witness's own knowledge and which are matters of information or belief, and (2) the source for any matters of information or belief (see para.32PD.18 above). As a rule, evidence to be relied on by a party should be reduced to witness statements and served on his opponents. Consequently, a deponent's compliance with para.18.2 should render any request for particulars from other parties unnecessary in the normal case. See further para.32.8.2 above. **33.2.4**

Circumstances in which notice of intention to rely on hearsay evidence is not required[1]

33.3 **33.3 Section 2(1) of the Civil Evidence Act 1995 (duty to give notice of intention to rely on hearsay evidence) does not apply—**

(a) to evidence at hearings other than trials;

(aa) to an affidavit or witness statement which is to be used at trial but which does not contain hearsay evidence;

(b) to a statement which a party to a probate action wishes to put in evidence and which is alleged to have been made by the person whose estate is the subject of the proceedings; or

(c) where the requirement is excluded by a practice direction.

Effect of rule

33.3.1 Section 2(1) of the Civil Evidence Act 1995 states that a party proposing to adduce hearsay evidence (i.e. evidence of a statement made otherwise than by a person while giving oral evidence in the proceedings which is tendered as evidence of the matters stated) shall give notice to the other parties. Section 2(2) states that provision may be made by rules of court specifying classes of proceedings or evidence in relation to which the duty to give notice imposed by s.2(1) on a party proposing to adduce hearsay evidence does not apply (see Vol.2, para.9B–1073). The provisions in r.33.3 are in exercise of this power.

Rule 33.2(1) states that a party intending to rely on hearsay evidence "at trial" should give notice. Rule 33.3(a) states that the duty to give notice does not apply where parties intend to rely on hearsay evidence at "hearings other than trials"; consequently, no duty arises in relation to interlocutory proceedings. As to the meaning of "trial" and "trials" in this context, see para.33.2.1 above. Normally, evidence adduced in interlocutory hearings will be in the form of witness statements or affidavits, and in relation to both forms of written evidence, attention should be drawn to any statements of information or belief, as distinct from statements made from the witness's own knowledge, and to this extent should draw attention to hearsay statements (see paras 32.8.2, 32.15.4 and 33.2.4 above).

The purpose of the exception of the hearsay notice requirement provided for by r.33.3(b) is obvious and is of long-standing (see former RSC O.38 r.21(3)(b), and CCR O.20 r.15(3)(b)). The significance of it is that notice is not required where it is proposed to adduce in a probate claim a statement made by the deceased as evidence of the matters asserted therein. Rules of court relating to probate claims are now found in CPR Pt 74.

Rule 33.3(c) states that any requirement to give notice of intention to rely on hearsay evidence may be excluded by practice direction. This provision enables the hearsay notice requirement to be suspended by practice direction where that should be desirable (a power that might have proved useful, for example, in the resolution of the controversy as to the use in evidence of Ogden tables).

Paragraph(aa) was inserted by the Civil Procedure (Amendment) Rules 1999 r.9.

Rule 33.3(aa) states that the duty to give notice of intention to rely on hearsay does not apply to an affidavit or witness statement "which is to be used at trial but which does not contain hearsay evidence". This is a curious provision. (Why should it be thought necessary to provide expressly that no hearsay notice need be given where the written evidence contains no hearsay statement?) In the CPR, r.33.3(aa) occupies a similar position to that occupied in the former rules by RSC O.38 r.21(3)(a), which stated that the requirement that a party proposing to adduce hearsay evidence at trial should give a hearsay notice did not apply to "evidence which is authorised to be given by or in an affidavit". Under the former rules, RSC O.41 r.5 stated the long-standing rule that an affidavit (for trial) could contain (unless the court ordered *otherwise*) "only such facts as the deponent is able of his own knowledge to prove"

[1] Amended by the Civil Procedure (Amendment) Rules (SI 1999/1008).

(but an affidavit sworn for interlocutory proceedings could contain statements of information or belief with the sources and grounds thereof). Thus, the effect of RSC O.38 r.21(3)(a) and O.41, r.5 (which had to be read together) in combination was (oddly) that no hearsay notice was required where it was proposed to adduce at trial an affidavit containing only such facts as the deponent was able of his own knowledge to prove. No comparable provision to O.41, r.5 is found in the CPR (*cf.*, Practice Direction (Written Evidence), para.4.2, see para.32PD.4 above). Consequently, in carrying forward former r.21(3)(a) to CPR, r.33.3(aa) the draftsman felt obliged to add "but which does not contain hearsay evidence". If the result seems odd the explanation is that the effect of the former rules was odd (at least after r.21 was amended following the repeal of the Civil Evidence Act 1968 by the Civil Evidence Act 1995).

Power to call witness for cross-examination on hearsay evidence

33.4—(1) Where a party— 33.4

(a) proposes to rely on hearsay evidence; and

(b) does not propose to call the person who made the original statement to give oral evidence,

the court may, on the application of any other party, permit that party to call the maker of the statement to be cross-examined on the contents of the statement.

(2) An application for permission to cross-examine under this rule must be made not more than 14 days after the day on which a notice of intention to rely on the hearsay evidence was served on the applicant.

Effect of rule

See former RSC O.38, r.22 and CCR O.20, r.16. 33.4.1

Rule 32.5 states that, if a party has served a witness statement and he wishes to rely at trial on the evidence of the witness who made the statement, he must call the witness to give oral evidence unless the court orders otherwise "or he puts in the statement as hearsay evidence". If the party is to put in the statement as hearsay evidence he must comply with the rules in Pt 33.

Rule 33.2 states that, where a party proposes to rely on hearsay evidence at trial, he must give notice to all other parties either by serving the witness statement (where the hearsay is contained in a witness statement) (r.33.2(1)) or by hearsay notice (in all other cases) (r.33.2(3)). Where notice is given by service of a witness statement and the party serving the statement does not propose to call the witness at trial he must inform all other parties of his intention in that respect. Where notice is given, not by service of a witness statement but by service of a hearsay notice, it will be obvious to the other parties that it is not the intention to call the maker of the statement.

The Civil Evidence Act 1995 s.3 states that rules of court may provide that where a party adduces hearsay evidence of a statement made by a person and does not call that person as a witness, any other party may, with the leave of the court, call that person as a witness and cross-examine him on the statement as if he had been called by the first-mentioned party and as if the hearsay statement were his evidence in chief (see Vol.2, para.9B–1073). The provisions in r.33.4 are made in exercise of this rule-making power. The main significance of these provisions is that they enable the party against whom the evidence is adduced to obtain the permission of the court to call the maker of the statement for cross-examination. This is a significant power because it enables a court, on the application of a party, to require evidence adduced by the other party to be properly tested rather than simply having to consider the weight to be attached to a written statement, particularly where the evidence in that statement is of importance in the trial. It should be noted that cross-examination is confined to "the contents of the statement". Application for permission must be made within 14 days after the day on which notice of intention to rely on the hearsay evidence was served.

The capacity of an "other party" to make effective use of r.33.4 may be dependent on the notice of intention required by r.33.2 being served timeously by the party proposing to rely on the hearsay evidence. Before r.33.4 came into effect, late service of hearsay notices in relation to makers of witness statements located abroad were commonplace in commercial cases, there being no effective opportunity then for the other party to seek to cross-examine the witness. Since the coming into effect of r.33.4 the position is different. Late service may unfairly prejudice the other party's right to apply for permission to cross-examine under r.33.4 (*Cottrell v General Cologne Re UK Limited* [2004] EWHC 2402 (Comm), October 20, 2004, unrep., Morison J. (application made in course of trial for extension of time for serving notice of intention refused)).

Where a party (D) takes advantage of r.32.5(5), and puts in as hearsay evidence a witness statement served by his opponent (C) and made by a third person (X), the court may, on the application of C under r.33.4 permit C to call X to be cross-examined on the contents of his statement (*Douglas v Hello! Ltd (No.5)* [2003] EWCA Civ 332; [2003] C.P. Rep. 42, CA).

In *Tsavliris Russ (Worldwide Salvage & Towage) Ltd v RL Baron Shipping Co SA (The Green Opal)* [2003] 1 Lloyd's Rep. 523, witness statements signed by a witness (Y) were served by the defendants (D) on the claimants (C). The statements contained opinion evidence and were accompanied by notices under r.33.2 indicating that D (1) intended to rely on the hearsay evidence contained in the statements but (2) did not intend to call Y to testify at the trial. However, after discussions between C and D, the trial began on the understanding that Y would be called by D to give evidence. Nevertheless, shortly afterwards D announced that they did not propose to call Y. C then applied under r.33.4 for permission call and to cross-examine Y on his witness statements. Thereupon, D withdrew the witness statements from evidence. The judge (Tomlinson J.) refused C's application holding that r.33.4 does not permit, because s.3 of the 1995 Act does not permit, the cross-examination by one party of a person upon whom the other party had indicated he proposed to rely where that person's statement is not in the event adduced in evidence. Although it was made clear at the outset of the trial that D intended to rely on Y's witness statements, they had not at that stage irrevocably adduced it or put it in evidence and adopted it as part of their case.

Former RSC O.38, r.22(2) and CCR O.20, r.16(2) said an application to call a witness for cross-examination on hearsay evidence had to be made "on notice to all other parties". Presumably, where permission to cross-examine is sought under r.33.4 copies of the application notice should be served, not just on the party proposing to rely on the hearsay, but on all other parties.

It may be noted that r.32.7(1) provides that, at a hearing other than a trial, where evidence is given in writing (whether hearsay or not), any party may apply to the court for permission to cross-examine the person giving the evidence. If permission is granted but the person in question does not attend for cross-examination his evidence may not be used unless the court gives permission (r.32.7(2)). Presumably, if the evidence of the person who fails to attend is hearsay the court is less likely to give permission for the evidence to be used.

Part 33 is silent as to what should happen if the court gives permission for cross-examination under r.33.4(1) and the person does not then attend as required. However, the lack of a provision in Pt 33 equivalent to r.32.7(2) (which is confined in its application to a hearing other than a trial) does not lead to the conclusion that the court cannot refuse to allow hearsay evidence, albeit not cross-examined, to be adduced. The court has ample powers under r.32.1 to exclude a hearsay statement in these circumstances, and to do so would not offend s.1 of the 1995 Act because the evidence would be excluded, not on the ground of hearsay, but because the witness refused to attend for cross-examination (*Polanski v Condé Nast Publications Ltd* [2003] EWCA Civ 1573; [2004] 1 W.L.R. 387, CA). If the court considers in all the circumstances that the person outside the jurisdiction should attend and be cross-examined at court in person, but the party intending to call him refuses to arrange for him to come to the English court, then the ordinary consequences of a refusal to obey an order of the court should follow. In such a case, the consequence would ordinarily be that the party would not be entitled to rely upon that evidence in any form (*ibid.*).

Credibility

33.5 ***33.5—(1)* Where a party—**

(a) proposes to rely on hearsay evidence; but

(b) does not propose to call the person who made the original statement to give oral evidence; and

(c) another party wishes to call evidence to attack the credibility of the person who made the statement,

the party who so wishes must give notice of his intention to the party who proposes to give the hearsay statement in evidence.

(2) A party must give notice under paragraph (1) not more than 14 days after the day on which a hearsay notice relating to the hearsay evidence was served on him.

Effect of rule

See former RSC O.38, r.23 and CCR O.20, r.17. 33.5.1

The Civil Evidence Act 1995 s.5(2) (see Vol.2, para.9B–1075) states that, where hearsay evidence is adduced and the maker of the original statement, or of any statement relied upon to prove another statement, is not called as a witness, evidence attacking the maker's credibility is admissible. This rule provides that a party who wishes to introduce such evidence must give notice of his intention to the party who proposes to give the hearsay statement in evidence within the time specified. The genesis of s.5(2) and of this rule pre-dates the introduction of rules requiring the mandatory exchange of witness statements. If a party wishes to introduce evidence attacking the credibility of the maker of a hearsay statement he will have to have served on other parties the witness statement of the witness who is going to provide such impeaching evidence.

Evidence tending to prove that the maker of the statement made any other statement inconsistent with it is also admissible for the purpose of showing that he had contradicted himself (s.5(2)). Rule 33.5 does not say that a party who wishes to introduce such evidence must give notice of his intention to the party who proposes to give the hearsay statement in evidence. If a party wishes to introduce evidence of an inconsistent statement he will have to have served on other parties the witness statement of the witness who is going to provide evidence of the inconsistent statement, thereby alerting the party relying on the hearsay of his intentions in this respect.

Use of plans, photographs and models as evidence

33.6—(1) This rule applies to evidence (such as a plan, photograph or model) which is not— 33.6

- **(a) contained in a witness statement, affidavit[GL] or expert's report;**
- **(b) to be given orally at trial; or**
- **(c) evidence of which prior notice must be given under rule 33.2.**

(2) This rule includes documents which may be received in evidence without further proof under section 9 of the Civil Evidence Act 1995.

(3) Unless the court orders otherwise the evidence shall not be receivable at a trial unless the party intending to put it in evidence has given notice to the other parties in accordance with this rule.

(4) Where the party intends to use the evidence as evidence of any fact then, except where paragraph (6) applies, he must give notice not later than the latest date for serving witness statements.

(5) He must give notice at least 21 days before the hearing at which he proposes to put in the evidence, if—

- **(a) there are not to be witness statements; or**
- **(b) he intends to put in the evidence solely in order to disprove an allegation made in a witness statement.**

(6) Where the evidence forms part of expert evidence, he must give notice when the expert's report is served on the other party.

(7) Where the evidence is being produced to the court for any reason other than as part of factual or expert evidence, he must give notice at least 21 days before the hearing at which he proposes to put in the evidence.

(8) Where a party has given notice that he intends to put in the evidence, he must give every other party an opportunity to inspect it and to agree to its admission without further proof.

Effect of rule

33.6.1 See former RSC O.38, r.5.

Unless the court orders otherwise, no plan, photograph or model is receivable at trial unless the party intending to use such material "as evidence of any fact" has given notice to other parties as required by the rule and given them an opportunity to inspect it and to agree its admission without further proof. The rule is designed to facilitate the proving of the fact that the plan, photograph or model is what it purports to be and to enable evidence as to this to be dispensed with at trial.

Where the party to whom notice of evidence in the form of a plan, photograph or model is given is dissatisfied with it, believing it to be (for example) misleading because it is inaccurate or incomplete, he may wish to prepare his own evidence, and for the purpose of doing so if necessary he may seek orders from the court permitting him to enter upon and to inspect property (see paras (c)(ii) and (d) of r.25.1(1)) (*Orford v Rasmi Electronics* [2002] EWCA Civ 1672; October 25, 2002, unrep., CA, per Brooke L.J.).

Proof of records of business or public authority

33.6.2 Rule 33.6(2) refers to the Civil Evidence Act 1995 s.9. That section simplifies the manner in which a party may prove that a document is part of the records of a business or public authority (see Vol.2, para.9B–1079). A document shall be taken to form part of such a record if there is produced to the court a certificate to that effect signed by an officer of the business or authority to which the records belong. Upon production to the court of such a certificate, no further proof that the document is what it purports to be is required. (The section also provides a simple means for proving the absence of an entry in the records of a business or public authority, s.9(3).)

The section is not concerned with the proof of any facts stated in a document forming part of the records of a business or public authority. Normally, proof of such facts will involve the adducing of documentary hearsay made admissible in evidence by the Civil Evidence Act 1995 s.1. A party wishing to adduce such evidence must give prior notice under r.33.2. The notice and inspection provisions in r.33.6 do not apply to evidence of which prior notice must be given under r.33.3 (r.33.6(c)) but yet the rule "includes a document which may be received in evidence without further proof" under s.9 (r.33.6(2)). The implications of this are not entirely clear. Where a party wishes to adduce documentary hearsay, and the document forms part of the records of a business or public authority, the question arises whether he is required to comply, not only with the notice requirements in r.33.2 but also with the notice and inspection requirements in r.33.6. This may be important because the consequences of failure to give notice are different. The consequence of a failure to give notice under r.33.2 is not that the evidence is inadmissible but that the court may take the failure into account (a) in considering "the exercise of its powers with respect to the course of proceedings and costs", and (b) as a matter affecting the weight to be given to the evidence in accordance with s.4 (s.2(4)). However, a failure to give notice under r.33.6 is that "the evidence shall not be receivable" unless the court orders otherwise (r.33.6(3)). It should also be noted that the court may, having regard to the circumstances of the case, direct that any of the provisions in s.9 do not apply to particular records (s.9(5)). This power might be used, for example, where the court has real doubt as to the genuineness of the certificate produced to the court and decides that further evidence to prove that the document is what it purports to be is required.

Evidence of finding on question of foreign law

33.7 **33.7—(1) This rule sets out the procedure which must be followed by a party who intends to put in evidence a finding on a**

question of foreign law by virtue of section 4(2) of the Civil Evidence Act 1972.[1]

(2) He must give any other party notice of his intention.

(3) He must give the notice—

(a) if there are to be witness statements, not later than the latest date for serving them; or

(b) otherwise, not less than 21 days before the hearing at which he proposes to put the finding in evidence.

(4) The notice must—

(a) specify the question on which the finding was made; and

(b) enclose a copy of a document where it is reported or recorded.

Effect of rule

See former RSC O.38, r.7 and CCR O.20, r.25. For Civil Evidence Act 1972 s.4(2), see Vol.2, para.9B–1063. **33.7.1**

Evidence of consent of trustee to act

33.8 A document purporting to contain the written consent of a person to act as trustee and to bear his signature verified by some other person is evidence of such consent. **33.8**

Effect of rule

See former RSC O.33, r.11. **33.8.1**

Human Rights[2]

33.9—(1) This rule applies where a claim is— **33.9**

(a) for a remedy under section 7 of the Human Rights Act 1998 in respect of a judicial act which is alleged to have infringed the claimant's Article 5 Convention rights; and

(b) based on a finding by a court or tribunal that the claimant's Convention rights have been infringed.

(2) The court hearing the claim—

(a) may proceed on the basis of the finding of that other court or tribunal that there has been an infringement but it is not required to do so, and

(b) may reach its own conclusion in the light of that finding and of the evidence heard by that other court or tribunal.

Effect of Rule

This rule was inserted by the Civil Procedure (Amendment No.4) Rules 2000. The Human Rights Act 1998 (see Vol.2, para.3D–1) provides that it is unlawful for a public authority (including a court or tribunal) to act in a way which is incompatible with a Convention right (s.6(1)). Article 5 of the Convention grants a right to liberty and security. A person who claims that a public authority has acted (or proposes to act) in a way which is made unlawful by s.6(1) may (a) bring proceedings against the authority **33.9.1**

---

[1] 1972 c.30.

[2] Introduced by the Civil Procedure (Amendment No.4) Rules 2000 (SI 2000/2092).

under the Act in the appropriate court or tribunal, or (b) rely on the Convention right or rights concerned in any legal proceedings (s.7(1)). Where a person chooses the former of these courses, proceedings in respect of a "judicial act" may be brought only (a) by exercising a right of appeal, or (b) on any application for judicial review, or (c) in such other forum as may be prescribed by rules. In this context, "judicial act" means a judicial act of a court and includes an act done on the instructions, or on behalf of, a judge (s.9(5)). Where a claimant applies for a remedy under s.7 in circumstances to which the provisions outlined immediately above obtain and the claimant's Convention rights have been infringed, then r.33.9 has effect and the court hearing the claim may proceed (but need not) on the basis of the finding of that other court or tribunal that there has been an infringement.

PRACTICE DIRECTION—CIVIL EVIDENCE ACT 1995

This Practice Direction supplements CPR Part 33

1. Section 16(3A) of the Civil Evidence Act 1995 (c.38) (as amended) provides that transitional provisions for the application of the provisions of the Civil Evidence Act 1995 to proceedings begun before 31 January 1997 may be made by practice direction. **33PD.1**

2. Except as provided for by paragraph 3, the provisions of the Civil Evidence Act 1995 apply to claims commenced before 31 January 1997.

3. The provisions of the Civil Evidence Act 1995 do not apply to claims commenced before 31 January 1997 if, before 26 April 1999:

(a) directions were given, or orders were made, as to the evidence to be given at the trial or hearing; or

(b) the trial or hearing had begun.

PART 34

WITNESSES, DEPOSITIONS AND EVIDENCE FOR FOREIGN COURTS

34.0.1 **Contents**

I. Witnesses and Depositions

II. Evidence for Foreign Courts

III. Taking of Evidence—Member States of the European Union

Editorial introduction

Part 34 consists of three sections. Section III was added with effect from January 1, 2004, by the Civil Procedure (Amendment No.4) Rules 2003 (SI 2003/2113) and there were consequential amendments to r.34.13 and r.34.16. **34.0.2**

Section I deals with two separate and distinct topics. The first topic is the attendance of witnesses. Rules 34.2 to 34.7 contain provisions designed to secure the attendance of witnesses to give evidence and produce documents. Formerly, the process for compelling attendance in the High Court was principally the writ of subpoena, and in the county courts the process was a witness summons. Rules 34.2 to 34.7 apply at both levels of Court. The second topic in Sect.I is evidence by deposition. In appropriate circumstances the evidence of a witness may be given, not *viva voce* by the witness at the hearing to which it relates, but in the form of a sworn deposition taken from the witness before the hearing by an examiner. Rules 34.8 to 34.15 contain provisions regulating the procedure for the taking of depositions (whether the witness is within, or without, the jurisdiction). The two topics are quite distinct. The rules securing the attendance of witnesses are of day-to-day importance in proceedings in the High Court and in the county courts. The rules as to the taking of depositions for use in English courts come into play rarely, and usually only in substantial High Court cases. (Rules as to the taking in England of evidence for use in foreign courts are found in Sect.II and Sect.III of Pt 34, see further below.)

Part 34 is supplemented by two Practice Directions. Practice Direction (Depositions and Court Attendance by Witnesses) (see para.34.PD.1 below) deals with witness summonses, depositions for use in the UK and abroad, and the taking of evidence between EU Member States. Practice Direction (Fees for Examiners of the Court) supplements r.34.14 in particular.

Section II (Evidence for Foreign Courts) was inserted in Pt 34 by the Civil Procedure (Amendment) Rules 2002 (SI 2002/2058) with effect from December 2, 2002. The provisions in Section II (rr.34.16 to 34.21) replace CPR Sch.1, RSC O.70.

Section III of Pt 34 (Taking Evidence—Member States of the European Union) makes provision about the procedure for requesting evidence to be taken in a State to which Council Regulation (EC) 1206/2001 on co-operation between the courts of the Member States of the European Union in the taking of evidence in civil or commercial matters (the Taking of Evidence Regulation) applies, and for dealing with requests by the courts of Regulation States for evidence to be taken in England and Wales. The Taking of Evidence Regulation, and hence Section III, does not apply to Denmark; see r.34.22(b) para.34.22. Applications for letters of request under the Proceeds of Crime Act 2002 are made under r.34.13(4) to (7) irrespective of where the proposed deponent is: see r.34.13A.

Attendance of witnesses

A witness summons is used to secure the attendance of the witness at the trial or at a hearing prior to trial; or to require the witness to produce documents to the court at the trial or at a hearing prior to trial (e.g. a "*Khanna* hearing", where the witness summons is used merely to obtain documents and prove their authenticity, the witness producing them not being relied on to give any other evidence. The practice is to specify a date for production of the documents which is earlier than the date fixed for the rest of the trial, see *Khanna v Lovell White Durrant* [1995] 1 W.L.R. 121; [1994] 4 All E.R. 267). **34.0.3**

Part 34 does not deal with penalties for non-compliance with a witness summons. In the High Court disobedience of a witness summons is a contempt of court under RSC O.52 (which is re-enacted in Sch.1 to the CPR). In the county courts the penalty is a fine (see s.55 of the County Courts Act 1984; and CCR O.34 which is re-enacted in Sch.2 to the CPR).

A witness summons is used not just to secure the attendance of a witness who is reluctant to come to court but also, for example, to enable the witness to produce evidence (e.g. to an employer) of the requirement to attend court or to secure priority so that the witness is not summonsed to appear elsewhere on the same day.

As to process for compelling attendance at High Court hearing of witness situated outside England and Wales but within United Kingdom, see Supreme Court Act 1981 s.36.

Depositions

Before applying for the evidence of a witness to be taken on deposition, consider whether there is a cheaper or better way: there usually is. **34.0.4**

At an examination (see rr.34.8 and 34.9) the evidence of the witness is taken before an "examiner" in the same way as if the witness were giving evidence at the trial. The deposition is then admitted in evidence at the trial. This procedure is necessarily expensive, especially if the witness is abroad. (The CCR contained no provision for depositions of witnesses outside England and Wales. The law was, and is, in s.56 of the County Courts Act 1984; and see now r.34.13(3)). Under the Taking of Evidence Regulation the county court has power to order the issue of a request to a Designated Court.

In practice, the taking of depositions outside England and Wales is restricted to substantial High Court cases. Even in such cases consider (as the court will—see the overriding objective in Pt 1) if there is a cheaper way. Three options are:

(1) If a witness statement has been obtained, rely on the statement itself without calling the witness at all (see Pt 33 and Civil Evidence Act 1995, especially r.33.2). If no witness statement has been obtained can an agent be employed to obtain one?

(2) Pay the witness his expenses to attend the trial. With the frequency and availability of modern air travel the cost of the journey and associated expenses is commonly less than that of an examination abroad.

(3) Obtain an order that the witness gives evidence by video link (see r.32.3).

In addition to depositions taken abroad for use in proceedings in England and Wales, Pt 34 also deals with depositions taken in England and Wales for use in the courts of England and Wales and depositions taken in England and Wales for use in courts abroad pursuant to a letter of request.

Related sources

34.0.5
- Practice Direction (Depositions and Court Attendance by Witnesses) (see para.34PD.1) and Practice Direction (Fees for the Examiners of the Court) (see para.34BPD.1)
- Civil Evidence Act 1995
- Supreme Court Act 1981 s.36
- County Courts Act 1984 ss.55 and 56
- RSC O.52 (see Sch.1 to CPR)
- Part 22 (Statement of Truth)
- Part 32 (Evidence)
- Part 33 (Miscellaneous Rules about Evidence)

Forms

34.0.6
- **N20** Witness summons
- **N21** Order for examination of deponent (before the hearing)
- **N93** Order under the Evidence (Proceedings in Other Jurisdictions) Act 1975
- **A** to **J** under the Taking of Evidence Regulations
- Annex A to the Practice Direction draft Letter of Request (where the Taking of Evidence Regulation does not apply).

I. Witnesses and Depositions

Scope of this Section[1]

34.1 **34.1—(1) This Section of this Part provides—**

(a) for the circumstances in which a person may be required to attend court to give evidence or produce a document; and

(b) for a party to obtain evidence before a hearing to be used at the hearing.

(2) In this Section, reference to a hearing includes a reference to the trial.

[1] Amended by the Civil Procedure (Amendment) Rules 2002 (SI 2002/2058).

Scope of Section I

Section I deals with the attendances of witnesses and depositions. In the provisions in Sect.I there are numerous references to "a hearing" (e.g. rr.34.2(4), 34.3(3), 34.5(3), 34.8(1), and 34.11). Rule 34.1(2) states that such a reference includes a reference "to the trial". Sometimes the context will expressly exclude a reference to the trial, or by expressly referring to the trial, will exclude a reference to any other hearing (e.g. r.34.3(2)). **34.1.1**

Applicability of Sect.I to arbitral proceedings

The Arbitration Act 1996 s.43 states that a party to arbitral proceedings "may use the same court procedures as are available in relation to legal proceedings" to secure the attendance before an arbitral tribunal of a witness in order to give oral testimony or to produce documents or other material evidence; this may only be done with the permission of the arbitral tribunal or the agreement of the other parties (see Vol.2, para.2E–188). As to tribunals other than arbitral tribunals, see further r.34.4 (Witness summons in aid of inferior court or tribunal). **34.1.2**

Witness summonses

34.2—(1) A witness summons is a document issued by the court requiring a witness to— **34.2**

(a) attend court to give evidence; or

(b) produce documents to the court.

(2) A witness summons must be in the relevant practice form.

(3) There must be a separate witness summons for each witness.

(4) A witness summons may require a witness to produce documents to the court either—

(a) on the date fixed for a hearing; or

(b) on such date as the court may direct.

(5) The only documents that a summons under this rule can require a person to produce before a hearing are documents which that person could be required to produce at the hearing.

"witness summons"

This term, already in use in county courts, has replaced the former term "*subpoena*" in the High Court. A separate witness summons is required for each witness and can require the witness to attend court to give evidence or produce documents to the court or both. **34.2.1**

In *Tajik Aluminium Plant v Hydo Aluminium AS* [2005] EWCA Civ 1218; [2006] 1 W.L.R. 767, CA; [2005] 4 All E.R. 1232, CA; the Court of Appeal stated that a witness summons to produce documents to the court under CPR r.34.2 involved the exercise of the court's coercive powers. The person to whom it is addressed is at risk of being in contempt of court if he fails to comply. Accordingly, the witness summons should either identify the documents individually or by reference to a class of documents or things so that it is possible to identify the documents to be produced with sufficient certainty to leave no real doubt in the mind of the person to whom the summons is addressed about what he is required to do. That is the test. Anything less was unfair to the witness; it also made supervision and enforcement by the court extremely difficult. The Court of Appeal stated that whether documents have been sufficiently identified is likely to depend, at least in part, on the particular circumstances of the case. The test is unlikely to be met if the documents are described simply by reference to a particular transaction or event which is itself described in broad terms, although in cases where the transaction is self-contained and sufficiently well defined that might be satisfactory. Doubts about the adequacy of the description should be resolved in favour of the witness.

"On such date as the court may direct"

It is clear from r.34.2(4) that a witness can be required to attend not only the trial itself but any other pre-trial hearing. However, permission is required to issue the witness summons if the hearing is not the trial itself (see r.34.3). **34.2.2**

Issue of a witness summons

34.3 **34.3—(1) A witness summons is issued on the date entered on the summons by the court.**

(2) A party must obtain permission from the court where he wishes to—

(a) have a summons issued less than 7 days before the date of the trial;

(b) have a summons issued for a witness to attend court to give evidence or to produce documents on any date except the date fixed for the trial; or

(c) have a summons issued for a witness to attend court to give evidence or to produce documents at any hearing except the trial.

(3) A witness summons must be issued by—

(a) the court where the case is proceeding; or

(b) the court where the hearing in question will be held.

(4) The court may set aside[GL] or vary a witness summons issued under this rule.

"issue of a witness summons"

34.3.1 A separate summons is required for each witness (see r.34.2(3)). Two copies of the witness summons are required; one is for sealing prior to service, the other is retained on the court file. See Practice Direction (Depositions and Court Attendance by Witnesses, para.1.1, and note paras 1.2 and 1.3 (see para.34PD.1 below). A witness summons must be in Form **N20** (to which the form for a certificate of service is attached).

Permission not required

34.3.2 Permission to issue a witness summons is not required provided that the summons is to attend, or produce documents at, the trial itself and the summons is issued 7 days or more before the trial.

Permission required

34.3.3 Permission to issue a witness summons is required in the three situations mentioned in r.34.3(2): this includes, for example, a pre-trial hearing whether in private or not. Where r.34.3(2)(a) applies (less than seven days before trial) see also r.34.5(2).

Pre-trial production of non-party's documents

34.3.4 Rule 34.3(2)(b) recognises and gives statutory effect to "*Khanna* hearings" (see *Khanna v Lovell White Durrant* [1995] 1 W.L.R. 121 referred to in the "Editorial Introduction", at para.34.0.2 above). A party who wishes to have sight of the documents of a non-party before the trial of the substantive issues can do so by obtaining an order for a witness summons to be served on that party and an order that the witness do then produce the documents at a hearing which is confined to receiving the documents, the subject of the witness summons, the remainder of the trial being adjourned to a date to be fixed. This practice is useful where the witness has no evidence to give other than proving the authenticity of the documents concerned. But it is usually preferable now that the power under CPR r.31.17 to make orders for discovery against non-parties applies to all proceedings to obtain such an order, rather than proceeding for a *Khanna* hearing.

"the court may set aside or vary a witness summons"

34.3.5 Applications to set aside a witness summons are made to the district judge or to the master. On such an application the court is concerned to see that parties do not abuse their privilege of summoning witnesses (*Raymond v Tapson* (1882) 22 Ch D 430, CA at 435). A witness served with a witness summons cannot have it set aside merely by swearing that he can give no material evidence; but if the court is satisfied that the witness summons has not been issued in good faith for the purpose of obtaining relevant evidence and that the witness named is in fact unable to give relevant evidence, it will set it aside. Such an order does not prejudice the power of the trial judge to order the witness to attend if he thinks his presence is necessary (*R. v Baines* [1909] 1 K.B. 258). The court will also set aside a witness summons which is oppressive, for example which relates to documents disclosure of which has been refused by the court (*Steele v Savory* [1891] W.N. 195; 8 T.L.R. 84), or which relates to documents protected by public interest immunity (*Bookbinder v Tebbit (No.2)* [1992] 1 W.L.R. 217).

A witness summons (or an application in the nature of such, e.g. to produce and show a film) may be set aside (or refused) where it appears that the request is irrelevant, fishing, speculative or oppressive: see *Senior v Holdsworth Ex p. Independent Television News Ltd* [1976] Q.B. 23; [1975] 2 All E.R. 1009, CA and *Re State of Norway's Application* [1987] Q.B. 433. In *Harrison v Bloom Camillin* (1999) L.T.L. May 14, Neuberger J. held that it was clear that r.34.3(4) allows the court to set aside or vary a witness summons but as no guidance is given as to what approach the court should take, regard is to be paid to the cases decided under the old rules. In *South Tyneside Borough Council v Wickes Building Supplies Ltd* [2004] EWHC 2428 (Comm) witness summonses had been issued by the Claimant against non-parties in a rent review arbitration and there was a confidentiality clause in the document sought. One of the non-parties was B&Q Plc a competitor of the Defendant. The witness summonses were set aside on the grounds that production of the documents was not necessary for the fair disposal of the arbitration (other comparables and materials were available to the arbitrator) and on the ground of confidentiality of the document. Gross J., summarised the law (of necessity derived from pre-CPR authorities) as follows:

"1. The object of a witness summons is to obtain production at trial of specified documents; accordingly, the witness summons must specifically identify the documents sought, it must not be used as an instrument to obtain disclosure and it must not be of a fishing or speculative nature.
2. The production of the documents must be necessary for the fair disposal of the matter or to save costs. The Court is entitled to take into account the question of whether the information can be obtained by some other means. It is to be remembered that, by its nature, a witness summons seeks to compel production from a non-party to the proceedings in question.
3. Plainly a witness summons will be set aside if the documents are not relevant to the proceedings; but the mere fact that they are relevant is not by itself necessarily decisive in favour of the witness summons.
4. The fact that the documents of which production is sought are confidential or contain confidential information is not an absolute bar to the enforcement of their production by way of witness summons; however, in the exercise of its discretion, the Court is entitled to have regard to the fact that documents are confidential and that to order production would involve a breach of confidence. While the Court's paramount concern must be the fair disposal of the cause or matter, it is not unmindful of other legitimate interests and that to order production of a third party's confidential documents may be oppressive, intrusive or unfair. In this connection, when documents are confidential, the claim that their production is necessary for the fair resolution of proceedings may well be subjected to particularly close scrutiny. The essential requirement of a witness summons have been further addressed by the Court of Appeal in *Tajik Aluminium v Hydro Aluminium* [2005] EWCA Civ 1218; [2006] 2 All E.R. (Comm) 295 in which the court stated that the summons should either identify the documents individually or by reference to a class of documents or things by which criteria the person to whom the the summons is addressed can know what obligation the court has imposed on him.

In some cases, a confidentiality clause may be overridden where, for example, a clear need for the documents is demonstrated and considerations of commercial sensitivity are not present or at least not present in acute form."

An unwilling expert may be released from attendance, see *Brown v Bennett (Witness Summons), The Times*, November 2, 2000 Neuberger J. In that case Neuberger J. said that it would only be in exceptional cases that an expert who could not expect to be paid would be compelled to give evidence.

Recovery of costs incurred in complying with witness summons

34.3.6 At the time of service of a witness summons, the witness must be offered or paid sums to cover his travelling expenses and to compensate him for loss of time (see r.34.7). Where the witness summons requires the witness to produce documents to the court, the witness may be faced with the prospect of incurring considerable expense, comparable to that which might be incurred by a non-party required to give disclosure of documents under the Supreme Court Act 1981 s.34 and CPR r.31.17. However, whereas a non-party subject to an order to disclose documents under r.31.17 is entitled to recover the costs of compliance, there is nothing in Pt 34 which provides for compensation for the costs of compliance incurred by a witness required to produce documents under a witness summons. Pt 34 assumes that, in complying with a summons to produce documents a witness will not normally be required to go to any significant trouble or expense in identifying, collating and bringing the documents to court. This was noted at first instance in *Individual Homes Ltd v Macbream Investments Ltd, The Times*, November 14, 2002. In that case, after the claim had been settled the judge ordered that a bank should be joined as a party to the proceedings for the purposes of costs (r.48.2) and that the claimant, who had issued a witness summons against one of the bank's employees, should pay the costs incurred by the bank in complying with the summons. In the circumstances were that, instead of issuing a witness summons against the employee, the claimants ought to have applied for an order against the bank under r.31.17. The judge expressed the view that, although no jurisdiction is given by Pt 34, the court has jurisdiction under the Supreme Court Act 1981 s.51 and CPR r.48.2 (Costs orders in favour of non-parties) to make an order for costs to compensate a witness for the costs incurred in complying with a witness summons to produce documents issued under r.34.2.

Witness summons in aid of inferior court or of tribunal

34.4 **34.4—(1) The court may issue a witness summons in aid of an inferior court or of a tribunal.**

(2) The court which issued the witness summons under this rule may set it aside.

(3) In this rule, "inferior court or tribunal" means any court or tribunal that does not have power to issue a witness summons in relation to proceedings before it.

"inferior court or tribunal"

34.4.1 This term is defined in r.34.4(3). Previously application was to the High Court but, as r.34.4(1) draws no distinction, either the High Court or a county court can issue the witness summons. An application to set aside (see commentary, para.34.3.5) must be to the court which issued the summons (r.34.4(2)). Whether or not a particular inferior court or tribunal has power to issue a witness summons itself is a question of construction of the statute which created it. Rule 34.4 is to assist such courts and tribunals which do not have such power. There is no extant list of the inferior courts or tribunals in relation to which it may be said (1) that they do have powers derived from elsewhere to issue summonses for the attendance of witnesses in relation to proceedings before them, or (2) that parties in proceedings before them may use the same court procedures as are available in relation to legal proceedings to secure the attendance of witnesses (as in the case of arbitral tribunals, see para.34.1.2 above). Consequently, there is no quick means of determining whether a tribunal is, within the meaning of r.34.4(3), a tribunal that does not have power to issue a witness summons in relation to proceedings before it and is, therefore, a tribunal for which a witness summons in aid may be issued under r.34.4. Certain statutory provisions deal with the matter expressly. The Solicitors Act 1974 s.46(11)) states that, for the purposes of any application or complaint made to the Solicitors Disciplinary Tribunal under that Act, the applicant or complainant "may issue writs of subpoena ad testificandum and duces tecum, but no person shall be compelled to produce any document which he could not be compelled to produce on the trial of an action". Similar statutory provisions apply to a number of other professional disciplinary bodies; e.g. in relation to professional conduct committees, the Medical Act 1983 Sch.4, para.2(1), the Dentists Act 1984 Sch.3, para.4(1), Nurses, Midwives and Health Visitors Act 1997, Sch.2, para.1. The Chairman of the Parole Board Panel is entitled to give directions under Rule 9 of the Parole Board Rules 1997 including a direction requiring a party to the proceedings (i.e., the prisoner or the Secretary of State) to apply for a witness summons from the county court or High Court under r.34.4; see *R. (Brooks) v Parole Board* [2004] EWCA Civ 80. The Upper Tribunal (which is not "an inferior court or tribunal" but a superior court of record) has power under its own rules to summon witnesses, etc. on the application of a party or on its own initiative (Tribunal Procedure (Upper Tribunal) Rules 2008 (SI 2008/2698) r.16). Rules applicable to the several Chambers of the First-tier Tribunal (which is not a superior court) contains similar provisions.

Arbitration porceedings

Section 43 of the Arbitration Act 1996 provides that a party to arbitral proceedings **34.4.2** may use the same court procedures as are available in relation to legal proceedings to secure the attendance before the tribunal of a witness in order to give oral testimony or to produce documents or other material evidence. This may only be done with the permission of the tribunal or the agreement of the other parties and the court procedures may only be used if the witness is in the United Kingdom, and the arbitral proceedings are being conducted in England and Wales or, as the case may be, Northern Ireland. Section 43(4) states that a person shall not be compelled by virtue of this section to produce any document or other material evidence which he could not be compelled to produce in legal proceedings. A party who wishes to rely on s.43 of the 1996 Act must apply for a witness summons in accordance with Pt 34; see para.7.1 of the Pt 62 Arbitration Practice Direction. There is no power under s.43 of the 1996 Act for a court to order disclosure against a non-party as opposed to issuing a witness summons for the production of specific documents; see *BNP Paribas v Deloitte &Touche LLP* [2003] EWHC 2874 (Comm); [2004] B.L.R. 90.

"court ... may set it aside"

A witness summons issued under r.34.4 is binding if it is served at least seven days **34.4.3** before the date on which the witness is required to attend (r.34.5(1)), but the court may abridge the time. Unless the court otherwise directs, an applicant must give at least two days notice to the party who issued the summons of his application under r.34.4(2) to set it aside (Practice Direction (Depositions and Court Attendance by Witnesses) para.2.4, see para.34PD.2 below). These provisions are designed to mitigate the inconvenience that may be caused by the service of a witness summons so near the date on which the witness is required to attend as to preclude an application being msde to set it aside. An application to set aside a witness summons issued under r.34.4 will be heard, in the High Court by a Master (at the Royal Courts of Justice) or by a district judge (at a district registry), and in a county court by a district judge (*ibid.* para.2.3).

Time for serving a witness summons

34.5—(1) The general rule is that a witness summons is binding if it is served at least 7 days before the date on which the witness is required to attend before the court or tribunal. **34.5**

(2) The court may direct that a witness summons shall be binding although it will be served less than 7 days before the date on which the witness is required to attend before the court or tribunal.

(3) A witness summons which is—

(a) served in accordance with this rule; and

(b) requires the witness to attend court to give evidence;

is binding until the conclusion of the hearing at which the attendance of the witness is required.

Effect of rule

Rule 34.5(1) is clear and requires the witness summons to be served at least seven **34.5.1** days before the date on which the witness must attend. For who is to serve, see r.34.6.

Permission is required to issue a witness summons less than seven days before the date of trial (see r.34.3(2)(a)) and a direction that the witness summons shall be binding pursuant to r.34.5(2) should be obtained at the same time.

"shall be binding" ... "will be served"

34.5.2 The use of the future tense in r.34.5(2) clearly envisages that a direction pursuant to that rule should be sought before the witness summons is served and not retrospectively.

Duration of witness summons

34.5.3 Rule 34.5(3) makes it clear that the witness summons continues to have effect until the conclusion of the trial or hearing at which the attendance is required. Thus, a new witness summons is not required if the hearing is adjourned, even if the adjournment is not to the next day. Of course, the trial judge can release the witness at some convenient point after the witness has given evidence. If for any reason the trial is abortive rather than adjourned, for example where a jury disagrees, a fresh witness summons would be required for a new trial.

Who is to serve a witness summons

34.6 **34.6—(1) A witness summons is to be served by the court unless the party on whose behalf it is issued indicates in writing, when he asks the court to issue the summons, that he wishes to serve it himself.**

(2) Where the court is to serve the witness summons, the party on whose behalf it is issued must deposit, in the court office, the money to be paid or offered to the witness under rule 34.7.

"a witness summons is to be served by the court ..."

34.6.1 Rule 34.6(1) creates a presumption that the court will serve the summons on the witness. Accordingly, r.6.3(2) applies and the court will decide which of the methods of service specified in r.6.2 is to be used. Having regard to the provisions of r.34.5(1) (witness summons to be served at least 7 days before the hearing) it is clearly necessary to issue in sufficient time for the court to effect service. See also r.34.7 and note that where the court is to effect service the money to be paid to the witness must be deposited in court pursuant to r.34.6(2).

In practice, however, the party usually prefers to serve a witness summons himself, and if he desires it served personally will have to serve himself. If the court serves the summons it will do so by first class post. Whether or not service by post is appropriate for a witness summons must depend on the circumstances of the case. If the witness summons is being served for a "non-hostile" reason (e.g. to enable a willing witness to obtain time off work or to enable an expert witness to break other commitments—see further "Editorial Introduction" to Pt 34, para.34.0.2) then service by post is likely to be sufficient. On the other hand, if the witness is refusing to attend and the witness summons is being issued to compel attendance, service by post is likely to be insufficient to impress the importance of his attendance on the witness. Personal service is not only more likely to create the appropriate impression but also more likely, as a consequence, to secure the attendance of the witness.

Thus, although personal service of a witness summons is no longer a prerequisite of the rule (unlike RSC O.38, r.17) in practice it is likely to be necessary to secure the attendance of a witness who has indicated his reluctance to attend or failed to confirm that he will attend and accordingly the extra cost of personal service is justified and likely to be allowed upon assessment of costs.

Personal service

34.6.2 Unlike RSC O.38, r.17, personal service is not a prerequisite of r.34.6. But see further commentary above.

"indicates in writing ... that he wishes to serve it himself"

34.6.3 The general rule is that the court will serve the witness summons. Often there will be good reason for the party issuing the witness summons to arrange personal service through a process server who will explain the summons and tender the necessary money to the witness (see para.34.0.3 above and r.34.7).

If the witness summons is being issued (as of right or after permission) through the post it is a simple matter for the letter requesting issue to also request return of the witness summons for personal service. But r.34.6(1) goes further than this. Even a party attending in person at the court office to issue a witness summons must indicate "in writing, when he asks the court to issue the summons, that he wishes to serve it himself".

"money to be paid to the witness"

See r.34.7. 34.6.4

Right of witness to travelling expenses and compensation for loss of time

34.7 At the time of service of a witness summons the witness must be offered or paid— 34.7

> **(a) a sum reasonably sufficient to cover his expenses in travelling to and from the court; and**
>
> **(b) such sum by way of compensation for loss of time as may be specified in the relevant practice direction.**

Conduct money

The term "conduct money" does not appear in Pt 34 but nor did it appear in RSC O.38 or CCR O.20. Conduct money is money given to a witness to defray his expenses of coming to, staying at, and returning from the place of trial. A witness was entitled to decline to attend or be sworn until his expenses were paid to him and the court would not entertain an application to commit or fine a witness for non-attendance unless it was proved that conduct money had been paid or tendered to that witness. 34.7.1

Rule 34.7 effects an important change in practice. In addition to "conduct money" (provided for by r.34.7(a)) at the time of service the witness must be offered or paid "such sum by way of compensation for loss of time as may be specified in the relevant practice direction" (r.34.7(b)). (The relevant practice direction is at para.34PD.1, see para 3.3 which provides that the sum in respect of the period during which earnings or benefits are lost, or such lesser sum as it may be proved that the witness will lose as a result of his attendance at court, is to be based on the sums payable to witnesses attending the Crown Court). The last "Guide to Allowances Under Part V of Costs in Criminal Cases (General) Regulations" was issued in June 2005 As from June 1, 2005 the maximum amount payable to an "ordinary witness" for financial loss for a period not exceeding 4 hours is £33.50 and if exceeding 4 hours, £67.00. With effect from August 1, 2001 the maximum subsistence allowance is £2.25 (for a period of absence not exceeding 5 hours); £4.50 (for a period exceeding 5 hours but not exceeding 10 hours); £9.75 (over 10 hours). The maximum overnight allowance is £95 for a hotel in London, Birmingham, Manchester, Leeds, Liverpool or Newcastle Upon Tyne city centres. With effect from the June 1, 2005 there is an additional £21 night subsistence allowance and £5 personal incidental allowance. Elsewhere, the overnight hotel allowance is £65 with the additional £21 night subsistence allowance and £5 personal incidental allowance from June 1, 2005. The overnight allowance is £25 only if staying with family or friends with effect from June 1, 2005. No one could accuse the regulations of generosity.

Evidence by deposition

34.8—(1) A party may apply for an order for a person to be examined before the hearing takes place. 34.8

(2) A person from whom evidence is to be obtained following an order under this rule is referred to as a "deponent" and the evidence is referred to as a "deposition".

(3) An order under this rule shall be for a deponent to be examined on oath before—

> **(a) a judge;**
>
> **(b) an examiner of the court; or**

(c) such other person as the court appoints.

(Rule 34.15 makes provision for the appointment of examiners of the court.)

(4) The order may require the production of any document which the court considers is necessary for the purposes of the examination.

(5) The order must state the date, time and place of the examination.

(6) At the time of service of the order the deponent must be offered or paid—

(a) a sum reasonably sufficient to cover his expenses in travelling to and from the place of examination; and

(b) such sum by way of compensation for loss of time as may be specified in the relevant practice direction.

(7) Where the court makes an order for a deposition to be taken, it may also order the party who obtained the order to serve a witness statement or witness summary in relation to the evidence to be given by the person to be examined.

(Part 32 contains the general rules about witness statements and witness summaries).

Purpose of rule

34.8.1 If a witness cannot attend trial it may be possible to obtain an order under this rule for the examination of the witness. In *Barratt v Shaw & Ashton and Another* [2001] EWCA Civ 137; [2001] C.P. Rep 57, the Court of Appeal said that the primary purpose of r.34.8 is the taking of evidence on deposition and introducing it in that form at the trial from a witness whom it would be impossible to bring to court for trial. However, that court was prepared to accept that it might be appropriate to order a deposition to be taken where justice required that the evidence to be given by the deponent be available prior to the hearing taking place. The example given was where a party wishes to pursue or resist an application for summary judgment under Pt 24, and he could not adduce the necessary evidence for that purpose without having the evidence taken on deposition—perhaps because the witness was refusing to provide a statement. The witness gives evidence before the examiner as if the examination were the trial itself. Thus there is full opportunity for cross-examination. The evidence is reduced to writing and the resulting document (the "deposition") is then received into evidence at the trial.

There are four distinct situations—

(1) Depositions taken in England and Wales for use as evidence in proceedings in courts in England and Wales (see para.4 of Practice Direction, at para.34PD.4).
(2) Depositions taken abroad for use as evidence in proceedings before courts in England and Wales where the Taking of Evidence Regulation does not apply (see para.5 of Practice Direction, at para.34PD.5).
(3) Depositions taken in England and Wales for use as evidence in proceedings abroad pursuant to letters of request where the Taking of Evidence Regulation does not apply (see para.6 of Practice Direction, at para.34PD.6).
(4) Taking of Evidence between Regulation States (see para.7 of Practice Direction, at para.34PD.7.

"before a judge; an examiner of the court; or such other person as the court appoints"

34.8.2 In England and Wales examination is usually before an examiner of the court appointed as such by the Lord Chancellor pursuant to r.34.15. Should there be no suitable examiner in the locality where the examination is to take place, a suitable person (formerly known as a "local special examiner") should be appointed pursuant to r.34.8(3)(c). An examination before a judge will only be ordered in the most exceptional cases and then only with the approval of the judge. Where an examination is sought before a master, the advice of the Senior Master or Chief Master should be sought either directly or through the Master's Secretary.

"date, time and place of the examination"

Anywhere suitable may be used, for example the residence of a witness too ill to attend elsewhere (*Re Bradbrook* (1889) 23 Q.B.D. 226, CA). Rule 34.8(5) requires the order for examination to state the date, time and place of it. **34.8.3**

conduct money

Note the requirement of r.34.8(6) to tender travelling expenses and a sum "by way of compensation for loss of time ...". The Practice Direction referred to is at para.34PD.1; but it does not differentiate between witness summonses and depositions. See further Commentary at para.34.7.1. **34.8.4**

"witness statement or witness summary"

Note the provisions of r.34.8(7) which replicates normal trial practice by requiring advance service of a witness statement or witness summary of the evidence to be given by the person to be examined: see rr.32.8 and 32.9. **34.8.5**

Evidence by video link

See r.32.3. As an alternative to obtaining a deposition, evidence by video link will be preferable (and probably cheaper) in some cases and has the further advantage that the trial judge will hear the evidence first hand. **34.8.6**

Conduct of examination

34.9—(1) Subject to any directions contained in the order for examination, the examination must be conducted in the same way as if the witness were giving evidence at a trial. **34.9**

(2) If all the parties are present, the examiner may conduct the examination of a person not named in the order for examination if all the parties and the person to be examined consent.

(3) The examiner may conduct the examination in private if he considers it appropriate to do so.

(4) The examiner must ensure that the evidence given by the witness is recorded in full.

(5) The examiner must send a copy of the deposition—

(a) to the person who obtained the order for the examination of the witness; and

(b) to the court where the case is proceeding.

(6) The party who obtained the order must send each of the other parties a copy of the deposition which he receives from the examiner.

"in the same way as if the witness were giving evidence at trial"

The main purpose of taking evidence on examination is to obtain the evidence of the witness as if the witness were giving evidence at trial. The examination takes place in the presence of the examiner, the parties and their counsel and solicitors. Modern trial practice is for a witness statement (if there is one) to stand as evidence in chief and the examiner will follow this practice if it is appropriate to do so. Cross-examination and re-examination follow. The examiner may allow a hostile witness to be treated as such by the party calling him (*Ohlsen v Terrero* (1875) L.R. 10 Ch. 127). **34.9.1**

"a person not named in the order"

Note the useful provision in r.34.9(2). **34.9.2**

"may conduct the examination in private"

34.9.3 The general rule is that all hearings are in public (r.39.2(1)) but this rule obviously requires exceptions in the case of depositions, for example if examination is taking place at the witness's home or at a nursing home. See further r.39.2(3). Examiners have always had a discretion (*Wright v Wilkin* (1858) 6 W.R. 643).

"evidence ... is recorded"

34.9.4 Rule 34.9(4) imposes a duty on the examiner to record the evidence. By arrangement, a shorthand writer may be and usually is employed. Alternatively, an audio recording can be made. Ordinarily the deposition will take the form of a verbatim transcript of question and answer this being the more accurate and convenient way of recording the evidence (see per Pennycuick V.-C. in *Lloyds Bank Ltd v Marcan* [1973] 1 W.L.R. 339 at 348; [1973] 2 All E.R. 359 at 371). The former practice of the deposition being taken down in narrative form, rather than in question and answer form, is no longer followed.

"In some cases video recordings have been used to record evidence ... for use in English courts" (per Evans J. in *J Barber & Sons v Lloyd's Underwriters* [1987] Q.B. 103) and this practice is growing in popularity (*cf.* r.32.3—evidence by video link). Paragraph 4.3 of the Practice Direction (see para.34PD.4) requires a written record as well as an audiotape or videotape recording.

Filing and serving of deposition

34.9.5 The examiner has the duty of filing the deposition with the court (r.34.9(5)(b)) and serving a copy on the person who obtained the order for examination (r.34.9(5)(a)): that party must serve other parties (r.34.9(6)).

Deponent objecting

34.9.6 If a deponent objects to answering any question or where objection is taken, see para.4.5 Practice Direction at para.34PD.4.

Enforcing attendance of witness

34.10 **34.10—(1) If a person served with an order to attend before an examiner—**

(a) fails to attend; or

(b) refuses to be sworn for the purpose of the examination or to answer any lawful question or produce any document at the examination,

a certificate of his failure or refusal, signed by the examiner, must be filed by the party requiring the deposition.

(2) On the certificate being filed, the party requiring the deposition may apply to the court for an order requiring that person to attend, or to be sworn or to answer any question or produce any document, as the case may be.

(3) An application for an order under this rule may be made without notice.

(4) The court may order the person against whom an order is made under this rule to pay any costs resulting from his failure or refusal.

Effect of rule

34.10.1 An order for the examination of a witness under r.34.8 is not an order on the witness to attend for examination (*Stuart v Balkis* (1884) 50 L.T. 479). Usually the witness is willing to attend and does attend his examination voluntarily. If he does not attend—or does attend but refuses to be sworn, answer a lawful question or produce any *document—the* examiner signs a certificate pursuant to r.34.10(1). Thereupon, the party seeking the deposition can apply without giving notice (r.34.10(3)) for an order "requiring that person to attend or be sworn ..., etc." (see r.34.10(2)). If the witness then fails to attend he is in contempt of court: an order for committal can be sought (see RSC O.52, re-enacted in Sch.1 to the CPR). Note r.34.10(4) regarding costs.

Use of deposition at a hearing

34.11—(1) A deposition ordered under rule 34.8 may be given in evidence at a hearing unless the court orders otherwise. 34.11

(2) A party intending to put in evidence a deposition at a hearing must serve notice of his intention to do so on every other party.

(3) He must serve the notice at least 21 days before the day fixed for the hearing.

(4) The court may require a deponent to attend the hearing and give evidence orally.

(5) Where a deposition is given in evidence at trial, it shall be treated as if it were a witness statement for the purposes of rule 32.13 (availability of witness statements for inspection).

Effect of rule

Having obtained a deposition a party is not obliged to use it as evidence. Indeed notice is required (see r.34.11(2) and (3)). There is nothing to prevent any party putting the deposition in evidence ("a party ...", r.34.11(2)) subject to the requirement of notice. A deposition given in evidence is available for inspection in the same way as a witness statement (see r.32.13 applied by r.34.11(5)). 34.11.1

An order pursuant to r.34.11(4) requiring the deponent to attend would be highly unusual. Even if a witness not expected to be available (hence the deposition) is now available, ordinarily the deposition will suffice. In *Barratt v Shaw & Ashton and Another* [2001] EWCA Civ 137; [2001] C.P.Rep 57 (CA), r.34.11(4) was described as "a fallback procedure for when it seems preferable that the trial judge should hear some of the evidence orally."

Restrictions on subsequent use of deposition taken for the purpose of any hearing except the trial

34.12—(1) Where the court orders a party to be examined about his or any other assets for the purpose of any hearing except the trial, the deposition may be used only for the purpose of the proceedings in which the order was made. 34.12

(2) However, it may be used for some other purpose—

(a) by the party who was examined;

(b) if the party who was examined agrees; or

(c) if the court gives permission.

Effect of rule

The title which has been given to r.34.12 is misleadingly wide. Rule 34.12(1) applies only to a deposition which resulted from an order requiring "a party to be examined about his or any other assets for the purpose of any hearing except the trial". 34.12.1

In *Dendron GmbH v University of California (Parallel Proceedings: Use of Evidence)* [2004] EWHC 589; [2005] 1 W.L.R. 200; [2004] I.L.Pr. 35, Laddie J., the court rejected the submission that r.34.12 was the only limitation on the use of depositions or that CPR Pt 34 was intended to be a definitive code in relation to the collateral use of evidence. Dealing with a deposition obtained through a court in the USA (see r.34.13) and a deposition obtained though a requested court in a Regulation State (see r.34.23), it was held that there exists an implied obligation not to use, without the permission of the (requesting) court or the consent of the witness, evidence obtained by compulsion under letters of request. A distinction was drawn with CPR Pt 31 (which is said to be a complete code relating to disclosure) on the basis that CPR Pt 31 was not concerned with the taking of evidence under compulsion. Although the *Dendron* case was concerned with evidence obtained under letters of request, it is strongly arguable that such an implied obligation also arises with depositions taken in England and Wales for use in England and Wales.

Where a person to be examined is out of the jurisdiction—letter of request

34.13 **34.13—(1) This rule applies where a party wishes to take a deposition from a person who is—**

(a) out of the jurisdiction; and

(b) not in a Regulation State within the meaning of Section III of this Part.

(1A) The High Court may order the issue of a letter of request to the judicial authorities of the country in which the proposed deponent is.

(2) A letter of request is a request to a judicial authority to take the evidence of that person, or arrange for it to be taken.

(3) The High Court may make an order under this rule in relation to county court proceedings.

(4) If the government of a country allows a person appointed by the High Court to examine a person in that country, the High Court may make an order appointing a special examiner for that purpose.

(5) A person may be examined under this rule on oath or affirmation or in accordance with any procedure permitted in the country in which the examination is to take place.

(6) If the High Court makes an order for the issue of a letter of request, the party who sought the order must file—

(a) the following documents and, except where paragraph (7) applies, a translation of them—

(i) a draft letter of request;

(ii) a statement of the issues relevant to the proceedings;

(iii) a list of questions or the subject matter of questions to be put to the person to be examined; and

(b) an undertaking to be responsible for the Secretary of State's expenses.

(7) There is no need to file a translation if—

(a) English is one of the official languages of the country where the examination is to take place; or

(b) a practice direction has specified that country as a country where no translation is necessary.

Effect of rule

34.13.1 Rule 34.13 is based on the former RSC O.39, r.3A. A "letter of request" issues only in the High Court but the High Court can make an order in a county court case (r.34.13(3)) though, in practice, the cost may be disproportionate in a county court case (consider r.1.1(2)(c)). "Letter of request" is defined in r.34.13(2). [Note that under the Taking of Evidence Regulation the county court has power to order the issue of a request to a Designated Court; see Section III below].

Paragraph (1) of this rule was substituted and para.(1A) inserted by the Civil Procedure (Amendment No.4) Rules 2003, with effect from January 1, 2004.

The rules provide the machinery for the examination of a person out of the *jurisdiction.* The exercise of the power under these rules is a matter of discretion, especially as the cost of taking evidence abroad is high and sometimes prohibitive. The Court is apt to look most favourably upon the application of a defendant resident abroad—who has not chosen an English forum (see, per Chitty J. in *Ross v Woodford* [1894] 1 Ch. 42; *New v Burns* (1894) 64 L.J. Q.B. 104, CA)—and least favourably upon the application of a claimant for his evidence to be taken abroad, for he has usually chosen his tribunal (*Ross v Woodford*; *Cock v Allcock* (1888) 21 Q.B.D. 178, CA; *Emanuel v Soltykoff* (1892) 8 T.L.R. 331). As regards other witnesses, a party cannot compel a witness in a foreign country to attend the trial, and therefore if the Court is satisfied that (1) he is unwilling or unable to be present (2) the application is made bona fide (*Re Boyse* (1882) 20 Ch.D. 760) and with such promptness as not to cause unreasonable delay (see *Langen v Tate* (1883) 24 Ch.D. 522, CA) and (3) the witness can give substantial evidence material to the issue (*Ehrmann v Ehrmann* [1896] 2 Ch. 511) an order is often made. But many other considerations may be relevant in all these cases. Reasonable attempts should first be made, in a proper case, to obtain the evidence in other ways—through a witness here (*Armour v Walker* (1883) 25 Ch.D. 673, CA; *Lawson v Vacuum Brake Co* (1884) 27 Ch D 137 CA; *Lewis v Kingsbury* (1888) 4 T.L.R. 629 at 639) by documents, by admissions or an order that the evidence may be given "by video link or by witness statement". Nowadays, the cost of a journey by air is commonly less than that of an examination abroad.

In *Honda Giken Kogyou Kabushiki Kaisha v KJM Superbikes Ltd* [2007] EWCA Civ 313, the Court of Appeal was concerned with an application under r.34.13 for the issue of a letter of request to the judicial authorities in the State of Victoria for the examination of two witnesses. The Court of Appeal adopted the approach of Sir Richard Scott V.-C. in *First American Corportation v Zayed* [1999] 1 W.L.R. 1154; [1998] 4 All E.R. 439, CA, a case concerned with the examination of witnesses in this jurisdiction for use in foreign courts (see paras 34.21.2 and 34.21.5). Allowing the appeal against the ruling of the deputy judge who had refused to grant the letters of request on the basis that the application was "fishing", it was said that the use of the term "fishing" as an objection to the grant of letters of request was not applicable to an intended witness who can reasonably be expected to give relevant evidence at trial. The Master of the Rolls set out four grounds where it might be appropriate to refuse an application to for the issue of a letter of request notwithstanding that the intended witness might have relevant evidence to give. The grounds were: (1) where the request is oppressive; (2) where the proposed letter of request is too wide; (3) other considerations, for example, where a case management judge concludes that the cost of obtaining the evidence would be disproportionate or that the evidence would not be necessary for the fair determination of the issues in the action (see: the considerations in para.34.3.5, cited with approval by the Master of the Rolls); and (4) delay; an application may be refused on the ground that it is made too late.

In *Peer International Corp v Termidor Music Publishers Ltd* [2005] EWHC 1048 (Ch), Lindsay J., drew a distinction between the taking of evidence abroad and the sitting of the High Court outside England and Wales which is not permitted by section 71 of the Supreme Court Act 1981. The point was made in that case that there have been many examples over the years of an English judge hearing evidence outside England and Wales. It was held that there was nothing in CPR r.34.13(4) which prevented a High Court judge who is hearing a case in England from appointing himself to be the special examiner. In that case the witnesses to be examined were based in Cuba and were willing witnesses on behalf of the Part 20 Defendant which was a Cuban company owned by the Cuban Government. The judge stated that so long as the Government of Cuba indicated that it would allow him, as a special examiner, to examine witnesses in Cuba, he would make an order appointing himself to that end. Furthermore, he held that in such circumstances, and assuming that the Government of Cuba did not insist on the formality of a letter of request, it was not necessary to obtain a letter of request.

It is to be noted that a letter of request would certainly be needed when it is necessary to obtain the evidence of witnesses under compulsion or when the government of a country might not readily consent to a special examiner taking evidence in its country. A special examiner does not have the coercive powers available to the judge sitting in his own jurisdiction. He has no power to compel the attendance of witnesses and no right to ask a government to procure the attendance of witnesses. In *Peer International*, the judge stressed that his sitting as a special examiner would represent no possible incursion into Cuba's dominion over its people and territory. Some other governments might not readily share that view.

As to the approach in England and Wales to the examination of *willing* witnesses by foreign diplomatic or consular officers or by other persons appointed by foreign courts or by legal representatives for the purpose of proceedings abroad; see 34.21.1.

Use of evidence

34.13.2 Evidence obtained by means of r.34.13 cannot be used, as of right, for collateral purposes, but there is a discretion in the court to allow such use in special circumstances and where the use would be just in all the circumstances, *Dendron GmbH v The Regents of the University of California* [2004] EWHC 589; [2005] 1 W.L.R 200; [2004] I.L.Pr. 35.

Practice Direction

34.13.3 See para.5 at para.34PD.5.

Not in a Regulation State

34.13.4 Note that a Regulation State is a Member State of the European Union except for Denmark. See r.34.22(b) at para.34.22.

34.13.5 *Non-Convention countries* —If it is desired to obtain the taking of evidence in a country with which no convention has been made, enquiry should be made of the Foreign Process Section (Room E10, R.C.J) as to whether the local law permits it. It is an available method in the case of Egypt, Japan and Sudan and (possibly) other countries. All states of the USA enforce the attendance of witnesses under this rule. The list of countries which permit examination by special examiner or by consular officer is subject to alteration.

34.13.6 *Scotland and Northern Ireland* —As to compelling attendance of witnesses in such cases, see *Campbell v Attorney General* (1867) 2 L.R. Ch.App. 571. A special examiner is appointed. A witness summons issued by the High Court runs throughout the United Kingdom, see s.36 of the Supreme Court Act 1981.

34.13.7 *Bilateral Convention countries* —In convention countries the taking of evidence before the British Consular Authority is permitted, but in most of these countries it is only permitted in respect of willing witnesses, and in Turkey only willing witnesses of British nationality.

If it is desired to designate as examiner a British consular officer in a foreign state the consent of H.M. Secretary of State for Foreign and Commonwealth Affairs must first be obtained, unless a convention has been entered into with the country in question, in which case no such consent is required. The applicant should apply to the Foreign Office. The answer will depend on whether the laws of the foreign State admit of such procedure and whether the consul proposed is willing to undertake the commission.

It is common practice for the order to designate "H.M. Consul (*or* Consul General) or his deputy."

Conventions have been made with the following countries:

Austria	Greece	Poland
Belgium	Hungary	Portugal
Croatia	Iraq	Serbia and Montenegro
Czech Republic	Israel	Slovakia
Denmark	Italy	Slovenia
Estonia	Latvia	Spain
Finland	Lithuania	Sweden
France	Netherlands	Turkey
Germany	Norway	Bosnia and Herzegovenia
Romania		

34.13.8 *Hague Convention countries* —The Hague Convention on the Taking of Evidence Abroad in Civil or Commercial Matters was concluded on March 18, 1970, and was ratified by the United Kingdom on July 16, 1976, and came into force on September 14, 1976 (see Cmnd. 6727 (1977)). The Convention provides for substantially the same matters of taking evidence abroad in civil or commercial matters as do the bilateral Conventions referred to above, but the Hague Convention is multilateral in its scope and operation.

The countries to which the Hague Convention applies are:

Argentina	Hungary	Russian Federation
Australia	India	Seychelles
Barbados	Israel	Singapore
Belarus	Italy	Slovakia
Bulgaria	Kuwait	Slovenia
China	Latvia	South Africa
Cyprus	Lithuania	Spain
Czech Republic	Luxembourg	Sri Lanka
Denmark	Mexico	Sweden
Estonia	Monaco	Switzerland
Finland	Norway	Turkey
France	Netherlands	Ukraine
Germany	Poland	United Kingdom and possessions
Greece	Portugal	United States and possessions
Romania	Venezuela	Bosnia and Herzegovina

An up to date list of countries to which the convention applies is published on the Hague Conventions website at *www.hcch.net*. This also sets out the reservations subject to which some of these countries have adhered to the convention. There is, of course, an overlap between signatories to the Hague Convention and Regulation States as defined in CPR r.34.22(b) Note that the Taking Of Evidence Regulation (see Sect.III below) prevails over provisions contained in bilateral or multilateral agreements and the Hague Convention; see art.21(1) of the said Regulation.

According to the Hague Convention website, the United Kingdom has not yet declared acceptance of the accession of the following countries: China, Hungary, Kuwait, Lithuania, Romania, Slovenia, Sri Lanka and Seychelles. The Special Administrative Regions of Hong Kong and Macao should no longer appear separately in the list. The Convention still applies to those regions but since Hong Kong and Macao have been restored to the Peoples' Republic of China by the United Kingdom and Portugal respectively, the information relating to these two regions (i.e. reservations, declarations, contact details of the authorities and dates of entry into force) has been added to the information for the Peoples' Republic of China.

Procedure on letter of request to Non-Convention and non-Regulation State countries

A letter of request is required from the High Court to a foreign Court to cause the evidence to be taken, and it may either ask for the interrogatories which accompany it to be put by the examiner (the usual procedure in many foreign Courts, where the Court alone puts the questions) or for the witnesses to be examined *viva voce* upon the matters in question. The method by letters of request is now available for all countries, including Her Majesty's Dominions, and in some countries (such as Egypt) it is the only available method. Letters of request are dealt with in the office of the Foreign Process Section, Room E10, R.C.J. **34.13.9**

Regulation State

Where the person to be examined is in a Regulation State, see rule 34.23 at para.34.23 and para.10.1 of the Practice Direction at para.34PD.7. **34.13.10**

Dominions

Where in a civil proceeding a commission, mandamus, order or request for examination of witnesses is addressed to any Court or Judge of a Court in Her Majesty's Dominions out of the jurisdiction of the Court ordering the examination, such Court or Judge may nominate a person to take the examination, and any depositions before him are admissible to the same extent as if taken before such Court or Judge. **34.13.11**

Eire

Letters of request appear to be the cheaper method. They are sent to the Minister **34.13.12** of Justice, who transmits them to the Master. The duty of taking evidence is usually assigned to the District Judge.

Practice in ChD and QBD

34.13.13 The application is made normally to the Master or District Judge on notice. The application for the Order is not made to the Senior Master, it is the subsequent application for the issue of a letter of request following the making of an order, which is made to the Senior Master. If the other side desire to join in the letters of request they can be allowed to do so at the hearing. Where it is desired to examine witnesses in different countries a separate application should be made in the case of each country.

In certain countries, including those with which conventions have been made, the evidence must be taken orally by examination and cross-examination. In such cases the names of agents of the parties are indorsed on the letters of request. Inquiry should be made at the Foreign and Commonwealth Office, whether evidence can be taken in this way.

Where the evidence is to be obtained by means of written questions, the questions to be asked on behalf of the applicant should be submitted to the other side in order that he may frame questions for cross-examination, and the questions to be asked in cross-examination should be submitted to the applicant to enable him to put further questions in re-examination. The Master will not entertain objections to the questions, they are left entirely to the parties; but objection may be made at the trial to admission of any of the evidence.

The letter of request is prepared by the solicitor and is taken to the Foreign Process Section, Room E10, together with the questions (if any) the order and a signed undertaking by the applicant to bear the expenses (see Form **PF78QB**). If the language of the country concerned is not English there must also be supplied translations of the letter of request and questions certified by the solicitor.

In cases within this rule the letter of request is then signed by the Senior Master and transmitted to the Foreign and Commonwealth Office, for transmission to the proper Court; but where the matter is urgent it may be sent direct to a Court in Her Majesty's Dominions.

On return of the evidence it is filed at the Central Office and notice given to the other side. If in a foreign language, a translation is made verified by the oath of the translator and filed.

Procedure on letters of request to Convention countries other than a Regulation State

34.13.14 Letters of request for the taking of evidence out of the jurisdiction in respect of proceedings in any division of the High Court are dealt with in the office of the Foreign Process Section, Room E10, Royal Courts of Justice, Strand, London, WC2A 2LL.

The conventions vary in details and should be consulted in each case; generally speaking, they provide for three alternative methods of obtaining evidence.

(a) By letter of request transmitted through the Foreign Office for execution by the foreign judicial authority which thereupon obtains the evidence giving effect so far as may be to any special procedure indicated in the letter of request; or (b) In the case of certain countries, by letter of request requesting the foreign judicial authority to cause the evidence to be taken by a British consular or diplomatic officer; the appointment of the consular officer is made by the English Court under r.2(2): witnesses will be compelled to attend; or (c) By a British consular officer or some other fit and proper person nominated by the English Court as a special examiner; attendance of witnesses will not usually be enforced. Under the conventions with France, the Czech Republic, Germany, Turkey, Hungary, Iraq, Croatia, Serbia, Slovakia and Slovenia a special examiner *must* be a consular authority. The practice generally corresponds to the procedure as between Letters of Request to non-Convention countries, except that the request under this rule is signed by the Senior Master, and the translation must be certified by the solicitor to the applicant. (Inquire from the Master's Secretary, Room E14).

Letter of request—Proceeds of Crime Act 2002[1]

34.13A—(1) This rule applies where a party to existing or contemplated proceedings in — 34.13A

(a) the High Court; or

(b) a magistrates' court,

under Part 5 of the Proceeds of Crime Act 2002 (civil recovery of the proceeds etc. of unlawful conduct) wishes to take a deposition from a person who is out of the jurisdiction.

(2) The High Court may, on the application of such a party, order the issue of a letter of request to the judicial authorities of the country in which the proposed deponent is.

(3) Paragraphs (4) to (7) of rule 34.13 shall apply irrespective of where the proposed deponent is, and rule 34.23 shall not apply in cases where the proposed deponent is in a Regulation State within the meaning of Section III of this Part.

Fees and expenses of examiner of the court

34.14—(1) An examiner of the court may charge a fee for the examination. 34.14

(2) He need not send the deposition to the court unless the fee is paid.

(3) The examiner's fees and expenses must be paid by the party who obtained the order for examination.

(4) If the fees and expenses due to an examiner are not paid within a reasonable time, he may report that fact to the court.

(5) The court may order the party who obtained the order for examination to deposit in the court office a specified sum in respect of the examiner's fees and, where it does so, the examiner will not be asked to act until the sum has been deposited.

(6) An order under this rule does not affect any decision as to the party who is ultimately to bear the costs of the examination.

Practice Direction

See Practice Direction—Fees for Examiners of the Court (para.34BPD.1). 34.14.1

Effect of rule

Ultimately the costs of an examination will be dealt with in the same way as other costs of the litigation (r.34.14(6)). But the examiner is entitled to be paid and need not file the deposition with the court under r.34.9(5) unless his fee is paid (r.34.14(2)). 34.14.2

See the Practice Direction at para.34BPD.1 which sets out how to calculate the fees an examiner may charge.

Examiners of the court

34.15—(1) The Lord Chancellor shall appoint persons to be examiners of the court. 34.15

(2) The persons appointed shall be barristers or solicitor-advocates who have been practising for a period of not less than three years.

---

[1] Introduced by the Civil Procedure (Amendment) Rules 2003 (SI 2003/3361).

(3) The Lord Chancellor may revoke an appointment at any time.

Effect of rule

34.15.1 Rule 34.15 is self-explanatory. The former RSC O.39, r.16 enabled the Lord Chancellor to appoint persons as examiners "for a period not exceeding five years at a time" but there is now no statutory period.

Examiners are used on a rota basis. In London the order for examination should be taken to the Master's Support Unit, Room E10, Royal Courts of Justice, and will be indorsed with the name of the examiner.

II. Evidence for foreign courts

Scope and interpretation[1]

34.16 **34.16—(1) This Section applies to an application for an order under the 1975 Act for evidence to be obtained, other than an application made as a result of a request by a court in another Regulation State.**

(2) In this Section—

(a) "the 1975 Act" means the Evidence (Proceedings in Other Jurisdictions) Act 1975[2]; and

(b) "Regulation State" has the same meaning as in Section III of this Part.

Editorial note

34.16.1 With effect from January 1, 2004 this rule was substituted by the Civil Procedure (Amendment No.4) Rules 2003 (SI 2003/2113). It must be noted that Denmark is not a Regulation State, see r.34.22. Accordingly, if the proceedings are in Denmark, the application is made under this Section. Applications made as a result of a request by a court in another Regulation State are made under Sect.III.

Application for order[3]

34.17 **34.17 An application for an order under the 1975 Act for evidence to be obtained—**

(a) must be—

(i) made to the High Court;

(ii) supported by written evidence; and

(iii) accompanied by the request as a result of which the application is made, and where appropriate, a translation of the request into English; and

(b) may be made without notice.

Examination[4]

34.18 **34.18—(1) The court may order an examination to be taken before—**

(a) any fit and proper person nominated by the person applying for the order;

---

[1] Amended by Civil Procedure (Amendment No.4) Rules 2003 (SI 2003/2113).
[2] 1975 c.34.
[3] Introduced by Civil Procedure (Amendment) Rules (SI 2002/2058).
[4] Introduced by Civil Procedure (Amendment) Rules (SI 2002/2058).

(b) an examiner of the court; or
(c) any other person whom the court considers suitable.

(2) Unless the court orders otherwise—
(a) the examination will be taken as provided by rule 34.9; and
(b) rule 34.10 applies.

(3) The court may make an order under rule 34.14 for payment of the fees and expenses of the examination.

Dealing with deposition[1]

34.19—(1) The examiner must send the deposition of the witness to the Senior Master unless the court orders otherwise. **34.19**

(2) The Senior Master will—
(a) give a certificate sealed with the seal of the Supreme Court for use out of the jurisdiction identifying the following documents—
(i) the request;
(ii) the order of the court for examination; and
(iii) the deposition of the witness; and
(b) send the certificate and the documents referred to in paragraph (a) to —
(i) the Secretary of State; or
(ii) where the request was sent to the Senior Master by another person in accordance with a Civil Procedure Convention, to that other person,

for transmission to the court or tribunal requesting the examination.

Claim to privilege[2]

34.20—(1) This rule applies where— **34.20**
(a) a witness claims to be exempt from giving evidence on the ground specified in section 3(1)(b) of the 1975 Act; and
(b) that claim is not supported or conceded as referred to in section 3(2) of that Act.

(2) The examiner may require the witness to give the evidence which he claims to be exempt from giving.

(3) Where the examiner does not require the witness to give that evidence, the court may order the witness to do so.

(4) An application for an order under paragraph (3) may be *made by the person who obtained* the order under section 2 of the 1975 Act.

(5) Where such evidence is taken —
(a) it must be contained in a document separate from the remainder of the deposition;

[1] Introduced by Civil Procedure (Amendment) Rules (SI 2002/2058).
[2] Introduced by Civil Procedure (Amendment) Rules (SI 2002/2058).

(b) the examiner will send to the Senior Master —

(i) the deposition; and

(ii) a signed statement setting out the claim to be exempt and the ground on which it was made.

(6) On receipt of the statement referred to in paragraph (5)(b)(ii), the Senior Master will —

(a) retain the document containing the part of the witness's evidence to which the claim to be exempt relates; and

(b) send the statement and a request to determine that claim to the foreign court or tribunal together with the documents referred to in rule 34.17.

(7) The Senior Master will —

(a) if the claim to be exempt is rejected by the foreign court or tribunal, send the document referred to in paragraph (5)(a) to that court or tribunal;

(b) if the claim is upheld, send the document to the witness; and

(c) in either case, notify the witness and person who obtained the order under section 2 of the foreign court or tribunal's decision.

Order under 1975 Act as applied by Patents Act 1977[1]

34.21 **34.21 Where an order is made for the examination of witnesses under section 1 of the 1975 Act as applied by section 92 of the Patents Act 1977[2] the court may permit an officer of the European Patent Office to—**

(a) attend the examination and examine the witnesses; or

(b) request the court or the examiner before whom the examination takes place to put specified questions to them.

Effect of 1975 Act and the rules

34.21.1 The 1975 Act and these rules should be read and applied in close conjunction, for together they provide a comprehensive, self-contained code for obtaining evidence in England for use in proceedings in foreign Courts in those cases where the proceedings are not taking place in a Regulation State. Where the proceedings are taking place in a Regulation State, reference must be made to Sect.III. The jurisdiction of the English courts to order persons within its jurisdiction to provide oral or documentary evidence in aid of proceedings in foreign Courts has always been exclusively statutory (*Rio Tinto Zinc Corp v Westinghouse Electric Corp* [1978] A.C. 547; [1978] 1 All E.R. 434, HL at 633 and 461, per Lord Diplock); and this jurisdiction and the powers of the High Court to make such orders are now contained in the 1975 Act, as supplemented by these rules. The Act is clear in its terms, so that references in aid of interpretation to the previous statutes which have been repealed are not required nor is any assistance to be gained from previous decisions of English Courts under the former statutes, though in practice it is almost inevitable that references will be so made.

The Act of 1975 applies to civil proceedings which are either pending or contemplated (s.1(b)). The application of the 1975 Act is not confined to countries which are parties to the Hague Convention; nor is the Act limited in its application to courts of law, but extends to tribunals as well (see, per Lord Diplock in *Rio Tinto Zinc Corp v Westinghouse Electric Corp*, above). On the other hand, the 1975 Act does not affect any of the bilateral Civil Procedure Conventions which the U.K. has with a number

[1] Introduced by Civil Procedure (Amendment) Rules (SI 2002/2058).
[2] 1975, c.37.

of foreign countries for the taking of evidence of a person within the jurisdiction for the assistance of courts or tribunals within those foreign countries (see r.3(b)).

It should perhaps be further noted that the 1975 Act does not affect the taking of evidence given *voluntarily* to foreign diplomatic or consular officers or other persons appointed by foreign courts to take evidence or to legal representatives taking evidence in this country for the purpose of proceedings abroad. There is in England no legal objection to the taking of evidence in this country for use outside the jurisdiction without the intervention of the High Court. A foreign Court is at liberty to appoint the consul in England of its own country, or any other person it desires, as an examiner to take evidence. So long as the witnesses are willing to attend to give evidence, the examination may be completed and the depositions returned to the foreign Court without the intervention of the Court in England. Thus American Courts often appoint some person in this country to take the evidence. On the other hand, the rules of this Order concern the power of the High Court to order such evidence to be taken, and they lay down the procedure.

General principles for compliance with foreign request for evidence

The general principle which is followed in England in relation to a request from a foreign Court for assistance in obtaining evidence for the purpose of proceedings in that Court is that the English Court will ordinarily give effect to such a request so far as is proper and practicable and to the extent that is permissible under English law. This principle reflects judicial and international comity (see, per Cooke J. in *Seyfang v G. D. Searle & Co* [1973] Q.B. 148 at 151; [1973] 1 All E.R. 290 at 293) and it conforms with the spirit of the Hague Convention and the 1975 Act as it conformed with the spirit of the former statutes. "We ought to afford foreign Courts the fullest benefit we can" (per Cockburn C.J. in *Desilla v Fells* (1879) 40 LT. 423 at 424). It is the duty and the pleasure of the English Court to do all it can to assist the foreign Court, just as the English Court would expect the foreign Court to help it in like circumstances (see, per Lord Denning M.R. in *Rio Tinto Zinc Corp v Westinghouse Electric Corp* [1978] A.C. 547 at 560; [1977] 3 All E.R. 703 at 708). **34.21.2**

In dealing with a request for evidence from a foreign Court, the English Court has first to decide whether it has jurisdiction to make an order to give effect to the request, and secondly, if it has, whether as a matter of discretion it ought to make or refuse to make such an order. As a matter of jurisdiction, in the ordinary way and in the absence of evidence to the contrary the English Court should be prepared to accept the statement of the foreign Court in its request that the evidence is required for the purposes of civil proceedings in that Court (see, per Lord Diplock in *Rio Tinto Zinc Corp v Westinghouse Electric Corp*, above). On the other hand, the form of the letter of request is not conclusive; the Court must examine the request objectively by the nature of the testimony sought (see, per Lord Wilberforce in *Rio Tinto Zinc Corp v Westinghouse Electric Corp*, above) and it has to look at the substance of the matter (see, per Lord Goddard in *Radio Corp of America v Rauland Corp* [1956] 1 Q.B. 618 at 641) but it may have regard to what was said in the foreign Court when the request for evidence was issued. If there is any doubt about the matter, the English Court may allow the parties to refer back to the foreign Court or Judge who issued the request for evidence (see *American Express Warehousing Ltd v Doe* [1967] 1 Lloyd's Rep. 222).

As a matter of discretion, again in the ordinary way, the English Court should exercise its discretion to make the order asked for unless it is satisfied that the application would be regarded as falling within the description of frivolous, vexatious or an abuse of the process of the Court (per Lord Diplock in *Rio Tinto Zinc Corp v Westinghouse Electric Corp*, above). Thus, the English Court will in its discretion refuse to order an expert to give evidence against his wishes in a case where he has had no connection with the facts or history of the matter in issue and still less to produce his working papers from which he had prepared published articles (*Seyfang v G. D. Searle & Co* [1973] Q.B. 148; [1973] 1 All E.R. 290).

The English Court has power to accept or reject the foreign request in whole or in part, whether as to oral or documentary evidence; and it can and should delete from the foreign request any parts that are excessive either as regards witnesses or as regards documents. The English Court will act on the principle that it should salve what it can, but should decline to comply with the foreign request in so far as it is not proper or permissible or practicable under English law to give effect to it. The English Court, moreover, ought not to embark on the process of re-structuring or re-casting or re-phrasing the foreign request so that it becomes different in substance from the original request. The Court has no power so to modify the original foreign request as to substitute a different category of documents for the category which had been requested by the foreign Court (see, per Lord Diplock in *Rio Tinto Zinc Corp v Westinghouse Electric Corp*, above) and see also *Minnesota v Philip Morris Inc* [1998] I.L.Pr. 170, CA, and *Golden Eagle Refinery v Associated International Insurance* [1998] EWCA Civ 293.

A request could not be denied on the ground of "fishing" if there was sufficient reason to believe that the witness could give relevant evidence to issues in the action and the issue of relevance fell to be determined by the foreign court. It was necessary however to protect witnesses from oppressive requirements such as submitting them to wide ranging examination while at the same time they were under threat of being added as defendants. The test of whether to disallow the request was similar to that applied in setting aside a domestic witness summons: *First American Corp v Al-Nahyan* [1999]1 W.L.R 1154 CA; [1998] 4 All E.R. 439, CA. The case of *USA v Philip Morris Inc* [2004] EWCA Civ 330, is an example to the court taking steps to protect the witness; see 34.21.4 below.

In *First American* (above) it was said that the court should first ask whether the intended witness can reasonably be expected to have relevant evidence to give on the topics mentioned in the requested testimony, and second whether the intention underlying the formulation of those topics is an intention to obtain evidence for use at the trial or is some other investigatory, and therefore impermissible intention; see Sir Richard Scott, Vice-Chancellor at p.1165D.

Evidence for civil proceedings

34.21.3 Under s.1 of the 1975 Act, the High Court has the powers conferred on it by the Act to render assistance to a foreign Court to obtain evidence in England and Wales for civil proceedings in that Court. Three conditions precedent must be fulfilled before the English Court can exercise the jurisdiction conferred upon it to make any order under the 1975 Act, namely:

(1) there must be an application to the Court for an order for evidence to be obtained in England and Wales;

(2) the Court must be satisfied that such application is made in pursuance of a request by or on behalf of a Court or tribunal described as "the requesting Court" exercising jurisdiction outside England and Wales (s.1(a)); and

(3) the Court must be satisfied that the evidence to which the application relates is to be obtained for the purposes of civil proceedings which either have been instituted before the requesting Court or where institution before that Court is contemplated (s.1(b)).

For this purpose, civil proceedings means proceedings in any civil or commercial matter, and request includes any commission, order or other process issued by or on behalf of the requesting Court, sometimes called "letters rogatory" (see s.9(1)).

The term "civil or commercial matter" is a wide general term, covering all kinds of suits, petitions, summonses, applications for orders and so forth, of which Courts are competent to take cognisance (per Chapman J. in *Re Extradition Act 1870 Ex p. Treasury Solicitor* [1969] 1 W.L.R. 12; sub nom. *Re Gross* [1968] 3 All E.R. 804). Civil proceedings include procedural steps taken in the course of proceedings from commencement to their conclusion; see *Rio Tinto Zinc Corportation v Westinghouse Electric Corp* [1978] A.C. 547 at 633; [1978] 1 All ER 703, HL at p.461.

Affiliation proceedings are a "civil matter" (*S. v E.* [1967] 1 Q.B. 367; [1967] 1 All E.R. 593).

For the purposes of civil proceedings, the English Court must be satisfied that the requesting Court is requiring the evidence for the purposes of proceedings which have been begun or are contemplated in that Court. What precisely is meant by 'contemplated' remains to be decided by an English court.

The English court will extend its assistance in obtaining evidence to be used for the enforcement of the revenue law of a foreign state in that state itself, since this will not breach the rule that the English courts will not assist in the direct or indirect enforcement in England of the revenue law of that foreign state (*Re State of Norway's Applications (Nos 1 & 2)* [1990] 1 A.C. 723).

In *Smith v Phillip Morris Companies Inc* [2006] EWHC 916 (QB), Andrew Smith J., an order for the oral examination of a non party to proceedings in Kansas was set aside where the letter of request seeking the order was couched in such wide terms that it amounted to an impermissible investigation and the letter of request could not properly be modified or made subject to conditions. The judgment contains a useful summary of the general principles which govern the approach of English courts to letters of request.

Powers of the Court

Under s.2 of the 1975 Act, the High Court is given extensive powers on an application under s.1 to make an order for obtaining the requested evidence in England or Wales. The Court may by its order make such provision for obtaining the requested evidence "as may appear to the Court appropriate for the purposes of giving effect to the request in pursuance of which the application is made" (s.2(1)) and the order may require a person specified therein to take such steps as the Court may consider appropriate for that purpose *(ibid.)*. **34.21.4**

In particular, the order of the Court may make provision for the examination of witnesses, either orally or in writing; the production of documents; the inspection, photographing, preservation, custody or detention of any property; the taking of samples of any property and the carrying out of any experiments on or with any property; the medical examination of any person, and the taking and testing of samples of blood from any person (s.2(2)).

In *USA v Philip Moris Inc* [2004] EWCA Civ 330, the judge at first instance included in his order a direction that the applicant (the Claimant) supply to the non-party witness and one of the defendants a paginated bundle of documents on which it intended to rely at the examination, together with a written indication of the proposed lines of questioning with reference to documents together with sample questions. He also fixed a directions hearing at which he would hear objections by the witness and the defendant and give further directions as appropriate. The Court of Appeal approved this approach. The case was complex, involved numerous documents and it was likely that the witness would raise issues of legal professional privilege.

Nevertheless, there are important limitations upon the powers of the English Court imposed by subss.(3) and (4) in making an order for obtaining evidence at the request of a foreign Court and by the common law. These limitations include:

(1) no order for general disclosure of documents;

(2) production only of particular documents specified in the foreign request; and

(3) breach of UK sovereignty.

In addition, of course, the Act of 1975 preserves the grounds of privilege of a witness from giving evidence or producing documents recognised under the law of England or of the requesting Court (s.3).

These limitations and the preservation of the recognised grounds of privilege are intended to protect and safeguard the position of a person, not a party to the foreign litigation, from giving evidence in aid of foreign proceedings, which according to the policy of English procedural law he ought not to be compelled to give. Note also that there is no power to order the taking of evidence from any person in his capacity as an officer or servant of the Crown; s.9(4) of the 1975 Act. As to evidence for pre-trial purposes see the next paragraph.

Distinction between evidence for trial or for pre-trial purposes

Under s.2(3), the English Court is prohibited from making an order requiring any particular steps to be taken unless they are steps which can be required to be taken by way of obtaining evidence for the purposes of civil proceedings in the English Court, whether or not they are proceedings of the same description as those to which the application for the order relates. This provision, which applies both to oral and documentary evidence recognises and gives effect to the distinction between evidence in the nature of proof to be used for the purposes of the trial and evidence in the nature of pre-trial disclosure to be used for the purposes of leading to a train of inquiry which might produce direct evidence for the trial. This distinction was in the mind of the draftsman of the Act of 1975 and was made the subject of an express declaration by Her Majesty's Government when ratifying the Hague Convention that the United Kingdom would "not execute letters of request issued for the purpose of obtaining pre-trial discovery of documents" (see Cmnd. 6727 (1976)); see 34.21.6 (below). **34.21.5**

Accordingly, the English Court could in the past refuse to make an order in aid of a foreign request for evidence if it appeared or to the extent to which it appeared that that evidence was required, not for the purpose of proof at the foreign trial, where it was admissible and relevant to the issues in those proceedings, but for the purpose of disclosure, something in the nature of a roving inquiry in which a party was seeking to "fish out" some material which might lead to obtaining admissible evidence at the trial, even though the procedure of the foreign Court permited such a practice, as, for example, rule 26 of the U.S. Federal Rules of Civil Procedure and the rules of many State Courts in the U.S.A., and rule 18 of the Nova Scotia Civil Procedure Rules (see *Radio Corp of America v Rauland Corp* [1956] 1 Q.B. 214; [1956] 1 All E.R. 549; DC; *Burchard v Macfarlane* [1891] 2 Q.B. 241; *Penn-Texas Corp v Murat Anstalt* [1964] 1 Q.B. 40; [1963] 1 All E.R. 258). On the other hand, if the foreign request is for evidence in the nature of proof to be adduced to the trial, the English Court will give effect to such request and it may do so subject to modifications as to the disallowances of certain witnesses or documents (*Rio Tinto Zinc Corp v Westinghouse Electric Corp* [1978] A.C. 547; [1978] 1 All ER. 434, HL, upholding the CA [1977] 3 W.L.R. 430; [1977] 3 All E.R. 703, though reversing the decision on other grounds; and see *American Express Warehousing Ltd v Doe* [1967] 1 Lloyd's Rep. 222, CA). The combined approach in relation to the Act of 1975 is set out by Waller L.J. in the decision of the Court of Appeal in *Genira Trade and Finance Inc v CS First Boston and Standard Bank (London) Ltd* [2001] EWCA Civ 1733, paras 28 to 32; [2002] C.L.C. 301. See also *First American Corp v Zayed and others* [1999] 1 W.L.R.1154; [1998] 4 All ER 439 CA; and see *Golden Eagle Refinery v Associated International Insurance* [1998] EWCA Civ 293, where the Court of Appeal upheld the orders for the examination of witnesses on terms that the examination "shall be for the purpose only of eliciting and recording testimony appropriate to be given at trial" and that "no question may be asked of the witness which in the opinion of the examiner is not a question of the nature that could properly be asked by counsel examining the witness in chief at trial before the High Court of England and Wales."

The Second Division of the Inner House of the Court of Session amended a letter of request from the Superior Court of the State of California which had the dual purpose of discovery and obtaining evidence for the use at trial by adding the words "for the purpose of his trial testimony only". The Court also directed that a legal representative of the witness should be allowed to be present at the examination with power to object to questions which appeared to be objectionable. It would then be for the examiner (in this case the Sheriff Principal of North Strathclyde) to rule upon these objections (*Lord Advocate v Murdoch* 1994 S.L.T. 852).

In relation to legal systems which do not recognise the distinction between the stages of pre-trial and trial, as in the case of many European Continental systems, it seems that the English Court may have to give effect to the request of the foreign Court, since all the material which such a Court gathers in the way of evidence forms part of the material on which that Court makes its final adjudication, so that the evidence is the equivalent of testimony at the trial. It remains to be seen how the more restrictive approach of the English courts to disclosure (Pt 31) is likely to effect the position given the extensive discretionary powers that remain.

No order for general disclosure of documents

34.21.6 Under s.2(4)(a) of the 1975 Act, the English Court is prohibited from making an order against a stranger to the proceedings requiring him to make general disclosure of documents, i.e. to state whether documents relevant to the proceedings to which the application for the order relates are or have been in his possession, custody or power. Such an order would be in the nature of a "fishing" expedition which is never allowed in the English Court (see, per Lord Goddard C.J. in *Radio Corp of America v Rauland Corp* [1956] 1 Q.B. 618, at 649; see also *Buchard v Macfarlane* [1891] 2 Q.B. 241). This provision was made pursuant to the express declaration of H.M. Government when modifying the Hague Convention (see Cmnd. 6727 (1976)). The words "possession, custody or power" are set out in the Act. CPR r.31.8 refers to "control".

Production of particular documents specified

34.21.7 Under s.2(4)(b) of the Act of 1975, the English court is prohibited from making an order against a stranger to the proceedings requiring him to produce any documents other than particular documents specified in the order as being documents appearing to the Court making the order to be, or be likely to be, in his possession, custody or *power.*

In making an order for the production of documents, the Court must first be satisfied that they are likely to be, in the control of the person against whom the order is made CPR r.31.8. The burden of proving this fact is upon the applicant, and there must be sufficient evidence supporting this ground.

Moreover, in applying this provision of the Act, the Court is limited to ordering the production of "particular documents specified," i.e. individual documents separately described, together with replies to letters where replies must have been sent (per Lord Diplock and per Lord Wilberforce respectively in *Rio Tinto Zinc Corp v Westinghouse Electric Corp*, above). General words like a request for "any memoranda, correspondence or other documents relevant thereto" or "any memoranda, correspondence or other documents referred to therein" are far too wide and will be struck out (*Rio Tinto Zinc Corp v Westinghouse Electric Corp*, above, negating to this extent *American Express Warehousing Ltd v Doe* [1967] 1 Lloyd's Rep. 222, CA). The analogy to be followed is, not what description of documents would be sufficient for the purposes of a witness summons to produce documents but what particular documents would fall within CPR r.31.12, for the production of "particular documents." Indeed, the Act of 1975 has not dealt more liberally than its predecessor with pre-trial discovery but it has taken a stricter line (see, per Lord Wilberforce in *Rio Tinto Zinc Corp v Westinghouse Electric Corp*, above).

The House of Lords has explained in *Re Asbestos Insurance Coverage Cases* [1985] 1 W.L.R. 331; [1985] 1 All ER. 716 that (1) "particular documents" means individual documents separately described; a compendious description of several documents (e.g. "monthly bank statements for August to December") may be used provided that the exact document in each case is clearly indicated. (2) A second test of "particular documents" is that they must be actual documents shown by evidence to exist or to have existed. Conjectural documents which may or may not exist, or have existed, do not satisfy this test (per Lord Fraser at 720–722).

On the other hand, documents to be produced under letters rogatory need not be ancillary to the oral evidence of witnesses (*Rio Tinto Zinc Corp v Westinghouse Electric Corp* [1978] A.C. 547).

In *Panayiotou v Sony Music* [1994] Ch 142; [1994] 1 All E.R. 755, 763, 764 a case concerning an outgoing letter of request under O.39, r.2, Nicholls V.-C. after discussing *Rio Tinto Zinc Corp v Westinghouse Electric Corp* and *Re Asbestos Insurance Coverage Cases*, above, considered that letters of request for the production of documents whether outgoing or incoming should be governed by a uniform standard and that standard was the standard applicable to a domestic summons to produce documents. See also hisdecision of the Court of Appeal in *First American Corp v Sheikh Zayed Al-Nahyan* [1999] I.L.Pr. 179.

Breach of UK sovereignty

Quite apart from the provisions of the 1975 Act, where it appears to the Court that **34.21.8** the Ministry or Department of another state, e.g. the USA has intervened in the letters rogatory proceedings with a view to the exercise by that State of extra-territorial jurisdiction in penal matters which in the view of Her Majesty's Government is prejudicial to the sovereignty of the UK, the Court will refuse to give effect to the letters rogatory; and in any event, such letters rogatory will have changed their character from being a request for evidence in proceedings for the foreign Court and converted into a request for evidence for the purpose of penal or grand jury investigation, e.g. under breaches of the US anti-trust legislation (*Rio Tinto Zinc Corp v Westinghouse Electric Corp*, above).

Privilege of witnesses

Under s.3(1) of the 1975 Act, a witness is entitled to claim privilege from giving any **34.21.9** evidence which he could not be compelled to give on any ground recognised under the law of England or under the law of the requesting Court. The claim to privilege against giving evidence extends not only to giving answers to any questions, whether oral or in writing but to producing any document (s.3(4)). Ordinarily, the English Court will make the order to give effect to the foreign request for evidence (see *Re Westinghouse Uranium Litigation* [1977] 3 W.L.R. 430; [1977] 3 All E.R. 703) and the claim to privilege must be properly taken by the witness at the time of his examination under the order or at the stage at which the relevant document is required to be produced (see *Re Westinghouse Uranium Litigation (No.2)* [1977] 3 W.L.R. 492; [1977] 3 All E.R. 717, CA).

The Court will give effect to the claim for privilege on any ground recognised by English law, even though it be a ground which is not recognised or known in the courts or territory of the requesting Court. Thus, in relation to letters rogatory from a US Federal Court, an English company was entitled to claim privilege against self-incrimination under s.14(1) of the Civil Evidence Act 1968 in respect of documents required to be produced, since such production would have exposed the company to fines imposed by the Commission of the European Communities under art.17 of reg.17 for intentionally or negligently acting in breach of art.85 of the Treaty of Rome, which formed part of the law of England, and such fines imposed by the Commission under this regulation constituted a "penalty" for the purposes of s.14 of the Civil Evidence Act 1968 and were recoverable by proceedings in England (*Rio Tinto Zinc Corp v Westinghouse Electric Corp* [1978] A.C. 547; [1978] 1 All E.R. 434, affirming [1977] 3 W.L.R. 492; [1977] 3 All E.R. 717, CA).

The Act provides a further ground entitling a witness who has been ordered to give evidence in aid of foreign proceedings to refuse to do so. By s.3(3), such a person will not be compelled to give any evidence, whether in answering any question or producing any document, if his doing so would be prejudicial to the security of the United Kingdom, and a certificate signed by or on behalf of the Secretary of State to this effect will be conclusive evidence of that fact. This provision is additional to the claim for privilege on the ground that disclosure of the document would be injurious to the public interest (see CPR r.31.19).

Privilege claimed under foreign law

34.21.10 Where the ground of privilege claimed is one not recognised by the law of England, but is recognised by the law of the country or territory of the requesting Court, the claim to privilege must either be supported by a statement contained in the request, whether unconditionally or subject to conditions which are fulfilled or it is conceded by the applicant for the order (s.3(2)(a) and (b)). If it is not so supported or conceded the witness may be required to give the evidence to which the claim relates but that evidence must not be transmitted to the requesting Court if that Court, on the matter being referred to it, upholds the claim (s.3(2) of the Act of 1975).

An example of such a claim for privilege would be the privilege afforded by the Fifth Amendment of the U.S. Constitution, which is available only to individuals and not to companies (see *Rio Tinto Zinc Corp v Westinghouse Electric Corp* [1978] A.C. 547).

When such a claim is made, the practice is that the examiner may, if he thinks fit, require the witness to give the evidence to which the claim relates and if the examiner does not do so the Court may do so, on the application without notice, of the person who obtained the order (see r.6(2)). If such evidence is taken then it must be contained in a document separate from the remainder of the deposition of the witness; the examiner must send to the Senior Master with the deposition a statement signed by the examiner setting out the claim and the ground on which it was made. On receipt of the statement the Senior Master must *retain* the document containing the part of the witness's evidence to which the claim relates, and he must send the statement and a request to determine the claim to the requesting Court with the rest of the deposition; and if the claim is rejected by the requesting Court, the Senior Master must send that Court the documents containing that part of the witness's evidence to which the claim relates, but if the claim is upheld, he must send the documents to the witness himself, and he must in either case notify the witness and the person who obtained the order for the examination of the Court's determination (see r.6(3)).

Evidence for criminal proceedings

34.21.11 Section 5 of the 1975 Act which enabled the High Court to make an order in pursuance of a foreign request for the evidence of a witness to be obtained for the purpose of criminal proceedings has been repealed with effect from July 1, 1991 by the Criminal Justice (International Co-operation) Act 1990.

Evidence for United Kingdom Court

34.21.12 Section 4 of the 1975 Act extends the powers of the High Court under SCA 1981 s.36 (previously s.49 of J.A. 1925) to order the issue of a summons in special form, enforceable throughout the United Kingdom, for the attendance of a witness at a trial, so as to enable the witness's attendance to be required before an examiner or commissioner appointed by the Court or Judge in any cause or matter in that Court, including an examiner or commissioner appointed to take evidence outside the jurisdiction of the Court.

Evidence for proceedings in the European Court of Justice

34.21.13 The 1975 Act has been made to apply to the Court of Justice of the European Communities with the modification that the person by whom a certificate may be given is the Registrar of that Court (see SI 1976/428). This enables evidence for proceedings before the European Court of Justice to be taken at the request of that Court in the United Kingdom.

Evidence for international proceedings

Section 6 of the 1975 Act enables the provisions of ss.1–3 of the Act to be extended by Order in Council to international proceedings of any description specified in the order including the International Court of Justice, or any other Court, tribunal, commission, body or authority referred to in s.6(3). **34.21.14**

Convention countries

For details of the countries that are parties to bilateral conventions and/or the Hague convention see paras and 34.13.7 and 34.13.8. **34.21.15**

Application for order by party

See r.34.17 and para.6.3 of the Practice Direction. The application for an order under s.2 of the Act of 1975 to give effect to a foreign request for evidence to be obtained in England and Wales for the purpose of civil proceedings in the foreign court is made to a Master of the Queen's Bench Division. **34.21.16**

The application for an order in Civil Proceedings must be made, without notice being served on every other party, and must be supported by witness statement or affidavit to which there must be exhibited in the request in pursuance of which the application is made, and if the request is not in the English language a translation must accompany the request and must be exhibited. As to sufficiency of letters of requests etc., see *Simpson v Hazard* [1887] W.N. 115.

Letters of request for evidence in foreign civil proceedings are dealt with in the office of the Foreign Process Section, Room E10, Royal Courts of Justice, Strand, London WC2A 2LL.

Application for order by Treasury Solicitor

Where a letter of request is received by the Senior Master from the Foreign Office or from a consul of a country with which a Civil Procedure Convention has been concluded, and no solicitors in this country have been instructed to act, the Senior Master calls upon the Treasury Solicitor to act and will then take the steps necessary to give effect to the letter of request. See para.6.4 of the Practice Direction at 34PD.6. It must be noted that in giving effect to the request, the Treasury Solicitor is not acting on behalf of the parties to the proceedings. **34.21.17**

It is unlikely that any legal representative of any of the parties to the proceedings will attend the examination. If, however, representatives (who may include counsel as well as solicitors) do attend, and a case officer on behalf of the Treasury Solicitor attends, the case officer will generally conduct conduct the examination-in-chief of the witness. Thereafter the witness may be cross-examined by the legal representative of the other party and re-examined by the representative of the party on whose behalf the examination has been sought. Finally, with the approval of the examiner the Treasury Solicitor may put further questions to the witness to elucidate any points remaining obscure. Care must be taken to see that all the questions asked of the witness are within the ambit of the letter of request.

Application to discharge order

As the order is made without notice being served on any other party, application may be made to vary or discharge the order. Such application must be made by Pt 23 application and should be supported by written evidence stating the grounds on which the order is sought to be discharged. A party in proceedings abroad has the right to be heard to challenge an order made under the Evidence (Proceedings in Other Jurisdictions) Act 1975, obtained in this country by the other party to the foreign proceedings and directed to a third party requiring the production of documents (*Boeing Co v P.P.G. Industries Inc* [1988] 3 All E.R. 839); see *Land Rover North America Inc v Windh* [2005] EWHC 432 (QB). **34.21.18**

Persons to take examination

The examination may be ordered to be taken before any fit and proper person nominated by the person applying for the order or before an examiner of the court or before such other qualified person as to the court seems fit (r.4(1)). The witness state- **34.21.19** ment or affidavit should therefore name the examiner where it is decided to appoint or ask for an examiner of the court to be appointed. If the examiner is named, the witness statement or affidavit should state that he is, in the dependant's opinion, a fit and proper person. A consular officer of the foreign country may be the examiner.

The court may make an order under CPR r.34.14, for the payment of the fees and expenses due to the examiner (see r.4(2)).

Because the 1975 Act sets limits on the extent of examination permitted which may give rise to the sort of difficulties discussed in subsequent paragraphs of the note, it is generally desirable that an English lawyer be appointed to conduct the examination. The wide discretion given to the Court under r.4 either to nominate or approve the nomination of the examiner does not preclude the nomination and approval of a foreign lawyer, but in many cases, particularly those of a complex nature, it is better practice that the examiner be a person familiar with English law and procedure. The court in the exercise of its discretion may require that such a person be nominated. It is open to the court to require that the examination is conducted by an examiner of the court.

Enforcing attendance of witnesses

34.21.20 Failure of a witness to attend is addressed in CPR r.34.10.

The witness is entitled both to conduct money and payment of expenses and loss of time as on attendance as a witness in civil proceedings before the court making the order (see s.2(5) of the 1975 Act).

Manner of taking examination

34.21.21 Subject to r.34.20 (claim to privilege), and to any special directions contained in the order for the examination of a witness, the examination must be taken in the manner provided by CPR, r.34.9 and 34.10. Normally, the examination will be conducted according to English law and procedure ("the English mode"). however, art.9 of the Hague Convention provides that a request that a special mode or procedure be followed should be complied with unless incompatible with the law of the state of execution.

Where a request is made by the foreign court as to the particular manner for taking depositions, that manner should be employed unless the manner proposed is so contrary to English established procedures that it should not be permitted and subject to the exercise of judicial discretion to permit it, and, therefore where the request is for tape or video recording of the depositions, which would be admissible in English courts if taken outside the court, the court will accede to that request and make such order accordingly (*J. Barber & Sons (a firm) v Lloyds Underwriters* [1986] 3 W.L.R. 515; [1986] 2 All E.R. 845).

The arrangements for the examination are made by the solicitor having conduct of the matter. Correspondence or oral communications passing between him and the witness will show whether it will be necessary to have an interpreter present at the examination. It will also be the duty of the solicitor to decide whether the evidence is likely to be of such length as will make it desirable to arrange for the evidence to be noted by shorthand. If a shorthand note is thought necessary the solicitor must arrange for the presence of a shorthand writer, but should first of all consult the examiner and any solicitors who he knows are going to attend.

The evidence can only be taken "in the English mode," but that does not mean that it is to be limited to what is admissible in English courts. The foreign Court should be afforded the fullest help it is possible to give. If its rules of evidence are known, effect should be given to them; if not, any questions should be admitted which may be expected to throw light on the matters in issue (per Cockburn C.J. in *Desilla v Fells* (1879) 40 L.T. 423–424). As the examination should be conducted in the English mode, a company cannot be ordered to attend for examination on oath (*Penn-Texas Corp v Murat Anstalt* [1964] 1 Q.B. 40; [1963] 1 All E.R. 258, CA) but a company or body corporate can be ordered to attend and produce specified documents by its proper officer (*Penn-Texas Corp v Murat Anstalt (No.2)* [1964] 2 Q.B. 647; [1964] 2 All E.R. 594, CA; *Panthalu v Ramnord Research Laboratories Ltd* [1966] 2 Q.B. 173; [1965] 2 All E.R. 921, CA).

At the examination the witness is questioned by the solicitor or counsel if he is instructed. The party who wishes to have the witness examined must restrict their questions to those appropriate for examination in chief and re-examination. If the other party to the proceedings attends or is represented, he or his representatives may cross-examine. The examiner must not permit the parties to raise questions beyond the questions or issues identified by the foreign court. The order of the court may provide that the person required to give testimony, either orally or in writing, may do so otherwise than on oath where this is asked for by the requesting court (see s.2(3) of the Act of 1975).

The witness giving evidence before an examiner has to give his own answers without the intervention of legal advice and is therefore not entitled to receive legal advice while being examined, but the examiner can, if he considers that the witness is not capable of an informed judgment, permit an independent adviser to object and formulate the grounds of objection to the questions put to the applicant (*R. v Rathbone Ex p. Dikko* [1985] Q.B. 630).

If the witness refuses to answer any question, that fact should be formally noted in the depositions, showing the ground of refusal, i.e. that he is not liable to answer. A witness willing to answer, notwithstanding his right to refuse, is entitled to do so and to have his answer recorded. Where a witness refuses to answer any question which he is liable to answer, a certificate of his refusal signed by the examiner must be filed and application may then be made to the court requiring the witness to answer (see para.34PD.6.8). The examination should, however, be completed in all other respects and adjourned generally.

An order for committal ought not to be made in the case of a witness examined under this Act, who refuses to produce material documents of which he has possession or control only in the character of servant to a master who is not a party to the proceedings and who has not forbidden him to produce the documents (*Eccles & Co v Louisville and Nashville Ry.* [1912] 1 K.B. 135, CA).

Blood and DNA tests

Occasionally a requesting court asks that a witness undergo a blood or DNA test. **34.21.22**
Blood tests are permissible under s.2 of the 1975 Act. Such a request should be included in the order but subject to the express provision that there should be no blood test without the the consent of the witness. The English court will not order a blood test without consent If the witness agrees to undergo a test the examiner should make a note of that fact in the deposition adding the words "provided that this is at no expense to myself." The witness should then be told that the Foreign Process Section will contact him direct to make the necessary arrangements.

Under s.20(1) of the Family Law Reform Act 1969 (as amended) the court may direct the taking of bodily samples for for the use of scientific tests in order to determine parentage. Sch.1 to the CPR RSC O.112 deals with applications for such directions. In the circumstances, the Senior Master is of the view that a DNA test can be sought by Letter of Request. Again, the consent of the witness would be required.

III. Taking of Evidence—Member States of the European Union

34.21.23

Editorial introduction

Section III was added to Pt 34 with effect from January 1, 2004 by the Civil Procedure (Amendment No.4) Rules 2003 (SI 2003/2113). The object of the Section is to give effect to the Council Regulation (EC) 1206/2001 of May 28, 2001 on co-operation between the courts of the Member States in the taking of evidence in civil and commercial matters ("the Taking of Evidence Regulation"). The Taking of Evidence Regulation applies to all Member States of the European Union except Denmark; r.34.22(b). A state to which the Taking of Regulation applies is defined as a Regulation State.

Apart from a short rule dealing with interpretation, Sect.III consists of two rules: a rule dealing with where the deposition is to be taken from a person who is in another Regulation State; and a rule dealing with where the deposition is to be taken within the jurisdiction for use for courts of other Regulation States. Whichever rule applies, the basic scheme is the same—a requesting court orders the issue of a request to a designated court ("the requested court") in the Regulation State in which the proposed deponent is situated. The object is to achieve direct transmission between the courts.

Section III is supplemented by paras 7 to 11 of the Practice Direction and The Taking of Evidence Regulation is annexed to the Practice Direction as Annex B. The requisite procedural forms are annexed to the Regulations. The Taking of Evidence

Regulation prevails over other provisions contained in bilateral or multilateral agreements and the Hague Convention; see art.21(1) of the Taking of Evidence Regulation. Accordingly, we have a complete code for the taking of evidence between Regulation States. This code requires careful study and what follows is merely a summary of some key features.

Designated Court or Requested Court

34.21.24 Each Regulation State has prepared a list of courts competent to take evidence. The designated courts in England and Wales are listed in Annex C to the Practice Direction. They are:

Area	Designated court
London and South Eastern Circuit	Royal Courts of Justice (Queen's Bench Division)
Midland Circuit	Birmingham Civil Justice Centre
Western Circuit	Bristol County Court
Wales Circuit	Cardiff Civil Justice Centre
Northern Circuit	Manchester County Court
North Eastern Circuit	Leeds County Court

Central Body

34.21.25 The Taking of Evidence Regulation requires each Regulation State to nominate a Central Body responsible for supplying information to courts; seeking solutions to any difficulties which may arise in respect of a request; and forwarding, in exceptional cases, at the request of a requesting court, a request to the competent court. The Senior Master has been nominated as the Central Body for England and Wales; see para.9 of the Practice Direction at 34PD.9.

Applications

34.21.26 An application for an order for the issue of a request to a designated court in another Regulation State should be made by application notice in accordance with Pt 23; see para.10.2 of the Practice Direction at 34PD.10. The form of request is prescribed as Form A in the Taking of Evidence Regulation. If the court grants an order it will send the form of request directly to the designated court. Note that it is the court where the proceedings are taking pace which orders the issue of a request and transmits the request directly to the requested court; see para.10.1 of the Practice Direction at 34PD.10 and art.2 of the Taking of Evidence Regulation. Accordingly, a county court may order the issue of a request. Where the person to be examined is not in a Regulation State, only the High Court may order the issue of a letter of request; see r.34.13(1A).

Evidence to be taken in England and Wales for use in another Regulation State

34.21.27 Where a designated court in England and Wales receives a request to take evidence from a court in a Regulation State, the court will send the request to the Treasury Solicitor. The Treasury Solicitor may, with the consent of the Treasury, apply for an order under r.34.24. An application to the court for an order must be accompanied by the Form of request to take evidence and any accompanying documents, translated if required under para.11.4 of the Practice Direction, see 34PD.11. The order for the deponent to attend and be examined together with the evidence on which the order was made must be served on the deponent. The provisions of paras 4.3 to 4.12 apply such depositions.

The Language

34.21.28 The United Kingdom has indicated that, in addition to English, it will accept French as a language in which documents may be submitted. Where the form or request and any accompanying documents are received in French they will be *translated into* English by the Treasury Solicitor. Otherwise documents must be translated into English.

Use of Post/Fax

34.21.29 Designated courts in England and Wales will accept a request by post or by fax.

Acknowledgment of Receipt

Within seven days of receipt the requested court must acknowledge receipt using Form B annexed to the Taking of Evidence Regulation. **34.21.30**

Incomplete Information

If a request cannot be executed because it does not contain all the information required by art.4, the requested court must within 30 days call for the missing information using Form C. **34.21.31**

Time for Execution of the Request

The request must be executed within 90 days of the receipt of a satisfactory request; see art.9 and art.10. If the request cannot be executed within 90 days, the requesting court must be informed using Form G. **34.21.32**

Special Procedures

Article 10 of the Taking of Evidence Regulation provides that a requesting court may ask for a special procedure to be used and this will be complied with unless it is incompatible with the law of the Regulation State of the requested court or by reason of major practical difficulties. This is not dissimilar to art.9 of the Hague Convention; see para.34.21.21 above. If the requested court does not comply with the request it shall inform the requesting court using Form E. **34.21.33**

Rights of Audience

The parties and their lawyers may attend and seek to participate. The requested court may law down conditions in accordance with art.10. **34.21.34**

Presence and Participation of the Requesting Court

The judges and representatives of the requesting court may attend and this may include a designated expert. They may apply to take part in the taking of the evidence. The requested court can lay down conditions upon which they may participate; see art.12. **34.21.35**

Witness summonses

These may be used to enforce the attendance of witnesses; see art.13. **34.21.36**

Refusal to Execute

Article 14 requires careful reading. It deals with the position where a person claims the right to refuse to give evidence or to be prohibited from giving evidence. **34.21.37**

Direct Taking of Evidence

A requesting court may seek to come to this jurisdiction to take the evidence itself. No witness summonses may be used in such circumstances and the witness must consent to give evidence; see art.17. A request to take evidence directly is made to the Senior Master as the Central Body. **34.21.38**

Interpretation[1]

34.22 In this Section— **34.22**

(a) "designated court" has the meaning given in the relevant practice direction;

(b) "Regulation State" has the same meaning as "Member State" *in the Taking of Evidence* Regulation, that is all Member States except Denmark;

(c) "the Taking of Evidence Regulation" means Council Regulation (EC) No. 1206/2001 of 28 May 2001 on co-operation between the courts of the Member States in the taking of evidence in civil and commercial matters.

[1] Introduced by Civil Procedure (Amendment No.4) Rules 2003 (SI 2003/2113).

Where a person to be examined is in another Regulation State[1]

34.23 **34.23—(1) Subject to rule 34.13A, this rule applies where a party wishes to take a deposition from a person who is in another Regulation State—**

(a) outside the jurisdiction; and

(b) in a Regulation State.

(2) The court may order the issue of a request to a designated court ("the requested court") in the Regulation State in which the proposed deponent is.

(3) If the court makes an order for the issue of a request, the party who sought the order must file—

(a) a draft Form A as set out in the annex to the Taking of Evidence Regulation (request for the taking of evidence);

(b) except where paragraph (4) applies, a translation of the form;

(c) an undertaking to be responsible for costs sought by the requested court in relation to—

(i) fees paid to experts and interpreters; and

(ii) where requested by that party, the use of special procedures or communications technology; and

(d) an undertaking to be responsible for the court's expenses.

(4) There is no need to file a translation if—

(a) English is one of the official languages of the Regulation State where the examination is to take place; or

(b) the Regulation State has indicated, in accordance with the Taking of Evidence Regulation, that English is a language which it will accept.

(5) Where article 17 of the Taking of Evidence Regulation (direct taking of evidence by the requested court) allows evidence to be taken directly in another Regulation State, the court may make an order for the submission of a request in accordance with that article.

(6) If the court makes an order for the submission of a request under paragraph (5), the party who sought the order must file—

(a) a draft Form I as set out in the annex to the Taking of Evidence Regulation (request for direct taking of evidence);

(b) except where paragraph (4) applies, a translation of the form; and

(c) an undertaking to be responsible for the court's expenses.

Note

34.23.1 See *Dendron GmbH v University of California (Parallel Proceedings: Use of Evidence)* [2004] EWHC 589; [2005] 1 W.L.R. 200; [2004] I.L.Pr. 35, Laddie J. (above).

[1] Introduced by Civil Procedure (Amendment No.4) Rules 2003 (SI 2003/2113) and amended by Civil Procedure (Amendment No.5) Rules 2003 (SI 2003/3361).

Proceeds of Crime Act 2002

An application for a letter of request under Part V of the Proceeds of Crime Act 2002 is made under paras (4) to (7) of r.34.13 irrespective of where the proposed deponent is and this rule does not apply; r.34.13A. **34.23.2**

Evidence for courts of other Regulation States[1]

34.24—(1) This rule applies where a court in another Regulation State ("the requesting court") issues a request for evidence to be taken from a person who is in the jurisdiction. **34.24**

(2) An application for an order for evidence to be taken—

(a) must be made to a designated court;

(b) must be accompanied by—

(i) the form of request for the taking of evidence as a result of which the application is made; and

(ii) where appropriate, a translation of the form of request; and

(c) may be made without notice.

(3) Rule 34.18(1) and (2) apply.

(4) The examiner must send—

(a) the deposition to the court for transmission to the requesting court; and

(b) a copy of the deposition to the person who obtained the order for evidence to be taken.

Use of evidence

Evidence obtained by means of the Taking of Evidence Regulations cannot be used, as of right, for collatoral purposes, but there is a discretion in the court to allow such use in special circumstances and where the use would be just in all the circumstances, *Dendron GmbH v The Regents of the Univeristy of California* [2004] EWHC 589; [2004] I.L.Pr. 35. **34.24.1**

Examination

Rule 34.24(3) states that r.34.18(1) and (2) apply. This rule deals with the examination. And r.34.18(2) states that unless the court orders otherwise, the examination will be taken as provided by r.34.9 and r.34.10 applies. Rule 34.9 states that subject to any direction contained in the order for examination, the examination must be conducted in the same way as if the witness were giving evidence at trial. This may pose a practical problem for the examiner given that most European courts adopt the practice of an inquisitorial inquiry by the judge (cf. the notes under para.34.21.21 dealing with the manner of taking the examination on letters of request from a non Regulation State). The questioning must be limited to the questions and issues raised under the request. **34.24.2**

Videotape recording and videoconferencing

Paragraph 11.8 of the Practice Direction states that the provisions of paras 4.3 to 4.12 of the Practice Direction apply to depositions under r.34.24. A requesting court may request that the evidence be recorded by videotape or that it be taken by using videoconference and teleconference; see art.10(4) of the Taking of Evidence Regulation. Where the deponent's evidence is recorded in this manner the deposition must always be recorded in writing by the examiner or by a competent shorthand writer or stenographer; see para.4.3 of the Practice Direction. **34.24.3**

Under art.17 of the Regulation a requesting court may request that it take evidence directly in another Member State; see para.34.21.38. The direct taking of evidence may be by videoconferencing. Evidence may be taken in this manner at a court in England and Wales with videoconferencing facilities—this is not limited to the

[1] Introduced by the Civil Procedure (Amendment No.4) Rules 2003 (SI 2003/2113).

designated or receiving court. The direct taking of evidence by the requesting court can only take place if it can be performed on a voluntary basis; see art.17(2) of the Regulation.

The requesting court will provide to the receiving court (together with Form A or I of the Regulation): the agreement in writing of the witness of his willingness to provide evidence by videoconference; a contact number for the witness; details of at which court the witness wishes to give evidence (the requesting court will be given a list of courts with the necessary equipment); the language in which the evidence will be taken (it is for the requesting court to deal with any translation issues); arrange for payment for the videoconference (the requesting court may require such costs; see art.18(2)) of the Regulation; and contact details for resolving any problems in relation to the videoconference. If the request is agreed, the designated or receiving court will send a copy of Form J to the requesting court and a copy and explanatory letter to the court at which the videoconferencing is to take place. A list of courts which have video-conferencing facilities is available from the Foreign Process section at the Royal Courts of Justice. The videoconferencing court, on receipt of the requesting court's call or letter, will agree arrangements for the videoconference which should, subject to the above matters, be made in accordance with Annex 3 of Practice Direction 32. The above is a summary of the instructions issued by the Senior Master (Master Turner) in August 2007.

PRACTICE DIRECTION—DEPOSITIONS AND COURT ATTENDANCE BY WITNESSES

This Practice Direction supplements CPR Part 34 **34PD.1**

Witness Summonses

Issue of witness summons

1.1 A witness summons may require a witness to:

(1) attend court to give evidence,

(2) produce documents to the court, or

(3) both,

on either a date fixed for the hearing or such date as the court may direct.[1]

1.2 Two copies of the witness summons[2] should be filed with the court for sealing, one of which will be retained on the court file.

1.3 A mistake in the name or address of a person named in a witness summons may be corrected if the summons has not been served.

1.4 The corrected summons must be re-sealed by the court and marked "Amended and Re-Sealed".

Witness summons issued in aid of an inferior court or tribunal

2.1 A witness summons may be issued in the High Court or a county court in aid of a court or tribunal which does not have the power to issue a witness summons in relation to the proceedings before it.[3] **34PD.2**

2.2 A witness summons referred to in paragraph 2.1 may be set aside by the court which issued it.[4]

2.3 An application to set aside a witness summons referred to in paragraph 2.1 will be heard:

(1) in the High Court by a Master at the Royal Courts of Justice or by a district judge in a District Registry, and

(2) in a county court by a district judge.

2.4 Unless the court otherwise directs, the applicant must give at least 2 days' notice to the party who issued the witness summons of the application, which will normally be dealt with at a hearing.

Travelling expenses and compensation for loss of time

3.1 When a witness is served with a witness summons he must be offered a sum to cover his travelling expenses to and from the court and compensation for his loss of time.[5] **34PD.3**

3.2 If the witness summons is to be served by the court, the party issuing the summons must deposit with the court:

(1) a sum sufficient to pay for the witness's expenses in travelling to the court and in returning to his home or place of work, and

[1] r.34.2(4).
[2] In Practice form **N20**.
[3] r.34.4(1).
[4] r.34.4(2).
[5] r.34.7.

(2) a sum in respect of the period during which earnings or benefit are lost, or such lesser sum as it may be proved that the witness will lose as a result of his attendance at court in answer to the witness summons.

3.3 The sum referred to in 3.2(2) is to be based on the sums payable to witnesses attending the Crown Court.[1]

3.4 Where the party issuing the witness summons wishes to serve it himself,[2] he must:

(1) notify the court in writing that he wishes to do so, and
(2) at the time of service offer the witness the sums mentioned in paragraph 3.2 above.

Depositions

To be taken in England and Wales for use as evidence in proceedings in courts in England and Wales

34PD.4 **4.1** A party may apply for an order for a person to be examined on oath before:

(1) a judge,
(2) an examiner of the court, or
(3) such other person as the court may appoint.[3]

4.2 The party who obtains an order for the examination of a deponent[4] before an examiner of the court[5] must:

(1) apply to the Foreign Process Section of the Masters' Secretary's Department at the Royal Courts of Justice for the allocation of an examiner,
(2) when allocated, provide the examiner with copies of all documents in the proceedings necessary to inform the examiner of the issues, and
(3) pay the deponent a sum to cover his travelling expenses to and from the examination and compensation for his loss of time.[6]

4.3 In ensuring that the deponent's evidence is recorded in full, the court or the examiner may permit it to be recorded on audiotape or videotape, but the deposition[7] must always be recorded in writing by him or by a competent shorthand writer or stenographer.

4.4 If the deposition is not recorded word for word, it must contain, as nearly as may be, the statement of the deponent; the examiner may record word for word any particular questions and answers which appear to him to have special importance.

4.5 If a deponent objects to answering any question or where any objection is taken to any question, the examiner must:

(1) record in the deposition or a document attached to it—

[1] Fixed pursuant to the Prosecution of Offences Act 1985 and the Costs in Criminal Cases (General) Regulations 1986.
[2] *r.34.6(1)*.
[3] r.34.8(3).
[4] See r.34.8(2) for explanation of "deponent" and "deposition".
[5] For the appointment of examiners of the court see r.34.15.
[6] r. 34.8(6).
[7] See r.34.8(2) for explanation of "deponent" and "deposition".

(a) the question,
(b) the nature of and grounds for the objection, and
(c) any answer given, and

(2) give his opinion as to the validity of the objection and must record it in the deposition or a document attached to it. The court will decide as to the validity of the objection and any question of costs arising from it.

4.6 Documents and exhibits must:

(1) have an identifying number or letter marked on them by the examiner, and

(2) be preserved by the party or his legal representative[1] who obtained the order for the examination, or as the court or the examiner may direct.

4.7 The examiner may put any question to the deponent as to:

(1) the meaning of any of his answers, or

(2) any matter arising in the course of the examination.

4.8 Where a deponent:

(1) fails to attend the examination, or

(2) refuses to:
(a) be sworn, or
(b) answer any lawful question, or
(c) produce any document,

the examiner will sign a certificate[2] of such failure or refusal and may include in his certificate any comment as to the conduct of the deponent or of any person attending the examination.

4.9 The party who obtained the order for the examination must file the certificate with the court and may apply for an order that the deponent attend for examination or as may be.[3] The application may be made without notice.[4]

4.10 The court will make such order on the application as it thinks fit including an order for the deponent to pay any costs resulting from his failure or refusal.[5]

4.11 A deponent who wilfully refuses to obey an order made against him under Part 34 may be proceeded against for contempt of court.

4.12 A deposition must:

(1) be signed by the examiner,

(2) have any amendments to it initialled by the examiner and the deponent,

(3) be endorsed by the examiner with—
(a) a statement of the time occupied by the examination, *and*
(b) a record of any refusal by the deponent to sign the deposition and of his reasons for not doing so, and

[1] For the definition of legal representative see r.2.3.
[2] r.34.10.
[3] r.34.10(2) and (3).
[4] r.34.10(3).
[5] r.34.10(4).

(4) be sent by the examiner to the court where the proceedings are taking place for filing on the court file.

4.13 Rule 34.14 deals with the fees and expenses of an examiner.

Depositions to be taken abroad for use as evidence in proceedings before Courts in England and Wales (where the Taking of Evidence Regulation does not apply)

34PD.5 **5.1** Where a party wishes to take a deposition from a person outside the jurisdiction, the High Court may order the issue of a letter of request to the judicial authorities of the country in which the proposed deponent is.[1]

5.2 An application for an order referred to in paragraph 5.1 should be made by application notice in accordance with Part 23.

5.3 The documents which a party applying for an order for the issue of a letter of request must file with his application notice are set out in rule 34.13(6). They are as follows:

(1) a draft letter of request in the form set out in Annex A to this practice direction,

(2) a statement of the issues relevant to the proceedings,

(3) a list of questions or the subject matter of questions to be put to the proposed deponent,

(4) a translation of the documents in (1), (2) and (3) above unless the proposed deponent is in a country of which English is an official language, and

(5) an undertaking to be responsible for the expenses of the Secretary of State.

In addition to the documents listed above the party applying for the order must file a draft order.

5.4 The above documents should be filed with the Masters' Secretary in Room E214, Royal Courts of Justice, Strand, London WC2A 2LL.

5.5 The application will be dealt with by the Senior Master of the Queen's Bench Division of the High Court who will, if appropriate, sign the letter of request.

5.6 Attention is drawn to the provisions of rule 23.10 (application to vary or discharge an order made without notice).

5.7 If parties are in doubt as to whether a translation under paragraph 5.3(4) above is required, they should seek guidance from the Foreign Process Section of the Masters' Secretary's Department.

5.8 A special examiner appointed under rule 34.13(4) may be the British Consul or the Consul-General or his deputy in the country where the evidence is to be taken if:

(1) there is in respect of that country a Civil Procedure Convention providing for the taking of evidence in that country for the assistance of proceedings in the High Court or other court in this country, or

(2) with the consent of the Secretary of State.

5.9 The provisions of paragraphs 4.1 to 4.12 above apply to the depositions referred to in this paragraph.

---

[1] r.34.13(1).

Depositions to be taken in England and Wales for use as evidence in proceedings before courts abroad pursuant to letters of request (where the Taking of Evidence Regulation does not apply)

6.1 Section II of Part 34 relating to obtaining evidence for foreign courts applies to letters of request and should be read in conjunction with this part of the practice direction. **34PD.6**

6.2 The Evidence (Proceedings in Other Jurisdictions) Act 1975 applies to these depositions.

6.3 The written evidence supporting an application under rule 34.17 (which should be made by application notice – see Part 23) must include or exhibit—

(1) a statement of the issues relevant to the proceedings;
(2) a list of questions or the subject matter of questions to be put to the proposed deponent;
(3) a draft order; and
(4) a translation of the documents in (1) and (2) into English, if necessary.

6.4(1) The Senior Master will send to the Treasury Solicitor any request—
(a) forwarded by the Secretary of State with a recommendation that effect should be given to the request without requiring an application to be made; or
(b) received by him in pursuance of a Civil Procedure Convention providing for the taking of evidence of any person in England and Wales to assist a court or tribunal in a foreign country where no person is named in the document as the applicant.

(2) In relation to such a request, the Treasury Solicitor may, with the consent of the Treasury—
(a) apply for an order under the 1975 Act; and
(b) take such other steps as are necessary to give effect to the request.

6.5 The order for the deponent to attend and be examined together with the evidence upon which the order was made must be served on the deponent.

6.6 Attention is drawn to the provisions of rule 23.10 (application to vary or discharge an order made without notice).

6.7 Arrangements for the examination to take place at a specified time and place before an examiner of the court or such other person as the court may appoint shall be made by the applicant for the order and approved by the Senior Master.

6.8 The provisions of paragraph 4.2 to 4.12 apply to the depositions referred to in this paragraph, except that the examiner must send the deposition to the Senior Master.

(For further information about evidence see Part 32 and the practice direction which supplements it.)

Taking of Evidence between EU Member States

Taking of Evidence Regulation

7.1 Where evidence is to be taken— **34PD.7**

(a) from a person in another Member State of the European Union for use as evidence in proceedings before courts in England and Wales; or
(b) from a person in England and Wales for use as evidence in proceedings before a court in another Member State,

Council Regulation (EC) No 1206/2001 of 28 May 2001 on co-operation between the courts of the Member States in the taking of evidence in civil or commercial matters ('the Taking of Evidence Regulation') applies.

7.2 The Taking of Evidence Regulation is annexed to this practice direction as Annex B.

7.3 The Taking of Evidence Regulation does not apply to Denmark. In relation to Denmark, therefore, rule 34.13 and Section II of Part 34 will continue to apply.

7.4 (Article 21(1) of the Taking of Evidence Regulation provides that the Regulation prevails over other provisions contained in bilateral or multilateral agreements or arrangements concluded by the Member States and in particular the Hague Convention of 1 March 1954 on Civil Procedure and the Hague Convention of 18 March 1970 on the Taking of Evidence Abroad in Civil or Commercial Matters)

7.5 Originally published in the official languages of the European Community in the *Official Journal of the European Communities* by the Office for Official Publications of the European Communities.

Meaning of 'designated court'

34PD.8 **8.1** In accordance with the Taking of Evidence Regulation, each Regulation State has prepared a list of courts competent to take evidence in accordance with the Regulation indicating the territorial and, where appropriate, special jurisdiction of those courts.

8.2 Where Part 34, Section III refers to a "designated court" in relation to another Regulation State, the reference is to the court, referred to in the list of competent courts of that State, which is appropriate to the application in hand.

8.3 Where the reference is to the "designated court" in England and Wales, the reference is to the appropriate competent court in the jurisdiction. The designated courts for England and Wales are listed in Annex C to this practice direction.

Central Body

34PD.9 **9.1** The Taking of Evidence Regulation stipulates that each Regulation State must nominate a Central Body responsible for—

(a) supplying information to courts;
(b) seeking solutions to any difficulties which may arise in respect of a request; and
(c) forwarding, in exceptional cases, at the request of a requesting court, a request to the competent court.

9.2 The United Kingdom has nominated the Senior Master, Queen's Bench Division, to be the Central Body for England and Wales.

9.3 The Senior Master, as Central Body, has been designated responsible for taking decisions on requests pursuant to Article 17 of the Regulation. Article 17 allows a court to submit a request to the Central Body or a designated competent authority in another Regulation State to take evidence directly in that State.

Evidence to be taken in another Regulation State for use in England and Wales

10.1 Where a person wishes to take a deposition from a person in another Regulation State, the court where the proceedings are taking place may order the issue of a request to the designated court in the Regulation State (Rule 34.23(2)). The form of request is prescribed as Form A in the Taking of Evidence Regulation. **34PD.10**

10.2 An application to the court for an order under rule 34.23(2) should be made by application notice in accordance with Part 23.

10.3 Rule 34.23(3) provides that the party applying for the order must file a draft form of request in the prescribed form. Where completion of the form requires attachments or documents to accompany the form, these must also be filed.

10.4 If the court grants an order under rule 34.23(2), it will send the form of request directly to the designated court.

10.5 Where the taking of evidence requires the use of an expert, the designated court may require a deposit in advance towards the costs of that expert. The party who obtained the order is responsible for the payment of any such deposit which should be deposited with the court for onward transmission. Under the provisions of the Taking of Evidence Regulation, the designated court is not required to execute the request until such payment is received.

10.6 Article 17 permits the court where proceedings are taking place to take evidence directly from a deponent in another Regulation State if the conditions of the article are satisfied. Direct taking of evidence can only take place if evidence is given voluntarily without the need for coercive measures. Rule 34.23(5) provides for the court to make an order for the submission of a request to take evidence directly. The form of request is Form I annexed to the Taking of Evidence Regulation and rule 34.23(6) makes provision for a draft of this form to be filed by the party seeking the order. An application for an order under rule 34.23(5) should be by application notice in accordance with Part 23.

10.7 Attention is drawn to the provisions of rule 23.10 (application to vary or discharge an order made without notice).

Evidence to be taken in England and Wales for use in another Regulation State

11.1 Where a designated court in England and Wales receives a request to take evidence from a court in a Regulation State, the court will send the request to the Treasury Solicitor. **34PD.11**

11.2 On receipt of the request, the Treasury Solicitor may, with the consent of the Treasury, apply for an order under rule 34.24.

11.3 An application to the court for an order must be accompanied by the Form of request to take evidence and any accompanying documents, translated if required under paragraph 11.4.

11.4 The United Kingdom has indicated that, in addition to English, it will accept French as a language in which documents may be submitted. Where the form or request and any accompanying documents are received in French they will be translated into English by the Treasury Solicitor.

11.5 The order for the deponent to attend and be examined together with the evidence on which the order was made must be served on the deponent.

11.6 Arrangements for the examination to take place at a specified time and place shall be made by the Treasury Solicitor and approved by the court.

11.7 The court shall send details of the arrangements for the examination to such of

(a) the parties and, if any, their representatives; or

(b) the representatives of the foreign court,

who have indicated, in accordance with the Taking of Evidence Regulation, that they wish to be present at the examination.

11.8 The provisions of paragraph 4.3 to 4.12 apply to the depositions referred to in this paragraph.

Annex A

Draft Letter of Request (where the Taking of Evidence Regulation does not apply)

34PD.12 To the Competent Judicial Authority of
in the of

I [*name*] Senior Master of the Queen's Bench Division of the Supreme Court of England and Wales respectfully request the assistance of your court with regard to the following matters.

1. A claim is now pending in the Division of the High Court of Justice in England and Wales entitled as follows [*set out full title and claim number*] in which [*name*] of [*address*] is the claimant and [*name*] of [*address*] is the defendant.
2. The names and addresses of the representatives or agents of [*set out names and addresses of representatives of the parties*].
3. The claim by the claimant is for:
   (a) [*set out the nature of the claim*]
   (b) [*the relief sought, and*]
   (c) [*a summary of the facts*.]
4. It is necessary for the purposes of justice and for the due determination of the matters in dispute between the parties that you cause the following witnesses, who are resident within your jurisdiction, to be examined. The names and addresses of the witnesses are as follows:

5. The witnesses should be examined on oath or if that is not possible within your laws or is impossible of performance by reason of the internal practice and procedure of your court or by reason of practical difficulties, they should be examined in accordance with whatever procedure your laws provide for in these matters.
6. Either/
The witnesses should be examined in accordance with the list of questions annexed hereto.
Or/
The witnesses should be examined regarding [*set out full details of evidence sought*]
N.B. Where the witness is required to produce documents, these should be clearly identified.
7. I would ask that you cause me, or the agents of the parties (if appointed), to be informed of the date and place where the examination is to take place.
8. Finally, I request that you will cause the evidence of the said witnesses to be reduced into writing and all documents produced on such examinations to be duly marked for identification and that you will further be pleased to authenticate such examinations by the seal of your court or in such other way as is in accordance with your procedure and return the written evidence and documents produced to me addressed as follows:

Senior Master of the Queen's Bench Division
Royal Courts of Justice
Strand
London WC2A 2LL
England

Annex B

Council Regulation (E.C.) No.1206/2001 of May 28 2001 on cooperation between the courts of the Member States in the taking of evidence in civil or commercial matters can be found in Volume 2 at para.5–331 *et seq*. **34PD.13**

Annex C

34PD.14

Designated courts in England and Wales under the Taking of Evidence Regulation
(see paragraph 8 above)

Area	**Designated court**
London and South Eastern Circuit	Royal Courts of Justice (Queen's Bench Division)
Midland Circuit	Birmingham Civil Justice Centre
Western Circuit	Bristol County Court
Wales Circuit	Cardiff Civil Justice Centre

Northern Circuit	Manchester County Court
North Eastern Circuit	Leeds County Court

CPR 34

PRACTICE DIRECTION—FEES FOR EXAMINERS OF THE COURT

This Practice Direction supplements CPR Part 34

Scope

1.1 This practice direction sets out— 34BPD.1

(1) how to calculate the fees an examiner of the court ("an examiner") may charge; and

(2) the expenses he may recover.

(CPR rule 34.8(3)(b) provides that the court may make an order for evidence to be obtained by the examination of a witness before an examiner of the court.)

1.2 The party who obtained the order for the examination must pay the fees and expenses of the examiner.

(CPR rule 34.14 permits an examiner to charge a fee for the examination and contains other provisions about his fees and expenses, and rule 34.15 provides who may be appointed as an examiner of the court.)

The examination fee

2.1 An examiner may charge an hourly rate for each hour (or part of an hour) that he is engaged in examining the witness. 34BPD.2

2.2 The hourly rate is to be calculated by reference to the formula set out in paragraph 3.

2.3 The examination fee will be the hourly rate multiplied by the number of hours the examination has taken. For example—

Examination fee = hourly rate × number of hours.

34BPD.3

How to calculate the hourly rate—the formula

3.1 Divide the amount of the minimum annual salary of a post within Group 7 of the judicial salary structure as designated by the Review Body on Senior Salaries,[19] by 220 to give "x"; and then divide "x" by 6 to give the hourly rate.

For example—

$$\frac{\text{minimum annual salary}}{220} = x$$

$$\frac{x}{6} = \text{hourly rate}$$

Single fee chargeable on making the appointment for examination

4.1 An examiner of court is also entitled to charge a single fee of twice the hourly rate (calculated in accordance with paragraph 3 above) as "the appointment fee" when the appointment for the examination is made. 34BPD.4

4.2 The examiner is entitled to retain the appointment fee where the witness fails to attend on the date and time arranged.

4.3 Where the examiner fails to attend on the date and time arranged he may not charge a further appointment fee for arranging a subsequent appointment.

(The examiner need not send the deposition to the court until his fees are paid—see CPR rule 34.14(2)).

Examiner's expenses

34BPD.5 **5.1** The examiner of court is also entitled to recover the following expenses—

(1) all reasonable travelling expenses;
(2) any other expenses reasonably incurred; and
(3) subject to paragraph 5.2, any reasonable charge for the room where the examination takes place.

5.2 No expenses may be recovered under sub-paragraph (3) above if the examination takes place at the examiner's usual business address.

(If the examiner's fees and expenses are not paid within a reasonable time he may report the fact to the court, see CPR rule 34.14(4) and (5)).

PART 35

Experts and Assessors

Contents 35.0.1

Editorial introduction

The provisions in Pt 35 cover much the same ground as those formerly found in RSC O.38, Pt IV. 35.0.2

In the Access to Justice Reports, expert evidence was identified as a major source of problems in the civil justice system (see Interim Report Chap. 23 and Final Report Chap. 13). It was said that the need to engage experts was a source of excessive expense, delay and, in some cases, increased complexity through the excessive or inappropriate use of experts. Concern was also expressed as to the failure of experts to maintain their independence from the parties by whom they had been instructed. The principal recommendation made in the Access to Justice Reports was that the calling of expert evidence should be subject to the complete control of the court through the exercise of the court's case management powers. In fact, under the Supreme Court and County Court rules, the court did have complete control over expert evidence but did not always exercise it.

This recommendation is carried into effect by the rules relating to the pre-trial directions which the court may give in cases proceeding on the fast track or the multi-track (see Pts 1, 3 and 26–29 and the Practice Directions supplementing those Parts).

The Protocol on Expert Evidence

In July 2005 the Civil Justice Council published the "Protocol for the Instruction of Experts to give Evidence in Civil Claims". This replaces the earlier Codes of Guidance on Expert Evidence produced by the Expert Witness Institute and the Academy of Experts. The Protocol offers guidance to experts and those who instruct them in compliance with CPR Pt 35. It is intended to assist in interpretation not to replace the Rule or Practice Direction. Much of the helpful guidance in the previous Codes is restated, but minus their occasional inaccuracies or idiosyncrasies. The Protocol does not apply to an expert who advises only pre-proceedings (whose advice will often 35.0.3

remain privileged) but does apply if the same expert is later instructed to prepare evidence for the litigation. The Protocol is annexed to the Pt 35 Practice Direction and experts and those instructing them are expected to have regard to the guidance it contains.

Expert evidence in small claims

35.0.4 In small claims the strict rules of evidence do not apply (r.27.8(3)). Further, generally, the provisions in Pt 35 dealing with expert evidence do not apply to small claims (r.27.2(1)(e)). The exceptions are: r.35.1 (Duty to restrict expert evidence), r.35.3 (Experts—overriding duty to the court) and r.35.8 (Instructions to a single joint expert). In small claims, the court has complete control over expert evidence. In such cases, no expert may give evidence, whether written or oral, without the permission of the court (r.27.5). There is also a limit on recoverable fees for an expert report of £200.

Expert evidence in High Court specialist divisions

35.0.5 In proceedings in the Commercial Court, the mercantile courts and in the Queen's Bench and Chancery Division, the provisions of Pt 35 and the supplementing Practice Direction are amplified by the Commercial Court and Chancery and Queen's Bench Guides and the Mercantile Court Guide, see "Related Sources," para.35.0.7 below.

Expert evidence at trial

35.0.6 In a number of cases decided since April 1999 the Court of Appeal has made it clear that attempts to introduce expert evidence late in the timetable, or the unavailability of the parties' chosen experts for the trial window or fixed trial date, will only very rarely be sufficient grounds to vary case management directions or trial dates.

In *Rollinson v Kimberly Clark Ltd* [2000] C.P. Rep. 85, the Court of Appeal said that it was not acceptable for a solicitor to instruct an expert shortly before trial without checking their availability for the trial date. In *Matthews v Tarmac Bricks and Tiles Ltd*, T.L.R., July 1, 1999, the Court of Appeal said that the court case managing an action needs to know specifically why an expert is not available for the trial date before the court will even begin to consider whether the date might be rearranged.

The new case-law on expert evidence has implications for the judiciary as well as for lawyers and experts: in *Flannery v Halifax Estate Agencies* [2000] 1 W.L.R. 377 the Court of Appeal emphasized that a judge has to give reasons for preferring the evidence of one expert to another, and that failure to do so may be valid grounds for an appeal and for remitting the case back for a re–trial. *Bennett v Smith* [2003] EWHC 1006 was decided similarly—here the judge had given adequate reasons and had been entitled to accept the opinions of one of the claimant's experts. In *English v Emery Reimbold & Strick Ltd* [2002] EWCA Civ 605, the Court of Appeal said that the judge should be invited to amplify the judgment before a decision is taken on the necessity of an appeal. In *X v Brown* [2003] EWCA Civ 181, the trial judge preferred the evidence of the defendant's psychiatrist that the claimant would have developed a disabling psychogenic illness in any event regardless of the accident to that of the claimant's expert. The Court of Appeal said the reasoning the judge had applied to his analysis of the expert evidence did not support his conclusions and adjusted the damages award.

In *Temple v South Manchester Health Authority* 2002 EWCA Civ 1406 it was held that a judge is entitled to prefer the evidence of one expert to that of another especially if the preferred expert's opinion is supported by other evidence but reasons should be given for the preference. *Smith v Southampton University Hospital NHS Trust* [2007] EWCA Civ 387 was a clinical negligence claim against two surgeons that was dismissed, in which there was a substantial amount of agreement between the two experts. The Court of Appeal held that the trial judge had failed to explain why she had rejected the evidence of one expert, and that it was not sufficient to say that the other expert was highly reputable and representative of a responsible body of medical opinion. However, in *Evans v Birmingham & Black Country Strategic Health Authority* [2007] EWCA Civ 1300 the Court of Appeal upheld the judge's decision, at a trial of the preliminary issue of causation in a clinical negligence case concerning alleged mismanagement of the claimant's birth, to accept the evidence of the defendant's expert witnesses as his preference for that evidence was fully reasoned in a careful and detailed judgment. In addition, in *Novartis Grimsby Ltd v John Cookson* [2007] EWCA Civ 1261 the Court of Appeal upheld the judge's decision that the major cause of the claimant's cancer was his exposure to carcinogenic amines when in the defendant's employment—he carefully explained his preference for one expert's evidence over the other. In *Devoran Joinery Co Ltd v Perkins (No.2)*, [2003] EWCA Civ 1241 the Court of Appeal overturned a first instance decision where a judge had "developed his own theory" on part of a defective building claim instead of recalling the claimant's expert to deal with the unsatisfactory elements of his evidence.

In *Woolley v Essex CC* [2006] EWCA Civ 753 the Court of Appeal decided that it was incumbent upon a trial judge to analyse an expert's report when it was readily apparent that a figure in the conclusions was a mistake and inconsistent with the body of the report. Additionally, in *Friarwood Ltd v Champagne Cattier SA* [2006] EWCA Civ 1106 a retrial was ordered when a judge had rejected expert evidence because he thought, incorrectly, that the expert had applied the wrong test.

A judge is entitled to prefer the evidence of a witness of fact to that of an expert witness but should give reasons to justify his views—see *Armstrong & Connor v First York* [2005] EWCA Civ 277, *Baird v Thurrock BC* [2005] EWCA Civ 1499, CA and *Montracon Ltd v Whalley* [2005] EWCA Civ 1383. Where the expert evidence is relevant to liability (e.g. the way in which an accident could have happened) the judge must consider that evidence at the time when he is reaching his conclusion on the credibility of the witness see *Jakto Transport Ltd v Hall* [2005] EWCA Civ 1327.

Related sources

35.0.7
- Part 1 (the Overriding Objective)
- Part 3 (Case Management)
- Part 18 (Further Information)
- Part 23 (General Rules About Applications for Court Orders)
- Part 25 (Interim Remedies)
- Parts 26 to 29 (Case Management on the Tracks)
- Part 32 (Evidence)
- Part 33 (Miscellaneous Rules About Evidence)
- Part 34 (Depositions and Court Attendance by Witnesses)
- Practice Direction (Experts and Assessors) (see para.35PD.1)
- Practice Direction (Fast Track) Appendix (para.28PD.13)
- Practice Direction (The Multi-Track), paras 4 & 5 (paras 29PD.4 & 29PD.5)
- Civil Evidence Act 1972 s.2 (Rules of court with respect to expert reports and oral expert evidence) (see Vol.2, para.9B–1057)
- Civil Evidence Act 1972 s.3 (Admissibility of expert opinion) (see Vol.2, para.9B–1060)
- Supreme Court Act 1981 s.70 (see Vol.2, para.9A–261)
- County Courts Act 1984 s.63, (see Vol.2, para.9A–537)
- Chancery Guide, paras 6.6 to 6.20 (Vol.2, paras 1–50 to 1–57)
- Mercantile Courts Guide, para.11 and B (Vol.2, para.2B–20).
- Queen's Bench Court Guide, para.7.9 (Vol.2, para.1B–49).
- Protocol for the Instruction of Experts to give Evidence in Civil Claims—see paras 35.16—35.38

Duty to restrict expert evidence

35.1 Expert evidence shall be restricted to that which is reasonably required to resolve the proceedings. 35.1

Effect of rule

The court may control the evidence by giving directions as to (a) the issues on which it requires evidence, (b) the nature of the evidence which it requires to decide those issues, and (c) the way in which the evidence is to be placed before the court (see r.32.1 and notes thereto). The general power to control evidence may be exercised to exclude evidence that would otherwise be admissible (*Grobbelaar v Sun Newspapers*—see above para.35.0.2) Rule 35.1 indicates that parties and court alike should seek to restrict the excessive or inappropriate use of expert evidence. Other rules seek to enforce this policy (e.g. r.35.4 (Court's power to restrict expert evidence)). Generally, subject to a few (but important) exceptions, the provisions of Pt 35 are disapplied in 35.1.1

cases proceeding on the small claims track. One of the exceptions is r.35.1 (the others are rr.35.3, 35.7 and 35.8) (see r.27.2(1)(e)).

The particular policy objective underlying r.35.1 is that of reducing the incidence of inappropriate use of experts to bolster cases (*Gumpo v Church of Scientology Religious Education College Inc*, July 26, 1999, unrep.; *Bandegani v Norwich Union Fire Insurance Society Ltd* [2001] C.L.Y. 1550—expert evidence is unnecessary on the value of a second-hand car worth approximately £1500. *Thermos Ltd v Aladdin Sales & Marketing Ltd* [2000] F.S.R. 402—where the issue in dispute, upon which the experts have been invited by the parties to report, is factual and "obvious" the court is unlikely to benefit from expert evidence). In *Heyward v Plymouth Hospital NHS Trust* [2005] EWCA Civ 939 the Court of Appeal upheld the first instance decision to restrict the expert evidence to one psychiatrist each in a relatively small stress at work claim—it would be open to the claimant to reapply for additional evidence if the defendant decided to rely upon quasi expert evidence of fact (see *ES v Chesterfield & North Derbyshire Royal Hospital NHS Trust* [2003] EWCA Civ 12844 and notes at para.35.7.1). In *J.P. Morgan Chase Bank v Springwell Navigation Corporation* [2006] EWHC 2755 (Comm), a claim for misrepresentation and negligence in relation to investment advice, the court concluded that the trial judge would not be assisted by an expert's report on portfolio analysis that covered the same ground as a report on private banking already admitted, or by a report on derivatives written by a lawyer, as the interpretation of commercial contracts was a question of law for the trial judge

In *Clarke (Executor of the Will of Francis Bacon) v Marlborough Fine Art (London) Ltd* [2002] EWHC 11 the claimant was refused permission to rely upon a lawyer specialising in art law on a contractual issue as this was a factual matter and not one for expert evidence-it was also said that the burden rests upon the party who seeks permission to adduce the expert evidence to show that it will assist the judge. And in *Miller v C and G Coach Services Ltd* 2003 EWCA Civ 442 the Court of Appeal commented that expert evidence could only provide guidelines within which the facts fell to be decided by a judge—in that case the likely speed of a coach involved in a road traffic accident.

If the parties instruct experts without waiting for the court to give permission they are at risk as to recovering the costs if the court subsequently decides that expert evidence is not necessary. In *Thomas Johnson Coker v Barkland Cleaning Co,* T.L.R., December 6, 1999, CA, where the issue was whether the claimant in a personal injury case had been hit by a machine on the factory floor, the claimant, who won the case, failed to recover the cost of instructing an expert instructing an expert as the court decided expert evidence was unnecessary.

In solicitors' negligence claims, expert evidence may be "reasonably required" to provide valuations of a loss of a chance claims *Mann v Chetty & Patel* [2001] C.P. Rep. 24, CA. In a dispute arising from a contract to supply an IT system the judge said it was unhelpful that no expert evidence was called *Peregrine Systems Ltd v Stena Ltd* [2004] EWHC 275, (TCC) and in *IPC Media Ltd v Highbury Leisure Publishing Ltd* [2004] EWHC 1967, (Ch) a copyright dispute, the parties were given permission only two months before trial to adduce expert evidence on the similarities between the design features of the two magazines.

In *Kearsley v Klarfield* [2005] EWCA Civ 1510 and *Casey v Cartwright* [2006] EWCA Civ 1280 the Court of Appeal gave guidance on the use of expert evidence in claims arising from low velocity road traffic accidents. The court may give the defendant permission to obtain their own medical report on causation only where the defendant alleges the claimant is fabricating their injuries, and the defendant has identified this as an issue, both pre-action and in the defence, and files and serves a witness statement within 21 days of the defence.

Interpretation

35.2 **35.2 A reference to an "expert " in this Part is a reference to an expert who has been instructed to give or prepare evidence for the purpose of court proceedings.**

Effect of rule

35.2.1 An expert is a person with a high degree of skill and knowledge in a particular subject, who has relevant and up to date expertise with regard to issues in the case, and sufficient education and communication skills to produce a clear written report, and, if necessary, to provide helpful oral evidence to the court. The relevant consideration is when the expert's duty to the court arises.

The effect of the CPR rules is to create a distinction between:

(1) An expert who advises a party on a specialist or technical matter within his/her expertise at any stage of a problem, dispute, or claim, and

(2) An expert witness who is instructed by a party during proceedings usually to prepare a written report for the court.

The difference is not purely semantic as an advisory expert may not be involved at all in the litigation, and their identity may not be known to the other party or to the court: whereas once a party has sought and obtained the approval of the court to rely upon the opinion evidence of an expert witness during the litigation, the CPR "cards on the table approach" means that the name and status of the expert witness, and invariably the written report, becomes disclosable to the other party and to the court. Difficulties may arise:

(1) When one or both parties have instructed an expert to advise at an early stage in a dispute, particularly when the value of the claim is not high, when subsequently the court decides that it would prefer evidence from a single joint expert (see the notes to rr.35.7 and 35.8 below).

(2) When one party seeks disclosure of the actual instructions given to the other party's expert witness, when part of those instructions were given at an early stage before litigation commenced (see the notes to r.35.10(5) Privilege).

Expert witnesses

The Civil Evidence Act 1972 s.3 states that, subject to rules of court made in pursuance of that Act, where a person is called as a witness in any civil proceedings, his opinion on any relevant matter on which he is qualified to give expert evidence shall be admissible in evidence. A statement of opinion by him on any relevant matter on which he is not qualified to give expert evidence, if made as a way of conveying relevant facts personally perceived by him is admissible as evidence of what he perceived. In this context, "relevant matter" includes an issue in the proceedings in question (see Vol.2, para.9B–1060). **35.2.2**

The functions of an expert witness may include giving assistance to the court on, for example, a technical or scientific matter, or specialist practice or procedure, and giving their opinion on specific matters in the dispute within their expertise. But it is not the function of an expert witness to give their opinion on the issues of law or fact which the judge or jury has to decide.

The court has the discretion whether to compel the appearance of expert witness having regard to his connection with the case, where he had other important work which might be disrupted where evidence could be gained from another source of equal authority (*Society of Lloyds v Clementson (No.2)*, *The Times*, February 29, 1996). In *Brown v Bennett (Witness Summons)*, *The Times*, November 2, 2000 an expert sought to set aside a witness summons because the party instructing her could no longer pay her fees. The court agreed, and said that only in exceptional cases would an expert who could not be paid be compelled to give evidence. See further Pt 34 (Depositions and court attendance by witnesses).

Lilly ICOS Ltd v Pfizer Ltd (No.2) [2002] EWCA Civ 2 decided that it is contrary to the public interest for a party and an expert to contract that the expert will not act as an expert witness for the other party.

Difficulties in securing the presence of an expert witness at trial, including where the expert is double-booked with other court work, can sometimes be overcome by cooperation between trial centres at diary manager or designated civil judge level.

Experts—overriding duty to the court

35.3—(1) It is the duty of an expert to help the court on the matters within his expertise. **35.3**

(2) This duty overrides any obligation to the person from whom he has received instructions or by whom he is paid.

Effect of rule

In the Interim Report it was said (p.182) that most of the problems with expert ev- **35.3.1** idence arise because the expert is initially recruited as part of the team which investigates and advances a party's contentions and then has to change roles and seek to provide the independent expert evidence which the court is entitled to expect. In the Final Report it was said (p.243) that a new approach was required which emphasises the expert's impartiality. Accordingly, it was recommended that rules of court should provide that where an expert is preparing evidence for court proceedings, or is giving evidence in court, his responsibility is to the court impartially on the matters within his expertise. This recommendation is implemented by r.35.3 and the Practice Direction General Requirements, paras 1.1 to 1.6 added in January 2002).

The trial judge may disregard expert evidence

35.3.2 If an expert witness completely disregards their duty to the court by failing to follow the court's directions, the court may rule that the party may not rely on that expert's evidence, the effect of which may mean that the party loses the entire action (see *Stevens v Gullis & Pile* [1999] B.L.R. 394 and [1999] 11 CL 47.

In *Pride Valley Foods Ltd v Hall and Partners* TCC, unrep, the judge was very critical of an expert witness in a construction case whose report was more than 200 pages in length, and which included opinions on issues outside his expertise: "his report offends the established basis on which an expert should give evidence".

But on occasions even when an expert's report is disproportionate and does not fully comply with the CPR the better solution might be to place it before the trial judge who could draw her own conclusions about its reliability (*Burgoyne v Pendlebury*, July 26, 2000, unrep.).

Duties and responsibilities of experts

35.3.3 The case law as to the duties and responsibilities of experts, in relation to the court and to the party was considered by Cresswell J. in *National Justice Compania Naviera SA v Prudential Assurance Co Ltd (The "Ikarian Reefer")* [1993] 2 Lloyd's Rep. 68. His lordship said (at 81–82) they included the following:

1. Expert evidence presented to the Court should be, and should be seen to be, the independent product of the expert uninfluenced as to the form or content by the exigencies of litigation (*Whitehouse v Jordan* [1981] 1 W.L.R. 246, HL, at 256, per Lord Wilberforce).
2. An expert witness should provide independent assistance to the court by way of objective unbiased opinion in relation to matters within his expertise (see *Pollivitte Ltd v Commercial Union Assurance Company Plc* [1987] 1 Lloyd's Rep. 379 at 386, per Garland J., and *Re J* (1990) F.C.R. 193, per Cazalet J. An expert witness in the High Court should never assume the role of an advocate.
3. An expert witness should state the facts or assumption on which his opinion is based. He should not omit to consider material facts which could detract from his concluded opinion (*Re J.*, above).
4. An expert witness should make it clear when a particular question or issue falls outside his expertise.
5. If an expert's opinion is not properly researched because he considers that insufficient data are available then this must be stated with an indication that the opinion is no more than a provisional one (*Re J.*, above). In cases where an expert witness who has prepared a report could not assert that the report contained the truth, the whole truth and nothing but the truth without some qualification that qualification should be stated in the report (*Derby & Co Ltd v Weldon (No.9), The Times*, November 9, 1990, CA, per Staughton L.J.
6. If, after exchange of reports, an expert witness changes his view on the material having read the other side's expert report or for any other reason, such change of view should be communicated (though legal representative) to the other side without delay and when appropriate to the court.
7. Where expert evidence refers to photographs, plans, calculations, analyses, measurements survey reports or other similar documents, these must be provided to the opposite party at the same time as the exchange of reports.

The requirements of this rule emphasise that it is to the court, that the overriding duty is owed irrespective of who instructed or called the expert. The other duties and responsibilities (above) remain to be fulfilled. The Practice Direction to Pt 35 now includes a paragraph which helpfully summarises Cresswell J.'s catalogue of duties and which emphasises in particular the need for experts to be independent, objective on matters within their expertise, and to consider all the material facts, including those which might deter from their opinion. See also the requirements as to the contents of an expert's report (r.32.11).

In *Anglo Group plc v Winther Browne and Co Ltd* [2000] 1 W.L.R. 820 it was said that expert witnesses should make it clear whether any question or issue falls outside their expertise, or their conclusions are based on inadequate evidence. When an expert receives new information she should be prepared to reconsider and even change her mind.

When an expert fails to comply with his duty

Royal & Sun Alliance Trust Co Ltd v Healey & Baker, October 13, 2000, New Law 100109601. Experts' duty to the court includes a duty to cover and give opinions upon the whole of the relevant subject matter and not to select only the evidence which supports the case of the party instructing him. (In this case the expert was an independent surveyor commenting on the letting potential of a property.) **35.3.4**

In *D v C* [2001] EWCA Civ 1511, CA, D sent a medico-legal report prepared for litigation against E, C's employer, to C's GP and to C's treating psychiatrist, without C's consent. The Court of Appeal ruled that this was a breach of confidence.

In *Liverpool Roman Catholic Archdiocesan Trustees Inc v Goldberg (No.2)* [2001] Lloyd's Rep. P.N. 518, CA, a claim against a tax barrister for negligent advice, it was held at first instance that there was no objection in principle to the defendant relying upon expert evidence from another tax barrister who was a colleague and friend, and it would be for the trial judge to decide if the evidence was cogent (the application objecting was made 14 months after the identity of the expert was known and only a few weeks before trial). A surprising decision in the light of art.6 of the ECHR. But this was overturned by the trial judge as the relationship could give the appearance of bias which is as important as whether the individual *could* act independently in circumstances of closeness.

In *Pearce v Ove Arup Partnership Ltd (Copying)* (2002) 25(2) I.P.D. 25011, an expert witness who appeared to the judge to be biased and irrational was reported to his professional body by the court. *Franks v Towse* [2001] EWCA Civ 9, CA decided that one person could not appear as an advocate and give expert opinion evidence (before the Lands Tribunal).

In *Cairnstores v Aktiebolaget Hassle* [2002] EWCA Civ 1504, the Defendant's expert was criticised by the judge for acting as an advocate because of "over-exposure" to their case having been involved with their side in similar litigation in several other countries.

In *SPE International v Professional Preparation Contractors Ltd* [2002] EWHC 881, the judge was critical of an expert witness who gave evidence on a report on a subject outside his expertise—calculation of losses in a very technical business dispute—without any written instructions and in ignorance of Pt 35. He was also not independent, as he acted as a management consultant to the claimant. The judge ruled his evidence inadmissible.

Great Future International Ltd v Sealand Housing Corp (No.6) [2002] EWCA Civ 1183 decided that it would have been appropriate for the trial judge to have allowed the defendant's advocate to put questions to the claimant's witnesses concerning an allegedly improper approach by a person working for the claimant to the defendant's expert witness suggesting that work for the experts' firm might be jeopardised by his appearing as an expert for the defendant.

In *Hussein v William Hill Group* [2004] EWHC 208, QB, a personal injury claim, two doctors who were friends of the claimant and who provided medical reports later in the proceedings which supported his claim were criticised by the judge and their reports were disregarded. The judge found that the claimant had greatly and deliberately exaggerated his injuries. The conduct of the doctors was referred to the General Medical Council.

C (A Child) (Immunisation: Parental Rights), Re & F (A Child) (Immunisation: Parental Rights), Re [2003] EWCA Civ 1148; [2003] 2 F.L.R. 1095 were disputes between parents concerning the immunisation of their children. The homeopath who gave evidence for the mothers (who were against the immunisation) was criticised by the judge for allowing her deeply held feelings about immunisation to overrule her duty to the court to give objective evidence.

In *Phillips v Symes (A Bankrupt)* [2004] EWHC 1887, Ch D the court had to decide as a preliminary issue whether the defendant had the mental capacity to participate in the litigation. The evidence was overwhelming that he did have capacity but an expert witness, a doctor, after meeting the defendant for only one hour, filed a report that said he had lacked capacity for many years. The judge said the doctor's opinion evidence lacked objectivity and offended common sense. (See also para.35.12.4 for additional notes on this case).

In *DN v Greenwich London Borough* [2004] EWCA Civ 1659 the Court of Appeal held that the child psychologist accused of negligence could give evidence as to why he considered that his conduct did not fall below the standard of care reasonably to be expected of him, and the fact that his evidence might lack the objectivity of an independent expert went to the issue of cogency and not admissibility.

In *Toth v Jarman* [2006] EWCA Civ 1028 the claimant raised for the first time on appeal that a medical expert had a conflict of interest because he was a member of the Cases Committee of the Medical Defence Union which had represented the defendant in the claim. The Court of Appeal held that this information could have been obtained before the trial, and would not have affected the outcome, as the doctor had ceased to be a member of the Committee some time before the trial. However the Court of Appeal said that experts' potential conflicts of interest should be disclosed at an early stage in proceedings, and experts might add to the declaration at the end of their report that they had no such conflict.

Court's power to restrict expert evidence

35.4 **35.4—(1) No party may call an expert or put in evidence an expert's report without the court's permission.**

(2) When a party applies for permission under this rule he must identify—

(a) the field in which he wishes to rely on expert evidence; and

(b) where practicable the expert in that field on whose evidence he wishes to rely.

(3) If permission is granted under this rule it shall be in relation only to the expert named or the field identified under paragraph (2).

(4) The court may limit the amount of the expert's fees and expenses that the party who wishes to rely on the expert may recover from any other party.

Effect of rule

35.4.1 Under former RSC O.38, r.4 the court had power to limit the number of expert witnesses who could be called at trial. The court's powers in this respect are now strengthened; perhaps it was too rarely used in the past.

The court has total control over the use of evidence (r.32.1), including expert evidence (subject to, from October 1, 2000, the provisions of the Human Rights Act 1998, particularly the right to a fair trial). The court must restrict it to that which is necessary to resolve the proceedings justly and the court may direct the manner in which the evidence is given (see r.35.5). There should be no expert evidence at all unless it will help the court, and no more than one expert in any one speciality unless this is necessary for some real purpose (Final Report, p.139).

In *Barings Plc (In Liquidation) v Coopers & Lybrand (No.2)* [2001] Lloyd's Rep. Bank. 85; [2001] Lloyd's Rep. P.N. 379; [2001] P.N.L.R. 22; (2001) 98(13) L.S.G. 40, Ch D, it was held that expert evidence was, prima facie, admissible where there was an acknowledged "body of expertise" that governed by established principles and rules of conduct which was pertinent to an issue to be decided by the court (here practice and procedure in investment banking), but the court has a discretion to exclude such evidence if it would not help the determination of the issues (the evidence was allowed).

It can be very difficult for the parties and their lawyers to anticipate in advance when the court will decide that expert evidence is necessary. The dilemma for a party is that he/she may need advice from an expert early in a dispute to help decide if there is a claim or defence to pursue, but if the court later decides that evidence from an expert witness is not necessary to assist the court in determining the issues in dispute at that stage, the costs incurred by a party in obtaining early advice from an expert may not be recoverable.

Confining expert evidence to one or two specialities may also cause difficulties, even when this seems justifiable on proportionality grounds, especially if the court has decided that a single joint expert will give evidence. It could encourage an expert to step outside his/her expertise, and to give opinion evidence on matters on which he/she is not really competent.

The options available to the court in giving directions as to expert evidence include the following (see Final Report, p.140):

(a) directing that no expert evidence is to be adduced at all, or no expert evidence of a particular type or relating to a particular issue;
(b) limiting the number of expert witnesses which each party may call, either generally or in a given speciality;
(c) directing that evidence is to be given by one or more experts chosen by agreement between the parties or, where they cannot agree, chosen by a method stated in r.35.7(3).

The uses which parties are permitted to make of expert evidence may vary depending on the nature of the case management track to which proceedings are allocated. The fact that expert evidence is to be relied on in a case, and the extent of that evidence, may affect the question whether a case is allocated to the fast track or to the multi-track. See, further, the provisions as to allocation of a case to an appropriate case management track in Pts 26 to 30 and the Practice Directions supplementing those Parts (see paras 26PD.1 *et seq.*); note also "Court's permission" below

There is no right under ECHR art.6(1) to call expert evidence where the court considers that such evidence would serve no useful purpose, unless such evidence is necessary to ensure the fairness of the proceedings: see, by analogy *H v France (A/162)* (1990) 12 E.H.R.R. 74, ECtHR.

Court's permission

Permission to call an expert to testify or to put in evidence an expert's report may be given in the court's own case management directions or in response to an application to the court by a party, the court will prompt the parties to consider their intentions regarding the use of expert evidence at an early stage. Parties are asked to state in the allocation questionnaire. (1) whether any party will be seeking to adduce expert evidence, if so (2) the name and other details of the expert whom the party wishes to use, and (3) whether any progress has been made towards the preparation of a single report by several experts (r.35.12) or the instruction of a single joint expert (r.35.7). **35.4.2**

In cases proceeding on the multi-track, the purpose of the case management conference is to set an agenda for the further progress of the case at the earliest possible stage and to ensure that procedures are followed and costs incurred that are proportionate to the case. This is likely to include exploring with the parties the extent to which the evidence of experts will be needed, the prospects for limiting the number of experts (perhaps to a single or joint expert), and whether it will be necessary for experts to give oral evidence at trial.

In fast track cases, the matters to be dealt with by directions under r.28.2(1) include expert evidence (r.28.3(1)(c)). In such cases, the principle of proportionality dictates that expert evidence should be particularly limited, generally restricting each party to two experts (r.26.6(6)(b)), with single joint experts being used wherever possible (see r.35.7) (Final Report, p.140).

Where a court is called upon to determine whether a person should be permitted to give expert evidence it should be provided with material by which it could assess (a) what the issues in the case were likely to be, and (b) the person's ability to deal with those issues (*Field v Leeds City Council*, *The Times*, January 18, 2000, CA, Court observing that in disrepair cases one expert should be appointed and indicating how parties should co-operate to achieve this). A properly qualified expert who understands that his primary duty is to the court is not necessarily disqualified from giving evidence by the fact that he is employed by one of the parties (*Admiral Management Services Ltd v Para-Protect Europe Ltd*, *The Times*, March 26, 2002 where the court said it would depend upon the employee's status as experts and the nature of the work carried out) or by having an indirect connection with a party (*Helical Bar PLC & another v Armchair*

Passenger Transport Ltd [2003] EWHC 367, QB where the expert was a market researcher on credit hire rates, and the claimant sought to overturn an order giving the defendant permission to rely on his report because the researcher had previously been employed by the hire company from which the claimant had hired his vehicle). In *Gallaher International Ltd v Tlais Enterprises Ltd* [2007] EWHC 464 (Comm) an expert report from an employee of a related company to the claimant was allowed to be put in evidence because the employer had taken steps to distance the employee from company business by seconding him to the proceedings for their duration and paying him only his usual salary, because the employee had relevant and scarce expertise in marketing cigarettes in the Middle East and clearly understood that his duty was to the court.

B (a minor) (sexual abuse: expert's report), Re [2000] 1 F.L.R. 871A, a psychiatrist who was treating a child following possible incidents involving the father, was not sufficiently independent to provide forensic evidence to the court in a contested contact case.

In two personal injury cases decided early in 2007 the Court of Appeal decided that a medical witness was a witness of fact not an expert. In *Kirkman v Euro Exide Corporation* [2007] EWCA Civ 66 a surgeon who had treated the claimant had given a view in his statement as to whether he would have recommended surgery on the claimant's troublesome knee but for the further damage caused to it in the accident. The court held that this was evidence of fact, not opinion evidence, and the trial judge should have allowed it to be admitted. *Gall v Chief Constable of the West Midlands* [2006] EWCA Civ 2638, a claim for assault by the police, in which the evidence in dispute was a short report from the claimant's GP describing the claimant's injuries, was decided similarly.

Preaction protocols and disclosure of expert reports

35.4.3 The pre-action protocols for personal injury and clinical negligence encourage the parties to identify the need for expert evidence at the stage of investigating the claim, and in fast track personal injury cases in particular to try to instruct a single expert in a particular discipline, rather than one expert per party. However, it should be noted that the protocols assume that the claimant will instruct the expert, giving the defendant the opportunity to comment on the identity of the expert in advance, and to ask questions on the report, while the CPR assumes, unless the court orders otherwise, that an expert will be jointly instructed by the parties (although they may write separate letters of instruction).

In *Carlson v Townsend* [2001] EWCA Civ 511 the Court of Appeal confirmed that the personal injury pre-action protocol does not require a medical expert, selected in accordance with the protocol, to be jointly instructed, or her report to be disclosed to the defendant. Such reports remain privileged and the court cannot order their production, although the claimant would need the court's permission before relying on another expert's report in the proceedings.

The pre-action protocol for professional negligence claims encourages parties to appoint a joint expert, but permits the defendant to instruct their own if the claimant has done so before contacting the defendant, and both parties to instruct their own if they cannot agree on the identity of the joint expert. The Preaction Protocol for Construction and Engineering has similar provisions. The Housing Disrepair Protocol provides for joint selection and instruction of a single joint expert in a similar way to the personal injury protocol.

Costs of expert evidence

35.4.4 Rule 35.4(4) states that the court may limit the amount of the expert's fees and expenses that the party who wishes to rely on the expert may recover from any other party. Thus, where the costs of an expert are payable by one party to another, the amount recovered by the receiving party may be less than full costs reasonably incurred.

When exercising its discretion as to costs, the court must have regard to all the circumstances, including the conduct of all the parties (r.44.3(4)(a)). In this context, the "conduct of the parties" could include the unreasonable raising and pursuing of issues requiring expert evidence and any failure to comply with any pre-action protocol relating to such evidence (r.44.3(5)). (Note also r.43.6 (factors to be taken into account in deciding amount of costs).)

The Rules, it would seem, do not preclude the court:

(1) capping the amount of experts' fees which may be recovered at a limit set by the budget of the less well-resourced party

(2) ordering the better resourced party to bear all the costs of obtaining expert evidence regardless of the outcome of the case.

In *Kranidiotes v Paschali* [2001] EWCA Civ 357; March 8, 2001, CA, the court limited the fee of an accountant single joint expert to be instructed to value a shareholding, to £10,000. The expert selected by the parties quoted a fee of £75,000. The court terminated these instructions as the cost was disproportionate and ordered that another expert should be instructed. The Court of Appeal dismissed the defendant's appeal as the decision was within the judge's case management powers.

In small claims cases, the court may order a party to pay all or part of an expert's fee. Such sum must not exceed the amount specified in the relevant practice direction (r.27.14(3)(d) currently £200).

In cases proceeding on the fast track, the court's power to award trial costs is limited in accordance with Pt 45 (r.28.2(5)).

Although not expressly covered by the Rules or Practice Direction, it would clearly not be acceptable to the court for an expert witness to be paid on any form of contingency arrangement, including where the lawyers are working on a conditional fee agreement. Contingency arrangements for an expert witness would undermine the appearance, and possibly the reality, of the "independence" and their overriding duty to the court. But in *R. (on the application of Factortame & others) v Secretary Of State for Transport, Environment & the Regions (No.2)* [2002] EWCA Civ 932, CA, the claimants were allowed to recover accountants' fees charged as "8% of the final settlement received", as the accountants were not retained to give opinion evidence but to carry out support work for the expert witnesses, that could have been undertaken by the claimant's solicitors, and they played no part in the final proceedings on liability. *Davis v Stena* [2005] EWHC 420 (QB) was a claim concerning a fatal accident at sea, in which the claimant's (the widow's) liability expert had been instructed initially on a contingency fee basis (the solicitor and expert were unaware this was not allowed). The defendant applied at the start of the trial (by which time the expert was instructed on a deferred fee basis) for the claimant's expert evidence to be excluded: the judge decided that the consequent adjournment would add significantly to the costs, and cause delay, and that the expert could be cross-examined on his independence and credibility.

Martin v Holland & Barrett [2002] 3 Costs L.R. 530 approved an expert charging cancellation fees when a claim settled 12 days before trial, as it is "not unreasonable to expect experts to lay down terms in advance if they were to commit to a day in court."

Standard directions

For standard directions as to experts which may given by the court in fast track cases, see Practice Direction (Fast Track), Appendix (para.28FD.13 above). In multi-track cases, agreed directions on allocation should include provision for expert evidence, see Practice Direction (The Multi-Track), paras 4.7(1)(d) and 4.8(4) (para.29PD.4 above). As to directions which may be given by the court in multi-track cases on allocation and subsequently, see *ibid.* paras 4.10 and 4.11, 5.3, 5,5 and 5.6 (see para.29PD.4 and 29PD.5). **35.4.5**

General requirement for expert evidence to be given in a written report

35.5—(1) Expert evidence is to be given in a written report unless the court directs otherwise. **35.5**

(2) If a claim is on the fast track, the court will not direct an *expert to attend a hearing* unless it is necessary to do so in the interests of justice.

Effect of rule

For form and contents of expert's reports, see Practice Direction (Experts and Assessors), paras 1.1 to 1.6 (see para.35PD.1); see further notes following r.35.10, below. The general rule is that expert evidence, insofar as it is permitted, is to be given in a written report. **35.5.1**

Usually, the court will only give permission, in the first instance, in the directions made after filing of the allocation questionnaire, for expert evidence to be given by a written report, particularly in a case allocated to the fast track. The lifting of the limitation on oral expert evidence will be considered (or reconsidered) by the court on a case management occasion, usually at listing questionnaire, or pre-trial review stage. The court will have to be satisfied that there is no scope for further minimising the matters in issue between the experts by discussions (r.35.12), written questions (r.35.6), etc. before lifting that limitation.

It is also the general rule that, where a party wishes to use an expert's report at trial, or, having obtained the court's permission, wishes to call the expert to give evidence orally, he must disclose the report to other parties (r.35.13). Prior to the CPR it was not unusual for expert evidence to be served very late, sometimes only days before or, even at trial. Except in highly unusual circumstances, such conduct will no longer be acceptable, and parties can expect that the court will rule that late expert evidence cannot be relied upon. (*Baron v Lovell, The Times*, September 14, 1999, CA).

The non acceptability of late expert evidence was emphasized in *Calenti v North Middlesex NHS Trust* L.T.L. April 14, 2001, QBD when a defendant sought permission to adduce medical evidence two weeks before trial.

But, on occasions, to "deal with a case justly ", the court will allow an expert to be instructed at a late stage and allow a party to amend their statement of case based on the expert report. In *Holmes v SGB Services Plc* [2001] EWCA Civ 354 202, CA no steps were taken by the claimant to obtain expert evidence until 9 months after the defendant's witness statements were served disputing that the personal injury accident could have happened in the way the claimant alleged. The single expert advanced a different possible explanation for the accident. The claimant was allowed to amend his particulars of claim and the trial date was vacated. The defendant's appeal was dismissed - the single expert's evidence took the case out of the run of ordinary case management decisions and it was for the first instance judge, not the Court of Appeal, to decide what weight to give to the various factors.

In *Kapadia v Lambeth LBC* [2000] I.R.L.R. 14 it was decided that once a medical expert had been instructed to prepare a personal injury report for the defence, with the claimant's agreement, neither the claimant nor the expert could decide not to release the report because the claimant was not happy with it, as this would defeat the objective of transparency of expert evidence.

In *UYB Ltd v British Railways Board, The Times*, November 15, 2000 the claimant argued that a draft expert report disclosed "without prejudice" to assist negotiations should have been admitted in evidence at the trial two years later when the claimant's entitlement to interest on damages was in dispute. The Court of Appeal confirmed that "without prejudice" documents, including draft expert reports, as under the previous roles, should not be referred to at trial, particularly as in this case the figures in the draft and final reports were quite different.

In *Gough v Mummery* [2002] EWCA Civ 1573 the trial judge refused to adjourn a trial to resolve which version of an expert's letter was the right one—both bore the same date but were quite different. One was signed and the other was not. The Court of Appeal said the judge was right in accepting the signed one especially as he took the view neither was crucial to his decision.

In *Beck v Ministry of Defence* [2003] EWCA Civ 1043 the Court of Appeal allowed the defendant to abandon their first expert's report, although this was favourable to their case, and to instruct a second expert, but on condition that the first expert's report was disclosed. It was emphasised that a party seeking to "replace" an expert has to provide good reasons particularly, as here, where a claimant may be subjected to another medical examination, but that the party does not have to disclose the first report until the court has decided the application for a further expert. But in *Hajigeorgiou v Vasiliou* [2005] EWCA Civ 236 the Court of Appeal held that permission was not needed for the defendant to instruct a different expert than had been canvassed at the case management conference because the judge's directions did not name the expert to be instructed. The decision in Beck (above) was confirmed where a proposed expert was named, or a report had been obtained from the intended expert i.e. that the first instructed expert's report must be disclosed as a pre-condition to instructing a second expert.

Carruthers v MP Fireworks, January 26, 2007, unrep., Bristol County Court: the claimant was injured by a defendant's exploding firework. Pre-proceedings the claimant instructed an expert to test the remains of the firework but did not disclose the report. After issue the District Judge ordered that the claimant could rely upon another expert provided he disclosed the previous report (following *Beck v MOD*). On appeal it was held that while the court could not usually order a party to disclose an expert's report obtained pre-action, as it was privileged (see *Carlson v Townsend* notes to para.35.4.3) where an expert had performed tests on an exhibit, open justice and fairness would usually demand that the results of those tests should be put before the other party and the court, particularly when there was some perception that the tests might have caused some alteration to the exhibit.

Calden v Nunn 2003 WL 270906 the Court of Appeal refused to allow the defendants to rely upon an additional expert very late in the proceedings, after all the other experts had met and largely reached agreement, and when the trial window, already twice postponed, was imminent. Instead questions arising from the "new" expert's report were to be put to the claimant's "like" expert.

The court has wide powers under its general powers of case management to make orders as to the exchange of experts' reports. This may be simultaneous or sequential. The court may order simultaneous exchange of some reports (e.g. on liability) and sequential exchange of others (e.g. a *quantum*). Such order may prescribe the time and date of such exchange and may spell out the consequences of non-compliance (rr.5.1(2) and 5.3). The court will usually impose a sensible but tight timetable for such matters as may include the exchange of experts' reports and for experts' discussions or meetings (as often as may be necessary having regard to the complexity of a case) as may be necessary in order to try to agree such matters as may be agreed, and to identify matters that cannot be agreed, giving a summary of reasons why not (see r.35.12).

Fast track claims

In fast track cases, the general rule is that expert evidence is to be given in a written report prepared by the expert and not, unless the court so directs, by the expert's oral evidence. However, in fast track cases the court will not give a direction "unless it is necessary to do so in the interests of justice" (r.35.5(2)) and the parties will be expected to make out a strong case for requiring oral expert evidence. **35.5.2**

Use of plans, photographs and models as evidence

Where evidence of this type forms part of expert evidence but is not contained in the expert's report, the party proposing to adduce such evidence must give notice to the other party when serving the expert's report (r.33.6(6)). **35.5.3**

Expert evidence as to foreign law

See r.33.7. **35.5.4**

Witness summonses

A witness may be required to attend court to give evidence or produce documents by a "witness summons"; see provisions in Pt 34 (Depositions and court attendance by witnesses. See also *Society of Lloyds v Clementson (No.2)*, *The Times*, February 29, 1996, referred to in notes following r.35.2. **35.5.5**

Expert witnesses often do not realise that service of a witness summons is not a hostile act but only a "prior booking system" to ensure that over-committed experts give evidence in court in one case rather than another. (See also the notes at para.35.2.2)

Inspection of written evidence

Where an expert witness is called to give evidence, generally his report will stand as his evidence in chief. Rule 32.13 provides that a witness statement which stands as evidence in chief is open to inspection unless the court directs otherwise. Any person may ask the court to direct that such a witness statement should not be open for inspection unless during the course of the trial. The court should not make a direction preventing inspection except on specific grounds, for example because of the nature of any expert medical evidence in the statement (r.32.13). Where the expert is not called to give oral evidence and his report is put in evidence it would be open to inspection. **35.5.6**

Written questions to experts

35.6—(1) A party may put to— **35.6**

(a) an expert instructed by another party; or

(b) a single joint expert appointed under rule 35.7,

written questions about his report.

(2) Written questions under paragraph (1)—

(a) may be put once only;

(b) must be put within 28 days of service of the expert's report; and

(c) must be for the purpose only of clarification of the report;

unless in any case—

(i) the court gives permission; or

(ii) the other party agrees.

(3) An expert's answers to questions put in accordance with paragraph (1) shall be treated as part of the expert's report.

(4) Where—

(a) a party has put a written question to an expert instructed by another party in accordance with this rule; and

(b) the expert does not answer that question,

the court may make one or both of the following orders in relation to the party who instructed the expert—

(i) that the party may not rely on the evidence of that expert; or

(ii) that the party may not recover the fees and expenses of that expert from any other party.

Effect of rule

35.6.1 The general rule is that, where expert evidence is permitted, it is to be given by written report without the maker of the report being called to testify. An expert's report must be disclosed to the other side (r.35.13), whether or not the expert is to give oral evidence. Under r.35.6 a party may put to an expert instructed by another party written questions about his/her report in accordance with the terms of the rule. (As to putting questions about a report prepared by a single joint expert see notes following r.35.7.) The answers form part of the report (r.35.6(3)). Where an expert does not answer a question put, r.35.6(4) comes into play.

This is a useful provision, perhaps particularly so in fast track cases (see r.35.5(2)). It enables a party to obtain clarification of a report prepared by an expert instructed by his opponent. In a given case, were it not possible to achieve such clarification or extension of a report, the court, for that reason alone, may feel obliged to direct that the expert witness should testify at trial.

MMR and MR Vaccine Litigation (No.4) [2002] EWHC 1213 (QB) clarified which expert reports are appropriate for questions: not reports in Group Litigation (see Pt 19) prepared for an interim application hearing to decide the issues for trial, but which were not intended to be relied upon at trial.

Written questions may be put once only (without the court's permission) and must be put within 28 days of receipt of the expert's report. Practice Direction (Experts and Assessors), para.4.2 (see para.35PD.1) states that, where a party sends a written question or questions direct to an expert and the other party is represented by solicitors, a copy of the questions should, at the same time, be sent to those solicitors.

The meaning of "clarification" is not explained in the Rule or Practice Direction. However, it would seem that questions should not be used to require an expert to carry out new investigations or tests, to expand significantly on his/her report, or to conduct a form of cross-examination by post, including on the expert's credibility unless the court gives express permission. In *Mutch v Allen* [2001] All E.R. D 121, CA, a medical expert in a personal injury claim was asked by the defendant whether the claimant's injuries would have less severe if he had been wearing a seat belt. At first instance it was accepted this was outside the scope of his instructions and report and was not therefore "clarification". The Court of Appeal said that the expert answering the question would assist 'the just disposal of the dispute', but either the expert should be called to give evidence and be cross-examined by both parties at trial. Or the parties could apply to the court for permission to obtain further expert evidence on this point.

If an expert receives a set of questions which he/she considers go beyond the spirit of the rule, the right approach, it is suggested, is for the expert to answer the clearly relevant questions, and only to decline to answer the remainder if:

(1) to do so would clearly be prejudicial to the instructing party's position or

(2) the time and cost of replying to the questions is disproportionate.

One approach to dealing with excessive or onerous questions is for the expert to exercise his/her right to ask the court for directions (see notes to r.35.14 below).

An omission from this rule is the time-scale within which an expert should reply to written questions. Parties should invite the court to include a suitable timescale in directions. In most circumstances 28 days would be reasonable.

In September 1999, the Practice Direction to Pt 35, para.4.3 (see below) was amended to require the party instructing the expert to pay any fees charged by the expert for answering questions put under r.35.6. Previously, it was the party asking the questions that paid the expert's fees. It would seem that the change was made at least partly for practical reasons to facilitate payment of an expert's fees.

Court's power to direct that evidence is to be given by a single joint expert

35.7—(1) Where two or more parties wish to submit expert evidence on a particular issue, the court may direct that the evidence on that issue is to be given by one expert only. 35.7

(2) The parties wishing to submit the expert evidence are called "the instructing parties".

(3) Where the instructing parties cannot agree who should be the expert, the court may—

(a) select the expert from a list prepared or identified by the instructing parties; or

(b) direct that the expert be selected in such other manner as the court may direct.

Effect of rule

Rule 35.7 provides that where several parties wish to submit expert evidence on "a particular issue" the court may direct that, instead of permitting each party to submit the evidence of an expert, the court may direct that the evidence "on that issue" should be given by one expert only. Such a direction may be given by the court on its own initiative (see r.3.3). This is yet another way in which the court may exercise its power to control expert evidence for the purpose of reducing costs and delay. (Obviously, the parties may agree to give joint instructions to a single expert without a direction by the court to that effect under r.35.7.) Rule 27.2(1)(e) states that r.35.7 shall apply in small claims. Practice Direction (Committal Applications), para.10 (see para.scpd52.6 below) states that the power given to the court by r.35.7 (or by r.35.8 or r.35.9) does not apply to an application to the court for an order for committal of a person to prison. 35.7.1

This discretionary power may be exercised at any time. It may be anticipated that the court is likely to direct that the evidence on a particular issue is to be given by a single joint expert where it appears to the court, on the information then available, that the issue falls within a substantially established area of knowledge and where it is not necessary for the court to sample a range of opinion. There is no presumption in favour of the appointment of a single joint expert, except in cases allocated to the fast track. The object is to do away with the calling of multiple experts where, given the nature of the issue over which the parties are at odds, that is not justified. This has the advantages of reducing costs and delays and of strengthening the impartial role of experts.

The main difficulty with this new rule is that the court is only involved in most disputes at a relatively late stage. On occasions, one or both parties may have needed, or chosen, to obtain advise from an expert before proceedings were issued. This can pose a dilemma for the case management judge when giving directions on expert evidence, especially in cases allocated to the fast track. While the court may perceive there to be significant advantages for evidence to be obtained from one single joint expert, the impact on the timetable of the action, and particularly on the costs incurred, may be disproportionate if the court orders the instruction of a new expert at directions stage, when one or both parties have already instructed their own expert. In some circumstances it will be more appropriate to allow the parties to retain their own expert, and for the court to seek to narrow the issues in dispute on the expert opinion evidence by requiring service of written questions on the experts, and by ordering an experts' discussion.

In *Sage v Feiven* [2002] C.L.Y. 430 the claimant obtained a report from an orthapaedic surgeon which was not disclosed (following *Carlton v Townsend* [2001] EWCA Civ 511, CA). When proceedings were issued the defendant invited the District Judge to order a report from the same surgeon as a single joint expert, and the D.J. did so, on proportionality grounds. This was overturned on appeal, because inevitably, privileged information would be disclosed to the defendant. The parties were ordered to instruct a new expert.

In *Mwamda v East London Bus & Coach Co Ltd* [2002] C.L.Y. 432 the claimant in a personal injury case was not allowed to rely upon a report obtained from a GP without following the pre-action protocol procedure and which did not comply with Pt 35 in several respects. The court ordered the instruction of a new single joint expert.

The single joint expert, however selected, is instructed by the parties concerned (see r.35.8).

In the light of his/her report, the parties may agree that the evidence of a single joint expert should not be given at the trial. If the evidence is to be used at trial it may be submitted as a written report without the expert being called. If a single joint expert is called to give oral evidence at trial, it is submitted, although the rule and the practice direction do not make this clear, that both parties will have the opportunity to cross-examine him/her, but with a degree of restraint, given that the expert has been instructed by the parties.

A direction that the evidence on a particular issue should be given by one expert only may be given by the court on its own initiative or on application. (Where the court proposes to make an order of its own initiative, it may give *any person* likely to be affected by it an opportunity to make representations, usually within seven days.) An application may be made, not only by one or other of the two or more parties wishing to submit expert evidence on the issue, but also by any other party.

Power of court to direct evidence from lead experts

35.7.2 Practice Direction (Experts and Assessors), para.5 (see para.35PD.5) states that, where the court has directed that the evidence on a particular issue is to be given by one expert only but there are a number of disciplines relevant to that issue, a leading expert in the dominant discipline should be identified as the single expert. He/she should prepare the general part of the report and be responsible for annexing or incorporating the contents of any reports from experts in other disciplines.

Experience since the implementation of the CPR suggests this power is only occasionally being exercised in more complex cases, where key liability or *quantum* experts, typically medical, accountancy, or care, are being instructed in effect to "coordinate" the work of other experts. This has clear advantages for the court but can pose difficulties for the lead expert, especially where the opinion evidence from the other experts conflicts or where the lead expert disagrees with some of the other experts' opinions.

Rule 35.6 states that a party may put to a single joint expert appointed under r.35.7 written questions about his report.

Court of Appeal guidance on rule 35.7

35.7.3 There have been a number of helpful decisions of the Court of Appeal in relation to r.35.7. In *S (a Minor) v Birmingham Health Authority* [2001] Lloyd's Rep Med 382, the first instance court had ordered a single joint expert to prepare opinion evidence on liability and causation in a clinical negligence claim. The claimant appealed on the basis that the issues to be covered in the expert's report were so important to the likely outcome of the case that the parties should be entitled to instruct an expert each: the appeal court agreed. In *Field v Leeds City Council* [2000] T.L.R. January 15, 2000, the appeal court said that an expert employed by a local authority is not necessarily disqualified by his employment from acting as an expert witness for the defendant in a housing disrepair claim, provided he understood that his role was an independent one, and that he had a duty to the court; but in many circumstances in this type of case it was preferable for the parties to jointly instruct a single expert. *Field* was followed in *Admiral Management Services Ltd v Para Protect Europe Ltd* [2002] EWHC 233, a dispute concerning the alleged poaching of employees and intellectual property. The Claimant, the first employer, was allowed in principle, to recover the costs of "expert" staff time in searching for, and analysing, material found on the defendant's, the second employer's computers.

In *ES v Chesterfield and North Derbyshire Royal Hospital NHS Trust* [2003] EWCA Civ 1284 the claimant in a clinical negligence claim wanted to instruct two opinion experts when the defendant had two from the same discipline as witnesses of fact. The Court of Appeal overturned the District Judge as the claim was worth £1.5 million, the issues were complex and in accordance with the overriding objective.

Piper v Clifford Kent Ltd [2003] EWCA Civ 1692 a claim in smell nuisance from a chicken farm, the single joint expert, upon whose evidence the judge had relied, had failed to measure the wind direction on his visit: on appeal the case was remitted back to the county court for a retrial. *Wright v Sullivan* [2005] EWCA Civ 656 decided that in a serious personal injury claim, a clinical case manager appointed to assist a severely injured person owed a duty of care to the patient claimant alone, if called to give evidence would be a witness of fact, and could not be jointly instructed as a single joint expert to give opinion evidence.

It is clear that the court can prefer the evidence of a witness of fact to an expert's opinion evidence. In *Regan v Chetwynd* December 15, 2000, unrep., the court agreed with the claimant that the single joint expert accident reconstruction expert's report should be viewed with caution, and in *Fuller v Strum* (2001) 98(6) L.S.G. 45 Ch D, in a case about an allegedly forged will, the judge preferred the evidence of the witnesses of fact to that of the handwriting expert who had concluded that the will was forged, as the expert was doing no more than drawing inferences from facts given to him.

Single joint experts and Article 6 of ECHR

Although, strictly speaking, the single joint expert is not a "court appointed expert" **35.7.4**
the appointment of an expert by the court is not in any event objectionable under ECHR art.6(1): *Brandstetter v Austria* (1993) 15 E.H.R.R. 378, ECtHR. The expert appointed by the court should be free from both actual and apparent bias (*Bonisch v Austria* (1987) 9 EHRR 191, ECtHR), although apparent bias may not always be sufficient to render a trial unfair: *Brandsetter v Austria* (1993) 15 E.H.R.R. 378, ECtHR.

The ECHR art.6(1) right to an adversarial procedure may require the parties to be actively involved in the process by which the expert prepares his report, including attending interviews and examining the documents on which the report is based: *Mantovanelli v France* (1997) 24 E.H.R.R. 370, ECHR. It is not contrary to art.6(1) for the court to allow a party to put additional questions to a joint expert following completion of her report: *D (A Child) v Walker*, [2000] 1 W.L.R. 1382, CA. Indeed the requirements of art.6(1) will not be satisfied where the court considers itself bound by conclusions reached by another person or body on material issues, thereby depriving itself of jurisdiction to determine matters which are crucial to the dispute: *Terra Woningen v Netherlands* (1997) 24 E.H.R.R. 456 (relating to the findings of fact).

Directions as to single joint expert

For directions as to the appointment of single joint experts which may given by the **35.7.5**
court in fast track cases, see Practice Direction (Fast Track), Appendix (para.28PD.13 above). In multi-track cases, where appropriate agreed directions on allocation should include provision for the use of a single joint expert, see Practice Direction (The Multi-Track), para.4.8(4) (para.29PD.4 above). In such cases, where the court gives directions on its own initiative in the circumstances stated in para.4.10 of this Practice Direction, its general approach will be to give directions for a single joint expert on any appropriate issue unless there is good reason not to do so (para.29PD.4 above).

For directions as to single joint expert in commercial cases, see Commercial Court Guide, para.H2.4.

For directions as to single joint expert in Chancery proceedings, see Chancery Guide, para.6.10 (Vol.2, para.1–48).

Obtaining further expert evidence

35.7.6 Where the parties give joint instructions to a single expert, whether as a result of a direction given by the court under r.35.7 or as a result of an agreement to that effect between the parties, it is conceivable that one of the parties may be unhappy with the report produced by the single joint expert. The question may then arise whether that party should be permitted to instruct another expert with a view to his obtaining a report which will enable him to make a decision as to whether or not there were aspects of the report of the single joint expert which he might wish to challenge. In *Daniels v Walker* [2000] 1 W.L.R. 1382, CA, it was held that, where the dissatisfied party's reasons were not fanciful, such permission may be granted, at least where the parties had agreed to give joint instructions to the single expert, and especially where a substantial sum was involved. Where it would be unjust, having regard to the overriding objective (r.1.1), not to allow that party to call the further expert evidence, then he must be allowed to call that evidence. The Court added that, in a given case the dissatisfied party's disagreement may be cleared up by written questions to the single joint expert (r.35.6). Where further expert evidence was obtained by the dissatisfied party (or, perhaps, both parties) then a decision would have to be made by the court as to what evidence should be called at trial. That decision should not be made until there had been a meeting between the experts involved (r.35.12). Factors that may be relevant to the question whether a party should be permitted to adduce further expert evidence were outlined in *Cosgrove v Pattison*, [2001] C.P. Rep. 68 (Neuberger J). But in *Popek v National Westminster Bank Plc* [2002] EWCA Civ 42 the Court of Appeal decided that the trial judge was not wrong to refuse the claimant's late application to adduce additional expert evidence to that of the single joint expert, not least because the claimant's case had no prospect of success. Also in *Peet v Mid Kent Healthcare Trust* [2001] EWCA Civ 1703, the Court of Appeal seemed to suggest a stiffer test for adducing additional expert evidence — that "good reasons" are needed — not just more than "fanciful reasons". But could the difference in the Court's reasoning be related to whether one or both parties in the litigation are publicly funded?

In *Sutton v Tesco Stores Plc* (2002) C.L. August Digest 57 the claimant, in a personal injury slipping claim, was allowed to rely upon a report from her treating psychiatrist obtained without discussion with the defendant or the court's permission, to challenge evidence from other experts, including single joint experts, that she was malingering, but not to recover the costs of the report, regardless of the outcome.

In *Smolen v Solon Co-operative Housing Services Ltd* [2003] EWCA Civ 1240 the Court of Appeal upheld the first instance decision to allow the appointment of a second single joint expert when the claimant objected to the first one, even though this was after his report was disclosed, because he had been instructed by the defendant's solicitor many times before: but the claimant was ordered to pay half the first expert's fee in the usual way and to pay the fees for the second expert into court.

In *Re W (a child) non-accidental injury: expert evidence* [2007] EWHC 136 (Fam) All E.R. (D) 159 it was held that in difficult or unusual cases a single joint expert should consider and if necessary make recommendations on the need for further expert evidence.

In *G. Saunder v Birmingham City Council* 2008 EAT May 21 the claimant, in a claim for severe psychiatric injury allegedly caused by unlawful discrimination, was allowed to rely upon a report from one of the two experts he had instructed to comment upon the report of the single joint expert, who had concluded that the onset of the illness pre-dated the discrimination. The EAT concluded that further expert evidence was justified as the issue of causation would have a significant effect on the amount of compensation, and as the claimant had already instructed the experts there would be no delay in allowing in evidence of one of them. The EAT also concluded that the claimant's allegation that the SJE was biased could be addressed by cross-examination at the trial.

Instructions to a single joint expert

35.8 **35.8—(1) Where the court gives a direction under rule 35.7 for a single joint expert to be used, each instructing party may give *instructions to* the expert.**

(2) When an instructing party gives instructions to the expert he must, at the same time, send a copy of the instructions to the other instructing parties.

(3) The court may give directions about—

(a) the payment of the expert's fees and expenses; and

(b) any inspection, examination or experiments which the expert wishes to carry out.

(4) The court may, before an expert is instructed—

(a) limit the amount that can be paid by way of fees and expenses to the expert; and

(b) direct that the instructing parties pay that amount into court.

(5) Unless the court otherwise directs, the instructing parties are jointly and severally liable[GL] for the payment of the expert's fees and expenses.

Effect of rule

The provisions of this rule are supplementary to the court's power to appoint a single joint expert given in r.35.7. The first two paragraphs in r.35.8 deal with the manner in which the single joint expert is to be instructed. The remaining paragraphs deal with the matter of the expert's fees and expenses. Rule 27.2(1)(e) states that r.35.8 shall apply in small claims. Practice Direction (Committal Applications), para.10 (see para.scpd52.6 below) states that the power given to the court by r.35.8 (or by r.35.7 or r.35.9 does not apply to an application to the court for an order for committal of a person to prison. **35.8.1**

Instructions to single joint expert

It is conceivable that the several parties may be able to agree on joint instructions to be given to the single joint expert. However, it has to be expected that they may not be able to agree. Rule 35.8 does not give the court the power in that event to order that joint instructions should be settled. Instead it is provided that each instructing party may give instructions to the expert provided that, when he does so, those instructions are revealed to the other instructing parties. **35.8.2**

In *Yorke v Katra* [2002] EWCA Civ 867 the Court of Appeal held that the District and Circuit judges were wrong to strike out the defence of a litigant in person in a building dispute on the small claims track because the defendant had disobeyed a court order to sign a letter of instruction to a single joint expert (drafted by the claimant's solicitor): he had amended it and then signed it. The Court of Appeal said he was entitled to send his own letter in accordance with CPR r.35.8. This was perhaps a surprising decision given that Pt 35 does not apply to cases on the small claims track (see CPR r.27.2) but understandable on the facts.

A potential difficulty for the expert is that the first party to instruct him may fail to tell him he is a single joint expert. The second letter of instruction from the other party will come as a surprise, and may even cause practical difficulties if the expert has begun work on the first set of instructions, and the two sets of instructions are very different.

An expert's report, including the report of a single joint expert, must state the substance of all material instructions, whether written or oral, on the basis of which the report was written (r.35.10(3)).

Where a single joint expert receives conflicting instructions from the parties, which cannot be resolved by discussion, the expert may wish to exercise his/her right to apply to the court for directions under r.35.14.

Single joint expert's fees and expenses

Under r.35.8, the parties are liable (jointly and severally) for the costs of the single joint expert's fees but the extent of their liability will depend on any order as to costs. Obviously, particularly where the parties have not been able to agree on the appointment of a single joint expert, it is important that they should be clear at the outset of the extent of their potential liability as to costs. Consequently, it is provided that the court may give directions about the payment of the expert's fees and expenses and may, before an expert is instructed, limit the amount that can be paid by way of fees and expenses to the expert. (Further, this is consistent with the other powers which **35.8.3** the court has to limit fees payable to experts.) The court may secure the payments of the expert's fees and expenses by instructing the parties to make a payment into court.

In practice, it can cause difficulties for an expert if each party is responsible for part of his/her fees. Some experts have reached arrangements that the first party to instruct him/her pays the entire fee and recovers the relevant share from the other party.

Directions as to inspection, etc.

35.8.4 In appointing a single joint expert, the court may give directions about any inspection, examination or experiments which the expert wishes to carry out (r.35.8(3)(b)).

Note also, r.33.6(8) (inspection of plans, models, photographs, etc.).

Conferences and meetings with single joint experts and their attendance at trial

35.8.5 In *Peet v Mid-Kent Healthcare Trust (Practice Note)* [2001] EWCA Civ 1703; [2002] 1 W.L.R. 210, CA, the claimant in a cerebral palsy clinical negligence case wanted a non-medical single joint expert to attend a conference with counsel in the absence of the other party. The Court of Appeal refused consent on the grounds that all contact with a single joint expert must be transparent, his report would usually be the only evidence he gave, and one party could not fairly be permitted to test it before trial without the involvement of the other party. It was also said, controversially, but obiter, that usually there should not be a need to amplify or test the report of a single joint expert at trial by cross-examination. But in *Austen v Oxford CC* [2002] All E.R. (D) 97 on appeal a single joint expert psychiatrist was ordered to give evidence at a disposal hearing because otherwise there could be an injustice and in *Layland v Fairview New Homes plc* [2002] EWHC 1350 it was held that the District Judge was wrong to give summary judgment based on a disputed single joint expert report (concerning the alleged reduction in value of a property located close to an incinerator). He should have allowed submissions and cross-examination on the report.

Childs v Vernon & Butcher [2007] EWCA Civ 305 concerned a boundary dispute. The expert had discussions with one party in the absence of the other. The Court of Appeal held this was wholly improper, but did not disturb the trial judge's finding as this was supported by factual evidence in addition to the expert's report.

Weight to be given to a single joint expert's report

35.8.6 In *Coopers Payen Ltd v Southampton Container Terminal Ltd* [2003] EWCA Civ 1223 the Court of Appeal decided that where a witness of fact gives evidence on an issue that is contrary to that of the single joint expert, the judge should make a considered choice as to which evidence to accept, but that it should be unusual to disregard the expert's evidence. But in *Richard Tucker v Rebecca Watt* [2005] EWCA Civ 1420 the Court of Appeal held that a trial judge had not erred in reaching a conclusion based upon the claimant's evidence when the defendant had resisted the calling of a joint expert to be cross-examined who had taken a different view on causation in his written report to the claimant's evidence.

Power of court to direct a party to provide information

35.9 **35.9 Where a party has access to information which is not reasonably available to the other party, the court may direct the party who has access to the information to—**

(a) prepare and file a document recording the information; and

(b) serve a copy of that document on the other party.

Effect of rule

35.9.1 In the Final Report it was said (p.146) that there should be, so far as possible, a level playing field between litigants of unequal financial or other resources. A particular problem arises when one party, often the defendant (e.g. a hospital or a large company), has an easily available source of expertise to which the other party does not have access (see also p.138). In the Final Report, it was suggested that a new procedure should be introduced enabling claimants to apply to the court (either before or after proceedings have started) for an order requiring a defendant with access to expertise to provide the claimant with an expert's report on a particular situation.

Rule 35.9 carries that recommendation into effect, but with modifications. The rule is careful to say that what is provided is not an expert's "report" but merely "information" but, presumably, information derived from a source of expertise.

Practice Direction (Committal Applications), para.10 (see para.scpd52.6 below) states that the power given to the court by r.35.9 (or by r.35.7 or r.35.8) does not apply to an application to the court for an order for committal of a person to prison.

In terms, r.35.9 contrasts with the proposed provisions of draft versions of the rule whereby a court could order a party to arrange for an expert to prepare a report on any matter and if appropriate to arrange for an examination in relation to the matter to be carried out. Rule 35.9 makes no express reference to examination, experiment or tests in relation to the matter in issue. The omission must be deliberate. A situation may arise wherein one party has researched and developed a technical process over a long period of time and is therefore possessed with the greatest expertise in that area. It might thus be reasonable for the court to require that party to share information as to those matters which might reasonably assist the opposing party's expert without the necessity of time-consuming and expensive research before he can form a view. Any direction under r.35.9 would have to take into account such matters as commercial confidentiality in the use of such information in connection with the proceedings. It is hard to conceive of circumstances whereby such information could be sought by a party before proceedings have commenced. There seems to be no basis upon which a court could order an examination, experiment or tests on the matter in issue before preparing and filing the document recording the information An application on notice in writing would be made to the court stating what order the applicant is seeking and the reasons relied upon by the applicant. Such an application may be supported by evidence from the applicant's expert setting out his particular difficulties in the absence of such information and the advantage that such information would have as to the just and expeditious resolution of the case. On the face of it, there is nothing to prevent a court of its own motion making such an order under this rule. If it was satisfied upon evidence before it that it was necessary to make such an order to enable the court to deal with the case justly considering its overriding objectives of ensuring so far as is practical that the parties are on equal footing expense could be saved and that the matter could be dealt with expeditiously.

Practice Direction (Expert and Assessors), para.3 (see para.35PD.3) states that where the court makes an order under this rule, the document to be prepared recording the information should set out sufficient details of any facts, tests or experiments which constitute the information to enable an assessment and understanding of the significance of the information to me made and obtained.

It does not seem that very much use has been made of this new rule as yet. Indeed in *Field v Leeds City Council, The Times*, January 18, 2000, CA, the Court of Appeal said that it is often preferable for the parties to instruct an independent single joint expert rather than for one party to obtain a report from an in-house expert.

Contents of report

35.10—(1) An expert's report must comply with the requirements set out in the relevant practice direction. 35.10

(2) At the end of an expert's report there must be a statement that—

(a) the expert understands his duty to the court; and

(b) he has complied with that duty.

(3) The expert's report must state the substance of all material *instructions, whether* written or oral, on the basis of which the report was written.

(4) The instructions referred to in paragraph (3) shall not be privileged[GL] against disclosure but the court will not, in relation to those instructions—

(a) order disclosure of any specific document; or

(b) permit any questioning in court, other than by the party who instructed the expert,

unless it is satisfied that there are reasonable grounds to consider the statement of instructions given under paragraph (3) to be inaccurate or incomplete.

Effect of rule

35.10.1 An expert's report must comply with the provisions of this rule and the requirements set out in the relevant practice direction (see para.35PD.1). The purpose of the requirement in r.35.10(2) is to remind the expert preparing a report that his duty to "help the court" overrides any obligation to the person from whom he has received instructions or by whom, he is paid (r.35.3(2)). Full compliance with this duty would include ensuring that the report includes everything which the expert regards as being relevant to the opinion which he has expressed, and that any matter which would affect the validity of that opinion has been drawn to the attention of the court. But this is not without controversy, as experts sometimes step outside their area of expertise and include in their reports matters which they may regard as being relevant to their opinion evidence but which the parties (and the court) do not and which, on occasions, may even be prejudicial to the instructing parties' positions.

An expert's report which is to be adduced in evidence should carry a statement of truth (see Practice Direction (Expert and Assessors), paras 1.3 and 1.4 (see para.35PD.1)) (see also Pt 22 (Statements of Truth)).

Form and content of expert's report

35.10.2 Practice Direction (Experts and Assessors), para.1.1 states that an expert's report should be addressed to the court and not to the party from whom the expert has received his instructions. The report must deal with the matters itemised in para.1.2 of that Practice Direction. In addition it should comply with the guidance in the Protocol for the Instruction of Experts to give Evidence in Civil Claims, paragraphs 13.1 to 13.15—see para.35.28.

Oldham MBC v GW, PW and KPW [2007] EWHC 136 (Fam) concerned care proceedings but the judge's guidance on the role of an expert and contents of reports has relevance to all contested proceedings where expert opinion evidence is important to the outcome. The judge emphasised that:

- experts need clear instructions and access to all relevant documents, not selected ones;
- the expert's report should set out the expert's analytical process, differentiate between facts, assumptions, deductions and note inconsistent or contradictory features of the case;
- the expert should identify the professional range of opinion and use a "balance sheet" approach to his own opinion;
- the expert should volunteer where an opinion from other expertise is likely to assist the parties and the court;
- the expert should not stray into the role of decision-maker.

Material instructions

35.10.3 The requirement that the expert's report must state the substance of all material instructions, whether written or oral, on the basis of which the report was written (r.35.10(3)) is an important innovation (see Practice Direction (Experts and Assessors), para.1.2(8), see para.35PD.1). From, the court's perspective, knowledge of the instructions adds considerably to the value to the court of the expert's report received. Further, the discipline of reciting instructions should serve to reinforce the expert's overriding duty to the court (r.35.3)). In this respect, the objective of the rules is to prevent the suppression of relevant opinions or factual material which does not support the case put forward by the party instructing the expert (Final Report, p.144).

In a given case, the drawing of a distinction between material and non-material instructions may be difficult especially where the expert was instructed early in a dispute when a party was still considering whether he/she had a claim and against *whom*. One view is that, in these circumstances, the expert should be sent fresh instructions once the court has given permission for expert evidence: this will usually be at directions stage following completion of the allocation questionnaires. Oral instructions can cause a particular problem: so it is important that parties, lawyers, and experts keep careful notes of all discussions which might amount to instructions.

Privilege

See Interim Report p.188 and Final Report p.144. **35.10.4**

In the Interim Report it was stated (p.144) that, once an expert has been instructed to prepare a report for use by the court, any communications between the expert and the client and the client or his advisers should no longer be privileged. In the Final Report (p.144) it was conceded that this was too sweeping and could lead to additional delay and expense. Consequently, under r.35.10(4) the withdrawal of privilege against disclosure is restricted to the material instructions on which the report is based (r.35.10(3)) (for guidance as to meaning of "privilege", see Glossary). The expert's report must recite the "substance" of those instructions. The significance of the withdrawal of privilege in relation to material instructions is that it opens up the possibility that the opposing party may be able to apply for disclosure of the actual instructions themselves and, perhaps, of related documents, and, further, that it exposes the expert to cross-examination at trial about his instructions. The objective is to ensure that the instructions are transparent and, normally, that should be achieved without disclosure of documents or cross-examination being required. Consequently, r.35.10(4) provides that the court will not, in relation to material instructions (a) order disclosure of any specific document, or (b) permit any questioning in court, other than by the party who instructed the expert, unless it is satisfied that there are reasonable grounds to consider that the statement of the substance of all material instructions given in the expert's report is inaccurate or incomplete. Practice Direction (Experts and Assessors), para.3 (see para.35PD.1) adds that, if the court is so satisfied, it will allow cross-examination "where it appears to be in the interests of justice to do so".

In *Morris v Bank of India* November 15, 2001, unrep., Ch D an expert's report in a banking dispute failed to reveal "all the material instructions" relied upon – here some witness statements. Their disclosure was ordered, relying upon r.35.10(4).

In *Salt v Consignia Plc* [2002] C.L.Y. 420 a solicitor's entire letters of instruction to a medical expert as far as they were material, were ordered to be disclosed (under CPR r.35.10(4) Salt's expert had referred to the letters in his report but had not stated the substance of all his material instructions andSalt's solicitor had only disclosed edited versions of the letters which in the event referred to other matters not directly part of the experts' instructions.

But in *Lucas v Barking, Havering and Redbridge Hospitals NHS Trust* [2003] EWCA Civ 1102 it was held that one party might not as a matter of course call under CPR r.35.10(4) for the immediate disclosure of documents constituting an expert's instructions or referred to in his report (here an earlier medical report and a witness statement). The court would only order their disclosure if there were grounds for believing the statement in the expert's report about the instructions was inaccurate or misleading. The Court also said that the mere mention of a privileged document in an expert's report does not necessarily waive privilege in the document, if the contents of the privileged document are not to be relied upon by the discloser and that CPR r.31.14 (which deals with inspection of documents referred to in other evidence disclosed) was unlikely to have been intended to change the law of privilege to require "automatic" disclosure.

In *Jackson v Marley Davenport Ltd* [2004] EWCA Civ 1225 the Court of Appeal decided, on similar principles to Lucas (above), that drafts of an expert's report remain privileged and the court has no power to order their disclosure failing any breach of r.35.10(4).

But if a party chooses to "deploy in court" letters to their expert by relying upon them in a witness statement in support of an interlocutory application, the party has waived privilege in the letters and they must be disclosed, see: *Dunlop Slazenger International v Joe Bloggs* [2003] EWCA Civ 901.

Literature to be served with reports

Wardlaw v Farrar [2003] EWCA Civ 1719 decided that in clinical negligence claims being conducted in the county courts or District Registries, the judges should adopt the standard direction of the Queens' Bench Masters that any material or literature upon which an expert wished to rely must be served either with his report or at the latest one month before trial. Permission would be needed from the trial judge before an expert witness could introduce additional material at trial. The point of principle is applicable to experts' reports in any discipline. **35.10.5**

Any literature relied upon by one party's expert should be reviewed by the other party's expert and be available for the trial judge. In *Breeze v Ahmad* [2005] EWCA Civ 223 the claimant was able to show that the literature relied upon by the defendant was "unwittingly portrayed inaccurately and/or incompletely" which led the judge to place more reliance upon it than he should have done—a retrial was ordered.

Use by one party of expert's report disclosed by another

35.11 **35.11 Where a party has disclosed an expert's report, any party may use that expert's report as evidence at the trial.**

Effect of rule

35.11.1 *Gurney Consulting Engineers v Gleeds Health and Safety Ltd* [2006] EWHC 43 (TCC) decided that it was not necessary for a party to seek permission to rely upon an expert's report which had been disclosed by a party who had ceased to be involved in the proceedings, even though the court had not given specific permission for the remaining parties to rely upon those reports, but the party seeking to so rely should advise the other remaining parties which reports they intended to rely upon and for what purpose. This was followed in *Shepherd & Neame v EDF Energy Networks (SPN) Plc* [2008] EWHC 123 TCC.

Discussions between experts[1]

35.12 **35.12—(1) The court may, at any stage, direct a discussion between experts for the purpose of requiring the experts to—**

(a) identify and discuss the expert issues in the proceedings; and

(b) where possible, reach agreed opinion on those issues.

(2) The court may specify the issues which the experts must discuss.

(3) The court may direct that following a discussion between the experts they must prepare a statement for the court showing—

(a) those issues on which they agree; and

(b) those issues on which they disagree and a summary of their reasons for disagreeing.[2]

(4) The content of the discussion between the experts shall not be referred to at the trial unless the parties agree.

(5) Where experts reach agreement on an issue during their discussions, the agreement shall not bind the parties unless the parties expressly agree to be bound by the agreement.

Effect of rule

35.12.1 Former RSC O.38, r.38 (applied in county courts by CCR O.20, r.27) gave the court power to direct that there should be a meeting without prejudice of the parties' expert witnesses for the purpose of identifying those parts of their evidence which are in issue. This procedural device applied infrequently.

Rule 35.12 does not stipulate that there should be a "meeting" between experts, but rather that there should be a "discussion". This indicates that, in the interest of saving costs, experts might use telephone conferencing and video conferencing techniques. Clearly these techniques will be more appropriate when: time is too short to arrange a meeting before trial, in lower value claims on proportionality grounds, when there are few differences between the two experts' reports and/or when the experts know one another.

In terms, r.35.12 differs in significant respects from former RSC O.38, r.38. The rules require the experts, not simply to identify those parts of their evidence which are in issue, but to identify the issues in the proceedings and, where possible, to "reach

[1] Amended by the Civil Procedure (Amendment No.5) Rules 2001 (SI 2001/4015).

[2] Sub-paras (a) and (b) substituted by the Civil Procedure (Amendment No.5) Rules 2001, in force March 25, 2002.

agreement on an issue". Further, the court may specify the issues which the experts must discuss. Narrowing, at an early stage, the issues to be put before the court, including issues of expert opinion, is one of the fundamental purposes of case management (r.1.4(2)(b)). The procedural judge conducting a case management conference should not only direct an experts' meeting but define, with the help of the parties and their legal representatives, the subject matter to be covered (Final Report p.148).

The former rule said, rather lamely, that, where a meeting of experts took place, the experts may prepare a joint statement indicating those parts of their evidence on which they are, and those on which they are not, in agreement. Rule 35.12 is much more prescriptive in this respect. The court may direct that the expert must prepare a statement for the court, not only showing areas of agreement and disagreement, but also giving a summary of their reasons for disagreeing. The meeting should cover only matters within the expert's professional competence; it is for the parties and their legal representatives to consider the effect of any agreement or disagreement on the future conduct of the case (Final Report p.148).

The duty owed by the experts to the court under CPR 35.3 requires that they should state in their joint statement the views which they themselves honestly hold. It is not for the parties to tell the experts what opinions they are allowed to hold. Interference of this sort by the parties with the experts in their complying with the directions given by the court may amount to a breach of the condition with the result that permission to adduce the expert's evidence at trial may be refused (*Robin Ellis Ltd v Malwright Ltd* [1999] B.L.R. 81; 15 Const.L.J. 141, per Judge Bowsher Q.C.).

Discussions between experts may be directed at any stage and either before or after the disclosure of their reports. It is important that experts should communicate at the earliest possible stage in the case to establish that they are answering the same questions or addressing the same issues.

A discussion may be most effective if there is an agenda agreed in advance between the parties' legal representatives and the experts. It is appropriate for the parties' solicitors in conjunction with their experts to identify matters in issue in order to determine items for the agenda.

There are two schools of thought on who should attend an experts' discussion. The more commonly held view is that lawyers and clients should not be present to enable the experts to debate their opinion issues in a full and frank way. (Certainly if one party sends a representative to the meeting the other should also be allowed to, in the spirit of a "level playing field" *Smith v Stephens* NLD May 15, 2001, QBD.) But the other view is that the presence of lawyers can be helpful: to answer questions on legal matters and procedure, to ensure fair play between the experts, and also to ensure that the agenda is followed and that the experts produce an agreed statement, as directed. There is also a view that on occasions the parties should attend an experts' discussion: particularly where liability experts are meeting in a clinical or professional negligence case as it can seem very unfair to a claimant in this type of action if two experts from the same profession as the person allegedly negligent, effectively decide important issues in the case in private.

In *H v Lambeth, Southwark and Lewisham HA* [2001] EWCA Civ 1455, the Court of Appeal decided that an experts' discussion in a clinical negligence claim does not engage the question of a right to a fair trial under ECHR art.6 because the court's power to order a discussion is discretionary and any agreement reached at the discussion is not binding on the parties, or on the court. In the same case the Court of Appeal declined to order that the lawyers should attend the discussion on the grounds that their input should be to a "well appointed agenda" but Hale L.J. suggested that when time and costs permitted the appointment of an independent legally qualified person to chair an experts' discussion might be considered.

The joint statement

The experts in conjunction with the other experts of like discipline should prepare a written note signed by each of them as to matters of opinion on which they are agreed. Whilst all experts may not agree particular point limited agreement should be explored. **35.12.2**

Rule 34.12(5) acknowledges that, where in the course of their discussions experts reach agreement on an issue, that agreement should not bind the parties unless they expressly agree to be bound by the agreement. As a practical matter, the rule could hardly state otherwise. The parties may give their consent either prospectively or retrospectively.

But in practice, it could be very difficult for a party dissatisfied with an agreement reached at a experts' discussion, to persuade the court that this agreement should, in effect, be set aside unless the party's expert had clearly stepped outside his expertise or brief, or otherwise had shown himself to be incompetent.

Rule 34.12.(4) provides that the contents of the discussion between the experts should be privileged in the sense that no part of their discussion should be referred to at trial unless the parties agree. The expert does not normally have authority to bind the client, but an expert should be aware of the extent of his authority and that matters which the expert agrees in a note of the meeting may be binding on him.

In *Transco Plc v Griggs* [2003] EWCA Civ 564 both parties' medical experts changed their minds following their discussion. The Court of Appeal said that an expert's willingness to change his opinion in the light of discussion with others, and the evidence as it develops, may be a sign of strength rather than weakness. But in *Stallwood v David and Adamson* [2006] EWHC 2600, QB, a personal injury claim in which the claimant's medical expert changed his opinion after a discussion with the defendant's expert and the statement then read that the experts agreed that the claimant's inability to work was unrelated to the accident, the claimant was allowed to call a second expert, partly because she had lost confidence in the first one, and partly because the judge had made gratuitous comments at the case management conference that heightened the claimant's sense of grievance.

In *Fifield v Denton Hall Legal Services* [2006] EWCA Civ 169 an expert who retracted his agreement to the signed joint statement because, he said, he had not properly checked the wording and because he had been pressurised on the telephone by the other expert, was criticised by the court—at best he had been somewhat thoughtless, and at worst he had made an unprincipled attempt to tailor his evidence to fit in with the claimant's case.

Content of experts' discussion "shall not be referred to at the trial"

35.12.3 As explained above, the joint statement prepared by experts in accordance with directions given under r.35.12 may contain matters that are agreed and matters that are not agreed. The parties may agree to be bound by matters agreed by the experts. Whether or not the parties have so agreed to be bound does not affect the admissibility of the experts' joint statement (whether interim or final); in particular lack of such agreement does not make the statement privileged (see *Robin Ellis Ltd v Malwright Ltd* [1999] B.L.R. 81; 15 Const.L.J. 141 (Judge Bowsher Q.C.) and authorities discussed there). In *Aird v Prime Meridian Ltd* [2006] EWCA Civ 1866 the Court of Appeal held that an experts' joint statement did not acquire without prejudice status because it was used at a mediation that failed.

Former RSC O.38, r.38 stated that the meeting of experts should be a meeting "without prejudice". The scope of "without prejudice" privilege was authoritatively determined in *Rush & Tomkins Ltd v Greater London Council* [1989] A.C. 1280, HL. This privilege is a joint privilege; its waiver requires the consent of both parties. Now, r.34.12(4) states that, where a discussion between experts is directed, "the content" of the discussion should be privileged in the sense that no part of their discussion should be referred to at trial unless the parties agree. This expressly retains the "without prejudice" privilege in relation to communications between experts engaged in discussions directed under r.35.12.

Expert witness immunity

35.12.4 An expert witness who gives evidence at trial is immune from suit in respect of anything he says in court and that immunity will extend to the contents of his report which adopts or incorporates his evidence. Where an expert gives evidence at the trial the immunity which he would enjoy in respect of that evidence is not to be circumvented by a suit based on the report itself. The question of expert witness immunity was considered in *Stanton v Callaghan* [1999] 2 W.L.R. 745, CA, a case involving former RSC O.38, r.38 in which some differences in judicial reasoning emerged. This case would seem to provide authority for the proposition that (for reasons that are not agreed) the immunity of an expert witness extends at least to immunity from suit by his own client in respect of work done in preparing a joint statement following a meeting with the opposite party's expert (whether ordered by the court or not) in the run up to trial, and revising his own witness statement in the light of such meeting.

Whether this immunity would survive without challenge seemed questionable in the light of the decisions of the court in *Stevens v Gullis* [1999] B.L.R. 394 when the incompetence of an expert witness effectively lost his instructing party the case, and in *Hall v Simons* [2000] T.L.R., July 2, 2000, when the House of Lords removed the long-established principle of advocates' immunity, particularly if and when an expert fails to comply with his duty to assist the court, e.g. by ignoring court orders in the particular case. But in *Paimano v Raiss* [2001] Lloyd's Rep. P.N. 341, QB, in an action against a surveyor expert for negligent advice, the court struck out those parts of the claim that concerned allegedly dishonest statements made by the expert under cross-examination about his expertise and qualifications in the previouslitigation, on the ground that an expert witness was entitled to immunity from suit on public policy grounds, even in respect of evidence which turned out to have been dishonest.

And in *Phillips v Symes (Costs No.2)* [2004] EWHC 2330, Ch D the court decided that an expert witness (whose report lacked objectivity and offended common sense—see the notes to 35.3.1) could be added as a party to enable the claimant's to make a wasted costs application against him, but that a high level of proof would be required to establish gross dereliction of duty or recklessness by the expert.

In *Meadow v General Medical Council* [2006] EWCA Civ 1390 at first instance Collins J. concluded that the General Medical Council did not have jurisdiction to hear a complaint concerning Sir Roy Meadow's evidence to the Crown Court in the case against Sally Clark (a solicitor accused and found guilty of murdering two of her three children) because expert witness immunity extends to professional disciplinary proceedings in relation to a professional's work as an expert witness, save in the very rare circumstance that a trial judge specifically requests the professional body to investigate the expert's conduct because it has fallen far below what is expected of him. The Court of Appeal, in a long judgment, overturned Collins J.'s decision on immunity and noted that:

1. the courts have shown a marked reluctance to extend expert's immunity;
2. none of the statutory procedures, for a wide variety of different professional regulatory and disciplinary bodies, contain a provision enabling the person being investigated to object to the jurisdiction on the ground that the complaint refers to evidence given in court which is immune from disciplinary proceedings, and it is not appropriate for the court to qualify professional bodies' statutory duties;
3. the purpose of professional disciplinary proceedings is different from civil litigation, in that it is to regulate the professions for the benefit of the public, not to punish the practitioner, and so it is appropriate that the totality of a practitioner's professional conduct should be subject to scrutiny;
4. it is for Parliament to decide whether any fresh immunities should be created, not for the courts;
5. it is not appropriate to impose a duty on trial judges to decide whether and which expert witnesses conduct should be investigated by their professional body, not least because this would be fraught with uncertainty.

Consequence of failure to disclose expert's report

35.13 A party who fails to disclose an expert's report may not use the report at the trial or call the expert to give evidence orally unless the court gives permission. **35.13**

Effect of rule

Expert evidence is to be restricted to that which is reasonably required to resolve the proceedings (r.35.1). Rule 35.4 states that no party may call an expert or put in evidence an expert's report without the court's permission. The general rule is that expert evidence is to be given in a written report. In terms, none of the rules in Pt 35 imposes on a party who has obtained the court's permission to call an expert or put in evidence an expert's report a duty to disclose that report, or to disclose it to particular persons within a particular time but, clearly, the court may impose directions to that effect and may vary or revoke them subsequently. Rule 35.13 assumes that a party has been directed to disclose an expert's report and has failed to do so. The rule imposes a sanction: that party may not use the report at trial or call the expert to give evidence orally unless the court gives permission. Rule 3.9 (Relief from sanctions) may be engaged where a party fails to comply with r.35.13, or with a practice direction or court order, relating to the pre-trial disclosure of an expert's report, and any sanction for such failure takes effect in accordance with r.3.8. **35.13.1**

In *Baron v Lovell* [1999] T.L.R., September 14, 1999, the Court of Appeal emphasised the importance of disclosing an expert report promptly. Holding back expert evidence until close to trial, at best will attract costs penalties, and at worst will prompt the court to make an order that the party cannot rely upon that evidence, which may substantially affect the outcome of the case. But serving expert evidence late may not be fatal, in *Meredith v Colleys Valuation Services Ltd* 2001 WL 1347050 – the Court of Appeal reversed the first instance decision, preventing a defendant from relying upon an expert report served two weeks late, because the delay was short, there was no unless order, the claimant had the report and costs penalties were a preferable alternative sanction.

In *R.C. Residuals v Linton Fuel Oils Ltd* [2002] EWCA Civ 911; [2002] 1 W.L.R. 2782, CA, both parties were late serving their expert evidence, and the trial was adjourned. The claimant served expert reports respectively 10 and 20 minutes beyond the time specified in an "unless" order. The judge struck out the evidence, but the Court of Appeal allowed the appeal as the defendant had refused service of the reports by email, and the new trial date would not be affected by so short a delay.

Increasingly the courts expect parties to organise their expert evidence early in the case. In *Ahmed v Stanley A Coleman & Hill (A Firm)* [2002] EWCA Civ 935 the claimant in a professional negligence claim arising from a personal injury claim, was refused permission to adduce on an appeal of a case management decision additional medical evidence, partly because there had been sufficient time for this application to be made before the case management hearing. In *Cassie v Ministry of Defence* [2002] EWCA Civ 838, the claimant's attempt to appeal the trial judge's award of damages, in a personal injury case, on the ground that the judge made repeated reference to the absence of psychological evidence, was refused because the claimant had not appealed an "on paper" refusal of permission to appeal a decision on the same issue.

In *Gower Chemicals Group Litigation v Gower Chemicals Ltd and Neath Port Talbot County Borough Council* [2008] EWHC 735 it was decided in a group action that settled after mediation, that if the claimants wished to recover the costs of obtaining expert reports that had not been disclosed, they must elect whether to disclose the reports if they wanted to pursue the costs claim, and that the costs judge was not wrong to so order without looking at the reports.

Expert's right to ask court for directions[1]

35.14 **35.14—(1) An expert may file a written request for directions to assist him in carrying out his function as an expert.**

(2) An expert must, unless the court orders otherwise, provide a copy of any proposed request for directions under paragraph (1)—

(a) to the party instructing him, at least 7 days before he files the request; and

(b) to all other parties, at least 4 days before he files it.

(3) The court, when it gives directions, may also direct that a party be served with a copy of the directions.[2]

Effect of rule

35.14.1 An expert, in carrying out his function, operates within a framework stipulated by the instructions he has received, by the directions, if any, given by the court, and by the rules in this Part. When, upon a party's application the court grants permission to adduce expert evidence, the court may attach directions (r.35.14). They may also be attached when the court gives a direction for a discussion between experts (r.35.12) and where it gives a direction under r.35.7 for a single joint expert to be used. Within this framework, it is the duty of the expert to help the court; this duty overrides his obligations to others (r.35.3).

In December 2001, r.35.14(2) was added.

[1] Amended by the Civil Procedure (Amendment No.5) Rules 2001 (SI 2001/4015).
[2] Amended by the Civil Procedure (Amendment No.5) Rules 2001, in force March 25, 2002.

An expert now has to copy any request to the court to his/her instructing party seven days, and to any other party four days, in advance of filing it. Previously such requests could be made without notice. The possible reason for the change is that the courts are experiencing difficulty with some experts' requests, especially if they arrive in letter form and not as Pt 23 applications, and therefore, prefer to rely on the instructing solicitors 'filtering' them. But this seems to devalue one of the purposes of the rule – to give experts, especially single joint experts, direct access to the case management judge to resolve an issue which the parties cannot. Allowing parties to see the expert's request in advance could mean, in effect, it will not reach the court at all, unless the expert is robust and determined.

Orders

In April 2005 a new para.6A was added to the Practice Direction requiring parties to serve upon experts copies of any order that requires an instructed expert to take a step in the proceedings or that otherwise affects the expert. **35.14A**

Assessors

35.15—(1) This rule applies where the court appoints one or more persons (an "assessor") under section 70 of the Supreme Court Act 1981[1] or section 63 of the County Courts Act 1984.[2] **35.15**

(2) The assessor shall assist the court in dealing with a matter in which the assessor has skill and experience.

(3) An assessor shall take such part in the proceedings as the court may direct and in particular the court may—

(a) direct the assessor to prepare a report for the court on any matter at issue in the proceedings; and

(b) direct the assessor to attend the whole or any part of the trial to advise the court on any such matter.

(4) If the assessor prepares a report for the court before the trial has begun—

(a) the court will send a copy to each of the parties; and

(b) the parties may use it at trial.

(5) The remuneration to be paid to the assessor for his services shall be determined by the court and shall form part of the costs of the proceedings.

(6) The court may order any party to deposit in the court office a specified sum in respect of the assessor's fees and, where it does so, the assessor will not be asked to act until the sum has been deposited.

(7) Paragraphs (5) and (6) shall not apply where the remuneration of the assessor is to be paid out of money provided by Parliament.

Effect of rule

See Interim Report p.187 and Final Report p.151. **35.15.1**

The Supreme Court Act 1981 s.70(1), states that the High Court may, if it thinks it expedient to do so, call in the aid of one or more assessors specially qualified "and hear and dispose of the cause or matter wholly or partially with their assistance" (see Vol.2, para.9A–261). Paragraphs (2) and (4) of s.70 deal with the remuneration of assessors. Former RSC O.33, r.6 said that such trial should take place "in such manner and on such terms as the court may direct" (note also RSC O.33, r.2). The County

[1] 1981 c.54.
[2] 1984 c.28 s.63 was amended by SI 1998/2940.

Courts Act 1984 s.63(1) is to similar effect and enables a county court judge to sit with assessors on an application of a party (see Vol.2, para.9A–537). Rules of court relevant to s.63(1) were found in former CCR O.13, r.11. For the purpose of implementing r.35.15 (and other provisions in the CPR), s.63 of the 1984 Act has been amended by the Modification of Enactments Order (SI 1998/2940) art.6(d).

As to assessors in the Admiralty Court, see Practice Direction (Admiralty) paras 20.1 and20.2 (see Vol.2).

In some other CPR provisions it is expressly provided that r.35.15 shall have effect where an assessor is appointed in particular proceedings; e.g. proceedings under the Sex Discrimination Act 1975 s.66(1), and the Telecommunications Act 1984, Sch.2, para.5 (see respectively, Sch.2, CCR O.49 rr.17 and 18A).

Under r.35.15, an assessor may be appointed by the court of its own initiative and the assessor's remuneration shall form part of the costs of the proceedings. The court may appoint several assessors, for example, where a case raises several matters calling for different skills and experiences.

Paragraphs (5) and (6) of r.35.15 deal with the assessor's remuneration (*cf.* r.35.8(4)(5) (remuneration of single joint expert)); note also para.(7).

Formerly, the appointment of assessors in Admiralty cases, and also in patent cases, was common. It is to be expected that the practice will be extended to other cases in the future under r.35.15.

The court may vary or revoke an order or direction made under this rule (r.3.1(7)).

In *Balcombe Group plc v London Development Agency* [2008] EWHC 1392 (TCC) the court refused an application by the defendant for the appointment of an assessor to assist the trial judge with the evaluation of sums due to the claimant for services provided to the defendant in the acquisition of land for the 2012 Olympics, because this would add another layer of costs in a relatively modest claim of £600,000 and the judge would be able to decide on the appropriate remuneration once the ODPM's Compensation Code had been explained to him.

Appointment of assessor

35.15.2 Practice Direction (Experts and Assessors), para.6.1 (see para.35PD.1) states that, not less than 21 days before appointing an assessor, the court will notify each party in writing of the name of the proposed assessor, of the matter in respect of which the assistance of the assessor will be sought, and of the qualifications of the assessor to give that assistance. Paragraph 6.2 states that objection to a proposed appointment of an assessor, either personally or in respect of his qualifications, may be taken by any party (County Courts Act 1984 s.63(5)). Objection must be made in writing and filed with the court within seven days of receipt of the notification from the court. The objection will be taken into account by the court in deciding whether or not to make the appointment.

Assessor advising court at trial (r.35.15(3)(b))

35.15.3 The court may direct the assessor to attend the trial to advise the court on any matter at issue in the proceedings. This is consistent with s.70(1) of the 1981 Act and s.63(1) of the 1984 Act. Both of these provisions envisage the assessor sitting with the judge at the trial or hearing.

Assessor preparing report for court (r.35.15(3)(a))

35.15.4 The court may direct the assessor to prepare a report for the court on any matter at issue in the proceedings. It would seem that this provision anticipates that the assessor may assist the judge without actually participating in the trial or hearing itself. (Conceivably, the assessor may prepare a report for the court and attend the trial to advise.) It is important that a clear distinction should be drawn between the expert witness and the assessor. The assessor has a judicial role, he is not an expert witness appointed by the court. He cannot be cross-examined.

The assessor assists the judge in discharging his judicial role. His function is to "educate" the judge and to enable him to reach a properly informed decision. An assessor is likely to be of particular assistance in a case raising complex technical issues. However, normally the use of an assessor in addition to the parties' expert witnesses would not be cost effective except in the heaviest of cases. Even in smaller cases, where technical issues are not agreed, the assistance of an assessor may provide the most economical way of disposing of the case and, in addition, may provide the parties with a decision no less satisfactory than that of a judge lacking the assessor's expertise.

Expense is incurred in the engaging of an assessor. In this respect, as in others, the court has to bear in mind the overriding objective, and especially the matter of cost to the parties (see r.1.1(2)(b) and (c)(i)). In a given case, the appointment of an assessor may result in substantial savings in the length of the hearing.

Rule 35.15(3) speaks of the assessor taking such part "in the proceedings as the court may direct". This seems wider than the former provisions and with the statutory provisions. Section 70(1) of the 1981 Act says the court "may hear and dispose" of the case "with their assistance" and s.63(1) of the 1984 Act says the assessor may "sit with the judge".

Practice Direction (Experts and Assessors), para.6.4 (see para.35PD.1) states that copies of any report prepared by the assessor will be sent to each of the parties but the assessor will not give oral evidence or be open to cross-examination or questioning.

In *Owners of the Bow Spring v Owners of the Manzanillo II* [2004] EWCA Civ 1007 a dispute arising from a nautical collision, the Court of Appeal, obiter, said that the judge was correct to invite counsel to comment upon the questions he intended to put to the nautical assessors but he should have done likewise with the assessors' answers before deciding whether to accept the assessors' advice.

In *Global Mariner v Atlantic Crusader* [2005] EWHC 380 (Admiralty) the judge expanded upon the Court of Appeal obiter comments in the Manzanillo case above, to recommend the following procedure in a nautical case when assessors have been appointed:

- The range of topics on which advice might be sought from the assessors should be canvassed with counsel, at the latest, by the stage of final submissions;
- Questions put by the judge, and the assessors' answers, should be disclosed to counsel before the draft judgment is handed down;
- Generally any further answers from the assessors, and the judge's decision, with reasons, in relation to that advice, will be recorded in the judgment without a further round of disclosure, on the grounds of proportionality.

PRACTICE DIRECTION—EXPERTS AND ASSESSORS

This Practice Direction supplements CPR Part 35

35PD.1 Part 35 is intended to limit the use of oral expert evidence to that which is reasonably required. In addition, where possible, matters requiring expert evidence should be dealt with by a single expert. Permission of the court is always required either to call an expert or to put an expert's report in evidence. There is annexed to this Practice Direction a protocol for the instruction of experts to give evidence in civil claims. Experts and those instructing them are expected to have regard to the guidance contained in the protocol.

Expert Evidence – General Requirements

1.1 It is the duty of an expert to help the court on matters within his own expertise: rule 35.3(1). This duty is paramount and overrides any obligation to the person from whom the expert has received instructions or by whom he is paid: rule 35.3(2).

1.2 Expert evidence should be the independent product of the expert uninfluenced by the pressures of litigation.

1.3 An expert should assist the court by providing objective, unbiased opinion on matters within his expertise, and should not assume the role of an advocate.

1.4 An expert should consider all material facts, including those which might detract from his opinion.

1.5 An expert should make it clear:

(a) when a question or issue falls outside his expertise; and

(b) when he is not able to reach a definite opinion, for example because he has insufficient information.

1.6 If, after producing a report, an expert changes his view on any material matter, such change of view should be communicated to all the parties without delay, and when appropriate to the court.

Form and Content of Expert's Reports

35PD.2 **2.1** An expert's report should be addressed to the court and not to the party from whom the expert has received his instructions.

2.2 An expert's report must:

(1) give details of the expert's qualifications;

(2) give details of any literature or other material which the expert has relied on in making the report;

(3) contain a statement setting out the substance of all facts and instructions given to the expert which are material to the opinions expressed in the report or upon which those opinions are based;

(4) make clear which of the facts stated in the report are within the expert's own knowledge;

(5) say who carried out any examination, measurement, test or experiment which the expert has used for the report, give the qualifications of that person, and say whether or not the test or experiment has been carried out under the expert's supervision;

(6) where there is a range of opinion on the matters dealt with in the report—

(a) summarise the range of opinion, and
(b) give reasons for his own opinion;

(7) contain a summary of the conclusions reached;

(8) if the expert is not able to give his opinion without qualification, state the qualification; and

(9) contain a statement that the expert understands his duty to the court, and has complied and will continue to comply with that duty.

2.3 An expert's report must be verified by a statement of truth as well as containing the statements required in paragraph 2.2(8) and (9) above.

2.4 The form of the statement of truth is as follows:

"I confirm that insofar as the facts stated in my report are within my own knowledge I have made clear which they are and I believe them to be true, and that the opinions I have expressed represent my true and complete professional opinion."

2.5 Attention is drawn to rule 32.14 which sets out the consequences of verifying a document containing a false statement without an honest belief in its truth.

(For information about statements of truth see Part 22 and the practice direction which supplements it.)

Information

3. Under Rule 35.9 the court may direct a party with access to information which is not reasonably available to another party to serve on that other party a document which records the information. The document served must include sufficient details of all the facts, tests, experiments and assumptions which underlie any part of the information to enable the party on whom it is served to make, or to obtain, a proper interpretation of the information and an assessment of its significance. **35PD.3**

Instructions

4. The instructions referred to in paragraph 2.2(3) will not be protected by privilege (see rule 35.10(4)). But cross-examination of the expert on the contents of his instructions will not be allowed unless the court permits it (or unless the party who gave the instructions consents to it). Before it gives permission the court must be satisfied that there are reasonable grounds to consider that the statement in the report of the substance of the instructions is inaccurate or incomplete. If the court is so satisfied, it will allow the cross-examination where it appears to be in the interests of justice to do so. **35PD.4**

Questions to experts

5.1 Questions asked for the purpose of clarifying the expert's report (see rule 35.6) should be put, in writing, to the expert not later than 28 days after receipt of the expert's report (see paragraphs 1.2 to 1.5 above as to verification). **35PD.5**

5.2 Where a party sends a written question or questions direct to an expert, a copy of the questions should, at the same time, be sent to the other party or parties.

5.3 The party or parties instructing the expert must pay any fees charged by that expert for answering questions put under rule 35.6. This does not affect any decision of the court as to the party who is ultimately to bear the expert's costs.

Single expert

35PD.6 **6.** Where the court has directed that the evidence on a particular issue is to be given by one expert only (rule 35.7) but there are a number of disciplines relevant to that issue, a leading expert in the dominant discipline should be identified as the single expert. He should prepare the general part of the report and be responsible for annexing or incorporating the contents of any reports from experts in other disciplines.

Orders

35PD.6A **6A.** Where an order requires an act to be done by an expert, or otherwise affects an expert, the party instructing that expert must serve a copy of the order on the expert instructed by him. In the case of a jointly instructed expert, the claimant must serve the order.

Assessors

35PD.7 **7.1** An assessor may be appointed to assist the court under rule 35.15. Not less than 21 days before making any such appointment, the court will notify each party in writing of the name of the proposed assessor, of the matter in respect of which the assistance of the assessor will be sought and of the qualifications of the assessor to give that assistance.

7.2 Where any person has been proposed for appointment as an assessor, objection to him, either personally or in respect of his qualification, may be taken by any party.

7.3 Any such objection must be made in writing and filed with the court within 7 days of receipt of the notification referred to in paragraph 6.1 and will be taken into account by the court in deciding whether or not to make the appointment (section 63(5) of the County Courts Act 1984).

7.4 Copies of any report prepared by the assessor will be sent to each of the parties but the assessor will not give oral evidence or be open to cross-examination or questioning.

Protocol for the Instruction of Experts to give evidence in civil claims

1. Introduction

35.16 Expert witnesses perform a vital role in civil litigation. It is essential that both those who instruct experts and experts themselves are given clear guidance as to what they are expected to do in civil proceedings. The purpose of this Protocol is to provide such guidance. It has been drafted by the Civil Justice Council and reflects the rules and practice directions current [in June 2005], replacing *the Code of Guidance* on Expert Evidence. The authors of the Protocol wish to acknowledge the valuable assistance they obtained by drawing on earlier documents produced by the Academy of Experts and the Expert Witness Institute, as well as suggestions made by the Clinical Dispute Forum. The Protocol has been approved by the Master of the Rolls.

2. Aims of Protocol

2.1 This Protocol offers guidance to experts and to those instructing them in the interpretation of and compliance with Part 35 of the Civil Procedure Rules (CPR 35) and its associated Practice Direction (PD35) and to further the objectives of the Civil Procedure Rules in general. It is intended to assist in the interpretation of those provisions in the interests of good practice but it does not replace them. It sets out standards for the use of experts and the conduct of experts and those who instruct them. The existence of this Protocol does not remove the need for experts and those who instruct them to be familiar with CPR 35 and PD35. **35.17**

2.2 Experts and those who instruct them should also bear in mind para 1.4 of the Practice Direction on Protocols which contains the following objectives, namely to:

- (a) encourage the exchange of early and full information about the expert issues involved in a prospective legal claim;
- (b) enable the parties to avoid or reduce the scope of litigation by agreeing the whole or part of an expert issue before commencement of proceedings; and
- (c) support the efficient management of proceedings where litigation cannot be avoided.

3. Application

3.1 This Protocol applies to any steps taken for the purpose of civil proceedings by experts or those who instruct them on or after 5th September 2005. **35.18**

3.2 It applies to all experts who are, or who may be, governed by CPR Part 35 and to those who instruct them. Experts are governed by Part 35 if they are or have been instructed to give or prepare evidence for the purpose of civil proceedings in a court in England and Wales (CPR 35.2).

3.3 Experts, and those instructing them, should be aware that some cases may be "specialist proceedings" (CPR 49) where there are modifications to the Civil Procedure Rules. Proceedings may also be governed by other Protocols. Further, some courts have published their own Guides which supplement the Civil Procedure Rules for proceedings in those courts. They contain provisions affecting expert evidence. Expert witnesses and those instructing them should be familiar with them when they are relevant.

3.4 Courts may take into account any failure to comply with this Protocol when making orders in relation to costs, interest, time limits, the stay of proceedings and whether to order a party to pay a sum of money into court.

3.5 Limitation

If, as a result of complying with any part of this Protocol, claims would or might be time barred under any provision in the Limitation Act 1980, or any other legislation that imposes a time limit for the bringing an action, claimants may commence proceedings without complying with this Protocol. In such circumstances, claimants who commence proceedings without complying with all, or any part, of this Protocol must apply, giving notice to all other parties, to the court for directions as to the timetable and form of procedure to be adopted, at the same time as they request the court to issue proceedings. The court may consider whether to order a stay of the whole or part of the proceedings pending compliance with this Protocol and may make orders in relation to costs.

4. Duties of experts

35.19 **4.1** Experts always owe a duty to exercise reasonable skill and care to those instructing them, and to comply with any relevant professional code of ethics. However when they are instructed to give or prepare evidence for the purpose of civil proceedings in England and Wales they have an overriding duty to help the court on matters within their expertise (CPR 35.3). This duty overrides any obligation to the person instructing or paying them. Experts must not serve the exclusive interest of those who retain them.

4.2 Experts should be aware of the overriding objective that courts deal with cases justly. This includes dealing with cases proportionately, expeditiously and fairly (CPR 1.1). Experts are under an obligation to assist the court so as to enable them to deal with cases in accordance with the overriding objective. However the overriding objective does not impose on experts any duty to act as mediators between the parties or require them to trespass on the role of the court in deciding facts.

4.3 Experts should provide opinions which are independent, regardless of the pressures of litigation. In this context, a useful test of 'independence' is that the expert would express the same opinion if given the same instructions by an opposing party. Experts should not take it upon themselves to promote the point of view of the party instructing them or engage in the role of advocates.

4.4 Experts should confine their opinions to matters which are material to the disputes between the parties and provide opinions only in relation to matters which lie within their expertise. Experts should indicate without delay where particular questions or issues fall outside their expertise.

4.5 Experts should take into account all material facts before them at the time that they give their opinion. Their reports should set out those facts and any literature or any other material on which they have relied in forming their opinions. They should indicate if an opinion is provisional, or qualified, or where they consider that further information is required or if, for any other reason, they are not satisfied that an opinion can be expressed finally and without qualification.

4.6 Experts should inform those instructing them without delay of any change in their opinions on any material matter and the reason for it.

4.7 Experts should be aware that any failure by them to comply with the Civil Procedure Rules or court orders or any excessive delay for which they are responsible may result in the parties who instructed them being penalised in costs and even, in extreme cases, being debarred from placing the experts' evidence before the court. In[1] *Phillips v Symes* Peter Smith J held that courts may also make orders for costs (under section 51 of the Supreme Court Act 1981) directly against expert witnesses who by their evidence cause significant expense to be incurred, and do so in flagrant and reckless disregard of their duties to the Court.

5. Conduct of Experts instructed only to advise

5.1 Part 35 only applies where experts are instructed to give **35.20**
opinions which are relied on for the purposes of court proceedings. Advice which the parties do not intend to adduce in litigation is likely to be confidential; the Protocol does not apply in these circumstances.[2,3]

5.2 The same applies where, after the commencement of proceedings, experts are instructed only to advise (e.g. to comment upon a single joint expert's report) and not to give or prepare evidence for use in the proceedings.

5.3 However this Protocol does apply if experts who were formerly instructed only to advise are later instructed to give or prepare evidence for the purpose of civil proceedings.

6. The Need for Experts

6.1 Those intending to instruct experts to give or prepare evidence **35.21**
for the purpose of civil proceedings should consider whether expert evidence is appropriate, taking account of the principles set out in CPR Parts 1 and 35, and in particular whether:

(a) it is relevant to a matter which is in dispute between the parties.

(b) it is reasonably required to resolve the proceedings (CPR 35.1);

(c) the expert has expertise relevant to the issue on which an opinion is sought;

(d) the expert has the experience, expertise and training appropriate to the value, complexity and importance of the case; and whether

(e) these objects can be achieved by the appointment of a single joint expert (see section 17 below).

6.2 Although the court's permission is not generally required to instruct an expert, the court's permission is required before experts can be called to give evidence or their evidence can be put in (CPR 35.4).

7. The appointment of experts

7.1 Before experts are formally instructed or the court's permis- **35.22**
sion to appoint named experts is sought, the following should be established:

(a) that they have the appropriate expertise and experience;

---

[1] *Phillips v Symes* [2004] EWHC 2330 (Ch).
[2] *Carlson v Townsend* [2001] 1 W.L.R. 2415.
[3] *Jackson v Marley Davenport* [2004] 1 W.L.R. 2926.

(b) that they are familiar with the general duties of an expert;

(c) that they can produce a report, deal with questions and have discussions with other experts within a reasonable time and at a cost proportionate to the matters in issue;

(d) a description of the work required;

(e) whether they are available to attend the trial, if attendance is required; and

(f) there is no potential conflict of interest.

7.2 Terms of appointment should be agreed at the outset and should normally include:

(a) the capacity in which the expert is to be appointed (e.g. party appointed expert, single joint expert or expert advisor);

(b) the services required of the expert (e.g. provision of expert's report, answering questions in writing, attendance at meetings and attendance at court);

(c) time for delivery of the report;

(d) the basis of the expert's charges (either daily or hourly rates and an estimate of the time likely to be required, or a total fee for the services);

(e) travelling expenses and disbursements;

(f) cancellation charges;

(g) any fees for attending court;

(h) time for making the payment; and

(i) whether fees are to be paid by a third party.

(j) if a party is publicly funded, whether or not the expert's charges will be subject to assessment by a costs officer.

7.3 As to the appointment of single joint experts, see section 17 below.

7.4 When necessary, arrangements should be made for dealing with questions to experts and discussions between experts, including any directions given by the court, and provision should be made for the cost of this work.

7.5 Experts should be informed regularly about deadlines for all matters concerning them. Those instructing experts should promptly send them copies of all court orders and directions which may affect the preparation of their reports or any other matters concerning their obligations.

7.6 Conditional and Contingency Fees

Payments contingent upon the nature of the expert evidence given in legal proceedings, or upon the outcome of a case, must not be offered or accepted. To do so would contravene experts' overriding *duty to the court* and compromise their duty of independence.

7.7 Agreement to delay payment of experts' fees until after the conclusion of cases is permissible as long as the amount of the fee does not depend on the outcome of the case.

8. Instructions

8.1 Those instructing experts should ensure that they give clear instructions, including the following: 35.23

(a) basic information, such as names, addresses, telephone numbers, dates of birth and dates of incidents;

(b) the nature and extent of the expertise which is called for;

(c) the purpose of requesting the advice or report, a description of the matter(s) to be investigated, the principal known issues and the identity of all parties;

(d) the statement(s) of case (if any), those documents which form part of standard disclosure and witness statements which are relevant to the advice or report;

(e) where proceedings have not been started, whether proceedings are being contemplated and, if so, whether the expert is asked only for advice;

(f) an outline programme, consistent with good case management and the expert's availability, for the completion and delivery of each stage of the expert's work; and

(g) where proceedings have been started, the dates of any hearings (including any Case Management Conferences and/or Pre-Trial Reviews), the name of the court, the claim number and the track to which the claim has been allocated.

8.2 Experts who do not receive clear instructions should request clarification and may indicate that they are not prepared to act unless and until such clear instructions are received.

8.3 As to the instruction of single joint experts, see section 17 below.

9. Experts' Acceptance of Instructions

9.1 Experts should confirm without delay whether or not they accept instructions. They should also inform those instructing them (whether on initial instruction or at any later stage) without delay if: 35.24

(a) instructions are not acceptable because, for example, they require work that falls outside their expertise, impose unrealistic deadlines, or are insufficiently clear;

(b) they consider that instructions are or have become insufficient to complete the work;

(c) they become aware that they may not be able to fulfil *any of the terms* of appointment;

(d) the instructions and/or work have, for any reason, placed them in conflict with their duties as an expert; or

(e) they are not satisfied that they can comply with any orders that have been made.

9.2 Experts must neither express an opinion outside the scope of their field of expertise, nor accept any instructions to do so.

10. Withdrawal

35.25 **10.1** Where experts' instructions remain incompatible with their duties, whether through incompleteness, a conflict between their duty to the court and their instructions, or for any other substantial and significant reason, they may consider withdrawing from the case. However, experts should not withdraw without first discussing the position fully with those who instruct them and considering carefully whether it would be more appropriate to make a written request for directions from the court. If experts do withdraw, they must give formal written notice to those instructing them.

11. Experts' Right to ask Court for Directions

35.26 **11.1** Experts may request directions from the court to assist them in carrying out their functions as experts. Experts should normally discuss such matters with those who instruct them before making any such request. Unless the court otherwise orders, any proposed request for directions should be copied to the party instructing the expert at least seven days before filing any request to the court, and to all other parties at least four days before filing it. (CPR 35.14).

11.2 Requests to the court for directions should be made by letter, containing:

(a) the title of the claim;
(b) the claim number of the case;
(c) the name of the expert;
(d) full details of why directions are sought; and
(e) copies of any relevant documentation.

12. Power of the Court to Direct a Party to Provide Information

35.27 **12.1** If experts consider that those instructing them have not provided information which they require, they may, after discussion with those instructing them and giving notice, write to the court to seek directions (CPR 35.14).

12.2 Experts and those who instruct them should also be aware of CPR 35.9. This provides that where one party has access to information which is not readily available to the other party, the court may direct the party who has access to the information to prepare, file and copy to the other party a document recording the information. If experts require such information which has not been disclosed, they should discuss the position with those instructing them without delay, so that a request for the information can be made, and, if not forthcoming, an application can be made to the court. Unless a document appears to be essential, experts should assess the cost and time involved in the production of a document and whether its provision would be proportionate in the context of the case.

13. Contents of Experts' Reports

35.28 **13.1** The content and extent of experts' reports should be governed by the scope of their instructions and general obligations, the contents of CPR 35 and PD35 and their overriding duty to the court.

13.2 In preparing reports, experts should maintain professional objectivity and impartiality at all times.

13.3 PD 35, para 2 provides that experts' reports should be addressed to the court and gives detailed directions about the form and content of such reports. All experts and those who instruct them should ensure that they are familiar with these requirements.

13.4 Model forms of Experts' Reports are available from bodies such as the Academy of Experts or the Expert Witness Institute.

13.5 Experts' reports must contain statements that they understand their duty to the court and have complied and will continue to comply with that duty (PD35 para 2.2(9)). They must also be verified by a statement of truth. The form of the statement of truth is as follows:

> "I confirm that insofar as the facts stated in my report are within my own knowledge I have made clear which they are and I believe them to be true, and that the opinions I have expressed represent my true and complete professional opinion."

This wording is mandatory and must not be modified.

13.6 Qualifications

The details of experts' qualifications to be given in reports should be commensurate with the nature and complexity of the case. It may be sufficient merely to state academic and professional qualifications. However, where highly specialised expertise is called for, experts should include the detail of particular training and/or experience that qualifies them to provide that highly specialised evidence.

13.7 Tests

Where tests of a scientific or technical nature have been carried out, experts should state:

(a) the methodology used; and

(b) by whom the tests were undertaken and under whose supervision, summarising their respective qualifications and experience.

13.8 Reliance on the work of others

Where experts rely in their reports on literature or other material and cite the opinions of others without having verified them, they must give details of those opinions relied on. It is likely to assist the court if the qualifications of the originator(s) are also stated.

Facts

13.9 When addressing questions of fact and opinion, experts should keep the two separate and discrete. **35.29**

13.10 Experts must state those facts (whether assumed or otherwise) upon which their opinions are based. They must distinguish clearly between those facts which experts know to be true and those facts which they assume.

13.11 Where there are material facts in dispute experts should express separate opinions on each hypothesis put forward. They should not express a view in favour of one or other disputed version of the facts unless, as a result of particular expertise and experience, they consider one set of facts as being improbable or less probable, in which case they may express that view, and should give reasons for holding it.

13.12 Range of opinion

If the mandatory summary of the range of opinion is based on published sources, experts should explain those sources and, where appropriate, state the qualifications of the originator(s) of the opinions from which they differ, particularly if such opinions represent a well-established school of thought.

13.13 Where there is no available source for the range of opinion, experts may need to express opinions on what they believe to be the range which other experts would arrive at if asked. In those circumstances, experts should make it clear that the range that they summarise is based on their own judgement and explain the basis of that judgement.

13.14 Conclusions

A summary of conclusions is mandatory. The summary should be at the end of the report after all the reasoning. There may be cases, however, where the benefit to the court is heightened by placing a short summary at the beginning of the report whilst giving the full conclusions at the end. For example, it can assist with the comprehension of the analysis and with the absorption of the detailed facts if the court is told at the outset of the direction in which the report's logic will flow in cases involving highly complex matters which fall outside the general knowledge of the court.

13.15 Basis of report: material instructions

The mandatory statement of the substance of all material instructions should not be incomplete or otherwise tend to mislead. The imperative is transparency. The term "instructions" includes all material which solicitors place in front of experts in order to gain advice. The omission from the statement of 'off-the-record' oral instructions is not permitted. Courts may allow cross-examination about the instructions if there are reasonable grounds to consider that the statement may be inaccurate or incomplete.

14. After receipt of experts' reports

35.30 **14.1** Following the receipt of experts' reports, those instructing them should advise the experts as soon as reasonably practicable whether, and if so when, the report will be disclosed to other parties; and, if so disclosed, the date of actual disclosure.

14.2 If experts' reports are to be relied upon, and if experts are to give oral evidence, those instructing them should give the experts the opportunity to consider and comment upon other reports within their area of expertise and which deal with relevant issues at the earliest opportunity.

14.3 Those instructing experts should keep experts informed of the progress of cases, including amendments to statements of case relevant to experts' opinion.

14.4 If those instructing experts become aware of material changes in circumstances or that relevant information within their control was not previously provided to experts, they should without delay instruct experts to review, and if necessary, update the contents of their reports.

15. Amendment of reports

15.1 It may become necessary for experts to amend their reports: 35.31

(a) as a result of an exchange of questions and answers;

(b) following agreements reached at meetings between experts; or

(c) where further evidence or documentation is disclosed.

15.2 Experts should not be asked to, and should not, amend, expand or alter any parts of reports in a manner which distorts their true opinion, but may be invited to amend or expand reports to ensure accuracy, internal consistency, completeness and relevance to the issues and clarity. Although experts should generally follow the recommendations of solicitors with regard to the form of reports, they should form their own independent views as to the opinions and contents expressed in their reports and exclude any suggestions which do not accord with their views.

15.3 Where experts change their opinion following a meeting of experts, a simple signed and dated addendum or memorandum to that effect is generally sufficient. In some cases, however, the benefit to the court of having an amended report may justify the cost of making the amendment.

15.4 Where experts significantly alter their opinion, as a result of new evidence or because evidence on which they relied has become unreliable, or for any other reason, they should amend their reports to reflect that fact. Amended reports should include reasons for amendments. In such circumstances those instructing experts should inform other parties as soon as possible of any change of opinion.

15.5 When experts intend to amend their reports, they should inform those instructing them without delay and give reasons. They should provide the amended version (or an addendum or memorandum) clearly marked as such as quickly as possible.

16. Written Questions to Experts

16.1 The procedure for putting written questions to experts (CPR 35.32
35.6) is intended to facilitate the clarification of opinions and issues after experts' reports have been served. Experts have a duty to provide answers to questions properly put. Where they fail to do so, the court may impose sanctions against the party instructing the expert, and, if, there is continued non-compliance, debar a party from relying on the report. Experts should copy their answers to those instructing them.

16.2 Experts' answers to questions automatically become part of their reports. They are covered by the statement of truth and form part of the expert evidence.

16.3 Where experts believe that questions put are not properly directed to the clarification of the report, or are disproportionate, or have been asked out of time, they should discuss the questions with those instructing them and, if appropriate, those asking the questions. Attempts should be made to resolve such problems without the need for an application to the court for directions.

16.4 Written requests for directions in relation to questions

If those instructing experts do not apply to the court in respect of questions, but experts still believe that questions are improper or out of time, experts may file written requests with the court for directions to assist in carrying out their functions as experts (CPR 35.14). See Section 11 above.

17. Single Joint Experts

35.33 **17.1** CPR 35 and PD35 deal extensively with the instruction and use of joint experts by the parties and the powers of the court to order their use (see CPR 35.7 and 35.8, PD35, para 5).

17.2 The Civil Procedure Rules encourage the use of joint experts. Wherever possible a joint report should be obtained. Consideration should therefore be given by all parties to the appointment of single joint experts in all cases where a court might direct such an appointment. Single joint experts are the norm in cases allocated to the small claims track and the fast track.

17.3 Where, in the early stages of a dispute, examinations, investigations, tests, site inspections, experiments, preparation of photographs, plans or other similar preliminary expert tasks are necessary, consideration should be given to the instruction of a single joint expert, especially where such matters are not, at that stage, expected to be contentious as between the parties. The objective of such an appointment should be to agree or to narrow issues.

17.4 Experts who have previously advised a party (whether in the same case or otherwise) should only be proposed as single joint experts if other parties are given all relevant information about the previous involvement.

17.5 The appointment of a single joint expert does not prevent parties from instructing their own experts to advise (but the costs of such expert advisers may not be recoverable in the case).

17.6 Joint instructions

35.34 The parties should try to agree joint instructions to single joint experts, but, in default of agreement, each party may give instructions. In particular, all parties should try to agree what documents should be included with instructions and what assumptions single joint experts should make.

17.7 Where the parties fail to agree joint instructions, they should try to agree where the areas of disagreement lie and their instructions should make this clear. If separate instructions are given, they should be copied at the same time to the other instructing parties.

17.8 Where experts are instructed by two or more parties, the terms of appointment should, unless the court has directed otherwise, or the parties have agreed otherwise, include:

(a) a statement that all the instructing parties are jointly and severally liable to pay the experts' fees and, accordingly, that experts' invoices should be sent simultaneously to all instructing parties or their solicitors (as appropriate); and

(b) a statement as to whether any order has been made limiting the amount of experts' fees and expenses (CPR 35.8(4)(a)).

17.9 Where instructions have not been received by the expert from one or more of the instructing parties the expert should give notice (normally at least 7 days) of a deadline to all instructing parties for the receipt by the expert of such instructions. Unless the instructions are received within the deadline the expert may begin work. In the event that instructions are received after the deadline but before the signing off of the report the expert should consider whether it is practicable to comply with those instructions without adversely affecting the timetable set for delivery of the report and in such a manner as to comply with the proportionality principle. An expert who decides to issue a report without taking into account instructions received after the deadline should inform the parties who may apply to the court for directions. In either event the report must show clearly that the expert did not receive instructions within the deadline, or, as the case may be, at all.

17.10 Conduct of the single joint expert

Single joint experts should keep all instructing parties informed of any material steps that they may be taking by, for example, copying all correspondence to those instructing them. **35.35**

17.11 Single joint experts are Part 35 experts and so have an overriding duty to the court. They are the parties' appointed experts and therefore owe an equal duty to all parties. They should maintain independence, impartiality and transparency at all times.

17.12 Single joint experts should not attend any meeting or conference which is not a joint one, unless all the parties have agreed in writing or the court has directed that such a meeting may be held [1] and who is to pay the experts' fees for the meeting.

17.13 Single joint experts may request directions from the court—see Section 11 above.

17.14 Single joint experts should serve their reports simultaneously on all instructing parties. They should provide a single report even though they may have received instructions which contain areas of conflicting fact or allegation. If conflicting instructions lead to different opinions (for example, because the instructions require experts to make different assumptions of fact), reports may need to contain more than one set of opinions on any issue. It is for the court to determine the facts.

17.15 Cross-examination

Single joint experts do not normally give oral evidence at trial but if they do, all parties may cross-examine them. In general written questions (CPR 35.6) should be put to single joint experts before requests are made for them to attend court for the purpose of cross-examination [2].

18. Discussions between Experts

18.1 The court has powers to direct discussions between experts for the purposes set out in the Rules (CPR 35.12). Parties may also agree that discussions take place between their experts. **35.36**

[1] *Peet v Mid Kent Area Healthcare NHS Trust* [2002] 1 WLR 210
[2] *Daniels v Walker* [2000] 1 WLR 1382

18.2 Where single joint experts have been instructed but parties have, with the permission of the court, instructed their own additional Part 35 experts, there may, if the court so orders or the parties agree, be discussions between the single joint experts and the additional Part 35 experts. Such discussions should be confined to those matters within the remit of the additional Part 35 experts or as ordered by the court.

18.3 The purpose of discussions between experts should be, wherever possible, to:

(a) identify and discuss the expert issues in the proceedings;

(b) reach agreed opinions on those issues, and, if that is not possible, to narrow the issues in the case;

(c) identify those issues on which they agree and disagree and summarise their reasons for disagreement on any issue; and

(d) identify what action, if any, may be taken to resolve any of the outstanding issues between the parties.

18.4 Arrangements for discussions between experts

Arrangements for discussions between experts should be proportionate to the value of cases. In small claims and fast-track cases there should not normally be meetings between experts. Where discussion is justified in such cases, telephone discussion or an exchange of letters should, in the interests of proportionality, usually suffice. In multi-track cases, discussion may be face to face, but the practicalities or the proportionality principle may require discussions to be by telephone or video conference.

18.5 The parties, their lawyers and experts should co-operate to produce the agenda for any discussion between experts, although primary responsibility for preparation of the agenda should normally lie with the parties' solicitors.

18.6 The agenda should indicate what matters have been agreed and summarise concisely those which are in issue. It is often helpful for it to include questions to be answered by the experts. If agreement cannot be reached promptly or a party is unrepresented, the court may give directions for the drawing up of the agenda. The agenda should be circulated to experts and those instructing them to allow sufficient time for the experts to prepare for the discussion.

18.7 Those instructing experts must not instruct experts to avoid reaching agreement (or to defer doing so) on any matter within the experts' competence. Experts are not permitted to accept such instructions.

35.37 **18.8** The parties' lawyers may only be present at discussions between experts if all the parties agree or the court so orders. If lawyers do attend, they should not normally intervene except to answer questions put to them by the experts or to advise about the law.[1]

18.9 The content of discussions between experts should not be referred to at trial unless the parties agree (CPR 35.12(4)). It is good practice for any such agreement to be in writing.

[1] *Hubbard v Lambeth, Southwark and Lewisham HA* [2001] EWCA 1455

18.10 At the conclusion of any discussion between experts, a statement should be prepared setting out:

(a) a list of issues that have been agreed, including, in each instance, the basis of agreement;

(b) a list of issues that have not been agreed, including, in each instance, the basis of disagreement;

(c) a list of any further issues that have arisen that were not included in the original agenda for discussion;

(d) a record of further action, if any, to be taken or recommended, including as appropriate the holding of further discussions between experts.

18.11 The statement should be agreed and signed by all the parties to the discussion as soon as may be practicable.

18.12 Agreements between experts during discussions do not bind the parties unless the parties expressly agree to be bound by the agreement (CPR 35.12(5)). However, in view of the overriding objective, parties should give careful consideration before refusing to be bound by such an agreement and be able to explain their refusal should it become relevant to the issue of costs.

19. Attendance of Experts at Court

19.1 Experts instructed in cases have an obligation to attend court if called upon to do so and accordingly should ensure that those instructing them are always aware of their dates to be avoided and take all reasonable steps to be available. **35.38**

19.2 Those instructing experts should:

(a) ascertain the availability of experts before trial dates are fixed;

(b) keep experts updated with timetables (including the dates and times experts are to attend) and the location of the court;

(c) give consideration, where appropriate, to experts giving evidence via a video-link.

(d) inform experts immediately if trial dates are vacated.

19.3 Experts should normally attend court without the need for the service of witness summonses, but on occasion they may be served to require attendance (CPR 34). The use of witness summonses does not affect the contractual or other obligations of the parties to pay experts' fees.

PART 36

OFFERS TO SETTLE

Contents

Editorial introduction

36.0.2 Part 36 concerns offers to settle made in accordance with its provisions and the consequences which follow if such offers do so comply. There is no prohibition against a party making an offer to settle in any way he chooses but if the offer does not comply with the provisions of Pt 36, the consequences specified in rr.36.10, 36.11 and 36.14 will not apply.

Part 36 applies not only to claims, but also to counterclaims and additional claims within Pt 20 (see CPR r.20(2) and (3)).

The present Pt 36 came into effect on April 6, 2007. There are transitional provisions in respect of Pt 36 offers and Pt 36 payments into court initiated before April 6, 2007 providing that if any such would have had the consequences set out in Pt 36 as it was in force immediately before April 6, 2007 it will have the consequences set out in rr.36.10, 36.11 and 36.14 after that date (see r.7(2) of the Civil Procedure (Amendment No.3) Rules 2006 (SI 2006/3435) set out at para.36.0.3 below and Practice Direction B supplementing Pt 36 set out at 36BPD.1 *et seq.* below.

Payment into Court no longer plays any role in the Pt 36 offer to settle procedure post April 6, 2007 but now where an offer is or includes an offer to pay a single sum of money that sum must be paid within 14 days of the date of acceptance or any delayed date where court involvement is required and if not so paid judgment may be entered for the unpaid sum (r.36.11(6) and (7)). Further r.36.11(8) also provides for the enforcement of any accepted but unhonoured term not being within r.36.11(6) without the need for a new claim.

The standard formalities of a Pt 36 offer are set out in r.36.2. Offers claims involving future pecuniary loss (r.36.5), provisional damages (r.36.6) and deductible benefits (r.36.15) must contain the further information required by such rules.

Rule 36.3 sets out a number of general provisions including the meaning of the concept of "the relevant period" which concept regulates a number of other provisions such as withdrawal or change of terms to be less advantageous (r.36.3(5) and (6) and the r.36.10 and r.36.11 consequences. It further provides that a Pt 36 offer may be made at any time including before the commencement of proceedings and in appeal proceedings (r.36.3(3)) and by r.36.3(3) provides that an offer of a monetary sum will be treated as inclusive of interest until the date specified therein.

Clarification of the terms of Pt 36 offer on request or by a Pt 23 application is provided for by r.36.8 and includes a requirement that if ordered by the Court a date when the offer is to be treated as having been made must be specified.

Acceptance (see r.36.9) can now and subject to certain circumstances where the court's permission is required (see r.36.9(3)) be made at any time unless the offeror serves notice of withdrawal on the offeree.

Rule 36.10 sets out the costs consequences of accepting a Pt 36 offer. The costs consequences very depending upon whether the acceptance is within the relevant period or where the defendant's offer relates to part only of the claim and at the time of acceptance within the relevant period the claimant abandons the balance of the claim or the offer is made less than 21 days before the start of the trial or the relevant period has expired.

The effect of acceptance is set out in r.36.11 and includes a stay, a stay delayed until court approval is forthcoming where court approval is required, the facility to enter judgment for any accepted but unpaid money sum and to enforce any accepted but unhonoured non-monetary terms without the need for a new claim.

The position where the offer is made by one or more but not all defendants is provided for by r.36.12 and depends upon whether they are "sued jointly or in the alternative" or are alleged to have "a several liability".

Restrictions on disclosure of a Pt 36 offer are contained in r.36.13.

Costs consequences following judgment in the light of a defendant's or a claimant's offer are set out in r.36.14. The entitlement (unless the court considers it unjust) to the enhancement provisions set out in r.36.14(3) is available however only to the claimant.

Rule 36.15 deals with the deduction of benefits and requires that the information set out in r.36.15 must be provided in any offer within r.36.15.

The transitional provisions

In respect of a Pt 36 offer or a Pt 36 payment made before April 6, 2007, the date upon which CPR, Pt 36 set out at para.36.1 *et seq.* below came into effect, the Civil Procedure (Amendment No.3) Rules 2006 (SI 2006/3435) enacts the following transitional provisions: **36.0.3**

"7.—(2) Where a Part 36 offer or Part 36 payment was made before 6th April 2007, if it would have had the consequences set out in the rules of court contained in Part 36 as it was in force immediately before 6th April 2007, it will have the consequences set out in rules 36.10, 36.11 and 36.14 after that date.

(3) Where a Part 36 offer or Part 36 payment was made before 6th April 2007, the permission of the court is required to accept that offer or payment, if permission would have been required under the rules of court contained in Part 36 as it was in force immediately before 6th April 2007.

(4) Rule 37.3 will apply to a Part 36 payment made before 6th April 2007 as if that payment into court had been made under a court order.

(5) Subject to paragraph (6), where a person has made a Part 36 offer or Part 36 payment less than 21 days before 6th April 2007—

(a) paragraphs (1) to (4) of this Rule shall not apply to the offer or payment; and

(b) the rules of court contained in Part 36 as it was in force immediately before 6th April 2007 shall continue to apply to that offer or payment as if they had not been revoked.

(6) Paragraph (5) ceases to apply to a Part 36 offer or Part 36 payment made less than 21 days before 6th April 2007 at the expiry of 21 days from the date that offer or payment was made unless the trial has started within that period.

(7) Where, before 6th April 2007, a person has made an offer to settle before commencement of proceedings which complied with rule 36.10 as it was in force immediately before 6th April 2007—

(a) the court will take that offer into account when making any order as to costs; and

(b) the permission of the court will be required to accept the offer after proceedings have been commenced."

See too the transitional provisions set out in Practice Direction B supplementing Part 36 at paras 36BPD.1 *et seq.* below.

For CPR Pt 36 pre-April 6, 2007 and its supplementary Practice Direction see the *White Book*, 2006 edn, Vol.1 at paras 36.1 *et seq.* together with the commentary thereon.

Related sources

36.0.4
- Practice Direction—Offers to Settle Pt 36 Practice Direction (see paras 36PD.1 *et seq.*)
- Practice Direction B suppplementing Part 36 (see paras 36BPD.1 *et seq.*)
- The Transitional Provisions—Civil Procedure (Amendment No.3) Rules 2006 (SI 2006/3435), para.7(2) to (7) (see para.36.0.3 above)
- CPR r.20.3 (Pt 20 claim to be treated as a claim for purposes inter alia of Pt 36)
- CPR r.21.10 (Compromise by or on behalf of a child or protected party)
- CPR r.41.2 (Order for an award of provisional damages)
- CPR r.41.3A (Apportionment by Court of FAA 1976 and/or LR(MP)A 1934 awards
- CPR r.44.3(4)(c) (Court to take into account any admissible offer to settle and which is not an offer to which costs consequences under Pt 36 apply)

Forms

36.0.5
- **N242A**

Scope of this Part[1]

36.1 **36.1—(1) This Part contains rules about—**

(a) offers to settle; and

(b) the consequences where an offer to settle is made in accordance with this Part.

(2) Nothing in this Part prevents a party making an offer to settle in whatever way he chooses, but if the offer is not made in accordance with rule 36.2, it will not have the consequences specified in rules 36.10, 36.11 and 36.14.

(Rule 44.3 requires the court to consider an offer to settle that does not have the costs consequences set out in this Part in deciding what order to make about costs)

General note

36.1.1 Part 36 provides a statutory procedure for settlement which is complete in itself. The need, therefore, to resort to a *Calderbank* letter (see *Calderbank v Calderbank* [1976] Fam. 93; [1975] 3 All E.R. 333, CA, has been largelyremoved. However, the concept of a *Calderbank* letter which does not in its terms comply with the provisions of Pt 36 and other non-complying offers is preserved though the consequences specified in rr.36.10, 36.11 and 36.14 will not follow. Such a non-complying offer is made by letter written "without prejudice save as to costs" or "without prejudice" but subject to an express reservation of the right to refer to the letter on the issue of costs should the claim proceed to judgment. However it should be noted that although the existence of a *Calderbank* type letter may be a very important consideration in the exercise of the Court's discretion with regards to costs and is a fact which the Court is required to take into account when exercising such discretion (see CPR r.44.3) it is not to be equated with a Pt 36 offer. The Court retains its discretion and the existence of a *Calderbank* letter should influence but not govern the exercise of the discretion (see *McDonnell v McDonnell* [1977] 1 W.L.R. 34; [1977] 1 All E.R. 766, CA).

Nature of a Part 36 offer

36.1.2 *Part 36 provides a* statutory procedure for settlement which is complete in its own right and by itself.

[1] Introduced by the Civil Procedure (Amendment No.3) Rules 2006 (SI 2006/3435).

In *Flynn v Scougall*; [2004] EWCA Civ 873 [2004] 1 W.L.R. 3069, CA, [2004] 3 All E.R. 609, CA, the court stated that Pt 36 payments (likewise offers) were not contractual in nature but wholly procedural and subject to the rules of court, re-affirming in terms of the CPR the approach in *Cumper v Pothecary* [1941] 2 K.B. 58, a RSC O.22 case.

In *Toprak Enerji Sanayi AS v Sale Tilney Technology Plc* [1994] 1 W.L.R. 840; [1994] 3 All E.R. 483; [1994] 1 Lloyd's Rep. 303, the court held that there was nothing in the former RSC O.22, r.1 to suggest that a payment into court was of its nature so personal to the claimant that in no circumstances could the payment be treated as available to an assignee, transferee or successor of the claimant. The whole structure of the rule is directed to matching payments to claims, not to identifying a payment as an offer made to the claimant personally. Further, it was held that a defendant who made a payment into court was not estopped from asserting that the claim form had not been duly served (*Towers v Morley* [1992] 1 W.L.R. 511, CA).

It is considered that a Pt 36 offer will be similarly treated by the courts. See too *Orton v Collins* [2007] EWHC 803(Ch); [2007] 1 W.L.R. 2953; [2007] 3 All E.R. 863 Ch D.

Scope of Part 36

Part 36 does not apply to small claims, see CPR r.27.2(1)(g). **36.1.3**

Part 36 offers can now be made at any time including before the commencement of proceedings and may be made in appeal proceedings (see r.36.3(2) below). However composite first instance and appeal offers to settle are not permissible and seperate offers must be made (see r.36.3(4) below).

For interplay of CPR r.36 and a case governed by the costs provisions of the Warsaw Convention and in particular art.22(4) thereof see *GKN West Helicopters Ltd v Korean Air Lines Ltd* [2003] EWHC 1120 (Comm); [2003] 2 Lloyd's Rep. 629.

Practice Directions

CPR r.36 is supplemented by Practice Direction—Offers to Settle (see paras 36PD.1 *et seq.*) and Practice Direction B supplementing Part 36 (see paras 36BPD.1 *et seq.*) which should be read in conjunction with Pt 36. **36.1.4**

Form and content of a Part 36 offer[1]

36.2—(1) An offer to settle which is made in accordance with this rule is called a Part 36 offer. **36.2**

(2) A Part 36 offer must—

(a) be in writing;

(b) state on its face that it is intended to have the consequences of Part 36;

(c) specify a period of not less than 21 days within which the defendant will be liable for the claimant's costs in accordance with rule 36.10 if the offer is accepted;

(d) state whether it relates to the whole of the claim or to part of it or to an issue that arises in it and if so to which part or issue; and

(e) state whether it takes into account any counterclaim.

(Rule 36.7 makes provision for when a Part 36 offer is made)

(3) Rule 36.2(2)(c) does not apply if the offer is made less than 21 days before the start of the trial.

***(4)* In *appropriate* cases, *a* Part 36 offer must contain such further information as is required by rule 36.5 (Personal injury claims for future pecuniary loss), rule 36.6 (Offer to settle a claim for provisional damages), and rule 36.15 (Deduction of benefits).**

(5) An offeror may make a Part 36 offer solely in relation to liability.

[1] Introduced by the Civil Procedure (Amendment No.3) Rules 2006 (SI 2006/3435).

General note

36.2.1 The Pt 36 offer must comply with the provisions of r.36.2(2) above and where appropriate contain the further information required by r.36(5) (personal injury claims for future pecuniary loss), by r.36.6 (offer to settle a claim for provisional damages) and by r.36.15 (deduction of benefits), see r.36.2(4). Clarity is required in the information given and if given will avoid the need for an application for clarification under r.36.8.

The general rule is that Pt 36 offers should be made not less than 21 days before the start of a trial as such will trigger the costs consequences without court involvement or further agreement as to the liability for costs set out in r.36.10(1) to (3). If made less than 21 days before the start of a trial or the offer is accepted after the expiry of "the relevant period" (see below r.36.3(1)(c)) then unless the parties agree the liability for costs, the Court will make an order as to costs, see r.36.10(4) and (5) below.

Form

36.2.2 A Pt 36 offer may be made using Form **N242A** (Practice Direction—Offers to Settle, para.1.1). Where a party is legally represented it must be served upon the legal representative (*ibid.* para.1.2).

Part 36 offers—general provisions[1]

36.3 **36.3—(1) In this part—**

(a) the party who makes an offer is the 'offeror';

(b) the party to whom an offer is made is the 'offeree'; and

(c) 'the relevant period' means—

(i) in the case of an offer made not less than 21 days before trial, the period stated under rule 36.2(2)(c) or such longer period as the parties agree;

(ii) otherwise, the period up to end of the trial or such other period as the court has determined.

(2) A Part 36 offer—

(a) may be made at any time, including before the commencement of proceedings; and

(b) may be made in appeal proceedings.

(3) A Part 36 offer which offers to pay or offers to accept a sum of money will be treated as inclusive of all interest until—

(a) the date on which the period stated under rule 36.2(2)(c) expires; or

(b) if rule 36.2(3) applies, a date 21 days after the date the offer was made.

(4) A Part 36 offer shall have the consequences set out in this Part only in relation to the costs of the proceedings in respect of which it is made, and not in relation to the costs of any appeal from the final decision in those proceedings.

(5) Before expiry of the relevant period, a Part 36 offer may be withdrawn or its terms changed to be less advantageous to the offeree, only if the court gives permission.

(6) After expiry of the relevant period and provided that the offeree has not previously served notice of acceptance, the offeror

[1] Introduced by the Civil Procedure (Amendment No.3) Rules 2006 (SI 2006/3435).

may withdraw the offer or change its terms to be less advantageous to the offeree without the permission of the court.

(7) The offeror does so by serving written notice of the withdrawal or change of terms on the offeree.

(Rule 36.14(6) deals with the costs consequences following judgment of an offer that is withdrawn)

Contents

A Pt 36 offer must contain the specific matters set out in r.36.2, set out at para.36.2 and commented upon at para.36.2 1 above. **36.3.1**

By r.36.3(4) interest will be treated as included in all offers to pay or to accept a sum of money until the dates specified in subsection (4) (q.v.).

Content limitations

It is still necessary to make a separate Pt 36 offer in respect of a first instance proceeding and another in respect of a subsequent appeal. A composite Pt 36 offer is not permissible. See r.36.3(2) and (4) and see *East West Corporation v Dampskibsselskabet AF (No.2); Utaniko Ltd v P&O Nedlloyd BV (No.2)* [2003] EWCA 174; [2003] 1 Lloyd's Rep. 265, CA. See too the following note in Pt 52 after r.52.12: **36.3.2**

> "(Rule 36.3 has the effect that a Part 36 offer made in proceedings in first instance will not have consequences in any appeal proceedings. Therefore, a fresh Part 36 offer needs to be made in appeal proceedings. However, rule 52.12 applies to a Part 36 offer whether made in the original proceedings or in the appeal.)"

Part 36 procedure contains its own provisions as to costs, thus proposed terms as to costs are not within the scope of a Pt 36 offer, *Mitchell v James* [2002] EWCA Civ 997; [2004] 1 W.L.R. 158; [2003] 2 All E.R. 1064. A party may however offer to settle in any way he wishes including a term as to costs and such will be taken into account when the court exercises its discretion in relation to inter parties costs at the end of the case. See too under "General Note" at para.36.1.1 above.

"the relevant period"

This is defined in r.36.3(1)(c) above and is of importance to Pt 36 procedure as it regulates the facility to withdraw or change to terms less advantageous to the offeree (see r.36.3(5) and (6)) and acceptance requires Court permission in a case within r.36.15(3)(b) (q.v.) where the relevant period has expired and further deductible benefits have been paid to the claimant since the date of the offer. **36.3.3**

Withdrawal/change of terms less favourable to offeree

Once the relevant period has expired then provided that the offeree has not previously served notice of acceptance, the offer may be withdrawn or its terms changed to be less favourable to the offeree without the permission of the court (r.36.3(6)). Before expiry of the relevant period withdrawal or change to less favourable terms can only take place with permission of the court (r.36.3(5)). **36.3.4**

Where court permission is required application should be made in accordance with Pt 23, see Practice Direction—Offers to Settle, para.2.2 (para.36PD.2 below).

In *Marsh v Frenchay Healthcare NHS Trust, The Times*, March 13, 2001 it was held that in application for permission to withdraw a payment under the former CPR r.36.6(5) case law in relation to the former RSC O.22, r.1(3) could be discarded in favour of the flexible new approach to deal justly with the case. But in *MRW Technologies Ltd v Cecil Holdings Ltd* June 22, 2001, unrep. it was held that although the court might now incline to a more flexible approach, the "change of circumstances" test stated in *Cumper v Pothercary* [1941] 2 K.B. 58, CA was consistent with the overriding objective of CPR r.1.1 and should be adopted. In *Capital Bank Plc v Stickland* [2004] EWCA Civ 1677; [2005] 1 W.L.R. 3914; [2005] 2 All E.R. 544, the Court of Appeal held that under the present rules the fact that there has been a change of circumstance is certainly relevant and may well be the most important factor to be taken into account in a particular case. The Court of Appeal also held that there was no justification for requiring a claimant making a Pt 36 offer to withdraw or reduce his offer (or to be treated as having done so) as a condition of his opposing a defendant's application for late acceptance of the offer.

Part 36 offers—defendants' offers[1]

36.4 **36.4—(1) Subject to rule 36.5(3) and rule 36.6(1), a Part 36 offer by a defendant to pay a sum of money in settlement of a claim must be an offer to pay a single sum of money.**

(2) But, an offer that includes an offer to pay all or part of the sum, if accepted, at a date later than 14 days following the date of acceptance will not be treated as a Part 36 offer unless the offeree accepts the offer.

Personal injury claims for future pecuniary loss[2]

36.5 **36.5—(1) This rule applies to a claim for damages for personal injury which is or includes a claim for future pecuniary loss.**

(2) An offer to settle such a claim will not have the consequences set out in rules 36.10, 36.11 and 36.14 unless it is made by way of a Part 36 offer under this rule.

(3) A Part 36 offer to which this rule applies may contain an offer to pay, or an offer to accept—

(a) the whole or part of the damages for future pecuniary loss in the form of

(i) a lump sum; or

(ii) periodical payments; or

(iii) both a lump sum and periodical payments;

(b) the whole or part of any other damages in the form of a lump sum.

(4) A Part 36 offer to which this rule applies—

(a) must state the amount of any offer to pay the whole or part of any damages in the form of a lump sum;

(b) may state—

(i) what part of the lump sum, if any, relates to damages for future pecuniary loss; and

(ii) what part relates to other damages to be accepted in the form of a lump sum;

(c) must state what part of the offer relates to damages for future pecuniary loss to be paid or accepted in the form of periodical payments and must specify—

(i) the amount and duration of the periodical payments;

(ii) the amount of any payments for substantial capital purchases and when they are to be made; and

(iii) that each amount is to vary by reference to the retail prices index (or to some other named index, or that it is not to vary by reference to any index); and

(d) must state either that any damages which take the form

[1] Introduced by the Civil Procedure (Amendment No.3) Rules 2006 (SI 2006/3435).
[2] Introduced by the Civil Procedure (Amendment No.3) Rules 2006 (SI 2006/3435).

of periodical payments will be funded in a way which ensures that the continuity of payment is reasonably secure in accordance with section 2(4) of the Damages Act 1996 or how such damages are to be paid and how the continuity of their payment is to be secured.

(5) Rule 36.4 applies to the extent that a Part 36 offer by a defendant under this rule includes an offer to pay all or part of any damages in the form of a lump sum.

(6) Where the offeror makes a Part 36 offer to which this rule applies and which offers to pay or to accept damages in the form of both a lump sum and periodical payments, the offeree may only give notice of acceptance of the offer as a whole.

(7) If the offeree accepts a Part 36 offer which includes payment of any part of the damages in the form of periodical payments, the claimant must, within 7 days of the date of acceptance, apply to the court for an order for an award of damages in the form of periodical payments under rule 41.8.

(A practice direction supplementing Part 41 contains information about periodical payments under the Damages Act 1996)

Offer to settle a claim for provisional damages[1]

36.6—(1) An offeror may make a Part 36 offer in respect of a claim which includes a claim for provisional damages. **36.6**

(2) Where he does so, the Part 36 offer must specify whether or not the offeror is proposing that the settlement shall include an award of provisional damages.

(3) Where the offeror is offering to agree to the making of an award of provisional damages the Part 36 offer must also state—

(a) that the sum offered is in satisfaction of the claim for damages on the assumption that the injured person will not develop the disease or suffer the type of deterioration specified in the offer;

(b) that the offer is subject to the condition that the claimant must make any claim for further damages within a limited period; and

(c) what that period is.

(4) Rule 36.4 applies to the extent that a Part 36 offer by a defendant includes an offer to agree to the making of an award of provisional damages.

(5) If the offeree accepts the Part 36 offer, the claimant must, within 7 days of the date of acceptance, apply to the court for an order for an award of provisional damages under rule 41.2.

Time when a Part 36 offer is made[2]

36.7—(1) A Part 36 offer is made when it is served on the offeree. **36.7**

(2) A change in the terms of a Part 36 offer will be effective when notice of the change is served on the offeree.

[1] Introduced by the Civil Procedure (Amendment No.3) Rules 2006 (SI 2006/3435).
[2] Introduced by the Civil Procedure (Amendment No.3) Rules 2006 (SI 2006/3435).

(Rule 36.3 makes provision about when permission is required to change the terms of an offer to make it less advantageous to the offeree)

Note

36.7.1 Times run from service of the relevant document. In the event of a clarification order being made under r.36.8 the court must specify the date when the Pt 36 offer is to be treated as having been made (see r.36.8(3)).

In the light of the change of terminology to "when it is served" as opposed to "when received" under the predecessor to the present provision it is unlikely that anything less than formal service under the rules will suffice whereas under the former provision informal service (i.e. receipt not complying with the provisions as to service contained in Pt 6) sufficed, see *Charles v NTL Group* [2002] EWCA Civ 2004; [2003] C.P. Rep. 44, CA.

Clarification of a Part 36 offer[1]

36.8 **36.8—(1) The offeree may, within 7 days of a Part 36 offer being made, request the offeror to clarify the offer.**

(2) If the offeror does not give the clarification requested under paragraph (1) within 7 days of receiving the request, the offeree may, unless the trial has started, apply for an order that he does so.

(Part 23 contains provisions about making an application to the court)

(3) If the court makes an order under paragraph (2), it must specify the date when the Part 36 offer is to be treated as having been made.

Provision of Information

36.8.1 In *Ford v GKR Construction Ltd* [2000] 1 W.L.R. 1397; [2000] 1 All E.R. 802, CA, Lord Woolf M.R. said that if the process of making Pt 36 offers before the commencement of litigation is to work in the way which the CPR intend, the parties must be provided with the information which they require in order to assess whether to make an offer or whether to accept that offer. Where offers are not accepted, the CPR make provision as to what are to be the cost consequences (CPR r.36.14 (q.v.)) which rule deals with the usual consequences of not accepting an offer which, when judged in the light of the litigation, should have been accepted.

Acceptance of a Part 36 offer[2]

36.9 **36.9—(1) A Part 36 offer is accepted by serving written notice of the acceptance on the offeror.**

(2) Subject to rule 36.9(3), a Part 36 offer may be accepted at any time (whether or not the offeree has subsequently made a different offer) unless the offeror serves notice of withdrawal on the offeree.

(Rule 21.10 deals with compromise etc. by or on behalf of a child or protected party.)

(3) The court's permission is required to accept a Part 36 offer where—

(a) rule 36.12(4) applies;

[1] Introduced by the Civil Procedure (Amendment No.3) Rules 2006 (SI 2006/3435).
[2] Introduced by the Civil Procedure (Amendment No.3) Rules 2006 (SI 2006/3435) and amended by the Civil Procedure (Amendment) Rules 2007 (SI 2007/2204) and the Civil Procedure (Amendment) Rules 2008 (SI 2008/2178).

(b) rule 36.15(3)(b) applies, the relevant period has expired and further deductible amounts have been paid to the claimant since the date of the offer;

(c) an apportionment is required under rule 41.3A; or

(d) the trial has started.

(Rule 36.12 deals with offers by some but not all of multiple defendants.)

(Rule 36.15 defines "deductible amounts".)

(Rule 41.3A requires an apportionment in proceedings under the Fatal Accidents Act 1976 and Law Reform (Miscellaneous Provisions) Act 1934.)

(4) Where the court gives permission under paragraph (3), unless all the parties have agreed costs, the court will make an order dealing with costs, and may order that the costs consequences set out in rule 36.10 will apply.

(5) Unless the parties agree, a Part 36 offer may not be accepted after the end of the trial but before judgment is handed down.

Note

Unless r.36.9(3) applies (q.v.) a Pt 36 offer may now be accepted at any time unless the offeror serves notice of withdrawal on the offeree (see r.36.9(2)). **36.9.1**

Application for court permission

Such is made by way of a Pt 23 application and must be made to a judge other than a trial judge unless the parties otherwise agree (see PD 36 paras 3.2 and 3.3 at para.36PD.3 below). **36.9.2**

When the application is one to which r.36.9(3)(b) above applies that application must contain the particulars set out in PD 36 para.3.3(1) and (2), see para.36PD.3.3 below.

Costs consequences of acceptance of a Part 36 offer[1]

36.10—(1) Subject to paragraph (2) and paragraph (4)(a), where a Part 36 offer is accepted within the relevant period the claimant will be entitled to the costs of the proceedings up to the date on which notice of acceptance was served on the offeror. **36.10**

(2) Where—

(a) a defendant's Part 36 offer relates to part only of the claim; and

(b) at the time of serving notice of acceptance within the relevant period the claimant abandons the balance of the claim,

the claimant will be entitled to the costs of the proceedings up to the date of serving notice of acceptance unless the court orders otherwise.

(3) Costs under paragraphs (1) and (2) of this rule will be assessed on the standard basis if the amount of costs is not agreed.

(Rule 44.4(2) explains the standard basis for assessment of costs.)

(Rule 44.12 contains provisions about when a costs order is

[1] Introduced by the Civil Procedure (Amendment No.3) Rules 2006 (SI 2006/3435) and amended by the Civil Procedure (Amendment) Rules 2008 (SI 2008/2178).

deemed to have been made and applying for an order under section 194(3) of the Legal Services Act 2007.)

(4) Where—

(a) a Part 36 offer that was made less than 21 days before the start of trial is accepted; or

(b) a Part 36 offer is accepted after expiry of the relevant period,

if the parties do not agree the liability for costs, the court will make an order as to costs.

(5) Where paragraph (4)(b) applies, unless the court orders otherwise—

(a) the claimant will be entitled to the costs of the proceedings up to the date on which the relevant period expired; and

(b) the offeree will be liable for the offeror's costs for the period from the date of expiry of the relevant period to the date of acceptance.

(6) The claimant's costs include any costs incurred in dealing with the defendant's counterclaim if the Part 36 offer states that it takes into account the counterclaim.

Costs under r.36.10(1) and (2)

36.10.1 Whilst a judge making an order for costs can disallow a proportion of a party's costs to reflect conduct, where an offer is accepted without needing the permission of the court, no order for costs is made by the court but an order entitling the accepting party to his costs is deemed to have been made. In such circumstances on an assessment the costs judge has no jurisdiction to disallow costs under CPR r.44.3 and the receiving party is entitled to 100 per cent of his costs as assessed: *Lahey v Pirelli Tyres Ltd* [2007] EWCA Civ 91; [2007] 1 W.L.R. 998, CA, a pre-April 6, 2007, Pt.36 case.

On its true construction r.36.10(2) gives the Court a complete discretion to deal with the costs at large. Thus the Court is empowered to deal with the costs of the whole action and not just the costs referable to the abandoned parts of the claim, *E Ivor Hughes Educational Foundation v Leach* [2005] EWHC 1317 (Ch), a case under the former r.36.13(2). Such costs will be assessed on the standard basis if not agreed, r.36.10(3).

A party entitled under rules to costs is entitled to interest on costs under s.17 of the Judgments Acts 1838, and s.74 of the County Courts Act 1984.

Interest payable pursuant to s.17 of the Judgments Act 1838 or s.74 of the County Courts Act 1984 on the costs deemed to have been ordered begins to run from the date on which the event which gave rise to the entitlement to costs occurred, see CPR r.44.12, para.44.12 below.

The effect of acceptance of a Part 36 offer[1]

36.11 **36.11—(1) If a Part 36 offer is accepted, the claim will be stayed[GL].**

(2) In the case of acceptance of a Part 36 offer which relates to the whole claim the stay[GL] will be upon the terms of the offer.

(3) If a Part 36 offer which relates to part only of the claim is accepted—

(a) the claim will be stayed[GL] as to that part upon the terms of the offer; and

(b) subject to rule 36.10(2), unless the parties have agreed

[1] Introduced by the Civil Procedure (Amendment No.3) Rules 2006 (SI 2006/3435).

costs, the liability for costs shall be decided by the court.

(4) If the approval of the court is required before a settlement can be binding, any stay[GL] which would otherwise arise on the acceptance of a Part 36 offer will take effect only when that approval has been given.

(5) Any stay[GL] arising under this rule will not affect the power of the court—

(a) to enforce the terms of a Part 36 offer;

(b) to deal with any question of costs (including interest on costs) relating to the proceedings.

(6) Unless the parties agree otherwise in writing, where a Part 36 offer by a defendant that is or that includes an offer to pay a single sum of money is accepted, that sum must be paid to the offeree within 14 days of the date of—

(a) acceptance; or

(b) the order when the court makes an order under rule 41.2 (order for an award of provisional damages) or rule 41.8 (order for an award of periodical payments), unless the court orders otherwise.

(7) If the accepted sum is not paid within 14 days or such other period as has been agreed the offeree may enter judgment for the unpaid sum.

(8) Where—

(a) a Part 36 offer (or part of a Part 36 offer) which is not an offer to which paragraph (6) applies is accepted; and

(b) a party alleges that the other party has not honoured the terms of the offer,

that party may apply to enforce the terms of the offer without the need for a new claim.

Note

The facility to enter judgment for any unpaid sum which has been offered and accepted but not paid within 14 days of acceptance or court order under r.41.2 (provisional damages) or r.41.8 (periodical payments) or within such other period as may be agreed is new and welcome. **36.11.1**

Rule 36.11(8) allows an accepting party to apply to enforce terms other than those within r.36.11(6) which have not been honoured without the need for a new claim.

Where the approval of the court is required before a settlement can be binding (as in the case of a claim involving a child or protected party) any stay hereunder will take effect only when that approval has been given (r.36.11(4)). Furthermore, the stay under this rule will not effect the powers of the court listed in r.36.11(5).

Acceptance of a Part 36 offer made by one or more, but not all, defendants[1]

36.12—(1) This rule applies where the claimant wishes to accept a Part 36 offer made by one or more, but not all, of a number of defendants. **36.12**

(2) If the defendants are sued jointly or in the alternative, the claimant may accept the offer if—

[1] Introduced by the Civil Procedure (Amendment No.3) Rules 2006 (SI 2006/3435).

(a) he discontinues his claim against those defendants who have not made the offer; and

(b) those defendants give written consent to the acceptance of the offer.

(3) If the claimant alleges that the defendants have a several liability^GL to him, the claimant may—

(a) accept the offer; and

(b) continue with his claims against the other defendants if he is entitled to do so.

(4) In all other cases the claimant must apply to the court for an order permitting him to accept the Part 36 offer.

Note

36.12.1 Whether defendants are sued jointly or in the alternative on the one hand, or as being severally liable, depends not upon the manner in which they are sued but upon the nature and quality of the liability alleged. See further *Townsend v Stone Toms and Partners* [1981] 1 W.L.R. 1153; [1981] 2 All E.R. 690, CA, a case under the former RSC and which contains examples of joint and of alternative liability.

Discretion to costs

36.12.2 SCA 1981 s.51 gives the court complete discretion as to costs. Rule 44.3(4)(c) provides that the court, when exercising its discretion as to costs, must have regard to any admissible offer to settle made by a party which is drawn to its attention, and which is not an offer to which the costs consequences under Pt 36 apply.

Restriction on disclosure of a Part 36 offer[1]

36.13 **36.13—(1) A Part 36 offer will be treated as 'without prejudice^GL except as to costs'.**

(2) The fact that a Part 36 offer has been made must not be communicated to the trial judge or to the judge (if any) allocated in advance to conduct the trial until the case has been decided.

(3) Paragraph (2) does not apply—

(a) where the defence of tender before claim^GL has been raised;

(b) where the proceedings have been stayed^GL under rule 36.11 following acceptance of a Part 36 offer; or

(c) where the offeror and the offeree agree in writing that it should not apply.

Interlocutory proceedings and a Part 36 offer (r.36.13(2))

36.13.1 The restriction on communication under para.(2) as formulated under the forerunner of this rule was held to have no application to interlocutory proceedings in the course of which it is often both necessary and desirable that the Court should know of [offers to settle] (*Williams v Boag* [1941] 1 K.B. 1, per Goddard L.J. at 71). Parties and their solicitors should be aware of the need for different approaches to references depending on whether the judge conducting the CMC or other interlocutory proceedings is, or could be, the trial judge. This is of particular importance where the Designated Civil Judge is conducting the CMC. The rule has been applied equally to the Court of Appeal (see CPR, r.52.12) and on an appeal as to the *quantum* of damage the Court of Appeal was not told the amount paid into Court (see the former practice in *Mason v Mason* [1966] 1 W.L.R. 767; [1965] 3 All E.R. 492 (Note)).

The rule is directory not compulsive and upon breach the court has a discretion whether to continue or to recuse. It will usually continue where to do so will cause no

[1] Introduced by the Civil Procedure (Amendment No.3) Rules 2006 (SI 2006/3435).

injustice, see *Millensted v Grosvenor House (Park Lane) Ltd* [1937] 1 K.B. 717. These principles were reaffirmed in *Garratt v Saxby* [2004] EWCA Civ 341; [2004] 1 W.L.R. 2152, CA, in which it was said that it was proper to take into account any additional time, cost and difficulty involved were the hearing to be aborted.

The position where there has been a split trial is not specifically addressed as it was under the forerunner of this provision, r.36.19(3)(c) and absent agreement under the present r.36.13(3)(c) a strictly literal interpretation of the phrase "until the case has been decided" would result in an embargo which might well result in the court being denied information material to deciding what order as to costs if any was appropriate at the split trial stage. Whereas in *HSS Hire Services Group plc v BMB Builders Merchants Ltd* [2005] EWCA Civ 626; [2005] 1 W.L.R. 3158; [2005] 3 All E.R. 486 (a former r.36.19(3)(c) case) the court held at para.35:

> "... r.36.19 does not allow for the disclosure of the amount of [an offer to settle]. On its language it allows simply the disclosure of the fact that there has been one or the fact that there has not. The consequences of that being the correct interpretation of r.36.19 seem to me to be as follows. If the court is told that there has been no [offer to settle], then the court is free to exercise its discretion to award costs in relation to the preliminary issue and there is no difficulty with r.44.3(4)(c). If however it is told that there has been [an offer], then, in any but perhaps the most exceptional case, I find it very difficult to think that there could be circumstances where if the issue of damages remains to be decided, the judge can do otherwise than to reserve the question of costs until after the determination of that issue."

Costs consequences following judgment[1]

36.14—(1) This rule applies where upon judgment being entered— 36.14

(a) a claimant fails to obtain a judgment more advantageous than a defendant's Part 36 offer; or

(b) judgment against the defendant is at least as advantageous to the claimant as the proposals contained in a claimant's Part 36 offer.

(2) Subject to paragraph (6), where rule 36.14(1)(a) applies, the court will, unless it considers it unjust to do so, order that the defendant is entitled to—

(a) his costs from the date on which the relevant period expired; and

(b) interest on those costs.

(3) Subject to paragraph (6), where rule 36.14(1)(b) applies, the court will, unless it considers it unjust to do so, order that the claimant is entitled to—

(a) interest on the whole or part of any sum of money (excluding interest) awarded at a rate not exceeding 10% above base rate[GL] for some or all of the period starting with the date on which the relevant period expired;

(b) his costs on the indemnity basis from the date on which the relevant period expired; and

(c) interest on those costs at a rate not exceeding 10% above base rate[GL].

(4) In considering whether it would be unjust to make the orders referred to in paragraphs (2) and (3) above, the court will take into account all the circumstances of the case including—

[1] Introduced by the Civil Procedure (Amendment No.3) Rules 2006 (SI 2006/3435).

(a) the terms of any Part 36 offer;

(b) the stage in the proceedings when any Part 36 offer was made, including in particular how long before the trial started the offer was made;

(c) the information available to the parties at the time when the Part 36 offer was made; and

(d) the conduct of the parties with regard to the giving or refusing to give information for the purposes of enabling the offer to be made or evaluated.

(5) Where the court awards interest under this rule and also awards interest on the same sum and for the same period under any other power, the total rate of interest may not exceed 10% above base rate[GL].

(6) Paragraphs (2) and (3) of this rule do not apply to a Part 36 offer—

(a) that has been withdrawn;

(b) that has been changed so that its terms are less advantageous to the offeree, and the offeree has beaten the less advantageous offer;

(c) made less than 21 days before trial, unless the court has abridged the relevant period.

(Rule 44.3 requires the court to consider an offer to settle that does not have the costs consequences set out in this Part in deciding what order to make about costs)

General Note

36.14.1 The rule now uses the expressions more advantageous than a defendant's Pt 36 offer and at least as advantageous to the claimant as the proposals contained in a claimant's Pt 36 offer. Different consequences follow. In particular the entitlement, unless the court considers it unjust, to the enhancement provisions of r.36.14(3) are not available to the defendant.

These provisions are designed as an incentive to encourage claimants to make and defendants to accept appropriate offers of settlement. Such incentive would be deprived of effect unless the non-acceptance of that which ultimately proves to have been a sufficient offer ordinarily will advantage the claimant in the respects set out in the rule. The enhancement provisions as to costs and interest are designed to redress any perceived unfairness if there was to be no difference between acceptance and non-acceptance. *McPhilemy v Times Newspapers Ltd (No.2)* [2001] EWCA Civ 933; [2002] 1 W.L.R. 934; [2001] 4 All E.R. 861, CA. Further, an order for indemnity costs under the former CPR r.36.21(3), now CPR r.36.14(3), is not penal and carries no stigma or implied disapproval of the defendant's conduct (*ibid.*). See too *Reid Minty v Taylor* [2001] EWCA Civ 1723; [2002] 1 W.L.R. 2800; [2002] 2 All E.R. 150, CA, moral lack of probity or conduct deserving of moral condemnation is not a requisite of jurisdiction to award indemnity costs.

The phrase "more advantageous" is a broad concept to be viewed in the light of all the circumstances of the case and one where a strict monetary comparison was not the governing criterion, *Carver v BAA Plc* [2008] EWCA Civ 412; *The Times*, June 4, 2008 CA. In *Multiplex Constructions (UK) Ltd v Cleveland Bridge UK Ltd* [2008] EWHC 2280 [TCC] the court set out how this principal should be applied in the overall costs decision making process.

In *Hertsmere Primary Trust Care Trust v Administrators of Balasubramanium's Estate* [2005] EWHC 320 (Ch); [2005] 3 All E.R. 274, the Court held that a technical error in complying with r.36.5 (now r.36.2) did not disentitle offeror from the full benefit of r.36.21 (now r.36.14) where the offeree in breach of its duty to co-operate refused to elucidate upon the nature of the error.

The amendments to s.17 of the Judgments Act 1838 enable the court to order interest to run on costs from a date earlier than the judgment (see r.44.3(6)(g)). That power may well be exercised where this Part applies to penalise further the refusal of a reasonable offer.

"...order interest ... at a rate not exceeding 10% above base rate ..."

The court will make in the circumstances specified in this rule such an order unless it considers it unjust to do so. The matters which the court is to consider are set out in para.(4). See *KR v Bryn Alyn Community (Holdings) Ltd (In Liquidation) (Permission to Amend)* [2003] EWCA Civ 383; [2003] P.I.Q.R. P30, CA. Further enhanced interest on any monetary award runs until date of trial judge's judgment and not any later Court of Appeal judgment date (*ibid.*). **36.14.2**

The words "his costs" in the former r.36.21(3)(a) (now r 36.14(3)(b)) mean such costs as would on the application of the principles set out in r.44.3 be awarded disregarding the effect of Pt 36, see *Kastor Navigation Co Ltd v AGF MAT (No.2), The Times*, March 29, 2003, affirmed on this point [2004] EWCA Civ 277.

Enhanced interest/costs

The power to award enhanced interest and costs arises upon judgment being entered. So long as judgment is entered it appears not to matter what particular steps or process (e.g. trial, summary judgment, breach of order or rule) led to judgment being entered. **36.14.3**

Unless it considers it unjust (r.36.14(2) and (3))

The court will doubtless take into account all the circumstances of the case including those specified under r.36.14(4). If an offeree fails to better the Pt 36 offer then the regime provides for an order for costs for the offeror post the period provided for acceptance. The party at risk is then required to establish grounds for rendering it unjust to make the order and such must be found by the court so as to deny the offeror his costs. Considering whether the offeree had reasonable grounds for not accepting as if there was an unfettered discretion as to costs is the incorrect approach and wrong in principle: *Matthews v Metal Improvements* [2007] EWCA Civ 215; [2007] CP Rep.27. In *Ford v GKR Construction* [2000] 1 W.L.R. 1397; [2000] 1 All E.R. 802, the Court of Appeal emphasised the need for parties to litigation to be provided with the information that they needed in order to be able to assess whether to make or to accept an offer to settle under Pt 36. **36.14.4**

In *Factortame v Secretary of State* [2002] EWCA Civ 22; [2002] 1 W.L.R. 2438; [2002] 2 All E.R. 838, CA, (a case involving the acceptance by a claimant of a Pt 36 offer following its significant amendment by the defendant to whom the relevant information had always been available) Walker L.J. (with whom Sedley and Simon Brown L.JJ. agreed) said at p.848, para.27:

> "Each case will turn on its own circumstances. It seems to me that so far as possible the judge should be trying to assess who in reality is the unsuccessful party and who has been responsible for the fact that costs have been incurred which should not have been. It is plainly right that a full-scale trial examining privileged material, and listening to ex post facto justification should be avoided. It furthermore does not seem to me to be right to seek to lay down rules as to where the onus will lie where a defendant is allowed to amend his case. As I have already said straightjackets in this area should be avoided. The starting point is that a claimant who fails to beat [an offer] will prima facie be liable for the costs. An amendment may be of such a character that a judge will feel that the onus should be firmly placed on the defendant to persuade him that the prima facie rule should continue to apply; on the other hand the judge may be quite clear by reference to his feel of the case that the amendment is being used as an excuse *[to accept an offer] that should* have been accepted when originally made. Some cases will lie between the two extremes, and the judge will have to adjust his assessment to give effect to possibilities which it would be inappropriate to try out and thus by reference to his overall view of the case."

Although r.36.14 is silent on whether indemnity costs could be awarded where the claimant fails to better a defendant's Pt 36 offer and although normally standard basis costs would follow, indemnity costs could be awarded if the circumstances of the case justified indemnity costs, *Excelsior Commercial Holdings v Salisbury Hamer Aspden & Johnson* [2002] EWCA Civ 879 and *Balmoral Group Ltd v Borealis (UK) Ltd* [2006] EWHC 2531 (Comm), October 17, unrep. (both cases under the former Pt 36 provision).

Deduction of benefits and lump sum payments[1]

36.15 **36.15 (1) In this rule and rule 36.9 —**

(a) "the 1997 Act" means the Social Security (Recovery of Benefits) Act 1997;

(b) "the 2008 Regulations" means the Social Security (Recovery of Benefits) (Lump Sum Payments) Regulations 2008;

(c) "recoverable amount" means—

(i) "recoverable benefits" as defined in section 1(4)(c) of the 1997 Act; and

(ii) "recoverable lump sum payments" as defined in regulation 4 of the 2008 Regulations;

(d) "deductible amount" means—

(i) any benefits by the amount of which damages are to be reduced in accordance with section 8 of, and Schedule 2 to the 1997 Act ("deductible benefits"); and

(ii) any lump sum payment by the amount of which damages are to be reduced in accordance with regulation 12 of the 2008 Regulations ("deductible lump sum payments"); and

(e) "certificate"—

(i) in relation to recoverable benefits is construed in accordance with the provisions of the 1997 Act; and

(ii) in relation to recoverable lump sum payments has the meaning given in section 29 of the 1997 Act as applied by regulation 2 of, and modified by Schedule 1 to the 2008 Regulations.

(2) This rule applies where a payment to a claimant following acceptance of a Part 36 offer would be a compensation payment as defined in section 1(4)(b) or 1A(5)(b) of the 1997 Act.

(3) A defendant who makes a Part 36 offer should state either—

(a) that the offer is made without regard to any liability for recoverable amounts; or

(b) that it is intended to include any deductible amounts.

(4) Where paragraph (3)(b) applies, paragraphs (5) to (9) of this rule will apply to the Part 36 offer.

(5) Before making the Part 36 offer, the offeror must apply for a certificate.

(6) Subject to paragraph (7), the Part 36 offer must state—

(a) the amount of gross compensation;

(b) the name and amount of any deductible amount by which the gross amount is reduced; and

(c) the net amount of compensation.

[1] Amended by the Civil Procedure (Amendment) Rules 2008 (SI 2008/2178).

(7) If at the time the offeror makes the Part 36 offer, the offeror has applied for, but has not received a certificate, the offeror must clarify the offer by stating the matters referred to in paragraphs (6)(b) and (6)(c) not more than 7 days after receipt of the certificate.

(8) For the purposes of rule 36.14(1)(a), a claimant fails to recover more than any sum offered (including a lump sum offered under rule 36.5) if the claimant fails upon judgment being entered to recover a sum, once deductible amounts identified in the judgment have been deducted, greater than the net amount stated under paragraph (6)(c).

"(Section 15(2) of the 1997 Act provides that the court must specify the compensation payment attributable to each head of damage. Schedule 1 to the 2008 Regulations modifies section 15 of the 1997 Act in relation to lump sum payments and provides that the court must specify the compensation payment attributable to each or any dependant who has received a lump sum payment.)

(9) Where—

(a) further deductible amounts have accrued since the Part 36 offer was made; and

(b) the court gives permission to accept the Part 36 offer,

the court may direct that the amount of the offer payable to the offeree shall be reduced by a sum equivalent to the deductible amounts paid to the claimant since the date of the offer.

(Rule 36.9(3)(b) states that permission is required to accept an offer where the relevant period has expired and further deductible benefits have been paid to the claimant)

"... but has not received a certificate of recoverable benefit" (r.36.15(7))

This is a provision allowing a defendant to make an offer to settle at a time when he has applied for but not received a certificate which will have the consequences set out in Pt 36. The conditions specified must be complied with to achieve such consequences. **36.15.1**

Rule 36.15(6) and (7)

Care must be taken to ensure that the amount of benefit received to be set-off is set-off only against the appropriate head of damage in respect of which the benefit has been paid (e.g. past loss of earnings) and not brought generally into account. Further, any adjustment of the certificated amount is a matter for the compensator to pursue, see *Williams v Devon CC* [2003] EWCA Civ 365; *The Times*, March 18, 2003. **36.15.2**

PRACTICE DIRECTION—OFFERS TO SETTLE

This Practice Direction supplements CPR Part 36

Formalities of Part 36 offers and other notices under this part

36PD.1 **1.1** A Part 36 offer may be made using Form **N242A**.

1.2 Where a Part 36 offer, notice of acceptance or notice of withdrawal or change of terms is to be served on a party who is legally represented, the document to be served must be served on the legal representative.

36PD.1.1 *Note* —Form **N242A** can be found in the *Civil Procedure Forms Volume*.

Application for permission to withdraw a Part 36 offer

36PD.2 **2.1** Rule 36.3(4) provides that before expiry of the relevant period a Part 36 offer may only be withdrawn or its terms changed to be less advantageous to the offeree with the permission of the court.

2.2 The permission of the court must be sought—

(1) by making an application under Part 23, which must be dealt with by a judge other than the judge (if any) allocated in advance to conduct the trial, unless the parties agree that such judge may hear the application;

(2) at a trial or other hearing, provided that it is not to the trial judge or to the judge (if any) allocated in advance to conduct the trial, unless the parties agree that such judge may hear the application.

36PD.2.1 *Note* — Rule 36.3(4) above should read 36.3(5).

Acceptance of a Part 36 offer

36PD.3 **3.1** Where a Part 36 offer is accepted in accordance with rule 36.9(1) the notice of acceptance must be served on the offeror and filed with the court where the case is proceeding.

3.2 Where the court's permission is required to accept a Part 36 offer, the permission of the court must be sought—

(1) by making an application under Part 23, which must be dealt with by a judge other than the judge (if any) allocated in advance to conduct the trial, unless the parties agree that such judge may hear the application;

(2) at a trial or other hearing, provided that it is not to the trial judge or to the judge (if any) allocated in advance to conduct the trial, unless the parties agree that such judge may hear the application.

3.3 Where rule 36.9(3)(b) applies, the application for permission to accept the offer must—

(1) state—

(a) the net amount offered in the Part 36 offer;

(b) the deductible amounts that had accrued at the date the offer was made;

(c) the deductible amounts that have subsequently accrued; and

(2) be accompanied by a copy of the current certificate.

Note on former PD 36 para.7.10 (the White Book 2006 edn) — Re para.7.10 of the pre-April 6, 2007 Pt 36 Practice Direction (in respect of payments made under this provision) see the *White Book* 2006 edn, Vol.1 at para.36PD.7. **36PD.3.1**

For the purposes of this provision "the date of acceptance" which is material to determine the distribution of interest accrued on monies paid in is the date of a valid acceptance which in the case of a minor or protected party is the date when the acceptance has been approved by the court: *Brennan v ECO Compositing Ltd* [2006] EWHC 3153 (QB); [2007] 1 W.L.R. 773; [2007] 3 All E.R. 67.

PRACTICE DIRECTION B SUPPLEMENTING PART 36

This Practice Direction supplements CPR Part 36

From 6th April 2007, new rules came into force concerning offers to settle, and Part 36, as it was in force immediately before 6th April 2007, was substituted by a new Part 36.

Rule 7 of the Civil Procedure (Amendment No.3) Rules 2006 that brought those new rules into force and replaced the previous rules contained some provisions that dealt with how the rules are to apply to offers and payments into court made before 6th April 2007.

This Practice Direction explains how those provisions will operate.

36BPD.0.1 *Note*—For r.7 of the Civil Procedure (Amendment No.3) Rules 2006 see para.36.0.3 above.

Offers and payments made before 6th April 2007

36BPD.1 **1.1** Paragraph (2) of rule 7 provides that where a Part 36 offer or Part 36 payment was made before 6th April 2007, if it would have had the consequences set out in the rules of court contained in Part 36 as it was in force immediately before 6th April 2007, it will have the consequences set out in rules 36.10, 36.11 and 36.14 after that date.

1.2 This provision makes clear that a Part 36 offer or Part 36 payment that was valid before 6th April 2007, will continue to be a valid Part 36 offer under the rules in force from 6th April 2007, and will have the consequences set out in those rules, specifically in relation to costs and the effect of acceptance.

Permission of the court

36BPD.2 **2.1** Paragraph (3) of rule 7 provides that where a Part 36 offer or Part 36 payment was made before 6th April 2007, the permission of the court is required to accept that offer or payment, if permission would have been required under the rules of court contained in Part 36 as it was in force immediately before 6th April 2007.

2.2 This provision preserves the requirement to obtain the permission of the court to accept an offer as it existed under the rules in force immediately before 6th April 2007. Therefore, if permission would have been required before 6th April 2007, it will be required after that date. But, if permission would not have been required because the parties have been able to agree liability for costs, or if a further offer has been made triggering a new period for acceptance, permission will not be required after 6th April 2007.

Payments into court made before 6th April 2007

36BPD.3 **3.1** Paragraph (4) of rule 7 provides that rule 37.3 will apply to a Part 36 payment made before 6th April 2007 as if that payment into court had been made under a court order.

3.2 Rule 37.3 applies to all payments under Part 37, including payments into court under order, and permission is required to take the money out of court.

3.3 By applying rule 37.3 to payments into court made before 6th April 2007, this provision preserves in particular the requirement that permission be obtained to withdraw such payment.

3.4 But, rule 37.3 also provides that money may be taken out of court without the court's permission where a Part 36 offer (including an offer underlying a Part 36 payment) is accepted without needing the permission of the court and the defendant agrees that the sum may be paid out in satisfaction of the offer. Paragraph 3.4 of the Practice Direction to Part 37 makes provision about how to take money out of court.

3.5 This exception to the permission requirement preserves the right under rule 37.2, as it was in force immediately before 6th April 2007, to treat a payment into court made under order or by way of a defence of tender before claim as a Part 36 payment.

3.6 This provision has the effect that a Part 36 payment made before 6th April 2007 may be taken out of court simply by filing a request for payment if the offer underlying the Part 36 payment is accepted without needing permission. In those circumstances, it may be assumed that the defendant agrees to the money being used in satisfaction of the sum offered, and the requirement in paragraph 3.4 of the Practice Direction to Part 37 to file a Form 202 will not apply.

Offers remaining open for acceptance

4.1 Paragraph (5) of rule 7 provides that the rules of court contained in Part 36 as it was in force immediately before 6th April 2007 shall continue to apply to a Part 36 offer or Part 36 payment made less than 21 days before 6th April 2007. **36BPD.4**

4.2 This provision preserves those rules in their entirety in relation to offers and payments made less than 21 days before 6th April 2007 for the period that they are expressed to remain open for acceptance.

4.3 Paragraph (6) of rule 7 provides that paragraph (5) ceases to apply at the expiry of 21 days from the date that the offer or payment was made, unless the trial has started within that period.

4.4 This provision has the effect that once the 21 day period has expired, the new regime (including the modifications at paragraphs (2), (3) and (4) of rule 7) will apply to the offer or payment.

4.5 If the trial has started within the 21 day period, the rules that were in force before 6th April 2007 will continue to apply to the offer or payment.

Offers made before commencement of proceedings

5.1 Paragraph (7) of rule 7 deals with the position where, before 6th April 2007, a person made an offer to settle before commencement of proceedings which complied with the provisions of rule 36.10 as it was in force immediately before 6th April 2007. **36BPD.5**

5.2 The court will take that offer into account when making any order as to costs. This preserves the discretion of the court to take into account an offer made before commencement of proceedings as it existed before 6th April 2007.

5.3 The permission of the court will be required to accept such an offer after proceedings have been commenced. This preserves the position under rule 36.10(4) as it was in force immediately before 6th April 2007.

5.4 If proceedings are commenced after 6th April 2007, the requirement to pay money into court in respect of a defendant's money offer under rule 36.10(3)(a) (as it was in force before 6th April 2007) will not an apply to a defendant's money offer made before the proceedings were commenced.

36BPD.5.1 *Note*—For r.36.10 as it was before see the *White Book*, 2006 edn, Vol.1, at para.36.10.

PART 37

Miscellaneous Provisions about Payments into Court

Contents

37.0.1

Editorial introduction

If money is paid into court under a court order notice of such payment must be given to every other party and such money may not be paid out without court order, see r.37.1(a) below, save as provided under r.37.3. 37.0.2

If a defendant wishes to rely upon a defence of tender he must make a payment into court of the amount he says was tendered, see r.37.2(1).

Money paid into court under a court order or in support of a defence of tender may not be paid out without court permission except where a Pt 36 offer is accepted without needing court permission and the defendant agrees that a sum paid into court by him should be used to satisfy the offer in whole or in part, see r.37.3.

Rule 37.4 provides that a Practice Direction may set out special provisions with regard to payments into court under various enactments. The Practice Direction (Miscellaneous Provisions about Payment into Court), supplementing Pt 37, is set out at para.37PD.1 *et seq.* below, and concerns payments into court under the Life Assurance Companies (Payment into Court) Act 1896, under the Trustee Act 1925, and under the Vehicular Access Across Common and Other Land (England) Regulations 2002 (SI 2002/1711). See further para.37.4.1 below.

Related sources

- Part 23 Applications to Court, see paras 23.0.1 *et seq.* 37.0.3
- Part 36 Offers to Settle, see paras 36.1 *et seq.*
- Practice Direction (Miscellaneous Provisions about Payments Into Court) (see paras 37PD.1 *et seq.*)

Forms

- **N244** 37.0.4
- **N244A**
- Court Funds Office Forms **Form 100**, **Form 201** and **Form 202**

Money paid into court under a court order[1]

37.1—(1) A party who makes a payment into court under a court order must— 37.1

(a) *serve notice* of the payment on every other party; and

(b) in relation to each such notice, file a certificate of service.

Formalities of payment into court under order

See PD 37 paras 1.1 to 1.2 (see para.37PD.1). 37.1.1

[1] Introduced By the Civil Procedure (Amendment No.3) Rules 2006 (SI 2006/3435).

Money paid into court where defendant wishes to rely on a defence of tender before claim[1]

37.2 **37.2—(1) Where a defendant wishes to rely on a defence of tender before claim[GL] he must make a payment into court of the amount he says was tendered.**

(2) If the defendant does not make a payment in accordance with paragraph (1), the defence of tender before claim will not be available to him until he does so.

Formalities of payment into court where defence of tender before claim

37.2.1 See PD 37 paras 1.1 and 1.2 (see para.37PD.1).

Payment out of money paid into court[2]

37.3 **37.3—(1) Money paid into court under a court order or in support of a defence of tender before claim[GL] may not be paid out without the court's permission except where—**

(a) a Part 36 offer is accepted without needing the permission of the court; and

(b) the defendant agrees that a sum paid into court by him should be used to satisfy the offer (in whole or in part).

(Rule 36.9 sets out when the court's permission is required to accept a Part 36 offer)

Formalities of payment out of court

37.3.1 See PD 37 paras 3.1 to 3.8 (see para.37PD.3, **Form 201** and **Form 202**).

Payment into court under enactments[3]

37.4 **37.4 A practice direction may set out special provisions with regard to payments into court under various enactments.**

Practice Direction—Miscellaneous Provisions About Payments into Court

37.4.1 This Practice Direction is set out at 37PD.1 *et seq.* below. It concerns the following enactments: the Life Assurance Companies (Payment into Court) Act 1896, the Trustee Act 1925, and the Vehicular Access Across Common and Other Land (England) Regulations 2002 (SI 2002/1711).

For the provisions in respect of the Fatal Accidents Act 1976 and the Law Reform (Miscellaneous Provisions) Act 1934, which hitherto appeared at r.37(4) of Pt 37 as it was pre-April 6, 2007, see now r.41.3A at para.41.3A above.

---

[1] Introduced by the Civil Procedure (Amendment No.3) Rules 2006 (SI 2006/3435).
[2] Introduced by the Civil Procedure (Amendment No.3) Rules 2006 (SI 2006/3435).
[3] Introduced by the Civil Procedure (Amendment No.3) Rules 2006 (SI 2006/3435).

PRACTICE DIRECTION—MISCELLANEOUS PROVISIONS ABOUT PAYMENTS INTO COURT

This Practice Direction supplements CPR Part 37

Payment into court under an order, etc

1.1 Except where paragraph 1.2 applies, a party paying money into court under an order or in support of a defence of tender before claim must— **37PD.1**

(1) send to the Court Funds Office—
  (a) the payment, usually a cheque made payable to the Accountant General of the Supreme Court;
  (b) a sealed copy of the order or a copy of the defence; and
  (c) a completed Court Funds Office form 100;

(2) serve a copy of the form 100 on each other party; and

(3) file at the court—
  (a) a copy of the form 100; and
  (b) a certificate of service confirming service of a copy of that form on each party served.

1.2 Instead of complying with paragraph 1.1(1), a litigant in person without a current account may, in a claim proceeding in a county court or District Registry, make a payment into court by—

(1) lodging the payment in cash with the court; and

(2) giving the court a completed Court Funds Office form 100.

Note —Form **100** can be found in the *Civil Procedure Forms Volume*. **37PD.1.1**

Applications relating to funds in court

2.1 This paragraph applies to an application relating to money or securities which have been paid into court other than an application for the payment out of the money or securities (for example, an application for money to be invested, or for payment of interest to any person). **37PD.2**

2.2 An application—

(1) must be made in accordance with Part 23; and

(2) may be made without notice, but the court may direct notice to be served on any person.

(Where money paid into court is accepted by or on behalf of a child or protected party, rule 21.11(1)(b) provides that the money shall be dealt with in accordance with directions given by the court under that rule and not otherwise. Paragraphs 8 to 13 of the practice direction supplementing Part 21 make further provision about how the money may be dealt with).

Note —For CPR r.21.11.(1)(b) and paras 8 to 13 of the Practice Direction supplementing Pt 21 see respectively para.21.11 and 21PD.8 *et seq.* above. **37PD.2.1**

Payment out of court

3.1 Rule 37.3 provides that the court's permission is required to take money out of court except where the defendant agrees that the money which has been paid into court should be used to satisfy a Part 36 offer. **37PD.3**

3.2 Permission may be obtained by making an application in accordance with Part 23. The application notice must state the grounds on which the order for payment out is sought. Evidence of any facts on which the applicant relies may also be necessary.

3.3 Where the court gives permission under rule 37.3, it will include a direction for the payment out of any money in court, including any interest accrued.

3.4 Where permission is not required to take money out of court, the requesting party should file a request for payment in Court Funds Office form 201 with the Court Funds Office, accompanied by a statement that the defendant agrees that the money should be used to satisfy the Part 36offer in Court Funds Office form 202.

(Paragraph 3.6 of Practice Direction B supplementing Part 36 provides that a defendant who made a Part 36 payment before 6th April 2007, and whose Part 36 offer underlying the payment is accepted without requiring the permission of the court, is not required to file form 202.).

3.5 The request for payment should contain the following details—

(1) where the party receiving the payment is legally represented—

(a) the name, business address and reference of the legal representative; and

(b) the name of the bank and the sort code number, the title of the account and the account number where the payment is to be transmitted;

(2) where the party is acting in person–

(a) his name and address; and

(b) his bank account details as in paragraph (1)(b) above; and

(3) whether the party receiving the payment is, or has been, in receipt of services funded by the Legal Services Commission as part of the Community Legal Service.

3.6 Where paragraph 3.4 applies, interest accruing up to the date of acceptance will be paid to the defendant.

(Rule 20.2 provides that in these Rules references to a claimant or defendant include a party bringing or defending an additional claim).

3.7 Subject to paragraph 3.8, if a party does not wish the payment to be transmitted into his bank account or if he does not have a bank account, he may send a written request to the Accountant-General for the payment to be made to him by cheque.

3.8 Where a party seeking payment out of court has provided the necessary information, the payment—

(1) where a party is legally represented, must be made to the legal representative;

(2) if the party is not legally represented but has given notice under paragraph 3.5(3), must be made to the Legal Services Commission.

37PD.3.1 *Note*—For CPR r.37.3 see para.37.3 above. Form **201** and Form **202** can be found in the *Civil Procedure Forms Volume*.

Payment into court by life assurance company

4.1 A company wishing to make a payment into court under the Life Assurance Companies (Payment into Court) Act 1896 ('the 1896 Act') must file a witness statement or an affidavit setting out— **37PD.4**

(1) a short description of the policy under which money is payable;

(2) a statement of the persons entitled under the policy, including their names and addresses so far as known to the company;

(3) a short statement of—
 (a) the notices received by the company making any claim to the money assured, or withdrawing any such claim;
 (b) the dates of receipt of such notices; and
 (c) the names and addresses of the persons by whom they were given;

(4) a statement that, in the opinion of the board of directors of the company, no sufficient discharge can be obtained for the money which is payable, other than by paying it into court under the 1896 Act;

(5) a statement that the company agrees to comply with any order or direction the court may make—
 (a) to pay any further sum into court; or
 (b) to pay any costs;

(6) an undertaking by the company to immediately send to the Accountant General at the Court Funds Office any notice of claim received by the company after the witness statement or affidavit has been filed, together with a letter referring to the Court Funds Office reference number; and

(7) the company's address for service.

4.2 The witness statement or affidavit must be filed at—

(1) Chancery Chambers at the Royal Courts of Justice, or

(2) a Chancery district registry of the High Court.

4.3 The company must not deduct from the money payable by it under the policy any costs of the payment into court, except for any court fee.

4.4 If the company is a party to any proceedings issued in relation to the policy or the money assured by it, it may not make a payment into court under the 1896 Act without the permission of the court in those proceedings.

4.5 If a company pays money into court under the 1896 Act, unless the court orders otherwise it must immediately serve notice of the payment on every person who is entitled under the policy or has made a claim to the money assured.

Application for payment out of money paid into court by life assurance company

5.1 Any application for the payment out of money which has been paid into court under the 1896 Act must be made in accordance with paragraph 3 of this practice direction. **37PD.5**

5.2 The application must be served on—

(1) every person stated in the written evidence of the company which made the payment to be entitled to or to have an interest in the money;

(2) any other person who has given notice of a claim to the money; and

(3) the company which made the payment, if an application is being made for costs against it, but not otherwise.

Payment into court under Trustee Act 1925

37PD.6 **6.1** A trustee wishing to make a payment into court under section 63 of the Trustee Act 1925 must file a witness statement or an affidavit setting out —

(1) a short description of—
  (a) the trust; and
  (b) the instrument creating the trust, or the circumstances in which the trust arose;

(2) the names of the persons interested in or entitled to the money or securities to be paid into court, with their address so far as known to him;

(3) a statement that he agrees to answer any inquiries which the court may make or direct relating to the application of the money or securities; and

(4) his address for service.

6.2 The witness statement or affidavit must be filed at—

(1) Chancery Chambers at the Royal Courts of Justice;

(2) a Chancery district registry of the High Court; or

(3) a county court.

6.3 If a trustee pays money or securities into court, unless the court orders otherwise he must immediately serve notice of the payment into court on every person interested in or entitled to the money or securities.

Application for payment out of funds paid into court by trustee

37PD.7 **7.1** An application for the payment out of any money or securities paid into court under section 63 of the Trustee Act 1925 must be made in accordance with paragraph 3 of this practice direction.

7.2 The application may be made without notice, but the court may direct notice to be served on any person.

Payment into court under Vehicular Access Across Common And Other Land (England) Regulations 2002

37PD.8 **8.1** In this section of this Practice Direction—

(1) expressions used have the meanings given by the Vehicular Access Across Common and Other Land (England) Regulations 2002; and

(2) a regulation referred to by number alone means the regulation so numbered in those Regulations.

8.2 Where the applicant wishes to pay money into a county court under regulation 14 he must file a witness statement or an affidavit when he lodges the money.

8.3 The witness statement or affidavit must—

(1) state briefly why the applicant is making the payment into court; and

(2) be accompanied by copies of—

(a) the notice served under regulation 6;

(b) any counter-notice served under regulation 8;

(c) any amended notice or counter-notice served under regulation 9;

(d) any determination of the Lands Tribunal of a matter referred to it under regulation 10; and

(e) any determination of the value of the premises by a chartered surveyor following the service of a valuation notice under regulation 12.

8.4 If an applicant pays money into court under regulation 14, he must immediately serve notice of the payment and a copy of the witness statement or affidavit on the land owner.

8.5 An application for payment out of the money must be made in accordance with paragraph 3 of this practice direction.

PART 38

DISCONTINUANCE

Contents

Editorial introduction

38.0.2 Discontinuance by the claimant terminates the claim in whole or in part (see r.38.2(1)).

Permission to discontinue is required by the claimant only in the situations prescribed by r.38.2(2).

A claimant who discontinues is liable for the defendant's costs unless the court orders otherwise (r.38.6).

Practice Direction

38.0.3 Part 38 is not supplemented by a Practice Direction.

Related sources

38.0.4 Part 17 Practice Direction (amendment) to Pt 39, para.4 (see para.39PD.1).

Forms

38.0.5 **N729** Notice of discontinuance

Scope of this Part

38.1 **38.1—(1) The rules in this Part set out the procedure by which a claimant may discontinue all or part of a claim.**

(2) A claimant who—

(a) claims more than one remedy; and

(b) subsequently abandons his claim to one or more of the remedies but continues with his claim for the other remedies,

is not treated as discontinuing all or part of a claim for the purposes of this Part.

(The procedure for amending a statement of case, set out in Part 17, applies where a claimant abandons a claim for a particular remedy but wishes to continue with his claim for other remedies.)

Effect of rule

38.1.1 The word "claim" in RSC O.21 was used in the sense of "cause of action" rather than a form of relief. Part 38 is clearly to like effect. Thus a claimant may discontinue *all or part of a claim* but a claimant who merely abandons one or more of the remedies sought is not treated as discontinuing for the purposes of Pt 38. (*cf.* the power to amend in Pt 17 which may result in the withdrawal of part of a claim.) A notice of discontinuance is a decision of the court for the purposes of the Companies Act 1989 s.394(7) (*Jarvis Plc v PricewaterhouseCoopers* [2001] B.C.C. 670, Ch D).

Right to discontinue claim

38.2—(1) A claimant may discontinue all or part of a claim at any time. 38.2

(2) However—

(a) a claimant must obtain the permission of the court if he wishes to discontinue all or part of a claim in relation to which—

(i) the court has granted an interim injunction[GL]; or

(ii) any party has given an undertaking to the court;

(b) where the claimant has received an interim payment in relation to a claim (whether voluntarily or pursuant to an order under Part 25), he may discontinue that claim only if—

(i) the defendant who made the interim payment consents in writing; or

(ii) the court gives permission;

(c) where there is more than one claimant, a claimant may not discontinue unless—

(i) every other claimant consents in writing; or

(ii) the court gives permission.

(3) Where there is more than one defendant, the claimant may discontinue all or part of a claim against all or any of the defendants.

Effect of rule

Rule 38.2 is clear. As a general rule it gives the claimant, a right to discontinue all or part of a claim at any time without having first to seek the permission of the court. Permission is required only in the special situations provided for by r.38.2(2). The claimant may discontinue all or part of a claim against all or any of the defendants. 38.2.1

For the procedure to discontinue see r.38.3 and for the costs consequences see r.38.6.

Permission to discontinue

Permission to discontinue under CPR r.38.2(a)(i) is only required where discontinuance is sought in relation to a party against whom an interim injunction has been obtained. It does not apply in relation to other parties to the action against whom no such relief has been granted (*KGM v Generali Kent Sigorta* June 25, 2002, unrep., QBD Commercial Court). 38.2.2

Procedure for discontinuing

38.3—(1) To discontinue a claim or part of a claim, a claimant must— 38.3

(a) file a notice of discontinuance; and

***(b) serve a copy* of it on every other party to the proceedings.**

(2) The claimant must state in the notice of discontinuance which he files that he has served notice of discontinuance on every other party to the proceedings.

(3) Where the claimant needs the consent of some other party, a copy of the necessary consent must be attached to the notice of discontinuance.

(4) Where there is more than one defendant, the notice of discontinuance must specify against which defendants the claim is discontinued.

Notice of discontinuance

38.3.1 Unless permission or consent is required (see r.38.2 above, all that is required to discontinue is for the claimant to file notice of discontinuance with the court and serve a copy of it on every other party to the proceedings. A notice of discontinuance must comply with r.38.3(2), (3) and (4) and must be in Form **N279**. A notice of discontinuance takes effect on the day that it is served (CPR, r.38.5 and *Jarvis Plc v PricewaterhouseCoopers*, [2001] B.C.C. 670, Ch D).

Discontinuance after the trial date is fixed

38.3.2 Practice Direction to Pt 39, para.4.1 provides that the listing officer must be informed immediately if a claim is discontinued after a date or "window" has been fixed for trial.

Right to apply to have notice of discontinuance set aside

38.4 **38.4—(1) Where the claimant discontinues under rule 38.2(1) the defendant may apply to have the notice of discontinuance set aside.**[GL]

(2) The defendant may not make an application under this rule more than 28 days after the date when the notice of discontinuance was served on him.

Effect of rule

38.4.1 The rule provides a procedure and time limit for a defendant to apply to have a notice of discontinuance set aside.

A court may set aside a notice of discontinuance as an abuse of the process of the court (*Ernst and Young v Butte Mining plc* [1996] 1 W.L.R. 1605; *Fakih Bros v Moller (Copenhagen)* [1994] 1 Lloyd's Rep. 103).

A defendant who would have opposed an application for permission must invoke r.38.4 and apply to have the notice of discontinuance set aside within 28 days of service of the notice upon him.

Application

38.4.2 Such an application should be made with notice and be supported by evidence (see Pt 23, Practice Direction to Pt 23, para.9 and r.32.2).

When discontinuance takes effect where permission of the court is not needed

38.5 **38.5—(1) Discontinuance against any defendant takes effect on the date when notice of discontinuance is served on him under rule 38.3(1).**

(2) Subject to rule 38.4, the proceedings are brought to an end as against him on that date.

(3) However, this does not affect proceedings to deal with any question of costs.

"Where permission of the court is not needed"

38.5.1 Permission to discontinue is not required as a general rule. However, permission is required in the special situations set out in r.38.2(2).

Effect of rule

38.5.2 Discontinuance takes effect on the date when notice of discontinuance is served. In a case where permission to discontinue is required pursuant to r.38.2(2) the order granting permission will provide for the date when discontinuance takes effect.

"question of costs"

See r.38.6. 38.5.3

Liability for costs[1]

38.6—(1) Unless the court orders otherwise, a claimant who discontinues is liable for the costs which a defendant against whom the claimant discontinues incurred on or before the date on which notice of discontinuance was served on the defendant. 38.6

(2) If proceedings are only partly discontinued—

(a) the claimant is liable under paragraph (1) for costs relating only to the part of the proceedings which he is discontinuing; and

(b) unless the court orders otherwise, the costs which the claimant is liable to pay must not be assessed until the conclusion of the rest of the proceedings.

(3) This rule does not apply to claims allocated to the small claims track.

(Rule 44.12 provides for the basis of assessment where the right to costs arises on discontinuance and contains provisions about when a costs order is deemed to have been made and applying for an order under section 194(3) of the Legal Services Act 2007.)

Effect of rule

The general rule is that a claimant is liable for the defendant's costs up to the date when notice of the discontinuance is served (CPR r.38.6(1)), see e.g. *Three Rivers DC v Governor and Company of the Bank of England* [2006] EWHC 816 (Comm), April 12, 2006 (Tomlinson J.) and in relation to proceedings under Landlord and Tenant Act 1954 s.24, *Lay v Drexler* [2007] EWCA Civ 464; *The Times*, June 20, 2007 (by filing an acknowledgement of service, tenants were in effect commencing their own proceedings. When they were terminated by the tenants' unilateral act, that was equivalent to a decision to discontinue and so the normal costs order should follow.). An order is deemed to have been made in the defendant's favour on the standard basis (see r.44.12(1)). For the procedure for assessing costs, see r.44.7.Statutory interest on costs runs from the date of service of the notice of discontinuance—see r.44.12(2). 38.6.1

A claimant who wishes to avoid an order for costs may apply under r.38.6. Where an application is made to discontinue, with some other order for costs, the burden is on the party making that application. See *In re Walker Wingsail Systems Plc, Walker v Walker* [2005] EWCA Civ 247; [2006] 1 W.L.R. 2194; [2005] C.P. Rep. 33 where the Court of Appeal found that there had been no change in circumstances since the issue of the claim and that there was nothing to show that it was fair to depart from the general rule. The fact that the claimant had become alive at a late stage to the commercial effect of factors, which were clear at the outset and, if properly evaluated could have led to a decision in 1999 that the proceedings were not worth pursuing, was not a good reason.

See too *R. v Bassettlaw DC Ex p. Aldergate Estates Ltd*, April 17, 2000, unrep., (Jackson J.) noted at *Civil Procedure News* Issue 6/2000 p.4 (good claim was withdrawn because it had become academic as a result of concession by another party); *Aegis Group plc v Inland Revenue [2005]* EWHC 1468 (Ch); May 13, 2005 (costs reduced to reflect the defendant's failure to comply with the judicial review pre action protocol); *In re the estate of Jean Wylde, deceased (Wylde v Culver)*, unrep., April 12, 2006, Ch D (G Bompas Q.C.) (no order as to costs where there was no evidence to show that the claimant had acted unreasonably or in bad faith in challenging the will);and *RBG Resources Plc (In Liquidation) v Viren Kumar Rastogi* [2004] EWHC 994 (ChD); May 24, 2005 (defendant's unreasonable and unjustified stance in negotiations for settlement, a good reason to

[1] Amended by the Civil Procedure (Amendment) Rules 2008 (SI 2008/2178).

order that he should be deprived of a proportion of his costs on discontinuance); *cf. Reid v The Capita Group Plc*, October 17, 2005, unrep., Ch D (claimant ordered to pay defendant's costs where the issue of proceedings was premature and there was insufficient notice of proceedings to defendant).

Note that the normal rule as to costs does not apply if a claimant in a case allocated to the small claims track serves a notice of discontinuance (r.38.6(3)) although it might be contended that costs should be awarded if a party has behaved unreasonably (r.27.14(2)(d)).

Basis for costs

38.6.2 In view of CPR r.44.12(1)(d) a costs order following service of a notice of discontinuance is deemed to be on the standard basis, but CPR r.38.6(1) which gives the court power to order otherwise, allows the court, where there are exceptional circumstances, to order costs on the indemnity basis (*Atlantic Bar and Grill Ltd v Posthouse Hotels Ltd* [2000] C.P. Rep. 32.

Discontinuance and subsequent proceedings

38.7 **38.7 A claimant who discontinues a claim needs the permission of the court to make another claim against the same defendant if—**

(a) he discontinued the claim after the defendant filed a defence; and

(b) the other claim arises out of facts which are the same or substantially the same as those relating to the discontinued claim.

Effect of rule

38.7.1 As a matter of common sense a claimant who has brought and then abandoned a claim ought not, as a general rule, to be allowed to start another claim arising out of the same facts.

A claimant who wishes to do so is first required to seek permission. The court is likely to give permission, for example, where the claimant was misled or tricked by the defendant, where important new evidence has come to light or where there has been a retrospective change in the law (e.g. a House of Lords case overruling a Court of Appeal decision which had led the claimant to discontinue). All these examples are, of course, exceptional cases and assume that the limitation period has still not expired.

Under the former practice of former RSC O.21, r.3 where leave to discontinue was required, the court would often impose terms as a condition of granting leave including a term that no new action be brought. Such an order is no longer required as r.38.7 puts the onus on the claimant to seek permission before making another claim against the same defendant arising out of the same facts.

The rule is silent as to how the claimant seeks permission. Therefore the general rules in Pt 23 apply. The application should be on notice with evidence.

Permission for another claim is not required if the claimant discontinues the first claim before the defendant filed a defence.

Stay of remainder of partly discontinued proceedings where costs not paid[1]

38.8 **38.8—(1) This rule applies where—**

(a) proceedings are partly discontinued;

(b) a claimant is liable to—

(i) pay costs under rule 38.6; or

(ii) make a payment pursuant to an order under section 194(3) of the Legal Services Act 2007; and

---

[1] Amended by the Civil Procedure (Amendment No.3) Rules 2000 (SI 2000/1317) and the Civil Procedure (Amendment) Rules 2008 (SI 2008/2178).

(c) the claimant fails to pay those costs or make the payment within 14 days of—

(i) the date on which the parties agreed the sum payable by the claimant; or

(ii) the date on which the court ordered the costs to be paid.

(2) Where this rule applies, the court may stay[GL] the remainder of the proceedings until the claimant pays the whole of the costs which the claimant is liable to pay under rule 38.6 or makes the payment pursuant to an order under section 194(3) of the Legal Services Act 2007.

(Rules 44.3C and 44.12 contain provisions about applying for an order under section 194(3) of the Legal Services Act 2007.)

Effect of rule

Rule 38.8 needs to be read in conjunction with r.38.6. Under r.38.6, if proceedings are only partly discontinued, the claimant is liable for the defendant's costs relating to the part of the proceedings which are discontinued, but, unless the court orders otherwise, the costs which the claimant is liable to pay must not be assessed until the conclusion of the rest of the proceedings. Rule 38.8 can only come into play, therefore, where the court has ordered otherwise under r.38.6(2)(b). If the court has ordered otherwise the claimant must pay the defendant's costs within 14 days (r.38.8(1)(c)) and if he fails to do so the court may stay the remainder of the proceedings until the costs have been paid. Rule 38.8(2) provides that the court "may stay" the remainder of the proceedings. Thus a stay is not automatic and an application to the court is required. 38.8.1

Note that the time for payment of costs was reduced form 21 days to 14 days by the Civil Procedure (Amendment No.3) Rules 2000 which came into effect on July 3, 2000.

PART 39

MISCELLANEOUS PROVISIONS RELATING TO HEARINGS

Contents

39.0.1

Editorial introduction

39.0.2 As its title suggests this Part sweeps up various remaining provisions concerning hearings, in particular setting out which hearings should be in public and which should be in private. There are two practice directions. Significantly the first Practice Direction (see para.39PD.1) deals with a number of subjects not dealt with in the Rules themselves, namely settlement or discontinuance after the fixing of a trial date, recording of proceedings and exhibits. The First Practice Direction was amended in May 1999 (new paras 5.2 to 5.5). The Second Practice Direction (39BPD.1) deals with court sittings in the High Court and Court of Appeal. It was amended in May 1999 (changes to paras 3.2 and 3.3(2)).

With effect from October 2, 2006, r.39.8 (Claims under the Race Relations Act 1976), which was inserted in this Part by the Civil Procedure (Amendment No.2) Rules 2001 (SI 2001/1388), was revoked by the Civil Procedure (Amendment) Rules 2006 (SI 2006/1689), together with the related provision of Sch.2 CCR O.49, r.17. Further, from the same date Practice Direction (Claims under the Race Relations Act 1976 (National Security)), which supplemented r.39.8, was omitted—see CPR Update 42. In effect, the provisions revoked and omitted were replaced by paras 5.1 to 5.5 of Practice Direction (Proceedings under Enactments Relating to Discrimination), first published in that Update (see para.B13–001 below).

Related sources

39.0.3
- Practice Directions to Pt 39 (see paras 39PD.1 and 39BPD.1.)
- Practice Direction 54D—Administrative Court (Venue) (para.54DPD.1 below)
- Human Rights Act 1998 Sch.1 art.6
- Rule 76.22
- Rule 79.17

Practice Directions

39.0.4 The first of the two practice directions supplementing this Part is concerned principally (but not exclusively) with the matters dealt with rr.39.2 to 39.6. The second has no direct connection with any rule in Pt 39 but is included in this Part for convenience. On the matter of court sittings, note also Practice Direction 54D—Administrative Court (Venue) (para.54DPD.1 below).

Interpretation

39.1 **39.1 In this Part, reference to a hearing includes a reference to the trial.**

"hearing" (r.39.1, r.39.2)

Apart from expressly providing that "hearing" includes trial, there is no further definition. It is clear that it includes interlocutory hearings (e.g. under Pt 23—see, e.g. the reference in r.39.2(3)(e)) and hearings of cases on the Small Claims Track (see, e.g. r.27.6(4) and r.27.8) as well as fast track and multi-track trials **39.1.1**

Conduct of hearings generally

The potential ECHR art.6(1) implications of the court's power to control evidence were considered at para.32.1.1, above. In relation to the court's control of the trial itself, the ECtHR has held that it is generally for national courts to regulate their own proceedings, including deciding on the time allowed for oral submissions: *Brown v United Kingdom* (1999) 28 E.H.R.R. CD 233, ECtHR, (3rd chamber). The court must ensure equality of arms between the parties, and must also ensure that the proceedings are properly adversarial: *Mantovanelli v France* (1997) 24 E.H.R.R. 370, ECtHR. See also *Pellegrini v Italy* (2002) 35 E.H.R.R. 2, para.44. **39.1.2**

Each party must have a genuine opportunity to respond to the evidence relied upon by the other side: *Van de Hurk v Netherlands* (1994) 18 E.H.R.R. 481, ECtHR and *WJ v Austria* (1999) 27 E.H.R.R. CD 83, ECtHR, (1st chamber). This may involve the disclosure to the other side of documents previously only made available to the court: *McMichael v United Kingdom* (1995) 20 E.H.R.R. 205, ECtHR and *Feldbrugge v Netherlands* (1986) 8 E.H.R.R. 425, ECtHR.

The court may also be required to take a broad approach to determining who should be heard during the proceedings, in order to ensure effective and adequate representation of third parties: *Keegan v Ireland* (1994) 18 E.H.R.R. 342, ECtHR. The court should ensure that the parties have a sufficient opportunity to respond to any submissions made by an *amicus curiae*, or by someone in a similar role: *Van Orshoven v Belgium* (1998) 26 E.H.R.R. 55, ECtHR and *Nwabueze v General Medical Council* [2000] 1 W.L.R. 1760, PC.

General rule—hearing to be in public[1]

39.2—(1) The general rule is that a hearing is to be in public. **39.2**

(2) The requirement for a hearing to be in public does not require the court to make special arrangements for accommodating members of the public.

(3) A hearing, or any part of it, may be in private if—

(a) publicity would defeat the object of the hearing;

(b) it involves matters relating to national security;

(c) it involves confidential information (including information relating to personal financial matters) and publicity would damage that confidentiality;

(d) a private hearing is necessary to protect the interests of any child or protected party;

(e) it is a hearing of an application made without notice and it would be unjust to any respondent for there to be a public hearing;

(f) it involves uncontentious matters arising in the administration of trusts or in the administration of a deceased person's estate; or

(g) the court considers this to be necessary, in the interests of justice.

(4) The court may order that the identity of any party or witness must not be disclosed if it considers non-disclosure necessary in order to protect the interests of that party or witness.

[1] Amended by the Civil Procedure (Amendment) Rules 2007 (SI 2007/2204).

"hearing to be in public" (r.39.2)

39.2.1 See Human Rights Act 1998 Sch.1 (incorporating the European Convention on Human Rights) where art.6 states:

> "In the determination of his civil rights and obligation ... everyone is entitled to a fair and public hearing within a reasonable time by an independent and impartial tribunal established by law. Judgment shall be pronounced publicly but the press and public may be excluded from all or part of the trial in the interest of morals, public order or national security in a democratic society, where the interests of juveniles or the protection of the private life of the parties so require, or to the extent strictly necessary in the opinion of the court in special circumstances where publicity would prejudice the interests of justice."

The general rule is that hearings are to be in public (see *Scott v Scott* [1913] AC 417 and *R. (on the application of Pelling) v Bow County Court (No.2)* [2001] U.K.H.R.R. 165, QBD Administrative Court). However that rule is not absolute. CPR, r.39.2(3) is facultative and permits certain limited exceptions, always assumed to that being subject to the interests of justice. CPR, r.39.2 is not unlawful or *ultra vires*. Nor does it breach ECHR Arts 6 or 10. (*The Queen on the application of Michael John Pelling v Bow County Court*, see above).

The exceptions are set out in r.39.2 and fleshed out in the Practice Direction (see para.39PD.1). For authority under ECHR art.6(1) on the right to a public hearing, see *Werner v Austria* (1998) 26 E.H.R.R. 310, ECtHR, *Diennet v France* (1996) 21 E.H.R.R. 554, ECtHR, and *Scarth v United Kingdom (33745/96)* (1998) 26 E.H.R.R. CD154, EComHR, comfirmed by ECtHR.

Note that one consequence of hearings in public is an automatic right to a transcript, subject to payment of the appropriate fee (Practice Direction, para.1.11, see 39PD.1) whereas if the hearing is in private, a member of the public who is not a party to the proceedings must seek the permission of the judge before obtaining a transcript of the judgment (Practice Direction, para.1.12, see 39PD.1). For the position under ECHR Article 6(1) in relation to public access to judgments see *Pretto v Italy* (1984) 6 E.H.R.R. 182, ECtHR, *Axen v Germany* (1984) 6 E.H.R.R. 195, ECtHR, and *Werner v Austria* (1998) 26 E.H.R.R. 310, ECtHR. The Convention draws a distinction between hearings, which may be held in private in certain circumstances, and judgments, which must be pronounced publicly. this means that they must be available to the public.

Note that the venue of a hearing and whether it is in public or private does not affect existing rights of audience (Practice Direction, para.1.14, see 39PD.1). As to the importance of the public having unihibited dues to public hearings in another context, see *Storer v British Gas Plc* [2000] 1 W.L.R. 1237, CA.

The Strasbourg institutions have generally taken the view that interlocutory hearings are not determinative of civil rights and obligations with the meaning of ECHR art.6 (1). These hearings are therefore generally not required to be public: *APIS v Slovakia to* (2000) 29 E.H.R.R. CD 105, decision of January 13, 2000, unrep., ECtHR, 2nd chamber (interim injunction), *Alsterlund v Sweden 12446/86*, (1988) 56 D.R. 229, EComHR (stay of execution), *Noviflora Sweden ab v Sweden (14369/88)* (1993) 15 E.H.R.R. CD6, decision of October 12, 1992, unrep., EComHR (search order), *Ewing v United Kingdom No.11224/84* (1998) 10 E.H.R.R. CD141.

"A hearing, or any part of it, may be in private" (r.39.2(3))

39.2.2 See too the Practice Direction (para.39PD.1). Paragraph 1.4 states that the decision as to whether to hold a hearing in public or in private must be made by the judge conducting the hearing having regard to any representations which may have been made to him. Paragraph 1.5 of the Practice Direction sets out types of hearings which shall in the first instance be listed in private. See too *Smithkline Beecham Plc v Generics (UK) Ltd* [2003] EWCA Civ 1109; *The Times*, August 25, 2003 (patent infringement claim—cross-examination on confidential documents in private).

For consideration of the application of ECHR art.6(1) to a refusal to admit a McKenzie friend to an ex parte hearing in private see *R. v Bow County Court Ex p. Pelling* [1999] 1 W.L.R. 1807, CA. The court should also bear in mind the ECHR principle of proportionality when deciding whether all or part of the hearing should be held in private.

In proceedings to which Pt 76 (Prevention of Terrorism Act 2005) applies, and in proceedings to which Pt 79 (Financial Restrictions Proceedings Under the Counter-Terrorism Act 2008) applies, the court is given special powers to hold hearings in private for particular purposes (see, respectively, r.76.22 and r.79.17(2)).

An inspector of court administration exercising rights of entry and inspection under the Courts Act 2003 s.61 is not entitled to be present when a county court is hearing proceedings in private.

"Publicity would defeat the object of the hearing" (r.39.2(3)(a))

For example, an application for a freezing injunction or a search order. See Practice Direction to Pt 25. **39.2.3**

"personal financial matters" (r.39.2(3)(c))

Practice Direction, para.1.5 (see para.39PD.1) provides that the following hearings shall in the first instance be listed in private, namely mortgage possession proceedings against individuals, landlord and tenant possession proceedings based on non-payment of rent, applications to suspend warrants where the ability to make payments is an issue, redetermination under r.14.13, applications to vary or suspend payment of judgment debts, applications for charging orders, garnishee orders, attachment of earnings orders, administration orders or the appointment of a receiver, oral examinations, determination of an assisted person's liability for costs under reg.127 of the Civil Legal Aid (General) Regulations 1989; the detemination of the liability of a LSC funded client under regs 9 and 10 of the Community Legal Service (Costs) Regulations 2000; applications for security for costs under Companies Act 1985 s.726(1), proceedings brought under Consumer Credit Act 1974, Inheritance (Provision for Family and Dependants) Act 1975 or Protection from Harassment Act 1997 and applications under the Variation of Trusts Act 1958 where no facts are in dispute. See too Practice Direction, para.1.7 (see para.39PD.1) and para.5.1 of the Practice Direction which supplements Pt 27 (see para.27PD.5) (hearing of claims in the small claims track). Note that a hearing of a small claim in premises other than a court is not a hearing in public (Practice Direction, para.1.7, see para.39PD.1). **39.2.4**

"child or protected party"

Where a claim by or on behalf of a child or protected party is compromised etc. by or on behalf of a child or a protected party the approval of the court is required as provided by r.21.10. Paragraph (3)(d) of r.39.2 states that a hearing, or any part of it, may be in private if that is necessary to protect the interest of any child or patient. Paragraph 1.6 of Practice Direction (Miscellaneous Provisions Relating to Hearings) (see para.39PD.1 below) explains that para.(3)(d) of r.39.2 includes the hearing of an application as required by r.21.10. In para.(3)(d), "protected party" was substituted for "patient" by the Civil Procedure (Amendment) Rules 2007 (SI 2007/2204) with effect from October 1, 2007 to reflect the change in nomenclature brought about by the Mental Capacity Act 2005, and para.1.6 of the Practice Direction was amended accordingly. **39.2.5**

"an application made without notice and it would be unjust to any respondent" (r.39.2(3)(e))

See r.23.4(2). **39.2.6**

"necessary in the interests of justice" (r.39.2(3)(g))

Clearly this gives the judge a wide discretion. See too r.1.1 (the overriding objective) and Practice Direction, para.1.8 (see para.39PD.1). The questions whether evidence should be excluded on the ground of public interest immunity and whether the court should sit in private are distinct; once it is determined that the immunity attaches the evidence is excluded as a matter of law and the court has no discretion to admit it on terms that it be heard in private (*Powell v Chief Constable of North Wales* [1999] EWCA Civ 2097; *The Times*, February 11, 2000, CA). **39.2.7**

Transcripts

See Practice Direction, paras 1.11 and 1.12 (para.39PD.1). **39.2.8**

Hearing in private, judgment in public

A judge, having heard proceedings in private, may give judgment in open court (e.g. *Wills v Mills & Co* [2005] EWCA Civ 591, May 3, 2005, unrep., CA), but is not obliged to do so, especially where the judgment cannot be anonymised or abridged (*Y. v Attorney General* [2003] EWHC 1462, Ch; June 24, 2003, unrep., Sir Andrew Morritt V.-C.). See further para.5.4B.5 above, and para.40.2.5 below (and cases referred to **39.2.9** there). Among the justifications that may be given for this is that copies of a Court of Appeal or High Court judgment given in private may be provided by the court's giving permission on application; see further under r.5.4C(2); see further para.5.4C.7 above. See also para.23.0.10 above (hearing of applications in private).

Private hearings and contempt

39.2.10 The Administration of Justice Act 1960 s.12(1) states that the publication of "information relating to proceedings" before any court sitting in private shall not of itself be contempt of court, except in certain circumstances. One of the circumstances is that the court (having power to do so) "expressly prohibits" publication. Section 12(2) refers to the publication of orders made by courts sitting in private and is to similar effect. Where a court simply makes an order under r.39.2(3) and a hearing is held in private, then (provided none of the other exceptional circumstances referred to in s.12(1) applies) publication of matters referred to in s.12 is not expressly prohibited and prohibition cannot be implied (*AF Noonan (Architectural Practice) v Bournemouth & Boscombe Athletic Community Football Club Ltd* [2007] EWCA Civ 848, July 2, 2007, unrep., CA).

Failure to attend the trial[1]

39.3 **39.3—(1) The court may proceed with a trial in the absence of a party but—**

(a) if no party attends the trial, it may strike out[GL] the whole of the proceedings;

(b) if the claimant does not attend, it may strike out his claim and any defence to counterclaim; and

(c) if a defendant does not attend, it may strike out his defence or counterclaim (or both).

(2) Where the court strikes out proceedings, or any part of them, under this rule, it may subsequently restore the proceedings, or that part.

(3) Where a party does not attend and the court gives judgment or makes an order against him, the party who failed to attend may apply for the judgment or order to be set aside.[GL]

(4) An application under paragraph (2) or paragraph (3) must be supported by evidence.

(5) Where an application is made under paragraph (2) or (3) by a party who failed to attend the trial, the court may grant the application only if the applicant—

(a) acted promptly when he found out that the court had exercised its power to strike out[GL] or to enter judgment or make an order against him;

(b) had a good reason for not attending the trial; and

(c) has a reasonable prospect of success at the trial.

"a party who failed to attend the trial" (r.39.3(3))

39.3.1 This must be read in conjunction with Practice Direction, paras 2.1–2.4 (see 39PD.1) (*cf.* RSC O.35, r.1 and CCR O.21).

In *Nelson v Clearsprings (Management) Limited* [2006] EWCA Civ 1252, [2007] 1 W.L.R. 962, the Court of Appeal stated that the whole of r.39.5 contemplates a trial in the absence of a party who has been properly served with a claim form in accordance with the relevant rules as to service (that is to say, a party who had formal notice of the proceedings), or in respect of whom service has been dispensed with. Where (1) the

[1] Amended by the Civil Procedure (Amendment No.4) Rules 2000 (SI 2000/2092).

party failing to attend trial is a defendant who has not had formal notice (because of a failure to effect proper service on him), and service on him has not been dispensed with, and (2) judgment is given against him in his absence, that party may apply to set the (irregular) judgment aside as of right; but in these circumstances, the court's jurisdiction is not derived from r.39.5 but from powers given by r.3.1(2)(m) and r.3.10. The particular significance of this is that the provisions of para.(5) of r.39.5 do not apply to an application by such a party (see further para.39.3.7 below).

Where a party does not attend a hearing, and the court refuses an adjournment and gives judgment or makes an order against him, it is an abuse of process for the party who failed to attend to appeal against the refusal of an adjournment where he also has the opportunity to apply to have the judgment or order set aside under CPR 39.3(3)— *Tennero Ltd v Arnold* [2006] EWHC 1530; [2007] 1 W.L.R. 1025, QB; July 6, 2006, (Jack J.).

"The court may ... strike out the whole of the proceedings" (r.39.3(1))

Note the power to restore: r.39.3(2). Any application to restore should be made in accordance with Pt 23: see Practice Direction, para.2.3 (see para.39PD.1). The court may not set aside an earlier order unless the requirements of CPR, r.39.3(5) are met. One requirement is that the applicant explain his or her non-attendance at trial. If there is no evidence in support of the reason for non-attendance the application must fail at that hurdle (*Southwark LBC v Joseph* March 2000, *Legal Action* 29, CA). **39.3.2**

There is no objection in principle under ECHR art.6(1) to the entering of judgment against a party who fails to attend a trial: *Probst v Germany*, No.19913/92, January 11, 1995, unrep., EComHR, provided that he has the opportunity to apply to have the judgment set aside and to explain his failure to attend: see, by analogy, *Poitrimol v France* (1994) 18 E.H.R.R. 130, ECtHR. See also *Barclays Bank Plc v Ellis* [2001] C.P. Rep. 50.

"counterclaim" (r.39.3(1))

See Pt 20. **39.3.3**

"If the claimant does not attend" (r.39.3(1)(b))

The Practice Direction, para.2.2 (see para.39PD.1) envisages that even though a defence to counterclaim may be struck out, the defendant will still have to prove his or her counterclaim, although this will normally only entail referring to the Pt 20 claim form (with statement of truth) or tendering witness statements: see Pt 32. **39.3.4**

For the purposes of CPR, r.39.3(1)(b) a party is "present" at a trial if his/her solicitor attends even if the person bringing or defending the claim is not at court (*Rouse v Freeman, The Times*, January 8, 2002, Gross J.).

"If the defendant does not attend" (r.39.3(1)(c))

The Practice Direction, para.2.2 (see para.39PD.1) envisages that even though a defence may be struck out, the claimant will still have to prove his or her claim, although this will normally only entail referring to the statement of case (with statement of truth) or tendering witness statements: see r.32.6(2) and r.22.1(1)(a). **39.3.5**

As to whether or not a party was absent at trial, see *Rouse v Freeman, The Times* January 8, 2002 Gross J. (whether individual claimant present through solicitor) and *Watson v Bluemoor Properties* [2002] EWCA Civ 1875; December 10, 2002 (whether defendant company present through director).

"the party who failed to attend may apply for the judgment or order to be set aside"

See Pt 23. Any application should be made on notice and be supported by evidence (r.39.3(4)) giving reasons for the failure to attend court and stating when the applicant found out about the order against him: see Practice Direction, para.2.4 (see para.39PD.1). Unlike CCR O.37, r.2, r.39.3(3) does not specify the judge who should hear the application (see too the reference to "court" in r.2.4). Although the aim of the rules is to provide maximum flexibility, as a matter of practice, if all other things are equal, it would be wise for any such application to be heard by the same judge or same level of judge as the one who made the original order. **39.3.6**

"the court may grant the application only if ..." (r.39.3(5))

Note that the wording of r.39.3(5) provides more stringent requirements than CCR O.37, r.2 which it replaced. The court no longer has a broad discretion. There is only **39.3.7** jurisdiction to set aside a regular judgment if the party seeking to have the order set aside can satisfy all three requirements in r.39.3(5). (This passage was quoted with approval by Simon Brown L.J. in *Regency Rolls Ltd v Carnall* [2000] EWCA Civ 379, October 16, 2000, CA, unrep., but noted in *Civil Procedure News*, April 23, 2001. See too *Barclays Bank Plc v Ellis* [2001] C.P. Rep. 50, CA.) In view of this, cases such as *Hayman v Rowlands* [1957] 1 W.L.R. 317, CA and *Grimshaw v Dunbar* [1953] 1 Q.B. 408, CA, no longer apply. The test is more similar to that set out in *Alpine Bulk Transport v Saudi Eagle Shipping* [1986] Lloyd's Rep. 721, CA, and *Shocked v Golschmidt* [1998] 1 All E.R. 372, CA

Note that if the judgment is a nullity (e.g. because the claim form has not been served) the defendant is entitled to have any order set aside as of right (ex debito justitiae)— *White v Weston* [1968] 2 Q.B. 647, CA. However this principle does not extend to a defendant who had notice of the proceedings, but was not notified of the trial date. Such a defendant is required by CPR, r.39.3(5) to show the court that he had a reasonable prospect of success at the trial (*Hackney LBC v Driscoll* [2003] EWCA Civ 1037; [2003] 1 W.L.R. 2602; [2003] 4 All E.R. 1205).

In *Nelson v Clearsprings (Management) Limited* [2006] EWCA Civ 1252, September 22, 2006, unrep., CA, the Court of Appeal stated that it was not intended that the more stringent requirements of r.39.3(5) should apply to judgments irregularly obtained, in the sense of being obtained without service of the claim form in accordance with the rules; see further para.39.3.1 above. In this case, the Court outlined (at para.56) the procedure that should be followed (until rules dealing specifically with the situation are enacted) in cases where judgment has been entered against a defendant, even though the defendant has never been served with the claim form at all, and that defendant applies to have the (irregular) judgment set aside.

"acted promptly"

39.3.7.1 See *Regency Rolls Ltd v Carnall* [2000] EWCA Civ 379; October 16, 2000, unrep., CA, but noted in *Civil Procedure News*, April 23, 2001, where an application to set aside was dismissed partly because the applicant had not acted promptly—the application under CPR r.39.3 was made over four weeks after the hearing. Arden L.J. pointed out that "The dictionary meaning of 'promptly' is 'with alacrity'". Simon Brown L.J. said:

> "I would accordingly construe 'promptly' here to require, not that an applicant has been guilty of no needless delay whatever, but rather that he has acted with all reasonable celerity in the circumstances."

The Court of Appeal has held that a company acted promptly when, in a case involving "a considerable amount of documentation", an application to set aside was issued six weeks after judgment (*Watson v Bluemoor Properties Ltd* [2002] EWCA Civ 1875; December 10, 2002).

"had a good reason for not attending the trial"

39.3.7.2 The court must be satisfied that the reason for not attending is genuine and honest. However, that in itself is not sufficient to make a 'good' reason. There are no fixed reasons that are good or bad and an over-analytical approach is inconsistent with the overriding objective of the CPR. The ordinary English meaning of the phrase 'good reason' is a sufficiently clear expression of the standard of acceptability to be supplied. If a defendant says that he or she was ignorant of a hearing, it is normally necessary to ask why that was so. The mere assertion that a party was unaware of the hearing date is unlikely to be sufficient to constitute a good reason. It is usually relevant to inquire whether the party was aware that proceedings had been issued and served. Once a party is aware that proceedings have been served, he or she has to be taken to expect to receive communications personally from the opposing party and/or the court. That includes notifications of hearing dates. If there is no system in place for ensuring that such communications are received, he or she is unlikely to be able to rely on the absence of such a system to say that there was a good reason for not attending the hearing. It is particularly difficult for a party to argue that there was a good reason for not attending if he or she deliberately avoided receiving such communications in order to frustrate the litigation process. However, there is no obligation to make oneself amenable to potential claims of which there is no notice (*Estate Acquisition and Development Limited v Wiltshire* [2006] EWCA Civ 533; [2006] C.P. Rep. 32).

The court has to consider each case in light of all the relevant factors for non-attendance and, looking at the matter in the round, determine whether the reason is sufficient for the court to exercise its discretion in favour of the defaulting party (*Brazil v Brazil* [2002] EWCA Civ 1135; (2003) C.P. Rep.7; *The Times*, October 18, 2002—in that case where the defendant was illiterate and acting in person, non-receipt of a notice of hearing sent to an incorrect address by the court was a good reason for the defendant's non-attendance. It was not cured by the subsequent receipt by him of the trial bundle). In *Attorney General of Zambia v Meer Care & Desai (a firm)* [2008] EWCA Civ 754; July 9, 2008, the Court of Appeal held that a defendant's account of why he had not realised that he was a defendant to the proceedings, and therefore had not taken any part in them, was one which was capable of belief and amounted to a good reason under CPR 39.3(5)(b). He relied on the absence of a letter before action or similar communication, his previous involvement as a witness and the voluminous documents in which two translated documents had been included.

Where insufficient notification from solicitors meant that the defendant was clearly unaware that the fixed trial date for both the claim against her and her counter claim had been moved to a different venue, it was appropriate to set aside the order made in her absence dismising her counterclaim (*Garland v Stedman*, December 7, 2000, unrep., CA, but noted by Lawtel). It has been held on an application to set aside judgment, following the refusal of an application to adjourn a trial on medical grounds due to the lack of a medical certificate, that it was wrong to reject evidence of a medical condition in the absence of the defendant's cross-examination, where there was no reason to infer untrustworthiness and where there was no proper basis to reject such evidence (*St Ermin's Property Company Ltd v Draper* [2004] EWHC 697, ChD, January 27, 2004).

"has a reasonable prospect of success at the trial"

The reasonable prospect of success condition in r.39.3(5) does not offend any fundamental principle of justice or any principle of ECHR jurisprudence (*Hackney LBC v Driscoll* [2003] EWCA Civ 1037; [2003] 1 W.L.R. 2602) See too *Regency Rolls Ltd v Carnall* [2000] EWCA Civ 379; October 16, 2000, unrep., CA, but noted in *Civil Procedure News*, April 23, 2001, where an application to set aside was dismissed partly because the applicant's version of events was inherently incapable of belief and he could not be described as having reasonable prospects of success. See too *Attorney General of Zambia v Meer Care & Desai (a firm)* [2008] EWCA Civ 754; July 9, 2008. **39.3.7.3**

Failure to attend hearing of application for summary judgment

In accordance with CPR Pt 24, on application for summary judgment the court may give summary judgment against a claimant or defendant. On such an application, the court may, instead of giving summary judgment, make other dispositive orders; in particular the court may (1) strike out or dismiss the claim, (2) dismiss the application, or (3) make a conditional order (Practice Direction (Summary Disposal of Claims), para.5.1, see para.24PD.5 above). The hearing of a summary judgment application is not a trial (although summary judgment may be given at trial). Consequently, where a party fails to attend the hearing of an application for summary judgment the court's power to set aside any judgment or order under r.39.3 does not avail him and relief must be sought under other provisions. See further para.24.6.8 above. **39.3.8**

Timetable for trial

39.4 When the court sets a timetable for a trial in accordance with rule 28.6 (fixing or confirming the trial date and giving directions—fast track) or rule 29.8 (setting a trial timetable and fixing or confirming the trial date or week—multi-track) it will do so in consultation with the parties. **39.4**

Timetable for trial

The Rules envisage that trial time tables (e.g. length of opening (if any), cross-examination and closing speeches of both parties) should be given at listing stage (see CPR r.28.6 and paras 28.6.4 and 28.6.5, and para.7.2(2)(b) to Practice Direction 28 in relation to fast track and CPR r.29.8(c)(i) and para.9.2(2)(b) to Practice Direction 29 in relation to multi track. Although there is power to revise such time tables (para.8.3 to Practice Direction 28 and para.10.3 to Practice Direction 29), in the Chancery Division, any revision has to be justified and a proper reason given since the court and the parties will have made their plans on the basis of the estimate previously submitted (*St Albans Court Ltd v Daldorch Estates Ltd*, *The Times*, May 24, 1999, Ch D). **39.4.1**

Trial bundles

39.5 **39.5—(1) Unless the court orders otherwise, the claimant must file a trial bundle containing documents required by—**

(a) a relevant practice direction; and

(b) any court order.

(2) The claimant must file the trial bundle not more than 7 days and not less than 3 days before the start of the trial.

Trial bundles (r.39.5)

39.5.1 This rule replaces CCR O.17, r.12 and RSC O.37, r.10. Note that unlike the former rules, responsibility lies solely on the claimant. Although the rules no longer state that defendants have an obligation to notify claimants of the documents that they want to have included in bundles, the parties should attempt to agree the contents of trial bundles where possible (Practice Direction, para.3.9, see para.39PD.3).

"file" (r.39.5(1))

39.5.2 See r.2.3.

"a relevant practice direction" (r.39.5(1)(a))

39.5.3 See Practice Direction, para.3.2 (see para.39PD.3) which sets out in detail the documents to be included unless the court orders otherwise. The originals of any documents contained in the trial bundles should be available at trial (Practice Direction, para.3.3, see para.39PD.3).

The preparation and production of the trial bundle, even where delegated to another person, is the responsibility of the legal representative who has conduct of the claim on behalf of the claimant (Practice Direction, para.3.4, see para.39PD.3).

Trial bundles should be paginated continuously throughout and indexed. Where the total number of pages is more than 100, numbered dividers should be placed at intervals between groups of documents (Practice Direction, para.3.5, see para.39PD.3). Bundles should normally be contained in ring binders or lever arch files. If there are numerous bundles, a core bundle should be prepared (Practice Direction, para.3.6, see para.39PD.3).

If a copy of a document is illegible a typed copy should be included in the bundle next to it (Practice Direction, para.3.8, see para.39PD.3).

The party filing the trial bundle should supply identical bundles to all parties to the proceedings and for the use of witnesses (Practice Direction, para.3.10). Note that there is no provision for payment.

In relation to fast track trial bundles, see the Appendix to Practice Direction to Pt 28 (para.28PD.13).

Where bundles have been filed, there is no principle which inhibits a judge from reading inadmissable material. What a judge decides to pre-read is a matter for his or her discretion. (*Barings Plc (In Liquidation) v Coopers & Lybrand (No.3)* [2001] EWCA Civ 1163, CA.)

"not more than 7 days and not less than 3 days" (r.39.5(2))

39.5.4 See r.2.8. Days means clear days.

Chancery Division and Queen's Bench Division

39.5.5 For guidance on the preparation of bundles in the Chancery Division, see The Chancery Guide, para.7.9 onwards at 1A–65 and *St Albans Court Ltd v Daldorch Estates Ltd, The Times*, May 24, 1999, Ch D) and for guidance on the preparation of bundles in the Queen's Bench Division, see The Queen's Bench Guide, para.7.11.7 onwards at 1B–51.

Representation at trial of companies or other corporations

39.6 **39.6 A company or other corporation may be represented at trial *by an employee if—***

(a) the employee has been authorised by the company or corporation to appear at trial on its behalf; and

(b) the court gives permission.

"Representation at trial of companies or other corporations" (r.39.6)

See *Charles P Kinnell & Co Ltd v Harding Wace & Co* [1918] 1 K.B. 405 at 413 where Swinfen Eady L.J. said: "As from its nature a company cannot appear in person, not having as a legal entity any visible person, it must appear by counsel or solicitor, or by leave of the judge some other person may be allowed to appear instead of the company to address the court which includes the examination of witnesses and generally conducting the case." In *"Access to Justice, Final Report"*, Lord Woolf M.R. stated: **39.6.1**

> "The court should normally exercise its discretion in favour of allowing an employee of a company to take any steps on behalf of the company which a litigant in person could take in High Court or county court proceedings." (Recommendation 153.)
>
> In *Watson v Bluemoor Properties Ltd* [2002] EWCA 1875; December 10, 2002, Sullivan J. said:
>
> "The CPR deliberately introduced a greater measure of flexibility into the ability of companies to choose their representative. They no longer have to be represented by directors, but may be represented by an authorised employee, whether or not that employee is a director, provided always that the court is prepared to grant permission."

Note PD to Pt 39, para.5.2 which sets out additional information to be included in the written statement giving details about representation at hearings where a company appears without solicitor or barrister.

The requirements contained in CPR, r.39.6 do not apply to claims allocated to the small claims track (see CPR, r.27.2(1)(h) and *Avinue Ltd v Sunrule Ltd* [2003] EWCA Civ 1942; [2004] 1 W.L.R. 634.

Representation

See also Practice Direction supplementing Pt 39 (see para.5.1)which provides that at any hearing a written statement with the name and address of each advocate, his qualification or entitlement to act as an advocate and the party for whom he acts should be provided for the court. **39.6.2**

Impounded documents

39.7—(1) Documents impounded by order of the court must not be released from the custody of the court except in compliance— **39.7**

(a) with a court order; or

(b) with a written request made by a Law Officer or the Director of Public Prosecutions.

(2) A document released from the custody of the court under paragraph (1)(b) must be released into the custody of the person who requested it.

(3) Documents impounded by order of the court, while in the custody of the court, may not be inspected except by a person authorised to do so by a court order.

Impounded documents (r.39.7)—Effect of rule

The effect of the rule is that, while the documents are in the custody of the Court, *they should not leave its custody* (*Re A Solicitor* (1892) 65 L.T. 584, in which leave to inspect was given, but not to make copies of the documents). **39.7.1**

In actions in Ch D, impounded documents are deposited in the Central Office, Filing Department. In actions in QBD they are retained by the Associate.

The Court has an inherent jurisdiction to take charge of a document material to a case once the document has come into its hands, if it is necessary to do so for the purposes of justice (e.g. because a document or the conduct of a party requires investigation by a Law Officer or the Director of Public Prosecutions and it is necessary to preserve the document pending such an investigation) notwithstanding the possible rights of third parties, although not in blind disregard of such rights (*Beck v Value*

Capital Ltd [1975] 1 W.L.R. 1; [1974] 3 All E.R. 437). In such case, it is open to the party who is entitled to possession of the document and who is not before the court, to apply for his release if he shows sufficient cause (*ibid.*).

Exhibits at trial

39.7.2 See Practice Direction, para.7 (see para.39PD.7). Exhibits handed in during a trial should be recorded on an exhibit list. They should be kept in the custody of the court until the conclusion of the trial unless the judge directs otherwise. At the conclusion of the trial it is the parties' responsibility to obtain their return.

Settlement or discontinuance after the trial date is fixed

39.7.3 See Practice Direction, para.4.1 (see para.39PD.4). In such circumstances the parties must ensure that the listing officer for the trial court is notified immediately.

Recording of proceedings

39.7.4 See Practice Direction, para.6.1 (see para.39PD.6). Judgments will be recorded unless judges direct otherwise. Oral evidence will normally be recorded also. No party or member of the public may use unofficial recording equipment without the permission of the court— i.e. the judge, master or district judge (see r.2.4). To do so without permission constitutes contempt of court.

Note PD to Pt 39, paras 6.3 to 6.5 which deal with transcripts.

As to the taking of photographs or making of drawings, see the Criminal Justice Act 1925 s.41.

Citation of Human Rights authorities

39.7.5 Note the provisions of PD39 para.8 and *Barclays Bank Plc v Ellis* [2001] C.P. Rep. 50, CA where Schiemann L.J. said that counsel who wished to rely on the provisions of the Human Rights Act 1998 should be in a position to provide the court with any decisions of the European Court of Human Rights on which they rely.

Memorandum from the Lord Chief Justice and the Attorney General

Requests for the Appointment of an Advocate to the Court

39.8.1

1. The memorandum has been agreed between the Attorney General and the Lord Chief Justice. It gives guidance about making a request for the appointment of an Advocate to the Court (formerly called an "amicus curiae").
2. In most cases, an Advocate to the Court is appointed by the Attorney General, following a request by the court. In some cases, an Advocate to the Court will be appointed by the Official Solicitor or the Children & Family Court Advisory Service (CAFCASS) (see paragraphs 11 and 12 below).

The role of an Advocate to the Court

39.8.2

3. A court may properly seek the assistance of an Advocate to the Court when there is a danger of an important and difficult point of law being decided without the court hearing relevant argument. In those circumstances the Attorney General may decide to appoint an Advocate to the Court.
4. It is important to bear in mind that an Advocate to the Court represents noone. His or her function is to give to the court such assistance as he or she is able on the relevant law and its application to the facts of the case. An Advocate to the Court will not normally be instructed to lead evidence, cross- examine witnesses, or investigate the facts. In particular, it is not appropriate for the court to seek assistance from an Advocate to the Court simply because a defendant in criminal proceedings refuses representation.
5. The following circumstances are to be distinguished from those where it will be appropriate for the court to seek the assistance of an Advocate to the Court:
   i. where a point of law which affects a government department is being argued in a case where the department is not represented and where the court believe that the department may wish to be represented;
   ii. where the Attorney believes it is necessary for him to intervene as a party in his capacity as guardian of the public interest;
   iii. where the court believes it is appropriate for a litigant in person to seek free (pro bono) assistance;

iv. where, in a criminal trial, the defendant is unrepresented and the Advocate to the Court would be duplicating the prosecutor's duty as a minister of justice "to assist the court on all matters of law applicable to the case";

v. where in a criminal case in relation to sentencing appeals there are issues of fact which are likely to arise and the prosecution ought to be represented, or it would be reasonable to ask the prosecutor to be present and address the court as to the relevant law.

6. In the first of these five cases, the court may invite the Attorney to make arrangements for the advocate to be instructed on behalf of the department. In the second, the court may grant the Attorney permission to intervene, in which case the advocate instructed represents the Attorney. In neither case is the advocate an Advocate to the Court.

7. In the third case the court may grant a litigant in person an adjournment to enable him or her to seek free (pro bono) assistance. In doing so, the court should bear in mind that it is likely to take longer to obtain free (pro bono) representation than funded representation. In contrast to an Advocate to the Court, a free (pro bono) legal representative will obtain his or her instructions from the litigant and will represent the interests of that party. His or her role before the court and duty to the court will be identical to that of any other representative of the parties. Accordingly it will not be appropriate for the court to take such a course where the type of assistance required is that provided by an Advocate to the Court.

8. In the fourth case the prosecutor's special duty is akin to an Advocate to the Court. In the fifth case, in relation to appeals against sentence where the defendant is represented, it may be preferable to request the attendance of the prosecutor who will be able to address the court on issues of fact and law. It would not be proper for an Advocate to the Court to take instructions from the prosecuting authority in relation to factual matters relating to the prosecution. An Advocate to the Court should only be asked to address the court as to the relevant law.

Making a request to the Attorney General

9. A request for an Advocate to the Court should be made by the Court as soon as convenient after it is made aware of the point of law which requires the assistance of an Advocate to the Court. The request should set out the circumstances which have occurred, identifying the point of law upon which assistance is sought and the nature of the assistance required. The court should consider whether it would be sufficient for such assistance to be in writing in the form of submissions as to the law, or whether the assistance should include oral submissions at the hearing. The request should ordinarily be made in writing and be accompanied by the papers necessary to enable the Attorney to reach a decision on the basis of a proper understanding of the case. **39.8.3**

10. The Attorney will decide whether it is appropriate to provide such assistance and, if so, the form such assistance should take. Before reaching a decision he may seek further information or assistance from the court. The Attorney will also ask the court to keep under review the need for such assistance. Where the circumstances which gave rise to the original request have changed, such that the court may now anticipate hearing all relevant argument on the point of law without the presence of an Advocate to the Court, either the Court or the Attorney may ask the Advocate to the Court to withdraw.

Requests to the Official Solicitor or CAFCASS

11. A request for an Advocate to the Court may be made to the Official Solicitor or CAFCASS (Legal Services and Special Casework) where the issue is one in which their experience of representing children and adults under disability gives rise to special experience. The division of responsibility between them is outlined in Practice Notes reported at [2001] 2 FLR 151 and [2001] 2 FLR 155. **39.8.4**

12. The procedure and circumstances for requesting an Advocate to the Court to be appointed by the Official Solicitor or CAFCASS are the same as those applying to requests to the Attorney General. In cases of extreme urgency, telephone requests may be made. In some cases, the Official Solicitor himself will be ap-

pointed as Advocate to the Court. He may be given directions by the Court authorising him to obtain documents, conduct investigations and enquiries and to advise the Court. He may appear by counsel or an in-house advocate.

The Attorney General
Lord Goldsmith QC

The Lord Chief Justice
The Right Hon. The Lord Woolf
19 December 2001

Requests for an Advocate to the Court should be addressed as follows:
The Legal Secretary,
The Legal Secretariat to the Law Officers,
Attorney General's Chambers,
9 Buckingham Gate,
London
SW1E 6JP
Telephone: 020 7271 2417 (criminal)
020 7271 2413 (civil)
Fax: 020 7271 2434

Official Solicitor to the Supreme Court,
81 Chancery Lane,
London
WC2A 1DD
Telephone: 020 7911 7127
Fax: 020 7911 7105

CAFCASS (Legal Services and Special Casework) Newspaper House,
8-16 Great New Street,
London
EC4A 3BN
Telephone: 020 7904 0867
Fax: 020 7904 0868/9

For information about free (pro bono) services:
Bar Pro Bono Unit,
7 Gray's Inn Square,
London
WC1R 5AZ
Telephone: 020 7831 9711
Fax: 020 7831 9733
Email: enquiries@barprobonounit.f9.co.uk

PRACTICE DIRECTION—MISCELLANEOUS PROVISIONS RELATING TO HEARINGS

This Practice Direction supplements CPR Part 39

Hearings

1.1 In Part 39, reference to a hearing includes reference to the trial.[1] **39PD.1**

1.2 The general rule is that a hearing is to be in public.[2]

1.3 Rule 39.2(3) sets out the type of proceedings which may be dealt with in private.

1.4 The decision as to whether to hold a hearing in public or in private must be made by the judge conducting the hearing having regard to any representations which may have been made to him.

1.4A The judge should also have regard to Article 6(1) of the European Convention on Human Rights. This requires that, in general, court hearings are to be held in public, but the press and public may be excluded in the circumstances specified in that Article. Article 6(1) will usually be relevant, for example, where a party applies for a hearing which would normally be held in public to be held in private as well as where a hearing would normally be held in private. The judge may need to consider whether the case is within any of the exceptions permitted by Article 6(1).

1.5 The hearings set out below shall in the first instance be listed by the court as hearings in private under rule 39.2(3)(c), namely:

(1) a claim by a mortgagee against one or more individuals for an order for possession of land,

(2) a claim by a landlord against one or more tenants or former tenants for the repossession of a dwelling house based on the non-payment of rent,

(3) an application to suspend a warrant of execution or a warrant of possession or to stay execution where the court is being invited to consider the ability of a party to make payments to another party,

(4) a redetermination under rule 14.13 or an application to vary or suspend the payment of a judgment debt by instalments,

(5) an application for a charging order (including an application to enforce a charging order), third party debt order, attachment of earnings order, administration order, or the appointment of a receiver,

(6) an order to attend court for questioning,

(7) the determination of the liability of an LSC funded client under regulations 9 and 10 of the Community Legal Service *(Costs) Regulations* 2000, or of an assisted person's liability for costs under regulation 127 of the Civil Legal Aid (General) Regulations 1989,

(8) an application for security for costs under section 726(1) of the Companies Act 1985, and

---

[1] r. 39.1.
[2] r.39.2(1).

(9) proceedings brought under the Consumer Credit Act 1974, the Inheritance (Provision for Family and Dependants) Act 1975 or the Protection from Harassment Act 1997,

(10) an application by a trustee or personal representative for directions as to bringing or defending legal proceedings.

1.6 Rule 39.2(3)(d) states that a hearing may be in private where it involves the interests of a child or protected party. This includes the approval of a compromise or settlement on behalf of a child or protected party or an application for the payment of money out of court to such a person.

1.7 Attention is drawn to paragraph 5.1 of the practice direction which supplements Part 27 (relating to the hearing of claims in the small claims track), which provides that the judge may decide to hold a small claim hearing in private if the parties agree or if a ground mentioned in rule 39.2(3) applies. A hearing of a small claim in premises other than the court will not be a hearing in public.

1.7A Attention is drawn to paragraph 24.5(8) of the practice direction supplementing Part 52, which provides that an appeal to a county court against certain decisions under the Representation of the People Act 1983 is to be heard in private unless the court orders otherwise. Attention is also drawn to paragraph 24.5(9) of that practice direction, which provides that an appeal to the Court of Appeal against such a decision of a county court may be heard in private if the Court of Appeal so orders.

1.8 Nothing in this practice direction prevents a judge ordering that a hearing taking place in public shall continue in private, or vice-versa.

1.9 If the court or judge's room in which the proceedings are taking place has a sign on the door indicating that the proceedings are private, members of the public who are not parties to the proceedings will not be admitted unless the court permits.

1.10 Where there is no such sign on the door of the court or judge's room, members of the public will be admitted where practicable. The judge may, if he thinks it appropriate, adjourn the proceedings to a larger room or court.

1.11 When a hearing takes place in public, members of the public may obtain a transcript of any judgment given or a copy of any order made, subject to payment of the appropriate fee.

1.12 When a judgment is given or an order is made in private, if any member of the public who is not a party to the proceedings seeks a transcript of the judgment or a copy of the order, he must seek the leave of the judge who gave the judgment or made the order.

1.13 A judgment or order given or made in private, when drawn up, must have clearly marked in the title:

"Before [*title and name of judge*] sitting in Private"

1.14 References to hearings being in public or private or in a judge's room contained in the Civil Procedure Rules (including the *Rules of the Supreme* Court and the County Court Rules scheduled to Part 50) and the practice directions which supplement them do not restrict any existing rights of audience or confer any new rights of audience in respect of applications or proceedings which under the rules previously in force would have been heard in court or in chambers respectively.

1.15 Where the court lists a hearing of a claim by a mortgagee for an order for possession of land under paragraph 1.5(1) above to be in private, any fact which needs to be proved by the evidence of witnesses may be proved by evidence in writing.

(CPR rule 32.2 sets out the general rule as to how evidence is to be given and facts are to be proved.)

Failure to attend the trial

2.1 Rule 39.3 sets out the consequences of a party's failure to attend the trial. **39PD.2**

2.2 The court may proceed with a trial in the absence of a party.[1] In the absence of:

(1) the defendant, the claimant may—
  (a) prove his claim at trial and obtain judgment on his claim and for costs, and
  (b) seek the striking out of any counterclaim,
(2) the claimant, the defendant may—
  (a) prove any counterclaim at trial and obtain judgment on his counterclaim and for costs, and
  (b) seek the striking out of the claim, or
(3) both parties, the court may strike out the whole of the proceedings.

2.3 Where the court has struck out proceedings, or any part of them, on the failure of a party to attend, that party may apply in accordance with Part 23 for the proceedings, or that part of them, to be restored and for any judgment given against that party to be set aside.[2]

2.4 The application referred to in paragraph 2.3 above must be supported by evidence giving reasons for the failure to attend court and stating when the applicant found out about the order against him.

Bundles of documents for hearings or trial

3.1 Unless the court orders otherwise, the claimant must file the trial bundle not more than 7 days and not less than 3 days before the start of the trial. **39PD.3**

3.2 Unless the court orders otherwise, the trial bundle should include a copy of:

(1) the claim form and all statements of case,
(2) a case summary and/or chronology where appropriate,
(3) requests for further information and responses to the requests,
(4) all witness statements to be relied on as evidence,
(5) any witness summaries,
(6) any notices of intention to rely on hearsay evidence under rule 32.2,

[1] r.39.3(1).
[2] r.Rule 39.3(2) and (3).

(7) any notices of intention to rely on evidence (such as a plan, photograph etc.) under rule 33.6 which is not—
   (a) contained in a witness statement, affidavit or experts' report,
   (b) being given orally at trial,
   (c) hearsay evidence under rule 33.2,

(8) any medical reports and responses to them,

(9) any experts' reports and responses to them,

(10) any order giving directions as to the conduct of the trial, and

(11) any other necessary documents.

3.3 The originals of the documents contained in the trial bundle, together with copies of any other court orders should be available at the trial.

3.4 The preparation and production of the trial bundle, even where it is delegated to another person, is the responsibility of the legal representative[1] who has conduct of the claim on behalf of the claimant.

3.5 The trial bundle should be paginated (continuously) throughout, and indexed with a description of each document and the page number. Where the total number of pages is more than 100, numbered dividers should be placed at intervals between groups of documents.

3.6 The bundle should normally be contained in a ring binder or lever arch file. Where more than one bundle is supplied, they should be clearly distinguishable, for example, by different colours or letters. If there are numerous bundles, a core bundle should be prepared containing the core documents essential to the proceedings, with references to the supplementary documents in the other bundles.

3.7 For convenience, experts' reports may be contained in a separate bundle and cross referenced in the main bundle.

3.8 If a document to be included in the trial bundle is illegible, a typed copy should be included in the bundle next to it, suitably cross-referenced.

3.9 The contents of the trial bundle should be agreed where possible. The parties should also agree where possible:

(1) that the documents contained in the bundle are authentic even if not disclosed under Part 31, and

(2) that documents in the bundle may be treated as evidence of the facts stated in them even if a notice under the Civil Evidence Act 1995 has not been served.

Where it is not possible to agree the contents of the bundle, a summary of the points on which the parties are unable to agree should be included.

3.10 The party filing the trial bundle should supply identical bundles to all the parties to the proceedings and for the use of the witnesses.

Settlement or discontinuance after the trial date is fixed

39PD.4 **4.1** Where:

[1] For the definition of legal representative see r. 2.3.

(1) an offer to settle a claim is accepted,
(2) or a settlement is reached, or
(3) a claim is discontinued, which disposes of the whole of a claim for which a date or "window" has been fixed for the trial, the parties must ensure that the listing officer for the trial court is notified immediately.

4.2 If an order is drawn up giving effect to the settlement or discontinuance, a copy of the sealed order should be filed with the listing officer.

Representation at hearings

5.1 At any hearing, a written statement containing the following information should be provided for the court: **39PD.5**

(1) the name and address of each advocate,
(2) his qualification or entitlement to act as an advocate, and
(3) the party for whom he so acts.

5.2 Where a party is a company or other corporation and is to be represented at a hearing by an employee the written statement should contain the following additional information:

(1) The full name of the company or corporation as stated in its certificate of registration.
(2) The registered number of the company or corporation.
(3) The position or office in the company or corporation held by the representative.
(4) The date on which and manner in which the representative was authorised to act for the company or corporation, e.g. ____19 ____: written authority from managing director; or ____19 ____: Board resolution dated ____19 ____.

5.3 Rule 39.6 is intended to enable a company or other corporation to represent itself as a litigant in person. Permission under rule 39.6(b) should therefore be given by the court unless there is some particular and sufficient reason why it should be withheld. In considering whether to grant permission the matters to be taken into acocunt include the complexity of the issues and the experience and position in the company or corporation of the proposed representative.

5.4 Permission under rule 39.6(b) should be obtained in advance of the hearing from, preferably, the judge who is to hear the case, but may, if it is for any reason impracticable or inconvenient to do so, be obtained from any judge by whom the case could be heard.

5.5 The permission may be obtained informally and without notice to the other parties. The judge who gives the permission should record in writing that he has done so and supply a copy to the company or corporation in question and to any other party who asks for one.

5.6 Permission should not normally be granted under Rule 39.6:

(a) in jury trials;
(b) in contempt proceedings.

Recording of proceedings

6.1 At any hearing, whether in the High Court or a county court, **39PD.6**

the proceedings will be tape recorded unless the judge directs otherwise.

6.2 No party or member of the public may use unofficial recording equipment in any court or judge's room without the permission of the court. To do so without permission constitutes a contempt of court.[1]

6.3 Any party or person may require a transcript or transcripts of the recording of any hearing to be supplied to him, upon payment of the charges authorised by any scheme in force for the making of the recording or the transcript.

6.4 Where the person requiring the transcript or transcripts is not a party to the proceedings and the hearing or any part of it was held in private under CPR rule 39.2, paragraph 6.3 does not apply unless the court so orders.

6.5 Attention is drawn to paragraph 7.9 of the Court of Appeal (Civil Division) Practice Direction which deals with the provision of transcripts for use in the Court of Appeal at public expense.

Exhibits at trial

39PD.7 **7.** Exhibits which are handed in and proved during the course of the trial should be recorded on an exhibit list and kept in the custody of the court until the conclusion of the trial, unless the judge directs otherwise. At the conclusion of the trial it is the parties' responsibility to obtain the return of those exhibits which they handed in and to preserve them for the period in which any appeal may take place.

Citation of Authorities Human Rights

39PD.8 **8.1** If it is necessary for a party to give evidence at a hearing of an authority referred to in section 2 of the Human Rights Act 1998—

(1) the authority to be cited should be an authoritative and complete report; and

(2) the party must give to the court and any other party a list of the authorities he intends to cite and copies of the reports not less than three days before the hearing.

(Section 2(1) of the Human Rights Act 1998 requires the court to take into account the authorities listed there)

(3) Copies of the complete original texts issued by the European Court and Commission either paper based or from the Court's judgment database (HUDOC), which is available on the Internet, may be used.

[1] S. 9 of the Contempt of Court Act 1981.

PRACTICE DIRECTION—COURT SITTINGS

This Practice Direction supplements CPR Part 39 **39BPD.1**

COURT SITTINGS

1.1(1) The sittings of the Court of Appeal and of the High Court shall be four in every year, that is to say

(a) the Michaelmas sittings which shall begin on 1st October and end on 21st December;

(b) the Hilary sittings which shall begin on 11th January and end on the Wednesday before Easter Sunday;

(c) the Easter sittings which shall begin on the second Tuesday after Easter Sunday and end on the Friday before the spring holiday; and

(d) the Trinity sittings which shall begin on the second Tuesday after the spring holiday and end on 31st July.

(2) In the above paragraph "spring holiday" means the bank holiday falling on the last Monday in May or any day appointed instead of that day under section 1(2) of the Banking and Financial Dealings Act 1971.

VACATIONS

The High Court

2.1(1) One or more judges of each Division of the High Court shall sit in vacation on such days as the senior judge of that Division may from time to time direct, to hear such cases, claims, matters or applications as require to be immediately or promptly heard and to hear other cases, claims, matters or applications if the senior judge of that Division determines that sittings are necessary for that purpose. **39BPD.2**

(2) Any party to a claim or matter may at any time apply to the Court for an order that such claim or matter be heard in vacation and, if the Court is satisfied that the claim or matter requires to be immediately or promptly heard, it may make an order accordingly and fix a date for the hearing.

(3) Any judge of the High Court may hear such other cases, claims, matters or applications in vacation as the Court may direct.

2.2 The directions in paragraph 3.1 shall not apply in relation to the trial or hearing of cases, claims, matters or applications outside the Royal Courts of Justice but the senior Presiding Judge of each Circuit, with the concurrence of the Senior Presiding Judge, and the Vice-Chancellor of the County Palatine of Lancaster and the Chancery Supervising Judge for Birmingham, Bristol and Cardiff, with the concurrence of the Vice-Chancellor, may make such arrangements for vacation sittings in the courts for which they are respectively responsible as they think desirable.

2.3(1) Subject to the discretion of the Judge, any appeal and any application normally made to a Judge may be made in the month of September.

(2) In the month of August, save with the permission of a Judge

or under arrangements for vacation sittings in courts outside the Royal Courts of Justice, appeals to a Judge will be limited to the matters set out in paragraph 3.5 below, and only applications of real urgency will be dealt with, for example urgent applications in respect of injunctions or for possession under RSC Order 113 (Schedule 1 to the CPR).

(3) It is desirable, where this is practical, that applications or appeals are submitted to a Master, District Judge or Judge prior to the hearing of the application or appeal so that they can be marked "fit for August" or "fit for vacation." If they are so marked, then normally the Judge will be prepared to hear the application or appeal in August, if marked "fit for August" or in September if marked "fit for vacation". A request to have the papers so marked should normally be made in writing, shortly setting out the nature of the application or appeal and the reasons why it should be dealt with in August or in September, as the case may be.

Chancery Masters

39BPD.3 **2.4** There is no distinction between term time and vacation so far as business before the Chancery Masters is concerned. The Masters will deal with all types of business throughout the year, and when a Master is on holiday his list will normally be taken by a Deputy Master.

Queen's Bench Masters

39BPD.4 **2.5**(1) An application notice may, without permission, be issued returnable before a Master in the month of August for any of the following purposes:

to set aside a claim form or particulars of claim, or service of a claim form or particulars of claim;
to set aside judgment; for stay of execution;
for any order by consent;
for judgment or permission to enter judgment;
for approval of settlements or for interim payment;
for relief from forfeiture; for charging order; for garnishee order;
for appointment or discharge of a receiver;
for relief by way of interpleader by a sheriff or High Court enforcement officer;
for transfer to a county court or for trial by Master;
for time where time is running in the month of August;

(2) In any case of urgency any other type of application notice (that is other than those for the purposes in (1) above), may, with the permission of a Master be issued returnable before a Master during the month of August.

PART 40

JUDGMENTS, ORDERS, SALE OF LAND ETC.

Contents 40.0.1

I. Judgments and Orders

II. Sale of land etc. and conveyancing counsel

III. Declaratory Judgments

Editorial introduction

The provisions in Pt 40 are divided into three Sects: I. Judgments and Orders, and II, Sale of Land etc. and Conveyancing Counsel, and III. Declaratory Judgments. The first section appeared in the original CPR brought into effect in April 1999, and the second was added by the Civil Procedure (Amendment) Rules 2000 (SI 2000/221) and came into effect on May 2, 2000. The third was added by the Civil Procedure (Amendment) Rules 2001 (SI 2001/256) and came into effect on March 26, 2001. 40.0.2

Judgments and orders

40.0.3 The rules in Sect.I of this Part replaced a number of provisions formerly found in the RSC and CCR; notably RSC O.42 (Judgments and Orders) and (in part) CCR O.22 (Judgments and Orders). Rules 8, 10, 11 and 13 of CCR O.22 are not so replaced but are re-enacted in Sch.2. The differences between the rules in Section I and the former RSC and CCR rules are mainly in form rather than in substance, but there are a few changes which are significant.

Rule 40.1 was amended by the Civil Procedure (Amendment No.4) Rules 2004 (SI 2004/3419).

The rules in Sect.I are supplemented by Practice Direction (Judgments and Orders) (see para.40BPD.1 *et seq* below). Among the matters dealt with by this practice direction are many that were dealt with formerly by rules contained in RSC O.42 (e.g. consent orders (para.3.1, formerly r.5A)). In a number of respects the directions are significantly different from the rules they replace.

A "slip rule" specifically directed at the correction of an accidental slip or omission in a judgment or order is expressly enacted in r.40.12 (note also Practice Direction (Judgments and Orders) paras 4.1 to 4.4; see para.40BPD.4 below). Compare r.3.10 (General power of the court to rectify matters where there has been an error of procedure).

Rule 40.1 was amended by the Civil Procedure (Amendment No.4) Rules 2004 (SI 2004/3419).

Accounts and inquiries

40.0.4 Former RSC O.43 contained rules dealing (1) with applications for summary orders for accounts and inquiries and (2) with the procedure to be followed after such orders were made. Sub-paragraph (o) of r.25.1(1) states that the court may grant an interim remedy in the form of an order directing any account to be taken or inquiry to be made by the court (note explanation in para.25.1.38 above); see also Pt 69 (Court's Power to Appoint a Receiver) and the practice direction supplementing that Part. The provisions in former RSC O.43 relating to the procedures for the taking of accounts and conducting inquiries under a judgment or order are not included in the rules in Pt 40 but are found (with some modifications and additions) in a practice direction supplementing this Part, that is to say, in Practice Direction (Accounts, Inquiries Etc.), paras 1 to 8 (see para.40PD.2 *et seq.* below). Until December 2, 2002, other provisions in that practice direction dealt with the application of Sch.1, RSC O.44 (Proceedings Under Judgments and Orders) to county court proceedings (effectively replacing former CCR O.23 (Accounts and Inquiries in Equity Proceedings)). With effect from that date, O.44 was revoked and substantially replaced with new paras 9.1 to 15 (applying to High Court and county court proceedings) then added to the practice direction (see paras 40PD.10 *et seq.* below). The effect of r.2 of O.44 is maintained by CPR r.19.7A.

Structured settlements

40.0.5 By the Civil Procedure (Amendment No.3) Rules 2004 (SI 2004/3129), Section II was added to CPR Pt 41. The provisions in that Section deal with the court's jurisdiction under the Damages Act 1996 to make orders for damages in the form (wholly or partly) of periodical payments (instead of lump sum payments) when awarding damages for future pecuniary loss in personal injury cases. That jurisdiction supplanted the jurisdiction of the court to approve, what were known as, "structured settlements". Consequently, the practice direction attached, not to Pt 41, but to Pt 40, and which contained a guide to the procedure to be followed where parties sought an order based on a structured settlement, was revoked.

Sale of land etc. and conveyancing counsel

40.0.6 Former RSC O.31 (Sales of Land by Order of Court, Etc.) was re-enacted in CPR Sch.1 and made applicable in county court as well as High Court proceedings. This Order was revoked by Civil Procedure (Amendment) Rules 2000 and replaced by the rules in Sect.II of this Part (rr.40.16 to 40.19). The provisions of Sect.II are supplemented by Practice Direction (Sale Etc. of Land by Order of Court and Conveyancing Counsel of the Court) (see paras 40DPD.1 *et seq.* below).

Declaratory judgments

40.0.7 Section III of this Part consists of one rule, r.40.20. It states that the court may make binding declarations whether or not any other remedy is claimed. The rule was added by the Civil Procedure (Amendment) Rules 2001 (SI 2001/256) r.13, and replaced former RSC O.15, r.16; see further para.40.20.1 below.

Reserved judgments

Practice Direction (Reserved Judgments) supplements this Part. It was originally issued by TSO CPR Update 40 October 2005, and came into effect on October 1, 2005. With effect from October 1, 2008, it was entirely substituted by TSO CPR Update 47.See further para.40.2.5 (Handing down written judgments) below. 40.0.8

Related sources

40.0.9
- Rule 59.12 (Judgments and Orders)
- Rule 57.15(2) (Proceedings in High Court)
- Rule 76.32 (Judgments)
- Rule 79.28 (Judgments)
- CCR O.22 (see para.cc22.8)
- Part 12 (Default judgments)
- Part 13 (Setting aside default judgments)
- Part 16 (Statements of case— r.16.4(1)(b) and r.16.4(2)—Interest)
- Practice Direction (Statements of Case), para.12.1 (see para.16PD.1)
- Practice Direction (Commercial Court), paras 14.1 & 14.2 (Judgments and orders) (see Vol.2, para.2A–35)
- Practice Direction (Mercantile Courts), para.11.1 (Judgments and orders) (see Vol.2, para.2B–16)
- *Practice Direction (Declaratory Proceedings: Incapacitated Adults)* [2002] 1 W.L.R. 325, Fam.D. (see para.21.0.6 above)
- *Practice Statement (Supreme Court: Judgments)* [1998] 1 W.L.R. 825 (see para.B5–001 below)
- *Practice Statement (Supreme Court: Judgments) (No.2)* [1999] 1 W.L.R. 1 (see para.B6–001 below)
- Queen's Bench Guide, para.10.3 (see Vol.2, para.1B–71)
- Chancery Guide, Ch.9 (see Vol.2, para.1A–85)
- Commercial Court Guide, Section J, para.12 (see Vol.2, para.2A–118)
- County Courts Act 1984 ss.69 to 72 (see Vol.2, paras 9A–554 to 9A–561)

Practice Directions

Part 40 is supplemented by Practice Directions: 40.0.10
- Accounts and Inquiries (see para.40PD.1 below)
- Judgments and Orders (see para.40BPD.1 below)
- Court's Powers in Relation to Land and Conveyancing Counsel (see para.40DPD.1 below)
- Reserved Judgments (see para.40EPD.1 below)

Note also:
- *Practice Direction (Declaratory Proceedings: Incapacitated Adults)* [2002] 1 W.L.R. 325, Fam.D. (See para.21.0.6 above)

I. Judgments and Orders

Scope of this section[1]

40.1 This Section sets out rules about judgments and orders which apply except where any other of these Rules or a practice direction makes a different provision in relation to the judgment or *order in question.* 40.1

Meaning of "judgment" and "order"

Under the RSC and the CCR a "judgment" was the final decision of the court in civil proceedings commenced in the High Court by writ (or in any other manner prescribed by rules of court), or brought in a county court on a plaint. Such a proceeding was an "action"; so a judgment was a final decision in an action (in the county 40.1.1

[1] Amended by the Civil Procedure (Amendment) Rules 2000 (SI 2000/221).

courts actions could be "fixed date" or "default"). In the High Court and the county courts, any civil proceeding that was not an action was a "matter". In the High Court a matter could be brought on various forms of originating process; in the county courts a matter was brought on an originating application. A final decision of a court on a matter was not a "judgment" but an "order". A decision of the court in an action or in a matter other than a final decision was also an "order". (A "cause" included an action and any criminal proceedings falling within the jurisdiction of the High Court).

These technical distinctions between a "judgment" and an "order" were derived in part from provisions defining some of the terms of art referred to in the previous paragraph as found in the definition provisions in the Supreme Court Act 1981 and the County Courts Act 1984 (see, respectively, s.151 and s.147, in Vol.2, paras 9A–391 and 9A–712), and in the RSC and CCR. (Once upon a time, the distinction was important when it came to enforcement, but that ceased to be the case a long time ago and dicta to the effect that it is doubtful whether there is still any distinction between the two terms have to be seen in that context, e.g. *Onslow v Commissioners of Inland Revenue* (1890) 25 QBD 465, per Lord Esher M.R.) One important reason for distinguishing a judgment from an order disappeared with the definition of "judgment" for the purposes of enforcement came to include "any judgment or order" (see Administration of Justice Act 1920 s.12(1)). It would seem that the terms "judgment" and "order", whether found in the CPR or in other legislation (whether primary or secondary), have to be defined in context. The proper definitions may be matters of considerable importance, as is illustrated by *Knight v Rochdale Healthcare NHS Trust* [2003] EWHC 1831; [2003] 4 All E.R. 416, (QB) (Crane J.) (where the question was whether a consent order was a judgment within the meaning of the Limitation Act 1980 s.10(3)); *Enron (Thrace) Exploration and Production B.V. v Clapp* [2005] EWHC 401 (Comm), March 22, 2005, unrep. (Aikens J.) (whether court had jurisdiction under r.3.1(7) to entertain second application to set aside default judgment); *R. (Jones) v Ceredigion CC* [2005] EWCA Civ 986; [2005] 1 W.L.R. 3626, CA (whether Court of Appeal had jurisdiction under the Supreme Court Act 1981 s.16(1) in circumstances where the appellant had been refused permission to appeal directly from the High Court to the House of Lords); *Bishlawi v Minrealm Ltd* [2007] EWHC 2204 (Ch); September 13, 2007, unrep. (Kitchin J.) (whether an undertaking an order within CPR Sch.1 RSC Ord.45, r.5).

Under the CPR, the various forms of originating process that previously existed are substituted by a single form, the claim, and "action" and "matter" cease to be terms of art (though "action" remains in some primary legislation). It no longer makes sense to say that a "judgment" is a final decision obtained in an action, and every other decision, whether obtained in an action or a matter, is an "order" (*Ex p. Chinery Onslow* (1884) 12 QBD 342). However, the terms "judgment" and "order" are used in many provisions in the CPR, sometimes in conjunction and sometimes not, and most of these provisions have been copied (apparently unthinkingly) from former RSC and CCR provisions in some of which the distinction between "judgment" and "order" was meaningful and was intended to have discriminating effects (see *Knight v Rochdale Healthcare NHS Trust* [2003] EWHC 1831; [2003] 4 All E.R. 416,(QB) (Crane J.)). It remains to be seen whether anything important has been lost, and whether any unwelcome problems have been caused, by maintaining in the CPR the expressions "judgment" and "order" when it appears that one is not a synonym for the other, but yet no basis for distinguishing between them can be derived from the rules themselves. Neither expression is mentioned in the interpretation provision of the CPR (r.2.3) or in the Glossary. It could be argued that, under the CPR, a "judgment" is a final decision of the court in a claim, and an "order" is any other decision. (The concept of "final decision" arises under the CPR in the context of appeals and has received judicial exposition; see *Roerig v Valiant Trawlers Ltd* [2002] EWCA Civ 21; [2002] 1 All E.R. 961, CA). In Pt 70 (General Rules About Enforcement), the expression "judgment or order" is given an extended definition (r.70.1(2)(c)), and in Practice Direction (Case Management-Preliminary Stage: Allocation and Re-allocation), para.12.1 it is given a restricted meaning for certain case management purposes (see para.26PD.2 above).

Generally, primary legislation granting rights of appeal in civil proceedings, grant the right in relation to a "judgment" or "order" of the lower court (e.g. Supreme Court Act 1981 ss.15 and 16, and County Courts Act 1984 s.77(7)). However, under the Access to Justice Act 1999 (Destination of Appeals) Order 2000, the term "decision" is used to encompass "any judgment, order or direction" of the High Court or a county court. This reflects the 1999 Act and the amendments made to other legislation by that Act (e.g. Supreme Court Act 1981 s.58). Unfortunately, whereas under the old rules of court, the expressions "judgment" and "order" were used accurately, throughout Pt 52 (Appeals), the terms "decision", "order", "order or judgment", and "order or decision", are used indiscriminately.

The rules in Sect.I of Pt 40 apply "except where any other of these Rules or a practice direction makes a different provision". The words "or a practice direction-"were added to this rule by the Civil Procedure (Amendment No.4) Rules 2004 (SI 2004/3419), with effect from April 1, 2005 (see further para.40.9.2 below).

Standard requirements[1]

40.2—(1) Every judgment or order must state the name and judicial title of the person who made it, unless it is— 40.2

(a) default judgment entered under rule 12.4(1) (entry of default judgment where judgment is entered by a court officer) or a default costs certificate obtained under rule 47.11;

(b) judgment entered under rules 14.4, 14.5, 14.6, 14.7 and 14.9 (entry of judgment on admission where judgment is entered by a court officer);

(c) a consent order under rule 40.6(2) (consent orders made by court officers);

(d) an order made by a court officer under rule 70.5 (orders to enforce awards as if payable under a court order); or

(e) an order made by a court officer under rule 71.2 (orders to obtain information from judgment debtors).

(2) Every judgment or order must—

(a) bear the date on which it is given or made; and

(b) be sealed[GL] by the court.

(3) Paragraph (4) applies where a party applies for permission to appeal against a judgment or order at the hearing at which the judgment or order was made.

(4) Where this paragraph applies, the judgment or order shall state—

(a) whether or not the judgment or order is final;

(b) whether an appeal lies from the judgment or order and, if so, to which appeal court;

(c) whether the court gives permission to appeal; and

(d) if not, the appropriate appeal court to which any further application for permission may be made.

(Paragraph 4.3B of the Practice Direction supplementing Part 52 deals with the court's power to adjourn a hearing where a judgment or order is handed down and no application for permission to appeal is made at that hearing)

Effect of judgment before entry—altering judgment

A judgment takes effect from the time when the judge pronounces it, and the subsequent entry of it is in obedience to the rules of court (*Holtby v Hodgson* (1889) 24 Q.B.D. 103). Accordingly, r.40.7 states that (except where r.40.10 applies) a judgment order takes effect from the day when it is given or made, or such later date as the **40.2.1**

[1] Amended by the Civil Procedure (Amendment) Rules 2000 (SI 2000/221), the Civil Procedure (Amendment No.4) Rules 2001 (SI 2001/2792) and the Civil Procedure (Amendment No.4) Rules 2005 (SI 2005/3515).

court may specify. But, as was confirmed by the Court of Appeal in *Re Barrell Enterprises* [1973] 1 W.L.R. 19, CA, it is within the powers of the judge to alter his judgment at any time before it is entered and perfected (see also *Pittalis v Sherefettin* [1986] 1 Q.B. 808, CA and cases referred to therein). The disclosure to the judge of a payment into court does not affect this right (*Millensted v Grosvenor House Ltd* [1937] 1 K.B. 717, CA).

After the coming into effect of the CPR, in *Stewart v Engel* [2000] 1 W.L.R. 2268; [2000] 3 All E.R. 518, CA, the Court of Appeal said there was nothing in the CPR abrogating the Barrell jurisdiction (*op. cit.* at p.2274 per Sir Christopher Slade). The jurisdiction was reviewed and endorsed in *Taylor v Lawrence* [2002] EWCA Civ 290, [2003] Q.B. 528, CA (a decision of the Court of Appeal consisting of five judges). In the *Re Barrell* case it was said that, when an oral judgment has been given, whether in a court of first instance or on appeal, the successful party ought "save in most exceptional circumstances to be able to assume that the judgment is a valid and effective one" (*op. cit.* at p.23 per Russell L.J.). In *Stewart v Engel*, the judges, whilst agreeing that the Barrell jurisdiction survived the CPR, were not agreed on the question whether the jurisdiction remains subject to the "exceptional circumstances" requirement as understood before the CPR came into effect. As a practical matter this difference may not be important. The pre- and post-CPR cases were carefully considered and explained by May L.J. in *Robinson v Bird* [2003] EWCA Civ 1820; *The Times*, January 20, 2004, CA, and by Rix L.J. in *Compaigne Noga d'Importation et d'Exploration S.A. v Abacha* [2001] 3 All E.R. 513. See also (*A v B Plc* [2002] EWCA Civ 337; [2003] Q.B. 195, CA).

First instance cases on the exercise of the Barrell jurisdiction decided since the coming into effect of the CPR include the following: *Charlesworth v Relay Roads Ltd* [2000] 1 W.L.R. 230 (Neuberger J.); *Spice Girls Ltd v Aprilia World Service BV (Permission to Appeal)*, 2000 S.L.T. 1272 (Arden J.); *Mamidoil-Jetoil Greek Petroleum S.A. v Okta Crude Oil Refinery AD (No.2)* [2001] 1 Lloyd's Rep. 591 (Thomas J.); *Read v Edmed* [2004] EWHC 3274, (QB), (Bell J.); *Enron (Thrace) Exploration and Production B.V. v Clapp* [2005] EWHC 401 (Comm), March 22, 2005, unrep. (Aikens J.). See also "Finality of judgments", Vol.2, para.9A–558.

The court has an inherent jurisdiction to vary its own orders to make the meaning and intention of the court clear (Practice Direction (Judgments and Orders), para.4.5, see para.40BPD.4 below. For correction of an accidental slip or omission in a judgment or order, see r.40.12 and notes following. For general power of court to vary or revoke order, see r.3.1(7), and para.40.9.3 below.

40.2.1.A *Recalling and re-considering judgment*

A party may make an application to a judge to reconsider a judgment whether given at the end of the trial of an action, or on a preliminary issue, or on ruling on an interlocutory application, or on making an order for costs (as in *Ultraframe (UK) v Fielding* [2006] EWCA Civ 1660; [2007] 2 All E.R. 983, CA), or in other circumstances. And such an application may be made where the judgment is the judgment of an appeal court (see further below). Where necessary, the court will give directions for the preparation and filing of skeletons, witness statements and documents (e.g. *Albon v Naza Motor Trading SDN BH* [2007] EWHC 2613 (Ch); November 9, 2007, unrep. (Lightman J.).)

In *Malmesbury (Earl of) v Strutt & Parker* [2007] EWHC 2199 (QB); October 9, 2007, unrep. (Jack J.), a professional negligence case, the trial judge was invited by the parties to confine his judgment to certain issues of liability. Subsequently, in refusing the claimant's application to reconsider certain findings, the judge stated that the jurisdiction should be exercised only where it is clear to the judge without prolonged inquiry that he reached the wrong conclusion.

In delivering the principal judgment in *Robinson v Bird, op cit.*, May L.J. made the following points (para.94, see also Peter Gibson L.J. at para.120). Once a judgment has been handed down or given, there are obvious reasons why the court should hesitate long and hard before making a material alteration to it. The cases acknowledge that there may very occasionally be circumstances in which a judge not only can, but should make a material alteration in the interests of justice. Reopening contentious matters or permitting one or more of the parties to add to their case or make a new case should rarely be allowed. Any attempt to do this is likely to receive summary rejection in most cases. It will only very rarely be appropriate for parties to attempt to do so. This necessarily means that the court would only be persuaded to do so in "exceptional circumstances", but that expression by itself is no more than a relatively uninformative label. It is not profitable to debate what it means in isolation from the facts of a particular case.

In delivering the principal judgment in *Robinson v Bird, op cit.*, May L.J. made the following points (para.94, see also Peter Gibson L.J. at para.120). Once a judgment has been handed down or given, there are obvious reasons why the court should hesitate long and hard before making a material alteration to it. The cases acknowledge that there may very occasionally be circumstances in which a judge not only can, but should make a material alteration in the interests of justice. Reopening contentious matters or permitting one or more of the parties to add to their case or make a new case should rarely be allowed. Any attempt to do this is likely to receive summary rejection in most cases. It will only very rarely be appropriate for parties to attempt to do so. This necessarily means that the court would only be persuaded to do so in "exceptional circumstances", but that expression by itself is no more than a relatively uninformative label. It is not profitable to debate what it means in isolation from the facts of a particular case.

In delivering the principal judgment in *Robinson v Bird, op cit.*, May L.J. made the following points (para.94, see also Peter Gibson L.J. at para.120). Once a judgment has been handed down or given, there are obvious reasons why the court should hesitate long and hard before making a material alteration to it. The cases acknowledge that there may very occasionally be circumstances in which a judge not only can, but should make a material alteration in the interests of justice. Reopening contentious matters or permitting one or more of the parties to add to their case or make a new case should rarely be allowed. Any attempt to do this is likely to receive summary rejection in most cases. It will only very rarely be appropriate for parties to attempt to do so. This necessarily means that the court would only be persuaded to do so in "exceptional circumstances", but that expression by itself is no more than a relatively uninformative label. It is not profitable to debate what it means in isolation from the facts of a particular case.

In delivering the principal judgment in *Robinson v Bird, op cit.*, May L.J. made the following points (para.94, see also Peter Gibson L.J. at para.120). Once a judgment has been handed down or given, there are obvious reasons why the court should hesitate long and hard before making a material alteration to it. The cases acknowledge that there may very occasionally be circumstances in which a judge not only can, but should make a material alteration in the interests of justice. Reopening contentious matters or permitting one or more of the parties to add to their case or make a new case should rarely be allowed. Any attempt to do this is likely to receive summary rejection in most cases. It will only very rarely be appropriate for parties to attempt to do so. This necessarily means that the court would only be persuaded to do so in "exceptional circumstances", but that expression by itself is no more than a relatively uninformative label. It is not profitable to debate what it means in isolation from the facts of a particular case.

In *A v B Plc* [2002] EWCA Civ 337; [2003] Q.B. 195, CA, at an *inter partes* hearing, the judge granted the claimant (C) an interim injunction restraining the defendants (D) from publishing confidential information. Subsequently, on ground of C's material non-disclosure, the judge discharged the injunction but, before the order carrying this decision into effect was perfected, at the request of C reconsidered his judgment and, on basis of evidence contained in an additional witness statement tendered on behalf of C, reversed his decision and continued the injunction. The Court of Appeal granted D's appeal on the merits and discharged the injunction. Consequently, the Court did not have to decide the other point raised by D on appeal, that is, whether the judge erred in reconsidering his judgment. However, having been persuaded that issues of principle were involved, in particular as to (1) when a decision can be reconsidered and (2) when additional evidence is or is not admissible, the Court expressed the opinion (albeit without the benefit of oral argument) that the judge had erred in that respect. But the Court rejected the suggestion that, in a case where the judgment in question is one granting an interim injunction, there are technicalities relevant to the issues of principle which require one outcome or another. Each application has to be decided on its merits, as to which the only guidance which is required is that contained in the overriding objective (see r.1.1).

It should be understood that circumstances may arise where a judge, in giving judgment, should not only recognise that, in the period between the delivery of the judgment and the moment when the order is sealed or otherwise perfected, there is jurisdiction in the court which enables him to reconsider and if necessary alter, the judgment order, but should anticipate that he may need to take advantage of the jurisdiction and should take steps to ensure that the order is not peremptorily perfected.

An example is provided by the situation where a judge gives judgment dismissing an application for summary judgment, and thereupon makes a conditional order requiring a party to pay money into court, but directs that the order should not be perfected until the party affected has had an opportunity of placing evidence of his means before the court (*Anglo-Eastern Trust Ltd v Kermanshahchi* [2002] EWCA Civ 198; February 22, 2002, unrep., CA, at para.71).

The exercise of the Barrell jurisdiction should be distinguished from the situation where a judgment is perfected but that judgment does not dispose of the issues between the parties. For example, where issues as to whether a claimant has "beaten" an offer and should enjoy the costs benefits granted by r.36.21 are not finally dealt with in a perfected judgment (*K.R. v Bryn Alyn Community (Holdings) Ltd* [2003] EWCA Civ 783, June 10, 2003, unrep., CA (jurisdiction of Court of Appeal to deal with Pt 36 appeals where damages increased on appeal bringing certain co-claimants within the net of r.36.21)). Where there is a split trial, for example with liability being dealt with before quantum, and the judgment of the former is perfected before the completion of the trial of the latter, issues dealt with in that judgment may not be re-litigated at the quantum hearing (*Barings Plc v Coopers & Lybrand* [2003] EWHC 2371 (Ch) October 17, 2003, unrep. (Evans-Lombe J.)).

Also, the exercise of the Barrell jurisdiction should be distinguished from the situation where a judgment order is perfected in circumstances where the order itself contemplates, and allows for the fact, that further argument before the court may be necessary. For example, where a judgment order discharges certain orders and anticipates that further argument might be necessary if the parties cannot agree what the consequences of that discharge should be (*Grupo Torras S.A. v Torras Hostench London Ltd* [2001] EWCA Civ 1370; July 30, 2001, unrep., CA).

Where an order carrying into effect a judgment is perfected, in dealing with an appeal made on the basis that the judge failed to make findings on particular issues, the circumstances may be such as to make it appropriate for the appeal court to take into consideration a subsequent supplementary judgment by the judge dealing with those issues where that judgment did not in any way alter the perfected order, rather than to remit the matter for further consideration by the trial court (*Roche v Chief Constable of Greater Manchester* [2005] EWCA Civ 1454).

40.2.1.B *Altering draft judgment*

Nowadays, in accordance with the modern practice in the High Court and the Court of Appeal, on a confidential basis judges routinely make available their written judgments to legal advisers in advance of the handing down hearing. The duties of counsel in these circumstances were stressed and explained in *Director of Public Prosecutions v P. (No.2)* [2007] EWHC 1144 (Admin); [2007] 4 All E.R. 648 (see further para.40.2.5 below). If a judge sends his written judgment to the advisers in draft, and they are able to agree the consequential orders, he may be able to excuse their attendance when he delivers the judgment formally in court, thereby making it available to the public and the media (if interested), but he cannot dispense completely with the formality of handing down his judgment in open court (*Owusu v Jackson* [2002] EWCA Civ 877; June 19, 2002, unrep., CA; *cf. Williams Corporate Finance Plc v Holland* [2001] EWCA Civ 1526; October 22, 2001, unrep., CA). In such circumstances, the judgment may be formally delivered by another judge. A draft judgment may be as good as judgment signed and sealed for the purpose of enforcing it (*Birmingham City Council v Yardley* [2004] EWCA Civ 1756).

The practice of circulating judgments before handing down may encourage parties to invoke the exercise of the Barrell jurisdiction. Examples of cases in which parties applied to the trial judge to reopen trial for purpose making further submissions on issues on which they had failed are *Markem Corporation v Zipher Limited* [2005] EWCA Civ 267, March 22, 2005, unrep., CA; *Navitaire Inc v Easy Jet Airline Company Ltd* [2004] EWHC 2271 (Ch); and [2005] EWHC 282 (Ch), March 11, 2005, unrep. (Pumfrey J.). In *Prudential Assurance Co Ltd v McBains Cooper* [2000] 1 W.L.R. 2000, CA; [2001] 3 All E.R. 1014, CA, the Court of Appeal said (1) where the practice of making a judgment available to parties in advance of its delivery is followed, at that time the judgment is not being "given or made" within the meaning of r.40.7, (2) the purpose of the practice is not to make available to the parties more material to help them settle their dispute, (3) the parties' agreement is just one factor which a judge should take into account in exercising his discretion in the public interest. In *Royal Brompton Hospital N.H.S. Trust v Hammond*, [2001] EWCA Civ 778; May 23, 2001, unrep., CA, the Court said (1) there is no logical reason why a judgment should be more readily altered after delivery to the parties, but before handing down, than during delivery of an oral judgment or immediately after delivery (this proposition was doubted in *Robinson v Bird, op cit.*, see further below), (2) the discretion to re-consider a judgment before it is sealed or otherwise perfected has to be exercised in accordance with the overriding objective, (3) accordingly, cases should be dealt with expeditiously and fairly, with an appropriate share of the court's resources being allotted to the case, (4) to achieve that, parties must place before the court the submissions they wish rely upon and it would only be in an exceptional case or for strong reasons that they would be allowed to re-open arguments after the process of delivering judgment has been initiated, (5) the practice of supplying parties with copies of judgments to be handed down was not adopted to encourage or facilitate re-opening of issues that were argued. See also *Watchtower Investments Ltd v Payne* [2001] EWCA Civ 1261, July 20, 2001, unrep., CA In *ISTIL Group Inc v Zahoor* [2003] EWHC 165 (Ch); [2003] 2 All E.R. 252, the draft judgment circulated by the judge in an interlocutory matter contained adverse findings concerning the honesty of the conduct of the claimants. As a result, the claimants asked the judge for permission to address him further on the matter and to adduce further evidence. In view of the serious nature of the findings, the judge (Lawrence Collins J.) granted permission. Where a significant decision of the Court of Appeal or the House of Lords becomes available before a judgment is formally handed down, a judge ought to be willing to reconsider his or her conclusions in the light of the decision in order to minimise the possibility of an appeal with its attendant delay and expense (*Hatton v Chafes (A Firm)* [2003] EWCA Civ 341; March 13, 2003, unrep., CA).

In *Robinson v Bird* [2003] EWCA Civ 1820; *The Times*, January 20, 2004, CA, in analysing the authorities relating to the application of the Barrell jurisdiction to the pre-handing down procedure provided for by Practice Statement (Supreme Court: Judgments) (see para.40.2.5 below), May L.J. examined the judgments of the Court of Appeal in *Prudential Assurance Co Ltd v McBains Cooper, op cit.*, and *Royal Brompton Hospital N.H.S. Trust v Hammond, op cit.* His lordship noted that, in the Royal Brompton Hospital case, the Court rejected the submission that a court would more readily alter its judgment before it was officially handed down than afterwards and said (obiter) that the same considerations arise in either instance. May L.J. doubted whether this was correct. His lordship said (para.91):

> "If a judgment has not been handed down or delivered, it has not been given. Until it is given, it is of no effect. Granted that there are obvious reasons why it would be unfortunate ... for a judge to alter a draft judgment which has been handed to the parties, it remains a draft judgment which, in my view, the judge is at liberty to alter. The jurisdiction to do so is not in doubt. The question is whether 'exceptional circumstances' or something less rigorous will enable him to do so in a particular case.'

In answering this particular question, May L.J. said (para.96) a judge should only exceptionally make other than typographical and minor corrections to a judgment given to parties under the pre-handing down procedure "so perhaps the uninformative label "exceptional circumstances" needs to be appended to the exercise of the jurisdiction". But his lordship again stressed that such expressions as "exceptional circumstances" and "strong reasons" are only labels. The question whether to exercise the jurisdiction to alter a draft judgment can only depend on the circumstances of the particular case.

In *Egan v Motor Services (Bath) Ltd* [2007] EWCA Civ 1002; [2008] 1 All E.R. 1156, CA the Court of Appeal (1) noted and deprecated the growing practice of counsel writing to the judge upon receipt of draft judgment, asking him to reconsider his conclusions, and (2) stated that, (a) circulation of a draft is not intended to provide counsel with an opportunity to re-argue the issues in the case, and (b) only in the most exceptional circumstances is it appropriate to ask the judge to reconsider a point of substance; for example, where counsel feels that the judge (i) had not given adequate reasons for some aspect of his decision, or (ii) had decided the case on a point which was not properly argued or has relied on an authority which was not considered.

Appellate courts, as well as trial courts, may recall judgments and reconsider them. (A dramatic illustration is the famous case of *Cutts v Head* [1984] Ch. 290, CA, where the Court of Appeal changed its mind completely.) *Robinson v Bird* was referred to in *Gravgaard v Aldridge & Brownlee, The Times*, December 2, 2004, CA, where, after circulation of the Court of Appeal's judgment before handing down, counsel made further written submissions to the appeal judges. The Court stated that, in these circumstances, counsel would only rarely be allowed (a) to reopen contentious matters, or (b) to attempt to add to their case or make a new case. In *Daniels v Thompson* [2004] EWCA Civ 307 March 18, 2003, unrep., CA, the Court of Appeal refused to give counsel permission to make further oral or written submissions after receiving the draft judgment; and in *Browning v Brachers* [2004] EWHC 16, (QB) February 13, 2004, unrep., the trial judge (Jack J.) refused to allow counsel to make further submissions as to the manner in which interest losses should be calculated. On the other hand, in *Director of Public Prosecutions v P. (No.2) (Note)* [2007] EWHC 1144 (Admin); [2007] 4 All E.R. 648, DC, upon circulating its draft judgment to the parties, in which a Divisional Court made certain obiter observations on a legal issue which had not been fully argued (and which lawyers representing the CPS in the case believed to be of wider importance), the court permitted the CPS to make further submissions and adjourned the handing down.

It is not unusual for judgments as handed down to contain passages indicating that the court has taken into account and dealt with comments and submissions made by counsel in response to their receipt of a copy of the judgment before handing down. Sometimes the response is simply an acknowledgment that they were received with no revision of the judgment being made, or merely revisions in the form of the correction of minor errors. At other times it is a reasoned response to submissions on substantive or procedural issues. See e.g. *Sinclair Investment Holdings S.A. v Cushnie* [2004] EWHC 218, (Ch) February 12, 2004, unrep. (Mann J.); *Reed Executive Plc v Reed Business Information Ltd* [2004] EWCA Civ 159, March 3, 2004, unrep., CA; *R. (Godmanchester Town Council) v Secretary of State for Environment, Food and Rural Affairs* [2004] EWHC 1217, (Admin), July 22, 2004, unrep.; *Slough BC v C.* [2004] EWHC 1759, (Admin), July 22, 2004, unrep. (Richards J.); *Tinsley v Sarkar* [2004] EWCA Civ 1098, July 23, 2004, unrep., CA; *Perotti v Collyer-Bristow (No.2)* [2004] EWCA Civ 1019; [2004] 4 All E.R. 72, CA; *Oakley Inc v Animal Limited* [2005] EWHC 210 (Ch), February 17, 2005, unrep. (Mr. Peter Prescott Q.C.); *Radu v Houston* [2006] EWCA Civ 1575, November 22, 2006, unrep., CA.

In the House of Lords, drafts of speeches to be delivered are provided to counsel in confidence with a request that counsel should identify any misprints, inadvertent errors of fact or ambiguities of expression. This is provided for by direction 20.3 of the Practice Directions Applicable to Civil Appeals (see Vol.2 para.4A–91 below). In *R. (Edwards) v Environment Agency* [2008] UKHL 22; *The Times* May 6, 2008, HL, solicitors for the appellant submitted a memorandum containing references to three European Directives not mentioned in the appellant's submission and repeating arguments that had already been considered. The Law Lords said that this was an abuse of the procedure of the House (see paras 66 and 73). Express provision for the making of new submissions to the House after the conclusion of argument is made in direction 38.1.

40.2.1.C *Clarifying or amplifying reasons*

Since the decision of the Court of Appeal in *Flannery v Halifax Estate Agencies Ltd* [2000] 1 W.L.R. 377, CA, applications to trial judges for permission to appeal against their decisions on the ground that the reasons given by the judge were insufficient in some material respects have become more common. It seems that, nowadays, trial judges are held to a more exacting standard. This has led to an increase in the instances in which counsel, upon receiving copies of reserved judgments before handing down, have invited judges to clarify or amplify their reasons in relation to particular conclusions (e.g. reasons for rejecting the evidence of an expert witness) (e.g. *Aerospace Publishing Limited v Thames Water Utilities Ltd* [2006] EWCA Civ 717, April 27, 2006, CA (where contended that judge's conclusions as to claimant's losses were inadequately supported by his reasons)). And it has led to the development of the practice of appeal courts, when considering applications for permission to appeal, inviting the judge to amplify his reasons (as explained in *Long v Sava* [2007] EWHC 2087 (Ch); September 28, 2007 (Mr. Peter Leaver Q.C.), and illustrated in *Hicks v Russell Jones & Walker* [2007] EWHC 2545 (Ch); November 5, 2007, unrep. (Henderson J.)) (see para.52.11.4 below). In *English v Emery Reimbold & Strick Ltd (Practice Note)* [2002] EWCA Civ 605; [2002] 1 W.L.R. 2409, CA, the Court of Appeal recommended that, where such an application is made to a trial judge after judgment has been given, the judge should consider whether his judgment is defective for lack of reasons, adjourning for that purpose should he find this necessary. It has been stated that, where a judge has handed down or delivered judgment in a complex case, for the purpose of avoiding the delay and costs of an appeal an advocate ought immediately draw the judge's attention to any material omission of which he is then aware or then believes exists, as it would be unsatisfactory to allow an omission by a judge to deal with a point in a judgment as grounds for an application for appeal if the matter had not be brought to the judge's attention when there was a ready opportunity to do so (*In re T. (A Child) (Contact: Alienation: Permission to Appeal)* [2002] EWCA Civ 1736; [2003] 1 F.L.R. 531, CA, at para.50 per Arden L.J.). In many cases, the advocate ought to raise such matter with the judge "in pursuance with his duty to assist the court to achieve the overriding objective" under r.1.3 (*ibid.*). Where, upon judgment being given, counsel believes that a judge has failed to deal with a material part of the case (e.g. the evidence of an expert), it is his responsibility to point out the alleged defect to the judge so that he may deal with it. See also *In re M (A Child) (Non accidental Injury: Burden of Proof)* [2008] EWCA Civ 1261; *The Times* December 16, 2008, CA, where the court (in remitting to the judge a passage of the judge's judgment for clarification) stressed that counsel has a positive duty in civil proceedings to raise with the judge at handing down, not only any alleged defect in the judge's reasoning, but also any genuine query or ambiguity which arose in the written judgment. In such circumstances it is not appropriate for counsel to draw the judge's attention to the alleged insufficiency by way of an application for permission to appeal (*In re S. (Children)* [2007] EWCA Civ 694; *The Times*, July 2, 2007, CA). See further para.35.0.6 above, and para.52.11.5 below.

Re-opening final determination of appeal

In *Taylor v Lawrence* [2002] EWCA Civ 90; [2002] 2 All E.R. 353, CA, the Court of Appeal held that, in exceptional circumstances, the Court has power, to avoid real injustice where there is no alternative effective remedy, to re-open an appeal after the order carrying its judgment into effect has been perfected. (In *Seray-Wurie v Hackney LBC* [2002] EWCA Civ 909; [2002] 3 All E.R. 448, CA, it was held that the High Court has a similar power.) This is not an example of the exercise of the Barrell jurisdiction, but a significant expansion of the Court's powers based ultimately on an implied jurisdiction to do that which is necessary to achieve its objectives as a court of justice. Following upon the decisions in *Taylor v Lawrence* and the *Seray-Wurie* case, the CPR were amended by the addition of r.52.17 (Reopening of final appeals) and this rule is supplemented by provisions in Section IV of Practice Direction (Appeals) (see further commentary to CPR Pt 52 below). In *Matlaszek v Bloom Camillin (A Firm)* [2003] EWHC 2728, Brooke L.J. observed that in the Court of Appeal during the previous 12 months over 200 applications had been made to invoke the exceptional *Taylor v Lawrence* jurisdiction but none had been granted. Some parties aggrieved by the decisions of circuit judges (sitting as appeal courts) refusing permission to appeal to them, and unable to appeal such decisions or to get them re-opened under this jurisdiction, have attempted to take advantage of the court's limited jurisdiction to quash such decisions on judicial review; see *R. (Sivasubramaniam) v Wandsworth CC* [2002] EWCA Civ 1738; [2003] 1 W.L.R. 475, CA; *Gregory v Turner* [2003] EWCA Civ 183; [2003] 1 W.L.R. 1149, CA. In *K.R. v Bryn Alyn Community (Holdings) Ltd* [2003] EWCA Civ 783, June 10, 2003, unrep., CA, (decided before r.52.17 came into effect), it was stressed that the jurisdiction to re-open the final determination of an appeal was exceptional but it was suggested that where a party is seeking to get some ancillary matter decided "the court should be much less reluctant to hold itself powerless". 40.2.1.1

Entry of judgment in foreign currency

The English court has power to give judgment for a sum of money expressed in a foreign currency (*Miliangos v George Frank (Textiles) Ltd* [1976] A.C. 443; [1975] 3 All E.R. 801, HL). This power may be exercised even where the foreign currency is payable under a contract the proper law of which is English law (*Barclays Bank International Ltd v Levin Brothers (Bradford) Ltd* [1977] Q.B. 270; [1976] 3 All E.R. 900 (dishonoured bills of exchange accepted payable in England but expressed in foreign currency)). The court has further power to award damages for breach of contract in foreign currency (*Kraut (Jean) A.G. v Albany Fabrics Ltd* [1977] Q.B. 182; [1977] 1 All E.R. 116) and to award damages for tort in a foreign currency (*Owner of the M.V. Eleftherotria v Owner of the M.V. Despina R., "The Despina R"*. [1978] Q.B. 396; [1979] 1 All E.R. 421; and in both cases to award damages in the currency that best expresses the plaintiff's loss (see *Services Europe Atlantique Sud SEAS v Stockholms Rederiaktiebolag SVEA, "The Folias"* [1979] A.C. 685; [1979] 1 All E.R. 421, HL). It does not matter whether the foreign currency is that of a Member State of the European Community (see *Schorsch Meier GmbH v Hennin* [1975] Q.B. 416; [1975] 1 All E.R. 152, CA) or the currency of any other State (*Miliangos v George Frank (Textiles) Ltd*). The judgment will be for payment of the amount of the foreign currency or its sterling equivalent (*ibid.*) converted 40.2.2

for the purposes of the enforcement of the judgment at the time of payment, i.e. the date on which enforcement process is taken or authorised in terms of sterling (*ibid.*).

Where a person applies to the High Court to enforce a European Enforcement Order expressed in a foreign currency in the circumstances provided for by Sect.V of Pt 74, the application must contain a certificate of the sterling equivalent as required by r.74.31(2).

Where a charterparty provides that demurrage is to be calculated in US dollars and does not provide for it to be paid in sterling the reasonable inference is that the money of payment as well as the money of account, is US dollars, even though the freight is payable in sterling and the contract is to be governed by English law, the rate of exchange for demurrage is that prevailing at the date of the payment of the demurrage and not at the date of the bill of lading, and therefore the owners are entitled to the difference between the amount of sterling actually paid at the date of the bill of lading and the sum required to be paid at the rate of exchange ruling at the date of payment and to have the balance awarded in US dollars (*George Veflings Rederi A/S v President of India* [1979] 1 W.L.R. 59; [1979] 1 All E.R. 380, CA).

In the case of liquidation of a company, the practice of converting a foreign currency judgment into sterling as at the date of its enforcement does not apply, but instead the foreign currency debt must not be proved according to its sterling value at the date of the commencement of the winding-up (*Lines Bros Ltd (In Liquidation), Re* [1982] Ch. 1; [1982] 2 All E.R. 183, CA), though in a wholly solvent liquidation, the liquidator should make good a shortfall in the full contractual foreign currency debt before he pays anything to the shareholders (*ibid.*, per Brightman L.J.).

Where there is more than one eligible foreign currency in which the judgment may be given, the applicable principles are those stated by Lord Wilberforce in *Services Europe Atlantique Sud (SEAS) v Stockholms Rederiaktiebolag SVEA, "The Folias"* [1979] A.C. 685; [1979] 1 All E.R. 421, and in the absence of an agreed currency of account and payment, the judgment would be expressed in the currency in which the plaintiff's loss was felt or which most expressed his loss (*Société Française Bunge SA v Belcan N.V.*; *The Federal Huron* [1985] 3 All E.R. 378). The principles emerging from Lord Wilberforce's judgment were summarised in *Barings Plc v Coopers & Lybrand* [2003] EWHC 2371, (Ch), October 17, 2003, unrep., at para.30 (Evans-Lombe J.).

In an action by a foreign national for damages for personal injuries suffered during a visit to England, the damages will be assessed in the currency of his country, since his loss is most closely linked with that currency, except that the damages for pain, suffering and loss of amenities will be assessed in sterling (*Hoffman v Sofaer* [1982] 1 W.L.R. 1350).

If the court does express its judgment for the payment of money in a foreign currency, the judgment will be entered in that currency or its sterling equivalent at the time of payment.

It is not clear whether the plaintiff has the *right* to elect that the judgment should be expressed in sterling or in a foreign currency. It would seem that the court retains a residual discretion to determine whether the judgment should be expressed in sterling or in a foreign currency and that it will exercise this discretion having regard to all the circumstances including the position of the parties and the fluctuations in the rates of exchange between the currency of the contract and sterling during the period between the date when the cause of action whether in contract or tort arose and the date of judgment. There may well be cases in which although the plaintiff may elect that the judgment should be expressed in sterling, yet the defendant may wish, or it might otherwise be just, that the judgment should be expressed in a foreign currency of the contract and vice versa.

Before the CPR came into effect, where a judgment creditor applied for a charging order to enforce a judgment expressed in a foreign currency, it was a requirement that the applicant's affidavit in support should include a certificate stating the sterling equivalent of the judgment. And it was the practice of the court, if granting the application, to make an order for the sterling equivalent of the judgment as so verified by the affidavit, but this was subject to any order or direction which the court may give or make in a particular case. The basis of this practice was *Practice Direction (Judgment: Foreign Currency), [1976]* 1 W.L.R. 83, issued by the Senior Master following the decision of the House of Lords in *Miliangos v George Frank (Textiles) Ltd*, [1976] A.C. 443, H.L. (see Supreme Court Practice 1999 Vol.2 para.2A-37). In *Carnegie v Giessen* [2005] EWCA Civ 191; [2005] 1 W.L.R. 2510, CA, the Court of Appeal held that this practice, and the court's jurisdiction to depart from it in a particular case (a power exercised by the Master in this case), have survived the coming into effect of the CPR. The Court said (1) the principle derived from the authorities is that conversion should be made as close as practicable to the date of payment, having regard to the realities of enforcement procedures, (2) there is nothing in s.1(1) or s.3(4) of the Charging Orders Act 1976 which assists the argument that a charging order may not be expressed in a foreign currency, (3) in departing from the normal practice the Master had exercised his discretion correctly in the circumstances of this case.

Foreign currency may only be lodged in court where the court so directs or permits (the Court Funds Rules 1987 r.38 (see Vol.2 para.6A–90).

Orders enforceable like judgments

By virtue of the provisions of this Part and CPR Pt 70, an order may be enforced in **40.2.3**
the same manner as a judgment, and therefore the express provision to this effect contained in the former O.42, r.24, has been omitted as being unnecessary. It is doubtful whether there is still any distinction between a "judgment" and an "order" (see, per Lord Esher M.R. in *Onslow v Commissioners of Inland Revenue* (1890) 25 Q.B.D. 465: "A judgment is a decision obtained in an action, and every other decision is an order"; *Ex p. Chinery* (1884) 12 Q.B.D. 342; *Ex p. Moore* (1885) 14 Q.B.D. 627; *cf. Shaw v Hertford CC* [1899] 2 Q.B. 282.

The term "order" includes, e.g. an order made by the Disciplinary Committee of the Law Society, pursuant to the Solicitors Act 1974 s.47(2).

An action will lie on an order against a solicitor to pay the costs of proceedings to strike him off the rolls, notwithstanding that an attempt to enforce the order by attachment has failed (*Godfrey v George* [1896] 1 Q.B. 48). And an action will lie on a garnishee order against garnishees, where payment cannot be obtained by execution (*Pritchett v English and Colonial Syndicate* [1899] 2 Q.B. 428).

A balance order can be enforced by execution as a judgment against a party within the jurisdiction. Where the contributory was out of the jurisdiction it was held that the company could bring an action for the recovery of the amount due, and leave was given to serve the writ in such action out of the jurisdiction (*Westmoreland, etc., Slate Co v Fielden* [1891] 3 Ch. 15). An award under a submission can (by order) be enforced as a judgment. See Arbitration Act 1996 s.66(1) (Vol.2, 2E–241).

Judgment of House of Lords

The jurisdiction to ante-date a judgment of the House of Lords can only be derived **40.2.4**
from the order itself; if this is silent the judgment can only speak from its date (*Nitrate Producers S.S. Co Ltd v Short Bros. Ltd* (1922) 127 L.T. 727; 91 L.J.K.B. 871).

Where on appeal to the House of Lords a judgment is reversed with the result that a sum of money then *for the first time* becomes payable, interest runs from the date of the judgment in the House of Lords. But if the effect of an appeal to the tribunal to restore a judgment of a court of first instance under which money was payable, interest runs from the date of that judgment.

Handing down written judgments

A judge is required to give reasons for his decision; that is to say, reasons for his **40.2.5**
judgment in the narrow sense. The expression "judgment" is commonly used to mean, not just the judge's decision, but his reasons for it. Judgments in this broad sense may be given orally or in writing. The general rule is that hearings, including the delivery of judgment, should be in public. But in permitted circumstances hearings may be in private (r.39.2) (see paras 5.4B.5 and 39.2.9 above). A judge, having heard proceedings in private may give judgment in open court, but is not obliged to do so. A judge, having delivered a judgment in private, may give permission for it to be reported. It is conceivable that part of a judgment will be confidential and the other not, with only the latter part being given in open court; e.g. *E.P.I. Environmental Technologies Inc v Symphony Plastic Technologies Plc (Practice Note)* [2004] EWHC 2945 (Ch); [2005] 1 W.L.R. 3456 (Peter Smith J.) (judgment in claim for breach of confidentiality agreement etc. relating to additive used in manufacturing process); *McKennitt v Ash* [2006] EWCA Civ 1714; [2007] 3 W.L.R. 194, CA (open judgment restraining further publication of book with confidential appendix in which actual enjoined material fully described); *Browne of Madingley (Lord) v Associated Newspapers Ltd* [2007] EWCA Civ 295; [2007] 3 W.L.R. 289, CA (private judgment granting interim injunction restraining publication of confidential information); *Madarassy v Nomura International Plc* [2006] EWHC 748 (QB), April 6, 2006, unrep. A hearing may be

in private, and the judgment handed down in private, but with the judge giving permission for it to be reported (e.g. *D.E. v Surrey County Council* [2006] EWHC 359 (Fam); December 29, 2006, unrep. (Munby J.)). (For an extensive discussion of the relevant law on the question whether judgments or summaries of them should remain private, see *Department of Economics, Policy and Development of the City of Moscow v Bankers Trust Co* [2004] EWCA Civ 314, [2005] Q.B. 207, CA; note also *Three Rivers DC v Bank of England* [2005] EWCA Civ 933, July 14, 2005, unrep., CA.)

Generally, where judgment is reserved in the Court of Appeal or in the High Court, the written judgment will be given to the parties' legal advisers on a confidential basis before the handing down hearing. Breach of this confidence may be contempt of court. The particular advantages of this practice are that it enables counsel in advance of the handing down hearing (1) to draw to the attention of the court any minor corrections or amendments that should be made to the judgment before it is handed down, (2) to prepare drafts of consequential orders (whether agreed or not) that will have to be made upon handing down, and (3) to prepare their submissions as to summary assessment of costs and for permission to appeal. The procedure is particularly useful in cases where it is very important that consequential orders be settled quickly (*In re M. (Child Abduction: Delay)* [2007] *The Times* August 28, 2007, CA). It may be appropriate for an appellate court to arrange for a written judgment to be given before handing down to an appellant in person (*Perotti v Collyer-Bristow (A Firm) (Vexatious Litigant: Directions: Corrections)* [2004] EWCA Civ 1019, CA). Under this practice the attendance of counsel at the handing down may be unnecessary and, where attendance is unnecessary the costs of attendance may be disallowed. Provisions reflecting and amplifying the points made immediately above are found in various places. Practice Direction (Reserved Judgments), which was added to Pt 40 in October 2005 and reissued with amendments in October 2008 (see para.40EPD.1 below) contains provisions that apply to all reserved judgments which the court intends to hand down in writing and which regulate the availability of such judgments before handing down, corrections to the draft judgment, orders consequential on judgment, and attendance at handing down. The changes made in October 2008 were designed to take account of the fact that, nowadays, before handing down routinely draft written judgments are circulated by electronic methods, and to deal with the concerns expressed in *Director of Public Prosecutions v P. (Practice Note)*, [2007] EWHC 1144 (Admin); [2008] 1 W.L.R. 1024, DC, and elsewhere. As a consequence, paras 15.13 to 15.21 of Practice Direction (Appeals), which dealt with draft Court of Appeal judgments, were omitted, and para.15.12 was substituted; see further para.52.12.8, below. Earlier provisions (still apparently extant) dealing with this matter are found in *Practice Statement (Supreme Court: Judgments)* [1998] 1 W.L.R. 825, as modified by *Practice Statement (Supreme Court: Judgments) (No.2)* [1999] 1 W.L.R. 1 (see Section B—Practice Directions and Practice Statements, below). Guidance on practice is found in several of the Court Guides; e.g. Queen's Bench Guide, para.10.3.5 (see Vol.2, para.1B–71), Chancery Guide, para.10.1 (see Vol.2, para.1A–85), Admiralty and Commercial Courts Guide, para.J12 (see Vol.2, para.2A–117), Patents Court Guide para.20 (see Vol.2, para.2F–130). See also Section D—Procedural Guides No.16. Reserved Judgments, (para.D16–001) below.

Following upon the coming into effect of Practice Direction (Reserved Judgments) (see above), principally for the purpose of ensuring that journalists understand the risks, it was stressed that, unless a specific order is made by the court, all "draft" judgments are embargoed and cannot be published until the "official" judgment is handed down; the publication of a draft judgment would be regarded as a contempt of court and the consequences of a breach of the practice direction might be severe (*Baigent v Random House Group Ltd* [2006] EWHC 1131 (Ch), May 3, 2006, unrep. (Peter Smith J.)). In *Director of Public Prosecutions v. P. (No.2) (Note)* [2007] EWHC 1144 (Admin); [2008] 1 W.L.R. 1024, DC, a Divisional Court stressed that, under the Practice Direction, disclosure of a draft judgment to solicitors is limited to the solicitors directly involved in the case. Such solicitors should not disclose a draft to other members of their firms or organisations (e.g. the CPS or government departments), save to the extent necessary for the taking of instructions in respect of the instant case. Any solicitor in doubt as to the propriety of a particular disclosure should request permission from the judge concerned (by email if that is convenient).

For alteration, either before or after handing down, of a judgment circulated to counsel before handing down as a result of counsel's further submissions, see para.40.2.1, above.

Where a draft judgment has been sent to parties, and the action is compromised thereafter, the judge has a discretion whether or not to publish the draft. Generally, if a draft judgment has not been sent to parties by the time they compromise, the court (particularly a trial court) will not publish that judgment (*Gurney Consulting Engineers v Gleeds Health and Safety Limited (No.2)* [2006] EWHC 536 (TCC), *The Times*, April 24, 2006 (Judge Peter Coulson Q.C.)).

In *Glaxo Group Limited v Genentech Inc* [2008] EWCA Civ 23; [2008] F.S.R. 23, CA, the claimants (C) brought a claim for the revocation of the defendant's (D) patent. D appealed against a judge's refusal of their application for a stay of these proceedings. At the end of the hearing the Court of Appeal announced its decision to dismiss D's appeal, but said that it would give its reasons at a later date. Before the court handed down judgment, D notified the court that they had decided to consent to the revocation of the patent. In handing down judgment the court stated that D's concession did not absolve the court from its duty to supply written reasons for its decision.

Judgments and orders to be dated

Under the CPR case management system, dates are important. Every judgment or order must "bear the date on which it is made" (r.40.2(2)(a)). Other dates are calculated on the basis of the judgment or order date (e.g. r.40.11 (Time for complying with a judgment or order)). It may be necessary to distinguish this date from other dates, including dates given in the body of the judgment or order itself. For example, under r.52.4(2)(b), notice of appeal must be filed within 14 days after "the date of the decision of the lower court"; that date is the date when the lower court gave its decision as recited in the perfected order, and not the date when the order was perfected (*Sayers v Clarke Walker* [2002] EWCA Civ 645; [2002] 3 All E.R. 490, CA, see also *Owusu v Jackson* [2002] EWCA Civ 877; June 19, 2002, CA). Note also r.40.7 (When judgment or order takes effect). For rules as to the calculation of any period of time for doing any act specified by a judgment or order of the court, see r.2.8. **40.2.6**

Judgments and orders to indicate appropriate route for appeal

Paragraphs (3) and (4) were added to r.40.2 by the Civil Procedure (Amendment No.4) Rules 2005 (SI 2005/3515) (with effect from April 6, 2006). Put shortly, these provisions require a judge to explain the routes of appeal where the losing party seeks permission to appeal and to state the prescribed route of appeal in granting permission. These additions to the standard requirements in judgments and orders were made in an effort to deal with practical problems that had arisen largely because of misunderstandings in the minds of court staff, practitioners and judges as to the modern (admittedly complicated) rules about the routes of appeal and about the circumstances in which permission to appeal may or may not be required. Some of the difficulties came about because judgments and orders subsequently the subject of appeal sometimes did not adequately state what exactly had been decided creating doubts as to how any appeal might be handled (especially by the Court of Appeal). In a number of judgments the Court of Appeal endeavoured to draw attention to these problems and urged the lower courts to take greater care in the drafting of orders and judgments. These amendments to r.40.2 were accompanied by amendments to para.2A of Practice Direction (Appeals) (supplementing Pt 52) designed to state the routes of appeal more clearly (see para.52PD.2A below) and by the addition of para.4.3A, which reflects paras (3) and (4) of r.40.2. **40.2.7**

Withholding judgment reasons

Part 76 contains rules dealing with the rather unusual procedure that applies to applications for control orders in proceedings under the Prevention of Terrorism Act 2005. Rule 76.32(1) states that, when the court gives judgment in any proceedings to which Pt 76 applies, it may withhold any or part of its reasons if and to the extent that it is not possible to give reasons without disclosing information contrary to the public interest. This power is different to the power of the court to give a judgment that is confidential (either in whole or in part) to the parties (see paras 5.4.11, 39.2.9 and 40.2.5). Similar provisions to those contained in r.76.32 are also found in r.79.28. That rule, and the other rules in Pt 79, apply to financial restrictions proceedings under the Counter-Terrorism Act 2008. **40.2.8**

Application to Enterprise Act 2002 warrants

It is expressly provided in Practice Direction (Application for a Warrant under the Enterprise Act 2002) para.7.2 (see para.B14–001, below) that the provisions of r.40.2 apply to a warrant under the Enterprise Act 2002 s.194. **40.2.9**

Drawing up and filing of judgments and orders[1]

40.3 **40.3—(1) Except as is provided at paragraph (4) below or by any Practice Direction, every judgment or order will be drawn up by the court unless—**

(a) the court orders a party to draw it up; or

(b) a party, with the permission of the court, agrees to draw it up;

(c) the court dispenses with the need to draw it up;

(d) it is a consent order under rule 40.6.

(2) The court may direct that—

(a) a judgment or an order drawn up by a party must be checked by the court before it is sealed^{GL}; or

(b) before a judgment or an order is drawn up by the court, the parties must file an agreed statement of its terms.

(3) Where a judgment or an order is to be drawn up by a party—

(a) he must file it no later than 7 days after the date on which the court ordered or permitted him to draw it up so that it can be sealed^{GL} by the court; and

(b) if he fails to file it within that period, any other party may draw it up and file it.

(4) Except for orders made by the court of its own initiative and unless the court otherwise orders, every judgment or order made in claims proceeding in the Queen's Bench Division at the Royal Courts of Justice, other than in the Administrative Court, will be drawn up by the parties, and rule 40.3 is modified accordingly.

Effect of rule

40.3.1 In paras 1.1 to 1.3 of Practice Direction (Judgments and Orders) the terms of paras (1) to (3) of r.40.3 are narrated and by para.1.4 an omission in the rule is made good (see para.40BPD.1 below). That paragraph states that, if the court directs under r.40.3(2)(b) that the parties should file an agreed statement of terms of an order which the court is to draw up, the parties must do so no later than seven days from the date the order was made, unless the court directs otherwise. Paragraph (1) of r.40.3 states that paras (1) to (3) apply except "as provided by paragraph (4)". Paragraph (4) was added by the Civil Procedure (Amendment No.3) Rules 2005 (SI 2005/2292) with effect from October 1, 2005. It modifies the general rule that judgments and orders will be drawn up by the court in relation to judgments and orders made in claims proceeding in the Queen's Bench Division at the RCJ (other than in the Administrative Court). Paragraph (1) of r.40.3 also states that the provisions of the rule shall apply except "as provided by any Practice Direction". The effect of r.40.1 is to make it possible for paras. (1) to (3) of r.40.3 to be modified by other CPR rules. Such other rules having the same effect as r.40.3(4) in particular contexts are: r.58.15(1) (Commercial Court), r.59.12(1) (Mercantile Courts), and r.60.7(1) (Technology and Construction Court) (see, respectively, Vol.2, paras 2A–21, 2B–15 & 2C–13). See also Practice Direction (Commercial Court) para.14, Practice Direction (Mercantile Courts) para.11.

In Pt 57 Sect.IV (claims under theInheritance (Provision for Family and Dependants) Act 1975), r.57.15(2) applies the CPR to claims under the Act issued in the Family Division, but in relation to the drawing up and service of orders, provides that the provisions of the Family Proceedings Rules 1991 relating to the drawing up and service of orders are to apply instead of CPR Pt 40 and its practice direction.

[1] Amended by the Civil Procedure (Amendment) Rules 2000 (SI 2000/221).

Service of judgments and orders[1]

40.4—(1) Where a judgment or an order has been drawn up by a party and is to be served by the court— 40.4

(a) the party who drew it up must file a copy to be retained at court and sufficient copies for service on him and on the other parties; and

(b) once it has been sealed[GL], the court must serve a copy of it on each party to the proceedings.

(2) Unless the court directs otherwise, any order made otherwise than at trial must be served on—

(a) the applicant and the respondent; and

(b) any other person on whom the court orders it to be served.

(Rule 6.21 sets out who is to serve a document other than the claim form.)

Effect of rule

Whereas there was no requirement in the former RSC to serve orders, this is now compulsory if the judgment or order is drawn by a party and filed with the court. The party doing so must provide sufficient copies for service on all the other parties. 40.4.1

Power to require judgment or order to be served on a party as well as his solicitor[2]

40.5 Where the party on whom a judgment or order is to be served is acting by a solicitor, the court may order the judgment or order to be served on the party as well as on his solicitor. 40.5

Effect of rule

Normally it is sufficient to serve the solicitor "on the record" as acting for a party, but this provision enables orders, likely to be "unless" orders, to be served on the party personally where such a party has to do some particular act. 40.5.1

Consent judgments and orders[3]

40.6—(1) This rule applies where all the parties agree the terms in which a judgment should be given or an order should be made. 40.6

(2) A court officer may enter and seal[GL] an agreed judgment or order if—

(a) the judgment or order is listed in paragraph (3);

(b) none of the parties is a litigant in person; and

(c) the approval of the court is not required by these Rules, a practice direction or any enactment before an agreed order can be made.

(3) The judgments and orders referred to in paragraph (2) are—

(a) a judgment or order for—

(i) the payment of an amount of money (including a

[1] Amended by the Civil Procedure (Amendment) Rules 2000 (SI 2000/221), the Civil Procedure (Amendment) Rules 2002 (SI 2002/2058) and the Civil Procedure (Amendment) Rules 2008 (SI 2008/2178).

[2] Amended by the Civil Procedure (Amendment) Rules 2000 (SI 2000/221).

[3] Amended by the Civil Procedure (Amendment) Rules 2000 (SI 2000/221).

judgment or order for damages or the value of goods to be decided by the court); or

(ii) the delivery up of goods with or without the option of paying the value of the goods or the agreed value.

(b) an order for—

(i) the dismissal of any proceedings, wholly or in part;

(ii) the stay[GL] of proceedings on agreed terms, disposing of the proceedings, whether those terms are recorded in a schedule to the order or elsewhere;

(iii) the stay[GL] of enforcement of a judgment, either unconditionally or on condition that the money due under the judgment is paid by instalments specified in the order;

(iv) the setting aside under Part 13 of a default judgment which has not been satisfied;

(v) the payment out of money which has been paid into court;

(vi) the discharge from liability of any party;

(vii) the payment, assessment or waiver of costs, or such other provision for costs as may be agreed.

(4) Rule 40.3 (drawing up and filing judgments and orders) applies to judgments and orders entered and sealed[GL] by a court officer under paragraph (2) as it applies to other judgments and orders.

(5) Where paragraph (2) does not apply, any party may apply for a judgment or order in the terms agreed.

(6) The court may deal with an application under paragraph (5) without a hearing.

(7) Where this rule applies—

(a) the order which is agreed by the parties must be drawn up in the terms agreed;

(b) it must be expressed as being "By Consent";

(c) it must be signed by the legal representative acting for each of the parties to whom the order relates or, where paragraph (5) applies, by the party if he is a litigant in person.

Effect of rule

40.6.1 This rule continues the useful provisions of former RSC O.42, r.5A and CCR O.22, r.7A but not all the former classes of judgments or orders have been repeated in this rule, namely possession of land where the claim does not relate to a dwelling-house.

The former rule did not apply to proceedings where any of the parties were under a disability but the consent of the court was and is still required in such cases (see Pt 21). Historically speaking, the significant feature of the rule is that it enables a judgments or order to be entered and sealed by an officer of the court without the intervention of a judicial officer (see para.2.5.3 above).

Consent orders not covered by this rule require an application to the court for approval. See further para.40BPD.3 and Queen's Bench Guide, para.9.3.2 (see Vol.2, para.1A–62). Rule 40.6 does not apply in claims proceeding in the Commercial Court or in a Mercantile Court (see r.58.15(3) and r.59.12(3)).

Where a claim is made by or on behalf of a child or patient, or against a child or patient, no settlement, compromise or payment and no acceptance of money paid into court shall be valid, so far as it relates to the claim by, on behalf of or against the child or patient, without the approval of the court (r.21.10). It has been suggested that 40.6 should be amended so as to provide that a request for a judgment or order by consent should expressly state that none of the parties is a child or a patient (*Bailey v Warren* [2006] EWCA Civ 51; *The Times* February 20, 2006, CA, at para.135 Arden L.J. (application by patient to set aside consent liability judgment)).

As to declarations by consent, see para.40.20.3 below.

Tomlin orders

There are various ways in which a claim can be disposed of when terms of settlement are arrived at. One method is known as the Tomlin form of order, suggested by Tomlin J. in *Practice Note* [1927] W.N. 290, following the decision in *Dashwood v Dashwood* (1927) 71 S.J. 911. Under such an order the proceedings are stayed on agreed terms to be scheduled to the order. These orders were discussed in *Horizon Technologies International v Lucky Wealth Consultants Ltd* [1992] 1 W.L.R 24, PC (see also *Green v Rozen* [1955] 1 W.L.R. 741). **40.6.2**

The Tomlin order has always been a useful device. Nowadays, under the case management system introduced by the CPR, more cases conclude with such an order.

Where proceedings are to be disposed by an order in Tomlin form, the order should read:

"The Claimant and the Defendant having agreed to the terms set out in the schedule hereto, IT IS ORDERED THAT all further proceedings in this claim be stayed except for the purpose of carrying such terms into effect. Liberty to apply as to carrying such terms into effect."

It is important to remember that the terms in the schedule are not part of the order as such. The terms in the schedule cannot be directly enforced as an order of the court. Thus there is no money judgment to be enforced and it does not carry statutory interest under Judgments Act 1838 s.17.

A provision seeking detailed assessment of a party's costs must be in the body of the order, not in the schedule, otherwise the costs judge will not be able to carry out the assessment (*Horizon Technologies International Ltd v Lucky Wealth Consultants Ltd, op cit.*).

Essentially, a Tomlin Order records terms of settlement agreed between the parties but those terms are not ordered by the court and are not enforceable as a judgment, at least not without a further order.

The terms contained in the schedule are not something for approval by a judge. The judge will, however, approve the order itself. The only orders which the court usually makes are:

(i) That the proceedings be stayed to enable the agreed terms to be put into effect.

(ii) That, if the agreed terms require it, there be payment out of monies paid into court and provision for accrued interest thereon.

(iii) For costs to be assessed, whether between the parties or out of public funds.

Terms in the schedule cannot be enforced on an application to commit: an injunction or an order for specific performance must first be obtained. Hence the need for "Liberty to apply for the purpose of carrying such terms into effect".

The effect of the terms of compromise recorded in a Tomlin order is that the defendant has irrevocably dedicated the property, the subject matter of the agreed terms, to the purposes of the compromise. The defendant would be required, if necessary by an order, for specific performance, to realise the property as agreed with the claimant. The compromise imposes an immediate trust (*Anders Utkilens Rederi A/S v O/Y Lovisa Stevedoring Co A/B* [1985] 2 All E.R. 669).

If the terms scheduled to a consent order are too vague the court will decline to enforce them under the "liberty to apply" provision of the order (*Wilson & Whitworth Ltd v Express and Independent Newspapers Ltd* [1969] 1 W.L.R. 197). Where the scheduled terms are clear an order to give effect to them can be obtained under the "liberty to apply" provision notwithstanding that they go beyond the ambit of the original dispute, could not have been obtained or enforced in the original action and that the obligation did not exist but arose for the first time under the compromise (*EF Phillips & Sons v Clarke* [1970] Ch. 322). Indeed one of the advantages of a Tomlin order is that the parties can include in the schedule provisions which could not have been ordered by the court and which go beyond the limitations of the dispute itself.

If it is intended to embody terms of settlement which can be enforced as an order the terms need to be in the order itself (not the schedule) and set out clearly. Such an order should not include provision for a stay of the proceedings as there would be no point to such a stay.

A Tomlin order is not necessary where all that is required is an order that one party shall pay money to the other. The order should say "The defendant will pay to the claimant £x in full and final settlement of his claim by [date]." (Add an order for assessment of costs, if required.) The court cannot order a party to accept so the order should not say, for example, "The claimant will accept £x in full and final settlement of the claim." Similarly, the court cannot order a party to discontinue a claim: the order should say, for example "Upon the claimant discontinuing the claim and the defendant discontinuing the counterclaim, it is ordered that there be no order for costs." An order to this effect is not a Tomlin order, but a Tomlin order would not be appropriate in such a case.

Practitioners need to decide whether the case requires an order of the court or a Tomlin order with the compromised terms set out in a schedule and take care to draft the order appropriately. The current experience of the courts is that too many proposed orders are having to be returned as being neither enforceable orders nor properly drafted Tomlin orders. A properly drafted Tomlin order is very short and simple (see above). A judge is not concerned with the terms in the schedule; still less is there power to make an order in different terms (*Noel v Becker* [1971] 1 W.L.R. 355, CA) but, of course, practitioners should ensure that the terms are clear and should consider how the proposed terms would be enforced in the event of default.

In *Wallace v Brian Gale & Associates, The Times* March 31, 1997, CA, P's action for damages for negligent survey of house compromised under a Tomlin order by which D agreed to carry out remedial work and to pay P's "costs of this action". It was held that D's liability for costs included any subsequent costs incurred by P for carrying the terms of the order into effect.

In *Islam v Askar, The Times*, October 20, 1994, CA, following agreement between P and D, county court proceedings for winding-up of their partnership were stayed by consent. P subsequently discovered that the terms of the schedule to the Tomlin order differed from the terms of agreement. It was held that the court had an inherent jurisdiction to rectify the order. In *Allied Irish Bank Plc v Hughes, The Times*, November 4, 1994,a Tomlin order was approved by the judge, with alterations made by him for purpose of greater clarity, and entered in court records. On application by P to enforce the order it was held that the order was not a nullity as, in the circumstances, D's consent to it in its altered form could be implied.

Setting aside consent judgments and orders

40.6.3 Rule 40.6 is restricted in its application to judgments and orders made in the circumstances listed in para.(3). In modern times, the grounds upon which (e.g. change in law, mistake as to law), and the procedural means by which (e.g. fresh action, appeal, application for re-hearing), a consent judgment (whether or not falling within r.40.6) may be set aside or varied under r.3.1(7) or some comparable provision, have been considered on a number of occasions in the context of orders made in ancillary relief proceedings. The relevant law was discussed in *S. v S. (Ancillary Relief: Consent Order)* [2002] EWHC 223 (Fam); [2003] Fam. 1 (Bracewell J.) (decided before Sch.2, CCR O.37 r.1 was revoked). The authorities demonstrate that the grounds for setting aside or varying a consent order fall into two categories. They are: (1) cases in which there was, at the date of the order an erroneous basis of fact; and (2) cases in which there has been a material or unforeseen changes in circumstances after the order so as to undermine or invalidate the basis of the order (*ibid*). For an example of variation being permitted on both grounds, see *Raja v Hoogstraten* [2005] EWHC 2668, Ch, November 23, 2005, unrep. (Lightman J.) (consent freezing order varied to include assets not disclosed). A consent order is an agreement between the parties and the court must be very careful in exercising a discretion to vary the terms of an order which represents a contract (*Weston v Dayman* [2006] EWCA Civ 1165, June 7, 2006, CA unrep. (Court of Appeal accepting without deciding that the court has under r.3.1(7) a residual discretion to vary a consent order not falling within either of the two categories)). See also *Ropac Ltd v Inntrepreneur Pub Co (CPC) Ltd* [2001] C.P. Rep. 201 (Neuberger J.) (variation of consent order extending time).

When judgment or order takes effect[1]

40.7—(1) A judgment or order takes effect from the day when it is given or made, or such later date as the court may specify. 40.7

(2) This rule applies to all judgments and orders except those to which rule 40.10 (judgment against a State) applies.

Effect of Rule

For reasons too numerous to mention, the fixing of the day when a judgment or order takes effect (or even the exact time within a day) may be important, not only to the parties but also to third parties affected by it. So it is important that there should be no room for doubt. Any such doubt may lead to further doubt; e.g. as to the time at which any sanction for failure to comply with an order took effect (see r.3.8(1)), or at which an interim injunction ceased to have effect by operation of r.25.11, or at which a claim was struck out (e.g. under r.29.6(3)) without any further order of the court. 40.7.1

In terms, r.40.7 speaks of a judgment or order taking effect at a "later date". This raises the question whether the date has to be specified, or whether it is sufficient if it is to be calculated by reference to a particular event. The rule was referred to in *Halabi v Camden LBC* [2008] EWHC 322 (Ch), The Times March 25, 2008 (Mr John Jarvis Q.C.), an order annulling a bankruptcy order was granted on terms that it should not take effect until the condition that the Official Receiver had notified the court that the debts had been paid was satisfied.

Where the practice of making a reserved judgment available to parties in advance of its delivery (see para.40.2.6 above) is followed, at that time the judgment is not being "given or made" within the meaning of r.40.7 (*Prudential Assurance Co Ltd v McBains Cooper* [2000] 1 W.L.R. 2000, CA).

It may be noted that, whereas former RSC O.42, r.3(2) provided that the court could direct that an order should be dated "as of some other earlier or later day" as the court may specify, r.40.7 confines the alternative date to "such later date" as the court may specify (*Rowan Companies Inc v Lambert Eggink Offshore Transport Consultants V.O.F.* [1999] 2 Lloyd's Rep. 443).

Note also r.40.2(2) (every judgment or order must bear the date on which it is made).

A property adjustment order in ancillary relief proceedings made under the Matrimonial Causes Act 1973 s.24(1)(a), directing a party to a marriage to transfer property to another person confers an equitable interest in the property on the person to whom it ordered the property to be transferred from the moment when the order takes effect (*Mountney v Treharne* [2002] EWCA Civ 1174; [2002] 3 W.L.R. 1760, CA).

Time from which interest begins to run[2]

40.8—(1) Where interest is payable on a judgment pursuant to section 17 of the Judgments Act 1838[3] or section 74 of the County Courts Act 1984,[4] the interest shall begin to run from the date that judgment is given unless— 40.8

(a) a rule in another Part or a practice direction makes different provision; or

(b) the court orders otherwise.

(2) The court may order that interest shall begin to run from a date before the date that judgment is given.

---

[1] Amended by the Civil Procedure (Amendment) Rules 2000 (SI 2000/221).
[2] Amended by the Civil Procedure (Amendment) Rules 2000 (SI 2000/221).
[3] 1838 c.110. S.17 was amended by SI 1998/2940.
[4] 1984 c.28. S.74 was amended by s.(2) of the Private International Law (Miscellaneous Provisions) Act 1995 (c.42).

Effect of rule

40.8.1 Rule 40.8 is concerned with the payment of interest on judgment debts. When the court gives a claimant judgment for a money sum, generally that award will include interest from the date when the cause of action arose until the date of the court's judgment. The cause of action including the claim for interest merges with the judgment, and interest on the principal sum ceases to run. The claimant is left with his judgment debt. As he will remain out-of-pocket until the judgment debt is satisfied, not unreasonably the law provides, by a combination of provisions in primary legislation and rules of court, that interest should run on the judgment debt. Rule 40.8 is concerned with the determination of the date from which interest on judgment debts should run in proceedings to which the CPR apply. Neither the former RSC nor the CPR contained a comparable provision to this rule. Before the CPR came into effect, there were important distinctions between, on the one hand, High Court judgments, and on the other, county court judgments, as to the circumstances in which interest on judgment debts could be ordered and, in particular, as to the periods by reference to which interest was to be calculated and paid. These distinctions largely remain and it was necessary to include in the CPR a provision in the terms of r.40.8 to ensure that they did. (The rule did not appear in the penultimate draft of the CPR published in November 1998 and was a very late addition.) So we have here, not a rule that has as its principal purpose the doing away with distinctions between High Court and county court procedure and practice, but one which maintains them. In terms the rule gives the court considerable flexibility in determining the periods by reference to which interest on judgment debts is to be calculated and paid, including the power to order that interest should begin to run from a date before the judgment is given (r.40.8(2)). The court's power to levy interest on a judgment debt should be distinguished from its power to order in a judgment for a money sum that that sum should include principal and interest, and that such interest should run from a particular date (usually the date when the cause of action arose) to the date of judgment.

Power to award interest

40.8.2 The Judgments Act 1838 s.17(1) applies to High Court proceedings and states that "every judgment debt shall carry interest". This provision envisages a single judgment which constitutes the "judgment debt" and which can only arise where the judgment itself quantifies the sum which the judgment debtor owes to the judgment creditor (*Thomas v Bunn* [1991] 1 A.C. 362, HL, at p.380 per Lord Ackner).

The County Courts Act 1984 s.74 applies to county court proceedings and states that sums made payable under judgments or orders (including sums payable by instalments) shall carry interest as provided for by Order (see Vol.2 para.9A–563). That power was not exercised until the County Courts (Interest on Judgment Debts) Order 1991 (SI 1991/1184) was enacted, implementing a recommendation made in the Report of the Civil Justice Review Body (Cm 394, 1988) that, subject to appropriate exclusions, High Court and county court remedies should be the same in this respect. The 1991 Order has been amended subsequently (see SI 1996/2516, SI 1998/2400). (For text of this Order, see Vol. 2 para.9B–70.)

It is the case that not all judgments or orders made in county courts proceedings carry interest; the exclusions are significant. Article 2(1) of the 1991 Order states the general rule that every judgment debt under "a relevant judgment", shall, to the extent that it remains unsatisfied, carry interest under the Order, and a "relevant judgment" means a judgment or order "for the payment of a sum of money (a) of not less than £5,000 or (b) in respect of a debt which is a qualifying debt for the purposes of the Late Payment of Commercial Debts (Interest) Act 1998" (art.1(2)). However, there are exceptions to the general rule. Interest shall not be payable under the Order where the relevant judgment (a) is given in proceedings to recover money due under an agreement regulated by the Consumer Credit Act 1974, or (b) grants the landlord or the mortgagee of a dwelling house a suspended possession order (art.2(3)) (note also art.2(4) (relevant judgment making financial provision for spouse or child)).

By operation of the Crown Proceedings Act 1947 s.24 (see Vol.2 para.9B–1147), the Judgments Act 1838 s.17 is applied "to judgment debts due from or to the Crown" without any qualification restricting such debts to judgment debts payable under judgments or orders given or made in the High Court. It would seem therefore that restrictions on the levying of interest on county court judgment debts imposed by the 1991 Order do not apply where such a debt is due from or to the Crown.

Under the usual form of a Tomlin order, where there is a term in the schedule providing for the payment of a sum of money, statutory interest on such sum does not become payable unless and until a judgment or order for payment of the sum is given under the liberty to apply (see further para.40.6.2 above).

The Judgments Act 1838 s.17(2) states that rules of court may provide that all or part of any interest otherwise payable under s.17(1) may be disallowed by the court. Examples of such rules in the CPR are para.(3) of r.47.8 (Sanction for failure to commence detailed assessment proceedings in time), and para.(5) of r.47.14 (Detailed assessment hearing); see further paras 40.8.11 and 40.8.12 below.

Where a party obtains permission under the Arbitration Act 1996 s.101 for an award, in terms not providing for post-award interest, to be enforced in the same manner as a judgment, interest under the Judgments Act 1838 s.17 becomes payable on the judgment (*Gater Assets Ltd v Nak Naftogaz Ukrainiy* [2008] EWHC 1108 (Comm), May 21, 2008, unrep. (Beatson J.)).

Statutory rate of interest

The Judgments Act 1838 s.17(1) states that every judgment debt shall carry interest "at the rate of 8 per cent per annum". By operation of the Administration of Justice Act 1970 s.44, the rate as fixed by s.17(1) may be varied by Order). The most recent exercise of this power was the enactment of the Judgment Debts (Rate of Interest) Order 1993 (SI 1993/564). By that Order, with effect from April 1, 1993, the rate of 8 per cent was substituted for the rate of 15 per cent (which had been the rate since April 16, 1985). **40.8.3**

The County Courts Act 1984 s.74 states that, where county court judgment debts carry interest, the rate of interest shall be prescribed by Order. The County Courts (Interest on Judgment Debts) Order 1991 (SI 1991/1184) art.5(1) states that the rate of interest is to be that for the time being specified in s.17(1) of the 1838 Act. Thus, the present rate of interest on such judgment debts is 8 per cent.

The statutory rate of interest may not be varied by the court (*Rocco Guiseppe & Figli v Tradex Export SA* [1984] 1 W.L.R. 742, *Thomas v Bunn* [1991] 1 A.C. 362, HL).

Old authority, apparently unaffected by the CPR, holds that, where a claim is brought under a contract to pay a debt with interest and judgment is obtained, the claimant is not entitled to levy under execution for interest at a rate higher than the statutory rate unless the contract (or subsequent agreement) states specifically that any judgment obtained for recovery of the debt shall carry interest at the higher rate, and in that event, the requirement to pay such interest should form part of the judgment (see *Re European Central Railway*, (1877) 4 Ch D 33; *Ex p. Ewings* (1883) 25 Ch D 338, *Arbuthnot v Bunsilall* (1890) 62 L.T. 234, *Economic Life Assurance Society v Usborne* [1902] A.C. 147).

Interest rate on claims in foreign currency

Where a judgment debt carries interest and has been given for a sum expressed in a currency other than sterling, the court may order that the rate of interest shall be such rate as the court thinks fit, instead of the statutory rate of interest otherwise applicable; see Administration of Justice Act 1970 s.44A, and the County Courts (Interest on Judgment Debts) Order 1991 (SI 1991/1184) art.5(2) (these provisions came into effect on November 1, 1996, following the enactment of the Private International Law (Miscellaneous Provisions) Act 1995, and do not apply to a judgment or order given before that date). **40.8.4**

Periods by reference to which interest is to be calculated and paid

The period during which a judgment debtor remains liable to the judgment creditor for interest awarded on a judgment debt ends when the debt is satisfied. The more difficult question is: when does the period of such liability begin? Rule 40.8(1) provides answers to this question in cases where interest is payable pursuant to the Judgments Act 1838 s.17(1) or the County Courts Act s.74. **40.8.5**

Judgment pursuant to s.17 of 1838 Act—The Judgments Act 1838 s.17(1) states that interest on a High Court judgment shall run "from such time as may be prescribed by rules of court until the same shall be satisfied". In relation to proceedings to which the CPR applies, the rules of court prescribing that time from which interest shall run are found in r.40.8. It is stated in r.40.8(1) that, subject to exceptions, the interest shall begin to run "from the date that judgment is given". The exceptions are (a) where a rule in another Part or a practice direction makes different provision, or (b) where the **40.8.6** court orders otherwise. Further, r.40.8(2) states that the court may order that interest shall begin to run from a date before that judgment is given. Thus, in relation to proceedings to which the CPR applies, the general rule is that interest should run from the date that judgment is given, rather than from the later date on which judgment is entered.

It may be noted that, until it was amended by the Civil Procedure (Modification of Enactments) Order 1998 (SI 1998/2940) for the purpose of facilitating the making of Civil Procedure Rules, s.17 of the 1838 Act stated that every judgment debt should carry interest "from the time of entering up the judgment". As a matter of language taken by itself that would mean the date which appears on the formal order of the court entering judgment. But in the nineteenth century it was authoritatively held that this was not the position and that the starting date for the running of interest was the date on which the judgment or order took effect. That date was the date on which it was pronounced unless the court ordered it to be dated earlier or later (see now CPR r.40.7, reenacting former RSC O.42, r.3). (For the history of s.17, confirming this construction, see *Thomas v Bunn* [1991] 1 A.C. 362, HL). Thus, in stating that interest shall begin to run "from the date that judgment is given", r.40.8(1) effected no change in the law as previously understood.

40.8.7 *Judgment pursuant to s.74 of 1984 Act* —The County Courts Act 1984 s.74(4)(c) states that the Order making power under s.74 includes power "to make provision for the manner in which and the periods by reference to which the interest is to be calculated and paid". A judgment on which interest is payable "pursuant to" s.74 (within the meaning of r.40.8) is a judgment to which that section applies, as elaborated by any Order made under the section. The Order made under s.74 is the County Courts (Interest on Judgment Debts) Order 1991 (SI 1991/1184), as amended (see Vol. 2 para.9B–80). (It should be noted that this Order is not confined to judgments given in proceedings to which the CPR are directly applied by r.2.1.) Article 2(1) of the 1991 Order states that "to the extent it remains unsatisfied" the judgment or order shall carry interest "from the date on which the relevant judgment was given". Article 2(2) states that, in the case of a judgment debt or order for the payment of a judgment debt, other than costs, the amount of which has to be determined at a later date, the judgment debt shall carry interest from that later date. Article 3 (Interest where payment deferred) states that, where under the terms of a relevant judgment payment of a judgment debt (a) is not required to be made until a specified date, or (b) is to be made by instalments, interest shall not accrue under this Order (i) until that date, or (ii) on the amount of any instalment, until it falls due, as the case may be". Note also art.4 (Interest and enforcement or other proceedings); see "Suspension of interest where judgment creditor takes enforcement proceedings" para.40.8.14 below.

40.8.8 *Different provision and court order otherwise* —From what has been said above, an answer may be gleaned to the question: when does the period of liability of a judgment debtor to the judgment creditor for interest awarded on a judgment debt begin to run? The answer provided by r.40.8(1) is that, subject to exceptions, it shall begin to run from the date that judgment is given. Presumably, insofar as the application of any provision in the 1991 Order may give a different answer, that different answer should prevail. Rule 40.8(1) allows that exceptions to the rule that interest shall begin to run from the date that judgment is given may be provided for "in a rule in another Part or a practice direction". Examples are found primarily in provisions relating to interest on costs orders; see "Interest on costs orders in substantive proceedings" see para.40.8.14 below.

Rule 40.8(1)(b) also provides, by way of exception to the rule that interest on a judgment debt shall run from the date that judgment is given, that the court may make a different order; that is to say, may order that such interest should run from some other date. And r.40.8(2) states that the court may order that interest shall begin to run, not from the date that judgment is given, but from a date before the judgment is given. Where express provision is made elsewhere, whether within the CPR or without (e.g. in the 1991 Order), to the effect that a date other than the date on which judgment is given should be the date from which interest shall begin to run, it is not obvious whether, how or why the court should have recourse to these exceptions.

The Judgments Act 1838 s.17(2) states that rules of court may provide for the court to disallow all or part of any interest otherwise payable under s.17(1). There is nothing in r.40.8 which is in express exercise of this particular rule-making power. However, it could be said that where a court, by selecting a later date than the date on which judgment was given, postpones the start of the period by reference to which interest payable on a judgment debt is to be calculated and paid, in effect the court has disallowed part of interest otherwise payable.

Distinction between interest on debts and damages and judgment debt interest

The Supreme Court Act 1981 s.35A and the County Courts Act 1984 s.69 (see Vol.2 paras 9A–122 and 9A–554) provide that, in proceedings before the High Court or a county court for the recovery or a debt or damages, the court may include in any sum for which judgment is given simple interest (see para.7.0.10 *et seq* above). In the case of any sum paid before judgment, interest runs up to "the date of payment" and in the case of a sum for which judgment is given, interest runs up to "the date of the judgment". (As to the period during which inclusive interest accrues on the sum stated in a Pt 36 offer, see CPR r.36.3(3).) Where there is a judgment for debt or damages, normally it will include the principal sum (say £50,000) plus any interest awarded by the court (say £5,000), and the total sum (£55,000) will constitute the judgment debt. Such judgment may be, not only a judgment given at the end of a contested trial, but a consent judgment, or a judgment on admissions (in which case r.14.14 (Interest) will apply), or a default judgment (in which case r.12.6 (Interest) will apply). Whether or not any interest at all is incorporated in the judgment will depend on the nature and details of the claim and any agreement between the parties. Generally, in cases where damages are claimed the damages are assessed as at when the cause of action arose (except where there is some future or continuing loss) and so the period by reference to which interest is to be calculated and paid will be the period between the date of the cause of action and the date of the judgment. In any event, in accordance with r.40.8, the resulting judgment debt (i.e. the £55,000) may carry interest until it is satisfied. In the normal case, the end of the period for which any interest payable under s.35A and s.69 runs will be followed immediately by the beginning of the period for which interest on the judgment debt will run. However, in some contexts complications can arise in fixing the former date (see paras 7.0.18 and 7.0.19 above), and are likely to be aggravated when the interest rates under the two regimes are significantly different. In a personal injury claim, damages are assessed, not at the date when such damages were first sustained, but at the date of trial. In *Thomas v Bunn* [1991] 1 A.C. 362, HL, it was held that, where, in a claim for damages in a personal injury case, liability is determined or agreed and on (say) January 1 a judgment or order is made by the court for damages to be assessed by the court, and subsequently the damages are assessed on (say) June 1, then "the date of the judgment" within the meaning of s.35A of the 1981 Act and s.69 of the 1984 Act is the latter date. Therefore, unless the court orders otherwise, any interest payable on the judgment debt in accordance with r.40.8 does not begin (as might be argued) on January 1, but on June 1. However, it should be noted that *Thomas v Bunn* was decided before s.17 of the 1838 Act was amended and before the coming into effect of the power given to the court under r.40.8 to order that the date from which judgment debt interest should begin to run should be other than the date on which judgment is given and, in particular, the power to order that such interest shall begin to run from a date before the date that judgment is given. **40.8.9**

Disallowance of statutory interest

As amended by the Civil Procedure (Modification of Enactments) Order 1998 (SI 1998/2940) for the purpose of facilitating the making of Civil Procedure Rules, s.17(2) of the 1838 Act states that rules of court may provide for the court to disallow all or part of any interest otherwise payable. Examples of rules in the CPR expressly giving the court power to disallow interest are r.47.8(3) and r.47.14(5); see "Interest on costs orders" *(paras 40.8.11 and 40.8.12 below)*. **40.8.10**

Interest on costs orders in substantive proceedings

In numerous respects, the matter of interest payable on costs orders are affected by special provisions found in CPR Pts 44 to 48, and r.40.8 has to be read in the light of those provisions. The matter need not be dealt with in detail here; it is sufficient to note a few points. Rules as to the court's discretion and circumstances to be taken into account when exercising its discretion as to costs are found in CPR r.44.3 and it is provided there that the orders which the court may make include an order that a party must pay interest on costs "from or until a certain date, including a date before **40.8.11** judgment" (r.44.3(6)(g)) (see para.44.3.14 below). (It was an anomaly under the pre-CPR law that an order for payment of costs to be assessed was construed as a judgment debt under the Judgments Act 1838 s.17 even though, before assessment, there was no sum for which execution could be levied (*Hunt v R.M. Douglas (Roofing) Ltd* [1990] 1 A.C. 398, HL). Now the court has a discretion which enables it to look at the dates when the costs were incurred, and to come to a conclusion in relation to the payment of interest that fits the justice of the circumstances of the particular case (*Powell v Herefordshire Health Authority* [2002] EWCA Civ 1786; [2003] 3 All E.R. 253, CA)).In cases where costs orders are deemed to have been made interest begins to run "from the date on which the event which gave rise to the entitlement to costs occurred" (r.44.12(2)) (see para.44.12.4 below). Certain rules in Pt 47 (Procedure for detailed assessment of costs and default provisions) give the court power to disallow all or part of the interest otherwise payable on costs orders in various circumstances; for example, as a sanction where a receiving party fails to commence detailed assessment proceedings within the period specified (r.47.8(3)) (see para.47.8.1 below), or fails to file a request where points of dispute are served (r.47.14(5)) (see para.47.14.1 below).

Interest on orders for costs of detailed assessment proceedings

40.8.12 Where costs are determined at detailed assessment proceedings, generally the receiving party is entitled to his costs of those proceedings (r.47.18) and any order to this effect may carry interest. Para.45.5 of Practice Direction (Costs) states that such interest shall begin to run "from the date of the default, interim or final costs certificate as the case may be" (see paras 47.8.1 and 47PD.17 below).

Enforcement of payment of interest due on judgment debt

40.8.13 The Judgments Act 1838 s.17(1) states that interest on a judgment debt "may be levied under a writ of execution". The County Courts Act 1984 s.74(3) states that payment of interest due "shall be enforceable as a sum payable under judgment or order". Where a judgment creditor is driven to take enforcement proceedings to enforce his judgment debt it is unlikely that the proceedings will be for the accrued interest alone. As to enforcement of judgments and orders generally, see CPR Pts 70 to 74 and related RSC and CCR provisions in CPR Schs 1 and 2.

Suspension of interest where judgment creditor takes enforcement proceedings

40.8.14 The County Courts (Interest on Judgment) Debts Order 1991 (SI 1991/1184) art.4(1) states that, where a judgment creditor takes proceedings in a county court to enforce payment under a "relevant judgment", the judgment debt shall cease to carry interest thereafter, except where those proceedings fail to produce any payment from the debtor in which case interest shall accrue as if those proceedings had never been taken. In this context, a "relevant judgment" means a judgment or order for the payment of a sum of money (a) of not less than £5,000 or (b) in respect of a debt which is a qualifying debt for the purposes of the Late Payment of Commercial Debts (Interest) Act 1998 (art.1(2)). For the purposes of art.4(1), enforcement proceedings include any proceedings for examining or summoning a judgment debtor or attaching a debt owed by him, but do not include proceedings under the Charging Orders Act 1979 (art.4(2)). Where an administration order, that is to say, an order under s.112 of the 1984 Act, or an attachment of earnings order is made, interest shall not accrue during the time the order is in force (art.4(3)).

Interest details in application to enforce judgment debt

40.8.15 Where a judgment creditor is claiming interest on a judgment debt, he must include in his application or request to issue enforcement proceedings in relation to that judgment the details required by para.6 of Practice Direction (Enforcement of Judgments and Orders), replacing former CCR O.25, r.5A (see para.70PD.6 below).

Post-judgment interest under consumer credit or hire agreement

40.8.16 Once a judgment is obtained under a loan agreement for a principal sum and judgment is entered, the contract merges in the judgment and the principal becomes owed *under* the judgment and not under the contract. If under the contract interest on any principal sum is due, then, absent special provisions, the contract is considered ancillary to the covenant to pay the principal, with the result that if judgment is obtained on the principal, the covenant to pay interest merges in the judgment. Thus, for as long as the judgment debt remains unsatisfied, interest will be payable, not on the principal, but on the judgment debt in the normal way. Commercial agreements routinely contain special provisions that avoid this result and under which the parties agree that a covenant to pay interest will not merge in any judgment for the principal sum due, and in that event interest may be charged under the contract on the principal sum due even after judgment for that sum ("post-judgment interest"). Thus, after judgment the judgment debtor may be liable, not only for interest on the judgment debt, but also for post-judgment interest. However, where a creditor or owner under a consumer credit agreement, or consumer hire agreement, wants to be able to recover from the debtor or hirer post-judgment interest in connection with a sum that is required to be paid under a judgment given in relation to the agreement, the conditions of the Consumer Credit Act 1974 s.130A apply (see Vol.2 para.3H–297). That section provides that a creditor or owner who wishes to obtain post-judgment interest payable under the agreement must first serve notice on the debtor or hirer in accordance with Regulations. The section was inserted in the 1974 Act by the Consumer Credit Act 2006 s.17, and may be seen as a legislative response to the decision of the House of Lords in *Director General of Fair Trading v First National Bank Plc.* [2001] UKHL 52; [2002] 1 A.C. 481, HL (where the argument that a contractual clause entitling a creditor to obtain post-judgment interest was unfair was rejected). The section applies to agreements whenever made but only in relation to sums that are required to be paid after the coming into force of s.17. (By the Consumer Credit Act 2006 (Commencement No.1) Order 2006 (SI 2006/1508) s.130A was brought into force on June 16, 2006, but only to the extent of enabling Regulations to be made.) Interest on a judgment debt is not payable under the County Courts (Interest on Judgment Debts) Order 1991 (SI 1991/1184) where the relevant judgment (as defined in art.1(1) of that Order) is given in proceedings to recover money due under an agreement regulated by the Consumer Credit Act 1974 (art.2(3)).

Who may apply to set aside or vary a judgment or order[1]

40.9 A person who is not a party but who is directly affected by a judgment or order may apply to have the judgment or order set aside or varied. 40.9

Effect of rule

A person who is a party to proceedings may, in circumstances far too numerous and varied to be easily succinctly and accurately stated, apply to have any judgment or order given or made in the proceedings set aside or varied. (Sometimes the application will take the form of an appeal, sometimes not). For obvious reasons, the bias of procedural law is against permitting parties to cause the court to go back on judgments and orders given and made, so the circumstances in which a party may succeed in such an application are bound to be, at least to an extent, restricted. 40.9.1

Rule 40.9 states that "a person who is not a party but who is directly affected by a judgment or order" (hereinafter "a non-party"), may apply to have the judgment set aside or varied. On the face of it, that is a strikingly wide proposition and the first thing to be said about it is that there is no general rule to the effect that a non-party may do what a party may not. As is the case with parties, the circumstances in which a non-party might succeed in an application to set aside or vary a judgment or order are restricted and cannot easily be stated succinctly. By stating that a "directly affected" non-party may apply to have a judgment set aside or varied, r.40.9 gives no clue as to when such an application may succeed. But there must be some circumstances in which it might, otherwise the rule would be otiose. (Historically speaking, the best known circumstance was where, after default judgment for possession of land was given to the plaintiff and the defendant put out, a person with a claim to possession, but who was not a party to the proceedings, was allowed in to defend as a party to the proceedings and the plaintiff's order for possession set aside, but without his judgment as against the defendant being disturbed.) The circumstances in which the court gives judgments and makes orders (procedural or otherwise) are legion. The questions whether, as a matter of law, a judgment or order may be varied or revoked, and whether, on the application of a party or of a non-party, it should be varied or revoked, must be determined in the contexts in which they arise. Generally, where a non-party

[1] Amended by the Civil Procedure (Amendment) Rules 2000 (SI 2000/221).

is likely to succeed in an application it will be in circumstances where, at least arguably, he is entitled to be made a party to the proceedings.

There is room for doubt as to whether "a person who is not a party" means (a) a person who is not a party to the proceedings in which the judgment or order was made, or (b) a person who is not (in some sense) a party to the judgment or order.

The stipulation that the non-party must be "directly affected" limits the scope of r.40.9. But it is necessary to consider further what is meant by "directly affected" and whether there are some types of judgment or order which may not be set aside or varied on the application of a non-party, whether directly affected or not.

It has been held at first instance that in the circumstances where (1) a defendant (D) had successfully defended a specific performance claim, but had been ordered to transfer to the claimant company (C) property previously transferred to him (D), not by C, but by another person (X) as part payment, and (2) D applied to vary the order to enable him to sell the property in order to recoup costs owed to him by C, X (who, although he was involved in the running of C, was not a party to the contract and had not been a party to the proceedings) could not apply under r.40.9 to have the order set aside or varied as he had no direct restitutionary claim against D, and for that reason he was not a person "directly affected" by the order (*Hepworht Group Ltd v Stockley* [2006] EWHC 3626 (Ch); [2007] All ER (Comm) 82).

In some situations, procedural rules require that certain persons must be made respondents or defendants to applications or claims, or that at least notice of the proceedings must be given to them, thereby enabling them to make a decision as to whether or not they wish to be joined as parties or to make representations; e.g. r.19.8A (Power to make judgment binding on non-parties) (implementing Administration of Justice Act 1985 s.47), Practice Direction (Possession Claims), paras 2.4 & 2.5(1) (see para.55PD.1 below), Practice Direction (Landlord and Tenant Claims and Miscellaneous Provisions About Land), paras 3.3, 3.4, 5.4, 5.5, 8.4 and 9.3 (see para.56PD.1 below). Where these requirements are not followed, and such persons are not joined as parties or given notice, as the case may be, then any judgment or order made in the proceedings may be irregular and liable to be set aside or varied on that ground and no recourse to r.40.9 would be necessary.

In the examples of a freezing injunction and of a search order annexed to Practice Direction (Injunctions) it is stated in, respectively, para.13 and para.27, that "anyone served with or notified of this order" would be a person "directly affected" by it. But clearly that is not the sole purpose of r.40.9.

It may be noted that, where the order in question is a search order made by the High Court, the rule is that, subject to an exception, a county court may not vary or revoke the order (County Court Remedies Regulations 1991 reg. 3(1), see Vol.2 para.9B–77). The exception is that a county court may vary such an order (but may not revoke it) where all the parties are agreed on the terms of the variation (*ibid.* reg. 3(4)(b)). These Regulations apply where the application to vary or revoke is made by a non-party as well as where it is made by a party.

Under the Damages Act 1996 s.2, in certain circumstances the court may make orders for damages in the form (wholly or partly) of periodical payments (instead of lump sum payment) when awarding damages for future pecuniary loss in respect of personal injury (see Sect.II of CPR Pt 41, and commentary there). Further, when making an order for periodical payments, the court may in addition provide in that order that it should be a "variable order". Conceivably, a person "who is not a party" may be "directly affected", within the meaning of r.40.9, by a periodical payments order with a variable order attached. However, the circumstances in which variable orders may be made and in which they may be invoked are governed by the statutory scheme based on s.2 and r.40.9 does not apply.

Other rules making different provision

40.9.2 According to r.40.1 (as amended in 2004), r.40.9 (and the other rules in Sect.I of Pt 40) applies "except where any other of these Rules or a practice direction makes a different provision in relation to the judgment or order in question". It is not immediately clear what it is that r.40.9 adds to the other provisions in the CPR providing for the setting aside or variation of judgments or orders. But perhaps r.40.9 is best understood if it is read in conjunction with those other provisions.

The other CPR rules providing for the setting aside or varying of judgments or orders are referred to in para.3.1.9 above. It will be noted that, in terms, some of them restrict the persons who may make applications to those who are parties to the order or judgment in question, and, therefore, would appear to leave no room for the operation of r.40.9, but others impose no such restriction, except possibly by necessary implication.

The other CPR rules providing for the setting aside or varying of judgments or orders and which in terms limit applicants to parties are as follows (for further information, see para.3.1.9 and the notes following these rules):

Rule 3.6 (Application by party against whom judgment without trial entered after striking out under r.3.5 to set judgment aside)

Rule 23.10(1) (Application to set aside or vary order made without notice)

Rule 23.11(2) (Application to relist application made by party failing to attend hearing at which order made)

Rule 39.3(3) (Application by party who failed to attend trial to set aside judgment or order made against him)

Rule 44.13(1B) (Application by party affected to vary deemed costs order)

Rule 44.18(7) (Application by party to vary costs capping order)

Rule 55.19 (Application by party to set aside or vary accelerated possession order for assured shorthold tenancy made by court without requiring the attendance of the parties)

CPR Sch. 2 CCR O.22, r.10 (Application by judgment debtor or creditor to vary date or rate of payment in money judgment or order)

To this list should be added, not another CPR rule, but Practice Direction (Summary Disposal of Claims), para.8.1 which states that, if an order for summary judgment under Pt 24 is made against a respondent who does not appear at the hearing of the application, the respondent may apply "for the order to be set aside or varied" (see para.24PD.8 above). In this context "order" includes judgment on the claim (*ibid.* para.5.1(1)). See further paras 24.6.8 & 39.3.8 above.

Mention should also be made of r.19.12(3) which states that, where a Group Litigation Order (GLO) is in place, a party to a claim entered on the group register after a judgment or order which is binding on him was given or made, may not apply for the judgment or order to be set aside, varied or stayed (and may not appeal), but may apply for an order that the judgment or order is not binding on him. Presumably, the restriction on the party imposed by this provision would also apply to a directly affected non-party.

The other CPR rules providing for the setting aside or variation of judgments or orders and which do not in terms limit applicants to parties (though it may be argued that they impliedly do so) and which, therefore, may leave scope for the operation of r.40.9, are as follows (for further information, see para.3.1.9 and the notes following these rules):

Rule 3.1(7) (Power of court to vary or revoke order made under CPR) (see further para.40.9.3 below)

Rule 13.2 (Cases where the court must set aside default judgment entered under Pt 12) (see further para.40.9.5 below)

Rule 13.3 (Cases where the court may set aside or vary default judgment entered under Pt 12) (see further para.40.9.5 below)

Rule 20.11(5) (Power of court to set aside or vary default judgments entered in certain Pt 20 claims)

Practice Direction (Admiralty), para.7.4 (Power of court to set aside or vary certain default judgments)

The Charging Orders Act 1979 s.3(5) (see Vol.2, para.9B–1022) and the Council Tax (Administration and Enforcement) Regulations 1992 reg. 51(4) provide that the court may at any time, on the application of the debtor, or any person interested in any property to which a charging order relates, or (where the 1992 Regulations apply) of the authority, make an order discharging or varying the order.Rules of court supporting this legislation are found in r.73.9. Under Pt 75 (Traffic Enforcement) orders may be revoked upon the respondent's application by statutory declaration made under the primary legislation to which that Part relates.Practice Direction (Appeals), para.13.1 states that an appeal court may set aside or vary the order of the lower court with consent and without determining the merits of the appeal, if it is satisfied that there are good and sufficient reasons for doing so (see para.52PD.47 below). Express powers to revoke an administration order are found in Sch.2, CCR O.39 rr.13A and 14 (see para.cc39.13A below).

Rule 3.5 states that, where a court makes an order which includes a term that the statement of case of a party shall be struck out if the party does not comply with the order, and the party against whom the order was made does not comply with it, then in claims of a certain type the other party may obtain judgment with costs simply by filing a request for judgment. Rule 3.6 states that, where, after the automatic striking out of a party's statement of case on the ground that he had failed to comply with a court order, the court gives judgment without trial against him under r.3.5 on a request for judgment, that party may apply to have the judgment set aside. One example of the circumstances envisaged by r.3.5 and r.3.6 would be where, on an application for summary judgment, the court makes a conditional order (as provided for by Practice Direction (The Summary Disposal of Claims), para.5.2, see para.24PD.5) imposing on the respondent a condition to the effect that he should take a specified step in relation to his defence and that his statement of case will be struck out if he does not comply, and the respondent fails to take the specified step. Provided the claim is of the variety covered by r.3.5(2) the applicant could then enter judgment with costs by filing a request for judgment. However, the respondent could apply under r.3.6 to set the judgment aside. In that event, the respondent must act within 14 days and, if he is to succeed, must surmount the onerous "relief from sanctions" conditions found in r.3.9.

General power to vary or revoke orders

40.9.3 Rule 3.1 lists certain of the court's "general powers of management" and does so in very broad terms. As indicated immediately above (para.40.9.2), r.3.1(7) states: "A power of the court under these Rules to make an order includes a power to vary or revoke the order". In terms it is not restricted to procedural orders. But it is restricted to a power to vary or revoke an order that the court has previously made, and does not extend to an order that is deemed to have been made by operation of the rules (*Lahey v Pirelli Tyres Ltd* [2007] EWCA Civ 91; [2007] 1 W.L.R. 998, CA). Whether an order may be, and whether it should be varied or revoked under the rule, are matters that must be determined in the context in which they arise. Any order varying or revoking the trial judge's post judgment orders must be sought and obtained on an appeal (*R + V Versicherung A.G. v Risk Insurance and Reinsurance Solutions S.A.* [2007] EWHC 79 (Comm); *The Times* February 26, 2007(Gloster J.) (where held, in the context of the case, the power can have no application to a final judgment at trial on the substantive merits of an issue)). The court's jurisdiction under r.3.1(7) is not a substitute for an appeal and it is exercisable where there is additional material before the court in the form of evidence (or, possibly, argument) (*Edwards v Golding* [2007] EWCA Civ 416; *The Times* May 22, 2007, CA (judge justified in setting aside Master's order, rather than requiring applicant to make an appeal out of time, as the case before him was essentially different, and in doing so the judge did not usurp the power of the Court of Appeal but rather corrected a fundamental procedural error)). The purpose of the rule is explained in para.3.1.9. For obvious reasons, it does not purport to stipulate the circumstances in which an application to vary or revoke an order should be granted, or by whom such an order may be made, whether by a party or a non-party (whether directly affected or not). Presumably, this particular power does not allow any court at any time "simply to reverse itself if it happens to change its mind" (*SCT Finance Ltd v Bolton* [2002] EWCA Civ 56; [2003] 3 All E.R. 434, CA, at para.58, per Waller L.J.). Under r.3.1(2)(a), the court may extend time, except where the CPR "provide otherwise". By stating that the court may "at any time" correct a slip, r.40.12 does not "provide otherwise" so as to enable a party to escape the normal rules as to the exercise of discretion to extend time for compliance with an order (*Omega Engineering Inc v Omega SA (Extension of Time)* [2003] EWHC 1482, (Pumfrey J.)).

Setting aside or varying summary possession orders

40.9.4 The powers of the High Court and a county court to set aside or vary orders made in summary proceedings for possession of land were found in Sch.1, RSC O.113 r.8, and Sch.2, CCR O.24 r.7. These provisions were revoked when Pt 55 (Possession Claims) was added to the CPR with effect from October 15, 2001, and were not expressly re-enacted in Pt 55. Consequently, the court's power to set aside an order for summary possession is derived from the general power to vary or revoke orders explained immediately above (see para.40.9.3). In summary proceedings for possession of land, it is not always clear at the outset who the interested parties are. In a given case, it may quickly become obvious that, because the facts are not as they initially appeared, orders made should be set aside or revoked (if not on the court's own initiative) either on the application of known parties or of other persons.

Default judgments

40.9.5 It would seem that the main relevance of r.40.9 is to applications to set aside or vary default judgments granted under r.13.2 and r.13.3 (see para.40.9.2 above). Normally (and for obvious reasons) an application to set aside a default judgment will be made by the defendant (i.e. the judgment debtor). However, neither r.13.2 nor r.13.3 stipulates that an application (in the case of r.13.2) to set aside or (in the case of r.13.3) to set aside or vary a default judgment should be made by a party to the claim (whether claimant or defendant) on which the judgment was given. Thus, in terms, the rules do not prevent an application to set aside or vary a default judgment being made by a non-party (or, indeed, by the court on its own motion). The former RSC and CCR rules on setting aside default judgments imposed no restriction on non-party applications either (see RSC O.13, r.9 and O.19, r.9, and CCR O.37, r.4), but limits were imposed by case law (see further below). CPR r.40.9 states, simply, that an application may be made by a person who, although not a party, is "directly affected by a judgment or order", a formulation that gives the court all of the flexibility necessary to accommodate the circumstances in which applications by non-parties to set aside or vary should be countenanced by the court in this context. (However, it should be noted that, although r.40.9 has this useful effect, in terms the rule is not restricted to applications to set aside or vary default judgments as it purports to apply to judgments generally and also to orders, except where any other rule in the CPR makes a different provision.)

Pre-CPR authorities make it clear that the rules that formerly played the role now played by r.13.2 and r.13.3, were not designed to give a *locus standi* to persons who had none, but rather to enable judgments by default to be set aside on terms by those who had or how could acquire a locus standi. Where judgment by default is entered against a defendant, a person who was not a party to the proceedings in which the judgment was given, may apply on notice to the claimant to set the judgment aside and for permission to defend in the defendant's name on such terms as the court may think reasonable or just. Obviously, such an application would not succeed except where the applicant can show that his interests are affected by the default judgment. (Whether or not the applicant can do so depends on the legal and factual issues arising and is not a procedural question.)

It is conceivable that the applicant may have the defendant's permission to use the defendant's name for such an application; indeed, the defendant may already have bound himself to give permission (e.g. where a policy holder is so bound to his insurers). The more difficult situation is where the applicant does not have the defendant's permission and cannot therefore apply in the defendant's name. In these circumstances the applicant may apply in his own name on notice to both the defendant and the plaintiff for leave to have the judgment set aside, and to be at liberty either (1) to defend the action for the defendant (on such terms of indemnifying the defendant as the judge may consider right), or (2) to intervene in the action in the same manner as he may have intervened had he been joined as a party before the default judgment was entered. This mode of proceeding was established by *Jacques v Harrison* (1884) 12 Q.B.D. 165, CA (where, on the application of equitable mortgagees, the Court of Appeal set aside judgments by default and writs of possession obtained against mortgagors on the grounds of their breaches of covenants in a lease), and was approved and followed by the House of Lords in *Employers Liability Assurance Corp Ltd v Sedgwick Collins & Co Ltd* [1927] A.C. 95, HL. The giving of notice of the application to the defendant is not a matter of mere form but is an essential requirement. "Until the applicant has made the defendant a party to the application by service upon him of the summons, the applicant remains a mere stranger to the action" (*ibid.* p.168 per Bowen L.J.). The point is that the defendant may have thought it more consistent with his own interests not to contest the claim further and to let judgment go by default. If the claim is to be revived at the instance of a "stranger to the action" the defendant (as well as the claimant) has the right to dispute the title of the applicant to interfere. Further, the defendant has the right to be heard on the question whether he should not be indemnified against any risks or costs to which he may be exposed by the revival of the claim.

In *Latif v Imaan Inc* [2007] EWHC 3179 (Ch), December 17, 2007, unrep. (Briggs J.), the facts were that, on December 6, 2007, in Chancery proceedings commenced in

2005, a company (C) obtained judgment against another company (D) for £8.9m. The judgment included a declaration that, for purposes of enforcement, all D's assets, including a particular London property, should be treated as subject to an equitable charge in C's favour. Beforehand, in separate Queen's Bench proceedings commenced in July 2007, a trading entity (X) brought a claim against D to recover a loan and, on September 18, 2007, obtained a default judgment in those proceedings. In addition, (1) on October 20, 2007, D purported to grant X charge over the London property as security for the loan (being a charge capable of ranking in priority to C's beneficial interest arising out of the judgment in the Chancery proceedings), and (2) a Queen's Bench Master made an interim third party debt order in relation to the property. C contended that the loan and the charge were devices put in place by the principal defendant in the Chancery proceedings in order to protect assets vested in D from enforcement. C, though not a party to the Queen's Bench proceedings, applied for an order setting aside X's default judgment obtained in those proceedings. In granting the application the judge held that (1) C was a person "directly affected" by the default judgment within the meaning of r.40.9, (2) C had sufficient interest in the matters recorded by the default judgment, namely the making of the loan and its non payment, to intervene to have that judgment set aside, (3) the existence or non existence of the loan was a highly material fact relevant to the validity or otherwise of X's charge over the property.

Note also, *Minet v Johnson* [1886-90] All E.R. 586, CA (default judgment for possession of land set aside on application of party in possession not made party to the action); *Windsor v Chalcraft* [1939] 1 K.B. 279; [1938] 2 All E.R. 751, CA (default judgment, which insurers were liable to satisfy, set aside and insurers given leave to defend in the defendant's name or their own name).

Judgment against a State in default of acknowledgment of service[1]

40.10 **40.10—(1) Where the claimant obtains default judgment under Part 12 on a claim against a State where the defendant has failed to file an acknowledgment of service, the judgment does not take effect until 2 months after service on the State of—**

(a) a copy of the judgment; and

(b) a copy of the evidence in support of the application for permission to enter default judgment (unless the evidence has already been served on the State in accordance with an order made under Part 12).

(2) In this rule, "State" has the meaning given by section 14 of the State Immunity Act 1978.[2]

Effect of rule

40.10.1 This rule gives effect to the provisions of s.12(5) of the State Immunity Act 1978 that the time for an application by the defendant state to set aside a default judgment entered against it with leave of the court shall begin to run two months after the date on which the copy of the judgment is served on the state. It would be contrary to international comity and indeed perhaps injurious to international relations to allow a foreign state to have a default judgment entered against it and *enforced* without prior warning. This rule therefore provides expressly that during such period of two months the default judgment will not take effect, i.e. it will not be enforceable and during that period it will be open to the state to apply to set aside the default judgment.

If, however, the claimant has duly served on the state a copy of the default judgment and a copy of any supporting affidavit to obtain leave to enter such judgment and two further months have expired, he will be entitled to proceed to enforce the judgment. Before doing so, it will be necessary for him to satisfy the court that such due service has been effected and that such two months has expired from the date of *service* so that the judgment has taken effect.

---

[1] Amended by the Civil Procedure (Amendment) Rules 2000 (SI 2000/221).
[2] 1978 c.33.

As to the extent to which a judgment or an award against a foreign state can be enforced, see s.13 of the State Immunity Act 1978.

Judgment of overseas country against a state

A judgment given by a court of an overseas country against a state other than the United Kingdom or the state to which that court belongs must be recognised and enforced in the United Kingdom if, and only if, (a) it would be so recognised and enforced if it had not been given against a state, and (b) that court would have had jurisdiction in the matter if it had applied rules corresponding to those applicable to such matters in the United Kingdom in accordance with ss.2 to 11 of the State Immunity Act 1978 (see Civil Jurisdiction and Judgments Act 1982 s.31(1)). For this purpose a judgment given against a state includes references to (a) judgments against the government, or a department of the government, of the state but not judgments against an entity which is distinct from the executive organs of government, unless such judgment is given in proceedings relating to anything done by that entity in the exercise of the sovereign authority of the state, and (b) judgments against the sovereign or head of state in his public capacity (*ibid.*, s.32(2)). The provisions of ss.12, 13 and 14(3) and (4) of the State Immunity Act, relating to the service of process and procedural privileges apply to proceedings for the recognition or enforcement in the United Kingdom of a judgment given by a court of an overseas country (*ibid.*, s.31(4)). In the case of a federal state, the term "state" includes any of its constituent territories (*ibid.*, s.31(5)). The recognition or enforcement of judgments given by a court of an overseas country is not affected by a judgment to which Pt I of the Foreign Judgments (Reciprocal Enforcement) Act 1933 applies by virtue of the relevant provisions of specified statutes (*ibid.*, s.31(3)). 40.10.2

Time for complying with a judgment or order[1]

40.11 A party must comply with a judgment or order for the payment of an amount of money (including costs) within 14 days of the date of the judgment or order, unless— 40.11

- **(a) the judgment or order specifies a different date for compliance (including specifying payment by instalments);**
- **(b) any of these Rules specifies a different date for compliance; or**
- **(c) the court has stayed the proceedings or judgment.**

(Parts 12 and 14 specify different dates for complying with certain default judgments and judgments on admissions.)

Effect of rule

This rule is amplified in Practice Direction (Judgments and Orders), para.9.1 (see para.40BPD.9). As to time for complying with an order for costs, see r.44.8. 40.11.1

For rules as to the calculation of any period of time for doing any act specified by the CPR, a practice direction, or a judgment or order of the court, see r.2.8.

Correction of errors in judgments and orders[2]

40.12—(1) The court may at any time correct an accidental slip or omission in a judgment or order. 40.12

***(2) A party may* apply for a correction without notice.**

The slip rule

The so-called "slip rule" is one of the most widely known but misunderstood rules. The rule applies only to "an accidental slip or omission in a judgment or order". Es- 40.12.1

[1] Amended by the Civil Procedure (Amendment) Rules 2000 (SI 2000/221).
[2] Amended by the Civil Procedure (Amendment) Rules 2000 (SI 2000/221).

sentially it is there to do no more than correct typographical errors (e.g. where the order says claimant when it means defendant; where it says 70 days instead of seven; where it says "January 2001" instead of "January 2002". Of course, such errors ought not to occur in important documents like a court order but they are regrettably common). Although not limited to errors by the court or court officers, the rule is limited to genuine slips and cannot be used to correct an error of substance nor in an attempt to get the court to add to its original order (e.g. to add a money judgment where none was sought, and none given at the trial).

Practice Direction (Judgments and Orders), para.4 (see para.40BPD.4 below) explains.

It is important that judgments and orders should be drawn up correctly. If a party believes it is not, then the proper procedure is for him to ascertain whether the court is prepared to correct it under the slip rule. Circumstances may arise where, whether the order remains as it is, or is altered to meet the party's complaint, is a matter that may affect the proper destination for an appeal from the court's decision; e.g. *Scribes West Ltd v Relsa Anstalt (No.2)* [2004] EWCA Civ 965, CA (the proper appeal court must be one that is readily ascertainable from the face of the lower court's order, and not one which would or might have been ascertainable if that court had made a different order).

The slip rule cannot be used to enable the court to have second thoughts or to add to its original order (see para.40.2.1 above). A judge does have the power to recall his order before it is issued but not afterwards. Once the order is drawn up, judicial mistakes have to be corrected by an appellate court. However, the court has an inherent jurisdiction to vary its own orders to make the meaning and intention of the court clear and can use the slip rule to amend an order to give effect to the intention of the court. See *Bristol-Myers Squibb v Baker Norton Pharmaceuticals Inc* [2001] EWCA Civ 414; applied in *Foenander v Foenander* [2004] EWCA Civ 1675 (Wall L.J.) (correction of order referring to civil restraint order). Under r.3.1(2)(a), the court may extend time, except where the CPR "provide otherwise". By stating that the court may "at any time" correct a slip, r.40.12 does not "provide otherwise" so as to enable a party to escape the normal rules as to the exercise of discretion to extend time for compliance with an order (*Omega Engineering Inc v Omega SA (Extension of Time)* [2003] EWHC 1482 (Ch); *The Times*, September 29, 2003 (Pumfrey J.)).

In *Markos v Goodfellow* [2002] EWCA Civ 1542; October 11, 2002, unrep., CA, on the ground that the matter was *de minimis*, the trial judge dismissed a county court claim for trespass to land and, on appeal, a High Court judge held that any degree of trespass was actionable and ordered that the judgment appealed should be corrected under the slip rule so as to state that the claimant should have judgment for a nominal sum. In allowing the defendant's appeal the Court of Appeal stressed that r.40.12 is limited to genuine slips, is only applicable to "an accidental slip or omission", and cannot be used to change the substance of a judgment. Each case must turn on its own facts. However, judgments dealing with the application of the slip rule often provide useful illustrations of its scope. Recent examples of cases in which the courts have declined to apply the slip rule include *Smithkline Beecham Plc. v Apotex Europe Ltd* [2005] EWHC 1655 (Ch); *The Times*, August 10, 2005 (Lewison J.) (co-defendants not named as potential beneficiaries of claimant's cross-undertaking attached to interim injunction to compensate defendant in damages); *Hajigeorgiou v Vasiliou* [2005] EWCA Civ 236; *The Times*, March 22, 2005, CA (in case management directions experts not named but identified only by field of expertise); *R + V Versicherung A.G. v. Risk Insurance and Reinsurance Solutions S.A.* [2007] EWHC 79 (Comm); *The Times* February 26, 2007 (Gloster J.) (alterations to judge's orders proposed matters of substance challenging the judge's judgment).

Cases where court gives judgment both on claim and counterclaim[1]

40.13 **40.13—(1) This rule applies where the court gives judgment for specified amounts both for the claimant on his claim and against the claimant on a counterclaim.**

(2) If there is a *balance* in favour of one of the parties, it may or-

[1] Amended by the Civil Procedure (Amendment) Rules 2000 (SI 2000/221).

der the party whose judgment is for the lesser amount to pay the balance.

(3) In a case to which this rule applies, the court may make a separate order as to costs against each party.

Judgment in favour of certain part owners relating to the detention of goods[1]

40.14—(1) In this rule "part owner" means one of two or more persons who have an interest in the same goods. 40.14

(2) Where—

(a) a part owner makes a claim relating to the detention of the goods; and

(b) the claim is not based on a right to possession,

any judgment or order given or made in respect of the claim is to be for the payment of damages only, unless the claimant had the written authority of every other part owner of the goods to make the claim on his behalf as well as for himself.

(3) This rule applies notwithstanding anything in subsection (3) of section 3 of the Torts (Interference with Goods) Act 1977, but does not affect the remedies and jurisdiction mentioned in subsection (8) of that section.

Effect of rule

This rule gives effect to the current rule of law that a person without an immediate right to the possession of goods cannot sue for wrongful detention for specific delivery or in conversion, but is confined to his remedy in damages limited to his "reversionary" interest in the goods. One of two or more co-owners of goods cannot therefore obtain an order for specific delivery of the goods or even their assessed value, unless he can show that he has the written authority of every other owner to sue on his or their behalf. 40.14.1

II. Sale of Land etc. and Conveyancing Counsel

Scope of this Section[2]

40.15—(1) This Section— 40.15

(a) deals with the court's power to order the sale, mortgage, partition or exchange of land; and

(b) contains provisions about conveyancing counsel.

(Section 131 of the Supreme Court Act 1981 provides for the appointment of the conveyancing counsel of the Supreme Court.)

(2) In this Section "land" includes any interest in, or right over, land.

Scope

See para.40.0.6 above. 40.15.1

Power to order sale etc.[3]

40.16 In any proceedings relating to land, the court may order the land, or part of it, to be— 40.16

[1] Amended by the Civil Procedure (Amendment) Rules 2000 (SI 2000/221).
[2] Amended by the Civil Procedure (Amendment) Rules 2000 (SI 2000/221).
[3] Amended by the Civil Procedure (Amendment) Rules 2000 (SI 2000/221).

(a) sold;
(b) mortgaged;
(c) exchanged; or
(d) partitioned.

Effect of rule

40.16.1 The Court is empowered to give such directions as are necessary, r.40.16. It applies to both the Chancery Division of the High Court and the County Court. Often the Court will direct a sale "in such manner as the parties may agree or the court may direct in default of agreement". The application is made by Pt 23 application notice.

Sale by personal representatives of real estate

40.16.2 See CPR 64.2 and PD to Pt 64 para.1(2).

Discharge of incumbrances on sale

40.16.3 Paragraph 1.2 of Pt 1 or PD D to Pt 40 provides that where land subject to any incumbrance is sold or exchanged any party may apply to the court for a direction under LPA 1925 s.50.

Applications

40.16.4 Applications in existing proceedings are made by application notice otherwise by the issue of a claim form under Pt 8 (Practice Direction, para.1.5).

Directions

40.16.5 The directions that in particular the court will make are set out in paras 1 and 2 of Pt 1 of PD to Pt 40.

Permission to bid

40.16.6 Under a sale directed by the Court any party to the claim, desiring to purchase, should obtain permission to bid before the sale; but the sale will not necessarily be set aside because such leave has not been obtained. Bid includes tender or offer.

Certifying result of sale

40.16.7 Paragraphs 4.1 and 4.2 of Part 1 or PD to Part 40 applies.

Partition

40.16.8 The power of the Court to direct a partition is rarely exercised. However, rule 40.16(d) expressly envisages such an order. Reference should be made to s.7 of the Trusts of Land and Appointment of Trustees Act 1996 (Partition by trustees) and to s.14 (Powers of court).

Power to order delivery up of possession etc.[1]

40.17 **40.17 Where the court has made an order under rule 40.16, it may order any party to deliver up to the purchaser or any other person—**

(a) possession of the land;
(b) receipt of rents or profits relating to it; or
(c) both.

Reference to conveyancing counsel[2]

40.18 **40.18—(1) The court may direct conveyancing counsel to investigate and prepare a report on the title of any land or to draft *any* document.**

[1] Amended by the Civil Procedure (Amendment) Rules 2000 (SI 2000/221).
[2] Amended by the Civil Procedure (Amendment) Rules 2000 (SI 2000/221).

(2) The court may take the report on title into account when it decides the issue in question.

(Provisions dealing with the fees payable to conveyancing counsel are set out in the practice direction relating to Part 44).

Fees of conveyancing counsel

Practice Direction (Costs), para.8.8 states that, where the court refers a matter to the conveyancing counsel of the court, the fees payable to counsel in respect of the work done or to be done will be assessed in accordance with r.44.3 (see para.44PD.2 below). **40.18.1**

Reference to conveyancing counsel

The usual practice is that the court when making an order does not specify the name of the conveyancing counsel (under 40DPD6.1) but refers to "conveyancing counsel of the court". The solicitor concerned will then write to the Chief Master enclosing a copyof the order and asking him to nominate a particular counsel (40DPD6(2)–(3)). There are currently three conveyancing counsels of the court. The Chief Master will nominate one of these and write to him, sending him a copy of the order (40DPD6(3)). At the same time the Chief Master will write back to the solicitor concerned, informing him of the name and address of the nominated counsel. **40.18.2**

Party may object to report[1]

40.19—(1) Any party to the proceedings may object to the report on title prepared by conveyancing counsel. **40.19**

(2) Where there is an objection, the issue will be referred to a judge for determination.

(Part 23 contains general rules about making an application).

Jurisdiction

Both the High Court and the County Court can refer any matter of title to conveyancing counsel. Part 2 of the Practice Direction deals with the mechanism of such references. This procedure is rarely used in practice. **40.19.1**

Where the court refers any matter to conveyancing counsel the fees payable to counsel will be assessed by the court in accordance with r.44.3: para.8.8(1) of PD to Pt 44.

III. Declaratory judgments

Declaratory Judgments[2]

40.20 The court may make binding declarations whether or not any other remedy is claimed. **40.20**

Effect of rule

Rule 40.20 is to the same effect as former RSC O.15, r.16, a provision which survived until March 2001 as one of the CPR "schedule" rules (see para.40.0.7 above). The history of the rule may be traced back to 1883. When introduced it was a remedial provision, designed to enable the courts to grant declaratory judgments in circumstances where that had not been possible previously. The rule established the proposition that the court's jurisdiction to make a declaration is not confined to cases in which the claimant has a complete and subsisting cause of action apart from the rule; thus, the court may make a declaration where no other relief is claimed or can be claimed (*Guaranty Trust Co of New York v Hannay* [1915] 2 K.B. 536, CA) (see further para.25.1.17 above). Because the remedy has been in place for so long, and because its **40.20.1**

[1] Amended by the Civil Procedure (Amendment) Rules 2000 (SI 2000/221).
[2] Introduced by the Civil Procedure (Amendment) Rules 2001 (SI 2001/256).

effects have become so familiar, a reminder of its purpose (surprising as it now seems) is necessary if r.40.20 is not to be regarded as otiose.

Rule 25.1(1)(b) states that the court may grant an interim declaration as an interim remedy, see para.25.1.17 above.

Jurisdiction to make declarations

40.20.2 The jurisdiction to grant remedies in the form of declarations is not derived from r.40.20, as that rule is concerned only with the short point that a declaration can be granted whether or not any other remedy is claimed. Claims for declarations alone are unusual. Generally, declarations are sought and granted together with other forms of relief (often in the form of injunctions). In judicial review proceedings, a declaration may be granted as provided by the Supreme Court Act 1981 s.31, and the Crown Proceedings Act 1947 s.21 provides that, in proceedings against the Crown, in certain circumstances the court shall not grant relief by way of injunction or specific performance but shall in lieu thereof "make an order declaratory of the rights of the parties" (e.g. *Getmapping Plc v Ordnance Survey* [2002] EWHC 1089; May 31, 2002, unrep. (Laddie J.)). Declarations as remedies should be distinguished from other forms of declaration, e.g. declarations under the Human Rights Act 1998 s.4 to the effect that primary legislation is incompatible with Convention rights (see Vol.2, para.3D-17 below).

The power to make declarations is a discretionary power.As between the parties to a claim, the court can grant a declaration as to their rights, or as to the existence of facts, or as to a principle of law (*Financial Services Authority v Rourke* [2002] C.P. Rep. 14 (Neuberger J.)). When considering whether to grant a declaration or not, the court should take into account justice to the claimant, justice to the defendant, whether the declaration would serve a useful purpose, and whether there are any other special reasons why or why not the court should grant the declaration (*ibid.*). The principles were considered at first instance in *Nokia Corp v InterDigital Technology Corp* [2006] EWHC 802 (Pat), April 12, 2006 unrep., (Pumfrey J.), and by the Court of Appeal in dismissing the appeal in that case [2006] EWCA Civ 1618; [2007] F.S.R. 23, CA; see also *Arrow Generics Ltd v Merck & Co Inc* [2007] EWHC 1900 (Pat); July 31, 2007, unrep. (Kitchin J.); *Hawkes v Cuddy* [2007] EWCA Civ 1072; *The Times* November 13, 2007, CA. (jurisdiction to grant declaration of criminal conduct on application to strike out claim).

In the Supreme Court Practice 1999, the commentary following RSC O.15 r.16, was extensive (see Vol.1, paras 15/16/1 to 15/16/10 and para.19/7/15). That material, much of which was illustrative of the exercise of the court's discretion in this respect, is not repeated here. In modern times, declaratory relief in relation to commercial disputes and judicial review has developed significantly, and much of the old authority should be treated with caution.

It may be noted that, whereas CPR, r.40.20 speaks of the court's jurisdiction to make "binding declarations", RSC O.15 r.16 spoke of the court making "binding declarations of right". The claim for a remedy in the form of a declaration is an important procedural device for ascertaining and determining the rights of parties and for the determination of points of law.

In *Amstrad Consumer Electronics Plc v The British Phonographic Industry Ltd* [1986] F.S.R. 159, a declaration of non-infringement of copyright was refused on the grounds that to grant it would be to prejudice a trial in the event of criminal proceedings being launched in respect of the infringement; *cf.*, *Financial Services Authority v Rourke* [2002] C.P. Rep. 14 (Neuberger J.) (giving special attention to the question whether the defendant's rights under art.6.2 and art.6.3 of the Human Rights Convention might be infringed).

A civil court ought not grant a "declaration of innocence" to a defendant in criminal proceedings which are properly instituted against him and are not vexatious or an abuse of the process of the court (*Imperial Tobacco Ltd v Attorney General* [1981] A.C. 718, HL).

Where a court awards provisional damages to a plaintiff for suffering asbestos-related disease, it has no power to make a declaration that his dependants are entitled, in the event of his death from such disease, to recover further damages under the Fatal Accidents Act 1976, since such event would only happen, if at all, in the future and moreover, the identity of the persons concerned could not presently be predicted (*Middleton v Elliot Turbomachinery, The Times*, October 29, 1990).

As to declarations of non-liability (negative declarations), both in transnational and domestic litigation, see *Messier-Dowty Ltd v Sabena SA* [2000] 1 W.L.R. 2040, CA, and the authorities cited there.

As to the question whether the court may or should grant a declaration (or any other remedy) where the issue between the parties is "hypothetical" or has become "academic", see Vol.2, para.9A–77.

As to the commencement of proceedings invoking the jurisdiction of High Court to grant declarations as to the best interests of incapacitated adults, see *Practice Direction (Declaratory Proceedings: Incapacitated Adults)* [2002] 1 W.L.R. 325, Fam.D. (para.21.0.6 above).

Declarations without trial (judgment by consent or default and summary judgment)

In *Wallersteiner v Moir* [1974] 1 W.L.R. 991, CA, the Chancery case of *Williams v Powell* [1894] W.N. 141, was cited as authority for the proposition that a declaration is a judicial act and ought not to be made on default of pleading, or on admissions of counsel, or by consent, but only if the court is satisfied by evidence. Buckley L.J. explained (at p.1029) that this rule is "a practice of very long standing" (see also *New Brunswick Railway Co Ltd v British & French Trust Corp Ltd* [1939] A.C. 1, and *Metzger v Department of Social Security* [1977] 3 All E.R. 444, at p.451, per Megarry V.-C.). In his lordship's opinion, where relief is to be granted without trial. whether on admissions or by agreement or in default of pleading, and it is necessary to make clear on what footing the relief is to be granted, the right course is not to make a declaration "but to state that the relief shall be such and such a footing without any declaration to the effect that that footing in fact reflects the legal situation". This rule of practice has been justified on various grounds, including the ground that declarations of legal right may affect third parties who are not bound by the declaration (a consideration that may have particular relevance in judicial review proceedings). **40.20.3**

The rule is a rule of practice and not of law. In *Wallersteiner v Moir*, Scarman L.J. said (at p.1030) that the power of the court to give declaratory relief without trial undoubtedly exists "but should be exercised only in cases in which to deny it would be to impose injustice on the claimant". Cases in which applications have been made for declarations without trial, and in which the court has held that the remedy should be granted because to deny it would impose injustice on the claimant, include *Patten v Burke Publishing Co Ltd* [1991] 1 W.L.R. 541 (Millett J.) (declaration that contract at end by reason of defendant's repudiation), *Aitbelaid v Nima*, *The Times*, July 19, 1991 (Leonard J.) (declarations as to certain documents and shares involved in the action).

In *Financial Services Authority v Rourke* [2002] C.P. Rep. 14 (Neuberger J.), the claimants claimed both injunctive and declaratory relief and applied for summary judgment. The declaration sought was to the effect that on numerous occasions the defendant had acted in breach of the Banking Act 1987. The judge held that the declaration could be granted provided the facts were established to the court's satisfaction on a balance of probabilities (and bearing in mind that the court would have to be strongly persuaded as to allegations of dishonesty). The judge found that, in the circumstances, there was no realistic possibility of the defendant showing that the facts alleged were wrong; consequently, although at the hearing of the summary judgment application there had been no disclosure of documents, no exchange of witness statements and no examination and cross-examination of witnesses, the factual basis for the declarations sought had been made out.

Practice Direction (Judicial Review), paras 17.1 to 17.3 (see para.54PD.17 below) provides that, in judicial review proceedings, if the parties are agreed about the final order to be made, the court will consider the documents which the claimant is required to file in these circumstances and, if satisfied that the order should be made, will make the order.If the court is not satisfied that the order should be made, a hearing date will be set. Where a draft agreed final order includes a declaration the rule of practice referred to above may persuade the court that the order should not be made without a hearing.

PRACTICE DIRECTION—ACCOUNTS, INQUIRIES ETC.

This Practice Direction supplements CPR Part 40

Accounts and inquiries: general

40PD.1 **1.1** Where the court orders any account to be taken or any inquiry to be made, it may, by the same or a subsequent order, give directions as to the manner in which the account is to be taken and verified or the inquiry is to be conducted.

1.2 In particular, the court may direct that in taking an account, the relevant books of account shall be evidence of their contents but that any party may take such objections to the contents as he may think fit.

1.3 Any party may apply to the court in accordance with CPR Part 23 for directions as to the taking of an account or the conduct of an inquiry or for the variation of directions already made.

1.4 Every direction for the taking of an account or the making of an inquiry shall be numbered in the order so that, as far as possible, each distinct account and inquiry is given its own separate number.

Verifying the account

40PD.2 **2.** Subject to any order to the contrary:

(1) the accounting party must make out his account and verify it by an affidavit or witness statement to which the account is exhibited,

(2) the accounting party must file the account with the court and at the same time notify the other parties that he has done so and of the filing of any affidavit or witness statement verifying or supporting the account.

Objections

40PD.3 **3.1** Any party who wishes to contend:

(a) that an accounting party has received more than the amount shown by the account to have been received, or

(b) that the accounting party should be treated as having received more than he has actually received, or

(c) that any item in the account is erroneous in respect of amount, or

(d) that in any other respect the account is inaccurate, must, unless the court directs otherwise, give written notice to the accounting party of his objections.

3.2 The written notice referred to in paragraph 3.1 must, so far as the objecting party is able to do so:

(a) state the amount by which it is contended that the account understates the amount received by the accounting party,

(b) state the amount which it is contended that the accounting party should be treated as having received in addition to the amount he actually received,

(c) specify the respects in which it is contended that the account is inaccurate, and

(d) in each case, give the ground on which the contention is made.

3.3 The contents of the written notice must, unless the notice contains a statement of truth, be verified by either an affidavit or a witness statement to which the notice is an exhibit.

(Part 22 and the Practice Direction that supplements it contain provisions about statements of truth).

Allowances

4. In taking any account all just allowances shall be made without any express direction to that effect. **40PD.4**

Management of proceedings

5. The court may at any stage in the taking of an account or in the course of an inquiry direct a hearing in order to resolve an issue that has arisen and for that purpose may order that points of claim and points of defence be served and give any necessary directions. **40PD.5**

Delay

6.1 If it appears to the court that there is undue delay in the taking of any account or the progress of any inquiry the court may require the accounting party or the party with the conduct of the inquiry, as the case may be, to explain the delay and may then make such order of the management of the proceedings (including a stay) and for costs as the circumstances may require. **40PD.6**

6.2 The directions the court may give under paragraph 6.1 include a direction that the Official Solicitor take over the conduct of the proceedings and directions providing for the payment of the Official Solicitor's costs.

Distribution

7. Where some of the persons entitled to share in a fund are known but there is, or is likely to be, difficulty or delay in ascertaining other persons so entitled, the court may direct, or allow, immediate payment of their shares to the known persons without reserving any part of those shares to meet the subsequent costs of ascertaining the other persons. **40PD.7**

Guardian's accounts

8. The accounts of a person appointed guardian of the property of a child (defined in CPR 21.1(2)) must be verified and approved in such manner as the court may direct. **40PD.8**

Accounts and inquiries to be conducted before Master or district judge

9. Unless the court orders otherwise, an account or inquiry will be taken or made— **40PD.9**

(1) by a Master or district judge, if the proceedings are in the High Court; and

(2) by a district judge, if the proceedings are in a county court.

Advertisements

10. The court may— **40PD.10**

(1) direct any necessary advertisement; and

(2) fix the time within which the advertisement should require a reply.

Examination of claims

40PD.11 **11.1** Where the court orders an account of debts or other liabilities to be taken, it may direct any party, within a specified time, to—

(1) examine the claims of persons claiming to be owed money out of the estate or fund in question.
(2) determine, as far as he is able, which of them are valid; and
(3) file written evidence—
(a) stating his findings and his reasons for them; and
(b) listing any other debts which are or may be owed out of the estate or fund.

11.2 Where the court orders an inquiry for next of kin or other unascertained claimants to an estate or fund, it may direct any party, within a specified time, to—

(1) examine the claims that are made;
(2) determine, as far as he is able, which of them are valid; and
(3) file written evidence stating his findings and his reasons for them.

11.3 If the personal representatives or trustees concerned are not the parties directed by the court to examine claims, the court may direct them to join with the party directed to examine claims in producing the written evidence required by this rule.

Consideration of claims by the court

40PD.12 **12.** For the purpose of considering a claim the court may—

(1) direct it to be investigated in any manner;
(2) direct the person making the claim to give further details of it; and
(3) direct that person to—
(a) file written evidence; or
(b) attend court to give evidence,

to support his claim.

Notice of decision

40PD.13 **13.** If—

(1) the court has allowed or disallowed any claim or part of a claim; and
(2) the person making the claim was not present when the decision was made,

the court will serve on that person a notice informing him of its decision.

Interest on debts

40PD.14 **14.**(1) Where an account of the debts of a deceased person is directed by any judgment, unless the deceased's estate is *insolvent* or the court orders otherwise, interest shall be allowed—

(a) on any debt which carries interest, at the rate it carries, and

(b) on any other debt, from the date of the judgment, at the rate payable on judgment debts at that date.

(2) Where interest on a debt is allowed under paragraph (1)(b), it shall be paid out of any assets of the estate which remain after payment of—

(a) any costs of the proceedings directed to be paid out of the estate;

(b) all the debts which have been established; and

(c) the interest on such of those debts as by law carry interest.

(3) For the purpose of this rule—

(a) 'debt' includes funeral, testamentary or administration expenses; and

(b) in relation to any expenses incurred after the judgment, paragraph (1)(b) applies as if, instead of the date of the judgment, it referred to the date when the expenses became payable.

Interest on legacies

15. Where an account of legacies is directed by any judgment, then, subject to— **40PD.15**

(a) any directions contained in the will or codicil in question; and

(b) any order made by the court,

interest shall be allowed on each legacy at the basic rate payable for the time being on funds in court or at such other rate as the court shall direct, beginning one year after the testator's death.

PRACTICE DIRECTION—JUDGMENTS AND ORDERS

This Practice Direction supplements CPR Part 40

Drawing up and filing of judgments and orders

40BPD.1 **1.1** Rule 40.2 sets out the standard requirements for judgments and orders and rule 40.3 deals with how judgments and orders should be drawn up.

1.2 A party who has been ordered or given permission to draw up an order must file it for sealing within 7 days of being ordered or permitted to do so.[1] If he fails to do so, any other party may draw it up and file it.[2]

1.3 If the court directs that a judgment or order which is being drawn up by a party must be checked by the court before it is sealed, the party responsible must file the draft within 7 days of the date the order was made with a request that the draft be checked before it is sealed.

1.4 If the court directs the parties to file an agreed statement of terms of an order which the court is to draw up,[3] the parties must do so no later than 7 days from the date the order was made, unless the court directs otherwise.

1.5 If the court requires the terms of an order which is being drawn up by the court to be agreed by the parties the court may direct that a copy of the draft order is to be sent to all the parties:

(1) for their agreement to be endorsed on it and returned to the court before the order is sealed, or

(2) with notice of an appointment to attend before the court to agree the terms of the order.

Preparation of deeds or documents under an order

40BPD.2 **2.1** Where a judgment or order directs any deed or document to be prepared, executed or signed, the order will state:

(1) the person who is to prepare the deed or document, and

(2) if the deed or document is to be approved, the person who is to approve it.

2.2 If the parties are unable to agree the form of the deed or document, any party may apply in accordance with Part 23 for the form of the deed or document to be settled.

2.3 In such case the judge may:

(1) settled the deed or document himself, or

(2) refer it to

(a) a master, or

(b) a district judge, or

(c) a conveyancing counsel of the Supreme Court to settle.

(See also the Sale of Land practice direction supplementing CPR Part 40)

Consent orders

40BPD.3 **3.1** Rule 40.6(3) sets out the types of consent judgments and orders

[1] r.40.3(3)(a).
[2] r.40.3(3)(b).
[3] r.40.3(2(b).

which may be entered and sealed by a court officer. The court officer may do so in those cases provided that:

(1) none of the parties is a litigant in person, and

(2) the approval of the court is not required by the Rules, a practice direction or any enactment.[1]

3.2 If a consent order filed for sealing appears to be unclear or incorrect the court officer may refer it to a judge for consideration.[2]

3.3 Where a consent judgment or order does not come within the provisions of rule 40.6(2):

(1) an application notice requesting a judgment or order in the agreed terms should be filed with the draft judgment or order to be entered or sealed, and

(2) the draft judgment or order must be drawn so that the judge's name and judicial title can be inserted.

3.4 A consent judgment or order must:

(1) be drawn up in the terms agreed,

(2) bear on it the words "By Consent", and

(3) be signed by

(a) solicitors or counsel acting for each of the parties to the order, or

(b) where a party is a litigant in person, the litigant.[3]

3.5 Where the parties draw up a consent order in the form of a stay of proceedings on agreed terms, disposing of the proceedings,[4] and where the terms are recorded in a schedule to the order, any direction for:

(1) payment of money out of court, or

(2) payment and assessment of costs

should be contained in the body of the order and not in the schedule.

Correction of errors in judgments and orders

4.1 Where a judgment or order contains an accidental slip or omission a party may apply for it to be corrected.[5] **40BPD.4**

4.2 The application notice (which may be an informal document such as a letter) should describe the error and set out the correction required. An application may be dealt with without a hearing:

(1) where the applicant so requests,

(2) with the consent of the parties, or

(3) where the court does not consider that a hearing would be appropriate.

4.3 The judge may deal with the application without notice if the *slip or omission is obvious* or may direct notice of the application to be given to the other party or parties.

4.4 If the application is opposed it should, if practicable, be listed

[1] r.40.6(2).
[2] r.3.2.
[3] r.40.6(7).
[4] r.40.6(3)(b)(ii).
[5] r.40.10.

for hearing before the judge who gave the judgment or made the order.

4.5 The court has an inherent power to vary its own orders to make the meaning and intention of the court clear.

Adjustment of final judgment figure in respect of compensation recovery payments

40BPD.5 **5.1** In a final judgment where some or all of the damages awarded—

(1) fall under the heads of damage set out in column 1 of Schedule 2 to the Social Security (Recovery of Benefits) Act 1997 ("the 1997 Act") in respect of recoverable benefits received by the claimant set out in column 2 of that Schedule; and

(2) where the defendant has paid to the Secretary of State the recoverable benefits in accordance with the certificate (as defined in rule 36.15(1)(e)),

there will be stated in the preamble to the judgment or order the amount awarded under each head of damage and the amount by which it has been reduced in accordance with section 8 of and Schedule 2 of the 1997 Act.

5.1A Where damages are awarded in a case where a lump sum payment (to be construed in accordance with section 1A of the 1997 Act) has been made to a dependant, then section 15 of the 1997 Act (as modified by Schedule 1 to the Social Security (Recovery of Benefits)(Lump Sum Payments) Regulations 2008 sets out what the court order must contain.

5.2 The judgment or order should then provide for entry of judgment and payment of the balance.

Adjustment of final judgment figure in respect of an interim payment

40BPD.6 **6.1** In a final judgment[1] where an interim payment has previously been made which is less than the total amount awarded by the judge, the judgment or order should set out in a preamble:

(1) the total amount awarded by the judge, and

(2) the amount and date of the interim payment(s).

6.2 The total amount awarded by the judge should then be reduced by the total amount of any interim payments, and the judgment or order should then provide for entry of judgment and payment of the balance.

6.3 In a final judgment where an interim payment has previously been made which is more than the total amount awarded by the judge, the judgment or order should set out in a preamble;

(1) the total amount awarded by the judge, and

(2) the amount and date of the interim payment(s).

6.4 An order should then be made for repayment, reimbursement, variation or discharge under rule 25.8(2) and for interest on an overpayment under rule 25.8(5).

[1] As in Note 1 above.

Statement as to service of a claim form

7.1 Where a party to proceedings which have gone to trial requires a statement to be included in the judgment as to where, and by what means the claim form issued in those proceedings was served, application should be made to the trial judge when judgment is given. **40BPD.7**

7.2 If the judge so orders, the statement will be included in a preamble to the judgment as entered.

Orders requiring an act to be done

8.1 An order which requires an act to be done (other than a judgment or order for the payment of an amount of money) must specify the time within which the act should be done. **40BPD.8**

8.2 The consequences of failure to do an act within the time specified may be set out in the order. In this case the wording of the following examples suitably adapted must be used:

(1) Unless the [claimant][defendant] serves his list of documents by 4.00pm on Friday, January 22, 1999 his [claim][defence] will be struck out and judgment entered for the [defendent-][claimant], or

(2) Unless the [claimant][defendant] serves his list of documents within 14 days of service of this order his [claim][defence] will be struck out and judgment entered for the [defendant][claimant].

Example (1) should be used wherever possible.

Non-compliance with a judgment or order

9.1 An order which restrains a party from doing an act or requires an act to be done should, if disobedience is to be dealt with by an application to bring contempt of court proceedings, have a penal notice endorsed on it as follows: **40BPD.9**

"If you the within-named [ ] do not comply with this order you may be held to be in contempt of court and imprisoned or fined, or [in the case of a company or corporation] your assets may be seized."

9.2 The provisions of paragraph 8.1 above also apply to an order which contains an undertaking by a party to do or not do an act, subject to paragraph 9.3 below.

9.3 The court has the power to decline to:

(1) accept an undertaking, and

(2) deal with disobedience in respect of an undertaking by contempt of court proceedings, unless the party giving the undertaking has made a signed statement to the effect that he understands the terms of his undertaking and the consequences of failure to comply with it.

9.4 The statement may be endorsed on the [court copy of the] order containing the undertaking or may be filed in a separate document such as a letter.

Foreign currency

10. Where judgment is ordered to be entered in a foreign currency, the order should be in the following form: **40BPD.10**

"It is ordered that the defendant pay the claimant (*state the sum in the foreign currency*) or the Sterling equivalent at the time of payment."

Costs

40BPD.11 **11.1** Attention is drawn to the costs practice direction and, in particular, to the court's power to make a summary assessment of costs and the provisions relating to interest in detailed assessment proceedings.

11.2 Attention is also drawn to costs rule 44.13(1) which provides that if an order makes no mention of costs, none are payable in respect of the proceedings to which it relates.

Judgments paid by instalments

40BPD.12 **12.** Where a judgment is to be paid by instalments, the judgment should set out:

(1) the total amount of the judgment,
(2) the amount of each instalment,
(3) the number of instalments and the date on which each is to be paid, and
(4) to whom the instalments should be paid.

Order to make an order of the House of Lords an order of the High Court

40BPD.13 **13.1** Application may be made in accordance with Part 23 for an order to make an order of the House of Lords an order of the High Court. The application should be made to the procedural judge of the Division, District Registry or court in which the proceedings are taking place and may be made without notice unless the court directs otherwise.

13.2 The application must be supported by the following evidence:

(1) details of the order which was the subject of the appeal to the House of Lords,
(2) details of the order of the House of Lords, with a copy annexed, and
(3) a copy annexed of the certificate of the Clerk of Parliaments of the assessment of the costs of the appeal to the House of Lords in the sum of £ ....

13.3 The order to make an order of the House of Lords an order of the High Court should be in Form **No. PF68**.

Examples of forms of trial judgment

40BPD.14 **14.1** The following general forms may be used;

(1) judgment after trial before judge without jury—Form **No. 45**,
(2) judgment after trial before judge with jury—Form **No. 46**,
(3) judgment after trial before a Master or district judge—Form **No. 47**,
(4) judgment after trial before a judge of the Technology and Construction court—Form **No. 47** but with any necessary modifications.

14.2 A trial judgment should, in addition to the matters set out in paragraphs 5, 6 and 7 above, have the following matters set out in a preamble:

(1) the questions put to a jury and their answers to those questions,
(2) the findings of a jury and whether unanimous or by a majority,
(3) any order made during the course of the trial concerning the use of evidence,
(4) any matters that were agreed between the parties prior to or during the course of the trial in respect of
 (a) liability,
 (b) contribution,
 (c) the amount of the damages or part of the damages, and
(5) the findings of the judge in respect of each head of damage in a personal injury case.

14.3 Form **No. 49** should be used for trial judgment against an Estate.

The forms referred to in this practice direction are listed in the practice direction which supplements Part 4 (Forms).

14.4 On any application or appeal concerning–
(i) a committal order;
(ii) a refusal to grant habeas corpus or
(iii) a secure accommodation order made under section 25 of the Children Act 1989,

if the court ordering the release of the person concludes that his Convention rights have been infringed by the making of the order to which the application or appeal relates, the judgment or order should so state. If the court does not do so, that failure will not prevent another court from deciding the matter.

For information about

(1) Orders for provisional damages: see Part 41 and the practice direction which supplements it. **40BPD.15**
(2) Orders in respect of children and protected parties: see Part 21 and the practice direction which supplements it.
(3) Orders containing directions for payment of money out of court: see Parts 36 and 37 and the practice directions which supplement them.
(4) Structured settlement orders: see the separate practice direction supplementing Part 40.
(5) Taking accounts and conducting inquiries under a judgment or order: see the separate practice direction supplementing Part 40.

[THE NEXT PARAGRAPH IS 40DPD.1.]

PRACTICE DIRECTION—1. COURT'S POWERS IN RELATION TO LAND. 2. CONVEYANCING COUNSEL OF THE COURT

40DPD.1 *This Practice Direction Supplements CPR Part 40*

Part 1

Court's powers in relation to land

Application to the court where land subject to an incumbrance

1.1 In this paragraph "incumbrance" has the same meaning as it has in section 205(1) of the Law of Property Act 1925.

1.2 Where land subject to any incumbrance is sold or exchanged any party to the sale or exchange may apply to the court for a direction under section 50 of the Law of Property Act 1925 (discharge of incumbrances by the court on sales or exchanges).

1.3 The directions a court may give on such an application include a direction for the payment into court of a sum of money that the court considers sufficient to meet—

(1) the value of the incumbrance; and

(2) further costs, expenses and interest that may become due on or in respect of the incumbrance.

(Section 50(1) of the Law of Property Act 1925 contains provisions relating to the calculation of these amounts.)

1.4 Where a payment into court has been made in accordance with a direction under section 50(1) the court may—

(1) declare the land to be freed from the incumbrance; and

(2) make any order it considers appropriate for giving effect to an order made under rule 40.16 or relating to the money in court and the income thereof.

1.5 An application under section 50 should—

(1) if made in existing proceedings, be made in accordance with CPR Part 23;

(2) otherwise, be made by claim form under CPR Part 8.

Directions about the sale etc.

40DPD.2 **2.** Where the court has made an order under rule 40.16 it may give any other directions it considers appropriate for giving effect to the order. In particular the court may give directions—

(1) appointing a party or other person to conduct the sale;

(2) for obtaining evidence of the value of the land;

(3) as to the manner of sale;

(4) settling the particulars and conditions of the sale;

(5) fixing a minimum or reserve price;

(6) as to the fees and expenses to be allowed to an auctioneer or estate agent;

(7) for the purchase money to be paid

(a) into court;

(b) to trustees; or

(c) to any other person;

(8) for the result of a sale to be certified;

(9) under rule 40.18.

Application for permission to bid

3.1 Where— 40DPD.3

(1) the court has made an order under rule 40.16 for land to be sold; and

(2) a party wishes to bid for the land,

he should apply to the court for permission to do so.

3.2 An application for permission to bid must be made before the sale takes place.

3.3 If the court gives permission to all the parties to bid, it may appoint an independent person to conduct the sale.

3.4 "Bid" in this paragraph includes submitting a tender or other offer to buy.

Certifying sale result

4.1 If— 40DPD.4

(1) the court has directed the purchase money to be paid into court; or

(2) the court has directed that the result of the sale be certified,

the result of the sale must be certified by the person having conduct of the sale.

4.2 Unless the court directs otherwise, the certificate must give details of

(1) the amount of the purchase price;

(2) the amount of the fees and expenses payable to any auctioneer or estate agent;

(3) the amount of any other expenses of the sale;

(4) the net amount received in respect of the sale;

and must be verified by a statement of truth.

(Part 22 sets out requirements about statements of truth.)

4.3 The certificate must be filed

(1) if the proceedings are being dealt with in the Royal Courts of Justice, in Chancery Chambers;

(2) if the proceedings are being dealt with anywhere else, in the court where the proceedings are being dealt with.

Fees and expenses of auctioneers and estate agents

5.1(1) Where the court has ordered the sale of land under rule 40.16, auctioneer's and estate agent's charges may, unless the court orders otherwise, include 40DPD.5

(a) commission;

(b) *fees for valuation* of the land;

(c) charges for advertising the land;

(d) other expenses and disbursements but not charges for surveys.

(2) The court's authorisation is required for charges relating to surveys.

5.2 If the total amount of the auctioneer's and estate agent's charges authorised under paragraph 5.1(1)

(1) does not exceed 2.5% of the sale price; and

(2) does not exceed the rate of commission that that agent would normally charge on a sole agency basis

the charges may, unless the court orders otherwise and subject to paragraph 5.3(3) and (4), be met by deduction of the amount of the charges from the proceeds of sale without the need for any further authorisation from the court.

5.3 If—

(1) a charge made by an auctioneer or estate agent (whether in respect of fees or expenses or both) is not authorised under paragraph 5.1(1);

(2) the total amount of the charges so authorised exceeds the limits set out in paragraph 5.2;

(3) the land is sold in lots or by valuation; or

(4) the sale is of investment property, business property or farm property

an application must be made to the court for approval of the fees and expenses to be allowed.

5.4 An application under paragraph 5.3 may be made by any party or, if he is not a party, by the person having conduct of the sale, and may be made either before or after the sale has taken place.

Part 2

Conveyancing counsel of the court

Reference to conveyancing counsel

40DPD.6 **6.1** When the court refers a matter under rule 40.18, the court may specify a particular conveyancing counsel.

6.2 If the court does not specify a particular conveyancing counsel, references will be distributed among conveyancing counsel in accordance with arrangements made by the Chief Chancery Master.

6.3 Notice of every reference under rule 40.18 must be given to the Chief Chancery Master.

6.4 The court will send a copy of the order, together with all other necessary documents, to conveyancing counsel.

6.5 A court order sent to conveyancing counsel under paragraph 6.4 will be sufficient authority for him to prepare his report or draft the document.

6.6(1) An objection under rule 40.19 to a report on title prepared by conveyancing counsel must be made by application notice.

(2) The application notice must state—

(a) the matters the applicant objects to; and

(b) the reason for the objection.

PRACTICE DIRECTION—RESERVED JUDGMENTS

This Practice Direction supplements Part 40 40EPD.1

Scope and interpretation

1.1 This Practice Direction applies to all reserved judgments which the court intends to hand down in writing.

1.2 In this Practice Direction—

(a) "relevant court office" means the office of the court in which judgment is to be given; and

(b) "working day" means any day on which the relevant court office is open.

Availability of reserved judgments before handing down

2.1 Where judgment is to be reserved the judge (or Presiding Judge) may, at the conclusion of the hearing, invite the views of the parties' legal representatives as to the arrangements made for the handing down of the judgment. 40EPD.2

2.2 Unless the court directs otherwise, the following provisions of this paragraph apply where the judge or Presiding Judge is satisfied that the judgment will attract no special degree of confidentiality or sensitivity.

2.3 The court will provide a copy of the draft judgment to the parties' legal representatives by 4 p.m. on the second working day before handing down, or at such other time as the court may direct.

2.4 A copy of the draft judgment may be supplied, in confidence, to the parties provided that—

(a) neither the draft judgment nor its substance is disclosed to any other person or used in the public domain; and

(b) no action is taken (other than internally) in response to the draft judgment, before the judgment is handed down.

2.5 Where a copy of the draft judgment is supplied to a party's legal representatives in electronic form, they may supply a copy to that party in the same form.

2.6 If a party to whom a copy of the draft judgment is supplied under paragraph 2.4 is a partnership, company, government department, local authority or other organisation of a similar nature, additional copies may be distributed in confidence within the organisation, provided that all reasonable steps are taken to preserve its confidential nature and the requirements of paragraph 2.4 are adhered to.

2.7 If the parties or their legal representatives are in any doubt about the persons to whom copies of the draft judgment may be distributed they should enquire of the judge or Presiding Judge.

2.8 Any breach of the obligations or restrictions under paragraph 2.4 or failure to take all reasonable steps under paragraph 2.6 may be treated as contempt of court.

2.9 The case will be listed for judgment, and judgment handed down at the appropriate time.

Corrections to the draft judgment

3.1 Unless the parties or their legal representatives are told otherwise when the draft judgment is circulated, any proposed cor- 40EPD.3

rections to the draft judgment should be sent to the clerk of the judge who prepared the draft with a copy to any other party.

Orders consequential on judgment

40EPD.4 **4.1** Following the circulation of the draft judgment the parties or their legal representatives must seek to agree orders consequential upon the judgment.

4.2 In respect of any draft agreed order the parties must—

(a) fax or e-mail a copy to the clerk to the judge or Presiding Judge (together with any proposed corrections or amendments to the draft judgment); and

(b) file four copies (with completed backsheets) in the relevant court office, by 12 noon on the working day before handing down.

4.3 A copy of a draft order must bear the case reference, the date of handing down and the name of the judge or Presiding Judge.

4.4 Where a party wishes to apply for an order consequential on the judgment the application must be made by filing written submissions with the clerk to the judge or Presiding Judge by 12 noon on the working day before handing down.

4.5 Unless the court orders otherwise—

(a) where judgment is to be given by an appeal court (which has the same meaning as in rule 52.1(3)(b)), the application will be determined without a hearing; and

(b) where judgment is to be given by any other court, the application will be determined at a hearing.

Attendance at handing down

40EPD.5 **5.1** If there is not to be an oral hearing of an application for an order consequential on judgment—

(a) the parties' advocates need not attend on the handing down of judgment; and

(b) the judgment may be handed down by a judge sitting alone.

5.2 Where paragraph 5.1(a) applies but an advocate does attend the handing down of judgment, the court may if it considers such attendance unnecessary, disallow the costs of the attendance.

PART 41

DAMAGES

CPR 41

Contents

I. Proceedings to which section 32A of the Supreme Court Act 1981 or section 51 of the County Courts Act 1984 applies **41.0.1**

Editorial introduction

Since the coming into effect of the Civil Procedure (Amendment No.3) Rules 2004 (SI 2004/3129), this Part has been divided into two Sections. **41.0.2**

Section I (rr.41.1 to 41.3) contains rules of court authorised to be made by the Supreme Court Act 1981 s.32A and by the County Courts Act 1984 s.51 (see Vol.2, para.9A–107 and para.9A–497) (see also Damages Act 1996 s.3) in relation to the jurisdiction of the court to make orders for provisional damages in actions for damages for personal injuries. This Section is supplemented by Practice Direction (Provisional Damages), see para.41PD.1 below.

Section II (rr.41.4 to 41.10) contains rules of court authorised to be made by the Damages Act 1996 ss.2, 2A and 2B (as substituted by the Courts Act 2003 s.100) in relation to the jurisdiction of the court to make orders for damages taking the form (wholly or partly) of periodical payments (instead of lump sum payments) when awarding damages for future pecuniary loss in respect of personal injury. This Section is supplemented by Practice Direction (Periodical Payments under the Damages Act 1996), see para.41BPD.1 below. Practice Direction (Structured Settlements), which formerly supplemented Pt 40, was revoked when this direction came into effect.

In the interests of bringing finality in personal injury litigation, it is the court's function to make a single award for damages, making the best assessment possible of future loss. The inherent difficulty in doing this is partly overcome by the court's power to order provisional damages or payment of damages by periodical payments as provided for by the legislation referred to above. This inherent difficulty can also create necessary delays in the final disposal of personal injury and wrongful death cases that have to be specially managed by the court (see para.1.3.4 above).

Related sources

- Supreme Court Act 1981 s.32A (see Vol.2, para.9A–107) **41.0.3**

- County Courts Act 1984 s.51 (see Vol.2 para.9A–497)
- Damages Act 1996 ss.2, 2A, 2B and 3
- Practice Direction (Provisional Damages, Procedure) [1985] 1 W.L.R. 961, as amended by the Lord Chief Justice, March 23, 1995
- Part 25
- Rule 36.2A
- Rule 16.4(1)(d)
- Practice Direction (Appeals) para.13.5 (see para.52PD.49)
- Practice Direction (Children and Patients) para.6.4 (see para.21PD.6)
- Practice Direction (Offers to Settle and Payments Into Court) para.12.1 (see para.36PD.12)
- Damages (Variation of Periodical Payments) Order 2004

I. Proceedings to which Section 32A of the Supreme Court Act 1981 or Section 51 of the County Courts Act 1984 applies

Application and definitions

41.1 **41.1—(1) This Section of this Part applies to proceedings to which SCA s.32A or CCA s.51 applies.**

(2) In this Section—

(a) "SCA s.32A" means section 32A of the Supreme Court Act 1981[1];

(b) "CCA, s.51" means section 51 of the County Courts Act 1984[2]; and

(c) "award of provisional damages" means an award of damages for personal injuries under which—

(i) damages are assessed on the assumption referred to in SCA s.32A or CCA s.51 that the injured person will not develop the disease or suffer the deterioration; and

(ii) the injured person is entitled to apply for further damages at a future date if he develops the disease or suffers the deterioration.

41.1.1 *Note*—Amended by Civil Procedure (Amendment No.3) Rules 2004 (SI 2004/3129): effective April 1, 2005, the date of entry into force of s.100 of the Courts Act 2003 (The Courts Act 2003 (Commencement No.10) Order (SI 2005/910)).

"award of provisional damages"

41.1.2 Provisional damages may be awarded in a claim for personal injuries where it is proved or admitted that there is a chance that at some time in the future the injured person will, as a result of the act or omission which gave rise to the cause of action, develop some serious disease or suffer some serious deterioration in his physical or mental condition (see Supreme Court Act 1981 s.32A and County Courts Act 1984 s.51). Orders for awards of provisional damages in personal injury claims should be distinguished from interim payment orders as provided by the Supreme Court Act 1981 s.32 and the County Courts Act 1984 s.50 (see para.25.6.1 above).

As to meaning of a "claim for personal injuries" in the CPR, see r.2.3(1) above and para.2.3.16.

The court may make, in addition to an order for the award of provisional damages (as provided for by Sect.I of Pt 41), an order for the payment of those damages, insofar as they relate to future pecuniary loss, by a periodical payment order (as

[1] 1981 c.54. S.32A was inserted by s.6(1) of the Administration of Justice Act 1982 (c.53).

[2] 1984 c.28.

provided by Sect.II of Pt 41); further, in these circumstances, the periodical payment order may be a variable order (see para.41.8.6, below).

Information included in Particulars of claim

Part 16 and Practice Direction to Pt 16 set out the information that must be included in particulars of claim if a claim for provisional damages is to be made. In particular see r.16.4(1)(d) and Practice Direction to Pt 16, para.4.4 which provide that the particulars of claim must state that the claimant is claiming provisional damages, that there is a chance that at some future time the claimant will develop a serious disease or deterioration in his physical or mental condition, what that disease or deterioration will be and the grounds for claiming provisional damages. **41.1.3**

Order for an award of provisional damages

41.2—(1) The court may make an order for an award of provisional damages if— **41.2**

- **(a) the particulars of claim include a claim for provisional damages; and**
- **(b) the court is satisfied that SCA s.32A or CCA s.51 applies.**

(Rule 16.4(1)(d) sets out what must be included in the particulars of claim where the claimant is claiming provisional damages.)

(2) An order for an award of provisional damages—

- **(a) must specify the disease or type of deterioration in respect of which an application may be made at a future date;**
- **(b) must specify the period within which such an application may be made; and**
- **(c) may be made in respect of more than one disease or type of deterioration and may, in respect of each disease or type of deterioration, specify a different period within which a subsequent application may be made.**

(3) The claimant may make more than one application to extend the period specified under paragraph (2)(b) or (2)(c).

An order for an award for provisional damages

The regime for provisional damages is confined to carefully defined circumstances by the relevant legislation. In other circumstances it may well be in the interests of justice that a final award of damages should not be made until sufficient time has elapsed for a reliable prognosis to be made of the claimant's medical condition and that the assessment hearing should be adjourned accordingly (*Adan v Securicor Custodial Services Ltd* [2004] EWHC 394 (QB), (Eady J.)) (see para.1.3.4 above). **41.2.1**

See the form for a provisional damages judgment in the Annex to the Practice Direction to Pt 41.

Note that when giving judgment the judge should:

(1) specify the disease or type of deterioration which for the award of immediate damages it has been assumed will not occur and will entitle the claimant to further damages if they do occur;

(2) give an award of immediate damages;

(3) specify the period within which an application for further damages may be made (an application may be made to extend the period. The period may be expressed as being for the duration of the life of the claimant); and

(4) direct what documents are to be filed and preserved. (See Practice Direction to Pt 41, paras 2.1 to 2.4).

The case file

41.2.2 See Practice Direction to Pt 41, paras 3.1 to 3.6.

Consent orders

41.2.3 See Practice Direction to Pt 41, paras 4.1 to 4.3.

Default judgment

41.2.4 See Practice Direction to Pt 41, paras 5.1 to 5.3.

"particulars of claim"

41.2.5 (r.41.2)—See rr.7.4 and 16.4.

Application for further damages

41.3 **41.3—(1) The claimant may not make an application for further damages after the end of the period specified under rule 41.2(2), or such period as extended by the court.**

(2) Only one application for further damages may be made in respect of each disease or type of deterioration specified in the award of provisional damages.

(3) The claimant must give at least 28 days' written notice to the defendant of his intention to apply for further damages.

(4) If the claimant knows—

(a) that the defendant is insured in respect of the claim; and

(b) the identity of the defendant's insurers,

he must also give at least 28 days' written notice to the insurers.

(5) Within 21 days after the end of the 28 day notice period referred to in paragraphs (3) and (4), the claimant must apply for directions.

(6) […]

"application"

41.3.1 (rr.41.2 and 41.3)—See Pt 23.

"28 days"

41.3.2 (r.41.3(3)–(5))—See r.28.

Causation of further damages

41.3.3 Where an order for an award of provisional damages is made, the damages are assessed on the basis that, although there is a chance that the claimant will at some definite or indefinite time in the future, as a result of the act or omission which gave rise to the cause of action, develop some serious disease or suffer some serious deterioration in his physical or mental condition, these conditions (to be specified in the order) have not arisen at the time when the order is made. Conceivably, an order for an award of provisional damages may be made either after a trial on liability or after the parties have settled that issue. It is plain from the words of the Supreme Court Act 1981 s.32A and the County Courts Act 1984 s.51 that those provisions are not limited to the risk of a deterioration in the claimant's existing condition or of the risk of the onset of a new condition consequent upon it, but also apply to the risk of any serious condition resulting from the "act or omission giving rise to the cause of action" (*Rothwell v Chemical & Insulating Co Ltd* [2006] EWCA Civ 27, January 26, 2006, unrep., CA, at para.130, per Smith L.J.). Where the claimant claims that the conditions have subsequently arisen, and applies under r.41.3 for further damages, issues as to whether the defendant's acts or omissions caused those conditions to arise may have to be determined. Thus, para.2.5 of Practice Direction (Provisional Damages) states: "Causation of any further damages within the scope of the order shall be determined when any application for further damages is made" (see para.41PD.2 below). In *Green v Vickers Defence Systems* [2003] EWCA Civ 904, *The Times* July 1, 2002, CA, the order for an award for provisional damages (made by consent) stated that the award was made "on a full liability basis". Following the death of the claimant, as a result of one of the conditions subsequently arising, his widow brought proceedings against the defendants, relying on the order. The Court of Appeal held that no issue of causation remained outstanding and the defendants were precluded from contesting the widow's claim on that ground.

Subsection (6) of r.40.3 was omitted by the Civil Procedure (Amendment No.4) Rules 2004 (SI 2004/3419), with effect from April 1, 2005. That sub-rule stated that the rules in Pt 25 about the making of an interim payment (viz. rr.25.6 to 25.9) applied where an application for further damages was made under r.41.3. The link between r.41.3 and Pt 25 was removed because it was thought that, in certain circumstances, it could impose conditions on applications for further damages which would result in unfairness.

41.3A—(1) Where—[1] 41.3A

(a) a claim includes claims arising under—

(i) the Fatal Accidents Act 1976; and

(ii) the Law Reform (Miscellaneous Provisions) Act 1934; and

(b) a single sum of money is ordered or agreed to be paid in satisfaction of the claims,

the court will apportion the money between the different claims.

(2) Where, in an action in which a claim under the Fatal Accidents Act 1976 is made by or on behalf of more than one person, a single sum of money is ordered or agreed to be paid in satisfaction of the claim, the court will apportion it between the persons entitled to it.

(3) Unless it has already been apportioned by the court, a jury or agreement between the parties, the court will apportion money under paragraphs (1) and (2)—

(a) when it gives directions under rule 21.11 (control of money received by a child or patient); or

(b) if rule 21.11 does not apply, on application by one of the parties in accordance with Part 23.

Effect of rule

This rule was added by the Civil Procedure (Amendment No.3) Rules 2006 (SI 2006/3435) and came into effect on April 6, 2007. The addition was made as a consequence of the substitution of Pt 36 by that statutory instrument. Rule 36 9(3)(c) states that the court's permission to accept a Pt 36 offer is required where an apportionment is required under r.41.3A. 41.3A.1

II. Periodical Payments under the Damages Act 1996

Scope and interpretation

41.4—(1) This Section of this Part contains rules about the *exercise of the court's powers* under section 2(1) of the 1996 Act to order that all or part of an award of damages in respect of personal injury is to take the form of periodical payments. 41.4

(2) In this Section—

(a) "the 1996 Act" means the Damages Act 1996[2];

[1] Introduced by the Civil Procedure (Amendment No.3) Rules 2006 (SI 2006/3435).
[2] 1996 c.48.

(b) "damages" means damages for future pecuniary loss; and

(c) "periodical payments" means periodical payments under section 2(1) of the 1996 Act.[1]

"order to take the form of periodical payments"

41.4.1 The Damages Act 1996 s.2 recognised that parties to actions for personal injuries may wish to structure the payment of any damages payable by the defendant to the claimant so that they were payable, either wholly or partly, by periodical payments (rather than by lump sum), and gave the court power to make orders to this effect where the parties consented. Section 2 was substituted by the Courts Act 2003 s.100 so as to provide that the court should have power to make orders for damages taking the form (wholly or partly) of periodical payments (instead of lump sum payments) when awarding damages for future pecuniary loss in respect of personal injury, and to do so whether the parties consented or not. Sections 2A and 2B were also inserted in the 1996 Act making further provision for such "periodical payments" and s.4 (Enhanced protection for periodical payments) and s.5 (Meaning of structured settlement) of the 1996 Act were replaced by a new s.4 (Enhanced protection for periodical payments). The Lord Chancellor may by Order enable a court to vary on order or settlement providing for periodical payments in specified circumstances (s.2B).

For further information as to the 1996 Act, see Vol.2, Section 3F (Personal Injury).

The rules in this Section of Pt 41 were inserted by the Civil Procedure (Amendment No.3) Rules 2004 (SI 2004/3129). These provisions, and the amendments to the Damages Act 1996 referred to above, came into effect on April 1, 2005, the date of entry into force of s.100 of the Courts Act 2003 (The Courts Act 2003 (Commencement No.10) Order (SI 2005/910)).The Courts Act 2003 (Transitional Provisions, Savings and Consequential Provisions) Order 2005 (SI 2005/911) stated that the powers exercisable by the subss. (1) and (2) of s.2 of the Damages Act 1996 "shall be exercisable in proceedings whenever begun".

Rules 41.8 to 41.10 are supplemented by Practice Direction (Periodical Payments Under the Damages Act 1996); see para.41BPD.1 below. The court's jurisdiction to make a periodical payments order should be distinguished from its power to order that a judgment should be paid by instalments.

Statement of case

41.5 **41.5—(1) In a claim for damages for personal injury, each party in its statement of case may state whether it considers periodical payments or a lump sum is the more appropriate form for all or part of an award of damages and where such statement is given must provide relevant particulars of the circumstances which are relied on.**

(2) Where a statement under paragraph (1) is not given, the court may order a party to make such a statement.

(3) Where the court considers that a statement of case contains insufficient particulars under paragraph (1), the court may order a party to provide such further particulars as it considers appropriate.

"each party...may state"

41.5.1 Provisions as to statements of case are found in CPR Pt 16 and in the practice direction supplementing that Part. Some of those provisions impose particular requirements where claims of certain types are being pleaded. Rule 41.5 adds to these requirements in personal injury claims. The interesting feature of this rule is that it gives the court power to order a party to give attention to the question whether a periodical payments order might be appropriate. This reflects the fact that the court may make an order for periodical payments, whether or not the parties consent to such an order (s.2 of the 1996 Act). See further r.41.6, below.

[1] S.21 is substituted by s.100 of the Courts Act 2003 (c.39).

For a claimant, the nature and extent of the defendant's liability insurance may be relevant to his forming a view on whether a periodical payments order or a lump sum was likely to be more appropriate for any award of damages and is a "matter" upon which clarification or additional information may be sought from the defendant under r.18.1 though not strictly "in dispute" (*Harcourt v Griffin* [2007] EWHC 1500 (QB); June 27, 2007, unrep. (Irwin J.).

Court's indication to parties

41.6 The court shall consider and indicate to the parties as soon as practicable whether periodical payments or a lump sum is likely to be the more appropriate form for all or part of an award of damages. 41.6

Factors to be taken into account

41.7 When considering— 41.7

(a) its indication as to whether periodical payments or a lump sum is likely to be the more appropriate form for all or part of an award of damages under rule 41.6; or

(b) whether to make an order under section 2(1)(a) of the 1996 Act,

the court shall have regard to all the circumstances of the case and in particular the form of award which best meets the claimant's needs, having regard to the factors set out in the practice direction.

"the court shall have regard"

Sections 2, 2A and 4 of the 1996 Act (as substituted by the Courts Act 2003) contain a highly detailed scheme for periodical payments and recourse must be made to those provisions whenever the court is considering whether to make a periodical payments order. The rules in Sect.II of CPR Pt 41 do no more than supplement those sections, as allowed by the 1996 Act itself. 41.7.1

Section 2A(1)(a) states that Civil Procedure Rules may require a court to take specified matters into account in considering whether to order periodical payments. Accordingly, r.41.7 states the factors to be taken into account by the court when considering, not only whether to order periodical payments when making an award of damages for future pecuniary loss in respect of personal injury, but also whether it should give an "indication to the parties" as provided by r.41.6. The rule states that the court shall have regard to all the circumstances of the case and in particular the form of award which best meets the claimant's needs "having regard to the factors set out in the practice direction". Those factors are found in para.1 of the practice direction supplementing this Section of Pt 41; see para.41BPD.1, below.

Rules 41.8 and 41.9 contain provisions as to matters that should be specified in an order for periodical payments

Section 2(3) expressly states that a court may not make an order for periodical payments unless satisfied that the continuity of payment under the order is reasonably secure. This is not repeated in r.41.7, but is implied in r.41.9(1) and is elaborated in the practice direction provision supplementing that rule (see further, para.41.9.1 below).

In a serious case in which liability is wholly or largely conceded, it is likely that, when the court turns its attention to the question whether a periodical payments order or a lump sum best meets the claimant's needs, the claimant will have already received substantial interim payments from the defendants (see r.25.6). In *Osunde v Guy's & St Thomas' Hospital* [2007] EWHC 2275 (QB); September 27, 2007, unrep. (Calvert Smith J.), a claimant's application for a further interim payment was resisted (in the event, unsuccessfully) by the defendants partly on the ground that, in the circumstances, the amount sought would make it extremely difficult for the judge trying the issue of quantum to make a periodical payments order, since there would not be sufficient left in the damages awarded to permit it.

In *Godbold v Mahmood* [2005] EWHC 1002 (QB), April 20, 2005, unrep. (Mitting J.), the judge concluded that the claimant's damages for future loss earnings should be awarded as a lump sum, but his award for recurring care and related costs should be paid by periodical payments. In doing so the judge was influenced by two main factors: (1) the uncertainty as to the claimant's life expectancy, and (2) his receiver's preference (making it easier for him to match income and expenditure). See also, *Walton v Calderdale Healthcare NHS Trust* [2005] EWHC 1053 (QB), May 18, 2005, unrep. (Silber J.) (determining level of peiodical payments for recurring care costs after claimant ceased to be a minor). In *Taylor v Chesworth* [2007] EWHC 1001 (QB), April 30, 2007, unrep. (Ramsey J.), after the outlining the relevant provisions and identifying the circumstances to be taken into account the judge concluded that certain parts of the claimant's care and case management costs should be awarded as lump sums and certain parts as a PPO.

The award

41.8 **41.8—(1) Where the court awards damages in the form of periodical payments, the order must specify—**

(a) the annual amount awarded, how each payment is to be made during the year and at what intervals;

(b) the amount awarded for future—

(i) loss of earnings and other income; and

(ii) care and medical costs and other recurring or capital costs;

(c) that the claimant's annual future pecuniary losses, as assessed by the court, are to be paid for the duration of the claimant's life, or such other period as the court orders; and

(d) that the amount of the payments shall vary annually by reference to the retail prices index, unless the court orders otherwise under section 2(9) of the 1996 Act.

(2) Where the court orders that any part of the award shall continue after the claimant's death, for the benefit of the claimant's dependants, the order must also specify the relevant amount and duration of the payments and how each payment is to be made during the year and at what intervals.

(3) Where an amount awarded under paragraph (1)(b) is to increase or decrease on a certain date, the order must also specify—

(a) the date on which the increase or decrease will take effect; and

(b) the amount of the increase or decrease at current value.

(4) Where damages for substantial capital purchases are awarded under paragraph (1)(b)(ii), the order must also specify—

(a) the amount of the payments at current value;

(b) when the payments are to be made; and

(c) that the amount of the payments shall be adjusted by reference to the retail prices index, unless the court order otherwise under section 2(9) of the 1996 Act.

"the order must specify"

41.8.1 Rule 41.8 details, in sub-rules (1), (3) and (4), matters that must be specified by the court when it orders that damages awarded are wholly or partly to take the form of periodical payments. It descends into practical details not prescribed by the 1996 Act. In part, the rule reflects s.2(8). That section states that an order for periodical payments shall be treated as providing for the amount of payments to vary by reference to the prices index (as defined) at such times, and in such manner, as may be determined by or in accordance with Civil Procedure Rules; but an order may disapply or modify the effect of this provision (s.2(9)). Further rules as to matters that must be specified in a periodical payments order are found in r.41.9 (see below).

In *Thompstone v Tameside Hospital NHS Foundation Trust* [2008] EWHC 2948 (QB), December 2, 2008, unrep. (Sir Christopher Holland) the court set out a "model schedule" which should be attached to periodical payments orders made under r.41.8. In that case the judge explained that, although the model did no more than offer a precedent for adaptation to meet the particular nature of the award, departure from it in future cases would have to be justified before being approved by the court. For form of the model schedule, see Vol.2, Sect.3F (Personal Injury).

"award shall continue after claimant's death"

In para.2.1 of the practice direction it is explained that an order may be made under r.41.8(2) where a dependant would have had a claimed under the Fatal Accidents Act 1976 s.1 if the claimant had died at the time of the accident (see para.41BPD.2, below). **41.8.2**

It is expected that authoritative guidance will be given shortly as to the circumstances in which one form of indexation or another should be used. In some cases, pending that guidance judges giving judgments in quantum hearings at first instance have calculated awards as lump sums and given directions for further hearings on the indexation issue (e.g. *Redhead v Rawcliffe* [2006] EWHC 2695 (QB), October 31, 2006, unrep. (Keith J.); *Iqbal v Whipps Cross University Hospital NHS Trust* [2006] EWHC 3111 (QB), December 8, 2006, unrep. (Sir Rodger Bell); *Taylor v Chesworth* [2007] EWHC 1001 (QB), April 30, 2007, unrep. (Ramsey J.)). In *Corbett v South Yorkshire Strategic HA* [2006] EWCA Civ 1797, December 6, 2006, CA, unrep., the Court of Appeal upheld an assigned trial judge's decision refusing the defendant's application for a direction that the indexation issue should not be determined at a forthcoming quantum trial. See further Vol.2, para.3F–48.

Payments "shall vary annually"

Where a claimant is compensated for future pecuniary loss by a lump sum, a guess has to be made as to the effects on that sum of future inflation. Where he is compensated by a periodical payments order that risk is removed. The award will provide him year by year with appropriate compensation, and the use of an appropriate index (generally the RPI) will protect him from the effects of future inflation. Section 2(8) of the Damages Act 1996 states that an order for periodical payments shall be treated as providing for the amount of payments to vary by reference to the retail prices index "at such times, and in such manner, as may be determined by or in accordance with Civil Procedure Rules" (see Vol.2 para.3F–44). Section 2(9) further states that an order for periodical payments may include provision disapplying s.2(8) or modifying the effect of that subsection. These provisions are reflected and slightly amplified in para.(1)(d) of r.41.8 where it is expressly stated that the amount of the payments "shall vary annually" by reference to the RPI. If a periodical payments order does not identify on its face the manner in which the amount of the payments is to vary (in order to maintain their real value), then s.2(8) prescribes that it is to be treated as providing for what is set out in that subsection unless the order contains provision of a type identified in s.2(9). In *Flora v Wakom (Heathrow) Ltd* [2006] EWCA Civ 1103; [2007] 1 W.L.R. 482, CA, the Court of Appeal said there is nothing in the language of these subsections to suggest that the power to make provision such as identified in s.2(9) may only be triggered in an exceptional case. Section 2(8) expresses the default position; by exercise of its powers under s.2(9) the court may make some other order whenever it appears just to do so. In *Sarwar v Ali* [2007] EWHC 1255 (QB), May 25, 2007, unrep. (Lloyd Jones J.), the judge ruled that the index ASHE 6115, rather than the RPI, should be used. Where an issue arises as to whether an index other than the RPI should be used expert evidence may be required so that the effects of using one index or another may be determined. In *Flora v Wakom* the Court of Appeal recognised that, if exceptionality was not the test under s.2(8) (and r.41.8(1)(d)), the trial courts faced the prospect of many trials at which a host of expensive expert witnesses would be called for each side in their efforts to persuade the courts to determine the question of the appropriate index in their favour. The Court anticipated that, as a result of their decision, there would be a number of trials **41.8.2.1** at which such evidence could be thoroughly tested and that then a group of appeals could be consolidated and brought to the Court enabling it to give (against the background of the decision in the Flora case) definitive guidance in the light of findings of fact made by a number of trial judges. Such a group of appeals came before the Court in *Thompstone v Tameside & Glossop Acute Services NHS Trust* [2008] EWCA Civ 5; [2008] 1 W.L.R. 2207; [2008] 2 All E.R. 553, CA. In this case the Court held (amongst other things) that indexation on the basis of ASHE 6115 was appropriate in cases where claimants had suffered catastrophic injuries. On the matter of the risk of trial courts being over-burdened with expert evidence of independent financial advisers the Court said that, if a claimant is advised by an experienced and responsible expert, it is likely that great weight will be given to what the expert advises. Generally, expert defence evidence will not be required but judges should have regard to the defendant's general preferences advanced on instructions without the need for evidence to be called. Some defence evidence might be required if a more specific point is to be made, for example, where a defendant wishes to avoid a periodical payments order (which it perceives is likely to be indexed to a measure other than RPI) and wants to argue that it would be impossible for it to make suitable financial provision, consistent with regulatory requirements.

See further, Vol.2, para.3F–45.

"increase or decrease" of amount awarded

41.8.3 Where the court specifies that an amount awarded for future loss of earnings and other income, and care and medical costs and other recurring or capital costs, should increase or decrease the further details required by r.41.8(3) must be specified in the order. Examples of the circumstances which might lead the court to order such an increase or decrease are given in para.2.2 of the practice direction (see para.41BPD.2, below).

Acceptance of offer to settle in form of periodical payments

41.8.4 In a personal injury claim including a claim for damagesfor future pecuniary loss, the claimant or the defendant may wish to make an offer to settle. That offer may contain an offer to pay, or an offer to accept, the whole or part of the damages for such loss in the form of (a) either a lump sum or periodical payments, or (b) both a lump sum and periodical payments. Special rules as to such offers are found in Pt 36, in particular in r.36.2A. Paragraph 6 of the practice direction states that, where the parties settle a claim to which r.36.2A applies, any consent order, whether made under r.40.6 (Consent judgments or orders) or on an application under Pt 23, must satisfy the requirements of r.41.8 and of r.41.9 (see para.41BPD.6, below).

Settlement or compromise on belhalf of child or patient

41.8.5 Paragraph 7 of the practice direction states that, where a claim for damages for personal injury is made by or on behalf of a child or patient is settled prior to the start of proceedings or before trial, the provisions of Practice Direction (Children and Patients) (see para.21PD.1, above) must be satisfied (see 41BPD.7, below). Paragraphs 6.6 et seq of the practice direction referred to state that, where in any personal injury case a claim for damages for future pecuniary loss made by a child or patient is dealt with by agreement after proceedings have commenced, and the court's approval of a consent order is sought, the court must be satisfied that the parties have considered whether the damages should wholly or partly take the form of periodical payments, and where the settlement includes provision for periodical payments, its terms must satisfy the requirements of r.41.8 and of r.41.9. Where a claim is settled prior to the start of proceedings, para.6.4 of that practice direction applies. Paragraph 13.2 of Practice Direction (Appeals) states that, where one of the parties is a child or patient, an agreement reached at the appeal stage to pay periodical payments requires the court's approval (see para.52PD.49).

Variation of orders and settlements

41.8.6 Section 2B(1) of the 1996 Act states that the Lord Chancellor may by order made by statutory instrument enable a court which has made an order for periodical payments to vary the order in specified circumstances, otherwise than in accordance with s.2(5)(d) (as to which, see para.41.9.2, below). By s.2B(2), the Lord Chancellor may by such order enable a court in specified circumstances to vary the terms on which a claim or action for damages for personal injury is settled between parties by agreement; being an agreement that provides for periodical payments, provided the agreement expressly permits a party to apply to a court for variation in those circumstances.

The Lord Chancellor exercised his powers in these respects in the Damages (Variation of Periodical Payments) Order 2004 (SI 2005/841) (see Vol. 2 para.3F–62). Articles 2 to 7 deal with the power of the court to make variable orders, and arts 10 to 12 with the procedure for applications for the variation of variable orders. The court may make a variable order in addition to an order for an award of provisional damages (art.4). The 2005 Order also makes provision for the variation of settlement agreements of the type referred to in s.2B(2) of the 1996 Act.

Article 2 of the 2005 Order states that, if there is proved or admitted to be a chance that at some definite or indefinite time in the future certain specified events affecting the claimant will occur, the court may, on the application of a party, with the agreement of all the parties, or of its own initiative, provide in an order for periodical payments that it may be varied. The specified events are that the claimant will (a) as a result of the act or omission which gave rise to the cause of action, develop some serious disease or suffer some serious deterioration, or (b) enjoy some significant improvement in his physical or mental condition where that condition had been adversely affected as a result of that act or omission.

Continuity of payment

41.9—(1) An order for periodical payments shall specify that the payments must be funded in accordance with section 2(4) of the 1996 Act, unless the court orders an alternative method of funding. 41.9

(2) Before ordering an alternative method of funding, the court must be satisfied that—

(a) the continuity of payment under the order is reasonably secure; and

(b) the criteria set out in the practice direction are met.

(3) An order under paragraph (2) must specify the alternative method of funding.

"continuity of payment ... is reasonably secure"

A claimant who is awarded damages in the form of a lump sum becomes himself responsible for the protection of that sum once it is paid to him. Where his award of damages takes the form (wholly or partly) of periodical payments care has to be taken to ensure that the party responsible for those payments does not default. Much of the statutory scheme in the 1996 Act is directed at "the security of the continuity of payment". For example, s.2(3) states that a court may not make an order for periodical payments unless satisfied that the continuity of payment under the order is reasonably secure. Continuity of payment is to be treated as secure in certain circumstances stated in s.2(4), but the court may approve other alternative arrangements as provided for in s.2(5). Section 2A(1)(b) states that Civil Procedure Rules may require a court to take specified matters into account in considering the security of the continuity of payment. 41.9.1

Rule 41.9 reflects subss.(3), (4) and (5) of s.2. Paragraph 3 of the practice direction stipulates criteria that must be met before the court orders an alternative method of funding under r.41.9(2); see para.41BPD.3, below.

Note also references in paras 41.8.4 and 41.8.5, above, to circumstances in which the requirements of r.41.9 should be satisfied.

Variation of provisions as to continuity of payment

Where an order for periodical payments includes the provisions as to continuity of payment referred to in s.2(5) of the 1996 Act it may also provide that a party may apply to the court for a variation of them (s.2(5)(d)). 41.9.2

Assignment or charge

41.10 **41.10 Where the court under section 2(6)(a) of the 1996 Act is satisfied that special circumstances make an assignment or charge of periodical payments necessary, it shall, in deciding whether or not to approve the assignment or charge, also have regard to the factors set out in the practice direction.**

"Special circumstances make it necessary"

41.10.1 Section 2(6) states that, where a person has a right to receive payments under an order for periodical payments, or where an arrangement is entered into in satisfaction of an order which gives a person a right to receive periodical payments, that person's right under the order or arrangement may not be assigned or charged without the approval of the court which made the order. A court shall not approve an assignment or charge unless satisfied that "special circumstances make it necessary" (s.2(6)(a)). Section 2A(1)(c) states that Civil Procedure Rules may require a court to take specified matters into account in considering whether to approve an assignment or charge. Those "specified matters", that is to say, the "special circumstances" referred to in s.2(6)(a), are not set out in r.41.10 but are found in para.4 of the practice direction; see para.41BPD.4, below.

PRACTICE DIRECTION—PROVISIONAL DAMAGES

This Practice Direction supplements CPR Part 41

Claims for provisional damages

1.1 CPR Part 16 and the practice direction which supplements it set out information which must be included in the particulars of claim if a claim for provisional damages is made. **41PD.1**

Judgment for an award of provisional damages

2.1 When giving judgment at trial the judge will: **41PD.2**

(1) specify the disease or type of deterioration, or diseases or types of deterioration, which
  (a) for the purpose of the award of immediate damages it has been assumed will not occur, and
  (b) will entitle the claimant to further damages if it or they do occur at a future date,

(2) give an award of immediate damages,

(3) specify the period or periods within which an application for further damages may be made in respect of each disease or type of deterioration, and

(4) direct what documents are to be filed and preserved as the case file in support of any application for further damages.

2.2 The claimant may make an application or applications to extend the periods referred to in paragraph 2.1(3) above.[1]

2.3 A period specified under paragraph 2.1(3) may be expressed as being for the duration of the life of the claimant.

2.4 The documents to be preserved as the case file ("the case file documents") referred to in paragraph 2.1(4) will be set out in a schedule to the judgment as entered.

2.5 Causation of any further damages within the scope of the order shall be determined when any application for further damages is made.

2.6 A form for a provisional damages judgment is set out in the Annex to this practice direction.

The case file

3.1 The case file documents must be preserved until the expiry of the period or periods specified or of any extension of them. **41PD.3**

3.2 The case file documents will normally include:

(1) the judgment as entered,

(2) the statements of case,

(3) a transcript of the judge's oral judgment,

(4) all medical reports relied on, and

(5) a transcript of any parts of the claimant's own evidence which the judge considers necessary.

3.3 The associate/court clerk will:

(1) ensure that the case file documents are provided by the parties where necessary and filed on the court file,

---

[1] See CPR r.41.2(3).

(2) endorse the court file
   (a) to the effect that it contains the case file documents, and
   (b) with the period during which the case file documents must be preserved, and

(3) preserve the case file documents in the court office where the proceedings took place.

3.4 Any subsequent order:

(1) extending the period within which an application for further damages may be made, or

(2) of the Court of Appeal discharging or varying the provisions of the original judgment or of any subsequent order under sub-paragraph (1) above,

will become one of the case file documents and must be preserved accordingly and any variation of the period within which an application for further damages may be made should be endorsed on the court file containing the case file documents.

3.5 On an application to extend the periods referred to in paragraph 2.1(3) above a current medical report should be filed.

3.6 Legal representatives are reminded that it is their duty to preserve their own case file.

Consent orders

41PD.4 **4.1** An application to give effect to a consent order for provisional damages should be made in accordance with CPR Part 23. If the claimant is a child or protected party the approval of the court must also be sought and the application for approval will normally be dealt with at a hearing.

4.2 The order should be in the form of a consent judgment and should contain:

(1) the matters set out in paragraph 2.1(1) to (3) above, and

(2) a direction as to the documents to be preserved as the case file documents, which will normally be
   (a) the consent judgment,
   (b) any statements of case,
   (c) an agreed statement of facts, and
   (d) any agreed medical report(s).

4.3 The claimant or his legal representative must lodge the case file documents in the court office where the proceedings are taking place for inclusion in the court file. The court file should be endorsed as in paragraph 3.3(2) above, and the case file documents preserved as in paragraph 3.3(3) above.

Default judgment

41PD.5 **5.1** Where a defendant:

(1) fails to file an acknowledgment of service in accordance with CPR Part 10, and

(2) fails to file a defence in accordance with CPR Part 15,

within the time specified for doing so, the claimant may not, unless he abandons his claim for provisional damages, enter judgment in default but should make an application in accordance with CPR Part 23 for directions.

5.2 The Master or district judge will normally direct the following issues to be decided:

(1) whether the claim is an appropriate one for an award of provisional damages and if so, on what terms, and

(2) the amount of immediate damages.

5.3 If the judge makes an award of provisional damages, the provisions of paragraph 3 above apply.

Annex

(Example of an Award of Provisional Damages after Trial)

(*Title of proceedings*) **41PD.6**

THIS CLAIM having been tried before [*title and name of judge*] without a jury at [the Royal Courts of Justice *or as may be*] and [*title and name of judge*] having ordered that judgment as set out below be entered for the claimant

IT IS ORDERED—

(1) that the defendant pay the claimant by way of immediate damages the sum of £ .... (being (i) £ .... for special damages and £ .... [agreed interest] [interest at the rate of .. from .... to ....] (ii) £ .... for general damages and £ .... [agreed interest] [interest at the rate of 2% from .... to ....] and (iii) £ .... for loss of future earnings and/or earning capacity) on the assumption that the claimant would not at a future date as a result of the act or omission giving rise to the claim develop the following disease/type of deterioration namely [*set out disease or type of deterioration*]

(2) that if the claimant at a further date does develop that [disease][type of deterioration] he should be entitled to apply for further damages provided that the application is made on or before [*set out period*]

(3) that the documents set out in the schedule to this order be filed on the court file and preserved as the case file until the expiry of the period set out in paragraph (2) above or of any extension of that period which has been ordered

(4) (costs).

Schedule

(*List documents referred to in paragraph (3)).* **41PD.7**

PRACTICE DIRECTION—PERIODICAL PAYMENTS UNDER THE DAMAGES ACT 1996

This Practice Direction supplements CPR Part 41

Factors to be taken into Account (Rule 41.7)

41BPD.1 **1.** The factors which the court shall have regard to under rule 41.7 include—

(1) the scale of the annual payments taking into account any deduction for contributory negligence;

(2) the form of award preferred by the claimant including—
  (a) the reasons for the claimant's preference; and
  (b) the nature of any financial advice received by the claimant when considering the form of award; and

(3) the form of award preferred by the defendant including the reasons for the defendant's preference.

The Award (Rule 41.8)

41BPD.2 **2.1** An order may be made under rule 41.8(2) where a dependant would have had a claim under section 1 of the Fatal Accidents Act 1976 if the claimant had died at the time of the accident.

2.2 Examples of circumstances which might lead the court to order an increase or decrease under rule 41.8(3) are where the court determines that—

(1) the claimant's condition will change leading to an increase or reduction in his or her need to incur care, medical or other recurring or capital costs;

(2) gratuitous carers will no longer continue to provide care;

(3) the claimant's educational circumstances will change;

(4) the claimant would have received a promotional increase in pay;

(5) the claimant will cease earning.

Continuity of Payment (Rule 41.9)

41BPD.3 **3.** Before ordering an alternative method of funding under rule 41.9(1), the court must be satisfied that the following criteria are met—

(1) that a method of funding provided for under section 2(4) of the 1996 Act is not possible or there are good reasons to justify an alternative method of funding;

(2) that the proposed method of funding can be maintained for the duration of the award or for the proposed duration of the method of funding; and

(3) that the proposed method of funding will meet the level of payment ordered by the court.

Assignment or Charge (Rule 41.10)

41BPD.4 **4.** The factors which the court shall have regard to under rule 41.10 include—

(1) whether the capitalised value of the assignment or charge represents value for money;

(2) whether the assignment or charge is in the claimant's best

interests, taking into account whether these interests can be met in some other way; and

(3) how the claimant will be financially supported following the assignment or charge.

Variation

5. The Damages (Variation of Periodical Payments) Order 2004 sets out provisions which enable the court in certain circumstances to provide in an order for periodical payments that it may be varied. **41BPD.5**

Settlement

6. Where the parties settle a claim to which rule 36.5 applies, any consent order, whether made under rule 40.6 or on an application under Part 23, must satisfy the requirements of rules 41.8 and 41.9. **41BPD.6**

Settlement or Compromise on behalf of Child or Protected Party

7. Where a claim for damages for personal injury is made by or on behalf of a child or protected party and is settled prior to the start of proceedings or before trial, the provisions of the Practice Direction which supplements Part 21 must be complied with. **41BPD.7**

PART 42

Change of Solicitor

Contents

42.0.1

Editorial introduction

42.0.2 In the time-honoured expression, a solicitor acting for a party is said to be "on the record". A solicitor who ceases to act for a party is removed "from the record".

To an opponent, the consequences of a party acting by solicitor are twofold: first, the solicitor's business address will be that party's address for service (see r.6.5(5) and r.6.13(2)); secondly, the signing by the solicitor of the claim form (which has replaced the High Court writ and County Court summons), acknowledgment of service or statement of case (the term which has replaced "pleadings": see r.2.3) notifies the opponent that the party will be claiming solicitor's costs. Part 42 deals with four distinct situations frequently arising in practice and one rare situation.

The common situations are:

(1) a new solicitor appointed to act instead of a previous solicitor;
(2) a solicitor being appointed by a party who has hitherto acted in person;
(3) a party who has previously employed a solicitor now deciding to act in person;
(4) a solicitor applying to the court for an order that he has ceased to act.

The first three do not require an order (merely a notice), the fourth does.

The rare situation is removal of a solicitor on application of another party.

Related sources

42.0.3

- Solicitors Act 1974 (Vol. 2, paras 7–1 *et seq.*)
- Civil Legal Aid (General) Regulations 1989 reg.83
- Community Legal Service (Costs) Regulations 2000 (SI 2000/441).
- Rules 6.23 and 6.24 (address for service)
- Part 48, Pt II (Costs relating to solicitors)
- Part 44 (General rules about costs)
- Practice Direction to Pt 42 (see para.42PD.1)
- Part 23 (applications)

Forms

42.0.4

- **N434** Notice of change of solicitor

Note also the Queen's Bench Masters Practice forms relevant to RSC O.67 (Change of Solicitor) can be adapted for use under Pt 42.

Solicitor acting for a party

42.1 **42.1 Where the address for service of a party is the business address of his solicitor, the solicitor will be considered to be acting for that party until the provisions of this Part have been complied with.**

(Part 6 contains provisions about the address for service.)

Effect of rule

42.1.1 Every party to proceedings in the High Court or County Court must have an address for service (see Pt 6—Service of Documents, especially r.6.5(5) (address for service) and r.6.13(2) (service of claim form)). Where a party employs a solicitor, the solicitor's business address will be the address for service. All documents served at that address by the Court or another party are properly served. Rule 42.1 emphasises that the solicitor will be considered to be acting for that party until he filed the notice of change with the court and served it upon every other party, including the former client (Practice Direction to Pt 42, para.12).

Change of solicitor—duty to give notice[1]

42.2—(1) This rule applies where— 42.2

(a) a party for whom a solicitor is acting wants to change his solicitor;

(b) a party, after having conducted the claim in person, appoints a solicitor to act on his behalf (except where the solicitor is appointed only to act as an advocate for a hearing); or

(c) a party, after having conducted the claim by a solicitor, intends to act in person.

(2) Where this rule applies, the party or his solicitor (where one is acting) must—

(a) file notice of the change; and

(b) serve notice of the change on every other party and, where paragraph (1)(a) or (c) applies, on the former solicitor.

(3) The notice must state the party's new address for service.

(4) The notice filed at court must state that notice has been served as required by paragraph (2)(b).

(5) Subject to paragraph (6), where a party has changed his solicitor or intends to act in person, the former solicitor will be considered to be the party's solicitor unless and until—

(a) notice is filed and served in accordance with paragraph (2); or

(b) the court makes an order under rule 42.3 and the order is served as required by paragraph (3) of that rule.

(6) Where the certificate of a LSC funded client or an assisted person[2] is revoked or discharged—

(a) the solicitor who acted for the that person will cease to be the solicitor acting in the case as soon as his retainer is determined–

(i) under regulation 4 of the Community Legal Service (Costs) Regulations 2000 or

(ii) under regulation 83 of the Civil Legal Aid (General) Regulations 1989; and

***(b)* *if that person wishes* to continue—**

(i) where he appoints a solicitor to act on his behalf paragraph (2) will apply as if he had previously conducted the claim in person; and

[1] Amended by the Civil Procedure (Amendment No.3) Rules 2000 (SI 2000/1317) and the Civil Procedure (Amendment) Rules 2008 (SI 2008/2178).

[2] SI 1989/339 to which there are amendments not relevant to these Rules.

(ii) where he wants to act in person he must give an address for service.

(Rules 6.23 and 6.24 contain provisions about a party's address for service.)

("LSC funded client" and "asssited person" are defined in rule 43.2).

(7) "Certificate" in paragraph (6) means a certificate–

(a) in the case of a LSC funded client, a certificate issued under the Funding Code (approved under section 9 of the Access to Justice Act 1999), or

(b) in the case of an assisted person, a certificate within the meaning of the Civil Legal Aid (General) Regulations 1989.

"duty to give notice"

42.2.1 Rule 42.2, where it applies, imposes a duty to give notice. This is emphasised by the use of the word "must" in r.42.2(2), 42.2(3) and 42.2(4).

"change of solicitor"

42.2.2 Rule 42.2 applies to three distinct situations set about in r.42.2(1), namely a party changing his solicitor; a party who has acted in person now appointing a solicitor; and a party having employed a solicitor who now intends to act in person. CPR r.42.2(1)(b) does not require notice where a party who has acted in person appoints a solicitor only to act as an advocate. CPR r.42.2 does not apply to a solicitor acting as agent for another solicitor.

"notice of the change"

42.2.3 In the case of the three situations to which r.42.2(1) applies, no order of the court is required. All that is required is that a notice of the appropriate change which complies with r.42.2(3) and (4) must be filed with the court and served on every other party and the former solicitor: r.42.2(2).

Rule 42.2(5) is not really necessary having regard to r.42.1, but suffices to emphasise the mandatory requirements of the rule and that once a solicitor is appointed to act, that solicitor is considered to be the party's solicitor unless and until the requirements of Pt 42 are complied with.

Revocation or discharge of legal aid certificate

42.2.4 Rule 42.2(6) is a reminder that under reg.4 of the Community Legal Service (Costs) Regulations 2000 and reg.83 of the Civil Legal Aid (General) Regulations 1989 a solicitor's retainer is determined upon revocation or discharge of his client's legal aid certificate. In accordance with the Regulations the solicitor must serve notice of the revocation/discharge on all other parties and file a copy with the court. This is sufficient to remove the solicitor from the record without further notice or order. The issue which then arises is whether the previously publicly funded party has abandoned the proceedings or whether he wishes to continue the case either by acting in person or appointing a solicitor as a private client. Hence r.42.2(6) which requires the "assisted person" (strictly, of course, the formerly assisted person) to give an address for service if he now intends to act in person and requires a new solicitor to give notice pursuant to r.42.2(2). Failure to do this may result in his statement of case being struck out—see r.34(2)(c). See too Practice Direction to Pt 42, paras 2.1 to 22.

Effect of change on lien

42.2.5 The effect of the change on the solicitor's lien depends on whether the solicitor discharges himself or is discharged by the client. If the solicitor discharges himself, as, for instance, by refusing to proceed absolutely or unless funds are provided, he may be ordered to hand over the papers to the new solicitor on the latter undertakingto hold them without prejudice to his lien, and to return them intact after the action is over, and to allow the former solicitor access to them in the meantime (*Robins v Goldingham* (1872) L.R. 13 Eq. 440; *Bluck v Lovering & Co* (1886) 35 W.R. 232). On the other hand, if the solicitor is discharged by the client he cannot, so long as his costs are unpaid, be compelled to produce or hand over (otherwise than for misconduct) the papers (*Hughes v Hughes* [1958] P.224; [1958] 3 All E.R. 179, CA, and see *Re Rapid Road Transit Co* [1909] 1 Ch. 96). He may, however, be compelled to produce them for some purposes (*Re Hawkes* [1898] 2 Ch. 1) as, for instance, the drawing up of an order (*Clifford v Turrill* (1848) 2 De G. & S. 1; *Simmonds v G. E. Ry. Co* (1868) L.R. 3 Ch. 797; *Ross v Laughton* (1813) 1 Ves. & B. 349; *Re Toleman and England* (1880) 13 Ch.D. 885), or the management of an estate by a receiver (*Belaney v Ffrench* (1873) L.R. 8 Ch. 918), or after the appointment of a receiver in a partnership action (*Dessau v Peters, Rushton & Co* [1922] 1 Ch. 1). The lien gives the solicitor no greater rights over the papers than his client would have had (*Re Hawkes*, below; *Re Capital Fire Insurance Association* (1883) 24 Ch.D. 408; *Re Caudery* (1910) 54 S.J. 444) and in administration and other representative actions a discharged solicitor cannot resist production at the instance of creditors or litigants other than his client of documents received for the purposes of the action (*Re Hawkes, Ackerman v Lockhart* [1898] 2 Ch. 1 at 24; *Re Boughton, Boughton v Boughton* (1883) 23 Ch.D. 169; *Re Hutchinson* (1886) 34 W.R. 637; *Re Caudery* (1910) 54 S.J. 444). A winding-up order does not defeat an existing lien (*Re Rapid Road Transport Co* [1909] 1 Ch. 96, above).

There is a distinction between papers received for the purposes of the action and papers received prior to and irrespective of the action, etc. (*Re Hawkes*, above, and *Boden v Hensby* [1892] 1 Ch. 101).

Where a client discharges a solicitor the court has no power to call upon the solicitor to hand over documents because the solicitor's lien to retain those documents endures. But where the solicitor discharges himself in the course of an action, his possessory lien over the documents becomes subject to the practice of the court under which the court will ordinarily order the documents to be handed over to the new solicitor against an undertaking by the new solicitor to preserve the former solicitor's lien, though in exceptional circumstances the court may be justified in imposing terms (*Gamlen Chemicals Co (UK) Ltd v Rochem Ltd* [1980] 1 W.L.R. 614; [1980] 1 All E.R. 1049, CA).

Order that a solicitor has ceased to act

42.3—(1) A solicitor may apply for an order declaring that he has ceased to be the solicitor acting for a party. 42.3

(2) Where an application is made under this rule—

(a) notice of the application must be given to the party for whom the solicitor is acting, unless the court directs otherwise; and

(b) the application must be supported by evidence.

(3) Where the court makes an order that a solicitor has ceased to act—

(a) a copy of the order must be served on every party to the proceedings; and

(b) if it is served by a party or the solicitor, the party or the solicitor (as the case may be) must file a certificate of service.

Effect of rule

Strictly, no order under r.42.3 should ever be necessary. Where a party has determined his solicitor's retainer, or the solicitor has notified the former client that the solicitor has determined the retainer, the party or the party's new solicitor should simply give notice of change pursuant to r.42.2. It has been common for that party to fail to do so. 42.3.1

Where the solicitor's retainer has been determined but no notice has been given in accordance with r.42.2, the solicitor can apply for a an order under r.42.3 declaring that he has ceased to act. Having regard to the provisions of r.42.1 and r.42.2(5), the solicitor should do so promptly upon determination of the retainer.

Solicitor ceasing to act for party

42.3.2 Under a general retainer, a solicitor is required to act for a client to the end of an action and to take all necessary steps to bring that action to a conclusion. Such a retainer is not determined by death of the client (*Donslans Ltd v Van Hoogstraten*, February 13, 2002, CA, unrep. Otherwise the retainer continues until the solicitor is discharged by the client. (*Underwood, Son & Piper v Lewis* [1894] 2 Q.B. 306, CA; *Court v Berlin* [1897] 2 Q.B. 396, CA; *Re Wingfield & Blew* [1904] 2 Ch. 655, CA). But the retainer is subject to implied terms enabling the solicitor to withdraw for good cause and upon reasonable notice, and enabling the client to withdraw the retainer at any time (*ibid.*). Thus, a solicitor may withdraw for good cause where the client fails to provide a reasonable sum of money for disbursements, or the solicitor is being burdened and prevented by the client in properly conducting the action, e.g. by failing to give instructions (*ibid.*; see also *Robins v Goldingham* (1872) L.R. 13 Eq. 440). See now the Solicitors Act 1974 s.65(2), *Civil Procedure*, Vol. 2, Section 7; it is now deemed to be good cause for a solicitor to withdraw from his retainer if his client, on being requested, fails within a reasonable time to make payment of a reasonable sum on account of past or future costs generally (see, *ibid.*, s.87(1)). The right to withdraw for non-payment is therefore no longer limited to cases where the non-payment by the client relates to disbursements by the solicitor but now extends to cases where the solicitor has not been paid sums on account of his own profit costs. If a solicitor refuses to proceed without good cause and without giving reasonable notice to the client to pay him money or give him instructions, etc., he commits a breach of contract and cannot sue for his fees (*ibid.*) and the Court may refuse to make an order under this rule. It has however been emphasised in an Australian case that the decision in *Underwood's* case, although cited in the context of the rule, has nothing to do with the operation of the rule itself. The concern of the rule is with the record of the court and the service of documents. It comes into play when, rightly or wrongly, a solicitor has ceased to act and the party has not given notice of change of solicitor or notice of intention to act in person. The court has a discretion whether or not to make the order, but unless there are special circumstances which render it expedient to retain the solicitor on the record, the order will generally be made as a matter of course upon proof that the solicitor has in fact ceased to act for the party and that no steps have been taken to take the solicitor's name off the record. The rule makes it plain that an order thereunder does not affect the rights or liabilities of a solicitor and a party as between themselves (*Plenty v Gladwin* (1986) 67 A.L.R. 26, High Court of Australia).

"order declaring that he has ceased to be the solicitor acting for a party"

42.3.3 Unlike r.42.2 where notice suffices, an order is required where r.42.3 applies.

"notice of the application"

42.3.4 Notice of the application must, pursuant to r.42.3(2), be served on the former client by the solicitor. Note that there is no requirement to serve any other party. Indeed other parties should not be served, for to do so might injure the client (*Re Creehouse Ltd* [1983] 1 W.L.R. 77; [1982] 3 All E.R. 659, CA). Proof of service on the client will be required if he does not attend the hearing of the application. This should be proved by filing a certificate of service—see r.6.10 and Form **N215**.

"supported by evidence"

42.3.5 Rule 42.3(2)(b) makes it clear that the application by the solicitor must be supported by evidence. Although the former practice was for the solicitor to file an affidavit, this is no longer necessary. Evidence may be contained on the notice of application itself, if the statement of truth is completed, or may be given in the form of a separate witness statement (see rr.22.1, 32.2 and 32.15). Copies should be served on the solicitor's client, but not on other parties—para.42.3.5 above.

"a copy of the order must be served on every party ..."

42.3.6 If a solicitor obtains an order declaring that he has ceased to be the solicitor acting for a party, pursuant to r.42.3(3) a copy of that order must be served "on every party to the proceedings". This does, of course, include the solicitors' former client who is still a "party to the proceedings". A certificate of service of the order must then be filed with the court if service is effected by the solicitor (as it usually will be) rather than by the court (see r.6.10 and Form **N215**). As to where to file the certificate see Practice Direction to Pt 42, paras 2.5 to 2.7.

Address for service of party whose solicitor is removed

Where an order has been made removing a solicitor from the record, his or her former client must give an address for service within the jurisdiction. **42.3.7**

Removal of solicitor who has ceased to act on application of another party

42.4—(1) Where— **42.4**

(a) a solicitor who has acted for a party—

(i) has died;

(ii) has become bankrupt;

(iii) has ceased to practice; or

(iv) cannot be found; and

(b) the party has not given notice of a change of solicitor or notice of intention to act in person as required by rule 42.2(2),

any other party may apply for an order declaring that the solicitor has ceased to be the solicitor acting for the other party in the case.

(2) Where an application is made under this rule, notice of the application must be given to the party to whose solicitor the application relates unless the court directs otherwise.

(3) Where the court makes an order made under this rule—

(a) a copy of the order must be served on every other party to the proceedings; and

(b) where it is served by a party, that party must file a certificate of service.

Effect of r.42.4

Rule 42.4 is derived from RSC O.67, r.5 and no doubt will be as rarely used in practice as was its predecessor. Nevertheless it is a necessary rule to deal with the four situations set out in r.42.4(1)(a) where no notice has been given in accordance with r.42.2(2). The rule itself is clear and self-explanatory. **42.4.1**

Address for service of party whose solicitor is removed

See note under this heading in Commentary at para.42.3.8. **42.4.2**

Appointment of new solicitors

In *SMC Engineering (Bristol) Ltd v Fraser, The Times*, January 26, 2001, CA, the Court of Appeal indicated that it was inappropriate for a judge to make an order requiring a company to appoint new solicitors. As to the power to grant an injunction to restrain a particular advocate or legal advisor from acting, see *Skjevesland v Geveran Trading Co Ltd* [2002] EWCA Civ 1567,October 30, 2002. **42.4.3**

PRACTICE DIRECTION—CHANGE OF SOLICITOR

This Practice Direction supplements CPR Part 42

Solicitor acting for a party

42PD.1 **1.1** Rule 42.1 states that where the address for service of a party is the business address [1] of that party's solicitor, the solicitor will be considered to be acting for that party until the provisions of Part 42 have been complied with.

1.2 Subject to rule 42.2(6) (where the certificate of LSC funded client or assisted person is revoked or discharged), where a party has changed his solicitor or intends to act in person, the former solicitor will be considered to be the party's solicitor unless or until;

(1) a notice of the change is

(a) filed with the court,[2] and

(b) served on every other party,[3] or

(2) the court makes an order under rule 42.3 and the order is served on every other party.[4]

The notice should not be filed until every other party has been served.

1.3 A solicitor appointed to represent a party only as an advocate at a hearing will not be considered to be acting for that party within the meaning of Part 42.

Notice of change of solicitor

42PD.2 **2.1** Rule 42.2(1) sets out the circumstances following which a notice of the change must be filed and served.

2.2 A notice of the change giving the last known address of the former assisted person must also be filed and served on every party where, under rule 42.2(6):

(1) the certificate of a LSC funded client or assisted person is revoked or discharged,

(2) the solicitor who acted for that person ceased to act on determination of his retainer under regulation 83 of those Regulations, and

(3) the LSC funded client or the assisted person wishes either to act in person or appoint another solicitor to act on his behalf.

2.3 In addition, where a party or solicitor changes his address for service, a notice of that change should be filed and served on every party.

2.4 A party who, having conducted a claim by a solicitor, intends to act in person must give in the notice an address for service that is within the United Kingdom.[5]

2.5 Practice Form **N434** should be used to give notice of any change. The notice should be filed in the court office in which the claim is proceeding.

---

[1] Rules 6.7 and 6.23 contain provisions about service on the business address of a solicitor.

[2] r.42.2(2)(a)

[3] r.42.2(2)(b).

[4] r.42.2(5).

[5] See r.6.5(3).

2.6 Where the claim is proceeding in the High Court the notice should be filed either in the appropriate District Registry or if the claim is proceeding in the Royal Courts of Justice, as follows;

(1) a claim proceeding in the Queen's Bench Division—in the Action Department of the Central Office,
(2) a claim proceeding in the Chancery Division—in Chancery Chambers,
(3) a claim proceeding in the Administrative Court—in the Administrative Court office,
(4) a claim proceeding in the Admiralty and Commercial Registry—in the Admiralty and Commercial Registry, and
(5) a claim proceeding in the Technology and Construction Court—in the Registry of the Technology and Construction Court.

2.7 Where the claim is the subject of an appeal to the Court of Appeal, the notice should also be filed in the Civil Appeals Office.

(The Costs Practice Direction supplementing Parts 43 to 48 contains details of the information required to be included when the funding arrangements for the claim change)

Application for an order that a solicitor has ceased to act

3.1 A solicitor may apply under rule 42.3 for an order declaring that he has ceased to be the solicitor acting for a party. **42PD.3**

3.2 The application should be made in accordance with Part 23[1] and must be supported by evidence.[2] Unless the court directs otherwise the application notice must be served on the party.[3]

3.3 An order made under rule 42.3 must be served on every party and takes effect when it is served. Where the order is not served by the court, the person serving must file a certificate of service in practice Form **N215**.

Application by another party to remove a solicitor

4.1 Rule 42.4 sets out circumstances in which any other party may apply for an order declaring that a solicitor has ceased to be the solicitor acting for another party in the proceedings. **42PD.4**

4.2 The application should be made in accordance with Part 23 and must be supported by evidence. Unless the court directs otherwise the application notice must be served on the party to whose solicitor the application relates.

4.3 An order made under rule 42.4 must be served on every other party to the proceedings. Where the order is not served by the court, the person serving must file a certificate of service in practice Form **N215**.

New address for service where order made under rules 42.3 or 42.4

5.1 Where the court has made an order under rule 42.3 that a solicitor has ceased to act or under rule 42.4 declaring that a solicitor **42PD.5**

---

[1] See Pt 23 and the Practice Direction which supplements it.
[2] See Pt 32 and the Practice Direction which supplements it for information about evidence.
[3] r.42.3(2).

has ceased to be the soloicitor for a party, the party for whom the solicitor was acting must give a new address for service to comply with rules 6.23(1) and 6.24.

(Rule 6.23 provides that a party must give an address for service within the United Kingdom.)

(Until such time as a new address for service is given rule 6.9 will apply)

PART 43

Scope of Cost Rules and Definitions

Contents

43.0.1

CPR 43

Editorial introduction

The rules relating to costs in Pts 43 to 48 deal with the main provisions as to costs and the way in which the court will award and assess costs. These parts do not however provide a complete self contained code and other provisions relating to costs may be found under other rules and particularly Pt 36 Offers of settlement 43.0.2

Transitional Provisions

Paragraph 18 of the Practice Direction supplemental to Pt 51 (see para.51PD.1) deals with the extent to which the Civil Procedure Rules apply to proceedings issued before April 26, 1999. 43.0.3

So far as costs are concerned all the provisions in the new costs rules apply from April 26, 1999, both as to the procedure to be adopted and also the way in which costs are to be assessed. It is recognised that litigation may well have been in progress for some considerable time before April 26, 1999 without the parties or their lawyers being aware that the new rules might alter the way in which the steps which they were undertaking would be viewed by the court at the time of assessment of costs. When the court is assessing costs of work done prior to April 26, 1999 the new rules will apply, but the judge dealing with the costs (whether by summary or detailed assessment) will not disallow anything in respect of that work which would not have been disallowed under the rules in force prior to April 26, 1999. The Costs Practice Direction deals with the detailed transitional provisions in respect of proceedings for taxation commenced prior to April 26, 1999 (see Sect.57 of the Costs Practice Direction para.48PD.8).

Costs Judges have all the powers of the court under the CPR and accordingly the overriding objective set out in Pt 1 and the court's general powers of management set out in Pt 3 apply equally to all questions of costs. Authorised court officers have all the powers of the court when making a detailed assessment except certain penal powers (see r.47.3).

Under the transitional provisions the court cannot ignore that the parties have been acting under the old regime, but the court is not constrained to reach the same decision as would have been made previously. The position under the CPR is fundamentally different from under the old regime. Rule 1.1 makes it clear that the CPR is a new procedural code whose overriding objective is to enable courts to deal with cases justly; *Biguzzi v Rank Leisure Plc* [1999]1 W.L.R. 1926, CA.

Scope of this Part

43.1 This Part contains definitions and interpretation of certain matters set out in the rules about costs contained in Parts 44 to 48. 43.1

(Part 44 contains general rules about costs; Part 45 deals with fixed costs; Part 46 deals with fast track trial costs; Part 47 deals with the detailed assessment of costs and related appeals and Part 48 deals with costs payable in special cases.)

Definitions and application[1]

43.2 **43.2—(1) In Parts 44 to 48, unless the context otherwise requires—**

(a) "costs" includes fees, charges, disbursements, expenses, remuneration, reimbursement allowed to a litigant in person under rule 48.6,any additional liability incurred under a funding arrangement and any fee or reward charged by a lay representative for acting on behalf of a party in proceedings allocated to the small claims track;

(b) "costs judge" means a taxing master of the Supreme Court;

(c) "costs officer" means—

(i) a costs judge;

(ii) a district judge; and

(iii) an authorised court officer;

(d) "authorised court officer" means any officer of—

(i) a county court;

(ii) a district registry;

(iii) the Principal Registry of the Family Division; or

(iv) the Supreme Court Costs Office; whom the Lord Chancellor has authorised to assess costs;

(e) "fund" includes any estate or property held for the benefit of any person or class of person and any fund to which a trustee or personal representative is entitled in that capacity as such;

(f) "receiving party" means a party entitled to be paid costs;

(g) "paying party" means a party liable to pay costs;

(h) "assisted person" means an assisted person within the statutory provisions relating to legal aid;

(i) "LSC funded client" means an individual who receives services funded by the Legal Services Commission as part of the Community Legal Service within the meaning of Part I of the Access to Justice Act 1999;

(j) "fixed costs" means the amounts which are to be allowed in respect of solicitors' charges in the circumstances set out in Section I of Part 45.

(k) "funding arrangement" means an arrangement where a person has—

(i) entered into a conditional fee agreement or a collective conditional fee agreement[2] which provides for a success fee within the meaning of section 58(2) of the Courts and Legal Services Act 1990;

---

[1] *Amended by the Civil* Procedure (Amendment No.3) Rules 2000 (SI 2000/1317), the Civil Procedure (Amendment) Rules 2001 (SI 2001/256), the Civil Procedure (Amendment No.2) Rules 2003 (SI 2003/1242) and the Civil Procedure (Amendment) Rules 2008 (SI 2008/2178).

[2] Amended by the Civil Procedure (Amendment) Rules 2001 (SI 2001/256).

(ii) taken out an insurance policy to which section 29 of the Access to Justice Act 1999 (recovery of insurance premiums by way of costs) applies; or

(iii) made an agreement with a membership organisation to meet that person's his legal costs;

(l) "percentage increase" means the percentage by which the amount of a legal representative's fee can be increased in accordance with a conditional fee agreement which provides for a success fee;

(m) "insurance premium" means a sum a money paid or payable for insurance against the risk of incurring a costs liability in the proceedings, taken out after the event that is the subject matter of the claim;

(n) "membership organisation" means a body prescribed for the purposes of section 30 of the Access to Justice Act 1999 (recovery where the body undertakes to meet costs liabilities);

(o) "additional liability" means the percentage increase, the insurance premium, or the additional amount in respect of provision made by a membership organisation, as the case may be; and

(p) "free of charge" has the same meaning as in section 194(10) of the Legal Services Act 2007;

(q) "pro bono representation" means legal representation provided free of charge; and

(r) "the prescribed charity" has the same meaning as in section 194(8) of the Legal Services Act 2007.

(2) The costs to which the rules in Parts 44 to 48 apply include—

(a) the following costs where those costs may be assessed by the court;

(i) costs of proceedings before an arbitrator or umpire;

(ii) costs of proceedings before a tribunal or other statutory body; and

(iii) costs payable by a client to his solicitor; and

(b) costs which are payable by one party to another party under the terms of a contract, where the court makes an order for an assessment of those costs.

(3) Where advocacy or litigation services are provided to a client under a conditional fee agreement, costs are recoverable under Parts 44 to 48 notwithstanding that the client is liable to pay his legal representative's fees and expenses only to the extent that sums are recovered in respect of the proceedings, whether by way of costs or otherwise.

(4) In paragraph (3), the reference to a conditional fee agreement is to an agreement which satisfies all the conditions applicable

to it by virtue of section 58 of the Courts and Legal Services Act 1990[1].

43.2.0 *Note* —Paragraphs (3) and (4) were inserted by the Civil Procedure (Amendment No.2) Rules 2003 (SI 2003/1242) with effect from June 2, 2003 para.(3) being further amended (by the substitution of "the proceedings" for "litigation" with effect from June 9, 2003 by the Civil Procedure (Amendment No.3) Rules 2003 (SI 2003/1329).

Comment

43.2.1 Assessment is the process by which the court decides the amount of any costs payable.

As to summary assessment see r.43.3 and as to detailed assessment r.43.4. For the purpose of these rules a Taxing Master of the Supreme Court is referred to as a "Costs Judge".

The Indemnity Principle and CFAs

43.2.1.1 The indemnity principle is fully discussed in Vol.1 at para.47.14.4. Put simply the indemnity principle ensures that an unsuccessful party cannot be held liable to pay costs to a successful party who is not legally liable to pay them. Costs payable by a client to the solicitor belong to the solicitor: Costs recovered between the parties belong to the client. It follows that the latter cannot exceed the former. This principle worked satisfactorily pre CPR and in the days of widely available legal aid. However,conditional fee agreements have become the normal way of funding much litigation, especially personal injury litigation. The indemnity principle and the CFA do not logically sit together. The rule and regulation changes recognise this and take the sensible and simple approach of abrogating the indemnity principle in appropriate cases. Thus solicitors can lawfully agree with clients not to seek to recover by way of costs anything in excess of costs agreed with, or ordered to be paid by the other party. Rules 43.2 (3) and (4) as amended provide that costs whose recovery is limited in this way are recoverable costs for the purposes of CPR Pts 44 to 48.

The Court of Appeal has given a number of important rulings on CFA's in six conjoined appeals reported as *Hollins v Russell* [2003] EWCA Civ 718. This judgment is in six parts summarised as follows—

Part 1 (paras 1 to 40)—a description of the history and evolution of the modern costs and CFA regime.

Part 2 (paras 41 to 50)—the issues raised by the appeals and by the interveners, which include The Law Society.

Part 3 (paras 51 to 67)—the substance of the judgment. In future where a receiving party relies on a CFA he must elect whether to disclose the CFA to the other party or endeavour to prove entitlement to costs by other means. Thus, in practice, disclosure of the CFA is the norm. However, attendance notes and other correspondence should not ordinarily be disclosed.

Part 4 (paras 88 to 116)—if it is alleged that a CFA is unenforceable, the Court should ask itself "has the particular departure from a regulation pursuant to s.53(3)(a) of the CLSA 1990, or a requirement in s.58, either on its own or in conjunction with any other such departure in this case, had a materially adverse effect either upon the protection afforded to the client or upon the proper administration of justice? If the answer is 'yes' the conditions have not been satisfied. If the answer is 'no' the departure is immaterial" (" … the law does not care about very little things … "para.226).

Part 5 (paras 117 to 218) applies the principles to the cases. There were held to be no material breaches in any of them.

Part 6 (paras 219 to 226)—summary of the Courts conclusions.

Part 7 (paras 227 to 228)—the results of each appeal.

This detailed judgment is more fully analysed at 7A–47 *et seq.*

Costs estimates

43.2.2 Section 6 of the Costs Practice Direction (43PD.6) deals with costs estimates and when they are to be provided. The Court of Appeal has expressed the hope that Judges conducting cases will make full use of their powers under the Practice Direc-

[1] 1990 c.41, as substituted by s.27(1) of the Access to Justice Act 1999 (c.22).

tion both to obtain estimates of costs and to exercise their powers in respect of costs and case management to keep costs within the bounds of the proportionate in accordance with the overriding objective *Solutia (UK) Ltd v Griffiths* [2001] EWCA Civ 736.

The Court of Appeal has held that the Costs Practice Direction s.6, relating to costs estimates, is expressed in clear mandatory terms: costs estimates must be provided. The court set out a non exhaustive guide as to the circumstances in which a costs estimate might be taken into account in determining the reasonableness of costs claimed, intended to assist judges in the application of the direction. First, estimates made by solicitors of the overall likely costs of litigation should usually provide a useful yardstick by which the reasonableness of the costs finally claimed may be measured. If there is a substantial difference between the estimated costs and the costs claimed that difference calls for an explanation. In the absence of a satisfactory explanation the court may conclude that the difference itself is evidence from which it can conclude that the costs claimed are unreasonable. Secondly, the court may take the estimated costs into account if the other party shows that it relied on the estimate in a certain way. Thirdly, the court may take the estimate into account in cases where it decides that it would probably have given different case management directions if a realistic estimate had been given. The court did not consider that it would be a correct use of the power conferred by the Costs Practice Direction to hold a party to his estimates simply in order to penalise him for providing an inadequate estimate. Thus if the estimate had not been relied on by the paying party; the court concludedthat even if the estimate had been close to the figure ultimately claimed its case management directions would not have been affected; and, the costs claimed were otherwise reasonable and proportionate, then it would be wrong to reduce the costs claimed simply because they exceed the amount of the estimate. The court considered that the Costs Judge should determine how, if at all, to reflect the costs estimates in the assessment before going on to decide whether, for reasons unrelated to the estimate, there are elements of the costs claimed which were unreasonably incurred or unreasonable in amount. This will avoid the danger of "double jeopardy" referred to by Lord Woolf C.J. in *Lownds* (see *Lownds v Home Office* [2002] EWCA Civ 365 at para.30; [2002] 1 W.L.R. 2450, CA; *Leigh v Michelin Tyre Plc* [2003] EWCA Civ 1766).

The Court of Appeal has subsequently considered whether a paying party may claim that his liability to the receiving party under an order for the payment of costs is discharged or that it should be reduced, if the solicitor for the receiving party has failed to give his client an estimate of costs in accordance with the Solicitors Costs Information and Client Care Code. The court considered the indemnity principle and the special status of the solicitor's certificate of accuracy attached to a bill of costs (see *Bailey v IBC Vehicles Ltd* [1998] 3 All E.R. 570, CA and *Hollins v Russell* [2003] EWCA Civ 718; [2003] 1 W.L.R. 2487). The Law Society was permitted to intervene and submitted that the effect of Practice Rule 15 properly construed was that a breach would not render the solicitor's fees irrecoverable, but that the failure to provide an estimate was likely to be relevant in determining what costs clients could reasonably be expected to pay. The court inferred that the Client Care Code is to protect the legitimate interests of the client and the administration of justice rather than to relieve paying parties of their obligations to pay costs which have been reasonably incurred. Arden L.J., with whom the other members of the court agreed, found that the contract of retainer is not rendered unenforceable by the failure to give an estimate. The Code, like the Solicitors Practice Rules, constitutes subordinate legislation for the purposes of the Solicitors Act 1974. That means that it is binding and has statutory effect, it does not mean however that any contract made or performed in breach of a requirement imposed by the Code is unenforceable. In those circumstances that is a question for the discretion of the Judge assessing costs whether to take into account any failure by the receiving party to provide an estimate in the circumstances and of the kind required by the Code. It is open to the paying party to submit that if the receiving party's work had been estimated in accordance with the requirements of the Code a lower amount of costs would have been incurred. In those circumstances he may ask the Costs Judge to require the receiving party to prove that such an estimate was given. The procedure established in *Pamplin v Express Newspapers Ltd* [1985] 1 W.L.R. 689, Hobhouse J. would then apply. The Costs Judge must however give weight to the certificate as to accuracy. The Costs Judge must be satisfied that there is some real basis for the paying party's contention that the receiving party should be required to prove that there was an estimate or an adequate estimate that is not (to quote the words of Hobhouse J. in *Pamplin*) a sham or fanciful dispute. In addition the Costs

Judge must be satisfied that the absence of an estimate as to costs could have had both a calculable effect and a not immaterial effect on the costs claimed.

The court gave some guidance as to how the Costs Judge should take the fact that there is no estimate into account. The Judge should consider whether, and if so to what extent, the costs claimed would have been significantly lower if there had been an estimate. If the situation is that an estimate was given but not updated the first part of the guidance given by the court in *Leigh v Michelin* [2003] EWCA Civ 1766; [2004] 1 W.L.R. 846 may be applied. Arden L.J. stressed that the guidance given was not exhaustive since it was impossible to foresee all the differing circumstances that might arise in any individual assessment: *Garbutt v Edwards* [2005] EWCA Civ 1206; [2006] 1 W.L.R. 2907; [2006] 1 All E.R. 553, CA.

Where a solicitor's bill to the client far exceeded an estimate which had been given, the court held that the estimate of costs was not a fixed quotation nor did it put an upper limit on costs. The retainer was subject to the Supply of Goods and Services Act 1982 s.15 and it was therefore an implied term that the solicitors would be paid reasonable remuneration for their services. Although the solicitors had informed the client that they would update the cost estimate, this was not a condition precedent to the solicitors recovering any sum in addition to the sum set out in the estimate. In deciding what sum should be payable the court could have regard to the estimate and it was a factor in assessing reasonableness. For this purpose it was relevant, as a matter of law, to ask what, in all the circumstances, it was reasonable for the client to be expected to pay. The cases cited (*Wong v Vizards* [1997] 2 Costs L.R. 46; *Leigh v Michelin Tyre Plc* [2003] EWCA Civ 1766; [2004] 1 W.L.R. 846 and *Garbutt v Edwards* [2005] EWCA Civ 1206; [2006] 1 W.L.R. 2907) were not authority for the proposition that the solicitors had any automatic entitlement to add a margin to the estimate or that the client could cap its liability at the estimate plus a margin (*MasterCigars Direct Ltd v Withers LLP* [2007] EWHC 2733 (Ch); [2008] 3 All E.R. 417, Morgan J.).

Following the decision in *MasterCigars* Tugenhat J. dealt with another appeal (*Reynolds v Stone Rowe Brewer* [2008] EWHC 497 (QB)) in which the costs judge at first instance held that the solicitor should be bound by an estimate of £18,000 to which he added a 15 per cent margin in accordance with *Wong v Vizards* [1997] 2 Costs L.R. 46. The costs judge also limited the claimant's liability for counsel's and expert's fees to the estimates which had been given. The judge held (para.63) that it could not be shown that there was any error of law on the part of the costs judge about which the solicitors could complain. The costs judge was entitled to have regard to the estimates. He did so by giving them an interpretation which, in effect, meant that he treated the estimates as being for a much higher sum than that which the solicitors themselves attributed to the estimates. The court held that the judge did not treat the estimate of £18,000 as a fixed quotation but merely treated it as a yard stick; the figure that the costs judge certified was a figure that it was reasonable to expect the claimant to pay in the case.

Rule 43.2(2) Application of CPR

Arbitration

43.2.3 As to costs in regard to arbitrations, see Arbitration Act 1996 ss.59– 65 (Vol.2, Sect.2E, paras 2E–224 to 2E–234). The Costs Judge is merely the delegate of the arbitrator or other tribunal assessing the amount (*Perkins (H.G.) Ltd v Best-Shaw* [1973] 1 W.L.R. 975; [1973] 2 All E.R. 924).

Family proceedings

43.2.4 The Family Proceedings Rules 1991 have been amended to provide that Pts 43, 44 (except rr.44.9 to 44.12), 47 and and 48 of the CPR shall apply. Rule 44.3(2) (costs follow the event) does not apply. Family Proceedings (Miscellaneous Amendments) Rules 1999 (SI 1999/1012).

The Family Proceedings Rules 1991 have been further amended to make provision about the costs of ancillary relief proceedings. The existing rules about costs in such proceedings are omitted and a new rule (2.71) inserted which sets out a general rule that the court will not make a costs order in ancillary relief proceedings unless it is appropriate to do so because of the conduct of one of the parties in relation to those proceedings. The new rules require the completion of a costs estimate at interim hearings and the completion of a detailed statement of costs at any final ancillary relief hearing. The new provisions apply to proceedings commenced after April 3, 2006.

The Family Proceedings (Costs) Rules 1991 are revoked. See President's Practice Directions 48BPD.1 *et seq*.

Insolvency proceedings

The Insolvency Rules 1986 are modified by the Insolvency (Amendment) (No.2) Rules 1999 (SI 1999/1022). Subject to any inconsistent provisions CPR Pt 43, Pt 44, Pt 45, Pt 47 and Pt 48 apply to insolvency proceedings with any necessary modifications. **43.2.5**

Mediation

Following mediation the parties compromised the claim and counterclaim on the basis that the claimant should pay the defendant's costs of the counterclaim and various subsidiary provisions. The Tomlin Order concluding the proceedings did not deal explicitly with the costs of the mediation itself. The defendant sought the costs of the mediation. Prior to the mediation the parties had entered into an agreement that the mediated fee would be borne equally by each party and that each would bear its own costs. It was held at first instance as a matter of general principle that costs incurred in a mediation could form part of the costs of the action, in the same way as the reasonable costs of negotiation (see Costs Practice Direction para.4 6(8)). On appeal the defendant argued that the Tomlin Order took precedence over the mediation agreement and that therefore the costs were recoverable. The judge held that the mediation agreement was binding on the parties and to argue that it was effectively discharged by the Tomlin Order was reading too much into the Tomlin Order. The defendant was therefore unable to recover its share of the mediator's fee or any of its costs of attending on the mediation: *NatWest Bank v Feeney* (QB), May 14, 2007, Eady J. **43.2.6**

Meaning of summary assessment

43.3 "Summary assessment" means the procedure by which the court, when making an order about costs, orders payment of a sum of money instead of fixed costs or "detailed assessment". **43.3**

Comment

Judges are required to assess the costs of a case if practicable. In cases lasting not more than one day, the parties are under an obligation to provide the court and their opponents with details of the costs which may be sought in the event of success (see Sect.13 of the Costs Practice Direction). See Guide to Summary Assessment of Costs, para.48.16. **43.3.1**

The court has a discretion as to whether or not to carry out a summary assessment and there is no implied general rule requiring detailed assessment of costs in hearings lasting longer than one day. Paragraph 13.1 of the Costs Practice Direction requires the court to consider making a summary assessment in every case: *Q v Q (Costs: Summary Assessment)* [2002] 2 F.L.R. 668, Wilson J.

Appeal

Appeals from summary assessment are dealt with under the ordinary rules relating to appeals (see CPR Pt 52 and Practice Direction supplementing that Part). **43.3.2**

Meaning of detailed assessment

43.4 "Detailed assessment" means the procedure by which the amount of costs is decided by a cost officer in accordance with Part 47. **43.4**

Comment

"Detailed assessment" is the name given to the procedure formerly known as taxation. (See Section 3 of the Costs Practice Direction and Part 47.) **43.4.1**

PRACTICE DIRECTION ABOUT COSTS

This Practice Direction supplements CPR Parts 43 to 48

Section 1 Introduction

43PD.1 **1.1** This Practice Direction supplements Parts 43 to 48 of the Civil Procedure Rules. It applies to all proceedings to which those Parts apply.

1.2 Paragraphs 57.1 to 57.9 of this Practice Direction deal with various transitional provisions affecting proceedings about costs.

1.3 Attention is drawn to the powers to make orders about costs conferred on the Supreme Court and any county court by Section 51 of the Supreme Court Act 1981.

1.4 In these Directions:

"counsel" means a barrister or other person with a right of audience in relation to proceedings in the High Court or in the County Courts in which he is instructed to act.

"LSC" means Legal Services Commission.

"solicitor" means a solicitor of the Supreme Court or other person with a right of audience in relation to proceedings, who is conducting the claim or defence (as the case may be) on behalf of a party to the proceedings and, where the context admits, includes a patent agent.

1.5 In respect of any document which is required by these Directions to be signed by a party or his legal representative the Practice Direction supplementing Part 22 will apply as if the document in question was a statement of truth. (The Practice Direction supplementing Part 22 makes provision for cases in which a party is a child, a protected party or a company or other corporation and cases in which a document is signed on behalf of a partnership).

Section 2 Scope of Costs Rules and Definitions

2.1 Rule 43.2 Definitions and Application

43PD.2 Where the court makes an order for costs and the receiving party has entered into a funding arrangement as defined in rule 43.2, the costs payable by the paying party include any additional liability (also defined in rule 43.2) unless the court orders otherwise.

2.2 In the following paragraphs—

"funding arrangement", "percentage increase", "insurance premium", "membership organisation" and "additional liability" have the meanings given to them by rule 43.2.

A "conditional fee agreement" is an agreement with a person providing advocacy or litigation services which provides for his fees and expenses, or part of them, to be payable only in specified circumstances, whether or not it provides for a success fee as mentioned in section 58(2)(b) of the Courts and Legal Services Act 1990.

"base costs" means costs other than the amount of any additional *liability.*

2.3 Rule 44.3A (1) provides that the court will not assess any additional liability until the conclusion of the proceedings or the part of the proceedings to which the funding arrangement relates. (As to the time when detailed assessment may be carried out see paragraph 27.1 below).

2.4 For the purposes of the following paragraphs of this practice direction and rule 44.3A proceedings are concluded when the court has finally determined the matters in issue in the claim, whether or not there is an appeal. The making of an award of provisional damages under Part 41 will also be treated as a final determination of the matters in issue.

2.5 The court may order or the parties may agree in writing that, although the proceedings are continuing, they will nevertheless be treated as concluded.

Section 3 Model Forms for Claims for Costs

Rule 43.3 Meaning of Summary Assessment

3.1 Rule 43.3 defines summary assessment. When carrying out a summary assessment of costs where there is an additional liability the court may assess the base costs alone, or the base costs and the additional liability. **43PD.3**

3.2 Form **N260** is a model form of Statement of Costs to be used for summary assessments.

3.3 Further details about Statements of Costs are given in paragraph 13.5 below.

Rule 43.4 Meaning of Detailed Assessment

3.4 Rule 43.4 defines detailed assessment. When carrying out a detailed assessment of costs where there is an additional liability the court will assess both the base costs and the additional liability, or, if the base costs have already been assessed, the additional liability alone.

3.5 Precedents A, B, C and D in the Schedule of Costs Precedents annexed to this Practice Direction are model forms of bills of costs to be used for detailed assessments.

3.6 Further details about bills of costs are given in the next section of these Directions and in paragraphs 28.1 to 49.1, below.

3.7 Precedents A, B, C and D in the Schedule of Costs Precedents and the next section of this Practice Direction all refer to a model form of bill of costs. The use of a model form is not compulsory, but is encouraged. A party wishing to rely upon a bill which departs from the model forms should include in the background information of the bill an explanation for that departure.

3.8 In any order of the court (whether made before or after 26 April 1999) the word "taxation" will be taken to mean "detailed assessment" and the words "to be taxed" will be taken to mean "to be decided by detailed assessment" unless in either case the context otherwise requires.

Section 4 Form and Contents of Bills of Costs

4.1 A bill of costs may consist of such of the following sections as may be appropriate: **43PD.4**

(1) title page;

(2) background information;

(3) items of costs claimed under the headings specified in paragraph 4.6;

(4) summary showing the total costs claimed on each page of the bill;

(5) schedules of time spent on non-routine attendances; and

(6) the certificates referred to in paragraph 4.15.

4.2 Where it is necessary or convenient to do so, a bill of costs may be divided into two or more parts, each part containing sections (2), (3) and (4) above. Circumstances in which it will be necessary or convenient to divide a bill into parts include:

(1) Where the receiving party acted in person during the course of the proceedings (whether or not that party also had a legal representative at that time) the bill must be divided into different parts so as to distinguish between;
(a) the costs claimed for work done by the legal representative; and
(b) the costs claimed for work done by the receiving party in person.

(1A) Where the receiving party had pro bono representation for part of the proceedings and an order under section 194(3) of the Legal Services Act 2007 has been made, the bill must be divided into different parts so as to distinguish between:
(a) the sum equivalent to the costs claimed for work done by the legal representative acting free of charge; and
(b) the costs claimed for work done by the legal representative not acting free of charge.

(2) Where the receiving party was represented by different solicitors during the course of the proceedings, the bill must be divided into different parts so as to distinguish between the costs payable in respect of each solicitor.

(3) Where the receiving party obtained legal aid or LSC funding in respect of all or part of the proceedings the bill must be divided into separate parts so as to distinguish between;
(a) costs claimed before legal aid or LSC funding was granted;
(b) costs claimed after legal aid or LSC funding was granted; and
(c) any costs claimed after legal aid or LSC funding ceased.

(4) Where value added tax (VAT) is claimed and there was a change in the rate of VAT during the course of the proceedings, the bill must be divided into separate parts so as to distinguish between;
(a) costs claimed at the old rate of VAT; and
(b) costs claimed at the new rate of VAT.

(5) Where the bill covers costs payable under an order or orders under which there are different paying parties the bill must be divided into parts so as to deal separately with the costs payable by each paying party.

(6) Where the bill covers costs payable under an order or orders, in respect of which the receiving party wishes to

claim interest from different dates, the bill must be divided to enable such interest to be calculated.

4.3 Where a party claims costs against another party and also claims costs against the LSC only for work done in the same period, the costs claimed against the LSC only can be claimed either in a separate part of the bill or in additional columns in the same part of the bill. Precedents C and D in the Schedule of Costs Precedents annexed to this Practice Direction show how bills should be drafted when costs are claimed against the LSC only.

4.4 The title page of the bill of costs must set out:

(1) the full title of the proceedings;

(2) the name of the party whose bill it is and a description of the document showing the right to assessment (as to which see paragraph 40.4, below);

(3) if VAT is included as part of the claim for costs, the VAT number of the legal representative or other person in respect of whom VAT is claimed;

(4) details of all legal aid certificates, LSC certificates and relevant amendment certificates in respect of which claims for costs are included in the bill.

4.5 The background information included in the bill of costs should set out:

(1) a brief description of the proceedings up to the date of the notice of commencement;

(2) a statement of the status of the solicitor or solicitor's employee in respect of whom costs are claimed and (if those costs are calculated on the basis of hourly rates) the hourly rates claimed for each such person.

It should be noted that "legal executive"means a Fellow of the Institute of Legal Executives.

Other clerks, who are fee earners of equivalent experience, may be entitled to similar rates. It should be borne in mind that Fellows of the Institute of Legal Executives will have spent approximately 6 years in practice, and taken both general and specialist examinations. The Fellows have therefore acquired considerable practical and academic experience. Clerks without the equivalent experience of legal executives will normally be treated as being the equivalent of trainee solicitors and para-legals.

(3) a brief explanation of any agreement or arrangement between the receiving party and his solicitors, which affects the costs claimed in the bill.

***4.6** The bill of costs* may consist of items under such of the following heads as may be appropriate:

(1) attendances on the court and counsel up to the date of the notice of commencement;

(2) attendances on and communications with the receiving party;

(3) attendances on and communications with witnesses including any expert witness;

(4) attendances to inspect any property or place for the purposes of the proceedings;

(5) attendances on and communications with other persons, including offices of public records;

(6) communications with the court and with counsel;

(7) work done on documents: preparing and considering documentation, including documentation necessary to comply with Practice Direction (Pre-Action Conduct) or a relevant pre-action protocols where appropriate, work done in connection with arithmetical calculations of compensation and/or interest and time spent collating documents;

(8) work done in connection with negotiations with a view to settlement if not already covered in the heads listed above;

(9) attendances on and communications with London and other agents and work done by them;

(10) other work done which was of or incidental to the proceedings and which is not already covered in the heads listed above.

4.7 In respect of each of the heads of costs:

(1) "communications" means letters out and telephone calls;

(2) communications, which are not routine communications, must be set out in chronological order;

(3) routine communications should be set out as a single item at the end of each head;

4.8 Routine communications are letters out, e-mails out and telephone calls which because of their simplicity should not be regarded as letters or e-mails of substance or telephone calls which properly amount to an attendance.

4.9 Each item claimed in the bill of costs must be consecutively numbered.

4.10 In each part of the bill of costs which claims items under head (1) (attendances on court and counsel) a note should be made of:

(1) all relevant events, including events which do not constitute chargeable items;

(2) any orders for costs which the court made (whether or not a claim is made in respect of those costs in this bill of costs).

4.11 The numbered items of costs may be set out on paper divided into columns. Precedents A, B, C and D in the Schedule of Costs Precedents annexed to this Practice Direction illustrate various model forms of bills of costs.

4.12 In respect of heads (2) to (10) in paragraph 4.6 above, if the number of attendances and communications other than routine communications is twenty or more, the claim for the costs of those items in that section of the bill of costs should be for the total only and should refer to a schedule in which the full record of dates and details is set out. If the bill of costs contains more than one schedule each schedule should be numbered consecutively.

4.13 *The bill of costs must* not contain any claims in respect of costs or court fees which relate solely to the detailed assessment proceedings other than costs claimed for preparing and checking the bill.

4.14 The summary must show the total profit costs and disbursements claimed separately from the total VAT claimed. Where the bill of costs is divided into parts the summary must also give totals for each part. If each page of the bill gives a page total the summary must also set out the page totals for each page.

4.15 The bill of costs must contain such of the certificates, the texts of which are set out in Precedent F of the Schedule of Costs Precedents annexed to this Practice Direction, as are appropriate.

4.16 The following provisions relate to work done by solicitors:

(1) Routine letters out and routine telephone calls will in general be allowed on a unit basis of 6 minutes each, the charge being calculated by reference to the appropriate hourly rate. The unit charge for letters out will include perusing and considering the relevant letters in and no separate charge should be made for in-coming letters.

(2) E-mails received by solicitors will not normally be allowed. The court may, in its discretion, allow an actual time charge for preparation of e-mails sent by solicitors, which properly amount to attendances provided that the time taken has been recorded. The court may also, in its discretion, allow a sum in respect of routine e-mails sent to the client or others on a unit basis of 6 minutes each, the charge being calculated by reference to the appropriate hourly rate.

(3) Local travelling expenses incurred by solicitors will not be allowed. The definition of "local" is a matter for the discretion of the court. While no absolute rule can be laid down, as a matter of guidance, "local" will, in general, be taken to mean within a radius of 10 miles from the court dealing with the case at the relevant time. Where travelling and waiting time is claimed, this should be allowed at the rate agreed with the client unless this is more than the hourly rate on the assessment.

(4) The cost of postage, couriers, out-going telephone calls, fax and telex messages will in general not be allowed but the court may exceptionally in its discretion allow such expenses in unusual circumstances or where the cost is unusually heavy.

(5) The cost of making copies of documents will not in general be allowed but the court may exceptionally in its discretion make an allowance for copying in unusual circumstances or where the documents copied are unusually numerous in relation to the nature of the case. Where this discretion is invoked the number of copies made, their purpose and the costs claimed for them must be set out in the bill.

(6) Agency charges as between a principal solicitor and his agent will be dealt with on the principle that such charges, where appropriate, form part of the principal solicitor's charges. Where these charges relate to head (1) in paragraph 4.6 (attendances at court and on counsel) they should be included in their chronological order in that head. In other cases they should be included in head (9) (attendances on London and other agents).

4.17(1) Where a claim is made for a percentage increase in addition to an hourly rate or base fee, the amount of the increase must be shown separately, either in the appropriate arithmetic column or in the narrative column. (For an example see Precedent A or Precedent B).

(2) Where a claim is made against the LSC only and includes enhancement and where a claim is made in family proceedings and includes a claim for uplift or general care and conduct, the amount of enhancement uplift and general care and conduct must be shown, in respect of each item upon which it is claimed, as a separate amount either in the appropriate arithmetic column or in the narrative column. (For an example, see Precedent C).

"Enhancement" means the increase in prescribed rates which may be allowed by a costs officer in accordance with the Legal Aid in Civil Proceedings (Remuneration) Regulations 1994 or the Legal Aid in Family Proceedings Regulations 1991.

Costs of preparing the bill

4.18 A claim may be made for the reasonable costs of preparing and checking the bill of costs.

Section 5 Special Provisions Relating to VAT

43PD.5 **5.1** This section deals with claims for value added tax (VAT) which are made in respect of costs being dealt with by way of summary assessment or detailed assessment.

VAT Registration Number

5.2 The number allocated by HM Revenue and Customs to every person registered under the Value Added Tax Act 1994 (except a Government Department) must appear in a prominent place at the head of every statement, bill of costs, fee sheet, account or voucher on which VAT is being included as part of a claim for costs.

Entitlement to VAT on Costs

5.3 VAT should not be included in a claim for costs if the receiving party is able to recover the VAT as input tax. Where the receiving party is able to obtain credit from HM Revenue and Customs for a proportion of the VAT as input tax, only that proportion which is not eligible for credit should be included in the claim for costs.

5.4 The receiving party has responsibility for ensuring that VAT is claimed only when the receiving party is unable to recover the VAT or a proportion thereof as input tax.

5.5 Where there is a dispute as to whether VAT is properly claimed the receiving party must provide a certificate signed by the solicitors or the auditors of the receiving party substantially in the form illustrated in Precedent F in the Schedule of Costs Precedents annexed to this Practice Direction. Where the receiving party is a litigant in person who is claiming VAT, reference should be made by him to HM Revenue and Customs and wherever possible a Statement to similar effect produced at the hearing at which the costs are assessed.

5.6 Where there is a dispute as to whether any service in respect of which a charge is proposed to be made in the bill is zero rated or exempt, reference should be made to HM Revenue and Customs and wherever possible the view of HM Revenue and Customs obtained and made known at the hearing at which the costs are assessed. Such application should be made by the receiving party. In the case of a bill from a solicitor to his own client, such application should be made by the client.

Form of bill of costs where VAT rate changes

5.7 Where there is a change in the rate of VAT, suppliers of goods and services are entitled by ss.88 (1) and 88(2) of the VAT Act 1994 in most circumstances to elect whether the new or the old rate of VAT should apply to a supply where the basic and actual tax points span a period during which there has been a change in VAT rates.

5.8 It will be assumed, unless a contrary indication is given in writing, that an election to take advantage of the provisions mentioned in paragraph 5.7 above and to charge VAT at the lower rate has been made. In any case in which an election to charge at the lower rate is not made, such a decision must be justified to the court assessing the costs.

Apportionment

5.9 All bills of costs, fees and disbursements on which VAT is included must be divided into separate parts so as to show work done before, on and after the date or dates from which any change in the rate of VAT takes effect. Where, however, a lump sum charge is made for work which spans a period during which there has been a change in VAT rates, and paragraphs 5.7 and 5.8 above do not apply, reference should be made to paragraphs 8 and 9 of Appendix F of Customs' Notice 700 (or any revised edition of that notice), a copy of which should be in the possession of every registered trader. If necessary, the lump sum should be apportioned. The totals of profit costs and disbursements in each part must be carried separately to the summary.

5.10 Should there be a change in the rate between the conclusion of a detailed assessment and the issue of the final costs certificate, any interested party may apply for the detailed assessment to be varied so as to take account of any increase or reduction in the amount of tax payable. Once the final costs certificate has been issued, no variation under this paragraph will be permitted.

Disbursements

5.11 Petty (or general) disbursements such as postage, fares etc *which are normally treated* as part of a solicitor's overheads and included in his profit costs should be charged with VAT even though they bear no tax when the solicitor incurs them. The cost of travel by public transport on a specific journey for a particular client where it forms part of the service rendered by a solicitor to his client and is charged in his bill of costs, attracts VAT.

5.12 Reference is made to the criteria set out in the VAT Guide (Customs and Excise Notice 700 - 1st August 1991 edition paragraph

83, or any revised edition of that Notice), as to expenses which are not subject to VAT. Charges for the cost of travel by public transport, postage, telephone calls and telegraphic transfers where these form part of the service rendered by the solicitor to his client are examples of charges which do not satisfy these criteria and are thus liable to VAT at the standard rate.

Legal Aid/LSC Funding

5.13(1) VAT will be payable in respect of every supply made pursuant to a legal aid/LSC certificate where—

(a) the person making the supply is a taxable person; and

(b) the assisted person/LSC funded client—

(i) belongs in the United Kingdom or another member state of the European Union; and

(ii) is a private individual or receives the supply for non-business purposes.

(2) Where the assisted person/LSC funded client belongs outside the European Union, VAT is generally not payable unless the supply relates to land in the United Kingdom.

(3) For the purpose of sub-paragraphs (1) and (2), the place where a person belongs is determined by section 9 of the Value Added Tax Act 1994.

(4) Where the assisted person/LSC funded client is registered for VAT and the legal services paid for by the LSC are in connection with that person's business, the VAT on those services will be payable by the LSC only.

5.14 Any summary of costs payable by the LSC must be drawn so as to show the total VAT on Counsel's fees as a separate item from the VAT on other disbursements and the VAT on profit costs.

Tax invoice

5.15 A bill of costs filed for detailed assessment is always retained by the Court. Accordingly if a solicitor waives his solicitor and client costs and accepts the costs certified by the court as payable by the unsuccessful party in settlement, it will be necessary for a short statement as to the amount of the certified costs and the VAT thereon to be prepared for use as the tax invoice.

Vouchers

5.16 Where receipted accounts for disbursements made by the solicitor or his client are retained as tax invoices a photostat copy of any such receipted account may be produced and will be accepted as sufficient evidence of payment when disbursements are vouched.

Certificates

5.17 In a costs certificate payable by the LSC, the VAT on solicitor's costs, Counsel's fees and disbursements will be shown separately.

Litigants acting in person

5.18 Where a litigant acts in litigation on his own behalf he is not treated for the purposes of VAT as having supplied services and therefore no VAT is chargeable in respect of work done by that litigant (even where, for example, that litigant is a solicitor or other legal representative).

5.19 Consequently in the circumstances described in the preceding paragraph, a bill of costs presented for agreement or assessment should not claim any VAT which will not be allowed on assessment.

Government Departments

5.20 On an assessment between parties, where costs are being paid to a Government Department in respect of services rendered by its legal staff, VAT should not be added.

Payment pursuant to an order under section 194(3) of the Legal Services Act 2007

5.21 Where an order is made under section 194(3) of the Legal Services Act 2007 any bill presented for agreement or assessment pursuant to that order must not include a claim for VAT.

Section 6 Estimates of Costs

6.1 This section sets out certain steps which parties and their legal representatives must take in order to keep the parties informed about their potential liability in respect of costs and in order to assist the court to decide what, if any, order to make about costs and about case management. **43PD.6**

6.2(1) In this Section an "estimate of costs" means—

(a) an estimate of costs of—

(i) base costs (including disbursements) already incurred; and

(ii) base costs (including disbursements) to be incurred,

which a party, if successful in the proceedings, intends to seek to recover from any other party under an order for costs; or

(b) in proceedings where the party has pro bono representation and intends, if successful in the proceedings, to seek an order under section 194(3) of the Legal Services Act 2007, an estimate of the sum equivalent to—

(i) the base costs (including disbursements) that the party would have already incurred had the legal representation provided to that party not been free of charge; and

(ii) the base costs (including disbursements) that the party would incur if the legal representation to be provided to that party were not free of charge.

('Base costs' are defined in paragraph 2.2 of this Practice Direction.)

(2) A party who intends to recover an additional liability (defined in rule 43.2) need not reveal the amount of that liability in the estimate.

6.3 The court may at any stage in a case order any party to file an estimate of costs and to serve copies of the estimate on all other parties. The court may direct that the estimate be prepared in such a way as to demonstrate the likely effects of giving or not giving a particular case management direction which the court is considering, for example a direction for a split trial or for the trial of a preliminary issue. The court may specify a time limit for filing and serving the estimate. However, if no time limit is specified the estimate should be filed and served within 28 days of the date of the order.

6.4(1) When—

(a) a party to a claim which is outside the financial scope of the small claims track files an allocation questionnaire; or

(b) a party to a claim which is being dealt with on the fast track or the multi track, or under Part 8, files a pre-trial check list (listing questionnaire),

he must also file an estimate of costs and serve a copy of it on every other party, unless the court otherwise directs. Where a party is represented, the legal representative must in addition serve an estimate on the party he represents.

(2) Where a party is required to file and serve a new estimate of costs in accordance with Rule 44.15(3), if that party is represented the legal representative must in addition serve the new estimate on the party he represents.

(3) This paragraph does not apply to litigants in person.

6.5 An estimate of costs should be substantially in the form illustrated in Precedent H in the Schedule of Costs Precedents annexed to the Practice Direction.

6.5A(1) If there is a difference of 20% or more between the base costs claimed by a receiving party on detailed assessment and the costs shown in an estimate of costs filed by that party, the receiving party must provide a statement of the reasons for the difference with his bill of costs.

(2) If a paying party—

(a) claims that he reasonably relied on an estimate of costs filed by a receiving party; or

(b) wishes to rely upon the costs shown in the estimate in order to dispute the reasonableness or proportionality of the costs claimed,

the paying party must serve a statement setting out his case in this regard in his points of dispute.

('Relevant person' is defined in paragraph 32.10(1) of the Costs Practice Direction)

6.6(1) On an assessment of the costs of a party, the court may have regard to any estimate previously filed by that party, or by any other party in the same proceedings. Such an estimate may be taken into account as a factor among others, when assessing the reasonableness and proportionality of any costs claimed.

(2) In particular, where—

(a) there is a difference of 20% or more between the base costs claimed by a receiving party and the costs shown in an estimate of costs filed by that party; and

(b) it appears to the court that—

(i) the receiving party has not provided a satisfactory explanation for that difference; or

(ii) the paying party reasonably relied on the estimate of costs;

the court may regard the difference between the costs claimed and the costs shown in the estimate as evidence that the costs claimed are unreasonable or disproportionate.

PART 44

General Rules about Costs

44.0.1 **Contents**

Scope of this Part[1]

44.1 **44.1 This Part contains general rules about costs, and entitlement to costs and orders in respect of pro bono representation.**

(The definitions contained in Part 43 are relevant to this Part).

Solicitor's duty to notify client

44.2 **44.2—(1) Where—**

(a) the court makes a costs order against a legally represented party; and

[1] Amended by the Civil Procedure (Amendment) Rules 2008 (SI 2008/2178).

(b) the party is not present when the order is made,

the party's solicitor must notify his client in writing of the costs order no later than 7 days after the solicitor receives notice of the order.

Comment

This rule is the result of Lord Woolf's view that one of the reasons for the expense of litigation was that the client was not aware of the costs being incurred in his name by his legal representatives. The original requirement that the client should attend every case management conference has been dropped, but the solicitor is under a duty to inform the client whenever an adverse costs order is made. Although the court is not given specific penal powers in relation to failure to notify the client, such failure, if deliberate, might amount to professional misconduct. See also the similar provision in relation to costs orders for misconduct, r.44.14. The court may require the solicitor to produce evidence showing that he took reasonable steps to comply with the rule. (See s.7 of the costs practice direction.) **44.2.1**

Court's discretion and circumstances to be taken into account when exercising its discretion as to costs[1]

44.3—(1) The court has discretion as to— **44.3**

(a) whether costs are payable by one party to another;

(b) the amount of those costs; and

(c) when they are to be paid.

(2) If the court decides to make an order about costs—

(a) the general rule is that the unsuccessful party will be ordered to pay the costs of the successful party; but

(b) the court may make a different order.

(3) The general rule does not apply to the following proceedings—

(a) proceedings in the Court of Appeal on an application or appeal made in connection with proceedings in the Family Division; or

(b) proceedings in the Court of Appeal from a judgment, direction, decision or order given or made in probate proceedings or family proceedings.

(4) In deciding what order (if any) to make about costs, the court must have regard to all the circumstances, including—

(a) the conduct of all the parties;

(b) whether a party has succeeded on part of his case, even if he has not been wholly successful; and

(c) any payment into court or admissible offer to settle made by a party which is drawn to the court's attention, and which is not an offer to which costs consequences under Part 36 apply.

(5) The conduct of the parties includes—

(a) conduct before, as well as during, the proceedings, and in particular the extent to which the parties followed the Practice Direction (Pre-Action Conduct) or any relevant pre-action protocol;

[1] Amended by the Civil Procedure (Amendment No.3) Rules 2006 (SI 2006/3435).

(b) whether it was reasonable for a party to raise, pursue or contest a particular allegation or issue;

(c) the manner in which a party has pursued or defended his case or a particular allegation or issue;

(d) whether a claimant who has succeeded in his claim, in whole or in part, exaggerated his claim.

(6) The orders which the court may make under this rule include an order that a party must pay—

(a) a proportion of another party's costs;

(b) a stated amount in respect of another party's costs;

(c) costs from or until a certain date only;

(d) costs incurred before proceedings have begun;

(e) costs relating to particular steps taken in the proceedings;

(f) costs relating only to a distinct part of the proceedings; and

(g) interest on costs from or until a certain date, including a date before judgment.

(7) Where the court would otherwise consider making an order under paragraph (6)(f), it must instead, if practicable, make an order under paragraph (6)(a) or (c).

(8) Where the court has ordered a party to pay costs, it may order an amount to be paid on account before the costs are assessed.

(9) Where a party entitled to costs is also liable to pay costs the court may assess the costs which that party is liable to pay and either;

(a) set off the amount assessed against the amount the party is entitled to be paid and direct him to pay any balance; or

(b) delay the issue of a certificate for the costs to which the party is entitled until he has paid the amount which he is liable to pay.

Comment

44.3.1 Although this rule preserves the general rule that the unsuccessful party will be ordered to pay the costs of the successful party, Lord Woolf M.R. was anxious to move away from the position that any success is sufficient to obtain an order for costs. He therefore envisaged far more partial orders for costs which more accurately reflect the level of success achieved by the receiving party; see *A.E.I. Rediffusion Music Ltd v Phonographic Performance Ltd* [1999] 1 W.L.R. 1507, CA.

Jackson J., at the end of a long running dispute concerning the construction of Wembley Stadium, gave a supplementary judgment on costs in which he reviewed the relevant current cases. From this review he derived the following eight principles:

"(i) In commercial litigation where each party has claims and asserts that a balance is owing in its own favour, the party which ends up receiving payment should generally be characterised as the overall winner of the entire action.

(ii) In considering how to exercise its discretion the court should take as its starting point the general rule that the successful party is entitled to an order for costs.

(iii) The judge must then consider what departures are required from that starting point, having regard to all the circumstances of the case.

(iv) Where the circumstances of the case require an issue-based costs order, that is what the judge should make. However, the judge should hesitate before doing so, because of the practical difficulties which this causes and because of the steer given by rule 44.3(7).

(v) In many cases the judge can and should reflect the relative success of the parties on different issues by making a proportionate costs order.

(vi) In considering the circumstances of the case the judge will have regard not only to any part 36 offers made but also to each party's approach to negotiations (insofar as admissible) and general conduct of the litigation.

(vii) If (a) one party makes an offer under part 36 or an admissible offer within rule 44.3(4)(c) which is nearly but not quite sufficient, and (b) the other party rejects that offer outright without any attempt to negotiate, then it might be appropriate to penalise the second party in costs.

(viii) In assessing a proportionate costs order the judge should consider what costs are referable to each issue and what costs are common to several issues. It will often be reasonable for the overall winner to recover not only the costs specific to the issues which he has won but also the common costs."

Multiplex Constructions (UK) Ltd v Cleveland Bridge UK Ltd and Cleveland Bridge Dorman Long Engineering Ltd [2008] EWHC 2280 (TCC) Jackson J.

As a result of the authorities since the decision in *Elgindata (No.2), Re* [1992] 1 W.L.R. 1207, CA it is no longer necessary to establish that a successful party has acted unreasonably or improperly in raising an issue in order for it to be deprived of its costs and ordered to pay the unsuccessful party's costs of that particular issue. The issue based approach requires the court to consider issue by issue where the costs in each discrete issue fall: *Summit Property Ltd v Pitmans* [2001] EWCA Civ 2020. In a case where the trial judge had made a global order which deprived the claimant of any costs, because the claimant had obtained very much less by way of damages than had originally been claimed, the Court of Appeal held that the judge had failed to explain why he had not chosen to adopt a conventional issue based approach and his approach was accordingly flawed, since it was not in accordance with the principles laid out in CPR r.44.3. On the facts the Court of Appeal substituted an order that the claimant should have 50 per cent of his costs up to the conclusion of the trial on liability and all his costs thereafter: *Aspin v Metric Group Ltd* [2007] EWCA Civ 922. For a case in which the court awarded costs including costs under CPR r.36.20 and in circumstances that reflected the fact that each party had won and lost on a substantial issue, see *Fulham Leisure Holdings Ltd v Nicholson Graham and Jones* [2006] EWHC 2428, Ch, Mann J.

Although the normal rule is that the unsuccessful party should be ordered to pay the successful party's costs, the court has a discretion to make a different order where it would be unjust to follow the normal rule. Where the successful party had fought a case on a number of distinct bases on which he had lost, including an improper allegation of fraud, it was appropriate to make an issue based split costs order requiring each party to pay 50 per cent of the other party's costs. The Court of Appeal would have been surprised if the judge had not found it appropriate to make an issue based order: *National Westminster Bank Plc v Kotonou* [2007] EWCA Civ 223.

The trial judge has a wide discretion to further the overriding objective. In exercising that discretion the judge should have regard to the factors set out in CPR r.44.3(4). Where a judge awarded the claimant an amount which reflected the defendant's contention of what was proper, the defendant was, on the facts, in reality the winner. The judgment sum awarded was of relative insignificance to the sum claimed by the claimant. The Court of Appeal held that the judge had failed to have regard to the fact that the defendant had won in principle and set aside the order that the defendant should pay the claimant's costs substituting no order as to costs: *Islam v Ali* [2003] EWCA Civ 612. Claimants, who had won on the central issue but lost on eight other issues, were awarded their full costs of the proceedings relating to liability. In respect of an estoppel issue, and also on the quantum issue which the claimant had lost, the court ordered that the claimants should bear their own costs and pay those of the defendant, where they related to the attendance of counsel and solicitors in court on the days on which the quantum evidence was given. The court recognised that awarding one party the costs of particular issues would make the assessment process impossibly difficult for the Costs Judge. *Travellers Casualty and Sureties Company of Canada v Sun Life Assurance Company of Canada UK Ltd* [2006] EWHC 2885 (Comm) Christopher Clarke J.

The Court of Appeal allowed an appeal by defendants but ordered them to pay the costs in any event because of the way in which the matter had been conducted in the court below (*Daniels v Walker* [2000] 1 W.L.R. 1382).

Whereas prior to the CPR a party who met with "substantial" success was entitled to all his costs, the situation has since changed. Rule 44.3 enables the court to do greater justice where a successful party has caused an unsuccessful party to incur costs on an issue which later fails. On the particular facts of the case the defendants were allowed the costs of a tenancy issue to be set off against the claimant's costs on a dissolution of partnership issue (*Winter v Winter*, November 10, 2000, unrep., CA). The Court of Appeal altered an order that there be no order as to costs, better to reflect the Claimant's degree of success on an application which had been granted but in an amended form from that originally sought: *Jim Ennis Construction Ltd v Thewlis* [2003] EWCA Civ 1273.

An award of costs that simply looks at the number of issues won and lost does not fairly reflect the realities of the case. Where successful claimants had lost a good many issues it was not unreasonable, in particular in the light of the misleading conduct of three of the defendants, for the claimants to have raised the issues that they did. The claimants were awarded a percentage of their costs: *Douglas v Hello Ltd* [2004] EWHC 63, Ch, Lindsay J.

Where a claimant succeeded on one issue at trial, but in reality the defendant was the winner, an order that the claimant should pay the defendants' costs reflected the overall justice of the case. The court accepted that there was no automatic rule requiring reduction of a successful party's costs if he lost on one or more issues. In any litigation, particularly complex litigation, a winning party was likely to fail on one or more issues in the case. The claimant was ordered to make an interim payment representing less than 60 per cent of the defendants' total costs and less than a third of its own costs. One defendant was also entitled to recover its costs against two other defendants who had supported the claimant, limited to the amount by which that defendant's costs had been increased by the participation of the other two defendants in the trial (*Kidsons v Lloyds Underwriters* [2007] EWHC 2699 (Comm) Gloster J.).

Where a claimant fundamentally amended the particulars of claim shortly before trial, as a result of which the costs in the case amounted to substantially more than the original amount claimed in the action, the unsuccessful party would still usually have to pay the costs of the successful party, taking into account the conduct of the parties, whether a realistic offer to settle was made and whether the circumstances dictated that a party should pay a proportion of the other party's costs or up to a specific point in the proceedings. On the facts of the particular case an order that the defendant should pay two thirds of the claimant's costs was upheld: *Professional Information Technology Consultants Ltd v Jones* [2001] EWCA Civ 2103.

It is not open to a defendant who has paid money into court to argue that if a claimant had been more reasonable he would have offered more money. The remedy is in the defendant's own hands. It was open to the defendant to pay into court the maximum sum he was prepared to pay. At first instance the judge had reduced the award of costs to nil on the basis of the claimant's failure to engage in negotiations, which was a failure to comply with the pre-action protocol. The Court of Appeal found that the judge had failed to take into account the extent to which that factor had already been dealt with in his reasoning, thus no further reduction should have been made. On the facts the claimant was awarded 60 per cent of his costs from the date of the Pt 36 offer (*Straker v Tudor Rose (A Firm)* [2007] EWCA Civ 368; [2007] CP Rep 32).

Where a claimant applies to discover a third party's identity (a *Norwich Pharmacal* application: *Norwich Pharmacal Co v Customs and Excise Commissioners* [1974] A.C. 133). Rule 44.3 cannot apply to such applications since they are not really *inter partes* disputes. The defendant in the case had not resisted the court making the order but had remained neutral on the application. Such applications are akin to applications for pre-action disclosure under r.48.3. In general the costs incurred should be recovered from the wrong doer and not from the party from whom disclosure is sought. In a normal case the applicant should be ordered to pay the costs of the party making disclosure including the costs of disclosure: *Totalise Plc v Motley Fool Ltd* [2001] EWCA Civ 1897; [2002] 1 W.L.R. 1233, CA.

In contentious probate proceedings two long-standing exceptions to the general rule that costs follow the event have survived the introduction of the CPR: i.e. if the person who made the will, or persons interested in the residue, had been the cause of the action or responsible for the litigation, a case could be made out for costs to come out of the estate. Secondly, if the circumstances led reasonably to an investigation of the matter, then the costs might be left to be borne by those who had incurred them (see *Spiers v English* [1907] P. 122 and *Re Cutcliffe's Estate* [1959] P. 6; *Kostic v Chaplin* [2007] EWHC 2909 (Ch) Henderson J.).

Orders for costs

The court has the powers contained in s.51 of the Supreme Court Act 1981 in relation to costs. See Section 8 of the Costs Practice Direction for the effect of some common orders for costs; in respect of the fees of counsel; and the fees of conveyancing counsel. **44.3.2**

The scope of a judge's discretion under r.44.3 entitles him to make a variety of orders where there was a split trial. A judge is not required by the rules to make an immediate decision on costs after a trial on liability and has a discretion to postpone it until quantum has been finally determined: *Shepherds Investments Ltd v Andrew Walters* [2007] EWCA Civ 292.

In an appeal where the point of law arising was of some importance but the cost of the repair works in issue was small and much less than the legal costs involved, and bearing in mind the proportionality element of the overriding objective, the Court of Appeal granted permission to appeal on condition that the appellant should pay all the costs in the Court of Appeal irrespective of the outcome of the proceedings: *Morris v Wrexham CBC* [2001] EWHC Civ 697. As to protective costs orders see 48.15.7.

Although r.44.3 gives the court a discretion when considering costs, the court cannot act as an appellate court in respect of its own order except where fraud has been shown in the original application for the order. The court has no discretion under r.44.3 to amend its own costs order: *Commissioners of Customs & Excise v Anchor Foods, The Times*, September 28, 1999, Neuberger J.

In an action for malicious prosecution where a jury fails to agree, the standard order should be costs in the case: *Camiller v Commissioner of Police for the Metropolis, The Times*, June 8, 1999, CA.

For a case in which the court awarded successful defendants less than full costs because of the circumstances and conduct of some of the defendants: see *Groupo Torras S.A. v Al-Sabah*, July 5, 1999, unrep. (Mance L.J.). The fourth defendant was awarded only 50 per cent of his costs (deliberate backdating of relevant documents to deceive auditors). The sixth defendant was awarded one third of his costs (conduct unsatisfactory and improper). The tenth defendant was awarded one third of his costs (untruthful evidence at trial).

Where a party effectively controlled the actions of other co-parties (in the particular case the co-defendant companies were described as the second defendant's "children"), and operated them to maximise the benefit to him, the court found him jointly liable for costs and did not limit the order to those issues which he had lost. *Quadrant Holdings (Cambridge) Ltd v Quadrant Research Foundation (Costs)* [1999] F.S.R. 918, Pumfrey J.

Where a claimant brought a money claim and the defendant was successful on a single determinative issue but lost on three other principal issues, the award of costs to the defendants was reduced by one quarter. The court applied the following criteria:

(a) the reasonableness of taking the point;
(b) the extra time taken up prior to trial in preparing to argue the point;
(c) the extra time taken in court to argue the point;
(d) the extent to which it was just in all the circumstances to deprive the successful party of its costs; and
(e) the extent to which the unsuccessful point was related to any successful point. (*Antonelli v Allen* [2001] Lloyd's Rep. P.N. 487, Neuberger J.).

Counsels' fees

Unless a rule specifically requires the court to give a certificate for Counsel, there is no longer any need for such a certificate. (See para.8.7 of the Costs Practice Direction.) **44.3.3**

Summary assessment

As to summary assessment see notes at paras 44.7.1 and 44.7.4 and s.13 of the Costs Practice Direction. **44.3.4**

Discretion as to costs

In *Aiden Shipping Ltd v Interbulk Ltd* [1986] A.C. 965; [1986] 2 All E.R. 409; the House of Lords (overruling the Court of Appeal) held that the discretionary power to award costs contained in SCA 1981 s.51(1) was expressed in wide terms leaving the rule-making authority to control its exercise by rules of court, if it saw fit to do so, and **44.3.5** the appellate courts to establish principles for its exercise; and there was no justification for implying a limitation to the effect that costs could only be ordered to be paid by parties to the proceedings.

Lord Goff of Chieveley (at 981), said that he did not, for his part, foresee any injustice flowing from the abandonment of the implied limitation and expressed the view that "Courts of first instance are ... well capable of exercising their discretion under the statute in accordance with reason and justice."

In *Re Gibson's Settlement Trusts* [1981] Ch. 179; [1981] 1 All E.R. 233, Sir Robert Megarry V.-C. considered the circumstances in which costs incurred prior to the commencement of proceedings could be allowed. Disputes antecedent to the proceedings which bear no real relation to the subject of the litigation, could not be regarded as part of the costs of the proceedings, but disputes which are in some degree relevant to the proceedings, as ultimately constituted and the other parties' attitude made it reasonable to apprehend that the litigation would include them, could be allowed.

There is no logical basis for saying that the claimant must have identified the precise claim that is in the event made, before costs can be potentially recoverable. Lord Harnworth in speaking of costs "ultimately proving of use and service in the action" and Megarry V.-C. talking of "a kind of legitimation by subsequent litigation" make clear that the matter is one of hindsight rather than foresight, per Kay J. in *Rentall Ltd v D. S. Willcock Ltd, Review of Taxation*, July 30, 1997, unrep.—decision given in Open Court.

Because of the terms of the consent order the Costs Judge was required, on a true construction of the order, to separate into distinct categories costs of the Pt 8 proceedings and costs incidental to them.The court had to consider whether the preparation for proceedings of one type could properly be regarded as giving rise to costs of and incidental to subsequent proceedings of a narrower scope.The court followed the guidance laid down in *Re Gibsons Settlement Trust* [1981] 1 Ch 179, Sir Robert McGarry VC. Applying those guidelines the court found that the word product created by the breach of trust expenditure was ultimately of some use and service in the Pt 8 proceedings, albeit less than originally anticipated.The breach of trust dispute was in some degree relevant to the subject matter of the Pt 8 proceedings and above all the attitude both of the Trustees and the other branches of the family at the time of the relevant expenditure made it reasonable for the claimants to apprehend that the litigation would in due course include that dispute. *Newall v Lewis* [2008] EWHC 910 (Ch), Briggs J.

Neither a costs judge nor the court on appeal can properly refuse to carry out an order for detailed assessment because it is considered to be wrong or ultra vires; the only remedy if the order be wrong, is an appeal from the order, per Megaw J. in *Cope v United Dairies (London) Ltd* [1963] 2 Q.B. 33. A defendant who consented to judgment with costs could not appeal on grounds of mistake as to the terms of the claimants solicitor's retainer. A separate action was necessary (*Skinner v Thames Valley & Aldershot Co Ltd*, July 7, 1995, unrep., CA).

In the absence of fraud, misrepresentation or mistake, the court does not have jurisdiction to revisit a consent order, which can only be set aside or amended in the most exceptional circumstances since it represents the contract between the parties: *Centrehigh Ltd v Amen*, July 18, 2001, unrep., Neuberger J.

Costs between parties are awarded as an indemnity to the party incurring them and a successful party cannot therefore recover a sum in excess of his liability to his own solicitor (*Gundry v Sainsbury* [1910] 1 K.B. 645). For the circumstances when costs can still be recovered even though it was never realistically expected that the successful party would pay his own solicitor, see *R. v Miller & Glennie* [1983] 1 W.L.R. 1056; [1983] 3 All E.R. 186, following *Adams v London Improved Motor Coach Builders Ltd* [1921] 1 K.B. 495; and *Commissioners of Customs and Excise v Valerian Raz and Portcullis (VAT Consultancy) Limited*, 1995 S.T.C. 14, Macpherson of Cluny J. See also *Hazlett v Sefton Metropolitan Borough Council*, [2000] 4 All E.R. 887, DC.

The Court of Appeal has repeatedly stated that, when making an order for costs, the judge should clearly state his reasons, particularly where the costs incurred are disproportionate to the amount in issue: see *English v Emery Reimbold & Strick Ltd* [2002] EWCA Civ 605; *Verrechia v Commissioner of Police for the Metropolis* [2002] EWCA Civ 605; [2002] 3 All ER 385 CA; *Lavelle v Lavelle* [2004] EWCA Civ 223, CA.

Rule 44.3(1)

It is open to a judge, where a split trial has been ordered, to reserve the question of costs of the trial on liability until after the determination of the remaining issues. The Court of Appeal stated that there was much to be said for the view that the incidence of costs should be the same whether or not there has been an order for a split trial. Where there is a split trial and it remains uncertain whether the claimant will recover more than nominal damages it may be proper for the trial judge to defer making any order for the costs of the liability trial until the final outcome is known (*Weill v Mean Fidler* [2003] EWCA Civ 1058). **44.3.6**

A public body (the CPS) is not insulated from the normal costs rules simply because it is a public body. In confiscation proceedings, where the CPS was held to have acted unreasonably in ignoring documentary evidence, the intervener was awarded her costs. The Court of Appeal stated that there was no need for a judge to refer to CPR r.44.3 provided that he followed the philosophy of it which required him to start with the proposition that the general rule was that the unsuccessful party should pay the costs of the successful party and then to consider whether any of the specific matters in r.44.3(4) took the case out of the ordinary rule and then to consider all the circumstances (*CPS v Grimes* [2003] EWCA Civ 1814).

Unless manifest injustice can be shown, the Court of Appeal will not disturb a costs order made by the judge at the invitation of the parties after they have settled their action save for costs. In all but straightforward cases a judge is entitled to say to the parties that if they have not reached an agreement on costs, they have not settled the dispute. Where the substantive issues have been compromised, the judge should be slow to embark on a determination of disputed facts solely in order to put himself in a position to make a decision about costs: *BCT Software Solutions Ltd v C Brewer & Sons Ltd* [2003] EWCA Civ 9399.

If, after a judge has given judgment one party submits that the judge has failed to deal with a point, the judge may make it clear that the submission is unsustainable but may decide to give a supplementary judgment in the interests of clarification. If the judge concludes that there is some substance in the party's point he should consider the materiality of the point and whether it undermines the decision reached. If necessary, the judge will have to give judgment again and may reach a different, or even the opposite conclusion. A judge is entitled to vary or reserve his order until the order is drawn. Accordingly he is entitled to give judgment again if the circumstances require that course: *Venture Finance Plc v Mead* [2005] EWCA Civ 325.

The Court of Appeal (Chadwick L.J.) offered further guidance for the future:

> "25. It does not, of course, follow that there will be no cases in which (absent a judgment after trial) the Judge will be in a position to make an order about costs. There will be cases (perhaps many cases) in which it will be clear that there was only one issue, that one party has been successful on that issue, and that conduct is not a factor which could displace the general rule. But, in such cases, the answer to the question which party should bear the costs of the litigation is likely to be so obvious that ... the Judge will not be asked to decide that question. It will be agreed as one of the terms of compromise."
>
> "26. The cases in which the Judge will be asked to decide questions of costs—following a compromise of the substantive issues—are likely to be those in which the answer is not obvious. And it may well be that, in many such cases, the answer is not obvious because it turns on facts which are not agreed between the parties and which have not been determined. The Judge should be slow to embark on the determination of disputed facts solely in order to put himself in a position to make a decision about costs ... the better course may be to require the parties to confront the realities of their litigation situation; to point out to them that, if they have not reached an agreement on costs, they have not settled their dispute and the action must proceed to judgment"

BCT Software above, quoted with approval in *Venture Finance Plc v Mead* [2005] EWCA Civ 325.

Where the subject matter of proceedings becomes academic during the course of the proceedings, leaving costs as the only issue, it is within the court's discretion whether or not it should consider the substantive issue in deciding any order as to costs. Unusual circumstances would have to exist before the court would consider an academic issue (*Arcadia Ventures Ltd v Longhurst* December 6, 2000, unrep., Mr T. Etherton, Q.C.).

There is no tradition that when a dispute is not judicially resolved the correct order is "no order as to costs". Thus where a claim settled without trial and the parties agreed the amount of profits to be paid by the defendant to the claimant without the necessity of an inquiry, the judge was entitled to make an order that the defendant should pay the claimants' costs: *Brawley v Marczynski* [2002] EWCA Civ 756.

Insolvency practitioners appealed against an order requiring them to pay personally the costs of an application by one of the creditors to remove them as administrators of a company. The judge, having read the evidence and heard full argument from counsel, made an order for the company to be compulsorily wound up, and terminated the administrators' appointment on their own application. Nothing remained of the creditor's application, except the question of costs. The judge ordered the administrators, and the managing director of the company, to pay the creditor's costs. The insolvency practitioners argued that the judge should not have made the order that he did without first giving them the opportunity of explaining the position from the witness box. On appeal the court held that the insolvency practitioners had no right to insist that before deciding the costs question the judge should hear oral evidence from and cross-examination of the witnesses. The judge was in principle entitled to embark on an assessment of the incidence of costs in a summary way: *Coyne v DRC Distribution Ltd* [2008] EWCA Civ 488; [2008] BCC 612 (CA).

Where a claimant obtained a without notice freezing order in an excessive amount which was the subject both of an application to discharge by the defendant and an application to vary by the claimant which failed, the claimant being ultimately successful in a smaller sum at trial, the court ordered that there should be no order as to costs in respect of the initial application for the freezing order, that the claimant should pay the defendant's costs of the application to discharge the order, that there be no order as to costs in respect of the claimant's unsuccessful application to vary and that the defendant should pay the claimant two thirds of its costs of trial: *Mr Biss v XOV Ltd* [2001] E.W. QBD, May 3, Holland J.

Judicial Review

44.3.7 The Administrative Court considered the powers of the court in relation to costs in judicial review proceedings concluded without a full hearing.The following principles were identified:

- (i) the court has power to make a costs order when the substantive proceedings have been resolved without a trial but the parties have not agreed about costs;
- (ii) it will normally be irrelevant that the claimant is LSC funded;
- (iii) the overriding objective is to do justice between the parties without incurring unnecessary court time and consequently additional cost;
- (iv) at each end of the spectrum there will be cases where it is obvious which side would have won had the substantive issues been fought to a conclusion. In between the position will, in differing degrees, be less clear. How far the court will be prepared to look into the previously unresolved substantive issues will depend on the circumstances of the particular case not least the amount of costs at that stage and the conduct of the parties;
- (v) in the absence of a good reason to make any other order, the fallback is to make no order as to costs;
- (vi) the court should take care to ensure that it does not discourage parties from settling judicial review proceedings, for example by a local authority making a concession at an early stage.

R. (Boxall) v Waltham Forest LBC (2001) 4 C.C.L. Rep. 258, Scott Baker J. This decision was approved in *R. (on the application of Kuzeva) v London Borough of Southwark* [2002] EWCA Civ 781; [2002] All E.R.(D) 488. (After *R. (Boxall) v Waltham Forest LBC* see also *Seray-Wurie v Attorney General*, March 22, 2007, unrep., P Girolami Q.C.)

The court has the power to make a costs order when the substantive proceedings have been resolved without a trial and the parties have not agreed about costs: *Bernard v Dudley MBC* [2003] EWHC 147 (Admin), Henriques J.

The Court of Appeal has given guidance on the proper approach to the award of costs against an unsuccessful claimant on an oral application for permission to apply for judicial review. The effect of CPR PD 54 (Judicial Review) para.8.6 is that a defendant who attends and successfully resists the grant of permission at a renewal hearing *should not* generally recover from the claimant his costs of and occasioned by doing so. The court, in considering an award against an unsuccessful claimant of the defendants' and/or any other interested party's costs at a permission hearing, should only depart from the general guidance in the Practice Direction if it considers there are exceptional circumstances for doing so. Exceptional circumstances may include:

(a) the hopelessness of the claim;
(b) the persistence in it by the claimant after its hopelessness has been demonstrated;
(c) the extent to which the court considers that the claimant has sought to abuse the process of judicial review;
(d) whether the unsuccessful claimant has had in effect the advantage of an early substantive hearing of the claim. A relevant factor for the court may be the extent to which the unsuccessful claimant has substantial resources which it has used to pursue the unfounded claim and which are available to meet an order for costs.

See *R. (on the application of Mount Cook Land Ltd) v Westminster City Council* [2003] EWCA Civ 1346; [2003] All E.R. (D) 222 and *R. (on the application of Payne) v Caerphilly CBC (Costs)* [2004] EWCA Civ 433.

The Court of Appeal has dealt with the question: whether as a matter of law or practice an order for costs made in favour of a successful respondent to judicial review proceedings includes costs incurred prior to the grant of the permission unless these are expressly excluded. The court gave the following guidelines:

1. On the conclusion of full judicial review proceedings in a defendant's favour, the nature and purpose of the particular claim is relevant to the exercise of the judges' discretion as to costs. In contrast to a judicial review claim brought wholly or mainly for commercial or proprietary reasons, a claim brought partly or wholly in the public interest, albeit unsuccessful, may properly result in a restricted or no order for costs.
2. If awarding costs against the claimant, the judge should consider whether they are to include preparation costs in addition to acknowledgment costs. It will be for the defendant to justify these. There may be no sufficient reason why such costs, if incurred, should be recoverable.
3. It is highly desirable that these questions should be dealt with by the trial judge and left to the Costs Judge only in relation to the reasonableness of individual items.
4. If at the conclusion of such proceedings the judge makes an undifferentiated order for costs in a defendant's favour:
   (a) the order has to be regarded as including any reasonably incurred preparation costs; but
   (b) the *Practice Statement (Judicial Review: Costs)* 2004 1 W.L.R. 1760 should be read so as to exclude any costs of opposing the grant of permission in open court, which should be dealt with on the Mount Cook principles (*R.. (on the application of Mount Cook Land Ltd) v Westminster City Council* [2003] EWCA Civ 1346). per Sedley L.J. in *R. (Davey) v Aylesbury Vale DC* [2007] EWCA Civ 1166; [2008] 1 W.L.R. 878, CA; [2008] 2 All E.R. 178, CA.

Sir Anthony Clarke MR held that an order for "the costs of the claim" means the "costs of and incidental to" the claim. Those costs can include costs incurred before issue of the proceedings.

The MR whilst agreeing with the guideline set out by Sedley L.J. added a note of caution, stating:

"29. It does seem to me that costs should ordinarily follow the event and that it is for the claimant who has lost to show that some different approach should be adopted on the facts of a particular case. That principle is supported by the decision and reasoning of Dyson J. in *R v Lord Chancellor ex p. Child Poverty Action Group* [1999] 1 WLR 347 at 355H–356E ... The basic rule he refers to is ... that costs follow the event in public law cases, as in others, because where an unsuccessful claim is brought against a public body, it imposes costs on that body which have to be met out of money diverted from the funds available to fulfil its primary public functions.

...

33. It seems to me that any defendant who incurs more cost at the permission stage than is contemplated by Carnwath L.J. will not be awarded such additional costs at the permission stage if the application is unsuccessful. Moreover, as I see it, the court should at that stage decline to look at anything which goes beyond the "summary of grounds" described in [*Ewing v Office of the Deputy Prime Minister* [2005] EWCA Civ 1583]. In these circumstances, I am not persuaded that the ap-

proach we have adopted in this case will give rise to a risk of defendants recovering more expense than is reasonable at the permission stage."

In a case where the claimant won on the single most important issue but failed on the facts, justice required that the second defendant should pay 35 per cent of her costs. The court held that the claimant had undoubtedly won a very real victory the fruits of which she would not have herself enjoyed but which would benefit those who came after her (*R. (Watts) v Bedford Primary Care Trust* [2003] EWHC 2401 (Admin) Mumby J.). Similarly in a test case on a point of construction of the Principal Civil Service Pension Scheme, the court held that it was wrong to leave the defendant, a man of insubstantial means, to bear his own costs and the Minister for the Civil Service was ordered to pay the defendant's costs of and incidental to the appeal (*Minister for the Civil Service v Oakes* [2003] EWHC 3314).

The Administrative Court has emphasised that practitioners should expect to observe the court operating a more robust approach to judicial review claims used inappropriately as a means of monitoring and regulating the performance by a public authority of its public duties and responsibilities. Practitioners could no longer expect the lenience shown in the instant case. Defaulting parties could expect to find their cases being summarily dismissed and lawyers to find themselves exposed to an application for wasted costs: *R. (on the application of B) v Lambeth LBC* [2006] EWHC 639, Admin, Munby J.

Rule 44.3(2)

44.3.8 The general rule is that the unsuccessful party will be ordered to pay the successful party's costs but different orders may be made. Relevant factors include: payments into court, offers to settle, the conduct of the parties and whether a party has lost an issue: *Firle Investments Ltd v Data Point International Ltd* [2001] EWCA Civ 1106, CA. The question of who was the successful party, or the unsuccessful party to an action could be determined by who ultimately wrote the cheque at the end: *Day v Day (Costs)* [2006] EWCA Civ 415.

A judge making an award of costs has essentially to determine whether to apply the general rule that costs follow the event, or award costs on an issue by issue basis. It is not appropriate to consider in that determination, a claimant's ability to recover damages in an action overall. In a case where the claimant had succeeded in two thirds of his pleaded causes of action and the trial had not been prolonged by the unsuccessful cause of action, it was appropriate that the costs should follow the event: *Fleming v Chief Constable of Sussex* [2004] EWCA Civ 643.

In a claim for professional negligence, in which the defendants were found to have been negligent and in breach of statutory duty but the claim had been dismissed since it was statute barred, the court held that the mere fact that the claimant had succeeded on some points did not of itself justify departing from the general rule. In the particular case the claimant's conduct was criticised, the various issues were intertwined and the court held that the case was not suitable for a split or issues based costs order. Nonetheless, using a broad brush approach, the court decided that it was appropriate to order the claimant to pay 75 per cent of the defendant's costs (*Shore v Sedgwick Financial Services Ltd* [2007] EWHC 3054 (QB) Beatson J.).

Where there is no clear overall successful or unsuccessful party the general rule that costs follow the event may not apply. Where there has been no unreasonable conduct by either party in the litigation, and both sides have made attempts at different times and stages to resolve the matter, it may be appropriate to make no order for costs: *Cantor Gaming Ltd v Gameaccount Global Ltd* [2007] EWHC 25 September (Ch) Daniel Alexander QC. Where a claimant sues two defendants in the alternative and succeeds against only one, the court has a discretion to order the unsuccessful defendant to pay the successful defendant's costs. This may be done by an order that the unsuccessful defendant pay the successful defendant's costs directly to him (a *Sanderson* Order: *Sanderson v Blyth Theatre Company* [1903] 2 K.B. 533, CA) or by an order that the claimant pay the successful defendant's costs to him and recover them from the unsuccessful defendant as part of the claimant's costs of the action (a *Bullock* Order: *Bullock v London General Omnibus Co* [1907] 1 K.B. 264, CA). There are no hard and fast rules as to when it is appropriate to make a *Sanderson* Order. The court will consider the extent to which the claimant has behaved reasonably in suing two defendants since it would be hard if the claimant ended up paying the costs of the defendant against whom he had not succeeded. Equally it is not reasonable to join one defendant because the action is practically unsustainable. It would be unjust to make a co-defendant pay that defendant's costs which should be borne by the claimant. Ultimately it is a question for the discretion of the trial judge. *Moon v Garrett* [2006] EWCA Civ 1121. A *Bullock* or *Sanderson* Order is appropriate only in those cases where the claimant did not know which party was at fault and it was inappropriate to make either order when both defendants had succeeded in defending a large part of the claim. It would also be contrary to the objective of CPR r.44.3 to make a qualified *Bullock* or *Sanderson* Order: *Whitehead v Searle & Hibbert Pownall & Newton* [2007] EWHC 2046 (QB), Griffith Williams J. A claimant in a libel action sued three defendants but failed to establish malice against two of them. The unsucessful defendant was ordered to pay two thirds of the claimant's costs on the standard basis but the claimant was ordered to pay one quarter of the sucessful defendants' costs (the proportion was reduced because of the conduct of one of the defendants). There had never been any question of any of the three defendants blaming the others: *Rackham v Sandy (Costs)* [2005] EWHC 1354. Where a claimant sued three defendants for personal injuries arising out of breach of statutory duty, the judge was entitled to conclude that the claimant should pay the costs of the two defendants against whom the claims had failed. The Court of Appeal held that the jurisdiction to make a Sanderson order had survived the introduction of the CPR. The judge had to be guided by the overriding objective and by CPR Pt 44 and it had to be recognised that it was capable of working injustice against a successful defendant. In deciding whether to order an unsuccessful defendant to pay the costs of a successful defendant the relevant factors included: whether the claim against the successful defendant had been made "in the alternative"; whether the causes of action had been connected with those on which the claimant had been successful; and whether it had been reasonable for the claimant to join and pursue a claim against the successful defendant. The fact that one defendant blamed another could be a significant factor, but whether it was reasonable to join that defendant and pursue the claim depended on the facts of the case and whether the claimant could in fact sustain such a claim: *Irvine v Commissioner of Police for the Metropolis* [2005] EWCA Civ 129. A defendant who was sued by an impecunious claimant joined another party as a Pt 20 defendant in order to protect its position. The claim against the defendant was dismissed and the Pt 20 claim also had to be dismissed. The defendant complained that if it were ordered to pay the Pt 20 defendants' costs it would be doubly out of pocket since there was no prospect of recovery from the claimant. The Court of Appeal referred to the decision in *Johnson v Ribbins* [1977] 1 W.L.R. 1458 where the Court of Appeal had found that it could not be right to deprive a third party of an order for costs, to which he was otherwise entitled against the defendant, because the defendant, when looking to the claimant for reimbursement, found a person "not worth powder and shot". In the ordinary run of cases under CPR the same principle will be applied. A successful Pt 20 defendant should not be deprived of his prima facie right to an order for costs against a Pt 20 claimant merely on the ground of the claimant's impecuniosity. On the facts of the case the court ordered that on the assessment of the defendants' and Pt 20 defendants' costs, an enquiry should be made into the costs incurred by certain parties in and about instructing experts, whether such experts were to act in an evidentiary or an advisory role, such costs to include the legal costs associated with giving such instructions. Once the total of those costs have been ascertained they should be borne equally as to one sixth share each, subject to that the six parties should bear their own costs both in the main proceedings and in the Pt 20 proceedings: *Arkin v Borchard Lines Ltd* [2005] EWCA Civ 555.

The court, when refusing to make a *Bullock Order*, pointed out that the CPR encouraged the court to make issue based costs orders that reflected a more detailed analysis of success and failure and in particular to make costs orders in respect of certain periods or by reference to certain issues or by way of percentages: *McGlinn v Waltham Contractors Ltd* [2007] EWHC 698 (TCC), Coulson J.

In judicial review proceedings the court stated that there were judicial review cases where public interest or analogous considerations made it inappropriate to require an unsuccessful claimant to pay a defendant's costs. There was however no bright line distinction between judicial review cases which did or did not involve a public interest challenge, nor was the presence or absence of any private interest a determining factor with regard to costs. A more flexible and nuanced approach was indicated by the statutory duty to have regard to all the circumstances. There could be different degrees under a wide spectrum of public interest mixed with what might be a greater or lesser amount of private interest: *Smeaton v Secretary of State for Health* [2002] EWHC 866 (Admin), Munby J.

The general rule may be set aside, for example at the conclusion of lengthy complex proceedings involving a mother and son with some moderation in favour of the claimant in the light of the particular circumstances: *Neave v Neave* [2002] EWHC 966, QB, Holland J. Where a disorganised testator had unintentionally lost or destroyed his will, giving rise to litigation on his death, the court held it appropriate to order that the costs of both sides should be paid out of the estate: *Rowe v Clarke* [2006] EWHC 1292 (Ch), May 10, 2006, Mark Herbert Q.C.

A Pt 36 payment or offer should be regarded as the best to which a party is prepared to go, and if a claimant recovers more than the payment, he is entitled to his costs and should not be deprived of them by reason of a comparison with his Pt 36 offer: *Quorum A/S v Schramm*, November 21, 2001, unrep., Thomas J.

In a case where a defendant was successful on its counterclaim but was held by the judge to have unreasonably pursued two discrete issues as part of its case and was therefore penalised in costs, the Court of Appeal held that although the defendant had not succeeded on the two issues identified by the judge it had not acted unreasonably in pursuing them. There was therefore nothing in the facts of the case which justified departure from the general rule that the successful party should be awarded the whole of its costs: *Spice Girls Ltd v Aprilla World Service BV* [2002] EWCA Civ 15.

Where the ordinary costs order is departed from it is incumbent on the judge to give reasons, albeit short, for that departure. *Brent LBC v Anienobe* November 24, 1999, unrep., CA.

The task for the judge is to take an overview of the case as a whole and reach a conclusion based on two questions: (i) who succeeded in the action and (ii) what order for costs does justice require? *B.C.C.I. SA v Ali (No.3)* (1999) 149 N.L.J. 1734.

Where a defendant company successfully defended a claim against it but the trial judge rejected all the oral evidence except for that of three witnesses including the defendant's major shareholder and effective director, it was appropriate to make an order for costs in the Defendant's favour since a restriction on the recovery of the defendant's costs would be to the detriment of the shareholders and the person whose conduct had been exonerated. A conventional order was therefore made under rule 44.3(2)(a): *International Commercial Finance (UK) Ltd v Knitwear Ltd* [2001] EWHC, Ch, June 18, 2001, Hedley J.

Where the court imposed an order for costs on setting aside a judgment in default of appearance, it was held on appeal that the decision to impose such a sanction on a party was a matter for the discretion of the judge hearing the application and would only be varied on appeal if the order was wrong in law or unjust by reason of a serious procedural or other irregularity in the proceedings before the judge: *Gore v Jones*, *The Times*, February 21, 2001, Pumfrey J.

Costs Against a Regulatory Body

44.3.8.1 A regulator brings proceedings in the public interest in the exercise of a public function which it is required to perform. In those circumstances the principles applicable to an award of costs differ from those in relation to private civil litigation. Absent dishonesty or a lack of good faith a costs order should not be made against such a regulator unless there is good reason to do so. That reason must be more than that the other party has succeeded. In considering making such an order the court must consider, on the one hand, the financial prejudice to the particular complainant, weighed against the need to encourage public bodies to exercise their public function of making reasonable and sound decisions, without fear of exposure to undue financial prejudice, if the decision is successfully challenged (see *Gorlov v Institute of Chartered Accountants* [2001] EWHC 220 (Admin), Jackson J., and *City of Bradford MDC v Booth* [2000] COD 338, Lord Bingham C.J.). On the facts the appellant was ordered to pay 60 per cent of The Law Society's costs before the tribunal. He had brought the proceedings upon himself, was unsuccessful and had been suspended. The Law Society had successfully vindicated the integrity of the profession: *Baxendale-Walker v The Law Society* [2006] EWHC 643 (Admin); [2006] 3 All E.R. 675, Moses L.J. and Stanley Burnton J. On appeal the Court of Appeal considered whether there was a conflict between the above decision and that in *Law Society v Adcock* [2006] EWHC 3212 (Admin). Having analysed the authorities the Court of Appeal agreed with Moses L.J. The order of the court below was not disturbed: *Baxendale-Walker v The Law Society* [2007] EWCA Civ 233; [2007] 3 All E.R. 330.

The Privy Council has held that the principles to be derived from the authorities (*Bradford MDC v Booth* [2000] 164 J.P. 485 DC; *R (on the application of Gorlov) v Institute of Chartered Accountants of England and Wales* [2001] EWHC Admin 220; [2001] A.C.D. 73; and *Baxendale-Walker v Law Society* [2007] EWCA Civ 233; [2008] 1 W.L.R. 426) concerned the different position of costs before disciplinary tribunals or before a court upon a first appeal against an administrative decision by, e.g. a regulatory authority. In a case in which the Disciplinary Committee of the Royal College of Veterinary Surgeons made no order for costs in respect of the proceedings before it which had not been challenged, the Board, in practice, made costs orders against the authority when an appeal succeeded and in favour of the authority in the case of unsuccessful appeals. Where appeals failed on liability, but succeeded on penalty, no orders for costs were made. There was no reason to depart from the Board's previous practice. The Board rejected an argument that a split order should be made because certain submissions had not been accepted and the fact that the appeal had been supported by an appeal fund raised by other members of the profession did not constitute a reason why the costs order should be less than complete (*Walker v Royal College of Veterinary Surgeons (Costs)* [2008] UKPC 20).

Official Solicitor

Where the Official Solicitor acted as a litigation friend to someone who was incapacitated it was in the court's discretion to order costs against the claimant even where the claimant had not been unsuccessful as such. The Official Solicitor brought his skill and experience to bear in such cases in the public interest. Although the costs burden to be borne by the paying party might be severe it was likely that it would only be involved in very few such cases. On the other hand the Official Solicitor was necessarily involved in every such case, and if he could not recover any costs from NHS Trusts the burden would be beyond his budget. The Official Solicitor had no enhanced right to seek his costs, but was entitled to apply for them in the usual way. In medical treatment cases it was usual for the claimant NHS Trust to pay a proportion of its costs and this would normally be one half: *X NHS Trust v J* [2005] EWHC 1273; [2006] Lloyds Rep Med 180 Munby J. (Fam). **44.3.8.2**

Admiralty Court

There is no rule or principle in Admiralty Court cases, where there is no counterclaim, that a claimant who is found at fault under ss.187(1) and (2) of the Merchant Shipping Act 1995 should recover its costs in proportion to the percentage of liability of the defendant. The fact that the claimant had recovered only 70 per cent of the claim, having been found 30 per cent to blame, was not sufficient reason within rule 44.3(4)(b) or otherwise to reduce the costs awarded to the claimant. There was no basis on which the court could legitimately make an issues based order and the defendant's conduct, including their failure to make an offer at any stage, their late change of case and the unsatisfactory evidence of their two main witnesses reinforced the award of costs in favour of the claimant: *"Krysia" Maritime Inc v Intership Ltd* [2008] EWHC 1880 (Admlty) Aikens J. **44.3.8.3**

Rule 44.3(4)(a) Conduct

The rule sets out the factors to which the court must have regard to when considering what order to make about costs. These factors include the conduct of all the parties which is further analysed at r.44.3(5). See the Directions relating to Pt 36 (see para.36PD.1) in respect of offers and payments under that Part. **44.3.9**

Litigants need to be encouraged to be selective as to the points they take and the extent of costs recovery is an incentive for responsible behaviour: *Base Metal Trading Ltd v Shamurin* [2003] EWHC 2419 (Comm) (Tomlinson J.) and see *Kastor Navigation Co Ltd v AGF MAT (The Kastor Too) (Costs)* [2003] EWHC 472 (Comm) (Tomlinson J.). and *Kastor Navigation Co Ltd v Axa Global Risks (UK) Ltd (The Kastor Too)* [2004] EWCA Civ 277.

Where the court found there were reasonable grounds for suspecting undue influence in proceedings to prove a will the unsuccessful defendant was required to pay only half the claimant's costs: in *Good (Deceased) (Costs), Re* [2002] EWHC 640, Rimer J.

The judge should consider whether or not the parties have conducted the litigation in accordance with a system of civil litigation which is designed to enable the parties to know where they stand at the earliest possible stage and at the lowest practicable cost, so that they may make informed decisions about their prospects and the sensible conduct of their cases. *Ford v GKR Construction Ltd*, [2000] 1 W.L.R. 1397, CA; see also note at 36.20.2; and *Amec Process & Energy Ltd v Stork Engineers and Contractors BV (Costs Order)* [2000] B.L.R. 70.

In proceedings arising out of a road accident the claimant made an offer, before the proceedings were commenced, to settle on the basis of 95% to 5 per cent split on liability. The defendant rejected this offer and the defendant was found to be 100 per cent liable at trial. At first instance the judge refused to award the claimant costs on the indemnity basis because the offer was unrealistic. The Court of Appeal found that this was irrelevant to the exercise of discretion under CPR r.36.21 and there was nothing unjust in allowing that rule to have its ordinary effect. The claimant was therefore awarded costs on the indemnity basis: *Huck v Robson* [2002] EWCA Civ 398; [2002] 3 All E.R. 263, CA.

In a successful claim brought by the client against the solicitors who had acted for him in litigation, the solicitors joined counsel instructed by them in the original action as a third party. On appeal the solicitors were found to be liable as to 80 per cent and counsel as to 20 per cent of the damages awarded. The solicitors argued that costs should be apportioned in the same percentages. The court held that the costs order should reflect the fact that the matter should not have been defended by the solicitors and that both the solicitors and counsel had entered into an unnecessary and costly mud slinging contest. The solicitors were ordered to pay the full costs of the trial. Counsel was ordered to pay 20 per cent of the Pt 20 proceedings. The solicitors were required to pay one third of their own costs of the appeal, the balance to be paid by counsel: *Moy v Pettman Smith (A Firm) (Costs)* [2003] EWCA Civ 467; [2003] P.N.L.R. 31, CA.

Exaggeration and false claims

44.3.10 The Court of Appeal has examined the position as to what costs, if any, are reasonably incurred by a claimant in pursuing a claim for damages for personal injuries which he or she knows (or must be taken to know) have not been suffered and also the practice as to how the paying party is to go about challenging the reasonableness of incurring costs, when this may depend upon disputed facts, but the case has quite properly been settled. Although the decision related to the proper approach under RSC Order 62 r.12 it is suggested that similar principles will apply under the CPR. The court stated that the Costs Judge should start by going through the bill of costs and ruling out all those items considered to be unjustified (for example almost all other medical fees, costs of retaining Leading Counsel, etc). This would leave some items which were plainly reasonable as items even if questionable in amount and other items where it would be difficult if not impossible to disentangle what was reasonable from what was unreasonable even having regard to the way in which the rule required that doubt to be resolved. The court stated that at that stage, but not at any earlier stage, it would be appropriate for the Costs Judge to consider awarding a percentage of the sum claimed. The percentage awarded would have to be such that, at the end of the exercise, the total sum awarded by way of costs could be regarded as reasonable having regard to the amount of damages obtained. The court quoted with approval Judge L.J. in *Ford v GKR Construction Ltd* [2000] 1 W.L.R. 1397:

> "If the judge had concluded that the claimant had been demonstrated by the video evidence to be a malinger, dishonestly exaggerating her symptoms, I have little doubt that he would have taken the view that, even if the video evidence had arrived late, the claimant should not be permitted to escape the consequences of the revelation, even late, of her attempted fraud ...
>
> Every case and every consequential costs order depends upon the individual facts of the case."

A claimant who pursues an exaggerated and inflated claim for damages must expect to bear the consequences when his costs come to be assessed. In the absence of special circumstances a claimant who knows, or must be taken to know, that his claim for damages is unsustainable, in whole or in part, cannot be heard to assert that a defendant who has disclosed evidence which establishes the unsustainability of the claim ought to have disclosed that evidence at an earlier stage in the proceedings: *Booth v Britannia Hotels Ltd* [2002] EWCA Civ 579.

A claimant who sought £3.75 million damages accepted an open offer of £38,000 with no interest, with the question of costs to be left to the court. The court, considering the claimant's conduct, stated that the correct order was no order as to costs. The claimant could not be said to have achieved a significant win. The claim had been exaggerated throughout and the particulars of claim were not properly based on expert evidence. The offer had been made as a nuisance payment to get rid of the action. *Hooper* v Biddle & Co [2006] EWHC 2995, October 1, 2006, Ch, Susan Prevezer Q.C.

The Court of Appeal upheld an order that an insolvency practitioner should pay half the costs of a creditor in an application to set aside an individual voluntary arrangement since the insolvency practitioner's conduct had fallen far below that of a reasonable practitioner. *Smurthwaite v Simpson-Smith* [2006] EWCA Civ 1183.

Where a claimant had been found intentionally to have exaggerated her claim, the fact that she was awarded more than the Pt 36 payment made by the defendant was not the guiding factor in awarding costs. The defendant could be viewed as the overall winning party since the court was bound to take into account the conduct of the parties and the absence by the claimant of any intention to settle the matter. A claimant who had made no attempt to negotiate should expect the court to take that failure into account when determining costs. To commence and lose a matter on the ground that the claim was exaggerated, without making any attempt to settle was a deciding factor. The defendant was ordered to pay the claimant's costs down to the date of payment into court and the claimant was ordered to pay all the defendant's costs thereafter: *Painting v University of Oxford* [2005] EWCA Civ 161; *The Times*, February 15, 2005 CA. A claimant who sought more than £1 million damages was found at trial to have exaggerated his disability. The defendant had made a Pt 36 offer of £50,000. At trial the judge awarded damages of £55,000 and ordered the defendant to pay 75 per cent of the claimant's costs. The Court of Appeal declined to amend the order, finding that the judge had not exercised his discretion in a manner that was plainly wrong. The court stated that it remained open for the defendant, at detailed assessment, to challenge any costs incurred by the claimant insofar as they were unreasonably incurred in pursuing the claim to the extent to which it was exaggerated: *Jackson v Ministry of Defence* [2006] EWCA Civ 46.

Where a claimant sought damages of £610,000 for breach of duty under a service agreement and accepted a payment into court of £5,000 and abandoned the remaining claim the claimant was ordered to pay the defendant's costs, save for that relating to the payment in, which the defendant was ordered to pay in accordance with CPR Pt 27: *E Ivor Hughes Education Foundation v Leach* [2005] EWHC 1317, Ch, Peter Smith J.

It is not open to a judge to cut down the costs of the successful party under CPR r.44.3(4) merely because that party had not done as well as he had hoped. In the particular case the initial exaggeration of the claim had had no real effect on the costs of the action. The defendant had not achieved any partial success which might entitle her to an abatement of the claimant's costs (*Hall v Stone* [2007] EWCA Civ 1354).

The Court of Appeal granted permission to appeal on costs where the judge at first instance had found that the parties who were the real "winners" had been guilty of serious dishonesty. He made an order for costs with a reduction to reflect the dishonesty which he had found. The Court of Appeal stated:

> "It is well worthy of consideration by the Court of Appeal whether, where an ultimately successful party has, on the way to success, lied and sought to maintain forgeries and in other ways been thoroughly dishonest and moreover has greatly lengthened the trial in having these matters exposed, the usual rules as to costs are displaced."

The court drew the attention of the parties to *Aaron v Shelton* [2004] EWHC 1162, Jack J, which seemed to indicate that if a paying party were going to rely on the conduct or misconduct of the receiving party in order to seek a reduction in the costs to be paid, the time to raise that factor was at the end of the trial and not before the Costs Judge at the time of the assessment. Although as a result of a concession the principle in *Aaron v Shelton* was no longer material in the appeal, the court went on to comment that the decision of Jack J. on the facts was correct in principle, but that the statement of principle could be said to go further than the decision in the case required and was too broadly stated. As to the correct approach the court stated:

> "33. Clearly there is no problem if the judge's order makes 'no order as to costs', but if the judge orders a reduction by say 20% without more, what would be the natural construction of that order? My view is that the natural construction of such an order, unless the contrary is expressly stated, is that the party guilty of dishonesty should not be entitled to say on the assessment, my costs incurred in seeking to make a dishonest case can be taken as reasonably incurred because the judge has made a reduction. If the dishonest party was entitled to succeed on such an argument, he will hardly suffer any penalty at all.
>
> 34. It seems to me that consideration of a party's conduct should normally take place both at the stage when the judge is considering what order for costs he should make, and then during assessment. But the court will want to ensure that

dishonesty is penalised but that the party is not placed in double jeopardy. Ultimately, the question is one of the proper construction of the order made by the judge. Thus it will be important for the judge who is asked to take dishonesty into account at the end of a trial when considering the order for costs, to consider what is likely to occur on assessment. Where dishonest conduct is being reflected in an order made by the trial judge, it must be wise for the future for judges to make clear whether they are making the order on the basis that, on the assessment, the paying party will still be entitled to raise the dishonesty in arguing that costs incurred in supporting the particular dishonesty were unreasonably incurred. Judges may also want to consider whether to make an order under Rule 44.14 and it would be wise to do that before considering precisely what order to make in relation to the costs of a trial generally."

Northstar Systems Ltd v Fielding [2006] EWCA Civ 1660.

The court has held that it is an abuse of process, to seek to raise before the Costs Judge on an assessment, matters that could and should have been litigated before the court. The paying party was not permitted to raise, by way of points of dispute, precisely the same allegations that it had made in the pre-action protocol procedure but had not pursued in the action after the protocol had run its course: *Drukker & Co v Pridie Brewster & Co* [2005] EWHC 2788, QB, Openshaw J. (see also 44.3.13).

Where a claimant with a back injury had sought damages of £150,000 and accepted a Pt 36 payment of £4,000, the defendants argued that the district judge should allow the claimant no more than 25 per cent of the costs claimed. The district judge correctly held that he had no power to do what was suggested but made significant reductions during the course of the assessment. On appeal the Court of Appeal upheld the decision at first instance and stated:

"20. There is a real distinction between (a) carrying out an assessment and deciding *as part of the assessment* to reduce the bill by a percentage, and (b) deciding *in advance of the assessment* that the receiving party will only receive a percentage of the assessed costs. The figure that results from (a) represents 100% of the assessed costs. In deciding as part of the assessment to reduce the bill by a percentage the Costs Judge is giving effect to an order that the successful party is entitled to his costs to be assessed if not agreed. The figure that results from (b) represents less than 100% of the assessed costs. In deciding in advance of the assessment that the receiving party will only receive a percentage of the assessed costs the Costs Judge is not giving effect to an order that the successful party is entitled to his costs to be assessed if not agreed."

Lahey v Pirelli [2007] EWCA Civ 91.

The Court of Appeal held that in a case where both the claim and the counterclaim were at the small claims level, the fact that the defendant had brought and persisted in an additional hopeless counterclaim which caused the action to be allocated to the multi track, the defendant's conduct had resulted in the claimant incurring substantially more costs than would otherwise have been the case and the judge at first instance was plainly wrong in not taking that into account as a relevant factor when he made no order as to costs. The defendant was ordered to pay 50 per cent of the claimant's costs from the date of allocation to the multi track: *Peakman v Linbrooke Services Ltd* [2008] EWCA Civ 1239.

Rule 44.3(4)(b) success

44.3.11 In deciding what order for costs to make following an action, the court is entitled to take into account whether a party has succeeded on part of the case even if not wholly successful; the other party's reasonableness in raising, pursuing or contesting a particular allegation or issue is not necessarily relevant or a pre-condition to taking that factor into account. The defendant having been successful on two out of three issues, the claimant was awarded a percentage its costs: *Stocznia Gdanska SA v Latvian Shipping Co, The Times*, May 8, 2001, Thomas J.

In deciding what order for costs to make, the court must take into account the extent to which a party has succeeded, both in respect of it counterclaim and the level of success in relation to the defence of the claimant's claim. The court must also take into account any open offer of settlement which has been made, as well as the conduct of the parties: *Dick Van Dijk v Wilkinson T/A HFF Construction* [2001] EWCA Civ 1780.

In a case where the claimant succeeded on some issues, failed on others and abandoned still others, the Court of Appeal held that it was open to the judge to award the claimant a proportion of the costs in respect of those issues in which it had succeeded, but in respect of the abandoned issues these should have been left to the Costs Judge. Those costs should be disallowed on detailed assessment as costs unreasonably incurred in the litigation. (*Shirley v Caswell* [2000] Lloyd's Rep. P.N. 955; [2001] 1 Costs L.R. 1.).

The Civil Procedure Rules permit an order to be made for payment of a proportion of a party's costs. The decision in *Shirley v Caswell* above did not limit the court's power to make such an order: *Dooley v Parker* [2002] EWCA Civ 1188, Dyson L.J. stated that he did not read *Shirley v Caswell* as laying down any broad statement of principle other than that an order should not penalise a party twice over. If an order is made disallowing part of a receiving party's costs then the Costs Judge must take account of that fact when making the assessment of costs, and take great care to make sure that a double penalty is not imposed. There should be no difficulty about this since the Costs Judge should know from the terms of the judgment ordering payment of a proportion of a party's costs that that is what the trial judge did and the reasons why it was done. In a case in which there was a claim (for the return of a motor vehicle) and a counterclaim (for the cost of repairs) and where the claimant abandoned various issues during the course of proceedings, resulting in judgment being entered for the defendant on the counterclaim, the Court of Appeal held that, given the nature of the abandoned allegations, there must have been a notional increase in the costs to both parties. The court ordered the claimant to pay one half of the defendant's costs after the date on which the Defendant had returned the claimant's property to him: *Darougar v Belcher* [2002] EWCA Civ 1262.

In the majority of cases the court will make an order that the claimant should pay the defendant's costs of a case which is struck out, but where the order is for the claimants to have their costs of the action up to a certain date *Shirley v Caswell* (above) requires that, unless the judge has some specific reason for interfering or intervening, he can make an order leaving the question of assessment to the Costs Judge. On an assessment the Costs Judge will in any event disallow the costs of any claims which were positively struck out as well as disallowing costs in respect of issues abandoned or not pursued: *Nugent v Michael Goss Aviation* [2002] EWHC 1281 (QB), Burton J.

The Court of Appeal has stated that the provisions of rule 44.3(4) are inconsistent with any inflexible rule governing the costs of claim and counterclaim such as that in *Medway Oil v Continental Contractors* [1929] A.C. 88. The court declined to comment as to what should be the general approach to such a situation or even whether there should be a general approach (rule 46.3(6) makes provision for the allowance of costs where at a fast track trial the claimant succeeds on the claim and the defendant succeeds on the counterclaim): *Gould v Armstrong* [2002] EWCA Civ 1159.

The court (Patten J.) has had to consider how to divide the common costs of action in a case where the trial judge had ordered the defendant to pay the claimant's costs of the action, save for three specific items of costs. Patten J. stated:

> "3. The CPR make no special provision for dealing with costs of this type and some of the difficulties in the assessment of these costs arise directly from a common failure by judges to appreciate the complexities which can be created by orders which seek to split the responsibility for costs between the parties other than by an order for the payment of a simple percentage or proportion of the total costs bill."

The parties agreed that the costs order did not differ materially in its terms from the type of order considered by the Court of Appeal in *Cinema Press Ltd v Pictures & Pleasures Ltd* [1945] K.B. 356 which in turn applied the earlier decision of the House of Lords in *Medway Oil & Storage Co v Continental Contractors Ltd* [1929] A.C. 88. Patten J. decided:

> "50. The decision in *Medway* applied in *Cinema Press* establishes that on a taxation of common costs ... it is appropriate to attribute part of a composite fee to the items of work which the fee was intended to cover ... The same goes for the time spent on preparing parts of witness statements which deal separately and exclusively with [a particular] issue. But what the decision in *Medway* does not do is to authorise the [Costs Judge] in a case like the present, to apportion the costs of work all of which is relevant to both claims."

The judge concluded:

> "57. ... Instead the Costs Judge must analyse all the work done and claimed for in accordance with the *Medway* principles set out."
>
> *Dyson Technology Ltd v Strutt* [2007] EWHC 1756, Ch, Patten J.

The correct approach in principle in money claims is that it is important to identify the party who has to pay money to another when deciding what order for costs to make where both the claim and counterclaim are successful. Where the value of a defendant's counterclaim amounted to one quarter of the claimant's claim the Court of Appeal quashed an order that the claimant should pay the defendant's costs on the counterclaim and ordered the defendant to pay 75 per cent of the claimant's costs of the claim and counterclaim taken together: *ACT Construction v Mackie* [2005] EWCA Civ 1336.

Rule 44.3(4)(c) offers to settle

44.3.12 The Civil Procedure (Amendment No.3) Rules 2006 make a significant amendment to r.44.3(4)(c) so that it applies only to an offer to which the costs consequences under Pt 36 do not apply. Accordingly the text below must be read as applying only to offers made before the date of the amendment (April 6, 2007). Note that a corresponding amendment has been made to para.8.4 of the Costs Practice Direction.

There are compelling reasons of principle and policy why those prepared to make genuine offers of monetary settlement should do so by way of Pt 36 payments rather than written offers. Pt 36 payments offer greater clarity and certainty about (1) genuineness; (2) ability to pay; (3) whether the offer was open or without prejudice; and (4) the terms on which the dispute could be settled.

Where the defendant permitted the claimant to accept the payment in but did not agree costs. The judge ruled that the claimant was entitled to recover part only of the costs. The Court of Appeal held that the presumption that a claimant who fails to better a Pt 36 payment should be treated as the unsuccessful party can be dislodged in special circumstances, as where the defendant has withheld material and not allowed the claimant to make a proper appraisal of the defendant's case, but there was no principle that a defendant, at fault for failure to amend his case in time, should provide the claimant with additional time for accepting the payment in: *Factortame Ltd v Secretary of State for Transport, Local Government and the Regions* [2002] EWCA Civ 22; [2002] 1 W.L.R. 2438, CA.

Where a defendant made a written offer to settle the claimant's claim and made two subsequent Pt 36 payments it was held to be an error of principle outside the wide discretion given by r.44.3 to treat the defendant's written offer as if it were a Pt 36 payment made in a case in which the defendant had succeeded on all issues of trial. The written offer was relevant to the exercise of the discretion and on the particular facts of the case the claimant was ordered to pay half of the defendant's costs for the period, and notwithstanding that no Pt 36 payment which exceeded the judgment had been made until a late date, in the light of the unreasonable manner in which the claimant had conducted the claim there was ample justification for depriving the claimant of his costs for the period: *Amber v Stacey* [2001] 1 W.L.R. 1225; [2001] 2 All E.R. 88; [2001] C.P. Rep. 26, CA.

Rule 44.3(5) more about conduct

44.3.13 In deciding how to apportion costs to reflect the conduct of the parties in proceedings the judge should structure the judgment on costs around the provisions of CPR r.44.3 which require the court to take into account "the conduct of the parties". The introduction of the CPR does not affect the pre-existing law which entitles a judge to consider any relevant aspect of the conduct of the parties including their conduct in relation to the matters which gave rise to the litigation (see *Donald Campbell & Co Ltd v Pollak* [1927] A.C. 732). Although the practice of the Commercial Court (see *Hall v Rover Financial Services (GB) Ltd* [2002] EWCA Civ 1514) is not to disallow a successful party its costs simply because of anterior dishonest conduct which "while it was part of the transaction which gave rise to the proceedings, could not be characterised as misconduct in relation to the proceedings themselves", that was no more than a matter of practice. On their proper construction CPR r.44.3(4)(a) and (5)(a) do not contain any limitation such as would shut out reliance, in an appropriate case, on misconduct in and about the matters which triggered the litigation (*Groupama Insurance Co Ltd v Overseas Partners Re Ltd (Costs)* [2003] EWCA Civ 1846).

It is a lawyer's duty to further the overriding objective under r.1.1. If parties *turned down* ADR out of hand they may suffer the consequences when costs come to be decided. Where a defendant had been confident of success and had therefore felt that there could be no benefit in resorting to ADR, it was not willing to do so. Although successful in the proceedings no order for costs was made: *Dunnett v Railtrack Plc* [2002] EWCA Civ 303; [2002] 1 W.L.R. 2434, CA.

Where a defendant government department had not stood by a formal pledge, given on behalf of all government departments, to settle by alternative dispute resolution whenever possible, it was found not to be entitled to its costs even though successful on the main issue. The court made no order as to costs *Royal Bank of Scotland v Secretary of State for Defence*, May 14, 2003, unrep. (Lewison J.).

However, this decision was disapproved in *Halsey v Milton Keynes General NHS Trust* below.

Where a successful party had refused to agree to ADR, despite the court's encouragement, that was a fact that the court would take into account when deciding whether his refusal was unreasonable. The court went on to decide that there was no basis for the court to discriminate against successful public bodies when deciding whether a refusal to agree to ADR should result in a cost penalty. The "ADR" pledge announced in March 2001 by the Lord Chancellor was no more than an undertaking that ADR would be considered and used whenever the other party accepts it in all suitable cases by all Government departments and agencies. It was difficult to see in what circumstances it would be right to give great weight to the pledge. The court's role was to encourage not compel ADR. It was likely that compulsion of ADR would be regarded by the European Court of Human Rights as an unacceptable constraint on the right of access to court and therefore a violation of art.6 ECHR.

Although the fact that the court could not order disclosure of without prejudice negotiations against the wishes of one of the parties, could mean that the court would not be able to decide whether a party had been unreasonable in refusing mediation, it was always open to a party to make open or Calderbank offers of ADR, and the other party could respond to such offers either openly or in Calderbank form. If a party gave a good reason why it thought ADR would not serve a useful purpose, that was one thing, if it failed to do so, that was a matter which the court might consider relevant although not conclusive in exercising its discretion as to costs. The reasonableness or otherwise of going to ADR could be fairly and squarely debated between the parties, and under the Calderbank procedure, made available to the court when the question of costs came to be considered (*Reed Executive Plc v Reed Business Information Ltd (No.2)* [2004] EWCA Civ 887; [2004] 4 All ER 942, CA).

In *Halsey v Milton Keynes General NHS Trust* [2004] EWCA Civ 576; [2004] 4 All E.R. 920, CA, the Court of Appeal addressed the question of ADR in greater detail. The court indicated that the burden was on the unsuccessful party to show why there should be a departure from the general rule on costs, in the form of an order to deprive the successful party of some or all of his costs on the grounds that he refused to agree to ADR. A fundamental principal was that such a departure was not justified unless it had been shown that the successful party had acted unreasonably in refusing to agree to ADR. In deciding whether a party had acted unreasonably the court should bear in mind the advantages of ADR over the court process and have regard to all the circumstances of the particular case. The factors that could be relevant included:

(i) the nature of the dispute;
(ii) the merits of the case;
(iii) the extent to which other settlement methods had been attempted;
(iv) whether the costs of ADR were disproportionately high;
(v) whether any delay in setting up and attending the ADR would have been prejudicial;
(vi) whether the ADR had a reasonable prospect of success.

In a case in which the respondents put before the court an extensive bundle of correspondence showing that they had made real efforts to settle the dispute, by making offers which were reasonable and generous, and had sought a round the table meeting, all of which were refused by the appellant, the respondents did not act unreasonably by refusing to enter into mediation. The fact that mediation was refused did not detract from the usual order that the unsuccessful appellant should pay the successful respondent's costs in resisting the appeal: *Valentine v Allen* [2003] EWCA Civ 915.

A barrister was justified in refusing to proceed to mediation in a professional negligence action where the attitude and character of the claimant made it most unlikely that the mediation would succeed. The court stated that this was an exceptional decision reflecting how seriously disturbed the claimant's judgment was in relation to the case. The fact that heavy costs had already been incurred, that the allegation was one of professional negligence and that the defendant believed he had a good defence were not reasons justifying refusal to mediate. The court accepted however that the mediation had no realistic prospect of success. The defendant was accordingly not penalised in costs: *Hurst v Leeming* [2002] EWHC 1051 (Ch), Lightman J.

The Administrative Court found that a Magistrates' Court had been wrong to order a local authority to pay a sum towards the costs of a company which was the subject of an abatement notice under the Environmental Protection Act 1990 s.80, but whose appeal against the abatement notice failed. The reason given was that the authority had not offered the company the option of reasonable discussions. The Administrative Court held that since the local authority had successfully contested the company's appeal, and the abatement notice had been upheld, it was, prima facie, entitled to its costs. The only reasonable discussions which might have taken place were in respect of an extension of time, but the company had never requested an extension or accepted that the notice was valid. The local authority had reasonably pursued its statutory duty at the public expense and had succeeded. The order for the payment of the company's costs were set aside: *R. (on the application of Chiltern District Council) v Wren Davis Ltd* [2008] EWHC 2164 (Admin) Sir George Newman.

The court found it appropriate to make an order for costs which reflected the paying party's inappropriate unwillingness to negotiate and the fact that there had been a fabrication of documents. The paying party was ordered to pay the applicant's costs subject to detailed assessment if not agreed, less, after assessment, the sum of £20,000 (*Gil v Baygreen Properties Ltd (in liquidation)* [2004] EWHC 2029 (Ch), Nicholas Davidson Q.C).

Where failure to mediate was due to the attitudes taken on either side it was not open to one party to claim that the failure should be taken into account in the order as to costs. A party who agreed to mediation but then took an unreasonable position in the mediation was in the same position as a party who unreasonably refused to mediate.That was something which the court should take into account in its costs order (*Earl of Malmesbury v Strutt & Parker* [2007] EWHC 424 (QB) Jack J.).

A party should not be able to obtain a tactical or costs advantage where, in substance, the principles of a pre-action protocol had been complied with. In a case where the claimant had sent a letter of claim under the protocol containing a clear summary of the facts setting out the basis on which the claim was made and identifying the principal contractual terms and statutory provisions relied on and the nature of the relief sought, the defendant was held to be well aware, before the proceedings were commenced, what the nature of the claim was against it. The defendant had been given every opportunity to attend meetings, to discuss matters and to settle the dispute. When the claimant, who had been seeking a contribution from the defendant in respect of other proceedings, settled those proceedings, the defendant had sought an order for costs against the claimant on the basis that the pre-action protocol had not been fully complied with (*TJ Brent Ltd v Black & Veatch Consulting Ltd* [2008] EWHC 1497 (TCC) Akenhead J.).

Where a claimant sued a main contractor in respect of goods sold to a subcontractor, subject to a retention of title clause, the claimant offered to submit to mediation which was rejected. The claim was for £70,000, the defendant made a Pt 36 payment of £6,000 and judgment was ultimately given for £387. The defendant sought an order for costs on the indemnity basis and the claimant argued there should be no order for costs for the period during which the defendant had failed to provide the claimant with information on its payments to the sub-contractor and because of the refusal to mediate. The court held that the defendant's rejection of mediation was unreasonable, as there would have been reasonable prospects of resolving the matter, at least until the Pt 36 payment. The court held that the defendant's conduct deprived the parties of the opportunity to resolve the case at minimal cost. The claimant was granted its costs up to a particular date and the defendant its costs thereafter: *P4 Ltd v Unite Integrated Solutions Plc* [2006] EWHC 2924, Ramsey J.

Where solicitors were defendants to a Pt 20 claim and declined to engage in mediation three weeks prior to trial, the solicitors, who were successful at the trial, were not deprived of any part of their costs. The court held that it was entirely reasonable for the solicitors not to participate in the mediation between the original claimant and defendant: *Société Internationale de Telecommunications Aeronautiques SC v Wyatt & Co (UK) Ltd [2002] EWHC 2401,* Park J.

In a case where a claimant successfully sued her solicitor and barrister for negligence, the solicitor was willing to settle the case before further costs were incurred, and urged the barrister to mediate. The claimant had made an offer of settlement but the barrister consistently refused to negotiate or enter into mediation and had valued the claim at a significantly lower figure than the settlement offer. By the time the matter reached trial considerable further costs had been incurred. The claimant recovered less than his offer of settlement and the solicitor submitted that the barrister should pay the whole of the claimant's costs after the date when the solicitor urged the barrister to mediate, because of the barrister's persistent refusal to negotiate or to enter into mediation. Although the court held that there was a strong possibility that a settlement could have been achieved close to the sum actually awarded had there been negotiation, the main issue was whether the barrister's view of his prospects was an unreasonable one, and whether the solicitor could demonstrate that this was so. Given the differing views of the claim, this was not demonstrated. It could not be right that, to avoid being vulnerable on costs, the defendant should always be prepared to pay more than the claim was worth, as that would enable claimants to put undue pressure on the defendant to settle at a higher figure than the claim merited: *Hickman v Blake Lapthorn and Fisher* [2006] EWHC 12 (QB), Jack J.

Where a claimant was slightly injured in a road traffic accident in respect of which the court awarded £500 damages (£1,000 plus having been claimed) the court on appeal limited the claimant's costs recovery to the costs to which he would have been entitled had he not exaggerated the extent of his injuries. The defendant was accordingly ordered to pay the fixed costs permitted under CPR r.27.14. The judge then went on to award a further £1,000 under CPR r.27.14(1)(d) in respect of the unreasonable behaviour of the defendant including the manner in which he had driven his car prior to the collision and his wish that the case should proceed on the multi track: *Devine v Franklin* [2002] EWHC 1846 (QB), Gray J.

It behoves parties in litigation to be sensible about applications by the other side (e.g. an amendment application that ought to have been consented to) and not unreasonably to refuse. The application to amend in the particular case had been made because the claimant had had to make it. It should not have been resisted, as demonstrated by the fact that the defendant ultimately consented. The defendant was ordered to pay the costs of the application: *La Chemise Lacoste SA v Sketchers USA Ltd* May 24, 2006, unrep., Ch D, Mann J. Where an application for interim injunctive relief was discontinued on undertakings given by the respondent, the first instance judge had erred, in principle, in awarding costs in favour of the respondent. The costs could have been avoided if the respondent had given a better response to the letter before action. Had the matter gone to a hearing, it was clear that the applicant would have been the winner: *Fox Gregory Ltd v Hamptons Group Ltd* [2006] EWCA Civ 1544.

There is a long line of authority pre-CPR to the effect that a court is entitled to take into account pre-proceedings conduct by a party when exercising its discretion over costs. Rule 44.3(5)(a) specifically includes a reference to pre-proceedings conduct. Any suggestion that the conduct had to be conduct within the proceedings themselves (as stated in *Hall v Rover Financial Services* [2002] EWCA Civ 1514) should be interpreted as no more than the description of the contemporary practice of judges of the Commercial Court where the court is used to dealing with business people who "not infrequently do not follow the Queensbury Rules in their dealings with each other": *Groupama Insurance v Overseas Partners & Aon Ltd* [2003] EWCA Civ 1846.

Where a party, who was ultimately successful, had persisted in pursuing an untenable position in the litigation the court found that the party ought reasonably to have negotiated a settlement, along the lines of the Tomlin order which was ultimately agreed, at a very much earlier stage. The successful party was awarded its costs up until an exchange of correspondence in which the defendants had accepted that the claimant would ultimately be successful. The claimant was ordered to pay the defendants' costs from the exchange of correspondence until the date of final settlement by Tomlin order (*Carlisle & Cumbria United Independent Supporters' Society Ltd v CUFC Holdings Ltd* [2008] EWHC 1783 (Ch) Peter Smith J.).

Where the trial judge awarded the successful defendant only 75 per cent of its costs on the grounds that the case was a test case, the Court of Appeal held that the grounds upon which the court could depart from the usual order was set out in r.44.3(4) and (5). The list is not exhaustive. It is wrong to deprive a successful defendant of part of its costs on the ground that the judgment might be of assistance to it in the future (*Pexton v The Wellcome Trust*, October 10, 2000, unrep., CA).

Rule 44.3(6) types of order

The rule sets out a list (which is not exhaustive) of orders which the court may **44.3.14**
make and r.44.3(7) provides that if the court is minded to make an order for costs re-

lating to a distinct part of the proceedings the court should, if practicable, make an order for a proportion (i.e. a percentage) of another party's costs or costs from or until a certain date.

The Court of Appeal refused to alter a judge's rejection of a defendant's argument that an issue based order should be made reflecting the success of the defendant on a number of issues, because matters in the claim and counterclaim were inextricably intertwined and because of the defendant's conduct in contesting various items, in particular a claim for VAT in respect of which the judge found that one of the defendants had lied (*Boynton v Willers* [2003] EWCA Civ 904).

The Court of Appeal has held that a judge has a discretion to make an order for costs subject to a cap. In the particular case the judge was held to have exercised his discretion wrongly because the reason he gave for imposing a cap was proportionality but proportionality was catered for by the costs orders he had made, all of which provided for the costs to be assessed on the standard basis. There were also additional matters in respect of which the judge was held to have acted incorrectly: *SCT Finance Ltd v Bolton* [2002] EWCA Civ 56; [2003] 3 All E.R. 434, CA.

Consideration of the relevant factors by a judge, when considering what form of order ought to be made in order properly to apply CPR r.44.3(7), will in most cases lead to the conclusion that an "issues based" order ought not to be made. Wherever practicable the judge should endeavour to form a view as to the percentage of costs to which the winning party should be entitled, or alternatively whether justice would be sufficiently done by awarding costs from or until a particular date only, as suggested by CPR r.44.3(6)(c). Whatever order for costs is made reasons should be given and may be given briefly in a judgment. It is the duty of the judge to produce a judgment which gives a clear explanation for the order: *English v Emery Reimbold & Strick Ltd* [2002] EWCA Civ 605; [2002] 1 W.L.R. 2409; *Verrechia v Commissioner of Police for the Metropolis* [2002] EWCA Civ 605; [2002] 3 All E.R. 385, CA.

The court should be more ready than before CPR to make costs orders which reflect not merely the overall outcome of the proceedings but also the loss of particular issues. It was not necessary for the court to make an issues based order to achieve that result. Rule 44.3(7) makes this plain and the court will not be forced into making an issues based order rather than a percentage order by the failure of the parties to provide the court with sufficient information about costs to achieve the correct percentage: *Budgen v Andrew Gardner Partnership* [2002] EWCA Civ 1125; [2003] C.P. Rep. 8; *The Times*, September 9, 2002, CA. As to the correct approach to making an issue based costs order, the Court of Appeal accepted the principle that a claimant is entitled to put his case at its highest. There is however a distinction between putting the case at its highest and advancing a basis for relief on a basis that fails (especially if it is entirely unsupportable). There was no reason why the losing party should bear the costs in relation to an issue which simply could not succeed. With regard to ATE insurance the duty on those advising claimants which existed where public funding was the issue is no different in respect of proceedings brought under a CFA with ATE insurance. If a point is a bad one that should be the advice that those advising should give. There is an overriding duty to the court not to run unarguable points. It is certainly not an argument for an order that an opponent should bear all the costs of the successful party that some bad points needed to be run in order to obtain ATE insurance. The courts should not be slow to make a reduction in the costs that a successful party should recover if they form the view that bad points have been argued and lost: *Kew v Bettamix Ltd* [2006] EWCA Civ 1535.

Rule 44.3(6)(g) enables the court to order interest on costs to run from a date other than the date of judgment. The court has the power to reach a conclusion as to interest suiting the particular circumstances of the case: *Powell v Herefordshire Health Authority* [2002] EWCA Civ 1786; [2003] 3 All E.R. 253, CA. "In any event in principle there seems no reason why the court should not [award interest] where a party has had to put up money paying its solicitor and been out of the use of that money in the meanwhile" per Waller L.J. in *Bim Kemi AB v Blackburn Chemicals Ltd (Costs)* [2003] *EWCA Civ 889. The court has* expressed the view that the appropriate dates, when seeking to measure the extent to which a party has been out of pocket, would be the dates on which the invoices were actually paid. The appropriate time for interest to stop would be when interest on costs is replaced by judgment interest: *Douglas v Hello Ltd* [2004] EWHC 63 (Ch) Lindsay J.

Rule 44.3(8) payment on account

The court has power to order an amount to be paid on account of costs even though the costs have not been assessed. Quite apart from the specific rule, the court has an inherent jurisdiction to control its own processes. Rule 3.1(1) expressly preserves the inherent powers of the court. Where the paying party had refused to comply with orders requiring him to make interim payments towards the receiving party's costs the Costs Judge had the power to make an unless order, stipulating that unless the order was complied with, the receiving party would be entitled to the full amount of the costs sought. In the particular case the paying party had served points of dispute. The court therefore ordered detailed assessment, but the paying party was not permitted to participate further, unless the payments already ordered were made together with interest: *Days Healthcare UK Ltd v Pihsiang Machinery Manufacturing Co Ltd* [2006] EWHC 1444 (QB); [2006] 4 All E.R. 233, Langley J. **44.3.15**

Where a defendant had failed to pay the costs of an interim application which had been summarily assessed, the court granted the claimant's application that unless the amount due was paid the defendant be debarred from defending the proceedings and that the claimant be entitled to enter judgment. The matter was dealt with under the inherent jurisdiction of the court. Since the defendant was not resident within the jurisdiction enforcement remedies available to the claimant were of limited value. The court held that unless there was some overwhelming consideration falling within art.6 of the ECHR, the normal consequences of a failure to comply with an interim costs order should be an order of the type applied for: *Crystal Decisions (UK) Ltd v Vedatech Corp* [2006] EWHC 3500 (Ch), Patten J. See also *Oil & Minerals Development Corp v Sajjad*, April 4, 2002, unrep. (and see para.3.4.4).

Where the resources of a party ordered to pay costs are limited, the court should not force the receiving party to engage in detailed assessment proceedings before receiving any money at all since this would merely require the expenditure of further money on a process which would produce no return. The judge awarded an interim payment in an amount which he regarded as the absolute bare minimum that the defendants could hope to recover on a detailed assessment: *Allason v Random House UK Ltd* [2002] EWHC 1030 (Ch), Laddie J.

The discretion to make *pre-emptive costs orders* (now called protective costs orders), even in cases involving public interest challenges, should be exercised only in the most exceptional circumstances. Necessary conditions were that the issues raised were truly ones of general public importance and that the court had sufficient appreciation of the merits of the claim that it could conclude that it was in the public interest to make the order. The court also had to have regard to the financial resources of the applicant and the respondent and the amount of costs likely to be in issue: *R. v Lord Chancellor, Ex p. Child Poverty Action Group*; *R. v DPP, Ex p. Bull* [1999] 1 W.L.R. 347, Dyson J.

The criteria set out by Dyson J. in *R v Lord Chancellor, Ex p. Child Poverty Action Group* above, were held to be consistent with the overriding objective by Richards J. in *R. v Hammersmith & Fulham LBC Ex p. CPRE London Branch*, October 26, 1999, unrep. See note at 48.15.6.1 for Court of Appeal re-statement of these critieria. The court granted such an order to a party representing all policy holders opposed to a scheme put forward by the claimant insurance company for the reorganisation of their insurance business. The application was granted on the basis that the opposing party was entitled to the order because his position was analogous with that of a shareholder bringing a derivative action and he was performing a service enabling the claimant's scheme to be fully tested in court. The court retained a discretion to disallow costs unreasonably incurred since the court retained a discretion to disallow costs unreasonably incurred in opposition: *AXA Equity & Law Life Assurance Society Plc (No.1), Re*, [2001] 2 B.C.L.C. 447, Evans-Lombe J.

In general an interim order for payment of costs prior to assessment should be made, but the court has to take into account all the circumstances in the particular case including the unsuccessful party's wish to appeal; the relative financial position of each party; the court's overriding objective to deal with cases justly. Where it was necessary to wait for a detailed assessment, making an order for a lesser amount which the successful party would almost certainly recover was a closer approximation to justice. Having considered the circumstances and the conduct of the parties the court came to the view that the successful claimant was likely to recover only 40 per cent of its costs, this figure was further reduced by the court in arriving at an interim payment figure: *Mars UK Ltd v Teknowledge Ltd (Costs)* [1999] 2 Costs LR 44; [1999] 2 Costs L.R. 44, Jacob J. The decision in *Mars* was accepted in *Beach v Smirnov* [2007] EWHC 3499 (QB) Ouseley J. The judge stated that the principle which must underlie the making of an interim payment is that set out in *Mars*. The principle is that the claimant is entitled to something by way of costs and he should be paid it without delay. The fact that there may be difficulties of assessment does not absolve the judge from the need to consider whether the justice that comes from not keeping somebody out of the money to which he is entitled, can only be achieved at too high a price to a defendant, putting him in a position where he has paid more than due. Justice requires that a sum of costs be paid provided there can be a reasonable assessment of the sum that is very likely to be awarded (*Dyson Ltd v Hoover Ltd* [2003] EWHC 624 (Ch) Laddie J. not followed).

Whilst the decision in *Mars UK v Teknowledge Ltd* might be the starting point after a full trial, where the court has not heard the trial, and has not had the opportunity to assess the issue of proportionality, and has no detailed knowledge of the nature and strength of the arguments, there should be no presumption that an order for an interim payment should be made (and no presumption against). The provisions concerning the making of an interim costs certificate under CPR r.47.15 meant that a Costs Judge's power to order an interim payment had to be preceded by steps that put him in a position to make an accurate assessment similar to that of the judge at the end of a trial. The court held that the sums involved in the case were too large to justify an attempt at assessment without full knowledge of the issues. It was preferable for a Costs Judge to consider the question of costs: *Dyson Appliances Ltd v Hoover Ltd* [2003] EWHC 624 (Ch); *The Times*, March 18, 2003, Laddie J.

In a case in which the successful claimant submitted that summary assessment was appropriate the defendant argued that in the absence of agreement between the parties it should be possible to have a detailed assessment of the costs in dispute provided that a substantial payment on account was ordered. On the facts the judge found that there appeared to be no grounds for reducing the claimant's costs and ordered the majority of the costs to be paid on account, the balance to be subject to detailed assessment: *Mabey & Johnson Ltd v Ecclesiastical Insurance Office Plc (Costs)* [2000] C.L.C. 1570, Morrison J. The court has held that it is right, in principle, for a payment on account to be ordered in judicial review proceedings before the Administrative Court: *R (London Oratory School) v The Schools Adjudicator* [2004] EWHC 3014 (Admin) Jackson J.

Rule 44.3(9) set off

44.3.16 The Court of Appeal in *Lockley v National Blood Transfusion Service* [1992] 1 W.L.R. 492, CA stated the following propositions:

1. A direction for the set-off of costs against damages or costs to which a legally aided person has become or becomes entitled in the action may be permissable.
2. The set-off is no different from and no more extensive than the set-off available to or against parties who are not legally aided.
3. The broad criterion for the application of set-off is that the claimant's claim and the defendant's claim are so closely connected that it would be inequitable to allow the claimant's claim without taking into account the defendant's claim. As it has sometimes been put the defendant's claim must in equity impeach the claimant's claim.
4. Set-off of costs or damages to which one party is entitled against costs or damages to which another party is entitled depends upon the application of the equitable criterion set out in the judgment. It was treated by May J. in *Currie & Co v Law Society* [1977] Q.B. 990, 1000, as a "question for the courts discretion". The court did not think that a set-off of damages against damages could be properly be described as a discretionary matter, nor that a set-off of costs against damages could be so described.
5. If and to the extent that a set off of costs awarded against a legally aided party against costs or damages to which the legally aided party is entitled cannot be justified as a set off:
   (i) the liability of the legally aided party to pay the costs awarded against it will be subject to s.17(i) of the Legal Aid Act 1988 [now s.11 of the Access to Justice Act 1999] and reg.124(1) of the Civil Legal Aid (General) Regulations 1989 [now reg.9 of the Community Legal Service (Costs) Regulations 2000]; and
   (ii) the s.16(6) of the 1989 Act charge [now s.10(7) of the 1999 Act] will apply to the costs or damages to which the legally aided party is entitled.

The Court of Appeal subsequently examined the propositions set out in *Lockley* above in *R. (Burkett) v London Borough of Hammersmith & Fulham* [2004] EWCA Civ 1342. The court found that the complications introduced by the language of Order LXV r.14 of the Rules annexed to the Supreme Court (Amendment) Act 1875 have disappeared since s.51 of the Supreme Court Act 1981 provides quite simply that: "subject to the provisions of this and any other enactment and to Rules of Court" the costs of and incidental to all proceedings in the High Court shall be in the discretion of the court. A set off as to costs is therefore essentially discretionary in nature, a discretion only to be withheld from a judge by specific rules of law (paras 41 and 42).

Arguments that the order for set off of costs lacked mutuality, or that one set of costs failed to impeach a claim to the other set of costs, were drawn from the jurisprudence of equitable set off as a defence to an action brought. The arguments were irrelevant (except possibly as a guide to the judge to the exercise of discretion) to the discretionary jurisdiction as to costs (para.47).

In relation to arguments concerning s.11 of the Access to Justice Act 1999 a set off does not place the person against whom it is asserted under any obligation to pay, but merely reduces the amount that he can recover. The court did not agree that the approach was artificial or contrary to the spirit of costs protection. Costs protection was not an absolute right but something carefully moderated by specific statutory provisions to which the judges in earlier cases (including *Lockley*) had made careful reference. If there was any artificiality it was for this principle to be introduced into a case where it was not the assisted party but their lawyers who were seeking to resist the set off (para.50).

In respect of an argument that the statutory provisions demonstrated that an order for costs was in favour of the LSC; that the LSC was the counterparty to it; that the defendant owed the costs only to the LSC; and thus that the order could not be set off against a liability of the applicant to the LSC the court found that this was not the case. On their very face the provisions emphasise that the costs are recovered by the client and that the costs order is made in favour of the client. This reflects the long standing principle that however litigation is funded, the party not the funder remains in control of the action and is to be treated by the court no differently from a non funded party (see s.22(4) Access to Justice Act 1999). Secondly, Parliament has provided that there should be special arrangements for the management of orders made in favour of assisted persons, not only payments of costs but also payments of damages. It had never been suggested that because of this provision damages also belonged to the LSC. If that were indeed the case there would be no need for the statutory charge. The fact that a funder has made a provision with his principal as to the disposition of that principal's recovery cannot affect the nature of the relationship between the principal and the other party to the litigation in which the principal takes part, even where those arrangements are created by the statutory rules governing public funding rather than by private treaty (paras 53, 54 and 55).

The court has an inherent jurisdiction to order a set off of costs. Where it was not a case of normal common law equitable or statutory set off, any strict rules governing those forms of set off did not apply. There was no analogy with the traditional approach of the court to set off which might prejudice a solicitor's lien because in the particular case there was a crystallised debt and an outright assignment rather than a mere lien: *Izzo v Philip Ross & Co*, [2002] B.P.I.R. 310, Neuberger J.

The court has confirmed that the position with regard to set off remains the same as it was before the introduction of the CPR. Whilst an assisted person remains protected against the making of enforceable orders for payment of costs, that protection is not available in respect of orders for costs to be used as a shield or set off (*Hill v Bailey* [2003] EWHC 2835 (Ch), Lightman J.).

Costs orders relating to funding arrangements[1]

44.3A—(1) The court will not assess any additional liability until the conclusion of the proceedings, or the part of the proceedings, to which the funding arrangement relates. **44.3A**

("Funding arrangement" and "additional liability" are defined in rule 43.2).

[1] Introduced by the Civil Procedure (Amendment No.3) Rules 2000 (SI 2000/1317).

(2) At the conclusion of the proceedings, or the part of the proceedings, to which the funding arrangement relates the court may—

(a) make a summary assessment of all the costs, including any additional liability;

(b) make an order for detailed assessment of the additional liability but make a summary assessment of the other costs; or

(c) make an order for detailed assessment of all the costs.

(Part 47 sets out the procedure for the detailed assessment of costs)

Comment

44.3A.1 Because it was felt that disclosure of full details of funding arrangements, particularly the percentage success fee in a conditional fee agreement, was prejudicial, the rules provide for limited information to be given to opposing parties until the final assessment (summary or detailed) is made. The rule provides that the court will not assess any additional liability until the conclusion of the relevant part of the proceedings. At that point the court may carry out a summary assessment of all the costs, make a summary assessment of the base costs only and order a detailed assessment of the additional liability, or make an order for detailed assessment of all the costs. For a case in which the judge assessed the additional liability (a success fee under a CFA) and ordered detailed assessment of the claimant's costs in relation to liability, see *Burton v Kingsley* [2005] EWHC 1034 (QB) Richards J.

See note on *Times Newspapers Ltd v Burstein* at 47.14.3.

Summary assessment

44.3A.2 When the court makes a summary assessment during the course of the proceedings the judge should state separately the amount allowed in respect of solicitors' charges, counsels' fees and other disbursements. This is so even though any additional liability is not at that stage assessed. The reason for this is that when the final assessment takes place it will be necessary to identify the total figures allowed to solicitors and counsel in order that any percentage increase (which may be different for solicitors and counsel) can be applied.

Recoverability of Success Fees and Insurance Premiums

44.3A.3 For notes on these and related topics see Vol.2, para.7A–62 *et seq.*

Limits on recovery under funding arrangements[1]

44.3B **44.3B—(1) A party may not recover as an additional liability—**

(a) any proportion of the percentage increase relating to the cost to the legal representative of the postponement of the payment of his fees and expenses;

(b) any provision made by a membership organisation which exceeds the likely cost to that party of the premium of an insurance policy against the risk of incurring a liability to pay the costs of other parties to the proceedings;

(c) any additional liability for any period in the proceedings during which he failed to provide information about a funding arrangement in accordance with a rule, practice direction or court order;

[1] Introduced by the Civil Procedure (Amendment No.3) Rules 2000 (SI 2000/1317).

(d) any percentage increase where a party has failed to comply with—

(i) a requirement in the costs practice direction; or

(ii) a court order,

to disclose in any assessment proceedings, the reasons for setting the percentage increase at the level stated in the conditional fee agreement.

(2) This rule does not apply in an assessment under rule 48.9 (assessment of a solicitor's bill to his client).

(Rule 3.9 sets out the circumstances the court will consider on an application for relief from a sanction for failure to comply with any rule practice direction or court order).

Comment

The rule sets out the limits on recovery under the funding arrangements. Any proportion of the percentage increase in a conditional fee agreement which relates to the fact that payment of fees and expenses is delayed is not recoverable. In relation to provision made by a membership organisation, no more than the cost of a premium of an insurance policy covering the risk of having to pay the costs of other parties to the proceedings is recoverable. Recovery of additional liability is not possible for any period where the party has failed to provide information about a funding arrangement. For further discussion of these topics see Vol.2, para.7A–55 *et seq*. **44.3B.1**

Relief from Sanction

Where there has been a failure to disclose, the application for relief from sanctions should be made as soon as the failure is discovered. If the fees recoverable by counsel are likely to be affected by the failure, counsel must also be given notice of the application for relief. Counsel is entitled to be heard on the solicitor's application. CPR r.3.9 sets out the circumstances which court may consider on an application to grant relief from a sanction. Where the paying party had from the outset the information to which it was entitled, in relation to funding arrangements, the court found that there was no prejudice to that party from breaches of the Practice Direction (no formal notice had been given) and the receiving party was entitled to relief from the sanction provided for by r.44.3B(1(c) and was not to be deprived of the opportunity, in principle, to recover the agreed success fee: *Montlake v Lambert Smith Hampton Group Ltd* [2004] EWHC 1503 (Comm), Langley J. **44.3B.2**

Relief from sanctions should not be granted lightly and any party who fails to comply with the CPR runs a significant risk that he will be refused relief. Thus, if a party does not have a good explanation, or the other side is prejudiced by his failure, relief from sanctions will usually be refused. It is vitally important to the administration of justice that the rules of procedure are observed (*Subperstone v Hurst* [2008] EWHC 735 (Ch) Floyd J.).

Orders in respect of pro bono representation[1] **44.3C**

44.3C—(1) **In this rule, "the 2007 Act" means the Legal Services Act 2007.**

(2) Where the court makes an order under section 194(3) of the 2007 Act—

***(a)* *the court may order* the payment to the prescribed charity of a sum no greater than the costs specified in Part 45 to which the party with pro bono representation would have been entitled in accordance with that Part and in respect of that representation had it not been provided free of charge; or**

[1] Inserted by the Civil Procedure (Amendment) Rules 2008 (SI 2008/2178).

(b) where Part 45 does not apply, the court may determine the amount of the payment (other than a sum equivalent to fixed costs) to be made by the paying party to the prescribed charity by—

(i) making a summary assessment; or

(ii) making an order for detailed assessment,

of a sum equivalent to all or part of the costs the paying party would have been ordered to pay to the party with pro bono representation in respect of that representation had it not been provided free of charge.

(3) Where the court makes an order under section 194(3) of the 2007 Act, the order must specify that the payment by the paying party must be made to the prescribed charity.

(4) The receiving party must send a copy of the order to the prescribed charity within 7 days of receipt of the order.

(5) Where the court considers making or makes an order under section 194(3) of the 2007 Act, Parts 43 to 48 apply, where appropriate, with the following modifications—

(a) references to "costs orders", "orders about costs" or "orders for the payment of costs" are to be read, unless otherwise stated, as if they refer to an order under section 194(3);

(b) references to "costs" are to be read, as if they referred to a sum equivalent to the costs that would have been claimed by, incurred by or awarded to the party with pro bono representation in respect of that representation had it not been provided free of charge; and

(c) references to "receiving party" are to be read, as meaning a party who has pro bono representation and who would have been entitled to be paid costs in respect of that representation had it not been provided free of charge.

44.3C.1 Section 194 of the Legal Services Act 2007 makes provision for the recovery of costs in pro bono cases from October 1, 2008. The court is enabled to make an order for costs against an unsuccessful opponent of a litigant who has been represented pro bono. The costs awarded will not be payable to the litigant's legal representatives but to a charity, The Access to Justice Foundation, whose objectives are to receive and distribute financial resources to be utilised in helping to provide pro bono legal advice or assistance to those who need it most, eg, through advice centres and law centres.

Section 194 sets out the criteria for making an order (see para.9B–550). Such an order may be made if one of the parties' legal representatives was not acting pro bono but an order may not be made against a party who has been wholly represented pro bono or with LSC funding. Rule 44.3C sets out the procedure in respect of orders in respect of pro bono representation. Consequential amendments have been made throughout Pts 43 to 47 to deal with the new situation. There have also been consequential amendments to the Costs Practice Direction Pts 4, 5 and 6 and a new s.10A has been inserted. The rules relating to the assessment of costs remain the same, although it is expected that summary assessment will be the norm in pro bono cases.

Mr Jeremy Morgan Q.C., writing in The Law Society Gazette of November 13, 2008, suggests that where there is a series of costs orders going either way, if the first order is made in favour of the Foundation, and the second in favour of the opponent, it will not be possible to direct a set-off of these orders as they lack the mutuality essential for ordering set-off as a later court has no general power to revoke an earlier order. Both will stand and be enforceable. He suggests that there is an obvious unfairness about such a result, and that the solution is to invite the court in pro bono cases to reserve costs until the trial or other final hearing, preferably with a note on the court file to indicate the order which would have been made but for this problem. The court conducting the final hearing can then make a single order one way or the other which reflects the justice of the case overall, including the interlocutory successes and failures.

Basis of assessment[1]

44.4—(1) Where the court is to assess the amounts of costs (whether by summary or detailed assessment) it will assess those costs— 44.4

(a) on the standard basis; or

(b) on the indemnity basis,

but the court will not in either case allow costs which have been unreasonably incurred or are unreasonable in amount.

(Rule 48.3 sets out how the court decides the amount of costs payable under a contract.)

(2) Where the amount of costs is to be assessed on the standard basis, the court will—

(a) only allow costs which are proportionate to the matters in issue; and

(b) resolve any doubt which it may have as to whether costs were reasonably incurred or reasonable and proportionate in amount in favour of the paying party.

(Factors which the court may take into account are set out in rule 44.5.)

(3) Where the amount of costs is to be assessed on the indemnity basis, the court will resolve any doubt which it may have as to whether costs were reasonably incurred or were reasonable in amount in favour of the receiving party.

(4) Where—

(a) the court makes an order about costs without indicating the basis on which the costs are to be assessed; or

(b) the court makes an order for costs to be assessed on a basis other than the standard basis or the indemnity basis, the costs will be assessed on the standard basis.

(5) Where the amount of a solicitor's remuneration in respect of non-contentious business is regulated by any general orders made under the Solicitors Act 1974, the amount of the costs to be allowed in respect of any such business which falls to be assessed by the court will be decided in accordance with those general orders rather than this rule and rule 44.5.

Comment

The test to be applied under each basis is whether or not the costs have been reasonably incurred or are reasonable in amount. On the standard basis the additional test of proportionality is imposed and the court will only allow costs which are proportionate to the matters in issue. Rule 44.5 sets out the factors which the court must take into account in deciding the amount of costs. 44.4.1

[1] Amended by the Civil Procedure (Amendment No.3) Rules 2000 (SI 2000/1317).

Where the assessment is on the indemnity basis proportionality is not mentioned in the rule. The overriding objective imports proportionality into all proceedings.

Proportionality has always been a target which the courts should aim at. Case management powers will allow a judge to exercise the powers of limiting costs either indirectly or even directly so that they are proportionate to the amount involved: per Sir Christopher Staughton, *Griffiths v Solutia UK Ltd* [2001] EWCA Civ 736.

As to proportionality see para.44.4.3 and s.11 of the Costs Practice Direction.

Rule 44.4(2)—Proportionality

44.4.2 The Court of Appeal has given guidance on proportionality. The court stated that the requirement of proportionality now applies to decisions as to whether an order for costs should be made and to the assessment of costs which should be paid when an order has been made. The court suggested that the considerations to be taken into account by the court when making an order for costs under r.44.3 are "redolent of proportionality".

Because of the central role that proportionality should have in the resolution of civil litigation it is essential that courts attach the appropriate significance to the requirement of proportionality when making orders for costs and when assessing the amount of costs.

> "...what is required is a two stage approach. There has to be a global approach and an item by item approach. The global approach will indicate whether the total sum claimed is or appears to be disproportionate having particular regard to the considerations which Part 44.5(3) states are relevant. If the costs as a whole are not disproportionate according to that test then all that is normally required is that each item should have been reasonably incurred and the costs for that item should be reasonable. If on the other hand the costs as a whole appear disproportionate then the court will want to be satisfied that the work in relation to each item was necessary and, if necessary, that the cost of the item was reasonable. If, because of lack of planning or due to other causes, the global costs are disproportionately high, then the requirement that the costs should be proportionate means that no more should be payable than would have been payable if the litigation had been conducted in a proportionate manner. This in turn means that reasonable costs will only be recovered for the items which were necessary if the litigation had been conducted in a proportionate manner."

The court expressed the view that costs judges are well equipped to assess which approach a particular case requires. In a case where proportionality is likely to be an issue a preliminary judgment as to the proportionality of the costs as a whole must be made at the outset. This will ensure that the costs judge applies the correct approach to the detailed assessment.

> "In considering that question the Costs Judge will have regard to whether the appropriate level of fee earner or counsel has been deployed, whether offers to settle have been made, whether unnecessary experts had been instructed and the other matters set out in Part 44.5(3). Once the decision is reached as to proportionality of costs as a whole, the judge will be able to proceed to consider the costs, item by item, applying the appropriate test to each item."

In considering what was necessary a sensible standard of necessity has to be adopted. This is a standard which takes fully into account the need to make allowances for the different judgments which those responsible for litigation can sensibly come to as to what is required. The danger of setting too high a standard with the benefit of hindsight has to be avoided. The threshold required to meet "necessity" is higher than that of "reasonable" but it is still a standard that a competent practitioner should be able to achieve without undue difficulty. When a practitioner incurs expenses which are reasonable but not necessary he may be able to recover his fees and disbursements from his client but the extra expense which results from conducting litigation in a disproportionate matter cannot be recovered from the other party.

In deciding what is necessary the conduct of the other party is highly relevant. A party who is unco-operative may render necessary, costs which would otherwise be un*necessary* and it is acceptable that he should pay the costs for the expense which he has made necessary.

Dealing with the situation where a claimant recovers significantly less than he has claimed the court stated that the following approach should be followed:

> "Whether the costs incurred were proportionate should be decided having regard

to what it was reasonable for the party in question to believe might be recovered, thus:

(i) the proportionality of the costs incurred by the claimant should be determined having regard to the sum that it was reasonable for him to believe that he might recover at the time he made his claim;

(ii) the proportionality of the costs incurred by the defendant should be determined having regard to the sum it was reasonable for him to believe that the claimant might recover should his claim succeed.

This is likely to be the amount that the claimant has claimed, for a defendant will normally be entitled to take a claim at its face value.

The rationale for this approach is that a claimant should be allowed to incur the cost necessary to pursue a reasonable claim but not allowed to recover costs increased or incurred by putting forward an exaggerated claim and a defendant should not be prejudiced if he assumes the claim which was made was one which was reasonable and incurs costs in contesting the claim on this assumption."

Home Office v Lownds [2002] EWCA Civ 365; [2002] 1 W.L.R. 2450; [2002] 4 All E.R. 775, CA.

Lord Scott of Foscote, dealing with an appeal relating to a freezing injunction, stated:

39. "... I think it needs to be understood that the difference between costs at the standard rate and costs on an indemnity basis is, according to the language of the relevant rules, not very great.... It is difficult to see much difference between the two sets of criteria, save that where an indemnity basis has been ordered the onus must lie on the payer to show any unreasonableness. The criterion of proportionality, which applies only to standard basis costs, seems to me to add very little to the reasonableness criterion. The concept of costs that were unreasonably but proportionately incurred, or are unreasonable but proportionate in amount, or vice versa, is one that I find difficult to comprehend." *Fourie v Le Roux* [2007] UKHL 1.

It is not clear from the opinions whether the judgment of Lord Woolf in *Lownds v Home Office* [2002] EWCA Civ 365; [2002] 1 W.L.R. 2450; [2002] 4 All E.R. 775 was brought to the attention of their Lordships.

The application of the decision in *Home Office v Lownds* (above) has been considered by Morland J.:

28. "... I do not accept that if a Costs Judge has ruled at the outset of a detailed assessment that the bill as a whole is not disproportionate he is precluded from decided that an item or a number of items are or appear disproportionate having regard to the 'matters in issue'.

...

30. ... The effect of a preliminary finding of dispropotionality is like unto traffic lights at red. The receiving party will then face a stringent test to justify with regard to each item that it has been 'proportionately and by a sensible standard necessarily incurred:' and 'proportionate and reasonable in amount'.

...

32. A preliminary finding of disproportionality must not be regarded as penalising the receiving party in terms of the amount ultimately awarded because the overriding objective requires that a case is dealt with justly and fairly.

33. The preliminary judgment of proportionality determines the manner of the detailed assessment. It does not determine the final sum payable to the receiving party but a finding of disproprotionality does entail the receiving party being put to a stringent test the duel test of sensible necessity and reasonableness of amount for each item ... In the unlikely event that a Costs Judge at the initial stage is unable to say whether the bill viewed as a whole is proportionate or disproportionate he will be obliged to carry out a detailed assessment applying the dual test.

...

37. ... The Court of Appeal never envisaged that a Costs Judge before giving a preliminary judgment on proportionality of the costs as a whole would plough through in detail this gargantuan mass of material.

38. In my judgment even in very complex group litigation an experienced Costs Judge if provided with succinct skeletons of the parties contentions beforehand should be able to determine overall proportionality within an hour or less ..."

The court went on to state that in considering whether the costs claimed were proportionate it would be wrong to leave out of account pre CPR costs since they must form part of the global view. The judge concluded:

"54. ... If certain facets of the bill of costs strike the judge as being disproportionate he is entitled ... to rule that the bills as a whole fail the proportionality test and carry out the detailed assessment on the basis of the dual test. Even if the Costs Judge has reached the preliminary view that the bill as a whole is proportionate, in my judgment that preliminary view does not disentitle the Costs Judge from concluding that certain items appear disproportionate and applying the dual test of sensible necessity and reasonableness to that item."

Giambrone v JMC Holidays Ltd (formerly t/a Sunworld Holidays Ltd) (Costs) [2002] EWHC 2932; [2003] 1 All E.R. 982.

The decision in Lownds (above) requires the Costs Judge to undertake a two stage process, firstly to assess whether the costs overall are proportionate and second to proceed to assess proportionality and reasonableness on an item by item basis. When giving a ruling it is not imperative for the Costs Judge to go through the items in r.44.5 as a check list: *Ortwein v Rugby Mansions Ltd* [2003] EWHC 2077 July 28, 2003 (Ch), Lloyd J.

In Patent proceedings the court was required to determine costs arising. The claimant had succeeded in revoking the Patent in issue but was also forced to revoke two of its own Patents which were the subject of an undefended attack by the defendant. The claimant's costs totalled £6 million and the defendants' £1.6 million. The defendants submitted that the claimant's costs should be kept at the same level as the defendants' costs. The court found that the claimant's expenditure was entirely disproportionate to what had been at stake. The claimant had repeatedly asserted that the issues had no real commercial significance and there was accordingly no justification for the costs rising above that which would commonly be expected for an action of this nature. The judgment of the court amounted to a finding of disproportionality and the Costs Judge was directed to assess the costs on an item by item basis and to allow the items claimed only if they were necessary and reasonable. *Research in Motion UK Ltd v Visto Corporation* [2008
EWHC 819 (Ch), Floyd J.

Rule 44.4(3)—Costs on the Indemnity Basis

44.4.3 The Court of Appeal declined to give guidance to judges intending to make orders for costs on the indemnity basis. There was an infinite variety of situations that might go before a court justifying the making of such an order. The court could do no more than draw the judge's attention to the extensive width of the discretion provided in CPR Pt 44. Issues of costs ought to be left to a judge's discretion following the rules provided in the CPR. The words of the CPR should not be replaced or supplemented with guidance notes from the Court of Appeal. The making of a costs order on the indemnity basis would be appropriate in circumstances where the facts of the case and/or the conduct of the parties was such as to take the situation away from the norm: *Excelsior Commercial and Industrial Holdings Ltd v Salisbury Ham Johnson* and *Betesh & Co v Salisbury Hammer Aspden & Johnson* [2002] EWCA Civ 879. Following *Excelsior Commercial and Industrial Holdings* it is appropriate to award costs on the indemnity basis where the conduct of a party has taken the situation away from the norm. It is not always necessary to show deliberate misconduct, in some cases unreasonable conduct to a high degree would suffice. The claimant's refusal of two reasonable offers to settle would have been enough in itself to warrant an order on the indemnity basis (*Franks v Sinclair (Costs)* [2006] EWHC 3656 (Ch) David Richards J.). Where the court is considering whether a losing party's conduct is such as to justify an order for costs on the indemnity basis, the minimum nature of the conduct required is, except in very rare cases, that there has been a significant level of unreasonableness or otherwise inappropriate conduct in its wider sense in relation to that party's pre-litigation dealings with the winning party, or in relation to the commencement or conduct of the litigation itself. In a case where a counterclaiming defendant alleged fraud which was shown to be deeply flawed from the very commencement of the counterclaim, and where the allegation rested on an assumption which was so improbable as to be far fetched, the court made an order for costs on the indemnity basis: *National Westminster Bank Plc v Rabobank Nederland* [2007] EWHC 1742 (Comm),Sir Anthony Colman. A losing claim where the claim had a solid basis and was not a frivolous one, and where the claimant's pre-action activity had not overstepped the mark, did not result in an award of costs on the indemnity basis. The claimant's expert evidence however, was deficient and led to unnecessary costs being incurred by the defendant. The court ordered that the costs incurred in respect of counsels' and solicitors' attendance on specific days, and the costs attributable to dealing with the expert evidence were to be assessed on the indemnity basis. *Balmoral Group Ltd v Borealis (UK) Ltd* [2006] EWHC 2531 (Comm) Christopher Clarke J. Following *Excelsior v Salisbury* the suggestion that an award of costs of an interlocutory application had to follow the event unless the matters specially set out in r.44.3(4) took the case outside the general rule was rejected: *Lifeline Gloves Ltd v Richardson* [2005] EWHC 1524, Ch, Pumfrey J.

An order for indemnity costs does not enable a claimant to receive more costs than he has incurred, its practical effect is to avoid the costs being assessed at a lesser figure. Even on the indemnity basis the receiving party is restricted to recovering only the amount of costs which have been incurred. (*Petrotrade Inc v Texaco Ltd* [2001] 4 All E.R. 86; [2002] 1 W.L.R. 947 (Note), CA). A party who has acted throughout on professional advice is not guilty of conduct such as to merit an award of indemnity costs. There is no sound reason why parties litigating on issues of costs should be more vulnerable to an order for costs on the indemnity basis: *Zissis v Lukomski* [2006] EWCA Civ 341.

When considering an application for the award of costs on the indemnity basis the court is concerned principally with the losing party's conduct of the case rather than the substantive merits of the position. The Guide to the Summary Assessment of Costs helps to clarify the distinction for the purposes of CPR Pt 44 between proportionality and reasonableness. Proportionality concerns the relationship of the costs claimed for such things as the amount of money at stake in the proceedings, the importance of the case, the complexity of the issues and the means of the parties. Whether the costs, proportionate or not, were reasonably incurred is therefore a different question. Although the two may overlap, the object of an indemnity costs order is to take proportionality out of the picture and to place on the paying party the burden of persuasion as to reasonableness: *Simms v Law Society* [2005] EWCA Civ 849; (2005) 155 N.L.J. 1124.

The Court of Appeal has held that it is incorrect for a judge to be guided by the many pre CPR cases. The award of costs on the indemnity basis is normally reserved to cases where the court wishes to indicate its disapproval of the conduct in the litigation of the party against whom the costs are awarded: *Reid Minty v Gordon Taylor* [2001] EWCA Civ 1723; [2002] 2 All E.R. 150, CA.

In group litigation where the defendants mounted a full frontal attack on medical evidence underpinning field research programmes which they themselves had helped to set up, the judge found that the defendants' experts, had lost intellectual and professional credibility. The court found that the decision to continue the challenge through the defendants' experts after the claimant's experts had completed their evidence amounted to unreasonable conduct of the litigation. Therefore on the generic medical issues it was directed that the defendants should pay the costs on the indemnity basis, whereas in respect of all other issues, in the cases where the claimants succeeded, costs should be on the standard basis: *The British Coal Respiratory Disease Litigation, Re*, January 23, 1998, unrep., Turner J. Where cross-examination of a claimant took the form of a totally uncalled for personal attack, the court made an order for costs on the indemnity basis in favour of the claimant for that portion of the trial, *Clark v Associated Newspapers Ltd* [1998] 1 W.L.R. 1558; *The Times*, January 28, 1998, Lightman J.

Where a party to litigation acted in a way that could be described as disgraceful or deserving of moral condemnation an order for costs on the indemnity basis could be made: *Wailes v Stapleton Construction & Commercial Services Ltd*; *Wailes v Unum Ltd* [1997] 2 Lloyds' Rep. 112, Newman J. Where claimants brought proceedings for an account of the defendant's dealings with the estate of the deceased and abandoned 9 out of 13 claims for damages during the course of the proceedings, the remainder of which were lost, it was held to be appropriate to order costs on the indemnity basis. *Mahmey Trust Reg v Lloyds TSB Bank Plc* [2006] EWHC 1782, Ch, Evans-Lombe J.

A judge was wrong to award costs on the indemnity basis against a claimant who had not acted improperly in availing himself of the opportunity presented by statute to apply to the court. The claimant had made an application under the provisions of s.263 of the Insolvency Act 1986. The application had failed on the basis that the claimant had no sufficient interest to make the application. The Court of Appeal found the claimant had not acted improperly and that the costs should be on the standard basis; *Raja v Rubin* [2000] Ch. 274; [1999] 3 W.L.R. 606, CA.

If a judge considers that a party has acted unreasonably in connection with the litigation in breach of a direction of the court, it might be appropriate to make an order for costs on the indemnity basis against that party, or to exercise the power to award interest on damages at a much higher rate than usual. *Baron v Lovell* [2000] P.I.Q.R. P20; *The Times*, September 14, 1999, CA.

The decisions of the Court of Appeal in *Raja v Rubin* and *Baron v Lovell* (above) show that the court had been concerned with some part of the paying party's conduct of the litigation which merited the disapproval of the court. The usual order on the standard basis should be made unless there is some element of a party's conduct of the case which deserves some mark of disapproval. It is not just to penalise a party for running litigation which it has lost. Advancing a case which is unlikely to succeed or which fails in fact is not a sufficient reason for an award of costs on the indemnity basis: *Shania Investment Corp v Standard Bank London Ltd* November 2, 2001, unrep.

Failure by a claimant to send a letter before action to the defendant, or to give any other warning of the intention to commence proceedings resulted in an order for costs on the indemnity basis against the claimant. The court stated that the letter before action is at least as necessary under the CPR as under the former rules: *Phoenix Finance Ltd v Federation Internationale de L'Automobile* [2002] EWHC 1242 (Ch), Sir Andrew Morritt V.-C. A party who presented a petition to wind up a company without first presenting a statutory demand in circumstances, where the petitioner knew there was a serious dispute over the quality of the goods supplied, was ordered to pay the costs on the indemnity basis. The presentation of a petition in those circumstances was an abuse of process (*Company (No.2507 of 2003), Re* [2003] EWHC 1484 (Ch)). A claimant who sought to "park" the proceedings, while attempting to negotiate a settlement, by pursuing the hopeless appeal was ordered to pay costs on the indemnity basis as the claimant's conduct was an abuse of process: *Sodeca SA v NE Investments Inc* [2002] EWHC 1700 (QB), Toulson J. Where a judge made an order for costs on the indemnity basis, having been misled as to the status of a Pt 36 offer the Court of Appeal intervened to substitute an order for costs on the standard basis: *Nash (t/a Elite Carcraft) v Daniel* [2002] EWCA Civ 1146.

The court also had the power, in attempting to achieve pragmatic fairness, to order that interest on costs should run from a date before the principal judgment in the action. The court could find no power in CPR to adjust the rate of interest that fell to be awarded: *ABCI v Banque Franco-Tunisienne (Costs)* [2002] EWHC 567 (Comm) HHJ, Chambers QC.

If a (commercial) party embarks upon, or brings upon itself and pursues, large scale litigation which results in a resounding defeat involving the rejection of much of the evidence adduced in support of its case that provides a proper basis on which to award costs on the indemnity basis. In the particular case the claimant had conducted itself throughout the relevant events on the basis that its commercial interest took precedence over the rights and wrongs of the situation and it was prepared to risk the outcome of the litigation: *Amoco UK Exploration Co v British American Off-Shore Ltd*, November 22, 2001, unrep., Langley J.

Accountants who successfully defended an action sought to rely on a clause in the claimant's articles of association, indemnifying auditors of companies against any liability incurred in defending any proceedings, as entitling them to an order for costs on the indemnity basis in those proceedings. The court held that any contractual right which the defendant might have was not formally an issue in the proceedings and they were not therefore entitled to their costs on the indemnity basis: *John v Pricewaterhouse-Coopers (formerly Price Waterhouse)* [2002] 1 W.L.R. 953, Ferris J.; *Gomba Holdings Ltd v Minories Finance*, [1993] Ch. 171, CA, distinguished.

Following the above judgment the defendants submitted that they were contractually entitled to be indemnified from the assets of each of the companies against the costs incurred in defending the proceedings. The court refused the application since no such application had been made at the time the judgment had been handed down. As to deferment of the issue of costs the court's jurisdiction under s.51 of the Supreme Court Act 1981 was exhausted. It was open to the defendant to seek to recover the costs in separate proceedings: *John v PriceWaterhouseCoopers (Costs)* [2002] 1 W.L.R. 953, *Ferris J.*

Part 36 offers

44.4.3.1 An order for costs on the indemnity basis made under r.36.21(3) is not penal and carries no stigma or implied disapproval of the defendant's conduct. The making of such an order indicates only that the court has not considered it unjust to make the order for indemnity costs for which the rule provides: *McPhilemy v Times Newspapers Ltd (No.2)* [2001] EWCA Civ 933; [2002] 1 W.L.R. 934; [2001] 4 All E.R. 861, CA.

The provisions of para.8.4 of the Costs Practice Direction are directed at offers to settle in the ordinary sense of the word. Part of the culture of the CPR is to encourage parties to avoid proceedings if it is reasonable to do so. The Pt 36 offer is aimed at a genuine offer to settle and not some tactical ploy for the purpose of advancing a claim under r.36.21. In the circumstances the claimants were entitled to recover indemnity costs and enhanced interest from the date of their Pt 36 offers, not from the date of their claims: *Utankio Ltd v P & O Nedlloyd BV*; *East West Corp v DKBS 1912 (Costs)* [2002] EWHC 253 (Comm), Thomas J.

A respondent wishing to protect himself against costs of an appeal cannot rely on an offer to settle made before trial. The particular appeal turned on a pure point of construction to which there could be only one answer. In those circumstances the claimant could not be expected to have offered to give up a substantial part of its judgment. The claimant was awarded costs on the indemnity basis with interest from the mid point between the lapse of the offer and the date of the appeal hearing: *CEL Group Ltd v Nedlloyd Lines UK Ltd (Costs)* [2003] EWCA Civ 1371.

The underlying rationale of r.36.21—to encourage claimants to make offers—has no counterpart with regard to defendants. Conduct, albeit falling short of misconduct, deserving of moral condemnation can be so unreasonable as to justify an order for indemnity costs. Such conduct would need to be unreasonable to a high degree, in this context that does not mean merely wrong or misguided in hindsight. An indemnity costs order made under r.44, rather than under r.36, does carry at least some stigma. It is of its nature penal rather than exhortatory: *Kiam v MGN Ltd (No.2)* [2002] EWCA Civ 66; [2002] 2 All E.R. 242, CA.

The court has a wide discretion under r.44.3. The fact that the claimant had made a Pt 36 offer to accept as much as it was awarded, was plainly an important factor, as was the fact that the offer had been made on appeal, the court below having awarded a lesser sum. Where the defendant had not acted unreasonably in seeking to resist the appeal, nor acted improperly in its conduct of the appeal, the court held that this was not one of those rare cases in which refusal of a settlement offer would attract, under CPR Pt 44, not merely an adverse order for costs but an order on the indemnity basis: *Ali Reza-Delta Transport Co Ltd v United Arab Shipping Co SAG (Costs)* [2003] EWCA Civ 811; [2003] 3 All E.R. 1297, CA.

In normal circumstances an order for costs under r.36.20(2) should be an order on the standard basis unless it is unjust to make such an order. Where a Pt 36 payment is not accepted by a claimant he should not automatically be liable for indemnity costs unless there is something in the conduct of the action or the circumstances of the case which takes the case out of the norm in a way which justifies an order for indemnity costs: *Excelsior Commercial and Industrial Holdings Ltd v Salisbury Hammer Aspden & Johnson* [2002] EWCA Civ 879.

Rule 44.4(4)

The court has held that r.44.4(3) merely provides what is to be the legal consequence of an unqualified order for indemnity costs: **44.4.4**

> "it in no way forecloses the court from making a qualified order for indemnity costs, that is to say, an order where the ordering provision is qualified by the imposition of the burden of proof of reasonableness on the third party entitled to the costs."

The court ordered that accountants should receive all their costs reasonably incurred in complying with an order for disclosure, but the burden of justifying and explaining the reasonableness of those costs should lie on them (*Westminster City Council v Porter (Third Party Disclosure: Costs Basis)* [2003] EWHC 2373). The terms of this order appear to cut directly across the provisions of r.44.4(4)(b) and may well result in the costs being assessed on the standard basis.

Family proceedings

A successful petitioning wife sought costs on the indemnity basis from the former husband who had unsuccessfully defended divorce proceedings. She argued that he had only defended in order to wear her down and make her behave as he wanted and that he had unreasonably pursued his defence. The court allowed the application stating that the test of reasonableness or otherwise of the husband's conduct had to be **44.4.5** given its natural meaning without any extra gloss. The husband had sent a calderbank letter to the wife shortly before the trial conceding that he saw no future in the marriage. From that point on it was wrong of the husband to continue to defend the petition on the basis that the marriage had not irretrievably broken down. The court found that the husband's conduct of the case was unreasonable and bordering on being dishonest: *Hadjimilitis v Tsavliris (Costs)* [2003] 1 F.L.R. 81 (Alison Ball Q.C.).

In proceedings concerning contact arrangements, the children's mother had sent a letter and medical certificate to the court explaining that she could not attend a hearing. Because of an administrative error of the court, the documents were not passed to the judge, who made an order against the mother on the indemnity basis, on the basis of her unreasonable action in not attending. On appeal the order was set aside. Although the judge did not have the document submitted to the court, he did have a copy of the letter sent to the husband's solicitors which indicated that she had communicated with the court. The Court of Appeal found that to condemn the mother's conduct out of hand in those circumstances was wholly unwarranted. In any event it was unthinkable that such an order should be made given how unusual the awarding of indemnity costs was in such cases: *Re B (Children)*, February 21, 2007, unrep.

Human Rights

44.4.6 For a case management decision on the proportionality of expert's fees see *Mann v Chetty & Patel* [2001] C.P. Rep. 24, CA and the note at para.44.5.4. See also the note at para.44.4.3.

The Court of Appeal expressed concern and gave guidance in relation to the procedures to be followed in relation to claims for damages under the Human Rights Act so that the costs of obtaining relief are proportionate to that relief. In relation to proceedings which include a claim for damages for maladministration under the Human Rights Act the court gave the following guidance:

"81. ...

(i) The court should look critically at any attempt to recover damages under the HRA for maladministration by any procedure other than judicial review in the Administrative Court.

(ii) A claim for damages alone cannot be brought by judicial review (Part 54.3(2)) but in this case the proceedings should still be brought in the Administrative Court by an ordinary claim.

(iii) Before giving permission to apply for judicial review the Administrative Court Judge should require the claimant to explain why it would not be more appropriate to use any available internal complaint procedure or proceed by making a claim to the PCA or LGO at least in the first instance. The complaint procedures of the PCA and the LGO are designed to deal economically (the claimant pays no costs and does not require a lawyer) and expeditiously with claims for compensation for maladministration. (From enquiries the court has made it is apparent that the time scale for resolving complaints compares favourably with that of litigation).

(iv) If there is a legitimate claim for other relief permission should, if appropriate, be limited to that relief and consideration given to deferring permission for the damages claim, adjourning or staying that claim until use has been made of ADR, whether by reference to a mediator or ombudsman or otherwise or remitting that claim to a District Judge or Master if it cannot be dismissed summarily on grounds that, in any event, an award of damages is not required to achieve just satisfaction.

(v) It is hoped that with the assistance of this judgment in future claims that have had to be determined by the courts can be determined by the appropriate level of judge in a summary manner by the judge reading the relevant evidence, the citing of more than three authorities should be justified and the hearing should be limited to half a day except in exceptional circumstances.

(vi) There are no doubt other ways in which the proportionate resolution of this type of claim for damages can be achieved. We encourage their use and do not intend to be prescriptive. What we want to avoid is any repetition of what has happened in the court below in relation to each of these appeals and before us and when we have been deluged with extensive written and oral arguments and citation from numerous lever arch files crammed to overflowing with authorities the exercise that has taken place may be justifiable on one occasion but it will be difficult to justify it again."

Anufrijeva v London Borough of Southwark and two other appeals [2003] EWCA Civ1406.

Factors to be taken into account in deciding the amount of costs

44.5—(1) The court is to have regard to all the circumstances in deciding whether costs were— 44.5

(a) if it is assessing costs on the standard basis—

(i) proportionately and reasonably incurred; or

(ii) were proportionate and reasonable in amount, or

(b) if it is assessing costs on the indemnity basis—

(i) unreasonably incurred; or

(ii) unreasonable in amount.

(2) In particular the court must give effect to any orders which have already been made.

(3) The court must also have regard to—

(a) the conduct of all the parties, including in particular—

(i) conduct before, as well as during, the proceedings; and

(ii) the efforts made, if any, before and during the proceedings in order to try to resolve the dispute;

(b) the amount or value of any money or property involved;

(c) the importance of the matter to all the parties;

(d) the particular complexity of the matter or the difficulty or novelty of the questions raised;

(e) the skill, effort, specialised knowledge and responsibility involved;

(f) the time spent on the case; and

(g) the place where and the circumstances in which work or any part of it was done.

(Rule 35.4(4) gives the court power to limit the amount that a party may recover with regard to the fees and expenses of an expert.)

Comment

Rule 44.3 sets out the circumstances which the court must take into account when exercising its discretion as to costs. Rule 44.5 sets out the factors to be taken into account when deciding the amount of costs whether on a summary or detailed assessment. The conduct of all the parties is again relevant to the amount to be allowed and that conduct may be before as well as during the proceedings and includes the efforts made before and during the proceedings to try to resolve the dispute. 44.5.1

Separate actions were brought by four claimants against several defendants. The actions were not consolidated but were tried together. Some costs incurred by the defendants were common to all four actions, other costs were specific to each claim. The actions were dismissed by the trial judge who carried out a summary assessment and found that the claimants were jointly and severally liable for the common costs: *Bairstow v Queens Moat Houses Plc* [2000] B.C.C. 1025, Nelson J.

Where four different commercial interests commenced separate proceedings against the same defendant, which were not consolidated, the court awarded the successful claimants their costs but directed that the Costs Judge was free to consider the four actions as if they had been consolidated at the date of the order for mutuality of evidence.

Regard had to be had to the reasonableness of the claimants maintaining separate representation and separate expert witnesses during the period after that order: *Cipla Ltd v Glaxo Group Ltd and other actions* [2004] EWHC 819 (Ch), Pumfrey J. The Court of Appeal has held that there is nothing fundamentally different or special about generic costs, they were simply costs that have been shared for the sensible purpose of keeping the costs of each claim down.

The Court of Appeal suggested that it would be good practice for a solicitor to mention in a client care letter that some of the work to be done would be for the benefit of a group of clients, and that the individual would be liable only for his share. It would also be sensible for a solicitor to keep records of the number of clients for whom he was acting at any time. Such records would help him to demonstrate, if need be, that the proportion claimed for any individual client was justified: *Brown v Russell Young & Co* [2007] EWCA Civ 43; [2007] 2 All E.R. 453, CA.

In *Francis v Francis and Dickerson* [1956] P. 87; [1953] 3 All E.R. 836, it was held that the correct viewpoint to be taken by a costs officer in considering whether any step was reasonable is that of a sensible solicitor considering what, in the light of his then knowledge, was reasonable in the interest of his client. It was further held that any step taken on the advice of a properly instructed counsel should rarely be disallowed, but the Court of Appeal in *Davy-Chiesman v Davy-Chiesman* [1984] 2 W.L.R. 291; [1984] 1 All E.R. 321 held that a solicitor did not abdicate his own responsibility by instructing counsel, and where counsel's advice was "glaringly wrong" the solicitor should have expressed his own views.

Where both claimant and defendant appealed against costs orders made in relation to injunctive proceedings. The Court of Appeal dismissed both appeals ordering each party to pay most of the other party's costs of the unsuccessful appeal. The costs judge was directed to apportion those costs between various applications. In the event, the costs judge awarded one party all its reasonable costs. The other party appealed on the basis that the costs judge had failed to carry out an apportionment as directed by the Court of Appeal. On appeal the court found that, in circumstances where costs had been incurred for two purposes, a broad apportionment of them had to be made between each of the two purposes. The approach of the costs judge was incorrect as a matter of law: *Fourie v Le Roux* [2006] EWHC 1840 (Ch), Warren J.

Failure to serve statement of costs

44.5.2 The failure of a party to comply with s.13 of the Costs Practice Direction by omitting to file and serve a copy of the statement of costs not less than 24 hours before the date fixed for the hearing did not warrant the wholesale disallowance of costs. Where the only factor against awarding costs was merely the failure to serve a statement of costs without aggravating factors a party should not be deprived of all his costs. The court would take the matter into account but its reaction should be proportionate. The court should ask itself what if any prejudice there had been to the paying party and how that prejudice should be dealt with, e.g. by allowing a short adjournment or adjourning the swnmary assessment to another date, or directing detailed assessment: *MacDonald v Taree Holdings Ltd*, *The Times*, December 28, 2000, Neuberger J.

Summary assessment

44.5.3 It is wrong in principle for a judge to conclude that, because the paying party's costs are much the same as the receiving party's, the latter's costs could be assumed to be costs that it was reasonable for the paying party to pay. The judge's task is to focus on the heads of costs he is being asked to assess and to form his best judgment of the proportion it was reasonable to require the paying party to pay: *Machinery Developments Ltd v St Merryn Meat Ltd* [2005] EWCA Civ 29.

The judge in a trademark dispute summarily assessed the costs at the end of the trial at £10,000 as against the £38,000 claimed. In carrying out the summary assessment the judge had not gone into any sort of detailed analysis of the objector's statement of costs but appeared to have applied his own tariff as to what costs were appropriate for a one day paper only appeal. That approach was wrong in principle: *1-800 Flowers Inc v Phonenames Ltd* [2001] EWCA Civ 721; *The Times*, July 9, 2001. In respect of a hearing for assessment of damages, the claimant successfully applied for an adjournment but no provision was made for costs. In those circumstances neither party was entitled to its costs relating to that order. Accordingly the defendant could not recover the consequential cost of his expert witnesses cancellation fee: *Beahan v Stoneham* [2001] 2 Q.R. 8 (Buckley J.).

In proceedings claiming damages of £9,000 it was ultimately decided, because of double counting and an error in the exchange rate calculation, that only one head of claim was made out in the sum of £2,502. Because of the complicated procedural history the case had never been allocated to a track. The District Judge awarded costs against the defendant and summarily assessed them on the basis that it was not a small claim. On appeal it was held that even on the most successful outcome from the claimant's point of view, an award in excess of £4,003 could not have been made. Non allocation to a track meant that the small claims costs regime did not follow as an automatic starting point but it did not preclude the court from considering whether it would be reasonable to make an assessment consistent with the small claims costs regime or to apply the regime to a claim which should never have exceeded and never was anything more than a small claim. In the absence of any specific factors suggesting otherwise, in a case where an allocation to the small claims track would normally have been made, the normal rule should be that the small claims costs regime should apply: *Voice & Script International Ltd v Alghafar* [2003] EWCA Civ 736.

Proportionality

The Court of Appeal considered the question of proportionality in relation to costs which were to be summarily assessed. The court quoted with approval the judgment of HHJ Alton in the Birmingham County Court on June 22, 2000 in an unnamed case: **44.5.4**

> "In modern litigation, with the emphasis on proportionality, it is necessary for parties to make an assessment at the outset of the likely value of the claim and its importance and complexity, and then to plan in advance the necessary work, the appropriate level of person to carry out the work, the overall time which will be necessary and appropriate to spend on the various stages in bringing the action to trial, and the likely overall cost. While it is not unusual for costs to exceed the amount in issue, it is, in the context of modern litigation such as the present case, one reason for seeking to curb the amount of work done, and the cost by reference to the need for proportionality."

The court expressed the view that for the future it would be helpful for a judge carrying out a summary assessment to express his reasoning in rather more detail than happened in the particular case: *Jefferson v National Freight Carriers Plc* [2001] EWCA Civ 2082; [2001] 2 Costs L.R. 313, CA; *Lownds v Home Office* [2002] EWCA Civ 365. See also note at para.44.4.3.

Where a respondent successfully opposed an application to the Court of Appeal for permission to appeal, the court awarded the respondent their costs of opposing the application which had lasted half a day. The claim for costs was £54,487 On summary assessment, on the basis of written submissions, the court held that the total claimed was disproportionate and would be a surprise to most members of the public. The question for the court was whether it was just to require the appellant to pay the large sums claimed as the price of losing. It was not the concern of the court whether a bill of this size was to be presented to the respondent by their solicitors. On assessment the costs were limited to £16,195. The court reduced the amount of time claimed for perusal and preparation of documents, the amount claimed for attendance of solicitors at court and the fees of leading and junior counsel (*Habib Bank Ltd v Ahmed* [2004] EWCA Civ 805).

Where a judge forms the view that the costs as claimed are disproportionate and then looks at each item in turn to consider whether it was necessary, it is wrong for the judge, if of the view that the costs are still disproportionate, to simply reduce the global figure further to reach a figure which appears proportionate. The correct approach was to have gone back over each item in turn again *Re Michaelides* [2003] EWHC 3029 (Ch); [2004] BPIR 613, Blackburne J.

Considering proportionality was a more complex exercise than simply comparing the amount of the costs with the amount that was recovered. The Appeal Court found that the amount of costs claimed was excessive when looked at globally. The fact that the Costs Judge had not expressly referred to each of the factors set out in CPR r.44.5(3) was not material. *Young v JR Smart (Builders) Ltd (Costs)* [2004] EWHC 103 (QB); [2004] 2 Costs LR 298, Henriques J. It is too simplistic to focus on the amount of financial compensation compared to the costs when considering proportionality. In defamation proceedings the claimant's main concern was the delivery up and destruction of photographs. The defendant had prolonged the length of time that the proceedings went on by pursuing bad points on liability. Settlement was only achieved

20 months after the cause of action arose and costs had built up in the intervening period. Furthermore one of the defendants was outside the jurisdiction which had caused problems. Thus, although the amount of financial compensation may provide a useful starting point in determining proportionality, there were cases where the need to press for other remedies would assume greater significance: *Cox v MGN Ltd* [2006] EWHC 1235, QB, Eady J.

As to the issue of conduct see note at 44.3.10above: *Northstar Systems Ltd v Fielding* [2006] EWCA Civ 1660 and see *Drukker & Co v Pridie Brewster & Co* [2005] EWHC 2788, QB, Openshaw J.

Costs Incurred in Foreign Jurisdictions

44.5.5 Costs incurred by a litigant in another jurisdiction should be assessed in accordance with the rules and procedure of that jurisdiction, see *Wentworth v Lloyd* (1866) LR2 EQ 607, *Slingsby v Attorney General* [1918] P236, *McCullie v Butler (No.2) (Costs: Taxation)* [1962] 2 Q.B.309. Whilst r.44.5 requires the court to have regard to all the circumstances and factors, the relevance of those factors will vary from case to case and item to item. When assessing costs incurred in a foreign jurisdiction, r.44.5(3)(g) assumes significant importance and other factors might not be a feature of assessment in other jurisdictions. This however, would not prevent a paying party from contending, on detailed assessment, that fees were disproportionate or unreasonable: *Societa Finanziaria Industie Turistiche SPA v. Di Balsorano*, June 30, 2006, unrep., SCCO, Master Gordon-Saker.

Fixed costs

44.6 **44.6 A party may recover the fixed costs specified in Part 45 in accordance with that Part.**

Procedure for assessing costs

44.7 **44.7 Where the court orders a party to pay costs to another party (other than fixed costs) it may either—**

(a) make a summary assessment of the costs; or

(b) order detailed assessment of the costs by a costs officer,

unless any rule, practice direction or other enactment provides otherwise.

(The costs practice direction sets out the factors which will affect the court's decision under this rule.)

Comment

44.7.1 Attention is drawn to ss.12, 13 and 14 of the Costs Practice Direction dealing with the procedure for assessment and the summary assessment of costs. The court will make a summary assessment of costs unless it is not practicable to do so at the conclusion of a trial of a case which has been dealt with on the fast track or at the conclusion of any other hearing which has lasted not more than one day. The parties are required to prepare and serve upon each other a statement of costs in the form of a statement. The statement must be filed at the court and served on the other parties as early as possible and in any event not less than 24 hours before the hearing at which the assessment will take place, and see note at 44.5.2.

Where costs are assessed at a separate hearing following the end of a trial, the costs hearing itself may be subject to the fair trial requirements of ECHR art.6(1): *Robins v United Kingdom* (1998) 26 E.H.R.R. 527.

Only the judge who hears a case is in a position to make a summary assessment of the costs, otherwise the issue of costs should be sent to a costs judge for consideration: *Mahmood v Penrose* [2002] EWCA Civ 457, CA. A claimant can in principle recover by way of costs sums in respect of work by its own employee experts carried out in relation to the claim. There is nothing unjust in the reasonable recovery of the costs of in-house experts. The court stated that it was not obvious why the costs of outside experts should be recoverable but not those of in-house experts. Whilst *Buckland v Watts* [1971] W.L.R. 70 appeared to suggest that such costs were irrecoverable that was in conflict with *Re Nossen's Letter Patent* [1969] 1 W.L.R. 638 and the decision of the Court of Appeal in *Field v Leeds City Council, The Times*, January 18, 2000, CA. *Admiral Management Services Ltd v Para-Protect Europe Ltd* [2002] EWHC 233, Ch D, Stanley Burnton J. The question was raised as to whether the successful claimant was entitled to recover, as damages, the costs of its internal management and staff time and internal overheads, due to the diversion of internal resources caused by the actionable wrong of the defendant. The court held that there should be no difference, in principle, between the recoverability of damages in respect of times spent by employees, in a department specifically set up to investigate and mitigate anticipated and actual breaches of the claimant's conditions of trade, and the recoverability of damages, in respect of time spent by employees investigating actual torts committed against the claimant, where there was no such department. (*Admiral Management Services* above disapproved). *R + V Versicherung AG v Risk Insurance and Reinsurance Solutions SA (No.3)* [2006] EWHC 42 (Comm) Gloster J.

The Court of Appeal has considered in detail the question of staff costs and whether, where properly incurred, they should be recoverable as damages or costs. In *Aerospace Publishing Ltd v Thames Water Utilities Ltd* [2007] EWCA Civ 3, the claimant claimed damages in respect of a private archive which had been damaged by a burst water main. As part of their claim for special damage the claimants included a claim for staff work necessarily undertaken in relation to and consequent upon the flood. The majority of the claim was in respect of work done by the claimants' employees, but part of it was in respect of two ex-employees who returned to work on a freelance basis. The defendant's position was that the freelance costs were costs of the action to be assessed. The court was referred to five authorities (*Tate & Lyle Food and Distribution Ltd v Greater London Council* [1982] 1 W.L.R. 149; *Standard Chartered Bank v Pakistan National Shipping Corporation* [2001] EWCA Civ 55; *Horace Holman Group Ltd v Sherwood International Group* [2001] All E.R. (D.) 83 (Nov); *Admiral Management Services Ltd v Para-Protect Europe Ltd* [2002] EWHC 233 (Ch); [2002] 1 W.L.R. 2722; and *R+V Versicherung Attorney General v Risk Insurance and Reinsurance Solutions SA* [2006] EWHC 42 (Comm)) of which *Admiral Management Services* and *R+V Versicherung* were the most recent. The court (Wilson L.J.) stated:

> "85. In my view the divide between the decisions of Stanley Burnton J in *Admiral Management Services* and of Gloster J in *R + V Versicherung AG* is not as stark as may appear. But, to the extent that there is a difference, I consider that the approach of Gloster J is preferable as being, unsurprisingly, more consonant with the decision of this court in Standard Chartered Bank not cited to Stanley Burnton J."

The court stated that the authorities established the following propositions:

> "86. ...
>
> (a) The fact and, if so, the extent of the diversion of staff time have to be properly established and, if in that regard evidence which it would have been reasonable for the claimant to adduce is not adduced, he is at risk of finding that they have not been established.
>
> (b) The claimant also has to establish that the diversion caused significant disruption to its business.
>
> (c) Even though it may well be that strictly the claim should be cast in terms of loss of revenue attributable to the diversion of staff time, nevertheless in the ordinary case, and unless the defendant can establish the contrary, it is reasonable for the court to infer from the disruption that, had their time not been thus diverted, staff would have applied it to activities which would, directly or indirectly, have generated revenue for the claimant in an amount at least equal to the costs of employing them during that time."

On that basis the court could see no error in the judge's allowance within the damages of the costs of the employees referable to the diversion: *Aerospace Publishing Ltd v Thames Water Utilities Ltd* (above).

A non-solicitor litigant in person, even if a professional, cannot recover costs in respect of his time spent, other than in respect of time spent on matters within his own professional expertise and requiring the attention of an expert. The position of an office holder (liquidator/administrator) is no different. Even if the office holder had to bring or defend litigation, that did not mean that it was part of his profession to conduct litigation, in the way that it was part of the profession of a solicitor to do so. Only that part of the firm's costs which related to in-house expert services carried out by experts doing work which was such as to require the exercise of that particular expertise could be brought into account on the detailed assessment: *Sisu Fund Ltd v Tucker* [2005] EWHC 2321 (Ch); [2006] 1 All E.R. 167, Warren J. (The appeal against this decision was subsequently withdrawn.)

In litigation arising out of the foot and mouth disease outbreak in February 2001 the claimant, which had been engaged by DEFRA to carry out cleansing and disinfecting work, sued the Department in respect of unpaid invoices. The action was compromised on the basis that the defendant would pay the claimant's costs "including the (claimant's) reasonable internal costs of the main claim ... to be subject to detailed assessment on the standard basis if not agreed." The question arose as to the meaning of "reasonable". The court found that it was a word in common use and quoted the definition from the Shorter Oxford English Dictionary. It was unusual to find a provision for "internal costs" in an order relating to costs and "internal costs" must refer to all the non legal costs incurred by the claimant. The court held that the parties must have intended that the claimant was entitled to recover such in-house costs and so "reasonable" must qualify the assessment of those costs. The words "to be subject to detailed assessment on the standard basis if not agreed" related to the claimants' costs as a whole and not to the internal costs only. The addition of the word "reasonable" was surplusage: *Ruttle Plant Hire Ltd v Department for Environment Food and Rural Affairs* [2007] EWHC 1633 (QB) Griffith Williams J.

Estimates of costs

44.7.2 On completing the allocation questionnaire and the pre-trial questionnaire the party must set out an estimate of costs incurred to date and an estimate of likely future costs s.6 of the Costs Practice Direction. deals with this. Considerable care and precision is required in the preparation of such estimates since the estimates of opposing parties are likely to be compared one with another. An over generous estimate may result in an opponent recovering a similar amount, while an under-generous estimate may result in a recovery on behalf of the client which does not reflect the actual costs involved.

Signing the Bill of Costs

44.7.3 In signing the bill or statement of costs the solicitor certifies that the contents of the bill are correct: "that signature is no empty formality, the bill specifies the hourly rates applied [...]. If an agreement between the receiving solicitor and his client [...] restricted (say) the hourly rate payable by the client, that hourly rate is the most that can be claimed or recovered on [assessment] [...]. The signature of the bill of costs under the rules is effectively the certificate of an officer of the court that the receiving party's solicitors are not seeking to recover in relation to any item more than they have agreed to charge their client". Per Henry L.J., in *Bailey v IBC Vehicles Ltd* [1998] 3 All E.R. 570, CA.

"[...] in view of the increasing interest taken in (the indemnity principle) by unsuccessful parties to litigation coupled with the developing practice in relation to conditional fees, the extension of the client care letter and contentious business agreements under s.60(3) (of the Solicitors Act 1974), in future a short written explanation [...] should normally be attached to the bill of costs. This will avoid skirmishes which add unnecessarily to the costs of litigation." Per Judge L.J., in *Bailey v IBC Vehicles Ltd* [1998] 3 All E.R. 570, CA.

See s.4 of the Costs Practice Direction.

Summary Assessment

44.7.4 See Guide to Summary Assessment of Costs, para.48.16.

Judges are required to assess the costs of a case if practicable, and in cases lasting more than one day, the parties are under an obligation to provide the court and their opponents with details of the costs which may be sought in the event of success (see s.13 of the Costs Practice Direction). A Registrar in Bankruptcy was wrong in law not to assess costs on the detailed breakdown of costs actually incurred, as shown by the successful party's statement of costs, and instead substituting his own tariff: *McLinden v Redbond* [2006] EWHC 234 (Ch), Evans-Lombe J.

An order for costs following a summary assessment, other than one made at a final hearing, is exempt from registration under the Register of County Court Judgments Regulations 1985, as amended by the Register of County Court Judgments (Amendment) Regulations 1999 (SI 1999/1845).

Where an interim injunction is granted the court will normally reserve the costs of the application until the determination of the substantive issue. *Desquenne et Giral UK Ltd v Richardso* [2001] F.S.R. 1, CA). The court's hands are not tied however and if special factors are present a different order may be made. *Picnic at Ascot Inc v Derigs* [2001] F.S.R. 2, Neuberger J.

Family Proceedings

There is no rebuttable presumption against summary assessment in relation to costs where hearings last longer than one day. The exercise of the power to make a summary assessment should be considered in every case. In family proceedings the aggravation of detailed assessment of costs could run counter to the design of reducing contention and achieving satisfactory resolution of disputes: *Q v Q (Costs: Summary Assessment)* [2002] 2 F.L.R. 668, Wilson J. **44.7.5**

Appeals relating to Summary Assessment

Such appeals are dealt with under the ordinary rules relating to appeals. (See Pt 52.) **44.7.6**

The court allowed a stay of execution pending appeal against an order for the payment of summarily assessed costs, where the hearing of the application for permission was near and the court hearing that application would have the time to investigate the situation. In addition to which the schedule of costs had not been signed, in clear breach of the rules: *Wilson v Howard Pawnbrokers* [2002] EWHC 1489 (Ch), Etherton J.

Detailed Assessment

For the practice and procedure of detailed assessment see Pt 47 and Sects 28 to 49 of the Costs Practice Direction. **44.7.7**

Time for complying with an order for costs[1]

44.8 A party must comply with an order for the payment of costs within 14 days of— **44.8**

(a) the date of the judgment or order if it states the amount of those costs;

(b) if the amount of those costs (or part of them) is decided later in accordance with Part 47, the date of the certificate which states the amount; or

(c) in either case, such later date as the court may specify.

(Part 47 sets out the procedure for detailed assessment of costs.)

Comment

All certificates (default costs certificates, interim certificates and final certificates) contain an order to pay. **44.8.1**

The court has a discretion under r.44.3 as to when costs are to be paid but, unless otherwise ordered, costs become payable within 14 days of the date of the order. If a party seeks an extension of time in which to pay the costs it is for that party to make an application supported by evidence. In the absence of any alternative order, r.44.8 applies and the costs are payable within 14 days of the original order (*Pepin v Watts* [2001] C.P.L.R. 9, CA).

Costs on the small claims track and fast track[2]

44.9—(1) Part 27 (small claims) and Part 46 (Fast track trial costs) contain special rules about— **44.9**

(a) liability for costs;

(b) the amount of costs which the court may award; and

[1] Amended by Civil Procedure (Amendment No.3) Rules 2000 (SI 2000/1317).
[2] Amended by SI 1999/1008.

(c) the procedure for assessing costs.

(2) Once a claim is allocated to a particular track, those special rules shall apply to the period before, as well as after, allocation except where the court or a practice direction provides otherwise.

Comment

44.9.1 The rules relating to small claims and fast track trial costs do not apply until a claim is allocated to a particular track (see ss.15 and 16 of the Costs Practice Direction). Rule 44.11(1) provides that any costs orders made before a claim is allocated will not be affected by the allocation. See also note at 44.5.3 *Voice & Script International Ltd v Alghafar* [2003] EWCA Civ 736.

44.9.2 The pre-action protocol requires the claim to be advanced initially in accordance with its terms, under a warning that there is likely to be a costs penalty if it is not complied with. The references to costs in the protocol clearly demonstrate that its object is to achieve settlement without recourse to litigation (the case concerned the pre-action protocol for housing disrepair cases). The protocol was not to operate as a means of preventing recovery of reasonably incurred legal costs. The court's powers are unrestricted in relation to pre-allocation costs. It is perfectly proper for the court to make an order in relation to them under r.44.9(2) if to do so was necessary to ensure that the protocol did not operate to prevent recovery of costs reasonably incurred. The costs would be calculated according to the track to which the claim would fall if it had been litigated (*Birmingham City Council v Lee* [2008] EWCA Civ 891).

Limitation on amount court may allow where a claim allocated to the fast track settles before trial

44.10 **44.10—(1) Where the court—**

(a) assesses costs in relation to a claim which—

(i) has been allocated to the fast track; and

(ii) settles before the start of the trial; and

(b) is considering the amount of costs to be allowed in respect of a party's advocate for preparing for the trial,

it may not allow, in respect of those advocate's costs, an amount that exceeds the amount of fast track trial costs which would have been payable in relation to the claim had the trial taken place.

(2) When deciding the amount to be allowed in respect of the advocate's costs, the court shall have regard to—

(a) when the claim was settled; and

(b) when the court was notified that the claim had settled.

(3) In this rule, "advocate" and "fast track trial costs" have the meanings given to them by Part 46.

(Part 46 sets out the amount of fast track trial costs which may be awarded.)

Comment

44.10.1 Lord Woolf's original intention was that all fast track costs should be fixed or capped. There are some fixed costs provisions affecting the fast track in Pt 45, Sects II and III. Also fast track trial costs are fixed and this is dealt with at Pt 46. "Fast track trial costs" means the costs of a party's advocate for preparing for and appearing at the trial (see r.46.1(2)(b)). Rule 44.10 deals only with the amount of costs to be allowed in respect of a party's advocate for preparing for a fast track trial which settles before the start of the trial. The costs which may be allowed in respect of that work may not exceed the amount which would have been payable in accordance with Pt 46 had the trial taken place.

Costs following allocation and reallocation

44.11 **44.11—(1) Any costs orders made before a claim is allocated will not be affected by allocation.**

(2) Where—

(a) a claim is allocated to a track; and

(b) the court subsequently re-allocates that claim to a different track,

then unless the court orders otherwise, any special rules about costs applying—

(i) to the first track, will apply to the claim up to the date of reallocation; and

(ii) to the second track, will apply from the date of reallocation.

(Part 26 deals with the allocation and reallocation of claims between tracks.)

Comment

The special rules which apply tc small claims and fast track trial costs do not apply until the claim is allocated to a particular track (see r.44.9(2)). Any costs orders which are made before the claim is allocated to a track are not affected by subsequent allocation. Where the claim is re-allocated to a different track the special rules apply, according to track, up to and after the re-allocation unless the court makes a different order. See s.16 of the Costs Practice Direction. **44.11.1**

Cases where costs orders deemed to have been made[1]

44.12—(1) Where a right to costs arises under— **44.12**

(a) rule 3.7 (defendant's right to costs where claim struck out for non-payment of fees);

(b) rule 36.10(1) or (2) (claimant's entitlement to costs where a Part 36 offer is accepted)

(c) [...]

(d) rule 38.6 (defendant's right to costs where claimant discontinues),

a costs order will be deemed to have been made on the standard basis.

(1A) Where such an order is deemed to be made in favour of a party with pro bono representation, that party may apply for an order under section 194(3) of the Legal Services Act 2007.

(2) Interest payable pursuant to section 17 of the Judgments Act 1838 or section 74 of the County Courts Act 1984 on the costs deemed to have been ordered under paragraph (1) shall begin to run from the date on which the event which gave rise to the entitlement to costs occurred.

Comment

In certain cases costs orders are deemed to have been made. Rule 3.7 introduces an automatic strike-out for non payment of fees which gives the defendant the right to costs. **44.12.1**

The Civil Procedure (Amendment No.3) Rules 2006 amend r.44.12(1)(b) to refer to r.36.10(1) or (2) being the relevant clauses of the amended Pt 36.

Rule 44.12(1)(c) (claimant's right to costs when defendant accepts the claimant's Pt 36 offer) is omitted altogether. The text below must be read as referring only to the rule as it applied prior to the date of amendment (April 6, 2007).

---

[1] Amended by the Civil Procedure (Amendment No.3) Rules 2006 (SI 2006/3435) and the Civil Procedure (Amendment) Rules 2008 (SI 2008/2178).

Rule 44.12(1)(b) Part 36

44.12.2 Paragraphs 7.1–7.11 of PD 36 deal with acceptance by a claimant of a defendant's Pt 36 offer or payment, or a defendant's acceptance of the claimant's Pt 36 offer. Rule 38.6 deals with a claimant's liability for costs where a claimant has discontinued wholly or in part. Part 38 gives the court power to order otherwise and an order for costs on the indemnity basis may therefore be made. *Atlantic Bar & Grill Ltd v Posthouse Hotels Ltd (Costs)* [2000] C.P. Rep. 32 (Ratee J.). Defendants, who made an offer under the Warsaw Convention, which was refused, and subsequently made a payment into court exceeding the offer, which was accepted, applied that the claimants should not be entitled to their costs and that no costs order should be deemed to have been made under r.44.12(1)(b). The court held that the payment in exceeded the defendants' earlier offer and fell within "the amount of damages awarded" in art.22.4 of the Convention. The exception contained in art.22.4 did not apply and there was therefore no conflict between the Convention and the provisions of the rule: *GKN Westland Helicopters Ltd v Korean Air Lines Co Ltd* [2003] EWHC 1120 (Comm); *The Times*, June 11, 2003 (Morison J.).

Where a claimant who had suffered a back injury sought damages of £150,000 the defendants made a pre-action offer of £5,000 inclusive of costs. The offer was rejected and proceedings were commenced. The defendant then paid into court £4,000, which the claimant accepted within 21 days, thereby becoming entitled to costs on the standard basis to be assessed if not agreed. The defendants argued that the District Judge should allow the claimant no more than 25 per cent of the costs claimed. On appeal to the Circuit Judge the District Judge's decision was upheld. On appeal to the Court of Appeal the court confirmed that the District Judge had no power to vary the deemed order giving the claimant his costs, or to decide that the claimant should only be entitled to 25 per cent of the assessed costs. The court continued:

> "20. There is a real distinction between (a) carrying out an assessment and deciding as part of the assessment to reduce the bill by a percentage and (b) deciding in advance of the assessment that the receiving party will only receive a percentage of the assessed costs. The figure that results from (a) represents 100% of the assessed costs. In deciding as part of the assessment to reduce the bill by percentage, the Costs Judge is giving effect to an order that the successful party is entitled to his costs, to be assessed if not agreed. The figure that results from (b) represents less than 100% of the assessed costs. In deciding in advance of the assessment that the receiving party will only receive a percentage of the assessed costs, the Costs Judge is not giving effect to an order that the successful party is entitled to his costs, to be assessed if not agreed." *Lahey v Pirelli Tyres Ltd* [2007] EWCA Civ 91.

Rule 44.12(1)(d) discontinuance

44.12.3 The court may feel able to deprive a defendant of costs where proceedings are discontinued in circumstances which include but are not limited to:

(a) where the claimant has obtained an advantage from suing the defendant against whom it is discontinuing; and

(b) where the claim to be discontinued has become academic by some act on the part of the defendant for some independent party.

On the facts of the case discontinuance could not be equated with defeat or acknowledgment of likely defeat. The court permitted discontinuance with no order as to costs: *Everton v WPBSA (Promotions) Ltd*, December 12, 2001, unrep., Gray J.

Where claimants deleted a claim for compensation by amendment, this amounted to discontinuance under CPR r.38.6. The claimants were therefore liable for the defendants' costs of the discontinued claim down to the date of the discontinuance: *Isaac v Isaac (No.2)* [2005] EWHC 435, Park J.

In circumstances where claimants were held to have been unreasonably trying to delay the trial of the action, and who then discontinued, the court ordered the claimants to pay the defendant's costs on the indemnity basis: *Naskaris v ANS Plc* [2002] EWHC 1782 (Ch), Blackburn J.

Where a judge granted a claimant permission to discontinue judicial review proceedings and ordered the respondents to pay the claimant's costs to be assessed if not agreed, held on appeal that the judge was wrong on assessment to limit the costs to one only of several issues raised in the claim. The original order for costs could only mean that the claimant had been awarded all their costs: *R. (Chorion Plc) v Westminster City Council* [2002] EWCA Civ 1126; *The Times*, October 21, 2002, CA.

Where a judicial review application was discontinued the defendant's costs were reduced to reflect the defendant's failure to comply with the judicial review pre action protocol: *Aegis, Re* ; *Aegis Group Plc v Inland Revenue Commissioners* [2005] EWHC 1468, Park J.

The general rule is that a claimant who has been granted an order discontinuing its action, is liable for the defendant's costs up to the date when notice of discontinuation is served. It was appropriate that the burden should be on the party seeking to persuade the court to make a different order. In a case where a claimant had become alive at a late stage to commercial factors, which were clear from the outset of the proceedings, it was held that there was nothing to show that it was fair to depart from the general rule. It was not just or fair to allow a liquidator to walk away from an action in which he had made allegations which would undoubtedly have been resisted and to leave the defendant to pay his own costs when there had been no material change since the proceedings had commenced: *Walker v Walker* [2005] EWCA Civ 247; [2006] 1 W.L.R. 2194; [2006] 1 All E.R. 272, CA.

The court has jurisdiction to entertain an application for costs to be paid on the indemnity basis even where the claimants had discontinued their action and offered to pay costs on the indemnity basis, although they did not accept that the defendant was entitled to such an order. On the facts one reason why it was appropriate to award costs on the indemnity basis was because there were circumstances that took the case out of the ordinary, including the pursuit of hopeless but widely publicised allegations of dishonesty against many officers of the defendant. The fact that the claimants denied that the defendant was entitled to such an order itself created a sufficient lis to justify dealing with the application: *Three Rivers DC v Bank of England (Indemnity Costs)* [2006] EWHC 816 (Comm), Tomlinson J.

The Court of Appeal has held that service on the court by tenants, of notice under the Landlord and Tenant Act 1954 stating that they did not want a new tenancy, was the equivalent of a notice of discontinuance of the proceedings in which the tenants had been seeking an order for a new tenancy. It therefore followed that the tenants were liable to pay the costs of the proceedings under CPR r.38.6(1) unless special circumstances justified a different order: *Lay v Drexler* [2007] EWCA Civ 464.

Rule 44.12(2) Interest

Interest under the Judgments Act 1838 s.17 or County Courts Act 1984 s.74 runs from the date on which the event giving rise to the entitlement to costs occurred or from such date as the court may order. Section 17(1) of the Judgments Act 1838 has been amended by the Civil Procedure (Modification of Enactments) Order 1998 (SI 1998/2940) to provide that interest will run from such time as is prescribed by rules of court. See r.44.3(6)(g). In a patent action the judge ordered the claimant to pay part of the defendant's costs. Interest on the amount of costs assessed was payable from the date of the judgment. The claimant appealed and the defendants cross-appealed against the limited order for costs The appeal was dismissed but the cross-appeal as to costs succeeded, on the basis that the trial judge had pre-judged the results of detailed assessment without considering the facts. The defendants were therefore entitled to recover costs as eventually assessed. The effect of this order setting aside the original order as to costs was to make interest payable from the date of the Court of Appeal order. It was held that, although the Court of Appeal could not, under the slip rule, order that interest should be recoverable on all costs from the date of the original judge's order, it was possible under that rule to give effect to the intention of the court. Interest was therefore to run from the date of the judge's order persuant to his original order and from the date of the Court of Appeal judgment pursuant to that order: *Bristol Myers Squibb Co v Baker Norton Pharmaceuticals Inc* [2001] EWCA Civ 414. 44.12.4

Costs-only proceedings[1]

44.12A—(1) This rule sets out a procedure which may be followed where— 44.12A

(a) the parties to a dispute have reached an agreement on

[1] Introduced by the Civil Procedure (Amendment No.3) Rules 2000 (SI 2000/1317) and amended by the Civil Procedure (Amendment) Rules 2002 (SI 2002/2058) and the Civil Procedure (Amendment No.4) Rules 2003 (SI 2003/2113).

all issues (including which party is to pay the costs) which is made or confirmed in writing; but

(b) they have failed to agree the amount of those costs; and

(c) no proceedings have been started.

(1A) [...]

(2) Either party to the agreement may start proceedings under this rule by a claim form in accordance with Part 8.

(3) The claim form must contain or be accompanied by the agreement or confirmation.

(4) Except as provided in paragraph (4A), in proceedings to which this rule applies the court—

(a) may

(i) make an order for costs to be determined by detailed assessment; or

(ii) dismiss the claim; and

(b) must dismiss the claim if it is opposed.

(4A) In proceedings to which Section II of Part 45 applies, the court shall assess the costs in the manner set out in that Section.

(5) Rule 48.3 (amount of costs where costs are payable pursuant to a contract) does not apply to claims started under the procedure in this rule.

(Rule 7.2 provides that proceedings are started when the court issues a claim form at the request of the claimant)

(Rule 8.1 (6) provides that a practice direction may modify the Part 8 procedure).

Comment

44.12A.1 This rule is designed to deal with the situation where parties have agreed the substantive issue between them and one party has agreed to pay the other's costs, but it has not been possible to agree the amount of those costs. An application is made under Pt 8 and a reduced fee is payable. Where the court makes an order for costs in an application under this rule it will order detailed assessment. There will normally be no need for the parties to attend court for the Pt 8 application. If the applicant does not satisfy the court as to the existence of an agreement or the application is opposed, it will be dismissed. Sub-paragraph (1)(c) of r.44.12A was substituted by, and paras (1A) and (4A) were inserted by the Civil Procedure (Amendment No.4) Rules 2003; these changes came into effect on October 6, 2003.

Order for Costs

44.12A.2 An order for costs made under this rule is treated as an order for the amount of costs to be decided by detailed assessment under Pt 47.

Offers to Settle in Costs Only Proceedings

44.12A.3 Paragraph 46.2 of the Costs Practice Direction states that any offer should specify whether or not it is inclusive of the costs of preparation of the bill, interest and VAT. If the offer is silent it is treated as including these items. Since the purpose of the offer is to avoid a detailed assessment hearing, the cost of that hearing is excluded from the offer. Until the time the substantive claim is settled, "the proceedings" relate to liability and the amount of any compensation. After the substantive claim is settled "the proceedings" relate to the assessment of costs the paying party has to pay. Even when Pt 8 proceedings have to be commenced in order to obtain a court order for detailed assessment the "costs of the proceedings" within the meaning of CPR r.47.19 still relate only to the costs leading up to the disposal (by agreement) of the substantive claim. They are "the proceedings which gave rise to the assessment proceedings" and the assessment proceedings cover the whole period of negotiations about the amount of costs payable through the Pt 8 proceedings to the ultimate disposal of those proceedings, whether by agreement or by a court order. If the Costs Judge considers that the receiving party ought to have accepted an offer made before the Pt 8 proceedings commenced then he is likely to conclude that the paying party should receive all his costs including any costs involved in the subsequent Pt 8 proceedings pursuant to CPR r.47.18(2). The substantive proceedings and the assessment proceedings are quite different: *Crosbie v Munroe* [2003] EWCA Civ 350; [2003] 1 W.L.R. 2033, CA.

Special situations[1]

44.13—(1) Where the court makes an order which does not mention costs— **44.13**

(a) subject to paragraphs (1A) and (1B), the general rule is that no party is entitled—

(i) to costs; or

(ii) to seek an order under section 194(3) of the Legal Services Act 2007, in relation to that order; but

(b) this does not affect any entitlement of a party to recover costs out of a fund held by that party as trustee or personal representative, or pursuant to any lease, mortgage or other security.[2]

(1A) Where the court makes—

(a) an order granting permission to appeal;

(b) an order granting permission to apply for judicial review; or

(c) any other order or direction sought by a party on an application without notice,

and its order does not mention costs, it will be deemed to include an order for applicant's costs in the case.

(1B) Any party affected by a deemed order for costs under paragraph (1A) may apply at any time to vary the order.

(2) The court hearing an appeal may, unless it dismisses the appeal, make orders about the costs of the proceedings giving rise to the appeal as well as the costs of the appeal.

(3) Where proceedings are transferred from one court to another, the court to which they are transferred may deal with all the costs, including the costs before the transfer.

(4) Paragraph (3) is subject to any order of the court which ordered the transfer.

Comment

Rule 44.13(1) makes it clear that where an order is silent as to costs no party is entitled to the costs in relation to that order. **44.13.1**

See the table at para.8.5 of the Costs Practice Direction as to the meaning of "Costs here and below" and the exception for the Divisional Court.

Where an action had been automatically struck out due to the claimant's delay and the claimant successfully applied for it to be reinstated, the order made on that application was silent as to costs between the parties. The question of wasted costs was reserved to the trial judge. When, at the trial the claimant was successful, the trial

[1] Amended by the Civil Procedure (Amendment No.5) Rules 2001 (SI 2001/4015) and the Civil Procedure (Amendment) Rules 2008 (SI 2008/2178).

[2] Paragraph (1) substituted by the Civil Procedure (Amendment No.5) Rules 2001 SI 2001/4015, in force March 25, 2002.

judge had no jurisdiction to vary the earlier order to make the defendant pay the costs arising out of the strike out and reinstatement application: *Griffiths v Commissioner of Police* [2003] EWCA Civ 313.

Court's powers in relation to misconduct[1]

44.14 **44.14—(1) The court may make an order under this rule where—**

(a) a party or his legal representative, in connection with a summary or detailed assessment, fails to comply with a rule, practice direction or court order; or

(b) it appears to the court that the conduct of a party or his legal representative, before or during the proceedings which gave rise to the assessment proceedings, was unreasonable or improper.

(2) Where paragraph (1) applies, the court may—

(a) disallow all or part of the costs which are being assessed; or

(b) order the party at fault or his legal representative to pay costs which he has caused any other party to incur.

(3) Where—

(a) the court makes an order under paragraph (2) against a legally represented party; and

(b) the party is not present when the order is made,

the party's solicitor must notify his client in writing of the order no later than 7 days after the solicitor receives notice of the order.

Comment

44.14.0 The provisions relating to misconduct now extend to the legal representative of a party as well as to the party personally. The provisions relate both to unreasonable or improper conduct before or during the proceedings giving rise to the assessment proceedings, and during the assessment proceedings themselves. The effect of this is that a costs officer may of his or her own initiative, or at the request of a party, investigate and make orders in respect of unreasonable or improper conduct by a party or a legal representative. This means that a legal representative who has been found to have acted unreasonably or improperly may be ordered personally to pay costs which another party has been caused to incur. This power is in addition to the power to make wasted costs orders in accordance with s.51(6) of the Supreme Court Act 1981 (see r.48.7). In matrimonial proceedings, where an adjournment was wrongly obtained, the court found that there had been a culpable failure on the part of the wife's solicitors to invite an opposing party's solicitors to agree to an adjournment and a culpable misrepresentation on their part to the Clerk of the Rules that all the relevant parties agreed. The judge made no order as to costs between the parties on the adjournment. On appeal, the court held that there was no legitimate reason for depriving either the husband or the other party of their costs. The wife's gross delays had precipitated an adjournment of what turned out to be in excess of a year. In respect of the opposing party, there was a further compelling reason for awarding her costs, namely that solicitors had made to the Clerk of the Rules the misrepresentation which had secured an adjournment of the matter without reference to the opposing party's solicitors and without giving them the opportunity to object to it. The wife was ordered to pay the opposing party's costs of the hearing before the judge at first instance and any other costs thrown away as a result of the adjournment of the substantive hearing. *Gamboa-Garzon v Langer* [2006] EWCA Civ 1246.

Where the court makes an order against a party who is legally represented (whether the order is against the party personally or against the legal representative personally) the party's solicitor must notify the client in writing within seven days of receipt of no-

[1] Amended by the Civil Procedure (Amendment No.3) Rules 2000 (SI 2000/1317).

tice of the order if the party was not present when the order was made. This provision is in terms similar to r.44.2 which refers to "a costs order" made against a legally represented party.

As to wasted costs orders see r.48.7.

Delay

Unsuccessful claimants applied for detailed assessment proceedings to be struck out or stayed on the grounds of delay and failing to comply with the Rules and Costs Practice Direction. The court held that to impose the sanction of disallowance of costs, pursuant to r.44.14, on the ground of misconduct would be disproportionate. The blame for the delay was not all on the side of the defendant. Although there was culpable delay on the defendant's part, the claimants had not availed themselves of the right to apply under r.47.8(1) for an order requiring the defendant to commence detailed assessment within a specified period. The delay had not prevented fair assessment of the defendant's costs. The court found the defendant's bill of costs was valid and in compliance with the relevant rules. Even if there was a technical non compliance it would have reasonable justification and would not be a sound basis for the imposition of sanctions for misconduct pursuant to r.44.14(1)(a). *Botham v Khan* [2004] EWHC 2602, QB, Richards J. **44.14.1**

The solicitor and counsel relationship

In *Davy-Chiesman v Davy-Chiesman* [1984] Fam. 48; [1984] 1 All E.R. 321, the Court of Appeal held that where the relief sought as advised by counsel was glaringly wrong, the solicitor had a duty to inform the legal aid authorities of the change of circumstances, and to express his own views, and did not abdicate his own responsibility by instructing counsel. He was ordered to pay the costs of both sides personally. **44.14.2**

In *Re A (A Minor)* (1988) 18 Fam. Law. 339, CA, solicitors were held personally responsible for the costs of four abortive hearings, in a case where it was apparent that counsel was not competent and the solicitors should have withdrawn the instructions (A wasted costs order might now have been made against counsel.)

Although solicitors cannot automatically shelter behind counsel, if the circumstances warrant it they may be justified in relying upon counsel's advice (*Swedac Ltd v Magnet & Southern plc* [1990] F.S.R. 89). In circumstances where there was no evidence that a solicitor had expertise in the field of judicial review, the proposition that a solicitor who acted on counsel's advice had to bear responsibility for that advice in all circumstances could not be supported: *R. v Luton Family Proceedings Court Justices, Ex p. R.* (1998) 4 C.L. 51, CA.

Counsel is under a duty to reassess any advice in the light of further information. Failure to do so may lead to a wasted costs order (*C v C (Wasted Costs Order)* [1994] 2 F.L.R. 34, Ewbank J.).

It was unreasonable for a barrister in sole practice to rely wholly on instructing solicitors to notify him of the dates and times of his cases. It was counsel's responsibility to adopt a system which enabled him to keep abreast of the listing arrangements for his cases (*Re A Barrister (Wasted Costs Order) (No.4 of 1992)*, *The Times*, March 15, 1994; *Independent*, March 15, 1994, CA (Criminal Division) and see *Re A Barrister (Wasted Costs Order) (No.4 of 1993)*, *The Times*, April 21, 1993, CA (Criminal Division)).

Where the conduct of both the barrister and the solicitor in a case are the subject of criticism, any investigation of their professional conduct should be conducted by a joint tribunal (*Vowles v Vowles*, *The Times*, October 4, 1990, CA).

Providing information about funding arrangements[1]

***44.15—(1)* A party who seeks to recover an additional liability must provide information about the funding arrangement to the court and to other parties as required by a rule, practice direction or court order.** **44.15**

(2) Where the funding arrangement had changed, and the infor-

[1] Introduced by the Civil Procedure (Amendment No.3) Rules 2000 (SI 2000/1317) and amended by the Civil Procedure (Amendment) Rules 2002 (SI 2002/2058).

mation a party has previously provided in accordance with paragraph (1) is no longer accurate, that party must file notice of the change and serve it on all other parties within 7 days.

(3) Where paragraph (2) applies, and a party has already filed—

(a) an allocation questionnaire; or

(b) a pre-trial check list (listing questionnaire),

he must file and serve a new estimate of costs with the notice.

(The costs practice direction sets out—

- **the information to be provided when a party issues or responds to a claim form, files an allocation questionnaire, a pre-trial check list, and a claim for costs;**
- **the meaning of estimate of costs and the information required in it)**

(Rule 44.3B sets out situations where a party will not recover a sum representing any additional liability)

Comment

44.15.1 The rule provides that any party who seeks to recover an additional liability must provide certain information about it and must also provide information where the funding arrangement changes. The information to be provided in the notice of funding, and in the estimate of costs, is limited. Much fuller disclosure of information is required when the final assessment of costs takes place. See s.19 of the Costs Practice Direction.

This rule and s.19 of the Costs Practice Direction are not retrospective in their effect. Therefore no rules of court requiring notice of funding to be given apply to defendants entering into insurance arrangements between April 1 and July 2, 2000: *Inline Logistics Ltd v UCI Logistics Ltd* [2002] EWHC 519, Ferris J.

Adjournment where legal representative seeks to challenge disallowance of any amount of percentage increase[1]

44.16 **44.16—(1) This rule applies where the Conditional Fee Agreements Regulations 2000 or the Collective Conditional Fee Agreements Regulations 2000 continues to apply to an agreement which provides for a success fee.**

(2) Where—

(a) the court disallows any amount of a legal representative's percentage increase in summary or detailed assessment proceedings; and

(b) the legal representative applies for an order that the disallowed amount should continue to be payable by his client,

the court may adjourn the hearing to allow the client to be—

(i) notified of the order sought; and

(ii) separately represented.

(Regulation 3(2)(b) of the Conditional Fee Agreements Regulations 2000, which applies to Conditional Fee Agreements entered into before 1st November 2005, provides that a conditional fee

[1] Introduced by the Civil Procedure (Amendment No.3) Rules 2000 (SI 2000/1317) and amended by the Civil Procedure (Amendment) Rules 2001 (SI 2001/256), Civil Procedure (Amendment) Rules 2002 (SI 2002/2058) and the Civil Procedure (Amendment No.4) Rules 2005 (SI 2005/3515).

agreement which provides for a success fee must state that any amount of a percentage increase disallowed on assessment ceases to be payable unless the court is satisfied that it should continue to be so payable. Regulation 5(2)(b) of the Collective Conditional Fee Agreements Regulations 2000, which applies to Collective Conditional Fee Agreements entered into before 1st November 2005, makes similar provision in relation to collective conditional fee agreements.)

Comment

The effect of reg.(3)(2)(b) of the Conditional Fee Agreements Regulations 2000 (now reversed) is to prevent a legal representative from recovering from the client more, in respect of a success fee than the court has ordered the paying party to pay. The Costs Practice Direction s.20 sets out how the court may resolve the conflict between the legal representatives and the client when such an order is made. Rule 44.3B(1)(a) provides that any percentage increase relating to the cost of the postponement of the payment of fees and expenses is not recoverable against another party. There is potential for an application to be made under this rule, in many cases supported by a conditional fee agreement. **44.16.1**

Procedure

Section 20 of the Costs Practice Direction sets out the procedure to be followed in the assessment proceedings. If in detailed assessment proceedings, the points of dispute disclose that any percentage increase claimed by counsel is challenged, the solicitors must within three days of service deliver to counsel a copy of the relevant points of dispute and the relevant part of the bill. Counsel then has seven days within which to inform the solicitor in writing whether or not the reduction sought is accepted or what reply he wishes to make. The solicitor must serve this reply on the paying party. The Practice Direction sets out the steps to be taken where solicitor or counsel wish to apply for an order that the amount of any percentage increase disallowed against the paying party shall continue to be paid by the client. It should be noted that if the client is present when the application is made and agrees that it should be dealt with straight away or the court is satisfied by evidence that the client consents to an order being made in his absence, the court may, if it thinks fit, deal with the application without adjourning. Section 74(3) of the Solicitors Act 1974 (which prevents a solicitor recovering from the client more than the amount recoverable from an opposing party) applies, unless the solicitor and client have a written agreement which expressly permits payment to the solicitor of a greater amount in accordance with r.48.8(1A). **44.16.2**

Application of costs rules[1]

44.17 This Part and Part 45 (fixed costs), Part 46 (fast track trial costs), Part 47 (procedure for detailed assessment of costs and default provisions) and Part 48 (special cases), do not apply to the assessment of costs in proceedings to the extent that— **44.17**

(a) section 11 of the Access to Justice Act 1999, and provisions made under that Act; or

(b) regulations made under the Legal Aid Act 1988;

make different provision.

(The costs practice direction sets out the procedure to be followed where a party was wholly or partially funded by the Legal Services Commission).

[1] Introduced by the Civil Procedure (Amendment No.3) Rules 2000 (SI 2000/1317).

Comment

44.17.1 Section 11 of the Access to Justice Act 1999 deals with orders for costs against a LSC funded client and the Legal Services Commission. The Costs Practice Directions ss.21 to 23 set out the procedure to be followed, which is similar to but not identical with detailed assessment. The Civil Legal Aid (General) Regulations 1989, as amended, continue to apply to the assessment of costs where a certificate has been issued by the Legal Aid Board or by the Legal Services Commission.

Section 11(1) of the 1999 Act provides that costs ordered against an assisted party should not exceed a reasonable amount. The protection of the sub-section does not apply to those whose conduct amounts to serious crime, e.g. pursuing fraudulent claims against insurers: *Jones v Congregational and General Insurance Plc* [2003] EWHC 1027 (QB); [2003] 1 W.L.R. 3001 (H.H.J. Chambers Q.C.).

Community Legal Service (Costs) Regulations 2000, reg.5

44.17.2 An order should be made for the determination of an appellant's liability to pay costs and for any application by the respondent for an order for payment of costs by the Legal Services Commission to be referred to the Costs Judge in accordance with Regulation 10 of the Costs Regulations. If the LSC took the point that the application was premature the Costs Judge had the power to adjourn until final resolution of the proceedings but that should not be necessary (see *General Accident Fire and Life Assurance Corporation Ltd v Foster* [1972] 3 All E.R. 877, CA) since the relevant proceedings were those in the Court of Appeal. The proceedings in the Court of Appeal had been finally determined and there was no difficulty in the exercise by a Costs Judge of his jurisdiction in relation to the costs of those proceedings: *Masterman-Lister v Brutton & Co* [2003] EWCA Civ 70. Nothing in r.44.3 prevents the court from applying the Community Legal Service (Costs) Regulations 2000 in considering whether, but for cost protection, the court would have made an order against the unsuccessful party in the context of an application under s.11(1) of the 1999 Act: *Portsmouth Hospital NHS Trust v Wyatt (Costs)* [2006] EWCA Civ 529.

The Court of Appeal has held that it is clear from the wording of s.11of the 1999 Act that the provisions concerning the assessment of costs apply only to those costs which were actually funded by the CLS. CPR Pts 44 to 48 apply generally in relation to costs in civil actions, whereas the s.11 regime relates exclusively to funded costs. Accordingly, where a paying party has been CLS funded only for part of the litigation s.11 and the Regulations made under it, apply to that part of the litigation costs that were funded, CPR Pt 47 applies to the remaining costs. The fact that the receiving party had lost the opportunity to seek costs for the period covered by CLS funding did not exclude her from seeking costs for the non funded period: *Re B (Children)* [2005] EWCA Civ 779.

Costs capping orders—General

44.18 **44.18—(1) A costs capping order is an order limiting the amount of future costs (including disbursements) which a party may recover pursuant to an order for costs subsequently made.**

(2) In this rule, "future costs" means costs incurred in respect of work done after the date of the costs capping order but excluding the amount of any additional liability.

(3) This rule does not apply to protective costs orders

(4) A costs capping order may be in respect of—

(a) the whole litigation; or

(b) any issues which are ordered to be tried separately.

(5) The court may at any stage of proceedings make a costs capping order against all or any of the parties, if—

(a) it is in the interests of justice to do so;

(b) *there is a substantial risk* that without such an order costs will be disproportionately incurred; and

(c) it is not satisfied that the risk in sub-paragraph (b) can be adequately controlled by—

(i) case management directions or orders made under Part 3; and

(ii) detailed assessment of costs.

(6) In considering whether to exercise its discretion under this rule, the court will consider all the circumstances of the case, including—

(a) whether there is a substantial imbalance between the financial position of the parties;

(b) whether the costs of determining the amount of the cap are likely to be proportionate to the overall costs of the litigation;

(c) the stage which the proceedings have reached; and

(d) the costs which have been incurred to date and the future costs.

(7) A costs capping order, once made, will limit the costs recoverable by the party subject to the order unless a party successfully applies to vary the order. No such variation will be made unless—

(a) there has been a material and substantial change of circumstances since the date when the order was made; or

(b) there is some other compelling reason why a variation should be made.

Comment

The Civil Procedure Rule Committee has codified the position with regard to costs capping orders. Rules 44.18, 44.19 and 44.20 set out the general principles, the procedure for applying for a costs capping order and for varying such an order. **44.18.1**

Rule 44.18(1)(2)

Costs capping orders can only be made in respect of costs (including disbursements) to be incurred in the future. The Rule Committee took the view that the costs capping order should not include any amount for any additional liability. It is necessary to distinguish between costs capping orders and protective costs orders, as to which see r.48.15.7. **44.18.2**

Rule 44.18(4)(4)

The court may make a costs capping order in respect of the whole of the litigation, or any particular issue or issues ordered to be tried separately. Although the court may make a costs capping order at any stage of the proceedings, if the application is made too late the costs capping order will be pointless, since the bulk of the costs will already have been incurred. **44.18.3**

Rule 44.18(5)(6)

The criteria which have to be satisfied before the court will make a costs capping order are, that it is in the interests of justice to do so; there is a substantial risk that without such an order costs will be disproportionately incurred; and it is not satisfied that that risk can be adequately controlled by case management directions and detailed assessment of the costs. The court is required to take into account all the circumstances of the case, including the factors set out at rule 48.18(6). **44.18.4**

Application for a costs capping order

44.19—(1) An application for a costs capping order must be made on notice in accordance with Part 23. **44.19**

(2) The application notice must—

(a) set out—

(i) whether the costs capping order is in respect of

the whole of the litigation or a particular issue which is ordered to be tried separately; and

(ii) why a costs capping order should be made; and

(b) be accompanied by an estimate of costs setting out—

(i) the costs (and disbursements) incurred by the applicant to date; and

(ii) the costs (and disbursements) which the applicant is likely to incur in the future conduct of the proceedings.

(3) The court may give directions for the determination of the application and such directions may—

(a) direct any party to the proceedings—

(i) to file a schedule of costs in the form set out in the Practice Direction supplementing this rule;

(ii) to file written submissions on all or any part of the issues arising;

(b) fix the date and time estimate of the hearing of the application;

(c) indicate whether the judge hearing the application will sit with an assessor at the hearing of the application; and

(d) include any further directions as the court sees fit.

Costs capping

44.19.1 When an application for a costs capping order is made the application must specify whether the order sought is in respect of the whole of the litigation or a particular issue which is ordered to be tried separately, or (although the rule does not specifically so state), up to a particular point in the proceedings. The application must be accompanied by an estimate of costs setting out the costs and disbursements incurred by the applicant to date, and the likely future costs and disbursements of the proceedings.

The order may be made by the judge to whom the application is made, or that judge may sit with an assessor who will normally be a Costs Judge or Regional Costs Judge.

For the procedure to be followed, and for the matters to be taken into account by the court, where a party makes an application for an order limiting the amount of future costs (including disbursements) which a party may recover pursuant to an order for costs subsequently made (a "costs capping order"), see rr.44.18 to 44.20, and Practice Direction (Costs) Sect. 23A.

In *AB v Leeds Teaching Hospitals NHS Trust* [2003] EWHC 1034 (QB) Gage J. put a cap on the costs to be incurred by the claimants; a practice adopted by some district judges ever since the CPR came into force. This reasoning was followed by Hallett J. in making a costs capping order in *Various Ledward Claimants v Kent and Medway HA* [2003] EWHC 2551; [2004] 1 Costs L.R. 101.

The purpose of a costs capping order is to enable the capped party to plan the appropriate level of expenditure to bring the case to trial, at a cost which is in line with amount of the cap. The imposition of a costs cap very close to trial, would in effect, penalise a claimant. The amount of cover and existence of material exclusions in a ATE policy are of obvious relevance to an opposing party who must be in a position to make informed choices as to the conduct of the litigation. On the facts, the application for a cap was refused. *Henry v British Broadcasting Corporation* [2005] EWHC 2503 (QB); [2006] 1 All E.R. 154, Gray J.

Although the court does have jurisdiction to make cost cap orders, where the claimant solicitors were experienced in the field and there was not a real and substantial risk that costs would be disproportionately or unreasonably incurred, a post trial detailed assessment was sufficient to ensure that costs did not become disproportionate. The risk could be managed by conventional case management and detailed assessment after trial. It was very unlikely that it would be appropriate for the court to adopt a practice of capping costs in the majority of clinical negligence cases other than where group litigation was involved. When such an application was made it should be supported by evidence showing a prima facie case that the conditions could be satisfied. The allocation and pre trial questionnaire should have attached estimates of the likely overall costs which should give a good guide; the court should be able to deal with an application at a comparatively short hearing; and the benefit of the doubt in respect of reasonableness of prospective costs should be resolved in favour of the party being capped (*Smart v East Cheshire NHS Trust* [2003] EWHC 2806 (QB) Gage J.).

In group litigation in which the LSC had withdrawn funding, a number of claimants wished to carry on either unconditionally or until the outcome of a further funding review. They sought a costs capping order against the defendants. The court expressed the view that a prospective costs capping order should only be contemplated where there are grounds for believing that a party may incur excessive or disproportionate legal costs and where the risk that excessive legal costs are being incurred unnecessarily will not be picked up by the court when exercising its case management functions or when conducting a detailed assessment of the costs after trial. Costs capping is a relatively dramatic course to take and will only be ordered on cogent evidence: *Sayers v SmithKline Beecham* [2004] EWHC 1899 (QB) Keith J.

In group litigation it is important for the parties to know and to budget for the costs consequences of losing. Where a judge is asked to make a costs capping order it is necessary to take a broad brush approach and to fix overall figures, having regard to the individual costs heads that make up each party's estimate. In the particular case the judge imposed a cap on both sides, which included a 5 per cent addition to allow for contingencies. The parties had agreed that any cap on the claimant's costs would not include any success fee element. The order made was limited up to the end of the trial of generic issues and the parties were at liberty to apply if circumstances unforeseeable and beyond their reasonable control should occur, giving rise to a genuine need to adjust the figures: *Multiple Claimants v Corby BC* [2008] EWHC 619 (TCC) Akenhead J.

In *Willis v Nicolson* [2007] EWCA Civ 199, a costs capping application in a catastrophic injury case, the Court of Appeal commented that the court would be careful before imposing a cap, particularly when those restricted were acting for a claimant who had suffered catastrophic injuries. To conduct the exercise properly the court would need reliable information about, and understanding of the nature of the particular case and the general demands of that type of litigation. For reasons both of fairness and of practicality a cap could not be imposed retrospectively, so that the enquiry must take place at a sufficiently early stage to have a real effect on the expenditure. There has therefore to be careful selection of the right moment in the litigation process for consideration of a costs cap. The court also pointed out that the exercise of costs capping should not be entered upon lightly, since the cap has to be determined by a Costs Judge, a scarce resource; and if the exercise is to be done properly it is likely, as in effect a substitute for final assessment, to be as expensive and time consuming as a final assessment itself. The Court of Appeal had considered giving a comprehensive set of guiding principles for costs capping cases, but after further consideration decided that such guidance should emanate from the Civil Procedure Rule Committee after consultation.

In *King v Telegraph Group Ltd* [2004] EWCA Civ 613, the Court of Appeal said that the view expressed by Gage J. in *AB v Leeds Teaching Hospitals NHS Trust* [2003] EWHC 1034 (QB), to the effect that the court possesses the power to make a costs capping order in an appropriate case, is correct. In the *King* case the court said:

> "The language of Section 51 of the Supreme Court Act 1981 is very wide and CPR 3.2(m) confers the requisite power. Needless to say, in deciding what order to make the court should take the principles set out in CPR 44.3 (which govern the retrospective assessment of costs) as an important point of reference."

In this case the court also referred to the judgment of Dyson L.J. in *Leigh v Michelin Tyre Plc* [2003] EWCA Civ 1766; [2004] 2 All E.R. 175, CA, where his lordship expressed the opinion that the prospective fixing of costs budgets was likely to achieve the objective of controlling the costs of litigation more effectively than estimates.

In dealing with a costs capping application in defamation proceedings the judge held that the amount allowed by the Costs Judge in respect of solicitors costs was too low. The court on appeal declined to interfere with the allowance in respect of counsel's fees, expressing the view that while it would not wish to endorse a decision which involved precluding the claimant from instructing leading counsel, whilst the defendant was free to do so, in the instant case the defendant had made a concession that it would instruct only junior counsel. In those circumstances it would not be so unfair as to be unreasonable that the claimant should be similarly confined: *Tierney v News Group Newspapers Ltd* [2006] EWHC 3275 (QB), Eady J. In a passing off action, where the claimant was represented on a CFA with no ATE cover, the court was not persuaded that this was in itself enough to justify a costs capping order. Notwithstanding that the defendants had demonstrated a significant risk of excessive or extravagant expenditure in two specific areas, the judge was not satisfied that excessive expenditure could not adequately be dealt with on detailed assessment: *Knight v Beyond Properties Pty Ltd* [2006] EWHC 1242 (Ch); [2007] 1 W.L.R. 625, Mann J.

Application to vary a costs capping order

44.20 **44.20 An application to vary a costs capping order must be made by application notice pursuant to Part 23.**

Application for costs capping order (rr.44.18 to 44.20)

44.20.1 Rules 44.18 to 44.20 were inserted in the CPR by Civil Procedure (Amendment No.3) Rules 2008 (SI 2008/3327) r.9(c) and came into effect on April 6, 2009. These provisions are supplemented by Practice Direction—Costs, Sect.23A: see para.44PD.18below. Paragraph 23A states that the estimate of costs required by rr.44.19 and 44.20(2) must be in the form illustrated in Precedent H in the Schedule of Costs Precedents annexed to this Practice Direction. For commentary on costs capping orders, see para.43.2.1.2 above.

If either party wishes to vary the costs capping order the application is made on notice pursuant to Pt 23. No variation will be made unless there has been a material and substantial change of circumstances since the day when the order was made, or there is some other compelling reason why a variation should be made (see r.44.18(7)).

DIRECTIONS RELATING TO PART 44—GENERAL RULES ABOUT COSTS

Section 7 Solicitor's Duty to Notify Client: Rule 44.2

7.1 For the purposes of rule 44.2 "client" includes a party for whom a solicitor is acting and any other person (for example, an insurer, a trade union or the LSC) who has instructed the solicitor to act or who is liable to pay his fees. **44PD.1**

7.2 Where a solicitor notifies a client of an order under that rule, he must also explain why the order came to be made.

7.3 Although rule 44.2 does not specify any sanction for breach of the rule the court may, either in the order for costs itself or in a subsequent order, require the solicitor to produce to the court evidence showing that he took reasonable steps to comply with the rule.

Section 8 Court's Discretion and Circumstances to be Taken Into Account When Exercising its Discretion as to Costs: Rule 44.3

8.1 Attention is drawn to the factors set out in this rule which may lead the court to depart from the general rule stated in rule 44.3(2) and to make a different order about costs. **44PD.2**

8.2 In a probate claim where a defendant has in his defence given notice that he requires the will to be proved in solemn form (see paragraph 8.3 of the practice direction supplementing Part 57), the court will not make an order for costs against the defendant unless it appears that there was no reasonable ground for opposing the will. The term 'probate claim' is defined in rule 57.1(2).

8.3(1) The court may make an order about costs at any stage in a case.

(2) In particular the court may make an order about costs when it deals with any application, makes any order or holds any hearing and that order about costs may relate to the costs of that application, order or hearing.

(3) Rule 44.3A(1) provides that the court will not assess any additional liability until the conclusion of the proceedings or the part of the proceedings to which the funding arrangement relates. (Paragraphs 2.4 and 2.5 above explain when proceedings are concluded. As to the time when detailed assessment may be carried out see paragraphs 28.1, below.)

8.4 In deciding what order to make about costs the court is *required* to have regard to all the circumstances including any payment into court or admissible offer to settle made by a party which is drawn to the court's attention, and which is not an offer to which costs consequences under Part 36 apply.

8.5 There are certain costs orders which the court will commonly make in proceedings before trial. The following table sets out the general effect of these orders. The table is not an exhaustive list of the orders which the court may make.

Term	Effect
• Costs • Costs in any event	The party in whose favour the order is made is entitled to the costs in respect of the part of the proceedings to which the order relates, whatever other costs orders are made in the proceedings.
• Costs in the case • Costs in the application	The party in whose favour the court makes an order for costs at the end of the proceedings is entitled to his costs of the part of the proceedings to which the order relates.
• Costs reserved	The decision about costs is deferred to a later occasion, but if no later order is made the costs will be costs in the case.
• Claimant's/ Defendant's costs in case/ application	If the party in whose favour the costs order is made is awarded costs at the end of the proceedings, that party is entitled to his costs of the part of the proceedings to which the order relates. If any other party is awarded costs at the end of the proceedings, the party in whose favour the final costs order is made is not liable to pay the costs of any other party in respect of the part of the proceedings to which the order relates.
• Costs thrown away	Where, for example, a judgment or order is set aside, the party in whose favour the costs order is made is entitled to the costs which have been incurred as a consequence. This includes the costs of — a) preparing for and attending any hearing at which the judgment or order which has been set aside was made; b) preparing for and attending any hearing to set aside the judgment or order in question; c) preparing for and attending any hearing at which the court orders the proceedings or the part in question to be adjourned; d) any steps taken to enforce a judgment or order which has subsequently been set aside.

Term	Effect
• Costs of and caused by	Where, for example, the court makes this order on an application to amend a statement of case, the party in whose favour the costs order is made is entitled to the costs of preparing for and attending the application and the costs of any consequential amendment to his own statement of case.
• Costs here and below	The party in whose favour the costs order is made is entitled not only to his costs in respect of the proceedings in which the court makes the order but also to his costs of the proceedings in any lower court. In the case of an appeal from a Divisional Court the party is not entitled to any costs incurred in any court below the Divisional Court.
• No order as to costs • Each party to pay his own costs	Each party is to bear his own costs of the part of the proceedings to which the order relates whatever costs order the court makes at the end of the proceedings.

8.6 Where, under rule 44.3(8), the court orders an amount to be paid before costs are assessed—

(1) the order will state that amount, and

(2) if no other date for payment is specified in the order rule 44.8 (Time for complying with an order for costs) will apply.

Fees of counsel

8.7(1) This paragraph applies where the court orders the detailed assessment of the costs of a hearing at which one or more counsel appeared for a party.

(2) Where an order for costs states the opinion of the court as to whether or not the hearing was fit for the attendance of one or more counsel, a costs officer conducting a detailed assessment of costs to which that order relates will have regard to the opinion stated.

(3) The court will generally express an opinion only where:

(a) the paying party asks it to do so;

(b) more than one counsel appeared for a party or,

(c) the court wishes to record its opinion that the case was not fit for the attendance of counsel.

Fees payable to conveyancing counsel appointed by the court to assist it

8.8(1) Where the court refers any matter to the conveyancing counsel of the court the fees payable to counsel in respect of the work done or to be done will be assessed by the court in accordance with rule 44.3.

(2) An appeal from a decision of the court in respect of the fees of such counsel will be dealt with under the general rules as to appeals set out in Part 52. If the appeal is against the decision of an authorised court officer, it will be dealt with in accordance with rules 47.20 to 47.23.

Section 9 Costs Orders Relating to Funding Arrangements: Rule 44.3A

44PD.3 **9.1** Under an order for payment of "costs" the costs payable will include an additional liability incurred under a funding arrangement.

9.2(1) If before the conclusion of the proceedings the court carries out a summary assessment of the base costs it may identify separately the amount allowed in respect of: solicitors' charges; counsels' fees; other disbursements; and any value added tax (VAT). (Sections 13 and 14 of this Practice Direction deal with summary assessment.)

(2) If an order for the base costs of a previous application or hearing did not identify separately the amounts allowed for solicitor's charges, counsel's fees and other disbursements, a court which later makes an assessment of an additional liability may apportion the base costs previously ordered.

Section 10 Limits on Recovery Under Funding Arrangements: Rule 44.3B

44PD.4 **10.1** In a case to which rule 44.3B(1)(c) or (d) applies the party in default may apply for relief from the sanction. He should do so as quickly as possible after he becomes aware of the default. An application, supported by evidence, should be made under Part 23 to a costs judge or district judge of the court which is dealing with the case. (Attention is drawn to rules 3.8 and 3.9 which deal with sanctions and relief from sanctions).

10.2 Where the amount of any percentage increase recoverable by counsel may be affected by the outcome of the application, the solicitor issuing the application must serve on counsel a copy of the application notice and notice of the hearing as soon as practicable and in any event at least 2 days before the hearing. Counsel may make written submissions or may attend and make oral submissions at the hearing. (Paragraph 1.4 contains definitions of the terms "counsel" and "solicitor".)

Section 10A Orders in respect of pro bono representation: Rule 44.3C

44PD.4.1 **10A.1** Rule 44.3C(2) sets out how the court may determine the amount of payment when making an order under section 194(3) of the Legal Services Act 2007. Paragraph 13.2 of this Practice Direction provides that the general rule is that the court will make a summary assessment of costs in the circumstances outlined in that paragraph unless there is good reason not to do so. This will apply to rule 44.3C(2)(b) with the modification that the summary assessment of the costs is to be read as meaning the summary assessment of the sum equivalent to the costs that would have been claimed by the party with pro bono representation in respect of that representation had it not been provided free of charge.

10A.2 Where an order under section 194(3) of the Legal Services Act 2007 is sought, to assist the court in making a summary assessment of the amount payable to the prescribed charity, the party who has pro bono representation must prepare, file and serve in accordance with paragraph 13.5(2) a written statement of the sum equivalent to the costs that party would have claimed for that legal representation had it not been provided free of charge.

Section 11 Factors to be Taken Into Account in Deciding The Amount of Costs: Rule 44.5

11.1 In applying the test of proportionality the court will have regard to rule 1.1(2)(c). The relationship between the total of the costs incurred and the financial value of the claim may not be a reliable guide. A fixed percentage cannot be applied in all cases to the value of the claim in order to ascertain whether or not the costs are proportionate. **44PD.5**

11.2 In any proceedings there will be costs which will inevitably be incurred and which are necessary for the successful conduct of the case. Solicitors are not required to conduct litigation at rates which are uneconomic. Thus in a modest claim the proportion of costs is likely to be higher than in a large claim, and may even equal or possibly exceed the amount in dispute.

11.3 Where a trial takes place, the time taken by the court in dealing with a particular issue may not be an accurate guide to the amount of time properly spent by the legal or other representatives in preparation for the trial of that issue.

11.4 Where a party has entered into a funding arrangement the costs claimed may, subject to rule 44.3B include an additional liability.

11.5 In deciding whether the costs claimed are reasonable and (on a standard basis assessment) proportionate, the court will consider the amount of any additional liability separately from the base costs.

11.6 In deciding whether the base costs are reasonable and (if relevant) proportionate the court will consider the factors set out in rule 44.5.

11.7 Subject to paragraph 17.8(2), when the court is considering the factors to be taken into account in assessing an additional liability, it will have regard to the facts and circumstances as they reasonably appeared to the solicitor or counsel when the funding arrangement was entered into and at the time of any variation of the arrangement.

11.8(1) In deciding whether a percentage increase is reasonable relevant factors to be taken into account may include:

(a) the risk that the circumstances in which the costs, fees or expenses would be payable might or might not occur;

(b) the legal representative's liability for any disbursements;

(c) what other methods of financing the costs were available to the receiving party.

11.9 A percentage increase will not be reduced simply on the ground that, when added to base costs which are reasonable and (where relevant) proportionate, the total appears disproportionate.

11.10 In deciding whether the cost of insurance cover is reasonable, relevant factors to be taken into account include:

(1) where the insurance cover is not purchased in support of a conditional fee agreement with a success fee, how its cost compares with the likely cost of funding the case with a conditional fee agreement with a success fee and supporting insurance cover;

(2) the level and extent of the cover provided;

(3) the availability of any pre-existing insurance cover;

(4) whether any part of the premium would be rebated in the event of early settlement;

(5) the amount of commission payable to the receiving party or his legal representatives or other agents.

11.11 Where the court is considering a provision made by a membership organisation, rule 44.3B(1)(b) provides that any such provision which exceeds the likely cost to the receiving party of the premium of an insurance policy against the risk of incurring a liability to pay the costs of other parties to the proceedings is not recoverable. In such circumstances the court will, when assessing the additional liability, have regard to the factors set out in paragraph 11.10 above, in addition to the factors set out in rule 44.5.

Section 12 Procedure for Assessing Costs: Rule 44.7

44PD.6 **12.1** Where the court does not order fixed costs (or no fixed costs are provided for) the amount of costs payable will be assessed by the court. This rule allows the court making an order about costs either

(a) to make a summary assessment of the amount of the costs, or

(b) to order the amount to be decided in accordance with Part 47 (a detailed assessment).

12.2 An order for costs will be treated as an order for the amount of costs to be decided by a detailed assessment unless the order otherwise provides.

12.3 Whenever the court awards costs to be assessed by way of detailed assessment it should consider whether to exercise the power in rule 44.3(8) (Courts Discretion as to Costs) to order the paying party to pay such sum of money as it thinks just on account of those costs.

Section 13 Summary Assessment: General Provisions

44PD.7 **13.1** Whenever a court makes an order about costs which does not provide for fixed costs to be paid the court should consider whether to make a summary assessment of costs.

13.2 The general rule is that the court should make a summary assessment of the costs:

(1) at the conclusion of the trial of a case which has been dealt with on the fast track, in which case the order will deal with the costs of the whole claim, and

(2) at the conclusion of any other hearing, which has lasted not more than one day, in which case the order will deal with the costs of the application or matter to which the hearing related. If this hearing disposes of the claim, the order may deal with the costs of the whole claim;

(3) in hearings in the Court of Appeal to which Paragraph 14 of the Practice Direction supplementing Part 52 (Appeals) applies;

unless there is good reason not to do so, e.g. where the paying party shows substantial grounds for disputing the sum claimed for costs that cannot be dealt with summarily or there is insufficient time to carry out a summary assessment.

13.3 The general rule in paragraph 13.2 does not apply to a mortgagee's costs incurred in mortgage possession proceedings or other proceedings relating to a mortgage unless the mortgagee asks the court to make an order for his costs to be paid by another party. Paragraphs 50.3 and 50.4 deal in more detail with costs relating to mortgages.

13.4 Where an application has been made and the parties to the application agree an order by consent without any party attending, the parties should agree a figure for costs to be inserted in the consent order or agree that there should be no order for costs. If the parties cannot agree the costs position, attendance on the appointment will be necessary but, unless good reason can be shown for the failure to deal with costs as set out above, no costs will be allowed for that attendance.

13.5(1) It is duty of the parties and their legal representatives to assist the judge in making a summary assessment of costs in any case to which paragraph 13.2 above applies, in accordance with the following paragraphs.

(2) Each party who intends to claim costs must prepare a written statement of the costs he intends to claim showing separately in the form of a schedule:

(a) the number of hours to be claimed,

(b) the hourly rate to be claimed,

(c) the grade of fee earner;

(d) the amount and nature of any disbursement to be claimed, other than counsel's fee for appearing at the hearing,

(e) the amount of solicitor's costs to be claimed for attending or appearing at the hearing,

(f) the fees of counsel to be claimed in respect of the hearing, and

(g) any value added tax (VAT) to be claimed on these amounts.

(3) The statement of costs should follow as closely as possible Form **N260** and must be signed by the party or his legal representative. Where a litigant is an assisted person or is a LSC funded client or is represented by a solicitor in the litigant's employment the statement of costs need not include the certificate appended at the end of Form **N260**.

(4) The statement of costs must be filed at court and copies of it must be served on any party against whom an order for payment of those costs is intended to be sought. The statement of costs should be filed and the copies of it should be

served as soon as possible and in any event not less than 24 hours before the date fixed for the hearing.

(5) Where the litigant is or may be entitled to claim an additional liability the statement filed and served need not reveal the amount of that liability.

13.6 The failure by a party, without reasonable excuse, to comply with the foregoing paragraphs will be taken into account by the court in deciding what order to make about the costs of the claim, hearing or application, and about the costs of any further hearing or detailed assessment hearing that may be necessary as a result of that failure.

13.7 If the court makes a summary assessment of costs at the conclusion of proceedings the court will specify separately

(1) the base costs, and if appropriate, the additional liability allowed as solicitor's charges, counsel's fees, other disbursements and any VAT; and

(2) the amount which is awarded under Part 46 (Fast Track Trial Costs).

13.8 The court awarding costs cannot make an order for a summary assessment of costs by a costs officer. If a summary assessment of costs is appropriate but the court awarding costs is unable to do so on the day, the court must give directions as to a further hearing before the same judge.

13.9 The court will not make a summary assessment of the costs of a receiving party who is an assisted person or LSC funded client.

13.10 A summary assessment of costs payable by an assisted person or LSC funded client is not by itself a determination of that person's liability to pay those costs (as to which see rule 44.17 and paragraphs 21.1 to 23.17 of this Practice Direction).

13.11

(1) The court will not make a summary assessment of the costs of a receiving party who is a child or protected party within the meaning of Part 21 unless the solicitor acting for the child or protected party has waived the right to further costs (see paragraph 51.1 below).

(2) The court may make a summary assessment of costs payable by a child or patient.

13.12

(1) Attention is drawn to rule 44.3A which prevents the court from making a summary assessment of an additional liability before the conclusion of the proceedings or the part of the proceedings to which the funding arrangement relates. Where this applies, the court should nonetheless make a summary assessment of the base costs of the hearing or application unless there is a good reason not to do so.

(2) Where the court makes a summary assessment of the base costs all statements of costs and costs estimates put before the judge will be retained on the court file.

13.13 The court will not give its approval to disproportionate and unreasonable costs. Accordingly:

(a) When the amount of the costs to be paid has been agreed between the parties the order for costs must state that the order is by consent.

(b) If the judge is to make an order which is not by consent, the judge will, so far as possible, ensure that the final figure is not disproportionate and/or unreasonable having regard to Part 1 of the CPR. The judge will retain this responsibility notwithstanding the absence of challenge to individual items in the make-up of the figure sought. The fact that the paying party is not disputing the amount of costs can however be taken as some indication that the amount is proportionate and reasonable. The judge will therefore intervene only if satisfied that the costs are so disproportionate that it is right to do so.

Section 14 Summary Assessment Where Costs Claimed Include an Additional Liability

Orders made before the conclusion of the proceedings

14.1 The existence of a conditional fee agreement or other funding arrangement within the meaning of rule 43.2 is not by itself a sufficient reason for not carrying out a summary assessment. **44PD.8**

14.2 Where a legal representative acting for the receiving party has entered into a conditional fee agreement the court may summarily assess all the costs (other than any additional liability).

14.3 Where costs have been summarily assessed an order for payment will not be made unless the court has been satisfied that in respect of the costs claimed, the receiving party is at the time liable to pay to his legal representative an amount equal to or greater than the costs claimed. A statement in the form of the certificate appended at the end of Form **N260** may be sufficient proof of liability. The giving of information under rule 44.15 (where that rule applies) is not sufficient.

14.4 The court may direct that any costs, for which the receiving party may not in the event be liable, shall be paid into court to await the outcome of the case, or shall not be enforceable until further order, or it may postpone the receiving party's right to receive payment in some other way.

Orders made at the conclusion of the proceedings

14.5 Where there has been a trial of one or more issues separately from other issues, the court will not normally order detailed assessment of the additional liability until all issues have been tried unless the parties agree.

14.6 Rule 44.3A(2) sets out the ways in which the court may deal with the assessment of the costs where there is a funding arrangement. Where the court makes a summary assessment of the base costs:

(1) The order may state separately the base costs allowed as (a) solicitor's charges, (b) counsel's fees, (c) any other disbursements and (d) any VAT;

(2) the statements of costs upon which the judge based his summary assessment will be retained on the court file.

14.7 Where the court makes a summary assessment of an additional liability at the conclusion of proceedings, that assessment must relate to the whole of the proceedings; this will include any additional liability relating to base costs allowed by the court when making a summary assessment on a previous application or hearing.

14.8 Paragraph 13.13 applies where the parties are agreed about the total amount to be paid by way of costs, or are agreed about the amount of the base costs that will be paid. Where they disagree about the additional liability the court may summarily assess that liability or make an order for a detailed assessment.

14.9 In order to facilitate the court in making a summary assessment of any additional liability at the conclusion of the proceedings the party seeking such costs must prepare and have available for the court a bundle of documents which must include—

(1) a copy of every notice of funding arrangement (Form **N251**) which has been filed by him;

(2) a copy of every estimate and statement of costs filed by him;

(3) a copy of the risk assessment prepared at the time any relevant funding arrangement was entered into and on the basis of which the amount of the additional liability was fixed.

Section 15 Costs on the Small Claims Track and Fast Track: Rule 44.9

44PD.9 **15.1**(1) Before a claim is allocated to one of those tracks the court is not restricted by any of the special rules that apply to that track.

(2) Where a claim has been allocated to one of those tracks, the special rules which relate to that track will apply to work done before as well as after allocation save to the extent (if any) that an order for costs in respect of that work was made before allocation.

(i) This paragraph applies where a claim, issued for a sum in excess of the normal financial scope of the small claims track, is allocated to that track only because an admission of part of the claim by the defendant reduces the amount in dispute to a sum within the normal scope of that track.

(3) (See also paragraph 7.4 of the practice direction supplementing CPR Part 26)

(ii) On entering judgment for the admitted part before allocation of the balance of the claim the court may allow costs in respect of the proceedings down to that date.

Section 16 Costs Following Allocation and Re-Allocation: Rule 44.11

44PD.10 **16.1** This paragraph applies where the court is about to make an order to re-allocate a claim from the small claims track to another track.

16.2 Before *making the order to* re-allocate the claim, the court must decide whether any party is to pay costs to any other party down to the date of the order to re-allocate in accordance with the rules about costs contained in Part 27(The Small Claims Track).

16.3 If it decides to make such an order about costs, the court will make a summary assessment of those costs in accordance with that Part.

Section 17 Costs-Only Proceedings: Rule 44.12A

17.1 A claim form under this rule should not be issued in the High Court unless the dispute to which the agreement relates was of such a value or type that had proceedings been begun they would have been commenced in the High Court. **44PD.11**

17.2 A claim form which is to be issued in the High Court at the Royal Courts of Justice will be issued in the Supreme Court Costs Office.

17.3 Attention is drawn to rule 8.2 (in particular to paragraph (b)(ii)) and to rule 44.12A(3). The claim form must:

(1) identify the claim or dispute to which the agreement to pay costs relates;

(2) state the date and terms of the agreement on which the claimant relies;

(3) set out or have attached to it a draft of the order which the claimant seeks;

(4) state the amount of the costs claimed; and,

(5) state whether the costs are claimed on the standard or indemnity basis. If no basis is specified the costs will be treated as being claimed on the standard basis.

17.4 The evidence to be filed and served with the claim form under Rule 8.5 must include copies of the documents on which the claimant relies to prove the defendant's agreement to pay costs.

17.5 A costs judge or a district judge has jurisdiction to hear and decide any issue which may arise in a claim issued under this rule irrespective of the amount of the costs claimed or of the value of the claim to which the agreement to pay costs relates. A costs officer may make an order by consent under paragraph 17.7, or an order dismissing a claim under paragraph 17.9 below.

17.6 When the time for filing the defendant's acknowledgement of service has expired, the claimant may by letter request the court to make an order in the terms of his claim, unless the defendant has filed an acknowledgement of service stating that he intends to contest the claim or to seek a different order.

17.7 Rule 40.6 applies where an order is to be made by consent. An order may be made by consent in terms which differ from those set out in the claim form.

17.8(1) An order for costs made under this rule will be treated as an order for the amount of costs to be decided by a *detailed assessment* to which Part 47 and the practice directions relating to it apply. Rule 44.4(4) (*determination* of basis of assessment) also applies to the order.

(2) In cases in which an additional liability is claimed, the costs judge or district judge should have regard to the time when and the extent to which the claim has been settled and to the fact that the claim has been settled without the need to commence proceedings.

17.9(1) For the purposes of rule 44.12A(4)(b)—

(a) a claim will be treated as opposed if the defendant files an acknowledgment of service stating that he intends to contest the making of an order for costs to seek a different remedy; and

(b) a claim will not be treated as opposed if the defendant files an acknowledgment of service stating that he disputes the amount of the claim for costs.

(2) An order dismissing the claim will be made as soon as an acknowledgment of service opposing the claim is filed. The dismissal of a claim under rule 44.12A(4) does not prevent the claimant from issuing another claim form under Part 7 or Part 8 based on the agreement or alleged agreement to which the proceedings under this rule related.

17.10(1) Rule 8.9 (which provides that claims issued under Part 8 shall be treated as allocated to the multi-track) shall not apply to claims issued under this rule. A claim issued under this rule may be dealt with without being allocated to a track.

(2) Rule 8.1(3) and Part 24 do not apply to proceedings brought under rule 44.12A.

17.11 Nothing in this rule prevents a person from issuing a claim form under Part 7 or Part 8 to sue on an agreement made in settlement of a dispute where that agreement makes provision for costs, nor from claiming in that case an order for costs or a specified sum in respect of costs.

Section 18 Court's Powers in Relation to Misconduct: Rule 44.14

44PD.12 **18.1** Before making an order under rule 44.14 the court must give the party or legal representative in question a reasonable opportunity to attend a hearing to give reasons why it should not make such an order.

18.2 Conduct before or during the proceedings which gave rise to the assessment which is unreasonable or improper includes steps which are calculated to prevent or inhibit the court from furthering the overriding objective.

18.3 Although rule 44.14(3) does not specify any sanction for breach of the obligation imposed by the rule the court may, either in the order under paragraph (2) or in a subsequent order, require the solicitor to produce to the court evidence that he took reasonable steps to comply with the obligation.

Section 19 Providing Information About Funding Arrangements: Rule 44.15

44PD.13 **19.1**(1) A party who wishes to claim an additional liability in respect of a funding arrangement must give any other party information about that claim if he is to recover the additional liability. There is no requirement to specify the amount of the additional liability separately nor to state how it is calculated until it falls to be assessed. That principle is reflected in rules 44.3A and 44.15, in the following paragraphs and in Sections 6, 13, 14 and 31 of this Practice Direction. Section 6 deals with estimates of costs, Sections 13 and 14 deal with summary assessment and Section 31 deals with detailed assessment.

(2) In the following paragraphs a party who has entered into a funding arrangement is treated as a person who intends to recover a sum representing an additional liability by way of costs.

(3) Attention is drawn to paragraph 57.9 of this Practice Direction which sets out time limits for the provision of information where a funding arrangement is entered into between March 31 and July 2, 2000 and proceedings relevant to that arrangement are commenced before July 3, 2000.

Method of giving information

19.2(1) In this paragraph, "claim form" includes petition and application notice, and the notice of funding to be filed or served is a notice containing the information set out in Form **N251**.

(a) A claimant who has entered into a funding arrangement before starting the proceedings to which it relates must provide information to the court by filing the notice when he issues the claim form.

(b) He must provide information to every other party by serving the notice. If he serves the claim form himself he must serve the notice with the claim form. If the court is to serve the claim form, the court will also serve the notice if the claimant provides it with sufficient copies for service.

(3) A defendant who has entered into a funding arrangement before filing any document

(a) must provide information to the court by filing notice with his first document. A "first document" may be an acknowledgement of service, a defence, or any other document, such as an application to set aside a default judgment.

(b) must provide information to every party by serving notice. If he serves his first document himself he must serve the notice with that document. If the court is to serve his first document the court will also serve the notice if the defendant provides it with sufficient copies for service.

(4) In all other circumstances a party must file and serve notice within 7 days of entering into the funding arrangement concerned.

(Practice Direction (Pre-Action Conduct) provides that a party should inform any other party as soon as possible about a funding arrangement entered into prior to the start of proceedings.)

Notice of change of information

19.3(1) Rule 44.15 imposes a duty on a party to give notice of change if the information he has previously provided is no longer accurate. To comply he must file and serve notice containing the information set out in Form N251. Rule44.15(3) may impose other duties in relation to new estimates of costs.

(2) Further notification need not be provided where a party has already given notice:

(a) that he has entered into a conditional fee agreement with a legal representative and during the currency of that agreement either of them enters into another such agreement with an additional legal representative; or

(b) of some insurance cover, unless that cover is cancelled or unless new cover is taken out with a different insurer.

(3) Part 6 applies to the service of notices.

(4) The notice must be signed by the party or by his legal representative.

Information which must be provided

19.4(1) Unless the court otherwise orders, a party who is required to supply information about a funding arrangement must state whether he has—

entered into a conditional fee agreement which provides for a success fee within the meaning of section 58(2) of the Courts and Legal Services Act 1990;

taken out an insurance policy to which section 29 of the Access to Justice Act 1999 applies;

made an arrangement with a body which is prescribed for the purpose of section 30 of that Act;

or more than one of these.

(2) Where the funding arrangement is a conditional fee agreement, the party must state the date of the agreement and identify the claim or claims to which it relates (including Part 20 claims if any).

(3) Where the funding arrangement is an insurance policy, the party must state the name and address of the insurer, the policy number and the date of the policy, and must identify the claim or claims to which it relates (including Part 20 claims if any).

(4) Where the funding arrangement is by way of an arrangement with a relevant body the party must state the name of the body and set out the date and terms of the undertaking it has given and must identify the claim or claims to which it relates (including Part 20 claims if any).

(5) Where a party has entered into more than one funding arrangement in respect of a claim, for example a conditional fee agreement and an insurance policy, a single notice containing the information set out in Form **N251** may contain the required information about both or all of them.

19.5 Where the court makes a Group Litigation Order, the court may give directions as to the extent to which individual parties should provide information in accordance with rule 44.15. (Part 19 deals with Group Litigation Orders.)

Section 20 Procedure Where Legal Representative Wishes to Recover From His Client an Agreed Percentage Increase Which has Been Disallowed or Reduced on Assessment: Rule 44.16

20.1(1) Attention is drawn to Regulation 3(2)(b) of the Conditional Fee Agreements Regulations 2000 and to Regulation 5(2)(b) of the Collective Conditional Fee Agreements Regulations 2000, which provide that some or all of a success fee ceases to be payable in certain circumstances. [Both sets of regulations were revoked by the Conditional Fee Agreements (Revocation) Regulations 2005 but continue to have effect in relation to conditional fee agreements and collective conditional fee agreements entered into before 1st November 2005.] **44PD.14**

(2) Rule 44.16 allows the court to adjourn a hearing at which the legal representative acting for the receiving party applies for an order that a disallowed amount should continue to be payable under the agreement.

20.2 In the following paragraphs 'counsel' means counsel who has acted in the case under a conditional fee agreement which provides for a success fee. A reference to counsel includes a reference to any person who appeared as an advocate in the case and who is not a partner or employee of the solicitor or firm which is conducting the claim or defence (as the case may be) on behalf of the receiving party.

Procedure following Summary Assessment

20.3(1) If the court disallows any amount of a legal representative's percentage increase, the court will, unless sub-paragraph (2) applies, give directions to enable an application to be made by the legal representative for the disallowed amount to be payable by his client, including, if appropriate, a direction that the application will be determined by a costs judge or district judge of the court dealing with the case.

(2) The court that has made the summary assessment may then and there decide the issue whether the disallowed amount should continue to be payable, if:

(a) the receiving party and all parties to the relevant agreement consent to the court doing so;

(b) the receiving party (or, if corporate, an officer) is present in court; and

(c) the court is satisfied that the issue can be fairly decided then and there.

Procedure following Detailed Assessment

20.4(1) Where detailed assessment proceedings have been commenced, and the paying party serves points of dispute (as to which see Section 34 of this Practice Direction), which show that he is seeking a reduction in any percentage increase charged by counsel on his fees, the solicitor acting for the receiving party must within 3 days of service deliver to counsel a copy of the relevant points of dispute and the bill of costs or the relevant parts of the bill.

(2) Counsel must within 10 days thereafter inform the solicitor in writing whether or not he will accept the reduction sought or some other reduction. Counsel may state any points he wishes to have made in a reply to the points of dispute, and the solicitor must serve them on the paying party as or as part of a reply.

(3) Counsel who fails to inform the solicitor within the time limits set out above will be taken to accept the reduction unless the court otherwise orders.

20.5 Where the paying party serves points of dispute seeking a reduction in any percentage increase charged by a legal representative acting for the receiving party, and that legal representative intends, if necessary, to apply for an order that any amount of the percentage disallowed as against the paying party shall continue to be payable by his client, the solicitor acting for the receiving party must, within 14 days of service of the points of dispute, give to his client a clear written explanation of the nature of the relevant point of dispute and the effect it will have if it is upheld in whole or in part by the court, and of the client's right to attend any subsequent hearings at court when the matter is raised.

20.6 Where the solicitor acting for a receiving party files a request for a detailed assessment hearing it must if appropriate, be accompanied by a certificate signed by him stating:

(1) that the amount of the percentage increase in respect of counsel's fees or solicitor's charges is disputed;

(2) whether an application will be made for an order that any amount of that increase which is disallowed should continue to be payable by his client;

(3) that he has given his client an explanation in accordance with paragraph 20.5; and,

(4) whether his client wishes to attend court when the amount of any relevant percentage increase may be decided.

20.7(1) The solicitor acting for the receiving party must within 7 days of receiving from the court notice of the date of the assessment hearing, notify his client, and if appropriate, counsel in writing of the date, time and place of the hearing.

(2) Counsel may attend or be represented at the detailed assessment hearing and may make oral or written submissions.

20.8(1) At the detailed assessment hearing, the court will deal with the assessment of the costs payable by one party to another, including the amount of the percentage increase, and give a certificate accordingly.

(2) The court may decide the issue whether the disallowed

amount should continue to be payable under the relevant conditional fee agreement without an adjournment if:

(a) the receiving party and all parties to the relevant agreement consent to the court deciding the issue without an adjournment,

(b) the receiving party (or, if corporate, an officer or employee who has authority to consent on behalf of the receiving party) is present in court, and

(c) the court is satisfied that the issue can be fairly decided without an adjournment.

(3) In any other case the court will give directions and fix a date for the hearing of the application.

Section 21 Application of Costs Rules: Rule 44.17

21.1 Rule 44.17(b) excludes the costs rules to the extent that regulations under the Legal Aid Act 1988 make different provision. The primary examples of such regulations are the regulations providing prescribed rates (with or without enhancement). **44PD.15**

21.2 Rule 44.17(a) provides that the procedure for detailed assessment does not apply to the extent that section 11 of the Access to Justice Act 1999 and provisions made under that Act make different provision.

21.3 Section 11 of the Access to Justice Act 1999 provides special protection against liability for costs for litigants who receive funding by the LSC (Legal Services Commission) as part of the Community Legal Service. Any costs ordered to be paid by a LSC funded client must not exceed the amount which is reasonable for him to pay having regard to all the circumstances including:

(a) the financial resources of all the parties to the proceedings, and

(b) their conduct in connection with the dispute to which the proceedings relate.

21.4 In this Practice Direction

"cost protection" means the limit on costs awarded against a LSC funded client set out in Section 11(1) of the Access to Justice Act 1999.

"partner" has the meaning given by the Community Legal Service (Costs) Regulations 2000.

21.5 Whether or not cost protection applies depends upon the "level of service" for which funding was provided by the LSC in accordance with the Funding Code approved under section 9 of the Access to Justice Act 1999. The levels of service referred to are:

(1) Legal Help — advice and assistance about a legal problem, not including representation or advocacy in proceedings.

(2) Help at Court — *advocacy at* a specific hearing, where the advocate is not formally representing the client in the proceedings.

(3) Family Mediation.

(4) Legal Representation — representation in actual or contemplated proceedings. Legal Representation can take the form of Investigative Help (limited to investigating the merits of a potential claim) or Full Representation.

(5) General Family Help and Help with Mediation.

21.6 Levels of service (4) and (5) are provided under a certificate (similar to a legal aid certificate). The certificate will state which level of service is covered. Where there are proceedings, a copy of the certificate will be lodged with the court.

21.7 Cost protection does not apply where—

(1) The LSC funded client receives Help at Court;

(2) The LSC funded client receives Legal Help only i.e. where the solicitor is advising, but not representing a litigant in person. However, where the LSC funded client receives Legal Help e.g. to write a letter before action, but later receives Legal Representation or General Family Help or Help with Mediation in respect of the same dispute, other than in family proceedings, cost protection does apply to all costs incurred by the receiving party in the funded proceedings or prospective proceedings;

(3) The LSC funded client receives General Family Help or Help with Mediation in family proceedings;

(4) The LSC funded client receives Legal Representation in family proceedings.

21.8 Where cost protection does not apply, the court may award costs in the normal way.

21.9 Where work is done before the issue of a certificate, cost protection does not apply to those costs, except where:

(1) pre-action Legal Help is given and the LSC funded client subsequently receives Legal Representation or General Family Help or Help with Mediation in respect of the same dispute, other than in family proceedings; or

(2) where urgent work is undertaken immediately before the grant of an emergency certificate, other than in family proceedings, when no emergency application could be made as the LSC's offices were closed, provided that the solicitor seeks an emergency certificate at the first available opportunity and the certificate is granted.

21.10 If a LSC funded client's certificate is revoked, costs protection does not apply to work done before or after revocation.

21.11 If a LSC funded client's certificate is discharged, costs protection only applies to costs incurred before the date on which funded services ceased to be provided under the certificate. This may be a date before the date on which the certificate is formally discharged by the LSC (*Burridge v Stafford*: *Khan v Ali* [2000] 1 W.L.R. 927; [1999] 4 All E.R. 660, CA).

21.11A Where an LSC funded client has cost protection, the procedure described in sections 22 and 23 of this Practice Direction applies. However that procedure does not apply in relation to costs claimed during any periods in the proceedings when the LSC funded client did not have cost protection, and the procedure set out in CPR *Parts* 45 to 47 will apply (as appropriate) in relation to those periods.

Assessing a LSC Funded Client's Resources

21.12 The first £100,000 of the value of the LSC funded client's interest in the main or only home is disregarded when assessing his or her financial resources for the purposes of S.11 and cannot be the subject of any enforcement process by the receiving party. The receiving party cannot apply for an order to sell the LSC funded client's home, but could secure the debt against any value exceeding £100,000 by way of a charging order.

21.13 The court may only take into account the value of the LSC funded client's clothes, household furniture, tools and implements of trade to the extent that it considers that having regard to the quantity or value of the items, the circumstances are exceptional.

21.14 The LSC funded client's resources include the resources of his partner, unless the partner has a contrary interest in the dispute in respect of which funded services are provided.

Party acting in a Representative, Fiduciary or Official Capacity

21.15(1) Where a LSC funded client is acting in a representative, fiduciary or official capacity, the court shall not take the personal resources of the party into account for the purposes of either a Section 11 order or costs against the Commission, but shall have regard to the value of any property or estate or the amount of any fund out of which the party is entitled to be indemnified, and may also have regard to the resources of any persons who are beneficially interested in the property, estate or fund.

(2) Similarly, where a party is acting as a litigation friend to a client who is a child or a protected party, the court shall not take the personal resources of the litigation friend into account in assessing the resources of the client.

(3) The purpose of this provision is to ensure that any liability is determined with reference to the value of the property or fund being used to pay for the litigation, and the financial position of those who may benefit from or rely on it.

Costs against the LSC

21.16 Regulation 5 of the Community Legal Service (Cost Protection) Regulations 2000 governs when costs can be awarded against the LSC. This provision only applies where cost protection applies and the costs ordered to be paid by the LSC funded client do not fully meet the costs that would have been ordered to be paid by him if cost protection did not apply.

21.17 In this Section and the following two Sections of this Practice Direction "non-funded party" means a party to proceedings who has not received LSC *funded services in relation* to these proceedings under a legal aid certificate or a certificate issued under the LSC Funding Code other than a certificate which has been revoked.

21.18 The following criteria set out in Regulation 5 must be satisfied before the LSC can be ordered to pay the whole or any part of the costs incurred by a non-funded party:

(1) the proceedings are finally decided in favour of a non-funded party;

(2) unless there is good reason for delay the non-funded party provides written notice of intention to seek an order against the LSC within three months of the making of the section 11(1) costs order;

(3) the court is satisfied that it is just and equitable in the circumstances that provision for the costs should be made out of public funds; and

(4) where costs are incurred in a court of first instance, the following additional criteria must also be met:

(i) the proceedings were instituted by the LSC funded client;

(ii) the non-funded party is an individual; and

(iii) the non-funded party will suffer financial hardship unless the order is made.

("Section 11(1) costs order" is defined in paragraph 22.1, below.)

21.19 In determining whether conditions (3) and (4) are satisfied, the court shall take into account the resources of the non-funded party and his partner, unless the partner has a contrary interest.

21.19A An order under Regulation 5 may be made in relation to proceedings in the Court of Appeal, High Court or a County Court, by a Costs Judge or a District Judge.

Effect of Appeals

21.20(1) An order for costs can only be made against the LSC when the proceedings (including any appeal) are finally decided. Therefore, where a court of first instance decides in favour of a non-funded party and an appeal lies, any order made against the LSC shall not take effect unless:

(a) where permission to appeal is required, the time limit for permission to appeal expires, without permission being granted;

(b) where permission to appeal is granted or is not required, the time limit for appeal expires without an appeal being brought.

(2) Accordingly, if the LSC funded client appeals, any earlier order against the LSC can never take effect. If the appeal is unsuccessful, an application can be made to the appeal court for a fresh order.

Section 22 Orders for Costs to Which Section 11 of the Access to Justice Act 1999 Applies

44PD.16 **22.1** In this Practice Direction:

"order for costs to be determined" means an order for costs to which Section 11 of the Access to Justice Act 1999 applies under which the amount of costs payable by the LSC funded client is to be determined by a costs judge or district judge under Section 23 of this Practice Direction.

"order specifying the costs payable" means an order for costs to which Section 11 of the Act applies and which specifies the amount which the LSC funded client is to pay.

"full costs" means, where an order to which Section 11 of the Act applies is made against a LSC funded client, the amount of costs which that person would, had cost protection not applied, have been ordered to pay.

"determination proceedings" means proceedings to which paragraphs 22.1 to 22.10 apply.

"Section 11(1) costs order" means an order for costs to be determined or an order specifying the costs payable other than an order specifying the costs payable which was made in determination proceedings.

"statement of resources" means

(1) a statement, verified by a statement of truth, made by a party to proceedings setting out:

(a) his income and capital and financial commitments during the previous year and, if applicable, those of his partner;

(b) his estimated future financial resources and expectations and, if applicable, those of his partner ("partner" is defined in paragraph 21.4 above);

(c) a declaration that he and, if applicable, his partner, has not deliberately foregone or deprived himself of any resources or expectations;

(d) particulars of any application for funding made by him in connection with the proceedings; and,

(e) any other facts relevant to the determination of his resources; or

(2) a statement, verified by a statement of truth, made by a client receiving funded services, setting out the information provided by the client under Regulation 6 of the Community Legal Service (Financial) Regulations 2000, and stating that there has been no significant change in the client's financial circumstances since the date on which the information was provided or, as the case may be, details of any such change.

"Regional Director" means any Regional Director appointed by the LSC and any member of his staff authorised to act on his behalf.

22.2 Regulations 8 to 13 of the Community Legal Service (Costs) Regulations 2000 as amended set out the procedure for seeking costs against a funded client and the LSC. The effect of these Regulations is set out in this section and the next section of this Practice Direction.

22.3 As from 5 June 2000, Regulations 9 to 13 of the Community Legal Service (Costs) Regulations 2000 as amended also apply to certificates issued under the Legal Aid Act 1988 where costs against the assisted person fall to be assessed under Regulation 124 of the Civil Legal Aid (General) Regulations 1989. In this section and the next section of this Practice Direction the expression "LSC funded client" includes an assisted person (defined in rule 43.2).

22.4 Regulation 8 of the Community Legal Service (Costs) Regulations 2000 as amended provides that a party intending to seek an order for costs against a LSC funded client may at any time file and serve on the LSC funded client a statement of resources. If that statement is served 7 or more days before a date fixed for a hearing at which an order for costs may be made, the LSC funded client must also make a statement of resources and produce it at the hearing.

22.5 If the court decides to make an order for costs against a LSC funded client to whom cost protection applies it may either:

(1) make an order for costs to be determined, or

(2) make an order specifying the costs payable.

22.6 If the court makes an order for costs to be determined it may also

(1) state the amount of full costs, or

(2) make findings of facts, e.g. concerning the conduct of all the parties which are to be taken into account by the court in the subsequent determination proceedings.

22.7 The court will not make an order specifying the costs payable unless:

(1) it considers that it has sufficient information before it to decide what amount is a reasonable amount for the LSC funded client to pay in accordance with Section 11 of the Act, and

(2) either

(a) the order also states the amount of full costs, or

(b) the court considers that it has sufficient information before it to decide what amount is a reasonable amount for the LSC funded client to pay in accordance with Section 11 of the Act and is satisfied that, if it were to determine the full costs at that time, they would exceed the amounts specified in the order.

22.8 Where an order specifying the costs payable is made and the LSC funded client does not have cost protection in respect of all of the costs awarded in that order, the order must identify the sum payable (if any) in respect of which the LSC funded client has cost protection and the sum payable (if any) in respect of which he does not have cost protection.

22.9 The court cannot make an order under Regulations 8 to 13 of the Community Legal Service (Costs) Regulations 2000 as amended except in proceedings to which the next section of this Practice Direction applies.

Section 23 Determination Proceedings and Similar Proceedings Under the Community Legal Service (Costs) Regulations 2000

44PD.17 **23.1** This section of this Practice Direction deals with

(1) proceedings subsequent to the making of an order for costs to be determined,

(2) variations in the amount stated in an order specifying the amount of costs payable,

(3) the late determination of costs under an order for costs to be determined, and

(4) appeals in respect of determination.

23.2 In this section of this Practice Direction "appropriate court office" means:

(1) the district registry or county court in which the case was being dealt with when the Section 11(1) order was made, or to which it has subsequently been transferred; or

(2) in all other cases, the Supreme Court Costs Office.

23.2A(1)This paragraph applies where the appropriate office is any of the following county courts:

Barnet, Bow, Brentford, Bromley, Central London, Clerkenwell, Croyden, Edmonton, Ilford, Kingston, Lambeth, Mayors and City of London, Romford, Shoreditch, Uxbridge, Wandsworth, West London, Willesden and Woolwich.

(2) Where this paragraph applies:—

(i) a receiving party seeking an order specifying costs payable by an LSC funded client and/or by the Legal Services Commission under this section must file his application in the Supreme Court Costs Office and, for all purposes relating to the application, the Supreme Court Costs Office will be treated as the appropriate office in that case; and

(ii) unless an order is made transferring the application to the Supreme Court Costs Office as part of the High Court, an appeal from any decision made by a costs judge shall lie to the Designated Civil Judge for the London Group of County Courts or such judge as he shall nominate. The appeal notice and any other relevant papers should be lodged at the Central London Civil Justice Centre.

23.3(1) A receiving party seeking an order specifying costs payable by an LSC funded client and/or by the LSC may within 3 months of an order for costs to be determined, file in the appropriate court office an application in Form **N244** accompanied by

(a) the receiving party's bill of costs (unless the full costs have already been determined);

(b) the receiving party's statement of resources (unless the court is determining an application against a costs order against the LSC and the costs were not incurred in the court of first instance); and

(c) if the receiving party intends to seek costs against the *LSC, written* notice to that effect.

(2) If the LSC funded client's liability has already been determined and is less than the full costs, the application will be for costs against the LSC only. If the LSC funded client's liability has not yet been determined, the receiving party must indicate if costs will be sought against the LSC if the funded client's liability is determined as less than the full costs.

(The LSC funded client's certificate will contain the addresses of the LSC funded client, his solicitor, and the relevant Regional Office of the LSC.)

23.4 The receiving party must file the above documents in the appropriate court office and (where relevant) serve copies on the LSC funded client and the Regional Director. In respect of applications for funded services made before 3 December 2001 a failure to file a request within the 3 months time limit specified in Regulation 10(2) is an absolute bar to the making of a costs order against the LSC. Where the application for funded services was made on or after 3 December 2001 the court does have power to extend the 3 months time limit, but only if the applicant can show good reason for the delay.

23.5 On being served with the application, the LSC funded client must respond by filing a statement of resources and serving a copy of it on the receiving party (and the Regional Director where relevant) within 21 days. The LSC funded client may also file and serve written points disputing the bill within the same time limit. (Under rule 3.1 the court may extend or shorten this time limit.)

23.6 If the LSC funded client fails to file a statement of resources without good reason, the court will determine his liability (and the amount of full costs if relevant) and need not hold an oral hearing for such determination.

23.7 When the LSC funded client files a statement or the 21 day period for doing so expires, the court will fix a hearing date and give the relevant parties at least 14 days notice. The court may fix a hearing without waiting for the expiry of the 21 day period if the application is made only against the LSC.

23.8 Determination proceedings will be listed for hearing before a costs judge or district judge. The determination of the liability on the LSC funded client will be listed as a private hearing.

23.9 Where the LSC funded client does not have cost protection in respect of all of the costs awarded, the order made by the costs judge or district judge must in addition to specifying the costs payable, identify the full costs in respect of which cost protection applies and the full costs in respect of which cost protection does not apply.

23.10 The Regional Director may appear at any hearing at which a costs order may be made against the LSC. Instead of appearing, he may file a written statement at court and serve a copy on the receiving party. The written statement should be filed and a copy served, not less than 7 days before the hearing.

Variation of an order specifying the costs payable

23.11(1) This paragraph applies where the amount stated in an order specifying the costs payable plus the amount ordered to be paid by the LSC is less than the full costs to which cost protection applies.

(2) The receiving party may apply to the court for a variation of the amount which the LSC funded client is required to pay on the ground that there has been a significant change in the client's circumstances since the date of the order.

23.12 On an application under paragraph 23.11, where the order specifying the costs payable does not state the full costs:

(1) the receiving party must file with his application the receiving party's statement of resources and bill of costs and copies of these documents should be served with the application.

(2) The LSC funded client must respond to the application by making a statement of resources which must be filed at court and served on the receiving party within 21 days thereafter. The LSC funded client may also file and serve written points disputing the bill within the same time limit.

(3) The court will, when determining the application assess the full costs identifying any part of them to which cost protection does apply and any part of them to which cost protection does not apply.

23.13 On an application under paragraph 23.11 the order specifying the costs payable may be varied as the court thinks fit. That variation must not increase:

(1) the amount of any costs ordered to be paid by the LSC, and

(2) the amount payable by the LSC funded client,

to a sum which is greater than the amount of the full costs plus the costs of the application.

23.14(1) Where an order for costs to be determined has been made but the receiving party has not applied, within the three month time limit under paragraph 23.2, the receiving party may apply on any of the following grounds for a determination of the amount which the funded client is required to pay:

(a) there has been a significant change in the funded client's circumstances since the date of the order for costs to be determined; or

(b) material additional information about the funded client's financial resources is available which could not with reasonable diligence have been obtained by the receiving party at the relevant time; or

(c) there were other good reasons for the failure by the receiving party to make an application within the time limit.

(2) An application for costs payable by the LSC cannot be made under this paragraph.

23.15(1) Where the receiving party has received funded services in relation to the proceedings, the LSC may make an application under paragraphs 23.11 and 23.14 above.

(2) In respect of an application under paragraph 23.11 made by the LSC, the LSC must file and serve copies of the documents described in paragraph 23.12(1).

23.16 An application under paragraph 23.11, 23.14 and 23.15 must be commenced before the expiration of 6 years from the date on which the court made the order specifying the costs payable, or (as the case may be) the order for costs to be determined.

23.17 Applications under paragraphs 23.11, 23.14 and 23.15 should be made in the appropriate court office and should be made in Form **N244** to be listed for a hearing before a costs judge or district judge.

Appeals

23.18(1) Save as mentioned above any determination made under Regulation 9 or 10 of the Costs Regulations is final (Regulation 11(1)). Any party with a financial interest in the assessment of the full costs, other than a funded party, may appeal against that assessment in accordance with CPR Part 52 (Regulation 11(2) and CPR rule 47.20).

(2) The receiving party or the Commission may appeal on a point of law against the making of a costs order against the Commission, against the amount of costs the Commission is required to pay or against the court's refusal to make such an order (Regulation 11(4)).

Section 23A Costs Capping Orders

When to make an application

44PD.18 **23A.1** The court will make a costs capping order only in exceptional circumstances.

23A.2 An application for a costs capping order must be made as soon as possible, preferably before or at the first case management hearing or shortly afterwards. The stage which the proceedings have reached at the time of the application will be one of the factors the court will consider when deciding whether to make a costs capping order.

Estimate of costs

23A.3 The estimate of costs required by rules 44.19 and 44.20(2) must be in the form illustrated in Precedent H in the Schedule of Costs Precedents annexed to this Practice Direction.

Schedule of costs

23A.4 The schedule of costs referred to in rule 44.19(3)—

(a) must set out—

(i) each sub-heading as it appears in the applicant's estimate of costs (column 1);

(ii) alongside each sub-heading, the amount claimed by the applicant in the applicant's estimate of costs (column 2); and

(iii) alongside the figures referred to in sub-paragraph (ii) the amount that the respondent proposes should be allowed under each sub-heading (column 3); and

(b) must be supported by a statement of truth.

Assessing the quantum of the costs cap

23A.5 When assessing the quantum of a costs cap, the court will take into account the factors detailed in rule 44.5 and the relevant provisions supporting that rule in this Practice Direction. The court may also take into account when considering a party's estimate of the costs they are likely to incur in the future conduct of the proceedings a reasonable allowance on costs for contingencies.

PART 45

Fixed Costs

45.0.1 **Contents**

Editorial introduction

Section II (Road Traffic Accidents—Fixed recoverable Costs in Costs-Only Proceedings) (rr.45.7 to 45.14) was added to Pt 45 by the Civil Procedure (Amendment No.4) Rules 2004 and came into effect on October 6, 2003 (see paras 45.7 *et seq.* below). The provisions in Sect.II introduce a scheme for providing that only specified costs are recoverable, other than in exceptional circumstances, where costs in costs-only proceedings under r.44.12A in relation to disputes arising out of road traffic accidents are settled for an amount of agreed damages exceeding £10,000. These provisions apply only to accidents occurring on or after October 6, 2003. **45.0.2**

Section III (Fixed Percentage Increase in Road Traffic Accident Claims) fixes the success fee other than in small claims in relation to accidents which occurred on or after October 6, 2003. The success fees are fixed for both consel and solicitors at all stages up to trial. There is provision for applying for an alternative success fee in cases where the damages exceed £500,000. See r.45.18.

Section IV sets out the success fees in Employer's Liability personal injury claims; and Sect.V, the success fees in Employer's Liability disease claims.

I. Fixed Costs

Scope of this Section

45.1—(1) This Section sets out the amounts which, unless the court orders otherwise, are to be allowed in respect of solicitors' charges in the cases to which this Section applies. **45.1**

(2) This Section applies where—

(a) the only claim is a claim for a specified sum of money where the value of the claim exceeds £25 and—

(i) judgment in default is obtained under rule 12.4(1);

(ii) judgment on admission is obtained under rule 14.4(3);

(iii) judgment on admission on part of the claim is obtained under rule 14.5(6);

(iv) summary judgment is given under Part 24;

(v) the court has made an order to strike out(GL) a defence under rule 3.4(2)(a) as disclosing no reasonable grounds for defending the claim; or

(vi) rule 45.3 applies;

(b) the only claim is a claim where the court gave a fixed date for the hearing when it issued the claim and judg-

ment is given for the delivery of goods, and the value of the claim exceeds £25;

(c) the claim is for the recovery of land, including a possession claim under Part 55, whether or not the claim includes a claim for a sum of money and the defendant gives up possession, pays the amount claimed, if any, and the fixed commencement costs stated in the claim form;

(d) the claim is for the recovery of land, including a possession claim under Part 55, where one of the grounds for possession is arrears of rent, for which the court gave a fixed date for the hearing when it issued the claim and judgment is given for the possession of land (whether or not the order for possession is suspended on terms) and the defendant—

(i) has neither delivered a defence, or counterclaim, nor otherwise denied liability; or

(ii) has delivered a defence which is limited to specifying his proposals for the payment of arrears of rent;

(e) the claim is a possession claim under Section II of Part 55 (accelerated possession claims of land let on an assured shorthold tenancy) and a possession order is made where the defendant has neither delivered a defence, or counterclaim, nor otherwise denied liability;

(f) the claim is a demotion claim under Section III of Part 65 or a demotion claim is made in the same claim form in which a claim for possession is made under Part 55 and that demotion claim is successful; or

(g) a judgment creditor has taken steps under Parts 70 to 73 to enforce a judgment or order.

(The practice direction supplementing rule 7.9 sets out the types of case where a court will give a fixed date for a hearing when it issues a claim)

(3) Any appropriate court fee will be allowed in addition to the costs set out in this Section.

(4) The claim form may include a claim for fixed commencement costs.

Comment

45.1.1 Part 45 is specifically applied to judgment in default (r.12.4(1)); judgment on admission in whole (r.14.4(3)) or in part (r.14.56(6)); summary judgment under Pt 24 strike out (r.3.4(2)(a)); or when the defendant is only liable for fixed commencement costs (r.45.3). Part 45 also applies to judgment for delivery of goods on a fixed date hearing. If the value of a claim does not exceed £25, Pt 45 does not apply.

In relation to a claim on the small claims track the court may not order a party to pay a sum to another party in respect of costs except the fixed costs payable under Pt 45 attributable to issuing the claim (see r.27.14(2)(a)). The Costs Practice Direction also provides for fixed costs to be paid on the issue of a default costs certificate. See ss.24 and 25 of the Costs Practice Direction.

The provisions of CPR 45.3 operate to apply the costs fixed by Sect.I of Pt 45 unless the court otherwise orders. On the particular facts of the case the court refused to exercise its discretion to allow more than the fixed costs, stating, among other reasons:

"this court has recognised the importance of a summary and prompt procedure to secure enforcement of adjudicators' decisions properly reached. A party which makes a 'without prejudice save as to costs' offer is not entitled in some way to have it responded to or to assume that threatened proceedings against it will or might be withheld. It would be different if the without prejudice correspondence had revealed some agreement by which the claimant undertook, at least temporarily, not to issue proceedings … It would not be fair to limit a successful claimant which complied with the steps called for in the rule and the [TCC] Guide."

The claimant was justified in issuing proceedings and the Pt 24 application following a threatened defence and an unqualified admission on the part of the defendant after issue (*Amber Construction Services Ltd v London Interspace HG Ltd* [2007] EWHC 3042 (TCC) Akenhead J.).

Amount of fixed commencement costs in a claim for the recovery of money or goods

45.2—(1) The amount of fixed commencement costs in a claim to which rule 45.1(2)(a) or (b) applies— 45.2

(a) shall be calculated by reference to Table 1; and

(b) the amount claimed, or the value of the goods claimed if specified, in the claim form is to be used for determining the band in Table 1 that applies to the claim.

(2) The amounts shown in Table 4 are to be allowed in addition, if applicable.

Amount of fixed commencement costs in a claim for the recovery of land or a demotion claim

45.2A—(1) The amount of fixed commencement costs in a claim to which rule 45.1(2)(c), (d) or (f) applies shall be calculated by reference to Table 2. 45.2A

(2) The amounts shown in Table 4 are to be allowed in addition, if applicable.

TABLE 1

FIXED COSTS ON COMMENCEMENT OF A CLAIM FOR THE RECOVERY OF MONEY OR GOODS

Relevant band	Where the claim form is served by the court or by any method other than personal service by the claimant	Where • the claim form is served personally by the claimant; and • there is only one defendant	Where there is more than one defendant, for each additional defendant personally served at separate addresses by the claimant

Where— • the value of the claim exceeds £25 but does not exceed £500	£50	£60	£15
Where— • the value of the claim exceeds £500 but does not exceed £1,000	£70	£80	£15
Where— • the value of the claim exceeds £1,000 but does not exceed £5,000; or • the only claim is for delivery of goods and no value is specified or stated on the claim form	£80	£90	£15
Where— • the value of the claim exceeds £5,000	£100	£110	£15

TABLE 2

FIXED COSTS ON COMMENCEMENT OF A CLAIM FOR THE RECOVERY OF LAND OR A DEMOTION CLAIM

Where the claim form is served by the court or by any method other than personal service by the claimant	Where • the claim form is served personally by the claimant; and • there is only one defendant	Where there is more than one defendant, for each additional defendant personally served at separate addresses by the claimant
£69.50	£77.00	£15.00

Comment

The tables provide different levels of fees depending upon the value of the claim, the method of service and the number of defendants. The relevant band is ascertained by reference to the amount claimed and the value of the goods in the claim form. **45.2.1**

When defendant only liable for fixed commencement costs[1]

45.3—(1) Where— **45.3**

(a) the only claim is for a specified sum of money; and

(b) the defendant pays the money claimed within 14 days after service of particulars of claim on him, together with the fixed commencement costs stated in the claim form,

the defendant is not liable for any further costs unless the court orders otherwise.

Costs on entry of judgment in a claim for the recovery of money or goods

45.4 Where— **45.4**

(a) the claimant has claimed fixed commencement costs under rule 45.2; and

(b) judgment is entered in a claim to which rule 45.1(2)(a) or (b) applies in the circumstances specified in Table 3, the amount to be included in the judgment for the claimant's solicitor's charges is the total of—

(i) the fixed commencement costs; and

(ii) the relevant amount shown in Table 3.

Comment

Table 3 sets out the fixed costs on entry of judgment. Different costs are payable in respect of cases above and below £5,000 and in different circumstances The amount which is included in the judgment is the aggregate of the fixed commencement costs (see Table 1, r.45.2) and the relevant figure in Table 2. **45.4.1**

Costs on entry of judgment in a claim for the recovery of land or a demotion claim

45.4A—(1) Where— **45.4A**

[1] Amended by the Civil Procedure (Amendment No.3) Rules 2006 (SI 2006/3435).

(a) the claimant has claimed fixed commencement costs under rule 45.2A; and

(b) judgment is entered in a claim to which rule 45.1(2)(d) or (f) applies, the amount to be included in the judgment for the claimant's solicitor's charges is the total of—

(i) the fixed commencement costs; and

(ii) the sum of £57.25.

(2) Where an order for possession is made in a claim to which rule 45.1(2)(e) applies, the amount allowed for the claimant's solicitor's charges for preparing and filing—

(a) the claim form;

(b) the documents that accompany the claim form; and

(c) the request for possession,

is £79.50.

TABLE 3

FIXED COSTS ON ENTRY OF JUDGMENT IN A CLAIM FOR THE RECOVERY OF MONEY OR GOODS

	Where the amount of the judgment exceeds £25 but does not exceed £5000	**Where the amount of the judgment exceeds £5000**
Where judgment in default of an acknowledgment of service is entered under rule 12.4(1) (entry of judgment by request on claim for money only)	£22	£30
Where judgment in default of a defence is entered under rule 12.4(1) (entry of judgment by request on claim for money only)	£25	£35
Where judgment is entered under rule 14.4 (judgment on admission), or rule 14.5 (judgment on admission of part of claim), and claimant accepts the defendant's proposal as to the manner of payment.	£40	£55

	Where the amount of the judgment exceeds £25 but does not exceed £5000	Where the amount of the judgment exceeds £5000
Where judgment is entered under rule 14.4 (judgment on admission), or rule 14.5 (judgment on admission on part of claim) and court decides the date or times of payment	£55	£70
Where summary judgment is given under Part 24 or the court strikes out a defence under rule 3.4(2)(a), in either case, on application by a party	£175	£210
Where judgment is given on a claim for delivery of goods under a regulated agreement within the meaning of the Consumer Credit Act 1974 and no other entry in this table applies	£60	£85

Miscellaneous fixed costs

45.5 Table 4 shows the amount to be allowed in respect of solicitor's charges in the circumstances mentioned. 45.5

TABLE 4

MISCELLANEOUS FIXED COSTS

For service by a party of any document required to be served personally including preparing and copying a certificate of service for each individual served	£15.00
Where service by an alternative method or at an alternative place is permitted by an order under rule 6.15 for each individual served	£53.25
Where a document is served out of the jurisdiction— (a) in Scotland, Northern Ireland, the Isle of Man or the Channel Islands (b) in any other place	 £68.25 £77.00

Comment

45.5.1 As to fixed costs on the issue of a Default Costs Certificate see Sect.25 of the Costs Practice Direction.

Table of Fixed Costs published by the Senior Master (Queen's Bench Division) and the Chief Master (Chancery Division)

45.5.2 This Table replaces the one approved on December 22, 2004 which is hereby cancelled.

The Table is compiled from Pt 45 and Sch.1 to Pt 50 (RSC O.62) of the Civil Procedure Rules 1998 (SI 1998/3132) and The Civil Proceedings Fees Order 2004 (SI 2004/3121) and takes effect from May 16, 2005. There is no VAT addition to this Table of Costs.

The Table sets out the amounts which, unless the court orders otherwise, are to be allowed in respect of solicitors' charges together with the court fee, where appropriate.

45.5.3 *A. Fixed Commencement Costs on Claim Form* —The following apply to all claim forms for a specified sum of money only

Where the claim form is served by the court or by any method other than personal service by the claimant and—	
the sum claimed exceeds £15,000 but does not exceed £50,000	£500.00
the sum claimed exceeds £50,000 but does not exceed £100,000	£800.00
the sum claimed exceeds £100,000 but does not exceed £150,000	£1,000.00
the sum claimed exceeds £150,000 but does not exceed £200,000	£1,200.00
the sum claimed exceeds £200,000 but does not exceed £250,000	£1,400.00
the sum claimed exceeds £250,000 but does not exceed £300,000	£1,600.00
the sum claimed exceeds £300,000 or not limited	£1,800.00
(the fee is included in the above figure)	
Where the claim form is served personally by the claimant and there is only one defendant and—	
the sum claimed exceeds £15,000 but does not exceed £50,000	£510.00
the sum claimed exceeds £50,000 but does not exceed £100,000	£810.00
the sum claimed exceeds £100,000 but does not exceed £150,000	£1,010.00
the sum claimed exceeds £150,000 but does not exceed £200,000	£1,210.00
the sum claimed exceeds £200,000 but does not exceed £250,000	£1,410.00
the sum claimed exceeds £250,000 but does not exceed £300,000	£1,610.00
the sum claimed exceeds £300,000 or not limited	£1,810.00
(the fee is included in the above figures)	
Additional costs	
Where the claim form is served personally by the claimant and *where there is more than one* defendant, for each additional defendant personally served at separate addresses by the claimant	£15.00

For service by a party of any document required to be served personally including preparing and copying a certificate of service for each individual served	£15.00*
Where service by an alternative method is permitted by an order under rule 6.8 for each individual served	£25.00*
Where a document is served out of the jurisdiction:	
(a) in Scotland, Northern Ireland, the Isle of Man or the Channel Islands	£65.00*
(b) in any other place	£75.00*
* *Add application fee if appropriate*	

B. Fixed Costs on Entry of Judgment —The following are to be **added** to the fixed commencement costs **45.5.4**

Where judgment in default of an acknowledgment of service is entered under rule 12.4(1) (entry of judgment by request on claim for money only)	£30.00
Where judgment in default of a defence is entered under rule 12.4(1) (entry of judgment by request on claim for money only)	£35.00
Where judgment is entered under rule 14.4 (judgment on admission) or rule 14.5 (judgment on admission of part of claim) and claimant accepts the defendant's proposal as to the manner of payment	£55.00
Where judgment is entered under rule 14.4 (judgment on admission) or rule 14.5 (judgment on admission on part of claim) and court decides the date or times of payment	£70.00
Where summary judgment is given under Part 24 or the court strikes out a defence under rule 3.4(2)(a), in either case, on application by a party (fee included)	£310.00

C. Costs on Judgment without Trial for Possession of Land —This section does not apply where the claimant is also entitled under the judgment to damages to be assessed, or where the claimant claims any remedy of the nature specified in Order 45 rule 3(2) (mortgage claims). **45.5.5**

Where the claim is for the possession of land, and the claimant obtains judgment under CPR Part 12 (default judgment) or CPR Part 24 (summary judgment) for possession of land and costs	
	£143.75 together with any court fee and additional costs (see Table below) where appropriate
Additional costs	
Where there is more than one defendant, in respect of each additional defendant served	£13.75

Where service by an alternative method is ordered and effected, in respect of each defendant served	£53.25*
Where service out of the jurisdiction is ordered and effected, in the case of service—	
(a) in Scotland, Northern Ireland, the Isle of Man or the Channel Islands	£68.25*
(b) in any other place out of the jurisdiction	£77.00*
In the case of default judgment under CPR Part 12 or summary judgment under CPR Part 24 the claimant makes an affidavit of service for the purpose of a judgment where the defendant failed to respond to the claim form (the allowance to include the search fee)	£20.50
In the case of summary judgment under CPR Part 24 where an affidavit of service of the summons is required	£20.50
In the case of summary judgment under CPR Part 24 for each adjournment of the application	£20.50
* *Add application fee if appropriate*	

45.5.6 *D. Enforcement Costs* —The following apply only where an amount in respect of solicitors' charges has been entered on the claim form under CPR Part 45 (see sections A and B above) or Schedule 1 (RSC O.62) (see section C above)

Scottish and Northern Ireland Money Judgments	
Where a certificate in respect of money provisions contained in a judgment is registered in the High Court in the Register of United Kingdom judgments under Schedule 6 to the Civil Jurisdiction and Judgments Act 1982,	
Costs of registration	£39.00
Recovery of Award	
For an application under rule 70.5(4) that an award may be enforced as if payable under a court order, where the amount outstanding under the award:	
exceeds £25 but does not exceed £250	£30.75
exceeds £250 but does not exceed £600	£41.00
exceeds £600 but does not exceed £2,000	£69.50
exceeds £2,000	£75.50
Orders to Obtain Information	
On attendance to question a judgment debtor (or officer of a company or other corporation) who has been ordered to attend court under rule 71.2 where the questioning takes place before a court officer, including attendance by a responsible representative of the solicitor	

	For each half hour or part, £15.00 (When the questioning takes place before a judge, he may summarily assess any costs allowed.) plus fee of £50.00
Third Party Debt Orders and Money in Court to credit of Judgment Debtor	
On the making of a final third party debt order under Rule 72.8(6)(a) or an order for the payment to the Judgment creditor of money in court under rule 72.10(1)(b):	
If the amount recovered is less than £150	one half of the amount recovered Plus fee of £100
Otherwise (including fee)	£198.50**
Charging Order	
On the making of a final charging order under Rule 73.8(2)(a) (including fee)	£210.00**
	The court may also allow reasonable disbursements in respect of search fees and the registration of the order.
Writ of Possession	
Where leave is given under Order 45 rule 3 to enforce a judgment or order for the giving of possession of land by writ of possession, if the costs are allowed on the judgment or order there shall be allowed the following costs, which shall be added to the judgment or order—	
Basic costs (including fee)	£92.50**
Where notice of the proceedings has been given to more than one person, in respect of each additional person	£2.75
Writ of Execution	
Where a writ of execution within the meaning of Order 46 rule 1 is issued against any party, there shall be allowed—	
Costs of issuing execution (including fee)	£101.75**
*** Remove application fee where appropriate (e.g. where fee exemption/remission certificate applies)*	

Approved the 16th day of May 2005

Fixed enforcement costs

45.6 Table 5 shows the amount to be allowed in respect of solicitors' costs in the circumstances mentioned. The amounts shown in Table 4 are to be allowed in addition, if applicable. 45.6

TABLE 5

FIXED ENFORCEMENT COSTS

For an application under rule 70.5(4) that an award may be enforced as if payable under a court order, where the amount outstanding under the award:	
exceeds £25 but does not exceed £250	£30.75
exceeds £250 but does not exceed £600	£41.00
exceeds £600 but does not exceed £2,000	£69.50
exceeds £2,000	£75.50
On attendance to question a judgment debtor (or officer of a company or other corporation) who has been ordered to attend court under rule 71.2 where the questioning takes place before a court officer, including attendance by a responsible representative of the solicitor	For each half hour or part, £15.00 (When the questioning takes place before a judge, he may summarily assess any costs allowed)
On the making of a final third party debt order under rule 72.8(6)(a) or an order for the payment to the judgment creditor of money in court under rule 72.10(1)(b):	
if the amount recovered is less than	one-half of the amount recovered
£150 otherwise	£98.50
On the making of a final charging order under rule 73.8(2)(a):	£110.00
	The court may also allow reasonable disbursements in respect of search fees and the registration of the order.
Where a certificate is issued and registered under Schedule 6 to the Civil Jurisdiction and Judgments Act 1982, the costs of registration	£39.00

Where permission is given under RSC Order 45, rule 3 to enforce a judgment or order giving possession of land and costs are allowed on the judgment or order, the amount to be added to the judgment or order for costs—	
(a) basic costs	£42.50
(b) where notice of the proceedings is to be to more than one person, for each additional person	£2.75
Where a writ of execution as defined in the RSC Order 46, rule 1, is issued against any party	£51.75
Where a request is filed for the issue of a warrant of execution under CCR Order 26, rule 1, for a sum exceeding £25	£2.25
Where an application for an attachment of earnings order is made and costs are allowed under CCR Order 27, rule 9 or CCR Order 28, rule 10, for each attendance on the hearing of the application	£8.50

II. Road Traffic Accidents—Fixed Recoverable Costs

Section II of Part 45 does not apply to any costs-only proceedings arising out of a dispute, where the road traffic accident which gave rise to the dispute occurred before 6th October 2003 (Civil Procedure (Amendment No.4) Rules 2003, r.1). 45.7

Scope and interpretation[1]

45.7—(1) **This Section sets out the costs which are to be allowed in—**

(a) costs-only proceedings under the procedure set out in rule 44.12A; or

(b) proceedings for approval of a settlement or compromise under rule 21.10(2),

in cases to which this Section applies.

(2) This Section applies where—

(a) the dispute arises from a road traffic accident;

(b) the agreed damages include damages in respect of personal injury, damage to property, or both;

(c) the total value of the agreed damages does not exceed £10,000; and

[1] Introduced by the Civil Procedure (Amendment No.4) Rules (SI 2003/2113).

(d) if a claim had been issued for the amount of the agreed damages, the small claims track would not have been the normal track for that claim.

(3) This Section does not apply where the claimant is a litigant in person.

(Rule 2.3 defines "personal injuries" as including any disease and any impairment of a person's physical or mental condition)

(Rule 26.6 provides for when the small claims track is the normal track)

(4) In this Section—

(a) "road traffic accident" means an accident resulting in bodily injury to any person or damage to property caused by, or arising out of, the use of a motor vehicle on a road or other public place in England and Wales;

(b) "motor vehicle" means a mechanically propelled vehicle intended for use on roads; and

(c) "road" means any highway and any other road to which the public has access and includes bridges over which a road passes.

Application of fixed recoverable costs[1]

45.8 **45.8 Subject to rule 45.12, the only costs which are to be allowed are—**

(a) fixed recoverable costs calculated in accordance with rule 45.9;

(b) disbursements allowed in accordance with rule 45.10; and

(c) a success fee allowed in accordance with rule 45.11.

(Rule 45.12 provides for where a party issues a claim for more than the fixed recoverable costs).

Amount of fixed recoverable costs[2]

45.9 **45.9—(1) Subject to paragraphs (2) and (3), the amount of fixed recoverable costs is the total of—**

(a) £800;

(b) 20% of the damages agreed up to £5,000; and

(c) 15% of the damages agreed between £5,000 and £10,000.

(2) Where the claimant—

(a) lives or works in an area set out in the relevant practice direction; and

(b) instructs a solicitor or firm of solicitors who practise in that area,

the fixed recoverable costs shall include, in addition to the costs specified in paragraph (1), an amount equal to 12.5% of the costs *allowable under that* paragraph.

[1] Introduced by the Civil Procedure (Amendment No.4) Rules (SI 2003/2113).
[2] Introduced by the Civil Procedure (Amendment No.4) Rules (SI 2003/2113).

(3) Where appropriate, value added tax (VAT) may be recovered in addition to the amount of fixed recoverable costs and any reference in this Section to fixed recoverable costs is a reference to those costs net of any such VAT.

The intention underlying r.45.7(14) is to provide an agreed scheme of recovery which is certain and easily calculated. The levels of remuneration may over reward in some cases and under reward in others, but are enough to be regarded as fair when taken as a whole. The court has found that the intention of the rule makers was that the indemnity principle should not apply to the *figures* which are recoverable and there is little reason why the indemnity principle should be assumed to have any application to rr.45.9 and 45.11. The court rejected the argument that there was an overriding need to enable the paying party to satisfy itself that the CFA is compliant to the regulations. Whilst this may result in some non-compliant agreements having effect, it would avoid wasteful arguments about whether there had or had not been substantial non compliance with what is required in these straightforward types of case. Rule 45.10 requires a different approach because there are no fixed figures for disbursements. In cases falling under Pt 45, Sect.II the receiving party does not have to demonstrate that there is a valid retainer between the solicitor and the client, merely that the conditions laid down under the rules have been complied with: *Nizami v Butt* [2006] EWHC 159 (QB), Simon J.; [2006] 1 W.L.R. 3307; [2006] 2 All E.R. 140. The decision in *Nizami v Butt* was approved by the Court of Appeal in *Lamont v Burton* [2007] EWCA Civ 429; [2007] 1 W.L.R. 2814; [2007] 3 All E.R. 173, CA. 45.9.1

Disbursements[1]

45.10—(1) The court— 45.10

(a) may allow a claim for a disbursement of a type mentioned in paragraph (2); but

(b) must not allow a claim for any other type of disbursement.

(2) The disbursements referred to in paragraph (1) are—

(a) the cost of obtaining—

(i) medical records;

(ii) a medical report;

(iii) a police report;

(iv) an engineer's report; or

(v) a search of the records of the Driver Vehicle Licensing Authority;

(b) the amount of an insurance premium; or, where a membership organisation undertakes to meet liabilities incurred to pay the costs of other parties to proceedings, a sum not exceeding such additional amount of costs as would be allowed under section 30 in respect of provision made against the risk of having to meet such liabilities;

("membership organisation" is defined in rule 43.2(1)(n)).

(c) where they are necessarily incurred by reason of one or more of the claimants being a child or protected party as defined in Part 21—

(i) fees payable for instructing counsel; or

[1] Introduced by the Civil Procedure (Amendment No.4) Rules 2003 (SI 2003/2113) and amended by the Civil Procedure (Amendment No.5) Rules 2003 (SI 2003/3361) and the Civil Procedure (Amendment) Rules 2007 (SI 2007/2204).

(ii) court fees payable on an application to the court;

(d) any other disbursement that has arisen due to a particular feature of the dispute.

("insurance premium" is defined in rule 43.2)

Allowance for disbursements

45.10.1 With effect from February 1, 2004, r.45.10(2) was amended by the Civil Procedure (Amendment No.5) Rules 2003 to clarify that, in costs-only proceedings brought under Sect.II of Pt 45 by a party funded by a body which indemnifies its members or other persons against liabilities for costs which they may incur in proceedings, the court may allow that party as a disbursement a sum not exceeding such amount as would be allowed under s.30 of the Access to Justice Act 1999.

Success fee[1]

45.11 **45.11—(1) A claimant may recover a success fee if he has entered into a funding arrangement of a type specified in rule 43.2(k)(i).**

(2) The amount of the success fee shall be 12.5% of the fixed recoverable costs calculated in accordance with rule 45.9(1), disregarding any additional amount which may be included in the fixed recoverable costs by virtue of rule 45.9(2).

Rule 43.2(k)(i) defines as funding arrangement as including a conditional fee agreement or collective conditional fee agreement which provides for a success fee)

Amount of success fee

45.11.1 With effect from March 1, 2004, r.45.11(2) was substituted by the Civil Procedure (Amendment No.5) Rules 2003, to specify the amount of the success fee which a claimant may recover in proceedings under Sect.II of Part 45 if he has entered into a conditional fee agreement or a collective conditional fee agreement which provides for a success fee.

The court has no discretion whether or not to allow a success fee or to apply a different level of success fee than that set out in the Rules even where the successful claimant had the benefit of a before the event insurance policy. Rule 45.11(1) provides that a claimant may recover a success fee, i.e. is entitled to claim a success fee, and Rule 45.11(2) lays down that the success fee "shall be" 12.5 per cent: *Kilby v Gawith* [2008] EWCA Civ 812.

Claims for an amount of costs exceeding fixed recoverable costs[2]

45.12 **45.12—(1) The court will entertain a claim for an amount of costs (excluding any success fee or disbursements) greater than the fixed recoverable costs but only if it considers that there are exceptional circumstances making it appropriate to do so.**

(2) If the court considers such a claim appropriate, it may—

(a) assess the costs; or

(b) make an order for the costs to be assessed.

(3) If the court does not consider the claim appropriate, it must make an order for fixed recoverable costs only.

[1] Introduced by the Civil Procedure (Amendment No.4) Rules 2003 (SI 2003/2113) and amended by the Civil Procedure (Amendment No.5) Rules 2003 (SI 2003/3361).

[2] Introduced by the Civil Procedure (Amendment No.4) Rules (SI 2003/2113).

Failure to acheive costs greater than fixed recoverable costs[1]

45.13—(1) This rule applies where— 45.13

(a) costs are assessed in accordance with rule 45.12(2); and

(b) the court assesses the costs (excluding any VAT) as being an amount which is less than 20% greater than the amount of the fixed recoverable costs.

(2) The court must order the defendant to pay to the claimant the lesser of—

(a) the fixed recoverable costs; and

(b) the assessed costs.

Costs of the costs-only proceedings or the detailed assessment[2]

45.14 Where— 45.14

(a) the court makes an order for fixed recoverable costs in accordance with rule 45.12(3); or

(b) rule 45.13 applies,

the court must—

(i) make no award for the payment of the claimant's costs in bringing the proceedings under rule 44.12A; and

(ii) order that the claimant pay the defendant's costs of defending those proceedings.

III. Fixed Percentage Increase in Road Traffic Accident Claims 45.15

Scope and interpretation

45.15—(1) This Section sets out the percentage increase which is to be allowed in the cases to which this Section applies.

(Rule 43.2(1)(l) defines "percentage increase" as the percentage by which the amount of a legal representative's fee can be increased in accordance with a conditional fee agreement which provides for a success fee).

(2) This Section applies where—

(a) the dispute arises from a road traffic accident; and

(b) the claimant has entered into a funding arrangement of a type specified in rule 43.2(k)(i).

(Rule 43.2(k)(i) defines a funding arrangement as including an arrangement where a person has entered into a conditional fee agreement or collective conditional fee agreement which provides for a success fee).

(3) *This Section* does not apply if the proceedings are costs only proceedings to which Section II of this Part applies.

(4) This Section does not apply—

(a) to a claim which has been allocated to the small claims track;

[1] Introduced by the Civil Procedure (Amendment No.4) Rules (SI 2003/2113).
[2] Introduced by the Civil Procedure (Amendment No.4) Rules (SI 2003/2113).

(b) to a claim not allocated to a track, but for which the small claims track is the normal track; or

(c) where the road traffic accident which gave rise to the dispute occurred before 6th October 2003.

(5) The definitions in rule 45.7(4) apply to this Section as they apply to Section II.

(6) In this Section—

(a) a reference to "fees" is a reference to fees for work done under a conditional fee agreement or collective conditional fee agreement;

(b) a reference to "trial" is a reference to the final contested hearing or to the contested hearing of any issue ordered to be tried separately;

(c) a reference to a claim concluding at trial is a reference to a claim concluding by settlement after the trial has commenced or by judgment; and

(d) "trial period" means a period of time fixed by the court within which the trial is to take place and where the court fixes more than one such period in relation to a claim, means the most recent period to be fixed.

Percentage increase of solicitors' fees

45.16 45.16—(1) Subject to rule 45.18, the percentage increase which is to be allowed in relation to solicitors' fees is—

(a) 100% where the claim concludes at trial; or

(b) 12.5% where—

(i) the claim concludes before a trial has commenced; or

(ii) the dispute is settled before a claim is issued.

Percentage increase of counsel's fees

45.17 45.17—(1) Subject to rule 45.18, the percentage increase which is to be allowed in relation to counsel's fees is—

(a) 100% where the claim concludes at trial;

(b) if the claim has been allocated to the fast track—

(i) 50% if the claim concludes 14 days or less before the date fixed for the commencement of the trial; or

(ii) 12.5% if the claim concludes more than 14 days before the date fixed for the commencement of the trial or before any such date has been fixed;

(c) if the claim has been allocated to the multi-track—

(i) 75% if the claim concludes 21 days or less before the date fixed for the commencement of the trial; or

(ii) 12.5% if the claim concludes more than 21 days before the date fixed for the commencement of the trial or before any such date has been fixed;

(d) 12.5% where—

(i) the claim has been issued but concludes before it has been allocated to a track; or

(ii) in relation to costs-only proceedings, the dispute is settled before a claim is issued.

(2) Where a trial period has been fixed, if—

(a) the claim concludes before the first day of that period; and

(b) no trial date has been fixed within that period before the claim concludes,

the first day of that period is treated as the date fixed for the commencement of the trial for the purposes of paragraph (1).

(3) Where a trial period has been fixed, if—

(a) the claim concludes before the first day of that period; but

(b) before the claim concludes, a trial date had been fixed within that period,

the trial date is the date fixed for the commencement of the trial for the purposes of paragraph (1).

(4) Where a trial period has been fixed and the claim concludes—

(a) on or after the first day of that period; but

(b) before commencement of the trial,

the percentage increase in paragraph (1)(b)(i) or (1)(c)(i) shall apply as appropriate, whether or not a trial date has been fixed within that period.

(5) For the purposes of this rule, in calculating the periods of time, the day fixed for the commencement of the trial (or the first day of the trial period, where appropriate) is not included.

Application for an alternative percentage increase where the fixed increase is 12.5%

45.18—(1) This rule applies where the percentage increase to be allowed— 45.18

(a) in relation to solicitors' fees under the provisions of rule 45.16; or

(b) in relation to counsel's fees under rule 45.17,

is 12.5%.

(2) A party may apply for a percentage increase greater or less than that amount if—

(a) the parties agree damages of an amount greater than £500,000 or the court awards damages of an amount greater than £500,000; or

(b) the court awards damages of £500,000 or less but would have awarded damages greater than £500,000 if it had not made a finding of contributory negligence; or

(c) the parties agree damages of £500,000 or less and it is reasonable to expect that if the court had made an award of damages, it would have awarded damages greater than £500,000, disregarding any reduction the

court may have made in respect of contributory negligence.

(3) In paragraph (2), a reference to a lump sum of damages includes a reference to periodical payments of equivalent value.

(4) If the court is satisfied that the circumstances set out in paragraph (2) apply it must—

(a) assess the percentage increase; or

(b) make an order for the percentage increase to be assessed.

Assessment of alternative percentage increase

45.19 **45.19—(1) This rule applies where the percentage increase of fees is assessed under rule 45.18(4).**

(2) If the percentage increase is assessed as greater than 20% or less than 7.5%, the percentage increase to be allowed shall be that assessed by the court.

(3) If the percentage increase is assessed as no greater than 20% and no less than 7.5%—

(a) the percentage increase to be allowed shall be 12.5%; and

(b) the costs of the application and assessment shall be paid by the applicant.

Comment

45.19.1 The third section of Pt 45 (fixed costs) lays down the success (percentage increase) which will be allowed to a successful claimant in a road traffic accident case conducted under a CFA with a success fee (as specified in CPR r.43.2(k)(i)). The provisions apply only where the road traffic accident giving rise to the dispute occurred on or after October 6, 2003. The provisions do not apply to a small claim, ie a claim on the small claims track or a claim for which that track is the normal track. If Sect.II of Pt 45 is applicable Sect.III does not apply

Different provisions are made in respect of the fees of solicitors and counsel. In respect of solicitors the percentage increase which is to be allowed is 100 per cent where the claim concludes at trial, or 12.5 per cent where the claim concludes before a trial has commenced or the dispute is settled before a claim is issued (CPR r.45.16). "Trial" is a reference to the final contested hearing or to the contested hearing of any issue ordered to be tried separately. A case which "concludes at trial" includes both a claim which settles after the trial has commenced or one which is decided by judgment (CPR r.45.15(6)).

In respect of counsels' fees the success fee is 100 per cent where the claim concludes at trial; if the claim is on the fast track 50 per cent, if the claim concludes 14 days or less before the date fixed for the commencement of the trial, or 12.5 per cent if it concludes more than 14 days before that date or before any such date has been fixed. On the multi track the success fee which will be allowed is 70 per cent, if the claim concludes 21 days or less before the date fixed for the commencement of the trial, or 12.5 per cent if it concludes more than 21 days before that date or before any such date has been fixed. Where a claim has been issued but concludes before it has been allocated to a track, or, in relation to costs only proceedings, the dispute is settled before a claim is issued, the success fee will be allowed at 12.5 per cent (CPR r.45.17(1)).

In order to cope with the different methods of listing on the fast track, the multi track and at the Royal Courts of Justice the Section lays down provisions for establishing *"the date fixed for the commencement* of the trial" (see CPR r.45.17(2) to (5)).

45.19.2 *Application for an alternative percentage increase*—Where the success fee which will be allowed either in respect of solicitors' fees or counsels' fees is 12.5 per cent, a party may, in certain circumstances, apply for a greater or lesser percentage. This may be done where the parties agree damages at an amount greater than £500,000 or the court makes an award greater than that figure; the court awards £500,000 or less but would have awarded more than £500,000 if it had not made a finding of contributory negligence; or the parties agree damages of £500,000 or less and "it is reasonable to expect" that, but for any finding of contributory negligence, the court would have awarded damages greater than £500,000 (CPR r.45.18(1) and (2)).

If the court is satisfied that the case falls within the relevant criteria it will assess the percentage increase or make an order for it to be assessed (by a Costs Judge or District Judge). If the percentage increase allowed is greater than 20 per cent or less than 7.5 per cent the percentage allowed will be that assessed by the court. If the percentage increase is assessed at no greater than 20 per cent and no less than 7.5 per cent the increase allowed will remain at 12.5 per cent and the costs of the application and assessment will be paid by the applicant (CPR rr.45.18(4) and 45.19).

IV. Fixed Percentage Increase in Employers Liability Claims 45.20

Scope and interpretation

45.20—(1) **Subject to paragraph (2), this Section applies where—**

(a) the dispute is between an employee and his employer arising from a bodily injury sustained by the employee in the course of his employment; and

(b) the claimant has entered into a funding arrangement of a type specified in rule 43.2(1)(k)(i).

(2) This Section does not apply—

(a) where the dispute—

(i) relates to a disease;

(ii) relates to an injury sustained before 1st October 2004; or

(iii) arises from a road traffic accident (as defined in rule 45.7(4)(a)); or

(iv) relates to an injury to which Section V of this Part applies; or

(b) to a claim—

(i) which has been allocated to the small claims track; or

(ii) not allocated to a track, but for which the small claims track is the normal track.

(3) For the purposes of this Section—

(a) "employee" has the meaning given to it by section 2(1) of the Employers' Liability (Compulsory Insurance) Act 1969[1]; and

(b) a reference to "fees" is a reference to fees for work done under a conditional fee agreement or collective conditional fee agreement.

Percentage increase of solicitors' and counsel's fees

45.21 In the cases to which this Section applies, subject to rule 45.22 the percentage increase which is to be allowed in relation to 45.21

[1] 1969 c.57.

solicitors' and counsel's fees is to be determined in accordance with rules 45.16 and 45.17, subject to the modifications that—

(a) the percentage increase which is to be allowed in relation to solicitors' fees under rule 45.16(b) is—

(i) 27.5% if a membership organisation has undertaken to meet the claimant's liabilities for legal costs in accordance with section 30 of the Access to Justice Act 1999; and

(ii) 25% in any other case; and

(b) the percentage increase which is to be allowed in relation to counsel's fees under rule 45.17(1)(b)(ii), (1)(c)(ii) or (1)(d) is 25%.

("membership organisation" is defined in rule 43.2(1)(n)).

Alternative percentage increase

45.22 **45.22—(1) In the cases to which this Section applies, rule 45.18(2)–(4) applies where—**

(a) the percentage increase of solicitors' fees to be allowed in accordance with rule 45.21 is 25% or 27.5%; or

(b) the percentage increase of counsel's fees to be allowed is 25%.

(2) Where the percentage increase of fees is assessed by the court under rule 45.18(4) as applied by paragraph (1) above—

(a) if the percentage increase is assessed as greater than 40% or less than 15%, the percentage increase to be allowed shall be that assessed by the court; and

(b) if the percentage increase is assessed as no greater than 40% and no less than 15%—

(i) the percentage increase to be allowed shall be 25% or 27.5%(as the case may be); and

(ii) the costs of the application and assessment shall be paid by the applicant.

V. Fixed Recoverable Success Fees in Employer's Liability Disease Claims

Scope and Interpretation

45.23 **45.23—(1) Subject to paragraph (2), this Section applies where—**

(a) the dispute is between an employee (or, if the employee is deceased, the employee's estate or dependants) and his employer (or a person alleged to be liable for the employer's alleged breach of statutory or common law duties of care); and

(b) the dispute relates to a disease with which the employee is diagnosed that is alleged to have been contracted as a consequence of the employer's alleged breach of *statutory or common* law duties of care in the course of the employee's employment; and

(c) the claimant has entered into a funding arrangement of a type specified in rule 43.2(1)(k)(i).

(2) This Section does not apply where—

(a) the claimant sent a letter of claim to the defendant containing a summary of the facts on which the claim is based and main allegations of fault before 1st October 2005; or

(b) rule 45.20(2)(b) applies.

(3) For the purposes of this Section—

(a) rule 45.15(6) applies;

(b) "employee" has the meaning given to it by section 2(1) of the Employers'Liability (Compulsory Insurance) Act 1969;

(c) "Type A claim" means a claim relating to a disease or physical injury alleged to have been caused by exposure to asbestos;

(d) "Type B claim" means a claim relating to—

(i) a psychiatric injury alleged to have been caused by work-related psychological stress;

(ii) a work-related upper limb disorder which is alleged to have been caused by physical stress or strain, excluding hand/arm vibration injuries; and

(e) "Type C claim" means a claim relating to a disease not falling within either type A or type B.

(The Table annexed to the Practice Direction supplementing Part 45 contains a non-exclusive list of diseases within Type A and Type B).

Percentage increase of Solicitors' Fees

45.24—(1) In the cases to which this Section applies, subject to rule 45.26, the percentage increase which is to be allowed in relation to solicitors' fees is— 45.24

(a) 100% if the claim concludes at trial; or

(b) where—

(i) the claim concludes before a trial has commenced; or

(ii) the dispute is settled before a claim is issued,

to be determined by rule 45.24(2).

(2) Where rule 45.24(1)(b) applies, the percentage increase which is to be allowed in relation to solicitors' fees is—

(a) in type A claims—

(i) 30% if a membership organisation has undertaken to meet the claimant's liabilities for legal costs in accordance with section 30 of the Access to Justice Act 1999; and

(ii) 27.5% in any other case;

(b) in type B claims, 100%; and

(c) in type C claims—

(i) 70% if a membership organisation has undertaken to meet the claimant's liabilities for legal

costs in accordance with section 30 of the Access to Justice Act 1999; and

(ii) 62.5% in any other case.

("Membership organisation" is defined in rule 43.2(1)(n)).

Percentage increase of counsel's fees

45.25 **45.25—(1) In the cases to which this Section applies, subject to rule 45.26, the percentage increase which is to be allowed in relation to counsel's fees is—**

(a) 100% if the claim concludes at trial; or

(b) where—

(i) the claim concludes before a trial has commenced; or

(ii) the dispute is settled before a claim is issued,

to be determined by rule 45.25(2).

(2) Where rule 45.25(1)(b) applies, the percentage increase which is to be allowed in relation to counsel's fees is—

(a) if the claim has been allocated to the fast track, the amount shown in Table 6; and

(b) if the claim has been allocated to the multi-track, the amount shown in Table 7.

(3) Where a trial period has been fixed, rules 45.17(2) to 45.17(5) apply for the purposes of determining the date fixed for the commencement of the trial.

TABLE 6

CLAIMS ALLOCATED TO THE FAST TRACK

	If the claim concludes 14 days or less before the date fixed for commencement of the trial	If the claim concludes more than 14 days before the date fixed for commencement of the trial or before any such date has been fixed
Type A claim	50%	27.5%
Type B claim	100%	100%
Type C claim	62.5%	62.5%

TABLE 7
CLAIMS ALLOCATED TO THE MULTI-TRACK

	If the claim concludes 21 days or less before the date fixed for commencement of the trial	If the claim concludes more than 21 days before the date fixed for commencement of the trial or before any such date has been fixed
Type A claim	75%	27.5%
Type B claim	100%	100%
Type C claim	75%	62.5%

Alternative percentage increase

45.26—(1) In cases to which this Section applies and subject to paragraph (2) below, rules 45.18(2) to (4) apply where the percentage increase is the amount allowed under rules 45.24 and 45.25. **45.26**

(2) For the purposes of this section, the sum of £250,000 shall be substituted for the sum of £500,000 in rules 45.18(2)(a) to (c).

(3) Where the percentage increase of fees is assessed by the court under rule 45.18(4), as applied by paragraph 1 above, the percentage increase to be allowed shall be the amount shown in Table 8.

(4) The percentage increase cannot be varied where the case concludes at trial.

TABLE 8

Type of claim	Amount Allowed	
A	If the percentage increase is assessed as greater than 40% or less than 15%, the percentage increase that is assessed by the court.	If the percentage increase is assessed as no greater than 40% and no less than 15%— (i) 27.5%; and (ii) the costs of the application and assessment shall be paid by the applicant.

Type of claim	Amount Allowed	
B	If the percentage increase is assessed as less than 75%, the percentage increase that is assessed by the court.	If the percentage increase is assessed as no less than 75%— (i) 100%; and (ii) the costs of the application and assessment shall be paid by the applicant.
C	If the percentage increase is assessed as greater than 75% or less than 50%, the percentage increase that is assessed by the court.	If the percentage increase is assessed as no greater than 75% and no less than 50%— (i) 62.5%; and (ii) the costs of the application and assessment shall be paid by the applicant.

PRACTICE DIRECTION RELATING TO PART 45

Fixed Costs

Section 24 Fixed Costs in Small Claims

24.1 Under Rule 27.14 the costs which can be awarded to a claimant in a small claims track case include the fixed costs payable under Part 45 attributable to issuing the claim. **45PD.1**

24.2 Those fixed costs shall be the sum of

(a) the fixed commencement costs calculated in accordance with Table 1 of Rule 45.2 and;

(b) the appropriate court fee or fees paid by the claimant.

Section 24A Claims to Which Part 45 Does Not Apply

24A In a claim to which Part 45 does not apply, no amount shall be entered on the claim form for the charges of the claimant's solicitor, but the words "to be assessed" shall be inserted. **45PD.2**

Section 25 Fixed Costs on the Issue of a Default Costs Certificate

25.1 Unless paragraph 24.2 applies or unless the court orders otherwise, the fixed costs to be included in a default costs certificate are £80 plus a sum equal to any appropriate court fee payable on the issue of the certificate. **45PD.3**

25.2 The fixed costs included in a certificate must not exceed the maximum sum specified for costs and court fee in the notice of commencement.

Section 25A — Road Traffic Accidents: Fixed Recoverable Costs in Costs-Only Proceedings

Scope

25A.1 Section II of Part 45 ('the Section') provides for certain fixed costs to be recoverable between parties in respect of costs incurred in disputes which are settled prior to proceedings being issued. The Section applies to road traffic accident disputes as defined in rule 45.7(4)(a), where the accident which gave rise to the dispute occurred on or after 6th October 2003. **45PD.4**

25A.2 The Section does not apply to diputes where the total agreed value of the damages is within the small claims limit or exceeds £10,000. Rule 26.8(2) sets out how the financial value of a claim is assessed for the purposes of allocation to track.

25A.3 Fixed recoverable costs are to be calculated by reference to the amount of agreed damages which are payable to the receiving party. In calculating the amount of these damages—

(a) account must be taken of both general and special damages and interest;

(b) any interim payments made must be included;

(c) where the parties have agreed an element of contributory negligence, the amount of damages attributed to that negligence must be deducted;

(d) any amount required by statute to be paid by the compensating party directly to a third party (such as sums paid by way of compensation recovery payments and National Health Service expenses) must not be included.

25A.4 The Section applies to cases which fall within the scope of the Uninsured Drivers Agreement dated 13 August 1999. The section does not apply to cases which fall within the scope of the Untraced Drivers Agreement dated 14 February 2003.

Fixed recoverable costs formula

45PD.5 **25A.5** The amount of fixed costs recoverable is calculated by totalling the following—

(a) the sum of £800;

(b) 20% of the agreed damages up to £5,000; and

(c) 15% of the agreed damages between £5,000 and £10,000.

For example, agreed damages of £7,523 would result in recoverable costs of £2,178.45 i.e.£800 + (20% of £5,000) + (15% of £2,523).

Additional costs for work in specified areas

45PD.6 **25A.6** The area referred to in rule 45.9(2) consists of (within London) the county court districts of Barnet, Bow, Brentford, Central London, Clerkenwell, Edmonton, Ilford, Lambeth, Mayors and City of London, Romford, Shoreditch, Wandsworth, West London, Willesden and Woolwich and (outside London) the county court districts of Bromley, Croydon, Dartford, Gravesend and Uxbridge.

Multiple claimants

45PD.7 **25A.7** Where there is more than one potential claimant in relation to a dispute and two or more claimants instruct the same solicitor or firm of solicitors, the provisions of the section apply in respect of each claimant.

Information to be included in the claim form

45PD.8 **25A.8** Costs only proceedings are commenced using the procedure set out in rule 44.12A. A claim form should be issued in accordance with Part 8. Where the claimant is claiming an amount of costs which exceed the amount of the fixed recoverable costs he must include on the claim form details of the exceptional circumstances which he considers justifies the additional costs.

25A.9 The claimant must also include on the claim form details of any disbursements or success fee he wishes to claim. The disbursements that may be claimed are set out in rule 45.10(1). If the disbursement falls within 45.10(2)(d) (disbursements that have arisen due to a particular feature of the dispute) the claimant must give details of the particular feature of the dispute and why he considers the disbursement to be necessary.

Disbursements and success fee

45PD.9 **25A.10** If the parties agree the amount of the fixed recoverable costs and the only dispute is as to the payment of, or amount of, a disbursement or as to the amount of a success fee, then proceedings should be issued under rule 44.12A in the normal way and not by reference to Section II of Part 45.

Section 25B—Fixed Recoverable Success Fees in Employer's Liability Disease Claims

45PD.10 **25B.1** The following table is a non-exclusive list of the conditions that will fall within Type A and Type B claims for the purposes of Rule 45.23.

Claim type	Description
A	Asbestosis
	Mesothelioma
	Bilateral Pleural Thickening
	Pleural Plaques
B	Repetitive Strain Injury/WRULD
	Carpal Tunnel Syndrome caused by Repetitive Strain Injury
	Occupational Stress

PART 46

Fast Track Trial Costs

Contents

46.0.1

Scope of this Part[1]

46.1 **46.1—(1) This Part deals with the amount of costs which the court may award as the costs of an advocate for preparing for and appearing at the trial of a claim in the fast track (referred to in this rule as "fast track trial costs").**

(2) For the purposes of this Part—

(a) "advocate" means a person exercising a right of audience as a representative of, or on behalf of, a party;

(b) "fast track trial costs" means the costs of a party's advocate for preparing for and appearing at the trial, but does not include—

(i) any other disbursements; or

(ii) any value added tax payable on the fees of a party's advocate; and

(c) "trial" includes a hearing where the court decides an amount of money or the value of goods following a judgment under Part 12 (default judgment) or Part 14 (admissions) but does not include—

(i) the hearing of an application for summary judgment under Part 24; or

(ii) the court's approval of a settlement or other compromise under rule 21.10.

(Part 21 deals with claims made by or on behalf of, or against, children and protected parties.)

Comment

46.1.1 Fast track trial costs are the costs of a party's advocate for preparing for and appearing at the trial. Trial is defined at r.46.1(2)(c) but does not include the hearing of an application for summary judgment under Pt 24, or approval of a settlement or compromise under r.21.10 (children and protected parties), see ss.26 and 27 of the Costs Practice Direction.

Amount of fast track trial costs[2]

46.2 **46.2—(1) The following table shows the amount of fast track trial**

[1] Amended by the Civil Procedure (Amendment) Rules 2007 (SI 2007/2204).
[2] Amended by the Civil Procedure (Amendment) Rules 2007 (SI 2007/2204).

costs which the court may award (whether by summary or detailed assessment).

Value of the claim	Amount of fast track trial costs which thecourt may award
No more than £3,000	£485
More than £3,000 but not more than £10,000	£690
More than £10,000 but not more than £15,000	£1,035
For proceedings issued on or after 6th April, 2009, more than £15,000	£1,650

(2) The court may not award more or less than the amount shown in the table except where—

(a) it decides not to award any fast track trial costs; or

(b) rule 46.3 applies;

but the court may apportion the amount awarded between the parties to reflect their respective degrees of success on the issues at trial.

(3) Where the only claim is for the payment of money—

(a) for the purpose of quantifying fast track trial costs awarded to a claimant, the value of the claim is the total amount of the judgment excluding—

(i) interest and costs; and

(ii) any reduction made for contributory negligence;

(b) for the purpose of quantifying fast track trial costs awarded to a defendant, the value of the claim is—

(i) the amount specified in the claim form (excluding interest and costs);

(ii) if no amount is specified, the maximum amount which the claimant reasonably expected to recover according to the statement of value included in the claim form under rule 16.3; or

(iii) more than £15,000, if the claim form states that the claimant cannot reasonably say how much is likely to be recovered.

(4) Where the claim is only for a remedy other than the payment of money the value of the claim is deemed to be more than £3,000 but not more than £10,000, unless the court orders otherwise.

(5) Where the claim includes both a claim for the payment of money and for a remedy other than the payment of money, the value of the claim is deemed to be the higher of—

(a) the value of the money claim decided in accordance with paragraph (3); or

(b) the deemed value of the other remedy decided in accordance with paragraph (4),

unless the court orders otherwise.

(6) Where—

(a) a defendant has made a counterclaim against the claimant;

(b) the counterclaim has a higher value than the claim; and

(c) the claimant succeeds at trial both on the claim and the counterclaim,

for the purpose of quantifying fast track trial costs awarded to the claimant, the value of the claim is the value of the defendant's counterclaim calculated in accordance with this rule.

Comment

46.2.1 This rule was amended by the Civil Procedure (Amendment No.3) Rules 2008 (SI 2008/3327) r.10 as a consequence of the amendment to r.26.6 increasing the financial limit of the fast track procedure from £15,000 to £25,000 for claims issued on or after April 6, 2009. For claims issued after that date which are worth more that £15,000 the amount of fast track cists which the court may award is £1,650.

The amount of fast track trial costs may not be exceeded or reduced except where the court decides not to award any fast track trial costs or the provisions of r.46.3 apply. These include where the court considers it necessary for a legal representative to attend to assist the advocate, when a further £250 may be awarded in accordance with r.46.3. In addition the court may apportion the amount between the parties to reflect their respective degrees of success on the issues at the trial but even where this is done, the total amount of fast track trial costs may not be exceeded.

Power to award more or less than the amount of fast track trial costs[1]

46.3 **46.3—(1) This rule sets out when a court may award—**

(a) an additional amount to the amount of fast track trial costs shown in the table in rule 46.2(1); and

(b) less than those amounts.

(2) If—

(a) in addition to the advocate, a party's legal representative attends the trial;

(b) the court considers that it was necessary for a legal representative to attend to assist the advocate; and

(c) the court awards fast track trial costs to that party,

the court may award an additional £345 in respect of the legal representative's attendance at the trial.

(Legal representative is defined in rule 2.3.)

(2A) The court may in addition award a sum representing an additional liability. (The requirements to provide information about a funding arrangement where a party wishes to recover any additional liability under a funding arrangement are set out in the costs practice direction)

("Additional liability" is defined in rule 43.2).

(3) If the court considers that it is necessary to direct a separate trial of an issue then the court may award an additional amount in

[1] Amended by the Civil Procedure (Amendment No.3) Rules 2000 (SI 2000/1317) and the Civil Procedure (Amendment) Rules 2007 (SI 2007/2204).

respect of the separate trial but that amount is limited in accordance with paragraph (4) of this rule.

(4) The additional amount the court may award under paragraph 3 must not exceed two-thirds of the amount payable for that claim, subject to a minimum award of £485.

(5) Where the party to whom fast track trial costs are to be awarded is a litigant in person, the court will award—

(a) if the litigant in person can prove financial loss, two thirds of the amount that would otherwise be awarded; or

(b) if the litigant in person fails to prove financial loss, an amount in respect of the time spent reasonably doing the work at the rate specified in the costs practice direction.

(6) Where a defendant has made a counterclaim against the claimant, and—

(a) the claimant has succeeded on his claim; and

(b) the defendant has succeeded on his counterclaim,

the court will quantify the amount of the award of fast track trial costs to which—

(i) but for the counterclaim, the claimant would be entitled for succeeding on his claim; and

(ii) but for the claim, the defendant would be entitled for succeeding on his counterclaim,

and make one award of the difference, if any, to the party entitled to the higher award of costs.

(7) Where the court considers that the party to whom fast track trial costs are to be awarded has behaved unreasonably or improperly during the trial, it may award that party an amount less than would otherwise be payable for that claim, as it considers appropriate.

(8) Where the court considers that the party who is to pay the fast track trial costs has behaved improperly during the trial the court may award such additional amount to the other party as it considers appropriate.

Comment

If the court is considering the award of an additional amount in respect of a party's legal representative, it should be noted that the test is one of necessity rather than reasonableness. **46.3.1**

Where a separate trial is directed an additional amount may be allowed but will not exceed two thirds of the amount payable in respect of the claim but will not be less than £350.

Travelling time does not fall within the exceptions to r.46.2(2) and is not separately recoverable.

Rule 46.3(5)—Litigant in Person

Where the litigant in person proves financial loss, two thirds of the amount which would otherwise be awarded is payable irrespective of the amount of time involved. If financial loss is not proved the court must decide an amount in respect of the time reasonably spent doing the work at the rate specified at s.52 of the Costs Practice Direction. Although the rule is not specific it would seem that a litigant in person who fails to prove financial loss cannot recover more than two thirds of the amount which would otherwise be awarded. **46.3.2**

Rule 46.3(7) and (8)—Misconduct

46.3.3 The court has powers in addition to those at r.44.14 (powers in relation to misconduct) and may allow less than it would otherwise have done, where the party has behaved unreasonably or improperly during the trial, or may award an additional amount where it considers that the party who is to pay fast track trial costs has behaved improperly during the trial. Note that the powers under these sub-rules are in respect of the party only and not in respect of the legal representative.

Fast track trial costs where there is more than one claimant or defendant

46.4 **46.4—(1) Where the same advocate is acting for more than one party—**

(a) the court may make only one award in respect of fast track trial costs payable to that advocate; and

(b) the parties for whom the advocate is acting are jointly entitled to any fast track trial costs awarded by the court.

(2) Where—

(a) the same advocate is acting for more than one claimant; and

(b) each claimant has a separate claim against the defendant,

the value of the claim, for the purpose of quantifying the award in respect of fast track trial costs is to be ascertained in accordance with paragraph (3).

(3) The value of the claim in the circumstances mentioned in paragraph (2) is—

(a) where the only claim of each claimant is for the payment of money—

(i) if the award of fast track trial costs is in favour of the claimants, the total amount of the judgment made in favour of all the claimants jointly represented; or

(ii) if the award is in favour of the defendant, the total amount claimed by the claimants;

and in either case, quantified in accordance with rule 46.2(3);

(b) where the only claim of each claimant is for a remedy other than the payment of money, deemed to be more than £3,000 but not more than £10,000; and

(c) where claims of the claimants include both a claim for the payment of money and for a remedy other than the payment of money, deemed to be—

(i) more than £3,000 but not more than £10,000; or

(ii) if greater, the value of the money claims calculated in accordance with sub-paragraph (a) above.

(4) Where—

(a) there is more than one defendant; and

(b) any or all of the defendants are separately represented,

the court may award fast track trial costs to each party who is separately represented.

(5) Where—

(a) there is more than one claimant; and

(b) a single defendant,

the court may make only one award to the defendant of fast track trial costs, for which the claimants are jointly and severally liable[GL].

(6) For the purpose of quantifying the fast track trial costs awarded to the single defendant under paragraph (5), the value of the claim is to be calculated in accordance with paragraph (3) of this rule.

Comment

Where the same advocate acts for more than one party there will be only one award in respect of fast track trial costs. Normally one advocate will represent all claimants but where defendants are represented separately the court may award fast track trial costs to each party who is separately represented. Rule 46.4(3) sets out how the value of the claim is to be calculated where the same advocate is acting for more than one claimant and each claimant has a separate claim against the defendant. The same method of calculation is also used for quantifying the fast track trial costs awarded to a single defendant against more than one claimant. **46.4.1**

PRACTICE DIRECTION RELATING TO PART 46

Fast Track Trial Costs

Section 26 Scope of Part 46: Rule 46.1

46PD.1 **26.1** Part 46 applies to the costs of an advocate for preparing for and appearing at the trial of a claim in the fast track.

26.2 It applies only where, at the date of the trial, the claim is allocated to the fast track. It does not apply in any other case, irrespective of the final value of the claim.

26.3 In particular it does not apply to:

(a) the hearing of a claim which is allocated to the small claims track with the consent of the parties given under rule 26.7(3); or

(b) a disposal hearing at which the amount to be paid under a judgment or order is decided by the court (see paragraph 12.8 of the Practice Direction which supplements Part 26 (Case Management—Preliminary Stage)).

Cases which settle before trial

26.4 Attention is drawn to rule 44.10 (limitation on amount court may award where a claim allocated to the fast track settles before trial).

Section 27 Power to Award More or Less than the Amount of Fast Track Trial Costs: Rule 46.3

46PD.2 **27.1** Rule 44.15 (providing information about funding arrangements) sets out the requirement to provide information about funding arrangements to the court and other parties. Section 19 of this Practice Direction sets out the information to be provided and when this is to be done.

27.2 Section 11, of this Practice Direction explains how the court will approach the question of what sum to allow in respect of additional liability.

27.3 The court has the power, when considering whether a percentage increase is reasonable, to allow different percentages for different items of costs or for different periods during which costs were incurred.

PART 47

Procedure for Detailed Assessment of Costs and Default Provisions

Contents 47.0.1

I. General Rules About Detailed Assessment

II. Costs Payable by One Party to Another—Commencement of Detailed Assessment Proceedings

III. Costs Payable by One Party to Another—Default Provisions

IV. Costs Payable by One Party to Another—Procedure Where Points of Dispute are Served

V. Interim Costs Certificate and Final Costs Certificate

VI. Detailed Assessment Procedure for costs of a LSC funded client or an assisted person where costs are payable out of the community legal service fund

Editorial introduction

47.0.2 Proceedings for detailed assessment are commenced by serving the bill and supporting documents on other interested parties. The court does not come into contact with the detailed assessment proceedings until either the receiving party seeks a default costs certificate, where the paying party has failed to serve points of dispute, or the receiving party requests a detailed assessment hearing.

Appeals are under Pt 52 to a judge of the next tier. Permission is required. Appeals from authorised court officers are to the costs judge or district judge under Pt 47, VIII. No Permission is required.

The court has power to order a party to make a payment on account before assessment takes place in accordance with r.44.3(8).

The court may also issue an interim certificate in accordance with r.47.15 at any time after the receiving party has filed a request for a detailed assessment hearing, for such sum as it considers appropriate. There is no requirement that the amount of the interim certificate should relate to an amount agreed between the parties or decided by detailed assessment.

All certificates (default, interim and final) include an order to pay the costs within 14 days (see r.44.8) and are therefore enforceable unless the court orders otherwise.

Costs officers have all the powers of the court except that authorised court officers are not permitted to exercise penal powers (see r.47.3(1)), see also r.2.4.

(The definitions contained in Pt 43 are relevant to this Part.)

I. General Rules about Detailed Assessment

Time when detailed assessment may be carried out

47.1 **47.1 The general rule is that the costs of any proceedings or any part of the proceedings are not to be assessed by the detailed pro-**

cedure until the conclusion of the proceedings but the court may order them to be assessed immediately.

(The costs practice direction gives further guidance about when proceedings are concluded for the purpose of this rule.)

Comment

See s.28 of the Costs Practice Direction in relation to deciding when proceedings are concluded. The Court of Appeal has held that, although the CPRprovides for payment of costs as the case goes along, for policy reasons, the normal approach is as set out in the rule. In respect of an appeal which was a discrete issue as to jurisdiction, the court ordered assessment of costs forthwith with no order for immediate payment. The question of payment to be deferred to await the outcome of an application for security for costs: *Saab v Saudi American Bank* [1999] 1 W.L.R. 1861. On another occasion the Court of Appeal stated: "It is certainly the practice ... in this court that, where the appeal is a discrete matter; the costs are ordered there and then and do not wait for the conclusion of the proceedings as a whole. That practice precedes the new rules." The court went on to dismiss the appeal with costs to be assessed and paid forthwith, i.e. within a period after the completion of the detailed assessment: *Morris v Bank of America National Trust (Appeal against Striking Out)* [2000] 1 All E.R. 954. **47.1.1**

As to set off, see note at 44.3.14.

A claimant whose claim for professional negligence against his solicitors had been struck out as an abuse of process was refused an order for immediate detailed assessment and payment of his costs on the ground that it would be unfair to the solicitors to order immediate assessment and payment of costs since the claimant was legally aided and there was a potential set off should the claimant be unsuccessful at trial. The normal course of ordering assessment in due course under r.47.1 was followed: *Hicks v Russell Jones & Walker* [2001] CP Rep. 25, CA; *Lockley v National Blood Transfusion Service* [1992] 1 W.L.R. 492, CA.

No stay of detailed assessment where there is an appeal

47.2 Detailed assessment is not stayed pending an appeal unless the court so orders. **47.2**

Comment

See s.29 of the Costs Practice Direction as to application to stay. **47.2.1**

Powers of an authorised court officer[1]

47.3—(1) An authorised court officer has all the powers of the court when making a detailed assessment, except— **47.3**

(a) power to make a wasted costs order as defined in rule 48.7;

(b) power to make an order under—

(i) rule 44.14 (powers in relation to misconduct)

(ii) rule 47.8 (sanction for delay in commencing detailed assessment proceedings);

(iii) paragraph (2) (objection to detailed assessment by authorised court officer); and

(c) power to make a detailed assessment of costs payable to a solicitor by his client, unless the costs are being assessed under rule 48.5 (costs where money is payable to a child or protected party).

(2) Where a party objects to the detailed assessment of costs be-

1 Amended by the Civil Procedure (Amendment) Rules 2007 (SI 2007/2204).

ing made by an authorised court officer, the court may order it to be made by a costs judge or a district judge.

(The costs practice direction sets out the relevant procedure.)

Comment

47.3.1 An authorised court officer has all the powers of the court except for the penal powers listed in the rule. Rule 2.4 confirms the position.

If a party wishes the detailed assessment to be conducted by somebody other than an authorised court officer an application must be made in accordance with Pt 23 (see s.30 of the Costs Practice Direction).

In the Supreme Court Costs Office authorised court officers are permitted to conduct detailed assessments up to £75,000 in the case of principal officers, and up to £30,000 in the case of SEO officers.

At the time of writing there are no authorised court officers outside the SCCO.

Venue for detailed assessment proceedings

47.4 **47.4—(1) All applications and requests in detailed assessment proceedings must be made to or filed at the appropriate office.**

(The costs practice direction sets out the meaning of "appropriate office" in any particular case.)

(2) The court may direct that the appropriate office is to be the Supreme Court Costs Office.

(3) A county court may direct that another county court is to be the appropriate office.

(4) A direction under paragraph (3) may be made without proceedings being transferred to that court.

(Rule 30.2 makes provision for any county court to transfer the proceedings to another county court for detailed assessment of costs).

Comment

47.4.1 See s.31 of the Costs Practice Direction as to the appropriate office in any particular case.

The court (including a County Court) may direct that the appropriate office is to be the Supreme Court Costs Office, in addition one County Court may direct another to be the appropriate office.

II. Costs Payable By One Party to Another—Commencement of Detailed Assessment Proceedings

Application of this Section[1]

47.5 **47.5 This Section of Part 47 applies where a cost officer is to make a detailed assessment of—**

(a) costs which are payable by one party to another; or

(b) the sum which is payable by one party to the prescribed charity pursuant to an order under section 194(3) of the Legal Services Act 2007.

Comment

47.5.1 For the practice where costs are payable by one party to another and also out of the legal aid fund at prescribed rates see ss.43 and 49 of the Costs Practice Direction.

[1] Amended by Civil Procedure (Amendment) Rules 2008 (SI 2008/2178).

Commencement of detailed assessment proceedings

47.6—(1) Detailed assessment proceedings are commenced by the receiving party serving on the paying party— 47.6

(a) notice of commencement in the relevant practice form; and

(b) a copy of the bill of costs.

(Rule 47.7 sets out the period for commencing detailed assessment proceedings.)

(2) The receiving party must also serve a copy of the notice of commencement and the bill on any other relevant persons, specified in the costs practice direction.

(3) A person on whom a copy of the notice of commencement is served under paragraph (2) is a party to the detailed assessment proceedings (in addition to the paying party and the receiving party).

(The costs practice direction deals with—

- **other documents which the party must file when he requests detailed assessment;**
- **the court's powers where it considers that a hearing may be necessary;**
- **the form of a bill; and**
- **the length of notice which will be given if a hearing date is fixed.)**

Comment

47.6.1 The procedure for commencing detailed assessment does not at that stage involve the court. The receiving party must serve on the paying party, and any other relevant persons, notice of commencement (see Form **N252**) and a copy of the bill of costs.

See ss.32 to 40 of the Costs Practice Direction as to the procedure, and s.4 relating to Pt 43 (paras 43BPD.1 *et seq.*) as to the form and contents of the bill of costs.

Where the successful party had had two firms of solicitors and agreed the amount of costs recoverable in respect of the second solicitors, it was not possible to claim a separate assessment in respect of the costs of the first solicitors The court (Christopher Clarke J.) stated:

> "33. The rules clearly provide that detailed assessment proceedings are commenced by the receiving party serving both a notice of commencement and the (not a) bill of costs. The bill is the receiving party's statement of what he claims is due to him pursuant to whatever order entitles him to costs. If the receiving party is entitled to recover his costs of instructing more than one solicitor the Practice Direction requires him to include the costs of each solicitor separately in the bill. If he fails to include the costs of his previous solicitor, and the Costs Judge completes his assessment of the costs without regard to the previous solicitor's costs and proceeds to a final certificate, the receiving party cannot *claim a further assessment*. The detailed assessment proceedings have been completed and an amount ordered to be paid. The receiving party cannot start again ..." (*Harris v Moat Housing Group-South Ltd* [2007] EWHC 3092 (QB); [2008] 1 W.L.R. 1578, Christopher Clarke J.).

Tomlin Orders

47.6.2 Many claims are settled on terms which are confidential, those terms being contained in a schedule to the Tomlin Order. Unless the order itself contains a provision for costs to be paid and assessed if not agreed, the right to detailed assessment does not arise.

Period for commencing detailed assessment proceedings[1]

47.7 **47.7 The following table shows the period for commencing detailed assessment proceedings.**

Source of right to detailed assessment	**Time by which detailed assessment proceedings must be commenced**
Judgment, direction, order, award or other determination	**3 months after the date of the judgment, etc. Where detailed assessment is stayed pending an appeal, 3 months after the date of the order lifting the stay**
Discontinuance under Part 38	**3 months after the date of service of notice of discontinuance under rule 38.3; or 3 months after the date of the dismissal of application to set the notice of discontinuance aside under rule 38.4**
Acceptance of an offer to settle under Part 36	**3 months after the date when the right to costs arose**

Comment

47.7.1 The table sets out the time by which detailed assessment proceedings must be commenced. The time is essentially three months after the event giving rise to the right to detailed assessment. See s.33 of the Costs Practice Direction.

Sanction for failure to commence in time[2]

47.8 **47.8—(1) Where the receiving party fails to commence detailed assessment proceedings within the period specified—**

(a) in rule 47.7; or

(b) by the direction of the court,

the paying party may apply for an order requiring the receiving party to commence detailed assessment proceedings within such time as the court may specify.

(2) On an application under paragraph (1), the court may direct that, unless the receiving party commences detailed assessment proceedings within the time specified by the court, all or part of the costs to which the receiving party would otherwise be entitled will be disallowed.

(3) If—

(a) the paying party has not made an application in accordance with paragraph (1); and

(b) the receiving party commences the proceedings later than the period specified in 47.7,

the court may disallow all or part of the interest otherwise payable to the receiving party under—

[1] Amended by the Civil Procedure (Amendment No.3) Rules 2006 (SI 2006/3435).
[2] Amended by Civil Procedure (Amendment No.3) Rules 2000 (SI 2000/1317).

(a) section 17 of the Judgments Act 1838; or

(b) section 74 of the County Courts Act 1984;

but must not impose any other sanction except in accordance with rule 44.14 (powers in relation to misconduct).

(4) Where the costs to be assessed in a detailed assessment are payable out of the Community Legal Service Fund, this rule applies as if the receiving party were the solicitor to whom the costs are payable and the paying party were the Legal Services Commission.

Comment

It is not necessary to obtain permission to commence detailed assessment proceedings out of time, but r.47.8 provides a sanction for delay. If the time for commencing detailed assessment proceedings has expired, the paying party may apply for an order under r.47.8(1) and if the receiving party does not comply with this, all or part of the costs may be disallowed. See s.34 of the Costs Practice Direction as to such applications. If the receiving party commences proceedings for detailed assessment out of time but before the paying party has made an application, the only sanction which the court may impose is to disallow all or part of the interest which would otherwise be payable. Section 17(1) of the Judgments Act 1838, as amended, provides that interest will run from the time prescribed by rules of court (see r.44.12(2)). The court may exercise its powers in relation to misconduct under r.44.14 if the circumstances warrant it. See Note Re delay at 44.14.1 (*Botham v Khan (Costs)* [2004] EWHC 2602, (QB), Richards J.). **47.8.1**

Delay (3 years) does not amount to a violation of the paying party's rights under art.6 ECHR since r.47.8 provides a mechanism for the paying party to bring the matter to the attention of the court in order to obtain a hearing within a reasonable time. If the paying party fails to take advantage of that mechanism, it cannot be said that he has been deprived of his rights under art.6. The court, by proceeding to the hearing, does not sanction continuance of a breach of art.6 but is taking remedial action to correct the consequences of the breach. If the court were to refuse to hear the detailed assessment, on the basis of a prior breach of art.6, the result would be to deprive the receiving party entirely of the benefit of the costs order made in its favour which would breach that party's own rights under art.6. On the facts there was nothing which would justify categorising the receiving party's conduct as unreasonable or improper to justify imposing a sanction under CPR, r.44.14(4): *Less v Benedict* [2005] EWHC 1643.

Rule 47.8(2)

The High Court has held in family proceedings that disallowing a substantial bill of costs in full was too drastic a penalty for delay on the part of the claimant, when the cause of their delay was neglect rather than intention, and the defendants had failed to co-operate when they could easily have done so. The defendants had applied two years later for an order that unless the claimant commenced detailed assessment proceedings within seven days the costs over and above the amount already paid should be disallowed in full. The order depriving the claimant of its costs failed sufficiently to balance the effect of the order on each party. Whilst there was some disadvantage to the defendant in assessing a bill three years after the event, the claimant was owed money subject to assessment. The court substituted an order that the claimant should recover 80 per cent of costs as assessed stating that this met sufficiently the seriousness of the delay, its failure to comply with a court order and the delay before it sought an extension of time: *Q v J*, March 2, 2003, unrep., Sumner J. **47.8.2**

In a dispute between members of a family in connection with the winding up of a family business, one member of the family refused to accept the receiver's report and final accounts. Other members did accept them. A payment into court to the credit of the action was made in 1982 and no payment out was ever made. The dispute itself was resolved in 1984 and the court ordered that the balance of the monies remaining after payment of the costs should be distributed in specified proportions. The costs had still not been determined by 2004. The sum in court had grown to approximately £400,000. On appeal it was held that the order which had been made against the second claimant had been made on the basis of material that he had never had an opportunity to meet, and in circumstances where the inference drawn from the material before the judge had not been an appropriate inference to draw. The judge's approach was flawed and the appropriate order was for the funds to be distributed on the basis that no party would bring in bills, either to be taxed or assessed before the apportionment. The time limits for the lodging of the bills of costs should not be extended. To impose an assessment of bills 40 years old upon a Costs Judge would be to impose a most extreme task, in circumstances where neither party had seen fit to take the necessary steps to protect themselves in accordance with the rules. *Weston v Weston* [2006] EWCA Civ 1554; All E.R. (D) 269 (Oct).

Rule 47.8(3)

47.8.2.1 There is no conflict or inconsistency between r.47.8 and r.44.14. The former relates to the disallowance of interest and the latter to the disallowance of costs. Where a party or his legal representative has been guilty of unreasonable or improper conduct in a case where there had been a delay of five years the court held there was no express reference to any causative connection being required in r.44.14(2)(a) nor was there a necessity to imply such a requirement. Rule 47.8(3) made it clear that the court may disallow interest but may not impose any other sanction, except in accordance with r.44.14. It could not be said that where the court disallowed interest it would only be in exceptional circumstances that it could disallow costs under r.44.14. Neither rule refers to "exceptional circumstances": *Haji-Ioannou v Frangos* [2006] EWHC 279, Ch, Lindsay J. On appeal it was held that there was a certain tension between r.44.14 and r.47.8, although failure to commence detailed assessment proceedings within three months was a failure to comply with a rule, not every failure to commence detailed assessment proceedings should be regarded as misconduct. "Misconduct" was the key to resolving the tension. A bad breach of a rule would enable a Costs Judge to exercise the power to disallow some or all of the costs which he was assessing. An inordinate and inexcusable delay which had prejudiced the paying party could come into that category. Excusable though inordinate delay might not, especially if it had caused no prejudice. The overriding objective required cases to be dealt with justly and therefore a penalty had to be proportional to the offence: *Haji-Ioannou v Frangos* [2006] EWCA Civ 1663; [2007] 3 All E.R. 938, CA; *Haji-Ioannou v Frangos (No.2)* [2006] EWCA Civ 1663; [2008] 1 W.L.R. 144, CA.

Rule 47.8(4)

47.8.3 Where costs are payable out of the Community Legal Services fund and there has been a delay in commencing detailed assessment proceedings, such delay is not infrequent and can cause difficulties for counsel who remain unpaid and cannot themselves commence detailed assessment proceedings. The rule enables the Legal Services Commission to make an application under r.47.8(1).

Points of dispute and consequence of not serving

47.9 **47.9—(1) The paying party and any other party to the detailed assessment proceedings may dispute any item in the bill of costs by serving points of dispute on—**

(a) the receiving party; and

(b) every other party to the detailed assessment proceedings.

(2) The period for serving points of dispute is 21 days after the date of service of the notice of commencement.

(3) If a party serves points of dispute after the period set out in paragraph (2) he may not be heard further in the detailed assessment proceedings, unless the court gives permission.

(The costs practice direction sets out requirements about the formof points of dispute.)

(4) *The receiving* party may file a request for a default costs certificate if—

(a) the period set out in rule 47.9(2) for serving points of dispute has expired; and

(b) he has not been served with any points of dispute.

(5) If any party (including the paying party) serves points of dispute before the issue of a default costs certificate the court may not issue the default costs certificate.

(Section IV of this Part sets out the procedure to be followed after points of dispute have been filed.)

Comment

Any person served with a copy of the bill and notice of commencement may serve points of dispute within 21 days after the date of service. If points of dispute are served after the time laid down in the rule that party may not be heard further unless the court gives permission. **47.9.1**

See s.35 of the Costs Practice Direction as to time limits, the form and contents of points of dispute.

Failure to serve points of dispute entitles the receiving party to request a default costs certificate in accordance with r.47.11. Even if points of dispute are served out of time the court may not subsequently issue a default costs certificate (see r.47.9(5)).

Procedure where costs are agreed[1]

47.10—(1) If the paying party and the receiving party agree the amount of costs, either party may apply for a costs certificate (either interim or final) in the amount agreed. **47.10**

(Rule 47.15 and Rule 47.16 contain further provisions about interim and final costs certificates respectively.)

(2) An application for a certificate under paragraph (1) must be made to the court which would be the venue for detailed assessment proceedings under rule 47.4.

Comment

It is open to the parties to agree all or part of the costs being claimed. Either party may apply for an appropriate certificate from the court; i.e. an interim certificate, if part of the costs are agreed or a final certificate, if all the costs are agreed (see rr.47.15 and 47.16). **47.10.1**

Except in the RCJ, if agreement is reached before the court has become involved in the detailed assessment proceedings, the application for a certificate is made to the court which gave the judgment or made the order giving the right to the detailed assessment proceedings, or if the proceedings have been transferred to another court to that court. In any other case the court will be the "appropriate office" ascertained in accordance with r.47.4. See s.36 of the Costs Practice Direction as to procedure where costs are agreed. In cases proceeding in the RCJ application should be made to the SCCO.

III. Costs Payable By One Party to Another—Default Provisions

Default costs certificate[2]

47.11—(1) Where the receiving party is permitted by rule 47.9 to obtain a default costs certificate, that party does so by filing a *request in the relevant practice* form. (The costs practice direction deals with the procedure by which the receiving party may obtain a default costs certificate.) **47.11**

(2) A default costs certificate will include an order to pay the costs to which it relates.

---

[1] Amended by the Civil Procedure (Amendment No.3) Rules 2000 (SI 2000/1317).
[2] Amended by the Civil Procedure (Amendment) Rules 2008 (SI 2008/2178).

(3) Where a receiving party obtains a default costs certificate, the costs payable to that party for the commencement of detailed assessment proceedings will be the sum set out in the costs practice direction.

(4) A receiving party who obtains a default costs certificate in detailed assessment proceedings pursuant to an order under section 194(3) of the Legal Services Act 2007 must send a copy of the default costs certificate to the prescribed charity.

Comment

47.11.1 As to the procedure for obtaining a default costs certificate see s.37 of the Costs Practice Direction. A default costs certificate, like all certificates, includes an order to pay the costs to which it relates. A party must comply with an order for payment within 14 days of the date of the certificate in accordance with r.44.8.

This will normally be the first occasion when the court has come into contact with the detailed assessment proceedings.

Amended by SI 1999/1008.

Setting aside default costs certificate[1]

47.12 **47.12—(1) The court must set aside a default costs certificate if the receiving party was not entitled to it.**

(2) In any other case, the court may set aside or vary a default costs certificate if it appears to the court that there is some good reason why the detailed assessment proceedings should continue.

(3) Where—

(a) the receiving party has purported to serve the notice of commencement on the paying party;

(b) a default costs certificate has been issued; and

(c) the receiving party subsequently discovers that the notice of commencement did not reach the paying party at least 21 days before the default costs certificate was issued;

the receiving party must—

(i) file a request for the default costs certificate to be set aside; or

(ii) apply to the court for directions.

(4) Where paragraph (3) applies, the receiving party may take no further step in

(a) the detailed assessment proceedings; or

(b) the enforcement of the default costs certificate,

until the certificate has been set aside or the court has given directions.

(The costs practice direction contains further details about the procedure for setting aside a default costs certificate and the matters which the court must take into account.)

(5) Where the court sets aside or varies a default costs certificate in detailed assessment proceedings pursuant to an order under section 194(3) of the Legal Services Act 2007, the receiving party must

[1] Amended by the Civil Procedure (Amendment) Rules 2008 (SI 2008/2178).

send a copy of the order setting aside or varying the default costs certificate to the prescribed charity.

Comment

The onus is on the receiving party to request that a default costs certificate be set aside, or to apply for directions where the notice of commencement did not reach the paying party at least 21 days before the default costs certificate was issued. 47.12.1

Either party may apply to the court to set aside or vary a default costs certificate for good reason. See s.38 of the Costs Practice Direction for the procedure for setting aside a default costs certificate and the matters which the court will take into account.

The court issuing the default costs certificate has, among its other powers, the power to stay enforcement of the certificate.

IV. Costs Payable By One Party to Another—Procedure Where Points of Dispute Are Served

Optional reply[1]

47.13—(1) Where any party to the detailed assessment proceedings serves points of dispute, the receiving party may serve a reply on the other parties to the assessment proceedings. 47.13

(2) He may do so within 21 days after service on him of the points of dispute to which his reply relates.

(The costs practice direction sets out the meaning of reply).

Comment

There is no obligation upon the receiving party to serve a reply but, if the receiving party fails to do so, this may be a factor taken into account under r.47.18(2) when the court is considering what order to make in respect of the costs of the detailed assessment proceedings. See s.39 of the Costs Practice Direction. 47.13.1

Detailed assessment hearing[2]

47.14—(1) Where points of dispute are served in accordance with this Part, the receiving party may file a request for a detailed assessment hearing. 47.14

(2) He must file a request within 3 months of the expiry of the period for commencing detailed assessment proceedings as specified—

(a) in rule 47.7; or

(b) by any direction of the court.

(3) Where the receiving party fails to file a request in accordance with paragraph (2), the paying party may apply for an order requiring the receiving party to file the request within such time as the court may specify.

***(4) On an application under* paragraph (3), the court may direct that, unless the receiving party requests a detailed assessment hearing within the time specified by the court, all or part of the costs to which the receiving party would otherwise be entitled will be disallowed.**

---

1 Amended by the Civil Procedure (Amendment No.3) Rules 2000 (SI 2000/1317).
2 Amended by the Civil Procedure (Amendment) Rules 2002 (SI 2002/2058).

(5) If—

(a) the paying party has not made an application in accordance with paragraph (3); and

(b) the receiving party files a request for a detailed assessment hearing later than the period specified in paragraph (2)

the court may disallow all or part of the interest otherwise payable to the receiving party under—

(i) section 17 of the Judgments Act 1838[1]; or

(ii) section 74 of the County Courts Act 1984,[2]

but must not impose any other sanction except in accordance with rule 44.14 (powers in relation to misconduct).

(6) No party other than—

(a) the receiving party;

(b) the paying party; and

(c) any party who has served points of dispute under rule 47.9,

may be heard at the detailed assessment hearing unless the court gives permission.

(7) Only items specified in the points of dispute may be raised at the hearing, unless the court gives permission.

(The costs practice direction specifies other documents which must be filed with the request for hearing and the length of notice which the court will give when it fixes a hearing date.)

Comment

47.14.1 If no application is made for a default costs certificate, the request for a detailed assessment hearing is likely to be the first occasion on which the court has come into contact with the detailed assessment proceedings.

If the receiving party does not apply for a detailed assessment hearing within the time specified, the paying party may make an application under r.47.14(3). Such an application enables the court to make an order which could result in the receiving party having disallowed all or part of the costs.

A claimant company sued five defendants, four of whom were represented by one firm of solicitors. Different heads of relief were claimed against each of the defendants; the judge allowed some and dismissed others. The three defendants were awarded their costs, but the solicitor's bill did not identify the costs incurred by each of them separately. On assessment the costs judge decided that the costs should be divided equally between them as there was no work which could be identified as being solely for the benefit of one or more of them but not the others. There was only one retainer letter addressed to a single defendant but there was no doubt that the solicitors had clearly acted for all three. On appeal it was held that, where there was no express agreement concerning division of costs, a general rule of thumb was to divide them equally between the relevant parties. This rule of thumb should not be allowed to produce injustice and, where costs could be shown to be attributable to one party only, the liability for those costs fell only on that party. Once it was established that a firm of solicitors was acting for a particular party a presumption arose that the client was liable to pay the solicitors and the onus was on the paying party to rebut that presumption. In order to do this it would have to be shown that there were no circumstances in which the solicitor would be able to look to the client for payment. In the same case a claim was made for the costs of work done by a property lawyer who had advised in relation to the transactions giving rise to the litigation. The court held

[1] 1838 c.110. Section 17 was amended by SI 1998/2940.

[2] S.74 was amended by s.(2) of the Private International Law (Miscellaneous Provisions) Act 1995 (c.42).

that the costs incurred by the lawyer in assistance or general preparation of the case as a solicitor, and the costs of his attendance at court were allowable. Work done by a legal team in producing a witness statement for the lawyer was not allowable, save to the extent that the work done was attributable to the lawyer in his capacity as a solicitor rather than in his capacity as a witness of fact (*Meretz Investments NV v ACP Ltd* [2007] EWHC 2635 (Ch) Warren J.).

Rule 47.14(5)—Interest

Where the receiving party files the request for a detailed assessment hearing out of time, but before any application by the paying party, the court may disallow interest for the period of the delay but may not impose any other sanction. The court's powers in relation to misconduct under r.44.14 are unaffected. **47.14.1.1**

Amended by SI 1999/1008.

Rule 47.14(6)—Who may be heard

The rule limits the number of parties who may be heard at the detailed assessment hearing and the matters which may be raised at the hearing unless the court gives permission. **47.14.2**

See s.40 of the Costs Practice Direction as to the documents which must be filed with request for hearing, the document giving the right to detailed assessment and procedure, including agreement, adjournment and amendment.

The court will give at least 14 days notice of the date of hearing.

Rule 47.14(7)—Privilege and the power to order disclosure

Where privileged documents are given to a Costs Judge in accordance with section 40 of the Costs Practice Direction privilege is not lost. The Costs Judge should direct the receiving party to produce a witness statement together with the relevant documents to the Costs Judge alone at first and should then decide whether the receiving party should be put to their election as to whether to disclose the documents in order to rely upon their contents or to decline disclosure and rely on witness statements alone: per Nelson J., *Giambrone v JMC Holidays* [2002] EWHC 495 (QB). **47.14.3**

> "The [Costs Judge] does not have any power to order discovery to be given: he does not have any power to override a right of privilege. But it is the duty of the [Costs Judge] if the respondent raises a factual issue, which is real and relevant and not a sham or fanciful dispute, to require the claimant to prove the facts upon which he relies. The claimant then has to choose what evidence and to what extent he will waive his privilege. That is a choice for the claimant alone. The [Costs Judge] then has to decide the issue of fact on the evidence. In considering whether he is satisfied by the evidence the [Costs Judge] will no doubt take into account that the claimant may have a legitimate interest in not adducing the most obvious or complete evidence, and may prefer only to rely on oral evidence rather than producing priviledged documents" *per* Hobhouse J. in *Pamplin v Express Newspapers Ltd (Costs)* [1985] 1 W.L.R. 689 at 697.
>
> "The Costs Officer is exercising a judicial function with substantial financial consequences for the parties if some feature of the case alerts him to the need to make further investigation he may seek further information. No doubt he would begin by asking for a letter or some form of written confirmation or reassurance as appropriate. If this were to prove inadequate he might then make orders for discovery or require evidence." *per* Judge L.J. in *Bailey v IBC Vehicles Ltd* [1998] 3 All E.R. 570.

Rimer J. found those views to be still valid, he continued:

> "I can, in any event,see no good reason why the client care letter and the payment calculations should not have been disclosed to the defendant, since I have not been persuaded that they were priviledged. But if anything in them might have been regarded as privileged one course which might at least have been considered was the redaction from them of the privileged parts . . . The claimant chose to prove his version of a disputed issue of fact by reference to certain documents. In my view, the basic principle is that, if he wanted to do so, fairness required him also to disclose the documents to the defendant."*Dickinson v Rushmer* [2002] 1 Costs L.R. 128.

Once the document is of sufficient importance to be taken into account in arriving at a conclusion as to recoverability, then, unless otherwise agreed, it must be shown to the paying party or the receiving party should be put to its election in respect of every document relied on regardless of its degree of relevance. It was expected that in the great majority of cases the paying party would be content to agree that the Costs Judge alone should see privileged documents. Only where it was necessary and proportionate should the receiving party be put to his election. The redaction and production of privileged documents or the adduing of further evidence would lead to additional delay and increase costs. The court considered that the applicable principle was an absolute one. Privilege would not be overridden by the court and must be waived by the party entitled to assert it. It followed that the terms of para.40.14 of the Costs Practice Direction were consistent with the requirements of the EHCR. The court expressed the view that the protection afforded to the receiving party by the rule that the waiver is for the purpose of the assessment only and that the document remains otherwise privileged should play a much more significant role than it appears to in the decision whether or not to waive privilege in a proper case, per Pumfrey J. *South Coast Shipping Co Ltd v Havant BC* [2002] 3 All E.R. 779. The court indicated that it should be standard practice where a client care letter was affirmatively relied on that it be produced to the paying party, per Gray J., *Adams v MacInnes*, November 8, 2001, unrep.

The court again considered the question of disclosure of documents on detailed assessment where the Costs Judge had ordered the receiving parties, the claimants in the litigation,to elect either to disclose certain experts' reports for which they were seeking costs, those reports not having previously been disclosed in the litigation, or to decline disclosure and rely on other evidence. The court reviewed the judgments in *Pamplin v Express Newspapers Ltd* [1985] 1 W.L.R. 689, Hobhouse J.; *Goldman v Hesper* [1988] 1 W.L.R. 1238, Taylor J.; *Dickinson v Rushmer* [2002] Costs L.R. 128, Rymer J.; and *South Coast Shipping Co Ltd v Havant BC* [2002] 3 All E R 779, Pumfrey J. The court held that the position in law was clear and the appeal was dismissed. *Gower Chemicals Group Litigation v Gower Chemicals Ltd* [2008] EWHC 735 (QB), Davis J.

> "When a party lodges a privileged document for detailed assessment in order to claim the costs of it; if the other party wishes to see it to dispute that claim for costs the claimant must be given the right to elect to withdraw it and not claim costs or he must disclose it."

Per Drake J., *Skuse v Granada Television Ltd* [1994] 1 W.L.R. 1156, see also *Pamplin v Express Newspapers Limited* [1985] 1 W.L.R. 689; *Goldman v Hesper* [1998] 1 W.L.R. 1238, CA and *Derby & Co v Weldon (No.7)* [1990] 1 W.L.R. 1156. Drake J. stated "Had I ordered disclosure ... of any part of the bundle I would have ordered that the document should be edited so as to remove the irrelevant material". It is permissible to blank out parts of documents disclosed on discovery on the ground that they are irrelevant to the issues in the action. See *G.E. Corporate Finance Group v Bankers Trust Co*, *The Times*, August 3, 1994, CA.

The court cannot order disclosure of "without prejudice" negotiations against the wishes of one of the parties to those negotiations. This may mean that in some cases the court, when it comes to the question of costs, cannot decide whether one side or the other was unreasonable in refusing mediation. The court does not have power to order any disclosure of the detail of the "without prejudice" negotiations for the purposes of deciding the question of costs: *Reed Executive Plc v Reed Business Information Ltd* [2004] EWCA Civ 887; [2004] 1 P&T 1087, CA. The rule in *Walker v Wilshire* [1889] 23 Q.B.D.335 remains good law.

Where documents were disclosed in the course of assessment proceedings, and the party to whom they were disclosed wished to use them in proceedings in the USA, the Court of Appeal decided that the documents were privileged and were disclosed for the purpose of assessment only. They were relevant to an issue and should have been disclosed in the interests of justice and an order for disclosure would have been made if sought. The privilege in them was waived only for the purposes of detailed assessment. The court rejected an argument that enforcing privilege amounted to interference with the US proceedings. It was for the US court to decide whether there had been a breach of US law and what to do about it. The documents were subject to an implied undertaking (*Prudential Insurance Co v Fountain Page Ltd* [1991] 1 W.L.R. 756) even though they were disclosed without an order. Special circumstances were required if the undertaking was to be released and this depended on all the facts (*Crest Homes Plc v Marks* [1997] 1 A.C. 829), *Bourns Inc v Raychem Corp* [1999] 3 All E.R. 154; *The Times*, May 12, 1999, CA.

In detailed assessment proceedings the paying party sought an order requiring the receiving party's solicitors to give full particulars of their dealings with their client both in relation to their original retention as his solicitors and in relation to a subsequent conditional fee agreement. Information was sought by way of disclosure of documents and otherwise to support the contention that there had in truth been an agreement whereby the client was liable to the solicitors' costs prior to a particular date and as to the validity of the CFA. In the event the receiving party's solicitors disclosed full details of the CFA and ultimately their file and attendance notes. The paying party argued that a retainer is or becomes champertous and therefore unlawful and unenforceable if a solicitor is or becomes aware at any time that his client could not possibly have afforded to pay his costs whatever might have been the formal agreement between them. and continues to act thereafter. The court held that the Costs Judge undoubtedly had jurisdiction to make the orders requested and if it had been necessary to make such orders in order to ensure a fair determination of the issue, the application should have been acceded to. The mere fact that the issue has been raised is not of itself sufficient if there is no prospect that cross examination could either undermine or further elucidate the receiving party's case. To refuse to accede to the application will not be unfair and will not breach the requirement of the overriding objective that the parties are on an equal footing but would save expense and deal with the issues proportionately and expeditiously: *Times Newspapers Ltd v Burstein* [2002] EWCA Civ 1739.

In cases involving vast amounts of documents, a party may sometimes reduce a document into an electronic form to ease management. The cost of the equipment necessary to undertake this work is not normally recoverable, although the actual work required to analyse the documents may be regarded as fee earners work. The party contemplating reducing documents into electronic form may apply to the court in advance for an order regulating the matter, including the basis of charge for electronic copies. The court has power to give directions as to whether inspection should be by electronic means or hard copy (*Grupo Torras SA v Al-Sabah (No.3)* [1997] C.L.C. 1553 *Jafter v Grupo Torras SA*, *The Times*, October 13, 1997, Mance J.). On the particular facts of that case the court directed that inspection should be by means of CD, which could be produced at a relatively modest cost, as against production of photostat copies of the documents themselves, which would have cost a very great deal of money. The actual work of assembling the database was a matter to be left to the outcome of the trial and subsequent assessment.

The Indemnity Principle

"Costs as between party and party are given by the law as an indemnity to the person entitled to them; they are not imposed as a punishment on the party who pays them, or given as a bonus to the party who receives them." (*Harold v Smith* [1860] 5 H. & N. 381, Bramwell B.). "It is of great importance to litigants who are unsuccessful, that they should not be oppressed into having to pay an excessive amount of costs ... the costs chargeable as between party and party are all that are necessary to enable the adverse party to conduct the litigation and no more. Any charges merely for conducting litigation more conveniently may be called luxuries and must be paid by the party incurring them" (*Smith v Buller* [1875] L.R. 19 Eq. 473, Sir Richard Malins V.-C.). The test is now one of reasonableness and proportionality rather than necessity. The purpose of assessment is to ascertain the amount payable to the party recovering costs not to fix the remuneration of solicitors. The order for costs may not be more than an indemnity, i.e. the amount which the successful party has to pay to his own solicitor (*Gundry v Sainsbury* [1910] 1 K.B. 99). **47.14.4**

The indemnity principle is to be applied on an item by item basis rather than on a global basis "where applicable the figures in a contentious business agreement provide both a measure and a ceiling for each recoverable item of costs", per Sir Brian Neill, *The General of Berne Insurance Co v Jardine Reinsurance Management* [1998] 2 All E.R. 301, CA. That judgment related to a contentious business agreement where the hourly rate was agreed. The principle applies even where there is no contentous business agreement: "In my judgment there should be no distinction between those cases where a formal contentious business agreement is in place and which are governed by s.60(3) of the Solicitors Act 1974 and other cases where there is an agreement partly evidenced in writing, an unwritten agreement or no agreement at all, but merely an understanding arising perhaps from a long established relationship ..."; *Nederlandse Reassurantie Groep Holding NV v Bacon & Woodrow* [1998] 2 Costs L.R. 32, Tucker J.

Re: Eastwood (deceased); *Lloyds Bank Ltd v Eastwood* [1975] Ch 112, established that the conventional method, appropriate to assessing the bill of a solicitor in private practice, was also appropriate for a bill of an in-house solicitor in all but special cases where it was reasonably plain that that method would infringe the indemnity principle. This had the merit of simplicity and of avoiding the burden of detailed enquiry. A special case would arise where a sum could be identified, different from that produced by a conventional approach, which was adequate to cover the actual cost incurred in doing all the work done. Such a sum might be identified by concession or by the factual assessment of the costs officer, but that possibility did not justify detailed investigation in every case (*Cole v British Telecommunications Plc* [2000] 2 Costs L.R. 310; July 4, 2000, CA). The decision in *London & Scottish Benefits Society v Chorley* [1883–84] 13 Q.B.D. 872 dealt with the costs of a solicitor appearing in person:

> "The unsuccessful adversary of a solicitor appearing in person cannot be charged for what does not exist. He cannot be charged for the solicitor consulting himself or instructing himself to attend upon himself. The true rule seems to me that when a solicitor brings or defends an action in person he is entitled to the same costs as an ordinary litigant appearing in person subject to this restriction that no costs which are really unnecessary can be recovered."

And see *Stubblefield v Kemp* [2001] 1 Costs L.R. 30, Arden J.

The liquidator of a football club commenced proceedings to set aside a legal charge. Before trial the defendant accepted that the charge was invalid. He was ordered to pay the costs of the liquidator. In the meantime the liquidator was in dispute with his former solicitors as to the fees payable. This dispute led to proceedings between the solicitors and the liquidator. Those proceedings were compromised on the basis that each party should pay his own costs and that the solicitors would seek no further fees from the liquidator, save what was recovered from the defendant in the proceedings relating to the legal charge. The paying party argued that under the indemnity principle he could not, in the light of that agreement, be ordered to pay any further costs. On appeal the judge held that the agreement between the liquidator and the former solicitors did not amount to a release from further liability of the liquidator to the solicitor, such a liability could exist notwithstanding that there was an agreement not to enforce the liability against the liquidator. The agreement was capable of being merely an agreement not to enforce liability in one particular way. No fees had been written off. The liquidator's liability had not been extinguished. The parties had merely limited its enforcement. Had the agreement been a CFA it would have been unenforceable if it contravened the relevant Regulations. It was however not a contingency fee agreement which, on the facts, was held not to be unlawful. At the date of the agreement the action in question was over and the result was known, all the fees had become payable. There was no conditionality in relation to them at the time that the retainer had been entered into or at the time it had been fulfilled. The liability for costs had accrued unconditionally and without reference to future events. No further liability could accrue: *Wakeling v Harrington* [2007] EWHC 1184 (Ch), Mann J.

The hourly rate

47.14.5 Evans J. examined the question of solicitors' hourly rates in *Johnson v Reed Corrugated Cases Ltd* [1992] 1 All E.R. 169. The judge quoted with approval the decisions in *Re Eastwood (dec'd.)* [1975] Ch. 112; *Leopold Lazarus Ltd v Secretary of State for Trade and Industry* (1976) 120 S.J. 268; *Stubbs v Royal National Orthopaedic Hospital*, December 21, 1988, unrep.; *Finlay v Glaxo Laboratories Ltd* , October 9, 1989, unrep. and *R. v Wilkinson* [1980] 1 All E.R. 597. The solicitors had submitted evidence as to their expense rate calculated in accordance with the Law Society's book, *The Expense of Time*, and the judge expressed the view that presenting such figures, requiring non-expert analysis, i.e. by persons who are not accountants, is misconceived as a means of assisting the court in a particular case. Assessing costs is not an exact science; neither is accountancy. Treating the latter as if it were, so that the results of an accountancy exercise can be used as a basis for the former, seemed to the judge to achieve the worst of both worlds. The costs officer's general knowledge and experience of local conditions and circumstances remains the only firm basis for reliable and consistent assessment.

Evans J. did not support any idea that part of the court's functions on an assessment is to discipline solicitors into charging less than they have done, or to regulate the amount of their charges to their clients. The court is not concerned with charges, only with costs; it is not concerned with any market, except indirectly, certainly not to influence any market. Its function is to assess the reasonable amount of costs for work reasonably done; that, and nothing else.

"If as the solicitors argue, the proper guide is that of the average solicitor employed by the average firm in the area concerned, then the Central London Law Societies' Survey, whilst not necessarily a perfect indication of that average, is, on the evidence in this case, the closest approach we have to that average", per Mr. Justice Lindsay in *Re A Company* 1989, C. No.4081; [1995] 2 All E.R. 155. Approach of Lindsay J. followed in *KPMG Peat Marwick McLintock v HLT Group Ltd* [1995] 2 All E.R. 180, Auld J.

The Guide to the Summary Assessment of Costs (issued by the SCCO) is of only limited assistance to the Judge in a case of, e.g. brain damage at birth, which is a particularly sensitive subject matter for litigation in which the specific demands placed on solicitors by clients and litigation friends varied from case to case. The guideline figures are not supposed to replace the experience and knowledge of those familiar with the local area and the field generally: *Higgs v Camden & Islington Health Authority* [2003] EWHC 15, QB; [2003] 2 Costs L.R. 211 (Fulford J.).

The question of whether a costs draftsman's fee for attending on detailed assessment should be treated as a disbursement or as part of the solicitors' profit costs, and thus attract a success fee, was considered by the Court of Appeal. At first instance the costs judge had decided that the fees were disbursements which did not attract a success fee. The court found that the costs draftsmen were doing work which the solicitors had themselves undertaken to their client to do. It was solicitors' work for which the solicitors were entitled to make their own direct charge. The majority of the court concluded that there was no reason in principle which compels the court to require parties who enter into CFAs to address, at the outset, the risk of costs proceedings, separately. There were clear reasons of policy for the court not to require this. The court expressed the view that there was general sense, if CFAs are to be a substantial means of financing civil litigation, that they should not be over complicated, that costs should be agreed wherever possible and that, if there are to be contested costs proceedings, the means whereby the winning solicitor finances litigation which he loses should extend to the costs proceedings at the same rate as the proceedings themselves if that is what has been agreed with the client (para.21). Maurice Kay L.J. dissented stating:

> "28. ... I resist the submission that we should adopt the concept of 'solicitors' work' as determinative taxonomy, regardless of whether the solicitor carries out the work. Nor am I persuaded that the potential liability of the solicitor to his client for the negligence of the costs consultant is decisive. In the event of such liability the solicitor would be able to seek an indemnity from the costs consultant.
> 29. I appreciate that this conclusion may seem anomalous and adventitious. The paying party has no control over whether the solicitor engages an independent costs consultant or carries out the work in-house, in which latter case the success fee would be payable. On the other hand, the solicitor may elect to instruct specialist costs counsel...on the assessment and in that case counsel's fee would be a disbursement and no success fee would become payable upon it, unless counsel had his own CFA. The anomalies are not all one way. For my part I prefer an anomalous conclusion to an unjust one." (*Crane v Cannons Leisure Centre* [2007] EWCA Civ 1352; [2008] 1 W.L.R. 2549).

Instructing distant solicitors

Where a claimant was injured in Sheffield and the union to which he belonged **47.14.6**
instructed solicitors in London, the trial being in Sheffield, it was submitted by the defendants that only the Sheffield rate should be allowed, and not the London solicitors' rate. It was decided, that given the undoubted expertise of the union's solicitors, it was reasonable to instruct them, the costs had therefore been reasonably incurred and were of a reasonable amount. The London rate was allowed (*Wraith v Sheffield Forgemasters Ltd [1996] 1 W.L.R. 617, Potter J.*). But on appeal, on the issue whether the liability of an unsuccessful party ordered to pay costs should be restricted to what a reasonable competent solicitor, practising in the area of the court (or in the area where the successful party lived) might have been expected to charge or whether the successful party should be entitled to recover the sums claimed by the solicitor who was in fact instructed on his behalf, the Court of Appeal, whilst upholding Potter J. in principle, took issue with the way the principle was applied to the facts of the case because the Trade Union knew or ought to have known what sort of legal fees it would have to expend to obtain competent services for the claimant who lived in Sheffield who had sustained a serious accident there. "It is the duty of Unions and Insur-

ers in each individual case to keep down the costs of litigation, this means that if they instruct London solicitors who charge London rates for a case which has no obvious connection with London and which does not require expertise only to be found there, they will, even if successful, recover less than the solicitors have charged" (*Wraith v Sheffield Forgemasters Ltd* [1998] 1 W.L.R. 132, CA). See also *A v Chief Constable of South Yorkshire* [2008] EWHC 1658 (Comm), Teare J. In another case heard at the same time as *Wraith*, solicitors acting for a wife in Family Proceedings wrongly applied for a Charging Order in Brighton County Court, they persisted with this application, having been told it was incorrect and ultimately the husband, having changed solicitors from a firm in East Grinstead, with whom he had become dissatisfied, to a firm in London was successful in having the order for sale struck out and obtaining a wasted costs order against the wife's solicitors. It was argued that the husband should have obtained the services of solicitors in Brighton or in Tunbridge Wells, where he lived. The court found that there were certain matters which were relevant when considering the reasonableness of the husband instructing the London firm:

> "(1) The importance of the matter to him, it was obviously of great importance, it threatened his home.
>
> (2) The legal and factualcomplexities insofar as he might reasonably be expected to understand them. Due to the incompetence of the wife's solicitors the matter had taken on an appearance of some complexity.
>
> (3) The location of his home, his place of work and the location of the court in which the relevant proceedings had been commenced.
>
> (4) The husband's possibly well-founded dissatisfaction with the solicitors he had originally instructed, which may well have resulted in a natural desire to instruct solicitors further afield who would not be inhibited in representing his interests.
>
> (5) The fact that he has sought advice as to who to consult and had been recommended to consult the London firm.
>
> (6) The location of the London firm, including their accessibility to him and their readiness to attend at the relevant court.
>
> (7) What, if anything he might reasonably be expected to know of the fees likely to be charged by the London firm as compared with the fees of other solicitors whom he might reasonably be expected to have considered."

Having applied those considerations to the facts, the court allowed the London rate for the solicitors (*Truscott v Truscott*, July 31, 1997, reported as *Wraith v Sheffield Forgemasters Ltd* [1998] 1 W.L.R. 132, CA). Where a firm outside London dealt only with specialised commercial cases for selected clients and was thus clearly outside the range of local solicitors, it was possible to allow a rate more than the broad average direct cost for that area. This would not be appropriate if the firm had engaged in a case which could reasonably have been handled by other local firms since the cost would not then have been reasonably incurred, i.e. it must have been reasonable to instruct a firm for the particular case (*Jones v Secretary of State for Wales and Vale of Glamorgan B.C.* [1997] 1 W.L.R. 1008, per Buckley J.).

In defamation proceedings the court found that it was not always necessary to instruct London specialist solicitors in order to have the necessary or proportionate expertise available. The court upheld a finding that it was not reasonable for the claimant to instruct London libel specialists rather than a local firm in Norwich in respect of a defamation claim against a national newspaper. The assessment of reasonableness had to be made by reference to the circumstances confronting the claimant when or shortly before he instructed the specialist solicitors. Although the Costs Judge had erred in deciding that the case was a Norfolk case, at the relevant time the likelihood was that the hearing would have been in London, the action being in respect of a grave libel published nationwide by defendants based in London. What was more important was the Judge's conclusion that by the time the claimant instructed the specialist solicitors the only live issue was damages and that the defendant had submitted uncontested evidence about there being local solicitors able to represent the claimant. The court found that it was important to recognise that in order to have the necessary or proportionate expertise available it was not always necessary to instruct London specialist solicitors. An important factor was that any competent litigation solicitor in the country could call upon specialist members of the Bar at very short notice. *Gazley v Wade & News Group Newspapers Ltd* [2004] EWHC 2675 (QB), Eady J.

In deciding whether or not it is disproportionate to instruct distant solicitors, the court should take into account other factors such as the fact that the solicitors were usually instructed by the clients on the particular type of case (e.g. infringement of trade mark), that the solicitors had knowledge of the client's products and the skill and resources available to operate speedily (to obtain a search order) and that when the solicitors had been instructed the defendant's location and the extent of its counterfeit operation might not have been known: *Mattel Inc v RSW Plc* [2004] EWHC 1610 (Ch), H.H.J. Hegarty Q.C.

If a party chooses a particular status or type of solicitor or counsel or one located in a particular area then the costs will have been reasonably incurred if, having regard to the circumstances, a reasonable choice has been made. The question to be asked is whether the solicitor chosen is the sort of solicitor that a person would have instructed with a view to the proper conduct of his case in minimising the costs of litigation. Per Hooper J. review of detailed assessment, *A v F Co Ltd*, unrep.; *S v F Co Ltd* (1996) SCTO Digest No.13.

In a case where a claimant was injured in an accident in the Manchester area and the union instructed London solicitors the Court of Appeal decided that the question to be determined was whether, objectively, the claimant acted reasonably in instructing London solicitors. The fact that a trade union habitually used a particular firm of solicitors was of only limited relevance. On the particular facts of the case there was no obvious connection to London and this factor became increasingly important when the case did not require expertise that could only be found there. The availability of expert medical witnesses in London could not give the case a connection with London. On the facts the case was pre-eminently a Manchester one that required no expertise that could be found only in London, *Sullivan v Cooperative Insurance Society Ltd* [1999] C.P.L.R. 487; [1999] 2 Costs L.R. 158; *The Times*, May 19, 1999, CA.

Rights of audience on detailed assessment

In detailed assessment proceedings, rights of audience may be exercised by any counsel properly instructed by solicitors, any solicitor or employee of a solicitor representing one of the parties to the proceedings. By virtue of the Association of Law Costs Draftsmen Order 2006, (SI 2006/3333), the Association of Law Costs Draftsmen is with effect from January 1, 2007, designated as an authorised body for the purposes of ss.27 and 28 of the Courts and Legal Services Act 1990, and is therefore in a position to authorise certain fellows to exercise rights of audience and limited rights to litigate. If the party is legally represented costs consultants, costs draftsmen and the like can only be heard on the basis that they are temporarily, and for the purpose of those detailed assessment proceeding, employees of the solicitors representing the party. The solicitors are responsible for the conduct of the detailed assessment proceedings and cannot avoid that responsibility merely by instructing a costs draftsman. **47.14.7**

> "A costs draftsman can appear on behalf of a party only as the duly authorised representative of the solicitor who has instructed him to be there. The scope of his apparent authority would be the same ... as any costs draftsman employed by the firm." *per* Evans L.J., *Waterson Hicks v Eliopoulos*, November 14, 1995, unrep., CA.

Where a party is a litigant in person the party may appear in person or may be assisted by an expert in accordance with r.48.6(3)(c). Expert assistance in those circumstances may be given by a barrister, solicitor, Fellow of the Institute of Legal Executives, Fellow of the Association of Law Costs Draftsmen, a law costs draftsman who is a member of the Academy of Experts or a law costs draftsman who is a member of the Expert Witness Institute (see s.52 of the Costs Practice Direction).

As to the use of McKenzie friends see: *R. v Bow County Court Ex p. Pelling* [1999] 4 All E.R. 751, CA and *Noueiri v Paragon Finance Ltd* [2001] EWCA Civ 1402; [2001] 1 W.L.R. 2357, CA. As to legally qualified representatives without rights of audience, see *Clarkson v Gilbert* [2000] C.P. Rep. 58, CA (husband—who had completed the Bar finals but had not been called to the Bar—given permission to represent his wife who was not present when the application was made but had given the power of attorney). The phrase "exceptional circumstances" as a qualification for the proper exercise of the court's discretion was intended to relate to similar situations where a person without statutory rights of audience nevertheless was carrying on the profession of providing legal assistance. It had not been meant to apply to a husband wishing to appear for his wife. The question was whether in all the circumstances of the case the court should exercise its discretion to grant rights of audience. See *D v S (rights of audience)* [1997] 1 F.L.R. 724.

The court must be able to rely implicitly on those appearing before it. Both barristers and solicitors have, as part of their Rules of Professional Conduct, the requirement that the court must not be misled. In certain limited circumstances a litigant in person may be entitled to rely on the advice of experts or the help of a MacKenzie Friend. Where a party is properly represented by solicitors throughout, it is the solicitors responsibility to arrange for appropriate representation at the detailed assessment proceedings and to supervise that representation. In a case where costs negotiators were instructed direct by the liability insurers, to the effective exclusion of solicitors on the record, the court found that the advocate instructed by the costs negotiators did not have a right of audience and could not be heard. In addition the terms of remuneration between the insurer and the costs negotiators, which were linked directly to the size of the reduction achieved in the receiving party's bill was champertous and unlawful: *Ahmed v Powell* [2003] P.N.L.R. 22, Senior Costs Judge.

47.14.8 In *Practice Note (Family Courts: McKenzie Friends) (No.2)* [2008] 1 W.L.R. 2757, Fam D, the President gave guidance as to the proper approach to the exercise of the court's discretion to allow an unrepresented party in family proceedings to have assistance from a lay person, sometimes called a McKenzie friend (MF). Amongst other things, the guidance states that a litigant in person wishing to have the help of a MF should be allowed such help unless the judge is satisfied that fairness and the interests of justice do not so require; the presumption in favour of permitting a MF is a strong one. Various factors that should not outweigh the presumption are listed. The guidance also refers to various matters of practice to be followed by parties applying for the assistance on an MF. Further, the guidance lists the things that a MF may do in assisting the unrepresented party, and what the MF may not do. Included in the latter category is examining witnesses and addressing the court, that is to say, exercising a right of audience. The court has a discretion to grant a lay person, whether an MF or not, a right of audience. The guidance refers to the exercise of this discretion in cases where a party wishes that his or her MF should be permitted to exercise such right. As to this last point, see further Vol.2 Section 13 (Rights of Audience) para.13–19.

The grant of rights of audience to an organisation is outside the scope of the court's discretionary power to grant rights of audience to individuals, which, under s.27 of the Courts and Legal Services Act 1990, is confined to individual applications made on a case by case basis. See *Gregory v Turner* [2003] 1 W.L.R. 1149, CA; *Izzo v Phillip Ross & Co* [2002] B.P.I.R. 310, Ch D, and *Cooper v Rhuscott Estates* [2004] EWCA Civ 673.

V. Interim Costs Certificate and Final Costs Certificate

Power to issue an interim certificate[1]

47.15 **47.15—(1) The court may at any time after the receiving party has filed a request for a detailed assessment hearing—**

(a) issue an interim costs certificate for such sum as it considers appropriate;

(b) amend or cancel an interim certificate.

(2) An interim certificate will include an order to pay the costs to which it relates, unless the court orders otherwise.

(3) The court may order the costs certified in an interim certificate, to be paid into the court.

(4) Where the court—

(a) issues an interim costs certificate; or

(b) amends or cancels an interim certificate,

in detailed assessment proceedings pursuant to an order under section 194(3) of the Legal Services Act 2007, the receiving party must send a copy of the interim costs certificate or the order amending or cancelling the interim costs certificate to the prescribed charity.

[1] Amended by the Civil Procedure (Amendment) Rules 2008 (SI 2008/2178).

Comment

There is no requirement that any of the costs be assessed or agreed prior to the issue of an interim costs certificate. The court is given complete discretion once a request for a detailed assessment hearing has been filed to issue an interim certificate for such sum as it considers appropriate. **47.15.1**

As with default costs certificates and final costs certificates the interim costs certificate includes an order to pay. Rule 44.8 provides that payment must be made within 14 days of the date of the certificate. The court issuing the certificate has the power to stay enforcement of it. See s.41 of the Costs Practice Direction.

The court may order that, instead of the certified amount being paid to the receiving party, it should be paid into court. This may be appropriate where the paying party is proving dilatory but where there is also an order for costs in favour of the paying party.

Final costs certificate[1]

47.16—(1) In this rule a completed bill means a bill calculated to show the amount due following the detailed assessment of the costs. **47.16**

(2) The period for filing the completed bill is 14 days after the end of the detailed assessment hearing.

(3) When a completed bill is filed the court will issue a final costs certificate and serve it on the parties to the detailed assessment proceedings.

(4) Paragraph (3) is subject to any order made by the court that a certificate is not to be issued until other costs have been paid.

(5) A final costs certificate will include an order to pay the costs to which it relates, unless the court orders otherwise.

(The costs practice direction deals with the form of a final costs certificate.)

(6) Where the court issues a final costs certificate in detailed assessment proceedings pursuant to an order under section 194(3) of the Legal Services Act 2007, the receiving party must send a copy of the final costs certificate to the prescribed charity.

Comment

Once the detailed assessment hearing has finished the receiving party is required to complete the bill by calculating the amounts due and to file it with the court within 14 days after the end of the detailed assessment hearing. **47.16.1**

See s.42 of the Costs Practice Direction as to completion of the bill and the form of the final costs certificate.

As with a default costs certificate and interim costs certificate, the final costs certificate will include an order to pay the costs. The time for payment, in accordance with r.44.8, is within 14 days of the date of the certificate. The court issuing the certificate has the power to stay enforcement of the certificate.

Amended by SI 1999/1008.

[1] Amended by the Civil Procedure (Amendment) Rules 2008 (SI 2008/2178).

VI. Detailed Assessment Procedure for Costs of a LSC funded client or an assisted person where costs are payable out of the community legal service fund

Detailed assessment procedure for costs of a LSC funded client or an assisted person where costs are payable out of the community legal service fund[1]

47.17 **47.17—(1) Where the court is to assess costs of a LSC funded client or an assisted person which are payable out of the community legal service fund, that person's solicitor may commence detailed assessment proceedings by filing a request in the relevant practice form.**

(2) A request under paragraph (1) must be filed within 3 months after the date when the right to detailed assessment arose.

(3) The solicitor must also serve a copy of the request for detailed assessment on the LSC funded client or the assisted person, if notice of that person's interest has been given to the court in accordance with community legal service or legal aid regulations.

(4) Where the solicitor has certified that the LSC funded client or that person wishes to attend an assessment hearing, the court will on receipt of the request for assessment, fix a date for the assessment hearing.

(5) Where paragraph (3) does not apply, the court will on receipt of the request for assessment provisionally assess the costs without the attendance of the solicitor, unless it considers that a hearing is necessary.

(6) After the court has provisionally assessed the bill, it will return the bill to the solicitor.

(7) The court will fix a date for an assessment hearing if the solicitor informs the court, within 14 days after he receives the provisionally assessed bill, that he wants the court to hold such a hearing.

Comment

47.17.1 This section of the rules deals with costs payable only out of the Community Legal Service Fund. (For the practice where costs are payable by one party to another and also out of the Community Legal Service Fund at prescribed rates see paras 49.1 to 49.8 of the Costs Practice Direction.)

The detailed assessment proceedings are commenced by filing a request for detailed assessment (in Form **N258A**). The time for filing the request is within three months after the date when the right to detailed assessment arose. A copy of the request must be served on the assisted person if the assisted person has a financial interest and wishes to attend the assessment hearing (see Civil Legal Aid (General) Regulations 1989 reg.119).

The court will give a date for the detailed assessment hearing in every case where the LSC funded client or the assisted person wishes to attend and may do so if it considers that a hearing is necessary. Otherwise the court will provisionally assess the costs without the attendance of the solicitor but, if the solicitor does not accept the provisional assessment the court will fix a date for a detailed assessment hearing, if the solicitor informs the court within 14 days that that is what is wanted. See s.43 of the *Costs Practice Direction* for these procedures.

[1] Amended by the Civil Procedure (Amendment No.3) Rules 2000 (SI 2000/1317) and the Civil Procedure (Amendment No.4) Rules 2000 (SI 2000/2092).

Detailed assessment procedure where costs are payable out of a fund other than the community legal service fund[1]

47.17A—(1) Where the court is to assess costs which are payable out of a fund other than the Community Legal Service Fund, the receiving party may commence detailed assessment proceedings by filing a request in the relevant practice form. 47.17A

(2) A request under paragraph (1) must be filed within 3 months after the date when the right to detailed assessment arose.

(3) The court may direct that the party seeking assessment serve a copy of the request on any person who has a financial interest in the outcome of the assessment.

(4) The court will, on receipt of the request for assessment, provisionally assess the costs without the attendance of the receiving party, unless it considers that a hearing is necessary.

(5) After the court has provisionally assessed the bill, it will return the bill to the receiving party.

(6) The court will fix a date for an assessment hearing if the party informs the court, within 14 days after he receives the provisionally assessed bill, that he wants the court to hold such a hearing.

Comment

This rule provides a procedure where costs are paid out of a fund other that the Community Legal Service Fund, it therefore covers cases in the Court of Protection, claims by trustees and the like. The Practice Direction provides that provisional assessment may take place and also provides for appropriate notice to be given to parties with a financial interest in the fund. Section 44 of the Costs Practice Direction. 47.17A.1

Costs payable out of a fund

Following the decision in *AG v Nethercote* [1841] 11 Sim 529 and *Marsden's Estate, Re* (1889) L.R. 40 Ch. D. 475 it is quite clear that whenever there are funds out of which costs are to be paid there is not an order which attracts interest. The reason for that is that there is not an order of the court in adversarial litigation. In the case of a Tomlin Order the provisions as to payment of costs in the schedule do not fall within the Judgments Act. On the facts of the case there was a contractual agreement between the parties and if interest was to be payable it should have been expressly included or excluded: *Wills v Crown Estate Commissioners* [2003] EWHC 1718 (Ch), Peter Smith J. 47.17A.2

VII. Costs of Detailed Assessment Proceedings

Liability for costs of detailed assessment proceedings[2]

47.18—(1) The receiving party is entitled to the costs of the detailed assessment proceedings except where— 47.18

(a) the provisions of any Act, any of these Rules or any relevant practice direction provide otherwise; or

(b) the court makes some other order in relation to all or part of the costs of the detailed assessment proceedings.

(1A) Paragraph (1) does not apply where the receiving party has pro bono representation in the detailed assessment proceedings but that party may apply for an order in respect of that representation under section 194(3) of the Legal Services Act 2007.

[1] Introduced by the Civil Procedure (Amendment No.3) Rules 2000 (SI 2000/1317).
[2] Amended by the Civil Procedure (Amendment) Rules 2008 (SI 2008/2178).

(2) In deciding whether to make some other order, the court must have regard to all the circumstances, including—

(a) the conduct of all the parties;

(b) the amount, if any, by which the bill of costs has been reduced; and

(c) whether it was reasonable for a party to claim the costs of a particular item or to dispute that item.

Comment

47.18.1 There is a presumption that the receiving party is entitled to the costs of the detailed assessment proceedings unless some provision to the contrary is in existence, or the court makes a different order in relation to all or part of the costs.

In deciding what order to make the court is required to have regard to: all the circumstances, including the conduct of all the parties (presumably this means conduct in relation to the detailed assessment proceedings rather than in the substantive proceedings); the amount of any reduction; and whether it was reasonable for a party to claim or dispute a particular item. The last two categories overlap to a certain extent and are aimed at unreasonable demands and/or unreasonable objections. See s.45 of the Costs Practice Direction.

See also r.44.14 as to misconduct in assessment proceedings.

47.18.2 The costs of detailed assessment fall to be dealt with under CPR r.47.18not under r.47.8 even where there has been substantial delay. Rule 47.18 raised a rebuttable presumption that a receiving party should have his costs of a detailed assessment subject to the right of the Costs Judge to make a different order: *Bufton v Hill* [2002] EWHC 977; [2002] 3 Costs L.R. 381.

Where taxation proceedings were commenced before the CPR came into force Order 62 of the Rules of the Supreme Court governed the taxation proceedings even though the final hearing took place after the coming into force of the CPR. The paying party had made an offer to settle the costs which the court held included interest as it was expressed to be in full settlement. On that basis the offer was not successful and the order that the receiving party should pay the costs of the taxation was set aside: *Morris v Wiltshire (Costs)* [2002] 1 Costs L.R.167, Roderick Evans J.

In family proceedings in which a party was legally aided, the question arose as to what was properly allowable in respect of the reasonable costs of preparing the bill of costs. The Legal Aid in Family Proceedings (Remuneration) Regulations 1991 laid down the maximum permitted. The Regulations were to be taken as setting the reasonable cost in the context in which they applied. This was distinguishable from the costs of preparing for and attending a taxation hearing in respect of which a further amount could be allowed: *A Local Authority v A (A Mother and Child)* [2001] 1 Costs L.R. 136; [2001] 1 F.L.R. 602; [2001] Fam. Law 260, CA.

Offers to settle without prejudice save as to costs of the detailed assessment proceedings[1]

47.19 **47.19—(1) Where—**

(a) a party (whether the paying party or the receiving party) makes a written offer to settle the costs of the proceedings which gave rise to the assessment proceedings; and

(b) the offer is expressed to be without prejudice[GL] save as to the costs of the detailed assessment proceedings, the court will take the offer into account in deciding who should pay the costs of those proceedings.

(2) The fact of the offer must not be communicated to the costs

[1] Amended by the Civil Procedure (Amendment No.3) Rules 2000 (SI 2000/1317) and the Civil Procedure (Amendment) Rules 2002 (SI 2002/2058).

officer until the question of costs of the detailed assessment proceedings falls to be decided.

(The costs practice direction provides that rule 47.19 does not apply where the receiving party is a LSC funded client or an assisted person, unless the court orders otherwise.)

Comment

The *Calderbank* procedure is retained in respect of the costs of detailed assessment proceedings. Either party may make a written offer and the court will take that offer into account in deciding who should pay the costs of the detailed assessment proceedings. **47.19.1**

See s.46 of the Costs Practice Direction in relation to such offers.

The rule does not apply where the receiving party is a LSC funded client or an assisted person, unless the court orders otherwise.

Technically speaking an offer made in these circumstances is not a Pt 36 offer. Note that r.36.19(1) does not prohibit the communication of the fact that an offer has been made as r.47.19(2) does. As to such offers in costs only proceedings, see para.44.12A.3.

Rule 47.19

The Costs Judge was right to consider the only offer which had been made which complied with r.47.19 and s.46 of the Costs Practice Direction in deciding what decision to reach in respect of the costs of detailed assessment and to ignore other offers which did not comply with those provisions: *Wills v Crown Estate Commissioners* [2003] EWHC 1718 (Ch), Peter Smith J. **47.19.2**

Privy Council

After a detailed assessment in the Privy Council the Judicial Taxing Officer had to deal with the fact that the paying party had made a written offer followed by an oral offer. The bill had been reduced to a figure between the two. The decision of the Judicial Taxing Officer was appealed and was considered by the Law Lords. Lord Hope of Craighead stated: **47.19.3**

> "The oral offer did not meet the requirements of CPR rule 47.19(1) as it was not made in writing, and it was not renewed after the expiry of the time limit to which it was made subject. It is true that the total amount which the Costs Judge allowed after taxation was substantially less than that claimed in the bill of costs. But that result was due as much to the disallowance of several large amounts as a whole as it was to the product of a detailed assessment. Their Lordships consider that, in the circumstances, this was not in itself a sufficient reason for holding that the appellant was not entitled to the costs of the taxation." *Horsford v Bird* [2006] UKPC 55.

VIII. Appeals from Authorised Court Officers in Detailed Assessment Proceedings

Right to appeal[1]

47.20—(1) Any party to detailed assessment proceedings may appeal against a decision of an authorised court officer in those *proceedings*. **47.20**

(2) For the purpose of this Section, a LSC funded client or an assisted person is not a party to detailed assessment proceedings.

(Part 52 sets out general rules about appeals)

[1] Amended by the Civil Procedure (Amendment No.2) Rules 2000 (SI 2000/940), the Civil Procedure (Amendment No.3) Rules 2000 (SI 2000/1317) and the Civil Procedure (Amendment No.4) Rules 2003 (SI 2003/2113).

Comment

47.20.1 As to appeals in both summary assessment and detailed assessment the provisions of Pt 52 apply. Appeals from costs judges and district judges of the High Court are to a High Court Judge; appeals from district judges of the County Court are to a Circuit Judge. See Access to Justice Act 1999 (Destination of Appeals) Order 2000. Permission is not required for an appeal from an authorised court officer to a costs judge or district judge of the High Court. Permission is required to appeal from a decision of a costs judge or district judge in such proceedings to a High Court Judge. *Tanfern Ltd v Cameron-MacDonald* [2000] 1 W.L.R. 1311, CA. See also *Dooley v Parker (Costs)*, [2002] EWCA Civ 1188. Rule 52.4(2) provides that the appellant must file the appellant's notice at the Appeal Court within such period as may be directed by the lower court, or where that court makes no such direction, 14 days after the date of the decision of the lower court that the appellant wishes to appeal. In detailed assessment proceedings the 14 days starts from the date of the particular decision complained of, even if the detailed assessment hearing continues over a number of days. The time does not run from the conclusion of the detailed assessment hearing: *Kasir v Darlington & Simpson Rolls Mills Ltd* [2001] 2 Costs L.R. 228, Popplewell J.

Where the High Court Judge refuses permission to appeal from a Costs Judge, the Court of Appeal has no jurisdiction to hear an appeal from that refusal, although the Court of Appeal could grant permission for an appeal from that part of the High Court Judge's order dealing with the summary assessment of costs: *Riniker v University College London* [2001] 1 W.L.R. 13, CA.

The High Court has jurisdiction to re-open an appeal that it has already determined so as to avoid real injustice in exceptional circumstances. The power will only be used where it is clearly established that a significant injustice has probably occurred and there is no alternative effective remedy: *Seray-Wurie v Hackney LBC* [2002] EWCA Civ 909; [2002] 3 All E.R. 448, CA.

The proper approach of the court to an appeal from a Costs Judge was considered by Buckley J. in *Mealing McLeod v Common Professional Examination Board (Assessment of Costs)* [2000] 2 Costs L.R. 223, March 30, 2000:

> "Broadly speaking a judge will allow an appeal ... if satisfied that the decision of the Costs Judge was wrong ... that is easy to apply to matters of principle or construction. However where the appeal includes challenges to the details of the assessment, such as hours allowed in respect of a particular item, the task in hand is one of assessment or judgment, rather than principle. There is no absolute answer. Notwithstanding that the judge to whom the appeal is made may sit with assessors ... the appeal is not a re-hearing and, given the nature of the Costs Judge's task and his expertise, I would usually regard it as undesirable for it to be so ... [S]ince the appeal is not a re-hearing I would regard it as inappropriate for the judge on appeal to be drawn into an exercise calculated to add a little here or knock off a little there. If the judge's attention is drawn to items which, with the advice of his assessors, he feels should in fairness be altered, doubtless he will act. That is a matter for his good judgment. Permission to appeal should not be granted simply to allow yet another trawl through the bill, in the absence of some sensible and significant complaint. If an appeal turns out to be no more than such an exercise the sanction of costs may be used."

In family proceedings (governed by the Family Proceedings Rules 1991) an appeal arising out of assessment of costs is dealt with under rr.47.20 to 47.23 where the appeal is against a decision of an authorised court officer and under Pt 52 in any other case: Family Proceedings (Amendment) Rules 2003 (SI 2003/184). The Access to Justice Act 1999 (Destination of Appeals) (Family Proceedings) Order 2005 (SI 2005/3276) provides different routes for appeals against decisions made in relation to adoption. In particular appeals from decisions by a District Judge of a County Court lie to a judge of that court, and appeals from decisions made by a District Judge of the High Court or of the Principal Registry of the Family Division or a Costs Judge lie to the High Court. These provisions apply to appeals in which notice is lodged after December 30, 2005.

Following a detailed assessment Holland J. gave permission to appeal and ordered a complete rehearing. The judge had however been seriously misled by the papers put before him. The Court of Appeal found that had he not been misled he would never have given permission to appeal and would certainly not have ordered a complete rehearing. In a separate application the paying party applied to amend their points of dispute. Treacy J. granted the application after brief argument. The Court of Appeal found that he could not possibly have known, by reference to the whole history of the proceedings, how great the expansion of the argument would be and how unfair it would be to the receiving party at this late stage, the paying party having deliberately drafted the points of dispute in their original narrow terms despite warnings from HHJ Seymour Q.C. and Master Seager Berry. The rulings of Treacy J. were set aside and the court then had to consider whether it had the power to revoke the permission to appeal granted by Holland J. The court was persuaded, by reference to CPR 52.10, that it had the power to revoke the grant of permission and did so: *Angel Airlines SA v Dean & Dean Solicitors* [2006] EWCA Civ 1505.

Court to hear appeal[1]

47.21 An appeal against a decision of an authorised court officer is to a costs judge or a district judge of the High Court. **47.21**

Comment

All appeals are to a judge of the next tier. Appeals from an authorised court officer go to a costs judge or district judge. At the time of writing authorised court officers only exist in the Supreme Court Costs Office. The Lord Chancellor has the power to appoint authorised court officers in any court. **47.21.1**

Appeal procedure[2]

47.22—(1) The appellant must file an appeal notice within 21 days after the date of the decision he wishes to appeal against. **47.22**

(2) On receipt of the appeal notice, the court will—

(a) serve a copy of the notice on the parties to the detailed assessment proceedings; and

(b) give notice of the appeal to those parties.

Comment

The party wishing to appeal must file an appeal notice within 21 days—there is no requirement to obtain permission or reasons but see s.48 of the Costs Paractice Direction as to providing a note of the decision. **47.22.1**

Powers of the court on appeal[3]

47.23 On an appeal from an authorised court officer the court will— **47.23**

(a) re-hear the proceedings which gave rise to the decision appealed against; and

(b) make any order and give any directions as it considers appropriate.

Comment

An appeal from an authorised court officer is a re-hearing and the court may make any order and give directions as it considers appropriate. **47.23.1**

---

[1] Amended by the Civil Procedure (Amendment No.2) Rules 2000 (SI 2000/940).

[2] Amended by the Civil Procedure (Amendment No.2) Rules 2000 (SI 2000/940), the Civil Procedure (Amendment No.3) Rules 2000 (SI 2000/1317) and the Civil Procedure (Amendment) Rules 2007 (SI 2007/2204).

[3] Amended by the Civil Procedure (Amendment No.2) Rules 2000 (SI 2000/940).

PRACTICE DIRECTIONS RELATING TO PART 47—PROCEDURE FOR DETAILED ASSESSMENT OF COSTS AND DEFAULT PROVISIONS

Section 28 Time when assessment may be carried out: Rule 47.1

47PD.1 **28.1**(1) For the purposes of rule 47.1, proceedings are concluded when the court has finally determined the matters in issue in the claim, whether or not there is an appeal.

(2) For the purposes of this rule, the making of an award of provisional damages under Part 41 will be treated as a final determination of the matters in issue.

(3) The court may order or the parties may agree in writing that, although the proceedings are continuing, they will nevertheless be treated as concluded.

(a) A party who is served with a notice of commencement (see paragraph 32.3 below) may apply to a costs judge or a district judge to determine whether the party who served it is entitled to commence detailed assessment proceedings.

(b) On hearing such an application the orders which the court may make include: an order allowing the detailed assessment proceedings to continue, or an order setting aside the notice of commencement.

(5) A costs judge or a district judge may make an order allowing detailed assessment proceedings to be commenced where there is no realistic prospect of the claim continuing.

Section 29 No stay of detailed assessment where there is an appeal: Rule 47.2

47PD.2 **29.1**(1) Rule 47.2 provides that detailed assessment is not stayed pending an appeal unless the court so orders.

(2) An application to stay the detailed assessment of costs pending an appeal may be made to the court whose order is being appealed or to the court who will hear the appeal.

Section 30 Powers of an authorised court officer: Rule 47.3

47PD.3 **30.1**(1) The court officers authorised by the Lord Chancellor to assess costs in the Supreme Court Costs Office and the Principal Registry of the Family Division are authorised to deal with claims for costs not exceeding £30,000 (excluding VAT) in the case of senior executive officers or their equivalent and £75,000 (excluding VAT) in the case of principal officers.

(2) In calculating whether or not a bill of costs is within the authorised amounts, the figure to be taken into account is the total claim for costs including any additional liability.

(3) Where the receiving party, paying party and any other party to the detailed assessment proceedings who has served points of dispute are agreed that the assessment *should not* be made by an authorised court officer, the receiving party should so inform the court when requesting a hearing date. The court will then list the hearing before a costs judge or a district judge.

(4) In any other case a party who objects to the assessment being made by an authorised court officer must make an application to the costs judge or district judge under Part 23 (General Rules about Applications for Court Orders) setting out the reasons for the objection and if sufficient reason is shown the court will direct that the bill be assessed by a costs judge or district judge.

Section 31 Venue for detailed assessment proceedings: Rule 47.4

31.1 For the purposes of rule 47.4(1) the "appropriate office" means **47PD.4**

(1) the district registry or county court in which the case was being dealt with when the judgment or order was made or the event occurred which gave rise to the right to assessment, or to which it has subsequently been transferred;

(1A) where a tribunal, person or other body makes an order for the detailed assessment of costs, a county court (subject to paragraph 31.1A(1)); or

(2) in all other cases including Court of Appeal cases, the Supreme Court Costs Office.

31.1A(1) This paragraph applies where the appropriate office is any of the following county courts:

Barnet, Bow, Brentford, Bromley, Central London, Clerkenwell, Croydon, Edmonton, Ilford, Kingston, Lambeth, Mayors and City of London, Romford, Shoreditch, Uxbridge, Wandsworth, West London, Willesden and Woolwich.

(2) Where this paragraph applies:—

(i) the receiving party must file any request for a detailed assessment hearing in the Supreme Court Costs Office and, for all purposes relating to that detailed assessment, the Supreme Court Costs Office will be treated as the appropriate office in that case; and

(ii) unless an order is made under rule 47.4(2) directing that the Supreme Court Costs Office as part of the High Court shall be the appropriate office, an appeal from any decision made by a costs judge shall lie to the Designated Civil Judge for the London Group of County Courts or such judge as he shall nominate. The appeal notice and any other relevant papers should be lodged at the Central London Civil Justice *Centre*.

31.2(1) A direction under rule 47.4(2) or (3) specifying a particular court, registry or office as the appropriate office may be given on application or on the court's own initiative.

(2) Before making such a direction on its own initiative the court will give the parties the opportunity to make representations.

(3) Unless the Supreme Court Costs Office is the appropriate

office for the purposes of Rule 47.4(1) an order directing that an assessment is to take place at the Supreme Court Costs Office will be made only if it is appropriate to do so having regard to the size of the bill of costs, the difficulty of the issues involved, the likely length of the hearing, the cost to the parties and any other relevant matter.

Section 32 Commencement of detailed assessment proceedings: Rule 47.6

47PD.5 **32.1** Precedents A, B, C and D in the Schedule of Costs Precedents annexed to this Practice Direction are model forms of bills of costs for detailed assessment. Further information about bills of costs is set out in Section 4.

32.2 A detailed assessment may be in respect of:

(1) base costs, where a claim for additional liability has not been made or has been agreed;

(2) a claim for additional liability only, base costs having been summarily assessed or agreed; or

(3) both base costs and additional liability.

32.3 If the detailed assessment is in respect of costs without any additional liability, the receiving party must serve on the paying party and all the other relevant persons the following documents:

(a) a notice of commencement;

(b) a copy of the bill of costs;

(c) copies of the fee notes of counsel and of any expert in respect of fees claimed in the bill;

(d) written evidence as to any other disbursement which is claimed and which exceeds £250;

(e) a statement giving the name and address for service of any person upon whom the receiving party intends to serve the notice of commencement.

32.4 If the detailed assessment is in respect of an additional liability only, the receiving party must serve on the paying party and all other relevant persons the following documents:

(a) a notice of commencement;

(b) a copy of the bill of costs;

(c) the relevant details of the additional liability;

(d) a statement giving the name and address of any person upon whom the receiving party intends to serve the notice of commencement.

32.5 The relevant details of an additional liability are as follows:

(1) In the case of a conditional fee agreement with a success fee:

(a) a statement showing the amount of costs which have been summarily assessed or agreed, and the percentage increase which has been claimed in respect of those costs;

(b) a statement of the reasons for the percentage increase given in accordance with Regulation 3(1)(a) of the Conditional Fee Agreements Regulations or Regulation 5(1)(c) of the Collective Conditional Fee Agreements Regulations 2000. [Both sets of regulations were revoked by the Conditional Fee Agreements (Revocation) Regulations 2005 but continue to have effect in relation to conditional fee agreements and collective conditional fee agreements entered into before 1st November 2005.]

(2) If the additional liability is an insurance premium: a copy of the insurance certificate showing whether the policy covers the receiving party's own costs; his opponent's costs; or his own costs and his opponent's costs; and the maximum extent of that cover, and the amount of the premium paid or payable.

(3) If the receiving party claims an additional amount under Section 30 of the Access of Justice Act 1999: a statement setting out the basis upon which the receiving party's liability for the additional amount is calculated.

32.6 Attention is drawn to the fact that the additional amount recoverable pursuant to section 30 of the Access to Justice Act 1999: in respect of a membership organisation must not exceed the likely cost of the premium of an insurance policy against the risk of incurring a liability to pay the costs of other parties to the proceedings as provided by the Access to Justice (Membership Organisation) Regulations 2000 Regulation 4 (for the purposes of arrangements entered into before 1st November 2005) and The Access to Justice (Membership Organisation) Regulations 2005 Regulation 5 (for the purposes of arrangements entered into on or after 1st November 2005).

32.7 If a detailed assessment is in respect of both base costs and an additional liability, the receiving party must serve on the paying party and all other relevant persons the documents listed in paragraph 32.3 and the documents giving relevant details of an additional liability listed in paragraph 32.5.

32.8(1) The Notice of Commencement should be in Form **N252**.

(2) Before it is served, it must be completed to show as separate items;

(a) the total amount of the costs claimed in the bill;

(b) the extra sum which will be payable by way of fixed costs and court fees if a default costs certificate is obtained.

32.9(1) This paragraph applies where the notice of commencement is to be served outside England and Wales.

(2) The date to be inserted in the notice of commencement for the paying party to send points of dispute is a date (not less than 21 days from the date of service of the notice) which must be calculated by reference to Section IV of Part 6 as if the notice were a claim form and as if the *date to be inserted* was the date for the filing of a defence.

32.10(1) For the purposes of rule 47.6(2) a "relevant person" means:

(a) any person who has taken part in the proceedings which gave rise to the assessment and who is directly liable under an order for costs made against him;

(b) any person who has given to the receiving party notice in writing that he has a financial interest in the outcome of the assessment and wishes to be a party accordingly;

(c) any other person whom the court orders to be treated as such.

(2) Where a party is unsure whether a person is or is not a relevant person, that party may apply to the appropriate office for directions.

(3) The court will generally not make an order that the person in respect of whom the application is made will be treated as a relevant person, unless within a specified time he applies to the court to be joined as a party to the assessment proceedings in accordance with Part 19 (Parties and Group Litigation).

32.11(1) This paragraph applies in cases in which the bill of costs is capable of being copied onto a computer disk.

(2) If, before the detailed assessment hearing, a paying party requests a disk copy of a bill to which this paragraph applies, the receiving party must supply him with a copy free of charge not more than 7 days after the date on which he received the request.

Section 33 Period for commencing detailed assessment proceedings: Rule 47.7

47PD.6 **33.1** The parties may agree under rule 2.11 (Time limits may be varied by parties) to extend or shorten the time specified by rule 47.7 for commencing the detailed assessment proceedings.

33.2 A party may apply to the appropriate office for an order under rule 3.1(2)(a) to extend or shorten that time.

33.3 Attention is drawn to rule 47.6(1). The detailed assessment proceedings are commenced by service of the documents referred to.

33.4 Permission to commence assessment proceedings out of time is not required.

Section 34 Sanction for delay in commencing detailed assessment proceedings: Rule 47.8

47PD.7 **34.1**(1) An application for an order under rule 47.8 must be made in writing and be issued in the appropriate office.

(2) The application notice must be served at least 7 days before the hearing.

Section 35 Points of dispute and consequences of not serving: Rule 47.9

47PD.8 **35.1** The parties may agree under rule 2.11 (Time limits may be varied by parties) to extend or shorten the time specified by rule 47.9 for service of points of dispute. A party may apply to the appropriate office for an order under rule 3.1(2)(a) to extend or shorten that time.

*35.2 Points of dispute sho*uld be short and to the point and should follow as closely as possible Precedent G of the Schedule of Costs Precedents annexed to this Practice Direction.

35.3 Points of dispute must—

(1) identify each item in the bill of costs which is disputed,
(2) in each case state concisely the nature and grounds of dispute,
(3) where practicable suggest a figure to be allowed for each item in respect of which a reduction is sought, and
(4) be signed by the party serving them or his solicitor.

35.4(1) The normal period for serving points of dispute is 21 days after the date of service of the notice of commencement.
(2) Where a notice of commencement is served on a party outside England and Wales the period within which that party should serve points of dispute is to be calculated by reference to Section IV of Part 6 as if the notice of commencement was a claim form and as if the period for serving points of dispute were the period for filing a defence.

35.5 A party who serves points of dispute on the receiving party must at the same time serve a copy on every other party to the detailed assessment proceedings, whose name and address for service appears on the statement served by the receiving party in accordance with paragraph 32.3 or 32.4 above.

35.6(1) This paragraph applies in cases in which Points of Dispute are capable of being copied onto a computer disk.
(2) If, within 14 days of the receipt of the Points of Dispute, the receiving party requests a disk copy of them, the paying party must supply him with a copy free of charge not more than 7 days after the date on which he received the request.

35.7(1) Where the receiving party claims an additional liability, a party who serves points of dispute on the receiving party may include a request for information about other methods of financing costs which were available to the receiving party.
(2) Part 18 (further information) and the Practice Direction Supplementing that part apply to such a request.

Section 36 Procedure where costs are agreed: Rule 47.10

36.1 Where the parties have agreed terms as to the issue of a costs certificate (either interim or final) they should apply under rule 40.6 (Consent judgments and orders) for an order that a certificate be issued in terms set out in the application. Such an application may be dealt with by a court officer, who may issue the certificate. **47PD.9**

36.2 Where in the course of proceedings the receiving party claims that the paying party has agreed to pay costs but that he will neither pay those costs nor join in a consent application under paragraph 36.1, the receiving party may apply under Part 23 (General Rules about Applications for Court Orders) for a certificate either interim or final to be issued.

36.3 An application under paragraph 36.2 must be supported by evidence and will be heard by a costs judge or a district judge. The respondent to the application must file and serve any evidence he relies on at least two days before the hearing date.

36.4 Nothing in rule 47.10 prevents parties who seek a judgment or order by consent from including in the draft a term that a party shall pay to another party a specified sum in respect of costs.

36.5(1) The receiving party may discontinue the detailed assessment proceedings in accordance with Part 38 (Discontinuance).

(2) Where the receiving party discontinues the detailed assessment proceedings before a detailed assessment hearing has been requested, the paying party may apply to the appropriate office for an order about the costs of the detailed assessment proceedings.

(3) Where a detailed assessment hearing has been requested the receiving party may not discontinue unless the court gives permission.

(4) A bill of costs may be withdrawn by consent whether or not a detailed assessment hearing has been requested.

Section 37 Default costs certificate: Rule 47.11

47PD.10 **37.1**(1) A request for the issue of a default costs certificate must be made in Form **N254** and must be signed by the receiving party or his solicitor.

(2) The request must be accompanied by a copy of the document giving the right to detailed assessment. (Section 40.4 of the Costs Practice Direction identifies the appropriate documents).

37.2 The request must be filed at the appropriate office.

37.3 A default costs certificate will be in Form **N255**.

37.4 Attention is drawn to Rules 40.3 (Drawing up and Filing of Judgments and Orders) and 40.4 (Service of Judgments and Orders) which apply to the preparation and service of a default costs certificate. The receiving party will be treated as having permission to draw up a default costs certificate by virtue of this Practice Direction.

37.5 The issue of a default costs certificate does not prohibit, govern or affect any detailed assessment of the same costs which are payable out of the Community Legal Service Fund.

37.6 An application for an order staying enforcement of a default costs certificate may be made either—

(1) to a costs judge or district judge of the court office which issued the certificate; or

(2) to the court (if different) which has general jurisdiction to enforce the certificate.

37.7 Proceedings for enforcement of default costs certificates may not be issued in the Supreme Court Costs Office.

37.8 The fixed costs payable in respect of solicitor's charges on the issue of the default costs certificate are £80.

Section 38 Setting aside default costs certificate: Rule 47.12

47PD.11 **38.1**(1) A court officer may set aside a default costs certificate at the request of the receiving party under rule 47.12(3).

(2) A costs judge or a district judge will make any other order or give any directions under this rule.

38.2(1) An application for an order under rule 47.12(2) to set aside or vary a default costs certificate must be supported by evidence.

(2) In deciding whether to set aside or vary a certificate under rule 47.12(2) the matters to which the court must have regard include whether the party seeking the order made the application promptly.

(3) As a general rule a default costs certificate will be set aside under rule 47.12(2) only if the applicant shows a good reason for the court to do so and if he files with his application a copy of the bill and a copy of the default costs certificate, and a draft of the points of dispute he proposes to serve if his application is granted.

38.3(1) Attention is drawn to rule 3.1(3) (which enables the court when making an order to make it subject to conditions) and to rule 44.3(8) (which enables the court to order a party whom it has ordered to pay costs to pay an amount on account before the costs are assessed).

(2) A costs judge or a district judge may exercise the power of the court to make an order under rule 44.3(8) although he did not make the order about costs which led to the issue of the default costs certificate.

38.4 If a default costs certificate is set aside the court will give directions for the management of the detailed assessment proceedings.

Section 39 Optional reply: Rule 47.13

39.1(1) Where the receiving party wishes to serve a reply, he must also serve a copy on every other party to the detailed assessment proceedings. The time for doing so is within 21 days after service of the points of dispute. **47PD.12**

(2) A reply means:

(i) a separate document prepared by the receiving party; or

(ii) his written comments added to the points of dispute.

(3) A reply must be signed by the party serving it or his solicitor.

Section 40 Detailed assessment hearing: Rule 47.14

40.1 The time for requesting a detailed assessment hearing is within 3 months of the expiry of the period for commencing detailed assessment proceedings. **47PD.13**

40.2 The request for a detailed assessment hearing must be in Form **N258**. The request must be accompanied by:

(a) a copy of the notice of commencement of detailed assessment proceedings;

(b) a copy of the bill of costs,

(c) the document giving the right to detailed assessment (see paragraph 40.4 below);

(d) a copy of the points of dispute, annotated as necessary in order to show which items have been agreed and their value and to show which items remain in dispute and their value;

(e) as many copies of the points of dispute so annotated as there are persons who have served points of dispute;

(f) a copy of any replies served;

(g) a copy of all orders made by the court relating to the costs which are to be assessed;

(h) copies of the fee notes and other written evidence as served on the paying party in accordance with paragraph 32.3 above;

(i) where there is a dispute as to the receiving party's liability to pay costs to the solicitors who acted for the receiving party, any agreement, letter or other written information provided by the solicitor to his client explaining how the solicitor's charges are to be calculated;

(j) a statement signed by the receiving party or his solicitor giving the name, address for service, reference and telephone number and fax number, if any, of –

(i) the receiving party;

(ii) the paying party;

(iii) any other person who has served points of dispute or who has given notice to the receiving party under paragraph 32.10(1)(b) above;

and giving an estimate of the length of time the detailed assessment hearing will take;

(k) where the application for a detailed assessment hearing is made by a party other than the receiving party, such of the documents set out in this paragraph as are in the possession of that party;

(l) where the court is to assess the costs of an assisted person or LSC funded client –

(i) the legal aid certificate, LSC certificate and relevant amendment certificates, any authorities and any certificates of discharge or revocation;

(ii) a certificate, in Precedent F(3) of the Schedule of Costs Precedents;

(iii) if the assisted person has a financial interest in the detailed assessment hearing and wishes to attend, the postal address of that person to which the court will send notice of any hearing;

(iv) if the rates payable out of the LSC fund are prescribed rates, a schedule to the bill of costs setting out all the items in the bill which are claimed against other parties calculated at the legal aid prescribed rates with or without any claim for enhancement: (further information as to this schedule is set out in Section 48 of this Practice Direction);

(v) a copy of any default costs certificate in respect of costs claimed in the bill of costs.

40.3(1) This paragraph applies to any document described in paragraph 40.2(i) above which the receiving party has filed in the appropriate office. The document must be the latest relevant version and in any event have been filed not more than 2 years before filing the request for a detailed assessment hearing.

(2) In respect of any documents to which this paragraph applies, the receiving party may, instead of filing a copy of it, specify in the request for a detailed assessment hearing the case number under which a copy of the document was previously filed.

40.4 "The document giving the right to detailed assessment" means such one or more of the following documents as are appropriate to the detailed assessment proceedings:

(a) a copy of the judgment or order of the court giving the right to detailed assessment;

(b) a copy of the notice served under rule 3.7 (sanctions for non-payment of certain fees) where a claim is struck out under that rule;

(c) a copy of the notice of acceptance where an offer to settle is accepted under Part 36 (Offers to settle);

(d) a copy of the notice of discontinuance in a case which is discontinued under Part 38 (Discontinuance);

(e) a copy of the award made on an arbitration under any Act or pursuant to an agreement, where no court has made an order for the enforcement of the award;

(f) a copy of the order, award or determination of a statutorily constituted tribunal or body;

(g) in a case under the Sheriffs Act 1887, the sheriff's bill of fees and charges, unless a court order giving the right to detailed assessment has been made;

(h) a notice of revocation or discharge under Regulation 82 of the Civil Legal Aid (General) Regulations 1989.

(i) In the county courts certain Acts and Regulations provide for costs incurred in proceedings under those Acts and Regulations to be assessed in the county court if so ordered on application. Where such an application is made, a copy of the order.

40.5 On receipt of the request for a detailed assessment hearing the court will fix a date for the hearing, or, if the costs officer so decides, will give directions or fix a date for a preliminary appointment.

40.6(1) The court will give at least 14 days' notice of the time and place of the detailed assessment hearing to every person named in the statement referred to in paragraph 40.2(j) above.

(2) The court will when giving notice, give each person who has served points of dispute a copy of the points of dispute annotated by the receiving party in compliance with paragraph 40.2(d) above.

(3) Attention is drawn to rule 47.14(6) & (7): apart from the receiving party, only those who have served points of

dispute may be heard on the detailed assessment unless the court gives permission, and only items specified in the points of dispute may be raised unless the court gives permission.

40.7(1) If the receiving party does not file a request for a detailed assessment hearing within the prescribed time, the paying party may apply to the court to fix a time within which the receiving party must do so. The sanction, for failure to commence detailed assessment proceedings within the time specified by the court, is that all or part of the costs may be disallowed (see rule 47.8(2)).

(2) Where the receiving party commences detailed assessment proceedings after the time specified in the rules but before the paying party has made an application to the court to specify a time, the only sanction which the court may impose is to disallow all or part of the interest which would otherwise be payable for the period of delay, unless the court exercises its powers under rule 44.14 (court's powers in relation to misconduct).

40.8 If either party wishes to make an application in the detailed assessment proceedings the provisions of Part 23 (General Rules about Applications for Court Orders) apply.

40.9(1) This paragraph deals with the procedure to be adopted where a date has been given by the court for a detailed assessment hearing and

(a) the detailed assessment proceedings are settled; or

(b) a party to the detailed assessment proceedings wishes to apply to vary the date which the court has fixed; or

(c) the parties to the detailed assessment proceedings agree about changes they wish to make to any direction given for the management of the detailed assessment proceedings.

(2) If detailed assessment proceedings are settled, the receiving party must give notice of that fact to the court immediately, preferably by fax.

(3) A party who wishes to apply to vary a direction must do so in accordance with Part 23 (General Rules about Applications for Court Orders).

(4) If the parties agree about changes they wish to make to any direction given for the management of the detailed assessment proceedings—

(a) they must apply to the court for an order by consent; and

(b) they must file a draft of the directions sought and an agreed statement of the reasons why the variation is sought; and

(c) the court may make an order in the agreed terms or in other terms without a hearing, but it may direct that a hearing is to be listed.

40.10(1) If a party wishes to vary his bill of costs, points of dispute or a reply, an amended or supplementary document must be filed with the court and copies of it must be served on all other relevant parties.

(2) Permission is not required to vary a bill of costs, points of dispute or a reply but the court may disallow the variation or permit it only upon conditions, including conditions as to the payment of any costs caused or wasted by the variation.

40.11 Unless the court directs otherwise the receiving party must file with the court the papers in support of the bill not less than 7 days before the date for the detailed assessment hearing and not more than 14 days before that date.

40.12 The following provisions apply in respect of the papers to be filed in support of the bill;

(a) If the claim is for costs only without any additional liability the papers to be filed, and the order in which they are to be arranged are as follows:

(i) instructions and briefs to counsel arranged in chronological order together with all advices, opinions and drafts received and response to such instructions;

(ii) reports and opinions of medical and other experts;

(iii) any other relevant papers;

(iv) a full set of any relevant pleadings to the extent that they have not already been filed in court;

(v) correspondence, files and attendance notes;

(b) where the claim is in respect of an additional liability only, such of the papers listed at (a) above, as are relevant to the issues raised by the claim for additional liability;

(c) where the claim is for both base costs and an additional liability, the papers listed at (a) above, together with any papers relevant to the issues raised by the claim for additional liability.

40.13 The provisions set out in Section 20 of this Practice Direction apply where the court disallows any amount of a legal representative's percentage increase, and the legal representative applies for an order that the disallowed amount should continue to be payable by the client in accordance with Rule 44.16.

40.14 The court may direct the receiving party to produce any document which in the opinion of the court is necessary to enable it to reach its decision. These documents will in the first instance be *produced to* the court, but the court may ask the receiving party to elect whether to disclose the particular document to the paying party in order to rely on the contents of the document, or whether to decline disclosure and instead rely on other evidence.

40.15 Costs assessed at a detailed assessment at the conclusion of proceedings may include an assessment of any additional liability in respect of the costs of a previous application or hearing.

40.16 Once the detailed assessment hearing has ended it is the responsibility of the legal representative appearing for the receiving party or, as the case may be, the receiving party in person to remove the papers filed in support of the bill.

Section 41 Power to issue an interim certificate: Rule 47.15

47PD.14 **41.1**(1) A party wishing to apply for an interim certificate may do so by making an application in accordance with Part 23 (General Rules about Applications for Court Orders).

(2) Attention is drawn to the fact that the court's power to issue an interim certificate arises only after the receiving party has filed a request for a detailed assessment hearing.

Section 42 Final costs certificate: Rule 47.16

47PD.15 **42.1** At the detailed assessment hearing the court will indicate any disallowance or reduction in the sums claimed in the bill of costs by making an appropriate note on the bill.

42.2 The receiving party must, in order to complete the bill after the detailed assessment hearing make clear the correct figures agreed or allowed in respect of each item and must re-calculate the summary of the bill appropriately.

42.3 The completed bill of costs must be filed with the court no later than 14 days after the detailed assessment hearing.

42.4 At the same time as filing the completed bill of costs, the party whose bill it is must also produce receipted fee notes and receipted accounts in respect of all disbursements except those covered by a certificate in Precedent F(5) in the Schedule of Costs Precedents annexed to this Practice Direction.

42.5 No final costs certificate will be issued until all relevant court fees payable on the assessment of costs have been paid.

42.6 If the receiving party fails to file a completed bill in accordance with rule 47.16 the paying party may make an application under Part 23 (General Rules about Applications for Court Orders) seeking an appropriate order under rule 3.1 (The court's general powers of management).

42.7 A final costs certificate will show:

(a) the amount of any costs which have been agreed between the parties or which have been allowed on detailed assessment;

(b) where applicable the amount agreed or allowed in respect of VAT on the costs agreed or allowed.

This provision is subject to any contrary provision made by the statutory provisions relating to costs payable out of the Community Legal Service Fund.

42.8 A final costs certificate will include disbursements in respect of the fees of counsel only if receipted fee notes or accounts in respect of those disbursements have been produced to the court and only to the extent indicated by those receipts.

42.9 Where the certificate relates to costs payable between parties a separate certificate will be issued for each party entitled to costs.

42.10 Form **N257** is a model form of interim costs certificate and Form **N256** is a model form of final costs certificate.

42.11 An application for an order staying enforcement of an interim costs certificate or final costs certificate may be made either:

(1) to a costs judge or district judge of the court office which issued the certificate; or

(2) to the court (if different) which has general jurisdiction to enforce the certificate.

42.12 Proceedings for enforcement of interim costs certificates or final costs certificates may not be issued in the Supreme Court Costs Office.

Section 43 Detailed assessment procedure where costs are payable out of the community legal service fund: Rule 47.17

43.1 The provisions of this section apply where the court is to assess costs which are payable only out of the community legal service fund. Paragraphs 39.1 to 40.16 and 49.1 to 49.8 apply in cases involving costs payable by another person as well as costs payable only out of the community legal service fund. **47PD.16**

43.2 The time for requesting a detailed assessment under rule 47.17 is within 3 months after the date when the right to detailed assessment arose.

43.3 The request for a detailed assessment of costs must be in Form **N258A**. The request must be accompanied by:

(a) a copy of the bill of costs;

(b) the document giving the right to detailed assessment (for further information as to this document, see paragraph 40.4 above);

(c) a copy of all orders made by the court relating to the costs which are to be assessed;

(d) copies of any fee notes of counsel and any expert in respect of fees claimed in the bill;

(e) written evidence as to any other disbursement which is claimed and which exceeds £250;

(f) the legal aid certificates, LSC certificates, any relevant amendment certificates, any authorities and any certificates of discharge or revocation;

(g) In the Supreme Court Costs Office the relevant papers in support of the bill as described in paragraph 40.12 above; in cases proceeding in District Registries and county courts this provision does not apply and the papers should only be lodged if requested by the costs officer.

(h) a statement signed by the solicitor giving his name, address for service, reference, telephone number, fax *number and, if* the assisted person has a financial interest in the detailed assessment and wishes to attend, giving the postal address of that person, to which the court will send notice of any hearing.

43.4 Rule 47.17 provides that the court will hold a detailed assessment hearing if the assisted person has a financial interest in the detailed assessment and wishes to attend. The court may also hold a detailed assessment hearing in any other case, instead of provisionally assessing a bill of costs, where it considers that a hearing is necessary. Before deciding whether a hearing is necessary under this rule, the court may require the solicitor whose bill it is, to provide further information relating to the bill.

43.5 Where the court has provisionally assessed a bill of costs it will send to the solicitor a notice, in Form **N253** annexed to this practice direction, of the amount of costs which the court proposes to allow together with the bill itself. The legal representative should, if the provisional assessment is to be accepted, then complete the bill.

43.6 The court will fix a date for a detailed assessment hearing if the solicitor informs the court within 14 days after he receives the notice of the amount allowed on the provisional assessment that he wants the court to hold such a hearing.

43.7 The court will give at least 14 days' notice of the time and place of the detailed assessment hearing to the solicitor and, if the assisted person has a financial interest in the detailed assessment and wishes to attend, to the assisted person.

43.8 If the solicitor whose bill it is, or any other party wishes to make an application in the detailed assessment proceedings, the provisions of Part 23 (General Rules about Applications for Court Orders) applies.

43.9 It is the responsibility of the legal representative to complete the bill by entering in the bill the correct figures allowed in respect of each item, recalculating the summary of the bill appropriately and completing the Community Legal Service assessment certificate (Form **EX80A**).

Section 44 Costs of detailed assessment proceedings where costs are payable out of a fund other than the Community Legal Service Fund: Rule 47.17A

47PD.17 **44.1** Rule 47.17A provides that the court will make a provisional assessment of a bill of costs payable out of a fund (other than the Community Legal Service Fund) unless it considers that a hearing is necessary. It also enables the court to direct under rule 47.17A(3) that the receiving party must serve a copy of the request for assessment and copies of the documents which accompany it, on any person who has a financial interest in the outcome of the assessment.

(a) A person has a financial interest in the outcome of the assessment if the assessment will or may affect the amount of money or property to which he is or may become entitled out of the fund.

(b) Where an interest in the fund is itself held by a trustee for the benefit of some other person, that trustee will be treated as the person having such a financial interest.

(c) 'Trustee' includes a personal representative, receiver or any other person acting in a fiduciary capacity.

44.3 The request for a detailed assessment of costs out of the fund should be in Form **N258B**, be accompanied by the documents set out at paragraph 43.3(a) to (e) and (g) above and the following;

(a) a statement signed by the receiving party giving his

name, address for service, reference, telephone number, fax number and,

(b) a statement of the postal address of any person who has a financial interest in the outcome of the assessment, to which the court may send notice of any hearing; and

(c) in respect of each person stated to have such an interest if such person is a child or protected party,a statement to that effect.

44.4 The court will decide, having regard to the amount of the bill, the size of the fund and the number of persons who have a financial interest, which of those persons should be served. The court may dispense with service on all or some of them.

44.5 Where the court makes an order dispensing with service on all such persons it may proceed at once to make a provisional assessment, or, if it decides that a hearing is necessary, give appropriate directions. Before deciding whether a hearing is necessary under this rule, the court may require the receiving party to provide further information relating to the bill.

44.6(1) Where the court has provisionally assessed a bill of costs, it will send to the receiving party, a notice in Form **N253** of the amount of costs which the court proposes to allow together with the bill itself. If the receiving party is legally represented the legal representative should, if the provisional assessment is to be accepted, then complete the bill.

(2) The court will fix a date for a detailed assessment hearing, if the receiving party informs the court within 14 days after he receives the notice in Form **N253** of the amount allowed on the provisional assessment, that he wants the court to hold such a hearing.

44.7 Where the court makes an order that a person who has a financial interest is to be served with a copy of the request for assessment, it may give directions about service and about the hearing.

44.8 The court will give at least 14 days' notice of the time and place of the detailed assessment hearing to the receiving party and, to any person who has a financial interest in the outcome of the assessment and has been served with a copy of the request for assessment.

44.9 If the receiving party, or any other party or any person who has a financial interest in the outcome of assessment, wishes to make an application in the detailed assessment proceedings, the provisions of Part 23 (General Rules about Applications for Court Orders) applies.

44.10 *If the receiving party* is legally represented the legal representative must in order to complete the bill after the assessment make clear the correct figures allowed in respect of each item and must recalculate the summary of the bill if appropriate.

Section 45 Liability for costs of detailed assessment proceedings: Rule 47.18

45.1 As a general rule the court will assess the receiving party's **47PD.18**

costs of the detailed assessment proceedings and add them to the bill of costs.

45.2 If the costs of the detailed assessment proceedings are awarded to the paying party, the court will either assess those costs by summary assessment or make an order for them to be decided by detailed assessment.

45.3 No party should file or serve a statement of costs of the detailed assessment proceedings unless the court orders him to do so.

45.4 Attention is drawn to the fact that in deciding what order to make about the costs of detailed assessment proceedings the court must have regard to the conduct of all parties, the amount by which the bill of costs has been reduced and whether it was reasonable for a party to claim the costs of a particular item or to dispute that item.

45.5(1) In respect of interest on the costs of detailed assessment proceedings, the interest shall begin to run from the date of the default, interim or final costs certificate as the case may be.

(2) This provision applies only to the costs of the detailed assessment proceedings themselves. The costs of the substantive proceedings are governed by rule 40.8(1).

Section 46 Offers to settle without prejudice save as to the costs of the detailed assessment proceedings: Rule 47.19

47PD.19 **46.1** Rule 47.19 allows the court to take into account offers to settle, without prejudice save as to the costs of detailed assessment proceedings, when deciding who is liable for the costs of those proceedings. The rule does not specify a time within which such an offer should be made. An offer made by the paying party should usually be made within 14 days after service of the notice of commencement on that party. If the offer is made by the receiving party, it should normally be made within 14 days after the service of points of dispute by the paying party. Offers made after these periods are likely to be given less weight by the court in deciding what order as to costs to make unless there is good reason for the offer not being made until the later time.

46.2 Where an offer to settle is made it should specify whether or not it is intended to be inclusive of the cost of preparation of the bill, interest and value added tax (VAT). The offer may include or exclude some or all of these items but the position must be made clear on the face of the offer so that the offeree is clear about the terms of the offer when it is being considered. Unless the offer states otherwise, the offer will be treated as being inclusive of all these items.

46.3 Where an offer to settle is accepted, an application may be made for a certificate in agreed terms, or the bill of costs may be withdrawn, in accordance with rule 47.10 (Procedure where costs are agreed).

46.4 Where the receiving party is an assisted person or an LSC funded client, an offer to settle without prejudice save as to the costs of the detailed assessment proceedings will not have the consequences specified under rule 47.19 unless the court so orders.

Section 47 Appeals from Authorised Court Officers in Detailed Assessment Proceedings—Right to Appeal: Rule 47.20

47.1 This Section and the next Section of this Practice Direction relate only to appeals from authorised court officers in detailed assessment proceedings. All other appeals arising out of detailed assessment proceedings (and arising out of summary assessments) are dealt with in accordance with Part 52 and the Practice Direction which supplements that Part. The destination of appeals is dealt with in accordance with the Access to Justice Act 1999 (Destination of Appeals) Order 2000. **47PD.20**

47.2 In respect of appeals from authorised court officers, there is no requirement to obtain permission, or to seek written reasons.

Section 48 Procedure on Appeal from Authorised Court Officers: Rule 47.22

48.1 The appellant must file a notice which should be in Form **N161**(an appellant's notice). **47PD.21**

48.2 The appeal will be heard by a costs judge or a district judge of the High Court, and is a re-hearing.

48.3 The appellant's notice should, if possible, be accompanied by a suitable record of the judgment appealed against. Where reasons given for the decision have been officially recorded by the court an approved transcript of that record should accompany the notice. Photocopies will not be accepted for this purpose. Where there is no official record the following documents will be acceptable:

(1) The officer's comments written on the bill.

(2) Advocates' notes of the reasons agreed by the respondent if possible and approved by the authorised court officer.

When the appellant was unrepresented before the authorised court officer, it is the duty of any advocate for the respondent to make his own note of the reasons promptly available, free of charge to the appellant where there is no official record or if the court so directs. Where the appellant was represented before the authorised court officer, it is the duty of his/her own former advocate to make his/her notes available. The appellant should submit the note of the reasons to the costs judge or district judge hearing the appeal.

48.4 The appellant may not be able to obtain a suitable record of the authorised court officer's decision within the time in which the appellant's notice must be filed. In such cases, the appellant's notice must still be completed to the best of the appellant's ability. It may however be amended subsequently with the permission of the costs judge or district judge hearing the appeal.

Section 49 Costs Payable By The LSC At Prescribed Rates

49.1 This section applies to a bill of costs of an assisted person or LSC funded client which is payable by another person where the costs which can be claimed against the LSC are restricted to prescribed rates (with or without enhancement). **47PD.22**

49.2 Where this section applies, the solicitor of the assisted person or LSC funded client must file a legal aid/ LSC schedule in accordance with Paragraph 40.2(l) above. The schedule should follow as closely as possible Precedent E of the Schedule of Costs Precedents annexed to this Practice Direction.

49.3 The schedule must set out by reference to the item numbers in the bill of costs, all the costs claimed as payable by another person, but the arithmetic in the schedule should claim those items at prescribed rates only (with or without any claim for enhancement).

49.4 Where there has been a change in the prescribed rates during the period covered by the bill of costs, the schedule (as opposed to the bill) should be divided into separate parts, so as to deal separately with each change of rate. The schedule must also be divided so as to correspond with any divisions in the bill of costs.

49.5 If the bill of costs contains additional columns setting out costs claimed against the LSC only, the schedule may be set out in a separate document or, alternatively, may be included in the additional columns of the bill.

49.6 The detailed assessment of the legal aid/ LSC schedule will take place immediately after the detailed assessment of the bill of costs.

49.7 Attention is drawn to the possibility that, on occasions, the court may decide to conduct the detailed assessment of the legal aid/ LSC schedule separately from any detailed assessment of the bill of costs. This will occur, for example, where a default costs certificate is obtained as between the parties but that certificate is not set aside at the time of the detailed assessment pursuant to the Legal Aid Act 1988 or regulations thereunder.

49.8 Where costs have been assessed at prescribed rates it is the responsibility of the legal representative to enter the correct figures allowed in respect of each item and to recalculate the summary of the legal aid/ LSC schedule.

Section 49A Costs Payable by the Trustee for Civil Recovery under a Recovery Order

47PD.23 **49A.1** In this section—

"the Act" means the Proceeds of Crime Act 2002;

"the Order in Council" means the Proceeds of Crime Act 2002 (External Requests and Orders) Order 2005; and

"the Regulations" means the Proceeds of Crime Act 2002 (Legal Expenses in Civil Recovery Proceedings) Regulations 2005.

49A.2 This section applies to the assessment of costs where the court has made a recovery order which provides for the payment by the trustee for civil recovery of a person's reasonable legal costs in respect of civil recovery proceedings. Such an order may be made under section 266(8A) of the Act or article 177(10) of the Order in Council. The procedure for obtaining a recovery order is set out in the Act and Order in Council, together with the Civil Recovery Proceedings Practice Direction.

49A.3 Where this section applies, costs are to be assessed in accordance with the procedure for detailed assessment under Part 47, subject to the modifications set out in Parts 4 and 5 of the Regulations.

49A.4 The detailed assessment will normally be made by a costs judge, even if the costs are within the authorised amounts specified in paragraph 30.1(1). The appropriate office for the purpose of rule 47.4(1) is the Supreme Court Costs Office.

CPR 47

49A.5 In detailed assessment proceedings to which this section applies—

(1) the paying party is the trustee for civil recovery;

(2) the receiving party is the person whose reasonable legal costs are payable pursuant to provision made in the recovery order under section 266(8A) of the Act or article 177(10) of the Order in Council; and

(3) the relevant persons for the purpose of rule 47.6(2) includes the enforcement authority or the appropriate officer as defined in paragraph 1.5 of the Civil Recovery Proceedings Practice Direction in addition to the persons referred to in paragraph 32.10.

49A.6 On commencing detailed assessment proceedings, the receiving party must, in addition to serving the documents listed in paragraph 32.3 on the paying party and all other relevant persons, serve a statement giving the date, amount and source of all interim payments which have been released in respect of any of those costs under Part 3 of the Regulations.

49A.7 By virtue of regulation 13(2) of the Regulations, detailed assessment proceedings must be commenced not later than 2 months after the date of the recovery order, and a request for a detailed assessment hearing must be filed not later than 2 months after the expiry of the period for commencing the detailed assessment proceedings.

49A.8 The documents which must accompany the request for a detailed assessment hearing shall include copies of all exclusions from property freezing orders or interim receiving orders made by the court for the purpose of enabling the receiving party to meet the costs which are to be assessed, and of every estimate of costs filed by the receiving party in support of an application for such an exclusion.

49A.9 The receiving party's costs will be assessed on the standard basis, subject to Part 5 of the Regulations (and in particular regulation 17, which specifies the hourly rates which may be allowed). Attention is also drawn to regulation 14, which provides that the amounts of any interim payments released in respect of the receiving party's costs will be deducted from the costs allowed in accordance with Part 5 of the Regulations.

PART 48

COSTS—SPECIAL CASES

Contents

48.0.1 *I. Costs Payable by or to Particular Persons*

II. Costs Relating to Solicitors and other Legal Representatives

(The definitions contained in Part 43 are relevant to this Part.)

I. Costs Payable by or to Particular Persons

Pre-commencement disclosure and orders for disclosure against a person who is not a party

48.1 ***48.1*—(1) This paragraph applies where a person applies—**

(a) for an order under—

(i) section 33 of the Supreme Court Act 1981; or

(ii) section 52 of the County Courts Act 1984,

(which give the court powers exercisable before commencement of proceedings); or

(b) for an order under—

(i) section 34 of the Supreme Court Act 1981; or

(ii) section 53 of the County Courts Act 1984,

(which give the court power to make an order against a non-party for disclosure of documents, inspection of property, etc.).

(2) The general rule is that the court will award the person against whom the order is sought his costs—

(a) of the application; and

(b) of complying with any order made on the application.

(3) The court may however make a different order, having regard to all the circumstances, including—

(a) the extent to which it was reasonable for the person against whom the order was sought to oppose the application; and

(b) whether the parties to the application have complied with any relevant pre-action protocols.

Comment

In relation to pre-commencement disclosure the court will normally award the costs of the application and the costs of complying with any order for disclosure, inspection, etc., in favour of the party against whom the order is sought If, however, that party has unreasonably opposed the application or failed to comply with any relevant pre-action protocol, the court may well make a different order. **48.1.1**

Rule 48.1(3)

Although there is a presumption under Rule 48.1(3) that the court will award the person against whom the order is sought, his costs of the application and of complying with any order made, the court is entitled, as a matter of discretion, to deprive that party of its costs on the basis that the application has been unreasonably and unsuccessfully resisted: *Bermuda International Securities Ltd v KPMG* [2001] EWCA Civ 269. **48.1.2**

There is a duty to disclose medical records to a person having parental responsibility for a child. The Data Protection Act 1998 does not prevent the disclosure of information nor does it require it. The court found that it was reasonable for a Trust to object to disclosure of a child's records but that it was for the Trust to indicate in what way those objections could be met. The Trust was entitled to present a proper argument to the court raising legitimate concerns. In the circumstances the court ordered that each party should pay its own costs: *Re R (a child)* [2004] EWHC 2085 (Fam) Sumner J.

Starting from the position set out in r.48.1(2) one would expect a court to order that the party producing the documents should bear the costs of the application only in a case where it was clearly unreasonable for the respondent to oppose the application, or where the manner of the opposition was so unreasonable as to make it appropriate to require him to bear the whole of the parties' costs. The Court of Appeal found on the facts that there was ample material to justify a departure from the general rule, but not to extent of ordering the respondent to pay the whole of the applicant's costs. An order of no order as to costs was substituted: *SES Contracting Ltd v UK Coal Plc* [2007] EWCA Civ 791.

Costs orders in favour of or against non-parties[1]

48.2—(1) Where the court is considering whether to exercise its **48.2**

[1] Amended by the Civil Procedure (Amendment No.3) Rules 2000 (SI 2000/1317).

power under section 51 of the Supreme Court Act 1981 (costs are in the discretion of the court) to make a costs order in favour of or against a person who is not a party to proceedings—

(a) that person must be added as a party to the proceedings for the purposes of costs only; and

(b) he must be given a reasonable opportunity to attend a hearing at which the court will consider the matter further.

(2) This rule does not apply—

(a) where the court is considering whether to—

(i) make an order against the Legal Services Commission;

(ii) make a wasted costs order (as defined in 48.7); and

(b) in proceedings to which 48.1 applies (pre-commencement disclosure and orders for disclosure against a person who is not a party).

Comment

48.2.1 Section 51 of the Supreme Court Act 1981 (see Vol.2, para.9A–199) gives the court full power to determine by whom and to what extent costs are to be paid. The Court of Appeal has laid down guidelines for the exercise of this power, see *Symphony Group Plc v Hodgson* 1993 4 All E.R. 143, CA. The following are material considerations.

(1) An order for the payment of costs by a non-party would always be exceptional. The judge should treat any application for such an order with considerable caution.

(2) It would be even more exceptional for an order for the payment of costs to be made against a non-party where the applicant had a cause of action against the non-party, and could have joined him as a party to the original proceedings.

(3) Even if the applicant could provide a good reason for not joining the non-party against whom he had a valid cause of action, he should warn the non-party at the earliest opportunity of the possibility that he might seek to apply for costs against him.

(4) An application for payment of costs by a non-party should normally be determined by the trial judge (see *Bahai v Rashidian* [1985] 1 W.L.R. 1337).

(5) The fact that the trial judge in the course of his judgment had expressed views on the conduct of the non-party, neither consistuted bias nor the appearance of bias.

(6) The procedure for the determination of costs is a summary procedure, not necessarily subject to all the rules that would apply in an action. Thus, subject to any relevant statutory exceptions, judicial findings are inadmissible as evidence of the facts upon which they were based in proceedings between one of the parties to the original proceedings and a stranger. Yet in the summary procedure for the determination of the liability of a solicitor to pay the costs of an action to which he was not a party, the judge's findings of fact may be admissible. This departure from basic principles can only be justified if the connection of the non-party with the original proceedings was so close that he will not suffer any injustice by allowing this exception to the general rule.

(7) In so far as the evidence of a witness in proceedings might lead to an application for the costs of those proceedings against him or his company, it introduced yet another exception to a valuable general principle.

(8) The fact that an employee of a company gave evidence in an action did not normally mean that the company was taking part in that action, in so far as that was an allegation relied upon by the party who applied for an order for costs against a non-party.

(9) The judge should be alert to the possibility that an application for costs against a non-party was motivated by a resentment of an inability to obtain an effective order for costs against a legally aided litigant.

Per Balcombe L.J. *Symphony Group Plc v Hodgson* [1993] 4 All E.R. 143, CA (the above is necessarily much reduced and reference should be made to the full judgment).

The discretion to award costs under s.51 of the Supreme Court Act 1981, did not confer jurisdiction on the Court to award costs other than those incurred in the proceedings before it (*Zanussi v Anglo Venezuelan Real Estate and Agricultural Development Ltd*, *The Times*, April 18, 1996).

An application for a non party costs order should be made to the trial judge, notwithstanding that the judge had expressed a view about the conduct of the non party. Unless the trial judge was precluded from hearing the application for some compelling reason, it was his duty to do so. The trial judge should not decline to hear an application for such an order without good reason. The immunity of a witness does not prevent that evidence being used on a subsequent application for a non party costs order: *Equitas Ltd v Horace Holman & Co Ltd* [2008] EWHC 2287 (Comm) Andrew Smith J.

The Court of Appeal has held that parties and their legal advisers should be well advised and cognisant of the dangers in terms of costs of litigating about comparatively small sums in a manner that was only commensurate with much larger issues. Litigation ought to be proportionate to the need for reasonable remedies, not an exercise in attrition: *Sims v Hawkins* [2007] EWCA Civ 1175.

It is relevant to the court's exercise of discretion, whether to make an order against a non party, for it to consider whether the non party has received notice before or during the litigation that he may be made subject to an order for costs. The discretion to award costs against non parties may be exercised in a variety of circumstances, such as whether the third party is considered to be the real party interested in the outcome of the litigation; or, where the third party has been responsible for bringing the proceedings and they have been brought in bad faith or for an ulterior purpose, or there is some other conduct that makes it just and reasonable to make an order (see Millett L.J. in *Metalloy Supplies Ltd (In Liquidation) v MA (UK) Ltd* [1997] 1 W.L.R. 1613 at 1619): *Barndeal Ltd v Richmond upon Thames LBC (Costs)* [2005] EWHC 1377 (QB), [2006] 1 Costs L.R. 47, Newman J.

Where appellants had failed to comply with orders to pay costs into court, the Court of Appeal ordered that unless the outstanding costs were paid within seven days the appeal would be dismissed. The court had jurisdiction to make such an order under CPR r.3.1(3). The appellants were being financed as to costs by a third party whose aim was to fund the litigation without incurring any liability for the other side's costs in the event that the appellants failed. There was no reason why the third party who had financed the trial and was financing the appeal should be allowed to conduct the litigation in such a way (*Contract Facilities v Rees* [2003] EWCA Civ 1105).

In the case of a sole or controlling director of an insolvent company such an order will not normally be made unless it can be shown that the director caused the company to bring or defend proceedings improperly. *Gardiner v FX Music Ltd*, March 27, 2000, unrep., Geoffrey Voss Q.C. In deciding whether to make an order for costs against a company director who was not a party to the proceedings, the crucial question is whether the relevant directors or director held a bona fide belief that:

(i) the company had an arguable defence; and

(ii) it was in the interests of the company to advance the defence.

On the particular facts of the case: the director had treated the companies as an extension of himself, and the money earned as his own, and had defended the petitions to protect his personal reputation and position, without seriously considering the interest of the companies and their creditors. The order that the director should be made personally responsible for the costs was properly made: *North West Holdings Plc (In Liquidation) (Costs), Re*, [2001] EWCA Civ 67, CA.

Where an individual funds litigation by an insolvent litigant, that individual could be held liable for the costs, especially where he had a personal interest in the outcome and was aware of the risks involved: *Fulton Motors Ltd v Toyota (GB) Ltd (Costs)* [2000] C.P. Rep. 24.

In circumstances where the judge at first instance had stayed an action because the claimant appeared to be funded by a non-party who would not or could not satisfactorily accept liability to pay the successful opponent's costs, the proper course was to allow the action to proceed to trial, and then, if the need arose, for the defendant to make an application for costs under s.51 of the Supreme Court Act 1981 (*Abraham v Thompson* [1997] 4 All E.R. 362, CA).

The Court refused to make an order for costs against a legal expenses insurance company since the insurers had not instigated or controlled the litigation and the circumstances did not make it reasonable and just that they should pay the defendants' costs (*Murphy v Young & Co's Brewery Plc* [1997] 1 W.L.R. 159, CA).

The court has jurisdiction to make an order for costs against a non party even where no order for costs as between the parties has been made. In proceedings where there was a clear case of wanton and vicious intermeddling with a dispute by a third party the court decided that the costs incurred by the parties were attributable to the intermeddling and two of the defendants would never have been involved in the litigation at all but for the role taken by the non party: *Nordstern Allgemeine Versicherungs AG v Internav Ltd*; *Same v Katsamas* [1999] 2 Lloyd's Rep. 139; *The Times*, June 8, 1999, CA.

Under r.48.2(1) there must be permission to join the non party and, where necessary, permission to serve outside the jurisdiction. It is implicit in the rule or inherent in the court's jurisdiction that, for purposes of service of a process on a non party joined for the purposes of costs, the court has power to give permission to serve out of the jurisdiction if satisfied that an appropriate case has been made out. Article 2 of the Brussels Convention is only intended to apply to a substantive cause of action of the kind which could support proceedings by itself and an application for the court to exercise the statutory discretion under s.51 of the Supreme Court Act 1981 was not such a claim (see *Murphy v Young & Co's Brewery Plc* above); *National Justice Compania Naviera SA v Prudential Assurance Co Ltd (The Ikarian Reefer (No.2))* [1999] 2 Lloyd's Rep. 621, Rix J.; affirmed [2000] 1 All E.R. 37, CA.

Where legal expenses insurers took over the defence of an action in circumstances where the defendant, a limited company, was in liquidation, the Court ordered the costs to be paid by the insurers. The decisive factor being, that the insurers took over the defence of the action and conducted it for their own benefit. The defendant took no further part. It could properly be said that the real defendants were the insurers. That factor outweighed any other factors pointing against the making of a costs order (*Pendennis Shipyard Ltd v Margrathea (Pendennis) Ltd (In liquidation)* [1998] 1 Lloyd's Rep. 315; *The Times*, August 27, 1997, QB, HHJ. Jack Q.C.). In a case where insurers of a negligent and impecunious defendant were found liable to indemnify the defendant and to pay the claimants' costs of the action, the liability for *inter partes* costs was independent of the policy limit and unrestricted, it flowed from the insurers' decision that the action should be defended (*T.G.A. Chapman Ltd v Christopher* [1998] 1 W.L.R. 12, CA). See also *Cormack v Washbourne (formerly t/a Washbourne & Co)* [1999] Lloyd's Rep. P.N. 389; [2000] C.P.L.R. 358.

Where an insurance company had funded, controlled and directed in its own interest the defence of a personal injury claim against its insured, the court found that it was appropriate to order the insurer to pay the costs. The court found it impossible to reconcile the assertion that the defence was being conducted in the mutual interests of a defendant and the insurer. Had the insurance company focussed at any stage on the defendant's commercial interest in the litigation it could only have concluded that its interests would best be served by a settlement of the claim. An offer to settle had been turned down without any reference to the defendant. The court inferred that the insurance company was not interested in a consideration of how the defence of the litigation might be conducted so as to achieve the best commercial outcome for the defendant. The defence had been conducted throughout on the basis that the only real interest being protected was that of the insurance company (*Palmer v The Estate of Kevin Palmer Deceased, MIB, PZP Ltd and Royal and Sun Alliance Insurance Plc* [2008] EWCA Civ 46).

The Court of Appeal indicated that *Globe Equities Ltd v Globe Legal Services Ltd* [1999] B.L.R. 232, CA is the leading authority on non party costs. Attention is also drawn to *SBJ Stephenson Ltd v Mandy (Interim Order)* [1999] C.P.L.R. 500 and *Locabail (UK) Ltd v Bayfield Properties Ltd (No.3)*, [2000] I.C.R. 612, Mr Lawrence Collins Q.C.; *Stocznia Gdanska SA v Latreefers Inc* [2000] C.P.L.R. 65; [2001] B.C.C. 174, CA. When considering whether a non-party insurer should be ordered to pay costs it does not necessarily always have to be shown that the insurer has acted out of self interest, unless there is sufficient conflict of interest. *Cormack v Washbourne (formerly t/a Washbourne & Co)* [1999] Lloyd's Rep. P.N. 389; [2000] C.P.L.R. 358, CA.

The rule does not apply where the court is making an order against the Legal Services Commission; making a wasted costs order (this is governed by r.48.7); or in relation to orders for pre-commencement disclosure against a person who is not a party (see r.48.1 above).

The Court of Appeal ordered the sole director and shareholder of a company, who was not a party to proceedings brought by the Secretary of State for Trade & Industry for winding-up his company, to pay costs because justice required that the non party should pay both the Trade Secretary's costs and the company's costs of the winding-up proceedings and that none of the company's costs should be paid directly or indirectly out of the company's assets until after the company's unsecured creditors had been paid. Justice required such an order because the scheme operated by the company was a swindle, the director was operating the swindle through the company and he was the controlling force behind the company's opposition to the winding-up order. (*Secretary of State for Trade and Industry v Aurum Marketing Ltd* [1999] 2 B.C.L.C. 498 CA). Where a successful respondent to an application to strike out was, on the facts, without remedy for consequential loss arising it was an impermissible shortcut to seek an order for costs against a non party who had had no control over the manner or timing of the proceedings, their conduct or conclusion: *Johnson v McKean* [2001] N.P.C. 179.

The key issues to be considered when the court is deciding whether to make an order against a director, are the bona fides of the pursuit of the action and whether the conduct of the director was so exceptional as to justify an order against him. Where successful defendants sought an order against the claimant's solicitors on the basis that they had acted as true funders of the litigation, the court held that deferring or limiting paying until the outcome of a case does not make the solicitor a funder, maintainer or financier. Even though the solicitors might have acted rashly or over generously they did not act outside their role as solicitors when they made these decisions. The Judge at first instance had found that the relationship between solicitor and client was very similar to that under a CFA.

> "[the solicitors] did not engage in an improper no win/no fee arrangement. They simply took a risk and extended credit to their client. It would be a sad day if solicitors could not extend credit, even to their litigation clients, without fear of vulnerability to a Section 51 order."

Per Hale L.J., *Floods of Queensferry v Shand* [2002] EWCA Civ 918.

The Court of Appeal held that a lawyer who had had a costs order made against him for personally intervening in an action against the first defendant could not be criticised for assisting the defendant financially in instructing solicitors of high standing and for assisting him in attempting to discharge his costs liabilities, particularly since a freezing order limited access to the defendant's own funds. There was no logical basis for finding that the lawyer's actions, which had the desired consequence of ensuring that the defendants' case did not go by default, so transformed the nature of the lawyer's involvement as to justify a costs order against him. There was no suggestion that the lawyer was personally interested in the outcome of the litigation: *Gulf Azov Shipping v Idisi* [2004] EWCA Civ 292.

Where an insurance company had funded, controlled and directed in its own interest the defence of a personal injury claim against its insured, the court found that it was appropriate to order the insurer to pay the costs. The court found it impossible to reconcile the assertion that the defence was being conducted in the mutual interests of a defendant and the insurer. Had the insurance company focussed at any stage on the defendant's commercial interest in the litigation it could only have concluded that its interests would best be served by a settlement of the claim. An offer to settle had been turned down without any reference to the defendant. The court inferred that the insurance company was not interested in a consideration of how the defence of the litigation might be conducted so as to achieve the best commercial outcome for the defendant. The defence had been conducted throughout on the basis that the only real interest being protected was that of the insurance company (*Palmer v The Estate of Kevin Palmer Deceased, MIB, PZP Ltd and Royal and Sun Alliance Insurance Plc* [2008] EWCA Civ 46).

Where a non party is shown to have intervened in litigation so as to take control of the prosecution or defence of a claim, substantially for his own purposes or benefit and the claim or defence fails, there is no requirement that a court, making a non party cost order against a director, should find that the director was guilty of some impropriety in the prosecution by the company of the claim: *BE Studios Ltd v Smith and Williamson Ltd* [2005] EWHC 2730 (Ch), Evans Lombe J.

It seems that, where (1) a person (a) is subject to a civil proceedings order, and (b) has been refused leave under the Supreme Court Act 1981 s.42 to enable him to institute or continue, or to make an application in, particular proceedings, and (2) the court finds that a non-party costs order should be made against him in relation to those proceedings, then (3) such order may be made without his being joined as a party to the proceedings under r.48.2(1)(a) (see *Ewing v Office of the Deputy Prime Minister* [2005] EWCA Civ 1583).

Where receivers were properly seeking to enforce a contractual right (breach of contract) there were no exceptional circumstances to warrant the making of a third party costs order. There was no element of impropriety or unreasonableness in the initiation and prosecution of the claim and no justification for making the order sought. The receivers did not fund the initial proceedings, nor did they benefit from them in any relevant sense. The receivers were held to be merely agents of the company in receivership: *Dolphin Quays Developments Ltd (in receivership) v Mills* [2007] EWHC 1180 (Ch), Sir Andrew Morritt, Chancellor; [2007] 4 All E.R. 503.

48.2.1.1 An application for an order to join a party would normally be expected to explain the nature of the claim against the intended party and the purpose to be served by joining that party. If it became clear that the joinder was an abuse of process the court would normally dismiss the application. At the stage of joinder it is not inappropriate to attempt a preliminary assessment of the merits in order to see whether an application for a non party costs order had any real prospect of success: *P R Records Ltd v Vinyl 2000 Ltd* [2007] EWHC 1721 (Ch), Morgan J.

A liability insurer appealed against the decision not to make a costs order against a witness alleged to be a party to a conspiracy to bring a dishonest insurance claim arising out of a road accident. Although the insurers could have joined the witness as a defendant to its counterclaim alleging that he was a co-conspirator they did not do so. At trial the claim was dismissed as fraudulent and the witness was then joined for the purpose of seeking a costs order against him, which was refused. The Court of Appeal held that the judge had wrongly fettered his own discretion in that he thought it had to be shown that the non-party was a funder or controller of the litigation before such an order could be made. The court declined to make a non-party costs order against the witness, stating that it would be exceptional for such an order to be made against the non-party where the applicant had a cause of action against that party and could have joined him to the original proceedings. The insurers remained free to sue the witness for his part in the dishonest conspiracy and if it succeeded the costs of successfully defending the primary claim would be recoverable as damages flowing from the conspiracy (*Oriakhel v Vickers; Groupama Insurance Co Ltd; Kahn; and Graham Coffey & Co* [2008] EWCA Civ 748).

Litigation funding

48.2.2 The court necessarily has the ancillary power to order a party to proceedings, or the solicitors who had been on the record for that party, to disclose to the other party the names of those who have financed the litigation. Where a power exists to grant a remedy there must be, inherent in that power, the power to make ancillary orders to make the remedy effective (see *Abraham v Thompson* [1997] 4 All E.R. 362, CA): *Raiffeisenzentralbank Osterreich AG v Crossseas Shipping Ltd* [2003] EWHC 1381 (Comm), Morrison J.

The Privy Council (Lord Brown of Eaton-Under-Heywood) has set out the principles to be derived from the English and Commonwealth authorities:

> "(1) Although costs orders against non parties are to be regarded as 'exceptional', exceptional in this context means no more than outside the ordinary run of cases where parties pursue or defend claims for their own benefit and at their own expense. The ultimate question in any such 'exceptional' case is whether in all the circumstances it is just to make the order …
>
> (2) Generally speaking the discretion will not be exercised against 'pure funders' described in paragraph 40 of *Hamilton v Al-Fayed* as:
>
> 'those with no personal interest in the litigation, who do not stand to benefit from it, are not funding it as a matter of business, and in no way seek to control its course'.

In that case the court's usual approach is to give priority to the public interest in the funded party getting access to justice over that of the successful unfunded party recovering his costs and so not having to bear the expense of vindicating his rights.

> (3) Where, however, the non party not merely funds the proceedings but substantially also controls or at any rate is to benefit from them, justice will ordinarily require that, if the proceedings fail, he will pay the successful party's costs. The non party in these cases is not so much facilitating access to justice by the party funded as himself gaining access to justice for his own purposes. He

himself is the 'real party' to the litigation, a concept repeatedly invoked throughout the jurisprudence—see, for example, Millett L.J.'s judgment in *Metalloy Supplies Ltd (In Liquidation) v MA (UK) Ltd* [1997] 1 W.L.R. 1613. Consistently with this approach, Phillips L.J. described the non party underwriters in *TGA Chapman Ltd v Christopher* [1998] 1 W.L.R. 12 as 'the defendants in all but name'. Nor, indeed, is it necessary that the non party be 'the only real party' to the litigation ... provided that he is 'a real party in ... very important and critical aspects'—see *Arundel Chiropractic Centre Pty Ltd v Deputy Commissioner of Taxation* [2001] 179 A.L.R. 406. Some reflection of this concept of 'the real party' is to be found in CPR r.25.13(2)(f) which allows a security for costs order to be made where 'the claimant is acting as a nominal claimant'.

(4) Perhaps the most difficult cases are those in which non parties, receivers or liquidators (or, indeed, financially insecure companies generally) in litigation designed to advance the funders own financial interests."

Dymocks Franchise Systems (NSW) Pty Ltd v Todd [2004] UKPC 39; [2004] 1 W.L.R. 2807; [2005] 4 All E.R. 195.

The Court of Appeal relying on that summary of principles stated the correct approach to making an order for costs in a case funded by third party commercial funders:

"38. While we do not dispute the importance of helping to ensure access to justice, we considered that the Judge was wrong not to give appropriate weight to the rule that costs should normally follow the event ... In our judgment the existence of this rule, and the reasons given to justify its existence, render it unjust that a funder who purchases a stake in an action for a commercial motive should be protected from all liability for the costs of the opposing party if the funded party fails in the action. Somehow or other a just solution must be devised whereby on the one hand a successful opponent is not denied all his costs, while on the other hand commercial funders who provide help to those seeking access to justice which they could not otherwise afford are not deterred by fear of disproportionate costs consequences if the litigation they are supporting does not succeed.

...

40. The approach that we are about to commend will not be appropriate in the case of a funding agreement that falls foul of the policy considerations that render an agreement champertous. A funder who enters into such an agreement will be likely to render himself liable for the opposing party's costs without limit should the claim fail ... Our approach is designed to cater for the commercial funder who is financing part of the costs of litigation in a manner which facilitates access to justice and which is not otherwise objectionable. Such funding will leave the claimant as the party primarily interested in the result of the litigation and the party in control of the conduct of the litigation.

41. We consider that a professional funder who finances part of a claimant's costs of litigation, should be potentially liable for the costs of the opposing party *to the extent of the funding provided*. The effect of this will of course be that if the funding is provided on a contingency basis of recovery, the funder will require, as the price of the funding, a greater share of the recovery should the claim succeed. In the individual case, the net recovery of the successful claimant will be diminished. While this is unfortunate, it seems to us that it is a cost that the impecunious claimant can reasonably be expected to bear. Overall justice will be better served than leaving defendants in a position where they have no right to recover any costs from a professional funder whose intervention has permitted the continuation of a claim which has ultimately proved to be without merit.

42. If the course which we have proposed becomes generally accepted it is likely to have the following consequences. Professional funders are likely to cap the funds that they provide in order to limit their exposure to a reasonable amount. This should have a salutary effect in keeping costs proportionate ... Professional funders will also have to consider with even greater care whether the prospects of the litigation are sufficiently good to justify the support that they are asked to give. This will also be in the public interest.

43. In the present appeal we are concerned only with the professional funder who has contributed a part of a litigant's expenses through a non champertous agreement in the expectation of reward if the litigant succeeds. We can see no reason in principle, however, why the solution we suggest should not be ap-

plicable where the funder has similarly contributed the greater part, or all, of the expenses with the action.

...

45. ...Accordingly, we propose to order that MPC pay £1.3 million by way of contribution to defence costs..."

Arkin v Borchard Lines Ltd [2005] EWCA Civ 655; [2005] 1 W.L.R. 3055.

Relying on *Dymocks Franchise Systems* and *Arkin v Bourchard Lines* above, it has been held that causation is no longer a necessary pre-condition to an order for costs against a non party, but an order for costs against a non party is exceptional. The facts of the case were held to be exceptional and justified the making of such an order against the main shareholder and manager of a company which he controlled and who had misled the court in respect of the status of the company after its merger with another company, and had concealed the merger from the court. These actions had effectively deprived the claimant company of any realistic opportunity of recovering its costs unless a third party costs order was made: *Total Spares & Supplies Ltd v Antares SRL* [2006] EWHC 1537, Ch, David Richards J. The Privy Council made an order against the principal shareholder and chairman of the appellant company on the basis that he had pursued the appeal in his own interests and at his own expense. The Board found that he was treating the company as "his creature" and preferring his own interests to those of the company. *Suisse Security Bank & Trust Ltd v Governor of the Central Bank of the Bahamas* [2006] UKPC 41.

Similarly the Court of Appeal upheld a decision to join an individual to the proceedings and make him jointly and severally liable for the costs of the successful defendants where that person had controlled proceedings brought by the claimant company who funded the proceedings and would have benefited from them had they been successful. The Court quoted with approval, the judgment of Rix L.J., in *Goodwood Recoveries Ltd v Breen* (see below) and added that the principles set out in that judgment are not confined to "directors" (per Longmore L.J.). Laws L.J. added that the exercise of the jurisdiction to award costs against non parties becomes over complicated by reference to authority and in his view had become over burdened: "Section 51 [of the Supreme Court Act 1981] confers a discretion not confined by specific limitations. While the learning is ... important in indicating the kind of considerations upon which the Court will focus, it must not be treated as a rulebook": *Petromec Inc v Petroleo Brasileiro SA v Petrobras* [2006] EWCA Civ 1038. If funds are provided to a litigant by way of a loan with no further involvement by the lender, and no interest in the litigation conferred on the lender, an order for costs against the lender is not normally appropriate. The Court found this approach to be correct as regards to ordinary commercial lenders. Loans made on non-commercial terms for ulterior purposes are in a different category and may, depending on the circumstances, constitute funding which can justify an order for costs against the lender *Vaughan v Jones and Fowler* [2006] EWHC 2123 (Ch), David Richards J.

The Court held that there was no reason in principle why a costs order should not be varied, provided there had been a change of circumstances, or where the Court had been misled in a material way e.g. as to the financial position of the party against whom the original order for costs was made. Similarly where it had become apparent that another party, against whom no order had been made, but who had controlled the litigation on behalf of the party ordered to pay the costs and had personally benefited from the litigation even though that benefit was not a financial one: *Latimer Management Consultants Ltd v Ellingham Investments Ltd* [2006] EWHC 3662 (Ch); [2007] 1 W.L.R. 2569; [2007] 3 All E.R. 485 Bernard Livesey Q.C.

48.2.2.1 Following the decision of the Court of Appeal in *Myatt v National Coal Board* [2006] EWCA Civ 1017 the respondent Coal Board sought its costs from the appellants' solicitors personally. Although the court found that the appellants had themselves a financial interest in the outcome of the appeal, the question to be decided was whether there was jurisdiction to order the solicitors to pay some or all of the respondents' costs and if so how that jurisdiction should be exercised. Having referred to *Symphony Group Plc v Hodgson* and *Dymocks v Todd* the court held that a solicitor who is "a real party ... in very important and critical respects" and who "not merely funds the proceedings but substantially also contributes, or at any rate, is to benefit from them" may be potentially liable. The court did not accept that the mere fact that a solicitor was on the record prosecuting proceedings for his or her client was fatal to an application by the successful opposing party under ss.51(1) and (3) of the Supreme Court Act 1981, that the solicitor should pay some or all of the costs. Had the appellants had no financial interest at all, the other party with an interest in the appeal would be the solicitors. In the judgment of the court they would undoubtedly be acting outside the role of solicitor. The court had no doubt that there was jurisdiction to make an order under s.51(3) of the 1981 Act against a solicitor where litigation was pursued by the client for the benefit or to a substantial degree for the benefit of the solicitor. Taking into account the fact that the respondents had not warned the solicitors that they might apply for an order for costs against them so that they had not had a reasonable opportunity for deciding whether or not to continue with the proceedings, the solicitors were ordered to pay 50 per cent of the respondents' costs of the appeal: *Myatt v National Coal Board* [2007] EWCA Civ 307.

The normal rule under CPR Pt 44 is that costs should follow the event. The question as to the costs consequences of a joinder whether under CPR Pt 19 or Pt 20 is a matter for the court's discretion. Whether or not the joinder was initiated by the court did not mean that a party should not bear the cost consequences of that decision making process. On the "almost unique" facts of the case the court found that the circumstances were exceptional and justified a departure from the normal rule. The defendant was ordered to pay the costs of the claimant and of the respondent solicitors who were joined to the proceedings. *Phillips v Symes (No.2)* [2004] EWHC 2330 (Ch), Peter Smith J. In the same proceedings the claimant applied for the determination of a preliminary issue as to whether an expert could be joined to proceedings as respondent for the purposes of costs only. The court found that the defendant had appropriate mental capacity in spite of a report by the expert which stated that as a result of a stroke the defendant had suffered in 1980 he lacked the necessary capacity. The expert had been called by the Official Solicitor to assist the court in determining the issue. The court held that the expert had an objective duty which did not change depending on the status of the client to complete with the expert duties that were imposed by the court. To fail to warn someone that their evidence could lead to a costs application against them was a denial of justice. Whether and how a person should be warned had to be approached on a case by case basis. At one end of the scale were legal representatives where there was no real reason to warn them of potential exposure to a wasted costs order. At the other end of the scale were lay witnesses where the court had to be alert to ensure that any cross examination was fair and not used as a stalking horse for subsequent costs applications. In between the two extremes were experts where the only warning required was the self evident one set out in the Civil Procedure Rules and the declaration that the experts signed. The high level of proof required to establish the breach of duty to the court could not be ignored, namely gross dereliction of duty or recklessness. It would be wrong of the court to remove from itself the power to make a costs order in appropriate circumstances against an expert who, by his evidence, caused significant expense to be incurred and did so in flagrant reckless disregard of his duties to the court. *Phillips v Symes (No.2)* [2004] EWHC 2330, (Ch); [2005] 1 W.L.R. 2043, Peter Smith J; [2005] 4 All E.R. 519. **48.2.3**

A non party director who could be described as the "real party" seeking his own benefit and controlling and/or funding the litigation, then, even where he had acted in good faith, or without any impropriety, justice might demand that he be liable in costs. On the facts of the particular case the costs of the litigation brought by the claimant company would not have been incurred without the director's involvement. The director was the party for whose benefit the litigation was brought. He controlled it throughout. The only reason he did not fund it was because it was funded under a CFA by the firm of solicitors for whom he acted as a consultant and in whose name he undertook the conduct of the litigation. In any event the whole of the costs of the litigation were caused by the director's dishonesty or impropriety, irrespective of whether he had any bona fide belief in the claim. It was therefore not necessary to decide whether there had to be a causal link between all the costs and the alleged impropriety: *Goodwood Recoveries Ltd v Breen* [2005] EWCA Civ 414; [2006] 1 W.L.R. 2723; [2006] 2 All E.R. 533, CA.

The court made an order that a controlling company director should be liable jointly and severally with the company for costs on the indemnity basis where the director was an evasive and untruthful witness who had sought to support a case that was advanced on a false basis. The company's pursuit of the claim was irresponsible and it was ordered to pay the costs on the indemnity basis. Those costs included the costs of mediation which failed. The judge held that the case was exceptional and it was therefore just to make the director personally liable jointly and severally with the company. The director was, in substance, the, or at least a, real party to the proceedings. The company was established by him and financed with his money. He had controlled and managed the pursuit of the proceedings from start to finish. The director's wife and co-director was held neither to be a real party nor to have funded the proceedings or been responsible for the pursuit of the hopeless counterclaim: *Chantrey Vellacott v Convergence Group Plc* [2007] EWHC 1774 (Ch), Rimer J.

The Court of Appeal held that where the interests of a company and its director were so close it was just to make a third party costs order against the director personally. Given the way the director conducted his affairs through the company it would be unjust to rely on the separate legal personality of the company to avoid liability for costs: *Alan Phillips Associates Ltd v Dowling* [2007] EWCA Civ 64.

48.2.3.1 Where a company sued another company for monies owed to it and obtained judgment but the respondent company entered a creditors' voluntary liquidation after judgment the claimant company applied for a third party costs order against the sole shareholders and directors of the company on the grounds that they had controlled and directed the conduct of the litigation with impropriety and dishonesty, the court held it was appropriate to make a third party costs order having regard to the shareholders' control of the defence and counterclaim, their funding of it to a substantial extent and the fact that its success would have been largely or entirely for their own personal benefit. The shareholders could not realistically be regarded as acting in the interests of the company and its creditors rather than in their own personal interests. A good deal of the evidence on which the shareholders relied was untrue. *I-Remit Inc v Far East Express Remittance Limited: I-Remit Incorporated v Ubando* [2008] EWHC 939 (Ch), David Richards J.

The court considered the question whether, when a Receiver appointed under a bank charge causes an insolvent company to sue, the action is unsuccessful and the successful parties are unable to recover costs against the company, the successful party may recover the costs from the Receiver under the jurisdiction in s.51 of the Supreme Court Act 1981 to award costs against a non-party. The argument that whenever an insolvent corporate litigant (including a defendant) is ordered to pay the costs of legal proceedings, the officer or agent responsible for their conduct should be directed to pay the costs, recovering if he can from his principal pursuant to such indemnity as he may have, was rejected. The court did not consider that Aden Shipping justified the judicial creation of a substantive rule that Receivers should be personally responsible for the costs of a successful party. The applicant would not have had to invoke the court's jurisdiction to make an order for costs against a non-party if he had been advised at an early stage to take the prudent routine step of invoking the court's discretion under CPR 25.13(2)(c) to make an order for security for costs against the company as claimant in the proceedings. There were ample grounds for believing that the company would be unable to pay the costs if it were not successful in the specific performance proceedings. A valid claim by the company would not have been stifled by an order for security as the Receivers were giving instructions in the name of the company and had sufficient assets in their hands which would have been used to back the claim directly for the benefit of the company, and indirectly for the benefit of the debenture holder, and over which the Receivers had a right of indemnity. *Mills v Birchal and Gilbertson* [2008] EWCA Civ 385.

Vexatious litigants

48.2.4 The Court of Appeal has given guidance on the procedure to be adopted in relation to applications for costs where a vexatious litigant has made an application for leave to bring proceedings at the same time as an application to be joined in a concurrent application for permission to seek Judicial Review. A vexatious litigant should not allow his name to be included on a claim form unless he had obtained the necessary leave. A vexatious litigant who had no sufficient interest in his own right did not improve his position by joining up with a competent litigant with equally little interest. The court had to be careful to ensure that the costs falling on the judicial review claimant were not disproportionately inflated by the involvement of other parties at the permission stage. The costs awarded against the appellant arose solely under the Judicial Review procedure. Even if the Judicial Review proceedings were treated as effective only in respect of the competent litigant, it was clear that the appellant was the main instigator. It did not matter whether or not technically he was treated as a party to the proceedings or was using the other litigant as a means of gaining access to justice for his own purposes and was therefore "the real party," that was sufficient for the purposes of costs: *Ewing v The Office of the Deputy Prime Minister* [2005] EWCA Civ 1583.

Amount of costs where costs are payable pursuant to a contract

48.3—(1) Where the court assesses (whether by the summary or detailed procedure) costs which are payable by the paying party to the receiving party under the terms of a contract, the costs payable under those terms are, unless the contract expressly provides otherwise, to be presumed to be costs which— 48.3

(a) have been reasonably incurred; and

(b) are reasonable in amount; and the court will assess them accordingly.

(The costs practice direction sets out circumstances where the court may make order otherwise.)

(2) This rule does not apply where the contract is between a solicitor and his client.

Comment

In respect of costs payable under a contract there is a presumption that the costs have been reasonably incurred and are reasonable in amount. However if the terms of the contract are manifestly unreasonable the presumption will be rebutted. In such a case the court may make a special order, for example, reducing or disallowing some or all of the costs recovered, see s.50 of the Costs Practice Direction. A mortgagee is allowed to reimbruse himself out of the mortgaged property for all costs, charges and expenses reasonably and properly incurred in enforcing or preserving his security. Often the process of enforcement or preservation makes it necessary for him to take or defend proceedings. In regard to such proceedings three propositions may be stated: 48.3.1

(i) The mortgagee's costs, reasonably and properly incurred, of proceedings between himself and the mortgagor or his surety are allowable.

(ii) Allowable also are the mortgagee's costs, reasonably and properly incurred, of proceedings between himself and a third party where what is impugned is the title to the estate.

(iii) But where a third party impugns the title to a mortgage, or the enforcement or exercise of some right or power accruing to the mortgagee thereunder, the mortgagee's costs of the proceedings, even though they be reasonable and properly incurred, are not allowable.

Per Nourse L.J. in *Parker-Tweedale v Dunbar Bank plc (No.2)* [1990] 2 All E.R. 588, CA at 591.

Propositions (i) and (ii) form the general rule (iii) is the exception to it. The general rule is to be found in *Detillin v Gale* [1802] 7 Ves. 583, 32 E.R. 234; *Dryden v Frost* [1838] 3 My. & Cr. 670; [1835–42] All E.R. Rep. 390; and *National Provincial Bank of England v Games* [1886] 31 Ch.D. 582.

The exception is to be found in *Owen v Crouch* [1857] 5 W.R. 545; *Parker v Watkins* [1859] John 133, 70 E.R. 369; and *Re Smith's Mortgage* [1931] 2 C.h. 168; *Harrison v Edwards* [1931] 2 Ch. 168; All E.R. Rep. 698. The decision of the Court of Appeal in *Re Leighton's Conveyance* [1936] 3 All E.R. 1033; [1937] Ch. 149, supports both propositions.

A mortgagee is entitled to recover, under the terms of the mortage deed, the actual costs, charges and expenses incurred, except for any costs that have not been reasonably incurred or were unreasonable in amount. But litigation and non-litigation costs may be referred to a Costs Judge for quantification and the mortgagee is contractually entitled to payment on the indemnity basis. The court's discretion as to the basis of assessment of a mortgagee's costs will normally be exercised so as to correspond with the contractual entitlement. It follows that the judge has power to order that the contractual costs, charges and expenses and the costs incurred in the litigation be assessed on the indemnity basis (*Gomba Holdings (UK) Limited v Minories Finance Limited (No.2)* [1992] 3 W.L.R. 723).

The Court of Appeal reviewed the law and set out principles which emerge:

(i) An order for the payment of costs of proceedings by one party to another party is always a discretionary order: s.51 of the Supreme Court Act 1981.

(ii) Where there is a contractual right to the costs the discretion should ordinarily be exercised, so as to reflect that contractual right.

(iii) The power of the Court to disallow a mortgagee's costs sought to be added to the mortgage security is a power that does not derive from s.51, but from the power of the Courts of Equity to fix the terms on which redemption will be allowed.

(iv) A decision by a Court to refuse costs in whole or in part to a mortgage litigant may be a decision in the exercise of the s.51 discretion; or a decision in the exercise of the power to fix the terms on which redemption will be allowed, or a decision as to the extent of a mortgagee's contractual right to add his costs to the security of a combination of two or more of these things. The pleadings in the case and the submissions made to the Judge may indicate which of the decisions has been made.

(v) A mortgagee is not to be deprived of a contractual or equitable right to add costs to the security, merely by reason of an order for payment of costs made without reference to the mortagee's contractual or equitable rights, and without any adjudication as to whether or not the mortgagee should be deprived of those costs (*Gomba Holdings UK Ltd v Minories Finance Ltd (No.2)* [1992] 3 W.L.R. 723) and see *Fairview Investments Ltd v Sharma*, October 14, 1999, unrep., CA.

If the mortgagees seek to deduct an excessive sum, the remedy of the defendant mortagor is to ask for an account and to challenge the figure which the claimant mortagees seek to charge for their costs. At that stage the Court would not be bound by the contractual provisions and would be entitled to say that the costs sought to be charged were excessive and could make the appropriate order at that point. This would however depend on the mortagees having behaved unreasonably. Per Balcombe L.J. in *Mortgage Funding Corporation plc v Kashef-Hamadani*, April 26, 1993, unrep., CA.

This rule does not apply to a contract between a solicitor and his client since this is governed by the Solicitors Act 1874 Pt III ss.56 to 75.

Limitations on court's power to award costs in favour of trustee or personal representative[1]

48.4 **48.4—(1) This rule applies where—**

(a) a person is or has been a party to any proceedings in the capacity of trustee or personal representative; and

(b) rule 48.3 does not apply.

(2) The general rule is that he is entitled to be paid the costs of those proceedings, insofar as they are not recovered from or paid by any other person, out of the relevant trust fund or estate.

(3) Where he is entitled to be paid any of those costs out of the fund or estate, those costs will be assessed on the indemnity basis.[2]

Comment

48.4.1 Amended by SI 1999/1008.

As a general rule a trustee or personal representative is entitled to the costs of any proceedings brought in that capacity on the indemnity basis. Frequently the court orders that such costs are payable out of the trust fund, see *Re Beddoe* [1893] 1 Ch. 547.

Where trustees are willing and able to bring proceedings to resolve a dispute

[1] Amended by the Civil Procedure (Amendment No.5) Rules 2001 (SI 2001/4015).

[2] Paragraphs (2) and (3) substituted by the Civil Procedure Amendment No.5 Rules (SI 2001/4015) (L.32), in force March 25, 2002.

concerning the trust, the fact that a claimant beneficiary succeeded in her claim did not necessarily result in an order for costs in the beneficiary's favour. A more robust attitude to costs was now appropriate under the new rules, although the guidelines set out in In *Re Buckton* [1907] 2 Ch 406 had not been superseded. (*D'Abo v Paget (No.2)*, *The Times*, August 10, 2000, Lawrence Collins Q.C.).

Where beneficiaries make a hostile claim against trustees or other beneficiaries a pre-emptive costs order should only be made where the court hearing the costs application is satisfied that no other order could properly be made by the court which is to hear the proceedings: *Chessels v British Telecommunications Plc* [2002] Pens. L.R. 141, Laddie J.

Costs where money is payable by or to a child or protected party[1]

48.5—(1) This rule applies to any proceedings where a party is a child or protected party and— **48.5**

(a) money is ordered or agreed to be paid to, or for the benefit of, that party; or

(b) money is ordered to be paid by him or on his behalf.

("Child" and "protected party" have the same meaning as in rule 21.1(2).)

(2) The general rule is that—

(a) the court must order a detailed assessment of the costs payable by or out of money belonging to, any party who is a child or protected party; and

(b) on an assessment under paragraph (a), the court must also assess any costs payable to that party in the proceedings, unless—

(i) the court has issued a default costs certificate in relation to those costs under rule 47.11; or

(ii) the costs are payable in proceedings to which Section II of Part 45 applies.

(3) The court need not order detailed assessment of costs in the circumstances set out in the costs practice direction.

(4) Where—

(a) a claimant is a child or protected party; and

(b) a detailed assessment has taken place under paragraph (2)(a), the only amount payable by the child or protected party is the amount which the court certifies as payable.

(This rule applies to a counterclaim by or on behalf of a child or protected party by virtue of rule 20.3.)

Comment

This rule is designed to protect money belonging to a child or protected party, and the court must therefore order detailed assessment of the costs payable by a child or protected party to his or her solicitor, and must also carry out an assessment of the costs payable to the child or protected party in the proceedings, unless a default costs certificate has been issued in respect of those costs. Where costs are recovered from a paying party on behalf of the child or protected party, solicitors frequently waive any further claim for costs, in which case there is no need for a detailed assessment of the solicitor and client costs. **48.5.1**

See s.51 of the Costs Practice Direction, as to the circumstances in which detailed assessment need not be ordered.

[1] Amended by the Civil Procedure (Amendment) Rules 2007 (SI 2007/2204).

The rule applies equally to a counterclaim by or on behalf of the child or protected party; see r.20.3.

A litigation friend who incurs expenses on behalf of a chid or protected party in any proceedings is entitled to recover the amount paid or payable out of any money recovered or paid into court to the extent that it has been reasonably incurred and is reasonable in amount, see CPR r.21.11A and PD 21.8A.

Litigants in person[1]

48.6 **48.6—(1) This rule applies where the court orders (whether by summary assessment or detailed assessment) that the costs of a litigant in person are to be paid by any other person.**

(2) The costs allowed under this rule must not exceed, except in the case of a disbursement, two-thirds of the amount which would have been allowed if the litigant in person had been represented by a legal representative.

(3) The litigant in person shall be allowed—

(a) costs for the same categories of—

(i) work; and

(ii) disbursements,

which would have been allowed if the work had been done or the disbursements had been made by a legal representative on the litigant in person's behalf;

(b) the payments reasonably made by him for legal services relating to the conduct of the proceedings; and

(c) the costs of obtaining expert assistance in assessing the costs claim.

(4) The amount of costs to be allowed to the litigant in person for any item of work claimed shall be—

(a) where the litigant can prove financial loss, the amount that he can prove he has lost for time reasonably spent on doing the work; or

(b) where the litigant cannot prove financial loss, an amount for the time reasonably spent on doing the work at the rate set out in the practice direction.

(5) A litigant who is allowed costs for attending at court to conduct his case is not entitled to a witness allowance in respect of such attendance in addition to those costs.

(6) For the purposes of this rule, a litigant in person includes—

(a) a company or other corporation which is acting without a legal representative; and

(b) a barrister, solicitor, solicitor's employee or other authorised litigator (as defined in the Courts and Legal Services Act 1990[2] who is acting for himself.

Comment

48.6.1 There is an absolute cap on the amount recoverable by a litigant in person, namely two thirds of the amount which would have been allowed if the litigant in person had been represented by a legal representative. Disbursements, if reasonable, may be

[1] Amended by the Civil Procedure (Amendment) Rules 2002 (SI 2002/2058).
[2] 1990 c.41.

recovered in full. Those disbursements may include payment by the litigant in person for legal services relating to the conduct of the proceedings. Lord Woolf envisaged a move towards the supply of partial legal services. A litigant in person may also recover the reasonable costs of obtaining expert assistance in connection with assessing the claim for costs, see s.52 of the Costs Practice Direction as to who may be an expert for these purposes.

The onus is on the litigant in person to prove financial loss in respect of any item of work and if he fails to do so the amount recoverable is that fixed periodically by statutory instrument (presently £9.25 per hour).

A litigant in person may now include a company or other corporation acting without a legal representative and a barrister, solicitor, solicitor's employee or other authorised litigator acting for himself. The previous exemption for a solicitor acting on his own behalf has been removed although para.52.5 of the Directions provides a way out of the difficulty. A company acting through an in-house legal representative who is in possession of a practising certificate or equivalent authorisation will not be treated as a litigant in person but the legal representative will be able to recover costs in the normal way on behalf of the company.

As to the use of a McKenzie friend see: *Re G (Chambers Proceedings: McKenzie friend)* (1999) 2 F.L.R. 59, CA, *R. v Bow County Court Ex p. Pelling* [1999] 4 All E.R. 751, CA and *Noueiri v Paragon Finance Ltd* [2001] EWCA Civ 1402; [2001] 1 W.L.R. 2357, CA.

The courts recognise the difficulty that litigants in person have in presenting cases, and for that reason they may have the assistance of a MacKenzie Friend in court. That person may sit beside them and give help and advice during the course of the proceedings but that person is not an advocate appearing on behalf of the litigant. The court may grant a right of audience to a person in relation to particular proceedings under s.27(2)(c) of the Courts and Legal Services Act 1990. It is for the litigant in person to indicate to the court why some other person is needed, who is not qualified as an advocate, to act on their behalf. In the ordinary way it is for the litigant to satisfy the court that it would be appropriate. (*Clarkson v Gilbert (Rights of Audience)* [2000] C.P. Rep. 58.)

Effect of Rule

Prior to the Litigants in Person (Costs and Expenses) Act 1975, a litigant in person could recover only out of pocket expenses (*Buckland v Watts* [1970] 1 Q.B. 27; [1969] 2 All E.R. 985, CA. See also Litigants in Person (Costs and Expenses) Act 1975. The Litigants in Person (Costs and Expenses) Order 1980 (SI 1980/1159) extended the scope to the Employment Appeal Tribunal. **48.6.2**

The Litigants in Person (Costs and Expenses) (Magistrates' Court) Order 2001 (SI 2001/3438) extends the scope to Magistrates' Courts in England and Wales in respect of civil proceedings in Magistrates' Courts.

In *Parikh v Midland Bank Ltd*, 1982, unrep., the Court of Appeal held that a payment made by a doctor litigant to a locum was not a disbursement of the purpose of costs. In *McLeod-Johnson-Hart v Aga Khan Foundation (UK)* [1984] 1 All E.R. 239 Lloyd J. held that a litigant was not entitled to a notional disbursement in respect of a brief fee in quantifying two-thirds of the daily attendance fee and also the claim must distinguish between leisure and pecuniary loss time. This decision was upheld by the Court of Appeal [1984] 1 W.L.R. 994; [1984] 2 All E.R. 439).

Although a litigant in person cannot be allowed a notional disbursement in respect of counsel who is not employed that does not mean the costs judge is required to disallow a disbursement actually incurred so as to avoid the necessity of employing not only a solicitor but also counsel; thus a successful defendant is entitled to travelling expenses (from South Africa) to conduct the case in person and to the reasonable costs of travelling in connection with the case (*Law Society v Persaud, The Times*, May 10, 1990).

Interest on money borrowed by a successful claimant to finance litigation is not costs, and cannot properly be included in an order for costs (*Mann v Eccott*, June 27, unrep., CA).

Calculating the costs of a litigant in person

The exercise is as follows. Find out, in respect of the item, what, at the litigant in person charging rate, the total is. Compare that with two thirds of the notional solicitor rate, give the lower of the two items. That does mean that the bill of costs drawn by the litigant in person must be gone through in some detail item by item. Per Jacob J. in *Morris v Wiltshire & Woodspring District Council*, January 16, 1998, unrep. A costs **48.6.3** officer should keep in mind that it is appropriate to allow a litigant in person more time for a particular task than would be allowed to a solicitor. *Mealing McLeod v Common Professional Examination Board (Assessment of Costs)* [2000] 2 Costs L.R. 223, March 30, 2000, unrep., Buckley J.

In principle a litigant in person is entitled to his time for researching his case at the rate fixed by statute subject to a cap of two thirds of what he would have recovered if legally represented. In a case in which the litigant had undertaken in excess of 1200 hours of research during the proceedings, and where there was evidence of an estimate given by a firm of solicitors that the costs of the action were likely to have been in excess of £15,000, the court, taking that figure as a rough estimate, allowed the litigant £10,460: *R. v Legal Services Commission Ex p. Wulfsohn* [2002] EWCA Civ 250; [2002] 3 Costs L.R. 341, CA.

Where a person with no legal qualifications gave assistance to a litigant in person the court had no jurisdiction to award costs for the work carried out by the non legally qualified person. CPR r.48.6(3)(a) dealt with the time spent by a litigant and disbursements made by him that would have been recoverable if made by a legal representative. Fees paid to a non legally qualified assistant were not disbursements since they would not have been paid had the litigant been legally represented: *United Building & Plumbing Contractors v Kajla* [2002] EWCA Civ 628.

The Bar operates a Licensed Access Scheme under which certain licensed bodies, e.g. members of the Institute of Taxation, may instruct counsel direct. The Bar Council has issued rules governing the way in which barristers instructed under the Licensed Access Scheme must conduct their business. This is a useful device for reducing costs, particularly in cases of a technical nature where the solicitor would otherwise be no more than a conduit between, e.g. a specialist tax practitioner and a specialist tax barrister. The scheme has however produced a difficulty in that a tax payer being advised by members of the Institute of Taxation and by counsel under the Licensed Access Scheme appealed from a decision of the Commissioners and thence to the Court of Appeal where the tax payer was successful. Although it was conceded that the tax payer was entitled to his costs, there was considerable argument as to the extent of those costs. The Court of Appeal found that the tax payer had been acting as a litigant in person (although he had in fact taken no active part in the proceedings), that counsel's fee was recoverable since it was a disbursement which would have been made had solicitors been instructed but that the fees of the tax advisers were not recoverable: *Agassi v Robinson (HMIT)* [2005] EWCA Civ 1507; [2006] 1 W.L.R. 2126; [2006] 1 All E.R. 900, CA.

A non-solicitor litigant in person, even if a professional, cannot recover costs in respect of his time spent, other than in respect of time spent on matters within his own professional expertise and requiring the attention of an expert. The position of an office holder (liquidator / administrator) is no different. Even if the office holder had to bring or defend litigation, that did not mean that it was part of his profession to conduct litigation, in the way that it was part of the profession of a solicitor to do so. Only that part of the firm's costs which related to in-house expert services carried out by experts doing work which was such as to require the exercise of that particular expertise could be brought into account on the detailed assessment: *Sisu Fund Ltd v Tucker* [2005] EWHC 2321 (Ch); [2006] 1 All E.R. 167, Warren J. (the appeal against this decision was subsequently withdrawn).

VAT Tribunal

48.6.4 A successful party in proceedings before a VAT tribunal is only entitled to out-of-pocket expenses, with no allowance for time spent, as there is no provision for this in r.29(1)(a) of the Value Added Tax Tribunals Rules 1986 (SI 1986/590) (*Commissioners of Customs & Excise v Ross* [1990] 2 All E.R. 65): Approved: *Nader v H.M. Customs & Excise* [1993] S.T.C. 806, CA.

Official Receiver

48.6.5 In a case in which the Official Receiver obtained disqualification orders in the High Court against three respondents, together with an order for the Official Receiver's costs, the issue arose, in respect of work done by the Official Receiver himself, whether he was entitled to be treated as a litigant in person or whether recovery was limited to out of pocket expenses. The Court of Appeal found that the Official Receiver, if unrepresented in the conduct of an application to disqualify a director, was himself a litigant in person for the purpose of assessing and recovering costs. The court also considered whether or not the Official Receiver had suffered financial loss. The court referred with approval to *Eastwood (Deceased), Re* [1975] Ch. 112; *Eastwood (Deceased), Re* [1973] 3 W.L.R. 795. The court found that the Official Receiver worked upon the case like the Treasury Solicitor and an employed solicitor. The costs, like the costs of the Treasury Solicitor in *Re Eastwood* were pecuniary in nature and therefore the amount recoverable should be that provided for by the rules. *Minotaur Data Systems Ltd, Re* [1999] 1 W.L.R. 1129 and *The Official Receiver v Brunt & Ors* [1999] 3 All E.R. 122, CA.

The decision in *Re: Eastwood* (above) was confirmed by the Court of Appeal in *Cole v British Telecommunications Plc* [2000] 2 Costs L.R. 310, CA.

Solicitors acting on own account

Solicitors who acted on their own account and were successful defendants in proceedings were allowed a lower hourly rate than that claimed (the accepted commercial rate) on the basis that the defendants whilst working on their own account did not in fact have any overheads. On the application for permission to appeal the court held that a paying party could not be charged for what did not exist: see *London Scottish Benefits Society v Chorley* [1883–1884] L.R. 13 Q.B.D. 872. In preventing a bonus out of an award of costs there was no inconsistency to the overridding principle of indemnity; the costs of the appeal were likely to be disproportionate: *Stubblefield v Kemp* [2001] 1 Costs L.R. 30, Arden J. **48.6.6**

The Court of Appeal examined the principle to be derived from *London Scottish Benefit Society* (above) in *Malkinson v Trim* [2002] EWCA Civ 1273. The court held that the principle did survive the Civil Procedure Rules and that a partner who is represented in legal proceedings by his firm incurs no liability to the firm but suffers a loss for which under the indemnity principle he ought to be compensated because the firm, of which he is a member, expends time and resources which would otherwise be devoted to other clients. The only sensible way in which effect can be given to the indemnity princple is by allowing those costs: " ..that is the solution which for over 100 years the courts have adopted as a rule of practice".

On the question of whether or not a solicitor could recover her costs of acting on her own behalf in a case, which spanned the pre and post CPR regime, the court found that although the solicitor was a practising solicitor, she was not a practising solicitor who was able to charge for her time. This was, in the judgment of the court, the defining criterion. She was therefore only entitled to recover costs as a litigant in person pre CPR. In followed that post CPR she was unable to take advantage of section 52.5 of the Costs Practice Direction, a provision which, in the view of the court, could not have been designed to do more than to preserve the rule in *London Scottish Benefit Society v Chorley* (see *Boyd & Hutchinson v Joseph* [2003] EWHC 413 (Ch), Patten J).

Costs where the court has made a group litigation order[1]

48.6A—(1) This rule applies where the court has made a Group Litigation Order ("GLO"). **48.6A**

(2) In this rule—

(a) "individual costs" means costs incurred in relation to an individual claim on the group register;

(b) "common costs" means—

(i) costs incurred in relation to the GLO issues;

(ii) individual costs incurred in a claim while it is proceeding as a test claim; and

(iii) costs incurred by the lead solicitor in administering the group litigation; and

(c) "group litigant" means a claimant or defendant, as the case may be, whose claim is entered on the group register.

[1] Introduced by the Civil Procedure (Amendment No.3) Rules 2000 (SI 2000/1317).

(3) Unless the court orders otherwise, any order for common costs against group litigants imposes on each group litigant several liability (GL) for an equal proportion of those common costs.

(4) The general rule is that where a group litigant is the paying party, he will, in addition to any costs he is liable to pay to the receiving party, be liable for—

(a) the individual costs of his claim; and

(b) an equal proportion, together with all the other group litigants, of the common costs.

(5) Where the court makes an order about costs in relation to any application or hearing which involved—

(a) one or more GLO issues; and

(b) issues relevant only to individual claims,

the court will direct the proportion of the costs that is to relate to common costs and the proportion that is to relate to individual costs.

(6) Where common costs have been incurred before a claim is entered on the group register, the court may order the group litigant to be liable for a proportion of those costs.

(7) Where a claim is removed from the group register, the court may make an order for costs in that claim which includes a proportion of the common costs incurred up to the date on which the claim is removed from the group register.

(Part 19 sets out rules about group litigation)

Comment

48.6A.1 Part 19 has been amended to incorporate rules relating to group litigation. This provides that, unless the court orders otherwise, group litigants are severally (not jointly) liable for an equal proportion of common costs. In addition a group litigant is liable for the individual costs of his or her own claim. A group litigant coming late to the group register may be ordered to be liable for a proportion of the costs incurred before that litigant's name is entered on the register.

The court refused to make an order to the effect that claimants (represented under conditional fee agreements), who were successful should be entitled to their costs, but in the event of failure all claimants who had been involved in any stage would be liable to pay any costs order on a pro rata basis. The proposal was rejected as it would encourage those with weaker cases to continue at all costs. The order should provide that both liability for and the benefit of costs, in relation to the issues common to all claimants, would be several rather than joint. It was not yet clear what would happen to an unsuccessful claimant at the end of group litigation conducted under a conditional fee agreement. *Hodgson v Imperial Tobacco Ltd (No.2)* [1998] 2 Costs L.R. 27, Wright J.

Taking the indemnity principle as a starting point, where several clients instruct the same solicitor in a group action, the liability of each is for the entirety of the individual costs of his claim and a per capita share of the common costs unless there were good evidential grounds for the court ordering otherwise: *AB v Liverpool City Council (Costs)* [2003] EWHC 1539 (QB). In the Vibration White Finger Litigation against British Coal (DTI) claims are handled under a claims handling agreement (CHA). A supervising Judge was appointed who held review hearings at regular intervals to enable the progress of the litigation to be supervised and to deal with any ad hoc issues. The supervising Judge found he had no jurisdiction to make an order for the payment of interest. The procedure was not group litigation but was merely designed to carry the terms of the CHA into effect. On appeal the Court held, to all intents and purposes the procedure is group litigation, although not formally group litigation (the procedures being devised before the current rules came into force), considerations as to ensuring that claims were processed fairly and efficiently, and promoting the just disposal of cases, applied as if it were group litigation: *A B and Others v British Coal Corporation (DTI)* [2006] EWCA Civ 1357.

Group Litigation

The courts are entitled to devise new procedures adapted to the circumstances of particular group litigation (*Horrocks v Ford Motor Company Ltd*, *The Times*, February 15, 1990, CA). There is nothing in the guidance given by appellate courts which precludes a costs sharing order, accordingly an order could be made that any cost incurred or ordered to be paid by any claimant should be paid equally by all claimants (*Chrzanowska v Glaxo Laboratories Ltd*, *Independent*, March 13, 1990). See *Davies (Joseph Owen) v Eli Lilley* [1987] 1 W.L.R. 1136; [1987] 3 All E.R. 94, for the procedure to be followed in cases where large numbers of claimants, including some who are legally aided, make related claims against the same defendants. (In essence, no difference should be drawn between parties who are legally aided and those who are funding the litigation on a private basis). In group proceedings in which common issues were raised, in lead actions chosen for trial of principal issues, costs sharing orders were made against other defendants (*Re Interest Rate Swap Litigation*, *The Times*, December 19, 1991). **48.6A.2**

In litigation, where the claimant building society issued proceedings involving hundreds of claims against various firms of solicitors, arising out of mortgage transactions, a number of claims were selected for trial as being representative of the various types of claim. Twenty-five claims were tried, together with a further 13 against a particular firm. Some claims were not disposed of at trial but were either discontinued or settled. At trial the claimant succeeded in 22 claims and the relevant defendant was ordered to pay the claimant's costs of the particular action and the appropriate share of the claimant's generic costs. In those cases where the claimant lost, the claimant was ordered to pay the defendant's costs including generic costs. The claimant argued that it had been largely successful in its claims and that the defendants should pay the generic costs. The court found that broadly speaking the claimant had succeeded in roughly 78 per cent of its claims and the defendants had succeeded in 11 per cent. The court ordered the defendants to pay the claimant 60 per cent of the claimant's generic costs: *Nationwide Building Society v Various Solicitors (No.4)*, *Independent*, October 25, 1999, Blackburne J.

In proceedings where two out of five lead cases went to trial and were dismissed, the claimants succeeding on certain issues only, the Court of Appeal ordered that all claimants succeeding should contribute to 75 per cent of the defendant's costs. It was impossible to say that the claimants and their advisors did not intend that the costs of the lead actions should be borne proportionately by all claimants, therefore there was no proper basis for making a distinction between the lead claimant and the other common claimants: *Ochwat v Watson Burton* [2000] C.P. Rep. 45.

If there is an agreement about the apportionment, between group litigants of costs of proceedings, like a test case, the existence of the agreement does not exclude the statutory discretion of the court to make its own order, including an order which binds group litigants who are not strictly parties to the test case. Where there are contractual rights and obligations the court's discretion should ordinarily be exercised so as to reflect those contractual rights and obligations (per Park J. *Bank of Credit and Commerce International SA (In Liquidation) v Ali (No.5)* [2000] 2 Costs L.R. 243.

Lead cases and test cases

It is sensible and consonant with justice that both the recoverability of common costs and the liability, if any, of discontinuing claimants for costs should be determined at the same time as orders for common costs were made in respect of those common issues. The court then had a full picture and could make whatever order was just in all the circumstances. There is an inherent injustice to claimants and an inappropriate advantage to defendants if an order making a discontinuing claimant liable for his individual costs, together with his share of the common costs incurred by the defendants up to the last day of the quarter in which he discontinued was allowed to remain the norm. A group action is essentially different from the typical action where the single claimant, or limited number of claimants, brought an action. To have a prima facie rule that any discontinuing claimant should have a crystallised liability to recover common costs and a potential liability for the common costs of defendants at the end of a quarter in which he discontinued was too blunt an instrument and was necessarily favourable to the defendants when it was as yet unknown whether the claimants as a whole were to be successful in the common issues which were to be tried: *Sayers v* **48.6A.3**

Smithkline Beecham Plc; XYZ v Schering Health Care Ltd; Afrika v Cape Plc [2001] EWCA Civ 2017; [2002] 1 W.L.R. 2274, CA.

In most group litigation cases there should be no need for any detailed assessment of costs until the conclusion of the group litigation. Claimants' solicitors are entitled to an adequate cash flow from the defendants once the general issue of liability has been admitted or determined in the claimants' favour. Similarly on determination of generic issues in the claimants' favour, and on the assessment or settlement of awards of damages to individuals or batches of claimants, the court expressed the hope that defendants' solicitors would agree to pay, at various stages in the group litigation, a realistic interim amount on account of a final detailed assessment of costs if necessary. If agreement could not be reached as to an interim payment it should be dealt with cheaply and shortly by the nominated trial Judge under his powers under r.44.3(8). If the Judge was provided beforehand with a written schedule of costs, together with a succinct skeleton of the issues, and the rival contentions of the party, it might be possible for the award of costs on account to be dealt with on paper: *Giambrone v JMC Holidays Ltd (formerly t/a Sunworld Holidays Ltd) (Costs)* [2002] EWHC 2932 (QB), Morland J.

II. Costs Relating to Solicitors and other Legal Representatives

Personal liability of legal representative for costs—wasted costs orders[1]

48.7 **48.7—(1) This rule applies where the court is considering whether to make an order under section 51(6) of the Supreme Court Act 1981[2] (court's power to disallow or (as the case may be) order a legal representative to meet "wasted costs" in cases to which this section applies.**

(2) The court must give the legal representative a reasonable opportunity to attend a hearing to give reasons why it should not make such an order.

(3) [Revoked]

(4) When the court makes a wasted costs order, it must—

(a) specify the amount to be disallowed or paid; or

(b) direct a costs judge or a district judge to decide the amount of costs to be disallowed or paid.

(5) The court may direct that notice shall be given to the legal representative's client, in such manner as the court may direct—

(a) of any proceedings under this rule; or

(b) of any order made under it against his legal representative.

(6) Before making a wasted costs order, the court may direct a costs judge or a district judge to inquire into the matter and report to the court.

(7) The court may refer the question of wasted costs to a costs judge or a district judge, instead of making a wasted costs order.

Comment

48.7.1 The wasted costs provisions are set out in s.51(6) of the Supreme Court Act 1981.

---

[1] Amended by the Civil Procedure (Amendment No.3) Rules 2000 (SI 2000/1317) and Civil Procedure (Amendment) Rules 2002 (SI 2002/2058).

[2] 1981 c.54. Section 51 was substituted by s.4(1) of the Courts and Legal Services Act 1990 (c.41).

See s.53 of the Costs Practice Direction as to the way in which the court will deal with wasted costs applications.

The court has power to order that the client be informed of any application for wasted costs and of any order made against the legal representative. Even if the court does not make such an order, r.44.2 has the effect of requiring the legal representative to notify the client of any adverse order made if the client was not present when it was made.

The court may refer the matter to a Costs Judge or District Judge for enquiry and report, or may leave it to the Costs Judge or District Judge to deal with the matter.

Supreme Court Act 1981 s.51

It is open to a litigant to seek a wasted costs order against the legal representatives of any party including his own representatives: *Brown v Bennett (Wasted Costs) (No.1)* [2002] 1 W.L.R. 713, Neuberger J. **48.7.2**

The House of Lords, approving *Brown v Bennett* above, confirmed that the court did have jurisdiction under s.51 of the Supreme Court Act 1981 (1) to make a wasted costs order against the legal representative of any opposing party; (2) a barrister could be liable for a wasted costs order in relation to conduct immediately relevant to the exercise of a right of audience although not involving advocacy. A court considering making a wasted costs order had to make full allowance for the inability of the respondent lawyers to tell the full story because of the privilege of the client. The court should therefore not make an order against a lawyer precluded by legal professional privilege from advancing his full answer to the complaint against him without satisfying itself that it was in all the circumstances fair to do so. Where counsel was drafting allegations of fraud it was not necessary for him to have admissible evidence of fraud but only material such as to lead responsible counsel to conclude that serious allegations could be based on it: *Medcalf v Weatherill* [2002] UKHL 27.

Under s.51(6) the court has power to order "the legal or other representative" to meet wasted costs. A "legal or other representative" is any person exercising a right to conduct litigation on the party's behalf. Solicitors who had failed to issue proceedings did not fall within the definition of persons exercising a right to conduct litigation in the proceedings. The court has to be satisfied that the conduct of the person against whom the wasted costs order is to be made was causative of the costs which have been incurred. In the absence of a causative link no wasted costs order could be made: *Byrne v South Sefton Health Authority* [2001] EWCA Civ 1904.

Wasted costs orders

The Court of Appeal has considered in detail the wasted costs jurisdiction introduced by the Courts and Legal Services Act 1990 (*Allen v Unigate Dairies Ltd*; *Ridehalgh v Horsefield*; *Philex plc v Golban*; *Watson v Watson*; *Antonelli v Wide Gery Farr (A Firm)*, [1994] Ch. 205; [1994] 3 W.L.R. 462, CA). The Court held that while litigants should not be financially prejudiced by the unjustifiable conduct of litigation by their or their opponent's lawyers, the courts in the exercise of the wasted costs jurisdiction, should be astute to control the threat of a new and costly form of satellite litigation. When a wasted costs order was contemplated a three stage test should be applied: **48.7.3**

(a) Had the legal representative of whom complaint was made acted improperly, unreasonably or negligently?
(b) If so, did such conduct cause the applicant to incur unnecessary costs?
(c) If so, was it, in all the circumstances, just to order the legal representative to compensate the applicant for the whole or part of the relevant costs?

The making of a wasted costs order does not breach ECHR, Protocol 1 art.1 (*X v Germany*, No.7544/76, 14 D.R. 60, EComHR), nor does it raise an issue under ECHR art.6 (1) (*B v United Kingdom*, No.10615/83, 38 D.R. 213, EComHR).

Improper, unreasonable or negligent —"Improper" covered, but was not confined to, conduct which would ordinarily be held to justify disbarment, striking off, suspension from practice or other serious professional penalty. **48.7.4**

"Unreasonable" aptly described conduct which was vexatious, designed to harass the other side, rather than advance the resolution of the case, and it made no difference that the conduct was the product of excessive zeal and not improprer motive.

"Negligence" should be understood in an untechnical way to denote failure to act with the competence reasonably expected of ordinary members of the profession. In adopting that approach the court firmly discountenanced any suggestion that an application for a wasted costs order needed to prove, under the negligence head, anything less than he would had to prove in an action for negligence. See *Saif Ali v Sydney Mitchell & Co* [1980] A.C. 198 at 218, 220 (see also *Sampson v John Boddy Timber Ltd, Independent*, May 17, 1995, CA; and *D. Walter & Co Ltd v Neville Eckley & Co* (1997) B.C.C. 331 per Sir Richard Scott, V.-C.).

Delay in the conduct of proceedings can give rise to a wasted costs order. When considering making such an order the judge is obliged to carry out some enquiry into the costs incurred but not a detailed enquiry. Provided the judge has made a reasoned assessment of the costs wasted he will make an order in broad terms. The judge should identify the conduct of the legal representative relating to the delay which is improper, unreasonable or negligent and then make an assessment of the costs actually wasted: *Kilroy v Kilroy* [1997] P.N.L.R. 66, CA.

In order for a wasted costs order to be made any impropriety should be a very serious one and there had to be something more than negligence. There had to be something akin to abuse of process. It is a necessary requirement of any wasted costs order that there should be a breach of the lawyer's duty to the court, there must be something more than mere negligence for the wasted costs jurisdiction to arise: *Persaud (Luke) v Persaud (Mohan)* [2003] EWCA Civ 394; [2003] P.N.L.R. 26, CA. Solicitors cannot be liable for wasted costs as a result of actions before the litigation has started, especially when the actions were no more than negligent and the solicitors never acted in the litigation once it started: *Byrne v Sefton HA* [2001] EWCA Civ 1904. Following a review of the authorities relied on in *Persaud*, the Court of Appeal did not accept that the meaning of "negligent" had been modified as suggested. In cases where the allegation is that the legal representative has pursued a hopeless case, the question is whether no reasonably competent legal representative would have continued with the action. This question could not be answered affirmatively unless the representative also acted unreasonably which is akin to establishing abuse of process. Where privilege was not waived and the judge did not have the benefit of seeing counsel's advice in relation to the claim which had proceeded, the court could not infer simply from the extension of legal aid for the trial, that the solicitors had asserted that there were good prospects of success: *Dempsey v Johnstone* [2003] EWCA Civ 1134. Unless an applicant for a wasted costs order can establish that the legal representative acted in a way that was not only "improper, unreasonable or negligent" but was also in some way in breach of any duty to the court, the court cannot make a wasted costs order. Where a legal representative had been found to have acted negligently, the act had occurred at a time when there were no legal proceedings on foot and therefore there could be no question of that negligence representing any sort of breach of any duty to the court: *Charles v Gillian Radford & Co* [2003] EWHC 3180, (Ch) Neuberger J.

Solicitors acting for a mining company sought an injunction against the Central Bank of Mongolia to restrain the bank from dealing with gold deposited by the claimant company. The injunction was refused on the basis that the bank was immune from proceedings, because of the effect of the State Immunity Act 1978. The solicitors then obtained a Norwich Pharmacal Order, but this was overturned by the Court of Appeal, again on the basis of the state immunity of the bank. Leave to appeal to the House of Lords was refused. The bank then applied for a wasted costs order against the solicitors, on the basis that their conduct was persistently negligent and unreasonable, since they should have appreciated that the bank was immune from suit because of the provisions of the State Immunity Act. The court found that the solicitors' conduct could not be categorised as negligent or unreasonable. The law relating to the liability of the bank to the company could not be said to be so straightforward that the claimant could be criticised for pursuing the claim. Neither the House of Lords nor the Court of Appeal had criticised the claimant, nor had the bank suffered any loss. The application was refused: *KOO Golden East Mongolia v Bank of Nova Scotia* [2008] EWHC 1120 (QB) Silber J.

Solicitors appealed against the making of a wasted costs order against them on the application of a local authority. The basis on which the authority had suggested the solicitors should pay wasted costs was that they were said to have acted "unreasonably". The solicitors acted for a person occupying council premises, in respect of which the council sought a possession order. At the hearing to set aside the possession order counsel asked for production of the request for the warrant. When the warrant was produced counsel raised a new point based on its irregularity. The matter had to be adjourned. The solicitors had been held vicariously liable for the costs consequences of the adjournment. It was not suggested that counsel had acted in any way unreasonably. The fact that it had not occurred to the solicitors that production of the request might open up a new avenue of argument was not such a shortcoming as could fairly be castigated as "unreasonable" conduct on the solicitors' part involving a breach of duty to the courts such as to justify a wasted costs order against them: Hallam-Peel & Co v *The London Borough of Southwark* [2008] EWCA Civ 1120.

A wasted costs order was upheld in a case which had not been merely the prosecution of a hopeless case on instructions, but where the solicitors had themselves been negligent, in failing to address the relevant test for the existence of a contract of employment to which the defendants' representatives had drawn its attention. A reasonably competent solicitor would have been expected to advise the claimant in clear terms that on the material available it had no claim. The solicitors could not explain or excuse its conduct by reference to the claimant's instructions. The involvement of counsel did not absolve the solicitors and the order could be made notwithstanding considerations arising from the fact that the claimant was publicly funded: *The Issacs Partnership v Omm Al-Jawaby Oil Service Co Ltd*, November 5, 2003, unrep. (Gross J.).

Pursuing a hopeless case —A personal representative was not to be held to have acted improperly and unreasonably or negligently simply because, he acted for a party who pursued a claim or defence which was plainly doomed to fail. The legal representatives would advise their clients of the perceived weakness of their case and of the risk of failure, but the clients were free to reject advice and insist that cases be litigated. **48.7.5**

It was rarely if ever safe for a court to assume that a hopeless case was being litigated on the advice of the lawyers involved. They were there to present the case and it was for the judge and not the lawyers to judge it.

It was not entirely easy to distinguish by definition between the hopeless case; and the case which amounted to an abuse of the process, but in practice it was not hard to say which was which, and if there was doubt the legal representative was entitled to the benefit of it. (See also *Re O (A Minor) (Wasted Costs Application)* [1994] 2 F.L.R. 842, Connell J.) (Where at a hearing counsel accepted that an application to suspend a warrant of possession was hopeless, and counsel, with a senior partner of the solicitors behind him, made no application for an adjournment nor gave an explanation of the conduct of the solicitors, it was held that the solicitors had had a reasonable opportunity to show cause why the order should not be made and, whilst the original application was doomed to failure, that did not of itself justify a wasted costs order but the absence of explanation suggested playing for time and the commonplace nature of the original application rendered it unnecessary for the judge to insist on a full investigation of the solicitors' motivation:*Woolwich Building Society v Finberg* [1998] P.N.L.R. 216, CA.)

The question which the judge must ask was whether or not a reasonably competent legal adviser would have evaluated the chances of success as being such as to justify continuing with the proceedings. In determining that question the judge may only come to a conclusion adverse to the legal advisers if he has had the opportunity of seeing counsel's advice. In the absence of waiver of privilege in respect of that advice it cannot be inferred that the evaluation of the claim was negligent in the relevant sense: *Dempsey v Johnstone* [2003] EWCA Civ 1134.

Where solicitors had been aware for over two months that an applicant's application had been rendered academic, the court refused to make a wasted costs order even though the claim had not been withdrawn until four days before the hearing. In circumstances where the solicitors had attempted to contact the claimant on a number of occasions without success, the solicitors conduct was not unreasonable: *R. (Latchman) v Secretary of State for the Home Department* [2004] EWHC 2795 (Admin), Bennett J.

Legal Aid —It was incumbent on the courts to which wasted costs applications were made to bear prominently in mind the peculiar vulnerability of legal representatives acting for assisted persons. *Symphony Group plc v Hodgson* [1993] 3 W.L.R. 830, 842. It would subvert the benevolent purposes of the legal aid legislation if such representatives were subject to any unusual personal risk, and they should bear prominently in mind that their advice and conduct was not to be tempered by the knowledge that their client was not their paymaster, and so no, in all probability, liable for the costs of the other side. (This view was endorsed by Otton L.J. in *Wall v Lefever* [1998] 1 F.C.R. 605; *The Times*, August 1, 1997, CA.) **48.7.6**

Where a party is legally aided the solicitor is under a duty (see Civil Legal Aid (General) Regulations 1989 reg.82(2)) to serve notice of revocation or discharge of legal aid on all other parties to the proceedings and also on counsel and on the Court hearing the matter. Failure to do so could amount to unreasonable behaviour and costs suffered by other parties as a result of the failure should not be borne by the LSC: *Banks v Woodhall Duckham Ltd (No.2)* [1997] P.I.Q.R. P464; *NG Ferguson & Co Ltd v Brown & Tawse (A Firm)*, 1918 S.C. (H.L.) 125; *Banks v Humphrey & Glasgow, sub nom. Re Stathams (Wasted Costs Order)* [1997] P.I.Q.R. P464, CA.

Where the Legal Aid Certificates of both parties in a partnership dispute, were discharged, and a wasted costs order was made against the claimant's representatives for pursuing the action pending appeal against discharge, the Court of Appeal held that the court should be slow to supplement statutory or supplementary duties by placing a higher standard on the parties. No order as to costs was substituted: *Tate v Hart* [1999] Lloyd's Rep. P.N. 566.

48.7.7 *Immunity*—A barrister and a solicitor acting as advocate is no longer immune from action for negligence at the suit of a client in respect of his conduct and management of a case in court, and the pre-trial work immediately connected with it (*Arthur JS Hall & Co v Simons* [2002] 1 A.C. 615).

If an advocate's conduct in court was improper, unreasonable or negligent he was liable to a wasted costs order.

A judge must make full allowance for the fact that an advocate in court often had to make decisions quickly and under pressure. Mistakes would inevitably be made, things done which the outcome showed to have been unwise. Advocacy was more an art than a science and it could not be conducted according to formulae. It was only when, with all allowances made, an advocate's conduct of court proceedings was quite plainly unjustifiable that it would be appropriate to make a wasted costs order against him.

48.7.8 *Privilege*—If the applicant's privileged communications were germane to the application he could waive privilege, and if he declined to do so, adverse inferences could be drawn. The respondent's lawyers were in a different position. The privilege was not theirs to waive. Judges invited to make such orders should make full allowance for the inability of the respondent lawyers to tell the whole story. Where there was room for doubt the respondent lawyers were entitled to the benefit of it. It was only when, with all allowances made, a lawyer's conduct of proceedings was quite plainly unjustifiable, that it could be appropriate to make the order.

A material factor in deciding the culpability of legal representatives' conduct is whether the client has waived legal professional privilege, if not the court must make assumptions in favour of those legal representatives: *Daly v Hubner* [2002] Lloyd's Rep. P.N. 461 (Ch), Etherton J.

Acting on instructions is no answer to a charge of abuse of process and breach of duty to the court. Refusal to waive privilege does not preclude a finding of abuse when the particular conduct admits of no reasonable explanation. In the particular case the solicitors had been under a duty to investigate the client's motives for issuing an appeal and had failed to do so: *Morris v Roberts (HMIT) (Wasted Costs Order)* [2005] EWHC 1040 (Ch); [2005] P.N.L.R. 41, Lightman J.

48.7.9 *Causation*—Demonstration of the causal link between the improper, unreasonable, or negligent conduct and the waste of costs was essential. Where conduct was proved but no waste of costs shown to have resulted the case might be referred to the appropriate disciplinary body or the legal aid authorities. It was not a matter for the exercise of the wasted costs jurisdiction.

48.7.10 *Reliance on counsel*—A solicitor did not abdicate his professional responsibility when he sought the advice of counsel. He had to apply his mind to the advice received. The more specialist the nature of the advice, the more reasonable it was likely to be for him to accept it (*Locke v Camberwell H.A.* [1991] 2 Med. L.R. 249) (and see *Reaveley v Safeway Stores plc* [1998] P.N.L.R. 526, CA).

48.7.11 *Threats to apply for wasted costs orders*—Such threats should not be made as a means of intimidation. If one side considered that the conduct of the other was improper, unreasonable or negligent, and was likely to cause a waste of costs it was not objectionale to alert the other side to that view.

Timing of the application —In general wasted costs application were best left until after the end of the trial (*Film Lab Systems International Ltd v Pennington* [1994] 4 All E.R. 673, DC). **48.7.12**

In family proceedings where the husband changed his legal advisers his former solicitors having taken no steps to prepare a case for trial despite issues having been identified, the wife's solicitors had to seek discovery of documents held by the husband's original solicitors, the trial was vacated and directions had neither been sought nor given. On the wife's application for a wasted costs order against her husband's legal team before the main trial began, the court held that a wasted costs application could be heard before the main trial, especially where the legal representatives had changed. Counsel was ordered to bear 75 per cent of the costs to reflect seniority and prime responsibilty, the solicitor being ordered to pay the remainder to reflect inattentiveness to the impact of the advice received: *B v B (Wasted Costs: abuse of process)* [2001] 1 F.L.R. 843, Wall J.

In proceedings in which the defendant was successful, an order was made for costs as between the parties. Prior to the detailed assessment the defendant sought wasted costs against the claimant's legal representative. On appeal it was held that the court did have jurisdiction to make a wasted costs order. The case was not concerned with revisiting costs with a view to a wasted costs order under s.51(6), but with revisiting a decision on costs as between the parties under s.51(1) of the Act. This involved the exercise of two separate discretions and the discretion in relation to a possible wasted costs order could be exercised at any time up until detailed assessment: *Melchior v Vettivel* [2002] C.P. Rep. 24, Patten J; *Commissioners for Customs & Excise v Anchor Foods, The Times*, September 28, 1999, Neuberger J. distinguished.

The applicant —The court itself might initiate the enquiry, but save in the most obvious case courts should be slow to initiate the enquiry. The courts would usually be well advised to leave an aggrieved party to make the application. The costs would then in the ordinary way follow the event between the parties. **48.7.13**

Procedure —The procedure to be followed was to be laid down by courts so as to the meet the requirements of the individual case before them. The overriding requirements were that any procedure had to be fair and as simple and summary as fairness permitted. The respondent lawyer was to be very clearly told what he was said to have done wrong and what was claimed. The requirements of simplicity and summariness meant that elaborate pleadings should in general be avoided. No formal process of discovery would be appropriate. The court could not imagine any circumstances in which the applicant should be permitted to interrogate the respondent lawyer or vice versa. Hearings should be measured in hours not days or weeks. Per Pumfrey J. in *S. v M. (Wasted Costs Order), The Times*, March 26, 1998. The question whether a wasted costs order should be made could only sensibly be answered if the scope of the costs sought was narrow and clear. If there was insufficient material for the judge to make a determination, and the costs recoverable would, in any event, be limited, it was not appropriate to make an order: *Regent Leisuretime Ltd v Skerrett* [2006] EWCA Civ 1032. **48.7.14**

When an application for a wasted costs order has been settled, the Court should be provided with a succinct written statement giving information as to matters relevant to the reputations of the lawyers which would otherwise not be brought to the Court's attention (*Manzanilla Ltd v Corton Property & Investments Ltd (No.2)* [1997] 3 F.C.R. 389, CA).

In finding that the appropriate court to deal with the wasted costs order was the court that had dealt with the proceedings to which the costs related, the Court of Appeal gave further guidance:

(1) The making of an order as to who should bear the costs and on what basis, in respect of proceedings which go to trial, are in principle part of the overriding order made by the court at the conclusion of the trial.
(2) In the absence of at least a good reason to the contrary, the costs of proceedings should be dealt with by the tribunal which determines the issue which disposes of the case immediately after the judgment in disposing of the case.
(3) In principle there is no difference between a costs order against a party and a costs order against a non party, they are all part of the judicial function involved in disposing of a case.
(4) Where a wasted costs order is sought in respect of an interlocutory matter before trial, it is often better for the application for wasted costs only to be made after the trial.

(5) It is not mandatory that the application for wasted costs be made at the end of the trial. In many cases a party considering an application for a wasted costs order will ask the judge for time to consider whether to make such an application, and, even if such an application is made, the normal course is for the court to give directions in relation to the disposal of the application rather than to deal with it straightaway.

(6) The application for a wasted costs order can be made after the order in relation to the proceedings has been drawn up, although the court hearing the application late will not necessarily grant it if there is no good reason for the delay: *Gray v Going Places Leisure Travel Ltd* [2005] EWCA Civ 189.

An application for a wasted costs order was held to be inappropriate where complicated proceedings requiring detailed investigation into the facts would ensue as the procedure was a summary one to be applied in uninvolved and clear cases where unnecessary costs were incurred. *Manzanilla Ltd v Corton Property* (above) followed. The summary procedure might also be inappropriate in circumstances where a solicitor was alleged to be in breach of his professional duty to his client. *Turner Page Music v Torres Design Associates Ltd*, *The Times*, August 3, 1998, CA.

A wasted costs application was refused where the likely costs of the investigation were disproportionate to the sums claimed. (Sum claimed £169,000: estimated costs of application £130,000) *Chief Constable of North Yorkshire v Audsley* [2000] Lloyd's Rep. PN 675, Keene J.

In deciding whether or not to make a wasted costs order on the basis of negligent non disclosure on an application without notice the court held that section 51(7) of the Supreme Court Act 1981 did not require knowing complicity of a legal representative. A solicitor did not have to know he was failing to make a disclosure which he ought to make, it was sufficient if he knew of a material fact which was not disclosed but negligently or unreasonably believed it was not material or negligently failed to make enquiries which would have revealed material matters; *Lowline (PSV) Ltd v Direct Aviation Ltd*, April 15, 1999, unrep., Rix J.

Rule 48.9(2) provides that the court must give the legal representative opportunity to show cause why an order should not be made. That should not be understood to mean that the burden was on the legal representative to exculpate himself. An order should not be made unless the applicants satisfied the court, or the court was itself satisfied that an order should be made. The rule clearly envisaged that the representative would not be called on to reply unless an apparently strong prima facie case had been made against him, and the language of the rule recognised a shift in the evidential burden.

48.7.15 *Discretion*—The jurisdiction to make a wasted costs order depended at two stages on the court's discretion

(a) At the stage of initial application when the court was invited to give the representative an opportunity to show cause. That was not something to be done automatically. The costs of the enquiries compared with the cost claimed would always be a relevant consideration. The discretion, like any other, was to be exercised judicially, but judges might not infrequently decide that further proceedings were not likely to be justified (and see *Re Freudiana Holdings Ltd*, *The Times*, December 4, 1995, CA).

(b) The final stage: even if the court were satisfied that legal representatives had acted improperly, unreasonably or negligently so as to waste costs, it was not bound to make an order, but would have to give sustainable reasons for the exercise of its discretion in that way.

Although a legal representative might not be liable for wasted costs under the Supreme Court Act 1981 s.51(6) if he is not acting for a party to the proceedings the Court nevertheless has a general power to order costs under s.51(3) even against someone not representing a party to the proceedings where the legal representative has acted improperly and unreasonably (*Kleinwort Benson v De Montenegro* [1994] N.P.C. 46, Aldous J.)

48.7.16 *General principles*—Save in exceptional circumstances, no application for a wasted costs order should in civil litigation be sought against a party's legal representative until after trial. The test to be applied on such an application has to be the same whether the legal representative was acting for a legally aided or for a paying client.

No lawyer who acts in the public interest by accepting legally aided clients should stand any greater risk of being ordered to pay costs, than if he acts for a paying client, per Aldous J. (*Filmlab Systems International Ltd v Pennington* [1994] 4 All E.R. 673, DC). Where a solicitor knew that his clients' sworn evidence in other proceedings meant that their originally pleaded defence was untenable, the solicitor could not avoid liability by a professed reliance on counsel. It was on the facts startlingly clear that the defence was not a true statement of the defendant's case nor of the issues for trial. The solicitor was liable for the wasted costs. *General Mediterranean Holdings SA v Patel* [2000] 1 W.L.R. 272.

Wasted Costs Orders Generally —Applicants for wasted costs orders must bear in mind the principle of proportionality. It is not proportionate for the court to spend more time on wasted costs proceedings than had been expended on the substantive proceedings. *Re Merc Property Ltd*, *The Times*, May 19, 1999, Lindsay J. **48.7.17**

The Court of Appeal summarised the principles derived from *Ridehalgh v Horsefield* [1994] Ch. 205; *Tolstoy-Miloslavsky v Aldington* [1996] 1 W.L.R. 736 and *Wall v Lefever* [1998] 1 F.C.R. 605; *The Times*, August 1, 1997. The power to make a wasted costs order is to be found in s.51 of the Supreme Court Act 1981 and the principles to be applied include:

(a) Improper conduct is that which would be so regarded "according to the consensus of professional (including judicial) opinion". Unreasonable conduct "aptly describes conduct which is vexatious, designed to harass the other side rather than advance the resolution of the case and it makes no difference that the conduct is the product of excessive zeal and not improper motive…the acid test is whether the conduct permits of a reasonable explanation". Negligent conduct was to be understood "in an untechnical way to denote failure to act with the competence reasonably to be expected of ordinary members of the profession". (*Ridehalgh*)

(b) "Legal representatives will…whether barristers or solicitors, advise clients of the perceived weakness of their case and of the risk of failure. But clients are free to reject their advice and insist that cases be litigated. It is rarely if ever safe for a Court to assume that a hopeless case is being litigated on the advice of the lawyers involved…it is however one thing for a legal representative to present on instructions a case which he regards as bound to fail, it is quite another to lend his assistance to proceedings which are an abuse of the process of the Court…it is not entirely easy to distinguish by definition between the hopeless case and the case which amounts to an abuse of the process, but in practice it is not hard to say which is which and if there is doubt the legal representative is entitled to the benefit of it." (*Ridehalgh*)

(c) "A solicitor does not abdicate his professional responsibility when he seeks the advice of counsel." (*Ridehalgh*) Where leading and junior counsel have put their signatures to a statement of claim this "did not exonerate the solicitors from their obligations to exercise their own independent judgment to consider whether the claim could properly be pursued, they were not entitled to follow counsel blindly". (*Tolstoy*)

(d) "The jurisdiction to make a wasted costs order must be exercised with care and only in clear cases." (*Tolstoy*) "It should not be used to create satellite litigation which is as expensive and as complicated as the original litigation. It must be used as a remedy in cases where the need for a wasted costs order is reasonably obvious. It is a summary remedy which is to be used in circumstances where there is a clear picture which indicates that a professional adviser has been negligent." (*Wall v Lefever*): *Fletamentos Maritimos SA v Effjohn International BV* [2003] Lloyd's Rep. P.N. 26.

For a decision relating to public law care proceedings, see *Re G (Minors) L (Care Proceedings: Wasted Costs)* [2000] 2 W.L.R. 1007, Wall J.

Where, on an appeal, the court found that solicitors had acted negligently in making the application at first instance, the court allowed the appeal and made a wasted costs order against the solicitors since it was their negligence which had led to proceedings being brought in a form which was inappropriate to determine a particular issue: *Sherman v Perkins* [2002] W.T.L.R. 603, David Mackie Q.C.

On an appeal against the refusal to make a wasted costs order the Court of Appeal was reluctant to interfere with the discretion of the judge, adding to that the court's views on proportionality, the case ought to be rejected. This was just the type of satellite litigation that should be discouraged at this stage: *White v White* [2003] EWCA Civ 156.

The fact that proceedings have been compromised by a *Tomlin* Order does not prevent the judge dealing with an application for wasted costs. It was not necessary to lift the stay on proceedings in order to pursue the wasted costs application. The court had jurisdiction under s.51(6) of the Supreme Court Act 1981 to make a wasted costs order "in any proceedings" which in that sub-section means "in connection with" or "in relation to": *Wagstaff v Colls* [2003] EWCA Civ 469; [2003] P.N.L.R. 29, CA.

A case which is not obviously hopeless, but which is quite proper to argue, will not provide an appropriate basis to make a wasted costs order against solicitors who had acted for a claimant, in an action which had been discontinued. The defendant had not shown that no reasonably competent solicitor could have concluded that the claimant had a realistic prospect of success: *EFI Marsh v Sofaer; Griffinhoofe & Co; Sofaer; Griffinhoofe & Co v Judkins* [2006] EWHC 1217 (Ch), David Richards J.

On an application for a wasted costs order against a solicitor, where the solicitor was alleged to have been negligent or in breach of duty in failing to obtain documents by way of disclosure in civil proceedings, the court held that, although it was a matter of good practice for a solicitor to take possession of and inspect a client's files which were relevant to the proceedings, failure to take those steps did not mean that he was in breach of his duty to the client or to the court. A solicitor was obliged to explain the obligation of disclosure to his client but was entitled to accept instructions to the effect that certain categories of documents had been lost in the absence of any matters casting doubt on those instructions or requiring further investigation (*Hedrich v Standard Bank London Ltd* [2007] EWHC 1656 (QB); [2007] P.N.L.R. 31, Field J.).

On appeal the decision at first instance was upheld. The Court of Appeal stated that the authorities established that there were two competing public interests involved in the wasted costs jurisdiction. On the one hand litigants should not suffer loss from the misconduct of litigation by legal representatives; but on the other hand: this form of satellite litigation was to be rigorously confined. (See *Ridehalgh v Horsfield* [1994] Ch. 205 CA and *Medcalf v Mardell (Wasted Costs Order)* [2002] UKHL 27, [2003] 1 A.C. 120; *Hedrich v Standard Bank London Ltd* [2008] EWCA Civ 905.)

A wasted costs order against the defendant's solicitors was refused, but the court disallowed part of the defendants' costs where its conduct in relation to disclosure had been lamentable and the costs were further reduced in respect of an issue where the defendant had allowed the claimant (in person) to proceed on an incorrect basis: *Wright v HSBC Bank Plc* [2006] EWHC 1473(QB), Jack J.

Wasted Costs Orders Against Counsel

48.7.18 The liability of a barrister for a wasted costs order is not limited to his conduct of the proceedings in court. A barrister is within the definition of a person "exercising a right of audience or a right to conduct litigation": *Brown v Bennett (Wasted Costs) (No.1)* [2002] 1 W.L.R. 713, Neuberger J.

The House of Lords, approving *Brown v Bennett* above, confirmed that the court did have jurisdiction under s.51 of the Supreme Court Act 1981 (1) to make a wasted costs order against the legal representative of any opposing party; (2) a barrister could be liable for a wasted costs order in relation to conduct immediately relevant to the exercise of a right of audience although not involving advocacy. A court considering making a wasted costs order had to make full allowance for the inability of the respondent lawyers to tell the full story because of the privilege of the client. The court should therefore not make an order against a lawyer precluded by legal professional privilege from advancing his full answer to the complaint against him without satisfying itself that it was in all the circumstances fair to do so. Where counsel was drafting allegations of fraud it was not necessary for him to have admissible evidence of fraud but only material such as to lead responsible counsel to conclude that serious allegations could be based on it: *Medcalf v Mardell (Wasted Costs Order)* [2002] UKHL 27.

Wasted Costs Orders Against a Solicitor Advocate

48.7.18.1 A respondent local authority submitted that the solicitor advocate had instigated, managed and maintained judicial review proceedings as part of a campaign, stepping outside the role of a legal representative and that it had therefore incurred wasted costs. The court held that although the solicitor advocate's behaviour throughout the proceedings was unreasonable and negligent, and the action was completely unnecessary and doomed to failure, no wasted costs order would be made. Having referred to the three stage test (see para.48.7.3, above) the third stage seemed to permit a consideration of the effect of the order upon the person against whom it was sought. On the facts, a wasted costs order would have carried a significant risk of causing the solicitor advocate to become bankrupt. That would be a disproportionate consequence of her unreasonable and negligent conduct in the litigation: R (on the application of Hide & Ors) v *Staffordshire County Council* [2007] EWHC 2441 (Admin) Wyn Williams J.

The Court's Inherent Jurisdiction

Where a court was persuaded that a solicitor had not acted negligently in continuing to act for a company which had been struck off the register, nonetheless the court was able to make an award of costs against the solicitor under its inherent jurisdiction, on the basis that the defendants were clearly in a position to know the status of the company: *Padhiar v Patel* [2001] Lloyd's Rep. P.N. 328. **48.7.19**

ECHR

A party which successfully appealed against the refusal of the Restrictive Practice Court to recuse itself on the grounds of apparent bias submitted that their right to a fair trial under art.6(1) ECHR had been infringed and that they were entitled to compensation for the wasted costs (estimated at about £1 million because the proceedings had to begin again) by the Lord Chancellor who was the emanation of the State responsible for providing impartial tribunals to conduct trials of civil litigation. The Court of Appeal held that the situation had been remedied by providing an impartial tribunal to determine the party's civil rights and obligations. There had therefore been no violation of the right to a fair trial which would give rise to compensation. The Lord Chancellor was therefore not liable to pay the costs of the wasted hearing before the Restrictive Practices Court: *Re Medicaments and Related Classes of Goods (No.4) The Times*, August 7, 2001, CA; *Director General of Fair Trading v Proprietary Association* [2002] EWCA Civ 1217; [2002] 1 All E.R. 853, CA. **48.7.20**

Basis of detailed assessment of solicitor and client costs[1]

48.8—(1) This rule applies to every assessment of a solicitor's bill to his client except a bill which is to be paid out of the Community Legal Service Fund under the Legal Aid Act 1988 or the Access to justice Act 1999; and— **48.8**

(1A) Section 74(3) of the Solicitors Act 1974(a) applies unless the solicitor and client have entered into a written agreement which expressly permits payment to the solicitor of an amount of costs greater than that which the client could have recovered from another party to the proceedings.

(2) Subject to paragraph (1A), costs are to be assessed on the indemnity basis but are to be presumed—

(a) to have been reasonably incurred if they were incurred with the express or implied approval of the client;

(b) to be reasonable in amount if their amount was expressly or impliedly approved by the client;

(c) to have been unreasonably incurred if—

(i) they are of an unusual nature or amount; and

(ii) the solicitor did not tell his client that as a result he might not recover all of them from the other party.

(3) Where the court is considering a percentage increase, whether on the application of the legal representative under rule

[1] Amended by the Civil Procedure (Amendment No.3) Rules 2000 (SI 2000/1317) and the Civil Procedure (Amendment) Rules 2001 (SI 2001/256).

44.16 or on the application of the client, the court will have regard to all the relevant factors as they reasonably appeared to the solicitor or counsel when the conditional fee arrangement was entered into or varied.

(4) In paragraph (3), "conditional fee arrangement" means an agreement enforceable under section 58 of the Courts and Legal Services Act 1990 at the date on which that agreement was entered into or varied. Paragraphs (3) and (4) are shown above as amended by the Civil Procedure (Amendment) Rules 2001 (SI 2001/256).

Comment

48.8.1 Since a detailed assessment of a solicitor and client bill is on the indemnity basis, no question of proportionality arises but the presumptions set out at r.48.8(2) apply. See s.54 of the Costs Practice Direction.

Costs payable out of the Community Legal Service Fund are not dealt with under this rule.

See s.55 of the Costs Practice Direction as to the way in which the court will approach detailed assessment of a conditional fee agreement entered into before April 1, 2000.

This rule preserves the freedom of the client and the solicitor to make whatever agreement they may desire for the supply of the solicitors services subject to the provisions of the Solicitors Act 1974 ss.59 *et seq.*, regarding contentious business agreements, and to the requirement in (2)(c) of the rule.

A client who retains a solicitor whose practice is carried on in a high cost area or in a manner which is plainly luxurious is generally presumed to have impliedly approved of the additional costs necessarily incurred in maintaining that type of practice.

Unusual expense includes special fees for counsel which are unusual or extraordinary or generous fees (*Canvendish v Strutt* [1904] 1 Ch. 524). On the other hand a party is entitled to be allowed a brief fee to Counsel which is the normal and reasonable fee for such a case, heard out of London, even if it is heard in a town where there are a few local members of the bar who are prepared to do the work for less: and this whether the party is legally aided or not (*Self v Self* [1954] P. 480; [1954] 2 All E.R. 550; *Young v Kohler* [1955] 1 W.L.R. 395; [1955] 1 All E.R. 796); and whether Counsel has another brief in the same Court on the same day (*Isaac v Isaac* [1955] P. 333; [1955] 2 All E.R. 811).

Rule 48.8(2)

48.8.2 Where a client had been provided with an estimate of costs on the basis of an hourly rate shortly prior to trial, it was held to be unreasonable that the client should then be charged a higher hourly rate than he was led to believe would be charged. The estimate of costs up to and including trial did not constitute a binding agreement but the correspondence amounted to a clear and considered indication of the client's maximum liability to the solicitors upon which the client was likely to and did rely. The Law Society's Guide to Professional Conduct of Solicitors indicates that the final amount payable should not vary substantially from an estimate given unless the client has been informed of the changed circumstances in writing. *Wong v Vizards* (1997) 2 Costs L.R. 46, Toulson J. In order for a solicitor's charging rates to be expressly or impliedly approved by the client, the client must have been given information adequate to make that approval "informed". Absent informed approval, there is no presumption sufficient to displace the figure arrived at by detailed assessment: *MacDougall v Boote Edgar Esterkin* [2001] 1 Costs L.R. 118, Holland J.

The position of legal representatives acting under conditional fee agreements

48.8.3 The existence of a conditional fee agreement does not alter the relationship between the legal adviser and the client. Legal representatives owe the client exactly the same duties and remain under the same duty to the client to disregard their own interests as if there were no conditional fee agreement. The legal representative also owes the same duties to the Court. There is no reason why the circumstances in which a legal representative acting under a conditional fee agreement can be made personally liable for the costs of a party other than his client should differ from those in which a legal representative who is not acting under a conditional fee agreement would be liable. The existence of a conditional fee agreement should make the legal representative's position as a matter of law no worse, so far as being ordered to pay costs is concerned, than it would be if there were no conditional fee agreement. Legal representatives acting under conditional fee agreements are under no more risk of paying costs personally than they would be if they were not so acting. Per Lord Woolf M.R. in *Hodgson v Imperial Tobacco Ltd*, [1998] 1 W.L.R. 1056, CA.

For a note as to Conditional Fee Agreements in arbitration cases see *Bevan Ashford v Geoff Yeandle (Contractors) Ltd (in liquidation)* [1999] Ch 239; [1998] 3 W.L.R. 172; *The Times*, April 23, 1998, Sir Richard Scott V.-C., para.7A–49.

Assessment procedure

48.10—(1) This rule sets out the procedure to be followed where the court has made an order under Part III of the Solicitors Act 1974 [1] for the assessment of costs payable to a solicitor by his client. 48.10

(2) The solicitor must serve a breakdown of costs within 28 days of the order for costs to be assessed.

(3) The client must serve points of dispute within 14 days after service on him of the breakdown of costs.

(4) If the solicitor wishes to serve a reply, he must do so within 14 days of service on him of the points of dispute.

(5) Either party may file a request for a hearing date—

(a) after points of dispute have been served; but

(b) no later than 3 months after the date of the order for the costs to be assessed.

(6) This procedure applies subject to any contrary order made by the court.

Comment

The present rule sets out the procedure where the court has made an order for the detailed assessment of costs payable to a solicitor by his client. See Costs Practice Direction s.56. 48.10.1

Where the court makes an order for detailed assessment the solicitor is required to serve a breakdown of the costs within 28 days of the order. This breakdown is not a detailed bill for the purposes of s.64(2) of the Solicitors Act 1974. If the client does not serve points of dispute no default costs certificate may be issued (Costs PD para.56.7). In the case of default by either party the other party may make an appropriate Pt 23 application.

The procedure set out in Pt 47 applies subject to the provisions of this rule and to any contrary order made by the court. (See s.56 of the Costs Practice Direction as to the procedure to be adopted.)

Amended by SI 1999/1008.

The court has indicated that it should be standard practice where a client care letter has been affirmatively relied on that it should be produced to the paying party: *Adams v MacInnes* November 8, 2001, unrep., Gray J.

VAT

For the provisions relating to VAT in relation to bills being dealt with by way of summary or detailed assessment see Costs Practice Direction s.5. 48.10.2

[1] 1974 c.47.

DIRECTIONS RELATING TO PART 48—COSTS—SPECIAL CASES

Section 50 Amount of costs where costs are payable pursuant to contract: Rule 48.3

48PD.1 **50.1** Where the court is assessing costs payable under a contract, it may make an order that all or part of the costs payable under the contract shall be disallowed if it is satisfied by the paying party that costs have been unreasonably incurred or are unreasonable in amount.

50.2 Rule 48.3 only applies if the court is assessing costs payable under a contract. It does not—

(1) require the court to make an assessment of such costs; or

(2) require a mortgagee to apply for an order for those costs that he has a contractual right to recover out of the mortgage funds.

50.3 The following principles apply to costs relating to a mortgage—

(1) An order for the payment of costs of proceedings by one party to another is always a discretionary order: section 51 of the Supreme Court Act 1981.

(2) Where there is a contractual right to the costs the discretion should ordinarily be exercised so as to reflect that contractual right.

(3) The power of the court to disallow a mortgagee's costs sought to be added to the mortgage security is a power that does not derive from section 51, but from the power of the courts of equity to fix the terms on which redemption will be allowed.

(4) A decision by a court to refuse costs in whole or in part to a mortgagee litigant may be-

(a) a decision in the exercise of the section 51 discretion;

(b) a decision in the exercise of the power to fix the terms on which redemption will be allowed;

(c) a decision as to the extent of a mortgagee's contractual right to add his costs to the security;

or

(d) a combination of two or more of these things.

The statements of case in the proceedings or the submissions made to the court may indicate which of the decisions has been made.

(5) A mortgagee is not to be deprived of a contractual or equitable right to add costs to the security merely by reason of an order for payment of costs made without reference to the mortgagee's contractual or equitable rights, and without any adjudication as to whether or not the mortgagee should be deprived of these costs.

50.4(1) Where the contract entitles a mortgagee to—

(a) add the costs of litigation relating to the mortgage to the sum secured by it;

(b) require a mortgagor to pay those costs, or

(c) both,

the mortgagor may make an application for the court to direct that an account of the mortgagee's costs be taken.

(Rule 25.1(1)(n) provides that the court may direct that a party file an account)

(2) The mortgagor may then dispute an amount in the mortgagee's account on the basis that it has been unreasonably incurred or is unreasonable in amount.

(3) Where a mortgagor disputes an amount, the court may make an order that the disputed costs are assessed under rule 48.3.

Section 50A Limitation on court's power to award costs in favour of trustee or personal representative: Rule 48.4

50A.1 A trustee or personal representative is entitled to an indemnity out of the relevant trust fund or estate for costs properly incurred, which may include costs awarded against the trustee or personal representative in favour of another party.

50A.2 Whether costs were properly incurred depends on all the circumstances of the case, and may, for example, depend on—

(1) whether the trustee or personal representative obtained directions from the court before bringing or defending the proceedings;

(2) whether the trustee or personal representative acted in the interests of the fund or estate or in substance for a benefit other than that of the estate, including his own; and

(3) whether the trustee or personal representative acted in some way unreasonably in bringing or defending, or in the conduct of, the proceedings.

50A.3 The trustee or personal representative is not to be taken to have acted in substance for a benefit other than of the fund by reason only that he has defended a claim in which relief is sought against him personally.

Section 51 Costs where money is payable by or to a child or protected party: Rule 48.5

51.1 The circumstances in which the court need not order the assessment of costs under rule 48.5(3) are as follows: **48PD.2**

(a) where there is no need to do so to protect the interests of the child or protected party or his estate;

(b) where another party has agreed to pay a specified sum in respect of the costs of the child or protected party and the solicitor acting for the child or protected party has waived the right to claim further costs;

(c) where the court has decided the costs payable to the child or protected party by way of summary assessment and the solicitor acting for the child or protected party has waived the right to claim further costs;

(d) where an insurer or other person is liable to discharge the costs which the child or protected party would otherwise be liable to pay to his solicitor and the court is satisfied that the insurer or other person is financially able to discharge those costs.

Section 52 Litigants in person: Rule 48.6

48PD.3 **52.1** In order to qualify as an expert for the purpose of rule 48.6(3)(c) (expert assistance in connection with assessing the claim for costs), the person in question must be a

(1) barrister,
(2) solicitor,
(3) Fellow of the Institute of Legal Executives,
(4) Fellow of the Association of Law Costs Draftsmen,
(5) law costs draftsman who is a member of the Academy of Experts,
(6) law costs draftsman who is a member of the Expert Witness Institute.

52.2 Where a litigant in person wishes to prove that he has suffered financial loss he should produce to the court any written evidence he relies on to support that claim, and serve a copy of that evidence on any party against whom he seeks costs at least 24 hours before the hearing at which the question may be decided.

52.3 Where a litigant in person commences detailed assessment proceedings under rule 47.6 he should serve copies of that written evidence with the notice of commencement.

52.4 The amount, which may be allowed to a litigant in person under rule 46.3(5)(b) and rule 48.6(4), is £9.25 per hour.

52.5 Attention is drawn to rule 48.6(6)(b). A solicitor who, instead of acting for himself, is represented in the proceedings by his firm or by himself in his firm name, is not, for the purpose of the Civil Procedure Rules, a litigant in person.

Section 53 Personal liability of legal representative for costs—wasted costs orders: Rule 48.7

48PD.4 **53.1** Rule 48.7 deals with wasted costs orders against legal representatives. Such orders can be made at any stage in the proceedings up to and including the proceedings relating to the detailed assessment of costs. In general, applications for wasted costs are best left until after the end of the trial.

53.2 The court may make a wasted costs order against a legal representative on its own initiative.

53.3 A party may apply for a wasted costs order—

(1) by filing an application notice in accordance with Part 23; or
(2) by making an application orally in the course of any hearing.

53.4 It is appropriate for the court to make a wasted costs order against a legal representative, only if—

(1) the legal representative has acted improperly, unreasonably or negligently;
(2) his conduct has caused a party to incur unnecessary costs, and
(3) it is just in all the circumstances to order him to compensate that party for the whole or part of those costs.

53.5 The court will give directions about the procedure that will be followed in each case in order to ensure that the issues are dealt with in a way which is fair and as simple and summary as the circumstances permit.

53.6 As a general rule the court will consider whether to make a wasted costs order in two stages—

(1) in the first stage, the court must be satisfied—
  (a) that it has before it evidence or other material which, if unanswered, would be likely to lead to a wasted costs order being made; and
  (b) the wasted costs proceedings are justified notwithstanding the likely costs involved.

(2) at the second stage (even if the court is satisfied under paragraph (1)) the court will consider, after giving the legal representative an opportunity to give reasons why the court should not make a wasted costs order, whether it is appropriate to make a wasted costs order in accordance with paragraph 53.4 above.

53.7 On an application for a wasted costs order under Part 23 the court may proceed to the second stage described in paragraph 53.6 without first adjourning the hearing if it is satisfied that the legal representative has already had a reasonable opportunity to give reasons why the court should not make a wasted costs order. In other cases the court will adjourn the hearing before proceeding to the second stage.

53.8 On an application for a wasted costs order under Part 23 the application notice and any evidence in support must identify—

(1) what the legal representative is alleged to have done or failed to do; and

(2) the costs that he may be ordered to pay or which are sought against him.

53.9 A wasted costs order is an order—

(1) that the legal representative pay a specified sum in respect of costs to a party; or

(2) for costs relating to a specified sum or items of work to be disallowed.

53.10 Attention is drawn to rule 44.3A(1) and (2) which respectively prevent the court from assessing any additional liability until the conclusion of the proceedings (or the part of the proceedings) to which the funding arrangement relates, and set out the orders the court may make at the conclusion of the proceedings.

Section 54 Basis of Detailed Assessment of Solicitor and Client Costs: *Rule 48.8*

54.1 A client and his solicitor may agree whatever terms they consider appropriate about the payment of the solicitor's charges for his services. If, however, the costs are of an unusual nature (either in amount or in the type of costs incurred) those costs will be presumed to have been unreasonably incurred unless the solicitor satisfies the court that he informed the client that they were unusual and, where the costs relate to litigation, that he informed the client they might **48PD.5**

not be allowed on an assessment of costs between the parties. That information must have been given to the client before the costs were incurred.

54.2(1) Costs as between a solicitor and client are assessed on the indemnity basis as defined by rule 44.4.

(2) Attention is drawn to the presumptions set out in rule 48.8(2). These presumptions may be rebutted by evidence to the contrary.

54.3 Rule 48.10 and Section 56 of this Practice Direction deal with the procedure to be followed for obtaining the assessment of a solicitor's bill pursuant to an order under Part III of the Solicitors Act 1974.

54.4 If a party fails to comply with the requirements of rule 48.10 concerning the service of a breakdown of costs or points of dispute, any other party may apply to the court in which the detailed assessment hearing should take place for an order requiring compliance with rule 48.10. If the court makes such an order, it may—

(a) make it subject to conditions including a condition to pay a sum of money into court; and

(b) specify the consequence of failure to comply with the order or a condition.

54.5(1) A client who has entered into a conditional fee agreement with a solicitor may apply for assessment of the base costs (which is carried out in accordance with rule 48.8(2) as if there were no conditional fee agreement) or for assessment of the percentage increase (success fee) or both.

(2) Where the court is to assess the percentage increase the court will have regard to all the relevant factors as they appeared to the solicitor or counsel when the conditional fee agreement was entered into.

48PD.6 **54.6** Where the client applies to the court to reduce the percentage increase which the solicitor has charged the client under the conditional fee agreement, the client must set out in his application notice:

(a) the reasons why the percentage increase should be reduced; and

(b) what the percentage increase should be.

54.7 The factors relevant to assessing the percentage increase include—

(a) the risk that the circumstances in which the fees or expenses would be payable might not occur;

(b) the disadvantages relating to the absence of payment on account;

(c) whether there is a conditional fee agreement between the solicitor and counsel;

(d) the solicitor's liability for any disbursements.

54.8 When the court is considering the factors to be taken into account, it will have regard to the circumstances as they reasonably appeared to the solicitor or counsel when the conditional fee agreement was entered into.

Section 56 Procedure on Assessment of Solicitor and Client Costs: Rule 48.10

56.1 The paragraphs in this section apply to orders made under Part III of the Solicitors Act 1974 for the assessment of costs. In these paragraphs "client" includes any person entitled to make an application under Part III of that Act. **48PD.7**

56.2 The procedure for obtaining an order under Part III of the Solicitors Act 1974 is by the alternative procedure for claims under Part 8, as modified by rule 67.3 and the Practice Direction supplementing Part 67. Precedent J of the Schedule of Costs Precedents annexed to this Practice Direction is a model form of claim form. The application must be accompanied by the bill or bills in respect of which assessment is sought, and, if the claim concerns a conditional fee agreement, a copy of that agreement. If the original bill is not available a copy will suffice.

56.3 Model forms of order, which the court may make, are set out in Precedents K, L and M of the Schedule of Costs Precedents annexed to this Practice Direction.

56.4 Attention is drawn to the time limits within which the required steps must be taken: *i.e.* the solicitor must serve a breakdown of costs within 28 days of the order for costs to be assessed, the client must serve points of dispute within 14 days after service on him of the breakdown, and any reply must be served within 14 days of service of the points of dispute.

56.5 The breakdown of costs referred to in rule 48.10 is a document which contains the following information:

(a) details of the work done under each of the bills sent for assessment; and

(b) in applications under Section 70 of the Solicitors Act 1974, an account showing money received by the solicitor to the credit of the client and sums paid out of that money on behalf of the client but not payments out which were made in satisfaction of the bill or of any items which are claimed in the bill.

56.6 Precedent P of the Schedule of Costs Precedents annexed to this Practice Direction is a model form of breakdown of costs. A party who is required to serve a breakdown of costs must also serve—

(1) copies of the fee notes of counsel and of any expert in respect of fees claimed in the breakdown, and

(2) written evidence as to any other disbursement which is claimed in the breakdown and which exceeds £250.

56.7 The provisions relating to default costs certificates (rule 47.11) do not apply to cases to which rule 48.10 applies.

56.8 Points of dispute should, as far as practicable, be in the form complying with paragraphs 35.1 to 35.7.

56.9 The time for requesting a detailed assessment hearing is within 3 months after the date of the order for the costs to be assessed.

56.10 The form of request for a hearing date must be in Form **N258C**. The request must be accompanied by copies of—

(a) the order sending the bill or bills for assessment;

(b) the bill or bills sent for assessment;
(c) the solicitor's breakdown of costs and any invoices or accounts served with that breakdown;
(d) a copy of the points of dispute, annotated as necessary in order to show which items have been agreed and their value and to show which items remain in dispute;
(e) as many copies of the points of dispute so annotated as there are other parties to the proceedings to whom the court should give details of the assessment hearing requested;
(f) a copy of any replies served;
(g) a statement signed by the party filing the request or his legal representative giving the names and addresses for service of all parties to the proceedings.

56.11 The request must include an estimate of the length of time the detailed assessment hearing will take.

56.12 On receipt of the request for a detailed assessment hearing the court will fix a date for the hearing or if the costs judge or district judge so decides, will give directions or fix a date for a preliminary appointment.

56.13(1) The court will give at least 14 days' notice of the time and place of the detailed assessment hearing to every person named in the statement referred to in paragraph 56.10(g) above.

(2) The court will when giving notice, give all parties other than the party who requested the hearing a copy of the points of dispute annotated by the party requesting the hearing in compliance with paragraph 56.10(e) above.

(3) Attention is drawn to rule 47.14(6) and (7): apart from the solicitor whose bill it is, only those parties who have served points of dispute may be heard on the detailed assessment unless the court gives permission, and only items specified in the points of dispute may be raised unless the court gives permission.

56.14(1) If a party wishes to vary his breakdown of costs, points of dispute or reply, an amended or supplementary document must be filed with the court and copies of it must be served on all other relevant parties.

(2) Permission is not required to vary a breakdown of costs, points of dispute or a reply but the court may disallow the variation or permit it only upon conditions, including conditions as to the payment of any costs caused or wasted by the variation.

56.15 Unless the court directs otherwise the solicitor must file with the court the papers in support of the bill not less than 7 days before the date for the detailed assessment hearing and not more than 14 days before that date.

56.16 Once the detailed assessment hearing has ended it is the responsibility of the legal representative appearing for the solicitor or, as the case may be, the solicitor in person to remove the papers filed in support of the bill.

56.17(1) Attention is drawn to rule 47.15 (power to issue an interim certificate).

(2) If, in the course of a detailed assessment hearing of a solicitor's bill to his client, it appears to the costs judge or district judge that in any event the solicitor will be liable in connection with that bill to pay money to the client, he may issue an interim certificate specifying an amount which in his opinion is payable by the solicitor to his client. Such a certificate will include an order to pay the sum it certifies unless the court orders otherwise.

56.18(1) Attention is drawn to rule 47.16 which requires the solicitor to file a completed bill within 14 days after the end of the detailed assessment hearing. The court may dispense with the requirement to file a completed bill.

(2) After the detailed assessment hearing is concluded the court will—

(a) complete the court copy of the bill so as to show the amount allowed;

(b) determine the result of the cash account;

(c) award the costs of the detailed assessment hearing in accordance with Section 70(8) of the Solicitors Act 1974; and

(d) issue a final costs certificate showing the amount due following the detailed assessment hearing.

56.19 A final costs certificate will include an order to pay the sum it certifies unless the court orders otherwise.

Section 57 Transitional Arrangements

57.1 In this section "the previous rules" means the Rules of the Supreme Court 1965 ("RSC") or County Court Rules 1981 ("CCR"), as appropriate. **48PD.8**

General Scheme of Transitional Arrangements concerning Costs Proceedings

57.2(1) Paragraph 18 of the Practice Direction which supplements Part 51 (Transitional Arrangements) provides that the CPR govern any assessments of costs which take place on or after 26th April 1999 and states a presumption to be applied in respect of costs for work undertaken before 26th April 1999.

(2) The following paragraphs provide five further transitional arrangements:

(a) to provide an additional presumption to be applied when assessing costs which were awarded by an order made in a county court before 26th April 1999 which allowed costs "on Scale 1" to be determined in accordance with CCR Appendix A, or "on the lower scale" to be determined in accordance with CCR Appendix C.

(b) to preserve the effect of CCR Appendix B Part III, paragraph 2;

(c) to clarify the approach to be taken where a bill of costs was provisionally taxed before 26th April 1999 and the receiving party is unwilling to accept the result of the provisional taxation.

(d) to preserve the right to carry in objections or apply for a reconsideration in all taxation proceedings commenced before 26th April 1999.

(e) to deal with funding arrangements made before 3 July 2000.

Scale 1 or lower scale costs

57.3 Where an order was made in county court proceedings before 26th April 1999 under which the costs were allowed on Scale 1 or the lower scale, the general presumption is that no costs will be allowed under that order which would not have been allowed in a taxation before 26th April 1999.

Fixed costs on the lower scale

57.4 The amount to be allowed as fixed costs for making or opposing an application for a rehearing to set aside a judgment given before 26th April 1999 where the costs are on lower scale is £11.25.

Bills provisionally taxed before 26th April 1999

57.5 In respect of bills of costs provisionally taxed before 26th April 1999:

(1) The previous rules apply on the question who can request a hearing and the time limits for doing so; and

(2) The CPR govern any subsequent hearing in that case.

Bills taxed before 26th April 1999

57.6 Where a bill of costs was taxed before 26th April 1999, the previous rules govern the steps which can be taken to challenge that taxation.

Other taxation proceedings

57.7(1) This paragraph applies to taxation proceedings which were commenced before 26th April 1999, were assigned for taxation to a Taxing Master or District Judge, and which were still pending on 26th April 1999.

(2) Any assessment of costs that takes place in cases to which this paragraph applies which is conducted on or after 26th April 1999, will be conducted in accordance with the CPR.

(3) In addition to the possibility of appeal under rules 47.20 to 47.23 and Part 52 any party to a detailed assessment who is dissatisfied with any decision on a detailed assessment made by a costs judge or district judge may apply to that costs judge or district judge for a review of the decision. The review shall, for procedural purposes, be treated as if it were an appeal from an authorised court officer.

(4) The right of review provided by paragraph (3) above, will not apply in cases in which, at least 28 days before the date of the assessment hearing, all parties were served

with notice that the rights of appeal in respect of that hearing would be governed by Part 47 Section VIII (Appeals from Authorised Court Officers in Detailed Assessment Proceedings) and Part 52 (Appeals).

(5) An order for the service of notice under sub-paragraph (4) above may be made on the application of any party to the detailed assessment proceedings or may be made by the court of its own initiative.

[**Note:** The court decided that paragraphs 57.6 and 57.7 are intended to keep the application of the RSC and the CPR separate. To hold otherwise would mean that a taxation shortly before 26 April 1999 carried out subject to the RSC, if subject to review after that date, would be subject to the CPR and potentially to considerations and powers not earlier available. It followed that whichever Code of Rules applied to the original taxation should apply also to the review procedure: *Morris v Wiltshire*, November 30, 2001 (unreported), Evans J.]

Transitional provisions concerning the Access to Justice Act 1999 sections 28 to 31

57.8(1) Sections 28 to 31 of the Access to Justice Act 1999, the Conditional Fee Agreements Regulations 2000, the Access to Justice (Membership Organisations) Regulations 2000, and the Access to Justice Act 1999 (Transitional Provisions) Order 2000 came into force on 1 April 2000. The Civil Procedure (Amendment No.3) Rules came into force on 3 July 2000. [The Conditional Fee Agreements Regulations 2000 were revoked by the Conditional Fee Agreements (Revocation) Regulations 2005 but continue to have effect in relation to conditional fee agreements entered into before 1 November 2005. The Access to Justice (Membership Organisation) Regulations 2000 were revoked by the Access to Justice (Membership Organisation) Regulations 2005 but continue to have effect in relation to arrangements entered into before 1st November 2005.]

(2) The Access to Justice Act 1999 (Transitional Provisions) Order 2000 provides that no conditional fee agreement or other arrangement about costs entered into before 1 April 2000 can be a funding arrangement, as defined in rule 43.2. The order also has the effect that where a conditional fee agreement or other funding arrangement has been entered into before 1 April 2000 and a second or subsequent funding arrangement of the same type is entered into on or after 1 April 2000, the second or subsequent funding arrangement does not give rise to a liability which is recoverable from a paying party.

(3) The Collective Conditional Fee Agreements Regulations 2000 came into force on 30 November 2000. The Regulations apply to agreements entered into between 30 November 2000 and 31 October 2005. Agreements

entered into before 30 November 2000 are treated as if the Regulations had not come into force. The Regulations do not apply to collective conditional fee agreements entered into on or after 1 November 2005.

[**Note**: Where a CFA was entered into prior to April 1, 2000 a success fee cannot be recovered against a paying party as a result of a subsequent CFA entered into after that date. However a success fee can be recovered if the funding arrangement prior to April 1, 2000 was of a different type.]

57.9(1) Rule 39 of the Civil Procedure (Amendment No. 3) Rules 2000 applies where between 1 April and 2 July 2000 (including both dates)—

a funding arrangement is entered into, and proceedings are started in respect of a claim which is the subject of that agreement.

(2) Attention is drawn to the need to act promptly so as to comply with the requirements of the Rules and the Practice Directions by 31 July 2000 (*i.e.* within the 28 days from 3 July 2000 permitted by Rule 39) if that compliance is to be treated as compliance with the relevant provision. Attention is drawn in particular to Rule 44.15 (Providing Information about Funding Arrangements) and Section 19 of this Practice Direction.

(3) Nothing in the legislation referred to above makes provision for a party who has entered into a funding arrangement to recover from another party any amount of an additional liability which relates to anything done or any costs incurred before the arrangement was entered into.

Civil Procedure (Amendment No. 3) Rules 2000

39 Transitional provision

48PD.9 (1) This rule applies where a person has—

(a) entered into a funding arrangement, and

(b) started proceedings in respect of a claim the subject of that funding arrangement

before the date on which these Rules come into force.

(2) Any requirement imposed—

(a) by any provision of the Civil Procedure Rules amended by these Rules, or

(b) by a practice direction

in respect of that funding arrangement may be complied with within 28 days of the coming into force of these Rules, and that compliance with the relevant rule or practice direction.

(3) For the purpose of this rule, "funding arrangement" means an arrangement where a person has—

(a) entered into a conditional fee agreement which provides for a success fee within the meaning of section 58(2) of the Courts and Legal Services Act 1990;

(b) taken out an insurance policy to which section 29 of the Access to Justice Act 1999 (recovery of insurance premiums by way of costs) applies; or

(c) made an agreement with a membership organisation prescibed for the purpose of section 30 of the Access to Justice Act 1999 (recovery where body undertakes to meet cost liabilities) to meet his legal costs.

Schedule of Costs Precedents

The following forms are annexed to this Practice Direction: **48PD.10**

- **Precedent A**—Model form of bill of costs (receiving party's solicitor and counsel on CFA terms)
- **Precedent B**—Model form of bill of costs (detailed assessment of additional liability only)
- **Precedent C**—Model form of bill of costs (payable by defendant and the LSC)
- **Precedent D**—Model form of bill of costs (alternative form, single column for amounts claimed, separate parts for costs payable by the LSC only)
- **Precedent E**—Legal Aid/ LSC Schedule of Costs
- **Precedent F**—Certificates for inclusion in bill of costs
- **Precedent G**—Points of Dispute
- **Precedent H**—Estimate of costs served on other parties
- **Precedent J**—Solicitors Act 1974: Part 8 claim form under Part III of the Act
- **Precedent K**—Solicitors Act 1974: order for delivery of bill
- **Precedent L**—Solicitors Act 1974: order for detailed assessment (client)
- **Precedent M**—Solicitors Act 1974: order for detailed assessment (solicitors)
- **Precedent P**—Solicitors Act 1974: breakdown of costs

Precedents B, C, D, E, H, K, L M and P follow this list. For Precedents A, F, G and J see the Appendix to The Supreme Court Costs Office Guide in Vol.2, section 1C. All of the Precedents can be found in the *Civil Procedure Forms Volume*.

Precedent B—Model form of bill of costs (detailed assessment of additional liability only)

48PD.10.1

SCHEDULE OF COSTS PRECEDENTS
PRECEDENT B

IN THE HIGH COURT OF JUSTICE 2000 - B - 9999

QUEEN'S BENCH DIVISION

BRIGHTON DISTRICT REGISTRY

BETWEEN

AB Claimant

- and -

CD Defendant

CLAIMANT'S BILL OF COSTS TO BE ASSESSED PURSUANT TO THE ORDER DATED 26th JULY 2001

V.A.T. No. 33 4404 90

In these proceedings the claimant sought compensation for personal injuries and other losses suffered in a road accident which occurred on Friday 1st January 1999 near the junction between Bolingbroke Lane and Regency Road, Brighton, East Sussex. The claimant had been travelling as a front seat passenger in a car driven by the defendant. The claimant suffered severe injuries when, because of the defendant's negligence, the car left the road and collided with a brick wall.

The defendant was later convicted of various offences arising out of the accident including careless driving and driving under the influence of drink or drugs.

In the civil action the defendant alleged that immediately before the car journey began the claimant had known that the defendant was under the influence of alcohol and therefore consented to the risk of injury or was contributorily negligent as to it. It was also alleged that, immediately before the accident occurred, the claimant wrongfully took control of the steering wheel so causing the accident to occur.

The claimant first instructed solicitors, E F & Co, in this matter in July 2000. The claim form was issued in October 1999 and in February 2000 the proceedings were listed for a two day trial commencing 25th July 2001. At the trial the defendant was found liable but the compensation was reduced by 25% to take account of contributory negligence by the claimant. The claimant was awarded a total of £78,256.83 plus £1,207.16 interest plus costs, and the base costs were summarily assessed

The claimant instructed E F & Co under a conditional fee agreement dated 8th July 2000 which specifies the following base fees and success fees.

Partner - £180 per hour plus VAT
Assistant Solicitor - £140 per hour plus VAT
Other fee earners - £85 per hour plus VAT
Success fees exclusive of disbursement funding costs: 40%
Success fee in respect of disbursement funding costs: 7.5% (not claimed in this bill)

Except where the contrary is stated the proceedings were conducted on behalf of the claimant by an assistant solicitor, admitted November 1999.

E F & Co instructed Counsel (Miss GH, called 1992) under a conditional fee agreement dated 5th June 2001 which specifies a success fee of 75% and base fees, payable in various circumstances, of which the following are relevant.

Fees for interim hearing whose estimated duration is up to 2 hours: £600
Brief for trial whose estimated duration is 2 days: £2,000
Fee for second and subsequent days: £650 per day

Item No.	Description of work done	V.A.T.	Disburse -ments	Profit Costs
	8th July 2000 - EF & Co instructed			
	22nd July 2000 - AEI with Eastbird Legal Protection Ltd			
1	Premium for policy		£ 120.00	
	9th February 2001 - Case management conference at which costs were awarded to the Claimant and the base costs were summarily assessed at £400			
2	Success fee on costs of case management conference (40% of £400) plus VAT	£ 28.00		£ 160.00
	28th June 2001 - Pre trial review: costs in the case (base costs included base costs at trial)			
	25th July 2001 - First day of trial			
	26th July 2001 - Second day of trial at which judgment was given for the claimant as follows: Compensation: £78,256.83 Interest thereon: £1,207.16 **Base costs to trial** Solicitor's fees: £12,500.00 plus £2187.50 VAT thereon Counsel's fees: £3,200.00 plus £560.00 VAT thereon Other disbursements: £2,300.00 plus £4.02 VAT thereon			
3	Success fee on solicitor's base costs awarded at trial (40% of £12,500) plus VAT	£ 875.00		£5,000.00
4	Success fee on Counsel's base costs awarded at trial (75% of £3,200) plus VAT	£ 420.00	£2,400.00	
	Other work done Preparing and checking bill Engaged: Solicitor - 0.25 hours £ 35.00 Engaged: Costs draftsman - 1.75 hours £ 148.75			
5	Total base fee for other work done plus **VAT** £	32.16		£ 183.75
6	**Success fee for other work done (40% of** £183.75) plus VAT	£ 12.87		£ 73.50
	Totals:	£1,368.03	£2,520.00	£5,417.25
	Profit Costs Disbursements VAT		£	£5,417.25 £2,520.00 1,368.03
	Grand total:			£9,305.28

Precedent C—Model form of bill of costs (payable by defendant and the LSC)

48PD.10.2

SCHEDULE OF COSTS PRECEDENTS
PRECEDENT C

IN THE HIGH COURT OF JUSTICE 1999 - B - 9999

QUEEN'S BENCH DIVISION

BRIGHTON DISTRICT REGISTRY

BETWEEN

AB Claimant

~ and ~

CD Defendant

CLAIMANT'S BILL OF COSTS TO BE ASSESSED PURSUANT TO THE ORDER DATED 26th JULY 2000 AND IN ACCORDANCE WITH REGULATION 107A OF THE CIVIL LEGAL AID (GENERAL) REGULATIONS 1989

Legal Aid Certificate No. 01. 01. 99. 32552X issued on 9th September 1999.

V.A.T. No. 33 4404 90

In these proceedings the claimant sought compensation for personal injuries and other losses suffered in a road accident which occurred on Friday 1st January 1999 near the junction between Bolingbroke Lane and Regency Road, Brighton, East Sussex. The claimant had been travelling as a front seat passenger in a car driven by the defendant. The claimant suffered severe injuries when, because of the defendant's negligence, the car left the road and collided with a brick wall.

The defendant was later convicted of various offences arising out of the accident including careless driving and driving under the influence of drink or drugs.

In the civil action the defendant alleged that immediately before the car journey began the claimant had known that the defendant was under the influence of alcohol and therefore consented to the risk of injury or was contributorily negligent as to it. It was also alleged that, immediately before the accident occurred, the claimant wrongfully took control of the steering wheel so causing the accident to occur.

The claimant first instructed solicitors, E F & Co, in this matter in July 1999. The claim form was issued in October 1999 and in February 2000 the proceedings were listed for a two day trial commencing 25th July 2000. At the trial the defendant was found liable but the compensation was **reduced by 25% to take account of contributory negligence by the claimant.** The claimant was awarded a total of £78,256.83 plus £1,207.16 interest plus costs.

The proceedings were conducted on behalf of the claimant by an assistant solicitor admitted November 1998. The bill is divided into two parts.

Part 1 Costs payable by the defendant to the date of grant of legal aid

This covers the period from 8th July 1999 to 8th September 1999. In this part the solicitor's time is charged at £140 per hour (including travel and waiting time) and letters out and telephone calls at £14.00 each.

Part 2 Costs payable by the defendant and L.S.C. from the date of grant of legal aid

This part covers the period from 9th September 1999 to the present time, the client having the benefit of a legal aid certificate covering these proceedings. In this part, solicitor's time in respect of costs payable by the defendant has been charged as in Part 1 plus costs draftsman's and trainee's time charged at £85 per hour. Solicitor's time in respect of costs payable by the LSC only are charged at the prescribed hourly rates plus enhancement of 50%.

Preparation: £74
Attending counsel in conference or at court: £36.40
Travelling and waiting: £32.70
Routine letters out: £7.40
Routine telephone calls: £4.10

	Description of work done	Payable by L.S.C. only			Payable by Defendant		
Item No.	**Part 1: COSTS TO DATE OF GRANT OF LEGAL AID.**	V.A.T.	Disburse-ments	Profit Costs	V.A.T.	Disburse-ments	Profit Costs
	Claimant						
1	8th July 1999 - First Instructions - 0.75 hours						£ 105.00
2	Routine Letters out - 3						£ 42.00
	Witnesses of Fact						
3	Routine Letters out - 2						£ 28.00
	The Defendant						
4	8th July 1999 - Timed letter sent - 0.5 hours						£ 70.00
5	VAT **on total profit costs (17.5% of** £245)				£ 42.88		
	To Summary				£ 42.88	£ -	£ 245.00
	Part 2: COSTS FROM DATE OF GRANT OF LEGAL AID						
	7th October 1999 - Claim issued						
6	Issue fee				-	£ 400.00	
	21st October 1999 - Particulars of claim served						
	25th November 1999 - Time for service of defence extended by agreement to 14th January 2000						
	17th January 2000 - Filing allocation questionnaire						
7	Fee on allocation				-	£ 80.00	
	20th January 2000 - Case allocated to multi track						
	9th February 2000 - Case management conference Engaged 0.75 hours £105.00 **Travel and waiting 2.00 hours** £280.00						
8	**Total solicitor's fee for attending**						£ 385.00
	23rd February 2000 - Claimant's list of documents						
	12th April 2000 - Payment into court of £25,126.33						
	13th April 2000 - Filing pre-trial checklist						
9	Fee on listing				-	£ 400.00	
	28th June 2000 - Pre-trial review Engaged 1.5 hours £210.00 **Travel and waiting 2.00 hours** £280.00						
10	Total solicitor's **fee for attending**						£ 490.00
11	Counsel's brief fee for attending pre-trial review (Miss GH)				£ 105.00	£ 600.00	
	To Summary	£ -	£ -	£ -	£ 105.00	£1,480.00	£ 875.00

	Description of work done	Payable by L.S.C. only			Payable by Defendant		
Item No.		V.A.T. ments	Disburse- Costs	Profit	V.A.T. ments	Disburse- Costs	Profit
	25th July 2000 - Attending first day of trial: adjourned part heard Engaged in court 5.00 hours £700.00 Engaged in conference 0.75 hours £105.00 **Travel and waiting 1.5 hours** £210.00						
12	Total solicitor's **fee for attending**						£1,015.00
13	Counsel's brief fee for trial (Miss GH)				£ 350.00	£2,000.00	
14	Fee of expert witness (Dr IJ)				-	£ 850.00	
15	Expenses of witnesses of fact				-	£ 84.00	
	26th July 2000 - Attending second day of trial when judgment was given for the claimant in the sum of £78,256.83 **plus £1,207.16 interest plus costs** Engaged in court 3.00 hours £420.00 Engaged in conference 1.5 hours £210.00 Travel and waiting 1.5 hours £210.00						
16	Total solicitor's fee for attending						£ 840.00
17	Counsel's fee for second day (Miss GH)				£ 113.75	£ 650.00	
	Claimant ~ (1) Payable by Defendant Timed attendances in person and by telephone - see Schedule 1						
18	Total fees for Schedule 1 - 7.50 hours						£1,050.00
19	Routine letters out and telephone calls - 26 (14 + 12)						£ 364.00
	Claimant ~ (2) Payable by LSC only **11th September 1999 - telephone call** Engaged 0.25 hours £18.50 Enhancement 50% £9.25						
20	Total solicitor's fee		£ 27.75				
	10th April 2000 - telephone call Engaged 0.1 hours £4.10 Enhancement 50% £2.05						
21	Total solicitor's fee		£ 6.15				
	Witnesses of fact Timed attendances in person, by letter **out and by telephone - see Schedule** 2						
22	Total fees for Schedule 2 - 5.2 hours		£				728.00
23	Routine letters out (including e mails) and telephone calls - 6 (4 + 2)						£ 84.00
24	Paid travelling on 9th October 1999				£ 4.02	£ 22.96	
	To Summary	£ -	£ -	£ 33.90	£ 467.77	£3,606.96	£4,081.00

	Description of work done	Payable by L.S.C. only			Payable by Defendant		
Item No.		V.A.T. ments	Disburse- Costs	Profit	V.A.T. ments	Disburse- Costs	Profit
	Medical expert (Dr IJ)						
25	11th September 1999 - long letter out 0.33 hours						£ 46.20
26	30th January 2000 - long letter out 0.25 hours						£ 35.00
27	23rd May 2000 - telephone call 0.2 hrs					£ 28.00	
28	Routine letters out and telephone calls - 10 (6 + 4)						£ 140.00
29	Dr IJ's fee for report				-	£ 350.00	
	Solicitors for the defendant						
30	19th February 2000 - telephone call 0.25 hours						£ 35.00
31	Routine letters out and telephone calls - 24 (18 + 6)						£ 336.00
	Communications with the court						
32	Routine letters out and telephone calls - 9 (8 + 1)						£ 126.00
	Communications with Counsel						
33	Routine letters out (including e mails) and telephone calls - 19 (11 + 8)						£ 266.00
	Legal Aid Board and LSC ~ Payable by LSC only **2nd August 2000 - Report on case** Engaged 0.5 hours £37.00 Enhancement 50% £18.50						
34	Total solicitor's fee			£ 55.50			
	Routine letters out and telephone calls Letters out - 2 £14.80 Telephones call - 4 £16.40						
35	Total solicitor's fee			£ 31.20			
	Work done on documents Timed attendances - see Schedule 3						
36	**Total fees for Schedule 3 - 45.25 hours** at £140 + 12 hours at £85						£7,355.00
	Work done on negotiations **23rd March 2000 - meeting at offices** of solicitors for the Defendant Engaged - 1.5 hours £210.00 **Travel and waiting 1.25 hours** £175.00						
37	Total solicitor'**s fee for meeting**						£ 385.00
	Other work done ~ (1) Payable by Defendant Preparing and checking bill Engaged: Solicitor - 1 hour £140.00 Engaged: Costs Draftsman - 4 hours £340.00						
38	Total on other work done (1)						£ 480.00
	To Summary	£ -	£ -	£ 86.70	£ -	£ 350.00	£9,232.20

	Description of work done	Payable by L.S.C. only			Payable by Defendant		
Item No.		V.A.T. ments	Disburse- Costs	Profit	V.A.T. ments	Disburse- Costs	Profit
	Other work done ~ (2) Payable by LSC only Preparing and checking bill Engaged: Solicitor - no claim Engaged: Costs Draftsman - 1 hour £74.00						
39	Total on other work done (2)			£ 74.00			
40	VAT on total profit costs payable by Defendant (17.5% of £14,176.20)			£2,480.84			
41	VAT on total profit costs payable by LSC only (17.5% of £205.60)	£ 35.98					
	To summary	£ 35.98	£ -	£ 74.00	£2,480.84	£ -	£ -
	SUMMARY						
	Part 1 - Pre Legal Aid						
	Page 3	£ -	£ -	£ -	£ 42.88	£ -	£ 245.00
	Part 2 - Costs since grant of legal aid	£					
	Page 3	£ -	£ -	£ -	£ 105.00	£ 1,480.00	£ 875.00
	Page 4	£ -	£ -	£ 33.90	£ 467.77	£3,606.96	£4,081.00
	Page 5	£ -	£ -	£ 86.70	£ -	£ 350.00	£9,232.20
	Page 6	£ 35.98	£ -	£ 74.00	£2,480.84	£ -	£ -
	Totals	£ 35.98	£ -	£ 194.60	£3,096.49	£5,436.96	£14,433.20
	Grand totals						
	Costs payable by Defendant						£22,966.65
	Costs payable by LSC only						£ 230.58
	Grand total:						£23,197.23

Precedent D—Model form of bill of costs (alternative form, single column for amounts claimed, separate parts for costs payable by the LSC only)

48PD.10.3

SCHEDULE OF COSTS PRECEDENTS
PRECEDENT D

IN THE HIGH COURT OF JUSTICE 1999 - B - 9999

QUEEN'S BENCH DIVISION

BRIGHTON DISTRICT REGISTRY

BETWEEN

AB Claimant

~ and ~

CD Defendant

CLAIMANT'S BILL OF COSTS TO BE ASSESSED PURSUANT TO THE ORDER DATED 26th JULY 2000 AND IN ACCORDANCE WITH REGULATION 107A OF THE CIVIL LEGAL AID (GENERAL) REGULATIONS 1989

Legal Aid Certificate No. 01. 01. 99. 32552X issued on 9th September 1999.

V.A.T. No. 33 4404 90

In these proceedings the claimant sought compensation for personal injuries and other losses suffered in a road accident which occurred on Friday 1st January 1999 near the junction between Bolingbroke Lane and Regency Road, Brighton, East Sussex. The claimant had been travelling as a front seat passenger in a car driven by the defendant. The claimant suffered severe injuries when, because of the defendant's negligence, the car left the road and collided with a brick wall.

The defendant was later convicted of various offences arising out of the accident including careless driving and driving under the influence of drink or drugs.

In the civil action the defendant alleged that immediately before the car journey began the claimant had known that the defendant was under the influence of alcohol and therefore consented to the risk of injury or was contributorily negligent as to it. It was also alleged that, immediately before the accident occurred, the claimant wrongfully took control of the steering wheel so causing the accident to occur.

The claimant first instructed solicitors, E F & Co, in this matter in July 1999. The claim form was issued in October 1999 and in February 2000 the proceedings were listed for a two day trial commencing 25th July 2000. At the trial the defendant was found liable but the compensation was **reduced by 25% to take account of contributory negligence by the claimant.** The claimant was awarded a total of £78,256.83 plus £1,207.16 interest plus costs.

The proceedings were conducted on behalf of the claimant by an assistant solicitor, admitted November 1998. The bill is divided into three parts.

Part 1 Costs payable by the defendant to the date of grant of legal aid

This covers the period from 8th July 1999 to 8th September 1999. In this part the solicitor's time is charged at £140 per hour (including travel and waiting time) and letters out and telephone calls at £14.00 each.

Part 2 Costs payable by the defendant from the date of grant of legal aid

This part covers the period from 9th September 1999 to the present time, the client having the benefit of a legal aid certificate covering these proceedings. In this part, solicitorís time in respect of costs payable by the defendant has been charged as in Part 1 plus costs draftsmanís and traineeís time charged at £85 per hour.

Part 3 Costs payable by the LSC only

This part covers the same period as Part 2. In this part solicitorís time in respect of costs payable by the LSC only are charged at the prescribed hourly rates plus enhancement of 50%.

Preparation: £74
Attending counsel in conference or at court: £36.40
Travelling and waiting: £32.70
Routine letters out: £7.40
Routine telephone calls: £4.10

Item No.	Item	Amount claimed	VAT	Amount allowed	VAT
	Part 1: COSTS PAYABLE BY THE DEFENDANT				
	Claimant				
1	8th July 1999 - First Instructions - 0.75 hours	£ 105.00	£ 18.38		
2	Routine Letters out - 3	£ 42.00	£ 7.35		
	Witnesses of Fact				
3	Routine Letters out - 2	£ 28.00	£ 4.90		
	The Defendant				
4	8th July 1999 - Timed letter sent - 0.5 hours	£ 70.00	£ 12.25		
	To Summary	£ 245.00	£ 42.88		
	Part 2: COSTS PAYABLE BY THE DEFENDANT				
	7th October 1999 - Claim issued				
5	Issue fee	£ 400.00	-		
	21st October 1999 - Particulars of claim served				
	25th November 1999 - Time for service of defence extended by agreement to 14th January 2000				
	17th January 2000 - Filing allocation questionnaire				
6	Fee on allocation	£ 80.00	-		
	20th January 2000 - Case allocated to multi track				
	9th February 2000 - Case management conference Engaged 0.75 hours £105.00 **Travel and waiting 2.00 hours** £280.00				
7	**Total solicitor**'s fee for attending	£ 385.00	£ 67.38		
	23rd February 2000 - Claimant's list of documents				
	12th April 2000 - Payment into court of £25,126.33				
	13th April 2000 - Filing pre-trial checklist				
8	Fee on listing	£ 400.00	-		
	28th June 2000 - Pre-trial review Engaged 1.5 hours £210.00 Travel and waiting 2.00 hours £280.00				
9	Total solicitor's fee for attending	£ 490.00	£ 85.75		
10	Counsel's brief fee for attending pre-trial review (Miss GH)	£ 600.00	£ 105.00		

Item No.	Item	Amount claimed	VAT	Amount allowed	VAT
	25th July 2000 - Attending first day of trial: adjourned part heard Engaged in court 5.00 hours £700.00 **Engaged in conference 0.75 hours £105.00** **Travel and waiting 1.5 hours** £210.00				
11	**Total solicitor**'s fee for attending	£1,015.00	£ 177.63		
12	Counsel's brief fee for trial (Miss GH)	£2,000.00	£ 350.00		
13	Fee of expert witness (Dr IJ)	£ 850.00			
14	Expenses of witnesses of fact	£ 84.00			
	26th July 2000 - Attending second day of trial when judgment 'was given for the claimant in the sum of £78,256.83 plus' '£1,207.16 interest plus costs' Engaged in court 3.00 hours £420.00 Engaged in conference 1.5 hours £210.00 Travel and waiting 1.5 hours £210.00				
15	Total solicitor's fee for attending	£ 840.00	£ 147.00		
16	Counsel's fee for second day (Miss GH)	£ 650.00	£ 113.75		
	Claimant				
	Timed attendances in person and by telephone - see Schedule 1				
17	Total fees for Schedule 1 - 7.50 hours	£1,050.00	£ 183.75		
18	Routine letters out and telephone calls - 26 (14 + 12)	£ 364.00	£ 63.70		
	Witnesses of fact				
	'Timed attendances in person, by letter out and by ' telephone - see Schedule 2				
19	Total fees for Schedule 2 - 5.2 hours	£ 728.00	£ 127.40		
20	Routine letters out (including e mails) and telephone calls - 6 (4 + 2) £	84.00	£ 14.70		
21	Paid travelling on 9th October 1999	£ 22.96	£ 4.02		
	Medical expert (Dr IJ)				
22	11th September 1999 - long letter out 0.33 hours	£ 46.20	£ 8.09		
23	30th January 2000 - long letter out 0.25 hours	£ 35.00	£ 6.13		
24	23rd May 2000 - telephone call 0.2 hours	£ 28.00	£ 4.90		
25	Routine letters out and telephone calls - 10 (6 + 4)	£ 140.00	£ 24.50		
26	Dr IJ's fee for report	£ 350.00	ó		
	Solicitors for the defendant				
27	19th February 2000 - telephone call 0.25 hours	£ 35.00	£ 6.13		
28	Routine letters out and telephone calls - 24 (18 + 6)	£ 336.00	£ 58.80		
	Communications with the court				
29	Routine letters out and telephone calls - 9 (8 + 1)	£ 126.00	£ 22.05		

Item No.	Item	Amount claimed	VAT	Amount allowed	VAT
	Communications with Counsel				
30	Routine letters out (including e mails) and telephone calls - 19 (11 + 8)	£ 266.00	£ 46.55		
	Work done on documents Timed attendances - see Schedule 3				
31	**Total fees for Schedule 3 - 45.25 hours at** £140 + 12 hours at £85	£7,355.00	£1,287.13		
	Work done on negotiations **23rd March 2000 - meeting at offices** of solicitors for the Defendant Engaged - 1.5 hours £210.00 Travel and waiting - 1.25 hours £175.00				
32	Total solicitor's fee for meeting	£ 385.00	£ 67.38		
33	**Other work done** Preparing and checking bill Engaged: Solicitor - 1 hour £140.00 Engaged: Costs Draftsman 4 hours £340.00 Total on other work done	£ 480.00	£ 84.00		
	To summary	£19,625.16	£3,055.70		
	Part 3: COSTS PAYABLE BY LSC ONLY **Claimant** 11th September 1999 - telephone call Engaged 0.25 hours £18.50 Enhancement 50% £9.25				
34	Total solicitor's fee	£ 27.75	£ 4.86		
	10th April 2000 - telephone call Engaged 0.1 hours £4.10 Enhancement 50% £2.05				
35	Total solicitor's fee	£ 6.15	£ 1.08		
	Legal Aid Board and LSC 2nd August 2000 - Report on case Engaged 0.5 hours £37.00 Enhancement 50% £18.50				
36	Total solicitor's fee	£ 55.50	£ 9.71		
	Routine letters out and telephone calls Letters out - 2 £14.80 Telephone calls - 4 £16.40				
37	Total solicitor's fee	£ 31.20	£ 5.46		
	Other work done Preparing and checking bill Engaged: Solicitor - no claim Engaged: Costs Draftsman - 1 hours £74.00				
38	Total on other work done	£ 74.00	£ 12.95		
	To summary	£ 194.60	£ 34.06		

Item No.	Item		Amount claimed	VAT	Amount allowed	VAT
	SUMMARY					
	Costs payable by the Defendant					
		Part 1	£ 245.00	£ 42.88		
		Part 2	£19,625.16	£3,055.70		
		Total costs payable by the Defendant	£19,870.16	£3,098.58		
	Costs payable by LSC only					
		Part 3	£ 194.60	£ 34.06		
	Grand Totals					
		Costs payable by the Defendant	£19,870.16	£3,098.58		
		Costs payable by LSC only	£ 194.60	£ 34.06		
		Grand total	£20,064.76	£3,132.63		

Precedent E—Legal Aid/ LSC Schedule of Costs

48PD.10.4

SCHEDULE OF COSTS PRECEDENTS
PRECEDENT E

Legal Aid/LSC Schedule of Costs

IN THE HIGH COURT OF JUSTICE 1999 - B - 9999

QUEEN'S BENCH DIVISION

BRIGHTON DISTRICT REGISTRY

BETWEEN

AB Claimant

~ and ~

CD Defendant

CLAIMANT'S BILL OF COSTS: LEGAL AID/LSC SCHEDULE

Item No.	Description of work done		V.A.T.	Disburse-ments	Profit Costs
6	Issue fee		-	£ 400.00	
7	Allocation fee		-	£ 80.00	
8	Solicitor's fee for hearing Engaged 0.75 hours Enhancement thereon at 50% Travel and waiting 2.00 hours Total solicitor's fee for attending	 £55.50 £27.75 £65.40			£ 148.65
9	Fee on listing	-		£ 400.00	
10	Solicitor's fee for hearing Engaged 1.5 hours Enhancement thereon at 50% Travel and waiting 2.00 hours Total solicitor's fee for attending	 £111.00 £55.50 £65.40			£ 231.90
11	Counsel's fee		£ 105.00	£ 600.00	
12	Solicitor's fee for trial Engaged in court 5.00 hours Engaged in conference 0.75 hours Enhancement thereon at 50% Travel and waiting 1.50 hours Total solicitor's fee for attending	 £182.00 £27.30 £104.65 £49.05			£ 363.00
13	Counsel's brief fee for trial		£ 350.00	£2,000.00	
14	Expert's fee for trial		-	£ 850.00	
15	Witnesses' expenses		-	£ 84.00	
	To summary		£ 455.00	£4,414.00	£ 743.55

Item No.	Description of work done		V.A.T.	Disburse-ments	Profit Costs
16	Solicitor's fee for trial (second day)				
	Engaged in court 3.00 hours	£109.20			
	Engaged in conference 1.50 hours	**£54.60**			
	Enhancement thereon at 50%	£81.90			
	Travel and waiting 1.50 hours	£49.05			
	Total solicitor's fee for attending				£ 294.75
17	Counsel's fee for second day of trial		£ 113.75	£ 650.00	
18	Timed attendances on Claimant (1)				
	7.5 hours	£555.00			
	Enhancement thereon at 50%	£277.50			£ 832.50
19	Routine communications with Claimant (1)				
	Letters out - 14	£103.60			
	Telephone calls - 12	£49.20			£ 152.80
22	Timed attendances on and communications with witnesses of fact				
	5.2 hours	£384.80			
	Enhancement thereon at 50%	£192.40			£ 577.20
23	Routine communications with witnesses of fact				
	Letters out - 4	£29.60			
	Telephone calls - 2	£8.20			£ 37.80
24	Paid travelling		4.02	22.96	
25	Timed attendance on medical expert				
	0.33 hours	£24.42			
	Enhancement thereon at 50%	**£12.21**			£ 36.63
26	Timed communications with medical expert				
	0.25 hours	£18.50			
	Enhancement thereon at 50%	£9.25			£ 27.75
27	Timed communications with medical expert				
	0.2 hours	£14.80			
	Enhancement thereon at 50%	£7.40			£ 22.20
28	Routine communications with medical expert				
	Letters out - 6	£44.40			
	Telephone calls - 4	£16.40			£ 60.80
29	Expert's fee for report		-	£ 350.00	
30	Timed communications with solicitors for Defendant				
	0.25 hours	£18.50			
	Enhancement thereon at 50%	£9.25			£ 27.75
31	Routine communications with solicitors for Defendant				
	Letters out - 18	£133.20			
	Telephone calls - 6	£24.60			£ 157.80
32	Routine communications with the court				
	Letters out - 8	£59.20			
	Telephone calls - 1	£4.10			£ 63.30
	To summary		£ 117.77	£ 1,022.96	£ 2,291.28

Item No.	Description of work done		V.A.T.	Disburse-ments	Profit Costs
33	Routine communications with Counsel				
	Letters out - 11	£81.40			
	Telephone calls - 8	£32.80			£ 114.20
36	Work done on documents				
	57.25 hours	£4,236.50			
	Enhancement thereon at 50%	£2,118.25			£6,354.75
37	Work done on negotiations				
	Engaged - 1.5 hours	£111.00			
	Enhancement thereon at 50%	£55.50			
	Travel and waiting - 1.25 hours	£40.88			£ 207.38
38	Other work done (1)				
	Preparing and checking bill				£ 370.00
40	VAT on total profit costs set out above (17.5% of £10,216.86)		£1,787.95		
	To summary		£1,787.95	£ -	£7,046.33
	SUMMARY				
		Page 1	£ 455.00	£4,414.00	£ 743.55
		Page 2	£ 117.77	£1,022.96	£2,291.28
		Page 3	£1,787.95	£ -	£7,046.33
		Totals:	£2,360.72	£5,436.96	£10,081.16
		Grand total:			£17,878.84

Precedent H—Estimate of costs served on other parties

48PD.10.5

SCHEDULE OF COSTS PRECEDENTS
PRECEDENT H

IN THE HIGH COURT OF JUSTICE 2000 - B - 9999

QUEEN'S BENCH DIVISION

BRIGHTON DISTRICT REGISTRY

BETWEEN

AB Claimant

and

CD Defendant

ESTIMATE OF CLAIMANT'S COSTS DATED 12th APRIL 2001

The claimant instructed E F & Co under a conditional fee agreement dated 8th July 2000 in respect of which the following hourly rates are recoverable as base costs

Partner - £180 per hour plus VAT
Assistant Solicitor - £140 per hour plus VAT
Other fee earners - £85 per hour plus VAT

Item No.	Description of work done	V.A.T.	Disburse-ments	Profit Costs
	PART 1: BASE COSTS ALREADY INCURRED			
	8th July 2000 - EF & Co instructed			
	7th October 2000 - Claim issued			
1	Issue fee	-	£ 400.00	
	21st October 2000 - Particulars of claim served			
	25th November 2000 - Time for service of defence extended by agreement to 14th January 2001			
2	Fee on allocation	-	£ 80.00	
	20th January 2001 - case allocated to multi-track			
	9th February 2001 - Case management conference at which costs were awarded to the claimant and the base costs were summarily assessed at £400 (paid on 24th February 2001)			-
	23rd February 2001 - Claimant's list of documents			
	ATTENDANCES, COMMUNICATIONS AND WORK DONE			
	Claimant			
3	0.75 hours at £180			£ 135.00
4	4.4 hours at £140			£ 616.00
	To Summary	£ -	£ 480.00	£ 751.00

Item No.	Description of work done	V.A.T.	Disburse-ments	Profit Costs
	Witnesses of Fact			
5	3.8 hours at £140			£ 532.00
6	Paid travelling on 9th October 2000	£ 4.02	£ 22.96	
	Medical expert (Dr. IJ)			
7	1.5 hours at £140			£ 210.00
8	Dr. IJ"s fee for report		£ 350.00	
	Defendant and his solicitor			
9	2.5 hours at £140			£ 350.00
	Court (communications only)			
10	0.4 hours at £140			£ 56.00
	Documents			
11	0.75 hours at £180 and 22.25 hours at £140			£3,250.00
	Negotiations			
12	2.75 hours at £140			£ 385.00
13	VAT on solicitor's base fees	£ 968.45		
	To Summary	£ 972.47	£ 372.96	£4,783.00
	PART2: BASE COSTS TO BE INCURRED			
14	Fee on listing		£ 400.00	
	Attendance at pre-trial review			
15	5 hours at £140			£ 700.00
16	Counsel's base fee for pre-trial review		£ 750.00	
	Attendance at trial			
17	20 hours at £140			£2,800.00
18	Counsel's base fee for trial including refresher		£3,000.00	
19	Fee of expert witness (Dr. IJ)	-	£ 1,000.00	
20	Expenses of witnesses of fact	-	£ 150.00	
	ATTENDANCES, COMMUNICATIONS AND WORK TO BE DONE			
	Claimant			
21	1 hour at £180			£ 180.00
22	8 hours at £140			£1,120.00
	Witnesses of fact			
23	5 hours at £140			£ 700.00
	Medical expert (Dr. IJ)			
24	1 hour at £140			£ 140.00
	Defendant and his solicitor			
25	2 hours at £140			£ 280.00
	To Summary	£ -	£ 5,300.00	£5,920.00

Item No.	Description of work done	V.A.T.	Disburse-ments	Profit Costs
	Court (communications only)			
26	1 hour at £140			£ 140.00
	Counsel (communications only)			
27	3 hours at £140			£ 420.00
	Documents			
28	1 hour at £180, 25 hours at £140 and 15 hours at £85			£4,995.00
	Negotiations			
29	5 hours at £140			£ 700.00
	Other work			
30	5 hours at £140			£ 700.00
31	VAT on solicitor's base fees	£2,253.13		
	To Summary	£2,253.13	£ -	£ 6,955.00
	SUMMARY			
	Part 1			
	Page 1	£ -	£ 480.00	£ 751.00
	Page 2	£ 972.47	**£ 372.96**	£4,783.00
	Total base costs already incurred	£ 972.47	£ 852.96	£5,534.00
	Part 2			
	Page 2	£ -	£ 5,300.00	£5,920.00
	Page 3	£2,253.13	£ -	**£6,955.00**
	Total base costs to be incurred	£2,253.13	£5,300.00	£12,875.00
	Total of base costs	£3,225.60	£6,152.96	£18,409.00
	Grand total			£27,787.56

Precedent K—Solicitors Act 1974: order for delivery of bill

48PD.10.6

SCHEDULE OF COST PRECEDENTS
PRECEDENT K
Solicitorís Act: order for delivery of bill

DATED the [DATE]

IN THE HIGH COURT OF JUSTICE [Claim No]

[DIVISION]

[JUDGE TYPE][JUDGE NAME]

BETWEEN:

[CLAIMANT]

Claimant

- and -

[DEFENDANT]

Defendant

UPON THE APPLICATION OF THE [PARTY]

[the parties and their representatives who attended]

AND UPON HEARING

AND UPON READING the documents on the Court File

IT IS ORDERED THAT

(1) The [PARTY] must within [NUMBER OF DAYS] deliver to the [PARTY], or to his solicitor, a bill of costs in **all causes and matters in which he has been concerned for the [PARTY]**

(2) The [PARTY] must give credit in that bill for all money received by him from or on account of the [PARTY]

Precedent L—Solicitors Act 1974: order for detailed assessment (client)

48PD.10.7

SCHEDULE OF COST PRECEDENTS
PRECEDENT L
Order on Client's Application for Detailed Assessment of Solicitor's Bill

DATED the [DATE]

IN THE HIGH COURT OF JUSTICE [Claim No]

[DIVISION]

[JUDGE TYPE][JUDGE NAME]

BETWEEN:

[CLAIMANT]

Claimant

- and -

[DEFENDANT]

Defendant

UPON THE APPLICATION OF THE [PARTY]

[the parties and their representatives who attended]

AND UPON HEARING

AND UPON READING the documents on the Court File

IT IS ORDERED THAT

(1) A detailed assessment must be made of the bill dated [ ] delivered to the claimant by the defendant.

(2) On making the detailed assessment, the court must also assess the costs of these proceedings and certify what is due to or from either party in respect of the bill and the costs of these proceedings.

(3) Until these proceedings are concluded the defendant must not commence or continue any proceedings against the claimant in respect of the bill mentioned above.

(4) Upon payment by the claimant of any sum certified as due to the defendant in these proceedings the defendant must deliver to the claimant all the documentation in the defendant's possession or control which belong to the claimant.

Precedent M—Solicitors Act 1974: order for detailed assessment (solicitors)

48PD.10.8

SCHEDULE OF COSTS PRECEDENTS
PRECEDENT M
Order on Solicitor's Application for Assessment Under the Solicitor's Act 1974 Part III

Upon hearing ... upon reading ...

IT IS ORDERED THAT

(1) A detailed assessment must be made of the bill dated [ ] delivered to the defendant by the claimant.

(2) If the defendant attends the detailed assessment the court making that assessment must also assess the costs of these proceedings and certify what is due to or from either party in respect of the bill and the costs of these proceedings.

(3) Until these proceedings are concluded the claimant must not commence or continue any proceedings against the defendant in respect of the bill mentioned above.

(4) Upon payment by the defendant of any sum certified as due to the claimant in these proceedings the claimant must deliver to the defendant all the documentation in the claimant's possession or control which belong to the defendant.

Precedent P—Solicitors Act 1974: breakdown of costs

48PD.10.9

SCHEDULE OF COSTS PRECEDENTS
PRECEDENT P

Solicitors Act: Breakdown of Costs

IN THE HIGH COURT OF JUSTICE — Claim Number

QUEEN'S BENCH DIVISION

SUPREME COURT COSTS OFFICE

BETWEEN

EF — Claimant

~ and ~

GH & Co — Defendants

BREAKDOWN OF DEFENDANT'S BILL OF COSTS DATED 26TH FEBRUARY 1999 TO BE ASSESSED PURSUANT TO THE ORDER DATED 27TH APRIL 1999

The claimant instructed the defendants in connection with a summons for careless or inconsiderate driving which had been served upon him. By letter dated 21st October 1998 the defendants wrote to the claimant setting out their terms of business including the hourly rates of the fee earners who would act on his instructions. On 23rd October 1998 the claimant dated and signed a copy of that letter and returned it to the defendants so indicating his acceptance of the terms set out.

The proceedings were of the highest importance to the claimant who feared losing his licence and who wished to defend any civil proceedings that might be taken against him as a result of the prosecution. The defendants entered into correspondence with the CPS and eventually obtained their witness statements and invited them to consent to an adjournment because of the absence overseas of an important witness for the claimant (Mr LM). Eventually the defendants successfully applied to the court for an adjournment, and also applied for and obtained a witness summons. At the trial the claimant was found guilty and was fined £300 and 4 points were endorsed on his driving licence.

Proceedings were conducted by an assistant solicitor admitted in 1990 whose time is charged at an agreed rate of £150 per hour with routine letters out and telephone calls at an agreed rate of £15 each. At the trial a trainee attended with counsel. The trainee's time is charged at an agreed rate of £75 per hour.

Cash account for client: EF

Received		**Paid**	
From client on account generally: 22nd October 1998	1,500.00	Refund to client: 26th February 1999	385.00
From client on account generally: 12th February 1999	**1,000.00**	Balancing Item	**2,115.00**
	2,500.00		**2,500.00**
Balance due to client EF:	**£2,115.00**		

	Item		V.A.T.	Disburse-ments	Profit Costs
	Attendances on Court and Counsel				
	5th November 1998 - application made for an adjournment for the convenience of a witness				
	13th November 1998 - contested hearing of the application				
	Engaged 10 minutes	£ 25.00			
	Travel and waiting 30 minutes	£ 75.00			
1	Total solicitor's fee for hearing		£ 17.50		£ 100.00
	17th November 1998 - conference with counsel				
	Engaged 45 minutes	£ 112.50			
	Travel and waiting 1 hour	£ 150.00			
2	Total solicitor's fee for conference		£ 45.94		£ 262.50
3	Counsel's fee for conference (paid: Miss JK)		£ 13.13	£ 75.00	
	15th February 1999 - Brief to counsel - 4 pages A4				
	23rd February 1999 - attending the trial				
	Trainee engaged in court 1 hour	£ 75.00			
	Engaged in conference 30 minutes	£ 37.50			
	Travel and waiting (apportioned) 45 minutes	£ 56.25			
4	**Total trainee solicitor**'s fee for trial		£ 29.53		£ 158.75
5	Counsel's brief fee (paid: Miss JK)		£ 17.50	£ 100.00	
	Claimant				
6	21st October 1998 - first instructions 1 hour		£ 26.25		£ 150.00
7	16th November 1998 - finalising proof of evidence 45 minutes		£ 19.69		£ 112.50
8	Routine letters out and telephone calls - 12 (9 + 3)		£ 31.50		£ 180.00
	Witness (Mr LM)				
	Personal attendance by trainee solicitor				
	Engaged 45 minutes	£ 56.25			
	Travel and waiting 1 hour	£ 75.00			
9	Total trainee solicitor's fee for attendance		£ 22.97		£ 131.25
10	Routine letters out - 6		£ 15.75		£ 90.00
	Other persons				
11	Routine letters out and telephone calls to the CPS - 8 (6 + 2)		£ 21.00		£ 120.00
	Communications with the court				
12	Routine letters out - 6		£ 15.75		£ 90.00
13	**Communications with Counsel**				
	Routine letters out and telephone calls - 8 (4 + 4)		£ 21.00		£ 120.00
	Work done on documents				
14	**Instructions to counsel - 30 minutes**		£ 13.13		£ 75.00
15	Attendance note of conference - 15 minutes		£ 6.56		£ 37.50
16	Brief to counsel - 30 minutes		£ **13.13**		£ 75.00
17	Attendance note of trial (trainee) - 45 minutes		£ 9.84		£ 56.25
			£ 340.17	£ 175.00	£1,768.75
	Summary				
	Total costs claimed in breakdown £1,943.75 + £340.17 VAT.				
	(Total costs billed £1899.00 + **£315.00** VAT)				

List of costs forms and form numbers

48PD.11 *[Please note that this list is not part of the Practice Direction]*

1. Statement of Costs (summary assessment) [Form **N260**]
2. Bill of Costs (detailed assessment)
3. Legal Aid Schedule of Costs
4. Certificate for inclusion in bills
5. Notice of Commencement of Assessment of Bill of Costs [Form **N252**]
6. Points of Dispute
7. Request for Default Costs Certificate [Form **N254**]

8A. Request for a Detailed Assessment Hearing (non-legal aid) [Form **N258**]

8B. Request for a Detailed Assessment Hearing (Legal aid only) [Form **N258A**]

9. Default Costs Certificate (County Court) [Form **N255**]
10. Default Costs Certificate (High Court) [Form **N255A**]
11. Interim Costs Certificate [Form **N257**]
12. Final Costs Certificate (County Court) [Form **N256**]
13. Final Costs Certificate (High Court) [Form **N256 HC**]
14. Notice of Amount Allowed on Provisional Assessment (Legal Aid only) [Form **N253**]
15. Legal Aid Assessment Certificate [Form **EX80A**]
16. Notice of Appeal [**CF16**]
17. Solicitors Act: Order for delivery of bill [**CF17**]
18. Solicitors Act: Order for detailed assessment (client) [**CF18**]
19. Solicitors Act: Order for detailed assessment (solicitors) [**CF19**]
20. Solicitors Act: Breakdown of costs [**CF20**]
21. Solicitors Act: Request for a hearing date [**CF21**]

PRACTICE DIRECTION—FAMILY DIVISION

It is directed that upon the coming into force on 26 April 1999 of the Civil Procedure Rules (CPR) and the Family Proceedings (Miscellaneous Amendments) Rules 1999 (SI 1999/1012): **48BPD.1**

(a) Paragraph 3.2 of the Practice Direction (Allocation of cases to levels of judiciary) shall apply to the Family Division. District judges (including district judges of the Principal Registry) shall have jurisdiction to hear and dispose of proceedings under the Inheritance (Provision for Family and Dependants) Act 1975 and under s.14 of the Trusts of Land and Appointment of Trustees Act 1996.

(b) The Practice Direction about costs supplementing CPR Pts 43 to 48 (the costs direction) (see *Civil Procedure 1999*, pp.467–522, paras 48PD.1 to 48PD.23) shall apply to family proceedings to which the Family Proceedings Rules 1991 (SI 1991/1247), apply and to proceedings in the Family Division. References in the costs direction to "claimant" and "defendant" are to be read as references to the equivalent terms used in family proceedings and other terms and expressions used in the costs direction shall be similarly treated. References to procedural steps and to other Parts of the CPR which have not yet been applied to family proceedings are to be read as referring to equivalent or similar procedures under the rules applicable to family proceedings, as the context may permit. The previous practice in relation to "costs reserved" will no longer be followed and such an order will have the effect specified in the costs direction. It should also be noted that the period for commencing detailed assessment proceedings will be as specified in CPR, r.47.7 (three months) in substitution for the period of six months previously applicable.

President's Direction

Issued with the approval and concurrence of the Lord Chancellor.

22nd April 1999. Sir Stephen Brown P.

President's Direction

The Principal Registry Of The Family Division Costs July 24, 2000 Civil Procedure Rules 1998 The President's Direction dated April 22, 1999 applied the (Civil Procedure) Practice Direction about Costs Supplementing Parts 43 to 48 of the Civil Procedure Rules ("the costs direction") to family proceedings (within the Family Proceedings Rules 1991) and to proceedings in the Family Division. A further edition of the costs direction (effective from July 3, 2000) has been published and it is hereby directed that the further edition (and all subsequent editions as and when they are published and come into effect) shall extend to family proceedings and to the extent applicable to such proceedings. The further edition of the costs direction includes provisions applicable to proceedings following changes in the manner in which legal services are funded pursuant *to the Access to Justice Act 1999. It sh*ould be noted that although the cost of the premium in respect of legal costs insurance (section 29) or the cost of funding by a prescibed membership organisation (section 30) may be recoverable, family proceedings (within section 58A(2) of the Courts and Legal Services Act 1990) cannot be the subject of an enforceable conditional fee agreement. Issued with the approval of the Lord Chancellor **48BPD.2**

Elizabeth Butler–Sloss

President

PRACTICE DIRECTION (ANCILLARY RELIEF: COSTS)

48BPD.3 **1** The Family Proceedings (Amendment) Rules 2006 make significant changes to the court's power to make costs orders in ancillary relief proceedings. The new rules will come into force on 3 April 2006. They will apply to an application for ancillary relief contained in a petition or answer filed on or after 3 April 2006, or to such an application which has not been made in a petition or answer but is made in Form A on or after that date. The rules will also apply to an application under section 10(2) of the Matrimonial Causes Act 1973 or under section 48(2) of the Civil Partnership Act 2004 made in Form B on or after that date. They do not however apply to such applications if they are to be heard by the court with an application which was made before that date.

2 Under the new rules the court will only have power to make a costs order in ancillary relief proceedings when this is justified by the litigation conduct of one of the parties: see new rule 2.71 of the Family Proceedings Rules 1991, as amended. When determining whether and how to exercise this power the court will be required to take into account the list of factors set out in the rules. The court will no longer be able to take into account any offers to settle expressed to be "without prejudice" or "without prejudice save as to costs" in deciding what, if any, costs order to make.

3 The new rules require the completion of Forms H and H1: see rule 2.61F of the Family Proceedings Rules 1991, as amended. Form H is to be used at interim hearings so that the court has available to it a realistic estimate of the costs incurred to date. Form H1 is for use at a final hearing to provide the court with accurate details of the costs which each party has incurred, or expects to incur, in relation to the ancillary relief proceedings. The purpose of this form is to enable the court to take account of the impact of each party's costs liability on their financial situations. Parties should ensure that the information contained in these forms is as full and accurate as possible and that any sums already paid in respect of a party's ancillary relief costs are clearly set out. Where relevant, any liability arising from the costs of other proceedings between the parties should continue to be referred to in the appropriate section of a party's Form E; any such costs should not be included in Forms H or H1.

4 Parties who intend to seek a costs order against another party in proceedings to which rule 2.71 of the Family Proceedings Rules 1991 applies should ordinarily make this plain in open correspondence or in skeleton arguments before the date of the hearing. In any case where summary assessment of costs awarded under rule 2.71 of the Family Proceedings Rules 1991 would be appropriate parties are under an obligation to file a statement of costs in CPR Form **N260**: see Practice Direction about Costs supplementing CPR Pts 43 to 48, section 13, and paragraph 6 below.

5 An order for maintenance pending suit which includes an element to allow a party to deal with legal fees (see *A v A (Maintenance Pending Suit: Payment of Legal Fees)* [2001] 1 WLR 605; *G v G (Maintenance Pending Suit: Costs)* [2002] 3 FCR 339; *McFarlane v McFarlane* [2005] Fam 171; and *Moses-Taiga v Taiga* [2005] EWCA Civ 1013) is an order made pursuant to section 22 of the Matrimonial Causes Act

1973, and is not a "costs order" within the meaning of rule 2.71 of the Family Proceedings Rules 1991.

6 The *President's Practice Direction (Family Proceedings: Allocation and Costs)* [1999] 1 WLR 1128 dated 22 April 1999 (as supplemented by the *President's Practice Direction (Family Proceedings: Costs)* [2000] 1 WLR 1781 dated 24 July 2000) makes provision in relation to the application of the Practice Direction about Costs supplementing CPR Pts 43 to 48 to family proceedings to which the Family Proceedings Rules 1991 apply. Those President's directions will apply to a costs order made under new rule 2.71 of the Family Proceedings Rules 1991, as amended, as though the reference to the Practice Direction about Costs supplementing CPR Pts 43 to 48 were a reference to that direction excluding section 6, paragraphs 8.1 to 8.4 and sections 15 and 16.

7 Issued with the concurrence of the Lord Chancellor.

GENERAL PRINCIPLES AND CASE LAW RELATING TO COSTS AND THEIR ASSESSMENT

Introductory note

48.11.1 This section is not intended to be a definitive work on the general principles of assessment, but a compilation of decisions and commentary which may from time to time need to be referred to.

Contents

48.11.2 *General Principles and Case Law relating to Costs and their Assessment*

1. Costs in specific courts and other tribunals

2. Costs relating to specific statutes

3. Costs relating to particular types of action or proceedings also general principles of assessment

4. Costs Relating to Particular Types of Parties and Miscellaneous

1. Costs in specific courts and other tribunals

Arbitration: reference costs

The words used in s.63(5) of the 1996 Act (see para.2E–236+) were familiar to all as the pre-CPR standard basis. It seems that when the CPR Costs Rules were introduced the wording of the Act and the new rules were not compared. Although the Act will take precedence over the rules, CPR 43.2(2) applies the Costs Rules to arbitration proceedings and the rules require proportionality to be taken into consideration by the court. Section 63 envisages: (1) the agreement of the parties; (3) determination by the Tribunal "on such basis as it thinks fit"; (4) and (5) determination by the court "on such basis as it thinks fit". This would seem to mean that the arbitrator under (1) and (3) may act as he pleases in accordance with (5); if the court becomes involved (5) is modified to mean the standard basis including proportionality. It should be borne in mind that any attempt to demonstrate a basis other than the standard basis would be caught by CPR 44.4(4)(b). **48.12.1**

The "costs of the reference" are those "which are incidental to the reference and incurred in bringing it about—costs of the arrangements, meetings, discussions, consultations, conferences and all that are necessary to bring the parties *ad idem* to a point on which they agree, but up to which there must be preliminary steps". Per Huddleston B. in *Autothreptic Steam Boiler Co Ltd v Townsend Hook and Co* (1888) 21 Q.B.D. 182. Section 47 of the 1996 Act enables the Tribunal to decide in its first award to deal with the costs of a preliminary hearing by a subsequent award. Section 47 confers an entirely general power to determine the issues arising in the reference in more than one award: see *Trade Maritime Corp v Hellenic Mutual War Risks Association (Bermuda) Ltd* [2006] EWHC 578 (Comm) Christopher Clarke J.

An agreement which has the effect that a party is to pay the whole or part of the costs of the arbitration in any event is only valid if made after the dispute in question has arisen (s.60 of the Arbitration Act 1996). *Everglade Maritime Inc v Schiffahrtsgesellschaft Detlaf Von Appen GmbH (The Maria)* [1993] 3 All E.R. 748, CA.

Where an arbitrator made a final award in which he ruled in favour of the applicants on some issues and in favour of the respondent on others and ordered the applicants to pay the respondents' costs, and in giving reasons for the decision relied on two matters which the parties had not raised, the Court found that the arbitrator had not acted in accordance with the general duty, under s.33 of the Act, to act fairly and impartially between the parties. His failure to raise these matters with the parties amounted to a serious irregularity within the meaning of s.63(2) of the Arbitration Act 1996. *Gbangbola v Smith & Sherriff Ltd* [1998] 3 All E.R. 730, TCC, Judge Lloyd, Q.C.

It is not improper for an arbitrator to propose to both parties an arrangement for payment of fees, including a commitment fee payable in advance of the hearing. It would probably constitute misconduct for an arbitrator to conclude an agreement as to fees with one party when the other refused to join in the agreement (*Norjar A/S v Hyundai Heavy Industries Co Ltd* [1991] 3 All E.R. 211). See also s.60(1) of the Arbitration Act 1996.

The parties are free to argue what costs of the arbitration are recoverable (s.63 of the Arbitration Act 1996). As to the recoverable fee and expenses of arbitrators, see *ibid.*, s.64.

Where a whole cause is referred to an arbitrator, and he awards "the costs of the action and of this my award," the costs of the reference are included in "the costs of the action" (*Patten v West of England Iron, etc, Co* [1894] 2 Q.B. 159). See also s.61 of the Arbitration Act 1996.

It is not competent for an arbitrator to deal with costs which might be incurred before the Divisional Court (*Higham v Havant and Waterloo U.D.C.* [1951] 2 K.B. 527, CA; (1951) 2 T.L.R. 87).

For the statutory provisions relating to the costs of arbitration see Arbitration Act 1996 ss.59– 65. Under the Arbitration Act 1950 s.18 (where the old law continues to apply) it is open to the arbitrator to assess the costs on a request made before the final award. Where an award was made which did not contain a direction that assessment should be by any specified tribunal it was still open to the arbitrator to carry out the assessment. The High Court has jurisdiction to assess the costs, and in the absence of a request to the arbitrator to tax, would deal with the matter. On the particular facts of the case the arbitrator had done nothing to lose the power to assess and remained obliged to do so pursuant to a request: *M/S Alghanim Industries Inc v Skandia International Insurance Corporation* [2001] 2 All E.R. 30, Ms B Dohmann Q.C.

Where a final arbitration award has been based upon a figure which the arbitrator was unaware was erroneous, that error amounted to an accidental slip for the purposes of s.57(3)(a) of the Arbitration Act 1996. The section was sufficiently wide to encompass correction of the award together with any consequent order as to costs: *Gannet Shipping Ltd v Eastrade Commodities Inc*; *East Trade Commodities Inc v Gannet Shipping Ltd* [2002] 1 All E.R. (Comm) 297, Langley J.

The rules of a trade association provided for an appeal against the finding in a first tier arbitration to the association's appeal board. In a case in which the chairman of the board arranged for the appointment of an assistant solicitor to act as a legal draftsman for the purpose of drafting the award the Commercial Court held that the role of such a draftsman was limited, given the role of the tribunal itself, and it was the duty of the tribunal to satisfy itself that the fee charged was fair and reasonable in the light of the sums in issue, the complexity of the legal argument and the attitude of the parties. Since the draftsman had not been employed as a legal adviser there was no need for him to have attended the hearing and accordingly the time spent by him was grossly excessive and could not be justified. The fees ordered to be paid in respect of the draftsman were reduced by approximately 50 per cent: *Agrimex Ltd v Tradigrain SA* [2003] EWHC 1656 (QB), Thomas J.

In adjudication proceedings, under the Construction Industries Council's model adjudication procedure, one clause of the agreement was modified to give the adjudicator power, in his discretion, to direct the payment of legal costs and expenses to one party by another as part of his decision. The adjudication did not proceed to a substantive decision. One party discontinued its claim and paid the adjudicator's fees and expenses to date. The other party claimed its legal costs up to the time of the discontinuance. The court of appeal held (on the basis of the amended clause) that the adjudicator's power to direct payment of costs was not limited to circumstances in which he had made a substantive contested decision on the dispute referred to him. The discontinuing party therefore had to comply with the adjudicator's direction that it should pay the other party's costs up to the date of discontinuance: *John Roberts Architects Ltd v Parkcare Homes (No.2) Ltd* [2006] EWCA Civ 64.

Calderbank Letters

48.12.2 If a party seeks to rely on an offer of settlement which is unclear as to how costs are to be dealt with, the arbitrator determining the award of costs at the conclusion of the hearing will be at a disadvantage. It is desirable that there should be clarity as to what provision in relation to costs is intended: see *Tramountana Armadora SA v Atlantic Shipping Co SA (The Vorros)* [1978] 2 All E.R. 870. Where an offer is framed in a way which enables the arbitrator to consider whether or not the offeree has gained by continuing with the arbitration rather than by accepting the offer, the arbitrator is entitled to consider the offer: *Lindner Ceilings Floors Partitions Plc v How Engineering Services Ltd* [2001] B.L.R. 90, Richard Seymour Q.C.

Arbitration costs of claims consultants

48.12.3 In *Piper Double Glazing Ltd v D.C. Contracts* [1994] 1 All E.R. 117, Potter J. answered in the affirmative the preliminary issue "where in an arbitration conducted in England or Wales in accordance with English law:

(*i*) a party is represented by a person who is neither a qualified solicitor, nor a barrister ('the unqualified person'), but who provides services and performs functions similar to those provided or performed by a solicitor or barrister, and;

(ii) an award is made by the Arbitrator in favour of that party which includes a direction that another party should pay the first party s costs of the arbitration; and

(iii) the award provides such for such costs to be [assessed] in the High Court, if not agreed [...] and

(iv) the arbitration agreement or reference to arbitration contains no provision excluding the recovery of such costs;

in proceedings for the [assessment] of costs pursuant to the award, does the Court on a proper construction of [Rules of Court] and or ss.20–25 of the Solicitors Act 1974, have power to allow any amount for the costs incurred by the unqualified person in relation to the conduct of the arbitration?"

The learned Judge refused to answer the second issue:

"If the Court does have power to allow amounts for the costs so incurred by the unqualified person in relation to the conduct of the arbitration, are those costs to be allowed or to be assessed on the basis set out by Master Hurst in *William Tarr & Co Ltd v Royal Insurance plc*, April 8, 1989, unrep., that being that the costs recovered cannot [...] be more than the amount recoverable had the arbitration been conducted by solicitor and counsel, and if not upon what basis should they be assessed or allowed?"

Copyright Tribunal

The Copyright Tribunal may at its discretion at any stage in the proceedings make an order in relation to the payment of costs by one party to another in respect of the whole or part of the proceedings. The Tribunal may direct payment of a lump sum by way of costs, or such a proportion of the costs as may be just, in which case the Tribunal may assess the sum to be paid or direct it to be assessed by the Chairman or by a Costs Judge of the Supreme Court (or the Taxing Master of the Supreme Court of Northern Ireland or the Auditor of the Court of Session) (Copyright Tribunal Rules 1989 r.48(1)(2)). Neither the Copyright, Design and Patents Act 1988 nor the 1989 Rules provide that costs should follow the event. The Tribunal has a very wide discretion as to costs under s.151 of the 1988 Act: *AEI Rediffusion Music Ltd v Phonographic Performance Ltd* [1999] 1 W.L.R. 1507. **48.12.4**

Administrative Court

The established practice of the Administrative Court is to make no order for costs against inferior courts or tribunals if they do not appear at the challenge in question to oppose the appeal. The two exceptions to that general proposition are: **48.12.5**

(a) where there is flagrant improper behaviour on the part of the inferior court or tribunal; and

(b) when the inferior court or tribunal has unreasonably declined or neglected to sign a consent order disposing of the proceedings (see *R (on the application of Davies) v HM Deputy Coroner for Birmingham (Costs)* [2004] EWCA Civ 207; [2004] 1 W.L.R. 2739): *LT v Cardiff Council & Anor* [2007] EWHC 2568 (Admin) Wyn Williams J.

The Administrative Court has no jurisdiction on an application for judicial review to award costs out of central funds to the successful applicant. Section 51 of the Contempt of Court Act 1981 gave the court a general and wide discretion to make such orders as to payments of costs as it thought fit. This power does not include the power to make an award out of central funds even where there is "no other possible source of costs" in an application for judicial review (*Holden & Co v CPS (No.2)* [1993] 2 W.L.R. 934, HL, reversing *R. v Bow Street Metropolitan Stipendiary Magistrate Ex p. Mirror Group Newspapers*; *R. v same Ex p. B.B.C.* [1992] 1 W.L.R. 412, DC).

In principle a defendant is entitled to recover the costs inevitably incurred in the preparation of grounds for opposing a judicial review application. A defendant who failed to comply with Pt 54 of the Rules would be unable to take part in any subsequent oral or interim applications without the permission of the court. In order to avoid a seperate application for costs it is appropriate for a defendant to include the application within the body of the acknowledgment of service: *Leach v Commissioner for Local Administration* [2001] EWHC 455 (Admin); *The Times*, August 2, 2001, Collins J.

An applicant for judicial review who abandons his application because he no longer requires relief from the court is not entitled to recover his costs. Under s.51(1) of the Supreme Court Act 1981 costs are only recoverable when there are proceedings before the court: an application for leave to move for judicial review cannot constitute proceedings (*R. v Test Valley Borough Council Ex p. Goodman* [1992] C.O.D. 101).

Solicitors Disciplinary Tribunal

48.12.6 The Solicitors Disciplinary Tribunal has the power to make an order for costs under s.47 of the Solicitors Act 1974 even if an allegation was not proved. The court rejected an argument that when more than one partner might have been at fault, but only one was brought before the Tribunal, it was not right to make those over whom the Tribunal had jurisdiction pay all the costs of the investigation and hearing simply because a solicitors former partner might have had some culpability did not mean there should be some discount for costs: *Singh v The Law Society* [2001] EWHC 1106 (Admin).

The Tribunal may make such order as to costs as it thinks fit including an order disallowing costs incurred unnecessarily. The Tribunal may order that costs be paid by any party judged to be responsible for wasted or unnecessary costs, whether arising through non-compliance with time limits or otherwise. The Tribunal may order that any party bear the whole or a part or a proportion of the costs. The amount of the costs to be paid may either be fixed by the tribunal or be subject to detailed assessment by a Costs judge (the Solicitors (Disciplinary Proceedings) Rules 2007 (SI 2007/3588) rr.18(1) to (3)).The Tribunal may also make an order as to costs where any application or allegation is withdrawn or amended, where no allegation of misconduct (including an application under s.43 of the Solicitors Act 1974) is proved against a respondent (the Solicitors (Disciplinary Proceedings) Rules 2007 (SI 2007/3588) r.18(4)).

Employment Appeal Tribunal

48.12.7 The Employment Appeal Tribunal Rules 1993 (SI 1993/2854) as amended, apply to all proceedings irrespective of when those proceedings were commenced. Costs ordered to be paid under those rules are in practice assessed in the Supreme Court Costs Office.

The Litigants in Person (Costs and Expenses) Act 1975 has been applied to the Employment Appeal Tribunal with effect from September 1, 1980 by the Litigants in Person (Costs and Expenses) Order 1980 (SI 1980/1159) and see Vol.2, 9B–1209. Where a litigant in person cannot prove financial loss, the litigant will be allowed an amount for the time which the tribunal considers reasonably spent on doing the work, at the rate of £25 per hour (this rate increases by the sum of £1 for every year commencing with April 6, 2006): Employment Appeal Tribunal Rules 1993 r.34D(4) and (5). An application for costs must be made either during or at the end of a relevant hearing, or in writing to the Registrar within 14 days of the sealing of the relevant order: Practice Direction (Employment Appeal Tribunal—Procedure) 2004 s.19.

In considering what order for costs is appropriate the Employment Tribunal should not take into account the means of the paying party. Once the threshold of unreasonable conduct has been crossed there is no reason why the misbehaving party should not be required to compensate his opponent for costs which he should not have had to incur.

In deciding whether or not to make an order for costs against a party who has acted unreasonably in conducting the proceedings, the crucial question is whether in all the circumstances of the case a claimant (e.g. who withdrew a claim), had conducted the proceedings unreasonably, not whether the withdrawal of the claim was in itself unreasonable. It would be wrong for Employment Tribunals to take the line that it was unreasonable conduct for claimants to withdraw claims, and unfortunate if claimants were deterred from withdrawing by the prospect of an order for costs which might well not have been made against them had they failed in their claim after a full hearing. Equally, tribunals should not follow a practice on costs which might encourage speculative claims by allowing claimants to start cases in the hope of receiving an offer to settle failing which they could drop the case without any risk of a costs sanction: *McPherson v BNP Paribas* [2004] EWCA Civ 569; [2004] 3 All E.R. 266, CA.

In considering the award of costs on appeal, the fact that a case has been allowed through at a preliminary hearing is not a bar to arguing that it is unnecessary. *Tesco Stores Ltd v Wilson*, January 12, 2000, unrep., EAT, H.H. Judge Clark.

The fact that an appeal has been sifted prior to a full hearing, or has been allowed to proceed after a preliminary hearing, does not preclude the possibility of costs being awarded if the appeal is subsequently held to have no reasonable prospect of success. It is not the practice to refuse to award costs simply because an appeal has survived a preliminary stage, a proposition which risked conflicting with the powers of the EAT to award costs under the EAT Rules 1993 r.34, *Iron and Steel Trades Confederation v ASW Ltd (in liquidation)* [2004] I.R.L.R. 926, Burton J.

The Employment Tribunal is entitled to award costs against an applicant on the basis that the proceedings brought against the employer had been misconceived and conducted unreasonably. Although costs orders under the Employment Tribunals (Constitution and Rules of Procedure) Regulations 2001 were exceptional or rare the decision was based on the conclusion that the claim was misconceived and had no real prospect of success. In addition the applicant had behaved unreasonably and the Tribunal had regard to the nature, gravity and effect of the unreasonable conduct as factors relevant to the exercise of its discretion: *Salinas v Bear Stearns International Holdings Inc* [2005] I.C.R. 1117, Burnton J.

The Employment Tribunal concluded that certain workers had acted unreasonably in bringing a claim against a company when they were in fact self employed and operated under a contract with another company. They were ordered to pay the respondents' costs. The respondents' counsel had a general qualification within the meaning of the Courts and Legal Services Act 1990 s.71, but their solicitor, who did not have a practising certificate, did not. The solicitor's fees could only be recovered by way of a preparation time order. Schedule 1, para.46(1) of the Employment Tribunal (Constitution and Rules of Procedure) Regulations 2004 precluded a Tribunal from making a preparation time order and a costs order in favour of the same party in the same proceedings. The decision of the Court of Appeal in *Agassi v Robinson (Inspector of Taxes) (Costs)* [2005] EWCA Civ 1507; [2006] 1 W.L.R. 2126 would apply in any detailed assessment proceedings and would bind the Costs Judge or District Judge: *Ramsey v Bowercross Construction Ltd* August 14, 2008, unrep. (EAT) Peter Clarke J.

The correct procedure when an Employment Tribunal is considering the making of a wasted costs order is that set out in Rule 48 of the Employment Tribunal Rules of Procedure. The correct test is a three-stage one: (a) Did the legal representative act improperly, unreasonably or negligently? (b) If so, did the conduct result in unnecessary costs? (c) Was it just to order the representative to compensate the applicant for all or part of the relevant costs? The idea that a wasted costs order could be made simply because the lawyer's client had pursued a hopeless case was entirely erroneous. *Ratcliffe Duce & Gammer v Binns* April 23, 2008, unrep. (EAT), Elias J.

The fact that a teacher had claimed the remedy of re-engagement and had succeeded in obtaining a finding of unfair dismissal did not entitle him, whatever the circumstances, to pursue that remedy long after it had become obvious that no such remedy was remotely practicable. The tribunal was entitled to find that the applicant had conducted the litigation unreasonably and an order for costs could accordingly be made against him: *Woolf v Kingston Upon Hull City Council* June 7, 2007, unrep. (EAT), Wilkie J. and two others.

The applicant, a former employee of the first respondent brought proceedings including for racial discrimination. The respondent's solicitor wrote to the applicant indicating that if she was unsuccessful an application for costs would be made. The claim of racial discrimination was dismissed and the solicitor issued an application for costs on the respondent's instructions. The application for costs was dismissed. The solicitor then wrote to the applicant indicating that the respondent intended to take disciplinary proceedings against the applicant. The applicant brought a second claim asserting that the respondent's application for costs, the terms of a settlement proposal and the subsequent pursuance of the application to the tribunal amounted to victimisation and that she had been victimised by the threat of disciplinary proceedings. She also claimed that there had been a breach of the Race Relations Act 1976 s.33. The Court of Appeal found that the decision to take disciplinary proceedings was the respondent's and that the solicitor did not take part in the decision but had merely advised that such action should be taken, but that did not begin to demonstrate that the decision was that of anybody other than the respondent. The solicitor was doing no more than acting on the respondent's instructions. The institution of proceedings was not to be treated as "aiding" for the purposes of s.33 of the 1976 Act: *Bird v Sylvester* [2007] EWCA Civ 1052.

Lands Tribunal

Where a claim for pre-reference costs is not quantified by the claimant, it will be sufficient for the sealed offer to agree to the payment of those costs in general terms. If **48.12.8** they are later quantified for the claimant, a revised sealed offer may be substituted. This is relevant for the purpose of deciding whether the award of costs of the proceedings before the Tribunal are controlled by s.4 of the Land Compensation Act 1961 or whether they are in the unfettered discretion of the Tribunal (*Day v Greater London Council* (1972) 122 New L.J. 23). Where the Lands Tribunal made an award of compensation in 1988 which was subsequently set aside and the matter remitted for redetermination, the Tribunal redetermining the compensation in 1991, interest on costs ran from the date of the 1991 award which was the only effective award on the reference: *Barclays Bank plc v Kent County Council* [1998] R.V.R. 74, CA.

The Lands Tribunal will usually apply the same principle as the High Court and County Courts even though the CPR do not directly apply to costs in the Tribunal. In a case where the Tribunal awarded the claimant 75 per cent of its costs on the basis that its claim had been exaggerated the Court of Appeal held that the principle of equivalence in land compensation cases required that a claimant was entitled to the reasonable and necessary expenses attributable to the compulsory acquisition of his land. There was a danger of a too literal application of the President's Practice Direction and the CPR jurisprudence could result in a breach of the principle of equivalence. Merely claiming a sum much greater than the amount awarded would not justify a reduction in costs. To the extent that the reduction in costs was a reflection of costs which were not reasonable and necessary then it would be justified. In the instant case a substantial amount of time had been spent on inappropriate comparables and the complainant had caused an adjournment. In the circumstances the Tribunal's award was upheld: *Purfleet Farms v Secretary of State for Transport* [2002] EWCA Civ 1430. As a general rule it would be fair for an applicant not to be at risk as to costs, at least until he had had an opportunity to consider the evidence relied upon by an objector as establishing his title. If the applicant, having had that opportunity, persisted in resisting the objector's claim and went on to lose then there was no reason why he should not pay the costs in accordance with the ordinary rule: *Winter v Traditional and Contemporary Contracts Ltd* [2006] EWCA Civ 1740.

The Lands Tribunal awarded a claimant compensation in respect of the freehold interest in a dwelling house. The local authority was ordered to pay 60 per cent of the total costs. The parties agreed the amount of compensation payable, which was less than the sealed offer but could not agree the costs. The local authority argued that it should only have to pay 60 per cent of the costs up to the date of the sealed offer as the claimant had unreasonably pursued a claim for loss of profit and that the claimant should pay the local authorities costs thereafter. The tribunal decided that the claimant was entitled to recover its costs up to the date of the sealed offer, but since the local authority had withdrawn its offer at a late stage that was a special reason in the claimant's favour and justified a departure from the usual practice which would have been to order the claimant to pay the local authority's costs after the date of the sealed offer. *Christos v Secretary of State for the Environment, Transport and the Regions (Costs)* [2004] R.V.R. 59, N J Rose.

Where a claimant had accepted an offer which did not provide for costs incurred after the offer was made, the tribunal retained jurisdiction over costs where they were not covered by the agreed terms and could therefore deal with costs as a matter of discretion in accordance with the Lands Tribunal Rules 1996 r.52: *Chapter Group Plc v London Regional Transport* [2006] R.V.R. 242, Judge Rich Q.C.

An applicant applied for an order under s.20C of the Landlord and Tenant Act 1985 that the costs incurred by the respondent landlord in connection with proceedings before the Leasehold Valuation Tribunal were not to be regarded as relevant costs to be taken into account in determining the amount of any service charge payable by the applicant. The Tribunal held that such an order could properly be made in favour of a particular tenant but that did not prevent the landlord from calculating the service charge of other tenants to include those costs. It was just and equitable that the applicant, who had been successful in the Tribunal, should not have to pay, through her service charge, any part of the landlord's costs: *Volosinovici v Corvan (Properties) Ltd Lands Tribunal*, 25 October 2007, HHJ Huskinson (unreported).

In relation to para.22.4 of the Lands Tribunal Practice Direction (Practice Direction (Lands Tr: Practice Directions) [2006] R v R 221) the Court of Appeal held that as a general rule it would seem fair for the applicant not to be at risk as to costs at least until he had had an opportunity to consider the evidence relied on by the objector as establishing his title. If the applicant, having had that opportunity, persisted in resisting the objector's claim and went on to lose then there was no reason why he should not pay the costs in accordance with the ordinary rule. Likewise if an objector had held up a potential development in reliance on a claimed right which he was unable to establish there was no reason why he should not pay the costs. A party claiming the costs of a preliminary dispute should make clear what precisely he was claiming and from when: *Winter v Traditional and Contemporary Contracts Ltd* [2006] EWCA Civ 1740; [2007] 2 All E.R. 343 CA.

Special Educational Needs Tribunal

To justify an order for costs against the Tribunal there must be shown perversity on the part of the Tribunal or a flagrant disregard for the principles of justice which is the threshold for a costs order to be made against justices or Tribunals. *R. v Lincoln Justices Ex p. Count* [1996] 8 Admin.L.R. 233, per Turner J.; *S. v Metropolitan Borough of Dudley*, December 10, 1999, unrep. **48.12.9**

Competition Appeal Tribunal

The Tribunal may, at any stage of proceedings, make any order it thinks fit in relation to payment of costs by one party to another in respect of the whole or part of the proceedings. In determining how much the party is required to pay the Tribunal may take into account the conduct of all the parties in relation to the proceedings. In this context "costs" means costs and expenses recoverable before the Supreme Court of England and Wales, the Court of Session or the Supreme Court of Northern Ireland. The Tribunal may assess the sum to be paid or may direct that it be assessed by the President, a Chairman or the Registrar or dealt with by the detailed assessment of a Costs Officer of the Supreme Court or a Taxing Officer of the Supreme Court of Northern Ireland or by the Auditor of the Court of Session. The power to award costs includes the power to direct any party to pay the Tribunal such sum as may be appropriate in reimbursement of any costs incurred by the Tribunal in connection with the summoning or citation of witnesses or the instruction of experts on the Tribunal's behalf. Any sum due as a result of such a direction may be recovered by the Tribunal as a civil debt due to the Tribunal: Competition Appeal Tribunal Rules (SI 2003/1372) r.55. **48.12.10**

The rules as to funding arrangements, made under the Civil Procedure Rules 1998 as amended, apply to proceedings before the Tribunal (*ibid*, r.65).

The Competition Appeal Tribunal decided that an unsuccessful appellant had not acted unreasonably in bringing an appeal. The submission of the Director General of the Office of Fair Trading that the appeal was manifestly inadmissible could not be sustained. In its previous decision the Tribunal had stated that many of the Appellants' arguments had considerable force and it was only due to exceptional circumstances that an appealable decision did not arise. The appellant's presentation of the notice of appeal and the documents did not in themselves justify an order for costs. A general rule that costs should be borne by the unsuccessful appellant would risk frustrating the objectives of the Competition Act 1998 by deterring appeals from smaller companies, representative bodies and consumers. The costs of the respondent Director would ultimately be passed on to the industry and to consumers. The costs were minuscule compared with the Water Industry's total revenues, whereas the burden of costs falling on a small complainant acting reasonably was likely to be disproportionately heavy. The system of regulation would work more effectively if there were no deterrents to complaints and appeals being made. The Director's costs in the appeal should be regarded as part of the general costs of regulation of the water services sector, *Aquavitae (UK) Ltd v Director General of Water Service (Costs)* [2003] CAT 23; [2004] Comp. A.R. 203, Sir Christopher Bellamy, President.

As to the costs of a company being treated as a litigant in person, see *Albion Water Ltd v Water Services Regulation Authority (formerly Director General of Water Services)* [2007] CAT 1, [2007] Comp A.R. 505, Sir Christopher Bellamy P., and *Albion Water Ltd v Water Services Regulation Authority (formerly Director General of Water Services)* [2007] CAT 2, [2007] Comp A.R. 553, Sir Christopher Bellamy P. It would be contrary to the public interest to potential new entrants to regulated sectors were deterred from bringing appeals if the Tribunal were regularly to render them liable for the Regulator's costs as well as their own, in the absence of unreasonable conduct or some other exceptional factor. The costs incurred by the Regulator in such cases were miniscule when compared with the costs of the industry taken as a whole, yet they could be disproportionately heavy if borne by an unsuccessful appellant (*Independent Water Co Ltd v Water Services Regulation Authority (Costs)* [2007] CAT 21, [2007] Comp A.R. 885, Marion Simons Q.C.).

The discretion to award costs must be exercised judicially avoiding the application of rigid rules. It might be necessary to make costs orders against unsuccessful applicants in cases involving penalties given that appeals presented a significant burden on the public purse. Where the victim of the abuse of dominant position intervened in two appeals successfully, and where its submissions had been distinct from those of the Director and of material assistance to the Tribunal, the correct approach was for the Tribunal to award costs to the intervener, which on the facts of the case were 60 per cent of the first appeal, and its full costs of the second appeal. *Aberdeen Journals Ltd v Office of Fair Trading (Costs)* [2003] CAT 21; [2004] Comp. A.R. 189, Sir Christopher Bellamy, President. See also *IBA Health Ltd v Office of Fair Trading (Costs)* [2004] CAT 6; [2004] Comp. A.R. 529, Sir Christopher Bellamy, President.

In general terms the application of the principles set out in *IBA Health Ltd v Office of Fair Trading* above would normally result in a successful party being awarded at least a proportion of its costs in s.120 of the Enterprise Act 2002 cases. On the facts, the successful party was awarded half its costs reasonably and proportionately incurred, excluding the costs incurred wholly or mainly as a result of a party intervening. The intervener had conducted itself in a reasonable and restrained manner and it would not be appropriate to make a costs order against it. The level of costs claimed by the successful party merited further consideration. The party was invited to supply the Tribunal with a detailed schedule supporting the amounts claimed and to indicate whether it wished the costs to be subject to assessment by the Tribunal or by a Costs Judge: *Unichem Ltd v Office of Fair Trading (Costs)* [2005] CAT 31; [2006] Comp. A.R.172 Sir Christopher Bellamy, President.

Although an appellant's success was the starting point for the exercise of a tribunal's discretion as to costs, other factors could lead to the conclusion that those costs should lie where they fell. Where parties had incurred costs needlessly because the OFT failed to give them notice of its intention to withdraw they were entitled to recover the reasonable and proportionate costs which they had incurred after the OFT had conceded that its defence was on a different basis from its decision. The costs incurred before that should lie where they fell because the work done could be of use in future administrative or legal proceedings: *Mastercard UK Members Forum Ltd v OFT (Costs)* [2006] CAT 15; [2006] Comp A.R. 607, Arthur Pryor, CAT.

There is no immutable rule as to the appropriate costs order and how the discretion contained in the Competition Appeal Tribunal Rules 2003 r.55, should be exercised. A successful appellant, who could fairly be identified as a "winner", was entitled to recover its costs, although such an appellant might be deprived of those costs referable to issues upon which it had failed or upon which its conduct had been unreasonable. The OFT was not entitled to any special protection from vulnerability to costs orders in favour of successful appellants. A second appellant was not entitled to recover any costs incurred in supporting or duplicating the arguments advanced by the first appellant: *Race Course Association v Office of Fair Trading (Costs)* [2006] CAT 1; [2006] Comp. A.R. 438 Rimer J.

VAT Tribunal

48.12.11 The general rule regarding costs that prevailed in the VAT Tribunal was that Commissioners would not seek costs against unsuccessful appellants unless (a) the appeal was exceptional in terms of its complexity and involved large sums of money; (b) if that was so whether it involved an important general point of law requiring clarification which took it out of (a); and (c) whether the appellant had misused the Tribunal procedure, for example bringing a frivolous or vexatious case, or failing to appear or not disclosing relevant evidence until the appeal hearing: *SFU Barbers Ltd v Revenue & Customs Commissioners* [2006] V.A.T. T.r. (Manchester); October 26, 2006, unrep.

2. Costs relating to specific statutes

Consumer Credit Act 1974

48.13 On an appeal to the Secretary of State under Pt III of the Act he may under s.41(3) direct any party to pay costs. Where such directions are made an order of the High Court under s.41(4) they are assessed by a Costs Judge.

Coroner's Act 1988

48.13.1 A woman died having given birth by caesarean section. The cause of death was a cerebral haemorrhage. Her husband sought an inquest on the basis that his wife had died an unnatural death, possibly as a result of negligence within the hospital. The coroner took the view that although it was arguable that lack of care might have been an effective cause of death, in that given proper care the haemorrhage might not have occurred, the death was nonetheless natural not unnatural. The Divisional Court directed an inquest, holding that if a patient was in hospital suffering from a condition which if not monitored and treated in a routine way would result in death, and for whatever reason, monitoring and treating was omitted, the coroner was under duty to hold an inquest, unless he could say there were no grounds for suspecting that the omission was an effective cause of death. The coroner was ordered to pay the costs. The order was consistent with the power in s.13(2)(b) of the Coroners Act 1988: *R. (on the application of Touche) v HM Coroner for Inner North London District* [2001] EWCA Civ 383; [2001] 2 All E.R. 752, CA.

The established practice of the court is to make no order for costs against an inferior court or tribunal which does not appear before it, except where there has been a flagrant incidence of improper behaviour or when the inferior court or tribunal unreasonably declined or neglected to sign a consent order disposing of the proceedings. The courts will treat an inferior court or tribunal which resists an application actively by way of argument, so as to make itself an active party to the litigation, as if it were such a party, so that in the normal course of events costs would follow the event. If, on the other hand, the inferior court or tribunal appeared in the proceedings in order to assist the court neutrally on questions of jurisdiction, procedure, specialist case law and the like the court would treat it as a neutral party and would not make an order for costs in its favour or against it whatever the outcome of the application. That approach might need to be modified so that a successful applicant who had to finance his own litigation might be fairly compensated out of a source of public funds and not be put to irrecoverable expense in asserting his rights, after a coroner (or other inferior tribunal) had gone wrong in law and where there was no other very obvious candidate available to pay his costs. An inferior tribunal which simply puts in a witness statement will not be at risk of an adverse costs order: *R. (Davies) v HM Deputy Coroner for Birmingham (No.2)* [2004] EWCA Civ 207; [2004] 1 W.L.R. 2739, CA (*Touche* above not followed).

Law of Property Act 1925

Under a lease, the lessees were obliged to pay all costs including solicitor's costs incurred by the landlord of and incidental to the preparation and service of a notice under s.146 of the 1925 Act and proceedings for the recovery of any rents reserved. Under that covenant the only costs recoverable were those that were "incidental to the preparation and service of" proceedings. That phrase includes little more than the costs incurred for the issue fee, preparation of witness statements and service: see *Wright v Bennet* [1948] 1 Q.B. 60. "Incidental" is to be treated as referring to costs that were subordinate to those of the action: *Contractreal Ltd v Davies* [2001] EWCA Civ 928. **48.13.2**

Local Government Act 1972 s.250—power to make orders for costs in planning cases

In deciding whether to make an order for costs against a planning authority which had raised objections to a planning application there is an evidential threshold which, if reached, is likely to put a planning authority beyond the risk of a finding that it has been guilty of unreasonable conduct (*R. v Secretary of State for the Environment Ex p. North Norfolk D.C.* [1994] 2 P.L.R. 78; and *R. v Secretary of State for the Environment Ex p. Chichester D.C.* [1993] 2 P.L.R. 1). "Sufficient evidential basis" means evidence not lacking real substance capable of belief and which, if accepted, would be capable of making good the plaintiff authority's objection (*R. v Secretary of State for the Environment Ex p. Wakefield Metropolitan B.C., The Times*, October 29, 1996). **48.13.3**

Magistrates' Court Act 1980

The proper approach to be adopted by a magistrates' court under s.61(1) of the 1980 Act when considering whether to make "such order as to costs...as it thinks just and reasonable" is as follows: **48.13.4**

(1) Section 64(1) confers a discretion on the magistrates' court to make such order as to costs as it thinks just and reasonable; that provision applies both to the quantum of the costs, if any, to be paid but also to the party, if any, which should pay them.

(2) What the court will think just and reasonable depends on all the relevant facts

and circumstances of the case before it. It might think it just and reasonable that costs should follow the event but need not think so in all the cases covered by the sub-section.

(3) Where a complainant has successfully challenged before justices an administrative decision made by a police or regulatory authority acting honestly, reasonably, properly and on grounds that reasonably appeared to be sound in exercise of its public duty the court should consider, in addition to any other relevant fact or circumstances, both:

(i) the financial prejudice to the particular complainant in the particular circumstances if an order for costs were not made in his favour; and

(ii) the need to encourage public authorities to make and stand by honest, reasonable and apparently sound administrative decisions made in the public interest without fear of exposure to undue financial prejudice if the decision was successfully challenged (*Bradford MDC v Booth* (2000) 164 J.P. 485; (2001) 3 L.G.L.R. 8; [2000] C.O.D. 338; (2000) 164 J.P.N. 801, DC).

The guidance given in *Bradford MDC v Booth* above is equally applicable in comparable cases where there is a statutory appeal from a decision of a local authority and the court has a broad discretion as to costs. Although as a matter of strict law the power of the court in such circumstances to award costs is not confined to cases where the local authority acted unreasonably and in bad faith, the fact that the local authority acted reasonably and in good faith in the discharge of its public function is plainly a most important factor: *R (on the application of Cambridge City Council) v Alex Nestling Ltd* [2006] EWHC 1374, (Admin).

The power of Justices to award costs under the Police Property Act 1997 is contained in s.64(1) of the Magistrates' Courts Act 1980. That section limits the power to award costs against a complainant (in this case the Chief Constable) to those occasions on which the complaint was dismissed in an application for Justices to determine which of two respondents were entitled to a sum of money. The fact that the Justices decided it should be returned to a particular respondent meant that the complaint was not dismissed and therefore no order for costs could be made: *R. (on the application of Chief Constable of Northamptonshire) v Daventry Justices* [2001] EWHC Admin 446.

Human Rights Act 1998

48.13.5 The respondent sought costs relying on HRA 1998 on the basis that there had been a breach of their rights under art.6 ECHR. It was held that the respondents were not a victim within art.3(4) ECHR or for the purposes of making an application under s.7(1) of the 1998 Act. The respondent could not complain of violation of any Convention rights because Restrictive Practices Court proceedings were not determinative of its civil rights and obligations within art.6(1) ECHR. It was clear from the case law of ECtHR that if a reviewing court has the power to quash an impugned decision and either to make the relevant decision afresh or to remit the case for a new decision by an impartial body, there would have been no breach of art.6(1): *Director General of Fair Trading v Proprietary Association of GB* [2001] EWCA Civ 1217.

Merchant Shipping Act 1995

48.13.6 The Secretary of State ordered a rehearing of formal investigation (RFI) of the MV Derbyshire under s.269 of the Merchant Shipping Act 1995. The investigation found that the minimum hatch cover strength requirements laid down for the forward hatches were seriously deficient. The ship builder, ship owner and classification society all applied for an order that they should recover their costs of the RFI from the Department of the Environment. The court exercised its discretion by reference to publice policy factors. There was not an invariable rule or presumption that costs lay where they fell. The ship owner was not involved in any continuing litigation arising out of the casualty and was exposed to the risk of adverse criticism. The owners were found to be free of fault, their evidence had made a contribution to the investigation and report. They played an important part in the meetings of experts. They were allowed 30 per cent of the aggregate of their solicitors' overall profit costs and disbursements including counsel's fees from public funds. The builders were made a party to the RFI by the court's order. They were exposed to the risk of criticism. They provided important evidence to the investigation. They played an important part in the meetings of experts. They were awarded 75 per cent of their costs from public funds. The classification society occupied an unique position in the RFI since its very existence was directed to ship safety which underlay the investigation and report but part of this work had been in the course of performing its function as a classification society. The court ordered that it should recover 15 per cent of its solicitor and counsel costs and disbursements and its in-house costs. *Rehearing of formal investigation into loss of MV Derbyshire* EWHC Q.B.D. (Admiralty), October 22, 2001, Colman J.

The Court of Appeal has jurisdiction over the costs of the proceedings below (SCA 1981 s.51) and may vary the order as to costs made in the Court below and make such order as it thinks fit. The general rule applies equally in a salvage suit, where the appellant succeeds in reducing substantially the amount of the salvage awarded, and in collision cases in admiralty (*The Toscana* [1905] P. 148; *The London* [1905] P. 152). The Court of Appeal, like any other Court, has jurisdiction over the costs of the proceedings, even though it may have no jurisdiction over their subject-matter (*Ecclesiastical Commissioners for England v National Provincial Bank Ltd* [1935] 1 K.B. 566 at 575, CA; *Diss Urban Sanitary Authority v Aldrich* (1877) 2 Q.B.D. 179; *Crowther v Boult* (1884) L.R. 13 Q.B.D. 680).

3. Costs relating to particular types of action or proceedings

Counsel

Evans J. examined the question of two counsel in some depth in *Juby v London Fire and Civil Defence Authority* and *Saunders v Essex CC*, April 24, 1990, unrep., Evans J. first listed the most likely factors affecting the decision whether or not to instruct a leader; they include: **48.14**

(a) the nature of the case, including in accident cases;
  (i) the nature and severity of the plaintiff's injury;
  (ii) the likely duration of the trial;
  (iii) difficult questions regarding the quantum of damages, including medical evidence and questions of law;
  (iv) difficult questions of fact, including expert engineering evidence, or issues as to causation;
(b) its importance for the client;
(c) the amount of damages likely to be recovered;
(d) the general importance of the case, e.g. as affecting other cases;
(e) any particular requirements of the case, e.g. the need for legal advice, or for special expertise, e.g. examining or cross examining witnesses; and
(f) other reasons why an experienced and senior advocate may be required.

The fact that the other party has instructed leading counsel or intends to do so cannot and should not be disregarded as a factor to be taken into account when deciding the question whether or not it is reasonable to have instructed leading counsel. It was treated as relevant though not conclusive in *British Metal Corp Ltd v Ludlow Brothers (1913) Ltd* [1938] Ch. 787.

With regard to the question of whether or not a junior should be instructed in addition to leading counsel, it must be answered by reference to the test of reasonableness. The test must be applied by the costs officer in the particular circumstances of each case. The correct approach is exemplified by The Code of Conduct (para.606): reasonableness of the decision to instruct junior counsel in addition to a leader must be judged from the point of view of the (lay) client's interests, which are paramount even on an assessment when it is the losing party (or the CLS fund) who is required to pay.

Particular reasons why a junior may be necessary for the proper conduct of the case, in the interests of the client include:

(a) to assist with the court proceedings either by taking an active part or by keeping a full note of the evidence, editing transcripts etc.;
(b) dealing with documents generally, particularly when the same junior counsel has taken part in discovery;
(c) to carry out legal or other research, e.g. on matters on which expert evidence is given;
(d) to assist leading counsel in negotiations with the other party, particularly when, as in many accident cases, junior counsel has already advised the injured person and has become known to him. The lay client might well fail to understand why the junior who has dealt with his case up to trial should no

longer be present when his claim is settled by negotiation or dealt with by judgment.

The fact that the solicitors are experienced in the type of litigation and able to present comprehensive and competent instructions to counsel is not relevant to the question whether it is reasonable to instruct junior counsel.

A balance has to be struck between the advantages of the more efficient presentation of the client's case and the extra expense involved in instructing leading counsel, or two counsel rather than one. The test laid down in *Francis v Francis and Dickerson* [1956] P. 87, has equal relevance to the assessment of standard basis costs today. This one CPR decision does not deal with proportionality.

With regard to the instruction of leading counsel the correct question is not whether the case was well within the capabilities of junior counsel but rather whether or not it was reasonable to instruct leading counsel (*R. v Dudley Magistrates' Court Ex p. Power City Stores Ltd* [1990] 140 N.L.J. 361).

Brief fee when incurred

48.14.1 The Court of Appeal, at the end of a successful appeal, made an order that the claimant should pay the first, second and fourth defendant's costs "of the trial commencing on October 6, 1998...[and] that there be no order as to costs for the period of August 23, 1998 to start of trial". The question arose whether this order did or did not include the brief fees paid to three counsel. Fees which had been staged and paid in full during the September prior to trial. Patten J. did not regard the words "commencing on October, 6" as the most obvious words of limitation holding that they appeared to be more descriptive of the trial and neither added to nor subtracted from the phrase "costs of the trial" since the brief fees were clearly part of the costs of the trial they were recoverable under the order: *Cantor Fitzgerald International v Tradition (UK) Ltd (Brief Fees)* [2003] EWHC 1907 (Ch), Patten J.

A publicly funded claimant refused an increased Pt 36 payment made after delivery of the brief to counsel. On the third day of the assessment of damages hearing the claimant accepted the payment in. The defendant was ordered to pay the claimant's costs down to the date of payment in, and the claimant to pay the costs thereafter. In deciding how the brief fee should be apportioned the court decided that as at the date of payment in counsel was entitled to a commitment fee equivalent to half the brief fee. The court does not appear to have been persuaded by the argument that a brief fee is normally incurred in full on the day on which it is delivered (*Baucutt v Walding*, October 14, 2003, unrep. Hallett J.). It is appropriate today to take a realistic and practical approach to the quantum of brief fee payable where the brief has been delivered well in advance of the trial and the case settled soon after delivery, rather than apply too rigidly the old rule that a brief fee becomes payable on delivery of the brief. *Miller v Hales* [2006] EWHC 1717 (QB) Jack J.

The court subsequently commented that although the more realistic modern approach to when counsel's brief fee is considered to have been incurred is to apportion it when a case settles early, where it settles at court or on the day before the hearing there should be no disallowance of any of the brief fee in the bill for that reason alone (*London & Oriental Homes Ltd v Hope (trading as Dawson Estate Agents)* December 11, 2007, unrep., Lewison J.).

Brief fee—quantum

48.14.2 In *Simpsons Motor Sales (London) Ltd v Hendon BC* [1965] 1 W.L.R. 112; [1964] 3 All E.R. 833, Pennycuick J., stated that a proper measure for counsel's fees was to estimate what fee a hypothetical counsel, capable of conducting the case effectively, but unable or unwilling to insist on the high fees sometimes demanded by counsel of pre-eminent reputation, would be content to take on the brief: but there was no precise standard of measurement, and the Costs Judge must, using his knowledge and experience, determine what was the proper figure.

In assessing counsel's brief fee it is always relevant to take into account what work that fee together with any refreshers has to cover. The brief fee covers all the work done by way of preparation for representation at the trial and attendance on the first day of the trial. But in heavy litigation, particularly where there is a team of barristers and experts, additional work is involved in ensuring that the client is properly represented and his case fully developed beyond simply appearing in court, such as counsel having to meet to consider strategy and tactics and prepare material and to meet experts prior to their going into the witness box to give evidence. Counsel is only entitled to charge for the work he has been instructed to do and where the work is done on legal aid, which has been authorised by the LSC certificate. Where legal aid authorisation is for representation at the trial, counsel will have to base his claim for remuneration on the delivery of the brief and what is required for the representation of the assisted party in court; in such cases, therefore, the remuneration should be the brief fee and daily refreshers calculated by reference to the time during which the trial is proceeding but not for days on which the court is not sitting. Counsel is not normally entitled to be remunerated separately for necessary work which is an incident of the proper representation of the client; rather, in a privately funded case a barrister must negotiate a brief fee sufficient to cover such work, while in legal aid work the barrister may, on the CLS assessment, require that the brief fee and the refresher rate properly reflect the amount of work that actually had to be done. On a CLS assessment the brief fee should be assessed and allowed having regard to the full history of the trial as known at the date of assessment. Although it should take into account any need for counsel to have meetings with each other and with experts out of court hours and to prepare final submissions, it should also take account of the fact that all heavy trials include such a need to a greater or lesser extent. Preparation by counsel of his examinations-in-chief and cross-examinations and of his final submissions is an ordinary part of his conduct of a trial on behalf of his client being all part of the work which counsel accepts an obligation to perform by accepting the brief and for which he is remunerated by the brief fee and the refreshers. Per Hobhouse J. *Loveday v Renton (No.2)* [1992] 3 All E.R. 184.

Written submissions

The court made observations on the subject of written closing submissions at the end of a lengthy review of a detailed assessment. **48.14.3**

> "In the hearing of the preliminary issue in this review of taxation the court was occupied for nine hearing days, a daily transcript was obtained and there were in excess of 5,000 documents including original documents before the court. The issues were complex and at the conclusion of the evidence the matter was adjourned so that written submissions could be prepared. These were detailed and of assistance to the court. As Mr Justice Hobhouse, as he then was, said in *Loveday v Renton (No.2)* [1992] 3 All E.R. 184 final submissions are an ordinary part of the conduct of a trial by a barrister on behalf of his client as part of the work which he accepts an obligation to perform in accepting the brief fee and for which he is remunerated by the brief fee and the agreed refreshers. Thus the preparation of final submissions, whether or not reduced into the form of a written document, is all work that has to be done in any event by counsel.
>
> There may however be circumstances where the case is properly regarded as sufficiently complex or exceptional not to have been covered by the brief fee, and hence for a separate fee to have been specifically agreed for the preparation of written submissions by counsel.
>
> Where such an agreement is made it would in my judgment be perfectly proper for the costs judge to consider it allowable in principle subject to detailed assessment of the amount when assessing the bill of costs."

Per Nelson J. *Chohan v Times Newspapers Ltd*, September 7, 1998, unrep.

House of Lords—Brief fee—quantum

For a discussion of the appropriate quantum of counsel's brief fee in the House of Lords, see *A.T.&T. Istel Ltd v Tully (No.2)* [1994] 1 W.L.R. 279; *R. v Reid (No.2)* [1994] 1 W.L.R. 279, HL. **48.14.4**

Brief fees and skeleton arguments in the Court of Appeal

The correct approach to assessing brief fees and skeleton argument fees for counsel in the Court of Appeal is in three stages. Stage 1: the fee for the skeleton argument should be assessed (largely by reference to the amount of time which counsel has reasonably and proportionately devoted to reading the documents, researching the law and drafting the skeleton arguments). Stage 2: the brief fee should be assessed. The exercise involves considering both the amount of time properly spent and other factors (see r.44.5 and the judgment of Hobhouse J. in *Loveday v Renton (No.2)* 1992 3 All E.R. 184 at 194). It is important to avoid double payment. Insofar as counsel prepared, whilst drafting the skeleton argument, that preparation should not be paid for in the brief fee. Stage 3: having arrived at an appropriate skeleton argument fee and **48.14.5** brief fee the two figures should be aggregated to see whether the total appears too large or too small for the overall conduct of the case in the Court of Appeal. If the total figure seems to be disproportionately large or small then an appropriate adjustment should be made (per Jackson J. in *Hornsby v Leventhal* [2000] 4 All E.R. 567).

Group actions: multiple representation in planning appeals.

48.14.6 The practice of awarding two sets of costs in certain types of planning appeal, notably where a decision of the Secretary of State in favour of the developer is challenged by the local authority, and the Secretary of State successfully defends his decision (in such cases the developer has usually been regarded as having a separate interest which he is entitled to protect at the local authority's expense), is recognised by the Court: *Waverley Borough Council v Secretary of State for the Environment* (1988) 55 P. & C.R. 111; [1987] J.P.L. 202, Simon Brown J. The House of Lords has reviewed the practice: As in all questions to do with costs the fundamental rule is that there are no rules. Costs are always in the discretion of the Court, and a practice however widespread and long standing must never be allowed to harden into a rule. The following propositions may be supported:

(1) The Secretary of State when successful in defending his decision will normally be entitled to the whole of his costs. He should not be required to share his award of costs by apportionment whether by agreement with other parties or by further Order of the Court. In so far as the Court of Appeal in *Wychavon District Council v Secretary of State for the Environment* [1994] C.O.D. 205; *The Times*, January 7, 1994, may have encouraged or sanctioned such a course, their Lordships disagreed.

(2) The developer will not normally be entitled to his costs, unless he can show that there was likely to be a separate issue on which he was entitled to be heard. That is to say, unless an issue not covered by Counsel for the Secretary of State; or unless he has an interest which requires separate representation. The mere fact that he is a developer will not of itself justify a second set of costs in every case.

(3) A second set of costs is more likely to be awarded at first instance, than in the Court of Appeal or House of Lords by which time the issues should have crystallised, and the extent to which they are indeed separate interests should have been clarified.

(4) An award of a third set of costs will rarely be justified even if there are in theory three or more separate interests; per Lord Lloyd of Berwick, *Bolton MDC v Secretary of State for the Environment* [1995] 1 W.L.R. 1176, HL.

An order of a government department as to costs on an enquiry will not be assessed in the High Court unless it is made a rule of Court under s.250(4) of the Local Government Act 1972.

In judicial review proceedings challenging a decision of the Secretary of State in respect of a statutory tidal defence scheme a developer was named as an interested party. The claim was dismissed and the claimant ordered to pay the costs of the Secretary of State, which it was argued should include the costs incurred by the interested party. The interested party had incurred the costs of providing evidence for the Secretary of State, for the defence of the claimant's claim and did not seek to incur any additional costs by way of obtaining separate representation at the hearing. The court held this was a convenient and sensible approach and that the interested party was entitled to its costs in providing the evidence, being costs which would have been recoverable by the Secretary of State had he obtained the evidence himself: *Issac v Secretary of State for the Environment, Food and Rural Affairs* [2002] EWHC 1983 (Admin), Forbes J.

Costs of test cases

48.14.7 The Court has jurisdiction to make an anticipatory costs order so that where lead cases were selected, the purpose should not be vitiated by having regard to the means and willingness of claimants to accept a high degree of risk as to costs rather than the issues in the particular actions (*Ward v Guiness Mahon & Co Ltd* [1996] 1 W.L.R. 894, CA). Where after the trial of test cases the answer to the question: who had been successful? was that the honours were even, it was appropriate for there to be no order for costs. *BCCI SA v Ali* (1999) 149 N.L.J. 1734 (No.4), unrep., Lightman J.

Costs incurred in foreign proceedings

The claimant and defendant were parties to a series of contracts each of which contained an English jurisdiction clause. The claimants commenced proceedings in England for sums due under the contracts. The defendants issued seperate proceedings in New York. The claimants successfully applied for those proceedings to be struck out as a breach of the jurisdiction clause. It was common ground that the claimants had not asked the New York court for its costs of that application since those costs were not recoverable. The claimants added a new claim to the English proceedings seeking to recover the costs of the New York proceedings as part of their damages for breach of contract. The Court of Appeal held, absent a separate cause of action, costs of foreign proceedings could not be recovered in separate proceedings in England. There was no policy reason why the claimants should not be entitled to pursue a seperate cause of action in England. In particular: 48.14.8

(i) international comity would not be breached by permitting such recovery;
(ii) there was no issue of res judicata because there was an independent cause of action and there had been no adjudication by the New York court;
(iii) the principle in *Henderson v Henderson* [1843] 3 Hare 100 (of issue estoppel) was manifestly inapplicable to the facts of the present case; and
(iv) the mere fact that the English courts had for many years proceeded on the presumption that such costs were not recoverable was no reason for allowing one party to a contract to escape liability for damages that he had caused by attempting to sue in a country where a different costs regime prevailed: *Union Discount Co Ltd v Robert Zoller* [2001] EWCA Civ 1755; [2002] 1 W.L.R. 1517; [2002] 1 All E.R. 693, CA.

It would give rise to a fundamentally unjust situation if the effect of the authorities was to prevent the recovery of costs by separate proceedings as damages, notwithstanding a breach of the arbitration or jurisdiction agreement. The court held that the successful party should not have to forego any part of its costs. Provided that it could be established by a successful application for a stay or an anti suit injunction as a remedy for breach of an arbitration or jurisdiction clause that the breach had caused the innocent party reasonably to incur legal costs, those costs should normally be recoverable on the indemnity basis: *A v B* [2007] EWHC 54 (Comm), Colman J.

Where the court is calculating damages, the costs of proceedings in a different jurisdiction should be calculated on the indemnity basis and not on the standard basis. In the particular case the innocent party had incurred legal costs to stifle a claim brought against it in another jurisdiction in breach of a promise not to sue. The party was held to have incurred loss of a kind reasonably foreseeable and therefore prima facie recoverable as damages for breach of contract, subject to ordinary principles of causation, remoteness and mitigation. Where there was a demonstrable disparity between what was recoverable in respect of costs in a foreign jurisdiction and what would be recovered as damages there was no policy reason for preventing proceedings in the English Courts to recover as damages any such shortfall: *National Westminster Bank Plc v Rabobank Nederland* [2007] EWHC 1742 (Comm) Sir Anthony Colman.

Note —Commentary continues after the Guidance Notes on the application of s.11 Access to Justice Act 1999. 48.14.8.1

GUIDANCE NOTES ON THE APPLICATION OF S.11 ACCESS TO JUSTICE ACT 1999 ISSUED BY THE SENIOR COSTS JUDGE

Introduction

48.14.9 **1.1** On April 1, 2000 the Access to Justice Act 1999 (the Act) replaced the former legal aid scheme with Community Legal Service funding under Part 1 of the Act and the Legal Services Commission took over the functions of the Legal Aid Board. Section 11 of the Act (Costs in funded cases) effectively replaces the Legal Aid Act 1988 Section 17 (Limit on costs against assisted party) and Section 18 (Costs of successful unassisted parties).

1.2 Section 11 of the Act and the regulations made thereunder have given rise to a certain amount of confusion and difficulty. These guidance notes (which have been approved by Lord Phillips of Worth Matravers, Master of the Rolls) are intended to assist judges, litigants and lawyers dealing with cases in the Court of Appeal, the High Court or in the County Court.

1.3 In these notes the expression "LSC funded client" includes an assisted person.

Section 11 of the Act

48.14.10 **2.1** The full text of Section 11 of the Act is set out in Appendix 1, below:

2.2 Attention is drawn to Section 11(4)(d): the power to require payment by the Commission to a party for whom services are not funded by the Commission, is now governed by the Regulations rather than, as under the former scheme, by the Statute itself. Under these Regulations the function of deciding whether or not a costs order could and should be made against the Commission is now expressly assigned to the Costs Judge or District Judge. He cannot make such an order unless and until the prescribed formalities have been completed. It is not open to the trial court to rule that it is just and equitable to make the order or to direct that the order is to be made before the prescribed formalities have been completed, although the trial court may record findings of fact as to the parties' conduct which must be taken into account in determining what amount the LSC funded client should pay.

The Regulations made under the Act

48.14.11 **3.1** The relevant regulations are the Community Legal Service (Costs) Regulations 2000 (S.I. 2000 No. 441 as amended by S.I. 2001 No. 822, the "Costs Regulations") and the Community Legal Service (Cost Protection) Regulations 2000 (S.I. 2000 No. 824 as amended by S.I. 2001 No. 823, the "Cost Protection Regulations").

3.2 The procedures for ordering costs against client and Commission are set out in Regulations 9 and 10 and 10A of the Costs Regulations 2000. Regulation 10A empowers the court to order a funded party to pay an amount on account of costs in certain circumstances.

3.3 The Cost Protection Regulations set out the circumstances in which costs orders against the LSC may be made. The full text of Regulation 5 is set out in Appendix 2, below.

3.4 The words shown in square brackets underlined in Regulation

5(3), as set out in Appendix 2 below are taken from draft Amendment Regulations, which it is currently proposed, will be laid before Parliament, to come into force on December 3, 2001.

3.5 Unless and until Regulation 5(3) is amended (see above) a formal request under Costs Regulation 10(2) for an order against the LSC cannot validly be made after the expiry of the 3 month deadline (see further, para.31(ii) of the judgment quoted in para.4.3 below).

3.6 Regulation 7 has the effect of excluding the possibility of an order for costs being made against the Commission under the broad and general power to order costs under Section 51(3) of the Supreme Court Act 1981.

The Procedure

4.1 The Costs Regulations and the Cost Protection Regulations form a self contained code of substantive law and procedural law governing orders for costs against assisted persons, LSC funded clients and the LSC. The ordinary rules governing the assessment of costs (*i.e.*, CPR Parts 44 to 48) do not apply (see CPR, r.44.17). **48.14.12**

4.2 The relevant parts of the Costs Practice Direction are Sections 21 to 23. In order to provide for the division of functions between the court awarding costs and the Costs Judge or District Judge who assesses them, the Costs Practice Direction gives definitions for the following terms (para.22.1):

"order for costs to be determined" means an order for costs to which Section 11 of the Access to Justice Act 1999 applies under which the amount of costs payable by the LSC funded client is to be determined by a costs judge or district judge under Section 23 of this Practice Direction.

"order specifying the costs payable" means an order for costs to which Section 11 of the Act applies and which specifies the amount which the LSC funded client is to pay.

"full costs" means, where an order to which Section 11 of the Act applies is made against a LSC funded client, the amount of costs which that person would, had cost protection not applied, have been ordered to pay.

"determination proceedings" means proceedings to which paragraphs 23.1 to 23.10 [of the Costs Practice Direction] apply.

"Section 11(1) costs order" means an order for costs to be determined or an order specifying the costs payable other than an order specifying the costs payable which was made in determination proceedings."

4.3 In *R v Secretary of State for the Home Department Ex Parte Gunn [2001] EWCA Civ 891*, the Master of the Rolls gave the judgment of the court and set out the procedure to be followed. The key passages are set out below:

"27. The new Regulations introduce a two stage process in relation to the recovery of costs in cases to which Section 11(1) of the 1999 Act applies. The procedure to be followed is primarily to be derived from the Costs Regulations. The scheme is as follows.

Stage 1

28. The first stage involves the Court dealing with the substance of the dispute, which we shall call the trial Court. The role of the trial Court is as follows:

(i) To decide whether to make an order for costs against a funded litigant ("the client"). (Regulation 9(1))

(ii) To decide whether it is in a position to specify the amount, if any, to be paid by the client. (Regulation 9(2)).

(iii) To make a costs order against the client which either

(a) Specifies the amount, if any, to be paid by the client and states the amount of the full costs, or

(b) Does not specify the amount to be paid by the client. (Regulation 9(3) and (4))

The order is described in the Regulations as a Section 11(1) costs order and is defined in both sets of regulations as a "costs order against a client where cost protection applies". "Cost protection" means "the limit set on costs awarded against a client set out in Section 11(1) of the Act".

(iv) Where the order does not specify the amount to be paid by the client, to make, if it sees fit, findings of fact, as to the parties conduct in the proceedings or otherwise, relevant to the determination of that amount. (Regulations 9(6))

Stage 2

29. Stage 2 consists of the procedure to be followed to ascertain the amount of costs to be paid by the client against whom the trial Court has made an order that does not specify the amount. Stage 2 also includes the procedure for determining whether an order for costs should be made against the Commission. (Regulation 9(5)). The Regulations in relation to Stage 2 allocate certain functions to "the Court". Regulation 10(10) provides that, in relation to proceedings in the Court of Appeal, High Court or County Court, the Court's functions "may be exercised" by a Costs Judge or a District Judge. While it is arguable that the High Court and the Court of Appeal also enjoy jurisdiction to exercise these functions we think it plain that the scheme does not envisage that they should do so.

30. Regulation 2 provides that "Costs Judge" has the same meaning as in the CPR. CPR 43.2(1)(b) provides that "Costs Judge" means a Taxing Master of the Supreme Court.

31. The procedure under Stage 2 is as follows:

(i) The party in whose favour the costs order has been made ("the receiving party") may, within three months of the making of the costs order, request a hearing to determine the costs payable to him. (Regulation 10(2))

(ii) The receiving party may, at the same time, seek a costs order against the Commission. (Regulation 10(3)(c)). We wish to take this opportunity to emphasise a fact that we understand is not generally appreciated. The three month time limit for seeking an order against the Commission is mandatory – there is no power to extend it.

(iii) The receiving party must, when making the request, file with the Court and serve on the client and the Regional Director of the Commission (if an order is sought against the Commission):

(a) A bill of costs;

(b) A statement of resources;

(c) A written notice that a costs order is sought against the Commission.

(Regulation 10(3) and (4))

(iv) The client must file a statement of resources and serve this on the receiving party and the Regional Director (where a claim is made on the Commission). (Regulation 10(6))

(v) The Court sets a date for the hearing. (Regulation 19(9))

(vi) The Court conducts the hearing, assesses the costs (if any) to be paid by the client and, where appropriate, makes a costs order against the Commission.

32. The Costs Regulations do not, in fact, expressly provide that the Costs Judge/District Judge shall carry out the functions set out under (vi) above, but it is plainly implicit that he should. That this is part of his role is confirmed by the explicit provisions of the Cost Protection Regulations.

33. The Cost Protection Regulations set out the circumstances in which the Costs Judge or District Judge may make a costs order against the Commission. Regulation 5(3) makes it plain that it is for the Costs Judge or District Judge to be satisfied that it is just and equitable (see Section 7 below) that provision for the costs should be made out of public funds and, in respect of proceedings at first instance, that the non-funded party will suffer severe financial hardship unless the order is made. In considering these matters the Costs Judge or District Judge is expressly required to have regard to the resources of the non-funded party and of his partner – Regulation 5(6)."

Note: Statement of resources —The Community Legal Service (Costs) (Amendment) Regulations 2003 (SI 2003/649) amends reg.10 from April 7, 2003 to the effect that the receiving party only has to make a statement of resources when he has to show financial hardship for the purposes of reg.5(3)(c) of the Cost Protection Regs (Order for Costs against the LSC in a court of first instance).

What Orders may the Court Awarding Costs Make?

5.1 An order for costs against an LSC funded client may or may not specify the amount of full costs and may or may not specify the amount payable by the LSC funded client. The court will not specify the amounts payable unless it has sufficient information before it to decide what is a reasonable amount for the client to pay in accordance with Section 11(1) of the 1999 Act. **48.14.13**

5.2 If the order does not specify the amount payable by the LSC funded client it may instead:

(i) make findings of fact relevant to the determination of the amount to be paid (Costs Regulation 9(6)); and/or

(ii) make an order under Costs Regulation 10A ordering the LSC funded client to pay an amount on account of the costs which are the subject of the order.

5.3 The court may order a payment on account under Costs Regulation 10A only if it has sufficient information before it to decide the minimum amount which the client is likely to be ordered to pay on a determination under Regulation 10 (Costs Regulation 10A(2)). An order for a payment on account must order the client to make the payment into court and the money must remain in court pending the determination of proceedings under Regulation 10. If the receiving party fails to commence such proceedings within the time permitted by Regulation 10(2) the payment on account must be repaid to the LSC funded client (see generally, Costs Regulation 10A (4) and (5)).

5.4 A specimen order for costs against a claimant who is an LSC funded client is set out in Appendix 3, below.

Subsequent Applications to a Costs Judge or District Judge

48.14.14 **6.1** Subsequent applications to the Costs Judge or District Judge of the relevant court should be made on Form **N244** within three months after a Section 11(1) Costs Order is made. Full details of the procedure is set out in Sections 21 to 23 of the Costs Practice Direction. Since June 5, 2000 this procedure also applies to applications against assisted persons and against the LSC in respect of old legal aid certificates (Access to Justice Act 1999 (Commencement No. 3:Transitional Provisions and Savings) Order 2000, para.8.3).

6.2 Depending upon the circumstances the application to the Costs Judge or District Judge may request the determination of:

(i) the amount of full costs;
(ii) the amount payable by the LSC funded client;
(iii) the amount payable by the LSC itself.

6.3 A specimen order for costs for use by a Costs Judge or District Judge is set out in Appendix 4, below.

Applying the "Just and Equitable" Test

48.14.15 **7.1** How should the Costs Judge or District Judge apply the "just and equitable" test set out in Costs Protection Regulation 5(3)(d)? In *Ex parte Gunn* the Court of Appeal expressed the view that the well established meaning of "just and equitable" did not require change by reason of the introduction of Regulation 5(6) of the Costs Protection Regulations, which requires the court to have regard to the resources of the non funded party. In courts of first instance the court must be satisfied that the proceedings were instituted by the funded client and that the non funded party will suffer severe financial hardship unless the order is made. The statement of resources filed by the non funded party in accordance with Regulation 10(3)(b) of the Costs Regulations may be of relevance to the just and equitable test but the Court of Appeal found that the requirement to provide a statement of resources was not intended to modify the practice based on the authorities in relation to applications in courts other than courts of first instance. The Court of Appeal went on to state:

> "50. *It seems* to us that this practice reflects reasoning that it will normally be just and equitable that when a costs order is made against a party who has been supported by public funds, the costs covered by the order should, insofar as they

cannot be recovered from the funded party, be defrayed out of public funds."

7.2 It is not open to the court awarding costs to make an order for costs against the LSC itself. However Costs Regulation 9(6) does permit the court awarding costs to make findings of fact relevant to the determination of the amount to be paid by the LSC funded client. In *Ex parte Gunn* the Court of Appeal considered that it must also be open to the trial Court to make any findings in relation to the conduct of the parties or facts that have emerged in the course of the proceedings, that have relevance to the application of the just and equitable test.

Costs Orders in Favour of a Public Body

8.1 Is it appropriate for the Costs Judge or District Judge to make an order against the LSC itself in favour of a public body? This question is unlikely to arise in practice as regards costs incurred in a court of first instance since, in such cases the public body is unlikely to be able to satisfy the financial hardship test set out in Costs Protection Regulation 5(3)(c). As regards costs of appeals, the financial hardship test does not apply. In *Ex parte Gunn* the Court of Appeal made it clear that it could detect no change in legislative intent in relation to the jurisdiction to make an order in favour of a public body and concluded that there is jurisdiction to make an order against the Commission in favour of a public body even if it is a Government Department. **48.14.16**

8.2 The Court referred to the judgment of Lord Woolf MR in *Re O (A Minor) (Costs: Liability of Legal Aid Board)* [1997] 1 F.L.R. 465 at page 470G:

> "If the court comes to a conclusion that in those circumstances it would make the hypothetical order for costs [what is now a section 11(1) order] then in the case of an appeal the court will usually conclude, in the absence of some special circumstance, that for the purposes of s.18(4)(c) [of the 1988 Act], it is just and equitable to make an order. Contrary to Mr Howard's submission, a local authority, because it is a public body, is not at a disadvantage as compared with any other litigant in seeking an order against the Board,"

8.3 The Court of Appeal considered that the practice laid down in *Re O*should be followed by Costs Judges and District Judges when applications are made to them for costs against the Commission, in respect of appeal costs incurred by non funded parties even if they are Government Departments. Costs Judges and District Judges should proceed on the premise that it is just and equitable that the LSC should stand behind the LSC funded client unless there are circumstances which render that result unjust or inequitable.

APPENDIX 1

Full Text of Access to Justice Act 1999, Section 11

(1) Except in prescribed circumstances, costs ordered against an individual in relation to any proceedings or part of proceedings funded for him shall not exceed the amount (if any) which is a reasonable one for him to pay having regard to all the circumstances including– **48.14.17**

(a) the financial resources of all the parties to the proceedings, and

(b) their conduct in connection with the dispute to which the proceedings relate;

and for this purpose proceedings, or a part of proceedings, are funded for an individual if services relating to the proceedings or part are funded for him by the Commission as part of the Community Legal Service.

(2) In assessing for the purposes of subsection (1) the financial resources of an individual for whom services are funded by the Commission as part of the Community Legal Service, his clothes and household furniture and the tools and implements of his trade shall not be taken into account, except so far as may be prescribed.

(3) Subject to subsections (1) and (2), regulations may make provision about costs in relation to proceedings in which services are funded by the Commission for any of the parties as part of the Community Legal Service.

(4) The regulations may, in particular, make provision–

(a) specifying the principles to be applied in determining the amount of any costs which may be awarded against a party for whom services are funded by the Commission as part of the Community Legal Service,

(b) limiting the circumstances in which, or extent to which, an order for costs may be enforced against such a party,

(c) as to the cases in which, and extent to which, such a party may be required to give security for costs and the manner in which it is to be given,

(d) requiring the payment by the Commission of the whole or part of any costs incurred by a party for whom services are not funded by the Commission as part of the Community Legal Service,

(e) specifying the principles to be applied in determining the amount of any costs which may be awarded to a party for whom services are so funded,

(f) requiring the payment to the Commission, or the person or body by which the services were provided, of the whole or part of any sum awarded by way of costs to such a party, and

(g) as to the court, tribunal or other person or body by whom the amount of any costs is to be determined and the extent to which any determination of that amount is to be final.

COSTS ORDER AGAINST COMMISSION

APPENDIX 2

Full Text of Regulation 5 of the Community Legal Service (Costs) Regulation 2000, as Amended

48.14.18 **(1)** The following paragraphs of this regulation apply where:

(a) funded services are provided to a client in relation to proceedings;

(b) those proceedings are finally decided in favour of a non-funded party; and
(c) cost protection applies.

(2) The court may, subject to the following paragraphs of this regulation, make an order for the payment by the Commission to the non-funded party of the whole or any part of the costs incurred by him in the proceedings (other than any costs that the client is required to pay under a section 11(1) costs order).

(3) An order under paragraph (2) may only be made if all the conditions set out in sub-paragraphs (a),(b),(c) and (d) are satisfied:

(a) a section 11(1) costs order is made against the client in the proceedings, and the amount (if any) which the client is required to pay under that costs order is less than the amount of the full costs;
(b) unless there is good reason for the delay, the non-funded party makes a request under regulation 10(2) of the Community Legal Service (Costs) Regulations 2000 within three months of the making of the section 11(1) costs order;
(c) as regards costs incurred in a court of first instance, the proceedings were instituted by the client, the non funded party is an individual and the court is satisfied that the non-funded party will suffer financial hardship unless the order is made; and
(d) in any case, the court is satisfied that it is just and equitable in the circumstances that provision for the costs should be made out of public funds.

(3A) An order under paragraph (2) may be made—

(a) in relation to proceedings in the House of Lords, by the Clerk to the Parliaments;
(b) in relation to proceedings in the Court of Appeal, High Court or a county court, by a costs judge or a district judge;
(c) in relation to proceedings in a magistrates' court, by a single justice or by the justices' clerk;
(d) in relation to proceedings in the Employment Appeal Tribunal, by the Registrar of that tribunal.

(4) Where the client receives funded services in connection with part only of the proceedings, the reference in paragraph (2) to the costs incurred by the non-funded party in the relevant proceedings shall be construed as a reference to so much of those costs as is attributable to the part of the proceedings which are funded proceedings.

(5) Where a court decides any proceedings in favour of the non-funded party and an appeal lies (with or without permission) against that decision, any order made under this regulation shall not take effect:

(a) where permission to appeal is required, unless the time limit for applications for permission to appeal expires without permission being granted;
(b) where permission to appeal is granted or is not required, unless the time limit for appeal expires without an appeal being brought.

(6) Subject to paragraph (7), in determining whether the conditions in paragraph (3)(c) and (d) are satisfied, the court shall have regard to the resources of the non-funded party and of his partner.

(7) The court shall not have regard to the resources of the partner of the non-funded party if the partner has a contrary interest in the funded proceedings.

(8) Where the non-funded party is acting in a representative, fiduciary or official capacity and is entitled to be indemnified in respect of his costs from any property, estate or fund, the court shall, for the purposes of paragraph (3), have regard to the value of the property, estate or fund and the resources of the persons, if any, including that party where appropriate, who are beneficially interested in that property, estate or fund.

SPECIMEN ORDER FOR COSTS AGAINST A CLAIMANT WHO IS AN LSC FUNDED CLIENT

APPENDIX 3

48.14.19 *IT IS ORDERED THAT*

1. The claim is dismissed.

2. The full costs of this claim which have been incurred by the defendant are [summarily assessed at £] [to be determined by a Costs Judge or District Judge].

3. The claimant (a party who was in receipt of services funded by the Legal Services Commission) do pay to the Defendant [nil] [£] [an amount to be determined by a Costs Judge or District Judge]. [When determining such costs the Costs Judge or District Judge should take into account the following facts:

[Here list any findings of fact as to the party's conduct in the proceedings or otherwise which are relevant to the determination of the costs payable by the LSC funded client]

4. On or before (date) the claimant must pay into court £ on account of the costs payable under paragraph 2, above.

5. There be a detailed assessment of the costs of the claimant which are payable out of the Community Legal Service Fund.

SPECIMEN ORDER FOR USE BY A COSTS JUDGE OR DISTRICT JUDGE

APPENDIX 4

48.14.20 *IT IS ORDERED THAT*

1. The full costs of the [defendant] herein, [including the costs of this application] are assessed at £

2. The amount of costs which it is reasonable for the [claimant] to pay to the [defendant] is [nil] [£ which sum is payable to the [defendant] on or before (date)].

3. The sum of £ paid into court on account of the costs specified in paragraph 2 above and any interest accruing thereon shall be paid out to the [defendant in part satisfaction] [claimant] as specified in the payment schedule to this Order.

4. The amount of costs payable by the Legal Services Commission to the [defendant] [including the costs of this application] is £ which sum is payable to the [defendant] on or before (date)

[Schedule in Form **200** *(see Court Funds Rules 1987)]*

An appellant who was granted a funding certificate which referred only to representation as an appellant was not covered in respect of the costs of a cross appeal. Costs protection under the CLS (Cost Protection) Regulations applies only to costs incurred after the issue of the certificate. The LSC had the power to amend a certificate retrospectively, but unless and until it did so, the appellant was only entitled to costs protection in respect of her own appeal. There was a powerful argument for saying that the LSC should not effect such an amendment without giving the other party an opportunity to object. In those circumstances it was insufficient for the other party to say she would be prejudiced by the amendment, in the sense that she would be worse off. It would be necessary to demonstrate that she might have acted in a significantly different way had the original certificate reflected the LSC's intention (*Hinde v Harbourne* [2003] EWHC 3109, (Ch), Neuberger J.; see also *R & T Thew Ltd v Reeves (No.1)* [1982] Q.B. 172 and *R v Legal Aid Board Ex p. Edwin Coe (A Firm)* [2000] 1 WLR 1909). **48.14.21**

[THE NEXT PARAGRAPH IS 48.14.30.]

Expert witnesses

See Pt 35 for the courts powers in respect of experts. **48.14.30**

The duties and responsibilities of expert witnesses in civil cases include:

1. Evidence should be and should be seen to be the independent product of the expert uninfluenced as to form or content by the exigencies of litigation. See *Whitehouse v Jordan* [1981] 1 All E.R. 276.

2. Independent assistance should be provided to the Court by way of objective unbiased opinion regarding matters within the expertise of the expert. See *Polivitte Limited v Commercial Union Assurance Co PLC* [1987] 1 Lloyd's Rep. 379, 386, per Garland J. and *Re J* [1990] F.C.R. 193, per Cazalet J. An expert witness in the High Court should never assume the role of advocate.

3. Facts or assumptions upon which the opinion is based should be stated together with material facts which could detract from the concluded opinion.

4. The witness should make it clear when a question or issue falls outside his experience.

5. If the opinion is not properly researched because it is considered that insufficient data was available that must be stated with an indication that the opinion is provisional (see *Re J.*) if the witness cannot assert that the report contains the truth the whole truth and nothing but the truth that qualification should be stated on the report. See *Derby &Co Ltd v Weldon (No.9)* [1991] 1 W.L.R. 652, per Staughton L.J.

6. If after exchange of reports an expert changes his mind on a material matter the change of view should be communicated to the other side through legal representatives without delay and when appropriate to the Court.

7. Photographs, plans, survey reports and other documents referred to in the expert evidence must be provided to the other side at the same time as the exchange of reports per Cresswell J. in *National Justice Compania Naviera SA v Prudential Assurance Company Limited (Ikarian Reefer)* [1993] 2 Lloyd's Rep. 68.

An agreement between a claimant and a firm of accountants that they would undertake work relating to litigation on the basis that their charges would be 8 per cent of the damages recovered was held not to be champertous because the accountants were not conducting litigation and did not themselves act as the expert witnesses. They had specifically employed experts whose fees they paid. They advised on and coordinated the evidence of loss and provided back-up services for the expert witnesses. If the accountants had not performed those services they would have had to be carried out by the claimants' solicitors at higher rates. The agreement was not a conditional fee agreement under s.58 of the Courts and Legal Services Act 1990 since that section applied only to agreements concluded by those conducting litigation or providing advocacy services. Section 58 does not apply to expert witnesses. For an expert to give evidence on a contingency fee basis would give the expert a significant financial interest in the outcome of the case which was highly undesirable and it would be very rare for the court to consent to an expert being instructed on that basis. The agreement was not contrary to public policy nor champertous: *R (on the application of Factortame) v The Secretary of State for Transport* [2002] EWCA Civ 932.

Marine claims recovery agents agreed to act on behalf of cargo insurers following the loss of a vessel on the basis of a fee of 5 per cent of recovery on a "no cure, no pay" basis. They carried out the initial work and then when proceedings became necessary solicitors were instructed. The successful claimants sought the recovery agent's fees either as damages or costs. The court found that the fees were not claimable as damages only costs. The arrangement was held not to be champertous (as asserted by the defendants) because:

(i) the bills of lading had stipulated for foreign law and it was not until a late stage that the application of English law was agreed.
(ii) the paying party was protected by the fact that it would only have to pay standard basis costs and the 5 per cent operated as a cap.
(iii) there was little scope for the agents to influence the outcome as solicitors and counsel were acting.
(iv) the majority of claims of this sort were compromised without lawyers.
(v) the agents were already acting for other underwriters.
(vi) the agreement was not exclusively concerned with litigation.

Papera Traders Co Ltd v Hyundai Merchant Marine Co Ltd (The Eurasian Dream) (No.2) [2002] EWHC 2130 Cresswell J.

Witness expenses

48.14.31 Where a Merchant bank, retained to advise a defendant, was the subject of a witness summons served by the claimant, the witness was entitled to the costs incurred in complying with the summons and was not limited to conduct money only. The costs could include taking legal advice, where it was reasonable to have done so. The court could decide whether the costs were payable on the standard or on the indemnity basis, any dispute being resolved by a Costs judge (*J. H. Shannon v Country Casuals Holdings Plc, The Times*, June 16, 1997, per Garland J.).

4. Costs relating to particular types of parties and miscellaneous

Bankruptcy

48.15 It is for a bankrupt's trustee in bankruptcy to decide whether to pursue an appeal. If he declines to do so the bankrupt may challenge the decision under the Insolvency Act 1986 s.303 and the Bankruptcy Court has the power to direct the trustee himself or to permit the bankrupt to conduct the appeal in the name of the trustee where security has been provided. Where no trustee had been appointed earlier costs orders were unenforceable and the bankrupt did not have any locus to pursue an appeal: *Dadurian Group International Inc v Simms* [2008] EWHC 723 (Ch), Warren J.

A creditor who serves a statutory demand, without judgment having already been given in his favour, does so at his own risk as to costs. The service of a statutory demand is a step in the bankruptcy proceedings and a cause of action in its own right. In *Re A Debtor (No.620 of 1997), The Times*, June 18, 1998, Hart J.

As to the principles to be considered when setting aside a statutory demand see: *Bayoil SA* [1999] 1 W.L.R. 147, provided the judge properly directs himself upon the matters to be considered costs are always discretionary. *A Debtor, Re (No.87 of 1999)*, January 17, 2000, unrep., per Rimer J.

Where it is sought to enforce an order for summarily assessed costs by invoking the bankruptcy regime (by issuing a statutory demand) the policy considerations of the CPR favouring summary assessment and the early recovery of costs have to be weighed against the operation of the bankruptcy regime, including the power of the court to set aside a statutory demand where the debtor appeared to have a counterclaim set off or cross demand. It would be an exceptional case in which the court would refuse to set aside a statutory demand where the debtor appeared to have such a claim, since in normal circumstances it would be unacceptable if a debtor was made bankrupt but within a short time was found that the petitioning credit was in fact a net debtor to the estate: *Cohen v TSB Bank Plc*, November 20, 2001, unrep., Etherton J.

When, following service of the petition, the debt is paid, the appropriate order for costs must reflect the ultimate success of the creditors but must also reflect any avoidable defects in the creditor's proceedings. Where substantial additional costs were incurred, quite unnecessarily by the debtor, because of e.g. adjournments, the proper order should be no order as to costs. In *Re A Debtor (No.510 of 1997), The Times*, June 18, 1998, Mr Stanley Burnton, Q.C.

In a bankruptcy in which the only real asset was a boat upon which the bankrupt lived, a trustee in bankruptcy applied for an order that his remuneration should be charged on the basis of time spent. The respondent creditor sought an order that the remuneration be fixed in a certain sum. The court held that its task was to arrive at a level of remuneration that balanced the various criteria of the value of the service rendered, the proportionality of the remuneration and a fair and reasonable remuneration for the work properly undertaken, as set out in Practice Statement (Fixing and approval of the remuneration of appointees). The court made a number of reductions, some substantial, to the remuneration claimed by the trustee, including a substantial reduction in the amount of time claimed for calculating the time costs themselves, which had amounted to a quarter of the total remuneration. Expenditure on that scale was grossly disproportionate (*Simion v Brown; Brown v Simion* [2007] EWHC 511 (Ch); [2007] B.P.I.R. 412 David Richards J.).

A costs order made against a discharged bankrupt in proceedings commenced prior to the bankruptcy was not a bankruptcy debt pursuant to s.382(1)(a) of the Insolvency Act 1986. The costs order was not a contingent liability at the date of the commencement of the bankruptcy. Until an order was made there could be no obligation to pay costs: *Glenister v Rowe*, *The Times*, April 28, 1999, CA. Where petitioning creditors issued a first statutory demand and then a petition for the debtor's bankruptcy, as a result of which a trustee in bankruptcy was appointed, on the compromise of the claim there was a dispute as to who should be liable for the trustee's costs. Since both parties were legally aided the court found that it was least unjust to order the creditors and the debtor to be jointly liable for the trustee's costs. *Butterworth v Soutter* [2000] B.P.I.R. 582.

A costs order made in family proceedings is not capable of creating a provable debt in bankruptcy proceedings because it is an obligation arising under an order made in family proceedings within r.12.3(2)(a) of the Insolvency Rules 1986 (*Levy v Legal Services Commission (formerly Legal Aid Board)* [2000] 1 F.L.R. 922, CA).

A bankruptcy petition is not barred by s.24 of the Limitation Act 1980 when the petition is based on costs orders pronounced more than six years before the petition because the relevant date from which the six year period starts to run is that when the judgment becomes enforceable, i.e. enforceable by action on the judgment. Thus the obligation to pay costs only becomes enforceable when the amount is certified after detailed assessment or otherwise quantified (*Debtor (No.2672 of 2000), Re, The Times*, December 5, 2000) (*Times Newspapers Ltd v Chohan, The Times*, December 5, 2000, Mr Anthony Mann Q.C., confirmed EWCA Civ 964; *The Times*, August 1, 2001, CA).

A costs certificate referring to the joint costs of three defendants represents a sufficiently detailed debt for the purpose of a statutory demand. The submission that three separate costs certificates should have been issued was rejected. The final costs certificate which had been issued referred to all three defendants jointly in respect of the total amount. Payment to one joint creditor would discharge the entire debt. A creditor was entitled to serve a statutory demand requiring payment of the whole sum of money to him: *Mahmood v Penrose* [2004] EWCA Civ 1254 (Ch), Mann J.

A resolution approving an IVA was subsequently set aside because the insolvency practitioner had admitted as a creditor the debtor's co-habitee on the basis of her beneficial interest in a property. This amounted to a material irregularity and invalidated the resolution. The insolvency practitioner was held personally liable for half of the costs of the issues on which an applicant for specific disclosure had succeeded, the conduct fell below that of an insolvency practitioner behaving reasonably: *Smurthwaite v Simpson-Smith; Mond v Smurthwaite* [2006] EWCA Civ 1183; [2006] B.P.I.R. 1504, CA.

Companies

The court has to be alert to the possibility that a company's decision to commence and continue proceedings might not be taken in good faith but could be used for some ulterior purpose. If an ulterior purpose was found to underlie the decision making process the court might be expected to express its disapproval by making orders for costs on the indemnity basis against those responsible (*Jarvis Plc v Pricewaterhouse-Coopers* [2001] B.C.C. 670). **48.15.1**

The general costs principle is applicable so that when a creditor is entitled to more than the statutory minimum debt, the debt is due and it is decided to be so either by concession or by the court, the creditor is entitled to payment of the costs of the winding-up petition and of any applications connected with the petition unless there is good reason to the contrary: *Ryan Developments Ltd, Re* [2002] EWHC 1121, Neuberger

J. The Courts do not, as a rule, make costs orders against objecting shareholders or creditors, where their objections are not frivolous and have been of assistance to the Court. The respondent company was ordered to pay the additional costs of the applicant company, incurred as a result of the respondent company's objections, based on security issues, when, as a stock holder, it had no interest in objecting and the rights carried by the stock were not arguably infringed: *In the matter of Peninsular and Oriental Steam Navigation Co* [2006] EWHC 389, October 6, 2006, (Ch) Warren J; see also: *In the matter of Alliance Insurance Co Ltd*, October 17, 2006, (Ch) David Richards J.

The Secretary of State presented petitions for two companies to be wound up in the public interest, which were by then insolvent. The Judge ordered the controlling shareholder to pay the costs of the Secretary of State not limited to those incurred directly as a result of opposing the petitions. The Judge found that the shareholder had conducted the company's affairs for his own personal benefit, had treated the company's money as his own and had defended the petition in his own rather than the company's interests. The Court of Appeal found that this was a sound basis for the conclusion that it would be just for the shareholder to pay the Secretary of State's costs although not a party to the proceedings: *North West Holdings Plc (In Liquidation) (Costs), Re* [2001] EWCA Civ 67, January 26 [2001], CA.

A similar order was made against the owner of 75 per cent of the shares of a company which had been operating a swindle and was wound up. Although the shareholder was not a director he was the moving force behind the company and its opposition to the winding-up order. The court held that as the shareholder was operating the swindle he could not be heard to say that he was resisting the winding-up order in the public interest or that of the creditors or the company. Although there was cash in hand it could not be assumed that the company was solvent. The shareholder was ordered to pay the costs of the Secretary of State and of the company. The company's costs were not to be paid out of the assets of the company until all the unsecured creditors had been paid in full. If the shareholder paid the costs of the Secretary of State and if all the other creditors were paid he would be entitled to seek recovery of the company's costs from the company: *Secretary of State for Trade and Industry v Liquid Acquisitions Ltd* [2002] EWHC 180 (Ch); [2003] 1 B.C.L.C. 375 (Lloyd J.).

Where a petition under s.459 of the Companies Act 1985 was struck out when it was found that documents disclosed by the petitioners had been forged by the person behind the first petitioner, the respondents sought their costs under s.51 of the Supreme Court Act 1981 against non parties, the petitioner having no money. The respondents argued that the non parties were not pure funders as they had an interest in the outcome of the proceedings other than merely the possible repayment of the sums which they had lent. The court found that they were pure funders and that it would not be just to make an order against them under s.51. They had lent money out of sympathy and friendship rather than to gain a commercial advantage: *Arrow Nominees Inc v Blackledge (Costs: Non-Parties)* [2003] EWHC 1516 (Ch), Lloyd J.

Where a company was in administration and received an offer for the sale of its factory premises, which the administrators wished to accept, the question arose as to what was to happen to a large quantity of machinery belonging to a different company under hire purchase agreements. Before the judge two valuations were produced, and the judge assessed the market value of the goods at a figure which fell mid way between the two valuations. The company which owned the machinery sought a review of the judge's decision, but the judge would only permit this if the company would pay the administrator's costs of any inquiry into the market value in any event. The company declined and the judge refused to review his decision. On appeal it was held that the judge had erred in principle in the exercise of his discretion by directing that the company would have to pay the costs in any event, which was not a proper condition for the judge to impose. It did not constitute compensation to the administrators for the costs thrown away: *Stanley Holmes & Sons Ltd v Davenham Trust Plc* [2006] EWCA Civ 1568.

A company voluntary arrangement (CVA) provided that one of the company directors would fund a legal action to pursue a breach of contract claim "all funds recovered after settlement of [the Director's] costs including legal costs of pursuing the claim will be made available to creditors" and a little later "upon settlement of the legal action the costs of [the director] in funding the pursuit of the claim will be discharged prior to the settlement of claims of the creditors". The Court of Appeal held:

41. "The references in the CVA to the 'costs', 'legal costs' and 'funding' the legal

action and the claim indicate that there were agreed limits to what [the director] was entitled to recover under the CVA. On the one hand, identifiable legal costs are clearly covered. On the other hand, there is no provision in the CVA which entitles [the director] to recover money simply on the ground that he spent it on running the company in order to pursue the claim. The crucial question is the extent to which he is entitled under the CVA to recover non legal costs and expenses ...

43. ... The legal basis of his entitlement to recovery of expenditure is governed by the terms of the CVA, as construed by the court, not by any general principle of reward for risk and effort or by application of a 'but for' test ...

44. ... In the absence of an agreed variation to cover particular items beyond legal costs, it is necessary to find a link between [the director's] costs and expenses and the funding of the claim. The application of the objective considerations of necessity and reasonableness, which feature in the question posed by the Judge are unavoidable ..."

Simpson v Bowker [2007] EWCA Civ 772.

Counterclaim

Where claim and counterclaim are both dismissed with costs, upon assessment the rule is that the claim should be treated as if it stood alone and the counterclaim should bear only the amount by which the costs of the proceedings have been increased by it. No costs not incurred by reason of the counterclaim can be costs of the counterclaim. In the absence of special directions by the Court, there should be no apportionment. The same principle applies where both the claim and the counterclaim have succeeded (*Medway Oil and Storage Co v Continental Contractors* [1929] A.C. 88, HL). But see *Millican v Tucker* [1980] 1 W.L.R. 640; [1980] 1 All E.R. 1083, where the Court of Appeal held it was well within the Judge's discretion *inter partes* to order the apportionment of the costs of claim and counterclaim equally. Costs can be awarded on the basis of the issues actually involved (see r.44.3(4)) so as to encourage good litigation practice. It is relevant to good litigation practice to consider the ways in which both sides could have protected themselves with regard to costs. *Universal Cycles Plc v Grangebriar Ltd* [2000] C.P.L.R. 42, CA. **48.15.2**

In a building dispute in which both the claim and the counterclaim succeeded, the Court of Appeal held that the Judge was wrong to order the claimant to pay the costs of the counterclaim and the defendants to pay the costs of the claim, because the defendants were, in reality, the unsuccessful parties and a just award was that the claimant should recover 60 per cent of its costs of all the proceedings: **48.15.3**

"30. ...The most obvious and frequently most desirable option is that signposted in CPR 44.3 paragraph 6(a) namely to order a proportion of the party's costs to be paid...Ordering a proportion of costs obviates all the difficulties... in an assessment of how much is properly to be allocated to each and every issue considered in isolation. Better by far to decide, despite the difficulty and imprecision of the calculation, that the relevant issue or issues should bear a percentage of the costs taken overall...

...

33. ...How,...does one decide who the unsuccessful party is? This was after all a form of commercial litigation where each side was claiming money from the other. Costs following the event is the general rule and in this kind of litigation the event is determined by establishing who writes the cheque at the end of the case. Here the defendants do. They were the unsuccessful parties and my starting point is that the claimant is entitled that the costs of the proceedings claim and counterclaim be taken together.

34. The circumstances of the case may justify a departure from the general rule *and so the conduct* of the parties, and questions of whether they have not been wholly successful become relevant. CPR 44.3(5) identifies specific aspects of conduct for the court to consider including conduct before as well as during the proceedings, the reasonableness of the parties raising, pursuing or contesting particular allegations or issues, the manner in which he has done so and the extent to which, though successful, he has exaggerated his claim."

Burchell v Bullard [2005] EWCA Civ 358.

Liquidation

In a liquidation, costs which fall properly within the ambit of the Insolvency Rules **48.15.4**

1986 r.4.218, are payable in priority to preferential debts. The costs of unsuccessful litigation do not fall within that rule nor can they be categorised as genuine expenses of the winding-up under the Insolvency Act 1986 s.175(2). Section 156 of the 1986 Act deals with orders for payments of expenses by the court and under that section there could be expenditure appropriately incurred which does not fall within the strict ambit of either of the other provisions and could include the costs of unsuccessful litigation; *Mond v Hammond Suddards (No.2)* [2000] Ch. 40; [1999] 3 W.L.R. 697; *The Times*, June 18, 1999, CA and see *Re M. C. Bacon Ltd (No.2)* [1991] Ch. 127. The Court retains a power to examine all aspects of the expenses of office holders, such as joint provisional liquidators, whether it be their own remuneration, that of their employees or disbursements in respect of third parties. *IPEE Jacob and Another v UIC Insurance Co Ltd* [2006] EWHC 2717 (Ch), Peter Smith J.

In the normal course of events any costs orders made against liquidators in relation to civil proceedings undertaken by them have priority over the general expenses of the liquidation (see *London Metallurgical Co, Re* [1895] 1 Ch 758): *Digital Equipment Co Ltd v Bower* [2003] EWHC 2895.

In hostile litigation involving the solvency of a company the court is required to be particularly cautious in making a pre-emptive costs order. To make such an order the court needs complete confidence that the administrator will win and that all costs would be properly incurred. A pre-emptive order may be made only on the strongest possible grounds. Once it is established that there is a more than negligible chance that the administrators might fail it is potentially unjust to make a pre-emptive costs order: *Ciro Citterio Menswear Plc* [2002] EWHC 662, Pumfrey J.

Where a former director of an insolvent company was required for examination under s.235 of the Insolvency Act 1986, but refused to provide an address and indicated that he would be out of the country for several months, the court ordered that the costs of the examination should be paid by the director, even though he voluntarily attended for examination. The correct test was whether the liquidator was reasonably entitled to conclude that there was a danger that an examinee would not attend for examination. The director's refusal was sufficient to give rise to reasonable suspicion in the mind of the liquidator that the director did not intend to co-operate (*Miller v Bain (Director's Breach of Duty)* [2002] 1 B.C.L.C. 266, November 28, 2000, Sir Andrew Morritt V.-C.). One of the two joint liquidators of a limited company sought legal advice as to the behaviour of two directors of the company and on the basis of that advice, and with the acquiescence of the small number of creditors whose views could be obtained, the liquidator commenced an action against the respondents for wrongly trading and misfeance. A preferential creditor emerged, which meant that the available funding for the litigation was diminished. The liquidator had already incurred £5,000 of costs and applied for an order for reimbursement of his costs to date, from the assets of the company. The court refused to make the order on the basis that it was premature until the outcome of the litigation was known. It was not at that time possible to decide whether the applicant had acted properly in commencing the litigation. The applicant did not need to know whether he was protected by an indemnity and had reached that stage in the litigation without an order from the court: *Romar Engineering Co Ltd, Re* [2003] B.C.C. 535.

A company was held to be entitled to its costs as against a respondent liquidator who, when acting as provisional liquidator of a company, had obtained a without notice freezing order against the applicant company which was subsequently discharged on the basis that there had been improper disclosure of material facts. The provisional liquidator had given an undertaking that he would be liable for any loss to the applicant company if the court found that the freezing order had occasioned such a loss. The court held that the company was entitled to recover its costs on the standard basis, and the costs were to be quantified in the same way as costs which were recoverable as damages. The fact that the provisional liquidator was innocent of any personal conscious failure was insufficient to absolve him from liability which would produce precisely the injustice which the undertaking was designed to guard against: *Apex Frozen Foods Ltd v Ali* [2007] EWHC 469, Warren J.

A company applying for an administration order also applied for an order that the costs of the application be an expense of the administration and also sought an order that one of its creditors, who had opposed the making of an administration order, should pay its costs from the time that evidence in opposition had been served. The judge held there was no reason why the costs of the company administration should not be an expense of the administration. It would require something out of the ordinary to justify an order that the costs of the unsuccessful creditor should be an expense of the administration. It was just in all the circumstances to order that the creditor should pay the company's costs to the extent that they had been increased by the creditor's unsuccessful opposition. The increased burden of costs fell directly on the company and indirectly on the creditors. The administration order had been made because it was in the interests of the creditors generally (*In the matter of Professional Computer Group Ltd* [2008] EWHC 1541 (Ch) Morgan J.)

Patents

The CPR and associated Practice Directions apply as much to patent actions as to any other actions, accordingly r.44.3 applies to how the court should exercise its discretion as to costs in a patents case. An issue by issue approach should be applied so far as it is reasonably possible. That approach should not be thought capable of achieving a "precise" figure of costs. The percentage awards of costs should reflect the overall justice of the case: *SmithKline Beecham Plc v Apotex Europe Ltd (Costs) (No.2)* [2004] EWCA Civ 1703. **48.15.5**

If the court was minded to move away from the general rule that the unsuccessful party should be ordered to pay the costs of the successful party an increasingly strong justification was required. If there was justification for ordering the otherwise successful party to pay the costs of a particular issue to the other it was a convenient rule of thumb to treat both parties' costs of an issue as being equal to and double the deduction, e.g. if a party failed to recover costs of an issue amounting to 15 per cent of his total costs, those costs should be reduced by 30 per cent if the court was of the view that he should also pay the costs of that issue to the other (*Monsanto Technology LLC v Cargill International SA* [2007] EWHC 3113 (Pat) Pumphrey L.J.).

Where the Court of Appeal dismissed the appellant's appeal without having to consider the respondent's notice the court rejected the losing appellant's argument that only part of the costs of the appeal should be awarded against them. The court held that the fact that it was able to resolve the appeal without coming to the respondent's notice saved time and costs. The appropriate award was therefore 100 per cent of the appropriate costs in the appeal. Parties to patent actions must realise that they are party to the same sort of rules as other people; that the size of the team should be proportionate to the job involved; that the more people put on the team the more likely it is that the costs will be increased by one member of a team talking to another. The court expressed the view that for a one, or a one day and a bit patent appeal the appropriate cost should be £50,000: *The Burnden Group Plc v Ultraframe UK Ltd* and *The Burnden Group Plc v Northstar Systems Ltd* [2005] EWCA Civ 1019.

In an action for infringement of a patent the defendant served a defence and counterclaim with particulars of objection. At a late stage the defendant sought to introduce further particulars of prior use. The claimant accepted that the amendment should be allowed and that if the allegations were proved it might elect to submit to an order for revocation. The claimant argued, relying on *See v Scott-Paine* (1933) 50 R.P.C. 56, that since the new allegations would render the earlier issues redundant, there should be an order for the claimant's costs in relation to those issues.

On the facts of the case the court found that there was no lack of due diligence by the defendants up to the time of the discovery of the new evidence and the delay following acquisition of the new evidence was not unreasonable. In any event the substance of the defendants' new allegations would have come as no surprise to the claimant, the claimant's application was accordingly refused: *CIL International Ltd v Vitrashop Ltd* [2002] F.S.R. 4.

In the Patent Office costs are usually awarded on a fixed scale set by the Office in consultation with its users. In a case where the successful party was denied costs outside the usual scale because of its own minor unreasonable behaviour, the court held that the hearing officer had been wrong to hold that a party alleging unreasonable behaviour had to have been blameless. Serious consideration should be given to an award of higher costs where a case was unarguable or where a party had unreasonably failed to consider what evidence was relevant before filing a large amount of irrelevant evidence: *Re Bud & Budweiser, Budbrau Trade Marks* [2002] R.P.C. 747, Simon Thorley Q.C.

In patent infringement proceedings the claimant made a Pt 36 offer before trial on liability which was not accepted. The defendant made a Pt 36 payment before the hearing of the inquiry as to damages which acceded the claimants original offer. The claimant accepting the payment in sought an order that the defendant should pay costs on the indemnity basis. The court held that it had no power to award costs on the indemnity basis since acceptance of the payment in amounted to an agreement to accept costs on the standard basis: *Dyson Appliances Ltd v Hoover Ltd* [2002] EWHC 2229 (Ch), Jacob J.

In patent proceedings the Judge ordered the claimant to pay 95 per cent of the defendants costs after a trial of the preliminary issues. £75,000 was ordered to be paid as an interim payment into a joint account in the names of the parties' solicitors. The Defendant subsequently went into administrative receivership and its solicitors obtained a charging order under s.73 of the Solicitors Act 1974 in respect of their costs in the preliminary issues. The court held that the money in the joint account represented a successful defence and as such was a valuable item that benefited both the defendant and its secured creditors in which the defendant solicitors had an interest by virtue of s.73. The claimants' application for a set off of costs against the sum held in the joint account was refused since to allow the set off would be detrimental to those other interests: *Rohm & Haas v Collag Ltd (No.2)* [2002] BPIR 837, Pumfrey J.

In patent proceedings concerning alleged infringement and invalidity which succeeded in part, the court make a percentage order. When such an order was made all costs were notionally allocated to the issues of infringement or invalidity, the successful party was assumed to recover all its reasonable costs of the action and the percentage deduction was made from that overall sum: *Apotex Europe Ltd v SmithKline Beecham Plc* [2004] EWHC 964, (Ch) Pumfrey J.

Pensions Ombudsman

48.15.6 Where the Pensions Ombudsman makes himself a party to an appeal following determination of a complaint he puts himself at risk as to an order for costs. In the case of appeals from tribunals other than the Pensions Ombudsman there is a settled practice that if the tribunal took no part in the appeal an order for costs would not be made against it, but if it did appear and made representations in support of its decision it made itself at least potentially liable for costs in the event that its decision was reversed. There is no reason to distinguish the position of the Pensions Ombudsman from that of other tribunals: *Moore's (Wallisdown) Ltd v Pensions Ombudsman* [2002] 1 W.L.R. 1649; [2002] 1 All E.R. 737, Ferris J.

Protective Costs Orders

48.15.7 For the procedure to be followed, and for the matters to be taken into account by the court, where a party makes an application for an order limiting the amount of future costs (including disbursements) which a party may recover pursuant to an order for costs subsequently made (a "costs capping order"), see rr.44.18 to 44.20 and commentary in para.43.2.1.2 above. That procedure does not apply to applications for protective costs orders (r.44.18(3)); see further paras 3.1.8 above and para.54.6.3 below, and note guidance on principles and procedure (both at first instance and on appeal) given by the Court of Appeal in *R. (Buglife-The Invertebrate Conservation Trust) v Thurrock Thames Gateway Development Corp* [2008] EWCA Civ 1209, November 4, 2008, CA, unrep.

The Court of Appeal has given a detailed judgment reviewing the relevant authorities, including the decision in *MacDonald v Horn* [1995] 1 All E.R. 961 under the following headings:

"The traditional approach to costs in private law litigation.
Some distinctive features relating to costs in public law litigation.
Protective costs orders: the historical setting.
Protective costs orders in the High Court and Court of Appeal.
Recent developments in Ireland, Canada and Australia.
Protective costs orders: the governing principles and some practical guidance."

The guidance given by the court is very extensive and can only be summarised here.

A protective costs order may be made at any stage of the proceedings on such conditions as the court thinks fit provided that the court is satisfied that:

(i) the issues raised are of general public importance;
(ii) the public interest requires that those issues should be resolved;
(iii) the applicant has no private interest in the outcome of the case;
(iv) having regard to the financial resources of the applicant and the respondents and to the amount of costs that are likely to be involved it is fair and just to make the order;

(v) if the order is not made the applicant will probably discontinue the proceedings and will be acting reasonably in so doing.

If those acting for the applicant are doing so pro bono this will be likely to enhance the merits of the application for a protected costs order.

It is for the court in its discretion to decide whether it is fair and just to make the order in the light of the considerations set out above: *R. (Corner House Research) v Secretary of State for Trade and Industry* [2005] EWCA Civ 192; [2005] 4 All E.R. 1.

The court went on to consider the decision in *R. v Lord Chancellor Ex p. Child Poverty Action Group; R. v DPP Ex p. Bull* [1999] 1 W.L.R. 347, which was approved, save in respect of the second guideline which set too high a test on the prospects of success required. A protective costs order may take a number of different forms and the choice of form is an important aspect of the judge's discretion. Where an applicant seeks an order for costs, if successful, the court should prescribe, by way of a capping order, a total amount of the recoverable costs which would allow for modest legal representation. A claimant should apply for a protective costs order in the claim form, which should include a schedule of the claimant's future cost of and incidental to the full judicial review application. A defendant should set out any reasons for resisting an order in its acknowledgement of service: *R. (Corner House Research) v Secretary of State for Trade and Industry* [2005] EWCA Civ 192; [2005] 4 All E.R. 1. The Court of Appeal indicated that a party contemplating making a request for a protected costs order would face a liability for the court fees and a liability for the costs of those who successfully resist the making of such an order on the papers (which should not generally exceed a proportion of a total of £2,000 in a multi party case) and a further liability if it requests the court to reconsider the matter at an oral hearing (which should not generally exceed the proportionate total of £5,000 in a multi party case).

Whilst, so far, Protective Costs Orders have been made only in favour of claimants in judicial review cases, there is no reason in principle why they should not, in an appropriate case, extend to protect the position of a defendant. Such an order would be unusual but might be made where an individual had a public law role and there was, for whatever reason, no protection given to him in relation to costs by any other body or person: *R. (Ministry of Defence) v Wiltshire & Swindon Coroner* [2005] EWHC 889 (Admin); [2005] All E.R. 40, Collins J.

Certain conditions have to be fulfilled to warrant the making of a protective costs order, one of these being that the applicant should have no private interest in the outcome of the case. Where the applicant was seeking compensation as part of the relief sought, that amounted to a private interest in the outcome, and the application was refused: *Weir v Secretary of State for Transport* [2005] EWHC 24, April (Ch), Lindsay J.

When making an application for a protective costs order for the first time at the appeal stage, there is no reason why different considerations from those set out in *R. (Corner House Research) v Secretary of State for Trade & Industry*, above, should be applied: *Goodson v HM Coroner for Bedfordshire and Luton (Protective Costs)* [2005] EWCA Civ 1172. See also para.48.15.9

Protective cost order applications must be considered in a comparatively summary fashion and at strictly limited expense by the Judge entertaining the application at the interlocutory stage. In a case where the Judge had concluded that the case did not raise sufficient issues of general public importance as to require in the public interest that they should be litigated at the expense of the NHS Trust, whether it succeeded or not, the Court of Appeal held that it was not arguable that the Judge had wrongly treated as an overarching preliminary test the requirement that a case be exceptional before a protective costs order could be made: *R. (on the application of Bullmore) v West Hertfordshire Hospitals NHS Trust* [2007] EWCA Civ 609.

In family proceedings, a protective costs order was refused but a costs cap was imposed, in circumstances where a petitioner sought a declaration that her same sex marriage was valid in the United Kingdom. The court held that the proceedings were essentially "quasi-public", in that they went to matters of status, were essentially directed to the matters of elucidation of public law, and might appropriately have been brought in the Administrative Court but for s.55 of the Family Law Act 1986. The court approached the application on the basis of the principles set out in *R. (on the application of Cornerhouse Research) v Secretary of State for Trade & Industry* [2005] EWCA Civ 192. On the facts, the proceedings did not raise issues of general public importance and it was not unreasonable that the petitioner should be at risk of at least a contribution to the costs of the Lord Chancellor as intervener: *Wilkinson & Kitzinger v HM Attorney General (The Lord Chancellor intervening)* [2006] EWHC 835 (Fam), Sir Mark Potter P.

The Court has inherent jurisdiction to control its own procedures and to make conditional costs orders. CPR 3.1(3)(a) provides that where the Court makes a case management order, it may do so subject to conditions, including a condition to pay a sum of money into Court. The Costs Judge accordingly has the jurisdiction to grant a final costs certificate where the respondent had failed to pay an interim costs order of £2 million. *Days Healthcare UK Ltd v Pihsiang Machinery Manufacturing Co Ltd* [2006] EWHC 1444, QB, Langley J.

Where a respondent company requested an inquiry as to damages for breach of contract, the Court held on the facts that the request should be granted, subject to paying the opposing local authority 50 per cent of its costs of the proceedings below and 90 per cent of its costs of the appeal. *Hampshire County Council v Supportways Community Services Ltd (No.2)* [2006] EWCA Civ 1170.

Once the main practical purpose of a case has gone the court should take into account the applicant's ability to finance it when deciding whether to allow it to continue. Where a party had suggested that the court could make a protective costs order, but had not made an application for one, it would have been wrong to make such an order without an opportunity for the affected parties to comment. It was however important that a means should be found to do this without the process itself becoming a source of additional cost. The appropriateness and workability of the criterion laid down in *Corner House* above, that an application for judicial review seeking a protective costs order should not have any private interest in the proceedings was doubtful. Different considerations may apply to a case where the applicant's "interests" were not private law interests but simply interests that he shared with other members of his group in the protection of the environment. In that context the provisions of the Aarhus Convention on Access to Justice in Environmental matters may also be relevant, see *R (on the application Burkett) v Hammersmith LBC* [2004] EWCA Civ 1342 and *R (on the application of England) v Tower Hamlets LBC* [2006] EWCA Civ 1742.

The decision in *Corner House* was examined in some detail by the Court of Appeal (*R (Compton) v Wiltshire Primary Care Trust* [2008] EWCA Civ 749). The applicant sought to prevent the closure of parts of a local hospital which affected a wide community. The court held that where that community had a real interest in the issues that arise being resolved it was certainly open to a judge to hold that there was public interest in resolution of the issues and that the issues were ones of general public importance.

> "23. ... The paragraphs in *Corner House* are not in my view to be read as statutory provisions, nor to be read in an over-restrictive way. Indeed it seems to me that there is already support for a non-rigorous approach exemplified by paragraph 19 of Lloyd Jones J's judgment in [*R (on the application of Bulmore) v West Hertfordshire Hospitals NHS Trust* [2007] EWHC 1350 (Admin)] where he said in relation to the criteria of 'no private interest':-
>
> 19. This particular requirement as formulated in *Corner House* has been diluted in the later case law. I have in mind particularly *Wilkinson v Kitzinger* [2006] EWHC 835 (Fam), [2006] 2 FCR 537, [2006] 2 FLR 397 (Fam), where Sir Mark Potter P said at paragraph 54:
>
> 'As to (1)(iii) I find the requirement that the applicant should have 'no private interest in the outcome' a somewhat elusive concept to apply in any case in which the applicant either in private or public law proceedings is pursuing a personal remedy, albeit his or her purpose is essentially representative of a number of persons with a similar interest. In such a case, it is difficult to see why, if a PCO is otherwise appropriate, the existence of the applicant's private or personal interest should disqualify him or her from the benefit of such an order. I consider that, the nature and extent of the 'private interest' and its weight or performance in the overall context should be treated as a flexible element in the court's consideration of the question whether it is fair and just to make the order. Were I to be persuaded that the remaining criteria are satisfied, I would not regard requirement 1(iii) as fatal to this application'.
>
> I note that passage was approved by the Court of Appeal in *R (England) v London Borough of Tower Hamlets and Others* at paragraph 14."

The court went on to express the view that "exceptionality" was not seen in *Corner House* as some additional criteria to the principles set out in para.74 but a prediction as to the effect of applying those principles. The court suggested that the word "general" did not mean that it must be of interest to all the public nationally, although it was accepted that a local group might be so small that issues in which they alone might be interested might not be of "general public importance". It is a question of degree and a question which *Corner House* would expect judges to resolve. The court expressed regret that the Rules Committee had not codified the procedure but declined to reconsider the guidance previously given in Corner House.

As to procedure, the court said this:

"47. . . . If the person benefiting from a PCO is the would-be appellant [the governing principles identified in paragraph 74 of *Corner House*] may however to be re-examined at the appellate stage. It may have become clear that no issue of general public importance arises or it may be clear there is no public interest in bringing the case to the Court of Appeal. If the beneficiary of a PCO has succeeded in the court of first instance it is difficult to think that some protection will not be appropriate in the Court of Appeal.

48. . . . So far as procedure is concerned if the recipient of a PCO in the court below is wishing to appeal, an application for a PCO should be lodged with the application for permission. The respondent should have an opportunity of providing written reasons why a PCO is now inappropriate. The decision will be taken on paper by the single Lord Justice. If a PCO is refused the applicant can apply orally. If it is granted then the respondent will need compelling reasons to set it aside.

49. . . . What about PCOs on appeals from a refusal to grant a PCO or from the granting of a PCO? The normal order should be that there will be no order for costs save in exceptional circumstances, for example where the application is an abuse of process. The appeals were dismissed. Buxton LJ gave a powerful dissenting judgment." (*R (Compton) v Wiltshire Primary Care Trust* [2008] EWCA Civ 749.)

On an application for a Protective Costs Order the Court of Appeal was faced on the one hand with stifling a substantive appeal, and on the other hand of causing some potential injustice to respondents who had joined themselves to the appeal. The court found that the appeal was a broad appeal which was a matter of public interest, covering not only the immediate parties to it but many other potential parties in the background as well. Taking into account the amount of money which had already been spent at the trial, which far outstripped any costs of the appeal so far as the additional respondents were concerned, the court decided to permit the appeal to proceed. This caused the least injustice in the case. The respondents were large companies acting in their own interests and were well able to look after themselves. The respondents were ordered to bear their own costs of the appeal regardless of its outcome: *Baker v Quantum Clothing Group Ltd* [2008] EWCA Civ 823.

The Court of Appeal has reviewed the law relating to Protective Costs Orders, including *R. (Cornerhouse Research) v SSTI* [2005] EWCA Civ 192; [2005] 1 W.L.R. 2600 and *R. (Compton) v Wiltshire Primary Care Trust* [2008] EWCA Civ 749. The procedure to be adopted at first instance is set out in *Corner House* and refined in Compton. The procedure to be adopted in the Court of Appeal was set out by Waller L.J. in *Compton*. The court found that there is some overlap between the issue whether to grant permission to appeal and the issue whether to grant a PCO. They both involve some consideration of the merits and should therefore be considered together. The general principle is that where permission to appeal is granted the court will not readily set the order aside. CPR r.52.9(2) expressly provides that it will only do so if there is compelling reason, and the cases show that it will only do so in very restricted circumstances. It was held not to be appropriate to do so in the particular case where Laws L.J. had formed the view that there was a sufficient public interest in the issues raised to require permission to be granted: *R.(on the application of Buglife-The Invertebrate Conservation Trust) v Thurrock Thames Gateway Development Corporation and Rosemound Developments Ltd* [2008] EWCA Civ 1209.

Receiver

As to remuneration of a receiver see CPR r.69.7. Receivers are personally bound by their contract with their solicitors and must pay the proper charges, but they should give close scrutiny to the solicitors' bills and whether such charges should be recovered from the estate would depend on whether they had acted properly in employing them for the tasks in question. Office holders such as Receivers were not normally expected to act voluntarily, but office holders who sought remuneration at a particular level had **48.15.8** to justify their claim as one aspect of their duty to account. They had to give full particulars and they ought to be remunerated on the basis of time spent. They had to do significantly more than giving the total number of hours spent by them or their staff and multiplying it by the charging rate of the individual whose time was spent. They should explain the nature of each task undertaken and why it was undertaken. The charging rate should be proved by evidence, they should keep records, the test being whether a reasonably prudent man, faced with the same circumstances in relation to his own affairs, would have done the same things (*Mirror Group Newspapers Plc v Maxwell (No.1)* [1998] B.C.C. 324, Ferris J.). The language of CPR 69.7 is confined to the remuneration of a receiver and cannot be stretched to include expenses of the receiver. Such expenses fall to be met from the realisable assets: *Capewell v Customs and Excise Commissioners (Costs)* [2005] EWCA Civ 964.

Trustees, personal representatives

48.15.9 *Powers of the court as to costs*—The court has jurisdiction to make an order as to the ultimate incidence of costs in the proceedings ahead of the trial of the action (*Re Wedstock Realizations Ltd* [1988] B.C.L.C. 354 at 358, 359). There is a discretion to make an order in terms which ensure that, win or lose, a litigant would be entitled to costs out of the property in dispute, before the facts have been fully explored and before the relevant law has been fully argued. That discretion is most frequently exercised in favour of trustees and executors (*Re Beddoe* [1893] 1 Ch. 547 at 557, 561 at 562).

A trustee who defends proceedings brought against him in a representative capacity without obtaining a Beddoe order will be at risk as to costs. If the court would not have given authority to defend the proceedings in accordance with the principles set out in *Beddoe, Re* [1893] 1 Ch. 547 it would not allow the costs to be paid out of the trust funds either even if the trustee was advised by counsel that he had a good defence to the claim: *Singh v Bhasin* [2000] W.T.L.R. 275; *The Times*, August 21, 1998, Mr Alan Boyle Q.C.

The discretion has also been exercised in favour of an executor who, on application to the court, has been authorised to bring or defend proceedings so that, even if unsuccessful, he would be entitled to be indemnified out of the estate for all the costs for which he might be liable (*Dallaway (Deceased), Re* [1982] 1 W.L.R. 756). The trustee of a family trust was held to have acted properly and reasonably on the advice of solicitors, in commencing and pursuing litigation on a trust matter, as the claims had a reasonable prospect of success. He had not acted in breach of trust by paying monies out of the trust fund in satisfaction of the costs of the action. His decision not to apply for a *Beddoe* order was not evidence of wilful wrongdoing and did not constitute a breach of trust at all. *Bonham v Blake Lapthorne Linell and Fishwick* [2006] EWHC 2513 (Ch), Kitchin J.

The court is much influenced by the fact that it is the duty of trustees and executors to protect the estate, that they are entitled to be indemnified for costs properly incurred for the benefit of the estate and Rules of Court expressly provide that executors and trustees are entitled to their costs out of the fund held by them in that capacity (*National Anti-Vivisection Society Ltd v Duddington, The Times*, November 23, 1989, per Mummery J.). Thus in *Westdock Realisations Ltd, Re* (above) an order was made that the costs of liquidation should be paid from the fund held by the receiver; but in *Charge Card Services Ltd, Re* [1987] Ch. 150, Hoffmann J. declined to make an order ahead of the final hearing of a liquidator's summons for directions.

The court may also exercise its discretion to make pre-emptive costs orders in the case of an action by a minority shareholder in a similar way to a trustee on a *Beddoe* application (*Wallersteiner v Moir* [1975] Q.B. 373 at 389 at 391–392, 403–405; *Smith v Croft* [1986] 1 W.L.R. 580).

The essence of the discretion depends on the facts of each case (*Re Evans (dec'd)*). [1986] 1 W.L.R. 101). However it is not necessarily limited to categories of case which have arisen to date (e.g. trustee, executor, liquidator, receiver, minority shareholder) but must be exercised judiciously having regard only to the relevant factors (*National Anti-Vivisection Society Ltd* (above)). The following factors have featured in decided cases as relevant to the court's jurisdiction to make pre-emptive costs orders:

(i) The merits.
(ii) The likely order for costs at trial.
(iii) The justice of the case.

(iv) Special factors.

(i) The merits. —The prospects of success of a claim or a defence is the most important question to be taken into account in considering whether the action or defence should be financed out of the estate or fund in dispute (*Re Evans (dec'd)* (above)). The fund in dispute should not be used to support contentions which were not made in good faith or on reasonable grounds.

(ii) The likely order for costs at trial. —Unless the court is satisfied that it is likely that an order would be made after trial, that the costs in question be paid out of the fund, it is not in general right to make such an order before trial (*Re Wedstock* [1988] B.C.L.C. 354 (above)). In the case of a trustee the court at trial will in general give effect to the trustee's right to indemnity out of the trust fund if he has acted properly for the benefit of the fund in the pursuit or defence of proceedings even if he is ultimately unsuccessful.

The Court held that, on a correct intrepretation of "costs" in RSC O.62 r.1(4) the remuneration of a receiver was not included, nor was the assessment of that remuneration "an assessment" in the Chancery Divison. It therefore followed that no fee was payable on the assessment of the remuneration by the costs judge. *Mirror Group Newspapers Plc v Maxwell (No.1)* [1998] B.C.C. 324, May 22, 2000, Ferris J.

(iii) The justice of the case. —A pre-emptive order should not be made if there is a real possibility of it acting unjustly. It might be unjust in a particular case for the successful claimant to the property in dispute to be placed in a position where even if he wins, property held to be his is burdened with payment of the unsuccessful parties' costs. That is a powerful consideration where the persons who would benefit from the pre-emptive order are all adult and *sui juris* (*Re Evans (dec'd)*).

(iv) Special factors. —Examples of other special factors which might make a pre-trial order appropriate include the following: Where it is essential for the due administration of justice for a liquidator or administrator to obtain the court's decision because there are large classes of persons, e.g. creditors, who might be affected by the decision (*Re Exchange Securities Ltd (No.2)* [1985] B.C.L.C. 392 at 395). Again the application might be a test case in which a decision is necessary on a point in order to resolve a number of pending cases (*Re Wedstock* [1988] B.C.L.C. 354 (above) at 360–361).

In a case which depends on the resolution of the question whether property is held in trust by the defendants for the claimant, the very existence of the trustee/beneficiary relationship is in issue in the action. Since that involves hostile litigation between two rival claimants it is wrong for the court to fetter the discretion of the trial judge by making a pre-emptive interlocutory order for costs in favour of the defendants, to be paid out of the property in dispute, which might operate unjustly against the claimant (*National Anti-Vivisection Society Ltd* (above)).

A pre-emptive costs order could be made in favour of employees who were representative claimants in an action against their employers and the trustees of relevant pension funds, where they had not the resources to pursue major litigation, and their claims were so strong that it was inconceivable that if an independent trustee were appointed he would not apply for and obtain such an order (*McDonald v Horn* [1995] 1 All E.R. 961, Vinelott J.

The Court of Appeal upheld the Judgment of Mr Justice Vinelott, stating that the point was one of considerable practical importance. Reference should be made to the full judgment for an analysis of the law.

Statutory Costs Jurisdiction: The Court's jurisdiction to deal with litigation costs is based upon s.51 of the Supreme Court Act 1981, this discretion must be exercised in accordance with the Rules of Court and established principles: *McDonald v Horn* [1995] 1 All E.R. 961 and see *Machin v National Power* [1998] O.P.L.R. 187; [2001] W.T.L.R. 741, Carnwath J.; *AXA Equity & Law Life Assurance Society Plc (No.1), Re* [2001] 2 B.C.L.C. 447, Evans-Lombe J.

The criteria set out by Dyson J. in *R. v Lord Chancellor Ex p. Child Poverty Action Group* [1999] 1 W.L.R. 347 were held to be consistent with the overriding objective by Richards J. in *R. v Hammersmith & Fulham LBC Ex p. CPRE London Branch* [2000] Env. L.R. 544. The court granted such an order to a party representing all policy holders opposed to a scheme put forward by the claimant insurance company for the reorganisation of their insurance business. The application was granted on the basis that the opposing party was entitled to the order because his position was analogous with that of a shareholder bringing a derivative action and he was performing a service enabling the claimant's scheme to be fully tested in court. The court retained a discretion to disallow costs unreasonably incurred since the court retained a discretion to disallow costs unreasonably incurred in opposition: *AXA Equity & Law Life Assurance Society Plc (No.1), Re* [2001] 2 B.C.L.C. 447, Evans-Lombe J. On an application for directions by trustees, it is normal practice for costs to be paid out of the trust funds (*Buckton (Costs), Re* [1907] 2 Ch. 406). CPR r.44.3(2) gives a wider discretion than was formerly the case, to diverge from that practice where appropriate. It was appropriate to depart from the normal procedure, where trustees had adopted a partisan role arguing positively for a specific outcome in the interests of one class of beneficiary against the interests of another class of beneficiary. The role adopted by the trustees was not neutral and they therefore had to accept that there might be costs consequences. The trustees were ordered to pay the costs personally, *Breadner v Granville-Grossman (Costs)* [2001] W.T.L.R. 377, Park J.

The court decided that it was reasonable to make a pre-emptive costs order in favour of a representative beneficiary joined as a defendant, where he represented a significant class of members (in respect of a pension scheme). There were two classes of beneficiary, and although there was no obvious conflict between them, seperate legal representation was requested. The court was entitled to take into account the suspicions existing between the two classes and the desirablility of having the ultimate decision (as to whether to merge two pension schemes) accepted with good grace. It was not necessary for an applicant for a pre-emptive costs order to show that no reasonable trial judge would have ordered otherwise, *British Airways Pension Schemes, Re* [2000] Pens. L.R. 311, Park J.; similarly see: *Stevens v Bell (Costs)* [2001] O.P.L.R. 123, Park J.

The Administrative Court made a pre-emptive costs order limited to £25,000 in favour of the campaign for nuclear disarmament in respect of its application for permission to apply for declaratory relief in relation to the Government's proposed initiation of hostilities against the Republic of Iraq. It was argued that the applicant was a private company limited by guarantee of modest resources which had had no opportunity to raise funds elsewhere and could not continue with the proceedings unless it had the certainty of a costs cap; the issues were of obvious public importance, the sum suggested would meet the applicants costs if it were unsuccessful in its application for permission to apply for judicial review if the applicant could not proceed for want of a pre-emptive costs order an alternative application would be found with or without public funding. The court held that it was particularly appropriate to make a pre-emptive costs order in such a case where the course to be ordered would secure a speedy determination against the claimants were it to be found non justiciable: *Campaign for Nuclear Disarmament, Re*, [2002] EWHC 2712 (Admin); [2003] C.P. Rep. 28, Simon Brown L.J., Maurice Kay J.

GUIDE TO THE SUMMARY ASSESSMENT OF COSTS 2005 EDITION

Introduction

1. Sections 13 and 14 of the Costs Practice Direction deal with the general provisions relating to summary assessment. Rule 43.2 defines costs and Rule 44.7 contains the court's power to make a summary assessment. (Appendix 1 contains extracts from the relevant Rules and Practice Directions.) **48.16**

2. The general rule is that the court should make a summary assessment of the costs:

(a) at the conclusion of the trial of a case which has been dealt with on the fast track, in which case the order will deal with the costs of the whole claim; and

(b) at the conclusion of any other hearing which has lasted not more than one day, in which case the order will deal with the costs of the application or matter to which the hearing related. If this hearing disposes of the claim, the order may deal with the costs of the whole claim.

3. If there is a conditional fee agreement or other funding arrangement, Rule 44.3A prevents the court from making a summary assessment of an additional liability before the conclusion of the proceedings or the part of the proceedings to which the funding arrangement relates. In such a case, the court should nonetheless make a summary assessment of the base costs of the hearing or application unless there is good reason not to do so. Where the court makes a summary assessment of the base costs, all statements of costs and estimates put before the Judge will be retained on the court file and the Judge carrying out a final assessment must be supplied with copies of all the costs orders previously made and, if required, be shown all the previous costs statements and estimates.

4. The court should not make a summary assessment of the costs of a receiving party who is an assisted person or LSC funded client. The court may make a summary assessment of costs payable by an assisted person or by a LSC funded client. Such an assessment is not by itself a determination of that person's liability to pay those costs (as to which see Rule 44.17 and paragraphs 20.1 to 22.33 of the Costs Practice Direction.

5. The court must not make a summary assessment of the costs of a receiving party who is a child or patient within Part 21 unless the solicitor acting for the child or patienthas waived the right to further costs. The court may make a summary assessment of costs payable by a child or patient.

6. The court awarding costs cannot make an order for the summary assessment to be carried out by a costs officer. If summary assessment of costs is appropriate but the court awarding costs is unable to carry out the assessment on the day it must give directions as to a further hearing before the same Judge or order detailed assessment.

The approach to costs

7. General approach to summary and detailed assessment should be the same. For the summary assessment to be accurate the Judge must be informed about previous summary assessments carried out in the case. This is particularly important where the Judge is assessing all the costs at the conclusion of a case. **48.17**

8. The court should not be seen to be endorsing disproportionate and unreasonable costs. Accordingly:

(a) when the amount of the costs to be paid has been agreed the court should make this clear by saying that the order is by consent

(b) If the Judge is to make an order which is not by consent, he will, so far as possible, ensure that the final figure is not disproportionate and/or unreasonable having regard to Part 1 of the CPR. He will retain this responsibility notwithstanding the absence of challenge to individual items comprised in the figure sought.

9. Where a case is simple and straightforward it is obviously easier to decide whether the final figure is disproportionate than where the case is more complex. For this reason, it is impossible to ignore the work on the case which has had to be done.

10. The fact that the paying party is not disputing the amount of costs can be taken as some indication that the amount is proportionate and reasonable. The Judge therefore will intervene only if satisfied that the costs are so disproportionate that it is right to do so.

11. The court can allow a sum which it considers to be proportionate as a payment on account whilst at the same time ordering detailed assessment.

The basis of assessment

The standard basis

48.18 12. Rule 44.4(1) and (2) (Appendix 1) provide that where the court assesses the amount of costs on the standard basis it will not allow costs which have been unreasonably incurred or are unreasonable in amount and will only allow costs which are proportionate to the matters in issue. The court will resolve in favour of the paying party any doubt which it may have as to whether the costs were reasonably incurred or were reasonable and proportionate in amount.

The indemnity basis

48.19 13. Rule 44.4(1) and (3) (Appendix 1) provide that where the court assesses the amount of costs on the indemnity basis it will not allow costs which have been unreasonably incurred or are unreasonable in amount and it will resolve in favour of the receiving party any doubt which it may have as to whether costs were reasonably incurred or were reasonable in amount. The test of proportionality is not mentioned in the definition of the indemnity basis.

Proportionality

48.20 14. "Proportionality" is not defined in the rules or the Practice Direction. Section 11 of the Costs Practice Direction indicates, however, that in applying the test of proportionality the court will have regard to rule 1.1(2)(c) by, so far as practicable, dealing with the case in ways which are proportionate:

(i) to the amount of money involved;
(ii) to the importance of the case;
(iii) to the complexity of the issues; and
(iv) to the financial position of each party.

15. Paragraphs 11.1 to 11.3 of the Practice Direction give the following warnings as to the test of proportionality.

(i) the relationship between the total costs incurred and the financial value of the claim may not be a reliable guide. A fixed percentage cannot be applied in all cases to the value of the claim in order to ascertain whether or not the costs are proportionate.
(ii) in any proceedings, there will be costs which will be inevitably be incurred and which are necessary for the successful conduct of the case. Solicitors are not required to conduct litigation at rates which are uneconomic. Thus in a modest claim the proportion of costs is likely to be higher than in a large claim and may even equal or possibly exceed the amount in dispute.
(iii) where a trial takes place the time taken by the court in dealing with the particular issue may not be an accurate guide to the amount of time properly spent by the legal or other representatives in preparation for the trial of that issue.

16. The Court of Appeal has given guidance on the correct approach to proportionality when assessing costs:

> "what is required is a two stage approach. There has to be a global approach and an item by item approach. The global approach will indicate whether the total sum claimed is or appears to be disproportionate having particular regard to the considerations which Part 44.5(3) states are relevant. If the costs as a whole are

not disproportionate according to that test then all that is normally required is that each item should have been reasonably incurred and the costs for that item should be reasonable. If on the other hand the costs as a whole appear disproportionate then the court will want to be satisfied that the work in relation to each item was necessary, and, if necessary, the cost of the item was reasonable"

(*Home Office v Lownds* [2002] EWCA Civ 365; [2002] 1 WLR 2450; [2002] 4 All ER 775 CA).

The text of rule 44.5(3) is included in Appendix 1 to this Guide.

17. The relevant costs for consideration at the first stage are the base costs only before VAT is added (CPD 11.5 and *Giambrone v JMC Holidays* [2003] 2 Costs LR 189).

18. The fact that, at the first stage, the costs as a whole appear to be proportionate does not prevent the court from finding individual items are disproportionate and applying the test of necessity to them alone (Giambrone).

Summary assessment where costs claimed include additional liability

19. Rule 44.3A deals with costs orders relating to funding arrangements. An order for payment of "costs" includes an additional liability incurred under a funding arrangement. Where the court carries out a summary assessment of base costs before the conclusion of proceedings it is helpful if the order identifies separately the amount allowed in respect of: solicitors charges; Counsel's fees; other disbursements; and any value added tax. If this is not done, the court which later makes an assessment of an additional liability, will have to apportion the base costs previously assessed. **48.21**

20. Rule 44.3B sets out the limits on recovery under funding arrangements. The court will consider the amount of any additional liability separately from the base costs and when considering the factors to be taken into account under rule 44.5 in assessing an additional liability the court will have regard to the facts and circumstances as they reasonably appeared to the solicitor or Counsel when the funding arrangement was entered into and at the time of any variation of the arrangement.

Orders made before the conclusion of proceedings

21. Where an order for costs is made before the conclusion of the proceedings and a legal representative for the receiving party has entered into a conditional fee agreement the court may summarily assess the base costs. An order for payment of those costs will not be made unless the court is satisfied that the receiving party is at the time liable to pay to his legal representative an amount equal to or greater than the costs claimed. If the court is not so satisfied it may direct that any costs, for which the receiving party may not in the final event be liable, be paid into court to await the outcome of the case or shall not be enforceable until further order, or the court may postpone the receiving party's right to receive payment in some other way. **48.22**

Orders made at the conclusion of proceedings

22. Where the court makes a summary assessment of an additional liability at the conclusion of the proceedings, that assessment must relate to the whole of the proceedings; this will include any additional liability relating to base costs allowed by the court when making a summary assessment on a previous application or hearing. **48.23**

Factors to be taken into account in deciding the amount of costs

23. Rule 44.5 (Appendix 1) sets out the factors to be taken into account. Those factors include: the conduct of all the parties, including in particular, conduct before as well as during the proceedings and the efforts made, if any, before and during the proceedings in order to try to resolve the dispute. **48.24**

24. In deciding whether the costs claimed are reasonable and (on the standard basis) proportionate, the court will consider the amount of any additional liability separately from the base costs.

25. The Judge, before commencing a summary assessment on the standard basis should, in accordance with the guidance in *Home Office v Lownds* [2002] EWCA Civ 365; [2002] 1 WLR 2450; [2002] 4 All ER 775 CA) (see paragraph 16 above), step back and consider the proportionality of the costs claimed. If the costs claimed overall appear proportionate they may be assessed applying a test of reasonableness. If on the other hand the costs appear to be disproportionate then the more stringent test of necessity should be applied. If previous orders for summarily assessed costs have been made then the Judge should, subject to paragraph 27, consider the proportionality of the total costs of the proceedings.

26. In considering what is necessary, a sensible standard of necessity has to be adopted. This is a standard which takes fully into account the need to make allowances for the different judgements which those responsible for litigation can sensibly come to as to what is required. The danger of setting too high a standard with the benefit of hindsight has to be avoided. The threshold required to meet "necessity" is higher than that of "reasonableness" but it is still a standard that a competent practitioner should be able to achieve without undue difficulty. In deciding what is necessary the conduct of the other party is highly relevant. A party who is unco-operative may render necessary costs which would otherwise be unnecessary. It is acceptable that that party should pay the costs for the expense which he has made necessary.

27. In arriving at a final figure the Judge should not reduce the costs of the receiving party on account of the costs awarded to that party under a previous summary assessment. To do so would impugn the decision of the earlier Judge. Where however the amount of costs previously ordered to be paid has been agreed by the parties with no judicial assessment there is nothing to prevent the court taking these figures into account when considering proportionality.

Conditional fee agreements with a success fee

48.25 28. The factors to be taken into account when deciding whether a percentage increase is reasonable may include:

(a) the risk that the circumstances in which the costs, fees or expenses would be payable might or might not occur;

(b) the legal representative's liability for any disbursements;

(c) what other methods of financing the costs were available to the receiving party.

The court has the power to allow different percentages for different items of costs or for different periods during which costs were incurred (CPD 11.8(2)). The court should have regard to the facts and circumstances as they reasonably appeared to the solicitor or Counsel when the funding arrangement was entered into, and at the time of any variation of the agreement (CPD 11.7).

29. A percentage increase should not be reduced simply on the ground that, when added to base costs which are reasonable and (where relevant) proportionate, the total appears disproportionate (CPD 11.9).

In road traffic accident claims where the accident occurred on or after 6 October 2003 the percentage increase to be allowed as a success fee is fixed by rules: see CPR 45 Section 111.

Insurance Premiums

48.26 *30. Relevant factors* to be taken into account when deciding whether the cost of insurance cover is reasonable include:

(a) where the insurance cover is not purchased in support of a conditional fee agreement with a success fee, how its cost compares with the likely cost of funding the case with a conditional fee agreement with a success fee and supporting insurance cover;

(b) the level and extent of the cover provided;

(c) the availability of any pre-existing insurance cover;

(d) whether any part of the premium would be rebated in the event of early settlement;

(e) the amount of commission payable to the receiving party or his legal representatives or other agents.

Membership organisation—additional amount

31. When considering a provision made by a membership organisation the court should not allow a provision which exceeds the likely cost to the receiving party of the premium of an insurance policy against the risk of incurring a liability to pay the costs of other parties to the proceedings. In those circumstances the court will have regard to the factors set out in paragraph 26 above in addition to the factors set out in rule 44.5 (Appendix 1). **48.27**

Success fee disputes between legal representative and client: procedure following the summary assessment

32. A court which has made a summary assessment which disallows or reduces a legal representative's percentage increase may then and there decide the issue whether the disallowed amount should continue to be payable. The court may do this if: **48.28**

(a) the receiving party and all parties to the relevant agreement consent to the court doing so;

(b) the receiving party (or, if corporate, a duly authorised officer) is present in court; and

(c) the court is satisfied that the issue can be fairly decided then and there.

33. In any other case the court will give directions to enable an application to be made by the legal representative for the disallowed amount to be payable by his client, including if appropriate a direction that the application will be determined by a Costs Judge or District Judge of the court dealing with the case.

General principles to be applied in summary assessment

The Indemnity Principle

34. A party in whose favour an order for costs has been made may not recover more than he is liable to pay his own solicitors. See *Harold v Smith* [1865] H & N 381, 385; and *Gundry v Sainsbury* [1910] 1 KB 645 CA. There are exceptions to the principle, notably costs funded by the Legal Services Commission and fees payable under certain types of conditional fee agreement. **48.29**

35. The statement of costs put before the court for summary assessment must be signed by the party or its legal representative. That form contains the statement:

> "The costs estimated above do not exceed the costs which the [party] is liable to pay in respect of the work which this estimate covers."

36. Following the decision of Lord Justice Henry in *Bailey v IBC Vehicles Ltd* [1998] 3 All ER 570 CA, the signature of a statement of costs (or a bill for detailed assessment) by a solicitor is, in normal circumstances, sufficient to enable the court to be satisfied that the indemnity principle has not been breached. A solicitor is an officer of the court and as Henry L.J. stated:

> "In so signing he certifies that the contents of the bill are correct. That signature is no empty formality. The bill specifies the hourly rates applied. If an agreement between the receiving solicitor and his client. restricted (say) the hourly rate payable by the client that hourly rate is the most that can be claimed or recovered on [assessment] . The signature of the bill of costs : is effectively the certificate of an officer of the court that the receiving party's solicitors are not seeking to recover in relation to any item more than they have agreed to charge their client."

Deferring payment of costs

48.30 37. As a general rule a paying party should be ordered to pay the amount of any summarily assessed costs within 14 days. Before making such an order the court should consider whether an order for payment of the costs might bring the action to an end and whether this would be just in all the circumstances.

Litigants in person

48.31 38. Where the receiving party is a litigant in person rule 48.6 (Appendix 1) governs the way in which the question of costs should be dealt with. A litigant in person may be allowed a sum in respect of costs at the rate of £9.25 for each hour reasonably spent in preparation and attendance. He may be allowed a reasonable sum in excess of that amount if he can show that his work on the case has caused him financial loss justifying a higher award.

39. In all cases there is an absolute cap on the amount recoverable by a litigant in person, namely the reasonable costs of disbursements plus two thirds of the amount which would have been allowed if the litigant in person had been legally represented. (rule 48.6(2)). The litigant in person is entitled to recover in addition: payments reasonably made for legal services relating to the conduct of the proceedings: and the costs of obtaining expert assistance in connection with assessing the claim for costs. This does mean that a litigant in person may be able to claim both the cost of obtaining legal advice and services as well as the cost of undertaking the litigation in person. Those qualified to give expert assistance in connection with assessing the claim for costs are: a barrister, a solicitor, Fellow of the Institute of Legal Executives, Fellow of the Association of Law Costs Draftsmen, a law costs draftsman who is a member of the Academy of Experts and a law costs draftsman who is a member of the Expert Witness Institute.

40. Although the definition of litigant in person includes a solicitor, a solicitor who instead of acting for himself is represented in the proceedings by his firm, or by himself in his firm name, is not, for the purpose of the Civil Procedure Rules, a litigant in person (see Section 52 of the Costs Practice Direction).

Guideline figures for solicitors' hourly rates

48.32 41. Guideline figures for solicitors charges (as at January 2005) are published in Appendix 2 to this Guide, which also contains some explanatory notes. The guideline rates are not scale figures: they are broad approximations only. In any particular area the Designated Civil Judge may supply more up to date guidelines for rates in that area. Costs and fees exceeding the guidelines may well be justified in an appropriate case and that is a matter for the exercise of discretion by the court.

42. The guideline figures are not intended to replace figures used by those with accurate local knowledge. They are intended to provide a starting point for those faced with summary assessment who do not have that local knowledge.

43. In substantial and complex litigation an hourly rate in excess of the guideline figures may be appropriate for grade A fee earners where other factors, including the value of the litigation, the level of the complexity, the urgency or importance of the matter, as well as any international element, would justify a significantly higher rate to reflect higher average costs.

Solicitor Advocates

48.33 44. Remuneration of solicitor advocates is based on the normal principles for remuneration of solicitors. It is not therefore appropriate to seek a brief fee and refreshers as if the advocate were a member of the Bar. If the cost of using a solicitor advocate is more than the cost of instructing Counsel, the higher cost is unlikely to be recovered. The figures properly recoverable by solicitor advocates should reflect the amount of preparation undertaken, the time spent in court and the weight and gravity of the case.

45. Where the solicitor advocate is also the solicitor who does the preparation work, the solicitor is entitled to charge normal solicitors' rates for that preparation, but once the solicitor advocate starts preparation for the hearing itself the fees recoverable should not exceed those which would be recoverable in respect of Counsel.

46. It is clearly wrong for the fees of a solicitor acting as a junior Counsel to exceed the fee appropriate for the leading Counsel.

Counsels' fees

47A. proper measure for Counsels' fees is to estimate what fee a hypothetical Counsel, capable of conducting the case effectively, but unable or unwilling to insist on the higher fees sometimes demanded by Counsel of pre-eminent reputation, would be content to take on the brief: but there is no precise standard of measurement and the judge must, using his or her knowledge and experience, determine the proper figure. (Per Pennycuick J. in *Simpsons Motor Sales (London) Ltd v Hendon Borough Council* [1965] 1 WLR 112.) **48.34**

Guideline figures

48. Appendix 2 contains a table of Counsels' fees relating to proceedings in run of the mill cases in the Queen's Bench and Chancery Divisions and in the Administrative Court. These figures are not recommended rates but it is hoped that Judges may find the figures of some help when they are called upon to assess Counsels' fees. It has not been possible to publish more specific guideline figures because of lack of sufficient data. **48.35**

49. The figures contained in the table in Appendix 2 are based upon figures supplied by the Bar and in broad terms the figures are averages based on the information supplied.

The time spent by solicitors and counsel

50. There can be no guidance as to whether the time claimed has been reasonably spent, and it is for the Judge in each case to consider the work properly undertaken by Solicitors and Counsel and to arrive at a figure which is in all circumstances reasonable. **48.36**

A model form of Statement of Costs

51. A model form of Statement of Costs is to be found in Appendix 3. **48.37**

Fast track trial costs

52. The amount of fast track trial costs is set out in the table to Rule 46.2. Rule 46.1(2) provides definitions of "advocate", "fast track trial costs" and "trial". The court may not award more or less than the amount shown in the table except where it decides not to award any fast track trial costs or where rule 46.3 applies. Rule 46.3 sets out the court's power to award more or less than the amount of fast track trial costs (Appendix 1). **48.38**

Summary assessment of costs in the Court of Appeal

53. The Practice Direction supplementing CPR Part 52 identifies five types of hearing at which costs are likely to be assessed by way of summary assessment and states that parties attending any of those hearings should be prepared to deal with the summary assessment. The Costs Practice Direction (paragraph 13.5) places a duty on the parties and their legal representatives to file and serve a statement of any costs they intend to claim in respect of such hearings. **48.39**

55. In this Guide the term "Counsel" includes a solicitor-advocate who is instructed by another solicitor.

Contested directions hearings: applications for permission to appeal at which the respondent is present and (4) appeals from case management decisions

48.40 56. The guidance given below in relation to contested directions hearings, applications for permission to appeal at which the respondent is present and appeals from case management decisions relates to hearings which, although important, are not difficult or complex and are not of general public importance and are listed either for a hearing not exceeding one hour or for a hearing not exceeding one half day.

57. If these hearings are attended by solicitor and Counsel the number of hours which it is reasonable to presume that the solicitor will undertake (in respect of preparation, attendance, travel in Central London and waiting) is 4 hours for a one hour appointment and 7.5 hours for a half day appointment. It is reasonable to presume that Counsel who has between 5 and 10 years' experience merits a fee of approximately £550 (exclusive of VAT) for a one hour appointment and merits a fee of approximately £880 (exclusive of VAT) for a half day appointment.

58. If these hearings were attended by a solicitor without Counsel it is reasonable to presume that the total number of hours the solicitor will spend (in respect of preparation, attendance, travel in Central London and waiting) is 5 hours for a one hour appointment and 10 hours for a half day appointment.

59. If these hearings are attended by a litigant in person it is reasonable to presume that the total number of hours the litigant in person will spend (in respect of preparation, attendance and waiting) is 9 hours for a one hour appointment and 14 hours for a half day appointment. In each case a further allowance should be made for time and expense in travelling to the appointment.

Dismissal list hearings at which the respondent is present

48.41 60. The guidance given below in relation to dismissal list hearings in the Court of Appeal at which the respondent is present, relates to cases which are listed for less than one hour and are of significantly less weight than the contested directions hearings, applications for permission to appeal and appeals from case management decisions described above.

61. If the hearing is attended by solicitor and Counsel (for the appellant or the respondent), it is reasonable to presume that the total number of hours to allow the solicitor (in respect of preparation, attendance, travel in Central London and waiting) is 2 hours, and it is reasonable to presume that Counsel who has between 5 and 10 years' experience merits a fee of approximately £385 (exclusive of VAT).

62. If an appeal is dismissed and costs are awarded to the respondent, it will probably be appropriate to allow further costs in respect of work previously done in responding to the appeal. Consideration should be given to whether it is in fact appropriate to carry out a summary assessment, depending on the amount of work done by the respondent.

63. Subject to paragraph 62, if the hearing is attended by a solicitor without Counsel it is reasonable to presume that the total number of hours to allow the solicitor (in respect of preparation, attendance, travel in Central London and waiting) is 3 hours.

64. Subject to paragraph 62, if the hearing is attended by a litigant in person it is reasonable to presume that the total number of hours to allow the litigant in person (in respect of preparation, attendance and waiting) is 6 hours with a further allowance for time and expense in travelling to the appointment.

Appeals listed for one day or less

48.42 65. Appeals listed for one day or less vary enormously as to weight, complexity and importance. Thus, it is not at present possible to give guidance as to the number of hours reasonably spent by solicitors (in respect of preparation, attendances, travel and waiting) in such appeals. The following general guidance is given:

(1) It may not be appropriate to carry out a summary assessment if a case lasts more than half a day or involves leading Counsel since in those circumstances the case is likely to be complex and weighty. It will often be unwise for the court summarily to assess costs in a matter which is not simple and straightforward, unless the difference between the parties is comparatively small, or unless the correct allowance appears clear.

(2) Where both Counsel and solicitors have been instructed, the reasonable fees of Counsel are likely to exceed the reasonable fees of the solicitor.

(3) The fact that the same Counsel appeared in the lower court does not greatly reduce the reasonable fee unless, for example, the lower court dealt with a great many more issues than are raised on the appeal. It is reasonable for Counsel to spend as much time preparing issues for the Court of Appeal hearing as he spent preparing those issues for the lower court hearing.

(4) If the case merits leading Counsel it may merit also the instruction of a junior to assist him. The junior's fees should be allowed at one half of the leader's fees unless:

- the junior is a senior junior and the case merited both a leader and a senior junior.
- The junior took a responsibility which was equal to or larger than that taken by the leader.
- The junior undertook work not covered by the brief.

(5) In many cases the largest element in the solicitors' reasonable fees for work in the Court of Appeal concerns instructing Counsel and preparing the appeal bundles. Time spent by the solicitor in the development of legal submissions will only be allowed where it does not duplicate work done by Counsel and is claimed at a rate the same or lower than the rate Counsel would have claimed.

(6) Although the solicitor may have spent many hours with the client, the client should have been warned that little of this time is recoverable against a losing party. Reasonable time spent receiving instructions and reporting events should not greatly exceed the time spent on attending the opponents.

(7) Given that the case will be presented by a barrister or a solicitor advocate there is usually no reason for any other solicitor to spend many hours perusing papers. A large claim for such perusal probably indicates that a new fee earner was reading in. Reading in fees are not normally recoverable from an opponent.

(8) Although it is usually reasonable to have a senior fee earner sitting with Counsel in the Court of Appeal, it is not usually reasonable to have two fee earners. The second fee earner may be there for training purposes only.

(9) In most appeals it will be appropriate to make an allowance for copy documents. The allowance for copying which is included in the solicitor's hourly rates will have already been used up or exceeded in the lower court. An hourly rate charge is appropriate for selecting and collating documents and dictating the indices. If the paperwork is voluminous much of this should be delegated to a trainee. Note that:

a. for the copying itself, a fair allowance is 10p per page, i.e. £100 per 1,000 sheets. This includes an allowance for checking the accuracy of the copying.

b. Time spent standing at the photocopier and time spent taking the papers to a local photocopy shop is not recoverable. Such work is not fee earner work; it is secretarial.

(10) It must be borne in mind that skeleton arguments will have been lodged at an early stage, and, in respect of floating appeals, the case may have come into and out of the list. In those circumstances it may be necessary to change Counsel which would inevitably increase the costs. New Counsel may decide to submit a different skeleton argument. Where this has occurred, detailed assessment is to be preferred.

Solicitors' charges in the Court of Appeal

66. Although many appointments in the Court of Appeal merit the attendance of a **48.43**

senior fee earner familiar with the case, the most minor appointments may not. For example, on an application in the dismissal list in a case tried in Newcastle, if Counsel who was briefed for the trial attends it may be unreasonable for a solicitor familiar with the case to travel from Newcastle to attend also. In order to arrive at a notional figure to represent the instruction of and costs of an agent, it may be appropriate to disallow most of the travel time and travelling expenses claimed by the solicitor.

67. The Court of Appeal has stated that it is the duty of litigators (particularly trade unions and insurers) to keep down the cost of litigation. This means that if they instruct London solicitors who charge London rates for a case which has no obvious connection with London and which does not require expertise only to be found there, they will, even if successful, recover less than the solicitors have charged (see *Wraith v Sheffield Forgemasters Ltd* [1998] 1 WLR 132 CA).

68. In relation to the first four types of hearing appropriate for summary assessment in the Court of Appeal, some guidance is given above suggesting the number of hours which may be reasonable for the solicitor to spend. That guidance should be used as a starting point only. The court should also have regard to the number of hours actually claimed.

Counsel's fees in the Court of Appeal

48.44 69. Counsel's fees depend upon the seniority of Counsel which it was reasonable to instruct and the market price for the item of work in question. It is not appropriate to specify an hourly rate for Counsel and to remunerate them at a multiple of that rate according to the number of hours reasonably spent. Such an approach would reward the indolent and penalise the expeditious.

70. In previous paragraphs (paragraphs 57 and 61), figures were suggested for brief fees for Counsel who has between 5 and 10 years' experience. For less experienced Counsel it may be appropriate to reduce these figures; for more experienced Counsel it may be appropriate to increase these figures. The guideline figures are a starting point only and the Court has the discretion to allow fees appropriate to the particular circumstances of the appeal.

Conditional fee agreements with success fees

48.45 71. Although it is not common for appellants to enter into such agreements, it is common for respondents (the successful party at first instance) whose claim or defence was conducted under a conditional fee agreement: such agreements often cover appeals brought by the opponent.

72. Attention is drawn to paragraph 3 of this Guide dealing with summary assessment of an additional liability at the conclusion of proceedings.

73. Paragraphs 27 and 28 set out the factors to be taken into account when deciding whether a percentage increase is reasonable.

Costs awarded to LIP

48.46 74. Attention is drawn to paragraphs 38 to 40 of this Guide.

Appendix 1

Civil Procedure Rules

48.47 For the text of Civil Procedure Rules mentioned in this Guide, please see the relevant CPR Part.

Appendix 2

Guideline Figures for the Summary Assessment of Costs Explanatory Notes

Solicitors hourly rates

The guideline rates for solicitors provided here are broad approximations only. In any particular area the Designated Civil Judge may supply more exact guidelines for rates in that area. Also the costs estimate provided by the paying party may give further guidance if the solicitors for both parties are based in the same locality. **48.48**

The following diagram shows guideline figures for each of three bands outside the London area, and a further three bands within the London area with a statement of the localities included in each band. In each band there are four columns specifying figures for different grades of fee earner.

Localities

The guideline figures have been grouped according to locality by way of general guidance only. Although many firms may be comparable with others in the same locality, some of them will not be. For example, a firm located in the City of London which specialises in fast track personal injury claims may not be comparable with other firms in that locality and vice versa. **48.48.1**

In any particular case the hourly rate it is reasonable to allow should be determined by reference to the rates charged by comparable firms. For this purpose the costs estimate supplied by the paying party may be of assistance The rate to allow should not be determined by reference to locality or postcode alone.

Grades of fee earner

The grades of fee earner have been agreed between representatives of the Supreme Court Costs Office, the Association of District Judges and the Law Society. The categories are as follows: **48.48.2**

1. Solicitors with over eight years post qualification experience including at least eight years litigation experience.
2. Solicitors and legal executives with over four years post qualification experience including at least four years litigation experience.
3. Other solicitors and legal executives and fee earners of equivalent experience.
4. Trainee solicitors, para legals and other fee earners.

"Legal Executive" means a Fellow of the Institute of Legal Executives. Those who are not Fellows of the Institute are not entitled to call themselves legal executives and in principle are therefore not entitled to the same hourly rate as a legal executive.

Unqualified clerks who are fee earners of equivalent experience may be entitled to similar rates and in this regard it should be borne in mind that Fellows of the Institute of Legal Executives generally spend two years in a solicitor's office before passing their Part 1 general examinations, spend a further two years before passing the Part 2 specialist examinations and then complete a further two years in practice before being able to become Fellows. Fellows have therefore possess considerable practical experience and academic achievement. Clerks without the equivalent experience of legal executives will be treated as being in the bottom grade of fee earner ie. trainee solicitors and fee earners of equivalent experience. Whether or not a fee earner has equivalent experience is ultimately a matter for the discretion of the court.

Rates to allow for senior fee earners

Many High Court cases justify fee earners at a senior level. However the same may not be true of attendance at pre-trial hearings with counsel. The task of sitting behind counsel should be delegated to a more junior fee earner in all but the most important pre-trial hearings. The fact that the receiving party insisted upon the senior's attendance, or the fact that the fee earner is a sole practitioner who has no juniors to delegate to, should not be the determinative factors. As with hourly rates the costs estimate supplied by the paying party may be of assistance. What grade of fee earner did they use? **48.48.3**

An hourly rate in excess of the guideline figures may be appropriate for Grade A fee earners in substantial and complex litigation where other factors, including the value of the litigation, the level of complexity, the urgency or importance of the matter as well as any international element would justify a significantly higher rate to reflect higher average costs.

Guideline Rates for Summary Assessment 2009

48.49 The following entries have been amended in the table (note that these rates are interim in nature in the sense that there remain some unresolved issues):

Band One				
Grade*	**A****	**B**	**C**	**D**
Guideline Rates	**213**	**189**	**158**	**116**
Aldershot, Farnham, Bournemouth (including Poole)				
Birmingham Inner				
Bristol				
Cambridge City, Harlow				
Canterbury, Maidstone, Medway & Tunbridge Wells				
Cardiff (Inner)				
Chelmsford South, Essex & East Suffolk				
Chester				
Fareham, Winchester				
Hampshire, Dorset, Wiltshire, Isle of Wight				
Kingston, Guildford, Reigate, Epsom				
Leeds Inner (within 2 kilometers radius of the City Art Gallery)				
Lewes				
Liverpool, Birkenhead				
Manchester Central				
Newcastle—City Centre (within a 2 mile radius of St Nicholas Cathedral)				
Norwich City				
Nottingham City				
Oxford, Thames Valley				
Southampton, Portsmouth				
Swindon, Basingstoke				
Watford				

Band Two				
Grade*	**A****	**B**	**C**	**D**
Guideline Rates	**198**	**174**	**144**	**116**
Bath, Cheltenham and Gloucester, Taunton, Yeovil				
Bury				
Chelmsford North, Cambridge County, Peterborough, Bury St E, Norfolk, Lowestoft				

Cheshire & North Wales

Coventry, Rugby, Nuneaton, Stratford and Warwick

Exeter, Plymouth

Hull (City)

Leeds Outer, Wakefield & Pontefract

Leigh

Lincoln

Luton, Bedford, St Albans, Hitchin, Hertford

Manchester Outer, Oldham, Bolton, Tameside

Newcastle (other than City Centre)

Nottingham & Derbyshire

Sheffield, Doncaster and South Yorkshire

Southport

St Helens

Stockport, Altrincham, Salford

Swansea, Newport, Cardiff (Outer)

Wigan

Wolverhampton, Walsall, Dudley & Stourbridge

York, Harrogate

Band Three				
Grade*	**A****	**B**	**C**	**D**
Guideline Rates	**198**	**174**	**144**	**109**
Birmingham Outer				
Bradford (Dewsbury, Halifax, Huddersfield, Keighley & Skipton)				
Cumbria				
Devon, Cornwall				
Grimsby, Skegness				
Hull Outer				
Kidderminster				
Northampton & Leicester				
Preston, Lancaster, Blackpool, Chorley, Accrington, Burnley, Blackburn, Rawenstall & Nelson				
Scarborough & Ripon				
Stafford, Stoke, Tamworth				
Teesside				
Worcester, Hereford, Evesham and Redditch				
Shrewsbury, Telford, Ludlow, Oswestry				
South & West Wales				

London Bands

Grade*	A**	B	C	D
City of London: EC1, EC2, EC3, EC4	402	291	222	136
Central London: W1, WC1, WC2, SW1	312	238	193	124
Outer London (All other London post codes: W, NW, N, E, SE, SW and Bromley, Croydon, Dartford, Gravesend and Uxbridge)	225–263	169–225	168	124

*There are four grades of fee earner:

A. Solicitors with over 8 years post qualification experience including at least 8 years litigation experience.
B. Solicitors and legal executives with over 4 years post qualification experience including at least 4 years litigation experience.
C. Other solicitors and legal executives and fee earners of equivalent experience.
D. Trainee solicitors, para legals and fee earners of equivalent experience.

Note: "Legal Executive" means a Fellow of the Institute of Legal Executives.

**An hourly rate in excess of the guideline figures may be appropriate for Grade A fee earners in substantial and complex litigation where other factors, including the value of the litigation, the level of complexity, the urgency or importance of the matter as well as any international element would justify a significantly higher rate to reflect higher average costs.

Counsel's Fees

48.50 The following table sets out figures based on Supreme Court Costs Office statistics dealing with run of the mill proceedings in the Queens Bench and Chancery Division and in the Administrative Court. The table gives figures for cases lasting up to an hour and up to half a day, in respect of counsel up to five years call, up to ten years call and over ten years call. It is emphasised that these figures are not recommended rates but it is hoped that they may provide a helpful starting point for judges when assessing counsel's fees. The appropriate fee in any particular case may be more or less than the figures appearing in the table, depending upon circumstances.

The table does not include any figures in respect of leading counsel's fees since such cases would self evidently be exceptional. Similarly, no figures are included for the Commercial Court or the Technology & Construction Court.

Table of Counsel's Fees

48.51

Queen's Bench	1 hour hearing	Half day hearing
Junior up to 5 years call	£259	£450
Junior 5—10 years call	£386	£767
Junior 10+ years call	£582	£1,164
Chancery Division	1 hour hearing	Half day hearing
Junior up to 5 years call	£291	£556
Junior 5—10 years call	£497	£931
Junior 10+ years call	£757	£1,397
Administrative Court	1 hour hearing	Halfday hearing
Junior up to 5 years call	£381	£582
Junior 5—10 years call	£698	£1,164
Junior 10+ years call	£989	£1,746

If the paying parties were represented by counsel, the fee paid to their counsel is an important factor but not a conclusive one on the question of fees payable to the receiving party's counsel.

In deciding upon the appropriate fee for the counsel the question is not simply one of counsel's experience and seniority but also of the level of counsel which the particular case merits.

Counsel's fees should not be allowed in cases in which it was not reasonable to have instructed counsel, but it must be borne in mind that, especially in substantial hearings, it may be more economical if the advocacy is conducted by counsel rather than a solicitor. In all cases the court should consider whether or not the decision to instruct counsel has led to an increase in costs and whether that increase is justifiable.

The Supreme Court Costs Office Guide

For the Supreme Court Costs Office Guide see Vol.2, Section 1C. **48.52**

PART 49

Specialist Proceedings

Contents

49.0.1

Editorial introduction

49.0.2 For application of CPR generally, see r.2.1 and commentary following that rule (para.2.1.1 above).

This rule expressly provides that the CPR shall apply to the proceedings listed therein, but "subject to the provisions of the relevant practice direction which applies to those proceedings". From time to time that list has been amended, most recently by the Civil Procedure (Amendment) Rules 2007 (SI 2007/2204).

"Specialist proceedings" should be distinguished from "specialist lists" (see para.2.3.14 above).

The relevant practice directions relating to the "specialist proceedings" referred to in r.49(2) are:

- Practice Direction—Applications under the Companies Acts and Related Legislation (see Vol.2 Sect.2G)
- Practice Direction—Order Under Section 127 Insolvency Act 1986 (see Vol.2 Sect.2G)

For detailed commentary on the effects of this rule, including an explanation of destinations in the CPR of proceedings originally listed in r.49(2), but since revoked, see Vol.2 Sect.12 (CPR: Application, Amendments and Interpretation), subss.C.2 and D.2 (paras 12–19 and 12–30).

Appeals in specialist proceedings

49.0.3 It should be noted that Practice Direction (Appeals) para.2A.1 refers to "specialist proceedings" in the form of proceedings "under the Companies Acts 1985 or 1989" (as distinct from in the form of proceedings as stated in r.49(2) and in the relevant practice directions). That paragraph indicates the routes of appeal that appeals from final decisions and other decisions made in the High Court or a county court (whether made by a Master, district judge, circuit judge or High Court judge) in such proceedings should take, subject to any permission requirements (see para.52PD.3.1 below).

49.1 **49—(1) These Rules shall apply to the proceedings listed in paragraph (2) subject to the provisions of the relevant practice direction which applies to those proceedings.**

(2) The proceedings referred to in paragraph (1) are proceedings under—

(a) the Companies Act 1985 [1];
(b) the Companies Act 1989 [2];
(c) the Companies Act 2006 [3]; and
(d) other legislation relating to companies.

---

[1] 1985 c.6.
[2] 1989 c.40.
[3] 2006 c.46.

PART 50

Application of the Schedules

Contents

 50.0.1

Editorial introduction

When originally enacted in 1998, the CPR ended with Pt 51. In this (then) penultimate, two Schedules to the CPR are introduced; Schedule 1 and Schedule 2 containing, respectively, certain RSC and CCR provisions (amended in various respects). In the years since, many of the "Schedule rules" have been revoked as new practice directions and rules replacing them (insofar as that has been necessary) have been given and enacted. 50.0.2

For a detailed explanation of the purpose and continuing effects of Pt 50 and the Schedules, including a list of the Schedule rules still in force, see Vol.2 Sect.12 (CPR: Application, Amendments and Interpretation), subs.C.3 (para.12–20 et seq).

50—(1) The Schedules to these Rules set out, with modifications, certain provisions previously contained in the Rules of the Supreme Court 1965 and the County Court Rules 1981. 50.1

(2) These Rules apply in relation to the proceedings to which the Schedules apply subject to the provisions in the Schedules and the relevant practice directions.

(3) A provision previously contained in the Rules of the Supreme Court 1965—

(a) is headed "RSC";

(b) is numbered with the Order and rule numbers it bore as part of the RSC; and

(c) unless otherwise stated in the Schedules or the relevant practice direction, applies only to proceedings in the High Court.

(4) A provision previously contained in the County Court Rules 1981—

(a) is headed "CCR";

(b) is numbered with the Order and rule numbers it bore as part of the CCR; and

(c) unless otherwise stated in the Schedules or the relevant practice direction, applies only to proceedings in the county court.

(5) A reference in a Schedule to a rule by number alone is a reference to the rule so numbered in the Order in which the reference occurs.

(6) A reference in a Schedule to a rule by number prefixed by "CPR" is a reference to the rule with that number in these Rules.

(7) In the Schedules, unless otherwise stated, "the Act" means—

(a) in a provision headed "RSC", the Supreme Court Act 1981; and

(b) in a provision headed "CCR", the County Courts Act 1984.

PART 51

Transitional Arrangements and Pilot Schemes

Contents

51.0.1

51.1 **51.1 A practice direction shall make provision for the extent to which these Rules shall apply to proceedings issued before 26 April 1999.**[1]

51.2 Practice directions may modify or disapply any provision of these rules—

(a) for specified periods; and

(b) in relation to proceedings in specified courts,

during the operation of pilot schemes for assessing the use of new practices and procedures in connection with proceedings.

Editorial introduction

51.1.1 Rule 51.2 was added to this Part by the Civil Procedure (Amendment No.4) Rules 2001 (SI 2001/2792) and by the same statutory instrument the heading to the Part was amended by the addition of the words "and Pilot Schemes". Thereafter this Part deals with two quite different matters, (1) the transitional arrangements affecting cases commenced before the CPR came into effect, and (2) pilot schemes under which particular variations of CPR practice and procedure could be tested.

Transitional arrangements in supplementing practice direction

51.1.2 The practice direction referred to in r.51.1 is Practice Direction (Transitional Arrangements) (see para.51PD.1 below). This supplementing practice direction was amended in March 1999 (adding para.19(3)(d)) and in May 2000 (adding para.19(4)). It contains transitional arrangements directed at proceedings issued before April 26, 1999, and not automatically stayed by the operation of para.19(1) of the practice direction (see para.51PD.19 below).

For a detailed explanation of the effect of those provisions, including information on applications under para.19(2) to lift automatic stays imposed by operation of para.19(1), see Vol.2 Sect.12 (CPR: Application, Amendments and Interpretation), Subsect.E (para.12–35 et seq).

Transitional arrangements in amending statutory instruments

51.1.3 Since they were enacted in 1998, the CPR have been amended by a number of statutory instruments. Some of those statutory instruments have contained within them transitional provisions affecting the particular amendments made by them.

For a complete list of amending statutory instruments, their commencement dates, and the complete texts of transitional provisions (if any) contained within them, see Vol.2 Sect.12 (CPR: Application, Amendments and Interpretation), Subsects. D.3 and D.4 (paras 12–31 and 12–32 et seq).

Pilot schemes

51.1.4 For details of practice directions modifying or disapplying CPR provisions during

---

[1] Amended by the Civil Procedure (Amendment No.4) Rules 2001 (SI 2001/2792). Rule 51.2 introduced by the Civil Procedure (Amendment No.4) Rules 2001 (SI 2001/2792).

the operation of pilot schemes, see Vol.2, Section 12 (CPR: Application, Amendments and Interpretation), subs.C.1 (para.12–18). Practice Direction—Automatic Orders Pilot Scheme was inserted in the CPR, as a practice direction supplementing Pt 51, by TSO CPR Update 47 (September 2008) (see para.51BPD.1 below).

Automatic strike out pilot scheme

By TSO CPR Update 47 (September 2008), Practice Direction (Automatic Orders **51.1.5** Pilot Scheme) was brought into effect. Initially, the scheme operates from October 1, 2008 to September 30, 2009 in the county courts at Chelmsford, Newcastle, Teeside, Watford and York.

The scheme provides that a party's claim, defence or counterclaim is automatically struck out if that party fails to file an allocation questionnaire or pre-trial checklist following notification by the court to do so. An automatic stay of one month will be granted if all the parties make such a request. The procedures set forth in the scheme affect the operation of various provisions in CPR Pt 26 (Case Management—Preliminary Stage) and Pt 28 (The Fast Track). They are modified accordingly by the practice direction.

PRACTICE DIRECTION—TRANSITIONAL ARRANGEMENTS

This Practice Direction supplements CPR Part 51

Contents of this Practice Direction

51PD.1 **1**(1) This Practice Direction deals with the application of the Civil Procedure Rules ("CPR") to proceedings issued before 26 April 1999 ("existing proceedings").

(2) In this Practice Direction "the previous rules" means as appropriate the Rules of the Supreme Court 1965 (" RSC") or County Court Rules 1981 (" CCR"), in force immediately before 26 April 1999.

General scheme of transitional arrangements

51PD.2 **2** The general scheme is—

(a) to apply the previous rules to undefended cases, allowing them to progress to their disposal; but

(b) to apply the CPR to defended cases so far as is practicable.

Where the previous rules will normally apply

General principle

51PD.3 **3** Where an initiating step has been taken in a case before 26 April 1999, in particular one that uses forms or other documentation required by the previous rules, the case will proceed in the first instance under the previous rules. Any step which a party must take in response to something done by another party in accordance with the previous rules must also be in accordance with those rules.

Responding to old process

51PD.4 **4** A party who is served with an old type of originating process (writ, summons etc.) on or after 26 April 1999 is required to respond in accordance with the previous rules and the instructions on any forms received with the originating process.

Filing and service of pleadings where old process served

51PD.5 **5** Where a case has been begun by an old type of originating process (whether served before or after 26 April 1999), filing and service of pleadings will continue according to the previous rules.

Automatic directions/discovery

51PD.6 **6**(1) *High Court*

Where the timetable for automatic directions under RSC Order 25, rule 8 or automatic discovery under RSC Order 24 has begun to apply to proceedings before 26 April 1999, those directions will continue to have effect on or after 26 April 1999.

(2) *County Court*

Where automatic directions under CCR Order 17, rule 11 have begun to apply to existing proceedings before 26 April 1999 or the court has sent out notice that automatic directions under CCR Order 17, rule 11 (Form **N450**) will apply (even if the timetable will not begin until 26 April 1999 or after), those directions will continue to have effect on or after 26 April 1999.

(3) However CCR Order 17, rule 11(9) will not apply and therefore proceedings will not be struck out where there has been no request for a hearing to be fixed within 15 months of the date when pleadings were deemed to close. (But see paragraph 19.)

(4) *High Court and County Court*

However, if the case comes before the court on or after 26 April 1999, the new rules may apply. (See paragraph 15.)

Default judgment

7(1) If a party wishes default judgment to be entered in existing proceedings, he must do so in accordance with the previous rules. **51PD.7**

(2) Where default judgment has been entered and there are outstanding issues to be resolved (e.g. damages to be assessed), the court officer may refer the proceedings to the judge, so that case management decisions about the proceedings and the conduct of the hearing can be made in accordance with the practice set out in paragraph 15.

(3) If a party needs to apply for permission to enter default judgment, he must make that application under CPR Part 23 (general rules about applications for court orders).

(4) An application to set aside judgment entered in default must be made under CPR Part 23 (general rules about applications for court orders) and CPR Part 13 (setting aside or varying default judgment) will apply to the proceedings as it would apply to default judgment entered under the CPR.

(5) CPR rule 15.11 (claims stayed if it is not defended or admitted) applies to these proceedings.

Judgment on admission in the county court

8(1) If a party to existing proceedings in the county court wishes to request judgment to be entered on an admission, he must do so in accordance with the previous rules. **51PD.8**

(2) Where judgment has been entered and there are outstanding issues to be resolved (e.g. damages to be assessed), the court officer may refer the proceedings to the judge, so that case management decisions about the proceedings and the conduct of the hearing can be made in accordance with the practice set out in paragraph 15.

(3) If a party needs to apply for permission to enter judgment, he must make that application under CPR Part 23 (general rules about applications for court orders).

Order inconsistent with CPR

9 Where a court order has been made before 26 April 1999, that order must still be complied with on or after 26 April 1999. **51PD.9**

Steps taken before 26 April 1999

51PD.10 **10**(1) Where a party has taken any step in the proceedings in accordance with the previous rules that step will remain valid on or after 26 April 1999.

(2) A party will not normally be required to take any action that would amount to taking that step again under the CPR. For example if discovery has been given, a party will not normally be required to provide disclosure under CPR Part 31.

Where the CPR will normally apply

General principle

51PD.11 **11 Where a new step is to be taken in any existing proceedings on or after 26 April 1999, it is to be taken under the CPR.**

Part 1 (Overriding objective) to apply

51PD.12 **12** Part 1 (Overriding objective) will apply to all existing proceedings from 26 April 1999 onwards.

Originating process

51PD.13 **13**(1) Only claim forms under the CPR will be issued by the court on or after 26 April 1999.

(2) If a request to issue an old type of originating process (writ, summons etc.) is received at the court on or after 26 April 1999 it will be returned unissued.

(3) An application made on or after 26 April 1999 to extend the validity of originating process issued before 26 April 1999 must be made in accordance with CPR Part 23 (general rules about applications for court orders), but the court will decide whether to allow the application in accordance with the previous law.

Application to the court

51PD.14 **14**(1) Any application to the court made on or after 26 April 1999 must be made in accordance with CPR Part 23 (General rules about applications for court orders).

(2) Any other relevant CPR will apply to the substance of the application, unless this practice direction provides otherwise. (See paragraphs 13(3) (application to extend the validity of originating process) and 18(2) (costs)).

(3) For example, a party wishing to apply for summary judgment must do so having regard to the test in CPR Part 24. A party wishing to apply for an interim remedy must do so under CPR Part 25 etc.

(4) Any other CPR will apply as necessary. For example, CPR Part 4 will apply as to forms and CPR Part 6 will apply to service of documents.

(5) If the pleadings have not been filed at court, the applicant must file all pleadings served when he files his application notice.

First time before a judge on or after 26 April 1999

15(1) When proceedings come before a judge (whether at a hearing or on paper) for the first time on or after 26 April 1999, he may direct how the CPR are to apply to the proceedings and may disapply certain provisions of the CPR. He may also give case management directions (which may include allocating the proceedings to a case management track). **51PD.15**

(2) The general presumption will be that the CPR will apply to the proceedings from then on unless the judge directs or this practice direction provides otherwise. (See paragraphs 13(3) (application to extend the validity of originating process) and 18(2) (costs)).

(3) If an application has been issed before 26 April 1999 and the hearing of the application has been set for a date on or after 26 April 1999, the general presumption is that the application will be decided having regard to the CPR. (For example an application for summary judgment issued before 26 April 1999, with a hearing date set for 1 May 1999, will be decided having regard to the test in CPR Part 24 (summary judgment).)

(4) When the first occasion on which existing proceedings are before a judge on or after 26 April 1999 is a trial or hearing of a substantive issue, the general presumption is that the trial or hearing will be conducted having regard to the CPR.

Where pleadings deemed to close on or after 26 April 1999

16(1) This paragraph applies to existing proceedings where pleadings are deemed to close on or after 26 April 1999. However, this paragraph does not apply to those county court proceedings where notice that automatic directions apply (Form **N450**) has been sent (in which case the automatic directions will apply—see paragraph 6). **51PD.16**

(2) CPR Part 26 (case management—preliminary stage) applies to these proceedings.

(3) If a defence is filed at court on or after 26 April 1999, the court will serve an allocation questionnaire where CPR rule 26.3 would apply, unless it dispenses with the need for one.

(4) If pleadings have not been filed at court (this will normally be the case in the Queen's Bench Division) the claimant must file copies of all the pleadings served within 14 days of the date that pleadings are deemed to close.

(5) Unless it dispenses with the need for one, the court will then serve an allocation questionnaire.

(6) In the previous rules pleadings are deemed to close:

(a) High Court—

(i) 14 days after service of any reply, or

(ii) if there is no reply, 14 days after service of the defence to counterclaim, or

(iii) if there is no reply or defence to counterclaim, 14 days after the service of the defence.

(b) County Court—

14 days after the delivery of a defence or, where a counterclaim is served with the defence, 28 days after the delivery of the defence.

(7) Where there are 2 or more defendants the court will normally wait until the claimant has filed copies of all the pleadings before serving an allocation questionnaire. However, the court may (in cases where there is a delay) serve allocation questionnaires despite the fact that pleadings have not closed in respect of any other defendant.

(8) The court will then allocate the proceedings in accordance with CPR, rule 26.5.

(9) The CPR will then apply generally to the proceedings.

Agreement to apply the CPR

51PD.17 **17** The parties may agree in writing that the CPR will apply to any proceedings from the date of the agreement. When they do so:

(a) all those who are parties at that time must agree,

(b) the CPR must apply in their entirety,

(c) the agreement is irrevocable,

(d) the claimant must file a copy of the agreement at court.

Costs

51PD.18 **18**(1) Any assessment of costs that takes place on or after 26 April 1999 will be in accordance with CPR Parts 43 to 48.

(2) However, the general presumption is that no costs for work undertaken before 26 April 1999 will be disallowed if those costs would have been allowed in a costs taxation before 26 April 1999.

(3) The decision as to whether to allow costs for work undertaken on or after 26 April will generally be taken in accordance with CPR Parts 43 to 48.

(The costs practice direction contains more information on the operation of the transitional arrangements in relation to costs.)

Existing proceedings after one year

51PD.19 **19**(1) If any existing proceedings have not come before a judge, at a hearing or on paper, between 26 April 1999 and 25 April 2000, those proceedings shall be stayed.

(2) Any party to those proceedings may apply for the stay to be lifted.

(3) Proceedings of the following types will not be stayed as a result of this provision:

(a) where the case has been given a fixed trial date which is after 25 April 2000,

(b) personal injury cases where there is no issue on liability but the proceedings have been adjourned by court order to determine the prognosis,

(c) where the court is dealing with the continuing administration of an estate or a trust or a receivership,

(d) applications relating to funds in court.

(4) For the purposes of this paragraph proceedings will not be "existing proceedings" once final judgment has been given.

PRACTICE DIRECTION—AUTOMATIC ORDERS PILOT SCHEME

51BPD.1 *This Practice Direction supplements CPR Part 26 and 28*

Contents of this Practice Direction

1.1 This Practice Direction is made under rule 51.2. It provides for a pilot scheme ("the Automatic Orders Pilot Scheme") to—

(1) operate from 1st October 2008 to 30th September 2009;

(2) operate in the county courts at Chelmsford, Newcastle, Teesside, Watford and York; and

(3) apply to claims started on or after 1st October 2008.

1.2 The Automatic Orders Pilot Scheme will apply to claims where—

(1) all parties request a stay of proceedings for one month;

(2) any party fails to file an allocation questionnaire; or

(3) in cases with only one claimant and one defendant and which are allocated to the fast track, a party fails to file a pre-trial checklist.

Amendments to Part 26 and Part 28

51BPD.2 **2** During the operation of the Automatic Orders Pilot Scheme—

Stay of proceedings for one month

(1) Rule 26.4 is modified by substituting for paragraph (2) the following—

"(2)(a) Where all parties request a stay under paragraph (1), the proceedings will be stayed for one month and the court will notify the parties to that effect.

(b) Any request for a further stay will be considered under rule 26.4(3).

(c) Where the court, of its own initiative, considers that such a stay would be appropriate, the court will direct that the proceedings, either in whole or in part, be stayed for one month, or for such specified period as the court considers appropriate.".

Failure by a party to file an allocation questionnaire

(2) Practice Direction (Case Management - Preliminary Stage: Allocation and Re-allocation) supplementing Part 26 is modified by substituting for paragraph 2.5 the following—

"2.5(1) Where a party does not file an allocation questionnaire within the time specified by Form N152, the court will serve a notice on that party requiring the allocation questionnaire to be filed within 7 days from service of the notice.

(2) Where a party does not file the allocation questionnaire within the period specified in the notice served pursuant to paragraph (1) then that party's claim, defence or counterclaim (as appropriate) will automatically be struck out without further order of the court.".

Failure to file a pre-trial checklist in a case allocated to the fast track

(3) Where there is only one claimant and one defendant and

the case is allocated to the fast track then rule 28.5 is modified by substituting for paragraphs (3) and (4) the following—

"(3) Where a party does not file a pre-trial checklist the court will serve a notice on that party requiring the pre-trial checklist to be filed within 7 days from service of the notice.

(4) Where that party does not file the pre-trial checklist within the period specified in the notice served pursuant to paragraph (3) then that party's claim, defence or counterclaim (as appropriate) will automatically be struck out without further order of the court.

(5) If—

(a) a party has failed to give all the information requested by the pre-trial checklist; or

(b) the court considers that a hearing is necessary to enable it to decide what directions to give in order to complete preparation of the case for trial,

the court may give such directions as it thinks appropriate.".

(4) Where there is only one claimant and one defendant and the case is allocated to the fast track then the Practice Direction supplementing Part 28 is modified by—

(a) substituting for paragraph 6.1(3) the following—

(3) When all the pre-trial checklists have been filed the court file will be placed before a judge for directions.";

and

(b) disapplying paragraphs 6.4 and 6.5.

PART 52

APPEALS

52.0.1 **Contents**

Editorial introduction

52.0.2 Under the former procedural rules the rights of appeal in civil litigation were extensive. A disappointed litigant could generally appeal to the Court of Appeal against a final decision, however inconsequential his litigation may be. In the case of "interlocutory" decisions two-stage appeals (first to the judge and then to the Court of Appeal) were commonplace. The requirement for leave to appeal was gradually extended over the years, but the philosophy remained that the litigant should generally have two bites at the cherry. Appeals from a district judge or master to a judge were full rehearings. Appeals to the Court of Appeal were limited rehearings.

Between 1994 and 2000 the reform of civil appeals was under active consideration. This review continued both during and after the Woolf Inquiry.

Woolf Report

Lord Woolf's final report on "Access to Justice" (HMSO, July 1996), which followed a two year inquiry, dealt with appeals at Ch.14. Lord Woolf defined the purpose of appeals in para.2 of that chapter: **52.0.3**

"Appeals serve two purposes: the private purpose, which is to do justice in particular cases by correcting wrong decisions, and the public purpose, which is to ensure public confidence in the administration of justice by making such corrections and to clarify and develop the law and to set precedents."

Lord Woolf urged that these purposes should be achieved without introducing unnecessary costs and delay. He recommended (amongst other matters) that leave to appeal should be required for all interlocutory appeals; that some appeals should lie to courts lower than the Court of Appeal; that all appeals should be of the "limited Court of Appeal rehearing type"; that there should be greater uniformity in the procedure for statutory appeal to the courts; and that the rules on appeals should be rationalised, so that there may be a single procedure for all appeals. Lord Woolf's recommendations on appeals were provisional, since in March 1996 the Lord Chancellor announced that a full review of the civil division of the Court of Appeal would be undertaken, starting two months after publication of the Woolf Report.

Bowman Report

In October 1996 a full review of the civil division of the Court of Appeal was instituted under the chairmanship of Sir Jeffery Bowman. The review team included Lord Woolf. Its report ("the Bowman Report") was published in September 1997. Its recommendations were along the lines foreshadowed by the Woolf Report, but were very much more detailed. The report was backed by statistical research into the manner in which applications and appeals currently arrived at the Court of Appeal: see the "mapping study" at Appendix 7 to the Bowman Report. The review team also surveyed the procedures operated by appellate courts in Ontario, New York, San Francisco and Washington DC. These procedures are summarised in Appendix 2 to the Bowman Report. **52.0.4**

Chapter 2 of the Bowman Report discussed the principles underlying a civil appeals system. The same considerations of justice, expedition and moderation of costs should apply to appeals as to first instance litigation. An appeal should not be seen as an automatic further stage in a case. A dissatisfied litigant's only "right" is to have his case looked at by a higher court (in the context of a permission application) to see if there appears to have been an injustice. If he crosses that threshold, then he should be allowed to appeal. The review team summarised the purpose of appeals in this way:

"There is a private and a public purpose of appeals in civil cases. The private purpose is to correct an error, unfairness or wrong exercise of discretion which has led to an unjust result. The public purpose is to ensure public confidence in the administration of justice and, in appropriate cases, to:

— Clarify and develop the law, practice and procedure; and

— Help maintain the standards of first instance courts and tribunals."

The review team accepted the principle of proportionality. Appeals should be dealt with in ways that are proportionate to the grounds of complaint and the subject matter of the dispute. The review team further considered that more than one level of appeal could not normally be justified, except where there was an important point of principle or practice involved.

The Bowman Report made 146 detailed recommendations, which were in line with the general philosophy set out in Ch.2 of the report. Many of these recommendations were implemented by the Access to Justice Act 1999 and CPR Pt 52, with effect from May 2, 2000.

Access to Justice Act 1999

The Access to Justice Act 1999 (Vol.2, Section 9A) paved the way for the reforms to civil appeals, which were introduced in May 2000. Section 54 enables rules of court to impose a "permission" requirement upon any appeal to a county court, the High Court or the Court of Appeal. Section 55 imposes restrictions upon second appeals. Only the Court of Appeal can grant permission for second appeals and the criteria for granting such permission are strict. **52.0.5**

Section 56 empowers the Lord Chancellor to provide for the destination of appeals by means of statutory instrument, after first consulting with the Heads of Divisions and the Master of the Rolls. The Lord Chancellor has exercised this power by making the Access to Justice Act 1999 (Destination of Appeals) Order 2000. The Order is set out in Vol.2, Section 9A. It is discussed below under the heading "Destination of Appeals". Section 57 enables appeals to junior appellate courts to be re-assigned to the Court of Appeal. Sections 58 and 59 amend provisions of the Supreme Court Act 1981 relating to the civil division of the Court of Appeal. More specific reference to the Access to Justice Act 1999 will be made in the commentary following individual rules.

CPR Part 52

52.0.6 Part 52, which came into force on May 2, 2000, created a uniform system of appeals. It replaced the former RSC O.55 (appeals to High Court from court, tribunal or person), O.56 (appeals to High Court by case stated), O.58 (appeals from masters, registrars, referees and judges), O.59 (appeals to the Court of Appeal), O.60 (appeals to the Court of Appeal from the Restrictive Practices Court) and O.61 (appeals from tribunals to Court of Appeal by case stated).

Part 52 regulates not only appeals from one court to another, but also appeals to the courts from tribunals and similar bodies pursuant to statute. Section III of the practice direction sets out provisions about specific appeals. These modify the general provisions of Pt 52, to the extent set out in paras 20 to 24 of the practice direction, but only in respect of specified appeals.

CPR r.2.1(2) states that the CPR do not apply to all civil proceedings, e.g. insolvency proceedings and family proceedings. It should be noted, however, that the ambit of Pt 52 is wider. Part 52 applies to some of the proceedings specified in r.2.1 as falling outside the scope of the CPR. See para.2 of the Practice Direction and the commentary following r.52.1 below.

General comments on the reforms introduced in May 2000

52.0.7 The changes which came into effect on May 2, 2000 were described by Brooke L.J. in *Tanfern Ltd v Cameron MacDonald (Practice Note)* [2000] 1 W.L.R. 1311 as "the most significant changes in the arrangements for appeals in civil proceedings in this country for 125 years" (judgment para.50). The reforms were, broadly speaking, welcomed by N.H. Andrews in "A new system of civil appeals and a new set of problems" [2000] C.L.J. 464. Andrews noted that the Court of Appeal's law–making role would be enhanced; that the changes would reduce the delay, expense and uncertainty of civil proceedings; and that there would be a greater incentive for litigants to "get it right first time round". However, these changes would reduce the chances of rectifying defective decisions. This is the price paid for achieving the impressive benefits of the new system of appeals. Andrews noted that there might be some tension between the effect of these reforms and the effect of the House of Lords' decision in *Arthur JS Hall & Co v Simons* [2002] 1 A.C. 615 (which was given on July 20, 2000).

Pre-2000 authority

52.0.8 The changes made in 2000 are so fundamental that citation of authority on the former rules is of limited assistance in resolving questions which arise concerning Pt 52. This does not, however, mean that experience gained from the old rules or judicial analysis of those rules should be ignored. The commentary to RSC Ords 55, 56, 58 and 59 in the Supreme Court Practice 1999 neatly distils the authorities and learning which accumulated over the last 125 years of the second millenium.

Terminology used in this commentary

52.0.9 In this commentary the terms "appeal", "appeal court", "lower court", "appellant", "respondent" and "appeal notice" have the meanings assigned to them in r.52.1(3). In addition:

"junior appellate court" means any appeal court below the level of the Court of Appeal;

"he" means "he or she";

(for the avoidance of doubt) "appeal" includes an appeal by a respondent, i.e. what has traditionally been called a cross-appeal.

"The Destination Order" means the Access to Justice Act 1999 (Destination of Appeals) Order 2000.

Overriding objective

52.0.10 Rule 1.2, which states that the court must seek to give effect to the overriding objective (see r.1.1) when it exercises any power given to it by the Rules, or interprets any rule, applies to the provisions of Pt 52 as to other parts of the CPR.

Destinations of appeals—routes of appeals

Section 16(1) of the Supreme Court Act 1981 provides that subject to certain exceptions (e.g. direct appeals to the House of Lords) the Court of Appeal shall have jurisdiction "to hear and determine appeals from any judgment or order of the High Court". Section 77(1) of the County Courts Act 1984 provides that, subject to specified exceptions, if a party to proceedings in a county court "is dissatisfied with the determination of the judge or jury, he may appeal from it to the Court of Appeal ..." These provisions are set out in Vol.2, s.9A. **52.0.11**

The Destination Order —In the exercise of his power under s.56 of the Access to Justice Act 1999 the Lord Chancellor made the Access to Justice Act 1999 (Destination of Appeals) Order 2000, which is referred to in this commentary as "the Destination Order". The Destination Order is reproduced at Vol.2, s.9A. The Destination Order provides that a number of appeals which (under the statutes referred to in the previous paragraph) would otherwise lie to the Court of Appeal shall now be dealt with by a lower court. The Destination Order also provides a summary of the destinations for different types of civil appeals.

The destination arrangements are restated in paras 2A.1 to 2A.5 of the practice direction, where they are supplemented by further guidance. The court or judge to which any appeal is to be made is set out in three tables attached to para.2A.1.

The general principle is that appeal lies to the next level of judge in the court hierarchy. See *Tanfern Ltd v Cameron-MacDonald (Practice Note)* [2000] 1 W.L.R. 1311 at para.15.

Article 2 of the Destination Order provides that in the High Court appeals lies from a master or district judge of the High Court to a High Court judge. Article 3 provides that appeal lies from a district judge of a county court to a judge of a county court (i.e. to a circuit judge), and that appeal lies from any other decision of a county court (i.e. from a circuit judge or recorder) to the High Court.

The effects of arts 4(a) and 4(b) —Article 4 of the Destination Order sets out two exceptions to the general provisions contained in arts 2 and 3. These two exceptions appear in art.4(a) and art.4(b). The general effect of these exceptions is to provide that appeals from county courts (other than in family proceedings) will lie to the High Court, rather than to the Court of Appeal.

The effect of art.4(a), as amended by the Civil Procedure (Modification of Enactments) Order 2003 (SI 2003/490), is as follows. The normal route of appeal will not be followed where a district judge or a circuit judge in a county court, or a master or a district judge in the High Court, gives the "final decision" in a multi-track claim made under CPR Pt 7 and allocated to the multi-track under those rules. In such a case appeal lies directly to the Court of Appeal. This exception is reflected in Table 1 attached to para.2A.1 in the practice direction.

It should be noted that art.4 (a) does not apply (and therefore the normal destination arrangements apply) to Pt 8 claims, which are allocated to the multi-track under r.8.9(c).

The exception in art.4(a) has no application to a case which was not allocated to the multi-track. This is so even if the district judge regarded the case as suitable for the multi-track and would have so allocated it, had he appreciated that the allocation was important. See *Clark (Inspector of Taxes) v Perks* [2001] 1 W.L.R. 17 at paras 7 and 54. The exception in art.4(a) does not apply to a case which was allocated to the multi-track after the decision under appeal had been made: *Milward v Three Rivers District Council* CAT, October 25, 2000.

The effect of art.4(b), as amended by the Civil Procedure (Modification of Enactments) Order 2002 (SI 2002/439) and the Civil Procedure (Modification of Enactments) Order 2003 (*op. cit.*), is as follows. Where a final decision is made in certain specialist proceedings, appeal lies directly to the Court of Appeal, whatever level of judge made the "final decision". This exception also is reflected in Table 1 attached to para.2A.1 in the practice direction.

The destination of any second appeal is governed by art.5 of the Destination Order. Any decision which was made on an appeal to a county court or the High Court (other than from an officer of the court authorised to assess costs) can only be appealed to the Court of Appeal.

The meaning of "final decision" —If the effects of the exceptions to the general principle stated in paras (a) and (b) of art.4 of the Destination Order are to be properly understood, it is necessary to be clear about what is meant by "final decision". This matter is dealt with by paras (2)(c) and (3) of art.1 of the Destination Order. As is explained immediately below, these paragraphs are repeated in and amplified by provisions in the practice direction. The application of these provisions has occasioned difficulty and the Court of Appeal has sought to explain them in a number of cases; notably in *Tanfern Ltd v Cameron-MacDonald (Practice Note), op. cit.*, *Lloyd Jones v T. Mobile (UK) Ltd* [2003] EWCA Civ 1162; [2003] 3 E.G.L.R. 55 and *Scribes West Ltd v Relsa Anstalt (Practice Note)* [2004] EWCA Civ 965; [2005] 1 W.L.R. 1839.

Paragraph (2)(c) of art.1 of the Destination Order states that "final decision" means a decision of a court "that would finally determine (subject to any possible appeal or detailed assessment of costs) the entire proceedings whichever way the court decided the issue before it". This includes, not only the court's decision on the merits of a claim, but also as to where the liability for the costs of the claim (or issue) should fall: see *Dooley v Parker* [2002] EWCA Civ 96. The terms of para.(2)(c) are repeated in para.2A.2 of the practice direction where in addition, by way of further explanation, it is stated (following what was said in the *Tanfern Ltd* case, *op. cit.*, para.18), that a case management decision, the grant or refusal of interim relief, a summary judgment, or a striking out, are not final decisions for the purpose of determining the appropriate route of appeal. For the avoidance of doubt, para.2A.4 of the practice direction states that an order made on a summary or detailed assessment of costs, or on an application to enforce a final decision, is not a final decision (see further *Tanfern Ltd*, *op. cit.*, para.17, as explained in *Dooley, op. cit.*, para.7).

Paragraph (3) of art.1 of the Destination Order states that a decision of a court "shall be treated as a final decision" where two conditions are met: first, the decision is made at the conclusion of part of a hearing or trial which has been split into parts, and secondly, the decision would, if made at the conclusion of that hearing or trial, be a final decision under para.(2)(c). This is repeated in para.2A.3 of the practice direction where in addition it is stated, again by way of further explanation (following what was said in the *Tanfern Ltd*. case, *op. cit.*, para.17), that a judgment on liability at the end of a split trial and a judgment at the conclusion of the assessment of damages following a judgment on liability, are both final decisions for this purpose. In *Persaud v Dulovic* [2002] EWHC 889 (QB); [2002] C.P. Rep. 56, it was held by Silber J. (partly on the basis that "split into parts" does not necessarily mean split by an order of the court) that an appeal from a county court judge's dismissal of an application by a party to proceedings for a wasted costs order, against the legal representative of his opponent in those proceedings made and dealt with after trial, was an appeal from a final decision and therefore the proper route for appeal was not to the High Court but to the Court of Appeal (see further *Persaud v Persaud* [2003] EWCA Civ 394; [2003] P.N.L.R. 26). Furthermore, where a judge having upheld a submission of no case to answer enters judgment for the defendant at "half time", that constitutes a final decision for the purposes of the Destination Order: see *Graham v Chorley BC* [2006] EWCA Civ 92.

Despite certain observations in *Roerig v Valiant Trawlers Ltd* [2002] EWCA Civ 21; [2002] 1 W.L.R. 2304, recourse should not be had to the pre-CPR case-law as an aid to interpreting or applying the Destination Order: *Scribes West Ltd v Relsa Anstalt (Practice Note)* [2004] EWCA Civ 965 at [22]–[25]; [2005] 1 W.L.R. 1839.

The further explanations given in para.2A.2 of the practice direction of what are not, and in para.2A.3 of what are, final decisions (going beyond art.4), were added when paras 2A.1 to 2A.5 were re-issued with effect from April 6, 2006. As indicated above, they take into account guidance given by the Court of Appeal in reported cases.

The Court of Appeal

52.0.12 The constitution, jurisdiction and powers of the Court of Appeal are governed by ss.1–3, 15–18 and 53–58 of the Supreme Court Act 1981. "The Court of Appeal is a statutory creation with the boundaries of its jurisdiction identified by, and subject to, restrictions imposed by statute": *Westminster City Council v O'Reilly* [2003] EWCA Civ 1007 at [6]; [2004] 1 W.L.R. 195.

The Court of Appeal's power to hear appeals from the High Court is derived from ss.16–18 of the Supreme Court Act 1981. The powers of the Court of Appeal in relation to appeals from county courts are set out in ss.77–81 of the County Courts Act 1984. Where statute provides that any order, judgment or decision of a court or tribunal is final, the Court of Appeal has no power to hear an appeal: see s.18(1)(c) of the Supreme Court Act 1981 and *Westminster City Council v O'Reilly* [2003] EWCA Civ 1007; [2004] 1 W.L.R. 195 (no appeal to Court of Appeal from decision of the High Court on an appeal by way of case stated from licensing justices pursuant to s.111 of the Magistrates' Courts Act 1980). In *Farley v Child Support Agency* [2005] EWCA Civ 869 the Court of Appeal handed down a judgment without jurisdiction, since all parties and the court had overlooked the above provisions. The court then used a highly accelerated judicial review procedure, in order to legitimise that judgment.

The relevant provisions of the Supreme Court Act 1981 and the County Courts Act 1984 are set out in Vol.2, Section 9A.

The Court of Appeal has jurisdiction to hear appeals in cases where the appellant has obtained a "leapfrog" certificate under Part 2 of the Administration of Justice Act 1969, but subsequently does not pursue his appeal to the House of Lords because of restrictions placed by the House of Lords upon its grant of leave to appeal: see *Jones v Ceredigion CC* [2005] EWCA Civ 986; [2005] 1 W.L.R. 3626.

In relation to issues of public importance, the Court of Appeal has power to entertain an appeal, with the consent of all parties, even though the dispute between those parties has been settled at the time of the hearing: *Bowman v Fels* [2005] EWCA Civ 226; [2005] 1 W.L.R. 383 at [11]–[18].

Appeals are against orders, not reasoned judgments

Section 16 of the Supreme Court Act 1981 provides: "Subject as otherwise provided **52.0.13**
by this or any other Act ... the Court of Appeal shall have jurisdiction to hear and determine appeals from any judgment or order of the High Court." Accordingly appeal lies against the order made by the lower court, not against the reasons which that court gave for its decision or the findings which it made along the way. Thus a party who has been wholly successful in obtaining or (as the case may be) resisting the relief sought cannot appeal against the judgment, in order to challenge findings made: *Lake v Lake* [1955] P 336, CA (a decision based upon s.27(1) of the Supreme Court of Judicature (Consolidation) Act 1925, which, so far as material, was in the same terms as s.16 of the Supreme Court Act 1981). If the court wishes to enable a party to appeal against a particular finding contained in the judgment, it may make a declaration embodying that finding. See *Compagnie Noga D'Importation Et D'Exportation SA v Australia and New Zealand Banking Group Ltd* [2002] EWCA Civ 1142; [2003] 1 W.L.R. 307.

By way of exception to the principles stated above, in *Morina v Secretary of State for Work and Pensions* [2007] EWCA Civ 749 the Court of Appeal held that it was not precluded from hearing appeals by the Secretary of State on jurisdictional points from a social security commissioner, even though the Secretary of State had "won" before the commissioner. In each of the two cases under consideration the Secretary of State had lost on the jurisdictional points, but won on the merits before the commissioner, with the result that the Secretary of State was the overall victor below. Nevertheless there was good reason for the jurisdictional points to be decided by the Court of Appeal.

A further consequence of section 16 of the Supreme Court Act 1981 is that no appeal against a judgment is possible unless and until the lower court makes the order which is foreshadowed by that judgment: *Re Mathew* [2001] B.P.I.R. 531.

No appeal from High Court to Court of Appeal in any criminal cause or matter

Section 18(1) of the Supreme Court Act 1981 provides: "No appeal shall lie to the **52.0.14**
Court of Appeal—(a) ... from any judgment of the High Court in any criminal cause or matter". In *Amand v Secretary of State for Home Affairs* [1943] A.C. 147 an order refusing *habeas corpus* to a person who had been arrested for the purpose of being handed over to a foreign state for trial was held to have been made in a "criminal cause or matter". Viscount Simon LC stated that the nature and character of the proceeding in which *habeas corpus* was sought provided the test. In *US Government v Montgomery* [2001] UKHL 3; [2001] 1 W.L.R. 196 proceedings under s.77 of the Criminal Justice Act 1988, which were commenced in consequence of orders made in criminal proceedings in the United States, were held not to be a "criminal cause or matter". Accordingly, the Court of Appeal had jurisdiction to hear the appeal. Lord Hoffmann (with whom Lord Cooke, Lord Hutton and Lord Scott agreed) stated at para 22:

"... the jurisdiction conferred upon the High Court under Pt VI of the 1988 Act is a civil jurisdiction, notwithstanding that that jurisdiction exists to enforce or determine disputes over the debts or proprietary rights created or consequent upon a confiscation order made by a criminal court."

In *R. (Mehmet) v Clerk to the Justices of Miskin, Cynon Valley & Merthyr Tydfil Petty Sessional Divisions* [2002] EWCA Civ 1248, the Court of Appeal held that an order of the Divisional Court refusing the claimant permission to seek judicial review of the assessment of his costs following acquittal in the magistrates' court was a "judgment of the High Court in a criminal cause or matter". Consequently the Court of Appeal had no jurisdiction to hear the claimant's application for permission to appeal. In reaching this conclusion Brooke L.J. applied the following dictum of Sir John Donaldson MR in *Carr v Atkins* [1987] Q.B. 963 at 967: "The nature of an order made or refused in judicial review proceedings must depend not upon that order but upon the order that is sought to be reviewed."

When the Administrative Court hears judicial review proceedings arising out of criminal matters, no appeal lies to the Court of Appeal: *R. (SW Yorkshire Mental Health NHS Trust) v Bradford Crown Court* [2003] EWCA Civ 1857; [2004] 1 W.L.R. 1664; *R. (Aru) v Chief Constable of Merseyside Police* [2004] EWCA Civ 199; [2004] 1 W.L.R. 1697.

Bail pending appeal

52.0.15 In *R. (Sezek) v SSHD* [2001] EWCA Civ 795 the question arose whether the Court of Appeal had jurisdiction to grant bail in civil proceedings concerning immigration. Peter Gibson L.J., giving the judgment of the court, stated at [16] that the High Court had power in judicial review proceedings to make ancillary orders temporarily releasing an applicant from detention. Accordingly, on an appeal in those proceedings by virtue of s.15(3) of the Supreme Court Act 1981 the Court of Appeal can make the like order. Nevertheless the Court of Appeal, in making such a decision, should give great weight to the fact that the Secretary of State has decided that the individual should be detained and to the reasons why the Secretary of State opposes release.

In an appeal to the Court of Appeal from the Special Immigration Appeals Commission ("SIAC") concerning certification, it was held that the court had no jurisdiction to hear an appeal against the grant or refusal of bail by *SIAC: G v Secretary of State for the Home Department* [2004] EWCA Civ 265; [2004] 1 W.L.R. 1349. However, the web of statutory provisions governing these matters is subject to frequent and continuing amendments.

The problem of vexatious litigation

52.0.16 In *Bhamjee v Forsdick (No.2)* [2003] EWCA Civ 1113; [2004] 1 W.L.R. 88 the Court of Appeal addressed the problem of vexatious litigants. These are a tiny minority of litigants who will not take "no" for an answer, and who bombard the courts with unmeritorious applications. A consequence of the reforms introduced in May 2000 is that respondents are generally not "vexed" by the appeals which such individuals launch. However, these appeals do impose a substantial burden on appeal courts, which have to process and, in due course, refuse the applications for permission to appeal.

The Court of Appeal in *Bhamjee* designed a new form of order, the "general civil restraint order", which will prevent litigants of the type described from commencing any action or making any application without prior permission from the court (to be dealt with in writing). The Court of Appeal further held that if a litigant subject to an extended civil restraint order or a general civil restraint order persists in making hopeless applications, then a High Court judge or a designated civil judge (or his deputy) may give a direction prohibiting him from applying for permission to appeal: see *Bhamjee* at [51]. The Rule Committee subsequently codified the effect of *Bhamjee*: see CPR r.3.11 and the practice direction on civil restraint orders supplementing r.3.11. Any judge proceeding under these provisions must allow the litigant a proper opportunity to prepare and present his case: *R (Kumar) v Secretary of State for Constitutional Affairs* [2006] EWCA Civ 990; [2007] 1 W.L.R. 536.

In *Perotti v Collyer-Bristow* [2004] EWCA Civ 639; [2004] 4 All E.R. 53 the claimant made a batch of hopeless applications to the Court of Appeal. In the previous seven years he had made 80 applications to the Court of Appeal, only two of which had been allowed. The Court of Appeal concluded that the existing extended civil restraint order provided insufficient protection against the nuisance posed by the claimant's litigious activities. The Court directed that for the next two years any application made by the claimant to the Court of Appeal in any matter not embraced by the extended civil restraint order should be considered only on paper by a judge of the Court of Appeal (unless that judge directed an oral hearing). The decision on paper would be final and not subject to reconsideration at an oral hearing. It should be noted, however, that (save in respect of family proceedings) the introduction of r.52.3(4A) in 2006 has removed the mischief with which *Perotti* was concerned.

Any appeal court dismissing an application for permission to appeal or an appeal, which it considers to be totally without merit, must (a) record that fact in its order and (b) consider whether to make a civil restraint order: see r.52.10 (5) and (6).

See further Vol.2, para.9A–150.

Publication of Court of Appeal judgments and related information

All substantive decisions of the Court of Appeal are now published, within three days of becoming available, on the website of the British and Irish Legal Information Institute: *http://www.bailii.org* [Accessed January 7, 2008]. **52.0.17**

Much useful information about the civil division of the Court of Appeal and its workings can be found on the court's website: *http://www.hmcourts-service.gov.uk/cms/civilappeals.htm* [Accessed January 7, 2008]. This website includes a simple interactive guide to routes of appeal.

I. General Rules about Appeals

Scope and interpretation[1]

52.1—(1) The rules in this Part apply to appeals to— **52.1**

(a) the civil division of the Court of Appeal;

(b) the High Court; and

(c) a county court.

(2) This Part does not apply to an appeal in detailed assessment proceedings against a decision of an authorised court officer.

(Rules 47.20 to 47.23 deal with appeals against a decision of an authorised court officer in detailed assessment proceedings)

(3) In this Part—

(a) "appeal" includes an appeal by way of case stated;

(b) "appeal court" means the court to which an appeal is made;

(c) "lower court" means the court, tribunal or other person or body from whose decision an appeal is brought;

(d) "appellant" means a person who brings or seeks to bring an appeal;

(e) "respondent" means—

(i) a person other than the appellant who was a party to the proceedings in the lower court and who is affected by the appeal; and

(ii) a person who is permitted by the appeal court to be a party to the appeal; and

(f) "appeal notice" means an appellant's or respondent's *notice.*

(4) This Part is subject to any rule, enactment or practice direction which sets out special provisions with regard to any particular category of appeal.

---

[1] Introduced by the Civil Procedure (Amendment) Rules 2000 (SI 2000/221) and amended by the Civil Procedure (Amendment No.4) Rules 2000 (SI 2000/2092) and the Civil Procedure (Amendment No.4) Rules 2005 (SI 2005/3515).

The broad scope of Part 52

52.1.1 The language of r.52.1.1 indicates the broad scope of Pt 52. Part 52 embraces appeals to county courts, the High Court and the Court of Appeal.

> "It encompasses, not only appeals where the lower court was itself a court, but also statutory appeals from the decisions of tribunals, ministers or other bodies or persons. Within the court system, it applies to an appeal from a district judge to a circuit judge, just as it applies to an appeal from a High Court judge to the Court of Appeal. Subject to rule 52.1 (4) and paragraph 17.1 (4) of the practice direction, it applies to a wide variety of statutory appeals where the nature of the decision appealed against and the procedure by which it was reached may differ substantially."

(Per May L.J. in *EI Dupont Nemours & Co v ST Dupont* [2003] EWCA Civ 1368 at [92]); [2006] 1 W.L.R. 2793).

The broad scope of CPR Pt 52 is also apparent from para.2A of the practice direction (re routes of appeal within the court system), sect.II of the practice direction (re statutory appeals and appeals by way of case stated) and sect.III of the practice direction (which makes detailed provision for a variety of specific appeals). See also the introductory commentary to Pt 52, set out above.

Part 52 also applies to an appeal under the Party Wall etc. Act 1996 from the decision of a surveyor appointed under that Act: see *Zissis v Lukomski* [2006] EWCA Civ 341; [2006] 1 W.L.R. 2778.

Part 52 applies to appeals in insolvency proceedings, only to the extent provided in the Insolvency Proceedings Practice Direction.

Part 52 applies to appeals in proceedings to which Pt 76 (Prevention of Terrorism Act 2005) relates and to appeals in proceedings to which Pt 79 relates, subject to certain modifications (see, respectively, r.76.16 and r.79.13).

Appeals in contempt proceedings

52.1.2 Section 13 of the Administration of Justice Act 1960 (which is set out in Vol.2, Section 9B) provides:

> "(1) Subject to the provisions of this section, an appeal shall lie under this section from any order or decision of a court in the exercise of jurisdiction to punish for contempt of court (including criminal contempt); and in relation to any such order or decision the provisions of this section shall have effect in substitution for any other enactment relating to appeals in civil or criminal proceedings.
>
> (2) An appeal under this section shall lie in any case at the instance of the defendant and, in the case of an application for committal or attachment, at the instance of the applicant; and the appeal shall lie...
>
> (b) from an order or decision of a county court ... to the civil division of the Court of Appeal..."

The effect of CPR r.52.1(4) is that the right of appeal to the Court of Appeal under s.13 of the Administration of Justice Act 1960 remains in effect: see *Hampshire CC v Gillingham* (CAT) June 22, 2000 and *L.B. Barnet v Hurst* [2002] EWCA Civ 1009; [2003] 1 W.L.R. 722. As to whether and when permission to appeal is required in contempt proceedings, see the commentary following r.52.3 below.

If a circuit judge in the county court makes a committal order or other order in contempt proceedings, appeal lies to the Court of Appeal under s.13(2) of the 1960 Act. If a district judge makes a committal order or other order in contempt proceedings, appeal will ordinarily lie to a circuit judge in the county court. Alternatively, and exceptionally, appeal may lie to the Court of Appeal either by application of *King v Read* [1999] 1 F.L.R. 425 or through the transfer operation contained in CPR r.52.14. The latter mechanism is to be preferred. See *L.B. Barnet v Hurst* [2002] EWCA Civ 1009 at [28]; [2003] 1 W.L.R. 722.

In dealing with an appeal under s.13 of the Administration of Justice Act 1960 the Court of Appeal has a complete discretion, fettered only by the need to do justice. The court must take into account the interests of (a) the contemnor, (b) the "victim" of the contempt and (c) other users of the court (for whom maintenance of the authority of the court is of supreme importance). The interests of the contemnor include ensuring that he has been informed in sufficiently clear terms of what has been found against him. See *Re Scriven* [2004] EWCA Civ 683 at [30]–[32].

When the civil division of the Court of Appeal is hearing appeals in contempt cases, it will adopt the same principles and approach in relation to sentencing as the criminal division of the Court of Appeal: see *Murray v Robinson* [2005] EWCA Civ 935 at [2]. The Court of Appeal will not interfere if the sentence fell within the permissible bracket: *Devjee v Patel* [2006] EWCA Civ 1211.

Meaning of "appellant"

In r.52.1(3)(d) "appellant" is defined as "a person who brings or seeks to bring an appeal". This definition is wide enough to embrace a person who was not party to the proceedings below, but who is adversely affected by the outcome. Thus in *MA Holdings Ltd v George Wimpey UK Ltd (1) and Tewkesbury BC (2)* [2008] EWCA Civ 12; [2008] 1 W.L.R. 1649, M was given permission to appeal, even though it had not been party to the proceedings below. In the proceedings below Wimpey had secured an order quashing the Council's decision to adopt the local plan, thereby directly affecting M's property interests. M "was no mere intermeddling busybody": per Dyson L.J. at [26]. **52.1.3**

Joinder of additional parties to appeal

The Court of Appeal has power to join additional parties to an appeal, even after the court's order has been sealed, if this is necessary for the purpose of dealing with ancillary orders: see *DK v Bryn Alyn Community (Holdings) Ltd (In Liquidation)* [2003] EWCA Civ 783. **52.1.4**

Costs appeals

Costs appeals fall into two categories: (i) appeals against the order for costs made by a lower court either as part of some wider judgment or in costs-only proceedings pursuant to r.44.12A; (ii) appeals against the detailed assessment of costs made pursuant to such an order. **52.1.5**

Appeals in category (i) all fall under the regime of CPR Pt 52. The general approach of appeal courts is one of reluctance to interfere with costs orders, unless the substantive judgment is being varied. "As is well known, orders for costs are very rarely disturbed" per Judge L.J. in *Voice & Script International Ltd v Alghafar* [2003] EWCA Civ 736. In *Adamson v Halifax Plc* [2002] EWCA Civ 1134 at [16]; [2003] 1 W.L.R. 60 Sir Murray Stuart Smith, giving the leading judgment, formulated the test as follows:

> "Costs are in the discretion of the trial judge and this court will only interfere with the exercise of that discretion on well-defined principles. As I said in *Roache v News Group Newspapers* [1998] EMLR 161, 172:
>
> 'Before the court can interfere it must be shown that the judge has either erred in principle in his approach, or has left out of account, or taken into account, some feature that he should, or should not, have considered, or that his decision is wholly wrong because the court is forced to the conclusion that he has not balanced the various factors in the scale.'"

Islam v Ali [2003] EWCA Civ 612 provides an example of circumstances in which the Court of Appeal was prepared to vary a costs order made by a circuit judge on the ground that he had erred in principle. (A had won on all substantive issues, although she was still ordered to pay a small sum to I, in respect of which she had failed to make a payment into court or Pt 36 offer. The judge's order that A pay I's costs was varied to no order as to costs.) Auld L.J. formulated the principles in such appeals as follows:

> "19. It is, as both counsel have acknowledged, a wide discretion, and the Court of Appeal should only interfere with the judge's exercise of it if he has "exceeded the generous ambit within which reasonable disagreement is possible", a familiar passage now taken from the judgment of Brooke LJ in *Tanfern v Cameron-MacDonald (Practice Note)* [2000] 1 W.L.R. 1311, at paragraph 32, citing Lord Fraser in *G v G (Minors: Custody Appeal)* [1985] 1 W.L.R.647, 652."

Auld L.J. also expressed agreement with the formulation of Sir Murray Stuart Smith in *Adamson v Halifax Plc* [2002] EWCA Civ 1134 at [16]; [2003] 1 W.L.R. 60.

An appeal court will also interfere with a costs order, if the lower court has failed to apply one or more of the rules in Pt 44 correctly: see e.g. *Winter v Winter* CAT, November 10, 2000.

The position in relation to appeals in category (ii) is as follows. If the assessment of costs was carried out by an authorised court officer, then the appeal against his decision is not subject to Pt 52: see r.52.1(2). An appeal against the detailed assessment of costs made by an authorised court officer lies to a costs judge, and permission is not required for such an appeal. The rules and procedures governing these appeals are set out in CPR Pt 47, rr.47.20 to 47.23 and in ss.47–48 of the corresponding practice direction. (These provisions are discussed in the commentary following rr.47.20 to 47.23.) On the other hand, if the detailed assessment of costs is made by a costs judge or a district judge, then any appeal from his decision falls under the regime of Pt 52 and permission to appeal is required. An appeal from a costs judge lies to a High Court judge. An appeal from a district judge lies to a circuit judge (in the county court) or to a High Court judge (in the High Court). In cases of sufficient importance a costs judge may direct (subject to the restrictions in r.52.14) that the first appeal should be heard by the Court of Appeal. Before taking this course, however, the costs judge will need to see detailed grounds of appeal and will require demonstration that those grounds raise matters of principle suitable for consideration by the Court of Appeal: see *Sharratt v London Central Bus Company* [2004] EWCA Civ 575 at [46].

An appeal from an authorised court officer to a costs judge is a complete rehearing. An appeal from a costs judge or a district judge to a High Court judge or a circuit judge is not a complete rehearing. For the extent to which an appeal court will interfere with the decision of a costs judge or a district judge in relation to the detailed assessment of costs, see *Hornsby v Clark Kenneth Leventhal* [2000] 4 All E.R. 567 at 570j–571f. It should be noted that where a costs judge hears an appeal against the detailed assessment of costs made by an authorised court officer, any appeal against that judge's decision is treated as a "first appeal", not a "second appeal": see art.5(a) of the Destination Order.

In proceedings concerning the detailed assessment of costs second appeals to the Court of Appeal are permitted, subject to the restrictions contained in s.55(1) of the Access to Justice Act 1999 and CPR r.52.13. (These restrictions are discussed in the commentary following r.52.13.) *Hollins v Russell* [2003] EWCA Civ 718; [2003] 1 W.L.R. 248 provides an example of assessment proceedings which raised issues of principle and were permitted to proceed to the Court of Appeal.

For a fuller and more comprehensive discussion of costs appeals, practitioners are referred to Ch.9 of *Civil Costs* by Senior Costs Judge P.T. Hurst (4th edn, Sweet & Maxwell, 2007).

Parties to comply with the practice direction[1]

52.2 **52.2 All parties to an appeal must comply with the relevant practice direction.**

Parties to comply with the Practice Direction

52.2.1 The "relevant practice direction" is at para.52PD.1. It will be referred to in this commentary simply as "the practice direction". The practice direction amplifies the provisions of Pt 52 in considerable detail. The practice direction was substantially amended on June 30, 2004. The Court of Appeal fully explained the nature and effect of those amendments in *Scribes West Ltd v Anstalt (No.1)* [2004] EWCA Civ 835.

The use of practice directions in this new form is discussed by J.A. Jolowicz in "Practice Directions and Civil Procedure Rules" [2000] C.L.J. 53. For the first time practice directions have a statutory basis, namely the Civil Procedure Act 1997: see s.1(2), s.5 and Sch.1 (Vol.2, Section 9A). Practice directions either add detail to the rules or, in some cases, contain free-standing provisions which might have appeared (but did not appear) in the rules. Practice directions can be amended more easily than the rules. However, no doubt the cautionary words of Professor Jolowicz will be borne in mind:

> "Practice directions should not be used as a cheap and easily amended form of legislation on matters for which proper legislation under the eye of Parliament is more appropriate."

The proper boundaries of practice directions have been recognised by the Court of Appeal on more than one occasion. See *Leigh v Michelin Tyre plc* [2003] EWCA Civ 1766 at [19]–[20] and the passages there cited. Practice directions were described as "at best a weak aid to the construction of the rules". In *KU v Liverpool City Council* [2005] EWCA Civ 475 at [48] Brooke L.J. stated that practice directions provide

[1] Introduced by the Civil Procedure (Amendment) Rules 2000 (SI 2000/221).

invaluable guidance on matters of practice, but in so far as they contain statements of law which are wrong they carry no authority at all.

Permission[1]

52.3—(1) An appellant or respondent requires permission to appeal— 52.3

(a) where the appeal is from a decision of a judge in a county court or the High Court, except where the appeal is against—

(i) a committal order;

(ii) a refusal to grant habeas corpus; or

(iii) a secure accommodation order made under section 25 of the Children Act 1989; or

(b) as provided by the relevant practice direction.

(Other enactments may provide that permission is required for particular appeals.)

(2) An application for permission to appeal may be made—

(a) to the lower court at the hearing at which the decision to be appealed was made; or

(b) to the appeal court in an appeal notice.

(Rule 52.4 sets out the time limits for filing an appellant's notice at the appeal court. Rule 52.5 sets out the time limits for filing a respondent's notice at the appeal court. Any application for permission to appeal to the appeal court must be made in the appeal notice (see rules 52.4(2) and 52.5(3).)

(Rule 52.13(1) provides that permission is required from the Court of Appeal for all appeals to that court from a decision of a county court or the High Court which was itself made on appeal.)

(3) Where the lower court refuses an application for permission to appeal, a further application for permission to appeal may be made to the appeal court.

(4) Subject to paragraph (4A), where the appeal court, without a hearing, refuses permission to appeal, the person seeking permission may request the decision to be reconsidered at a hearing.

(4A) Where the Court of Appeal refuses permission to appeal without a hearing, it may, if it considers that the application is totally without merit, make an order that the person seeking permission may not request the decision to be reconsidered at a hearing.

(4B) Rule 3.3(5) will not apply to an order that the person seeking permission may not request the decision to be reconsidered at a hearing made under paragraph (4A).

(5) A request under paragraph (4) must be filed within 7 days after service of the notice that permission has been refused.

(6) Permission to appeal may be given only where—

(a) the court considers that the appeal would have a real prospect of success; or

[1] Introduced by the Civil Procedure (Amendment) Rules 2000 (SI 2000/221) and amended by the Civil Procedure (Amendment No.4) Rules 2005 (SI 2005/3515) and the Civil Procedure (Amendment) Rules 2006 (SI 2006/1689).

(b) there is some other compelling reason why the appeal should be heard.

(7) An order giving permission may—

(a) limit the issues to be heard; and

(b) be made subject to conditions.

(Rule 3.1(3) also provides that the court may make an order subject to conditions.)

(Rule 25.15 provides for the court to order security for costs of an appeal.)

Requirement for permission

52.3.1 A party requires permission to appeal against a county court or High Court decision, unless the order complained of is a committal order, a refusal to grant *habeas corpus* or a secure accommodation order under s.25 of the Children Act 1989: see r.52.3(1)(a). In relation to committal orders (r.52.3 (1)(a)(i)), only the contemnor is exempted from the requirement to seek permission to appeal: see *L.B. Barnet v Hurst* [2002] EWCA Civ 1009; [2003] 1 W.L.R. 722; *Kynaston v Carroll* [2004] EWCA Civ 1434; *Poole Borough Council v Hambridge* [2007] EWCA Civ 990 (disapproving *Wood v Collins* [2006] EWCA Civ 743).

Other exceptions to the permission requirement are discussed in *Tanfern Ltd v Cameron-MacDonald (Practice Note)* [2000] 1 W.L.R. 1311 at paras 24–26. The justification for this almost universal requirement for permission is to be found in Ch.3 of the Bowman report. The anomalies in the old rules are swept away. Unmeritorious appeals are filtered out at an early stage, thus protecting both parties from unnecessary costs. Also a convenient opportunity is provided for case management at an early stage.

Rule 52.3(1)(b) allows further categories of appeal requiring permission to be specified in the practice direction. At the moment no such categories are specified.

Appeals in insolvency proceedings fall under a different regime, as set out in the Insolvency Proceedings Practice Direction. The permission requirement in relation to first appeals is set out in para.17.6 of the Insolvency Proceedings Practice Direction,Vol.2, para.3E–18.

A judge exercising jurisdiction under Pt 7 of the Mental Health Act 1983 falls outside the ambit of r.52.3(1). Accordingly permission is not required for an appeal against the decision of such a judge: see *In the Matter of MB (a patient)* [2005] EWCA Civ 1293; [2006] 1 W.L.R. 287.

Appeals in contempt proceedings

52.3.2 The possible routes of appeal against orders made in contempt proceedings have been outlined above in the commentary following r.52.1. If a judge makes a committal order in contempt proceedings, then no permission is required to appeal against that order: see r.52.3(1)(a)(i). If a judge makes any other form of order in contempt proceedings (e.g. an order that the defendant pay the claimant's costs), that is not a "committal order" and permission to appeal is required: see *Government of Sierra Leone v Davenport* [2002] EWCA Civ 230 and *L.B. Barnet v Hurst* [2002] EWCA Civ 1009 at [25]–[27]; [2003] 1 W.L.R. 722.

If a circuit judge, on appeal, upholds a committal order made by a district judge, then any appeal from the circuit judge is a second appeal. Thus it is caught by art.5 of the Destination Order and CPR r.52.13. Permission is always required for such an appeal. See *L.B. Barnet v Hurst* [2002] EWCA Civ 1009 at [29]–[30]; [2003] 1 W.L.R. 722.

Statutory appeals

52.3.3 A "statutory appeal" is an appeal to the court from a Minister of State, government department, tribunal or other person (see para.17.1(1) of the practice direction). Neither Pt 52 of the CPR nor the practice direction imposes a general requirement for permisssion to appeal in respect of statutory appeals. In *Colley v Council for Licensed Conveyancers* [2001] EWCA Civ 1137; [2002] 1 W.L.R. 160, the Court of Appeal rejected the contention that para.17.2 of the practice direction imposed a requirement for permission to appeal in all statutory appeals. Nevertheless permission is required for an appeal from the Lands Tribunal to the Court of Appeal: see *Girls Day School Trust (1872) v Dadak* [2001] EWCA Civ 380.

When and where should the application for permission be made?

An application for permission should be made to the lower court orally at the hearing at which the decision to be appealed against is made. If no such application is made or if the lower court refuses permission, then the application for permission may be made to the appeal court in the appeal notice. See r.52.3(2) and (3) and paras 4.6 and 4.7 of the practice direction. **52.3.4**

The language of r.52.3(2) (note the word "or") and of para.4.6 of the practice direction (note the word "should", rather than "shall" or "must") indicates that a party, who fails to apply for permission to the lower court but goes directly to the appeal court, suffers no sanction. This situation may arise where a party has a change of heart or a change of advice after the hearing at which he has been unsuccessful.

Despite the lack of compulsion, a litigant with arguable grounds for appeal would generally be well advised to apply for permission to the lower court at the time of judgment for five reasons:

(a) The judge below is fully seized of the matter and so the application will take minimal time. Indeed the judge may have already decided that the case raises questions fit for appeal.
(b) An application at this stage involves neither party in additional costs.
(c) No harm is done if the application fails. The litigant enjoys two bites at the cherry.
(d) If the application succeeds and the litigant subsequently decides to appeal, he avoids the expensive and time-consuming permission stage in the appeal court.
(e) No harm is done if the application succeeds, but the litigant subsequently decides not to appeal.

It should be noted that the guidance in this paragraph was firmly endorsed by the Court of Appeal in *T (A Child)* [2002] EWCA Civ 1736 at [12]–[13].

If the unsuccessful party requires further time before making its application to the lower court for permission to appeal, the court may adjourn the hearing for that purpose: see para.4.3B of the practice direction.

A more difficult question is whether the lower court has power (in appropriate circumstances) to order such an adjournment retrospectively—for example, where the unsuccessful party decides to appeal a day or two later and costs may be saved by going back to the original judge. The opening words of para.4.3B ("Where no application for permission to appeal has been made") suggest that there may be such a power, but the latter part of the paragraph suggests otherwise. There are two first instance decisions on this question, but unfortunately they come to opposite conclusions: see *Balmoral Group Ltd v Borealis (UK) Ltd* [2006] EWHC 2228 (Comm) and *Multiplex Construction (UK) Ltd v Honeywell Control Systems Ltd* [2007] EWHC 236 (TCC). *Balmoral* was not cited to the judge in the second case, so the two decisions were reached in isolation.

If the judge hands down a reserved judgment in the absence of the parties and is aware that one party wishes to appeal, he should formally adjourn the hearing to enable that party to apply for permission to appeal: *Jackson v Marina Homes Ltd* [2007] EWCA Civ 1404 at [8].

If one ground of appeal is that the judge has failed to deal with a particular point, the judge should be given an opportunity to deal with that point at the hearing before the application for permission is made: see *English v Emery Reimbold & Strick Ltd* [2002] EWCA Civ 605; [2002] 1 W.L.R. 2409 at [25] and *In the matter of S (Children)* [2007] EWCA Civ 694 at [23]–[25]. These authorities are discussed further in the commentary following r.52.11.

Duty of the lower court when an application for permission to appeal is made

Where a party applies to the lower court for permission to appeal against a decision in accordance with r.52.3(2)(a), the judge must state (a) whether the judgment or order is final, (b) whether an appeal lies and, if so, to which court, (c) whether the lower court gives permission to appeal, and (d) if not, the appropriate appeal court to which any further application may be made. See para.4.3A of the practice direction. CPR r.40.2 (4) requires these same matters to be stated in the order which the court draws up following the hearing. **52.3.5**

Where no application for permission is made on the occasion when judgment is given, but the unsuccessful party requests further time to make such an application, the lower court may adjourn the hearing to give that party the opportunity to do so. See para.4.3B of the practice direction.

If the lower court purports to grant permission outside the time limit for appealing, then (absent any extension of time) such "permission" is ineffective: *Lloyd Jones v T Mobile (UK) Ltd* [2003] EWCA Civ 1162.

How the appeal court deals with such applications

52.3.6 The appeal court can, and in many cases will, determine applications for permission on paper. See para.4.11 of the practice direction. However, cases of particular difficulty or cases raising special problems are generally referred by the appeal court for oral hearing, without any intermediate consideration on paper. Likewise, cases in which it is thought likely that the appellant would in any event exercise his right to an oral hearing (as to which see the following paragraph) are generally listed for oral hearing at the outset. If permission is granted on paper, then the appeal will proceed to the next stage (see para.4.12 of the practice direction), save in those rare cases where an application to set aside permission is appropriate under r.52.9.

If the appeal court refuses permission on paper, then (save in respect of appeals to the Court of Appeal which are totally without merit) the appellant is entitled to have the matter reconsidered at an oral hearing. See r.52.3(4) and para.4.13 of the practice direction. The request for such an oral hearing must be filed within seven days after service of the notice that permission has been refused. See r.52.3(5) and para.4.14 of the practice direction. However, the appeal court has power under r.3.1 (2)(a) to extend the 7 day period for requesting reconsideration at an oral hearing: see *Slot v Isaac* [2002] EWCA Civ 481 at [15]. The procedure to be followed after the appellant has requested an oral hearing is set out in paras 4.14A–4.17 of the practice direction.

The overall effect of these provisions is that (save in respect of appeals to the Court of Appeal which are totally without merit) every disappointed litigant at first instance can, one way or another, achieve at least a brief hearing in the appeal court, so that the main thrust of his complaint can be ventilated orally.

In the case of appeals to the Court of Appeal which are totally without merit, the lord justice refusing permission on paper may make an order debarring the applicant from requesting reconsideration at an oral hearing.

Furthermore the Court of Appeal will refuse to entertain an application for permission to appeal (and will not list such an application for hearing) if it is obvious that the court has no jurisdiction. See *Jolly v Jay* [2002] EWCA Civ 277 at [19] and *Bulled v Kayat* [2002] EWCA Civ 804 at [9]–[11].

Any decision refusing permission to appeal must be adequately reasoned, in order to comply with art.6 of the European Convention on Human Rights. Thus an unparticularised assertion that the appellant has not complied with the practice direction is insufficient. See *Hyams v Plender* [2001] 1 W.L.R. 32 at para.17.

The basic criteria for granting permission

52.3.7 Permission to appeal may be given only where (a) the appeal appears to have a real prospect of success or (b) there is some other compelling reason why the appeal should be heard. See r.52.3(6). The word "may" in r.52.3(6) indicates that the court has a discretion. This discretion must be exercised in accordance with the overriding objective (see r.1.1).

The first ground ("real prospect of success") presents no conceptual problems. It is precisely the same test as that which the courts apply when considering summary judgment: see r.24.2. The rationale is the same. If a claim or defence has no real prospect of success, the court will prevent the litigant from pursuing it. Likewise if an appeal has no real prospect of success, the court will prevent the litigant from pursuing it. The main practical difference is that (for obvious reasons) more appeals are weeded out by this process, than first instance claims or defences.

In *Swain v Hillman* [2001] 1 All E.R. 91 Lord Woolf M.R. discussed the meaning of "real prospect of succeeding" in r.24.2. The court had to consider whether there was a realistic, as opposed to a fanciful, prospect of success. In *Tanfern Ltd v Cameron-MacDonald (Practice Note)* [2000] 1 W.L.R. 1311 at para.21, Brooke L.J. cited *Swain v Hillman* and stated that the same approach should be adopted in relation to r.52.3(6)(a).

The second ground ("some other compelling reason") is more difficult. On a semantic analysis, the word "or" is disjunctive. See *Morris v Bank of India* [2004] EWCA Civ 1286 at [9]–[10]. Ground (b) often (but not invariably) arises for consideration if the proposed appeal has no real prospect of succeeding. But what "compelling reason" can there be for allowing a litigant, who has lost at first instance, to throw away yet more costs on an appeal which has no real prospect of success? Or for subjecting a successful litigant to the stress and irrecoverable costs of defending a hopeless appeal?

The origins of ground (b) can be traced to paragraphs 37–38 of Ch.3 of the Bowman Report, which quoted with approval the following passage from the judgment of the Court of Appeal in *Smith v Cosworth Casting Processes Ltd* [1997] 1 W.L.R. 1538:

> "There can be many reasons for granting leave even if the court is not satisfied that the appeal has any prospect of success. For example, the issue may be one which the court considers should in the public interest be examined by this court or, to be more specific, this court may take the view that the case raises an issue where the law requires clarifying."

The theoretical difficulty with the passage just quoted is that if the case raises an issue where the law requires clarifying, then by definition the appeal *does* have a real prospect of success. Such clarification might operate in favour of the appellant. If the "clarification" cannot affect the outcome of the appeal, then in many cases it may be inappropriate to grant permission.

Experience has shown, however, that ground (b) constitutes a valuable reserve power to permit certain appeals to proceed to the Court of Appeal, even though it is not possible to say that there is a "real prospect of success". In one case, for example, a major developer (which was well able to bear both sides' costs) was permitted to pursue an appeal with slender prospects of success, because the appeal was likely to result in the elucidation of an important point of planning law. In some instances the appellant (e.g. a public authority) is pursuing its appeal, in order to obtain an authoritative decision on a point of general application. In such cases the Court of Appeal may grant permission to appeal but on condition that the appellant pays both parties' costs in any event.

In cases where the current appeal is hopeless because of binding authority, but a further appeal to the House of Lords might succeed, then special considerations arise. The appellant has, ultimately, a real prospect of success. It may be appropriate for the Court of Appeal to grant permission, but to dismiss the appeal immediately. This course spares the parties unnecessary costs and leaves it open to the appellant to seek permission to appeal to the House of Lords. The Court of Appeal, in effect, took this course in *Beedell v West Ferry Printers Ltd* [2001] EWCA Civ 400; *The Times*, April 5, 2001.

In relation to junior appellate courts, the position would appear to be different. It is difficult to conceive of any reason (compelling or otherwise) why an appeal should be allowed to proceed to the junior appellate court, if it has no real prospect of success. Even if the unpromising appeal raises questions of public interest or general policy, the junior appellate court is hardly the forum to address such matters. Accordingly, in relation to appeals to junior appellate courts (where no question of transfer under r.52.14 arises), it is suggested that ground (a) alone is relevant, namely "real prospect of success".

For the meaning of the phrase "some other compelling reason" in the context of second appeals, see the commentary following rule 52.13 below.

The effect of refusal of permission

Refusal of permission is, effectively, the end of the road: see *Moyse v Regal Partnerships Ltd* [2004] EWCA Civ 1269 at [31]. If both the lower court and the appeal court **52.3.8** refuse permission to appeal, it is not possible to appeal to a higher court (e.g. the Court of Appeal) against that refusal of permission. This is the effect of s.54(4) of the Access to Justice Act 1999 and of para.4.8 of the practice direction. These provisions *cannot, save in exceptional circumstances,* be circumvented by an application to the Administrative Court for judicial review of the decision of a junior appellate court, refusing permission to appeal: see *R. (Mahon) v Taunton County Court* [2001] EWHC Admin 1078; [2002] A.C.D. 192; *R. (Messer) v Cambridge County Court* [2002] EWCA Civ 1355; *Sivasubramaniam v Wandsworth County Court* [2002] EWCA Civ 1738 at [49]–[56]; [2003] 1 W.L.R. 475. Judicial review of a junior appellate court's refusal of permission to appeal is only available where (a) there has been some fundamental departure from the correct procedures or (b) the judge refusing permission to appeal has acted in complete disregard of his duties: see *Gregory v Turner* [2003] EWCA Civ 183 at [38]–[45]; [2003] 1 W.L.R. 1149.

The Court of Appeal, whose jurisdiction is wholly statutory, has no inherent jurisdiction to hear an appeal against the decision of a junior appellate court refusing permission to appeal (unless it can truly be said that there was no decision at all). See *Riniker v University College London* [2001] 1 W.L.R. 13 and *Clark (Inspector of Taxes) v Perks* [2001] 1 W.L.R. 17 at para.20. The only exception to this principle of finality is that in extremely rare cases the Court of Appeal or the High Court pursuant to r.52.17 may re-open an appeal after it has refused permission.

If, at the same time as refusing permission to appeal, a junior appellate court makes an order for costs or some other ancillary order, then there is a right of appeal against that order. If the order is made by a circuit judge, then such an appeal lies to a High Court judge as a "first appeal". See *Jolly v Jay* [2002] EWCA Civ 277 at [51]–[52]; *Moyse v Regal Mortgages Ltd Partnership* [2004] EWCA Civ 1269.

Permission will be granted more sparingly to appeal against case management decisions

52.3.9 This aspect is dealt with in paras 4.4 and 4.5 of the practice direction. The court considering a permission application must take into account the significance of the appeal, the likely costs, the delay or disruption which would be entailed and whether the issue could more conveniently be determined at or after trial. The justification of this approach is to be found in para.38 of Ch.3 of the Bowman Report. The review team recommended "that an additional element is required in the case of interlocutory appeals, which can cause substantial delays in the progress of cases at first instance." The review team went on to recommend that a balance be struck in determining whether appeals should be allowed at that stage.

The court should also bear in mind at the permission stage the high threshold which an appellant seeking to overturn a case management decision within the judge's discretion must cross: see *Royal & Sun Alliance v T & N Ltd* [2002] EWCA Civ 1964 at [38]; *Walbrook Trustee (Jersey) Ltd v Fattal* [2008] EWCA Civ 427 at [33].

Permission will be granted more sparingly for second appeals (and only by the Court of Appeal)

52.3.10 A decision of the High Court or of a county court made on the hearing of an appeal may be the subject of a further appeal, but this is subject to restrictions. In particular, the Court of Appeal is the only court that can hear a second appeal. Only the Court of Appeal can grant permission for a second appeal. See paras 4.9 and 4.10 of the practice direction.

The circumstances in which the Court of Appeal will grant permission for a second appeal are restricted both by statute and by the CPR. See the commentary following r.52.13 below.

Permission will be granted more sparingly for appeals from specialist tribunals

52.3.11 In *Cooke v Secretary of State for Social Security* [2001] EWCA Civ 734; [2002] 3 All E.R. 279 the Court of Appeal considered the criteria which should be applied in relation to applications for permission to appeal from the Social Security Commissioner. Hale L.J., giving the principal judgment, said that although s.55 (1) of the Access to Justice Act 1999 did not in terms apply, many of the policy considerations underlying that section were applicable.

> "Firstly, this is a highly specialised area of law which many lawyers—indeed, I would suspect most lawyers—rarely encounter in practice. Secondly, there is an independent two-tier appellate structure. ... After the initial decision there is a fresh hearing before a specialist tribunal which is chaired by a lawyer and has an appropriate balance of experience and expertise amongst its members. After that there is an appeal on a point of law to a highly expert and specialized legally qualified body, the Social Security Commissioners." (Paragraph 15)

Hale L.J. accepted that such appeal structures should have a link to the ordinary court system. Nevertheless the courts "should approach such cases with an appropriate degree of caution". The Social Security Commissioners will have a more comprehensive understanding of social security principles than the courts. Hale L.J. added that, subject to the qualifications mentioned in para.18, her comments were also relevant to other similar appeal structures.

In *Napp Pharmaceutical Holdings Ltd v Director General of Fair Trading* [2002] EWCA Civ 976; [2002] 4 All E.R. 376 the Court of Appeal refused the claimant permission to appeal against a decision of the Competition Commission Appeal Tribunal. Buxton

L.J. said that the Tribunal's findings (concerning abusive pricing policy and abnormal conduct) did not involve points of law and could not be reviewed in the Court of Appeal. He added:

> "But even if we did have authority to review such findings, as the conclusion of an expert and specialist tribunal, specifically constituted by Parliament to make judgments in an area in which judges have no expertise, they fall exactly into the category identified by Hale L.J. in *Cooke v Secretary of State for Social Security* [2001] EWCA Civ 734, as an area which this court would be very slow indeed to enter."

See also *Hinchy v Secretary of State for Work and Pensions* [2005] UKHL 16.

In relation to appeals from the Asylum and Immigration Appeals Tribunal, the approach of the Court of Appeal is as set out in *SSHD v Akaeke* [2005] EWCA Civ 947 at [28]–[30] and in *R. (Iran) v SSHD* [2005] EWCA Civ 982 at [92]–[93]. The Court of Appeal will be slow to grant permission to appeal from the Asylum and Immigration Appeals Tribunal for broadly the same reasons that it is slow to grant permission to appeal from other specialist tribunals.

In relation to appeals from the Lands Tribunal, the Court of Appeal adopts a broadly similar approach to that set out by Hale L.J. in *Cooke v Secretary of State for Social Security* [2001] EWCA Civ 734; [2002] 3 All E.R. 279. However, the Court of Appeal will be less reluctant to grant permission to appeal where the question raised is one of construction not requiring the specialist expertise of the Lands Tribunal. See *Cawsand Fort Management Co Ltd v Stafford* [2007] EWCA Civ 231. (The subsequent appeal in that case was unsuccessful: see *Cawsand Fort Management Co Ltd v Stafford* [2007] EWCA Civ 1187; [2008] 1 W.L.R. 371.)

Permission will be granted more sparingly for appeals on questions of fact from the Technology and Construction Court

Under the former Rules of the Supreme Court there was a more restrictive regime for appeals from decisions of official referees than for appeals from decision of other courts. The rationale was explained by Lord Bingham M.R. in *Virgin Management Ltd v De Morgan Group* (1994) 68 B.L.R. 26 at 33: **52.3.12**

> "The reason why rights of appeal against factual decisions of official referees have been subject to special restrictions and conditions is obvious. Official referees were originally appointed to conduct protracted and painstaking enquiries into complex and detailed factual issues. The investigation of multifarious claims and cross-claims arising out of building contracts is one example...It was clearly felt that the factual minutiae with which official referees were required to deal were not suitable matters for reconsideration on appeal. It was better that, for better or worse, their decisions on such matters should stand, rather as if they were arbitrators. If personal or professional reputations were at stake, that was a different matter."

This more restrictive approach to factual appeals from TCC judges has survived the introduction of the CPR. In *Skanska Construction UK Ltd v Egger (Barony) Ltd* [2002] EWCA Civ 1914 Lawrence Collins J (with whom Thorpe and Latham L.JJ. agreed) said:

> "But the decisions of the Technology and Construction Court have special characteristics which affect the readiness of the Court of Appeal to reconsider them on appeal. First, the findings of fact often fall within an area of specialist expertise, where the evidence is of a technical nature and given by experienced experts, and which is evidence of a kind which judges of the Technology and Construction Court are particularly well placed to assess. Second, the conclusions of fact will frequently involve an assessment or evaluation of a number of different factors which have to be weighed against each other, which is often a matter of degree. Third, the decisions may deal with factual minutiae not easily susceptible of reconsideration on appeal."

The Court of Appeal endorsed the above approach in *Yorkshire Water Services v Taylor Woodrow Construction Northern Ltd* [2005] EWCA Civ 894; [2005] B.L.R. 395. The Court of Appeal dismissed in robust terms an application for leave to appeal from the decision of Forbes J. (the judge in charge of the Technology and Construction Court) in a highly complex action concerning claims for defects, delay and loss and expense. May L.J., delivering the judgment of the court, said at para.27:

> "I do not consider that the advent of Part 52 of the CPR has altered this court's approach to applications for permission to appeal from factual decisions of TCC

judges…The policy has been somewhat relaxed, and findings of fact such as Lord Bingham described on page 35 in *Virgin Management* are not no-go areas. The burden on a prospective appellant in these areas is nevertheless hard to discharge. In my view, the more complicated and technical the facts, the harder generally speaking is the burden. The reason again is obvious. The more complicated and technical the facts, the longer and more expensive would be this court's enquiry, whether by review or re-hearing, and the more disproportionate would be the whole exercise for the parties and the court alike…"

Permission to appeal may be granted more readily in patent cases

52.3.13 In *Pozzoli SPA v BDMO SA* [2007] EWCA Civ 588 the Court of Appeal granted permission to appeal against a decision that Pozzoli's patent was invalid, but went on to dismiss the appeal. The Court of Appeal held that art.32 of the TRIPS Agreement (an international treaty) did not compel the grant of permission to appeal in any case where a patent had been declared invalid. At [10] Jacob L.J. (with whom Mummery and Keene L.J.J. agreed) stated:

"I would add this about permission to appeal in patent cases generally. Unless the case is very clear and can be understood sufficiently readily in an hour or so, the better course is normally for permission to be granted by the trial judge. For, unlike the trial judge, the Court of Appeal judge(s) who have to decide whether permission should be granted (where the trial judge has refused it) will not be immersed in the technology and evidence in the same way as the trial judge. Faced with but an incomplete understanding and a plausible skeleton argument seeking permission, the Court of Appeal will generally be likely to grant permission, even if it later discerns that the case is indeed clear."

At first blush, the difference between the Court of Appeal's approach to (a) appeals in patent cases and (b) appeals in other cases involving specialist or technical expertise may seem surprising. However, this approach has been authoritatively laid down and its rationale explained.

Limited permission

52.3.14 An order giving permission to appeal may limit the issues to be heard: see r.52.3(7)(a). This power will be exercised where the appellant includes some hopeless points among his grounds of appeal. It is in the interests of all parties (including the appellant) that these be weeded out at the start. Paragraph 4.18 of the practice direction provides that where limited permission is granted, the court will either (a) refuse permission on any remaining issues or (b) reserve the question of permission on any remaining issues to the court hearing the appeal. In the latter event, the procedure to be followed thereafter is set out in para.4.19 of the practice direction.

If the appeal court refuses permission to appeal on the remaining issues after consideration on paper, then the appellant can renew his application for permission in respect of those issues at an oral hearing, in accordance with para.4.20 of the practice direction. On the other hand, if the appeal court refuses permission to appeal on the remaining issues at or after an oral hearing, then the appellant cannot renew his application for permission in respect of those issues at the hearing of the appeal. This is the consequence of s.54(4) of the Access to Justice Act 1999. See *Fieldman v Markovic* [2001] C.P. Rep. 119; *James v Baily Gibson & Co* [2002] EWCA Civ 1690 and para.4.21 of the practice direction.

Conditional permission

52.3.15 An order giving permission to appeal may be made subject to conditions: see r.52.3(7)(b). The power is expressed broadly and it may be used in order to do justice between the parties. In *Morris v Wrexham CBC* [2001] EWHC Admin 697 the appellant wished to appeal in order to obtain clarification of the law. Leave to appeal was granted on condition that the appellant paid the respondent's costs of the appeal in any event. In *Lloyd Jones v T Mobile (UK) Ltd* [2003] EWCA Civ 1162 at [26] the Court of Appeal granted permission to appeal (coupled with a five months extension of time) on condition that the appellant should not be entitled to the costs of the appeal, even *if it* succeeded. One reason for imposing this condition was that the appellant was a large corporation, which had incurred substantial costs on the appeal because the matter was important to its business, whereas the respondents were a group of individual objectors.

In *Ungi v Liverpool City Council* [2004] EWCA Civ 1617 the defendant wished to appeal on grounds not argued (or not fully argued) below. The proposed appeal raised important points of practice, which called out for the guidance of the Court of Appeal. The court permitted the appeal to proceed, but on condition that (a) the orders for costs in the court below should remain undisturbed and (b) the appellant should pay both parties' costs of the appeal.

Where the proposed appellant has failed to comply with orders of the court below, it may be appropriate to make such compliance a condition of permission to appeal. In *Day's Medical Aids Ltd v Pihsiang Machinery Manufacturing Co Ltd* [2004] EWCA Civ 993 there was no stay of execution pending the defendant's appeal, but the defendant (a Taiwanese company) had failed to comply with the judgment. The Court of Appeal made it a condition of permission to appeal that the defendant pay to the claimants the judgment sum plus costs and interest. In reaching this decision Dyson L.J. proceeded on the basis that the court should only impose conditions on permission to appeal where there was a compelling reason to do so (see para.5). He also accepted that there was no general rule that compliance with the judgment below should be a condition of permission to appeal (see para.25). The decision was based upon the particular circumstances of that case.

The appeal court has power to vary the conditions attached to permission to appeal: see r.52.9(1)(c) and the commentary following that provision.

Advocacy at permission hearing

The oral hearing of an application for permission will be of limited duration. Also it will often be attended by one party only. Although the judge or lord justice will have pre-read the relevant documents, he is unlikely to be as familiar with the details of the case as the judge below or the advocates who appeared below. The advocate appearing at the permission hearing should use his limited time wisely, focussing on his best points clearly and fairly. Any necessary exposition should be succinct and to the point. Also, assuming that the other parties are absent, the advocate must remember his duty to draw attention to any adverse authorities or factors. The rules governing permission to appeal have the potential to protect litigants from enormous cost and delay. If they are to achieve this objective without causing injustice, there must be both careful preparation by the court and high standards of preparation and presentation by the advocates. **52.3.16**

The appellant's advocate should ensure that para.4.14A of the practice direction is complied with. In particular, at least four days before the hearing he must lodge a brief written statement identifying (a) the points which he proposes to raise and (b) why he contends that permission should be granted, despite the reasons previously given for refusing permission.

The role of respondents in relation to permission applications

In *Jolly v Jay* [2002] EWCA Civ 277 the Court of Appeal gave guidance as to the role of respondents at the permission stage. A respondent should only file submissions at this early stage, if they are addressed to the point that the appeal would not meet the relevant threshold test or tests, or if there is some material inaccuracy in the papers placed before the court (para.44). In general respondents should not make submissions on the merits at the permission stage (para.45). Respondents will not be prejudiced at the appeal itself by such restraint at the permission stage, since this is essentially a "without notice" procedure (para.46). **52.3.17**

Where a permission application is to be determined on paper, any submissions from the respondent should be in writing. Even at an oral permission hearing, it may well suffice for the respondent's submissions to be made in writing. See *Jolly v Jay* [2002] EWCA Civ 277 at [47]. The respondent is unlikely to recover his costs of submitting written submissions or attending an oral hearing at the permission stage, unless such submissions or attendance are specifically requested by the court. Much of the effect of *Jolly v Jay* is now codified in paras 4.22–4.24 of the practice direction.

If the court requests the respondent's attendance at the permission hearing, then the respondent will receive a copy of the appeal bundle from the appellant: see para.4.16 of the practice direction.

Position of judge who has initially refused permission on paper

A judge who has initially refused permission to appeal to the Court of Appeal on consideration of the papers is entitled (absent special circumstances) to sit as a member of the court hearing the substantive appeal: see *Sengupta v Holmes* [2002] EWCA Civ **52.3.18**

1104; *The Times*, August 19, 2002, CA; *Dŵr Cymru Cyfyngedig v Albion Water* [2008] EWCA Civ 97, January 14, 2008, CA, unrep. It is, however, quite often the practice of the Court of Appeal to direct that the lord justice who refused permission on paper should not be a member of the constitution which hears the substantive appeal (where, for example, he expressed his adverse views strongly on paper).

In relation to junior appellate courts, different considerations may arise. On the one hand, it may be thought undesirable that the only judge hearing a substantive appeal is one who has previously expressed the view in writing that the appeal has no real prospect of success. On the other hand, the reasoning in *Sengupta v Holmes* would seem to be equally applicable to junior appellate courts. Furthermore, in practice, designated civil judges try to deal with CPR appeals themselves, in order to achieve consistency of approach. There would therefore be practical problems if circuit judges were precluded from hearing substantive appeals in cases where they had initially refused permission on paper. There might also be practical problems if High Court judges were precluded from hearing substantive appeals in cases where they had initially refused permission on paper. It is quite often the case on circuit that, owing to pressure of criminal work, only one High Court judge is available to hear civil appeals. See further, Vol.2 para.9A–48 (Judicial bias).

Procedure after permission

52.3.19 This is dealt with in paras 6.1 to 6.6 of the practice direction. In the case of appeals to the Court of Appeal, the appellant will receive an appeal questionnaire from the court and must respond to it within 14 days.

Change in appellant's case or change in circumstances after grant of permission

52.3.20 Where the appellant's case changes after the grant of permission, the appellant's representatives should write to the appeal court and to the other party, indicating the proposed nature of the changed case. The court should be asked to indicate whether it will deal with the matter at the beginning of the hearing of the appeal or whether it will give directions on an earlier date. After being informed of the respondent's attitude, the court can decide whether to shut out the new grounds or allow them to be argued: see *Shire v Secretary of State for Work and Pensions* [2003] EWCA Civ 1465 at [6]–[7]. See also the commentary following r.52.8.

Where there is a material change in circumstances after the grant of permission, which would affect the question of whether permission should have been given, the applicant should inform the court in writing: *Walbrook Trustee (Jersey) Ltd v Fattal* [2008] EWCA Civ 427 at [49].

Time estimates

52.3.21 One of the most important elements of the appeal questionnaire is the estimate of time for the hearing of the appeal, which must be made by the appellant's advocate. The respondent's advocate must consider this estimate. If he takes a different view, his own estimate of time must be sent to the court within seven days. See para.6.6 of the practice direction. Two general points need to be made about time estimates. First, accurate estimation is crucial to the efficient planning and listing of hearings. Secondly, accurate estimation is sometimes difficult. Not all judges pre-read with equal devotion to detail. Points have a habit of cropping up or fading away at appeals, with the effect of either shortening or elongating the hearing. Despite these handicaps, the opposing advocates must exercise judgment, draw on their own experience and, most importantly, talk to each other about the likely course and length of the hearing. Advocates who make no serious effort to estimate the length of an appeal hearing are in dereliction of their duty to the court.

In respect of appeals to the Court of Appeal, the appellant's advocate must state his time estimate for the hearing of the appeal in para.1 of his skeleton argument: see para.5.10(7) of the practice direction.

The effect of a "leapfrog" certificate

52.3.22 Where a judge grants a "leapfrog" certificate under s.12 of the Administration of Justice Act 1969 to any party, that party may apply to the House of Lords for leave to appeal directly from the High Court to the House of Lords. Section 13 of the 1969 Act provides that, if the House of Lords grants such leave, "no appeal from the decision of the judge to which the certificate relates shall lie to the Court of Appeal". Thus any permission to appeal to the Court of Appeal which the judge may have granted is overridden. If, however, the House of Lords grants permission to appeal subject to conditions and the appellant does not accept those conditions, then his right of appeal to the Court of Appeal revives: *R (Jones) v Ceredigion County Council* [2007] UKHL 24; [2007] 1 W.L.R. 1400.

Appellant's notice[1]

52.4—(1) Where the appellant seeks permission from the appeal court it must be requested in the appellant's notice. 52.4

(2) The appellant must file the appellant's notice at the appeal court within—

(a) such period as may be directed by the lower court (which may be longer or shorter than the period referred to in sub-paragraph (b)); or

(b) where the court makes no such direction, 21 days after the date of the decision of the lower court that the appellant wishes to appeal.

(3) Unless the appeal court orders otherwise, an appellant's notice must be served on each respondent—

(a) as soon as practicable; and

(b) in any event not later than 7 days,

after it is filed.

Time for appellant's notice

The appellant's notice must be filed within 21 days after the date of the decision under appeal, unless the lower court directs a different period. Before r.52.4(2) was amended by the Civil Procedure (Amendment No.4) Rules 2005 (SI 2005/3515) (with effect from April 6, 2006) the period was 14 days. The brevity of the time allowed reflects a clear policy decision in favour of finality. Any party seeking to challenge a judicial decision must move with expedition. In the immediate aftermath of the judgment below both the party and his advisers are fully seized of the case. They can be expected to formulate any grounds of appeal without delay. The background to this rule is set out by Brooke L.J. in *Sayers v Clarke Walker* [2002] EWCA Civ 645 at [12]–16]; [2002] 1 W.L.R. 3095. The Bowman Report (1997) recommended in respect of appeals to the Court of Appeal that the time limit for appeals against final decisions should be six weeks and that the time limit for appeals against procedural decisions should be seven days (see Ch.7, paras 7 and 8). The Civil Procedure Rule Committee rejected these recommendations. It adopted a uniform time limit of, initially, 14 days only for all appeals, save in respect of judicial review permission appeals, where the time limit is seven days (see r.52.15 below). However, as explained above, the 14 day time limit was subsequently increased by the Civil Procedure Rule Committee to 21 days. 52.4.1

If a party has good reason for seeking a longer period in which to appeal, he should apply to the lower court on the occasion when judgment is given (unless that hearing is adjourned pursuant to para.4.3B of the practice direction). An example of a good reason for seeking a modest extension of time may be that the appellant (through no fault of its own) has an unwieldy decision-making process, such as a board of trustees which needs to be convened. Another example may be that a national holiday period is about to begin. Another example may be that an approved transcript of judgment or a perfected written judgment may reasonably be required before the notice of appeal can be prepared. It should be noted, however, that the lower court will not normally extend time for the notice of appeal by more than 14 days: see para.5.19 of the practice direction.

An application to the lower court to extend time pursuant to r.52.4(2)(a) may be made on a date after judgment was given, although this course involves additional and

[1] Introduced by the Civil Procedure (Amendment) Rules 2000 (SI 2000/221) and amended by the Civil Procedure (Amendment No.4) Rules 2005 (SI 2005/3515).

avoidable expense. Indeed such an application may even be made after expiry of the 21 day period: see *Dalkia Utilities Services plc v Celtech International Ltd (No.2)* [2006] EWHC 63_2 (Comm). Although *Dalkia* was decided under the old regime, when the relevant time limit was 14 days (not 21 days), the statements of principle in paras 5–6 remain valid. Nevertheless, once the appellant's notice has been filed (albeit out of time), the lower court should not exercise its discretion to extend time. The matter should be left for the appeal court to consider in accordance with r.52.6. See *Aujla v Sanghera* [2004] EWCA Civ 121 at [14]–[21].

If an extension of time is needed beyond the period specified by the lower court (or beyond the 21 day period mentioned in r.52.4(2)(b)), then the appellant should apply to the appeal court. See r.52.6(1). The application must be made in the appellant's notice. See para.5.2 of the practice direction. The notice should state the reason for the delay and the steps taken prior to the application being made. The respondent has a right to be heard on this application. See para.5.3 of the practice direction. This perilous course for appellants (which is discussed further in the commentary on r.52.6) emphasises: (a) the importance of complying with time limits in the first place; (b) the wisdom of applying *prospectively* to the lower court for any extension of time which really is necessary.

It should be noted that specific time limits for particular categories of appeal, whether imposed by statute, rule or practice direction, may override the general 21 day time limit imposed by r.52.4(2): see r.52.1(4). Paragraphs 16 to 24 of the practice direction set out the applicable time limits for statutory appeals, appeals by way of case stated and a variety of specific appeals.

Date when time starts to run

52.4.2 Time starts to run on the date when the judge below makes his decision, not on the date when the order reflecting that decision is drawn up. See *Sayers v Clarke Walker* [2002] EWCA Civ 645 at [5]; [2002] 1 W.L.R. 3095. The problems which arise when the judge below (wrongly) dispenses with the formality of handing down judgment are discussed in *Owusu v Jackson* [2002] EWCA Civ 877 at [24]–[27].

In the case of appeals from the Upper Tribunal to the Court of Appeal time starts to run on the date on which the Upper Tribunal's decision on permission to appeal is given: see paras 17.4A (1) and (2) of the practice direction.

Content of appellant's notice

52.4.3 If permission has not already been granted by the lower court, the appellant's notice must include an application for permission. See r.52.4(1) and para.5.1 of the practice direction. The appellant's notice must be in Form **N161**. The grounds of appeal (s.7 of Form **N161**) should set out clearly why it is said (a) that the decision of the lower court is wrong or (b) that the decision of the lower court is unjust because of a serious procedural or other irregularity. In respect of each ground, the appellant must specify whether the ground raises an appeal on a point of law or is an appeal against a finding of fact. See r.52.11(3) and para.3.2 of the practice direction. If the appellant is raising any human rights points, he must comply with para.5.1A of the practice direction.

Skeleton argument

52.4.4 Every appellant who is represented is required (and other appellants are encouraged) to prepare a skeleton argument. If it is short it can be fitted into s.8 of the appellant's notice. Otherwise, the skeleton argument should be a separate document accompanying the appellant's notice. If that is not practicable, the skeleton argument must be lodged and served within 14 days after filing the appellant's notice. See para.5.9 of the practice direction.

The content of skeleton arguments is dealt with in para.5.10 of the practice direction. This paragraph incorporates the relevant requirements of the *Practice Direction (Citation of Authorities)* [2001] 1 W.L.R. 1001. Paragraph 5.10 is clear and specific in its requirements and there are costs consequences for non-compliance: see para.5.10(6). The skeleton argument is a vital document and must be prepared with great care. It will perform two functions. First, it will assist the appeal court in its case management function. (Hence the need for its early production). Secondly, it will be the document upon which the appellant relies at the full hearing, as a summary of his submissions.

In addition to his skeleton argument, the appellant should also provide a chronology (if appropriate, as it usually is) and, if necessary, a list of persons featuring in the case, and/or a glossary of technical terms: see para.5.11 of the practice direction.

Documents to be lodged with the appellant's notice

In the case of small claims being appealed to a circuit judge or a High Court judge, the documents which the appellant must file are set out in para.5.8 of the practice direction. **52.4.5**

In the case of all other appeals, the documents which an appellant must file are those set out in paras 5.6 and 5.6A of the practice direction. These comprise a small number of specified documents and also an appeal bundle. The appeal bundle shall consist of the documents identified in para.5.6A(1) (a)–(k) (the appellant's notice, the order being appealed and so forth) and also:

"(l) any other documents which the appellant reasonably considers necessary to enable the appeal court to reach its decision on the hearing of the application or appeal; and (m) such other documents as the court may direct".

Paragraph 5.6A(2) specifically requires that all documents extraneous to the issues be excluded. Where the appellant is represented, his representative must sign and place in the bundle a certificate stating that he has read and understood para.5.6A(2) of the practice direction and that the composition of the bundle complies with it (see para.5.6A(3)). This certificate will

> "act as an important reassurance ... that the bad old days of unthinkingly copying the trial bundle are over, and that only those that are directly relevant to the subject-matter of the appeal will have been included in an appeal bundle."

See *Scribes West Ltd v Anstalt (No.1)* [2004] EWCA Civ 835 at [11].

Paragraph 5.7 of the practice direction sets out the procedure to be followed if any relevant document is not available when the appellant's notice is filed.

Paragraph 6.3A of the practice direction specifies the documents which must be added to, or removed from, the appeal bundle after the appeal court has dealt with the question of permission.

Paragraphs 20–24 of the practice direction include requirements in respect of documents to be filed in support of specific appeals.

Where an appeal is proceeding in the Court of Appeal, there are additional requirements to be complied with. These are set out in paras 15.1 to 15.4 of the practice direction. Paragraph 15.1 deals with the filing and service of documents. Paragraphs 15.2 and 15.3 provide for the subsequent preparation of a core bundle in any case where the appeal bundle exceeds 500 pages. Paragraph 15.4 sets out precisely how bundles must be prepared for the Court of Appeal. The sanctions for non-compliance range from disallowance of costs or rejection of the proffered bundles to dismissal of the entire appeal or application.

Practitioners would be well advised (and may be encouraged by their insurers) to study the above provisions with care and to heed them scrupulously. The current provisions concerning appeal bundles were introduced into the practice direction on June 30, 2004. These provisions were introduced in response to a number of cases in which practitioners had been woefully lax in the preparation of bundles (leading to a wastage of time and costs) and had been subject to criticism by the Court of Appeal.

Any plan, map, diagram or photograph should be in such form, or accompanied by such explanation, that it is readily intelligible to the judge or lord justice who is pre-reading the papers: see *Hunte v E. Bottomley & Sons Ltd* [2007] EWCA Civ 1168.

Practice where the proposed appeal court lacks jurisdiction

Paragraph 2A.5 of the practice direction states the practice to be followed by a court officer in giving notice to an applicant who has attempted to file an appellant's notice in circumstances where the appeal court does not have jurisdiction to issue the notice. Where that officer is an officer of the Court of Appeal (civil division), r.52.16(5) is disapplied, with the effect that the applicant may not request the court under that rule to review the officer's decision. **52.4.6**

Respondent's notice[1]

52.5 **52.5—(1) A respondent may file and serve a respondent's notice.**

(2) A respondent who—

(a) is seeking permission to appeal from the appeal court; or

(b) wishes to ask the appeal court to uphold the order of the lower court for reasons different from or additional to those given by the lower court,

must file a respondent's notice.

(3) Where the respondent seeks permission from the appeal court it must be requested in the respondent's notice.

(4) A respondent's notice must be filed within—

(a) such period as may be directed by the lower court; or

(b) where the court makes no such direction, 14 days, after the date in paragraph (5).

(5) The date referred to in paragraph (4) is—

(a) the date the respondent is served with the appellant's notice where—

(i) permission to appeal was given by the lower court; or

(ii) permission to appeal is not required;

(b) the date the respondent is served with notification that the appeal court has given the appellant permission to appeal; or

(c) the date the respondent is served with notification that the application for permission to appeal and the appeal itself are to be heard together.

(6) Unless the appeal court orders otherwise a respondent's notice must be served on the appellant and any other respondent—

(a) as soon as practicable; and

(b) in any event not later than 7 days,

after it is filed.

Obligation on respondents

52.5.1 Rule 52.5 should be read in conjunction with s.7 and para.15.6 of the practice direction. In the case of appeals to the Court of Appeal the respondent must, within 21 days after notification that permission has been granted (or that the application for permission and the appeal will be heard together), notify the Civil Appeals Office and the appellant whether he intends (a) to file a respondent's notice or (b) to rely on the reasons given by the lower court. Failure to comply with this obligation can cause considerable difficulties for the court: see *Mlauzi v SSHD* [2005] EWCA Civ 128 at [30]–[31].

The passive respondent

52.5.2 If the respondent seeks only to uphold the judgment of the court below for the reasons given by that court, then he is not obliged to serve a respondent's notice.

Respondent relying upon further reasons

52.5.3 If the respondent seeks to uphold the order of the court below for additional reasons or different reasons from those given by that court, then he must file and

[1] Introduced by the Civil Procedure (Amendment) Rules 2000 (SI 2000/221).

serve a respondent's notice. The respondent's notice should be in Form **N162**. The respondent should state the additional or different grounds upon which he relies in s.6.

Respondent seeking to vary the order of the court below

If the respondent seeks to vary the order of the court below, then he must (a) file and serve a respondent's notice and (b) apply for permission to appeal. The criteria and procedure for granting permission to appeal have been discussed above. In practice, however, respondents may find it somewhat easier to obtain permission than appellants. Once one party has obtained permission to re-open the case upon appeal, it may be inappropriate to tie the other party to the terms of the original judgment. If the appeal and cross-appeal are linked (e.g. the defendant disputes the finding of liability and the claimant responds by challenging the level of contributory negligence), it will often be illogical to grant permission to one party and refuse it to the other. **52.5.4**

Time for respondent's notice

The time for filing a respondent's notice is set out in r.52.5(4) and (5). In essence, the respondent has 14 days after the date on which, one way or another, it becomes clear that the appellant's appeal will proceed. The lower court may direct a period longer or shorter that 14 days. An important consequence flows from these provisions. If one party applies to the lower court for permission to appeal (whether or not successfully), the other party/parties should immediately consider how long might be required for a respondent's notice (in the event that permission to appeal is granted either by the lower court or by the appeal court) and make any appropriate application to the lower court. Finally, a respondent's notice must be served on all other parties as soon as practicable and in any event within seven days after being filed. See r.52.5(6)). If the respondent requires any extension of time from the appeal court, then he should request this in the respondent's notice: see para.7.5 of the practice direction. **52.5.5**

Respondent's skeleton argument

Paragraph 7.6 of the practice direction obliges the respondent to provide a skeleton argument "in all cases where he proposes to address arguments to the court". If it is short, it can be accommodated in s.7 of the respondent's notice. Otherwise, the skeleton argument should be a separate document. It must either accompany the respondent's notice or else be lodged and served within 14 days after filing the notice. See para.7.7 of the Practice Direction. The respondent's skeleton argument is required at this early stage to assist case management decisions: see p.86 of the Bowman Report and the judgment of Brooke L.J. in *Philosophy Inc v Ferretti Studios SRL* [2002] EWCA Civ 921. **52.5.6**

The content of a respondent's skeleton argument is dealt with in para.7.8 of the practice direction. This is a crucial document, which will repay care and thought in its preparation. It will have three important functions. First, it will assist the appeal court in case management. Secondly, it may inspire some of the court's questions or interruptions when the appellant's advocate is opening his appeal (thus helping to focus the oral hearing at an early stage). Thirdly, it will be the document upon which the respondent (if called upon) relies as a summary of his submissions.

Where the appeal relates to a claim on the small claims track or the respondent is not represented, the respondent is not obliged to provide a skeleton argument, but he is entitled to do so. See para.7.7A of the practice direction.

In cases where there is no respondent's notice, the respondent need not serve his skeleton argument until seven days before the appeal hearing: see para.7.7(2) of the practice direction. However, if an appeal to the Court of Appeal is allocated to the short warned list, the respondent's skeleton argument may be required at short notice: see *Scribes West Ltd v Anstalt (No.1)* [2004] EWCA Civ 835 at [24].

Documents to be filed by the respondent

Paragraphs 7.10–7.13 explain what documents the respondent must file and serve. If the respondent maintains that additional documents merit inclusion in the appeal bundle, then there is an obligation on the representatives of both parties to focus on this question and to endeavour to reach a sensible agreement. It is in the interests of the clients on both sides (as well as the court) to end up with a bundle which contains all documents relevant to the issues in the appeal and no other documents. **52.5.7**

Variation of time[1]

52.6 **52.6—(1) An application to vary the time limit for filing an appeal notice must be made to the appeal court.**

(2) The parties may not agree to extend any date or time limit set by—

(a) these Rules;

(b) the relevant practice direction; or

(c) an order of the appeal court or the lower court.

(Rule 3.1(2)(a) provides that the court may extend or shorten the time for compliance with any rule, practice direction or court order (even if an application for extension is made after the time for compliance has expired).)

(Rule 3.1(2)(b) provides that the court may adjourn or bring forward a hearing.)

Consequences of refusal to extend time

52.6.1 If a circuit judge or a High Court judge declines to extend time for appealing against the decision of a lower court, that decision does not have the same finality as a refusal of permission to appeal. The disappointed party may (if he obtains permission) appeal against the decision that time should not be extended. See *Foenander v Bond Lewis & Co* [2001] EWCA Civ 759; [2002] 1 W.L.R. 525.

The practical consequences of this decision need to be borne in mind by judges dealing with applications under r.52.6(1). These consequences were spelt out by Brooke L.J. in *Foenander* at para.19:

> "The logic of this decision is that if a circuit judge or a High Court judge sitting in an appeal court has the choice of disposing of a belated and unmeritorious appeal either by refusing to extend time for appealing or by refusing permission to appeal, he/she should bear in mind that taking the latter course will bring the appellate proceedings to an end. The adoption of the former course, on the other hand, may entail further expense and delay while a challenge is launched at a higher appeal court against the decision not to extend time for appealing."

Criteria to be applied on applications to extend time

52.6.2 On applications under r.52.6 to extend time for appealing after expiry of the time limit, it is necessary to have regard to the checklist in r.3.9. This is because the applicant has not complied with r.52.4(2) and, in the absence of relief, the applicant will be unable to appeal: see *Sayers v Clarke Walker* [2002] EWCA Civ 645 at [21]; [2002] 1 W.L.R. 3095. In cases where the arguments for granting or refusing an extension of time are otherwise evenly balanced, the court should evaluate the merits of the proposed appeal in order to form a judgment on what the applicants will be losing if time is not extended: see *Sayers v Clarke Walker* at [34]. In *Smith v Brough* [2005] EWCA Civ 261 the Court of Appeal, in the course of refusing to extend time by 39 months, stressed the importance of finality in litigation.

In *Smith v Kvaerner Cementation Foundations Ltd* [2006] EWCA Civ 242; [2007] 1 W.L.R. 370 the claimant was granted permission to appeal, despite his delay of four years in applying to the Court of Appeal. The paramount consideration in that case was that the claimant at trial had been denied his right under ECHR art.6 to a fair hearing before an independent and impartial tribunal. There was also a good explanation for his failure to pursue an appeal earlier.

If an application to extend time for appealing is made in time (i.e. it is made prospectively), then r.3.9 does not apply: see the reasoning of the Court of Appeal in *Robert v Momentum Services Ltd* [2003] EWCA Civ 299; [2003] 2 All E.R. 74.

Applications for extension of time by asylum seekers

52.6.3 If an asylum seeker fails before the Asylum and Immigration Tribunal (AIT), but

[1] Introduced by Civil Procedure (Amendment) Rules 2000 (SI 2000/221).

obtains leave from the AIT to appeal to the Court of Appeal, his notice of appeal should be lodged within 14 days: see para.21.7 (3) of the practice direction. If he fails to meet that time limit, he will require an extension of time. The principles upon which an application for such an extension of time should be dealt with were summarised as follows by the Court of Appeal in *BR (Iran) v SSHD* [2007] EWCA Civ 198 at [23]; [2007] 1 W.L.R. 2278:

"(i) There should be a presumption that where the AIT has granted permission to appeal to this court the appeal ought to be heard.

(ii) If a procedural fault causes this court to have to consider whether the appeal should proceed, the presumption may be displaced if it can be shown that the decision of the SIJ was plainly wrong, in the sense that it is clear that failure to pursue the appeal would not lead to the United Kingdom being in breach of its international obligations. ...

(iii) Length of delay, when caused by legal representatives, should not be relevant.

(iv) Where delay has been caused by the applicant, the court is likely to look carefully at the light that that sheds on the credibility of the assertion that the applicant has a good claim for international protection. At the same time, the court will remind itself that if after that scrutiny such a claim is established, then the claimant is indeed entitled to international protection despite the domestic court's disapproval of his conduct or his way of promoting his case. ..."

Stay[GL1]

52.7 Unless— 52.7

(a) the appeal court or the lower court orders otherwise; or

(b) the appeal is from the Asylum and Immigration Tribunal,

an appeal shall not operate as a stay of any order or decision of the lower court.

General approach

52.7.1 Neither the commencement of an appeal nor the grant of permission to appeal affects the enforceability of the judgment below. If the appellant desires a stay, he must apply for it and put forward solid grounds why such a stay should be granted. This is true even in judicial review cases concerning immigration or asylum, where the appellant faces deportation as a consequence of the High Court's decision: see *R. (Pharis) v SSHD* [2004] EWCA Civ 654; [2004] 1 W.L.R. 2590.

Under RSC O.59 (which governed appeals prior to May 2000) the courts had established the principle that a successful litigant should not generally be deprived of the fruits of his litigation pending appeal, unless there was some good reason for this course. This general principle still applies. "The normal rule is for no stay ..." per Potter L.J. in *Leicester Circuits Ltd v Coates Brothers plc* [2002] EWCA Civ 474 at [13].

The balancing exercise

52.7.2 If an appellant puts forward solid grounds for seeking a stay, the court must then consider all the circumstances of the case. It must weigh up the risks inherent in granting a stay and the risks inherent in refusing a stay. See, e.g. *R. (Van Hoogstraten) v Governor of Belmarsh Prison* [2002] EWHC 2015 (Admin); *Gater Assets Ltd v Nak Naftogaz Ukrainiy* [2008] EWCA Civ 51. In *Hammond Suddard Solicitors v Agrichem International Holdings Ltd* [2001] EWCA Civ 2065, December 18, 2001, unrep., CA, Clarke L.J. described the correct approach as follows at [22]:

"Whether the court should exercise its discretion to grant a stay will depend upon all the circumstances of the case, but the essential question is whether there is a risk of injustice to one or both parties if it grants or refuses a stay. In particular, if a stay is refused what are the risks of an appeal being stifled? If a stay is granted and the appeal fails, what are the risks that the respondent will be unable to enforce the judg-

[1] Introduced by the Civil Procedure (Amendment) Rules 2000 (SI 2000/221) and amended by the Civil Procedure (Amendment) Rules 2006 (SI 2006/1689).

ment? On the other hand, if a stay is refused and the appeal succeeds, and the judgment is enforced in the meantime, what are the risks of the appellant being able to recover any monies paid from the respondent?" (The last sentence might be more felicitous if the word "able" is changed to "unable").

In considering whether, absent a stay, the appeal would be stifled, the court does not look only at the means of the appellant. It also considers whether the money can be raised from the appellant's directors, shareholders, other backers or interested persons: see *Contract Facilities Ltd v Estate of Rees (deceased)* [2003] EWCA Civ 465 at [10].

A stay may be granted subject to conditions. For example, in *Contract Facilities Ltd v Estate of Rees (deceased)* [2003] EWCA Civ 465 the appellant claimant obtained a stay of the costs order below, on condition that he paid into a joint account of the two firms of solicitors 50 per cent of the costs claimed by the defendant.

Where the lower court orders a stay of proceedings

52.7.3 A stay of proceedings ordered by the lower court does not preclude an appeal against the order imposing the stay: see *Aoun v Bahri* [2002] EWCA Civ 1141 at [20]–[23].

Appeals from the Asylum and Immigration Tribunal

52.7.4 The Asylum and Immigration Tribunal ("AIT") is the body which replaced the Immigration Appeal Tribunal with effect from April 2005. Pursuant to r.52.7(b) an appeal from the AIT operates as an automatic stay of the AIT's order or decision.

Where a party applies to the Court of Appeal for permission to appeal out of time against a decision of the AIT, that application does not give rise to an automatic stay of the AIT's order. Nevertheless the Court of Appeal has inherent jurisdiction to order the Secretary of State to refrain from removing the applicant until the application for permission has been determined. When this jurisdiction is exercised a very important factor will be the court's assessment of the likelihood that the applications for an extension of time and for permission to appeal will be granted. See *YD (Turkey) v SSHD* [2006] EWCA Civ 52; [2006] 1 W.L.R. 1646.

Appeals against possession orders

52.7.5 In *Admiral Taverns (Cygnet) Ltd v Daniel* [2008] EWHC 1688 (QB) Teare J. held that s.89 of the Housing Act 1980 did not prevent an appeal court from staying a possession order until the application to appeal or, alternatively, the appeal had been determined.

Amendment of appeal notice[1]

52.8 **52.8 An appeal notice may not be amended without the permission of the appeal court.**

Point raised below

52.8.1 If the proposed amendment raises a point which was argued in the lower court, the question may arise why this was not included in the original appeal notice. Nevertheless, if the amendment is sought timeously, it may not prejudice other parties. Such an amendment may well be permitted, subject to the general principles governing amendments. See the commentary to Pt 17.

Point not raised below

52.8.2 If the appellant seeks to raise a new point or to withdraw a concession made below, then different considerations arise. In *Jones v MBNA International Bank* June 30, 2000, unrep. the Court of Appeal refused the claimant's application to make amendments raising new grounds of claim. May L.J. stated at para.52:

> "Civil trials are conducted on the basis that the court decides the factual and legal issues which the parties bring before the court. ... Normally a party cannot

[1] Introduced by the Civil Procedure (Amendment) Rules 2000 (SI 2000/221).

raise in subsequent proceedings claims or issues which could and should have been raised in the first proceedings. Equally, a party cannot, in my judgment, normally seek to appeal a trial judge's decision on the basis that a claim, which could have been brought before the trial judge, but was not, would have succeeded if it had been so brought. The justice of this as general principle is, in my view, obvious. It is not merely a matter of efficiency, expediency and cost, but of substantial justice. Parties to litigation are entitled to know where they stand. The parties are entitled, and the court requires, to know what the issues are. Upon this depends a variety of decisions, including, by the parties, what evidence to call, how much effort and money it is appropriate to invest in the case, and generally how to conduct the case; and, by the court, what case management and administrative decisions to make and give, and the substantive decision of the case itself. Litigation should be resolved once and for all, and it is not, generally speaking, just if a party who successfully contested a case advanced on one basis should be expected to face on appeal, not a challenge to the original decision, but a new case advanced on a different basis. There may be exceptional cases in which the court would not apply the general principle which I have expressed."

Arden L.J. expressed similar views in *Crane T/A Indigital Satellite Services v Sky In-Home Ltd* [2008] EWCA Civ 978 at [18]–[22]. Arden L.J. identified a number of factors which would be fatal to an application to raise a new point on appeal, such as the fact that different evidence would have been called at trial.

As to the procedure, which should be followed where the nature of the claimant's case changes after the grant of permission, see the commentary following r.52.3.

If the appellant wishes to raise a new point on appeal, this may necessitate amendment of the original pleadings. The Court of Appeal has power in an appropriate (and, it is submitted, exceptional) case to allow such an amendment, even if it was not sought in the court below: see *Islington LBC v UCKAC* [2006] EWCA Civ 340 at [36]–[41]. Nevertheless, in the absence of permission to amend, the court's jurisdiction is constrained by what is in the grounds of appeal and in the grant of permission: see *Gover v Propertycare Ltd* [2006] EWCA Civ 286 at [10].

Striking out[GL] appeal notices and setting aside or imposing conditions on permission to appeal[1]

52.9—(1) The appeal court may— **52.9**

(a) strike out the whole or part of an appeal notice;

(b) set aside[GL] permission to appeal in whole or in part;

(c) impose or vary conditions upon which an appeal may be brought.

(2) The court will only exercise its powers under paragraph (1) where there is a compelling reason for doing so.

(3) Where a party was present at the hearing at which permission was given he may not subsequently apply for an order that the court exercise its powers under sub-paragraphs (1)(b) or (1)(c).

The appeal court's power

Under r.52.9(1) the appeal court has power to strike out the whole or part of an **52.9.1** appeal notice; to set aside permission to appeal in whole or in part; or to impose or vary conditions upon the bringing of an appeal. As to the court's power to order that permission to appeal should be made subject to conditions, see r.52.3(7)(b).

Cautionary note

This tempting provision should not lure advocates into tactical skirmishing or into **52.9.2** manoeuvres designed to wear down the opposition. Save in exceptional circumstances, it is a misuse of the court's resources and a waste of costs for the court to consider the

[1] Introduced by the Civil Procedure (Amendment) Rules 2000 (SI 2000/221).

substance of an appeal on some intermediate date between the permission hearing and the full appeal. This paragraph of commentary was cited by the Court of Appeal, apparently with approval, in *Nathan v Smilovitch* [2002] EWCA Civ 759 at [8].

Rule 52.9(2) provides that the power will only be exercised where there is "a compelling reason". There would be a compelling reason, if the materials previously before the judge were so inaccurate or incomplete that the judge had granted permission, when otherwise he would not have done: see *Hertsmere BC v Harty* [2001] EWCA Civ 1238 at [2]; *Angel Airlines SA v Dean & Dean* [2006] EWCA Civ 1505. In *Nathan v Smilovitch* [2002] EWCA Civ 759 at [9] Longmore L.J. said:

> "For my part, unless the nature of the application shows that some decisive authority or decisive statutory provision has been overlooked by the lord justice granting permission to appeal, an applicant would normally have to show that the single lord justice had actually been misled in the course of the presentation of an application."

In *Barings Bank plc (in liquidation) v Coopers & Lybrand* [2002] EWCA Civ 1155 a differently constituted Court of Appeal agreed with that formulation. In *Barings Bank* events since the grant of permission reduced the importance of the appeal, so that it was relevant to costs only. The Court held that this was not a compelling reason for setting aside the grant of permission and declined to do so. Laws L.J. said:

> "It seems to me to be of the highest importance that the court should very firmly discourage the bringing of satellite litigation under the guise of an application under CPR r.52.9. The rule is there to cater for the rare case in which the lord justice granting permission to appeal has actually been misled. If he has, the court's process has been abused and that is of course a special situation. There may also be cases where, as Longmore L.J. indicated in *Nathan v Smilovitch* [2002] EWCA Civ 759, some decisive authority or statute has been overlooked by the lord justice granting permission. But where such a state of affairs is asserted, the learning in question must in my view be plainly and unarguably decisive of the issue. If there is anything to argue about, an application to set aside the grant of permission will be misconceived."

In the rare cases in which it is appropriate to make an application to set aside the grant of permission to appeal or to impose conditions on the grant of permission, such application should be made promptly: see *Okta Crude Oil Refinery AD v Moil-Coal Trading Co Ltd* [2003] EWCA Civ 617 at [10]–[11]. The application should not be made at the substantive hearing of the appeal: see *Tradigrain SA v Intertek Testing Services (ITS) Canada Ltd* [2007] EWCA Civ 154.

If the respondent was present on the occasion when permission was granted, then he cannot subsequently apply to set aside or vary that permission. See r.52.9(3).

In *Athletic Union of Constantinople v National Basketball Association (No.2)* [2002] EWCA Civ 830; [2002] 1 W.L.R. 2863 the Court of Appeal set aside permission to appeal previously granted by a single lord justice, for want of jurisdiction.

Striking out an appeal notice

52.9.3 It is now unlikely that an appeal notice will be struck out on grounds of lack of merit. If permission to appeal has been granted (and that permission is not to be set aside), it follows that the appeal has a real prospect of success or that there is some other compelling reason why the appeal should be heard: see r.52.3(6). If the appeal notice has been amended after the permission stage, such amendment must have been approved by the court: see r.52.8. Accordingly the power to strike out is more likely to be used for other purposes, for example as a sanction for non-compliance with orders. See e.g. *Carr v Bower Cotton* [2002] EWCA Civ 789 at [36]; *Taiga v Taiga* [2004] EWCA Civ 1399.

In *Turner v Haworth Associates* [2001] EWCA Civ 370 a circuit judge struck out a notice of appeal from an order of a district judge on the ground that the notice of appeal was frivolous, vexatious and an abuse of process. The Court of Appeal upheld the circuit judge's decision. Chadwick L.J. (with whom Hale L.J. agreed) said at [28]: "... the practice which is now embodied in CPR r.52.9 reflects the jurisdiction which a court must have in order to safeguard its own proceedings from abuse; and to deal with an appeal in a summary manner if it thinks that appropriate." It should be noted, however, that the appeal against the district judge's order in *Turner* was commenced before May 2, 2000, and thus was not subject to a permission requirement. If the appeal had been commenced after May 2, 2000, neither the district judge nor the circuit judge would have given permission to appeal and thus no question of striking out would have arisen.

Imposition of conditions

Rule 52.9(1)(c) enables conditions to be imposed, when such conditions were not attached to the original grant of permission pursuant to r.52.3(7)(b). In *Hammond Suddard Solicitors v Agrichem International Holdings Ltd* [2001] EWCA Civ 2065, December 18, 2001, CA, unrep., the Court of Appeal pursuant to r.52.9(1)(c) required the appellant defendant to pay into court the amount of the judgment debt plus costs as a condition of proceeding with its appeal. The appellant in that case was a foreign limited company, which appeared (a) to have ample assets overseas (so that the new condition would not stifle the appeal) but (b) to be unlikely to honour the original judgment if its appeal failed. In *Bell Electric Ltd v Aweco Appliance Systems GmbH & Co KG (Application to Stay Appeal)* [2002] EWCA Civ 1501; [2003] 1 All E.R. 344 the Court of Appeal required the appellant defendant to give security for the judgment sum, as a condition of prosecuting its appeal, despite the absence of any perceptible future problems in enforcing the judgment debt. This was because of the appellant's deliberate breach of an earlier order to pay the judgment sum. In *Dunford Trading AG v OAO Atlantrybflot* [2004] EWCA Civ 1265 Clarke L.J. indicated that if the appellant were deliberately dissipating its assets in order to avoid paying a judgment, that might justify adding a condition to the leave to appeal, requiring payment of the judgment debt into court. On the other hand, in *Wittman (UK) Ltd v Willdav Engineering SA* [2007] EWCA Civ 521 the Court of Appeal refused to impose a condition that the appellant defendant should pay the amount of the judgment debt into court. The appellant had obtained a stay of execution pending appeal. It was uncertain whether the appellant would be able to meet the judgment debt, but "mere impecuniosity" was not a sufficient ground for imposing such a condition (see [10]). Furthermore the respondent had delayed in making its application. **52.9.4**

The principles which emerge from the above cases are:

(i) An application by a respondent for an order that the appellant do give security as a condition of proceeding with his appeal need not involve consideration of the merits of the appeal at an intermediate stage between the permission hearing and the full appeal. So it does not infringe the cautionary note set out above. See *Bell Electric* at [19].

(ii) In determining whether there is a "compelling reason" to impose such a condition the court should consider the justice of the case and all the circumstances.

(iii) Any application for the imposition of such a condition should be made promptly.

In *Masri v Consolidated Contractors International (UK) Ltd* [2007] EWCA Civ 702 Lloyd L.J. followed *Hammond Suddard* and rejected the submission that such an approach was contrary to ECHR art.6. In *Peer International Corporation v Termidor Music Publishers* [2007] EWCA Civ 1308 Lloyd L.J. followed *Hammond Suddard* and held that there was a "compelling reason" to vary the terms upon which permission to appeal had been given by imposing a condition that the appellant do comply with certain costs orders (which were not challenged in the appeal).

For another example of conditions being imposed later upon permission to appeal, see the commentary on r.52.3(7)(b) above.

The effect of rule 52.9(3)

Rule 52.9(3) should not be construed as barring an appellant from challenging a condition, which would prevent him from obtaining access to the court: *Kuwait Airways Corporation v Iraqi Airways Co (Application for Permission to Appeal)* [2005] EWCA Civ 934 at [73]–[74]. Indeed r.52.9(3) does not apply to the appellant at all: see *Kuwait Airways* at [75]–[81]. **52.9.5**

Statutory appeals which do not require permission

Rule 52.9 applies to statutory appeals which do not require permission: see *Calltel Telecom Ltd v HM Revenue & Customs* [2008] EWHC 2107 (Ch). At [34]–[35] Briggs J. questioned what the "compelling reason" requirement contained in r.52.9 (2) added in relation to such appeals. **52.9.6**

Appeal court's powers[1]

52.10 **52.10—(1) In relation to an appeal the appeal court has all the powers of the lower court. (Rule 52.1(4) provides that this Part is subject to any enactment that sets out special provisions with regard to any particular category of appeal—where such an enactment gives a statutory power to a tribunal, person or other body it may be the case that the appeal court may not exercise that power on an appeal.)**

(2) The appeal court has power to—

(a) affirm, set aside or vary any order or judgment made or given by the lower court;

(b) refer any claim or issue for determination by the lower court;

(c) order a new trial or hearing;

(d) make orders for the payment of interest;

(e) make a costs order.

(3) In an appeal from a claim tried with a jury the Court of Appeal may, instead of ordering a new trial—

(a) make an order for damages[GL]; or

(b) vary an award of damages made by the jury.

(4) The appeal court may exercise its powers in relation to the whole or part of an order of the lower court.

(Part 3 contains general rules about the court's case management powers.)

(5) If the appeal court—

(a) refuses an application for permission to appeal;

(b) strikes out an appellant's notice; or

(c) dismisses an appeal,

and it considers that the application, the appellant's notice or the appeal is totally without merit, the provisions of paragraph (6) must be complied with.

(6) Where paragraph (5) applies—

(a) the court's order must record the fact that it considers the application, the appellant's notice or the appeal to be totally without merit; and

(b) the court must at the same time consider whether it is appropriate to make a civil restraint order.

Security for costs of proceedings below

52.10.1 The Court of Appeal has power under this rule to make an order for security in respect of the costs of the proceedings below: *Dar International FEF Co v Aon Ltd* [2003] EWCA Civ 1833; [2004] 1 W.L.R. 1395.

Power to refer before substantive hearing of appeal

52.10.2 Under r.52.10 (2)(b) the appeal court has power to refer any claim or issue back to the lower court for determination. The appeal court may exercise this power even before the substantive hearing of the appeal. Thus the appeal court may invite the judge below to address points which contingently arise in the event that the appeal succeeds on the issue for which permission to appeal has been granted. See *Hicks v Russell Jones & Walker* [2007] EWCA Civ 844 at [15]–[25].

[1] Introduced by the Civil Procedure (Amendment) Rules 2000 (SI 2000/221).

Court of Appeal's power to award interest

In *Multiplex Construction Ltd v Cleveland Bridge Ltd* [2008] EWCA Civ 133 the Court of Appeal, having allowed in part CB's appeal in respect of preliminary issue 11, ordered that the costs of the hearing below in respect of preliminary issue 11 be reserved to the trial judge; the court further ordered that the payment on account of costs previously made by the partially successful appellant be repaid with interest. May L.J. (with whom Smith L.J. agreed) held that the Court of Appeal's power to award interest in those circumstances arose under r.52.10(2)(d), alternatively under r.52.10(1) (Court of Appeal has all the powers of the lower court) read in conjunction with r.44.3(6)(g) and 44.3(8). 52.10.3

Court of Appeal's power to refer issues to lower court

The Court of Appeal's power under r.52.10(2)(b) to refer issues for determination by the lower court may be exercised even before the appeal has been heard. In *Hicks v Russell Jones & Walker* [2007] EWCA Civ 844; [2008] 2 All E.R. 1089 the respondents considered that, if one of the grounds of appeal succeeded, additional findings would be required from the judge on matters which had been fully covered before him. The judge indicated that he was willing to make such findings, subject to the approval of the Court of Appeal. The Court of Appeal directed the judge to address the points which contingently arose in relation to the ground of appeal for which permission had been granted. 52.10.4

Where the lower court comprised judge and jury

Under r.52.10(3) the Court of Appeal has power either to order a new trial or, in effect, to take a short cut. In the latter event the Court of Appeal itself may make an order for damages or vary an award of damages made by the jury. This latter course bypasses the jury, but it has the potential to save both parties substantial costs. 52.10.5

Where the lower court's error arises from some misdirection by the judge, no conceptual problem arises. Where, however, there is an appeal against the verdict of a jury, properly directed, special considerations arise. First, the reasoning process by which the jury reached its verdict is not disclosed and may be a matter for speculation. Secondly, the jury is "an integral and honourable part of the justice system" (per Lord Hobhouse in *Grobbelaar v News Group Newspapers Ltd* [2002] UKHL 40 at [60]; [2002] 1 W.L.R. 3024), whose verdict has a special status. Accordingly the Court of Appeal ought not to find the verdict of a jury on liability to be perverse, unless there was no rational explanation for it: *Grobbelaar v News Group Newspapers Ltd* [2002] UKHL 40; [2002] 1 W.L.R. 3024. In *Grobbelaar* the House of Lords restored the jury's defamation verdict in favour of the plaintiff (which had been quashed by the Court of Appeal) but reduced damages from £85,000 to £1.

Need for clarity in drafting the court's order

Where an appeal court orders a rehearing, the court should make clear on the face of its order whether it is ordering a rehearing at appeal court level (in which case any subsequent appeal would be a second appeal) or a rehearing of the original matter at first instance: *Fowler de Pledge (A Firm) v Smith* [2003] EWCA Civ 703 at [39]. The facts of that case illustrate the confusion and costs which can arise when there is doubt about the character of the rehearing which takes place. The confusion which arises from lack of clarity in the judge's order is also illustrated by *Hackney LBC v Driscoll* [2003] EWCA Civ 1037 and *Southern & District Finance plc v Turner* [2003] EWCA Civ 1574. 52.10.6

Hearing of appeals[1]

52.11—(1) Every appeal will be limited to a review of the decision of the lower court unless— 52.11

(a) a practice direction makes different provision for a particular category of appeal; or

(b) the court considers that in the circumstances of an individual appeal it would be in the interests of justice to hold a re-hearing.

[1] Introduced by the Civil Procedure (Amendment) Rules 2000 (SI 2000/221).

(2) Unless it orders otherwise, the appeal court will not receive—

(a) oral evidence; or

(b) evidence which was not before the lower court.

(3) The appeal court will allow an appeal where the decision of the lower court was—

(a) wrong; or

(b) unjust because of a serious procedural or other irregularity in the proceedings in the lower court.

(4) The appeal court may draw any inference of fact which it considers justified on the evidence.

(5) At the hearing of the appeal a party may not rely on a matter not contained in his appeal notice unless the appeal court gives permission.

Review or re-hearing?

52.11.1 Rule 52.11(1) provides that every appeal will be limited to a review of the decision of the lower court, unless (a) a practice direction makes different provision or (b) in the circumstances of an individual appeal "it would be in the interests of justice to hold a re-hearing."

As to r.52.11(1)(a), the most relevant provision of the practice direction is para.9.1. This requires a re-hearing if the appeal is from a minister, person or other body who

> "(1) did not hold a hearing to come to that decision; or (2) held a hearing to come to that decision, but the procedure adopted did not provide for the consideration of evidence".

In addition, specific categories of appeal may be required by statute and/or the practice direction to take the form of re-hearings: see e.g. paras 22.2, 22.3 and 24.3 of the practice direction. Thus an appeal to the Administrative Court from the Fitness to Practise Panel of the General Medical Council is required to be by way of re-hearing.

As to r.52.11(1)(b), the decision whether to review or to re-hear will be heavily conditioned by the facts of particular cases, although (where the practice direction does not require a re-hearing) the normal practice will be to review. See *Asiansky Television plc v Bayer Rosin* [2001] EWCA Civ 1792. Ward L.J. observed in *Ealing LBC v Richardson* [2005] EWCA Civ 1798 at [20]:

> "It is, after all, firmly to be accepted that a re-hearing is an exception to the general rule; that some injustice must have occurred, and a simple failure to put one's case before the first court is not ordinarily to be cured by a re-hearing."

In *Secretary of State for Trade and Industry v Lewis* [2001] 2 B.C.L.C. 597 at 600e–g, Neuberger J. said that generally the fact that the court below had not given reasons was not a ground for holding a re-hearing, rather than a review. It would be otherwise if the court below had been asked to give its reasons and had refused to do so or if there was some good reason for not asking the court below to give its reasons.

In *Audergon v La Baguette Ltd* [2002] EWCA Civ 10 the Court of Appeal reversed the decision of a Chancery judge because, on hearing an appeal from a master, the judge had conducted a re-hearing whereas he should have conducted a review. Jonathan Parker L.J. (with whom Tuckey and Pill L.JJ. agreed) formulated at [83] five general observations with regard to the discretion to hold a re-hearing:

> "(1) The general rule is that appeals at all levels will be by way of review... (2) A decision to hold a re-hearing will only be justified where the appeal court considers that in the circumstances of the individual appeal it is in the interests of justice to do so. (3) It is undesirable to attempt to formulate criteria to be applied by the appeal court in deciding whether to hold a re-hearing. ... (4) In a case involving some procedural or other irregularity in the lower court it will be material for the appeal court, when considering whether to hold a re-hearing, to have regard to the fact that an appeal will be allowed where the decision of the lower court is rendered "unjust because of serious procedural or other irregularity" ... (5) The word "will" in the opening words of CPR r.52.11(3) throws no light on the approach to be adopted in deciding whether to hold a re-hearing under CPR r.52.11(1)(b)."

Appeals from the Registrar of Trade Marks will normally proceed by way of review rather than rehearing: see *Dyson Ltd v Registrar of Trade Marks* [2003] EWHC 1062 (Ch) at [4]–[14]; [2003] 1 W.L.R. 2406; *EI Du Pont Nemours & Co v ST Du Pont* [2003] EWCA Civ 1368 at [96]; [2006] 1 W.L.R. 2793. An appeal from a hearing officer to the High Court under s.74B of the Patents Act 1977 (as amended by the Patents Act 2004) generally proceeds by way of review rather than re-hearing: see *DLP Ltd's Patent, Re* [2007] EWHC 2669 (Pat); [2008] 1 All E.R. 839.

Where an application for extension of time is made prospectively under r.3.1(2)(a) to the district judge, any appeal against his decision should normally be by way of review. A rehearing would only be appropriate if the district judge's decision was so inadequately reasoned that the losing party does not know why he lost: see *Robert v Momentum Services Ltd* [2003] EWCA Civ 299 at [28]; [2003] 2 All E.R. 74.

The decision of the Court of Appeal in *Assicurazioni Generali SpA v Arab Insurance Group* [2002] EWCA Civ 1642; [2003] 1 W.L.R. 577 contains a thoughtful discussion as to what the difference is between "review" and "rehearing" in the context of r.52.11(1). Both Clarke L.J. and Ward L.J. conclude that in a case where the appeal court is being asked to reverse findings of fact based upon oral evidence which the judge has heard, the approach of the appeal court is the same, whether it proceeds by way of review or rehearing. On the other hand, where the judge's evaluation of the facts or exercise of discretion is challenged, then the difference between a review and a rehearing will be of considerable importance. In *Datec Electronic Holdings Ltd v United Parcels Service Ltd* [2007] UKHL 23; 1 W.L.R. 1325 at [46] the House of Lords approved the judgment of Clarke L.J. in *Assicurazioni Generali SpA*.

The Court of Appeal re-examined the difference between "review" and "re-hearing" in *E.I. Du Pont Nemours & Co v S.T. Du Pont* [2003] EWCA Civ 1368; [2006] 1 W.L.R. 2793. May L.J. made five important points in his judgment on this issue:

(i) Because r.52.11 applies to a wide range of possible appeals, it "contains a degree of flexibility necessary to enable the court to achieve the overriding objective of dealing with individual cases justly". See [92]–[93]. In other words, the precise meaning and application of "review" and "re-hearing" will depend upon the circumstances of the case.

(ii) In r.52.11(1) "re-hearing" means a re-hearing in the fullest sense of the word. That is the sort of re-hearing which used to take place upon an appeal from a master or registrar to a judge in chambers pursuant to the former RSC O.58 r.1. See [89] and [96].

(iii) In r.52.11(1) "review" is not to be equated with judicial review. "It is closely akin to, although not conceptually identical with, the scope of an appeal to the Court of Appeal under the former Rules of the Supreme Court. The review will engage the merits of the appeal. It will accord appropriate respect to the decision of the lower court. Appropriate respect will be tempered by the nature of the lower court and its decision making process. There will also be a spectrum of appropriate respect depending on the nature of the decision of the lower court which is challenged. At one end of the spectrum will be decisions of primary fact reached after an evaluation of oral evidence where credibility is in issue and purely discretionary decisions. Further along the spectrum will be multi-factorial decisions often dependent on inferences and an analysis of documentary material". See [94].

(iv) The power of the appeal court to receive fresh evidence pursuant to r.52.11(2) arises both on a re-hearing and on a review. See [95].

(v) May L.J. agreed with the judgment of Clark L.J. in *Assicurazioni Generali SpA*, subject to one gloss: "The attribution of the label "rehearing" is not, other than exceptionally, necessary to enable the court upon a hearing by way of review to make the evaluative judgments necessary to determine whether the decision under appeal was or was not wrong". See [97].

In an appeal by way of re-hearing from a profession's regulatory or disciplinary tribunal, the court will have to decide how much deference it should accord to the decision of the tribunal members. In *CRHCP v General Medical Council* [2004] EWCA Civ 1356; [2005] 1 W.L.R. 717 the Court of Appeal formulated the approach as follows at para.78:

> "Where all material evidence has been placed before the disciplinary tribunal and it has given due consideration to the relevant factors, ... the court should place weight on the expertise brought to bear in evaluating how best the needs of the public and the profession should be protected. Where, however, there has

been a failure of process, or evidence is taken into account on appeal that was not placed before the disciplinary tribunal, the decision reached by that tribunal will inevitably need to be re-asssessed."

In *General Medical Council v Meadow* [2006] EWCA Civ 1390 the Fitness to Practise Panel of the GMC found that M was guilty of serious professional misconduct, the Administrative Court on appeal reversed that finding and the Court of Appeal, by a majority, upheld the decision of the Administrative Court on that issue. Auld L.J. (with whom Thorpe L.J. agreed at para.282) noted that the courts had begun to distance themselves from earlier expressions of deference to specialist regulatory and disciplinary bodies. This was more a question of emphasis than clear definition. The courts should still accord such bodies an appropriate measure of respect. "However, the courts should be ready in appropriate cases and, if necessary, to substitute their own view for that of disciplinary bodies." See para.120.

Fresh evidence

52.11.2 The appeal court will not receive fresh evidence (oral or written) "unless it orders otherwise". See r.52.11(2). The principles upon which this power will be exercised are not spelt out in the rule or the practice direction.

Prior to May 2000, after there had been a trial on the merits, the Court of Appeal would only receive further evidence "on special grounds" (RSC O.59, r.10(2)). Subject to certain established exceptions, the "special grounds" were those set out in *Ladd v Marshall* [1954] 1 W.L.R. 1489. They were: (1) the evidence could not have been obtained with reasonable diligence for use at the trial; (2) the evidence must be such that, if given, it would probably have an important influence on the result of the case, though it need not be decisive; (3) the evidence must be such as is presumably to be believed; it must be apparently credible, though it need not be incontrovertible. See Denning L.J. at 1491. For a detailed discussion of the *Ladd v Marshall* conditions, see Vol.1 of the Supreme Court Practice 1999, pp.1063–1064.

In *Hertfordshire Investments Ltd v Bubb* [2000] 1 W.L.R. 2318, the Court of Appeal noted that r.52.11(2) did not retain the former requirement for "special grounds". Nevertheless the principles reflected in *Ladd v Marshall* remain relevant. They are matters which the Court of Appeal must consider in the exercise of its discretion, when deciding whether to receive fresh evidence. See the judgment of Hale L.J. at 2325.

In *Hamilton v Al-Fayed (Joined Party)* [2001] E.M.L.R. 15 the Court of Appeal approved the guidance given in *Hertfordshire Investments Ltd*. Lord Phillips M.R., giving the judgment of the Court, said this at para.11:

> "We consider that under the new, as under the old, procedure special grounds must be shown to justify the introduction of fresh evidence on appeal. In a case such as this, which is governed by the transitional provisions, we do not consider that we are placed in the straightjacket of previous authority when considering whether such special grounds have been demonstrated. That question must be considered in light of the overriding objective of the new CPR. The old cases will, nonetheless remain powerful persuasive authority, for they illustrate the attempts of the courts to strike a fair balance between the need for concluded litigation to be determinative of disputes and the desirability that the judicial process should achieve the right result. That task is one which accords with the overriding objective."

This approach was followed in *Riyad Bank v Ahli United Bank (UK) plc* [2005] EWCA Civ 1419 and *Toth v Jarman* [2006] EWCA Civ 1028, cases which mark a further stage in the rehabilitation of *Ladd v Marshall*. In *Al-Koronky v Time Life Entertainment Group* [2006] EWCA Civ 1123 the Court of Appeal refused to admit fresh evidence in an appeal against an order for security for costs. The proposed evidence concerning the claimants' impecuniosity could and should have been put before the judge at the original hearing. The proposed evidence concerning the claimants' likelihood of success at trial was highly contentious.

> "We are forced to conclude that it would be wrong and contrary to the interests of justice to admit it at this stage. We would, in effect, be conducting a new and very different hearing from that which occurred at first instance, and such a departure from the well established principles is not justified."

(See the judgment of the court, para.20.)

The Court of Appeal adopts a similar approach towards applications to adduce fresh evidence in the context of appeals against summary judgment under r.24.2 or striking out orders under r.3.4: see *Aylwen v Taylor Joynson Garrett* [2001] EWCA Civ 1171 at [47]–[49]; [2002] P.N.L.R. 1.

Junior appellate courts generally adopt a similar approach to that of the Court of Appeal in relation to applications to adduce fresh evidence.

In trade mark appeals the same principles govern the reception of fresh evidence as in other appeals. However, the nature of trade mark appeals may give rise to a particular application of those principles which is somewhat more relaxed. See *EI Du Pont Nemours & Co v ST Du Pont* [2003] EWCA Civ 1368 at [100]–[104]; [2006] 1 W.L.R. 2793.

Rule 52.11(2), unlike its predecessor (RSC O.59, r.10(2)), contains no qualification concerning matters which have occurred after the date of the trial or hearing. Under the former law, the express (but exceptional) power to admit further evidence as to matters occurring after the date of the trial or hearing was exercised sparingly and with due regard to the need for finality in litigation. See *Hughes v Singh*, *The Times*, April 21, 1989. The position under the CPR was summarised in *R. (Iran) v SSHD* [2005] EWCA Civ 982 at [34]–[37]. It remains the case that evidence of changed circumstances since the date of the original decision should only be sparingly admitted. Examples of cases in which it was appropriate to admit such evidence were given by Brooke L.J. at [34].

Case management of appeal hearing

Any appellate court will seek to use its resources in the most efficacious manner and may take any proper "short cut" which becomes available. This is in accordance with the overriding objective (CPR Pt 1). **52.11.3**

If the appellant has to succeed on two grounds in order to overturn the first instance judgment, the appellate court may decide to hear argument first on one ground only (e.g. because that ground will take less time or because it poses particular difficulties for the appellant). If that course is taken and the appellant loses on the first ground, he cannot insist upon ventilating the second ground simply to improve his position in relation to costs: see *Palfrey v Wilson* [2007] EWCA Civ 94 at [4]–[5].

Grounds for allowing appeal

Rule 52.11(3) provides two grounds upon which an appeal "will" be allowed: (a) that the decision of the lower court was wrong; (b) that the decision of the lower court was unjust because of a serious procedural or other irregularity. **52.11.4**

In r.52.11(3)(a) "wrong" presumably means that the court below (i) erred in law or (ii) erred in fact or (iii) erred (to the appropriate extent) in the exercise of its discretion.

The distinction between these different categories of appeal is important. Practitioners should not confuse the approach to reviewing an exercise of discretion with the approach to reviewing a judge's findings of fact: see *Manning v Stylianou* [2007] EWCA Civ 1655 at [19].

In relation to alleged errors of fact by the lower court, the Court of Appeal gave valuable guidance as to the approach to be adopted in *Assicurazioni Generali SpA v Arab Insurance Group* [2002] EWCA Civ 1642; [2003] 1 W.L.R. 577 at [6]–[23] per Clarke L.J. and [193]–[197] per Ward L.J. The degree of deference which is due to the findings of primary fact made by the judge below will depend upon the nature and circumstances of the case. The approach of the court in this kind of case (absent any fresh evidence) should be the same, whether it is conducting a review or a re-hearing. On the other hand, where the judge's evaluation of the facts is challenged, such cases may be closely analogous to the exercise of a discretion and appellate courts should approach such cases in a similar way (as to which, see the following paragraph).

In *Manning v Stylianou* [2007] EWCA Civ 1655 the Court of Appeal was entitled to (and did) reverse the trial judge's decision as to where the claimant's accident had occurred. This was because the interpretation of photographs was crucial to that decision and the Court of Appeal was in just as good a position as the trial judge to interpret the photographs. On the other hand, in *Designers Guild Ltd v Russell Williams (Textiles) Ltd* [2000] 1 W.L.R. 2416 the House of Lords held that the Court of Appeal had erred in substituting its own assessment of the evidence for that made by the trial judge. The trial judge's decision on the issue of substantiality in a copyright infringement claim was restored. The extent of the Immigration Appeal Tribunal's former power to interfere with findings of fact in immigration appeals is addressed in *Subesh v SSHD* [2004] EWCA Civ 56 at [40]–[50].

As to what constitutes a sufficient error in the exercise of discretion to warrant interference by the appeal court, see *Tanfern Ltd v Cameron MacDonald* [2000] 1 W.L.R. 1311, para.32. Brooke L.J. suggested that guidance might be gained from the speech of Lord Fraser in *G. v G. (Minors: Custody Appeal)* [1985] 1 W.L.R. 647 at 652. In the latter part of the passage cited by Brooke L.J., Lord Fraser stated:

> "... the appellate court should only interfere when they consider that the judge of first instance has not merely preferred an imperfect solution which is different from an alternative imperfect solution which the Court of Appeal might or would have adopted, but has exceeded the generous ambit within which a reasonable disagreement is possible."

An alternative formulation of the threshold test for interference with the exercise of discretion by the appeal court is that stated by Lord Woolf M.R. in *Phonographic Performance Ltd v AEI Rediffusion Music Ltd* [1999] 1 W.L.R. 1507 at 1523:

> "Before the court can interfere it must be shown that the judge has either erred in principle in his approach or has left out of account or has taken into account some feature that he should, or should not, have considered, or that his decision was wholly wrong because the court is forced to the conclusion that he has not balanced the various factors fairly in the scale."

This passage was cited and applied by the Court of Appeal in *Price v Price (t/a Poppyland Headware)* [2003] EWCA Civ 888 at [26]–[27]; [2003] 3 All E.R. 911.

There are some cases where the first instance judge has made a decision which involved the assessment and balancing of a large number of factors, for example determining whether an action constitutes abuse of process. Such a decision is not an exercise of discretion, because there is only one right answer to the question before the judge. The Court of Appeal is reluctant to interfere with such a decision. However, the Court of Appeal will interfere if the judge has taken into account immaterial factors, omitted to take into account material factors, erred in principle or come to a decision that was impermissible: see *Aldi Stores Ltd v WSP Group plc* [2007] EWCA Civ 1260 at [16]; [2008] 1 W.L.R. 748. The Court of Appeal will also interfere if the judge's decision was "plainly wrong": see *Stuart v Goldberg* [2008] EWCA Civ 2 at [76] and [81].

In determining whether the decision of the lower court was "wrong" for the purposes of r.52.11(3)(a), regard must be had to the way in which the parties' cases were formulated below: see *King v Telegraph Group Ltd* [2004] EWCA Civ 613 at [54].

The ground in r.52.11(3)(b) is onerous. The procedural or other irregularity must be a serious one. Furthermore it must have caused the decision of the lower court to be unjust. However, this ground does not depend upon the decision of the lower court being "wrong". In other words ground (b) may apply even if the lower court would have reached the same decision, absent any procedural or other irregularity. *Storer v British Gas Plc* [2000] 1 W.L.R. 1237 (which pre-dated the new Pt 52 by 3 months) affords a good illustration of such a case. The Court of Appeal in *Storer* allowed an appeal because the industrial tribunal had not sat in public. Nevertheless, in the majority of cases an appeal on ground (3)(b) is unlikely to succeed unless the irregularity has had a significant impact upon the proceedings below; for example, the wrongful exclusion of evidence or wrongful restriction of cross-examination on matters crucial to the case: *Hayes v Transco plc* [2003] EWCA Civ 1261. In *Breeze v Ahmad* [2005] EWCA Civ 192; [2005] C.P. Rep. 29 the Court of Appeal allowed an appeal and ordered a retrial, because the effect of two technical papers (which had not been produced to the court) had been unwittingly misrepresented to the court.

Failure to give reasons

52.11.5 In *Flannery v Halifax Estate Agencies Ltd* [2000] 1 W.L.R. 377 the Court of Appeal allowed an appeal on the ground that the judge had failed to give reasons for preferring the expert evidence of one party to that of the other. In *English v Emery Reimbold & Strick Ltd* [2002] EWCA Civ 605; [2002] 1 W.L.R. 2409 the Court of Appeal enumerated why a trial judge must give adequate reasons. Reasons are necessary in order to render practicable the exercise of any right of appeal. Justice must be seen to be done. It must be apparent both to the parties and to the public why one party has won and the other has lost. The giving of reasons provides a necessary discipline for judges and it contributes to the setting of precedents for the future. The judge does not have to deal with every argument presented, but must make plain the principles on which he has acted and the reasons which led him to his decision.

In *English* at [25] the Court of Appeal said that at the permission stage the judge may take, or be given, the opportunity to provide additional reasons for his decision. This course could lead to a considerable saving of costs, especially where the outcome of any appeal may be an order for a retrial. The same principle applies in family proceedings: see *T (A Child)* [2002] EWCA Civ 1736 at [49]. The correct sequence is that first the judge should be invited to deal with whatever point it is said he has failed to deal with; secondly, and in the light of any elaboration given by the judge, the applicant should consider whether he still wishes to appeal; if so, thirdly he should apply to the judge for permission to appeal: see *In the matter of S (Children)* [2007] EWCA Civ 694 at [23]–[25]. In the case of *In re M (A Child) (Non accidental Injury: Burden of Proof)* [2008] EWCA Civ 1261, *The Times* December 16, 2008, CA, the Court of Appeal (in remitting to the judge a passage of the judge's judgment for clarification) stressed that counsel has a positive duty in civil proceedings to raise with the judge at handing down, not only any alleged defect in the judge's reasoning, but also any genuine query or ambiguity which arose in the written judgment. See further para.40.2.1.C.

It is, however, inappropriate to go back to the trial judge for clarification or amplification at a later stage, many months after the original judgment was delivered (*Michael Hyde Associates Ltd v J D Williams & Co Ltd* [2001] P.N.L.R. 233) or where there is a danger of ex post facto rationalisation (*Aerospace Publishing Ltd v Thames Water Utilities Ltd* [2006] EWCA Civ 717). The Court of Appeal does not have power to invite the Asylum and Immigration Tribunal to provide additional reasons for a decision which is under appeal: see *Hatungimana v SSHD* [2006] EWCA Civ 231.

If a judge volunteers further reasons for his decision in a second judgment, the Court of Appeal may take those further reasons into account: see *Roche v Chief Constable of Greater Manchester* [2005] EWCA Civ 1454 at [23]–[27].

Uniform approach of all appeal courts

The most radical change made by r.52.11 is to unify the approach of all appeal courts. Prior to May 2000 an appeal from a district judge or master to a judge in chambers was a complete re-hearing, with a fairly relaxed approach towards the admission of fresh evidence. The uniform approach which is now to be adopted by all appeal courts accords with recommendation 181 of the Woolf Report. Under the new approach the decision of the lower court attracts much greater significance. See *Tanfern Ltd v Cameron-MacDonald* [2000] 1 W.L.R. 1311, para.31. **52.11.6**

Non-disclosure of Part 36 offers and payments[1]

52.12—(1) The fact that a Part 36 offer or payment into court has been made must not be disclosed to any judge of the appeal court who is to hear or determine— **52.12**

(a) an application for permission to appeal; or

(b) an appeal,

until all questions (other than costs) have been determined.

(2) Paragraph (1) does not apply if the Part 36 offer or payment into court is relevant to the substance of the appeal.

(3) Paragraph (1) does not prevent disclosure in any application in the appeal proceedings if disclosure of the fact that a Part 36 offer or a payment into court has been made is properly relevant to the matter to be decided.

(Rule 36.3 has the effect that a Part 36 offer made in proceedings at first instance will not have consequences in any appeal proceedings. Therefore, a fresh Part 36 offer needs to be made in appeal proceedings. However, r.52.12 applies to a Part 36 offer whether made in the original proceedings or in the appeal.)

Note

In *Garrett v Saxby* [2004] EWCA Civ 341; [2004] 1 W.L.R. 2152; the Court of Appeal **52.12.1**

[1] Introduced by the Civil Procedure (Amendment) Rules 2000 (SI 2000/221), amended by the Civil Procedure (Amendment No.5) Rules 2003 (SI 2003 No.3361) and by the Civil Procedure (Amendment No.3) Rules 2006 (SI 2006/3435).

discussed what should be done when, through inadvertence, there has been a breach of r.52.12(1). Dyson L.J., giving the principal judgment, reviewed the pre-CPR authorities, which he considered to be of continuing persuasive force. His conclusions at [20] appear to be equally applicable both to appeal courts and to first instance judges:

> "It is for the judge to decide in each case whether the disclosure of a Part 36 offer or payment makes a fair trial impossible and whether justice demands that he recuse himself. But judges should not be too ready to reach such a conclusion; the delay and extra cost occasioned by a recusal may be very considerable. Moreover, when exercising their discretion, judges should remind themselves that they ought to have little difficulty in analysing and deciding the issues in the case on their merits without being influenced by their knowledge of the amount of the Part 36 offer or payment".

Statutory appeals—court's power to hear any person[1]

52.12A **52.12A—(1) In a statutory appeal, any person may apply for permission—**

(a) to file evidence; or

(b) to make representations at the appeal hearing.

(2) An application under paragraph (1) must be made promptly.

Statutory appeals

52.12A.1 A statutory appeal is an appeal to the court from a minister, government department, tribunal or other person pursuant to statute: see para.17.1 (1) of the practice direction. Provisions governing statutory appeals are set out in para.17 and following of the practice direction.

Rule 52.12A enables someone other than a party, if granted permission, to file evidence or to make representations at the hearing of a statutory appeal. The procedures to be followed in an application under r.52.12A are set out in paras 17.7 to 17.11 of the practice direction.

II. Special Provisions Applying to the Court of Appeal

Introduction

52.12.1.1 A number of special provisions apply to proceedings in the Court of Appeal, Civil Division. These are set out in rr.52.13–52.16 and in para.15 of the practice direction. Applications and appeals to that court, and other relevant documents, are filed in the Civil Appeals Office Registry, Room E307, Royal Courts of Justice, Strand, London WC2A 2LL (telephone 020 7947 7882 and 020 7947 6533): see para.15.1 of the practice direction. The work of that office is conducted under the direction of the Master and Head of Civil Appeals. Rule 52.16 (amplified by para.15.5 of the practice direction) provides for the judicial powers which he and his deputies may exercise.

The Court of Appeal's website includes a wealth of valuable practical guidance about Court of Appeal practice. Such guidance is to be found in particular under the headings "Forms and guidance", "Legal, Personal and Practical Support" and "Questions and Answers".

The day to day management of cases is carried out by lawyers in the Civil Appeals Office under the general direction of the court, and particularly under the direction of the appropriate supervising lord justice. The prefix of the reference number assigned to each case that is filed in the Court of Appeal, denotes the responsible section within the office.

In applications before the Court of Appeal which are likely to last half an hour or less, consideration should be given to the use of video-conference facilities. See *Black v Pastouna* [2005] EWCA Civ 1389.

Filing Documents

52.12.2 The documents required to be filed in the Civil Appeals Office in respect of an ap-

[1] Introduced by the Civil Procedure (Amendment) Rules 2007 (SI 2007/2204).

peal proceeding in the Court of Appeal are set out in s.5, s.7 and paras 15.1–15.4 and 15.11B of the practice direction. These requirements have been discussed and emphasised in the commentaries following rr.52.4 and 52.5 above. Suffice it to say, at this stage, that these requirements must be scrupulously observed or sanctions are likely to follow. The Court of Appeal will refuse to make orders by consent administratively, if the requirements of the practice direction are broken. Instead the parties will be required to attend before the court and to explain what has happened and why: *Jayapragash v SSHD* [2004] EWCA Civ 1260.

For guidance on filing documents by (a) email or (b) electronically using the online forms service, see paras 15.1A and 15.1B of the practice direction.

Lists and Citation of Authorities

When citing reported cases, the parties and their representatives should follow the guidance given in s.8 of *Practice Statement (Supreme Court: Judgments)* [1998] 1 W.L.R. 825. In particular, if a case is reported in the official Law Reports published by the Incorporated Council of Law Reporting for England and Wales, that report should be cited. These are the most authoritative reports and they contain a summary of argument. When a decision of the Court of Appeal given after January 10, 2001 is cited, the system of neutral citation must be used as set out in *Practice Direction (Judgments: Form and Citation)* [2001] 1 W.L.R. 194. When a decision of the High Court given after January 13, 2002 is cited, the system of neutral citation must be used as set out in *Practice Direction (Judgments: Neutral Citations)* [2002] 1 W.L.R. 346. **52.12.3**

In April 2001 the Court of Appeal issued a practice direction, which still remains in force, with a view to limiting the citation of cases to those which are relevant and useful to the court: *Practice Direction (Court of Appeal: Citation of Authorities)* [2001] 1 W.L.R. 1001 ("the 2001 Practice Direction").

Paragraph 15.11 of the Pt 52 practice direction requires the appellant's representative to file a bundle of authorities with the court at least seven days before the hearing. The rules governing the bundle of authorities are clearly set out in para.15.11 and they must be scrupulously observed. Paragraph 15.11 (5) requires the advocates who will argue the case to certify that the requirements of para.5.10(3)–(5) of the practice direction have been complied with. These provisions encapsulate the most pertinent parts of the 2001 Practice Direction.

Supplementary skeleton arguments

Paragraph 15.11A of the practice direction permits the filing of supplementary skeleton arguments. The appellant's skeleton argument must be filed at least 14 days before the hearing. The respondent's skeleton argument must be filed at least seven days before the hearing. Any argument which is not contained in the original or supplementary skeleton arguments (timeously served) may be shut out by the court: see para.15.11A(4) of the practice direction. The background and effect of these provisions were set out in *Scribes West Ltd v Resla Anstalt (No.1)* [2004] EWCA Civ 835; June 29, 2004, unrep., CA, at paras 25 to 27. In *AIC Ltd v ITS Testing Services (UK) Ltd (The "Kriti Palm")* [2006] EWCA Civ 1601; [2007] 1 Lloyd's Rep. 555, CA, Buxton L.J. explained (at para.393) that, in para.15.11A, "supplementary" means what it says, and permits the filing of a further skeleton argument to provide for lately decided or (within limits) discovered authority, for changes of underlying factual circumstances, or for the brief answering of points in the other side's argument that genuinely do not arise out of the original grounds of appeal. The provision does not permit the late submission of a skeleton argument raising a completely revised and expanded case. Should an appellant party find itself wishing to make a very much expanded case, requiring an extension of the time already allocated by the court for the hearing of the appeal, that party should, at the earliest date at which that becomes apparent, give the court full details making entirely clear what is wanted and why it is wanted (ibid). **52.12.4**

The ultimate sanction

It can be seen from the provisions summarised above that, one way or another, all documents needed for an appeal hearing must be filed with the Court of Appeal at least seven days before the hearing ("the cut-off date"). There is good reason for this requirement, namely the fact that at some point during the final seven-day period (and the precise date will depend upon pressure of other business) each of the lords justices will do his or her pre-reading for the hearing. The Court of Appeal operates under huge pressure, and it is the duty of the parties and their representatives to co-operate with the court by ensuring that all documents are filed by the cut-off date. **52.12.5**

Paragraph 15.11B of the practice direction contains the ultimate sanction. If any document is lacking 10 days before the hearing, a reminder will be sent out by the Civil Appeals Office. If any document is still lacking at the cut-off date, then the defaulting party may be required to attend before the presiding lord justice and may be debarred from pursuing or opposing the appeal, as the case may be. The defaulting party would do well to ensure that all documents have been filed before that encounter takes place. See *Scribes West Ltd v Anstalt (No.1)* [2004] EWCA Civ 835 at [31]–[32].

Listing of applications and appeals

52.12.6 The constituent elements of the Civil Appeals List of the Court of Appeal and the arrangements for its management are set out at paras 15.7–15.9A of the practice direction.

A permission hearing which has been listed by the Court of Appeal will not generally be adjourned for the convenience of counsel. However, the court is sometimes able to list a permission hearing at 9.00 or 9.30am for the assistance of counsel who is in another court later that day. See *In the Matter of N and N (Children)* [2006] EWCA Civ 1562.

Hear-by Dates and Listing Windows

52.12.7 The hear-by dates applicable to all appeals and applications filed after March 1, 2003 are set out in *Practice Note (Court of Appeal: Listing Windows) (No.2)* [2003] 1 W.L.R. 838.

The Court of Appeal will strive to ensure that appeals are generally heard within their listing windows. Applications for a hearing to be fixed beyond the hear-by date will be determined by a single lord justice or the master, but will be granted only for the most compelling reasons. See para.2 of *Practice Note (Court of Appeal: Listing Windows)* [2001] 1 W.L.R. 1517, which remains in force (as stated in para.2 of the 2003 practice note).

Handed down judgments

52.12.8 Where the Court of Appeal reserves judgment and later hands down judgment in writing, the procedure to be followed is set out in the practice direction on "Reserved Judgments" supplementing Pt 40.

Notification of settlement

52.12.9 It is the duty of counsel and solicitors on both sides to notify the Court of Appeal immediately, if a case which is listed for hearing settles. Even if the settlement occurs over a weekend, the Court should still be notified immediately. The Royal Courts of Justice has a 24 hour switchboard and arrangements can be made to inform the lords justices of the settlement. If counsel or solicitors fail promptly to notify the Court of a settlement, they are likely to be criticised. See *Tasyurdu v SSHD* [2003] EWCA Civ 447; *Yell Ltd v Garton* [2004] EWCA Civ 87.

If negotiations are in progress, which may well lead to the settlement of an appeal listed for hearing in the near future, again the Court of Appeal should be informed promptly. Such information will be treated as "given on a without prejudice basis". The listing will not be altered until it is confirmed that the application or appeal will be withdrawn. See *Tasyurdu* at [13] and *Yell* at [2] and [6].

If an appeal is settled at a late stage, but the requirements of the practice direction have not been complied with, the Court of Appeal will refuse to grant a consent order administratively. Instead the court will require the parties to attend and explain any breach of the practice direction. See *R. (Jeyapragash) v Immigration Appeal Tribunal* [2004] EWCA Civ 1260.

The procedures to be followed in obtaining a consent order following the settlement of an appeal (whether in favour of appellant or respondent) are set out in paras 12 and 13 of the practice direction.

Urgent cases

52.12.10 In cases of genuine urgency an "aspiring appellant" (i.e. one who needs permission) may approach the Court of Appeal by telephone, usually on notice to the other party. If necessary the approach can even be made out of court hours, first through the security officers of the Royal Courts of Justice and thence through a deputy master to a lord justice. See *In the Matter of N (a Child)* [2007] EWCA Civ 899 at [27].

II. Special Provisions Applying to the Court of Appeal

Second appeals to the Court[1]

52.13—(1) Permission is required from the Court of Appeal for any appeal to that court from a decision of a county court or the High Court which was itself made on appeal. 52.13

(2) The Court of Appeal will not give permission unless it considers that—

(a) the appeal would raise an important point of principle or practice; or

(b) there is some other compelling reason for the Court of Appeal to hear it.

Statutory restrictions on second appeals

The Bowman Report recommended in Chs 2 and 4 that one level of appeal should be the norm. This principle reflects the need for certainty, reasonable expense and proportionality. The review team considered that where there has already been an appeal to some court below the Court of Appeal, a further appeal should only be allowed in special circumstances. This recommendation was adopted in s.55(1) of the Access to Justice Act 1999, which provides: 52.13.1

"Where an appeal is made to a county court or the High Court in relation to any matter, and on hearing the appeal the court makes a decision in relation to that matter, no appeal may be made to the Court of Appeal from that decision unless the Court of Appeal considers that—

(a) the appeal would raise an important point of principle or practice, or

(b) there is some other compelling reason for the Court of Appeal to hear it."

This provision is substantially repeated in r.52.13.

The Bowman Report highlighted as a particular problem the situation in which the same party brought successive appeals and lost at each stage (see Ch.4, paras 7 and 8). However, the reforms made have gone further than that. Section 55(1) of the Access to Justice Act 1999 has effect even if the would-be appellant won at first instance before losing in the junior appellate court.

The purpose and effect of s.55(1) of the Access to Justice Act 1999 were considered by the Court of Appeal in *Tanfern Ltd v Cameron-MacDonald (Practice Note)* [2000] 1 W.L.R. 1311 at paras 41–46. Brooke L.J. (with whom Lord Woolf M.R. and Peter Gibson L.J. agreed) stated that judges of the quality of lords justices of appeal were a scarce and valuable resource and it was important that they were used effectively. It would no longer be possible to pursue a second appeal to the Court of Appeal merely because the appeal was "properly arguable" or had a "real prospect of success". In *Clark (Inspector of Taxes) v Perks* [2001] 1 W.L.R. 17 the Court of Appeal re-emphasised the general guidance which it had given in *Tanfern*. The Court of Appeal in *Clark* gave a single judgment in which it stated (at para.17):

"...the whole thrust of the new appellate reforms ... is to use the time and resources of the judges of the Court of Appeal, and of the lawyers and staff who support them, on matters which really merit the attention of a court of this stature in the judicial hierarchy."

In relation to the unusual situation where some of the matters sought to be raised constitute a first appeal and others constitute a second appeal, the approach of the Court of Appeal in *Convergence Group plc v Vellacott* [2005] EWCA Civ 290 will probably be followed.

What constitute "first" and "second" appeals for these purposes

For the purposes of s.55 of the 1999 Act and CPR r.52.13, the following are to be treated as appeals to the county court or the High Court (i.e. as "first" appeals): (a) An 52.13.2

[1] Introduced by the Civil Procedure (Amendment) Rules 2000 (SI 2000/221).

appeal to the High Court on a point of law pursuant to s.11 of the Tribunals and Inquiries Act 1992; (b) Any appeal to the High Court which can colloquially be categorised as an appeal by way of case stated; (c) An appeal to a county court on a point of law from a decision of a local housing authority pursuant to s.204 of the Housing Act 1996; (d) Any other appeal to the High Court or to a county court from any tribunal or other body or person. See *Clark (Inspector of Taxes) v Perks* [2001] 1 W.L.R. 17 at para.13 and (in respect of appeals under s.204 of the Housing Act 1996) *Azimi v London Borough of Newham* (2001) 33 H.L.R. 51. An appeal from a decision of the High Court or of a county court in any of the above cases is to be treated as a second appeal and subject to the restrictions of s.55 of the 1999 Act and r.52.13.

A more difficult problem is whether an appeal from the High Court to the Court of Appeal pursuant to s.69(8) of the Arbitration Act 1996 is a "second appeal" to which the restrictions contained in s.55 of the Access to Justice Act 1999 apply. This question was discussed by the Court of Appeal obiter but after full argument in *Henry Boot Construction (UK) Ltd v Malmaison Hotel (Manchester) Ltd* [2001] Q.B. 388. Waller and Swinton Thomas L.JJ considered that s.55 of the Access to Justice Act 1999 had no effect in relation to an appeal to the Court of Appeal under s.69(8) of the Arbitration Act 1996. Once a party has obtained the leave of a High Court judge pursuant to s.69(8) of the Arbitration Act 1996 to appeal to the Court of Appeal, he is not subsequently required to seek permission from the Court of Appeal (pursuant to s.55 of the Access to Justice Act 1999 and CPR r.52.13) to pursue that same appeal. Arden J. took a different view on this issue.

In *Athletic Union of Constantinople v National Basketball Association (No.2)* [2002] EWCA Civ 830; [2002] 1 W.L.R. 2863 a differently constituted Court of Appeal unanimously approved the majority view in *Henry Boot*. Under ss.67(4) and 69(8) of the Arbitration Act 1996 the High Court could grant or refuse permission to appeal to the Court of Appeal. The Court of Appeal had no jurisdiction to override such grant or refusal of permission. The only exception would be in very rare cases where the judge gave inadequate reasons for refusal of permission or where the judge's decision was arbitrary: see *North Range Shipping Ltd v Seatrans Shipping Corp* [2002] EWCA Civ 405; [2002] 1 W.L.R. 2397; *CGU International Insurance plc v AstraZeneca Insurance Co Ltd* [2006] EWCA Civ 1340. It should be noted that a judge's decision that the parties have, or alternatively that they have not, entered into an exclusion agreement for the purposes of s.69 of the Arbitration Act 1996 is not the same as a grant or refusal of leave to appeal under s.69. Accordingly such a decision is not caught by the restrictions on appeal imposed by that section. See *Sumakan Ltd v The Commonwealth Secretariat* [2007] EWCA Civ 243; *The Times*, April 13, 2007.

The second appeals provisions in s.55 of the 1999 Act and CPR r.52.13 do not apply to appeals under s.97(3) of the Patents Act 1977: *Smith International Inc v Specialised Petroleum Services Group Ltd* [2005] EWCA Civ 1357; [2006] 1 W.L.R. 252.

What constitutes "an important point of principle or practice"?

52.13.3 The first criterion for granting permission for a second appeal is stated in s.55(1)(a) of the 1999 Act and CPR r.52.13(2)(a), namely that the appeal would raise an important point of principle or practice. This means an important point of principle or practice that has not yet been established. An appeal concerning the correct application of a principle or practice whose meaning and scope has already been determined by a higher court does not satisfy s.55(1)(a) or r.52.13(2)(a). See *Uphill v BRB (Residuary) Ltd* [2005] EWCA Civ 60 at [18]; [2005] 1 W.L.R. 2070.

The meaning of "some other compelling reason"

52.13.4 The second criterion for granting permission for a second appeal is stated in s.55(1)(b) of the 1999 Act and CPR r.52.13(2)(b), namely that there is "some other compelling reason" for the Court of Appeal to hear the appeal. In *Major v Lamyman* [2003] EWCA Civ 1701 a High Court judge allowed an appeal on very thin grounds in a substantial matter, without referring to the only two criteria which permitted him to interfere with a judgment following a trial on the facts. The Court of Appeal granted permission for a second appeal on the basis that the appeal raised an important point of practice, alternatively that there was some other compelling reason.

In *Uphill v BRB (Residuary) Ltd* [2005] EWCA Civ 60 at [19]–[25]; [2005] 1 W.L.R. 2070 the Court of Appeal discussed the meaning of the phrase "some other compelling reason" in the context of r.52.13(2)(b). The court did not specifically refer to s.55(1)(b) of the Access to Justice Act 1999, but the court's observations must be equally applicable to that statutory provision. It should be remembered that the phrase "some other compelling reason" is of statutory origin, not the creature of the Rule Committee. Dyson L.J., giving the judgment of the court, elucidated the meaning of that phrase in para.24:

"(1) A good starting point will almost always be a consideration of the prospects of success. It is unlikely that the court will find that there is a compelling reason to give permission for a second appeal unless it forms the view that the prospects of success are very high...

(2) ...the fact that the prospects of success are very high will not necessarily be sufficient to provide a compelling reason for giving permission to appeal. An examination of all the circumstances of the case may lead the court to conclude that, despite the existence of very good prospects of success, there is no compelling reason for giving permission to appeal...

(3) There may be circumstances where there is a compelling reason to grant permission to appeal even where the prospects of success are not very high. The court may be satisfied that there are good grounds for believing that the hearing was tainted by some procedural irregularity so as to render the first appeal unfair..."

Nevertheless the guidance given in *Uphill* should not be allowed to ossify into rule. The Court of Appeal should be flexible in its interpretation of r.52.13, depending on the provenance of the proposed appeal. See *Cramp v Hastings BC* [2005] EWCA Civ 1005 at [64]–[67]. In *Esure Insurance Ltd v Direct Line Insurance Plc* [2008] EWCA Civ 842 the complexity of the case and the real prospect of showing that the judge had incorrectly exercised his appellate function were held to constitute "compelling reasons" for permitting a second appeal: see the judgment of Arden L.J. at [65], with whom Jacob and Maurice Kay L.JJ. agreed.

Consequence of purported grant of permission by junior appellate court

If a junior appellate court (in disregard of s.55 of the 1999 Act, CPR r.52.13(1) and para.4.9 of the practice direction) purports to give permission for a second appeal, that grant of permission is a nullity. See *Clark (Inspector of Taxes) v Perks* [2001] 1 W.L.R. 17 at para.16. **52.13.5**

Assignment of appeals to the Court of Appeal[1]

52.14—"(1) Where the court from or to which an appeal is made or from which permission to appeal is sought ("the relevant court") considers that— **52.14**

(a) an appeal which is to be heard by a county court or the High Court would raise an important point of principle or practice; or

(b) there is some other compelling reason for the Court of Appeal to hear it,

the relevant court may order the appeal to be transferred to the Court of Appeal.

(The Master of the Rolls has the power to direct that an appeal which would be heard by a county court or the High Court should be heard instead by the Court of Appeal—see section 57 of the Access to Justice Act 1999).

***(2) The Master of the Rolls or the Court* of Appeal may remit an appeal to the court in which the original appeal was or would have been brought."**

Leapfrog procedure

Section 57 of the Access to Justice Act 1999 provides: **52.14.1**

[1] Introduced by the Civil Procedure (Amendment) Rules 2000 (SI 2000/221).

(1) Where in any proceedings in a county court or the High Court a person appeals, or seeks permission to appeal, to a court other than the Court of Appeal or House of Lords—

(a) the Master of the Rolls, or

(b) the court from which or to which the appeal is made, or from which permission to appeal is sought,

may direct that the appeal shall be heard instead by the Court of Appeal.

(2) The power conferred by subsection (1)(b) shall be subject to rules of court.

The provisions of r.52.14 comprise the "rules of court" referred to in s.57(2) of the Access to Justice Act 1999. The criteria for leapfrogging an appeal direct to the Court of Appeal are (a) an important point of principle or practice or (b) some other compelling reason. In the context of r.52.14(1)(b) what is meant by the phrase "some other compelling reason"? Presumably this is directed to the importance of the case itself, as opposed to the importance of the issues upon which the appeal will turn. Perhaps if a master gives summary judgment for a very large sum of money, based upon his interpretation of an ambiguous one-off contract, that might be a "compelling reason" for the appeal to lie straight to the Court of Appeal.

In *Clark (Inspector of Taxes) v Perks* [2001] 1 W.L.R 17 at para.9 the Court of Appeal suggested that the lower court's power to transfer a first appeal to the Court of Appeal should be sparingly used. In any case of doubt the matter should be referred to the Master of the Rolls for consideration, since s.57 of the Access to Justice Act 1999 has conferred an identical power on him.

In *In the Matter of Claims Direct Test Cases* [2002] EWCA Civ 428 at [23] Lord Phillips M.R. stated his conclusion that s.57 of the Access to Justice Act 1999 "does not permit the "leapfrogging" of an application for permission to appeal, as opposed to an appeal in respect of which permission has been granted".

If the lower court refuses permission to appeal, it does not have jurisdiction (either under s.57 of the Access to Justice Act 1999 or under r.52.14) to direct that any appeal which may subsequently be permitted should go to the Court of Appeal as opposed to a junior appellate court: see *7E Communications Ltd v Vertex Antennentechnik GmbH* [2007] EWCA Civ 140; [2007] 1 W.L.R. 2175.

Paragraph 10.1 of the practice direction provides that the Court of Appeal may give such directions as are considered appropriate, following receipt of an appeal under the leapfrog procedure.

Judicial review appeals[1]

52.15 **52.15—(1) Where permission to apply for judicial review has been refused at a hearing in the High Court, the person seeking that permission may apply to the Court of Appeal for permission to appeal.**

(2) An application in accordance with paragraph (1) must be made within 7 days of the decision of the High Court to refuse to give permission to apply for judicial review.

(3) On an application under paragraph (1), the Court of Appeal may, instead of giving permission to appeal, give permission to apply for judicial review.

(4) Where the Court of Appeal gives permission to apply for judicial review in accordance with paragraph (3), the case will proceed in the High Court unless the Court of Appeal orders otherwise.

Application for permission to appeal against refusal of permission below

52.15.1 Where a claimant is refused permission under r.54.4 to proceed in a claim for judicial review, he may seek permission to appeal against that refusal. Rule 52.15

[1] Introduced by the Civil Procedure (Amendment) Rules 2000 (SI 2000/221).

modifies the general provisions about permission to appeal (r.52.3 and s.4 of the practice direction) in relation to judicial review appeals.

The risk of escalating costs

There is an obvious danger that cost-saving mechanisms (viz. the requirements for permission from an Administrative Court judge and from the Court of Appeal) may end up multiplying costs. Before his claim for judicial review gets under way the applicant might have undergone three preliminary hearings, namely (1) a permission hearing before an Administrative Court judge, (2) a permission hearing before the Court of Appeal and (3) a substantive hearing before the Court of Appeal. **52.15.2**

The solution

Rule 52.15(3) empowers the Court of Appeal to cut the Gordian knot and, instead of granting permission to appeal, to grant permission to apply for judicial review. It is respectfully suggested that (except in cases where the court needs to adjourn in order to hear the respondent) this power should generally be exercised, essentially for three reasons: (1) If there is a real prospect of success on the appeal, almost by definition the underlying claim for judicial review must be arguable. (2) It is undesirable that the merits of a judicial review claim should be scrutinised at a full hearing before two or three lords justices before it is adjudicated upon by a first instance judge. (3) It may be thought oppressive to make the claimant pay a third set of costs before his claim reaches the starting line. **52.15.3**

The true nature of the application

Although in substance the claimant is trying to persuade the Court of Appeal to grant permission to apply for judicial review, the legal basis of his application should not be overlooked. It is, and can only be, an application for permission to appeal to the Court of Appeal against the refusal by the High Court to grant permission to apply for judicial review. Where (as sometimes happens) the Court of Appeal states that it is refusing permission to apply for judicial review, this is by necessary implication a refusal of permission to appeal to the Court of Appeal. Furthermore, since the only application before the Court of Appeal is an application for permission to appeal, an adverse decision on that application (however formulated) cannot be the subject of an appeal to the House of Lords. See *R. v Secretary of State for Trade and Industry, ex p. Eastaway* [2000] 1 W.L.R. 2222. If, on the other hand, the Court of Appeal grants permission to appeal but then refuses permission to apply for judicial review at the substantive hearing, there is potentially a right of appeal to the House of Lords. See *R. (Burkett) v Hammersmith LBC* [2002] 1 W.L.R. 1593; *R. (Werner) v Commissioners of Inland Revenue* [2002] EWCA Civ 979 per Brooke L.J. at [33]. **52.15.4**

Where the court wishes to hear the respondent

It is sometimes necessary to hear the respondent, in order to determine whether the original claim is fit for consideration at a substantive judicial review hearing. In those circumstances the normal course is to adjourn the application for permission to appeal to be heard on notice, with the appeal to follow if permission is granted. See *R. (Werner) v Commissioners of Inland Revenue* [2002] EWCA Civ 979 at [28]–[32]. **52.15.5**

Time limit for application to Court of Appeal

The time limit for applying to the Court of Appeal is seven days: see r.52.15 (2). The principles governing the grant of any extension of time are as set out in the notes to r.52.6 above. Where the claimant has been refused permission to apply for judicial review of a decision of the Immigration Appeal Tribunal, the Court of Appeal will only grant an extension of time in exceptional circumstances: see *R. (Awan) v Immigration Appeal Tribunal* [2004] EWCA Civ 922 at [69]–[76]. **52.15.6**

Possible transfer to Upper Tribunal

Pursuant to s.31A of the Supreme Court Act 1981 (inserted by s.19 of the Tribunals, Courts and Enforcement Act 2007) (a) certain categories of judicial review applications must be transferred to the Upper Tribunal and (b) certain categories of judicial review applications may be transferred to the Upper Tribunal if this appears to be "just and convenient". A fuller explanation of these provisions is set out in the commentary on Part 54 below. **52.15.7**

If the Court of Appeal grants permission to apply for judicial review, then in the exercise of its powers under r.52.15(4) the Court of Appeal should go on to consider the question of transfer to the Upper Tribunal.

Who may exercise the powers of the Court of Appeal[1]

52.16 **52.16—(1) A court officer assigned to the Civil Appeals Office who is—**

(a) a barrister; or

(b) a solicitor

may exercise the jurisdiction of the Court of Appeal with regard to the matters set out in paragraph (2) with the consent of the Master of the Rolls.

(2) The matters referred to in paragraph (1) are—

(a) any matter incidental to any proceedings in the Court of Appeal;

(b) any other matter where there is no substantial dispute between the parties; and

(c) the dismissal of an appeal or application where a party has failed to comply with any order, rule or practice direction.

(3) A court officer may not decide an application for—

(a) permission to appeal;

(b) bail pending an appeal;

(c) an injunction[GL];

(d) a stay[GL] of any proceedings, other than a temporary stay of any order or decision of the lower court over a period when the Court of Appeal is not sitting or cannot conveniently be convened.

(4) Decisions of a court officer may be made without a hearing.

(5) A party may request any decision of a court officer to be reviewed by the Court of Appeal.

(6) At the request of a party, a hearing will be held to reconsider a decision of—

(a) a single judge; or

(b) a court officer,

made without a hearing.

(6A) A request under paragraph (5) or (6) must be filed within 7 days after the party is served with notice of the decision.

(7) A single judge may refer any matter for a decision by a court consisting of two or more judges.

(Section 54(6) of the Supreme Court Act 1981 provides that there is no appeal from the decision of a single judge on an application for permission to appeal.)

(Section 58(2) of the Supreme Court Act 1981 provides that there is no appeal to the House of Lords from decisions of the Court of Appeal that—

[1] Introduced by the Civil Procedure (Amendment) Rules 2000 (SI 2000/221) and amended by the Civil Procedure (Amendment No.5) Rules 2003 (SI 2003/3361).

(a) are taken by a single judge or any officer or member of staff of that court in proceedings incidental to any cause or matter pending before the civil division of that court; and

(b) do not involve the determination of an appeal or of an application for permission to appeal,

and which may be called into question by rules of court. Rules 52.16(5) and (6) provide the procedure for the calling into question of such decisions).

The Court

In s.54 of the Supreme Court Act 1981 the "court" means a court of the civil division of the Court of Appeal: s.54(1). The court may consist of one or more judges of the Court of Appeal: s.54(2). Directions may be given as to the minimum number of judges of which a court must consist for particular types of proceedings: s.54(3) and (4). The effect of these provisions is that where a hearing takes place before a single lord justice, that lord justice constitutes the court. Accordingly a hearing to review or reconsider the decision of a court officer pursuant to r.52.16(5) or (6) may take place before one or more lords justices. **52.16.1**

Hearing to reconsider a decision of a single lord justice

If a single lord justice reaches a decision on paper, that decision may be reconsidered by the court at an oral hearing: see r.52.16(6)(a). On the other hand, if a single lord justice makes a decision at a hearing, that decision cannot be reconsidered by a court comprising two or more lord justices. This is because the lord justice on the first occasion constitutes the "court": *Paragon Finance plc v Noueiri* [2001] EWCA Civ 1114. **52.16.2**

Time limit for request

A request for reconsideration pursuant to r.52.16(5) or (6) should be made within seven days: see r.52.16(6A). **52.16.3**

III. Provisions about Reopening Appeals

Reopening of final appeals[1]

52.17—(1) The Court of Appeal or the High Court will not reopen a final determination of any appeal unless— **52.17**

(a) it is necessary to do so in order to avoid real injustice;

(b) the circumstances are exceptional and make it appropriate to reopen the appeal; and

(c) there is no alternative effective remedy.

(2) In paragraphs (1), (3), (4) and (6), "appeal" includes an application for permission to appeal.

(3) This rule does not apply to appeals to a county court.

(4) Permission is needed to make an application under this rule to reopen a final determination of an appeal even in cases where *under rule 52.3(1)* permission was not needed for the original appeal.

(5) There is no right to an oral hearing of an application for permission unless, exceptionally, the judge so directs.

(6) The judge will not grant permission without directing the

[1] Introduced by the Civil Procedure (Amendment No.4) Rules 2003 (SI 2003/2113).

application to be served on the other party to the original appeal and giving him an opportunity to make representations.

(7) There is no right of appeal or review from the decision of the judge on the application for permission, which is final.

(8) The procedure for making an application for permission is set out in the practice direction.

Background

52.17.1 Part 52 in its original form did not provide for the re-opening of an appeal after it had been concluded. Nevertheless in *Taylor v Lawrence* [2002] EWCA Civ 90; [2003] QB 528 a five-judge Court of Appeal comprising Lord Woolf C.J., Lord Phillips M.R., Ward L.J., Brooke L.J. and Chadwick L.J. decided that such jurisdiction did exist. The Lord Chief Justice, giving the judgment of the Court, reasoned as follows. The Court of Appeal has two objectives: (a) to correct wrong decisions; (b) to clarify and develop the law and set precedents (see the general introduction to the *White Book* commentary on Pt 52). An appellate court has the implicit powers to do that which is necessary to achieve those dual objectives. Accordingly the Court of Appeal has a residual jurisdiction to re-open an appeal, in order to avoid real injustice in exceptional circumstances. The Court stressed that this jurisdiction would seldom be exercised. "What will be of the greatest importance is that it should be clearly established that a significant injustice has probably occurred and that there is no alternative remedy" (Judgment para.55). The Court also said that the jurisdiction would only be exercised in a case where the House of Lords would not give leave to appeal.

There is no discussion in *Taylor v Lawrence* of the position of junior appellate courts. This was addressed in *Seray-Wurie v Hackney LBC* [2002] EWCA Civ 909; [2003] 1 W.L.R. 257. Brooke L.J. (with whom Dyson and Simon Brown L.JJ agreed) said:

> "It appears to me that the same logic which drove the Court of Appeal in *Taylor v Lawrence*...to hold that the Court of Appeal possessed such a power must also drive us to hold that the High Court, which also possesses an inherent jurisdiction to do what it needs must have power to do in order to maintain its character as a court of justice, possesses a similar power. The restrictions on the exercise of the power will be precisely the same."

This jurisdiction appears to have been widely misunderstood. In the first year after the decision in *Taylor v Lawrence* more than 200 applications to re-open appeals were made to the Court of Appeal, all of them without merit: see *Matlaszek v Bloom Camillin* [2003] EWCA Civ 154 at [30] and *Gregory v Turner* [2003] EWCA Civ 183 at [28]; [2003] 1 W.L.R. 1149. It was noted in *Bhamjee v Forsdick (No.1)* [2003] EWCA Civ 799 that the flow of unmeritorious applications to re-open appeals was imposing an unacceptable burden on the resources of the Court of Appeal.

During 2003 the Civil Procedure Rule Committee formulated a procedure to regulate the exercise of the new jurisdiction which the Court of Appeal had identified in *Taylor v Lawrence*. This procedure is set out in r.52.17, which came into force on October 6, 2003.

Scope of the rule

52.17.2 The power to re-open an appeal after it has been finally determined is vested only in the Court of Appeal and the High Court. The county courts have no such power. Thus in *Gregory v Turner* [2003] EWCA Civ 183; [2003] 1 W.L.R. 1149, where it appeared that a circuit judge had wrongly refused leave to appeal against the decision of a deputy district judge, no redress was available to the disappointed party.

Rule 52.17 is drafted in highly restrictive terms, reflecting the reasoning of the Court of Appeal in *Taylor v Lawrence*. The circumstances described in r.52.17(1) are truly exceptional. Both practitioners and litigants should note the high hurdle to be surmounted and should refrain from applying to re-open the general run of appellate decisions, about which (inevitably) one or other party is likely to be aggrieved.

The first successful application to re-open an appeal came in May 2004: *Couwenbergh v Valkova* [2004] EWCA Civ 676, in which it was alleged that the original decision had been achieved by means of deceit and perverting the course of justice. That case proceeded to a full appeal in which the appellant was successful: see *Couwenbergh v Valkova* [2005] EWCA Civ 145.

In *In re Uddin (A Child)* [2005] EWCA Civ 52; [2005] 1 W.L.R. 2398 the Court of

Appeal refused to re-open an appeal on the grounds of fresh evidence. Dame Elizabeth Butler-Sloss P. observed that the hurdle to be surmounted was much greater than the normal test for admitting fresh evidence on appeal.

> "...the *Taylor v Lawrence* jurisdiction can in our judgment only be properly invoked where it is demonstrated that the integrity of the earlier litigation process, whether at trial or at the first appeal, has been critically undermined." (para 18)
>
> "In our judgment it must at least be shown, not merely that the fresh evidence demonstrates a real possibility that an erroneous result was arrived at in the earlier proceedings (first instance or appellate), but that there exists a powerful probability that such a result has in fact been perpetrated. That, in our view, is a necessary but by no means a sufficient condition..." (para 22).

The Court of Appeal adopted a similarly restrictive approach in *Richmond upon Thames LBC v Secretary of State for Transport* [2006] EWCA Civ 193 (application to re-open appeal against costs orders in the light of subsequent decision of the European Court of Human Rights refused).

In *Feakins v DEFRA* [2006] EWCA Civ 699 the Court of Appeal gave permission to re-open an appeal which had been heard five years previously. This was an unusual case, in which the Court of Appeal at the original hearing had been misled by untrue evidence. It was "highly likely" that, if the court had known the true position at the original hearing, it would have reached a different decision: see para.38.

In *Sir William Jaffray v The Society of Lloyd's* [2007] EWCA Civ 586; [2008] 1 W.L.R. 75 the Court of Appeal expressed reservation about *Couwenbergh v Valkova, In re Uddin (A Child)* and other decisions which proceeded on the basis that the *Taylor v Lawrence*-jurisdiction was available in cases of fraud. Buxton L.J. (delivering the judgment of the court) noted binding authority to the effect that where a judgment is obtained by fraud on the court, the remedy is not an appeal or a re-opened appeal but a collateral action. Nevertheless, reluctantly assuming that the Court of Appeal had jurisdiction to re-open a determined appeal on the grounds of fraud, Buxton L.J. went on to set out strict limitations on the exercise of that jurisdiction. In the light of those limitations the application to re-open the *Jaffray* appeal was refused. Ten days after *Jaffray* a different constitution the Court of Appeal considered similar issues obiter. The court (without reference to *Jaffray*) inclined to the view that the *Taylor v Lawrence* jurisdiction would be available in cases of fraud, but left the question open: see *Bassi v Anas* [2007] EWCA Civ 903.

Procedure

Permission is required to apply to re-open an appeal after it has been finally **52.17.3**
determined. The application for permission must be made in writing in accordance with para.25.4 of the practice direction. A copy of the application for permission must not be served on any other party, unless the court so directs: see para.25.5 of the practice direction. The great majority of such permission applications are refused upon consideration of the papers, without any need to hold an oral hearing or to notify any other party.

In those rare cases where it might actually be appropriate to re-open an appeal, the judge will direct that the application be served on the other party and will give him the opportunity to make representations: see r.52.17(6) and para.25.6 of the practice direction. Those rare cases in which the other party is invited to make representations may well also fall into the exceptional category in which an oral hearing of the permission application is directed under r.52.17(5).

Where permission to appeal has been granted on some issues only

Where permission to appeal has been granted on some issues but refused on other **52.17.4**
issues, the appellant may rely upon the *Taylor v Lawrence* jurisdiction and r.52.17 in order to seek to re-open issues upon which permission to appeal has been refused. However, the court will apply a similarly restrictive approach to such applications by an appellant: see *Indicii Salus Ltd v Chandrasekaran* [2008] EWCA Civ 67 at [28]–[29].

IV. Statutory Rights of Appeal

Appeals under the Law of Property Act 1922[1]

52.18 **52.18 An appeal lies to the High Court against a decision of the Secretary of State under paragraph 16 of Schedule 15 to the Law of Property Act 1922 [2].**

Editorial note

52.18.1 This rule replaced RSC Order 93 r.9 with effect from October 1, 2007: see the Civil Procedure (Amendment) Rules 2007 (SI 2007/2204). Appeals under this rule are assigned to the Chancery Division: see para.23.2 of the practice direction.

Appeals from certain tribunals[3]

52.19 **52.19—(1) A person who was a party to proceedings before a tribunal referred to in section 11(1) of the Tribunals and Inquiries Act 1992 [4] and is dissatisfied in point of law with the decision of the tribunal may appeal to the High Court.**

(2) The tribunal may, of its own initiative or at the request of a party to the proceedings before it, state, in the form of a special case for the decision of the High Court, a question of law arising in the course of the proceedings.

Editorial note

52.19.1 This rule replaced RSC Order 94 rr.8(1) and 9(1) with effect from October 1, 2007: see the Civil Procedure (Amendment) Rules 2007 (SI 2007/2204). In an appeal under this rule the appellant must serve his appellant's notice not only on the respondents, but also upon the person or body appealed from in accordance with para.17.5 of the practice direction.

Appeals under certain planning legislation[5]

52.20 **52.20—(1) Where the Secretary of State has given a decision in proceedings on an appeal under Part VII of the Town and Country Planning Act 1990 [6] against an enforcement notice—**

(a) the appellant;

(b) the local planning authority; or

(c) another person having an interest in the land to which the notice relates,

may appeal to the High Court against the decision on a point of law.

(2) Where the Secretary of State has given a decision in proceedings on an appeal under Part VIII of that Act against a notice under section 207 of that Act—

(a) the appellant;

(b) the local planning authority; or

[1] Introduced by the Civil Procedure (Amendment) Rules 2007 (SI 2007/2204).

[2] 1922 c.16. Sch.15, para.16 was amended by the Law of Property (Amendment) Act 1924 (c.5), s.2 and Sch.2, para.5(8) and SI 2002/794, art.5(1) and Sch.1, para.1(a).

[3] Introduced by the Civil Procedure (Amendment) Rules 2007 (SI 2007/2204).

[4] 1992 c.53.

[5] Introduced by the Civil Procedure (Amendment) Rules 2007 (SI 2007/2204).

[6] 1990 c.8.

(c) any person (other than the appellant) on whom the notice was served,

may appeal to the High Court against the decision on a point of law.

(3) Where the Secretary of State has given a decision in proceedings on an appeal under section 39 of the Planning (Listed Buildings and Conservation Areas) Act 1990 [1] against a listed building enforcement notice—

(a) the appellant;

(b) the local planning authority; or

(c) any other person having an interest in the land to which the notice relates,

may appeal to the High Court against the decision on a point of law.

Editorial note

This rule replaced RSC Order 94 rr.12 and 13 with effect from October 1, 2007: see the Civil Procedure (Amendment) Rules 2007 (SI 2007/2204). Further procedural rules governing planning appeals (with effect from October 1, 2007) are set out in paras 22.6C and 22.8A of the practice direction. **52.20.1**

[1] 1990 c.9.

PRACTICE DIRECTION—APPEALS

52PD.1 *This Practice Direction supplements CPR Part 52*

Contents of this Practice Direction

1.1 This Practice Direction is divided into four sections:

- Section I – General provisions about appeals
- Section II – General provisions about statutory appeals and appeals by way of case stated
- Section III – Provisions about specific appeals
- Section IV – Provisions about reopening appeals

Section I

General provisions about appeals

52PD.2 **2.1** This practice direction applies to all appeals to which Part 52 applies except where specific provision is made for appeals to the Court of Appeal.

2.2 For the purpose only of appeals to the Court of Appeal from cases in family proceedings this Practice Direction will apply with such modifications as may be required.

Routes of Appeal

52PD.3 **2A.1** The court or judge to which an appeal is to be made (subject to obtaining any necessary permission) is set out in the tables below:

Table 1[1] addresses appeals in cases other than insolvency proceedings and those cases to which Table 3 applies;

Table 2 addresses insolvency proceedings; and

Table 3 addresses certain family cases to which CPR Part 52 may apply.

The tables do not include so-called "leap frog" appeals either to the Court of Appeal pursuant to section 57 of the Access to Justice Act 1999 or to the House of Lords pursuant to section 13 of the Administration of Justice Act 1969.

(An interactive routes of appeal guide can be found on the Court of Appeal's website at *http://www.hmcourts-service.gov.uk/infoabout/coa_civil/routes_app/index.htm*)

Table 1

52PD.3.1 In this Table, reference to—

(a) a 'Circuit judge' includes a recorder or a district judge who is exercising the jurisdiction of a circuit judge with the permission of the designated civil judge in respect of that case (see Practice Direction 2B (Allocation of cases to levels of judiciary), paragraph 11.1(d));

(b) 'the Destinations of Appeal Order" means the Access to Justice Act 1999 (Destination of Appeals) Order 2000; and

(c) 'final decision' has the meaning for the purposes of this table as set out in paragraphs 2A.2 and 2A.3.

[1] Reproduced with the kind permission of Tottel Publishing, publisher of *Manual of Civil Appeals*.

Court	Track/nature of claim	Judge who made the decision	Nature of the decision under appeal	Appeal court
County	Part 7 claim	District judge	Interim decision	Circuit judge in the county court
County	Part 7 claim, other than a claim allocated to the multi-track	District judge	Final decision	Circuit judge in the county court
County	Part 7 claim, allocated to the multi-track	District judge	Final decision	Court of Appeal
County	Part 8 claim	District judge	Any decision	Circuit judge in the county court
County	Claims or originating or pre-action applications started otherwise than by a Part 7 or Part 8 claim (for example an application under Part 23)	District judge	Any decision	Circuit judge in the county court
County	Specialist proceedings (under the Companies Act 1985 or the Companies Act 1989 or to which Sections I or II of Part 57 or any of Parts 60, 62 or 63 apply)	District judge	Interim decision	Circuit judge in the county court

County	Specialist proceedings (under the Companies Act 1985 or the Companies Act 1989 or to which Sections I or II, of Part 57 or any of Parts 60, 62 or 63 apply)	District judge	Final decision	Court of Appeal
County	Part 7 claim	Circuit judge	Interim decision	Single judge of the High Court
County	Part 7 claim, other than a claim allocated to the multi-track	Circuit judge	Final decision	Single judge of the High Court
County	Part 7 claim allocated to the multi-track	Circuit judge	Final decision	Court of Appeal
County	Part 8 claim	Circuit judge	Any decision	Single judge of the High Court
County	Claims or originating or pre-action applications started otherwise than by a Part 7 or Part 8 claim (for example an application under Part 23)	Circuit judge	Any decision	Single judge of the High Court
County	Specialist proceedings (under the Companies Act 1985 or the Companies Act 1989 or to which Sections I or II of Part 57 or any of Parts 60, 62 or 63 apply)	Circuit judge	Interim decision	Single judge of the High Court

CPR 52

County	Specialist proceedings (under the Companies Act 1985 or the Companies Act 1989 or to which Sections I or II of Part 57 or any of Parts 60, 62 or 63 apply)	Circuit judge	Final decision	Court of Appeal
High	Part 7 claim	Master, district judge sitting in a district registry or any other judge referred to in article 2 of the Destination of Appeals Order (where appropriate)	Interim decision	Single judge of the High Court
High	Part 7 claim, other than a claim allocated to the multi-track	Master, district judge sitting in a district registry or any other judge referred to in article 2 of the Destination of Appeals Order (where appropriate)	Final decision	Single judge of the High Court
High	Part 7 claim, allocated to the multi-track	Master, district judge sitting in a district registry or any other judge *referred* to in article 2 of the Destination of Appeals Order (where appropriate)	Final decision	Court of Appeal

High	Part 8 claim	Master, district judge sitting in a district registry or any other judge referred to in article 2 of the Destination of Appeals Order (where appropriate)	Any decision	Single judge of the High Court
High	Claims or originating or pre-action applications started otherwise than by a Part 7 or Part 8 claim (for example an application under Part 23)	Master, district judge sitting in a district registry or any other judge referred to in article 2 of the Destination of Appeals Order (where appropriate)	Any decision	Single judge of the High Court
High	Specialist proceedings (under the Companies Act 1985 or the Companies Act 1989 or to which Sections I, II, or III of Part 57 or any of Parts 58 to 63 apply)	Master, district judge sitting in a district registry or any other judge referred to in article 2 of the Destination of Appeals Order (where appropriate)	Interim decision	Single judge of the High Court

High	Specialist proceedings (under the Companies Act 1985 or the Companies Act 1989 or to which Sections I, II or III of Part 57 or any of Parts 58 to 63 apply)	Master, district judge sitting in a district registry or any other judge referred to in article 2 of the Destination of Appeals Order (where appropriate)	Final decision	Court of Appeal
High	Any	High Court judge	Any decision	Court of Appeal

Table 2: Insolvency proceedings

In this Table references to a "Circuit judge" include a recorder or a district judge who is exercising the jurisdiction of a circuit judge with the permission of the designated civil judge in respect of that case (see: Practice Direction 2B, paragraph 11.1(d)). **52PD.3.2**

COURT	TRACK/ NATURE OF CLAIM	JUDGE WHO MADE DECISION	NATURE OF DECISION UNDER APPEAL	APPEAL COURT
County	Insolvency	District judge or circuit judge	Any	Single judge of the High Court
County	Insolvency	Registrar	Any	Single judge of the High Court
High Court	Insolvency	High Court judge	Any	Court of Appeal

Table 3: Proceedings which may be heard in the Family Division of the High Court and to which the CPR may apply

The proceedings to which this table will apply include proceedings under the Inheritance (Provision for Family and Dependants) Act 1975 and proceedings under the Trusts of Land and Appointment of Trustees Act 1996. **52PD.3.3**

For the meaning of "final decision" for the purposes of this table see paragraphs 2A.2 and 2A.3 below.

COURT	TRACK/ NATURE OF CLAIM	JUDGE WHO MADE DECISION	NATURE OF DECISION UNDER APPEAL	APPEAL COURT
High Court Principal Registry of the Family Division	Proceedings under CPR Pt 8 (if not allocated to any track or if simply treated as allocated to the multi-track under CPR 8.9(c))	District judge	Any decision	High Court judge of the Family Division
High Court Principal Registry of the Family Division	Proceedings under CPR Pt 8 specifically allocated to the multi-track by an order of the court	District judge	Any decision	High Court judge of the Family Division
High Court Principal Registry of the Family Division	Proceedings under CPR Part 7	District judge	Any decision other than a final decision	High Court judge of the Family Division
High Court Principal Registry of the Family Division	Proceedings under CPR Part 7 and allocated to the multi-track	District judge	Final decision	Court of Appeal
High Court Family Division	Proceedings under CPR Part 7 or 8	High Court judge	Any	Court of Appeal

2A.2 A "final decision" is a decision of a court that would finally determine (subject to any possible appeal or detailed assessment of costs) the entire proceedings whichever way the court decided the issues before it. Decisions made on an application to strike-out or for summary judgment are not final decisions for the purpose of determining the appropriate route of appeal (Art. 1 Access to Justice Act 1999 (Destination of Appeals) Order 2000). Accordingly:

(1) a case management decision;

(2) the grant or refusal of interim relief;

(3) a summary judgment;

(4) a striking out,

are not final decisions for this purpose.

2A.3 *A decision* of a court is to be treated as a final decision for routes of appeal purposes where it:

(1) is made at the conclusion of part of a hearing or trial which has been split into parts; and

(2) would, if it had been made at the conclusion of that hearing or trial, have been a final decision.

Accordingly, a judgment on liability at the end of a split trial is a "final decision" for this purpose and the judgment at the conclusion of the assessment of damages following a judgment on liability is also a "final decision" for this purpose.

2A.4 An order made:

(1) on a summary or detailed assessment of costs; or

(2) on an application to enforce a final decision,

is not a "final decision" and any appeal from such an order will follow the routes of appeal set out in the tables above.

(Section 16(1) of the Supreme Court Act 1981 (as amended); section 77(1) of the County Courts Act 1984 (as amended); and the Access to Justice Act 1999 (Destination of Appeals) Order 2000 set out the provisions governing routes of appeal).

2A.5(1) Where an applicant attempts to file an appellant's notice and the appeal court does not have jurisdiction to issue the notice, a court officer may notify the applicant in writing that the appeal court does not have jurisdiction in respect of the notice.

(2) Before notifying a person under paragraph (1) the court officer must confer—

(a) with a judge of the appeal court; or,

(b) where the Court of Appeal, Civil Division is the appeal court, with a court officer who exercises the jurisdiction of that Court under rule 52.16.

(3) Where a court officer in the Court of Appeal, Civil Division notifies a person under paragraph (1), rule 52.16(5) shall not apply.

Destination of appeals

Paragraph 2A of the practice direction sets out the effect of the provisions of the Access to Justice Act 1999 (Destination of Appeals) Order 2000 (referred to in this commentary as "the Destination Order") and supplements those provisions. The Destination Order is set out in Vol.2, Sect.9A. The operation of the Destination Order and of para.2A of the practice direction are discussed above in the introductory commentary to Pt 52, under the heading "Destination of appeals". **52PD.4**

The tables in para.2A.1 do not specifically mention recorders sitting in county courts. The routes of appeal from such recorders are the same as the routes of appeal from circuit judges, subject to the gloss set out in para.8.13(1A) of the practice direction. The gist of this paragraph is that a designated civil judge (provided that he is authorised to sit as a deputy High Court judge, as is usually the case) may hear an appeal from such a recorder.

Grounds for appeal

3.1 *Rule 52.11(3)(a) and (b) sets out the circumstances in which the* appeal court will allow an appeal. **52PD.5**

3.2 The grounds of appeal should—

(1) set out clearly the reasons why rule 52.11(3)(a) or (b) is said to apply; and

(2) specify, in respect of each ground, whether the ground raises an appeal on a point of law or is an appeal against a finding of fact.

Permission to appeal

52PD.6 **4.1** Rule 52.3 sets out the circumstances when permission to appeal is required.

4.2 The permission of—

(1) the Court of Appeal; or

(2) where the lower court's rules allow, the lower court,

is required for all appeals to the Court of Appeal except as provided for by statute or rule 52.3.

(The requirement of permission to appeal may be imposed by a practice direction—see rule 52.3(b))

4.3 Where the lower court is not required to give permission to appeal, it may give an indication of its opinion as to whether permission should be given.

(Rule 52.1(3)(c) defines "lower court".)

4.3A(1) This paragraph applies where a party applies for permission to appeal against a decision at the hearing at which the decision was made.

(2) Where this paragraph applies, the judge making the decision shall state—

(a) whether or not the judgment or order is final;

(b) whether an appeal lies from the judgment or order and, if so, to which appeal court;

(c) whether the court gives permission to appeal; and

(d) if not, the appropriate appeal court to which any further application for permission may be made.

(Rule 40.2(4) contains requirements as to the contents of the judgment or order in these circumstances.)

4.3B Where no application for permission to appeal has been made in accordance with rule 52.3(2)(a) but a party requests further time to make such an application, the court may adjourn the hearing to give that party the opportunity to do so.

Appeals from case management decisions

52PD.7 **4.4** Case management decisions include decisions made under rule 3.1(2) and decisions about:

(1) disclosure

(2) filing of witness statements or experts' reports

(3) directions about the timetable of the claim

(4) adding a party to a claim

(5) security for costs.

4.5 Where the application is for permission to appeal from a case management decision, the court dealing with the application may take into account whether:

(1) the issue is of insufficient significance to justify the costs of an appeal;

(2) the procedural consequences of an appeal (e.g. loss of trial date) outweigh the significance of the case management decision;

(3) it would be more convenient to determine the issue at or after trial.

Court to which permission to appeal application should be made

4.6 An application for permission should be made orally at the hearing at which the decision to be appealed against is made. **52PD.8**

4.7 Where:

(a) no application for permission to appeal is made at the hearing; or

(b) the lower court refuses permission to appeal,

an application for permission to appeal may be made to the appeal court in accordance with rules 52.3(2) and (3).

4.8 There is no appeal from a decision of the appeal court to allow or refuse permission to appeal to that court (although where the appeal court, without a hearing, refuses permission to appeal, the person seeking permission may request that decision to be reconsidered at a hearing). See section 54(4) of the Access to Justice Act and rule 52.3(2), (3), (4) and (5).

Second appeals

4.9 An application for permission to appeal from a decision of the High Court or a county court which was itself made on appeal must be made to the Court of Appeal. **52PD.9**

4.10 If permission to appeal is granted the appeal will be heard by the Court of Appeal.

Consideration of permission without a hearing

4.11 Applications for permission to appeal may be considered by the appeal court without a hearing. **52PD.10**

4.12 If permission is granted without a hearing the parties will be notified of that decision and the procedure in paragraphs 6.1 to 6.6 will then apply.

4.13 If permission is refused without a hearing the parties will be notified of that decision with the reasons for it. The decision is subject to the appellant's right to have it reconsidered at an oral hearing. This may be before the same judge.

4.14 A request for the decision to be reconsidered at an oral hearing must be filed at the appeal court within 7 days after service of the notice that permission has been refused. A copy of the request must be served by the appellant on the respondent at the same time.

Permission hearing

4.14A(1) This paragraph applies where an appellant, who is represented, makes a request for a decision to be reconsidered at an oral hearing. **52PD.11**

(2) The appellant's advocate must, at least 4 days before the hearing, in a brief written statement—

(a) inform the court and the respondent of the points which he proposes to raise at the hearing;

(b) set out his reasons why permission should be granted notwithstanding the reasons given for the refusal of permission; and

(c) confirm, where applicable, that the requirements of paragraph 4.17 have been complied with (appellant in receipt of services funded by the Legal Services Commission).-

4.15 Notice of a permission hearing will be given to the respondent but he is not required to attend unless the court requests him to do so.

4.16 If the court requests the respondent's attendance at the permission hearing, the appellant must supply the respondent with a copy of the appeal bundle (see paragraph 5.6A) within 7 days of being notified of the request, or such other period as the court may direct. The costs of providing that bundle shall be borne by the appellant initially, but will form part of the costs of the permission application.

Appellants in receipt of services funded by the Legal Services Commission applying for permission to appeal

52PD.12 **4.17** Where the appellant is in receipt of services funded by the Legal Services Commission (or legally aided) and permission to appeal has been refused by the appeal court without a hearing, the appellant must send a copy of the reasons the appeal court gave for refusing permission to the relevant office of the Legal Services Commission as soon as it has been received from the court. The court will require confirmation that this has been done if a hearing is requested to reconsider the question of permission.

Limited permission

52PD.13 **4.18** Where a court under rule 52.3(7) gives permission to appeal on some issues only, it will—

(1) refuse permission on any remaining issues; or
(2) reserve the question of permission to appeal on any remaining issues to the court hearing the appeal.

4.19 If the court reserves the question of permission under paragraph 4.18(2), the appellant must, within 14 days after service of the court's order, inform the appeal court and the respondent in writing whether he intends to pursue the reserved issues. If the appellant does intend to pursue the reserved issues, the parties must include in any time estimate for the appeal hearing, their time estimate for the reserved issues.

4.20 If the appeal court refuses permission to appeal on the remaining issues without a hearing and the applicant wishes to have that decision reconsidered at an oral hearing, the time limit in rule 52.3(5) shall apply. Any application for an extension of this time limit should be made promptly. The court hearing the appeal on the issues for which permission has been granted will not normally grant, at the appeal hearing, an application to extend the time limit in rule 52.3(5) for the remaining issues.

4.21 If the appeal court refuses permission to appeal on remaining issues at or after an oral hearing, the application for permission to appeal on those issues cannot be renewed at the appeal hearing. See section 54(4) of the Access to Justice Act 1999.

Respondents' costs of permission applications

52PD.14 **4.22** In most cases, applications for permission to appeal will be determined without the court requesting—

(1) submissions from, or
(2) if there is an oral hearing, attendance by

the respondent.

4.23 Where the court does not request submissions from or attendance by the respondent, costs will not normally be allowed to a respondent who volunteers submissions or attendance.

4.24 Where the court does request—

(1) submissions from; or

(2) attendance by the respondent,

the court will normally allow the respondent his costs if permission is refused.

Appellant's notice

5.1 An appellant's notice must be filed and served in all cases. Where an application for permission to appeal is made to the appeal court it must be applied for in the appellant's notice. **52PD.15**

Human Rights

5.1A(1) This paragraph applies where the appellant seeks— **52PD.16**

(a) to rely on any issue under the Human Rights Act 1998; or

(b) a remedy available under that Act,

for the first time in an appeal.

(2) The appellant must include in his appeal notice the information required by paragraph 15.1 of the practice direction supplementing Part 16.

(3) Paragraph 15.2 of the practice direction supplementing Part 16 applies as if references to a statement of case were to the appeal notice.

5.1B CPR rule 19.4A and the practice direction supplementing it shall apply as if references to the case management conference were to the application for permission to appeal.

(The practice direction to Part 19 provides for notice to be given and parties joined in certain circumstances to which this paragraph applies).

Extension of time for filing appellant's notice

5.2 Where the time for filing an appellant's notice has expired, the appellant must— **52PD.17**

(a) file the appellant's notice; and

(b) include in that appellant's notice an application for an extension of time.

The appellant's notice should state the reason for the delay and the steps taken prior to the application being made.

5.3 Where the appellant's notice includes an application for an *extension of time and permission* to appeal has been given or is not required the respondent has the right to be heard on that application. He must be served with a copy of the appeal bundle (see paragraph 5.6A). However, a respondent who unreasonably opposes an extension of time runs the risk of being ordered to pay the appellant's costs of that application.

5.4 If an extension of time is given following such an application the procedure at paragraphs 6.1 to 6.6 applies.

Applications

52PD.18 **5.5** Notice of an application to be made to the appeal court for a remedy incidental to the appeal (e.g. an interim remedy under rule 25.1 or an order for security for costs) may be included in the appeal notice or in a Part 23 application notice.

(Rule 25.15 deals with security for costs of an appeal)

(Paragraph 11 of this practice direction contains other provisions relating to applications)

Documents

52PD.19 **5.6**(1) This paragraph applies to every case except where the appeal—

(a) relates to a claim allocated to the small claims track; and

(b) is being heard in a county court or the High Court.

(Paragraph 5.8 applies where this paragraph does not apply)

(2) The appellant must file the following documents together with an appeal bundle (see paragraph 5.6A) with his appellant's notice—

(a) two additional copies of the appellant's notice for the appeal court; and

(b) one copy of the appellant's notice for each of the respondents;

(c) one copy of his skeleton argument for each copy of the appellant's notice that is filed (see paragraph 5.9);

(d) a sealed copy of the order being appealed;

(e) a copy of any order giving or refusing permission to appeal, together with a copy of the judge's reasons for allowing or refusing permission to appeal;

(f) any witness statements or affidavits in support of any application included in the appellant's notice;

(g) a copy of the order allocating a case to a track (if any).

5.6A(1) An appellant must include in his appeal bundle the following documents:

(a) a sealed copy of the appellant's notice;

(b) a sealed copy of the order being appealed;

(c) a copy of any order giving or refusing permission to appeal, together with a copy of the judge's reasons for allowing or refusing permission to appeal;

(d) any affidavit or witness statement filed in support of any application included in the appellant's notice;

(e) a copy of his skeleton argument;

(f) a transcript or note of judgment (see paragraph 5.12), and in cases where permission to appeal was given by the lower court or is not required those parts of any transcript of evidence which are directly relevant to any question at issue on the appeal;

(g) the claim form and statements of case (where relevant to the subject of the appeal);

(h) any application notice (or case management documentation) relevant to the subject of the appeal;
(i) in cases where the decision appealed was itself made on appeal (eg from district judge to circuit judge), the first order, the reasons given and the appellant's notice used to appeal from that order;
(j) in the case of judicial review or a statutory appeal, the original decision which was the subject of the application to the lower court;
(k) in cases where the appeal is from a Tribunal, a copy of the Tribunal's reasons for the decision, a copy of the decision reviewed by the Tribunal and the reasons for the original decision and any document filed with the Tribunal setting out the grounds of appeal from that decision;
(l) any other documents which the appellant reasonably considers necessary to enable the appeal court to reach its decision on the hearing of the application or appeal; and
(m) such other documents as the court may direct.

(2) All documents that are extraneous to the issues to be considered on the application or the appeal must be excluded. The appeal bundle may include affidavits, witness statements, summaries, experts' reports and exhibits but only where these are directly relevant to the subject matter of the appeal.

(3) Where the appellant is represented, the appeal bundle must contain a certificate signed by his solicitor, counsel or other representative to the effect that he has read and understood paragraph (2) above and that the composition of the appeal bundle complies with it.

5.7 Where it is not possible to file all the above documents, the appellant must indicate which documents have not yet been filed and the reasons why they are not currently available. The appellant must then provide a reasonable estimate of when the missing document or documents can be filed and file them as soon as reasonably practicable.

Small claims

5.8(1) This paragraph applies where— **52PD.20**
(a) the appeal relates to a claim allocated to the small claims track; and
(b) the appeal is being heard in a county court or the High Court.

(1A) An appellant's notice must be filed and served in Form **N164**.

(2) The appellant must file the following documents with his appellant's notice—
(a) a sealed copy of the order being appealed; and
(b) any order giving or refusing permission to appeal, together with a copy of the reasons for that decision.

(3) The appellant may, if relevant to the issues to be determined on the appeal, file any other document listed in paragraph

5.6 or 5.6A in addition to the documents referred to in sub-paragraph (2).

(4) The appellant need not file a record of the reasons for judgment of the lower court with his appellant's notice unless sub-paragraph (5) applies.

(5) The court may order a suitable record of the reasons for judgment of the lower court (see paragraph 5.12) to be filed—

(a) to enable it to decide if permission should be granted; or

(b) if permission is granted to enable it to decide the appeal.

Skeleton arguments

52PD.21 **5.9**(1) The appellant's notice must, subject to (2) and (3) below, be accompanied by a skeleton argument. Alternatively the skeleton argument may be included in the appellant's notice. Where the skeleton argument is so included it will not form part of the notice for the purposes of rule 52.8.

(2) Where it is impracticable for the appellant's skeleton argument to accompany the appellant's notice it must be filed and served on all respondents within 14 days of filing the notice.

(3) An appellant who is not represented need not file a skeleton argument but is encouraged to do so since this will be helpful to the court.

Content of skeleton arguments

52PD.22 **5.10**(1) A skeleton argument must contain a numbered list of the points which the party wishes to make. These should both define and confine the areas of controversy. Each point should be stated as concisely as the nature of the case allows.

(2) A numbered point must be followed by a reference to any document on which the party wishes to rely.

(3) A skeleton argument must state, in respect of each authority cited—

(a) the proposition of law that the authority demonstrates; and

(b) the parts of the authority (identified by page or paragraph references) that support the proposition.

(4) If more than one authority is cited in support of a given proposition, the skeleton argument must briefly state the reason for taking that course.

(5) The statement referred to in sub-paragraph (4) should not materially add to the length of the skeleton argument but should be sufficient to demonstrate, in the context of the argument—

(a) the relevance of the authority or authorities to that argument; and

(b) that the citation is necessary for a proper presentation of that argument.

(6) The cost of preparing a skeleton argument which—

(a) does not comply with the requirements set out in this paragraph; or

(b) was not filed within the time limits provided by this Practice Direction (or any further time granted by the court),

will not be allowed on assessment except to the extent that the court otherwise directs.

(7) A skeleton argument filed in the Court of Appeal, Civil Division on behalf of the appellant should contain in paragraph 1 the advocate's time estimate for the hearing of the appeal.

5.11 The appellant should consider what other information the appeal court will need. This may include a list of persons who feature in the case or glossaries of technical terms. A chronology of relevant events will be necessary in most appeals.

Suitable record of the judgment

5.12 Where the judgment to be appealed has been officially recorded by the court, an approved transcript of that record should accompany the appellant's notice. Photocopies will not be accepted for this purpose. However, where there is no officially recorded judgment, the following documents will be acceptable: **52PD.23**

Written judgments

(1) Where the judgment was made in writing a copy of that judgment endorsed with the judge's signature. **52PD.24**

Note of judgment

(2) When judgment was not officially recorded or made in writing a note of the judgment (agreed between the appellant's and respondent's advocates) should be submitted for approval to the judge whose decision is being appealed. If the parties cannot agree on a single note of the judgment, both versions should be provided to that judge with an explanatory letter. For the purpose of an application for permission to appeal the note need not be approved by the respondent or the lower court judge. **52PD.25**

Advocates' notes of judgments where the appellant is unrepresented

(3) When the appellant was unrepresented in the lower court it is the duty of any advocate for the respondent to make his/her note of judgment promptly available, free of charge to the appellant where there is no officially recorded judgment *or if the court so directs.* Where the appellant was represented in the lower court it is the duty of his/her own former advocate to make his/her note available in these circumstances. The appellant should submit the note of judgment to the appeal court. **52PD.26**

Reasons for judgment in Tribunal cases

(4) A sealed copy of the Tribunal's reasons for the decision. **52PD.27**

5.13 An appellant may not be able to obtain an official transcript or other suitable record of the lower court's decision within the time within which the appellant's notice must be filed. In such cases the appellant's notice must still be completed to the best of the appellant's ability on the basis of the documentation available. However it may be amended subsequently with the permission of the appeal court.

Advocates' notes of judgments

52PD.28 **5.14** Advocates' brief (or, where appropriate, refresher) fee includes:

(1) remuneration for taking a note of the judgment of the court;
(2) having the note transcribed accurately;
(3) attempting to agree the note with the other side if represented;
(4) submitting the note to the judge for approval where appropriate;
(5) revising it if so requested by the judge,
(6) providing any copies required for the appeal court, instructing solicitors and lay client; and
(7) providing a copy of his note to an unrepresented appellant.

Transcripts or Notes of Evidence

52PD.29 **5.15** When the evidence is relevant to the appeal an official transcript of the relevant evidence must be obtained. Transcripts or notes of evidence are generally not needed for the purpose of determining an application for permission to appeal.

Notes of evidence

52PD.30 **5.16** If evidence relevant to the appeal was not officially recorded, a typed version of the judge's notes of evidence must be obtained.

Transcripts at public expense

52PD.31 **5.17** Where the lower court or the appeal court is satisfied that—

(1) an unrepresented appellant; or
(2) an appellant whose legal representation is provided free of charge to the appellant and not funded by the Community Legal Service;

is in such poor financial circumstances that the cost of a transcript would be an excessive burden the court may certify that the cost of obtaining one official transcript should be borne at public expense.

5.18 In the case of a request for an official transcript of evidence or proceedings to be paid for at public expense, the court must also be satisfied that there are reasonable grounds for appeal. Whenever possible a request for a transcript at public expense should be made to the lower court when asking for permission to appeal.

Transcripts of judgments at public expense

52PD.32 Paragraph 5.17 of the practice direction relates principally to transcripts of judgments. In *Perotti v Westminster City Council (Application for Permission to Appeal)* [2005] EWCA Civ 581 the Court of Appeal upheld an order that P's application for a transcript at public expense should not be considered until after he had furnished detailed grounds of appeal. In some cases this is an appropriate course, in order to prevent the fruitless expenditure of public funds.

Filing and service of appellant's notice

5.19 Rule 52.4 sets out the procedure and time limits for filing and serving an appellant's notice. The appellant must file the appellant's notice at the appeal court within such period as may be directed by the lower court which should not normally exceed 35 days or, where the lower court directs no such period, within 21 days of the date of the decision that the appellant wishes to appeal.

(Rule 52.15 sets out the time limit for filing an application for permission to appeal against the refusal of the High Court to grant permission to apply for judicial review)

5.20 Where the lower court judge announces his decision and reserves the reasons for his judgment or order until a later date, he should, in the exercise of powers under rule 52.4(2)(a), fix a period for filing the appellant's notice at the appeal court that takes this into account.

5.21(1) Except where the appeal court orders otherwise a sealed copy of the appellant's notice, including any skeleton arguments must be served on all respondents in accordance with the timetable prescribed by rule 52.4(3) except where this requirement is modified by paragraph 5.9(2) in which case the skeleton argument should be served as soon as it is filed.

(2) The appellant must, as soon as practicable, file a certificate of service of the documents referred to in paragraph (1).

5.22 Unless the court otherwise directs a respondent need not take any action when served with an appellant's notice until such time as notification is given to him that permission to appeal has been given.

5.23 The court may dispense with the requirement for service of the notice on a respondent. Any application notice seeking an order under rule 6.28 to dispense with service should set out the reasons relied on and be verified by a statement of truth.

5.24(1) Where the appellant is applying for permission to appeal in his appellant's notice, he must serve on the respondents his appellant's notice and skeleton argument (but not the appeal bundle), unless the appeal court directs otherwise.

(2) Where permission to appeal—

(a) has been given by the lower court; or

(b) is not required,

the appellant must serve the appeal bundle on the respondents with the appellant's notice.

Amendment of Appeal Notice

5.25 An appeal notice may be amended with permission. Such an application to amend and any application in opposition will normally be dealt with at the hearing unless that course would cause unnecessary expense or delay in which case a request should be made for the application to amend to be heard in advance. **52PD.34**

Procedure after permission is obtained

6.1 This paragraph sets out the procedure where: **52PD.35**

(1) permission to appeal is given by the appeal court; or
(2) the appellant's notice is filed in the appeal court and—
(a) permission was given by the lower court; or
(b) permission is not required.

6.2 If the appeal court gives permission to appeal, the appeal bundle must be served on each of the respondents within 7 days of receiving the order giving permission to appeal.

(Part 6 (service of documents) provides rules on service.)

6.3 The appeal court will send the parties—
(1) notification of—
(a) the date of the hearing or the period of time (the 'listing window') during which the appeal is likely to be heard; and
(b) in the Court of Appeal, the date by which the appeal will be heard (the 'hear by date');
(2) where permission is granted by the appeal court a copy of the order giving permission to appeal; and
(3) any other directions given by the court.

6.3A(1) Where the appeal court grants permission to appeal, the appellant must add the following documents to the appeal bundle—
(a) the respondent's notice and skeleton argument (if any);
(b) those parts of the transcripts of evidence which are directly relevant to any question at issue on the appeal;
(c) the order granting permission to appeal and, where permission to appeal was granted at an oral hearing, the transcript (or note) of any judgment which was given; and
(d) any document which the appellant and respondent have agreed to add to the appeal bundle in accordance with paragraph 7.11.
(2) Where permission to appeal has been refused on a particular issue, the appellant must remove from the appeal bundle all documents that are relevant only to that issue.

Appeal Questionnaire in the Court of Appeal

52PD.36 **6.4** The Court of Appeal will send an Appeal Questionnaire to the appellant when it notifies him of the matters referred to in paragraph 6.3.

6.5 The appellant must complete and file the Appeal Questionnaire within 14 days of the date of the letter of notification of the matters in paragraph 6.3. The Appeal Questionnaire must contain:
(1) if the appellant is legally represented, the advocate's time estimate for the hearing of the appeal;
(2) where a transcript of evidence is relevant to the appeal, confirmation as to what parts of a transcript of evidence have been ordered where this is not already in the bundle of documents;

(3) confirmation that copies of the appeal bundle are being prepared and will be held ready for the use of the Court of Appeal and an undertaking that they will be supplied to the court on request. For the purpose of these bundles photocopies of the transcripts will be accepted;

(4) confirmation that copies of the Appeal Questionnaire and the appeal bundle have been served on the respondents and the date of that service.

Time estimates

6.6 The time estimate included in an Appeal Questionnaire must be that of the advocate who will argue the appeal. It should exclude the time required by the court to give judgment. If the respondent disagrees with the time estimate, the respondent must inform the court within 7 days of receipt of the Appeal Questionnaire. In the absence of such notification the respondent will be deemed to have accepted the estimate proposed on behalf of the appellant. **52PD.37**

Respondent

7.1 A respondent who wishes to ask the appeal court to vary the order of the lower court in any way must appeal and permission will be required on the same basis as for an appellant. **52PD.38**

(Paragraph 3.2 applies to grounds of appeal by a respondent.)

7.2 A respondent who wishes only to request that the appeal court upholds the judgment or order of the lower court whether for the reasons given in the lower court or otherwise does not make an appeal and does not therefore require permission to appeal in accordance with rule 52.3(1).

(Paragraph 7.6 requires a respondent to file a skeleton argument where he wishes to address the appeal court)

7.3(1) A respondent who wishes to appeal or who wishes to ask the appeal court to uphold the order of the lower court for reasons different from or additional to those given by the lower court must file a respondent's notice.

(2) If the respondent does not file a respondent's notice, he will not be entitled, except with the permission of the court, to rely on any reason not relied on in the lower court.

7.3A Paragraphs 5.1A, 5.1B and 5.2 of this practice direction (Human Rights and extension for time for filing appellant's notice) also apply to a respondent and a respondent's notice.

Time limits

7.4 The time limits for filing a respondent's notice are set out in *rule 52.5(4) and (5)*. **52PD.39**

7.5 Where an extension of time is required the extension must be requested in the respondent's notice and the reasons why the respondent failed to act within the specified time must be included.

7.6 Except where paragraph 7.7A applies, the respondent must file a skeleton argument for the court in all cases where he proposes to address arguments to the court. The respondent's skeleton argument may be included within a respondent's notice. Where a skeleton argument is included within a respondent's notice it will not form part of the notice for the purposes of rule 52.8.

7.7(1) A respondent who—
(a) files a respondent's notice; but
(b) does not include his skeleton argument within that notice,
must file and serve his skeleton argument within 14 days of filing the notice.

(2) A respondent who does not file a respondent's notice but who files a skeleton argument must file and serve that skeleton argument at least 7 days before the appeal hearing.

(Rule 52.5(4) sets out the period for filing and serving a respondent's notice)

7.7A(1) Where the appeal relates to a claim allocated to the small claims track and is being heard in a county court or the High Court, the respondent may file a skeleton argument but is not required to do so.

(2) A respondent who is not represented need not file a skeleton argument but is encouraged to do so in order to assist the court.

7.7B The respondent must—
(1) serve his skeleton argument on—
(a) the appellant; and
(b) any other respondent,
at the same time as he files it at the court; and
(2) file a certificate of service.

Content of skeleton arguments

52PD.40 **7.8** A respondent's skeleton argument must conform to the directions at paragraphs 5.10 and 5.11 with any necessary modifications. It should, where appropriate, answer the arguments set out in the appellant's skeleton argument.

Applications within respondent's notices

52PD.41 **7.9** A respondent may include an application within a respondent's notice in accordance with paragraph 5.5 above.

Filing respondent's notices and skeleton arguments

52PD.42 **7.10**(1) The respondent must file the following documents with his respondent's notice in every case:
(a) two additional copies of the respondent's notice for the appeal court; and
(b) one copy each for the appellant and any other respondents.

(2) The respondent may file a skeleton argument with his respondent's notice and—
(a) where he does so he must file two copies; and
(b) where he does not do so he must comply with paragraph 7.7.

7.11 If the respondent wishes to rely on any documents which he reasonably considers necessary to enable the appeal court to reach its decision on the appeal in addition to those filed by the appellant, he must make every effort to agree amendments to the appeal bundle with the appellant.

7.12(1) If the representatives for the parties are unable to reach agreement, the respondent may prepare a supplemental bundle.

(2) If the respondent prepares a supplemental bundle he must file it, together with the requisite number of copies for the appeal court, at the appeal court—

(a) with the respondent's notice; or

(b) if a respondent's notice is not filed, within 21 days after he is served with the appeal bundle.

7.13 The respondent must serve—

(1) the respondent's notice;

(2) his skeleton argument (if any); and

(3) the supplemental bundle (if any),

on—

(a) the appellant; and

(b) any other respondent,

at the same time as he files them at the court.

Appeals to the High Court

Application

8.1 This paragraph applies where an appeal lies to a High Court judge from the decision of a county court or a district judge of the High Court. **52PD.43**

8.2 The following table sets out the following venues for each circuit—

(a) Appeal centres – court centres where appeals to which this paragraph applies may be filed, managed and heard. Paragraphs 8.6 to 8.8 provide for special arrangements in relation to the South Eastern Circuit.

(b) Hearing only centres – court centres where appeals to which this paragraph applies may be heard by order made at an appeal centre (see paragraph 8.10).

Circuit	Appeal Centres	Hearing Only Centres
Midland Circuit	Birmingham Nottingham	Lincoln Leicester Northampton Stafford
North Eastern Circuit	Leeds Newcastle Sheffield	Teesside
Northern Circuit	Manchester Liverpool Preston Chester	Carlisle

Circuit	Appeal Centres	Hearing Only Centres
Wales Circuit	Cardiff Swansea Mold	Caernarfon
Western Circuit	Bristol Exeter Winchester	Truro Plymouth
South Eastern Circuit	Royal Courts of Justice Lewes Luton Norwich Reading Chelmsford St Albans Maidstone Oxford	

Venue for appeals and filing of notices on circuits other than the South Eastern Circuit

8.3 Paragraphs 8.4 and 8.5 apply where the lower court is situated on a circuit other than the South Eastern Circuit.

8.4 The appellant's notice must be filed at an appeal centre on the circuit in which the lower court is situated. The appeal will be managed and heard at that appeal centre unless the appeal court orders otherwise.

8.5 A respondent's notice must be filed at the appeal centre where the appellant's notice was filed unless the appeal has been transferred to another appeal centre, in which case it must be filed at that appeal centre.

Venue for appeals and filing of notices on the South Eastern Circuit

52PD.44 **8.6** Paragraphs 8.7 and 8.8 apply where the lower court is situated on the South Eastern Circuit.

8.7 The appellant's notice must be filed at an appeal centre on the South Eastern Circuit. The appeal will be managed and heard at the Royal Courts of Justice unless the appeal court orders otherwise. An order that an appeal is to be managed or heard at another appeal centre may not be made unless the consent of the Presiding Judge of the circuit in charge of civil matters has been obtained.

8.8 A respondent's notice must be filed at the Royal Courts of Justice unless the appeal has been transferred to another appeal centre, in which case it must be filed at that appeal centre.

General provisions

52PD.45 **8.9** The appeal court may transfer an appeal to another appeal centre (whether or not on the same circuit). In deciding whether to do so the court will have regard to the criteria in rule 30.3 (criteria for a transfer order). The appeal court may do so either on application by a party or of its own initiative. Where an appeal is transferred under this paragraph, notice of transfer must be served on every person on whom the appellant's notice has been served. An appeal may not be transferred to an appeal centre on another circuit, either for management or hearing, unless the consent of the Presiding Judge of that circuit in charge of civil matters has been obtained.

8.10 Directions may be given for—

(a) an appeal to be heard at a hearing only centre; or

(b) an application in an appeal to be heard at any other venue,

instead of at the appeal centre managing the appeal.

8.11 Unless a direction has been made under 8.10, any application in the appeal must be made at the appeal centre where the appeal is being managed.

8.12 The appeal court may adopt all or any part of the procedure set out in paragraphs 6.4 to 6.6.

8.13 Where the lower court is a county court:

(1) subject to paragraph (1A), appeals and applications for permission to appeal will be heard by a High Court Judge or by a person authorised under paragraphs (1), (2) or (4) of the Table in section 9(1) of the Supreme Court Act 1981 to act as a judge of the High Court;

(1A) an appeal or application for permission to appeal from the decision of a Recorder in the county court may be heard by a Designated Civil Judge who is authorised under paragraph (5) of the Table in section 9(1) of the Supreme Court Act 1981 to act as a judge of the High Court; and

(2) other applications in the appeal may be heard and directions in the appeal may be given either by a High Court Judge or by any person authorised under section 9 of the Supreme Court Act 1981 to act as a judge of the High Court.

8.14 In the case of appeals from Masters or district judges of the High Court, appeals, applications for permission and any other applications in the appeal may be heard and directions in the appeal may be given by a High Court Judge or by any person authorised under section 9 of the Supreme Court Act 1981 to act as a judge of the High Court.

Appeals to a judge of a county court from a district judge

8A.1 The Designated Civil Judge in consultation with his Presiding Judges has responsibility for allocating appeals from decisions of district judges to circuit judges. **52PD.46**

Re-hearings

9.1 The hearing of an appeal will be a re-hearing (as opposed to a review of the decision of the lower court) if the appeal is from the decision of a minister, person or other body and the minister, person or other body— **52PD.47**

(1) did not hold a hearing to come to that decision; or

(2) held a hearing to come to that decision, but the procedure adopted did not provide for the consideration of evidence.

Appeals transferred to the Court of Appeal

10.1 Where an appeal is transferred to the Court of Appeal under **52PD.48**

rule 52.14 the Court of Appeal may give such additional directions as are considered appropriate.

Applications

52PD.49 **11.1** Where a party to an appeal makes an application whether in an appeal notice or by Part 23 application notice, the provisions of Part 23 will apply.

11.2 The applicant must file the following documents with the notice

(1) one additional copy of the application notice for the appeal court and one copy for each of the respondents;

(2) where applicable a sealed copy of the order which is the subject of the main appeal;

(3) a bundle of documents in support which should include:

(a) the Part 23 application notice; and

(b) any witness statements and affidavits filed in support of the application notice.

Disposing of applications or appeals by consent

Dismissal of applications or appeals by consent

52PD.50 **12.1** These paragraphs do not apply where—

(1) any party to the proceedings is a child or protected party; or

(2) the appeal or application is to the Court of Appeal from a decision of the Court of Protection.

12.2 Where an appellant does not wish to pursue an application or an appeal, he may request the appeal court for an order that his application or appeal be dismissed. Such a request must contain a statement that the appellant is not a child or protected party and that the appeal or application is not from a decision of the Court of Protection. If such a request is granted it will usually be on the basis that the appellant pays the costs of the application or appeal.

12.3 If the appellant wishes to have the application or appeal dismissed without costs, his request must be accompanied by a consent signed by the respondent or his legal representative stating—

(1) that the respondent is not a child or protected party and that the appeal or application is not from a decision of the Court of Protection; and

(2) that he consents to the dismissal of the application or appeal without costs.

12.4 Where a settlement has been reached disposing of the application or appeal, the parties may make a joint request to the court stating that—

(1) none of them is a child or protected party; and

(2) the appeal or application is not from a decision of the Court of Protection, and asking that the application or appeal be dismissed by consent. If the request is granted the application or appeal will be dismissed.

('Child' and 'protected party' have the same meaning as in rule 21.1(2).)

Allowing unopposed appeals or applications on paper

13.1 The appeal court will not normally make an order allowing an appeal unless satisfied that the decision of the lower court was wrong, but the appeal court may set aside or vary the order of the lower court with consent and without determining the merits of the appeal, if it is satisfied that there are good and sufficient reasons for doing so. Where the appeal court is requested by all parties to allow an application or an appeal the court may consider the request on the papers. The request should state that none of the parties is a child or protected party and that the application or appeal is not from a decision of the Court of Protection and set out the relevant history of the proceedings and the matters relied on as justifying the proposed order and be accompanied by a copy of the proposed order. **52PD.51**

Procedure for consent orders and agreements to pay periodical payments involving a child or protected party or in applications or appeals to the Court of Appeal from a decision of the Court of Protection

13.2 Where one of the parties is a child or protected party or the application or appeal is to the Court of Appeal from a decision of the Court of Protection— **52PD.52**

(1) a settlement relating to an appeal or application;

(2) in a personal injury claim for damages for future pecuniary loss, an agreement reached at the appeal stage to pay periodical payments or

(3) a request by an appellant for an order that his application or appeal be dismissed with or without the consent of the respondent,

requires the court's approval.

Child

13.3 In cases involving a child a copy of the proposed order signed by the parties' solicitors should be sent to the appeal court, together with an opinion from the advocate acting on behalf of the child. **52PD.53**

Protected party

13.4 Where a party is a protected party the same procedure will be adopted, but the documents filed should also include any relevant reports prepared for the Court of Protection. **52PD.54**

('Child' and 'protected party' have the same meaning as in rule 21.1(2).)

Periodical payments

13.5 Where periodical payments for future pecuniary loss have been negotiated in a personal injury case which is under appeal, the documents filed should include those which would be required in the case of a personal injury claim for damages for future pecuniary loss dealt with at first instance. Details can be found in the Practice Direction which supplements Part 21. **52PD.55**

Summary assessment of costs

14.1 Costs are likely to be assessed by way of summary assessment at the following hearings: **52PD.56**

(1) contested directions hearings;
(2) applications for permission to appeal at which the respondent is present;
(3) dismissal list hearings in the Court of Appeal at which the respondent is present;
(4) appeals from case management decisions; and
(5) appeals listed for one day or less.

14.2 Parties attending any of the hearings referred to in paragraph 14.1 should be prepared to deal with the summary assessment.

Other special provisions regarding the Court of Appeal

Filing of documents

52PD.57 **15.1**(1) The documents relevant to proceedings in the Court of Appeal, Civil Division must be filed in the Civil Appeals Office Registry, Room E307, Royal Courts of Justice, Strand, London, WC2A 2LL.

(2) The Civil Appeals Office will not serve documents and where service is required by the CPR or this practice direction it must be effected by the parties.

15.1A(1)A party may file by email—

(a) an appellant's notice;
(b) a respondent's notice;
(c) an application notice,

in the Court of Appeal, Civil Division, using the email account specified in the "Guidelines for filing by Email" which appear on the Court of Appeal, Civil Division website at *www.hmcourts-service.gov.uk/cms/civilappeals.htm*.

(2) A party may only file a notice in accordance with paragraph (1) where he is permitted to do so by the "Guidelines for filing by Email".

15.1B(1)A party to an appeal in the Court of Appeal, Civil Division may file—

(a) an appellant's notice;
(b) a respondent's notice; or
(c) an application notice,

electronically using the online forms service on the Court of Appeal, Civil Division website at *www.civilappeals.gov.uk*.

(2) A party may only file a notice in accordance with paragraph (1) where he is permitted to so do by the 'Guidelines for filing electronically'. The Guidelines for filing electronically may be found on the Court of Appeal, Civil Division website.

(3) The online forms service will assist the user in completing a document accurately but the user is responsible for ensuring that the rules and practice directions relating to the document have been complied with. Transmission by the service does not guarantee that the document will be accepted by the Court of Appeal, Civil Division.

(4) A party using the online forms service in accordance with

this paragraph is responsible for ensuring that the transmission or any document attached to it is filed within any relevant time limits.

(5) Parties are advised not to transmit electronically any correspondence or documents of a confidential or sensitive nature, as security cannot be guaranteed.

(6) Where a party wishes to file a document containing a statement of truth electronically, that party should retain the document containing the original signature and file with the court a version of the document on which the name of the person who has signed the statement of truth is typed underneath the statement.

Core Bundles

15.2 In cases where the appeal bundle comprises more than 500 pages, exclusive of transcripts, the appellant's solicitors must, after consultation with the respondent's solicitors, also prepare and file with the court, in addition to copies of the appeal bundle (as amended in accordance with paragraph 7.11) the requisite number of copies of a core bundle. **52PD.58**

15.3(1) The core bundle must be filed within 28 days of receipt of the order giving permission to appeal or, where permission to appeal was granted by the lower court or is not required, within 28 days of the date of service of the appellant's notice on the respondent.

(2) The core bundle—

(a) must contain the documents which are central to the appeal; and

(b) must not exceed 150 pages.

Preparation of bundles

15.4 The provisions of this paragraph apply to the preparation of appeal bundles, supplemental respondents' bundles where the parties are unable to agree amendments to the appeal bundle, and core bundles. **52PD.59**

(1) **Rejection of bundles.** Where documents are copied unnecessarily or bundled incompletely, costs may be disallowed. Where the provisions of this Practice Direction as to the preparation or delivery of bundles are not followed the bundle may be rejected by the court or be made the subject of a special costs order.

(2) **Avoidance of duplication.** No more than one copy of any document should be included unless there is a good reason for doing otherwise (such as the use of a separate core bundle—see paragraph 15.2).

(3) **Pagination**

(a) Bundles must be paginated, each page being numbered individually and consecutively. The pagination used at trial must also be indicated. Letters and other documents should normally be included in chronological order. (An exception to consecutive page numbering arises in the case of core bundles where it may be preferable to retain the original numbering).

(b) Page numbers should be inserted in bold figures at the bottom of the page and in a form that can be clearly distinguished from any other pagination on the document.

(4) **Format and presentation**

(a) Where possible the documents should be in A4 format. Where a document has to be read across rather than down the page, it should be so placed in the bundle as to ensure that the text starts nearest the spine.

(b) Where any marking or writing in colour on a document is important, the document must be copied in colour or marked up correctly in colour.

(c) Documents which are not easily legible should be transcribed and the transcription marked and placed adjacent to the document transcribed.

(d) Documents in a foreign language should be translated and the translation marked and placed adjacent to the document translated. The translation should be agreed or, if it cannot be agreed, each party's proposed translation should be included.

(e) The size of any bundle should be tailored to its contents. A large lever arch file should not be used for just a few pages nor should files of whatever size be overloaded.

(f) Where it will assist the Court of Appeal, different sections of the file may be separated by cardboard or other tabbed dividers so long as these are clearly indexed. Where, for example, a document is awaited when the appeal bundle is filed, a single sheet of paper can be inserted after a divider, indicating the nature of the document awaited. For example, 'Transcript of evidence of Mr J Smith (to follow)'.

(5) **Binding**

(a) All documents, with the exception of transcripts, must be bound together. This may be in a lever arch file, ring binder or plastic folder. Plastic sleeves containing loose documents must not be used. Binders and files must be strong enough to withstand heavy use.

(b) Large documents such as plans should be placed in an easily accessible file. Large documents which will need to be opened up frequently should be inserted in a file larger than A4 size.

(6) **Indices and labels**

(a) An index must be included at the front of the bundle listing all the documents and providing the page references for each. In the case of documents such as letters, invoices or bank statements, they may be given a general description.

(b) Where the bundles consist of more than one file, an index to all the files should be included in the first file and an index included for each file. Indices should, if possible, be on a single sheet. The full name of the case should not be inserted on the index if this would waste space. Documents should be identified briefly but properly.

(7) **Identification**

(a) Every bundle must be clearly identified, on the spine and on the front cover, with the name of the case and the Court of Appeal's reference. Where the bundle consists of more than one file, each file must be numbered on the spine, the front cover and the inside of the front cover.

(b) Outer labels should use large lettering eg 'Appeal Bundle A' or 'Core Bundle'. The full title of the appeal and solicitors' names and addresses should be omitted. A label should be used on the front as well as on the spine.

(8) **Staples etc.** All staples, heavy metal clips etc, must be removed.

(9) **Statements of case**

(a) Statements of case should be assembled in 'chapter' form – i.e claim followed by particulars of claim, followed by further information, irrespective of date.

(b) Redundant documents, eg particulars of claim overtaken by amendments, requests for further information recited in the answers given, should generally be excluded.

(10) **New Documents**

(a) Before a new document is introduced into bundles which have already been delivered to the court, steps should be taken to ensure that it carries an appropriate bundle/page number so that it can be added to the court documents. It should not be stapled and it should be prepared with punch holes for immediate inclusion in the binders in use.

(b) If it is expected that a large number of miscellaneous new documents will from time to time be introduced, there should be a special tabbed empty loose-leaf file for that purpose. An index should be produced for this file, updated as necessary.

(11) **Inter-solicitor correspondence.** Since inter-solicitor correspondence is unlikely to be required for the purposes of an appeal, only those letters which will need to be referred to should be copied.

(12) **Sanctions for non-compliance.** If the appellant fails to comply with the requirements as to the provision of bundles of documents, the application or appeal will be referred for consideration to be given as to why it should not be dismissed for failure to so comply.

Master in the Court of Appeal, Civil Division

15.5 When the Head of the Civil Appeals Office acts in a judicial capacity pursuant to rule 52.16, he shall be known as Master. Other **52PD.60**

eligible officers may also be designated by the Master of the Rolls to exercise judicial authority under rule 52.16 and shall then be known as Deputy Masters.

Respondent to notify Civil Appeals Office whether he intends to file respondent's notice

52PD.61 **15.6** A respondent must, no later than 21 days after the date he is served with notification that—

(1) permission to appeal has been granted; or

(2) the application for permission to appeal and the appeal are to be heard together,

inform the Civil Appeals Office and the appellant in writing whether—

(a) he proposes to file a respondent's notice appealing the order or seeking to uphold the order for reasons different from, or additional to, those given by the lower court; or

(b) he proposes to rely on the reasons given by the lower court for its decision.

(Paragraph 15.11B requires all documents needed for an appeal hearing, including a respondent's skeleton argument, to be filed at least 7 days before the hearing)

Listing and hear-by dates

52PD.62 **15.7** The management of the list will be dealt with by the listing officer under the direction of the Master.

15.8 The Civil Appeals List of the Court of Appeal is divided as follows:

- *The applications list* —applications for permission to appeal and other applications.
- *The appeals list* —appeals where permission to appeal has been given or where an appeal lies without permission being required where a hearing date is fixed in advance. (Appeals in this list which require special listing arrangements will be assigned to the special fixtures list)
- *The expedited list* —appeals or applications where the Court of Appeal has directed an expedited hearing. The current practice of the Court of Appeal is summarised in *Unilever plc v. Chefaro Proprietaries Ltd* (Practice Note) [1995]1 W.L.R. 243.
- *The stand-out list* —Appeals or applications which, for good reason, are not at present ready to proceed and have been stood out by judicial direction.
- *The second fixtures list* —[see paragraph 15.9A(1) below].
- *The second fixtures list* —if an appeal is designated as a 'second fixture' it means that a hearing date is arranged in advance on the express basis that the list is fully booked for the period in question and therefore the case will be heard only if a suitable gap occurs in the list.
- *The short-warned list* —appeals which the court considers may be prepared for the hearing by an advocate other than the one originally instructed with a half day's notice, or such other period as the court may direct.

Special provisions relating to the short-warned list

15.9(1) Where an appeal is assigned to the short-warned list, the Civil Appeals Office will notify the parties' solicitors in writing. The court may abridge the time for filing any outstanding bundles in an appeal assigned to this list. **52PD.63**

(2) The solicitors for the parties must notify their advocate and their client as soon as the Civil Appeals Office notifies them that the appeal has been assigned to the short-warned list.

(3) The appellant may apply in writing for the appeal to be removed from the short-warned list within 14 days of notification of its assignment. The application will be decided by a Lord Justice, or the Master, and will only be granted for the most compelling reasons.

(4) The Civil Appeals Listing Officer may place an appeal from the short-warned list 'on call' from a given date and will inform the parties' advocates accordingly.

(5) An appeal which is 'on call' may be listed for hearing on half a day's notice or such longer period as the court may direct.

(6) Once an appeal is listed for hearing from the short warned list it becomes the immediate professional duty of the advocate instructed in the appeal, if he is unable to appear at the hearing, to take all practicable measures to ensure that his lay client is represented at the hearing by an advocate who is fully instructed and able to argue the appeal.

Special provisions relating to the special fixtures list

15.9A(1) The special fixtures list is a sub-division of the appeals list and is used to deal with appeals that may require special listing arrangements, such as the need to list a number of cases before the same constitution, in a particular order, during a particular period or at a given location. **52PD.64**

(2) The Civil Appeals Office will notify the parties' representatives, or the parties if acting in person, of the particular arrangements that will apply. The notice—

(a) will give details of the specific period during which a case is scheduled to be heard; and

(b) may give directions in relation to the filing of any outstanding documents.

(3) The listing officer will notify the parties' representatives of the precise hearing date as soon as practicable. While every effort will be made to accommodate the availability of counsel, the requirements of the court will prevail.

Requests for directions

15.10 To ensure that all requests for directions are centrally monitored and correctly allocated, all requests for directions or rulings (whether relating to listing or any other matters) should be made to the Civil Appeals Office. Those seeking directions or rulings **52PD.65**

must not approach the supervising Lord Justice either directly, or via his or her clerk.

Bundles of authorities

52PD.66 **15.11**(1) Once the parties have been notified of the date fixed for the hearing, the appellant's advocate must, after consultation with his opponent, file a bundle containing photocopies of the authorities upon which each side will rely at the hearing.

(2) The bundle of authorities should, in general—

(a) have the relevant passages of the authorities marked;

(b) not include authorities for propositions not in dispute; and

(c) not contain more than 10 authorities unless the scale of the appeal warrants more extensive citation.

(3) The bundle of authorities must be filed—

(a) at least 7 days before the hearing; or

(b) where the period of notice of the hearing is less than 7 days, immediately.

(4) If, through some oversight, a party intends, during the hearing, to refer to other authorities the parties may agree a second agreed bundle. The appellant's advocate must file this bundle at least 48 hours before the hearing commences.

(5) A bundle of authorities must bear a certification by the advocates responsible for arguing the case that the requirements of sub-paragraphs (3) to (5) of paragraph 5.10 have been complied with in respect of each authority included.

Supplementary skeleton arguments

52PD.67 **15.11A**(1) A supplementary skeleton argument on which the appellant wishes to rely must be filed at least 14 days before the hearing.

(2) A supplementary skeleton argument on which the respondent wishes to rely must be filed at least 7 days before the hearing.

(3) All supplementary skeleton arguments must comply with the requirements set out in paragraph 5.10.

(4) At the hearing the court may refuse to hear argument from a party not contained in a skeleton argument filed within the relevant time limit set out in this paragraph.

Papers for the appeal hearing

52PD.68 **15.11B**(1) All the documents which are needed for the appeal hearing must be filed at least 7 days before the hearing. Where a document has not been filed 10 days before the hearing a reminder will be sent by the Civil Appeals Office.

(2) Any party who fails to comply with the provisions of paragraph (1) may be required to attend before the Presiding Lord Justice to seek permission to proceed with, or to oppose, the appeal.

Disposal of bundles of documents

15.11C(1) Where the court has determined a case, the official transcriber will retain one set of papers. The Civil Appeals Office will destroy any remaining sets of papers not collected within 21 days of— **52PD.69**

(a) where one or moreparties attend the hearing, the date of the court's decision;

(b) where there is no attendance, the date of the notification of court's decision.

(2) The parties should ensure that bundles of papers supplied to the court do not contain original documents (other than transcripts). The parties must ensure that they—

(a) bring any necessary original documents to the hearing; and

(b) retrieve any original documents handed up to the court before leaving the court.

(3) The court will retain application bundles where permission to appeal has been granted. Where permission is refused the arrangements in sub-paragraph (1) will apply.

(4) Where a single Lord Justice has refused permission to appeal on paper, application bundles will not be destroyed until after the time limit for seeking a hearing has expired.

Reserved Judgments

15.12 The Practice Direction supplementing Part 40 (Reserved Judgments) contains provisions relating to reserved judgments. **52PD.70**

[THE NEXT PARAGRAPH IS 52PD.76.]

Section II

General provisions about statutory appeals and appeals by way of case stated

16.1 This section of this practice direction contains general provisions about statutory appeals (paragraphs 17.1–17.11) and appeals by way of case stated (paragraphs 18.1–18.20). **52PD.76**

16.2 Where any of the provisions in this section provide for documents to be filed at the appeal court, these documents are in addition to any documents required under Part 52 or section 1 of this practice direction.

Statutory appeals

17.1 This part of this section— **52PD.77**

(1) applies where under any enactment an appeal (other than by way of case stated) lies to the court from a Minister of State, government department, tribunal or other person ("statutory appeals"); and

(2) is subject to any provision about a specific category of appeal in any enactment or Section III of this practice direction.

Part 52

52PD.78 **17.2** Part 52 applies to statutory appeals with the following amendments:

Filing of appellant's notice

52PD.79 **17.3** Subject to paragraph 17.4A, the appellant must file the appellant's notice at the appeal court within 28 days after the date of the decision of the lower court being appealed.

17.4 Where a statement of the reasons for a decision is given later than the notice of that decision, the period for filing the appellant's notice is calculated from the date on which the statement is received by the appellant.

17.4A(1) Where the appellant wishes to appeal against a decision of the Administrative Appeals Chamber of the Upper Tribunal, the appellant's notice must be filed within 42 days of the date on which the Upper Tribunal's decision on permission to appeal to the Court of Appeal is given.

(2) Where the appellant wishes to appeal against a decision of any other Chamber of the Upper Tribunal, the appellant's notice must be filed within 28 days of the date on which the Upper Tribunal's decision on permission to appeal to the Court of Appeal is given.

Service of appellant's notice

52PD.80 **17.5**(1) Subject to sub-paragraph (1A), in addition to the respondents to the appeal, the appellant must serve the appellant's notice in accordance with rule 52.4(3) on the chairman of the tribunal, Minister of State, government department or other person from whose decision the appeal is brought.

(1A) Sub-paragraph (1) does not apply to an appeal against a decision of the Upper Tribunal.

(2) In the case of an appeal from the decision of a tribunal that has no chairman or member who acts as a chairman, the appellant's notice must be served on the member or members of the tribunal.

Right of Minister etc. to be heard on the appeal

52PD.81 **17.6** Where the appeal is from an order or decision of a Minister of State or government department, the Minister or department, as the case may be, is entitled to attend the hearing and to make representations to the court.

Rule 52.12A Statutory appeals—court's power to hear any person

52PD.81.1 **17.7** Where all the parties consent, the court may deal with an application under rule 52.12A without a hearing.

52PD.81.2 **17.8** Where the court gives permission for a person to file evidence or to make representations at the appeal hearing, it may do so on conditions and may give case management directions.

52PD.81.3 **17.9** An application for permission must be made by letter to the relevant court office, identifying the appeal, explaining who the applicant is and indicating why and in what form the applicant wants to participate in the hearing.

17.10 If the applicant is seeking a prospective order as to costs, the letter must say what kind of order and on what grounds. **52PD.81.4**

17.11 Applications to intervene must be made at the earliest reasonable opportunity, since it will usually be essential not to delay the hearing. **52PD.81.5**

Appeals by way of case stated

18.1 This part of this section— **52PD.82**

(1) applies where under any enactment—

(a) an appeal lies to the court by way of case stated; or

(b) a question of law may be referred to the court by way of case stated; and

(2) is subject to any provision about to a specific category of appeal in any enactment or Section III of this practice direction.

Part 52

18.2 Part 52 applies to appeals by way of case stated subject to the following amendments. **52PD.83**

Case stated by Crown Court or Magistrates' Court

Application to state a case

18.3 The procedure for applying to the Crown Court or a Magistrates' Court to have a case stated for the opinion of the High Court is set out in the Crown Court Rules 1982 and the Magistrates' Courts Rules 1981 respectively. **52PD.84**

Filing of appellant's notice

18.4 The appellant must file the appellant's notice at the appeal court within 10 days after he receives the stated case. **52PD.85**

Documents to be lodged

18.5 The appellant must lodge the following documents with his appellant's notice: **52PD.86**

(1) the stated case;

(2) a copy of the judgment, order or decision in respect of which the case has been stated; and

(3) where the judgment, order or decision in respect of which the case has been stated was itself given or made on appeal, a copy of the judgment, order or decision appealed from.

Service of appellant's notice

18.6 The appellant must serve the appellant's notice and accompanying documents on all respondents within 4 days after they are filed or lodged at the appeal court. **52PD.87**

Case stated by Minister, government department, tribunal or other person

Application to state a case

52PD.88 **18.7** The procedure for applying to a Minister, government department, tribunal or other person ("Minister or tribunal etc.") to have a case stated for the opinion of the court may be set out in—

(1) the enactment which provides for the right of appeal; or

(2) any rules of procedure relating to the Minister or tribunal etc.

Signing of stated case by Minister or tribunal etc.

52PD.89 **18.8**

(1) A case stated by a tribunal must be signed by—

(a) the chairman;

(b) the president; or

(c) in the case where the tribunal has neither person in sub-paragraph (a) or (b) nor any member who acts as its chairman or president, by the member or members of the tribunal.

(2) A case stated by any other person must be signed by that person or by a person authorised to do so.

Service of stated case by Minister or tribunal etc.

52PD.90 **18.9** The Minister or tribunal etc. must serve the stated case on—

(1) the party who requests the case to be stated; or

(2) the party as a result of whose application to the court, the case was stated.

18.10 Where an enactment provides that a Minister or tribunal etc. may state a case or refer a question of law to the court by way of case stated without a request being made, the Minister or tribunal etc. must—

(1) serve the stated case on those parties that the Minister or tribunal etc. considers appropriate; and

(2) give notice to every other party to the proceedings that the stated case has been served on the party named and on the date specified in the notice.

Filing and service of appellant's notice

52PD.91 **18.11** The party on whom the stated case was served must file the appellant's notice and the stated case at the appeal court and serve copies of the notice and stated case on—

(1) the Minister or tribunal etc. who stated the case; and

(2) every party to the proceedings to which the stated case relates,

within 14 days after the stated case was served on him.

18.12 Where paragraph 18.10 applies the Minister or tribunal etc. must—

(1) file an appellant's notice and the stated case at the appeal court; and

(2) serve copies of those documents on the persons served under paragraph 18.10

within 14 days after stating the case.

18.13 Where—

(1) a stated case has been served by the Minister or Tribunal etc. in accordance with paragraph 18.9; and

(2) the party on whom the stated case was served does not file an appellant's notice in accordance with paragraph 18.11,

any other party may file an appellant's notice with the stated case at the appeal court and serve a copy of the notice and the case on the persons listed in paragraph 18.11 within the period of time set out in paragraph 18.14.

18.14 The period of time referred to in paragraph 18.13 is 14 days from the last day on which the party on whom the stated case was served may file an appellant's notice in accordance with paragraph 18.11.

Amendment of stated case

18.15 The court may amend the stated case or order it to be returned to the Minister or tribunal etc. for amendment and may draw inferences of fact from the facts stated in the case. **52PD.92**

Right of Minister etc. to be heard on the appeal

18.16 Where the case is stated by a Minister or government department, that Minister or department, as the case may be, is entitled to appear on the appeal and to make representations to the court. **52PD.93**

Application for order to state a case

18.17 An application to the court for an order requiring a minister or tribunal etc. to state a case for the decision of the court, or to refer a question of law to the court by way of case stated must be made to the court which would be the appeal court if the case were stated. **52PD.94**

18.18 An application to the court for an order directing a Minister or tribunal etc. to—

(1) state a case for determination by the court; or

(2) refer a question of law to the court by way of case stated,

must be made in accordance with CPR Part 23

18.19 The application notice must contain—

(1) the grounds of the application;

(2) the question of law on which it is sought to have the case stated; and

(3) any reasons given by the minister or tribunal etc. for his or its refusal to state a case.

18.20 The application notice must be filed at the appeal court and served on—

(1) the minister, department, secretary of the tribunal or other person as the case may be; and

(2) every party to the proceedings to which the application relates,

within 14 days after the appellant receives notice of the refusal of his request to state a case.

Section III

Provisions about specific appeals

20.1 This section of this Practice Direction provides special provi- **52PD.95**

sions about the appeals to which the following table refers. This Section is not exhaustive and does not create, amend or remove any right of appeal.

20.2 Part 52 applies to all appeals to which this section applies subject to any special provisions set out in this section.

20.3 Where any of the provisions in this section provide for documents to be filed at the appeal court, these documents are in addition to any documents required under Part 52 or sections I or II of this practice direction.

52PD.96

Appeals to the Court of Appeal	Paragraph
Articles 81 and 82 of the EC Treaty and Chapters I and II of Part I of the Competition Act 1998	21.10A
Asylum and Immigration Tribunal	21.7
Civil Partnership—conditional order for dissolution or nullity	21.1
Competition Appeal Tribunal	21.10
Contempt of Court	21.4
Court of Protection	21.12
Decree nisi of divorce	21.1
Lands Tribunal	21.9
Nullity of marriage	21.1
Patents Court on appeal from Comptroller	21.3
Proscribed Organisations Appeal Commission	21.11
Revocation of patent	21.2
Special Commissioner (where the appeal is direct to the Court of Appeal)	21.8
Value Added Tax and Duties Tribunals (where the appeal is direct to the Court of Appeal)	21.6

52PD.97

Appeals to the High Court	Paragraph
Agricultural Land Tribunal	22.7
Architects Act 1997, s.22	22.3
Charities Act 1993	23.8A
Chiropractors Act 1994, s.31	22.3
Clergy Pensions Measure 1961 s.38(3)	23.2
Commons Registration Act 1965	23.9
Consumer Credit Act 1974	22.4
Dentists Act 1984, s.20 or s.44	22.3
Employment Tribunals Act 1996	22.6E
Extradition Act 2003	22.6A
Friendly Societies Act 1974	23.7
Friendly Societies Act 1992	23.7
Industrial and Provident Societies Act 1965	23.2, 23.7
Industrial Assurance Act 1923	23.2, 23.7

Industrial Assurance Act 1923, s.17	23.6
Inheritance Tax Act 1984, s.222	23.3
Inheritance Tax Act 1984, s.225	23.5
Inheritance Tax Act 1984 , ss.249(3) and 251	23.4
Land Registration Act 1925	23.2
Land Registration Act 2002	23.2, 23.8B
Law of Property Act 1922, para.16 of Sched.15	23.2
Medical Act 1983, s.40	22.3
Medicines Act 1968, ss.82(3) and 83(2)	22.3
Mental Health Review Tribunal	22.8
Merchant Shipping Act 1995	22.2
National Health Service Act 1977	22.6D
Nurses, Midwives and Health Visitors Act 1997, s.12	22.3
Opticians Act 1989, s.23	22.3
Osteopaths Act 1993, s.31	22.3
Pensions Act 1995, s.97	23.2
Pension Schemes Act 1993, ss.151 and 173	23.2
Pharmacy Act 1954	22.3
Planning (Listed Buildings and Conservation Areas) Act 1990, s.65 (appeal)	22.6C
Planning (Listed Buildings and Conservation Areas) Act 1990, s.65 (case stated)	22.8A
Social Security Administration Act 1992	22.6
Stamp Duty Reserve Tax Regulations 1986, reg.10	23.5
Taxes Management Act 1970, ss.53 and 100C(4)	23.4
Town and Country Planning Act 1990, s.289 (appeal)	22.6C
Town and Country Planning Act 1990, s.289 (case stated)	22.8A
Taxes Management Act 1970, s.56A	23.5
Value Added Tax and Duties Tribunal	23.8
Water Resources Act 1991, s.205(4)	23.2

52PD.98

Appeals to the County Court	**Paragraph**
Local Government (Miscellaneous Provisions) *Act 1976*	24.1
Housing Act 1996, ss.204 and 204A	24.2
Immigration and Asylum Act 1999, Pt II	24.3
Representation of the People Act 1983, s.56	24.4 to 24.6
UK Borders Act 2007, s.11	24.7

Appeal against decree nisi of divorce or nullity of marriage or conditional dissolution or nullity order in relation to civil partnership

52PD.99 **21.1**(1) The appellant must file the appellant's notice at the Court of Appeal within 28 days after the date on which the decree was pronounced or conditional order made.

(2) The appellant must file the following documents with the appellant's notice—

(a) the decree or conditional order; and

(b) a certificate of service of the appellant's notice.

(3) The appellant's notice must be served on the appropriate district judge (see sub-paragraph (6)) in addition to the persons to be served under rule 52.4(3) and in accordance with that rule.

(4) The lower court may not alter the time limits for filing of the appeal notices.

(5) Where an appellant intends to apply to the Court of Appeal for an extension of time for serving or filing the appellant's notice he must give notice of that intention to the appropriate district judge (see sub-paragraph 6) before the application is made.

(6) In this paragraph "the appropriate district judge" means, where the lower court is—

(a) a county court, the district judge of that court;

(b) a district registry, the district judge of that registry;

(c) the Principal Registry of the Family Division, the senior district judge of that division.

Appeal against order for revocation of patent

52PD.100 **21.2**(1) This paragraph applies where an appeal lies to the Court of Appeal from an order for the revocation of a patent.

(2) The appellant must serve the appellant's notice on the Comptroller-General of Patents, Designs and Trade Marks (the "Comptroller") in addition to the persons to be served under rule 52.4(3) and in accordance with that rule.

(3) Where, before the appeal hearing, the respondent decides not to oppose the appeal or not to attend the appeal hearing, he must immediately serve notice of that decision on—

(a) the Comptroller; and

(b) the appellant

(4) Where the respondent serves a notice in accordance with paragraph (3), he must also serve copies of the following documents on the Comptroller with that notice—

(a) the petition;

(b) any statements of claim;

(c) any written evidence filed in the claim.

(5) Within 14 days after receiving the notice in accordance with paragraph (3), the Comptroller must serve on the appellant a notice stating whether or not he intends to attend the appeal hearing.

(6) The Comptroller may attend the appeal hearing and oppose the appeal—

(a) in any case where he has given notice under paragraph (5) of his intention to attend; and

(b) in any other case (including, in particular, a case where the respondent withdraws his opposition to the appeal during the hearing) if the Court of Appeal so directs or permits.

Appeal from Patents Court on appeal from Comptroller

21.3 Where the appeal is from a decision of the Patents Court which was itself made on an appeal from a decision of the Comptroller-General of Patents, Designs and Trade Marks, the appellant must serve the appellant's notice on the Comptroller in addition to the persons to be served under rule 52.4(3) and in accordance with that rule. **52PD.101**

Appeals in cases of contempt of court

21.4 In an appeal under section 13 of the Administration of Justice Act 1960 (appeals in cases of contempt of court), the appellant must serve the appellant's notice on the court or the Upper Tribunal from whose order or decision the appeal is brought in addition to the persons to be served under rule 52.4(3) and in accordance with that rule. **52PD.102**

Appeals from Social Security or Child Support Commissioners

21.5 [...] **52PD.103**

Appeals from commissioners

Appeals from commissioners as formerly provided for by para.21.5 are now dealt with within the new Tribunal system, established with effect from November 3, 2008. Accordingly, para.21.5 has been omitted. **52PD.103.1**

[THE NEXT PARAGRAPH IS 52PD.105.]

Appeals from Value Added Tax and Duties Tribunals

21.6(1) An application to the Court of Appeal for permission to appeal from a value added tax and duties tribunal direct to that court must be made within 28 days after the date on which the tribunal certifies that its decision involves a point of law relating wholly or mainly to the construction of— **52PD.105**

(a) an enactment or of a statutory instrument; or

(b) any of the Community Treaties or any Community Instrument,

which has been fully argued before and fully considered by it.

(2) The application must be made by the parties jointly filing at the Court of Appeal an appellant's notice that—

(a) contains a statement of the grounds for the application; and

(b) is accompanied by a copy of the decision to be appealed, endorsed with the certificate of the tribunal.

(3) The court will notify the appellant of its decision and—

(a) where permission to appeal to the Court of Appeal is given, the appellant must serve the appellant's notice on the chairman of the tribunal in addition to the persons to be served under rule 52.4(3) within 14 days after that notification.

(b) where permission to appeal to the Court of Appeal is refused, the period for appealing to the High Court is to be calculated from the date of the notification of that refusal.

Asylum and Immigration Appeals

52PD.106 **21.7**(1) This paragraph applies to appeals—

(a) from the Immigration Appeal Tribunal under section 103 of the Nationality, Immigration and Asylum Act 2002 ('the 2002 Act'); and

(b) from the Asylum and Immigration Tribunal under the following provisions of the 2002 Act—

(i) section 103B (appeal from the Tribunal following reconsideration); and

(ii) section 103E (appeal from the Tribunal sitting as a panel).

(2) The appellant is not required to file an appeal bundle in accordance with paragraph 5.6A of this practice direction, but must file the documents specified in paragraphs 5.6(2)(a) to (f) together with a copy of the Tribunal's determination.

(3) The appellant's notice must be filed at the Court of Appeal within 14 days after the appellant is served with written notice of the decision of the Tribunal to grant or refuse permission to appeal.

(4) The appellant must serve the appellant's notice in accordance with rule 52.4(3) on—

(a) the persons to be served under that rule; and

(b) the Asylum and Immigration Tribunal.

(5) On being served with the appellant's notice, the Asylum and Immigration Tribunal must send to the Court of Appeal copies of the documents which were before the relevant Tribunal when it considered the appeal.

52PD.107 **21.7A**(1) This paragraph applies to appeals from the Asylum and Immigration Tribunal referred to the Court of Appeal under section 103C of the Nationality, Immigration and Asylum Act 2002.

(2) On making an order referring an appeal to the Court of Appeal, the High Court shall send to the Court of Appeal copies of—

(a) that order and any other order made in relation to the application for reconsideration; and

(b) the application notice, written submissions and other documents filed under rule 54.29

(3) Unless the court directs otherwise, the application notice filed under rule 54.29 shall be treated as the appellant's notice.

(4) The respondent may file a respondent's notice within 14 days after the date on which the respondent is served with the order of the High Court referring the appeal to the Court of Appeal.

(5) The Court of Appeal may give such additional directions as are appropriate.

21.7B(1) This paragraph applies to appeals from the Asylum and Immigration Tribunal which—

(a) would otherwise be treated as abandoned under section 104(4A) of the Nationality, Immigration and Asylum Act 2002 (the "2002 Act"); but

(b) meet the conditions set out in section 104(4B) or section 104(4C) of the 2002 Act.

(2) Where section 104(4A) of the 2002 Act applies and the appellant wishes to pursue his appeal, the appellant must file a notice at the Court of Appeal—

(a) where section 104(4B) of the 2002 Act applies, within 28 days of the date on which the appellant received notice of the grant of leave to enter or remain in the United Kingdom for a period exceeding 12 months; or

(b) where section 104(4C) of the 2002 Act applies, within 28 days of the date on which the appellant received notice of the grant of leave to enter or remain in the United Kingdom.

(3) Where the appellant does not comply with the time limits specified in paragraph (2) the appeal will be treated as abandoned in accordance with section 104(4) of the 2002 Act.

(4) The appellant must serve the notice filed under paragraph (2) on the respondent.

(5) Where section 104(4B) of the 2002 Act applies, the notice filed under paragraph (2) must state—

(a) the appellant's full name and date of birth;

(b) the Court of Appeal reference number;

(c) the Home Office reference number, if applicable;

(d) the date on which the appellant was granted leave to enter or remain in the United Kingdom for a period exceeding 12 months; and

(e) that the appellant wishes to pursue the appeal in so far as it is brought on the ground relating to the Refugee Convention specified in section 84(1)(g) of the 2002 Act.

(6) Where section 104(4C) of the 2002 Act applies, the notice filed under paragraph (2) must state—
(a) the appellant's full name and date of birth;
(b) the Court of Appeal reference number;
(c) the Home Office reference number, if applicable;
(d) the date on which the appellant was granted leave to enter or remain *in the United Kingdom*; and
(e) that the appellant wishes to pursue the appeal in so far as it is brought on the ground relating to section 19B of the Race Relations Act 1976 specified in section 84(1)(b) of the 2002 Act.

(7) Where an appellant has filed a notice under paragraph (2) the Court of Appeal will notify the appellant of the date on which it received the notice.

(8) The Court of Appeal will send a copy of the notice issued under paragraph (7) to the respondent.

Jurisdiction to hear appeals from the Asylum and Immigration Tribunal

52PD.108 It should be noted that appeals only lie from the Asylum and Immigration Tribunal to the Court of Appeal where the underlying adjudicator's decision was made in England or Wales. If the adjudicator's decision was made in Scotland, then appeal lies from the Asylum and Immigration Tribunal to the Court of Session: see *Gardi v SSHD* (No.2) (Note) [2002] EWCA Civ 1560; [2002] 1 W.L.R. 3282.

Appeal from Special Commissioners

52PD.109 **21.8**(1) An application to the Court of Appeal for permission to appeal from the Special Commissioners direct to that court under section 56A of the Taxes Management Act 1970 must be made within 28 days after the date on which the Special Commissioners certify that their decision involves a point of law relating wholly or mainly to the construction of an enactment which has been fully argued before and fully considered before them.

(2) The application must be made by the parties jointly filing at the Court of Appeal an appellant's notice that—
(a) contains a statement of the grounds for the application; and
(b) is accompanied by a copy of the decision to be appealed, endorsed with the certificate of the tribunal.

(3) The court will notify the parties of its decision and—
(a) where permission to appeal to the Court of Appeal is given, the appellant must serve the appellant's notice on the Clerk to the Special Commissioners in addition to the persons to be served under rule 52.4(3) within 14 days after that notification.
(b) where permission to appeal to the Court of Appeal is refused, the period for appealing to the High Court is to be calculated from the date of the notification of that refusal.

Appeal from Lands Tribunal

52PD.110 **21.9** The appellant must file the appellant's notice at the Court of Appeal within 28 days after the date of the decision of the tribunal.

Appeal from Competition Appeal Tribunal

21.10(1) Where the appellant applies for permission to appeal at the hearing at which the decision is delivered by the tribunal and— **52PD.111**

(a) permission is given; or

(b) permission is refused and the appellant wishes to make an application to the Court of Appeal for permission to appeal,

the appellant's notice must be filed at the Court of Appeal within 14 days after the date of that hearing.

(2) Where the appellant applies in writing to the Registrar of the tribunal for permission to appeal and—

(a) permission is given; or

(b) permission is refused and the appellant wishes to make an application to the Court of Appeal for permission to appeal,

the appellant's notice must be filed at the Court of Appeal within 14 days after the date of receipt of the tribunal's decision on permission.

(3) Where the appellant does not make an application to the tribunal for permission to appeal, but wishes to make an application to the Court of Appeal for permission, the appellant's notice must be filed at the Court of Appeal within 14 days after the end of the period within which he may make a written application to the Registrar of the tribunal.

Appeals relating to the application of Articles 81 and 82 of the EC Treaty and Chapters I and II of Part I of the Competition Act 1998

21.10A(1) This paragraph applies to any appeal to the Court of Appeal relating to the application of— **52PD.112**

(a) Article 81 or Article 82 of the Treaty establishing the European Community; or

(b) Chapter I or Chapter II of Part I of the Competition Act 1998.

(2) In this paragraph—

(a) 'the Act' means the Competition Act 1998;

(b) 'the Commission' means the European Commission;

(c) 'the Competition Regulation' means Council Regulation (EC) No. 1/2003 of 16 December 2002 on the implementation of the rules on competition laid down in Articles 81 and 82 of the Treaty;

(d) 'national competition authority' means—

(i) the Office of Fair Trading; and

(ii) any other person or body designated pursuant to Article 35 of the Competition Regulation as a national competition authority of the United Kingdom;

(e) 'the Treaty' means the Treaty establishing the European Community.

(3) Any party whose appeal notice raises an issue relating to

the application of Article 81 or 82 of the Treaty, or Chapter I or II of Part I of the Act, must—

(a) state that fact in his appeal notice; and

(b) serve a copy of the appeal notice on the Office of Fair Trading at the same time as it is served on the other party to the appeal (addressed to the Director of Competition Policy Co-ordination, Office of Fair Trading, Fleetbank House, 2-6 Salisbury Square, London EC4Y 8JX).

(4) Attention is drawn to the provisions of article 15.3 of the Competition Regulation, which entitles competition authorities and the Commission to submit written observations to national courts on issues relating to the application of Article 81 or 82 and, with the permission of the court in question, to submit oral observations to the court.

(5) A national competition authority may also make written observations to the Court of Appeal, or apply for permission to make oral observations, on issues relating to the application of Chapter I or II.

(6) If a national competition authority or the Commission intends to make written observations to the Court of Appeal, it must give notice of its intention to do so by letter to the Civil Appeals Office at the earliest opportunity.

(7) An application by a national competition authority or the Commission for permission to make oral representations at the hearing of an appeal must be made by letter to the Civil Appeals Office at the earliest opportunity, identifying the appeal and indicating why the applicant wishes to make oral representations.

(8) If a national competition authority or the Commission files a notice under sub-paragraph (6) or an application under sub-paragraph (7), it must at the same time serve a copy of the notice or application on every party to the appeal.

(9) Any request by a national competition authority or the Commission for the court to send it any documents relating to an appeal should be made at the same time as filing a notice under sub-paragraph (6) or an application under sub-paragraph (7).

(10) When the Court of Appeal receives a notice under sub-paragraph (6) it may give case management directions to the national competition authority or the Commission, including directions about the date by which any written observations are to be filed.

(11) The Court of Appeal will serve on every party to the appeal a copy of any directions given or order made—

(a) on an application under sub-paragraph (7); or

(b) under sub-paragraph (10).

(12) Every party to an appeal which raises an issue relating to the application of Article 81 or 82, and any national competition authority which has been served with a copy of a

party's appeal notice, is under a duty to notify the Court of Appeal at any stage of the appeal if they are *aware* that—

(a) the Commission has adopted, or is contemplating adopting, a decision in relation to proceedings which it has initiated; and

(b) the decision referred to in (a) above has or would have legal effects in relation to the particular agreement, decision or practice in issue before the court.

(13) Where the Court of Appeal is aware that the Commission is contemplating adopting a decision as mentioned in sub-paragraph (12)(a), it shall consider whether to stay the appeal pending the Commission's decision.

(14) Where any judgment is given which decides on the application of Article 81 or 82, the court shall direct that a copy of the transcript of the judgment shall be sent to the Commission.

Judgments may be sent to the Commission electronically to comp-amicus@cec.eu.int or by post to the European Commission—DG Competition, B–1049, Brussels.

Appeal from Proscribed Organisations Appeal Commission

21.11(1) The appellant's notice must be filed at the Court of Appeal within 14 days after the date when the Proscribed Organisations Appeal Commission— **52PD.113**

(a) granted; or

(b) where section 6(2)(b) of the Terrorism Act 2000 applies, refused permission to appeal.

Appeal from the Court of Protection

21.12 **52PD.113.1**

(1) In this paragraph—

(a) 'P' means a person who lacks, or who is alleged to lack, capacity within the meaning of the Mental Capacity Act 2005 to make a decision or decisions in relation to any matter that is subject to an order of the Court of Protection;

(b) 'the person effecting notification' means—

(i) the appellant;

(ii) an agent duly appointed by the appellant; or

(iii) such other person as the Court of Protection may direct,

who is required to notify P in accordance with this paragraph; and

(c) 'final order' means a decision of the Court of Appeal that finally determines the appeal proceedings before it.

(2) Where P is not a party to the proceedings, unless the Court of Appeal directs otherwise, the person effecting notification must notify P—

(a) that an appellant's notice has been filed with the Court of Appeal and—

(i) who the appellant is;
(ii) what final order the appellant is seeking;
(iii) what will happen if the Court of Appeal makes the final order sought by the appellant; and
(iv) that P may apply under rule 52.12A by letter for permission to file evidence or make representations at the appeal hearing;

(b) of the final order, the effect of the final order and what steps P can take in relation to it; and
(c) of such other events and documents as the Court of Appeal may direct.

(Paragraphs 17.7 to 17.11 of this practice direction contain provisions on how a third party can apply for permission to file evidence or make representations at an appeal hearing.)

(3) The person effecting notification must provide P with the information specified in sub-paragraph (2)
(a) within 14 days of the date on which the appellant's notice was filed with the Court of Appeal;
(b) within 14 days of the date on which the final order was made; or
(c) within such time as the Court of Appeal may direct,
as the case may be.

(4) The person effecting notification must provide P in person with the information specified in sub-paragraph (2) in a way that is appropriate to P's circumstances (for example, using simple language, visual aids or any other appropriate means).

(5) Where P is to be notified as to—
(a) the existence or effect of a document other than the appellant's notice or final order; or
(b) the taking place of an event,
the person effecting notification must explain to P—
(i) in the case of a document, what the document is and what effect, if any, it has; or
(ii) in the case of an event, what the event is and its relevance to P.

(6) The person effecting notification must, within 7 days of notifying P, file a certificate of notification (form N165) which certifies—
(a) the date on which P was notified; and
(b) that P was notified in accordance with this paragraph.

(7) Where the person effecting notification has not notified P in accordance with this paragraph, he must file with the Court of Appeal a certificate of non-notification (form N165) stating the reason why notification has not been effected.

(8) Where the person effecting notification must file a certificate of non-notification with the Court of Appeal, he must file the certificate within the following time limits—
(a) where P is to be notified in accordance with sub-paragraph (2)(a) (appellant's notice), within 21 days of

the appellant's notice being filed with the Court of Appeal;

(b) where P is to be notified in accordance with sub-paragraph (2)(b) (final order), within 21 days of the final order being made by the Court of Appeal; or

(c) where P is to be notified of such other events and documents as may be directed by the Court of Appeal, within such time as the Court of Appeal directs.

(9) The appellant or such other person as the Court of Appeal may direct may apply to the Court of Appeal seeking an order—

(a) dispensing with the requirement to comply with the provisions of this paragraph; or

(b) requiring some other person to comply with the provisions of this paragraph.

(10) An application made under sub-paragraph (9) may be made in the appellant's notice or by Part 23 application notice.

(Paragraph 12 contains provisions about the dismissal of applications or appeals by consent. Paragraph 13 contains provisions about allowing unopposed appeals or applications on paper and procedures for consent orders and agreements to pay periodical payments involving a child or protected party or in appeals to the Court of Appeal from a decision of the Court of Protection.)

Appeals in relation to serious crime prevention orders

21.13(1) This paragraph applies where the appeal is in relation to a serious crime prevention order and is made under section 23(1) of the Serious Crime Act 2007 or section 16 of the Supreme Court Act 1981. **52PD.113.2**

(2) The appellant must serve the appellant's notice on any person who made representations in the proceedings by virtue of section 9(1), (2) or (3) of the Serious Crime Act 2007 in addition to the persons to be served under rule 52.4(3) and in accordance with that rule.

Appeals to the High Court—Queen's Bench Division

22.1 The following appeals are to be heard in the Queen's Bench Division. **52PD.114**

Statutory Appeals

Appeals under the Merchant Shipping Act 1995

22.2(1) This paragraph applies to appeals under the Merchant Shipping Act 1995 and for this purpose a re-hearing and an application under section 61 of the Merchant Shipping Act 1995 are treated as appeals. **52PD.115**

(2) The appellant must file any report to the Secretary of State containing the decision from which the appeal is brought with the appellant's notice.

(3) Where a re-hearing by the High Court is ordered under

sections 64 or 269 of the Merchant Shipping Act 1995, the Secretary of State must give reasonable notice to the parties whom he considers to be affected by the re-hearing.

Appeals against decisions affecting the registration of architects and health care professionals

52PD.116 **22.3**(1) This paragraph applies to an appeal to the High Court under—

(a) section 22 of the Architects Act 1997;
(b) section 82(3) and 83(2) of the Medicines Act 1968;
(c) section 12 of the Nurses, Midwives and Health Visitors Act 1997;
(cc) article 38 of the Nursing and Midwifery Order 2001;
(d) section 10 of the Pharmacy Act 1954;
(e) section 40 of the Medical Act 1983;
(f) section 29 or section 44 of the Dentists Act 1984;
(g) section 23 of the Opticians Act 1989;
(h) section 31 of the Osteopaths Act 1993; and
(i) section 31 of the Chiropractors Act 1994.

(2) Every appeal to which this paragraph applies must be supported by written evidence and, if the court so orders, oral evidence and will be by way of re-hearing.

(3) The appellant must file the appellant's notice within 28 days after the decision that the appellant wishes to appeal.

(4) In the case of an appeal under an enactment specified in column 1 of the following table, the persons to be made respondents are the persons specified in relation to that enactment in column 2 of the table and the person to be served with the appellant's notice is the person so specified in column 3.

1 **Enactment**	2 **Respondents**	3 **Person to be served**
Architects Act 1997, s.22	The Architects' Registration Council of the United Kingdom	The registrar of the Council
Medicines Act 1968, s.82(3) and s.83(2)	The Pharmaceutical Society of Great Britain	The registrar of the Society
Nurses, Midwives and Health Visitors Act 1997, s.12; Nursing and Midwifery Order 2001, art.38	The Nursing and Midwifery Council	The Registrar of the Council
Pharmacy Act 1954, *s.10*	The Royal Pharmaceutical Society of Great Britain	The registrar of the Society

Medical Act 1983, s.40	The General Medical Council	The Registrar of the Council
Dentists Act 1984, s.29 or s.44	The General Dental Council	The Registrar of the Council
Opticians Act 1989, s.23	The General Optical Council	The Registrar of the Council
Osteopaths Act 1993, s.31	The General Osteopathic Council	The Registrar of the Council
Chiropractors Act 1994, s.31	The General Chiropractic Council	The Registrar of the Council

Consumer Credit Act 1974: appeal from Secretary of State

22.4(1) A person dissatisfied in point of law with a decision of the Secretary of State on an appeal under section 41 of the Consumer Credit Act 1974 from a determination of the Office of Fair Trading who had a right to appeal to the Secretary of State, whether or not he exercised that right, may appeal to the High Court. **52PD.117**

(2) The appellant must serve the appellant's notice on—

(a) the Secretary of State;

(b) the original applicant, if any, where the appeal is by a licensee under a group licence against compulsory variation, suspension or revocation of that licence; and

(c) any other person as directed by the court.

(3) The appeal court may remit the matter to the Secretary of State to the extent necessary to enable him to provide the court with such further information as the court may direct.

(4) If the appeal court allows the appeal, it shall not set aside or vary the decision but shall remit the matter to the Secretary of State with the opinion of the court for hearing and determination by him.

The Pensions Appeal Tribunal Act 1943

22.5 [Omitted] **52PD.118**

The Social Security Administration Act 1992

22.6(1) Any person who by virtue of section 18 or 58(8) of the Social Security Administration Act 1992 ("the Act") is entitled and wishes to appeal against a decision of the Secretary of State on a question of law must, within the prescribed period, or within such further time as the Secretary of State may allow, serve on the Secretary of State a notice requiring him to state a case setting out— **52PD.119**

(a) his decision; and

(b) the facts on which his decision was based.

(2) Unless paragraph (3) applies the prescribed period is 28 days after receipt of the notice of the decision.

(3) Where, within 28 days after receipt of notice of the decision, a request is made to the Secretary of State in accordance with regulations made under the Act to furnish a statement of the grounds of the decision, the prescribed period is 28 days after receipt of that statement.

(4) Where under section 18 or section 58(8) of the Act, the Secretary of State refers a question of law to the court, he must state that question together with the relevant facts in a case.

(5) The appellant's notice and the case stated must be filed at the appeal court and a copy of the notice and the case stated served on—

(a) the Secretary of State; and

(b) every person as between whom and the Secretary of State the question has arisen,

within 28 days after the case stated was served on the party at whose request, or as a result of whose application to the court, the case was stated.

(6) Unless the appeal court otherwise orders, the appeal or reference shall not be heard sooner than 28 days after service of the appellant's notice.

(7) The appeal court may order the case stated by the Secretary of State to be returned to the Secretary of State for him to hear further evidence.

Appeals under the Extradition Act 2003

52PD.120 **22.6A**(1) In this paragraph, 'the Act' means the Extradition Act 2003.

(2) Appeals to the High Court under the Act must be brought in the Administrative Court of the Queen's Bench Division.

(3) Where an appeal is brought under section 26 or 28 of the Act—

(a) the appellant's notice must be filed and served before the expiry of 7 days, starting with the day on which the order is made;

(b) the appellant must endorse the appellant's notice with the date of the person's arrest;

(c) the High Court must begin to hear the substantive appeal within 40 days of the person's arrest; and

(d) the appellant must serve a copy of the appellant's notice on the Crown Prosecution Service, if they are not a party to the appeal, in addition to the persons to be served under rule 52.4(3) and in accordance with that rule.

(4) The High Court may extend the period of 40 days under paragraph (3)(c) if it believes it to be in the interests of justice to do so.

(5) Where an appeal is brought under section 103 of the Act, the appellant's notice must be filed and served before the expiry of 14 days, starting with the day on which the Sec-

retary of State informs the person under section 100(1) or (4) of the Act of the order he has made in respect of the person.

(6) Where an appeal is brought under section 105 of the Act, the appellant's notice must be filed and served before the expiry of 14 days, starting with the day on which the order for discharge is made.

(7) Where an appeal is brought under section 108 of the Act the appellant's notice must be filed and served before the expiry of 14 days, starting with the day on which the Secretary of State informs the person that he has ordered his extradition.

(8) Where an appeal is brought under section 110 of the Act the appellant's notice must be filed and served before the expiry of 14 days, starting with the day on which the Secretary of State informs the person acting on behalf of a category 2 territory, as defined in section 69 of the Act, of the order for discharge.

(Section 69 of the Act provides that a category 2 territory is that designated for the purposes of Part 2 of the Act).

(9) Subject to paragraph (10), where an appeal is brought under section 103, 105, 108 or 110 of the Act, the High Court must begin to hear the substantive appeal within 76 days of the appellant's notice being filed.

(10) Where an appeal is brought under section 103 of the Act before the Secretary of State has decided whether the person is to be extradited—

- (a) the period of 76 days does not start until the day on which the Secretary of State informs the person of his decision; and
- (b) the Secretary of State must, as soon as practicable after he informs the person of his decision, inform the High Court—
  - (i) of his decision; and
  - (ii) of the date on which he informs the person of his decision.

(11) The High Court may extend the period of 76 days if it believes it to be in the interests of justice to do so.

(12) Where an appeal is brought under section 103, 105, 108 or 110 of the Act, the appellant must serve a copy of the appellant's notice on—

- (a) the Crown Prosecution Service; and
- (b) the Home Office,

if they are not a party to the appeal, in addition to the persons to be served under rule 52.4(3) and in accordance with that rule.

Editorial note

In interpreting para.22.6A of the practice direction and the underlying provisions of the Extradition Act 2003, reference should be made to the standard text books on **52PD.120.1** extradition. It should be noted that the time limits in para.22.6A(3)(a) (seven days in respect of category 1 territories) and para.22.6A(5)(14 days in respect of category 2 territories) apply to both filing and serving the notice of appeal. These time limits are mandatory and cannot be extended by the court. See *Mucelli v Government of Albania, Moulai v Deputy Public Prosecutor in Creteil, France* [2009] UKHL 2.

Appeals under section 49 of the Solicitors Act 1974

52PD.121 **22.6B**(1) This paragraph applies to appeals from the Solicitors Disciplinary Tribunal ('the Tribunal') to the High Court under section 49(1)(b) of the Solicitors Act 1974 ('the Act'). The procedure for appeals to the Master of the Rolls under section 49(1)(a) of the Act is set out in the Master of the Rolls (Appeals and Applications) Regulations 2001.

(2) Appeals to the High Court under section 49(1)(b) of the Act must be brought in the Administrative Court of the Queen's Bench Division.

(3) The appellant's notice—

(a) must state in the heading that the appeal relates to a solicitor, or a solicitor's clerk, and is made under section 49 of the Act;

(b) must be filed within 14 days after the date on which the Tribunal's statement of its findings was filed with the Law Society in accordance with section 48(1) of the Act; and

(c) must be accompanied by copies of the order appealed against and the statement of the Tribunal's findings required by section 48(1) of the Act; and

(d) unless the court orders otherwise, must be served by the appellant on—

(i) every party to the proceedings before the Tribunal; and

(ii) the Law Society.

(4) The court—

(a) may order an appellant to give security for the costs of an appeal only if he was the applicant in the proceedings before the tribunal; and

(b) may not order any other party to give security for costs.

(5) The court may direct the Tribunal to provide it with a written statement of their opinion on the case, or on any question arising in it. If the court gives such a direction, the clerk to the Tribunal must as soon as possible—

(a) file the statement; and

(b) serve a copy on each party to the appeal.

(6) The court may give permission for any person to intervene to be heard in opposition to the appeal.

(7) An appellant may at any time discontinue his appeal by—

(a) serving notice of discontinuance on the clerk to the Tribunal and every other party to the appeal; and

(b) filing a copy of the notice.

(8) Unless the court orders otherwise, an appellant who discontinues is liable for the costs of every other party to the appeal.

Appeals under s 289(6) of the Town and Country Planning Act 1990 and s 65(5) of the Planning (Listed Buildings and Conservation Areas) Act 1990

22.6C (1) An application for permission to appeal to the High Court under section 289 of the Town and Country Planning Act 1990 ('the TCP Act') or section 65 of the Planning (Listed Buildings and Conservation Areas) Act 1990 ('the PLBCA Act') must be made within 28 days after notice of the decision is given to the applicant. **52PD.121.1**

(2) The application—

(a) must be in writing and must set out the reasons why permission should be granted; and

(b) if the time for applying has expired, must include an application to extend the time for applying, and must set out the reasons why the application was not made within that time.

(3) The applicant must, before filing the application, serve a copy of it on the persons referred to in sub-paragraph (11) with the draft appellant's notice and a copy of the witness statement or affidavit to be filed with the application.

(4) The applicant must file the application in the Administrative Court Office with—

(i) a copy of the decision being appealed;

(ii) a draft appellant's notice;

(iii) a witness statement or affidavit verifying any facts relied on; and

(iv) a witness statement or affidavit giving the name and address of, and the place and date of service on, each person who has been served with the application. If any person who ought to be served has not been served, the witness statement or affidavit must state that fact and the reason why the person was not served.

(5) An application will be heard—

(a) by a single judge; and

(b) unless the court otherwise orders, not less than 21 days after it was filed at the Administrative Court Office.

(6) Any person served with the application is entitled to appear and be heard.

(7) Any respondent who intends to use a witness statement or affidavit at the hearing—

(a) must file it in the Administrative Court Office; and

(b) must serve a copy on the applicant as soon as is practicable and in any event, unless the court otherwise allows, at least 2 days before the hearing.

(8) The court may allow the applicant to use a further witness statement or affidavit.

(9) Where on the hearing of an application the court is of the opinion that a person who ought to have been served has not been served, the court may adjourn the hearing, on such terms as it directs, in order that the application may be served on that person.

(10) Where the court grants permission—

(a) it may impose terms as to costs and as to giving security;

(b) it may give directions; and

(c) the relevant appellant's notice must be served and filed within 7 days of the grant.

(11) The persons to be served with the appellant's notice are—

(a) the Secretary of State;

(b) the local planning authority who served the notice or gave the decision, as the case may be, or, where the appeal is brought by that authority, the appellant or applicant in the proceedings in which the decision appealed against was given;

(c) in the case of an appeal brought by virtue of section 289(1) of the TCP Act or section 65(1) of the PLBCA Act, any other person having an interest in the land to which the notice relates; and

(d) in the case of an appeal brought by virtue of section 289(2) of the TCP Act, any other person on whom the notice to which those proceedings related was served.

(12) The appeal will be heard and determined by a single judge unless the court directs that the matter be heard and determined by a Divisional Court.

(13) The court may remit the matter to the Secretary of State to the extent necessary to enable him to provide the court with such further information in connection with the matter as the court may direct.

(14) Where the court is of the opinion that the decision appealed against was erroneous in point of law, it will not set aside or vary that decision but will remit the matter to the Secretary of State for re-hearing and determination in accordance with the opinion of the court.

(15) The court may give directions as to the exercise, until an appeal brought by virtue of section 289(1) of the TCP Act is finally concluded and any re-hearing and determination by the Secretary of State has taken place, of the power to serve, and institute proceedings (including criminal proceedings) concerning—

(a) a stop notice under section 183 of that Act; and

(b) a breach of condition notice under section 187A of that Act.

Planning appeals

52PD.121.1.1 This paragraph replaced certain parts of RSC Order 94 rr.12 and 13 (i.e. parts which were not re-enacted in r.52.20) with effect from October 1, 2007. RSC Order 94 rr.12 and 13 were revoked by the Civil Procedure (Amendment) Rules 2007 (SI 2007/2204).

The permission requirement in respect of planning appeals was introduced by s.289 of the Town and Country Planning Act 1990 and s.65 (5) of the Planning (Listed Buildings and Conservation Areas) Act 1990. The procedure for obtaining such permission is now set out in para.22.6C of the practice direction.

If permission is granted, the appeal will be heard by a single judge of the Administrative Court, unless the court directs that such appeal be heard by a Divisional Court: see para.22.6C (12) of the Practice Direction.

An appeal by way of case stated will be heard by a single judge of the Administrative Court, unless the court directs that such appeal be heard by a Divisional Court: see para.22.8A of the Practice Direction (which replaces the former RSC Order 94 r.13 (4)).

National Health Service Act 1977: appeal from tribunal

22.6D(1) This paragraph applies to an appeal from a tribunal constituted under section 46 of the National Health Service Act 1977. **52PD.121.2**

(2) The appellant must file the appellant's notice at the High Court within 14 days after the date of the decision of the tribunal.

Employment Tribunals Act 1996: appeal from tribunal

22.6E(1) This paragraph applies to an appeal from a tribunal constituted under section 1 of the Employment Tribunals Act 1996. **52PD.121.3**

(2) The appellant must file the appellant's notice at the High Court within 42 days after the date of the decision of the tribunal.

(3) The appellant must serve the appellant's notice on the secretary of the tribunal.

Appeals by way of case stated

Reference of question of law by Agriculture Land Tribunal

22.7(1) A question of law referred to the High Court by an Agricultural Land Tribunal under section 5 of the Agriculture (Miscellaneous Provisions) Act 1954 shall be referred by way of case stated by the Tribunal. **52PD.122**

(2) Where the proceedings before the tribunal arose on an application under section 11 of the Agricultural Holdings Act 1986, an—

(a) application notice for an order under section 6 that the tribunal refers a question of law to the court; and

(b) appellant's notice by which an appellant seeks the court's determination on a question of law,

must be served on the authority having power to enforce the statutory requirement specified in the notice in addition to every other party to those proceedings and on the secretary of the tribunal.

(3) Where, in accordance with paragraph (2), a notice is served on the authority mentioned in that paragraph, that authority may attend the appeal hearing and make representations to the court.

Case stated by Mental Health Review Tribunal

52PD.123 **22.8**(1) In this paragraph "the Act" means the Mental Health Act 1983 and "party to proceedings" means—

(a) the person who initiated the proceedings; and

(b) any person to whom, in accordance with rules made under section 78 of the Act, the tribunal sent notice of the application or reference or a request instead notice of reference.

(2) A party to proceedings shall not be entitled to apply to the High Court for an order under section 78(8) of the Act directing the tribunal to state a case for determination by court unless—

(a) within 21 days after the decision of the tribunal was communicated to him in accordance with rules made under section 78 of the Act he made a written request to the tribunal to state a case; and

(b) either the tribunal

(i) failed to comply with that request within 21 days after it was made; or

(ii) refused to comply with it.

(3) The period for filing the application notice for an order under section 78(8) of the Act is—

(a) where the tribunal failed to comply with the applicant's request to state a case within the period mentioned in paragraph (2)(b)(i), 14 days after the expiration of that period;

(b) where the tribunal refused that request, 14 days after receipt by the applicant of notice of the refusal of his request.

(4) A Mental Health Review Tribunal by whom a case is stated shall be entitled to attend the proceedings for the determination of the case and make representations to the court.

(5) If the court allows the appeal, it may give any direction which the tribunal ought to have given under Part V of the Act.

Case stated under section 289 of the Town and Country Planning Act 1990 or section 65 of the Planning (Listed Buildings and Conservation Areas) Act 1990

52PD.123.1 **22.8A** A case stated under section 289(3) of the Town and Country Planning Act 1990 or section 65(2) of the Planning (Listed Buildings and Conservation Areas) Act 1990 will be heard and determined by a single judge unless the court directs that the matter be heard and determined by a Divisional Court.

Editorial note

52PD.123.1.1 See the commentary following para.22.6C of the practice direction, above.

Appeals to the High Court—Chancery Division

52PD.124 **23.1** The following appeals are to be heard in the Chancery Division.

Determination of appeal or case stated under various Acts

23.2 Any appeal to the High Court, and any case stated or question referred for the opinion of that court under any of the following enactments shall be heard in the Chancery Division— **52PD.125**

(1) paragraph 16 of Schedule 15 to the Law of Property Act 1922;
(2) the Industrial Assurance Act 1923;
(3) the Land Registration Act 1925;
(4) section 205(4) of the Water Resources Act 1991;
(5) section 38(3) of the Clergy Pensions Measure 1961;
(6) the Industrial and Provident Societies Act 1965;
(7) section 151 of the Pension Schemes Act 1993;
(8) section 173 of the Pensions Schemes Act 1993;
(9) section 97 of the Pensions Act 1995;
(10) the Charities Act 1993;
(11) section 13 and 13B of the Stamp Act 1891;
(12) section 705A of the Income and Corporation Taxes Act 1988;
(13) regulation 22 of the General Commissioners (Jurisdiction and Procedure) Regulations 1994;
(14) section 53, 56A or 100C(4) of the Taxes Management Act 1970;
(15) section 222(3), 225, 249(3) or 251 of the Inheritance Tax Act 1984;
(16) regulation 8(3) or 10 of the Stamp Duty Reserve Tax Regulations 1986;
(17) the Land Registration Act 2002;
(18) regulation 74 of the European Public Limited-Liability Company Regulations 2004.

(This list is not exhaustive);

Statutory appeals

Appeal under section 222 of the Inheritance Tax Act 1984

23.3(1) This paragraph applies to appeals to the High Court under section 222(3) of the Inheritance Tax Act 1984 (the "1984 Act") and regulation 8(3) of the Stamp Duty Reserve Tax Regulations 1986 (the "1986 Regulations"). **52PD.126**

(2) The appellant's notice must—

(a) state the date on which the Commissioners for HM Revenue and Customs (the "Board") gave notice to the appellant under section 221 of the 1984 Act or *regulation 6 of the 1986* Regulations of the determination that is the subject of the appeal;

(b) state the date on which the appellant gave to the Board notice of appeal under section 222(1) of the 1984 Act or regulation 8(1) of the 1986 Regulations and, if notice was not given within the time permitted, whether the Board or the Special Commissioners have given their consent to the appeal being brought out of time, and, if they have, the date they gave their consent; and

(c) either state that the appellant and the Board have agreed that the appeal may be to the High Court or contain an application for permission to appeal to the High Court.

(3) The appellant must file the following documents with the appellant's notice—

(a) 2 copies of the notice referred to in paragraph 2(a);

(b) 2 copies of the notice of appeal (under section 222(1) of the 1984 Act or regulation 8(1) of the 1986 Regulations) referred to in paragraph 2(b); and

(c) where the appellant's notice contains an application for permission to appeal, written evidence setting out the grounds on which it is alleged that the matters to be decided on the appeal are likely to be substantially confined to questions of law.

(4) The appellant must—

(a) file the appellant's notice at the court; and

(b) serve the appellant's notice on the Board,

within 30 days of the date on which the appellant gave to the Board notice of appeal under section 222(1) of the 1984 Act or regulation 8(1) of the 1986 Regulations or, if the Board or the Special Commissioners have given consent to the appeal being brought out of time, within 30 days of the date on which such consent was given.

(5) The court will set a date for the hearing of not less than 40 days from the date that the appellant's notice was filed.

(6) Where the appellant's notice contains an application for permission to appeal—

(a) a copy of the written evidence filed in accordance with paragraph (3)(c) must be served on the Board with the appellant's notice; and

(b) the Board—

(i) may file written evidence; and

(ii) if it does so, must serve a copy of that evidence on the appellant, within 30 days after service of the written evidence under paragraph (6)(a).

(7) The appellant may not rely on any grounds of appeal not specified in the notice referred to in paragraph (2)(b) on the hearing of the appeal without the permission of the court.

Appeals under section 53 and 100C(4) of the Taxes Management Act 1970 and section 249(3) or 251 of the Inheritance Tax Act 1984

52PD.127 **23.4**(1) The appellant must serve the appellant's notice on—

(a) the General or Special Commissioners against whose decision, award or determination the appeal is brought; and

(b) (i) in the case of an appeal brought under section 100C(4) of the Taxes Management Act 1970 or section 249(3) of the Inheritance Tax Act 1984 by any party other than the defendant in the proceedings before the Commissioners, that defendant; or

(ii) in any other case, the Commissioners for HM Revenue and Customs.

(2) The appellant must file the appellant's notice at the court within 30 days after the date of the decision, award or determination against which the appeal is brought.

(3) Within 30 days of the service on them of the appellant's notice the General or Special Commissioners, as the case may be, must—

(a) file 2 copies of a note of their findings and of the reasons for their decision, award or determination at the court; and

(b) serve a copy of the note on every other party to the appeal.

(4) Any document to be served on the General or Special Commissioners may be served by delivering or sending it to their clerk.

Appeals under section 56A of the Taxes Management Act 1970, section 225 of the Inheritance Tax Act 1984 and regulation 10 of the Stamp Duty Reserve Tax Regulations 1986

23.5(1) The appellant must file the appellant's notice— **52PD.128**

(a) where the appeal is made following the refusal of the Special Commissioners to issue a certificate under section 56A(2)(b) of the Taxes Management Act 1970, within 28 days from the date of the release of the decision of the Special Commissioners containing the refusal;

(b) where the appeal is made following the refusal of permission to appeal to the Court of Appeal under section 56A(2)(c) of that Act, within 28 days from the date when permission is refused; or

(c) in all other cases within 56 days after the date of the decision or determination that the appellant wishes to appeal.

Appeal under section 17 of the Industrial Assurance Act 1923

23.6 The appellant must file the appellant's notice within 21 days after the date of the Commissioner's refusal or direction under section 17(3) of the Industrial Assurance Act 1923. **52PD.129**

Appeals affecting industrial and provident societies etc.

23.7(1) This paragraph applies to all appeals under— **52PD.130**

(a) the Friendly Societies Act 1974;

(b) the Friendly Societies Act 1992;

(c) the Industrial Assurance Act 1923; and

(d) the Industrial and Provident Societies Act 1965.

(2) At any stage on an appeal, the court may—

(a) direct that the appellant's notice be served on any person;

(b) direct that notice be given by advertisement or otherwise of—

(i) the bringing of the appeal;

(ii) the nature of the appeal; and

(iii) the time when the appeal will or is likely to be heard; or

(c) give such other directions as it thinks proper to enable any person interested in—

(i) the society, trade union, alleged trade union or industrial assurance company; or

(ii) the subject matter of the appeal,

to appear and be heard at the appeal hearing.

Appeal from Value Added Tax and Duties Tribunal

52PD.131 **23.8**(1) A party to proceedings before a Value Added Tax and Duties Tribunal who is dissatisfied in point of law with a decision of the tribunal may appeal under section 11(1) of the Tribunals and Inquiries Act 1992 to the High Court.

(2) The appellant must file the appellant's notice—

(a) where the appeal is made following the refusal of the Value Added Tax and Duties Tribunal to grant a certificate under article 2(b) of the Value Added Tax and Duties Tribunal Appeals Order 1986, within 28 days from the date of the release of the decision containing the refusal;

(b) in all other cases within 56 days after the date of the decision or determination that the appellant wishes to appeal.

Appeal against an order or decision of the Charity Commissioners

23.8A(1) In this paragraph—

'the Act' means the Charities Act 1993; and

'the Commissioners' means the Charity Commissioners for England and Wales.

(2) The Attorney-General, unless he is the appellant, must be made a respondent to the appeal.

(3) The appellant's notice must state the grounds of the appeal, and the appellant may not rely on any other grounds without the permission of the court.

(4) Sub-paragraphs (5) and (6) apply, in addition to the above provisions, where the appeal is made under section 16(12) of the Act.

(5) If the Commissioners have granted a certificate that it is a proper case for an appeal, a copy of the certificate must be filed with the appellant's notice.

(6) If the appellant applies in the appellant's notice for permission to appeal under section 16(13) of the Act—

(a) the appellant's notice must state—

(i) that the appellant has requested the Commissioners to grant a certificate that it is a proper case for an appeal, and they have refused to do so;

(ii) the date of such refusal;

(iii) the grounds on which the appellant alleges that it is a proper case for an appeal; and

(iv) if the application for permission to appeal is made with the consent of any other party to the proposed appeal, that fact;

(b) if the Commissioners have given reasons for refusing a certificate, a copy of the reasons must be attached to the appellant's notice;

(c) the court may, before determining the application, direct the Commissioners to file a written statement of their reasons for refusing a certificate;

(d) the court will serve on the appellant a copy of any statement filed under sub-paragraph (c).

Appeal against a decision of the adjudicator under section 111 of the Land Registration Act 2002

23.8B(1) A person who is aggrieved by a decision of the adjudicator and who wishes to appeal that decision must obtain permission to appeal. **52PD.132**

(2) The appellant must serve on the adjudicator a copy of the appeal court's decision on a request for permission to appeal as soon as reasonably practicable and in any event within 14 days of receipt by the appellant of the decision on permission.

(3) The appellant must serve on the adjudicator and the Chief Land Registrar a copy of any order by the appeal court to stay a decision of the adjudicator pending the outcome of the appeal as soon as reasonably practicable and in any event within 14 days of receipt by the appellant of the appeal court's order to stay.

(4) The appellant must serve on the adjudicator and the Chief Land Registrar a copy of the appeal court's decision on the appeal as soon as reasonably practicable and in any event within 14 days of receipt by the appellant of the appeal court's decision.

Appeals under regulation 74 of the European Public Limited-Liability Company Regulations 2004

23.8C(1) In this paragraph— **52PD.133**

(a) "the 2004 Regulations" means the European Public Limited-Liability Company Regulations 2004;

(b) "the EC Regulation" means Council Regulation (EC)

No 2157/2001 of 8 October 2001 on the Statute for a European company (SE);

(c) "SE" means a European public limited-liability company (Societas Europaea) within the meaning of Article 1 of the EC Regulation.

(2) This paragraph applies to appeals under regulation 74 of the 2004 Regulations against the opposition—

(a) of the Secretary of State or national financial supervisory authority to the transfer of the registered office of an SE under Article 8(14) of the EC Regulation; and

(b) of the Secretary of State to the participation by a company in the formation of an SE by merger under Article 19 of the EC Regulation.

(3) Where an SE seeks to appeal against the opposition of the national financial supervisory authority to the transfer of its registered office under Article 8(14) of the EC Regulation, it must serve the appellant's notice on both the national financial supervisory authority and the Secretary of State.

(4) The appellant's notice must contain an application for permission to appeal.

(5) The appeal will be a review of the decision of the Secretary of State and not a re-hearing. The grounds of review are set out in regulation 74(2) of the 2004 Regulations.

(6) The appeal will be heard by a High Court judge.

Appeals by way of case stated

Proceedings under the Commons Registration Act 1965

52PD.134 **23.9** (1) A person aggrieved by the decision of a Commons Commissioner who requires the Commissioner to state a case for the opinion of the High Court under section 18 of the Commons Registration Act 1965 must file the appellant's notice within 42 days from the date on which notice of the decision was sent to the aggrieved person.

(2) Proceedings under that section are assigned to the Chancery Division.

Appeals to a County Court

Local Government (Miscellaneous Provisions) Act 1976

52PD.135 **24.1** Where one of the grounds upon which an appeal against a notice under sections 21, 23 or 35 of the Local Government (Miscellaneous Provisions) Act 1976 is brought is that—

(a) it would have been fairer to serve the notice on another person; or

(b) that it would be reasonable for the whole or part of the expenses to which the appeal relates to be paid by some other person, that person must be made a respondent to the appeal, unless the court, on application of the appellant made without notice, otherwise directs.

Appeals under sections 204 and 204A of the Housing Act 1996

24.2(1) An appellant should include appeals under section 204 and 204A of the Housing Act 1996 in one appellant's notice.

(2) If it is not possible to do so (for example because an urgent application under section 204A is required) the appeals may be included in separate appellant's notices.

(3) An appeal under section 204A may include an application for an order under section 204A(4)(a) requiring the authority to secure that accommodation is available for the applicant's occupation.

(4) If, exceptionally, the court makes an order under section 204A(4)(a) without notice, the appellant's notice must be served on the authority together with the order. Such an order will normally require the authority to secure that accommodation is available until a hearing date when the authority can make representations as to whether the order under section 204A(4)(a) should be continued.

Appeal under Part II of the Immigration and Asylum Act 1999 (carriers' liability)

24.3(1) A person appealing to a county court under section 35A or section 40B of the Immigration and Asylum Act 1999 ("the Act") against a decision by the Secretary of State to impose a penalty under section 32 or a charge under section 40 of the Act must, subject to paragraph (2), file the appellant's notice within 28 days after receiving the penalty notice or charge notice.

(2) Where the appellant has given notice of objection to the Secretary of State under section 35(4) or section 40A(3) of the Act within the time prescribed for doing so, he must file the appellant's notice within 28 days after receiving notice of the Secretary of State's decision in response to the notice of objection.

(3) Sections 35A and 40B of the Act provide that any appeal under those sections shall be a re-hearing of the Secretary of State's decision to impose a penalty or charge, and therefore rule 52.11(1) does not apply.

Representation of the People Act 1983—appeals against decisions of registration officers

24.4 (1) This paragraph applies in relation to an appeal against a decision of a registration officer, being a decision referred to in section 56(1) of the Representation of the People Act 1983 ('the Act').

(2) Where a person ('the appellant') has given notice of such

an appeal in accordance with the relevant requirements of section 56, and of the regulations made under section 53 ('the Regulations'), of the Act, the registration officer must, within 7 days after he receives the notice, forward—

(a) the notice; and

(b) the statement required by the Regulations,

by post to the county court.

(3) The respondents to the appeal will be—

(a) the registration officer; and

(b) if the decision of the registration officer was given in favour of any other person than the appellant, that other person.

(4) On the hearing of the appeal—

(a) the statement forwarded to the court by the registration officer, and any document containing information submitted to the court by the registration officer pursuant to the Regulations, are admissible as evidence of the facts stated in them; and

(b) the court—

(i) may draw any inference of fact that the registration officer might have drawn; and

(ii) may give any decision and make any order that the registration officer ought to have given or made.

(5) A respondent to an appeal (other than the registration officer) is not liable for nor entitled to costs, unless he appears before the court in support of the registration officer's decision.

(6) Rule 52.4, and paragraphs 5, 6 and 7 of this practice direction, do not apply to an appeal to which this paragraph applies.

Representation of the People Act 1983—special provision in relation to anonymous entries in the register

24.5(1) In this paragraph—

'anonymous entry' has the meaning given by section 9B(4) of the Representation of the People Act 1983;

'appeal notice' means the notice required by regulation 32 of the Representation of the People (England and Wales) Regulations 2001.

(2) This paragraph applies to an appeal to a county court to which paragraph 24.4 applies if a party to the appeal is a person—

(a) whose entry in the register is an anonymous entry; or

(b) who has applied for such an entry.

(3) This paragraph also applies to an appeal to the Court of Appeal from a decision of a county court in an appeal to which paragraph 24.4 applies.

(4) The appellant may indicate in his appeal notice that he

has applied for an anonymous entry, or that his entry in the register is an anonymous entry.

(5) The respondent or any other person who applies to become a party to the proceedings may indicate in a respondent's notice or an application to join the proceedings that his entry in the register is an anonymous entry, or that he has applied for an anonymous entry.

(6) Where the appellant gives such an indication in his appeal notice, the court will refer the matter to a district judge for directions about the further conduct of the proceedings, and, in particular, directions about how the matter should be listed in the court list.

(7) Where the court otherwise becomes aware that a party to the appeal is a person referred to in sub-paragraph (2), the court will give notice to the parties that no further step is to be taken until the court has given any necessary directions for the further conduct of the matter.

(8) In the case of proceedings in a county court, the hearing will be in private unless the court orders otherwise.

(9) In the case of proceedings in the Court of Appeal, the hearing may be in private if the court so orders.

Representation of the People Act 1983—appeals selected as test cases

24.6(1) Where two or more appeals to which paragraph 24.4 applies involve the same point of law, the court may direct that one appeal ("the test-case appeal") is to be heard first as a test case.

(2) The court will send a notice of the direction to each party to all of those appeals.

(3) Where any party to an appeal other than the test-case appeal gives notice to the court, within 7 days after the notice is served on him, that he desires the appeal to which he is a party to be heard—

(a) the court will hear that appeal after the test-case appeal is disposed of;

(b) the court will give the parties to that appeal notice of the day on which it will be heard; and

(c) the party who gave the notice is not entitled to receive any costs of the separate hearing of that appeal unless the judge otherwise orders.

(4) Where no notice is given under sub-paragraph (3) within the period limited by that paragraph—

(a) the decision on the test-case appeal binds the parties to each of the other appeals;

(b) without further hearing, the court will make, in each other appeal, an order similar to the order in the test-case appeal; and

(c) the party to each other appeal who is in the same interest as the unsuccessful party to the selected appeal is liable for the costs of the test-case appeal in the same manner and to the same extent as the unsuccessful party to that appeal and an order directing him to pay such costs may be made and enforced accordingly.

(5) Sub-paragraph (4)(a) does not affect the right to appeal to the Court of Appeal of any party to an appeal other than the test-case appeal.

Appeals under section 11 of the UK Borders Act 2007

52PD.135.1 **24.7**(1) A person appealing to a county court under section 11 of the UK Borders Act 2007 ("the Act") against a decision by the Secretary of State to impose a penalty under section 9(1) of the Act, must, subject to paragraph (2), file the appellant's notice within 28 days after receiving the penalty notice.

(2) Where the appellant has given notice of objection to the Secretary of State under section 10 of the Act within the time prescribed for doing so, the appellant's notice must be filed within 28 days after receiving notice of the Secretary of State's decision in response to the notice of objection.

Section IV

Provisions about Reopening Appeals

Reopening of Final Appeals

52PD.136 **25.1** This paragraph applies to applications under rule 52.17 for permission to reopen a final determination of an appeal.

25.2 In this paragraph, "appeal" includes an application for permission to appeal.

25.3 Permission must be sought from the court whose decision the applicant wishes to reopen.

25.4 The application for permission must be made by application notice and supported by written evidence, verified by a statement of truth.

25.5 A copy of the application for permission must not be served on any other party to the original appeal unless the court so directs.

25.6 Where the court directs that the application for permission is to be served on another party, that party may within 14 days of the service on him of the copy of the application file and serve a written statement either supporting or opposing the application.

25.7 The application for permission, and any written statements supporting or opposing it, will be considered on paper by a single judge, and will be allowed to proceed only if the judge so directs.

52PD.137 *Note* —Amended by Civil Procedure (Amendment No.3) Rules 2004 (SI 2004/3129) which came into force April 1, 2005 (SI 2005/910).

PART 53

DEFAMATION CLAIMS

Contents

53.0.1

Editorial introduction

This short Part, with its relatively extensive accompanying Practice Direction, conveniently gathers together in one place all the material rules which apply specifically to defamation actions. Pt 53 itself contains rules, made under s.10 of the Defamation Act 1996, for summary disposal of defamation actions, and a provision to protect sources of information. The Practice Direction brings together rules for offer of amends under ss.2–4 of the Defamation Act 1996 and for summary disposal, rules for limiting pleaded meanings, and a number of rules which give guidance to the practitioner on points of pleading. Note that Pt 24 (summary judgment) has now assumed a greater importance in defamation practice than summary disposal under Pt 53 and the 1996 Act. 53.0.2

Scope of this Part[1]

53.1 This Part contains rules about defamation claims. 53.1

Summary disposal under the Defamation Act 1996[2]

53.2—(1) This rule provides for summary disposal in accordance with the Defamation Act 1996 ("the Act"). 53.2

(2) In proceedings for summary disposal under sections 8 and 9 of the Act, rules 24.4 (procedure), 24.5 (evidence) and 24.6 (directions) apply.

(3) An application for summary judgment under Part 24 may not be made if—

(a) an application has been made for summary disposal in accordance with the Act, and that application has not been disposed of; or

(b) summary relief has been granted on an application for summary disposal under the Act.

(4) The court may on any application for summary disposal direct the defendant to elect whether or not to make an offer to make amends under section 2 of the Act.

(5) When it makes a direction under paragraph (4), the Court *will specify the time by which* and the manner in which—

(a) the election is to be made; and

(b) notification of it is to be given to the court and the other parties.

---

[1] Introduced by the Civil Procedure (Amendment) Rules 2000 (SI 2000/221).
[2] Introduced by the Civil Procedure (Amendment) Rules 2000 (SI 2000/221).

Summary disposal

53.2.1 This rule gives effect to the regime for summary disposal of defamation claims introduced by ss.8 to 10 of the Defamation Act 1996. The summary disposal procedure enables the court to consider the strength of claim and defence at any stage and to dispose of the claim summarily at the instance of either party. It provides an alternative to summary judgment under Pt 24.

Both procedures share the same basic test, namely whether there is a prospect of success which is not fanciful: *James Gilbert Ltd v MGN Ltd* [2000] E.M.L.R. 680; *Mosley v Focus Magazin Verlag GmbH* [2001] EWCA Civ 1030. See also Lord Woolf's analysis of Pt 24's "no real prospect of success" in *Swain v Hillman* [2001] 1 All E.R. 91.

In other respects, the two procedures differ markedly. The main differences are these:

1. Under the Act, a claimant may obtain summary relief, which (by s.9) means such of the following as may be appropriate: (a) a declaration that the offending statement was false and defamatory of the claimant; (b) an order that the defendant publish a suitable correction and apology; (c) damages not exceeding £10,000, and (d) an injunction. By contrast, under Pt 24 there is no mechanism for obtaining an order for an apology, but equally there is no statutory limit on damages, which, once liability is established, may be assessed by a jury in the normal way.
2. Pt 24 cannot be used to determine any question which s.69 of the Supreme Court Act 1981 provides should be decided by a jury, and in particular the questions of whether the words complained of are defamatory and what meaning or meanings they bear: *Safeway Stores v Tate* [2001] Q.B. 1120, CA. But that does not prevent the judge from concluding that the evidence, taken at its highest, is such that a properly directed jury could not reach a necessary factual conclusion: in that case, the judge will withdraw the issue from the jury (*Alexander v Arts Council of Wales* [2001] 1 W.L.R. 1840, CA; *Miller v Associated Newspapers Ltd* [2003] EWHC 2799, [2004] E.M.L.R. 33 at [13], Eady J).
3. While both procedures allow an action to go to trial if there is some reason (under Pt 24, a "compelling" reason) why it should do so, s.8(4) of the Act obliges the court in considering whether a claim should be tried to have regard to a number of factors (whether all the persons who are or might be defendants are before the court; whether summary disposal of the claim against another defendant would be inappropriate; the extent to which there is a conflict of evidence; the seriousness of the defamation; and whether it is justifiable in the circumstances to proceed to a full trial). There is no equivalent obligation under Pt 24.
4. Pt 24 applications (commonly coupled with an application to strike out under CPR r.3.4(2)) may be used to attack part of a claim (for example, a plea of qualified privilege), whereas applications under the Act are intended to dispose of the claim in its entirety.

The summary disposal regime has proved less popular than its Pt 24 sibling, and applications have been relatively rare in recent times. Their object may be to dispose of a defence and obtain judgment on the claim (e.g. *Downtex v Flatley* [2003] EWCA Civ 1282, where the Court of Appeal was persuaded that a defence of qualified privilege was bound to fail), or to force the claimant to have his claim disposed of summarily rather than by jury trial, in which case the defendant must waive any substantive defence (see e.g. *Milne v Telegraph Group Ltd (No.2)* [2001] E.M.L.R. 30). On a defendant's application, the court must be satisfied that summary relief (in particular, the £10,000 damages ceiling) will adequately compensate the claimant: see s.8(3), *Burstein v Times Newspapers Ltd* [2001] 1 W.L.R. 579 and *Mawdsley v Guardian Newspapers Ltd* [2002] EWHC 1780 at [16], [56].

Where it makes no practical difference which procedure is to be followed, the application should be made (at least where it is the defendant's application) solely under Pt 24 (*Clarke v Davey* [2002] EWHC 2342, QB, Gray J.). Gray J. said in that case that the effect of Pt 53.2(3) is to bar concurrent applications under s.8 and Pt 24, and that if both are made, the applicant will be put to election: see also Sedley L.J. in *Hassan v Holburn* [2004] EWCA Civ 789.Nonetheless, the practice of combining a s.8 application with one under Pt 24 was noted without disapproval by the CA (although the point was not argued) in *Downtex v Flatley* [2003] EWCA Civ 1282 [3] and applications have been combined without comment: see e.g. *Blackwell v Bates* [2007] EWHC 3098 (QB).On any view, however, the s.8 application must be heard and disposed of before that under Pt 24 can be heard.

Procedure and evidence

The rules governing procedure, evidence and directions in Pt 24 applications are expressly imported into the statutory regime. However, whereas under Pt 24 a claimant may generally not apply until the defendant has filed an acknowledgment of service or a defence, under Pt 53 the application may be made by either party after service of particulars of claim (see para.5.2 of the Practice Direction, para.53PD.14 below). Claimants' applications where the relief sought includes an order for publication of an apology or an injunction to restrain further publication should be made direct to the Judge, as should applications in particularly serious matters (see para.53PD.14.2). The application notice, whether under s.8 or Pt 24, should set out the grounds of the application in clear terms so that the repondent is not taken by surprise: *Armstrong v Times Newspapers Ltd* [2005] EWCA Civ 1007; [2005] E.M.L.R. 33. **53.2.2**

Direction to elect whether or not to make offer of amends

This rule was expressly envisaged by s.10(2)(f) of the Act. It was considered by Gray J. in *Green v Times Newspapers Ltd*, January 17, 2001, unrep. For the offer of amends procedure, see paras 3.1 to 3.3 and para.7 of the Practice Direction (para.53PD.37 below). **53.2.3**

Sources of information[1]

53.3 Unless the court orders otherwise, a party will not be required to provide further information about the identity of the defendant's sources of information. **53.3**

(Part 18 provides for requests for further information.)

Sources of information

This is the successor of RSC O.82, r.6, which prohibited interrogatories as to the defendant's sources of information or grounds of belief where defences of fair comment or privilege were pleaded. With the advent of the CPR, and the assimilation of interrogatories with requests for further and better particulars under the rubric of "Further Information" (Pt 18), O.82, r.6 acquired a wider potency at the very time when its utility was most in doubt. In its current form, the scope of the rule is wider still, for it is not limited to cases where fair comment or privilege are in issue. The rule sits uneasily with the importance in common law qualified privilege of the source of the defendant's information, the status of that information and the steps taken to verify it (see *Reynolds v Times Newspapers* [2001] 2 A.C. 127), and may debar claimants from obtaining further information about what will often be a critical part of a defendant's case. In practice, its importance is limited, given the statutory protection of journalists' sources provided by s.10 of the Contempt of Court Act 1981. For the kinds of difficulties which can arise with sources when Reynolds privilege is pleaded, see *Loutchansky v Times Newspapers* [2001] E.M.L.R. 39 at paras 50 *et seq.*, per Gray J. **53.3.1**

[1] Introduced by the Civil Procedure (Amendment) Rules 2000 (SI 2000/221).

PRACTICE DIRECTION—DEFAMATION CLAIMS

This Practice Direction supplements CPR Part 53

General

53PD.1 **1** This practice direction applies to defamation claims.

Statements of case

53PD.2 **2.1** Statements of case should be confined to the information necessary to inform the other party of the nature of the case he has to meet. Such information should be set out concisely and in a manner proportionate to the subject matter of the claim.

2.2(1) In a claim for libel the publication the subject of the claim must be identified in the claim form.

(2) In a claim for slander the claim form must so far as possible contain the words complained of, and identify the person to whom they were spoken and when.

Libel: identifying the publication in the claim form

53PD.3 "Publication" is used in the technical sense of the instance of libel (e.g. the particular document, or broadcast programme) which is complained of. So the pleader should claim, e.g. "Damages for libel published by the Defendant on page—of the issue of the Daily Trumpet dated January 1, 2000".

Slander

53PD.4 It is good practice to provide similar particulars in the case of a slander. The requirement used to be that the claim form should give sufficient detail of the words complained of, including to whom they were spoken and when, to enable them to be identified. So it was enough, e.g. to claim "Damages for slander published by the defendant to Fred Smith on January 1, 2000". Paragraph 2.2(2) goes further, and appears to oblige the pleader to set out the actual words complained of on the claim form. This is more than is required in the case of a libel. This is a very curious requirement, because until public access to statements of case was greatly widened in December 2006 it was bad practice to set out the words complained of in the Claim Form. That was because the public could inspect and copy it, and the media could report it under the cloak of qualified privilege, while the Particulars of Claim could only be inspected with the court's permission. Thus it was that Gray J. described setting out the libel in the writ as "unwise" in *Carpenter v Associated Newspapers* November 26, 2001, unrep. However, with effect from December 18, 2006 r.5.4C has given non-parties access to all statements of case filed at court after October 2, 2006. It may follow that discretion in drafting the Claim Form is no longer necessary. But it should be noted that CPR 5.4C(4) empowers the court, on the application of a party or of a person identified in a statement of case, to make an order limiting or excluding access to particular documents. Such applications are made in defamation cases where a damaging libel or slander has been published to only a few people, and where the new rule would otherwise serve only to aggravate the damage suffered. It may be that the court will be readier to make such an order in the case of Particulars of Claim (which were not previously available to public inspection) than in the case of Claim Forms (which always were available).

53PD.5 **2.3**(1) The claimant must specify in the particulars of claim the defamatory meaning which he alleges that the words or matters complained of conveyed, both

(a) as to their natural and ordinary meaning; and

(b) as to any innuendo meaning (that is a meaning alleged to be conveyed to some person by reason of knowing facts extraneous to the words complained of).

(2) In the case of an innuendo meaning, the claimant must also identify the relevant extraneous facts.

Pleading the meaning

Modern practice is to plead the meaning which the claimant contends that the words bear, however obvious it may be. Pleading the meaning is a difficult art: the meaning should be as high and as specific as possible, but not strained and not too wide. Too narrow or too low a meaning, and the claimant will be constrained in opening the case to the jury; too high, and he may face an adverse ruling under para.4 of this Practice Direction (see Pt 53, Practice Direction, para.53PD.31 below); too wide, and he may let in a wider defence of justification than would otherwise have been possible (see the cautionary tale of *Bookbinder v Tebbit* [1989] 1 W.L.R. 640). **53PD.6**

Natural and ordinary and innuendo meanings

Where words are defamatory on their face, they are said to be defamatory in their natural and ordinary meaning; where they are defamatory only by reason of some special facts known to the person who read or heard them (the "publishee"), they are said to be defamatory in an innuendo meaning, often referred to in the authorities as a "legal" innuendo. (Note that confusion has been caused in the past by the use of the word "innuendo", sometimes qualified with the words "popular" or "false", to refer to a natural and ordinary meaning which arises by implication or inference; that usage is best avoided). **53PD.7**

Innuendo meanings: extraneous facts

When a legal innuendo is pleaded, para.2.3(2) requires the pleader to set out the special or extraneous facts which are relied on as giving the words their defamatory meaning. The special facts must be matters outside the libel: *Grubb v Bristol United Press* [1963] 1 Q.B. 309. They may be the explanation of a slang word or a technical term, which was understood by the publishee but might not have made sense to most people who heard it; or they may be some additional facts, known to the publishee, which gave the words a defamatory sense. It is usually necessary to identify the publishees who knew the special facts and therefore would have understood the words to bear the innuendo meaning; but it may be possible to rely on inference in suitable cases (see *Fullam v Newcastle Chronicle* [1977] 1 W.L.R. 651). The claimant cannot rely on special facts which occur or are discovered after the words have been published, because the cause of action is complete on publication: *Grapelli v Block* [1981] 1 W.L.R. 822. An advantage of the legal innuendo is that counsel may ask publishees at trial what they understood the words to mean, which is not permissible where only a natural and ordinary meaning is pleaded. **53PD.8**

2.4 In a claim for slander the precise words used and the names of the persons to whom they were spoken and when must, so far as possible, be set out in the particulars of claim, if not already contained in the claim form. **53PD.9**

Slander: setting out the actual words

This requirement reflects the law as it has stood for centuries: see for example *Cook v Cox* (1814) 3 M&S 110 at 113, per Lord Ellenborough C.J. (the actual words must be set out "in order that the defendant may know the certainty of the charge, and be able to shape his defence"). The oddity about this paragraph is that it does not refer to libel, and it would be quite wrong to argue from that omission that the actual words of a libel need not be set out in the particulars of claim. The rule in libel was always the same as in slander: **53PD.10**

> "In libel and slander everything may turn on the form of words. ... It is not the fact of the defendant having used defamatory expressions, but the fact of his having used those defamatory expressions alleged, which is the fact on which the case depends"

per Lord Coleridge C.J., *Harris v Warre* (1879) 4 C.P.D. 125 at 128.

The words "so far as possible" do not remove the well-established requirement for the claimant to plead his case in slander with sufficient particularity to enable the defendant to know how to formulate his case, and it remains impermissible to plead the effect or gist of the words in the hope of fishing for disclosure: exactly what is required of the pleader will to some extent depend on the facts of the case. The exact words should always be pleaded if possible, but the words must at the least be set out with reasonable precision (*Best v Charter Medical of England Ltd* [2002] E.M.L.R. 335, CA).

53PD.11 **2.5** Where a defendant alleges that the words complained of are true he must:

(1) specify the defamatory meanings he seeks to justify; and
(2) give details of the matters on which he relies in support of that allegation.

Specifying the meaning to be justified

53PD.12 Justification (proving that the words complained of are true) is a defence to a claim in libel or in slander. It is open to a defendant to justify a libel or slander (i.e. to prove it to be true) in any meaning which a jury could properly find the words to bear (see e.g. *Prager v Times Newspapers* [1988] 1 W.L.R. 77 at 86; *Polly Peck v Trelford* [1986] Q.B. 1000). But in doing so, the defendant must specify the meaning in which he is justifying, i.e. the meaning in which he says that the words are true (see *Lucas-Box v News Group* [1986]1 W.L.R. 147, CA).

For example, a defence of justification might typically use words such as these, e.g.: "The words complained of are true in the following meaning, namely that in January 2000 the claimant defrauded the X Bank of a substantial sum of money". The defendant will then go on (see below) to set out the particulars of justification, namely the material facts on which he relies in support of his plea. For the so-called "three tiers" of defamatory meaning, and more detailed guidance on pleading justification, see *Gatley on Libel & Slander* (11th edn), paras 29.5ff and 32.6.

As para.2.5(1) makes clear, the meaning to be justified must be a defamatory meaning: see, e.g. *Broadcasting Corporation of NZ v Crush* [1988] 2 N.Z.L.R. 234 at 237 (proving the truth of a non-defamatory meaning would be a "pointless exercise"), and *Maxwell v Bower*, Michael Davies J., April 10, 1990, unrep.

Note the "somewhat subtle" distinction (*Prager v Times Newspapers* [1988] 1 W.L.R. 77 at 91, per Nicholls L.J.) between pleading the meaning in which the defendant justifies the libel or slander, which he is obliged to do, and pleading the meaning which—quite apart from any plea of justification—he says the words bear, which he is not obliged to do.

Details of the matters relied on in support of a plea of justification

53PD.13 Once the defendant has decided on the meaning in which he intends to prove that the libel or slander is true, he must set out, plainly and unambiguously, the material facts which he relies on in support of that case. They are known as "Particulars of Justification".

53PD.14 **2.6** Where a defendant alleges that the words complained of are fair comment on a matter of public interest he must:

(1) specify the defamatory meaning he seeks to defend as fair comment on a matter of public interest; and
(2) give details of the matters on which he relies in support of that allegation.

Fair comment

53PD.15 As with justification (see para.2.5 above) so with fair comment, the defendant is now obliged to set out the meaning that he intends to defend. This rule stems from the decision in *Control Risks v New English Library* [1990] 1 W.L.R. 183. It is trite that fair comment must be based on facts truly stated. However, this does not confine the defendant to facts stated in the words complained of. What matters is that the reader can distinguish fact from comment. Facts not stated can be relied on as long as they existed at the time of publication and were known—at least in general terms—to the commentator (*Lowe v Associated Newspapers* [2006] EWHC 320, QB; [2007] 1 Q.B. 580).

Details of the matters relied on in support of a plea of fair comment

53PD.16 The defendant must always give details of the facts on which the comment is based. Since the comment must relate to a matter of public interest he should also, although the Practice Direction does not state it, specify the matter of public interest relied on.

2.7 Where a defendant alleges that the words complained of were published on a privileged occasion he must specify the circumstances he relies on in support of that contention. 53PD.17

Qualified privilege

This requirement is particularly important in the context of recent developments in the common law of qualified privilege. Defendants pleading qualified (or absolute) privilege have always been obliged to set out the facts giving rise to the privilege, but in the light of *Reynolds v Times Newspapers* [2001] 2 A.C. 127 it will usually be necessary, at least when the defamation has been widely disseminated, to plead a number of circumstantial matters, such as the seriousness of the allegation and the extent to which it is a matter of public concern, the source and status of the information, the steps taken to verify it, the urgency of the matter, and the steps taken to obtain and print the plaintiff's side of the story, and in addition the reasonable belief of those responsible for publication that the story was true: *Jameel v Wall Street Journal* [2005] EWCA Civ 74; [2005] Q.B. 904 at [18] and [27] (this point was not addressed by the HL on appeal). See also *Loutchansky v Times Newspapers Ltd (Nos 2–5)* [2002] Q.B. 783, CA, for the requirement of responsible journalism, and *Jameel v Wall Street Journal* [2006] UKHL 44; [2007] 1 A.C. 359. 53PD.18

2.8 Where a defendant alleges that the words complained of are true, or are fair comment on a matter of public interest, the claimant must serve a reply specifically admitting or denying the allegation and giving the facts on which he relies. 53PD.19

Reply to defence of justification or fair comment

It used to be the case that the claimant did not have to plead to the particulars of justification or fair comment, which had the result that the whole plea was in issue (although the power to order him to do so was confirmed in *Morrell v International Thomson Publishing*, July 18, 1990, unrep., CA, giving rise to the expression "Morrell particulars"). Now, the pleader is obliged to plead to each of the particulars of justification or fair comment. 53PD.20

2.9 If the defendant contends that any of the words or matters are fair comment on a matter of public interest, or were published on a privileged occasion, and the claimant intends to allege that the defendant acted with malice, the claimant must serve a reply giving details of the facts or matters relied on. 53PD.21

Malice

Claimants used to allege in particulars of claim that the defendant "falsely and maliciously" published the words complained of. That form of words was not just stilted: it was otiose. That is because falsity is presumed in the claimant's favour, and malice is not a necessary element of his cause of action. Malice should only be pleaded in the particulars of claim where it is relied on as aggravating damage. 53PD.22

Otherwise, and this is the object of this paragraph, malice must be pleaded in the reply, in answer to a defence of fair comment or qualified privilege. In either case, the claimant must give full particulars in his reply of all the facts and matters from which malice is to be inferred. The normal practice is to allege that the defendant published the words complained of with "express malice", and to follow that general plea with particulars of the facts which show, or from which it is to be inferred, that the defendant was driven by some dominant improper motive, or knew that (or was recklessly indifferent as to whether) his words were false, or was otherwise malicious (for malice in relation to qualified privilege, see *Horrocks v Lowe* [1975] A.C. 135; for malice in relation to fair comment, see the judgment of Lord Nicholls in *Cheng v Tse* [2001] E.M.L.R. 777, Court of Final Appeal, Hong Kong). Note that malice is a dead letter in *Reynolds* privilege (see note at 53PD.18 above) "because the propriety of the conduct of the defendant is built into the conditions under which the material is privileged" (*Jameel v Wall Street Journal* [2006] UKHL 44; [2007] 1 A.C. 359, per Lord Hoffmann at [46].

53PD.23 **2.10**(1) A claimant must give full details of the facts and matters on which he relies in support of his claim for damages.

(2) Where a claimant seeks aggravated or exemplary damages he must provide the information specified in rule 16.4(1)(c).

Damages

53PD.24 There is no obligation to give particulars where the claimant relies only on the law's presumption of damage; in such cases he will simply plead words to the effect that by reason of the publication of the words complained of, he has suffered distress and injury to his reputation. But where he relies on any factor which goes beyond the normal damage presumed to follow from publication of defamatory words, he must plead it, so that the defendant knows the case he has to meet and is given some assistance in calculating a payment into court.

That will include any factors which have aggravated damages, including anything relevant to the impact of the libel or slander on the claimant's feelings, such as the way others treated the claimant as a result, and the defendant's own behaviour (e.g. refusal to apologise, repetition of the libel, and malicious conduct, such as spreading a libel with no belief that it is true), and any unusual feature relied on as increasing damage: see, e.g. *Slipper v BBC* [1991] 1 Q.B. 283. The modern practice is to plead fully the claimant's case on general damage, and the pleader should ensure that he includes every matter of substance which has contributed to the damage done to the claimant's reputation and feelings. If, as often happens, the defendant's conduct after proceedings have begun is relied on as aggravating damage, the claimant should amend to plead it, although that principle should be tempered with common sense: for example, it will not be necessary to amend at trial in order to rely on a hostile and persistent cross-examination.

Rule 16.4(1)(c) obliges the claimant to state if he is seeking aggravated or exemplary damages and to state his grounds for doing so.

53PD.25 **2.11** A defendant who relies on an offer to make amends under section 2 of the Defamation Act 1996 as his defence must—

(1) state in his defence—

(a) that he is relying on the offer in accordance with section 4(2) of the Defamation Act 1996; and

(b) that it has not been withdrawn by him or been accepted, and

(2) attach a copy of the offer he made with his defence.

Offer of amends as a defence

53PD.26 The fact that an offer of amends has been made but not accepted is a defence to a defamation claim (s.4(2)), except where the offeror knew or had reason to believe that the statement complained of (a) referred to the claimant or was likely to be understood as doing so, and (b) was both false and defamatory of the claimant (s.4(3)). This imports a bad faith or malice test, which will rarely be satisfied: see *Milne v Express Newspapers* [2002] EWHC 2564, QB; [2003] 1 W.L.R. 927, Eady J., affirmed [2004] EWCA (Civ) 664; [2005] 1 W.L.R. 772. Where the defence of offer of amends is relied on, no other defence may be pleaded: s.4(4).

Court's Powers in Connection with an Offer of Amends

53PD.27 **3.1** Sections 2 to 4 of the Defamation Act 1996 make provision for a person who has made a statement which is alleged to be defamatory to make an offer of amends. Section 3 provides for the court to assist in the process of making amends.

3.2 A claim under section 3 of the Defamation Act 1996 made other than in existing proceedings may be made under CPR Part 8—

(1) where the parties agree on the steps to make amends, and

the sole purpose of the claim is for the court to make an order under section 3(3) for an order that the offer be fulfilled; or

(2) where the parties do not agree—

(a) on the steps to be taken by way of correction, apology and publication (see section 3(4));

(b) on the amount to be paid by way of compensation (see section 3(5)); or

(c) on the amount to be paid by way of costs (see section 3(6)).

(Applications in existing proceedings made under section 3 of the Defamation Act 1996 must be made in accordance with CPR Part 23.)

3.3(1) A claim or application under section 3 of the Defamation Act 1996 must be supported by written evidence.

(2) The evidence referred to in paragraph (1) must include—

(a) a copy of the offer of amends;

(b) details of the steps taken to fulfil the offer of amends;

(c) a copy of the text of any correction and apology;

(d) details of the publication of the correction and apology;

(e) a statement of the amount of any sum paid as compensation;

(f) a statement of the amount of any sum paid for costs;

(g) why the offer is unsatisfactory.

(3) Where any step specified in section 2(4) of the Defamation Act 1996 has not been taken, then the evidence referred to in paragraph (2)(c) to (f) must state what steps are proposed by the party to fulfil the offer of amends and the date or dates on which each step will be fulfilled and, if none, that no proposal has been made to take that step.

Offer of amends

This procedure allows a person who has published a statement alleged to be defamatory of another to offer to make amends. An offer of amends must be in writing, must be expressed to be an offer of amends under s.2 and must state whether or not it is qualified (i.e. limited to a specific defamatory meaning which the offeror accepts that the statement conveys); but whatever else the offer may contain, s.2(4) provides that it will be taken to include an offer to make a suitable correction and apology, before service of defence, to publish the correction and apology in a manner that is reasonable and practicable in the circumstances, and to pay the aggrieved party (who need not have issued proceedings) such compensation (if any) and costs as may be agreed or determined. **53PD.28**

The section 3 procedure

If the offer is accepted, the s.3 procedure applies. The party accepting the offer may neither bring nor continue defamation proceedings against the offeror in respect of the libel or slander concerned, but he can enforce the offer. To do so, any of a number of applications to the court may have to be made. If both parties agree on the steps to be taken to fulfil the offer, the person accepting the offer may apply to the court for an order that the other party should fulfil the offer by taking those steps. If they do not agree, other consequences flow. If they disagree about the steps to be taken by way of correction, apology and their publication, the offeror may make the correction and apology by statement in court in terms approved by the court, and give an undertak- **53PD.29** ing to the court as to the manner in which they are to be published. If the parties disagree about the amount of compensation, the court must determine the amount according to the usual principles applying to defamation damages. The same applies, *mutatis mutandis*, if they disagree about costs. For the principles to be applied on assessment of damages, and the need to avoid a "rough and ready" approach, see *Kareem Abu v MGN Ltd* [2003] 2 All E.R. 864, Eady J. and *Nail v News Group Newspapers Ltd* [2004] EWCA Civ 1708; [2005] 1 All E.R. 1040; and for guidance on the practical need for informal discussion between the parties to avoid applications to the court, see *Cleese v Clark* [2003] EWHC 137, QB; [2004] E.M.L.R. 3, Eady J. It appears that it is not open to a defendant who has made an unqualified offer to argue that that the claimant's meanings are untenable: such a challenge should be flagged up by use of a qualified offer (see *Nail v News Group* [2004] EWHC 647, QB; [2004] E.M.L.R. 20, approved [2004] EWCA Civ 1708; [2005] 1 All E.R. 1040).

Paragraph 3.2 provides that s.3 applications before proceedings have been issued must be made under CPR Pt 8, while applications made after the issue of proceedings should be made under Pt 23; and para.3.3 sets out the requirements for written evidence in support of a s.3 application. Note that while para.3.3(2)(e) requires that the amount of any sum actually paid as compensation must be included in the supporting evidence, it is preferable for the judge not to be told the competing figures advanced by the parties in without prejudice correspondence: *Cleese v Clark*, above.

Note that there is no provision for "rejection" of the offer, which is either accepted or not accepted. A failure to accept may be construed as non-acceptance. The onus is squarely on the claimant to decide promptly whether or not to accept: see *Loughton Contracts plc v Dun & Bradstreet Ltd* [2006] EWHC 1224 (QB). However, a reasonable time will be allowed: *Tesco Stores v Guardian News & Media Ltd*, Eady J., July 29, 2008. Once an offer is accepted, the defendant may not resile from it except in rare and special circumstances so different from those contemplated that it would be appropriate to release him from his obligation: *Warren v Random House Group Ltd* [2008] EWCA Civ 834.

A claimant may obtain disclosure of an identified and specific document which is relevant to a pleaded issue and highly material to the decision whether or not to accept the offer of amends, but that is not to sanction routine or wide-ranging applications by claimants faced with that decision: *Rigg v Associated Newspapers Ltd* [2003] EWHC 710, QB; [2004] E.M.L.R. 4, Gray J.

The section 4 procedure

53PD.30 If the offer is not accepted, the fact that it was made is a defence (if the offer was qualified, then a partial defence) to defamation proceedings in respect of the publication in question. But there is no defence if the offeror knew or had reason to believe that the allegation complained of referred to the claimant or was likely to be understood as referring to him, and was both false and defamatory of him.

The offer of amends regime (which is much used by the media) is intended to provide an exit route for journalists who have made a mistake and want to put their hands up. It is only intended to shut out those who have acted in bad faith, i.e. maliciously (see *Milne v Express Newspapers* [2002] EWHC 2564, QB; [2003] 1 W.L.R. 927, Eady J., affirmed [2004] EWCA (Civ) 664; [2005] 1 W.L.R. 772.

Ruling on Meaning

53PD.31 **4.1** At any time the court may decide—

(1) whether a statement complained of is capable of having any meaning attributed to it in a statement of case;

(2) whether the statement is capable of being defamatory of the claimant;

(3) whether the statement is capable of bearing any other meaning defamatory of the claimant.

4.2 An application for a ruling on meaning may be made at any time after the service of particulars of claim. Such an application should be made promptly.

(This provision disapplies for these applications the usual time restriction on making applications in rule 24.4.1.)

4.3 Where an application is made for a ruling on meaning, the application notice must state that it is an application for a ruling on meaning made in accordance with this practice direction.

4.4 The application notice or the evidence contained or referred to in it, or served with it, must identify precisely the statement, and the meaning attributed to it, that the court is being asked to consider.

(Rule 3.3 applies where the court exercises its powers of its own initiative.)

(Following a ruling on meaning the court may exercise its power under rule 3.4.)

(Section 7 of the Defamation Act 1996 applies to rulings on meaning.)

Ruling on meaning

The question whether words are capable of bearing a particular meaning has always been a question of law for the judge at trial or, more recently, beforehand: see *Lewis v Daily Telegraph* [1964] A.C. 234. The judge will lay down the limits of the range of the possible defamatory meanings of which the words are capable, whereas it is for the jury to determine the actual meaning of the words within that permissible range (*Mapp v News Group Newspapers* [1998] Q.B. 520 at 523). **53PD.32**

This procedure has been used to valuable effect, and a corpus of authority has grown up on the criteria for determining whether words are capable of bearing a particular meaning (see, e.g. *Mapp v News Group Newspapers* (above); *Cruise v Express Newspapers* [1999] Q.B. 931). As to whether words are capable of being defamatory at all, see *Berkoff v Burchill* [1997] E.M.L.R. 139, and for the question of whether they contain two or more distinct stings, see *Cruise v Express Newspapers* above. There is less reason for a pre-emptive ruling on meaning where the defence is qualified privilege: see *Jameel v Wall Street Journal* [2004] E.M.L.R. 6, CA. For recent consideration of the principles, see *Jameel v Wall Street Journal* (above) and *Jameel v Times Newspapers Ltd* [2004] EWCA Civ 983; [2004] E.M.L.R. 31, where the taxonomy of different levels of meaning is considered.

Who may apply

Either party may apply: this means that a claimant may apply for a ruling as to whether a defendant's "Lucas-Box" meaning (the meaning which the defendant is setting out to justify: see *Lucas-Box v News Group Newspapers* [1986] 1 W.L.R. 147) is one which the words are capable of bearing (see, e.g. *Venables v Bose*, Sir Maurice Drake, November 6, 1996, unrep.); and a party may even apply for a ruling on his own meaning (see *Parry v Express Newspapers*, March 9, 1995, unrep., CA). **53PD.33**

Timing of application

Any application for a ruling on meaning should be made at the earliest opportunity (*Ibe v LWT* December 4, 1998, unrep., Popplewell J.). **53PD.34**

Appeals

Note that the Court of Appeal discourages appeals from rulings as to meaning except in cases which are clearly fit for argument in that court, although it will be less reluctant to interfere with a judge's decision where a meaning has been ruled out once and for all (see *Cruise v Express Newspapers* [1999] Q.B. 931 at 936), and where the judge has erred on the side of unnecessary restriction of meaning (*Berezovsky v Forbes Inc* [2001] E.M.L.R. 1030, CA). **53PD.35**

Master or Judge?

Until the advent of the CPR, the practice was always to list applications for rulings on meaning before the judge in charge of the jury list or a judge nominated by him (in accordance with the Listing Statement issued by Drake J. as judge in charge of the jury list on May 22, 1995). That accorded with the original wording of the rule, which provided for applications to be made to a judge in chambers, and with its origins as a device for bringing forward a ruling which was for the trial judge to make. Although **53PD.36** the wording of the rule on its face permits applications to be made to a Master or district judge, it is doubtful whether this result was intended, in view of the fact that a ruling on a meaning is substantive, not procedural, and binds the trial judge. No doubt for that reason, the practice is to list the application directly before the judge in charge of the jury list.

Summary Disposal

53PD.37 **5.1** Where an application is made for summary disposal, the application notice must state—

(1) that it is an application for summary disposal made in accordance with section 8 of the Defamation Act 1996;

(2) the matters set out in paragraph 2(3) of the practice direction to Part 24; and

(3) whether or not the defendant has made an offer to make amends under section 2 of the Act and whether or not it has been withdrawn.

5.2 An application for summary disposal may be made at any time after the service of particulars of claim.

(This provision disapplies for these applications the usual time restriction on making applications in rule 24.4.1).

5.3(1) This paragraph applies where—

(a) the court has ordered the defendant in defamation proceedings to agree and publish a correction and apology as summary relief under section 8(2) of the Defamation Act 1996; and

(b) the parties are unable to agree its content within the time specified in the order.

(2) Where the court grants this type of summary relief under the Act, the order will specify the date by which the parties should reach agreement about the content, time, manner, form and place of publication of the correction and apology.

(3) Where the parties cannot agree the content of the correction and apology by the date specified in the order, then the claimant must prepare a summary of the judgment given by the court and serve it on all the other parties within 3 days following the date specified in the order.

(4) Where the parties cannot agree the summary of the judgment prepared by the claimant they must within 3 days of receiving the summary—

(a) file with the court and serve on all the other parties a copy of the summary showing the revisions they wish to make to it; and

(b) apply to the court for the court to settle the summary.

(5) The court will then itself settle the summary and the judge who delivered the judgment being summarised will normally do this.

Procedure and evidence

53PD.38 Applications for summary disposal should be made by Pt 23 notice in the usual way. However, the notice must state that it is an application for summary disposal under s.8 of the Defamation Act 1996. That is to ensure that there is no confusion with the Pt 24 summary judgment procedure. It has been said that if the two procedures are invoked in tandem, the applicant may be put to election: see r.53.2(3), and *Clarke v Davey* [2002] EWHC 2342 (QB), Gray J. (although a combined application was noted without disapproval by the Court of Appeal in *Downtex v Flatley* [2003] EWCA Civ 1282 and has since been made without comment: *Blackwell v Batos* [2007] EWHC 3098 (QB)). *Clarke v Davey* shows that (at least on a defendant's application) where it makes no practical difference whether the s.8 or Pt 24 procedure is followed, the application should be made solely under Pt 24. The notice must also state whether or not the defendant has made an offer of amends under s.2 of the 1996 Act and if made, whether or not it has been withdrawn. As with a Pt 24 application for summary judgment, the notice (or the accompanying evidence) must, in accordance with Pt 24, Practice Direction, para.2(3)(qv), identify any point of law or provision in a document on which the applicant relies, and/or state that the application is made because the applicant believes that the respondent has no real prospect of success on the claim, defence or issue in question, and state that the applicant knows of no other reason why disposal of the claim or issue should await trial.

In making that statement, the applicant would be wise to consider carefully the factors to which the court is obliged, by s.8(4) of the 1996 Act, to have regard in considering whether a claim should go to trial, namely whether all the persons who are or might be defendants are before the court; whether summary disposal of the claim against another defendant would be inappropriate; the extent to which there is a conflict of evidence; the seriousness of the alleged wrong (as regards both the content of the statement and the extent of publication); and whether it is justifiable in the circumstances to proceed to a full trial.

Paragraph 5.2 states that an application may be made at any time after service of particulars of claim, and confirms that the usual time restriction for Pt 24 summary judgment applications does not apply. By r.24.4(1), a claimant may generally not make a Pt 24 application until the defendant (the respondent to the application) has filed an acknowledgement of service or a defence: so the claimant seeking summary disposal under Pt 53 may issue his application without waiting 14 days for the acknowledgement of service or defence. The application may even be made after judgment on liability: see *Loutchansky v Times Newspapers Ltd (Nos 2-5)* [2002] Q.B. 783, where the Court of Appeal upheld Gray J.'s order for summary disposal of assessment of damages following trial of the issues of liability by a jury.

In other respects the procedural requirements of r.24.4 apply to a r.53.2 application, as do the provisions for evidence (r.24.5) and directions (r.24.6): see r.53.2(2). So the respondent must be given at least 14 days' notice of the date fixed for the hearing and the issues to be decided (r.24.4(3)); the respondent must file and serve any written evidence at least 7 days before the hearing (r.24.5(1)), and any evidence in reply must be filed and served at least 3 days before (r.24.5(2)). The application notice must set out the grounds of the application in clear terms: *Armstrong v Times Newspapers Ltd* [2005] EWCA Civ 1007; [2005] E.M.L.R. 33.

Tribunal

The relief which the court may give to a claimant by way of summary disposal of a claim includes a mandatory injunction (s.9(1)(b): an order that the defendant publish or cause to be published a suitable correction and apology) and an injunction to restrain further publication (s.9(1)(d)). The court may also grant a declaration of falsity under s.9(1)(a), but see *Mahfouz v Brisard* [2006] EWHC 1191, QB for reasons why it may be reluctant to do so. Neither a Master nor a district judge has jurisdiction to grant such relief, so such applications should be made direct to the judge. Applications in serious matters (e.g. actions involving the media, police officers or public office holders, or serious or high profile allegations) should also be made to the judge. If the judge (or Master) thinks that the application should be heard at a lower (or higher) level, the parties may be asked to argue the point. **53PD.39**

Correction and apology

Paragraph 5.3 provides a mechanism for the enforcement of orders for publication of corrections and apologies as part of the grant of summary relief under s.9 of the 1996 Act. Section 9(2) provides that the content of any correction and apology and the time, manner, form and place of publication are for the parties to agree, but that if they cannot agree the court may direct the defendant to publish a summary of the court's judgment to be agreed by the parties or settled by the court. **53PD.40**

Statements in Open Court

6.1 This paragraph only applies where a party wishes to accept a Part 36 offer or other offer of settlement in relation to a claim for **53PD.41**

(1) libel;

(2) slander.

6.2 A party may apply for permission to make a statement in open court before or after he accepts the Part 36 offer in accordance with rule 36.9(1) or other offer to settle the claim.

6.3 The statement that the applicant wishes to make must be submitted for the approval of the court and must accompany the notice of application.

6.4 The court may postpone the time for making the statement if other claims relating to the subject matter of the statement are still proceeding.

(Applications must be made in accordance with Part 23).

Statement in court

53PD.42 This is a valuable means of vindication for a claimant in a libel or slander action, because it can be reported freely under the privilege which protects fair and accurate reports of proceedings heard in public and will normally receive some press and media coverage, even if only in the claimant's home district. It may be unilateral (where the claimant alone makes a statement) or bilateral (where the defendant joins in the making of a statement in agreed terms). The bilateral statement is far more effective, because it almost invariably demands an acceptance by the defendant that his words were false, and a suitable expression of contrition.

Procedure

53PD.43 Statements in court are made in two main situations: one is where a party wishes to accept a Pt 36 offer, and the other is where the action has settled, and (generally) one of the terms of settlement provides for a bilateral statement to be made in agreed terms. In either case, the applicant issues an application notice under CPR Pt 23 seeking permission to make a statement in terms approved by the court. The practice is now to make the application not to the judge but to the Senior Master, but the judge retains the right to approve the statement, since it is read in the judge's court. In the case of an agreed statement, if the Senior Master gives permission, the order is sealed and a setting down number is obtained from the Clerk of the Lists. A date convenient for both parties is arranged between counsel's clerks or between solicitors, and the signed statement is released to the judge for mention. It is unusual for a bilateral statement to be refused by the court, but the court will refuse permission if informed that one of the parties proposing to join in the statement believes that it is false:

> "It is one thing for the court to be unable to guarantee that all its judgments or verdicts are the whole truth. It is quite another for the court to permit itself to be used for the making of a statement that the maker is at the same time declaring he believes to be untrue" (per Tugendhat J., *Adelson v Associated Newspapers Ltd (No.3)* [2008] EWHC 278 (QB) [67], [70]).

An application for permission to make a unilateral statement is also made to the Senior Master, but if it is opposed or not agreed he will generally refer the application to the judge (see *Phillips v Associated Newspapers Ltd* [2004] EWHC 190; [2004] 1 W.L.R. 2106). If it is known to be opposed, it should be made direct to the judge (see *Phillips, ibid*).

Where a statement is opposed

53PD.44 When the claimant applies to make a statement, the defendant has the right to be heard and to object to its wording (see for instance *Charlton v EMAP*, *The Times*, June 11, 1993, where the defendant was not allowed to insist on a reference to a payment in having been made for "commercial reasons"). Subject to a defendant's objections, the court will generally give permission to make a statement, particularly when the libel has been widely publicised, although if the sum offered is very small compared with the gravity of the libel permission may be refused (see for instance *Church of Scientology v North News* (1973) 117 S.J. 566, where the plaintiff accepted a payment of £50 and was refused leave to make a statement). It would be quite exceptional for the court to refuse permission for the making of a reasonable and proportionate statement: see *Phillips v Associated Newspapers Ltd* [2004] EWHC 190; [2004] 1 W.L.R. 2106. Note that in that case Eady J. held that where a claimant has accepted a Pt 36 offer, the costs of any application to make a unilateral statement, and of the making of the statement itself, will generally fall to be paid by the defendant as an integral part of the costs of the action.

Where the action has settled, the terms of the statement will usually be agreed, but a second defendant who is not party to the settlement may wish to be heard (as in *Barnet v Crozier* [1987] 1 W.L.R. 272). Where parties reach a bona fide settlement, and ask for permission to make a statement in court, permission ought to be granted unless, taking into account the interests of all parties affected and the risk of prejudice to the fair trial of any outstanding issue, sufficient reason appears from the material before the judge for it to be refused (*ibid.*). It appears that a third party affected by a statement also has standing to apply to the court not to approve it: see *Virgin Atlantic Airways v British Airways* January 11, 1993, unrep., in which Drake J. allowed a third party to make representations and to make his own statement challenging what was said.

Offer of amends

A statement may also be made where an offer of amends is accepted by the aggrieved party, but there is no agreement on the steps to be taken by way of correction, apology and publication. In that case, the offeror may make the correction and apology by a (presumably unilateral) statement in terms approved by the court: Defamation Act 1996 s.3(4). However, such a statement would not fall within the terms of para.6 of the Practice Direction. **53PD.45**

Transitional Provision Relating to Section 4 of the Defamation Act 1952

7. Paragraph 3 of this practice direction applies, with any necessary modifications to an application to the court to determine any question as to the steps to be taken to fulfil an offer made under section 4 of the Defamation Act 1952. **53PD.46**

(Section 4 of the Defamation Act 1952 is repealed by the Defamation Act 1996. The commencement order bringing in the repeal makes transitional provision for offers which have been made at the date the repeal came into force.)

Offer of amends under section 4 of the Defamation Act 1952

This paragraph is a dead letter. There cannot now be any outstanding offers of amends made before February 28, 2000, under the 1952 Act, a procedure which in any event was unusable and unused. **53PD.47**

PART 54

JUDICIAL REVIEW AND STATUTORY REVIEW

Contents

54.0.1

I. Judicial Review

II. Statutory Review under the Nationality, Immigration and Asylum Act 2002

III. Applications for Statutory Review under section 103A of the Nationality, Immigration and Asylum Act 2002

Editorial introduction

Section 31 of the Supreme Court Act 1981 and Pts 8 and 54 of the Civil Procedure Rules deal with the rules applicable to judicial review. SCA 1981 s.31 provides that an application to the High Court for (a) a quashing order, a mandatory or prohibiting order (formerly known as certiorari, mandamus or prohibition respectively), (b) a declaration or injunction (in the circumstances set out in s.31(2)) and (c) an application for an injunction under s.30 restraining a person from acting in an office to which that section applies when he is not entitled to do so shall be made in accordance with rules of court by a procedure to be known as "an application for judicial review" (Civil Procedure, Vol.2, para.9A–101). **54.0.2**

Part 8 of the CPR, as modified by Pt 54, read with SCA 1981 s.31 now contains the procedural rules governing claims for judicial review. These rules govern the way that the courts exercise their supervisory jurisdiction over the proceedings and decisions of bodies performing public law duties or functions. They replace the former RSC O.53, introduced in 1977, which previously set out the rules governing the making of applications for judicial review and which is now revoked.

A claim for judicial review is a two-stage process. The claimant must first seek permission to apply for judicial review (see r.54.4). The claimant must file and serve a claim form on the defendant and interested parties who in turn must file and serve an acknowledgement of service setting out in summary the grounds for contesting the claim. The court then decides, on the basis of those documents, whether to grant permission. Then, if permission is granted, the claim can proceed, the defendant and any interested party may put in written evidence and there will be a hearing of the substantive claim for judicial review.

The changes to the judicial review procedure were introduced following a review of the Crown Office under Sir Jeffrey Bowman. The report of the review team was submitted to the Lord Chancellor in March 2000.

Part III deals with applications for an order requiring the Asylum and Immigration Tribunal ("AIT") to reconsider a decision made by it on an appeal under ss.82 and 83 of the Nationality, Immigration and Asylum Act 2002 ("the 2002 Act"). Such orders may only be made where the Administrative Court considers that the AIT may have made an error of law and there is a real possibility that the AIT would make a different decision on reconsideration: see s.103A of the 2002 Act and r.54.33. There is a filter provision whereby such applications are first considered by a member of the AIT who may grant or refuse an order requiring consideration: see para.30 of Sch.2 to the Asylum (Treatment of Claimants, etc.) Act 2004. Where an order is refused, the claimant may make an application to the Administrative Court in accordance with s.103A of the 2002 Act and r.54.31.

Entry into force and Transitional Provisions

Part 54 I of the CPR was introduced by the Civil Procedure (Amendment No.4) Rules 2000 (SI 2000/2092) which came into force on October 2, 2000. **54.0.3**

Rule 22 and Sch.1 to the rules insert Pt 54 into the CPR. Rule 23 revokes the former RSC O.53. Part 54, however, only applies to applications for permission (and the related application for judicial review) made on or after October 2, 2000. Where a person has filed an application for permission to make an application for judicial review before October 2, 2000 in accordance with RSC O.53, Pt 54 does not apply and RSC O.53 continues to apply to the application for permission and the related application for judicial review: see r.30 of the Civil Procedure (Amendment No.4) Rules 2000.

Part 54, Sect.II was introduced by the Civil Procedure Rules 2003 (SI 2003/364). It deals with appeals to the former Immigration Appeal Tribunal under s.101(2) of the Nationality, Immigration and Asylum Act 2002. That section ceased to have effect from April 4, 2005 but there are transitional provisions for applications in relation to appeals made under that section: see SI 2005/565. Part 54, Sect.III was introduced by the Civil Procedure (Amendment Rules) 2005 (SI 2005/352) and came into force on April 4, 2005.

Practice directions

54.0.4 This Part is supplemented by four practice directions. The first is of general application and the second and third deal with specific types of claim. The last of them, Practice Direction 54D (Administrative Court (Venue)), was first published in TSO CPR Update 49 and came into effect on April, 6, 2009. It contains provisions dealing with the place in which a claim before the Administrative Court should be started and administered and the venue at which it will be determined. A practice direction has also been issued renaming the Crown Office List and the Crown Office as the Administrative Court and Administrative Court Office respectively: Practice Direction (Administrative Court: Establishment) [2000] 1 W.L.R. 1654. There is a practice direction on termination of proceedings: see Practice Direction (Administrative Proceedings [2008] 1 W.L.R. 1377.

Pre-action Protocol

54.0.5 A pre-action protocol has been adopted for judicial review claims with effect from March 4, 2002.

Related sources

54.0.6
- Supreme Court Act 1981 s.31 (Vol.2, para.9A–101.)
- CPR Pt 8
- CPR r.52.15 (judicial review appeals)
- Nationality, Immigration and Asylum Act 2002
- Courts, Tribunal and Enforcement Act 2007

I. Judicial Review

Scope and interpretation[1]

54.1 **54.1—(1) This Section of this Part contains rules about judicial review.**

(2) In this Section—

(a) a "claim for judicial review" means a claim to review the lawfulness of-

(i) an enactment; or

(ii) a decision, action or failure to act in relation to the exercise of a public function.

(e) "the judicial review procedure" means the Part 8 procedure as modified by this Section;

(f) "interested party" means any person (other than the claimant and defendant) who is directly affected by the claim; and

[1] Introduced by the Civil Procedure (Amendment No.4) Rules 2000 (SI 2000/2092) and amended by the Civil Procedure Rules 2003 (SI 2003/364).

(g) "court" means the High Court, unless otherwise stated.
(Rule 8.1(6)(b) provides that a rule or practice direction may, in relation to a specified type of proceedings, disapply or modify any of the rules set out in Part 8 as they apply to those proceedings)

Amendment—r.54.1

In r.54.1(2), sub-paras (b), (c) and (d) were omitted by Civil Procedure (Amendment No.5) Rules 2003 (SI 2003/3361), which came into force on May 1, 2004. **54.1.1A**

Introduction: scope of judicial review

Judicial review is generally understood as describing the process by which the courts exercise a supervisory jurisdiction over the acts or omissions of public bodies in the field of public law. Judicial review is available only against public bodies, that is bodies exercising a power, or performing a duty, which involves "a public element" per Sir John Donaldson M.R. in *R. v Panel on Takeover and Mergers Ex p. Datafin* [1987] Q.B. 815 at p.838E. Judicial review is also available only where an issue of public law arises; a claim for judicial review cannot be used merely to enforce private law rights against a public body: *R. v East Berkshire Health Authority Ex p. Walsh* [1985] Q.B. 152 at p.162. A claim for judicial review may be brought only by a person with a sufficient interest in the matter to which the application relates: SCA 1981 s.31(3). **54.1.1**

That approach to the scope of judicial review is reflected in the definition of a claim for judicial review in r.54.1(2)(a) which provides that a claim for judicial review means a claim to review the lawfulness of an enactment or a decision, action or failure to act in relation to the exercise of a public function. That definition effectively encapsulates the scope of judicial review in English public law.

In the light of the provisions of r.54.1, the provisions of SCA 1981 s.31 and previous case law, the principal questions which arise in determining whether it is appropriate to bring a claim by way of a claim for judicial review, are namely,

(1) Against what persons or bodies does judicial review lie?
(2) Is the measure, action or omission challenged one that is amenable to judicial review?
(3) On what grounds does judicial review lie?
(4) Who can apply for judicial review?

Supreme Court Act 1981, s.29 was amended by the Civil Procedure Modification of Supreme Court Act 1981) Order 2004 (SI 2004/1033) and the prerogative orders were renamed quashing orders, mandatory orders and prohibiting orders. Consequently, with effect from May 1, 2004, r.54.1(2) was amended by the Civil Procedure (Amendment No.5) Rules 2003, so as to omit sub-paras (b), (c) and (d). Similar amendments were made to CPR Sch.1 RSC Ords 45, 79 and 93. Rule 54 3 was also amended by that statutory instrument (see para.54.3.9 below).

Against whom does judicial review lie

A claim for judicial review may be brought against an inferior court or tribunal or any person or body performing public duties or functions. Persons exercising powers or performing duties derived from statute or the prerogative are generally seen as public bodies for these purposes and actions and omissions done in the exercise of their statutory functions are generally amenable to judicial review (see, e.g. on statute, *R. v Secretary of State for Trade and Industry Ex p. Vardy* [1993] 1 C.M.L.R. 721; on the prerogative, *R. v Criminal Injuries Compensation Board Ex p. Lain* [1967] 2 Q.B. 864; *Council of Civil Service Unions v Minister for the Civil Service* [1985] A.C. 374—powers derived from the prerogative are public law powers amenable to judicial review provided they raise issues which are justiciable). **54.1.2**

Powers which are not derived from statute or the prerogative may, however, involve a sufficient public element to render the exercise of those powers amenable to judicial review. In *R. v Panel on Take-overs and Mergers Ex p. Datafin Ltd* [1987] Q.B. 815, the Court of Appeal held that judicial review did lie against the Take-over Panel, even though it was part of the self-regulatory system operated by the City, and did not derive its authority from statute or the exercise of the prerogative. The extent to which the activities of a body are underpinned by statute or is operating under the authority of the government or is woven into the fabric of governmental regulation are both relevant considerations in determining whether a body is a public body for the purposes of judicial review (see *R. v Panel on Take-overs and Mergers Ex p. Datafin Ltd* [1987] Q.B. 815). Other examples of non-statutory and non-prerogative powers being amenable to judicial review include, *R. v Advertising Standards Authority Ex p. The Insurance Service plc*, *The Times*, July 14, 1989 (the Advertising Standards Authority) and *R. v Code of Practice Committee of the British Pharmaceutical Ex p. Professional Counselling Aids Ltd* (1990) 10 B.M.L.R. 21. Conversely, judicial review was not available against bodies dealing with the affairs of purely religious bodies or bodies regulating horseracing, football or travel agents as there was no suggestion that those bodies were part of a system of government regulation of those activities or that the government would regulate the activities if those bodies did not exist: see, e.g. *R. v Chief Rabbi of the United Hebrew Congregations of Great Britain and the Commonwealth Ex p. Wachmann* [1992] 1 W.L.R. 1036; *R. v Disciplinary Committee of the Jockey Club Ex p. The Aga Khan* [1993] 1 W.L.R. 909; *R. v Football Association Ex p. Football League* [1993] 2 All E.R. 833. The courts have left open the position in relation to the Press Complaints Commission (*R. v Press Complaints Commission Ex p. Stewart-Brady* (1997) 9 Admin. L.R. 2742) and the BBC (*R. v BBC Ex p. Referendum Party* [1997] E.M.L.R. 605). In addition, where a public body is under a statutory duty to make arrangements to provide a particular service, and it makes arrangements by means of a contract with a company, then that company does not owe any public law duties and its actions are not amenable to judicial review. Thus, where a local authority discharged its duty to make arrangements to provide residential accomodation to vulnerable groups by means of a contract with a private company whereby the company provided residential accomodation, that private company was not subject to judicial review: the company did not owe its existence or its ability to enter into a contract to any statutory provision and there was insufficient statutory underpinning of its activities to make its functions public law functions: see *R. v Servite Houses and Wandsworth LBC Ex p. Goldsmith* [2001] L.G.R. 55. Nor do such companies exercise public functions for the purpose of s.6 of the Human Rights Act 1998: see *Johnson v Birmingham City Council (Secretary of State for Constitutional Affairs intervening)* [2008] 1 A.C. 95.

The courts have also consistently held that a body which derives its authority from contract or from a consensual submission to the jurisdiction by the parties to its jurisdiction will not normally be a public body and cannot be made the subject of a claim for judicial review: see *Law v National Greyhound Racing Club* [1983] 1 W.L.R. 1302; *R. v Disciplinary Committee of the Jockey Club Ex p. Aga Khan* [1993] 1 W.L.R. 909 (domestic tribunals or sporting bodies acquiring jurisdiction by contract not amenable to judicial review; quaere whether a decision which did not in fact derive from any agreement or contract between the body and the individual seeking to challenge it could be the subject of judicial review).

The current approach is conveniently summarised in the decision of the Divisional Court in *R. v Insurance Ombudsman Bureau Ex p. Aegon Life Insurance Limited*, *The Times* January 7, 1994. The court held that judicial review would not lie against a body whose birth and constitution owed nothing to any exercise of governmental power; a body could be classed as public only if it had been woven into the fabric of public regulation or into a system of governmental control, or was integrated into a system of statutory regulation or, but for its existence, a governmental body would assume control. Judicial review did not lie against a body whose powers derived from the agreement of the parties and when private law remedies were available against the body concerned. The Insurance Ombudsman Bureau fell into the latter category because it was a body whose jurisdiction was dependent on the contractual consent of its members and its decisions were of a private law arbitrative nature. See generally, Ch.2 of Lewis, *Judicial Remedies in Public Law* (3rd edn).

Judicial review is available to control the lawfulness of acts or omissions of inferior courts and tribunals. The superior courts, however, such as the High Court, Court of Appeal, and Judicial Committee of the House of Lords, are not amenable to judicial review. The Crown Court is amenable to judicial review except in matters relating to trial on indictment (see SCA 1981 s.29(3)).

Judicial review is only available as against public bodies in relation to their public functions. It is not available to enforce purely private law rights against public bodies. Thus, a claim to enforce a purely private law right, such as a contractual right, against a public body cannot be brought by way of a claim for judicial review: see, e.g. *R. v East Berkshire Health Authority Ex p. Walsh* [1985] Q.B. 152. That restriction is reflected in the wording of Pt 54.1(2)(ii) which deals with claims relating to the lawfulness of decisions, actions or failures to act in relation to the exercise of a public function. That wording is not apt to encompass a claim to enforce a purely private law right.

Is the measure, action or omission challenged one that is amenable to judicial review?

Rule 54.1(2)(a) defines a claim for judicial review as a claim to review the lawfulness of an enactment or a decision, action or failure to act. So far as primary legislation is concerned, the courts have jurisdiction to determine whether an Act of Parliament is compatible with European Union law and, if it conflicts with any directly effective provision of European Union law, it must disapply the provisions of the Act of Parliament and give precedence to the relevant provisions of European Union law: see *R. v Secretary of State for Transport Ex p. Factortame (No.2)* [1990] 1 A.C. 603; *R. v Secretary of State for Employment Ex p. Equal Opportunities Commission* [1995] 1 A.C. 1. Under the Human Rights Act 1998, the courts also have jurisdiction to determine whether an Act of Parliament is compatible with certain rights derived from the European Convention on Human Rights. The courts may only grant a declaration that the legislation is incompatible; they cannot set aside or disapply legislation which conflicts with a Convention right: see ss.3 and 4 of the Human Rights Act 1998. Subject to those qualifications, the constitutional position is that the courts have no jurisdiction to review the lawfulness of Acts of Parliament as the Queen-in-Parliament is sovereign and there are no restrictions on its competence: see, e.g. *Manuel v Attorney General* [1983] Ch. 77. Similarly, the courts will not investigate the internal proceedings of Parliament to determine whether or not its internal procedures were observed: see *Pickin v British Railways Board* [1974] A.C. 765. See also *R. (Jackson) v Attorney General* [2006] 1 A.C. 262 (court able to determine whether Parliament Act 1949 was within scope of the acts that could be enacted in accordance with the provisions of the Parliament Act 1911 by the Queen and Commons alone). **54.1.3**

Enactments also include subordinate legislation. This takes a variety of forms such as Orders in Council or regulations made by statutory instruments. Judicial review is available to review the lawfulness of subordinate legislation on the usual grounds of error of law, procedural impropriety or irrationality. Exceptionally, the courts will not review subordinate legislation to determine whether it is irrational where that subordinate legislation involves the formulation or implementation of national economic policy and can only take effect once approved by the House of Commons unless there is an element of bad faith, improper purpose or manifest absurdity: see *R. v Secretary of State for the Environment Ex p. Hammersmith and Fulham LBC* [1991] 1 A.C. 521. The courts may, exceptionally, review the lawfulness of subordinate legislation even before it is laid before Parliament: see, e.g. *R. v HM Treasury Ex p. Smedley* [1985] Q.B. 657; *R. v Boundary Commission for England Ex p. Foot* [1983] Q.B. 600.

Rule 54.1(2) also defines a claim for judicial review as including a claim to review the lawfulness of a decision, action or failure to act. This definition is a reflection of the existing scope of English public law, that is, it is intended to enable the courts to control unlawful exercises of public power or unlawful failures to perform public duties. The courts have taken a broad view of the measures that may be subject to judicial review, and the width of that jurisdiction is reflected in the words in Pt 54 which provide for review of a decision, action or failure to act. It is unlikely that Pt 54 was intended in any way to restrict the existing jurisdiction (and, if it had sought to do so, it may well have been ultra vires). The measures in respect of which judicial review lies include a wide range of decisions affecting a person's liberty or his rights, interests, or expectations or claims for benefits. They also include preliminary and procedural decisions. The courts have also granted judicial review of a number of other types of measures, such as recommendations (e.g. *R. v Hallstrom Ex p. W* [1986] Q.B. 1090), reports (e.g. *Mahon v Air New Zealand* [1984] A.C. 808), advice or guidance (e.g. *R. v Secretary of State for the Environment Ex p. London Borough of Tower Hamlets* [1993] Q.B. 632 and *R. v Secretary of State for the Environment Ex p. Lancashire CC* [1994] 4 All E.R. 165; *Gillick v West Norfolk and Wisbech Area Health Authority* [1986] A.C. 112) and policies of central and local government and other public bodies (e.g. *R. v Secretary of State for the Home Department Ex p. Simms* [2000] 2 A.C. 115; *R. v Lewisham London BC Ex p. Shell U.K.* [1988] 1 All E.R. 938). All these measures constitute "action .. in relation to the exercise of a public function" and would equally be reviewable under the definition of a claim for judicial review in Pt 54.1(2)(ii).

Failure to act where there is a duty on a public body to act is also subject to judicial review. This may occur where a public body, such as an inferior court or tribunal, wrongly refuses to exercise its jurisdiction or where a public body wrongly refuses to carry out a public duty.

Where the courts consider that judicial review is inappropriate in relation to a particular type of public law power, the current trend is to regard judicial review as available in principle but likely to be granted only in exceptional circumstances (e.g. *R. v Lord Chancellor Ex p. Maxwell* [1997] 1 W.L.R. 104, judicial review of decision by Lord Chancellor as to which judges should hear a trial available in principle but, given the width of the statutory discretion, were unlikely to succeed in practice; *R. v DPP Ex p. C* (1994) 7 Admin. L. Rep. 385, judicial review of a decision to prosecute only likely to be reviewed in exceptional circumstances: see *Sharma v Brown-Antoine* [2007] 1 W.L.R. 780 at para.14(5) and cases cited there). Alternatively, the courts may refuse permission to apply for judicial review as a matter of discretion rather than holding that they have no jurisdiction to grant judicial review (e.g. *R. v Secretary of State for the Environment Ex p. Kensington and Chelsea RLBC* (1987) 19 H.L.R. 161: challenge to a decision of a planning inspector to refuse to admit evidence during a planning inquiry would normally be premature and permission for judicial review refused, as there were exceptional reasons in that case, however, permission was granted). Or the court may hold that a particular exercise of power raises issues that are not justiciable in that they raise issues which, by their nature, the courts are unable to resolve (e.g. *Council for Civil Service Unions v Minister for the Civil Service* [1984] A.C. 374, exercise of a power for reasons of national security not justiciable and *R. (Campaign for Nuclear Disarmament) v Prime Minister* [2002] EWHC 2777, December 17, 2002 (questions of foreign policy and the deployment of the armed forces, and in particular whether military action against Iraq was permitted under UN Resolution 1441, were not justiciable) *R. (Gentle) v Prime Minister* [2006] EWCA Civ 1689; [2007] 2 W.L.R. 195. See generally, Ch.4 of Lewis, *Judicial Remedies in Public Law* for a description of the acts and omissions of public bodies which are subject to judicial review.

On what grounds does judicial review lie?

54.1.4 The circumstances in which judicial review can be granted is a vast topic and in a commentary of this kind is it not practicable to give more than a brief outline (for a detailed analysis of the principles and authorities see de Smith, Jowell and Woolf, *Judicial Review of Administrative Action* and Wade and Forsyth, *Administrative Law*). In general, judicial review is concerned with reviewing not the merits of the decision in respect of which the application for judicial review is made, but the lawfulness of the decision-making process itself. The court is concerned with identifying whether or not one or more of the grounds of judicial review have been established. The court does not act as a "court of appeal" from the body concerned, nor will it interfere with the exercise of power or discretion by a public body unless that body has acted unlawfully in the sense that it has breached one of the relevant principles of public law developed by the courts to ensure that public bodies do not exceed or abuse their powers. In summary, the grounds upon which judicial review lies may be grouped under the following main headings.

Error of law

54.1.5 Judicial review will lie where an inferior court or tribunal or other public authority makes an error of law in exercising its powers or performing its duties. In the past, the courts have been troubled by the question of whether every error of law amounted to a jurisdictional error which the court was entitled to correct on judicial review or whether some questions of law were matters for the inferior court, tribunal or public authority to determine so that errors did not take them outside their jurisdiction and did not enable the courts to intervene by way of judicial review. The general approach of the courts at present is to regard almost every error of law by a public body as being amenable to judicial review (*R. v Bedwellty Justices Ex p. Williams* [1997] A.C. 225, summarising the relevant case law beginning with *Anisminic Ltd v Foreign Compensation Commission (No.2)* [1969] 2 A.C. 147 and continuing with *South East Asia Fire Bricks Sdn Bhd v Non Metallic Mineral Products Manufacturing Employees Union* [1981] A.C. 363 and *Re Racal Communications Ltd* [1981] A.C. 374; see also *R. v Lord President of the Privy Council Ex p. Page* [1993] A.C. 682 esp. at p.701). In addition, the courts historically had jurisdiction in respect of errors of law within jurisdiction which appeared on the face of the record (*R. v Northumberland Compensation Appeal Tribunal Ex p. Shaw* [1952] 1 K.B. 338; *Baldwin & Francis Ltd v Patents Appeal Commission* [1959] A.C. 663). What constitutes the record has now been widely interpreted and is not confined to the formal order but extends to the reasoning given by the judge in his or her written or oral judgment (*R. v Knightsbridge Crown Court Ex p. International Sporting Club (London)* [1982] Q.B. 304). The importance of review for errors of law on the face of the record has now declined as the courts have accepted that any error of law by a public body is normally subject to judicial review.

Procedural Impropriety

Judicial review will lie where there has been a breach of the common law rules of natural justice or procedural fairness (*Ridge v Baldwin* [1964] A.C. 40) or where there has been a failure to comply with any statutory procedural obligation, such as an obligation to consult prior to taking action. Broadly, the rules of natural justice require that a person be given a fair hearing before a decision affecting him is taken and that the decision maker is unbiased in the sense that there is no real danger that the decision maker will unfairly favour or disfavour that person *R. v Gough* [1993] A.C. 646; *Re Medicaments and Related Classes of Goods (No.2)* [2001] 1 W.L.R. 700 and *Porter v Magill* [2002] 2 A.C. 357. Whether the rules of natural justice or procedural fairness apply to a particular decision-making process, and what the actual requirements of fairness require, depends on the circumstances of the particular case. "The rules of natural justice - or of fairness - are not cut and dried. They vary infinitely" (*R. v Secretary of State for the Home Department Ex p. Santillo* [1981] Q.B. 778 per Lord Denning M.R.). The rules of natural justice will normally apply where the decision concerned affects a person's liberty or his rights as where his property is being taken or where he is dismissed from a public office (as in *Ridge v Baldwin* [1964] A.C. 40 where a chief constable was dismissed by the police authority). A person may also have a legitimate expectation that he will be given a hearing or consulted before a decision is taken (even if the decision is not one that would normally attract the duty to observe the principles of natural justice). Such a legitimate expectation might arise either because of a promise that a person would be consulted or a past practice of consulting or, if a person has enjoyed a benefit, he may have a legitimate expectation that he will be consulted before the benefit is removed: see, generally, *Council for Civil Service Unions v Minister for the Civil Service* [1984] A.C. 374. **54.1.6**

Irrationality and the Wednesbury principle

Decisions of public authorities are liable to be quashed or otherwise dealt with by an appropriate order in judicial review proceedings if the court concludes that no person properly directing itself as to the relevant law could reasonably have reached that decision on the material before it or if the decision is otherwise irrational: *Associated Picture Houses Ltd v Wednesbury Corp* [1948] 1 K.B. 223. **54.1.7**

The heightened "super-Wednesbury" standard of review applied in fundamental rights cases has been held to be an ineffective remedy under ECHR art.13, for at least some human rights matters (see *Smith & Grady v United Kingdom* (2000) 29 E.H.R.R. 493).

Abuse of power generally

The courts have developed other principles of public law enforceable by way of judicial review to ensure that public bodies do not abuse their powers. Some of these principles can be seen as aspects of the grounds of judicial review already discussed; others have a seperate role to play. These principles include ensuring that public bodies exercise their powers in order to further the statutory purpose for which the powers were conferred and do not act for an improper or ulterior purpose (*Padfield v Minister of Agriculture Fisheries & Food* [1968] A.C. 997). Public bodies must take into account relevant considerations, i.e. ones that are expressly or impliedly relevant to the exercise of the discretion in question or which are drawn to their attention. They must not take into account irrelevant considerations. They may adopt general policies governing the way in which they will exercise their discretion but they may not fetter their discretion by applying the policy unduly rigidly (*British Oxygen Co v Minister of Technology* [1971] A.C. 610; *R. v North West Lancashire Health Authority Ex p. A* [2000] 1 W.L.R. 977). They may not unlawfully delegate their powers. if they propose to delegate powers to committee or officers, they must ensure that they have express or implied powers to do so and have, in fact, properly delegated the decision-making power to the committee or official in question. In exceptional circumstances, where a public body has created a legitimate expectation that a person would be entitled to a particular benefit, it may be so unfair as to amount to an abuse of power for the public **54.1.8** body to act in a way which breached that legitimate expectation (*R. v Inland Revenue Commissioners Ex p. Unilever plc* [1996] S.T.C. 681; *R. v Inland Revenue Commissioners Ex p. Preston* [1985] A.C. 835). In such circumstances, the person concerned may use the concept of legitimate expectations to ensure that a substantive benefit is concurred (*R. v North and East Devon Health Authority Ex p. Coughlan* [2001] Q.B. 213). Generally, such circumstances arise where the public body has made a clear, unambiguous and unqualified representation that it will act in a particular way, the person concerned has relied upon that representation to his detriment in some way and there is no overriding public interest justifying the decision to resile from the representation (*R. v IRC Ex p. MFK Underwriting Ltd* [1990] 1 W.L.R. 1545; *R. v Secretary of State for Education and Employment Ex p. Begbie* [2000] 1 W.L.R. 1115 and *Nadarajah v Secretary of State for the Home Department* [2005] EWCA Civ 1363).

In general, decisions on matter of fact are for the public body decision-maker. The courts may, however, review a decision where the public body has made an error of jurisdictional fact, i.e. an error as to the existence of some precedent fact which must exist before the public body acquires the power to act (*R. v Secretary of State Ex p. Khawaja* [1984] A.C. 74). The courts have also begun to consider whether judicial review should be allowed generally because of some mistake of fact (see *R. v Criminal Injuries Compensation Board Ex p. A* [1999] 2 A.C. 330 and *E v Secretary of State for the Home Department* [2004] EWCA Civ 49; [2004] Q.B. 1044).

There is no general duty at common law at present to provide reasons for decisions (*R. v Secretary of State for the Home Department Ex p. Doody* [1994] 1 A.C. 531). Reasons may, however, be required in certain cases because of the importance of the interests at stake or because the decision appears to be so aberrant that some explanation is called for (*R. v Higher Education Funding Council Ex p. Institute of Dental Surgery* [1994] 1 W.L.R. 242). In addition, particular statutes frequently impose obligations on particular tribunals or bodies to give reasons for their decision. Where reasons for a decision are given, they must be proper, adequate and intelligible reasons dealing with the main points raised (*South Bucks DC v Porter (No.2)* [2004] UKHL 33; [2004] 1 W.L.R. 1593).

Human Rights Act 1998

54.1.9 This Act incorporates certain of the rights contained in the European Convention on Human Rights into domestic law. Most of the relevant provisions of the Act came into force on October 2, 2000. Challenges may be brought against public bodies by way of claims for judicial review alleging that their actions have violated a person's Convention rights. Where such a claim is made, that fact must be stated in the claim form and precise details of the Convention right relied upon and the relief sought must be given: see para.5.3 of the Practice Direction—Judicial Review.

Court's discretion

54.1.10 Even if the claimant establishes one of the grounds of judicial review, the court is not bound to grant a remedy. The remedies are discretionary and, whilst a court will usually grant an appropriate remedy if the claimant establishes that the public body has acted unlawfully, there are cases where the courts may decline to grant a remedy see *R (Edwards) v Environment Agency* [2008] UKHL 22 at para.63.Grounds for refusing to grant a remedy include the following: where there was undue delay in making a claim but the courts have extended the time limits (see r.54.5 below), the courts may still refuse a remedy if granting a remedy would cause substantial hardship to or substantially prejudice the rights of any person or would be detrimental to good administration (SCA 1981 s.31(6)). A remedy may, exceptionally, even be refused if the claim was filed in time if granting a remedy would cause undue prejudice to third parties or the wider public interest (*R. v Brent LBC Ex p. O'Malley* (1998) 30 H.L.R. 328 but see cases in para.54.5.7). The courts may decline to grant a remedy if a remedy is no longer necessary because the issues have become academic or are no longer of practical significance (although the courts may still grant declaratory relief, particularly if the claim raises an issue which it is in the public interest to resolve and which is likely to arise in other cases in the near future (*R. v Secretary of State for the Home Department Ex p. Salem* [1999] A.C. 450)). The courts may refuse a remedy if they are satisfied that the individual has in fact suffered no prejudice by the error complained of or, if the court is satisfied that the public body would reach the same decision irrespective of the error. However, it is only in exceptional circumstances that the courts will reach such a conclusion (see *R (Smith) v NE Derbyshire Primary Care Trust* [2006] 1

W.L.R. 3315 and *Berkeley v Secretary of State for the Environment* [2001] 2 A.C. 603). The courts may refuse a remedy if it transpires that there was an adequate alternative remedy available which the claimant should have used rather than bringing a claim for judicial review, see, e.g. *R. v Secretary of State for the Home Department Ex p. Swati* [1986] 1 W.L.R. 477; [1986] 1 All E.R. 717; *R. v Birmingham City Council Ex p. Ferrero* [1993] 1 All E.R. 530; (1991) 155 J.P. 721; *R. (on the application of G) v Immigration Appeal Tribunal* [2005] EWCA Civ 1731; [2005] 1 W.L.R. 1445 and *R (Sinclair Gardens Investments Kensingston Ltd v Lands Tribunal* [2006] 3 All E.R. 650.

Standing: Who may apply for judicial review

A court may not grant permission to make an application for judicial review unless the claimant has sufficient interest in the matter to which the claim relates (SCA 1981 s.31(3)). The question of what is a sufficient interest is a mixed question of fact and law; a question of fact and degree having regard to the relationship between the claimant and the matter to which the claim relates and all the other circumstances of the case (*R. v Inland Revenue Commissioners Ex p. National Federation of Self Employed and Small Businesses Ltd* [1982] A.C. 617). **54.1.11**

If the claimant has a direct personal interest in the outcome of the claim, he will normally be regarded as having a sufficient interest in the matter. The term interest is not given a narrow construction but includes any connection, association or interrelation between the claimant and the matter to which the claim relates. If his interest is not direct or personal, but is a general or public interest, it will be for the courts to determine whether or not he has standing. The courts have recognised that a public spirited citizen may be allowed to seek judicial review where there is a serious issue of public importance to be tried (*R. v Secretary of State for Foreign and Commonwealth Affairs Ex p. Lord Rees-Mogg* [1994] Q.B. 552). Claims for judicial review are often made by public interest groups established to represent particular interests or campaign on particular issues. The courts have adopted an increasingly liberal approach to questions of standing over recent years. They consider a number of factors in deciding whether bodies have sufficient interest to bring a challenge including the merits of the challenge, the importance of vindicating the rule of law, the importance of the issue raised, the likely absence of any other responsible challenger, the nature of the breach and the role played by the group or body in respect of the issues in question (*R. v Secretary of State for Foreign and Commonwealth Affairs Ex p. World Development Movement Ltd* [1995] 1 W.L.R. 386).

The SCA 1981 s.31(3) requires the claimant to establish a "sufficient interest" at the stage of the application for permission. The House of Lords has held that the test for standing involves a two-stage process. At the permission stage, the question for the court is whether a sufficient interest has been shown to justify granting permission. Except in simple cases where it is appropriate at the earliest stage to find that the applicant has no standing, because for example, he is really no more than a "meddlesome busybody" (per Lord Donaldson M.R. in *R. v Monopolies and Mergers Commission, Ex p. Argyll Group Plc* [1986] 1 W.L.R. 763), it is generally undesirable for the courts to consider standing in detail as a preliminary issue, since the question of sufficient interest must be taken together with the legal and factual context of the claim and whether there has been a breach or failure to carry out statutory or other public duties: see *R. v Inland Revenue Commissioners Ex p. National Federation of Self Employed and Small Businesses Ltd* [1982] A.C. 617. If permission is granted, standing can be considered again at the substantive hearing to consider whether the claimant has sufficient interest to maintain his claim for a particular remedy. At this stage, questions of standing frequently overlap with the discretion of the court to grant or refuse a remedy (*R. v Secretary of State for Health Ex p. Presvac Engineering Ltd* (1991) 4 Admin. L.Rep. 121).

Prerogative remedies renamed

Supreme Court Act 1981, s.29 as amended by the Civil Procedure (Modification of the Supreme Court Act 1981) Order 2004 also renames the former prerogative remedies so that an order of mandamus is now called "a mandatory order", an order of prohibition a "prohibiting order" and an order of *certiorari* a "quashing order". **54.1.12**

Parties

The parties to a judicial review claim will be the claimant, the defendant and interested parties. The defendant will usually be the public body whose decision, action or failure to act is under challenge. An "interested party" is defined in r.54.1(1)(f) **54.1.13** as any person "who is directly affected by the claim". Under the former RSC O.53, r.5(3), applications for judicial review had to be served on persons directly affected and it is likely that the same definition of that term will apply to Pt 54. A person is directly affected if he is affected simply by reason of the grant of a remedy (*R. v Liverpool City Council Ex p. Muldoon* [1996] 1 W.L.R. 1103). In *Ex p. Muldoon*, the Secretary of State was not directly affected by a challenge to a decision of the local housing authority refusing to pay the applicant housing benefit. He was indirectly affected, in that he would be liable to pay 95 per cent of the benefit if the refusal to pay was quashed, but he was not directly affected by the grant of a remedy. Examples of persons directly affected include the recipient of a planning permission where an individual seeks to challenge the lawfulness of the grant of planning permission. The grant of a remedy, such as the quashing of the decision to grant planning permission, would directly affect the rights of the person with the benefit of the planning permission. The courts also have power to allow any other person to file evidence or appear at a judicial review hearing (CPR r.54.17).

Meaning of judicial review procedure

54.1.14 The judicial review procedure, for the purposes of Pt 54, means the Pt 8 procedure for bringing a claim as modified by Pt 54 (CPR r.54.1(1)(e)).

When this section must be used[1]

54.2 **54.2 The judicial review procedure must be used in a claim for judicial review where the claimant is seeking—**

(a) a mandatory order;

(b) a prohibiting order;

(c) a quashing order; or

(d) an injunction under section 30 of the Supreme Court Act 1981 (restraining a person from acting in any office in which he is not entitled to act).

Judicial review remedies

54.2.1 The judicial review procedure must be used when the claimant is seeking one of the prerogative orders, now known as a quashing order, a mandatory order or a prohibiting order. These remedies were developed to enable the courts to exercise its supervisory jurisdiction to review the lawfulness of the acts of inferior courts, tribunals and public bodies. These remedies can only be used challenges to public bodies which raise public law issues. All the prerogative remedies are discretionary.

A quashing order is an order which brings up into the High Court a decision of an inferior court, tribunal or other public authority for it to be quashed or set aside. Thus, where in judicial review proceedings, the court concludes that a decision of an inferior court, tribunal or other public authority should be set aside, a quashing order would normally be the appropriate order. Where the court quashes a decision, it has power to remit the matter to the decision-maker: see r.54.19.

A mandatory order is an order requiring an inferior court, tribunal or other public body charged with a public duty to carry out its judicial or other public duty. A mandatory order may, therefore, be granted requiring an inferior court or tribunal to hear a case where it wrongly held that it has no jurisdiction to hear a case. It may also be granted where an inferior court or tribunal is obliged to state a case but is refusing to do so. In addition, there are statutory provisions under which a mandatory order, requiring a case to be stated, may be directed to the Crown Court (s.29(3) of the Supreme Court Act 1981) or a magistrates' court (s.111(6) of the Magistrates' Courts Act 1980). A mandatory order can issue to require a public body such as a minister or local authority, to carry out a specific act, if it is under a statutory duty to do that act. In practice, the courts do not generally grant a mandatory order against public bodies in such circumstances, but grant a declaration setting out the scope of the public body's duty and rely upon the public authority to comply.

---

[1] Introduced by the Civil Procedure (Amendment No.4) Rules 2000 (SI 2000/2092) and amended by the Civil Procedure Rules 2003 (SI 2003/364).

A mandatory order cannot be made against the Crown (s.40 of the Crown Proceedings Act 1947) but it will lie against an officer of the Crown, including a minister, who is obliged by statute to perform a duty (see, dicta of Lord Woolf in *M v Home Office* [1994] 1 A.C. 377 at p.425).

A prohibiting order is an order restraining an inferior court, tribunal or other public body from acting outside its jurisdiction or from otherwise abusing its powers. Thus, for example, where a tribunal is proposing to adjudicate upon some matter which is not within its jurisdiction, a prohibiting order may be granted on a claim for judicial review to restrain the tribunal from acting. A prohibiting order may be granted before the inferior court, tribunal or other public authority has made any decision: *R. v Electricity Commissioners* [1924] K.B. 171; *R. v Minister of Health* (1929) 45 T.L.R. 176.

An application for an injunction under s.30 of the Supreme Court Act 1981 restraining a person from acting in a public office can also only be sought by means of a claim for judicial review.

When this section may be used[1]

54.3—(1) The judicial review procedure may be used in a claim for judicial review where the claimant is seeking— 54.3

(a) a declaration; or

(b) an injunction(GL).

(Section 31(2) of the Supreme Court Act 1981 sets out the circumstances in which the court may grant a declaration or injunction in a claim for judicial review)

(Where the claimant is seeking a declaration or injunction in addition to one of the remedies listed in rule 54.2, the judicial review procedure must be used)

(2) A claim for judicial review may include a claim for damages, restitution or the recovery of a sum due but may not seek such a remedy alone.

(Section 31(4) of the Supreme Court Act 1981 sets out the circumstances in which the court may award damages, restitution or the recovery of a sum due on a claim for judicial review)

Cases when the judicial review procedure may be used

The jurisdiction to grant injunctions is contained in s.37 of the Supreme Court Act 1981. Declarations and injunctions may be sought in a claim for judicial review either alongside of, or instead of, the prerogative remedies. SCA 1981 s.31(2) provides that the courts may grant a declaration or injunction instead or in addition to one of the prerogative remedies where it is just and convenient to do so, having regard to (a) the nature of the matters in respect of which relief may be granted by mandatory orders, quashing orders and prohibiting orders (b) the nature of the body against whom relief may be granted by such orders and (c) all the circumstances of the case. The prerogative orders lie against a public body where issues of public, as opposed to purely private, law arise. Similarly, declarations and injunctions may only be sought by way of the judicial review procedure in such public law cases. Thus the judicial review procedure may not be used to seek a declaration or injunction against a body which derives its jurisdiction over others from contract and which is not a public body: see, e.g. *Law v National Greyhound Racing Club* [1983] 1 W.L.R. 1302. Similarly, the judicial review procedure cannot be used to enforce purely private law rights against a public body: see, e.g. *R. v East Berkshire Health Authority Ex p. Walsh* [1985] Q.B. 152. 54.3.1

Distinction between public law and private law

The judicial review procedure has special provisions designed to protect public bodies, most notably, a short time limit and the need to obtain permission. Declara- 54.3.2

[1] Introduced by the Civil Procedure (Amendment No.4) Rules 2000 (SI 2000/2092) and amended by the Civil Procedure Rules 2003 (SI 2003/364).

tions and injunctions remain available by way of an ordinary Pt 7 or Pt 8 claim where these restrictions do not apply. The courts have had to consider the extent to which a declaration or injunction may be sought by way of an ordinary claim when the claim raises public law issues that could have been brought by way of a claim for judicial review.

The House of Lords has held that, as a general rule, it is contrary to public policy and as such an abuse of process for a person seeking to establish that a decision or action of a person or body infringes rights which are entitled to protection under public law, to proceed by way of an ordinary claim rather than the judicial review procedure, thereby evading the provisions intended to protect public authorities (*O'Reilly v Mackman* [1983] 2 A.C. 237; this dealt with the provisions of the former RSC O.53, but the relevant provisions of Pt 54 are materially identical and there is no reason to believe that the law in relation to Pt 54 is any different from that previously applicable). If a person commences an ordinary Pt 7 claim in circumstances where he should have complied with the judicial review procedure (that is, Pt 8 as modified by Pt 54), the claim will be struck out. Thus ordinary proceedings by prisoners seeing declarations that the decisions of the Board of Visitors of a prison were unlawful on the grounds that they failed to comply with the rules of natural justice were struck out as they raised public law issues which should have been challenged by way of judicial review (*O'Reilly v Mackman* above).

The precise scope of the rule in *O'Reilly v Mackman* is still a matter of debate. Two main approaches have been canvassed in the case law. One approach is that the rule does not apply to claims which are brought to vindicate private law rights even though they involve a challenge to a public law decision or action and may involve determining questions of public law. If this approach is adopted, then the aggrieved person will only be forced to proceed by way of a claim for judicial review where private law rights are not at stake, that is in a case which only raises issues of public law. The alternative approach is that the rule in *O'Reilly v Mackman* applies to all cases where the claim involves a challenge to a public law decision or action or involves determining questions of public law (subject to certain limited exceptions) whether or not the ultimate aim of the proceedings is to vindicate a private law right. In *Roy v Kensington and Chelsea and Westminster Family Practitioner Committee* [1992] 1 A.C. 624, the House of Lords left open the question of which of these approaches should be adopted but indicated a preference for the first approach. There, the House held that a claim by a general medical practitioner that the Family Practitioner Committee had acted unlawfully in deciding to reduce the amount that he was paid by way of a practice allowance under the NHS regulations was a claim that could be litigated by way of an ordinary claim notwithstanding the fact that the claim involved a challenge to a public law decision said to be unlawful on public law grounds. The claimant had not therefore abused the process of the court by not making an application for judicial review and his claim would not be struck out. The House of Lords said that, even assuming that the rule in *O'Reilly v Mackman* generally required all challenges to public law decisions or actions to be brought by way of judicial review, subject to certain exceptions, this case was either not within the rule or was excepted from it because the claimant's claim was based either on a contractual or statutory private law right to be paid his remuneration in accordance with his terms of service. Accordingly, private law rights dominated the proceedings and the order sought (payment of the full amount of the practice allowance) was one which could not be made in judicial review proceedings. In *Mercury Ltd v Telecommunications Director* [1996] 1 W.L.R. 48, the House of Lords said that it was important to retain flexibility, that the precise limits of what is called private law and public law are by no means worked out, and that private law proceedings should only be struck out if they are an abuse of the process of the court. For further discussion, see also *Gillick v West Norfolk & Wisbech Area Health Authority* [1986] A.C. 112 and *Trustees of Dennis Rye Pension Fund v Sheffield City Council* [1998] 1 W.L.R. 1629. See generally Ch.3 in Lewis, *Judicial Remedies in Public Law*.

In *Clark v University of Lincolnshire and Humberside* [2000] 1 W.L.R. 1988, the Court of Appeal again indicated that a claim based on an alleged breach of a contractual relationship between the claimant and the public authority defendant should not be struck out simply because the issues raised could have been litigated by means of a claim for judicial review. Such claims could be brought by way of an ordinary claim, but the Court of Appeal indicated that the courts could use their powers under the CPR to strike out such claims where there had been an abuse of process. One of the most significant differences between ordinary claim proceedings and judicial review is the time-limit for instituting proceedings: in ordinary claims, the time-limit is usually six years whilst in judicial review a claimant must apply for permission promptly and in any event within three months. The Court of Appeal indicated in *Clark* that, whilst commencing proceedings within the statutory limitation period for bringing ordinary private law proceedings would not of itself be an abuse, the court could have regard to the delay in commencing proceedings if in fact the claim was one that would normally have been brought by way of judicial review. The courts could, therefore, strike out a claim if, having regard to the entirety of the circumstances, including the availability of judicial review and the delay in commencing proceedings, the court's process was being misused or if it was clear that, because of the lapse of time or other circumstances, no worthwhile relief would be granted in the ordinary proceedings.

There are recognised exceptions to the rule in *O'Reilly v Mackman*, whatever its proper scope. Thus, it is permissible to litigate public law issues in ordinary private law claims where, for instance, the invalidity of a public law decision arises as a collateral issue in a claim for the infringement of a private law right or where none of the parties objects to the proceedings being continued by way of ordinary claim (*O'Reilly v Mackman*). The invalidity of a public law action or decision, which is an integral part of a public body's claim, may also be raised as a substantive defence in civil proceedings (*London Borough of Wandsworth v Winder* [1985] A.C. 461) although a challenge merely to the decision by a public body to institute civil proceedings should be brought by way of judicial review (*Avon CC v Buscott* [1988] Q.B. 656 but see dicta in *Doherty v Birmingham City Council* [2008] UKHL 57 suggesting that these issues can be raised by way of a defence to possession proceedings.). Where a person is charged with contravening a public law measure such as subordinate legislation or a byelaw, he may generally raise the invalidity of that measure as a defence to the criminal charge (*Boddington v British Transport Police* [1999] 2 A.C. 143). The exception to this rule arises only in those rare circumstances where the provisions creating the criminal offence make it an offence to comply with a particular measure, whether or not that measure is invalid (*R. v Wicks* [1998] 2 A.C. 92).

See also the decision of the Court of Appeal in *Wandsworth London BC v A.* [2000] 1 W.L.R. 1246 on the extent to which a defendant may raise the invalidity of the actions of a public body as a defence to a claim by a public authority.

Injunctions

It is now clear that injunctions, including interim injunctions, are available against **54.3.3**
all public bodies including ministers and Crown servants acting in their official capacity (*M. v Home Office* [1994] 1 A.C. 377).

Interim Remedies

At any time in the course of judicial review proceedings, the court may grant any **54.3.4**
interim remedy in accordance with Pt 25 of the CPR, in particular interim injunctions (CPR r.25.1(a)) and interim declarations (CPR r.25.1(b)). In addition, the court has inherent jurisdiction to grant a stay (see CPR r.54.10) or certain other forms of interim relief such as bail.

Procedure for claiming interim relief

A claim for such interim relief ought to be included in the claim for judicial review **54.3.5**
(CPR r.54.6). Interim relief can be granted at any time, including, in urgent cases, before proceedings are started (CPR r.25.2). Thus, interim relief may be granted in urgent cases before permission to apply for judicial review is given (as was the case under RSC O.53: *M v Home Office* [1994] 1 A.C. 377). If a claimant seeks interim relief after the grant of permission, the procedure in CPR Pt 25 applies. Practical problems may arise if the claimant wishes to have a claim for interim relief determined before or *at the same time* as the grant of permission is being considered and guidance on this has now been issued: Practice Statement (Administrative Court: Listing and Urgent Cases) [2002] 1 W.L.R. 810: see para.54.4.1 below.

Test in considering whether to grant an interim injunction

The courts will consider whether the claim raises a serious issue to be tried, and if **54.3.6**
so where the balance of convenience, including the wider public interest, lies. The availability of damages is unlikely to be determinative of the grant of interim injunctions in most public law cases as they will either not be available or will not be an adequate remedy. In considering the balance of convenience as a whole, the courts must

have regard to the wider public interest (*Smith v Inner London Education Authority* [1978] 1 All E.R. 411; *Sierbein v Westminister City Council* (1987) 86 L.G.R. 431). See generally CPR Pt 25.

Interim Relief to give effect to European Union law

54.3.7 In *R. v Secretary of State for Transport Ex p. Factortame (No.2)* [1991] 1 A.C. 603, the European Court of Justice held that a national court must have jurisdiction to grant interim relief in order to ensure the full and effective protection of directly effective rights derived from European Community law. Where the claim is that domestic legislation contravenes European Community law, the test for determining whether to grant relief is, it seems at present, a matter for the national courts to decide. The House of Lords held that in such cases that:

(1) the balance of convenience was likely to be the deciding factor as there was unlikely to be an adequate remedy in damages available to either side;

(2) generally, the court should not restrain a public authority from enforcing apparently authentic national legislation unless the court was satisfied, having regard to all the circumstances, that the challenge to the law is, prima facie, so firmly based as to justify so exceptional a course being taken; but it is always a matter of discretion; and

(3) on the facts of the instant case, the applicants' challenge was, prima facie, a strong one and the balance of convenience came down in favour of the grant of the interim injunction sought.

Different considerations apply where the claimant is challenging the validity of European Union legislation such as a Directive or Regulation. Only the European Court of Justice can rule on the validity of such measures. If a national court has doubts as to the validity of such a measure, the proper course is for that court to refer the question of the validity of the measure to the European Court under art.234 of the EC Treaty *Foto-frost v Hauptzollamt Lubeck-Ost (Case C-314/85)* [1987] E.C.R. 4199). The national court should only grant interim relief suspending the operation of the measure pending the preliminary ruling of the European Court if they are satisfied that there are serious doubts as to the validity of the measure and there is an urgent need for interim relief in order to avoid serious and irreparable damage to the party seeking interim relief (*Atlanta Fruchthandelsgesellschaft mbH v Bundesamt fur Ernahrung und Forstwirtschaft (C465/93)* [1996] All E.R. (E.C.) 31; [1995] E.C.R. I-3761 and see *R.. (on the application of ABNA Ltd) v Secretary of State for Health* [2003] EWHC 2420; [2004] Eu. L.R. 88). The Court of Appeal has also held that a similar test applies in considering whether to grant interim relief to suspend domestic legislation intended to implement European Union legislation pending a ruling on the validity of the measure (*R. v Secretary of State for Health Ex p. Imperial Tobacco* [2001] 1 W.L.R. 127). By the time that the matter reached the House of Lords, the matter had become academic as the government had undertaken not to make any national regulations to implement a Directive in the light of the opinion of the Advocate General that the relevant European Directive was ultra vires. Three members of the House of Lords, however, expressed the view that it was at least arguable that the appropriate test was the European Community law test set out in *Atlanta* and, if they had had to decide the issue, they would have referred the matter to the European Court under art.234 EC. Two of their Lordships considered that the appropriate test in these circumstances for determining whether to grant interim relief was the domestic law test set out in *American Cyanamid*, not the European test, and considered that the matter was *acte clair* so that no reference would have been necessary. See *R. v Secretary of State for Health Ex p. Imperial Tobacco Limited* [2001] 1 W.L.R. 127.

Damages

54.3.8 A claim for damages may be included in a claim for judicial review (SCA s.31(4), CPR r.54.1(2)). Such a claim may, however, only be included in addition to a claim for one of the prerogative remedies or a declaration or injunction; a claimant may not seek damages alone in a claim for judicial review. Furthermore, damages may only be awarded if they could have been awarded in an ordinary claim, that is the claimant must be able to establish a private law cause of action or a claim under the Human *Rights Act 1998* (see, e.g. *R. (Bernard) v Enfield BC* [2002] EWHC 2282; [2003] U.K.H.R.R. 148; *Anufrijeva v Southwark LBC* [2003] EWCA Civ 1406; [2004] Q.B. 1124; and *R. (Greenfield) v Secretary of State for the Home Department* [2005] 1 W.L.R. 673). The judicial review procedure does not create any new right or remedy in damages; it simply provides that, if a claim for damages exists in private law, it may, in appropriate cases, be claimed in the judicial review procedure alongside the claim for a prerogative or other remedy to vindicate a public law right.

Restitution and award of liquidated sum

54.3.9 With effect from May 1, 2004, r.54.3 was amended by the Civil Procedure (Amendment No.5) Rules 2003, to allow the remedies of restitution and the award of a liquidated sum to be sought on a claim for judicial review.

Permission required[1]

54.4 **54.4 The court's permission to proceed is required in a claim for judicial review whether started under this Section or transferred to the Administrative Court.**

Procedure for determining applications for permission

54.4.1 Claims for judicial review may only be brought where the court has first granted the claimant permission to bring such a claim. Pt 54 introduces significant changes to the procedure for applying for permission. Before applying for permission, however, a claimant should normally comply with the pre-action protocol for judicial review. That requires the claimant to send a letter before action to the defendant. The letter should identify the decision, act or omission being challenged, set out a summary of the facts and the reasons for the challenge. A standard form letter is set out at Annex A to the pre-action protocol. The defendant should normally respond within 14 days, giving its response to the claim and indicating which parts of the claim, if any, is conceded. A standard form letter setting out the information that should be provided is set out at Annex B to the pre-action protocol. The claim should not normally be made until the 14 days for the reply has passed. However, the pre-action protocol does not affect the time-limit for filing a claim form and, if the time-limit is approaching, the safest course of action is to file and serve the claim form with an explanation of why the pre-action protocol was not followed. To make a claim, the claimant must first file a claim form in the Administrative Court Office. The claim form must contain the matters set out in CPR rr.8.3 and 54.6 (see para.54.6.1 below) together with the material required by the Practice Direction—Judicial Review. That claim form must also be served on the defendant and any interested person within seven days of being issued by the Administrative Court Office (CPR r.54.7). They must then file an acknowledgement of service (form **N462**) within 21 days and serve it as soon as reasonably practicable and not later than seven days on the claimant and any interested person (CPR r.54.8(2)). The acknowledgement of service must set out a summary of the grounds for contesting the claim (CPR r.54.8(4)).

The rules contemplate that the court will, in the first instance, deal with the application for permission by considering the papers alone and there will not generally be an oral hearing (see also para.8.4 of the Practice Direction). In particular, the claimant no longer has a right to have the permission determined at an oral hearing, although he has a right to request that any decision to refuse or limit the grant of permission be reconsidered at an oral hearing (CPR r.54.12(3)).

Difficulties have arisen where a claimant needs to have the application for permission considered urgently. The judicial review procedure in Pt 54 contemplates that applications for permission will be dealt with on the papers and after service of the claim form and the 21 days for filing the acknowledgment of service have passed. The Administrative Court has issued a practice statement giving guidance on this matter. Where there is a need for the application to be dealt with as a matter of urgency, the claimant should complete the prescribed form stating the need for urgency, the time scale sought for the consideration of the permission application and the date by which the substantive hearing needs to take place. The claim form and the request for urgent consideration must be faxed to the defendant and the interested parties who should be advised of the application. A judge will then consider the application for permission within that time scale: see Practice Statement (Administrative Courts: Lis-

[1] Introduced by the Civil Procedure (Amendment No.4) Rules 2000 (SI 2000/2092) and amended by the Civil Procedure Rules 2003 (SI 2003/364).

ing and Urgent Cases) [2002] 1 W.L.R. 810. The prescribed form for a Request for Urgent Consideration is form **N463**.

Difficulties may also arise where a claimant wishes to obtain interim relief or to obtain expedition. If interim relief is sought in judicial review proceedings, that application may need to be dealt with more quickly than the normal judicial review procedure allows for and would normally require an oral hearing (see, for the former practice under RSC O.53, *R. v Kensington & Chelsea Royal London Borough Ex p. Hammell* [1989] Q.B. 518 indicating that an oral hearing with notice to the other side would be required except in cases of urgency). The Practice Statement provides that where an interim injunction is sought then, in the Request for Urgent Consideration, the claim must, in addition to the information referred to above, provide a draft order and the grounds for seeking an injunction. The judge will then consider the application within the time requested and may make such order as he or she considers appropriate. The judge may also direct that an oral hearing take place within a specified time: see *Practice Statement* [2002] 1 W.L.R. 810. The preferable course of action would be to direct that the application for interim relief be listed for an oral hearing, if possible, with notice of the hearing to the defendant and interested parties so that all parties may attend and make representations. There may, of course, be situations of real urgency where this is not feasible. Here, the court could grant an interim order for a short period and direct that the matter be listed for an oral hearing before the end of that period or grant interim relief with liberty to the defendant to apply to discharge the order. See *R (Lawler) v Restormel BC* [2008] A.C.D. 3. The court may either grant permission to apply for judicial review at the time that it considers the request for urgent consideration (leaving only the application for interim relief to be dealt with at the oral hearing) or it may direct that both the application for permission and the application for interim relief be heard orally.

Test for granting permission

54.4.2 The purpose of the requirement for permission is to eliminate at an early stage claims which are hopeless, frivolous or vexatious and to ensure that a claim only proceeds to a substantive hearing if the court is satisfied that there is a case fit for further consideration. The requirement that permission is required is designed to "prevent the time of the court being wasted by busybodies with misguided or trivial complaints of administrative error, and to remove the uncertainty in which public officers and authorities might be left as to whether they could safely proceed with administrative action while proceedings for judicial review of it were actually pending although misconceived" (*R. v Inland Revenue Commissioners Ex p. National Federation of Self-employed and Small Businesses Ltd* [1982] A.C. 617 at p.642 per Lord Diplock). Permission will be granted only where the court is satisfied that the papers disclose that there is an arguable case that a ground for seeking judicial review exits which merits full investigation at a full oral hearing with all the parties and all the relevant evidence (*R. v Legal Aid Board Ex p. Hughes* (1992) 5 Admin. L. Rep. 623; *R. v Secretary of State for the Home Department Ex p. Rukshanda Begum and Angur Begum* [1990] C.O.D. 107 and *Sharma v Brown-Antoine* [2007] 1 W.L.R. 780 at para.14(4)).

Delay

54.4.3 In addition, the courts may refuse permission if there has been delay in filing a claim (CPR r.54.5 and para.54.5.1 below).

Discretion

54.4.4 The court may also refuse permission in the exercise of its discretion. In particular, the courts will not normally grant permission to apply for judicial review where an adequate alternative remedy existed which the claimant could use or could have used (*R. v Chief Constable of Merseyside Police Ex p. Calveley* [1986] Q.B. 424; *R. v Secretary of State for the Home Department Ex p. Swati* [1986] 1 W.L.R. 477 and *R. (on the application of G) v Immigration Appeal Tribunal* [2004] EWHC 588 (Admin); [2005] 1 W.L.R. 1445; *R. (on the application of Sivasubramaniam) v Wandsworth County Court* [2002] EWEA Civ 1738; [2004] 1 W.L.R. 2953; *R (Carnell) v Regents Park College and the Conference of Colleges Appeal Tribunal* [2008] EWHC 739 (Admin); [2008] E.L.R. 268 at paras 31–34). The courts may, however, grant permission to apply for judicial review in exceptional circumstances, or where the alternative remedy is not adequate in the circumstances or where there is some other reason which makes judicial review proceedings particularly appropriate (see, e.g. *R. v Hereford Magistrates Court Ex p. Rowlands* [1998] Q.B. 110).

Permission may also be refused, for example, if the claim is academic or if the claimant has not, in fact suffered any injustice.

Limited permission

The claim for judicial review will, usually, set out a number of grounds upon which it said that the public body has acted unlawfully. It is now generally accepted that the court may either grant permission for all the grounds to be argued or, alternatively, may refuse permission to argue certain grounds, because, for example, a particular ground of challenge does not raise an arguable point (*R. v Staffordshire CC Education Appeals Committee Ex p. Ashworth* (1996) Admin L. Rep. 373; *R. v Advertising Standards Authority Ex p. City Trading* [1997] C.O.D. 202). Part 54 implicitly recognises the power of the court to grant permission on certain grounds only as it expressly provides for a claimant to be able to request that a decision granting limited permission only be reconsidered at a hearing (CPR r.54.12). Similarly, where more than one decision is challenged, the court may grant permission to apply for judicial review of one or more decisions but refuse permission in respect of others. **54.4.5**

Time limit for filing claim form[1]

54.5—(1) The claim form must be filed— **54.5**

(a) promptly; and

(b) in any event not later than 3 months after the grounds to make the claim first arose.

(2) The time limit in this rule may not be extended by agreement between the parties.

(3) This rule does not apply when any other enactment specifies a shorter time limit for making the claim for judicial review.

Time limits and delay

A claim for judicial review must be made promptly and in any event within 3 months from the date upon which grounds of the claim arose. The test is promptness and a claim will not necessarily be made promptly simply because it has been made within the three months period (*R. v Independent Television Commission Ex p. TV NI Ltd*, *The Times*, December 30, 1991; *R. v Cotswold DC Ex p. Barrington Parish Council* (1997) 75 P & C.R. 515 at pp.523–523). The House of Lords has left open the question of whether the "promptness" test satisfies the requirement of European Union law and the European Convention on Human Rights: see *R. v Hammersmith and Fulham LBC Ex. p. Burkett* [2002] 1 W.L.R. 1593. Claimants should, however, operate on the basis that the rule is compatible until declared incompatible, *R. (Young) v Oxford City Council* [2002] EWCA Civ 990, judgment June 27, 2001 and see also *R. (Hardy) v Pembrokeshire CC* [2006] EWCA Civ 240; [2006] Env. L.R. 28. See also *Lemm v United Kingdom*, Application 41671/98 ECHR, unrep., July 5, 2002. The obligation to comply with the pre-action protocol by sending a letter before action and giving the defendant 14 days to reply does not remove the obligation to bring the claim promptly and certainly if it means that the claim would be lodged outside the three month period, the sensible course of action would be to lodge the claim and to explain, in the claim form, why the need for urgency meant that it was not possible to comply with the pre-action protocol. **54.5.1**

The time limit begins to run from the date when the grounds for the claim first arose. The time does not run from the date when the claimant first learnt of the decision or action under challenge nor from the date when the claimant considers that he had adequate information to bring the claim. Such matters may be relevant to the separate question of whether an extension of the time limit should be granted (*R. v Secretary of State for Transport Ex p. Presvac Engineering Ltd* at pp.133–134).

If the claim is for a quashing order in respect of a judgment, order or conviction, the time-limit runs from the date of that judgment, order or conviction (Practice Direction, para.4.1). If the challenge is to a particular decision or action, the time limit will usually run from the date when the decision or action was taken. The claimant

[1] Introduced by the Civil Procedure (Amendment No.4) Rules 2000 (SI 2000/2092).

must, however, challenge the substantive decision that is the real basis of his complaint. A claimant may, for example, fail to bring a challenge to a particular decision, and may then seek to challenge some later ancillary or consequential decision or approval of the earlier decision on the ground that the later decision is unlawful as it is based on the original decision which is also unlawful. In such situations the courts may find that the time-limit begins to run from the date of the earlier decision. The High Court has held, for example, that where a local education authority published proposals to close a school and the claimant wished to claim that the local education authority had acted unlawfully in publishing proposals (as the wrong committee within the authority took the decision), the time limit ran from the date of the earlier decision, not the date of the decision of the school organisation committee approving the proposals. As the claimant was out of time to challenge the earlier decision, the validity of that decision could not found a challenge to the lawfulness of the later decision of the school organisation committee: *R. (Louden) v Bury School Organisation Committee* [2002] EWHC 2749 (Admin) judgment, December 19, 2002. Different considerations may arise where one body takes a decision which is conditional on some other event occuring. Thus, in planning a local planning authority may resolve to grant planning permission on condition that some other requirement is first met. The House of Lords has held that: the time-limit begins to run from the actual grant of planning permission, not from the date of the resolution to grant permission: *R. v Hammersmith and Fulham LBC Ex. p. Burkett* [2002] 1 W.L.R. 1593.

A court may grant an extension of time under CPR Pt 3.1(2)(a) (previously, RSC O.53 itself provided that the court could extend the time if there was good reason to do so). The likelihood is that the courts will continue to apply the previous case law on RSC O.53 on whether there was a good reason for extending the time in deciding whether or not to grant an extension of time under CPR r.3.1 in a judicial review claim. The courts have always recognised that public law claims are unlike ordinary civil litigation and require strict adherence to the time limits contained in the rules governing judicial review (*R. v Institute of Chartered Accountants in England and Wales Ex p. Andreou* (1996) 8 Admin L.R. 557). The courts are likely to require that there is a good reason or adequate explanation for the delay and that extending the time limit will not cause substantial hardship or substantial prejudice or be deteremental to good administration. Under the former provisions of RSC O.53, r.4 the courts refused to accept that there was good reason for extending the time for making a judicial review application where the delay was the fault of the applicant's lawyers (*R. v Secretary of State for Health Ex p. Furneaux* [1994] 2 All E.R. 652). The courts have accepted that there was good reason for the delay if the applicant was unaware of the decision provided that he applied expeditiously once he became aware of it (*R. v Secretary of State for the Home Department Ex p. Ruddock* [1987] 1 W.L.R. 1482; *R. v Secretary of State for Foreign and Commonwealth Affairs Ex p. World Development Movement Ltd* [1995] 1 W.L.R. 386 at p.402). The fact that the claim raises issues of general public importance may be a reason for extending the time-limit (*R. v Secretary of State for the Home Department Ex p. Ruddock* [1987] 1 W.L.R. 1482; *S (Application for Judicial Review), Re* [1998] 1 F.L.R. 790). Delay caused by factors outside the applicant's control, such as delay in obtaining legal aid, may be excusable (*R. v Stratford-upon-Avon DC Ex p. Jackson* [1985] 1 W.L.R. 1319.

SCA 1981 s.31(6), provides that:

> "Where the High Court considers that there has been undue delay in making an application for judicial review, the court may refuse to grant (a) leave for the making of an application or (b) any relief sought on the application, if it considers that the granting of the relief sought would be likely to cause substantial hardship to, or substantially prejudice the rights of, any person or would be detrimental to good administration."

The House of Lords has considered the relationship between SCA 1981 s.31(6) and the former RSC O.53, r.3(4). The House has held that, if an application was not made promptly or within three months, there was undue delay for the purposes of SCA 1981 s.31(6). Consequently, even if there were good reasons for granting an extension, SCA 1981 s.31(6) applied and courts could either refuse permission or refuse a remedy at the substantive hearing if there were the requisite prejudice, hardship or detriment (*R. v Dairy Produce Quota Tribunal for England and Wales Ex p. Caswell* [1990] 2 A.C. 738. The courts are likely to take the same view of the relationship between SCA 1981 s.31(6) and CPR r.3.1(2)(a) and r.54.5. The matter is unlikely to be significant in practice as the courts retain a discretion to refuse permission or a remedy even if the claim is brought within time if it considers it appropriate to do so because of the prejudice to third parties or the detriment to good administration (*R. v Brent LBC Ex p. O'Malley* (1998) 30 H.L.R. 328 at pp.293–294; *R. v Gateshead MBC Ex p. Nichol* 87 L.G.R. 435).

A finding that there was undue delay in bringing the claim but that an extension of time is appropriate is final and cannot be re-opened by the defendant at the substantive hearing (*R. v Criminal Injuries Compensation Board Ex p. A.* [1999] 2 A.C. 330 dealing with RSC O.53 but the same reasoning would apply to CPR r.3.1(2)(a)). A defendant who wishes to allege that delay is a bar to the claim must therefore raise that issue in the acknowledgement of service and, if appropriate, may need to file written evidence to deal with the matter. This is a situation where the courts commonly direct that a paper application be dealt with at an oral hearing with both the claimant, defendant and interested parties appearing to make representations on the delay issue.

The Court of Appeal has added a qualification to the decision of the House of Lords in *Ex p. A*. The court has held that, where a court grants permission on the basis that the claim was brought promptly, the court dealing with the substantive hearing may still consider the question of whether the claim was made without undue delay for the purpose of deciding whether the discretionary grounds for refusing a remedy set out in s.31(6) of the Supreme Court Act 1981 apply. However, the Court of Appeal held that the defendant should only be able to recanvass the question of undue delay in such circumstances where (1) the judge hearing the initial application has expressly so indicated (2) if new and relevant material is produced at the substantive hearing (3) if, exceptionally, the issues as they have developed at the substantive hearing put a different aspect on the issue of promptness or (4) the judge has plainly overlooked a relevant matter or reached a decision *per incuriam*: see *R. (on the application of Lichfield Securities Ltd) v Lichfield DC* [2001] EWCA Civ 304.

Claim form[1]

54.6—(1) In addition to the matters set out in rule 8.2 (contents of the claim form) the claimant must also state- **54.6**

(a) the name and address of any person he considers to be an interested party;

(b) that he is requesting permission to proceed with a claim for judicial review; and

(c) any remedy (including any interim remedy) he is claiming.

Part 25 sets out how to apply for an interim remedy)

(2) The claim form must be accompanied by the documents required by the relevant practice direction.

Procedure for bringing a claim

A claim for judicial review is to be headed "The Queen on the application of (name of applicant) Claimant, versus the public body against whom the proceedings are brought Defendant" (*Practice Direction: The Administrative Court* [2000] 1 W.L.R. 1654). The appropriate claim form is Form **N461**. The claim form must contain (1) the claimant's name and his solicitors' name and address (or the claimant's address); (2) the name and address of any defendant; (3) the name of any interested parties; (3) the fact that the claimant is applying for permission to apply for judicial review; (4) the remedies sought (including any interim remedy or a stay); (5) a detailed statement of the grounds for bringing the claim; (6) a statement of the facts relied upon; (7) any application for an extension of time for filing the claim form; (8) any application for directions (e.g. that expedition and abridgment of the time for service of the detailed grounds of resistance and written evidence if permission is granted); and (9) a time estimate for the substantive hearing of the application for judicial review if permission is granted (see generally, CPR Pt 8.2 and Pt 54.6 and Practice Direction, paras 5.1 and 5.6). The claim form should indicate that the pre-action protocol has been complied **54.6.1**

[1] Introduced by the Civil Procedure (Amendment No.4) Rules 2000 (SI 2000/2092).

with or reasons for non-compliance must be given in the form: *Practice Statement (Administrative Court: Listing and Urgent Cases)* [2002] 1 W.L.R. 810. If the claimant is raising a devolution issue, the claim form must specify that fact and contain a summary of the facts, circumstances and points of law upon which it is said that a devolution issue arises (see Practice Direction, para.5.4). If the claimant is seeking to raise an issue or claim a remedy under the Human Rights Act 1998, the claim form must specify that fact and give precise details of the Convention right alleged to have been infringed and specify the relief sought (see Practice Direction, para.5.3).

The claim form must be accompanied by any written evidence in support of the claim or of any application to extend the time-limit for filing the claim form. It must also be accompanied by a copy of any order that the claimant seeks to have quashed and, if the claim relates to a decision of a court or tribunal, an approved copy of the reasons for reaching the decision. The claim form must also be accompanied by any documents upon which the claimant proposes to rely. These will usually be annexed to the witness statement and, where the claimant is seeking judicial review of a decision, will include a copy of the decision or decision letter under challenge together with the other relevant documentation. Copies of relevant statutory provisions and a list of essential reading must also be lodged with the claim form. The claimant is required to lodge two copies of a paginated and indexed bundle containing the claim form, the written evidence and accompanying documents and the relevant statutory material. See generally Practice Direction, paras 5.7–5.10.

The claim form should provide sufficient information to enable the defendant and interested parties to be able to provide an acknowledgement of service. Equally importantly, the claim form should enable a court, which will be dealing with the application for permission on the papers, to identify what the alleged claim is about and whether or not there is an arguable case. In practice, in describing the grounds of the claim, it is often useful to provide a brief introductory paragraph identifying the enactment, decision or action challenged or the failure to act that is complained of and a summary of the basis of the challenge. Then the claim should record the essential facts, followed by a description of the legislative framework and then set out the specific grounds of challenge, i.e. identifying the error of law made by the public body or the relevant principles of public law that the public body has breached. Questions of delay, alternative remedies, statutory provisions ousting the jurisdiction of the courts and any issues relating to standing also need to be dealt with. A non-party may obtain a copy of the Claim form from the court: *R. (Corner House Research) v Director of Serious Fraud Office* [2008] A.C.D. 246.

Duty to make full and frank disclosure

54.6.2 The claimant is under a duty to disclose all material facts. These include all material facts known to the claimant and those he would have known had he made the appropriate inquiries prior to applying for permission (*R. v Lloyd's of London, Ex p. Briggs* [1993] 1 Lloyd's Rep. 176; *R. v Secretary of State for the Home Department, Ex p. Ketowoglo The Times*, April 6, 1992; *R. v Jockey Club Licensing Committee, Ex p. Barrie Wright* [1991] C.O.D. 306). Non-disclosure is a sufficient reason for refusing the remedy sought or refusing permission (*R. v Kensington General Commissioners, ex. p. Polignac* [1917] 1 K.B. 486).

Protected Costs Orders

54.6.3 In general, costs follow the event and an unsuccessful claimant will be ordered to pay the successful defendant's costs. A claimant may, however, wish to apply for a protective costs order, that is, an order that a claimant is not liable to pay the costs of a successful defendant or that his liability is restricted to a particular amount. The court will not generally make such orders unless the public law challenges raised are ones of general public importance, the public interest requires that those issues should be resolved, the claimant has no financial interest in the outcome of the case, it is fair and just to make the order having regard to the financial resources of the claimant and the defendant and to the amount of costs that were likely to be involved and the claimant would probably discontinue proceedings and would be acting reasonably in so doing if such an order were refused; see *R. (Corner House Research) v Secretary of State for Trade and Industry, [2005] EWHC* Civ 192; [2005] 1 W.L.R. 2600; R. (*Compton*) *v Wiltshire Primary Care Trust* [2008] EWCA Civ 749; *R. v Lord Chancellor Ex p. Child Poverty Action Group* [1999] 1 W.L.R. 347. An application for a protected costs order should normally be included in the claim form and supported by the requisite evidence including a full schedule of the claimant's likely future costs. A defendant who wishes to resist such an order should do so in the acknowledgment of service. The matter would normally be dealt with on the paper by the judge who considers the application for permission. If such an order is refused, it may be renewed at an oral hearing. See generally, *R (Corner House Research) v Secretary of State for Trade and Industry*, [2005] EWCA Civ 192; [2005] 1 W.L.R. 2600 and *R. (Buglife-the Invertebrate Conservation Trust) v Thurrock Thames Gateway Development Corp* [2008] EWCA Civ 1209.

For the procedure to be followed, and for the matters to be taken into account by the court, where a party makes an application for an order limiting the amount of future costs (including disbursements) which a party may recover pursuant to an order for costs subsequently made (a "costs capping order"), see rr.44.18 to 44.20, and commentary in para.43.2.1.2 above. That procedure does not apply to applications for protective costs orders (r.44.18(3)); see further paras 3.1.8 and 48.15.7 above, and note guidance on principles and procedure (both at first instance and on appeal) given by the Court of Appeal in *R. v (Corner House Research) v Secretary of State for Trade and Industry* [2005] EWCA Civ 192; [2005] 1 W.L.R. 2600, CA, and *R. (Buglife-the Invertebrate Conservation Trust) v Thurrock Thames Gateway Development Corp.* [2008] EWCA Civ 1209, November 4, 2008, CA, unrep.

Service of claim form[1]

54.7 The claim form must be served on— 54.7

(a) the defendant; and

(b) unless the court otherwise directs, any person the claimant considers to be an interested party,

within 7 days after the date of issue.

The claimant must file the claim form in the Administrative Court Office. The claimant must also serve the claim form on the defendant and, unless the court otherwise directs, on any person that the claimant considers to be an interested party within 7 days of the issue of the claim form. On the definition of the parties see para.54.1.13 above. 54.7.1

Acknowledgment of service[2]

54.8—(1) Any person served with the claim form who wishes to take part in the judicial review must file an acknowledgment of service in the relevant practice form in accordance with the following provisions of this rule. 54.8

(2) Any acknowledgment of service must be—

(a) filed not more than 21 days after service of the claim form; and

(b) served on—

(i) the claimant; and

(ii) subject to any direction under rule 54.7(b), any other person named in the claim form, as soon as practicable and, in any event, not later than 7 days after it is filed.

(3) The time limits under this rule may not be extended by agreement between the parties.

(4) The acknowledgment of service—

(a) must—

(i) where the person filing it intends to contest the claim, set out a summary of his grounds for doing so; and

[1] Introduced by the Civil Procedure (Amendment No.4) Rules 2000 (SI 2000/2092).
[2] Introduced by the Civil Procedure (Amendment No.4) Rules 2000 (SI 2000/2092).

(ii) state the name and address of any person the person filing it considers to be an interested party; and

(b) may include or be accompanied by an application for directions.

(5) Rule 10.3(2) does not apply

Acknowledgment of service.

54.8.1 The defendant and any interested party wishing to take part in the judicial review must file an acknowledgment of service in the Administrative Court Office within 21 days after service on them of the claim form. The appropriate form is form **N462**. The defendant must serve the acknowledgment on the claimant and any person named in the claim form as soon as reasonably practicable after filing it and in any event within seven days. An interested party must serve an acknowledgment of service on the claimant, defendant and any other interested party named in the claim form in the same time limit. The parties cannot agree an extension of time (CPR r.54.8(3)).

The requirement of service and the opportunity for the defendant to put in a response are among the most significant changes introduced by the Pt 54 of the CPR. The assumption is that the court will decide the application on the papers, those papers including both the claim and the defendant's summary response. Previously, the rules provided that the application for permission was to be made without notice to the respondent and there was no requirement that the application for permission be served on the proposed respondent (although in practice, respondents should have been informed that the applicant was considering applying for judicial review and were frequently served with a copy of the application for permission and, if an oral hearing was held, frequently attended and made representations). A non-party may obtain a copy of the acknowledgment of service from the court: *R. (Corner House Research) v Director of Serious Fraud Office* [2008] A.C.D. 246.

Content

54.8.2 The acknowledgment of service must set out a summary of the grounds upon which the claim is contested and the names and addresses of any person considered to be an interested party. It may also include an application for directions. A defendant who wishes to apply for an order for the costs of filing an acknowledgment of service if permission is refused should include this application: see para.54.12.5 below.

Neither the rules nor provisions in the practice direction supplementing Pt 54 expand on what is meant by the "summary of grounds" required by r.54.8(4) to be included in the acknowledgment of service where the person filing it intends to defend the claim. This summary must be contrasted with the necessarily more elaborate "detailed grounds for contesting the claim" and supporting "written evidence" required by r.54.14 following the grant of permission. The purpose of the r.54.8(4) summary is not to provide the basis for full argument of the substantive merits, but rather to assist the judge in deciding whether to grant permission and, if so, on what terms. Where appropriate, it may be helpful to draw attention to any points fatal to the claim or to procedural bars, and to the practical and financial consequences for other parties (if any) which may (for example) be relevant to directions for expedition. It should be possible to do what is necessary at this stage without incurring substantial expense (*Ewing v Office of the Deputy Prime Minister* [2005] EWCA Civ 1583; [2006] 1 W.L.R. 1260 at para.37 per Carnwath L.J.). Where the defendants' resistance is successful at the permission stage they may be awarded the costs of the acknowledgment of service (*Mount Cook Land Limited v Westminster City Council* [2003] EWCA Civ 1346; [2004] 2 P. & C.R. 22, CA), see 54.12.5 below.

Written evidence

54.8.3 There is no express provision for the defendant or interested party to file and service written evidence at this stage in the judicial review procedure but, equally, there seems no reason, in principle, why this should not be done in appropriate cases or, more usually, crucial documents may be attached to the acknowledgement of service. Previously, under the former RSC O.53, it was common for the proposed respondent *to file evidence about* delay (which was particularly important since that matter could only be dealt with at the permission stage and could not be re-argued at the substantive hearing if permission was granted: *R. v Criminal Injuries Compensation Board Ex p. A* [1999] 2 A.C. 330) to draw attention to an alternative appeal procedure, or to set out a fuller version of the facts, in an attempt to persuade the court that permission should not be granted. The court usually had regard to that evidence, provided that the claimant had had the opportunity to deal with it. The practice of admitting such evidence, in general, proved beneficial. It may, however, add to the time for consideration of the permission application (since the claimant may need time to respond) and it may result in applications for permission being adjourned to open court.

Failure to file acknowledgment of service[1]

54.9—(1) Where a person served with the claim form has failed to file an acknowledgment of service in accordance with rule 54.8, he- 54.9

(a) may not take part in a hearing to decide whether permission should be given unless the court allows him to do so; but

(b) provided he complies with rule 54.14 or any other direction of the court regarding the filing and service of-

(i) detailed grounds for contesting the claim or supporting it on additional grounds; and

(ii) any written evidence,

may take part in the hearing of the judicial review.

(2) Where that person takes part in the hearing of the judicial review, the court may take his failure to file an acknowledgment of service into account when deciding what order to make about costs.

(3) Rule 8.4 does not apply.

Consequences

This rule sets out the consequences for a defendant or an interested party of failing to file an acknowledgment of service in accordance with r.54.8. That person cannot take part in any hearing to consider whether permission should be granted unless the court allows him to do so. There will only be a hearing if permission has been refused and the applicant requests a reconsideration of that decision under CPR r.54.12 (or if the court adjourns the application to a hearing). If permission is granted at that hearing, then the defendant or interested party can take part in the substantive hearing of the application, provided they comply with the requirements to file detailed grounds for contesting the claim and any written evidence under CFR r.54.14. 54.9.1

Costs

If a person does take part in the substantive hearing of the judicial review application, the failure to provide a written acknowledgment of service may also be taken into account when deciding what costs order should be made. The implication is that, if the defendant could have made it clear from the outset that the claim would not succeed, then the defendant may not be able to recover his costs if he wins and, conceivably, could even be made to bear the costs of the claimant (at least up to the point when detailed grounds for resistance were filed and it should have been clear that the claim could not succeed and should be withdrawn). Costs are, however, discretionary and depend on all the circumstances of the case. 54.9.2

Permission given[2]

54.10—(1) Where permission to proceed is given the court may also give directions. 54.10

(2) Directions under paragraph (1) may include a stay$^{(GL)}$ of proceedings to which the claim relates.

[1] Introduced by the Civil Procedure (Amendment No.4) Rules 2000 (SI 2000/2092).
[2] Introduced by the Civil Procedure (Amendment No.4) Rules 2000 (SI 2000/2092).

(Rule 3.7 provides a sanction for the non-payment of the fee payable when permission to proceed has been given)

Directions

54.10.1 The court may also give directions when granting permission. Amongst the most common directions are likely to be directions that that the hearing of the substantive matter be expedited and that the time limit for written evidence be abridged

Stays

54.10.2 A court may also direct that the proceedings to which the claim relates be stayed. In *R. v Secretary of State for Education Ex p. Avon CC* [1991] 1 Q.B. 558, the Court of Appeal held the power to grant a stay is not limited to cases where the judicial review application relates to judicial or quasi-judicial proceedings, but enables the court to impose a stay on the "process by which the challenged decision has been reached, including the decision itself". Thus the court could grant a stay of an administrative decision making process (if it has not yet been completed) being undertaken by a public body such as a local authority or minister, or could stay the implementation of a decision by such a body (if the decision has already been taken): see *R. v Ashworth Hospital Authority, Ex p. H.* [2003] 1 W.L.R. 127. The Privy Council has, however, indicated that a stay is an order which puts a stop to further proceedings before a court or tribunal and so cannot be used to prevent the implementation of a decision made by a minister in the exercise of statutory powers (*Minister of Foreign Affairs, Trade and Industry v Vehicles and Supplies Ltd* [1991] 1 W.L.R. 550. Stays are only appropriate to restrain a public body from acting. They are not appropriate to compel a public body to act.

Procedure for applying

54.10.3 A claim for a stay ought to be included in the claim form.

Test for granting a stay

54.10.4 The criteria for granting a stay and, in particular, the relationship between stays and interim remedies, remains to be worked out. At present, given the decision in *Ex p. Avon*, the grant of a stay can, in theory, achieve much of what is usually sought to be done by way of interim injunctions in that it can be directed to stop an administrative body from continuing its decision-making process or to prevent the implementation of a decision. Where a grant of a stay against a public body will detrimentally affect a third party, the Court of Appeal has held that the proper approach is to treat the matter as an application for an interim injunction against the third party (*R. v HM Inspectorate of Pollution Ex p. Greenpeace Ltd (No.1)* [1994] 1 W.L.R. 570). In particular, the claimant will normally be expected to give a cross-undertaking in damages to the third party and there will be a reluctance to grant a stay in the absence of an appropriate cross-undertaking (see, e.g. *R. v Secretary of State for the Environment Ex p. Royal Society for the Protection of Birds* (1995) 7 Admin L. Rep. 434; *R. v HM Inspectorate of Pollution Ex p. Greenpeace Ltd (No.1)* [1994] 1 W.L.R. 570). On the procedure and test for interim relief, see paras and above).

Where the grant of a stay concerns only the claimant and the defendant, but the effect of the stay will, in substance, operate to restrain a public body from continuing an administrative process or from implementing a decision (assuming that *Ex p. Avon* is correctly decided), there is also much to be said for treating question of a stay as if it were an application for an interim injunction and applying the same procedure and the same principles as would apply to a claim for such an injunction (on the procedure and test for interim relief see paras 54.3.5–54.3.6 above).

Service of order giving or refusing permission[1]

54.11 **54.11 The court will serve—**

(a) the order giving or refusing permission; and

(b) any directions,

[1] Introduced by the Civil Procedure (Amendment No.4) Rules 2000 (SI 2000/2092).

CPR 54

on—

(i) the claimant;

(ii) the defendant; and

(iii) any other person who filed an acknowledgment of service.

Notification of the decision

The court will serve the order giving or refusing or granting permission, and any directions, on the claimant, and any interested party who served an acknowledgement of service. There is no longer any requirement for the claimant to enter and service a notice of motion following the grant of permission. The grant of permission itself triggers the next stage in the judicial review procedure, which is the filing of a detailed response and written evidence by the defendant and interested parties under r.54.13. This rule applies, it seems, both to decisions taken on the papers only or after an oral hearing. **54.11.1**

The court will also serve on the parties its reasons for granting or refusing permission (r.54.12(2)).

Permission decision without a hearing[1]

54.12—(1) This rule applies where the court, without a hearing— **54.12**

(a) refuses permission to proceed; or

(b) gives permission to proceed—

(i) subject to conditions; or

(ii) on certain grounds only.

(2) The court will serve its reasons for making the decision when it serves the order giving or refusing permission in accordance with rule 54.11.

(3) The claimant may not appeal but may request the decision to be reconsidered at a hearing.

(4) A request under paragraph (3) must be filed within 7 days after service of the reasons under paragraph (2).

(5) The claimant, defendant and any other person who has filed an acknowledgment of service will be given at least 2 days' notice of the hearing date.

Reconsideration of a refusal of permission

If the judge has determined the application for permission without a hearing, and permission has been refused or granted on certain grounds only or is subject to conditions, the claimant cannot appeal against the decision but there is provision for the claimant to request that the decision be reconsidered at a hearing (CPR r.54.12(2)). The request for reconsideration must be filed in the Administrative Court Office within seven days of service of the reasons for refusal (r.54.12(4)). The claimant and any person who has filed an acknowledgement of service must be given at least two days' notice of a hearing date. The clear implication is, therefore, that there will be an oral hearing at which the claimant and the defendant and other interested persons will be able to attend and make representations. **54.12.1**

Appeals against refusal of permission to the Court of Appeal

Where permission has been refused in a civil (i.e. non-criminal) case after a hearing in the High Court, the person seeking permission may apply to the Court of Appeal within seven days of the decision of the High Court refusing permission (CPR r.52.15) The Court of Appeal may, on considering that application, grant permission to apply for judicial review and, if so, the claim will proceed in the High Court in the usual way (CPR r.52.15(3) and (4)). **54.12.2**

[1] Introduced by the Civil Procedure (Amendment No.4) Rules 2000 (SI 2000/2092).

Appeals to the House of Lords

54.12.3 In *Re Poh* [1983] 1 W.L.R. 2, the House of Lords held that there can be no appeal to the House of Lords against a decision of the Court of Appeal refusing permission to apply for judicial review. The reasoning in *Re Poh* had been doubted by the Privy Council in *Kemper Reinsurance Co v Minister of Finance* [1998] 3 W.L.R. 630. The House of Lords has, however, upheld the decision in *Re Poh* and confirmed that the House of Lords has no jurisdiction to entertain an appeal against the refusal of permission to apply for judicial review: *R. v Secretary of State for Trade and Industry Ex p. Eastaway* [2000] 1 W.L.R. 2222. The House of Lords reasoned that the Court of Appeal only had jurisdiction to entertain an appeal against a decision of the High Court refusing permission to apply for judicial review. If the Court of Appeal refused permission to appeal, then such a decision was covered by the rule in *Lane v Esdaile* and there could not be an appeal against that refusal of permission to appeal. Where, however, the Court of Appeal grants permission to appeal, but then refuses to grant permission to apply for judicial review (because of the alleged delay in filing the claim), the House of Lords has held that it does have jurisdiction to hear an appeal against the refusal to grant permission to apply: *R. v Hammersmith and Fulham LBC Ex p. Burkett* [2002] 1 W.L.R. 1593.

Appeals in non-criminal cases

54.12.4 There can be no appeal to the Court of Appeal against the refusal by the High Court to grant permission to apply for judicial review in a criminal case (SCA 1981 s.18(1)(a)). The decision in *Re Poh* would prevent a refusal of permission by the High Court being appealed to the House of Lords. Where the High Court considers that the possibility of an appeal to the House of Lords should be preserved, the usual course is for the High Court to grant permission, to dismiss the substantive application and to certify that a question of general public importance arises. The claimant may then petition the House of Lords for permission to appeal against the decision to dismiss the claim (*R. v DPP Ex p. Camelot plc* (1998) 10 Admin L.Rep. 93 at 105).

Costs at the permission stage

54.12.5 The courts have discretion under SCA 1981 s.51 to award costs on an application for permission for judicial review (*R. v Camden LBC Ex p. Martin* [1997] 1 W.L.R. 359). Where the claimant is granted permission, the costs will be costs in the case unless the judge granting permission makes a different order: *Practice Statement (QBD (Admin Ct): Judicial Review: Costs)* [2004] 1 W.L.R. 1760. Costs will usually follow the event with the unsuccessful party being ordered to pay the costs of the successful party. If the defendant successfully resists the claim, those costs will include the costs of dealing with the claim after the grant of permission and also other costs reasonably incurred by the defendant prior to the grant of permission (including the acknowledgment of service but excluding the costs of any oral permission hearing) unless the court makes an alternative order: see *R (Davey) v Aylesbury Vale DC (Practice Note)* [2008] 1 W.L.R. 878. If the claimant is refused permission, whether there has or has not been a hearing, he will generally have to bear his own costs. There may be exceptional circumstances where the defendant takes the action sought in the judicial proceedings after the claim form is served and thereby avoids the need for judicial review but where it is appropriate to award the claimant his costs to that point. Such exceptional circumstances arose in *R. v Kensington and Chelsea Royal BC Ex p. Ghebregiogis* (1994) 27 H.L.R. 602 where the claimant had sent a clear letter before action, the point of law was simple and the defendant had simply failed to pay any attention to it, thereby forcing the claimant to incur the costs of applying for permission. The principles governing the award of costs where the claim for judicial review does not proceed to a full hearing of the substantive application have been usefully summarised in *R. (Boxall) v Mayor and Burgesses of Waltham Forest LBC* (2001) 4 C.C.L. Rep. 258 and see *R (Scott) v London Borough of Hackney*, January 21, 2009 and *DB v Worcestershire CC* [2006] EWHC 2613 (Admin). The court retains a power to make a costs order where the substantive hearing has not proceeded to a trial. It will ordinarily be irrelevant that the claimant is legally aided. The overall objective will be to do justice between the parties without unnecessarily using court time or incurring further costs. At each end of the spectrum, there will be cases where it is obvious which side would have won (and costs can be awarded accordingly). In between, the position will be less clear. The extent to which the court will be prepared to consider the unresolved substantive issues will depend on the circumstances of the case and, in particular, the amount of the costs at stake and the conduct of the parties. In the absence of a good reason to make any other order, the fallback position is that there should be no order as to costs. The court should also take care to ensure that it does not discourage parties from settling proceedings, for example by discouraging the public authority defendant from making a concession at an early stage (because it would be concerned about the possible costs implications of such a concession). Where the defendant has taken steps to deal with the subject matter of the challenge because it has recognised that it is likely to lose, then the defendant may be ordered to pay the claimant's costs. Where, however, the challenge becomes academic because the defendant decides to short circuit the proceedings (for example, by doing what is requested) because the defendant has decided to avoid the expense, inconvenience or uncertainty of proceedings, without accepting the likelihood of their succeeding, then the defendant should not be liable for the claimant's costs and the appropriate order will generally be no order for costs.

The Court of Appeal has also reviewed the position in relation to the award of costs against a claimant who is unsuccessful at the permission stage: see *R. (on the application of Mount Cook Land Ltd) v Westminster City Council* [2003] EWCA Civ 1346; [2004] 2 P. & C. R. 405. A defendant who has complied with the pre-action protocol and who has filed an acknowledgment of service should, generally, be able to recover the costs of filing an acknowledgment of service from an unsuccessful claimant where permission is refused: see paragraph 76(1) of the judgment in *R. (on the application of Mount Cook Land Ltd) v Westminster City Council* [2003] EWCA Civ 1346; [2004] 2 P. & C. R. 405 and *Leach, Re* [2001] EWHC Admin 455; *The Times*, August 2, 2001. Defendants who wish to claim such costs should normally make an application for costs in the body of the acknowledgment of service and provide details of the amount claimed. In *R. (on the application of Mount Cook Land Ltd) v Westminster City Council*, the Court of Appeal appeared to go further and indicated that an interested party who complied with the pre-action protocol and served an acknowledgement of service ought also to be able to recover the costs of doing so against an unsuccessful claimant, although strictly, that issue did not arise in that case.

The court should not order an unsuccessful claimant to pay the costs of a defendant or an interested party attending an oral hearing and successfully resisting an application for permission except in exceptional circumstances. Such circumstances may consist in the presence of one or more of the following factors: (a) the hopelessness of the claim; (b) the persistence by the claimant in the claim after having been alerted to facts or the law demonstrating its hopelessness; (c) the extent to which the court considers that the claimant has sough to abuse the process of judicial review for collateral purposes; (d) whether, as a result of full argument and the deployment of documentary evidence, the claimant has, in effect, had the advantage of an early substantive hearing of the claim. The court may also consider the extent to which the unsuccessful claimant has substantial resources which he has used to pursue the unfounded claim and which are available to meet an order for courts. See *R. (on the application of Mount Cook Land Ltd) v Westminster City Council* [2003] EWCA Civ 1346; [2004] 2 P. & C. R. 405 at para.76 of the judgment and para.8.6 of the Practice Direction. The Court of Appeal did not have to deal specifically with the position of an interested party and it may be that, even if there were exceptional circumstances justifying the award of costs in favour of a defendant, that the court would not, generally, order the unsuccessful claimant to pay the costs of an interested party unless there was some separate issue or some separate interest calling for the interested party to appear: see *Bolton MDC v Secretary of State for the Environment (Costs)* [1995] 1 W.L.R. 1176 and para.54.16.7 below. See above for applications for protected costs orders.

In *Ewing v Office of the Deputy Prime Minister* [2005] EWCA Civ 1583; [2006] 1 W.L.R. 1260; December 12, 2005, CA, unrep., the Court of Appeal suggested that an opportunity should be found as soon as possible to introduce a specific rule or practice direction governing the procedure for applications for costs at the permission stage, and the principles to be applied. The court said it would be helpful if, at the same time, there could be clarification of what is required to be incorporated in the acknowledgment of service by way of "summary grounds" as required by r.54.8(4) (see para.54.8.2 above) and whether it is necessary to impose the same requirement on all parties in this respect, or whether distinctions should be drawn between defendants and interested parties.

Pending any new rules or directions, the court stated that the following procedure should be followed (*ibid.* at para.37 per Carnwath L.J.):

1. where a proposed defendant or interested party wishes to seek costs at the

permission stage, the acknowledgment of service should include an application for costs and should be accompanied by a schedule setting out the amount claimed;

2. the judge refusing permission should include in the refusal a decision whether to award costs in principle, and (if so) an indication of the amount which he proposes to assess summarily;
3. the claimant should be given 14 days to respond in writing and should serve a copy on the defendant;
4. the defendant shall have seven days to reply in writing to any such response, and to the amount proposed by the judge;
5. the judge will then decide and make an award on the papers.

The court also said that, where a claimant does not follow the Pre-Action Protocol procedure, he must expect to put his opponents to greater expense in preparing the summary of grounds and this may be reflected in any order for costs against him if permission is refused (*ibid.* at para.54 per Brooke L.J.).

Defendant etc. may not apply to set aside(GL)[1]

54.13 **54.13 Neither the defendant nor any other person served with the claim form may apply to set aside(GL) an order giving permission to proceed.**

Applications to set aside

54.13.1 The court has an inherent jurisdiction to set aside orders, including orders granting permission to apply for judicial review, which have been made without notice being given to the defendant or other interested party (*R. v Secretary of State for the Home Department Ex p. Chinoy* (1992) 4 Admin L. Rep. 457). That jurisdiction continues to exist in relation to permission granted under CPR Pt 54. Where, however, the claim form has been served on the defendant or an interested party, so that they had the opportunity of filing an acknowledgment of service setting out a summary of the grounds of resistance, that defendant or interested party cannot apply to set aside the grant of permission (CPR r.54.13). As the claim form must be served on such persons, applications to set aside the grant of permission are likely now to be rare and to occur only when by oversight or some other reason a defendant or interested party was not served or where, for some reason, permission was granted before the defendant had filed his acknowledgment of service and before the time for doing so had expired see, e.g. *R. on the application of Webb v Bristol City Council* [2001] EWHC Admin 696. Even where an application to set aside can be made, the courts generally have discouraged such applications and have indicated that the jurisdiction to set aside should only be exercised sparingly and in a very plain case (*R. v Secretary of State for the Home Department Ex p. Chinoy* (1992) 4 Admin L.Rep. 457).

Response[2]

54.14 **54.14—(1) A defendant and any other person served with the claim form who wishes to contest the claim or support it on additional grounds must file and serve—**

(a) detailed grounds for contesting the claim or supporting it on additional grounds; and

(b) any written evidence,

within 35 days after service of the order giving permission.

(2) The following rules do not apply—

(a) rule 8.5(3) and 8.5 (4)(defendant to file and serve written evidence at the same time as acknowledgment of service); and

(b) rule 8.5(5) and 8.5(6) (claimant to file and serve any reply within 14 days).

[1] Introduced by the Civil Procedure (Amendment No.4) Rules 2000 (SI 2000/2092).
[2] Introduced by the Civil Procedure (Amendment No.4) Rules 2000 (SI 2000/2092).

Response and written evidence

The defendant and any person served with the claim form who wishes to contest the claim must file and serve a response setting out their detailed grounds for contesting the claim and any written evidence within 35 days of service of the order giving permission. The defendant's evidence should be served on the claimant and all other persons known to be interested parties and the interested party's evidence served on the claimant, the defendant and any other person known to be an interested party. An interested person may wish to support the claim, rather than contest it. Such a person may support the claim on additional grounds by serving a detailed response setting out the additional grounds and any written evidence within 35 days of service. Should that occur, the defendant may need to respond to that additional evidence. The court has a discretion to allow a defendant to rely on further written evidence under CPR r.54.16. **54.14.1**

The defendant will need to provide sufficient information to enable the court to determine whether it has acted lawfully. In *R. v Lancashire CC Ex p. Huddleston* [1986] 2 All E.R. 941, Sir John Donaldson M.R. described this obligation on the defendant as a "duty to make full and fair disclosure" (at p.945) while Purchas L.J. stated that the defendant "should set out fully what they did and why so so far as is necessary fully and fairly to meet the challenge" made by the claimant (at p.947). See also *Tweed v Parades Commission for Northern Ireland* [2007] 1 A.C. 650 at paras 31 and 54.Where the defendant has already given reasons for the decision or action taken, it may adduce evidence to clarify, elucidate or supplement those reasons but may not adduce evidence to contradict the reasoning in the original decision (*Re C and C* [1992] C.O.D. 29; *R. v Legal Aid Area Appeal Committee Ex p. Angell* [1990] C.O D. 355; *R. v Westminster City Council Ex p. Ermakov* [1996] 2 All E.R. 302) and *R. (on the application of Leung) v Imperial College of Science, Technology and Medicine* [2002] EWHC 1358; [2002] E.L.R. 653.

The claimant and his legal advisers have a duty, once the defendant's evidence is received, to reconsider the claim for judicial review and to consider whether there is sufficient merit to justify continuing the judicial review procedure (*R. v Liverpool Justices Ex p. P* [1998] C.O.D. 453; *R. v Inland Revenue Commissioners Ex p. Continental Shipping* [1996] C.O.D. 335). A non-party may obtain a copy of the detailed grounds from the courts: *R. (Corner House Research) v Director of Serious Fraud Office* [2008] A.C.D. 246.

Where claimant seeks to rely on additional grounds[1]

54.15 The court's permission is required if a claimant seeks to rely on grounds other than those for which he has been given permission to proceed. **54.15**

This rule allows the court to grant permission to a claimant to add additional grounds of claim to those for which the claimant was originally given permission. Paragraph 11.1 of the Practice Direction deals with the service of notice of amendments and requires notice to be served seven clear days before the hearing. The court can, in the exercise of its inherent jurisdiction, also allow the claimant to amend the claim to claim different remedies from those originally included in the claim form. **54.15.1**

The power to permit additional grounds to be argued is particularly appropriate in respect of new grounds which did not form part of the original claim for judicial review. Where, however, permission to argue a particular ground has been expressly refused at an oral permission hearing, a claimant wishing to challenge that refusal should normally do so by appealing against the refusal to the Court of Appeal. Exceptionally, however, the court hearing the substantive application of the grounds where permission was given, may exercise its discretion under CPR r.54.15 to permit the claimant to argue the specific ground where permission was refused if there has been a significant change of circumstances or the claimant has become aware of significant new facts which he could not reasonably have known or found out about at the time of the permission hearing or if a proposition of law is now maintainable which was not previously open to the claimant (for example, where the Court of Appeal has overturned a decision of the High Court) or where is some other substantial justifica-

[1] Introduced by the Civil Procedure (Amendment No.4) Rules 2000 (SI 2000/2092).

tion for allowing the point to be argued: see *R. (on the application of Opoku) v Southwark College Principal* [2002] EWHC 2092; [2003] 1 W.L.R. 234; *R. (Smith) v Parole Board* [2003] 1 W.L.R. 2548.

Evidence[1]

54.16 **54.16—(1) Rule 8.6(1) does not apply.**

(2) No written evidence may be relied on unless—

(a) it has been served in accordance with any—

(i) rule under this Section; or

(ii) direction of the court; or

(b) the court gives permission.

Evidence

54.16.1 No party may rely on written evidence unless it has been served in accordance with the rules or direction of the court, or the court gives permission for it to be used. It is common for additional evidence to be served in the following circumstances. A claimant may seek to serve written evidence in reply to that of the defendant or interested party. Furthermore, the factual situation may change and further relevant events may occur after the time for serving evidence but before the substantive hearing. It is common practice for the courts to allow the claimant or the defendant or interested party to file and serve additional written evidence to inform the court of subsequent events, providing that the other parties have adequate time to consider and deal with that evidence.

By Civil Procedure (Amendment) Rules 2002 (SI 2002/2058) r.21, in para.(1) of r.54.16. "Rule 8.6(1)" is substituted for "Rule 8.6". This amendment came into effect December 2, 2002. It brings the rule into line with the construction already placed on the rule (see *R. (on the application of G) v Ealing LBC (No.2)* [2002] EWHC 250 (Admin); [2002] EWHC 250, Munby J.).

Interlocutory applications

54.16.2 Cross-examination was available under the former RSC O.53 judicial review procedure but was rarely ordered. The task of finding the primary facts was largely a matter for the decision-maker and the courts acted as a supervisory body ensuring that the decision-maker acted lawfully on the facts as found. There were, however, rare occasions when facts were in dispute, such as what procedure was followed before a decision was taken or what factors were taken into account by the decision-maker. Cross-examination could, exceptionally, be appropriate in such circumstances. Even here, the courts may refuse cross-examination and proceed on the basis of the written evidence and the contemporaneous documents (*R. v Chief Constable of Thames Valley Ex p. Cotton* [1990] I.R.L.R. 344). CPR r.8.6(1) provides for the court to give directions requiring the attendance of a person who has given written evidence for the purposes of cross-examination. CPR r.54.16 provides, however, that r.8.6(1) does not apply to the judicial review procedure. It is unclear whether this rule was intended to restrict the availability of cross-examination. The courts will regard themselves as able to order cross-examination in the exercise of their inherent jurisdiction in any event although there will be few judicial review cases where cross-examination will be appropriate see *R (G) v Ealing LBC, The Times*, March 18, 2002.

In certain cases under the Human Rights Act 1998, the judicial review court may be required to conduct a merits review on the evidence, for which purpose cross-examination may be necessary: see *R. (Wilkinson) v Responsible Medical Officer Broadmoor Hospital & others* [2002] 1 W.L.R. 419.

Disclosure

54.16.2.1 The courts may make an order for the disclosure of specific documents or for standard disclosure i.e. disclosure of documents upon which the claimant relies or ones which adversely affect his case (CPR rr.31.6 and 31.12). In principle, the question is

[1] Introduced by the Civil Procedure (Amendment No.4) Rules 2000 (SI 2000/2092) and amended by the Civil Procedure Rules 2003 (SI 2003/364).

whether disclosure of a document is necessary in order to deal fairly and justly with the case taking account of all the facts and circumstances of the particular case (see *Tweed v Parades Commission of Northern Ireland* [2006] UKHL 53; [2007] 2 W.L.R. 1 at paras 3 and 32). Disclosure is not automatic. In many judicial review cases, an order for disclosure will not be necessary as the claim will raise issues of law. Facts will be agreed or will appear from the documents that are exhibited and it will be the legal consequences of those facts that will be in issue. In such cases disclosure is unlikely to be required: see *Tweed* at paras 2 and 32. Furthermore, the defendant public authority will frequently have exhibited the main documents as a matter of practice or in order to comply with its duty of candour. The courts will not allow "fishing expeditions" where a claimant seeks disclosure in the hope that something will emerge which may form the basis for a claim: *R. v Secretary of State for the Environment Ex p. Islington LBC and London Lesbian and Gay Centre* [1992] C.O.D. 67; *Tweed* at para.56. Even where an order for disclosure is made, it will, generally, be an order for disclosure of specific documents rather than an order for standard disclosure.

The need for disclosure is likely to be greater in cases involving claims that action taken by a public authority infringes a Convention right and is not justified because it is disproportionate. The courts may need to see the main documentation upon which the decision of the public authority concerned was based in order to assess the merits of such a claim and the courts are likely to show a "somewhat greater readiness than hitherto" to order disclosure of the main documents in such cases: see *Tweed* at paras 39 and 57. Disclosure in judicial review cases is still not automatic, however, and even in such cases the need and particularly the extent of disclosure will depend on all the circumstances of the case.

Where a public authority defendant relies on a document as significant to its decision, it will ordinarily be good practice to exhibit the document to a witness statement not merely summarise its contents in the witness statement. If the public authority does not exhibit such a document, and an application is made for disclosure, the court will need to consider whether or not disclosure of that document is necessary for dealing fairly and justly with the case. The former practice, whereby claimants were unable to obtain disclosure of documents in order to ascertain whether statements made in the written evidence were correct unless there was some evidence outside the written evidence which suggested that the statements were inaccurate, misleading or incomplete in some material respect, is no longer to be followed. Rather, a more flexible and less prescriptive principle, depending on whether disclosure is necessary for fairly and justly disposing of the case, is to be applied: see *Tweed* at paras 4–5, 32 and 56. Where objections to disclosure are made, for example, on grounds of confidentiality or the volume of the material concerned, it may be necessary for the court to consider the material first. A court may have to determine whether or not the information was imparted in confidence and, if so, whether it adds materially to the summaries given in the witness statements.

Listing of judicial review claims

Claims for judicial review are included in the Crown Office List (now the Administrative Court). When a case is ready to be heard, a date is found by the Administrate Court office. Expedited users take precedence. There is also a short current list of cases which are not given a fixed date but may be called on at short notice. Guidance on listing is given in the Practice Statement (Administrative Courts: Listing and Urgent Cases) [2002] 1 W.L.R. 810. **54.16.3**

Bundles and skeletons arguments

The claimant must file and serve a skeleton argument not less than 21 working days before the date of hearing. The defendant and any other party wishing to make representations at the hearing must file and serve skeletons not less than 14 working days before the hearing. Skeleton arguments must include a time estimate, a list of issues, a list of legal points to be taken, a chronology of events (with page references), a list of persons referred to, and a list of essential reading (with a time estimate for the reading): see Practice Direction, para.15. The claimant must also file a paginated, indexed bundle of all relevant documents. It must include those documents required by the claimant, the defendant and any other party wishing to make representations. See Practice Direction, para.16. The bundle will usually comprise the order granting permission, the claim form, the claimant's written evidence and documents, the defendant's acknowledgement of service and detailed grounds of resistance, written **54.16.4** evidence and documents and any interested party's acknowledgment of service, detailed grounds of resistance and written evidence and documents.

Hearing of substantive judicial review claims

54.16.5 The hearing of a claim for judicial review is normally before a single judge in open court.

Fresh evidence

54.16.6 The principles on which fresh evidence can be admitted in judicial review proceedings are: (1) the court can receive evidence to show what material was before the inferior court, tribunal or public body; (2) where the jurisdiction of the inferior court, tribunal or public depends upon a question of fact or where the question is whether essential procedural requirements were observed, the court may receive and consider additional evidence to determine the question of jurisdictional fact or procedural error; and (3) where the decision-making process is tainted by misconduct on the part of a member of the inferior court, tribunal or public body, or one of the parties before such a body, fresh evidence is available to prove the particular misconduct alleged. Examples of such misconduct are bias by the decision-making body or fraud or perjury by a party. Where a party deliberately suppressed material with the intention of misleading, it would be for the court to consider whether the conduct of the party could be described as fraudulent so as to permit the fresh evidence (*R. v Secretary of State for the Environment Ex p. Powis* [1981] 1 W.L.R. 584).

Where it is sought to adduce fresh evidence before the Court of Appeal which was not before the court which considered the matter below, fresh evidence will not normally be admitted unless the three conditions laid down in *Ladd v Marshall* [1954] 1 W.L.R. 1489 are satisfied. Whilst *Ladd v Marshall* does not, strictly, apply to appeals in judicial review proceedings, and the Court of Appeal has a wider discretion to admit fresh evidence than exists in ordinary civil litigation, the Court of Appeal will adopt a similar approach to that in *Ladd v Marshall* in the interests of achieving finality in litigation (*Momin Ali v Secretary of State for the Home Department* [1984] 1 W.L.R. 663 and *E v Secretary of State for the Home Department* [2004] EWCA Civ 49; [2004] Q.B. 1044).

The Court of Appeal has held that the principles underlying *Ladd v Marshall* continue to apply after the introduction of the CPR: *R. v Secretary of State for Education and Employment Ex p. Amraf Training plc*, *The Times*, June 28, 2001.

Costs

54.16.7 The court has a discretion in regard to costs generally (SCA 1981 s.51). Costs in judicial review generally follow the event and the unsuccessful party will generally be ordered to pay the costs of the unsuccessful party. The defendant, i.e. the public body whose action, decision, or failure to act is under challenge, will normally be ordered to pay the costs of the successful claimant. The established practice of the courts is, however, not to exercise its discretion to order an inferior court or tribunal to pay costs to a successful claimant where the court or tribunal does not appear (except where there has been a flagrant instance of improper behaviour or it unreasonably declines or neglects to sign a consent order). Nor will the courts generally order an inferior court or tribunal to pay costs where it appears in order to assist the court neutrally on questions of jurisdiction, procedure, specialist case and the like (although the courts may depart from this practice in appropriate cases). Where a court or tribunal makes itself an active party to the litigation and actively resists the claim, it will be liable in costs in the normal way. See *R. (Davies) v Birmingham Deputy Coroner* [2004] EWCA Civ 207; [2004] 1 W.L.R. 2739. The claimant will normally be ordered to pay the costs of the defendant who successfully resists the claim for judicial review. The courts do not, generally, order an unsuccessful claimant to pay two sets of costs, i.e. the defendant's costs and the costs of any interested party served with the claim form (*Bolton MDC v Secretary of State for the Environment* [1995] 1 W.L.R. 1176). The courts may award two sets of costs where the interested party deals with a separate issue not dealt with by the defendant or where the defendant and the interested party have separate and distinct interests which require separate representation (*Bolton MDC v Secretary of State for the Environment* [1995] 1 W.L.R. 1176).

Appeals

54.16.8 In civil cases, the unsuccessful party can seek permission to appeal against the decision to the Court of Appeal (see, generally, CPR Pt 52). There is no appeal to the Court of Appeal in criminal cases. There may be an appeal to the House of Lords where the High Court certifies that the case raises a point of general public importance and either the High Court or the House of Lords grants permission to appeal (Administration of Justice Act 1960 s.1).

Court's powers to hear any person[1]

54.17—(1) Any person may apply for permission- **54.17**

(a) to file evidence; or

(b) make representations at the hearing of the judicial review.

(2) An application under paragraph (1) should be made promptly.

Effect of rule

This rule gives the court power to allow any person to apply to file evidence or make representations at the judicial review hearing, whether in support of, or in opposition to the claim. The court may give permission on terms, such as that the person bear his own costs in any event, or that the time for making oral representations be limited or that representations be limited to written representations. **54.17.1**

Judicial review may be decided without a hearing[2]

54.18 The court may decide the claim for judicial review without a hearing where all the parties agree. **54.18**

Effect of rule

This rule permits the court to decide the claim without a hearing where all parties agree. Parties here presumably means the claimant, the defendant and an interested party within the meaning of r.54.1(f). The rule appears to be directed towards a situation where there is a dispute between the parties but all sides agree that the matter can be determined on the papers only. **54.18.1**

Court's powers in respect of quashing orders[3]

54.19—(1) This rule applies where the court makes a quashing order in respect of the decision to which the claim relates. **54.19**

(2) The court may—

(a) (i) remit the matter to the decision-maker; and

(ii) direct it to reconsider the matter and reach a decision in accordance with the judgment of the court.

(b) in so far as any enactment permits, substitute its own decision for the decision to which the claim relates.

Remitting

Where the court quashes a decision, it may also remit the matter to the decision-maker to reconsider and reach a decision in accordance with the judgment of the court. **54.19.1**

Decision-taking

CPR r.54.19(2) provides that in so far as any enactment permits, the court may **54.19.2**

---

[1] Introduced by the Civil Procedure (Amendment No.4) Rules 2000 (SI 2000/2092).
[2] Introduced by the Civil Procedure (Amendment No.4) Rules 2000 (SI 2000/2092).
[3] Introduced by the Civil Procedure (Amendment No.4) Rules 2000 (SI 2000/2092) and amended by the Civil Procedure (Amendment) Rules 2008 (SI 2008/2178).

substitute its decision. Statute provides powers for the court to vary rather than merely quash and remit a decision, as is the case, for example, in criminal cases where the courts have power to vary the sentence imposed by an inferior court (Supreme Court Act 1981 s.43). Section 31(5A) of the Supreme Court Act 1981 as amended by the Courts, Tribunals and Enforcement Act 2007 s.141, provides powers for the court to substitute a decision but only if the decision was one of a court or tribunal, it was quashed on the grounds of error of law and, without the error, there was only one decision to which the court or tribunal could have come.

Transfer[1]

54.20 **54.20 The court may—**

(a) order a claim to continue as if it had not been started under this Section; and

(b) where it does so, give directions about the future management of the claim.

(Part 30 (transfer) applies to transfers to and from the Administrative Court)

Transfer

54.20.1 This rule empowers the court to order that a claim brought by means of the judicial review procedure (that is, is a claim for judicial review under CPR Pt 8 as modified by Pt 54) to continue as if it had been it had not been brought under this Part. The purpose of this rule is to enable claims that were brought by judicial review to continue as ordinary civil claims under CPR Pt 7. The power may be used where a claimant seeks both public law remedies and also damages, e.g. a quashing order to set aside a detention and damages for the tort of false imprisonment. The claim for damages may be stood over until the public law claim is heard and then the private law claim for damages can be dealt with. The rule is also intended to enable claims that are, in fact, private law claims but which are inadvertently brought by way of a claim for judicial review to continue as an ordinary Pt 7 claims (*R. v East Berkshire Health Authority Ex p. Walsh* [1985] Q.B. 152 at p.166 on the predecessor to this rule under RSC O.53, r.9(5) and dicta of *O'Reilly v Mackman* [1983] 2 A.C. 237 at pp.283–284 but see, also, *R. v Secretary of State for the Home Office Ex p. Dew* [1987] 1 W.L.R. 881 giving a narrow scope to the rule). The court may also give directions about the future management of the claim.

II. Statutory Review under the Nationality, Immigration and Asylum Act 2002

Scope and interpretation[2]

54.21 **54.21—(1) This Section of this Part contains rules about applications to the High Court under section 101(2) of the Nationality, Immigration and Asylum Act 2002[3] for a review of a decision of the Immigration Appeal Tribunal on an application for permission to appeal from an adjudicator.**

(2) In this Section—

(a) 'the Act' means the Nationality, Immigration and Asylum Act 2002;

(b) 'adjudicator' means an adjudicator appointed for the purposes of Part 5 of the Act;

[1] Introduced by the Civil Procedure (Amendment No.4) Rules 2000 (SI 2000/2092) and amended by the Civil Procedure Rules 2003 (SI 2003/364).
[2] Introduced by the Civil Procedure Rules 2003 (SI 2003/364).
[3] 2002 c.41.

(c) 'applicant' means a person applying to the High Court under section 101(2) of the Act;

(d) 'other party' means the other party to the proceedings before the Tribunal; and

(e) 'Tribunal' means the Immigration Appeal Tribunal.

Application for review[1]

54.22—(1) An application under section 101(2) of the Act must be made to the Administrative Court. 54.22

(2) The application must be made by filing an application notice.

(3) The applicant must file with the application notice—

(a) the immigration or asylum decision to which the proceedings relate, and any document giving reasons for that decision; and

(b) the grounds of appeal to the adjudicator;

(c) the adjudicator's determination;

(d) the grounds of appeal to the Tribunal together with any documents sent with them;

(e) the Tribunal's determination on the application for permission to appeal; and

(f) any other documents material to the application which were before the adjudicator.

(4) The applicant must also file with the application notice written submissions setting out—

(a) the grounds upon which it is contended that the Tribunal made an error of law; and

(b) reasons in support of those grounds.

(5) [Revoked]

Application for review

Applications should normally be made under this procedure and not by a claim for judicial review: *R. (on the application of G) v Immigration Appeal Tribunal* [2004] EWCA Civ 1731; [2005] 1 W.L.R. 1445 (inappropriate to pursue a claim for judicial review when the grounds were or could have been brought by a statutory application). The applicant is under a duty to disclose all material facts. In exceptional circumstances, such as gross procedural unfairness, judicial review may still be available: *R. (AM (Cameroon) v Asylum and Immigration Tribunal* [2008] EWCA Civ 100; [2008] 1 W.L.R. 2062. 54.22.1

Time limit for application[2]

54.23—(1) The application notice must be filed not later than 14 days after the applicant is deemed to have received notice of the Tribunal's decision in accordance with rules made under section *106 of the Act*. 54.23

(2) The court may extend the time limit in paragraph (1) in exceptional circumstances.

(3) An application to extend the time limit must be made in the

[1] Introduced by the Civil Procedure Rules 2003 (SI 2003/364).
[2] Introduced by the Civil Procedure Rules 2003 (SI 2003/364).

application notice and supported by written evidence verified by a statement of truth.

Service of application[1]

54.24 **54.24—(1) The applicant must serve on the Asylum and Immigration Tribunal copies of the application notice and written submissions.**

(2) Where an application is for review of a decision by the Tribunal to grant permission to appeal, the applicant must serve on the other party copies of—

(a) the application notice;

(b) the written submissions; and

(c) all the documents filed in support of the application, except for documents which come from or have already been served on that party.

(3) Where documents are required to be served under paragraphs (1) and (2), they must be served as soon as practicable after they are filed.

Determining the application[2]

54.25 **54.25—(1) The application will be determined by a single judge without a hearing, and by reference only to the written submissions and the documents filed with them.**

(2) If the applicant relies on evidence which was not submitted to the adjudicator or the Tribunal, the court will not consider that evidence unless it is satisfied that there were good reasons why it was not submitted to the adjudicator or the Tribunal.

(3) The court may—

(a) affirm the Tribunal's decision to refuse permission to appeal;

(b) reverse the Tribunal's decision to grant permission to appeal; or

(c) order the Asylum and Immigration Tribunal to reconsider the adjudicator's decision on the appeal.

(4) Where the Tribunal refused permission to appeal, the court will order the Asylum and Immigration Tribunal to reconsider the adjudicator's decision on the appeal only if it is satisfied that—

(a) the Tribunal may have made an error of law; and

(b) there is a real possibility that the Asylum and Immigration Tribunal would make a different decision from the adjudicator on reconsidering the appeal (which may include making a different direction under section 87 of the 2002 Act).

(5) Where the Tribunal granted permission to appeal, the court will reverse the Tribunal's decision only if it is satisfied that there is no real possibility that the Asylum and Immigration Tribunal, on

[1] Introduced by the Civil Procedure Rules 2003 (SI 2003/364).
[2] Introduced by the Civil Procedure Rules 2003 (SI 2003/364).

reconsidering the adjudicator's decision on the appeal, would make a different decision from the adjudicator.

(6) The court's decision shall be final and there shall be no appeal from that decision or renewal of the application.

Service of order[1]

54.26—(1) The court will send copies of its order to— 54.26

- **(a) the applicant, except where paragraph (2) applies;**
- **(b) the other party; and**
- **(c) the Asylum and Immigration Tribunal.**

(2) Where—

- **(a) the application relates, in whole or in part, to a claim for asylum;**
- **(b) the Tribunal refused permission to appeal; and**
- **(c) the court affirms the Tribunal's decision,**

the court will send a copy of its order to the Secretary of State, who must serve the order on the applicant.

(3) Where the Secretary of State has served an order in accordance with paragraph (2), he must notify the court on what date and by what method the order was served.

(4) If the court issues a certificate under section 101(3)(d) of the Act, it will send a copy of the certificate together with the order to—

- **(a) the persons to whom it sends the order under paragraphs (1) and (2); and**
- **(b) if the applicant is in receipt of public funding, the Legal Services Commission.**

Costs[2]

54.27 The court may reserve the costs of the application to be determined by the Asylum and Immigration Tribunal. 54.27

III. Applications for Statutory Review under section 103A of the Nationality, Immigration and Asylum Act 2002 54.28

Scope and interpretation[3]

54.28—(1) This Section of this Part contains rules about applications to the High Court under section 103A of the Nationality, Immigration and Asylum Act 2002[4] for an order requiring the Asylum and Immigration Tribunal to reconsider its decision on an appeal.

(2) In this Section—

- **(a) "the 2002 Act" means the Nationality, Immigration and Asylum Act 2002;**

---

[1] Introduced by the Civil Procedure Rules 2003 (SI 2003/364).
[2] Amended by the Civil Procedure Rules 2003 (SI 2003/364).
[3] Amended by the Civil Procedure (Amendment No.4) Rules 2005 (SI 2005/3515).
[4] 2002 c.41.

(b) "the 2004 Act" means the Asylum and Immigration (Treatment of Claimants, etc.) Act 2004[1];

(c) "appellant" means the appellant in the proceedings before the Tribunal;

(d) "applicant" means a person applying to the High Court under section 103A;

(e) "asylum claim" has the meaning given in section 113(1) of the 2002 Act;

(ea) "fast track case" means any case in relation to which an order made under section 26(8) of the 2004 Act provides that the time period for making an application under section 103A(1) of the 2002 Act or giving notification under paragraph 30(5) of Schedule 2 to the 2004 Act is less than 5 days;

(f) "filter provision" means paragraph 30 of Schedule 2 to the 2004 Act;

(g) "order for reconsideration" means an order under section 103A(1) requiring the Tribunal to reconsider its decision on an appeal;

(h) "section 103A" means section 103A of the 2002 Act;

(i) "Tribunal" means the Asylum and Immigration Tribunal.

(3) Any reference in this Section to a period of time specified in—

(a) section 103A(3) for making an application for an order under section 103A(1); or

(b) paragraph 30(5)(b) of Schedule 2 to the 2004 Act for giving notice under that paragraph,

includes a reference to that period as varied by any order under section 26(8) of the 2004 Act.

(4) Rule 2.8 applies to the calculation of the periods of time specified in—

(a) section 103A(3); and

(b) paragraph 30(5)(b) of Schedule 2 to the 2004 Act.

(5) Save as provided otherwise, the provisions of this Section apply to an application under section 103A regardless of whether the filter provision has effect in relation to that application.

Representation of applicants while filter provision has effect[2]

54.28A **54.28A—(1) This rule applies during any period in which the filter provision has effect.**

(2) An applicant may, for the purpose of taking any step under rule 54.29 or 54.30, be represented by any person permitted to provide him with immigration advice or immigration services under section 84 of the Immigration and Asylum Act 1999.[3]

[1] *2004 c.19.*

[2] Introduced by the Civil Procedure (Amendment No.4) Rules 2005 (SI 2005/3515).

[3] 1999 c.33. Part V of that Act has been amended by the Nationality, Immigration and Asylum Act 2002 (c.41), s.140, and the Asylum and Immigration (Treatment of Claimants, etc.) Act 2004 (c.19), ss.37 to 41 and 47, and Sch.4.

(3) A representative acting for an applicant under paragraph (2) shall be regarded as the applicant's legal representative for the purpose of rule 22.1 (Documents to be verified by a statement of truth) regardless of whether he would otherwise be so regarded.

Service of documents on appellants within the jurisdiction[1]

54.28B—(1) In proceedings under this Section, rules 6.7 and 6.23(2)(a) do not apply to the service of documents on an appellant who is within the jurisdiction. 54.28B

(2) Where a representative is acting for an appellant who is within the jurisdiction, a document must be served on the appellant by—

(a) serving it on the appellant's representative; or

(b) serving it on the appellant personally or sending it to the appellant's address by first class post (or an alternative service which provides for delivery on the next business day),

but if the document is served on the appellant under sub-paragraph (b), a copy must also at the same time be sent to the appellant's representative.

Application for review[2]

54.29—(1) Subject to paragraph (5), an application for an order for reconsideration must be made by filing an application notice— 54.29

(a) during a period in which the filter provision has effect, with the Tribunal at the address specified in the relevant practice direction; and

(b) at any other time, at the Administrative Court Office.

(2) During any period in which the filter provision does not have effect, the applicant must file with the application notice—

(a) the notice of the immigration, asylum or nationality decision to which the appeal related;

(b) any other document which was served on the appellant giving reasons for that decision;

(c) the grounds of appeal to the Tribunal;

(d) the Tribunal's determination on the appeal; and

(e) any other documents material to the application which were before the Tribunal.

(2A) During any period in which the filter provision has effect, the applicant must file with the application notice a list of the documents referred to in paragraph (2)(a) to (e).

(3) The applicant must also file with the application notice written submissions setting out—

(a) the grounds upon which it is contended that the

[1] Introduced by the Civil Procedure (Amendment No.4) Rules 2005 (SI 2005/3515) and amended by the Civil Procedure (Amendment) Rules 2006 (SI 2006/1689)and the Civil Procedure (Amendment) Rules 2008 (SI 2008/2178).

[2] Amended by the Civil Procedure (Amendment No.4) Rules 2005 (SI 2005/3515).

Tribunal made an error of law which may have affected its decision; and

(b) reasons in support of those grounds.

(4) Where the applicant—

(a) was the respondent to the appeal; and

(b) was required to serve the Tribunal's determination on the appellant,

the application notice must contain a statement of the date on which, and the means by which, the determination was served.

(5) Where the applicant is in detention under the Immigration Acts, the application may be made either—

(a) in accordance with paragraphs (1) to (3); or

(b) by serving the documents specified in paragraphs (1) to (3) on the person having custody of him.

(6) Where an application is made in accordance with paragraph (5)(b), the person on whom the application notice is served must—

(a) endorse on the notice the date that it is served on him;

(b) give the applicant an acknowledgment in writing of receipt of the notice; and

(c) forward the notice and documents within 2 days

(i) during a period in which the filter provision has effect, to the Tribunal; and

(ii) at any other time, to the Administrative Court Office.

Application to extend time limit

54.30 **54.30** An application to extend the time limit for making an application under section 103A(1) must—

(a) be made in the application notice;

(b) set out the grounds on which it is contended that the application notice could not reasonably practicably have been filed within the time limit; and

(c) be supported by written evidence verified by a statement of truth.

Procedure while filter provision has effect[1]

54.31 **54.31—(1)** This rule applies during any period in which the filter provision has effect.

(2) Where the applicant receives notice from the Tribunal that it—

(a) does not propose to make an order for reconsideration; or

(b) does not propose to grant permission for the application to be made outside the relevant time limit,

and the applicant wishes the court to consider the application, *the applicant must* file a notice in writing at the Administrative

[1] Amended by the Civil Procedure (Amendment) Rules 2006 (SI 2006/1689).

Court Office in accordance with paragraph 30(5)(b) of Schedule 2 to the 2004 Act.

(2A) The applicant must file with the notice—

(a) a copy of the Tribunal's notification that it does not propose to make an order for reconsideration or does not propose to grant permission for the application to be made outside the relevant time limit (referred to in CPR rule 54.31(2));

(b) any other document which was served on the applicant by the Tribunal giving reasons for its decision in paragraph (a);

(c) written evidence in support of any application by the applicant seeking permission to make the application outside the relevant time limit, if applicable;

(d) a copy of the application for reconsideration under section 103A of the 2002 Act (Form AIT/103A), as submitted to the Tribunal (referred to in Rule 54.29(1)(a)).

(3) Where the applicant—

(a) was the respondent to the appeal; and

(b) was required to serve the notice from the Tribunal mentioned in paragraph (2) on the appellant,

the notice filed in accordance with paragraph 30(5)(b) of Schedule 2 to the 2004 Act must contain a statement of the date on which, and the means by which, the notice from the Tribunal was served.

(4) A notice which is filed outside the period specified in paragraph 30(5)(b) must—

(a) set out the grounds on which it is contended that the notice could not reasonably practicably have been filed within that period; and

(b) be supported by written evidence verified by a statement of truth.

(5) If the applicant wishes to respond to the reasons given by the Tribunal for its decision that it—

(a) does not propose to make an order for reconsideration; or

(b) does not propose to grant permission for the application to be made outside the relevant time limit,

the notice filed in accordance with paragraph 30(5)(b) of Schedule 2 to the 2004 Act must be accompanied by written submissions setting out the grounds upon which the applicant disputes any of the reasons given by the Tribunal and giving reasons in support of those grounds.

Procedure in fast track cases while filter provision does not have effect[1]

54.32—(1) This rule applies only during a period in which the filter provision does not have effect. 54.32

[1] Amended by the Civil Procedure (Amendment No.4) Rules 2005 (SI 2005/3515).

(2) Where a party applies for an order for reconsideration in a fast track case—

(a) the court will serve copies of the application notice and written submissions on the other party to the appeal; and

(b) the other party to the appeal may file submissions in response to the application not later than 2 days after being served with the application.

Determination of the application by the Administrative Court

54.33 **54.33—(1) This rule, and rules 54.34 and 54.35, apply to applications under section 103A which are determined by the Administrative Court.**

(2) The application will be considered by a single judge without a hearing.

(3) Unless it orders otherwise, the court will not receive evidence which was not submitted to the Tribunal.

(4) Subject to paragraph (5), where the court determines an application for an order for reconsideration, it may—

(a) dismiss the application;

(b) make an order requiring the Tribunal to reconsider its decision on the appeal under section 103A(1) of the 2002 Act; or

(c) refer the appeal to the Court of Appeal under section 103C of the 2002 Act.

(5) The court will only make an order requiring the Tribunal to reconsider its decision on an appeal if it thinks that—

(a) the Tribunal may have made an error of law; and

(b) there is a real possibility that the Tribunal would make a different decision on reconsidering the appeal (which may include making a different direction under section 87 of the 2002 Act).

(6) Where the Court of Appeal has restored the application to the court under section 103C(2)(g) of the 2002 Act, the court may not refer the appeal to the Court of Appeal.

(7) The court's decision shall be final and there shall be no appeal from that decision or renewal of the application.

Editorial note

54.33.1 Applications to challenge decisions of the asylum immigration tribunal should be brought by an application for review and not by judicial review save in exceptional circumstances, see *F (Mongolia) v Secretary of State for the Home Department* [2007] EWCA Civ 679; [2007] 1 W.L.R. 2523. For an example of exceptional circumstances justifying judicial review see *R. (AM Grunereous) v AIT* [2006] EWCA Civ 100.For the role and powers of the asylum immigration tribunal when considering an order to review its decision, see *DK (Serbia) v Secretary of State for the Home Department* [2008] 1 W.L.R. 1246.

Service of order[1]

54.34 ***54.34*—(1) The court will send copies of its order to—**

[1] Amended by the Civil Procedure (Amendment No.4) Rules 2005 (SI 2005/3515).

CPR 54

(a) the applicant and the other party to the appeal, except where paragraph (2) applies; and
(b) the Tribunal.

(2) Where the appellant is within the jurisdiction and the application relates, in whole or in part, to an asylum claim, the court will send a copy of its order to the Secretary of State.

(2A) Paragraph (2) does not apply in a fast track case.

(3) Where the court sends an order to the Secretary of State under paragraph (2), the Secretary of State must—
(a) serve the order on the appellant; and
(b) immediately after serving the order, notify—
(i) the court; and
(ii) where the order requires the Tribunal to reconsider its decision on the appeal, the Tribunal,

on what date and by what method the order was served.

(4) The Secretary of State must provide the notification required by paragraph (3)(b) no later than 28 days after the date on which the court sends him a copy of its order.

(5) If, 28 days after the date on which the court sends a copy of its order to the Secretary of State in accordance with paragraph (2), the Secretary of State has not provided the notification required by paragraph (3)(b)(i), the court may serve the order on the appellant.

(5A) Where the court serves an order for reconsideration under paragraph (5), it will notify the Tribunal of the date on which the order was served.

(6) If the court makes an order under section 103D(1) of the 2002 Act, it will send copies of that order to—
(a) the appellant's legal representative; and
(b) the Legal Services Commission.

(7) Where paragraph (2) applies, the court will not serve copies of an order under section 103D(1) of the 2002 Act until either—
(a) the Secretary of State has provided the notification required by paragraph (3)(b); or
(b) 28 days after the date on which the court sent a copy of its order to the Secretary of State,

whichever is the earlier.

Costs

54.35 The court shall make no order as to the costs of an application under this Section except, where appropriate, an order under section 103D(1) of the 2002 Act. 54.35

Continuing an application in circumstances in which it would otherwise be treated as abandoned[1]

54.36—(1) This rule applies to an application under section 103A of the 2002 Act which— 54.36

[1] Introduced by the Civil Procedure (Amendment) Rules 2006 (SI 2006/1689).

(a) would otherwise be treated as abandoned under section 104(4A) of the 2002 Act; but

(b) meets the conditions set out in section 104(4B) or section 104(4C) of the 2002 Act.

(2) Where section 104(4A) of the 2002 Act applies and the applicant wishes to pursue the application, the applicant must file a notice at the Administrative Court Office—

(a) where section 104(4B) of the 2002 Act applies, within 28 days of the date on which the applicant received notice of the grant of leave to enter or remain in the United Kingdom for a period exceeding 12 months; or

(b) where section 104(4C) of the 2002 Act applies, within 28 days of the date on which the applicant received notice of the grant of leave to enter or remain in the United Kingdom.

(3) Where the applicant does not comply with the time limits specified in paragraph (2), the application will be treated as abandoned in accordance with section 104(4) of the 2002 Act.

(4) The applicant must serve the notice filed under paragraph (2) on the other party to the appeal.

(5) Where section 104(4B) of the 2002 Act applies, the notice filed under paragraph (2) must state—

(a) the applicant's full name and date of birth;

(b) the Administrative Court reference number;

(c) the Home Office reference number, if applicable;

(d) the date on which the applicant was granted leave to enter or remain in the United Kingdom for a period exceeding 12 months; and

(e) that the applicant wishes to pursue the application insofar as it is brought on grounds relating to the Refugee Convention specified in section 84(1)(g) of the 2002 Act.

(6) Where section 104(4C) of the 2002 Act applies, the notice filed under paragraph (2) must state—

(a) the applicant's full name and date of birth;

(b) the Administrative Court reference number;

(c) the Home Office reference number, if applicable;

(d) the date on which the applicant was granted leave to enter or remain in the United Kingdom; and

(e) that the applicant wishes to pursue the application insofar as it is brought on grounds relating to section 19B of the Race Relations Act 1976 specified in section 84(1)(b) of the 2002 Act.

(7) Where an applicant has filed a notice under paragraph (2) the court will notify the applicant of the date on which it received the notice.

(8) The court will send a copy of the notice issued under paragraph (7) to the other party to the appeal.

PRACTICE DIRECTION 54A—JUDICIAL REVIEW

Section I—General provisions relating to judicial review

This Practice Direction supplements CPR Part 54 **54APD.1**

1.1 In addition to Part 54 and this practice direction attention is drawn to:

- section 31 of the Supreme Court Act 1981; and
- the Human Rights Act 1998

The Court

2.1 Part 54 claims for judicial review are dealt with in the Administrative Court. **54APD.2**

(Practice Direction 54D (Administrative Court (Venue)) contains provisions about where a claim for judicial review may be started, administered and heard.)

Judicial Review Claims in Wales

3.1 [Omitted; see now Practice Direction 54D—Administrative Court (Venue)] **54APD.3**

3.2 [Omitted]

Rule 54.5—Time Limit for Filing Claim Form

4.1 Where the claim is for a quashing order in respect of a judgment, order or conviction, the date when the grounds to make the claim first arose, for the purposes of rule 54.5(1)(b), is the date of that judgment, order or conviction. **54APD.4**

Rule 54.6—Claim Form

Interested parties

5.1 Where the claim for judicial review relates to proceedings in a court or tribunal, any other parties to those proceedings must be named in the claim form as interested parties under rule 54.6(1)(a) (and therefore served with the claim form under rule 54.7(b)). **54APD.5**

5.2 For example, in a claim by a defendant in a criminal case in the Magistrates or Crown Court for judicial review of a decision in that case, the prosecution must always be named as an interested party.

Human rights

5.3 Where the claimant is seeking to raise any issue under the Human Rights Act 1998, or seeks a remedy available under that Act, the claim form must include the information required by paragraph 15 of the practice direction supplementing Part 16.

Devolution issues

5.4 Where the claimant intends to raise a devolution issue, the claim form must:

(1) specify that the applicant wishes to raise a devolution issue and identify the relevant provisions of the Government of Wales Act 2006, the Northern Ireland Act 1998 or the Scotland Act 1998; and

(2) contain a summary of the facts, circumstances and points of law on the basis of which it is alleged that a devolution issue arises.

5.5 In this practice direction "devolution issue" has the same meaning as in paragraph 1, Schedule 9 to the Government of Wales Act 2006, paragraph 1, Schedule 10 to the Northern Ireland Act 1998; and paragraph 1, Schedule 6 to the Scotland Act 1998.

Claim form

5.6 The claim form must include or be accompanied by—

(1) a detailed statement of the claimant's grounds for bringing the claim for judicial review;
(2) a statement of the facts relied on;
(3) any application to extend the time limit for filing the claim form;
(4) any application for directions.

5.7 In addition, the claim form must be accompanied by

(1) any written evidence in support of the claim or application to extend time;
(2) a copy of any order that the claimant seeks to have quashed;
(3) where the claim for judicial review relates to a decision of a court or tribunal, an approved copy of the reasons for reaching that decision;
(4) copies of any documents on which the claimant proposes to rely;
(5) copies of any relevant statutory material;
(6) a list of essential documents for advance reading by the court (with page references to the passages relied on).

5.8 Where it is not possible to file all the above documents, the claimant must indicate which documents have not been filed and the reasons why they are not currently available.

Bundle of documents

5.9 The claimant must file two copies of a paginated and indexed bundle containing all the documents referred to in paragraphs 5.6 and 5.7.

5.10 Attention is drawn to rules 8.5(1) and 8.5(7).

Rule 54.7—Service of Claim Form

54APD.6 **6.1** Except as required by rules 54.11 or 54.12(2), the Administrative Court will not serve documents and service must be effected by the parties.

6.2 Where the defendant or interested party to the claim for judicial review is the Asylum and Immigration Tribunal, the address for service of the claim form is the Asylum and Immigration Tribunal, Official Correspondence Unit, PO Box 6987, Leicester, LE1 6ZX or fax number 0116 249 4131. (Part 6 contains provisions about the service of claim forms.)

Rule 54.8—Acknowledgment of Service

54APD.7 **7.1** Attention is drawn to rule 8.3(2) and the relevant practice direction and to rule 10.5.

Rule 54.10—Permission Given

Directions

8.1 Case management directions under rule 54.10(1) may include directions about serving the claim form and any evidence on other persons. 54APD.8

8.2 Where a claim is made under the Human Rights Act 1998, a direction may be made for giving notice to the Crown or joining the Crown as a party. Attention is drawn to rule 19.4A and paragraph 6 of the Practice Direction supplementing Section I of Part 19.

8.3 [Omitted]

Permission without a hearing

8.4 The court will generally, in the first instance, consider the question of permission without a hearing.

Permission hearing

8.5 Neither the defendant nor any other interested party need attend a hearing on the question of permission unless the court directs otherwise.

8.6 Where the defendant or any party does attend a hearing, the court will not generally make an order for costs against the claimant.

Rule 54.11—Service of Order Giving or Refusing Permission

9.1 An order refusing permission or giving it subject to conditions or on certain grounds only must set out or be accompanied by the court's reasons for coming to that decision. 54APD.9

Rule 54.14—Response

10.1 Where the party filing the detailed grounds intends to rely on documents not already filed, he must file a paginated bundle of those documents when he files the detailed grounds. 54APD.10

Rule 54.15—Where Claimant Seeks to Rely on Additional Grounds

11.1 Where the claimant intends to apply to rely on additional grounds at the hearing of the claim for judicial review, he must give notice to the court and to any other person served with the claim form no later than 7 clear days before the hearing (or the warned date where appropriate). 54APD.11

Rule 54.16—Evidence

12.1 Disclosure is not required unless the court orders otherwise. 54APD.12

Rule 54.17—Court's Powers to Hear Any Person

13.1 Where all the parties consent, the court may deal with an application under rule 54.17 without a hearing. 54APD.13

13.2 Where the court gives permission for a person to file evidence or make representations at the hearing of the claim for judicial review, it may do so on conditions and may give case management directions.

13.3 An application for permission should be made by letter to the Administrative Court office, identifying the claim, explaining who the applicant is and indicating why and in what form the applicant wants to participate in the hearing.

13.4 If the applicant is seeking a prospective order as to costs, the letter should say what kind of order and on what grounds.

13.5 Applications to intervene must be made at the earliest reasonable opportunity, since it will usually be essential not to delay the hearing.

Rule 54.20—Transfer

54APD.14 **14.1** Attention is drawn to rule 30.5.

14.2 In deciding whether a claim is suitable for transfer to the Administrative Court, the court will consider whether it raises issues of public law to which Part 54 should apply.

Skeleton arguments

54APD.15 **15.1** The claimant must file and serve a skeleton argument not less than 21 working days before the date of the hearing of the judicial review (or the warned date).

15.2 The defendant and any other party wishing to make representations at the hearing of the judicial review must file and serve a skeleton argument not less than 14 working days before the date of the hearing of the judicial review (or the warned date).

15.3 Skeleton arguments must contain:

(1) a time estimate for the complete hearing, including delivery of judgment;
(2) a list of issues;
(3) a list of the legal points to be taken (together with any relevant authorities with page references to the passages relied on);
(4) a chronology of events (with page references to the bundle of documents (see paragraph 16.1);
(5) a list of essential documents for the advance reading of the court (with page references to the passages relied on) (if different from that filed with the claim form) and a time estimate for that reading; and
(6) a list of persons referred to.

Bundle of documents to be filed

54APD.16 **16.1** The claimant must file a paginated and indexed bundle of all relevant documents required for the hearing of the judicial review when he files his skeleton argument.

16.2 The bundle must also include those documents required by the defendant and any other party who is to make representations at the hearing.

Agreed final order

54APD.17 **17.1** If the parties agree about the final order to be made in a claim for judicial review, the claimant must file at the court a document (with 2 copies) signed by all the parties setting out the terms of the proposed agreed order together with a short statement of the matters relied on as justifying the proposed agreed order and copies of any authorities or statutory provisions relied on.

17.2 The court will consider the documents referred to in paragraph 17.1 and will make the order if satisfied that the order should be made.

17.3 If the court is not satisfied that the order should be made, a hearing date will be set.

17.4 Where the agreement relates to an order for costs only, the parties need only file a document signed by all the parties setting out the terms of the proposed order.

Section II—Applications for permission to apply for judicial review in immigration and asylum cases—challenging removal

18.1(1) This Section applies where— **54APD.18**

(a) a person has been served with a copy of directions for his removal from the United Kingdom by the Immigration and Nationality Directorate of the Home Office and notified that this Section applies; and

(b) that person makes an application for permission to apply for judicial review before his removal takes effect.

(2) This Section does not prevent a person from applying for judicial review after he has been removed.

(3) The requirements contained in this Section of this Practice Direction are additional to those contained elsewhere in the Practice Direction.

18.2(1) A person who makes an application for permission to apply for judicial review must file a claim form and a copy at court, and the claim form must—

(a) indicate on its face that this Section of the Practice Direction applies; and

(b) be accompanied by—

(i) a copy of the removal directions and the decision to which the application relates; and

(ii) any document served with the removal directions including any document which contains the Immigration and Nationality Directorate's factual summary of the case; and

(c) contain or be accompanied by the detailed statement of the claimant's grounds for bringing the claim for judicial review; or

(d) if the claimant is unable to comply with paragraph (b) or (c), contain or be accompanied by a statement of the reasons why.

(2) The claimant must, immediately upon issue of the claim, send copies of the issued claim form and accompanying documents to the address specified by the Immigration and Nationality Directorate.

(Rule 54.7 also requires the defendant to be served with the claim form within 7 days of the date of issue. Rule 6.5(8) provides that service on a Government Department must be effected on the solicitor acting for that Department, which in the case of the Immigration and Nationality Directorate is the Treasury Solicitor. The address for the Treasury Solicitor may be found in the Annex to Part 66 of these Rules.)

18.3 Where the claimant has not complied with paragraph 18.2(1)(b) or (c) and has provided reasons why he is unable to comply, and the court has issued the claim form, the Administrative Court—

(a) will refer the matter to a Judge for consideration as soon as practicable; and

(b) will notify the parties that it has done so.

18.4 If, upon a refusal to grant permission to apply for judicial review, the Court indicates that the application is clearly without merit, that indication will be included in the order refusing permission.

CPR 54

PRACTICE DIRECTION—APPLICATIONS FOR STATUTORY REVIEW UNDER SECTION 103A OF THE NATIONALITY, IMMIGRATION AND ASYLUM ACT 2002

This Practice Direction supplements section III of CPR Part 54

1 Attention is drawn to: **54BPD.1**

- Sections 103A, 103C and 103D of the Nationality, Immigration and Asylum Act 2002 (inserted by section 26(6) of the Asylum and Immigration (Treatment of Claimants, etc.) Act 2004); and
- (2) Paragraph 30 of Schedule 2 to the 2004 Act.

The Court

2.1 Applications for review under section 103A(1) of the 2002 Act are dealt with in the Administrative Court, subject to the transitional filter provision in paragraph 30 of Schedule 2 of the 2004 Act which provides that they shall initially be considered by a member of the Tribunal. **54BPD.2**

2.2 During any period in which the filter provision has effect, the address for filing section 103A applications shall be the Asylum and Immigration Tribunal, P.O. Box 6987, Leicester LE1 6ZX.

2.3 Where a fast track order within the meaning of Rule 54.32(3) applies to a section 103A application, paragraph 2.2 shall not apply and the address for filing the application shall be the address specified in the Tribunal's determination of the appeal.

Access to Court Orders Served on the Appellant by the Secretary of State

3.1 Where the court sends a copy of its order on a section 103A application to the Secretary of State but not the appellant in accordance with Rule 54.34(2), then Rules 5.4(3)(b) and 5.4(5)(a)(ii) are modified as follows. **54BPD.3**

3.2 Neither the appellant nor any other person may obtain from the records of the court a copy of the court's order on the section 103A application, or of any order made under section 103D(1) of the 2002 Act in relation to that application, until either the Secretary of State has given the court the notification required by Rule 54.34(3)(b) or 28 days after the date on which the court sent a copy of the order to the Secretary of State, whichever is the earlier.

Referral to Court of Appeal

4.1 Where the court refers an appeal to the Court of Appeal, its order will set out the question of law raised by the appeal which is of such importance that it should be decided by the Court of Appeal. **54BPD.4**

4.2 Paragraph 21.7A of the practice direction supplementing Part 52 makes provision about appeals which are referred to the Court of Appeal.

PRACTICE DIRECTION 54C—REFERENCES BY THE LEGAL SERVICES COMMISSION

54CPD.1 **1.1** This Practice Direction applies where the Legal Services Commission ("the Commission") refers to the High Court a question that arises on a review of a decision about an individual's financial eligibility for a representation order in criminal proceedings under the Criminal Defence Service (Financial Eligibility) Regulations 2006.

1.2 A reference of a question by the Legal Services Commission must be made to the Administrative Court.

1.3 Part 52 does not apply to a review under this paragraph.

1.4 The Commission must—

(a) file at the court—

(i) the individual's applications for a representation order and for a review, and any supporting documents;

(ii) a copy of the question on which the court's decision is sought; and

(iii) a statement of the Commission's observations on the question; and

(b) serve a copy of the question and the statement on the individual.

1.5 The individual may file representations on the question at the court within 7 days after service on him of the copy of the question and the statement.

1.6 The question will be decided without a hearing unless the court directs otherwise.

PRACTICE DIRECTION 54D—ADMINISTRATIVE COURT (VENUE)

This Practice Direction supplements Part 54

Scope and purpose

1.1 This Practice Direction concerns the place in which a claim before the Administrative Court should be started and administered and the venue at which it will be determined. **54DPD.1**

1.2 This Practice Direction is intended to facilitate access to justice by enabling cases to be administered and determined in the most appropriate location. To achieve this purpose it provides flexibility in relation to where claims are to be administered and enables claims to be transferred to different venues.

Venue—general provisions

2.1 The claim form in proceedings in the Administrative Court may be issued at the Administrative Court Office of the High Court at— **54DPD.2**

(1) the Royal Courts of Justice in London; or

(2) at the District Registry of the High Court at Birmingham, Cardiff, Leeds, or Manchester unless the claim is one of the excepted classes of claim set out in paragraph 3 of this Practice Direction which may only be started and determined at the Royal Courts of Justice in London.

2.2 Any claim started in Birmingham will normally be determined at a court in the Midland region (geographically covering the area of the Midland Circuit); in Cardiff in Wales; in Leeds in the North-Eastern Region (geographically covering the area of the North Eastern Circuit); in London at the Royal Courts of Justice; and in Manchester, in the North-Western Region (geographically covering the Northern Circuit).

Excepted classes of claim

3.1 The excepted classes of claim referred to in paragraph 2.1(2) are— **54DPD.3**

(1) proceedings to which Part 76 or Part 79 applies, and for the avoidance of doubt—

(a) proceedings relating to control orders (within the meaning of Part 76);

(b) financial restrictions proceedings (within the meaning of Part 79);

(c) proceedings relating to terrorism or alleged terrorists (where that is a relevant feature of the claim); and

(d) proceedings in which a special advocate is or is to be instructed;

(2) proceedings to which RSC Order 115 applies;

(3) proceedings under the Proceeds of Crime Act 2002;

(4) appeals to the Administrative Court under the Extradition Act 2003;

(5) proceedings which must be heard by a Divisional Court; and

(6) proceedings relating to the discipline of solicitors.

3.2 If a claim form is issued at an Administrative Court office other than in London and includes one of the excepted classes of claim, the proceedings will be transferred to London.

Urgent applications

54DPD.4 **4.1** During the hours when the court is open, where an urgent application needs to be made to the Administrative Court outside London, the application must be made to the judge designated to deal with such applications in the relevant District Registry.

4.2 Any urgent application to the Administrative Court during the hours when the court is closed, must be made to the duty out of hours High Court judge by telephoning 020 7947 6000.

Assignment to another venue

54DPD.5 **5.1** The proceedings may be transferred from the office at which the claim form was issued to another office. Such transfer is a judicial act.

5.2 The general expectation is that proceedings will be administered and determined in the region with which the claimant has the closest connection, subject to the following considerations as applicable—

(1) any reason expressed by any party for preferring a particular venue;

(2) the region in which the defendant, or any relevant office or department of the defendant, is based;

(3) the region in which the claimant's legal representatives are based;

(4) the ease and cost of travel to a hearing;

(5) the availability and suitability of alternative means of attending a hearing (for example, by videolink);

(6) the extent and nature of media interest in the proceedings in any particular locality;

(7) the time within which it is appropriate for the proceedings to be determined;

(8) whether it is desirable to administer or determine the claim in another region in the light of the volume of claims issued at, and the capacity, resources and workload of, the court at which it is issued;

(9) whether the claim raises issues sufficiently similar to those in another outstanding claim to make it desirable that it should be determined together with, or immediately following, that other claim; and

(10) whether the claim raises devolution issues and for that reason whether it should more appropriately be determined in London or Cardiff.

5.3(1) When an urgent application is made under paragraph 4.1 *or 4.2, this will* not by itself decide the venue for the further administration or determination of the claim.

(2) The court dealing with the urgent application may direct that the case be assigned to a particular venue.

(3) When an urgent application is made under paragraph 4.2, and the court does not make a direction under sub-paragraph (2), the claim will be assigned in the first place to London but may be reassigned to another venue at a later date.

5.4 The court may on an application by a party or of its own initiative direct that the claim be determined in a region other than that of the venue in which the claim is currently assigned. The considerations in paragraph 5.2 apply.

5.5 Once assigned to a venue, the proceedings will be both administered from that venue and determined by a judge of the Administrative Court at a suitable court within that region, or, if the venue is in London, at the Royal Courts of Justice. The choice of which court (of those within the region which are identified by the Presiding Judge of the circuit suitable for such hearing) will be decided, subject to availability, by the considerations in paragraph 5.2.

5.6 When giving directions under rule 54.10, the court may direct that proceedings be reassigned to another region for hearing (applying the considerations in paragraph 5.2). If no such direction is given, the claim will be heard in the same region as that in which the permission application was determined (whether on paper or at a hearing).

PART 55

Possession Claims

55.0.1 **Contents**

I. General Rules

II. Accelerated Possession Claims of Property Let on an Assured Shorthold Tenancy

III. Interim Possession Orders

Editorial introduction

The Civil Procedure (Amendment) Rules 2001 (SI 2001/256) introduced Civil Procedure Rule Pt 55 which deals exclusively with possession claims. It came into force on October 15, 2001. It provides a new procedural code for possession claims. It applies to all possession claims issued on or after that date. (Civil Procedure (Amendment) Rules 2001 (SI 2001/256), para.31) Pt 55 is accompanied by a Practice Direction. New prescribed forms have also been drafted. 55.0.2

Part 55 does not apply to claims issued before October 15, 2001—the rules of court in force immediately before that date apply as if they had not been amended or revoked (Civil Procedure (Amendment) Rules 2001 (SI 2001/256) para.31).

Pt 55, Sect.III

By the Civil Procedure (Amendment) Rules 2002 (SI 2002/2058) r.22 and Sch.3, Sect.III (Interim possession orders) (rr.55.20 to 55.28) is added to this Part and various minor consequential amendments are made to r.55.2. As a result of the insertion of Sect.III, Sch.2, CCR O.24, Pt II (Interim possession orders) is revoked (para.cc24.8 below). These changes came into effect on December 2, 2002. 55.0.2.1

Related sources

- Part 1 (Overriding Objective) 55.0.3
- Part 3 (Case Management)
- Part 6 (Service)
- Part 16 (Particulars of Claim)
- Part 26 (Case Management – Preliminary Stage)
- Part 65 and PD65 (Proceedings Relating to Anti-Social Behaviour and Harassment)
- Anti-Social Behaviour Act 2003
- Housing Acts 1980, 1985, 1988 and 1996
- Criminal Justice and Public Order Act 1994 ss.75 and 76
- Criminal Law Act 1977 s.12
- CCR O.24, r.6 (warrants of possession and restitution)
- CCR O.26, r.17 (warrants of possession)

Forms

- **N5** Claim form for possession of property 55.0.4
- **N5A** Claim form for relief against forfeiture
- **N5B** Claim form for possession of property (accelerated possession procedure) (assured shorthold tenancy)(PD55.1.5)
- **N5C** Notes for the claimant (accelerated possession procedure)
- **N6** Claim for demotion of tenancy (PD65.5.2)
- **N7** Notes for defendant (mortgaged residential premises)
- **N7A** Notes for defendant (rented residential premises)
- **N7B** Notes for defendant—forfeiture of the lease (residential premises)
- **N7D** Notes for defendant—demotion claim
- **N11** Form of defence
- **N11B** Defence to possession claim—accelerated procedure
- **N11M** Defence form—mortgaged residential premises
- **N11R** Defence form (rented residential premises)
- **N26** Order for possession
- **N26A** Order—accelerated procedure
- **N27** Order for possession (forfeiture)
- **N28** Order for possession (rented residential premises)(suspended)
- **N28A** Order for possession (rented premises)(postponed)
- **N119** Particulars of claim for possession (rented residential premises)
- **N120** Particulars of claim—mortgaged residential premises
- **N121** Particulars of claim—trespassers

- **N130** Application for interim possession order
- **N133** Witness statement of defendant to oppose making of an interim possession order
- **N134** Interim possession order
- **N136** Order for possession (after IPO)
- **N206A** Notice of Issue
- **N206B** Notice of Issue

I. General Rules

Interpretation[1]

55.1 **55.1 In this Part—**

(a) "a possession claim" means a claim for the recovery of possession of land (including buildings or parts of buildings);

(b) "a possession claim against trespassers" means a claim for the recovery of land which the claimant alleges is occupied only by a person or persons who entered or remained on the land without the consent of a person entitled to possession of that land but does not include a claim against a tenant or sub-tenant whether his tenancy has been terminated or not;

(c) "mortgage" includes a legal or equitable mortgage and a legal or equitable charge and "mortgagee" is to be interpreted accordingly;

(d) "the 1985 Act" means the Housing Act 1985[2];

(e) "the 1988 Act" means the Housing Act 1988[3];

(f) "a demotion claim" means a claim made by a landlord for an order under section 82A of the 1985 Act or section 6A of the 1988 Act ("a demotion order");

(g) "a demoted tenancy" means a tenancy created by virtue of a demotion order; and

(h) "a suspension claim" means a claim made by a landlord for an order under section 121A of the 1985 Act.

55.1.1 **Housing Act 1985** See para.3A–325.
Housing Act 1988 See para.3A–711+.
demotion claims See Housing Act 1985 s.82A (para.3A–349) and Housing Act 1988 s.6A (para.3A–765 and 65.11.3).

Scope[4]

55.2 **55.2—(1) The procedure set out in this Section of this Part must be used where the claim includes—**

(a) a possession claim brought by a—

(i) landlord (or former landlord);

(ii) mortgagee; or

(iii) licensor (or former licensor);

---

[1] *Introduced by the Civil* Procedure (Amendment) Rules 2001 (SI 2001/256).
[2] 1985 c.68.
[3] 1988 c.50.
[4] Introduced by the Civil Procedure (Amendment) Rules 2001 (SI 2001/256) and amended by the Civil Procedure (Amendment) Rules 2002 (SI 2002/2058).

(b) a possession claim against trespassers; or
(c) a claim by a tenant seeking relief from forfeiture.

(Where a demotion claim or a suspension claim (or both) is made in the same claim form in which a possession claim is started, this Section of this Part applies as modified by rule 65.12. Where the claim is a demotion claim or a suspension claim only, or a suspension claim made in addition to a demotion claim, Section III of Part 65 applies).

(2) This Section of this Part—
(a) is subject to any enactment or practice direction which sets out special provisions with regard to any particular category of claim;
(b) does not apply where the claimant uses the procedure set out in Section II of this Part; and
(c) does not apply where the claimant seeks an interim possession order under Section III of this Part except where the court orders otherwise or that Section so provides.

Scope of Section 1—r.55.2

Rule 55.2 is printed as amended by Civil Procedure (Amendment) Rules 2002 (SI 2002/2058) r.22(b). That statutory instrument divides Pt 55 into three Sections by adding Sect.III (Interim Possession Orders). This addition, and the revocation of Scheduled Rules related to it, came into force on December 2, 2002. **55.2.1**

A possession claim against trespassers

See CPR r.55.1(b). **55.2.2**

Mortgage

See CPR r.55.1(c). **55.2.3**

Application of Part 55

Part 55 must be used where court proceedings include a possession claim brought by a landlord, a lender or a licensor (CPR r.55.2). Part 55 must also be used in a claim brought against trespassers. It replaces CCR O.24 and RSC O.113 so that the procedure for bringing claims against trespassers, including those whose names are unknown, is brought within the main Pt 55 procedure, albeit with certain modifications. **55.2.4**

A possession claim against trespassers means a claim for the recovery of land which the claimant alleges is occupied only by a person or persons who entered or remained on the land without the consent of a person entitled to possession of that land. The definition therefore includes a former licensee whose licence has expired or which has been validly determined but does not include a claim against a tenant or sub-tenant whether the tenancy has been terminated or not (CPR r.55.1(b)). In this respect the new rule is different to the former position whereby CCR O.24 and RSC O.113 could be used against unlawful subtenants (see *Moore Properties (Ilford) Ltd v McKeon* [1976] 1 W.L.R. 1278, Ch D). A claim, which is not a possession claim, may be brought under the Pt 55 procedure if it is started in the same claim form as a possession claim (see PD55, para.1.7).

Demotion claims

See Housing Act 1985 s.82A (para.3A–349) and Housing Act 1988 s.6A (para.3A–765). See too the commentary at 65.11.3. **55.2.5**

Starting the claim[1]

55.3—(1) The claim must be started in the county court for the **55.3**

[1] Introduced by the Civil Procedure (Amendment) Rules 2001 (SI 2001/256).

district in which the land is situated unless paragraph (2) applies or an enactment provides otherwise.

(2) The claim may be started in the High Court if the claimant files with his claim form a certificate stating the reasons for bringing the claim in that court verified by a statement of truth in accordance with Rule 22.1(1).

(3) The practice direction refers to circumstances which may justify starting the claim in the High Court.

(4) Where, in a possession claim against trespassers, the claimant does not know the name of a person in occupation or possession of the land, the claim must be brought against "persons unknown" in addition to any named defendants.

(5) The claim form and form of defence sent with it must be in the forms set out in the relevant practice direction.

A possession claim against trespassers

55.3.1 See CPR r.55.1(b).

Form of defence

55.3.2 See CPR r.55.7.

Which court?

55.3.3 The basic rule is that possession claims must be started in the county court for the district where the property is situated (CPR r.55.3(1)). However a claimant may start a possession claim in the High Court if there are exceptional circumstances (PD55, para.2.1), e.g. where:

— there are complicated disputes of fact;
— there are points of law of general importance; or
— there is a claim against trespassers where there is a substantial risk of public disturbance or of serious harm to persons or property which requires immediate determination.

The value of the property and the amount of the financial claim may be relevant circumstances, but they alone will not normally justify starting the claim in the High Court. The Practice Direction points out the consequences of issuing in the High Court when it is not justified. In such circumstances, courts will normally either strike out the claim or transfer it to the county court on its own initiative. This is likely to result in delay and the court will normally disallow the costs of starting the claim in the High Court and of any transfer.

The Claim Form

55.3.4 See Forms **N5** and **N5B**.. The claim form must be in prescribed form (PD55, para.2.6) and must be verified by a statement of truth (CPR, r.22.1). In a claim against trespassers, if the claimant does not know the name of a person in occupation, the claim must be brought against "persons unknown" in addition to any named defendants (CPR r.55.3(4)). If proceedings are issued in the High Court, the claim form must be accompanied by a certificate stating the reasons for bringing the claim in the High Court, verified by a statement of truth.

It has been held at first instance (*Birmingham CC v Hosey*, December 2002, unrep. (H.H.J. MacDuff Q.C.)) that a statement of truth in a possession claim form which had not been signed personally, but which bore the rubber stamp of a signature of an employee in the claimant's legal services department who had no personal knowledge of the case, had not been signed within the meaning of CPR r.22.1. The requirement in *CPR r.22.1*(a) for the statement of case to be signed is not a mere technicality or a matter of form. Courts need to be able to rely upon documents bearing statements of truth. It is essential that statements of case should be properly verified. See too PD 22, para.3.

Possession claims online

For the procedure for the issue of possession claims online, see Practice Direction 55B. **55.3.5**

Particulars of claim[1]

55.4 The particulars of claim must be filed and served with the claim form. **55.4**

(The relevant practice direction and Part 16 provide details about the contents of the particulars of claim)

Particulars of Claim

Particulars of Claim must be filed and served with the claim form. All Particulars of Claim must: **55.4.1**

- comply with CPR Pt 16. This means that they must contain a concise statement of facts and, if interest is sought, give details;
- identify the land to which the claim relates (PD55, para.2.1(1));
- state whether it is residential property (PD55, para.2.1(2));
- state the ground on which possession is claimed (PD55, para.2.1(3));
- give full details of any mortgage or tenancy agreement (PD55, para.2.1(4)); and
- give details of every person who, to the best of the claimant's knowledge, is in possession of the property (PD55, para.2.1(5)).

PD16, para.7.3(1) requires that a copy of any written agreement upon which the claim is based should be attached to or served with the Particulars of Claim.

Mortgage

See CPR r.55.1(c). **55.4.2**

Proceedings against residential tenants

There are additional requirements for Particulars of Claim where the subject matter of the claim is a tenancy of residential premises (PD55, para.2.3). If the possession claim relies on a statutory ground or grounds for possession, the particulars of claim must specify the ground or grounds relied on (PD55 , para.2.4B). If the claim is based upon non–payment of rent, the particulars of claim form must be in Form **N119** (see PD55, para.1.5 as amended by the 25th update to the rules) and must state: **55.4.3**

- the amount due at the start of proceedings;
- in schedule form, the dates when arrears of rent arose, all amounts of rent due, the dates and amounts of all payments made and a running total of the arrears. In general the schedule should cover the preceding two years, or if the first date of default occurred less than two years before the date of issue, it should cover the period from the first date of default. However if the claimant wishes to rely on a history of arrears which is longer than two years, this should be stated in the particulars and a full schedule should be exhibited to a witness statement;
- a daily rate of any rent and interest;
- any previous steps taken to recover arrears, with full details of any court proceedings;
- any relevant information about the defendant's circumstances, including details about benefits and payments direct.

The Particulars of Claim must also give the name of any person known to be *entitled to apply for relief* from forfeiture. The claimant must file a copy of the Particulars of Claim for service upon such a person (*PD* 55, para.2.4). Note that there are different requirements where possession claims are issued through Possession Claims Online (see PD 55B.).

Proceedings against Mortgagors

See r.55.1(c). There are additional requirements for Particulars of Claim where **55.4.4**

[1] Introduced by the Civil Procedure (Amendment) Rules 2001 (SI 2001/256).

they relate to a mortgage of residential premises (PD 55, para.2.5). In such circumstances, they must be in Form **N120** (see PD 55, para.1.5 as amended by the 25th update to the rules) and give details as to:

- whether a Class F land charge has been registered, or whether a notice under the Matrimonial Homes Act 1983 has been entered or whether a notice under the Family Law Act 1996 has been registered. If this is the case, the claimant must serve notice of the proceedings on any such person; and
- the state of the mortgage account, including the amount of the advance, periodic payments and interest required, the amount needed to redeem the mortgage including solicitors' costs and administration charges and the rate of interest payable. If the mortgage is a regulated consumer credit agreement, they must state the total amount outstanding.

If the claim is based on arrears the Particulars of Claim must set out:

- in schedule form, the dates when the arrears arose, all amounts due, the dates and amounts of all payments made and a running total of the arrears. In general the schedule should cover the preceding two years, or if the first date of default occurred less than two years before the date of issue, it should cover the period from the first date of default. However if the claimant wishes to rely on a history of arrears which is longer than two years, this should be stated in the particulars and a full schedule should be exhibited to a witness statement;
- details of all other payments to be made and claimed;
- any relevant information about the defendant's circumstances, including details about benefits and payments direct; and
- any previous steps taken to recover arrears, with full details of any court proceedings.

Note that there are different requirements where possession claims are issued through Possession Claims Online (see PD 55B).

Proceedings against trespassers

55.4.5 See CPR r.55.1(b). Where the claim is brought against trespassers (PD 55, para.2.6), the Particulars of Claim must state the claimant's interest in the land and the circumstances in which it was occupied without licence or consent. In a claim against trespassers (CPR r.55.1(b)), a separate unoccupied area should be included in a possession order if, and only if, the land owner is entitled to an injunction quia timet against occupants in relation to the separate area (*Drury v Secretary of State for the Environment, Food and Rural Affairs* [2004] EWCA Civ 200; *The Times*, March 15, 2004; *Ministry of Agriculture, Fisheries & Food v Heyman* (1990) 59 P. & C.R. 48, QBD; and *University of Essex v Djemal* [1980] 1 W.L.R. 1301, CA. The threshold requirement is for convincing evidence of a real danger of actual violation. The inclusion in a possession order of an unoccupied area should be exceptional. The necessary evidence should usually take the form of an intention to decamp to the other area, of a history of movement between the two areas from which a real danger of repetition can be inferred, or of such propinquity and similarity between the two areas as to command the inference of a real danger of decampment from one to the other.

Demotion claims

55.4.5.1 PD65, para.5.1 provides that if a demotion order is sought as an alternative to possession, the particulars of claim must—

(1) state whether the demotion claim is a claim under Housing Act 1985 s.82A(2) or under Housing Act 1988 s.6A(2);

(2) state whether the claimant is a local housing authority, a housing action trust or a registered social landlord;

(3) provide details of any statement of express terms of the tenancy served on the tenant under Housing Act 1985 s.82A(7) or under Housing Act 1988 s.6A(10), as applicable; and

(4) state details of the conduct alleged.

Forms

55.4.6 See **N119** (Particulars of Claim for possession—rented residential premises), **N120** (Particulars of Claim—mortgaged premises), and **N121** (Particulars of Claim—trespassers).

Failure to comply with CPR r.55.4

Rule 3.10 deals with the effect of an error of procedure or a failure to comply with any Civil Procedure Rule. The error does not invalidate the step taken and the court may make an order to remedy the error. In considering such matters, the court should have regard to the overriding objective (r.1.1). In some situations dealing "with cases justly" will involve adjourning proceedings to enable the claimant to complete and serve the correct form and to allow the defendant to respond to the information contained in it. In other cases, where the defect is purely technical and there is no prejudice to the defendant, the court is likely to waive the defect. If the failure on the part of the claimant amounts to an abuse of process, the court may strike out the claim (rr.3.1 and 3.4). See, in another context, *Gwynedd CC v Grunshaw* [2000] 1 W.L.R 494, CA. **55.4.7**

Hearing date[1]

55.5—(1) The court will fix a date for the hearing when it issues the claim form. **55.5**

(2) In a possession claim against trespassers the defendant must be served with the claim form, particulars of claim and any witness statements—

(a) in the case of residential property, not less than 5 days; and

(b) in the case of other land, not less than 2 days,

before the hearing date.

(3) In all other possession claims—

(a) the hearing date will be not less than 28 days from the date of issue of the claim form;

(b) the standard period between the issue of the claim form and the hearing will be not more than 8 weeks; and

(c) the defendant must be served with the claim form and particulars of claim not less than 21 days before the hearing date.

(Rule 3.1(2)(a) provides that the court may extend or shorten the time for compliance with any Rule)

A possession claim against trespassers

See r.55.1(b). **55.5.1**

Five days... two days

See r.2.8. "Days" means "clear days". **55.5.2**

Hearings

Courts should fix a date for the hearing on the issue of the claim form (r.55.5(1)). **55.5.3** The time between service of the claim form and the hearing must be at least 21 days in all possession claims apart from those against trespassers. In addition Pt 55 provides that the hearing date will be not less than 28 days from the date of issue (r.55.5(3)(a)) and that the standard period between issue and the hearing will be not more than eight weeks (r.55.5(3)(c)). There must be a minimum of two days between service and the hearing in claims against trespassers of non-residential land and five days where trespassers are alleged to be in possession of residential premises (r.55.5(2) and (3)).

These times may be shortened in accordance with the normal provisions for extending or shortening time contained in r.3.1(2)(a). The Practice Direction states that particular consideration should be given to shortening time where:

— the defendant, or a person for whom the defendant is responsible, has assaulted or threatened to assault the landlord, a member of the landlord's staff, or another tenant;

[1] Introduced by the Civil Procedure (Amendment) Rules 2001 (SI 2001/256).

— there are reasonable grounds for fearing such an assault; or
— the defendant, or a person for whom the defendant is responsible, has caused serious damage or threatened to cause serious damage to the property or to the home or property of another resident (PD 55, para.3.2).

If the Claimant wishes to seek an order abridging time for the first hearing, an **N244** Application Notice giving appropriate reasons should accompany the claim form and Particulars of Claim.

Service of claims against trespassers[1]

55.6 **55.6 Where, in a possession claim against trespassers, the claim has been issued against "persons unknown", the claim form, particulars of claim and any witness statements must be served on those persons by—**

(a) (i) attaching copies of the claim form, particulars of claim and any witness statements to the main door or some other part of the land so that they are clearly visible; and

(ii) if practicable, inserting copies of those documents in a sealed transparent envelope addressed to "the occupiers" through the letter box; or

(b) placing stakes in the land in places where they are clearly visible and attaching to each stake copies of the claim form, particulars of claim and any witness statements in a sealed transparent envelope addressed to "the occupiers".

A possession claim against trespassers

55.6.1 See r.55.1(b).

Persons unknown

55.6.2 See r.55.3(4).

Service generally

55.6.3 The normal rules in CPR Pt 6, which deals with service, apply to Pt 55 claims. Note in particular rr.6.12 to 6.16. Service may be effected by personal service, first class post, leaving documents at the defendant's last known address and in some circumstances via the document exchange or by fax by the court. There are special rules in the Companies Act 1985 for service on companies.

Service upon trespassers

55.6.4 Where the claim is brought against trespassers who are persons unknown service should be effected by attaching the claim form and any witness statements to the main door or some other part of the building where it is clearly visible and by placing it them through the letter box in a sealed transparent envelope, addressed to "to the occupiers". Where the premises are not residential, service may be effected by placing stakes (to which the claim form and any witness statements are is attached) in the land at prominent positions. If these methods are to be used, the claimant must supply the court with sufficient stakes and transparent envelopes (PD 55, para.4.1).

Possession orders against trespassers

55.6.5 In *Drury v Secretary of State for the Environment, Food and Rural Affairs* [2004] EWCA Civ 200; [2004] 1 W.L.R. 1906, para.21 Wilson J. said that:

"*the inclusion in* a possession order of an area of land owned by the claimant

[1] Introduced by the Civil Procedure (Amendment) Rules 2001 (SI 2001/256).

which has not yet been occupied by the defendants should be exceptional. Although it would be foolish to be prescriptive about the nature of the necessary evidence, it seems safe to say that it will usually take the form either of an expression of intention to decamp to the other area or of a history of movement between the two areas from which a real danger of repetition can be inferred or… of such propinquity and similarity between the two areas as to command the inference of a real danger of decampment from one to the other" (para.17).

After quoting that passage, in *Secretary of State for the Environment, Food and Rural Affairs v Meier* [2008] EWCA Civ 903, July 31, 2008 Arden L.J. stated that in such a case the court has a general discretion, but it should only exercise its discretion to refuse an order in exceptional circumstances. There was no reason why "exceptional circumstances" should not, in an appropriate case, include the failure to perform an obligation imposed by public law.

Defendant's response[1]

55.7—(1) An acknowledgment of service is not required and Part 10 does not apply. 55.7

(2) In a possession claim against trespassers rule 15.2 does not apply and the defendant need not file a defence.

(3) Where, in any other possession claim, the defendant does not file a defence within the time specified in rule 15.4, he may take part in any hearing but the court may take his failure to do so into account when deciding what order to make about costs.

(4) Part 12 (default judgment) does not apply in a claim to which this Part applies.

A possession claim against trespassers

See r.55.1(b). 55.7.1

Acknowledgement of service

See CPR Pt 10. 55.7.2

Defence

See CPR Pt 9. 55.7.3

The Defendant's response

CPR r.55 contains modifications to the normal rules for defendants who wish to respond to claims. CPR Pt 10 (acknowledgement of service) does not apply (r.55.7(1)). Nor does CPR Pt 12 (default judgment) (r.55.7(4)). It is not possible for a landlord to obtain a possession order by default if the tenant fails to file or serve a defence. This is not only because CPR Pt 55 expressly disapplies such a remedy, but also because it would preclude the court from considering reasonableness where a landlord relies upon a discretionary ground for possession (see, e.g. *R. v Bloomsbury and Marylebone CC, ex. p. Blackburne* (1985) 275 E.G. 1273, CA; *Hounslow LBC v McBride* (1999) 31 H.L.R. 143, CA and *R. v Birmingham CC, Ex p. Foley*, March 2001, Legal Action 29, QBD). 55.7.4

Forms

The defendant's response must be in the form annexed to the Practice Direction (*PD 55, para.*1.5). In practice this means that the defendant or the defendant's solicitor must complete **N11R** (Defence form—rented residential premises) or **N11M** (Defence form—mortgaged premises). 55.7.5

Failure to file or serve a Defence

CPR r.15.2, which states that a defendant who wishes to defend must file a Defence within 14 days, applies to most Pt 55 claims. However failure to file or serve a Defence 55.7.6

[1] Introduced by the Civil Procedure (Amendment) Rules 2001 (SI 2001/256).

does not prevent the defendant from taking part in the proceedings. Failure to file or serve a Defence may though be taken into account when deciding what costs order to make (r.55.7(2)). The requirement to file and serve a Defence does not apply in claims against trespassers (r.55.7(2)).

Consumer Credit Act 1974

55.7.7 See Civil Procedure, Vol.2, para.3B–235. In Consumer Credit Act 1974 cases, the borrower may apply for a time order (s.129) in the Defence or by making an application in proceedings (PD55, para.7.1).

Costs

55.7.8 Fixed costs apply to certain types of possession claims—unless the court orders otherwise. CPR r.45.1 provides that fixed costs apply where—

- The defendant gives up possession and pays the amount claimed (if any) and the fixed commencement costs;
- One of the grounds for possession is arrears of rent, the court gave a fixed date for hearing, a possession order is made (whether suspended or not) and the defendant has either failed to deliver a defence or the defence is limited to specifying proposals for payment of arrears; and
- The claim is brought under the accelerated procedure (Pt 55, Section 2) against an assured shorthold tenant, a possession order is made and the defendant has neither delivered a defence nor otherwise denied liability
- The claim is a demotion claim or a demotion claim is made in the same claim form in which a possession claim is made and the demotion claim is successful.

The amounts of fixed costs are set out in CPR r.45.2A, Table 2, and CPR r.45.4A.

The hearing[1]

55.8 **55.8—(1) At the hearing fixed in accordance with rule 55.5(1) or at any adjournment of that hearing, the court may—**

(a) decide the claim; or

(b) give case management directions.

(2) Where the claim is genuinely disputed on grounds which appear to be substantial, case management directions given under paragraph (1)(b) will include the allocation of the claim to a track or directions to enable it to be allocated.

(3) Except where—

(a) the claim is allocated to the fast track or the multi-track; or

(b) the court orders otherwise,

any fact that needs to be proved by the evidence of witnesses at a hearing referred to in paragraph (1) may be proved by evidence in writing.

(Rule 32.2(1) sets out the general rule about evidence. Rule 32.2(2) provides that rule 32.2 (1) is subject to any provision to the contrary)

(4) Subject to paragraph (5), all witness statements must be filed and served at least 2 days before the hearing.

(5) In a possession claim against trespassers all witness statements on which the claimant intends to rely must be filed and served with the claim form.

(6) Where the claimant serves the claim form and particulars of

[1] Introduced by the Civil Procedure (Amendment) Rules 2001 (SI 2001/256) and amended by the Civil Procedure (Amendment) Rules 2008 (SI 2008/2178).

claim, the claimant must produce at the hearing a certificate of service of those documents and rule 6.17(2)(a) does not apply.

A possession claim against trespassers

See r.55.1(b). **55.8.1**

Case management

At the hearing or any adjournment, the court may decide the claim or, give case management directions (r.55.8(1)). If the claim is genuinely disputed on grounds which appear to be substantial, directions will include allocation to track or directions to enable it to be allocated. **55.8.2**

Allocation to track

See r.55.9 and r.26.8. **55.8.3**

Two days

See r.2.8. "Days" means "clear days". **55.8.4**

Witness statements

See CPR Pt 32. **55.8.5**

Certificate of service

See r.6.10. **55.8.6**

Preparation for and evidence at the hearing

Except in claims against trespassers, all witness statements must be filed and served at least two days before the hearing. They should include evidence of arrears up to the date of the hearing, if necessary by including a daily rate. However this does not prevent any arrears statement from being brought up to date at the hearing (PD 55, para.5.2). **55.8.7**

Defendants should give evidence about the amount of any outstanding benefits and the state of any benefit claims (PD 55, para.5.3).

In mortgage possession claims, the claimant must, within 5 days of receiving notification of the date of the hearing by the court, send a notice addressed "to the occupiers" of the property giving details of the hearing. The claimant should also produce a copy and evidence of service at the hearing (r.55.10). It used to be the practice for courts to insist that mortgagees produce the original charge certificate at possession hearings, but now an official copy of the Charges Register issued by the Land Registry is admissible in evidence to the same extent as the original. (See Land Registration Act 2002 s.67 and Land Registration Rules (SI 2003/1417).) Courts normally also expect claimants in mortgage possession claims to produce an official search certificate giving the result of a search under Family Law Act 1996 s.56(3). (See Land Registration Rules SI 2003/1417, reg.159).

Where the claimant serves the claim form and the Particulars of Claim, the claimant must produce a certificate of service at the hearing (r.55.8(6)).

If the claim has not been allocated to track, or has been allocated to the small claims track, any fact that needs to be proved may be proved by evidence in writing—either in the form of a witness statement or the claim form with its statement of truth (r.55.8(3)). However if the evidence is disputed and the maker of the witness statement is not present, the court will normally adjourn so that oral evidence can be given (PD55, para.5.4).

Level of judiciary

District judges have jurisdiction to hear possession claims, even if allocated to the multi-track—see PD2B, para.11.1(b). **55.8.8**

Orders fixing a date for possession

In many possession claims against secure tenants based upon rent arrears, courts make orders for possession where possession is postponed or enforcement suspended on terms that tenants pay current rent and a regular sum towards arrears. Traditionally such orders have been made in Form N28. However, in *Harlow DC v Hall* [2006] EWCA Civ 156; [2006] 1 W.L.R. 2116, the Court of Appeal held that orders made in **55.8.9** the Form **N28** ("suspended possession order") in use between 2001 and 2006 terminated secure tenancies on the date specified and converted occupants into tolerated trespassers even if they complied with the terms of the order. In *Bristol CC v Hassan; Bristol CC v Glastonbury* [2006] EWCA Civ 656; [2006] 1 W.L.R. 2582, the Court of Appeal held that courts do not have to use Form **N28** and sanctioned a form of postponed order which does not specify a date on which possession is to be given up and so allows secure tenancies to continue even after breach of the terms of the possession order. For a more detailed discussion of the effect of various forms of suspended and postponed possession orders, see 3A–380. As a result of these Court of Appeal decisions, PD 55 has been amended, by inserting paras 10.1 to 10.10, and two new forms of order introduced—a modified Form **N28** in similar form to that put forward by the DCA in spring 2006 (see para.3A–380) and a Form **N28A** "Order for possession (rented premises)(postponed)" in similar form to that set out in *Bristol CC v Hassan* which does not specify a date for possession. Breach of an order in Form **N28** results in secure tenants becoming trespassers. However, secure tenancies continue despite breach of the terms of an order in Form **N28A**. Practice Direction 55, para.10.2 provides that if a tenant breaches the terms of an order in Form **N28A** and the landlord wants the court to fix a date for possession, the landlord can make an application to the court following a warning notice to the tenant. That notice must be sent at least 14 days and not more than three months before applying for an order. It must:

(1) state that the claimant intends to apply for an order fixing the date upon which the defendant is to give up possession of the property;
(2) record the current arrears and state how the defendant has failed to comply with the order (by reference to a statement of the rent account enclosed with the notice);
(3) request that the defendant reply to the claimant within seven days, agreeing or disputing the stated arrears; and
(4) inform the defendant of his or her right to apply to the court for a further postponement of the date for possession or to stay or suspend enforcement.

The application to the court to fix a date can be made on a "without notice" basis, but the claimant must file the following documents with the application notice:

(1) a copy of the warning notice;
(2) a copy of the defendant's reply, if any, and any relevant subsequent correspondence between the claimant and the defendant; and
(3) a statement of the rent account showing the arrears that have accrued since the first failure to pay in accordance with the order or the arrears that have accrued during the period of two years immediately preceding the date of the application notice, where the first such failure to pay occurs more than two years before that date.

The application should be referred to a district judge who should normally determine the application without a hearing by fixing the date for possession as the next working day, but, if the judge considers that a hearing is necessary, a date should be fixed for the application to be heard and the defendant should be served with the application notice and supporting evidence.

Allocation[1]

55.9 **55.9—(1) When the court decides the track for a possession claim, the matters to which it shall have regard include—**

(a) the matters set out in rule 26.8 as modified by the relevant practice direction;
(b) the amount of any arrears of rent or mortgage instalments;
(c) the importance to the defendant of retaining possession of the land;
(d) the importance of vacant possession to the claimant; ***and***

[1] Introduced by the Civil Procedure (Amendment) Rules 2001 (SI 2001/256).

(e) if applicable, the alleged conduct of the defendant.

(2) The court will only allocate possession claims to the small claims track if all the parties agree.

(3) Where a possession claim has been allocated to the small claims track the claim shall be treated, for the purposes of costs, as if it were proceeding on the fast track except that trial costs shall be in the discretion of the court and shall not exceed the amount that would be recoverable under rule 46.2 (amount of fast track costs) if the value of the claim were up to £3,000.

(4) Where all the parties agree the court may, when it allocates the claim, order that rule 27.14 (costs on the small claims track) applies and, where it does so, paragraph (3) does not apply.

Mortgage

See r.55.1(c). **55.9.1**

Small claims track

See CPR Pt 27. **55.9.2**

Fast track

See CPR Pt 28. **55.9.3**

Fast track trial costs

See CPR Pt 46. **55.9.4**

Allocation to track

See too r.26.8. As possession claims are no longer brought under Pt 8, they are no longer deemed to be allocated to the multi-track in the absence of specific directions. Judges should normally allocate them to the fast or multi-track. They may only be allocated to the small claims track if all parties agree (r.55.9(2)). If a possession claim is allocated to the small claims track, the fast track costs regime applies, but the trial costs are in the discretion of the judge. They should not exceed the amount of fast track costs allowable in r.46.2 if the value were up to £3,000—i.e. currently £350 (r.55.9(3)). **55.9.5**

In considering allocation, courts should take into account the normal criteria contained in r.26.8 (value, remedy sought, complexity, number of parties, etc.). In addition they should take into account the amount of arrears of rent or mortgage instalments, the importance to the defendant of retaining possession and the importance of vacant possession to claimant. In cases of anti-social behaviour, it may be relevant to consider the interests of persons other than the parties (r.26 8(1)(g)).

Possession claims relating to mortgaged residential property[1]

55.10—(1) This rule applies where a mortgagee seeks possession of land which consists of or includes residential property. **55.10**

(2) The claimant must send a notice to the property addressed to "the occupiers" within 5 days of receiving notification of the date of the hearing by the court.

(3) The notice referred to in paragraph (2) must—

(a) state that a possession claim for the property has started;

(b) show the name and address of the claimant, the defendant and the court which issued the claim form; and

(c) give details of the hearing.

[1] Introduced by the Civil Procedure (Amendment) Rules 2001 (SI 2001/256).

(4) The claimant must produce at the hearing—

(a) a copy of the notice; and

(b) evidence that he has served it.

Mortgage

55.10.1 See r.55.1(c) and, generally, the annotations to r.55.8.

Mortgage Pre-Action Protocol

55.10.2 A new pre-action protocol for possession claims based on residential mortgage arrears came into force on November 19, 2008. See C12–001 and the annotations thereto. The Protocol does not alter the parties' contractual or statutory rights and obligations, but does describe the behaviour the court will normally expect of the parties prior to the start of possession claims. It aims to ensure that lenders and borrowers act fairly and reasonably with each other in resolving any matter concerning mortgages and encourages more pre-action contact between lenders and borrowers in an effort to seek agreement, and where this cannot be reached, to enable efficient use of the court's time and resources. For example, it provides that

- lenders should consider reasonable requests from borrowers to change the date of regular payment or the method of payment;
- lenders should respond promptly to any proposal for payment made by borrowers. If lenders do not agree to such a proposal they should give reasons in writing;
- if lenders submit proposals for payment, borrowers should be given a reasonable period of time in which to consider such proposals; and
- if borrowers can demonstrate that reasonable steps have been or will be taken to market the property at an appropriate price in accordance with reasonable professional advice, lenders should consider postponing starting possession claims.

The protocol does not contain any specific sanctions, but concludes "Parties should be able, if requested by the court, to explain the actions that they have taken to comply with this protocol." However, if non-compliance has led to the commencement of proceedings which might otherwise not have needed to be commenced, or has led to costs being incurred in the proceedings that might otherwise not have been incurred, the court has the power to make the orders in relation to costs and interest set out in para 2.3 of the Practice Direction on Protocols (see C1–002), although when doing so, the court should bear in mind the contractual rights and obligations of the parties under the mortgage deed.

Electronic issue of certain possession claims

55.10A **55.10A—(1) A practice direction may make provision for a claimant to start certain types of possession claim in certain courts by requesting the issue of a claim form electronically.**

(2) The practice direction may, in particular—

(a) provide that only particular provisions apply in specific courts;

(b) specify—

(i) the type of possession claim which may be issued electronically;

(ii) the conditions that a claim must meet before it may be issued electronically;

(c) specify the court where the claim may be issued;

(d) enable the parties to make certain applications or take further steps in relation to the claim electronically;

(e) specify the requirements that must be fulfilled in relation to such applications or steps;

(f) enable the parties to correspond electronically with the court about the claim;

(g) specify the requirements that must be fulfilled in relation to electronic correspondence;

(h) provide how any fee payable on the filing of any document is to be paid where the document is filed electronically.

(3) The Practice Direction may disapply or modify these Rules as appropriate in relation to possession claims started electronically.

II. Accelerated Possession Claims of Property Let on an Assured Shorthold Tenancy

When this section may be used[1]

55.11—(1) The claimant may bring a possession claim under this Section of this Part where— 55.11

(a) the claim is brought under section 21 of the 1988 Act[2] to recover possession of residential property let under an assured shorthold tenancy; and

(b) subject to rule 55.12(2), all the conditions listed in rule 55.12(1) are satisfied.

(2) The claim must be started in the county court for the district in which the property is situated.

(3) In this Section of this Part, a "demoted assured shorthold tenancy" means a demoted tenancy where the landlord is a registered social landlord.

(By virtue of section 20B of the 1988 Act, a demoted assured shorthold tenancy is an assured shorthold tenancy)

The 1988 Act

The Housing Act 1988—see r.55.1(d). **55.11.1**

Accelerated possession procedure

The accelerated possession procedure allows landlords to obtain possession orders without a hearing in undisputed claims. It applies only to claims brought under Housing Act 1988 s.21 to recover possession against assured shorthold tenants after service of two months notice (r.55.11). Such claims must be started in the county court for the district in which the property is situated. **55.11.2**

Assured shorthold tenancy

See Housing Act 1988 ss.19A to 21. Civil Procedure, Vol.2, paras 3A–822 to 3A–851. **55.11.3**

Demoted assured shorthold tenancy

See Housing Act 1988 s.20B (para.3A–614) and the commentary at 65.11.3. **55.11.3.1**

Requirements for use of the accelerated possession procedure

Landlords who wish to use the accelerated procedure must satisfy the court that the conditions set out in r.55.12 have been complied with. These requirements are that: **55.11.4**

(a) the tenancy was entered into on or after January 15, 1989;

(b) the only purpose of the proceedings is to recover possession—no other claim may be made, except for costs;

[1] Introduced by the Civil Procedure (Amendment) Rules 2001 (SI 2001/256).

[2] 1988 c.50; Section 21 was amended by the Local Government and Housing Act 1989 (c.42) s.194(1) and Sch.11, para.103 and by the Housing Act 1996 (c.52) ss.98 and 99.

(c) the tenancy did not immediately follow an assured tenancy which was not an assured shorthold tenancy;

(d) the tenancy was an assured shorthold tenancy in accordance with the Housing Act 1988 s.19A or s.20(1)(a) to (c);

(e) the tenancy is subject to a written agreement, or follows a tenancy where there was a written agreement; and

(f) a Housing Act 1988 s.21(1) or s.21(4) notice giving at least two months' notice has been served.

Note also that Housing Act 2004 s.215(1) provides that if a tenancy deposit (see Housing Act s.212(8)) has been paid in connection with an assured shorthold tenancy, no s.21 notice may be given in relation to the tenancy at any time when (a) the deposit is not being held in accordance with an authorised scheme (see Housing Act 2004 s.213(4)), or (b) the initial requirements of such a scheme (see s.213(4)) have not been complied with in relation to the deposit. See para.3A–894.

Conditions[1]

55.12 55.12

(1) The conditions referred to in rule 55.11(1)(b) are that—

(a) the tenancy and any agreement for the tenancy were entered into on or after 15 January 1989;

(b) the only purpose of the claim is to recover possession of the property and no other claim is made;

(c) the tenancy did not immediately follow an assured tenancy which was not an assured shorthold tenancy;

(d) the tenancy fulfilled the conditions provided by section 19A or 20(1)(a) to (c) of the 1988 Act[2];

(e) the tenancy—

(i) was the subject of a written agreement;

(ii) arises by virtue of section 5 of the 1988 Act but follows a tenancy that was the subject of a written agreement; or

(iii) relates to the same or substantially the same property let to the same tenant and on the same terms (though not necessarily as to rent or duration) as a tenancy which was the subject of a written agreement; and

(f) a notice in accordance with sections 21(1) or 21(4) of the 1988 Act[3] was given to the tenant in writing.

(2) If the tenancy is a demoted assured shorthold tenancy, only the conditions in paragraph (1)(b) and (f) need be satisfied.

The 1988 Act

55.12.1 The Housing Act 1988—see r.55.1(d).

Demoted assured shorthold tenancy

55.12.2 See Housing Act 1988 s.20B (para.3A–668+) and the commentary at 65.11.3.

---

[1] *Introduced* by the Civil Procedure (Amendment) Rules 2001 (SI 2001/256).

[2] 1988 c.50; Section 19A was inserted by the Housing Act 1996 (c.52), s.96(1); s.20(1) was amended by s.104 and Sch.8, para.2(3) of that Act.

[3] 1988 c.50; Section 21(1) and 21(4) were amended by the Housing Act 1996 (c.52), s.98.

Claim form[1]

55.13—(1) The claim form must— 55.13

(a) be in the form set out in the relevant practice direction; and

(b) (i) contain such information; and

(ii) be accompanied by such documents,

as are required by that form.

(2) All relevant sections of the form must be completed.

(3) The court will serve the claim form by first class post (or an alternative service which provides for delivery on the next working day).

Claim form

The claim form in accelerated possession proceedings must be in the form set out in the Practice Direction (Form **N5B**). It must contain all the information and be accompanied by all the documents required in that form. All sections of the form must be completed. 55.13.1

Defence[2]

55.14—(1) A defendant who wishes to— 55.14

(a) oppose the claim; or

(b) seek a postponement of possession in accordance with rule 55.18,

must file his defence within 14 days after service of the claim form.

(2) The defence should be in the form set out in the relevant practice direction.

Defence

See CPR Pt 9. A defendant who wishes to oppose the claim must file a Defence within 14 days after service of the claim form (r.55.14). The Defence must be in the form set out in the Practice Direction (Form **N11B**). 55.14.1

Claim referred to judge[3]

55.15—(1) On receipt of the defence the court will— 55.15

(a) send a copy to the claimant; and

(b) refer the claim and defence to a judge.

(2) Where the period set out in rule 55.14 has expired without the defendant filing a defence—

(a) the claimant may file a written request for an order for possession; and

(b) the court will refer that request to a judge.

(3) Where the defence is received after the period set out in rule 55.14 has expired but before a request is filed in accordance with paragraph (2), paragraph (1) will still apply.

---

[1] Introduced by the Civil Procedure (Amendment) Rules 2001 (SI 2001/256) and amended by the Civil Procedure (Amendment No.4) Rules 2005 (SI 2005/3515).

[2] Introduced by the Civil Procedure (Amendment) Rules 2001 (SI 2001/256).

[3] Introduced by the Civil Procedure (Amendment) Rules 2001 (SI 2001/256).

(4) Where—

(a) the period set out in rule 55.14 has expired without the defendant filing a defence; and

(b) the claimant has not made a request for an order for possession under paragraph (2) within 3 months after the expiry of the period set out in rule 55.14,

the claim will be stayed.

Claim referred to judge

55.15.1 Accelerated possession claims should be referred to a judge, either on receipt of a Defence, or on the request of the claimant after the expiry of fourteen days (r.55.15). The judge can still consider any Defence if it is received out of time but before the landlord's request is received. If the defendant does not file a Defence and the claimant does not request a possession order within three months after service, the claim will be stayed.

Consideration of the claim[1]

55.16 **55.16—(1) After considering the claim and any defence, the judge will—**

(a) make an order for possession under rule 55.17;

(b) where he is not satisfied as to any of the matters set out in paragraph (2)—

(i) direct that a date be fixed for a hearing; and

(ii) give any appropriate case management directions; or

(c) strike out the claim if the claim form discloses no reasonable grounds for bringing the claim.

(2) The matters referred to in paragraph (1)(b) are that—

(a) the claim form was served; and

(b) the claimant has established that he is entitled to recover possession under section 21 of the 1988 Act against the defendant.

(3) The court will give all parties not less than 14 days' notice of a hearing fixed under paragraph (1)(b)(i).

(4) Where a claim is struck out under paragraph (1)(c)—

(a) the court will serve its reasons for striking out the claim with the order; and

(b) the claimant may apply to restore the claim within 28 days after the date the order was served on him.

The 1988 Act

55.16.1 The Housing Act 1988—see r.55.1(d).

Fourteen days

55.16.2 See r.2.8. "Days" means "clear days".

Consideration of the claim

55.16.3 After considering the claim, the judge should either:

(a) make an order for possession without a hearing; or

(b) if he or she is not satisfied that the claim was served or that the claimant is

[1] Introduced by the Civil Procedure (Amendment) Rules 2001 (SI 2001/256).

entitled to possession, fix a hearing date and give case management directions. At least 14 days notice of the hearing must be given; or

(c) strike out the claim if it discloses no reasonable grounds for bringing claim.

If the claim is struck out, reasons must be given with the order. In those circumstances, the claimant may, within 28 days, apply to restore claim (r.55.16).

It should be remembered that the Court of Appeal has described the accelerated possession procedure as:

> "a robust machinery. It depends upon district judges rigorously considering the documents which have been filed. Some replies may be little more than a plea, however genuine for mercy. But if, on the face of the reply, a matter has been raised which, if true, might arguably raise a defence; or if the documents filed by the claimant might arguably disclose a defect in his claim, then the district judge must necessarily be "not satisfied" within the meaning of [the rules]." (*Manel v Memon* [2000] 33 E.G. 74; (2001) 33 H.L.R. 24, CA).

In that case the Court of Appeal set aside a possession order made under the accelerated procedure by a district judge where a landlord was relying upon a defective s.21 notice. Holman J. expressed concern that the district judge had adopted the accelerated possession procedure and made a possession order without giving the tenant the opportunity to make representations at an oral hearing. Although this case was decided under CCR O.49, r.6A, exactly the same considerations apply to CPR Pt 55.

Possession order[1]

55.17 Except where rules 55.16(1)(b) or (c) apply, the judge will make an order for possession without requiring the attendance of the parties. 55.17

Costs

Where a judge makes a possession order under the accelerated possession procedure, fixed costs may apply. CPR r.45.1(2)(e) provides that fixed costs apply where the claim is brought under the accelerated procedure, a possession order is made and the defendant has neither delivered a defence nor otherwise denied liability – unless the court orders otherwise. The amounts of fixed costs are set out in CPR r.45.4A. 55.17.1

Postponement of possession[2]

55.18—(1) Where the defendant seeks postponement of possession on the ground of exceptional hardship under section 89 of the Housing Act 1980[3], the judge may direct a hearing of that issue. 55.18

(2) Where the judge directs a hearing under paragraph (1)—

(a) the hearing must be held before the date on which possession is to be given up; and

(b) the judge will direct how many days' notice the parties must be given of that hearing.

(3) Where the judge is satisfied, on a hearing directed under paragraph (1), that exceptional hardship would be caused by requiring possession to be given up by the date in the order of possession, he may vary the date on which possession must be given up.

Postponement of possession

When making orders against assured shorthold tenants under the Housing Act 1988 s.21, judges must order possession to be given within fourteen days, unless 55.18.1

[1] Introduced by the Civil Procedure (Amendment) Rules 2001 (SI 2001/256).
[2] Introduced by the Civil Procedure (Amendment) Rules 2001 (SI 2001/256).
[3] 1980, c.51.

exceptional hardship would be caused, in which case the maximum time that can be allowed is 42 days (Housing Act 1980 s.89). Claimants may indicate in accelerated possession claim forms that they are content for the judge to consider postponing the date on which possession is to be given without a hearing. In that case the judge may order possession in six weeks without a hearing (r.55.18).

Otherwise, if the defendant seeks postponement on the ground of exceptional hardship, the judge must make an order for possession within fourteen days, but direct a hearing on the issue of postponement. The hearing must be before the date on which possession is to be given up. If at the hearing, the judge is satisfied that there will be exceptional hardship, he or she may vary the date on which possession must be given up. However the date can be no more than six weeks after the date on which the original order was made (PD55, para.8.4 and Housing Act 1980 s.89).

Application to set aside or vary[1]

55.19 **55.19 The court may—**

(a) on application by a party within 14 days of service of the order; or

(b) of its own initiative,

set aside or vary any order made under rule 55.17.

III. Interim Possession Orders

When this section may be used[2]

55.20 **55.20—(1) This Section of this Part applies where the claimant seeks an Interim Possession Order.**

(2) In this Section—

(a) "IPO" means Interim Possession Order; and

(b) "premises" has the same meaning as in section 12 of the Criminal Law Act 1977.[3]

(3) Where this Section requires an act to be done within a specified number of hours, rule 2.8(4) does not apply.

Editorial note

55.20.1 This Section of Pt 55 was added to the CPR by Civil Procedure (Amendment) Rules 2002 (SI 2002/2058) r.22(c), Sch.3, Pt II. The provisions of this Section came into force on December 2, 2002. On that date, certain minor amendments made to r.55.2 also came into effect. Criminal Justice and Public Order Act 1994 ss.75 and 76 created interim possession orders (IPOs). Originally the procedure to be followed was contained in CCR O.24, but it is now incorporated in Pt 55.

IPOs can only be granted against trespassers. Failure to comply with an IPO is a criminal offence. The IPO procedure can only be used if: (1) the claimant is only seeking possession. A claimant cannot seek an IPO if there is a claim for another remedy (e.g. damages); (2) the claimant has an immediate right to possession and has had such a right throughout the period of unlawful occupation; (3) the defendants entered the premises as trespassers. It cannot be used against former licensees, tenants or subtenants.

If an IPO has been made and served, any person who is present on the premises as a trespasser at any time during the currency of the order commits an offence unless he or she leaves the premises within 24 hours of service of the order (and does not return) or a copy of the order is not fixed to the premises. It is also an offence if a person who was on the premises when the order was served and who has left then re-

---

[1] Introduced by the Civil Procedure (Amendment) Rules 2001 (SI 2001/256).
[2] Introduced by the Civil Procedure (Amendment) Rules 2002 (SI 2002/2058).
[3] 1977, c.45.

enters or attempts to do so as a trespasser after the expiry of the order but within one year of the date of service of the order. Offences are triable summarily.

Premises

See Criminal Law Act 1977 s.12(1) which states: 55.20.2

"(a) 'premises' means any building, any part of a building under separate occupation, any land ancillary to a building, the site comprising any building or buildings together with any land ancillary thereto..."

Section 12(2) provides that references to a building shall apply also to any structure other than a movable one, and to any movable structure, vehicle or vessel designed or adapted for use for residential purposes. Part of a building is under separate occupation if anyone is in occupation or entitled to occupation of that part as distinct from the whole. Land is ancillary to a building if it is adjacent to it and used (or intended for use) in connection with the occupation of that building or any part of it.

Conditions for IPO application[1]

55.21—(1) An application for an IPO may be made where the following conditions are satisfied — 55.21

(a) the only claim made is a possession claim against trespassers for the recovery of premises;

(b) the claimant —

(i) has an immediate right to possession of the premises; and

(ii) has had such a right throughout the period of alleged unlawful occupation; and

(c) the claim is made within 28 days of the date on which the claimant first knew, or ought reasonably to have known, that the defendant (or any of the defendants), was in occupation.

(2) An application for an IPO may not be made against a defendant who entered or remained on the premises with the consent of a person who, at the time consent was given, had an immediate right to possession of the premises.

Premises

See Criminal Law Act 1977 s.12, summarised at para.55.20.2. 55.21.1

The application[2]

55.22—(1) Rules 55.3(1) and (4) apply to the claim. 55.22

(2) The claim form and the defendant's form of witness statement must be in the form set out in the relevant practice direction.

(3) When he files his claim form, the claimant must also file—

(a) an application notice in the form set out in the relevant practice direction; and

(b) written evidence.

(4) The written evidence must be given—

(a) by the claimant personally; or

(b) where the claimant is a body corporate, by a duly authorised officer.

[1] Introduced by the Civil Procedure (Amendment) Rules 2002 (SI 2002/2058).
[2] Introduced by the Civil Procedure (Amendment) Rules 2002 (SI 2002/2058).

(Rule 22.1(6)(b) provides that the statement of truth must be signed by the maker of the witness statement)

(5) The court will—

(a) issue—

(i) the claim form; and

(ii) the application for the IPO; and

(b) set a date for the hearing of the application.

(6) The hearing of the application will be as soon as practicable but not less than 3 days after the date of issue.

The application

55.22.1 See Forms N5 (claim form, specified in PD55.13) and N130 which comprises both the application and the statement in support of the application. The written evidence (i.e. the statement) must be made personally by the claimant (not by a solicitor or agent) unless the claimant is a corporate body in which case an authorised officer may make it. It includes an undertaking to reinstate the defendant and to pay damages if ordered by the court.

The court should list a hearing as soon as possible after the documents have been filed, but not less than three days after the date on which the application for an IPO is issued. "Three days" means three clear days and Saturdays, Sundays, Bank Holidays, Christmas Day and Good Friday do not count—see CPR r.2.8.

Service[1]

55.23 **55.23—(1) Within 24 hours of the issue of the application, the claimant must serve on the defendant—**

(a) the claim form;

(b) the application notice together with the written evidence in support; and

(c) a blank form for the defendant's witness statement (as set out in the relevant practice direction) which must be attached to the application notice.

(2) The claimant must serve the documents listed in paragraph (1) in accordance with rule 55.6(a).

(3) At or before the hearing the claimant must file a certificate of service in relation to the documents listed in paragraph (1) and rule 6.17(2)(a) does not apply.

Service

55.23.1 Service of the N5, the completed N130 and a blank form of defendant's witness statement (Form N133) must take place within 24 hours after issue. This should be done by fixing a copy to the main door or other conspicuous part of the premises and, if practicable, inserting a copy in a sealed and transparent envelope addressed to the occupiers through the letter box in accordance with CPR r.55.6.

Defendant's response[2]

55.24 **55.24—(1) At any time before the hearing the defendant may file a witness statement in response to the application.**

(2) The witness statement should be in the form set out in the relevant practice direction.

[1] Introduced by the Civil Procedure (Amendment) Rules 2002 (SI 2002/2058) and amended by the Civil Procedure (Amendment) Rules 2008 (SI 2008/2178).

[2] Introduced by the Civil Procedure (Amendment) Rules 2002 (SI 2002/2058).

Witness statement

See Form N133. 55.24.1

Hearing of the application[1]

55.25—(1) In deciding whether to grant an IPO, the court will have regard to whether the claimant has given, or is prepared to give, the following undertakings in support of his application— 55.25

(a) if, after an IPO is made, the court decides that the claimant was not entitled to the order to—

(i) reinstate the defendant if so ordered by the court; and

(ii) pay such damages as the court may order; and

(b) before the claim for possession is finally decided, not to

(i) damage the premises;

(ii) grant a right of occupation to any other person; and

(iii) damage or dispose of any of the defendant's property.

(2) The court will make an IPO if—

(a) the claimant has—

(i) filed a certificate of service of the documents referred to in rule 55.23(1); or

(ii) proved service of those documents to the satisfaction of the court; and

(b) the court considers that—

(i) the conditions set out in rule 55.21(1) are satisfied; and

(ii) any undertakings given by the claimant as a condition of making the order are adequate.

(3) An IPO will be in the form set out in the relevant practice direction and will require the defendant to vacate the premises specified in the claim form within 24 hours of the service of the order.

(4) On making an IPO the court will set a date for the hearing of the claim for possession which will be not less than 7 days after the date on which the IPO is made.

(5) Where the court does not make an IPO—

(a) the court will set a date for the hearing of the claim;

(b) the court may give directions for the future conduct of the claim; and

(c) subject to such directions, the claim shall proceed in accordance with Section I of this Part.

Undertakings

In deciding whether or not to grant an IPO the court should have regard to whether or not the owner has given the undertakings in the prescribed Form N133 to 55.25.1

[1] Introduced by the Civil Procedure (Amendment) Rules 2002 (SI 2002/2058).

reinstate the occupier and pay damages if the court subsequently finds that the IPO should not have been granted. Before making a final order, the court should have regard to whether or not the claimant has undertaken not to damage the premises or the defendant's belongings or to grant any right of occupation to any other person pending the final hearing.

Making an IPO

55.25.2 The court must make an IPO if:

— satisfied as to service (see CPR r.55.25(2)(a) and CPR r.55.6(a));

— the claimant is only seeking possession, has an immediate right to possession and has had such a right throughout the period of unlawful occupation and the defendant entered the premises as a trespassers (see CPR r.55.21); and

— adequate undertakings have been given (see CPR r.55.25(1)).

A final hearing should be listed not less than seven days after the date on which the IPO is made.

Interim possession order

55.25.3 See Form N134.

Service and enforcement of the IPO[1]

55.26 **55.26—(1) An IPO must be served within 48 hours after it is sealed.**

(2) The claimant must serve the IPO on the defendant together with copies of—

(a) the claim form; and

(b) the written evidence in support,

in accordance with rule 55.6(a).

(3) CCR Order 26, rule 17 does not apply to the enforcement of an IPO.

(4) If an IPO is not served within the time limit specified by this rule, the claimant may apply to the court for directions for the claim for possession to continue under Section I of this Part.

Service and enforcement

55.26.1 If an IPO is made in Form N134, it must be served upon the trespassers with a copy of the claimant's Forms N5 and N130 within 48 hours of it being sealed. Under s.76 it is a criminal offence to be "present on the premises as a trespasser at any time during the currency of the order" but no offence is committed if the trespasser leaves the premises within 24 hours and does not return. Similarly no offence is committed if a copy of the order is not fixed to the premises.

CCR Order 26, rule 17

55.26.2 CCR O.26, r.17 (warrants of possession) does not apply if an IPO has been made.

After IPO made[2]

55.27 **55.27—(1) Before the date for the hearing of the claim, the claimant must file a certificate of service in relation to the documents specified in rule 55.26(2).**

(2) The IPO will expire on the date of the hearing of the claim.

(3) At the hearing the court may make any order it considers appropriate and *may, in particular*—

---

[1] Introduced by the Civil Procedure (Amendment) Rules 2002 (SI 2002/2058).
[2] Introduced by the Civil Procedure (Amendment) Rules 2002 (SI 2002/2058).

(a) make a final order for possession;
(b) dismiss the claim for possession;
(c) give directions for the claim for possession to continue under Section I of this Part; or
(d) enforce any of the claimant's undertakings.

(4) Unless the court directs otherwise, the claimant must serve any order or directions in accordance with rule 55.6(a).

(5) CCR Order 24, rule 6 applies to the enforcement of a final order for possession.

After an IPO has been made

If an IPO is made, the court fixes a return day which is not less than seven days after the initial hearing. The IPO lapses on the return day. This means that once the return day has arrived, it is no longer a criminal offence for trespassers to be on the premises. At the return day hearing, the court may either make a final possession order, dismiss the claim, give further directions or enforce any of the claimant's undertakings. A final order for possession is made in Form **N136**. **55.27.1**

CCR Order 24, rule 6

CCR O.24, r.6 (warrants of possession and restitution) applies if a final order for possession is made. **55.27.2**

Application to set aside IPO[1]

55.28—(1) If the defendant has left the premises, he may apply on grounds of urgency for the IPO to be set aside before the date of the hearing of the claim. **55.28**

(2) An application under paragraph (1) must be supported by a witness statement.

(3) On receipt of the application, the court will give directions as to—
(a) the date for the hearing; and
(b) the period of notice, if any, to be given to the claimant and the method of service of any such notice.

(4) No application to set aside an IPO may be made under rule 39.3.

(5) Where no notice is required under paragraph (3)(b), the only matters to be dealt with at the hearing of the application to set aside are whether—
(a) the IPO should be set aside; and
(b) any undertaking to re-instate the defendant should be enforced,
and all other matters will be dealt with at the hearing of the claim.

(6) The court will serve on all the parties—
(a) a copy of the order made under paragraph (5); and
(b) where no notice was required under paragraph (3)(b), a copy of the defendant's application to set aside and the witness statement in support.

[1] Introduced by the Civil Procedure (Amendment) Rules 2002 (SI 2002/2058).

(7) Where notice is required under paragraph (3)(b), the court may treat the hearing of the application to set aside as the hearing of the claim.

Setting aside IPOs

55.28.1 If occupiers have vacated premises they may apply to set aside an IPO which has been made before the return day. Any such application should be supported by a witness statement.

PRACTICE DIRECTION — POSSESSION CLAIMS

This Practice Direction supplements CPR Part 55 55PD.1

Section I General Rules

55.3 — Starting the claim

1.1 Except where the county court does not have jurisdiction, possession claims should normally be brought in the county court. Only exceptional circumstances justify starting a claim in the High Court.

1.2 If a claimant starts a claim in the High Court and the court decides that it should have been started in the county court, the court will normally either strike the claim out or transfer it to the county court on its own initiative. This is likely to result in delay and the court will normally disallow the costs of starting the claim in the High Court and any transfer.

1.3 Circumstances which may, in an appropriate case, justify starting a claim in the High Court are if—

(1) there are complicated disputes of fact;

(2) there are points of law of general importance; or

(3) the claim is against trespassers and there is a substantial risk of public disturbance or of serious harm to persons or property which properly require immediate determination.

1.4 The value of the property and the amount of any financial claim may be relevant circumstances, but these factors alone will not normally justify starting the claim in the High Court.

1.5 The claimant must use the appropriate claim form and particulars of claim form set out in Table 1 to Part 4 Practice Direction. The defence must be in form **N11**, **N11B**, **N11M** or **N11R**, as appropriate.

1.6 High Court claims for the possession of land subject to a mortgage will be assigned to the Chancery Division.

1.7 A claim which is not a possession claim may be brought under the procedure set out in Section I of Part 55 if it is started in the same claim form as a possession claim which, by virtue of rule 55.2(1) must be brought in accordance with that Section.

(Rule 7.3 provides that a claimant may use a single claim form to start all claims which can be conveniently disposed of in the same proceedings)

1.8 For example a claim under paragraphs 4, 5 or 6 of Part I of Schedule 1 to the Mobile Homes Act 1983 may be brought using the procedure set out in Section I of Part 55 if the claim is started in the same claim form as a claim enforcing the rights referred to in section 3(1)(b) of the Caravan Sites Act 1968 (which, by virtue of rule 55.2(1) must be brought under Section I of Part 55).

1.9 Where the claim form includes a demotion claim, the claim must be started in the county court for the district in which the land is situated.

55.4 — Particulars of claim

2.1 In a possession claim the particulars of claim must: 55PD.2

(1) identify the land to which the claim relates;

(2) state whether the claim relates to residential property;
(3) state the ground on which possession is claimed;
(4) give full details about any mortgage or tenancy agreement; and
(5) give details of every person who, to the best of the claimant's knowledge, is in possession of the property.

Residential property let on a tenancy

55PD.3 **2.2** Paragraphs 2.3. to 2.4B apply if the claim relates to residential property let on a tenancy.

2.3 If the claim includes a claim for non-payment of rent the particulars of claim must set out:

(1) the amount due at the start of the proceedings;
(2) in schedule form, the dates and amounts of all payments due and payments made under the tenancy agreement for a period of two years immediately preceding the date of issue, or if the first date of default occurred less than two years before the date of issue from the first date of default and a running total of the arrears;
(3) the daily rate of any rent and interest;
(4) any previous steps taken to recover the arrears of rent with full details of any court proceedings; and
(5) any relevant information about the defendant's circumstances, in particular:
 (a) whether the defendant is in receipt of social security benefits; and
 (b) whether any payments are made on his behalf directly to the claimant under the Social Security Contributions and Benefits Act 1992.

2.3A If the claimant wishes to rely on a history of arrears which is longer than two years, he should state this in his particulars and exhibit a full (or longer) schedule to a witness statement.

2.4B If the possession claim relies on a statutory ground or grounds for possession, the particulars of claim must specify the ground or grounds relied on.

2.4 If the claimant know of any person (including a mortgagee) entitled to claim relief against forfeiture as underlessee under section 146(4) of the Law of Property Act 1925 (or in accordance with section 38 of the Supreme Court Act 1981, or section 138(9C) of the County Courts Act 1984):

(1) the particulars of claim must state the name and address of that person; and
(2) the claimant must file a copy of the particulars of claim for service on him.

2.4A If the claim for possession relates to the conduct of the tenant, the particulars of claim must state details of the conduct alleged.

Land subject to a mortgage

55PD.4 **2.5** If the claim is a possession claim by a mortgagee, the particulars of claim must also set out:

(1) if the claim relates to residential property whether:

(a) a land charge of Class F has been registered under section 2(7) of the Matrimonial Homes Act 1967;
(b) a notice registered under section 2(8) or 8(3) of the Matrimonial Homes Act 1983 has been entered and on whose behalf; or
(c) a notice under section 31(10) of the Family Law Act 1996 has been registered and on whose behalf; and

if so, that the claimant will serve notice of the claim on the persons on whose behalf the land charge is registered or the notice or caution entered.

(2) the state of the mortgage account by including:
(a) the amount of:
(i) the advance;
(ii) any periodic repayment; and
(iii) any payment of interest required to be made;
(b) the amount which would have to be paid (after taking into account any adjustment for early settlement) in order to redeem the mortgage at a stated date not more than 14 days after the claim started specifying the amount of solicitor's costs and administration charges which would be payable;
(c) if the loan which is secured by the mortgage is a regulated consumer credit agreement, the total amount outstanding under the terms of the mortgage; and
(d) the rate of interest payable:
(i) at the commencement of the mortgage;
(ii) immediately before any arrears referred to in paragraph (3) accrued;
(iii) at the commencement of the proceedings.

(3) if the claim is brought because of failure to pay the periodic payments when due:
(a) in schedule form, the dates and amounts of all payments due and payments made under the mortgage agreement or mortgage deed for a period of two years immediately preceding the date of issue, or if the first date of default occurred less than two years before the date of issue from the first date of default and a running total of the arrears;
(b) give details of:
(i) any other payments required to be made as a term of the mortgage (such as for insurance premiums, legal costs, default interest, penalties, administrative or other charges);
(ii) any other sums claimed and stating the nature and amount of each such charge; and
(iii) whether any of these payments is in arrears and whether or not it is included in the amount of any periodic payment.

(4) whether or not the loan which is secured by the mortgage is

a regulated consumer credit agreement and, if so, specify the date on which any notice required by sections 76 or 87 of the Consumer Credit Act 1974 was given;

(5) if appropriate details that show the property is not one to which section 141 of the Consumer Credit Act 1974 applies;

(6) any relevant information about the defendant's circumstances, in particular:

(a) whether the defendant is in receipt of social security benefits; and

(b) whether any payments are made on his behalf directly to the claimant under the Social Security Contributions and Benefits Act 1992;

(7) give details of any tenancy entered into between the mortgagor and mortgagee (including any notices served); and

(8) state any previous steps which the claimant has taken to recover the money secured by the mortgage or the mortgaged property and, in the case of court proceedings, state:

(a) the dates when the claim started and concluded; and

(b) the dates and terms of any orders made.

55PD.4A **2.5A** If the claimant wishes to rely on a history of arrears which is longer than two years, he should state this in his particulars and exhibit a full (or longer) schedule to a witness statement.

Possession claim against trespassers

55PD.5 **2.6** If the claim is a possession claim against trespassers, the particulars of claim must state the claimant's interest in the land or the basis of his right to claim possession and the circumstances in which it has been occupied without licence or consent.

Possession claim in relation to a demoted tenancy by a housing action trust or a local housing authority

55PD.5A **2.7** If the claim is a possession claim under section 143D of the Housing Act 1996 (possession claim in relation to a demoted tenancy where the landlord is a housing action trust or a local housing authority), the particulars of claim must have attached to them a copy of the notice to the tenant served under section 143E of the 1996 Act.

55.5 — Hearing date

55PD.6 **3.1** The court may exercise its powers under rules 3.1(2)(a) and (b) to shorten the time periods set out in rules 55.5(2) and (3).

3.2 Particular consideration should be given to the exercise of this power if:

(1) the defendant, or a person for whom the defendant is responsible, has assaulted or threatened to assault:

(a) the claimant;

(b) a member of the claimant's staff; and

(c) another resident in the locality;

(2) there are reasonable grounds for fearing such an assault; or

(3) the defendant, or a person for whom the defendant is responsible, has caused serious damage or threatened to

cause serious damage to the property or to the home or property of another resident in the locality.

3.3 Where paragraph 3.2 applies but the case cannot be determined at the first hearing fixed under rule 55.5, the court will consider what steps are needed to finally determine the case as quickly as reasonably practicable.

55.6 — Service in claims against trespassers

4.1 If the claim form is to be served by the court and in accordance with rule 55.6(b) the claimant must provide sufficient stakes and transparent envelopes. **55PD.7**

55.8 — The Hearing

5.1 Attention is drawn to rule 55.8(3). Each party should wherever possible include all the evidence he wishes to present in his statement of case, verified by a statement of truth. **55PD.8**

5.2 If relevant the claimant's evidence should include the amount of any rent or mortgage arrears and interest on those arrears. These amounts should, if possible, be up to date of the hearing (if necessary by specifying a daily rate of arrears and interest). However, rule 55.8(4) does not prevent such evidence being brought up to date orally or in writing on the day of the hearing if necessary.

5.3 If relevant the defendant should give evidence of:

(1) the amount of any outstanding social security or housing benefit payments relevant to rent or mortgage arrears; and

(2) the status of:

(a) any claims for social security or housing benefit about which a decision has not yet been made; and

(b) any applications to appeal or review a social security or housing benefit decision where that appeal or review has not yet concluded.

5.4 If:

(1) the maker of a witness statement does not attend the hearing; and

(2) the other party disputes material evidence contained in his statement,

the court will normally adjourn the hearing so that oral evidence can be given.

Allocation

6.1 [Revoked] **55PD.9**

Consumer Credit Act claims relating to the recovery of land

7.1 Any application by the defendant for a time order under *section 129 of the Consumer Credit Act* 1974 may be made: **55PD.10**

(1) in his defence; or

(2) by application notice in the proceedings.

Enforcement of Charging Order by Sale

7.2 A party seeking to enforce a charging order by sale should follow the procedure set out in rule 73.10 and the Part 55 procedure should not be used. **55PD.11**

Section II Accelerated possession claims of property let on an assured shorthold tenancy

55.18 Postponement of possession

55PD.12 **8.1** If the judge is satisfied as to the matters set out in rule 55.16(2), he will make an order for possession in accordance with rule 55.17, whether or not the defendant seeks a postponement of possession on the ground of exceptional hardship under section 89 of the Housing Act 1980.

8.2 In a claim in which the judge is satisfied that the defendant has shown exceptional hardship, he will only postpone possession without directing a hearing under rule 55.18(1) if—

(1) he considers that possession should be given up 6 weeks after the date of the order or, if the defendant has requested postponement to an earlier date, on that date; and

(2) the claimant indicated on his claim form that he would be content for the court to make such an order without a hearing.

8.3 In all other cases if the defendant seeks a postponement of possession under section 89 of the Housing Act 1980, the judge will direct a hearing under rule 55.18(1).

8.4 If, at that hearing, the judge is satisfied that exceptional hardship would be caused by requiring possession to be given up by the date in the order of possession, he may vary that order under rule 55.18(3) so that possession is to be given up at a later date. That later date may be no later than 6 weeks after the making of the order for possession on the papers (see section 89 of the Housing Act 1980).

Section III Interim Possession Orders

55PD.13

9.1 The claim form must be in form **N5**, the application notice seeking the interim possession order must be in form **N130** and the defendant's witness statement must be in form **N133**.

9.2 The IPO will be in form **N134** (annexed to this practice direction).

Section IV Orders fixing a date for possession

55PD.14 **10.1** This paragraph applies where the court has made an order postponing the date for possession under section 85(2)(b) of the Housing Act 1985 (secure tenancies) or under section 9(2)(b) of the Housing Act 1988 (assured tenancies).

10.2 If the defendant fails to comply with any of the terms of the order which relate to payment, the claimant, after following the procedure set out in paragraph 10.3, may apply for an order fixing the date upon which the defendant has to give up possession of the property. Unless the court further postpones the date for possession, the defendant will be required to give up possession on that date.

10.3 At least 14 days and not more than 3 months before applying for an order under paragraph 10.2, the claimant must give written notice to the defendant in accordance with paragraph 10.4.

10.4 The notice referred to in paragraph 10.3 must—

(1) state that the claimant intends to apply for an order fixing the date upon which the defendant is to give up possession of the property;

(2) record the current arrears and state how the defendant has failed to comply with the order referred to in paragraph 10.1 (by reference to a statement of the rent account enclosed with the notice);

(3) request that the defendant reply to the claimant within 7 days, agreeing or disputing the stated arrears and

(4) inform the defendant of his right to apply to the court—
(a) for a further postponement of the date for possession; or
(b) to stay or suspend enforcement.

10.5 In his reply to the notice, the defendant must:

(1) where he disputes the stated arrears, provide details of payments or credits made;

(2) where he agrees the stated arrears, explain why payments have not been made.

10.6 An application for an order under paragraph 10.2 must be made by filing an application notice in accordance with Part 23. The application notice must state whether or not there is any outstanding claim by the defendant for housing benefit.

10.7 The claimant must file the following documents with the application notice—

(1) a copy of the notice referred to in paragraph 10.3;

(2) a copy of the defendant's reply, if any, to the notice and any relevant subsequent correspondence between the claimant and the defendant;

(3) a statement of the rent account showing:
(a) the arrears that have accrued since the first failure to pay in accordance with the order referred to in paragraph 10.2; or
(b) the arrears that have accrued during the period of two years immediately preceding the date of the application notice, where the first such failure to pay occurs more than two years before that date.

10.8 Rules 23.7 (service of a copy of an application notice) and 23.10 (right to set aside or vary an order made without service of the application notice) and paragraphs 2.3, 2.4 and 2.5 of the Practice Direction supplementing Part 23 (dealing with applications without a hearing) do not apply to an application under this Section.

10.9 On being filed, the application will be referred to the District Judge who—

(1) will normally determine the application without a hearing by fixing the date for possession as the next working day; but

(2) if he considers that a hearing is necessary—
(a) will fix a date for the application to be heard; and
(b) direct service of the application notice and supporting evidence on the defendant.

10.10 The court does not have jurisdiction to review a decision that it was reasonable to make an order for possession.

PRACTICE DIRECTION—POSSESSION CLAIMS ONLINE

55BPD.1 *This Practice Direction supplements rule 55.10A*

Scope of this Practice Direction

1.1 This practice direction provides for a scheme ('Possession Claims Online') to operate in specified county courts—

(1) enabling claimants and their representatives to start certain possession claims under CPR Part 55 by requesting the issue of a claim form electronically via the PCOL website; and

(2) where a claim has been started electronically, enabling the claimant or defendant and their representatives to take further steps in the claim electronically as specified below.

1.2 In this practice direction—

(1) 'PCOL website' means the website www.possessionclaim.gov.uk which may be accessed via Her Majesty's Courts Service website (www.hmcourts-service.gov.uk) and through which Possession Claims Online will operate; and

(2) 'specified court' means a county court specified on the PCOL website as one in which Possession Claims Online is available.

Information on the PCOL Website

55BPD.2 **2.1** The PCOL website contains further details and guidance about the operation of Possession Claims Online.

2.2 In particular the PCOL website sets out—

(1) the specified courts; and

(2) the dates from which Possession Claims Online will be available in each specified court.

2.3 The operation of Possession Claims Online in any specified court may be restricted to taking certain of the steps specified in this practice direction, and in such cases the PCOL website will set out the steps which may be taken using Possession Claims Online in that specified court.

Security

55BPD.3 **3.1** Her Majesty's Courts Service will take such measures as it thinks fit to ensure the security of steps taken or information stored electronically. These may include requiring users of Possession Claims Online—

(1) to enter a customer identification number or password;

(2) to provide personal information for identification purposes; and

(3) to comply with any other security measures,

before taking any step online.

Fees

55BPD.4 **4.1** A step may only be taken using Possession Claims Online on payment of the prescribed fee where a fee is payable. Where this practice direction provides for a fee to be paid electronically, it may be paid by—

(1) credit card;

(2) debit card; or
(3) any other method which Her Majesty's Courts Service may permit.

4.2 A defendant who wishes to claim exemption from payment of fees must do so through an organisation approved by Her Majesty's Courts Service before taking any step using PCOL which attracts a fee. If satisfied that the defendant is entitled to fee exemption, the organisation will submit the fee exemption form through the PCOL website to Her Majesty's Courts Service. The defendant may then use PCOL to take such a step.

(Her Majesty's Courts Service website contains guidance as to when the entitlement to claim an exemption from payment of fees arises. The PCOL website will contain a list of organisations through which the defendant may claim an exemption from fees).

Claims which may be started using Possession Claims Online

5.1 A claim may be started online if— **55BPD.5**
(1) it is brought under Section I of Part 55;
(2) it includes a possession claim for residential property by—
(a) a landlord against a tenant, solely on the ground of arrears of rent (but not a claim for forfeiture of a lease); or
(b) a mortgagee against a mortgagor, solely on the ground of default in the payment of sums due under a mortgage.

relating to land within the district of a specified court;
(3) it does not include a claim for any other remedy except for payment of arrears of rent or money due under a mortgage, interest and costs;
(4) the defendant has an address for service in England and Wales; and
(5) the claimant is able to provide a postcode for the property.

5.2 A claim must not be started online if a defendant is known to be a child or protected party.

Starting a Claim

6.1 A claimant may request the issue of a claim form by— **55BPD.6**
(1) completing an online claim form at the PCOL website;
(2) paying the appropriate issue fee electronically at the PCOL website or by some other means approved by Her Majesty's Courts Service.

6.2 The particulars of claim must be included in the online claim form and may not be filed separately. It is not necessary to file a copy of the tenancy agreement, mortgage deed or mortgage agreement with the particulars of claim.

6.2A In the case of a possession claim for residential property that relies on a statutory ground or grounds for possession, the claimant must specify, in section 4(a) of the online claim form, the ground or grounds relied on.

6.3 Subject to paragraphs 6.3A and 6.3B, the particulars of claim must include a history of the rent or mortgage account, in schedule form setting out—

(1) the dates and amounts of all payments due and payments made under the tenancy agreement, mortgage deed or mortgage agreement either from the first date of default if that date occurred less than two years before the date of issue or for a period of two years immediately preceding the date of issue; and

(2) a running total of the arrears.

6.3A Paragraph 6.3B applies where the claimant has, before commencing proceedings, provided the defendant in schedule form with—

(1) details of the dates and amounts of all payments due and payments made under the tenancy agreement, mortgage deed or mortgage account—

(a) for a period of two years immediately preceding the date of commencing proceedings; or

(b) if the first date of default occurred less than two years before that date, from the first date of default; and

(2) a running total of the arrears.

6.3B Where this paragraph applies the claimant may, in place of the information required by paragraph 6.3, include in his particulars of claim a summary only of the arrears containing at least the following information—

(1) The amount of arrears as stated in the notice of seeking possession served under either section 83 of the Housing Act 1985 or section 8 of the Housing Act 1988, or at the date of the claimant's letter before action, as appropriate;

(2) the dates and amounts of the last three payments in cleared funds made by the defendant or, if less than three payments have been made, the dates and amounts of all payments made;

(3) the arrears at the date of issue, assuming that no further payments are made by the defendant.

6.3C Where the particulars of claim include a summary only of the arrears the claimant must—

(1) serve on the defendant not more than 7 days after the date of issue, a full, up-to-date arrears history containing at least the information required by paragraph 6.3; and

(2) either

(a) make a witness statement confirming that he has complied with sub-paragraph (1) or (2) of paragraph 6.3A as appropriate, and including or exhibiting the full arrears history; or

(b) verify by way of oral evidence at the hearing that he has complied with sub-paragraph (1) or (2) of paragraph 6.3A as appropriate and also produce and verify the full arrears history.

(Rule 55.8(4) requires all witness statements to be filed and served at least 2 days before the hearing.)

6.4 If the claimant wishes to rely on a history of arrears which is longer than two years, he should state this in his particulars and exhibit a full (or longer) schedule to a witness statement.

6.5 When an online claim form is received, an acknowledgment of receipt will automatically be sent to the claimant. The acknowledgment does not constitute notice that the claim form has been issued or served.

6.6 When the court issues a claim form following the submission of an online claim form, the claim is 'brought' for the purposes of the Limitation Act 1980 and any other enactment on the date on which the online claim form is received by the court's computer system. The court will keep a record, by electronic or other means, of when online claim forms are received.

6.7 When the court issues a claim form it will—

(1) serve a printed version of the claim form and a defence form on the defendant; and

(2) send the claimant notice of issue by post or, where the claimant has supplied an e-mail address, by electronic means.

6.8 The claim shall be deemed to be served on the fifth day after the claim was issued irrespective of whether that day is a business day or not.

6.9 Where the period of time within which a defence must be filed ends on a day when the court is closed, the defendant may file his defence on the next day that the court is open.

6.10 The claim form shall have printed on it a unique customer identification number or a password by which the defendant may access the claim on the PCOL website.

6.11 PCOL will issue the proceedings in the appropriate county court by reference to the post code provided by the claimant and that court shall have jurisdiction to hear and determine the claim and to carry out enforcement of any judgment irrespective of whether the property is within or outside the jurisdiction of that court.

(CPR 30.2(1) authorises proceedings to be transferred from one county court to another.)

Defence

7.1 A defendant wishing to file— **55BPD.7**

(1) a defence; or

(2) a counterclaim (to be filed together with a defence) to a claim which has been issued through the PCOL system,

may, instead of filing a written form, do so by—

(a) completing the relevant online form at the PCOL website; and

(b) if the defendant is making a counterclaim, paying the appropriate fee electronically at the PCOL website or by some other means approved by Her Majesty's Courts Service.

7.2 Where a defendant files a defence by completing the relevant online form, he must not send the court a hard copy.

7.3 When an online defence form is received, an acknowledgment of receipt will automatically be sent to the defendant. The acknowledgment does not constitute notice that the defence has been served.

7.4 The online defence form will be treated as being filed—

(1) on the day the court receives it, if it receives it before 4 p.m. on a working day; and

(2) otherwise, on the next working day after the court receives the online defence form.

7.5 A defence is filed when the online defence form is received by the court's computer system. The court will keep a record, by electronic or other means, of when online defence forms are received.

Statement of Truth

55BPD.8 **8.1** CPR Part 22 requires any statement of case to be verified by a statement of truth. This applies to any online claims and defences and application notices.

8.2 CPR Part 22 also requires that if an applicant wishes to rely on matters set out in his application notice as evidence, the application notice must be verified by a statement of truth. This applies to any application notice completed online that contains matters on which the applicant wishes to rely as evidence.

8.3 Attention is drawn to—

(1) paragraph 2 of the practice direction supplementing CPR Part 22, which stipulates the form of the statement of truth; and

(2) paragraph 3 of the practice direction supplementing CPR Part 22, which provides who may sign a statement of truth; and

(3) CPR 32.14, which sets out the consequences of making, or causing to be made, a false statement in a document verified by a statement of truth, without an honest belief in its truth.

Signature

55BPD.9 **9.1** Any provision of the CPR which requires a document to be signed by any person is satisfied by that person entering his name on an online form.

Communication with the Court Electronically by the Messaging Service

55BPD.10 **10.1** If the PCOL website specifies that a court accepts electronic communications relating to claims brought using Possession Claims Online the parties may communicate with the court using the messaging service facility, available on the PCOL website ('the messaging service').

10.2 The messaging service is for brief and straightforward communications only. The PCOL website contains a list of examples of when it will not be appropriate to use the messaging service.

10.3 Parties must not send to the court forms or attachments via the messaging service.

10.4 The court shall treat any forms or attachments sent via the messaging service as not having been filed or received.

10.5 The court will normally reply via the messaging service where—

(1) the response is to a message transmitted via the messaging service; and

(2) the sender has provided an e-mail address.

Electronic Applications

55BPD.11 **11.1** Certain applications in relation to a possession claim started online may be made electronically ('online applications'). An online application may be made if a form for that application is published on the PCOL website ('online application form') and the application is made at least five clear days before the hearing.

11.2 If a claim for possession has been started online and a party wishes to make an online application, he may do so by—

(1) completing the appropriate online application form at the PCOL website; and

(2) paying the appropriate fee electronically at the PCOL website or by some other means approved by Her Majesty's Courts Service.

11.3 When an online application form is received, an acknowledgment of receipt will automatically be sent to the applicant. The acknowledgment does not constitute a notice that the online application form has been issued or served.

11.4 Where an application must be made within a specified time, it is so made if the online application form is received by the court's computer system within that time. The court will keep a record, by electronic or other means, of when online application forms are received.

11.5 When the court receives an online application form it shall—

(1) serve a copy of the online application endorsed with the date of the hearing by post on the claimant at least two clear days before the hearing; and

(2) send the defendant notice of service and confirmation of the date of the hearing by post; provided that

(3) where either party has provided the court with an e-mail address for service, service of the application and/or the notice of service and confirmation of the hearing date may be effected by electronic means.

Request for Issue of Warrant

12.1 Where— 55BPD.12

(1) the court has made an order for possession in a claim started online; and

(2) the claimant is entitled to the issue of a warrant of possession without requiring the permission of the court

the claimant may request the issue of a warrant by completing an online request form at the PCOL website and paying the appropriate fee electronically at the PCOL website or by some other means approved by Her Majesty's Courts Service.

12.2 A request under paragraph 12.1 will be treated as being filed—

(1) *on the* day the court receives the request, if it receives it before 4 p.m. on a working day; and

(2) otherwise, on the next working day after the court receives the request.

(CCR Order 26 rule 5 sets out certain circumstances in which a warrant of execution may not be issued without the permission of the court. CCR Order 26 rule 17(6) applies rule 5 of that Order with necessary modifications to a warrant of possession.)

Application to Suspend Warrant of Possession

55BPD.13 **13.1** Where the court has issued a warrant of possession, the defendant may apply electronically for the suspension of the warrant, provided that:

(1) the application is made at least five clear days before the appointment for possession; and

(2) the defendant is not prevented from making such an application without the permission of the court.

13.2 The defendant may apply electronically for the suspension of the warrant, by—

(1) completing an online application for suspension at the PCOL website; and

(2) paying the appropriate fee electronically at the PCOL website or by some other means approved by Her Majesty's Courts Service.

13.3 When an online application for suspension is received, an acknowledgment of receipt will automatically be sent to the defendant. The acknowledgment does not constitute a notice that the online application for suspension has been served.

13.4 Where an application must be made within a specified time, it is so made if the online application for suspension is received by the court's computer system within that time. The court will keep a record, by electronic or other means, of when online applications for suspension are received.

13.5 When the court receives an online application for suspension it shall—

(1) serve a copy of the online application for suspension endorsed with the date of the hearing by post on the claimant at least two clear days before the hearing; and

(2) send the defendant notice of service and confirmation of the date of the hearing by post; provided that

(3) where either party has provided the court with an e-mail address for service, service of the application and/or the notice of service and confirmation of the hearing date may be effected by electronic means.

Viewing the Case Record

55BPD.14 **14.1** A facility will be provided on the PCOL website for parties or their representatives to view—

(1) an electronic record of the status of claims started online, which will be reviewed and, if necessary, updated at least once each day; and

(2) all information relating to the case that has been filed by the parties electronically.

14.2 In addition, where the PCOL website specifies that the court has the facility to provide viewing of such information by electronic means, the parties or their representatives may view the following information electronically—

(1) court orders made in relation to the case; and

(2) details of progress on enforcement and subsequent orders made.

PART 56

LANDLORD AND TENANT CLAIMS AND MISCELLANEOUS PROVISIONS ABOUT LAND

CPR 56

Contents

I. Landlord and Tenants Claims **56.0.1**

II. Miscellaneous Provisions About Land

Editorial introduction

Part 56 was introduced by the Civil Procedure (Amendment) Rules (SI 2001/256) and came into force on October 15, 2001. It is accompanied by a Practice Direction. Together the rule and PD 56 deal with a number of "landlord and tenant claims" as defined in r.56.1(1), primarily claims under Pt II of the Landlord and Tenant Act 1954, and other miscellaneous provisions about land. **56.0.2**

These provisions were substantially amended as a consequence of the reforms to Pt II of the 1954 Act which were brought into force on June 1, 2004 by the Regulatory Reform (Business Tenancies) (England and Wales) Order 2003 (SI 2003/3096) (see para.3B–91). The amendments to Part 56 were made by the Civil Procedure (Amendment) Rules 2004 (SI 2004/1306). Part 56 and PD 56 are reproduced as amended.

Contracting out and surrender: Pt 56 in its original form provided for a joint claim to be made by a landlord and tenant to authorise an agreement (for contracting out or surrender) under s.38(4) to be started in the High Court or any county court (CPR 56.2(4)—in its original form). Section 38(4) was repealed and replaced by s.38A which has set up a new system for contracting out and surrender that does not use the courts (3B–235). Except for one transitional case, it has not therefore been possible since June 1, 2004 for the court to authorise an agreement under s.38(4). The transitional case applies where there is an agreement for a lease entered into before June 1, 2004 which has not been completed. In such a case the old arrangements for joint applications to the court have been preserved (see art.29(4) of the 2003 Reform Order (at 3B–93) and r.20(1) of the Civil Procedure (Amendment) Rules 2004 (SI 2004/1306) (below)). As before the application may be made to the High Court or any court no matter where the property is situated.

Lease renewal, termination and interim rent: As originally drafted Pt 56 and PD 56 left much to be desired in relation to lease renewal claims. However, the new ability for the landlord as well as the tenant to apply for renewal and for the landlord to apply to terminate the continuation tenancy, as well as the new provisions relating to interim rent, have required substantial changes to Pt 56 and PD 56 so that they now look very different. The criticisms that were made of the old provisions have also been taken on board. Note also that the provision for a three month stay that used to be in CPR 56.3 has gone. This is no longer necessary because s.29B of the 1954 Act now allows parties to agree extensions of time for applying to the court (see vol.2, para.3B–165). The new provisions contained in Pt 56 and PD 56 apply to claims for termination or renewal, or interim rent, where the s.25 notice or s.26 request was served on or after June 1, 2004 (see para.29(1) of the 2003 Reform Order—reproduced at 3B–93) and r.20(1) of the Civil Procedure (Amendment) Rules 2004 (SI 2004/1306), see below:

Transitional provisions

20.—(1) In the circumstances where article 29(1) or (4) of the Regulatory Reform (Business Tenancies) (England and Wales) Order 2003 applies—

(a) the amendments to Part 56 made by rules 15 and 16 of these Rules shall not apply; and

(b) Part 56 shall continue to apply on and after 1st June 2004 as if those amendments had not been made.

Related sources

56.0.3
- CPR Part 8.
- The Landlord and Tenant Act 1927.
- TheLeasehold Property (Repairs) Act 1938.
- The Landlord and Tenant Act 1954.
- The Landlord and Tenant Act 1985.
- The Landlord and Tenant Act 1987 .
- The Chancel Repairs Act 1932.
- The Leasehold Reform Act 1967.
- The Access to Neighbouring Land Act 1992.
- The Leasehold Reform, Housing and Urban Development Act 1993.
- The Commonhold and Leasehold Reform Act 2002.
- The Regulatory Reform (Business Tenancies) (England and Wales) Order 2003 (SI 2003/3096).
- The Housing Act 2004.

Forms

56.0.4
- **N1** Pt 8 claim form.
- **N208** Pt 8 claim form.
- **N9** Acknowledgment of service—Pt 7 claim.
- **N210** Acknowledgment of service—Pt 8 claim.

Protocols

56.0.5 No protocol has been formally approved for use in connection with landlord and tenant claims. However PD to Protocols, para.4, provides that in cases not covered by an approved protocol, courts will expect parties, in accordance with the overriding objective, to act reasonably in exchanging information and documents to try to avoid the necessity for the start of proceedings. Parties to a potential dispute should also follow a reasonable procedure, suitable to their particular circumstances, which is intended to avoid litigation. The procedure should not be regarded as a prelude to inevitable litigation. It should normally include (a) the claimant writing to give details of the claim; (b) defendant acknowledging the claim letter promptly; (c) defendant giving within a reasonable time a detailed written response; and (d) parties conducting genuine and reasonable negotiations with a view to settling the claim economically and without court proceedings. Paragraph 4 also sets out further details as to how the parties should behave in order to achieve these aims, some of which will be suitable to landlord and tenant claims. Of particular relevance to many landlord and tenant claims is the following statement: "If an expert is needed, the parties should wherever possible and to save expense engage an agreed expert."

I. Landlord and Tenant Claims

Scope and interpretation[1]

56.1 **56.1—(1) In this Section of this Part "landlord and tenant claim" means a claim under—**

[1] Introduced by the Civil Procedure (Amendment) Rules 2001 (SI 2001/256) and amended by the Civil Procedure (Amendment) Rules 2008 (SI 2008/2178).

(a) the Landlord and Tenant Act 1927;
(b) the Leasehold Property (Repairs) Act 1938;
(c) the Landlord and Tenant Act 1954;
(d) the Landlord and Tenant Act 1985;
(e) the Landlord and Tenant Act 1987; or
(f) section 214 of the Housing Act 2004.

(2) A practice direction may set out special provisions with regard to any particular category of landlord and tenant claim.

The Landlord and Tenant Act 1927

For Pt I (compensation for improvements and goodwill on the termination of business tenancies) see *Halsbury's Statutes*, Vol.23 and *Woodfall Landlord and Tenant* Vol.2, Appendix C1 and for Pt II (principally provisions relating to covenants to repair and not to assign, etc.), see Vol.2, Sect.3B (Business Tenancies) of this work; *Halsbury's Statutes*, Vol.23; and *Woodfall Landlord and Tenant*, Vol.1, Appendix A1. Note that in proceedings brought under the Act: **56.1.1**

- the Pt 8 procedure must be used (PD 56, para 2.1) so that claim form N208 must be used;
- the required contents of the claim form are set out in PD 56, para.5.2.
- the defendant's immediate landlord must be a defendant to the claim (PD56, para.5.4);
- the court will fix a date for a hearing when it issues the claim form (PD56, para.5.3). In most cases, this will be a short directions hearing;
- evidence need not be filed with the claim form or acknowledgment of service (PD56, para.5.6). In most cases directions relating to evidence will be given by the District Judge as part of the "box work" or sometimes at a hearing.

The Leasehold Property (Repairs) Act 1938

The Act restricts the enforcement by landlords of obligations to repair and similar covenants. See *Halsbury's Statutes*, Vol.23 and *Woodfall Landlord and Tenant*, Vol.1, Appendix A1. **56.1.2**

The Landlord and Tenant Act 1954

For Pt I (security of tenure for tenants with low rents) see *Halsbury's Statutes*, Vol 23 and *Woodfall Landlord and Tenant*, Vol.3, Appendix D1 and for Pt II (which allows some tenants occupying premises for business or professional purposes to obtain new tenancies), see *Halsbury's Statutes*, Vol.23 and *Woodfall Landlord and Tenant*, Vol.2, Appendix C1; and Vol.2, para.3B–90 of this work. **56.1.3**

The Landlord and Tenant Act 1985

Section 31C of the 1985 Act used to allow for the transfer of service charge (and some other cases), to the leasehold valuation tribunal and PD 56 para.6.1 contains provisions relating to the transfer of such claims. However, s.31C was repealed and replaced by the Commonhold and Leasehold Reform Act 2002. Paragraph 3 of Sch.12 to the 2002 Act now contains power to transfer service charge and other claims to the tribunal and the procedural rules for transfer are contained in PD 56 para.15.1. **56.1.4**

The Landlord and Tenant Act 1987

The 1987 Act gives tenants the right of first refusal in certain cases where the landlord wishes to sell the reversion. The enforcement provisions are dealt with by the court (s.19). It also provides for the compulsory acquisition of the landlord's interests in certain circumstances under Pt III although the provisions in that Part have been made largely redundant by collective enfranchisement in the Leasehold Reform and Urban Development Act 1993 and the no fault right to manage introduced by the Commonhold and Leasehold Reform Act 2002. Paragraphs 7 and 8 of the practice direction set out the procedural requirements for applications under this Act which must be commenced under Pt 8 using Form N208 (PD 56 para.2.1), generally in the county court for the district in which the property is situated (CPR 56.2 and PD 56 para.2). **56.1.5**

Housing Act 2004

56.1.6 Section 214 of the 2004 Act is concerned with proceedings relating to tenancy deposits. Under that section an application may be made to the county court where the initial requirements of an authorised scheme have not been complied with or where it has not been possible to obtain confirmation from the scheme administrator that the deposit is being held in accordance with the scheme. The court has power under the section, depending on the circumstances, to order repayment of the deposit, order it to be paid into a designated account under a custodial scheme and to order the landlord to pay to the applicant a sum equivalent to three times the amount of the deposit. It can also order the return of deposits that were not made in money. See further paras 3A–1622 and 3A–1627.

Sect.II of Pt 56 relates to miscellaneous other provisions about land—some of which also have landlord and tenant content (see para.56.4). The statutes covered are:

- the Chancel Repairs Act 1832;
- the Leasehold Reform Act 1967;
- the Access to Neighbouring Land Act 1992;
- the Leasehold Reform, Housing and Urban Development Act 1993; and
- the Commonhold and Leasehold Reform Act 2002.

Starting the claim[1]

56.2 **56.2—(1) The claim must be started in the county court for the district in which the land is situated unless paragraph (2) applies or an enactment provides otherwise.**

(2) Unless an enactment provides otherwise, the claim may be started in the High Court if the claimant files with the claim form a certificate stating the reasons for bringing the claim in that court verified by a statement of truth in accordance with rule 22.1(1).

(3) The practice direction refers to circumstances which may justify starting the claim in the High Court.

(4) [revoked]

Which court?

56.2.1 The basic rule is that landlord and tenant claims must be started in the county court for the district where the property is situated (CPR r.56.2(1)). Unless an enactment provides otherwise a claimant may only start a landlord and tenant claim in the High Court if there are exceptional circumstances (PD56, para.2.4), e.g where:

— there are complicated disputes of fact; or
— there are points of law of general importance.

The value of the property and the amount of the financial claim may be relevant circumstances, but they alone will not normally justify starting the claim in the High Court (PD56, para.2.5). The Practice Direction points out the consequences of issuing in the High Court when it is not justified. In such circumstances, courts normally either strike out claims or transfer them to the county court on its own initiative. This is likely to result in delay and courts normally disallow the costs of starting the claim in the High Court and of any transfer (PD56, para.2.3).

Practice Direction

56.2.2 It is para.2 of the Practice Direction that refers to the circumstances that may justify starting the claim in the High Court.

Contracting out—old regime

56.2.3 It is only in transitional cases where the court still retains jurisdiction to authorise agreements under s.38(4) of the Landlord and Tenant Act 1954 (prior to its amendment on June 1, 2004) that the joint application may be issued in the High Court or any county court wherever the property is situated (see para.56.0.2).

[1] Introduced by the Civil Procedure (Amendment) Rules 2001 (SI 2001/256) and amended by the Civil Procedure (Amendment) Rules 2008 (SI 2008/2178).

Claims for a new tenancy under section 24 and for the termination of a tenancy under section 29(2) of the Landlord and Tenant Act 1954[1] 56.3

56.3—(1) This rule applies to a claim for a new tenancy under section 24 and to a claim for the termination of a tenancy under section 29(2) of the 1954 Act.

(2) In this rule—

(a) "the 1954 Act" means the Landlord and Tenant Act 1954;

(b) "an unopposed claim" means a claim for a new tenancy under section 24 of the 1954 Act in circumstances where the grant of a new tenancy is not opposed;

(c) "an opposed claim" means a claim for—

(i) a new tenancy under section 24 of the 1954 Act in circumstances where the grant of a new tenancy is opposed; or

(ii) the termination of a tenancy under section 29(2) of the 1954 Act.

(3) Where the claim is an unopposed claim—

(a) the claimant must use the Part 8 procedure, but the following rules do not apply—

(i) rule 8.5; and

(ii) rule 8.6; and

(b) [...]

(c) the court will give directions about the future management of the claim following receipt of the acknowledgment of service.

(4) Where the claim is an opposed claim the claimant must use the Part 7 procedure.

(The practice direction to this Part contains provisions about evidence, including expert evidence in opposed claims)

Opposed and unopposed claims

Part 56 divides lease renewal claims under s.24 and claims for termination under s.29(2) of Pt II of the 1954 Act (Vol.2, paras 3B–104 and 3B–151) into opposed claims and unopposed claims. Opposed claims are dealt with under Pt 7; and unopposed claims are dealt with under Pt 8. (CPR 56.3; PD 56 paras 2.1A and 3.1). 56.3.1

Service

Prior to October 1, 2008, there were special provisions about service in lease renewal claims, requiring the claim form to be served two months after the date of issue. These provisions were deleted by para.29 of the Civil Procedure (Amendment) Rules 2008. Deletion of these provisions means that the normal rules of service (themselves substantially amended on October 1, 2008) now apply. Thus, the period for service of a claim form in a lease renewal claim is four months (see CPR r.7.5). 56.3.2

In addition to service on the defendant the claim form must also be served on any person named in the claim form in accordance with PD 56, 3.5(6) or 3.7 (3) (see PD 56, 3.6 and 3.8).

[1] Amended by the Civil Procedure (Amendment) Rules 2008 (SI 2008/2178).

Other matters

56.3.3 Further details, relating to the persons who are to be joined as defendants, contents required of the claim forms, form and contents of acknowledgments of service, evidence and other matters relating to the management of the claim are set out in the practice direction.

II. Miscellaneous Provisions About Land

Scope[1]

56.4 **56.4 A practice direction may set out special provisions with regard to claims under the following enactments—**

(a) the Chancel Repairs Act 1932;

(b) the Leasehold Reform Act 1967;

(c) the Access to Neighbouring Land Act 1992;

(d) the Leasehold Reform, Housing and Urban Development Act 1993; and

(e) the Commonhold and Leasehold Reform Act 2002.

Practice Direction

56.4.1 Section II of PD 56 does set out special provisions with regard to claims under these Acts (PD 28, para.56).

The Chancel Repairs Act 1932

56.4.2 See *Halsbury's Statutes*, Vol.14. PD56, para.12.1 provides that a claimant seeking to recover a sum required to put a chancel in proper repair must use the Pt 8 procedure.

The Leasehold Reform Act 1967

56.4.3 See *Halsbury's Statutes*, Vol.23 and *Woodfall Landlord and Tenant*, Vol.4, Appendix E1. PD56, paras 13.1 to 13.3 contain provisions that apply if a tenant wishes to pay money into court under ss.11(4), 13(1) or 13(3) and provisions about the procedure where claims are transferred to the Leasehold Valuation Tribunal under s.21(3).

The Access to Neighbouring Land Act 1992

56.4.4 See *Halsbury's Statutes*, Vol.37 and *Woodfall Landlord and Tenant*, Vol.1, Chap. 15. PD56, paras 11.1 to 11.3 provide that the Pt 8 procedure must be used and set out requirements relating to the contents of the claim form and state that the owner and occupant of the servient land must be defendants.

The Leasehold Reform, Housing and Urban Development Act 1993

56.4.5 See *Halsbury's Statutes*, Vol.23 and *Woodfall Landlord and Tenant*, Vol.4, Appendix G1. The Act provides for the collective enfranchisement for some lessees of flats and for the individual rights of some lessees of flats to acquire new leases. PD56, paras 14.1 to 14.7 deal with the procedure on applications to the court in respect of collective enfranchisement, what should be done if a person wishes to pay money into court under s.27(3) or s.51(3) and for the procedure on transfer to a leasehold valuation tribunal under s.91(4).

The Commonhold and Leasehold Reform Act 2002

56.4.6 The 2002 Act gave leasehold valuation tribunals extended jurisdiction to deal with various matters. In particular, they are no longer confined to determining whether or not service charges are reasonable. They may also decide contractual questions, i.e. whether a service charge is payable and if so, the person by whom it is payable, the person to whom it is payable, the amount, the date at or by which it is payable and the manner in which it is payable (see s.155 of the 2002 Act; Vol.2). Other matters which can be transferred to a leasehold valuation tribunal are administration charges (s.158), estate management charges (s.159), the determination of whether or not a breach entitling a landlord to serve a s.146 notice has occurred (s.168 of the 2002 Act). *Paragraph 3 of Sch.12 of the 2002* Act provides that where in any proceedings before

[1] Introduced by the Civil Procedure (Amendment) Rules 2001 (SI 2001/256).

a court there falls for determination a question falling within the jurisdiction of a leasehold valuation tribunal the court may by order transfer the proceedings so far as they relate to that question to a leasehold valuation tribunal (see further Vol.2). (This provision was brought into force in England on September 30, 2003 as a result of the Commonhold and Leasehold Reform Act 2002 (Commencement No.2 and Savings) (England) Order 2003 (SI 2003/1986); and in Wales on March 30, 2004 as a result of the Commonhold and Leasehold Reform Act 2002 (Commencement No.2 and Savings) (Wales) Order (SI 2004/669)(W.62)).

PD 56 para.15.1 sets out the procedure for transfer.

PRACTICE DIRECTION—LANDLORD AND TENANT CLAIMS AND MISCELLANEOUS PROVISIONS ABOUT LAND

56PD.1 *This Practice Direction supplements CPR Part 56*

Section I

Landlord and Tenant Claims

1.1 In this section of this practice direction—

(1) "the 1927 Act" means the Landlord and Tenant Act 1927;

(2) "the 1954 Act" means the Landlord and Tenant Act 1954;

(3) "the 1985 Act" means the Landlord and Tenant Act 1985; and

(4) "the 1987 Act" means the Landlord and Tenant Act 1987.

Introduction

56PD.2 Section 1 of the Practice Direction expands on the rules in Sect.1 of CPR Pt 56 and applies to the four statutes mentioned above. It also presumably applies to claims under the Leasehold Property (Repairs) Act 1938 where appropriate, which is defined as a "landlord and tenant claim" in CPR para.56.1, although not specifically mentioned here.

Part II of the 1954 Act

56PD.3 Most of the provisions of this part of the practice direction relate to claims under Pt II of the 1954 Act and have been more complicated since June 1, 2004 as they need to accommodate the various changes made to Pt II of the Act by the Regulatory Reform (Business Tenancies) (England and Wales) Order 2003. As mentioned in the introduction to CPR Pt 56 the practice direction is reproduced as amended but only applies in its amended form to claims for termination or renewal where the s.25 notice or s.26 request was served on or after June 1, 2004 (para.56.0.2).

56.2—Starting the claim

56PD.4 **2.1** Subject to paragraph 2.1A, the claimant in a landlord and tenant claim must use the Part 8 procedure as modified by Part 56 and this practice direction.

2.1A Where the landlord and tenant claim is a claim for—

(1) a new tenancy under section 24 of the 1954 Act in circumstances where the grant of a new tenancy is opposed; or

(2) the termination of a tenancy under section 29(2) of the 1954 Act,

the claimant must use the Part 7 procedure as modified by Part 56 and this practice direction.

2.2 Except where the county court does not have jurisdiction, landlord and tenant claims should normally be brought in the county court. Only exceptional circumstances justify starting a claim in the High Court.

2.3 If a claimant starts a claim in the High Court and the court decides that it should have been started in the county court, the court will normally either strike the claim out or transfer it to the county court on its own initiative. This is likely to result in delay and the court will normally disallow the costs of starting the claim in the High Court and of any transfer.

2.4 Circumstances which may, in an appropriate case, justify starting a claim in the High Court are if—

(1) there are complicated disputes of fact; or

(2) there are points of law of general importance.

2.5 The value of the property and the amount of any financial claim may be relevant circumstances, but these factors alone will not normally justify starting the claim in the High Court.

2.6 A landlord and tenant claim started in the High Court must be brought in the Chancery Division.

Introduction

Paragraph 2 of the Practice Direction: **56PD.5**

- provides that most landlord and tenant claims including unopposed claims for renewal under Pt II of the 1954 Act must be begun using Pt 8 as modified;
- provides that opposed lease renewal claims and claims for termination under s.29(2) of Pt II of the 1954 Act must be begun under Pt 7 as modified (see also CPR r.56.3);
- repeats and expands upon the provision in CPR r.56.2 requiring that landlord and tenant claims should normally be brought in the county court;
- states that a landlord and tenant claim started in the High Court must be brought in the Chancery Division.

Time limits—1954 Act claims

The time limits for claims for lease renewal under s.24 of Pt II of the 1954 Act and termination under s.29(2) are set out in ss.29A and 29B of that Act (see Vol.2, para.3B–161). **56PD.6**

Withdrawing a claim

The landlord may not withdraw an application for a new lease unless the tenant consents to its withdrawal (s.24(2C); Vol.2, 3B–104). Nor may the landlord withdraw an application to terminate a tenancy under s.29(2) unless the tenant consents to its withdrawal (s.29(6); Vol.2, para.3B–151). **56PD.7**

Claims for a new tenancy under section 24 and termination of a tenancy under section 29(2) of the 1954 Act

3.1 This paragraph applies to a claim for a new tenancy under section 24 and termination of a tenancy under section 29(2) of the 1954 Act where rule 56.3 applies and in this paragraph— **56PD.8**

(1) "an unopposed claim" means a claim for a new tenancy under section 24 of the 1954 Act in circumstances where the grant of a new tenancy is not opposed;

(2) "an opposed claim" means a claim for—

(a) a new tenancy under section 24 of the 1954 Act in circumstances where the grant of a new tenancy is opposed; or

(b) the termination of a tenancy under section 29(2) of the 1954 Act; and

(3) "grounds of opposition" means—

(a) the grounds specified in section 30(1) of the 1954 Act on which a landlord may oppose an application for a new tenancy under section 24(1) of the 1954 Act or make an application under section 29(2) of the 1954 Act; or

(b) any other basis on which the landlord asserts that a new tenancy ought not to be granted.

Introduction

Under the reforms to Pt II of the 1954 Act, brought about by the 2003 Reform Order, either the landlord or the tenant is able to apply for an order that the tenant be granted a new lease under s.24; and the landlord is able to apply for an order under **56PD.9** s.29(2) that the continuation tenancy be terminated relying upon one of the grounds in s.30. He does not have to wait for the tenant to apply and then oppose. (See Vol.2, para.3B–149.)

Opposed and unopposed claims

56PD.10 This paragraph of the Practice Direction repeats the definitions of "opposed" and "unopposed" claims originally found in r.56.3 and goes on to explain that the phrase "ground of opposition" means (i) one of the grounds specified in s.30 of the 1954 Act and (ii) "any other basis on which the landlord asserts that a new tenancy ought not to be granted". For example, a landlord may object to a claim for a new tenancy on the basis that Pt II of the 1954 Act has ceased to apply because the tenant is no longer occupying the premises for the purposes of his business (s.23 of the Act; Vol.2, para.3B–94). This would be a basis upon which the landlord might object to a new tenancy other than a s.30 ground.

Where the landlord is seeking termination under s.29(2) or opposing renewal under s.24 he must set out his grounds of opposition and full details of those grounds in his claim form or acknowledgment of service as appropriate (PD 56 para.3.9 and 3.12).

Precedence of claim forms where there is more than one application to the court under section 24(1) or section 29(2) of the 1954 Act

56PD.11 **3.2** Where more than one application to the court under section 24(1) or section 29(2) of the 1954 Act is made, the following provisions shall apply—

(1) once an application to the court under section 24(1) of the 1954 Act has been served on a defendant, no further application to the court in respect of the same tenancy whether under section 24(1) or section 29(2) of the 1954 Act may be served by that defendant without the permission of the court;

(2) if more than one application to the court under section 24(1) of the 1954 Act in respect of the same tenancy is served on the same day, any landlord's application shall stand stayed until further order of the court;

(3) if applications to the court under both section 24(1) and section 29(2) of the 1954 Act in respect of the same tenancy are served on the same day, any tenant's application shall stand stayed until further order of the court; and

(4) if a defendant is served with an application under section 29(2) of the 1954 Act ("the section 29(2) application") which was issued at a time when an application to the court had already been made by that defendant in respect of the same tenancy under section 24(1) of the 1954 Act ("the section 24(1) application"), the service of the section 29(2) application shall be deemed to be a notice under rule 7.7 requiring service or discontinuance of the section 24(1) application within a period of 14 days after the service of the section 29(2) application.

Preventing multiple claims

56PD.12 Given that either a landlord or tenant may apply for a new tenancy; or a landlord may apply to terminate a continuation tenancy the possibility arises that both the landlord and the tenant may each make an application without the other knowing about it. In order to avoid a multiplicity of actions there are therefore various provisions in Pt II of the 1954 Act, as amended by the 2003 Reform Order, to deal with these potential situations. Those provisions are supplemented by this paragraph of the practice direction. The position is as follows:

- The landlord may not apply to terminate the continuation tenancy if either he or the tenant has applied to renew (s.29(3) of the 1954 Act; Vol.2 para.3B–151). The issues between the parties will be determined on the application to renew and if the tenant is unsuccessful his current tenancy will come to an end (generally) three months hence in accordance with s.64 (Vol.2, 3B–282).
- Neither the tenant nor the landlord may make an application to renew under s.24 if the other has made such an application and the application has been served (s.24(2A)).
- Nor may an application for renewal be made (by the landlord or the tenant) if the landlord has issued and served an application for termination of the current tenancy under s.29(2) and (s.24(2B)). If the landlord fails in his application to terminate the tenancy the court is required at the end of the case to make an order for the grant of a new tenancy (s.29(4)(b)).

The reason (in each of the latter two cases above) for providing that the application must be served, and not just issued, is to prevent abuse by landlords. There was some fear that a landlord might issue the application (which would prevent the tenant from applying) and then fail to serve the application within the two months provided for service by r.56.3(4). The landlord's application would fall and because the landlord had already made an application, the tenant would be unable to do so and so would lose the right to renew.

The requirement that the application be served before the other party is prevented from making his or her own application gives rise to a risk that the other party could make an application during a period in which normal service of the first application was taking place. It is this risk that PD 56 para.3.2 is designed to address. The position is as follows:

- If the application to renew has been served the landlord cannot serve his application to renew or terminate without permission (PD 3.2(1)).
- If the landlord and the tenant both serve their respective applications to renew on the same day the landlord's application is stayed until further order of the court (PD 3.2(2)).
- If the landlord's application to terminate and the tenant's application to renew are served on the same day the tenant's application to renew is stayed until further order (PD 3.2(3)).
- If the tenant issues but does not serve an application to renew and the landlord then issues and serves an application to terminate, the landlord's service of his application is deemed to be a notice under CPR r.7.7 requiring service or discontinuance of the tenant's application to renew within a period of 14 days after service of the application to terminate. If the tenant fails to comply with the deemed notice the court may on the application of the landlord (a) dismiss the tenant's claim or (b) make any other order it thinks just (CPR r.7.7). If the tenant's claim is dismissed it will then be possible for the landlord's claim for termination to proceed.

Situations can be envisaged that are not covered by any of the above provisions. For example, the landlord may issue but not serve his application to terminate. The tenant may then issue his application to renew without knowledge of the application to terminate. This is not invalid because the landlord's application to terminate was not served—i.e. s.24(2B) does not apply. Nor is the situation dealt with in PD56, para.3.2(4). In a situation such as this the court will probably stay the tenant's application and proceed on the basis of the landlord's application to terminate (being first in time). Either way it does not matter very much because if the landlord is unsuccessful in the application to terminate the court will order the grant of a new tenancy (s.29(4)(b); Vol.2, para.3B–151).

Defendant where the claimant is the tenant making a claim for a new tenancy under section 24 of the 1954 Act

3.3 Where a claim for a new tenancy under section 24 of the 1954 Act is made by a tenant, the person who, in relation to the claimant's current tenancy, is the landlord as defined in section 44 of the 1954 Act must be a defendant. **56PD.13**

Defendant

56PD.14 The person who is "the landlord" as defined by s.44 (Vol.2, para.3B–272) must be made a defendant to the tenant's application for a new tenancy. This person is not necessarily the tenant's immediate landlord.

Contents of the claim form in all cases

56PD.15 **3.4** The claim form must contain details of—

(1) the property to which the claim relates;

(2) the particulars of the current tenancy (including date, parties and duration), the current rent (if not the original rent) and the date and method of termination;

(3) every notice or request given or made under sections 25 or 26 of the 1954 Act; and

(4) the expiry date of—

(a) the statutory period under section 29A(2) of the 1954 Act; or

(b) any agreed extended period made under section 29B(1) or 29B(2) of the 1954 Act.

Comment

56PD.16 There are certain particulars that are required in all claims, whether it is the landlord or the tenant applying for the new lease; or the landlord for termination. These are set out in this paragraph. There are then further, different, particulars that are required depending upon whether or not the claim is being brought by the tenant (para.3.5) or the landlord (para.3.7) (renewal cases); or termination (para.3.9).

Claim form where the claimant is the tenant making a claim for a new tenancy under section 24 of the 1954 Act

56PD.17 **3.5** Where the claimant is the tenant making a claim for a new tenancy under section 24 of the 1954 Act, in addition to the details specified in paragraph 3.4, the claim form must contain details of—

(1) the nature of the business carried on at the property;

(2) whether the claimant relies on section 23(1A), 41 or 42 of the 1954 Act and, if so, the basis on which he does so;

(3) whether the claimant relies on section 31A of the 1954 Act and, if so, the basis on which he does so;

(4) whether any, and if so what part, of the property comprised in the tenancy is occupied neither by the claimant nor by a person employed by the claimant for the purpose of the claimant's business;

(5) the claimant's proposed terms of the new tenancy; and

(6) the name and address of—

(a) anyone known to the claimant who has an interest in the reversion in the property (whether immediate or in not more than 15 years) on the termination of the claimant's current tenancy and who is likely to be affected by the grant of a new tenancy; or

(b) if the claimant does not know of anyone specified by *sub-paragraph* (6)(a), anyone who has a freehold interest in the property.

3.6 The claim form must be served on the persons referred to in paragraph 3.5(6)(a) or (b) as appropriate.

Claim form where the claimant is the landlord making a claim for a new tenancy under section 24 of the 1954 Act

3.7 Where the claimant is the landlord making a claim for a new tenancy under section 24 of the 1954 Act, in addition to the details specified in paragraph 3.4, the claim form must contain details of— **56PD.18**

(1) the claimant's proposed terms of the new tenancy;
(2) whether the claimant is aware that the defendant's tenancy is one to which section 32(2) of the 1954 Act applies and, if so, whether the claimant requires that any new tenancy shall be a tenancy of the whole of the property comprised in the defendant's current tenancy or just of the holding as defined by section 23(3) of the 1954 Act; and
(3) the name and address of—
   (a) anyone known to the claimant who has an interest in the reversion in the property (whether immediate or in not more than 15 years) on the termination of the claimant's current tenancy and who is likely to be affected by the grant of a new tenancy; or
   (b) if the claimant does not know of anyone specified by sub-paragraph (3)(a), anyone who has a freehold interest in the property.

3.8 The claim form must be served on the persons referred to in paragraph 3.7(3)(a) or (b) as appropriate.

Claim form where the claimant is the landlord making an application for the termination of a tenancy under section 29(2) of the 1954 Act

3.9 Where the claimant is the landlord making an application for the termination of a tenancy under section 29(2) of the 1954 Act, in addition to the details specified in paragraph 3.4, the claim form must contain— **56PD.19**

(1) the claimant's grounds of opposition;
(2) full details of those grounds of opposition; and
(3) the terms of a new tenancy that the claimant proposes in the event that his claim fails.

Acknowledgment of service where the claim is an unopposed claim and where the claimant is the tenant

3.10 Where the claim is an unopposed claim and the claimant is the tenant, the acknowledgment of service is to be in form N210 and must state with particulars— **56PD.20**

(1) whether, if a new tenancy is granted, the defendant objects to any of the terms proposed by the claimant and if so—
   (a) the terms to which he objects; and
   (b) the terms that he proposes in so far as they differ from those proposed by the claimant;
(2) whether the defendant is a tenant under a lease having less than 15 years unexpired at the date of the termination of the claimant's current tenancy and, if so, the name and address of any person who, to the knowledge of the defendant, has an interest in the reversion in the property expectant (whether immediate or in not more than 15 years from that date) on the termination of the defendant's tenancy;

(3) the name and address of any person having an interest in the property who is likely to be affected by the grant of a new tenancy; and

(4) if the claimant's current tenancy is one to which section 32(2) of the 1954 Act applies, whether the defendant requires that any new tenancy shall be a tenancy of the whole of the property comprised in the claimant's current tenancy.

Amending acknowledgement to include new clause

56PD.20.1 In *Benchmark Group Plc v Davies Attbrook (Chemists) Ltd, The Times*, November 24, 2005 Lewison J. held that the trial judge should have allowed the landlord to amend the acknowledgement of service the day before the trial so as to seek a landlord's redevelopment clause. It is not uncommon for things to change in the course of an application for the grant of a new tenancy, which is concerned with the future relationship of the parties. (See also the discussion of the case in Property Law Journal, February 20, 2006, p.23—"Making up your mind..." by Kate Andrews.)

Comment

56PD.21 Where the claimant is the tenant, making an application for a new lease, and the claim is unopposed the landlord must use Form N210 for his acknowledgment of service and state with particulars the matters set out in this paragraph. None of the sections of Form N210 are particularly appropriate for these particulars but no doubt inserting them in section A or on a separate sheet attached to and referred to in the acknowledgment will be considered sufficient.

Section 32(2) of the 1954 Act can be found in Vol.2, para.3B–195).

Acknowledgment of service where the claim is an unopposed claim and the claimant is the landlord

56PD.22 **3.11** Where the claim is an unopposed claim and the claimant is the landlord, the acknowledgment of service is to be in form *N210* and must state with particulars—

(1) the nature of the business carried on at the property;

(2) if the defendant relies on section 23(1A), 41 or 42 of the 1954 Act, the basis on which he does so;

(3) whether any, and if so what part, of the property comprised in the tenancy is occupied neither by the defendant nor by a person employed by the defendant for the purpose of the defendant's business;

(4) the name and address of—

(a) anyone known to the defendant who has an interest in the reversion in the property (whether immediate or in not more than 15 years) on the termination of the defendant's current tenancy and who is likely to be affected by the grant of a new tenancy; or

(b) if the defendant does not know of anyone specified by sub-paragraph (4)(a), anyone who has a freehold interest in the property; and

(5) whether, if a new tenancy is granted, the defendant objects to any of the terms proposed by the claimant and, if so—

(a) the terms to which he objects; and

(b) the terms that he proposes in so far as they differ from those proposed by the claimant.

Comment

Where the claim is for a new tenancy brought by the landlord and is unopposed (see definition of "unopposed claim" in para.3.1) the acknowledgment of service must be in Form N210 and must state the particulars required by this paragraph. See the comment under para.3.10 in relation to completion of this form. 56PD.23

If a landlord brings a claim for a new lease that the tenant does not want the court will dismiss the landlord's application "if the tenant informs the court that he does not want a new tenancy" (s.29(5) of the 1954 Act; Vol.2, para.3B–151). A simple letter to the court from the tenant or his solicitor will no doubt suffice.

Section 32(2) of the 1954 Act can be found in Vol.2 at para.3B–195).

Acknowledgment of service and defence where the claim is an opposed claim and where the claimant is the tenant

3.12 Where the claim is an opposed claim and the claimant is the tenant— 56PD.24

(1) the acknowledgment of service is to be in form *N9*; and
(2) in his defence the defendant must state with particulars—
  (a) the defendant's grounds of opposition;
  (b) full details of those grounds of opposition;
  (c) whether, if a new tenancy is granted, the defendant objects to any of the terms proposed by the claimant and if so—
    (i) the terms to which he objects; and
    (ii) the terms that he proposes in so far as they differ from those proposed by the claimant;
  (d) whether the defendant is a tenant under a lease having less than 15 years unexpired at the date of the termination of the claimant's current tenancy and, if so, the name and address of any person who, to the knowledge of the defendant, has an interest in the reversion in the property expectant (whether immediately or in not more than 15 years from that date) on the termination of the defendant's tenancy;
  (e) the name and address of any person having an interest in the property who is likely to be affected by the grant of a new tenancy; and
  (f) if the claimant's current tenancy is one to which section 32(2) of the 1954 Act applies, whether the defendant requires that any new tenancy shall be a tenancy of the whole of the property comprised in the claimant's current tenancy.

Comment

Where the claim is an opposed claim for a new lease brought by the tenant the acknowledgment of service must be in form N9, the standard acknowledgment for Part 7 claims; and the defence must contain the particulars set out in this paragraph. 56PD.25

Section 32(2) of the 1954 Act can be found in Vol.2, para.3B–195).

Acknowledgment of service and defence where the claimant is the landlord making an application for the termination of a tenancy under section 29(2) of the 1954 Act

3.13 Where the claim is an opposed claim and the claimant is the landlord— 56PD.26

(1) the acknowledgment of service is to be in form N9; and
(2) in his defence the defendant must state with particulars—

(a) whether the defendant relies on section 23(1A), 41 or 42 of the 1954 Act and, if so, the basis on which he does so;
(b) whether the defendant relies on section 31A of the 1954 Act and, if so, the basis on which he does so; and
(c) the terms of the new tenancy that the defendant would propose in the event that the claimant's claim to terminate the current tenancy fails.

Comment

56PD.27 The appropriate acknowledgement of claim form is Form N9, the standard acknowledgement for Pt 7 claims (PD 3.13). In his defence the tenant must state *with particulars*—

- Whether the tenant relies on s.23(1A) (relating to companies; see Vol.2, para.3B–94); s.41 (trusts; para.3B–251) or s.42 (groups of companies; para.3B–261) and if so, the basis on which he does so. There is no reference in the practice direction to s.41A (partnerships—para.3B–256) but if relevant it is suggested that appropriate details are included.
- Whether the tenant relies on s.31A (relevant to ground (f) claims; Vol.2, para.3B–190) and, if so, the basis on which he does so.
- The terms of the new tenancy that the defendant would propose in the event that the landlord's claim to terminate the tenancy fails. (Under s.29(4)(b) if the court dismisses the landlord's application to terminate it will make an order for the grant of a new tenancy; Vol.2, para.3B–151. As to the trial of preliminary issues see PD 56 para.3.16 below).

Evidence in an unopposed claim

56PD.28 **3.14** Where the claim is an unopposed claim, no evidence need be filed unless and until the court directs it to be filed.

Expert Evidence

56PD.29 This paragraph makes it clear that it is not necessary to file any evidence until the court orders it. In unopposed claims for lease renewal the dispute will usually be about the amount of the rent and expert evidence will be required.

There is some dispute as to the extent to which the court should order single joint experts, and this applies to lease renewal claims as much as any other. However, it is increasingly the practice of the courts to do so and this is strongly encouraged by the rules and the court of appeal (CPR 35.7 see also *Peet v Mid-Kent Healthcare Trust* [2001] EWCA Civ 1703; [2002] 1 W.L.R. 211; [2002] 3 All E.R. 688). The days when the landlord's expert always specified a high rent and the tenant's expert always specified a low rent (each backed up by different comparables) are surely over? There may be the risk that each party will employ his own expert to check on the reports of the joint expert. However, that risk is no greater in lease renewal claims than in other cases. Indeed, if the parties address the issue of an expert at an early stage (as required by para.4 of the PD to the Protocols) it is likely to be less of a problem. It is also true that, traditionally at least, the primary role of the experts in lease renewal claims has been to negotiate on behalf of the parties and then only when those negotiations have broken down have they become experts in the true sense. However, their pre-existing role has surely prejudiced their position making them unsuitable to be experts with a primary duty to the court. Perhaps the bottom line is that court procedures are just not suitable for determining issues relating, in particular, to the level of rent and that parties should consider alternative methods of dispute resolution such as "PACT" (Professional Arbitration on Court Terms—a scheme jointly run by the RICS and the Law Society) or mediation. Details of the PACT scheme can be obtained by telephoning 020 7334 3806, emailing drs@rics.org.uk or from the RICS website at *http://www.rics.org* [Accessed December 18, 2008]—type "PACT" into the search function.

Separate experts

56PD.30 If the court does allow separate experts for each party they will invariably be required to discuss the issues, reach agreement where possible and list the remaining unresolved items (CPR r.35.12). The direction should provide for any expert evidence as to rent not to be prepared until after the other terms have been agreed or determined. This follows from the requirement of s.34(1) of the 1954 Act that the rent payable shall be such sum at which having regard to the terms of the tenancy (other than those relating to rent) the holding might reasonably be expected to be let in the open market. If the parties cannot agree on the other terms first it may be necessary to come back for further directions.

Allocation of unopposed claims

An unopposed claim is brought under Pt 8 and so is automatically "treated as allocated to the multi-track and therefore Pt 26 does not apply' (CPR Pt 8.9(c)). **56PD.31**

Which level of judge?

High Court claims are brought in the Chancery Division (PD56, 2.6). In that division a Master or District Judge may not make a final order under Pt II of the 1954 Act without the consent of the Chancellor of the High Court except by consent (PD 2B para 5.1(j) as amended on June 1, 2004). **56PD.32**

In the county court the District Judge may hear the claim if the Designated Civil Judge (DCJ) gives permission. This follows from PD 2B para 11.1(d).

The argument in favour of the view that the district judge may hear such a claim with permission of the DCJ is as follows:

- Items (i) to (vii) in paragraph (a) of para 11.1 of PD2B are exceptions to the deemed multi-track cases in (a). (As stated above, an unopposed claim is deemed to be allocated to the multi-track.)
- The "other proceedings" in (d) refer to proceedings other than those in (a), (b) and (c) of para 11.1.
- The exceptions listed in (a) are therefore part of the "other proceedings" because they are not part of (a)—having been excepted from it.
- As these are "other proceedings" the DCJ can give permission for a district judge to hear the claim.

Although district judges have jurisdiction if the DCJ gives permission, it does seem that at case management stage these claims are usually listed before circuit judges. (See also para.56PD.38).

Evidence in an opposed claim

3.15 Where the claim is an opposed claim, evidence (including expert evidence) must be filed by the parties as the court directs and the landlord shall be required to file his evidence first. **56PD.33**

Evidence

As with opposed claims, this paragraph (although with slightly different wording) makes it clear that evidence, including expert evidence, will be filed in accordance with court directions. In an opposed claim the landlord must file his evidence first. For example, if the landlord is seeking to terminate the tenancy or oppose a claim for a new lease by relying upon the development ground in s.30(1)(f) he will be required to file evidence supporting that ground before the tenant will be required to rely to it. **56PD.34**

Other matters relating to the management of the case are dealt with under para.3.16 below.

Grounds of opposition to be tried as a preliminary issue

3.16 Unless in the circumstances of the case it is unreasonable to do so, any grounds of opposition shall be tried as a preliminary issue. **56PD.35**

Preliminary Issue

As stated in the paragraph, any ground of opposition will normally be treated as a preliminary issue. Once that has been determined the court will go on to consider the terms of a new lease if the ground of opposition is rejected (s.29(4)(b) of the 1954 Act). **56PD.36**

Allocation

An unopposed claim is brought under Pt 8 and so is automatically treated as allocated to the multi-track (CPR Pt 8.9(c)). However, an opposed claim is brought **56PD.37** under Pt 7 and so needs to be assigned to a track. There are no specific rules in Pt 56 relating to allocation. Thus, the usual rules in Pt 26 apply—although opposed claims under Pt 56 may not be allocated to the small claims track (PD 26 8.1 as amended on June 1, 2004). In deciding the track the court should have regard to the factors set out in CPR r.26.8 (see 26.7), i.e.:

- the financial value, if any, of the claim;
- the nature of the remedy sought;
- the likely complexity of the facts, law or evidence;
- the number of parties or likely parties;
- the value of any counterclaim or other Pt 20 claim and the complexity of any matters relating to it;
- the amount of oral evidence which may be required;
- the importance of the claim to persons who are not parties to the proceedings;
- the views expressed by the parties; and
- the circumstances of the parties.

Which level of judge?

56PD.38 See 56PD.32. However, note that if the claim is allocated to the multi-track (as opposed to there being a deemed allocation, which occurs where the claim is unopposed) para 11.1(a) of PD 2B has no relevance and a district judge in the county court can clearly only hear the claim if the DCJ gives permission (2B, para 11.1(d)). This gives strength to the argument that a district judge may hear an unopposed claim with the consent of the DCJ. If the contrary were true the odd position would arise whereby a district judge could hear an opposed claim (albeit with permission of the DCJ) but not an unopposed claim.

Judgment in default

56PD.39 Where the claim is an opposed claim it is brought under Pt 7. Thus, it would seem that the normal default judgments provisions apply. If the defendant fails to acknowledge service or file a defence within time and the claimant wishes to obtain a default judgment he must make an application in accordance with Pt 23 (CPR r.12.4(2)(a)).

A county court judge has held that a landlord was entitled to judgment in default of a defence on his application to terminate the continuation tenancy under s.29(2) of the 1954 Act. On an appeal that was not pursued the tenant for the first time raised an argument that judgment in default is not possible in the light of s.29(4)(a) which states: "If he [the landlord] establishes, to the satisfaction of the court, any of the grounds...[for termination], the court shall make an order for termination of the current tenancy". The issue was not resolved because the case settled before the appeal. (See the article: "In default of a defence" by David Stevens, Maples Teesdale, *Estates Gazette*, September 24, 2005, p.137—the author of the article suggests that landlords would be prudent to combine an application for default judgment with an application for summary judgment).

Applications for interim rent under section 24A to 24D of the 1954 Act

56PD.40 **3.17** Where proceedings have already been commenced for the grant of a new tenancy or the termination of an existing tenancy, the claim for interim rent under section 24A of the 1954 Act shall be made in those proceedings by—

(1) the claim form;

(2) the acknowledgment of service or defence; or

(3) an application on notice under Part 23.

3.18 Any application under section 24D(3) of the 1954 Act shall be made by an application on notice under Part 23 in the original proceedings.

3.19 Where no other proceedings have been commenced for the grant of a new tenancy or termination of an existing tenancy or where such proceedings have been disposed of, an application for interim rent under section 24A of the 1954 Act shall be made under the procedure in Part 8 and the claim form shall include details of—

(1) the property to which the claim relates;

(2) the particulars of the relevant tenancy (including date, parties and duration) and the current rent (if not the original rent);

(3) every notice or request given or made under sections 25 or 26 of the 1954 Act;

(4) if the relevant tenancy has terminated, the date and mode of termination; and

(5) if the relevant tenancy has been terminated and the landlord has granted a new tenancy of the property to the tenant—

(a) particulars of the new tenancy (including date, parties and duration) and the rent; and

(b) in a case where section 24C(2) of the 1954 Act applies but the claimant seeks a different rent under section 24C(3) of that Act, particulars and matters on which the claimant relies as satisfying section 24C(3).

Interim rent

The statutory provisions relating to interim rent were substantially revised by Regulatory Reform (Business Tenancies) (England and Wales) Order and are to be found in Vol.2, s.3B, paras 110 to 119. The changes brought about by the 2003 Reform Order (and these paragraphs of PD56) do not apply where the landlord gave the tenant a s.25 notice before June 1, 2004 or the tenant made a s.26 request before that date (the 2003 Reform Order, art.29(1); 56.0.2). **56PD.41**

Qualifications of the usual order

The references to s.24C are references to the situation where one of the parties argues that the usual figure to be awarded as the interim rent where the landlord does not oppose the grant of a new tenancy (i.e. a sum equivalent to the rent payable under the new lease) should not be awarded because one of the qualifications set out in that section applies; i.e. that there has been a substantial change in market conditions between the date upon which interim rent becomes payable and the date of the grant of the new tenancy; or the terms are very different; or both. (See further s.24C at Vol.2, para.3B–118.) **56PD.42**

Independent application

The application for interim rent is an independent application and so will continue even if the tenant's application to renew/the landlord's application to terminate is withdrawn (*Coates Brothers v General Accident Life Assurance* [1991] 1 W.L.R. 712; [1991] 3 All E.R. 929). **56PD.43**

Estoppel

A tenant who has made a claim for a new tenancy but later changes his mind will not be permitted to defeat a landlord's claim for an interim rent by subsequently denying that the Act applies. The law will not permit a party to "approbate and reprobate" (*Benedictus v Jalaram Ltd* [1989] 1 EGLR 251; see also *Bell v General Accident Fire & Life Assurance Corp Ltd* [1998] L. & T.R. 1). **56PD.44**

Other claims under Part II of the 1954 Act

4.1 The mesne landlord to whose consent a claim for the determination of any question arising under paragraph 4(3) of Schedule 6 to the 1954 Act shall be made a defendant to the claim. **56PD.45**

4.2 If any dispute as to the rateable value of any holding has been referred under section 37(5) of the 1954 Act to the Commissioners for HM Revenue and Customs for decision by a valuation officer, any document purporting to be a statement of the valuation officer of his decision is admissible as evidence of the matters contained in it.

Claim for compensation for improvements under Part I of the 1927 Act

56PD.46 **5.1** This paragraph applies to a claim under Part I of the 1927 Act.

Part 1 of the 1927 Act

56PD.47 The provisions of this statute can be found in Vol.2, para.3B–1 onwards.

The claim form

56PD.48 **5.2** The claim form must include details of:

(1) the nature of the claim or the matter to be determined;
(2) the property to which the claim relates;
(3) the nature of the business carried on at the property;
(4) particulars of the lease or agreement for the tenancy including:
  (a) the names and addresses of the parties to the lease or agreement;
  (b) its duration;
  (c) the rent payable;
  (d) details of any assignment or other devolution of the lease or agreement;
(5) the date and mode of termination of the tenancy;
(6) if the claimant has left the property, the date on which he did so;
(7) particulars of the improvement or proposed improvement to which the claim relates;
(8) if the claim is for a payment of compensation, the amount claimed.

5.3 The court will fix a date for a hearing when it issues the claim form.

Defendant

56PD.49 **5.4** The claimant's immediate landlord must be a defendant to the claim.

5.5 The defendant must immediately serve a copy of the claim form and any document served with it and of his acknowledgment of service on his immediate landlord. If the person so served is not the freeholder, he must serve a copy of these documents on his landlord and so on from landlord to landlord.

Evidence

56PD.50 **5.6** Evidence need not be filed—with the claim form or acknowledgment of service.

Certification under section 3 of the 1927 Act

56PD.51 **5.7** If the court intends to certify under section 3 of the 1927 Act that an improvement is a proper improvement or has been duly executed, it shall do so by way of an order.

Compensation under section 1 or 8 of the 1927 Act

5.8 A claim under section 1(1) or 8(1) of the 1927 Act must be in writing, signed by the claimant, his solicitor or agent and include details of—

(1) the name and address of the claimant and of the landlord against whom the claim is made;
(2) the property to which the claim relates;
(3) the nature of the business carried on at the property;
(4) a concise statement of the nature of the claim;
(5) particulars of the improvement, including the date when it was completed and costs; and
(6) the amount claimed.

5.9 A mesne landlord must immediately serve a copy of the claim on his immediate superior landlord. If the person so served is not the freeholder, he must serve a copy of the document on his landlord and so on from landlord to landlord.

(Paragraphs 5.8 and 5.9 provide the procedure for making claims under section 1(1) and 8(1) of the 1927 Act—"claims" do not, at this stage, relate to proceedings before the court).

Transfer to leasehold valuation tribunal under 1985 Act

6.1 If a question is ordered to be transferred to a leasehold valuation tribunal for determination under section 31C of the 1985 Act the court will: **56PD.52**

(1) send notice of the transfer to all parties to the claim; and
(2) send to the leasehold valuation tribunal:
  (a) copies certified by the district judge of all entries in the records of the court relating to the question;
  (b) the order of transfer; and
  (c) all documents filed in the claim relating to the question.

(Paragraph 6.1 no longer applies to proceedings in England but continues to apply to proceedings in Wales.)

Section 31C of the 1985 Act has in fact been repealed by the Commonhold and Leasehold Reform Act 2002. The repeal came into effect in England on September 30, 2003 as a result of the Commonhold and Leasehold Reform Act 2002 (Commencement No.2 and Savings) (England) Order 2003 (SI 2003/1986); and in Wales on March 30, 2004 as a result of the Commonhold and Leasehold Reform Act 2002 (Commencement No.2 and Savings) (Wales) Order 2004 (SI 2002/669)(W.62). Instead para.3 of Sch.12 to the 2002 Act now contains power to transfer service charge and other claims to the tribunal and the procedural rules for transfer are contained in PD 56 15.1 (below). **56PD.53**

Claim to enforce obligation under Part I of the 1987 Act

7.1 A copy of the notice served under section 19(2)(a) of the 1987 Act must accompany the claim form seeking an order under section 19(1) of that Act. **56PD.54**

Claim form for acquisition order under section 28 of the 1987 Act

8.1 This paragraph applies to a claim for an acquisition order under section 28 of the 1987 Act. **56PD.55**

Claim form

8.2 The claim form must: **56PD.56**

(1) identify the property to which the claim relates and give details to show that section 25 of the 1987 Act applies;
(2) give details of the claimants to show that they constitute the requisite majority of qualifying tenants;
(3) state the names and addresses of the claimants and of the landlord of the property, or, if the landlord cannot be found or his identity ascertained, the steps taken to ascertain his identity;
(4) state the name and address of:
   (a) the person nominated by the claimants for the purposes of Part III of the 1987 Act; and
   (b) every person known to the claimants who is likely to be affected by the application, including (but not limited to), the other tenants of flats contained in the property (whether or not they could have made a claim), any mortgagee or superior landlord of the landlord, and any tenants' association (within the meaning of section 29 of the 1985 Act); and
(5) state the grounds of the claim.

Notice under section 27

56PD.57 **8.3** A copy of the notice served on the landlord under section 27 of the 1987 Act must accompany the claim form unless the court has dispensed with the requirement to serve a notice under section 27(3) of the 1987 Act.

Defendants

56PD.58 **8.4** The landlord of the property (and the nominated person, if he is not a claimant) must be defendants.

Service

56PD.59 **8.5** A copy of the claim form must be served on each of the persons named by the claimant under paragraph 8.2(4)(b) together with a notice that he may apply to be made a party.

Payment into court by nominated person

56PD.60 **8.6** If the nominated person pays money into court in accordance with an order under section 33(1) of the 1987 Act, he must file a copy of the certificate of the surveyor selected under section 33(2)(a) of that Act.

Claim for an order varying leases under the 1987 Act

56PD.61 [...]

56PD.62 *Note*—The power to vary leases under the 1987 Act has been transferred to the leasehold valuation tribunal (s.163 of the Commonhold and Leasehold Reform Act 2002) in England on September 30, 2003 (the Commonhold and Leasehold Reform Act 2002 (Commencement No.2 and Savings) (England) Order 2003 (SI 2003/1986)) and in Wales on March 30, 2004 (the Commonhold and Leasehold Reform Act 2002 (Commencement No.2 and Savings) (Wales) Order 2004 (SI 2004/669)(W.62)). *Paragraphs 9.1 to 9.6 of the PD have therefore been omitted.*

Service of documents in claims under the 1987 Act

56PD.63 **10.1** All documents must be served by the parties.

10.2 If a notice is to be served in or before a claim under the 1987 Act, it must be served—

(1) in accordance with section 54, and
(2) in the case of service on a landlord, at the address given under section 48(1).

Section II

Miscellaneous provisions about land

Access to Neighbouring Land Act 1992

11.1 The claimant must use the Part 8 procedure. 56PD.64

11.2 The claim form must set out:

(1) details of the dominant and servient land involved and whether the dominant land includes or consists of residential property;
(2) the work required;
(3) why entry to the servient land is required with plans (if applicable);
(4) the names and addresses of the persons who will carry out the work; and
(5) the proposed date when the work will be carried out; and
(6) what (if any) provision has been made by way of insurance in the event of possible injury to persons or damage to property arising out of the proposed work.

11.3 The owner and occupier of the servient land must be defendants to the claim.

Chancel Repairs Act 1932

12.1 The claimant in a claim to recover the sum required to put a chancel in proper repair must use the Part 8 procedure. 56PD.65

12.2 A notice to repair under section 2 of the Chancel Repairs Act 1932 must—

(1) state—
  (a) the responsible authority by whom the notice is given;
  (b) the chancel alleged to be in need of repair;
  (c) the repairs alleged to be necessary; and
  (d) the grounds on which the person to whom the notice is addressed is alleged to be liable to repair the chancel; and
(2) call upon the person to whom the notice is addressed to put the chancel in proper repair.

12.3 The notice must be served in accordance with Part 6.

Leasehold Reform Act 1967

13.1 In this paragraph a section or schedule referred to by number means the section or schedule so numbered in the Leasehold Reform Act 1967. 56PD.66

13.2 If a tenant of a house and premises wishes to pay money into court under sections 11(4), 13(1) or 13(3)—

(1) he must file in the office of the appropriate court an application notice containing or accompanied by evidence stating—
(a) the reasons for the payment into court;
(b) the house and premises to which the payment relates;
(c) the name and address of the landlord; and
(d) so far as they are known to the tenant, the name and address of every person who is or may be interested in or entitled to the money;

(2) on the filing of the witness statement the tenant must pay the money into court and the court will send notice of the payment to the landlord and every person whose name and address are given in a witness statement;

(3) any subsequent payment into court by the landlord under section 11(4) must be made to the credit of the same account as the payment into court by the tenant and subparagraphs (1) and (2) will apply to the landlord as if he were a tenant; and

(4) the appropriate court for the purposes of paragraph (a) is the county court for the district in which the property is situated or, if the payment into court is made by reason of a notice under section 13(3), any other county court as specified in the notice.

13.3 If an order is made transferring an application to a leasehold valuation tribunal under section 21(3), the court will:

(1) send a notice of the transfer to all parties to the application; and

(2) send to the tribunal copies of the order of transfer and all documents filed in the proceedings.

(Paragraph 13.3 no longer applies to proceedings in England but continues to apply to proceedings in Wales)

13.4 A claim under section 17 or 18 for an order for possession of a house and premises *must be made in accordance with Part 55*.

13.5 *In a claim under section 17 or 18, the defendant must:*

(1) immediately after being served with the claim form, serve on every person in occupation of the property or part of it under an immediate or derivative sub-tenancy, a notice informing him of the claim and of his right under paragraph 3(4) of Schedule 2 take part in the hearing of the claim with the permission of the court; and

(2) within 14 days after being served with the claim form, file a defence stating the ground, if any, on which he intends to oppose the claim and giving particulars of every such sub-tenancy.

13.6 An application made to the High Court under section 19 or 27 shall be assigned to the Chancery Division.

Leasehold Reform, Housing and Urban Development Act 1993

56PD.67 ***14.1*** In this paragraph:

(1) "the 1993 Act" means the Leasehold Reform, Housing and Urban Development Act 1993; and

(2) a section or schedule referred to by number means the section or schedule so numbered in the 1993 Act

14.2 If a claim is made under section 23(1) by a person other than the reversioner:

(1) on the issue of the claim form in accordance with Part 8, the claimant must send a copy to the reversioner; and

(2) the claimant must promptly inform the reversioner either:
(a) of the court's decision; or
(b) that the claim has been withdrawn.

14.3 Where an application is made under section 26(1) or (2) or section 50(1) or (2):

(1) it must be made by the issue of a claim form in accordance with the Part 8 procedure which need not be served on any other party; and

(2) the court may grant or refuse the application or give directions for its future conduct, including the addition as defendants of such persons as appear to have an interest in it.

14.4 An application under section 26(3) must be made by the issue of a claim form in accordance with the Part 8 procedure and:

(1) the claimants must serve the claim form on any person they know or have reason to believe is a relevant landlord, giving particulars of the claim and the hearing date and informing that person of his right to be joined as a party to the claim;

(2) the landlord whom it is sought to appoint as the reversioner must be a defendant, and must file an acknowledgment of service;

(3) a person on whom notice is served under paragraph (1) must be joined as a defendant to the claim if he gives notice in writing to the court of his wish to be added as a party, and the court will notify all other parties of the addition.

14.5 If a person wishes to pay money into court under section 27(3), section 51(3) or paragraph 4 of Schedule 8—

(1) he must file in the office of the appropriate court an application notice containing or accompanied by evidence stating—
(a) the reasons for the payment into court,
(b) the interest or interests in the property to which the payment relates or where the payment into court is made under section 51(3), the flat to which it relates;
(c) details of any vesting order;
(d) the name and address of the landlord; and
(e) so far as they are known to the tenant, the name and address of every person who is or may be interested in or *entitled to the money*;

(2) on the filing of the witness statement the money must be paid into the court and the court will send notice of the payment to the landlord and every person whose name and address are given in the witness statement;

(3) any subsequent payment into court by the landlord must be made to the credit of the same account as the earlier payment into court;

(4) the appropriate court for the purposes of paragraph (1) is–
   (a) where a vesting order has been made, the county court that made the order; or
   (b) where no such order has been made, the county court in whose district the property is situated.

14.6 If an order is made transferring an application to a leasehold valuation tribunal under section 91(4), the court will:

(1) send notice of the transfer to all parties to the application; and

(2) send to the tribunal copies of the order of transfer and all documents filed in the proceedings.

(Paragraph 14.6 no longer applies to proceedings in England but continues to apply to proceedings in Wales)

14.7 If a relevant landlord acts independently under Schedule 1, paragraph 7, he is entitled to require any party to claims under the 1993 Act (as described in paragraph 7(1)(b) of Schedule 1) to supply him, on payment of the reasonable costs of copying, with copies of all documents which that party has served on the other parties to the claim.

Transfer to leasehold valuation tribunal under the Commonhold and Leasehold Reform Act 2002

56PD.68 **15.1** If a question is ordered to be transferred to a leasehold valuation tribunal for determination under paragraph 3 of Schedule 12 to the Commonhold and Leasehold Reform Act 2002 the court will—

(1) send notice of the transfer to all parties to the claim; and

(2) send to the leasehold valuation tribunal—
   (a) the order of transfer; and
   (b) all documents filed in the claim relating to the question.

(Paragraph 15.1 applies to proceedings in England but does not apply to proceedings in Wales)

PART 57

PROBATE AND INHERITANCE

Contents

Editorial introduction

Part 57 is in four sections. The first section deals with contentious probate. The second and third sections are concerned with matters other than contentious probate, namely rectification of wills and the removal or substitution of personal representatives. The fourth deals with claims under the Inheritance (Provision for Family and Dependants) Act 1975. The four sections are all contained within one part because they share an underlying theme: death. **57.0.2**

Scope of this Part and definitions

57.1—(1) This Part contains rules about— **57.1**

CPR 57

(a) probate claims;

(b) claims for the rectification of wills;

(c) claims and applications to—

(i) substitute another person for a personal representative; or

(ii) remove a personal representative; and

(d) claims under the Inheritance (Provision for Family and Dependants) Act 1975.

(2) In this Part:

(a) "probate claim" means a claim for—

(i) the grant of probate of the will, or letters of administration of the estate, of a deceased person;

(ii) the revocation of such a grant; or

(iii) a decree pronouncing for or against the validity of an alleged will;

not being a claim which is non-contentious (or common form) probate business;

(Section 128 of the Supreme Court Act 1981 defines non-contentious (or common form) probate business.)

(b) "relevant office" means—

(i) in the case of High Court proceedings in a Chancery district registry, that registry;

(ii) in the case of any other High Court proceedings, Chancery Chambers at the Royal Courts of Justice, Strand, London, WC2A 2LL; and

(iii) in the case of county court proceedings, the office of the county court in question;

(c) "testamentary document" means a will, a draft of a will, written instructions for a will made by or at the request of, or under the instructions of, the testator, and any document purporting to be evidence of the contents, or to be a copy, of a will which is alleged to have been lost or destroyed;

(d) "will" includes a codicil.

I. Probate Claims

Editorial note

57.1.1 Probate claims follow the Pt 7 procedure with the following modifications:

- a defendant must acknowledge service;
- the time for acknowledging service is 28 days after service of the particular claim;
- the time for filing the defence is also 28 days after the service of the particulars of claim.

Testamentary documents. It is essential that the rule about testamentary documents (r.57.5) is adhered to so that the court has available to it as soon as possible the material necessary to decide whether the existing parties are the correct parties, whether new parties should be added and whether notice of proceedings should be served on non-parties. The rule is that unless the court directs otherwise the claimant must file his evidence and lodge his documents when he issues his claim and the defendant must do so when he acknowledges service (which is why the normal time for acknowledging service is extended in probate claims to 28 days). The rule about testamentary documents applies only to Probate Claims (i.e. claims falling under section I). It does not apply to the other three sections of Pt 57 (i.e. rectification of wills, removal or substitution of personal representatives and claims under the Inheritance (Provision for Family and Dependants) Act 1975). Similarly Practice Direction 2.1 only applies to Probate Claims, and therefore claims under the other three sections of Pt 57 should not be marked "In the estate of [*name*] deceased (Probate)".

County Courts. The county court has jurisdiction only where (a) an application for a grant has been made through the Principal Registry or a district probate registry and (b) the value of the net estate after payment of expenses and debts does not exceed the county court limit, currently £30,000 (see s.32 of the County Courts Act 1984 and the County Courts Jurisdiction Order 1981). Even where a county court does have jurisdiction the claim can only be brought in a county court where there is also a High Court Chancery District Registry—that is to say, in Birmingham, Bristol, Caernarfon, Cardiff, Leeds, Liverpool, Manchester, Mold, Newcastle upon Tyne and Preston or in the Central London County Court (which has a Chancery List). The reason is that probate claims require specialist Chancery knowledge and it is therefore desirable that they are dealt with by Chancery district judges and Chancery Circuit Judges. That being so, and consistent with the wording of r.57.2(3), if a probate claim is commenced in the High Court because the county court has no jurisdiction, but the High Court thinks it appropriate to use its power under s.40(2) of the County Courts Act 1984 to transfer the claim to a county court—see *National Westminster Bank plc v King* [2008] EWHC 280 (Ch) —it will transfer the claim to a county court where there is also a Chancery District Registry or to the Central London County Court (Chancery List).

Forms

- **N1P** Claim form probate. 57.1.2
- Probate Claim: Notes for claimant on completing a claim form.
- **N4** Acknowledgment of service (probate claim)
- **N205D** Notice of issue (probate).
- Probate Claim: Notes for the defendant.

General

57.2—(1) This Section contains rules about probate claims. 57.2

(2) Probate claims in the High Court are assigned to the Chancery Division.

(3) Probate claims in the county court must only be brought in—

(a) a county court where there is also a Chancery district registry; or

(b) the Central London County Court.

(4) All probate claims are allocated to the multi-track.

How to start a probate claim

57.3 A probate claim must be commenced— 57.3

(a) in the relevant office; and

(b) using the procedure in Part 7.

Acknowledgment of service and defence[1]

57.4—(1) A defendant who is served with a claim form must file an acknowledgment of service. 57.4

[1] Amended by the Civil Procedure (Amendment) Rules 2008 (SI 2008/2178).

(2) Subject to paragraph (3), the period for filing an acknowledgment of service is—

(a) if the defendant is served with a claim form which states that particulars of claim are to follow, 28 days after service of the particulars of claim; and

(b) in any other case, 28 days after service of the claim form.

(3) If the claim form is served out of the jurisdiction under rule 6.32 or 6.33, the period for filing an acknowledgment of service is 14 days longer than the relevant period specified in rule 6.35 or Practice Direction B supplementing Part 6.

(4) Rule 15(4) (which provides the period for filing a defence) applies as if the words "under Part 10" were omitted from rule 15.4(1)(b).

Lodging of testamentary documents and filing of evidence about testamentary documents

57.5 **57.5—(1) Any testamentary document of the deceased person in the possession or control of any party must be lodged with the court.**

(2) Unless the court directs otherwise, the testamentary documents must be lodged in the relevant office—

(a) by the claimant when the claim form is issued; and

(b) by a defendant when he acknowledges service.

(3) The claimant and every defendant who acknowledges service of the claim form must in written evidence—

(a) describe any testamentary document of the deceased of which he has any knowledge or, if he does not know of any such testamentary document, state that fact, and

(b) if any testamentary document of which he has knowledge is not in his possession or under his control, give the name and address of the person in whose possession or under whose control it is or, if he does not know the name or address of that person, state that fact.

(A specimen form for the written evidence about testamentary documents is annexed to the practice direction.)

(4) Unless the court directs otherwise, the written evidence required by paragraph (3) must be filed in the relevant office—

(a) by the claimant, when the claim form is issued; and

(b) by a defendant when he acknowledges service.

(5) Except with the permission of the court, a party shall not be allowed to inspect the testamentary documents or written evidence lodged or filed by any other party until he himself has lodged his testamentary documents and filed his evidence.

(6) The provisions of paragraphs (2) and (4) may be modified by a practice direction under this Part.

Revocation of existing grant

57.6 **57.6—(1) In a probate claim which seeks the revocation of a grant** of probate or letters of administration every person who is entitled, or claims to be entitled, to administer the estate under that grant must be made a party to the claim.

(2) If the claimant is the person to whom the grant was made, he must lodge the probate or letters of administration in the relevant office when the claim form is issued.

(3) If a defendant has the probate or letters of administration under his control, he must lodge it in the relevant office when he acknowledges service.

(4) Paragraphs (2) and (3) do not apply where the grant has already been lodged at the court, which in this paragraph includes the Principal Registry of the Family Division or a district probate registry.

Contents of statements of case

57.7—(1) The claim form must contain a statement of the nature of the interest of the claimant and of each defendant in the estate. **57.7**

(2) If a party disputes another party's interest in the estate he must state this in his statement of case and set out his reasons.

(3) Any party who contends that at the time when a will was executed the testator did not know of and approve its contents must give particulars of the facts and matters relied on.

(4) Any party who wishes to contend that—

(a) a will was not duly executed;

(b) at the time of the execution of a will the testator lacked testamentary capacity; or

(c) the execution of a will was obtained by undue influence or fraud,

must set out the contention specifically and give particulars of the facts and matters relied on.

(5) (a) A defendant may give notice in his defence that he does not raise any positive case, but insists on the will being proved in solemn form and, for that purpose, will cross-examine the witnesses who attested the will.

(b) If a defendant gives such a notice, the court will not make an order for costs against him unless it considers that there was no reasonable ground for opposing the will.

Editorial note

In *O'Brien v Seagrave* [2007] EWHC 788 (Ch); [2007] 3 All E.R. 633 (Judge Mackie Q.C.) it was held that the claimant's right to bring proceedings under the 1975 Act was a sufficient interest to permit her to proceed with a probate claim seeking revocation of a grant in common form for the purposes of r.57.7(1). **57.7.1**

Counterclaim

57.8—(1) A defendant who contends that he has any claim or is entitled to any remedy relating to the grant of probate of the will, or letters of administration of the estate, of the deceased person must serve a counterclaim making that contention. **57.8**

(2) If the claimant fails to serve particulars of claim within the time allowed, the defendant may, with the permission of the court, serve a counterclaim and the probate claim shall then proceed as if the counterclaim were the particulars of claim.

Probate counterclaim in other proceedings

57.9 **57.9—(1) In this rule "probate counterclaim" means a counterclaim in any claim other than a probate claim by which the defendant claims any such remedy as is mentioned in rule 57.1(2)(a).**

(2) Subject to the following paragraphs of this rule, this Part shall apply with the necessary modifications to a probate counterclaim as it applies to a probate claim.

(3) A probate counterclaim must contain a statement of the nature of the interest of each of the parties in the estate of the deceased to which the probate counterclaim relates.

(4) Unless an application notice is issued within 7 days after the service of a probate counterclaim for an order under rule 3.1(2)(e) or 3.4 for the probate counterclaim to be dealt with in separate proceedings or to be struck out, and the application is granted, the court shall order the transfer of the proceedings to either—

- **(a) the Chancery Division (if it is not already assigned to that Division) and to either the Royal Courts of Justice or a Chancery district registry (if it is not already proceeding in one of those places); or**
- **(b) if the county court has jurisdiction, to a county court where there is also a Chancery district registry or the Central London County Court.**

(5) If an order is made that a probate counterclaim be dealt with in separate proceedings, the order shall order the transfer of the probate counterclaim as required under paragraph (4).

Failure to acknowledge service or to file a defence

57.10 **57.10—(1) A default judgment cannot be obtained in a probate claim and rule 10.2 and Part 12 do not apply.**

(2) If any of several defendants fails to acknowledge service the claimant may—

- **(a) after the time for acknowledging service has expired; and**
- **(b) upon filing written evidence of service of the claim form and (if no particulars of claim were contained in or served with the claim form) the particulars of claim on that defendant;**

proceed with the probate claim as if that defendant had acknowledged service.

(3) If no defendant acknowledges service or files a defence then, *unless on the* application of the claimant the court orders the claim to be discontinued, the claimant may, after the time for acknowledging service or for filing a defence (as the case may be) has expired, apply to the court for an order that the claim is to proceed to trial.

(4) When making an application under paragraph (3) the claimant must file written evidence of service of the claim form and (if no particulars of claim were contained in or served with the claim form) the particulars of claim on each of the defendants.

(5) Where the court makes an order under paragraph (3), it may direct that the claim be tried on written evidence.

Discontinuance and dismissal

57.11—(1) Part 38 does not apply to probate claims. 57.11

(2) At any stage of a probate claim the court, on the application of the claimant or of any defendant who has acknowledged service, may order that—

(a) the claim be discontinued or dismissed on such terms as to costs or otherwise as it thinks just; and

(b) a grant of probate of the will, or letters of administration of the estate, of the deceased person be made to the person entitled to the grant.

II. Rectification of Wills

Rectification of Wills

57.12—(1) This Section contains rules about claims for the rectification of a will. 57.12

(Section 20 of the Administration of Justice Act 1982 provides for rectification of a will. Additional provisions are contained in rule 55 of the Non-Contentious Probate Rules 1987).

(2) Every personal representative of the estate shall be joined as a party.

(3) The practice direction makes provision for lodging the grant of probate or letters of administration with the will annexed in a claim under this Section.

III. Substitution and Removal of Personal Representatives

Substitution and Removal of Personal Representatives

57.13—(1) This Section contains rules about claims and applications for substitution or removal of a personal representative. 57.13

(2) Claims under this Section must be brought in the High Court and are assigned to the Chancery Division.

(Section 50 of the Administration of Justice Act 1985 gives the High Court power to appoint a substitute for, or to remove, a personal representative).

(3) Every personal representative of the estate shall be joined as a party.

(4) The practice direction makes provision for lodging the grant of probate or letters of administration in a claim under this Section.

(5) If substitution or removal of a personal representative is sought by application in existing proceedings, this rule shall apply

with references to claims being read as if they referred to applications.

IV. Claims under the Inheritance (Provision for Family and Dependants) Act 1975

Scope of this section

57.14 **57.14 This Section contains rules about claims under the Inheritance (Provision for Family and Dependants) Act 1975 ("the Act").**

Editorial note

57.14.1 Claims under the Inheritance (Provision for Family and Dependants) Act 1975 ("the Act") are not probate claims. The procedure for claims under the Act is to be found in the fourth section of Pt 57 at CPR 57.14 to 57.16 and in 57 PD 15 to 18. It was previously contained in CPR Sch.1 RSC O.99. The procedure is quite separate from that laid down in the first section of Pt 57 for probate claims.

Proceedings in the High Court

57.15 **57.15—(1) Proceedings in the High Court under the Act shall be issued in either —**

(a) the Chancery Division; or

(b) the Family Division.

(2) The Civil Procedure Rules apply to proceedings under the Act which are brought in the Family Division, except that the provisions of the Family Proceedings Rules 1991 relating to the drawing up and service of orders apply instead of the provisions in Part 40 and its practice direction.

Jurisdiction

57.15.1 Proceedings in the High Court under the Act must be issued in either the Chancery Division or the Family Division: CPR 57.15(1). There is concurrent jurisdiction.

The CPR applies to proceedings under the Act which are brought in the Family Division, except that the provisions of the Family Proceedings Rules 1991 relating to the drawing up and service of orders apply instead of the provisions in Pt 40 and its practice direction: CPR 57.15(2).

Section 25 of the County Courts Act 1984 (Vol.2 at 9A–452) as amended by the High Court and County Courts Jurisdiction Order (SI 1991/724) art.2(8) and Sch., Pt 1 confers on the county court an unlimited jurisdiction to hear and determine claims under the Act.

Procedure for claims under section 1 of the Act[1]

57.16 **57.16—(1) A claim under section 1 of the Act must be made by issuing a claim form in accordance with Part 8.**

(2) Rule 8.3 (acknowledgment of service) and rule 8.5 (filing and serving written evidence) apply as modified by paragraphs (3) to (5) of this rule.

(3) The written evidence filed and served by the claimant with the claim form must have exhibited to it an official copy of —

(a) the grant of probate or letters of administration in respect of the deceased's estate; and

---

[1] Amended by the Civil Procedure (Amendment) Rules 2008 (SI 2008/2178).

(b) every testamentary document in respect of which probate or letters of administration were granted.

(4) Subject to paragraph (4A), the time within which a defendant must file and serve —

(a) an acknowledgment of service; and

(b) any written evidence,

is not more than 21 days after service of the claim form on him.

(4A) If the claim form is served out of the jurisdiction under rule 6.32 or 6.33, the period for filing an acknowledgment of service and any written evidence is 7 days longer than the relevant period specified in rule 6.35 or Practice Direction B supplementing Part 6.

(5) A defendant who is a personal representative of the deceased must file and serve written evidence, which must include the information required by the practice direction.

Procedure

Claims under the Act must be made by issuing a Pt 8 claim form: CPR 57.16(1). Practice Form **N208** should be used. The proceedings should be entitled "In the matter of the Inheritance (Provision for Family and Dependants) Act 1975". **57.16.0**

If permission is required to bring the claim out of time under s.4 of the Act, such permission should be asked for in a separate paragraph of the claim form.

The written evidence filed and served by the claimant with the claim form must have exhibited to it an official copy of the grant of probate or letters of administration in respect of the deceased's estate and every testamentary document in respect of which probate or letters of administration were granted: CPR 57.16(3).

CPR Pt 8.3 (acknowledgement of service) and r.8.5 (filing and serving written evidence) apply as modified by CPR 57.16 (3) to (5). Defendants served within the jurisdiction must file and serve an acknowledgement of service not later than 21 days after service of the Pt 8 claim. Any written evidence (subject to any extension of time that is agreed or directed) must likewise be filed and served not more than 21 days after service. In the case of a Defendant served out of the jurisdiction, the time for filing an acknowledgement of service and any written evidence is seven days longer than the relevant period specified in r.6.22: CPR 57.16(4A).

A defendant who is a personal representative who wishes to remain neutral in relation to the claim and agrees to abide by any decision which the court may make should state this in Section A of the acknowledgement of service form. It is normally appropriate for a personal representative who is not a beneficiary to adopt a neutral stance in relation to a claim issued within time.

A defendant who is a personal representative is required to file and serve written evidence which includes the information required by 57PD.16(1) to (4) within 21 days of the service of the claim form on him. This evidence must include full details of the size and nature of the deceased's "net estate" as defined in s.25 of the Act.

The normal rules as to, and the criteria for, the transfer of claims between High Court and County Court and within the High Court apply to claims under the Act.

In the High Court claims under the Act may be tried by a Master (Chancery Division) or District Judge (Family Division): Practice Direction—Allocation of Cases to Levels of Judiciary 2 BPD 4.1.

On the hearing of a claim under the 1975 Act the personal representatives must produce the original grant of representation to the deceased's estate. If the court makes an order under the Act, the original grant together with a sealed copy of the order must be sent to the Principal Registry of the Family Division, First Avenue House, 42–49 High Holborn, London WC1V 6NP for a memorandum of the order to be endorsed on or permanently annexed to the grant.

Time-limit for applications

By s.4 of the Act an application under s.2 shall not, except with the permission of the court, be made after the end of the period of six months from the date on which a **57.16.0.1** grant of representation to the estate of the deceased is first taken out. Section 23 of the Act clarifies the date when representation is first taken out for the purposes of s.4. The rules contemplate that a grant of representation will have been taken out prior to proceedings under the Act being commenced. In *Re McBroom* [1992] 2 F.L.R. 49 proceedings issued prior to any grant were held to be premature and struck out (although *Re Searle, Searle v Siems* [1949] Ch 73 a decision under the Inheritance (Family Provision) Act 1938 (since repealed by the Act) does not appear to have been cited to the judge). The purpose of s.4 appears to be to prevent applications being made too late rather than too early, but the making of an application before the grant of representation gives rise to procedural complications and should be avoided.

Compromise of claims under the Act

57.16.1 A personal representative does not have power under s.15 of the Trustee Act 1925 to compromise claims under the Act as a claim under the Act is not a claim against the estate but a claim to become a beneficiary, or to obtain an increased beneficial interest, in the estate. A compromise requires the consent of the claimant and all beneficiaries whose interests are affected by its terms. For that reason it is important to ensure that all such beneficiaries are made parties to the claim.

A master or district judge has power to approve compromises under the Act without financial limit: 2BPD 5.1(a).

Where a claim under the Act is compromised and an order is sought under s.2 of the Act, the court must be satisfied not only that the order is within its jurisdiction but also one which may properly be made. This applies especially if more than two years have elapsed since the death of the deceased and where the effect of the order is to confer a substantial advantage on the parties at the expense of the revenue: *In re Goodchild* [1997] 1 W.L.R. 1216 at 1231D–E per Morritt L.J.

Where the approval of the court is sought to a compromise of a claim under the Act on behalf of a child or protected party an opinion on the merits of the compromise given by counsel or solicitor acting for the child or protected party must be obtained and a copy of that opinion and the instructions on which it was given lodged with the court. Such approval may be sought before proceedings are begun under CPR 21.10(2). However, where an order is sought under s.2 of the Act varying the dispositions of the deceased's estate (whether effected by will or occurring on intestacy) it would seem to be necessary for proceedings under the Act to have been issued in order to invoke the statutory jurisdiction and be effective for tax purposes.

Every final order embodying terms of compromise made in proceedings under the Act must contain a direction that a memorandum of the order should be endorsed on or permanently annexed to the probate or letters of administration and that a copy of the order be sent to the Principal Registry of the Family Division with the relevant grant of probate or letters of administration for endorsement: 57 PD para.18.3.

Combining claims under the Act with other claims

57.16.2 As claims under the Act are required to be made by issuing a Pt 8 claim, they cannot be combined in one claim form with other claims which are likely to involve substantial disputes of fact and for which the Pt 8 procedure is not appropriate or which, as in the case of probate claims, must be commenced using the Pt 7 procedure. An application may instead be made in an appropriate case for a claim under the Act to be tried together with another claim under CPR Pt 3.1(2)(h).

Civil Partnership Act 2004

57.16.3 The categories of persons permitted to apply under the Act has been extended by the Civil Partnership Act 2004 s.71, Sch.4 Pt 2 paras 15(1) and (2) to include a civil partner and a former civil partner of the deceased. The 2004 Act came into force on December 5, 2005.

PRACTICE DIRECTION—PROBATE

This Practice Direction supplements CPR Part 57 **57PD.1**

I. Probate Claims

General

1.1 This Section of this practice direction applies to contentious probate claims.

1.2 The rules and procedure relating to non-contentious probate proceedings (also known as "common form") are the Non-Contentious Probate Rules 1987 as amended.

How to start a probate claim

2.1 A claim form and all subsequent court documents relating to a probate claim must be marked at the top "In the estate of [*name*] deceased (Probate)". **57PD.2**

2.2 The claim form must be issued out of—

(1) Chancery Chambers at the Royal Courts of Justice; or
(2) one of the Chancery district registries; or
(3) if the claim is suitable to be heard in the county court—
  (a) a county court in a place where there is also a Chancery district registry; or
  (b) the Central London County Court.

There are Chancery district registries at Birmingham, Bristol, Caernarfon, Cardiff, Leeds, Liverpool, Manchester, Mold, Newcastle upon Tyne and Preston.

(Section 32 of the County Courts Act 1984 identifies which probate claims may be heard in a county court).

2.3 When the claim form is issued, the relevant office will send a notice to Leeds District Probate Registry, Coronet House, Queen Street, Leeds, LS1 2BA, DX 26451 Leeds (Park Square), telephone 0113 243 1505, requesting that all testamentary documents, grants of representation and other relevant documents currently held at any probate registry are sent to the relevant office.

2.4 The commencement of a probate claim will, unless a court otherwise directs, prevent any grant of probate or letters of administration being made until the probate claim has been disposed of.

(Rule 45 of the Non-Contentious Probate Rules 1987 makes provision for notice of the probate claim to be given, and section 117 of the Supreme Court Act 1981 for the grant of letters of administration pending the determination of a probate claim. Paragraph 8 of this practice direction makes provision about an application for such a grant).

Testamentary documents and evidence about testamentary documents

3.1 Unless the court orders otherwise, if a testamentary document is held by the court (whether it was lodged by a party or it was previously held at a probate registry) when the claim has been disposed of the court will send it to the Leeds District Probate Registry. **57PD.3**

3.2 The written evidence about testamentary documents required by this Part—

(1) should be in the form annexed to this practice direction; and

(2) must be signed by the party personally and not by his solicitor or other representative (except that if the party is a child or protected party the written evidence must be signed by his litigation friend).

3.3 In a case in which there is urgent need to commence a probate claim (for example, in order to be able to apply immediately for the appointment of an administrator pending the determination of the claim) and it is not possible for the claimant to lodge the testamentary documents or to file the evidence about testamentary documents in the relevant office at the same time as the claim form is to be issued, the court may direct that the claimant shall be allowed to issue the claim form upon his giving an undertaking to the court to lodge the documents and file the evidence within such time as the court shall specify.

Case management

57PD.4 **4.** In giving case management directions in a probate claim the court will give consideration to the questions—

(1) whether any person who may be affected by the claim and who is not joined as a party should be joined as a party or given notice of the claim, whether under rule 19.8A or otherwise; and

(2) whether to make a representation order under rule 19.6 or rule 19.7.

Summary judgment

57PD.5 **5.1** If an order pronouncing for a will in solemn form is sought on an application for summary judgment, the evidence in support of the application must include written evidence proving due execution of the will.

5.2 If a defendant has given notice in his defence under rule 57.7(5) that he raises no positive case but—

(1) he insists that the will be proved in solemn form; and

(2) for that purpose he will cross-examine the witness who attested the will;

any application by the claimant for summary judgment is subject to the right of that defendant to require those witnesses to attend court for cross-examination.

Settlement of a probate claim

57PD.6 **6.1** If at any time the parties agree to settle a probate claim, the court may—

(1) order the trial of the claim on written evidence, which will lead to a grant in the solemn form;

(2) order that the claim be discontinued or dismissed under rule 57.11, which will lead to a grant in common form; or

(3) pronounce for or against the validity of one or more wills under section 49 of the Administration of Justice Act 1985.

(For a form of order which is also applicable to discontinuance and which may be adapted as appropriate, see Practice Form No. CH38)

(Section 49 of the Administration of Justice Act 1985 permits a probate claim to be compromised without a trial if every 'relevant beneficiary', as defined in that section, has consented to the proposed order. It is only available in the High Court).

6.2 Applications under section 49 of the Administration of Justice Act 1985 may be heard by a master or district judge and must be supported by written evidence identifying the relevant beneficiaries and exhibiting the written consent of each of them. The written evidence of testamentary documents required by rule 57 5 will still be necessary.

Application for an order to bring in a will, etc.

7.1 Any party applying for an order under section 122 of the Supreme Court Act 1981 ("the 1981 Act") must serve the application notice on the person against whom the order is sought. **57PD.7**

(Section 122 of the 1981 Act empowers the court to order a person to attend court for examination, and to answer questions and bring in documents, if there are reasonable grounds for believing that such person has knowledge of a testamentary document. Rule 50(1) of the Non-Contentious Probate Rules 1987 makes similar provision where a probate claim has not been commenced).

7.2 An application for the issue of a witness summons under section 123 of the 1981 Act—

(1) may be made without notice; and

(2) must be supported by written evidence setting out the grounds of the application.

(Section 123 of the 1981 Act empowers the court, where it appears that any person has in his possession, custody or power a testamentary document, to issue a witness summons ordering such person to bring in that document. Rule 50(2) of the Non-Contentious Probate Rules makes similar provision where a probate claim has not been commenced).

7.3 An application made under section 122 or 123 of the 1981 Act should be made to a master or district judge.

7.4 A person against whom a witness summons is issued under section 123 of the 1981 Act who denies that the testamentary document referred to in the witness summons is in his possession or under his control may file written evidence to that effect.

Administration pending the determination of a probate claim

8.1 An application under section 117 of the Supreme Court Act 1981 for an order for the grant of administration pending the determination of a probate claim should be made by application notice in the probate claim. **57PD.8**

8.2 If an order for a grant of administration is made under section 117 of the 1981 Act—

(1) Rules 69.4 to 69.7 shall apply as if the administrator were a receiver appointed by the court;

(2) if the court allows the administrator remuneration under rule 69.7, it may make an order under section 117(3) of the 1981 Act assigning the remuneration out of the estate of the deceased; and

(3) every application relating to the conduct of the administration shall be made by application notice in the probate claim.

8.3 An order under section 117 may be made by a master or district judge.

8.4 If an order is made under section 117 an application for the grant of letters of administration should be made to the Principal Registry of the Family Division, First Avenue House, 42–49 High Holborn, London WC1V 6NP.

8.5 The appointment of an administrator to whom letters of administration are granted following an order under section 117 will cease automatically when a final order in the probate claim is made but will continue pending any appeal.

II. Rectification of wills

Scope of this Section

57PD.9 **9.** This section of this practice direction applies to claims for the rectification of a will.

Lodging the grant

57PD.10 **10.1** If the claimant is the person to whom the grant was made in respect of the will of which rectification is sought, he must, unless the court orders otherwise, lodge the probate or letters of administration with the will annexed with the court when the claim form is issued.

10.2 If a defendant has the probate or letters of administration in his possession or under his control, he must, unless the court orders otherwise, lodge it in the relevant office within 14 days after the service of the claim form on him.

Orders

57PD.11 **11.1** A copy of every order made for the rectification of a will shall be sent to the Principal Registry of the Family Division for filing, and a memorandum of the order shall be endorsed on, or permanently annexed to, the grant under which the estate is administered.

III. Substitution and removal of personal representatives

Scope of this Section

57PD.12 **12.** This section of this practice direction applies to claims and applications for substitution or removal of a personal representative. If substitution or removal of a personal representative is sought by application in existing proceedings, this Section shall apply with references to the claim, claim form and claimant being read as if they referred to the application, application notice and applicant *respectively*.

Starting the claim

57PD.13 **13.1** The claim form must be accompanied by:

(1) a sealed or certified copy of the grant of probate or letters of administration; and

(2) written evidence containing the grounds of the claim and the following information so far as it is known to the claimant—

(a) brief details of the property comprised in the estate, with an approximate estimate of its capital value and any income that is received from it;

(b) brief details of the liabilities of the estate;

(c) the names and addresses of the persons who are in possession of the documents relating to the estate;

(d) the names of the beneficiaries and their respective interests in the estate; and

(e) the name, address and occupation of any proposed substituted personal representative.

13.2 If the claim is for the appointment of a substituted personal representative, the claim form must be accompanied by—

(1) a signed or (in the case of the Public Trustee or a corporation) sealed consent to act; and

(2) written evidence as to the fitness of the proposed substituted personal representative, if an individual, to act.

Production of the grant

14.1 On the hearing of the claim the personal representative must produce to the Court the grant of representation to the deceased's estate. **57PD.14**

14.2 If an order is made substituting or removing the personal representative, the grant (together with a sealed copy of the order) must be sent to and remain in the custody of the principal Registry of the Family Division until a memorandum of the order has been endorsed on or permanently annexed to the grant.

IV. Claims under the Inheritance (Provision for Family and Dependants) Act 1975

Acknowledgment of service by personal representative—rule 57.16(4)

15 Where a defendant who is a personal representative wishes to remain neutral in relation to the claim, and agrees to abide by any decision which the court may make, he should state this in Section A of the acknowledgment of service form. **57PD.15**

Written evidence of personal representative—rule 57.16(5)

16 The written evidence filed by a defendant who is a personal representative must state to the best of that person's ability— **57PD.16**

(1) full details of the value of the deceased's net estate, as defined in section 25(1) of the Act;

(2) the person or classes of persons beneficially interested in the estate, and—

(a) the names and (unless they are parties to the claim) addresses of all living beneficiaries; and

(a) the value of their interests in the estate so far as they are known.

(3) whether any living beneficiary (and if so, naming him) is a child or a person who lacks capacity (within the meaning of the Mental Capacity Act 2005); and

(4) any facts which might affect the exercise of the court's powers under the Act.

Separate representation of claimants

57PD.17 **17** If a claim is made jointly by two or more claimants, and it later appears that any of the claimants have a conflict of interests—

(1) any claimant may choose to be represented at any hearing by separate solicitors or counsel, or may appear in person; and

(2) if the court considers that claimants who are represented by the same solicitors or counsel ought to be separately represented, it may adjourn the application until they are.

Production of the grant

57PD.18 **18.1** On the hearing of a claim the personal representative must produce to the court the original grant of representation to the deceased's estate.

18.2 If the court makes an order under the Act, the original grant (together with a sealed copy of the order) must be sent to the Principal Registry of the Family Division for a memorandum of the order to be endorsed on or permanently annexed to the grant in accordance with section 19(3) of the Act.

18.3 Every final order embodying terms of compromise made in proceedings under the Act, whether made with or without a hearing, must contain a direction that a memorandum of the order shall be endorsed on or permanently annexed to the probate or letters of administration and a copy of the order shall be sent to the Principal Registry of the Family Division with the relevant grant of probate or letters of administration for endorsement.

Annex

A Form of Witness Statement or Affidavit about Testamentary Documents (CPR Rule 57.5)

57PD.19

(*Title of the claim*)

I [*name and address*] the claimant/defendant in this claim state [on oath] that I have no knowledge of any document—

(i) being or purported to be or having the form or effect of a will or codicil of [*name of deceased*] whose estate is the subject of this claim;

(ii) being or purporting to be a draft or written instructions for any such will or codicil made by or at the request of or under the instructions of the deceased;

(iii) being or purported to be evidence of the contents or a copy of any such will or codicil which is alleged to have been lost or destroyed, except ... [*describe any testamentary document of the deceased, and if any such document is not in your control, give the name and address of the person who you believe has possession of control of it, or state that you do not know the name and address of that person*] ...

[I believe that the facts stated in this witness statement are true] [*or jurat for affidavit*]
(*NOTE: "testamentary document" is defined in* CPR rule 57.1)

57PD.20 *Note* —CPR Pts 58– 63 and supplementary Practice Directions are reproduced in Section 2 of Vol.2 as follows:

- Part 58 Commercial Court, para.2A–1
- Part 59 Mercantile Court, para.2B–1
- Part 60 Technology and Construction Court, para.2C–1
- Part 61 Admiralty Claims, para.2D–1
- Part 62 Arbitration Claims, para.2E–1
- Part 63 Patents and Other Intellectual Property Claims, para.2F–1

PART 64

ESTATES, TRUSTS AND CHARITIES

Contents

64.0.1

Editorial introduction

64.0.2 This Part was added to the CPR by Civil Procedure (Amendment) Rules 2002 (SI 2002/2058), r.26(a) and Sch.5. The provisions of this Part came into force on December 2, 2002. On that date, provisions in the schedule rules dealing with the matters now covered by Pt 64 were revoked. The principal Scheduled Rules revocations brought about by the addition of this Part and the practice directions supplementing it include: RSC O.85 (Administration and Similar Actions), RSC O.93 (Applications and Appeals Under Various Acts to the High Court: Chancery Division) rr.6 and 21, and RSC O.108 (Proceedings relating to charities: the Charities Act 1993).

Related sources

64.0.3
- Part 8 (Alternative Procedure for Claims)
- Part 23 (General Rules about Applications for Court Orders)
- Part 40 (Judgments, Orders, Sale of Land etc.)
- Part 52 (Appeals)
- Part 57 (Probate and Inheritance)
- Chancery Guide 2005 (Vol.2, para.1A–0)

The following Chancery Practice Forms are relevant to this Part:

- **PF7CH** Inquiry for persons entitled to the property of an intestate
- **PF8CH** Application Notice after Master's findings on kin inquiry (Re Benjamin order) giving permission to distribute estate upon footing(s)
- **PF9CH** Order giving permission to distribute estate upon footing(s) (Re Benjamin)
- **PF10CH** Judgment in beneficiaries' administration action
- **PF11CH** Judgment in creditors' administration action
- **PF27CH** Affidavit/witness statement verifying accounts and answering usual inquiries in administration action
- **PF28CH** Executors' (or administrators') account, being account A referred to in **PF27CH**

CPR 64

General[1]

64.1—(1) This Part contains rules— 64.1

(a) in Section I, about claims relating to—

(i) the administration of estates of deceased persons, and

(ii) trusts; and

(b) in Section II, about charity proceedings.

(2) In this Part and its practice directions, where appropriate, references to trustees include executors and administrators.

(3) All proceedings in the High Court to which this Part applies must be brought in the Chancery Division.

I. Claims Relating to the Administration of Estates and Trusts

Scope of this Section[2]

64.2 This Section of this Part applies to claims— 64.2

(a) for the court to determine any question arising in—

(i) the administration of the estate of a deceased person; or

(ii) the execution of a trust;

(b) for an order for the administration of the estate of a deceased person, or the execution of a trust, to be carried out under the direction of the court ("an administration order");

(c) under the Variation of Trusts Act 1958; or

(d) under section 48 of the Administration of Justice Act 1985[3].

Applications under r.64.2(a) to determine any question arising in the administration of the estate of a deceased person or execution of a trust

Examples of claims under r.64.2(a) are set out in PD 64 para.1. Applications for directions by trustees or personal representatives must be made by Pt 8 claim form. The proceedings will normally be heard in private (BPD 64 para.3, r.39.2(3)(f) and PD 39, para.1.5). If the trustees consider it appropriate they may apply to the court under r.8.2A for permission to issue the claim form without naming any defendants (BPD 64 para.4.2). Detailed guidance as to the procedure for applying to the court for directions in relation to the administration of a trust are given in the Practice Direction, BPD 64; see also Chapter 26 of the Chancery Guide, paras 26.3–26.26. 64.2.1

Prospective Costs Orders in relation to applications under r.64.2(a)

Where one or more beneficiaries makes an application under r.64.2(a), the court has power to direct in advance of the hearing that the beneficiaries' costs should be paid out of the trust fund on the indemnity basis in any event. See *Re Buckton* [1907] 2 Ch. 406 at 414, which set out the criteria for making such an order. Such an order will only be made if it is considered inevitable that the trial judge would order the beneficiaries costs out of the estate (*McDonald v Horn* [1995] 1 All E.R. 961). The court may order the costs to be paid from time to time on an interim basis. An application for a prospective costs order, which should be made by Pt 23 Application Notice supported by evidence given by witness statement, will be dealt with on paper in an ordinary case 64.2.2

[1] Introduced by the Civil Procedure (Amendment) Rules 2002 (SI 2002/2058).
[2] Introduced by the Civil Procedure (Amendment) Rules 2002 (SI 2002/2058).
[3] 1985 c.61. S.48 has been amended by the Courts and Legal Services Act 1990 (c.41).

(BPD 64 para.6.5). Trustees should in every case consider whether the application is suitable to be dealt with without a hearing. If a hearing is considered necessary the Pt 23 Application Notice should seek a hearing and in Part C or in evidence explain the position. Detailed guidance on the procedure to be followed is given in PD 64 para.6, to which is annexed a model form of order. See also Chancery Guide, para.26.30.

Beddoe applications under 64.2 (a)

64.2.3 Trustees or executors may bring applications for directions as to whether or not to bring or defend proceedings, *Re Beddoe, Downes v Cottam* [1893] 1 Ch. 547. Although a trustee or executor is entitled to an indemnity out of the trust fund against all charges and expenses properly incurred by him he will be deprived of his indemnity if it is held that the expenses were not properly incurred. Therefore an executor or trustee is at risk of being deprived of his costs of defending or bringing a claim if he does so without either the consent of all his beneficiaries, or in default of such consent the direction of the court. The application must be made by Pt 8 claim, independently of the main litigation, to a Master other than the assigned Master. The Master's jurisdiction is limited to making orders in plain cases and practitioners should therefore consider the appropriate level of judiciary under the Pt 2 Practice Direction—Allocation of Cases to Levels of Judiciary. All *Beddoe* applications must be supported by evidence including the advice of a suitably qualified lawyer as to the prospects of success and other relevant matters including costs estimates. A draft order must be filed. No separate Application Notice is necessary for the claim to be decided. On issue of the Pt 8 claim the court office should be asked for a hearing date or alternatively, in a very simple case, for the claim to be put before the Master for consideration as to whether an order can be made without a hearing (BPD 64 paras 7.2 to 7.3).

Other more usual forms of application under 64.2(a)

64.2.4 These include: absence of power (the sanctioning of acts being done by trustees which they themselves have no power to do); purchase by trustees of part of the trust estate; orders for partial distribution to known beneficiaries; kin inquiries; and Benjamin orders (authorising the distribution of the fund on the footing that a beneficiary predeceased the testator or intestate (*Re Benjamin, Neville v Benjamin* [1902] 1 Ch. 723). See form **PF8CH**).

Applications for permission to distribute the estate of a deceased Lloyd's name

64.2.5 These are made under r.64.2 (a). The procedure for this is governed by a Practice Statement dated May 25, 2001 ([2001] 3 All E.R. 765), following *Re Yorke (deceased)* [1997] 4 All E.R. 907, which enables the personal representatives of a deceased Lloyd's name to distribute the estate on the footing that no, or no further, provision need be made for Lloyd's creditors. The application must be made by Pt 8 claim form, which may be issued without naming any other party. The Practice Statement includes a form of witness statement and draft order, both of which should accompany the claim form. The procedure is set out in the Chancery Guide, paras 26.50–26.55 and Appendix 11. If the deceased was involved in underwriting activities through a limited liability vehicle, this should be drawn to the court's attention.

Administration orders

64.2.6 An application may be made under r.64.2(b) for an order for the administration of an estate or the execution of a trust to be carried out under the direction of the court. It may occasionally be found desirable to take a full administration order so that the court is ready to deal with any situation which may emerge in the course of proceedings relating to the estate of a deceased person or a trust. The order can expressly stipulate that no account or inquiry not immediately required shall be taken or made without permission. An administration order enures for the protection of the general body of creditors as well as beneficiaries. The issue of an application for a general administration order does not interfere with any power or discretion vested in any executor, administrator or trustee except to such extent as must necessarily be involved in a particular relief sought. After an order for general administration they can only exercise their powers subject to the sanction of the court (*Re Furness* [1943] Ch.415).

Administration actions are of two kinds: creditor's administration actions and beneficiary's administration actions. Normally, a creditor's administration action is for the administration of a deceased person's estate. A beneficiary's administration action in respect of the estate of a deceased person or a trust may be brought by a beneficiary or by the executors, administrators or trustees as the case may be. All the executors, administrators or trustees must be made parties and any of them who does not consent to being joined as a claimant must be made a defendant. See forms **PF10CH** and **PF11CH** for beneficiaries' actions and creditors' actions respectively.

Where the estate is insolvent the proceedings should be commenced by a creditor as claimant against the personal representative as defendant. The personal representative is not entitled to commence proceedings against a creditor who is unwilling to be made a defendant. In such a case the proper course is for the personal representative to present a petition under the Insolvency Act 1986. But, it would seem that the proceedings would be properly constituted if brought against a creditor who was willing to be joined as a defendant (*Re Bradley* [1956] Ch. 615; [1956] 3 All E.R. 113). Where the usual order has been made for administration in a beneficiary's action, and, by reason of insolvency, beneficiaries are no longer interested, the action must be reconstituted and carried on by creditors as claimants. See *Re Van Oppen* [1935] W.N. 51; 179 L.TJ. 255. The application is then treated on the same footing as any other application for a creditor's administration order in case of insolvency and is dealt with by the Master without reference to the judge. For a form of order see PF22CH.

Variation of Trusts Act 1958—r.64.2(c)

Claims under the Variation of Trusts Act were previously dealt with by RSC O.93, r.6. Claims must be made by Pt 8 claim form (CPR r.64.3) and will normally be heard by the judge in private (CPR r.39.2(3)(f)). Applications under the Variation of Trusts Act may be listed for hearing in the General List without any direction by the Master, upon lodgment of a certificate of readiness signed by the advocates for all the parties (Chancery Guide, para.6.28). PD 64 para.4 sets out the requirements as to the evidence that must be filed where any children or unborn beneficiaries will be affected by a proposed arrangement under the Act. A written opinion of the advocate who will appear at the hearing may be required, particularly in complicated cases. (See also Chancery Guide, paras 26.23–26.34). Attention is drawn to CPR r.64.4(2), which specifies the parties to be joined in such proceedings. **64.2.7**

Administration of Justice Act 1985 s.48—r.64.2(d)

Claims under s.48 of the Administration of Justice Act (power of the High Court to authorise action to be taken in reliance on written legal opinion as to the construction of a will or trust document) were previously dealt with by RSC O.93, r.21. Claims must be made by Pt 8 claim form (CPR r.64.3) without naming the defendant under CPR r.8.2A and no separate application for permission under r.8.2A need be made (PD 64 para.5).The legal opinion must be given by a person who has a 10-year High Court qualification within the meaning of s.71 of the Courts and Legal Services Act 1990. The claim should be supported by a witness statement or affidavit stating the names of all persons affected by the order sought, the surrounding circumstances admissible and relevant to construction of the document, details of the qualification and experience of the writer of the opinion, the approximate value of the fund or property in question and the details of any dispute known to exist. There should be exhibited to the witness statement or affidavit copies of all relevant documents, instructions to the writer of the opinion, the opinion itself and a draft order. If the judge directs service of notices under r.19.8A and any acknowledgment of service is received, the claimant should apply to the Master, on notice to the parties who acknowledged service, for directions (see Chancery Guide, paras 26.37–26.42). **64.2.8**

Claim form[1]

64.3 A claim to which this Section applies must be made by issuing a Part 8 claim form. **64.3**

Parties[2]

64.4—(1) In a claim to which this Section applies, other than an **64.4**

[1] Introduced by the Civil Procedure (Amendment) Rules 2002 (SI 2002/2058).
[2] Introduced by the Civil Procedure (Amendment) Rules 2002 (SI 2002/2058).

application under section 48 of the Administration of Justice Act 1985—

(a) all the trustees must be parties;

(b) if the claim is made by trustees, any of them who does not consent to being a claimant must be made a defendant; and

(c) the claimant may make parties to the claim any persons with an interest in or claim against the estate, or an interest under the trust, who it is appropriate to make parties having regard to the nature of the order sought.

(2) In addition, in a claim under the Variation of Trusts Act 1958, unless the court directs otherwise any person who—

(a) created the trust; or

(b) provided property for the purposes of the trust,

must, if still alive, be made a party to the claim.

(The court may, under rule 19.2, order additional persons to be made parties to a claim.)

II. Charity Proceedings

Scope of this Section and Interpretation[1]

64.5 **64.5—(1) This Section applies to charity proceedings.**

(2) In this Section—

(a) "the Act" means the Charities Act 1993;

(b) "charity proceedings" has the same meaning as in section 33(8) of the Act; and

(c) "the Commissioners" means the Charity Commissioners for England and Wales.

II. Charity Proceedings—Editorial introduction

64.5.1 This section deals with applications to the High Court, under s.33(5) of the Charities Act 1993, for permission to start charity proceedings, following refusal by the Charity Commissioners to authorise proceedings. "Charity proceedings" are defined in CPR r.64.2(b) by reference to s.33.8 of the Charities Act 1993. This subsection states: "'charity proceedings' means proceedings in any court in England or Wales brought under the court's jurisdiction with respect to charities, or brought under the court's jurisdiction with respect to trusts in relation to the administration of a trust for charitable purposes." The procedures for these applications, which were previously in RSC O.108, are now to be found partly in CPR r.64.6 and partly in PD 64, paras 9 and 10.

RSC O.108 was also concerned with applications for permission to appeal against an order of the Charity Commissioners under s.16(13) of the Act. These applications are now dealt with in PD 52, para.23.8A.

In the case of a charitable trust the Attorney General must be joined as a defendant if he is not a claimant (PD 64 para.7) and will usually be the only defendant (BPD 64 para.4.4).

Application for permission to take charity proceedings[2]

64.6 **64.6—(1) An application to the High Court under section 33(5) of the Act for permission to start charity proceedings must be made**

[1] Introduced by the Civil Procedure (Amendment) Rules 2002 (SI 2002/2058).
[2] Introduced by the Civil Procedure (Amendment) Rules 2002 (SI 2002/2058).

within 21 days after the refusal by the Commissioners of an order authorising proceedings.

(2) The application must be made by issuing a Part 8 claim form, which must contain the information specified in the practice direction.

(3) The Commissioners must be made defendants to the claim, but the claim form need not be served on them or on any other person.

(4) The judge considering the application may direct the Commissioners to file a written statement of their reasons for their decision.

(5) The court will serve on the applicant a copy of any statement filed under paragraph (4).

(6) The judge may either—

(a) give permission without a hearing; or

(b) fix a hearing.

Permission to commence proceedings

Application for an order under s.33(2) of the 1993 Act authorising charity proceedings should be made in the case of a charity to the Secretary, Charity Commission, Harmsworth House, 13-15 Bouverie Street, London EC4Y 8D and should include the material specified in PD 64 para.9.1. **64.6.1**

PRACTICE DIRECTION—ESTATES, TRUSTS AND CHARITIES

64PD.1 *This Practice Direction supplements CPR Part 64*

I. Claims relating to the administration of estates and trusts

Examples of claims under rule 64.2(a)

1 The following are examples of the types of claims which may be made under rule 64.2(a)—

(1) a claim for the determination of any of the following questions—

(a) any question as to who is included in any class of persons having—

(i) a claim against the estate of a deceased person;

(ii) a beneficial interest in the estate of such a person; or

(iii) a beneficial interest in any property subject to a trust;

(b) any question as to the rights or interests of any person claiming—

(i) to be a creditor of the estate of a deceased person;

(ii) to be entitled under a will or on the intestacy of a deceased person; or

(iii) to be beneficially entitled under a trust;

(2) a claim for any of the following remedies—

(a) an order requiring a trustee—

(i) to provide and, if necessary, verify accounts;

(ii) to pay into court money which he holds in that capacity; or

(iii) to do or not to do any particular act;

(b) an order approving any sale, purchase, compromise or other transaction by a trustee; or

(c) an order directing any act to be done which the court could order to be done if the estate or trust in question were being administered or executed under the direction of the court.

Applications by trustees for directions

64PD.2 **2** A separate practice direction contains guidance about applications by trustees for directions.

Administration orders—rule 64.2(b)

64PD.3 **3.1** The court will only make an administration order if it considers that the issues between the parties cannot properly be resolved in any other way.

3.2 If, in a claim for an administration order, the claimant alleges that the trustees have not provided proper accounts, the court may—

(1) stay the proceedings for a specified period, and order them to file and serve proper accounts within that period; or

(2) if necessary to prevent proceedings by other creditors or persons claiming to be entitled to the estate or fund, make

an administration order and include in it an order that no such proceedings are to be taken without the court's permission.

3.3 Where an administration order has been made in relation to the estate of a deceased person, and a claim is made against the estate by any person who is not a party to the proceedings—

(1) no party other than the executors or administrators of the estate may take part in any proceedings relating to the claim without the permission of the court; and

(2) the court may direct or permit any other party to take part in the proceedings, on such terms as to costs or otherwise as it thinks fit.

3.4 Where an order is made for the sale of any property vested in trustees, those persons shall have the conduct of the sale unless the court directs otherwise.

Applications under the Variation of Trusts Act 1958—rule 64.2(c)

4.1 Where children or unborn beneficiaries will be affected by a proposed arrangement under the Act, the evidence filed in support of the application must— **64PD.4**

(1) show that their litigation friends or the trustees support the arrangements as being in the interests of the children or unborn beneficiaries; and

(2) unless paragraph 4.3 applies or the court orders otherwise, be accompanied by a written opinion to this effect by the advocate who will appear on the hearing of the application.

4.2 A written opinion filed under paragraph 4.1(2) must—

(1) if it is given on formal instructions, be accompanied by a copy of those instructions; or

(2) otherwise, state fully the basis on which it is given.

4.3 No written opinion needs to be filed in support of an application to approve an arrangement under section 1(1)(d) of the Act (discretionary interests under protective trusts).

4.4 Where the interests of two or more children, or two or more of the children and unborn beneficiaries, are similar, only a single written opinion needs to be filed.

Applications under section 48 of the Administration of Justice Act 1985—rule 64.2(d)

5 A Part 8 claim form for an application by trustees under section 48 of the Administration of Justice Act 1985 (power of High Court to authorise action to be taken in reliance on legal opinion) may be issued without naming a defendant, under rule 8.2A. No separate application for permission under rule 8.2A need be made. **64PD.5**

Prospective costs orders

6.1 These paragraphs are about the costs of applications under rule 64.2(a). **64PD.6**

6.2 Where trustees have power to agree to pay the costs of a party to such an application, and exercise such a power, rule 48.3 applies. In such a case, an order is not required and the trustees are entitled to recover out of the trust fund any costs which they pay pursuant to the agreement made in the exercise of such power.

6.3 Where the trustees do not have, or decide not to exercise, a power to make such an agreement, the trustees or the party concerned may apply to the court at any stage of proceedings for an order that the costs of any party (including the costs of the trustees) shall be paid out of the fund (a "prospective costs order").

6.4 The court, on an application for a prospective costs order, may—

(a) in the case of the trustees' costs, authorise the trustees to raise and meet such costs out of the fund;

(b) in the case of the costs of any other party, authorise or direct the trustees to pay such costs (or any part of them, or the costs incurred up to a particular time) out of the trust fund to be assessed, if not agreed by the trustees, on the indemnity basis or, if the court directs, on the standard basis, and to make payments from time to time on account of such costs. A model form of order is annexed to this Practice Direction.

6.5 The court will always consider whether it is possible to deal with the application for a prospective costs order on paper without a hearing and in an ordinary case would expect to be able to do so. The trustees must consider whether a hearing is needed for any reason. If they consider that it is they should say so and explain why in their evidence. If any party to the application referred to in paragraph 6.1 above (or any other person interested in the trust fund) considers that a hearing is necessary (for instance because he wishes to oppose the making of a prospective costs order) this should be stated, and the reasons explained, in his evidence, if any, or otherwise in a letter to the court.

6.6 If the court would be minded to refuse the application on a consideration of the papers alone, the parties will be notified and given the opportunity, within a stated time, to ask for a hearing.

6.7 The evidence in support of an application for a prospective costs order should be given by witness statement. The trustees and the applicant (if different) must ensure full disclosure of the relevant matters to show that the case is one which falls within the category of case where a prospective costs order can properly be made.

6.8 The model form of order is designed for use in the more straightforward cases, where a question needs to be determined which has arisen in the administration of the trust, whether the claimants are the trustees or a beneficiary. The form may be adapted for use in less straightforward cases, in particular where the proceedings are hostile, but special factors may also have to be reflected in the terms of the order in such a case.

II. Charity Proceedings

Role of Attorney-General

64PD.7 **7** The Attorney-General is a necessary party to all charity proceedings, other than any commenced by the Charity Commissioners, and must be joined as a defendant if he is not a claimant.

Service on Charity Commissioners or Attorney-General

8 Any document required or authorised to be served on the Commissioners or the Attorney-General must be served on the Treasury Solicitor in accordance with paragraph 2.1 of the Practice Direction supplementing Part 66. **64PD.8**

Applications for permission to take charity proceedings—rule 64.6

9.1 The claim form for an application under section 33(5) of the Act must state— **64PD.9**

(1) the name, address and description of the applicant;
(2) details of the proceedings which he wishes to take;
(3) the date of the Commissioners' refusal to grant an order authorising the taking of proceedings;
(4) the grounds on which the applicant alleges that it is a proper case for taking proceedings; and
(5) if the application is made with the consent of any other party to the proposed proceedings, that fact.

9.2 If the Commissioners have given reasons for refusing to grant an order, a copy of their reasons must be filed with the claim form.

Appeals against orders of the Charity Commissioners

10 Part 52 applies to any appeal against an order of the Charity Commissioners. Section III of the practice direction supplementing Part 52 contains special provisions about such appeals. **64PD.10**

Appendix

64PD.11

Model form of prospective costs order

UPON THE APPLICATION etc.
AND UPON HEARING etc.
AND UPON READING etc.
AND UPON the Solicitors for the .... Defendant undertaking to make the repayments mentioned in paragraph 2 below in the circumstances there mentioned

IT IS [BY CONSENT] ORDERED THAT:

1. The Claimants as trustees of ....("the [Settlement/Scheme]") do-

(a) pay from the assets of the [Settlement/Scheme] the costs of and incidental to these proceedings incurred by the .... Defendant such costs to be subject to a detailed assessment on the indemnity basis if not agreed and (for the avoidance of doubt) to-

(i) include costs incurred by the .... Defendant from and after [*date*] in anticipation of being appointed to represent any class of persons presently or formerly beneficially interested under the trusts of the [Settlement/Scheme] irrespective of whether [he/she] is in fact so appointed; and

(ii) exclude (in the absence of any further order) costs incurred in prosecuting any Part 20 claim or any appeal;

(b) indemnify the .... Defendant in respect of any costs which he may be ordered to pay to any other party to these proceedings in connection therewith.

2. Until the outcome of the detailed assessment (or the agreement regarding costs) contemplated in paragraph 1 above, the Claimants as trustees do pay from the assets of the [Settlement/Scheme] to the Solicitors for the .... Defendant monthly (or at such other intervals as may be agreed) such sums on account of the costs referred to in paragraph 1(a) of this Order as the Solicitors for the .... Defendant shall certify-

(i) to have been reasonably and properly incurred and not to exceed such amount as is likely in their opinion to be allowed on a detailed assessment on the indemnity basis; and

(ii) to have accured on account of the present roceedings in the period prior to the date of such certificate and not to have been previously provided for under this Order.

PROVIDED ALWAYS that the Solicitors for the .... Defendant shall repay such sums (if any) as, having been paid to them on account, are disallowed on a detailed assessment or are otherwise agreed to be repaid and any such sums shall be repaid together with interest at 1% above the base rate for the time being of [Barclays] Bank plc from and including the date of payment to those Solicitors up to and including the date of repayment, such interest to accrue daily.

3. Any party may apply to vary or discharge paragraphs 1 and 2 of this Order but only in respect of costs to be incurred after the date of such application.

Note: this form of order assumes that the trustees are the claimants. If the claimant is a beneficiary and the trustees are defendants, references to the parties need to be adapted accordingly.

PRACTICE DIRECTION—APPLICATIONS TO THE COURT FOR DIRECTIONS BY TRUSTEES IN RELATION TO THE ADMINISTRATION OF THE TRUST

This Practice Direction supplements Section I of CPR Part 64 **64BPD.1**

1 This Practice Direction is about applications to the court for directions by trustees in relation to the administration of the trust.

Contents of the claim form

2 If confidentiality of the directions sought is important (for example, where the directions relate to actual or proposed litigation with a third party who could find out what directions the trustees are seeking through access to the claim form under CPR, rule 5.4) the statement of the remedy sought, for the purposes of CPR, rule 8.2(b), may be expressed in general terms. The trustees must, in that case, state specifically in the evidence what it is that they seek to be allowed to do. **64BPD.2**

Proceedings in private

3 The proceedings will in the first instance be listed in private (see paragraph 1.5 of the Practice Direction supplementing Part 39 and rule 39.2(3)(f)). Accordingly the order made, as well as the other documents among the court records (apart from a claim form which has been served), will not be open to inspection by third parties without the court's permission (rule 5.4(2)). If the matter is disposed of without a hearing, the order made will be expressed to have been made in private. **64BPD.3**

Joining defendants or giving notice to those interested

4.1 Rule 64.4(1)(c) deals with the joining of beneficiaries as defendants. Often, especially in the case of a private trust, it will be clear that some, and which, beneficiaries need to be joined as defendants. Sometimes, if there are only two views of the appropriate course, and one is advocated by one beneficiary who will be joined, it may not be necessary for other beneficiaries to be joined since the trustees may be able to present the other arguments. Equally, in the case of pension trust, it may not be necessary for a member of every possible different class of beneficiaries to be joined. **64BPD.4**

4.2 In some cases the court may be able to assess whether or not to give the directions sought, or what directions to give, without hearing from any party other than the trustees. If the trustees consider that their case is in that category they may apply to the court to issue the claim form without naming any defendants under rule 8.2A. They must apply to the court before the claim form is issued (rule 8.2A(2)) and include a copy of the claim form that they propose to issue (rule 8.2A(3)(b)).

4.3 In other cases the trustees may know that beneficiaries need to be joined as defendants, or to be given notice, but may be in doubt as to which. Examples could include a case concerning a pension scheme with many beneficiaries and a number of different categories of interest, especially if they may be differently affected by the action for which directions are sought, or a private trust with a large class of discretionary beneficiaries. In those cases the trustees may apply to issue the claim form without naming any defendants under rule 8.2A. The application may be combined with an application to the court for directions as to which persons to join as parties or to give notice to under rule 19.8A.

4.4 In the case of a charitable trust the Attorney-General is always the appropriate defendant, and almost always the only one.

Case management directions

64BPD.5 **5.1** The claim will be referred to the master or district judge once a defendant has acknowledged service, or otherwise on expiry of the period for acknowledgment of service, (or, if no defendant is named, as soon as the claimants' evidence has been filed) to consider directions for the management of the case. Such directions may be given without a hearing in some cases; these might include directions as to parties or as to notice of proceedings, as mentioned in paragraph 4 above.

Proceeding without a hearing

64BPD.6 **6.1** The court will always consider whether it is possible to deal with the application on paper without a hearing. The trustees must always consider whether a hearing is needed for any reason. If they consider that it is they should say so and explain why in their evidence. If a defendant considers that a hearing is needed, this should be stated, and the reasons explained, in his evidence, if any, or otherwise in a letter to the court.

6.2 If the court would be minded to refuse to give the directions asked for on a consideration of the papers alone, the parties will be notified and given the opportunity, within a stated time, to ask for a hearing.

6.3 In charity cases, the master or district judge may deal with the case without a hearing on the basis of a letter by or on behalf of the Attorney-General that sets out his attitude to the application.

Evidence

64BPD.7 **7.1** The trustees' evidence should be given by witness statement. In order to ensure that, if directions are given, the trustees are properly protected by the order, they must ensure full disclosure of relevant matters, even if the case is to proceed with the participation of beneficiaries as defendants.

7.2 Applications for directions whether or not to take or defend or pursue litigation should be supported by evidence including the advice of an appropriately qualified lawyer as to the prospects of success and other matters relevant to be taken into account, including a cost estimate for the proceedings and any known facts concerning the means of the opposite party to the proceedings, and a draft of any proposed statement of case. There are cases in which it is likely to be so clear that the trustees ought to proceed as they wish that the costs of making the application, even on a simplified procedure without a hearing and perhaps without defendants, are not justified in comparison with the size of the fund or the matters at issue.

7.3 References in this practice direction to an appropriately qualified lawyer mean one whose qualifications and experience are appropriate to the circumstances of the case. The qualifications should be stated. If the advice is given on formal instructions, the instructions should always be put in evidence as well, so that the court can see the basis on which the advice was given. If it is not, the advice must state fully the basis on which it is given.

7.4 All applications for directions should be supported by evidence showing the value of the trust assets, the significance of the proposed litigation or other course of action for the trust, and why the court's directions are needed. In the case of a pension trust the evidence should include the latest actuarial valuation, and should describe the membership profile and, if a deficit on winding up is likely, the priority provisions and their likely effect.

7.5 On an application for directions about actual or possible litigation the evidence should also state whether (i) the Practice Direction (Pre-Action Conduct) or any relevant Pre-Action Protocol has been complied with; and (ii) the trustees have proposed or undertaken, or intend to propose, mediation by ADR, and (in each case) if not why not.

7.6 If a beneficiary of the trust is a party to the litigation about which directions are sought, with an interest opposed to that of the trustees, that beneficiary should be a defendant to the trustees' application, but any material which would be privileged as regards that beneficiary in the litigation should be put in evidence as exhibits to the trustees' witness statement, and should not be served on the beneficiary. However if the trustees' representatives consider that no harm would be done by the disclosure of all or some part of the material, then that material should be served on that defendant. That defendant may also be excluded from part of the hearing, including that which is devoted to discussion of the material withheld.

Consultation with beneficiaries

7.7 The evidence must explain what, if any, consultation there has **64BPD.8**
been with beneficiaries, and with what result. In preparation for an application for directions in respect of litigation, the following guidance is to be followed:

(1) If the trust is a private trust where the beneficiaries principally concerned are not numerous and are all or mainly adult, identified and traceable, the trustees will be expected to have canvassed with all the adult beneficiaries the proposed or possible courses of action before applying for directions.

(2) If it is a private trust with a larger number of beneficiaries, including those not yet born or identified, or children, it is likely that there will nevertheless be some adult beneficiaries principally concerned, with whom the trustees must consult.

(3) In relation to a charitable trust the trustees must have consulted the Attorney-General, through the Treasury Solicitor, as well as the Charity Commissioners whose consent to the application will have been needed under section 33 of the Charities Act 1993.

(4) In relation to a pension trust, unless the members are very

few in number, no particular steps by way of consultation with beneficiaries (including, where relevant, employers) or their representatives are required in preparation for the application, though the trustees' evidence should describe any consultation that has in fact taken place. If no consultation has taken place, the court could in some cases direct that meetings of one or more classes of beneficiaries be held to consider the subject matter of the application, possibly as a preliminary to deciding whether a member of a particular class ought to be joined as a defendant, though in a case concerning actual or proposed litigation, steps would need to be considered to protect privileged material from too wide disclosure.

7.8(1) If the court gives directions allowing the trustees to take, defend or pursue litigation it may do so up to a particular stage in the litigation, requiring the trustees, before they carry on beyond that point, to renew their application to the court. What stage that should be will depend on the likely management of the litigation under the CPR. If the application is to be renewed after disclosure of documents, and disclosed documents need to be shown to the court, it may be necessary to obtain permission to do this from the court in which the other litigation is proceeding.

(2) In such a case the court may sometimes direct that the case be dealt with at that stage without a hearing if the beneficiaries obtain and lodge the written advice of an appropriately qualified lawyer stating that he or they support the continuation of the directions. Any such advice will be considered by the court and, if thought fit, the trustees will be given a direction allowing them to continue pursuing the proceedings without a hearing.

7.9 In a case of urgency, such as where a limitation period or period for service of proceedings is about to expire, the court may be able to give directions on a summary consideration of the evidence to cover the steps which need to be taken urgently, but limiting those directions so that the application needs to be renewed on fuller consideration at an early stage.

7.10 In any application for directions where a child is a defendant, the court will expect to have put before it the instructions to and advice of an appropriately qualified lawyer as to the benefits and disadvantages of the proposed, and any other relevant, course of action from the point of view of the child beneficiary.

7.11 The master or district judge may give the directions sought though, if the directions relate to actual or proposed litigation, only if it is a plain case, and therefore the master or district judge may think it appropriate to give the directions without a hearing: see the Practice Direction supplementing Part 2: Allocation of Cases to Levels of the Judiciary, para.4.1 and para.5.1(e), and see also paragraph 6 above. Otherwise the case will be referred to the judge.

7.12 Where a hearing takes place, if the advice of a lawyer has been put in evidence in accordance with paragraph 7.2 or 7.10, that lawyer should if possible appear on the hearing.

PART 65

Proceedings Relating to Anti-Social Behaviour and Harassment

Contents

65.0.1

Editorial introduction

65.0.2 Part 65 and its Practice Direction were introduced by the Civil Procedure (Amendment) Rules 2004 (see SI 2004/1306). They came into effect on June 30, 2004. Their main purpose is to update procedure to allow claims for anti-social behaviour injunctions and demotion of tenancies in the light of the amendments to substantive law (especially Housing Act 1996—see para.3A–1033) introduced by the Anti-Social Behaviour Act 2003. However they also deal with anti-social behaviour orders (ASBOs) and injunctions under the Protection from Harassment Act 1997.

Section VI of Pt 65 (6.31 to 6.36) contained rules about applications for drink banning orders and interim drinking banning orders under the Violent Crime Reduction Act 2006 (c.38) ss.4 9. This Section was inserted into Pt 65 by the Civil Procedure (Amendment No.3) Rules 2006 (SI 2006/3435) and was supplemented by Practice Direction—Anti-Social Behaviour and Harassment Sect.VI (paras 15.1 and 15.2). However, upon it becoming apparent that the implementation of the relevant provisions of the underpinning legislation had been delayed indefinitely, Sect.VI of Pt 65 was omitted by the Civil Procedure (Amendment) Rules 2008 (SI 2008/2187), and Sect.VI of 65PD was omitted by TSO CPR Update 47, both with effect from October 1, 2008.

Related sources

65.0.3
- PD 2B (Allocation of cases to levels of judiciary)
- Part 7 (How to start proceedings – the claim form)

- Part 8 (Alternative Procedure for claims)
- Part 10 (Acknowledgement of Service)
- Part 12 (Default Judgment)
- Part 16 (Statements of Case)
- Part 19 (Parties and Group Litigation)
- Part 23 (General Rules about Applications for Court Orders)
- Part 55 (Possession Claims)
- RSC Order 52
- CCR Order 29
- Housing Act 1996, as amended by Anti-Social Behaviour Act 2003
- Protection from Harassment Act 1997
- Crime and Disorder Act 1998 (as amended by Police Reform Act 2002 and the Anti-Social Behaviour Act 2003)

Forms

- **N6** Claim form for demotion of tenancy 65.0.4
- **N7D** Notes for defendant to a demotion claim
- **N11D** Defence form to a claim for a demotion order, and
- **N16** Injunction Order
- **N16A** Application for injunction (general form)
- **N110A** Anti-social behaviour injunction power of arrest
- **N113** (Anti-social behaviour order)
- **N122** Particulars of claim for demotion order
- **N142** Guardianship Order (Housing Act 1996, Mental Health Act 1983)
- **N143** Interim Hospital Order (Housing Act 1996, Mental Health act 1983)
- **N206D** Notice of Issue (demotion claim)
- **N244** (Application Notice)

Scope of this Part[1]

65.1 This Part contains rules— 65.1

(a) in Section I, about injunctions under the Housing Act 1996[2];

(b) in Section II, about applications by local authorities under section 91(3) of the Anti-Social Behaviour Act 2003[3] for a power of arrest to be attached to an injunction;

(c) in Section III, about claims for demotion orders under the Housing Act 1985[4] and Housing Act 1988[5] and proceedings relating to demoted tenancies;

(d) in Section IV, about anti-social behaviour orders under the Crime and Disorder Act 1998[6];

(e) in Section V, about claims under section 3 of the Protection from Harassment Act 1997 [7]; and

(f) [...]

---

[1] Amended by the Civil Procedure (Amendment) Rules 2007 (SI 2007/2204) and the Civil Procedure (Amendment) Rules 2008 (SI 2008/2178).
[2] 1996 c.52.
[3] 2003 c.38.
[4] 1985 c.68.
[5] 1988 c.50.
[6] 1998 c.37.
[7] 1997 c.40.

(g) in Section VII, about parenting orders under sections 26A and 26B of the Anti-Social Behaviour Act 2003 [1].

Note

65.1.1
- **injunctions under the Housing Act 1996** See para.3A–1195.
- **applications by local authorities under section 91(3) of the Anti-Social Behaviour Act 2003 for a power of arrest** See para.3A–1200.
- **claims for demotion orders** See paras 3A–360 and 3A–757.
- **proceedings relating to demoted tenancies** See para.3A–11104.
- **anti-social behaviour orders under the Crime and Disorder Act 1998** See 3A–1401.1.

I. Housing Act 1996 injunctions

Scope of this Section and interpretation

65.2 **65.2—(1) This Section applies to applications for an injunction and other related proceedings under Chapter III of Part V of the Housing Act 1996 (injunctions against anti-social behaviour).**

(2) In this Section "the 1996 Act" means the Housing Act 1996.

Injunctions under the Housing Act 1996

65.2.1 See para.3A–1195. In particular Housing Act 1996 s.153A gives "relevant landlords" (as defined in s.153E) power to apply for free-standing anti-social behaviour injunctions irrespective of whether or not there is any other common law or statutory cause of action. Anti-social behaviour injunctions may prohibit the person in respect of whom they are granted from engaging in housing-related anti-social conduct of a kind specified in the injunction. "Anti-social conduct" means conduct anywhere which is capable of causing nuisance or annoyance to some person (who need not be a particular identified person). "Housing-related" means directly or indirectly relating to or affecting the housing management functions of a relevant landlord. Such injunctions may be granted if the person against whom the injunction is sought is engaging, has engaged or threatens to engage in housing-related conduct capable of causing a nuisance or annoyance to:

(a) a person with a right to reside in or occupy housing accommodation owned or managed by a relevant landlord,

(b) a person with a right to reside in or occupy other housing accommodation in the neighbourhood of housing accommodation mentioned in paragraph (a),

(c) a person engaged in lawful activity in, or in the neighbourhood of, housing accommodation mentioned in paragraph (a), or

(d) a person employed (whether or not by a relevant landlord) in connection with the exercise of a relevant landlord's housing management functions.

Applications for an injunction

65.3 **65.3—(1) An application for an injunction under Chapter III of Part V of the 1996 Act[2] shall be subject to the Part 8 procedure as modified by this rule and the relevant practice direction.**

(2) The application must be—

(a) made by a claim form in accordance with the relevant practice direction;

(b) commenced in the court for the district in which the

---

[1] s.24 of the Police and Justice Act 2006 (c.48) inserts ss.26A, 26B and 26C into the Anti-Social Behaviour Act 2003.

[2] 1996 c.52. These sections were inserted by s.13 of the Anti-Social Behaviour Act 2003.

defendant resides or the conduct complained of occurred; and

(c) supported by a witness statement which must be filed with the claim form.

(3) The claim form must state—

(a) the matters required by rule 8.2; and

(b) the terms of the injunction applied for.

(4) An application under this rule may be made without notice and where such an application without notice is made—

(a) the witness statement in support of the application must state the reasons why notice has not been given; and

(b) the following rules do not apply—

(i) 8.3;

(ii) 8.4;

(iii) 8.5(2) to (6);

(iv) 8.6(1);

(v) 8.7; and

(vi) 8.8.

(5) In every application made on notice, the application notice must be served, together with a copy of the witness statement, by the claimant on the defendant personally.

(6) An application made on notice may be listed for hearing before the expiry of the time for the defendant to file an acknowledgement of service under rule 8.3, and in such a case—

(a) the claimant must serve the application notice and witness statement on the defendant not less than two days before the hearing; and

(b) the defendant may take part in the hearing whether or not he has filed an acknowledgment of service.

Editorial introduction

Applications for injunctions under ss.153A, 153B or 153D must be made in Form **N16A** and follow the Pt 8 procedure. They must be made in the court for the district in which the defendant resides or the conduct complained of occurred (CPR r.65.3; PD65, para.1). All applications must state the terms of the injunction applied for and be supported by written evidence. They must be made on two days notice unless the court otherwise directs (see CPR r.65.3(6)(a)). The defendant must be served personally. If the application is made without notice the affidavit should explain why notice has not been given (CPR r.65.3(4)(a)). Unless otherwise directed applications made on notice should be heard in public (CPR r.39.2) Applications for injunctions must be made in Form **N16A** (PD65, para.1). Injunctions should be in Form **N16**. Wherever possible the claimant should file a draft of the order sought with the application and a disc with the draft order should be available to the court (PD25, para.2.4). Injunctions must be "framed in terms appropriate and proportionate to the facts of the case". *If there is a* risk of significant harm to a particular person or persons it is usually appropriate for the injunction to identify that person or those persons. However, in order to justify granting a wider injunction, restraining someone from causing a nuisance or annoyance to "a person of a similar description", it is normally necessary for the judge to make a finding that there has been use or threats of violence to persons of a similar description, and that there is a risk of significant harm to persons of a similar description if an injunction is not granted in respect of them (*Manchester City Council v Lee* [2003] EWCA Civ 1256; [2004] 1 W.L.R. 349). Rule 65.3(2)(c) was amended (see Civil Procedure (Amendment No.2) Rules 2004 (SI 2004/2072) (L.11)) to enable the use of witness statements in place of affidavits in applica- **65.3.1** tions for injunctions under Housing Act 1996, ss.153A-E. The amendment took effect on September 1, 2004.

Application for an injunction under section 153A, 153B or 153D

65.3.2 See paras 3A–1195, 3A–1200 and 3A–1205.

Claim form

65.3.3 See Form **N16A** which, under Pt 65, is to be treated as the Pt 8 claim form (PD 65.1). In particular, the claimant must state the remedy sought, the legal basis for the claim to that remedy and the enactment under which the remedy is sought.

Court for the district in which the defendant resides or the conduct complained of occurred

65.3.4 *c.f.* CPR r.55.3 and r.56.2. In the light of CPR r.3.10, issue in the wrong court is likely to be seen as an error of procedure which does not invalidate the step taken. In most cases judges would correct the error by transferring to the appropriate court. See, in another context, *Gwynedd CC v Grunshaw* [2000] 1 W.L.R. 494, CA.

The following rules do not apply

65.3.5 Unlike most Pt 8 claims,

(a) there is no requirement for an acknowledgement of service (*c.f.* CPR r.8.3 and 8.4);

(b) the normal Pt 8 provisions for filing of evidence do not apply (i.e. Pt 8.5(2) to (6) and 8.6(1)), but N.B. the requirement for affidavit evidence in CPR r.65.3(2)(b); and

(c) the procedure for objecting to the Pt 8 procedure does not apply (*c.f.* Pt 8.8).

Application notice and witness statement

65.3.6 See Form **N16A** (PD 65.1). If the application for an injunction is made without notice, the witness statement in support of the application must state the reasons why notice has not been given.

Jurisdiction

65.3.7 See PD 2B as amended. The former position was that the jurisdiction of the court under repealed ss.152 and 153 could be exercised by district judges as well as circuit judges. PD 2B, paras 8.1 and 8.3, as amended, make it clear that district and deputy district judges have jurisdiction to grant anti-social behaviour injunctions and to commit for contempt. There is no longer any requirement that district judges and deputy district judges have to have had appropriate training before exercising the jurisdiction (*c.f.* the Practice Direction made by the Lord Chancellor on August 28, 1997 which has been revoked and not replaced.) Notwithstanding the suggestion in some quarters that the former rule giving district judges jurisdiction was ultra vires, it is now accepted that this is not the case—see County Courts Act 1984 s.75(3)(d), repealed by Civil Procedure Act 1997 Sch.2, but Sch.1 to that Act provides that the Civil Procedure Rules may deal with the subjects contained in the former rules.

Injunction containing provisions to which a power of arrest is attached

65.4 **65.4—(1) In this rule "relevant provision" means a provision of an injunction to which a power of arrest is attached.**

(Sections 153C(3) and 153D(4) of the 1996 Act[1] confer powers to attach a power of arrest to an injunction)

(2) Where an injunction contains one or more relevant provisions—

(a) each relevant provision must be set out in a separate *paragraph of the injunction*; and

[1] 1996 c.52. These sections were inserted by s.13 of the Anti-Social Behaviour Act 2003.

(b) subject to paragraph (3), the claimant must deliver a copy of the relevant provisions to any police station for the area where the conduct occurred.

(3) Where the injunction has been granted without notice, the claimant must not deliver a copy of the relevant provisions to any police station for the area where the conduct occurred before the defendant has been served with the injunction containing the relevant provisions.

(4) Where an order is made varying or discharging any relevant provision, the claimant must—

(a) immediately inform the police station to which a copy of the relevant provisions was delivered under paragraph (2)(b); and

(b) deliver a copy of the order to any police station so informed.

Power of arrest

See Housing Act 1996 ss.153C and 153D at paras 3A–1200 and 3A–1205. A power of arrest should made be in Form N110A. If a power of arrest is sought, each provision which is to be subject to the power of arrest must be set out in a separate clause of the injunction (CPR r.65.4). Powers of arrest may be sought in claim forms, acknowledgements of service or Pt 23 applications. They must be supported by written evidence. If made on notice, not less than two days notice must be given (CPR r.65.9). It is important to spell out in the injunction the specific activities which are forbidden and confine the power of arrest to those specific activities alone. Under ECHR law, citizens must be able, if necessary with appropriate advice, to foresee to a reasonable degree the consequences that a given action may produce (*Silver v UK* (1983) 5 E.H.H.R. 347, at paras 87-8). Summary arrest and detention are clearly an extremely serious interference with a person's private life, which can only be justified by an order which is "particularly precise" (*Kopp v Switzerland* (1999) 27 E.H.R.R. 91, at para.72). See too *Manchester CC v Lee* [2003] EWCA Civ 1256; [2004] 1 W.L.R. 349 and, in a domestic violence context, *Hale v Tanner* [2000] 1 W.L.R. 2377, CA, which suggests a power of arrest be attached only to paragraphs prohibiting violence or physical proximity. This is confirmed by s.153C. 65.4.1

The claimant must deliver a copy an injunction with a Power of Arrest to any police station for the area where the conduct occurred—but if it was granted without notice, only after service on the defendant (CPR r.65.4). The claimant must immediately inform the police station if an injunction containing a power of arrest is varied or discharged.

Application for warrant of arrest under section 155(3) of the 1996 Act[1]

65.5—(1) An application for a warrant of arrest under section 155(3) of the 1996 Act must be made in accordance with Part 23 and may be made without notice. 65.5

(2) An applicant for a warrant of arrest under section 155(3) of *the 1996 Act must*—

(a) file an affidavit setting out grounds for the application with the application notice; or

(b) give oral evidence as to the grounds for the application at the hearing.

---

[1] 1996 c.52. This section was amended by s.13 of the Anti-Social Behaviour Act 2003.

Housing Act 1996 s.155

65.5.1 See para.3A–1216.

Warrant

65.5.2 A warrant of arrest under s.155(3) shall not be issued unless the application is substantiated on oath and the judge has reasonable grounds for believing that the defendant has failed to comply with the injunction (see PD 65, para.2.1).

Proceedings following arrest

65.6 **65.6—(1) This rule applies where a person is arrested pursuant to—**

(a) a power of arrest attached to a provision of an injunction; or

(b) a warrant of arrest.

(2) The judge before whom a person is brought following his arrest may—

(a) deal with the matter; or

(b) adjourn the proceedings.

(3) Where the proceedings are adjourned the judge may remand the arrested person in accordance with section 155(2)(b) or (5) of the 1996 Act.

(4) Where the proceedings are adjourned and the arrested person is released—

(a) the matter must be dealt with (whether by the same or another judge) within 28 days of the date on which the arrested person appears in court; and

(b) the arrested person must be given not less than 2 days' notice of the hearing.

(5) An application notice seeking the committal for contempt of court of the arrested person may be issued even if the arrested person is not dealt with within the period mentioned in paragraph (4)(a).

(6) CCR Order 29, rule 1 shall apply where an application is made in a county court to commit a person for breach of an injunction, as if references in that rule to the judge included references to a district judge.

(For applications in the High Court for the discharge of a person committed to prison for contempt of court see RSC Order 52, rule 8. For such applications in the county court see CCR Order 29, rule 3).

Power of arrest

65.6.1 See Housing Act 1996 ss.153C and 153D at paras 3A–1200 and 3A–1205 and CPR r.65.4 above.

Warrant of arrest

65.6.2 See CPR r.65.5 above.

***Dealing with* breaches of anti-social behaviour injunctions**

65.6.3 The judge before whom an arrested person is brought may deal with the matter or adjourn proceedings (CPR r.65.6). In such circumstances the arrested person may be remanded or released. If the person is released, the matter shall be dealt with by the same or another judge within 28 days of the date the arrested person appears in court. At least two days notice of the adjourned hearing must be given (CPR r.65.6).

Applications for bail

65.6.4 An application for bail made by a person arrested under a power of arrest attached to an injunction or a warrant of arrest issued under s.155(3) may be made either orally or in an application notice. An application notice seeking bail must contain (1) the full name of the person making the application; (2) the address of the place where the person making the application is detained; (3) the address where s/he would reside if bail were granted; (4) the amount of any proposed recognizance; and (5) the grounds for the application and, where a previous application has been refused, full details of any change in circumstances which has occurred since that refusal. A copy of the application notice must be served on the person who obtained the injunction (PD 65, para.3). If a person is bailed, subject to a recognizance, the recognizance may subsequently be taken by a judge, a justice of the peace, a justice's clerk, a senior police officer or the governor of a prison (CPR r.65.7).

Jurisdiction

65.6.5 See PD 2B as amended. The former position was that the jurisdiction of the court under repealed ss.152 and 153 could be exercised by district judges as well as circuit judges. The amendment to PD 2B makes it clear that district and deputy district judges have jurisdiction to grant anti-social behaviour injunctions and to commit for contempt. There is no longer any requirement that district judges and deputy district judges have to have had appropriate training before exercising the jurisdiction (*c.f.* the Practice Direction made by the Lord Chancellor on August 28, 1997 which has been revoked and not replaced). Notwithstanding the suggestion in some quarters that the former rule giving district judges jurisdiction was ultra vires, it is now accepted that this is not the case—see County Courts Act 1984 s.75(3)(d), repealed by Civil Procedure Act 1997 Sch.2, but Sch.1 to that Act provides that the Civil Procedure Rules may deal with the subjects contained in the former rules. See too CPR r.65.6(6) which provides that CCR O.29, r.1 applies on an application to commit for breach of an anti-social behaviour injunction, as if references in that rule to the judge included references to a district judge.

Recognizance

65.7 **65.7—(1) Where, in accordance with paragraph 2(2)(b) of Schedule 15 to the 1996 Act, the court fixes the amount of any recognizance with a view to it being taken subsequently, the recognizance may be taken by—**

(a) a judge;

(b) a justice of the peace;

(c) a justices' clerk;

(d) a police officer of the rank of inspector or above or in charge of a police station; or

(e) where the arrested person is in his custody, the governor or keeper of a prison,

with the same consequences as if it had been entered into before the court.

***(2) The person having* custody of an applicant for bail must release him if satisfied that the required recognizances have been taken.**

Housing Act 1996, Sch.15

65.7.1 See para.3A–1397.

Recognizance

65.7.2 See commentary to CPR r.65.6, above.

II. Applications by local authorities for power of arrest to be attached to an injunction

Scope of this Section and interpretation[1]

65.8 **65.8—(1) This Section applies to applications by local authorities under section 91(3) of the Anti-Social Behaviour Act 2003 [2] or under section 27(3) of the Police and Justice Act 2006 [3] for a power of arrest to be attached to an injunction.**

(Section 91 of the 2003 Act and section 27 of the 2006 Act apply to proceedings in which a local authority is a party by virtue of section 222 of the Local Government Act 1972) [4] (power of local authority to bring, defend or appear in proceedings for the promotion or protection of the interests of inhabitants in their area)

(2) In this Section "the 2003 Act" means the Anti-social Behaviour Act 2003.

(3) In this Section "the 2006 Act" means the Police and Justice Act 2006.

Editorial introduction

65.8.1 Local Government Act 1972 s.222, gives local authorities power to bring civil proceedings "for the promotion or protection of the interests of the inhabitants of their area". In *Nottingham City Council v Zain* [2001] EWCA Civ 1248; [2002] 1 W.L.R. 607, the Court of Appeal held that a local authority has the power to institute proceedings under s.222 in its own name for injunctive relief to restrain a public nuisance provided that it considers it expedient for the promotion and protection of the interests of the inhabitants of its area. Anti-Social Behaviour Act 2003 s.91 provides that if the court grants a s.222 injunction which prohibits conduct which is capable of causing nuisance or annoyance, it may attach a power of arrest to any provision of the injunction if the court thinks that either the conduct consists of or includes the use or threatened use of violence, or there is a significant risk of harm to the person mentioned in that subsection. Harm includes serious ill-treatment or abuse (whether physical or not).

Applications under section 91(3) of the 2003 Act or section 27(3) of the 2006 Act for a power of arrest to be attached to any provision of an injunction[5]

65.9 **65.9—(1) An application under section 91(3) of the 2003 Act or section 27(3) of the 2006 Act for a power of arrest to be attached to any provision of an injunction must be made in the proceedings seeking the injunction by—**

(a) the claim form;

(b) the acknowledgment of service;

(c) the defence or counterclaim in a Part 7 claim; or

(d) application under Part 23.

(2) Every application must be supported by written evidence.

(3) Every application made on notice must be served personally, together with a copy of the written evidence, by the local authority

---

[1] Amended by the Civil Procedure (Amendment) Rules 2007 (SI 2007/2204).
[2] 2003 c.38.
[3] 2006 c.48.
[4] 1972 c.70.
[5] Amended by the Civil Procedure (Amendment) Rules 2007 (SI 2007/2204).

on the person against whom the injunction is sought not less than 2 days before the hearing.

(Attention is drawn to rule 25.3(3)—applications without notice).

Anti-social Behaviour Act 2003 s.91

See commentary to CPR r.65.8. 65.9.1

Power of arrest

See commentary at para.65.8.1. 65.9.2

Injunction containing provisions to which a power of arrest is attached[1]

65.10—(1) Where a power of arrest is attached to a provision of an injunction on the application of a local authority under section 91(3) of the 2003 Act, the following rules in Section I of this Part shall apply— 65.10

(a) rule 65.4; and

(b) paragraphs (1), (2), (4) and (5) of rule 65.6.

(1A) Where a power of arrest is attached to a provision of an injunction on the application of a local authority under section 27(3) of the 2006 Act, the following rules in Section I of this Part apply—

(a) rule 65.4;

(b) paragraphs (1), (2), (4) and (5) of rule 65.6;

(c) paragraph (1) of rule 65.7, as if the reference to paragraph 2(2)(b) of Schedule 15 to the Housing Act 1996 [2] was a reference to paragraph 2(2)(b) of Schedule 10 to the 2006 Act; and

(d) paragraph (2) of rule 65.7.

(2) CCR Order 29, rule 1 shall apply where an application is made in a county court to commit a person for breach of an injunction.

Anti-Social Behaviour Act 2003 s.91

See commentary to CPR r.65.8. 65.10.1

Power of arrest

See the commentary to CPR r.65.4 and r.65.6 above. 65.10.2

Jurisdiction

See commentary at para.65.3.6 and para.65.6.5 above. 65.10.3

III. Demotion claims, proceedings related to demoted tenancies and applications to suspend the right to buy

Scope of this Section and interpretation

65.11—(1) This Section applies to— 65.11

(a) claims by a landlord for an order under section 82A of

[1] Amended by the Civil Procedure (Amendment) Rules 2007 (SI 2007/2204).
[2] 1996 c.52

the Housing Act 1985[1] or under section 6A of the Housing Act 1988[2] ("a demotion order");

(aa) claims by a landlord for an order under section 121A of the Housing Act 1985 ("a suspension order"); and

(b) proceedings relating to a tenancy created by virtue of a demotion order.

(2) In this Section—

(a) "a demotion claim" means a claim made by a landlord for a demotion order; and

(b) "a demoted tenancy" means a tenancy created by virtue of a demotion order;

(c) "suspension claim" means a claim made by a landlord for a suspension order; and

(d) "suspension period" means the period during which the suspension order suspends the right to buy in relation to the dwelling house.

Editorial introduction

65.11.1 The Anti-Social Behaviour Act 2003 amended the Housing Acts, 1985, 1988 and 1996 to give county courts power to change secure or assured tenancies into demoted tenancies, lacking the rights that are associated with secure and assured tenancies. Applications for demoted tenancies may be made by local housing authorities, housing action trusts and registered social landlords. The court can only grant a demotion order if—

(a) a notice seeking a demotion order has been served or it is just and equitable to dispense with that requirement;

(b) it is satisfied that the tenant or a person residing in or visiting the dwelling-house has engaged or has threatened to engage in conduct to which Housing Act 1996 s.153A or s.153B (anti-social behaviour or use of premises for unlawful purposes) applies; and

(c) it is reasonable to make the order.

A demotion order—

(a) terminates the secure or assured tenancy with effect from the date specified in the order;

(b) if the tenant remains in occupation, creates a demoted tenancy; and

(c) makes it a term of the demoted tenancy that any arrears of rent payable at the termination of the secure tenancy become payable under the demoted tenancy. A demoted tenancy lacks security of tenure but before bringing a possession claim, a local authority landlord of a former secure demoted tenant must serve on the tenant a notice of proceedings which—

  (i) states that the court will be asked to make a possession order;

  (ii) sets out the reasons for the landlord's decision to apply for the order; and

  (iii) specifies the date after which proceedings for the possession of the dwelling-house may be begun.

Housing Act 1996 s.143F provides a procedure for an internal review of the decision to seek possession.

If the former tenancy was an assured tenancy, the tenant becomes a demoted assured shorthold tenant. If the landlord wishes to recover possession, it need only comply with Housing Act 1988 s.21 (para.3A–879). There is no right to a review.

Housing Act 1985 s.82A

65.11.2 See para.3A–360.

[1] 1985 c.68. This section was inserted by s.14 of the Anti-Social Behaviour Act 2003.
[2] 1988 c.50. This section was inserted by s.14 of the Anti-Social Behaviour Act 2003.

Housing Act 1985 s.6A

See para.3A–757. 65.11.3

Demotion claims or suspension claims made in the alternative to possession claims

65.12 Where a demotion order or suspension order (or both) is claimed in the alternative to a possession order, the claimant must use the Part 55 procedure and Section I of Part 55 applies, except that the claim must be made in the county court for the district in which the property to which the claim relates is situated. 65.12

A demotion order

See CPR r.65.11. 65.12.1

Part 55 procedure

A demotion claim may be sought as an alternative to possession. In those circumstances, Pt 55, the normal procedure for possession claims, applies. See CPR r.55.3, the paragraphs which follow and the commentary thereto. If the landlord only seeks demotion, Pt 65 applies—see below—although the procedure is very similar to that provided for by Pt 55. 65.12.2

The county court for the district in which the property to which the claim relates is situated

CPR r.55.3 gives a landlord the option of starting a possession claim in the High Court in certain circumstances. That option is disapplied in relation to demotion claims by CPR r.62.12. 65.12.3

Other demotion or suspension claims

65.13 Where a demotion claim or suspension claim (or both) is made other than in a possession claim, rules 65.14 to 65.19 apply. 65.13

Demotion claim

See CPR r.65.11. If demotion is sought as an alternative to possession, CPR Pt 55, the normal procedure for possession claims, applies. If the landlord only seeks demotion, Pt 65 applies, although the procedure is very similar to that provided for by Pt 55. 65.13.1

Starting a demotion or suspension claim

65.14—(1) The claim must be made in the county court for the district in which the property to which the claim relates is situated. 65.14

(2) The claim form and form of defence sent with it must be in the forms set out in the relevant practice direction.

(The relevant practice direction and Part 16 provide details about the contents of the particulars of claim).

Demotion claim

See CPR r.65.11. 65.14.1

Court for the district in which the defendant resides or the conduct complained of occurred

See too *PD 65, para.6.1; c.f.* CPR rr.55.3, 56.2 and 65.3. In the light of CPR r 3.10, issue in the wrong court is likely to be seen as an error of procedure which does not invalidate the step taken. In most cases judges would correct the error by transferring to the appropriate court. See, in another context, *Gwynedd CC v Grunshaw* [2000] 1 W.L.R. 494, CA. 65.14.2

Particulars of claim

65.15 The particulars of claim must be filed and served with the claim form. 65.15

Claim form

65.15.1 See PD 65, para.6.2 and Form N6.

Particulars of claim

65.15.2 See PD 65, para.6.2 and Form N122. PD 65, para.7.1 provides that the particulars of claim must—

(1) state whether the demotion claim is made under Housing Act 1985 s.82A(2) or Housing Act 1988 s.6A(2);
(2) state whether the claimant is a local housing authority, a housing action trust or a registered social landlord;
(3) identify the property to which the claim relates;
(4) provide details about the tenancy, including the parties, the period of the tenancy, the rent, the dates on which the rent is payable and any statement of express terms of the tenancy served on the tenant under s.82A(7) or under s.6A(10); and
(5) state details of the conduct alleged.

PD 65, para.9.1 provides that each party should wherever possible include all the evidence he or she wishes to present in his statement of case, verified by a statement of truth.

Hearing date

65.16 **65.16—(1) The court will fix a date for the hearing when it issues the claim form.**

(2) The hearing date will be not less than 28 days from the date of issue of the claim form.

(3) The standard period between the issue of the claim form and the hearing will be not more than 8 weeks.

(4) The defendant must be served with the claim form and the particulars of claim not less than 21 days before the hearing date.

(Rule 3.1(2)(a) provides that the court may extend or shorten the time for compliance with any rule and rule 3.1(2)(b) provides that the court may adjourn or bring forward a hearing).

Hearing date

65.16.1 These provisions are exactly the same as the comparable provisions which apply to possession claims—see CPR r.55.5(1) and (3) and the commentary at para.55.5.3. Note that PD 65, para.8.2 provides that particular consideration should be given to abridging time between service and the hearing if—

(1) the defendant has assaulted or threatened to assault the claimant, a member of the claimant's staff or another resident in the locality;
(2) there are reasonable grounds for fearing such an assault; or
(3) the defendant has caused serious damage or threatened to cause serious damage to the property or to the home or property of another resident in the locality.

Defendant's response

65.17 **65.17—(1) An acknowledgement of service is not required and Part 10 does not apply.**

(2) Where the defendant does not file a defence within the time specified in rule 15.4 he may take part in any hearing but the court may take his failure to do so into account when deciding what order to make about costs.

(3) Part 12 (default judgment) does not apply.

Defence

See Form N11D. These provisions are exactly the same as the comparable provisions which apply to possession claims—see CPR r.55.7(1) and (3) and the commentary at para.55.7.4. **65.17.1**

The hearing[1]

65.18—(1) At the hearing fixed in accordance with rule 65.16(1) or at any adjournment of that hearing the court may— **65.18**

(a) decide the claim; or

(b) give case management directions.

(2) Where the claim is genuinely disputed on grounds which appear to be substantial, case management directions given under paragraph (1)(b) will include the allocation of the claim to a track or directions to enable it to be allocated.

(3) Except where—

(a) the claim is allocated to the fast track or the multi-track; or

(b) the court directs otherwise,

any fact that needs to be proved by the evidence of witnesses at a hearing referred to in paragraph (1) may be proved by evidence in writing.

(Rule 32.2(1) sets out the general rule about evidence. Rule 32.2(2) provides that rule 32.2(1) is subject to any provision to the contrary).

(4) All witness statements must be filed and served at least two days before the hearing.

(5) Where the claimant serves the claim form and particulars of claim, the claimant must produce at the hearing a certificate of service of those documents and rule 6.17(2)(a) does not apply.

Demotion claim

See CPR r.65.11. **65.18.1**

The hearing

These provisions are almost exactly the same as the comparable provisions which apply to possession claims—see CPR r.55.8 and the commentary at para.55.8.7. **65.18.2**

Jurisdiction

District judges have jurisdiction to try demotion claims—see PD 2B, para.11.1(b). **65.18.3**

Evidence

See PD 65, para.6.3. The claimant's evidence should include details of the conduct alleged. **65.18.4**

Costs

Fixed costs may apply where a demotion order is claimed and made, either in stand alone proceedings under CPR Pt 65 or where it is sought in a possession claim form under *CPR Pt 55—unless* the court orders otherwise. The amounts of fixed costs are set out in CPR r.45.2A, Table 2, and CPR r.45.4A. **65.18.5**

Allocation

65.19 When the court decides the track for the claim, the matters to which it shall have regard include— **65.19**

[1] Amended by the Civil Procedure (Amendment) Rules 2008 (SI 2008/2178).

(a) the matters set out in rule 26.8; and

(b) the nature and extent of the conduct alleged.

Demotion claim

65.19.1 See CPR r.65.11.

Allocation

65.19.2 *c.f.* CPR r.55.9. See the commentary at para.26.8.4.

Proceedings relating to demoted tenancies

65.20 **65.20 A practice direction may make provision about proceedings relating to demoted tenancies.**

Demoted tenancy

65.20.1 See CPR r.65.11.

A practice direction

65.20.2 PD 65, para.11.1 provides that proceedings as to whether a statement supplied in pursuance to Housing Act 1996 s.143M(4)(b) (see para.3A–1133—written statement of certain terms of tenancy) is accurate must be brought under the Pt 8 procedure.

IV. Anti-social behaviour orders under the Crime and Disorder Act 1998

Scope of this Section and interpretation

65.21 **65.21—(1) This Section applies to applications in proceedings in a county court under sub-sections (2), (3) or (3B) of section 1B of the Crime and Disorder Act 1998[1] by a relevant authority, and to applications for interim orders under section 1D of that Act.**

(2) In this Section—

(a) "the 1998 Act" means the Crime and Disorder Act 1998;

(b) "relevant authority" has the same meaning as in section 1(1A) of the 1998 Act; and

(c) "the principal proceedings"means any proceedings in a county court.

Crime and Disorder Act 1998, s.1B

65.21.1 See 3A–1401.1.

Editorial introduction

65.21.2 Part I of the Crime and Disorder Act 1998, as amended, includes provisions which enable Magistrates Courts to grant anti-social behaviour orders ("ASBOs"), parenting orders, child safety orders and intervention orders. Among the grounds for the grant of an ASBO is a finding that "the person has acted in an anti-social manner, that is to say, in a manner that caused or was likely to cause harassment, alarm or distress to one or more persons not of the same household as himself". An ASBO may only be granted if such an order is necessary to protect relevant persons from further anti-social acts (s.1(1)). When considering whether a person's conduct has caused or is likely to cause harassment, alarm or distress to others within the meaning of Crime and Disorder Act 1998 s.1(1)(a) "likely" means "more probable than not". The likelihood has to be proved to the criminal standard (see *Chief Constable of Lancashire v Pot-*

---

[1] 1998 c.37. Sections 1(1A) and 1B were amended by s.85 of the Anti-Social Behaviour Act 2003 (c.38).

ter [2003] EWHC 2272 and *R. (on the application of McCann) v Manchester Crown Court* [2002] UKHL 39; [2003] 1 A.C. 787; [2002] 3 W.L.R. 1313). An ASBO may prohibit the defendant from doing anything described in the order. The prohibitions that may be imposed by an ASBO are "those necessary for the purpose of protecting persons (whether relevant persons or persons elsewhere in England and Wales) from further anti-social acts by the defendant" (s.1(4) and (6)). ASBOs have effect for the period (not less than two years) specified in the order or until further order (s.1(7)). Breach of an ASBO may be punished on summary conviction by imprisonment for a term not exceeding six months or a fine or both; or on conviction on indictment, by imprisonment for a term not exceeding five years or to a fine, or to both (s.1(10)). Breach of such orders amounts to a criminal offence.

The power to grant ASBOs has been extended to county courts since April 1, 2003—see Police Reform Act 2002 s.63 , inserting s.1B into the Crime and Disorder Act 1998 and the Police Reform Act 2002 (Commencement No.4) Order 2003 (SI 2003/808). Anti-Social Behaviour Act 2003 s.85 also amends s.1B to allow a relevant authority which considers that a person who is not a party to county court proceedings has acted in an anti-social manner, and that those anti-social acts are material to the proceedings, to apply for that person to be joined to the county court proceedings so that the county court may make an ASBO. A relevant authority may also apply to be joined to county court proceedings if it is not already a party so that it may apply for an ASBO. These changes came into effect on March 31, 2004.

A relevant authority

See the Crime and Disorder Act 1998 s.1(1A), as amended by the Crime and Disorder Act 1998 (Relevant Authorities and Relevant Persons) Order 2006 SI 2006/2137 namely the council for a local government area, a county council, the chief officer of police of any police force maintained for a police area, the chief constable of the British Transport Police Force, a social landlord who provides or manages any houses or hostel which is registered under the Housing Act 1996 s.1 a housing action trust (see Housing Act 1988 s.62), the Environment Agency or Transport for London. 65.21.3

Service

PD 65, para.13.1 provides that an ASBO made under s.1B(4) or an interim order under s.1D must be served personally on the defendant. 65.21.4

Jurisdiction

PD 2B, para.8.1A provides that district judges have jurisdiction to make ASBOs under s.1B and interim ASBOs under s.1D. 65.21.5

Application where the relevant authority is a party in principal proceedings

65.22—(1) Subject to paragraph (2)— 65.22

(a) where the relevant authority is the claimant in the principal proceedings, an application under section 1B(2) of the 1998 Act for an order under section 1B(4) of the 1998 Act must be made in the claim form; and

(b) where the relevant authority is a defendant in the principal proceedings, an application for an order must be made by application notice which must be filed with the defence.

(2) Where the relevant authority becomes aware of the circumstances that lead it to apply for an order after its claim is issued or its defence filed, the application must be made by application notice as soon as possible thereafter.

(3) Where the application is made by application notice, it should normally be made on notice to the person against whom the order is sought.

Relevant Authority

65.22.1 See CPR r.65.21 and the Crime and Disorder Act 1998 s.1(1A) (para.3A–1503) as amended by the Crime and Disorder Act 1998 (Relevant Authorities and Relevant Persons) Order 2006 SI 2006/2137, namely the council for a local government area, a county council, the chief officer of police of any police force maintained for a police area, the chief constable of the British Transport Police Force, a social landlord who provides or manages any houses or hostel which is registered under Housing Act 1996 s.1 a housing action trust (see Housing Act 1988 s.62), the Environment Agency or Transport for London.

Principal proceedings

65.22.2 See the Crime and Disorder Act 1998 s.1B (para.3A–1512) and CPR r.65.21—i.e. any proceedings in a county court.

Application notice

65.22.3 See CPR r.23.3 and Form **N244**. An application must be made as soon as possible after the authority becomes aware of the circumstances that lead it to apply for an order—see CPR r.65.22(2) . Such an application should normally be made on notice in accordance with CPR r.23.7—i.e. at least three days before the court is to deal with the application—but see CPR r.23.4 .

Application by a relevant authority to join a person to the principal proceedings

65.23 **65.23—(1) An application under section 1B(3B) of the 1998 Act by a relevant authority which is a party to the principal proceedings to join a person to the principal proceedings must be made—**

- **(a) in accordance with Section I of Part 19;**
- **(b) in the same application notice as the application for an order under section 1B(4) of the 1998 Act against the person; and**
- **(c) as soon as possible after the relevant authority considers that the criteria in section 1B(3A) of the 1998 Act are met.**

(2) The application notice must contain—

- **(a) the relevant authority's reasons for claiming that the person's anti-social acts are material in relation to the principal proceedings; and**
- **(b) details of the anti-social acts alleged.**

(3) The application should normally be made on notice to the person against whom the order is sought.

Part 19

65.23.1 See in particular CPR r.19.4.

Relevant authority

65.23.2 See CPR r.65.21 and the Crime and Disorder Act 1998 s.1(1A) as amended by the Crime and Disorder Act 1998 (Relevant Authorities and Relevant Persons) Order 2006 SI 2006/2137, namely the council for a local government area, a county council, the chief officer of police of any police force maintained for a police area, the chief constable of the British Transport Police Force, a social landlord who provides or manages any houses or hostel which is registered under Housing Act 1996 s.1 a housing action trust (see Housing Act 1988 s.62), the Environment Agency or Transport for London.

***Principal** proceedings*

65.23.3 See Crime and Disorder Act 1998 s.1B and CPR r.65.21—i.e. any proceedings in a county court.

Application to join a person

See Crime and Disorder Act 1998 s.1B(3C) at 3A–1512. A person may only be joined if his or her anti-social acts are material in relation to the principal proceedings. The application should be made in Form **N244** and must contain the relevant authority's reasons for claiming that the person's anti-social acts are material in relation to the principal proceedings and details of the anti-social acts alleged. Such applications should normally be made on notice in accordance with CPR r.23.7—i.e. at least three days before the court is to deal with the application—but see CPR r.23.4. **65.23.4**

Application where the relevant authority is not party in principal proceedings

65.24—(1) Where the relevant authority is not a party to the principal proceedings— **65.24**

(a) an application under section 1B(3) of the 1998 Act to be made a party must be made in accordance with Section I of Part 19; and

(b) the application to be made a party and the application for an order under section 1B(4) of the 1998 Act must be made in the same application notice.

(2) The applications—

(a) must be made as soon as possible after the authority becomes aware of the principal proceedings; and

(b) should normally be made on notice to the person against whom the order is sought.

Relevant authority

See CPR r.65.21 and the Crime and Disorder Act 1998 s.1(1A) as amended by the Crime and Disorder Act 1998 (Relevant Authorities and Relevant Persons) Order 2006 SI 2006/2137, namely the council for a local government area, a county council, the chief officer of police of any police force maintained for a police area, the chief constable of the British Transport Police Force, a social landlord who provides or manages any houses or hostel which is registered under Housing Act 1996 s.1 a housing action trust (see Housing Act 1988 s.62), the Environment Agency or Transport for London. **65.24.1**

Principal proceedings

See Crime and Disorder Act 1998 s.1B and CPR r.65.21—i.e. any proceedings in a county court. **65.24.2**

Part 19

See in particular CPR r.19.4. **65.24.3**

Application to be joined

See Crime and Disorder Act 1998 s.1B(3) at para.3A–1512. The application should be made in Form **N244**. It should normally be made on notice in accordance with CPR r.23.7—i.e. at least three days before the court is to deal with the application—but see CPR r.23.4. **65.24.4**

Evidence

65.25 An application for an *order under* section 1B(4) of the 1998 Act must be accompanied by written evidence, which must include evidence that section 1E of the 1998 Act has been complied with. **65.25**

Written evidence

This may either be contained in Pt C of the application notice in Form N244 or in a separate witness statement. **65.25.1**

An order under Crime and Disorder Act 1998, s.1B(4)

65.25.2 i.e. an ASBO. See 3A–1512.

Crime and Disorder Act 1998, s.1E

65.25.3 Section 1E imposes consultation requirements—see para.3A–1522 and *McC v Wigan MBC*, October 30, 2003, unrep. where the lead role in seeking ASBOs was taken by a management company, which, although solely owned by the council, was a separate entity to the council. As such, in the absence of authorisation from the council, it was not authorised to consult. It was also apparent that there was a lack of knowledge on the part of the tenancy relations manager about the Home Office Guidance and an unstructured approach to the process. However these failings did not result in a substantial failure to comply with the consultation requirements. The requirement for consultation between the police and local authority in s.1E is fulfilled by substantial compliance, even though there may not have been full compliance. Information had been exchanged before making the application.

Application for an interim order

65.26 **65.26—(1) An application for an interim order under section 1D of the 1998 Act must be made in accordance with Part 25.**

(2) The application should normally be made—

(a) in the claim form or application notice seeking the order; and

(b) on notice to the person against whom the order is sought.

Interim order

65.26.1 See Crime and Disorder Act 1998 s.1D. The court may make an interim ASBO if it considers that it is just to make such an order pending the determination of the main application. Interim ASBOs should be made for a fixed period, but may be varied, renewed or discharged.

Jurisdiction

65.26.2 PD 2B, para.8.1A provides that district judges have jurisdiction to make an interim ASBO under s.1D.

Service

65.26.3 PD 65, para.13.1 provides that an order under s.1B(4) or an interim order under s.1D must be served personally on the defendant.

V. Proceedings under the Protection from Harassment Act 1997

Scope of this Section

65.27 **65.27 This Section applies to proceedings under section 3 of the Protection from Harassment Act 1997[1] ("the 1997 Act").**

Editorial introduction

65.27.1 Protection from Harassment Act 1997 s.1(1) provides that a person must not pursue a course of conduct (a) which amounts to harassment of another, and (b) which he knows or ought to know amounts to harassment of the other—i.e. if a reasonable person in possession of the same information would think the course of conduct amounted to harassment of the other. Such conduct is a criminal offence. In addition county courts may grant injunctions and award damages. Breach of an injunction is an *arrestable criminal offence*.

[1] 1997 c.40.

General approach

For the general approach of the Courts to the tort of harassment, before the passing of the Protection from Harassment Act 1997, see *Burris v Azadani* [1995] 4 All E.R. 802, CA. **65.27.2**

Section 3(3) of the 1997 Act provides:

"where—

(a) in such proceedings the High Court or a county court grants an injunction for the purpose of restraining the defendant from pursuing any conduct which amounts to harassment, and

(b) the plaintiff considers that the defendant has done anything which he is prohibited from doing by the injunction, the plaintiff may apply for the issue of a warrant for the arrest of the defendant."

The test under s.1(2) of the Protection from Harassment Act 1997, namely whether a reasonable person would think the conduct complained of amounted to harassment is objective. The mental illness of an offender is not, therefore, a defence. *R. v C (Sean Peter)*, [2001] EWCA Crim 1251 (Kennedy L.J., Curtis and Hughes JJ.).

Before the Protection from Harassment Act 1997 the common law had not reached the point of recognising a tort of international harassment, see *Wong v Parkside Health NHS Trust*, [2001] EWCA Civ 1721 (Brooke, Hale, L.JJ. and David Steel, J.). A company cannot be the victim of harassment under the Act and cannot bring a claim under it. However individuals who were non-corporate claimants, such as directors and employees, could be entitled to the protection of the Act and may institute proceedings: *Daiichi UK Ltd v Stop Huntingdon Animal Cruelty* [2003] EWHC 2337 (Owen J).

A director of a company may bring proceedings on behalf of employees of the company as being the most convenient and expeditious way of enabling the Court to protect their interests: *Emerson Developments Ltd v Avery* [2004] EWHC 194 (Field J.).

An employer may be held vicariously liable under s.3 of the 1997 Act for harassment in breach of s.1 of the Act by one of its employees in the course of his employment: *Majrowski v Guy's & St Thomas's NHS Trust The Times*, March 21, 2005 (Auld, May and Scott Baker L.JJ.).

In proceedings under s.3 of the 1997 Act the appropriate standard of proof is the civil standard *Hipgrave v Jones* [2004] EWHC 2901 (QB), Tugendhat J.

The power to vary a restraining order under s.5(4) of the Act includes a power to extend the duration of the order, provided there is some change of circumstances to justify such an extension: *DPP v Hall* [2006] 3 All E.R.170 (Scott Baker L.J. and Rafferty J. (Divisional Court)).

Claims under section 3 of the 1997 Act

65.28 A claim under section 3 of the 1997 Act — **65.28**

(a) shall be subject to the Part 8 procedure; and

(b) must be commenced—

(i) if in the High Court, in the Queen's Bench Division;

(ii) if in the county court, in the court for the district in which the defendant resides or carries on business or the court for the district in which the claimant resides or carries on business.

Subject to the Part 8 procedure

One effect of this is that claims must be issued in Form **N208**. They are automatically allocated to the multi-track. However *PD 2B*, *para.8.1* provides that district judges have jurisdiction to grant injunctions under Protection from Harassment Act 1997 s.3. However they do not have jurisdiction to make orders committing a person to prison for breach of a Protection from Harassment Act 1997 injunction. See PD 2B, para.8.3 and CCR O.29, r.1. In that context "judge" means "circuit judge". **65.28.1**

Court for the district in which the defendant or claimant resides or carries on business

c.f. CPR, rr.55.3 and 56.2. In the light of CPR r.2.10, issue in the wrong court is **65.28.2** likely to be seen as an error of procedure which does not invalidate the step taken. In most cases judges would correct the error by transferring to the appropriate court. See, in another context, *Gwynedd CC v Grunshaw* [2000] 1 W.L.R. 494, CA.

Applications for issue of a warrant of arrest under section 3(3) of the 1997 Act

65.29 **65.29—(1) An application for a warrant of arrest under section 3(3) of the 1997 Act—**

(a) must be made in accordance with Part 23; and

(b) may be made without notice.

(2) The application notice must be supported by affidavit evidence which must—

(a) set out the grounds for the application;

(b) state whether the claimant has informed the police of the conduct of the defendant as described in the affidavit; and

(c) state whether, to the claimant's knowledge, criminal proceedings are being pursued.

Warrant

65.29.1 PD 65, para.14.1 provides that a warrant of arrest under s.3(3) may only be issued if the application is substantiated on oath and the judge has reasonable grounds for believing that the defendant has done anything prohibited by the injunction.

Proceedings following arrest

65.30 **65.30—(1) The judge before whom a person is brought following his arrest may—**

(a) deal with the matter; or

(b) adjourn the proceedings.

(2) Where the proceedings are adjourned and the arrested person is released—

(a) the matter must be dealt with (whether by the same or another judge) within 28 days of the date on which the arrested person appears in court; and

(b) the arrested person must be given not less than 2 days' notice of the hearing.

Jurisdiction

65.30.1 District judges do not have jurisdiction to make orders committing a person to prison for breach of a Protection from Harassment Act 1997 injunction. See PD 2B, para.8.3 and CCR O.29, r.1. In that context "judge" means "circuit judge".

VI. Drinking Banning Orders under the Violent Crime Reduction Act 2006

65.31 [...][1]

[THE NEXT **PARAGRAPH IS 65.37.]**

[1] Deleted by the Civil Procedure (Amendment) Rules 2008 (SI 2008/2178).

VII. Parenting Orders under the Anti-Social Behaviour Act 2003

Scope of this Section and interpretation[1]

65.37—(1) This Section of this Part applies in relation to applications for parenting orders under sections 26A and 26B of the Anti-Social Behaviour Act 2003 by a relevant authority. 65.37

(2) In this Section—

(a) "the 2003 Act" means the Anti-Social Behaviour Act 2003; and

(b) "relevant authority" has the same meaning as in section 26C of the 2003 Act.

Editorial note

The Police and Justice Act 2006 Pt 3 contains new housing provisions (incorporated into the Anti-Social Behaviour Act 2003) enabling public and social landlords to enter into parenting contracts with tenants and seek parenting orders from the courts. These provisions were brought into force June 29, 2007 by the Police and Justice Act 2006 (Commencement No.3) Order 2007 SI 2007/1614 (C.65) 65.37.1

Applications for parenting orders[2]

65.38—(1) Subject to paragraph (2)— 65.38

(a) where the relevant authority is the claimant in the proceedings, an application for an order under section 26A or 26B of the 2003 Act must be made in the claim form; and

(b) where the relevant authority is a defendant in the proceedings, an application for such an order must be made by application notice which must be filed with the defence.

(2) Where the relevant authority becomes aware of the circumstances that lead it to apply for an order after its claim is issued or its defence filed, the application must be made by application notice as soon as possible thereafter.

(3) Where the application is made by application notice, it must normally be made on notice to the person against whom the order is sought.

"relevant authority"

See the Anti-Social Behaviour Act 2003 s.26C. 65.38.1

"claim form"

See para.65.3.3. 65.38.2

"application notice "

See para.65.3.6. Where the applicant is a registered social landlord, the application must be supported by evidence that the relevant local authority has been consulted in accordance with Anti-Social Behaviour Act 2003 s.26B(8) (PD65, para.16.1). 65.38.3

Applications by the relevant authority to be joined to proceedings[3]

65.39—(1) Where the relevant authority is not a party to the proceedings— 65.39

[1] Introduced by the Civil Procedure (Amendment) Rules 2007 (SI 2007/2204).
[2] Introduced by the Civil Procedure (Amendment) Rules 2007 (SI 2007/2204).
[3] Introduced by the Civil Procedure (Amendment) Rules 2007 (SI 2007/2204).

(a) an application under section 26C(2) of the 2003 Act to be made a party must be made in accordance with Section I of Part 19; and

(b) the application to be made a party and the application for an order under section 26A or 26B of the 2003 Act must be made in the same application notice.

(2) The applications—

(a) must be made as soon as possible after the relevant authority becomes aware of the proceedings; and

(b) must normally be made on notice to the person against whom the order is sought.

"relevant authority"

65.39.1 See the Anti-Social Behaviour Act 2003 s.26C.

Applications by the relevant authority to join a parent to proceedings[1]

65.40 **65.40—(1) An application under section 26C(3) of the 2003 Act by a relevant authority which is a party to the proceedings to join a parent to those proceedings must be made—**

(a) in the same application notice as the application for an order under section 26A or 26B of the 2003 Act; and

(b) as soon as possible after the relevant authority considers that the grounds for the application are met.

(2) Rule 19.2 does not apply in relation to an application made by a relevant authority under section 26C(3) of the 2003 Act to join a parent to the proceedings.

(3) The application notice must contain—

(a) the relevant authority's reasons for claiming the anti-social behaviour of the child or young person is material in relation to the proceedings; and

(b) details of the behaviour alleged.

(4) The application must normally be made on notice to the person against whom the order is sought.

"relevant authority"

65.40.1 See the Anti-Social Behaviour Act 2003 s.26C.

"application to join a person"

65.40.2 An application by a relevant authority under s.26C(3) to join a person to the proceedings may only be made against a person aged 18 or over (PD 65, para.16.3).

Evidence[2]

65.41 **65.41 An application under section 26A, 26B or 26C of the 2003 Act must be accompanied by written evidence.**

"written evidence"

65.41.1 See CPR Pt 32.

[1] Introduced by the Civil Procedure (Amendment) Rules 2007 (SI 2007/2204).
[2] Introduced by the Civil Procedure (Amendment) Rules 2007 (SI 2007/2204).

"service of order"

An order under the Anti-Social Behaviour Act 2003 s.26A or 26B must be served personally on the defendant (PD65, para.16.2). 65.41.2

PRACTICE DIRECTION—ANTI-SOCIAL BEHAVIOUR AND HARASSMENT

This Practice Direction supplements CPR Part 65

I. Housing Act 1996 Injunctions

Issuing the Claim

65PD.1 **1.1** An application for an injunction under section Chapter III of Part V of the 1996 Act must be made by form N16A and for the purposes of applying the practice direction that supplements Part 8 to applications under Section I of Part 65, form N16A shall be treated as the Part 8 claim form.

Warrant of Arrest on an Application under Section 155(3) of the 1996 Act

65PD.2 **2.1** In accordance with section 155(4) of the 1996 Act, a warrant of arrest on an application under section 155(3) of that Act shall not be issued unless—

(1) the application is substantiated on oath; and

(2) the judge has reasonable grounds for believing that the defendant has failed to comply with the injunction.

Application for Bail

65PD.3 **3.1** An application for bail by a person arrested under—

(1) a power of arrest attached to an injunction under Chapter III of Part V of the 1996 Act; or

(2) a warrant of arrest issued on an application under section 155(3) of that Act,

may be made either orally or in an application notice.

3.2 An application notice seeking bail must contain—

(1) the full name of the person making the application;

(2) the address of the place where the person making the application is detained at the time when the application is made;

(3) the address where the person making the application would reside if he were to be granted bail;

(4) the amount of the recognizance in which he would agree to be bound; and

(5) the grounds on which the application is made and, where previous application has been refused, full details of any change in circumstances which has occurred since that refusal.

3.3 A copy of the application notice must be served on the person who obtained the injunction.

Remand for Medical Examination and Report

65PD.4 **4.1** Section 156(4) of the 1996 Act provides that the judge has power to make an order under section 35 of the Mental Health Act 1983 in certain circumstances. If he does so attention is drawn to section 35(8) of that Act, which provides that a person remanded to hospital under that section may obtain at his own expense an independent report on his mental condition from a registered medical practitioner chosen by him and apply to the court on the basis of it for his remand to be terminated under section 35(7).

II. Applications by Local Authorities for Power of Arrest to be Attached to an Injunction

Application for Bail under the 2006 Act

4A.1 The following paragraphs of Section I of this practice direction apply in relation to an application for bail by a person arrested under a power of arrest attached to an injunction under section 27 of the 2006 Act— **65PD.4.1**

(1) paragraph 3.1(1), as if a reference to Chapter III of Part V of the Housing Act 1996 was a reference to section 27 of the 2006 Act;

(2) paragraph 3.2; and

(3) paragraph 3.3.

Remand for Medical Examination and Report

4A.2 Paragraph 4.1 of Section I of this practice direction applies in relation to section 27 of the 2006 Act, as if a reference in paragraph 4.1 to section 156(4) of the Housing Act 1996 was a reference to section 27(11) of the 2006 Act.

III. Demotion or Suspension Claims

Demotion Claims Made in the Alternative to Possession Claims

(Suspension claims may be made in England, but may not be made in Wales). **65PD.5**

5.1 If the claim relates to residential property let on a tenancy and if the claim includes a demotion claim, the particulars of claim must—

(1) state whether the demotion claim is a claim under section 82A(2) of the 1985 Act or under section 6A(2) of the 1988 Act;

(2) state whether the claimant is a local housing authority, a housing action trust or a registered social landlord;

(3) provide details of any statement of express terms of the tenancy served on the tenant under section 82A(7) of the 1985 Act or under section 6A(10) of the 1988 Act, as applicable; and

(4) state details of the conduct alleged.

Suspension Claims Made in the Alternative to Possession Claims

5A.1 If the claim relates to a residential property let on a tenancy and if the claim includes a suspension claim, the particulars of claim must— **65PD.5A**

(1) state that the suspension claim is a claim under section 121A of the 1985 Act;

(2) state which of the bodies the claimant's interest belongs to in order to comply with the landlord condition under section 80 of the 1985 Act;

(3) state details of the conduct alleged; and

(4) explain why it is reasonable to make the suspension order, having regard in particular to the factors set out in section 121A(4) of the 1985 Act.

Other Demotion or Suspension Claims

65PD.6 **6.1** Demotion or suspension claims, other than those made in the alternative to possession claims, must be made in the county court for the district in which the property to which the claim relates is situated.

6.2 The claimant must use the appropriate claim form and particulars of claim form set out in Table 1 to the Part 4 practice direction. The defence must be in form N11D as appropriate.

6.3 The claimant's evidence should include details of the conduct alleged, and any other matters relied upon.

Particulars of Claim

65PD.7 **7.1** In a demotion claim the particulars of claim must—

(1) state whether the demotion claim is a claim under section 82A(2) of the 1985 Act or under section 6A(2) of the 1988 Act;

(2) state whether the claimant is a local housing authority, a housing action trust or a registered social landlord;

(3) identify the property to which the claim relates;

(4) provide the following details about the tenancy to which the demotion claim relates—

(a) the parties to the tenancy;

(b) the period of the tenancy;

(c) the amount of the rent;

(d) the dates on which the rent is payable; and

(e) any statement of express terms of the tenancy served on the tenant under section 82A(7) of the 1985 Act or under section 6A(10) of the 1988 Act, as applicable; and

(5) state details of the conduct alleged.

7.2 In a suspension claim, the particulars of claim must—

(1) state that the suspension claim is a claim under section 121A of the 1985 Act;

(2) state which of the bodies the claimant's interest belongs to in order to comply with the landlord condition under section 80 of the 1985 Act;

(3) identify the property to which the claim relates;

(4) state details of the conduct alleged; and

(5) explain why it is reasonable to make the order, having regard in particular to the factors set out in section 121A(4) of the 1985 Act.

Hearing Date

65PD.8 **8.1** The court may use its powers under rules 3.1(2)(a) and (b) to shorten the time periods set out in rules 65.16(2), (3) and (4).

8.2 Particular consideration should be given to the exercise of this power if—

(1) the defendant, or a person for whom the defendant is responsible, has assaulted or threatened to assault—
(a) the claimant;
(b) a member of the claimant's staff; or
(c) another resident in the locality;

(2) there are reasonable grounds for fearing such an assault; or

(3) the defendant, or a person for whom the defendant is responsible, has caused serious damage or threatened to cause serious damage to the property or to the home or property of another resident in the locality.

8.3 Where paragraph 8.2 applies but the case cannot be determined at the first hearing fixed under rule 65.16, the court will consider what steps are needed to finally determine the case as quickly as reasonably practicable.

The Hearing

9.1 Attention is drawn to rule 65.18(3). Each party should wherever possible include all the evidence he wishes to present in his statement of case, verified by a statement of truth. **65PD.9**

9.2 The claimant's evidence should include details of the conduct to which section 153A or 153B of the 1996 Act applies and in respect of which the claim is made.

9.3 If—

(1) the maker of a witness statement does not attend a hearing; and

(2) the other party disputes material evidence contained in the statement,

the court will normally adjourn the hearing so that oral evidence can be given.

III. Proceedings Relating To Demoted Tenancies

Proceedings for the Possession of a Demoted Tenancy

10.1 Proceedings against a tenant of a demoted tenancy for possession must be brought under the procedure in Part 55 (Possession Claims). **65PD.10**

Proceedings in Relation to a Written Statement of Demoted Tenancy Terms

11.1 Proceedings as to whether a statement supplied in pursuance to section 143M(4)(b) of the 1996 Act (written statement of certain terms of tenancy) is accurate must be brought under the procedure in Part 8. **65PD.11**

Recovery of Costs

12.1 Attention is drawn to section 143N(4) of the 1996 Act which provides that if a person takes proceedings under Chapter 1A of the 1996 Act in the High Court which he could have taken in the county court, he is not entitled to recover any costs. **65PD.12**

IV. Anti-Social Behaviour Orders under the Crime and Disorder Act 1998

Service of an Order under Sections 1B(4) or 1D of the 1998 Act

13.1 An order under section 1B(4) or an interim order under section 1D of the 1998 Act must be served personally on the defendant. **65PD.13**

Application to join a person to the principal proceedings

13.2 Except as provided in paragraph 13.3, an application by a relevant authority under section 1B(3B) of the 1998 Act to join a person to the principal proceedings may only be made against a person aged 18 or over.

Pilot scheme: application to join a child to the principal proceedings

13.3(1) A pilot scheme shall operate from 1st October 2004 to 30th September 2006 in the county courts specified below, under which a relevant authority may—

(a) apply under section 1B(3B) of the 1998 Act to join a child to the principal proceedings; and

(b) if that child is so joined, apply for an order under section 1B(4) of the 1998 Act against him.

(2) In this paragraph, "child" means a person aged under 18.

(3) The county courts in which the pilot scheme shall operate are Bristol, Central London, Clerkenwell, Dewsbury, Huddersfield, Leicester, Manchester, Oxford, Tameside, Wigan and Wrexham.

(4) Attention is drawn to the provisions of Part 21 and its practice direction: in particular as to the requirement for a child to have a litigation friend unless the court makes an order under rule 21.2(3),and as to the procedure for appointment of a litigation friend. The Official Solicitor may be invited to act as litigation friend where there is no other willing and suitable person.

(5) Rule 21.3(2)(b) shall not apply to an application under the pilot scheme, and sub-paragraph (6) shall apply instead.

(6) A relevant authority may not, without the permission of the court, take any step in an application to join a child to the principal proceedings, except—

(a) filing and serving its application notice; and

(b) applying for the appointment of a litigation friend under rule 21.6,

unless the child has a litigation friend.

V. Proceedings under the Protection from Harassment Act 1997

Warrant of Arrest on Application under Section 3(3) of the 1997 Act

65PD.14 **14.1** In accordance with section 3(5) of the 1997 Act, a warrant of arrest on an application under section 3(3) of that Act may only be issued if—

(1) the application is substantiated on oath; and

(2) the judge has reasonable grounds for believing that the defendant has done anything which he is prohibited from doing by the injunction.

VI. Drinking Banning Orders under the Violent Crime Reduction Act 2006

65PD.15 [...] [Omitted; see para.65.0.2 above.]

VII. Parenting Orders under the Anti-Social Behaviour Act 2003

Applications for Parenting Orders

65PD.16 **16.1** Where the applicant is a registered social landlord, the application must be supported by evidence that the relevant local authority has been consulted in accordance with section 26B(8) of the 2003 Act.

16.2 An order under section 26A or 26B of the 2003 Act must be served personally on the defendant.

16.3 An application by a relevant authority under section 26C(3) of the 2003 Act to join a person to the proceedings may only be made against a person aged 18 or over.

PART 66

Crown Proceedings

Contents

Editorial introduction

66.0.2 This new Part, which came into effect on October 1, 2005 replaces, in its entirety, the former RSC Order 77—Proceedings by and Against the Crown, which conferred on the Crown a number of procedural privileges in civil proceedings. The new provisions are intended to create a more equal regime, with a much wider discretion conferred on the Court.

Civil proceedings by and against the Crown are, still, governed by the Crown Proceedings Act 1947, as amended. Such proceedings are defined by ss.23(1) and 23(2) of the Act.

Principle changes — Formerly where the Crown acknowledged service in the Central Office the proceedings were automatically transferred to the Royal Courts of Justice. Now under CPR and the criteria for a transfer order under Pt 30(3) includes:

> "(h) in the case of civil proceedings by or against the Crown, as defined in rule 66.1(2), the location of the relevant government department or offices of the Crown and, where appropriate, any relevant public interest that the matter should be tried in London."

In relation to the contents of the claim form CPR 16.2 has been amended to provide:

"(1A) In civil proceedings against the Crown as defined in rule 66.1(2) the claim form must also contain:—

(a) the names of the government departments and officers of the Crown concerned: and

(b) brief details of the circumstances in which it is alleged that the liability of the Crown arose."

As to service on the Crown this is governed by Section 18 of the CPA 1947 but CPR rr.6.4 and 6.5 now provide that service on a government department should be made on the solicitor acting for that department.

Summary judgments—Under RSC O.77 there was a general prohibition on summary judgment against the Crown. This is now modified by CPR r.24.4(1A).

The provisions in relation to judgment in default are also now amended, by CPR r.23.12(10).The new provisions in relation to enforcement against the Crown and money due are to be found in r.66.6(7).

Scope of this Part and Interpretation

66.1 **66.1—(1) This Part contains rules for civil proceedings by or against the Crown, and other civil proceedings to which the Crown is a party.**

(2) In *this Part*—

(a) "the Act" means the Crown Proceedings Act 1947;

(b) "civil proceedings by the Crown" means the civil

proceedings described in section 23(1) of the Act, but excluding the proceedings described in section 23(3);

(c) "civil proceedings against the Crown" means the civil proceedings described in section 23(2) of the Act, but excluding the proceedings described in section 23(3);

(d) "civil proceedings to which the Crown is a party" has the same meaning as it has for the purposes of Parts III and IV of the Act by virtue of section 38(4).

Application of the Civil Procedure Rules

66.2 These Rules and their practice directions apply to civil proceedings by or against the Crown and to other civil proceedings to which the Crown is a party unless this Part, a practice direction or any other enactment provides otherwise. 66.2

Action on behalf of the Crown

66.3—(1) Where by reason of a rule, practice direction or court order the Crown is permitted or required— 66.3

(a) to make a witness statement,

(b) to swear an affidavit,

(c) to verify a document by a statement of truth;

(d) to make a disclosure statement; or

(e) to discharge any other procedural obligation,

that function shall be performed by an appropriate officer acting on behalf of the Crown.

(2) The court may if necessary nominate an appropriate officer.

Counterclaims, other Part 20 claims, and set-off

66.4—(1) In a claim by the Crown for taxes, duties or penalties, the defendant cannot make a counterclaim or other Part 20 claim or raise a defence of a set-off. 66.4

(2) In any other claim by the Crown, the defendant cannot make a counterclaim or other Part 20 claim or raise a defence of set-off which is based on claim for repayment of taxes, duties or penalties.

(3) In proceedings by or against the Crown in the name of the Attorney-General, no counterclaim or other Part 20 claim can be made or defence of set-off raised without the permission of the court.

(4) In proceedings by or against the Crown in the name of a government department, no counterclaim or other Part 20 claim can be made or defence of set-off raised without the permission of the court unless the subject-matter relates to that government department.

Applications in revenue matters

66.5—(1) This rule sets out the procedure under section 14 of the Act, which allows the Crown to make summary applications in the High Court in certain revenue matters. 66.5

(2) The application must be made in the High Court using the Part 8 procedure.

(3) The title of the claim form must clearly identify the matters which give rise to the application.

Enforcement against the Crown

66.6 66.6—(1) The following rules do not apply to any order against the Crown—

(a) Parts 69 to 73;
(b) RSC Orders 45 to 47 and 52; and
(c) CCR Orders 25 to 29.

(2) In paragraph (1), "order against the Crown" means any judgment or order against the Crown, a government department, or an officer of the Crown as such, made—

(a) in civil proceedings by or against the Crown;
(b) in proceedings in the Administrative Court;
(c) in connection with an arbitration to which the Crown is a party; or
(d) in other civil proceedings to which the Crown is a party.

(3) An application under section 25(1) of the Act for a separate certificate of costs payable to the applicant may be made without notice.

Money due from the Crown

66.7 66.7—(1) None of the following orders—

(a) a third party debt order under Part 72;
(b) an order for the appointment of a receiver under Part 69; or
(c) an order for the appointment of a sequestrator under RSC Order 45,

may be made or have effect in respect of any money due from the Crown.

(2) In paragraph (1), "money due from the Crown" includes money accruing due, and money alleged to be due or accruing due.

(3) An application for an order under section 27 of the Act—

(a) restraining a person from receiving money payable to him by the Crown; and
(b) directing payment of the money to the applicant or another person,

may be made under Part 23.

(4) The application must be supported by written evidence setting out the facts on which it is based, and in particular identifying the debt from the Crown.

(5) Where the debt from the Crown is money in a National Savings Bank account, the witness must if possible identify the number of the account and the name and address of the branch where it is held.

(6) Notice of the application, with a copy of the written evidence, must be served—

(a) on the Crown, and

(b) on the person to be restrained,

at least 7 days before the hearing.

(7) Rule 72.8 applies to an application under this rule as it applies to an application under rule 72.2 for a third party debt order, except that the court will not have the power to order enforcement to issue against the Crown.

PRACTICE DIRECTION—CROWN PROCEEDINGS

This Practice Direction supplements CPR Part 66

Transfer

66PD.1 **1.1** Rule 30.3(2) sets out the circumstances to which the court must have regard when considering whether to make an order under section 40(2), 41(1) or 42(2) of the County Courts Act 1984 (transfer between the High Court and County Court), rule 30.2(1) (transfer between county courts) or rule 30.2(4) (transfer between the Royal Courts of Justice and the district registries).

1.2 From time to time the Attorney General will publish a note concerning the organisation of the Government Legal Service and matters relevant to the venue of Crown proceedings, for the assistance of practitioners and judges. When considering questions of venue under rule 30.3(2), the court should have regard to the Attorney General's note in addition to all the other circumstances of the case.

Service of Documents

66PD.2 **2.1** In civil proceedings by or against the Crown, documents required to be served on the Crown must be served in accordance with rule 6.10 or 6.23(7).

(The list published under section 17 of the Crown Proceedings Act 1947 of the solicitors acting for the different government departments on whom service is to be effected, and of their addresses is annexed to this Practice Direction).

ANNEX 1

DISPUTES AS TO VENUE—FACTORS TO BE TAKEN INTO CONSIDERATION
ATTORNEY GENERAL'S NOTE TO SUPPLEMENT THE PRACTICE DIRECTION

Introduction

66PD.3 Until the recent rule changes, the Crown was entitled in High Court matters to insist that venue was the Royal Courts of Justice in London (RCJ) (RSC O77, rule 2). This rule has now been revoked. A new rule 30.3(2)(h) provides that in cases involving civil proceedings by or against the Crown, when considering whether to order a transfer of those proceedings, the court must have regard to, "the location of the relevant government department or officers of the Crown and, where appropriate, any relevant public interest that the matter should be tried in London."

The Practice Direction to Part 66, at paragraph 2, provides that the Attorney-General will publish a note concerning the organisation of the Government Legal Service and matters relevant to the venue of Crown Proceedings, for the assistance of practitioners and judges. When considering questions of venue under rule 30.3(2), the court should have regard to the Attorney-General's note in addition to all the other circumstances of the case.

This note sets out the further factors to be taken into consideration where there is a dispute as to venue between a claimant and a government department. Where there is such a dispute, it should be dealt with at a case management conference.

Organisation of the Government Legal Service

The Government Legal Service (GLS) has the responsibility for advising the Government about its legal affairs and has the conduct of civil litigation on its behalf. The Treasury Solicitor conducts this litigation for the majority of Government Departments but lawyers in HM Revenue and Customs, the Department for the Environment, Food and Rural Affairs and the Department for Work and Pensions (which also acts for the Department of Health and the Food Standards Agency) have the conduct of litigation for their Departments. All Government litigation lawyers are based in London with the exception of HM Revenue and Customs, whose personal injury lawyers are in Manchester. A full list of addresses for service is annexed to the Practice Direction accompanying Part 66 of the CPR.

Factors be taken into account generally

Location

Whilst a number of government departments have offices outside London, central government bodies are based in London and the GLS is geared towards processing claims in the RCJ (see above). Where there is a High Court claim, many witnesses as well as lawyers and officials are London based and there may be a disproportionate cost in transferring them to a venue outside London. That is not to say, bearing in mind the overriding objective, that the Crown would oppose transfer away from the RCJ where it was appropriate, for example in personal injury disputes.

Precedent value

Some cases have important precedent value or are of general importance to the public, which may make them more suitable for being heard in the RCJ.

Special Considerations in relation to HM Revenue and Customs

HM Revenue and Customs has no lawyers outside London, except for those personal injury lawyers based in Manchester.

The work of HM Revenue and Customs is very specialised, needing in many cases to be dealt with by specialist judges in the Chancery Division familiar, for example, with tax work.

There is also the public interest to consider. All revenue cases (including those of HM Revenue and Customs) have important precedent value that applies across the entire tax system, with implications for the Exchequer.

ANNEX 2

CROWN PROCEEDINGS ACT 1947

List of Authorised Government Departments and the names and addresses for service of the person who is, or is acting for the purposes of the Act as, Solicitor for such Departments, published by the Minister for the Civil Service in pursuance of Section 17 of the Crown Proceedings Act 1947. **66PD.4**

This list supersedes the list published on 6 January 2004

AUTHORISED GOVERNMENT DEPARTMENTS	SOLICITOR AND ADDRESSES FOR SERVICE
Advisory, Conciliation and Arbitration Service)	The Treasury Solicitor One Kemble Street London WC2B 4TS (see Notes (1) and (2))
Assets Recovery Agency)	
Board of Trade)	
Cabinet Office)	
Central Office of Information)	
Crown Prosecution Service)	
Department for Culture, Media and Sport)	
Department for Education and Skills)	
Department for International Development)	

Department for Transport)
Department of Trade and Industry)
Export Credits Guarantee Department)
Foreign and Commonwealth Office)
Government Actuary's Department)
Health and Safety Executive)
Her Majesty's Chief Inspector of Schools in England)
Her Majesty's Chief Inspector of Schools in Wales)
Her Majesty's Treasury)
Home Office)
The International Rail Regulator)
Ministry of Defence)
Ministry of Justice)
National Savings and Investments)
Northern Ireland Office)
Office of the Deputy Prime Minister)
Office of Rail Regulation)
Ordnance Survey)
Privy Council Office)
Public Record Office)
Public Works Loan Board)
Royal Mint)
Serious Fraud Office)
Wales Office (Office of the Secretary of State for Wales) (see Note (4)))

Crown Estate Commissioners	Head of Legal The Crown Estate 16 Carlton House Terrace London SW1Y 5AH
Department for Environment, Food and Rural Affairs (see Note (4)) Forestry Commissioners	The Solicitor to the Department for Environment, Food and Rural Affairs Nobel House 17 Smith Square London SW1P 3JR
Department of Health Department for Work and Pensions Food Standards Agency Office for National Statistics	The Solicitor to the Department for Work and Pensions and the Department of Health New Court 48 Carey Street London WC2A 2LS
Director General of Water Services	Head of Legal Services The Office of Water Services Centre City Tower 7 Hill Street Birmingham B5 4UA

Gas and Electricity Markets Authority	General Counsel Office of Gas and Electricity Markets 9 Millbank London SW1P 3GE
Her Majesty's Revenue and Customs	The Solicitor to Her Majesty's Revenue and Customs Somerset House The Strand London WC2R 1LB
National Assembly for Wales	The Director of Legal Services to the Welsh Assembly Government Cathays Park Cardiff CF10 3NQ
Office of Fair Trading	The Solicitor to the Office of Fair Trading Fleetbank House 2–6 Salisbury Square London EC4Y 8JX
Postal Services Commission	The Chief Legal Adviser Postal Services Commission Hercules House 6 Hercules Road London SE1 7DB

Notes

(1) Section 17(3) and section 18 of the Crown Proceedings Act 1947 provide as follows: **66PD.5**

17.—(3) Civil proceedings against the Crown shall be instituted against the appropriate authorised Government department, or, if none of the authorised Government departments is appropriate or the person instituting the proceedings has any reasonable doubt whether any and if so which of those departments is appropriate, against the Attorney General.

18. All documents required to be served on the Crown for the purpose of or in connection with any civil proceedings by or against the Crown shall, if those proceedings are by or against an authorised Government department, be served on the solicitor, if any, for that department, or the person, if any, acting for the purposes of this Act as solicitor for that department, or if there is no such solicitor and no person so acting, or if the proceedings are brought by or against the Attorney General, on the Solicitor for the affairs of His Majesty's Treasury.

(2) The above-mentioned provisions do not apply to Scotland, where in accordance with the Crown Suits (Scotland) Act 1857, as amended by the Scotland Act 1998, civil proceedings against the Crown (other than the Scottish Administration) or any Government Department (other than the Scottish Executive) may be directed against the Advocate General for Scotland. The Advocate General's address for service is the Office of the Solicitor to the Advocate General for Scotland, Victoria Quay, Edinburgh EH6 6QQ. Civil proceedings against the Scottish Administration may be directed against the Scottish Ministers at St.Andrew's House, Edinburgh EH1 3DG, or against the Lord Advocate for and on behalf of the Scottish Executive. The Lord Advocate's address for service is 25 Chambers Street, Edinburgh, EH1 1LA.

(3) The reference to the Department for Constitutional Affairs includes a reference to the Lord Chancellor's Department.

(4) The Solicitor and address for service for the purposes of or in connection with civil proceedings brought by or against the Crown which relate to those matters for which the Secretary of State is responsible in Wales and for which the Secretary of State for Environment, Food and Rural Affairs is responsible is the Solicitor to the Department for Environment, Food and Rural Affairs, Nobel House, 17 Smith Square, London, SW1P 3JR. The Treasury Solicitor is the Solicitor acting for the Wales Office

(Office of the Secretary of State for Wales) in all other civil proceedings affecting that Office.

CABINET OFFICE
WHITEHALL
LONDON SW1

(Signed) SIR GUS O'DONNELL

PART 67

Proceedings Relating to Solicitors

Contents

67.0.1

Editorial introduction

The rules in this Order are concerned with the Court's exercise of jurisdiction in matters concerning solicitors under Pt III (Remuneration of solicitors) and Sch.1 (Powers exercisable on intervention in solicitor's practice) of the Solicitors Act 1974. They replace RSC O.106. **67.0.2**

Related sources

- Solicitors Act 1974 (Vol.2, Section 7, para.7–1) **67.0.3**
- CPR rr.48.8, 48.10 and Related Directions

Forms

The following forms are relevant to Precedents J, K, L, M and P of the Schedule of Costs Precedents, para.48PD.10; N208 Pt 8 Application, N244 Application Notice (Pt 23). **67.0.4**

Scope and interpretation

67.1—(1) This Part contains rules about the following types of proceedings relating to solicitors— **67.1**

(a) proceedings to obtain an order for a solicitor to deliver a bill or cash account and proceedings in relation to money or papers received by a solicitor (rule 67.2);

(b) proceedings under Part III of the Solicitors Act 1974[1] relating to the remuneration of solicitors (rule 67.3); and

(c) proceedings under Schedule 1 to the Solicitors Act 1974[2] arising out of the Law Society's intervention in a solicitor's practice (rule 67.4).

(2) In this Part—

"the Act" means the Solicitors Act 1974; and

"LLP" means limited liability partnership.

(Part 48 and Section 56 of the Costs Practice Direction contain provisions about the procedure and basis for the detailed assessment of solicitor and client costs under Part III of the Act).

---

[1] 1974 c.47.

[2] 1974 c.47. The relevant provisions of Sch.1 to the Solicitors Act 1974 were amended by the Criminal Justice Act 1982 (c.48), ss.37, 38 and 46; the Administration of Justice Act 1985 (c.61), s.8 and para.13 of Sch.1; and the Postal Service Act 2000 (Consequential Modifications No.1) Order 2001 (SI 2001/1149), art.3 and para.39 of Sch.1.

(The practice direction supplementing Part 52 contains provisions about appeals to the High Court from the Solicitors Disciplinary Tribunal under section 49 of the Act).

Power to order solicitor to deliver cash account etc.

67.2 **67.2—(1) Where the relationship of solicitor and client exists or has existed, the orders which the court may make against the solicitor, on the application of the client or his personal representatives, include any of the following—**

(a) to deliver a bill or cash account;

(b) to pay or deliver up any money or securities;

(c) to deliver a list of the moneys or securities which the solicitor has in his possession or control on behalf of the applicant;

(d) to pay into or lodge in court any such money or securities.

(2) An application for an order under this rule must be made—

(a) by Part 8 claim form; or

(b) if the application is made in existing proceedings, by application notice in accordance with Part 23.

(3) If the solicitor alleges that he has a claim for costs against the applicant, the court may make an order for—

(a) the detailed assessment and payment of those costs; and

(b) securing the payment of the costs, or protecting any solicitor's lien.

67.2.1 A client was successful on an application, but the Master made no order as to the costs in relation to the Pt 8 claim. On appeal it was held that the Master had failed to attach any significant weight to the fact that the client had been largely successful in relation to the relief sought, although a significant amount of time had been taken up with argument on matters which were either not resolved, or in respect of which there was no outright winner, the court awarded the client 75 per cent of his costs of the application, as well as the costs of the appeal: *Raj Tankaria v Morgan* [2006] EWHC 3090 (Ch), Kitchin J.

Proceedings under Part III of the Act

67.3 **67.3—(1) A claim for an order under Part III of the Act for the assessment of costs payable to a solicitor by his client—**

(a) which—

(i) relates to contentious business done in a county court; and

(ii) is within the financial limit of the county court's jurisdiction specified in section 69(3) of the Act[1],

may be made in that county court;

(b) in every other case, must be made in the High Court.

(Rule 30.2 makes provision for any county court to transfer the proceedings to another county court for detailed assessment of costs).

[1] The limit in s.69(3) of the Act was amended by the High Court and County Courts Jurisdiction Order 1991 (SI 1991/724), art.2(7) and (8) and Sch., Pt 1.

(Provisions about the venue for detailed assessment proceedings are contained in rule 47.4, Section 31 of the Costs Practice Direction and the Costs Pilot Scheme Practice Direction supplementing Part 47).

(2) A claim for an order under Part III of the Act must be made—

(a) by Part 8 claim form; or

(b) if the claim is made in existing proceedings, by application notice in accordance with Part 23.

(A model form of claim form is annexed to the Costs Practice Direction).

(3) A claim in the High Court under Part III of the Act may be determined by—

(a) a High Court judge;

(b) a Master, a costs judge or a district judge of the Principal Registry of the Family Division; or

(c) a district judge, if the costs are for—

(i) contentious business done in proceedings in the district registry of which he is the district judge;

(ii) contentious business done in proceedings in a county court within the district of that district registry; or

(iii) non-contentious business.

Proceedings under Schedule 1 to the Act

67.4—(1) Proceedings in the High Court under Schedule 1 to the Act must be brought— 67.4

(a) in the Chancery Division; and

(b) by Part 8 claim form, unless paragraph (4) below applies.

(2) The heading of the claim form must state that the claim relates to a solicitor and is made under Schedule 1 to the Act.

(3) Where proceedings are brought under paragraph 6(4) or 9(8) of Schedule 1 to the Act, the court will give directions and fix a date for the hearing immediately upon issuing the claim form.

(4) If the court has made an order under Schedule 1 to the Act, any subsequent application for an order under that Schedule which has the same parties may be made by a Part 23 application in the same proceedings.

(5) The table below sets out who must be made a defendant to each type of application under Schedule 1.

TABLE 1
DEFENDANTS TO APPLICATIONS UNDER SCHEDULE 1 TO THE ACT

Paragraph of Schedule 1 under which the application is made	*Defendant to application*
Paragraph 5	if the application relates to money held on behalf of an individual solicitor, the solicitor if the application relates to money held on behalf of a firm, every partner in the firm if the application relates to money held on behalf of a LLP or other corporation, the LLP or other corporation
Paragraph 6(4) or 9(8)	the Law Society
Paragraph 8, 9(4), 9(5) or 9(6)	the person against whom the Law Society is seeking an order
Paragraph 9(10)	the person from whom the Law Society took possession of the documents which it wishes to dispose of or destroy
Paragraph 10	if the application relates to postal packets addressed to an individual solicitor, the solicitor if the application relates to postal packets addressed to a firm, every partner in the firm if the application relates to postal packets addressed to a LLP or other corporation, the LLP or other corporation
Paragraph 11	the trustee whom the Law Society is seeking to replace and, if he is a co-trustee, the other trustees of the trust

(6) At any time after the Law Society has issued an application for an order under paragraph 5 of Schedule 1 to the Act, the court may, on an application by the Society—

- **(a) make an interim order under that paragraph to have effect until the hearing of the application; and**
- **(b) order the defendant, if he objects to the order being continued at the hearing, to file and serve written evidence showing cause why the order should not be continued.**

PRACTICE DIRECTION—PROCEEDINGS RELATING TO SOLICITORS

This Practice Direction supplements CPR Part 67

General

67PD.1

1 This Practice Direction applies to proceedings under Rule 67.2 and to the following types of claim under Rule 67.3 and Part III of the Solicitors Act 1974 ('the Act'):

(1) an application under section 57(5) of the Act for a costs officer to enquire into the facts and certify whether a non-contentious business agreement should be set aside or the amount payable under it reduced;

(2) a claim under section 61(1) of the Act for the court to enforce or set aside a contentious business agreement and determine questions as to its validity and effect;

(3) a claim by a client under s 61(3) of the Act for a costs officer to examine a contentious business agreement as to its fairness and reasonableness;

(4) where the amount agreed under a contentious business agreement has been paid, a claim under section 61(5) of the Act for the agreement to be re-opened and the costs assessed;

(5) proceedings under section 62 of the Act for the examination of a contentious business agreement, where the client makes the agreement as a representative of a person whose property will be chargeable with the amount payable;

(6) proceedings under section 63 of the Act where, after some business has been done under a contentious business agreement, but before the solicitor has wholly performed it:
(a) the solicitor dies or becomes incapable of acting; or
(b) the client changes solicitor;

(7) where an action is commenced on a gross sum bill, an application under section 64(3) of the Act for an order that the bill be assessed;

(8) a claim under section 68 of the Act for the delivery by a solicitor of a bill of costs and for the delivery up of, or otherwise in relation to, any documents;

(9) an application under section 69 of the Act for an order that the solicitor be at liberty to commence an action to recover his costs within one month of delivery of the bill;

(10) a claim under section 70(1) of the Act, by the party chargeable with the solicitor's bill, for an order that the bill be assessed and that no action be taken on the bill until the assessment is completed;

(11) a claim under section 70(2) of the Act, by either party, for an order that the bill be assessed and that no action be commenced or continued on the bill until the assessment is completed;

(12) a claim under section 70(3) of the Act, by the party chargeable with the bill, for detailed assessment showing special circumstances;

(13) a claim under section 71(1) of the Act, by a person other than the party chargeable with the bill, for detailed assessment;

(14) a claim under section 71(3) of the Act, by any person interested in any property out of which a trustee, executor or administrator has paid or is entitled to pay a solicitor's bill, for detailed assessment; and

(15) a claim by a solicitor under section 73 of the Act for a charging order.

Proceedings in the Supreme Court Costs Office

67PD.2 **2.1** Where a claim to which this practice direction applies is made by Part 8 claim form in the High Court in London—

(1) if the claim is of a type referred to in paragraphs 1(1) to (5), it must be issued in the Supreme Court Costs Office;

(2) in any other case, the claim may be issued in the Supreme Court Costs Office.

2.2 A claim which is made by Part 8 claim form in a district registry or by Part 23 application notice in existing High Court proceedings may be referred to the Supreme Court Costs Office.

Jurisdiction and Allocation of Claims Between Judiciary

67PD.3 **3.1** Rule 67.3(3) makes provision about jurisdiction to determine claims under Part III of the Act.

3.2 Claims for any of the orders listed in paragraph 1 should normally be made to a Master, costs judge or district judge. Only exceptional circumstances will justify making the claim directly to a High Court Judge.

3.3 Paragraph 1 of the practice direction supplementing Part 23 sets out the circumstances in which a matter may be referred to a judge.

Evidence in Proceedings for Order for Detailed Assessment

67PD.4 **4.** Where a Part 8 claim is brought for an order for the detailed assessment of a solicitor's bill of costs, the parties are not required to comply with Rule 8.5 unless:

(1) the claim will be contested; or

(2) the court directs that the parties should comply with Rule 8.5.

Drawing up and Service of Orders

67PD.5 **5.** Unless the court orders otherwise, an order in proceedings in the Supreme Court Costs Office to which this practice direction applies shall be drawn up and served by the party who made the relevant claim or application.

PART 68

REFERENCES TO THE EUROPEAN COURT

Contents 68.0.1

Editorial introduction

This Part was added to the CPR by Civil Procedure (Amendment) Rules 2002 (SI 2002/2058), r.26(b) and Sch.6. The provisions of this Part came into force December 2, 2002. On that date, provisions found in Schs 1 and 2 of the CPR now covered by Pt 68, in particular RSC O.114 and CCR O.19, r.15, were revoked. 68.0.2

Interpretation[1]

68.1 In this Part— 68.1

(a) "the court" means the court making the order;

(b) "the European Court" means the Court of Justice of the European Communities;

(c) "order" means an order referring a question to the European Court for a preliminary ruling under—

(i) article 234 of the Treaty establishing the European Community;

(ii) article 150 of the Euratom Treaty;

(iii) the Protocol of 3 June 1971 on the interpretation by the European Court of the Convention of 27 September 1968 on Jurisdiction and the Enforcement of Judgments in Civil and Commercial Matters[2]; or

(iv) the Protocol of 19 December 1988 on the interpretation by the European Court of the Convention of 19 June 1980 on the Law applicable to Contractual Obligations.[3]

Making of order of reference[4]

68.2—(1) An order may be made at any stage of the proceedings— 68.2

(a) by the court of its own initiative; or

(b) on an application by a party in accordance with Part 23.

(2) *An order may not be made*—

(a) in the High Court, by a Master or district judge;

(b) in a county court, by a district judge.

---

[1] Introduced by the Civil Procedure (Amendment) Rules 2002 (SI 2002/2058).
[2] Set out in Sch.2 to the Civil Jurisdiction and Judgments Act 1982 (c.27).
[3] Set out in Sch.3 to the Contracts (Applicable Law) Act 1990 (c.36).
[4] Introduced by the Civil Procedure (Amendment) Rules 2002 (SI 2002/2058).

(3) The request to the European Court for a preliminary ruling must be set out in a schedule to the order, and the court may give directions on the preparation of the schedule.

Effect of rule

68.2.1 An order may be made "at any stage of the proceedings". Where legal or factual issues remain to be resolved it may be, but not necessarily need be, premature for the court to order a reference. In *McCall v Poulton & Motor Insurer's Bureau* [2008] EWCA Civ 1313, November 21, 2008, CA, unrep., a circuit judge sitting in county court proceedings granted the interveners' application for an order of reference, but granted the second defendants permission to appeal. In the Court of Appeal the second defendant's opposition, to the extent that it was based on a submission that a reference would be premature, fell away and the court considered the matter afresh. But, in dismissing the appeal the court stated that the judge could not be criticised for making the reference order.

The ECJ's preliminary reference procedure does not permit interventions by private parties. The only parties entitled to participate (by submitting written observations or appearing at the oral hearing) are the parties to the action pending before the national court. The question whether or not a person is a party to that action must be decided according to the criteria of the national law. Rule 19.2(2)(a) provides that a person may be added as a new party if it is desirable to add the new party so that the court can resolve all issues in dispute in the proceedings: see para.19.2.2 above. In *Football Association Premier League Ltd. v QC Leisure* [2008] EWHC 2897 (Ch), November 13, 2008, unrep. (Kitchin J.), a heavy intellectual property case, the judge ordered that certain questions should be referred to the ECJ for preliminary ruling ([2008] EWHC 1411 (Ch)). Subsequently, the judge granted an application under r.19.2 made by five companies to be joined as co-claimants. In doing so the judge explained that, under r.19.2(2)(a), it does not have to be shown that there is an issue involving the new party and an existing party.

Transmission to the European Court[1]

68.3 **68.3—(1) The Senior Master will send a copy of the order to the Registrar of the European Court.**

(2) Where an order is made by a county court, the proper officer will send a copy of it to the Senior Master for onward transmission to the European Court.

(3) Unless the court orders otherwise, the Senior Master will not send a copy of the order to the European Court until—

(a) the time for appealing against the order has expired; or

(b) any application for permission to appeal has been refused, or any appeal has been determined.

Stay of proceedings[2]

68.4 **68.4 Where an order is made, unless the court orders otherwise the proceedings will be stayed until the European Court has given a preliminary ruling on the question referred to it.**

[1] Introduced by the Civil Procedure (Amendment) Rules 2002 (SI 2002/2058).
[2] Introduced by the Civil Procedure (Amendment) Rules 2002 (SI 2002/2058).

PRACTICE DIRECTION—REFERENCES TO THE EUROPEAN COURT

This Practice Direction supplements CPR Part 68 **68PD.1**

Wording of References

1.1 Where the court intends to refer a question to the European Court it will welcome suggestions from the parties for the wording of the reference. However the responsibility for settling the terms of the reference lies with the English court and not with the parties.

1.2 The reference should identify as clearly and succinctly as possible the question on which the court seeks the ruling of the European Court. In choosing the wording of the reference, it should be remembered that it will need to be translated into many other languages.

1.3 The court will incorporate the reference in its order. Scheduled to the order should be a document—

(1) giving the full name of the referring court;
(2) identifying the parties;
(3) summarising the nature and history of the proceedings, including the salient facts, indicating whether these are proved or admitted or assumed;
(4) setting out the relevant rules of national law;
(5) summarising the relevant contentions of the parties;
(6) explaining why a ruling of the European Court is sought; and
(7) identifying the provisions of Community law which it is being requested to interpret.

1.4 Where, as will often be convenient, some of these matters are in the form of a judgment, passages of the judgment not relevant to the reference should be omitted.

Transmission to the European Court

2.1 The order containing the reference, and the document scheduled to it, should be sent to The Senior Master, Room E115, Queen's Bench Division, Royal Courts of Justice, Strand, London WC2A 2LL, for onward transmission to the European Court. **68PD.2**

2.2 The relevant court file should also be sent to the Senior Master at the above address.

European Court Information Note

3. There is annexed to this Practice Direction an Information Note issued by the European Court. The reference in the opening passage to Article 177 of the EC Treaty should now be read as a reference to Article 234. **68PD.3**

Information Note on References from National Courts for a Preliminary Ruling

1. The preliminary ruling system is a fundamental mechanism of European Union law aimed at enabling national courts to ensure uniform interpretation and application of that law in all the Member States. **68PD.4**
2. The Court of Justice of the European Communities has juris-

diction to give preliminary rulings on the interpretation of the law of the European Union and on the validity of acts of secondary legislation. That general jurisdiction is conferred on it by Article 234 of the EC Treaty and, in certain specific cases, by other provisions.

3. The preliminary ruling procedure being based on cooperation between the Court and national courts, it may be helpful, in order to ensure that that cooperation is effective, to provide the national courts with the following information.
4. This practical information, which is in no way binding, is intended to provide guidance to national courts as to whether it is appropriate to make a reference for a preliminary ruling and, should they proceed, to help them formulate and submit questions to the Court.

The role of the Court in the preliminary ruling procedure

5. Under the preliminary ruling procedure, the Court's role is to give an interpretation of Community law or to rule on its validity, not to apply that law to the factual situation underlying the main proceedings, which is the task of the national court. It is not for the Court to decide issues of fact raised in the main proceedings or to resolve differences of opinion on the interpretation or application of rules of national law.
6. In ruling on the interpretation or validity of Community law, the Court makes every effort to give a reply which will be of assistance in resolving the dispute, but it is for the referring court to draw the appropriate conclusions from that reply, if necessary by disapplying the rule of national law in question.

The decision to submit a question to the Court

The originator of the question

7. Under Article 234 of the EC Treaty and Article 150 of the EAEC Treaty, any court or tribunal of a Member State, in so far as it is called upon to give a ruling in proceedings intended to arrive at a decision of a judicial nature, may as a rule refer a question to the Court for a preliminary ruling. The status of that court or tribunal is interpreted by the Court as a self-standing concept of the Community law.
8. However, in the specific sphere of acts of the institutions in Title IV of Part Three of the EC Treaty on visa, asylum, immigration and other policies related to free movement of persons—in particular jurisdiction and the recognition and enforcement of judicial decisions—a reference may be made only by courts or tribunals against the decisions of which there is no appeal, in accordance with Article 68 of the EC Treaty.
9. Likewise, under Article 35 of the Treaty on European Union, acts of the institutions in the area of police and judicial cooperation in criminal matters may be the subject of a reference for a preliminary ruling only from courts in the Member States which have accepted the jurisdiction of the Court, each Member State specifying whether that right of referral to the

Court applies to any court or tribunal of that State or only to those against the decisions of which there is no appeal.

10. It is not necessary for the parties in the case to raise the question; the national court may do so of its own motion.

References on interpretation

11. Any court or tribunal **may** refer a question to the Court on the interpretation of a rule of Community law if it considers it necessary to do so in order to resolve a dispute brought before it.

12. However, courts or tribunals against whose decisions there is no judicial remedy under national law must, as a rule, refer such a question to the Court, unless the Court has already ruled on the point (and there is no new context that raises any serious doubt as to whether that case-law may be applied), or unless the correct interpretation of the rule of Community law is obvious.

13. Thus, a court or tribunal against whose decisions there is a judicial remedy may, in particular when it considers that sufficient clarification is given by the case-law of the Court, itself decide on the correct interpretation of Community law and its application to the factual situation before it. However, a reference for a preliminary ruling may prove particularly useful, at an appropriate stage of the proceedings, when there is a new question of interpretation of general interest for the uniform application of Community law throughout the Union, or where the existing case-law does not appear to be applicable to a new set of facts.

14. It is for the national court to explain why the interpretation sought is necessary to enable it to give judgment.

References on determination of validity

15. Although national courts may reject pleas raised before them challenging the validity of Community acts, the Court has exclusive jurisdiction to declare such acts invalid.

16. All national courts **must** therefore refer a question to the Court when they have doubts about the validity of a Community act, stating the reasons for which they consider that the Community act may be invalid.

17. If a national court has serious doubts about the validity of a Community act on which a national measure is based, it may exceptionally suspend application of that measure temporarily or grant other interim relief with respect to it. It must then refer the question of validity to the Court of Justice, stating the reasons for which it considers the Community act to be invalid.

The stage at which to submit a question for a preliminary hearing

18. A national court or tribunal may refer a question to the Court of Justice for a preliminary ruling as soon as it finds that a ruling on the point or points of interpretation or validity is necessary to enable it to give judgment; it is the national court which is in the best position to decide at what stage of the proceedings such a question should be referred.

19. It is, however, desirable that a decision to seek a preliminary ruling should be taken when the proceedings have reached a stage at which the national court is able to define the factual and legal context of the question, so that the Court has available to it all the information necessary to check, where appropriate, that Community law applies to the main proceedings. It may also be in the interests of justice to refer a question for a preliminary ruling only after both sides have been heard.

The form of the reference for a preliminary ruling

20. The decision by which a national court or tribunal refers a question to the Court of Justice for a preliminary ruling may be in any form allowed by national law as regards procedural steps. It must however be borne in mind that it is that document which serves as the basis of the proceedings before the Court and that it must therefore contain such information as will enable the latter to give a reply which is of assistance to the national court. Moreover, it is only the actual reference for a preliminary ruling which is notified to the parties entitled to submit observations to the Court, in particular the Member States and the institutions, and which is translated.

21. Owing to the need to translate the reference, it should be drafted simply, clearly and precisely, avoiding superfluous detail.

22. A maximum of about ten pages is often sufficient to set out in a proper manner the context of a reference for a preliminary ruling. The order for reference must be succinct but sufficiently complete and must contain all the relevant information to give the Court and the parties entitled to submit observations a clear understanding of the factual and legal context of the main proceedings. In particular, the order for reference must:

- include a brief account of the subject-matter of the dispute and the relevant findings of fact, or, at least, set out the factual situation on which the question referred is based;
- set out the tenor of any applicable national provisions and identify, where necessary, the relevant national case-law, giving in each case precise references (e.g. page of an official journal or specific law report, with any internet reference);
- identify the Community provisions relevant to the case as accurately as possible;
- explain the reasons which prompted the national court to raise the question of the interpretation or validity of the Community provisions, and the relationship between those provisions and the national provisions applicable to the main proceedings;
- include, where appropriate, a summary of the main arguments of the parties.

In order to make it easier and refer to the document, it is

helpful if the different points or paragraphs of the order for reference are numbered.

23. Finally, the referring court may, if it considers itself to be in a position to do so, briefly state its view on the answer to be given to the questions referred for a preliminary ruling.
24. The question or questions themselves should appear in a separate and clearly identified section of the order for reference, generally at the beginning or the end. It must be possible to understand them without referring to the statement of the grounds for the reference, which however provides the necessary background for a proper assessment.

The effects of the reference for a preliminary ruling on the national proceedings

25. A reference for a preliminary ruling in general calls for the national proceedings to be stayed until the Court has given its ruling.
26. However, the national court may still order protective measures, particularly in a reference on determination of validity (see point 17 above).

Costs and legal aid

27. Proceedings for a preliminary ruling before the Court are free of charge and the Court does not rule on the costs of the parties to the main proceedings; it is for the national court to rule on those costs.
28. If a party has insufficient means and where possible under national rules, the national court may grant that party legal aid to cover the costs, including those of lawyers' fees, which it incurs before the Court. The Court itself may also grant legal aid.

Communication between the national court and the Court of Justice

29. The order for reference and the relevant documents (including, where applicable, the case file or a copy of the case file) are to be sent by the national court directly to the Court of Justice, by registered post (addressed to the Registry of the Court of Justice of the European Communities, L-2925 Luxembourg, telephone + 352-4303-1).
30. The Court Registry will stay in contact with the national court until a ruling is given and will send copies of the procedural documents.
31. The Court will send its ruling to the national court. It would welcome information from the national court on the action *taken upon its ruling in* the national proceedings and, where appropriate, a copy of the national court's final decision.

PART 69

COURT'S POWER TO APPOINT A RECEIVER

Contents

69.0.1

Editorial introduction

69.0.2 The rules in this Part deal with the powers of the Court to appoint receivers and applies to both the High Court and the county courts. The power to appoint a receiver is discretionary and accordingly the court will do so whenever it appears to it to be just and convenient to do so.

This Part was added by the Civil Procedure (Amendment) Rules 2002 (SI 2002/2058) and came into force on December 2, 2002. On that day the provisions found in the scheduled RSC O.30 (Receivers) and RSC O.51 (Receivers: Equitable Execution) were revoked.

Part 69 and its PD provides a comprehensive procedural code dealing with the appointment by the court of receivers and managers including provisions relating to the application for appointment, the evidence required on such application, security and renumeration. The rules emphasise that renumeration of a receiver must be authorised by the court and on the basis specified in the court's order. Part 69 also deals with such matters as receiver's accounts and discharge or termination of the receiver's appointment. The rules cover the appointment of receivers appointed for the purpose of preserving property during the course of litigation as well as the appointment of receivers by way of equitable execution, a procedure which is comparitively rare nowadays because of the availability of charging orders. Earlier commentary to RSC O.51 pointed out that execution against, for example, life interests in trust funds or in land is more convenient by way of appointment of a receiver. In practice the appointment of a receiver by way of equitable execution is designed to enable a judgment creditor to obtain payment of his debt when legal execution is not available because of the nature of the judgment debtor's interest in the property.

Special provisions apply to receivers under (1) the Insolvency Act 1986 (2) s.109 of the Law of Property Act 1925 and (3) the Mental Capacity Act 2005. Receivers were formerly appointed under the Pt 7 of the Mental Health Act 1983, now repealed by s.66 of the Mental Capacity Act 2005. Schedule 5 contains transitional provisions in relation to Pt 7 of the 1985 Act. Receivers, called deputies, are appointed by the court under s.19 of the 2005 Act. In the High Court proceedings in which a receiver is appointed other than by way of equitable execution are usually commenced in the Chancery Division.

Related sources

69.0.3
- Chancery Guide (paras 22.5–22.6 and Appendix 10)
- Queen's Bench Guide (Receivers: equitable execution, paras 12.7.1–12.7.8)

Forms

- PF30CH 69.0.4

Scope of this Part[1]

69.1—(1) This Part contains provisions about the court's power to appoint a receiver. 69.1

(2) In this Part "receiver" includes a manager.

Court's power to appoint receiver[2]

69.2—(1) The court may appoint a receiver— 69.2

(a) before proceedings have started;

(b) in existing proceedings; or

(c) on or after judgment.

(2) A receiver must be an individual.

(3) The court may at any time—

(a) terminate the appointment of a receiver; and

(b) appoint another receiver in his place.

(The practice direction describes the powers for the court to appoint a receiver.)

Rules 69.1 and 69.2 are to be read in conjunction with paras 1, 2 and 3 of the PD to Pt 69. Paragraph 1.1 of the PD sets out the statutory powers of the High Court and County Court. Accordingly, ss.37(1) and (2) of the Supreme Court Act 1981 give the High Court power to appoint a receiver in all cases in which it appears just and convenient and to do so conditionally or unconditionally. Section 107 of the County Courts Act 1984 provides that the power of the County Court to appoint a receiver by way of equitable execution shall operate in relation to all legal estates and interests in land and whether or not a charge has been imposed under s.1 of the Charging Orders Act 1979. Additionally, the High Court has power to appoint a receiver under Pt VI of the Criminal Justice Act 1988 (confiscation of the Proceeds of an Offence) in respect of realisable property (s.80(2)). This jurisdiction was examined by the HL in *Capewell v Revenue and Customs Commissioners* [2007] UKHL 2; [2007] 1 W.L.R. 386, HL. 69.2.1

In the usual situation the Court will appoint a receiver (who must be an individual: r.69.2(2)) in the course of existing proceedings but rule 69.2 makes it clear that the court may appoint a receiver before proceedings have commenced and on or after judgment. Paragraph 2.1 of the PD is important: the court will not normally consider an application for the appointment of a receiver before proceedings have commenced unless the application has been served. In practice this means that the Pt 23 application notice in the intended claim will need to be served on the persons identified in r.69.4.

Injunctions: if the application for the appointment of a receiver is joined with an application for an injunction, for example, for the detention, custody or preservation of relevant property then the second PD to Pt 2 (Allocation of Cases to Levels of Judiciary) is relevant. The master or district judge may grant an injunction relating to an order appointing a receiver by way of equitable execution (para.3.1 of PD to Pt 69). If an application is made for an injunction at the same time an application notice must be used.

Rule 69.2(3) provides that the court may at any time terminate the appointment of a receiver and appoint another in his place. This rule should be read in conjunction with r.69.9. The general principle is that the court is astute to see that the most suitable person acts as receiver. When appointed as manager, for example, in partnership claims, the same will apply.

[1] Introduced by the Civil Procedure (Amendment) Rules 2002 (SI 2002/2058).
[2] Introduced by the Civil Procedure (Amendment) Rules 2002 (SI 2002/2058).

How to apply for the appointment of a receiver[1]

69.3 **69.3 An application for the appointment of a receiver—**

(a) may be made without notice; and

(b) must be supported by written evidence.

69.3.1 Rule 69.3(a) provides that an application for the appointment of a receiver may be made without notice and by r.69.3(b) must be supported by written evidence. Although the application, which should be a Pt 23 application in Form **N244**, may be made without notice that will not be in the ordinary case. In the usual case theapplication notice should be served on the person to be appointed receiver and every other party to the claim. A without notice application may be suitable in cases of urgency or other special circumstances warranting it. In that event the court is likely to grant an interim order only with the usual permission to all parties to apply to vary or discharge the order.

Paragraph 4.1 of the PD sets out comprehensively what the written evidence in support of the application must contain and careful attention is to be paid to it. This evidence will be given by witness statement referred to in the Pt 23 application notice. The witness statement must contain a statement of truth.

Security: if the applicant is seeking permission for the receivert to act without giving security or before security is given then the evidence will be given by way of witness statement from a person who knows the receiver (described here as the nominee) and his or her belief of fitness. Paragraph 4.2(3) provides that the consent of the nominee to act must be available to the court.

Paragraphs 4.3 and 4.4 of the PD deals with situations where the applicant for the appointment of a receiver does not nominate a person to be appointed or where the court in its discretion decides not to nominate the person suggested, in either case this will be dealt with in the order made.

When an order has been made appointing a receiver it will in the usual case be necessary to apply thereafter for directions by a Pt 23 application notice. Paragraph 6 of the PD to Pt 69 lists the matters on which directions will be usually given. A draft order should accompany the application. This will not be the case if the original order appointing the receiver gives comprehensive directions.

The Chancery Division issues *A Guide for Receivers in the Chancery Division* (amended 2003) which is available from the Court Manager, Chancery Chambers, Room TM 6.06. The Guide is printed at Appendix 10 in the Chancery Guide.

Service of order appointing receiver[2]

69.4 **69.4 An order appointing a receiver must be served by the party who applied for it on—**

(a) the person appointed as receiver;

(b) unless the court orders otherwise, every other party to the proceedings; and

(c) such other persons as the court may direct.

Security[3]

69.5 **69.5—(1) The court may direct that before a receiver begins to act or within a specified time he must either—**

(a) give such security as the court may determine; or

(b) file and serve on all parties to the proceedings evidence that he already has in force sufficient security,

to cover his liability for his acts and omissions as a receiver.

[1] Introduced by the Civil Procedure (Amendment) Rules 2002 (SI 2002/2058).
[2] Introduced by the Civil Procedure (Amendment) Rules 2002 (SI 2002/2058).
[3] Introduced by the Civil Procedure (Amendment) Rules 2002 (SI 2002/2058).

(2) The court may terminate the appointment of the receiver if he fails to—

(a) give the security; or

(b) satisfy the court as to the security he has in force,

by the date specified.

Rule 69.5 is to be read in conjunction to para.7 of the PD to Pt 69. The general position is that the court is likely to require the receiver to give security by guarantee or bond before he begins to act or within a specified time unless there is sufficient evidence that he has already in force sufficient security to cover any liability for acts and omissions as receiver. Paragraph 7.2 of the PD is important in connection with situations where the person to be appointed is a licensed insolvency practitioner in which case security is given by bond provided under the Insolvency Practioner Regulations 1990. A form of guarantee is Form **PF30CH**. In the Chancery Division the executed guarantee i.e. signed by the receiver and sealed by the bank is lodged in Room TM 7.09, Royal Courts of Justice, WC2A 2LL. It will then be produced to the Master and placed on the Court file: similarly if security is given by bond. **69.5.1**

Rule 69.5(2) provides that the court may terminate a receiver's appointment if there has been a failure to give security or to satisfy the court that security is in force by the date given in the order. The order appointing the receiver will provide that the appointment is determined unless security is given as set out in the order. Good practice suggests that a draft order should in every case be available to the judge together with details of the bond to be given or as the case may be a draft guarantee with a clearing bank or the insurance company, listed in Appendix 2 to *A Guide for Receivers in the Chancery Division*(amended 2003).

Receiver's application for directions[1]

69.6—(1) The receiver may apply to the court at any time for directions to assist him in carrying out his function as a receiver. **69.6**

(2) The court, when it gives directions, may also direct the receiver to serve on any person—

(a) the directions; and

(b) the application for directions.

(The practice direction makes provision for the form of applications by, and directions to, a receiver.)

This rule and para.8 of the PD provide in general terms that the receiver can at any time apply to the court for directions in connection with the carrying out of his functions as receiver. The receiver will wish to obtain the court's permission for any action that is not covered by the order appointing him. Paragraphs 8.1 and 8.2 of the PD gives guidance as to when a Pt 23 application notice is or is not appropriate. If the application by the receiver is of substance and particularly if it is likely to be opposed or require close scrutiny by the court then such an application should be by a Pt 23 application notice supported by a witness statement. If, as the PD says, the application is unlikely to be contentious or unimportant to the parties then the receiver may apply to the court by letter. The Master or district judge will then consider the matter and may reply by letter, alternatively make an order, alternatively may direct that a Pt 23 application should be issued. Paragraph 8.2 of the PD provides that a receiver applying for directions by letter need not serve the letter or the court's reply on the parties unless the court otherwise directs. However the court will be astute to ensure transparency of all dealings with it such that the parties are aware of approaches to it. **69.6.1**

[1] Introduced by the Civil Procedure (Amendment) Rules 2002 (SI 2002/2058).

Receiver's remuneration[1]

69.7 **69.7—(1) A receiver may only charge for his services if the court—**

- **(a) so directs; and**
- **(b) specifies the basis on which the receiver is to be remunerated.**

(2) The court may specify—

- **(a) who is to be responsible for paying the receiver; and**
- **(b) the fund or property from which the receiver is to recover his remuneration.**

(3) If the court directs that the amount of a receiver's remuneration is to be determined by the court—

- **(a) the receiver may not recover any remuneration for his services without a determination by the court; and**
- **(b) the receiver or any party may apply at any time for such a determination to take place.**

(4) Unless the court orders otherwise, in determining the remuneration of a receiver the court shall award such sum as is reasonable and proportionate in all the circumstances and which takes into account—

- **(a) the time properly given by him and his staff to the receivership;**
- **(b) the complexity of the receivership;**
- **(c) any responsibility of an exceptional kind or degree which falls on the receiver in consequence of the receivership;**
- **(d) the effectiveness with which the receiver appears to be carrying out, or to have carried out, his duties; and**
- **(e) the value and nature of the subject matter of the receivership.**

(5) The court may refer the determination of a receiver's remuneration to a costs judge.

69.7.1 This rule makes it clear that a receiver may only charge for his services if the court has so authorised and that authorisation will be given in an order. A receiver may only, therefore, charge for services if the court so directs and specifies the basis on which he is to be remunerated. The court will also be likely in its order to specify who is to be responsible for the receiver's charges and identify the fund or property from which such remuneration is to be taken.

Rule 69(3) provides that if the amount of a receiver's remuneration is to be determined by the court then such remuneration shall not be recoverable without a determination by the court: accordingly the receiver will not be paid or entitled to recover his costs until after such determination.

Rule 69.7(4) and para.9.2 of the PD provides for the matters to be taken into account in determining the remuneration to be authorised on the basis of what is reasonable and proportionate. Pts 43–48 (costs) do not apply. Significantly rule 69.7(5) provides that the court may refer the determination of a receiver's remuneration to a costs judge. The court may take such a course if the remuneration is substantial and if it feels that the costs judge is best placed to determine amounts. The court is further empowered to appoint an assessor under r.35.15 to assist the court in determining a receiver's remuneration (para.9.5(2) of PD to Pt 69).

[1] Introduced by the Civil Procedure (Amendment) Rules 2002 (SI 2002/2058).

Paragraph 9.4 of the PD sets out the written evidence that a receiver must provide when seeking determination of his remuneration including the basis on which it is claimed and a certificate signed by the receiver that he considers that the remuneration claimed is reasonable and proportionate. The court is able to require the receiver to provide further information in support of his claim to remuneration (para.9.5(1) of PD to Pt 69). Nothing in the new Pt 69 appears to detract from the previous good practice of submitting to the parties the receiver's remuneration claim for approval before seeking the court's determination and approval; however the provisions of the PD remain to be nonetheless observed including the evidence set out in para.9.4 of the PD.

Expenses incurred by a receiver in carrying out his functions are not part of his remuneration but should be accounted for as part of his accounts for the assets recovered by him (para.9.6 of PD to Pt 69). Carnworth L.J. in *Capewell v Customs & Excise Commissioners* [2006] C.P. Rep. 36 at 43 considered expenses in connection with r.69.7(2) and observed that the PD confirmed the distinction between remuneration and expenses The HL in *Capewell* reversed the decision of the CA on other grounds. Lord Walker concluded that CPR Pt 69 sets out a procedural code applicable to receiverships of all types but did not override the provisions of the Criminal Justice Act 1988 referable to all receivers. Paragraph 6.3(4) of the PD provides that the court may give directions authorising a receiver to incur an expense. In an appropriate case a receiver should consider whether it is appropriate to seek the court's approval in respect of expenses, particularly if such expenses may be contentious or require scrutiny.

Interim orders: as under the previous procedure there appears to be no reason why the court cannot in an appropriate case make an interim order authorising a receiver's remuneration; equally in a suitable case an interim order specifying how the remuneration is to be determined and who is responsible for paying the receiver or the fund from which the remuneration is to be recovered.

Accounts[1]

69.8—(1) The court may order a receiver to prepare and serve accounts. (The practice direction contains provisions about directions for the preparation and service of accounts.) 69.8

(2) A party served with such accounts may apply for an order permitting him to inspect any document in the possession of the receiver relevant to those accounts.

(3) Any party may, within 14 days of being served with the accounts, serve notice on the receiver—

(a) specifying any item in the accounts to which he objects;

(b) giving the reason for such objection; and

(c) requiring the receiver, within 14 days of receipt of the notice, either—

(i) to notify all the parties who were served with the accounts that he accepts the objection; or

(ii) if he does not accept the objection, to apply for an examination of the accounts in relation to the contested item.

(4) When the receiver applies for the examination of the accounts he must at the same time file—

(a) the accounts; and

(b) a copy of the notice served on him under this rule.

(5) If the receiver fails to comply with paragraph (3)(c) of this rule, any party may apply to the court for an examination of the accounts in relation to the contested item.

---

[1] Introduced by the Civil Procedure (Amendment) Rules 2002 (SI 2002/2058).

(6) At the conclusion of its examination of the accounts the court will certify the result.

(The practice direction supplementing Part 40 provides for inquiries into accounts.)

69.8.1 The court may order the receiver to prepare and serve accounts. The order can require the receivver to do so by a specified date or at specified intervals and identify those upon whom the accounts are to be served: usually half-yearly and to be served within one month of the accounting period.

Rule 69.8 and the PD to Pt 69 contains provisions concerning the preparation and service by the receiver of accounts. In practice however the court will not become involved in the receiver's accounts if the accounts are agreed by the parties, after service of the accounts, or if no objection is taken by them.

The entitlement of parties served with the accounts to object to items in it is set out. A person served with the accounts may apply for an order permitting him to inspect any document in the possession of the receiver relevant to the accounts (r.69.8(2)) but such an application (a Pt 23 application) should not be made without first asking the receiver to permit inspection without an order (para.10.2 of the PD to Pt 69).

Non-compliance by receiver[1]

69.9 **69.9—(1) If a receiver fails to comply with any rule, practice direction or direction of the court the court may order him to attend a hearing to explain his non-compliance.**

(2) At the hearing the court may make any order it considers appropriate, including—

(a) terminating the appointment of the receiver;

(b) reducing the receiver's remuneration or disallowing it altogether; and

(c) ordering the receiver to pay the costs of any party.

(3) Where—

(a) the court has ordered a receiver to pay a sum of money into court; and

(b) the receiver has failed to do so,

the court may order him to pay interest on that sum for the time he is in default at such rate as it considers appropriate.

69.9.1 The rules here set out the various orders that the court may make in the event of non-compiance and including non-compliance with any order that the court has made in the receivership.

Application for discharge of receiver[2]

69.10 **69.10—(1) A receiver or any party may apply for the receiver to be discharged on completion of his duties.**

(2) The application notice must be served on the persons who were required under rule 69.4 to be served with the order appointing the receiver.

---

[1] Introduced by the Civil Procedure (Amendment) Rules 2002 (SI 2002/2058).

[2] Introduced by the Civil Procedure (Amendment) Rules 2002 (SI 2002/2058) and amended by the Civil Procedure (Amendment) Rules 2004 (SI 2004/1306).

Order discharging or terminating appointment of receiver[1]

69.11—(1) An order discharging or terminating the appointment of a receiver may— 69.11

(a) require him to pay into court any money held by him; or

(b) specify the person to whom he must pay any money or transfer any assets still in his possession; and

(c) make provision for the discharge or cancellation of any guarantee given by the receiver as security.

(2) The order must be served on the persons who were required under rule 69.4 to be served with the order appointing the receiver.

This rule is to be read in conjunction with r.69.10 (Application for discharge by receiver). In practice an order will be made at the conclusion of the receivership on the application by the receiver supported by a witness statement made by him, and it will deal with the monies held by him, the assests of the receivership and the cancellation of any bond or guarantee given by him. The order must be served on all parties to the proceedings (r.69.11(2)). 69.11.1

After the order is made, the guarantee and a duplicate order will be endorsed to that effect for return to the bank or insurance company for cancellation.

[1] Introduced by the Civil Procedure (Amendment) Rules 2002 (SI 2002/2058).

PRACTICE DIRECTION—COURT'S POWER TO APPOINT A RECEIVER

This Practice Direction supplements CPR Part 69

Court's power to appoint receiver

69PD.1 **1.1** The court's powers to appoint a receiver are set out in—

(1) section 37 of the Supreme Court Act 1981 (powers of the High Court with respect to injunctions and receivers);

(2) section 38 of the County Courts Act 1984 (remedies available in county courts); and

(3) section 107 of the County Courts Act 1984 (receivers by way of equitable execution).

Applications before proceedings are started—rule 69.2(1)(a)

69PD.2 **2.1** The court will normally only consider an application for the appointment of a receiver before proceedings are started after notice of the application has been served.

2.2 Rule 25.2(2) contains provisions about the grant of an order before proceedings are started.

Related injunctions

69PD.3 **3.1** If a person applies at the same time for—

(1) the appointment of a receiver; and

(2) a related injunction,

he must use the same claim form or application notice for both applications.

3.2 The second practice direction supplementing Part 2 (Allocation of Cases to Levels of Judiciary) sets out who may grant injunctions. Among other things, it provides that a Master or a District Judge may grant an injunction related to an order appointing a receiver by way of equitable execution.

Evidence in support of an application—rule 69.3

69PD.4 **4.1** The written evidence in support of an application for the appointment of a receiver must—

(1) explain the reasons why the appointment is required;

(2) give details of the property which it is proposed that the receiver should get in or manage, including estimates of—

(a) the value of the property; and

(b) the amount of income it is likely to produce;

(3) if the application is to appoint a receiver by way of equitable execution, give details of—

(a) the judgment which the applicant is seeking to enforce;

(b) the extent to which the debtor has failed to comply with the judgment;

(c) the result of any steps already taken to enforce the judgment; and

(d) why the judgment cannot be enforced by any other method; and

(4) if the applicant is asking the court to allow the receiver to act—

(a) without giving security; or
(b) before he has given security or satisfied the court that he has security in place,

explain the reasons why that is necessary.

4.2 In addition, the written evidence should normally identify an individual whom the court is to be asked to appoint as receiver ('the nominee'), and should—

(1) state the name, address and position of the nominee;
(2) include written evidence by a person who knows the nominee, stating that he believes the nominee is a suitable person to be appointed as receiver, and the basis of that belief; and
(3) be accompanied by written consent, signed by the nominee, to act as receiver if appointed.

4.3 If the applicant does not nominate a person to be appointed as receiver, or if the court decides not to appoint the nominee, the court may—

(1) order that a suitable person be appointed as receiver; and
(2) direct any party to nominate a suitable individual to be appointed.

4.4 A party directed to nominate a person to be appointed as receiver must file written evidence containing the information required by paragraph 4.2 and accompanied by the written consent of the nominee.

Appointment of receiver to enforce a judgment

5. Where a judgment creditor applies for the appointment of a receiver as a method of enforcing a judgment, in considering whether to make the appointment the court will have regard to— **69PD.5**

(1) the amount claimed by the judgment creditor;
(2) the amount likely to be obtained by the receiver; and
(3) the probable costs of his appointment.

Court's directions

6.1 The court may give directions to the receiver when it appoints him or at any time afterwards. **69PD.6**

6.2 The court will normally, when it appoints a receiver, give directions in relation to security – see paragraph 7 below

6.3 Other matters about which the court may give directions include—

(1) whether, and on what basis, the receiver is to be remunerated for carrying out his functions;
(2) the preparation and service of accounts—see rule 69.8(1) *and paragraph 10 below;*
(3) the payment of money into court; and
(4) authorising the receiver to carry on an activity or incur an expense.

Directions relating to security—rule 69.5

7.1 An order appointing a receiver will normally specify the date by which the receiver must— **69PD.7**

(1) give security; or

(2) file and serve evidence to satisfy the court that he already has security in force.

7.2 Unless the court directs otherwise, security will be given—

(1) if the receiver is an authorised insolvency practitioner, by the bond provided by him under the Insolvency Practitioners Regulations 1990 or the Insolvency Practitioners Regulations 2005 extended to cover appointment as a court appointed receiver; or

(2) in any other case, by a guarantee.

7.3 Where the court has given directions about giving security, then either—

(1) written evidence of the bond, the sufficiency of its cover and that it includes appointment as a court appointed receiver must be filed at court; or

(2) a guarantee should be prepared in a form, and entered into with a clearing bank or insurance company, approved by the court.

Receiver's application for directions—rule 69.6

69PD.8 **8.1** An application by a receiver for directions may be made by filing an application notice in accordance with Part 23.

8.2 If the directions sought by the receiver are unlikely to be contentious or important to the parties, he may make the application by letter, and the court may reply by letter. In such cases the receiver need not serve his letter or the court's reply on the parties, unless the court orders him to do so.

8.3 Where a receiver applies for directions by letter, the court may direct him to file and serve an application notice.

Receiver's remuneration—rule 69.7

69PD.9 **9.1** A receiver may only charge for his services if the court gives directions permitting it and specifying how the remuneration is to be determined.

9.2 The court will normally determine the amount of the receiver's remuneration on the basis of the criteria in rule 69.7(4). Parts 43 to 48 (costs) do not apply to the determination of the remuneration of a receiver.

9.3 Unless the court orders otherwise, the receiver will only be paid or be able to recover his remuneration after the amount of it has been determined.

9.4 An application by a receiver for the amount of his remuneration to be determined must be supported by—

(1) written evidence showing—

(a) on what basis the remuneration is claimed; and

(b) that it is justified and in accordance with this Part; and

(2) a certificate signed by the receiver that he considers that the remuneration he claims is reasonable and proportionate.

9.5 The court may, before determining the amount of a receiver's remuneration—

(1) require the receiver to provide further information in support of his claim; and
(2) appoint an assessor under rule 35.15 to assist the court.

9.6 Paragraphs 9.1 to 9.5 do not apply to expenses incurred by a receiver in carrying out his functions. These are accounted for as part of his account for the assets he has recovered, and not dealt with as part of the determination of his remuneration.

Accounts—rule 69.8

10.1 When the court gives directions under rule 69.8(1) for the receiver to prepare and serve accounts, it may— **69PD.10**
(1) direct the receiver to prepare and serve accounts either by a specified date or at specified intervals; and
(2) specify the persons on whom he must serve the accounts.

10.2 A party should not apply for an order under rule 69.8(2) permitting him to inspect documents in the possession of the receiver, without first asking the receiver to permit such inspection without an order.

10.3 Where the court makes an order under rule 69.8(2), it will normally direct that the receiver must—
(1) permit inspection within 7 days after being served with the order; and
(2) provide a copy of any documents the subject of the order within 7 days after receiving a request for a copy from the party permitted to inspect them, provided that party has undertaken to pay the reasonable cost of making and providing the copy.

PART 70

General Rules about Enforcement of Judgments and Orders

Contents

70.0.1

Editorial introduction

70.0.2 Parts 70 to 73 were added by the Civil Procedure (Amendment) Rules 2001 (SI 2001/2792). Some amendments were effected by the Civil Procedure (Amendment No.5) Rules 2001 (SI 2001/4015). These new Parts, as amended came into force on March 25, 2002.

The law on enforcement of judgments is unsatisfactory and in need of reform. Reforms enacted by the Tribunals Courts and Enforcement Act 2007 now appear unlikely to be implemented before 2011.

Unfortunately Pt 70, does not even incorporate the whole of Sch.1, RSC O.45 and Sch.2, CCR O.25. Thus we have CPR Pt 70—General Rules about Enforcement of Judgments and Orders, Sch.1, RSC O.45—Enforcement of Judgment and Orders: General and Sch.2, CCR O.25—Enforcement of Judgments and Orders: General.

It is a feature of civil justice that the court does not automatically enforce its judgments nor even help decide how they should be enforced. It is up to the judgment creditor. The relevant procedures are now contained in Pts 70 to 73, Sch.1, RSC Ords. 45, 46, 47, 51 and 52 and Sch.2, CCR Ords. 25 to 29. Pt 70 is supplemented by a comprehensive practice direction (see para.70PD.1). Paragraph 1 of the Practice Direction lists all available methods of enforcement.

Related sources

70.0.3

- Practice Direction—Enforcement of Judgments and Orders (70PD.1)
- Part 69—Court's power to appoint a Receiver
- Part 71—Orders to obtain information from judgment debtors
- Part 72—Third Part Debt Orders
- Part 73—Charging Orders, Stop Orders and Stop Notices
- RSC O.45—Enforcement of Judgments and Orders: General
- RSC O.46—Writs of Execution: General
- RSC O.47—Writs of Fieri Facias
- RSC O.52—Committal
- CCR O.25—Enforcement of Judgments and Orders: General
- CCR O.26—Warrants of Execution, Delivery and Possession
- CCR O.27—Attachment of Earnings
- CCR O.28—Judgment Summons
- CCR O.29—Committal for Breach of Order or Undertaking

Forms

70.0.4

- **N322** Order for recovery of money awarded by tribunal
- **N322A** Application to enforce an award

- **N322H** Request to register a High Court judgment or order for enforcement

Register of Judgments, Orders and Fines

A Register of County Court Judgments was created in 1852 and was held by the Lord Chancellor's Department. The Register could—for a fee—be searched, for example, to ascertain whether a prospective borrower had previously been sued to judgment. Since 1986 the Register has been held by Registry Trust Ltd. **70.0.5**

As from April 6, 2006 a new Register of Judgments, Orders and Fines is held pursuant to the Register of Judgments, Orders and Fines Regulations 2005 (SI 2005/3595). Subject to the regulations, and the exemptions in reg.9, the new register records all county court judgments, administration orders and Child Support Agency liability orders and, as from April 6, 2006, High Court judgments and fine defaulters. The Registry can be contacted at 173–175 Cleveland Street, London W1T 6QR and at *http://www.registry-trust.org.uk*. [Accessed October 29, 2007]

Scope of this Part and interpretation[1]

70.1—(1) This Part contains general rules about enforcement of judgments and orders. (Rules about specific methods of enforcement are contained in Parts 71 to 73, Schedule 1, RSC Orders 45 to 47 and 52 and Schedule 2, CCR Orders 25 to 29). **70.1**

(2) In this Part and in Parts 71 to 73—

(a) "judgment creditor" means a person who has obtained or is entitled to enforce a judgment or order;

(b) "judgment debtor" means a person against whom a judgment or order was given or made;

(c) "judgment or order" includes an award which the court has—

(i) registered for enforcement;

(ii) ordered to be enforced; or

(iii) given permission to enforce

as if it were a judgment or order of the court, and in relation to such an award, "the court which made the judgment or order" means the court which registered the award or made such an order; and

(d) "judgment or order for the payment of money" includes a judgment or order for the payment of costs, but does not include a judgment or order for the payment of money into court.

Change of terminology

Note the change of terms. After the court has given judgment parties are no longer "claimant" or "defendant" (although some court forms wrongly continue to describe them as such).The party entitled to enforce the judgment is the "judgment creditor" and the party against whom it can be enforced is the "judgment debtor". **70.1.1**

As if it were a judgment or order of the court

—see r.70.5. **70.1.2**

Judgment or order for the payment of costs

The amount of costs payable must have been decided before enforcement. A successful party who wishes to obtain a payment prior to assessment of costs should use r.44.3(8) or r.47.15. An order under either of these rules can be enforced. **70.1.3**

---

[1] Introduced by the Civil Procedure (Amendment No.4) Rules 2001 (SI 2001/2792) and amended by the Civil Procedure (Amendment) Rules 2002 (SI 2002/2058).

Payment of money into court

70.1.4 If the court has ordered a payment into court (see r.3.1(3)) but it has not been paid it is not possible to enforce the payment by execution. Instead an application must be made for imposition of a sanction such as strike out of the claim or defence as appropriate.

Methods of enforcing judgments or orders[1]

70.2 **70.2—(1) The relevant practice direction sets out methods of enforcing judgments or orders for the payment of money.**

(2) A judgment creditor may, except where an enactment, rule or practice direction provides otherwise—

- **(a) use any method of enforcement which is available; and**
- **(b) use more than one method of enforcement, either at the same time or one after another.**

Methods of enforcement

70.2.1 The following methods are available:

Writ of *fieri facias* (RSC Ords. 46 & 47)
Warrant of execution (CCR O.26)
Third party debt order (Pt 72)
Charging order, stop order or stop notice (Pt 73)
Attachment of earnings (CCR O.27)
Appointment of a receiver (Pt 69)
Committal if permitted by a rule and the Debtors Acts 1869 & 1878 (RSC O.45, r.5 & O.52; CCR Ords.28 &29)
Sequestration (RSC O.45, r.5)

Only the first two (writ of *fi-fa* and warrant of execution) of these methods is a wholly administrative process requiring no judicial decision.

See further the rules mentioned and commentary thereon.

Simultaneous enforcement

70.2.2 Rule 70.2(2)(b) provides welcome clarification. It has always been the law that a judgment creditor need not attempt to enforce his judgment sequentially by trying one method of enforcement after another but can attempt to enforce by more than one method simultaneously. However, many court officers seemed unsure of this. Whilst obviously the judgment creditor can only be paid once the rule confirms that he can use more than one method of enforcement at the same time. A judgment creditor who is unsure which method to use should first consider Pt 71.

Note the obligation imposed on judgment creditors by para.7 of PD 70 to notify the court in writing (or the Enforcement Officer in the case of a High Court writ of execution) of any payment received between the date of issue of the enforcement process and the hearing (execution). This would, of course, include any payment received under another enforcement process.

Interest on judgment debts

70.2.3 —see para.6 of PD 70.

Payment of judgment debt after issue of enforcement proceedings

70.2.4 —see para.7 of PD 70.

Transfer of proceedings for enforcement[2]

70.3 **70.3—(1) A judgment creditor wishing to enforce a High Court judgment or order in a county court must apply to the High Court for an order transferring the proceedings to that county court.**

[1] Introduced by the Civil Procedure (Amendment No.4) Rules 2001 (SI 2001/2792).
[2] Introduced by the Civil Procedure (Amendment No.4) Rules 2001 (SI 2001/2792).

(2) A practice direction may make provisions about the transfer of proceedings for enforcement.

(CCR Order 25, rule 13 contains provisions about the transfer of county court proceedings to the High Court for enforcement.)

Transfer to county court for enforcement

The most common reason for transferring from the High Court to the county court for enforcement purposes is that the County Court has exclusive jurisdiction to make an order under the Attachment of Earnings Act 1971 (See Sch.2, CCR O.27). **70.3.1**

The procedure to transfer is explained at para.3 of PD 70

Transfer to High Court for enforcement

The most common reason for transferring from the county court to the High Court for enforcement is to use a High Court Enforcement Officer to levy execution. Only where the sum which it is sought to enforce is less than £600 or the judgment arises out of an agreement regulated by the Consumer Credit Act 1974 must the judgment be enforced in the county court. In other cases the judgment can—and if it is sought to enforce £5000 or more must—be enforced in the High Court. See further commentary to RSC Ords 45 and 56 and to CCR Ords 25 and 26. **70.3.2**

Transfer from one county court to another

—see para.2 of PD 70. **70.3.3**

Enforcement of judgment or order by or against non–party[1]

70.4 If a judgment or order is given or made in favour of or against a person who is not a party to proceedings, it may be enforced by or against that person by the same methods as if he were a party. **70.4**

By or against a non party

Orders in favour of or against a non-party are rare but do arise (see r.48.2 and commentary thereon). Such orders can be enforced as if the non-party were a party. **70.4.1**

Enforcement of decisions of bodies other than the High Court and county courts and compromises enforceable by enactment[2]

70.5—(1) This rule applies, subject to paragraph (2), where an enactment provides that— **70.5**

(a) a decision of a court, tribunal, body or person other than the High Court or a county court; or

(b) a compromise,

may be enforced as if it were a court order or that any sum of money payable under that decision or compromise may be recoverable as if payable under a court order.

(2) This rule does not apply to—

(a) any judgment to which Part 74 applies;

(b) arbitration awards; or

(c) any order to which RSC Order 115 applies; or

---

[1] Introduced by the Civil Procedure (Amendment No.4) Rules 2001 (SI 2001/2792).

[2] Introduced by the Civil Procedure (Amendment No.4) Rules 2001 (SI 2001/2792) and amended by the Civil Procedure (Amendment No.5) Rules 2001 (SI 2001/4015), the Civil Procedure (Amendment) Rules 2002 (SI 2002/2058) , the Civil Procedure (Amendment No.4) Rules 2003 (SI 2003/2113) and the Civil Procedure (Amendment No.3) Rules 2008 (SI 2008/3327).

(d) proceedings to which Part 75 (traffic enforcement) applies.

(2A) Unless paragraph (3) applies, a party may enforce the decision or compromise by applying for a specific method of enforcement under Parts 71 to 73, Schedule 1 RSC Orders 45 to 47 and 52 and Schedule 2 CCR Orders 25 to 29 and must—

(a) file with the court a copy of the decision or compromise being enforced; and

(b) provide the court with the information required by the practice direction supplementing this Part.

(3) If an enactment provides that a decision or compromise is enforceable or a sum of money is recoverable if a court so orders, an application for such an order must be made in accordance with paragraphs (4)to (7) of this rule.

(4) The application—

(a) may, unless paragraph (4A) applies, be made without notice; and

(b) must be made to the court for the district where the person against whom the order is sought, resides or carries on business, unless the court otherwise orders.

(4A) Where a compromise requires a person to whom a sum of money is payable under the compromise to do anything in addition to discontinuing or not starting proceedings ("a conditional compromise"), an application under paragraph (4) must be made on notice.

(5) The application notice must—

(a) be in the form; and

(b) contain the information

required by the practice direction supplementing this Part.

(6) A copy of the decision or compromise must be filed with the application notice.

(7) An application other than in relation to a conditional compromise may be dealt with by a court officer without a hearing.

(7A) Where an application relates to a conditional compromise, the respondent may oppose it by filing a response within 14 days of service of the application notice and if the respondent—

(a) does not file a response within the time allowed, the court will make the order; or

(b) files a response within the time allowed, the court will make such order as appears appropriate.

(8) If an enactment provides that a decision or compromise may be enforced in the same manner as an order of the High Court if it is registered, any application to the High Court for registration must be made in accordance with the practice direction supplementing this Part.

Enforcement of decisions of tribunals, etc.

70.5.1 Many tribunals are created by statute to deal with particular types of dispute. Hearings before a tribunal often result in an order for the payment of money. As a tribunal has no machinery for enforcement, r.70.5 provides the machinery of the courts. The statute which creates the tribunal will be the relevant enactment for the purpose of r.70.5(3). See further paras 4 and 5 of PD 70.

Paragraphs (1), (2) and (3) were amended by, and para.(8) was inserted by the Civil Procedure (Amendment No.4) Rules 2003 with effect from October 6, 2003, primarily for the purpose of making necessary adjustments to the rule following upon the addition of rr.37 and 38 to Sch.1, RSC O.115. The rule was further amended by the Civil Procedure (Amendment No.3) Rules 2008 (SI 2008/3327). That statutory instrument added paras (2A), (4A) and (7A) to the rule, and these additions were accompanied by amendments to para.4 and 5 of PD70 (published in TSO CPR Update 49) (see para.70PD.4). The main purpose of these amendments was to provide that, where a compromise agreement includes a payment of a sum of money and it requires no action by the creditor other than to discontinue or not start proceedings, the recovery of the sum of money may be enforceable under r.70.5(1) as if it were a sum payable under a court order. In part, these changes were precipitated by the coming into effect of the Employment Tribunals Act 1996 s.19A (Conciliation: recovery of sum payable under compromises).

An application under rule 70.5(3) for an order to enforce a decision or compromise must be made by filing an application notice in practice form N322A (see para.4.2 of PD70).

Enforcement of decisions of VAT and Duties Tribunals

—see r.70.5(8) and para.5 of PD 70. **70.5.2**

Other than the high court and county courts

This includes the House of Lords (see para.13 of PD 40B). **70.5.3**

Effect of setting aside judgment or order[1]

70.6 If a judgment or order is set aside, any enforcement of the judgment or order shall cease to have effect unless the court otherwise orders. **70.6**

Setting aside—costs

Costs, including significant court fees, will have been incurred in the obtaining of the judgment and in issuing the enforcement process. Who will pay these costs and when is an issue which should be addressed at the hearing of the application to set aside judgment. It may be appropriate to set aside on terms as to costs. There are three main possibilities: costs to be paid by judgment debtor (the usual order when settling aside a regular judgment); costs to be paid by judgment creditor (the usual order when setting aside an irregular judgment); or costs in the case. **70.6.1**

"unless the court otherwise orders"

The use of these words in r.70.6 enables the court to keep an enforcement process "on hold" when a judgment is set aside. Thus, for example, a judgment creditor who has obtained priority and security by a charging order (see Pt 73) could be allowed to retain it as a condition of setting aside judgment. **70.6.2**

[1] Introduced by the Civil Procedure (Amendment No.4) Rules 2001 (SI 2001/2792).

PRACTICE DIRECTION—ENFORCEMENT OF JUDGMENTS AND ORDERS

70PD.1 *This Practice Direction supplements CPR Part 70*

Methods of enforcing money judgments—rule 70.2

1.1 A judgment creditor may enforce a judgment or order for the payment of money by any of the following methods:

(1) a writ of *fieri facias* or warrant of execution (see RSC Orders 46 and 47 and CCR Order 26);

(2) a third party debt order (see Part 72);

(3) a charging order, stop order or stop notice (see Part 73);

(4) in a county court, an attachment of earnings order (see CCR Order 27);

(5) the appointment of a receiver (see Part 69).

1.2 In addition the court may make the following orders against a judgment debtor—

(1) an order of committal, but only if permitted by—

(a) a rule; and

(b) the Debtors Acts 1869 and 1878

(See RSC Order 45, rule 5 and CCR Order 28. The practice direction on committal applications applies to an application for committal of a judgment debtor); and

(2) in the High Court, a writ of sequestration, but only if permitted by RSC Order 45, rule 5.

1.3 The enforcement of a judgment or order may be affected by—

(1) the enactments relating to insolvency; and

(2) county court administration orders.

Transfer of county court proceedings to another county court for enforcement—rule 70.3

70PD.2 **2.1** If a judgment creditor is required by a rule or practice direction to enforce a judgment or order of one county court in a different county court, he must first make a request in writing to the court in which the case is proceeding to transfer the proceedings to that other court.

2.2 On receipt of such a request, a court officer will transfer the proceedings to the other court unless a judge orders otherwise.

2.3 The court will give notice of the transfer to all the parties.

2.4 When the proceedings have been transferred, the parties must take any further steps in the proceedings in the court to which they have been transferred, unless a rule or practice direction provides otherwise.

(Part 52 and its practice direction provide to which court or judge an appeal against the judgment or order, or an application for permission to appeal, must be made.)

Enforcement of High Court judgment or order in a county court—rule 70.3

70PD.3 **3.1** If a judgment creditor wishes to enforce a High Court judgment or order in a county court, he must file the following documents in the county court with his application notice or request for enforcement—

(1) a copy of the judgment or order;
(2) a certificate verifying the amount due under the judgment or order;
(3) if a writ of execution has previously been issued in the High Court to enforce the judgment or order, a copy of the relevant enforcement officer's return to the writ; and
(4) a copy of the order transferring the proceedings to the county court.

3.2

In this paragraph and paragraph 7—

(1) "enforcement officer" means an individual who is authorised to act as an enforcement officer under the Courts Act 2003; and
(2) "relevant enforcement officer" means—
  (a) in relation to a writ of execution which is directed to a single enforcement officer, that officer;
  (b) in relation to a writ of execution which is directed to two or more enforcement officers, the officer to whom the writ is allocated.

Enforcement of decisions of bodies other than the High Court and county courts and compromises enforceable by enactment

4.1 The information referred to in rule 70.5(2A) must— **70PD.4**

(a) be included in practice form N322B;
(b) specify the statutory provision under which enforcement or the recovery of a sum of money is sought;
(c) state the name and address of the person against whom enforcement or recovery is sought;
(d) where the decision or compromise requires that person to pay a sum of money, state the amount which remains unpaid; and
(e) confirm that, where a sum of money is being recovered pursuant to a compromise, the compromise is not a conditional compromise.

4.2 An application under rule 70.5(3) for an order to enforce a decision or compromise must be made by filing an application notice in practice form N322A.

4.3 The application notice must state—

(a) the name and address of the person against whom the order is sought;
(b) how much remains unpaid or what obligation remains to be performed; and
(c) where the application relates to a conditional compromise, details of what under the compromise the applicant is required to do and has done under the compromise in addition to discontinuing or not starting proceedings.

4.4 Where—

(a) the application relates to a conditional compromise; and

(b) the application notice is served by the applicant on the respondent, the applicant must file a certificate of service with the court within 7 days of service of the application notice.

Registration of decisions in the High Court for enforcement—rule 70.5(8)

70PD.5 **5.1** An application to the High Court under an enactment to register a decision for enforcement must be made in writing to the head clerk of the Action Department at the Royal Courts of Justice, Strand, London WC2A 2LL.

5.2 The application must—

(1) specify the statutory provision under which the application is made;

(2) state the name and address of the person against whom it is sought to enforce the decision;

(3) if the decision requires that person to pay a sum of money, state the amount which remains unpaid.

Interest on judgment debts

70PD.6 **6.** If a judgment creditor is claiming interest on a judgment debt, he must include in his application or request to issue enforcement proceedings in relation to that judgment details of—

(1) the amount of interest claimed and the sum on which it is claimed;

(2) the dates from and to which interest has accrued; and

(3) the rate of interest which has been applied and, where more than one rate of interest has been applied, the relevant dates and rates.

(Interest may be claimed on High Court judgment debts under section 17 of the Judgments Act 1838. The County Courts (Interest on Judgment Debts) Order 1991 specifies when interest may be claimed on county court judgment debts).

Enforcing a judgment or order against a partnership

70PD.6A **6A.1** A judgment or order made against a partnership may be enforced against any property of the partnership within the jurisdiction.

6A.2 Subject to paragraph 6A.3, a judgment or order made against a partnership may be enforced against any person who is not a limited partner and who—

(1) acknowledged service of the claim form as a partner;

(2) having been served as a partner with the claim form, failed to acknowledge service of it;

(3) admitted in his statement of case that he is or was a partner at a material time; or

(4) was found by the court to have been a partner at a material time.

6A.3 A judgment or order made against a partnership may not be enforced against a limited partner or a member of the partnership who was ordinarily resident outside the jurisdiction when the claim form was issued unless that partner or member—

(1) acknowledged service of the claim form as a partner;
(2) was served within the jurisdiction with the claim form as a partner; or
(3) was served out of the jurisdiction with the claim form, as a partner, with the permission of the court given under Section IV of Part 6.

6A.4 A judgment creditor wishing to enforce a judgment or order against a person in circumstances not set out in paragraphs 6A.2 or 6A.3 must apply to the court for permission to enforce the judgment or order.

Payment of debt after issue of enforcement proceedings

7.1 If a judgment debt or part of it is paid— **70PD.7**

(1) after the judgment creditor has issued any application or request to enforce it; but
(2) before—
   (a) any writ or warrant has been executed; or
   (b) in any other case, the date fixed for the hearing of the application;

the judgment creditor must, unless paragraph 7.2 applies, immediately notify the court in writing.

7.2 If a judgment debt or part of it is paid after the judgment creditor has applied to the High Court for a writ of execution, paragraph 7.1 does not apply, and the judgment creditor must instead immediately notify the relevant enforcement officer in writing.

PART 71

Orders To Obtain Information From Judgment Debtors

Contents

71.0.1

Editorial introduction

71.0.2 Part 71 has replaced Sch.1, RSC O.48 and Sch.2, CCR O.25, rr.3 and 4 as from March 25, 2002 and deals with the procedure usually referred to as "oral examination". The scope of Pt 71 is clearly spelled out in r.71.1. It represents a tidying-up and simplification of the old rules but does not effect fundamental changes.

As noted in the Editorial Introduction to Pt 70, it is for the judgment creditor, not the court, to enforce the judgment. Enforcement can be expensive and abortive enforcement is just throwing good money after bad. Part 71 enables the judgment creditor to obtain information from the judgment debtor for the purpose of being able to better decide which method or methods of enforcement to use (sequentially or simultaneously, see r.70.2). There must, of course, be a judgment: this procedure is not available pre-action. Note the requirements of service in r.71.3 and to pay travelling expenses if requested in r.71.4. Rule 71.8 simplifies and clarifies the procedure if the debtor fails to comply with the order as doubts had been expressed as to whether the former rules were compatible with art.5 of the European Convention on Human Rights. Part 71 is supplemented by a Practice Direction.

Related sources

71.0.3

- Practice Direction—Orders to Obtain Information from Judgment Debtor (para.71PD.1)
- Practice Direction—Enforcement of Judgments and Orders (para.70PD.1)
- Part 70 CPR, and related sources thereto (para.70.0.3)

Forms

71.0.4

- **N316** Application for order that debtor attend court for examination
- **N316A** Application for order that officer of debtor company attend court for questioning
- **N39** Order to attend court for questioning
- **N40** Warrant of arrest and committal for disobedience (order to attend court for questioning)
- **N40A(HC)** Warrant of arrest for disobedience (order to attend court for questioning)
- **N40B(HC)** Warrant of committal for disobedience (order to attend court for questioning)
- **N40B** Warrant of committal for disobedience (order to attend court for questioning)
- **N79A** Suspended committal order for disobedience (order to attend court for questioning)
- **EX140** Record of examination (individual)
- **EX141** Record of examination (officer of company or corporation)

Scope of this Part[1]

71.1 This Part contains rules which provide for a judgment debtor to be required to attend court to provide information, for the purpose of enabling a judgment creditor to enforce a judgment or order against him. 71.1

Scope of Part 71

The purpose of Pt 71 is set out in r.71.1 and explained above at 71.0.2. The Part is not confined to money judgments. For example, a judgment debtor who has not complied with an order for the return of specific goods can be questioned pursuant to this Part. 71.1.1

Order to attend court[2]

71.2—(1) A judgment creditor may apply for an order requiring— 71.2

(a) a judgment debtor; or

(b) if a judgment debtor is a company or other corporation, an officer of that body,

to attend court to provide information about—

(i) the judgment debtor's means; or

(ii) any other matter about which information is needed to enforce a judgment or order.

(2) An application under paragraph (1)—

(a) may be made without notice; and

(b)

(i) must be issued in the court which made the judgment or order which it is sought to enforce, except that

(ii) if the proceedings have since been transferred to a different court, it must be issued in that court.

(3) The application notice must—

(a) be in the form; and

(b) contain the information

required by the relevant practice direction.

(4) An application under paragraph (1) may be dealt with by a court officer without a hearing.

(5) If the application notice complies with paragraph (3), an order to attend court will be issued in the terms of paragraph (6).

(6) A person served with an order issued under this rule must—

(a) attend court at the time and place specified in the order;

(b) when he does so, produce at court documents in his *control* which are described in the order; and

(c) answer on oath such questions as the court may require.

(7) An order under this rule will contain a notice in the following terms —

[1] Introduced by the Civil Procedure (Amendment No.4) Rules 2001 (SI 2001/2792).
[2] Introduced by the Civil Procedure (Amendment No.4) Rules 2001 (SI 2001/2792).

"You must obey this order. If you do not, you may be sent to prison for contempt of court."

Application Notice

71.2.1 See para.1 of PD71. Application is in Form N316 or N316A (as appropriate). No hearing is required (see r.71.2(4)).

Penal notice

71.2.2 Note the requirement of r.71.2(7) as to the endorsement of words usually referred to as a "penal notice". This is important if the order needs to be enforced (see further r.71.8) which provides for the order to require the debtor to attend the county court for the district where he resides or carries on business unless a judge decides otherwise. Any request for the judge so to order should be made on issuing the application.

Venue

71.2.3 Rule 71.2(2) deals with the court of issue. Application is made without notice to the court which made the judgment or order except where the proceedings have been transferred to a different court in which case it must be issued in that court. As to the court where the examination will be conducted see para.2.1, PD71.

"answer on oath such questions as the court may require"

71.2.4 The purpose of Pt 71 is clear from its title and r.71.1. A judgment debtor who does not answer questions is in contempt of court (see further r.71.8). A former procedure of oral examination was held to be "not only intended to be an examination, but a cross-examination and that of the severest kind" (*Republic of Costa Rica v Stronsberg* (1880) 16 Ch.D. 8) and this remains so under the modern procedure.

Overseas assets

71.2.5 When a judgment debtor is being examined regarding any debts owing to him and his assets he is required to answer questions relating to assets outside the jurisdiction. (*Interpool Ltd v Galani* [1988] Q.B. 738)

"an officer"

71.2.6 In interpreting identical words in a previous rule it was held that "an officer" included former officers (*Société Générale v J.M.Farin & Co* [1904] 1 K.B. 794).

"will be issued"

71.2.7 The former rule gave the court a discretion ("may, on an application made ex parte, order…") but the new rule gives the judgment creditor a right to issue. In *Sturges v Countess of Warwick* (1914) 30 T.L.R. 112 it was held that a further examination could be ordered in special circumstances. The new rule places no restriction on repeat examinations no doubt relying on the courts case management and costs powers to prevent abuse.

Despite the mandatory wording of the rule, the court officer always has power to refer cases of doubt to the judge (r.3.2) and the judge can refuse to issue (or require a hearing) where the application is misconceived eg. because time for payment has not yet expired (see *White Son & Pill v Stennings* [1911] 2 K.B. 418).

Service of order[1]

71.3 **71.3—(1) An order to attend court must, unless the court otherwise orders, be served personally on the person ordered to attend the court not less than 14 days before the hearing.**

(2) If the order is to be served by the judgment creditor, he must inform the court not less than 7 days before the date of the *hearing if he has* been unable to serve it.

[1] Introduced by the Civil Procedure (Amendment No.4) Rules 2001 (SI 2001/2792).

"must...be served personally"

See para.3 of PD71. In the county court bailiff service is now available only to an individual litigant in person. In all other cases personal service must be by the judgment creditor or someone acting on his behalf. **71.3.1**

"unless the court otherwise orders"

Service by an alternative method is dealt with in r.6.8. Usually there will have to be an attempt at personal service first. **71.3.2**

Costs

Fixed costs are prescribed by r.45.6. In addition, r.45.5 prescribes a fee of £15 for effecting personal service. This figure is disproportionately low as an enqiry agent will charge more than this and it is hardly adequate recompense for the creditor's own time. Yet the new rule requires personal service. **71.3.3**

Travelling expenses[1]

71.4—(1) A person ordered to attend may, within 7 days of being served with the order, ask the judgment creditor to pay him a sum reasonably sufficient to cover his travelling expenses to and from court. **71.4**

(2) The judgment creditor must pay a sum if requested.

Conduct money

The former requirement to tender conduct money has gone and is replaced by this simplified rule to pay travelling expenses if requested. **71.4.1**

Judgment creditor's affidavit[2]

71.5—(1) The judgment creditor must file an affidavit[GL] or affidavits— **71.5**

(a) by the person who served the order (unless it was served by the court) giving the details of how and when it was served;

(b) stating either that—

(i) the person ordered to attend court has not requested payment of his travelling expenses

(ii) the judgment creditor has paid a sum in accordance with such a request; and

(c) stating how much of the judgment debt remains unpaid.

(2) The judgment creditor must either—

(a) file the affidavit[GL] or affidavits not less than 2 days before the hearing; or

(b) produce it or them at the hearing.

Proof of service

Proof that the judgment debtor has been served is essential. This is no mere formality as a debtor who fails to attend can be committed to prison for contempt of court; see r.71.8. Thus formal proof of service is essential and r.71.5 is one of the few rules in the CPR which requires an affidavit. **71.5.1**

Conduct of the hearing[3]

71.6—(1) The person ordered to attend court will be questioned on oath. **71.6**

[1] Introduced by the Civil Procedure (Amendment No.4) Rules 2001 (SI 2001/2792).
[2] Introduced by the Civil Procedure (Amendment No.4) Rules 2001 (SI 2001/2792).
[3] Introduced by the Civil Procedure (Amendment No.4) Rules 2001 (SI 2001/2792).

(2) The questioning will be carried out by a court officer unless the court has ordered that the hearing shall be before a judge.

(3) The judgment creditor or his representative—

(a) may attend and ask questions where the questioning takes place before a court officer; and

(b) must attend and conduct the questioning if the hearing is before a judge.

Questioning

71.6.1 All questioning is carried out by a court officer initially. Only if there is a difficulty which requires the greater authority of a judge will the examination be heard by a judge (see para.2.2 of PD71). The judgment creditor may attend before the court officer but must attend and conduct the questioning if the hearing is before a judge. "Judge" includes masters, district judges and deputies (r.2.3(1)). See further *Republic of Costa Rica v Stronsberg* (1880) 16 Ch.D.8, noted at para.71.2.2.

Questioning by a court officer follows the standard format of completing Form EX140 or EX141 prescribed by PD71. (The forms are in the Forms Volume). These forms will not be used when questioning is conducted by or on behalf of the judgment creditor before the judge.

Adjournment of the hearing[1]

71.7 **71.7 If the hearing is adjourned, the court will give directions as to the manner in which notice of the new hearing is to be served on the judgment debtor.**

Adjournment

71.7.1 If the hearing is adjourned e.g. for the debtor to produce documents—the better practice is for the debtor to be given the date and time of the new hearing before leaving court. Additionally or alternatively the debtor should be asked to agree to postal service of notice of the new date. The expense of further personal service should be avoided if possible.

Failure to comply with order[2]

71.8 **71.8—(1) If a person against whom an order has been made under rule 71.2—**

(a) fails to attend court;

(b) refuses at the hearing to take the oath or to answer any question; or

(c) otherwise fails to comply with the order,

the court will refer the matter to a High Court judge or circuit judge.

(2) That judge may, subject to paragraphs (3) and (4), make a committal order against the person.

(3) A committal order for failing to attend court may not be made unless the judgment creditor has complied with rules 71.4 and 71.5.

(4) If a committal order is made, the judge will direct that—

(a) the order shall be suspended provided that the person—

[1] Introduced by the Civil Procedure (Amendment No.4) Rules 2001 (SI 2001/2792).
[2] Introduced by the Civil Procedure (Amendment No.4) Rules 2001 (SI 2001/2792) and amended by Civil Procedure (Amendment No.5) Rules 2001 (SI 2001/4015).

(i) attends court at a time and place specified in the order; and

(ii) complies with all the terms of that order and the original order; and

(b) if the person fails to comply with any term on which the committal order is suspended he shall be brought before a judge to consider whether the committal order should be discharged.

Suspended committal order

The most common of the three types of non-compliance listed in r.71.8(1) is the debtor's failure to attend court to be examined. The examination itself would have been before a court officer or district judge. That person certifies the debtor's non-attendance (para.8, PD71). The High Court judge or circuit judge, in reliance on that certificate then makes a committal order (r.71.8(2)) but suspends it provided that the debtor attends on a subsequent occasion. If the debtor immediately does so, the examination then takes place, and the suspended committal order is thereupon discharged. **71.8.1**

If the debtor fails to attend pursuant to the suspended committal order a warrant for his arrest is then issued (see para.8, PD71) but instead of being taken to prison to serve the committal sentence he is brought before the court pursuant to r.71.8(4)(b) This hearing can be before a master or district judge (para.8.4, PD71). The judge's task is to consider whether the committal order should be discharged (e.g. because of irregularity). In practice the order is invariably discharged because the debtor agrees to be examined there and then thus completing the purpose of Pt 71.

If for any reason the judge decides not to discharge the committal order (e.g. because the debtor refuses to answer questions) then a warrant of committal is issued immediately (para.8.6, PD71) and thereupon the debtor is conveyed to prison to serve the sentence. The judge must be satisfied beyond reasonable doubt as required by para.8 of PD71.

Some commentators have suggested that the new procedure is not compliant with the European Convention on Human Rights. There is nothing in Strasbourg jurisprudence to prevent civil courts having a proper machinery in place for the purpose of enforcing its orders.

The new procedure is clearly intended to be ECHR compliant and it is submitted that it is.

In practice actual committal to prison is rare. The bringing of the debtor to court is invariably sufficient to complete the purpose of Pt 71.

Contumelious conduct

In order to be efficacious the procedure under Pt 71 is necessarily robust. Even so, as the Court of Appeal points out in *Islamic Investment Company of the Gulf (Bahamas) Ltd v Symphony Gems* [2008] EWCA Civ 389, to make a committal order, even a suspended committal order, is a serious matter which requires a cautious approach and proof that the debtor has been contumacious with the court. In that case there was some suggestion that the alleged contemnor was in India and was subject to an order of the Indian court prohibiting him from being out of India on the date of the hearing in England that he failed to attend. Accordingly the evidence did not show to the criminal standard of proof that he had been contumacious with the court so a suspended committal order ought not to have been made. (In the event the cross-examination as to means was taking place in another room as the Court of Appeal was hearing the appeal). **71.8.2**

PRACTICE DIRECTION—ORDERS TO OBTAIN INFORMATION FROM JUDGMENT DEBTORS

71PD.1 *This Practice Direction supplements CPR Part 71*

Application notice—rule 71.2

1.1 An application by a judgment creditor under rule 71.2(1) must be made by filing an application notice in Practice Form **N316** if the application is to question an individual judgment debtor, or **N316A** if the application is to question an officer of a company or other corporation.

1.2 The application notice must—

(1) state the name and address of the judgment debtor;

(2) identify the judgment or order which the judgment creditor is seeking to enforce;

(3) if the application is to enforce a judgment or order for the payment of money, state the amount presently owed by the judgment debtor under the judgment or order;

(4) if the judgment debtor is a company or other corporation, state—

(a) the name and address of the officer of that body whom the judgment creditor wishes to be ordered to attend court; and

(b) his position in the company;

(5) if the judgment creditor wishes the questioning to be conducted before a judge, state this and give his reasons;

(6) if the judgment creditor wishes the judgment debtor (or other person to be questioned) to be ordered to produce specific documents at court, identify those documents; and

(7) if the application is to enforce a judgment or order which is not for the payment of money, identify the matters about which the judgment creditor wishes the judgment debtor (or officer of the judgment debtor) to be questioned.

1.3 The court officer considering the application notice—

(1) may, in any appropriate case, refer it to a judge (rule 3.2); and

(2) will refer it to a judge for consideration, if the judgment creditor requests the judgment debtor (or officer of the judgment debtor) to be questioned before a judge.

Order to attend court—rule 71.2

71PD.2 **2.1** The order will provide for the judgment debtor (or other person to be questioned) to attend the county court for the district in which he resides or carries on business, unless a judge decides otherwise.

2.2 The order will provide for questioning to take place before a judge only if the judge considering the request decides that there are compelling reasons to make such an order.

Service of order to attend court—rule 71.3

71PD.3 **3** Service of an order to attend court for questioning may be carried out by—

(a) the judgment creditor (or someone acting on the judgment creditor's behalf);
(b) a High Court enforcement officer; or
(c) a county court bailiff.

Attendance at court: normal procedure—rule 71.6

4.1 The court officer will ask a standard series of questions, as set out in the forms in Appendixes A and B to this practice direction. The form in Appendix A will be used if the person being questioned is the judgment debtor, and the form in Appendix B will be used if the person is an officer of a company or other corporation. **71PD.4**

4.2 The judgment creditor or his representative may either—
(1) attend court and ask questions himself; or
(2) request the court officer to ask additional questions, by attaching a list of proposed additional questions to his application notice.

4.3 The court officer will—
(1) make a written record of the evidence given, unless the proceedings are tape recorded;
(2) at the end of the questioning, read the record of evidence to the person being questioned and ask him to sign it; and
(3) if the person refuses to sign it, note that refusal on the record of evidence.

Attendance at court: procedure where the order is to attend before a judge—rule 71.6

5.1 Where the hearing takes places before a judge, the questioning will be conducted by the judgment creditor or his representative, and the standard questions in the forms in Appendixes A and B will not be used. **71PD.5**

5.2 The proceedings will be tape recorded and the court will not make a written record of the evidence.

Failure to comply with order: reference to judge—rule 71.8(1)

6 If a judge or court officer refers to a High Court judge or circuit judge the failure of a judgment debtor to comply with an order under rule 71.2, he shall certify in writing the respect in which the judgment debtor failed to comply with the order. **71PD.6**

Suspended committal order—rules 71.8(2) and (4)(a)

7.1 A committal order will be suspended provided that the person attends court at a time and place specified in the order (rule 71.8(4)(a)(i)). The appointment specified will be— **71PD.7**
(1) before a judge, if—
  (a) the original order under rule 71.2 was to attend before a judge; or
  (b) the judge making the suspended committal order so directs; and
(2) otherwise, before a court officer.

7.2 Rule 71.3 and paragraph 3 of this practice direction (service of order), and rule 71.5(1)(a) and (2) (affidavit of service), apply with the necessary changes to a suspended committal order as they do to an order to attend court.

Breach of terms on which committal order is suspended—rule 71.8(4)(b)

71PD.8 8.1 If—

(1) the judgment debtor fails to attend court at the time and place specified in the suspended committal order; and

(2) it appears to the judge or court officer that the judgment debtor has been duly served with the order,

the judge or court officer will certify in writing the debtor's failure to attend.

8.2 If the judgment debtor fails to comply with any other term on which the committal order was suspended, the judge or court officer will certify in writing the non-compliance and set out details of it.

8.3 A warrant to bring the judgment debtor before a judge may be issued on the basis of a certificate under paragraph 8.1 or 8.2.

8.4 The hearing under rule 71.8(4)(b) may take place before a master or district judge.

8.5 At the hearing the judge will discharge the committal order unless he is satisfied beyond reasonable doubt that—

(1) the judgment debtor has failed to comply with—

(a) the original order to attend court; and

(b) the terms on which the committal order was suspended; and

(2) both orders have been duly served on the judgment debtor.

8.6 If the judge decides that the committal order should not be discharged, a warrant of committal shall be issued immediately.

Editorial note

71PD.9 The following forms which are annexed to this PD can be found in the *Civil Procedure Forms Volume*:

- **EX140**
- **EX141**

PART 72

Third Party Debt Orders

Contents 72.0.1

Editorial introduction

Third Party Debt Orders, introduced as from March 25, 2002 replaced the familiar method of enforcement known as "garnishee proceedings". The new Part is clear and straightforward and the basic purpose remains unchanged. Put simply, if a judgment debtor is owed money by a third party the judgment creditor can obtain an order that the third party should pay the judgment creditor. The order is obtained without notice on an interim basis. A hearing follows when the court decides whether or not to make a final third party debt order. 72.0.2

A bank account in credit is a debt due by the bank to its customer. Consequently a judgment creditor who has the bank details of the judgment debtor (possibly as a result of obtaining information pursuant to Pt 71) can obtain a third party debt order against the bank.

The procedure requires the third party bank or building society to search and disclose information to the court and judgment creditor (r.72.6). Any third party, or judgment debtor, who objects to the making of the order must file and serve written evidence stating the grounds for the objection (r.72.8).

Rule 72.7 enables the judgment debtor to obtain "a hardship payment order".

Hearings are before a master or district judge. Part 72 is supplemented by a practice direction.

Related sources

- Practice Direction—Third Party Debt Orders (para.72PD.1) 72.0.3
- Practice Direction—Enforcement of Judgments and Orders (para.70PD.1)
- Supreme Court Act 1981 ss.40 and 139 (Vol.2, Section 9A)
- Banking Act 1987
- *Sch.1, RSC O.77, r.16—Proceedings* by and against the Crown, attachment of debts
- Sch.2, CCR O.27—Attachment of earnings
- Sch.2, CCR O.42, r.14—Attachment of debts etc.

Forms

- **N349** Application for third party debt order 72.0.4
- **N84** Interim third party debt order
- **N85** Final third party debt order

Scope of this Part and interpretation[1]

72.1 **72.1—(1) This Part contains rules which provide for a judgment creditor to obtain an order for the payment to him of money which a third party who is within the jurisdiction owes to the judgment debtor.**

(2) In this Part "bank or building society" includes any person carrying on a business in the course of which he lawfully accepts deposits in the United Kingdom.

"Within the jurisdiction"

72.1.1 The Rule requires the third party to be within the jurisdiction. There is no power to make an order under this Rule if he is not. Temporary physical presence within the jurisdiction at the time of the interim order will suffice; and if the third party has agreed to submit to the jurisdiction for the purpose of the application, that will be sufficient even though he has left the jurisdiction before the interim order has been made (*SCF Finance Co Ltd v Masri (No.3)* [1987] Q.B. 1028). There is no requirement that the third party debt must be properly recoverable within the jurisdiction. As a matter of discretion, however, the court will not attach a third party debt order where, although the third party is within the jurisdiction, the debt is recoverable outside the jurisdiction, if to do so is likely to expose the third party to the risk of having to pay the debt twice over (*Martin v Nadel* [1906] 2 KB 26; *SCF Finance Co Ltd v Masri (No.3)* [1987] Q.B. 1028; *Interpool Limited v Galani* [1988] Q.B. 738). To resist an order the third party must show that such a risk is real or substantial (*Swiss Bank Corp v Boehmische Industrial Bank* [1923] 1 K.B. 673 —where a statement in an affidavit that an order to pay the debt would leave the third party "*liable to an action to recover the same debt brought in a competent court in a foreign place*", which specified neither the "*competent court*" nor the "*foreign place*" was held to be too vague to establish a risk of double payment).

It is an integral feature of third party debt proceedings that on compliance the third party is discharged from liability to the judgment debtor to the extent of his payment. It is for this reason that the House of Lords overruled the Court of Appeal in *Societe Eram Shipping Co Ltd v Hong Kong & Shanghai Banking Corporation Ltd* [2003] UKHL 30; [2004] 1 A.C. 260. (A Hong Kong bank with a branch in London is "within the jurisdiction".)

The House of Lords also overruled the Court of Appeal in *Kuwait Oil Tanker Co SAK v UBS AG* [2003] UKHL 31; [2004] 1 A.C. 300. The judgment creditor sought to attach debts due to the judgment debtor from a Swiss bank with a branch in London. However, the debtor had an account in Switzerland, not London,and the House of Lords held that as the third party debt proceedings were enforcement against a debt due in Switzerland, under art.16(5) of the Lugano Convention the Swiss courts had exclusive jurisdiction.

"Lawfully accepts deposits in the United Kingdom"

72.1.2 Section 6 of the Banking Act 1987 describes a "*deposit taking business*" as one where (a) in the course of business money received by way of deposit is lent to others or (b) any other activity of the business is financed, wholly or to any material extent, out of the capital of or the interest on money received by way of deposit. For the meaning of "deposit" see s.5 of that Act. (For a case examining whether there was a deposit taking business see *SCF Finance Co Limited v Masri (No.2)* [1987] QB 1002). Section 3 of the Banking Act 1987 imposes restrictions on the acceptance of deposits in the course of carrying on a deposit taking business unless either the person accepting the deposit is an institution authorised by the Bank of England or, by s.4, is exempt from the provisions of s.3. Schedule II to the Act lists institutions which are exempt and therefore may be regarded as deposit taking institutions and so subject to third party debt orders.

---

[1] Introduced by the Civil Procedure (Amendment No.4) Rules 2001 (SI 2001/2792) and amended by the Civil Procedure (Amendment No.5) Rules 2001 (SI 2001/4015).

The National Savings Bank

Although the National Savings Bank is listed in Sch.II of the Banking Act 1987 and is therefore to be regarded as a "*deposit taking institution*" it retains its anomalous status as being under the control of the Crown. Therefore, a third party debt order under Pt 72 cannot be obtained against the National Savings Bank. See however instead an analogous procedure under r.66.7 (Section 139(2) of the SCA 1981 enables the Lord Chancellor to order that s.27 of the Crown Proceedings Act 1947 should not apply to the National Savings Bank but no such order has been made). 72.1.3

Third party debt order[1]

72.2—(1) Upon the application of a judgment creditor, the court may make an order (a "final third party debt order") requiring a third party to pay to the judgment creditor— 72.2

- **(a) the amount of any debt due or accruing due to the judgment debtor from the third party; or**
- **(b) so much of that debt as is sufficient to satisfy the judgment debt and the judgment creditor's costs of the application.**

(2) The court will not make an order under paragraph 1 without first making an order (an "interim third party debt order") as provided by rule 72.4(2).

(3) In deciding whether money standing to the credit of the judgment debtor in an account to which section 40 of the Supreme Court Act 1981 or section 108 of the County Courts Act 1984 relates may be made the subject of a third party debt order, any condition applying to the account that a receipt for money deposited in the account must be produced before any money is withdrawn will be disregarded.

(Section 40(3) of the Supreme Court Act 1981 and section 108(3) of the County Courts Act 1984 contain a list of other conditions applying to accounts that will also be disregarded.)

"Any debt due or accruing due"

It is essential that the relationship of creditor and debtor should exist between the judgment debtor and the third party respectively. If the judgment debtor could sue the third party for the amount and recover it, it is plain that there is an attachable debt, but this is not an infallible test. 72.2.1

There must be money "*due*" to the judgment debtor. In the case, for example, of a building contract in the RIBA form where the builder is paid on the certificate of the architect, money in the hands of the building owner cannot be attached until a certificate is issued and then only for the amount mentioned in that certificate (*Dunlop and Rankin Limited v Hendall Steel Structures Pitchers (Garnishees)* [1957] 1 W.L.R. 1102). A third party debt order cannot accelerate the time for payment of the debt. Where the debt is not due there is nothing to be attached (*Webb v Stenton* (1883) 11 Q.B.D. 518; *Re Greenwood* [1901] 1 Ch 887). A judgment creditor cannot, by means of a third party debt order, stand in a better position as regards a third party than did the judgment debtor; "*he can only obtain what the judgment debtor could honestly give him*" (*Re General Horticultural Co Ex p. Whitehouse* (1886) 32 Ch.D. 512).

***Section 40 Supreme Court Act 1981*/Section 108 County Courts Act 1984**

These Sections greatly extended the earlier restricted position in relation to the attachment of deposit accounts. The Sections apply to the following accounts: 72.2.2

- (a) Any deposit account with a bank or other deposit taking institution; and
- (b) Any withdrawable share account with any deposit taking institution.

---

[1] Introduced by the Civil Procedure (Amendment No.4) Rules 2001 (SI 2001/2792).

The Sections enable certain conditions to be ignored e.g. conditions that notice is required before money can be withdrawn; that a personal application must be made; that a bank passbook be produced. Section 40 of the Supreme Court Act 1981 is in Vol.2 at para.9A–142 and s.108 of the County Courts Act 1984 is at Vol.2, para.9A–628.

Rent

72.2.3 Rent due can be attached (*Mitchell v Lee* (1866–7) L.R. 2 Q.B. 259). But though it accrues from day to day under the Apportionment Act 1870, it is not attachable until it becomes payable by the tenant (*Barnett v Eastman* (1898) 67 L.J. Q.B. 517). Subject to the amount of the judgment debt—and the rent—the more usual way to attach rent is the appointment of a receiver (see Pt 69).

Joint judgment against two or more persons

72.2.4 A judgment creditor with a judgment against two or more persons can attach a debt owing to any of his judgment debtors (*Miller v Mynn* (1859) 23 L.J. Q.B. 324).

Debt of unascertained amount

72.2.5 The fact that the amount of a debt or accruing debt is not ascertained will not prevent an interim third party debt order being made (*Lucy v Wood* [1884] WN 58; *De Pass v Capital and Industries Corp* [1891] 1 Q.B. 216). In *O'Driscoll v Manchester Insurance Committee* [1915] 3 K.B. 499 money payable to a doctor by an insurance committee was held to be attachable after receipt by the committee of funds received by them to pay the doctor even though the precise sum due to him had not been ascertained. The garnishee (now called a third party) was found as a fact to be indebted in a specified sum at the date of the enquiry by the court. While this did not represent the entire indebtedness it was the actual amount ascertained and proved to be due at the date of the enquiry.

Debt already paid by cheque

72.2.6 Where the judgment debtor has been paid by a cheque which is stopped by the third party upon being served with an interim third party order, there will be an attachable debt (*Cohen v Hale* (1878) 3 Q.B.D. 371). But the third party is not under any duty to stop a cheque already sent by him at the time of service of the interim third party debt order and if he does not do so there will be no debt to be attached (*Elwell v Jackson* (1885) 1 T.L.R. 454; *cf. Ex p. Richdale* (1881–2) 19 Ch.D. 409).

Executors and personal representatives

72.2.7 When a third party who was indebted to the judgment debtor has died, an order can be served upon his executors or personal representatives but must be directed to them as such and not personally (*Stevens v Phelips* (1874–5) L.R. 10 Ch App 417).

Bill of exchange before maturity

72.2.8 Money which will become payable by the third party when a bill of exchange matures is attachable. The order will suspend execution until maturity and restrain the judgment debtor by injunction from dealing with the bill in the interim (*Hyam v Freeman* (1890) 35 S.J. 87).

Funds derived under international treaty

72.2.9 In *Philipp Brothers Limited v Republic of Sierra Leone* [1995] 1 Lloyd's Rep. 289, the judgment debtor held monies in a bank account representing funds provided by the EC under a programme of financial aid. It was held that the transactions under which the judgment debtor received the funds were governed not by municipal law but by international treaty. Obligations arising thereunder were not justiciable in an English court and no trust or other equitable right under English law arose. The account was a debt due from the bank and the garnishee order absolute (now a third party debt order) was upheld.

Wages and pensions

72.2.10 These cannot be attached by third party debt orders. See instead Attachment of Earnings Act *1971* and Sch.2, CCR O.27.

Debts due from the Crown

72.2.11 The Pt 72 procedure cannot be used against the Crown as third party. An alternative procedure is provided by Crown Proceedings Act 1947, s.27 and is governed by Pt 66. For the position of the National Savings Bank see para.72.1.3.

Effect of third party debt order on an assigned debt

It seems that where a judgment debtor assigned the debt to a fourth party before the interim order was served there is no debt due to him from the third party to attach even though the order was served before the third party had notice of the assignment (*Holt v Heatherfield* [1942] 2 K.B. 1). **72.2.12**

Debt recoverable outside the jurisdiction

In *Kuwait Oil Tanker Co SAK v Qabazard* [2003] UKHL 31; [2004] 1 A.C. 300, the judgment creditor sought to attach debts due to the judgment debtor from a Swiss Bank with a London Branch. However, the debtor had an account in Switzerland not London and the House of Lords held that as the third party debt proceedings were enforcement against a debt due in Switzerland, under art.16(5) of the Lugano Convention the Swiss courts had exclusive jurisdiction. See also *Société Eram Shipping Co Ltd v Compagnie Internationale de Navigation* noted at para.72.1.1 above. **72.2.13**

General principles

See the general principles discussed para.73.4.5. The general principles applied by the courts in third party debt orders and charging orders are the same. **72.2.14**

Debt due to judgment debtor and another

In *Hirschon v Evans* [1938] 2 K.B. 801 it was held that it was not possible to obtain a garnishee order (now a third party debt order) against a bank account in the joint names of the debtor and his wife. This is in contrast to execution; see para.sc46.1.2.1 and *Cohen v Cohen* (1982) 12 Fam Law 251. **72.2.15**

Trust funds

Only rarely can trust funds be attached through a third party debt order. Money held by trustees cannot be attached by a creditor of the settlor (*Vyse v Brown* (1884) 13 QBD 199). A trustee is not a debtor of the beneficiary unless he holds money which it is his duty to pay to the beneficiary (*Webb v Stenton* (1883) 11 QBD 518). Money held by a bank for a trustee is not a debt due to a beneficiary (*AIG Capital Partners Inc v Republic of Kazakhstan* [2005] EWHC 2239 (Comm); [2006] 1W.L.R. 1420, Aikens J). In these situations consider instead whether a receiver could be appointed under Part 69. **72.2.16**

A third party debt order will not be made if money isdue to the judgment debtor as trustee for another (*Roberts v Death* (1881) 8 QBD 319).

Application for third party debt order[1]

72.3—(1) An application for a third party debt order— **72.3**

(a) may be made without notice; and

(b)

(i) must be issued in the court which made the judgment or order which it is sought to enforce except that

(ii) if the proceedings have since been transferred to a different court, it must be issued in that court.

(2) The application notice must—

(a)

(i) be in the form; and

(ii) contain the information

required by the relevant practice direction; and

(b) be verified by a statement of truth.

[1] Introduced by the Civil Procedure (Amendment No.4) Rules 2001 (SI 2001/2792).

Form N349

72.3.1 The new rule clarifies and simplifies the procedure. An affidavit is no longer necessary. Form **N349** is drafted so as to require all necessary information and a statement of truth which must be signed by the judgment creditor or his solicitor.

Without notice

72.3.2 Applications for Third Party Debt Orders are made without notice. They are treated as urgent business and placed before the district judge or master on the same day as received and as soon as possible.

Venue

72.3.3 Note that the application must be issued in the court which made the judgment or, if proceedings have already been transferred, in the transferee court. This court may not be the judgment debtor's or the third party's local court. There is no provision for automatic transfer.

Speculative applications

72.3.4 As is made clear by para.1.3 of PD 72, applications must be informative and supported by evidence. The court will not grant speculative applications. In an appropriate case,the judgment creditor should consider an application under Pt 71.

Interim third party debt order[1]

72.4 **72.4—(1) An application for a third party debt order will initially be dealt with by a judge without a hearing.**

(2) The judge may make an interim third party debt order—

(a) fixing a hearing to consider whether to make a final third party debt order; and

(b) directing that until that hearing the third party must not make any payment which reduces the amount he owes the judgment debtor to less than the amount specified in the order.

(3) An interim third party debt order will specify the amount of money which the third party must retain, which will be the total of—

(a) the amount of money remaining due to the judgment creditor under the judgment or order; and

(b) an amount for the judgment creditor's fixed costs of the application, as specified in the relevant practice direction.

(4) An interim third party debt order becomes binding on a third party when it is served on him.

(5) The date of the hearing to consider the application shall be not less than 28 days after the interim third party debt order is made.

Form N84

72.4.1 An interim third party debt order is in Form **N84**. In addition to complying with the requirements of r.72.4 it also gives the judgment debtor information on "hardship payment orders" (as to which, see r.72.7).

Service of interim order[2]

72.5 **72.5—(1) Copies of an interim third party debt order, the ap-**

[1] Introduced by the Civil Procedure (Amendment No.4) Rules 2001 (SI 2001/2792).
[2] Introduced by the Civil Procedure (Amendment No.4) Rules 2001 (SI 2001/2792).

plication notice and any documents filed in support of it must be served—

(a) on the third party, not less than 21 days before the date fixed for the hearing; and

(b) on the judgment debtor not less than—

(i) 7 days after a copy has been served on the third party; and

(ii) 7 days before the date fixed for the hearing.

(2) If the judgment creditor serves the order, he must either—

(a) file a certificate of service not less than 2 days before the hearing; or

(b) produce a certificate of service at the hearing.

Service

Service is governed by Pt 6. See in particular r.6.3(2) for methods of service on a company and the table inr.6.9. Rule 72.5 requires service on the third party at least 21 days before the hearing and on the judgment debtor at least seven days before the hearing and seven days after the third party has been served. This is sensible. If the judgment debtor were to be served first it might be possible for him to defeat the application by assigning the debt. Further, in any case, there is always the risk that the third party acting in good faith will pay the debt (or, in the case of a bank account, that the funds will be withdrawn) thereby preventing it being attached. Accordingly service on the third party must be regarded as urgent. **72.5.1**

Service on a bank

Banks and other deposit taking institutions will invariably be incorporated. Thus they should be served at the principal office of the company or "*any place of business of the company within the jurisdiction which has a real connection with the claim*". The better and safer practice is to formally serve the bank at its registered office and also to send copy of the order etc to any branch where it is known or suspected that the debtor has an account. As to the obligations of a bank or building society on being served with an interim third party debt order, see r.72.6. **72.5.2**

Obligations of third parties served with interim order[1]

72.6—(1) A bank or building society served with an interim third party debt order must carry out a search to identify all accounts held with it by the judgment debtor. **72.6**

(2) The bank or building society must disclose to the court and the creditor within 7 days of being served with the order, in respect of each account held by the judgment debtor—

(a) the number of the account;

(b) whether the account is in credit; and

(c) if the account is in credit—

(i) whether the balance of the account is sufficient to cover the amount specified in the order;

(ii) the amount of the balance at the date it was served with the order, if it is less than the amount specified in the order; and

(iii) whether the bank or building society asserts any right to the money in the account, whether pur-

[1] Introduced by the Civil Procedure (Amendment No.4) Rules 2001 (SI 2001/2792), and amended by the Civil Procedure (Amendment No.5) Rules 2001 (SI 2001/4015).

suant to a right of set-off or otherwise, and if so giving details of the grounds of that assertion.

(3) If—

(a) the judgment debtor does not hold an account with the bank or building society; or

(b) the bank or building society is unable to comply with the order for any other reason (for example, because it has more than one account holder whose details match the information contained in the order, and cannot identify which account the order applies to),

the bank or building society must inform the court and the judgment creditor of that fact within 7 days of being served with the order.

(4) Any third party other than a bank or building society served with an interim third party debt order must notify the court and the judgment creditor in writing within 7 days of being served with the order, if he claims—

(a) not to owe any money to the judgment debtor; or

(b) to owe less than the amount specified in the order.

Scope of provision

72.6.1 Rule 72.6 codifies into rule form obligations which had been placed on third parties by case law. Banks and building societies are subject to rr.72.6(1), (2) and (3), whereas all other third parties are subject to rr.72.6(4).

It is to be hoped that the third party will comply with his obligations under this Rule (which are clearly spelt out on Form **N84**, the interim third party debt order), but the inevitable question arises what if he does not? In the case of a third party other than a bank or building society the answer is straightforward. If he has not complied with r.72.6(4) the court will be entitled to assume that the debt is not disputed and to make a final third party debt order.

Experience in practice is that, despite the short time limit, banks do comply with the requirements of the rule.

Service of an interim third party debt order does not operate as a transfer of the property in the debt but is an equitable charge on the debt. The third party cannot pay the debt to anybody without incurring the risk of having to pay it over again (*Galbraith v Grimshaw* [1910] A.C. 508). In *Reskin v Severo Sibrisko etc. and the Bank for Russian Trade Ltd* [1933] 1 K.B. 47, it was held that service of an interim order on the third party (the judgment debtor's bank) operated as a revocation of the debtor's instruction to close the account and transfer funds.

Obligations of third party

72.6.2 The order must name the debtor so as to establish his identity as the third party's creditor or it will not bind the third party (*Koch v Mineral Ore Syndicate* (1910) 54 S.J. 600, CA). A third party should not pay the judgment creditor merely upon an interim order (*Re Webster* [1907] 1 K.B. 623).He must inform the court of any claim to, or lien upon, the debt; and if with knowledge thereof he pays the judgment creditor he will still have to pay the person entitled to the claim or lien (*The Leader* (1867–9) L.R. 2 A. & E. 314). As all debts"due or accruing" are attached the third party must not appropriate any part of his debt to any other purpose, even though he owes more to the debtor than the latter's liability to the judgment creditor: thus a banker served with an interim order may dishonour any cheque drawn upon him by the judgment debtor (*Rogers v Whiteley* [1892] A.C. 118).

If a third party receives notice that the debtor has assigned the surplus of the debt that would remain after satisfying a final third party debt order, he may not appropriate such surplus in satisfaction of another third party debt order served after notice of the assignment (*Yates v Terry* [1902] 1 K.B. 527).

Banks and Building Societies need to comply with the obligations of r.72.6.

Unauthorised payment

The third party should not pay the creditor upon service of an interim order but should await the court's decision on whether or not the order is to be made final. If the third party does so and the order is not then made final, the third party runs the risk of having to pay twice as the bank had to in *Crantrave Ltd v Lloyds Bank Plc* [2000] Q.B. 917. **72.6.3**

Accounts in joint names

To be successfully attached all account holders must be judgment debtors; see para.72.2.15. A bank is under no obligation to disclose or freeze an account in the name of the judgment debtor and another (such as a spouse, civil partner or business partner). **72.6.4**

Arrangements for debtors in hardship[1]

72.7—(1) If— **72.7**

(a) a judgment debtor is an individual;

(b) he is prevented from withdrawing money from his account with a bank or building society as a result of an interim third party debt order; and

(c) he or his family is suffering hardship in meeting ordinary living expenses as a result,

the court may, on an application by the judgment debtor, make an order permitting the bank or building society to make a payment or payments out of the account ("a hardship payment order").

(2) An application for a hardship payment order may be made—

(a) in High Court proceedings, at the Royal Courts of Justice or to any district registry; and

(b) in county court proceedings, to any county court.

(3) A judgment debtor may only apply to one court for a hardship payment order.

(4) An application notice seeking a hardship payment order must—

(a) include detailed evidence explaining why the judgment debtor needs a payment of the amount requested; and

(b) be verified by a statement of truth.

(5) Unless the court orders otherwise, the application notice—

(a) must be served on the judgment creditor at least 2 days before the hearing; but

(b) does not need to be served on the third party.

(6) A hardship payment order may—

(a) permit the third party to make one or more payments out of the account; and

(b) specify to whom the payments may be made.

Hardship payment orders

Hardship payment orders are an innovation of the CPR. The service of an interim third party debt order on a bank or building society has the effect of freezing the account. The third party bank or building society cannot pay any of the judgment debtor's cheques or allow him to withdraw cash without authority of the court. Clearly this is capable of working hardship to the judgment debtor if, for example, he is unable to pay his mortgage or rent or buy food for himself and his family. There will be **72.7.1**

[1] Introduced by the Civil Procedure (Amendment No.4) Rules 2001 (SI 2001/2792).

inevitably some time delay prior to service of the interim third party debt order and the hearing to decide whether it should be made final. The third party is entitled to at least 21 days notice but in practice may receive much more. The provision for a hardship payment order seeks to strike a balance between the rights of the judgment creditor and the rights of the judgment debtor and enables the judgment debtor to apply to the court for specified payments to be made to him notwithstanding that the account has been frozen by the interim third party debt order.

Venue

72.7.2 The debtor does not have to make application to the court which made the interim order and the application will not be transferred (see para.5.2 PD 72) and will be dealt with by the court to which application is made. As noted at para.72.3.3 the creditor's application will not necessarily be in the debtor's local court. Thus r.72.7 enables the debtor to apply to any court though he can apply to only one court.

Service

72.7.3 Although the general rule is that any application for a hardship payment order has to be served on the creditor at least two days before the hearing (r.72.7(5)) the court can order otherwise. See further para.5 PD 72 which enables the court to deal with the application without notice and to allow the creditor to make representations by telephone.

Evidence

72.7.4 The judgment debtor should file documentary evidence in support of his application (see para.5.6 PD 72) unless the debtor wishes to oppose the application for a third party debt order and has requested a transfer (pursuant to para.4 of PD 72) to the court where the application for a hardship payment order is pending.

Advancing the hearing to further consider the application...

72.7.5 Where the application for the third party debt order and the application for the hardship payment order are both proceeding in the same court it is generally preferable to advance the hearing date of the further consideration required by r.72.8 to be heard simultaneously with debtor's application. Costs are saved and all issues can be resolved at one hearing. Judgment creditors should ask the court to do this if the court has not already done so of its own initiative. Unfortunately, this is not possible where both applications are in different courts (*cf.* r.72.3(1)(b) and paras 5.2 and 5.3 of PD 72).

Further consideration of the application[1]

72.8 **72.8—(1) If the judgment debtor or the third party objects to the court making a final third party debt order, he must file and serve written evidence stating the grounds for his objections.**

(2) If the judgment debtor or the third party knows or believes that a person other than the judgment debtor has any claim to the money specified in the interim order, he must file and serve written evidence stating his knowledge of that matter.

(3) If—

(a) the third party has given notice under rule 72.6 that he does not owe any money to the judgment debtor, or that the amount which he owes is less than the amount specified in the interim order; and

(b) the judgment creditor wishes to dispute this,

the judgment creditor must file and serve written evidence setting out the grounds on which he disputes the third party's case.

(4) *Written* evidence under paragraphs (1), (2) or (3) must be

[1] Introduced by the Civil Procedure (Amendment No.4) Rules 2001 (SI 2001/2792).

filed and served on each other party as soon as possible, and in any event not less than 3 days before the hearing.

(5) If the court is notified that some person other than the judgment debtor may have a claim to the money specified in the interim order, it will serve on that person notice of the application and the hearing.

(6) At the hearing the court may—

(a) make a final third party debt order;

(b) discharge the interim third party debt order and dismiss the application;

(c) decide any issues in dispute between the parties, or between any of the parties and any other person who has a claim to the money specified in the interim order; or

(d) direct a trial of any such issues, and if necessary give directions.

The hearing

Having made the interim third party debt order on a without notice basis there must now be a hearing to decide whether that order should be discharged or whether a final third party debt order should be made. In practice most cases are straightforward. The third party is not prejudiced by the making of an order (see r.72.9). The third party owes the money anyway and is merely directed to pay it to the judgment creditor instead of the judgment debtor and to the same extent receives discharge of his obligations. In all cases the third party should have given notice to the court pursuant to r.72.7. **72.8.1**

Rule 72.8 requires written evidence if either the judgment debtor or third party objects to the final order.

Rule 72.8(6) makes it clear that the District Judge or Master can decide the issues raised by the parties. Only exceptionally will it be necessary to give directions and order a trial pursuant to r.72.8(6)(d).

Often it will not be worthwhile for the judgment creditor to contest an issue and he may prefer to cut his losses and abandon the application either prior to or at the hearing; in which case he may be liable in costs (*Wintle v Williams* (1858) 3 H & N 288; 27 L.J. Exch. 311).

Transfer

A judgment debtor who wishes to oppose the application may seek a transfer to another court; see para.4 of PD 72. **72.8.2**

"The court may"

The use of the word "may" indicates that there is a discretionary power. In *Newman v Rook* (1858) 4 C.B. 434 it was held that a garnishee (now a third party) must set up a prima facie case before the court would order trial of an issue. **72.8.3**

In particular a final order will be refused where it would be inequitable (*Roberts Petroleum Ltd v Bernard Kenny Ltd* [1983] A.C. 192). It may be inequitable to prefer one creditor over another where the judgment debtor is clearly insolvent (*Pritchard v Westminster Bank Limited* [1969] 1 W.L.R. 547). However it may not be inequitable to prefer a creditor who is actively pursuing his debt when others are not (*FG Hemisphere Associates v Republic of Congo* (2006) *The Times*, February 27, 2006, Cooke J). In considering whether or not to exercise its discretion to make a final order the court must bear in mind not only the position of the judgment creditor, the judgment debtor and the third party but also the position of the other creditors. The court would not make a final order if there are proceedings underway for distribution of available assets of the judgment debtor among all creditors on a percentage basis (*D Wilson (Birmingham) Limited v Metropolitan Property Developments Limited* [1975] 2 All E.R. 814; *Rainbow v Moorgate Properties Limited* [1975] 2 All E.R. 821—a case on charging orders in which identical considerations apply). If there is doubt whether the estate of a deceased is insolvent the money in the hands of the third party can be ordered to be paid into court pending an enquiry whether or not the estate is insolvent (*George Lee and Sons (Builders) Limited v Olink* [1972] 1 W.L.R. 214).

An order will not be made if the money is due to the judgment debtor as trustee for another (*Roberts v Death* (1881) 8 Q.B.D. 319). Similarly the court would not make an order if the third party can prove that he would still be liable in a foreign court (*Martin v Nadel* [1906] 2 K.B. 26 and see para.72.1.1).

Effect of final third party order[1]

72.9 **72.9—(1) A final third party debt order shall be enforceable as an order to pay money.**

(2) If—

(a) the third party pays money to the judgment creditor in compliance with a third party debt order; or

(b) the order is enforced against him,

the third party shall, to the extent of the amount paid by him or realised by enforcement against him, be discharged from his debt to the judgment debtor.

(3) Paragraph (2) applies even if the third party debt order, or the original judgment or order against the judgment debtor, is later set aside.

"Enforceable as an order to pay money"

72.9.1 It would be extremely unusual for a third party to refuse or fail to comply with a final order. If he considers that the order should not have been made and was present at the hearing his remedy is to appeal it. If he was not present or if new information has come to light he should promptly apply for the order to be set aside. A final order is a valid judgment of the court which can be enforced in the same way as any other order and thus, for example, the judgment creditor can issue execution to enforce payment by the third party.

"Effect of order"

72.9.2 The amount owed *to* the judgment debtor by the third party is reduced by what the third party pays under the order *and* any costs and expenses to which the third party is entitled (see para.72.11.2).

The amount owed *by* the judgment debtor to the judgment creditor is reduced by what the third party pays under the order *less* the judgment creditor's costs of the application including the court fee.

Money in court[2]

72.10 **72.10—(1) If money is standing to the credit of the judgment debtor in court—**

(a) the judgment creditor may not apply for a third party debt order in respect of that money; but

(b) he may apply for an order that the money in court, or so much of it as is sufficient to satisfy the judgment or order and the costs of the application, be paid to him.

(2) An application notice seeking an order under this rule must be served on—

(a) the judgment debtor; and

(b) the Accountant General at the Court Funds Office.

[1] Introduced by the Civil Procedure (Amendment No.4) Rules 2001 (SI 2001/2792).
[2] Introduced by the Civil Procedure (Amendment No.4) Rules 2001 (SI 2001/2792).

(3) If an application notice has been issued under this rule, the money in court must not be paid out until the application has been disposed of.

Effect of rule

It is not appropriate for the court itself to be the subject of court proceedings and therefore it is not, and never has been, possible to obtain a third party debt order in respect of money in court. However where there is money in court standing to the credit of the judgment debtor r.72.10 provides a simple and alternative procedure which a judgment creditor can use. **72.10.1**

It has been held (unreported) that money paid into court in other pending proceedings is not "money standing to the credit of the judgment debtor in court" as it remains subject to the direction of the court in those proceedings.

Costs[1]

72.11 If the judgment creditor is awarded costs on an application for an order under rule 72.2 or 72.10— **72.11**

(a) he shall, unless the court otherwise directs, retain those costs out of the money recovered by him under the order; and

(b) the costs shall be deemed to be paid first out of the money he recovers, in priority to judgment debt.

Scope of provision

Rule 72.11 deals only with costs of the judgment creditor who has made a successful application. (If he has made an unsuccessful application he may be ordered to pay costs especially of a third party who has been put to expense.) The effect of the rule is to reduce the judgment debt by the net amount received after deducting costs of the third party debt proceedings. **72.11.1**

Bank's expenses

Deposit taking institutions, independently of any award of costs, have a statutory right to deduct a sum for administrative expenses from the balance in their hands when complying with an interim third party debt order (see s.40A SCA 1981 at para.9A–144 and s.109 CCA 1984 at para.9A–631). The sum is £55.00 (see Attachment of Debts (Expenses) Order 1996 (SI 1996/3098)). **72.11.2**

[1] Introduced by the Civil Procedure (Amendment No.4) Rules 2001 (SI 2001/2792).

PRACTICE DIRECTION—THIRD PARTY DEBT ORDERS

72PD.1 *This Practice Direction supplements CPR Part 72*

Application notice—rule 72.3

1.1 An application for a third party debt order must be made by filing an application notice in Practice Form **N349**.

1.2 The application notice must contain the following information—

(1) the name and address of the judgment debtor;
(2) details of the judgment or order sought to be enforced;
(3) the amount of money remaining due under the judgment or order;
(4) if the judgment debt is payable by instalments, the amount of any instalments which have fallen due and remain unpaid;
(5) the name and address of the third party;
(6) if the third party is a bank or building society—
  (a) its name and the address of the branch at which the judgment debtor's account is believed to be held; and
  (b) the account number;
 or, if the judgment creditor does not know all or part of this information, that fact;
(7) confirmation that to the best of the judgment creditor's knowledge or belief the third party—
  (a) is within the jurisdiction; and
  (b) owes money to or holds money to the credit of the judgment debtor;
(8) if the judgment creditor knows or believes that any person other than the judgment debtor has any claim to the money owed by the third party—
  (a) his name and (if known) his address; and
  (b) such information as is known to the judgment creditor about his claim;
(9) details of any other applications for third party debt orders issued by the judgment creditor in respect of the same judgment debt; and
(10) the sources or grounds of the judgment creditor's knowledge or belief of the matters referred to in (7), (8) and (9).

1.3 The court will not grant speculative applications for third party debt orders, and will only make an interim third party debt order against a bank or building society if the judgment creditor's application notice contains evidence to substantiate his belief that the judgment debtor has an account with the bank or building society in question.

Interim third party debt order—rule 72.4

72PD.2 **2.** An interim third party debt order will specify the amount of money which the third party must retain (rule 72.4(3)). This will include, in respect of the judgment creditor's fixed costs of the application, the amount which would be allowed to the judgment creditor under rule 45.6 if the whole balance of the judgment debt were recovered.

Interim orders relating to bank or building society accounts—rule 72.6(1)–(3)

3.1 A bank or building society served with an interim third party debt order is only required by rule 72.6, unless the order states otherwise— **72PD.3**

(1) to retain money in accounts held solely by the judgment debtor (or, if there are joint judgment debtors, accounts held jointly by them or solely by either or any of them); and

(2) to search for and disclose information about such accounts.

3.2 The bank or building society is not required, for example, to retain money in, or disclose information about—

(1) accounts in the joint names of the judgment debtor and another person; or

(2) if the interim order has been made against a firm, accounts in the names of individual members of that firm.

Attachment of debts owed by a partnership

3A.1 This paragraph relates to debts due or accruing due to a judgment creditor from a partnership. **72PD.3A**

3A.2 An interim third party debt order under rule 72.4(2) relating to such debts must be served on—

(1) a member of the partnership within the jurisdiction;

(2) a person authorised by a partner; or

(3) some other person having the control or management of the partnership business.

3A.3 Where an order made under rule 72.4(2) requires a partnership to appear before the court, it will be sufficient for a partner to appear before the court.

Transfer

4. The court may, on an application by a judgment debtor who wishes to oppose an application for a third party debt order, transfer it to the court for the district where the judgment debtor resides or carries on business, or to another court. **72PD.4**

Applications for hardship payment orders—rule 72.7

5.1 The court will treat an application for a hardship payment order as being made— **72PD.5**

(1) in the proceedings in which the interim third party debt order was made; and

(2) under the same claim number,

regardless of where the judgment debtor makes the application.

5.2 An application for a hardship payment order will be dealt with by the court to which it is made.

(Rule 72.7(2) provides that an application may be made—

- in High Court proceedings, in the Royal Courts of Justice or to any district registry; and
- in county court proceedings, to any county court.)

5.3 If the application is made to a different court from that dealing with the application for a third party debt order—

(1) the application for a third party debt order will not be transferred; but

(2) the court dealing with that application will send copies of—

(a) the application notice; and

(b) the interim third party debt order

to the court hearing the application for a hardship payment order

5.4 Rule 72.7(3) requires an application for a hardship payment order to be served on the judgment creditor at least 2 days before the court is to deal with the application, unless the court orders otherwise. In cases of exceptional urgency the judgment debtor may apply for a hardship payment order without notice to the judgment creditor and a judge will decide whether to—

(1) deal with the application without it being served on the judgment creditor; or

(2) direct it to be served.

5.5 If the judge decides to deal with the application without it being served on the judgment creditor, where possible he will normally—

(1) direct that the judgment creditor be informed of the application; and

(2) give him the opportunity to make representations,

by telephone, fax or other appropriate method of communication.

5.6 The evidence filed by a judgment debtor in support of an application for a hardship payment order should include documentary evidence, for example (if appropriate) bank statements, wage slips and mortgage statements, to prove his financial position and need for the payment.

Final orders relating to building society accounts

72PD.6 **6.** A final third party debt order will not require a payment which would reduce to less than £1 the amount in a judgment debtor's account with a building society or credit union.

PART 73

Charging Orders, Stop Orders and Stop Notices

CPR 73

Contents 73.0.1

Editorial introduction

73.0.2 Part 73 came into force on March 25, 2002 replacing Sch.1, RSC O.50 and Sch.2, *CCR O.31. It contains the necessary* procedural rules to give effect to the Charging Orders Act 1979: the Act is in Vol.2, para.9B–1016. Section 1 Charging Orders Act 1979 provides that where a judgment debtor is required to pay a sum of money to a judgment creditor then, for the purpose of enforcing that judgment or order, the "appropriate court" may make an order (a "charging order") imposing on such property of the debtor as may be specified in the order, a charge for securing the payment of any money due under the judgment or order. Such an order must be in accordance with the provisions of the 1979 Act.

Broadly, there are three kinds of charging order: a charging order on land (the most common); a charging order on securities; and a charge over the debtor's interest in partnership property.

A charging order on land provides the judgment creditor with security equivalent to a mortgage over the land specified in the order. It is, of course, subject to any prior mortgages and charges. The charging order does not affect the accrual of judgment interest on High Court or County Court judgments (Judgments Act 1838: County Courts (Interest on Judgment Debts) Order 1991 (SI 1991/1184)). Subsequently, the judgment creditor can apply for an order for sale so that, subject to prior encumbrances, he can be paid his judgment debt (and accrued interest) out of the proceeds of sale.

Most charging orders are made in the County Court. The High Court jurisdiction is limited by s.1 of the Charging Orders Act 1979. The only situation where the High Court has exclusive jurisdiction is where the property to be charged is a fund lodged in the High Court. In all other cases where there is a High Court judgment the County Court has a concurrent jurisdiction to make charging orders. In the case of a County Court judgment (or a fund lodged in a County Court), the County Court has exclusive jurisdiction.

The jurisdiction of the County Court to make a charging order over land is unlimited: as to which County Court, see r.73.3(2).

The order is obtained in a two stage process similar to the former procedure of a charging order nisi and charging order absolute. An "interim charging order" (see r.73.4) is obtained without notice. A hearing follows where the interim order is made final or discharged (see r.73.8).

Information on land owned by the judgment debtor, if not already known by the judgment creditor, can be obtained at a hearing held pursuant to Pt 71—Orders to Obtain Information from Judgment Debtors. Further, since December 3, 1990 (when the Land Registration Act 1988 came into force) leave to inspect the Land Register is not necessary and anyone can search against any property. An official copy is frequently used as evidence of the judgment debtor's ownership. Searches can, of course, be made on the internet.

Related sources

73.0.3

- Practice Direction—Charging Orders, Stop Orders and Stop Notices (see para.73PD.1)
- Practice Direction—Enforcement of Judgments and Orders (see para.70PD.1)
- Charging Orders Act 1979 (see Vol.2, para.9B–1016)
- Council Tax (Administration and Enforcement) Regulations 1992 (SI 1992/613)
- Section 23, County Courts Act 1984 (see Vol.2, para.9A–448)
- Fixed Costs—Sch.2, CCR O.38, Appendix B

Forms

73.0.4

- **N379** Application for charging order on land or property
- **N380** Application for charging order on securities
- **N86** Interim charging order
- **N87** Final charging order
- **No 79** Stop order on capital and income of funds in court
- **No 80** Witness Statement and Stop Notice
- **No 81** Order on claim to restrain transfer of stock

Charging order on matrimonial home

73.0.5

(1) If the property is in the sole name of the judgment debtor—or owned jointly by spouses who are both judgment debtors—the charge will be against the land itself.

(2) A charging order can be made in respect of land which the debtor owns jointly with another (e.g. a spouse, see *National Westminster Bank Ltd v Stockman* [1981] 1 W.L.R. 67). However, the order ranks as a charge on the debtor's beneficial interest rather than upon the land itself.

(3) No rule specifically requires service of the application or interim order on a *spouse.* However, invariably a spouse will be served under one of the following provisions:

(a) as a "creditor" under r.73.5(1)(b) if there are pending proceedings under, e.g., the Matrimonial Causes Act 1973;

(b) as a "trustee" under r.73.5(1)(c);

(c) as a person "in possession" under para.4.3(6) of PD 73;

(d) as a person who has registered a Class F land charge, or notice under s.31(10) Family Law Act 1996;

(e) as a person specifically directed to be served by the court. In practice virtually all courts so direct so as to be able to consider "all the circumstances of the case" as required by s.1(5) Charging Orders Act 1979.

(4) Where an interim order has been made after a petition for divorce the court will usually order that the application for a final order is heard alongside the ancillary relief proceedings in the divorce and if necessary transfer the application to the divorce court for that purpose (*Harman v Glencross* [1986] Fam. 81).

(5) Where an interim order has been made but there are no divorce proceedings there is no reason for refusing a final order. A spouse's right of occupation can be adequately protected under s.14 Trusts of Land and Appointment of Trustees Act 1996 in the event of proceedings to enforce the charge.

(6) A judgment creditor is justified in expecting that an interim order over one spouse's beneficial interest will be made final. The court must consider if there is any point in denying the creditor his charge if in any event a spouse's right of occupation could be defeated by the creditor making the judgment debtor bankrupt (*First National Securities Ltd v Hegerty* [1985] Q.B. 850).

(7) As a general rule, in any contest between a judgment creditor and a joint owner of the property or any adult or child resident therein, the interests of the judgment creditor will, sooner or later, prevail (see *Harman v Glencross* [1986] Fam. 81; *Austin-Fell v Austin-Fell* [1990] Fam. 172; *re Citro (a bankrupt)* [1991] Ch. 142; *Lloyds Bank Plc v Byrne & Byrne* [1991] 23 H.L.R. 472).

Scope of this Part and interpretation[1]

73.1—(1) This Part contains rules which provide for a judgment creditor to enforce a judgment by obtaining— **73.1**

(a) a charging order (Section I)

(b) a stop order (Section II)

(c) a stop notice (Section III)

over or against the judgment debtor's interest in an asset.

(2) In this Part—

(a) "the 1979 Act" means the Charging Orders Act 1979;

(b) "the 1992 Regulations" means the Council Tax (Administration and Enforcement) Regulations 1992;

(c) "funds in court" includes securities held in court;

(d) "securities" means securities of any kinds specified in section 2(2)(b) of the 1979 Act;

I. Charging Orders

Scope of this Section[2]

73.2 *This Section applies to an application* by a judgment creditor for a charging order under— **73.2**

(a) section 1 of the 1979 Act; or

(b) regulation 50 of the 1992 Regulations.

[1] Introduced by the Civil Procedure (Amendment No.4) Rules 2001 (SI 2001/2792).
[2] Introduced by the Civil Procedure (Amendment No.4) Rules 2001 (SI 2001/2792).

Application for charging order[1]

73.3 **73.3—(1) An application for a charging order may be made without notice.**

(2) An application for a charging order must be issued in the court which made the judgment or order which it is sought to enforce, unless—

- **(a) the proceedings have since been transferred to a different court, in which case the application must be issued in that court;**
- **(b) the application is made under the 1992 Regulations, in which case it must be issued in the county court for the district in which the relevant dwelling (as defined in regulation 50(3)(b) of those Regulations) is situated;**
- **(c) the application is for a charging order over an interest in a fund in court, in which case it must be issued in the court in which the claim relating to that fund is or was proceeding; or**
- **(d) the application is to enforce a judgment or order of the High Court and it is required by section 1(2) of the 1979 Act to be made to a county court.**

(3) Subject to paragraph (2), a judgment creditor may apply for a single charging order in respect of more than one judgment or order against the same debtor.

(4) The application notice must—

(a)

(i) be in the form; and

(ii) contain the information,

required by the relevant practice direction; and

(b) be verified by a statement of truth.

"required by section 1(2) of the 1979 Act to be made to a county court"

73.3.1 Section 1(2) is in Vol.2, para.9B–1017. The limit in s.1(2)(c) is now £5000 (see para.9B–1020). See also para.73.0.2.

Form

73.3.2 The application is in Form **N379** (land) or **N380** (securities). The prescribed forms provide for all required information and a statement of truth which can be given by the judgment creditor or his solicitor. An affidavit in support of the application is no longer required.

Venue

73.3.3 Note the court of issue as prescribed by r.73.3(2) which, as a general rule is the court which made the judgment or order which it is sought to enforce. However, prior to applying for the order, the judgment creditor could request transfer pursuant to Sch.2, CCR O.25, r.2.

Interim charging order[2]

73.4 **73.4—(1) An application for a charging order will initially be dealt with by a judge without a hearing.**

[1] Introduced by the Civil Procedure (Amendment No.4) Rules 2001 (SI 2001/2792).
[2] Introduced by the Civil Procedure (Amendment No.4) Rules 2001 (SI 2001/2792).

(2) The judge may make an order (an "interim charging order")—

(a) imposing a charge over the judgment debtor's interest in the asset to which the application relates; and

(b) fixing a hearing to consider whether to make a final charging order as provided by rule 73.8(2)(a).

"Judgment debtor's interest"

If the judgment debtor is the sole owner of the land the order should charge his legal and beneficial interest in it. If joint debtors hold the whole beneficial interest in the land then the legal estate held by the trustees (invariably the debtors themselves) should be charged (see s.2 of the Charging Orders Act 1979, Vol.2, para.9B–1021; *Clark v Chief Land Registrar* [1994] CH 370). If the judgment debtor is co-owner with someone else who is not a joint debtor, only the debtor's beneficial interest may be charged (*National Westminster Bank Limited v Stockman* [1981] 1 W.L.R. 67). **73.4.1**

"may make an order"

The use of the word "may" clearly imports a discretion, though of course a judicial one. The order is likely to be refused if it would be oppressive for example if the debt appears too small to justify the remedy. Thus if the judgment creditor considers that it is a case of "won't pay" rather than "can't pay" he should provide evidence of this in para.7 of his application. Similarly para.7 should contain any relevant information concerning abortive use of other methods of enforcement such as execution. In the past the most common reason for refusal of a charging order nisi was failure to supply the information required by the Rules. This problem ought not to occur with the simplified procedures and new forms under Pt 73. **73.4.2**

Registration

To be effective it is essential that the charging order be registered otherwise, as with any unregistered charge, it would be defeated by sale to a bona fide purchaser for value without notice. The interim charging order is registerable under s.3 of the Charging Orders Act 1979 (see Vol.2, para.9B–1022). In the case of land with a registered title a notice or restriction will be entered pursuant to the Land Registration Act 2002. It has always been a vexed question as to whether there should be two registrations i.e. initially of the interim charging order and then, if made, of the final charging order. Although the process under the COA 1979 produces two separate orders there is, in reality, only one charge.The charge takes effect conditionally when the court makes the interim charging order and becomes unconditional on the making of the final charging order. The interim charging order can be registered pursuant to s.3 of the Charging Orders Act 1979 and either the Land Charges Act 1972 or Land Registration Act 2002 as appropriate (but see "judgment debtors interest" above). Strictly, as all that a final charging order does is to confirm the interim charging order, no further registration is necessary. Nevertheless Land Registry practice is to accept separate registrations of the interim and final orders and, as these orders often remain in force for many years, it is certainly clearer and tidier if registration of the final charging order is effected to show beyond doubt that a final order was in fact made. A charging order against the legal estate of registered land is protected by agreed notice or unilateral notice (in Land Registry form AN1 or UN1 respectively). A charging order over a beneficial interest in registered land is protected by a restriction in form K of Sch.4 to the Land Registration Rules 2003 (SI 2003/1417). Apply in Land Registry form RX1. **73.4.3**

Standard and Non-standard restrictions

Unfortunately, the standard wording of a restriction in Form K is perceived by many judgment creditors to give inadequate protection to their charge. If land subject to a restriction is sold all that is required at the Land Registry to effect registration in the name of a new proprietor is confirmation that notice of the transfer has been given to the creditor. In theory, there is nothing to prevent such notice being given after the transfer has taken place when it is too late for the creditor to re-act. (In practice, the new proprietor is likely to insist that the charge is removed by paying the creditor but the restriction does not guarantee that this will happen). Consequently, many creditors seek an order of the court pursuant to s.46 of the Land Registration Act 2002 requir- **73.4.3.1** ing the Land Registrar to register a "non-standard restriction" instead of the standard restriction. The purpose of the non-standard restriction is to ensure that notice of any proposed sale, mortgage or re-mortgage is given to the creditor in good time (usually 14 days) before any such transaction takes place. If an application for a non-standard restriction is to be made it should be made at the hearing to consider whether the interim order should be made final rather than subsequently.

The present position is unsatisfactory and consideration needs to be given to amending the Land Registration Rules 2003 to improve the wording of the restriction to be registered in order to give better effect to the Charging Orders Act 1979. Alternatively the CPR and Form N87 (final charging order) could be amended to authorise a non-standard restriction in all cases.

Right to charging order where judgment debt payable by instalments

73.4.4 Section 1(1) of the Charging Orders Act 1979 empowers the Court to order a charge "*for securing the payment of any money due or to become due*" under a judgment or order. Hence, when a judgment debt is payable by instalments, the Court has power to make a charging order to secure the whole debt and not merely arrears of instalments. However, in the High Court the fact that a debtor is up-to-date in complying with an order for payment by instalments is likely to be a relevant factor in the exercise of the Court's discretion to make or refuse a charging order (*Mercantile Credit Co Ltd v Ellis* [1987] C.L.Y. 2917 CA; *Independent*, March 17, 1987, CA). Where, however, the interim charging order is obtained prior to the instalment order the court can—and usually does—confirm the charging order; *Ropaigealach v Allied Irish Bank* [2001] EWCA Civ 1790. Moreover the better view hitherto is that the effect of s.86(1) of the County Courts Act 1984 is to prevent the making of a charging order where a county court has made an order for payment of any sum by instalments until after default in payment of one or more instalments. However, s.93 of the Tribunals Courts and Enforcement Act 2007 (not yet in force) inserts new subsections into s.1 of the Charging Orders Act 1979. The new s.1(6) applies ss.1(7) and (8) to High Court and county court judgment debts payable by instalments. Section 1(7) provides:

> "The fact that there has been no default in payment of the instalments does not prevent a charging order from being made in respect of that sum".

Section 1(8) obliges the court, when considering all the circumstances, to take into account the fact that there has been no default.

General principles

73.4.5 The general principles governing the exercise of the discretion to make an order may be summarised as follows:

(1) The question whether an interim order should be made final is one for the discretion of the court.

(2) The burden of showing cause why an interim order shall not be made final is on the judgment debtor.

(3) For the purpose of the exercise of the Court's discretion there is no material difference between third party debt orders and changing orders.

(4) In exercising its discretion the Court must take into account all the relevant circumstances whether they arose before or after the interim order.

(5) The Court should exercise its discretion equitably having regard to the interests of all parties involved, including other unsecured creditors, as well as those of the judgment creditor and the judgment debtor.

(The above principles, stated in *Roberts Petroleum Ltd v Bernard Kenny Ltd* [1982] 1 W.L.R. 301, CA are not affected by the reversal of the case by the House of Lords, [1983] A.C. 192).

(6) The liquidation of a company, whether by resolution or by order for compulsory winding up brings into operation a statutory scheme for dealing with the company's assets and accordingly if a winding up occurs before the final order the Court will decline to make a final order (*Roberts Petroleum Ltd v Bernard Kenny Ltd* [1983] A.C. 192, HL). The same principle would apply if an individual is made bankrupt after the interim order but before the final order.

(7) It would not normally be a proper exercise of discretion to make a charging order on an asset of substantial value in respect of a small debt (per Simmonds J. in *Robinson v Bailey* [1942] Ch. 268 at p.271).

(8) The Court has a discretion which will not be interfered with on appeal unless exercised on a wrong principle (*Wicks v Shanks* (1893) 67 L.T. 109).

(9) Where execution by writ of *fi.-fa.* has been stayed on terms that the defendant pays by instalments (or similarly, where the court has ordered payment by instalments pursuant to r.40.11) and where the defendant is complying and thus is not in arrears, the High Court may properly exercise discretion not to make a charging order (*Mercantile Credit Co Ltd v Ellis* Independent, March 17, 1987, CA). In the county court s.86(1) County Courts Act 1984 prevents the making of a charging order where the County Court has ordered payment by instalments until after default in payment.

(10) For the considerations which arise on an application to *discharge* a final order upon supervening bankruptcy see *Jelle Zwemstra Ltd v Walton and Stuart* [1997] 6 C.L. 347 (and see para.73.4.6).

Effect of bankruptcy or liquidation of judgment debtor

By ss.346 and 183 of the Insolvency Act 1986, a judgment creditor may retain the benefit of a charging order provided that the final order was made before the commencement of the bankruptcy or winding up (see para.73.4.5). **73.4.6**

"asset to which the application relates"

A judgment creditor may apply in a single application notice for charging orders over more than one asset (see para.1.3 of PD 73) but a separate order will be made in respect of each asset charged. **73.4.7**

Interest and Costs

It has been held that although a charging order did not expressly provide for payment of interest and costs it did extend to both (*Ezekiel v Orakpo* [1997] 1 W.L.R. 340). It was further held that interest falling due more than six years before the commencement of the instant proceedings was recoverable under the charge. The principle is that costs incurred after judgment can be recouped under the charge if they would have been recouped under an equitable mortgage (*Holder v Supperstone* [2000] 1 All E.R. 473). **73.4.8**

Foreign currency

Practice Direction (Judgments: Foreign Currency [1976] 1 W.L.R. 83 remains in force. Subject to the court's discretion, where the judgment is in a foreign currency, the charge will be expressed in its sterling equivalent For a case where the court exercised its discretion to order the charge to be in the foreign currency see *Carnegie v Giessen* [2005] EWCA Civ 191; [2005] 1 W.L.R. 2510 discussed at para.73.10.8 and at para.40.2.2. **73.4.9**

Service of interim order[1]

73.5—(1) Copies of the interim charging order, the application notice and any documents filed in support of it must, not less than 21 days before the hearing, be served on the following persons— **73.5**

(a) the judgment debtor;

(b) such other creditors as the court directs;

(c) if the order relates to an interest under a trust, on such of the trustees as the court directs;

(d) if the interest charged is in securities other than the securities held in court, then—

(i) in the case of stock for which the Bank of England *keeps the register, the* Bank of England;

(ii) in the case of the government stock to which (i) does not apply, the keeper of the register;

(iii) in the case of stock of any body incorporated within England and Wales, that body;

[1] Introduced by the Civil Procedure (Amendment No.4) Rules 2001 (SI 2001/2792).

(iv) in the case of stock of any body incorporated outside England and Wales or of any state or territory outside the United Kingdom, which is registered in a register kept in England and Wales, the keeper of that register;

(v) in the case of units of any unit trust in respect of which a register of the unit holders is kept in England and Wales, the keeper of that register; and

(e) if the interest charged is in funds in court, the Accountant General at the Courts Funds Office.

(2) If the judgment creditor serves the order, he must either—

(a) file a certificate of service not less than 2 days before the hearing; or

(b) produce a certificate of service at the hearing.

"Such other creditors as the court directs"

73.5.1 The court has a discretion whether or not to make a charging order. It may not be equitable to do so where there are other creditors, the judgment debtor is insolvent, and there is or is about to be an arrangement to distribute available assets among the creditors pro rata (*D Wilson (Birmingham) Limited v Metropolitan Property Developments Limited* [1975] 2 All E.R. 814; *Rainbow v Moorgate Properties Ltd* [1975] 2 All E.R. 821). Accordingly, in the application, the judgment creditor is required to state other creditors of the judgment debtor of which he is aware and the Court has power to direct service on them. A debtor's spouse would be regarded as a creditor where an application for ancillary relief has been registered against the property (see generally, *Harman v Glencross* [1986] 1 All E.R. 545).

Service

73.5.2 The normal rules as to service in Pt 6 apply. This includes the rules for service out of the jurisdiction (see CPR r.6.30) which can be used if, for example, the judgment debtor no longer has an address for service within the jurisdiction but has a known address abroad.

Service on the debtor

73.5.3 In all cases the general rule is that the court will serve the debtor; see r.6.21.

Service on other creditors

73.5.4 If the court orders service on other creditors (as it usually does pursuant to r.73.5(1)(b)) it can also direct the applicant creditor to effect such service on them. However,if the court has not directed the applicant creditor to serve, then the court itself must effect service in accordance with r.6.21.

Service on the debtor's spouse

73.5.5 Surprisingly, there is no express rule requiring service of the interim charging order on the judgment debtor's spouse. Nevertheless, it is good practice to effect such service and the court frequently orders it. Another rule may in fact require such service; see further para.73.0.5.

Effect of interim order in relation to securities[1]

73.6 **73.6—(1) If a judgment debtor disposes of his interest in any securities, while they are subject to interim charging order which has been served on him, that disposition shall not, so long as that order *remains in force*, be valid as against the judgment creditor.**

[1] Introduced by the Civil Procedure (Amendment No.4) Rules 2001 (SI 2001/2792).

(2) A person served under rule 73.5(1)(d) with an interim charging order relating to securities must not, unless the court gives permission—

(a) permit any transfer of any of the securities; or

(b) pay any dividend, interest or redemption payment relating to them.

(3) If a person acts in breach of paragraph (2), he will be liable to pay to the judgment creditor—

(a) the value of the securities transferred or the amount of the payment made (as the case may be); or

(b) if less, the amount necessary to satisfy the debt in relation to which the interim charging order was made.

Effect of interim order in relation to funds in court[1]

73.7 If a judgment debtor disposes of his interest in funds in court while they are subject to an interim charging order which has been served on him and on the Accountant General in accordance with rule 73.5(1), that disposition shall not, so long as that order remains in force, be valid as against the judgment creditor. 73.7

Further consideration of the application[2]

73.8—(1) If any person objects to the court making a final charging order, he must— 73.8

(a) file; and

(b) serve on the applicant;

written evidence stating the grounds of his objections, not less than 7 days before the hearing.

(2) At the hearing the court may—

(a) make a final charging order confirming that the charge imposed by the interim charging order shall continue, with or without modification;

(b) discharge the interim charging order and dismiss the application;

(c) decide any issues in dispute between the parties, or between any of the parties and any other person who objects to the court making a final charging order; or

(d) direct a trial of any such issues, and if necessary give directions.

(3) If the court makes a final charging order which charges securities other than securities held in court, the order will include a stop notice unless the court otherwise orders.

(*Section III of this* Part contains provisions about stop notices.)

(4) Any order made at the hearing must be served on all the persons on whom the interim charging order was required to be served.

---

[1] Introduced by the Civil Procedure (Amendment No.4) Rules 2001 (SI 2001/2792).
[2] Introduced by the Civil Procedure (Amendment No.4) Rules 2001 (SI 2001/2792).

General principles

73.8.1 See para.73.4.5.

"Written evidence stating the grounds of his objections"

73.8.2 The requirement in r.73.8(1) is new. A judgment debtor should not just turn up at the hearing to oppose the interim charging order being confirmed but should comply with this Rule.

"Decide any issues in dispute between the parties"

73.8.3 The wording of r.73.8(2)(c) makes it clear that the District Judge or Master can determine the issues there and then at the initial hearing. Only exceptionally will it be appropriate to direct a trial of any such issues as provided for by r.73.8(2)(d).

Issue directed

73.8.4 If the title to the stock or shares is disputed, an issue may be directed to be tried, in which case the practice is to adjourn the application to make the charging order absolute until after the decision of the issue.

This note was expressly approved by the Court of Appeal in *Rosseel NV v Oriental Commercial and Shipping (UK) Ltd* [1991] E.G.C.S. 94, CA. What is said applies equally where the dispute is one of the fact:the normal course will be for the Court to exercise its discretion to direct an issue to be tried (*ibid.*).

Effect of insolvency

73.8.5 Once a bankruptcy petition has been presented any disposition of property made by the debtor would be void if the debtor is then adjudged bankrupt at the hearing of the petition (see s.284 of the Insolvency Act 1986). One purpose of a bankruptcy order is to provide for a rateable sharing of the debtor's assets among all creditors. Accordingly, once a petition has been presented the court is unlikely to make to make a final charging order as this would prefer one creditor; see *Roberts Petroleum Ltd v Bernard Kenny Ltd* [1982] 1 W.L.R. 301 at para.73.4.5 above and *Rainbow v Moorgate Properties Ltd* [1975] 2 All E.R. 821 at para.73.5.1 above. Similarly, as the judgment creditor can retain the benefit of a charging order only if the final order was made before presentation of the petition (see ss.183 and 346 of the Insolvency Act 1986) there is little point in an interim charging order being made after that date (though a creditor could ask the court to make an interim order and list the date for consideration of a final order after the date of hearing of the bankruptcy petition. The interim order would be discharged if the debtor is adjudged bankrupt but could be made final if the petition were dismissed).

Effect of IVA

73.8.6 Individual Voluntary Arrangements ("IVA") are governed by Pt Vlll of the Insolvency Act 1986 and are an alternative to bankruptcy. If the debtor obtains an "interim order" under s.252 of the Insolvency Act 1986 its effect is to impose a moratorium on proceedings against an insolvent debtor. Accordingly, the court would not make either an interim charging order or a final charging order while such an order is in force (though the court could leave an existing interim charging order in place pending the decision of the creditors whether or not to approve the IVA). The aim of s.252 is to prevent a viable proposal being destroyed by a selfish creditor. In *Peake, Re* [1987] CLY 215 an interim order under s.252 was used to prevent a sheriff from completing the execution process. Similarly it could be used to prevent one creditor obtaining priority by getting a charging order.

Costs

73.8.7 The costs allowed *inter partes*—i.e. against the judgment debtor—are fixed by r.45.6 at £110 plus reasonable disbursements in respect of search fees and the registration of the order (only one registration fee: see para.73.4.3). Affidavit fees are no longer necessary (see para.73.3.2).

Restraint orders

73.8.8 Sections 40 to 49 of the Proceeds of Crime Act 2002 provide for restraint orders. Formerly made by the High Court they are now made and administered by the Crown Court. They are normally made before criminal proceedings are completed in anticipation of a confiscation order (see further *Archbold* at 5–601).

The effect of a restraint order is to prohibit any person specified in the order from dealing with any "realisable property" held by him. The order may apply generally to all property.

By s.58(5) of the Proceeds of Crime Act 2002, if a court in which proceedings are pending is satisfied that a restraint order has been applied for or made in respect of the property the court may either stay the proceedings or allow them to continue on terms. Further, by s.58(6) the court must give an opportunity to be heard to the applicant for the restraint order or any appointed receiver.

It sometimes comes to light after a creditor has obtained an interim charging order that the Crown has obtained a restraint order on the same property. In order to preserve the Crown's priority it is submitted that a final charging order should not be made in such circumstances. Instead the court should adjourn, leaving the interim order in place, until such time as a confiscation order is made (whereupon the interim order is discharged) or the application for a confiscation order is refused (whereupon a final charging order could be made).

Discharge or variation of order[1]

73.9—(1) Any application to discharge or vary a charging order must be made to the court which made the charging order. (Section 3(5) of the 1979 Act and regulation 51(4) of the 1992 Regulations provide that the court may at any time, on the application of the debtor, or of any person interested in any property to which the order relates, or (where the 1992 Regulations apply) of the authority, make an order discharging or varying the charging order). 73.9

(2) The court may direct that—

(a) any interested person should be joined as a party to such an application; or

(b) the application should be served on any such person.

(3) An order discharging or varying a charging order must be served on all the persons whom the charging order was required to be served.

Discharge

See para.73.4.5 (*Jelle Zwemstra Ltd v Walton and Stuart* [1997] 6 C.L. 347) and para.73.4.6. 73.9.1

"any interested person"

A creditor who did not receive notice of the making of an interim order may well be an "interested person". This could include the debtor's spouse in a case where ancillary relief proceedings are pending (see generally, *Harman v Glencross* [1986] 1 All E.R. 545). Often the competing interests of creditor, debtor and spouse are such that all applications are heard together. 73.9.2

Limitation Act 1980

In *Yorkshire Bank Finance Ltd v Mulhall* [2008] EWCA Civ 1156 the judgment debtor sought to set aside a 16 year old charging order on the grounds that it could no longer be enforced. The application was dismissed: neither s.20(1) nor 24(1) of the Limitation Act 1980 apply to charging orders and the judgment creditor continued to enjoy rights as a secured creditor. 73.9.3

Enforcement of charging order by sale[2]

73.10—(1) Subject to the provisions of any enactment, the court may, upon a claim by a person who has obtained a charging order 73.10

[1] Introduced by the Civil Procedure (Amendment No.4) Rules 2001 (SI 2001/2792).
[2] Introduced by the Civil Procedure (Amendment No.4) Rules 2001 (SI 2001/2792).

over an interest in property, order the sale of the property to enforce the charging order.

(2) A claim for an order for sale under this rule should be made to the court which made the charging order, unless that court does not have jurisdiction to make an order for sale.

(A claim under this rule is a proceeding for the enforcement of a charge, and section 23(c) of the County Courts Act 1984 provides the extent of the county court's jurisdiction to hear and determine such proceedings).

(3) The claimant must use the Part 8 procedure.

(4) A copy of the charging order must be filed with the claim form.

(5) The claimant's written evidence must include the information required by the relevant practice direction.

Sale

73.10.1 It is one thing to make a charging order giving security to the judgment creditor and quite another thing to order a sale of the judgment debtor's property. Just as the Court has a discretion whether or not to make the charging order so it has discretion whether or not to order the sale. It would be an extreme sanction and all circumstances would have to be considered. Where the property is the debtor's home the Court will have to consider the provisions of art.8 European Convention on Human Rights (see Sch.1 of the Human Rights Act 1988 in Vol.2, para.3D–37). To order sale is a draconian step to satisfy a simple debt and is likely to be ordered for example, in a case of the judgment debtor's contumelious neglect or refusal to pay or in a case where in reality without a sale the judgment debt will not be paid (see, e.g. *Barclay's Bank v Hendricks (Ch.D)* [1996] 1 FLR 258 where the court ordered a sale even though the proceeds would amount to only about 20 per cent of the debt). Even where a sale is ordered the Court could suspend the order on terms as to payment by instalments, or postpone the sale until a specified future date (see e.g. *Austin-Fell v Austin-Fell* [1990] 2 All E.R. 455). Of course different considerations would apply if it were not the debtor's home and he held the property as a second home or as an investment. In all cases relevant factors will include the size of the judgment debt and the value of the property.

Section 23—County Courts Act 1984

73.10.2 This Section—in Vol.2, para.9A–448—limits the equity jurisdiction of the County Court. The limit, which is still £30,000 applies to "proceedings for enforcing any charge where the amount owing in respect of the .charge .does not exceed the County Court limit". Thus where the charged judgment debt exceeds £30,000 proceedings for an order for sale must be in the High Court. In all cases, the Pt 8 procedure must be used. See further, PD 73, para.4. However, if it is appropriate to do so, the High Court has the power to transfer the proceedings to a county court under s.40(2) of the County Courts Act 1984 (CPR r.30.3 sets out the matters to which the High Court must have regard when considering a transfer). In effect jurisdiction is conferred on the county court by the High Court transferring the proceedings (*National Westminster Bank plc v King* [2008] EWCA 280 (Ch), David Richards J.).

Procedure

73.10.3 In all cases proceedings to enforce a charging order by sale require separate proceedings using the Pt 8 procedure (r.73.10(3)). A common mistake is to name only the judgment debtor as defendant in a case where the application is made pursuant to the Trusts of Land and Appointment of Trustees Act 1996. See paras 73.10.5 to 73.10.7. Note the information to be provided by written evidence required by para.4.3 of PD 73. A new para.4.4 (inserted as from December 8, 2003) requires the claimant to take reasonable steps, before issuing the claim for an order for sale, to obtain the infomation required by para.4.3. In some cases it will be necessary, therefore, to apply under Pt 71 before applying for an order for sale under r.73.10. See generally para.4 of PD 73.

Applications in the High Court

Paragraph 4.2 of PD 73 says "A claim in the High Court for an order for sale of land to enforce a charging order must be started in Chancery Chambers at the Royal Courts of Justice or a Chancery district registry". However, in *Harlow and Milner Ltd v Teasdale* [2006] EWHC 1708 (TCC) Judge Peter Coulson Q.C. pointed out that r.73.10 contains no such requirement and held that an order for sale could be made in the Technology and Construction Court. Thus although generally such orders are sought in the Chancery Division in an appropriate case the claim can be brought elsewhere. **73.10.4**

Form of order for sale

Sample forms of order are set out in Appendix A to PD 73 (see PD 73, para.4.5; these are not prescribed forms and may be adapted or varied to meet the requirements of each case). There are two sample forms (1) Order for sale following a charging order (property owned solely by judgment debtor): (2) Order for sale following a charging order (property owned by judgment debtor and another person). **73.10.5**

Section 14 Trusts of Land and Appointment of Trustees Act 1996

Any person who is a trustee of land or has an interest in property subject to a trust of land may make an application to the court under s.14. If what has been charged under the charging order is the beneficial interest of the judgment debtor (which will be the case where the judgment debtor is a joint owner with another who is not a judgment debtor) the judgment creditor has sufficient standing to make an application for an order for sale under s.14 (see e.g. *Midland Bank Plc v Pike* [1988] 2 All E.R. 434; a case on s.30 Law of Property Act 1925 which has been replaced by s.14 Trusts of Land and Appointment of Trustees Act 1996). Section 14 is not relevant where the land itself is charged as it will be in a case where the judgment debtor is the sole owner (*Pickering v Wells* [2002] EWHC 273). **73.10.6**

Note the different forms of Order for sale in Appendix A to PD 73. In a case where the debtor is sole owner he will be the sole defendant to the Pt 8 application for an order for sale under r.73.10 whereas the co-owner(s) will have to be joined as defendants to the Pt 8 application under s.14.

Section 15 Trusts of Land and Appointment of Trustees Act 1996

Section 15 sets out the matters to which the court is to have regard in determining an application for an order under s.14 (see para.73.10.5 above). This section gives the court a greater discretion than it had under the former Law of Property Act 1925 s.30. For the courts general approach see the judgment of Neuberger J. in *Mortgage Corporation v Shaire* [2001] Ch. 743. The section does enable the court to give greater weight than was formerly the case to the welfare of a minor who lives at the property. However it is a powerful consideration that a creditor is being kept out of his money and is not receiving proper recompense; see *Bank of Ireland Home Mortgages Ltd v Bell* [2001] 2 F.L.R. 809 where a sale was ordered. **73.10.7**

Sections 14 and 15 are irrelevant in a case where the judgment debtor is the sole owner of the land subject to a charging order (*Pickering v Wells* [2002] EWHC 273—a case on the former RSC O.88 which, it is submitted is clearly correct and applies with equal force to r.73.10).

Judgment in foreign currency

In *Carnegie v Giessen* [2005] EWCA Civ 191 the judgment creditor obtained judgment and then a charging order expressed in dollars. At the hearing of an application for an order for sale the creditor applied for the judgment to be restated in its sterling equivalent (because of currency fluctuations). That application was refused and the refusal was upheld on appeal. The Court of Appeal held that the application was governed by *Practice Direction (Judgment: Foreign Currency)* [1976] 1 W.L.R. 83 (which is unaffected by the CPR) and although the Master had jurisdiction to revise his order retrospectively, he was entitled, in the exercise of his discretion to refuse to do so. **73.10.8**

Effect of the "banking crisis"

At the time of this edition the UK is in recession. Two banks have been nationalised and others have received Government help. Lenders are concerned about their balance sheets. **73.10.9**

A debt which would otherwise be a bad debt but which is then secured by a charging order will now appear on the balance sheet as an asset. This has led to many courts being inundated with applications for charging orders. The courts will make the order, subject to normal principles, but generally do so merely to give security rather than as a prelude to an order for sale. Unfortunately many courts are now receiving many unmeritorious applications for an order for sale often made by an assignee in respect of small or modest debts (such as credit card debts) purchased at a knock down price. Such applications are likely to be dismissed as totally without merit and subject to an adverse costs order.

II. Stop Orders

Interpretation[1]

73.11 **73.11 In this Section, "stop order" means an order of the High Court not to take, in relation to funds in court or securities specified in the order, any of the steps listed in section 5(5) of the 1979 Act.**

"section 5(5) of the 1979 Act"

73.11.1 —is in Vol.2, para.9B–1024.

"stop order"

73.11.2 The stop order is defined in s.5 Charging Orders Act 1979 (COA) (Vol.2, para.9B–1024) and in r.73.11. A stop order has the effect of preventing dealings in the various securities over which a charging order may be obtained (and in funds in court, see r.73.7) until further order.Its purpose is to give the applicant an opportunity to make whatever further application he considers appropriate to secure his judgment (usually a charging order on the securities; see s.2(2) of the COA 1979, Vol.2, para.9B–1021). See further rr.73.6 and 73.7.

For stop notices see rr.73.16 *et seq.*

Application for stop order[2]

73.12 **73.12—(1) The High Court may make—**

(a) a stop order relating to funds in court, on the application of any person—

(i) who has a mortgage or charge on the interest of any person in the funds; or

(ii) to whom that interest has been assigned; or

(iii) who is a judgment creditor of the person entitled to that interest; or

(b) a stop order relating to securities other than securities held in court, on the application of any person claiming to be beneficially entitled to an interest in the securities.

(2) An application for a stop order must be made—

(a) by application notice in existing proceedings; or

(b) by Part 8 claim form if there are no exisitng proceedings in the High Court.

(3) The application notice or claim form must be served on—

(a) every person whose interest may be affected by the order applied for; and

(b) either—

[1] Introduced by the Civil Procedure (Amendment No.4) Rules 2001 (SI 2001/2792).
[2] Introduced by the Civil Procedure (Amendment No.4) Rules 2001 (SI 2001/2792).

(i) the Accountant General at the Court Funds Office, if the application relates to funds in court; or

(ii) the person specified in rule 73.5(1)(d), if the application relates to securities other than securities held in court.

Effect of rule

See commentary at para.73.13.1. **73.12.1**

Stop order relating to funds in court[1]

73.13 A stop order relating to funds in court shall prohibit the transfer, sale and delivery out, payment or other dealing with— **73.13**

(a) the funds or any part of them; or

(b) any income on the funds.

Effect of rule

A judgment creditor can obtain a stop order on a fund in court in the Ch D without first obtaining a charging order in the Division in which the judgment was recovered (*Shaw v Hudson* (1879) 48 L.J. Ch 689; *Hopwell v Barnes* (1876) 1 Ch. 630). As to the equitable jurisdiction of the county court, see s.23 of the County Courts Act 1984 (Vol.2, para.9A–448); it is still limited to £30,000. **73.13.1**

A stop order may be obtained on a fund ordered to be paid in court, though it has not actually been paid in (*Shaw v Hudson*, above) but not where there is no fund in court and no order for bringing in any fund (*Wellesley v Mornington* (1863) 11 W.R. 17).

Application

The application must be made under CPR Pt 23 in pending proceedings (r.73.12(2)(a)) or by claim form under Pt 8 if there are no pending proceedings (r.73.12(2)(b)). **73.13.2**

Stop orders should distinguish between capital and income affected by them (*Mack v Postle* [1894] 2 Ch. 449).

A certificate of funds issued by the Accountant General must state particulars of any charges or restraints on the fund of which the Accountant General is aware: Court Funds Rules 1987 r.63(1) (Vol.2, Section 6A).

Parties

Unless the assignor joins in the application, he must be served with the application, whether the assignment is absolute or by way of mortgage (*Parsons v Groome* (1842) 4 Beav. 521). **73.13.3**

Evidence

It is necessary on an application for a stop order to give evidence of the title of the assignor generally (which, however, will usually appear from the proceedings in the cause) and of the assignment, unless the assignor appears and admits the execution (*Wood v Vincent* (1842) 4 Beav. 419; *Quarman v Williams* (1842) 5 Beav. 133); a certificate of the fund being in court should also be produced. **73.13.4**

Effect of stop order

By granting a stop order nothing is decided as to the rights of the parties (*Lucas v Peacock* (1846) 9 Beav. 177). As to effect on priorities, see "Priority acquired by stop order", para.73.13.8 below. **73.13.5**

The effect of a stop order, however general in its terms, is confined to the specific portion of the fund in respect of a dealing with which the order is made (*Macleod v Buchanan* (1864) 33 Beav. 234).

[1] Introduced by the Civil Procedure (Amendment No.4) Rules 2001 (SI 2001/2792).

Fund carried to separate account

73.13.6 The effect of an order carrying a fund to a separate account is to release it from the general questions in the cause, and incumbrancers advancing money on the faith of such an order are entitled to priority over a claim made in respect of a breach of trust against the person to whose account such fund is carried (*Re Eyton* (1887) 45 Ch.D. 458).

Funds improperly paid out of court

73.13.7 Unless a stop order has been obtained on a fund in court the Accountant General is not guilty of default so as to give rise to a claim against public funds if the money has been paid out in disregard of the creditor's possible rights (*Bath v Bath* [1901] 1 Ch. 460).

Priority acquired by stop order

73.13.8 The priorities on a fund in court are generally determined by the priorities of the respective stop orders, rather than by the date or nature of the charge (*Greening v Beckford* (1832) 5 Sim. 195; *Swayne v Swayne* (1849) 11 Beav. 463). Therefore, a mortgagee obtaining a stop order after the bankruptcy of the mortgagor has priority over the trustees in bankruptcy who have not obtained one (*Stuart v Cockerell* (1869) L.R. 8 Eq. 607; *Palmer v Locke* (1882) 18 Ch.D. 381). But one incumbrancer, by obtaining a stop order on a fund after it has been carried to the account of the mortgagor and his incumbrancers, does not obtain priority over a stop order obtained before the fund was carried over (*Lister v Tidd* (1867) L.R. 4 Eq. 462). When money has been paid into court, an incumbrance upon it can afterwards be perfected only by obtaining a stop order, the date of which governs priority.

This is the case where part only of the fund is in court. A subsequent incumbrancer does not lose his priority by reason of his having had notice of the previous incumbrance when he obtained the stop order, provided he had no notice of it when he took his security (*Mutual Life Ass. Soc. v Langley* (1886) 32 Ch.D. 460). But see *Stephens v Green* [1895] 2 Ch. 148.

But if proper notice has been given before the fund is in court, the priority is not lost by a stop order obtained after transfer of the fund into court (*Livesey v Harding* (1857) 23 Beav. 141; *Re Anglesey* [1903] 2 Ch. 727 at 732).

Where the mortgage to a subsequent mortgagee, who obtained a stop order, recited a prior mortgage, it was held that the priority of the prior mortgagee was not affected by the stop order (*Re Holmes* (1885) 29 Ch.D. 786).

But an order appointing a receiver by way of equitable execution has priority over a subsequent stop order (*Re Anglesey* [1903] 2 Ch. 727).

No personal representative

73.13.9 Where the person who obtained the stop order is dead and has no English personal representative, the Court may proceed in the absence of any representative of his estate where the proposed transaction does not affect his interest: e.g. payment out of another share in the fund: or may appoint someone to represent his estate (see CPR r.19.8).

Equitable assignment—stop order

73.13.10 See *Montefiore v Guedalla* [1903] 2 Ch. 26, CA.

Stop order relating to securities[1]

73.14 **73.14—(1) A stop order relating to securities other than securities held in court may prohibit all or any of the following steps—**

(a) the registration of any transfer of the securities;

(b) the making of any payment by way of dividend, interest or otherwise in respect of the securities; and

(c) in the case of units of a unit trust, any acquisition of or other dealing with the units by any person or body exercising functions under the trust.

[1] Introduced by the Civil Procedure (Amendment No.4) Rules 2001 (SI 2001/2792).

(2) The order shall specify—

(a) the securities to which it relates;

(b) the name in which the securities stand;

(c) the steps which may not be taken; and

(d) whether the prohibition applies to the securities only or to the dividends or interest as well.

Variation or discharge of order[1]

73.15—(1) The court may, on the application of any person claiming to have a beneficial interest in the funds or securities to which a stop order relates, make an order discharging or varying the order. 73.15

(2) An application notice seeking the variation or discharge of a stop order must be served on the person who obtained the order.

III. Stop Notices

General[2]

73.16 In this Section— 73.16

(a) "stop notice" means a notice issued by the court which requires a person or body not to take, in relation to securities specified in the notice, any of the steps listed in section 5(5) of the 1979 Act, without first giving notice to the person who obtained the notice; and

(b) "securities" does not include securities held in court.

"section 5(5) of the 1979 Act"

Reproduced in Vol.2 at paras 9B–1024 *et seq.* 73.16.1

"stop notice"

The stop notice is defined in COA 1979 s.5 (Vol.2, paras 9B–1024 *et seq.*) and in r.73.16. The stop notice prevents dealings in the securities, without first giving notice to the person (usually a judgment creditor) who has served the stop notice. This gives that person the opportunity to apply to court for whatever order he considers appropriate to protect his interests (usually a charging order on the securities; see COA 1979 s.2(2), Vol.2, para.9B–1021). 73.16.2

"securities held in court"

See para.73.7. A stop notice cannot be served in respect of "securities held in court" (r.73.16(b)) but a stop order can be obtained (r.73.12). 73.16.3

Form of stop notice

A form of stop notice is in Appendix B to PD 73. 73.16.4

Request for stop notice[3]

***73.17*—(1) The High Court may, on the request of any person claiming to be benficially entitled to an interest in securities, issue a stop notice.** 73.17

[1] Introduced by the Civil Procedure (Amendment No.4) Rules 2001 (SI 2001/2792).
[2] Introduced by the Civil Procedure (Amendment No.4) Rules 2001 (SI 2001/2792).
[3] Introduced by the Civil Procedure (Amendment No.4) Rules 2001 (SI 2001/2792).

(A stop notice may also be included in a final charging order, by either the High Court or a county court, under rule 73.8(3)).

(2) A request for a stop notice must be made by filing—

(a) a draft stop notice; and

(b) written evidence which—

(i) identifies the securities in question;

(ii) describes the applicant's interest in the securities; and

(iii) gives an address for service for the applicant.

(A sample form of stop notice is annexed to the relevant practice direction.

(3) If a court officer considers that the request complies with paragraph (2), he will issue a stop notice.

(4) The applicant must serve copies of the stop notice and his written evidence on the person to whom the stop notice is addressed.

Effect of rule

73.17.1 This rule provides the procedure for a stop notice in respect of securities which are not in court. The "stop notice" replaced the old writ of *distringas* (and is sometimes referred to in older cases as "a notice in lieu of *distringas*").

The applicant must be a person who claims to be beneficially interested in such securities. There must therefore be a beneficial interest in the stock sought to be affected, comprised in some document or legal instrument in writing. A beneficial interest is created by deposit of a certificate of shares as security for a debt and interest, without a transfer or memorandum (*Harrold v Plenty* [1901] 2 Ch. 314).

A judgment creditor who has obtained a charging order absolute upon the contingent equitable interest of a judgment debtor in Government and Bank of England Stock standing in the name of a trustee, can issue a stop notice under these rules. In *Adam v Bank of England* (1908) 52 S.J. 682, it was held that the Bank was bound to transfer stock on the direction of the legal owner, notwithstanding a charging order obtained against a person equitably entitled (following *Churchill v Bank of England* (1843) 11 M. & W. 323). Subsequently to this decision Joyce J. (November 9, 1908) authorised the issue in a Chancery action of a *distringas* notice based upon a charging order absolute.

Effect of stop notice

73.17.2 The effect of the stop notice is to prevent a fund being dealt with without the person who issues it having an opportunity of asserting his claim. "Where there is a *distringas* on stock, the Bank of England gives notice (after application to deal with the stock) to the issuer that unless he takes proceedings in a short time to assert his right the *distringas* will be disregarded, but a trustee has no such right" (*per* Stuart V.-C., *Wilkins v Sibley* (1863) 4 Giff. 442, 446–7). The effect of the writ of *distringas*, therefore, was, and by these rules the effect of a notice under the new procedure is, merely temporary, and the person issuing it must proceed to obtain a restraining order under r.12, or an injunction in a suit against a person in whose name the stock stands; as to which modes of procedure see *Re Blakeley's Trusts* (1883) 23 Ch.D. 549; *Re Prynne* (1885) 53 L.T. 465; *Société Générale de Paris v Tramways Union Co* (1885) 14 Q.B.D. 424 at 453, *per* Lindley L.J.; *Hobbs v Wayet* (1887) 36 Ch.D. 256, *per* Kekewich J.

Failure to give notice under r.11, does not affect priorities, for it will not postpone an assignee of shares, who has given notice (apart from r.11) to the company of an assignment to him as against a subsequent assignee, nor prevent the company from registering a transfer to such prior assignee (*Peat v Clayton* [1906] 1 Ch. 659).

Service of notice and affidavit as to stock comprised in legacy by legatee does not prevent a subsequent disclaimer of the legacy (*Hobbs v Wayet* (1887) 36 Ch.D. 256).

Where the bank gave notice that an application had been made to allow the transfer of stock and to pay the dividends thereon, and an application without notice was made to restrain the bank from dealing with the stock, the Court granted an interim injunction, and required notice of the order to be served on the legal owner or stock (*Re Blakeley's Trusts* (1883) 23 Ch.D. 549).

An application to restrain a transfer of funds belonging to the estate of a testator should be entitled in the matter of the trusts of the will (*Re Pike* [1902] W.N. 42).

Presumptive next of kin contingently entitled and those claiming under them have no sufficient interest to enable them to apply for an injunction to restrain the transfer of stock standing in the names of trustees (*Re Ashton* [1900] W.N. 109).

Effect of stop notice[1]

73.18—(1) A stop notice— 73.18

(a) takes effect when it is served in accordance with rule 73.17(4); and

(b) remains in force unless it is withdrawn or discharged in accordance with rule 73.20 or 73.21

(2) While a stop notice is in force, the person on whom it is served—

(a) must not—

(i) register a transfer of the securities described in the notice; or

(ii) take any other step restrained by the notice,

without first giving 14 days' notice to the person who obtained the stop notice; but

(b) must not, by reason only of the notice, refuse to register a transfer or to take any other step, after he has given 14 days' notice under paragraph (2)(a) and that period has expired.

Amendment to stop notice[2]

73.19—(1) If any securities are incorrectly described in a stop notice which has been obtained and served in accordance with rule 73.17, the applicant may request an amended stop notice in accordance with that rule. 73.19

(2) The amended stop notice takes effect when it is served.

Withdrawal of stop notice[3]

73.20—(1) A person who has obtained a stop notice may withdraw it by serving a request for its withdrawal on— 73.20

(a) the person or body on whom the stop notice was served; and

(b) the court which issued the stop notice.

(2) The request must be signed by the person who obtained the stop notice, and his signature must be witnessed by a practising solicitor.

---

[1] Introduced by the Civil Procedure (Amendment No.4) Rules 2001 (SI 2001/2792).
[2] Introduced by the Civil Procedure (Amendment No.4) Rules 2001 (SI 2001/2792).
[3] Introduced by the Civil Procedure (Amendment No.4) Rules 2001 (SI 2001/2792).

Discharge or variation of stop notice[1]

73.21 **73.21—(1) The court may, on the application of any person claiming to be beneficially entitled to an interest in the securities to which a stop notice relates, make an order discharging or varying the notice.**

(2) An application to discharge or vary a stop notice must be made to the court which issued the notice.

(3) The application notice must be served on the person who obtained the stop notice.

73.22 **73.22 The practice direction supplementing this Part makes provision for the procedure to be followed when applying for an order under section 23 of the Partnership Act 1890.[2]**

* * * *

Partnership Act 1890

Procedure against partnership property for a partner's separate judgment debt

73.22.1 **23.**—(1) A writ of execution shall not issue against any partnership property except on a judgment against the firm.

(2) The High Court, or a judge thereof, a county court, may, on the application by summons of any judgment creditor of a partner, make an order charging that partner's interest in the partnership property and profits with payment of the amount of the judgment debt and interest thereon, and may by the same or a subsequent order appoint a receiver of that partner's share of profits (whether already declared or accruing), and of any other money which may be coming to him in respect of the partnership, and direct all accounts and inquiries, and give all other orders and directions which might have been directed or given if the charge had been made in favour of the judgment creditor by the partner, or which the circumstances of the case may require.

(3) The other partner or partners shall be at liberty at any time to redeem the interest charged, or in case of a sale being directed, to purchase the same.

(4) […]

(5) This section shall not apply to Scotland.

* * * *

[1] Introduced by the Civil Procedure (Amendment No.4) Rules 2001 (SI 2001/2792).
[2] Introduced by the Civil Procedure (Amendment) Rules 2006 (SI 2006/1689).

PRACTICE DIRECTION—CHARGING ORDERS, STOP ORDERS AND STOP NOTICES

This Practice Direction supplements CPR Part 73

Section I—Charging Orders

Application notice—rule 73.3

1.1 An application for a charging order must be made by filing an application notice in Practice Form **N379** if the application relates to land, or **N380** if the application relates to securities. **73PD.1**

1.2 The application notice must contain the following information—

(1) the name and address of the judgment debtor;
(2) details of the judgment or order sought to be enforced;
(3) the amount of money remaining due under the judgment or order;
(4) if the judgment debt is payable by instalments, the amount of any instalments which have fallen due and remain unpaid;
(5) if the judgment creditor knows of the existence of any other creditors of the judgment debtor, their names and (if known) their addresses;
(6) identification of the asset or assets which it is intended to charge;
(7) details of the judgment debtor's interest in the asset; and
(8) the names and addresses of the persons on whom an interim charging order must be served under rule 73.5(1).

1.3 A judgment creditor may apply in a single application notice for charging orders over more than one asset, but if the court makes interim charging orders over more than one asset, it will draw up a separate order relating to each asset.

High Court and county court jurisdiction

2. The jurisdiction of the High Court and the county court to make charging orders is set out in section 1(2) of the 1979 Act. **73PD.2**

Transfer

3. The court may, on an application by a judgment debtor who wishes to oppose an application for a charging order, transfer it to the court for the district where the judgment debtor resides or carries on business, or to another court. **73PD.3**

Enforcement of charging orders by sale—rule 73.10

4.1 A county court has jurisdiction to determine a claim under rule 73.10 for the enforcement of a charging order if the amount owing under the charge does not exceed the county court limit. **73PD.4**

4.2 A claim in the High Court for an order for sale of land to enforce a charging order must be started in Chancery Chambers at the Royal Courts of Justice, or a Chancery district registry.

(There are Chancery district registries at Birmingham, Bristol, Caernarfon, Cardiff, Leeds, Liverpool, Manchester, Mold, Newcastle upon Tyne and Preston.)

4.3 The written evidence in support of a claim under rule 73.10 must —

(1) identify the charging order and the property sought to be sold;

(2) state the amount in respect of which the charge was imposed and the amount due at the date of issue of the claim;

(3) verify, so far as known, the debtor's title to the property charged;

(4) state, so far as the claimant is able to identify—

(a) the names and addresses of any other creditors who have a prior charge or other security over the property; and

(b) the amount owed to each such creditor; and

(5) give an estimate of the price which would be obtained on sale of the property.

(6) if the claim relates to land, give details of every person who to the best of the claimant's knowledge is in possession of the property; and

(7) if the claim relates to residential property—

(a) state whether—

(i) a land charge of Class F; or

(ii) a notice under section 31(10) of the Family Law Act 1996, or under any provision of an Act which preceded that section,

has been registered; and

(b) if so, state—

(i) on whose behalf the land charge or notice has been registered; and

(ii) that the claimant will serve notice of the claim on that person.

4.4 The claimant must take all reasonable steps to obtain the information required by paragraph 4.3(4) before issuing the claim.

4.5 Sample forms of orders for sale are set out in Appendix A to this practice direction for guidance. These are not prescribed forms of order and they may be adapted or varied by the court to meet the requirements of individual cases.

73PD.4.1 *Note* —In reference to PD 73 para.4.2 see commentary at para.73.10.4.

73PD.4A **4A.1** A charging order or interim charging order may be made against any property, within the jurisdiction, belonging to a judgment debtor that is a partnership.

4A.2 For the purposes of rule 73.5(1)(a) (service of the interim order), the specified documents must be served on—

(1) a member of the partnership within the jurisdiction;

(2) a person authorised by a partner; or

(3) some other person having the control or management of the partnership business.

4A.3 Where an order requires a partnership to appear before the court, it will be sufficient for a partner to appear before the court.

Section II—Stop Notices

73PD.5 **5.** A sample form of stop notice is set out in Appendix B to this practice direction.

Section III—Applications for orders made under section 23 of the Partnership Act 1890

6.1 This paragraph relates to orders made under section 23 of the Partnership Act 1890 ("Section 23"). **73PD.6**

6.2 The following applications must be made in accordance with Part 23—

(1) an application for an order under Section 23 of the 1890 Act made by a judgment creditor of a partner;

(2) an application for any order by a partner of the judgment debtor in consequence of any application made by the judgment creditor under Section 23.

6.3 The powers conferred on a judge by Section 23 may be exercised by—

(1) a Master;

(2) the Admiralty Registrar; or

(3) a district judge.

6.4 Every application notice filed under this paragraph by a judgment creditor, and every order made following such an application, must be served on the judgment debtor and on any of the other partners that are within the jurisdiction.

6.5 Every application notice filed under this paragraph by a partner of a judgment debtor, and every order made following such an application, must be served—

(1) on the judgment creditor and the judgment debtor; and

(2) on the other partners of the judgment debtor who are not joined in the application and who are within the jurisdiction.

6.6 An application notice or order served under this paragraph on one or more, but not all, of the partners of a partnership shall be deemed to have been served on all the partners of that partnership.

73PD.7

Order for sale following a charging order

(property solely owned by judgment debtor)

In the

Claim No.

Appn. No.

Claimant

Defendant

On the ___________ 20 _, ______________ sitting at ___________

heard ______________________________

The claimant is entitled to an equitable charge upon the defendant's interest in the property ______

____

____

____

____

[registered at H.M. Land Registry under Title No. ________________]

("the property") __________________________________

under a charging order made on the ____________________

in the ________________ in Claim No. _________________

and the court orders that

1. The remainder of this order will not take effect if the defendant by 4.00 p.m. on the 20 ___ pays to the claimant the judgment debt of £______ secured by the charge and his costs to date of this application assessed at £______, making together £______ [together ______ with interest at the rate of £______ per day from the date of this order until payment is received by the claimant].

2. The property shall be sold without further reference to the court at a price not less than £______, unless that figure is changed by a further order of the court.

3. The [claimant] [claimant's solicitor] will have conduct of the sale.

4. To enable the claimant to carry out the sale, there be created and vested in the claimant pursuant to section 90 of the Law of Property Act 1925 a legal term in the property of [3000 years] [one day less than the remaining period of the term created by the lease under which the defendant holds the property].

5. The defendant must deliver possession of the property to the claimant [on or before the _____ 20 __] [within [______] days of this order being served on him].

6. The claimant shall first apply the proceeds of sale of the property –

(i) to pay the costs and expenses of effecting the sale; and

(ii) to discharge any charges or other securities over the property which have priority over the charging order.

7. Out of the remaining proceeds of sale the claimant shall –

(i) retain the amount due to him as stated in paragraph 1; and

(ii) pay the balance (if any) [to the Defendant] [to ______________________________] [into court].

8. Either party may apply to the court to vary any of the terms of this order, or for further directions about the sale or the application of the proceeds of sale, or otherwise

73PD.8

Order for sale
Following a charging order (property owned by judgment debtor and another person)

In the
Claim No.

Claimant

Defendants

On the 20 , sitting at

heard

The claimant is entitled to an equitable charge upon the first defendant's interest in the property

[registered at H.M. Land Registry under Title No.]
("the property")
under a charging order made on the
in the in Claim No.

and the court orders that

1. The remainder of this order will not take effect if the first defendant by 4.00 p.m. on the 20 pays to the claimant the judgment debt of £ secured by the charge and his costs to date of this application assessed at £ , making together £ [together with interest at the rate of £ per day from the date of this order until payment is received by the claimant].

2. The property shall be sold without further reference to the court at a price not less than £ , unless that figure is changed by a further order of the court.

3. The [claimant] [claimant's solicitor] will have conduct of the sale.

4. The court pursuant to section 50 of the Trustee Act 1925 appoints the [claimant] [claimant's solicitor] to convey the property.

5. The defendants must deliver possession of the property to the claimant [on or before the 20] [within [ ] days of this order being served on him].

6. The claimant shall first apply the proceeds of sale of the property –

(i) to pay the costs and expenses of effecting the sale; and

(ii) to discharge any charges or other securities over the property which have priority over the charging order.

7. The claimant shall then divide the remaining proceeds of sale into two equal shares and –

(i) pay one equal share to the second defendant; and

(ii) out of the other equal share, retain the amount due to him as stated in paragraph 1, and pay the balance (if any) [to the first defendant] [to] [into court].

8. Any party may apply to the court to vary any of the terms of this order, or for further directions about the sale or the application of the proceeds of sale, or otherwise.

73PD.9

Stop Notice

CPR rule 73.17

To *[insert name of person or body to whom the notice is addressed]*

TAKE NOTICE that
[insert name and address]

claims to be beneficially entitled to an interest in the following securities –

[specify the securities, giving the name(s) in which they stand]

This Notice requires you to refrain from –

(1) registering a transfer of the securities specified above; or

(2) paying any dividend or interest in respect of the securities *[delete if inappropriate]*;

without first giving 14 days' notice in writing to the said *[insert name]* of the above address.

PART 74

ENFORCEMENT OF JUDGMENTS IN DIFFERENT JURISDICTIONS

74.0.1

Contents

V. European Enforcement Orders

Related sources

74.0.2
- Practice Direction Part 74
- Foreign Judgments (Reciprocal Enforcement) Act 1920
- Administration of Justice Act 1933
- Brussels Convention 1968
- European Communities (Enforcement of Community Judgments) Order 1972 (SI 1972/1590)
- Section 5 Protection of Trading Interests Act 1980
- Civil Jurisdiction and Judgments Act 1982
- Merchant Shipping (Liner Conferences) Act 1982
- Section 725 Companies Act 1985
- Civil Jurisdiction and Judgments Order 2001 (SI 2001/3929)
- Council Regulation (EC) No 44/2001 of 22 December 2000 (The Judgments Regulation)
- Council Regulation (EC) No 805/2004 of 21 April 2004 (European Enforcement Order)
- Part 23
- Part 52

Forms

74.0.3
- **PF154** Order for perrnission to register a foreign judgment
- **PF155** Certificates under section 1 0 of the Foreign Judgments (Reciprocal Enforcement) Act 1 93 3
- **PF156** Evidence in support of application for registration of a Community Judgment
- **PF157** Order for registration of a Community judgment
- **PF158** Notice of Registration of a Community Judgment
- **PF159** Evidence in support of application for Registration of a Judgment of another contracting state
- **PF160** Order for registration of a Judgment of another contracting state
- **PF161** Notice of Registration of a Judgment of another contracting state
- **PF163** Evidence in support of application for a certified copy of a judgment for enforcement in another contracting state
- **PF164** Evidence in support of application for certificate as to money provisions contained in a Judgment of the High Court for registration elsewhere in the *United Kingdom*
- **PF165** Evidence in support of application for registration in the High Court of a Judgment of a court in another part of the United Kingdom containing non-money provisions

Editorial introduction

This Part was added to the CPR by Civil Procedure (Amendment) Rules 2002 (SI 2002/2058), r.29(a) and Sch.8. The provisions of this Part came into force on December 2, 2002. On that date, provisions found in Schs 1 and 2 of the CPR dealing with the matters covered by Pt 74, were revoked. The principal Scheduled Rules revocations brought about by the addition of this Part and the practice directions which supplements it are: RSC O.71 (Reciprocal Enforcement of Judgments etc.) (and the practice directions supplementing that Order), and CCR O.35 (Enforcement of County Court Judgments Outside England and Wales). **74.0.4**

In the RSC, this Order and Ords 69 and 70 were grouped under the heading "Provisions as to Foreign Proceedings". Order 71 was divided into five Parts. When the RSC were re-published in their substantially revised form in 1965, O.71 contained the rules under which the court exercised the powers conferred on it by the Administration of Justice Act 1920 Pt II, and the Foreign Judgments (Reciprocal Enforcement) Act 1933 Pt I. The Order also contained a rule dealing with the registration of certificates under the Judgments Extension Act 1868 (r.14). At common law, a foreign judgment, though creating an obligation that is actionable in England, cannot be enforced here except by the institution of fresh legal proceedings in which the foreign judgment is, in effect, the cause of action. The Act of 1920 and the Act of 1933, both of which remain in force, and other legislation constitute important statutory exceptions to the common law doctrine and enable a judgment creditor to register a foreign judgment here and then to proceed to enforce the judgment as if it were an English judgment.

In the years since 1965, O.71 was considerably expanded by the addition of 43 individual rules marshalled in four further Parts to the Order. Part II, entitled Enforcement of European Community Judgments (rr.15–24), was added in 1972 following the accession of the United Kingdom to the European Communities. Part III, entitled (Reciprocal Enforcement: The Civil Jurisdiction and Judgments Act 1982 rr.25–39), was added in 1983 to make provision for the recognition and enforcement of judgments under the 1982 Act. Part IV, entitled (Enforcement of Recommendations etc. under the Merchant Shipping (Liner Conferences) Act 1982 rr.40– 44), was added in 1986 when that Act came into force. The language of the above rules was then adapted to reflect that of the new CPR although no substantive changes were made. Part V, entitled Reciprocal Enforcement: Council Regulation (EC) No.44/2001, December 22, 2000 on Jurisdiction and the Recognition and Enforcement of Judgments in Civil and Commercial Matters (rr.45–57) is ancillary to the Judgments Regulation.

The new Pt 74 represents a radical departure from the old approach of adding new provisions to earlier texts. Section I operates as a code for the enforcement within the jurisdiction of judgments of foreign courts albeit making necessary reference to any governing provision.

Section I

The Administration of Justice Act of 1920 makes provision, by a system of registration, for the enforcement within the United Kingdom of judgments obtained in a superior court of any part of the Commonwealth. The Foreign Judgments (Reciprocal Enforcement) Act 1933 extended the principle of registration to foreign countries generally. The provisions of both Acts are extended, as the case may be, to Commonwealth and foreign jurisdictions, by Orders in Council. The rules are purely procedural and do not deal with substantive issues, such as the circumstances upon which the court should or should not register the foreign judgment **74.0.5**

The rules in respect of judgments from Contracting States deal both with judgments that are subject to the Civil Jurisdiction and Judgments Act 1982 (as amended) and with the Judgment Regulations. The exercise of the powers under the 1982 Act and, one assumes, the Regulation is limited to those cases where the defendant has been served with proceedings in the original jurisdiction and has had time to arrange his defence (see *EMI Records Ltd v Modern Music Karl-Ulrich Walterbach GmbH* [1992] Q.B. 115; [1992] 1 All E.R. 616 where Hobhouse J. set aside an order registering an injunction obtained without notice in Germany. (And see note at 74.11.28.)

Interim relief —The court is empowered by s.25(1) and (2) of the 1982 Act to grant interim relief where proceedings have been or are to be commenced in a Brussels or Lugano Contracting State. (This includes interim relief in relation to an "Authentic Instrument" which under art. 50 can be enforced without proceedings: *S & T Bautrad-*

ing v Nordling [1997] 3 All E.R. 718.) Following the full implementation of s.25 of the 1982 Act by SI 1997/415 the jurisdiction to grant interim relief is not confined to the territories of Contracting States.

Section II

74.0.6 This section deals with outgoing judgments from the High Court and County Courts of England and Wales.

Section III

74.0.7 This section helpfully gives separate treatment to the enforcement of United Kingdom judgments in other parts of the United Kingdom. NB., the "United Kingdom" includes only England and Wales, Scotland and Northern Ireland. It does not include other parts of "Great Britain" such as the Channel Islands and the Isle of Man.

Section IV

74.0.8 The rules in this Section prescribe the procedure for giving effect to Community judgments enforceable in the High Court in accordance with the functions assigned to the court by the European Communities (Enforcement of Community Judgments) Order 1972 (SI 1972/1590). The judgments to which the 1972 Order applies are not those of the national courts of the Member States of the European Community but rather the judgments of the courts and institutions of the Community itself. That is to say, judgments by the European Court of Justice, and decisions of the Arbitration Committee of the European Atomic Energy Committee, of the High Authority of the European Coal & Steel Community which impose a pecuniary obligation, and of the Council of the Commission of the European Economic Community which impose a pecuniary obligation on persons other than States. Any Community judgment to which the Secretary of State has appended an order for enforcement shall be registered by the court if application is made by the person entitled to enforce it. Provision is made in this Part for the registration of such judgments, for notification to persons against whom they are given, and for applications to vary or cancel registration by reason of the judgment being satisfied and to register an order of the European Court of Justice suspending execution of a registered judgment. Part II also provides for the registration and enforcement of Euratom inspection orders.

The judgments, etc., of the three Community institutions referred to above have validity in the UK by virtue of the treaties by which the institutions were established. The necessary ancillary legislation required to ensure that the judgments, etc., could be enforced in the UK was contained in the European Communities (Enforcement of Community Judgments) Order 1972. The rules are supplementary to that statutory instrument and the expressions used in the rules have the same meanings as in that instrument, unless the context otherwise requires.

Section V

74.0.9 This section was introduced by the Civil Procedure (Amendment No.3) Rules 2005 (SI 2005/2292). It makes provision for the certification of judgments of the courts of England and Wales as European Enforcement Orders, and for the recognition and enforcement in England and Wales of judgments of other Contracting States that have been certified as European Enforcement Orders, under Council Regulation (EC) No 805/2004 creating a European Enforcement Order for uncontested claims (Official Journal L 143, 30/04/2004 P 0015-0039).

Council Regulation 1896/2006 of December 12, 2006

74.0.10 This regulation came into force on December 12, 2008 save Arts 28, 29, 30 and 31 which came into force on June 12, 2008. Its intention is to simplify and reduce the costs of litigation in cross-border cases concerning uncontested pecuniary claims by creating a European order for payment procedure; and to permit the free circulation of European orders for payment throughout the Member States by laying down minimum standards, compliance with which renders unnecessary any intermediate proceedings in the Member State of enforcement prior to recognition and enforcement.

Textbooks

74.0.11 The purpose of the notes that follow is only to make the rule intelligible; they are not a detailed commentary. For detailed commentaries on the rules see the leading textbooks, e.g. Dicey & Morris, *Conflict of Laws* (14th edn, 2006) and Briggs & Rees *Civil Jurisdictions and Judgments* (3rd edn).

Scope of this Part and interpretation[1]

74.1—(1) Section I of this Part applies to the enforcement in England and Wales of judgments of foreign courts. 74.1

(2) Section II applies to the enforcement in foreign countries of judgments of the High Court and of county courts.

(3) Section III applies to the enforcement of United Kingdom judgments in other parts of the United Kingdom.

(4) Section IV applies to the enforcement in England and Wales of European Community judgments and Euratom inspection orders.

(4A) Section V applies to—

- **(a) the certification of judgments and court settlements in England and Wales as European Enforcement Orders; and**
- **(b) the enforcement in England and Wales of judgments, court settlements and authentic instruments certified as European Enforcement Orders by other Member States.**

(5) In this Part—

- **(a) "the 1920 Act" means the Administration of Justice Act 1920;**
- **(b) "the 1933 Act" means the Foreign Judgments (Reciprocal Enforcement) Act 1933;**
- **(c) "the 1982 Act" means the Civil Jurisdiction and Judgments Act 1982[2];**
- **(d) "the Judgments Regulation" means Council Regulation (EC) No.44/2001 of 22nd December 2000 on jurisdiction and the recognition and enforcement of judgments in civil and commercial matters, as amended from time to time and as applied by the Agreement made on 19th October 2005 between the European Community and the Kingdom of Denmark on jurisdiction and the recognition and enforcement of judgments in civil and commercial matters [3];**
- **(e) "the EEO Regulation" means Council Regulation (EC) No 805/2004 creating a European Enforcement Order for uncontested claims.**

(A copy of the EEO Regulation is annexed to Practice Direction 74B European Enforcement Orders and can be found at *http://europa.eu.int/eur-lex/pri/en/oj/dat/2004/1_143/1_14320040430en00150039.pdf*)

---

[1] Introduced by the Civil Procedure (Amendment) Rules 2002 (SI 2002/2058) and amended by the Civil Jurisdiction and Judgments Regulations 2007 (SI 2007/1655).

[2] 1982 c.27, as amended by the Civil Jurisdiction and Judgments Act 1991 (c.12) and by SI 1989/1346, SI 1990/2591, SI 1993/603, SI 2000/1824 and SI 2001/3929.

[3] Amended by s.31 of the Civil Jurisdiction and Judgments Regulations 2007, SI 2007/1655.

I. Enforcement in England and Wales of Judgments of Foreign Courts

Interpretation[1]

74.2 **74.2—(1) In this Section—**

(a) "Contracting State" has the meaning given in section 1(3) of the 1982 Act;

(b) "Regulation State" means a Member State [2];

(c) "judgment" means, subject to any other enactment, any judgment given by a foreign court or tribunal, whatever the judgment may be called, and includes—

(i) a decree;

(ii) an order;

(iii) a decision;

(iv) a writ of execution; and

(v) the determination of costs by an officer of the court;

(d) "State of origin", in relation to any judgment, means the State in which that judgment was given.

(2) For the purposes of this Section, "domicile" is to be determined—

(a) in an application under the 1982 Act, in accordance with sections 41 to 46 that Act;

(b) in an application under the Judgments Regulation, in accordance with paragraphs 9 to 12 of Schedule 1 to the Civil Jurisdiction and Judgments Order 2001.

Note

74.2.1 The Judgments Regulation applies also to Denmark from July 1, 2007, pursuant to the Civil Jurisdiction and Judgments Order 2001, amending the Civil Jurisdiction and Judgments Act 1982 ss.1(1) and 1(3). Part 74.1(5)(d) and 74.2(1)(b) have been amended to reflect this.

Applications for registration[3]

74.3 **74.3—(1) This Section provides rules about applications under—**

(a) section 9 of the 1920 Act, in respect of judgments to which Part II of that Act applies;

(b) section 2 of the 1933 Act, in respect of judgments to which Part I of that Act applies;

(c) section 4 of the 1982 Act; and

(d) the Judgments Regulation,

for the registration of foreign judgments for enforcement in England and Wales.

(2) Applications—

(a) must be made to the High Court; and

(b) may be made without notice.

---

[1] *Introduced* by the Civil Procedure (Amendment) Rules 2002 (SI 2002/2058) and amended by the Civil Jurisdiction and Judgments Regulations 2007 (SI 2007/1655).

[2] Amended by the s.31 of the Civil Jurisdiction and Judgments Regulations 2007, SI 2007/1655.

[3] Introduced by the Civil Procedure (Amendment) Rules 2002 (SI 2002/2058).

Evidence in support[1]

74.4—(1) An application for registration of a judgment under the 1920, 1933 or 1982 Act must be supported by written evidence exhibiting— 74.4

(a) the judgment or a verified or certified or otherwise authenticated copy of it; and
(b) where the judgment is not in English, a translation of it into English—
  (i) certified by a notary public or other qualified person; or
  (ii) accompanied by written evidence confirming that the translation is accurate.

(2) The written evidence in support of the application must state—

(a) the name of the judgment creditor and his address for service within the jurisdiction;
(b) the name of the judgment debtor and his address or place of business, if known;
(c) the grounds on which the judgment creditor is entitled to enforce the judgment;
(d) in the case of a money judgment, the amount in respect of which it remains unsatisfied; and
(e) where interest is recoverable on the judgment under the law of the State of origin—
  (i) the amount of interest which has accrued up to the date of the application, or
  (ii) the rate of interest, the date from which it is recoverable, and the date on which it ceases to accrue.

(3) Written evidence in support of an application under the 1920 Act must also state that the judgment is not a judgment—

(a) which under section 9 of that Act may not be ordered to be registered; or
(b) to which section 5 of the Protection of Trading Interests Act 1980 applies.

(4) Written evidence in support of an application under the 1933 Act must also—

(a) state that the judgment is a money judgment;
(b) confirm that it can be enforced by execution in the State of origin;
(c) confirm that the registration could not be set aside under section 4 of that Act;
(d) confirm that the judgment is not a judgment to which section 5 of the Protection of Trading Interests Act 1980 applies;
(e) where the judgment contains different provisions, some but not all of which can be registered for enforcement,

[1] Introduced by the Civil Procedure (Amendment) Rules 2002 (SI 2002/2058).

set out those provisions in respect of which it is sought to register the judgment; and

(f) be accompanied by any further evidence as to—

(i) the enforceability of the judgment in the State of origin, and

(ii) the law of that State under which any interest has become due under the judgment,

which may be required under the relevant Order in Council extending Part I of the 1933 Act to that State.

(5) Written evidence in support of an application under the 1982 Act must also exhibit—

(a) documents which show that, under the law of the State of origin, the judgment is enforceable on the judgment debtor and has been served;

(b) in the case of a judgment in default, a document which establishes that the party in default was served with the document instituting the proceedings or with an equivalent document; and

(c) where appropriate, a document showing that the judgment creditor is in receipt of legal aid in the State of origin.

(6) An application for registration under the Judgments Regulation must, in addition to the evidence required by that Regulation, be supported by the evidence required by paragraphs (1)(b) and (2)(e) of this rule.

Security for costs[1]

74.5 74.5—(1) Subject to paragraphs (2) and (3), section II of Part 25 applies to an application for security for the costs of—

(a) the application for registration;

(b) any proceedings brought to set aside the registration; and

(c) any appeal against the granting of the registration,

as if the judgment creditor were a claimant.

(2) A judgment creditor making an application under the 1982 Act or the Judgments Regulation may not be required to give security solely on the ground that he is resident out of the jurisdiction.

(3) Paragraph (1) does not apply to an application under the 1933 Act where the relevant Order in Council otherwise provides.

Security for costs

74.5.1 The Order in Council which applies the Act to France prevents any application being made for security for costs on the registration of a French judgment (see note "Application of Act of 1933 to foreign countries", para.sc71.1.5). And r.29, below, considerably modifies this rule in cases of registration under the Civil Jurisdiction and Judgments Act 1982.

74.5.2 By s.3 of the Act, rules may be made under JA 1925 s.99 (now SCA 1981 s.87), for making provision with respect to the giving of security for costs to persons applying

[1] Introduced by the Civil Procedure (Amendment) Rules 2002 (SI 2002/2058).

for the registration of judgments. As to the International Conventions affecting security for costs see this n. at paras 25.13.3–25.13.4.

The procedure for enforcing judgments under Pt II of AJA 1920, and the Foreign Judgments (Reciprocal Enforcement) Act 1933, makes it necessary for claimants residing in those countries to which those Acts apply to give security (*Kohn v Rinson and Stafford (Brod.) Ltd* [1948] 1 K.B. 327). Although see the position for Contracting States stated at para.25.13.3.

Registration orders[1]

74.6—(1) An order granting permission to register a judgment ("registration order") must be drawn up by the judgment creditor and served on the judgment debtor— **74.6**

(a) by delivering it to the judgment debtorpersonally;

(b) as provided by—

(i) section 725 of the Companies Act 1985; or

(ii) the Companies Act 2006; or

(c) in such other manner as the court may direct.

(2) Permission is not required to serve a registration order out of the jurisdiction, and rules 6.40, 6.42, 6.43 and 6.46 apply to such an order as they apply to a claim form.

(3) A registration order must state—

(a) full particulars of the judgment registered;

(b) the name of the judgment creditor and his address for service within the jurisdiction;

(c) the right of the judgment debtor—

(i) in the case of registration following an application under the 1920 or the 1933 Act, to apply to have the registration set aside;

(ii) in the case of registration following an application under the 1982 Act or under the Judgments Regulation, to appeal against the registration order;

(d) the period within which such an application or appeal may be made; and

(e) that no measures of enforcement will be taken before the end of that period, other than measures ordered by the court to preserve the property of the judgment debtor.

The 1920 and 1933 Acts

The methods of enforcement in this country of judgments obtained outside the jurisdiction are as follows: **74.6.1**

(i) Judgments obtained in the superior Courts in many parts of HM Dominions outside the UK, by registration under Pt II of AJA 1920;

(ii) Judgments obtained in the superior Courts of any foreign country to which the Foreign Judgments (Reciprocal Enforcement) Act 1933 has been applied, by registration under Pt I of that Act;

(iii) By action on the judgment, but subject to s.6 of the Foreign Judgments (Reciprocal Enforcement) Act 1933 which restricts the method of enforcement of

---

[1] Introduced by the Civil Procedure (Amendment) Rules 2002 (SI 2002/2058) and amended by the Civil Procedure (Amendment) Rules 2008 (SI 2008/2178).

judgments to which the Act applies to proceedings by way of registration only (see *Yukon Gold, Ltd v Clark* [1938] 2 K.B. 241, CA).

The court may include interest when giving summary judgment for the enforcement of a foreign judgment even though the foreign law under which the judgment was obtained makes no provision for interest (*Midland International Services Ltd v Sudairy*, *Financial Times*, May 2, 1990).

Administration of Justice Act 1920

74.6.2 Part II of AJA 1920, enabled certain judgments of superior courts in any part of Her Majesty's Dominions outside the United Kingdom to be registered in the High Court (or High Court of Northern Ireland or Court of Session in Scotland) and such judgment has the same effect so far as it relates to execution as a judgment of the registering court. The Act, however, did not operate until an Order in Council applied it to (a) any part of the British Dominions, and such Order could only be made when reciprocal provisions had been made by the Legislature of that part for registration of English, Scottish and Irish judgments; or (b) to any territory under British protection or being administered under mandate.

Section 9(2) specified certain limitations on the judgments to be registered. Thus no judgment could be registered if (a) the original court acted without jurisdiction; or (b) the judgment debtor, being a person who was neither carrying on business nor ordinarily resident within the jurisdiction of the original court, did not voluntarily appear or otherwise submit or agree to submit to the jurisdiction of that court; or (c) the judgment debtor, being the defendant in the proceedings, was not duly served with the process of the original court, and did not appear, notwithstanding that he was ordinarily resident or was carrying on business within the jurisdiction of that court or agreed to submit to the jurisdiction of that court; or (d) the judgment was obtained by fraud; or (e) the judgment debtor satisfied the registering court either that an appeal was pending, or that he was entitled and intended to appeal against the judgment; or (f) the judgment was in respect of a cause of action which for reasons of public policy or for some other similar rule could not have been entertained by the registering court. Leave of the court was required in all cases and had to be applied for within 12 months, though this limit might be extended. For the purposes of the Act "judgment" meant any judgment or order in any civil proceedings before or after the Act whereby any sum of money was made payable, and included an award in proceedings on an arbitration if the award was enforceable as a judgment in the place where it was made. The powers of the Act might be exercised by a Judge.

Section 7 of the Foreign Judgments (Reciprocal Enforcement) Act 1933, provided that Pt II of AJA 1920, shall cease to have effect *except in relation to the Dominions to which it extended at the date of the Order in Council applying the 1933 Act to H.M. Dominions*.

Section 10 of the Act provides for the issue to a judgment creditor under a judgment obtained in the United Kingdom of a certified copy of the judgment on proof that the judgment debtor resides in some part of the British Dominions to which the Act applies.

Extension of Act of 1920 by Orders in Council

74.6.3 The provisions of Pt II of AJA 1920, have been extended by Orders in Council.

No further extensions of Pt II have been permissible since 1933, see s.7 of the 1933 Act.

These Orders in Council may, however, be consolidated if they are in force when the consolidating Order is made (Civil Jurisdiction and Judgments Act 1982 s.35(3) This consolidation took place by SI 1984/129 and Pt II of AJA 1920 extends to the countries specified in Sch.I to that Order which has been amended by the Judgments (Administration of Justice Act 1920, Pt II) (Amendment) Order 1985 (SI 1985/1994) and further amended by the Reciprocal Enforcement of Judgments (Administration of Justice Act 1920, Pt II) (Amendment) Order 1997 (SI 1997/2601) and the Civil Jurisdiction and Judgments Act 1982 (Gibraltor Order 1997) (SI 1997/2602), and now reads as follows:

Anguilla
Antigua and Barbuda
Bahamas
Barbados

Belize
Bermuda
Botswana
British Indian Ocean Territory
British Virgin Islands
Cayman Islands
Christmas Island
Cocos (Keeling) Islands
Dominica
Falkland Islands
Fiji
The Gambia
Ghana
Grenada
Guyana
Jamaica
Kenya
Kiribati
Lesotho
Malawi
Malaysia
Mauritius
Montserrat
New Zealand
Nigeria
Territory of Norfolk Island
Papua New Guinea
St Christopher and Nevis
St Helena
St Lucia
St Vincent and the Grenadines
Seychelles
Sierra Leone
Singapore
Solomon Islands
Sovereign Base Area of Akrotiri and Dhekelia in Cyprus
Sri Lanka
Swaziland
Tanzania
Tasmania
Trinidad and Tobago
Turks and Caicos Islands
Tuvalu
Uganda
Zambia
Zimbabwe

The 1920 Act no longer applies to Hong Kong and there is no provision for registration of Hong Kong judgments in England or English judgments in Hong Kong. Enforcement of such judgments is by action on the judgment.

Gibraltar is now subject to SI 1997/2602 and covered by the Civil Jurisdiction and Judgments Act 1982.

Foreign Judgments (Reciprocal Enforcement) Act 1933

The following is a brief summary of the provisions of this Act. By s.1 the Queen may, by Order in Council, direct that (subject to the terms of the Order) the provisions of the Act which relate to the registration of foreign judgments may extend to any foreign country which is prepared to give reciprocity of treatment to judgments **74.6.4** given in the courts of the United Kingdom. A "judgment" of a "court" of a foreign country—both terms are defined in the Act and the particular Order—may be registered provided it is final and conclusive, and there is payable thereunder a sum of money not being in respect of taxes, fines or penalties (s.1(2) and s.11(1) of the Act). Application to register may (by virtue of s.2) be made within six years of the date of the judgment, but not if it has been wholly satisfied or if it could not be enforced by execution in the country of the original court.

Broadly speaking, a foreign judgment when registered can be treated as if it were the judgment of an English court (s.2(1)). If expressed in the currency of a foreign country it will be registered in that currency or its sterling equivalent at the time of payment. Interest and the reasonable cost of registration may be added to the judgment when registered (*ibid.*, (6)). This addition will depend upon the direction in the Master's order which may be for a sum fixed or summarily assessed. Section 3 of the Act confers power to make rules for registration.

The cases in which the registration of a judgment may be set aside are specified in s.4 of the Act.

The circumstances in which the court of the country of origin are deemed to have had jurisdiction are set out in s.4(2) and (3). If an appeal is pending when application is made to set aside registration, the court may either set aside the registration or adjourn the application (s.5(1)). Section 8 of the Act defines the circumstances in which a judgment of that foreign court is to be recognised as conclusive in the English courts whether registered or not. By virtue of s.8, a foreign judgment is conclusive between the parties in English proceedings as to the matter thereby adjudicated upon. Moreover, by virtue of s.3 of the Foreign Limitation Periods Act 1984, the determination of the foreign court based upon the law relating to the limitation of actions whether of its own or any other country, including England and Wales, is deemed to be a determination on the merits, so that it will be treated as final and conclusive between the parties (statutorily negativing *Black-Clawson International Ltd v Papierwerke Waldhof-Aschaffenburg A.G.* [1975] A.C. 591; [1975] 1 All E.R. 810, HL).

The 1933 Act and the Conventions under it probably do not apply to matrimonial causes affecting status (*Vervaeke v Smith; Messina and Attorney General Intervening* [1981] Fam. 77; [1981] 1 All E.R. 55, CA).

Application of Act of 1933 to Foreign Countries

74.6.5 Austria— SI 1962/1339.

Belgium— S.R. & O. 1936 No.1169.

France— S. R. & O. 1936 No.609.

Federal Republic of Germany and West Berlin— SI 1961/1199.

The territory formerly incorporated within the German Democratic Republic and East Berlin now forms part of the German Federal Republic.

Israel— SI 1971/1039.

Italy— SI 1973/1894.

The Netherlands— SI 1969/1063.

The Netherlands Antilles, where the following courts will be deemed superior courts, namely The Hoge Raad der Nederlanden; The Hof Van Justitie der Nederlandse Antillen; The Gerecht in Eerste Aanleg—SI 1969/1063, as amended by the Reciprocal Enforcement of Foreign Judgments (The Netherlands) (Amendment) Order 1977—SI 1977/2149.

Norway— SI 1962/636.

Suriname— SI 1981/735.

Tonga— SI 1980/1523.

All the above countries except Israel, Suriname and Tonga are now parties to the Brussels or Lugano Conventions and applications in relation to Convention countries and matters should be made under the appropriate provisions.

Application of Act of 1933 to Commonwealth Territories

74.6.6 Although Pt I of the Foreign Judgments (Reciprocal Enforcement) Act 1933, was made applicable generally to H.M. Dominions, etc., by an Order in Council dated November 10, 1933 (under the provisions of s.7 of the Act) the application of the Act to any particular part of the Commonwealth Territories is dependent upon substantial reciprocity being assured by such places (s.1) when the Act may be brought into operation for such particular place by a further Order in Council (*Yukon Consolidated Gold*

Corp Ltd v Clark [1938] 2 K.B. 241). Orders have been made applying the Act to the following places in the Commonwealth:

Australia—SI 1994/1901.

Australian Capital Territory—SI 1955/559.

Canada: the Federal Court of Canada and any court to the Province of British Columbia, Manitoba, New Brunswick, Nova Scotia, Ontario, Prince Edward Island, Saskatchewan or the Yukon Territory—SI 1987/468 as amended by SI 1987/2211, SI 1988/1304 and SI 1988/1853. Northwest Territories: SI 1989/987. Newfoundland: SI 1991/1724, in force August 1, 1991; Alberta: SI 1992/1731, in force August 13, 1992. For amendments consequential on the accession of the United Kingdom to the Lugano Convention— SI 1995/2708.

Island of Guernsey—SI 1973/610.

Isle of Man—SI 1973/611.

Jersey, Bailiwick of—SI 1973/612.

Republic of India, the territories named in the schedule to the Order in Council—SI 1958/425.

Pakistan: SI 1958/141 and see Pakistan Act 1990.

Where Pt I of the Foreign Judgments (Reciprocal Enforcement) Act 1933, is extended to a part of H.M. Dominions or other territory to which Pt II of AJA 1920, extends, modifications are made by AJA 1956 s.51.

Countries currently covered for reciprocal enforcement under the Civil Jurisdiction and Judgments Act 1982

Denmark 74.6.7
Gibralter
Iceland
Northern Ireland
Norway
Scotland
Switzerland

Judgments Regulation

The Member States to which this applies are, as from July 1, 2007: 74.6.8

Austria
Belgium
Czech Republic
Denmark
Estonia
Finland
France
Germany
Greece
Greek Cyprus
Hungary
Italy
Latvia
Lithuania
Luxembourg
Malta
Netherlands
Poland
Portugal
Republic of Ireland
Slovakia
Slovenia
Spain
Sweden

Registration practice

74.6.9 The application to register a judgment either under the 1920 Act or the 1933 Act should be made without notice supported by a witness statement or affidavit to the Master. It should be lodged in Room E17. It will then be checked in the Action Department before being submitted to a Master for him or her to consider the application who may, instead of dealing with the application without notice being served on any other party, direct that a claim form be filed and served. Whether this is a Pt 7 or Pt 8 claim is likely to depend upon whether there are contested issues of fact.

The decision of the court whether to order registration of a foreign judgment under the 1920 Act or the 1933 Act is an adjudicative act for the purposes of the State Immunity Act 1978, as defined by Lord Denning in *Alcom Ltd v The Republic of Columbia* [1984] A.C. 580: *AIC Limited v The Federal Government of Nigeria* [2003] EWHC 1357 (QB).

Forms

74.6.10 The title of the witness statement or affidavit should expressly state whether it is made, "In the Matter of the Administration of Justice Act 1920 Part II", "In the Matter of the Foreign Judgments (Reciprocal Enforcement) Act 1933" or "In the Matter of the Civil Jurisdiction and Judgments Act 1982": and in each case, the title of the witness statement or affidavit should also identify the judgment by reference to the court in which it was obtained and its date.

Rate of exchange

74.6.11 Following the decision in *Miliangos v George Frank (Textiles) Ltd* [1976] A.C. 443; [1975] 3 All E.R. 801, and the repeal of s.2(3) of the Foreign Judgments (Reciprocal Enforcement) Act 1933 by s.4 of AJA 1977, the witness statement or affidavit in support of the application for the registration of a foreign judgment must not convert the amount of the foreign currency into United Kingdom currency at the rate of exchange prevailing at the date of that judgment. The foreign judgment will be registered in the foreign currency in which it is expressed, or its sterling equivalent at the time of payment. There is no power entitling the claimant to convert the currency of the foreign judgment at the rate of exchange prevailing at any earlier or other date except the date of payment.

This applies also to judgments under AJA 1920 Pt II, to which the relevant provision of the Act of 1933 had been extended, so negativing the case of *East India Trading Co Inc v Carmel Exporters and Importers Ltd* [1952] 2 Q.B. 439.

On the other hand, it should be remembered that when it comes to enforcing the foreign judgment so registered it will become necessary to convert the foreign currency at the date of enforcement according to the method of enforcement employed in accordance with the Queen's Bench Guide para.11.2.4.

Costs

74.6.12 Application may be made to enforce a judgment or order for costs given or made in any country to which the Act of 1920 or the Act of 1933 applies.

Judgment in respect of different matters under the Act of 1933

74.6.13 By s.4(5) of the Act of 1933, if the judgment is in respect of different matters, and some but not all of the provisions of the judgment are such that if they had been in separate judgments they could have been registered, the judgment may be registered in respect of such provisions.

Entitlement to enforce the judgment

74.6.14 A technical defect in the form of a foreign judgment, e.g. omission of certain words prescribed by the foreign law, does not render that judgment a nullity but only makes it voidable, and so long as it stands, it is enforceable by execution in that country, and is therefore capable of being registered in this country (*S.A. Consortium General Textiles v Sun and Sand Agencies Ltd* [1978] Q.B. 279; [1978] 2 W.L.R. 1; [1978] 2 All E.R. 339, CA).

Moreover, the power of a foreign court, e.g. in France, to award an additional compensatory sum for "resistance abusive", e.g. for failure to comply with the obligations of a mercantile transaction is not "a fine or other penalty" within s.1(2)(b) of the Act of 1933 and it is not contrary to public policy in England under s.4(1)(a)(ii) as being the equivalent of "exemplary damages" which are not generally awardable in England, and therefore such a foreign judgment is entitled to be enforced and capable of being registered in England (*ibid.*).

No submission to foreign court by appearance

For the purposes of determining whether a judgment given by a court of an overseas country should be recognised or enforced in England and Wales or Northern Ireland, the person against whom the judgment was given will not be regarded as having submitted to the jurisdiction of the court by reason only of the fact that he appeared (conditionally or otherwise) in the proceedings for all or any one or more of the following purposes, namely (a) to contest the jurisdiction of the court; (b) to ask the court to dismiss or stay the proceedings on the ground that the dispute in question should be submitted to arbitration or to the determination of the courts of another country; (c) to protect, or obtain the release of, property seized or threatened with seizure in the proceedings (see Civil Jurisdiction and Judgments Act 1982 s.33(1). The effect of this provision is to negative the decisions in *Henry v Geoprosco International Ltd* [1976] Q.B. 726, CA and in *Harris v Taylor* [1915] 2 K.B. 580, CA, (*Tracomin SA v Sudan Oil Seeds Ltd (Nos 1 and 2)* [1983] 1 W.L.R. 1026; [1983] 3 All E.R. 137 affirming [1983] 1 W.L.R. 662; [1983] 1 All E.R. 404). It should be remembered that such a judgment may still be recognised and enforced by the courts of the country in which it was rendered. Where contesting the jurisdiction involves a requirement to plead to the merits this will not be regarded as a submission to the jurisdiction (*Starlight International Inc v A.J. Bruce* [2002] EWHC 374; [2002] I.L.Pr. 35). **74.6.15**

See in particular *Harada v Turner* [2003] EWCA Civ 1695, judgments of Solomon Brown L.J. at paragraphs 22–35 and 38 and Mance L.J. at paragraphs 54–56, referring also to *Elefanten Schuh GMBH v Pierre Jacqmain* [1981] E.C.R. 171 and *ETS. Rohr SA v Dina Ossberger* (Case 27/81) 1981 E.C.R. 2431.

This provision will not affect the recognition or enforcement in England and Wales or Northern Ireland of a judgment which is required to be recognised or enforced there under the 1968 Convention on Jurisdiction and the Enforcement of Judgments in Civil and Commercial matters (see the 1982 Act s.2(2)(c) and Sch.1) (*ibid.*, s.33(2)).

Effect of registration

A foreign judgment, when registered, may form the basis of a bankruptcy notice (*Re A Judgment Debtor (No.2176 of 1938)* [1939] Ch. 601; [1939] 1 All E.R. 1). **74.6.16**

Applications to set aside registration[1]

74.7—(1) An application to set aside registration under the 1920 or the 1933 Act must be made within the period set out in the registration order. **74.7**

(2) The court may extend that period; but an application for such an extension must be made before the end of the period as originally fixed or as subsequently extended.

(3) The court hearing the application may order any issue between the judgment creditor and the judgment debtor to be tried.

Application to set aside registration

The circumstances in which registration may be set aside are set forth in s.4 of the of Act 1933. By subs. (1)(a) it *shall* be set aside if the court is satisfied: **74.7.1**

(i) that the judgment is not a judgment to which Pt I of the Act applies or was registered in contravention of the provisions of the Act; or
(ii) that the courts of the country of the original court had no jurisdiction in the circumstances of the case; or
(iii) that the judgment debtor, being the defendant in the proceedings in the original court, did not (notwithstanding that process may have been duly served on him in accordance with the law of the country of the original court) receive notice of those proceedings in sufficient time to enable him to defend the proceedings and did not appear; or
(iv) that the judgment was obtained by fraud; or
(v) that the enforcement of the judgment would be contrary to public policy in this country; or

[1] Introduced by the Civil Procedure (Amendment) Rules 2002 (SI 2002/2058).

(vi) that the rights under the judgment are not vested in the person by whom the application for registration was made:

By subs.1(b), a judgment *may* be set aside if the registering court is satisfied that the matter in dispute in the proceedings in the original court had previous to those proceedings been the subject of a final and conclusive judgment by a court having jurisdiction in the matter.

The circumstances in which the courts of the country of the original court shall be deemed to have had, or not to have had, jurisdiction are set forth in s.4(2) and (3) of the Act.

The Act of 1933 is based on reciprocity, and not on the comity of nations; and therefore if the defendant does not submit to the jurisdiction of the foreign court, even though he has been duly served with process of that court under its powers to serve its process outside its own jurisdiction, the registration of the foreign judgment obtained against him in default will be set aside (*Société Coopérative Sidmetal v Titan International Ltd* [1966] 1 Q.B. 828; [1965] 3 All E.R. 494). If, however, the defendant who does not appear in the proceedings before the foreign court and suffers a default judgment to be entered against him but then applies to that court to appeal out of time and further appeals from the refusal of the foreign court to extend his time, and his solicitors had stated that all disputes between the parties had to be before that foreign court, he will be treated as having agreed to submit to the jurisdiction of that court under s.4(2)(a)(ii) of the of Act 1933 (*SA Consortium General Textiles v Sun and Sand Agencies Ltd* [1978] Q.B. 279; [1978] 2 W.L.R. 1; [1978] 2 All E.R. 339). On the other hand, submission under s.4(2)(a)(iii) of the Act of 1933 to "Courts of the country of that Court" can arise only where there is an express submission to the courts of a country rather than to an individual court, though Lord Denning M.R. expressed the view that the subsection should be construed widely, so that a submission to the jurisdiction of any one of the courts of the country should be treated as the equivalent to a submission to the jurisdiction of any of the other courts of that country (*ibid.*).

It has been held that the registration of a French judgment which could have been enforced by execution in France at the time of the registration is valid, although at a later date it could not have been so enforced (*Re A Debtor (No.11 of 1939)* [1939] 2 All E.R. 400, CA). In that case the court emphasised the importance of applying to set aside a registration without delay.

Fraud

74.7.2 In an application to set aside on the ground that the judgment was obtained by fraud, it is immaterial that the facts on which the defendants relied to establish fraud were known to them and could have been raised in the original proceedings, and the defendants are entitled to have tried the issue of fraud (*Syal v Heyward* (1948) 64 T.L.R. 476). No order for a payment into court can be made as a condition of trial (*ibid.*).

The jurisdiction to set aside a foreign judgment obtained by fraud under s.9(2) of the 1920 Act and s.4(1)(a) of the 1933 Act has been considered by the House of Lords. The House ruled in favour of the long established common law principle that there was a special defence on a foreign judgment namely that it had been obtained by fraud (see *Abouloff v Oppenheimer* (1882) 10 Q.B.D. 295 and *Vadala v Lawes* (1890) 25 Q.B.D. 310. The rule of law that a domestic judgment could only be set aside for fraud on fresh evidence that was not available at the trial did not apply to a foreign judgment and the position had not been changed by the 1920 and 1933 Acts. International comity might require that foreign judgments should be given the same degree of finality as English judgments, but that was a matter for Parliament and not the courts (*Owens Bank Ltd v Bracco* [1992] 2 A.C. 443).

Public Policy

74.7.3 See *Habib Bank Ltd v Ahmed, The Times*, November 2, 2000 to the effect that where a party seeks to set aside a foreign judgment upon the basis that it should no longer be recognised because of political upheavals subsequent to judgments of that state coming within the 1933 Act, the English court should allow the Foreign Office to make representations (appeal allowed on other grounds [2002] 1 Lloyd's Rep. 444).

Liao v Burswood Nominees Limited [2004] SGCA 45; [2005] 4 LRC 8 is a decision of the Singapore Court of Appeal refusing an appeal against the setting aside of registration of an Australian judgment. In that case the court refused to accept the appellant's submissions that registration of a judgment for a gambling debt should be set aside on grounds that it was against public policy. It was held that public policy operated with less vigour in the conflict of laws than in domestic law.

Appeals[1]

74.8—(1) An appeal against the granting or the refusal of registration under the 1982 Act or the Judgments Regulation must be made in accordance with Part 52, subject to the following provisions of this rule. 74.8

(2) Permission is not required—

(a) to appeal; or

(b) to put in evidence.

(3) If—

(a) the judgment debtor is not domiciled within a Contracting State or a Regulation State, as the case may be, and

(b) an application to extend the time for appealing is made within two months of service of the registration order,

the court may extend the period for filing an appellant's notice against the order granting registration, but not on grounds of distance.

(4) The appellant's notice must be served—

(a) where the appeal is against the granting of registration, within—

(i) one month; or

(ii) where service is to be effected on a party not domiciled within the jurisdiction, two months,

of service of the registration order;

(b) where the appeal is against the refusal of registration, within one month of the decision on the application for registration.

Appeals

Article 37(1) of the Brussels Convention provides, insofar as relevant, that an appeal against the decision authorising enforcement shall be lodged in accordance with the rules governing procedure in contentious matters in the United Kingdom. In England and Wales, that is with the High Court of Justice, or in the case of a maintenance judgment, with the Magistrates' Court. 74.8.1

After the appeal has been lodged, the appellant may apply for a stay of proceedings if an ordinary appeal has been lodged against the judgment in the State of origin, or if the time for such an appeal has not yet expired (art.38(1) of the Brussels Convention). However, as the Convention has established an enforcement procedure which constitutes an autonomous and complete system independent from the legal systems of the Contracting States, the provisions relating to the stay of proceedings pending appeal against registration must be restrictively and uniformly applied so as to avoid derogation from the Convention's object of establishing a simple and rapid machinery for the enforcement of judgments enforceable in the State of origin. Only the court seised of the appeal (the appeal under Arts 36 and 37(1) of the Convention) has the power to stay the proceedings (Jenard Report, OJ 1979 C 59, p.52).

There is no appeal from the decision to grant or refuse a stay made in such an application: Case C–183/90 *van Dalfsen v van Loon* [1991] E.C.R. I-4743. By art.37(2) of the Brussels Convention, the judgment given on the appeal may be contested only by a single further appeal on a point of law. art.37(2) and art.38(1) have been interpreted as meaning that a decision by which a court of a Contracting State, seised of an appeal

[1] Introduced by the Civil Procedure (Amendment) Rules 2002 (SI 2002/2058).

against authorization to enforce an enforceable judgment of a court in another Contracting State, refuses a stay or lifts a stay previously ordered, cannot be contested by an appeal in cassation or similar form of appeal limited to points of law only. Moreover, the court seised of such an appeal on a point of law under art.37(2) of the Brussels Convention does not have jurisdiction to impose or reimpose such a stay: Case C–432/93 *Société d'Informatique Service Réalisation Organisation v Ampersand Software BV* [1995] E.C.R. I-2269, para.42.

In *Citibank NA v Rafidian Bank* [2003] EWHC 1950 (QB) it was held that the two month time limit under r.74.8 was not unfair and was compliant with art.6 ECHR. In *Verdoliva v BM Van der Hoeven BV ECJ C–3/05*; [2006] All E.R. (D) 205 Feb, the European Court held that the time limit for appealing was 'strict and mandatory', and that service of the decision authorising enforcement in accordance with the procedural rules of the contracting state in which enforcement was sought.

In *Orams v Apostolides* [2006] EWHL 2226, QB, the House of Lords allowed the appeal against registration of a default judgment of a court in Nicosia in the Turkish controlled part of Cyprus against British citizens who had purchased land in the Turkish controlled part of Cyprus from a Turkish Cypriot. The respondent was a Greek Cypriot whose family had originally owned the land but who had been forced to flee as a result of the Turkish invasion of Cyprus in 1974, who had obtained a default judgment for damages for trespass and delivery up of the land. It was held that by virtue of the European Council's decision given effect to in protocol 10 to the Treaty of Accession the legislation of the EU was suspended in the Turkish controlled part of Cyprus, so that registration of the judgment could not be effected under the Judgment Regulation.

In *La Caisse Regional du Credit Agricole Nord du France v Ashdown* [2007] EWHC 528 (QB) Tugendhat J. allowed an appeal from an order for registration under the Judgments Regulation. Two judgments were under appeal. The defendant's submission that only one judgment should have been registered because only one was referred to in the application notice, although both were referred to in the witness statement in support and copied in exhibits, was rejected. The judge held that "the rules do not require the application to be in any particular form, other than as required by CPR r.74.4. The November 4 judgment is referred to in the evidence submitted pursuant to CPR r.4.4. That counts as an application." However, the claimant's appeal on the earlier judgment was allowed, on the defendant adducing evidence, not challenged by the claimant bank, from a French lawyer that the judgment was not enforceable in France.

Protective Measures

74.8.2 In *Banco Nacional de Comercio Exterior S.N.C. v Empresa de Telecomunicaciones de Cuba S.A.* [2007] EWHC 2322 (Comm) the court refused either to grant a stay of appeal or to grant an appeal against registration of a judgment of the First Civil Section of the Ordinary Court of Turin in favour of the claimant. The application for a stay relied on art.46.1 of the Judgments Regulation, as giving the English court jurisdiction to grant a stay. Tomlinson J. declined to grant the stay, the Turin court having already considered and rejected that application. The only ground relied upon for the appeal against registration was that pursuant to art.43 of the Judgments Regulation, namely that recognition was manifestly contrary to public policy in the Member State in which recognition was sought. The appellants relied upon the fact that an appeal was pending of the Turin judgment on grounds that an arbitration award in Paris, upon which the Turin proceedings were based, had been annulled. Tomlinson J., citing *Interdesco S.A. v Nullifire Limited* [1992] 1 Lloyd's Rep. 180 as giving guidance as to "the correct approach", held that it would normally be appropriate for the defendant to pursue his remedy in the foreign court. He relied also on Arts 36 and 45(2), which prevent a review of the judgment of the foreign court as to its substance.

The case of *Banco Nacional de Comercio Exterior SNC v Empresa de Telecomunicaciones de Cuba SA* (2007) EWHC 19 (Comm) concerned the enforcement of an Italian judgment, registered in England pursuant to art.38(2) of the Judgments Regulation. David Steel J. considered whether any protective measures must be limited to assets within England. It was held that where a foreign judgment has been registered in England under the Judgments Regulation, art.47 provides "an unrestricted and discrete code for the granting of provisional or protective measures in the context of enforcement", and there was no basis for restricting protective measures to the freezing or disclosure of domestic assets.

Enforcement[1]

74.9—(1) No steps may be taken to enforce a judgment— 74.9

(a) before the end of the period specified in accordance with rule 74.6(3)(d), or that period as extended by the court; or

(b) where there is an application under rule 74.7 or an appeal under rule 74.8, until the application or appeal has been determined.

(2) Any party wishing to enforce a judgment must file evidence of the service on the judgment debtor of—

(a) the registration order; and

(b) any other relevant order of the court.

(3) Nothing in this rule prevents the court from making orders to preserve the property of the judgment debtor pending final determination of any issue relating to the enforcement of the judgment.

Protection of Trading Interests Act 1980

Section 5 of the Act prohibits the recovery of multiple damages pursuant to a foreign judgment. However, the prohibition does not prevent the recovery of ordinary compensatory damages for private causesof action similar to those available under English law: *Lewis v Eliades (No.2)* [2003] EWCA Civ 1758. **74.9.1**

Execution

A stay of execution of a foreign judgment duly registered will not be granted, simply because the defendants bring or continue another action against the claimant, at any rate in the absence of special circumstances which render it inexpedient to enforce the judgment under O.47, r.1 (*Wagner (Ferdinand) v Laubocher Brothers & Co* [1970] 2 Q.B. 313; [1970] 2 W.L.R. 1019, CA). **74.9.2**

While retaining a discretion in the matter, the English court should give "full faith and credit" to the foreign judgment, even though there may be arguable grounds for disputing it or raising a counterclaim against it, and should not therefore in its discretion set the registration aside or adjourn the application to set it aside pending the defendants' appeal to the foreign court, still less pending the trial of an action in the foreign court of a claim by the defendant for damages for breach of contract (*SA Consortium General Textiles v Sun and Sand Agencies Ltd* [1978] Q.B. 279; [1978] 2 W.L.R. 1; [1978] 2 All E.R. 339, CA).

Article 46 (and art.37) of the Judgments Regulation give a discretion to the court to stay enforcement of a judgment if an appeal against judgment is pending. It follows that the court has a discretion to permit enforcement of a judgment subject to the Judgments Regulation even though an appeal is pending in the member state where judgment was given. See *B.J. van Dalfsen v Van Loon* [1991] ECJ C-183/90, *Peteteit v Babcock International Holdings Limited* [1990] 1 W.L.R. 350 and *Banco Nacional de Comercio Exterior S.N.C. v Empresa de Telecomunicaciones de Cuba S.A.* [2007] EWHC 2322 (Comm). **74.9.3**

Recognition[2]

74.10—(1) Registration of a judgment serves as a decision that the judgment is recognised for the purposes of the 1982 Act and the Judgments Regulation. 74.10

(2) An application for recognition of a judgment is governed by the same rules as an application for registration of a judgment

[1] Introduced by the Civil Procedure (Amendment) Rules 2002 (SI 2002/2058).
[2] Introduced by the Civil Procedure (Amendment) Rules 2002 (SI 2002/2058).

under the 1982 Act or under the Judgments Regulation, except that rule 74.4(5)(a) and (c) does not apply.

Recognition of Judgments under the Judgments Regulation

74.10.1 Article 33 of the Judgments Regulation that a judgment given in a Contracting State shall be recognised in the other Contracting States without any special procedure being required.

In *Prudential Assurance Co Ltd v Prudential Insurance Co of America* [2003] EWCA Civ 327, the Court of Appeal considered whether art.26 of the Brussels Convention (art.33 Judgments Regulation) requires a court in the United Kingdom to dismiss proceedings for infringement of a national trade mark registered in the United Kingdom register, where the infringement alleged is the use in the United Kingdom of a similar mark which has been registered as a national trade mark in the French register, in circumstances where there has been a judgment of a court in France rejecting opposition to the registration of that mark. The court held (per Chadwick L.J.) that the answer to that question is plainly "No" in a case such as this where the court in the United Kingdom is seised on the basis that the validity of its own national mark is in issue (see Arts 16(4) and 28 of the Brussels Convention). But, if the validity of the national mark is not in issue in the action before the court in the United Kingdom, it seemed to the Court of Appeal that the answer is much less clear.

Purpose of recognition

74.10.2 Recognition under art.33 of the Judgments Convention includes enforcement but also includes recognition for the purpose of cause of action estoppel and issue estoppel (*Berkeley Administration Inc v McClelland (No.2)* [1995] I.L.Pr. 201).

Judgment

74.10.3 The definition of judgment is to be found in art.32 of the Judgments Regulation where it is stated that "for the purposes of this Regulation, 'judgment' means any judgment given by a court or tribunal of a Member State, whatever the judgment may be called, including a decree, order, decision or writ of execution, as well as the determination of costs or expenses by an officer of the court."

Judgment refers solely to judicial decisions actually given by a court or tribunal of a Contracting State, and such decisions must emanate from a judicial body of a Contracting State deciding on its own authority on the issues between the parties: Case C–414/92 *Solo Kleinmotoren GmbH v Emilio Boch* [1994] E.C.R. I-2237, paras 15 and 17.

The determination of costs by an officer of the court is treated as a judgment since the registrar acts as an officer of the court which decided on the substance of the matter and, in the event of a challenge to the registrar's decision, the court decides the issue (see Report of the Committee of Experts on the Convention (OJ 1979 C 59, at the foot of p.42)).

The similar German Zahlungsbefehl procedure is also enforceable: Case 166/80 *Klomps v Michel* [1981] E.C.R. 1593.

An order obtained without notice to the defendant does not qualify as a judgment for the purposes of art.32 of the Judgments Convention, at least until the defendant has applied unsuccessfully for it to be set aside: Case 125/79 *Denilauler v Couchet Frères* [1980] E.C.R. 1553.

A settlement is not a judgment for the purposes of art.25 of the Brussels Convention, (art.32 of Judgments Convention) even if it was reached in the court of a Contracting State and brings legal proceedings to an end (see *Solo Kleinmotoren GmbH* at para.18). Settlements in court are essentially contractual in that their terms depend first and foremost on the parties' intention (Report of the Committee of Experts on the Convention *op. cit.*, p.56).

The definition of "judgment" given in art.25 of the Brussels Convention and art.32 of the Judgments Regulation applies to all the provisions of the respective instruments in which that term is used.

Article 34: Denial of recognition

74.10.4 Notwithstanding art.36 of the Judgments Regulation) which provides that "under no circumstances may a foreign judgment be reviewed as to its substance", there are a number of circumstances where the court of the State in which recognition is sought must not recognise a judgment. These are set out in art.34 of the Judgments Regulation) as follows:

(1) Recognition is contrary to public policy in the State in which recognition is sought.

(2) Where the judgment was given in default of appearance, if the defendant was not duly served with the document which instituted the proceedings or with an equivalent document in sufficient time to enable him to arrange for his defence.

(3) If the judgment is irreconcilable with a judgment given in a dispute between the same parties in the State in which recognition is sought.

(4) If the judgment is irreconcilable with an earlier judgment given in a non-contracting State involving the same cause of action and between the same parties, provided that this latter judgment fulfils the conditions necessary for its recognition in the state addressed.

Public Policy

The public policy clause in art.34(1) of the Judgments Regulation "ought to operate only in exceptional cases" (see the Report on the Convention on jurisdiction and the enforcement of judgments in civil and commercial matters, O.J. 1979 C59, p.1, at 44). Recourse to it is in any event precluded when the issue must be resolved on the basis of a specific provision such as art.27(2): see, in connection with art.27(2), Case C–172/91 *Sonntag v Waidmann* [1993] E.C.R. I-1963 paras 23–24 and in connection with art.27(3), Case 145/86 *Hoffmann v Kreig* [1988] E.C.R. 645 para.21 and *Hendrikman v Druck* [1996] E.C.R. I–4945 at para.23. **74.10.5**

The public policy exception does not generally allow a foreign judgment to be challenged on the grounds that it was obtained by fraud, unlike the position at common law and under the Administration of Justice Act 1920 and the Foreign Judgments (Reciprocal Enforcement) Act 1933. In *Interdesco v Nullifire Ltd.* [1992] 1 Lloyd's Rep. 180, it was held that where registration of a foreign judgment under the Convention is challenged on the ground that the foreign court has been fraudulently deceived, the English court should first consider whether a remedy lies in the foreign court in question. If so, it would normally be appropriate to leave the defendant to pursue his remedy in that jurisdiction.

A judgment obtained in a Contracting State in breach of an anti-suit injunction would not be enforced in England as against public policy (*Philip Alexander Securities and Futures Ltd v Bamberger* [1997] EuLR 63, I.L.Pr. 73, CA).

Although the public policy clause is narrowly construed, recourse to it must be regarded as being possible in exceptional circumstances, such as where there is a manifest breach of a rule of law regarded as essential in the legal order of the State in which enforcement is sought. Where a defendant was unaware that the trial had been reactivated 12 years after it was stayed until even the time for an appeal had passed, he was manifestly denied a fair trial within Article 6 of the Human Rights Convention, and it was contrary to public policy to enforce the claimant's judgment against him (*Maronier v Larmer* [2002] EWCA Civ 774; [2003] Q.B. 620). Further, in Case C–7/98 *Dieter Krombach v André Bamberski* [2000] E.C.R. I-1935; [2001] Q.B. 709 the European Court of Justice held that the court of the State in which enforcement is sought can, with respect to a defendant domiciled in that State and prosecuted for an intentional offence, take account, in relation to the public policy clause in art.27(1) of the Brussels Convention, of the fact that the court of the State of origin refused to allow that person to have his defence presented unless he appeared in person. The court found that the guarantees laid down in the State of origin and in the Convention itself were insufficient to protect a defendant from a manifest breach of his right to defend himself before the court of origin, as recognised by the ECHR.

However, the court of the State in which enforcement is sought cannot refuse recognition of a decision emanating from another Contracting State solely on the ground that it considers that national or Community law was misapplied in that decision. In Case C–38/98 *Regie Nationale des Usines Renault SA v Maxicar SpA (C38/98)* [2000] E.C.R. I-2973, Renault applied to the Italian Appeal Court for a declaration of enforceability of a judgment of the French Court of Cassation. Maxicar challenged enforceability on the grounds that as the judgment recognised the existence of an intellectual property right in body parts for cars and conferred on the holder of that right protection by enabling him to prevent third parties trading in another Contracting State from manufacturing, selling, transporting, importing or exporting in that Contracting State such body parts, it was contrary to public policy under art.27(1) (now art.34(1)). The European Court of Justice held that since an error of law such as the one alleged did not constitute a manifest breach of a rule of law regarded as essential in the legal order of the State in which enforcement is sought, art.27(1) could not be relied upon.

In *Banco Nacional de Comercio Exterior S.N.C. v Empresa de Telecomunicaciones de Cuba S.A.* [2007] EWHC 2322 (Comm) the court refused either to grant a stay of appeal or to grant an appeal against registration of a judgment of the First Civil Section of the Ordinary Court of Turin in favour of the Claimant. The application for a stay relied on art.46.1 Judgments Regulation, as giving the English court jurisdiction to grant a stay. Tomlinson J. declined to grant the stay, the Turin court having already considered and rejected that application. The only ground relied upon for the appeal against registration was that pursuant to art.43 of the Judgments Regulation, namely that recognition was manifestly contrary to public policy in the Member State in which recognition was sought. The appellants relied upon the fact that an appeal was pending of the Turin judgment on grounds that an arbitration award in Paris, upon which the Turin proceedings were based, had been annulled. Tomlinson J., citing *Interdesco S.A. v Nullifire Limited* [1992] 1 Lloyd's Reports 180 as giving guidance as to 'the correct approach', held that it would normally be appropriate for the defendant to pursue his remedy in the foreign court. He relied also on art.36 and 45(2), which prevent a review of the judgment of the foreign court as to its substance.

Judgment in default of appearance

74.10.6 (art.34(2) of the Judgments Regulation denies recognition to a judgment given in default of appearance if the defendant "was not duly served with the document which instituted the proceedings or with an equivalent document in sufficient time to enable him to arrange for his defence". Its purpose is to ensure that a judgment is not recognised or enforced under the Regulation if the defendant has not had an opportunity of defending himself before the court first seised: Case 166/80 *Klomps v Michel* [1981] E.C.R. 1593 para.9, and Case C–172/91 *Sonntag v Waidmann* [1993] E.C.R. I-1963 para.38. This provision is to be strictly complied with and if service does not comply with the *lex loci executionis* the judgment cannot be enforced: Case C–123/91 *Minalment GmbH v Brandeis Ltd* [1992] E.C.R. I -5661.

In *British Seafood Limited v Kruk* [2008] EWHC 1528 (QB), Coulson J. dismissed an appeal against registration of a judgment given in default of appearance. The judge considered the effect of art.34.2 of the Judgments Regulation, under which recognition of a foreign judgment given in default of appearance must be refused if the judgment debtor was not given sufficient notice of the proceedings.

It was held that the court should adopt a practical approach, and look to function rather than form. If, for practical purposes, the judgment debtor had been informed of the proceedings and knew that it was necessary to arrange for a defence, then art.34.2 was not engaged.

Default of appearance

74.10.7 In Case C–172/91 *Sonntag v Waidmann* [1993] E.C.R. I-1963, the Court of Justice considered a number of questions referred to it by the Bundesgerichtschof concerning Arts 1, 27(2) and 37(2) of the Brussels Convention arising out of proceedings regarding the enforcement in Germany of the civil law provisions of a judgment given by an Italian criminal court. In response to the question regarding art.27(2), the European Court of Justice stated that non-recognition of a judgment for the reasons set out in art.27(2) of the Brussels Convention is possible only where the defendant was in default of appearance in the original proceedings. Consequently, that provision may not be relied upon where the defendant appeared. A defendant is deemed to have appeared for the purposes of art.27(2) of the Brussels Convention (art.34(2) of the Judgments Regulation) where, in connection with a claim for compensation joined to criminal proceedings, he answered at the trial, through counsel of his own choice, to the criminal charges but did not express a view on the civil claim, on which oral argument was also submitted in the presence of his counsel. (This does not appear to exclude the possibility that a defendant, whilst contesting the criminal proceedings, might refuse to enter an appearance for the purpose of the civil proceedings.)

Where proceedings are initiated against a person without his knowledge and a lawyer appears before the court first seised on his behalf but without his authority, such a person is quite powerless to defend himself, and must be regarded as "a defendant in default of appearance" within the meaning of art.27(2) of the Brussels Convention. art.27(2) of the Convention (art.34(2) of the Judgments Regulation) therefore applies to judgments given against a defendant who was not duly served with, or notified of, the document instituting proceedings in sufficient time and who was not validly represented during those proceedings, albeit that the judgments were not given in default of appearance because someone purporting to represent the defendant appeared before the court first seised: Case C–78/95 *Hendrikman and Feyen v Magenta Druck & Verlag GmbH* [1996] E.C.R. I-4943, paras 18–21.

The courts of some Contracting and Regulation States have been reluctant to recognise and enforce 'default judgments' which have been obtained in the English courts. For this reason it has been common practice for a claim which it is ultimately intended to enforce in a Brussels/Lugano Convention Contracting or a Regulation State to be taken to trial where the defendant is in default: *Berliner Bank AG v Karageorgis and another* [1996] 1 Lloyd's Rep. 426. In such a case the court should be invited to make an express finding of the facts on which its jurisdiction is based under art.28 of the Convention (art.35(2) of the Judgments Regulation). It has been considered to be advisable to rely on affidavit evidence rather than witness statements. The position should be simplified by the European Enforcement Order, (Regulation (EC) No.805/2004 of the European Parliament and of the Council of April 21, 2004), which came into force on October 21, 2005. This creates a simplified method of enforcement for uncontested claims throughout the EU Member States (except Denmark). (See Sect.V).

Duly served

The requirements of due service and service in sufficient time constitute two separate and concurrent safeguards for a defendant who fails to appear, and the absence of one of those safeguards is therefore a sufficient ground for refusal to recognise a foreign judgment. Questions concerning the curing of defective service are governed by the law of the Contracting State in which judgment was given, including any international agreements: Case C–305/88 *Lancry SA v Peters und Sickert KG* [1990] E.C.R. I-2725. **74.10.8**

In *Noirhomme v Walklate* [1992] 1 Lloyd's Rep. 427, Belgian process was served by post on a defendant in England, following which the defendant did not enter an appearance and the claimant entered a default judgment. The judgment was subsequently registered in England and the defendant appealed on the ground that he had not been duly served. H.H. Judge Kershaw, Q.C. held that such service complied with both art.27 of the Brussels Convention and art.15 of the Hague Convention. The court further held that it had power to stay the execution of such a judgment under O.47, r.1.

Served with the document which instituted the proceedings

In Case C–474/93 *Firma Hengst Import BV v Anna Maria Campese* [1995] E.C.R. I-2113 the Court of Justice held that an order against a defendant for payment (the decreto ingiuntivo) which was obtained without notice (Procedimento d'ingiunzione) and which was served on the defendant along with an application by the plaintiff, together constituted a "document which instituted the proceedings or an equivalent document" within the meaning of art.27(2) of the Brussels Convention, because the joint service of the documents started time running for the defendant to oppose the order, and the plaintiff could not obtain an enforceable order before the expiry of the time-limit. **74.10.9**

In sufficient time

The requirement that service of the document which instituted the proceedings should have been effected in sufficient time is applicable even where service was effected within a period prescribed by the court of the state in which the judgment was given or where the defendant resided, exclusively or otherwise, within the jurisdiction or that court or in the same country as that court. For a consideration of this requirement, see Case 166/80 *Klomps v Michel* [1981] E.C.R. 1593. To avoid interpreting the requirement of service in a restrictive and formalistic manner, in examining whether service was effected in sufficient time, the court in which enforcement is sought may take account of exceptional circumstances which arose *after* service was duly effected, such as the fact that the fact that the claimant was aware of the defendant's new address after service was effected, and that the defendant was responsible for the failure of the duly served document to reach the claimant: Case 49/84 *Debaecker v Bouwman* [1985] E.C.R. 1779. **74.10.10**

In *TSN Kunststoffrecycling GmbH v Jurgens* [2002] EWCA Civ 11; [2002] I.L.Pr. 34, the proceedings before the Court of Appeal concerned the registration of a German default judgment. The defendant had had two weeks to enter an appearance in the German proceedings, which he had failed to do, and a default judgment was issued five weeks after service. The Court of Appeal held that the defendant did have sufficient time to arrange his defence within art.27(2) of the Brussels Convention. Where, as in that case, the German procedural law was that notice of appearance at any time before judgment issued would have prevented issue, the relevant period was the whole period until judgment issued in default.

Irreconcilable with a judgment in a dispute between the same parties in State in which recognition sought

74.10.11 In order to ascertain whether two judgments are irreconcilable within the meaning of art.34(3) of the Judgments Regulation (art.27(3) of the Brussels Convention), the Court of Justice has held that it should be examined whether they entail legal consequences that are mutually exclusive (see Case 145/86 *Hoffmann* [1988] ECR 645, para.22).

In a reference from the Bundesgerichtshof (Germany), the Court of Justice gave a preliminary ruling in proceedings concerning a company, Italian Leather, who were seeking to prohibit WECO from using its brand name for the marketing of leather products after another German court had dismissed an identical application made by the same claimant against the same defendant. In Case C–80/00 *Italian Leather SpA* (judgment of the court of June 6, 2002), it was held that on a proper construction of art.27(3) of the Brussels Convention, a foreign decision on interim measures ordering an obligor not to carry out certain acts is irreconcilable with a decision on interim measures refusing to grant such an order in a dispute between the same parties in the State where recognition is sought. It was also held that where a court of the State in which recognition is sought finds that a judgment of a court of another State is irreconcilable with a judgment given by a court of the former State in a dispute between the same parties, it is required to refuse to recognise the foreign judgment.

Article 34(3) of the Judgments Convention (art 27(3) of the Brussels Convention) must be interpreted strictly, which means that an enforceable settlement reached before a court of the State in which recognition is sought in order to settle legal proceedings which are in progress does not constitute a "judgment" within the meaning of that provision: Case C–414/92 *Solo Kleinmotoren GmbH v Emilio Boch* [1994] E.C.R. I-2237 para.20.

The words "irreconcilable judgment" used in art.27(3) of the Convention do not have the same meaning as the same words used in art.22: Case C–406/92 *The Maciej Rataj* [1994] E.C.R. I-5439.

Rights in property arising out of a matrimonial relationship

74.10.12 A distinction has to be drawn between an order regulating rights of a property arising out of the matrimonial relationship which is not enforceable (art.1(1) of the Convention and art.1(2)(a) of the Regulation) and a maintenance order which is enforceable (art.5(2) of the Regulation). On a reference from the Arrondissementrechtbank Amsterdam in Case C–220/95 *Boogaard v Laumen* [1997] E.C.R. I-1147, the Court of Justice considered an application for enforcement, in the Netherlands, of a judgment in divorce proceedings given by the High Court of England and Wales which ordered payment of a lump sum and transfer of ownership in certain property by Boogaard to his former wife, Laumen. The Court of Justice held that if a provision awarded is designed to enable one spouse to provide for himself or herself or if the needs and resources of each of the spouses are taken into consideration in the determination of its amount, the decision will be concerned with maintenance. On the other hand, where the provision awarded is solely concerned with dividing property between spouses, the decision will be concerned with rights in property arising out of a matrimonial relationship and will not therefore be enforceable.

A decision which does both these things may, in accordance with art.42 of the Brussels Convention (in an amended form as art.48 of the Judgments Convention), be enforced in part if it clearly shows the aims to which the different parts of the judicial provision correspond (*Boogaard* at para.22).

Enforcement

74.10.13 The general rule, set out in art.38 of the Judgments Regulation, is that a judgment given in a Member State and enforceable in that State is to be enforced in another Contracting State when, on the application of any interested party, the order for its enforcement has been issued there.

Article 45.1 of the Judgments Regulation provides that:

"The court with which an appeal is lodged ... shall refuse or revoke a declaration of enforceability only on one of the grounds specified in Articles 34 and 354". Article 41 of the Judgments Regulation provides that the judgments shall be declared enforceable immediately on completion of the formalities in art.53 without any review under Arts 34 and 35. The party against whom enforcement is sought shall not at this stage of the proceedings be entitled to make any submissions on the application.

Issue of execution

In Case C–267/97 *Coursier v Fortis Bank SA* [1999] E.C.R. I-2543 the Court of Justice held that the requirement under art.31 of the Brussels Convention (Article 38 of the Judgments Regulation) that a foreign judgment be enforceable in the court of the State of origin, referred solely to the enforceability, in formal terms, of foreign decisions, and not to the circumstances in which such decisions may be executed in the State of origin. The judgment had become unenforceable in the court of the State of origin because of the insolvency of the judgment debtor there. It is for the court of the State in which enforcement is sought, in appeal proceedings brought under art.36 of the Brussels Convention (art.43 of the Judgments Regulation), to determine, in accordance with its domestic law including the rules of private international law, the legal effects of a decision given in the State of origin in relation to a court-supervised liquidation. **74.10.14**

Article 46 (and art.37) Judgments Regulation give a discretion to the court to stay enforcement of a judgment if an appeal against judgment is pending. It follows that the court has a discretion to permit enforcement of a judgment subject to the Judgments Regulation even though an appeal is pending in the member state where judgment was given. See *B.J. van Dalfsen v Van Loon* [1991] ECJ C–183/90, *Peteteit v Babcock International Holdings Limited* [1990] 1 W.L.R. 350 and *Banco Nacional de Comercio Exterior S.N.C. v Empresa de Telecomunicaciones de Cuba S.A.* [2007] EWHC 2322 (Comm).

Authentic instruments and approved court settlements

Article 50 of the Brussels Convention (art.57 of the Judgments Regulation as amended) provides that an "Authentic Instrument" which is enforceable in one Contracting State shall have an order for enforcement made in another Contracting State on application being made in accordance with the procedures provided for in art.31 *et seq.* (art.38 *et seq.* of the Judgments Regulation). Article 51 of the Brussels Convention (in an amended form as art.58 of the Judgments Regulation) applies the same procedure to "Settlements approved by a Court in the course of proceedings and enforceable in the State in which it is concluded." Section 13(1) of the Civil Jurisdiction and Judgments Act 1982 enabled Her Majesty by Order in Council to apply the Act to authentic instruments and court settlements with "such modifications as may be specified in the Order". The court was faced with the problem that s.2 of the 1982 Act gives the Conventions the force of law and the Conventions clearly make authentic instruments and court settlements enforceable as judgments. In the absence of an Order, the court had been allowing registration where the case that enforcement under the domestic law was permitted was clearly made out. This problem was resolved by the Civil Jurisdiction and Judgments (Authentic Instruments and Court Settlements) Order 1993 (SI 1993/604) which came into force on April 1, 1993. **74.10.15**

An authentic instrument or a court settlement is now to be treated "as if it was a judgment which had been originally given" (para.2(2)).

In the application of s.11 of the 1982 Act to authentic instruments there shall be substituted for s.11(a) the following:

"A document purporting to be a copy of an authenticated instrument drawn up or registered, and enforceable, in a Contracting State other than the United Kingdom is duly authenticated for the purpose of this section if it purports to be certified to be a true copy of such an instrument by a person duly authorised in that Contracting State to do so" (para.4(2)).

An example of when an application for recognition of a judgment may be made is where the judgment is for a declaration. **74.10.16**

The case of *Phillips v Avena* [2005] EWHC 3333 (Ch); *The Times*, November 22, 2005, [2005] All E.R. (D.) 118 (Dec) considered whether there should be recognition of a judgment of a court in Alberta, Canada, in relation to the assets of a deceased person's estate. The Alberta court found in favour of the Claimant. In a later judgment, on the without notice application of the First Defendant to a court in Panama, the Panama court made an order in the First Defendant's favour which was inconsistent with the judgment of the Alberta court, in relation to certain assets. It was held that a foreign judgment given in a foreign country with jurisdiction to give that judgment, where that judgment was not impeachable, might be enforced if the judgment was for a debt or definite sum of money and was final and conclusive. Where there were two competing judgments, the judgment that was earlier in time should be given effect to, rather than the latter of the two.

Recognition

74.10.17 Recognition under art.26 of the Conventions includes enforcement but also includes recognition for the purpose of cause of action estoppel and issue estoppel (*Berkeley Administration Inc v McClelland (No.2)* [1995] I.L.Pr. 201).

Authentic instruments and court settlements[1]

74.11 **74.11 The rules governing the registration of judgments under the 1982 Act or under the Judgments Regulation apply as appropriate and with any necessary modifications for the enforcement of—**

(a) authentic instruments which are subject to—

(i) article 50 of Schedule 1 to the 1982 Act;

(ii) article 50 of Schedule 3C to the 1982 Act; and

(iii) article 57 of the Judgments Regulation; and

(b) court settlements which are subject to—

(i) article 51 of Schedule 1 to the 1982 Act;

(ii) article 51 of Schedule 3C to the 1982 Act; and

(iii) article 58 of the Judgments Regulation.

II. Enforcement in Foreign Countries of Judgments of the High Court and County Courts

Application for a certified copy of a judgment[2]

74.12 **74.12—(1) This Section applies to applications—**

(a) to the High Court under section 10 of the 1920 Act;

(b) to the High Court or to a county court under section 10 of the 1933 Act;

(c) to the High Court or to a county court under section 12 of the 1982 Act; or

(d) to the High Court or to a county court under article 54 of the Judgments Regulation.

(2) A judgment creditor who wishes to enforce in a foreign country a judgment obtained in the High Court or in a county court must apply for a certified copy of the judgment.

(3) The application may be made without notice.

Evidence in support[3]

74.13 **74.13—(1) The application must be supported by written evidence exhibiting copies of—**

---

[1] Introduced by the Civil Procedure (Amendment) Rules 2002 (SI 2002/2058).
[2] Introduced by the Civil Procedure (Amendment) Rules 2002 (SI 2002/2058).
[3] Introduced by the Civil Procedure (Amendment) Rules 2002 (SI 2002/2058).

(a) the claim form in the proceedings in which judgment was given;
(b) evidence that it was served on the defendant;
(c) the statements of case; and
(d) where relevant, a document showing that for those proceedings the applicant was an assisted person or an LSC funded client, as defined in rule 43.2(1)(h) and (i).

(2) The written evidence must—
(a) identify the grounds on which the judgment was obtained;
(b) state whether the defendant objected to the jurisdiction and, if he did, the grounds of his objection;
(c) show that the judgment—
(i) has been served in accordance with Part 6 and rule 40.4, and
(ii) is not subject to a stay of execution;
(d) state—
(i) the date on which the time for appealing expired or will expire;
(ii) whether an appeal notice has been filed;
(iii) the status of any application for permission to appeal; and
(iv) whether an appeal is pending;
(e) state whether the judgment provides for the payment of a sum of money, and if so, the amount in respect of which it remains unsatisfied;
(f) state whether interest is recoverable on the judgment, and if so, either—
(i) the amount of interest which has accrued up to the date of the application, or
(ii) the rate of interest, the date from which it is recoverable, and the date on which it ceases to accrue.

Judgment entered in the High Court

Not every judgment of the High Court can be made the subject of a certificate. The rule applies to "a judgment under which a sum of money is payable, not being a sum payable in respect of taxes or other charges of a like nature or in respect of a fine or other penalty" (1933 Act s.10). **74.13.1**

It applies to an order to pay costs in divorce proceedings.

The enlargement of the County Court jurisdiction following the Courts and Legal Services Act 1990 raises the question of whether judgments transferred to the High Court for enforcement and which are to be treated "for all purposes" as a judgment or order of the High Court can be granted certificates for enforcement abroad under this rule and the 1920 and 1933 Acts. As these Acts are based on reciprocity it cannot be assumed that countries with which these reciprocal arrangements exist will enforce judgments other than those of the "High Court" or "Superior Court" as defined in the Acts, however they are described in subsequent domestic legislation which includes the repeal of references to the "Superior Court" in the 1933 Act by s.54 of the Civil Jurisdiction and Judgments Act 1982. A number of countries to which the 1933 Act applies are parties to the Brussels and Lugano Conventions (incorporated into English, Scottish and Northern Irish Law by the 1982 Act) under which the certification of county court judgments raises no problems and in such cases applications for certificates should be made to the county court. In respect of countries not party to these conventions it can only be stated with reasonable certainty that the Isle of Man will enforce under the 1933 Act county court judgments transferred to the High Court for enforcement and certified under this rule by the High Court (*Stapleford Flying Club v Kreisky*, April 18, 1991, unrep., High Court of the Isle of Man, Deemster Corrin). In all cases under the 1933 Act that do not fall within s.10, application for certificates should be made in the High Court on the transferred county court judgment, though there is a risk, other than in the Isle of Man, that the certificate will be rejected by the receiving country. The Royal Court of Jersey has in fact rejected registration of an English county court judgment transferred to the High Court for enforcement. The basis of rejection was the absence of reciprocity in that a judgment of the Jersey Petty Debts Court would not be amenable to registration in England. Bailiff Bailhache commented that though the English courts might be bound to regard the judgment of the county court as a judgment of the High Court for all purposes, it was not a judgment "given in a superior court" for the purposes of the Jersey legislation (*Re Hardwick* [1995] The Jersey Law Reports 245). The position under the 1920 Act remains unchanged and permits a certificate to be issued only in respect of judgments "obtained in the High Court" which leaves open the question of whether the receiving court will consider a transferred county court judgment to be such a judgment.

No orders have been made under s.32 of the Civil Jurisdiction and Judgments Act 1982 applying all or any part of that Act to the Isle of Man, Channel Islands, Gibraltar or the Cyprus sovereign bases.

"State that the time for appealing has expired"

74.13.2 These words are inapplicable to a judgment signed in default of acknowledgment of service or defence under Pt 12. The witness statement or affidavit in such a case must show that no application has been made to set aside the judgment. The form of certificate will then state that the defendant may apply to set the judgment aside although he has not yet done so (Practice Direction, July 17, 1962 seems to be the authority for this practice followed by the Judgment and Orders Section of the Central Office of the Royal Courts of Justice). For default judgments intended to be enforced in European Member States the more appropriate procedure may be to apply for a European Enforcement Certificate (see Sect.V), if the judgment falls within the relevant criteria.

Legislation for foreign public documents

74.13.3 See the Convention for abolishing this requirement (Cmnd. 2617) in the case of certain public documents.

Where the application should be made

74.13.4 Applications for certified copies of the High Court should be made to a High Court Master, save that applications for certified copies of judgments entered in District Registries should be made to the District Registry concerned where the District Judge may exercise the powers of a Master under this rule: see CPR r.2.4. This brings the procedure under the 1933 Act into line with the procedure under the Brussels Convention and Judgments Regulation regime.

III. Enforcement of United Kingdom Judgments in other parts of the United Kingdom

Interpretation[1]

74.14 **74.14 In this Section—**

(a) "money provision" means a provision for the payment of one or more sums of money in a judgment whose enforcement is governed by section 18 of, and Schedule 6 to, the 1982 Act; and

(b) "non-money provision" means a provision for any relief

[1] Introduced by the Civil Procedure (Amendment) Rules 2002 (SI 2002/2058).

or remedy not requiring payment of a sum of money in a judgment whose enforcement is governed by section 18 of, and Schedule 7 to, the 1982 Act.

Registration of money judgments in the High Court[1]

74.15—(1) This rule applies to applications to the High Court under paragraph 5 of Schedule 6 to the 1982 Act for the registration of a certificate for the enforcement of the money provisions of a judgment— 74.15

(a) which has been given by a court in another part of the United Kingdom, and

(b) to which section 18 of that Act applies.

(2) The certificate must within six months of the date of its issue be filed in the Central Office of the Supreme Court, together with a copy certified by written evidence to be a true copy.

Registration of non-money judgments in the High Court[2]

74.16—(1) This rule applies to applications to the High Court under paragraph 5 of Schedule 7 to the 1982 Act for the registration for enforcement of the non-money provisions of a judgment— 74.16

(a) which has been given by a court in another part of the United Kingdom, and

(b) to which section 18 of that Act applies.

(2) An application under paragraph (1) may be made without notice.

(3) An application under paragraph (1) must be accompanied—

(a) by a certified copy of the judgment issued under Schedule 7 to the 1982 Act; and

(b) by a certificate, issued not more than six months before the date of the application, stating that the conditions set out in paragraph 3 of Schedule 7 are satisfied in relation to the judgment.

(4) Rule 74.6 applies to judgments registered under Schedule 7 to the 1982 Act as it applies to judgments registered under section 4 of that Act.

(5) Rule 74.7 applies to applications to set aside the registration of a judgment under paragraph 9 of Schedule 7 to the 1982 Act as it applies to applications to set aside registrations under the 1920 and 1933 Acts.

Certificates of High Court and county court money judgments[3]

74.17—(1) *This rule applies to applications* under paragraph 2 of Schedule 6 to the 1982 Act for a certificate to enable the money provisions of a judgment of the High Court or of a county court to be enforced in another part of the United Kingdom. 74.17

[1] Introduced by the Civil Procedure (Amendment) Rules 2002 (SI 2002/2058).
[2] Introduced by the Civil Procedure (Amendment) Rules 2002 (SI 2002/2058).
[3] Introduced by the Civil Procedure (Amendment) Rules 2002 (SI 2002/2058).

(2) The judgment creditor may apply for a certificate by filing at the court where the judgment was given or has been entered written evidence stating—

(a) the name and address of the judgment creditor and, if known, of the judgment debtor;

(b) the sums payable and unsatisfied under the money provisions of the judgment;

(c) where interest is recoverable on the judgment, either—

(i) the amount of interest which has accrued up to the date of the application, or

(ii) the rate of interest, the date from which it is recoverable, and the date on which it ceases to accrue;

(d) that the judgment is not stayed;

(e) the date on which the time for appealing expired or will expire;

(f) whether an appeal notice has been filed;

(g) the status of any application for permission to appeal; and

(h) whether an appeal is pending.

Certified copies of High Court and county court non-money judgments[1]

74.18 **74.18—(1) This rule applies to applications under paragraph 2 of Schedule 7 to the 1982 Act for a certified copy of a judgment of the High Court or of a county court to which section 18 of the Act applies and which contains non-money provisions for enforcement in another part of the United Kingdom.**

(2) An application under paragraph (1) may be made without notice.

(3) The applicant may apply for a certified copy of a judgment by filing at the court where the judgment was given or has been entered written evidence stating—

(a) full particulars of the judgment;

(b) the name and address of the judgment creditor and, if known, of the judgment debtor;

(c) that the judgment is not stayed;

(d) the date on which the time for appealing expired or will expire;

(e) whether an appeal notice has been filed;

(f) the status of any application for permission to appeal; and

(g) whether an appeal is pending.

Application for stay of enforcement of a money judgment

74.18.1 Under para.9 of Sch.6 to the 1982 Act an application may be made to stay the enforcement of the certificate issued under r.74.15. On such an application the registering court has to be satisfied that the applicant is entitled and intends to apply to the judgment court to set aside or stay the judgment and if the registering court is

[1] Introduced by the Civil Procedure (Amendment) Rules 2002 (SI 2002/2058).

so satisfied it may stay the enforcement proceedings on such terms as it thinks fit for such period as may be reasonably sufficient to enable the application in the judgment court to be disposed of.

Where the English High Court is the registering court, though there is no settled procedure, it is suggested that the best practice would be to make the application to stay execution by application notice supported by witness statement so that the court has evidence before it on which it "may be satisfied" of the matters referred to in the paragraph. Such an application should follow the procedure under Sch.1, RSC O.47, r.1 and where an immediate stay is required the initial application should be without notice being served on any other party to the practice master.

IV. Enforcement in England and Wales of European Community Judgments

Interpretation[1]

74.19 In this Section— 74.19

(a) "Community judgment" means any judgment, decision or order which is enforceable under—

(i) article 244 or 256 of the Treaty establishing the European Community;

(ii) article 18, 159 or 164 of the Euratom Treaty;

(iii) article 44 or 92 of the ECSC Treaty;

(iv) article 82 of Council Regulation (EC) 40/94 of 20 December 1993 on the Community trade mark; or

(v) article 71 of Council Regulation (EC) 6/2002 of 12 December 2001 on Community designs;

(b) "Euratom inspection order" means an order made by the President of the European Court, or a decision of the Commission of the European Communities, under article 81 of the Euratom Treaty;

(c) "European Court" means the Court of Justice of the European Communities;

(d) "order for enforcement" means an order under the authority of the Secretary of State that the Community judgment to which it is appended is to be registered for enforcement in the United Kingdom.

Application for registration of a Community judgment[2]

74.20 An application to the High Court for the registration of a Community judgment may be made without notice. 74.20

Evidence in support[3]

74.21—(1) An application for registration must be supported by *written evidence exhibiting*— 74.21

(a) the Community judgment and the order for its enforcement, or an authenticated copy; and

[1] Introduced by the Civil Procedure (Amendment) Rules 2002 (SI 2002/2058) and amended by the Civil Procedure (Amendment No.5) Rules 2003 (SI 2003/3361).

[2] Introduced by the Civil Procedure (Amendment) Rules 2002 (SI 2002/2058).

[3] Introduced by the Civil Procedure (Amendment) Rules 2002 (SI 2002/2058).

(b) where the judgment is not in English, a translation of it into English—

(i) certified by a notary public or other qualified person; or

(ii) accompanied by written evidence confirming that the translation is accurate.

(2) Where the application is for registration of a Community judgment which is a money judgment, the evidence must state—

(a) the name of the judgment creditor and his address for service within the jurisdiction;

(b) the name of the judgment debtor and his address or place of business, if known;

(c) the amount in respect of which the judgment is unsatisfied; and

(d) that the European Court has not suspended enforcement of the judgment.

Registration orders[1]

74.22 **74.22—(1) A copy of the order granting permission to register a Community judgment ("the registration order") must be served on every person against whom the judgment was given.**

(2) The registration order must state the name and address for service of the person who applied for registration, and must exhibit—

(a) a copy of the registered Community judgment; and

(b) a copy of the order for its enforcement.

(3) In the case of a Community judgment which is a money judgment, the registration order must also state the right of the judgment debtor to apply within 28 days for the variation or cancellation of the registration under rule 74.23.

Application to vary or cancel registration[2]

74.23 **74.23—(1) An application to vary or cancel the registration of a Community judgment which is a money judgment on the ground that at the date of registration the judgment had been partly or wholly satisfied must be made within 28 days of the date on which the registration order was served on the judgment debtor.**

(2) The application must be supported by written evidence.

Enforcement[3]

74.24 **74.24 No steps may be taken to enforce a Community judgment which is a money judgment—**

(a) before the end of the period specified in accordance with rule 74.23(1); or

[1] Introduced by the Civil Procedure (Amendment) Rules 2002 (SI 2002/2058).
[2] Introduced by the Civil Procedure (Amendment) Rules 2002 (SI 2002/2058).
[3] Introduced by the Civil Procedure (Amendment) Rules 2002 (SI 2002/2058).

(b) where an application is made under that rule, until it has been determined.

Application for registration of suspension order[1]

74.25—(1) Where the European Courthas made an order that the enforcement of a registered Community judgment should be suspended, an application for the registration of that order in the High Court is made by filing a copy of the order in the Central Office of the Supreme Court. **74.25**

(2) The application may be made without notice.

Registration and enforcement of a Euratom inspection order[2]

74.26—(1) Rules 74.20, 74.21(1), and 74.22(1) and (2), which apply to the registration of a Community judgment, also apply to the registration of a Euratom inspection order but with the necessary modifications. **74.26**

(2) An application under article 6 of the European Communities (Enforcement of Community Judgments) Order 1972 to give effect to a Euratom inspection order may be made on written evidence, and—

(a) where the matter is urgent, without notice;

(b) otherwise, by claim form.

Community judgments enforceable in the UK

The provisions of Sect. IV of Pt 74 (added to the CPR by the Civil Procedure (Amendment) Rules 2002) replaced the rules previously found in CPR Sch.1, RSC O.71, Sect. II. **74.26.1**

For the purposes of the Order in Council and of this Order, "Community judgment" means any decision, judgment or order which is enforceable under or in accordance with art.187 or 192 of the EEC Treaty, Arts 18, 159 or 164 of the Euratom Treaty, or Arts 44 or 92 of the ECSC Treaty, and "Euratom inspection order" means an order made by or in the exercise of the functions of the President of the European Court or by the Commission of the European Communities under art.81 of the Euratom Treaty (see art.2(1) of the Order in Council).

The most likely Community judgments enforceable under the provisions of the Community Treaties which would require to be registered and enforced in the United Kingdom are decisions of the Commission of the European Communities imposing fines or penalties, either of lump sums expressed in "units of account" or percentages of the offending firm's turnover, e.g. under EEC Regulation 17/62 relating to restrictive practices and monopolies, under EEC Regulation 1017/68 applying the rules of competition to transport by rail, road and inland waterway and under EEC Regulation 11 (June 27, 1960) relating to the abolition of discrimination in transport charges and conditions: see also art.65(5) of the ECSC Treaty concerning competition. If the European Court upholds an appeal from the decision of the Commission to impose a fine or penalty, the judgment of the European Court becomes itself enforceable under the relevant provisions of the Treaties; and of course the European Court's orders for costs and fines for non-attendance of witnesses are also enforceable in the same way.

The party entitled to enforce a Community judgment will normally be the Commission itself, either because it imposed the fine or penalty in question or because, by virtue of the Treaties, it represents the Communities in legal proceedings.

The Order in Council provides for the automatic registration in the High Court of Community judgments to which the Secretary of State has duly appended the order

[1] Introduced by the Civil Procedure (Amendment) Rules 2002 (SI 2002/2058).
[2] Introduced by the Civil Procedure (Amendment) Rules 2002 (SI 2002/2058).

for enforcement and of Euratom inspection orders (see art.3(1) of the Order in Council).

Order for enforcement

74.26.2 By virtue of art.2(1) of the Order in Council, an order for enforcement means an order by or under the authority of the Secretary of State that the Community judgment to which it is appended is to be registered for enforcement in the United Kingdom. It is the function of the Secretary of State to verify the formal authenticity of any Community judgment sought to be registered, and an order will be made by him or under his authority that it be registered for enforcement in the United Kingdom.

Application for registration of Community judgment

74.26.3 The application to register for enforcement of a Community judgment is made in the first instance without notice being served on any other party to the Practice Master in the QBD who may exercise the powers assigned to the High Court by the Order in Council.

As a result of the repeal, by s.4 of the A.J.A. 1977, of art.3(2) of the Order in Council (which led to an amendment of former RSC O.71, r.18), there is no requirement that a community judgment in a foreign currency must be converted into sterling at the date when the judgment was originally given.

Effect of registration of Community judgment

74.26.4 Upon registration, a Community judgment becomes fully enforceable pursuant to art.4 of the Order in Council which provides as follows:

> "A Community judgment registered in accordance with art.3 shall, for all purposes of execution, be of the same force and effect, and proceedings may be taken on the judgment and any sum payable under the judgment shall carry interest, as if the judgment had been a judgment or order given or made by the High Court on the date of registration."

Notice of registration

74.26.5 Upon registration, the proper officer of the High Court must forthwith send notice of the registration to every person against whom the judgment or order is enforceable (see r.74.22). Such notice must comply with the requirements of r.74.22(2) and (where relevant) r.74.22(3). The judgment debtor may apply within 28 days, or thereafter with the leave of the court for the variation or cancellation of the registration on the ground that the judgment had been partly or wholly satisfied at the date of registration (see r.74.23).

An application for such variation or cancellation must be made by summons supported by witness statement or affidavit (r.74.23(2)).

Issue of execution

74.26.6 Although a Community judgment is enforceable immediately it is registered, nevertheless execution must not issue without the permission of the court on a pecuniary Community judgment until the expiration of 28 days after the date of the notice of registration of the judgment or the determination of any application for the variation or cancellation of the registration.

Application for registration of suspension order

74.26.7 Article 5 of the Order in Council makes the registration of an order of the European Court suspending the enforcement of a Community judgment automatic, as in the case of a Community judgment itself. An application for the registration of such suspension order must be made without notice being served on any other party to the Practice Master in the Q.B.D. by lodging a copy of the order in the Central Office (see r.74.25).

Application for enforcement of Euratom inspection order

74.26.8 By virtue of art.6 of the Order in Council, upon the registration of a Euratom inspection order in accordance with art.3, the High Court may make such order as it thinks fit against any person for the purpose of ensuring that effect is given to that order. The mode of application for such order is provided by r.74.26.

V. European Enforcement Orders

Interpretation

74.27 In this Section— 74.27

(a) "European Enforcement Order" has the meaning given in the EEO Regulation;

(b) "EEO" means European Enforcement Order;

(c) "judgment", "authentic instrument", "member state of origin", "member state of enforcement", and "court of origin" have the meanings given by Article 4 of the EEO Regulation; and

(d) "Regulation State" has the same meaning as "Member State" in the EEO Regulation, that is all Member States except Denmark.

Certification of Judgments of the Courts of England and Wales

74.28 An application for an EEO certificate must be made by filing the relevant practice form in accordance with Article 6 of the EEO Regulation. 74.28

An application should be made in Form **N219** or **N219A** depending upon whether the Judgment was by agreement/admission/settlement or in default of defence or objection, for a European Enforcement Order Certificate. The application may be made without notice and will be dealt with without a hearing, unless the Master orders a hearing. 74.28.1

Applications for a certificate of lack or limitation of enforceability

74.29 An application under Article 6(2) of the EEO Regulation for a certificate indicating the lack or limitation of enforceability of an EEO certificate must be made to the court of origin by application in accordance with Part 23. 74.29

Applications for rectification or withdrawal

74.30 An application under Article 10 of the EEO Regulation for rectification or withdrawal of an EEO certificate must be made to the court of origin and may be made by application in accordance with Part 23. 74.30

Enforcement of European Enforcement Orders in England and Wales[1]

74.31—(1) A person seeking to enforce an EEO in England and Wales must lodge at the court in which enforcement proceedings are to be brought the documents required by Article 20 of the EEO Regulation. 74.31

(2) Where a person applies to enforce an EEO expressed in a foreign currency, the application must contain a certificate of the sterling equivalent of the judgment sum at the close of business on the date nearest preceding the date of the application.

[1] Amended by the Civil Procedure (Amendment) Rules 2008 (SI 2008/2178).

(Part 70 contains further rules about enforcement.)

74.31.1

An EEO from another member state for enforcement in England and Wales should be lodged in the Judgments and Orders Section and is assigned a case number. The judgment will have to be translated into the language of the member state where enforcement is sought. (See art.202(c) of the EEO Regulation.)

Refusal of Enforcement[1]

74.32 **74.32—(1) An application under Article 21 of the EEO Regulation that the court should refuse to enforce an EEO must be made by application in accordance with Part 23 to the court in which the EEO is being enforced.**

(2) The judgment debtor must, as soon as practicable, serve copies of any order made under Article 21(1) on—

(a) all other parties to the proceedings and any other person affected by the order ("the affected persons"); and

(b) any court in which enforcement proceedings are pending in England and Wales ("the relevant courts").

(3) Upon service of the order on the affected persons, all enforcement proceedings under the EEO in the relevant courts will cease.

Stay of or limitation of enforcement[2]

74.33 **74.33—(1) Where an EEO certificate has been lodged and the judgment debtor applies to stay or limit the enforcement proceedings under Article 23 of the EEO Regulation, such application must be made in accordance with Part 23 to the court in which the EEO is being enforced.**

(2) The judgment debtor shall, as soon as practicable, serve a copy of any order made under the Article on—

(a) all other parties to the proceedings and any other person affected by the order; and

(b) any court in which enforcement proceedings are pending in England and Wales;

and the order will not have effect on any person until it has been served in accordance with this rule and they have received it.

[1] Amended by the Civil Procedure (Amendment) Rules 2008 (SI 2008/2178).
[2] Amended by the Civil Procedure (Amendment) Rules 2008 (SI 2008/2178).

PRACTICE DIRECTION—ENFORCEMENT OF JUDGMENTS IN DIFFERENT JURISDICTIONS

This Practice Direction supplements CPR Part 74 **74PD.1**

1 This practice direction is divided into two sections—
(1) Section I—Provisions about the enforcement of judgments
(2) Section II—The Merchant Shipping (Liner Conferences) Act 1982

I. Enforcement of judgments

Meaning of "judgment"

2 In rule 74.2(1)(c), the definition of 'judgment' is 'subject to any other enactment'. Such provisions include— **74PD.2**
(1) section 9(1) of the 1920 Act, which limits enforcement under that Act to judgments of superior courts;
(2) section 1(1) of the 1933 Act, which limits enforcement under that Act to judgments of those courts specified in the relevant Order in Council;
(3) section 1(2) of the 1933 Act, which limits enforcement under that Act to money judgments.

Registers

3 There will be kept in the Central Office of the Supreme Court at the Royal Courts of Justice, under the direction of the Senior Master— **74PD.3**
(1) registers of foreign judgments ordered by the High Court to be enforced following applications under—
(a) section 9 of the 1920 Act;
(b) section 2 of the 1933 Act;
(c) section 4 of the 1982 Act; or
(d) the Judgments Regulation;
(2) registers of certificates issued for the enforcement in foreign countries of High Court judgments under the 1920, 1933 and 1982 Acts, and under article 54 of the Judgments Regulation;
(3) a register of certificates filed in the Central Office of the High Court under rule 74.15(2) for the enforcement of money judgments given by the courts of Scotland or Northern Ireland;
(4) a register of certificates issued under rule 74.16(3) for the enforcement of non-money judgments given by the courts of Scotland or Northern Ireland;
(5) registers of certificates issued under rules 74.17 and 74.18 for the enforcement of High Court judgments in Scotland or Northern Ireland under Schedule 6 or Schedule 7 to the 1982 Act; and
(6) a register of Community judgments and Euratom inspection orders ordered to be registered under article 3 of the European Communities (Enforcement of Community Judgments) Order 1972.

Making an application

74PD.4 **4.1** Applications for the registration for enforcement in England and Wales of—

(1) foreign judgments under rule 74.3;

(2) judgments of courts in Scotland or Northern Ireland under rule 74.15 or 74.16; and

(3) European Community judgments under rule 74.20,

are assigned to the Queen's Bench Division and may be heard by a Master.

4.2 An application under rule 74.12 for a certified copy of a High Court or county court judgment for enforcement abroad must be made—

(1) in the case of a judgment given in the Chancery Division or the Queen's Bench Division of the High Court, to a Master or district judge;

(2) in the case of a judgment given in the Family Division of the High Court, to a district judge of that Division;

(3) in the case of a county court judgment, to a district judge.

4.3 An application under rule 74.17 or 74.18 for a certificate or a certified copy of a High Court or county court judgment for enforcement in Scotland or Northern Ireland must be made—

(1) in the case of a judgment given in the Chancery Division or the Queen's Bench Division of the High Court, to a Master or district judge;

(2) in the case of a judgment given in the Chancery Division or the Queen's Bench Division of the High Court, to a Master or district judge;

(3) in the case of a county court judgment, to a district judge.

4.4 The following applications must be made under Part 23—

(1) applications under rule 74.3 for the registration of a judgment;

(2) applications under rule 74.7 to set aside the registration of a judgment;

(3) applications under rule 74.12 for a certified copy of a judgment;

(4) applications under section III for a certificate for enforcement of a judgment;

(5) applications under rule 74.20 for the registration of a Community judgment;

(6) applications under rule 74.23 to vary or cancel the registration of a Community judgment; and

(7) applications under rule 74.25 for the registration of an order of the European Court that the enforcement of a registered Community judgment should be suspended.

Applications under the 1933 Act

74PD.5 **5** Foreign judgments are enforceable in England and Wales under the 1933 Act where there is an agreement on the reciprocal enforcement of judgments between the United Kingdom and the country in which the judgment was given. Such an agreement may contain particular provisions governing the enforcement of judgments (for example limiting the categories of judgments which are enforceable, or the courts whose judgments are enforceable). Any such specific limitations will be listed in the Order in Council giving effect in the United Kingdom to the agreement in question, and the rules in Section I of Part 74 will take effect subject to such limitations.

Evidence in support of an application under the Judgments Regulation: rule 74.4(6)

6.1 Where a judgment is to be recognised or enforced in a Regulation State, the Judgments Regulation applies. **74PD.6**

6.2 As a consequence of article 38(2) of the Judgments Regulation, the provisions in Chapter III of that Regulation relating to declaring judgments enforceable are the equivalent, in the United Kingdom, of provisions relating to registering judgments for enforcement.

6.3 Chapter III of, and Annex V to, the Judgments Regulation are annexed to this practice direction. They were originally published in the official languages of the European Community in the *Official Journal of the European Communities* by the Office for Official Publications of the European Communities.

6.4 Sections 2 and 3 of Chapter III of the Judgments Regulation (in particular articles 40, 53, 54 and 55, and Annex V) set out the evidence needed in support of an application.

6.5 The Judgments Regulation is supplemented by the Civil Jurisdiction and Judgments Order 2001, S.I. 2001 No.3929. The Order also makes amendments, in respect of that Regulation, to the Civil Jurisdiction and Judgments Act 1982.

Certified copies of judgments issued under rule 74.12

7.1 In an application by a judgment creditor under rule 74.12 for the enforcement abroad of a High Court judgment, the certified copy of the judgment will be an office copy, and will be accompanied by a certificate signed by a judge. The judgment and certificate will be sealed with the Seal of the Supreme Court. **74PD.7**

7.2 In an application by a judgment creditor under rule 74.12 for the enforcement abroad of a county court judgment, the certified copy will be a sealed copy, and will be accompanied by a certificate signed by a judge.

7.3 In applications under the 1920, 1933 or 1982 Acts, the certificate will be in Form 110, and will have annexed to it a copy of the claim form by which the proceedings were begun.

7.4 In an application under the Judgments Regulation, the certificate will be in the form of Annex V to the Regulation.

Certificates under section III of Part 74

8.1 *A certificate of a money* judgment of a court in Scotland or Northern Ireland must be filed for enforcement under rule 74.15(2) in the Action Department of the Central Office of the Supreme Court, Royal Courts of Justice, Strand, London WC2A 2LL. The copy will be sealed by a court officer before being returned to the applicant. **74PD.8**

8.2 A certificate issued under rule 74.17 for the enforcement in Scotland or Northern Ireland of a money judgment of the High Court or of a county court will be in Form 111.

8.3 In an application by a judgment creditor under rule 74.18 for the enforcement in Scotland or Northern Ireland of a non-money judgment of the High Court or of a county court, the certified copy of the judgment will be a sealed copy to which will be annexed a certificate in Form 112.

Material additional to section IV of Part 74

74PD.9 **9.1** Enforcement of Community judgments and of Euratom inspection orders is governed by the European Communities (Enforcement of Community Judgments) Order 1972, S.I. 1972 No.1590.

9.2 The Treaty establishing the European Community is the Treaty establishing the European Economic Community (Rome, 1957); relevant amendments are made by the Treaty of Amsterdam (1997, Cm. 3780).

9.3 The text of the Protocol of 3 June 1971 on the interpretation by the European Court of the Convention of 27 September 1968 on Jurisdiction and the Enforcement of Judgments in Civil and Commercial Matters is set out in Schedule 2 to the Civil Jurisdiction and Judgments Act 1982.

9.4 The text of the Protocol of 19 December 1988 on the interpretation by the European Court of the Convention of 19 June 1980 on the Law applicable to Contractual Obligations is set out in Schedule 3 to the Contracts (Applicable Law) Act 1990.

II. The Merchant Shipping (Liner Conferences) Act 1982

Content of this Section

74PD.10 **10** The Merchant Shipping (Liner Conferences) Act 1982 ('the Act') contains provisions for the settlement of disputes between liner conferences, shipping lines and shippers. This Section of the Practice Direction deals with the enforcement by the High Court under section 9 of the Act of recommendations of conciliators, and determinations and awards of costs.

Exercise of powers under the Act

74PD.11 **11** The powers of the High Court under the Act are exercised by the Commercial Court.

Applications for registration

74PD.12 **12.1** An application under section 9 of the Act for the registration of a recommendation, determination or award is made under Part 23.

12.2 An application for the registration of a recommendation must be supported by written evidence exhibiting—

(1) a verified or certified or otherwise authenticated copy of—
  (a) the recommendation;
  (b) the reasons for it; and
  (c) the record of settlement;

(2) where any of those documents is not in English, a translation of it into English—
  (a) certified by a notary public or other qualified person; or

(b) accompanied by written evidence confirming that the translation is accurate; and

(3) copies of the acceptance of the recommendation by the parties on whom it is binding, or otherwise verifying the acceptance where it is not in writing.

12.3 The evidence in support of the application must—

(1) give particulars of the failure to implement the recommendation; and

(2) confirm that none of the grounds which would render it unenforceable is applicable.

12.4 An application for the registration of a determination of costs or an award of costs must be supported by written evidence—

(1) exhibiting a verified or certified or otherwise authenticated copy of the recommendation or other document containing the determination or award; and

(2) stating that the costs have not been paid.

Order for registration

13.1 The applicant must draw up the order giving permission to register the recommendation, determination or award. **74PD.13**

13.2 The order must include a provision that the reasonable costs of the registration should be assessed.

Register of recommendations

14 There will be kept in the Admiralty and Commercial Registry at the Royal Courts of Justice, under the direction of the Senior Master, a register of the recommendations, determinations and awards ordered to be registered under section 9 of the Act, with particulars of enforcement. **74PD.14**

Appendix (Chapter III and Annex V of Council Regulation (EC) No.44/2001)

Chapter III and Annex V of Council Regulation (EC) No.44/2001 of 22 December 2000 on jurisdiction and the recognition and enforcement of judgments in civil and commercial matters can be found in Vol.2 at para.5–249*et seq.* **74PD.15**

PRACTICE DIRECTION—EUROPEAN ENFORCEMENT ORDERS

This Practice Direction supplements Section V of Part 74

Council Regulation

74BPD.1 **1.1** Certification and enforcement of European Enforcement Orders is governed by Council Regulation (EC) No 805/2004 creating a European Enforcement Order for uncontested claims.

1.2 The EEO Regulation is annexed to this practice direction and can be found at *http://europa.eu.int/eur-lex/pri/en/oj/dat/2004/1__143/1__14320040430en00150039.pdf*. It was originally published in the official languages of the European Community in the Official Journal of the European Communities by the Office for Official Publications of the European Communities.

1.3 Section V of Part 74 sets out the procedure for enforcement under the EEO Regulation. A claim that does not meet the requirements of the EEO Regulation, or which the judgment creditor does not wish to enforce using the EEO Regulation, may be enforceable using another method of enforcement.

74.28 Certification of Judgments of the Courts of England and Wales

74BPD.2 **2.1** An application under rule 74.28 for a certificate of a High Court or county court judgment for enforcement in another Regulation State must be made using Form N219 or Form N219A—

(1) in the case of a judgment given in the Chancery or Queen's Bench Division of the High Court, or in a district registry, to a Master or district judge; or

(2) in the case of a county court judgment, to a district judge.

2.2 Where the application is granted, the court will send the EEO certificate and a sealed copy of the judgment to the person making the application. Where the court refuses the application, the court will give reasons for the refusal and may give further directions.

74.29 Applications for a certificate of lack of enforceability

74BPD.3 **3.1** An application must be supported by written evidence in support of the grounds on which the judgment has ceased to be enforceable or its enforceability has been suspended or limited.

74.30 Application for rectification or withdrawal

74BPD.4 **4.1** An application must be supported by written evidence in support of the grounds on which it is contended that the EEO should be rectified or withdrawn.

74.31 Enforcement of European Enforcement Orders in England and Wales

74BPD.5 **5.1** When an EEO is lodged at the court in which enforcement proceedings are to be brought, it will be assigned a case number.

5.2 A copy of a document will satisfy the conditions necessary to establish its authenticity if it is an official copy of the courts state of origin.

5.3 If judgment is set aside in the court of origin, the judgment creditor must notify all courts in which enforcement proceedings are pending in England and Wales under the EEO as soon as reasonably practicable after the order is served on the judgment creditor. Notification may be by any means available including fax, e-mail, post or telephone.

74.32 Rule 74.32—An application for refusal of enforcement

6.1 An application must be accompanied by an official copy of the earlier judgment, any other documents relied upon and any translations required by the EEO Regulation and supported by written evidence showing— **74BPD.6**

(1) why the earlier judgment is irreconcilable with the judgment which the judgment creditor is seeking to enforce; and

(2) why the irreconcilability was not, and could not have been, raised as an objection in the proceedings in the court of origin.

74.33 Stay or limitation of enforcement

7.1 Unless the court orders otherwise, an application must be accompanied by evidence of the application in the court of origin, including— **74BPD.7**

(1) the application (or equivalent foreign process) or a copy of the application (or equivalent foreign process) certified by an appropriate officer of the court of origin; and

(2) where that document is not in English, a translation of it into English—

(a) certified by a notary public or person qualified to certify a translation in the Member State of the court of origin under Article 20(2)(c) of the EEO Regulation; or

(b) accompanied by written evidence confirming that the translation is accurate.

7.2 The written evidence in support of the application must state—

(1) that an application has been brought in the member state of origin;

(2) the nature of that application; and

(3) the date on which the application was filed, the state of the proceedings and the date by which it is believed that the application will be determined.

Annex

Regulation (EC) No.805/2004 of the European Parliament and of the Council of 21 April 2004 creating a European Enforcement Order for uncontested claims can be found in Vol.2 at para.5–356 *et seq.* **74BPD.8**

PART 75

TRAFFIC ENFORCEMENT

Contents

75.0.1

Editorial introduction

75.0.2 The Road Traffic Act 1991 established a new regime for enforcement of parking charges thereby de-criminalising such proceedings and removing them from the magistrates' courts. That Act is now replaced by the Traffic Management Act 2004.

The county court has a very limited role in traffic enforcement. Penalties are levied by local authorities. An aggrieved person makes representations to the authority. Appeal is to the Parking and Traffic Appeals Service.

Part 75 applies to the recovery of those matters listed in para.1.2 of PD75. In summary these are parking penalties; bus lane penalties; vehicle emission penalties and penalty charges under a road user charging scheme. Penalties are enforceable as if they were a county court judgment. Once the local authority has gone through the Pt 75 procedure for obtaining a court order it can proceed to enforcement.

Warrants of execution are executed by a bailiff certified in accordance with the Enforcement of Road Traffic Debts (Certificated Bailiffs) Regulations 1993 (SI 1993/2073). Article 4 provides that relevant sections of the CCA 1984 apply to certificated bailiffs as if they were bailiffs of the court. Article 6 disapplies Sect.86 CCA 1984.

Enforcement is through the Traffic Enforcement Centre at Northampton County Court. It is important to appreciate that Pt 75 is not an appeal procedure to the court. An application to the court by a respondent can only be for permission to apply to file witness statement out of time. To avoid enforcement the respondent must pay the total sum due or file a witness statement. There are only four grounds for making a statement namely that the penalty has been paid; that no penalty charge notice was received; that representations were made to the local authority but no reply was received and that an appeal was made to the Parking and Traffic Appeals Service but no response was received.

An application can be made to extend time for filing a witness statement. This is considered by a court officer at the Traffic Enforcement Centre. If the request is refused the respondent can request a review of that decision by a district judge. A new procedure from April 2009 entitles the respondent to a paper review by a district judge (which will be done at Northampton) or a hearing before a district judge in which case the application will be transferred to the respondent's local county court.

By the Civil Procedure (Amendment No.3) Rules 2008 (SI 2008/3327) r.75.5 (Functions of court officer) was substituted and r.75.5A (Review of decision of court officer) was added, and these changes (which came into effect on April 6, 2009) were accompanied by amendments to para.6 of PD75 (published in TSO CPR Update 49). The purpose of these alterations was to enable requests for a review by a district judge of a court officer's decision to be determined without an oral hearing, unless the person making the request asks for a hearing or the court orders a hearing.

The function of the district judge is extremely limited (see para.6.3 of PD75). It is a review of the decision to refuse the application for further time for filing a witness statement. It is not a review of the validity of the penalty notice.

Further details are explained in PD75 including the various relevant statutory provisions and details of the relevant forms and how to obtain them.

Under amendments to Pt 21 which came into force on October 1, 2007 drivers under the age of 18 do not require a litigation friend for Pt 75 proceedings.

Scope and interpretation[1]

75.1—(1) The practice direction supplements this Part— 75.1

(a) sets out the proceedings to which this Part applies; and

(b) may apply this Part with modifications in relation to any particular category of those proceedings.

(Rule 21.1(c) provides that Part 21 (children and protected parties) does not apply to proceedings under this Part where one of the parties is a child.)

(2) In this Part—

(a) "the Centre" means the Traffic Enforcement Centre established under the direction of the Lord Chancellor;

(b) "no relevant return to the warrant" means that—

(i) the bailiff has been unable to seize goods because the bailiff has been denied access to premises occupied by the defendant or because the goods have been removed from those premises;

(ii) any goods seized under a warrant of execution are insufficient to satisfy the debt and the cost of execution; or

(iii) the goods are insufficient to cover the cost of their removal and sale.

(c) "the 1993 Order" means the Enforcement of Road Traffic Debts Order 1993[2];

(d) "relevant period", in relation to any particular case, means—

(i) the period allowed for serving a statutory declaration or witness statement, as the case may be, under any enactment which applies to that case; or

(ii) where an enactment permits the court to extend that period, the period as extended;

(e) "specified debts" means the debts specified in article 2 of the 1993 Order or treated as so specified by any other enactment; and

(f) "the authority", "notice of the amount due", "order" and "the respondent" have the meaning given by the practice direction supplementing this Part..

The Centre[3]

75.2—(1) Proceedings to which this Part applies must be started in the Centre. 75.2

[1] Introduced by the Civil Procedure (Amendment) Rules 2002 (SI 2002/2058).
[2] SI 1993/2073 as amended by SI 2001/1386.
[3] Introduced by the Civil Procedure (Amendment) Rules 2002 (SI 2002/2058).

(2) For any purpose connected with the exercise of the Centre's functions—

(a) the Centre is deemed to be part of the office of the court whose name appears on the documents to which the functions relate or in whose name the documents are issued; and

(b) any officer of the Centre, in exercising its functions, is deemed to act as an officer of that court.

Request[1]

75.3 **75.3—(1) The authority must file a request in the appropriate form scheduling the amount claimed to be due.**

(2) The authority must, in that request or in another manner approved by the court officer—

(a) certify—

(i) that 14 days have elapsed since service of the notice of the amount due;

(ii) the date of such service;

(iii) the number of the notice of the amount due; and

(iv) that the amount due remains unpaid;

(b) specify the grounds (whether by reference to the appropriate code or otherwise), as stated in the notice, on which the authority claims to be entitled to claim that amount; and

(c) state—

(i) the name, title and address of the respondent;

(ii) the registration number of the vehicle concerned;

(iii) the authority's address for service;

(iv) the court fee; and

(v) such other matters as required by the practice direction supplementing this Part.

(3) On receipt of a request that meets the requirements of paragraphs (1) and (2), the court officer will order that the amount due may be recovered as if it were payable under a county court order by registering the request and returning it to the authority.

(4) On receipt of a registered request the authority may draw up an order and must attach to it a form of statutory declaration for the respondent's use.

(a) insert in the order the date by which the respondent must comply with it or file a statutory declaration or witness statement (as the case may be); and

(b) attach to the order a form of the statutory declaration or witness statement for the respondent's use.

(5) The authority must serve in accordance with Part 6 the order (and the form of statutory declaration or witness statement) on

[1] Introduced by the Civil Procedure (Amendment) Rules 2002 (SI 2002/2058) and amended by the Civil Procedure (Amendment No.4) Rules 2005 (SI 2005/3515).

the respondent within 15 days of the date on which the request is registered by the court.

Electronic delivery of documents[1]

75.4—(1) Where the authority is required to file any document other than the request, that requirement is satisfied if the information which would be contained in the document is delivered in computer-readable form. 75.4

(2) For the purposes of paragraph (1), information which would be contained in a document relating to one case may be combined with information of the same nature relating to another case.

(3) Where a document is required to be produced, that requirement will be satisfied if a copy of the document is produced from computer records.

Functions of court officer[2]

75.5 The practice direction supplementing this Part sets out the circumstances in which a court officer may exercise the functions of the court. 75.5

Review of decision of court officer[3]

75.5A—(1) Any party may request any decision of a court officer to be reviewed by a district judge. 75.5A

(2) Such a request must be made within 14 days of service of the decision.

(3) Unless—

(a) the party requesting the review requests an oral hearing; or

(b) the court orders an oral hearing,

a request for a review under paragraph (2) will be dealt with without an oral hearing.

Enforcement of orders[4]

75.6 Subject to the 1993 Order and this rule the following rules apply to the enforcement of specified debts— 75.6

(a) Parts 70 to 73;

(b) CCR Order 25, rule 1;

(c) CCR Order 26, rule 5; and

(d) CCR Order 27, rules 1 to 7, 7A, 7B, 9 to 16 and 18 to 22.

(Rule 30.2 provides for the transfer between courts in order to enforce a judgment).

---

[1] Introduced by the Civil Procedure (Amendment) Rules 2002 (SI 2002/2058).

[2] Introduced by the Civil Procedure (Amendment) Rules 2002 (SI 2002/2058) and amended by the Civil Procedure (Amendment No.3) Rules 2008 (SI 2008/3327).

[3] Introduced by the Civil Procedure (Amendment No.3) Rules 2008 (SI 2008/3327).

[4] Introduced by the Civil Procedure (Amendment) Rules 2002 (SI 2002/2058).

Warrant of execution[1]

75.7 **75.7—(1) An authority seeking the issue of a warrant of execution must file a request—**

(a) certifying the amount remaining due under the order;

(b) specifying the date of service of the order on the respondent; and

(c) certifying that the relevant period has elapsed.

(2) The court will seal the request and return it to the authority.

(3) Within 7 days of the sealing of the request the authority must prepare the warrant in the appropriate form.

(4) No payment under a warrant will be made to the court.

(5) For the purposes of execution a warrant will be valid for 12 months beginning with the date of its issue.

(6) An authority may not renew a warrant issued in accordance with this Part beyond the 12 month validity period but, subject to paragraph (7), an authority may request the reissue of a warrant during the 12 month validity period.

(7) Where the address of the respondent has changed since the issue of the warrant, the authority may request the reissue of the warrant by filing a request—

(a) specifying the new address of the respondent;

(b) providing evidence that the new address for the respondent does relate to the respondent named in the order and against whom enforcement is sought; and

(c) certifying that the amount due under the order remains unpaid.

(8) Where the court is satisfied that the new address of the respondent given in the request for the reissue of the warrant relates to the respondent named in the order, it will seal the request and return it to the authority.

(9) The authority must prepare the reissued warrant in the appropriate form within 7 days of the sealing of the request to reissue.

(10) A reissued warrant will only be valid for the remainder of the 12 month period beginning with the date it was originally issued.

Revocation of order[2]

75.8 **75.8 Where, in accordance with any enactment, an order is deemed to have been revoked following the filing of a statutory declaration or a witness statement—**

(a) the court will serve a copy of the statutory declaration or witness statement on the authority;

(b) any execution issued on the order will cease to have effect; and

(c) if appropriate, the authority must inform any bailiff

[1] Introduced by the Civil Procedure (Amendment) Rules 2002 (SI 2002/2058).
[2] Introduced by the Civil Procedure (Amendment) Rules 2002 (SI 2002/2058).

instructed to levy execution of the withdrawal of the warrant as soon as possible.

Transfer for enforcement[1]

75.9 Where the authority requests the transfer of proceedings to another county court for enforcement, the request must— 75.9

(a) where the authority has not attempted to enforce by execution, give the reason why no such attempt was made;

(b) certify that there has been no relevant return to the warrant of execution;

(c) specify the date of service of the order on the respondent; and

(d) certify that the relevant period has elapsed.

Further information required[2]

75.10 An application for— 75.10

(a) an attachment of earnings order;

(b) an order to obtain information from a debtor;

(c) a third party debt order; or

(d) a charging order,

must, in addition to the requirements of Parts 71, 72 or 73 or CCR Order 27—

(i) where the authority has not attempted to enforce by execution, give the reason why no such attempt was made;

(ii) certify that there has been no relevant return to the warrant of execution;

(iii) specify the date of service of the order on the respondent; and

(iv) certify that the relevant period has elapsed.

Combining requests[3]

75.11 Where the court officer allows, the authority may combine information relating to different orders against the same respondent in any request or application made under rules 75.9 or 75.10. 75.11

[1] Introduced by the Civil Procedure (Amendment) Rules 2002 (SI 2002/2058).
[2] Introduced by the Civil Procedure (Amendment) Rules 2002 (SI 2002/2058).
[3] Introduced by the Civil Procedure (Amendment) Rules 2002 (SI 2002/2058).

PRACTICE DIRECTION—TRAFFIC ENFORCEMENT

This Practice Direction supplements CPR Part 75

Interpretation and scope

75PD.1 **1.1** In this Practice Direction—

(1) 'the 1991 Act' means the Road Traffic Act 1991;

(2) 'the 1996 Act' means the London Local Authorities Act 1996;

(3) 'the Road User Charging Regulations' means the Road User Charging (Enforcement and Adjudication) (London) Regulations 2001;

(4) 'the Vehicle Emissions (England) Regulations' means the Road Traffic (Vehicle Emissions) (Fixed Penalty) (England) Regulations 2002;

(5) 'the Vehicle Emissions (Wales) Regulations' means the Road Traffic (Vehicle Emissions) (Fixed Penalty) (Wales) Regulations 2003;

(6) 'the 2003 Act' means the London Local Authorities and Transport for London Act 2003;

(7) the Civil Enforcement of Parking (England) Regulations' means the Civil Enforcement of Parking Contraventions (England) General Regulations 2007;

(8) 'the Civil Enforcement of Parking (Wales) Regulations' means the Civil Enforcement of Parking Contraventions (Penalty Charge Notices, Enforcement and Adjudication) (Wales) Regulations 2008;

(9) 'the Representations and Appeals (England) Regulations' means the Civil Enforcement of Parking Contraventions (England) Representations and Appeals Regulations 2007;

(10) 'the Representations and Appeals (Wales) Regulations' means the Civil Enforcement of Parking Contraventions (Representations and Appeals) (Wales) Regulations 2008.

1.2 Part 75 applies to proceedings for the recovery of—

(1) increased penalty charges provided for in parking charge certificates issued under paragraph 6 of Schedule 6 to the 1991 Act;

(2) amounts payable by a person other than an authority under an adjudication of a parking adjudicator pursuant to section 73 of the 1991 Act;

(3) increased penalty charges provided for in a charge certificate issued under paragraph 8 of Schedule 1 to the 1996 Act (relating to a contravention or failure to comply with an order made under a provision referred to in section 4(2) of that Act reserving all or part of a carriageway of a road as a bus lane);

(4) increased fixed penalties to which regulation 17(6) of the Vehicle Emissions (England) Regulations refer;

(5) amounts payable by a person other than an authority under an adjudication pursuant to the Schedule to the Road User Charging Regulations;

(6) increased penalty charges provided for in charge certificates

issued under regulation 17 of the Road User Charging Regulations;

(7) increased fixed penalties to which regulation 17(6) of the Vehicle Emissions (Wales) Regulations refer;

(8) increased penalty charges provided for in charge certificates issued under regulation 21 of the Civil Enforcement of Parking (England) Regulations;

(9) increased penalty charges provided for in charge certificates issued under regulation 13 of the Civil Enforcement of Parking (Wales) Regulations;

(10) amounts payable by a person other than an authority under an adjudication pursuant to the Representations and Appeals (England) Regulations; and

(11) amounts payable by a person other than an authority under an adjudication pursuant to of the Representations and Appeals (Wales) Regulations.

1.3 In Part 75 and this practice direction—

(1) "authority" means the authority entitled to recover amounts due under the enactments referred to in paragraph 1.2;

(2) "notice of the amount due" means, as the case may be—

(a) a parking charge certificate issued under paragraph 6 of Schedule 6 to the 1991 Act;

(b) a charge certificate issued under paragraph 8 of Schedule 1 to the 1996 Act;

(c) a fixed penalty notice issued under regulations 10 or 13 of the Vehicle Emissions (England) Regulations;

(d) a charge certificate issued under regulation 17 of the Road User Charging Regulations;

(e) a fixed penalty notice issued under regulations 10 or 13 of the Vehicle Emissions (Wales) Regulations; or

(f) a charge certificate issued under regulation 21 of the Civil Enforcement of Parking (England) Regulations; or

(g) a charge certificate issued under regulation 13 of the Civil Enforcement of Parking (Wales) Regulations;

(3) "order" means an order made under—

(a) paragraph 7 of Schedule 6 to the 1991 Act;

(b) paragraph 9 of Schedule 1 to the 1996 Act;

(c) section 73(15) of the 1991 Act;

(d) regulation 21 of the Vehicle Emissions (England) Regulations;

(e) regulation 7 of the Road User Charging Regulations;

(f) regulation 18 of the Road User Charging Regulations;

(g) regulation 21 of the Vehicle Emissions (Wales) Regulations;

(h) regulation 22 of the Civil Enforcement of Parking (England) Regulations;

(i) regulation 14 of the Civil Enforcement of Parking (Wales) Regulations;

(j) regulation 15(3)(a) of the Representations and Appeals (England) Regulations; or

(k) regulation 12(3)(a) of the Representations and Appeals (Wales) Regulations; and

(4) "respondent" means—

(a) the person on whom the notice of the amount due was served; or

(b) the person (other than an authority) by whom the amount due under an adjudication is payable.

Traffic Enforcement Centre

75PD.2 **2.1** All claims to which Part 75 applies must be started in the Traffic Enforcement Centre ('the Centre') at Northampton County Court.

Request

75PD.3 **3.1** Where an order in respect of amounts payable by a person other than an authority under an adjudication pursuant to—

(a) section 73 of the 1991 Act;

(b) the Representations and Appeals (England) Regulations;

(c) the Representations and Appeals (Wales) Regulations; or

(d) the Schedule to the Road User Charging Regulations, is sought, rule 75.3 applies with the necessary modifications and, in addition, the request must—

(i) state the date on which the adjudication was made;

(ii) provide details of the order made on the adjudication; and

(iii) certify the amount awarded by way of costs and that the amount remains unpaid.

Service of Order

75PD.3.1 **3A.1** Rule 75.3(5) requires the authority to serve the order within 15 days of the date on which the request is registered with the court. For clarity, the respondent must be served within 15 days and attention is drawn to the provisions of Part 6, particularly the provisions relating to deemed service.

Functions of court officer

75PD.4 **4.1** A court officer may exercise the functions of—

(1) the district judge under—

(a) paragraphs 8(4) and (5)(d) of Schedule 6 to the 1991 Act;

(b) paragraphs 10(4) and (5)(d) of Schedule 1 to the 1996 Act;

(c) regulations 19(4) and 19(5)(d) of the Road User Charging Regulations;

(d) regulations 23(4) and 23(5)(d) of the Civil Enforcement of Parking (England) Regulations; and

(e) regulations 15(4) and 15(5)(d) of the Civil Enforcement of Parking (Wales) Regulations, and

(2) the court under—

(a) paragraph 23(3) of the Vehicle Emissions (England) Regulations; and

(b) paragraph 23(3) of the Vehicle Emissions (Wales) Regulations.

Application for longer period for filing of statutory declaration or witness statement

5.1 Paragraphs 5.2 to 5.5 apply where the respondent applies for an order allowing a longer period than 21 days to serve— **75PD.5**

(1) a statutory declaration pursuant to—
 (a) paragraph 8(3) of Schedule 6 to the 1991 Act;
 (b) paragraph 10(3) of Schedule 1 to the 1996 Act;
 (c) regulation 23(3) of the Vehicle Emissions (England) Regulations;
 (d) regulation 19(3) of the Road User Charging Regulations;
 (e) regulation 23(3) of the Vehicle Emissions (Wales) Regulations, or

(2) a witness statement pursuant to—
 (a) regulation 23(3) of the Civil Enforcement of Parking (England) Regulations; or
 (b) regulation 15(3) of the Civil Enforcement of Parking (Wales) Regulations.

5.2 The respondent must send to the Centre—

(1) a completed application notice (form PE 2 may be used for applications relating to statutory declarations and form TE 7 may be used for applications relating to witness statements); and

(2) a completed—
 (a) statutory declaration in form PE 3; or
 (b) witness statement in form TE 9.

(Forms PE 2, PE 3, TE 7 and TE 9 can be obtained from the Centre at Northampton County Court, Bulk Centre, 21/27 St. Katherine's Street, Northampton NN1 2LH. (Telephone number: 08457 045007)).

5.3 The court will serve a copy of the application notice and a copy of the statutory declaration or witness statement on the authority that obtained the court order seeking representations on the application.

5.4 A court officer will deal with the application without a hearing. The matter will not be dealt with until at least 14 days after the date on which the application notice and statutory declaration or witness statement were served on the authority.

5.5 If the proceedings have been transferred to another court the Centre will transfer the application to that court.

5.6 Paragraphs 5.3 to 5.5 do not apply where the court receives an application notice that is accompanied by a statutory declaration that is invalid by virtue of paragraph 8(2A) of Schedule 6 to the 1991 Act as inserted by section 15 of the 2003 Act.

Application to review order made by court officer

6.1 Where any order is made by a court officer it will contain a statement of the right of either party to request a review of the decision by a district judge. **75PD.6**

6.2 Attention is drawn to rule 75.5A.

6.3 Attention is drawn to the limited powers of a district judge where a request is made to review an order of a court officer refusing an application for further time for filing a statutory declaration or witness statement. Any review of that order by a district judge will only be a review of the decision to refuse the application for further time for filing a statutory declaration or witness statement. The review will not be a review of the validity of the notice of the amount due or any order within the meaning of paragraph 1.3(3) of this Practice Direction.

Hearing

75PD.7 **7.1** When a hearing is to be held, the proceedings will be transferred to the county court for the district in which the respondent's address for service is situated. This transfer is only for the purposes of holding the hearing and serving any orders made as a result of the hearing.

7.2 The respondent's address for service is the address for service shown on the last of the following documents filed at court by the respondent—

(1) the application notice or, if more than one, the latest application notice; and

(2) the appellant's notice.

7.3 The court where the hearing is held will serve any orders made as a result of the hearing before returning the papers to the Centre, or, if the proceedings have been transferred, to the court where the proceedings have been transferred.

7.4 Evidence at any hearing may be given orally or by witness statement.

Applications to suspend a warrant of execution

75PD.8 **8.1** Where—

(1) the respondent makes an application under paragraph 5; and

(2) before that application is determined, a warrant of execution is issued,

the local authority must suspend enforcement of the warrant of execution until the application for an extension order is determined.

(Rule 75.8(b) provides that, where a court order is deemed to have been revoked following the filing of a statutory declaration or witness statement, any execution issued on the order will cease to have effect.)

PART 76

PROCEEDINGS UNDER THE PREVENTION OF TERRORISM ACT 2005

CPR 76

Contents

76.0.1

I. Application of this Part

II. Applications to the High Court relating to derogating control orders

III. Permission applications, references and appeals to the High Court relating to non-derogating control orders

IV. Appeals to the Court of Appeal

V. General provisions

Editorial introduction

76.0.2 The Prevention of Terrorism Act 2005 provides for the making of "control orders" imposing obligations on individuals suspected of involvement in terrorism-related activity. This legislation draws a distinction between a "derogating control order" and a "non-derogating control order". The procedure for making a control order of either variety is instigated by the Secretary of State and involves the exercise of jurisdiction by the High Court.

Part 76 was inserted in the CPR by the Civil Procedure (Amendment No.2) Rules 2005 (SI 2005/656) and came into effect on March 11, 2005. This Part contains rules about control order proceedings in the High Court, and appeals to the Court of Appeal against orders in such proceedings, made under the 2005 Act. This Act extended the power to make Civil Procedure Rules. It also modified the procedure by which Civil Procedure Rules are normally made for the particular purpose of the first exercise of the extended rule-making power.

Part 76 is divided into five sections. Rules relating to derogating control orders, non-derogating control orders, and appeals are found, respectively, in ss.2, 3 and 4. General provisions are found in s.5. In certain respects, rules found in these sections disapply, supersede or modify provisions found elsewhere in the CPR, including provisions as to evidence and disclosure, as to judgments, and as to appeals. Where an application made under s.2, Pt 23 is disapplied (r.76.3(2)). Rule 5.4 (Supply of court documents—general) does not apply to proceedings to which Pt 76 applies, unless the court otherwise directs. Paragraph 4(3) of the Schedule to the 2005 Act requires that rules of court should provide for the disclosure by the Secretary of State of material that might be of assistance of anotherparty in relation to a matter under consideration by the Court in the proceedings; so-called "exculpatory material". Such provisions are found in s.5. The legislation provides for the appointment of a special advocate and rules in s.5 apply in this event.

Rule 76.2(2) states that the court must ensure that information is not disclosed contrary to the public interest. Rules 76.2(1) states that, where Pt 76 applies, the overriding objective in CPR Pt 1, and so far as relevant any other rule, must be read and given effect in a way which is compatible with the duty stated in r.76.2(2). By r.3 of the Civil Procedure (Amendment No.2) Rules 2005, CPR r.1.2 (Application by the court of the overriding objective) is amended, making it subject to r.76.2.

Rule 76.34 suspends the normal rules as to the supply by the court to parties and non-parties of copies of documents in court records. A consequential amendment was made to this rule by the Civil Procedure (Amendment) Rules 2006 to reflect the substitution of rr.5.4, 5.4B and 5.4C for r.5.4.

Related sources

76.0.3
- Prevention of Terrorism Act 2005
- Part 1 (Overriding objective)
- Part 52 (Appeals)

I. Application of this Part

Scope and interpretation

76.1—(1) This Part contains rules about— 76.1

(a) control order proceedings in the High Court; and

(b) appeals to the Court of Appeal against an order of the High Court in such proceedings.

(2) In the case of proceedings brought by virtue of section 11(2) of the Act, the rules in this Part shall apply with any modification which the court considers necessary.

(3) In this Part—

(a) "the Act" means the Prevention of Terrorism Act 2005;

(b) "closed material" means any relevant material that the Secretary of State objects to disclosing to a relevant party;

(c) "control order proceedings" has the same meaning as in section 11(6) of the Act;

(d) "controlled person" has the same meaning as in section 15(1) of the Act;

(e) "legal representative" is to be construed in accordance with paragraph 11 of the Schedule to the Act;

(f) "open material" means any relevant material that the Secretary of State does not object to disclosing to a relevant party;

(g) "relevant law officer" has the same meaning as in paragraph 7(6) of the Schedule to the Act;

(h) "relevant material" has the same meaning as in paragraph 4(5) of the Schedule to the Act;

(i) "relevant party" has the same meaning as in paragraph 11 of the Schedule to the Act;

(j) "special advocate" means a person appointed under paragraph 7 of the Schedule to the Act.

(4) For the purposes of this Part, disclosure is contrary to the public interest if it is made contrary to the interests of national security, the international relations of the United Kingdom, the detection and prevention of crime, or in any other circumstances where disclosure is likely to harm the public interest.

Modification to the overriding objective

76.2—(1) Where this Part applies, the overriding objective in 76.2 Part 1, and so far as relevant any other rule, must be read and given effect in a way which is compatible with the duty set out in paragraph (2).

(2) The court must ensure that information is not disclosed contrary to the public interest.

(3) Subject to paragraph (2), the court must satisfy itself that the material available to it enables it properly to determine proceedings.

II. Applications to the High Court relating to derogating control orders

Scope of this section

76.3—(1) This section of this Part contains rules about applica- 76.3 tions relating to derogating control orders.

(2) Part 23 does not apply to an application made under this section of this Part.

Applications for the making of a derogating control order

76.4 **76.4 An application for the making of a derogating control order under section 4(1) of the Act must be made by the Secretary of State by filing with the court—**

(a) a statement of reasons to support the application for—

(i) making such an order, and

(ii) imposing each of the obligations to be imposed by that order;

(b) all relevant material;

(c) any written submissions; and

(d) a draft of the order sought.

Directions for a full hearing on notice

76.5 **76.5—(1) When the court makes a derogating control order under section 4(3) of the Act it must—**

(a) immediately fix a date, time and place for a further hearing at which the controlled person, his legal representative and a special advocate (if one has been appointed) can be present; and

(b) unless the court otherwise directs, that date must be no later than 7 days from the date that the order is made.

(2) At the hearing referred to in paragraph (1)(a) the court must give directions—

(a) for the holding of a full hearing under section 4(1)(b) of the Act to determine whether to confirm the control order (with or without modifications) or to revoke it; and

(b) specifying the date and time by which the parties and special advocate must file and serve any written evidence or written submissions in accordance with rule 76.30.

(3) When giving directions under paragraph (2), the court must have regard to the need to expedite the full hearing.

Applications on notice

76.6 **76.6—(1) An application under section 4(9) for the renewal, or under section 7(4) of the Act, for the revocation of a control order or for the modification of obligations imposed by such an order, must be made in accordance with this rule.**

(2) An application by the Secretary of State must be made by—

(a) filing with the court—

(i) a statement of reasons to support the application,

***(ii) all* relevant material,**

(iii) any written submissions, and

(iv) a draft of the order sought; and

(b) serving on the controlled person or his legal representative any open material.

(3) An application by the controlled person must be made by filing with the court and serving on the Secretary of State—

(a) a statement of reasons to support the application;
(b) any written evidence upon which he relies;
(c) any written submissions; and
(d) where appropriate, a draft of the order sought.

(4) If the controlled person wishes to oppose an application made under this rule, he must as soon as practicable file with the court, and serve on the Secretary of State, any written evidence and any written submissions upon which he relies.

(5) If the Secretary of State wishes to oppose an application made under this rule, he must as soon as practicable—

(a) file with the court—
  (i) all relevant material, and
  (ii) any written submissions; and
(b) serve on the controlled person any open material.

(Attention is drawn to rule 76.18 relating to the address for issuing proceedings in the High Court. Rules 76.28 and 76.29 will apply where any closed material is filed by the Secretary of State).

III. Permission applications, references and appeals to the High Court relating to non-derogating control orders

Scope of this section

76.7 This section of this Part contains rules about— 76.7

(a) applications under section 3(1)(a) of the Act (application for permission to make a non-derogating control order);
(b) references under section 3(3) of the Act (reference of a non-derogating control order made without permission); and
(c) appeals to the High Court under section 10 of the Act (appeals relating to non-derogating control orders).

Application for permission to make non-derogating control order

76.8 An application under section 3(1)(a) for permission to make a non-derogating control order must be made by the Secretary of State by filing with the court— 76.8

(a) a statement of reasons to support the application;
(b) all relevant material;
(c) any written submissions; and
(d) the proposed control order.

References under section 3(3) of the Act

76.9—(1) This rule applies where the Secretary of State makes a reference under section 3(3) of the Act (reference of a non-derogating control order). 76.9

(2) The Secretary of State must promptly file with the court—

(a) a statement of the reasons for—

(i) making the control order,

(ii) imposing the obligations imposed by that order;

(b) all relevant material; and

(c) any written submissions.

Directions for hearing on application for permission or on a reference

76.10 **76.10**—(1) This rule applies where the court gives directions under section 3(2)(c) or (6)(b) or (c) of the Act.

(2) The court must immediately—

(a) fix a date, time and place for a further hearing at which the controlled person, his legal representative and a special advocate (if one has been appointed) can be present; and

(b) unless the court otherwise directs, that date must be no later than 7 days from the date that the order is made.

(3) At the hearing referred to in paragraph (2), the court must give directions—

(a) for a hearing under section 3(10); and

(b) specifying the date and time by which the parties and special advocate must file and serve any written evidence or written submissions in accordance with rule 76.30.

(4) When giving directions under paragraph (3), the court must have regard to the need to expedite that hearing.

(Rules 76.28 and 76.29 will apply where any closed material is filed by the Secretary of State).

Appeals under section 10 of the Act

76.11 **76.11** This rule and rules 76.12 to 76.15 apply to an appeal under section 10 of the Act (appeals relating to a non-derogating control order).

Modification of Part 52 (appeals)

76.12 **76.12**—(1) Part 52 (appeals) applies to an appeal under section 10 of the Act, subject to—

(a) rule 76.2;

(b) the rules in section 5 of this Part; and

(c) the modifications set out in paragraphs (2) and (3) of this rule.

(2) The following rules do not apply to appeals under section 10 of the Act—

(a) rule 52.3 (permission);

(b) rule 52.4 (appellant's notice);

(c) rule 52.5 (respondent's notice); and

(d) rule 52.11 (hearing of appeals).

(3) Rule 52.2 (all parties to comply with the practice direction) applies, but the parties shall not be required to comply with paragraphs 5.6, 5.6A, 5.7, 5.9 and 5.10 of that practice direction.

Notice of appeal

76.13—(1) The controlled person must give notice of appeal by— 76.13

(a) filing it with the court; and

(b) serving a copy of the notice and any accompanying documents on the Secretary of State.

(2) The notice of appeal must—

(a) set out the grounds of the appeal; and

(b) state the name and address of—

(i) the controlled person, and

(ii) any legal representative of that person.

(3) A notice of appeal may include an application for an order under rule 76.19 requiring anonymity.

(4) The notice of appeal must be filed with—

(a) a copy of the order that is the subject of the appeal;

(b) a copy of the Secretary of State's decision on an application for the revocation of the control order, or for the modification of an obligation imposed by such an order.

(Attention is drawn to rule 76.18 relating to the address for issuing proceedings in the High Court).

Time limit for appealing

76.14—(1) Subject to paragraph (2), the controlled person must give notice of appeal no later than 28 days after receiving notice of— 76.14

(a) the order that is the subject of the appeal; or

(b) the decision by the Secretary of State on an application for the revocation of the control order, or for the modification of an obligation imposed by such an order.

(2) In a case where the Secretary of State has failed to determine an application for the revocation of the control order, or for the modification of an obligation imposed by such an order, the controlled person must file the notice of appeal—

(a) no earlier than 28 days; and

(b) no later than 42 days;

after the date the application was made.

Secretary of State's reply

76.15 If the Secretary of State wishes to oppose an appeal made under section 10 of the Act, he must no later than 14 days after he is served with the notice of appeal— 76.15

(a) file with the court—

(i) all relevant material, and

(ii) any written submissions; and

(b) serve on the controlled person any open material.

IV. Appeals to the Court of Appeal

Modification of Part 52 (appeals)

76.16 **76.16**—(1) Part 52 (appeals) applies to an appeal to the Court of Appeal against an order of the High Court in control order proceedings, subject to—

(a) rule 76.2;

(b) the rules in section 5 of this Part;and

(c) paragraphs (2) and (3) of this rule.

(2) The following rules do not apply to appeals to the Court of Appeal—

(a) rule 52.4(1) (appellant's notice); and

(b) rule 52.5 (respondent's notice); but

the provisions of rules 76.13 and 76.15 shall apply with appropriate modifications.

(3) Rule 52.2 (all parties to comply with the practice direction) applies, but the parties shall not be required to comply with paragraphs 5.6, 5.6A, 5.7, 6.3A, 15.2, 15.3, 15.4 and 15.6 of that practice direction.

IV. General provisions

Scope of this section

76.17 **76.17** This section of this Part applies to—

(a) control order proceedings in the High Court; and

(b) appeals to the Court of Appeal against an order of the High Court in such proceedings.

Address for issuing proceedings in the High Court

76.18 **76.18** Any control order proceedings must be issued at the Administrative Court Office, Room C315, Royal Courts of Justice, Strand, London, WC2A 2LL.

Applications for anonymity

76.19 **76.19**—(1) The controlled person or the Secretary of State may apply for an order requiring the anonymity of the controlled person.

(2) An application under paragraph (1) may be made at any time, irrespective of whether any control order proceedings have been commenced.

(3) An application may be made without notice to the other party.

(4) References in this rule to an order requiring anonymity for the controlled person are to be construed in accordance with paragraph 5(3) of the Schedule to the Act.

Notification of hearing

76.20 **76.20** Unless the court orders otherwise, it must serve notice of the date, time and place fixed for any hearing on—

(a) every party, whether or not entitled to attend that hearing; and
(b) if one has been appointed for the purposes of the hearing, the special advocate or those instructing him.

Hearings

76.21—(1) The following proceedings must be determined at a hearing— **76.21**

(a) a hearing pursuant to directions given under section 4(1)(b) of the Act (derogating control orders);
(b) a hearing pursuant to directions given under sections 3(2)(c) or (6)(b) or (c) of the Act (non-derogating control orders);
(c) an appeal under section 10 of the Act (appeal relating to a non-derogating control order);
(d) an appeal to the Court of Appeal from an order of the High Court made in any of the above proceedings; and
(e) a hearing under rule 76.29(2) (consideration of Secretary of State's objection).

(2) Paragraph (1)(c) and (d) do not apply where—

(a) the appeal is withdrawn by the controlled person;
(b) the Secretary of State consents to the appeal being allowed; or
(c) the controlled person is outside the United Kingdom or it is impracticable to give him notice of a hearing and, in either case, he is unrepresented.

Hearings in private

76.22—(1) If the court considers it necessary for any relevant party and his legal representative to be excluded from a hearing or part of a hearing in order to secure that information is not disclosed contrary to the public interest, it must— **76.22**

(a) direct accordingly; and
(b) conduct the hearing, or that part of it from which the relevant party and his legal representative are excluded, in private.

(2) The court may conduct a hearing or part of a hearing in private for any other good reason.

Appointment of a special advocate

76.23—(1) Subject to paragraph (2), the Secretary of State must immediately give notice of the proceedings to the relevant law officer upon— **76.23**

(a) making an application under section 4(1) of the Act (relating to a derogating control order);
(b) making an application under section 3(1)(a) of the Act (application for permission to make a non-derogating control order);

(c) making a reference under section 3(3) of the Act (reference of a non-derogating control order made without permission); or

(d) being served with a copy of any application, claim, or notice of appeal in proceedings to which this Part applies.

(2) Paragraph (1) applies unless—

(a) the Secretary of State does not intend to—

(i) oppose the appeal or application; or

(ii) withhold closed material from a relevant party; or

(b) a special advocate has already been appointed to represent the interests of the relevant party in the proceedings and that special advocate is not prevented from communicating with that party by virtue of rule 76.25.

(3) Where notice is given to the relevant law officer under paragraph (1), the relevant law officer may appoint a special advocate to represent the interests of the relevant party in the proceedings.

(4) Where any proceedings to which this Part apply are pending but no special advocate has been appointed, a relevant party or the Secretary of State may request the relevant law officer to appoint a special advocate.

Functions of special advocate

76.24 76.24 The functions of a special advocate are to represent the interests of a relevant party by—

(a) making submissions to the court at any hearings from which the relevant party and his legal representatives are excluded;

(b) cross-examining witnesses at any such hearings; and

(c) making written submissions to the court.

Special advocate: communicating about proceedings

76.25 76.25—(1) The special advocate may communicate with the relevant party or his legal representative at any time before the Secretary of State serves closed material on him.

(2) After the Secretary of State serves closed material on the special advocate, the special advocate must not communicate with any person about any matter connected with the proceedings, except in accordance with paragraph (3) or a direction of the court pursuant to a request under paragraph (4).

(3) The special advocate may, without directions from the court, communicate about the proceedings with—

(a) the court;

(b) the Secretary of State, or any person acting for him;

(c) the relevant law officer, or any person acting for him; or

(d) any other person, except for the relevant party or his legal representative, with whom it is necessary for administrative purposes for him to communicate about matters not connected with the substance of the proceedings.

(4) The special advocate may request directions from the court authorising him to communicate with the relevant party or his legal representative or with any other person.

(5) Where the special advocate makes a request for directions under paragraph (4)—

(a) the court must notify the Secretary of State of the request; and

(b) the Secretary of State must, within a period specified by the court, file with the court and serve on the special advocate notice of any objection which he has to the proposed communication, or to the form in which it is proposed to be made.

(6) Paragraph (2) does not prohibit the relevant party from communicating with the special advocate after the Secretary of State has served material on him as mentioned in paragraph (1), but—

(a) the relevant party may only communicate with the special advocate through a legal representative in writing; and

(b) the special advocate must not reply to the communication other than in accordance with directions of the court, except that he may without such directions send a written acknowledgment of receipt to the legal representative of the relevant party.

Modification of the general rules of evidence and disclosure

76.26—(1) Part 31 (disclosure and inspection of documents), Part 32 (evidence) and Part 33 (miscellaneous rules about evidence) do not apply to any proceedings to which this Part applies. 76.26

(2) Subject to the other rules in this Part, the evidence of a witness may be given either—

(a) orally, before the court; or

(b) in writing, in which case it shall be given in such manner and at such time as the court directs.

(3) The court may also receive evidence in documentary or any other form.

(4) The court may receive evidence that would not, but for this rule, be admissible in a court of law.

(5) Every party shall be entitled to adduce evidence and to cross-examine witnesses during any part of a hearing from which he and his legal representative are not excluded.

(6) The court may require a witness to give evidence on oath.

Filing and service of relevant material

76.27 The Secretary of State is required to make a reasonable 76.27

search for relevant material and to file and serve that material in accordance with the rules in this Part.

Closed material

76.28 **76.28—(1) The Secretary of State—**

(a) must apply to the court for permission to withhold closed material from a relevant party or his legal representative in accordance with this rule; and

(b) may not rely on closed material at a hearing on notice unless a special advocate has been appointed to represent the interests of the relevant party.

(2) The Secretary of State must file with the court and serve, at such time as the court directs, on the special advocate—

(a) the closed material;

(b) a statement of his reasons for withholding that material from the relevant party; and

(c) if he considers it possible to summarise that material without disclosing information contrary to the public interest, a summary of that material in a form which can be served on the relevant party.

(3) The Secretary of State may at any time amend or supplement material filed under this rule, but only with—

(a) the agreement of the special advocate; or

(b) the permission of the court.

Consideration of Secretary of State's objection

76.29 **76.29—(1) This rule applies where the Secretary of State has—**

(a) objected under rule 76.25(5)(b) to a proposed communication by the special advocate; or

(b) applied under rule 76.28 for permission to withhold closed material.

(2) The court must fix a hearing for the Secretary of State and the special advocate to make oral representations, unless—

(a) the special advocate gives notice to the court that he does not challenge the objection or application;

(b) the court has previously considered—

(i) an objection under rule 76.25(5)(b), or

(ii) an application under rule 76.28(1) for permission to withhold the same or substantially the same material, and

is satisfied that it would be just to uphold that objection or to give permission without a hearing; or

(c) the Secretary of State and the special advocate consent to the court deciding the issue without a hearing.

(3) If the special advocate does not challenge the objection or ***the application, he must*** **give notice of that fact to the court and the Secretary of State within 14 days, or such other period as the court may direct, after the Secretary of State serves on him a notice under rule 76.25(5)(b) or material under rule 76.28(2).**

(4) Where the court fixes a hearing under this rule, the Secretary of State and the special advocate must before the hearing file with the court a schedule identifying the issues which cannot be agreed between them, which must—

(a) list the items or issues in dispute;
(b) give brief reasons for their contentions on each; and
(c) set out any proposals for the court to resolve the issues in contention.

(5) A hearing under this rule shall take place in the absence of the relevant party and his legal representative.

(6) Where the court gives permission to the Secretary of State to withhold closed material, the court must—

(a) consider whether to direct the Secretary of State to serve a summary of that material on the relevant party or his legal representative; but
(b) ensure that no such summary contains information or other material the disclosure of which would be contrary to the public interest.

(7) Where the court has not given permission to the Secretary of State to withhold closed material from, or has directed the Secretary of State to serve a summary of that material on, a relevant party or his legal representative—

(a) the Secretary of State shall not be required to serve that material or summary; but
(b) if he does not do so, at a hearing on notice the court may—
(i) if it considers that the material or anything that is required to be summarised might be of assistance to the relevant party in relation to a matter under consideration by the court, direct that the matter be withdrawn from its consideration, and
(ii) in any other case, direct that the Secretary of State shall not rely in the proceedings on that material or (as the case may be) on what is required to be summarised.

(8) The court must give permission to the Secretary of State to withhold closed material where it considers that the disclosure of that material would be contrary to the public interest.

Order of filing and serving material and written submissions

76.30 Subject to any directions given by the court, the parties must file and serve any material and written submissions, and the special advocate must file and serve any written submissions, in the following order— 76.30

(a) the Secretary of State must file with the court all relevant material;
(b) the Secretary of State must serve on—
(i) the relevant party or his legal representative; and
(ii) the special advocate (as soon as one is appointed) or those instructing him,

any open material;

(c) the relevant party must file with the court and serve on the Secretary of State and special advocate (if one is appointed) or those instructing him any written evidence which he wishes the court to take into account at the hearing;

(d) the Secretary of State must file with the court any further relevant material;

(e) the Secretary of State must serve on—

(i) the relevant party or his legal representative, and

(ii) the special advocate (as soon as one is appointed) or those instructing him,

any open material filed with the court under paragraph (d);

(f) the Secretary of State must serve on the special advocate (if one has been appointed) any closed material;

(g) the parties and the special advocate (if one has been appointed) must file and serve any written submissions as directed by the court.

(Rules 76.28 and 76.29 will apply where any closed material is filed by the Secretary of State).

Failure to comply with directions

76.31 76.31—(1) Where a party or the special advocate fails to comply with a direction of the court, the court may serve on him a notice which states—

(a) the respect in which he has failed to comply with the direction;

(b) a time limit for complying with the direction; and

(c) that the court may proceed to determine the proceedings before it, on the material available to it, if the party or the special advocate fails to comply with the relevant direction within the time specified.

(2) Where a party or special advocate fails to comply with such a notice, the court may proceed in accordance with paragraph (1)(c).

Judgments

76.32 76.32—(1) When the court gives judgment in any proceedings to which this Part applies, it may withhold any or part of its reasons if and to the extent that it is not possible to give reasons without disclosing information contrary to the public interest.

(2) Where the judgment of the court does not include the full reasons for its decision, the court must serve on the Secretary of State and the special advocate a separate written judgment including those reasons.

Application by Secretary of State for reconsideration of decision

76.33 76.33—(1) This rule applies where the court proposes, in any proceedings to which this Part applies, to serve notice on a relevant party of any

(a) order or direction made or given in the absence of the Secretary of State; or

(b) any judgment.

(2) Before the court serves any such notice on the relevant party, it must first serve notice on the Secretary of State of its intention to do so.

(3) The Secretary of State may, within 5 days of being served with notice under paragraph (2), apply to the court to reconsider the terms of the order or direction or to review the terms of the proposed judgment if he considers that—

(a) his compliance with the order or direction; or

(b) the notification to the relevant party of any matter contained in the judgment, order or direction;

would cause information to be disclosed contrary to the public interest.

(4) Where the Secretary of State makes an application under paragraph (3), he must at the same time serve a copy of it on the special advocate, if one has been appointed.

(5) Rule 76.29 (except for paragraphs (6) and (7)) shall, if a special advocate has been appointed, apply with any necessary modifications to the consideration of an application under paragraph (3) of this rule.

(6) The court must not serve notice on the relevant party as mentioned in paragraph (1) before the time for the Secretary of State to make an application under paragraph (3) has expired.

Supply of court documents[1]

76.34 Unless the court otherwise directs, rule 5.4 (Register of Claims), rule 5.4B (Supply of documents from court records—a party) and rule 5.4C (Supply of documents from court records—a non-party) do not apply to any proceedings to which this Part applies. 76.34

[1] Amended by the Civil Procedure (Amendment) Rules 2006 (SI 2006/1689).

PART 77

Miscellaneous Provisions in Support of Criminal Justice

Contents

77.0.1

Editorial introduction

77.0.2 The Serious Crime Act 2007 enables the Director of Public Prosecutions, Crown Prosecutors to whom the DPP has delegated powers under Sch.2 and a number of other prosecuting authorities to apply to the High Court for a "Serious Crime Prevention Order". The Act also enables the parties or other persons affected to apply for the variation or discharge of such orders. The Crown Court also has power to grant such an order but an application to vary or discharge an order made in the Crown Court is made to the High Court.

The Act is a continuation of a clear trend of providing civil remedies in respect of criminal behaviour. The grounds for making an order are: (a) that the defendant has been involved in serious crime and (b) that the order would protect the public by preventing, restricting or disrupting his involvement in serious crime. To prove limb (a) it must be shown that the defendant has committed a serious offence *or* that he has facilitated the commission of a serious offence or that he has conducted himself in a way that was likely to facilitate the commission of a serious offence. A person is treated as having *committed* a serious offence if, and only if, he has been convicted of it but not necessarily in England and Wales. The other two methods of proving his involvement in serious crime are more open-ended and will no doubt give rise to extensive legal argument.

There are various different forms of SCPO and the restrictions that can be imposed are extensive; see s.1(3). An application must be accompanied by a draft of the particular order sought. "Serious Crime" is defined in Sch.1. Orders can be made against individuals, companies and partnerships. The Home Office envisages between thirty and fifty such orders each year. Properly used the Act could be, and is intended to be, a valuable means of fighting crime. Improperly used it is a potential means of oppression but the new Part and Practice Direction clearly strive to ensure that adequate safeguards are in place. The Part and PD are clear and self explanatory: the complications are in the Act.

Presumably, given the title of Pt 77 it is intended in due course to include within it other provisions in support of criminal justice currently found elsewhere within the rules. For example, the provisions found in CPR Sch.1 RSC Orders 79, 115 and 116 could be sensibly moved into it.

Scope and interpretation

77.1 **77.1—(1) This Part contains rules about—**

(a) applications for a serious crime prevention order under section 8 of the Serious Crime Act 2007(); and

(b) related applications under sections 9, 17 and 18 of that Act.

(2) In this Part—

(a) 'the 2007 Act' means the Serious Crime Act 2007; and

(b) 'SCPO' means a serious crime prevention order under section 1 or section 19 of the 2007 Act.

Applications for a SCPO

77.2 An application under section 8 of the 2007 Act for a SCPO must be started in accordance with Part 8 as modified by the practice direction supplementing this Part. 77.2

Applications by third parties to make representations and applications to vary or discharge a SCPO made by the High Court

77.3 An application under— 77.3

(1) section 9 of the 2007 Act; or

(2) section 17 or 18 of the 2007 Act to vary or discharge a SCPO made by the High Court,

must be made in accordance with Part 23 as modified by the practice direction supplementing this Part.

Applications to vary or discharge a SCPO made by the Crown Court

77.4 An application under section 17 or 18 of the 2007 Act to vary or discharge a SCPO made by the Crown Court must be started in accordance with Part 8. 77.4

Where to make an application

77.5 Applications under this Part must be made to the Queen's Bench Division of the High Court. 77.5

PRACTICE DIRECTION—APPLICATIONS FOR AND RELATING TO SERIOUS CRIME PREVENTION ORDERS

77PD.1 *This Practice Direction supplements CPR Part 77*

Claim form—application for a SCPO

1.1 An application for a SCPO must be started by way of a Part 8 claim form, although the court may decide during the proceedings that it would be more appropriate to continue the proceedings in accordance with Part 7.

(Rule 8.1(3) allows the court to make an order that the claim continue as if the claimant had not used the Part 8 procedure.)

1.2 The claim form must—

(1) identify which provisions of section 2(1) of the 2007 Act the applicant relies on and under each provision identified, set out the details of the allegations that the respondent has been involved in serious crime (whether in England and Wales or elsewhere);

(2) set out the applicant's grounds for contending that the proposed terms of the SCPO are appropriate for the purpose of protecting the public in accordance with section 1(3) of the 2007 Act; and

(3) include details of any third party whom the applicant believes is likely to be significantly adversely affected by the SCPO and the nature of that adverse effect.

1.3 The claim form must be accompanied by a draft of the SCPO for which the application is made. The terms of the draft SCPO must include any proposed dates, including those upon which the applicant proposes that the SCPO should come into force and cease to be in force.

1.4 Where it is alleged that the respondent has committed a serious offence, the claim form must be accompanied by evidence that the respondent has been convicted of the offence. Where a certificate of conviction can be obtained, this must be put in evidence.

1.5 Where it is alleged that the respondent has been convicted of an offence in another jurisdiction, the applicant must put in evidence—

(a) a document from the appropriate public authority in the jurisdiction concerned certifying that the respondent has after due process of law been convicted of the offence; and

(b) where the document is not in English, a translation of that document into English—

(i) certified by a notary public or other qualified person; or

(ii) accompanied by written evidence confirming that the translation is accurate.

Applications by third parties to make representations

2.1 The evidence in support of an application made under section 9 of the 2007 Act must contain details of why the third party believes the proposed order would be likely to have a significant adverse effect on that third party.

Applications to vary or discharge a SCPO

3.1 The application notice or claim form must contain—

(1) where the applicant is the person who is the subject of the SCPO, details of the change of circumstances affecting the SCPO;

(2) where the applicant seeks to vary the SCPO, any grounds advanced by the applicant for contending that the terms of the SCPO as varied would protect the public in accordance with section 17(1) of the 2007 Act;

(2A) where the applicant for the SCPO seeks to vary the SCPO—
(a) details of any third party whom the applicant believes is likely to be significantly adversely affected by the proposed variation to the SCPO; and
(b) details of the nature of that adverse effect;

(3) where the applicant seeks to vary the SCPO and is a third party or the person who is the subject of the SCPO—
(a) particulars of why the applicant believes the applicant is significantly adversely affected by the SCPO;
(b) particulars of how condition A or B in section 17 of the 2007 Act is met; and
(c) particulars relied upon to establish that the purpose of the application is not to make the SCPO more onerous on the person who is the subject of the order; and

(4) where the application is for the discharge of the SCPO and the applicant is a third party or the person who is the subject of the SCPO, particulars of—
(a) why the applicant believes the applicant is significantly adversely affected by the SCPO; and
(b) how condition A or B in section 18 of the 2007 Act is met.

3.2 Where the application is to vary or discharge a SCPO made by the Crown Court, the claim form must be accompanied by a copy of the SCPO made by the Crown Court.

Where to make an application

4.1 An application for a SCPO or relating to a SCPO must be started and heard in the Queen's Bench Division of the High Court at—

(a) the Royal Courts of Justice; or
(b) at one of the following district registries—
(i) Cardiff;
(ii) Birmingham;
(iii) Bristol;
(iv) Leeds;
(v) Manchester;
(vi) Newcastle; or
(vii) Nottingham.

PART 78

European Order for Payment and European Small Claims Procedures

Contents

78.0.1

Scope of this Section and interpretation[1]

78.1 **78.1. (1) Section I contains rules about European orders for payment made under Regulation (EC) No 1896/2006 of the European Parliament and of the Council of 12 December 2006 creating a European order for payment procedure(a).**

(2) Section II contains rules about the European small claims procedure under Regulation (EC) No 861/2007 of the European

[1] Introduced by the Civil Procedure (Amendment) Rules 2008 (SI 2008/2178).

Parliament and of the Council of 11 July 2007 establishing a European small claims procedure(b).

(3) In this Part—

(a) unless otherwise stated, a reference to an Annex is to an Annex to the Practice Direction supplementing this Part; and

(b) "Service Regulation" means Regulation (EC) 1393/2007 on service, within the same meaning as rule 6.31(e).

(c)

(4) Except where—

(a) the EOP Regulation (which has the same meaning as in rule 78.2(2)(a));

(b) the ESCP Regulation (which has the same meaning as in rule 78.12(2)(a)); or

(c) the Service Regulation

makes different provisions about the certification or verification of translations, every translation required by this Part or such Regulation must be accompanied by a statement by the person making it that it is a correct translation. The statement must include that person's name, address and qualifications for making the translation.

Section I—European Order for Payment Procedure

Scope of this Section and interpretation[1]

78.2.—(1) This Section applies to applications for European orders for payment and other related proceedings under Regulation (EC) No 1896/2006 of the European Parliament and of the Council of 12 December 2006 creating a European order for payment procedure. 78.2

(2) In this Section—

(a) "EOP Regulation" means Regulation (EC) No 1896/2006 of the European Parliament and of the Council of 12 December 2006 creating a European order for payment procedure. A copy of the EOP Regulation can be found at Annex 1;

(b) "court of origin" has the meaning given by article 5(4) of the EOP Regulation;

(c) "EOP" means a European order for payment;

(d) "EOP application" means an application for an EOP;

(e) "EOP application form A" means the Application for a European order for payment form A, annexed to the EOP Regulation at Annex I to that Regulation;

(f) "European order for payment" means an order for payment made by a court under article 12(1) of the EOP Regulation;

(g) "Member State" has the meaning given by article 2(3) of the EOP Regulation;

[1] Introduced by the Civil Procedure (Amendment) Rules 2008 (SI 2008/2178).

(h) "Member State of origin" has the meaning given by article 5(1) of the EOP Regulation;

(i) "statement of opposition" means a statement of opposition filed in accordance with article 16 of the EOP Regulation.

Editorial Introduction

78.2.1 The EC Regulations for both new procedures are annexed to the new rule and PD. They need to be studied carefully when making or responding to an application. Guidance and a checklist on procedure are being prepared to assist court staff with checking whether applications comply with the regulations.

The procedures cannot be used for certain types of claims (art.2)—these include individual's status; capacity personality or defamation claims; property rights arising from marriage and divorce or the tenancy of a property; social security; arbitration; and employment law (sic). The use of the procedure by claimants is optional. Claims within scope will be decided in accordance with the law of the member state of issue.

European Order for Payment (EOP) Procedure—Editorial Introduction

78.2.2 EC Regulation 1896/2006 created the European order for payment procedure that came into force on December 12, 2008. The aim is to enable efficient recovery of uncontested specific money claims cross-border within the EU (except Denmark). One party must be domiciled or habitually resident in a member state other than the member state of the court.

A claim is made using a new standard form application. If the application complies with the Regulations and the form is properly completed, an EOP is issued and served on the defendant with proof of receipt (which can be done electronically). If a statement of opposition is not sent to the court by the defendant within 30 days of service of the EOP (allowing for an appropriate time for the statement to arrive at court) the court shall declare the order enforceable. If the defendant opposes the claim, then, unless the claimant asks that the case ceases, the case will be transferred to the national system, and proceed in accordance with the CPR.

In exceptional cases the defendant can apply for a review for refusal, stay or limitation of enforcement. But the Regulations do not provide a right of appeal. Most applications of any type will be dealt with on paper, but oral hearings are not ruled out.

The Ministry of Justice originally proposed that all EOP applications would be dealt with by the county court regardless of value, but after discussion, the Civil Procedure Rule Committee decided that the High Court (QB and Chancery) and county court would have joint jurisdiction.

It is very unclear by whom and how often the procedure may be used but possible problems will be:

- The language of the Directive and Regulations is not easy to follow.
- The descriptions of claims not in scope are "economical", e.g. what does "employment law" mean—does it include contractual claims which in this jurisdiction can be issued in the county court, does the tenancy of a property include a holiday let? Yet this decision will generally be one for court staff to take , but no doubt District Judges and Masters will be asked to interpret the Regulations.
- Post to and from some parts of Europe can take seven to ten days but the time limits for responding run from dispatch, not receipt, and are not generous, so applications for review (or to set aside "default judgments" by any other name) seem likely.
- The requirement to conduct the case in English and provide translations could well be a deterrent to some parties.
- Determining defendants' applications to set aside the order (e.g. disputes about service), for a review, or for a stay: invariably this will a matter for the judges.

Application for a European Order for Payment[1]

78.3. Where a declaration provided by the claimant under article 7(3) of the EOP Regulation contains any deliberate false statement, rule 32.14 applies as if the EOP application form A were verified by a statement of truth. 78.3

(An EOP application is made in accordance with the EOP Regulation and in particular article 7 of that Regulation.)

Withdrawal of EOP application[2]

78.4.—(1) At any stage before a statement of opposition is filed, the claimant may notify the court that the claimant no longer wishes to proceed with the claim. 78.4

(2) Where the claimant notifies the court in accordance with paragraph (1)—

(a) the court will notify the defendant that the application has been withdrawn; and

(b) no order as to costs will be made.

Transfer of proceedings where an EOP application has been opposed[3]

78.5.—(1) Where a statement of opposition is filed in accordance with article 16 of the EOP Regulation and the claimant has not opposed the transfer of the matter— 78.5

(a) the EOP application will be treated as if it had been started as a claim under Part 7 and the EOP application form A will be treated as a Part 7 claim form including particulars of claim; and

(b) thereafter, these Rules apply with necessary modifications and subject to this rule and rules 78.6 and 78.7.

(2) When the court notifies the claimant in accordance with article 17(3) of the EOP Regulation the court will also—

(a) notify the claimant—

(i) that the EOP application form A is now treated as a Part 7 claim form including particulars of claim; and

(ii) of the time within which the defendant must respond under rule 78.6; and

(b) notify the defendant—

(i) that a statement of opposition has been received;

(ii) that the application will not continue under Part 78;

(iii) that the application has been transferred under article 17 of the EOP Regulation;

[1] Introduced by the Civil Procedure (Amendment) Rules 2008 (SI 2008/2178).
[2] Introduced by the Civil Procedure (Amendment) Rules 2008 (SI 2008/2178).
[3] Introduced by the Civil Procedure (Amendment) Rules 2008 (SI 2008/2178).

(iv) that the EOP application form A is now treated as a Part 7 claim form including particulars of claim; and

(v) of the time within which the defendant must respond under rule 78.6.

Filing of acknowledgment of service and defence where an EOP application is transferred under article 17 of the EOP Regulation[1]

78.6 **78.6.—(1) The defendant must file a defence within 30 days of the date of the notice issued by the court under rule 78.5(2)(b).**

(2) If the defendant wishes to dispute the court's jurisdiction, the defendant must instead—

(a) file an acknowledgment of service within the period specified in paragraph (1); and

(b) make an application under Part 11 within the period specified in that Part.

(3) Where this rule applies, the following rules do not apply—

(a) rule 10.1(3);

(b) rule 10.3; and

(c) rule 15.4(1).

Default judgment[2]

78.7 **78.7.—(1) If—**

(a) the defendant fails to file an acknowledgment of service within the period specified in rule 78.6(2)(a); and

(b) does not within that period—

(i) file a defence in accordance with Part 15 (except rule 15.4(1)) and rule 78.6(1); or

(ii) file an admission in accordance with Part 14,

the claimant may obtain default judgment if Part 12 allows it.

(2) Where this rule applies, rule 10.2 does not apply.

Review in exceptional cases[3]

78.8 **78.8. An application for a review under article 20 of the EOP Regulation must be made in accordance with Part 23.**

ENFORCEMENT OF EOPS IN ENGLAND AND WALES

Enforcement of European orders for payment[4]

78.9 **78.9.—(1) A person seeking to enforce an EOP in England and Wales must file at the court in which enforcement proceedings are to be brought the documents required by article 21 of the EOP Regulation.**

[1] Introduced by the Civil Procedure (Amendment) Rules 2008 (SI 2008/2178).
[2] Introduced by the Civil Procedure (Amendment) Rules 2008 (SI 2008/2178).
[3] Introduced by the Civil Procedure (Amendment) Rules 2008 (SI 2008/2178).
[4] Introduced by the Civil Procedure (Amendment) Rules 2008 (SI 2008/2178).

(2) Where a person applies to enforce an EOP expressed in a foreign currency, the application must contain a certificate of the sterling equivalent of the judgment sum at the close of business on the date nearest preceding the date of the application.

(Parts 70 to 74 contain further rules about enforcement.)

Refusal of enforcement[1]

78.10.—(1) An application under article 22 of the EOP Regulation that the court should refuse to enforce an EOP must be made in accordance with Part 23 to the court in which the EOP is being enforced. 78.10

(2) The judgment debtor must, as soon as practicable, serve copies of any order made under article 22 on—

(a) all other parties to the proceedings and any other person affected by the order ("the affected persons"); and

(b) any court in which enforcement proceedings of the EOP are pending in England and Wales ("the relevant courts").

(3) Upon service of the order on the affected persons, all enforcement proceedings of the EOP in the relevant courts will cease.

Stay of or limitation on enforcement[2]

78.11.—(1) Where the defendant has sought a review and also applies for a stay of or limitation on enforcement in accordance with article 23 of the EOP Regulation, such application must be made in accordance with Part 23 to the court in which the EOP is being enforced. 78.11

(2) The defendant must, as soon as practicable, serve a copy of any order made under article 23 on—

(a) all other parties to the proceedings and any other person affected by the order; and

(b) any court in which enforcement proceedings are pending in England and Wales,

and the order will not have effect on any person until it has been served in accordance with this rule and they have received it.

Section II—European Small Claims Procedure

Scope of this Section and interpretation[3]

78.12.—(1) This Section applies to the European small claims procedure under Regulation (EC) No 861/2007 of the European Parliament and of the Council of 11 July 2007 establishing a European small claims procedure. 78.12

[1] Introduced by the Civil Procedure (Amendment) Rules 2008 (SI 2008/2178).
[2] Introduced by the Civil Procedure (Amendment) Rules 2008 (SI 2008/2178).
[3] Introduced by the Civil Procedure (Amendment) Rules 2008 (SI 2008/2178).

(2) In this Section—

(a) "ESCP Regulation" means Regulation (EC) No 861/2007 of the European Parliament and of the Council of 11 July 2007 establishing a European small claims procedure. A copy of the ESCP Regulation can be found at Annex 2;

(b) "defendant's response" means the response to the ESCP claim form;

(c) "ESCP" means the European small claims procedure established by the ESCP Regulation;

(d) "ESCP claim form" means the claim form completed and filed in the ESCP;

(e) "ESCP counterclaim" has the meaning given to counterclaim by recital 16 of the ESCP Regulation;

(f) "ESCP judgment" means a judgment given in the ESCP;

(g) "Member State" has the meaning given by article 2(3) of the ESCP Regulation;

(h) "Member State of enforcement" is the Member State in which the ESCP judgment is to be enforced;

(i) "Member State of judgment" is the Member State in which the ESCP judgment is given.

European Small Claims Procedure (ESCP)—Editorial Introduction

78.12.1 EC Regulation 861/2007, establishing a cross-border European Small Claims Procedure (ESCP) was implemented in all member states on January 1, 2009. The aim is to improve access to justice by introducing a simple universal procedure for cross-border claims for less than 2000 euros (excluding interest, costs and disbursements), provided at least one party is domiciled or habitually resident in the state where the action is brought and the other party in another member state.

The Regulations include provision for judgments to recognised and be enforceable in other member states without the need for a declaration of enforceability.

The small claims track rules apply, except 27.14 in relation to costs.

The claimant issues the claim on new standard Form A. The claim, response and other communications with the court must be in English, and other documents on which the parties wish to rely, translated, if required, by an authorised identified translator.

If the claim is outside the art.2 scope (by value or subject—see comments on EOP above) the court will tell the claimant, who has the option to withdraw (within 21 days of the date of the court's notice). If the claim is unclear or the form is incorrectly completed the court may invite the claimant to put this right within 30 days (again from the date of the notice). If the claim appears to be "clearly unfounded or the application inadmissible" (not defined in the Regulations, but could include where no cause of action is identified) the claim will be dismissed.

A properly completed admissible claim within scope will be send to the defendant by ordinary post. He has 30 days to respond on Form B (from the date of dispatch by the court). His response will be sent to the claimant. If the defendant makes a counterclaim that exceeds 2000 euros (unless this is obviously deliberately inflated) the claim and the counterclaim are transferred out of the ESCP procedure into the regular CPR system (AQs, allocation to track etc.).

The Regulations require the court to decide the claim within 30 days (of receipt of the response). This may be on paper, but if an oral hearing is necessary this will usually be by telephone or video-conference.

If a judgment is entered against a defendant who has not responded, he may apply for a "review" if he was served with the claim too late to respond in time or prevented from doing so by "force majeure" or exceptional circumstances.

The unsuccessful party bears the costs of the necessarily incurred and proportionate costs and disbursements of the procedure (hence r.7.14 being disapplied).

Parties are likely to have problems with the Directive and Pt 78 because:

- The language of the Directive and Regulations is not easy to follow.
- The descriptions of claims not in scope are "economical", e.g. what does "employment law" mean—does it include contractual claims which in this jurisdiction can be issued in the county court, does the tenancy of a property include a holiday let? Yet this decision will generally be one for court staff to take , but no doubt District Judges and Masters will be asked to interpret the Regulations.
- Post to and from some parts of Europe can take seven to ten days but the time limits for responding run from dispatch, not receipt, and are not generous, so applications for review (or to set aside "default judgments" by any other name) seem likely.
- The requirement to conduct the case in English and provide translations could well be a deterrent to some parties.
- Determining defendants' applications to set aside the order (e.g. disputes about service), for a review, or for a stay: invariably this will be a matter for the judges.

For ESCP in particular other potential problems appear to be:

- Most defendants will have no knowledge of the England and Wales small claims track rules.
- Making decisions on paper in small claims is not easy when parties are not familiar with proving a claim with evidence. In the ESCP procedure there is no provision at all for disclosure of documents or witness statements, although as Pt 27 applies (apart from costs) the court could order this.
- Setting up hearings by telephone or video will not be easy if both parties are in person, taking into account time differences.
- Oral hearings, whether in person or by telephone, may be hampered by language problems and ordering interpreters at a distance will be impracticable.
- Unlike small claims track cases, ESCP claims attract costs—but will parties claim interest and file cost schedules, that include, e.g. costs of translation and of the telephone hearing? These could well exceed the value of the claim—would that be disproportionate when the rules require them?
- Enforcement—the claimant will have to be prepared to follow that through in the defendant's member state, which will not be easy, and may incur more costs.

Given the above the procedure will not be well used except perhaps by those returning from holidays or business trips in Europe having bought goods that prove to be faulty.

ESCP CLAIMS MADE IN A COURT IN ENGLAND AND WALES

78.13. Where a declaration provided by the claimant in the ESCP claim form contains any deliberate false statement, rule 32.14 applies as if the ESCP claim form were verified by a statement of truth. 78.13

(An ESCP claim form is completed and filed in accordance with the ESCP Regulation, in particular article 4(1), and in accordance with this paragraph.)

Allocation of ESCP claims[1]

78.14.—(1) ESCP claims are treated as if they were allocated to the small claims track. 78.14

(2) Part 27 applies, except rule 27.14.

[1] Introduced by the Civil Procedure (Amendment) Rules 2008 (SI 2008/2178).

Transfer of proceedings where the claim is outside the scope of the ESCP Regulation—article 4(3) of the ESCP Regulation[1]

78.15 **78.15.—(1) Where the court identifies that the claim is outside the scope of the ESCP Regulation, the court will notify the claimant of this in a transfer of proceedings notice.**

(2) If the claimant wishes to withdraw the claim, the claimant must notify the court of this within 21days of the date of the transfer of proceedings notice.

(3) Where the claimant has notified the court in accordance with paragraph (2), the claim is automatically withdrawn.

(4) Where the claimant has not notified the court in accordance with paragraph (2) and the claim is instead to be transferred under article 4(3) of the ESCP Regulation—

(a) the claim will be treated as if it had been started as a claim under Part 7 and the ESCP claim form will be treated as a Part 7 claim form including particulars of claim; and

(b) thereafter, these Rules apply with necessary modifications and subject to this rule,

and the court will notify the claimant of the transfer and its effect.

Defendant's response[2]

78.16 **78.16. Where a declaration provided by the defendant in the defendant's response contains any deliberate false statement, rule 32.14 applies as if the defendant's response were verified by a statement of truth.**

(The defendant's response is made in accordance with the ESCP Regulation and in particular article 5(3) of the ESCP Regulation.)

Transfer of proceedings where the defendant claims that the non-monetary claim exceeds the limit set in article 2(1) of the ESCP Regulation—article 5(5) of the ESCP Regulation[3]

78.17 **78.17.—(1) This rule applies where, under article 5(5) of the ESCP Regulation, the defendant claims that the value of a non-monetary claim exceeds the limit in article 2(1) of the ESCP Regulation.**

(2) When the court dispatches the defendant's response to the claimant, it will—

(a) notify the claimant that the court is considering whether the claim is outside the scope of the ESCP Regulation in a consideration of transfer notice; and

(b) send a copy of the notice to the defendant.

(3) If the claimant wishes to withdraw the claim in the event that the court decides that the claim is outside the scope of the ESCP

[1] Introduced by the Civil Procedure (Amendment) Rules 2008 (SI 2008/2178).
[2] Introduced by the Civil Procedure (Amendment) Rules 2008 (SI 2008/2178).
[3] Introduced by the Civil Procedure (Amendment) Rules 2008 (SI 2008/2178).

Regulation the claimant must notify the court and the defendant of this within 21 days of the date of the consideration of transfer notice.

(4) The court will notify the defendant as well as the claimant of its decision whether the claim is outside the scope of the ESCP Regulation.

(Article 5(5) of the ESCP Regulation provides that the court shall decide within 30 days of dispatching the defendant's response to the claimant, whether the claim is within the scope of the ESCP Regulation.)

(5) If the court decides that the claim is outside the scope of the ESCP Regulation and the claimant has notified the court and defendant in accordance with paragraph (3), the claim is automatically withdrawn.

(6) If the court decides that the claim is outside the scope of the ESCP Regulation and the claimant has not notified the court and defendant in accordance with paragraph (3)—

(a) the claim will be treated as if it had been started as a claim under Part 7 and the ESCP claim form will be treated as a Part 7 claim form including particulars of claim;

(b) the defendant's response will be treated as a defence; and

(c) thereafter, these Rules apply with necessary modifications and subject to this rule, and the court will notify the parties.

(7) This rule applies to an ESCP counterclaim as if the counterclaim were an ESCP claim.

Transfer of proceedings where the ESCP counterclaim exceeds the limit set in article 2(1) of the ESCP Regulation—article 5(7) of the ESCP Regulation[1]

78.18.—(1) Where the ESCP counterclaim exceeds the limit set in article 2(1) of the ESCP Regulation, the court will— 78.18

(a) notify the defendant of this in a transfer of proceedings notice; and

(b) send a copy of the notice to the claimant,

when the court dispatches the defendant's response to the claimant.

(2) If the defendant wishes to withdraw the ESCP counterclaim, the defendant must notify the court and the claimant of this within 21 days of the date of the transfer of proceedings notice.

(3) If the defendant notifies the court and claimant under paragraph (2), the ESCP counterclaim is automatically withdrawn.

(4) If the defendant does not notify the court and claimant in accordance with paragraph (2)—

(a) the claim will be treated as if it had been started as a

[1] Introduced by the Civil Procedure (Amendment) Rules 2008 (SI 2008/2178).

claim under Part 7 and the ESCP claim form will be treated as a Part 7 claim form including particulars of claim;

(b) the defendant's response and ESCP counterclaim are to be treated as the defence and counterclaim; and

(c) thereafter, these Rules apply with necessary modifications and subject to this rule, and the court will notify the parties.

Review of judgment[1]

78.19 **78.19.** An application for a review under article 18 of the ESCP Regulation must be made in accordance with Part 23.

ENFORCEMENT OF ESCP JUDGMENTS IN ENGLAND AND WALES

Enforcement of an ESCP judgment[2]

78.20 **78.20.—(1)** A person seeking to enforce an ESCP judgment in England and Wales must file at the court in which enforcement proceedings are to be brought the documents required by article 21 of the ESCP Regulation.

(2) Where a person applies to enforce an ESCP judgment expressed in a foreign currency, the application must contain a certificate of the sterling equivalent of the judgment sum at the close of business on the date nearest preceding the date of the application.

(Parts 70 to 74 contain further rules about enforcement.)

Refusal of enforcement[3]

78.21 **78.21.—(1)** An application under article 22 of the ESCP Regulation that the court should refuse to enforce an ESCP judgment must be made in accordance with Part 23 to the court in which the ESCP judgment is being enforced.

(2) The judgment debtor must, as soon as practicable, serve copies of any order made under article 22 on—

(a) all other parties to the proceedings and any other person affected by the order ("the affected persons"); and

(b) any court in which enforcement proceedings are pending in England and Wales ("the relevant courts").

(3) Upon service of the order on the affected persons, all enforcement proceedings of the ESCP judgment in the relevant courts will cease.

Stay of or limitation on enforcement[4]

78.22 **78.22.—(1)** An application by the defendant under article 23 of

[1] Introduced by the Civil Procedure (Amendment) Rules 2008 (SI 2008/2178).
[2] Introduced by the Civil Procedure (Amendment) Rules 2008 (SI 2008/2178).
[3] Introduced by the Civil Procedure (Amendment) Rules 2008 (SI 2008/2178).
[4] Introduced by the Civil Procedure (Amendment) Rules 2008 (SI 2008/2178).

the ESCP Regulation must be made in accordance with Part 23 to the court in which the ESCP judgment is being enforced.

(2) The defendant must, as soon as practicable, serve a copy of any order made under article 23 on—

- **(a) all other parties to the proceedings and any other person affected by the order; and**
- **(b) any court in which enforcement proceedings are pending in England and Wales,**

and the order will not have effect on any person until it has been served in accordance with this rule and they have received it.

PRACTICE DIRECTION—EUROPEAN ORDER FOR PAYMENT AND EUROPEAN SMALL CLAIMS PROCEDURE

78PD.1 *This Practice Direction supplements CPR Part 78*

EOP Regulation and application of the Civil Procedure Rules

1.1 EOP applications are primarily governed by the EOP Regulation. Where the EOP Regulation is silent, the Civil Procedure Rules apply with necessary modifications.

Rule 78.3 Application for a European order for payment

78PD.2 **2.1** An EOP application form A must be—

(1) completed in English or accompanied by a translation into English; and

(2) filed at court in person or by post.

2.2 An EOP application made to the High Court will be assigned to the Queen's Bench Division, but that will not prevent the application being transferred where appropriate.

Filing documents at court other than the EOP application form A

78PD.3 **3** Documents other than the EOP application form A that are filed at or sent to the court in the EOP proceedings, including statements of opposition, may be filed, in addition to by post or in person, by—

(1) fax; or

(2) other electronic means where the facilities are available.

Service

78PD.4 **4** Where the EOP Regulation is silent on service, the Service Regulation and the Civil Procedure Rules apply as appropriate.

Article 9 of the EOP Regulation—completion or rectification of the EOP application form A

78PD.5 **5.1** Article 9 of the EOP Regulation makes provision for the completion or rectification of the EOP application form A within a specified time.

5.2 The time specified for the purposes of article 9 will normally be within 30 days of the date of the request by the court to complete or rectify the EOP application form A (using form B annexed to the EOP Regulation).

Applications under Part 23

78PD.6 **6.1** Where an application is made under Section I of Part 78, there will not normally be an oral hearing.

6.2 Where an oral hearing is to be held, it will normally take place by telephone or video conference.

Rule 78.9 Enforcement of European orders for payment

78PD.7 **7.1** When an EOP is filed at the High Court or county court in which enforcement proceedings are to be brought, it will be assigned a case number.

7.2 A *copy of a document* will satisfy the conditions necessary to establish its authenticity if it is an official copy of the court of origin.

7.3 If judgment is set aside in the court of origin, the judgment creditor must notify all courts in which enforcement proceedings are pending in England and Wales under the EOP as soon as reasonably practicable after the order is served on the judgment creditor. Notification may be by any means available including fax, e-mail, post or telephone.

Rule 78.10 An application for refusal of enforcement

8.1 An application must be accompanied by an official copy of the earlier judgment, any other documents relied upon and any translations required by the EOP Regulation. **78PD.8**

8.2 Where the applicant relies on article 22(1) of the EOP Regulation, the application must be supported by written evidence showing—

(1) why the earlier judgment is irreconcilable with the judgment which the claimant is seeking to enforce; and

(2) why the irreconcilability was not, and could not have been, raised as an objection in the proceedings in the court of or

8.3 Where the applicant relies on article 22(2), the application must be supported by written evidence of the extent to which the defendant has paid the claimant the amount awarded in the EOP.

Rule 78.11 Stay of or limitation on enforcement

9.1 Unless the court orders otherwise, an application must be accompanied by evidence of the review application in the court of origin, including— **78PD.9**

(1) the review application or a copy of the review application certified by an appropriate officer of the court of origin; and

(2) where that document is not in English, a translation of it into English.

9.2 The written evidence in support of the application must state—

(1) that a review application has been brought in the Member State of origin;

(2) the nature of that review application; and

(3) the date on which the review application was filed, the stage the application has reached and the date by which it is believed that the application will be determined.

ESCP Regulation and application of the Civil Procedure Rules

10 Claims under the ESCP are primarily governed by the ESCP Regulation. Where the ESCP Regulation is silent, the Civil Procedure Rules apply with necessary modifications. In particular, Part 52 applies to any appeals. **78PD.10**

Rule 78.13 Filing an ESCP claim form

11 An ESCP claim form must be filed at court in person or by post. **78PD.11**

Article 4(4) of the ESCP Regulation—inadequate or insufficient information

12 Article 4(4) of the ESCP Regulation makes provision for— **78PD.12**

(1) the completion or rectification of the claim form;

(1) the supply of supplementary information or documents; or

(1) the withdrawal of the claim,

within a specified time.

Article 4(4) of the ESCP Regulation—inadequate or insufficient information

78PD.12.1 **12.1** Article 4(4) of the ESCP Regulation makes provision for—

(1) the completion or rectification of the claim form;

(2) the supply of supplementary information or documents; or

(3) the withdrawal of the claim,

within a specified time.

12.2 The time specified for the purposes of article 4(4) is within 30 days of the date of the request by the court to complete or rectify the claim form (using Form B annexed to the ESCP Regulation).

Rule 78.14 Allocation of ESCP claims

78PD.13 **13.1** Rule 78.14(1) provides that ESCP claims are treated as if they were allocated to the small claims track. However, rule 78.14(2) disapplies rule 27.14 on costs because recital 29 to the ESCP Regulation contains different provisions on costs.

within a specified time.

13.2 Rule 26.6(1) (scope of the small claims track) is also disapplied because article 2(1) of the ESCP Regulation has a different financial limit.

Filing documents at court other than the ESCP claim form

78PD.14 **14** Documents other than the ESCP claim form that are filed at or sent to the court in the ESCP proceedings, including the defendant's response, may be filed, in addition to by post or in person, by—

(1) fax; or

(2) other electronic means where the facilities are available.

Service

78PD.15 **15** Where the ESCP Regulation is silent on service, the Service Regulation and the Civil Procedure Rules apply as appropriate.

Rule 78.17 Transfer of proceedings where the defendant claims that the nonmonetary claim exceeds the limit set in article 2(1) of the ESCP Regulation—article 5(5) of the ESCP Regulation

78PD.16 **16.1** Rule 78.17(7) applies to counterclaims as if the counterclaim were an ESCP claim because the second paragraph of article 5(7) of the ESCP Regulation applies certain provisions about claims in the ESCP Regulation, including article 5(5), to ESCP counterclaims.

16.2 Attention is also drawn to the first paragraph of article 5(7) of the ESCP Regulation (transfer of claim and counterclaim in certain circumstances).

Oral hearing under article 8 of the ESCP Regulation

78PD.17 **17.1** Attention is drawn to article 5(1) of the ESCP Regulation, which sets out limitations on when oral hearings may be held.

17.2 Where an oral hearing is to be held, it will normally take place by telephone or video conference.

Applications under Part 23

78PD.18 **18.1** Where an application is made under Section II of Part 78 there will not normally be an oral hearing.

18.2 Where an oral hearing is to be held, it will normally take place by telephone or video conference.

Rule 78.20 Enforcement of an ESCP judgment

19.1 When an ESCP judgment is filed at the High Court or county court in which enforcement proceedings are to be brought, it will be assigned a case number. **78PD.19**

19.2 A copy of a document will satisfy the conditions necessary to establish its authenticity if it is an official copy of the courts of the Member State of judgment.

19.3 If judgment is set aside in the Member State of judgment, the judgment creditor must notify all courts in which proceedings are pending in England and Wales to enforce the ESCP judgment as soon as reasonably practicable after the order is served on the judgment creditor. Notification may be by any means available including fax, e-mail, post or telephone.

Rule 78.21 Application for refusal of enforcement

20.1 An application must be accompanied by an official copy of the earlier judgment, any other documents relied upon and any translations required by the ESCP Regulation. **78PD.20**

20.2 The application must be supported by written evidence showing—

(1) why the earlier judgment is irreconcilable with the judgment which the claimant is seeking to enforce; and

(2) why the irreconcilability was not, and could not have been, raised as an objection in the proceedings in the Member State of judgment.

Annex 1—The EOP Regulation

REGULATION (EC) No 1896/2006 OF THE EUROPEAN PARLIAMENT AND OF THE COUNCIL of 12 December 2006 creating a European order for payment procedure

Article 1—Subject matter

1. The purpose of this Regulation is: **78PD.21**

(a) to simplify, speed up and reduce the costs of litigation in cross-border cases concerning uncontested pecuniary claims by creating a European order for payment procedure; and

(b) to permit the free circulation of European orders for payment throughout the Member States by laying down minimum standards, compliance with which renders unnecessary any intermediate proceedings in the Member State of enforcement prior to recognition and enforcement.

2. This Regulation shall not prevent a claimant from pursuing a claim within the meaning of Article 4 by making use of another procedure available under the law of a Member State or under Community law.

Article 2—Scope

1. This Regulation shall apply to civil and commercial matters in **78PD.22**

cross-border cases, whatever the nature of the court or tribunal. It shall not extend, in particular, to revenue, customs or administrative matters or the liability of the State for acts and omissions in the exercise of State authority ('acta iure imperii'). 2. This Regulation shall not apply to:

(a) rights in property arising out of a matrimonial relationship, wills and succession;
(b) bankruptcy, proceedings relating to the winding-up of insolvent companies or other legal persons, judicial arrangements, compositions and analogous proceedings;
(c) social security;
(d) claims arising from non-contractual obligations, unless:
  (i) they have been the subject of an agreement between the parties or there has been an admission of debt, or
  (ii) they relate to liquidated debts arising from joint ownership of property.

3. In this Regulation, the term 'Member State' shall mean Member States with the exception of Denmark.

Article 3—Cross-border cases

78PD.23 1. For the purposes of this Regulation, a cross-border case is one in which at least one of the parties is domiciled or habitually resident in a Member State other than the Member State of the court seised. 2. Domicile shall be determined in accordance with Articles 59 and 60 of Council Regulation (EC) No 44/2001 of 22 December 2000 on jurisdiction and the recognition and enforcement of judgments in civil and commercial matters[1]. 3. The relevant moment for determining whether there is a cross-border case shall be the time when the application for a European order for payment is submitted in accordance with this Regulation.

Article 4—European order for payment procedure

78PD.24 The European order for payment procedure shall be established for the collection of pecuniary claims for a specific amount that have fallen due at the time when the application for a European order for payment is submitted.

Article 5—Definitions

78PD.25 For the purposes of this Regulation, the following definitions shall apply:

(1) 'Member State of origin' means the Member State in which a European order for payment is issued;
(2) 'Member State of enforcement' means the Member State in which enforcement of a European order for payment is sought;
(3) 'court' means any authority in a Member State with competence regarding European orders for payment or any other related matters;
(4) 'court of origin' means the court which issues a European order for payment.

[1] OJ L 12, 16.1.2001, p. 1. Regulation as last amended by Commission Regulation (EC) No 2245/2004 (OJ L 381, 28.12.2004, p. 10).

Article 6—Jurisdiction

1. For the purposes of applying this Regulation, jurisdiction shall be determined in accordance with the relevant rules of Community law, in particular Regulation (EC) No 44/2001. 2. However, if the claim relates to a contract concluded by a person, the consumer, for a purpose which can be regarded as being outside his trade or profession, and if the defendant is the consumer, only the courts in the Member State in which the defendant is domiciled, within the meaning of Article 59 of Regulation (EC) No 44/2001, shall have jurisdiction. **78PD.26**

Ariticle 7—Application for a European order for payment

1. An application for a European order for payment shall be made using standard form A as set out in Annex I. 2. The application shall state: **78PD.27**

(a) the names and addresses of the parties, and, where applicable, their representatives, and of the court to which the application is made;
(b) the amount of the claim, including the principal and, where applicable, interest, contractual penalties and costs;
(c) if interest on the claim is demanded, the interest rate and the period of time for which that interest is demanded unless statutory interest is automatically added to the principal under the law of the Member State of origin;
(d) the cause of the action, including a description of the circumstances invoked as the basis of the claim and, where applicable, of the interest demanded;
(e) a description of evidence supporting the claim;
(f) the grounds for jurisdiction; and
(g) the cross-border nature of the case within the meaning of Article 3.

3. In the application, the claimant shall declare that the information provided is true to the best of his knowledge and belief and shall acknowledge that any deliberate false statement could lead to appropriate penalties under the law of the Member State of origin.

4. In an Appendix to the application the claimant may indicate to the court that he opposes a transfer to ordinary civil proceedings within the meaning of Article 17 in the event of opposition by the defendant. This does not prevent the claimant from informing the court thereof subsequently, but in any event before the order is issued.

5. The application shall be submitted in paper form or by any other means of communication, including electronic, accepted by the Member State of origin and available to the court of origin.

6. The application shall be signed by the claimant or, where applicable, by his representative. Where the application is submitted in electronic form in accordance with paragraph 5, it shall be signed in accordance with Article 2(2) of Directive 1999/93/EC of the European Par-

liament and of the Council of 13 December 1999 on a Community framework for electronic signatures[1]. The signature shall be recognised in the Member State of origin and may not be made subject to additional requirements.

However, such electronic signature shall not be required if and to the extent that an alternative electronic communications system exists in the courts of the Member State of origin which is available to a certain group of pre-registered authenticated users and which permits the identification of those users in a secure manner. Member States shall inform the Commission of such communications systems.

Article 8—Examination of the application

78PD.28 The court seised of an application for a European order for payment shall examine, as soon as possible and on the basis of the application form, whether the requirements set out in Articles 2, 3, 4, 6 and 7 are met and whether the claim appears to be founded. This examination may take the form of an automated procedure.

Article 9—Completion and rectification

78PD.29 1. If the requirements set out in Article 7 are not met and unless the claim is clearly unfounded or the application is inadmissible, the court shall give the claimant the opportunity to complete or rectify the application. The court shall use standard form B as set out in Annex II. 2. Where the court requests the claimant to complete or rectify the application, it shall specify a time limit it deems appropriate in the circumstances. The court may at its discretion extend that time limit.

Article 10—Modification of the application

78PD.30 1. If the requirements referred to in Article 8 are met for only part of the claim, the court shall inform the claimant to that effect, using standard form C as set out in Annex III. The claimant shall be invited to accept or refuse a proposal for a European order for payment for the amount specified by the court and shall be informed of the consequences of his decision. The claimant shall reply by returning standard form C sent by the court within a time limit specified by the court in accordance with Article 9(2). 2. If the claimant accepts the court's proposal, the court shall issue a European order for payment, in accordance with Article 12, for that part of the claim accepted by the claimant. The consequences with respect to the remaining part of the initial claim shall be governed by national law. 3. If the claimant fails to send his reply within the time limit specified by the court or refuses the court's proposal, the court shall reject the application for a European order for payment in its entirety.

[1] OJ L 13, 19.1.2000, p. 12.

Article 11—Rejection of the application

1. The court shall reject the application if: 78PD.31

(a) the requirements set out in Articles 2, 3, 4, 6 and 7 are not met;

or

(b) the claim is clearly unfounded;

or

(c) the claimant fails to send his reply within the time limit specified by the court under Article 9(2);

or

(d) the claimant fails to send his reply within the time limit specified by the court or refuses the court's proposal, in accordance with Article 10.

The claimant shall be informed of the grounds for the rejection by means of standard form D as set out in Annex IV.

2. There shall be no right of appeal against the rejection of the application.

3. The rejection of the application shall not prevent the claimant from pursuing the claim by means of a new application for a European order for payment or of any other procedure available under the law of a Member State.

Article 12—Issue of a European order for payment

1. If the requirements referred to in Article 8 are met, the court shall issue, as soon as possible and normally within 30 days of the lodging of the application, a European order for payment using standard form E as set out in Annex V. The 30-day period shall not include the time taken by the claimant to complete, rectify or modify the application. 2. The European order for payment shall be issued together with a copy of the application form. It shall not comprise the information provided by the claimant in Appendices 1 and 2 to form A. 3. In the European order for payment, the defendant shall be advised of his options to: 78PD.32

(a) pay the amount indicated in the order to the claimant; or

or

(b) oppose the order by lodging with the court of origin a statement of opposition, to be sent within 30 days of service of the order on him.

4. In the European order for payment, the defendant shall be informed that:

(a) the order was issued solely on the basis of the information which was provided by the claimant and was not verified by the court;

(b) the order will become enforceable unless a statement of opposition has been lodged with the court in accordance with Article 16;

(c) where a statement of opposition is lodged, the proceedings shall continue before the competent courts of the Member State of origin in accordance with the rules of ordinary civil procedure unless the claimant has explicitly requested that the proceedings be terminated in that event.

5. The court shall ensure that the order is served on the defendant in accordance with national law by a method that shall meet the minimum standards laid down in Articles 13, 14 and 15.

Article 13—Service with proof of receipt by the defendant

78PD.33 The European order for payment may be served on the defendant in accordance with the national law of the State in which the service is to be effected, by one of the following methods:

(a) personal service attested by an acknowledgement of receipt, including the date of receipt, which is signed by the defendant;

(b) personal service attested by a document signed by the competent person who effected the service stating that the defendant has received the document or refused to receive it without any legal justification, and the date of service;

(c) postal service attested by an acknowledgement of receipt, including the date of receipt, which is signed and returned by the defendant;

(d) service by electronic means such as fax or e-mail, attested by an acknowledgement of receipt, including the date of receipt, which is signed and returned by the defendant.

Article 14—Service without proof of receipt by the defendant

78PD.34 1. The European order for payment may also be served on the defendant in accordance with the national law of the State in which service is to be effected, by one of the following methods:

(a) personal service at the defendant's personal address on persons who are living in the same household as the defendant or are employed there;

(b) in the case of a self-employed defendant or a legal person, personal service at the defendant's business premises on persons who are employed by the defendant;

(c) deposit of the order in the defendant's mailbox;

(d) deposit of the order at a post office or with competent public authorities and the placing in the defendant's mailbox of written notification of that deposit, provided that the written notification clearly states the character of the document as a court document or the legal effect of the notification as effecting service and setting in motion the running of time for the purposes of time limits;

(e) postal service without proof pursuant to paragraph 3 where the defendant has his address in the Member State of origin;

(f) (e) postal service without proof pursuant to paragraph 3 where the defendant has his address in the Member State of origin;

2. For the purposes of this Regulation, service under paragraph 1 is not admissible if the defendant's address is not known with certainty.

3. Service pursuant to paragraph 1(a), (b), (c) and (d) shall be attested by:

(a) a document signed by the competent person who effected the service, indicating:

(i) the method of service used;

and

(ii) the date of service;

and

(iii) where the order has been served on a person other than the defendant, the name of that person and his relation to the defendant;

or

(b) an acknowledgement of receipt by the person served, for the purposes of paragraphs (1)(a) and (b).

Article 15—Service on a representative

Service pursuant to Articles 13 or 14 may also be effected on a defendant's representative. **78PD.35**

Article 16—Opposition to the European order for payment

1. The defendant may lodge a statement of opposition to the European order for payment with the court of origin using standard form F as set out in Annex VI, which shall be supplied to him together with the European order for payment. 2. The statement of opposition shall be sent within 30 days of service of the order on the defendant. 3. The defendant shall indicate in the statement of opposition that he contests the claim, without having to specify the reasons for this. 4. The statement of opposition shall be submitted in paper form or by any other means of communication, including electronic, accepted by the Member State of origin and available to the court of origin. 5. The statement of opposition shall be signed by the defendant or, where applicable, by his representative. Where the statement of opposition is submitted in electronic form in accordance with paragraph 4, it shall be signed in accordance with Article 2(2) of Directive 1999/93/EC. The signature shall be recognised in the Member State of origin and may not be made subject to additional requirements. However, such electronic signature shall not be required if and to the extent that an alternative electronic communications system exists in the courts of the Member State of origin which is available to a certain group of pre-registered authenticated users and which permits the identification of those users in a secure manner. Member States shall inform the Commission of such communications systems. **78PD.36**

Article 17—Effects of the lodging of a statement of opposition

1. If a statement of opposition is entered within the time limit laid down in Article 16(2), the proceedings shall continue before the competent courts of the Member State of origin in accordance with the rules of ordinary civil procedure unless the claimant has explicitly requested that the proceedings be terminated in that event. Where the claimant has pursued his claim through the European order for payment procedure, nothing under national law shall prejudice his position in subsequent ordinary civil proceedings. 2. The transfer to **78PD.37**

ordinary civil proceedings within the meaning of paragraph 1 shall be governed by the law of the Member State of origin. 3. The claimant shall be informed whether the defendant has lodged a statement of opposition and of any transfer to ordinary civil proceedings.

Article 18—Enforceability

78PD.38 1. If within the time limit laid down in Article 16(2), taking into account an appropriate period of time to allow a statement to arrive, no statement of opposition has been lodged with the court of origin, the court of origin shall without delay declare the European order for payment enforceable using standard form G as set out in Annex VII. The court shall verify the date of service. 2. Without prejudice to paragraph 1, the formal requirements for enforceability shall be governed by the law of the Member State of origin. 3. The court shall send the enforceable European order for payment to the claimant.

Article 19—Abolition of exequatur

78PD.39 A European order for payment which has become enforceable in the Member State of origin shall be recognised and enforced in the other Member States without the need for a declaration of enforceability and without any possibility of opposing its recognition.

Article 20—Review in exceptional cases

78PD.40 1. After the expiry of the time limit laid down in Article 16(2) the defendant shall be entitled to apply for a review of the European order for payment before the competent court in the Member State of origin where:

(a)

(i) the order for payment was served by one of the methods provided for in Article 14,

(ii) service was not effected in sufficient time to enable him to arrange for his defence, without any fault on his part,

or

(d) (b) the defendant was prevented from objecting to the claim by reason of force majeure or due to extraordinary circumstances without any fault on his part, provided in either case that he acts promptly.

2. After expiry of the time limit laid down in Article 16(2) the defendant shall also be entitled to apply for a review of the European order for payment before the competent court in the Member State of origin where the order for payment was clearly wrongly issued, having regard to the requirements laid down in this Regulation, or due to other exceptional circumstances.

3. If the court rejects the defendant's application on the basis that none of the grounds for review referred to in paragraphs 1 and 2 apply, the European order for pay*ment* shall remain in force.

If the court decides that the review is justified for one of the reasons laid down in paragraphs 1 and 2, the European order for payment shall be null and void.

Article 21—Enforcement

1. Without prejudice to the provisions of this Regulation, enforcement procedures shall be governed by the law of the Member State of enforcement. A European order for payment which has become enforceable shall be enforced under the same conditions as an enforceable decision issued in the Member State of enforcement. 2. For enforcement in another Member State, the claimant shall provide the competent enforcement authorities of that Member State with: **78PD.41**

(a) a copy of the European order for payment, as declared enforceable by the court of origin, which satisfies the conditions necessary to establish its authenticity;
and

(b) where necessary, a translation of the European order for payment into the official language of the Member State of enforcement or, if there are several official languages in that Member State, the official language or one of the official languages of court proceedings of the place where enforcement is sought, in conformity with the law of that Member State, or into another language that the Member State of enforcement has indicated it can accept. Each Member State may indicate the official language or languages of the institutions of the European Union other than its own which it can accept for the European order for payment. The translation shall be certified by a person qualified to do so in one of the Member States.

3. No security, bond or deposit, however described, shall be required of a claimant who in one Member State applies for enforcement of a European order for payment issued in another Member State on the ground that he is a foreign national or that he is not domiciled or resident in the Member State of enforcement.

Article 22—Refusal of enforcement

1. Enforcement shall, upon application by the defendant, be refused by the competent court in the Member State of enforcement if the European order for payment is irreconcilable with an earlier decision or order previously given in any Member State or in a third country, provided that: **78PD.42**

(a) the earlier decision or order involved the same cause of action between the same parties; and

(b) the earlier decision or order fulfils the conditions necessary for its recognition in the Member State of enforcement; and

(c) the irreconcilability could not have been raised as an objection in the court proceedings in the Member State of origin.

to the extent that the defendant has paid the claimant the amount awarded in the European order for payment.

3. Under no circumstances may the European order for payment be reviewed as to its substance in the Member State of enforcement.

Article 23—Stay or limitation of enforcement

Where the defendant has applied for a review in accordance with **78PD.43**

Article 20, the competent court in the Member State of enforcement may, upon application by the defendant:

(a) limit the enforcement proceedings to protective measures; or

(b) make enforcement conditional on the provision of such security as it shall determine; or

(c) under exceptional circumstances, stay the enforcement proceedings.

Article 24—Legal representation

78PD.44 Representation by a lawyer or another legal professional shall not be mandatory:

(a) for the claimant in respect of the application for a European order for payment;

(b) for the defendant in respect of the statement of opposition to a European order for payment.

Article 25—Court fees

78PD.45 1. The combined court fees of a European order for payment procedure and of the ordinary civil proceedings that ensue in the event of a statement of opposition to a European order for payment in a Member State shall not exceed the court fees of ordinary civil proceedings without a preceding European order for payment procedure in that Member State. 2. For the purposes of this Regulation, court fees shall comprise fees and charges to be paid to the court, the amount of which is fixed in accordance with national law.

Article 26—Relationship with national procedural law

78PD.46 All procedural issues not specifically dealt with in this Regulation shall be governed by national law.

Article 27—Relationship with Regulation (EC) No 1348/2000

78PD.47 This Regulation shall not affect the application of Council Regulation (EC) No 1348/2000 of 29 May 2000 on the service in the Member States of judicial and extrajudicial documents in civil and commercial matters[1].

Article 28—Information relating to service costs and enforcement

78PD.48 Member States shall cooperate to provide the general public and professional circles with information on:

(a) costs of service of documents;

and

(b) which authorities have competence with respect to enforcement for the purposes of applying Articles 21, 22 and 23,

in particular via the European Judicial Network in civil and commercial matters established in accordance with Council Decision 2001/470/EC[2].

---

[1] OJ L 160, 30.6.2000, p. 37.
[2] OJ L 174, 27.6.2001, p. 25.

Article 29—Information relating to jurisdiction, review procedures, means of communication and languages

1. By 12 June 2008, Member States shall communicate to the Commission: 78PD.49

(a) which courts have jurisdiction to issue a European order for payment;
(b) the review procedure and the competent courts for the purposes of the application of Article 20;
(c) the means of communication accepted for the purposes of the European order for payment procedure and available to the courts;
(d) languages accepted pursuant to Article 21(2)(b).

Member States shall apprise the Commission of any subsequent changes to this information.

2. The Commission shall make the information notified in accordance with paragraph 1 publicly available through publication in the Official Journal of the European Union and through any other appropriate means.

Article 30—Amendments to the Annexes

The standard forms set out in the Annexes shall be updated or technically adjusted, ensuring full conformity with the provisions of this Regulation, in accordance with the procedure referred to in Article 31(2). 78PD.50

Article 31—Committee

1. The Commission shall be assisted by the committee established by Article 75 of Regulation (EC) No 44/2001. 2. Where reference is made to this paragraph, Article 5a(1)–(4) and Article 7 of Decision 1999/468/EC shall apply, having regard to the provisions of Article 8 thereof. 3. The Committee shall adopt its Rules of Procedure. 78PD.51

Article 32—Review

By 12 December 2013, the Commission shall present to the European Parliament, the Council and the European Economic and Social Committee a detailed report reviewing the operation of the European order for payment procedure. That report shall contain an assessment of the procedure as it has operated and an extended impact assessment for each Member State. To that end, and in order to ensure that best practice in the European Union is duly taken into account and reflects the principles of better legislation, Member States shall provide the Commission with information relating to the cross-border operation of the European order for payment. This information shall cover court fees, speed of the procedure, efficiency, ease of use and the internal payment order procedures of the Member States. The Commission's report shall be accompanied, if appropriate, by proposals for adaptation. 78PD.52

Article 33—Entry into force

This Regulation shall enter into force on the day following the date of its publication in the Official Journal of the European Union. 78PD.53

It shall apply from 12 December 2008, with the exception of Articles 28, 29, 30 and 31 which shall apply from 12 June 2008.

78PD.54 This Regulation shall be binding in its entirety and directly applicable in the Member States in accordance with the Treaty establishing the European Community.Done at Strasbourg,
12 December 2006.

For the European Parliament The President J. BORRELL FONTELLES
For the Council The President M. PEKKARINEN

Editorial note

78PD.55.0 The annexes consist of seven forms I to VII and are printed hereunder commencing at para.78PD.55.

Annexes

78PD.55

30.12.2006 EN Official Journal of the European Union L 399/11

ANNEX I

Application for a European order for payment

Form A Article 7 (1) of Regulation (EC) No 1896/2006 of the European Parliament and of the Council creating a European order for payment procedure

Please ensure that you read the guidelines on the last page – they will help you to understand this form!

Please note in particular that this form must be completed in the language or one of the languages accepted by the court to be seised. The form is available in all official languages of the European Union; this may help you fill in the form in the required language.

1. Court		
Court		
Address		
Postal code	City	Country

Case number (to be completed by the court)
Received by the court

2. Parties and their representatives

Codes: 01 Claimant; 02 Defendant; 03 Claimant's representative *; 04 Defendant's representative *; 05 Claimant's legally authorised representative **; 06 Defendant's legally authorised representative **

Code	Surname, first name/Name of company or organisation			Identification code (if applicable)	
	Address		Postal code	City	Country
	Phone ***	Fax ***		e-Mail ***	
	Occupation ***		Other details ***		
Code	Surname, first name/Name of company or organisation			Identification code (if applicable)	
	Address		Postal code	City	Country
	Phone ***	Fax ***		e-Mail ***	
	Occupation ***		Other details ***		
Code	Surname, first name/Name of company or organisation			Identification code (if applicable)	
	Address		Postal code	City	Country
	Phone ***	Fax ***		e-Mail ***	
	Occupation ***		Other details ***		
Code	Surname, first name/Name of company or organisation			Identification code (if applicable)	
	Address		Postal code	City	Country
	Phone ***	Fax ***		e-Mail ***	
	Occupation ***		Other details ***		

* e.g. lawyer ** e.g. parent, guardian, managing director *** optional

L 399/12 EN Official Journal of the European Union 30.12.2006

3. Grounds for the court's jurisdiction

Codes:

01 Domicile of the defendant or co-defendant
02 Place of performance of the obligation in question
03 Place of the harmful event
04 Where a dispute arises out of the operations of a branch, agency or other establishment, the place in which the branch, agency or other establishment is situated
05 Domicile of the trust
06 Where a dispute arises concerning the payment of remuneration claimed in respect of the salvage of a cargo or freight, the place of the court under the authority of which the cargo or freight is or could have been arrested
07 Domicile of the policyholder, the insured or the beneficiary in insurance matters
08 Domicile of the consumer
09 Place where the employee carries out his work
10 Place where the business which engaged the employee is situated
11 Place where the immovable property is situated
12 Choice of court agreed by the parties
13 Domicile of the maintenance creditor
14 Other (please specify)

Code	Specification only for code 14

4. Cross-border nature of the case

Codes:

01 Belgium	06 Spain	11 Lettland	16 The Netherlands	21 Slovakia
02 Czech Republic	07 France	12 Litauen	17 Austria	22 Finland
03 Germany	08 Ireland	13 Luxemburg	18 Poland	23 Sweden
04 Estonia	09 Italy	14 Ungarn	19 Portugal	24 United Kingdom
05 Greece	10 Cyprus	15 Malta	20 Slovenia	25 other (please specify)

Domicile or habitual residence of claimant	Domicile or habitual residence of defendant	Country of the court

5. Bank details (optional)

5.1 Payment of court fees by the claimant

Codes: 01 By bank transfer; 02 By credit card; 03 Collection by court from claimant's bank account; 04 Legal aid; 05 Other (please specify)

If you choose code 02 or 03, please fill in the bank details in Appendix 1

Code	If you choose code 05, please specify

5.2 Payment by defendant of amount awarded

Account holder	Bank name (BIC) or other relevant bank code
Account number	International bank account number (IBAN)

30.12.2006 EN Official Journal of the European Union L 399/13

EUR	Euro	CYP	Cypriot Pound	CZK	Czech Koruna	EEK	Estonian Kroon	GBP	Pound sterling
HUF	Hungarian Forint	LTL	Lithuanian Litas	LVL	Latvian Lats	MTL	Maltese Lira	PLN	Polish Zloty
SEK	Swedish Krona	SIT	Slovenian Tolars	SKK	Slovak Koruna	Other (according to international banking code)			

6. Principal

Currency	Total value of principal, excluding interest and costs

The claim relates to (Code 1)

01 Sales contract
02 Rental agreement - movable property
03 Rental agreement - immovable property
04 Rental agreement - commercial lease
05 Contract of service - electricity, gas, water, phone
06 Contract of service - medical services
07 Contract of service - transport
08 Contract of service - legal, tax, technical advice
09 Contract of service - hotel, restaurant
10 Contract of service - repair
11 Contract of service - brokerage
12 Contract of service - other (please specify)
13 Building contract
14 Insurance contract
15 Loan
16 Guarantee or other collateral(s)
17 Claims arising from non-contractual obligations if they are subject to an agreement between the parties or an admission of debt (e.g. damages, unjust enrichment)
18 Claims arising from joint ownership of property
19 Damages - contract
20 Subscription agreement (newspaper, magazine)
21 Membership fee
22 Employment agreement
23 Out-of-court settlement
24 Maintenance agreement
25 Other (please specify)

Circumstances invoked (Code 2)

30 Non-payment
31 Insufficient payment
32 Late payment
33 Non-delivery of goods or services
34 Delivery of defective goods or poor services
35 Goods or services not in conformity with the order
36 Other (please specify)

Other details (Code 3)

40 Place of purchase
41 Place of delivery
42 Date of purchase
43 Date of delivery
44 Type of goods or services concerned
45 Address of immovable property
46 In case of loan, purpose: Consumer credit
47 In case of loan, purpose: Mortgage credit
48 Other detail (please specify)

ID	Code 1	Code 2	Code 3	Explanatory statement	Date (or period)	Amount
ID	Code 1	Code 2	Code 3	Explanatory statement	Date (or period)	Amount
ID	Code 1	Code 2	Code 3	Explanatory statement	Date (or period)	Amount
ID	Code 1	Code 2	Code 3	Explanatory statement	Date (or period)	Amount

The claim has been assigned to the claimant by (if applicable)

Surname, first name/Name of company or organisation		Identification code (if applicable)	
Address	Postal code	City	Country

Additional specifications for claims relating to consumer contracts (if applicable)

The claim concerns matters relating to consumer contracts	If yes, the defendant is the consumer	If yes, the defendant is domiciled within the meaning of Article 59 of Council Regulation (EC) No 44/2001 in the Member State where the court is seised
yes no	yes no	yes no

7. Interest

Codes (please combine number with letter):

01 Statutory — 02 Contractual — 03 Capitalisation of interest — 04 Interest rate on a loan ** — 05 Amount calculated by the claimant — 06 Other ***

A per year — B per half year — C per quarter — D per month — E Other ***

ID *	Code	Interest rate (%)	% over base rate (ECB)	on (amount)	Starting from	to
ID *	Code	Zinssatz (%)	% über dem Basissatz der EZB	auf (Betrag)	Ab	bis
ID *	Code	Zinssatz (%)	% über dem Basissatz der EZB	auf (Betrag)	Ab	bis
ID *	Code	Zinssatz (%)	% über dem Basissatz der EZB	auf (Betrag)	Ab	bis
ID *	Please specify in case of Code 6 and/or E					

* Fill in corresponding claim ID ** taken out by the claimant at least in the amount of the principal *** Please specify

8. Contractual penalties (if applicable)

Amount	Please specify

9. Costs (if applicable)

Codes: 01 Court fees — 02 Other (please specify)

Code	Specification only for code 02	Currency	Amount
Code	Specification only for code 02	Currency	Amount
Code	Specification only for code 02	Currency	Amount
Code	Specification only for code 02	Currency	Amount

10. Evidence available in support of the claim

Codes: 01 Written evidence — 02 Oral evidence — 03 Expert evidence — 04 Inspection of an object or site — 05 Other (please specify)

ID *	Code	Description of evidence	Date (day/month/year)
ID *	Code	Description of evidence	Date (day/month/year)
ID *	Code	Description of evidence	Date (day/month/year)
ID *	Code	Description of evidence	Date (day/month/year)

* Fill in corresponding claim ID

30.12.2006 EN Official Journal of the European Union L 399/15

11. Additional statements and further information (if necessary)		

Ihereby request the court to order the defendant(s) to pay to the claimant(s) the sum of the above principal plus interest, contractual penalties and costs. **I declare that to the best of my knowledge and belief the information provided is true.** **I acknowledge that any deliberate false statement could lead to appropriate penalties under the law of the Member State of origin.**		
Done at	Date (day/month/year)	Signature and/or stamp

L 399/16 EN Official Journal of the European Union 30.12.2006

Appendix 1 to the application for a European order for payment

Bank details for the purposes of payment of court fees by the claimant

Code 02 By credit card 03 Collection by court from claimant's bank account

Code	Account holder	Bank name (BIC) or other relevant bank code / Credit card company
Account number / Credit card number		International bank account number (IBAN) / Expiry date and security number of credit card

30.12.2006 EN Official Journal of the European Union L 399/17

Appendix 2 to the application for a European order for payment **Opposition to a transfer to ordinary civil proceedings** Case number (to be completed if this Appendix is sent to the court separately from the application form)		
Done at	Date (day/month/year)	Signature and/or stamp

GUIDELINES FOR FILLING IN THE APPLICATION FORM

Important information

This form must be filled in in the language or one of the languages accepted by the court to be seised. Please note that the form is available in all official languages of the European Union; this may help you fill in the form in the required language.

If the defendant lodges an opposition to your claim, proceedings will continue before the competent courts in accordance with the rules of ordinary civil procedure. If you do not wish to continue proceedings in that event, you should also fill in Appendix 2 to this form. This appendix should reach the court before the European order for payment is issued.

If the application concerns a claim against a consumer relating to a consumer contract, it must be lodged with the competent court of the Member State in which the consumer is domiciled. In other cases, the application must be lodged with the court having jurisdiction in accordance with the rules of Council Regulation (EC) No 44/2001 on jurisdiction and the recognition and enforcement of judgments in civil and commercial matters. Information on the rules of jurisdiction can be found on the European Judicial Atlas (http://ec.europa.eu/justice_home/judicialatlascivil/html/index.htm).

Please make sure you duly sign and date the form on the last page.

Guidelines

At the start of each section you will find specific codes that should be inserted, as appropriate, in the relevant boxes.

1. Court When deciding which court to choose, you need to consider the grounds for the court's jurisdiction.

2. Parties and their representatives This field must identify the parties and their representatives, if any, in accordance with the codes indicated on the form. The box [Identification code] should refer, where applicable, to the special number which solicitors have in certain Member States for the purposes of electronic communication with the court (see Art. 7(6), second subparagraph, of Regulation (EC) No 1896/2006), to the registration number for companies or organisations or to any applicable identification number for natural persons. The box [Other details] may contain any other information that helps to identify the person (e.g. date of birth, position of the named person in the company or organisation concerned). If there are more than four parties and/or representatives, please use field [11].

3. Grounds for the court's jurisdiction See 'Important information' above.

4. Cross-border nature of the case For you to be allowed to use this European order for payment procedure, at least two of the boxes in this field must refer to different States.

5. Bank details (optional) In field [5.1], you may inform the court by what means you intend to pay the court fees. Please note that not all methods of payment in this field are necessarily available at the court to which you are making this application. You should verify which method of payment will be accepted by the court. You can do this by contacting the court concerned or by consulting the website of the European Judicial Network in civil and commercial matters (http://ec.europa.eu/civiljustice/). If you choose to pay by credit card or to allow the court to collect the fees from your bank account, you should give the necessary credit card/bank account details in Appendix 1 to this form.

In field [5.2], you may indicate by what means you wish to receive payment from the defendant. If you wish to be paid by bank transfer, please give the necessary bank details.

6. Principal This field must contain a description of the principal and the circumstances forming the basis of the claim in accordance with the codes indicated on the form. You need to use an identification number ('ID') for each claim, numbering them from 1 through 4. Each claim must be specified on the line of the box following the ID number, by filling in the relevant numbers of codes 1, 2, and 3. If you need more space, please use field [11]. The box [Date (or period)] refers, for instance, to the date of the contract or harmful event or to the period of the rent.

7. Interest If interest is demanded, this should be specified for each claim as identified in field [6] in accordance with the codes indicated on the form. The code must contain both the relevant number (first row of the codes) and the letter (second row of the codes). For instance, if the interest rate has been agreed by contract and covers annual periods, the code is 02A. If interest is demanded up to the decision by the court, the last box [to] should be left blank. Code 01 refers to an interest rate laid down by statute. Code 02 refers to an interest rate agreed by the parties. If you use Code 03 (capitalisation of interest), the amount indicated should be the basis for the remainder of the term to be covered. Capitalisation of interest refers to the situation where the accrued interest is added to the principal and is taken into account for purposes of calculating further interest. Please note that in commercial transactions as referred to in Directive 2000/35/EC of 29 June 2000 on combating late payments, the statutory interest rate is the sum of the interest rate applied by the European Central Bank to its most recent main refinancing operation carried out before the first calendar day of the half-year in question ('the reference rate'), plus at least seven percentage points. For a Member State which is not participating in the third stage of economic and monetary union, the reference rate referred to above is the equivalent rate set at national level (e.g. by the national central bank). In both cases the reference rate in force on the first calendar day of the half-year in question will apply for the following six months (see Art. 3(1)(d) of Directive 2000/35/EC). The 'base rate (ECB)' refers to the interest rate applied by the European Central Bank to its main refinancing operations.

8. Contractual penalties (if applicable)

9. Costs (if applicable) If reimbursement of costs is demanded, these must be described using the codes indicated on the form. The box [specification] must be used only for code 02, i.e. when reimbursement of costs other than court fees is demanded. These other costs could include, for instance, fees of a claimant's representative or prelitigation costs. If you request reimbursement of the court fees but you do not know the exact amount, you must fill in the box [Code] 01 but you may leave the box [Amount] blank and it will be filled in by the court.

10. Evidence available in support of the claim This field must specify the evidence available in support of each claim using the codes indicated on the form. The box [Description of evidence] will contain, for instance, the title, name, date and/or reference number of the document concerned, the amount mentioned on the document concerned, and/or the name of the witness or expert.

11. Additional statements and further information (if necessary) You may use this field if you need more space for any of the fields above or, if necessary, to provide additional information useful to the court. For instance, if there are several defendants each being liable for a portion of the claim, you should indicate here the amount individually owed by each defendant.

Appendix 1 Here you must indicate the details of your credit card or bank account if you choose to pay the court fees by credit card or if you allow the court to collect the fees from your bank account. Please note that not all methods of payment in this field are necessarily available at the court to which you are making this application. Please note that the information given in Appendix 1 will not be sent to the defendant.

Appendix 2 Here you must inform the court if you do not wish to continue proceedings in the event of the defendant opposing the claim. If you send this information to the court after having sent the application form, please make sure you fill in the case number given by the court. Please note that the information given in Appendix 2 will not be sent to the defendant.

L 399/20 EN Official Journal of the European Union 30.12.2006

ANNEX II

Request to the claimant to complete and/or rectify an application for a European order for payment

Form B Article 9 (1) of Regulation (EC) No 1896/2006 of the European Parliament and of the Council creating a European order for payment procedure

1. Court		
Court		
Address		
Postal code	City	Country

Case number	
Done at	Date (day/month/year)
Signature and/or stamp	

2. Parties and their representatives

Codes: 01 Claimant; 02 Defendant; 03 Claimant's representative *; 04 Defendant's representative *; 05 Claimant's legally authorised representative **; 06 Defendant's legally authorised representative **

Code	Surname, first name/Name of company or organisation			Identification code (if applicable)	
	Address		Postal code	City	Country
	Phone ***	Fax ***		e-Mail ***	
	Occupation***		Other details ***		
Code	Surname, first name/Name of company or organisation			Identification code (if applicable)	
	Address		Postal code	City	Country
	Phone ***	Fax ***		e-Mail ***	
	Occupation***		Other details ***		
Code	Surname, first name/Name of company or organisation			Identification code (if applicable)	
	Address		Postal code	City	Country
	Phone ***	Fax ***		e-Mail ***	
	Occupation***		Other details ***		
Code	Surname, first name/Name of company or organisation			Identification code (if applicable)	
	Address		Postal code	City	Country
	Phone ***	Fax ***		e-Mail ***	
	Occupation***		Other details ***		

* e.g. lawyer ** e.g. parent, guardian, managing director *** optional

30.12.2006 EN Official Journal of the European Union L 399/21

Following the examination of your application for a European order for payment, please complete and/or rectify the attached application as indicated below as soon as possible and in any event by ____/____/____

Your initial application should be completed and/or rectified in the language or in one of the languages accepted by the court seised.
The court will reject the application, under the conditions provided for in the Regulation, if you fail to complete and/or rectify the application within the time limit set out above.

Your application has not been filled in in the correct language. Please fill it in in one of the following languages:

01 Czech	05 Greek	09 Lithuanian	13 Polish	17 Finnish
02 German	06 French	10 Hungarian	14 Portuguese	18 Swedish
03 Estonian	07 Italian	11 Maltese	15 Slovak	19 English
04 Spanish	08 Latvian	12 Dutch	16 Slovene	20 other (please specify)

Language code	Language specification (only for code 20)

The following items must be completed and/or rectified:

Codes:

01 Parties and their representatives	04 Bank details	07 Contractual penalties	10 Additional statements
02 Grounds of jurisdiction	05 Principal	08 Costs	11 Signature
03 Cross border nature of the case	06 Interest	09 Evidence	

Code	Please specify
Code	Please specify
Code	Please specify
Code	Please specify
Code	Please specify

L 399/22 EN Official Journal of the European Union 30.12.2006

ANNEX III

Proposal to the claimant to modify an application for a European order for payment

Form C

Article 10 (1) of Regulation (EC) No 1896/2006 of the European Parliament and of the Council creating a European order for payment procedure

1. Court

Court		
Address		
Postal code	City	Country

Case number	
Done at	Date (day/month/year)
Signature and/or stamp	

2. Parties and their representatives

Codes: 01 Claimant
02 Defendant
03 Claimant's representative *
04 Defendant's representative *
05 Claimant's legally authorised representative **
06 Defendant's legally authorised representative **

Code	Surname, first name/Name of company or organisation		Identification code (if applicable)	
	Address	Postal code	City	Country
	Phone ***	Fax ***	e-Mail ***	
	Occupation ***		Other details ***	
Code	Surname, first name/Name of company or organisation		Identification code (if applicable)	
	Address	Postal code	City	Country
	Phone ***	Fax ***	e-Mail ***	
	Occupation ***		Other details ***	
Code	Surname, first name/Name of company or organisation		Identification code (if applicable)	
	Address	Postal code	City	Country
	Phone ***	Fax ***	e-Mail ***	
	Occupation ***		Other details ***	
Code	Surname, first name/Name of company or organisation		Identification code (if applicable)	
	Address	Postal code	City	Country
	Phone ***	Fax ***	e-Mail ***	
	Beruf ***		Sonstige Angaben ***	

* e.g. lawyer ** e.g. parent, guardian, managing director *** optional

30.12.2006 EN Official Journal of the European Union L 399/23

After examination of your application for a European order for payment, the court considers that the necessary requirements are met for only a part of the claim. Therefore, the court proposes the following modification to the application:

Please send your reply to the court as soon as possible and in any event by ____/____/____

If you fail to send your reply to the court within the time limit set out above or refuse this proposal, the court will reject your application for a European order for payment, under the conditions provided for in the Regulation, in its entirety.
If you accept this proposal, the court will issue a European order for payment for that part of the claim. It depends on the national law of the Member State where the court is seised whether you will be able in further proceedings, to recover the remaining part of your initial claim not covered by the European order for payment.

☐ I accept the above proposal by the court		☐ I refuse the above proposal by the court
Done at	Date (day/month/year)	Surname, first name Signature and/or stamp

L 399/24 EN Official Journal of the European Union 30.12.2006

ANNEX IV

Decision to reject the application for a European order for payment

Form D Article 11(1) of Regulation (EC) No 1896/2006 of the European Parliament and of the Council creating a European order for payment procedure

1. Court

Court		
Address		
Postal code	City	Country

Case number	
Done at	Date (day/month/year)
Signature and/or stamp	

2. Parties and their representatives

Codes: 01 Claimant 02 Defendant 03 Claimant's representative * 04 Defendant's representative * 05 Claimant's legally authorised representative ** 06 Defendant's legally authorised representative **

Code	Surname, first name/Name of company or organisation			Identification code (if applicable)	
	Address		Postal code	City	Country
	Phone ***	Fax ***		e-Mail ***	
	Occupation ***		Other details ***		
Code	Surname, first name/Name of company or organisation			Identification code (if applicable)	
	Address		Postal code	City	Country
	Phone ***	Fax ***		e-Mail ***	
	Occupation ***		Other details ***		
Code	Surname, first name/Name of company or organisation			Identification code (if applicable)	
	Address		Postal code	City	Country
	Phone ***	Fax ***		e-Mail ***	
	Occupation ***		Other details ***		
Code	Surname, first name/Name of company or organisation			Identification code (if applicable)	
	Address		Postal code	City	Country
	Phone ***	Fax ***		e-Mail ***	
	Occupation ***		Other details ***		

* e.g. lawyer ** e.g. parent, guardian, managing director *** optional

30.12.2006 EN Official Journal of the European Union L 399/25

The court has examined your application for a European order for payment, in accordance with Article 8 of Regulation (EC) No 1896/2006 and rejects it on the following ground(s):

01 The application does not fall within the scope of Article 2 of the Regulation (Article 11(1)(a)).
02 The application does not concern a cross-border case within the meaning of Article 3 of the Regulation (Article 11(1)(a)).
03 The application does not concern a pecuniary claim for a specific amount that has fallen due as referred to in Article 4 of the Regulation (Article 11(1)(a)).
04 The court does not have jurisdiction in accordance with Article 6 of the Regulation (Article 11(1)(a)).
05 The application does not fulfil the requirements set out in Article 7 of the Regulation (Article 11(1)(a)).
06 The claim is clearly unfounded (Article 11(1)(b)).
07 The application was not completed or rectified within the time limit specified by the court (Article 9(2) and Article 11(1)(c)).
08 The application was not modified within the time limit specified by the court (Article 10 and Article 11(1)(c)).

Ground(s) for rejection (please use code)

Code
Further information, where necessary

Code
Further information, where necessary

Code
Further information, where necessary

Code
Further information, where necessary

There is no right of appeal against this rejection. However, this does not preclude a new application for a European order for payment or any other procedure available under the law of a Member State.

L 399/26 EN Official Journal of the European Union 30.12.2006

ANNEX V

European order for payment

Form E Article 12 (1) of Regulation (EC) No 1896/2006 of the European Parliament and of the Council creating a European order for payment procedure

1. Court		
Court		
Adress		
Postal code	City	Country

Case number	
Done at	Date (day/month/year)
Signature and/or stamp	

2. Parties and their representatives

Codes: 01 Claimant | 02 Defendant | 03 Claimant's representative * | 04 Defendant's representative * | 05 Claimant's legally authorised representative ** | 06 Defendant's legally authorised representative **

Code	Surname, first name/Name of company or organisation			Identification code (if applicable)	
	Address		Postal code	City	Country
	Phone ***	Fax ***		e-Mail ***	
	Occupation ***		Other details ***		
Code	Surname, first name/Name of company or organisation			Identification code (if applicable)	
	Address		Postal code	City	Country
	Phone ***	Fax ***		e-Mail ***	
	Occupation ***		Other details ***		
Code	Surname, first name/Name of company or organisation			Identification code (if applicable)	
	Address		Postal code	City	Country
	Phone ***	Fax ***		e-Mail ***	
	Occupation ***		Other details ***		
Code	Surname, first name/Name of company or organisation			Identification code (if applicable)	
	Address		Postal code	City	Country
	Phone ***	Fax ***		e-Mail ***	
	Occupation ***		Other details ***		

* e.g. lawyer ** e.g. parent, guardian, managing director *** optional

30.12.2006 EN Official Journal of the European Union L 399/27

EUR	Euro	CYP	Cypriot Pound	CZK	Czech Koruna	EEK	Estonian Kroon	GBP	Pound sterling
HUF	Hungarian Forint	LTL	Lithuanian Litas	LVL	Latvian Lats	MTL	Maltese Lira	PLN	Polish Zloty
SEK	Swedish Krona	SIT	Slovenian Tolars	SKK	Slovak Koruna	Other (according to international banking code)			

In accordance with Article 12 of Regulation (EC) No 1896/2006, the court has issued this European order for payment on the basis of the attached application. By virtue of this decision, you are ordered to pay the claimant the following amount:

Defendant 1 Surname, first name/Name of company or organisation	Currency	Amount	Date (day/month/year)
Principal			
Interest (as of)			
Contractual penalties			
Costs			
Total amount			
Defendant 2 Surname, first name/Name of company or organisation	Currency	Amount	Date (day/month/year)
Principal			
Interest (as of)			
Contractual penalties			
Costs			
Total amount			
Joint liability			

IMPORTANT INFORMATION FOR THE DEFENDANT

You are hereby advised that:

a. You have the option to:
   i. pay the amount indicated in this order to the claimant; or
   ii. oppose the order by lodging a statement of opposition with the court that issued this order within the time limit indicated in (b);

b. The statement of opposition must be sent to the court within 30 days of service of this order on you. This 30-day period starts on the day following that on which this order was served. This period includes Saturdays, Sundays and public holidays. Where the last day of such a period is a Saturday, a Sunday or a public holiday, the period will expire on the following working day (see Council Regulation (EEC, Euratom) No 1182/71 of 3 June 1971 *). The public holidays to be taken into account are those of the Member State where the court is situated;

c. This order has been issued solely on the basis of the information provided by the claimant. That information has not been verified by the court;

d. This order will become enforceable unless a statement of opposition has been lodged with the court within the time limit indicated in (b);

e. Where a statement of opposition is lodged, the proceedings will continue before the competent courts of the Member State where this order was issued in accordance with the rules of ordinary civil procedure unless the claimant has explicitly requested that the proceedings be terminated in that event.

* OJ L 124, 8.6.1971, p. 1 (de, fr, it, nl).
English special edition: Series I Chapter 1971(II), p. 354.
Greek special edition: Chapter 01 Volume 1, p. 131.
Portuguese and Spanish special editions: Chapter 01 Volume 1, p. 149.
Finnish and Swedish special editions: Chapter 1 Volume 1, p. 71.
Czech, Estonian, Hungarian, Latvian, Lithuanian, Maltese, Polish, Slovak and Slovene special editions: Chapter 01 Volume 1, p. 51.

30.12.2006 EN Official Journal of the European Union L 399/29

ANNEX VI

Opposition to a European order for payment

Form F

Article 16 (1) of Regulation (EC) No 1896/2006 of the European Parliament and of the Council creating a European order for payment procedure

1. Court		
Court		
Address		
Postal code	Ort	Land

Case number (to be completed by the court)	
Received by the court	

2. Parties and their representatives

Codes: 01 Claimant; 02 Defendant; 03 Claimant's representative *; 04 Defendant's representative *; 05 Claimant's legally authorised representative **; 06 Defendant's legally authorised representative **

Code	Surname, first name/Name of company or organisation			Identification code (if applicable)	
	Address		Postal code	City	Country
	Phone ***	Fax ***		e-Mail ***	
	Occupation ***		Other details ***		
Code	Surname, first name/Name of company or organisation			Identification code (if applicable)	
	Address		Postal code	City	Country
	Phone ***	Fax ***		e-Mail ***	
	Occupation ***		Other details ***		
Code	Surname, first name/Name of company or organisation			Identification code (if applicable)	
	Address		Postal code	City	Country
	Phone ***	Fax ***		e-Mail ***	
	Occupation ***		Other details ***		
Code	Surname, first name/Name of company or organisation			Identification code (if applicable)	
	Address		Postal code	City	Country
	Phone ***	Fax ***		e-Mail ***	
	Occupation ***		Other details ***		

* e.g. lawyer ** e.g. parent, guardian, managing director *** optional

L 399/30 EN Official Journal of the European Union 30.12.2006

I hereby lodge a statement of opposition against the European order for payment issued on ____/____/____		
Done at	Date (day/month/year)	Surname, first name
		Signature and/or stamp

30.12.2006 EN Official Journal of the European Union L 399/31

ANNEX VII

Declaration of enforceability

Form G Article 18(1) of Regulation (EC) No 1896/2006 of the European Parliament and of the Council creating a European order for payment procedure

1. Court		
Court		
Address		
Postal code	City	Country

Case number	
Done at	Date (day/month/year)
Signature and/or stamp	

2. Parties and their representatives

Codes: 01 Claimant; 02 Defendant; 03 Claimant's representative *; 04 Defendant's representative *; 05 Claimant's legally authorised representative **; 06 Defendant's legally authorised representative **

Code	Surname, first name/Name of company or organisation			Identification code (if applicable)	
	Address		Postal code	City	Country
	Phone ***	Fax ***		e-Mail ***	
	Occupation ***		Other details ***		
Code	Surname, first name/Name of company or organisation			Identification code (if applicable)	
	Address		Postal code	City	Country
	Phone ***	Fax ***		e-Mail ***	
	Occupation ***		Other details ***		
Code	Surname, first name/Name of company or organisation			Identification code (if applicable)	
	Address		Postal code	City	Country
	Phone ***	Fax ***		e-Mail ***	
	Occupation ***		Other details ***		
Code	Surname, first name/Name of company or organisation			Identification code (if applicable)	
	Address		Postal code	City	Country
	Phone ***	Fax ***		e-Mail ***	
	Occupation ***		Other details ***		

*e.g. lawyer ** e.g. parent, guardian, managing director *** optional

L 399/32 EN Official Journal of the European Union 30.12.2006

The court hereby declares that the attached European order for payment, issued on ______/______/______ and served on ______/______/______ is enforceable in accordance with Article 18 of Regulation (EC) No 1896/2006.

Important information

This European order for payment is automatically enforceable in all Member States of the European Union except Denmark, without the need for an additional declaration of enforceability in the Member State where enforcement is sought and without any possibility of opposing its recognition. The enforcement procedures are governed by the law of the Member State of enforcement, except where the Regulation provides otherwise.

Annex 2—The ESCP Regulation

REGULATION (EC) No 861/2007 OF THE EUROPEAN PARLIAMENT AND OF THE COUNCIL of 11 July 2007 establishing a European Small Claims Procedure

CHAPTER I—SUBJECT MATTER AND SCOPE

Article 1—Subject matter

This Regulation establishes a European procedure for small claims (hereinafter referred to as the European Small Claims Procedure), intended to simplify and speed up litigation concerning small claims in cross-border cases, and to reduce costs. The European Small Claims Procedure shall be available to litigants as an alternative to the procedures existing under the laws of the Member States. This Regulation also eliminates the intermediate proceedings necessary to enable recognition and enforcement, in other Member States, of judgments given in one Member State in the European Small Claims Procedure. **78PD.56**

Article 2—Scope

1. This Regulation shall apply, in cross-border cases, to civil and commercial matters, whatever the nature of the court or tribunal, where the value of a claim does not exceed EUR 2 000 at the time when the claim form is received by the court or tribunal with jurisdiction, excluding all interest, expenses and disbursements. It shall not extend, in particular, to revenue, customs or administrative matters or to the liability of the State for acts and omissions in the exercise of State authority (acta jure imperii). 2. This Regulation shall not apply to matters concerning: **78PD.57**

(a) the status or legal capacity of natural persons;
(b) rights in property arising out of a matrimonial relationship, maintenance obligations, wills and succession;
(c) bankruptcy, proceedings relating to the winding-up of insolvent companies or other legal persons, judicial arrangements, compositions and analogous proceedings;
(d) social security;
(e) arbitration;
(f) employment law;
(g) tenancies of immovable property, with the exception of actions on monetary claims;.

or

(h) violations of privacy and of rights relating to personality, *including defamation.*

3. In this Regulation, the term 'Member State' shall mean Member States with the exception of Denmark.

Article 3—Cross-border cases

1. For the purposes of this Regulation, a cross-border case is one in which at least one of the parties is domiciled or habitually resident in a Member State other than the Member State of the court or tribunal **78PD.58**

seised. 2. Domicile shall be determined in accordance with Articles 59 and 60 of Regulation (EC) No 44/2001. 3. The relevant moment for determining whether there is a cross-border case is the date on which the claim form is received by the court or tribunal with jurisdiction.

CHAPTER II—THE EUROPEAN SMALL CLAIMS PROCEDURE

Article 4—Commencement of the Procedure

78PD.59 1. The claimant shall commence the European Small Claims Procedure by filling in standard claim Form A, as set out in Annex I, and lodging it with the court or tribunal with jurisdiction directly, by post or by any other means of communication, such as fax or e-mail, acceptable to the Member State in which the procedure is commenced. The claim form shall include a description of evidence supporting the claim and be accompanied, where appropriate, by any relevant supporting documents. 2. Member States shall inform the Commission which means of communication are acceptable to them. The Commission shall make such information publicly available. 3. Where a claim is outside the scope of this Regulation, the court or tribunal shall inform the claimant to that effect. Unless the claimant withdraws the claim, the court or tribunal shall proceed with it in accordance with the relevant procedural law applicable in the Member State in which the procedure is conducted. 4. Where the court or tribunal considers the information provided by the claimant to be inadequate or insufficiently clear or if the claim form is not filled in properly, it shall, unless the claim appears to be clearly unfounded or the application inadmissible, give the claimant the opportunity to complete or rectify the claim form or to supply supplementary information or documents or to withdraw the claim, within such period as it specifies. The court or tribunal shall use standard Form B, as set out in Annex II, for this purpose. Where the claim appears to be clearly unfounded or the application inadmissible or where the claimant fails to complete or rectify the claim form within the time specified, the application shall be dismissed. 5. Member States shall ensure that the claim form is available at all courts and tribunals at which the European Small Claims Procedure can be commenced.

Article 5—Conduct of the Procedure

78PD.60 1. The European Small Claims Procedure shall be a written procedure. The court or tribunal shall hold an oral hearing if it considers this to be necessary or if a party so requests. The court or tribunal may refuse such a request if it considers that with regard to the circumstances of the case, an oral hearing is obviously not necessary for the fair conduct of the proceedings. The reasons for refusal shall be given in writing. The refusal may not be contested separately. 2. After receiving the properly filled in claim form, the court or tribunal shall fill in Part I of the standard answer Form C, as set out in Annex III. A copy of the claim form, and, where applicable, of the supporting documents, together with the answer form thus filled in, shall be served on the defendant in accordance with Article 13. These documents shall be dispatched within 14 days of receiving the properly filled in claim form. 3. The defendant shall submit his re-

sponse within 30 days of service of the claim form and answer form, by filling in Part II of standard answer Form C, accompanied, where appropriate, by any relevant supporting documents, and returning it to the court or tribunal, or in any other appropriate way not using the answer form. 4. Within 14 days of receipt of the response from the defendant, the court or tribunal shall dispatch a copy thereof, together with any relevant supporting documents to the claimant. 5. If, in his response, the defendant claims that the value of a non-monetary claim exceeds the limit set out in Article 2(1), the court or tribunal shall decide within 30 days of dispatching the response to the claimant, whether the claim is within the scope of this Regulation. Such decision may not be contested separately. 6. Any counterclaim, to be submitted using standard Form A, and any relevant supporting documents shall be served on the claimant in accordance with Article 13. Those documents shall be dispatched within 14 days of receipt. The claimant shall have 30 days from service to respond to any counterclaim. 7. If the counterclaim exceeds the limit set out in Article 2(1), the claim and counterclaim shall not proceed in the European Small Claims Procedure but shall be dealt with in accordance with the relevant procedural law applicable in the Member State in which the procedure is conducted. Articles 2 and 4 as well as paragraphs 3, 4 and 5 of this Article shall apply, *mutatis mutandis*, to counterclaims.

Article 6—Languages

1. The claim form, the response, any counterclaim, any response to a counterclaim and any description of relevant supporting documents shall be submitted in the language or one of the languages of the court or tribunal. 2. If any other document received by the court or tribunal is not in the language in which the proceedings are conducted, the court or tribunal may require a translation of that document only if the translation appears to be necessary for giving the judgment. 3. Where a party has refused to accept a document because it is not in either of the following languages: **78PD.61**

(a) the official language of the Member State addressed, or, if there are several official languages in that Member State, the official language or one of the official languages of the place where service is to be effected or to where the document is to be dispatched; or

(b) a language which the addressee understands,

the court or tribunal shall so inform the other party with a view to that party providing a translation of the document.

Article 7—Conclusion of the Procedure

1. Within 30 days of receipt of the response from the defendant or the claimant within the time limits laid down in Article 5(3) or (6), the court or tribunal shall give a judgment, or: **78PD.62**

(a) demand further details concerning the claim from the parties within a specified period of time, not exceeding 30 days;

(b) take evidence in accordance with Article 9; or

(c) (c) summon the parties to an oral hearing to be held within 30 days of the summons.

2. The court or tribunal shall give the judgment either within 30 days of any oral hearing or after having received all information necessary for giving the judgment. The judgment shall be served on the parties in accordance with Article 13.

3. If the court or tribunal has not received an answer from the relevant party within the time limits laid down in Article 5(3) or (6), it shall give a judgment on the claim or counterclaim.

Article 8—Oral hearing

78PD.63 The court or tribunal may hold an oral hearing through video conference or other communication technology if the technical means are available.

Article 9—Taking of evidence

78PD.64 1. The court or tribunal shall determine the means of taking evidence and the extent of the evidence necessary for its judgment under the rules applicable to the admissibility of evidence. The court or tribunal may admit the taking of evidence through written statements of witnesses, experts or parties. It may also admit the taking of evidence through video conference or other communication technology if the technical means are available. 2. The court or tribunal may take expert evidence or oral testimony only if it is necessary for giving the judgment. In making its decision, the court or tribunal shall take costs into account. 3. The court or tribunal shall use the simplest and least burdensome method of taking evidence.

Article 10—Representation of parties

78PD.65 Representation by a lawyer or another legal professional shall not be mandatory.

Article 11—Assistance for the parties

78PD.66 The Member States shall ensure that the parties can receive practical assistance in filling in the forms.

Article 12—Remit of the court or tribunal

78PD.67 1. The court or tribunal shall not require the parties to make any legal assessment of the claim. 2. If necessary, the court or tribunal shall inform the parties about procedural questions. 3. Whenever appropriate, the court or tribunal shall seek to reach a settlement between the parties.

Article 13—Service of documents

78PD.68 1. Documents shall be served by postal service attested by an acknowledgement of receipt including the date of receipt. 2. If service in accordance with paragraph 1 is not possible, service may be effected by any of the methods provided for in Articles 13 or 14 of Regulation (EC) No 805/2004.

Article 14—Time limits

1. Where the court or tribunal sets a time limit, the party concerned shall be informed of the consequences of not complying with it. 2. The court or tribunal may extend the time limits provided for in Article 4(4), Article 5(3) and (6) and Article 7(1), in exceptional circumstances, if necessary in order to safeguard the rights of the parties. 3. If, in exceptional circumstances, it is not possible for the court or tribunal to respect the time limits provided for in Article 5(2) to (6) and Article 7, it shall take the steps required by those provisions as soon as possible. **78PD.69**

Article 15—Enforceability of the judgment

1. The judgment shall be enforceable notwithstanding any possible appeal. The provision of a security shall not be required. 2. Article 23 shall also apply in the event that the judgment is to be enforced in the Member State where the judgment was given. **78PD.70**

Article 16—Costs

The unsuccessful party shall bear the costs of the proceedings. However, the court or tribunal shall not award costs to the successful party to the extent that they were unnecessarily incurred or are disproportionate to the claim. **78PD.71**

Article 17—Appeal

1. Member States shall inform the Commission whether an appeal is available under their procedural law against a judgment given in the European Small Claims Procedure and within what time limit such appeal shall be lodged. The Commission shall make that information publicly available. 2. Article 16 shall apply to any appeal. **78PD.72**

Article 18—Minimum standards for review of the judgment

Minimum standards for review of the judgment 1. The defendant shall be entitled to apply for a review of the judgment given in the European Small Claims Procedure before the court or tribunal with jurisdiction of the Member State where the judgment was given where: (a) (i) the claim form or the summons to an oral hearing were served by a method without proof of receipt by him personally, as provided for in Article 14 of Regulation (EC) No 805/2004; and (ii) service was not effected in sufficient time to enable him to arrange for his defence without any fault on his part, or (b) the defendant was prevented from objecting to the claim by reason of force majeure, or due to extraordinary circumstances without any fault on his part, provided in either case that he acts promptly. 2. If the court or tribunal rejects the review on the basis that none of the grounds referred to in paragraph 1 apply, the judgment shall remain in force. If the court or tribunal decides that the review is justified for one of the reasons laid down in paragraph 1, the judgment given in the European Small Claims Procedure shall be null and void. **78PD.73**

Article 19—Applicable procedural law

Subject to the provisions of this Regulation, the European Small Claims Procedure shall be governed by the procedural law of the Member State in which the procedure is conducted. **78PD.74**

CHAPTER III—RECOGNITION AND ENFORCEMENT IN ANOTHER MEMBER STATE

Article 20—Recognition and enforcement

78PD.75 1. A judgment given in a Member State in the European Small Claims Procedure shall be recognised and enforced in another Member State without the need for a declaration of enforceability and without any possibility of opposing its recognition. 2. At the request of one of the parties, the court or tribunal shall issue a certificate concerning a judgment in the European Small Claims Procedure using standard Form D, as set out in Annex IV, at no extra cost.

Article 21—Enforcement procedure

78PD.76 1. Without prejudice to the provisions of this Chapter, the enforcement procedures shall be governed by the law of the Member State of enforcement. Any judgment given in the European Small Claims Procedure shall be enforced under the same conditions as a judgment given in the Member State of enforcement. 2. The party seeking enforcement shall produce:

(a) a copy of the judgment which satisfies the conditions necessary to establish its authenticity; and

(b) a copy of the certificate referred to in Article 20(2) and, where necessary, the translation thereof into the official language of the Member State of enforcement or, if there are several official languages in that Member State, the official language or one of the official languages of court or tribunal proceedings of the place where enforcement is sought in conformity with the law of that Member State, or into another language that the Member State of enforcement has indicated it can accept. Each Member State may indicate the official language or languages of the institutions of the European Union other than its own which it can accept for the European Small Claims Procedure. The content of Form D shall be translated by a person qualified to make translations in one of the Member States.

3. The party seeking the enforcement of a judgment given in the European Small Claims Procedure in another Member State shall not be required to have:

(a) an authorised representative; or

(b) a postal address

in the Member State of enforcement, other than with agents having competence for the enforcement procedure. 4. No security, bond or deposit, however described, shall be required of a party who in one Member State applies for enforcement of a judgment given in the European Small Claims Procedure in another Member State on the ground that he is a foreign national or that he is not domiciled or resident in the Member State of enforcement.

Article 22—Refusal of enforcement

78PD.77 1. Enforcement shall, upon application by the person against whom enforcement is sought, be refused by the court or tribunal with jurisdiction in the Member State of enforcement if the judgment given in the European Small Claims Procedure is irreconcilable with an earlier judgment given in any Member State or in a third country, provided that:

(a) the earlier judgment involved the same cause of action and was between the same parties;
(b) the earlier judgment was given in the Member State of enforcement or fulfils the conditions necessary for its recognition in the Member State of enforcement; and
(c) the irreconcilability was not and could not have been raised as an objection in the court or tribunal proceedings in the Member State where the judgment in the European Small Claims Procedure was given.

2. Under no circumstances may a judgment given in the European Small Claims Procedure be reviewed as to its substance in the Member State of enforcement.

Article 23—Stay or limitation of enforcement

Where a party has challenged a judgment given in the European Small Claims Procedure or where such a challenge is still possible, or where a party has made an application for review within the meaning of Article 18, the court or tribunal with jurisdiction or the competent authority in the Member State of enforcement may, upon application by the party against whom enforcement is sought: **78PD.78**

(a) limit the enforcement proceedings to protective measures;
(b) make enforcement conditional on the provision of such security as it shall determine; or
(c) under exceptional circumstances, stay the enforcement proceedings.

CHAPTER IV—FINAL PROVISIONS

Article 24—Information

The Member States shall cooperate to provide the general public and professional circles with information on the European Small Claims Procedure, including costs, in particular by way of the European Judicial Network in Civil and Commercial Matters established in accordance with Decision 2001/470/EC. **78PD.79**

Article 25—Information relating to jurisdiction, means of communication and appeals

1. By 1 January 2008 the Member States shall communicate to the Commission: **78PD.80**

(a) which courts or tribunals have jurisdiction to give a judgment in the European Small Claims Procedure;
(b) which means of communication are accepted for the purposes of the European Small Claims Procedure and available to the courts or tribunals in accordance with Article 4(1);
(c) whether an appeal is available under their procedural law in accordance with Article 17 and with which court or tribunal this may be lodged;
(d) which languages are accepted pursuant to Article 21(2)(b); and
(e) which authorities have competence with respect to enforce-

ment and which authorities have competence for the purposes of the application of Article 23.

Member States shall apprise the Commission of any subsequent changes to this information.

2. The Commission shall make the information notified in accordance with paragraph 1 publicly available through publication in the Official Journal of the European Union and through any other appropriate means.

Article 26—Implementing measures

78PD.81 The measures designed to amend non-essential elements of this Regulation, including by supplementing it, relating to updates or technical amendments to the forms in the Annexes shall be adopted in accordance with the regulatory procedure with scrutiny referred to in Article 27(2).

Article 27—Committee

78PD.82 1. The Commission shall be assisted by a Committee. 2. Where reference is made to this paragraph, Article 5a(1) to (4), and Article 7 of Decision 1999/468/EC shall apply, having regard to the provisions of Article 8 thereof.

Article 28—Review

78PD.83 By 1 January 2014, the Commission shall present to the European Parliament, the Council and the European Economic and Social Committee a detailed report reviewing the operation of the European Small Claims Procedure, including the limit of the value of the claim referred to in Article 2(1). That report shall contain an assessment of the procedure as it has operated and an extended impact assessment for each Member State. To that end and in order to ensure that best practice in the European Union is duly taken into account and reflects the principles of better legislation, Member States shall provide the Commission with information relating to the cross-border operation of the European Small Claims Procedure. This information shall cover court fees, speed of the procedure, efficiency, ease of use and the internal small claims procedures of the Member States.

The Commission's report shall be accompanied, if appropriate, by proposals for adaptation.

Article 29—Entry into force

78PD.84 This Regulation shall enter into force on the day following its publication in the Official Journal of the European Union. It shall apply from 1 January 2009, with the exception of Article 25, which shall apply from 1 January 2008.

78PD.85 This Regulation shall be binding in its entirety and directly applicable in the Member States in accordance with the Treaty establishing the European Community.

Done at Strasbourg, 11 July 2007.

For the European Parliament The President H.-G. PÖTTERING
For the Council The President M. LOBO ANTUNES

Editorial Note

78PD86.0 The annexes consist of four forms I to IV and are printed hereunder commencing at para.78PD.86.

ANNEX I

EUROPEAN SMALL CLAIMS PROCEDURE

FORM A

CLAIM FORM

(Article 4(1) of Regulation (EC) No 861/2007 of the European Parliament and of the Council establishing a European Small Claims Procedure)

Case number (*):
Received by the court/tribunal on: ___/___/_____ (*)
(*) To be filled in by the court/tribunal.

IMPORTANT INFORMATION

PLEASE READ THE GUIDELINES AT THE BEGINNING OF EACH SECTION – THEY WILL HELP YOU TO FILL IN THIS FORM

Language

Fill in this form in the language of the court/tribunal to which you are sending your application. Please note that the form is available in all official languages of the institutions of the European Union on the website of the European Judicial Atlas at http://ec.europa.eu/justice_home/judicialatlascivil/html/index_en.htm. This may help you in filling in the form in the required language.

Supporting documents

Please note that the claim form should be accompanied, where appropriate, by any relevant supporting documents. However, this does not prevent you from submitting, where appropriate, further evidence during the procedure.

A copy of the claim form and, where appropriate, of the supporting documents, will be served on the defendant. The defendant will have an opportunity to submit a response.

1. *Court/tribunal*

In this field you should identify the court/tribunal before which you are making your claim. When deciding which court/tribunal to choose, you need to consider the grounds for the court's/tribunal's jurisdiction. A non-exhaustive list of possible grounds of jurisdiction is included in section 4.

1.	*Before which court/tribunal are you making your claim?*
1.1.	Name:
1.2.	Street and number/PO box:
1.3.	City and postal code:
1.4.	Country:

2. *Claimant*

This field must identify you as the claimant and your representative, if any. Please note that it is not mandatory to be represented by a lawyer or another legal professional.

It may not be sufficient in some countries to give only a PO Box as the address and you should therefore include the street name and number with a postcode. Failure to do so may result in the document not being served.

'Other details' may contain information that helps to identify you, for example, your date of birth, occupation, position in the company, personal ID code and the company registry code in certain Member States.

Where there is more than one claimant, please use additional sheets.

2.	*The claimant's details*
2.1.	Surname, first name/name of company or organisation:
2.2.	Street and number/PO box:
2.3.	City and postal code:
2.4.	Country:
2.5.	Telephone (*):
2.6.	E-mail (*):
2.7.	Claimant's representative, if any, and contact details (*):
2.8.	Other details (*):

3. *Defendant*

In this field you should identify the defendant and, if known, his representative. Please note that it is not mandatory for the defendant to be represented by a lawyer or another legal professional.

It may not be sufficient in some countries to give only a P.O. Box as the address and therefore you should include the street name and number with a postcode. Failure to do so may result in the document not being served.

'Other details' may contain information that helps to identify the person, for example the date of birth, occupation, position in the company, personal ID code and company registry code in certain Member States. If there is more than one defendant, please use additional sheets.

3.	*The defendant's details*
3.1.	Surname, first name/name of company or organisation:
3.2.	Street and number/PO box:
3.3.	City and postal code:
3.4.	Country:
3.5.	Telephone (*):
3.6.	E-mail (*):
3.7.	Defendant's representative, if known, and contact details (*):
3.8.	Other details (*):

4. *Jurisdiction*

Your application must be lodged with the court/tribunal that has jurisdiction to deal with it. The court/ tribunal must have jurisdiction in accordance with the rules of Council Regulation (EC) No 44/2001 on jurisdiction and the recognition and enforcement of judgments in civil and commercial matters.

This section includes a non-exhaustive list of possible grounds for jurisdiction.

Information on the rules of jurisdiction can be found on the website of the European Judicial Atlas at http://ec.europa.eu/justice_home/judicialatlascivil/html/index_en.htm.

You can also look at http://ec.europa.eu/civiljustice/glossary/glossary_en.htm for an explanation of some of the legal terms employed.

(*) Optional.

L 199/12 EN Official Journal of the European Union 31.7.2007

4.	*On what ground do you consider the court/tribunal to have jurisdiction?*	
4.1.	Domicile of the defendant	☐
4.2.	Domicile of the consumer	☐
4.3.	Domicile of the policyholder, the insured or the beneficiary in insurance matters	☐
4.4.	Place of performance of the obligation in question	☐
4.5.	Place of the harmful event	☐
4.6.	Place where the immovable property is situated	☐
4.7.	Choice of court/tribunal agreed by the parties	
4.8.	Other (please specify): ____________________	

5. *Cross-border nature of the case*

In order to make use of the European Small Claims Procedure, your case must be of a cross-border nature. A case is of a cross-border nature if at least one of the parties is domiciled or habitually resident in a Member State other than the Member State of the court/tribunal.

5.	*Cross-border nature of the case*
5.1.	Country of domicile or habitual residence of claimant: ____________________
5.2.	Country of domicile or habitual residence of defendant: ____________________
5.3.	Member State of the court/tribunal: ____________________

6. *Bank details (optional)*

In field 6.1. you may inform the court/tribunal by which means you intend to pay the application fee. Please note that not all methods are necessarily available at the court/tribunal to which you are sending your application. You should verify which methods of payment will be accepted by the court/tribunal. You can do this by contacting the court/tribunal concerned or by consulting the website of the European Judicial Network in Civil and Commercial Matters at http://ec.europa.eu/civiljustice.

If you choose to pay by credit card or to allow the court/tribunal to collect the fee from your bank account, you should give the necessary credit card or bank account details in the Appendix to this form. The Appendix will be for the information of the court/tribunal only and will not be forwarded to the defendant.

In field 6.2. you are given the possibility of indicating by which means you wish to receive payment from the defendant, for example if the defendant wishes to pay immediately even before the judgment is given. If you wish to be paid by bank transfer please give the necessary bank details.

6.	*Bank details* (*)	
6.1.	How will you pay the application fee?	
6.1.1.	By bank transfer	☐
6.1.2.	By credit card	☐ (please fill in the Appendix)
6.1.3.	Direct debit from your bank account	☐ (please fill in the Appendix)
6.1.4.	Other (please specify):	
6.2.	To which account do you wish the defendant to pay any amount claimed or awarded?	
6.2.1.	Account holder:	
6.2.2.	Bank name, BIC or other relevant bank code:	
6.2.3.	Account number/IBAN:	

31.7.2007 EN Official Journal of the European Union L 199/13

7. *Claim*

Scope: Please note that the European Small Claims Procedure has a limited scope. No claims of a value higher than EUR 2000 or which are listed in Article 2 of Regulation (EC) No 861/2007 of the European Parliament and of the Council establishing a European Small Claims Procedure can be dealt with under this procedure. If your claim does not relate to an action within the scope of that Regulation in accordance with Article 2, proceedings will continue before the courts/tribunals with jurisdiction in accordance with the rules of ordinary civil procedure. If you do not wish to continue proceedings in that event, you should withdraw your application.

Monetary or other claim: You should indicate whether you are claiming money and/or something else (non-monetary claim), for example, delivery of goods, and then fill in respectively either 7.1. and/or 7.2. If your claim is not for money, please indicate the estimated value of your claim. In the case of a non-monetary claim, you should indicate whether you have a secondary claim for compensation if it is not possible to satisfy the original claim.

If you wish to claim the costs of the proceedings (e.g. translation costs, lawyers' fees, costs relating to the service of documents etc.), then you should indicate this in 7.3. Please note that rules regarding the costs which courts/tribunals can award vary between different Member States. Details of categories of costs in the Member States can be found on the website of the European Judicial Network in Civil and Commercial Matters at http://ec.europa.eu/civiljustice.

If you wish to claim any contractual interest, for example on a loan, you should indicate the rate and from what date it runs. The court/tribunal may award statutory interest on your claim, if you are successful. If you wish to claim interest, please indicate this and the date from which the interest should run.

7. *About your claim*

☐ 7.1. Claim for money

7.1.1. Amount of principal (excluding interest and costs): ____________

7.1.2. Currency

☐ Euro (EUR)	☐ Bulgarian lev (BGN)	☐ Cypriot pound (CYP)
☐ Czech koruna (CZK)	☐ Estonian kroon (EEK)	☐ Pound Sterling (GBP)
☐ Hungarian forint (HUF)	☐ Latvian lats (LVL)	☐ Lithuanian litas (LTL)
☐ Maltese lira (MTL)	☐ Polish zloty (PLN)	☐ Romanian leu (RON)
☐ Swedish kronor (SEK)	☐ Slovak koruna (SKK)	

☐ Other (please specify): ____________

☐ 7.2. Other claim:

7.2.1. Please specify what you are claiming: ____________

7.2.2. Estimated value of the claim: ____________

Currency:

☐ Euro (EUR)	☐ Bulgarian lev (BGN)	☐ Cypriot pound (CYP)
☐ Czech koruna (CZK)	☐ Estonian kroon (EEK)	☐ Pound Sterling (GBP)
☐ Hungarian forint (HUF)	☐ Latvian lats (LVL)	☐ Lithuanian litas (LTL)
☐ Maltese lira (MTL)	☐ Polish zloty (PLN)	☐ Romanian leu (RON)
☐ Swedish kronor (SEK)	☐ Slovak koruna (SKK)	

☐ Other (please specify): ____________

7.3. Are you claiming the costs of proceedings?

7.3.1. Yes ☐

7.3.2. No ☐

7.3.3. If yes, please specify which costs and indicate the amount claimed or incurred so far:

L 199/14 EN Official Journal of the European Union 31.7.2007

7.4. Are you claiming interest?
Yes ☐
No ☐
If yes, is the interest:
Contractual? ☐ If so, go to 7.4.1
Statutory? ☐ If so, go to 7.4.2

7.4.1. If contractual
(1) the rate is:
☐ ____ %
☐ ____ % above the base rate of the ECB
☐ other: ____________________
(2) the interest should run from: ___/___/_____ (date)

7.4.2. If statutory
the interest should run from: ___/___/_____ (date)

8. *Details of claim*

In 8.1. you should describe briefly the substance of your claim.

In 8.2. you should describe any relevant supporting evidence. This could, for example, be written evidence (e.g. contracts, receipts, etc.) or oral or written statements from witnesses. For each piece of evidence, please indicate which aspect of your claim it is intended to support.

If space is insufficient, you can add additional sheets.

8. *Details of claim*

8.1. Please give reasons for your claim, for example what happened, where and when.

8.2. Please describe the evidence you wish to put forward to support your claim and state which points of the claim it supports. Where appropriate, you should add relevant supporting documents.

8.2.1. Written evidence ☐ please specify below

8.2.2. Witnesses ☐ please specify below

8.2.3. Other ☐ please specify below

Oral hearing: Please note that the European Small Claims Procedure is a written procedure. However, you can request, in this form or at a later stage, that an oral hearing be held. The court/tribunal may decide to hold an oral hearing if it considers it necessary for the fair conduct of the proceedings or it may refuse it, having regard to all the circumstances of the case.

8.3. Do you want an oral hearing to be held?
Yes ☐
No ☐
If yes, please indicate reasons (*)

9. *Certificate*

A judgment given in a Member State in the European Small Claims Procedure can be recognised and enforced in another Member State. If you intend to ask for recognition and enforcement in a Member State other than that of the court/tribunal, you can request in this form that the court/tribunal, after having made a decision in your favour, issue a certificate concerning that judgment.

9. *Certificate*

I ask the court/tribunal to issue a certificate concerning the judgment

Yes ☐

No ☐

10. *Date and signature*

Please make sure that you write your name clearly and sign and date your application at the end.

10. *Date and signature*

I hereby request that the court/tribunal give a judgment against the defendant on the basis of my claim.

I declare that the information provided is true to the best of my knowledge and is given in good faith.

Done at: ______________________

Date: ___/___/_____

Name and signature:

L 199/16 EN Official Journal of the European Union 31.7.2007

Appendix to the claim form (Form A)

Bank details (*) for the purposes of payment of the application fee

Account holder/credit card holder:
Bank name, BIC or other relevant bank code/credit card company:
Account number or IBAN/credit card number, expiry date and security number of the credit card:

(*) Optional.

31.7.2007 EN Official Journal of the European Union L 199/17

ANNEX II

EUROPEAN SMALL CLAIMS PROCEDURE

FORM B

REQUEST BY THE COURT OR TRIBUNAL TO COMPLETE AND/OR RECTIFY THE CLAIM FORM

(Article 4(4) of Regulation (EC) No 861/2007 of the European Parliament and of the Council establishing a European Small Claims Procedure)

To be filled in by the court/tribunal

Case number:

Received by the court/tribunal on: ___/___/_____.

1. *Court/tribunal*

1.1. Name:

1.2. Street and number/PO box:

1.3. City and postal code:

1.4. Country:

2. *Claimant*

2.1. Surname, first name/name of company or organisation:

2.2. Street and number/PO box:

2.3. City and postal code:

2.4. Country:

2.5. Telephone (*):

2.6. E-mail (*):

2.7. Claimant's representative, if any, and contact details (*):

2.8. Other details (*):

3. *Defendant*

3.1. Surname, first name/name of company or organisation:

3.2. Street and number/PO box:

3.3. City and postal code:

3.4. Country:

3.5. Telephone (*):

3.6. E-mail (*):

3.7. Defendant's representative, if any, and contact details (*):

3.8. Other details (*):

(*) Optional.

L 199/18 EN Official Journal of the European Union 31.7.2007

The court/tribunal has examined your claim form and considers it to be inadequate or insufficiently clear or not properly filled in: please complete and/or rectify your form in the language of the court/tribunal as indicated below as soon as possible and at the latest by ______________________.

The court/tribunal shall dismiss your application under the conditions provided for in Regulation (EC) No 861(*)/2007 if you fail to complete and/or rectify it within the time limit set out above.

Your claim form has not been filled in the correct language. Please fill it in one of the following languages.

Bulgarian	☐	Czech	☐	German	☐
Estonian	☐	Spanish	☐	Greek	☐
French	☐	Irish	☐	Italian	☐
Latvian	☐	Lithuanian	☐	Hungarian	☐
Maltese	☐	Dutch	☐	Polish	☐
Portuguese	☐	Romanian	☐	Slovak	☐
Slovene	☐	Finnish	☐	Swedish	☐
English	☐	Other: (please specify) ______________			

The following sections of the claim form must be completed and/or rectified as stated below:

—

—

—

—

Done at:

Date: ___/___/______

Signature and/or stamp:

31.7.2007 EN Official Journal of the European Union L 199/19

ANNEX III

EUROPEAN SMALL CLAIMS PROCEDURE

FORM C

ANSWER FORM

(Article 5(2) and 5(3) of Regulation (EC) No 861/2007 of the European Parliament and of the Council establishing a European Small Claims Procedure)

IMPORTANT INFORMATION AND GUIDELINES FOR THE DEFENDANT

A claim as set out in the attached claim form has been submitted against you using the European Small Claims Procedure.

You can answer by filling in Part II of this form and returning it to the court/tribunal, or in any other appropriate way, within 30 days after the claim form has been served on you together with the answer form.

Please note that if you do not answer within 30 days, the court/tribunal shall give a judgment.

Please make sure that you write your name clearly and sign and date the answer form at the end.

You should also read the guidelines included in the claim form; these may help you to prepare your response.

Language: You should reply to the claim in the language of the court/tribunal which has sent you this form.

Please note that the form is available in all official languages of the institutions of the European Union on the website of the European Judicial Atlas at http://ec.europa.eu/justice_home/judicialatlascivil/html/index_en.htm. This may help you in filling in the form in the required language.

Oral hearing: Please note that the European Small Claims Procedure is a written procedure. However, you can ask for an oral hearing to be held. Please be aware that having regard to the circumstances of the case, the court/tribunal can refuse this request.

Supporting documents: You can indicate possible means of evidence, and add, where appropriate, supporting documents.

Counterclaim: If you want to make a claim against the claimant (counterclaim), you should fill in and attach a separate Form A which you can find on the Internet at http://ec.europa.eu/justice_home/judicialatlascivil/html/fillinginformation_en.htm or obtain from the court/tribunal which sent you this form. Please note that for the purposes of the counterclaim you are considered to be the claimant.

Correcting your details: You can also correct or supplement information about yourself (e.g. contact details, representative etc.) in section 6 'Other information'.

Extra space: If space is insufficient, you can add additional sheets.

Part I (to be filled in by the court/tribunal)

Name of claimant:

Name of defendant:

Court/tribunal:

Claim:

Case number:

L 199/20 EN Official Journal of the European Union 31.7.2007

Part II (to be filled in by the defendant)

1. Do you accept the claim?
   Yes ☐
   No ☐
   Partially ☐
   If you have answered 'no' or 'partially', please indicate reasons:
   The claim is outside the scope of the European Small Claims Procedure ☐
   please specify below
   Other ☐
   please specify below
2. If you do not accept the claim please describe the evidence you wish to put forward to contest it. Please state which points of your answer the evidence supports. Where appropriate, you should add relevant supporting documents.
   2.1. Written evidence ☐ please specify below
   2.2. Witnesses ☐ please specify below
   2.3. Other ☐ please specify below
3. Do you want an oral hearing to be held?
   Yes ☐
   No ☐
   If yes, please indicate reasons (*):
4. Are you claiming the costs of proceedings?
   4.1. Yes ☐
   4.2. No ☐
   4.3. If yes, please specify which costs and if possible, indicate the amount claimed or incurred so far:
5. Do you want to make a counterclaim?
   5.1. Yes ☐
   5.2. No ☐
   5.3. If yes, please fill in and attach a separate Form A
6. Other information (*)
7. Date and signature
   I declare that the information provided is true to the best of my knowledge and is given in good faith.
   Done at: __________
   Date: ___/___/_____
   Name and signature:

(*) Optional.

31.7.2007 EN Official Journal of the European Union L 199/21

ANNEX IV

EUROPEAN SMALL CLAIMS PROCEDURE

FORM D

CERTIFICATE CONCERNING A JUDGMENT IN THE EUROPEAN SMALL CLAIMS PROCEDURE

(Article 20(2) of Regulation (EC) No 861/2007 of the European Parliament and of the Council establishing a European Small Claims Procedure)

To be filled in by the court/tribunal

1. *Court/tribunal*
1.1. Name:
1.2. Street and number/PO box:
1.3. City and postal code:
1.4. Country:

2. *Claimant*
2.1. Surname, first name/name of company or organisation:
2.2. Street and number/PO box:
2.3. City and postal code:
2.4. Country:
2.5. Telephone (*):
2.6. E-mail (*):
2.7. Claimant's representative, if any, and contact details (*):
2.8. Other details (*):

3. *Defendant*
3.1. Surname, first name/name of company or organisation:
3.2. Street and number/PO box:
3.3. City and postal code:
3.4. Country:
3.5. Telephone (*):
3.6. E-mail (*):
3.7. Defendant's representative, if any, and contact details (*):
3.8. Other details (*):

(*) Optional.

L 199/22 EN Official Journal of the European Union 31.7.2007

4. *Judgment*

4.1. Date:

4.2. Case number:

4.3. The substance of the judgment:

4.3.1. The court/tribunal has ordered __________ to pay to __________

(1) Principal:

(2) Interest:

(3) Costs:

4.3.2. The court/tribunal has made an order against __________ to __________

(If the judgment was given by an appeal courtor in the case of a review of a judgment.)

This judgment supersedes the judgment given on ___/___/_____, case number __________, and any certificate relative thereto.

THE JUDGMENT WILL BE RECOGNISED AND ENFORCED IN ANOTHER MEMBER STATE WITHOUT THE NEED FOR A DECLARATION OF ENFORCEABILITY AND WITHOUT ANY POSSIBILITY OF OPPOSING ITS RECOGNITION.

Done at: __________

Date: ___/___/_____

Signature and/or stamp

PART 79

Financial Restrictions Proceedings Under the Counter-Terrorism Act 2008

79.0.1 **Contents**

Editorial introduction

The Civil Procedure (Amendment No.2) Rules (SI 2008/3085) were made on December 2, 2008, laid before Parliament on December 3, 2008 and came into force on December 4, 2008. The rules were made by the Lord Chancellor, not the CPR Committee (though the Committee now has responsibility for them and will make any required amendments). The rules insert Pt 79 into the CPR. Part 79 gives effect to certain provisions in the Counter Terrorism Act 2008. That Act received Royal Assent on November 26, 2008 and most of it came into force immediately. The Act gives very wide powers of the sort only previously encountered during wartime. Part 5 of the Act ("Terrorist Financing and Money Laundering") confers powers on "the Treasury" (query why "the Treasury" and not the DPP or the Attorney General?) to direct persons operating in the financial sector to take certain actions in respect of transactions or business with persons in a country of money laundering, terrorist financing or proliferation concern. Part 6 of the Act ("Financial Restrictions Proceedings") creates a statutory basis for a person affected by these Treasury decisions to apply to have them set aside. Part 6 applies to Treasury Decisions under (i) the UN Terrorism Orders, (ii) Pt 2 of the Anti-Terrorism, Crime and Security Act 2001 and (iii) under Sch.7 of the 2008 Act. It provides for rules of court (hence CPR Pt 79) to make provision about such application, in particular for the procedure which is to apply where the reason for the Treasury's decision cannot be disclosed to the applicant because disclosure would be contrary to the public interest (i.e. it involves "closed source material"). Closed source material relevant to the Treasury's decision is considered at a closed hearing where a "special advocate" (who has been security vetted) represents the interests of the applicant. Application is made to the High Court. **79.0.2**

1. Application of this Part

Scope and interpretation

79.1—(1) This Part contains rules about— **79.1**

(a) financial restrictions proceedings in the High Court; and

(b) appeals to the Court of Appeal against an order of the High Court in such proceedings.

(2) In this Part—

(a) "the Act" means the Counter-Terrorism Act 2008;

(b) "financial restrictions decision" means a decision to which section 63(1) of the Act applies;

(c) "financial restrictions proceedings" has the same meaning as in section 65 of the Act;

(d) "closed material" means—

(i) material, evidence or submissions to the court upon which the Treasury wish to rely in proceedings;

(ii) material which adversely affects the Treasury's case or supports another party's case; or

(iii) information which the Treasury are required to file pursuant to an order under rule 79.11(7),

but which the Treasury object to disclosing to another party and that party's legal representative;

(e) "legal representative" in relation to a party to proceed-

ings other than the Treasury does not include a special advocate;

(f) "material" means anything in which information of any description is recorded;

(g) "party" includes the Treasury unless otherwise stated or unless the context otherwise requires;

(h) "special advocate" means a person appointed under section 68 of the Act; and

(i) "specially represented party" means a party, other than the Treasury, whose interests a special advocate represents.

Modification to the overriding objective

79.2 **79.2—(1) Where this Part applies, the overriding objective in Part 1, and so far as relevant any other rule, must be read and given effect in a way which is compatible with the duty set out in paragraph (2).**

(2) The court will ensure that information is not disclosed contrary to the public interest.

(3) Without prejudice to paragraph (2), the court will satisfy itself that the material available to it enables it properly to determine the proceedings.

2. Application to Set Aside a Financial Restrictions Decision

Scope of this Section

79.3 **79.3. This Section applies to an application to set aside a financial restrictions decision.**

Where to make an application

79.4 **79.4. An application under this Section must be started and heard in the Administrative Court.**

Applications (general) and modification of Part 8

79.5 **79.5—(1) An application to set aside a financial restrictions decision must be made pursuant to Part 8, as modified by this Part, and subject to paragraph (2).**

(2) The following rules do not apply to an application under this Section—

(a) rule 8.1(3);

(b) rule 8.2A (issue of claim form without naming defendants);

(c) rule 8.4 (consequence of not filing an acknowledgment of service);

(d) rule 8.5 (filing and serving written evidence);

(e) rule 8.6 (evidence – general); and

(f) rule 8.8 (defendant objects to use of Part 8).

Application to set aside

79.6 **79.6—(1) An application to set aside a financial restrictions decision must be started by a claim form.**

(2) The claim form must set out—

(a) the details of the financial restrictions decision;

(b) details of how the claimant is affected by the financial restrictions decision; and

(c) the grounds on which the claimant seeks to set aside the decision.

(3) The claimant must file with the claim form—

(a) a copy of—

(i) the written notice of the relevant financial restrictions decision made by the Treasury; or

(ii) where relevant, any direction, order or licence made under Schedule 7 to the Act or any freezing order made under Part 2 of the Anti-terrorism, Crime and Security Act 2001; and

(b) any evidence, including witness statements, on which the claimant relies at that stage.

Fixing of directions hearing date

79.7 When the court issues the claim form it will fix a date for a directions hearing. (2) Unless the court directs otherwise, the directions hearing will be not less than 14 days but not more than 28 days after the date of issue of the claim form. 79.7

Service of the claim form and accompanying documents

79.8—(1) The court will— 79.8

(a) serve on the Treasury and any special advocate (if one has been appointed)—

(i) the claim form; and

(ii) the documents specified in rule 79.6(3); and

(b) send to all parties and any special advocate a notice of the directions hearing date (where such date is not endorsed on the claim form).

Acknowledgment of service

79.9—(1) Where a special advocate has been appointed, the Treasury must serve on that special advocate a copy of the acknowledgment of service filed under rule 8.3. 79.9

Directions hearing

79.10 At the directions hearing the court may give case management directions, in particular— 79.10

(a) for the holding of a further hearing to determine the application;

(b) fixing a date, time and place for the further hearing at which the parties, their legal representatives (if any) and any special advocate can be present; and

(c) as to the order in which, and the time within which, the following are to be filed and served—

(i) any response to the application to be filed and served by the Treasury under rule 79.11(1), (2) and (4);
(ii) any application to be made under rule 79.11(5);
(iii) any information to be filed and served by the Treasury pursuant to an order under rule 79.11(7);
(iv) any evidence to be filed and served by the claimant under rule 79.12(1);
(v) any evidence to be filed and served by the Treasury under rule 79.12(2);
(vi) any application by the Treasury under rule 79.11(3), 79.11(8) or 79.12(3); and
(vii) any further evidence, including witness statements, written submissions or skeleton arguments, to be filed and served by the parties and any special advocate.

Response by the Treasury

79.11 79.11—(1) Where the Treasury intend to oppose the application to set aside the financial restrictions decision, they must file with the court—

(a) the grounds for contesting the application; and
(b) any relevant evidence of which they are aware at that stage.

(2) Unless the Treasury object to the grounds and evidence in paragraph (1) being disclosed to the claimant and the claimant's legal representative, the Treasury must serve a copy of the grounds and evidence on the claimant at the same time as filing the grounds.

(3) Where the Treasury object to the grounds and evidence in paragraph (1) being disclosed to the claimant and the claimant's legal representative, the Treasury must make an application in accordance with rule 79.25.

(4) Where a special advocate has been appointed, the Treasury must serve on that special advocate a copy of the grounds and evidence filed under paragraph (1).

(5) The claimant and any special advocate may apply to the court for an order directing the Treasury to file and serve further information about the Treasury's grounds filed under paragraph (1)(a).

(6) The application under paragraph (5) must set out—

(a) what information is sought; and
(b) why the information sought is necessary for the determination of the application to set aside the financial restrictions decision.

(7) The court may make an order on an application under paragraph (5) where it considers that the information sought is—

(a) necessary for the determination of the application to set aside the financial restrictions decision; and
(b) may be provided without disproportionate cost, time or effort.

(8) Where the Treasury object to serving on the claimant and the claimant's legal representative the information sought under

paragraph (5), the Treasury must make an application in accordance with rule 79.25.

Filing and service of evidence

79.12—(1) Where the claimant wishes to rely on evidence in support of the application to set aside the financial restrictions decision and— 79.12

- **(a) such evidence was not filed with the court with the claim form; or**
- **(b) such evidence was filed with the court with the claim form but the claimant wishes to rely on further evidence,**

the claimant must file and serve that evidence, including any witness statement, on the Treasury and any special advocate.

(2) Where the claimant serves evidence in support of the application, the Treasury must file and serve, subject to paragraph (3), any further evidence, including any witness statement, on the claimant and any special advocate.

(3) Where the Treasury seek to withhold disclosure of any closed material from the claimant and the claimant's legal representative, the Treasury must make an application in accordance with rule 79.25.

(4) The Treasury must serve any closed material upon the special advocate.

(5) The parties and, where relevant, any special advocate must file and serve any further evidence, including witness statements, written submissions or skeleton arguments as directed by the court.

3. Appeal to the Court of Appeal

Modification of Part 52 (appeals)

79.13 Part 52 (appeals) applies to an appeal to the Court of Appeal against an order of the High Court in financial restrictions proceedings, subject to— 79.13

- **(a) rule 79.2; and**
- **(b) Section 4 of this Part.**

Service of appellant's notice on special advocate

79.14 The appellant must serve a copy of the appellant's notice on any special advocate. 79.14

4. General Provisions

Scope of this Section

79.15 This Section applies to all proceedings specified in rule 79.1(1). 79.15

Notification of hearing

79.16—(1) Unless the court orders otherwise, the court will serve any notice of the date, time and place fixed for a hearing on— 79.16

(2) every party, whether or not a party is entitled to attend that hearing; and

(3) if one has been appointed for the purposes of the proceedings, the special advocate or those instructing the special advocate.

Hearings

79.17 79.17—(1) All proceedings to which this Part applies must be determined at a hearing except where—

(a) the claimant withdraws the claim or application;
(b) the Treasury consent to the claim or application being allowed;
(c) the appellant withdraws the appeal against a decision of the High Court;
(d) the respondent to the appeal consents to the appeal being allowed; or
(e) the parties agree to a determination without a hearing.

(2) Where the court considers it necessary for a party other than the Treasury and that party's legal representative to be excluded from a hearing or part of a hearing in order to secure that information is not disclosed contrary to the public interest, the court will—

(a) direct accordingly; and
(b) conduct the hearing, or that part of it from which the party and that party's legal representative are excluded, in private but attended by a special advocate to represent the interests of the excluded party.

Appointment of a special advocate

79.18 79.18—(1) Subject to paragraph (2), the Treasury must immediately give notice of the proceedings to the Attorney General—

(a) upon being served with any claim form, application notice or appeal notice; or
(b) where the Treasury intend to file an appeal notice,

in proceedings to which this Part applies.

(2) Paragraph (1) applies unless—

(a) the Treasury do not intend to—
  (i) oppose the claim, application or appeal; or
  (ii) apply for permission to withhold closed material from a party and that party's legal representative; or
(b) a special advocate has already been appointed to represent the interests of a party other than the Treasury and that special advocate is not prevented from communicating with that party by virtue of rule 79.20.

(3) Where any proceedings to which this Part applies are pending but no special advocate has been appointed, any party may request the Attorney General to appoint a special advocate.

Function of a special advocate

79.19 79.19—(1) The function of a special advocate is to represent the interests of a party other than the Treasury by, for example—

(a) making submissions to the court at any hearing from which the party and that party's legal representative are excluded;
(b) adducing evidence and cross-examining witnesses at such a hearing;
(c) making applications to the court or seeking directions from the court where necessary; and
(d) making written submissions to the court.

Special advocate: communicating about proceedings

79.20—(1) The special advocate may communicate with the specially represented party or that party's legal representative at any time before the Treasury serve closed material on the special advocate. **79.20**

(2) After the Treasury serve closed material on the special advocate, the special advocate must not communicate with any person about any matter connected with the proceedings, except in accordance with paragraph (3) or a direction of the court pursuant to a request under paragraph (4).

(3) The special advocate may, without directions from the court, communicate about the proceedings with—
(a) the court;
(b) the Treasury and any persons acting for them;
(c) the Attorney General and any persons acting for the Attorney General; and
(d) any other person, except for—
(i) the specially represented party and that party's legal representative; and
(ii) any other party to the proceedings (other than the Treasury) and that party's legal representative,

with whom it is necessary for administrative purposes for the special advocate to communicate about matters not connected with the substance of the proceedings.

(4) The special advocate may request directions from the court authorising the special advocate to communicate with the specially represented party or that party's legal representative or with any other person.

(5) Where the special advocate makes a request for directions under paragraph (4)—
(a) the court will notify the Treasury of the request; and
(b) the Treasury must, within a period specified by the court, file and serve on the special advocate notice of any objection which they have to the proposed communication, or to the form in which it is proposed to be made.

(6) Paragraph (2) does not prohibit the specially represented party from communicating with the special advocate after the Treasury have served closed material on the special advocate as mentioned in paragraph (1), but—

(a) that party may only communicate with the special advocate through a legal representative in writing; and
(b) the special advocate must not reply to the communication other than in accordance with directions given by the court, except that the special advocate may without such directions send a written acknowledgment of receipt to the specially represented party's legal representative.

Consideration of the Treasury's objection

79.21 **79.21—(1)** Where the Treasury object under rule 79.20(5)(b) to a proposed communication by the special advocate the court will fix a hearing for the Treasury and the special advocate to make oral representations, unless—
(a) the special advocate gives notice to the court that the special advocate does not challenge the objection;
(b) the court—
(i) has previously considered an objection under rule 79.20(5)(b) to the same or substantially the same communication; and
(ii) is satisfied that it would be just to uphold or dismiss that objection without a hearing; or
(c) the Treasury and the special advocate consent to the court deciding the issue without a hearing.

(2) If the special advocate does not challenge the objection, the special advocate must give notice of that fact to the court and to the Treasury—
(a) within 14 days after the Treasury serve on the special advocate a notice under rule 79.20(5)(b); or
(b) within such other period as the court may direct.

(3) Where the court fixes a hearing under paragraph (1)—
(a) the special advocate may file with the court and serve on the Treasury a reply to the Treasury's objection;
(b) the Treasury may file with the court and serve on the special advocate a response to the special advocate's reply; and
(c) the Treasury and the special advocate must file with the court at least 7 days before the hearing a schedule identifying the issues which cannot be agreed between them and which must—
(i) give brief reasons for their contentions on each issue in dispute; and
(ii) set out any proposals for the court to resolve the issues in dispute.

(4) A hearing under this rule must take place in the absence of the specially represented party and that party's legal representative.

Modification of the general rules of evidence and disclosure

79.22 **79.22—(1)** Part 31 (disclosure and inspection of documents),

Part 32 (evidence) and Part 33 (miscellaneous rules about evidence) do not apply to any proceedings to which this Part applies.

(2) Subject to the other rules in this Part and to any directions of the court, the evidence of a witness may be given either—

- **(a) orally before the court; or**
- **(b) in a witness statement.**

(3) The court may also receive evidence in documentary or any other form.

(4) A party is entitled to adduce evidence and to cross-examine witnesses during any part of a hearing from which a party and that party's legal representative are not excluded.

(5) The court may require a witness to give evidence on oath or by affirmation.

Search for, filing of and service of material

79.23—(1) A party (the disclosing party) must— 79.23

- **(a) make a reasonable search for material relevant to the matters under consideration in the proceedings to which this Part applies; and**
- **(b) file and serve on the other party and any special advocate material other than closed material—**
  - **(i) on which the disclosing party relies;**
  - **(ii) which adversely affects the disclosing party's case;**
  - **(iii) which adversely affects the other party's case; or**
  - **(iv) which supports the other party's case.**

(2) The factors relevant in deciding the reasonableness of a search under paragraph (1)(a) include—

- **(a) the amount of material involved;**
- **(b) the nature and complexity of the proceedings;**
- **(c) whether the material is in the control of the party making the search;**
- **(d) the ease and expense of retrieval of any material; and**
- **(e) the significance of any material which is likely to be located during the search.**

(3) The duty to search for, file and serve material under paragraph (1) continues until the proceedings to which this Part applies have been determined.

(4) Where material, other than closed material, to which the duty under paragraph (1) extends comes to a party's attention before the proceedings to which this Part applies have been determined, that party must immediately—

- **(a) file it with the court;**
- **(b) serve it on the other party; and**
- **(c) serve it on any special advocate.**

Redacted material

79.24 Where the Treasury serve on another party any evidence 79.24

(including a witness statement) or material which has been redacted on grounds other than those of legal professional privilege, the Treasury must—

(a) notify the party that the evidence or material has been redacted and on what grounds it has been redacted;

(b) file the evidence or material with the court in an unredacted form together with an explanation of the redaction.

Application to withhold closed material

79.25 **79.25—(1) The Treasury—**

(a) must apply to the court for permission to withhold closed material from another party and that party's legal representative in accordance with this rule; and

(b) may not rely on closed material at a hearing unless a special advocate has been appointed and attends the hearing to represent the interests of that party.

(2) The Treasury must file with the court and serve, at such time as the court directs, on the special advocate—

(a) the closed material;

(b) a statement of the reasons for withholding that material from the specially represented party; and

(c) if the Treasury consider it possible to summarise that material without disclosing information contrary to the public interest, a summary of that material in a form which can be served on the specially represented party or that party's legal representative.

(3) Where the Treasury serve on the special advocate any closed material which has been redacted on grounds other than those of legal professional privilege—

(a) the Treasury must file with the court the material in an unredacted form together with an explanation of the redactions; and

(b) the court will give a direction to the Treasury as to what may be redacted and what, if any, must be served on the special advocate in an undredacted form.

(4) The Treasury may at any time amend or supplement material filed under this rule, but only with—

(a) the agreement of the special advocate; or

(b) the permission of the court.

Consideration of the Treasury's application

79.26 **79.26—(1) Where the Treasury apply in accordance with rule 79.25 for permission to withhold closed material the court will fix a hearing for the Treasury and the special advocate to make oral representations, unless—**

(a) the special advocate gives notice to the court that the special advocate does not challenge the application;

(b) the court—

(i) has previously considered an application for

permission to withhold the same or substantially the same material; and

(ii) is satisfied that it would be just to give permission without a hearing; or

(c) the Treasury and the special advocate consent to the court deciding the issue without a hearing.

(2) If the special advocate does not challenge the application, the special advocate must give notice of that fact to the court and to the Treasury—

(a) within 14 days after the Treasury serve on the special advocate the material under rule 79.25(2); or

(b) within such other period as the court may direct.

(3) Where the court fixes a hearing under paragraph (1)—

(a) the special advocate may file with the court and serve on the Treasury a reply to the Treasury's application;

(b) the Treasury may file with the court and serve on the special advocate a response to the special advocate's reply; and

(c) the Treasury and the special advocate must file with the court at least 7 days before the hearing a schedule identifying the issues which cannot be agreed between them and which must—

(i) give brief reasons for their contentions on each issue in dispute; and

(ii) set out any proposals for the court to resolve the issues in dispute.

(4) A hearing under this rule must take place in the absence of the specially represented party and that party's legal representative.

(5) The court will give permission to the Treasury to withhold closed material where it considers that disclosure of that material would be contrary to the public interest.

(6) Where the court gives permission to the Treasury to withhold closed material, the court will—

(a) consider whether to direct the Treasury to serve a summary of that material on the specially represented party or that party's legal representative; but

(b) ensure that such a summary does not contain material, the disclosure of which would be contrary to the public interest.

(7) Where the court does not give permission to the Treasury to withhold closed material from, or directs the Treasury to serve a summary of that material on, the specially represented party or that party's legal representative—

(a) the Treasury are not required to serve that material or summary; but

(b) if they do not do so, at a hearing on notice, the court may—

(i) where it considers that the material or anything that is required to be summarised might ad-

versely affect the Treasury's case or supports the case of the specially represented party, direct that the Treasury must not rely on such material in their case, or must make such concessions or take such other steps, as the court may specify; or

(ii) in any other case, direct that the Treasury do not rely on the material or (as the case may be) on that which is required to be summarised.

Failure to comply with directions

79.27 **79.27—(1) Where a party or special advocate fails to comply with a direction of the court, the court may serve on that party or the special advocate a notice which states—**

(a) the respect in which that party or special advocate has failed to comply with the direction;

(b) a time limit for complying with the direction; and

(c) that the court may proceed to determine the proceedings before it, on the material available to it, if the party or special advocate fails to comply with the relevant direction within the time specified.

(2) Where a party or special advocate fails to comply with such a notice, the court may proceed in accordance with paragraph (1)(c).

Judgments

79.28 **79.28—(1) When the court gives judgment in any proceedings to which this Part applies, it may withhold all or some of its reasons if and to the extent that it is not possible to give reasons without disclosing information contrary to the public interest.**

(2) Where the judgment of the court does not include the full reasons for its decision, the court will serve on the Treasury and the special advocate a separate written judgment including those reasons.

(3) Where the court serves a separate written judgment under paragraph (2), the special advocate may apply to the court to amend that judgment and the judgment under paragraph (1) on the grounds that the separate written judgment under paragraph (2) contains material not in the judgment under paragraph (1) the disclosure of which would not be contrary to the public interest.

(4) The special advocate must serve a copy of the application under paragraph (3) on the Treasury.

(5) The court will give the special advocate and the Treasury an opportunity to file written submissions and may determine the application with or without a hearing.

Application by Treasury for reconsideration of order, direction or *judgment*

79.29 **79.29—(1) This rule applies where the court proposes, in any proceedings to which this Part applies, to serve on a party other than the Treasury—**

(a) notice of any order or direction made or given in the absence of the Treasury; or
(b) any written judgment.

(2) Before the court serves any such notice or judgment on a party other than the Treasury, it will first serve notice on the Treasury of its intention to do so.

(3) The Treasury may, within 5 days of being served with notice under paragraph (2), apply to the court to reconsider the terms of the order or direction or to review the terms of the proposed judgment if they consider—

(a) their compliance with the order or direction; or
(b) the notification to another party of any matter contained in the judgment, order or direction,

would cause information to be disclosed contrary to the public interest.

(4) Where the Treasury make an application under paragraph (3), they must at the same time serve on a special advocate, if one has been appointed—

(a) a copy of the application;
(b) a copy of the relevant document referred to in paragraph (1)(a) or (b); and
(c) a copy of the notice served on the Treasury pursuant to paragraph (2).

(5) If a special advocate has been appointed, rule 79.26 (except for paragraphs (6) and (7)) will apply with any necessary modifications to the consideration of an application under paragraph (3) of this rule.

(6) The court will not serve notice on a party other than the Treasury as mentioned in paragraph (1) before the time for the Treasury to make an application under paragraph (3) has expired.

Supply of court documents

79.30 Unless the court directs otherwise, rule 5.4 (Register of Claims), rule 5.4B (Supply of documents from court records—a party) and rule 5.4C (Supply of documents from court records—a non-party) do not apply to any proceedings to which this Part applies or to any document relating to such proceedings. 79.30

SCHEDULE 1

RSC ORDER 17—INTERPLEADER

Contents sc17.0.1

Editorial introduction

Interpleader proceedings arise where a person, who himself makes no claim to property, faces competing claims from others to the property The interpleader action is commenced by the party facing the claims with the objective of removing himself from the dispute and protecting himself from the competing claims; the court then decides the rival claims. **sc17.0.2**

There are two categories of interpleader action; those arising during the execution of a judgment (in the High Court this is termed the "sheriffs interpleader" and in the County Court this is the "interpleader under execution") and those arising other than by execution for example where the proceedings are issued by a stakeholder. Interpleader under execution or sheriffs interpleader arises where a bailiff or sheriff seeks to levy execution on goods in the possession of the judgment debtor but which are claimed by another. The bailiff or sheriff will notify the execution creditor of the claim. The interpleader process follows unless the creditor admits the claim. Examples of stakeholder interpleader would be a solicitor or estate agent holding a deposit which is claimed by both the seller or the buyer or a carrier holding goods which are claimed by two or more persons alleging title.

In the High Court, interpleader proceedings are governed by RSC O.17 (CPR Sch.1.) and the County Court by CCR O.33 (CPR Sch.2). Although the procedures both have the same underlying objective they remain distinct, despite the introduction of the CPR. It has not been possible to create a unified procedural code because of the anomalous function of the district judge as the high bailiff in the county court (the County Courts Act 1984 (Sch.3, para.7) preserves the status of the district judge (formerly registrar) as the high bailiff of the County Court; the district judge is responsible for the acts and defaults of the himself and of the bailiffs appointed to assist him: s.123 of County Courts Act 1984.). Where an interpleader dispute arises during execution in the High Court the application is issued by the sheriff; the dispute is usually determined by the high court master or if the action is in the District Registry by the district judge (the dispute may be resolved by the summary procedure especially where the dispute is one of law alone (RSC O.17, r.5(2)(c))). In the County Court it is the district judge who issues the interpleader under execution and the matter is *heard by a circuit judge*. It follows that as long as s.123 of the County Courts Act 1984 remains in force, the procedure for interpleader actions arising by way of execution (CCR O.33, r.4) will differ in the High Court and County Court.

Features of interpleader actions—High Court and County Court

(i) application is made by claim form (the Pt 8 procedure is used in CPR PD 8B, Section A) unless made in existing proceedings when it is made by application under Pt 23 (RSC O.17, r.3) **sc17.0.3**

(ii) the layout of RSC O.17 and CCR O.33 is different The High Court rule is drafted so that the procedures arising by way of execution and those arising out of a stakeholders interpleader are combined but the County Court rule is in two parts; Pt 1 deals with interpleader proceedings under execution and Pt II with claims other than under execution (see the introduction above for the substantive difference in the rules because of the role of the district judge and the effect of s.123 of the County Courts Act 1984).

(iii) during the execution of a judgment the execution creditor has an opportunity to admit the competing claim and if he does so the sheriff or bailiff may withdraw and the interpleader will not be required (RSC O.17, r.(2) and CCR O.33, r.4(1)).

(iv) in a stakeholders interpleader the application must be supported by evidence (RSC O.17, r.3(4) and CCR O.33, r.6(3)) ; evidence is not required where the application is made by a sheriff or district judge during the execution of a judgment

(v) in a stakeholders interpleader the applicant must specify in his application that he has no claims in the subject matter in dispute other than for charges and costs and that he does not collude with any of the interpleader claimants plus the applicant must be willing to pay the subject matter into court or to dispose of it as the court may direct (RSC O.17, r.3(4)(a) to (c) and CCR O.33, r.6(3)(a) to (c))

(vi) the court gives directions for the conduct of the interpleader action which will include for example specifying which of the parties is to be treated as interpleader claimant and which as defendant and where the dispute is suitable for the summary procedure (RSC O.17, r.(1)(b))

(vii) in a stakeholders interpleader the relief is available where the applicant has been sued by rival claimants or expects to be sued (RSC O.17, r.1(1) (a) and CCR O.33, r.6(1))

(viii) the relief is available where the property in dispute is a debt or goods (RSC O.17, r.1(1) (a) and CCR O.33, r.6(1))

(ix) the interpleader action is a separate action distinct from the execution process or the original action (*James v Ricknell* (1888) 20 Q.B.D. 64; thus a solicitor acting under an ordinary retainer in the action is not authorised to engage in interpleader proceedings without first obtaining instructions to act from his client)

(x) a key difference between the High Court and county court procedures is that during the execution of a judgment the interpleader is issued by the sheriff and in the county court it is issued by the district judge.

History of Rules

sc17.0.4 Before the Interpleader Act 1831 (now repealed and replaced by RSC O.17) a party faced with competing claims would have had to defend both actions or a file a 'bill in equity' (called a bill of interpleader). RSC O.17 and CCR O.33 were subject to some cosmetic amendment with the introduction of the Civil Procedure Rules; more radical amendment is anticipated when the procedures come under review as part of the Enforcement Review; but there must be a statutory provision to disapply s.123 of the County Courts Act 1984 (see reference to the role of the District Judge as high bailiff in the editorial introduction (above)).

Courts Act 2003

sc17.0.5 The Courts Act 2003 abolished the responsibilities and liabilities if the sheriff for execution of High Court judgments and transferred them to High Court enforcement officers. Unfortunately RSC O.17 has not been amended to reflect this change and still refers to the sheriff. We reproduce the rule as it still appears. However, for practical purposes the term "sheriff" needs to be read as if the term "High Court enforcement officer" were used.

Related sources

sc17.0.6
- CPR Part 3—The courts case management powers
- CPR Part 8—Alternative Procedure for claims
- *CPR Part 23—General* Rules about applications for Court Orders
- CCR O.33—Interpleader Proceedings
- Crown Proceedings Act 1947 s.16 (Vol.2, Section 9B)

Forms

- **PF23QB** Notice of claim to goods taken in execution sc17.0.7
- **PF24QB** Notice by claimant of admission or dispute of title of interpleader claimant
- **PF25QB** Interpleader application by defendant
- **PF26QB** Interpleader application by sheriff
- **PF27QB** Evidence in support at interpleader application
- **PF28QB** Interpleader order (1) claim barred where sheriff interpleads
- **PF29QB** Interpleader order (1a) sheriff to withdraw
- **PF30QB** Interpleader order (2) interpleader claimant substituted as defendant
- **PF31QB** Interpleader order (3) trial of issue
- **PF32QB** Interpleader order (4) conditional order for sheriff to withdraw and trial of issue
- **PF34QB** Interpleader order (6) summary disposal
- **N276** Notice of hearing of Interpleader Proceedings transferred from High Court
- **N277** Notice of Pre-trial Review of Interpleader Proceedings transferred from High Court

Entitlement to relief by way of interpleader[1]

1.—(1) Where— sc17.1

(a) a person is under a liability in respect of a debt or in respect of any money, goods or chattels and he is, or expects to be, sued for or in respect of that debt or money or those goods or chattels by two or more persons making adverse claims thereto, or

(b) claim is made to any money, goods or chattels taken or intended to be taken by a sheriff in execution under any process, or to the proceeds or value of any such goods or chattels, by a person other than the person against whom the process is issued,

the person under liability as mentioned in sub-paragraph (a) or (subject to rule 2) the sheriff, may apply to the court for relief by way of interpleader.

(2) References in this Order to a sheriff shall be construed as including references to—

(a) an individual authorised to act as an enforcement officer under the Courts Act 2003; and

(b) any other officer charged with the execution of process by or under the authority of the High Court.

"Applicability of Rule"

These rules apply to both sheriffs interpleader and those arising other than by execution (Contrast CCR Order 33 where the rules concerning the different types of interpleader are in separate parts of the rule). sc17.1.1

"where a person is under a liability in respect of a debt"

The applicant may interplead as to so much of a debt as he admits, the dispute as to the residue being settled separately (*Reading v London School Board* (1886) 16 Q.B.D. 686). A liability to unliquidated damages is not a "debt" for this purpose (*Walter v Nicholson* (1838) 6 Dowl. 517; *Ingham v Walker* (1887) 3 T.L.R. 448, CA. *cf. Attenborough v London and St. Katharine's Dock Co* (1878) 3 C.P.D. 450, CA, where a separate claim for damages was reserved, and *cf. Ex p. Mersey Docks* [1899] 1 Q.B. 546, CA). A debt due but not yet payable is presumably within the words of the rule (*Reading v London School Board*). The Court will not entertain proceedings to determine the right to winnings sc17.1.2

[1] Amended by the Civil Procedure (Amendment No.5) Rules 2003 (SI 2003/3361).

under a gaming contract (*Shoolbred v Roberts* [1900] 2 Q.B. 497 at 501 and 502; and see *Applegarth v Colley* (1842) 2 Dowl. 223; *Dowson v Macfarlane* (1899) 81 L.T. 67; *Hill v William Hill (Park Lane Ltd)* [1949] A.C. 530).

"goods, or chattels"

sc17.1.3 Chattels is "one of the widest words known to the law in its relation to personal property" (per Fry L.J. in *Robinson v Jenkins* (1890) 24 Q.B.D. 275, at 279). It includes shares in a company (*ibid.*) and, *semble,* title deeds to property (*Roberts v Bell* (1857) 7 E. & B. 323). "Liability in respect of any goods or chattels" includes a claim by a claimant to a mere lien over or a right to possession of goods (*Jennings v Mather* [1902] 1 K.B. 1, CA).

"expects to be sued ... by two or more persons"

sc17.1.4 There must be a real foundation for the expectation (*Harrison v Payne* (1836) 2 Hodges 107; *Diplock v Hammond* (1854) 23 L.J.Ch. 550; *Watson v Park Royal Caterers* [1961] 1 W.L.R. 727). A person cannot protect himself by interpleader proceedings against a claim on which the claimant has obtained judgment (*Stevenson & Son, Ltd v Brownell* [1912] 2 Ch. 344 (a judgment by consent); *Randall v Lithgow* (1884) 12 Q.B.D. 525 (a garnishee order absolute)). The fact, however, that the applicant may be legally liable to both defendants may be a ground for refusing him relief (*Farr v Ward* (1837) 2 M. & W. 244; *Crawford v Fisher* (1842) 1 Hare 436, at 441; *Victor Söhne v British, etc., Steam Navigation* [1888] W.N. 84; *Sablicich v Russell* (1866) L.R. 2 Eq. 441. Compare *Ex p. Mersey Docks* [1899] 1 Q.B. 546 where relief was given, the question of an estoppel in favour of one claimant being reserved).

"making adverse claims thereto"

sc17.1.5 There must be adverse claims to the same property or debt (*Greatorex v Shackle* [1895] 2 Q.B. 249, where two auctioneers were each claiming a commission under a separate contract on the same sale of the same house, and relief was refused; *Wright v Freeman* (1879) 48 L.J. C.P. 276; *Wright v Freeman* (1879) 48 L.J.C.P. 276; *Sun Insurance Office v Galinsky* [1914] K.B. 545).

"claim is made to any money, goods, or chattels"

sc17.1.6 The claim must be actual and not merely anticipated (*Isaac v Spilsbury* (1833) 2 Dowl. 211; *Bentley v Hook* (1834) 2 Dowl. 339; *Salmon v James* (1832) 1 Dowl. 369; *Day v Waldock* (1833) 1 Dowl. 523). A claim to a lien or right of possession over the goods, and not to the absolute property, is within these words (see *Ford v Baynton* (1832) 1 Dowl. 357; *Green v Stevens* (1857) 2 H. & N. 146)—for example, a claim by the hirer under a hiring or hire-purchase agreement.

"taken or intended to be taken ... in execution under any process"

sc17.1.7 There must have been either an actual seizure or an intention of the sheriff to seize (*Day v Carr* (1852) 7 Ex. 883; *Lea v Rossi* (1855) 11 Ex. 13). The fact that the goods are seized in the possession of the claimant or a third person and not in that of the judgment debtor does not, of course, affect the sheriff's right to interplead (*Allen v Gibbon* (1833) 2 Dowl. 292; *Aylwin v Evans* (1883) 52 L.J. Ch. 105). But if the sheriff, after seizure, has withdrawn from possession (*Moore v Hawkins* (1894) 43 W.R. 235) or delivered up the goods seized to the claimant (*Braine v Hunt* (1834) 2 Dowl. 391) or sold them and paid the proceeds to the execution creditor (*Anderson v Calloway* (1833) 1 Dowl. 636; *Inland v Bushell* (1836) 5 Dowl. 147) the court will not grant him relief (except under r.2(3)).

"or to the proceeds or value of any such goods or chattels"

sc17.1.8 Where a claimant pays the sheriff out under protest, the amount paid is "the proceeds or vaue of" the goods within this rule (*Smith v Critchfield* (1885) 14 Q.B.D. 873, CA) but the claimant cannot succeed unless he was entitled to the goods (*Plant v Collins* [1913] 1 K.B. 242).

"by a person other than the person against whom the process is issued"

sc17.1.9 The claim may be by the execution debtor if he claims not in his own right but as executor or trustee (*Fenwick v Laycock* (1841) 6 Jur. 341). A beneficiary under a trust may claim without joining trustees (*Schroeder v Hanrott* (1873) 28 LT 704).

"may apply to the Court for relief"

The application is usually heard and determined by the Master or district judge in the High Court. See also rr.3 and 5 **sc17.1.10**

Crown

These rules apply to the Crown: s.16 of the Crown Proceedings Act 1947 (Vol.2, Section 9B). **sc17.1.11**

Equitable rights

Equitable claims and rights can be asserted and protected by interpleader: see *Jennings v Mather* [1901] 1 K.B. 108 at 115 and cases there cited. **sc17.1.12**

Landlords

If the rent is owing to the landlord of the premises upon which goods are seized in execution, the sheriff is prohibited by the Landlord and Tenant Act 1709 from removing the goods after having notice of rent being due, until the rent owing (up to one year's arrears) has been paid. Should he remove or sell them before such rent has been paid, he would be liable to an action founded on the statute. Though the execution creditor could not compel him to sell, it became the practice for the sheriff to sell and pay the landlord out of the proceeds; but a sheriff is entitled to withdraw and return *nulla bona,* when it becomes clear that neither the execution creditor nor the tenant will pay the landlord. (See Lindley L.J., at pp.573–576 in *Re Mackenzie* [1899] 2 Q.B. 566, CA). A sheriff, therefore, upon the landlord claiming, cannot interplead (*Clarke v Lord* (1833) 2 Dowl. 55, 227; *cf. Bateman v Farnsworth* (1860) 29 L.J.Exch. 365). **sc17.1.13**

RSC

Claim by co-owner or partner

If goods are the property of A and B, who hold them jointly or as tenants in common, the sheriff can seize and sell them on a judgment against A and B or a judgment against either of them (subject to the question of the distribution of the proceeds)—see *Farrar v Beswick* (1836) 1 M. & W. 682, *per* Parke, B. p. 685; *Mayhew v Herrick* (1849) 7 C.B. 229 at 240, 248 and 250. The same applied to partnership property, but now, on a judgment against one partner, execution will not issue against partnership property (Partnership Act 1890 s.23) and instead a charging order can be obtained on the partner's interest (*ibid.*). If, on execution being levied on a judgment against one partner, another partner sets up the partnership, and the execution creditor disputes the partnership or denies that the goods seized are property of the partnership, the dispute is proper subject-matter for interpleader (see *Peake v Carter* [1916] 1 K.B. 652, *per* Swinfen Eady L.J. at 655–656). If the goods are admitted to be partnership property, the sheriff will be ordered to withdraw. **sc17.1.14**

Claim by debenture-holders

A debenture usually creates a floating charge on a company's assets, and only where the charge has been crystallised—e.g. by appointment of a receiver—before the completion of an execution by seizure and sale do the rights of the debenture holders have priority over those of the execution creditor (*Re Standard Manufacturing Co* [1891] 1 Ch. 627, CA; *Re Opera* [1891] 3 Ch. 260, CA; and see *Taunton v Sheriff of Warwickshire* [1895] 2 Ch. 319, CA; *Evans v Rival Granite Quarries* [1910] 2 K.B. 979, CA; *Robinson v Burnell's Bakery* [1904] 2 K.B. 624; *Heaton & Dugard v Cutting Bros.* [1925] 1 K.B. 655). **sc17.1.15**

Claim to goods, etc., taken in execution

2.—(1) Any person making a claim to or in respect of any money, goods or chattels taken or intended to be taken in execution under process of the court, or to the proceeds or value of any such goods or chattels, must give notice of his claim to the sheriff charged with the execution of the process and must include in his notice a statement of his address, and that address shall be his address for service. **sc17.2**

(2) On receipt of a claim made under this rule the sheriff must forthwith give notice thereof to the execution creditor and the execution creditor must, within seven days after receiving the notice, give notice to the sheriff informing him whether he admits or disputes the claim.

An execution creditor who gives notice in accordance with this paragraph admitting a claim shall only be liable to the sheriff for any fees and expenses incurred by the sheriff before receipt of that notice.

(3) Where—

(a) the sheriff receives a notice from an execution creditor under paragraph (2) disputing a claim, or the execution creditor fails, within the period mentioned in that paragraph, to give the required notice, and

(b) the claim made under this rule is not withdrawn,

the sheriff may apply to the court for relief under this order.

(4) A sheriff who receives a notice from an execution creditor under paragraph (2) admitting a claim made under this rule shall withdraw from possession of the money, goods or chattels claimed and may apply to the court for relief under this Order of the following kind, that is to say, an order restraining the bringing of a claim against him for or in respect of his having taken possession of that money or those goods or chattels.

"address for service"

sc17.2.1 See r.6.5 of CPR 1998.

"may apply to the court for relief"

sc17.2.2 No particular formality is required *Christopher Newman (trading as Mantella Publishing) and Modern Bookbinders Ltd* [2000] 1 W.L.R. 2559; [2000] 2 All E.R. 814; *Independent*, February 3, 2000, CA; however sufficient detail should be provided to the bailiff for him to identify which particular goods are claimed and why; the judge is not obliged to hear the interpleader if the particulars of claim are insufficient *Boswick v Boffey* (1854) 9 Exch 315.

Claim in respect of goods protected from seizure

sc17.2A 2A.—(1) Where a judgment debtor whose goods have been seized, or are intended to be seized, by a sheriff under a writ of execution claims that such goods are not liable to execution by virtue of section 138(3A) of the Act, he must within 5 days of the seizure give notice in writing to the sheriff identifying all those goods in respect of which he makes such a claim and the grounds of such claim in respect of each item.

(2) Upon receipt of a notice of claim under paragraph (1), the sheriff must forthwith give notice thereof to the execution creditor and to any person who has made a claim to, or in respect of, the goods under rule 2(1) and the execution creditor and any person who has made claim must, within 7 days of receipt of such notice, inform the sheriff in writing whether he admits or disputes the judgment debtor's claim in respect of each item.

(3) The sheriff shall withdraw from possession of any goods in respect of which the judgment debtor's claim is admitted or if the execution creditor or any person claiming under rule 2(1) fails to notify him in accordance with paragraph (2) and the sheriff shall so inform the parties in writing.

(4) Where the sheriff receives notice from—

(a) the execution creditor; or

(b) any such person to whom notice was given under paragraph (2),

that the claim or any part thereof is disputed, he must forthwith seek the directions of the court and may include therein an application for an order restraining the bringing of any claim against him for, or in respect of, his having seized any of those goods or his having failed so to do.

(5) The sheriff's application for directions under paragraph (4) shall be made by an application in accordance with CPR Part 23 and, on the hearing of the application, the court may—

(a) determine the judgment debtor's claim summarily; or

(b) give such directions for the determination of any issue raised by such claim as may be just.

(6) A Master and a district judge of a district registry shall have power to make an order of the kind referred to in paragraph (4) and the reference to Master shall be construed in accordance with rule 4.

Mode of application

3.—(1) An application for relief under this order must be made by claim form unless made in an existing claim, in which case it must be made in accordance with CPR Part 23. **sc17.3**

(2) Where the applicant is a sheriff who has withdrawn from possession of money, goods or chattels taken in execution and who is applying for relief under rule 2(4) the claim form must be served on any person who made a claim under that rule to or in respect of that money or those goods or chattels, and that person may attend the hearing of the application.

(4) Subject to paragraph (5) a claim form or application notice under this rule must be supported by evidence that the applicant—

(a) claims no interest in the subject-matter in dispute other than for charges or costs,

(b) does not collude with any of the claimants to that subject-matter; and

(c) is willing to pay or transfer that subject-matter into court or to dispose of it as the court may direct.

(5) Where the applicant is a sheriff, he shall not provide such evidence as is referred to in paragraph (4) unless directed by the court to do so.

(6) Any person who makes a claim under rule 2 and who is served with a claim form under this rule shall within 14 days serve on the execution creditor and the sheriff a witness statement or affidavit specifying any money and describing any goods and chattels claimed and setting out the grounds upon which such claim is based.

(7) Where the applicant is a sheriff a claim form under this rule must give notice of the requirement in paragraph (6).

"claim form"

The Pt 8 procedure is used. PD 8, Table 1, Section A. **sc17.3.1**

"in accordance with Part 23"

Part 23, and its supplementing Practice Direction (para.23PD.1) contain general rules about applications for court orders in existing proceedings. The application notice can be in Form **N244** (see para.2.1 of the Practice Direction). Note the requirement for an application notice to be verified by a statement of truth—see Pt 22. **sc17.3.2**

"must be served"

sc17.3.3 See generally, Pt 6. Service by the court is the general rule and service by post the general method (rr.6.2 and 6.3). The claim form or application notice must be served on each interpleader claimant otherwise no order can be made affecting him (*Lambert v Townsend* (1832) 1 L.J. Exch. 113) and only interpleader claimants who are parties as claimant or defendant (claim form) or applicant or respondent (application notice under Pt 23) will be heard (*Clarke v Lord* (1833) 2 Dowl. 53). For service out at the jurisdiction see CPR Pt 6, Sect.III and *Attenborough v London and St Katharine's Dock Co* (1877–78) L.R. 3 C.P.D. 450.

Authority of solicitor

sc17.3.4 A solicitor, retained in the case, has no implied authority to conduct interpleader proceedings (*James v Ricknell* (1888) 20 Q.B.D. 64).

"must be supported by evidence"

sc17.3.5 The evidence is best reduced to writing and given in the form of a witness statement of affidavit. Interpleader proceedings are unique in that the person seeking relief must be a truly disinterested party: hence the need for such evidence as required by O.17, r.3(4). In a sheriff's interpleader the sheriff is assumed to be disinterested and is thus not required to provide evidence in the first instance (O.17, r.3(5)). see *Fairfax Gerrard Holdings Ltd v Rasool Zargam* [2004] EWHC 2079 QB; a case decided on its individual facts and an example of a situation where the interpleader was rejected because the right was not promptly asserted and the supporting evidence implausible and poorly documented.

"other than for charges or costs"

sc17.3.6 A lien over goods for charges for storage, or over the proceeds of sale for commission on the sale, does not disentitle the applicant to relief (*Cotter v Bank of England* (1833) 2 Dowl. 728; *Best v Hayes* (1863) 1 Hurl. & C. 718; *De Rothschild Frères v Morrison, Kekewich & Co* (1890) 24 Q.B.D. 750, CA).

"that the applicant does not collude"

sc17.3.7 "Collusion" does not here necessarily entail anything morally wrong, but means "playing the same game" as one of the claimants (*Murietta v South American Co*; *Tucker v Morris* (1832) 1 C. & M. 73; 2 L.J.Exch. 1; and see, as to sheriffs, *Duddin v Long* (1834) 3 Dowl. 139); *Fredericks and Pelhams Timber Buildings v Wilkins, Read (Claimant)* [1971] 1 W.L.R. 119 at 1204; [1971] 3 All E.R. 545 at 550–551, CA) and where the applicant has agreed to do so, or has taken an indemnity from that claimant (*Murietta v South America Co*; *Thopson v Wright* (1884) 13 Q.B.D. 632) though that claimant cannot complain, there is collusion (*ibid.*). Similarly where the applicant has placed himself in the position of being sued at the request and in the interests of one claimant (*Belcher v Smith* (1832) 9 Bing. 82).

"any person who makes a claim"

sc17.3.8 Any person who claims the property or debt is required to serve a witness statement or affidavit within 14 days of service. O.17, r.3(6), in its present form imposes this requirement on such a person "who is served with a claim form". This should read (as does r.3(4)) "claim form or application notice": see r.3(1)—the application must be by application notice in accordance with Pt 23 if made in existing proceedings.

The witness statement or affidavit should be by the person who makes the claim and who will give evidence in support of the claim and not, e.g. by his solicitor (*Wood v Lyne* (1850) 4 DeG & Sm 16; *Nelson v Barker* (1864) 2 H. & M. 334). The person who makes the claim cannot call on the sheriff for particulars of the goods seized so as to assist him to make out his claim (*Bauly v Crook* (1891) 65 L.T. 377). Particulars of the claim must be stated with such precision as to enable the opposing claimant or the execution creditor to decide whether to oppose it, and the court to make an appropriate order (*Powell v Lock* (1835) 3 A. & E. 315; *Webster v Delafield* (1849) 7 C.B. 187).

To whom Sheriff may apply for relief

sc17.4 4. An application to the court for relief under this order may, if the applicant is a sheriff, be made—

(a) where the claim in question is proceeding in the Royal Courts of Justice, to a Master or, if the execution to which the application relates has been or is to be levied in the district of a District Registry, either to a Master or to the district judge of that Registry;

(b) where the claim in question is proceeding in a District Registry, to the district judge of that Registry or, if such execution has been or is to be levied in the district of some other District Registry or outside the district of any District Registry, either to the said district judge or to the district judge of that other Registry or to a Master as the case may be.

Where the claim in question is proceeding in the Admiralty Court or the Family Division, references in this rule to a Master shall be construed as references to the Admiralty Registrar or to a Registrar of that Division.

Powers of Court hearing claim

5.—(1) Where on the hearing of a claim under this order all the persons by whom adverse claims to the subject-matter in dispute (hereafter in this order referred to as "the interpleader claimants") appear, the court may order— **sc17.5**

(a) that any interpleader claimant be made a defendant in any claim pending with respect to the subject-matter in dispute in substitution for or in addition to the applicant for relief under this order, or

(b) that an issue between the interpleader claimants be stated and tried and may direct which of the interpleader claimants is to be claimant and which defendant.

(2) Where—

(a) the applicant under this order is a sheriff; or

(b) all the interpleader claimants consent or any of them so requests; or

(c) the question at issue between the interpleader claimants is a question of law and the facts are not in dispute,

the court may summarily determine the question at issue between the interpleader claimants and make an order accordingly on such terms as may be just.

(3) Where an interpleader claimant, having been duly served with a claim form under this order, does not appear at the hearing or, having appeared, fails or refuses to comply with an order made in the proceedings, the court may make an order declaring the interpleader claimant, and all persons claiming under him, for ever barred from prosecuting his claim against the applicant for such relief and all persons claiming under him, but such an order shall not affect the rights of the interpleader claimants as between themselves.

"the court may order"

On the hearing of the application the Master or district judge may make one of the following orders:— **sc17.5.1**

1. Dismiss the application —e.g. on the ground that the conditions of rr.1 and 3 are not satisfied. **sc17.5.2**

2. Decide the issue summarily —Summary disposal is the most usual and consent to a summary disposal is not required where the applicant is the sheriff (r.5(2)(a)). Summary disposal contrasts with ordering an issue to be stated and tried (see 3 below). **sc17.5.3**

Summary disposal is the course usually taken in straightforward cases and in sheriff's interpleaders. However, if the goods are of considerable value and difficult questions of law may arise, summary disposal is not appropriate even if the parties consent (*Fredericks and Pelhams Timber Buildings v Wilkins, Read (Claimant)* [1971] 1 W.L.R. 1197; [1971] 3 All E.R. 545, CA).

If the Master or district judge is to decide the case summarily it is usually necessary to adjourn to a fixed date giving all necessary case-management directions—e.g. as to evidence, disclosure or other interim steps. If the value of the goods justifies it, he may order the sheriff to prepare, file and serve an inventory (*Fredericks and Pelhams Timber Buildings v Wilkins, Read (Claimant)*). At the hearing the modern practice is for witness statements (or affidavits) to stand as evidence-in-chief upon which rival claimants can cross-examine. If supporting witnesses are to be called directions should be sought at the initial hearing as for filing and service of witness statements.

sc17.5.4 *3. Order that an issue be stated and tried* —Even if the issue is not tried summarily it is usual for the parties to consent to trial by the Master or district judge to save delay and costs.The order defines the issue which is to be tried, e.g. "whether the goods are the property of A (the claimant in the issue) as against B (the defendant in the issue)". The court can direct which of the rival interpleader claimants is to be claimant and which defendant (r.5(1)(b)). In a sheriff's interpleader the execution creditor is usually made defendant but will be made claimant if the goods were in the possession of the interpleader-claimant at the time of seizure.

The burden of proof is on the party made claimant to prove title to the goods. If he proves merely that they belonged to a third person, the defendant is entitled to succeed (*Richards v Jenkins* (1887) 18 Q.B.D. 451, CA; *Re Bordon v Westminster Bank* (1933) 49 T.L.R. 414, CA).

Where the applicant for relief is not the sheriff similar considerations apply. Where a bailee holds goods in the name of one of the interpleader claimants, that person will generally be made defendant (*De la Rue v Hernu, Peron and Stockwell Ltd* [1936] 2 K.B. 164, CA).

sc17.5.5 *4. Transfer the issue/proceedings to the county court* —The whole proceedings, or the issue, can be transferred to the county court for trial by a circuit judge. This was not commonly done in the past but is more likely under the unified CPR. In the High Court a sheriff's interpleader is usually summarily determined by the Master/district judge (see 2 above) but a bailiff's interpleader (the county court equivalent) must be heard by a circuit judge as—anomalously—the county court district judge (as successor to the high bailiff) is in the same position as the sheriff and is therefore, technically, the applicant for relief. In practice, interpleader proceedings are rarely before a High Court judge and are suitable for release to a circuit judge under s.9 of the SCA 1981. Transfer to the county court is thus a sensible alternative.

sc17.5.6 *5. Refer the dispute to arbitration* —If all interpleader claimants are parties to an arbitration agreement, the Court may order the issue between them to be determined under that agreement (see s.5 of the Arbitration Act 1950; Arbitration Act 1996; *Re Phoenix Timber Co Ltd's Application* [1958] 2 Q.B. 1; [1958] 1 All E.R. 815). In any event the court must further the overring objective by "encouraging the parties to use an alternative dispute resolution procedure ..."; r.1.4(2)(e) of the CPR 1998.

Payment into court

sc17.5.7 The court will wish to release the applicant for relief—the "stakeholder"—from the interpleader proceedings as soon as possible. Where the dispute concerns a debt or a sum of money the applicant can be released by ordering him to pay the sum into court having deducted his assessed (or agreed) costs of the application: these costs will ultimately be paid by the unsuccessful interpleader claimant.

Sale or deposit of goods

sc17.5.8 For the purpose of saving costs and sheriff's charges, and especially where the goods are perishable, an order may be made for the sale of the goods under r.6 (*Paquin v Robinson (1901) 85* L.T. 5, CA) or under r.8. Alternatively the court can order sale unless a payment into court is made or security given by the interpleader claimant (see Form **PF32QB**).

Where it is not appropriate for the goods to be sold (e.g. the dispute concerns a specific chattel) the court can order the property to be deposited in the joint names of the solicitors for the parties. Alternatively, it may release the property to one of the interpleader claimants on his giving security or paying into court a sum representing the value of the goods.

Power to order sale of goods taken in execution

6. Where an application for relief under this order is made by a sheriff who has taken possession of any goods or chattels in execution under any process, and an interpleader claimant alleges that he is entitled, under a bill of sale or otherwise, to the goods or chattels by way of security for debt, the court may order those goods or chattels or any part thereof to be sold and may direct that the proceeds of sale be applied in such manner and on such terms as may be just and as may be specified in the order. **sc17.6**

Effect of rule

See "sale or deposit of goods" at para.sc17.5.8. **sc17.6.1**

Seizure of mortgaged goods

The sheriff is not bound to seize under a writ of *fi. fa.* goods in which the judgment debtor's interest is only an equitable one, but can, on ascertaining this, withdraw and make a return of *nulla bona* (*Scarlett v Hanson* (1884) 12 Q.B.D. 213, CA). He can, however, on claim being made to such goods so seized by him, interplead, and if he does so, the jurisdiction to make an order for sale under this rule arises. The object of the rule is, whilst protecting the rights of the secured creditor, to render any surplus realised, after due protection of such rights, available to satisfy the claim of the execution creditor (see *per*Lindley M.R. in *Stern v Tegner* [1898] 1 Q.B. 37 at 41). If the security is plainly enough to leave a surplus for the execution creditor, the bill of sale holder will not be allowed to defeat him: a sale will be ordered. If the security is plainly deficient, the sheriff will be ordered to withdraw. But if it is doubtful whether the security is or is not sufficient to pay off the secured creditor, the court will refuse to order a sale unless the execution creditor guarantees the secured creditor against loss by sale (*ibid.*). **sc17.6.2**

Power to stay proceedings

7. Where a defendant to a claim applies for relief under this Order in the claim, the court may by order stay all further proceedings in the claim. **sc17.7**

Effect of rule

The rule gives express power to stay. If the applicant for relief (the "stakeholder") is already being sued and is therefore defendant in an existing case, and the claimant in that case and a third person (the interpleader claimant) both claim from him the same money or goods, the simplest course may be to substitute the interpleader claimant as defendant in the existing case: see Form **PF30QB**. **sc17.7.1**

Other powers

8.—(1) Subject to the foregoing rules of this Order, the court may in or for the purposes of any interpleader proceedings make such order as to costs or any other matter as it thinks just. **sc17.8**

(2) Where the interpleader claimant fails to appear at the hearing, the Court may direct that the sheriff's and execution creditor's costs shall be assessed by a master or, where the hearing was heard in a district registry, by a district judge of that registry and the following CPR rules shall apply—

(a) 44.4 (basis of assessment);

(b) 44.5 (factors to be taken into account in deciding the amount of costs);

(c) 48.4 (limitations on court's power to award costs in favour of trustee or personal representative); and

(d) 48.6 (litigants in persons).

(3) Where the claim in question is proceeding in the Admiralty Court or the Family Division, references in this rule to a Master shall be construed as references to the Admiralty Register or to a Registrar of that Division.

"order as to costs"

sc17.8.1 In a sheriff's interpleader, where the interpleader claimant fails the sheriff is entitled to his costs (including possession money) from the time of notice of the claim or from sale, whichever is earlier. Where the interpleader claimant succeeds, the sheriff is entitled to his costs as against the execution creditor from the time when the creditor made it necessary for the sheriff to interplead. However, in either case, as a general rule, the sheriff recovers his costs from the execution creditor who, if successful, has a remedy over against the interpleader claimant. A successful interpleader claimant will generally be awarded costs against the execution creditor.

In a stakeholders interpleader, the applicant is usually required to pay the disputed sum into court (see "Payment into Court" at para.sc17.5.7) having deducted his assessed costs to date leaving open the issue (now to be determined) which of the interpleader claimants will ultimately bear those costs (*Searle v Matthews* (1887) 19 Q.B.D. 79; *Smith v Darlow* (1884) 26 Ch. D. 605, CA). Costs are discretionary and in an appropriate case the stakeholder can be refused costs (*Elder Dempster Lines v Ishag, The Lycaon* [1983] 2 Lloyd's Rep. 538).

The amount of costs will generally be assessed by summary assessment (see CPR Part 43 and Practice Direction About Costs, see para.48PD.1).

"order as to ... any other matter"

sc17.8.2 "Other matters" include the charges (referred to in r.8) of a stakeholder, e.g. a warehouseman with whom the goods have been stored; and the unsuccessful claimant who stored them may be ordered to pay his charges (*De Rothschild Frères v Morrison, Kekewich & Co* (1890) 24 Q.B.D. 750). If the execution creditor fails in the issue, the sheriff will not be allowed to retain the amount of his charges out of the proceeds of sale. The powers of the court are wide and may be exercised notwithstanding that the order may interfere with property rights (*B.P. Benzin und Petroleum A.G. v European-American Banking Corp* [1978] 1 Lloyd's Rep. 364).

"Other matters" also include the sale of the goods pending the decision of the interpleader (*Paguin v Robinson* (1901) 85 L.T. 5, CA). In *P. B. J. Davis Manufacturing Co v Fahn, Fahn (Claimant)* [1967] 1 W.L.R. 1059; [1967] 2 All E.R. 1274, CA, the claim had been allowed by the Master and the CA ordered a new trial and directed that the sheriff do retake posession and his possession be deemed to have continued without interruption, and that he was not to be liable for any dealings with the goods in the meantime.

Orders barring future actions

sc17.8.3 Power is given under r.2(4) or under this rule to order that no action may be brought against a sheriff who has interpleaded and such an order—"no action"—is ordinarily made. It may be refused if the court thinks that it would be unjust to deprive an injured party of a right of action, as, for instance if the sheriff has acted oppressively or if the claimant has a substantial grievance against the sheriff. The principles have been explained by the Court of Appeal in *Neumann v Bakeway Ltd* [1983] 1 W.L.R. 1016; [1983] 2 All E.R. 935, and by Glidewell J. in *The Observer Ltd v Gordon* [1983] 1 W.L.R. 1008; [1983] 2 All E.R. 945.

A sheriff who acts in good faith will be protected by s.138B of the Supreme Court Act 1981, accordingly the claimant must show an arguable claim which would override the Sheriff's defences (*ibid.*).

There may also be power to bar an action against the execution creditor (*Carpenter v Pearce* (1858) 27 L.J.Exch. 143), but there has been no such order for very many years; generally speaking the execution creditor is not liable for the sheriff's acts (*Barclays Bank Ltd v Roberts* [1954] 1 W.L.R. 1212; [1954] 3 All E.R. 107, following *Williams v Williams & Nathan* [1937] 2 All E.R. 559).

One order in several proceedings

9. Where the court considers it necessary or expedient to make an order in any interpleader proceedings in several proceedings pending in several Divisions, or before different Judges of the same Division, the court may make such an order; and the order shall be entitled in all those causes or matters and shall be binding on all the parties to them. **sc17.9**

Disclosure

10. CPR Parts 31 and 18 shall, with the necessary modifications, apply in relation to an interpleader issue as they apply in relation to any other proceedings. **sc17.10**

Trial of interpleader issue

11.—(1) CPR Part 39 shall, with the necessary modifications, apply to the trial of an interpleader issue as it applies to the trial of a claim. **sc17.11**

(2) The court by whom an interpleader issue is tried may give such judgment or make such order as finally to dispose of all questions arising in the interpleader proceedings.

RSC ORDER 45—ENFORCEMENT OF JUDGMENTS AND ORDERS: GENERAL

Contents

sc45.0.1

Editorial introduction

The methods of enforcement of judgments and orders of the High Court are now contained in Sch.1, RSC Ords 45, 46, 47 and 52 and in Pts 70 to 74. They should be read together as comprising the various ways in which the successful party (now the "judgment creditor") can employ the machinery of the High Court towards obtaining satisfaction of its judgment or compelling compliance therewith or obedience thereto. It is still a feature of the civil justice system that judgments are not enforced automatically by the court. It is for the judgment creditor to decide when and how to enforce the judgment. **sc45.0.2**

The rules on enforcement do not apply against the Crown (CPR r.66.6 and see *Franklin v The Queen (No.2)* [1974] Q.B. 205; [1973] 3 All E.R. 861).

The rules do apply to a judgment or order of the Court of Appeal as they apply to the High Court (Supreme Court Act 1981 s.1(4)). For enforcement of House of Lords judgments see para.13 of PD 40B and CPR r.70.5.

Although the term "writ" is no longer used for originating process (see Pt 7) it continues in use in the context of enforcement.

See further Practice Direction—Enforcement of Judgments and Orders at para.70PD.1.

Related sources

sc45.0.3

- Practice Direction—Enforcement of Judgments and Orders (see para.70PD.1)
- Part 70—General Rules about Enforcement of Judgments and Orders
- Part 71—Order to obtain information from judgment debtors
- Part 72—Third Party Debt Orders
- Part 73—Charging Orders, Stop Orders and Stop Notices
- RSC O.17—Interpleader
- RSC O.46—Writs of Execution: General
- RSC O.47—Writs of Fieri Facias
- RSC O.51—Receivers: Equitable Execution
- RSC O.52—Committal
- CCR O.25—Enforcement of Judgments and Orders: General
- Queen's Bench Guide, Section 11, Vol.2, para.1A–71

Forms

sc45.0.4 The following forms (formerly included amongst the Prescribed Forms in Appendix A to the RSC) are relevant to O.45. These forms are included in Table 2 (Practice Forms) attached to Practice Direction (Forms) at para.4PD.1.

- **No.50** Judgment for defendant's costs on discontinuance (r.15)
- **No.51** Judgment for costs after acceptance of money paid into court (r.15)
- **No.53** Writ of *fieri facias* (r.12)
- **No.54** Writ of *fieri facias* on order for costs (r.12)
- **No.55** Notice of Seizure (r.2)
- **No.56** Writ of *fieri facias* after levy of part (r.12)
- **No.57** Writ of *fieri facias* against personal representative (r.12)
- **No.58** Writ of *fieri facias* de bonis ecclesiastics (r.12)
- **No.59** Writ of sequestrari de bonis ecclesiasticis (r.12)
- **No.62** Writ of *fieri facias* to enforce Northern Irish or Scottish judgment
- **No.63** Writ of *fieri facias* to enforce foreign registered judgment
- **No.64** Writ of delivery: delivery of goods, damages and costs (r.12)
- **No.65** Writ of delivery: delivery of goods or value, damages, costs (r.12)
- **No.66** Writ of possession (r.12)
- **No.66A** Writ of possession under Order 113 (r.12)
- **No.67** Writ of sequestration (r.12)
- **PF86** Praecipe for writ of *fieri facias*
- **PF87** Praecipe for writ of sequestration (O.45)
- **PF88** Praecipe for writ of possession (O.45)
- **PF89** Praecipe for writ of possession and *fieri facias* combined (O.45)
- **PF90** Praecipe for writ of delivery (O.45)
- **PF141** Evidence of personal service of judgment or order (O.45, r.7)

High Court Enforcement Officers

sc45.0.5 Since April 1, 2004 High Court Enforcement Officers, and not the Sheriff, have been responsible for the execution of High Court writs of execution. The forms of writ were changed to reflect this and are now addressed to the HCEO. Officers are subject to the High Court Enforcement Officers Regulations 2004 (SI 2004/400). These regulations can be found in Vol.2 Section 9B at para.9B–1247 *et seq.*

Editorial note

Most of RSC O.45, r.1 was revoked by Civil Procedure (Amendment No.4) Rules 2001 which introduced Pts 70 to 73. The matters previously dealt with by O.45, r.1 are now dealt with in Pt 70 and its supplementing Practice Direction. However, save for the fact that they are now executed by High Court Enforcement Officers and not Sheriff's Officers, there have been no changes to writs of *fi-fa*, the most common method of enforcement. The detailed commentary on writ of *fi-fa*, which previously appeared as commentary to RSC O.45 is now to be found in the commentary to RSC O.46. **sc45.1.1**

Interpretation[1]

1A. Rule 1A in this Order, and in RSC Orders 46 and 47— **sc45.1A**

(a) "enforcement officer" means an individual who is authorised to act as an enforcement officer under the Courts Act 2003; and

(b) "relevant enforcement officer" means—

(i) in relation to a writ of execution which is directed to an single enforcement officer, that officer;

(ii) in relation to a writ of execution which is directed to two or more enforcement officers, the officer to whom the writ is allocated.

High Court Enforcement Officers

By s.99 and Sch.7 Courts Act 2003, Sheriffs are no longer responsible for enforcement of High Court writs of execution. Enforcement is now undertaken by High Court Enforcement Officers. (The High Court Enforcement Officers Regulations 2004 (SI 2004/400) (which include prescribed fees) are in Vol.2 at Section 9B). One important change is that the judgment creditor (rather than, as formerly, the Under-Sheriff) can choose which HCEO to instruct to enforce the writ. No doubt, over time, solicitors will develop a working relationship with particular HCEOs. The HCEO is no longer confined to a particular bailiwick. Bailiwicks are abolished and the country is divided into areas by post-code but the jurisdiction of a HCEO is not confined to a particular area. On issue, the writ can be addressed to a particular HCEO for the relevant post-code of the judgment debtor. **sc45.1A.1**

A complete list of HCEOs appears in Vol.2, Appendix 1 paras AP–10 and AP–12.

The High Court Enforcement Officers Association website at *www.hceoa.org.uk* has a search facility by name of HCEO and by post code. All Court Offices have a copy of the Directory of HCEOs but court officers cannot give advice or recommend a particular HCEO. There is an option of putting the postal area on the writ instead of the name of a particular HCEO in which case the writ will be allocated in strict rotation through the HCEOA's central database.

Notice of seizure[2]

2. When first executing a writ of fieri facias, the Sheriff or his officer or the relevant enforcement officer shall deliver to the debtor or leave at each place where execution is levied a notice in Form **No. 55** in the relevant Practice Direction informing the debtor of the execution. **sc45.2**

Writ of fieri facias

See detailed commentary at paras sc46.1.1 *et seq*. **sc45.2.1**

Enforcement of judgment for possession of land

3.—(1) Subject to the provisions of these rules, a judgment or order for the giving of possession of land may be enforced by one or more of the following means, that is to say— **sc45.3**

(a) writ of possession;

[1] Introduced by Civil Procedure (Amendment No.5) Rules 2003 (SI 2003/3361).
[2] Amended by Civil Procedure (Amendment No.5) Rules 2003 (SI 2003/3361).

RSC

(b) in a case in which rule 5 applies, an order of committal;

(c) in such a case, writ of sequestration.

(2) A writ of possession to enforce a judgment or order for the giving of possession of any land shall not be issued without the permission of the court except where the judgment or order was given or made in proceedings by a mortgagee or mortgagor or by any person having the right to foreclose or redeem any mortgage, being proceedings in which there is a claim for—

(a) payment of moneys secured by the mortgage;

(b) sale of the mortgaged property;

(c) foreclosure;

(d) delivery of possession (whether before or after foreclosure or without foreclosure) to the mortgagee by the mortgagor or by any person who is alleged to be in possession of the property;

(e) redemption;

(f) reconveyance of the land or its release from the security; or

(g) delivery of possession by the mortgagee.

(2A) In paragraph (2) "mortgage" includes a legal or equitable mortgage and a legal or equitable charge, and reference to a mortgagor, a mortgagee and mortgaged land is to be interpreted accordingly.

(3) Such permission as is referred to in paragraph (2) shall not be granted unless it is shown—

(a) that every person in actual possession of the whole or any part of the land has received such notice of the proceedings as appears to the court sufficient to enable him to apply to the court for any relief to which he may be entitled, and

(b) if the operation of the judgment or order is suspended by subsection (2) of section 16 of the Landlord and Tenant Act, 1954, that the applicant has not received notice in writing from the tenant that he desires that the provisions of paragraphs (a) and (b) of that subsection shall have effect.

(4) A writ of possession may include provision for enforcing the payment of any money adjudged or ordered to be paid by the judgment or order which is to be enforced by the writ.

History of rule

sc45.3.1 Amended by the Civil Procedure (Amendment) Rules 2001 (SI 2001/256).

Effect of rule

sc45.3.2 Under this rule, permission is required to enforce a judgment or order for the giving of possession of land, subject to the important exceptions (which, in practice, cover the majority of cases) listed in the amended r.3(2).

Permission to issue a writ of possession cannot be given on an interlocutory application but only to enforce a final judgment or order for possession (*Manchester Corp v Connolly* [1970] Ch. 420; [1970] 1 All E.R. 961, CA).

A judgment or order to give possession of land will not be enforceable by an order of committal or by writ of sequestration unless it specifies the time within which this act is required to be done, and the defendant refuses or neglects to do it within that time (see r.5(1)). Accordingly, as a judgment or order to give possession of land will not in practice specify the time within which this act is required to be done, it will not ordinarily be enforceable by an order of committal or by writ of sequestration, but only by a writ of possession, which will normally be sufficient to enforce the judgment. If, however, in an extreme case, it is desired to enforce the judgment against a recalcitrant defendant by an order of committal or writ of sequestration, it will be necessary first to apply to the court under r.6, for an order to fix the time within which the defendant is required to give possession of the land, and to serve that order upon the defendant under r.7, and then to apply under r.5, for the order of committal (see O.52) or writ of sequestration.

Writ of possession

For form of writ of possession, see Form **No. 66**. The writ of possession may be combined with the writ of *fi. fa.* (para.(4) and see Form **No. 53**). **sc45.3.3**

The writ of possession contains a recital of the judgment or order that the defendant "do give" to the claimant possession of the land. It must therefore contain a description of the property of which possession is to be given. General words will not do, and if necessary the writ of possession may have to be altered by inserting a sufficient description (*Thynne v Sarl* [1891] 2 Ch. 79).

The writ of possession does not require the enforcement officer to make a "return," but he is directed to indorse it immediately after execution with a statement of the manner in which he has executed it, and to send a copy of such statement to the claimant. This, however, is a mere formal matter of procedure and is not necessary in order to complete a seizure under the writ (*Re Hobson* (1886) 33 Ch D 493).

A second writ of possession for the giving of the same property cannot be issued until the first writ has been duly indorsed by the enforcement officer, showing that possession has not been given to the claimant of the whole property of which possession has been given under the judgment.

Housing Acts 1988/1996

All tenancies created on or after January 29, 1989 in respect of dwellings are governed by the Housing Act 1988. Consequently there are now relatively few tenancies governed by the Rent Act 1977 or its predecessors. See generally Vol.2, Section 3A—Residential Tenancies. **sc45.3.4**

The granting of a possession order always requires the exercise of a judicial discretion. Consequently, in relation to a dwelling a writ of possession will not issue to enforce a default judgment or order for possession (*Peachey Property Corp Ltd v Robinson* [1967] 2 Q.B. 543; [1966] 2 All E.R. 981, CA, applying *Smith v Poulter* [1947] K.B. 339). Nor will such a writ issue to enforce a judgment or order obtained by consent, since in such cases the question whether "it is reasonable to make such an order" has not been considered by a court. (Such a consent order should not, of course, be made.)

In relation to premises let as a dwelling on a lease which is subject to a right of re-entry or forfeiture, that right cannot be enforced otherwise than by proceedings in the court while any person is lawfully residing in the premises or part of them (Protection from Eviction Act 1977 s.2) and equally where any premises have been let as a dwelling under a tenancy to which the Rent Act/Housing Act does not apply the owner is not entitled to recover possession of the premises or part of them, at the termination of the former tenancy, otherwise than by proceedings in the court (Protection from Eviction Act 1977 s.3). For these purposes, the court is the county court where it has jurisdiction in respect of the recovery of these premises, otherwise it is the High Court (see Protection from Eviction Act 1977 s.9(1)). Where the right of forfeiture is being enforced by proceedings, the court can make an order so limited as to produce only a forfeiture and not procure delivery of the premises to the landlord (see *Wolmer Securities Ltd v Corne* [1966] 2 Q.B. 243; [1966] 2 W.L.R. 1381; [1966] 2 All E.R. 691, CA).

In relation to a dwelling-house to which Pt I or Pt II of the Landlord and Tenant Act 1954 applies, or which is held under a tenancy of an agricultural holding, the right to recover possession, otherwise than by virtue of the right of re-entry or forfeiture under the lease, must be enforced in the county court, and therefore in such a case also, the writ of possession will not issue (see Protection from Eviction Act 1977 ss.3(1), 9(1)).

In relation to a dwelling-house, whether it is a protected tenancy or not, the claimant may not enter into possession himself, even peaceably, and he can only enter into possession under a writ of possession (Protection from Eviction Act 1977 s.3) negativing to this extent *Aglionby v Cohen* [1955] 1 Q.B. 558; [1955] 1 All E.R. 785.

On the other hand, in relation to land or premises which did not come within the Rent Act 1968 or Pt I or Pt II of the Landlord and Tenant Act 1954, or were not let as a dwelling under a tenancy of an agricultural holding, the claimant may obtain a writ of possession to enforce his judgment or order for possession; and he may, having such a judgment for possession, enter at his own risk without issuing out a writ of possession, if he can do so without force (*Aglionby v Cohen*, above).

Reserve and Auxiliary Forces (Protection of Civil Interests) Act 1951

sc45.3.5 In the cases covered by this Act no judgment or order for recovery of possession of land in default of payment of rent may be enforced without the leave of the court (s.2(3)). This Act is of renewed practical importance given the policy of using the Territorial Army on active service. See paras 9A–1to 9A–408+

Permission to issue writ of possession

sc45.3.6 Permission to issue a writ of possession is necessary, except in a mortgage action for in that case the position of every person in occupation is known before an order for possession is made (see *Leicester Permanent Building Society v Shearley* [1951] Ch. 90; [1950] 2 All E.R. 738).

Where (as often happens) the property consists of a house of which various parts are sublet to, or in the occupation of, different persons, the evidence should show the nature and length of the notice which has been given to the various occupiers. Where the defendant or any other person is in actual possession of the premises the evidence must contain, inter alia, the following information:—(a) whether the premises or any part thereof is a dwelling-house; (b) if so (i) what is the rateable value of the dwelling-house; (ii) whether it is let furnished or unfurnished and, if furnished, what is the amount of furniture therein; (c) any other matters which will assist the Master in determining whether any occupier is protected by the Rent Acts (*Practice Direction* [1955] 1 W.L.R. 1314; [1955] 3 All E.R. 646).

Permission is required to issue execution on a suspended order for possession, see para.sc46.4.1.

Stay of writ of possession

sc45.3.7 The court has no power to grant a stay of a writ of possession as against a trespasser and a stay against a former tenant or service occupier would normally be limited to between four and six weeks (*McPhail v Persons' Names Unknown* [1973] Ch. 447, CA) However in a serious and substantial dispute between parties of commercial strength a period of three months or even longer may be granted (*Bain & Co v Church Commissioners for England* [1989] 1 W.L.R. 24).

Notice of the proceedings

sc45.3.8 Where the defendant is the only person in possession of the premises the claimant must give the defendant notice of the judgment or order, and call upon him to give up possession under the judgment or order. Where there are other persons (not parties to the proceedings) in actual possession it is also necessary to serve them with such written notice as will give them a reasonable opportunity of applying to the court.

The combined effect of O.45 and O.46 is that notice of an application for a warrant of possession must be given to a tenant and the writ of execution should not be issued without the tenant having an opportunity to apply to the court for relief (*Leicester City Council v Aldwinkle, The Times*, April 5, 1991, CA).

It should be observed that the rule does not confer any *new* rights on a tenant or other occupier. Its only effect is to give those who may apply for relief an opportunity of doing so.

In the course of winding-up proceedings, the Companies Court has jurisdiction to make an order for possession against the company where there is no defence to the claim for the forfeiture of the lease, but the Companies Court has no jurisdiction to entertain an application by a sub-tenant or mortgagee for relief from forfeiture under s.146 of the Law of Property Act 1925, since a winding-up proceeding is not "an action" and therefore relief from forfeiture has to be applied for by a separate proceeding (*Re Blue Jeans Sales Ltd* [1979] 1 W.L.R. 362; [1979] 1 All E.R. 641).

Landlord and Tenant Act 1954

sc45.3.9 In order to obtain the benefit of the provisions of s.16 a tenant, against whom an order for possession has been made, has not only to give notice in writing to the immediate landlord that he desires that the provisions of paras (a) and (b) of s.16(2) shall have effect, but also to file a copy of the notice in court. In such a case the order will not have effect except if and so far as it provides for the payment of costs

Wrongful or irregular execution of writ of possession

Enforcement officers executing a judgment (e.g. by causing an eviction) however wrong the judgment, or however they may be mistaken as to its effect, are not liable in an action for damages. Nor is the landlord rendered liable by his mere presence at the time of the eviction (*Williams v Williams & Nathan* [1937] 2 All E.R. 559, CA). Nor is the character and quality of the actions of the enforcement officer altered because he acted on the advice of the landlord's solicitors, unless at the very least he has made it plain that his subsequent actions were undertaken only on the basis of the landlord assuming responsibility therefore (*Barclays Bank Ltd v Roberts* [1954] 1 W.L.R. 1212; [1954] 3 All E.R. 107, CA). **sc45.3.10**

Costs

See Sch.1, RSC O.62, App. 3, "Fixed Costs" (see para.sc62 A3 below). No costs of application are given where no costs are allowed on the judgment. **sc45.3.11**

Writ of restitution

This writ is a writ of execution in aid of the writ of possession. See RSC O.46, r.3. The writ is in Form **No. 68**. **sc45.3.12**

RSC

Enforcement of judgment for delivery of goods

4.—(1) Subject to the provisions of these rules, a judgment or order for the delivery of any goods which does not give a person against whom the judgment is given or order made the alternative of paying the assessed value of the goods may be enforced by one or more of the following means, that is to say— **sc45.4**

(a) writ of delivery to recover the goods without alternative provision for recovery of the assessed value thereof (hereafter in this rule referred to as a "writ of specific delivery");

(b) in a case in which rule 5 applies, an order of committal;

(c) in such a case, writ of sequestration.

(2) Subject to the provisions of these rules, a judgment or order for the delivery of any goods or payment of their assessed value may be enforced by one or more of the following means, that is to say—

(a) writ of delivery to recover the goods or their assessed value;

(b) by order of the court, writ of specific delivery;

(c) in a case in which rule 5 applies, writ of sequestration.

An application for an order under sub-paragraph (b) shall be made in accordance with CPR Part 23, which must be served on the defendant against whom the judgment or order sought to be enforced was given or made.

(3) A writ of specific delivery, and a writ of delivery to recover any goods or their assessed value, may include provision for enforcing the payment of any money adjudged or ordered to be paid by the judgment or order which is to be enforced by the writ.

(4) A judgment or order for the payment of the assessed value of any goods may be enforced by the same means as any other judgment or order for the payment of money.

Effect of rule

This rule makes a sharp distinction between a judgment or order for delivery of **sc45.4.1** goods (1) which does *not* give the defendant the option of retaining them by paying their assessed value and (2) which *does* give the defendant such an option. In the case of a judgment or order in the first form, the method of enforcement is by writ of specific delivery, for the issue of which no permission of the court is required. In the case of a judgment or order in the second form, the method of enforcement is by a writ of delivery to recover the goods or their assessed value, for which again no permission is required, but in the case of such a judgment, if it is desired to enforce it by a writ of specific delivery, i.e. by depriving the defendant of the option of paying the assessed value of the goods, then the permission of the court must first be obtained (see para.2(b)).

A judgment or order to deliver goods which does not give the defendant the option of retaining them by paying their assessed value will not be enforceable by an order of committal or by writ of sequestration unless it specifies the time within which this act is required to be done and the defendant refuses or neglects to do it within that time (see r.5(1); and a judgment or order to deliver goods or to pay their assessed value will not be enforceable by writ of sequestration unless it specifies the time within which the delivery of the goods or the payment of the assessed value is required to be done and the defendant refuses or neglects to do either such act within that time (see r.5(1)). Accordingly, as a judgment or order to deliver goods, whether or not it gives the defendant the option of paying their assessed value, will not in practice specify the time within which the act is required to be done it will not ordinarily be enforceable by an order of committal or by writ of sequestration, but only by a writ of specific delivery or a writ of delivery. If, however, in an extreme case, it is desired to enforce the judgment or order by an order of committal or writ of sequestration, as the case may be, it will be necessary first to apply to the court under r.6, or in the case of a judgment or order for the delivery of goods or payment of their assessed value under r.5(3) for an order for a writ of specific delivery under r.4(2)(b) which will fix the time within which the defendant is required to deliver the goods and to serve such order upon the defendant with the requisite penal notice indorsed thereon under r.7, and then to apply under r.5, for order of committal (see O.52) or under this rule for a writ of sequestration, as the case may be.

Writ of delivery

sc45.4.2 For forms of writs of delivery, see Forms **No.64** and **No.65**. It should be observed that there is no writ named as "a writ of specific delivery", but Form **No.64**, is the form of a writ of delivery of goods which does not give the defendant the option of paying their assessed value and it is referred to in this rule as a "writ of specific delivery."

The writ of delivery may be combined with a writ of *fi. fa.* (para.(3) and see Forms **No.64** and **No.65**).

The writ of delivery contains a recital of the judgment or order that the defendant "do deliver" the goods to the claimant. It must therefore contain sufficient description of the goods which are to be so delivered.

Where a writ of delivery is issued for the delivery up of goods which are not in the custody of the defendant or for payment of their value, it is the duty of the defendant to take proper steps to make effective the delivery of the goods wherever they are to the claimant and for this purpose at least inform the claimant and any other persons concerned that the goods, being the property of the claimant, were at his disposal, otherwise the claimant is entitled to issue a writ of *fi. fa.* for the assessed value of the goods (*Metals and Ropes Co Ltd v Tattersall* [1966] 1 W.L.R. 1500; [1966] 3 All E.R. 401, CA).

Permission to issue writ of delivery

sc45.4.3 Where the judgment creditor has obtained a judgment or order for the delivery of the goods which does not give to the judgment debtor the option of paying their assessed value, he is entitled to issue a writ of specific delivery (Form **No. 64**) without the permission of the court, and without the previous assessment of their value (see *per* Collins M.R. in *Hymas v Ogden* [1905] 1 K.B. 246, CA).

For the actual delivery a writ of assistance may issue with permission (Form **No. 69**) (see *O.46*, r.3).

Where the judgment creditor has obtained a judgment or order for the delivery of the goods or the payment of their assessed value, he must first proceed to the assessment of the value, and then he may issue the writ of delivery (Form **No. 65**) for the delivery of the goods or their assessed value, and he is entitled to do so without permission.

On the other hand, where the judgment creditor has obtained a judgment or order for the delivery of the goods, or the payment of their assessed value, and he desires to proceed to recover the goods without giving the judgment debtor the option of paying their value, he must apply for an order of the court to issue a writ of specific delivery under r.4(2)(b). The court has a discretion whether to grant such permission to issue a writ for specific delivery (see *Whiteley Ltd v Hilt* [1918] 2 K.B. 808, CA; *Cohen v Roche* [1927] 1 K.B. 169).

Reserve and Auxiliary Forces (Protection of Civil Interests) Act 1951

In the cases covered by this Act no judgment or order for delivery of any property other than mortgaged property by reason of a default in payment of money may be enforced without the permission of the court (s.2(3)). This Act is of renewed importance given the current policy of using reserve forces on active duty. See paras 9A–1 to 9A–408+. **sc45.4.4**

Costs

See Sch.1 RSC O.62, App.3, "Fixed costs" in Sch.1 (see para.sc62.A3 below). **sc45.4.5**

Enforcement of judgment to do or abstain from doing any act

5.—(1) Where— **sc45.5**

(a) a person required by a judgment or order to do an act within a time specified in the judgment or order refuses or neglects to do it within that time or, as the case may be, within that time as extended or abridged under a court order or CPR, rule 2.11; or

(b) a person disobeys a judgment or order requiring him to abstain from doing an act,

then, subject to the provisions of these rules, the judgment or order may be enforced by one or more of the following means, that is to say—

(i) with the permission of the court, a writ of sequestration against the property of that person;

(ii) where that person is a body corporate, with the permission of the court, a writ of sequestration against the property of any director or other officer of the body;

(iii) subject to the provisions of the Debtors Act 1869 and 1878, an order of committal against that person or, where that person is a body corporate, against any such officer.

(2) Where a judgment or order requires a person to do an act within a time therein specified and an order is subsequently made under rule 6 requiring the act to be done within some other time, references in paragraph (1) of this rule to a judgment or order shall be construed as references to the order made under rule 6.

(3) Where under any judgment or order requiring the delivery of any goods the person liable to execution has the alternative of paying the assessed value of the goods, the judgment or order shall not be enforceable by order of committal under paragraph (1), but the court may, on the application of the person entitled to enforce the judgment or order, make an order requiring the first mentioned person to deliver the goods to the applicant within a time specified in the order, and that order may be so enforced.

Effect of rule

sc45.5.1 This rule governs the methods for the enforcement by the court of its judgments or orders in circumstances amounting to a contempt of court. It applies to both positive and negative judgments or orders, i.e. those which require a party to do an act as well as those which require a party to abstain from doing an act, subject, however, to this important qualification that the coercive methods of enforcement under this rule cannot be employed to enforce a judgment or order to do an act unless that act is required to be done, but is not done, within a specified time which has been fixed either by the original judgment or order, or by a subsequent order extending or abridging such time under CPR r.3.1(2)(a) or fixing such time under r.6.

An order made by a court of unlimited jurisdiction, even though irregular, must be obeyed unless and until it is set aside, and therefore disobedience to an interlocutory injunction which is irregular amounts to a contempt of court (*Isaacs v Robertson* [1985] A.C. 97; [1984] 3 W.L.R. 705; [1984] 3 All E.R. 140, PC).

The effect of the qualification is, that a judgment or order to pay money to some other person or to give possession of land or to deliver goods which need not, and will not as a general rule, specify the time within which such act is required to be done will not come within this rule, and so will not be enforceable by writ of sequestration or order of committal, unless and until time is specified for the doing of that Act (see para.(2) and r.6).

The methods of enforcement under the rule are

(i) by writ of sequestration, see O.46, r.5; and

(ii) by order of committal, see O.52, which is additional to the powers of the court under the Debtors Acts 1869 and 1878, under r.1, which, however, are curtailed by s.11 of AJA 1970.

This rule must be read together with r.7, under which as a general rule, enforcement under this rule cannot be obtained unless a copy of the order is served personally on the person in default with the requisite penal notice indorsed thereon.

Enforcing judgment requiring act to be done

sc45.5.2 A judgment or order requiring any act to be done must state the time within which the act is to be done before it can be enforced by the methods provided by this rule. Such time may be specified either by the original judgment or order (see Practice Direction (Judgments and Orders) para.8.1 (40BPD.8)) as extended or abridged under CPR r.3.1(2)(a), or by agreement of the parties under CPR r.2.11, or by a supplemental order made subsequently under r.6 (see para.(2)).

A further requirement for the enforcement under this rule of a judgment or order requiring an act to be done is due compliance with r.7.

An act required to be done may be directed to be done by the party by whom the judgment or order was obtained or by some other person appointed by the court, and at the expense of the disobedience party (see r.8).

A person practising as a solicitor but not duly qualified, who has been ordered to deliver up documents and to pay money, may be committed for breach of the order under this rule (*Re Hulm & Lewis* [1892] 2 Q.B. 261).

A declaratory order is not a coercive order, and refusal of a party to comply with its terms does not amount to a contempt of court (*Webster v Southwark London BC* [1983] Q.B. 698).

Breach of an undertaking

sc45.5.3 An undertaking given to the court is equivalent to an injunction, and its breach may be punished in the same way as the breach of an injunction (*L. & Birm. Ry. v Grand Junction Canal Co* (1835) 1 Ry. Ca. 224; *Neath Canal Co v Ynisarwed Resolven Coll. Co* (1875) L.R. 10 Ch. 450; *Milburn v Newton Colliery Ltd* (1908) 52 S.J. 317); *Northern Counties Securities Ltd v Jackson and Steeple Ltd* [1974] 1 W.L.R. 1133, p.1143; [1974] 2 All E.R. 625 at 634; *Re British Concrete Pipe Association's Agreement (Note)* [1983] I.C.R. 215, CA; *Gandolfo v Gandolfo* [1981] Q.B. 359). In family cases, see further s.46, Family Law Act 1996.

Although an undertaking given to the court in lieu of an injunction is recorded in a formal order, nevertheless it is the undertaking itself and not the order which requires the person giving it to comply with its terms and therefore failure to do so does not constitute disobedience to the order; and moreover, although such an undertaking is as binding and effective as an order, it differs from it in a fundamental way in that an undertaking is voluntary rather than imposed, and the person giving it is presumed to know of it. For these reasons the procedural requirements for the enforcement of an undertaking are not as strict as those applying to the enforcement of a judgment or order, and where the court is satisfied that the person giving it knew and understood its effect, it is not necessary for a copy of the order recording the undertaking to be served on him or to be indorsed with a penal notice (*Hussain v Hussain* [1986] Fam. 134; [1986] 2 W.L.R. 801; [1986] 1 All E.R. 961, CA; see also *Camden London BC v Alpenoak* (1985) 135 New L.J. 1209. The best practice to be adopted, however, in enforcing an undertaking given in lieu of an injunction is (1) that it should be included as a recital or preamble to an order of the court; (2) that the order incorporating the undertaking should be issued and served on the person who gave it; and (3) that the order should be indorsed with a suitably worded notice explaining the consequences of a breach of the undertaking (per Neill L.J. in *Hussain v Hussain*, above). This best practice is given added emphasis by para.9.3 of 40BPD (see para.40BPD.9).

The court has jurisdiction, on the application by a person to whom a solicitor gives an undertaking in his capacity as a solicitor, to exercise its summary procedure to compel the solicitor to carry out the undertaking, even though the applicant is not the client of the solicitor, and the undertaking was not given in the course of legal proceedings, and there is no suggestion of dishonourable or discreditable conduct on the part of the solicitor (*United Mining and Finance Corp Ltd v Becher* [1910] 2 K.B. 296; as to enforcing undertaking after action has come to an end through death, see *Coleman v Coleman* [1920] P. 71). As to whether a director who has neither aided nor abetted the contempt can be liable under the rule for breach by the company of its undertaking, given to the court and embodied in a written order see *Biba Ltd v Stratford Investments Ltd* [1973] 1 Ch. 281.

Where a defendant has voluntarily given an undertaking it is not necessary to serve on him the order containing the undertaking (*D v A &Co* [1900] 1 Ch. 484). (See also *Re Launder* (1908) 98 L.T. 554.) But it is the better practice to do so, see para.9.3 of 40BPD (see para.40BPD.9).

An undertaking to give bail to avoid arrest of a vessel cannot be withdrawn by substituting the vessel for the bail (*The Borre* [1921] P. 390).

The court will not vary an undertaking given by a party to a suit, but may release him if sufficient reason is shown (*Cutler v Wandsworth Stadium Ltd* (1945) 172 L.T. 207, CA).

Enforcement against body corporate

The remedies under this rule for enforcement of a judgment or order against a body corporate are (1) by writ of sequestration against the corporate property of that body; (2) by writ of sequestration against the personal property of any director or other officer of the body; and (3) by an order of committal against any director or other officer of that body. For position of directors on an undertaking, see *Biba Ltd v Stratford Investments* [1973] 1 Ch. 281. **sc45.5.4**

Where a company disobeys an injunction, a director or other officer of the company will not be liable in contempt to be committed or have his property sequestrated merely by virtue of his office or his knowledge of the order but will only be liable if he can be shewn to be in contempt under the general law of contempt and accordingly, in the absence of *mens rea* or an *actus reus*, such a director or other officer will not be liable in contempt (*Director General of Fair Trading v Buckland* [1990] 1 W.L.R. 920; [1990] 1 All E.R. 545).

See also *Attorney General for Tuvalu v Philatelic Distribution Corp Ltd* [1990] 1 W.L.R. 926 where the Court of Appeal clarified and explained *Director General of Fair Trading v Buckland* [1990] 1 W.L.R. 920. Where a company had been restrained from doing certain acts a director is under a duty to take reasonable care to secure compliance. If he failed to take adequate steps to ensure that those to whom relevant matters had been delegated had not misunderstood or overlooked the company's continuing obligations and the company breached the order he would be liable to be punished for contempt even though he had not personally participated in the breach.

"Refuses or neglects or disobeys"

The remedies under this rule may be applied where the person "refuses or neglects" to do an act within the time specified by the judgment or order, or where he "disobeys" a judgment or order requiring him to abstain from doing an act. Such refusal, neglect or disobedience must, however, be of a character or quality to constitute a contempt of **sc45.5.5** court. See *per* Lord Wilberforce in *Heatons Transport (St Helens) Ltd v Transport and General Workers' Union* [1973] A.C. 15 at 109; [1972] 3 All E.R. 101 at 117.

A person or corporation commits a breach of the injunction requiring him to abstain from doing an act, and is liable for process of contempt, if he or it does the act, and it is no answer to say that the act was not contumacious in the sense that, in doing it, there was no direct intention to disobey the order, and only those acts will be excluded from constituting a breach of the injunction which are casual or accidental and unintentional (*Heatons Transport (St. Helens) Ltd v Transport and General Workers' Union*, above. Lack of intention to disobey, may however affect the penalty (*Chelsea Man Plc v Chelsea Girl Ltd (No.2)* [1988] F.S.R. 217). It has been held that it is not necessary to show a wilful intention to disobey a court order but merely an intention to do a prohibited act knowing the consequences (*P v P (Contempt of Court: Mental Capacity* [1999] 2 F.L.R. 897).

It is not a defence that the claimant's application is stale, though delay in bringing proceedings may affect any penalty (*Chanel Ltd v F.G.M. Cosmetics* [1981] F.S.R. 471). A question of contempt must be decided even if it is virtually a decision of the matter in question in the action between the parties (*ibid.*). Whilst there may be jurisdiction to dismiss a contempt application for want of prosecution, such an application failed in *Japan Capsule Computers (UK) Ltd v Sonic Games Sales* [1988] F.S.R. 256. See also *Spectravest Inc v Aperknit Ltd* [1988] F.S.R. 161. However, when the breach alleged is of an interlocutory order, subsistence and ownership of the rights claimed must be assumed (*ibid.*).

Disobedience means refusal by the corporation or its servants (*Attorney General v Walthamstow U.D.C.* (1895) 11 T.L.R. 533) or neglect by its servants (*Stancomb v Trowbridge U.D.C.* [1910] 2 Ch. 190) to do the things which the corporation has been ordered to do. In the two cases cited the writ of sequestration was ordered to lie in the office for a period of nine and six months respectively; and see *Lee v Aylesbury Urban DC* (1902) 19 T.L.R. 106. A person is deemed to do a relevant act "by his servants or agents" if (a) the persons who did the acts were his servants or agents (b) the acts were done in the course of the service or agency and (c) he either (i) authorised the acts or (ii) could reasonably have foreseen the possibility of such acts and failed to take all reasonable steps to prevent them (*Hone v Page* [1980] F.S.R. 500). Accidental and unintentional results of an act may be sufficient to cause that act to constitute disobedience if repeated (*Davis v Rhayader Granite Quarries Ltd* (1911) 131 L.T.J. 79). Moreover, the failure to carry out an undertaking cannot be regarded as casual, accidental or unintentional, but will amount to a refusal or neglect or even disobedience under this rule, and will constitute a contempt of court, for which sequestration may issue, though if the disregard of the order is not obstinate a fine may be imposed in lieu of sequestration (*Steiner Products Ltd v Willy Steiner Ltd* [1966] 1 W.L.R. 986; [1966] 2 All E.R. 387).

As to the enforcement of a declaratory order by the process of sequestration, see *Webster v Southwark London BC* [1983] Q.B. 698.

Costs may be awarded on the indemnity basis (*Attorney General v Walthamstow U.D.C.* (1895) 11 T.L.R. 533; *Lee v Aylesbury U.D.C.* (1902) 19 T.L.R. 106; and *Stancomb v Trowbridge U.D.C.* [1910] 2 Ch. 190. This may be a sufficient punishment where there have been minor breaches of the order because the defendants did not take sufficient care to comply with its terms (*G.C.T. (Management) Ltd v The Laurie Marsh Group Ltd* [1973] R.P.C. 432, distinguishing *Plating Co v Farquharson* (1881) 17 Ch D 49).

Judgment or order requiring delivery of goods

sc45.5.6 Where the judgment or order for the delivery of goods gives the defendant the option either to deliver the goods or to pay their assessed value, it cannot be enforced by an order of committal (para.(3) and r.4(2)). In such a case, however, an order may be obtained under para.(3) for the delivery of the goods to the claimant within a specified time, and upon the making of such order, enforcement may be obtained by order of committal. Such order, however, can only be obtained by application to the Master, which should be served upon the defendant. If, however, it is desired to proceed by writ of sequestration, the proper course is to apply for an order for the issue of a writ of specific delivery, see r.4(2)(b) and (c). It is a question of construction of the order whether the defendants are required to deliver up only articles which were in their possession at the time of the order and not articles coming into their possession subsequently; (*Spectravest Inc v Aperknit Ltd* [1988] F.S.R. 161).

Judgment or order referring to legal basis of order

Where an order refers to the legal right involved (e.g. passing-off) as well as the acts not to be done these words are not otiose, and there is no breach of the order unless the acts relied on are in fact breaches of the legal right; but though no question of *res judicata* is involved, the matter being purely one of construction of the order, the terms of the order may presuppose a wide range of the acts now complained of as constituting an invasion of the legal right (*Chelsea Man Plc v Chelsea Girl Ltd (No.2)* [1988] F.S.R. 217 following *Calor Gas (Distributing) Co Ltd v G. Cooper* [1962] R.P.C. 16). And it is only the defendant's acts that must be proved beyond reasonable doubt; it may be a question for the impression of the court whether the facts amount in law to a breach of the court order (*Chelsea Man Plc v Chelsea Girl Ltd (No.2)* [1988] F.S.R. 217). **sc45.5.7**

Judgment, etc. requiring act to be done: order fixing time for doing it

6.—(1) Notwithstanding that a judgment or order requiring a person to do an act specifies a time within which the act is to be done, the court shall, have power to make an order requiring the act to be done within another time, being such time after service of that order, or such other time, as may be specified therein. **sc45.6**

(2) Where a judgment or order requiring a person to do an act does not specify a time within which the act is to be done, the court shall have power subsequently to make an order requiring the act to be done within such time after service of that order, or such other time, as may be specified therein.

(3) An application for an order under this rule must be made in accordance with CPR Part 23 and the application notice must, be served on the person required to do the act in question.

Effect of rule

This rule logically follows through the scheme under which judgments for the payment of money to a person or for giving possession of land or for delivery of goods are expressed in the form of requiring the defendant to do an act and while such judgments may not as a general rule in the first instance specify the time within which the required act is to be done, this rule provides that the court may specify such a time subsequently by a supplemental order made upon an application issued for this purpose The modern practice is to specify both a date and a time by which the act is to be done (CPR r.2.9). **sc45.6.1**

This rule only applies to a judgment or order which requires an act to be done. It does not apply to merely prohibitive orders (*Selous v Croydon Rural Sanitary Authority* (1885) 53 L.T. 209). Nor does this Rule apply to an order made under the Inheritance (Provision for Family and Dependants) Act 1975 *Re Jennery (dec'd.)* [1967] Ch. 280; [1967] 1 All E.R. 691, CA.

Paragraph (1) of the rule states the present practice, under which a judgment or order which specifies the time within which an act is required to be done may, by supplemental order of the court made subsequently, fix another time for the required act to be done. The practice extends to an order containing a positive undertaking to do a certain act within a specified time (*D v A & Co* [1900] 1 Ch. 484; *Re Launder* (1908) 98 L.T. 554). Thus where the undertaking was to do an act forthwith (*Halford v Hardy* (1900) 81 L.T. 721) or where no time was fixed (*Carter v Roberts* [1903] 2 Ch. 312) orders were made fixing a time. In *Cotton v Heyl* [1930] 1 Ch. 510, where the undertaking was to "pay out of the first moneys received", the court made a similar order.

Paragraph (2) of the rule empowers the court to make an order specifying the time within which the required act is to be done in two cases, namely (1) where the judgment or order does not itself specify such a time whether by omission or inadvertence or otherwise: and (2) where the judgment or order is to pay money to some other person, or to give possession of land or to deliver goods, and the time within which such act is to be done is not, as it generally would not be, specified by the judgment or order. (This paragraph accordingly negatives the former practice, under which in the case of a judgment for the recovery of money, the court had no jurisdiction to add a limitation of time within which payment was to be made and so formed a right to sequestration in default of payment (*Hulbert v Cathcart* [1894] 1 Q.B. 244) nor subsequently to make a supplemental order to fix a time for payment by a certain day (*Re Oddy* [1906] 1 Ch. 93; *cf. Drewett v Edwards* (1878) 37 L.T. 622).

The time within which the court may under the rule specify that the required act is to be done may be fixed by reference to the sense of the order, or it may be such other time as the court may think fit. It is, however, desirable that the time should be stated in the order with precision, e.g. "on or before (*or* not later than) the 31st May, 2009," *or* "before noon (*or* 4 p.m. *or as may be*) on —— day, the —— day of ——, 2009."

Service of copy of judgment, etc., prerequisite to enforcement under rule 5

sc45.7 7.—(1) In this rule references to an order shall be construed as including references to a judgment.

(2) Subject to paragraphs (6) and (7) of this rule, an order shall not be enforced under rule 5 unless—

(a) a copy of the order has been served personally on the person required to do or abstain from doing the act in question; and

(b) in the case of an order requiring a person to do an act, the copy has been so served before the expiration of the time within which he was required to do the act.

(3) Subject as aforesaid, an order requiring a body corporate to do or abstain from doing an act shall not be enforced as mentioned in rule 5(1)(b)(ii) or (iii) unless—

(a) a copy of the order has also been served personally on the officer against whose property permission is sought to issue a writ of sequestration or against whom an order of committal is sought; and

(b) in the case of an order requiring the body corporate to do an act, the copy has been so served before the expiration of the time within which the body was required to do the act.

(4) There must be prominently displayed on the front of the copy of an order served under this rule a warning to the person on whom the copy is served that disobedience to the order would be a contempt of court punishable by imprisonment, or (in the case of an order requiring a body corporate to do or abstain from doing an act) punishable by sequestration of the assets of the body corporate and by imprisonment of any individual responsible.

(5) With the copy of an order required to be served under this rule, being an order requiring a person to do an act, there must also be served a copy of any order or agreement under CPR, rule 2.11 extending or abridging the time for doing the act and, where the first-mentioned order was made under rule 5(3) or 6 of this order, a copy of the previous order requiring the act to be done.

(6) An order requiring a person to abstain from doing an act may be enforced under rule 5 notwithstanding that service of a copy of the order has not been effected in accordance with this rule if the court is satisfied that pending such service, the person against whom or against whose property is sought to enforce the order has had notice thereof either—

(a) by being present when the order was made, or

(b) by being notified of the terms of the order, whether by telephone, telegram or otherwise.

(7) The court may dispense with service of a copy of an order under this rule if it thinks it just to do so.

Effect of rule

The rule makes explicit the conditions precedent to the enforcement of a judgment or order by writ of sequestration or by order of committal under rule by specifying (1) the requisite document(s) to be served; (2) the time within which such document(s) must be served; (3) the person on whom such document(s) must be served; and (4) the terms of the penal notice to be indorsed. The rule also recognises the present practice under which the court may dispense with service of the requisite document(s). **sc45.7.1**

By paragraph (6) the court has the power to proceed to the enforcement of a negative order by writ of sequestration or by order of committal even though the original order has not yet been served in accordance with the requirements of this rule, provided however that the court is satisfied that the person or party in question has had notice of it either by being present when the order was made or by being notified of its terms by telephone, fax or in such other manner as the court may deem sufficient. A negative order is often made without notice in circumstances of great urgency to preserve the status quo, and it would be highly inconvenient if it could not be enforced until it was first served as required by this rule. Paragraph (6) is designed to enable the court, if necessary before service, to prevent disobedience or further disobedience or to compel obedience to a negative order.

RSC

Documents required to be served

The document or documents which are required by this rule to be served as a condition precedent to enforcement by writ of sequestration or order of committal under r.5 are: **sc45.7.2**

(a) in the case of a judgment or order to abstain from doing an act, a copy of that judgment or order;

(b) in the case of a judgment or order to do an act:

(i) a copy of that judgment, whether or not it specifies the time within which the required act is to be done; and

(ii) a copy of any order extending or shortening time under CPR r.3.1(2)(a) or of any written agreement to extend a time limit made under CPR r.2.11; and

(iii) if an order is subsequently made, whether or not the original judgment or order specified the time within which the required act was to be done, specifying the time within which such required act is to be done under r.6, or r.5(3) a copy of that order also (see para.(5) and *Re Seal* [1903] 1 Ch. 87).

Method of service

In every case the requisite document or documents must be served personally on the person required to do or abstain from doing the act in question, or on the officer of the body corporate against whom it is sought to enforce an order requiring that body to do or abstain from doing the act in question. The court, however, has power to order service of the requisite documents "by an alternative method" (see CPR r.6.8). **sc45.7.3**

Time for service of documents

Where a specified time is limited for doing the act required, the order must be served within that time (para.2(b) and para.3(b): *Iberian Trust Ltd v Founders Trust and Investment Co Ltd* [1932] 2 K.B. 87); or else a supplemental order extending the time fixed must be obtained (*Treherne v Dale* (1884) 27 Ch D 66; *Re Seal* [1903] 1 Ch. 87). **sc45.7.4**

Person on whom documents to be served

In the case of a judgment or order requiring an individual to do or abstain from doing an act, the requisite documents must be served on that person personally. **sc45.7.5**

Where an order is made against parties jointly and severally liable (as e.g. trustees) and one of them cannot be served with the requisite documents, service against the other is sufficient to found committal against him (*Re Ellis* (1906) 54 W.R. 526).

In the case of a judgment or order requiring a body corporate to do or abstain from doing an act, the requisite documents must be served on the body corporate in order to found an application for a writ of sequestration against the corporate property, and if it is sought to proceed by way of a writ of sequestration against the property of any director or other officer of that body or by way of committal against the person of such director or other officer, the requisite documents must be served personally on that director or officer.

Indorsement of penal notice or order

sc45.7.6 It is a necessary condition for the enforcement of a judgment or order under r.5 by way of sequestration or committal, that the copy of the judgment or order served under this rule should have the requisite penal notice prominently indorsed thereon.

This must be indorsed on the copy for service of all orders which are required to be served, whether personally or not, (*Hampden v Wallis* (1884) 26 Ch. D. 746) and this rule applies, even where the "defendant" is a limited liability company (*Benabo v William Jay & Partners Ltd* [1941] Ch. 52; [1940] W.N. 330). A similar memorandum has to be indorsed on orders in divorce proceedings requiring a person to do an act under O.45, r.7(4) (High Court Cases) or CCR O.29, r.1 (county court cases).

Although it was doubted in *Evans v Evans* (1893) 67 L.T. 719, whether a citation to bring in a grant in Probate proceedings was within this rule, it is the practice for it to be indorsed hereunder. It is also the practice to indorse a witness summons to bring in scripts (*Re Bristow* (1892) 66 L.T. 60).

The indorsement on the front of the order should be in the following words or in words to the following effect:—

In the case of a judgment or order requiring a person to do an act within a specified time or to abstain from doing an act:

> "If you, the within named A.B. neglect to obey this judgment (*or* order) by the time stated (*or in the case of an order to abstain from doing an act*, "If you, the within named A.B. disobey this judgment (*or* order)), you may be held to be in contempt of Court and liable to imprisonment."

In the case of a judgment (*or* order) requiring a body corporate to do within a specified time or to abstain from doing an act:

> "If you, the within named A.B., Ltd neglect to obey this judgment (*or* order) by the time stated (*or in the case of an order to abstain from doing an act*, "If you, the within named A.B., Ltd disobey this judgment (*or* order)), you may be held to be in contempt of Court and liable to sequestration of your assets."

In the case of a judgment (*or* order) requiring a body corporate to do or to abstain from doing an act, but it is sought to take enforcement proceedings against a director or other officer of that body:—

> "If A.B., Ltd neglect to obey this judgment (*or* order) by the time stated (*or in the case of an order to abstain from doing an act*, "If A.B., Ltd disobey this judgment (*or* order)), you, X.Y. (a director or officer of the said A.B., Ltd) may be held to be in contempt of Court and liable to imprisonment."

The court has a discretion under O.45, r.7(6) to dispense with the failure to incorporate a penal notice in a judgment or order requiring a person to abstain from doing an act but it has no such discretion to dispense with the penal notice where the judgment or order requires the person to do an act (*Dempster v Dempster, The Independent*, November 9, 1990, CA). Nevertheless, as liberty of the subject is involved, strict compliance with the rule is desirable and it is unwise to rely on this discretion.

The court had no discretion to dispense with the requirement for the display on the front of the copy order in a prominent manner of the warning that disobedience would be a contempt of court punishable with imprisonment (*Moerman-Lenglet v Henshaw, The Times*, November 23, 1992).

Dispensing with service of documents

sc45.7.7 Paragraph (7) embodies the former practice under which the court has power to dispense with the service of the requisite documents in order to found an order for sequestration or committal.

An order to sign judgment unless a sum is paid before a day named need not be served on the defendant before judgment is signed upon it (*Hopton v Robertson* (1884) W.N. 77; 23 Q.B.D. 126(n)).

An order of committal of a person for disobedience to an order requiring him to do a given act within a given time will not be directed unless a copy of the order, with a proper indorsement, has been personally served upon him in due time, or unless he has had notice of the order and is evading service thereof. The fact that the person was present in court when the order was made is not sufficient to dispense with service of the order (*Re Tuck; Century Insurance Co v Larkin* [1910] 1 Ir.R. 91); but in *Haydon v Haydon* [1911] 2 K.B. 191, CA, on an application under the Debtors Acts, an order for committal was made although the debtor had not been personally served with the order disobeyed, but he was in court when it was made and was present when the order was made for his committal.

Effect of notice of injunction

Where the injunction is to restrain the doing of an act, the person restrained, or a person who chooses to step into his place to do the act enjoined against (*Avory v Andrews* (1882) 51 L.J.Ch. 414) may be committed for breach of the injunction if he has in fact had notice of the granting of the injunction, either by his presence in court at the time of granting the injunction (*Hearn v Tennant* (1807) 14 Ves. 136; *Husson v Husson* [1962] 1 W.L.R. 1434; [1962] 3 All E.R. 1056); or by telegram (*Anon.*, cited by Malins, V.-C., in *Heywood v Wait* (1869) 18 W.R. 205; *Re Bryant* (1877) 4 Ch. D. 98). Telegrams are now abolished but consider whether fax, text message or email would now be sufficient for this purpose. But if the person charged with breach of the injunction swears positively that he did not believe the injunction had been granted, and is not cross-examined on that point, he will not be committed for contempt (*Kimpton v Eve* (1813) 2 V & B. 349; *Ex p. Langley* (1879) 13 Ch. D. 110). **sc45.7.8**

Where notice of an injunction had been obtained from the Press Association by newspapers subscribing to the Association, they were shown to have sufficient notice of the injunction and could be in contempt of court if they published material subject to an injunction since personal service could be dispensed with if unpracticable (*Cleveland CC v W., The Independent,* May 5, 1988).

Receipt by a person who has been restrained by injunction from receiving it, of money from the Crown, which is not bound by the injunction, is a contempt (*Eastern Trust Co v McKenzie, Mann & Co* [1915] A.C. 750).

Court may order act to be done at expense of disobedient party

8. If a mandatory order, an injunction or a judgment or order for the specific performance of a contract is not complied with, then, without prejudice to its powers under section 39 of the Act and its powers to punish the disobedient party for contempt, the court may direct that the act required to be done may, so far as practicable, be done by the party by whom the order or judgment was obtained or some other person appointed by the court, at the cost of the disobedient party, and upon the act being done the expenses incurred may be ascertained in such manner as the court may direct and execution may issue against the disobedient party for the amount so ascertained and for costs. **sc45.8**

History of rule

Amended by Civil Procedure (Amendment No.5) Rules 2003 (SI 2003/3361). **sc45.8.1**

Effect of rule

Under the SCA 1981 s.39 the court has power to order a conveyance, contract or other document to be executed or a negotiable instrument to be indorsed by a person nominated by the court in place of the party who has neglected or refused to comply with a judgment or order directing him to do so, and such conveyance, contract, document or instruments executed and indorsed will operate and be available for all purposes as if it had been executed or indorsed by the party directed to do so. For the practice under this section, see Vol.2, paras 9A–136 *et seq*. Rule 8 is expressly without prejudice to the court's powers under s.39. **sc45.8.2**

Where a party fails to carry out an undertaking (e.g. to remove a wall) permission may be given to the other party to do the work and apply for an order for payment of his expenses (*Mortimer v Wilson* (1885) 33 W.R. 927).

Upon an application to rectify the register of a company, where it appeared that there was no one having authority to carry out the order of the court, Kekewich J., refused to make an order under this rule in the first instance, but made a mandatory order on the company to rectify, leaving the parties to make a subsequent application in case of non-compliance (*Re L.L.Syndicate* (1901) 17 T.L.R. 711; *cf. Manihot Plantations* (1919) 63 S.J. 827).

Matters occurring after judgment: stay of execution, etc.

sc45.11 11. Without prejudice to Order 47, rule 1, a party against whom a judgment has been given or an order made may apply to the court for a stay of execution of the judgment or order or other relief on the ground of matters which have occurred since the date of the judgment or order, and the court may by order grant such relief, and on such terms, as it thinks just.

Forms of writs

sc45.12 12.—(1) A writ of fieri facias must be in such of the Forms Nos. 53 to 63 in the relevant practice direction as is appropriate in the particular case.

(2) A writ of delivery must be in Form **No. 64** or **No. 65** in the relevant practice direction, whichever is appropriate.

(3) A writ of possession must be in Form **No. 66** or **No. 66A** in the relevant practice direction, whichever is appropriate.

(4) A writ of sequestration must be in Form **No. 67** in the relevant Practice Direction.

Forms of writs

sc45.12.1 The forms of writs of execution are listed at para.4PD.1. These forms must be used where applicable and appropriate in the particular case, but of course with such variations as the circumstances of the particular case require. The form must be followed, having regard to the directions contained in the judgment or order itself (*Boswell v Coaks* (1887) 36 W.R. 65). The writ is directed to a High Court Enforcement Officer.

The more important forms of writs of *fi. fa.* are: the writ of *fi. fa.*, employed to enforce a judgment or order for the payment of money to a person (Form **No. 53**); the writ of *fi. fa.* on an order for costs (Form **No. 54**); the writ of *fi. fa.* after levy of part (Form **No. 56**); and the writ of *fi. fa.* against personal representative (Form **No. 57**).

Form **No. 64** is the writ of specific delivery and is the appropriate writ to enforce a judgment or order for the specific delivery of goods without the alternative of paying the assessed the value (see r.4(1)): whereas the writ of delivery in Form No. 65 is appropriate to enforce a judgment or order for the delivery of goods or the payment of their value.

Form **No. 66** is the general writ of possession of land, and Form No. 66A is the writ of possession for the recovery of land which will issue only under an order for possession made under O.113.

In addition to the writs of execution mentioned in the rule, *contains the* prescribed form of the writ of restitution (Form **No. 68**) and the writ of assistance (Form **No. 69**) see O.46, r.3.

RSC ORDER 46—WRITS OF EXECUTION: GENERAL

Contents

RSC

Editorial introduction

A writ of execution is the most commonly used method of enforcement in the High Court. For enforcement purposes the term "writ" survives the "Access to Justice" reforms (see also editorial introduction to RSC O.45). sc46.0.2

In addition to the writs of execution mentioned in r.1, the Order applies to the writs of execution in aid of those mentioned, namely, the writ of assistance, the writ of restitution, the writ of *venditioni exponas*, and the writ of *distringas nuper vicecomitem* (see r.3). The Order probably also applies to the writ of *fieri facias de bonis ecclesiasticis*, and the writ of *sequestrari de bonis ecclesiasticis* (see O.47, r.5). It would not appear to apply to a writ of attachment, since the power to punish for contempt of court is now to be exercised by an order of committal (see O.52, r.1(1)). The Order does not apply to the appointment of a receiver (*Norburn v Norburn* [1894] 1 Q.B. 448).

Related sources

- RSC O.45 Enforcement of Judgments and Orders: General sc46.0.3
- Part 70 General Rules about Enfocement of Judgments and Orders
- County Courts Act 1984 s.89 (Vol.2, Section 9A, para.9A–591)
- County Courts Act 2003 s.99 and Sch.7 (Vol.2, para.9A–932+)
- CCR O.26 (Warrants of execution, delivery and possession)
- Costs on judgment without trial for possession of land (Sch.1, RSC O.62, Appendix 3).

Forms

See Forms listed at para.and note in addition sc46.0.4

- **No.68** Writ of restitution
- **No.69** Writ of assistance
- **No.71** Notice of renewal of writ of execution

Definition

1. In this order, unless the context otherwise requires, "writ of execution" includes a writ of *fieri facias*, a writ of possession, a writ of delivery, a writ of sequestration and any further writ in aid of any of the aforementioned writs. sc46.1

Time for issue of writ of fi. fa.

The writ of *fi. fa.* may issue to enforce a judgment or order for the payment to, or for the recovery by, any person, of money or costs. The practice is clear, that a writ of *fi. fa.* may issue immediately upon payment becoming due and as a matter of course without permission and without the necessity for prior notice to, or for prior service of the judgment or order, upon the debtor (see *Land Credit Company of Ireland v Fermoy* (1870) L.R. 5 Ch. 323; *Hopton v Robertson* (1884) W.N. 77; 23 Q.B.D. 126n.; *Re A Solicitor* (1884) 33 W.R. 131). Accordingly, a judgment in the ordinary form of requiring the judgment debtor to pay money to a person, is enforceable by writ of *fi. fa.*, immediately it is entered, even though no time is specified for the payment to be made sc46.1.1

and even though notice of the judgment, still less the judgment itself, has not been served on the debtor. On the other hand, where the judgment or order directs payment within a specified time, the writ will issue immediately after, but not before, such time has expired; and where the judgment or order directs payment within a certain time after service on the debtor, the writ will issue immediately after, but not before, due service has been effected upon the debtor and proof of such service duly lodged with the Court. Similarly, if the judgment or order is conditional, the writ will issue immediately after, but not before, there has been default in complying with the condition. CPR r40.7(1) now expressly states that a judgment or order takes effect from the day when it is given or made, or such later date as the court may specify.

Where the judgment or order is for the payment (or recovery) of money and costs to be assessed, separate writs of *fi. fa.* may issue to enforce payment of the judgment debt and the costs after they have been assessed (see O.47, r.3).

It is wrongful to issue a writ of *fi. fa.* after payment, and therefore a person (including the solicitor for a party) who issues execution after payment (*Clissold v Cratchley* [1910] 2 K.B. 244) or after a valid tender (*Cubitt v Gamble* (1919) 35 T.L.R. 223) is liable to trespass. Ignorance of the payment is no defence. Similarly, it is submitted that it is wrongful to issue a writ of *fi. fa.* for a sum greater than the amount actually due at the time of its issue.

If neither the judgment creditor nor a person authorised by him is in England to receive the money, a stay of execution will be granted on payment into Court (*Re A Debtor*) [1912] 1 K.B. 53).

Nature of writ of fi. fa.

sc46.1.2 The writ of *fi. fa.* is the mode for the enforcement of a money judgment by the seizure and sale of the debtor's goods and chattels sufficient to satisfy the judgment debt and costs of the execution. The writ is expressed in the general form of a royal direction to a named High Court Enforcement Officer or the enforcement officers for the district in which it is desired to levy (if this second option is chosen the writ must be sent to the National Information Centre for Enforcement for allocation on a rota basis) to seize in execution such of the goods of the debtor as may be sufficient to satisfy the amount of the judgment debt together with the current rate of interest thereon until payment and the costs of the execution including the enforcement officer's costs and charges. The writ further directs the enforcement officer to pay the judgment creditor the amount levied (other than his own costs and charges) and to indorse on the writ a statement of how he has executed it, sending a copy of such statement to the judgment creditor.

For forms of writs of *fi. fa.* see Practice Direction (Forms) Table 2 at para.4PD.4.

The prescribed forms must be used wherever applicable with such variations as the circumstances of the particular case require (CPR r.4(2)), i.e. having regard to the directions contained in the judgment or order itself (*Boswell v Coaks* (1887) 36 W.R. 65). Variation will be required in the case of a judgment expressed in foreign currency.

The writ must correspond with the judgment in the names of the parties and to the subject-matter of the judgment, and should be directed to the proper person.

A list of enforcement officers to whom a writ may be directed is kept at the RCJ, all District Registries and all county courts. An edited list is in Vol.2 at Appendix 1 paras AP–10 and AP–12.

The writ must bear the date of the day and the hour of its issue.

The writ must be indorsed with the name and address of the solicitor actually issuing it out, and if he is acting as agent for another solicitor, the name and address of such other solicitor. Where there has been a change of solicitor, the new solicitor must place his name on the record before he can issue execution in the action. (See Pt 42.)

The writ must also be indorsed with the place of residence or business of the judgment creditor, whether he is acting in person or not.

The writ as amended in 2004 requires the address[es] for enforcement, including county and postcode to be given. Enforcement officers are allocated to post code areas and not, as previously, to bailiwicks. Bear in mind that in the case of a company, although process may have been properly served at a registered office that address could be, for example, an accountant's office and useless for levy purposes. The officer needs business addresses where goods can be seized. In practice the officer welcomes any information which will assist him to levy.

Enforcement of judgment debt in foreign currency by writ of fi. fa.

Where the judgment creditor desires to proceed to enforce a judgment expressed in a foreign currency by the issue of a writ of *fi. fa.* the *praecipe* for the issue of the writ must first be indorsed and signed by or on behalf of the solicitor for the judgment creditor or by the judgment creditor if he is acting in person with the requisite certificate (see para.11(a) of the *Practice Direction (QBD: Judgment: Foreign Currency) (No.1)* [1976] 1 W.L.R. 83; [1976] 1 W.L.R. 83. The amount so certified will then be entered in the writ of *fi. fa.* by adapting Form **No. 53** to meet the circumstances of the case but substituting the requisite recital (see *ibid.*, para.11(b)). **sc46.1.3**

Effect of writ of fi. fa.

The SCA 1981 s.138 has been repealed and replaced by Courts Act 2003, s.99 and Sch.7. The enforcement officer must endorse the writ with the date and time of its receipt. The writ binds the property in the goods of the execution debtor from the time when the writ is received by the person who is under a duty to enforce it (see Courts Act 2003, Sch.7, para.8). Similarly, in the county court, the bailiff must indorse on the back of the warrant of execution the hour, day, month and year when he received the application for it (County Courts Act 1984 s.99(3)). **sc46.1.4**

Such a writ will not prejudice the title to such goods acquired by any person in good faith and for valuable consideration, unless such person has at the time when he acquired his title notice that such writ or any other writ, by virtue of which the goods of the execution debtor might be seized or attached, had been delivered to and remained unexecuted in the hands of the enforcement officer.

In the county court, the time at which the application for a warrant is made, and not the time at which it was delivered to the bailiff for execution, is the time to be regarded under s.138 (*Murgatroyd v Wright* [1907] 2 K.B. 333)

The question whether there is an effective seizure of the goods by the enforcement officer under the writ of execution is a question of fact and there may be such a seizure even though the debtor refuses to sign a possession agreement, and even though the enforcement officer leaves the premises in which the goods are, and although the debtor may pass a good title to a purchaser who buys in good faith and for valuable consideration without notice of the writ or seizure under Courts Act 2003, Sch.7, para.8(2), the goods remain subject to the enforcement officer's rights, and therefore any sale by such purchaser, though it may pass a good title, will be in breach of the implied warranties as to quiet possession and freedom from encumbrances for which he will be liable in damages (*Lloyds and Scottish Finance Ltd v Modern Cars and Caravans (Kingston)* [1966] 1 Q.B. 764; [1964] 2 All E.R. 732).

The term of this section "binds the property in the goods of the execution debtor" simply means that on delivery of the goods to him, the enforcement officer acquires a legal right to seize sufficient of the debtor's goods to satisfy the account specified in the writ but from such delivery the goods become, as it were, impressed with the superimposed right of the enforcement officer (see *Samuel v Duke* (1838) 3 M & W 622). Thereafter, the debtor cannot deal with his goods except by sale to a bona fide purchaser for value and without notice of the delivery of the writ.

It has been held that notice to the judgment debtor of the delivery of the writ of execution to the enforcement officer was notice to the trustees of a deed of assignment for the benefit of his creditors, subsequently resolved upon and executed by the judgment debtors (*Ehlers v Kauffman* (1883) 49 L.T. 806).

If a deed of assignment to a trustee for creditors is revocable, as not having been communicated to any of them, at the time when the writ of execution is delivered to the enforcement officer the execution creditors are entitled to the goods (*Ellis & Co v Cross* [1915] 2 K.B. 654).

The property in the goods remains in the debtor until sale (*Giles v Grover* (1832) 1 Cl. & Fin. 72).

Priority of writs of fi. fa.

The priority as between writs of *fi. fa.* depends upon the time each is delivered to the enforcement officer for execution (see Courts Act 2003, Sch.7, para.7 and above). **sc46.1.5**

As between writs issued out of the High Court and warrants of execution issued from a county court against the same party, the priority to the goods seized is determined by the priority of the time of the delivery of the writ to the enforcement officer to be executed, which will be found indorsed on the back of the writ or the time at which the warrant is received by the bailiff of the enforcing county court, which will be found indorsed on the back of the warrant, see County Courts Act 1984, s.99 and

Courts Act 2003, Sch.7. Sch.7 has replaced SCA 1981, s.138 which, in turn had replaced Sale of Goods Act 1893, s.26 as to the effect of the writ on property.

Duties of enforcement officer

sc46.1.6 The High Court Enforcement Officer has inherited all the traditional duties, powers, rights, privileges and liabilities of the Sheriff (Courts Act 2003, Sch.7, s.99). As a rule, an enforcement officer in executing a writ must have regard to the interests and instructions of the execution creditor as far as compatible with his duty (*Re Crook* (1894) 63 L.J.Q.B. 756).

The truth is that the enforcement officer though for some purposes is an agent of the party who puts the writ in his hands, is not a mere agent. He is a public functionary having indeed duties to perform towards those who set him in motion analogous, in many respects, to those of an agent towards his principal; but he also has duties towards others and particularly towards those against whom the writs in his hands are directed (see *per* Lord Cranworth L.C. in *Hooper v Lane* (1857) 6 HLCas. 443, 549–550, cited in *Re A Debtor (No.2 of 1977) Ex p. the Debtor v Goacher* [1979] 1 W.L.R. 956; [1979] 1 All E.R. 870).

Where the writ has been withdrawn, the enforcement officer cannot re-enter without further instructions from the execution creditor, and, if a second execution creditor subsequently issues a writ against the same debtor the enforcement officer is justified in executing it without notice to the former execution creditor (*Shaw v Kirby* (1888) 52 J.P. 182).

Although an execution creditor or his solicitor, after delivery of the writ to the enforcement officer, may withdraw the execution or postpone the sale of chattels seized under it, there is no implied power in the managing clerk of the solicitor to do so (*Whyte v Nutting* [1897] 2 Ir.R. 241).

Sale by enforcement officer without notice of claim

sc46.1.7 Where the enforcement officer sells goods in the possession of the judgment debtor which he has seized under an execution without any claim having been made to such goods, the enforcement officer is protected from any liability (by Courts Act 2003, Sch.7, s.99 replacing the Supreme Court Act 1981 s.138B(1) which in turn re-enacted the Bankruptcy and Deeds of Arrangement Act 1913 s.15) unless it is proved that he had notice or ought by making reasonable inquiry have ascertained that the goods were not the property of the judgment debtor (*The Observer Ltd v Gordon* [1983] 1 W.L.R. 1008; [1983] 2 All E.R. 945).

Moreover, where the claimant has a "substantial grievance" on the ground that the enforcement officer has wrongfully, but without misconduct, seized his goods under a writ of *fi.fa.* and sold them at auction at a price greatly under their value, the onus is on him to show that there was a substantial difference between the value of the goods at the date of the sale and the price in fact realised, and in the absence of such proof, the enforcement officer is entitled to an order protecting him from proceedings by the claimant (*Neumann v Bakeaway Ltd* [1983] 1 W.L.R. 1016, CA).

Forcible entry

sc46.1.8 The enforcement officer is not entitled to break open the outer door in order to levy execution (*Semayne's Case* (1604) 5 Co. 91) nor to force his way in for the purpose of gaining entry (*Vaughan v McKenzie* [1969] 1 Q.B. 557; [1968] 1 All E.R. 1154, DC). But he may break open the outer door of the judgment debtor's workshop or other building not being his dwelling-house, nor connected with the dwelling-house (*Hodder v Williams* [1895] 2 Q.B. 663). This applies as well to distress for rent as to execution (*American Concentrated Must Corp v Hendry* [1893] W.N. 67, 82).

An enforcement officer already with walking possession of goods may lawfully break the lock to gain access to a house to seize the goods (*McLeod v Butterwick, The Times*, March 12, 1996).

Landlord

sc46.1.9 As to the rights of a landlord to payment of arrears of rent by a judgment creditor, *see* Insolvency Act 1986 s.347(6). Sections 6 and 7 of Landlord and Tenant Act 1709 did not apply as against execution creditors in favour of persons entitled to distrain (*Lewis v Davies* [1914] 2 K.B. 469, CA). As to the effect of petition for winding up, see *Re British Salicylates Ltd* [1919] 2 Ch. 155.

Possession, abandonment of

Where an enforcement officer, who has seized goods under a writ of *fi. fa.* goes out of possession, the question whether in so doing he has abandoned possession or not is always a question of fact (*Bagshawes v Deacon* [1898] 2 Q.B. 173; *National Commercial Bank of Scotland v Arcam Demolition, etc.* [1966] 2 Q.B. 593; [1966] 3 All E.R. 113, CA). See also *Lloyds and Scottish Finance Ltd v Modern Cars and Caravans (Kingston)* [1966] 1 Q.B. 764; [1964] 2 All E.R. 732. **sc46.1.10**

Wrongful seizure by enforcement officer

Where an enforcement officer, being misled by an indorsement put upon a writ of *fi. fa.* by the solicitor of the execution creditor, seized goods of the wrong person, it was held that the execution creditor was liable in an action of trespass (*Morris v Salberg* (1889) 22 Q.B.D. 614; see, too, *Jarmain v Hooper* (1843) 6 M. & G. 827; *Smith v Keal* (1882) 9 Q.B.D. 340; *Lee v Rumilly* (1891) 7 T.L.R. 303; *Hewitt v Spiers & Pond* (1897) 13 T.L.R. 64). But where there is nothing untrue in the directions in the indorsement so as to mislead the enforcement officer, the action is not maintainable against the judgment creditor (*Condy v Blaiberg* (1891) 7 T.L.R. 424, where the enforcement officer seized the goods of a third person). As to the exemption of a enforcement officer from penalties for an innocent mistake, see *Lee v Dangar* [1892] 2 Q.B. 337; and as to exemption from liability for the wrongful act of his own officer, see *Bagge v Whitehead* [1892] 2 Q.B. 355. **sc46.1.11**

Where neither the premises on which the goods are seized, nor the goods, belong to the execution debtor, the enforcement officer may, upon interpleader proceedings, be protected against an action for trespass as well as for wrongful seizure, if no substantial grievance has been done to the person whose premises are wrongfully entered (*Smith v Critchfield* (1885) 14 Q.B.D. 873) and the evidence shows that the enforcement officer has made all necessary and proper inquiries (*Salberg v Morris* (1888) 4 T.L.R. 47). But the enforcement officer was held not to be entitled to protection against an action of trespass where a substantial grievance had been done (*De Coppett v Barnett* (1901) 17 T.L.R. 273).

As to the protection of an enforcement officer selling goods of a third party in the possession of a judgment debtor see Courts Act 2003, Sch.7, s.99 replacing the Supreme Court Act 1981 s.138B(1)(b) which had re-enacted the Bankruptcy Act 1913 s.15.

Receiver, interference with possession of

The Court will not protect an enforcement officer who executes process after notice from a receiver that he is in possession (*Try v Try* (1851) 13 Beav 422; *Rock v Cook* (1848) 2 Ph. 691). An enforcement officer who seizes goods in the possession of a receiver is guilty of a contempt of Court (*Lane v Sterne* (1862) 3 Giff. 629) and may be committed. **sc46.1.12**

Reserve and Auxiliary Forces (Protection of Civil Interests) Act 1951

A judgment or order for the payment or recovery of a sum of money may not (except in certain specified cases) without the leave of the Court be enforced by execution or otherwise against a person protected by this Act (s.2(1)). See also, para.sc45.3.5. **sc46.1.13**

Crown

Save as provided by s.25(1)–(3) of the Crown Proceedings Act 1947, no execution or attachment or process in the nature of execution or attachment can issue for enforcing payment by the Crown of money or costs, and no person can be made individually liable under any order for payment by the Crown, or any government department, or any officer of the Crown as such, for any such money or costs (*ibid.*, subs (4) (Vol.2, Section 9B)). See r.66.6. **sc46.1.14**

Foreign sovereign

A sovereign state does not by initiating proceedings in this country render its property within the jurisdiction liable to execution to enforce an order for payment of costs (*Duff Dev Co v Kelantan* [1923] 1 Ch. 385). See also State Immunity Act 1978 s.20. **sc46.1.15**

Goods liable to seizure under writ of fi. fa.

At common law, only the goods and chattels of the judgment debtor could be taken in execution under a writ of *fi. fa.* By Courts Act 2003, Sch.7, para.9 an officer may seize "any goods of the execution debtor that are not exempt goods" and "any money, **sc46.1.16** banknotes, bills of exchange, promissory notes, bonds, specialties or securities for money belonging to the execution debtor". Thus, e.g. a pawnbroker's interest in redeemable pledges can be subject to execution under a writ of *fi-fa* (*Re Rollason* (1887) 34 Ch D 495).

An agreement that the wearing apparel of the wife provided by the husband is to remain his property is valid against execution creditors of the wife (*Rondeau v Marks* [1918] 1 K.B. 75).

Exempt goods

sc46.1.17 "Exempt goods" are now defined by Courts Act 2003, Sch.7, para.9. It means (a) such tools, books, vehicles and other items of equipment as are necessary to the execution debtor for use personally by him in his employment,business or vocation; (b) such clothing, bedding, furniture, household equipment and provisions as are necessary for satisfying the basic domestic needs of the execution debtor and his family.

What were "tools" or "implements" of trade within the Bankruptcy Act 1883 s.44(2) was a question of fact in each case. The hired cab of a cab driver was held as exempt within County Courts Act 1888 s.147 (*Lavell v Ritching* [1906] 1 K.B. 480). "The general principle is that prima facie all the judgment debtor's goods are liable to seizure under a writ of *fieri facias*. If a judgment debtor claims the benefit of a statutory exemption, the burden of showing that the exemption applies rests squarely on him" (per Steyn L.J. in *Toseland Building Supplies Ltd v Bishop (t/a Bishop Groundworks)*, October 28, 1993, unrep., CA). See also *Brookes v Harris* [1995] 1 W.L.R. 918 where a disc jockey's records were held to be "tools of his trade".

Equitable interest in chattels

sc46.1.18 The general rule is that a judgment creditor cannot under a *fi. fa*. seize chattels in which the judgment debtor has only an equitable interest; but this rule does not extend to cases where the whole beneficial interest is vested in the judgment debtors, e.g. where furniture has been assigned to trustees upon trust to allow one of two judgment debtors to use it during the joint lives of himself and his wife (the other judgment debtor) and after the death of either upon trust for the survivor (*Stevens v Hince* [1914] W.N. 148).

Where the goods seized are held by the defendant under another name

sc46.1.19 The form of *fi. fa*. relates to "the goods and chattels and other property .authorised by law". Cases have been known where a defendant has been sued as "John Brown", and the officer, when about to execute a writ of *fi. fa*., finds that all the goods are claimed by "Smith & Co.", under which name J. Brown carries on business. In such a case the judgment creditor should issue an application (see Pt 23) supported by evidence seeking permission to enforce against "Smith & Co.". As to enforcing a judgment or order against a firm see r.70.6A.

Goods of third persons

sc46.1.20 An enforcement officer may be restrained by injunction from remaining in possession of, and from selling goods, which do not belong to the judgment debtor; but the execution creditor should either be made a party to the action, or at least notice of it should be served upon him before the injunction is granted (*Hilliard v Hanson* (1882) 21 Ch. D. 69). In the usual case of the enforcement officer receiving a third party claim which is disputed by the execution creditor, he will issue interpleader proceedings under RSC O.17 for the issue as to ownership to be decided by the Court.

Where goods belonging to a builder were seized in execution, and such goods were subject to an agreement under which the building owner would have a lien on them on giving a notice in writing to the builder, but such notice was not given until seizure by the enforcement officer, it was held that the intervening seizure prevented the building owner's rights of lien from being effectual (*Byford v Russell* [1907] 2 K.B. 522). Where execution is sought to be levied against certain classes of goods, which experience has shown might belong to third persons or be subject to a hire purchase agreement, e.g. motor cars, caravans, motor boats, it may be advisable, where other enquiries have failed to make enquiry of H.P. Information Ltd.

Goods owned by debtor and third person

sc46.1.21 Where two persons own chattels as co-owners (whether joint tenants or tenants in common) each is entitled to possession and to sell without the consent of the other. Accordingly the enforcement officer acting under a *fi. fa.* upon a judgment against one co-owner is in no worse position and so can seize and sell the whole of the property (see *Farrar v Beswick* (1836) 1 M. & W. 682; *Mayhew v Herrick* (1849) 7 C.B. 229). In such a case, upon the enforcement officer interpleading, the Court or a Judge would order the enforcement officer to divide the proceeds of the sale accordingly between the judgment debtor and the co-owner claimant (*cf. The James W. Elwell* [1921] P.351).

The position is different in garnishee proceedings (now called Third Party Debt Orders; see Pt 72 CPR): an action upon a debt owing to two creditors jointly must be brought in their joint names, and therefore such a debt could not be attached under a judgment against one only of the joint creditors (*Macdonald v Tacquah Gold Mines* (1884) 13 Q.B.D. 535, *per* Bowen L.J., at 539; *Beasley v Roney* [1891] 1 Q.B. 509, *per* Pollock, B., at 512; *Hirschorn v Evans* [1938] 2 K.B. 801).

When two persons have separate and different interests in a chattel (e.g. one is owner subject to another's charge or lien) the enforcement officer may seize if the judgment debtor is entitled to possession, but may only sell the debtor's interest.

Goods of a company

As to seizure of property of a company comprised in debentures issued by such company, see *Re Opera Ltd* [1891] 3 Ch. 260; *Taunton v Sheriff of Warwickshire* [1895] 1 Ch. 734; 2 Ch. 319. **sc46.1.22**

RSC

A seizure of goods comprised in debentures constituting a floating charge on the property of a company is not a dealing with them in the ordinary course of business, and the fact that the moneys secured by the debentures have not become payable, does not debar the holders of them from intervening to protect their security as against an execution creditor (*Davey v Williamson* [1898] 2 Q.B. 194). But they must intervene in such a way as to cause the whole security to crystallise; they cannot claim a specific asset against the execution creditor while allowing the security to remain a floating charge *qua* the other assets (*Evans v Rival Granite Quarries Ltd* [1910] 2 K.B. 979, CA).

Under the Companies Act 1985 s.621 (which is analogous to the Insolvency Act 1986 s.346) where execution has issued against a company, and the company is subsequently wound up, the creditor cannot retain the benefit of the execution against the liquidator unless he has completed the execution before the commencement of the winding up, but the section gives the Court a discretion to defeat the rights conferred on the liquidator, either wholly or partially, according to what is right and fair in the circumstances of the case (*Re Grosvenor Metal Co Ltd* [1950] Ch. 63). As to completion by the appointment of a receiver, see AJA 1956 s.36(4).

By the CA 1985 s.622, where any goods of a company are taken in execution, and before sale or completion of the execution, notice is served on the enforcement officer that a provisional liquidator has been appointed or a winding-up order made, etc., the enforcement officer, on being required, is to deliver up the goods or money seized to the liquidator, but the costs of the execution are a first charge on the goods or money so delivered, and the liquidator may sell the goods or a sufficient part of them to satisfy that charge. The "costs" referred to in this section only include costs incurred by the enforcement officer himself. They do not include any costs of the execution creditor (*Re Woods (Bristol) Ltd* (1931) 75 S.J. 458), *cf.* Insolvency Act 1986 s.346 and "Bankruptcy of debtor", para.46.1.25.

Where a company contracts to issue debentures charging its property under such circumstances that equity would decree specific performance of the contract, and before the debentures are actually issued goods intended to be comprised therein are seized in execution, the intended debenture-holder stands practically in the same position, for the purpose of asserting his priority over the execution, as if the debentures had actually been issued; for an execution creditor takes subject to all equities (*Simultaneous Colour Printing Syndicate v Foweraker* [1901] 1 K.B. 771; and see *Re Standard Manufacturing Co* [1891] 1 Ch. 627; *Duck v Tower Galvanising Co* [1901] 2 K.B. 314; *Re London Pressed Hinge Co* [1905] 1 Ch. 576). But, where goods of a company were seized under a *fi. fa.*, and, in order to avoid a sale, the company, with the assent of the execution creditor, agreed that in consideration of his not selling they would pay a sum to the enforcement officer out of the daily takings, it was held that the judgment creditor was entitled to retain the moneys against the debenture holders of the company (*Robinson v Burnell's Vienna Bakery Co* [1904] 2 K.B. 624).

So where, in order to get rid of a man in possession, the managing director of a company paid out the enforcement officer who had seized goods to satisfy a judgment in respect of an ordinary trade debt but before the enforcement officer paid over to the execution creditors debenture-holders, who had a floating charge, had secured the appointment of a receiver, it was held that as the company had an implied licence from the debenture-holders to pay trade debts, the execution creditors were entitled to the money in the hands of the enforcement officer (*Heaton and Dugard Ltd v Cutting Bros Ltd* [1925] 1 K.B. 655).

Ship

sc46.1.23 Where the debtor owns some only of the shares in a foreign ship the enforcement officer is entitled to seize the ship as a whole and sell the shares (*The James W. Elwell* [1921] P. 351); *quaere* whether this procedure is applicable to an English ship, the shares in which are transferable by bill of sale (*ibid*., at 368). The possession of the enforcement officer does not deprive the marshall of his power to arrest in actions *in rem*. The maritime lien of the Master for wages even after seizure has priority to the claims of the execution creditor, but where the enforcement officer has seized before arrest by the marshal, the execution creditors have priority over necessaries men (*ibid*.); and the Master's lien has priority over the claim of the enforcement officer in respect of his costs of execution (*The Ile de Ceylan* [1922] P. 256). As to priority of a claim under a French *hypothèque* to a claim by necessaries men, see *Hills, etc., Co Ltd v Owners of Colorado* (1923) 39 T.L.R. 216.

Though judgment creditors cannot proceed *in rem* in respect of a judgment for an amount exceeding the bail given for release of the vessel, they may proceed by *fi. fa.* (*The Joannis Vatis* [1922] P. 213).

Goods of a patient in control of Court of Protection

sc46.1.24 When the property of a patient has become subject to the control of the Court of Protection by the appointment of a receiver, it cannot be seized under a writ of *fi. fa.* by an execution creditor of the patient (*Re Winkle* [1894] 2 Ch. 519, distinguished in *Davies v Thomas* [1900] 2 Ch. 462). But where, before the appointment of a receiver, the goods of a debtor who is a mental patient are taken in execution under a *fi. fa.*, there is no jurisdiction to order a sale of the goods for maintenance of the debtor in priority to the claims of the execution creditor (*Re Clarke* [1898] 1 Ch. 336; see now Mental Health Act 1983 s.96).

Bankruptcy of debtor

sc46.1.25 In order to entitle an execution creditor to retain the benefit of his execution against the trustee in bankruptcy of the debtor, he must have completed the execution by seizure and sale before the commencement of the bankruptcy (see Insolvency Act 1986 s.346).

A payment made by the debtor to the enforcement officer even if made before a bankruptcy order is made against him, operates in satisfaction of a judgment creditor's debt only when the judgment creditor is in a position to maintain an action against the enforcement officer for money had and received (*Re A Debtor (No.2 of 1977) Ex p. the Debtor v Goacher* [1979] 1 W.L.R. 956; [1979] 1 All E.R. 870).

The effect of the provisions of the Insolvency Act 1986 s.346, is that the title of the trustee will prevail over that of the execution creditor unless (1) the execution has been completed by seizure and sale or receipt of the full amount of the levy in the case of goods (*Figg v Moore* [1894] 2 Q.B. 690) or by a return of *nulla bona* as in *Re Fairley Ex p. Low and Bonar Ltd* [1922] 2 Ch. 791, or in the case of land by seizure or appointment of a receiver or payment; (2) the completion has taken place before the commencement of the bankruptcy (see *Burns v Brown* [1895] 1 Q.B. 324). The execution is completed by seizure and sale where, after execution, the enforcement officer has sold under authority given on an interpleader issue and paid the money into Court (*Re Chiandetti* (1921) 91 L.J.K.B. 70).

For the purposes of s.346 of the Insolvency Act 1986, and s.621 of the CA 1985, an execution against goods is completed by seizure and sale or by the making of a charging order under s.1 of the Charging Orders Act 1979 (see Charging Orders Act 1979 s.4; and O.50, r.1).

The execution is not "completed" within s.346 of the Insolvency Act 1986, unless payment has been made direct to the enforcement officer: payment of the amount of the levy to the creditor direct does not amount to such completion (*Re Godding* [1914] 2 K.B. 70; *Re Pollock* (1902) 87 L.T. 238). Where by arrangement certain goods supposed to be the property of the debtor's wife were withdrawn and sold before notice of the act of bankruptcy and the proceeds were paid after such notice, it was held that execution was not completed within the section (*Re Evans* [1916] H.B.R. 111).

An enforcement officer failed to execute a writ of *fi. fa.* if he did no more than call at the debtor's house and report his inability to gain access and such failure was not "a formal defect or irregularity" in insolvency proceedings capable of remedy under r.7.55 of the Insolvency Rules (*Re A Debtor (No.340 of 1992), The Times*, July 19, 1993).

If a debtor pays money in order to avoid a sale of goods taken in execution by the enforcement officer under a writ of *fi. fa.* it will be treated as "money in order to avoid sale" under s.346 of the Insolvency Act 1986, and not for "money received in part satisfaction of the execution" under s.346 of the Act, and accordingly such money becomes vested in the execution creditor and his title to it is subject to defeasance only if within 14 days of its receipt the enforcement officer receives notice of the debtor's bankruptcy (*Marley Tile Co Ltd v Burrows* [1978] Q.B. 241; [1978] 1 All E.R. 657, CA).

Debtors Act 1869 s.4

Decrees and orders for payment or recovery of a sum of money were formerly enforced in the first place by attachment of the debtor, and then by sequestration of his effects but they cannot as a rule be now enforced by committal, by reason of the Debtors Act 1869 s.4 of which provides as follows: **sc46.1.26**

"Abolition of imprisonment for debt, with exceptions

With the exceptions hereinafter-mentioned, no person shall, after the commencement of this Act, be arrested or imprisoned for making default in payment of a sum of money. **sc46.1.27**

There shall be excepted from the operation of the above enactment:
1. Default in payment of a penalty, or sum in the nature of a penalty other than a penalty in respect of any contract:
2. Default in payment of any sum recoverable summarily before a justice or justices of the peace:
3. Default by a trustee or person acting in a fiduciary capacity and ordered to pay by a Court of Equity [High Court of Justice] any sum in his possession or under his control:
4. Default by an attorney or solicitor in payment of costs when ordered to pay costs for misconduct as such, or in payment of a sum of money when ordered to pay the same in his character of an officer of the Court making the order:
5. Default in payment for the benefit of creditors of any portion of a salary or other income in respect of the payment of which any Court having jurisdiction in bankruptcy is authorised to make an order:
6. Default in payment of sums in respect of the payment of which orders are in this Act authorised to be made:
Provided, first, that no person shall be imprisoned in any case excepted from the operation of this section for a longer period than one year; and, secondly, that nothing in this section shall alter the effect of any judgment or order of any Court for payment of money except as regards the arrest and imprisonment of the person making default in paying such money."

The order of committal must accurately specify under which exception the default is included (*Re Wilde* [1910] W.N. 128, CA).

Crown debts

This section applies to sums of money payable and debts due to the Crown, including such sums payable in respect of any of the taxes, contributions or liabilities specified in Sch.4 to AJA 1970, see s.11(b)(ii) of that Act (Vol.2, para.9B–50), and Crown Proceedings Act 1947 s.26(2) (Vol.2, para.9B–362). **sc46.1.28**

Party in default

Though default in payment of a sum ordered to be paid cannot be punished by committal, the default remains a contempt, and the court has a discretion whether or not to allow the party in default to take any further proceeding in the action in which payment was ordered (*Leavis v Leavis* [1921] P. 299). This discretion is given added emphasis by CPR Pt 3 (see, in particular, r.3.4(2)(c)). **sc46.1.29**

"Penalty"

Penalty includes penal interest ordered to be paid by a trustee in bankruptcy under a financial provision under Sch.9, para.21 to the Insolvency Act 1986, but not the costs **sc46.1.30** of the order (*Re Nicholson* (1890) 63 L.T. 322) and see, *per* Morton L.J. in *Attorney General v Randall* [1944] K.B. 709; (1944) 60 T.L.R. 523 at 524.

"Sum recoverable before a justice"

sc46.1.31 Costs which have been awarded by a Crown Court against one of the parties to an appeal, or which by the Magistrates' Courts Act 1980 s.110 may be enforced before a justice by warrant of distress, and in default of distress by warrant of commitment, are within the second exception (*R. v Pratt* (1870) L.R. 5 Q.B. 176).

A committal to prison by a magistrate under the Distress for Rates Act 1849 s.2, is punitive in character and the Court cannot, under s.285 of the Insolvency Act 1986, order the debtor's release when proceedings on a bankruptcy petition are pending or an individual has been adjudged bankrupt (*Re Edgcome* [1902] 2 K.B. 403, CA).

"Trustee or person acting in a fiduciary capacity"

sc46.1.32 The words "person acting in a fiduciary capacity" in the third exception include any person who stands in a fiduciary relation towards any other person who may be entitled to call on him to pay, whether such other person is or is not a claimant in the action (per Jessel M.R. in *Marris v Ingram* (1880) 13 Ch. D. 338); and have been applied to an agent who received bills that he might discount them and hand the proceeds to the owner (*Hutchinson v Hartmont* [1877] W.N. 29); to a London agent making default in payment of a balance found due to the country solicitor (*Litchfield v Jones* (1887) 36 Ch. D. 530); to an auctioneer in respect of proceeds of goods intrusted to him for sale (*Crowther v Elgood* (1887) 34 Ch. D. 691); to a receiver who had made default in payment of a sum found to be due from him, even where he had been discharged before the order for payment (*Re Gent* (1889) 40 Ch. D. 190); to an executor indebted to his testator's estate, who having means to pay the debt due from him had persistently evaded payment (*Re Bourne* [1906] 1 Ch. 697, CA); and to a trustee who has received money in connection with the sale of heirlooms (*Re Berwick (Lord), Re Lord Berwick* (1900) 81 L.T. 797); but they have been held, under the circumstances, not to include a director or promoter of a company (*Metcalfe's Case* (1880) 13 Ch. D. 815; *Phosphate, etc. Co v Hartmont* (1887) 25 W.R. 743); nor a creditor ordered to repay money received by way of fraudulent preference (*Ex p. Hooson* (1873) L.R. 8 Ch. 231; *Re Bishop* (1891) 7 T.L.R. 610). They do not apply to the case of a partner who has received moneys on behalf of his firm (*Piddocke v Burt* [1894] 1 Ch. 343) even if he has given an undertaking (*Carter v Roberts* [1903] 2 Ch. 312, at 321).

The remedy is only intended to be given as between trustee and *cestuis que trust*, and is not a remedy for a mere creditor for whom the person against whom he seeks to assert the remedy is not a trustee (*per* Kay J., *Re Firmin* (1887) 57 L.T. 45); but a debtor who has admitted that a sum is due from him and submitted to an order directing him to hold it upon certain trusts is within the exception (*Preston v Etherington* (1887) 37 Ch. D. 104; and see *Taaffe v Fitzsimmons* [1894] 1 Ir.R.63).

Where a sole creditor in an administration action takes an order against an executor for personal payment of his certified debt the fiduciary relationship between them is at an end, and the creditor cannot bring the executor within the third exception in s.4 of the Debtors Act 1869 (*Re Thomas* [1912] 2 Ch. 348, CA).

"Possession or control"

sc46.1.33 A trustee who has without moral delinquency lost the trust moneys (*Middleton v Chichester* (1871) L.R. 6 Ch. 152) or has innocently suffered his co-trustee to appropriate and misapply them (*Evans v Bear* (1875) L.R. 10 Ch. 76) is within the third exception (see s.4, Debtors Act 1869 above); but not a trustee who has omitted to get in the trust moneys (*Ferguson v Ferguson* (1875) L.R. 10 Ch. 661) or is not proved to have ever had them in his possession (*Re Hincks Ex p. Cuddeford* (1878) 45 L.J. Bk. 127; *Re Hickey* (1866) 35 W.R. 53; *Re Fewster* [1901] 1 Ch. 447; and see *Phosphate, etc., Co v Hartmont* (1887) 25 W.R. 743; *Re Hind* (1878) 37 L.T. 168; *Harper v McIntyre* (1908) 99 L.T. 191).

An order on a defendant to pay into Court the alleged value of bonds previously directed to be deposited in Court cannot be enforced by committal, as there is no breach of an order to pay money in defendant's possession or under his control (*Cronin v Twinberrow* [1887] W.N. 201); nor can a judgment directing a trustee to make good the difference between the value of bonds at the date when he improperly sold them and their value at the date of judgment (*Re Walker* (1891) 60 L.J.Ch. 25).

An executor may be attached for default in payment of a debt due from him to the testator in his lifetime, but not for default in payment of such a debt and interest (not distinguished) because the interest could not be "in his possession or under his control" (*Re Hickey* (1886) 35 W.R. 53).

The exception applies only where there has been actual receipt of the money by the person sought to be imprisoned (*Re Fewster* [1901] 1 Ch. 447; *Re Wilkins* [1901] W.N. 202; and see *Re Underwood* (1903) 51 W.R. 335).

Privilege of Parliament

Privilege of parliament cannot be claimed by a person liable to imprisonment, as having acted in a fiduciary capacity (*Re Gent* (1889) 40 Ch. D. 190). Whether privilege of parliament can be set up where the trustee has been guilty of no moral culpability, *quaere* (*Aylesford v Poulett* [1892] 2 Ch. 60). **sc46.1.34**

Bankruptcy Order

Where a "receiving order" under the Bankruptcy Act 1914 (now replaced by a "bankruptcy order" under the Insolvency Act 1986) was made against a person within the exceptions to s.4, Debtors Act 1869 (see above) he was held not to be protected from committal under that section (see *Re Smith* [1893] 2 Ch. 1; *Re Edye* (1891) 63 L.T. 762 not following *Re Simes* (1890) 62 L.T. 721 and *Cobham v Dalton* (1875) L.R. 10 ChD 655. See also above note "Bankruptcy of debtor" at para.46.1.25. **sc46.1.35**

Service, where necessary

Where the order is for payment within a certain time after service, the trustee is not in default until the order has been served on him, and cannot be restrained by writ *ne exeat regno* from going out of the jurisdiction (*Colverson v Bloomfield* (1885) 29 Ch. D. 341). **sc46.1.36**

Terms of order

It need not be stated in the order required to be enforced that the person ordered to pay is a trustee or person in a fiduciary capacity, and that the money is in his possession or under his control, but such matters may be proved *aliunde* (*Brewster v Prior* (1887) 3 T.L.R. 590). **sc46.1.37**

The amount to be paid must be specified in the order for payment (*Re Spicer* [1881] W.N. 85).

"Default by an attorney or solicitor", etc.

As to an order of committal of a solicitor for non-payment of costs under the fourth exception in s.4, Debtors Act 1869 (see sc45.1.30), see *Tilney v Stansfeld* (1880) 28 W.R. 582. A committal may issue for default in payment of a balance found due following a detailed assessment (formerly "taxation") of costs (*Re Rush* (1870) L.R. 9 Eq. 147; *Re White* (1871) 19 W.R. 39) including the costs of the detailed assessment *Re A Solicitor* [1895] 2 Ch. 66; *Re N., A Solicitor* [1917] W.N. 138); but not where the solicitor is liable to pay costs as an ordinary litigant (*Re Hope* (1872) L.R. 7 Ch. 523; see *Jenkins v Fereday* (1872) L.R. 7 C.P. 358). The order must distinguish between the sum due for costs and the sum due from the solicitor as money in his hands (*Re Wilde* [1910] W.N. 128, CA). **sc46.1.38**

The sum ordered to be paid must be accurately defined (see *Re Weatherley* (1918) 88 L.J.K.B. 482, CA).

An order enforceable by committal for payment of money received by a solicitor for his client may be made, notwithstanding judgment has been obtained against him for the amount (*Re Grey* [1892] 2 Q.B. 440).

As to committal of a solicitor ordered to pay a sum of money belonging to a client and improperly dealt with by him, see *Re Dudley* (1883) 12 Q.B.D. 44.

Quaere, whether a London agent making default in payment of a balance found due on taking account between him and his principals is within the fourth exception, though he is certainly within the third exception *per* North J., *Litchfield v Jones* (1887) 36 Ch. D. 530). See *Re Farman* (1897) 14 T.L.R. 20.

After an order striking a solicitor off the roll has been made he may be attached for disobedience to a direction in the same order for payment of money due from him (*Re Strong* (1886) 32 Ch. D. 342).

Service

sc46.1.39 It is not necessary to serve on the solicitor the order to tax along with the certificate of the result of taxation before an order for attachment can issue against him for the balance found due, provided that the order to tax has been previously duly served on him (*Re Wilde* [1910] W.N. 105, 128, CA). (The term "taxation" has now been replaced by "detailed assessment".)

Waiver

sc46.1.40 Giving time and accepting part payment was held not to amount to a waiver of the right of attachment (*Re Fereday* [1895] 2 Ch. 437).

"For a longer period than one year"

sc46.1.41 In case of re-arrest, the period of imprisonment must end with the twelve months from date of the original imprisonment, inclusive of the time the debtor has been at liberty (*Church's Trustee v Hibbard* [1902] 2 Ch. 784, CA).

Discretion in cases within exceptions 3 and 4

sc46.1.42 The Debtors Act 1878 provides that in any case coming within the third and fourth exceptions in s.4 of the Debtors Act 1869, the Court may inquire into the case, and "may grant or refuse, either absolutely or upon terms, any application for a writ of attachment, or other process or order of arrest or imprisonment, and any application to stay the operation of any such writ, process or order, or for discharge from arrest or imprisonment thereunder."

Policy of Debtors Act

sc46.1.43 In *Barrett v Hammond* (1879) 10 Ch. D. 285, it was held by Bacon V.-C. (following *Street v Hope* (1879) 10 Ch. D. 287n., *per* Malins V.-C.) that the policy of the Debtors Act 1869 s.4, was not vindictive, and that the Court, in the exercise of its discretion under the Debtors Act 1878, would not order the imprisonment of a defaulting trustee, unless it was likely to be productive of payment; but Jessel M.R. in *Marris v Ingram* (1880) 13 Ch. D. 338, held that the Act of 1869 was intended for the punishment of fraudulent or dishonest debtors and declined to exercise the discretion given him by the Act of 1878, as he was not satisfied that defendant was unable to pay; and see *Re Knowles* (1883) 52 L.J.Ch. 685, *per* Kay J.; *Re Dudley* (1883) 12 Q.B.D. 44; *Re Freston* (1883) 11 Q.B.D. 545; *Re Gent* (1889) 40 Ch. D. 190; *Church's Trustee v Hibbard* [1902] 2 Ch. 784, CA; *Re Edgcome* [1902] 2 K.B. 403; *Re Wray* (1887) 36 Ch. D. 138 (where it was held that a receiving order against a defaulting solicitor did not prevent an order of committal issuing) followed in *Re Edye* (1891) 63 L.T. 762.

It is not necessary, in order to commit a defaulting trustee, to show that he has been guilty of fraud (*Preston v Etherington* (1888) 37 Ch. D. 104 at 110); but where there is no fraud the Court may decline to make an order of committal where the defaulting trustee executes a charge upon his property (*cf. Holroyde v Garnett* (1882) 20 Ch. D. 532).

Where there was no moral culpability involved in the misapplication of trust funds, the Court exercised its discretion in favour of the debtor (*Aylesford v Poulett* [1892] 2 Ch. 60).

Discretion of Judge

sc46.1.44 The Court of Appeal will not readily interfere with the conclusion of the Court below as to the debtor's ability or inability to pay (*Esdaile v Visser* (1880) 13 Ch. D. 421; but on this case see *Chard v Jervis* (1882) 9 Q.B.D. 178); or generally with the discretion of the Court below under the above section in refusing or granting an order of committal (*Re Wray* (1887) 36 Ch. D. 138 at 145; *Preston v Etherington* (1888) 37 Ch. D. 104; and see *Crowther v Elgood* (1887) 34 Ch. D. 691); unless the discretion is shown to have been exercised on an erroneous ground (*Re Smith* [1893] 2 Ch. 1 at 18). See further, Pt 52—Appeals.

Debtors Act 1869 s.5

sc46.1.45 The jurisdiction given by s.5 to commit to prison a person who makes default in payment of a debt or instalment of a debt due from him in pursuance of an order or judgment is exercisable by the High Court only in respect of a High Court maintenance order AJA 1970 s.11(a). This jurisdiction will therefore only be exercised by the Family Division of the High Court; see Family Proceedings Rules 1991 rr.7.4– 7.6.

In *Mubarak v Mubarak* [2001] 1 F.L.R. 698 the Court of Appeal held that the procedure under s.5 of the 1869 Act was not compatible with the European Convention on

Human Rights. Accordingly s.5 has been amended by the Civil Procedure (Modification of Enactments) Order 2002 (SI 2002/439). The section as amended is at para.cc28.0.3. Also Sch.2, CCR O.28 – Judgment Summonses was amended by the Civil Procedure (Amendment No.5) Rules 2001.

Debtors Act 1869 s.6

Its material parts provide as follows: **sc46.1.46**

"*Where the plaintiff in any action in any of Her Majesty's superior Courts of law at Westminster in which, if brought before the commencement of this Act, the defendant would have been liable to arrest, proves at any time before final judgment by evidence on oath, to the satisfaction of a judge of one of those Courts, that the plaintiff has good cause of action against the defendant to the amount of £50 or upwards, and that there is probable cause for believing that the defendant is about to quit England unless he be apprehended, and that the absence of the defendant from England will materially prejudice the plaintiff in the prosecution of his action, such judge may in the prescribed manner order such defendant to be arrested and imprisoned for a period not exceeding six months, unless and until he has sooner given the prescribed security, not exceeding the amount claimed in the action, that he will not go out of England without the leave of the Court ...*"

The application for an order under this section is made to the Judge in Chambers; it may be made without notice, at any time after the issue of the claim form and before final judgment; and it must be supported by affidavit evidence establishing the existence of the necessary conditions to the satisfaction of the Judge according to the high standard of proof required.

An order can be made under this section only if the following four conditions are satisfied, namely:

(1) the action is one in which the defendant would formerly, i.e. before the Debtors Act 1869 have been liable to arrest at law;
(2) a good cause of action for at least £50 is established;
(3) there is "probable cause" for believing that the defendant is about to quit England unless he is arrested; and
(4) "the absence of the defendant from England will materially prejudice the plaintiff in the prosecution of the action."

The making of an order under this section is discretionary (*Re Lehman Ex p. Hasluck* (1890) 6 T.L.R. 435).

It should be noted that an order under this section is available before judgment, and not after; it is designed to assist in obtaining a judgment and it is not a form of process of execution. For an examination of the history and the relevant authorities, see *per* Megarry J. in *Felton v Callis* [1969] 1 Q.B. 200; [1968] 3 All E.R. 673.

Writ ne exeat regno

This writ, which is in the nature of equitable bail, is still extant but by analogy can issue only if the requirements of s.6 of the Debtors Act 1869 are satisfied (*Felton v Callis* [1969] 1 Q.B. 200; [1968] 3 All E.R. 673 where the authorities are fully examined by Megarry J.). **sc46.1.47**

This writ, which has the effect of restraining the defendant from departing out of the jurisdiction, is ordered to issue to assist the claimant in obtaining judgment and not in executing it, and therefore it may properly issue in an action to recover a large sum of money belonging to clients of the claimant firm which the defendant had wrongfully converted to his own use and to secure full disclosure from the defendant as to what happened to such monies and a full inquiry into his monetary accounts (*Lipkin Gorman (a firm) v Cass, The Times*, May 29, 1985,). In practical terms the writ will require the passport of the defendant to be impounded (*ibid.*).

The writ may be issued in support of a "Freezing Injunction" (formerly referred to as a "*Mareva injunction*"; see CPR Pt 25) and should be directed to the Tipstaff (and not to a High Court enforcement officer) with the direction to bring the arrested defendant before the Judge forthwith or as soon as possible (*Al Nahkel for Contracting and Trading Ltd v Lowe* [1986] Q.B. 235; [1986] 1 All E.R. 729).

Even where the conditions for the issue of the writ *ne exeat regno* are not or cannot be fulfilled, the Court has power, sitting in private, to grant an injunction on an application without notice to restrain the defendant from leaving England and Wales and forthwith to deliver his passport to the person serving the order on him, where it appears just and convenient to do so, or when it is necessary to protect the claimant's rights pending the hearing of the action and to obtain information ordered to be disclosed under a Search Order and/or Freezing Injunction (see Pt 25), but such injunction should run only for so long as it is necessary to give effect to such orders (*Bayer A.G. v Winter* [1986] 1 W.L.R. 497; [1986] 1 All E.R. 733, CA). It will not be allowed to issue if its true purpose is to facilitate execution in the event of the claimant's action succeeding, and not to prevent the defendant leaving the country and thereby prejudicing the claimant in prosecuting his claim (*Allied Arab Bank v Hajjar* [1988] Q.B. 787).

In the interest of the ward of Court to know his or her true identity if that can be established by a DNA test (which, in practice has replaced the blood test) the Court will grant an injunction to restrain the mother from leaving the jurisdiction until the completion of the tests (*Re I. (A Minor), The Times*, May 22, 1987).

The application for the writ *ne exeat regno* is made without notice at any time before final judgment.

County court judgments

sc46.1.48 By virtue of s.42 of the County Courts Act 1984 (as amended by the Courts and Legal Services Act 1990), provision is made for specific judgments of the county court to be transferred to the High Court for enforcement, see Vol.2, paras 9A–482 *et seq.* for the County Courts Act 1984. See also Sch.2, CCR O.25, r.13. A judgment so transferred may be enforced in the High Court as if it were a judgment or order of High Court and must be treated as a judgment or order of the High Court for all purposes, except the power to set aside, correct, vary or quash the judgment or order or to appeal against it shall continue as if it were a county court judgment or order and not a High Court judgment or order.

By virtue of art.8 of the High Court and County Court Jurisdiction Order 1991 (SI 1991/724), a judgment or order of a county court for the payment of a sum of money which it is sought to enforce wholly or partially by execution against goods:

(a) shall be enforced only in the High Court where the sum which it is sought to enforce is £5,000 or more and the proceedings in which the judgment or order was obtained did not arise out of an agreement regulated by the Consumer Credit Act 1974;

(b) shall be enforced only in the county court where the sum which it is sought to enforce is less than £600;

(c) in any other case may be enforced in either the High Court or in a county court.

Magistrates' courts

sc46.1.49 The Magistrates' Courts Act 1980 s.87, provides that payment of a sum adjudged to be paid by a conviction of a magistrates' court may be enforced by the High Court or a county court (otherwise than by issue of a writ of *fi. fa.* or other process against goods or by imprisonment or attachment of earnings) as if the sum were due to the clerk of the magistrates' court in pursuance of a judgment or order of the High Court or county court, as the case may be.

So far as the Central Office is concerned, the Senior Master issued a Practice Direction dated November 22, 1967, setting out the following procedure to be followed for this purpose:

1. The applicant will bring an affidavit, framed for the purpose of the particular type of execution desired and exhibiting the authority of the magistrates' court to take the proceedings (M.C. Forms Rules 1981, Form **No. 63**). The authority will recite the conviction, the amount outstanding and the nature of the proceedings authorised to be taken. An extra copy of the exhibit will be required for filing in the Central Office.

2. Attendance will be made in the first place in the alphabetical section of the judgment department appropriate to the surname of the applicant. The copy of the exhibit will be lodged there and a reference number will be assigned to the matter, which will later be entered by the judgment clerk in a special register.

3. If the application is being made without notice (e.g. a charging order nisi or garnishee order *nisi*) the affidavit and original exhibit will then be taken to the Masters' Secretary's Office (Room E214) and lodged in the usual way.

4. Any other application will be initiated in the usual way after a reference number has been assigned.

High Court Enforcement Officers

By s.99 and Sch.7 Courts Act 2003 the former responsibilities of the Sheriff for executing High Court writs of enforcement now vest in High Court Enforcement Officers. sc46.1.50

Any High Court judgment and any county court judgment for over £600 (except where the judgment arises from a regulated agreement under the Consumer Credit Act 1974) can be enforced in the High Court. A county court judgment needs to be transferred to the High Court for enforcement purposes (use Form N293A). Many of the larger HCEO offices offer a transfer up service to assist judgment creditors to turn their county court judgment into a writ for enforcement in the High Court. Enquiries can be made of the HCEO where the writ of execution is to be sent; many arrange transfer up without charge (there is a court fee). Those not wanting to issue writs themselves and wishing to use a transfer up service can speed things up by getting the certificate of judgment stamped by the appropriate county court on Pt 2 of the N293A before sending it to the transfer up service provider. As ever, any practical information about assets available for seizure should be provided to the HCEO.

When permission to issue any writ of execution is necessary

2.—(1) A writ of execution to enforce a judgment or order may not issue without the permission of the court in the following cases, that is to say:— sc46.2

- (a) where 6 years or more have elapsed since the date of the judgment or order;
- (b) where any change has taken place, whether by death or otherwise, in the parties entitled or liable to execution under the judgment or order;
- (c) where the judgment or order is against the assets of a deceased person coming to the hands of his executors or administrators after the date of the judgment or order, and it is sought to issue execution against such assets;
- (d) where under the judgment or order any person is entitled to a remedy subject to the fulfilment of any condition which it is alleged has been fulfilled;
- (e) where any goods sought to be seized under a writ of execution are in the hands of a receiver appointed by the court or a sequestrator.

(2) Paragraph (1) is without prejudice to section 2 of the Reserve and Auxiliary Forces (Protection of Civil Interests) Act, or any other enactment or rule by virtue of which a person is required to obtain the permission of the court for the issue of a writ of execution or to proceed to execution on or otherwise to the enforcement of a judgment or order.

(3) Where the court grants permission, whether under this rule or otherwise, for the issue of a writ of execution and the writ is not issued within one year after the date of the order granting such permission, the order shall cease to have effect, without prejudice, however, to the making of a fresh order.

Effect of rule

The requirement of leave to issue execution under this rule applies to all writs of execution and is additional to the requirement of leave to issue particular writs of execution under other rules, e.g. O.45, r.3 (writ of possession); O.45, r.4(2) (writ of specific delivery of goods); O.46, r.3 (writs of execution in aid of other writs); O.46, r.5 (writ of sequestration); O.81, r.5(2) (execution against a person as a partner upon a judgment against a firm); O.81, r.6 (execution in actions between partners). sc46.2.1

The rule is also without prejudice to any other enactment or rule requiring leave to issue execution, e.g. leave to enforce an award under the Arbitration Act 1996 s.66 (see Vol.2, Section 2E, para.2E–252) under which leave is only given in a clear case (*Grech v Board of Trade* [1923] W.N. 235).

The order granting leave to issue execution shall be operative for one year after which it will cease to have effect, though a new order may be made.

Judgment over six years old—practice

sc46.2.2 Application for permission to issue execution on a judgment more than six years old should be made without notice supported by evidence (usually a witness statement or affidavit of facts by the applicant or his solicitor). The evidence should state (1) the date of the judgment (2) the amount of the original judgment debt (3) the amount remaining due (4) the causes of delay (5) that the applicant is entitled to execution, i.e. that there has been no change of parties or devolution of interest (or, if there has been the precise nature of it). The master/district judge may decline to deal with the application without notice to the judgment debtor and require the application for permission to be served and heard on notice.

An application to issue or to extend the time for execution under a judgment was not an "action" within the meaning of s.38(1) of the Limitation Act 1980, hence to do so did not come within the provisions of s.24(1) prohibiting the bringing of an action on a judgment after the expiration of six years (*National Westminster Bank v Powney* [1991] Ch. 339; [1990] 2 All E.R. 416, CA).

A garnishee order absolute is effective although more than six years have elapsed since the judgment (*Fellows v Thornton* (1885) 14 Q.B.D. 335). (Garnishee Orders are now replaced by "Third Party Debt Orders", see Pt 72.)

Dismissal of an application under this rule does not make a second application impossible, but the later application should not be granted unless it is founded on material which was not before the Court on the first application (*W. T. Lamb & Sons v Rider* [1948] 2 K.B. 331).

Obtaining permission to enforce by execution a judgment over six years old is no mere formality. Permission may be refused (see e.g. *Patel v Singh* [2002] All E.R. (D) 453) unless the applicant discharges the burden of proving that it is demonstrably just to grant it (*Duer v Frazer* [2001] 1 W.L.R. 919). The test is whether there are facts which take the case out of the general rule that execution would not be allowed after six years; see *Society of Lloyds v Longtin* [2005] EWHC 2471 (Comm).

Change of parties

sc46.2.3 (1) Where the judgment creditor has died the application should be without notice (see *Mercer v Lawrence* (1878) 26 W.R. 506, for form of order). In an Irish case (*Meehan v Tynan* [1915] 2 Ir.R. 52) where notice was given to the debtor, no costs were allowed.

(2) Where the judgment debtor has died, notice of the application must be served on the personal representative (see *Re Shephard* (1890) 43 Ch. D. 131 at 137; commented on in *Thompson v Gill* [1903] 1 K.B. 760, CA).

(3) Where there has been an assignment of the judgment debt it appears that the application must be properly made without notice as was the case in *Re Bagley* [1911] 1 K.B. 317, CA; the Irish practice is otherwise (see *Meehan v Tynan*, above); *Donohoe v Flavelle* [1916] 2 Ir.R. 192).

(4) Where a surety is seeking to enforce a judgment which he has obtained on assignment, permission to issue execution must be obtained under this rule (*Kayley v Hothersall* [1925] 1 K.B. 607). The master/district judge will often direct an application to be made on notice (see Pt 23).

Death of judgment debtor

sc46.2.4 The rule does not apply to an executor *de son tort* (*Lord Westmeath v Coyne* [1896] 2 Ir.R. 436).

Permission given under this rule to issue execution against the executor of a deceased debtor does not operate as a judgment against the executor. It dispenses with the necessity of recovering judgment against him (*Stewart v Rhodes* [1900] 1 Ch. 386). A charging order *nisi* against the interest of a deceased judgment debtor is not valid as against his executor (see *Scott v Scott* [1952] W.N. 522; [1952] 2 All E.R. 890).

Death of judgment creditor

sc46.2.5 Until the executors have obtained permission under this rule, they cannot issue a statutory demand under the Insolvency Act 1986 (see Ex p. Woodall (1884) 13 Q.B.D. 479, a case involving a "bankruptcy notice" which has now been superceded by the "statutory demand"). Executors can obtain permission and issue the demand without being added as parties: CPR r.19.2: *Re Bagley* [1911] 1 K.B. 317.

On the death of one of several partners, the survivors are entitled to an order hereunder for execution (*Davis v Andrews* [1884] W.N. 94).

Asking for appointment of a receiver and injunction is not asking for permission to issue execution within this rule (see *Morgan v Hart* [1914] 2 K.B. 183, CA, and *Re A Company* [1915] 1 Ch. 520 at 527). The executors of a deceased creditor are therefore not entitled to obtain an order for appointment of a receiver of the judgment debtor's property under this rule (*Norburn v Norburn* [1894] 1 Q.B. 448). *Semble*, the proper course in such a case is for the party becoming entitled to enforce the judgment to apply first to be added as a party to the proceedings under O 15, r.7, see *Re Shephard* (1890) 43 Ch. D. 131 at 135; *Salt v Cooper* (1880) 16 Ch. D. 544 at 552, 553.

Presentation of a winding-up petition by a judgment creditor is not execution on a judgment (*Re A Company*, above).

Bankruptcy of judgment creditor

The trustee in bankruptcy of a judgment creditor cannot petition for a bankruptcy order to be made until he has obtained an order under this rule; for, until that is done, he is not a petitioning creditor to whom the debt is owed (Insolvency Act 1986 s.120(1) *Re Clements* [1901] 1 K.B. 260); but the trustee can obtain an order under this rule without being added as a party under CPR r.19.2 and when he had done so he is a person entitled to sign judgment (*Re Bagley* [1911] 1 K.B. 317). **sc46.2.6**

Assignment

The assignment of part of judgment does not effect such a change of parties to enable the assignee to issue execution. Execution can only be levied in respect of the whole judgment (*Forster v Baker* [1910] 2 K.B. 636, CA; see *Rothschild v Fisher* [1920] 2 K.B. 243, CA; *Chung Kwok Hotel Co v Field* [1960] 1 W.L.R. 1112 at 1115; [1960] 3 All E.R. 143 at 145). **sc46.2.7**

An assignee of a judgment debt must apply for leave to issue execution under this rule; he need not obtain an order adding him as a party under CPR r.19.2 (*Re Bagley* [1911] 1 K.B. 317, CA). It is submitted that an application to be so added would be improper.

Where a surety has paid a judgment debt and has obtained an assignment of the judgment under the Mercantile Law Amendment Act 1856 s.5, he must obtain the permission of the Court before he can issue execution against his co-surety to enforce contribution (*Kayley v Hothersall* [1925] 1 K.B. 607, CA, following a *dictum* of Parker J. in *Dale v Powell* (1911) 105 L.T. 291 at 292).

Conditional judgment or order

An application for permission to issue execution upon the fulfilment of any condition subject to which the judgment or order was made should be made without notice supported by evidence (usually a witness statement or affidavit sworn by the applicant). The Master/district judge may direct that the application be made on notice. **sc46.2.8**

Partner, retirement of

Where judgment is recovered by a firm, the retirement of a partner does not amount to a change in the parties entitled to execution within this rule (*Re Frank Hill* [1921] 2 K.B. 831). **sc46.2.9**

Goods in hands of receiver appointed by Court of sequestrator

Paragraph (1)(e) requires that permission must first be obtained to issue execution against goods in the hands of a receiver appointed by the Court or a sequestrator. This provision is necessary because otherwise an enforcement officer who seizes goods in the possession of a receiver appointed by the Court is guilty of contempt (see *Lane v Sterne* (1862) 3 Giff. 629; *Edwards v Edwards* (1876) 2 Ch. D. 291; and see also *Angel v Smith* (1804) 9 Ves. 335 (sequestrator) and *Russell v E. Anglian Ry.* (1850) 3 Mac. & G. 104). **sc46.2.10**

Reserve and Auxiliary Forces (Protection of Civil Interests) Act 1951

A judgment or order for the payment or recovery of a sum of money may not (except in certain specified cases) without the permission of the Court be enforced against a person protected by this Act (s.2(1)). See paras 9A–1to 9A–408+. **sc46.2.11**

Remedy barred by Limitation Act 1980

sc46.2.12 By virtue of the 1980 Act s.24(1) which applies to judgments generally, not merely those which operate as charges on land (*Jay v Johnstone* [1893] 1 Q.B. 25, 189, CA; see also *Watson v Birch* (1847) 15 Sim. 523; *Hebblethwaite v Peever* [1892] 1 Q.B. 124) no action may be brought upon any judgment after the expiration of six years from the date on which the judgment became enforceable. An action on any judgment can be an abuse of the process of the Court where there is an effective alternative method of obtaining satisfaction (*Pritchett v English & Colonial Syndicate* [1899] 2 Q.B. 428). It was held in *Brew v Brew* [1899] 2 Ir.R. 163, that where a judgment was obtained against A and B, and two years later execution was issued against A, and part of the debt levied, such execution kept the judgment debt alive against both A and B for a further period of six years, and the judgment creditor was entitled under the corresponding Irish rule to an order to issue execution, though more than twelve years had elapsed since the date of the judgment. See *Taylor v Hollard* [1902] 1 K.B. 676, as to when a payment of part is sufficient to take the case out of the statute. But the right to sue on a judgment is quite distinct from the right to levy execution under it and the abovementioned section does not enable execution to be issued without the permission of the Court at any time within six years of the judgment (*W. T. Lamb & Sons v Rider* [1948] 2 K.B. 331, CA) and see *Berliner Industrie-bank A.G. v Jost* [1971] 2 Q.B. 463; [1971] 2 All E.R. 1513, CA.

An application for permission to issue execution on a judgment or to extend the process of execution was not an action within the Limitation Act 1980 s.38(1) (*National Westminster Bank Plc v Powney* [1990] 2 W.L.R. 1084; [1990] 2 All E.R. 416, CA following *W. T. Lamb & Sons v Rider* [1948] 2 K.B. 331, CA and not following *Lougher v Donovan* [1948] 2 All E.R. 11, CA).

Duration of order

sc46.2.13 Paragraph (3) adopts the current practice under which, where permission to issue execution has been given, it was considered to endure for one year only. This was by analogy to a practice of long standing (approved by Stirling J., in *Kemp v Abraham*, July 1888) under which the Masters required an affidavit explaining the delay before the issue of a writ of attachment upon an order which was more than a year old.

If the Master gives permission he may impose terms, e.g. that the writ of execution be issued within a specified time.

Execution against property of foreign or commonwealth states

sc46.2.14 In cases where judgment has been obtained against a foreign or Commonwealth state and it is sought to execute the judgment by writ of *fieri facias*, charging order or garnishee order, the provisions of Queen's Bench Practice Direction No.37 apply. This Practice Direction applies also in the Chancery Division.

NO.37 EXECUTION AGAINST PROPERTY OF FOREIGN OR COMMONWEALTH STATES

Practice Direction was issued by the Senior Master and by the Chief Master on July 28, 1994

1. This Practice Direction applies in the Central Office of the Supreme Court, Chancery Chambers and in all District Registries.
2. In cases where judgment has been obtained against a Foreign or Commonwealth State and it is sought to execute such judgment by any one or more of the following methods namely, writ of *fieri facias*, charging order or garnishee order, then paragraphs 3, 4, 5 and 6 of this Practice Direction shall apply.
3. Before the writ of *fieri facias*, is issued, the Master or District Judge must be informed in writing and his direction sought. In cases where application is made for a charging order nisi or a garnishee order nisi, the affidavit in support of the application must include a statement that the execution is sought against a foreign or Commonwealth State.
4. A Master or District Judge having been made aware of any of the matters set out at paragraph 3 of this Practice Direction shall, so soon as is reasonably practicable inform the Foreign and Commonwealth Office (FCO) of the application and shall not permit the issue of the writ of *fieri facias*, nor grant an order nisi until the FCO has been so informed.

5. Protocol Division, Head of Diplomatic Missions and International Organisations Unit, tel. 020 7008 0991, fax. 020 7008 0978.
6. Having regard to all the circumstances of the case, the Master or District Judge may postpone the decision whether to issue the writ or grant an order nisi for so long as he considers reasonable for the purpose of enabling the FCO to furnish further information relevant to his decision, but not for longer than three days from the time of his contacting the FCO under paragraph 5 of this Practice Direction. In the event that no further information is received from the FCO within 24 hours of its being informed, then the writ of *fieri facias*, may be issued or the order nisi may be sealed without further delay.
7. This Practice Direction is issued with the approval of the Lord Chief Justice and the Vice-Chancellor and comes into force from October 1, 1994.

Permission required for issue of writ in aid of other writ

3. A writ of execution in aid of any other writ of execution shall not issue without the permission of the court. **sc46.3**

Effect of rule

In practice the writ of restitution (warrant of restitution in the county court) is the most commonly used writ "in aid of any other writ of execution". Permission to issue a writ "in aid of" another should be sought without notice supported by evidence usually in the form of an affidavit sworn by someone with knowledge of the relevant facts. **sc46.3.1**

Writ of assistance

The Court still has power to order a writ of assistance to issue, and will do so in certain cases where the writ of delivery has proved or will probably prove to be fruitless. The permission of the Court must first be obtained by application made without notice supported by a witness statement or affidavit, which must prove that the order for the specific delivery of goods has been served and not complied with (*Webster v Taylor* (1854) 18 Jur. 869). **sc46.3.2**

Writ of restitution

Where, after entry of the enforcement officer under a writ of possession, or after the claimant has been put in possession by the enforcement officer, the defendant forcibly or by stratagem resumes possession of the property, the claimant may have a writ of restitution (*Pitcher v Roe* (1841) 9 Dowl. 971). This is the normal procedure and not an application to commit for contempt (*Alliance Building Society v Austen* [1951] 2 All E.R. 1068). Application for the writ should be made without notice to a Master supported by evidence such as a witness statement or affidavit of facts, and an order will be made for the writ to issue. **sc46.3.3**

Similarly, where a claimant has entered under a judgment for possession and a writ of possession issued thereunder and where the judgment is subsequently set aside and the application nevertheless fails to restore possession to the defendant: the defendant should apply to a Master for an order setting aside the writ of possession and ordering possession to be given by the claimant to the defendant and giving permission then (or subsequently on without notice application) to issue a writ of restitution. Similarly, where possession has been obtained under an irregular writ of possession, or of more land than is properly covered by the writ of possession (*ibid.*).

Where an order for possession has been made under RSC O.113, (see now CPR Pt 55) the Court has power, on the claimant's application to order the issue of a writ of restitution, even if not all the people then in possession of the land were in such possession when the order for possession under O.113 was obtained provided that there is a plain and sufficient nexus between the original recovery of possession and the need to effect recovery of the same land (*Wiltshire CC v Frazer (No.2)* [1986] 1 W.L.R. 109; [1986] 1 All E.R. 65).

Writ of venditioni exponas

This is a writ in aid of execution by writ of *fi. fa.* It can only be issued after the enforcement officer has made a return that he has seized goods under the writ of *fi. fa.* which he has not sold or has been unable to sell "for want of buyers." There is now no need to file such return but the affidavit in support of the without notice application for the writ should exhibit such return. **sc46.3.4**

Writ of caplas ad satisfaciendum

sc46.3.5 This writ is abolished (see SCA 1981 s.141).

Application for permission to issue writ

sc46.4 4.—(1) An application for permission to issue a writ of execution may be made in accordance with CPR, Part 23 but the application notice need not be served on the respondent unless the court directs.

(2) Such an application must be supported by a witness statement or affidavit—

(a) identifying the judgment or order to which the application relates and, if the judgment or order is for the payment of money, stating the amount originally due thereunder and the amount due thereunder at the date the application notice is filed;

(b) stating, where the case falls within rule 2(1)(a) the reasons for the delay in enforcing the judgment or order;

(c) stating, where the case falls within rule 2(1)(b), the change which has taken place in the parties entitled or liable to execution since the date of the judgment or order;

(d) stating, where the case falls within rule 2(1)(c) or (d), that a demand to satisfy the judgment or order was made on the person liable to satisfy it and that he has refused or failed to do so;

(e) giving such other information as is necessary to satisfy the court that the applicant is entitled to proceed to execution on the judgment or order in question and that the person against whom it is sought to issue execution is liable to execution on it.

(3) The court hearing such application may grant permission in accordance with the application or may order that any issue or question, a decision on which is necessary to determine the rights of the parties, be tried in any manner in which any question of fact or law arising in proceedings may be tried and, in either case, may impose such terms as to costs or otherwise as it thinks just.

Permission to issue execution on suspended orders of possession

sc46.4.1 There is still a significant (but surely unnecessary) distinction between enforcing suspended orders for possession in the High Court and the county courts (in the county courts see CCR O.26 in Sch.2). In the High Court a suspended possession order is an order under which a person is entitled to relief subject to the fulfilment of a condition for the purposes of r.1.2(1)(d) and accordingly r.4 applies. Therefore an application on notice supported by evidence is required. Permission to issue execution must not be given without first allowing the defendant an opportunity of being heard. (*Fleet Mortgage and Investment Co Ltd v Lower Maisonette, 46 Eaton Place Ltd* [1972] 1 W.L.R. 765; [1972] 2 All E.R. 737).

Although permission is not required to issue a warrant of possession in the county court the defendant can apply to suspend the warrant.

Application for permission to issue writ of sequestration

sc46.5 5.—(1) Notwithstanding anything in rules 2 and 4, an application for permission to issue a writ of sequestration must be made in accordance with CPR, Part 23 and be heard by a Judge.

(2) Subject to paragraph (3) the application notice, stating the

grounds of the application and accompanied by a copy of the witness statement or affidavit in support of the application, must be served personally on the person against whose property it is sought to issue the writ.

(3) The court may dispense with service of the application notice under this rule if it thinks it just to do so.

(4) The judge hearing an application for permission to issue a writ of sequestration may sit in private in any case in which, if the application were for an order of committal, he would be entitled to do so by virtue of Order 52, rule 6 but, except in such a case, the application shall be heard in public.

Sequestration

Sequestration is a form of contempt proceedings available only in the High Court (see PD 70 para.1.2). It can be used only in respect of orders in the nature of an injunction and therefore only rarely concerns money judgments. **sc46.5.1**

Effect of rule

As sequestration is a form of contempt (*Pratt v Inman* (1890) 43 Ch. D. 175) the rule requires that a writ of sequestration can issue only with permission of the court granted by a judge on an application duly served and supported by evidence. **sc46.5.2**

Where the disobedience to the order of the Court is not obstinate and the breaches have been remedied, the Court may impose a fine in lieu of the sequestration of the assets of a company or other corporate body, especially where such sequestration would adversely affect the livelihood of innocent parties (*Steiner Products Ltd v Willy Steiner Ltd* [1966] 1 W.L.R. 986; [1966] 2 All E.R. 387).

Judgments enforceable by sequestration

The judgments or orders that may be enforced by writ of sequestration are (1) those that require a person "to do an act" within a specified time, extended if necessary, and (2) those that require a person to abstain from "doing an act" (see RSC O.45, r.5(1)). Negative orders are now therefore enforceable by sequestration by virtue of express provision of O.45, r.5(1)(b). **sc46.5.3**

The overriding condition subject to which a positive judgment or order may be enforced by sequestration is that it must specify the time within which the required act must be done. In the usual case, no such time will be specified in a judgment or order to pay money to some other person, or to give possession of land, or to deliver goods, and such time will not generally be specified unless the person required to such an act is shown to be wilfully refusing or neglecting to do it. It is therefore likely to be as rare in the future as it has been in the past for the writ of sequestration to be available to issue or to issue in the case of the ordinary common law judgments for the payment of money to another person or for delivery of possession of land or goods.

Similarly it is not the practice to limit the time for payment of costs and therefore sequestration is unlikely to be used as a method of enforcing an order for the payment of costs.

Nevertheless, although O.45, r.5 refers to the power of the Court to grant permission to issue a writ of sequestration where a party refuses or neglects to comply with or disobeys a coercive order of the Court, the Court nevertheless has inherent power to ensure that its orders are carried out where the interests of justice demand that they be complied with, and therefore, in the case of a declaratory order, where a party knowingly adopts and continues a policy of refusing, neglecting or disobeying to comply with its terms, the Court has power under its inherent jurisdiction to give permission to issue a writ of sequestration (*Webster v Southwark London BC* [1983] Q.B. 698).

For instances where an order to pay money or costs has been enforced by sequestration see *Knill v Dumergue* [1911] 2 Ch. 199 (where the facts are inaccurately stated) a vendor's action for specific performance; *Re Slade* (1881) 18 Ch. D. 653 (damages and costs); *Willcock v Terrell* (1878) 3 Ex. D. 323 (an order to pay by instalments); *Capron v Capron* [1927] W.N. 178 (alimony).

On the other hand, sequestration may be issued to enforce a judgment or order for the payment of money into court, which must specify the time within which such act is to be done.

Sequestration may be issued against a child (see Pt 21); or against a defendant who has become a patient since the date of the order (*Robinson v Galland* [1889] W.N. 108)).

Sequestration of course does not lie to enforce a judgment against the Crown (O.77, r.15(1)); nor against third persons who are not parties to the suit (per Gorell Barnes J. in *Craig v Craig* [1896] P. 171 at 174).

Form of writ

sc46.5.4 See Form **No. 67**. The writ is addressed to four persons named in it and chosen by the person presenting the judgment or order. They need not be professional persons and are not required to give security for what they may receive.

Effect of writ

sc46.5.5 The writ binds real property (*Re Lush* (1870) L.R. 10 Eq. 442) and personal property in possession from the time it is issued (*Burdett v Rockley* (1682) 1 Vern. 58; *Dixon v Rowe* (1876) 35 L.T. 548) but creates no charge on land unless it is registered (Land Charges Act 1972 s.6); in case of a chose in action the mere issue of the writ, and the service of it on the party indebted to the judgment debtor, is not enough to create a charge on the chose in action (*Ex p. Nelson* (1880) 14 Ch. D. 41; *Re Pollard* (1903) 87 L.T. 61); an order for payment must be obtained. See too, as to the effect and operation of a sequestration, the judgment of Romer L.J. in *Re Pollard* [1903] 2 K.B.41 at 47, 48, CA.

The issue of the writ, coupled with the receipt of the money of the debtor by the sequestrator, does not in itself make the creditor a secured creditor within the meaning of the Bankruptcy Act 1914 (*Re Hastings* (1892) 67 L.T. 234; *Re Pollard* [1903] 2 K.B. 41, CA) or the Insolvency Act 1986.

The title of a sequestrator will prevail over that of a mortgagee under a mortgage made with notice, and in order to avoid the effect, of a writ of a sequestration (*Ward v Booth* (1872) L.R. 14 Eq. 195).

As to the effect of the writ upon the death of the person whose estate has been sequestrated, see *Pratt v Inman* (1890) 43 Ch. D. 175.

In relation to a writ of sequestration, the position of a third party is analogous to that of a third party in relation to an injunction, i.e. that he is subject to a duty not knowingly to take any action which will obstruct compliance with the terms of the writ of sequestration which requires the sequestrators to take possession of the assets of the contemnor (*Eckman v Midland Bank Ltd* [1973] Q.B. 519; [1973] 1 All E.R. 609, N.I.R.C., not following *Re Pollard*, above).

Where sequestration of a contemnor's assets has been ordered, anyone who knowingly takes any action which prevents the sequestrators from carrying out their duty will be treated as obstructing a Court order and therefore technically in contempt of Court. Any proper and necessary request addressed by the sequestrators to the contemnor's accountants to give information concerning details of the contemnor's assets must be answered, and the accountants must divulge the information asked for, even in the absence of the contemnor's consent which is irrelevant (*Messenger Newspaper Group Ltd v National Graphical Association* [1984] 1 All E.R. 293, CA).

Land

sc46.5.6 The writ should be registered, so far as it affects land under the Land Charges Act 1972 s.6(1)(a), or the Land Registration Act 2002 as appropriate.

Property liable to sequestration

sc46.5.7 The writ includes the rents and profits of real estate and all personal estate (see Form **No. 67**). The pension of a retired naval officer (*Dent v Dent* (1867) L.R. 1 P.& D. 366); of a Judge (*Willcock v Terrell* (1878) 3 Ex.D. 323); and of a civil servant (*Sansom v Sansom* (1879) 4 P.D. 69); money received in commutation of a pension (*Crowe v Price* (1889) 22 Q.B.D. 429); a deposit on appeal, ordered to be returned (*Conn v Garland* (1874) L.R. 9 Ch. 101); a rentcharge (*Wilson v Metcalfe* (1839) 1 Beav. 263); a pension under the East India Annuity Funds Act 1874 (*Knill v Dumergue* [1911] 2 Ch. 199, CA); and a balance in a bank (*Miller v Huddlestone* (1883) 22 Ch. D. 233; *Guerrine v Guerrine* [1959] 1 W.L.R. 760; [1959] 2 All E.R. 594) have been held liable to sequestration; but not the pension of an officer in the army (*Birch v Birch* (1883) 8 P.D. 163; *Lucas v Lucas* (1887) 18 Q.B.D. 127. However, in divorce cases see now Matrimonial Causes Act 1973, s.25 as amended by the Welfare Reform and Pensions Act 1999). The liability of property to sequestration may be determined by application under Pt 23 (*Knill v Dumergue* [1911] 2 Ch. 199).

The expression "personal estate" in the writ of sequestration includes both legal and equitable choses in action, e.g. surplus of proceeds of sale held on trust (*Bucknell v Bucknell* [1969] 1 W.L.R. 1204; [1969] 2 All E.R. 998).

In a clear and simple case, a third party from whom the sequestrators claim a chose in action belonging to the contemnor does not need a specific order of the Court to give him protection to make such payment and if he unreasonably compels the sequestrators to seek such an order, he may himself be liable for the costs of such proceedings (*ibid.*, and see *Eckman v Midland Bank Ltd* [1973] Q.B. 519; [1973] 1 All E.R. 609, N.I.R.C.).

Enforcement of order

Bankers holding a balance belonging to the person against whom sequestration has been issued may be ordered, upon application in the original action, to verify the amount by affidavit and pay it into Court (*Miller v Huddlestone* (1883) 22 Ch. D. 233 *q.v.*, for form of order). **sc46.5.8**

Discovery in aid of sequestration

See *Re Suarez (No.3)* (1918) 88 L.J.Ch. 10. **sc46.5.9**

Injunction in aid of sequestration

The judgment debtor may be restrained from receiving the fund, if necessary to make the sequestration effectual (*Willcock v Terrell* (1878) 3 Ex D. 323). **sc46.5.10**

Injunction in lieu of sequestration

Where an undertaking had been broken, an injunction was granted in lieu of sequestration, the defendants being ordered to pay costs as between solicitor and client (*Marsden & Sons Ltd v Old Silkstone Collieries Ltd* (1915) 13 L.G.R. 642). The modern equivalent is costs on the indemnity basis. **sc46.5.11**

Application of proceeds

The property sequestered may be applied to meet the demand of the party prosecuting the writ, but an application to the Court for the sale thereof is necessary. **sc46.5.12**

Where there is a fund in Court representing proceeds of a sequestration, the Court has jurisdiction to order payment out of the fund to the judgment creditor of costs which the judgment debtor has been ordered to pay to him (*Etherington v Big Blow Gold Mines* [1897] W.N. 21).

Costs of unsuccessful claim

Though sequestrators act under an order of the Court, they are liable for the costs of an issue to determine their claim to property, if they fail on such issue (*Wiebalck v Told* (1913) 29 T.L.R.741). **sc46.5.13**

Forms

See Form **No. 67**. **sc46.5.14**

Discharge of sequestration

Where the person whose property has been sequestered has purged his contempt, an order may be obtained on application for the discharge of the sequestration, and directing the sequestrators to withdraw from possession, and to pass their final accounts, and, after retaining their costs, charges and expenses, and any payments properly made by them, to pay the balance to him, and for the discharge therefrom of the sequestrators from all liability in respect of their office. **sc46.5.15**

Where after a writ of sequestration had been issued the person whose property had been sequestered committed an act of bankruptcy but had not purged his contempt, it was held that the trustee in bankruptcy was not entitled to have the writ discharged (*Coles v Coles* [1957] P. 68; [1956] 3 All E.R. 542).

Issue of writ of execution

6.—(1) Issue of a writ of execution takes place on its being sealed by a court officer of the appropriate office. **sc46.6**

(2) Before such a writ is issued, a praecipe for its issue must be filed.

(3) The praecipe must be signed by or on behalf of the solicitor of the person entitled to execution or, if that person is acting in person, by him.

(4) No such writ shall be sealed unless at the time of the tender thereof for sealing—

(a) the person tendering it produces—

(i) the judgment or order on which the writ is to issue, or an office copy thereof;

(ii) where the writ may not issue without the permission of the court, the order granting such permission or evidence of the granting of it;

(iii) where judgment on failure to acknowledge service has been entered against a State, as defined in section 14 of the State Immunity Act 1978, evidence that the State has been served in accordance with CPR, rule 40.10 and that the judgment has taken effect; and

(b) the court officer authorised to seal it is satisfied that the period, if any, specified in the judgment or order for the payment of any money or the doing of any other act thereunder has expired.

(5) Every writ of execution shall bear the date of the day on which it is issued.

(6) In this rule "the appropriate office" means—

(a) where the proceedings in which execution is to issue are in a District Registry, that Registry;

(b) where the proceedings are in the Principal Registry of the Family Division, that Registry;

(c) where the proceedings are Admiralty proceedings or commercial proceedings which are not in a District Registry, the Admiralty and Commercial Registry;

(ca) where the proceedings are in the Chancery Division, Chancery Chambers;

(d) in any other case, the Central Office of the Supreme Court.

[THE NEXT PARAGRAPH IS sc46.8.]

Duration and renewal of writ of execution[1]

sc46.8 8.—(1) For the purpose of execution, a writ of execution is valid in the first instance for 12 months beginning with the date of its issue.

(2) Where a writ has not been wholly executed the court may by order extend the validity of the writ from time to time for a period of 12 months at any one time beginning with the day on which the order is made, if an application for extension is made to the court before the day next following that on which the writ would otherwise expire or such later day, if any, as the court may allow.

(3) *Before a writ* the validity of which had been extended under

[1] Amended by Civil Procedure (Amendment No.5) Rules 2003 (SI 2003/3361).

paragraph (2) is executed either the writ must be sealed with the seal of the office out of which it was issued showing the date on which the order extending its validity was made or the applicant for the order must serve a notice (in Form **No. 71** in the relevant practice direction) sealed as aforesaid, on the enforcement officer to whom the writ is directed or the relevant enforcement officer informing him of the making of the order and the date thereof.

(4) The priority of a writ, the validity of which has been extended under this rule, shall be determined by reference to the date on which it was originally delivered to the enforcement officer or the relevant enforcement officer.

(5) The production of a writ of execution, or of such a notice as is mentioned in paragraph (3) purporting in either case to be sealed as mentioned in that paragraph, shall be evidence that the validity of that writ, or, as the case may be, of the writ referred to in that notice, has been extended under paragraph (2).

(6) If, during the validity of a writ of execution, an interpleader summons is issued in relation to an execution under that writ, the validity of the writ shall be extended until the expiry of 12 months from the conclusion of the interpleader proceedings.

Effect of rule

This rule provides for extending the validity of the writ of execution which is to be valid for 12 months from the date of its issue. This change in terminology makes no material change in practice. **sc46.8.1**

Practice on extending validity of writ of execution

The application is made without notice supported by a witness statement or an affidavit stating the reason why the writ has not been executed. **sc46.8.2**

It is not the usual practice to extend the validity of a writ of execution under this rule, except in cases where priority of date is important. After the year has expired the ordinary course is to issue a new writ on the certificate of a solicitor that nothing has been levied under the first writ.

In a case proceeding in a District Registry, the application to extend the validity of a writ of execution is to be made there to the District Judge.

The renewal of a writ of execution under para.(2)should not be granted as a matter of course, and especially after the year has expired, good cause should be shown for such renewal. This is all the more important where questions of priority may arise as between two or more judgment creditors. On an application for renewal of a writ of execution the Court should be informed as to whether there are any other judgment creditors who have delivered writs of execution to the enforcement officer, and the next subsequent judgment creditor or creditors ought to be heard and if necessary he or they ought to be allowed to intervene for this purpose on the question whether he or they will suffer any, and if so what prejudice if the writ of execution is renewed, which would deprive him or them of priority in the execution process.

Extension of writ of fi. fa.

Rule 8(6) was added to ensure that interpleader proceedings were not frustrated by the inadvertence of the execution creditor to renew the relevant writ of *fi. fa.*; hence if an interpleader summons is issued in relation to an execution under a writ of execution, then the validity of the writ is automatically extended for 12 months from the conclusion of the interpleader proceedings by virtue of r.8(6). **sc46.8.3**

Lost writ of fi. fa.

There is no provision in these rules for the issue of a duplicate writ of *fi. fa.* should the original be lost or destroyed before coming into the hands of the enforcement officer and which is within a year of issue. In such a case an application made without notice supported by evidence (usually an affidavit sworn by the judgment creditor's solicitor) setting out the circumstances under which the loss or destruction occurred **sc46.8.4** should be made to the master/district judge for the issue of a duplicate writ. A statement from the enforcement officer that the original writ has not been delivered to him for execution should also be submitted. A solicitor should undertake to return the original for cancellation in the event of it being found.

Return to writ of execution[1]

sc46.9 9.—(1) Any party at whose instance or against whom a writ of execution was issued may serve a notice on the enforcement officer to whom the writ was directed or the relevant enforcement officer requiring him, within such time as may be specified in the notice, to indorse on the writ a statement of the manner in which he has executed it and to send to that party a copy of the statement.

(2) If a sheriff or the relevant enforcement officer on whom such a notice is served fails to comply with it the party by whom it was served may apply to the court for an order directing the enforcement officer or the relevant enforcement officer to comply with the notice.

Effect of rule

sc46.9.1 A sheriff was formerly required to make a "return" to a writ. This is no longer required and accordingly r.9 makes provision for the execution creditor to serve notice requiring the enforcement officer "to indorse on the writ a statement of the manner in which he has executed it ...". In practice such notice is not usually required as the enforcement officer will inform the execution creditor of the action he has taken.

An execution creditor has no right to a return whilst interpleader is pending (*Angell v Baddeley* (1877) 3 Ex.D. 49, CA).

[1] Amended by Civil Procedure (Amendment No.5) Rules 2003 (SI 2003/3361).

PRACTICE DIRECTION—EXECUTION

This Practice Direction Supplements (RSC Order 46 Schedule 1 to the CPR) and (CCR Order 26 Schedule 2 to the CPR) scpd46.1

Levying Execution on Certain Days

1.1 Unless the Court orders otherwise, a writ of execution or a warrant of execution to enforce a judgment or order must not be executed on a Sunday, Good Friday or Christmas Day.

1.2 Paragraph 1.1 does not apply to an Admiralty claim *in rem*.

RSC ORDER 47—WRITS OF FIERI FACIAS

Contents

sc47.0.1

Editorial introduction

This Order contains special rules relating to execution by writ of *fieri facias*. See also O.45 and O.46 and, in particular commentary at para.sc46.1.1 *et seq.* Rule 1 confers express power on the court to stay execution by writ of *fieri facias*. (The bulk of the notes in this Order are concerned with this matter.) Rule 2 enables a judgment creditor to issue two or more writs to enforce a single judgment and r.3 states that separate writs may be issued for the judgment debt and for costs. sc47.0.2

Previously, unlike the CCR, the RSC contained no provision for the court itself to order payment by instalments at the time when the judgment or order was pronounced. Thus, to achieve payment by instalments in the High Court it was necessary for the judgment debtor to apply to the court under RSC O.47 for a stay of execution on terms. By contrast the county court could order payment by instalments on pronouncing judgment or at any time thereafter. See now CPR Pt 40. By r.40.11 both the High Court and county court have power to order payment by instalments and at the time when judgment is given. Unless the court orders otherwise a party must comply with a judgment or order for the payment of money within 14 days of the date of the judgment or order (CPR r.40.11).

Related sources

- Part 70—General Rules about Enforcement of Judgments and Orders sc47.0.3
- Supreme Court Act 1981 s.138A (Vol.2, Section 9A)
- RSC O.45—Enforcement of Judgments and Orders: General
- RSC O.46—Writs of Execution: General
- CCR O.25—Enforcement of Judgments and Orders: General
- CCR O.26—Warrants of Execution, Delivery and Possession
- CPR Part 40—Judgments and Orders

Forms

The following Queen's Bench Masters' Practice Forms (now listed in Table 2 (Practice Forms) of Practice Direction (Forms)) are relevant to O.47. See also list of forms at para.sc45.0.4. sc47.0.4

- **PF86** Praecipe for writ of *fieri facias* (r.6)
- **PF97** Order for sale by sheriff by private contract (r.6)
- **No. 53** Writ of *fieri facias*
- **N293A** Combined Certificate of Judgment and Request for Writ of *fieri facias* (Note: in the case of a High Court Judgment use Form *PF86* to request a *fi-fa*: in the case of a county court judgment,which is being registered in the High Court for the purpose of issuing a *fi-fa*, use Form **N293A**)

Fees chargeable by enforcement officers

sc47.0.5 Fees chargeable by enforcement officers are prescribed by the High Court Enforcement Officers Regulations 2004 (SI 2004/400), reg. 13 and Sch.3. These are in Vol 2 at Section 9B paras 9B–1238+ and 9B–1244+.

Power to stay execution by writ of fieri facias

sc47.1 1.—(1) Where a judgment is given or an order made for the payment by any person of money, and the court is satisfied, on an application made at the time of the judgment or order, or at any time thereafter, by the judgment debtor or other party liable to execution—

(a) that there are special circumstances which render it inexpedient to enforce the judgment or order, or

(b) that the applicant is unable from any cause to pay the money,

then, notwithstanding anything in rule 2 or 3, the court may by order stay the execution of the judgment or order by writ of fieri facias either absolutely or for such period and subject to such conditions as the court thinks fit.

(2) An application under this rule, if not made at the time the judgment is given or order made, must be made in accordance with CPR Part 23 and may be so made notwithstanding that the party liable to execution did not acknowledge service of the claim form or serve a defence or take any previous part in the proceedings.

(3) The grounds on which an application under this rule is made must be set out in the application notice and be supported by a witness statement or affidavit made by or on behalf of the applicant substantiating the said grounds and, in particular, where such application is made on the grounds of the applicant's inability to pay, disclosing his income, the nature and value of any property of his and the amount of any other liabilities of his.

(4) The application notice and a copy of the supporting witness statement or affidavit must, not less than 4 clear days before the hearing, be served on the party entitled to enforce the judgment or order.

(5) An order staying execution under this rule may be varied or revoked by a subsequent order.

Effect of rule

sc47.1.1 This rule confers express power on the court to stay execution by writ of *fi. fa.* either absolutely or for such period and subject to such conditions as the court thinks fit, provided that the applicant can satisfy either (a) or (b) in r.1(1). Previously applications were very common as the High Court, unlike the county court, had no power to order payment by instalments but see now CPR r.40.11. If execution has been issued clearly a judgment debtor may need to apply for a stay pursuant to O.47, r.1. If, however, execution has not yet been issued it may be preferable to apply to vary the judgment to provide for payment by instalments (or lower instalments) see, e.g. CPR r.40.11 and CPR r.13.4.

The usual form of order granting a stay of execution under this rule is as follows: "stay of execution (under O.47, r.1) so long as the defendant pays the judgment debt and costs by instalments at the rate of £—— *per* month on the —— day of each month, the first instalment to commence on the —— day of ——, 20—, provided that if he should make default in the payment of the said instalments or any part thereof on the due date, the stay be forthwith removed in respect of the whole outstanding balance at the time of such default and the judgment creditor do have permission forthwith to issue execution by writ of *fi. fa.* on the said judgment and costs" (see *Chitty and Jacob's Queen's Bench Forms*, Form 1124).

Paragraph (2) makes it clear that the judgment debtor is entitled to apply for a stay of execution by *fi. fa.*, notwithstanding that he has not acknowledged the service of the claim form or taken part in the proceedings.

It should perhaps be emphasised that the court has power to order a stay of execution by writ of *fi. fa.* either absolutely or for such period and subject to such conditions as the court thinks fit. If the debtor is the owner of premises the court has power there and then to impose a final charging order on the premises provided the judgment debtor agrees, so that the judgment creditor need not go through the machinery of obtaining such a charging order absolute under Pt 73, and in the absence of such agreement the court should endeavour as far as possible to maintain a fair and proper balance between the needs of the judgment debtor to be granted a stay of execution and the needs of the judgment creditor to obtain due and prompt satisfaction of his judgment debt. In any application for a stay of execution the starting point is that there has to be a good reason to deny the judgment creditor the immediate fruits of his judgment (*Winchester Cigarette Machinery Ltd v Payne (No.2), The Times*, December 15, 1993).

The terms of this rule give the court sufficiently wide discretion, if the circumstances of the case warrant it, for the court to pierce the corporate veil, and to look behind the incorporated companies involved in the dispute so as to ascertain the identity of the persons who controlled the companies and in a proper case, the court will grant a stay of execution (*Canada Enterprises Corp v MacNab Distilleries Ltd* [1987] 1 W.L.R. 813; [1981] Com.L.R. 167, CA). The court has jurisdiction to order a stay of execution under this rule, where as a result of a particular transaction a judgment debt is owed by a subsidiary company to a third party and that subsidiary's parent company has a claim against the same third party which also arises from that transaction. In such circumstances, it is right for the court to look behind the fact that there are companies concerned and to consider the parties who are controlling those companies (*Burnet v Francis Industries Plc* [1987] 1 W.L.R. 802; [1987] 2 All E.R. 323, CA. The factors to be considered in deciding special circumstances are set out in the judgment of Bingham L.J.).

The power to stay execution under this rule is separate and distinct from the power to stay execution pending an appeal under CPR Pt 52 (*Ellis v Scott (Practice Note)* [1964] 1 W.L.R. 976; [1964] 2 All E.R. 987).

A stay of execution of a judgment, including a foreign judgment duly registered in England, will not ordinarily be granted simply because the judgment debtor brings a cross-claim in another action against the judgment creditor, or at any rate in the absence of special circumstances rendering it inexpedient to enforce the judgment (*Wagner v Laubscher Brothers & Co* [1970] 2 Q.B. 313, CA).

It is open to the court to grant a stay of execution by a judgment creditor against a statutory body (*Marine, etc., Ass. Soc. v Feltwell* [1945] K.B. 394 at 398).

Practice under this rule

The application must be made in accordance with Pt 23. **sc47.1.2**

Setting aside execution

If execution has been improperly issued it may be set aside even after execution has **sc47.1.3**
been levied. If the court sets aside a default judgment pursuant to Pt 13 it will be necessary for the order to deal with payment of the costs of execution. These will have to be paid by the judgment debtor if the judgment was regular.

Creditor out of jurisdiction

It is the duty of the judgment debtor to find the creditor if the latter is within the **sc47.1.4**
jurisdiction; but if neither the creditor nor anyone authorised to receive payment is within the jurisdiction a stay of execution may be obtained (*Re A Debtor (1838 of 1911)* [1912] 1 K.B. 53 at 62, CA).

Bankruptcy of debtor

The Insolvency Act 1986 s.285(3), provides that after the making of a bankruptcy **sc47.1.5**
order, no creditor to whom the debtor is indebted in respect of any debt provable in bankruptcy shall have any remedy against the property or person of the debtor in respect of the debt, or shall commence any action or other legal proceedings unless with the leave of the court and on such terms as the court may impose.

This includes a judgment debt due to a creditor where a proof has been rejected in bankruptcy; execution cannot be levied after the bankruptcy has been annulled (*Brandon v McHenry* [1891] 1 Q.B. 538).

A covenant to pay money out of the estate of the covenantor after his birth is a debt provable in bankruptcy within this section (*Barnett v King* [1891] 1 Ch. 4).

Under Insolvency Act 1986 s.285(1) "at any time when proceedings on a bankruptcy petition are pending or an individual has been adjudged bankrupt, the court may stay any action, execution or other legal process against the property or person of the debtor or as the case may be, the bankrupt."

The presentation of a petition for a bankruptcy order protects a debtor from arrest as soon as it is "made" (Insolvency Act 1986 s.285(1) and (2)) i.e. pronounced (*Re Manning* (1885) 30 Ch. D. 480); but it does not protect a debtor who is within the exceptions to s.4 of Debtors Act 1869, and the court will not, without a good reason, interfere to prevent committal of a person who has filed a petition to avoid consequences of an order to pay into court money in his hands in a fiduciary capacity (*Re Mackintosh Ex p. Mackintosh* (1884) 13 Q.B.D. 235).

Where an enforcement officer had been unable to gain access to a debtor's house and the creditors had countermanded the execution and the enforcement officer had returned the writ marked "unsatisfied in whole", the execution had not been "returned unsatisfied in whole or in part" within the meaning of s.268(1)(b) of the Insolvency Act 1986 as to entitle the creditors to present a bankruptcy petition (*Re A Debtor (No.340 of 1992), The Times*, March 6, 1995). Of course, the creditor could still serve a statutory demand and petition for bankruptcy pursuant to s.268(1)(a)

Stays of execution and bankruptcy petitions

sc47.1.6 (1) A stay of execution by writ of *fi. fa.* under O.47, r.1 will not prevent a creditor's petition being presented because, although execution by this particular means would be stayed, the judgment debt would in theory remain "payable" and would be enforceable by other means. (See r.70.2. The general rule is that methods of enforcement can be used concurrently.)

(2) In practice neither the High Court Bankruptcy Registrars nor District Judges will normally make a bankruptcy order while a stay is in force but will adjourn the petition (if necessary from time to time) so long as the stay persists.

(3) If a general stay of execution (e.g. pending appeal) is in existence *at the date* of the presentation of the petition, this will be regarded as an obstacle to the acceptance of the petition or as grounds for immediate dismissal of the petition because there would not then be any debt payable in existence at the date of the petition. If a general stay comes into existence *after* the presentation of the petition it could provide grounds for dismissal of the petition or (more likely) for adjournment during the operation of the stay.

(4) Once a bankruptcy order has been made, the Insolvency Act 1986 s.285(3) provides that after the making of a bankruptcy order, no creditor to whom the debtor is indebted in respect of any debt provable in bankruptcy, shall have any remedy against the property or person of the debtor in respect of the debt or shall commence any action or other legal proceedings unless with the leave of the court and upon such terms as the court may impose.

(5) An interim order made by a bankruptcy court under s.252 of the Insolvency Act operates as a general stay of all proceedings and execution in any other court.

(6) Under the Insolvency Act 1986 s.285(1), "At any time when proceedings on a bankruptcy petition are pending or an individual has been adjudged bankrupt, the [Bankruptcy] Court may stay any action, execution or other legal process against property or person of the debtor or, as the case may be, of the bankrupt."

Further under s.254(1) of the Act, the Bankruptcy Court has jurisdiction to stay any particular proceedings or execution while an application for an interim order is pending, similar to the jurisdiction under s.285(1) while a bankruptcy petition is pending.

Winding up of defendant company

sc47.1.7 The court may, at any time after the presentation of a petition for winding up a company and before making an order for winding up the company, restrain further proceedings in any action, suit or proceeding against the company, and in the case of a company registered in pursuance of s.680 of the CA 1985, or of an unregistered company, against any contributory of the company, upon such terms as the court thinks fit (CA 1985 ss.521(1), (2) and 672). A stay will, in ordinary circumstances be ordered although a winding up is not in immediate prospect, e.g. pending approval of a scheme of arrangement (*Bowkett v Fuller's United Electric Works Ltd* [1923] 1 K.B. 160, CA) but after execution levied a stay may be refused (*Booth v Walkden Spinning Co* [1909] 2 K.B. 368). However where the primary form of relief sought by a claimant is injunctive, a stay will not generally be ordered (*Landi Den Hartog B.V. v Stopps* [1976] F.S.R. 497).

Where an order has been made for winding up a company under the CA 1985, no suit, action, or other proceeding shall be proceeded with or commenced against the company, and in the case of a company registered under s.680 of the CA 1985, or of an unregistered company, against any contributory of the company in respect of any debt of the company except with the leave of the court, and subject to such terms as the court may impose (Insolvency Act 1986 s.130).

Where any company is being wound up by the court, or subject to the supervision of the court, any attachment, sequestration, distress, or execution put in force against the estate or effects of the company after the commencement of the winding-up shall be void to all intents and purposes (Insolvency Act 1986 s.128).

As to the effect of these sections, see *Re Zoedone Co* (1884) 32 W.R. 312; *Re The Opera Ltd* [1891] 3 Ch. 260. The rule under which the court gives effect to the rights of an execution creditor when the enforcement officer is in possession at the date of the commencement of the winding-up applies in favour of other execution creditors, who prior to such commencement, have lodged their writs with the enforcement officer in possession (*Re Hille India Rubber Co* [1897] W.N. 20).

Where the enforcement officer is in possession at the date of a winding up order under an execution to recover a sum due under a judgment of the QBD, application to stay a sale by him should be made to the QBD not in the winding-up (*Re Twentieth Century Equitable Friendly Society* [1910] W.N. 236).

Voluntary liquidation

The court has the same jurisdiction to stay execution in the case of a voluntary as of a compulsory winding-up (*Westbury v Twigg & Co* [1892] 1 Q.B. 77); a stay will in some cases be refused (*Currie v Consolidated Kent Collieries Corp Ltd* [1906] 1 K.B. 134, CA). **sc47.1.8**

Where the creditors had been induced to postpone issuing execution by a trick on the part of the defendant company, the CA refused to prevent the creditors from proceeding with their execution after a resolution for voluntary winding-up had been passed (*Armorduct Manufacturing Co Ltd v General Incandescent Co Ltd* [1911] 2 K.B. 143, CA) but this will be done only in exceptional circumstances. The fact that the only right of the company to recover the money claimed from certain garnishees was based upon the company's liability to the judgment creditors is not such an exceptional circumstance as to take the case out of the general rule (*Anglo-Baltic Bank v Barber* [1924] 2 K.B. 410 at 418, CA).

Matters occurring after judgment

See Sch.1, RSC O.45, r.11. **sc47.1.9**

Two or more writs of fi-fa

The general rule of practice is summed up in the maxim "One judgment, one execution," i.e. judgment creditor cannot issue a series of small executions upon his judgment, making in the aggregate the amount of the judgment debt; upon one judgment he can issue only one execution (*Forster v Baker* [1910] 2 K.B. 636, CA, *per* Vaughan Williams L.J. at 641; *Rothschild v Fisher* [1920] 2 K.B. 243, CA). For this reason assignees of part of a judgment debt cannot issue execution. (For the position in the county court, see Sch.2, *CCR O.26*) **sc47.1.10**

If however, the judgment or order is for the recovery or payment of money, and at the same time for the recovery of property other than money, the appropriate writs for the enforcement of the two parts of the judgment or order may issue simultaneously or successively. The order in which writs of execution may be issued is in no way affected by the CPR.

Two or more writs of fieri facias

2. [revoked] **sc47.2**

History of rule

sc47.2.1 Revoked by Civil Procedure (Amendment No.5) Rules 2003 (SI 2003/3361).

Separate writs to enforce payment of costs, etc.

sc47.3 3.—(1) Where only the payment of money, together with costs to be assessed in accordance with CPR Part 47 (detailed costs assessment) is adjudged or ordered, then, if when the money becomes payable under the judgment or order the costs have not been assessed, the party entitled to enforce that judgment or order may issue a writ of fieri facias to enforce payment of the sum (other than for costs) adjudged or ordered and, not less than 8 days after the issue of that writ, he may issue a second writ to enforce payment of the assessed costs.

(2) A party entitled to enforce a judgment or order for the delivery of possession of any property (other than money) may, if he so elects, issue a separate writ of fieri facias to enforce payment of any damages or costs awarded to him by that judgment or order.

Effect of rule

sc47.3.1 This rule entitles a judgment creditor to enforce a judgment immediately without waiting for a detailed assessment of his costs under Pt 47. Once costs have been assessed he can issue a second writ to enforce payment of the costs—see r.3(1).

The costs referred to in para.(2) are of course the costs of the action. In the case of the writ of delivery of goods (see Form **No. 64** and **No. 65**) the costs of execution are included. On the other hand, in the case of the writ of delivery of possession of land (see Form **No. 66**) notwithstanding the form of the writ, the costs of the execution relating to the possession of the land are not included in the writ; and normally such costs are not recoverable by the writ of possession, which relates only to land. Such costs may, however, be awarded on application to the Master (see *Dartford Brewery Co v Moseley* [1906] 1 K.B. 462, CA).

An order for payment of costs to be taxed (now called assessment) was a judgment debt within the Judgments Act 1838 s.17, and the principle established since the enactment of the Rules of the Supreme Court 1883, following the common law rule, that interest on costs ran from the date of the judgment had not been altered by the revision of the Rules in 1965, notwithstanding that the footnote to that effect had been omitted from the prescribed form of the writ of *fieri facias*; accordingly a party who had been awarded costs in an action was entitled to interest on the amount of the costs from the date upon which judgment was pronounced (*Hunt v R. M. Douglas (Roofing) Ltd* [1990] 1 A.C. 398; [1988] 3 All E.R. 823, HL). See further CPR r.40.8 and para.40.8.1.

No expenses of execution in certain cases[1]

sc47.4 4. Where a judgment or order is for less than £600 and does not entitle the claimant to costs against the person against whom the writ of fieri facias to enforce the judgment or order is issued, the writ may not authorise the enforcement officer or enforcement officer to whom it is directed to levy any fees, poundage or other costs of execution.

Effect of rule

sc47.4.1 This rule will rarely apply in practice. Generally, a claim for money may only be commenced in the High Court if "the financial value of the claim" exceeds that value fixed by the High Court and County Jurisdiction Order 1991 art.4A (initially £15,000) (see Vol.2, para.9B–935). The "no costs of execution" rule only applies where the judgment is far "less than £600" *and* does not entitle the claimant to costs. If the judgment did award costs the execution creditor is entitled to costs of execution. In any event, where the sum which it is sought to enforce is less than £600 enforcement must be by execution in the county court and not by writ of *fi-fa*. (High Court and County *Courts Jurisdiction Order 1991*, para.8, see Vol.2 at 9B–939).

[1] Amended by Civil Procedure (Amendment No.5) Rules 2003 (SI 2003/3361).

Entitlement of enforcement officer to his fees and poundage

The former responsibilities of sheriffs are now those of High Court Enforcement Officers. See further paras sc45.0.5; sc45.0.6 and sc45.1A. Fees chargeable by enforcement officers are prescribed by Sch.3 of the High Court Enforcement Officers Regulations 2004 (SI 2004/400). **sc47.4.2**

The provision entitling the judgment creditor to "levy the poundage, fees and expenses of execution over and above the sum recovered" is contained in the prescribed forms of writs of *fi. fa.* (see generally Forms at para.4PD.1).

In the execution of a writ of *fi. fa.*, where the money has been obtained by the seizure of the goods, although there has been no sale, the enforcement officer has a right to his poundage (*Mortimore v Cragg* (1878) 3 C.P.D. 216) but there must be an actual seizure (*Bissicks v Bath Colliery Co* (1878) 3 Ex.D. 174). When after seizure the execution creditor becomes disentitled to recover the judgment debt, the enforcement officer cannot sell the goods for the purpose of realising his possession money, fees and expenses (*Sneary v Abdy* (1876) 1 Ex.D. 299); but the debtor's bankruptcy and an injunction restraining a sale do not affect the enforcement officer's right to payment by the trustee in bankruptcy of the necessary expenses of possession (*Re Craycraft* (1878) 8 Ch. D. 596).

The enforcement officer is not entitled to poundage unless he has actually obtained the money by compulsion from the judgment debtor, and has it ready to hand over to the judgment creditor (per Cave J., *Re Ludmore* (1884) 13 Q.B.D. 415 at 417). So, where two seizures were made under different writs in different counties, poundage was disallowed under one of the writs because the whole debt was realised under the other writ (*Lee v Dangar* [1892] 1 Q.B. 231; 2 Q.B. 337). The enforcement officer is not entitled to charge for more than one seizure in one place (*Re Wells Ex p. Sheriff of Kent* (1893) 68 L.T. 231). Nor is he entitled to poundage where, after seizure, a bankruptcy order is made against the execution debtor, and the goods are delivered to the Official Receiver under s.346 of the Insolvency Act 1986 (*Re Thomas* [1899] 1 Q.B. 460). The High Court Enforcement Officers Regulations 2004 (SI 2004/400) see in particular reg. 13 and Sch.3—are in Vol.2 Section 9B at paras 9B–1238+ *et seq.*

If the execution is stayed before the sale, the execution creditor is liable to pay the enforcement officer his fees, unless the order staying the execution provides otherwise. or unless the sale is stopped at the instance of the trustee in bankruptcy or the Official Receiver, who are in such cases liable for the fees; the order as to fees made under the Sheriffs Act 1887, does not alter the former law on the subject (*Montague v Davies, Benachi & Co* [1911] 2 K.B. 595).

Where, by a bona fide accident the enforcement officer levied too much for poundage, he was held not liable to the penalty under s.29 of the Sheriffs Act 1887 (*Shoppee v Nathan* [1892] 1 Q.B. 245).

The right of the enforcement officer to charge poundage where no sale took place was recognised in *Re Thomas Ex p. Sheriff of Middlesex* [1899] 1 Q.B. 460, *per* Lindley M.R. at p.462, "the Sheriff has seized no doubt but he has not sold. It has been by law settled for years that he is not entitled to poundage. I am aware there has been a qualification on that where the Sheriff has seized but has not sold in consequence of a compromise between the parties; there the law regards him as having secured the money for the creditor and gives him poundage".

Fees of High Court Enforcement Officers

The former responsibilities of sheriffs are now those of High Court Enforcement Officers. **sc47.4.3**

The opportunity has been taken to introduce a more transparent and simplified fee structure. See High Court Enforcement Officers Regulations 2004 (SI 2004/400) reg. 13 and Sch.3 in Vol.2 at Section 9B paras 9B–1238+ and 9B–1244+.

Writ of fieri facias de bonis ecclesiasticis, etc.[1]

5.—(1) Where it appears upon the return of any writ of fieri facias that the person against whom the writ was issued has no goods or chattels in the county of the sheriffs to whom the writ was directed or the district of the relevant enforcement officer but that he is the **sc47.5**

[1] Amended by Civil Procedure (Amendment No.5) Rules 2003 (SI 2003/3361).

incumbent of a benefice named in the return, then, after the writ and return have been filed, the party by whom the writ of fieri facias was issued may issue a writ of fieri facias de bonis ecclesiasticis or a writ of sequestrari de bonis ecclesiasticis directed to the bishop of the diocese within which that benefice is.

(2) Any such writ must be delivered to the bishop to be executed by him.

(3) Only such fees for the execution of any such writ shall be taken by or allowed to the bishop or any diocesan officer as are for the time being authorised by or under any enactment, including any measure of the General Synod.

Practice

sc47.5.1 These writs cannot be obtained until there has been an actual return of *nulla bona* under the former writ (*Rabbitts v Woodward* (1869) 20 L.T. 693, 778); and the enforcement officer must certify that the person against whom execution is issued is a beneficed clerk, and has no lay fee.

Forms

sc47.5.2 For forms, see Forms **No.58** and **No.59**. These forms are preserved by Table 2 of 4PD and can be found in the *Civil Procedure Forms Volume*.

Order for sale otherwise than by auction[1]

sc47.6 6.—(1) An order of the court under paragraph 10 of Schedule 7 to the Courts Act 2003 that a sale of goods seized under an execution may be made otherwise than by public auction may be made on the application of—

(a) the person at whose instance the writ of execution under which the sale is to be made was issued;

(b) the person against whom that writ was issued (in this rule referred to as "the judgment debtor");

(c) if the writ was directed to a sheriff, that sheriff; and

(d) if the writ was directed to one or more enforcement officers, the relevant enforcement officer;

(2) Such an application must be made in accordance with CPR Part 23 and the application notice must contain a short statement of the grounds of the application.

(3) Where the applicant for an order under this rule is not the sheriff or enforcement officer, the sheriff or enforcement officer must, on the demand of the applicant, send to the applicant a list stating

(a) whether he has notice of the issue of another writ or writs of execution against the goods of the judgment debtor; and

(b) so far as is known to him, the name and address of every creditor who has obtained the issue of another such writ of execution,

and where the sheriff or enforcement officer is the applicant, he must prepare such a list.

(4) Not less than 4 clear days before the hearing the applicant *must serve the* application notice on each of the other persons by

[1] Amended by Civil Procedure (Amendment No.5) Rules 2003 (SI 2003/3361).

whom the application might have been made and on every person named in the list under paragraph (3).

(5) Service of the application notice on a person named in the list under paragraph (3) is notice to him for the purpose of paragraph 10(3) of Schedule 7 to the Courts Act 2003.

(Paragraph 10(3) provides that if the person who seized the goods has notice of another execution or other executions, the court must not consider an application for leave to sell privately until the notice prescribed by Civil Procedure Rules has been given to the other execution creditor or creditors).

(6) The applicant must produce the list under paragraph (3) to the court on the hearing of the application.

(7) Every person on whom the summons was served may attend and be heard on the hearing of the application.

Effect of rule

This rule enables the enforcement officer himself to apply for an order for sale otherwise than by auction; it is his duty to get the best price he can for the goods, and he is the person who may be likely to know whether and when this can be achieved by a private sale. **sc47.6.1**

Sale of goods by enforcement officer

The former responsibilities of sheriffs are now those of High Court Enforcement Officers. See further paras sc45.0.5; sc45.0.6 and sc45.1A. **sc47.6.2**

Courts Act 2003, para.10, Sch.7 (replacing SCA 1981, s.138A(1)) requires goods seized by an enforcement officer under a High Court execution to be sold by public auction unless the court otherwise orders.

An application for permission to sell the debtor's goods by private contract is made by application notice as prescribed by O.47, r.6.

If the enforcement officer has notice of another execution the court must not consider an application for permission to sell privately until notice has been given to the other execution creditor(s).

Protection of High Court Enforcement Officer

The former responsibilities of sheriffs are now those of High Court Enforcement Officers. Protection of officers selling seized goods is now governed by Courts Act 2003, reg. 11, Sch.7 (replacing SCA 1981, s.138A(1)). **sc47.6.3**

Where the enforcement officer charged with enforcement of a process of execution sells goods in the possession of the debtor at the time of seizure, the purchaser of such goods acquires a good title and no person can recover against such sheriff or officer except as provided by the Insolvency Act for any sale or payment of proceeds prior to the receipt of claim for the same, unless it is proved that the person against whom recovery is sought had notice or might by making reasonable inquiry have ascertained that the goods were not the property of the judgment debtor. As to the object and effect of this section see *Curtis v Maloney* [1951] 1 K.B. 736; [1950] 2 All E.R. 982, CA.

RSC ORDER 52—COMMITTAL

Contents **sc52.0.1**

Editorial introduction

sc52.0.2 The court's power to punish for contempt of court may be exercised by an order for committal to prison (r.1) or by other means such as a fine (r.9). However, in punishing a contempt the court's powers are limited and the full range of sentencing options available to a criminal court are not available: for example, there is no power to impose a community penalty. The common law power to commit for an indefinite term has been abolished and committal must be for a fixed term which cannot exceed two years (Contempt of Court Act 1981 s.14).

Contempt can be either a civil contempt (e.g. disobedience of a court order) or a criminal contempt (e.g. disrupting court proceedings) and can take a multiplicity of different forms—see further Summary of types of contempt in commentary to O.52, r.1.

The rules in O.52 provide that in certain circumstances a committal order may be made only by a Divisional Court (rr.2 and 3) but in others may be made by a single judge (rr.1 and 4). In certain cases the application may be heard in private (r.6). Execution of an order may be suspended (r.7): this means, for example, that a sentence of imprisonment can be suspended and the restrictions which govern such sentences in the criminal courts do not apply. The court may summarily commit for contempt "in the face of the court" (r.5).

The court has power to discharge a contemnor prior to completion of sentence (r.8). There is a right of appeal which, in the case of civil contempt, is available to both applicant and contemnor (see the Administration of Justice Act 1960 s.13. Permission to appeal is not required for an appeal against a committal order (CPR r.52.3(1)(a)). O.52 is supplemented by a Practice Direction—Committal Applications; see para.scpd52.1. It applies to any application for an order for committal of a person to prison for contempt of court (a "committal application"). Where an alleged contempt concerns the county court the application may be made to the county court in question but otherwise to the High Court—see Practice Direction, paras 1.1 to 1.3, see para.scpd52.1.

Related sources

sc52.0.3

- Contempt of Court Act 1981 (Vol.2, section 3C)
- Criminal Justice Act 1991 s.45 (Vol.2, section 9B)
- Administration of Justice Act 1960 s.13
- CPR r.31.22 (False disclosure statements)
- CPR r.32.14 (False statements)
- RSC O.45, r.5 (Enforcement of judgment to do or abstain from doing any act)
- RSC O.57 (Divisional Court proceedings, etc: supplementary provisions)
- RSC O.109 (Administration of Justice Act 1960)
- CCR O.29 (Committal for Breach of Order or Undertaking)
- Practice Direction (Committal Applications) (see para.scpd52.1)

Forms

sc52.0.4 The following Prescribed Forms (formerly included amongst the Prescribed Forms in Appendix A to the RSC) are relevant to O.52. These forms are included in Table 2 (Practice Forms) attached to Practice Direction (Forms) (and may be found in the *Civil Procedure Forms Volume*):

- ***No. 85** Order of committal* (O.52)

The following Queen's Bench Masters' Practice Forms (now listed in Table 2 (Practice Forms) attached to Practice Direction (Forms)) are relevant to O.52:

- **PF103** Warrant of committal (general) (O.52)

- **PF104** Warrant of committal (in face of court) (O.52)
- **PF105** Warrant for committal (failure of witness to attend) (O.52)

Committal for contempt of court

1.—(1) The power of the High Court or Court of Appeal to punish for contempt of court may be exercised by an order of committal. sc52.1

(2) Where contempt of court—

(a) is committed in connection with—

(i) any proceedings before a Divisional Court of the Queen's Bench Division; or

(ii) criminal proceedings, except where the contempt is committed in the face of the court or consists of disobedience to an order of the court or a breach of an undertaking to the court; or

(iii) proceedings in an inferior court; or

(b) is committed otherwise than in connection with any proceedings,

then, subject to paragraph (4), an order of committal may be made only by a Divisional Court of the Queen's Bench Division.

This paragraph shall not apply in relation to contempt of the Court of Appeal.

(3) Where contempt of Court is committed in connection with any proceedings in the High Court, then, subject to paragraph (2), an order of committal may be made by a single judge of the Queen's Bench Division except where the proceedings were assigned or subsequently transferred to some other Division, in which case the order may be made only by a single judge of that other Division.

The reference in this paragraph to a single judge of the Queen's Bench Division shall, in relation to proceedings in any court the judge or judges of which are, when exercising the jurisdiction of that court, deemed by virtue of any enactment to constitute a court of the High Court, be construed as a reference to a judge of that court.

(4) Where by virtue of any enactment the High Court has power to punish or take steps for the punishment of any person charged with having done any thing in relation to a court, tribunal or person which would, if it had been done in relation to the High Court, have been a contempt of that court, an order of committal may be made—

(a) on an application under section 88 of the Charities Act 1993 [1], by a single judge of the Chancery Division; and

(b) in any other case, by a single judge of the Queen's Bench Division.

"The power ... to punish for contempt of court"

The term "contempt of court" is of ancient origin having been used in England *certainly since* the thirteenth century and probably earlier. It is based not on any exaggerated notion of the dignity of individuals be they judges, witnesses or others but on the duty of preventing any attempt to interfere with the administration of justice (see *Attorney General v Times Newspapers Ltd* [1991] 2 W.L.R. 994, HL). sc52.1.1

Although a finding of contempt cannot be made against the Crown directly it may be made against a government department or against a minister of the Crown both in his official and personal capacity (*Re M* [1993] 3 W.L.R. 433). For a consideration of

[1] 1993 c.10.

the authorities on the mental element of contempt see *Adam Phones Ltd v Goldschmidt* [1999] 4 All E.R. 486 (Jacob J.). If an application for a committal order is a wholly disproportionate response to a trivial or blameless breach of an order the court will dismiss the application with costs.

For the purposes of the Human Rights Act 1998 an application to commit for contempt, for an alleged breach of a worldwide search and seizure order, will constitute criminal proceedings for the purposes of the Convention. To deprive a defendant of his right to apply for public funding for the purposes of obtaining legal representation will contravene his rights under art.6(1) and 6(3)(c) of the Convention. A proper opportunity to exercise that right should outweigh other considerations, such as the convenience of other parties or the use of the court's resources. See *Berry Trade Ltd v Moussavi* [2002] 1 W.L.R. 1910 (Potter, Mummery and Arden L.JJ.).

Civil and criminal contempts

sc52.1.2 In *Attorney General v Newspaper Publishing Plc* [1988] Ch. 333, Sir John Donaldson M.R. said:

> "Despite its protean nature, contempt has been classified under two heads, 'civil contempt' and 'criminal contempt'. Whatever the value of this classification in earlier times, I venture to think that it now tends to mislead rather than assist, because the standard of proof is the same, namely the criminal standard and there are now common rights of appeal. Of greater assistance is a reclassification as (a) conduct which involves a breach, or assisting in the breach, of a court order and (b) any other "conduct which involves an interference with the due administration of justice, either in a particular case, or more generally, as a continuing process, the first category being a special form of the latter, such interference being a characteristic common to all contempts; *per*Lord Diplock in *Attorney General v Leveller Magazine Ltd* [1979] AC 440 at 449. What distinguishes the two categories is that in general conduct which involves a breach, or assisting in the breach, of a court order is treated as a matter for the parties to raise by complaint to the court, whereas other forms of contempt are in general considered to be a matter for the Attorney General to raise. In doing so he acts not as a government minister or legal adviser, but as the guardian of the public interest in the due administration of justice."

Civil contempt is not a criminal offence (*Cobra Golf Ltd v Rata* [1998] Ch. 109) but the standard of proof in all forms of contempt is the criminal standard, i.e. proof beyond a reasonable doubt (*Dean v Dean* [1987] 1 F.L.R. 517; *Attorney General v Newspaper Publishing Plc* [1988] Ch. 333, above). The chief instance of civil contempt (or "contempt in procedure") is disobedience to an order of the court by a party to the proceedings; the chief instances of criminal contempt are contempt *in facie curiae* by any person (e.g. by hurling abuse or an object at the court) and conduct obstructing or calculated to prejudice the due administration of justice (see the cases as to this distinction collected in *Re Bahama Islands* [1893] A.C. 138 at 146; and *Seldon v Wilde* [1911] 1 K.B. 701, CA; *Miller v Knox* (1838) 4 Bing. N.C. 574, at 587 *et seq.*). The distinction remains in force (a) in regard to privilege from arrest (as to which see para.sc52.7.5); (b) in regard to the principle (rarely heard of) that the prerogative of the Crown extends to remission of a sentence for criminal, not civil contempt: and (c) in regard to the principle that a civil contempt can be waived, for if the party for whose benefit an order was made is content that it should not be performed, the court has generally no interest to interfere (see *Roberts v Albert Bridge Co* (1873) L.R. 8 Ch. 753; *Anon.* (1809) 15 Ves. Jr. 174; *Woodward v Twinaine* (1840) 8 Sim. 301; and *R. v Newton* (1903) 19 T.L.R. 627, a criminal contempt).

Committal proceedings in the High Court are not "criminal proceedings" within ss.23 to 26 of the Criminal Justice Act 1988 but civil proceedings governed by the Civil Evidence Act 1995 and RSC O.52 as amended and appended by the CPR, for the purposes of admitting hearsay evidence. While the proceedings are subject to art.6 of the ECHR, the jurisprudence of the ECtHR supported a flexible approach to the admission of hearsay evidence, rather than its exclusion on principle: *Daltel Europe Ltd v Makki* [2006] EWCA Civ 94; [2006] 1 W.L.R. 2704, CA.

Where a contemnor is dealt with for contempt in relation to an assault in domestic proceedings in the County Court, parallel criminal proceedings in a magistrates court for assault do not amount to an abuse of process. *Crown Prosecution Service v Tweddell* [2001] EWHC Admin 188 (Latham L.J. and Astill L.J.). Contempt proceedings invariably proceed quicker than criminal proceedings arising out of the same incident. The first court need not concern itself with what the second court might do. It is for the second court to take into account the sentence of the first court (see *Lomas v Parle* [2003] EWCA Civ 1804; [2004] 1 W.L.R. 1642 Butler-Sloss P. Thorpe and Mance L.J.J.). Where a party alleges a failure to comply with an undertaking or order, the burden of proof will lie on that party. The standard of proof however will depend on the purpose for which the allegation is made. Where it is for the purpose of establishing a fresh allegation of contempt and a fresh committal it will be to the criminal standard, but if it is for some other purpose it will be to the civil standard: *Phillips v Symes* [2003] EWCA Civ 1769 (Waller, Hale and Carnwath L.JJ.).

Order of committal

This is a process under which the contemnor is seized, under order of the court, by a court official (normally the tipstaff or his deputy, or, if a tipstaff is not available, an usher) or by a police officer acting as his assistant, and taken to prison. **sc52.1.3**

Form of order of committal

The form required to be used for a committal order for contempt of court requires that the contempt be stated. That requirement must be strictly complied with by setting out in detail the acts constituting the contempt (*Chiltern DC v Keane* [1985] 1 W.L.R. 619; [1985] 2 All E.R. 118, CA). The period of imprisonment must be stated in the order. Each act of contempt admitted or proved must have its own sentence to be served concurrently or consecutively as ordered. **sc52.1.4**

In particular the following points should be noted: the order must state the contempt and must make clear to whom the order is directed and what that person must do to comply with it (*C (A Minor), Re The Times*, July 22, 1985); the contemnor must be able to see from the face of the order what it is that he is being committed for (*Parra v Rones* (1986) 16 Fam. Law 262, CA); the particulars of the contempt set out in the order must not contain references to matters not comprised in the affidavits in support of the application for committal, since the contemnor has had no notice of those matters (*Tabone v Seguna* [1986] 1 F.L.R. 591, CA) and must conform with the oral judgment given by the court making the order (*Re C (A Minor)* (above)). An order for committal which fails to specify the contempt for which it has been made is fundamentally defective and the Court of Appeal may decline to cure the defect by exercising its powers under RSC O.59, r.10(3): *Linkleter v Linkleter* (1988) 18 Fam Law 93 but see further *per* Lord Woolf MR in *Nicholls v Nicholls* [1997] 1 W.L.R. 314. If the contemnor was present at the committal proceedings the Court of Appeal may decide to rectify the order; if he was not it is likely to order a re-trial.

A committal order based on contempts proved by the judge which are not set out in the committal notice is invalid (*Javadi-Babreh v Javadi Babreh*, *The Independent*, November 16, 1992 (Stuart-Smith, Simon Brown L.JJ.)).

Recent authorities make clear that CPR r.52.11(4) (formerly RSC O.59, r.10(3)) and s.13(3) of the Administration of Justice Act 1960 give a court the power to rectify procedural defects both in the procedure leading up to the making of the order and after it has been made. That discretion must be exercised so as to best reflect the requirements of justice. The court must not only take into account the interests of the contemnor but also the interests of the other parties and the interest of upholding the reputation of civil justice in general. It is no longer appropriate to regard an order for committal as being no more than a form of execution available to another party. The court itself has a very substantial interest in seeing that its orders are upheld. If orders are set aside on purely technical grounds this will undermine the system of justice and the credibility of court orders. As long as the order made by the judge is valid the approach of the court will be to uphold the order in the absence of any prejudice or injustice to the contemnor (*Nicholls v Nicholls* [1997] 1 W.L.R. 314 (Lord Woolf M.R., Auld and Ward L.JJ.)).

Other remedies for contempt of court

See r.9 below. Apart from the power to imprison for contempt, there is jurisdiction to fine or to take security for good behaviour. For the latter power, see *Skipworth and the Defendant's Case* (1873) L.R. 9 Q.B. 230 at 241. Information or indictment is also applicable in a case of criminal contempt (*Schreiber v Lateward* (1781) 2 Dickens 592; *R. v Gray* [1900] 2 Q.B. 36; *R. v Ribbits* [1902] 1 K.B. 77 at 87; *Attorney General v Butterworth* [1963] 1 Q.B. 696 at 728; [1962] 3 All E.R. 326 at 334, CA; but see *R. v Parke* [1903] 2 K.B. 442 at 443; *R. v Davies* [1906] 1 K.B. 32 at 41); and the court, instead of **sc52.1.5** committing, may take the more lenient course of granting an injunction against repetition of the act of contempt (*Kitcat v Sharp* (1882) 52 L.J.Ch. 134; *Coats v Chadwick* [1894] 1 Ch. 347 at 349; *Cronmire v Daily Bourse* (1892) 9 T.L.R. 101); and the injunction may be granted against a person not a party to the action (*Lewis v James* (1887) 3 T.L.R. 527). It has been held that the remedy against a stranger to the action, for aiding and abetting a breach of an injunction or undertaking, is to apply for committal or sequestration and not an injunction, even though the court may take the more lenient course of granting an injunction instead. All that is required is that the aiders and abettors should be given notice of the terms of the injunction or undertaking (*Elliott v Klinger* [1967] 1 W.L.R. 1165; [1967] 3 All E.R. 141). The assets of a company may be sequestrated. A witness damnified by contemptuous conduct may even have a civil claim for damages (*Attorney General v Butterworth*, above, 696 at 719; but see *Chapman v Honig* [1963] 2 Q.B. 502; [1963] 2 All E.R. 513, CA). But a breach of an undertaking given by a party to the court does not necessarily give rise to a cause of action by the other party against him (see *Re Hudson* [1966] Ch. 207; [1966] 1 All E.R. 110).

It is a general principle that process by way of contempt should not be lightly employed, and not in aid of a civil remedy where some other method of achieving justice is available (*Re Clement* (1877) 46 L.J.Ch. 375; *Danchevsky v Danchevksy* [1975] Fam. 17; [1974] 3 All E.R. 9334, CA).

Contempt proceedings and criminal proceedings arising from same facts

sc52.1.6 It is a well-established principle that the jurisdiction of the court in contempt proceedings arises out of its inherent jurisdiction to enforce its own orders and is quite separate from any criminal proceedings, notwithstanding that they arise out of the same set of facts, and therefore, since contempt proceedings should be dealt with swiftly and decisively, the court should not generally adjourn the contempt proceedings until any pending criminal proceedings arising out of the same circumstances have been completed (*Szczepanski v Szczepanski* [1985] F.L.R. 468, CA; *Caprice v Boswell* (1986) 16 Fam. Law 52, CA). In particular contempt proceedings for breach of a non molestation order should be dealt with swiftly and decisively and should not be adjourned pending the outcome of the criminal proceedings where no real risk of prejudice has been established *Keeber v Keeber*, *The Times*, July 14, 1995 (Butler-Sloss and Otton L.JJ.)). The first court to sentence must not anticipate or allow for a likely further sentence. It is for the second court to reflect the prior sentence to ensure that the contemnor is not punished twice for the same act. (see *Lomas v Parle* [2004] 1 W.L.R. 1642, Butler-Sloss P., Thorpe and Mance L.JJ.).

Where a party seeks to uphold a non-molestation order on the grounds of threatened violence, and where the contempt warranted the top range of sentences, it was appropriate to bring proceedings under the Protection from Harassment Act 1997 (rather than the Family Law Act 1996) since the maximum sentence, up to five years imprisonment, was higher. *Robinson v Murray* [2005] EWCA Civ 935 (Lord Woolf C.J., Thorpe and Lloyd L.JJ.).

Summary of types of contempt

sc52.1.7 For a modern summary of contempt, see *Attorney General v Times Newspapers Ltd* [1992] 1 A.C. 191. For criminal contempt see further *Archbold: Criminal Pleading Evidence and Practice 2004*. In the following summary those lettered A to H inc. are civil; the remainder are criminal (note letter I, contempt pursuant to r.32.14 CPR).

sc52.1.8 *A. Failure to carry out an undertaking given to the court*—Service of the order containing the undertaking is not necessary in order to enforce the undertaking by committal; it is sufficient that the defendant has notice of the order (*D v A & Co* [1900] 1 Ch. 484). The fact that a party who is in breach of an undertaking has acted on legal advice may be regarded as a mitigating circumstance, but cannot be relied upon as a matter of course as complete mitigation (*Re Mileage Conference Group of the Tyre Manufacturers' Conference Ltd's Agreement* [1966] 1 W.L.R. 1137; [1966] 2 All E.R. 849, RPC). In order to establish a contempt of court by a party it is sufficient to prove that his conduct is intentional and that he knows all the facts which make it a breach of the undertaking or order; it is not necessary to prove that he appreciates that his conduct is in fact a breach of the undertaking or order (*Spectravest Inc v Aperknit Ltd* [1988] F.S.R. 161). Where, by an undertaking or interlocutory order, a defendant is required to refrain from "infringing the plaintiff's copyright," this means the copyright which the plaintiff claims to have, and requires the subsistence and ownership of the copyright to be assumed; it is not open to the defendant to argue questions relating to the subsistence and ownership of the copyright in committal proceedings (*ibid.*).

In order to establish a contempt of court by way of a breach of an injunction it is unnecessary to show that the contemnor had a wilful intention to disobey a court order, but merely a wilful and deliberate intention to do what he knew he must not do, knowing what the consequences would be. *P v P (Contempt of Court: Mental Capacity), The Times*, July 21, 1999 (Butler-Sloss, Judge and Sedley L.JJ.).

In order to enforce a negative undertaking it is not necessary that the order containing the undertaking should be drawn, indorsed with a penal notice and served personally in accordance with O.45. Such an undertaking is a promise to the court, as a result of which the court has taken a particular course, whether by judgment or order or otherwise, and the court has the same power to punish a breach of the undertaking as a contempt as it has to punish a breach of an injunction. Therefore the court can enforce a negative undertaking by using the appropriate remedies for contempt, provided only that the alleged contemnor knows of the undertaking given on his behalf (*Camden BC v Alpenoak Ltd* (1985) 135 New L.J. 1209). As to procedure on an application to commit for breach of an undertaking, see para.52.4.3 below, "Service of notice".

Where an undertaking is unqualified in its terms, and it is proved that the party giving the undertaking has not complied with it, it is no answer to a contempt charge to prove that the non-compliance was casual, inadvertent or accidental, rather than deliberate; such features go only to the question of what, if any, penalty should be imposed (*West Oxfordshire DC v Beratec Ltd, The Times*, October 30, 1986).

A fine imposed jointly and severally on a company and one of its directors for contempt for breaches of undertakings, is wrong in principle. Each defendant should be considered separately (*McMillan Graham Printers Ltd v RR (UK) Ltd, The Times*, March 19, 1993 (Nourse, Stuart-Smith and Waite L.JJ.)).

Great care should be taken in drawing up orders to ensure that undertakings are drafted in clear and precise terms so as to avoid long arguments about whether breaches have occurred (*O'Neill v Murray, The Times*, October 15, 1990, CA).

A breach of an undertaking to the court may constitute a contempt and an abuse of its process, irrespective of the contemnor's intentions (*Miller v Scorey* [1996] 1 W.L.R. 1122; [1996] 3 All E.R. 18) even where, for example, a client is in ignorance of the effect of an implied undertaking given by his solicitor (*Watkins v A. J. Wright (Electrical) Ltd, The Times*, July 15, 1996, *per* Blackburn J.).

B. Failure of a solicitor to carry out an undertaking given by him in his capacity as solicitor —even if not given to or in the presence of the court or to a party to the suit or **sc52.1.9**
to his own client (see Vol.2, Section 7, Solicitors, "Jurisdiction to enforce undertakings given by solicitors", para.7–223).

For the purpose of an application to commit a solicitor for contempt for breach of an order restraining him from destroying or altering any document, the word "document" includes information stored in the hard disk of a computer and the word "page" includes "screen". (*Alliance and Leicester Building Society v Ghahramani* [1992] RVR 198; *The Independent*, March 9, (Hoffmann J.).

C. Disobedience to a judgment or order for the payment of money (other than for the payment of money into court) within a time specified —subject to the provisions of the **sc52.1.10**
Debtors Acts 1869 and 1878 (RSC O.45, rr.1(1) and 5(1)(a)).

D. Disobedience to a judgment or order for the payment of money into court within a time specified —(subject as in C.) (RSC O.45, rr.1(2) and 5(1)(a)). **sc52.1.11**

E. Disobedience to a judgment or order to do any act within a time specified (RSC O.45, r.5(1)(a)). —Such order would include an order of mandamus (see, e.g. *R. v Leicester Guardians* (1899) 81 L.T. 559; *R. v Worcester Corp* (1903) 98 J.P. 130) or an order **sc52.1.12**
to attend for cross-examination if, but only if, conduct money has been tendered (*In the estate of Harvey* [1907] P. 239). Casual or unintentional disobedience to an order will not usually justify an order of committal; it must be contumacious (*Fairclough v Manchester Ship Canal Co* [1897] W.N. 7, CA; *Steiner Products Ltd v Willy Steiner, Ltd* [1966] 1 W.L.R. 986; [1966] 2 All E.R. 387). Thus an applicant who seeks to commit a person for breach of an injunction must establish a deliberate or wilful breach of a

RSC

court order beyond reasonable doubt (*Deborah Building Equipment v Scaffco*, *The Times*, November 5, 1986). Before a party launches proceedings against an opponent for committal for contempt (which necessarily invokes the possibility of the imprisonment of the respondent) something more must be involved than a mere technicality, especially since the coming into operation of the Civil Procedure Rules. An application which is a wholly disproportionate response to a trivial or blameless breach of a court's order will be likely to be dismissed with costs. *Adam Phones Ltd v Goldschmidt*, *The Times*, August 17, 1999 (Jacob J.). The High Court also has however a discretionary power to commit a contemnor to prison for negligently failing to comply with an injunction. It is not therefore automatically available at the demand of the claimant whose rights have been infringed. Thus it had been rightly refused to evict gypsies from green belt land where no other site was available because of the County Council's failure to perform its statutory duty to provide suitable caravan sites for gypsies (*Guildford BC v Valler*, *The Times*, October 15, 1993 (Russell, Staighton and Steyn L.JJ.)).

Where the judgment or order is against a body corporate, a director or other officer of the body may be committed (r.5(1)(iii)). The company itself cannot be committed but it can be fined (*R. v Hammond & Co Ltd* [1914] 2 K.B. 866). Since a company is not a physical person it can only act by its agents and falls to be judged by its actions and not simply by its words. A company can be held to be in contempt where an order is disobeyed as a result of a deliberate act by one of its employees (*Director General of Fair Trading v Pioneer Concrete (U.K.) Ltd* [1994] 3 W.L.R. 1249).

Failure to comply with certain orders, etc., peculiar to probate matters is punishable by committal—e.g. a citation to take a grant when the citee (an executor) has intermeddled in the estate (*Mordaunt v Clarke* (1869) 1 P. & D. 592; *Re Lister* (1894) 70 L.T. 812; *Re Coates* (1898) 78 L.T. 820); a subpoena to bring in a will (*Simmons v Deane* (1858) 27 L.J.P. 103; *Parkinson v Thornton* (1868) 37 L.J.P. 3); a citation to bring in a grant (*Evans v Evans* (1893) 67 L.T. 719); and an order to file an inventory (*Baker v Baker* (1860) 2 S. & T. 380; *Marsham v Brookes* (1863) 32 L.J.P. 95).

sc52.1.13 *F. Disobedience to a judgment or order to abstain from doing an act (RSC O.45, r.5(1)(b)).* —Where the judgment or order is against a body corporate, a director or other officer may be committed (O.45, r.5(1)(iii)).

sc52.1.14 *G. Disobedience to a judgment or order for the giving of possession of land within a time specified (RSC O.45, r.3)* —subject to the requirement of the leave of the court to issue a writ of possession, except in a mortgage action to which O.88 applies.

sc52.1.15 *H. Disobedience to a judgment or order for the delivery of any goods within a time specified which does not give the alternative of paying the assessed value (RSC O.45, r.4(1)).* —Where there is a breach of an order to do an act by a certain date, such as the delivery of goods, and non-compliance has been visited with imprisonment for contempt, a continuing breach cannot thereafter be the subject matter of a further committal under the same order. If the failure by the alleged contemnor has continued it is necessary to return to court and obtain a new order (*Kumari v Jalal* [1997] 1 W.L.R. 97, CA; [1996] 4 All E.R. 65).

sc52.1.16 *I. Making a false statement in a document verified by a statement of truth* —(see CPR r.32.14). CPR r.32.14 provides that contempt of court proceedings may be brought against a person who makes, or causes to be made, a false statement in a document verified by a statement of truth, without an honest belief in its truth. Such proceedings may be brought only (a) by the Attorney General or (b) with the permission of the court. The use of statements of truth does not introduce a new category of contempt, or change the substantive law of contempt, which requires that a false statement is likely to interfere with the course of justice. However it is important that flagrant breaches of the obligation to verify documents by statements of truth should be policed and enforced if necessary by committal proceddings. *Malgar Ltd v RE Leach (Engineering) Ltd*, [2000] C.P. Rep. 39 (Sir Richard Scott V.-C.).

sc52.1.17 *J. Contempt in the face of the court.* —The summary procedure to deal with contempt *in the face* of the court is unique in English law (see Mustill L.J. in *R. v Griffin* 88 Cr.App R 63 at 67). The nature of the jurisdiction was reviewed in *Balogh v St Albans Crown Court* [1975] Q.B. 73; [1974] 3 All E.R. 283, CA. Examples of this type of contempt are: assaulting (*Re Cosgrave* (1887)) or insulting (*R. v Jordan* (1888) 36 W.R.

797, CA) the presiding Judge; seizing a document in the hands of the court during the hearing and carrying it away in defiance of the court (*Watt v Ligertwood* (1874) L.R. 2 HL(Sc.) 361); a barrister becoming a party to a fraud and conducting his case so as intentionally to deceive the court (*Linwool v Andrews* (1888) 58 L.T. 612); a solicitor deceiving the court (*R. v Weisz Ex p. Macdonald (Hectar)* [1951] 2 K.B. 661; [1951] 2 All E.R. 408); assault on a solicitor within the precincts of the court (*Re Johnson* (1887) 20 Q.B.D. 68); and see *Apted v Apted and Bliss* [1930] P. 246; *Kirk v Kirk and Gundy* (1934) 150 L.T. 514, and rr.1(1) and 5. Service of process within the precincts of the court is not necessarily contempt (*R. v Jones Ex p. McVittie* [1931] 1 K B. 664).

The procedure to be followed by a judge faced with a contempt in the face of the court is now set out in Pt II of PD—Committal Applications: see para.scpd52.17. The Practice Direction has clearly been distilled from a series of Court of Appeal decisions. Although the judge does have the options of referring the contempt to the Attorney General or to another judge it is not a breach of art.6 ECHR for the judge to deal with the contempt himself (*Wilkinson v S* [2003] 1 W.L.R. 1254) and this is usually the best course provided that the procedure in the Practice Direction is followed.

The provisions of s.12 of the Contempt of Court Act 1981 give a good indication of the type of behaviour which may amount to contempt in the face of the court at common law. Thus a wolf whistle directed at a juror returning into court was potentially insulting, offensive and a serious interference with the administration of justice. Jurors did not come to courts in order to have comments made about their personal appearance. The appropriate penalty was a moderate fine or detention until the end of the day or over the luncheon adjournment (*R. v Powell, The Times*, June 3, 1993 (Staughton L.J., Popplewell and Laws JJ.)). Threats and obscenities directed at a jury by a member of a defendant's family, as a verdict was being returned, amounted to a serious contempt punishable with imprisonment. Such outbursts had become all too common in recent years and would not be tolerated: *R. v Britton* [2006] EWCA Crim 2082 (Gage L.J., Dobbs J. and Judge Mettyear).

Since the power summarily to commit a person to prison must be a matter of last resort, it is incumbent on the judge to consider whether some lesser alternative to protect the court processes may be deployed. In the heat of the moment there may be a perception in the judge of the need for speedy action and condign punishment, but the judge should give himself time for quiet reflection. If that opportunity is taken overnight, whilst the contemnor is in custody, that very opportunity may itself provide the solution: *R v Huggins* [2007] 2 Cr. App. R. 8 (Moses LJ, Nelson J and Sir Charles Mantell).

A judge is entitled to defer taking action on a prima facie contempt and may adjourn the issue of whether any contempt has been committed and of any punishment until later. An offender's refusal to obey a judge's order to hear sentence passed upon him constitutes a contempt: *R. v Santiago, The Times*, March 16, 2005 (Hooper L.J., Silber J. and Judge Paget Q.C.).

Contempt committed before a Judge in Chambers, Master or District Judge is punishable by a Judge in Court.

The procedure to be followed in the case of contempt of a Magistrate's Court is set out in a Practice Note issues by Lord Woolf C.J. on May 23, 2001 ([2001] 3 All E.R. 94).

In cases of alleged contempt, for example where it is suggested that a witness was approached and intimidated, the judge has a discretion whether to pursue:

- (i) the truly "summary" procedure of the type described in *Griffin* (1989) 88 Cr.App.R. 63;
- (ii) the "formal procedure", following deferral until the conclusion of the trial;
- (iii) referring the matter to the prosecuting authorities for prosecution as a substantive offence.

See *R v AS* [2008] EWCA Crim 138; February 8, 2008 (Thomas L.J., Davis and Clarke JJ.).

K. Words, written or spoken, scandalising the court —"Personal scurrilous abuse of a Judge as Judge"—very rare in fact—is contempt (*R. v Gray* [1900] 2 Q.B. 36; *McLeod v St Aubyn* [1899] A.C. 549 at 551). Statements to the effect that the accused in a criminal case will not get a fair trial are a contempt (*Skipworth's Case* (1873) L.R. 9 Q.B. 230) but libellous or misleading criticisms on the conduct of a Judge after the trial, are not necessarily contempt (*Re Bahama Islands* [1893] A.C. 138; *Dunn v Bevan* [1922] 1 Ch. 276). **sc52.1.18**

Criticism of the Court or its decisions, in the course of the exercise of the right of free speech, even if it is inaccurate is not a contempt of court (*R. v Commissioners of Police of the Metropolis Ex p. Blackburn (No.2)* [1968] 2 Q.B. 150; [1968] 1 All E.R. 763, CA). See also *R. v Lefroy* (1873) L.R.Q.B. 134; *Re Sarbadhicary* (1906) 23 T.L.R. 180, PC; *R. v Editor of New Statesman* (1928) 44 T.L.R. 301). Communications by letter to a Judge or officer of the court intended to influence a decision are a contempt (*Lechmere Charlton's Case* (1837) 2 My. & Cr. 316; and see *Martin's Case* (1747) 2 Russ. & M. 674; *Re Dyce Sombre* (1844) 1 Mac. & G. 116, 122).

sc52.1.19 *L. Words written or spoken, calculated to interfere with the course of justice*—This branch of the subject has given rise to some controversy as it involves restriction upon freedom of speech. The law has been discussed and explained in *Attorney General v Times Newspapers Ltd* [1974] A.C. 273; [1973] 3 All E.R. 54, HL and *F. (orse A.) (A Minor)* [1977] Fam. 58; [1976] 3 All E.R. 74, CA.

Two distinct types of contempt are involved:

(a) Publications which create a substantial risk that the course of justice in proceedings that are active will be impeded or prejudiced. This type of contempt is now dealt with by the Contempt of Court Act 1981 (see Vol.2, Section 3C) which should be consulted. To impede is to retard, slow down, delay, hinder or obstruct. To prejudice is to say or do that which is detrimental or injurious to the interests of that thing or person (see *Attorney General v British Broadcasting Corp* [1992] C.O.D. 264). The consent of the Attorney General is required for proceedings to punish contempt of this kind (s.7 *ibid.*). For the defence of bona fide discussion of public affairs, see s.5, *ibid.*, and *Attorney General v English* [1983] A.C. 116; [1982] 2 All E.R. 903, HL. Such prejudice may be by influencing the tribunal, or potential jurors for or against a party, or by putting pressure on parties or witnesses or by other means. Examples are: (i) publication by a newspaper before the trial of the result of its own investigation into a crime (*R. v Evening Standard* (1924) 40 T.L.R. 833); (ii) inciting public opinion against a party so as to affect his conduct of the case or the assertion of his rights (*Attorney General v Times Newspapers Ltd*, above; publications of the amount paid into court by a defendant (*R. v Wealdstone News and Harrow News* [1925] W.N. 154); (iii) publishing, during the course of a criminal trial before a jury, information revealing that the accused had committed other offences besides those for which he was being tried (*R. v Border Television Ltd Ex p. Attorney General* (1978) 122 S.J. 162). The mischief is the risk of prejudice to a fair trial; the court requires to be satisfied that the proceedings are genuine (*R. v Editor of the Daily Mail Ex p. Factor* (1928) 44 T.L.R. 303) and that risk of prejudice is real (*R. v Ingrams Ex p. Goldsmith* [1976] 10 C.L. 309a; (1976) 120 S.J. 835). It is a defence, by section 3 of the Contempt of Court Act 1981, to show that the publisher of offending material, having taken all reasonable care, did not know and had no reason to believe that proceedings were active.

(b) Publication of matters which the law or the court has decided should be kept confidential in the interests of justice. Even when sitting in open court the court may direct, in the interests of justice, that some matter should not be published; knowingly to frustrate a clear direction, properly given, will be a contempt (*Attorney General v Leveller Magazine Ltd* [1979] A.C. 440; [1979] 1 All E.R. 745, HL). The mischief is the unauthorised disclosure of confidential matter, irrespective of whether it will prejudice the fair trial of proceedings. It is necessary to establish that the offender had guilty knowledge, that is, knew, or must be taken to have known, that publication was not permitted (*F. (orse A.) (A Minor)*, above). The court has a discretion to permit disclosure of evidence given in camera (*Re R. (M. J.)* [1975] Fam. 89; [1975] 2 All E.R. 749). However where no express order has been made pursuant to s.12(1)(e) of the AJA 1960 prohibiting publication of information relating to proceedings heard in private, pursuant to an order under CPR r.39.2, allegations of contempt concerning publication of information relating to the proceedings were incapable of amounting to contempt: *A F Noonan (Architectural Practice) Ltd v Bournemouth & Boscombe Athletic Football Club Ltd* [2007] 1 W.L.R. 2614 (Sir Anthony Clarke M.R., Sir Igor Judge PQBD and Buxton L.J.)

The Contempt of Court Act 1981 has given to courts express power to order the postponement of publication of their proceedings of such publication and might create *a substantial risk* of prejudice to the administration of justice in those proceedings (s.4(2)); a court may also prohibit publication of any matter (such as a name) which it allowed to be withheld from the public during the proceedings (s.14). It appears reasonably clear from the judgments of Shaw and Ackner L.JJ. in *R. v Horsham JJ. Ex p.*

Farquharson [1982] Q.B. 762; [1982] 2 All E.R. 269 that a disregard of any such order or prohibition would be a contempt of court.

Where the court is contemplating the making or continuance of an order under s.4(2) of the 1981 Act, prohibiting the publication of any matter, it has a discretionary power to hear representations from the press, and should ordinarily do so when the press ask to be heard (*R. v Clerkenwell Magistrates' Court Ex p. The Telegraph Plc* [1993] 2 W.L.R. 233 (Mann L.J. and Leonard J.)).

In an application under s.4(2) of the Contempt of Court Act 1981, the court must first consider whether there is a substantial risk of prejudice and then, secondly, whether it was necessary to make an order for avoiding such a risk. In determining whether publication of matter would cause a substantial risk of prejudice to a future trial, a court should credit the jury with the will and ability to abide by the judge's direction to decide the case only on the evidence before them. The court should also bear in mind that the staying power and detail of publicity, even in cases of notoriety, are limited and that the nature of a trial is to focus the jury's minds on the evidence put before them, rather than on matters outside the courtroom. The Court of Appeal's function on an appeal under s.159 of the Criminal Justice Act 1988 was to form its own view on the material before it (*Ex p. The Telegraph Plc* [1993] 1 W.L.R. 980 (Lord Taylor of Gosforth C.J., Auld and Curtiss JJ.)).

In cases where no active steps had been taken in any prosecution against a plaintiff (so that the strict liability rule under ss.1 and 2 of the Contempt of Court Act 1981 did not apply), but it was sought to restrain publication of material on the ground of contempt of court at common law, it is necessary for the court to be sure that (a) publication would create a risk of real prejudice if and when the prosecution proceeded and (b) the material would be published with the specific intention of causing that risk (*Coe v Central Television, Cook and Thorne* , *The Independent*, August 11, 1993 (Glidewell, Butler-Sloss and Kennedy L.JJ.)).

The purpose of granting an interlocutory injunction is to prevent the restrained act from being done, pending a decision by the court on the claims in the proceedings. Third parties were therefore in contempt of court if they wilfully interfered with the administration of justice by thwarting the achievement of that purpose. See *Attorney General v Punch Ltd* [2002] UKHL 50; [2003] 1 A.C. 1046; [2003] 2 W.L.R. 49.

M. Acts calculated to prejudice the due course of justice—may constitute contempt, whether committed before, during or after the proceedings (*Attorney General v Butterworth* [1963] 1 Q.B. 696; [1962] 3 All E.R. 326). So, interference with solicitors (*Re Johnson* (1887) 20 Q.B.D. 68, CA); parties (*Smith v Lakeman* (1856) 2 Jur.(n.s.) 1202); *Attorney General v Times Newspapers Ltd* [1974] A.C. 273; witnesses (*Bromilow v Phillips* (1891) 40 W.R. 220)—for example, by victimising persons who have given evidence (*Attorney General v Butterworth*; *Chapman v Honig* [1963] 2 Q.B. 502; [1963] 2 All E.R. 513, CA)—or are likely to give evidence, or by publishing the name of a witness in a blackmail case contrary to the order of the judge (*R. v Socialist Worker Printers, etc. Ltd* [1975] Q.B. 637; [1975] 1 All E.R. 142). Interference with jurors or the impersonation of a juror may be contempt and the principles set out in *A.G. v Butterworth* apply equally to jurors. *Attorney General v Jackson* [1994] C.O.D. 169 (Mann L.J. and Holland J.); *Attorney General v Judd* [1995] C.O.D. 15 (Steyn L.J. and Kay J.). An offer of money to a bankrupt to suppress evidence at his public examination is a contempt (*Re Hooley, Rucker's Case* (1899) 79 L.T. 306). A third person aiding a party to flout an injunction may be guilty of contempt (*Seaward v Paterson* [1897] 1 Ch. 545, CA; *Hubbard v Woodfield* (1913) 57 S.J. 529). **sc52.1.20**

A person seeking by threats to induce a prosecutor to withdraw a private prosecution may be guilty of contempt (*R. v Martin*, *The Times*, April 23, 1986).

The Contempt of Court Act 1981 s.8 has made it a contempt of court to violate, or to attempt to violate, the confidentiality of a jury's deliberations. A letter by a juror to a defendant's mother disclosing aspects of the jury's deliberations was a clear and deliberate breach of s.8 of the Contempt of Court Act 1981, (which provision is entirely compatible with the Human Rights Act 1998) punishable in this case with a suspended sentence of imprisonment, and the making of an order for costs, however, he would not have been in contempt had he written directly or indirectly to the Crown Court or the Court of Appeal: *Attorney General v Scotcher* [2005] 1 W.L.R. 1867 (Scott Baker LJ and Pitchford J). It has also, by s.9, made it a contempt of court to bring into court, or to use in court, a tape recorder, except with the leave of the court, or to publish to the public any recordings made in court or to use any recordings in contravention of any conditions imposed by the court in granting such leave.

Intimidation of jurors in or immediately outside the court also constitutes contempt and may be dealt with by the judge summarily and of his own motion (*R. v Gough, The Times*, November 15, 1982).

Disclosure of the deliberations of a jury amounts to a contempt under s.8(1) of the Contempt of Court Act 1981, notwithstanding that the information has been obtained indirectly, since the section is aimed at keeping the secrets of the jury room inviolate in the interests of justice (*Attorney General v Associated Newspapers Ltd* [1993] 2 All E.R. 535 (Beldam L.J. and Tudor Evans J.)).

A fear of reprisal may amount to a defence in proceedings for contempt where the contempt consists of a refusal to give evidence against a defendant by whom the alleged contemnor claimed to have been attacked (*R. v Lewis* (1993) 96 Cr.App.R. 412 (Beldam L.J., Ian Kennedy and Morland JJ.)). For guidance on sentencing in such circumstances see *R. v Montgomery* [1995] 2 All E.R. 28.

Where a shorthand writer used a tape recorder in court without leave, contrary to s.9(1) of the Contempt of Court Act 1981, it had to be shown that her conduct contained some element of defiance or was otherwise intolerable before she could be punished under s.12 of the Act. Moreover a court should be very slow to act in a contempt matter without giving reasonable thought to the problem and without giving the alleged contemnor an opportunity to take advice and to apologise (*Re Hooker* [1993] C.O.D. 190 (Kennedy L.J. and Waterhouse J.)).

A threat to an officer of the court, such as a solicitor, can amount to a contempt of court in the same way as a threat to a witness (*R. v Osbourne, The Independent*, September 28, 1992). The prohibition on interfering with witnesses extends also to interference with proper and reasonable attempts by a party's legal adviser to identify and interview potential witnesses (*Connolly v Dale, The Times*, July 13, 1995.

The invasion of the papers of counsel or solicitors when they are in court acting for a party, may constitute a contempt (*Re Griffin (Paul), The Times*, November 6, 1996).

A juror's contumacious refusal to reach a verdict because of a reluctance to judge another may establish the actus reus of contempt but the *mens rea*, namely an intention to impede or create a real risk of prejudicing the administration of justice, must also be proved. When a judge has already expressed a view about a juror's conduct in relation to an alleged contempt it may be appropriate to refer the matter to another judge at the Crown Court or to invite the Attorney General to bring proceedings under RSC O.52 (*R. v Schot & Barclay, The Times*, May 14, 1997 (Rose L.J., Forbes and Keene JJ.)).

In the case of an allegation of interference with a prosecution witness the Crown Court has no power to remand an alleged contemnor in custody. If a judge wishes to ensure that an alleged contemnor is not at liberty he must either adjourn the trial, so as to deal with the matter himself, or refer the matter to another judge. He may not remand the alleged contemnor in custody pending the decision of the Attorney General (*Re Stevens and Holness, The Independent*, June 9, 1997).

A physical assault on a court official, engaged in official business in the administration of justice, is a contempt, *Re de Court, The Times*, November 27, 1997 (Sir Richard Scott V.-C.).

Illegal photography in court has the potential gravely to prejudice the administration of criminal justice. The taking of photographs using mobile phones in court had become a major problem in both Magistrates Courts and the Crown Court, and was also a matter of concern in civil courts. In an appropriate case an immediate sentence of imprisonment was likely: *R. v D (Contempt of Court; illegal photography), The Times*, May 13, 2004 (Lord Woolf C.J., Aikens and Fulford JJ.).

Draft judgments. Unless an order is made to the contrary all draft judgments are embargoed until the official judgment is handed down. The publication of a draft judgment is therefore a contempt of court: *Baigent v Random House & The Lawyer* [2006] EWHC 1131 (Ch) (Peter Smith J.).

sc52.1.21 *N. Interference with receivers may be contempt* —(see *Helmorev Smith* (1887) 35 Ch D. 449; *Dixon v Dixon* [1904] 1 Ch. 161; *Re New Gold Coast Exploration Co* [1901] 1 Ch. 860; *King v Dopson* (1911) 56 S.J. 51; *Re Seaton* [1928] W.N. 307). Interference with other officers of the court may also be contempt.

sc52.1.22 *O. Interference with property under arrest in an admiralty action in rem* —*The Petrel* (1836) 3 Hagg. 299; *The Harmonie* (1841) 1 Wm. Rob. 179, as, e.g. by removing the ship from the jurisdiction (breaking arrest) *The Seraglio* (1885) 10 P.D. 120; *The Jarlinn*

[1965] 1 W.L.R. 1098; [1965] 3 All E.R. 36. In *The Rhenania*, *The Times*, November 12, 1909, the motion for committal, for failure to bring the ship into port after service within the three-mile limit, was made by the Official Solicitor, as it was in *The Selina Stanford*, *The Times*, November 17, 1908.

P. Impeding the service of process may be contempt—(*Price v Hutchison* (1870) L.R. 9 Eq. 534; *Lewis v Owen* [1894] 1 Q.B. 102). Preventing the execution of a writ of possession may be contempt (*Lacon v De Groat* (1894) 10 T.L.R. 24; *Alliance Building Society v Austen* [1951] 2 All E.R. 1068). **sc52.1.23**

Q. Forging or altering the process of the court—is contempt (2 Hawk. P.C. 8th ed., pp.207, 212; *Re Jacobs*, *The Times*, June 13, 1874). **sc52.1.24**

Neglect of duty by sheriffs and other officers of the court may be contempt—See Sheriffs Act 1887 s.29; *Bagge v Whitehead* [1892] 2 Q.B. 355, CA. As to receivers see notes to CPR Pt 69. A liquidator or a trustee under a deed of arrangement, who fails to deliver accounts pursuant to orders of the Board of Trade, is punishable for contempt (*Re Allen* [1935] Ch. 74; *Re Grantham Wholesale Fruit, etc., Merchants Ltd* [1972] 1 W.L.R. 559). **sc52.1.25**

RSC

S. Disobedience to a writ of habeas corpus by the person to whom it is directed—is a contempt punishable by committal, if the original writ is personally served (*R. v Rowe* (1895) 71 L.T. 578). **sc52.1.26**

T. Disobedience to a subpoena ad testificandum or duces tecum though not wilful—(*R. v Daye* [1908] 2 K.B. 333) or refusal of a witness to answer a question (*Ex p. Fernandez* (1861) 30 L.J.C.P. 321; and see *Attorney General v Clough* [1963] 1 Q.B. 773; [1963] 1 All E.R. 420) may be contempt. Parties and witnesses summoned to attend before a Master are liable to process of contempt in case of default. However, a witness will not be in contempt for failing to attend court to give evidence unless a witness summons has first been issued on application under s.2 of the Criminal Procedure and Investigations Act 1996: *R. v Wang* [2005] EWCA Crim 476 (Pill L.J., Curtis and Pitchford JJ.). **sc52.1.27**

Section 3(1) of the Criminal Procedure (Attendance of Witnesses) Act 1965 provides that it is a contempt to disobey a witness order, without just excuse. The disobedience need not be wilful or deliberate since the offence is absolute, save for the qualification as to the just excuse, and culpable forgetfulness of the order could therefore amount to a contempt (*R. v Lennock* (1993) 97 Cr.App.R. 228).

While there is an obligation to tender conduct money to a witness who is to attend proceedings to give evidence, where such money is refused or waived, the witness cannot thereafter rely on its absence as a defence to contempt proceedings brought in consequence of his failure to attend. *H.M. Coroner for Kent v Terrill* [2001] A.C.D. 27, (Laws L.J. and Silber J.).

Under the CPR the term "witness summons" has superseded "subpoena"; see Pt 34.

U. Acting as solicitor, though unqualified—is contempt under the Solicitors Act 1974 s.20. See *Abercrombie v Jordan* (1881) 8 QBD 187; *Re Simmons* (1885) 15 QBD 348; *Re Panton* [1901] P. 239; *Re Ainsworth* [1905] 2 K.B. 103; *Davies v Davies* (1913) 29 T.L.R. 513. The sanction is committal, indictment or action for penalties. Committal may issue for breach of an order directing a person who professed to be a solicitor, but was not qualified, to deliver up documents and pay money (*Re Hulm & Lewis* [1892] 2 Q.B. 261). **sc52.1.28**

Ministers and civil servants

Ministers and civil servants are amenable to the court's contempt jurisdiction when acting in discharge or purported discharge of their official duties, provided the factual basis and the necessary intention are proved beyond all reasonable doubt (*M. v Home Office* [1993] 3 W.L.R. 433). **sc52.1.29**

Effect of party being in contempt

The court has a discretion whether to hear a contemnor who has not purged his contempt. However where a contemnor not only fails to comply with an order of the court but, for example, makes it clear that he will continue to defy the court's author- **sc52.1.30** ity whatever the outcome of an appeal, the court is entitled to exercise its discretion to decline to entertain his appeal (*X. Ltd v Morgan-Grampian (Publishers) Ltd* [1990] 2 W.L.R. 1000; [1990] 2 All E.R. 1, HL). A court's power to refuse to hear an alleged contemnor in support of an appeal against the order in respect of which he is said to be in contempt, should be exercised only exceptionally. The proper approach is first to decide whether he has an arguable case and, if so, to decide whether the judgment should be set aside or the contempt proceedings should be adjourned until the appeal has been heard (*Atlantic Capital Corp v Johnson* Independent, September 26, 1994, CA (Glidewell and Legatt L.JJ. and Sir Michael Kerr)). The court will exercise discretion to hear contemnors who have not purged their contempt where the contemnors are trustees, and it is in the interest of the beneficiaries under the trust that the application should be heard (*Clarke v Heathfield* [1985] I.C.R. 203, CA). Moreover, a contemnor who appeals against an order committing him for contempt on the ground of lack of jurisdiction in the court to make the original order, has, of course, a right to be heard (*Gordon v Gordon* [1904] P. 163, CA). It is now recognised that there is no general rule that a court will not hear an application for a contemnor's own benefit unless he has first purged his contempt. It was wrong for a judge to proceed with an effective hearing of an application to commit, where he knew that the contemnor wished to be heard in person but was prevented from attending for reasons over which he had no control. *Raja v Van Hoogstraten* [2004] EWCA Civ 968; [2004] All E.R. 793 (Pill, Chadwick and May L.JJ.).

For the origins of the learning on this branch of the law see *Chuck v Cremer* (1846) Coop. temp. Cott. 205 and 338, and *Hodkinson v Hodkinson* [1952] P. 285, CA and the old authorities therein cited.

Para.(2)—orders of committal by a Divisional Court of the QBD

sc52.1.31 This paragraph in effect restates the practice which has existed for many years (see Short & Mellor, *Crown Practice*, 2nd ed., pp.341 *et seq.* and former rules of court) except for the change instituted by para.(3) *q.v.*

sc52.1.32 *(a)(i) "contempt ... in connection with any proceedings before a Divisional Court of the QBD"* —For example, disobedience to a writ of habeas corpus, or to an order of mandamus (*R. v Poplar BC (No.2)* [1922] 1 K.B. 95) prohibition or certiorari (*Mungean v Wheatley* (1851) 6 Ex. 88). In these cases the court is punishing as contempt the disobedience to its own order.

sc52.1.33 *(ii) "contempt ... in connection with criminal proceedings"* —If the contempt is *in facie curiae*, or consists of disobedience to an order of the court or a breach of an undertaking to the court, that court will usually punish the contempt itself. In such cases a single Judge has jurisdiction, and in cases of disobedience to a Master's order on the application is made by motion to a Judge. There remains the wide and important jurisdiction of the QBD, exercised by the Divisional Court, to punish by committal or fine conduct calculated (*R. v Odhams Press Ltd* [1957] 1 Q.B. 73; [1956] 3 All E.R. 494; *R. v Griffiths* [1957] 2 Q.B. 192; [1957] 2 All E.R. 379; Administration of Justice Act 1960 s.11) to interfere with the due administration of justice in criminal proceedings; though the Crown Court has power to commit for contempt, the QBD has residual jurisdiction and is the appropriate court in respect of contempt of Magistrates' Courts and Courts-martial (see *R. v Davies*; *R. v Evening Standard Co*; *R. v Daily Mail Ex p. Famsworth* [1921] 2 K.B. 733). Disobedience of a witness summons issued by a Magistrates' Court cannot be punished as a contempt by a Divisional Court of the QBD, whereas disobedience to a Crown Office subpoena, issued in connection with the same proceedings, would be so punishable under para.2(a) (*R. v Judge* [1931] 2 K.B. 442).

An application to commit a person for breach of restraint and charging orders made under the Drug Trafficking Offences Act 1986 ss.8 and 9, and RSC O.115, r.3, relates to breach of an order made in civil proceedings, albeit closely connected to criminal proceedings; hence such application must be made to a single judge and not to the Divisional Court (*Re H, The Times*, April 1, 1988, CA). Where both the Crown Court and the Divisional Court have power to punish for contempt see the guidance provided by the Divisional Court in relation to O.52, r.1 in *DPP v Channel 4 Television Co Ltd [1993]* C.O.D. 6 and *Attorney General v Martonia* [1993] C.O.D. 9 (Woolf L.J. and Pill J.).

A trial judge in the Crown Court has jurisdiction to try an application by the prosecution for a defendant to be committed for contempt for allegedly breaching a restraint order. See *R v M (Restraint Order: Jurisdiction)* [2008] EWCA Crim 1901; *The Times*, October 24, 2008 (Toulson L.J., Andrew Smith and Bean JJ.).

(iii) "contempt … in connection with proceedings in an inferior Court"—Thirdly, just as the QBD has inherent power to supervise the proceedings of inferior courts, so it has power to protect them from acts calculated to interfere with the administration of justice by them, as for example, by punishing as a contempt any publication in a newspaper calculated to have that effect (*R. v Davies* [1906] 1 K.B. 32; *R. v Daily Herald* [1932] 2 K.B. 402 (proceedings in a Consistory Court); *R. v Evening Standard Co Ltd* [1954] 1 Q.B. 578; [1954] 1 All E.R. 1026) or any act obstructing process issued by order of such a court (*R. v Edwards* (1933) 49 T.L.R. 383). Where an inferior court is scandalised, the appropriate proceeding is by committal under the present rule, although it may also be dealt with on summary process for committal (*R. v Bairstow Ex p. DPP* [1941] W.N. 104). **sc52.1.34**

A county court has jurisdiction to commit for a contempt in the face of the court and for breach of its injunctions or other similar orders or undertakings. Any other contempt in connection with proceedings in a county court is punishable only by an order of committal in the QBD (*G (A Child) (Contempt: Committal Order), Re* [2003] EWCA Civ 489). (Para 1.1 of Practice Direction (Family Proceedings: Committal) [2001] 1 W.L.R. 1253 is incorrect).Where he lacks jurisdiction the county court judge should refer the matter to the Attorney General who will consider whether it needs to be raised in the Divisional Court (*Bush v Green* [1985] 1 W.L.R. 1143). See s.118 of the County Courts Act 1984 for the power to punish contempt in the face of the court. A county court does have power, derived from s.38 of the same act to order sequestration of a company's assets to compel obedience to its order (*Rose v Laskington Ltd* [1989] 3 W.L.R. 873; [2003] 3 All E.R. 306).

"Court" for this purpose means a court of law; a court dealing with matters of administration, such as local valuation courts, and not within the scope of O.52, r.1 (*Attorney General v BBC* [1981] A.C. 303; [1980] 3 All E.R. 161, HL). An employment tribunal is an inferior court for the purposes of r.1(2)(a)(iii) and the Divisional Court therefore has jurisdiction to punish for contempt of that tribunal (*Peach Grey & Co (A Firm) v Sommers* [1995] 2 All E.R. 513 (Rose L.J. and Tuckey J.)).

The power of a county court judge to punish for contempt under s.118 of the County Courts Act 1984 is not limited to dealing with contempts committed in the face of the court but extends to situations where a witness is wilfully insulted on his way to or from court, *Manchester City Council v McCann, The Times*, November 28, 1998 (Lord Woolf M.R., Henry and Clarke L.JJ.).

The Professional Conduct Committee of the General Medical Council is not part of the judicial system of the state and does not therefore fall within the definition of a "court" for the purposes of contempt proceedings: *General Medical Council v British Broadcasting Corp* [1998] 3 All E.R. 426 (Stuart-Smith, Aldous and Robert Walker L.JJ.).

The power to deal with an allegation of contempt, consisting of a breach of a restraint order made in the Crown Court, lies with that court, and not by way of an application to the Divisional Court: *R. v M* [2008] EWCA Crim 1901 (Toulson L.J., Andrew Smith and Bean J.J.).

Defendants who fail to attend the Crown Court in response to a summons should not be convicted and sentenced for offences under the Bail Act 1976 or for contempt of court, if they were not on bail or had received no notice of the summons: *R. v Noble The Times*, 21 July 2008 (Maurice Kay L.J., Plender J. and Judge Stokes Q.C.)

(b) "contempt … committed otherwise than in connection with any proceedings"—For example, the offence of scandalising the High Court or a Judge thereof, or any *particularly outrageous conduct* amounting to a contempt of that Court, without reference to any particular proceedings (see *M'Leod v St Aubyn* [1899] A.C. 549 at 551; *R. v Gray* [1900] 2 Q.B. 36). **sc52.1.35**

Para.(3)—orders of committal by a single judge of the QBD

This paragraph was introduced by RSC 1965. **sc52.1.36**

The first sentence enables a single judge of the QBD to punish contempt of Court committed in connection with any civil proceedings in that Division (not being proceedings before a Divisional Court) even though the contempt is not in face of the Court and does not consist of disobedience to an order of the Court. The practice, therefore, of the QBD and the other divisions is the same in this respect.

Para.(4)—contempt of other tribunals

sc52.1.37 See the Tribunals of Inquiry (Evidence) Act 1921 s.1(2); the Army Act 1955 s.101; the Air Force Act 1955 s.101; the Naval Discipline Act 1957 s.65; the Nuclear Installations (Licensing and Insurance) Act 1959 Sch.1, para.7; and the Pipe Lines Act 1962 Sch.5, para.7. Under each of these Acts, if any person does anything which, if the tribunal were a court of law having power to commit for contempt, would have been a contempt of court, his offence may be certified to the High Court, which may punish in like manner as for a contempt of the High Court (see as to the Tribunals of Inquiry (Evidence) Act 1921, *Attorney General v Clough* [1963] 1 Q.B. 773; [1963] 1 All E.R. 420; *Attorney General v Mullholland & Foster* [1963] 2 Q.B. 477; [1963] 1 All E.R. 767, CA). By virtue of Orders in Council made under s.8 of the Visiting Forces Act 1952, the above service enactments apply to service courts of certain visiting forces.

Treatment of contempt prisoners

sc52.1.38 Persons committed to prison for contempt of court are subject to special treatment under the Prison Rules 1999 (SI 1999/728); see r.7. Broadly speaking they are treated as unconvicted prisoners (remand prisoners). As to the special statutory regime governing early release of contempt prisoners, see para.sc52.8.2.

Sentence

sc52.1.39 Subject to any statute which imposes a lesser maximum (e.g. s.118 CCA 1984), the maximum sentence which can be imposed on one occasion for a contempt is two years (Contempt of Court Act 1981) including any activation of a previously suspended sentence (*Villiers v Villiers* [1994]1 W.L.R. 493). Guidance on sentencing was given by the Court of Appeal in *Hale v Tanner* [2000] 1 W.L.R. 2377 as amended by *Lomas v Parle* [2003] EWCA Civ 1804. Any sentence of imprisonment must bear a reasonable relationship to the maximum of two years. Where a serious contempt has been established by the evidence, the appropriate sanction in principle is a short period of imprisonment: *LTE Scientific Ltd v Thomas* [2005] EWHC 7 (Richards J.).

A sentence of four months' imprisonment for contempt was appropriate where, in a trial for drugs offences, the appellant, having given evidence in chief, refused to answer questions in cross examination. The general principles were set out in *Montgomery* (1995) 16 Cr.App.R.(S.) 274. While the maximum sentence for failing to comply with a witness order was three months, that should not inhibit the court from imposing a substantially longer sentence for a blatant contempt by a witness in the face of the court. Relevant considerations were, among others, the gravity of the offence being tried, the effect of the refusal, the reason for the refusal and whether it was aggravated by impertinent defiance of the judge: *R. v Dean Phillip Robinson* [2006] EWCA Crim 613; [2006] 2 Cr.App.R.(S.) 88.

Time on remand

sc52.1.40 There is no inherent power to remand in custody in the county court and only a very limited power in the High Court (e.g. overnight, see *Wilkinson v S* [2003] 1 W.L.R. 1254). If the contemnor is remanded in custody under a statutory power (e.g. Sch.5 to the Family Law Act 1996) the sentencing judge must take this into consideration (*The Queen, on the application of Sevketoglu v Sevketoglu* [2003] EWCA Civ 1570).

Early Release

sc52.1.41 As soon as the contemnor has served one-half of the sentence "it shall be the duty of the Secretary of State to release him unconditionally" (Criminal Justice Act 2003 s.258). Further, a contemnor may apply at any time to purge his contempt. Such an application should be heard by the sentencing judge if at all possible. The judge can say "yes", "no" or "not yet" but cannot suspend the remainder of the sentence (*Harris v Harris* [2001] EWCA Civ 1645; [2002] 1 F.L.R. 248).

Appeal

sc52.1.42 An appeal lies from an order punishing an offender for contempt of court. If the Court making the order is the Crown Court, the appeal lies to the criminal division of the Court of Appeal; in all other cases it lies to the civil division of that Court

(Administration of Justice Act 1960 s.13; SCA 1981 s.53). Where the Court of Appeal Criminal Division has jurisdiction to entertain an appeal under s.13 of the 1960 Act that is the route to be followed, rather than an application for judicial review. Section 13(1) of the 1960 Act applies not only when a contemnor has been convicted or sentenced for contempt but also to orders made in the course of the proceedings; thus the Crown Court has jurisdiction to grant bail pending determination of the proceedings for contempt: *R. v Seramuga* [2005] 1 W.L.R. 3366 (Mauurice Kay L.J., Davis and Field JJ.).

Where there has been no unfairness or material irregularity in the committal proceedings, and where there has been nothing more than an irregularity in the drawing up of the committal order, the irregularity can be corrected on appeal by virtue of the Administration of Justice Act 1960 s.13(3), and the sentence varied to make it a just sentence (*Linnett v Coles* [1987] Q.B. 555; [1986] 3 All E.R. 652, CA; *Wright v Jess* [1987] 1 W.L.R. 1076; [1987] 2 All E.R. 1067, CA). See further *per* Lord Woolf M.R. in *Nicholls v Nicholls* [1997] 1 W.L.R. 314.

Where there is a defect in the committal application rather than in the committal order, the Court should be cautious before exercising its power under s.13(3) of the Administration of Justice Act 1960 to substitute a new order, since a defect in the application can affect materially the fairness of the proceedings and render it unjust for the Court to use such power (*Harmsworth v Harmsworth* [1987] 1 W.L.R. 1676; [1987] 3 All E.R. 816, CA).

Section 13(3) of the Administration of Justice Act 1960 enables the Court of Appeal to correct errors in orders made by lower courts, but in cases of contempt this power will be used only in exceptional circumstances; while the court will not permit a technical infringement of the rules to prevent justice being done, it will not use the power to correct orders where requirements affecting important rights of contemnors have not been complied with (*Clarke v Clarke* [1990] 2 F.L.R. 115, CA). Thus where a committal order is not served on a contemnor until after he has been imprisoned for the contempt, and does not set out the lower court's findings so as to enable the contemnor to challenge them, the Court of Appeal will not intervene to correct the errors (*ibid.*).

On appeal from a committal order for a civil contempt, leave to adduce fresh evidence will be given if it is necessary or expedient in the interests of justice by analogy with s.23 of the Criminal Appeal Act 1968 (see for example *R. v Lattimore* (1975) 62 Cr.App.R. 53). There is no obligation on the appellant to fulfil the requirements set out in *Ladd v Marshall* [1954] 1 W.L.R. 1489 (*Irtelli v Squatriti* [1992] 3 W.L.R. 218 (Sir Donald Nicholls V.-C., Taylor and Farquharson L.JJ.)). There is no jurisdictional bar to prevent an *applicant* in committal proceedings from applying to the Court of Appeal under s.13(2) of the Administration of Justice Act 1960 for a redetermination of the sentence passed on a contemnor by a county court, where it is said that the sentence failed properly to reflect the seriousness of the contempt. However the Court of Appeal will only interfere in exceptional circumstances and where the decision of the court below was plainly wrong: *Wilson v Webster* [1998] 1 F.L.R. 1097 (Sir Stephen Brown P. and Sir Patrick Russell). Thus either party may appeal a committal order and the right of appeal is not therefore limited to the contemnor: *Wood v Collins*, *The Times*, June 26, 2006 (Thorpe, Gage L.JJ. and Hedley J.).

The right of appeal to the Court of Appeal, Civil Division, conferred by s.13 of the Administration of Justice Act 1960 is unaffected by s.56 of the Access to Justice Act 1999 and the Access to Justice Act 1999 (Destination of Appeals) Order 2000 and therefore lies as of right, and without the need to obtain permission to appeal. *Hampshire CC v Gillingham* (Sedley and Latham L.JJ.) June 20, 2000.

CPR r.52.3(1)(a)(i) provides that permission to appeal is not required where the appeal is against a committal order. However, for the purposes of the CPR appellate regime, a distinction must be drawn between an order by which a party is committed to prison, where permission to appeal is not required, and any other order or decision made by a court in the exercise of its jurisdiction to punish for contempt, where permission to appeal will be required; see *London Borough of Barnet v Hurst* [2002] EWCA Civ 1009, Simon Browne, Brooke and Dyson L.JJ. A claimant who seeks to appeal a decision that a defendant has purged his contempt will require permission to appeal: *Poole Borough Council v Hambridge* [2007] EWCA Civ 990 (Pill, Buxton and Lloyd L.JJ.). An application for habeas corpus is not the appropriate remedy to challenge a committal for contempt (*Rayne, Re* [2004] EWCA Civ 543 (Tuckey and Laws L.JJ.)).

Application to Divisional Court

sc52.2 2.—(1) No application to a Divisional Court for an order of committal against any person may be made unless permission to make such an application has been granted in accordance with this rule.

(2) An application for such permission must be made without notice to a Divisional Court, except in vacation when it may be made to a judge in chambers, and must be supported by a statement setting out the name and description of the applicant, the name, description and address of the person sought to be committed and the grounds on which his committal is sought, and by an affidavit, to be filed before the application is made, verifying the facts relied on.

(3) The applicant must give notice of the application for permission not later than the preceding day to the Crown Office and must at the same time lodge in that office copies of the statement and affidavit.

(4) Where an application for permission under this rule is refused by a judge in chambers, the applicant may make a fresh application for such permission to a Divisional Court.

(5) An application made to a Divisional Court by virtue of paragraph (4) must be made within 8 days after the judge's refusal to give permission or, if a Divisional Court does not sit within that period, on the first day on which it sits thereafter.

Effect of rule

sc52.2.1 The rule requires permission to be obtained by application made without notice (see Practice Direction, para.2.4, see para.scpd52.2 and CPR r.23.2(4)) supported by affidavit before an order of committal is sought from the Divisional Court. See further commentary to O.52, r.4.

Application for order after leave to apply granted

sc52.3 3.—(1) When permission has been granted under rule 2 to apply for an order of committal, the application for the order must be made to a Divisional Court and, unless the court or judge granting permission has otherwise directed, there must be at least 14 clear days between the service of the claim form and the day named therein for the hearing.

(2) Unless within 14 days after such permission was granted, the claim form is issued the permission shall lapse.

(3) Subject to paragraph 4, the claim form, accompanied by a copy of the statement and affidavit in support of the application for permission, must be served personally on the person sought to be committed.

(4) Without prejudice to the powers of the court or judge under Part 6 of the CPR, the court or judge may dispense with service under this rule if it or he thinks it just to do so.

General

sc52.3.1 The date on which and the name of the judge by whom the requisite permission was granted must be stated on the claim form or application notice by which the commital application is commenced: See Practice Direction, para.2.4, para.scpd52.2.

Personal service

sc52.3.2 No order will be issued for the committal of a person unless he is aware of the order, disobedience to which is said to constitute the contempt, and usually this requires proof that he has been personally served with it. If the order is directed to a group of persons or a corporation, some appropriate person must be personally served. An applicant must give each person sought to be committed the fullest notice that an application is being made for his committal (*R. v Poplar BC (No.2)* [1922] 1 K.B. 95)—e.g. by inserting his name in the claim form and personally serving him with it and the affidavit in support. O.52, r.3(4) gives express power to dispense with service, e.g. where the alleged contemnor is evading service. Service may be dispensed with only where there is no other course available to uphold the authority of the Court and protect the applicant: the dispensation should be recorded in the committal order (*Wright v Jess* [1987] 1 W.L.R. 1076; [1987] 2 All E.R. 1067, CA).

Failure to comply with a proper procedure, such as personal service, is not necessarily fatal to the lawfulness of a contempt order. The court has complete discretion, under s.13(3) of the Administration of Justice Act 1960 to perfect an invalid committal order in a contempt case, but that power should only be used in exceptional cases and should be dictated by the need to do justice having regard to the interests of the contemnor, the victim of the contempt and other court users. Where a contemnor has not suffered any injustice by the failure to follow the proper procedures (such as service) the committal order could stand subject to variation to take account of any technical or procedural defects (*M v P* (Contempt of Court: Committal Order, *Butler v Butler*) [1992] 3 W.L.R. 813; [1992] 4 All E R. 833 (Lord Donaldson of Lymington, M.R. Nolan and Scott L.JJ.) *Nicholls v Nicholls* [1997] 1 W.L.R. 314.

Where a new or adjourned date is fixed for the hearing of the notice of motion, personal service ought also to be affected of notification of the date (*Phonographic Performance Ltd v Tsang* (1985) 82 L.S Gaz. 2331, CA). Where a contemnor had been shown every latitude, but his attitude remained one of contumacious defiance and he had deliberately stayed away from the committal proceedings, there was no failure of due process giving rise to such injustice or unfairness as would warrant the exercise of the court's appellate power under s.13 of the 1960 Act. *Scriven, Re* [2004] EWCA Civ 683 (Clarke and Sedley LJ.J).

"14 clear days"

Both r.3(1) and r.3(2) refer to "14 days". Prior to its incorporation into Sch.1 to the CPR r.3(1) used to provide for eight clear days. **sc52.3.3**

"claim form"

Rule 3(3) now requires service of a claim form rather than a notice of motion. The application for permission is made in accordance with sc52.2 (see above). **sc52.3.4**

Application to court other than Divisional Court

4.—(1) Where an application for an order of committal may be made to a court other than a Divisional Court, the application must be made by claim form or application notice and be supported by an affidavit. **sc52.4**

(2) Subject to paragraph (3) the claim form or application notice, stating the grounds of the application and accompanied by a copy of the affidavit in support of the application, must be served personally on the person sought to be committed.

(3) Without prejudice to its powers under Part 6 of the CPR, the court may dispense with service under this rule if it thinks it just to do so.

(4) This rule does not apply to committal applications which under rules 1(2) and 3(1) should be made to a Divisional Court but which, in vacation, have been properly made to a single judge in accordance with RSC Order 64, rule 4.

Claim form on application notice

Generally a committal application must be commenced by the issue of a Part 8 claim form (see Practice Direction, para.2.1, see para.scpd52.2) but if the committal application is made in existing proceedings it may be commenced by filing an application notice in those proceedings. The application notice must state that it is made in those existing proceedings and include the title and reference number of those proceedings (see Practice Direction, para.2.2). **sc52.4.1**

A claim form, together with copies of all written evidence in support must, unless the court otherwise directs, be served personally on the respondent (see Practice Direction, para.2.5(1)). It must set out in full the grounds on which the committal application is made and should identify, separately and numerically, each alleged act of contempt (see Practice Direction, para.2.5(2)). An amendment may be made only with the permission of the court (see Practice Direction, para.2.5(3)).

If the committal application is commenced by the filing of an application notice CPR Pt 23 applies as amended by the Practice Direction. There is a similar requirement as to service and as to the provision of particulars and amendment (see Practice Direction, para.2.6).

There is no requirement to make the application to the judge who made the original order which is alleged to have been breached but it is preferable to do so if this can be done conveniently and without delay. If the contempt is of an Order of the Court of Appeal made on appeal, the application should be made to the Court below (*Fortescue v McKeown* [1914] 1 Ir.R.30; *Pott v Stuteley* [1935] W.N. 140); otherwise to the Court of Appeal.

The application must specify the breaches of the injunction or undertaking which are relied on (*Chanel Ltd v FGM Cosmetics Ltd* [1981] F.S.R. 471).

Service of the order

sc52.4.2 If the order requires a positive act to be done, the evidence must prove service of the order alleged to have been disobeyed. The order must be indorsed with a penal notice under O.45, r.7. In the case of a company, the penal notice must be directed to the company even though it may be desired to enforce it against the directors; the order may be served on the company as provided in s.725 of the CA 1985 but must be served personally on any director against whom it is intended to proceed (*Iberian Trust v Founder's Trust* [1932] 2 K.B. 87; *Bernabo v William Jay & Partners Ltd* [1941] Ch. 52). If the order is to abstain from doing an act, it is sufficient to prove that the person against whom it is desired to proceed for contempt had notice of, and disregarded, the prohibition (*Ronson Products Ltd v Ronson Furniture Ltd* [1966] R.P.C. 497 (enforcement against a director) not following *Redwing Ltd v Redwing Forest Products Ltd* (1947) 177 L.T. 387). Service of the order is, of course, the best way of giving notice of it, and must be effected if possible (see O.45, r.7).

Service of application to commit

sc52.4.3 The claim form/application notice must be served personally on the alleged contemnor (even if he has an address for service) unless the Court dispenses with such service (see r.4(2) and (3) and Practice Direction (Committal Applications), paras 2.5 and 2.6 see para.scpd52.2.) In *Mander v Falcke* [1891] 3 Ch. 488 it was held that the attendance of the contemnor at the hearing did not waive the necessity for service but it is submitted that this decision is not consistent with the modern procedure having regard to RSC O.52, r.4(3) and Part I CPR. Service is not an end in itself but a means of bringing to the attention of persons concerned notice that a hearing is to take place. Personal service is always preferable but the Court will dispense with it in appropriate cases, e.g. upon evidence that the contemnor is evading service. The Court can not only dispense with service but can dispense with service altogether see Practice Direction (Committal Applications), paras 2.5(1) and 2.6(1) at para.scpd52.2. In *O'Donovan v O'Donovan* [1955] 1 W.L.R. 1086 a committal order was made against a person out of the jurisdiction who had not been served with notice. Similarly in *Favard v Favard* (1896) 75 LT 664 where a respondent, in flagrant disobedience to an order, removed a child from the jurisdiction.

The general rule, however, is that an alleged contemnor is entitled to know, before the hearing of the committal application, of what he is accused and the supporting evidence. Thus where he had not been served with the application to commit him, and did not know until the day of the hearing (save indirectly) what was alleged against him, the judge erred in law in refusing an adjournment for the service of the relevant documents. Even where an alleged contemnor is legally represented he must nevertheless be given the opportunity to mitigate the proposed penalty, where the judge has the intention of imposing a term of imprisonment (*Taylor v Persico, The Times, February 12, 1992*, CA (Parker, Stocker L.JJ. and Sir David Croom-Johnson)).

A claimant who lived in China, but had commenced proceedings in England, had thereby submitted to the incidents of that litigation and to the jurisdiction of the court. A defendant did not therefore require permission to serve out of the jurisdiction an application for the claimant's committal for contempt: *Marketmaker Technology Ltd v CMC Group Plc* [2008] EWHC 1556 QB (Teare J.).

Undertakings

An undertaking given to the Court, although as binding and effective as an order, differs from an order in that it is volunteered rather than imposed; hence the person giving the undertaking is presumed to know of it, and proof of service of the order reciting the undertaking is not required prior to enforcement (*Hussain v Hussain* [1986] 2 W.L.R. 805; [1986] 1 All E.R. 961, CA). **sc52.4.4**

Grounds of the application

Where committal is sought for breach of an injunction, it must be made clear what the defendant is alleged to have done and that it is a breach. So, if the injunction is in general terms, restraining the defendant from disclosing or making use of any confidential information acquired by him in the course of his employment with the claimant, the latter must show what information is alleged to have been disclosed or used, and that it was confidential (*P. A. Thomas & Co v Mould* [1968] 2 Q.B. 913; [1968] 1 All E.R. 963). An alleged contemnor is not a compellable witness, even in proceedings for civil contempt, but he may be cross-examined upon an affidavit (*Comet Products U.K. Ltd v Hawker Plastics Ltd* [1971] 2 Q.B. 67; [1971] 1 All E.R. 1141). **sc52.4.5**

The application notice must state exactly what the alleged contemnor has done or omitted to do which constitutes a contempt of court with sufficient particularity to enable him to meet the charge (*Chiltern DC v Keane* [1985] 1 W.L.R. 619; [1985] 2 All E.R. 118, CA). The necessary information must be given in the application itself; if lengthy particulars are required it is permissible to include them in a schedule or addendum to the application, provided that they form part of the application itself; it is not permissible to refer in the application to an affidavit or other separate document for particulars which ought to be in the application (*Harmsworth v Harmsworth* [1987] 1 W.L.R. 1676; [1987] 3 All E.R. 816, CA).

Evidence

The standard of proof required at committal proceedings is the criminal standard (*Dean v Dean* [1987] F.L.R. 517). Proceedings for committal for contempt of court for breach of an injunction or undertaking are however, civil proceedings. Evidence is governed by Pt 32 CPR and its Supplementing Practice Direction. For affidavits see CPR r.32.15 and paras 2 *et seq.* of the Practice Direction at para.32PD.2. The Court will require the best available evidence of the alleged breach and the applicant must bear in mind that the burden of proof is on him. **sc52.4.6**

The rule of practice in criminal cases that no comment may be made by the prosecution on the defendant's failure to give evidence does not apply, however, to an application for committal for contempt for refusal to comply with an Anton Piller order, and the judge is entitled to draw appropriate inferences from the absence of any explanation by the person served with the order as to the non-production of documents within its scope (*Bhimji v Chatwani* [1991] 1 All E.R. 705). The Court has power to direct a respondent to a committal summons to swear affidavits or produce statements of witnesses of fact upon which he might wish to rely and to file and serve such evidence in convenient time before the hearing in order to permit proper presentation of evidence in reply. Although the respondent nevertheless retains the right not to have such evidence adduced at the hearing the wise course, generally speaking, is either to make a full and frank admission of the contempt or, if it is denied, to set out his case clearly and in detail (*Re B (A Minor) (Contempt Evidence)*, *The Times*, November 15, 1995 (Wall J.)).

As to the relationship generally between the rules of criminal procedure and the procedure applicable to civil proceedings to commit for contempt, see *Barclays De Zoete Wedd Securities Ltd v Nadir*, *The Times*, March 25, 1992 (Knox J.).

A finding of contempt in summary proceedings should not be based upon hearsay evidence given by a police officer concerning what he had been told by someone who was not a witness before the court (*R. v Shokoya* (1992), *The Times* June 10, 1992 (Russel L.J., Schiemann and Ebsworth JJ.)).

Committal proceedings in the High Court are civil proceedings governed by the Civil Evidence Act 1995 and RSC O.52, as amended and appended by the CPR, and the jurisprudence of the ECtHR supports a flexible approach to the admission of hearsay evidence, rather than its exclusion on principle: *Daltel Europe Ltd v Makki* [2006] EWCA Civ 94; [2006] 1 W.L.R. 2704, CA.

Re B (a Minor) (Contempt Evidence) [1996] 1 W.L.R. 627, contains an extensive review of the authorities.

Proceedings for a civil contempt are proceedings for the "recovery of a penalty" within s.14(1) of the Civil Evidence Act 1968 in respect of which the privilege against self incrimination applies. However, s.72 of the Supreme Court Act 1981 has the effect of withdrawing that privilege in relation to proceedings for infringement of intellectual property rights or passing off (*Cobra Golf Ltd v Rata* [1997] 2 All E.R. 150, Rimer J.). Where in proceedings for a freezing order a defendant had been ordered to attend for cross examination on his affidavit, the privilege against self–incrimination is available to him in respect of the risk of contempt proceedings in that action. *Memory Corp Plc v Sidhu* [2000] 1 All E.R. 434 (Arden J.).

Saving for power to commit without application for purpose

sc52.5 5. Nothing in the foregoing provisions of this order shall be taken as affecting the power of the High Court or Court of Appeal to make an order of committal of its own initiative against a person guilty of contempt of court.

Effect of rule

sc52.5.1 The rule enables the court to commit without any formal application to do so. In its original form the rule was confined to a contempt "in the face of the court" and although no longer so confined that is still the best example of when the court is likely to act of its own initiative. Another example would be disobedience of an order made in wardship proceedings (*R. v Gray* [1900] 2 Q.B. 36; *Bernstein v Bernstein* [1960] Ch. 120; *Hipgrave v Hipgrave* [1962] P.91; *Warwick Corp v Russell* [1964] 1 W.L.R. 613. The summary power to deal with contempt is unique in English law; see Mustill L.J. in *R. v Griffin*, 88 Cr.AppR. 63 at 67. Since O.52, r.5 provides for the High Court to make an order of committal of its own motion by virtue of s.38 of the County Courts Act 1984 that power applies equally to the County Court. Accordingly a Judge of the County Court has power to initiate contempt proceedings of his own motion, but such a procedure should only be used sparingly and as a last resort: *M (a minor)* [1999] 2 W.L.R. 810 (Evans and Ward L.JJ.).

The Court also has power to issue a witness summons of its own initiative in order to ascertain the facts (*Yianni v Yianni* [1966] 1 W.L.R. 120).

Provisions as to hearing

sc52.6 6.—(1) Subject to paragraph (2), the court hearing an application for an order of committal may sit in private in the following cases, that is to say—

(a) where the application arises out of proceedings relating to the wardship or adoption of an infant or wholly or mainly to the guardianship, custody, maintenance or upbringing of an infant, or rights of access to an infant;

(b) where the application arises out of proceedings relating to a person suffering or appearing to be suffering from mental disorder within the meaning of the Mental Health Act 1983;

(c) where the application arises out of proceedings in which a secret process, discovery or invention was in issue;

(d) where it appears to the court that in the interests of the administration of justice or for reasons of national security the application should be heard in private;

but, except as aforesaid, the application shall be heard in public.

(2) If the court hearing an application in private by virtue of paragraph (1) decides to make an order of committal against the person sought to be committed, it shall in public state—

(a) the name of that person;

(b) in general terms the nature of the contempt of court in respect of which the order of committal is being made; and

(c) the length of the period for which he is being committed.

(3) Except with the permission of the court hearing an application for an order of committal, no grounds shall be relied upon at the hearing except the grounds set out in the statement under rule 2 or, as the case may be, in the claim form or application notice under rule 4.

(4) If on the hearing of the application the person sought to be committed expresses a wish to give oral evidence on his own behalf, he shall be entitled to do so.

History of Rule

Amended by Civil Procedure (Amendment) Rules 1999 (SI 1999/1008) **sc52.6.1**

Effect of rule

The applicant for the committal order must obtain a hearing date from the Court when he files his application—see Practice Direction, para.4.1, para.scpd52.4. Unless the Court otherwise directs there must be 14 clear days between service and hearing—see Practice Direction, para.4.2. The Court may however at any time give case management directions. The general rule is that all hearings are to be in public (CPR r.39.2). O.52.6 provides the limited exceptions where application for an order of committal may be in private (r.6(1)). If the court, having heard an application in private finds the respondent guilty of contempt of court, the judge must state in public (1) the name of the respondent, (2) the nature of the contempt and (3) the penalty, if any, imposed: see r.6(2) and Practice Direction, para.9, scpd52.5. An order of committal is for a fixed term (s.14 of the Contempt of Court Act 1981). **sc52.6.2**

Power to suspend execution of committal order

7.—(1) The court by whom an order of committal is made may by order direct that the execution of the order of committal shall be suspended for such period or on such terms or conditions as it may specify. **sc52.7**

(2) Where execution of an order of committal is suspended by an order under paragraph (1), the applicant for the order of committal must, unless the court otherwise directs, serve on the person against whom it was made a notice informing him of the making and terms of the order under that paragraph.

Warrant for arrest[1]

7A A warrant for the arrest of a person against whom an order of committal has been made shall not, without further order of the court, be enforced more than 2 years after the date on which the warrant is issued. **sc52.7A**

Suspended committal order

O.52, r.7 does not of itself confer jurisdiction but merely prescibes the procedure for the exercise of an existing power of suspension. *Lee v Walker* [1985] Q.B. 1191. **sc52.7.1**

There is nothing in r.7 to suggest that it is the invariable practice to suspend a committal order only for a finite period. Thus a committal order may be suspended for so long as the contemnor complies with another order expressed to last "until further order", notwithstanding that the effect will be to suspend a sentence of imprisonment indefinitely. *Griffin v Griffin*, *The Times*, April 28, 2000 (Simon Brown and Hale L.JJ.).

[1] Introduced by the Civil Procedure (Amendment No.5) Rules 2003 (SI 2003/3361).

The courts power to suspend an order of committal to prison for contempt of court derives from this rule (and is not affected by the need for "exceptional circumstances" before a suspended sentence can be passed in a criminal case: s.22 of the Powers of Criminal Courts Act 1973 as amended). If a committal order is made for a fixed period but the sentence is suspended subject to the contemnor's compliance with a condition, and it is subsequently found that he has not complied with it, the power of the Court is not limited to declaring that the committal order is now operative: it retains a discretion to do whatever is just in the circumstances (*Re W (B) (An Infant)* [1969] 2 Ch. 50; [1969] 1 All E.R. 594, CA). If committal is suspended and the contemnor is then found guilty of another breach the court can activate the suspended sentence and impose another sentence to be served consecutively. However, the maximum sentence is still subject to the overall limit of two years prescribed by s.14 of the Contempt of Court Act 1981 (*Villiers v Villiers* [1994] 2 All E.R.149).

Where a contemnor applies to the court to purge his contempt the court has no power to suspend the unserved part of the sentence of imprisonment. On an application to purge the judge may only say "Yes", "No" or "Not Yet". While arguably a sentence partly immediate and partly suspended might be a useful refinement the gain would be outweighed by the introduction of complications which would influence a contemnor's judgment on whether to apply to purge his contempt. *Harris v Harris* [2002] 1 All E.R. 185 (Thorpe, Waller and Mantell, L.JJ.).

Where a comprehensive application to commit for contempt was made, and a substantial term of imprisonment imposed, it would normally be wrong to leave over for possible future activation any suspended sentence or consideration of other breaches of alleged contempts. *Phillips v Symes (No.3)* [2005] 1 W.L.R. 2986 (Pill and Longmore L.JJ.)

Committal order

sc52.7.2 Pursuant to the Practice Direction of January 30, 1961 the committal order is executed by the tipstaff or, if there is none, by the usher or some other official to whom the order of the Court is addressed, on the authority of a warrant signed by the Judge, or one of the Judges of the Court, making the order (*ibid.*).

If the contemnor is present the tipstaff takes him to prison. If the contemnor is absent but has a settled, known address, the tipstaff travels thither with the order and arrests him; if not, or if the contemnor moves or is likely to move, the tipstaff communicates with the local police who hold him and put him in the cells at the police station till the tipstaff arrives and conveys him to the gaol specified in the warrant (in London, Pentonville or Holloway, according to sex).

Appeal

sc52.7.3 See para.sc52.1.42.

Arrest

sc52.7.4 In all cases where an order is made for the committal of any person by reason of his contempt of court, it is the duty of the officer charged with the execution of such order, if necessary, and after the notice, to break open the outer door of the house of the party to be arrested (see *Burdett v Abbot* (1811) 14 East 1; *Re Freston* (1883) 11 Q.B.D. 545; *Harvey v Harvey* (1884) 26 Ch. D. 644).

Privilege from arrest

sc52.7.5 There is no privilege from arrest where a committal is granted for a contempt of Court which is of a criminal nature (*Re Freston*; *Stourton v Stourton* [1963] P. 302; [1963] 1 All E.R. 606); e.g. for disobedience by a solicitor to an order of the Court made against him as an officer of the Court (*Re Freston*; *Re Dudley* (1883) 12 Q.B.D. 44; *Re Grey* [1892] 2 Q.B. 440); or for disobedience by a receiver, even though a member of Parliament, to an order against him to pay his balance into Court (*Re Gent* (1889) 40 Ch. D. 190) or for disobedience by any person to an order of the Court for his attendance before an examiner (*Re Hunt* [1959] 2 Q.B. 69; [1959] 2 All E.R. 252).

Where, however, a committal is granted merely for the purpose of enforcing judgments in civil disputes, and where the breach of the order to do or not to do something cannot be said to be in the nature of an offence, then privilege may be successfully claimed (*Re Freston, per* Brett M.R.; *Stourton v Stourton*, above); e.g. by Members of Parliament (see *Onslow and Whalley's Case* (1874) L.R. 9 Q.B. 219, 228; *cf.* also *Ex p. Lindsay* [1892] 1 Q.B. 327) even until the expiration of 40 days after the prorogation and dissolution of Parliament, although the member claiming privilege has not been re-elected (*Re Anglo-French Co-operative Soc.* (1880) 14 Ch. D. 533); and, *semble*, by peers of the realm whether Parliament is sitting or not (*Stourton v Stourton*, above). But the jurisdiction of the Court was held not to be ousted where the act constituting the breach had occurred in the precincts of the House of Commons but was not connected with any proceedings in Parliament (*Rivlin v Bilainkin* [1953] 1 Q.B. 485; [1953] 1 All E.R. 534). See also *Re Gent* (1889) 40 Ch. D. 190, p.196. Privilege may also be claimed by barristers and solicitors going to or returning from professional attendance at Court, including a Magistrates' Court (*Re Freston*, above).

Although CCR O.42, r.1, providing that officers and attendants upon the Court, suitors, and witnesses, were to have privilege *eundo, redeundo, et morando* for their necessary attendance, and making it a contempt of Court to arrest them at such times, was repealed, and not re-enacted, still, it is conceived, the privilege of such persons remains unaffected according to the rules at common law (see Bac. Abr. Courts (E.); *Meekins v Smith* (1791) 1 H.Bl. 636). A witness in a suit arrested under a warrant of commitment for non-payment of poor rates immediately after leaving Court, was discharged from custody (*Hobern v Fowler* (1893) 62 L.J.Q.B. 49). See *Young v Young* (1896) 12 T.L.R. 503. But in the case of ordinary contempt the only privilege from arrest is the privilege of the Court to ensure that justice is done; and therefore arrest in Court is not wrongful (*Re Hunt* [1959] 2 Q.B. 69; [1959] 2 All E.R. 252, CA).

RSC

Discharge of person committed

8.—(1) The court may, on the application of any person committed to prison for any contempt of court, discharge him. **sc52.8**

(2) Where a person has been committed for failing to comply with a judgment or order requiring him to deliver any thing to some other person or to deposit it in court or elsewhere, and a writ of sequestration has also been issued to enforce that judgment or order, then, if the thing is in the custody or power of the person committed, the commissioners appointed by the writ of sequestration may take possession of it as if it were the property of that person and, without prejudice to the generality of paragraph (1), the court may discharge the person committed and may give such directions for dealing with the thing taken by the commissioners as it thinks fit.

(RSC Order 46 rule 5 contains rules relating to writs of sequestration.)

Effect of rule

The rule permitting the court to discharge a person committed for contempt used to be very important in the days when a person could be committed *sine die* (i.e. indefinitely or until he had purged his contempt). The rule survives even though committal must be for a fixed period not exceeding two years (which in any event is subject to early release—see below) including activation of any suspended sentence (*Villiers v Villiers* [1994] 2 All E.R. 149). **sc52.8.1**

In practice a contempt prisoner is told of his right to "purge his contempt" and apply for early discharge by the prison authorities. The Official Solicitor is also notified of all committals.

Under r.52.8(1) the court has a wide power to order the release of a contemnor notwithstanding that he had not purged his contempt: *Enfield LBC v Mahoney* [1983] 1 W.L.R. 749. That power existed even where the penal element of the contemnor's sentence has not been completed, but only in exceptional circumstances. Where the term imposed also contained a coercive element, that view should not be changed unless good reasons later emerged which had not been available at the time of the committal. *Shalson v Russo*, March 1, 2002, unrep., Neuberger, J.

Early release

Persons committed to prison for contempt of court are subject to the early release provisions of the Criminal Justice Act 2003. By s.258(2) as soon as a contemnor has served one-half of the term for which he was committed "it shall be the duty of the Secretary of State to release him unconditionally". Note that release is unconditional **sc52.8.2** and not on licence. Thus there can be no recall to prison if the contempt is repeated and fresh committal proceedings would be required. A judge cannot circumvent the statutory early release provisions by ordering that a contemnor should not be released until a specified date; *Thompson v Mitchell* [2004]EWCA Civ 1271 (Keene and Wall L.JJ.). Sentence must always be for a fixed term of which only half will be served.

Mode of application

sc52.8.3 The application for discharge should, if possible, be made to the tribunal which made the order for an order of committal, but such applications are now dealt with by any Judge of the Division in which the order was made, if the particular Judge who made it is not available. Application should now be by application notice. The Judge hearing the application for discharge has a complete discretion. The application can be granted resulting in immediate release: refused resting in the original release date remaining unchanged: or the Judge can order release on a future date (*Yager v Musa* [1961] 2 Q.B. 214.

Release by mistake

sc52.8.4 There is no jurisdiction to make a second order for committal for the same default, though the release has been made by mistake, but *semble* an order for re-arrest may be made under the original order (*Church's Trustee v Hibbard* [1902] 2 Ch. 784, CA).

Saving for other powers

sc52.9 9. Nothing in the foregoing provisions of this order shall be taken as affecting the power of the court to make an order requiring a person guilty of contempt of court, or a person punishable by virtue of any enactment in like manner as if he had been guilty of contempt of the High Court, to pay a fine or to give security for his good behaviour, and those provisions, so far as applicable, and with the necessary modifications, shall apply in relation to an application for such an order as they apply in relation to an application for an order of committal.

Effect of rule

sc52.9.1 The rule preserves the power to fine or give security for good behaviour. In many cases a fine will be more effective than imprisonment. The court does not have the full range of sentencing options available to a criminal court. In fixing the amount of a fine the judge can take judicial notice of previous breaches of undertakings given in similar cases (*Mullen v Hackney London BC* [1997] 2 All E.R. 906).

Striking out

sc52.9.2 The Court may, on the application of the respondent or on its own initiative, strike out a committal application if no reasonable grounds are disclosed, or if it is an abuse of process or likely to obstruct the just disposal of proceedings—or if there has been a failure to comply with a rule, practice direction or court order—see Practice Direction (Committal Applications), para.5 at para.scpd52.5.

Miscellaneous

sc52.9.3 Some provisions of the CPR regime are disapplied including CPR r.35.7 (power to direct that evidence be given by a single joint expert), r.35.8 (instructions to a single joint expert), r.35.9 (power to direct the provision of information) and r.18.1 (order for a party to give additional information) see Practice Direction (Committal Applications), paras 6 and 7, para.52PD.3.

A committal application may not be discontinued without the permission of the court, see Practice Direction (Committal Applications), para.8, para.scpd52.6.

Any procedural defect in the commencement or conduct of a committal application may be waived by the court if it is satisfied that no injustice has been caused to the respondent by the defect: PD para.10.

Except where under any enactment a Master or district judge has power to make a committal order such an order can only be made (1) in High Court proceedings by a High Court Judge or a person authorised to act as such and (2) in county court proceedings by a circuit judge or a person authorised to act or capable by virtue of his office of acting as such: Practice Direction (Committal Application), para.11, para.scpd52–011.

To strike out a claimant's case solely because he was in contempt would be an improper exercise of the court's powers, provided that a fair trial could follow, and would be likely to be a breach of art.6.1of the ECHR. *Arrow Nominees Inc v Blackledge* [2000] 1 B.C.L.C. 709 (Evans–Lombe J.).

Committal applications in family proceedings

As from March 16, 2001 the Practice Direction—Committal Applications Supplemental to RSC O.52 (Sch.1 to the CPR) and CCR O.29 (Sch.2 to the CPR) shall apply to all applications in family proceedings for an order of committal, in the same manner and to the same extent as it applies to proceedings governed by the CPR but subject to the Family Proceedings Rules 1991 and the rules applied by those rules and appropriate modifications consequent upon the limited application of the CPR to family proceedings. Practice Direction issued by Dame Elizabeth Butler-Sloss P., March 16, 2001 [2001] 2 All E.R. 704. **sc52.9.4**

A judge was entitled to make a custodial order against a parent, in this case the mother, who persistently refused to comply with an order for contact. *S (a Child) (Contact dispute: Committal), Re* [2004] EWCA Civ 1790 *Times*, December 9, 2004, (Thorpe, Arden and Neuberger L.JJ.).

PRACTICE DIRECTION—COMMITTAL APPLICATIONS

This Practice Direction supplements RSC Order 52 (Schedule 1 to the CPR) and CCR Order 29 (Schedule 2 to the CPR)

General

scpd52.1 **1.1** Part 1 of this practice direction applies to any application for an order for committal of a person to prison for contempt of court (a "committal application"). Part II makes additional provision where the committal application relates to a contempt in the face of the court.

1.2 Where the alleged contempt of court consists of or is based upon disobedience to an order made in a county court or breach of an undertaking given to a county court or consists of an act done in the course of proceedings in a county court, or where in any other way the alleged contempt is a contempt which the county court has power to punish, the committal application may be made in the county court in question.

1.3 In every other case, (other than one within Part II of this practice direction), a committal application must be made in the High Court.

1.4 In all cases, the Convention rights of those involved should particularly be borne in mind. It should be noted that the burden of proof, having regard to the possibility that a person may be sent to prison, is that the allegation be proved beyond reasonable doubt. (Section 1 of the Human Rights Act defines "the Convention rights")

Part I

Commencement of committal proceedings

scpd52.2 **2.1** A committal application must, subject to paragraph 2.2, be commenced by the issue of a Part 8 claim form. (see paragraph 2.5).

2.2(1) If the committal application is made in existing proceedings it must be commenced by the filing of an application notice in those proceedings

(2) An application to commit for breach of an undertaking or order must be commenced by the filing of an application notice in the proceedings in which the undertaking was given or the order was made.

(3) The application notice must state that the application is made in the proceedings in question and its title and reference number must correspond with the title and reference number of those proceedings.

2.3 If the committal application is one which cannot be made without permission, the claim form or application notice, as the case may be, may not be issued or filed until the requisite permission has been granted.

2.4 If the permission of the court is needed in order to make a committal application:

(1) the permission must be applied for by filing an application notice (see CPR, rule 23.2(4));

(2) the application notice need not be served on the respondent;

(3) the date on which and the name of the judge by whom the requisite permission was granted must be stated on the claim form or application notice by which the committal application is commenced;

(4) the permission may only be granted by a judge who, under paragraph 11, would have power to hear the committal application if permission were granted; and

(5) CPR, rules 23.9 and 23.10 do not apply.

2.5 If the committal application is commenced by the issue of a claim form, CPR Part 8 shall, subject to the provisions of this practice direction, apply as though references to "claimant" were references to the person making the committal application and references to "defendant" were references to the person against whom the committal application is made (in this practice direction referred to as "the respondent") but:

(1) the claim form together with copies of all written evidence in support must, unless the court otherwise directs, be served personally on the respondent,

(2) the claim form must set out in full the grounds on which the committal application is made and must identify, separately and numerically, each alleged act of contempt, including, if known, the date of each alleged act,

(3) an amendment to the claim form can be made with the permission of the court but not otherwise.

(4) CPR, rule 8.4 does not apply, and

(5) the claim form must contain a prominent notice stating the possible consequences of the court making a committal order and of the respondent not attending the hearing. A form of notice, which may be used, is annexed to this practice direction.

2.6 If a committal application is commenced by the filing of an application notice, CPR Part 23 shall, subject to the provisions of this practice direction, apply, but:

(1) the application notice together with copies of all written evidence in support must, unless the court otherwise directs, be served personally on the respondent,

(2) the application notice must set out in full the grounds on which the committal application is made and must identify, separately and numerically, each alleged act of contempt, including, if known, the date of each of the alleged acts,

(3) an amendment to the application notice can be made with the permission of the court but not otherwise,

(4) the court may not dispose of the committal application without a hearing, and

(5) the application notice must contain a prominent notice stating the possible consequences of the cort making a committal order and of the respondent not attending the hearing. A form of notice, which may be used, is annexed to this practice direction.

Written evidence

3.1 Written evidence in support of or in opposition to a committal application must be given by affidavit. **scpd52.3**

3.2 Written evidence served in support of or in opposition to a committal application must, unless the court otherwise directs, be filed.

3.3 A respondent, may give oral evidence at the hearing whether or not he has filed or served any written evidence. If he does so, he may be cross-examined.

3.4 A respondent may, with the permission of the court, call a witness to give oral evidence at the hearing whether or not the witness has sworn an affidavit.

Case management and date of hearing

scpd52.4 **4.1** The applicant for the committal order must, when lodging the claim form or application notice with the court for issuing or filing, as the case may be, obtain from the court a date for the hearing of the committal application.

4.2 Unless the court otherwise directs, the hearing date of a committal application shall be not less than 14 days after service of the claim form or of the application notice, as the case may be, on the respondent. The hearing date must be specified in the claim form or application notice or in a Notice of Hearing or Application attached to and served with the claim form or application notice.

4.3 The court may, however, at any time give management decisions, including directions for the service of written evidence by the respondent and written evidence in reply by the applicant, or may hold a directions hearing.

4.4 The court may on the hearing date:

(1) give case management directions with a view to a hearing of the committal application on a future date, or

(2) if the committal application is ready to be heard, proceed forthwith to hear it.

4.5 In dealing with any committal application, the court will have regard to the need for the respondent to have details of the alleged acts of contempt and the opportunity to respond to the committal application.

4.6 The court should also have regard to the need for the respondent to be—

(1) allowed a reasonable time for responding to the committal application including, if necessary, preparing a defence;

(2) made aware of the availablity of assistance from the Community Legal Service and how to contact the Service;

(3) given the opportunity, if unrepresented, to obtain legal advice; and

(4) if unable to understand English, allowed to make arrangements, seeking the assistance of the court if necessary, for an interpreter to attend the hearing.

Striking out

scpd52.5 **5.** The court may, on application by the respondent or on its own initiative, strike out a committal applicatiaon if it appears to the court:

(1) that the committal application and the evidence served in

support of it disclose no reasonable ground for alleging that the respondent is guilty of a contempt of court,

(2) that the committal application is an abuse of the court's process or, if made in existing proceedings, is otherwise likely to obstruct the just disposal of those proceedings, or

(3) that there has been a failure to comply with a rule, practice direction or court order.

(CPR Part 3 contains general powers for the management by the court).

Miscellaneous

6. CPR, rules 35.7 (Court's power to direct that evidence is to be given by a single joint expert), 35.8 (Instructions to single joint expert) and 35.9 (Power of court to direct a party to provide information) do not apply to committal applications. **scpd52.6**

RSC

7. An order under CPR, rule 18.1 (order for a party to give additional information) may not be made against a respondent to a committal application.

8. A committal application may not be discontinued without the permission of the court.

9. A committal application should normally be heard in public (see CPR, rule 39.2), but if it is heard in private and the court finds the respondent guilty of contempt of court, the judge shall, when next sitting in public, state:

(1) the name of the respondent,

(2) in general terms the nature of the contempt or contempts found proved, and

(3) the penalty (if any) imposed.

10. The court may waive any procedural defect in the commencement or conduct of a committal application if satisfied that no injustice has been caused to the respondent by the defect.

11. Except where under an enactment a Master or district judge has power to make a committal order, a committal order can only be made:

(1) in High Court proceedings, by a High Court Judge or a person authorised to act as such, or

(2) in county court proceedings by a Circuit Judge or a person authorised to act or capable by virtue of his office of acting as such.

Part II

12. Where the committal application relates to a contempt in the face of the court the following matters should be given particular attention. Normally, it will be appropriate to defer consideration of the behaviour to allow the respondent time to reflect on what has occurred. The time needed for the following procedures should allow such a period of reflection. **scpd52.7**

13. A Part 8 claim form and an application notice are not required for Part II, but other provisions of this practice direction should be applied, as necessary, or adapted to the circumstances. In addition the judge should:

(1) tell the respondent of the possible penalty he faces;

(2) inform the respondent in detail, and preferably in writing, of the actions and behaviour of the respondent which have given rise to the committal application;

(3) if he considers that an apology would remove the need for the committal application, tell the respondent;

(4) have regard to the need for the respondent to be–

(a) allowed a reasonable time for responding to the committal application, including, if necessary, preparing a defence;

(b) made aware of the availability of assistance from the Community Legal Service and how to contact the Service;

(c) given the opportunity, if unrepresented, to obtain legal advice;

(d) if unable to understand English, allowed to make arrangements, seeking the court's assistance if necessary, for an interpreter to attend the hearing; and

(e) brought back before the court for the committal application to be heard within a reasonable time.

(5) allow the respondent an opportunity to–

(a) apologise to the court;

(b) explain his actions and behaviour and;

(c) if the contempt is proved, to address the court on the penalty to be imposed on him;

(6) if there is a risk of the appearance of bias, ask another judge to hear the committal application;

(7) where appropriate, nominate a suitable person to give the respondent the information.

(It is likely to be appropriate to nominate a person where the effective communication of information by the judge to the respondent was not possible when the incident occurred.)

14. Where the committal application is to be heard by another judge, a written statement by the judge before whom the actions and behaviour of the respondent which have given rise to the committal application took place may be submitted as evidence of those actions and behaviour.

Annex

scpd52.8 IMPORTANT NOTICE The Court has power to send you to prison and to fine you if it finds that any of the allegations made against you are true and amount to a contempt of court. **You must attend court** on the date shown on the front of this form. It is in your own interest to do so. You should bring with you any witnesses and documents which you think will help you put your side of the case. If you consider the allegations are not true you must tell the court why. If it is established that they are true, you must tell the court of any good reason why they do not amount to a contempt of court, or, if they do, why you should not be punished. If you need advice you should show this document at once to your solicitor or go to a Citizens' Advice Bureau.

RSC ORDER 54—APPLICATIONS FOR WRIT OF HABEAS CORPUS

Contents **sc54.0.1**

Editorial introduction

The writ of habeas corpus may take various forms (see, generally, Gordon, *Judicial Review and Crown Office Proceedings*). The writ of habeas corpus *ad subjiciendum*, which is used to test the validity in the commitment of a prisoner, or want of jurisdiction to hold him, is the most important of all of the writs of this denomination. These rules provide the procedure for the granting of this writ. Two further forms of the writ of habeas corpus consist of habeas corpus *ad testificandum* (to bring up a prisoner to give evidence), and habeas corpus *ad respondendum* (to bring up a prisoner to answer a criminal charge). They are referred to in r.9. Forms for these three varieties of the writ are found in Appendix A and must be used as appropriate (r.10). The Court may direct that a claim form shall be used, being a modified Form **No. 87**. These and other matters are covered by a Practice Direction, *post*. **sc54.0.2**

Forms

The following Prescribed Forms (formerly included amongst the Prescribed Forms in Appendix A to the RSC) are relevant to O.54. These forms are included in Table 2 (Practice Forms) attached to Practice Direction (Forms): **sc54.0.3**

- **No. 87** Notice of motion for writ of habeas corpus *ad subjiciendum* (O.54, r.2)
- **No. 88** Notice directed by Court of adjourned application for writ of habeas corpus (O.54, r.2)
- **No. 89** Writ of habeas corpus *ad subjiciendum* (O.54, r.10)
- **No. 90** Notice to be served with writ of habeas corpus *ad subjiciendum* (O.54, r.6)
- **No. 91** Writ of habeas corpus *ad testificandum* (O.54, r.10)
- **No. 92** Writ of habeas corpus *ad respondendum* (O.54, r.10)

Application for writ of habeas corpus ad subjiciendum

1.—(1) Subject to rule 11, an application for a writ of habeas corpus *ad subjiciendum* shall be made to a judge in court, except that— **sc54.1**

(a) it shall be made to a Divisional Court of the Queen's Bench Division if the court so directs;

(b) it may be made to a judge otherwise than in court at any time when no judge is sitting in court; and

(c) any application on behalf of a child must be made in the first instance to a judge otherwise than in court.

(2) An application for such writ may be made without notice be-

ing served on any other party and, subject to paragraph (3) must be supported by a witness statement or affidavit by the person restrained showing that it is made at his instance and setting out the nature of the restraint.

(3) Where the person restrained is unable for any reason to make the witness statement or affidavit required by paragraph (2) the witness statement or affidavit may be made by some other person on his behalf and that witness statement or affidavit must state that the person restrained is unable to make the witness statement or affidavit himself and for what reason.

History of Rule

sc54.1.1 Amended by SI 1971/1269 and SI 1980/2000.

Habeas corpus

sc54.1.2 The writ of habeas corpus *ad subjiciendum* (commonly known as habeas corpus) remains of the highest constitutional importance, for by it the liberty of the subject is vindicated and his release from any manner of unjustifiable detention assured. It is a prerogative writ familiar to the common law at least as long ago as the thirteenth century, and its efficiency has been furthered by a number of statutes (the Habeas Corpus Acts of 1640, 1679 and 1816). It is a writ of right and granted *ex debito justitiae,* but not as of course (see e.g. *Re Corke* [1954] 1 W.L.R. 899; [1954] 2 All E.R. 440) and may be refused where another remedy lies whereby the validity of the restraint can be effectively questioned.

Formerly the writ might be issued to any part of the Dominions of the Crown, but now by the Habeas Corpus Act 1862, it is enacted that no writ of habeas corpus shall issue out of England by authority or any Judge or Court of justice therein into any colony or foreign dominion of the Crown where Her Majesty has a lawfully established Court of Justice having authority to grant and issue the writ and to ensure its due execution throughout such colony or dominion. The writ will not issue to Scotland (*R. v Cowle* (1759) 2 Burr. 856) nor to Northern Ireland (*Re Keenan* [1972] 1 Q.B. 533; [1971] 3 All E.R. 884) but it will to the Isle of Man (being a "dominion" but not a "foreign dominion" *Ex p. Brown* (1864) 33 L.J.Q.B. 193). As regards Jersey it appears that before 1862 a writ of habeas corpus could be enforced there if so ordered by the Privy Council (*Re Belson* (1850) 7 Moore P.C. 114). But this is probably no longer so, since Jersey is, historically a "foreign dominion". It may issue to a protectorate which is not a dominion of the Crown if the authority in fact exercised by the Crown makes this just and convenient (*R. v Crewe (Earl) Ex p. Sekgome* [1910] 2 K.B. 576; *Re Ning Yi-Ching*, 56 T.L.R. 3; *Re Mwenya* [1960] 1 Q.B. 241; [1959] 3 All E.R. 525 CA). It will not issue against any person who is abroad and out of the jurisdiction (*R. v Pinckney* [1904] 2 K.B. 84) or who is upon a public vessel of a foreign State, nor will it issue in respect of an alien detained in this country in the embassy or legation of the State of which he is a subject (*Re Sun Yat* (1896), cited in Short and Mellor, *Crown Office Practice* (1908). But see also *R. v Secretary of State for Foreign and Commonwealth Office Ex p. Bancoult* [2001] A.C.D. 101, (Law and Gibbs L.JJ.) as to whether, in a proper case, habeas corpus might issue beyond the seas "to any place under the subjection of the Crown".

The purpose of the writ is that the body may be produced before the Court, so that release from restraint may be secured—and not that someone who has unlawfully detained or unlawfully parted with the custody may be punished; and therefore the writ is not granted after the release of the person detained (*Bernardo v Ford, Gossage's Case* [1892] A.C. 326, disagreeing with the contrary view expressed in *R. v Barnardo, Tye's Case* [1889] 23 Q.B.D. 305; see also *R. v Secretary of State for Home Affairs Ex p. O'Brien* [1923] 2 K.B. 361; [1923] A.C. 603). The writ is used to test any alleged invalidity in the commitment of a prisoner, or want of jurisdiction to hold him in custody—as, for example, where he is held under military arrest without being brought to trial, or is detained under order of a naval, military or ecclesiastical Court. In *Re Maychell, The Independent*, February 26, 1993 (Kennedy L.J. and Clark J.) a person's detention by military authorities for 75 days was held to be lawful in circumstances where there had to be proper investigation of serious allegations. *R. v Royal Army Service Corp, Colchester Ex p. Elliott* [1949] 1 All E.R. 373 is authority for the proposition that the Divisional Court's powers extend to a person held in military custody, even where the military authorities are satisfied that the custody was lawful. It is used on behalf of a person committed without jurisdiction under the Extradition Acts (see s.11 of the 1870 Act, and *R. v Governor of Brixton Prison* [1924] 1 K.B. 455; *Re Kolczynski* [1955] 1 Q.B. 540; [1955] 1 All E.R. 31; *R. v Governor of Brixton Prison Ex p. Schtraks* [1964] A.C. 556; [1962] 3 All E.R. 529, HL) or under the Fugitive Offenders Act 1881 ss.5, 7, and *R. v Governor of Brixton Prison Ex p. Mourat Mehmet* [1962] 2 Q.B. 1; [1962] 1 All E.R. 463). In all these cases the writ is equally available on behalf of a British subject or friendly or enemy alien, provided he is within the realm and under the protection of the Crown (contrast *R. v Bottrill* [1947] K.B. 41, the case of an alien enemy interned by order of the Crown, and *Re Ning Yi-Ching*). On the other hand, the writ does not in general lie in respect of a person who is in execution on a criminal charge, or committed by a Court of record for a contempt or by Parliament for a contempt or breach of privilege. In the former case, the right to be discharged must be tested by appeal (see *Ex p. Corke*; *Re Featherstone* (1953) 37 Cr.App.R. 146; *Re Wring* [1960] 1 W.L.R. 138; [1960] 1 All E.R. 536n.; *Re Philpot* [1960] 1 W.L.R. 115; [1960] 1 All E.R. 165, 166) or certiorari, and in the other cases, the Court is the proper Judge of what is contempt of itself (see *Re Hunt of Middlesex Case* (1840) 11 A. & E. 273). Applications by parents or guardians as to the custody or care of infants are made to the Family Division (SCA 1981 s.61, Sch.1, para.3). Applications to the High Court for bail are made by summons before a Judge in Chambers to show cause why the defendant should not be admitted to bail.

Whether a person is detained is a question of objective fact which does not depend on the presence or absence of consent or knowledge. A person is detained in law if those who have control over the premises in which he is have the intention that he shall not be permitted to leave those premises and have the ability to prevent him from leaving: *R. v Bournewood Community and Mental Health NHS Trust Ex p.* [1998] 1 All E.R. 635 (Lord Woolf M.R., Phillips and Chadwick L.JJ.).

RSC

Application for the writ

Under the present procedure the application is made without notice in the first instance (to this extent a return to the practice in force till about 1780). Except in applications on behalf of a child, upon the hearing, if the Court gives leave, the application is usually adjourned for notice to be served on such persons as the Court directs; and upon the adjourned hearing, if the application succeeds, the writ is ordered to issue. **sc54.1.3**

The applications for a writ of habeas corpus must, subject to r.11, be made to a Judge in Court (r.1) except that if the Court so directs it must be made to a Divisional Court of the QBD (r.1(a)) and it may be made to a Judge otherwise than in Court at any time when no Judge is sitting in Court (r.1(b)).

On a criminal application for habeas corpus an order for the release of the person restrained can be refused only by a Divisional Court of the QBD (see s.14(1) of AJA 1960) so that in such a case, a single Judge has no power to refuse an application for habeas corpus.

Applications on behalf of a minor must be made to a Judge in Chambers whether in term time or in vacation (see r.1(c)) who, if he thinks fit, directs a summons to issue, and if the applicant is successful the issue of the writ is ordered. For Forms, see Vol.2, Section 1A.

However it is not open to the court to issue a writ of habeas corpus, at the instance of a third person, when the subject of the application is *sui juris* and had plainly stated in an affidavit that he was not being unlawfully detained (*In the matter of M* [1995] C.O.D. 64 (Sir Stephen Brown P.)).

So far does the law lean in favour of the liberty of the subject that the application is entitled to precedence over virtually all other court business (*R. v Home Secretary Ex p. Cheblak* [1991] 1 W.L.R. 890 at 894). The Court of Appeal (which is not part of the High Court) has no original jurisdiction in the matter, nor has any judge of the High Court sitting in the Court of Appeal (*Stoneham v Woods* [1914] W.N. 202; *Carroll, Re* [1931] 1 K.B. 104; *Ex p. Chapple* (1950) 66 T.L.R. (Pt 2) 932).

When an application for habeas corpus has once been made in a civil or criminal matter no such application may be made on the same grounds in respect of the same person to any other court or judge unless fresh evidence is adduced in support of the application (AJA 1960 s.14(2)). The Lord Chancellor has no original or appellate jurisdiction to grant habeas corpus (see AJA 1960 s.14(2) and *Kray, Re* [1965] Ch. 736).

Section 14(2) does no more than allow successive applications for habeas corpus on the same grounds provided fresh evidence is adduced in support of each application. The court retains jurisdiction to control its own procedures so as to prevent them being used vexatiously or in abuse of process and may thus strike out proceedings in an appropriate case (*R. v Governor of Brixton Prison Ex p. Osman (No.4)* [1992] 1 All E.R. 579).

When the Home Secretary considers that an application for a writ of habeas corpus by a person awaiting extradition does not comply with the requirements of s.14(2) of the AJA 1960 he may proceed with arrangements for that applicant's return to the requesting state. Where there is argument as to whether s.14(2) has been complied with no doubt the Secretary of State will consider it prudent to await the decision of the court. Where the applicant is fearful that the Secretary of State might not do so application can be made to the court for the sort of interim relief envisaged in *R. v Secretary of State for the Home Department Ex p. Muboyayi* [1992] Q.B. 244; *R. v Secretary of State for the Home Department Ex p. Osman (No.2)*, *The Times*, November 26, 1992 (Kennedy L.J and Waterhouse J.). The approach adopted by the court in relation to detention by order of the Secretary of State under the Immigration Act 1971 is exemplified in *Re Mahmod* [1994] C.O.D. 404 where Laws J., ordering the writ to issue forthwith, observed: "while, of course, Parliament is entitled to confer powers of administrative detention without trial, the courts will see to it that where such a power is conferred the statute that confers it will be strictly and narrowly construed and its operation and effect will be supervised by the court according to high standards".

A challenge to the decision of a District Judge, in proceedings under a European arrest warrant, lies "only by means of an appeal" under s.34 of the Extradition Act 2003, and not by way of proceedings for habeas corpus *Re Hilali, House of Lords* [2008] UKHL 3; [2008] 2 All E.R. 207. However, if there is fresh evidence to demonstrate that the appeal decision was wrong in some fundamental aspect, the proper course is to apply under CPR 52.17 to re-open the determination of the Divisional Court, since that rule embodies the principles set out in *Taylor v Lawrence* [2003] Q.B. 528, and not to seek to challenge the applicant's detention by way of an application for habeas corpus. See *Ignaoua v The Judicial Authority of the Courts of Milan* [2008] EWHC 2619 (Admin), (Keene L.J. and Owen J.)

In general, on an application for a writ of habeas corpus, fresh evidence will not be admitted. Therefore, where the applicant did not raise any issue or call any evidence before the magistrates that he would, if sent back to Ireland, be prosecuted or detained for an offence of a political character, he is precluded from raising this issue or adducing evidence on the matter before a higher Court (*Nobbs, Re* [1978] 1 W.L.R. 1302; [1978] 3 All E.R. 390, DC).

Where the order for detention and removal of a person as an illegal entrant is completely in order, it is prima facie good, and the burden is on the applicant for habeas corpus to challenge its validity and to show that he is being unlawfully detained, e.g. by proving that his passport had been stamped with lawful authority (*R. v Secretary of State for the Home Department Ex p. Choudhary* [1978] 1 W.L.R. 1177; [1978] 2 All E.R. 790, CA).

In an application for habeas corpus the court will adopt the sort of "special responsibility" and "most anxious scrutiny" as was proposed for asylum cases in *Bugdaycay v Home Secretary* [1987] 1 A.C. 514; *R. v Secretary of State for Ex p. Osman* [1993] C.O.D. 39 (Woolf L.J. and Pill J.).

In considering an application for habeas corpus in a deportation case the court may see all the evidence available to the Secretary of State, even if it is hearsay, but it will be for the court to decide what weight to attach to it. Generally in such cases the remedies in proceedings for judicial review will be more appropriate (*Re Saidur Rahman* [1996] C.O.D. 465, *per* Collins J.; and in the Court of Appeal, *The Times*, December 24, 1996).

Where an applicant persists in making hopelessly misconceived applications for habeas corpus, in respect of a particular conviction, constituting a plain abuse of process, the court may direct that no further such applications are to be accepted or processed by the Crown Office in respect of that conviction: *Re Leachman* [1998] C.O.D. 466 (Simon Brown L.J. and Mance J.).

Where an applicant had unsuccessfully challenged a number of immigration decisions by way of applications for judicial review it was an abuse of process to seek to challenge those decisions by way of an application for *habeas corpus*. Although the doctrine of *res judicata* does not apply to an application for *habeas corpus*, the principle that it was an abuse of process to raise in subsequent proceedings matters which could, and therefore should, have been litigated in earlier proceedings was applicable. In these circumstances the court will not depart from the general principle in relation to the finality of litigation. *Sheikh, Re, The Independent*, December 12, 2000 (Schiemann, Tuckey L.JJ. and Sir Swinton Thomas).

Habeas Corpus is available after the completion of the statutory appeal process contained in Part I of the Extradition Act 2003 providing the applicant's continued detention pursuant to the extradition process had subsequently become unlawful due to a fundamental change in circumstances in which the lawful order had been made: *Hilali v Governor of Whitemoor Prison* [2007] 3 W.L.R. 621 (Smith L.J. and Irwin J.).

Application for discharge from committal order

The High Court has power, without prejudice to any other jurisdiction of the Court, to order the person committed to stand charges abroad to be discharged from custody if it appears to the Court that it would, having regard to all the circumstances be unjust or oppressive to return him to the country seeking his return either (a) by reason of the trivial nature of the offence of which he is accused, or (b) by reason of the passage of time since he is alleged to have committed it or (c) because the accusation against him is not made in good faith in the interests of justice (see the Extradition Act 1989 s.11(3)). In ordering discharge under this provision the Court is not exercising a separate and distinct statutory power to mitigate what is in fact a lawful detention, but on the contrary is granting relief by way of habeas corpus and is dealing with the application as a true habeas corpus application, i.e. discharge from unlawful detention (*R. v Governor of Pentonville Prison Ex p. Tarling* [1979] 1 W.L.R. 1417; [1979] 2 All E.R. 1103, DC, distinguishing *R. v Governor of Brixton Prison Ex p. Savarkan* [1910] 2 K.B. 1056). The date of "the passage of time" is to be considered on a second application for the writ as the date of that application, but the passage of time resulting from bona fide appeals even to the House of Lords affords no ground for holding that it would be unjust or oppressive or make it unfair to return the applicant to face the charge on which he has been committed (*ibid.*). **sc54.1.4**

Habeas corpus or judicial review

See generally *R. v Secretary of State for the Home Department Ex p. Khawaja* [1984] A.C. 74. Where the power to detain is dependent upon the existence of a precedent fact, and the existence of that fact is challenged by or on behalf of the person detained, a challenge to the detention may be mounted by means of an application for a writ of habeas corpus even if there are alternative procedures available. **sc54.1.5**

"A writ of habeas corpus will issue where someone is detained without any authority or the purported authority is beyond the powers of the person authorising the detention and so is unlawful. The remedy of judicial review is available where the decision or action sought to be impugned is within the powers of the person taking it but, due to procedural error, a misappreciation of the law, a failure to take account of relevant matters, or taking account of irrelevant matters or the fundamental unreasonableness of the decision or action, it should never have been taken", *per* Lord Donaldson of Lymington M.R. in *R. v Home Secretary Ex p. Cheblak* [1991] 1 W.L.R. 890 at 894.

In certain circumstances habeas corpus may serve to prevent the removal of an applicant from the jurisdiction. Thus the Court will not permit a would-be immigrant to be compulsorily removed from its jurisdiction if he has sought the protection and assistance of the Court. Since any compulsory removal necessarily involves some deprivation of liberty a writ of habeas corpus is an alternative remedy to a "stay" under O.53, r.3(10)(a). The effect of service of such a writ is to make the "gaoler" responsible to the Court in place of the authority which ordered the detention, leaving it to the Court to determine on the return of the writ whether the detention should continue.

"If it be objected, and shown, that the use of a writ of *habeas corpus quia timet* is a novelty, so be it. Thus, the greatest and oldest of all prerogative writs, is quite capable of adapting itself to the circumstances of the times. An alternative might be to adapt the writ of *ne exeat regno* which was designed to prevent debtors fleeing the country, to suit a situation in which far from wishing to leave the jurisdiction someone is being compulsorily removed therefrom," *per* Lord Donaldson of Lymington M.R. in *R. v Secretary of State for the Home Department Ex p. Muboyayi* [1991] 3 W.L.R. 442. Glidewell L.J. expressed no concluded view on this point but Taylor L.J. agreed with the Master of the Rolls. See also *M. v Home Office and Kenneth Baker* [1992] 2 W.L.R. 73.

It is usually a sufficient response to an application for habeas corpus to satisfy the court that there is, *ex facie*, a statutory authority for the detention. If the legal or factual merits of the underlying processes which had led to the detention could be entertained, there would be no distinction between habeas corpus and judicial review: *Re Mulcahy (Eleanor)* [1993] C.O.D. 223 (Laws J.).

Where a defendant has been invalidly arraigned but judicial review may not be available by reason of s.29(3) of the Supreme Court Act 1981 (matters relating to trial on indictment) habeas corpus may issue (*R. v Maidstone Crown Court Ex p. Clark* [1995] 1 W.L.R. 831 (Glidewell LJ. and Curtis J.)).

Where a person is committed to custody by justices by means of a defective warrant for failing to pay a fine, the appropriate remedy is judicial review rather than habeas corpus. In judicial review proceedings the court has wider powers of disposal and the challenge is properly directed at the justices, rather than at the prison governor whose involvement is, in truth, immaterial. (*Re Crawley*, *The Times*, December 7, 1995 (Simon Brown L.J., Scott Baker and Latham JJ.)).

Where the object is to show that there was no jurisdiction to detain a patient under the Mental Health Act 1983, because the relevant procedures had not been properly complied with, rather than to overturn an administrative decision, the appropriate remedy is habeas corpus, and not judicial review (*Re S-C (Mental patient: Habeas Corpus)*, *The Times*, December 4, 1995 (Sir Thomas Bingham M.R., Neill and Hirst L.JJ.)). In relation to the Mental Health Act 1983, where many requirements are so precise, the court will be cautious in implying a need for procedural precision in relation to detention under the Act, where none has been specifically expressed (*Re Whitbread (Mental patient: Habeas Corpus)*, *The Times*, July 14, 1997; and *Re A W* [1997] C.O.D. 269 at first instance).

Where a challenge is made to an allegedly defective warrant of commitment the appropriate procedure is by way of an application for judicial review and not an application for habeas corpus. In judicial review the court has wider powers of disposal. And see also, generally, on the question whether habeas corpus or judicial review, and for an extensive examination of the authorities (*R. v Oldham Justices Ex p. Cawley* [1996] 2 W.L.R. 681).

Where an application is made by way of habeas corpus, in circumstances which would have been best dealt with by an application for judicial review, the court will not simply reject it out of hand if the matter can be put into decent procedural shape so as to enable the issue to be resolved: *Re John (Julie)* [1998] C.O.D. 306 (Latham J.).

It was sometimes thought that habeas corpus had advantages over judicial review because of the difference in the burden of proof but in practice that had no practical consequences. Judicial review had advantages over habeas corpus because of the range of remedies available. If a person wrongly detained was released prior to an order for habeas corpus there was no relief which the court could grant, whereas in the case of judicial review it could grant an injunction and, in appropriate cases, damages. In *Re S-C (Mental Patient: Habeas Corpus)* [1996] Q.B. 599, an application for judicial review would have been equally appropriate and would even have had advantages over habeas corpus. Applications for habeas corpus were to be discouraged unless it was clear that no other relief would be required. If both applications were lodged every effort should be made to harmonise the proceedings and the same affidavits should be used. At any interlocutory and final hearing both set of proceedings should be before the court, and in the event of an appeal the same notice of appeal would suffice: *Re Barker*; *R. v BHB Community Healthcare NHS Trust Ex p. Barker*, *The Times*, October 14, 1998 (Lord Woolf M.R., Hobhouse and Thorpe L.JJ.).

An application for habeas corpus, by an applicant seeking to impugn a three year old decision of the Secretary of State that he was an illegal immigrant, after an application for judicial review had been rejected, was an abuse of the process of the Court, *R. v Secretary of State for the Home Department Ex p. Sheik*, *The Times*, December 22, 2000 (Schiemann, Tuckey L.JJ. and Sir Swinton Thomas).

Bail

sc54.1.6 An immigrant on whom a deportation order had been served was not to be granted bail pending determination of an application for habeas corpus. Even if the Court hearing a civil application for habeas corpus had jurisdiction to grant bail the fear that he would remain out of sight justified his being kept in custody (*R. v Governor of Haslar Prison Ex p. Egbe*, *The Times*, June 4, 1991 (Parker and Taylor L.JJ. and Sir Roualeyn Cumming-Bruce).

Appeals

The applicant may, however, go to the CA by way of appeal, unless it is in a criminal cause or matter, that is to say, unless the direct outcome of the proceedings may be the trial of the applicant and his possible punishment for an alleged offence by an (English or foreign) Court claiming jurisdiction (*Amand v Home Secretary and Minister of Defence of Royal Netherlands Government* [1943] A.C. 147, *per* Viscount Simon at p.156; *Ex p. Woodhall* (1888) 20 Q.B.D. 832; *Ex p. Savarkar* [1910] 2 K.B. 1036) or unless the question is whether the sentence for a criminal offence is being duly carried out (*R. v Governor of Maidstone Prison Ex p. Maguire* (1925) 41 T.L.R. 554; *Re Hastings (No.3)* [1959] Ch. 368; [1959] 1 All E.R. 698), or the person in respect of whom the application is made is restrained as a person liable, or treated under an enactment as liable, to be detained under certain provisions of the Mental Health Act 1983 (see AJA 1960 s.14(3)). From an order of a single Judge in a criminal matter there is no appeal (SCA 1981 s.18(1)(a) and AJA 1960 s.15(2)); but from a decision of a Divisional Court in such a matter appeal now lies to the House of Lords under the provisions of ss.1 and 15 of the 1960 Act, subject to leave being obtained from the Divisional Court or the House of Lords. The conditions contained in s.1(2) restricting the grant of such leave by the Divisional Court or the House of Lords, are not applicable to appeals in habeas corpus proceedings (s.15(3)) or proceedings under s.10 of the Fugitive Offenders Act 1881 (*Zacharia v Republic of Cyprus* [1963] A.C. 634; [1962] 2 All E.R. 438). An application to the Divisional Court for leave to appeal to the House of Lords must be made within fourteen days after its decision (AJA 1960 s.2(1)) but the time may be extended in all cases on application by the defendant (ss.2(3) and 15(3)). In criminal or civil matters appeal now lies in all cases (subject to what is stated above) from an order for the release of the person restrained as well as against the refusal of such an order (s.15(1)) and from an order in proceedings on behalf of a child (*Barnado v McHugh* [1891] A.C. 388) as well as in other cases. In civil matters, from any decision of a Judge appeal lies to the CA; and from a Divisional Court to the CA; in each case without leave. **sc54.1.7**

The effect of s.15(4) of the Administration of Justice Act 1960 is to provide that once a judge at first instance has granted a writ of habeas corpus, a successful appeal by the person having had custody of the applicant cannot render the applicant liable to detention, unless an interim order for detention or release on bail was made, by the Divisional Court under s.5 of the Act (*R. v Secretary of State for the Home Department Ex p. Vink, Taggar, Vink and Singh* [1996] C.O.D. 134).

Extradition proceedings under the Extradition Act 1989 are criminal proceedings for the purposes of an application for habeas corpus (*Re Levin* [1997] 3 W.L.R. 117, HL), and an order relating to the obtaining of evidence under the Criminal Justice (International Co-operation) Act 1990 for the purposes of such proceedings is likewise a criminal cause or matter and the Court of Appeal, Civil Division therefore has no jurisdiction (*Cuoghi v Governor of Brixton Prison*, *The Times*, July 24, 1997).

Costs

In the discretion of the Court (*R. v Mansell-Jones or Jones* [1894] 2 Q.B. 382); either the applicant or the respondent may be ordered to pay the costs. **sc54.1.8**

Forms generally

See Forms Nos 87–92. **sc54.1.9**

The application

The application should, as a rule, be made by counsel, but litigants may for sufficient reason be allowed to apply in person for this and the other prerogative writs (*Re Newton* (1855) 16 C.B. 97; *Cobbett v Hudson* (1855) 15 Q.B. 988; *Re Greene* (1941) 57 T.L.R. 533; Practice Note [1947] W.N. 218; *Re Wring* [1960] 1 W.L.R. 138; [1960] 1 All E.R. 536). In *Pharoah* unrep. CO/1279/87 (Schiemann J.), the applicant was a patient under s.3 of the Mental Health Act 1983. He submitted an application for habeas corpus challenging the psychiatric diagnosis. The Health Authority declined to produce him for the purpose of the hearing of his application unless directed to do so by the Court. The Court refused to order his production but invited the Official Solicitor to produce a report which disclosed that in 1985 the applicant had been made subject to an order of the Court of Protection. In refusing his application, Schiemann J. expressed himself satisfied that the applicant was lawfully detained, but in any event the applicant was not entitled to apply for habeas corpus because (i) he was a patient of the Court of Protection and thus, by operation of O.80, r.2, he could only bring proceedings by his next friend and (ii) he was not represented by counsel. See also **sc54.1.10** more generally *R. v Secretary of State for the Home Department Ex p. Wynne* [1992] C.O.D. 74; *The Times*, December 27, 1991.

The application need not be in the name of a person detained, but may be made by any other person at his instance, or by a person entitled to his custody, or, where no communication has been possible, by a relative or friend on his behalf (contrast *Ex p. Child* (1854) 15 C.B. 238); and the witness statement or affidavit in support of the application should depose to the facts on this head, as well as to the facts on which the intervention of the Court is sought. Three copies of the witness statement or affidavit are required for the use of the Court, to be lodged, if possible, the day before the application. An application can be initiated after an extradition warrant has been signed only in the most exceptional circumstances (see *R. v Governor of Pentonville Prison Ex p. Tarling* [1979] 1 W.L.R. 1417, and *Re Hagan and Croft* [1993] C.O.D. 215). It is to be noted that Rule 54 now allows for the provision of a witness statement or affidavit.

Northern Ireland

sc54.1.11 The writ does not run to Northern Ireland (*Re Keenan* [1972] 1 Q.B. 523; [1971] 3 All E.R. 883, CA).

Power of Court to whom application made without notice being served on any other party

sc54.2 2.—(1) The court or judge to whom an application under rule 1 is made without notice being served on any other party may make an order forthwith for the writ to issue, or may—

(a) where the application is made to a judge otherwise than in court, direct the issue of a claim form seeking the writ, or that an application therefor be made by claim form to a Divisional Court or to a judge in court;

(b) where the application is made to a judge in court, adjourn the application so that notice thereof may be given, or direct that an application be made by claim form to a Divisional Court;

(c) where the application is made to a Divisional Court, adjourn the application so that notice thereof may be given.

(2) The claim form must be served on the person against whom the issue of the writ is sought and on such other persons as the court or judge may direct, and, unless the court or judge otherwise directs, there must be at least 8 clear days between the service of the claim form and the date named therein for the hearing of the application.

History of Rule

sc54.2.1 Reproduces the former RSC 1938 O.59, rr.16 and 17.

Practice

sc54.2.2 Where the court directs that a claim form is to be used it must be in Form 87 modified in accordance with the guidance set out in the forms Practice Direction—see Practice Direction, para.3.1, para.scpd54.3. Where an application is adjourned for service of the notice of the application a suitably modified Form 88 must be used. As to the former practice directions which still apply, see the Practice Direction which supplements RSC O.54, para.7.1, see para.scpd54.7. Although there is power by this rule to make an order forthwith for the issue of the writ on the without notice application, it is only exercised where there is a likelihood that delay may defeat justice, or where the facts and law are clear. In other cases the Court or the Judge makes one of the other orders mentioned in the rule, in which event the person detained must not be ordered to be released meanwhile. He may, however, be admitted to bail, in which case the jurisdiction of the Court is unaffected (*Re Amand* [1941] 2 K.B. 239 at 249).

The summons is issued at the Administrative Court Office, and the motion entered for hearing in that department (RSC O.57, r.2). Three copies of the notice, affidavits and exhibits must be lodged for use of the Divisional Court.

Persons to be served

The notice of adjourned hearing and the claim form should as a rule be directed to the person having control of the body (for example, the prison governor, not the Secretary of State); but (*semble*) it may be addressed to a person who has such control that he can order the gaoler to release the prisoner (*R. v Crewe (Earl) Ex p. Sekgome* [1910] 2 K.B. 576 at 592, 604, CA). Further, the Court may direct service on any other person whom it considers interested or desires to hear, or may hear him without such direction (e.g. in extradition proceedings, the requisitioning government (*R. v Governor of Brixton Prison Ex p. Minervini* [1959] 1 Q.B. 155; [1958] 3 All E.R. 318). The notice may be directed to a corporation (see *Re Carroll* [1931] 1 K.B. 104) but it is better directed to an officer thereof. See Practice Direction, para.5.1, see para.scpd54.5 as to service. The claim form must be served, together with the writ and notice—Form 90 as modified. An overwhelming reason must be shown before the Divisional Court will direct service on other persons, although different considerations may possibly apply in proceedings before the House of Lords. In *Re Pinochet Ugarte*, *The Times*, February 16, 2000, (Rose L.J. and Smith J.). **sc54.2.3**

RSC

Copies of witness statements or affidavits to be supplied

3. Every party to an application under rule 1 must supply to every other party on demand and on payment of the proper charges copies of the witness statements or affidavits which he proposes to use at the hearing of the application. **sc54.3**

Power to order release of person restrained

4.—(1) Without prejudice to rule 2(1), the court or judge hearing an application for a writ of habeas corpus ad subjiciendum may in its or his discretion order that the person restrained be released, and such order shall be a sufficient warrant to any governor of a prison, constable or other person for the release of the person under restraint. **sc54.4**

(2) Where such an application in a criminal proceedings is heard by a judge and the judge does not order the release of the person restrained, he shall direct that the application be made by claim form to a Divisional Court of the Queen's Bench Division.

History of Rule

Reproduces in substance the former RSC 1938 O.59, r.19. **sc54.4.1**

Practice

The prisoner will not be brought up on the adjourned application or hearing of the motion unless the Court or Judge, who heard the application in the first instance, has so directed, or the Court so orders in the course of the hearing. At the hearing an order may be made for the writ to issue in accordance with r.5, but a modern practice has grown up of making an order for release as provided by r.4 (see *Chitty and Jacobs Queen's Bench Forms*, Form 1756) in which case the writ is not formally issued: the Master of the Crown Office writes to the prison governor directing the discharge of the prisoner, and the return to the writ need not show the cause of detainer but merely the fact of release. **sc54.4.2**

Directions as to return to writ

5. Where a writ of habeas corpus ad subjiciendum is ordered to issue, the court or judge by whom the order is made shall give directions as to the court or judge before whom, and the date on which, the writ is returnable. **sc54.5**

History of Rule

Reproduces in substance the previous RSC 1938 O.59, r.20, but omits to provide that "every such writ shall be returnable immediately". **sc54.5.1**

Form of order

sc54.5.2 This is made by a Judge in Chambers.

Service of writ and notice

sc54.6 6.—(1) Subject to paragraphs (2) and (3), a writ of habeas corpus ad subjiciendum must be served personally on the person to whom it is directed.

(2) If it is not possible to serve such writ personally, or if it is directed to a governor of a prison or other public official, it must be served by leaving it with a servant or agent of the person to whom the writ is directed at the place where the person restrained is confined or restrained.

(3) If the writ is directed to more than one person, the writ must be served in manner provided by this rule on the person first named in the writ, and copies must be served on each of the other persons in the same manner as the writ.

(4) There must be served with the writ a notice (in Form 90 of the relevant practice direction) stating the court or judge before whom and the date on which the person restrained is to be brought and that in default of obedience proceedings for committal of the party disobeying will be taken.

Return to the writ

sc54.7 7.—(1) The return to a writ of habeas corpus ad subjiciendum must be indorsed on or annexed to the writ and must state all the causes of the detainer of the person restrained.

(2) The return may be amended, or another return substituted therefor, by permission of the court or judge before whom the writ is returnable.

Form of return

sc54.7.1 This is indorsed on the writ, and if it is too long for indorsement a schedule should be attached as follows—

"The return to (or execution of) this writ appears by the Schedule annexed hereto (or, by affidavit of X. Y. filed herein)."

The Schedule

sc54.7.2 I, X. Y. (the person ordered to produce the body) in obedience to the writ herewith do certify and return that A. B. is detained in my custody under and by virtue of a (warrant of commitment, order, etc.) as follows. (Set out verbatim its terms.)

It appears to be doubtful whether a return to an applicant for habeas corpus which merely specifies that the applicant is being detained under a particular section of the Immigration Act 1971 is sufficient, since the rule requires that the return "must state all the causes of the detainer of the person restrained" see *R. v Secretary of State for the Home Department Ex p. Iqbal* [1978] Q.B. 264; [1979] 1 All E.R. 675.

"The causes of the prisoner's detainer"

sc54.7.3 The Court has power to examine by affidavit evidence the truth of the facts alleged in the return, but does not act as a Court of appeal. If the detainer is under an order or conviction of a judicial authority, it will enquire if there was any evidence to justify it; if there was, it cannot be disturbed; if there was not, the Court can release on habeas corpus or quash on certiorari (*R. v Board of Control Ex p. Rutty* [1956] 2 Q.B. 109; [1956] 1 All E.R. 769).

Onus of proof

sc54.7.4 If the return to the writ on its face shows a valid authority for the detention, it is for the applicant to show, that the detention is, prima facie, *illegal* (*R. v Governor of Risley Remand Centre Ex p. Hassan* [1976] 1 W.L.R. 971; [1976] 2 All E.R. 123, DC).

Where the return to an applicant for habeas corpus appears valid on its face but is subsequently found to contain some material error, the Court is entitled, as part of its inquiry under s.3 of the Habeas Corpus Act 1816 into the truth of the facts stated in the return, to go behind the wording on the face of the return and see whether there were in fact good grounds for the detention of the applicant and is not restricted to merely examine the reasons for the detention given in the return (*R. v Secretary of State for the Home Department Ex p. Iqbal* [1978] Q.B. 264; [1979] 1 All E.R. 675).

Where applicants had established, prima facie, that they were the beneficiaries of a valid pardon which would render their detention relating to offences covered by that pardon unlawful, it is for the prosecution to justify their detention and the applicants were entitled to a writ of habeas corpus as of right so that the lawfulness of their imprisonment could be determined (*Phillip v DPP of Trinidad and Tobago* [1992] 2 W.L.R. 211; [1992] All E.R. 665).

RSC

Procedure at hearing of writ

8. When a return to a writ of habeas corpus ad subjiciendum is made, the return shall first be read, and motion then made for discharging or remanding the person restrained or amending or quashing the return, and where that person is brought up in accordance with the writ, his counsel shall be heard first, then the counsel for the Crown, and then one counsel for the person restrained in reply. **sc54.8**

History of Rule

Reproduces r.23 of the former RSC 1938 O.59. **sc54.8.1**

Form of order of discharge

If the respondent does not appear, and the body is not produced, application may be made to the Court, supported by affidavit of service and disobedience, for committal for contempt, or to a Judge for the issue of a bench warrant. **sc54.8.2**

Bringing up prisoner to give evidence, etc.

9.—(1) An application for a writ of habeas corpus ad testificandum or of habeas corpus ad respondendum must be made on witness statement or affidavit to a judge. **sc54.9**

(2) An application for an order to bring up a prisoner, otherwise than by writ of habeas corpus, to give evidence in any proceedings, civil or criminal, before any court, tribunal or justice, must be made on witness statement or affidavit to a judge.

History of Rule

Reproduces the former RSC 1938 O.36, r.35, and RSC 1938 O.59, rr.24, 25. **sc54.9.1**

Habeas corpus ad testificandum and ad respondendum

The writ of habeas corpus *ad testificandum* is granted by a Judge of the High Court under common law powers, and, for the purposes of trials in the High Court, under the Habeas Corpus Act 1804. It is issued for bringing up a prisoner to give evidence before a Court. See Short and Mellor's, *Crown Office Practice* (2nd ed.), pp.332–334 for the relevant decisions. Under s.12(5) of Arbitration Act 1950, the High Court or a Judge (and a Master under r.73, r.3(1)) may order the issue of the writ to bring up a prisoner for examination before an arbitrator or umpire. A similar case is provided for by Sch.11, para.13 to the Agricultural Holdings Act 1986. The writ of habeas corpus *ad respondendum* is granted at common law, and, in regard to Courts-martial and proceedings before commissioners in bankruptcy, under the Habeas Corpus Act 1803. It issues to bring up a prisoner for trial or to be examined (see Short & Mellor (2nd ed.), p.334). **sc54.9.2**

By the Criminal Procedure Act 1853 s.9, power is given to the Judge to compel the attendance of a prisoner under sentence or commitment (*except under civil process*) by warrant or order.

In QBD the attendance of a prisoner in custody on civil process is enforced by issue of a writ of habeas corpus *ad testificandum* at the Action Department, Central Office, on the order of a Judge at Chambers under the Habeas Corpus Act 1804. The order for the writ to issue is obtained without notice on affidavit.

In Ch D, in a case of *Jenks v Ditton* (1897) 76 L.T. 591, on an application for a habeas corpus to bring up a prisoner detained under civil process Stirling J., declined to order a habeas corpus to issue, and made an order on the governor of the prison to bring up the prisoner.

In QBD, applications under the Criminal Procedure Act 1853, for an order for attendance of a prisoner detained under criminal process are made without notice to a Judge on an affidavit stating whether the prisoner is confined under sentence, or under commitment for trial, or otherwise, and giving the name of the prison in which he is confined, and stating that his evidence is necessary, and when and where required. The order is drawn up at the Crown Office (Short and Mellor's *Crown Office Practice*, p.335).

A party requiring the attendance of a prisoner to give evidence in a civil suit must tender the reasonable expenses of the prisoner and his escort (*Becker v Home Office* [1972] 2 Q.B. 407; [1972] 2 All E.R. 676, CA). The Court cannot grant a habeas corpus to a party to a suit, who is in custody, to enable him to appear in Court merely for the purpose of arguing his case in person (*Weldon v Neal* (1887) 15 Q.B.D. 471; *R. v Secretary of State for the Home Department Ex p. Wynne* [1992] C.O.D. 74).

Obtaining attendance of prisoner in custody

sc54.9.3 Section 29 of the Criminal Justice Act 1961 provides that the Secretary of State, if satisfied that the attendance at any place in the United Kingdom of a person detained in any part of the United Kingdom in a prison, youth custody centre, remand centre, detention centre or remand home, is desirable in the interests of justice, may direct that person to be taken to that place. The threshold is not what is *necessary* in the interests of justice but what is *desirable*—that being a lower threshold, see *Ex p. Wynne*, above.

Applications under this section for attendance at a civil Court are normally made by the solicitor acting for the party at whose instance the prisoner is required. Owing to the increasing number of litigants acting in person, it is likely that a Court will occasionally find it necessary to give some guidance to such a person.

An application for the production of a prisoner should be made in the first instance to the prison governor but in case of difficulty enquiry may be made of the Home Office's Tactical Management and Planning Unit, telephone 0121 4559855.

In some instances the Home Office may require confirmation from the Court that the attendance of the prisoner is essential. It is suggested that in those instances the applicant attend before the District Judge to give his reason for the request. If the District Judge is satisfied that the request ought to be granted, the Court should then communicate direct with the Home Office to this effect (Direction issued by the Lord Chancellor's Department, March 3, 1978).

Form of writ

sc54.10 10. A writ of habeas corpus must be in Form No. 89, 91 or 92 in the relevant practice direction, whichever is appropriate.

Applications relative to the custody, etc., of child

sc54.11 11. An application by a parent or guardian of a child for a writ of habeas corpus ad subjiciendum relative to the custody, care or control of the child must be made in the Family Division, and this order shall accordingly apply to such applications with the appropriate modifications.

History of Rule

sc54.11.1 Added by SI 1971/1269.

Effect of rule

sc54.11.2 This rule gives effect to the provisions of s.1(2) and Sch.1 to AJA 1970 (now replaced by SCA 1981 s.61, Sch.1, para.3) under which there are assigned to the Family Division, "proceedings in which a parent or guardian of a minor applies for a writ of habeas corpus *ad subjiciendum* relative to the custody, care or conduct of the minor". The effect of this rule, together with the amendment of r.1, which makes it subject to this rule, is to apply O.54 to such applications with the appropriate modifications.

PRACTICE DIRECTION—SCHEDULE 1, ORDER 54 (APPLICATION FOR WRIT OF HABEAS CORPUS)

scpd54.1 *This Practice Direction supplements CPR Part 50 and Schedule 1 to the CPR*

Terminology

1.1 In this practice direction—

(1) "Order 54" means those provisions contained in Schedule 1, RSC Order 54 which were previously contained in the Rules of the Supreme Court (1965);

(2) a reference to a rule or Part prefixed with CPR is a reference to a rule or Part contained in the CPR rules; and

(3) a reference to a rule number alone is a reference to the rule so numbered in Order 54.

Scope

scpd54.2 **2.1** This practice direction supplements Order 54 (which sets out how to apply for a writ of habeas corpus) by providing further detail about the application.

2.2 This practice direction must be read together with Order 54.

2.3 It also lists at paragraph 7 other practice directions which governed procedure relating to Order 54 before 26 April 1999 and which will continue to do so.

Form to be used where court directs claim form to be used

scpd54.3 **3.1** Where the court directs that an application be made by claim form, under—

(1) rule 2 (on hearing application under rule 1); or

(2) rule 4(2) (application in criminal proceedings ordered to be made to Divisional Court of the Queen's Bench Division),

the claimant must use Form 87 modified in accordance with the guidance set out in the Forms practice direction.

Form to be used for Notice of adjourned application directed by court

scpd54.4 **4.1** Where the court directs under rule 2(1)(c) that an application made under rule 1 is adjourned to allow for service of notice of the application, such notice must be given in modified Form 88.

Service

scpd54.5 **5.1** The party seeking the writ must serve—

(1) the claim form in accordance with rule 2.2; and

(2) the writ of habeas corpus ad subjiciendum and notice in Form 90, as modified, in accordance with rule 6.

(CPR, rule 6.3 provides that the court will normally serve a document which it has issued or prepared).

The Administrative Court

scpd54.6 **6.1** When the court directs that an application is to be made by claim form under—

(1) rule 2(1) (powers of court to whom application made under rule 1); or

(2) rule 4(2) (power of court where application made in criminal proceedings)

the application must be entered in the Administrative Court List in accordance with Practice Direction (Crown Office List) 1987 1 W.L.R. 232; [1987] 1 All E.R. 368.

(In Schedule 1, RSC Order 57 rule 2 provides for the entry of claims in the appropriate office and for the filing of copy documents for the use of the court)

Practice Directions etc., which apply to Order 54

7.1 On and after 26 April 1999, the Practice Directions, Statements and Practice Notes set out in Table 1 continue to apply to proceedings under Order 54. **scpd54.7**

TABLE 1

scpd54.8

Practice Direction etc.	Content
Practice Note [1983] 2 All E.R. 1020	Urgent matters outside London—consultation of Crown Office and continuation in London;
Practice Note (Crown Office List) [1987] 1 All E.R. 1184	Need for accuracy in time estimates
Practice Direction (Crown Office List) [1987] 1 W.L.R. 232; [1987] 1 All ER 368	Parts of the List.
Practice Direction (Crown Office List: Preparation for hearings) [1994] 4 All E.R. 671; [1994] 1 W.L.R. 1551 (18th November 1994)	Preparation for hearings; Documentation; Time limits; Skeleton arguments; amendment of grounds.
Practice Direction (Crown Office List; Consent Orders) [1997] 1 W.L.R. 825	Consent orders
Practice Statement (Supreme Court; Judgments) [1998] 1 W.L.R. 825; [1998] 2 All E.R. 638	Judgments

Editorial note

The proper citations and dates of the practice directions listed in Table 1 above are as shown immediately below. These practice directions are printed in the SCP 1999 at the places indicated. **scpd54.9**

- *Practice Direction (Crown Office List: Criminal Proceedings)* [1983] 1 W.L.R. 925; *sub nom. Practice Note (Crown Office List: Uncontested Proceedings: Applications Outside London: Delay)* [1983] 2 All E.R. 1020 (July 21, 1983) (see Queen's Bench Practice Direction No.23 (part), SCP 1999, Vol.2, paras 2C–164 to 2C–167)
- Practice Note (Crown Office List: Estimated Length of Hearing) [1987] 1 All E.R. 1184 (April 3, 1987)
- *Practice Direction (Crown Office List)* [1987] 1 W.L.R. 232; *sub nom. Practice Note (Crown Office List: Arrangement,* [1987] 1 All E.R. 368 (February 3, 1987) (see Queen's Bench Practice Direction No.24, SCP 1999, Vol.2, para.2C–168)
- *Practice Direction (QBD: Crown Office List: Preparation for Hearings)* [1994] 1 W.L.R. 1551; *sub nom. Practice Note (Crown Office List: Penalties for Late Papers)* [1994] 4 All E.R. 671 (October 25, 1994) (see Queen's Bench Practice Direction No.26, SCP 1999, Vol.2, paras 2C–173 to 2C–175)
- *Practice Direction (Crown Office List: Consent Orders)* [1997] 1 W.L.R. 825; *sub nom. Practice Note (Crown Office List: Uncontested Proceedings)* [1997] 2 All E.R. 799 (May 12, 1997) (see Queen's Bench Practice Direction No.27, SCP 1999, Vol.2, paras 2C–176 to 2C–179)

- Practice Statement (Supreme Court: Judgments) [1998] 1 W.L.R. 825; *sub nom. Practice Statement (Royal Courts of Justice: Judgments)* [1998] 2 All E.R. 667 (April 22, 1998); as modified by Practice Statement (Supreme Court: Judgments) (No.2) [1999] 1 W.L.R. 1; *sub nom. Practice Note (Royal Courts of Justice: Judgments)* [1999] 1 All E.R. 125; November 25, 1998)

RSC ORDER 64—SITTINGS, VACATIONS AND OFFICE HOURS

Contents

sc64.0.1

Divisional Court business during vacation

sc64.4 4. Proceedings which require to be immediately or promptly heard and which by virtue of the following provisions must be brought in a Divisional Court may, in vacation, be brought before a single judge:

(a) Order 52, rules 1(2) and 3(1).

History of rule

sc64.4.1 Amended by Civil Procedure (Amendment) Rules 2000 (SI 2000/221).

RSC ORDER 79—ESTREAT OF RECOGNIZANCES

Contents

sc79.0.1

Editorial introduction

sc79.0.2 Rules 1 to 7 of this Order were revoked in 1971 when the Crown Court was established by the Courts Act 1971 as part of the Supreme Court of England and Wales and given exclusive jurisdiction to try criminal cases arising on indictment. The rules that remain support the exercise of the High Court's jurisdiction in relation to certain matters on the criminal side, particularly the granting of bail (r.9). Rules relating to the powers of the High Court to set aside witness summonses and to issue warrants to secure the attendance of witnesses are contained in rr.10 and 11. It should be noted that those powers were granted by the Criminal Procedure (Attendance of Witnesses) Act 1965 ss.2 and 4 but have been removed by the Criminal Procedure and Investigations Act 1996 ss.66 and 67.

Section 17 of the Criminal Justice Act 2003 provides that the inherent power of the High Court to entertain an application in relation to bail, determined by a magistrates court or the Crown Court is abolished. However, it should be noted that in *R.(M.)* v Isleworth Crown Court and HM Customs & Excise [2005] EWHC 263 (Admin) the Divisional Court held that judicial review may lie in respect of the decision of the Crown court to refuse bail—and that such decisions do not fall within the exclusion of "matters relating to trial on indictment" in s.29(3) of the Supreme Court Act 1981. That jurisdiction will however be exercised sparingly.

Related sources

sc79.0.3

- Criminal Procedure (Attendance of Witnesses) Act 1965 ss.2 and 4
- Criminal Justice Act 1967 s.22
- RSC O.115 (Confiscation and forfeiture in connection with criminal proceedings)

Forms

sc79.0.4 The following Prescribed Forms (formerly included amongst the Prescribed Forms in Appendix A to the RSC) are relevant to O.79. These forms are included in Table 2 *(Practice Forms)* attached to Practice Direction (Forms):

- **No. 97** Summons to grant bail (O.79, r.9)
- **No. 97A** Summons to vary arrangements for bail in a criminal proceeding (O.79, r.9)

- **No. 98** Order of judge in chambers to release prisoner on bail (O.79, r.9)
- **No. 98A** Order of judge varying arrangements for bail (O.79, r.9)
- **No. 101** Witness summons—Crown Court (O.79, r.10)
- **No. 103** Witness summons—Crown Court (O.79, r.10)

Estreat of recognizances

8.—(1) No recognizance acknowledged in or removed into the Queen's Bench Division shall be estreated without the order of a judge. **sc79.8**

(2) Every application to estreat a recognizance in the Queen's Bench Division must be made by claim form by a judge and must be supported by a witness statement or affidavit showing in what manner the breach has been committed and proving that the claim form was duly served.

(2A) When it issues the claim form the court will fix a date for the hearing of the application.

(3) A claim form under this rule must be served at least 2 clear days before the day named therein for the hearing.

(4) On the hearing of the application the judge may, and if requested by any party shall, direct any issue of fact in dispute to be tried by a jury.

(5) If it appears to the judge that a default has been made in performing the conditions of the recognizance, the judge may order the recognizance to be estreated.

Enforcement of fines and forfeited recognizances

The machinery for the enforcement of fines and forfeited recognizances is provided by SCA 1981 s.140, see Vol.2, Section 9A, para.9A–386. **sc79.8.1**

Bail

9.—(1)Subject to the provisions of this rule, every application to the High Court in respect of bail in any criminal proceeding– **sc79.9**

(a) where the defendant is in custody, must be made by claim form to a judge [1]to show cause why the defendant should not be granted bail;

(b) where the defendant has been admitted to bail, must be made by claim form to a judge [2] to show cause why the variation in the arrangements for bail proposed by the applicant should not be made.

(2) Subject to paragraph (5), the claim form (in Form **No. 97** or **No. 97A** in the relevant practice direction) must, at least 24 hours before the day named therein for the hearing, be served–

(a) where the application was made by the defendant, on the prosecutor and on the Director of Public Prosecutions, if the prosecution is being carried on by him;

(b) where the application was made by the prosecutor or a constable under section 3(8) of the Bail Act 1976[3], on the defendant.

---

[1] Amended by the Civil Procedure (Amendment) Rules (SI 1999/1008) r.62(f).
[2] Amended by the Civil Procedure (Amendment) Rules (SI 1999/1008) r.62(f).
[3] Section 3(8) was amended by the Criminal Law Act 1977 (c.45) s.65(4) and Sch.12.

(3) Subject to paragraph (5), every application must be supported by witness statement or affidavit.

(4) Where a defendant in custody who desires to apply for bail is unable through lack of means to instruct a solicitor, he may give notice in writing to the [court] stating his desire to apply for bail and requesting that the official solicitor shall act for him in the application, and the [court may] assign the official solicitor to act for the applicant accordingly.

(5) Where the official solicitor has been so assigned the [court may] dispense with the requirements of paragraphs (1) to (3) and deal with the application in a summary manner.

(6) Where the [court] grants the defendant bail, the order must be in Form **No. 98** in the relevant Practice Direction and a copy of the order shall be transmitted forthwith—

(a) where the proceedings in respect of the defendant have been transferred to the Crown Court for trial or where the defendant has been committed to the Crown Court to be sentenced or otherwise dealt with, to the appropriate officer of the Crown Court;

(b) in any other case, to the designated officerwhich committed the defendant.

(6A) The recognizance of any surety required as a condition of bail granted as aforesaid may, where the defendant is in a prison or other place of detention, be entered into before the governor or keeper of the prison or place as well as before the person specified in section 8(4) of the Bail Act 1976.

(6B) Where under section 3(5) or (6) of the Bail Act 1976[1] [the court] imposes a requirement to be complied with before a person's release on bail, [it] may give directions as to the manner in which and the person or persons before whom the requirement may be complied with.

(7) A person who in pursuance of an order for the grant of bail made by [the court] under this rule proposes to enter into a recognizance or give security must, unless [the court] otherwise directs, give notice (in Form **No. 100** in the relevant Practice Direction) to the prosecutor at least 24 hours before he enters into the recognizance or complies with the requirements as aforesaid.

(8) Where in pursuance of such an order as aforesaid a recognizance is entered into or requirement complied with before any person, it shall be the duty of that person to cause the recognizance or, as the case may be, a statement of the requirement complied with to be transmitted forthwith—

(a) where the proceedings in respect of the defendant have been transferred to the Crown Court for trial or where the defendant has been committed to the Crown Court to be sentenced or otherwise dealt with, to the appropriate officer of the Crown Court;

(b) in any other case, to the designated officer which committed the defendant,

[1] Section 3(6) was amended by the Criminal Justice and Public Order Act 1994 (c.33) ss.27(2), 168(3), Sch.11.

and a copy of such recognizance or statement shall at the same time be sent to the governor or keeper of the prison or other place of detention in which the defendant is detained, unless the recognizance was entered into or the requirement complied with before such governor or keeper.

(10) An order varying the arrangements under which the defendant has been granted bail shall be in Form **No. 98A** in the relevant practice direction and a copy of the order shall be transmitted forthwith—

(a) where the proceedings in respect of the defendant have been transferred to the Crown Court for trial or where the defendant has been committed to the Crown Court to be sentenced or otherwise dealt with, to the appropriate officer of the Crown Court;

(b) in any other case, to the designated officer which committed the defendant.

(11) Where in pursuance of an order of [the High Court or the Crown Court] a person is released on bail in any criminal proceedings pending the determination of an appeal to the High Court or House of Lords or an application for an order of certiorari, then, upon the abandonment of the appeal or application, or upon the decision of the High Court or House of Lords being given, any justice (being a justice acting for the same petty sessions area as the magistrates' court by which that person was convicted or sentenced) may issue process for enforcing the decision in respect of which such appeal or application was brought or, as the case may be, the decision of the High Court or House of Lords.

(12) If an applicant to the High Court in any criminal proceedings is refused bail, the applicant shall not be entitled to make a fresh application for bail to any other judge or to a Divisional Court.

(13) The record required by section 5 of the Bail Act 1976 [1] to be made by the High Court shall be made by including in the file relating to the case in question a copy of the relevant order of the Court and shall contain the particulars set out in Form **No. 98** or **No. 98A** in the relevant Practice Direction, whichever is appropriate, except that in the case of a decision to withhold bail the record shall be made by inserting a statement of the decision on the Court's copy of the relevant claim form and including it in the file relating to the case in question.

(14) In the case of a person whose return or surrender is sought under the Extradition Act 1989, this rule shall apply as if references to the defendant were references to that person and references to the prosecutor were references to the State seeking the return or surrender of that person.

Amendment—sc79.9

Following the introduction of Civil Procedure (Amendment No 5) Rules 2003 (SI 2003/3361) the following amendment to RSC O.79.9 came into force on May 1, 2004: "an order of certiorari" is to be substituted by "a quashing order". **sc79.9.1A**

[1] Section 5 was amended by the Criminal Justice Act 1982 (c.48), s.60; and by the Criminal Law Act 1977 (c.45) s.65(4), Sch.12; and by the Criminal Justice and Public Order Act 1994 (c.33) s.27(4) and Sch.3, para.1.

History of rule

sc79.9.1 Amended by SI 1967/1809; SI 1971/1955; SI 1978/251 and SI 1989/1307. Further amended by SI 1995/2206—this amendment shall not apply where the defendant has been committed to the Crown Court for trial and the relevant provisions of Order 79 shall continue to apply to such proceedings as if this amendment had not been made.

RSC ORDER 93—APPLICATIONS AND APPEALS TO HIGH COURT UNDER VARIOUS ACTS: CHANCERY DIVISION

Editorial introduction

sc93.0.1 The remaining provisions of Order 93, namely rules 4, 5, 9, 10, 16, 17, 18 and 19, were revoked, with effect from October 1, 2007, by the Civil Procedure (Amendment) Rules 2007 (SI 2007/2204). Those provisions that remain relevant were (with one exception mentioned below) incorporated by the 45th Update, with effect from October 1, 2007, into the main body of the CPR.

The exception, r.93.4 (proceedings under the Trustee Act 1925) has now been incorporated into PD 8 para.9.4, and the proceedings assigned to the Chancery Division, by the 46th Update, with effect from April 6, 2008.

The various provisions of O.93 may now be found in the CPR as follows:

1.	Notice of Petition under s.55 of the National Debt Act 1870	23BPD para.2
2.	Application under the Public Trustee Act 1906 (free-standing proceedings)	8PD para.9.4 Table and Section C para.12
4.	Proceedings under the Trustee Act 1925	8PD para 9.4 Table
5.	Application under s.2 (3) of the Public Order Act 1936	8PD para.9.4 Table and Section C para.13
9.	Right of Appeal under para.16 of schedule 15 to the Law of Property Act 1922	52PD para.23.2(1)
10.	Determination of Appeal under the Land Registration Act 1925	52PD para.23.2(3)
16.	Proceedings under s.14 or 18 of the Commons Registration Act 1965	s.14: 8PD para.9.4 Table
17.	Proceedings under s.21 or s.25 of the Law of Property Act 1925	8PD para.9.4 Table
18.	Proceedings under s.86 of the Civil Aviation Act 1982	8PD para.9.4 Table and Section C para.15A
19.	Proceedings under the Control of Misleading Advertisements Regulations 1988	8PD para 9.4 Table (Note: s.85(7) of the Fair Trading Act 1973 has been repealed).
22.	Proceedings under the Financial Services and Markets Act 2000	8PD para.9.4 Table and Section C para.21

Note: PD 8 para.9.4, which was introduced in the 45th Update, specifies in a Table the Division to which applications in the High Court are assigned. All the proceedings formerly in O.93 are assigned to the Chancery Division. Where appropriate, the procedure to be followed is set out in PD 8 Section C, as specified above.

RSC ORDER 94—APPLICATIONS AND APPEALS TO HIGH COURT UNDER VARIOUS ACTS: QUEEN'S BENCH DIVISION

Note

sc94.1 The rules remaining in this Order, viz., 4, 5, 8, 9, 12 and 13, were revoked by Civil Procedure (Amendment) Rules 2007 (SI 2007/2204) r.20(a), with the result that the whole of the Order was revoked. In so far as it was necessary to do so, the effects of those rules were continued by new CPR provisions, mainly in r.52.19 and r.52.20, and in Practice Direction (Alternative Procedure for Claims) (supplementing Pt 8) and in Practice Direction (Appeals) (supplementing Pt 52).

RSC ORDER 109—THE ADMINISTRATION OF JUSTICE ACT 1960

Contents **sc109.0.1**

Applications under Act

1.—(1) Any of the following applications, that is to say— **sc109.1**

(a) an application under section 2 of the Administration of Justice Act 1960, or under that section as applied by section 13 of that Act, to extend the time within which an application may be made to a Divisional Court for permission to appeal to the House of Lords under section 1 of that Act, or section 13 thereof, from an order or decision of that court, and

(b) an application by a defendant under section 9(3) of that Act to a Divisional Court for permission to be present on the hearing of any proceedings preliminary or incidental to an appeal to the House of Lords under section 1 of that Act from a decision of that court

must be made to a Divisional Court except in vacation when it may be made to a judge.

(2) Any such application to a Divisional Court, if not made in the proceedings before the Divisional Court from whose order or decision the appeal in question is brought, must be made by the issue of a claim form.

(3) Any such application to a judge must, in the case of such an application as is referred to in paragraph (1)(a) be made by the issue of a claim form and, in the case of such an application as is referred to in paragraph (1)(b) need not be served on any other person unless, in the latter case, the judge otherwise directs.

(4) No application notice or copy of the claim form (as the case may be) by which such an application as is referred to in paragraph (1)(b) is made need be given to any party affected thereby unless the Divisional Court otherwise directs.

(5) Where any application to which this rule applies is made in vacation to a single judge and the judge refuses the application, the applicant shall be entitled to have the application determined by a Divisional Court.

Editorial note

Applications under this rule are made using the Pt 8 procedure—CPR PD 8 para.9.1. **sc109.1.1**

Appeals under section 13 of Act

2.—(1) An appeal to a Divisional Court of the High Court under section 13 of the Administration of Justice Act 1960, shall be heard and determined by a Divisional Court of the Queen's Bench Division. **sc109.2**

(3) [...]

(4) Unless the court gives permission, there shall be not more than 4 clear days between the date on which the order or decision appealed against was made and the day named in the notice of appeal for the hearing of the appeal.

(5) The notice must be served, and the appeal entered, not less than one clear day before the day named in the notice for the hearing of the appeal.

History of rule

sc109.2.1 Amended by SI 2000/221. Applications under this rule are made using the Pt 8 procedure—CPR PD 8 para.9.1 and cf. CPR PD 52 para.21.4.

Release of appellant on bail

sc109.3 3.—(1) Where, in the case of an appeal under section 13 of the Administration of Justice Act 1960, to a Divisional Court or to the House of Lords from a Divisional Court, the appellant is in custody, the High Court may order his release on his giving security (whether by recognizance, with or without sureties, or otherwise and for such reasonable sum as the court may fix) for his appearance, within 10 days after the judgment of the Divisional Court or, as the case may be, of the House of Lords, on the appeal before the court from whose order or decision the appeal is brought unless the order or decision is reversed by that judgment.

(2) Order 79 rule 9(1) to (6) and (8) shall apply in relation to an application to the High Court for bail pending an appeal under the said section 13 to which this rule applies, and to the admission of a person to bail in pursuance of an order made on the application, as they apply in relation to an application to that court for bail in criminal proceedings, and to the admission of a person to bail in pursuance of an order made on the application, but with the substitution, for references to the defendant, of references to the appellant, and, for references to the prosecutor, of references to the court officer of the court from whose order or decision the appeal is brought and to the parties to the proceedings in that court who are directly affected by the appeal.

Release of appellant on bail by the Court of Appeal

sc109.4 4.—(1) Where, in the case of an appeal under section 13 of the Administration of Justice Act 1960 to the Court of Appeal or to the House of Lords from the Court of Appeal, the appellant is in custody, the Court of Appeal may order his release on his giving security (whether by recognisance, with or without sureties, or otherwise and for such reasonable sum as that court may fix) for his appearance within 10 days after the judgment of the Court of Appeal or, as the case may be, of the House of Lords on the appeal shall have been given, before the court from whose order or decision the appeal is brought unless the order or decision is reversed by that judgment.

(2) An application for the release of a person under paragraph (1) pending an appeal to the Court of Appeal or House of Lords under the said section 13 must be made in accordance with CPR Part 23, *and the application* notice must, at least 24 hours before the day named therein for the hearing, be served on the court from whose order or decision the appeal is brought and on all parties to the proceedings in that court who are directly affected by the appeal.

(3) Order 79 rules 9(6), (6A), (6B) and (8) shall apply in relation to the grant of bail under this rule by the Court of Appeal in a case of criminal contempt of court as they apply in relation to the grant of bail in criminal proceedings by the High Court, but with the substitution for references to a judge of references to the Court of Appeal and for references to the defendant of references to the appellant.

(4) When granting bail under this rule in a case of civil contempt of court, the Court of Appeal may order that the recognisance or other security to be given by the appellant or the recognisance of any surety shall be given before any person authorised by virtue of section 119(1) of the Magistrates' Court Act 1980 to take recognisance where a magistrates' court having power to take it has, instead of taking it, fixed the amount in which the principal and his sureties, if any, are to be bound. An order by the Court of Appeal granting bail as aforesaid must be in Form **No. 98** in the relevant Practice Direction with the necesssary adaptations.

(5) Where in pursuance of an order of the Court of Appeal under paragraph (4) of this rule a recognisance is entered into or other security given before any person, it shall be the duty of that person to cause the recognisance of the appellant or any surety or, as the case may be, a statement of the other security given, to be transmitted forthwith to the designated officer which committed the appellant; and a copy of such recognisance or statement shall at the same time be sent to the governor or keeper of the prison or other place of detention in which the appellant is detained, unless the recognisance or security was given before such governor or keeper.

(6) The powers conferred on the Court of Appeal by paragraphs (1), (3) and (4) of this rule may be exercised by a single judge.

RSC

History of rule

Added by SI 2000/221. This rule allows the Court of Appeal to grant bail on appeal to that court or to the House of Lords but it is the more usual practice on appeals to the Court of Appeal to request directions in the appeal notice for an expedited hearing where the appellant is in custody. **sc109.4.1**

RSC ORDER 113—SUMMARY PROCEEDINGS FOR POSSESSION OF LAND

Contents

 sc113.0.1

Editorial introduction

RSC O.113 used to provide a summary procedure for eviction of trespassers. With the introduction of CPR Pt 55 these provisions have been repealed. The only remaining provision (RSC O.113, r.7) deals with writs for possession against persons who entered land as trespassers—see CPR 55.1(b) and RSC 45.12. **sc113.0.2**

If trespassers move back onto land after eviction, land owners may seek a writ of restitution in Form No.68—see RSC 46.3.

Forms

- **No. 66A** Writ of possession under O.113 **sc113.0.3**

Writ of possession

7.—(1) Order 45, rule 3(2) shall not apply in relation to an order for possession in a possession claim against trespassers under Part 55 **sc113.7** but no writ of possession to enforce such an order shall be issued after the expiry of three months from the date of the order without the permission of the court. An application for permission may be made without notice being served on any other party unless the court otherwise directs.

(2) The writ of possession shall be in Form **No. 66A**.

RSC ORDER 115—CONFISCATION AND FORFEITURE IN CONNECTION WITH CRIMINAL PROCEEDINGS

Contents

sc115.0.1

I. Drug Trafficking Act 1994 and Criminal Justice (International Co-operation) Act 1990

II. Part IV of the Criminal Justice Act 1988

Editorial introduction

In 1986, this Order was added to the RSC to provide rules necessary for the exercise by the High Court of its jurisdiction in support of certain criminal proceedings under provisions in the Drug Trafficking Offences Act 1986. The 1986 Act was replaced by the Drug Trafficking Act 1994 ("the 1994 Act"). The orders which the Court may make in exercise of the jurisdiction relate to the freezing and realisation of property under the control of defendants in criminal cases. In the years since, the machinery laid down in 1986, with some additions and amendments, has been pressed into service for the purpose of providing rules for the exercise of the Court's jurisdiction in support of criminal proceedings under the Criminal Justice Act 1988 Pt VI ("the 1988 Act"), the Prevention of Terrorism (Temporary Provisions) Act 1989 (subsequently replaced by the Terrorism Act 2000) and the Criminal Justice (International Co-operation) Act 1990, and for the purpose of permitting the enforcement of orders in accordance with the International Criminal Court Act 2001. The result is that the rules in the Order (there are now 38 of them) are not readily comprehended at first read. The rules have to be read in conjunction with the statutory provisions to which they relate. **sc115.0.2**

The rules governing the procedure of the Court when exercising its jurisdiction under the 1994 Act and the 1990 Act are grouped together in Pt I (rr.1 to 21A). In Pt II (rr.22 and 23) the rules in Pt I are applied *mutatis mutanais* to the exercise of the Court's jurisdiction under the 1988 Act. Therefore in the commentary to the rules in Pt I, reference will be made as appropriate to the 1988 Act. Rules relating to the Court's jurisdiction under the 2000 Act are found in Pt III (rr 24 to 36) and under the 2001 Act in Pt IV (rr.35 and 36).

The impact of the Proceeds of Crime Act 2002

The Proceeds of Crime Act 2002 (c.29) has now come into effect. It is necessary briefly to explain the effects of that Act and of two practice directions published. **sc115.0.3**

The Proceeds of Crime Act 2002 provides for the confiscation of the assets of persons convicted of criminal offences. It largely replaces the 1994 Act and the 1988 Act. Part 1 of the Act created an Assets Recovery Agency. Part 2 of the Act contains the statutory framework for the making of confiscation orders by the criminal courts of England and Wales (and is mirrored by Pts 3 and 4, which apply to Scotland and Northern Ireland). Part 5 introduces a new procedure of "civil recovery" under which

RSC

property obtained through unlawful conduct may be recovered in the High Court from a person notwithstanding that he has not been convicted of any offence with reference to the property. Part 8 provides for three types of investigation into matters related to confiscation; they are (1) confiscation investigation, (2) civil recovery investigation, and (3) money laundering investigation.

When contrasted with the legislation it replaces, the 2002 Act gives a greater role to the Crown Court (and to a lesser extent to the magistrates' courts) than to the High Court. Following the 2002 Act coming into force, applications for a restraint order or the appointment of a receiver which would previously have been made to the High Court under Pt VI of the 1988 Act or Pt 1 of the 1994 Act will instead be made to the Crown Court. As a result, the provisions of CPR Sch.1 RSC O.115 insofar as they apply to proceedings in the High Court as provided for by the 1988 Act and the 1994 Act will cease to be of use. However, as the provisions of the 1988 Act and the 1994 Act will continue to apply to pending and transitional cases the rules found in RSC O.115 will continue to have effect; the 1988 Act and the 1994 Act continue to apply to cases where any of the criminal acts were carried out before March 2003 (SI 2003/333, and see *RCPO v Hill* [2005] EWCA Crim 3271). In these cases restraint and receivership applications continue to be made to the High Court under CPR Sch.1 RSC O.115. With effect from February 17, 2002, RSC O.115 was supplemented by Practice Direction (Restraint Orders and Appointment of Receivers in Connection with Criminal Proceedings and Investigations) (see para.scpd115.1 below). The scope of this practice direction (which was first published in February 2003) is explained in para.1.1 and it should be noted that it applies, not only to applications to the High Court for a restraint order or the appointment of a receiver under the 1988 Act and the 1994 Act, but also under Sch.4 to the Terrorism Act 2000 (see O.115, rr.24 *et seq*).

Under Pt 5 (s.240 *et seq*) of the 2002 Act the High Court has jurisdiction under the "civil recovery" procedure provided for by that Part, in particular the procedure under which the State may recover property which is, or which represents, property obtained through unlawful conduct. Under Pt 8 (s.340 *et seq*) of the 2002 Act the High Court has jurisdiction to make orders for the purpose of civil recovery investigations. Directions supporting the exercise by the High Court of its various jurisdictions under Pts 5 and 8 are provided by the Practice Direction—Civil Recovery Proceedings). These directions came into force on the commencement of Ch.2 of Pt 5 and Ch.2 of Pt 8 of the 2002 Act. See para.B11–001 for the Practice Direction and a full commentary on the civil recovery powers in the 2002 Act. RSC O.115 has no application to any proceedings brought under the 2002 Act.

O.115, Pt I (rr.1 to 21A)

sc115.0.4 The Drug Trafficking Act 1994 is a consolidating Act, and came into force on February 3, 1995. By s.67 and Sch.2, para.1 of the Act, subordinate legislation for the purposes of any provision overtaken by the Act continues to have effect in relation to any corresponding provision in the Act; and the various references to subordinate legislation which follow must be read with that in mind. The Act provides that, where a person appears before the Crown Court to be sentenced for a drug trafficking offence and has benefited from such trafficking, that Court may make a "confiscation order" to recover his proceeds (ss.2 to 5). The Act further provides for charging and restraint orders to be made by the High Court on the application of the prosecution in respect of property which is held by a person against whom a confiscation order may be made or has been made by the Crown Court.

This Part of the Order, which was added by RSC (Amendment No.3) (SI 1986/2289), provides for the applications that may be made to the High Court for such charging and restraint orders. The provisions of the Order must be read with the relevant provisions of the 1994 Act.

The rules in Pt I of this Order are not restricted in their application to High Court proceedings arising under the 1994 Act. The explanation for this is as follows.

The Criminal Justice (International Co-operation) Act 1990 s.9 states that, by Order in Council, provision may be made for the enforcement in the United Kingdom of orders made by overseas courts for the forfeiture of property used in the commission of an offence which corresponds to, or is similar to, specified offences. For the purpose of enforcement in England and Wales, the offences specified include offences under *the Misuse of Drugs Act 1971*, a drug trafficking offence as defined by the Drug Trafficking Act 1994 or an offence to which the Criminal Justice Act 1988 Pt VI applies. An Order in Council under the section may authorise the making of rules of court (see s.10(3)). The Criminal Justice (International Co-operation) Act 1990 (Enforcement of

Overseas Forfeiture Orders) Order 1991 (SI 1991/1463) was made in exercise of the power in s.9.

O.115, Pt II (rr.22 and 23)

Pt VI of the Criminal Justice Act 1988 is modelled on the provisions of the Drug Trafficking Offences Act 1986 and gives the criminal courts powers to confiscate the proceeds of other highly profitable crimes. The offences to which Pt VI applies are prescribed by s.71(9)(c) and comprise offences listed in Sch.4 and, if not so listed, any indictable offence other than a drug trafficking offence. Under s.71, the Crown Court and the magistrates' courts may make confiscation orders. Supporting powers, similar to those given to the High Court by what is now the 1994 Act, are given to the Court by provisions in Pt VI. Thus the jurisdiction of the Court under the 1988 Act derives from s.77 (restraint orders), s.78 (charging orders), s.80 (appointment of receivers to realise property), s.81 (application of proceeds of realisation), s.83 (variation of confiscation orders) and s.89 (compensation of defendants not convicted etc.). Therefore in the commentary to the rules in Pt 1, reference will be made as appropriate to the 1988 Act. **sc115.0.5**

O.115, Pt III (rr.24 to 36)

This Part was added to O.115 by SI 1989/1307, following the coming into force on March 22, 1989, of Pt III of the Prevention of Terrorism (Temporary Provisions) Act 1989. The 1989 Act re-enacted and created certain criminal offences relating to the giving of financial assistance to terrorism. The 1989 Act was temporary in the sense that its provisions had to be renewed by Parliament from year to year (see s.27). The 1989 Act was replaced by the Terrorism Act 2000 (2000 c.11). Pt III of the 2000 Act corresponds with Pt III of the 1989 Act. However, whereas the 1989 Act was limited to terrorism connected with Northern Ireland, and with international terrorism, the 2000 Act is concerned with terrorism as more widely defined (see s.1). Part III of the 2000 Act reflects recommendations made in Chapter 13 of the Inquiry into Legislation Against Terrorism (Cm 3420, 1996) (the "Lloyd Report"). Offences in relation to terrorist property contained in Pt III include fund raising (s.15), use and possession (s.16), funding arrangements (s.17) and money laundering (s.18). Section 23 of the 2000 Act states that the court by or before which a person is convicted of an offence under any of ss.15 to 18 may make an order for the forfeiture of money or property related to such offences, and, in certain cases, other money or property in the defendant's possession or control at the time of the offence which is to be used for terrorist purposes. (Forfeiture orders of this variety should be distinguished from an order made under s.28 for the forfeiture of cash seized and detained under s.25.) Schedule 4 to the Act provides the procedural machinery for the making of a forfeiture order. This Schedule provides, not only for the making of a forfeiture order by a criminal court, but also for the making by the High Court (1) of an order restraining dealings in property in respect of which a forfeiture order has been or could be made (a restraint order), (2) of an order for compensation where a restraint order is discharged, and (3) of an order enforcing a forfeiture order (including orders made elsewhere in the British Islands and in designated foreign countries). (In addition, the Schedule provides for the making of Orders in Council for the enforcement in the United Kingdom of forfeiture orders made in designated countries.) Rules of court relevant to the exercise by the High Court of its jurisdiction in this respect are found in Pt III of O.115. **sc115.0.6**

Part III of O.115, which needs to be read in the context of Pt III of and Sch.4 to the Act, contains provisions similar to but not the same as the provisions of Pts I and II of this Order relating, respectively to the Drug Trafficking Act 1994 and Pt VI of the Criminal Justice Act 1988. The provisions of Pt III of the Order are in some respects more limited in extent and, in particular, do not provide for charging orders to be made over the property of a defendant.

The Order was subsequently amended by RSC (Amendment No.2) 1989 (SI 1989/386) by the addition of rules to take account of proceedings arising under the 1988 Act. Further amendments, by addition, were made by RSC (Amendment No.3) 1989 (SI 1989/1307) when the 1989 Act came into force. The enactment of the 1990 Act and a related Order in Council necessitated the amendments to the Order brought about by RSC (Amendment No.3) 1991 (SI 1991/1884); this SI also amended the title of O.115. See too SI 1995/2206. After the coming into effect of the Terrorism Act 2000, the provisions of Pt III of O.115 were amended by the the Civil Procedure (Amendment No.2) Rules 2001, and, after the coming into affect of the Anti-terrorism, Crime and Security Act 2001, they were further amended by the Civil Procedure (Amendment No.6) Rules 2001 (SI 2001/4016).

O.115, Pt IV (rr. 37 and 38)

sc115.0.7 This Part was added by the Civil Procedure (Amendment No.4) Rules 2003 (SI 2003/2113), following the coming into effect of certain provisions of the International Criminal Court Act 2001.

Related sources

sc115.0.8
- Pt 23 (General rules about applications for court orders)
- Pt 32.6 (Evidence in proceedings other than at trial)
- Pt 32.15 (Affidavit evidence)
- Pt 69 (Court's power to appoint receiver)
- Practice Direction (CPR Pt 8 and Sch.1 and Sch.2 to the CPR) (see para.8PD.1 above)
- Terrorism Act 2000 s.23 and Sch.4

I. Drug Trafficking Act 1994 and Criminal Justice (International Co-operation) Act 1990

Interpretation

sc115.1 1.—(1) In this Part of this Order, "The Act" means the Drug Trafficking Act 1994 and a section referred to by number means the section so numbered in the Act.

(2) Expressions used in this Part of this Order which are used in the Act have the same meanings in this Part of this Order as in the Act and include any extended meaning given by the Criminal Justice (Confiscation) (Northern Ireland) Order 1990.

Assignment of proceedings

sc115.2 2. Subject to rule 12, the jurisdiction of the High Court under the Act shall be exercised by a judge of the Chancery Division or of the Queen's Bench Division.

"jurisdiction of the High Court"

sc115.2.1 The jurisdiction of the High Court under the 1994 Act is derived principally from the following provisions: s.19 (confiscation order where defendant has absconded or died) (see r.2B); ss.26 and 27 (application for restraint and/or appointment of receiver or charging order) (see rr.3, 8 and 9); s.16 (increase in realisable property) (see r.9A); s.17 (variation of confiscation order where realisable property inadequate) (see r.9); ss.18 and 22 (compensation for defendants not convicted etc.) (see rr.10 and 11A); ss.25, 26 and 27 (discharge or variation of restraint orders and charging orders) (see r.5); s.21 (variation of confiscation order made under s.19); s.29 (application for appointment of receiver) (see rr.7 and 8); s.30 (application of proceeds of realisation) (see r.7); and s.59 (disclosure of information held by government departments) (see r.11)

The High Court has precisely the same jurisdiction in non drugs cases under the 1988 Act, except under the 1988 Act there is no power equivalent to s.19 (confiscation order where defendant dies or absconded) or s.16 (increase in realisable property).

The jurisdiction of the High Court as conferred by the predecessor to the 1994 Act, that is to say, by the Drug Trafficking Offences Act 1986, was analysed by Lord Hobhouse in the case of *Norris (Clifford), Re*, [2001] 1 W.L.R. 1388, HL. In all material respects the provisions granting jurisdiction to the High Court found in the 1994 Act and the 1988 Act are the same as those found in the 1986 Act.

In practice, the jurisdiction of the High Court is most likely to be invoked in one of two situations. First, on application by the prosecutor for a restraint order and possibly receiver pursuant to s.26 of the 1994 Act or s.77 of the 1988 Act. Such an application may be made from any time when a person is to be charged with an offence (s.25 of the 1994 Act; s.76 of the 1988 Act). Secondly, on application by the prosecutor for the appointment of a receiver to enforce any confiscation order made by the Crown Court (s.29 of the 1994 Act; s.80 of the 1988 Act).

"Subject to rule 12"

This rule is concerned with the exercise of jurisdiction under ss.37 to 40 of the Act, see para.sc115.12.2 below. **sc115.2.2**

Assignment

By a practice note issued by Watkins L.J. on January 22, 1987, it was provided that all applications under RSC O.115 in the first instance should be made to the judge of the Crown Office List. By Practice Direction (Administrative Court: Establishment) [2001] 1 W.L.R. 1654, issued in July 2000, the Crown Office List was renamed the Administrative Court. Thereafter, proceedings which would have previously been issued in the Crown Office have been issued in the Administrative Court. **sc115.2.3**

"shall be exercised by a judge"

Formerly, various provisions in O.115 stated that hearings were to be "in chambers". Now, the CPR provide that, as a general rule, hearings should be in public but, in certain circumstances, may be "in private"; see, generally, CPR r.39.2. Accordingly, amendments have been made in O.115; see, in addition to r.2, r.25(1). **sc115.2.4**

Title of proceedings

2A. An application made in accordance with CPR Part 23, or a claim form issued in relation to proceedings under this Part of this order shall be entitled in the matter of the defendant, naming him, and in the matter of the Act, and all subsequent documents in the matter shall be so entitled. **sc115.2A**

Originating process

Formerly, proceedings under RSC O.115 were commenced by originating motion. Where previously the originating process was in the form of an originating motion the rules in O.115 now provide that a claim form shall be used (see rr.2B(1), 3(1), 7(2), 17(2), 26(1)(3), and 33(2)). **sc115.2A.1**

A claim form under Pt 8 should therefore be used to commence any proceedings under O.115. Any subsequent application against, or in relation to the same defendant should be made by application notice issued in accordance with Pt 23 subject to any specific provision in O.115 in relation to the particular application in question.

Provisions in O.115 making express reference to application notices and Pt 23 are: rr.2B(1), 5(1), 6(1), 7(1), 8(3) and (5), 9(1), 10, 11(1), 11A(1), 13, 14, 15(1), 18, 23(e), 28(1) and (3) 29, 30 and 34.

Application for confiscation order

2B.—(1) An application by the prosecutor for a confiscation order under section 19 shall be made in accordance with CPR Part 23, where there have been proceedings against the defendant in the High Court, and shall otherwise be made by the issue of a claim form. **sc115.2B**

(2) The application shall be supported by a witness statement or affidavit giving full particulars of the following matters—

(a) the grounds for believing that the defendant has died or absconded;
(b) the date or approximate date on which the defendant died or absconded;
(c) where the application is made under section 19(2), the offence or offences of which the defendant was convicted, and the date and place of conviction;
(d) where the application is made under section 19(4), the proceedings which have been initiated against the defendant (including particulars of the offence and the date and place of institution of those proceedings); and
(e) where the defendant is alleged to have absconded, the steps taken to contact him.

(3) The prosecutor's statement under section 11 shall be exhibited to the witness statement or affidavit and shall include the following particulars—
(a) the name of the defendant;
(b) the name of the person by whom the statement is given;
(c) such information known to the prosecutor as is relevant to the determination whether the defendant has benefited from drug trafficking and to the assessment of the value of his proceeds of drug trafficking.

(4) Unless the court otherwise orders, a witness statement or affidavit under paragraph (2) may contain statements of information and belief, with their sources and grounds.

(5) The application and the witness statement or affidavit in support shall be served not less than 7 days before the date fixed for the hearing of the application on—
(a) the defendant (or on the personal representatives of a deceased defendant);
(b) any person who the prosecutor reasonably believes is likely to be affected by the making of a confiscation order; and
(c) the receiver, where one has been appointed in the matter.

"confiscation order"

sc115.2B.1 The expression "confiscation order" is a misnomer, as such an order is a financial order ordering a defendant convicted of a crime to pay a sum of money to the state; see *Norris (Clifford), Re* [2001] 1 W.L.R. 1388 (HL), *per* Lord Hobhouse. The amount to be recovered under a confiscation order shall be the amount the court assesses to be the value of the defendant's proceeds of crime (s.5(1)), unless the defendant shows that his assets are worth less than this amount (s.5(3)) in which case the confiscation order must be in this lesser amount (see *R. v Comiskey* (1991) 93 Cr.App.R. 227 and *R. v Barwick* [2001] 1 Cr.App.R.(S.) 445).

"under section 19"

sc115.2B.2 Under s.19 of the 1994 Act, the power of the High Court to make a confiscation order is restricted to the cases (1) of a defendant (charged with a drug trafficking offence) who absconds for a period of two years (whether convicted or not) and (2) of a defendant who is convicted of a drug trafficking offence but who dies before the Crown Court can make a confiscation order. Sections 20 to 24 supplement s.19 and include power to vary a confiscation order made under s.19 (see s.21 and r.11A). The power now found in s.19 was introduced by the 1994 Act and rr.2B and 11A were added to O.115 when that Act came into force.

Application for restraint order or charging order

3.—(1) An application for a restraint order under section 26 or for a charging order under section 27 (to either of which may be joined an application for the appointment of a receiver) may be made by the prosecutor by the issue of a claim form notice of which need not be served on any other party. **sc115.3**

(2) An application under paragraph (1) shall be supported by a witness statement or affidavit, which shall—

(a) give the grounds for the application; and

(b) to the best of the witness's ability, give full particulars of the realisable property in respect of which the order is sought and specify the person or persons holding such property.

(3) Unless the court otherwise directs, a witness statement or affidavit under paragraph (2) may contain statements of information or belief with the sources and grounds thereof.

"restraint order ... charging order"

1994 Act—Under the 1994 Act, where a person is convicted of a drug trafficking offence in the Crown Court and the prosecutor requires it, the Court must carry out the function of establishing in what amount a confiscation order must be made. In general terms, it must be made in an amount equal to the lower of either i) the value of the defendant's proceeds of drug trafficking or ii) the value of his assets, including gifts caught by the Act (s.2(5)). **sc115.3.1**

1988 Act—Similarly, under the 1988 Act where the defendant is convicted of financial crime in the criminal court and the prosecutor requires it, the court must make a confiscation order in an amount calculated with similar ceilings. For an explanation of the provisions see *R. v Benjafield; R. v Rezvi* [2003] 1 A.C. 1099, HL.

The powers conferred on the High Court by s.26 and s.27 of the 1994 Act or ss.77 and 78 of the 1988 Act are exercisable where (a) proceedings have been instituted in England and Wales against the defendant, (b) the proceedings have not been concluded (see s.41 of the 1994 Act and s.102 of the 1988 Act for when proceedings are concluded), and (c) the court is satisfied that there is reasonable cause to believe that the defendant has benefited from the relevant crime. Those powers are also exercisable where the court is satisfied (a) that whether by the laying of an information or otherwise, a person is to be charged, and (b) that there is reasonable cause to believe that he has benefited from the relevant crime. Under s.26 of the 1994 Act or s.77 of the 1988 Act the High Court may make a restraint order prohibiting any person from dealing with any realisable property, subject to such conditions and exceptions as may be specified in the order (see further para.sc115.4.2 below). Under s.27 of the 1994 Act or s.78 of the 1988 Act the High Court may make a charging order on realisable property for securing payment to the Crown (a) where a confiscation order has not been made, of amount equal to the value from time to time of the property charged, and (b) in any other case, of an amount not exceeding the amount payable under the confiscation order.

If these conditions are satisfied, the court may, not must, make a restraint order. Whether to make such an order is a question of judicial discretion. The principles which govern that discretion are similar to those applicable to CPR Pt 25 freezing orders (*SFO v X* [2005] EWCA Civ 1564). In particular, the applicant must demonstrate a risk of dissipation of assets, otherwise the restraint order has no proper purpose and would amount to a disproportionate interference with property rights conferred by art.1 of protocol 1 of the European Convention on Human Rights (see *Jennings v CPS* [2006] 1 W.L.R. 182; *R v B* [2008] EWCA Crim 1374).

Appointment of a receiver

Both the 1994 Act and the 1988 Act provide the power for the High Court to ap- **sc115.3.2** point a receiver (1994 Act s.26(7) and 1988 Act s.77(8)). This power may also be exercised at any stage from when a person is to be charged with criminal proceedings. Such a receiver at this stage is to manage the property not to realise it (*P (Restraint Order; Sale of Assets), Re* [2000] 1 W.L.R. 473; [1999] 4 All E.R. 473). The Acts contain a seperate power to appoint receivers to realise assets after a confiscation order has been made following conviction (1994 Act s.29; 1988 Act s.80). See r.8 for consequences of appointment of a receiver.

Application to external confiscation orders and proceedings in designated countries

sc115.3.3 Under s.39 of the 1994 Act and s.96 of the 1988 Act, by Order in Council, subject to necessary modifications, the Acts may be applied to an *external confiscation order* (as defined in s.39(2) of the 1994 Act and s.96(2) of the 1988 Act) made by a court in a designated country and to proceedings which have been or are to be instituted in a designated country and may result in such order being made there. The principal Orders in Council are the Drug Trafficking Act 1994 (Designated Countries and Territories) Order 1996 (SI 1996/2880) and the Criminal Justice Act 1988 (Designated Countries and Territories) Order 1991 (SI 1991/2873) (see further paras sc115.12.2 and sc115.13.2 below).

Application to external forfeiture orders and proceedings in designated countries

sc115.3.4 Under r.21A, applications may be made for restraint ordes and charging orders and the appointment of receivers in support of *external forfeiture orders* made by courts of designated countries or where such an order may be made in proceedings in such countries as provided for by Order in Council made under the Criminal Justice (International Co-operation) Act 1990; see para.sc115.21A.1.

"realisable property"

sc115.3.5 Section 6 of the 1994 Act defines "realisable property" as meaning subject to certain exceptions set out in s.6, (a) any property held by the defendant, and (b) any property held by a person to whom the defendant has directly or indirectly made a gift caught by the Act (as to which see s.8).

Any such assets may be made subject to an order, e.g. *R. v Buckman* (1977) 1 Cr.App.R.(S.) 325, CA; *R. v Clark* [1997] 1 W.L.R. 557, CA; and *R. v Brett (Terence David), The Times*, October 13, 1997.

Application "supported by a witness statement or affidavit"

sc115.3.6 See also paras sc115.11A.2, sc115.15.3, sc115.26.2 and sc115.31.1. Under the CPR, the general rule is that evidence at hearings other than the trial is to be by witness statement unless the court, a practice direction or any other enactment requires otherwise (CPR r.32.6). As to form of witness statement, see CPR r.32.8. Evidence must be given by affidavit, instead of or in addition to, a witness statement if this is required by the court, a provision contained in any rule, a practice direction or any other enactment (CPR r.32.15(1)). The rules have been amended so as to provide that applications may be supported by witness statements or affidavits (see rr.2B(2), 3(2), 6(2), 7(3), 11(2), 11A, 14, 15(1), 18, 26(2), 28(3), 31(1) and 34). It may be doubted whether it was intended that throughout O.115 witness statements should be regarded as an acceptable alternative form of written evidence to affidavits; note 6 to Practice Direction (Written Evidence), para.1.4 (see 32PD.1) adds to the uncertainty. However, in practice, evidence in such cases (save in applications to commit for contempt of court) is given by witness statement.

Rule 3(3) re-states the rule that, unless the Court otherwise directs, the witness statement or affidavit may contain statements of information or belief provided the sources of information and grounds for belief are set out. The grounds for belief that a defendant has benefited from crime may, therefore, properly be stated by the deponent as being information received from police officers who are members of a drug squad that they have kept observation on the defendant's home and a description of the observations made by them. The obligation to give full and frank disclosure to the Court does not require the naming of individual police officers concerned or the precise times at which they kept observation (*Re A Defendant, Independent*, April 2, *1987*).

Rules 3(2) and 3(3) should not be regarded as an exhaustive list of matters which should be included in the evidence in support of a restraint, charging or receivership order under s.26 or s.27 of the 1994 Act or s.77 or s.78 of the 1988 Act. Wherever such an application is made without notice, the prosecutor is under a duty of full and frank disclosure to reveal matters which undermine the application. For the principles see *Jennings v CPS* [2006] 1 W.L.R. 182. There is now an example restraint order annexed to the Restraint Order practice direction (scpd115). It is suggested that if this restraint order is departed from, such departure is drawn to the Court's attention in the evidence in support of the application.

If the evidence is also in support of an application to appoint a management receiver, see *Capewell v Customs and Excise Commissioners* [2004] EWCA Civ 1628; [2005] All E.R. 900 where the Court of Appeal set out a "checklist" of requirements.

Practice

Applications for a restraint order under ss.25 and 26 of the 1994 Act or for a charging order under ss.25 to 27 should be made by claim form to a judge sitting in private (see rr.2 and 2B) and will be made without notice in the first instance by the prosecutor where there is reason to think that otherwise assets will be dissipated (see *Jennings v CPS* [2006] 1 W.L.R. 182). Such without notice applications are made on paper without an oral hearing. Any subsequent application should be by application notice. The application should be supported by written evidence dealing with all the matters listed in sub-paras (a) to (e) of para.(2) of this rule. Rules 2B and 3(1) are listed in Table 2 of Practice Direction (CPR Pt 8, Sch.1 and Sch.2 to CPR) (see para.8BPD.7). Consequently, s.B of that Practice Direction takes effect where claims are brought under r.2B and r.3(1) with the result that the Pt 8 procedure applies subject to any special or contrary provisions in O.115 and as modified in paras B.6 to B.15 of the Practice Direction. **sc115.3.7**

Committal for contempt

An application to commit a person for breach of restraining and charging orders relates to breach of an order made in civil proceedings; hence such applications must be made to a single judge and not to the Divisional Court (*Re H, The Times*, April 1, 1988, CA. See further CPR Sch.1, O.52 and O.45 for procedure and evidence in relation to contempt applications. **sc115.3.8**

Restraint order and charging order

4.—(1) A restraint order may be made subject to conditions and exceptions, including but not limited to conditions relating to the indemnifying of third parties against expenses incurred in complying with the order, and exceptions relating to living expenses and legal expenses of the defendant, but the prosecutor shall not be required to give an undertaking to abide by any order as to damages sustained by the defendant as a result of the restraint order. **sc115.4**

(2) Unless the court otherwise directs, a restraint order made where notice of it has not been served on any person shall have effect until a day which shall be fixed for the hearing where all parties may attend on the application and a charging order shall be an order to show cause, imposing the charge until such day.

(3) Where a restraint order is made the prosecutor shall serve copies of the order and of the witness statement or affidavit in support on the defendant and on all other named persons restrained by the order and shall notify all other persons or bodies affected by the order of its terms.

(4) Where a charging order is made the prosecutor shall serve copies of the order and of the witness statement or affidavit in support on the defendant and, where the property to which the order relates is held by another person, on that person and shall serve a copy of the order on such of the persons or bodies specified in CPR rule 73.5(1)(c) to (e) as shall be appropriate.

Effect of rule

See para.sc115.3.1 above. By r.23 this rule is applied to applications for restraint orders under the 1988 Act. **sc115.4.1**

Return date

sc115.4.2 A restraint order made without notice should normally be "until further order" not fix a return date on notice for the order to be continued (*Ahmed v Ahmed* July 21, 1998, unrep., CA). If a return date is fixed, it should not normally be more than 14 days after the order is made (see Practice Direction scpd 115.7).

Service of charging order nisi

sc115.4.3 The requirements of this order are similar to those of Sch.1, RSC O.50, r.2. Copies of the order and supporting affidavit or witness statement must be served on the defendant, and, where the property in question is governed or other stock, on the keeper of the register, or where the order relates to a fund in Court, on the Accountant General, or where the order relates to an interest under a trust, on such of the trustees as the Court may direct.

Restraint order

sc115.4.4 Under s.26 of the 1994 Act, or s.77 of the 1988 Act, the Court may make a restraint order prohibiting any person from dealing with any realisable property (as defined in s.6 of the 1994 Act of s.74 of the 1988 Act) subject to such conditions and exceptions as may be specified in the order.

The High Court's power to make a restraint order is not confined to making a restraint order against the prosecuted person, but against "any person", provided the person has any interest in the defendant's assets or is a recipient of a gift caught by the Act (s.26 of the 1994 Act; s.77 of the 1988 Act, combined with the definition of "realisable property" in s.6 of the 1994 Act or s.74 of the 1988 Act, and *Re G* [2001] EWHC Admin 606). However, to restrain a third party the prosecutor must demonstrate a "good arguable case" that the property is realisable property (*CPS v Compton* [2002] EWCA Civ 720). For the proper amount in which to restrain see the Practice Direction (scpd115.3).

A restraint order should normally permit a business to run (see scpd.115.6).

A restraint order may also restrain persons from dealing with assets outside the jurisdiction as the Acts apply to property wherever situated (1994 Act s.62(2); 1988 Act s.102(3)). If the person to be restrained is outside the jurisdiction of the Court (wherever the property is situated) then a restraint order may be made, but permission to serve the order outside the jurisdiction must be obtained pursuant to Pt 6.36 para.3.1 of 6PDB—Service Out of the Jurisdiction.

The Court's jurisdiction to make or vary restraint orders is closely analogous to its jurisdiction to make or vary "freezing injunctions" (formerly Mareva injunctions) (*Serious Fraud Office v X* [2005] EWCA Civ 1564). The object in each case is to strike a balance at the interlocutory stage between keeping the defendant's assets available to satisfy any confiscation order which may be made in the event of conviction, and meeting the defendant's reasonable requirements in the meantime (*Peters, Re* [1988] Q.B. 871). Accordingly, a restraint order ought not to be varied by providing for capitalisation of maintenance and school fees to enable the defendant to make a lump sum payment to his son, pursuant to a consent order in divorce proceedings, since such a provision involves the anticipatory discharge of future liabilities, thereby reducing the assets which may become available to satisfy any confiscation order (*Re Peters* [1988] Q.B. 871). Similar considerations apply to a restraint order as to a freezing injunction when the Court is determining whether sums should be released for specific purposes. Thus, where a defendant appeals against conviction for drugs offences and against a confiscation order for a large sum made at the conclusion of the trial, the Court has power to vary a restraint order made against him prior to his conviction so as to enable assets to be released to fund his appeal (*Customs Excise Commissioners v Norris* [1991] 2 Q.B. 293; [1991] 2 All E.R. 395, CA), even though community funding may be available (*In the matter of William Briggs-Price* [2006] EWCA Civ 1477).

In the exercise of its jurisdiction to make a restraint order the Court has an inherent power to make ancillary orders to ensure that the exercise of its jurisdiction is effective to achieve its purpose (*In Re O* [1991] 2 Q.B. 520, CA, power to order disclosure of assets; *DPP v Scarlett* [2000] 1 W.L.R. 515, CA, ancillary order requiring defendant to repatriate moneys in foreign bank account).

A restraint order, however, is not in all respects equivalent to a freezing injunction. There is no jurisdiction either under the statute or the Court's inherent jurisdiction to provide for the payment of compensation to innocent third parties (sc.115.4(1)). A landlord who has not been given notice that his tenant's assets are subject to a restraint order seeking to distrain on machinery and premises demised to the tenant in respect of rent which is due, is entitled to determine the lease but is not entitled to keep the proceeds of the realisation of any property subject to the restraint order (*Re R. (Restraint Order)* [1990] Q.B. 307; [1990] 2 All E.R. 569).

Where a restraint order is made and expressed to be subject to an exception related to the defendant's legal expenses, it is proper for the order to direct assessment of his legal costs after verdict. However, despite the close analogy to freezing injunctions, restraint orders are not required to stipulate a fixed or maximum sum for such costs (*Re P. and Re W., The Times*, April 11, 1990, CA). It may also be appropriate to permit the prosecutor to police the amount of legal costs and insist on an assessment (*L (Restraint Order: Legal Costs), Re, The Times*, July 10, 1996, Latham J.). In order to obtain an exception to a restraint order to pay legal expenses, the defendant must show that it is just to do so. The Court is not bound to vary the order if there are other assets which could be used to pay legal expenses (*Serious Fraud Office v X* [2005] EWCA Civ 1564).

Although neither the 1994 Act nor the 1988 Act contains any express provision empowering the Court to order a defendant to make full disclosure of all his assets, there is (as referred to above) inherent in the statutes a power to make any order necessary to make a restraint order effective, including a power to order a defendant to make such disclosure. This power, however, is discretionary and is exercisable subject to certain conditions and exceptions. The Acts do not abrogate the common law rule against self-incrimination and hence it will be appropriate to make any such disclosure under subject to the condition that any disclosure made thereunder may not be used in criminal proceedings against the defendant or his spouse (*O. (Disclosure Order), Re* [1991] 2 Q.B. 520, CA). Such a disclosure order may be made against any person not just the prosecuted defendant (*D (Restraint Order: Non Party), Re, The Times*, January 26, 1995, Turner J). The provisions of the Acts which confer jurisdiction on the Court to make restraint and charging orders are civil in character and any appeal from a judge's order made thereunder lies properly to the Civil Division of the Court of Appeal (*Re O (ibid.)*).

In the absence of agreement to the contrary, a bank has a common law right to combine different accounts held by the same customer in order to establish the overall indebtedness of the bank to the customer, or the customer to the bank. The exercise by the bank of this right of combination, or any contractual right of set-off, did not constitute a disposal or diminution of the assets of the customer or a breach of a restraint order (*Re K. (Restraint Order)* [1990] 2 All E.R. 562).

In an early case in the jurisdiction, the High Court held that a restraint order should never be varied to enable a third party judgment creditor to be paid (*W, Re. The Times*, November 15, 1990; *Independent*, November 26, 1990 (C.S.)). However in *X (Restraint Order; Variation), Re* [2004] 3 W.L.R. 906, Davis J held that *W, Re* was wrongly decided and that the High Court had a discretion to vary a restraint order in such circumstances. It is thought that *Re X* is to be preferred. There is obiter support for such a preference in *Serious Fraud Office v Lexi Holdings Plc* [2008] EWCA Crim 1443.

Application to commit for contempt for breach of order

See note at para.sc115.3.10. **sc115.4.5**

Discharge or variation of order

5.—(1) Any person or body on whom a restraint order or a charging order is served or who is notified of such an order may make an application in accordance with CPR Part 23 to discharge or vary the order. **sc115.5**

(2) The application notice and any witness statement or affidavit in support shall be lodged with the court and served on the prosecutor and, where he is not the applicant, on the defendant, not less than two clear days before the date fixed for the hearing of the application.

(3) Upon the court being notified that proceedings for the offences have been concluded or that the amount, payment of which is secured by a charging order has been paid into court, any restraint order or charging order, as the case may be, shall be discharged.

(4) The court may also discharge a restraint order or a charging order upon receiving notice from the prosecutor that it is no longer appropriate for the restraint order or the charging order to remain in place.

Effect of rule

sc115.5.1 After its incorporation in CPR, Sch.1, minor amendments were made to this rule by the Civil Procedure (Amendment) Rule 1999 (SI 1999/1008), r.59(a) for the purpose of correcting mistakes in para.(2).

This rule is confined to the discharge or variation of a restraint order or a charging order. As to the discharge or variation of a confiscation order made under s.19 and r.2B, see r.11A below.

It is only necessary to issue an application under this provision if agreement cannot be reached with the prosecutor (and any other interested party). If agreement can be reached, then the restraint order may be varied under the terms of the original order (if it is made in such a way which allows agreement to be reached without application to the Court). Even if the restraint order does not allow variation to it by agreement between the parties, an application under Pt 23 is unnecessary if the parties are agreed on the terms of the variation. In such a case, a consent order can be drawn up, signed by the parties and sent to the Court under Pt 40.

If a third party (i.e. a person not being prosecuted) applies to vary a restraint order on the grounds that the property is not realisable property (i.e. not property in which the prosecuted defendant has any interest and the third party is not in receipt of a gift caught by the Act), the court should apply the "good arguable case" test (*CPS v Compton* [2003] EWCA Civ 720; *The Times*, December 11, 2002 (CA)). Alternatively, the Court could decide to order a trial of the issue in accordance with the principles set out in *SCF Finance v Masri* [1985] 1 W.L.R. 876.

"Proceedings ... concluded"

sc15.5.2 Proceedings are not concluded until the confiscation order is paid or no confiscation order is made (1994 Act s.41(3); 1988 Act s.102(12)). In practice, when proceedings are concluded, the prosecutor will write to the court which then makes an order discharging the retraint order.

Further application by prosecutor

sc115.6 6.—(1) Where a restraint order or a charging order has been made the prosecutor may apply by an application in accordance with CPR Part 23 with notice or, where the case is one of urgency or the giving of notice would cause a reasonable apprehension of dissipation of assets, without notice—

(a) to vary such order; or
(b) for a restraint order or a charging order in respect of other realisable property; or
(c) for the appointment of a receiver.

(2) An application under paragraph (1) shall be supported by a witness statement or affidavit which, where the application is for a restraint order or a charging order, shall to the best of the witness's ability give full particulars of the realisable property in respect of which the order is sought and specify the person or persons holding such property.

(3) The application and witness statement or affidavit in support shall be lodged with the court and served on the defendant and, where one has been appointed in the matter, on the receiver, not less than two clear days before the date fixed for the hearing of the application.

(4) Rule 4(3) and (4) shall apply to the service of restraint orders and charging orders respectively made under this rule on persons other than the defendant.

Effect of rule

After its incorporation in CPR Sch.1, a minor amendment was made to this rule by the Civil Procedure (Amendment) Rule 1999 (SI 1999/1008) r.59(b) for the purpose of correcting a mistake in para.(3). **sc115.6.1**

"application ... without notice"

Formerly, this rule provided that, in case of urgency application could be made ex parte. Throughout the CPR, "without notice", or some other phrase to similar effect, is preferred to "ex parte". Other rules similarly amended in O.115 are: rr.13, 27(2), 28(1) and 30. For urgent applications without notice generally, see CPR Pts 23 and 25. **sc115.6.2**

Realisation of property

7.—(1) An application by the prosecutor under section 29 shall, where there have been proceedings against the defendant in the High Court, be made by an application in accordance with CPR Part 23 and shall otherwise be made by the issue of a claim form. **sc115.7**

(2) The application notice or claim form, as the case may be, shall be served with the evidence in support not less than 7 days before the date fixed for the hearing of the application or claim on—

(a) the defendant;

(b) any person holding any interest in the realisable property to which the application relates; and

(c) the receiver, where one has been appointed in the matter.

(3) The application shall be supported by a witness statement or affidavit, which shall, to the best of the witness's ability, give full particulars of the realisable property to which it relates and specify the person or persons holding such property, and a copy of the confiscation order, of any certificate issued by the Crown Court under section 5(2) and of any charging order made in the matter shall be exhibited to such witness statement or affidavit.

(4) The Court may, on an application under section 29—

(a) exercise the power conferred by section 30(2) to direct the making of payments by a receiver;

(b) give directions in respect of the property interests to which the application relates; and

(c) make declarations in respect of those interests.

"application ... under section 29"

Pursuant to r.23 this rule also applies to applications under s.80 of the 1988 Act to appoint a receiver. **sc115.7.1**

Section 29 states that, where a confiscation order (a) has been made under the Act, (b) is not satisfied, and (c) is not subject to appeal, the High Court may, on an application by the prosecutor, appoint a receiver in respect of realisable property and exercise certain other powers in respect of such receivership. As para.(4) of this rule states, in addition the Court may exercise powers conferred by s.30 concerning the application of proceeds of realisation and other sums in the hands of a receiver. Section 80 of the 1988 Act is to similar effect.

The application notice or claim form must be served on, in addition to the defendant, any person holding an interest in the realisable property (r.7(2)(b)). Section 29(8) of the Act s.80(8) of the 1988 Act, provides that a reasonable opportunity must be given for persons holding any interest in the property to make representations to the Court. As to the assertion of an interest by a third party, see *Re Norris* [2001] UKHL 34; [2001] 1 W.L.R. 1388, HL (third party not precluded from asserting interest before High Court by reason of having previously given evidence in criminal proceedings when confiscation order made).

On application under s.29 of the 1994 Act or s.80 of the 1988 Act, the Court is bound to apply the mandatory statutory language of s.31 of the 1994 Act or s.82 of the 1988 Act. These require the Court to exercise its powers to protect the bona fide property rights of third parties who have not been convicted and are not the recipient of gifts caught by the Act; but subject to that the Court must exercise its powers with a view to satisfying any confiscation that has been made. In practice, therefore the High Court is pointed strongly towards appointing a receiver in all cases where an amount is outstanding on a confiscation order, subject to the rights and interests of third parties (see for example *MN & HN* [2005] EWHC 2987 (Admin)). The delay principles enshrined in art.6 of the European Convention on Human Rights apply to an application to appoint a receiver. If there has been unreasonable delay in breach of art.6, this does not justify, in itself, a refusal to appoint a receiver as the court must consider in every case the appropriate remedy for the delay. An appropriate remedy may be for example public pronouncement of the breach, but nonetheless the appointment of a receiver. See *CPS v Bentham* [2005] EWHC 2013 (Admin) where this course was taken and the principles were explained. In an extreme case, however the court may refuse to appoint a receiver; or, if one is appointed yet substantial delays in enforcement occur, the court may exercise its powers to strike out the proceedings (*Re F* [2007] EWHC 2874 Admin).

Generally a third party's rights are confined to protection of property rights. However, the Acts do not override the family court's jurisdiction uner the Matrimonial Causes Act 1973. Therefore in an appropriate case, the Court can order the transfer of the convicted person's property to his spouse under the 1973 Act even if that reduces the assets over which a receiver may be appointed (*HM Customs and Excise v MCA* [2003] Fam. 55 (CA)). The court will not normally, however, transfer property which represents the proceeds of crime to the innocent spouse, particularly where the proposed transferee is aware of its source (*CPS v Richards* [2006] EWCA Civ 849). Procedurally, the same judge should hear both matters. Therefore any family proceedings should be transferred to the Family Division of the High Court and heard with the confiscation matters by a judge authorised to sit in the Family Division and the Administrative Court (see *W&H v HM Customs and Excise* [2004] EWHC 526 (Fam/Admin where Munby J. also gave guidelines on the form of order which should be made on transfer to the Family Division).

For the remuneration and expenses of a receiver appointed to realise assets, see para.sc115.8.2.

"certificate issued ... under section 5(2)"

sc115.7.2 This provision states that if the Crown Court, in making a confiscation order, is satisfied as to any matter relevant for determining the amount that might be realised at the time of the order it may, and in certain circumstances shall, issue a certificate giving the court's opinion as to those matters.

Application to external confiscation orders and proceedings in designated countries

sc115.7.3 Section 29 of the 1994 Act and s.80 of the 1988 Act are modified by the Orders in Council referred to in para.sc115.3.3.

Practice

sc115.7.4 Applications under r.7 should be made by claim form if there are no proceedings against the defendant (for example a restraint order) otherwise the prosecutor should commence the application by application notice. The application should be supported by written evidence dealing with all the matters stated in para.(3) of this rule. Rule 7(1) is listed in Table 2 of Practice Direction (CPR Pt 8, Sch.1 and Sch.2 to CPR) (see para.8BPD.7). Consequently, Section B of that Practice Direction takes effect where application is made by claim form with the result that the Pt 8 procedure applies subject to any special or contrary provisions in O.115 and as modified in paras B.6 to B.15 of the Practice Direction. See also para.sc115.3.9 above.

Receivers

sc115.8 8.—(1) Subject to the provisions of this rule, the provisions of CPR Part 69 shall apply where a receiver is appointed in pursuance of a charging order or under sections 26 or 29.

(2) Where the receiver proposed to be appointed has been ap-

pointed receiver in other proceedings under the Act, it shall not be necessary for a witness statement or affidavit of fitness to be sworn or for the receiver to give security, unless the court otherwise orders.

(3) Where a receiver has fully paid the amount payable under the confiscation order and any sums remain in his hands, he shall make an application to the court for directions in accordance with CPR Part 23, as to the distribution of such sums.

(4) An application under paragraph (3) shall be served with any evidence in support not less than 7 days before the date fixed for the hearing of the application on—

(a) the defendant; and

(b) any other person who held property realised by the receiver.

(5) A receiver may apply for an order to discharge him from his office by making an application in accordance with CPR Part 23, which shall be served, together with any evidence in support, on all persons affected by his appointment not less than 7 days before the day fixed for the hearing of the application.

Effect of rule

Applications under Pt 23 are made on application notice. By r.23 this rule is applied to applications to appoint a receiver under s.77 or s.80 of the 1988 Act. **sc115.8.1**

"where a receiver is appointed"

A distinction must be drawn between a receiver appointed under s.26 of the 1994 Act or s.77 of the 1988 Act on one hand (a management receiver) and one appointed unders.29 of the 1994 Act or s.80 of the 1988 Act on the other (an enforcement receiver). **sc115.8.2**

A management receiver may be appointed before the making of a confiscation order to manage and preserve the relevant assets. Such a receiver's task is not to realise the assets but to preserve them from dissipation (*Re P (Restraint Order) (Sale of Assets)* [2000] 1 W.L.R. 473; [1999] 4 All E.R. 473). As the defendant at this stage is unconvicted the court should carefully balance the interests of the preservation of the property against the interests of the defendant, particularly the costs of the receivership (*Capewell v Customs and Excise Commissioners* [2004] EWCA Civ 1628, where guidance was also given on the evidence in support of a management receiver and to such receivers on their reporting and accounting functions). A management receiver should be paid out of the assets over which he is appointed (*Hughes v Customs and Excise Commissioners* [2002] EWCA Civ 734). The issue in *Hughes* was re-argued in *Capewellv Revenue and Customs Commissioners* [2007] UKHL 2; [2007] 1 W.L.R. 386, HL, following the implementation of Pt 69 of the CPR which is applied in part to receivers appointed under the confiscation legislation by r.8(1). The House of Lords reached the same conclusion as in *Hughes* explaining that the assets within a management receivership are liable for payment of the receiver's remuneration and expenses. These should be distinguished from the "receiver's costs", an expression which should be confined in meaning to litigation costs. There is no power for the court to order that a receiver's remuneration and expenses should be paid by any party to the proceedings, in particular the prosecutor/claimant. An order for the appointment of a management receiver without notice should normally limit the functions of the receiver to that which is urgently necessary. Further powers should be applied for by the receiver on notice (see the Practice Direction scpd 115.8).

Where a receiver is appointed as an enforcement receiver, different considerations apply. The defendant is convicted and a confiscation order has been made. The receiver's task is to realise the assets. Section 31 of the 1994 Act or s.82 of the 1988 Act normally requires a receiver to be appointed, subject to recognition by the court of innocent third party interests in the property (see *MN & HM* [2005] EWHC 2987 (Admin) and see *Norris, Re* [2001] UKHL 34; [2001] 1 W.L.R. 1388).

Section 81 of the 1988 Act and s.30 of the 1994 Act require a receiver appointed to enforce a confiscation order to pay the proceeds of realisation to the magistrates' court. The confiscation order liability against the defendant is reduced by the amount so paid. A question arises as to the incidence of receivership remuneration and expenses. Generally, the structure of s.81/s.30 is that the magistrates' court pays the receiver's remuneration and expenses out of the sums paid to it by the receiver after reduction of the defendant's confiscation liability. In this way receivership expenses are not an additional burden on the defendant. However, the court has a discretion when appointing a receiver (or on later application) to direct that the receiver should pay his own remuneration and expenses before applying an amount in payment of the confiscation order (s.81(1) of the 1988 Act/s.30(1) of the 1994 Act). This discretion might be exercised if a defendant has sufficient assets to pay both the confiscation order and receivership remuneration and expenses (see *MN and HN* [2005] EWHC 2982 (Admin)). In order for the receiver to pay himself first, there must be a clear direction under s.81(1)/s.30(1) (*Hansford v Southampton magistrates' court* [2008] EWHC 67 (Admin)). Where a receiver is appointed as a management receiver before a confiscation order is made, the normal order is that receivership remuneration and expenses is payable out of the assets on a regular basis, normally every three months (see the reference to *Hughes* and *Capewell* (above)). Where such an order is made and then a confiscation order is made and the receiver is given powers to realise assets to pay the order, the original order for the payment of remuneration and expenses will operate as a direction under s.81(1) of the 1988 Act/s.30(1) of the 1994 Act, thus authorising the receiver to pay his costs and expenses before paying the confiscation order (*In Re A* [2008] EWCA Civ 573).

A receiver (whether management or enforcement) may be appointed over assets held in the name of a company, even where the company is not prosecuted. This may depend upon the lifting of the corporate veil; which the court will do in an appropriate case, for example where the company has been used to perpetuate a fraud (*HM Customs and Excise and H and others* [1996] 2 All E.R. 391 (CA); *CPS v Compton* [2002] EWCA Civ 720; *The Times* December 11, 2002 (CA)).

Application to external confiscation orders and proceedings in designated countries

sc115.8.3 Sections 26 to 29 of the 1994 Act and s.77 of the 1988 Act are modified by the Orders in Council referred to in para.sc115.3.3 above.

Certificate of inadequacy

sc115.9 9.—(1) The defendant or a receiver appointed under section 26 or 29or in pursuance of a charging order may apply in accordance with CPR Part 23 for a certificate under section 17(1).

(2) An application under paragraph (1) shall be served with any supporting evidence not less than 7 days before the date fixed for the hearing of the application on the prosecutor and, as the case may be, on either the defendant or the receiver (where one has been appointed).

"certificate under section 17(1)"

sc115.9.1 This rule is applied to applications for a certificate of inadequacy under s.83 of the 1988 Act by virtue of r.23.

These sections state that, if on the application by the defendant in respect of a confiscation order, the High Court is satisfied that the realisable property is indequate for the payment of any amount remaining to be recovered under the order, the court shall issue a certificate to that effect, giving the court's reasons. The obtaining of such a certificate does not, by itself, effect a reduction in the confiscation order. To do so the defendant must return to the Crown Court, armed with his certificate.

An application for a certificate of inadequacy is not an opportunity to appeal against the reasoning behind the making of the confiscation order. To obtain a certificate the defendant must accept the findings of the Crown Court and then demonstrate what has happened to his realisable property since the confiscation order was made (*Gokal v Serious Fraud Office* [2001] EWCA Civ 368; *O'Donoghue* [2004] EWCA Civ 1800; *Farwell, Re [2003] EWCA Civ 1608, McKinsley v CPS* [2006] EWCA Civ 1092; [2006] 1 W.L.R. 3420 and *Telli v Revenue and Customs Prosecutions Office* [2007] EWCA Civ 1385).

A defendant does not have to realise all assets he has in order to be granted a certificate (*E v Revenue and Customs Prosecution Office* [2006] EWHC 2154).

Certificate under section 16

9A. An application under section 16(2) (increase in realisable property) shall be served with any supporting evidence not less than 7 days before the date fixed for the hearing of the application on the defendant and, as the case may be, on either the prosecutor or (where one has been appointed in the matter) on the receiver. sc115.9A

Compensation

10. An application for an order under section 18 shall be made in accordance with CPR Part 23, which shall be served, with any supporting evidence, on the person alleged to be in default and on the relevant authority under section 18(5) not less than 7 days before the date fixed for the hearing of the application. sc115.10

"application ... under section 18"

This section states that, if proceedings are instituted against a person for a drug trafficking offence and he is not convicted, or if convicted his conviction is quashed or he is pardoned, the High Court may on an application by a person who held property which was realisable property, order compensation to be paid to the applicant. See also r.29. sc115.10.1

"person ... in default"

See s.19(4). sc.115.10.2

"the relevant authority"

The relevant authority under s.18 of the 1994 Act is, if the appropriate police force, or, if he is a member of the Crown Prosecution Service, the Director of Public Prosecutions, or, if he is an officer within the meaning of the Customs and Excise Management Act 1979, the Commissioners of Customs and Excise. sc115.10.3

Disclosure of information

11.—(1) An application by the prosecutor under section 59 shall be made in accordance with CPR Part 23 and the application notice shall state the nature of the order sought and whether material sought to be disclosed is to be disclosed to a receiver appointed under section 26 or 29 or in pursuance of a charging order or to a person mentioned in section 59(8). sc115.11

(2) The application notice and witness statement or affidavit in support shall be served on the authorised Government Department in accordance with Order 77, rule 4 not less than 7 days before the date fixed for the hearing of the application.

(3) The witness statement or affidavit in support of an application under paragraph (1) shall state the grounds for believing that the conditions in section 59(4) and, if appropriate, section 59(7) are fulfilled.

"application ... under section 59"

This section provides a procedure which may lead to the disclosure of material held by a government department in cases where it would be possible for the High Court to make a restraint order under ss.25 to 28 or a charging order under s.6. An order requiring production to the High Court may be made without a hearing of an officer of the department holding the material being allowed. However, a further order for the disclosure of the material (e.g. to a receiver) may not be made unless the department concerned has been given an opportunity to make representations. sc115.11.1

Application "supported by a witness statement or affidavit"

sc115.11.2 See para.sc115.3.8 above.

Compensation for, discharge and variation of confiscation order

sc115.11A 11A.—(1) An application under section 21, 22 or 23 shall be made in accordance with CPR Part 23 which, together with any evidence in support, shall be lodged with the court and served on the prosecutor not less than 7 days before the day fixed for the hearing of the application.

(2) Notice shall also be served on any receiver appointed in pursuance of a charging order or under section 26 or 29.

(3) An application for an order under section 22 shall be supported by a witness statement or affidavit giving details of—

(a) the confiscation order made under section 19(4);
(b) the acquittal of the defendant;
(c) the realisable property held by the defendant; and
(d) the loss suffered by the applicant as a result of the confiscation order.

(4) An application for an order under section 23 shall be supported by a witness statement or affidavit giving details of—

(a) the confiscation order made under section 19(4);
(b) the date on which the defendant ceased to be an absconder;
(c) the date on which proceedings against the defendant were instituted and a summary of the steps taken in the proceedings since then; and
(d) any indication given by the prosecutor that he does not intend to proceed against the defendant.

(5) An application made under section 21 shall be supported by a witness statement or affidavit giving details of—

(a) the confiscation order made under section 19(4);
(b) the circumstances in which the defendant ceased to be an absconder; and
(c) the amounts referred to in section 21(2).

(6) Where an application is made for an order under section 23(3) or 24(2)(b), the witness statement or affidavit shall also include—

(a) details of the realisable property to which the application relates; and
(b) details of the loss suffered by the applicant as a result of the confiscation order.

(7) Unless the court otherwise orders, a witness statement or affidavit under paragraphs (3) to (6) may contain statements of information and belief, with the sources and grounds thereof.

"under section 21, 22 or 23"

sc115.11A.1 Under s.19 of the Act, the High Court may make a confiscation order in restricted circumstances (see para.sc115.2B.2 above). One circumstance is where a defendant (charged with a drug trafficking offence) has absconded. Sections 21, 22 and 23 supplement s.19 where a confiscation order has been made in this circumstance and, provide, respectively, for the variation of a confiscation order where a defendant has ceased to be an absconder, and for the discharge of an order and compensation where an absconder returns.

Exercise of powers under sections 37 and 40

sc115.12 12. The powers conferred on the High Court by sections 37 and 40 may be exercised by a judge or a Master of the Queen's Bench Division.

Effect of rule

Formerly, this rule stated that the powers conferred on the High Court judge were to be exercised "in chambers". When O.115 was re-enacted in CPR Sch.1, "in private" was substituted for "in chambers" and, subsequently, by Civil Procedure (Amendment) Rule 1999 (SI 1999/1008) r.59(b), the substitution was excised. The result is that, in a given case, the question whether a judge or a master should sit in public or in private when exercising these powers is to be resolved according to the general rules (see CPR r.39.2). **sc115.12.1**

"powers conferred ... by sections 37 and 40"

This rule also applies to section 97 of the 1988 Act by virtue of r.23. **sc115.12.2**

The exercise of jurisdiction provided for by r.2 is subject to this rule.

Section 37 enables provision to be made by Order in Council for the registration in the High Court and the enforcement in England and Wales of orders made in Scotland in connection with the confiscation of the proceeds of drug trafficking under the Criminal Justice (Scotland) Act 1987 Pt I. The relevant Order in Council is the Drug Trafficking Offences (Enforcement in England and Wales) Order 1988 (SI 1988/593).

Section 40 of the 1994 Act and s.97 of the 1988 Act state that, on an application made by or on behalf of the Government of a designated country, the High Court may register an external confiscation order made there. Such an order is an order made by a court in a country designated by Order in Council made under s.39 of the 1994 Act or s.96 of the 1988 Act for the purpose of recovering payments or other rewards received in connection with the relevant crime or their value (see s.39 of the 1994 Act or s.96 of the 1988 Act). The principal relevant orders are the The Drug Trafficking Act 1994 (Designated Countries and Territories) Order 1996 (SI 1996/2880) and the Criminal Justice Act 1988 (Designated Countries and Territories) Order 1991 (SI 1991/2873). For the registration and enforcement of external forfeiture orders, see r.21A below.

Procedural effect of Orders in Council made under sections 37 and 40

It should be noted that r.21 says that rr.12 to 20 of this Order shall have effect subject to the provisions of the Orders in Council made under s.37 and s.40. **sc115.12.3**

Application for registration

13. An application for registration of an order specified in an Order in Council made under section 37 or of an external confiscation order under section 40(1) may be made in accordance with CPR Part 23, and may be made without notice. **sc115.13**

"order specified in an Order in Council"

The relevant Orders in Council are the Drug Trafficking Offences (Enforcement in England and Wales) Order 1988 (SI 1988/593) and the Proceeds of Crime (Scotland) Act (Enforcement of Scottish Confiscation Orders in England and Wales) Order 2001 (SI 2001/953). Article 4 of this Order provides, inter alia, that certain orders made by the Scottish Court of Session under the Criminal Justice (Scotland) Act 1987 Pt I, including for example restraint orders, shall be registered in the High Court if application for registration is made in accordance with the relevant rules of court (including r.12 below). Article 3 provides that, upon such registration of a Scottish order, it may be enforced by the High Court as if it had originally been made in that court, providing it is done in accordance with the provisions of the 1988 or 2001 Order mentioned above and any rules of court relating to enforcement. **sc115.13.1**

"external confiscation order"

External confiscation orders are provided for by the Drug Trafficking Act 1994 (Designated Countries and Territories) Order (SI 1996/2880) made under s.39 of the 1994 Act, see para.sc115.12.2 above. Section 40(1) of the 1994 Act and s.97 of the 1988 Act says that, on an application, the High Court may register an external confiscation order made in a designated country if (a) it is satisfied that at the time of registration the order is in force and not subject to appeal (see further s.40(2)), (b) it is satisfied, where the person against whom the order is made did not appear in the proceedings, that he received notice of the proceedings in sufficient time to enable him to defend them; and (c) it is of the opinion that enforcing the order in England and Wales would **sc115.13.2** not be contrary to the interests of justice. An external confiscation order can be registered even if it is an order made *in rem* in foreign civil proceedings (*Re S.L.* [1995] 3 W.L.R. 830 (CA)).

External forfeiture orders

sc115.13.3 By virtue of r.21A, external forfeiture orders may also be registered, see para.sc115.21A.2 below.

Application for registration

sc115.13.4 In most applications to register it will be unnecessary to refer in detail to the jurisprudence on art.6 of the Convention (*Government of the United States of America v Montgomery (No.2)* [2004] 1 W.L.R. 2241, HL (application of "fugitive disentitlement doctrine" in proceedings in American court not making it unjust to register that court's confiscation order)).

An application for registraion cannot be defended by seeking to re-litigate facts already found against the defendant in the foreign proceedings (*Quattrocchi, Re* [2004] EWCA Civ 40).

Evidence in support of application under section 37

sc115.14 14. An application for registration of an order specified in an Order in Council made under section 37 must be made in accordance with CPR Part 23, and be supported by a witness statement or affidavit—

(i) exhibiting the order or a certified copy thereof, and

(ii) stating, to the best of the witness's knowledge, particulars of what property the person against whom the order was made holds in England and Wales, giving the source of the witness's knowledge.

"Order in Council made under section 37"

sc115.14.1 See para.sc115.12.3 above.

Evidence in support of application under section 40(1)

sc115.15 15.—(1) An application for registration of an external confiscation order must be made in accordance with CPR Part 23, and be supported by a witness statement or affidavit—

(a) exhibiting the order or a verified or certified or otherwise duly authenticated copy thereof and, where the order is not in the English language, a translation thereof into English certified by a notary public or authenticated by witness statement or affidavit, and

(b) stating—

(i) that the order is in force and is not subject to appeal;

(ii) where the person against whom the order was made did not appear in the proceedings, that he received notice thereof in sufficient time to enable him to defend them;

(iii) in the case of money, either that at the date of the application the sum payable under the order has not been paid or the amount which remains unpaid, as may be appropriate, or, in the case of other property, the property which has not been recovered; and

(iv) to the best of the witness's knowledge, particulars of what property the person against whom the order was made holds in England and Wales, giving the source of the witness's knowledge.

(2) Unless the court otherwise directs, a witness statement or affidavit for the purposes of this rule may contain statements of information or belief with the sources and grounds thereof.

Proof of certification

The Drug Trafficking Act 1994 (Designated Countries and Territories) Order 1990 (SI 1996/2880) arts 4 and 5 makes special provision for the proof of any order made or judgment given by a court in a designated country and for the certification of various matters arising in the proceedings in that country which may be relevant to registration in the High Court. **sc115.15.1**

Application "supported by a witness statement or affidavit"

See also para.sc115.3.8 above. **sc115.15.2**

Register of orders

16.—(1) There will be kept in the Central Office at the Royal Courts of Justice in London under the direction of the Master of the Administrative Court a register of the orders registered under the Act. **sc115.16**

(2) There shall be included in such register particulars of any variation or setting aside of a registration and of any execution issued on a registered order.

Notice of registration

17.—(1) Notice of the registration of an order must be served on the person against whom it was obtained by delivering it to that person personally or by sending it to that person's usual or last known address or place of business or in such other manner as the court may direct. **sc115.17**

(2) Permission is not required to serve a notice out of the jurisdiction and CPR rules 6.40, 6.42 and 6.46 shall apply in relation to such a notice as they apply in relation to a claim form.

History of rule

Amended by SI 2000/221 and SI 2008/2178. **sc115.17.1**

Application to vary or set aside registration

18. An application made in accordance with CPR Part 23 by the person against whom an order was made to vary or set aside the registration of an order must be made to a judge and be supported by witness statement or affidavit. **sc115.18**

Statutory provisions

Section 40 of the 1994 Act states that the High Court shall cancel the registration of an external confiscation order if it appears to the court that the order has been satisfied by payment of the amount due under it or by the person against whom it was made serving imprisonment in default of payment or by other means. The Criminal Justice (International Co-operation) Act 1990 (Enforcement of Overseas Forfeiture Orders) (Scotland) Order 1999 art.10(3) says that the court shall cancel the registration of an external forfeiture order in similar circumstances. See also, in relation to Scottish orders, the Drug Trafficking Offences (Enforcement in England and Wales) Order 1988. **sc115.18.1**

Enforcement of order

19.—(2) If an application is made under rule 18, an order shall not be enforced until after such application is determined. **sc115.19**

Effect of rule

sc115.19.1 Paragraph (1) of this rule was omitted in 1981.

Variation, satisfaction and discharge of registered order

sc115.20 20. Upon the court being notified by the applicant for registration that an order which has been registered has been varied, satisfied or discharged, particulars of the variation, satisfaction or discharge, as the case may be, shall be entered in the register.

Rules to have effect subject to Orders in Council

sc115.21 21. Rules 12 to 20 shall have effect subject to the provisions of the Order in Council made under section 37 or, as the case may be, of the Order in Council made under section 39.

Criminal Justice (International Co-operation) Act 1990: external forfeiture orders

sc115.21A 21A. The provisions of this Part of this order shall, with such modifications as are necessary and subject to the provisions of any Order in Council made under section 9 of the Criminal Justice (International Co-operation) Act 1990, apply to proceedings for the registration and enforcement of external forfeiture orders as they apply to such proceedings in relation to external confiscation orders. For the purposes of this rule, an external forfeiture order is an order made by a court in a country or territory outside the United Kingdom which is enforceable in the United Kingdom by virtue of any such Order in Council.

"Order in Council made under section 9"

sc115.21A.1 The Criminal Justice (International Co-operation) Act 1990 s.9 provides for the enforcement of overseas court orders for the forfeiture of property used in commission of an offence which corresponds to, or is similar to, the offences specified in s.9(6). Any Order in Council made under the section may authorise the making of rules of court (see s.10). The relevant Orders in Council are the Criminal Justice (International Co-operation) Act 1990 (Enforcement of Overseas Forfeiture Orders) Order 1991 (SI 1991/1463), as amended by SI 1992/1721, SI 1993/1791, SI 1993/3148; the Criminal Justice (International Co-operation) Act 1990 (Enforcement of Overseas Forfeiture Orders) (Northern Ireland) Order 1991 (SI 1991/1464) as amended by SI 1992/1721, SI 1993/1791, SI 1993/3148, SI 1994/1640, SI 1997/2977; and the Criminal Justice (International Co-operation) Act 1990 (Enforcement of Overseas Forfeiture Orders) (Scotland) Order 1991 (SI 1991/1468) as amended by SI 1992/1734, SI 1993/1807, SI 1993/3155, and as otherwise amended from time to time. The relevant Order in Council is the Criminal Justice (International Co-operation) Act 1990 (Enforcement of Overseas Forfeiture Orders) Order 1991 (SI 1991/1463). This Order provides for the enforcement in England and Wales of orders made by a court in a designated country or territory for the forfeiture and destruction or other disposal of property (referred to as external forfeiture orders) used in connection with the commission of a drug trafficking offence. The powers given apply to proceedings which have been or are to be instituted in a designated country or territory and may result in such an order being made there. Article 4 and Sch.2 to the Order designated countries and territories for the purposes of enforcement of forfeiture orders of courts in those countries and territories and proceedings which may lead to such an order being made there.

"registration of ... external forfeiture orders"

Article 10 of the Order in Council made under s.9 of the 1990 Act is in similar terms to s.40 of the 1994 Act and states that on an application the High Court may register an external forfeiture order made in a designated country if (a) it is satisfied that at the time of registration the order is in force and not subject to appeal (see further art.10(2)), (b) it is satisfied, where the person against whom the order is made did not appear in the proceedings, that he received notice of the proceedings in sufficient time to enable him to defend them; and (c) it is of the opinion that enforcing the order in England and Wales would not be contrary to the interests of justice. **sc115.21A.2**

"The provisions of this Part shall ... apply"

The rule states that the provisions of this Part shall apply to proceedings for the registration and enforcement of external forfeiture orders as they apply to such proceedings in relation to external confiscation orders. For the manner in which the rules of this Part apply to external confiscation orders, see paras sc115.12.2 and sc115.13.2 above. The rules of this Part provide, not only for the registration of orders, but also for applications for restraint orders, charging orders and the appointment of receivers. It should be noted, in relation to external forfeiture orders, that the Order in Council made under s.9 of the 1990 Act contains important provisions concerning these applications to which the rules of this Part, by the clear terms of r.21A, are subject; for example, arts 5 and 6 (restraint orders). It should also be noted that the Order of Council in arts 11 and 12 makes special provision for the proof of any order made or judgment given by a court in a designated country and for the certification of various matters arising in the proceedings in that country which may be relevant to registration and other proceedings in the High Court. **sc115.21A.3**

II. Part VI of the Criminal Justice Act 1988

Interpretation

22.—(1) In this Part of this order, "the 1988 Act" means the Criminal Justice Act 1988 and a section referred to by number means the section so numbered in that Act. **sc115.22**

(2) Expressions which are used in this Part of this order which are used in the 1988 Act have the same meanings in this Part of this order as in the 1988 Act and include any extended meaning given by the Criminal Justice (Confiscation) (Northern Ireland) Order 1990.

Effect of rule

See para.sc115.0.4 above. **sc115.22.1**

Application of Part I of Order 115

23. Part I of Order 115 (except rule 11) shall apply for the purposes of proceedings under Part VI of the 1988 Act with the necessary modifications and, in particular— **sc115.23**

(a) references to drug trafficking offences and to drug trafficking shall be construed as references to offences to which Part VI of the 1988 Act applies and to committing such an offence;

(b) references to the Drug Trafficking Act 1994 shall be construed as references to the 1988 Act and references to sections 5(2), 26, 27, 29, 30(2), 17(1), 18, 18(5), 39 and 40 of the 1994 Act shall be construed as references to sections 73(6), 77, 78, 80, 81, 81(1), 83(1), 89, 89(5), 96 and 97 of the 1988 Act respectively;

(c) rule 3(2) shall have effect as if the following sub-paragraphs were substituted for sub-paragraphs (a) and (b)—

"(a) state, as the case may be, either that proceedings have been instituted against the defendant for an offence to which Part VI of the 1988 Act applies (giving particulars of the offence) and that they have not been concluded or that, whether by the laying of an information or otherwise, a person is to be charged with such an offence;

(b) state, as the case may be, either that a confiscation order has been made or the grounds for believing that such an order may be made;"

(d) rule 7(3) shall have effect as if the words "certificate issued by a magistrates' court or the Crown Court" were substituted for the words "certificate issued by the Crown Court";

(e) rule 8 shall have effect as if the following paragraph were added at the end—

"(6) Where a receiver applies in accordance with CPR Part 23 for the variation of a confiscation order, the application notice shall be served, with any supporting evidence, on the defendant and any other person who may be affected by the making of an order under section 83 of the 1988 Act, not less than 7 days before the date fixed for the hearing of the application.";

(f) rule 11 shall apply with the necessary modifications where an application is made under section 93J of the 1988 Act for disclosure of information held by government departments.

"Part I ... shall apply"

sc115.23.1 This rule applies the provisions of Pt I of this Order (other than r.11) to High Court proceedings under Pt VI of the 1988 Act. Thus, these provisions need to be read in conjunction with ss.76 and 97 of the 1988 Act and in accordance with the particular modifications referred to in this rule.

"Sections 96 and 97 of the 1988 Act"

sc115.23.2 In the 1988 Act, these sections correspond with ss.39 and 40 of the 1994 Act (see paras sc115.12.2 and sc115.13.2 above). They deal with the registration and enforcement of external confiscation orders made by courts of designated countries and with the making of orders where confiscation orders may be made in proceedings in designated countries. These matters may be provided for by Order in Council made under s.96. The relevant Order in Council is the Criminal Justice Act 1988 (Designated Countries and Territories) Order 1991 (SI 1991/2873), as amended. This Order in Council, for the purpose of applying the provisions of Pt VI to orders and proceedings in designated countires, makes certain modifications to those provisions. Some of these modifications relate to sections in Pt VI giving jurisdiction to the High Court (e.g. the Order modifies the court's powers under s.77 (restraint orders) and s.78 (charging orders)) and others alter the effect of rules in Pt I of O.115 (e.g. the Order inserts s.79A which modifies r.3(2) as applied by r.23 and r.23(c) to Pt VI applications). Thus, where the jurisdiction of the High Court is being invoked in these circumstances, the provisions of Pt VI of the 1988 Act and the rules in Pt I of O.115 have to be read in conjunction with the Order in Council made under s.96.

III. Terrorism Act 2000

Interpretation

sc115.24 24. In this Part of this Order—

(a) "the Act" means the Terrorism Act 2000;
(b) "Schedule 4" means Schedule 4 to the Act;
(ba) "the prosecutor" means the person with conduct of proceedings which have been instituted in England and Wales for an offence under any of sections 15 to 18 of the Act, or the person who the High Court is satisfied will have the conduct of any proceedings for such an offence; and
(c) other expressions used have the same meanings as they have in Schedule 4 to the Act.

Effect of rule

This rule and rr.26, 27, 29 and 35 were amended by Civil Procedure (Amendment No.2) Rules 2001 to take account of the coming into effect of the Terrorism Act 2000; see further para.sc115.0.5 above and para.sc115.25.1 below. **sc115.24.1**

Rules 24, 26 and 27 were amended by the Civil Procedure (Amendment No.6) Rules 2001 (SI 2001/4016) to take account of the coming into effect of the Anti-terrorism, Crime and Security Act 2001. The 2001 Act made substantial amendments to Sch.4 of the Terrorism Act 2000.

Practice Direction (Restraint Orders and Appointment of Receivers in Connection with Criminal Proceedings and Investigations) (see para.scpd115.1 below), which now supplements RSC O.115, applies to applications to the High Court for a restraint order or the appointment of a receiver under Sch.4 to the Terrorism Act 2000 (see para sc115.0.2.1 above).

Assignment of proceedings

25.—(1) Subject to paragraph (2), the jurisdiction of the High Court under the Act shall be exercised by a judge of the Queen's Bench Division or of the Chancery Division. **sc115.25**

(2) The jurisdiction conferred on the High Court by paragraph 9 of Schedule 4 may also be exercised by a Master of the Queen's Bench Division.

"paragraph 9 of Schedule 4"

As explained above (see para sc115.24.1), rules in Sect.III of RSC O.115 were amended by the Civil Procedure (Amendment No.2) Rules 2001 to take account of the coming into effect of the Terrorism Act 2000. It would seem that, at that time, "paragraph 9 of Schedule 4" in r.25(2) should have been altered so as to read "paragraph 13 of Schedule 4". Paragraph 9 of Sch.4 to the Prevention of Terrorism (Temporary Provisions) Act 1989, dealt with the registration for enforcement of forfeiture and restraint orders made elsewhere in the British Islands. The effect of para.9 is retained by paras 12 and 13 of Sch.4 of the 2000 Act. Paragraph 12 contains definitions. Paragraph 13 provides for the registration and enforcement, in accordance with the terms of para.13 and rules of court, of such orders. Rule 25(2) states that the jurisdiction of the High Court in this respect may be exercised by a Master of the Queen's Bench Division. **sc115.25.1**

"shall be exercised by a judge"

See further para.sc115.2.4 above. **sc115.25.2**

Application for restraint order

26.—(1) An application for a restraint order under paragraph 5 of Schedule 4 may be made by the prosecutor by a claim form, which need not be served on any person. **sc115.26**

(2) An application under paragraph (1) shall be supported by a witness statement or affidavit, which shall—

(a) state, as the case may be, either—

(i) that proceedings have been instituted against a person for an offence under any of sections 15 to 18 of the Act and that they have not been concluded; or

(ii) that a criminal investigation has been started in England and Wales with regard to such an offence,

and in either case give details of the alleged or suspected offence and of the defendant's involvement;

(b) where proceedings have been instituted, state, as the case may be, that a forfeiture order has been made in the proceedings or the grounds for believing that such an order may be made;

(ba) where proceedings have not been instituted—

(i) indicate the state of progress of the investigation and when it is anticipated that a decision will be taken on whether to institute proceedings against the defendant;

(ii) state the grounds for believing that a forfeiture order may be made in any proceedings against the defendant; and

(iii) verify that the prosecutor is to have the conduct of any such proceedings;

(c) to the best of the witness's ability, give full particulars of the property in respect of which the order is sought and specify the person or persons holding such property and any other persons having an interest in it;

(3) A claim form under paragraph (1) shall be entitled in the matter of the defendant, naming him, and in the matter of the Act, and all subsequent documents in the matter shall be so entitled.

(4) Unless the court otherwise directs, a witness statement or affidavit under paragraph (2) may contain statements of information or belief with the sources and grounds thereof.

Restraint order

sc115.26.1 Rule 26 was amended by the Civil Procedure (Amendment No.6) Rules 2001 (SI 2001/4016) to take account of the coming into effect of amendments made to Sch.4 of the Terrorism Act 2000 by the Anti-terrorism, Crime and Security Act 2001. The amendments to Sch.4 extended the circumstances in which a prosecutor may apply to the High Court for a restraint order. As a result, an application may be made where a criminal investigation has been started in England and Wales with regard to a suspected offence under ss.15 to 18 of the 2000 Act.

See further, paras sc115.0.5, sc115.3.1 and sc115.4.3, above.

Application "supported by a witness statement or affidavit"

sc115.26.2 See para.sc115.3.8 above.

Practice

sc115.26.3 Paragraph 5(4) of Sch.4 to the 2000 Act states that an application for a restraint order (see further para.sc115.27.1 below) "may be made to a judge in chambers without notice". Applications under r.26 should be made by claim form or by application notice. The application should be supported by written evidence dealing with all the *matters stated in* paragraph (2) of this rule. Rule 26(1) is listed in Table 2 of Practice Direction (CPR Pt 8, Sch.1 and Sch.2 to CPR) (see para.8BPD.7). Consequently, s.B of that Practice Direction takes effect where application is made by claim form with the result that the Pt 8 procedure applies subject to any special or contrary provisions in

O.115 and as modified in paras B.6 to B.15 of the Practice Direction. See also para.sc115.3.9 above.

Restraint order

27.—(1) A restraint order may be made subject to conditions and exceptions, including but not limited to conditions relating to the indemnifying of third parties against expenses incurred in complying with the order, and exceptions relating to living expenses and legal expenses of the defendant, but the prosecutor shall not be required to give an undertaking to abide by any order as to damages sustained by the defendant as a result of the restraint order. **sc115.27**

(2) Unless the court otherwise directs, a restraint order made without notice of the application for it being served on any person shall have effect until a day which shall be fixed for the hearing where all parties may attend on the application.

(3) Where a restraint order is made the prosecutor shall serve copies of the order and, unless the court otherwise orders, of the witness statement or affidavit in support on the defendant and on all other persons affected by the order.

Restraint order

See further, paras sc115.0.5, sc115.3.1 and sc115.4.3, above. **sc115.27.1**

For the circumstances in which the High Court may make a restraint order, see sub-paras (1) and (2) of para.5 to Sch.4 of the 2000 Act. Paragraph 5(3) states that a restraint order:

> "prohibits a person to whom notice of it is given, subject to any conditions and exceptions specified in the order, from dealing with property in respect of which a forfeiture order has been or could be made in proceedings referred to in sub-paragraphs (1) or (2)".

A restraint order shall provide for notice of it to be given to any person affected by the order (*ibid.* para.6(1)). For the discharge or variation of a restraint order, see r.28 below.

Legal expenses

A defendant against whom a restraint order has been made may be permitted to draw on the fund which is subject to the order so as to enable him to meet the costs of legal representation, Those costs being taxed on the indemnity basis (*Re L., The Times*, July 10, 1996). **sc115.27.2**

Discharge or variation of order

28.—(1) Subject to paragraph (2), an application to discharge or vary a restraint order shall be made in accordance with CPR Part 23. **sc115.28**

(2) Where the case is one of urgency, an application under this rule by the prosecutor may be made without notice.

(3) The application and any witness statement or affidavit in support shall be lodged with the court and, where the application is made in accordance with CPR Part 23 the application notice, shall be served on the following persons (other than the applicant)—

- (a) the prosecutor;
- (b) the defendant; and
- (c) all other persons restrained or otherwise affected by the order;

not less than two clear days before the date fixed for the hearing of the application.

(4) Where a restraint order has been made and has not been discharged, the prosecutor shall notify the court when proceedings

for the offence have been concluded, and the court shall thereupon discharge the restraint order.

(5) Where an order is made discharging or varying a restraint order, the applicant shall serve copies of the order of discharge or variation on all persons restrained by the earlier order and shall notify all other persons affected of the terms of the order of discharge or variation.

Effect of rule

sc115.28.1 Sub-paragraph (2) of para.6 to Sch.4 of the 2000 Act states that a restraint order may be discharged or varied by the High Court on the application of a person affected by it. Sub-paragraph (3) of para.6 states that, where a restraint order was made by the court before a person was charged it shall be discharged if proceedings in respect of the offence "are not instituted within such time as the High Court considers reasonable" (para.6(2)(a)). In any case, a restraint order shall be discharged "if the proceedings for the offence have been concluded" (para.6(2)(b)). Where a restraint order is discharged, compensation may be payable, see r.29 below and notes following.

Compensation

sc115.29 29. An application for an order under paragraph 9 or 10 of Schedule 4 shall be made in accordance with CPR Part 23, and the application notice, shall be served, with any supporting evidence, on the person alleged to be in default and on the person or body by whom compensation, if ordered, will be payable under paragraph 9(6) or 10(4) not less than 7 days before the date fixed for the hearing of the application.

"application ... under paragraph 9 or 10 of Schedule 4"

sc115.29.1 Paragraphs 9 and 10 of Sch.4 to the 2000 Act state that, in certain circumstances, a person who had an interest in any property which was the subject of a forfeiture order or a restraint order may apply to the High Court for compensation. Paragraph 9 applies where the restraint order was discharged in accordance with para.6(3)(a) of that Schedule. That is to say, where the restraint order was made before criminal proceedings were instituted and was discharged because such proceedings were not instituted within a reasonable time. Paragraph 9 also applies where a forfeiture order or a restraint order is made in or in relation to proceedings for an offence under any of ss.15 to 18 of the Act (see para.sc115.0.5 above) which (a) do not result in conviction under any of those sections, (b) result in conviction for an offence under any of those sections in respect of which the person convicted is subsequently pardoned, or (c) result in conviction for an offence under any of those sections which is subsequently quashed. Sub-paragraphs (4), (5) and (6) of para.9 state the matters which the court must take into account when considering an application for compensation in these circumstances.

Paragraph 10 applies where an application for compensation is made in circumstances where a forfeiture order or a restraint order is made in or in relation to proceedings for an offence under any of ss.15 to 18 of the 2000 Act (see para.sc115.0.5 above) and the proceedings result in a conviction which is subsequently quashed on an appeal under s.7(2) or (5) of that Act.

Application for registration

sc115.30 30. An application for registration of a Scottish order, a Northern Ireland order or an Islands order must be made in accordance with CPR Part 23 and may be made without notice.

Evidence in support of application

sc115.31 31.—(1) An application for registration of any such order as is *mentioned in rule 30 must* be supported by a witness statement or affidavit—

(a) exhibiting the order or a certified copy thereof; and
(b) which shall, to the best of the witness's ability, give

particulars of such property in respect of which the order was made as is in England and Wales, and specify the person or persons holding such property.

(2) Unless the court otherwise directs, a witness statement or affidavit for the purposes of this rule may contain statements of information or belief with the sources and grounds thereof.

Application "supported by a witness statement or affidavit"

See also para.sc115.3.8 above. **sc115.31.1**

Register of orders

32.—(1) There will be kept in the Central Office at the Royal Courts of Justice in London under the direction of the Master of the Administrative Court a register of the orders registered under the Act. **sc115.32**

(2) There shall be included in such register particulars of any variation or setting aside of a registration, and of any execution issued on a registered order.

Effect of Rule

The registration for purposes of enforcement of forfeiture orders made elsewhere in the British islands is provided for by paras 12 and 13 of Sch.4 to the 2000 Act. Paragraph 13(3) states that, on an application made in accordance with rules of court for registration of a Scottish, Northern Ireland or Islands order, the High Court shall direct that the order shall, in accordance with such rules, be registered in that court. (Enforcement of orders made in designated countries is provided for by Order in Council, see para.14 of Sch.4.) **sc115.32.1**

Notice of registration

33.—(1) Notice of the registration of an order must be served on the person or persons holding the property referred to in rule 31(1)(b) and any other persons appearing to have an interest in that property. **sc115.33**

(2) Permission is not required to serve such a notice out of the jurisdiction and CPR rules 6.40, 6.42 and 6.46 shall apply in relation to such a notice as they apply in relation to a claim form.

History of rule

Amended by SI 2000/221 and SI 2008/2178. **sc115.33.1**

Application to vary or set aside registration

34. An application to vary or set aside the registration of an order must be made to a judge in accordance with CPR Part 23 and be supported by a witness statement or affidavit. This rule does not apply to a variation or cancellation under rule 36. **sc115.34**

Effect of rules

See generally, para.13 of Sch.4 to the 2000 Act (Enforcement of orders made *elsewhere in the British islands*) (para.sc115.32.1 above) and note in particular para.13(4) (rules of court shall make provision for cancelling or varying registration). **sc115.34.1**

Enforcement of order

35.—(2) If an application is made under rule 34, an order shall not be enforced until after such application is determined. **sc115.35**

(3) This rule does not apply to the taking of steps under paragraph 7 or 8 of Schedule 4, as applied by paragraph 13(6) of that Schedule.

Effect of rule

sc115.35.1 Paragraph (1) of this rule was omitted in 1991.

Paragraph 13(6) of Sch.4 to the 2000 Act states that, if a Scottish, Northern Ireland or Islands restraint order is registered in the High Court under para.13, paras 7 and 8 of Sch.4 "shall apply as they apply to a restraint order under para.5". Rule 35(3) makes it clear that the making of an application under r.34 to set aside or vary the registration of an order does not prevent the taking of steps under paras 7 or 8 of Sch.4. Paragraph 7 provides that a constable may seize any property subject to a restraint order for the purpose of preventing its being removed from Great Britain. Paragraph 8 applies provisions of the Land Charges Act 1972 and the Land Registration Act 1925 to restraint orders as they apply to orders affecting land made by the court for the purposes of enforcing judgments.

Variation and cancellation of registration

sc115.36 36. If effect has been given (whether in England or Wales or elsewhere) to a Scottish, Northern Ireland or Islands order, or if the order has been varied or discharged by the court by which it was made, the applicant for registration shall inform the court and—

(a) if such effect has been given in respect of all the money or other property to which the order applies, or if the order has been discharged by the court by which it was made, registration of the order shall be cancelled;

(b) if such effect has been given in respect of only part of the money or other property, or if the order has been varied by the court by which it was made, registration of the order shall be varied accordingly.

IV. International Criminal Court Act 2001: fines, forfeitures and reparation orders

Interpretation

sc115.37 37. In this Part of this Order—

(a) "the Act" means the International Criminal Court Act 2001[1];

(b) "the ICC" means the International Criminal Court;

(c) "an order of the ICC" means—

(i) a fine or forfeiture ordered by the ICC; or

(ii) an order by the ICC against a person convicted by the ICC specifying a reparation to, or in respect of, a victim.

Registration of ICC orders for enforcement

sc115.38 38.—(1) An application to the High Court to register an order of the ICC for enforcement, or to vary or set aside the registration of an order, may be made to a judge or a Master of the Queen's Bench Division.

(2) Rule 13 and rules 15 to 20 in Part I of this Order shall, with such modifications as are necessary and subject to the provisions of any regulations made under section 49 of the Act, apply to the registration for enforcement of an order of the ICC as they apply to the registration of an external confiscation order.

Effect of rule

sc115.38.1 See para.sc115.0.6 above. Rules 37 and 38 came into effect on October 6, 2003.

[1] 2001 c.17.

PRACTICE DIRECTION—RESTRAINT ORDERS AND APPOINTMENT OF RECEIVERS IN CONNECTION WITH CRIMINAL PROCEEDINGS AND INVESTIGATIONS

This practice direction supplements RSC Order 115 **scpd115.1**

This Practice Direction, supplementing RSC O.115, was first published in HMSO Update 30, February 2003. See further para.sc115.0.2.1 above.

Scope and interpretation

1.1 This practice direction applies to applications to the High Court for a restraint order or the appointment of a receiver under—

(1) Part VI of the Criminal Justice Act 1988 ('the 1988 Act');
(2) Part I of the Drug Trafficking Act 1994 ('the 1994 Act'); or
(3) Schedule 4 to the Terrorism Act 2000 ('the 2000 Act').

(Part VI of the 1988 Act and Part I of the 1994 Act are repealed by the Proceeds of Crime Act 2002 from a day to be appointed, but will continue to apply to pending and transitional cases. Following their repeal, applications for a restraint order or the appointment of a receiver which would previously have been made under those Acts will instead be made to the Crown Court under Part 2 of the 2002 Act.)

1.2 In this practice direction—

(1) 'the prosecutor' means the person applying for a restraint order or the appointment of a receiver; and
(2) 'the defendant' means the person against whom criminal proceedings have been brought or a criminal investigation is taking place, and against whom a confiscation order or forfeiture order has been or might be made.

Section I—Restraint Orders

Form of restraint order

2. An example of a restraint order is annexed to this practice direction. This example may be modified as appropriate in any particular case. **scpd115.2**

Amount under restraint

3.1 A restraint order may, where appropriate, apply to— **scpd115.3**

(1) all of the defendant's realisable property;
(2) the defendant's realisable property up to a specified value; or
(3) one or more particular specified assets.

3.2 Where—

(1) a confiscation order or forfeiture order has already been made against the defendant in a particular amount; or
(2) the prosecutor is able to make a reasonably accurate estimate of the amount of any confiscation order or forfeiture order that might be made against him,

and, in either case, it is clear that the defendant's realisable property is greater in value than the amount or estimated amount of that order, the court will normally limit the application of the restraint order in accordance with paragraph 3.1(2) or (3).

3.3 In such cases the prosecutor's draft order should normally either include an appropriate financial limit or specify the particular assets to which the order should apply.

Living expenses and legal fees

scpd115.4 **4.** A restraint order will normally, unless it is clear that a person restrained has sufficient assets which are not subject to the order, include an exception to the order permitting that person to spend assets—

(1) in the case of an individual, for reasonable living expenses; and

(2) in the case of either an individual or a company, to pay reasonable legal fees so that they may take advice in relation to the order and if so advised apply for its variation or discharge.

Restraint orders against third parties

scpd115.5 **5.1** Where a restraint order applies to property held in the name of a person other than the defendant—

(1) the order must be addressed to that person in addition to the defendant; and

(2) in applying for the order, the prosecutor must consider the guidance given in the matter of G (restraint order) [2001] EWHC Admin 606.

5.2 Examples of additional persons to whom an order must, where appropriate, be addressed include—

(1) a person who has a joint bank account with the defendant;

(2) in proceedings under the 1988 Act or the 1994 Act, a person to whom the defendant is alleged to have made a gift which may be treated as realisable property of the defendant under the provisions of the relevant Act; or

(3) a company, where the prosecutor alleges that assets apparently belonging to the company are in reality those of the defendant.

5.3 However, an order should not normally be addressed—

(1) to a bank with whom a defendant has an account; or

(2) to the business name of a defendant who carries on an unincorporated business (such business not being a separate legal entity from the defendant).

Restraint orders against business

scpd115.6 **6.** If an application for a restraint order is made against a company, partnership or individual apparently carrying on a legitimate business—

(1) the court will take into account the interests of the employees, creditors and customers of the business and, in the case of a company, any shareholders other than the defendant, before making an order which would or might prevent the business from being continued; and

(2) any restraint order made against that person will normally contain an exception enabling it to deal with its assets in the ordinary course of business.

Duration of order made on application without notice—rules 4(2) and 27(2)

7.1 RSC Order 115 rules 4(2) and 27(2) provide that, unless the court otherwise directs, a restraint order made without notice shall have effect until a day which shall be fixed for a further hearing where all parties may attend ('the return date'). **scpd115.7**

7.2 Where a return date is fixed, it will normally be no more than 14 days after the date of the order.

7.3 Where no return date is fixed, the court will always include in the order a provision giving the defendant or anyone affected by the order permission to apply to vary or discharge the order (see paragraph 14 of the sample form of order).

Section II—Appointment of Receiver

scpd115.8

8.1 CPR Part 69, and the practice direction supplementing that Part, apply to the appointment of a receiver under the 1988, 1994 or 2000 Act, subject to the provisions of RSC Order 115, rule 8 and rule 23(e) where applicable.

8.2 In particular, CPR rule 69.7, and paragraph 9 of the practice direction supplementing Part 69, apply in relation to the remuneration of the receiver.

8.3 Where no confiscation or forfeiture order has been made—

(1) an application for the appointment of a receiver should not be made without notice, unless the application is urgent or there is some other good reason for not giving notice to the defendant; and

(2) if the application is made without notice, the prosecutor's written evidence should explain the reasons for doing so.

8.4 Where the court appoints a receiver on an application without notice in the circumstances set out in paragraph 8.3, the order will normally limit the receiver's powers to manage, deal with or sell property (other than with the defendant's consent) to the extent that is shown to be urgently necessary. If the receiver seeks further powers, he should apply on notice for further directions.

scpd115.9

RESTRAINT ORDER PROHIBITING DISPOSAL OF ASSETS

IN THE HIGH COURT OF JUSTICE
QUEEN'S BENCH DIVISION
[ADMINISTRATIVE COURT]

Before The Honourable Mr Justice [ ] sitting in private

Claim No.

Dated

IN THE MATTER OF [ ] (Defendant)

AND IN THE MATTER OF THE [CRIMINAL JUSTICE ACT 1988] [DRUG TRAFFICKING ACT 1994] [TERRORISM ACT 2000]

TO: [(1)] [*the Defendant*]
[(2) Y]
[(3) Z LIMITED]

PENAL NOTICE

If you [ ] disobey this order you may be held to be in contempt of court and may be imprisoned, fined or have your assets seized.

Any other person who knows of this order and does anything which helps or permits the Defendant [or Y or Z Ltd] to breach the terms of this order may also be held to be in contempt of court and may be imprisoned, fined or have their assets seized.

THIS ORDER

1. This is a Restraint Order made against [ ] ("the Defendant") [and Y and Z Ltd] on [ ] by Mr Justice [ ] on the application of [ ] ("the Prosecutor"). The Judge read the witness statements listed in Schedule A and accepted the undertakings set out in Schedule B at the end of this order.

2. This order was made at a hearing without notice to the Defendant [or to Y and Z Ltd]. The Defendant [and Y and Z Ltd] has a right to apply to the court to vary or discharge the order – see paragraph 15 below.

[3. There will be a further hearing of this matter on [insert date] ("the return date") when the Prosecutor will apply for the continuation of this order. The Defendant [and Y and Z Ltd] and any other person affected by this order are entitled to appear and to object to the continuation of this order or to ask for it to be varied.][1]

[1] Include this paragraph if the court fixes a return date.

DISPOSAL OF OR DEALING WITH ASSETS

4. The Defendant must not [until further order of the court]-

(1) remove from England and Wales[2] any of his assets which are in England and Wales [up to the value of £]; or

(2) in any way dispose of, deal with or diminish the value of any of his assets whether they are in or outside England and Wales [up to the same value].

5. Paragraph 4 applies to all the Defendant's assets whether or not they are in his own name and whether they are solely or jointly owned. For the purpose of this order the Defendant's assets include any asset which he has the power, directly or indirectly, to dispose of or deal with as if it were his own. The Defendant is to be regarded as having such power if a third party holds or controls the asset in accordance with his direct or indirect instructions.

6. This prohibition includes the following assets in particular-

(a) the property known as *[title/address]* or the net sale money after payment of any mortgages if it has been sold;

(b) the property and assets of the Defendant's business [known as *[name]*] [carried on at *[address]*] or the sale money if any of them have been sold; and

(c) any money in the account numbered *[account number]* at *[title/address]*.

[7. (1) If the total value free of charges or other securities ("unencumbered value") of the Defendant's assets in England and Wales exceeds £ , the Defendant may remove any of those assets from England and Wales or may dispose of or deal with them so long as the total unencumbered value of the Respondent's assets still in England and Wales remains above £ .

(2) If the total unencumbered value of the Defendant's assets in England and Wales does not exceed £ , the Defendant must not remove any of those assets from England and Wales and must not dispose of or deal with any of them. If the Defendant has other assets outside England and Wales, he may dispose of or deal with those assets outside England and Wales so long as the total unencumbered value of all his assets

[2] In orders made under Schedule 4 to the Terrorism Act 2000, this paragraph should be amended by substituting a prohibition on removing assets from Great Britain.

RSC

whether in or outside England and Wales remains above £ .]

8. [Y must not in any way dispose of or deal with or diminish the value of *[insert description of property]*.][3]

9. [Z Ltd must not in any way dispose of or deal with or diminish the value of any of its property or assets.]

PROVISION OF INFORMATION[4]

10. The Defendant must serve a witness statement certified by a statement of truth on the Prosecutor within [ ] days after this order has been served on him setting out all his assets and all assets under his control whether in or outside England and Wales and whether in his own name or not and whether solely or jointly owned, giving the value, location and details of all such assets. The witness statement must include:

(1) the name and address of all persons including financial institutions holding any such assets;

(2) details of the Defendant's current salary or other form of income, identifying the amounts paid, by whom they are paid and the account or accounts into which such sums are paid;

(3) the names and numbers of all accounts held by or under the control of the Defendant, together with the name and address of the place where the account is held and the sums in the account;

(4) details (including addresses) of any real property in which the Defendant has any interest, including an interest in any of the net sale money if the property were to be sold. These details must include details of any mortgage or charge on the property;

(5) details of all National Savings Certificates, unit trusts, shares or debentures in any company or corporation, wherever incorporated in the world, owned or controlled by the Defendant or in which he has an interest;

(6) details of all trusts of which the Defendant is a beneficiary, including the name and address of every trustee;

(7) particulars of any income or debt due to the Defendant including the name and address of the debtor;

---

[3] It may, depending on the circumstances, be appropriate for the order to include more detailed provisions restraining a third party, corresponding with paragraphs 4 to 7 above.

[4] This section of the order is optional, although it will usually be included in orders made under the 1988 or 1994 Acts.

(8) details of all assets over £1,000 in value transferred by the Defendant, or anyone on his behalf, to others since [*date*], identifying the name and address of all persons to whom such property was transferred.

11. (1) Subject to any further order of the court any information given in compliance with this order shall only be used-

(a) for the purpose of these proceedings;

(b) if the Defendant is convicted, for the purposes of any confiscation hearing that may take place; and

(c) if a confiscation order is made, for the purposes of enforcing that order, including any receivership proceedings.

(2) There shall be no disclosure of any material disclosed in compliance with this order to any co-defendant in the criminal proceedings.

(3) However, nothing in this paragraph shall make inadmissible any disclosure made by the Defendant in any proceedings for perjury relating to that disclosure.

EXCEPTIONS TO THIS ORDER

12. (1) This order does not prohibit the Defendant [or Y] from spending up to £ a week towards his ordinary living expenses and up to £ [*or* a reasonable sum] on legal advice and representation in connection with this order. But before spending any money the Defendant [or Y] must tell the Prosecutor where the money is to come from.

[(2) This order does not prohibit the Defendant [or Y] from spending any money they may receive by way of state benefit from the Department of Social Security.]

[(3) This order does not prohibit the Defendant from spending towards his ordinary living expenses any sum earned by him whilst he is in prison.]

[(4) This order does not prohibit Z Ltd from spending up to £ [*or* a reasonable sum] on legal advice and representation. But before spending any money Z Ltd must tell the Prosecutor where the money is to come from.]

(5) The Defendant [or Y or Z Ltd] may agree with the Prosecutor that the above spending limits be varied or that this Order be

varied in any other respect in relation to them, but any such agreement must be in writing.

(6) This order does not prevent-

(a) any person from paying any money in satisfaction of the whole or part of any confiscation order which may be made against the Defendant; or

(b) the levy of distress upon any goods subject to this order for the purpose of enforcement of any confiscation order which may be made against the Defendant.

COSTS

13. The costs of this order are reserved.

VARIATION OR DISCHARGE OF THIS ORDER

14. Anyone affected by this order may apply to the court at any time to vary or discharge this order (or so much of it as affects that person), but they must first inform the Prosecutor and the Defendant [and Y and Z Ltd] giving two clear days' notice. If any evidence is to be relied upon in support of the application, the substance of it must be communicated in writing to the Prosecutor in advance.

INTERPRETATION OF THIS ORDER

15. A person who is an individual who is ordered not to do something must not do it himself or in any other way. He must not do it through others acting on his behalf or on his instructions or with his encouragement.

16. A person which is not an individual which is ordered not to do something must not do it itself or by its directors, officers, partners, employees or agents or in any other way.

PARTIES OTHER THAN THE DEFENDANT

17. **Effect of this order**

It is a contempt of court for any person notified of this order knowingly to assist in or permit a breach of this order. Any person doing so may be imprisoned, fined or have their assets seized. He is also at risk of prosecution for a money laundering offence.

18. **Set off by banks**

This order does not prevent any bank from exercising any right of set off it may have in respect of any facility which it gave to the Defendant before it was notified of this order.

19. **Withdrawals by the Defendant**

No bank need enquire as to the application or proposed application of any money withdrawn by the Defendant if the withdrawal appears to be permitted by this order.

20. **Persons outside England, Wales and Scotland**

(1) Except as provided in paragraph (2) below, the terms of this order do not affect or concern anyone outside the jurisdiction of this court or Scotland.

(2) The terms of this order will affect the following persons in a country or state outside the jurisdiction of this court or Scotland-

(a) a person to whom this order is addressed or the officer or agent appointed by power of attorney of such a person;

(b) any person who-
(i) is subject to the jurisdiction of this court or Scotland;
(ii) has been given written notice of this order at his residence or place of business within the jurisdiction of this court or Scotland; and
(iii) is able to prevent acts or omissions outside the jurisdiction of this court or Scotland which constitute or assist in a breach of the terms of this order; and

(c) any other person, only to the extent that this order is declared enforceable by or is enforced by a court in that country or state.

21. **Enforcement in Scotland**

This order shall have effect in the law of Scotland, and may be enforced there, if it is registered under section 35 of the Proceeds of Crime (Scotland) Act 1995.

[22. **Assets located outside England and Wales**

Nothing in this order shall, in respect of assets located outside England and Wales, prevent any third party from complying with-

(1) what it reasonably believes to be its obligations, contractual or otherwise, under the laws and obligations of the country or state in which those assets are situated or under the proper law of any contract between itself and the Respondent; and

(2) any orders of the courts of that country or state, provided that reasonable notice of any application for such an order is given to the Applicant's solicitors;

unless those assets are situated in Scotland and this order has been registered there, in which case this order must be obeyed there.]

COMMUNICATIONS WITH THE COURT

All communications to the court about this order should be sent to-

The Administrative Court Office, Royal Courts of Justice, Strand, London WC2A 2LL quoting the case number. The office is open between 10 a.m. and 4.30 p.m. Monday to Friday. The telephone number is 0207 947 6653.

SCHEDULE A

WITNESS STATEMENTS

SCHEDULE B

UNDERTAKINGS GIVEN TO THE COURT BY THE PROSECUTOR

(1) The Prosecutor will serve upon the Defendant [and Y and Z Ltd] -
  (a) a copy of this order; and
  (b) a copy of the witness statement containing the evidence relied upon by the Prosecutor, and any other documents provided to the court on the making of the application;

(2) Anyone notified of this order will be given a copy of it by the Prosecutor.

(3) The Prosecutor will pay the reasonable costs of anyone other than the Defendant [and Y and Z Ltd] which are incurred as a result of this order including the costs of finding out whether that person holds any of the Defendant's assets, save that the Prosecutor will not without an order of the court be obliged to pay any legal or accountancy costs so incurred unless the Prosecutor first gives its consent in writing.

ADDRESS OF THE PROSECUTOR FOR SERVICE AND ANY COMMUNICATION IN RESPECT OF THESE PROCEEDINGS

[*Address, reference, fax and telephone numbers*]"

RSC ORDER 116—THE CRIMINAL PROCEDURE AND INVESTIGATIONS ACT 1996

Contents

sc116.0.1

Editorial introduction

This Order was contained in Appendix 1 to the Civil Procedure (Amendment) Rules 1999 and was inserted after CPR Sch.1, O.115 by r.60 of those Rules. The Order came into force on April 26, 1999. **sc116.0.2**

The Order stipulates in considerable detail the procedure to be followed where an application is made to the High Court under s.54 of the Criminal Procedure and Investigations Act 1996; in effect, it is a self-contained procedural code as to matters of notice, service and evidence. Under that section, the High Court may make an order quashing the acquittal of a person acquitted by a criminal court (so-called "tainted acquittals").

The section applies where (a) a person has been acquitted of an offence (whether before or after the appointed day), and (b) a person has been convicted of "an administration of justice offence" involving interference with or intimidation of a juror or a witness (or potential witness) in any proceedings which led to the acquittal (s.54(1)). For these purposes, the administration of justice offenders are: (1) perverting the course of justice, (2) intimidation etc., of witnesses, jurors and others (Criminal Justice and Public Order Act 1994 s.51(1)), and (3) aiding, abetting etc., another person to commit an offence under the Perjury Act 1911 s.1 (s.54(6)).

Where it appears to the court before which the person was convicted that there is a real possibility that, but for the interference or intimidation, the acquitted person would not have been acquitted, "the court shall certify that it so appears" (s.54(2)), but the court should not so certify if, because of lapse of time or for any other reason, it would be contrary to the interests of justice to take proceedings against the acquitted person for the offence of which he was acquitted (s.54(5)).

Where a court makes an order under s.54(2) certifying that an acquittal was tainted, an application may be made to the High Court for an order quashing the acquittal (s.54(3)). The provisions of RSC O.116 govern the procedure to be followed on such an application. Rule 5(1) states that an application shall be made by claim form which shall be issued out of the Crown Office by the prosecutor; that is to say, by the individual or body which acted as prosecutor in the proceedings which led to the acquittal (r.2). Rule 5(1) is listed in Table 2 of Practice Direction (CPR Pt 8 and Sch.1 and Sch.2 to the CPR) (see para.8BPD.7). Consequently, Section B of that Practice Direction applies and the applicant must use the Pt 8 claim form procedure as modified therein.

On an application being made the court shall make an order quashing the acquittal if (but shall not do so unless) the four conditions in s.55 are satisfied (s.54(3)).

The four conditions stated in s.55 are as follows:

(1) that it appears to the High Court likely that, but for the interference or intimidation, the acquitted person would not have been acquitted;

(2) that it does not appear to the court that, because of lapse of time or for any other reason, it would be contrary to the interests of justice to take proceedings against the acquitted person for the offence of which he was acquitted;

(3) that it appears to the court that the acquitted person has been given a reasonable opportunity to make written representations to the court;

(4) that it appears to the court that the conviction of the person convicted for the administration of justice offence will stand.

In applying the fourth condition the court shall take into account all the information before it, but ignore the possibility of new factors coming to light (s.55(5)). Accordingly, the fourth condition has the effect that the court shall not make an order under s.54(3) if (for instance) it appears to the court that any time allowed for giving notice of appeal has not expired or that an appeal is pending (s.55(6)).

Related sources

sc116.0.3
- Criminal Procedure and Investigations Act 1996 ss.54 to 57
- CPR Pt 8 (Alternative procedure for claims)
- Practice Direction (CPR Pt 8 and Sch.1 and Sch.2 to the CPR) (see para.8BPD.1).

Application

sc116.1 1. This Order shall apply in relation to acquittals in respect of offences alleged to be committed on or after 15th April 1997.

Interpretation

sc116.2 2. In this Order, unless the context otherwise requires—

"the Act" means the Criminal Procedure and Investigations Act 1996;

"acquitted person" means a person whose acquittal of an offence is the subject of a certification under section 54(2) of the Act, and "acquittal" means the acquittal of that person of that offence;

"magistrates' court" has the same meaning as in section 148 of the Magistrates' Courts Act 1980;

"prosecutor" means the individual or body which acted as prosecutor in the proceedings which led to the acquittal.

"record of court proceedings" means—

(a) (where the proceedings took place in the Crown Court) a transcript of the evidence, or

(b) a note of the evidence made by the justices' clerk, in the proceedings which led to the conviction for the administration of justice offence referred to in section 54(1)(b) of the Act or, as the case may be, the proceedings which led to the acquittal.

"single judge" means a judge of the Queen's Bench Division.

"witness" means a witness whose evidence is contained in a witness statement or affidavit filed under rule 5, 7, 8 or 9;

Assignment of proceedings

sc116.3 3. The jurisdiction of the High Court under section 54(3) of the Act shall be exercised by a single judge.

Time limit for making application

sc116.4 4. An application under section 54(3) of the Act shall be made not later than 28 days after—

(a) the expiry of the period allowed for appealing (whether by case stated or otherwise), or making an application for leave to appeal, against the conviction referred to in section 54(1)(b) of the Act; or

(b) where notice of appeal or application for leave to appeal against the conviction is given, the determination of the appeal or application for leave to appeal and, for this purpose, "determination" includes abandonment (within the meaning of rule 10 of the Criminal Appeal Rules 1968 or, as the case may be, rule 11 of the Crown Court Rules 1982).

Application

sc116.5 5.—(1) An application under section 54(3) of the Act shall be made by claim form which shall be issued out of the Crown Office by the prosecutor.

(2) The application shall be accompanied by—

(a) a witness statement or affidavit which deals with the conditions in section 55(1), (2), and (4) of the Act and which exhibits any relevant documents (which may include a copy of any record of court proceedings);

(b) a copy of the certification under section 54(2) of the Act.

Notice to the acquitted person

6.—(1) The prosecutor shall, within 4 days of the issue of the application, serve written notice on the acquitted person that the application has been issued. **sc116.6**

(2) The notice given under paragraph (1) shall—

(a) specify the date on which the application was issued;

(b) be accompanied by a copy of the application and of the documents which accompanied it;

(c) inform the acquitted person that—

(i) the result of the application may be the making of an order by the High Court quashing the acquittal, and

(ii) if he wishes to respond to the application, he must, within 28 days of the date of service on him of the notice, file in the Crown Office any witness statement or affidavit on which he intends to rely.

Witness statement or Affidavit of Service on Acquitted Person

7. The prosecutor shall, as soon as practicable after service of the notice under rule 6, file at the Crown Office a witness statement or affidavit of service which exhibits a copy of the notice. **sc116.7**

Response of acquitted person

8.—(1) If the acquitted person wishes to respond to the application, he shall, within 28 days of service on him of notice under rule 6, file in the Crown Office a witness statement or affidavit which— **sc116.8**

(a) deals with the conditions in section 55(1), (2), and (4) of the Act; and

(b) exhibits any relevant documents (which may include a copy of any record of court proceedings).

(2) The acquitted person shall, within 4 days of the filing of the documents mentioned in paragraph (1), serve copies of them on the prosecutor.

Evidence

9.—(1) A witness statement or affidavit filed under rule 5, 7, 8 of this rule may contain statements of information or belief with the sources and grounds thereof. **sc116.9**

(2) The prosecutor may, not later than 10 days after expiry of the period allowed under rule 8(1), apply for an order granting permission to file further evidence without notice being served on any other party.

(3) If the single judge grants permission, the order shall specify a period within which further evidence or records are to be filed, and the Crown Office shall serve a copy of the order on the prosecutor and on the acquitted person.

(4) The prosecutor shall, within 4 days of filing further evidence in the Crown Office, serve a copy of that evidence on the acquitted person.

Determination of the application

sc116.10 10.—(1) Subject to paragraph (3), the single judge shall determine whether or not to make an order under section 54(3) of the Act on the basis of the written material provided under rules 5, 7, 8 and 9 in the absence of the prosecutor, the acquitted person, or of any witness.

(2) The determination shall not be made, and any hearing under paragraph (3) shall not take place, before the expiry of—

(a) 10 days after the expiry of the period allowed under rule 8(1), or

(b) 10 days after the expiry of the period allowed by any order made under rule 9(3).

(3) The single judge may, of his own initiative or on the application of the prosecution or acquitted person, order a hearing of the application if he thinks fit.

(4) An application under paragraph (3) shall state whether a hearing is desired in order for a deponent for the other party to attend and be cross-examined, and, if so, the reasons for wishing the witness to attend.

(5) An application under paragraph (3) shall be made no later than 7 days after the expiry of the period allowed—

(a) under rule 8(1) or

(b) by any order made under rule 9(3).

(6) Where a hearing is ordered, the single judge may, of his own initiative or on the application of the prosecutor or acquitted person, order a witness to attend in order to be cross-examined.

(7) The prosecutor or the acquitted person, as the case may be, shall within 4 days after filing the application under paragraph (3), serve a copy of it on the other party, and file in the Crown Office a witness statement or affidvit of service.

(8) A party served under paragraph (7) shall, within 5 days of service, file any representations he wishes to make as to whether or not a hearing should be ordered.

(9) Subject to paragraph (10) below—

(a) the single judge shall not determine an application for a hearing under paragraph (3) unless—

(i) a witness statement or affidavit of service has been filed as required by paragraph (7), and

(ii) the period for filing representations allowed under paragraph (8) has elapsed; or

(iii) representations have been filed under paragraph (8).

(b) The requirements imposed by sub-paragraph (a)(i) and (iii) are satisfied even though the witness statement or affidavit of service or, as the case may be, the representations are filed outside the time limits allowed.

(10) Where after an application for a hearing has been made—

(a) no witness statement or affidvit of service has been filed and

(b) no representations under paragraph (8) have been received after the expiry of 7 days from the filing of the application,

the single judge may reject the application.

(11) Where after a hearing is ordered, either the prosecution or the acquitted person desires a witness for the other party to attend the hearing in order to be cross-examined, he must apply for an order under paragraph (5) giving his reasons without notice being served on any other party.

(12) The Crown Office shall serve notice on the prosecutor and the acquitted person of any order made under the foregoing paragraphs of this rule and, where a hearing is ordered, the notice shall—

(a) set out the date, time and place of the hearing, and

(b) give details of any witness ordered to attend for cross-examination.

(13) A hearing ordered under paragraph (3) above shall be in public unless the single judge otherwise directs.

(14) The Crown Office shall serve notice of any order made under section 54(3) of the Act quashing the acquittal or of a decision not to make such an order on the prosecutor, the acquitted person and—

(a) where the court before which the acquittal or conviction occurred was a magistrates' court, on the designated officer;

(b) where the court before which the acquittal or conviction occurred was the Crown Court, on the appropriate officer of the Crown Court sitting at the place where the acquittal or conviction occurred.

Schedule 2

CCR ORDER 1—CITATION, APPLICATION AND INTERPRETATION

Contents

Application of RSC to county court proceedings

6. Where by virtue of these rules or section 76 of the Act or otherwise any provision of the RSC is applied in relation to proceedings in a county court, that provision shall have effect with the necessary modifications and in particular— **cc1.6**

(b) any reference in that provision to a Master, district judge of the Principal Registry of the Family Division, the Admiralty registrar, or a district judge or taxing officer shall be construed as a reference to the district judge of the county court; and

(d) any reference in that provision to an office of the Supreme Court having the conduct of the business of a division or court or a district registry shall be construed as a reference to the county court office.

Effect of rule

The CCR never were a comprehensive procedural code for the county courts. Section 76 of the CCA states that "in any case provided for by or in pursuance of this Act, the general principles of practice of the High Court may be adopted and applied to proceedings in a county court". The only surviving rule in CCR O.1, r.6, applies the RSC "with the necessary modifications". This principle has often been relied on. For example, *Grepe v Loam* (1888) 37 Ch.D. 168 is authority for the proposition that a judge in the county court has power—as in the High Court—to order that a litigant be prohibited from making any further application in the proceedings without permission. See now CPR r.3.11 (Power of the court to make civil restraint orders) and PD 3C. The rule remains important in interpreting and applying the remaining rules of the CCR in Sch.2 which still contains rules in daily use such as those dealing with enforcement of judgments. Therefore, all commentary to the CCR includes cross references to the cognate rule in the RSC. **cc1.6.1**

CCR ORDER 16—TRANSFER OF PROCEEDINGS

Contents

Interpleader proceedings under execution

7.—(1) This rule applies to interpleader proceedings under an execution which are ordered to be transferred from the High Court. **cc16.7**

(1A) In this rule references to the sheriff shall be interpreted as including references to an individual authorised to act as an enforcement officer under the Courts Act 2003.

(2) Notice of the hearings or pre-trial review of the proceedings

shall be given by the court officer to the sheriff as well as to every other party to the proceedings.

(3) The interpleader claimant shall, within 8 days of the receipt by him of the notice referred to in paragraph (2), file in triplicate particulars of any goods alleged to be his property and the grounds of his interpleader claim and the court officer shall send a copy to the execution creditor and to the sheriff, but the judge may hear the proceedings or, as the case may be, the district judge may proceed with the pre-trial review, if he thinks fit, notwithstanding that the particulars have not been filed.

(4) Subject to any directions in the order of the High Court, damages may be claimed against the execution creditor in the same manner as in interpleader proceedings commenced in a county court.

(5) On any day fixed for the pre-trial review of the proceedings or for the hearing of any application by the sheriff or other party for directions the court may order the sheriff—

(a) to postpone the sale of the goods seized;

(b) to remain in possession of such goods until the hearing of the proceedings; or

(c) to hand over possession of such goods to the district judge,

and, where a direction is given under sub-paragraph (c), the district judge shall be allowed reasonable charges for keeping possession of the goods, not exceeding those which might be allowed to the sheriff, and, if the district judge is directed to sell the goods, such charges for the sale as would be allowed under an execution issued by the county court.

(6) No order made in the proceedings shall prejudice or affect the rights of the sheriff to any proper charges and the judge may make such order with respect to them as may be just.

(7) The charges referred to in paragraphs (5) and (6) shall ultimately be borne in such manner as the judge shall direct.

(8) The order made at the hearing of the proceedings shall direct how any money in the hands of the sheriff is to be disposed of.

Related sources

cc16.7.1
- Schedule 1, RSC O.17—Interpleader
- Schedule 2, CCR O.33—Interpleader Proceedings

Effect of rule

cc16.7.2 Schedule 2, CCR O.16, r.7 applies only to interpleader proceedings under an execution which are transferred from the High Court to the county court. Generally, it is not convenient so to order. In the High Court interpleaders are heard by a master or district judge. In the county court the district judge (as successor to the "high bailiff") cannot hear an interpleader under execution. Although there is no reason for this limitation on transfer from the High Court (a High Court Enforcement Officer not a *county court bailiff, will have* levied) O.16, r.7 clearly envisages the hearing being before a circuit judge. Section 67 of the Tribunals Courts and Enforcement Act 2007 (not yet in force) will remove all responsibilities for execution from the district judge.

See further commentary to Sch.1, RSC O.17 and Sch.2, CCR O.33.

CCR ORDER 22—JUDGMENTS AND ORDERS

Contents

Certificate of judgment

8.—(1) Any person who wishes to have a certificate of any judgment or order given or made in a claim shall make a request in writing to the court stating— **cc22.8**

(a) if he is a party to the claim, whether the certificate—

(i) is required for the purpose of taking proceedings on the judgment or order in another court;

(ii) is required for the purpose of enforcing the judgment or order in the High Court; or

(iii) is for the purpose of evidence only;

(b) if he is not a party to the claim, the purpose for which the certificate is required, the capacity in which he asks for it and any other facts showing that the certificate may properly be granted.

(1A) Where the certificate is required for the purpose of enforcing the judgment or order in the High Court, the applicant shall also either—

(a) state that—

(i) it is intended to enforce the judgment or order by execution against goods; or

(ii) the judgment or order to be enforced is an order for possession of land made in a possession claim against trespassers; or

(b) confirm that an application has been made for an order under section 42 of the Act (transfer to High Court by order of a county court) and attach a copy of the application to the request for a certificate.

(2) Where the request is made by a person who is not a party to the claim, the request shall be referred to the district judge, who may, if he thinks fit, refer it to the judge.

(3) Without prejudice to paragraph (2), for the purposes of section 12(2) of the Act a certificate under this rule may be signed by the court manager or any other officer of the court acting on his behalf.

Related sources

- Article 8— High Court and County Courts Jurisdiction Order 1991 (See Vol.2 at Section 9B) **cc22.8.1**
- Civil Jurisdiction and Judgments Act 1982 (Vol.2, para.5–7)
- Schedule 4—Title II of 1958 Convention as Modified for Allocation of Jurisdiction within UK (Vol.2, para.5–145+)
- Part 40—CPR
- Part 74 Enforcement of Judgments in Different Jurisdictions

Forms

- N293 Certificate of Judgment or Order **cc22.8.2**
- No.111 Certificate of money provisions contained in a judgment for registration in another part of the UK (Sch 6 CJJA 1982)
- No.112 Certificate issued in respect of non-money provisions for registration in another part of the UK (Sch 7 CJJA 1982)

Effect of rule

cc22.8.3 Schedule 2, CCR O.22, r.8 is a self-contained and straightforward procedure for obtaining a certificate of judgment. In practice, such a certificate is required for the purpose of enforcing the judgment either elsewhere within the UK (i.e. outside England and Wales) or abroad.

The most common reason for requesting a certificate is to be able to enforce a county court judgment in the High Court (see CPR Pt 70 and commentary thereon). Confusingly and unhelpfully some statutes (and therefore some rules of court) refer to a "certificate of judgment" and others to a "certified copy of the judgment". These are not the same thing and care is required to ensure that the correct one is obtained.

Variation of payment

cc22.10 10.—(1) Where a judgment or order has been given or made for the payment of money, the person entitled to the benefit of the judgment or order or, as the case may be, the person liable to make the payment (in this rule referred to as "the judgment creditor" and "the debtor" respectively) may apply in accordance with the provisions of this rule for a variation in the date or rate of payment.

(2) The judgment creditor may apply in writing, without notice being served on any other party, for an order that the money, if payable in one sum, be paid at a later date than that by which it is due or by instalments or, if the money is already payable by instalments, that it be paid by the same or smaller instalments, and the court officer may make an order accordingly unless no payment has been made under the judgment or order for 6 years before the date of the application in which case he shall refer the application to the district judge.

(3) The judgment creditor may apply to the district judge on notice for an order that the money, if payable in one sum, be paid at an earlier date than that by which it is due or, if the money is payable by instalments, that it be paid in one sum or by larger instalments, and any such application shall be made in writing stating the proposed terms and the grounds on which it is made.

(4) Where an application is made under paragraph (3)—

(a) the proceedings shall be automatically transferred to the debtor's home court if the judgment or order was not given or made in that court; and

(b) the court officer shall fix a day for the hearing of the application before the district judge and give to the judgment creditor and the debtor not less than 8 days' notice of the day so fixed,

and at the hearing the district judge may make such order as seems just.

(5) The debtor may apply for an order that the money, if payable in one sum, be paid at a later date than that by which it is due or by instalments or, if the money is already payable by instalments, that it be paid by smaller instalments, and any such application shall be in the appropriate form stating the proposed terms, the grounds on which it is made and including a signed statement of the debtor's means.

(6) Where an application is made under paragraph (5), the court officer shall—

(a) send the judgment creditor a copy of the debtor's application (and statement of means); and

(b) require the judgment creditor to notify the court in writing, within 14 days of service of notification upon him, giving his reasons for any objection he may have to the granting of the application.

(7) If the judgment creditor does not notify the court of any objection within the time stated, the court officer shall make an order in the terms applied for.

(8) Upon receipt of a notice from the judgment creditor under paragraph (6), the court officer may determine the date and rate of payment and make an order accordingly.

(9) Any party affected by an order made under paragraph (8) may, within 14 days of service of the order on him and giving his reasons, apply on notice for the order to be re-considered and, where such an application is made—

(a) the proceedings shall be automatically transferred to the debtor's home court if the judgment or order was not given or made in that court; and

(b) the court officer shall fix a day for the hearing of the application before the district judge and give to the judgment creditor and the debtor not less than 8 days' notice of the day so fixed.

(10) On hearing an application under paragraph (9), the district judge may confirm the order or set it aside and make such new order as he thinks fit and the order so made shall be entered in the records of the court.

(11) Any order made under any of the foregoing paragraphs may be varied from time to time by a subsequent order made under any of those paragraphs.

Effect of rule

It has always been a feature of the county courts to provide for payment of a judgment debt by instalments. It used not to be possible for a High Court judgment to provide for payment by instalments (though a similar result could be achieved by applying for a stay of execution pursuant to RSC O.47, r.1) but it is now (see CPR r.40.11(a)). **cc22.10.1**

Inevitably changes of circumstances can occur which render it appropriate to review an order for payment by instalments. Schedule 2 , CCR O.22, r.10 provides for either a creditor or debtor to seek a review of an instalment order. Subject to the provisions of the rule, an application is considered by the "court officer" or, if necessary, by the district judge.

An application to vary does not act as a stay of enforcement. Accordingly, as a seperate matter, consideration needs to be given to need to apply for a stay especially if enforcement proceedings have already been issued.

Set-off of cross-judgments

11.—(1) An application under section 72 of the Act for permission to set off any sums, including costs, payable under several judgments or orders each of which was obtained in a county court shall be made in accordance with this rule. **cc22.11**

(2) Where the judgments or orders have been obtained in the same county court, the application may be made to that court on the day when the last judgment or order is obtained, if both parties are present, and in any other case shall be made on notice.

(3) Where the judgments or orders have been obtained in different county courts, the application may be made to either of them on notice, and notice shall be given to the other court.

(4) The district judge of the court to which the application is made and the district judge of any other court to which notice is given under paragraph (3) shall forthwith stay execution on any judgment or order in his court to which the application relates and any money paid into court under the judgment or order shall be retained until the application has been disposed of.

(5) The application may be heard and determined by the court and any order giving permission shall direct how any money paid into court is to be dealt with.

(6) Where the judgments or orders have been obtained in different courts, the court in which an order giving permission is made shall send a copy of the order to the other court, which shall deal with any money paid into that court in accordance with the order.

(7) The court officer or, as the case may be, each of the court officers affected shall enter satisfaction in the records of his court for any sums ordered to be set off, and execution or other process for the enforcement of any judgment or order not wholly satisfied shall issue only for the balance remaining payable.

(8) Where an order is made by the High Court giving permission to set off sums payable under several judgments and orders obtained respectively in the High Court and a county court, the court officer of the county court shall, on receipt of a copy of the order, proceed in accordance with paragraph (7).

"section 72 of the Act"

cc22.11.1 See Vol.2, para.9A–561—"set off in cases of cross judgments in county courts and High Court". The section deals with the situation where parties have obtained judgments against one another ("cross-judgments"), one obtained in a county court and the other in a county court or in the High Court.

Order of appellate court

cc22.13 13. Where the Court of Appeal or High Court has heard and determined an appeal from a county court, the party entitled to the benefit of the order of the Court of Appeal or High Court shall deposit the order or an office copy thereof in the office of the county court.

CCR ORDER 24 – SUMMARY PROCEEDINGS FOR THE RECOVERY OF LAND

Contents

cc24.0.1

Revocation of Part (CCR O.24, Pt II)

cc24.0.1.1 The provisions of Pt II of this Order (viz., rr.12 to 15) were revoked by the Civil Procedure (Amendment) Rules 2002 (SI 2002/2058), r.36 and Sch.10. In effect, these provisions were replaced by Sect.III of CPR Pt 55 (Possession Claims) inserted in the CPR by r.22(c) and Pt II of Sch.3 of that statutory instrument.

Editorial introduction

cc24.0.2 CCR O.24, in its original form, provided for a fast and economical procedure for obtaining an order for possession against squatters. The procedure still exists but since October 2001 has been incorporated into the main body of the CPR as Pt 55. The rump of O.24 is confined to warrants of possession against persons who entered land as trespassers—see CPR r.55.1(b).

Forms

- **N51** Warrant of restitution (O.24, r.6(1)) **cc24.0.3**

Warrant of possession

6.—(1) Subject to paragraphs (2) and (3), a warrant of possession to enforce an order for possession, in a possession claim against trespassers under Part 55, may be issued at any time after the making of the order and subject to the provisions of order 26, rule 17, a warrant of restitution may be issued in aid of the warrant of possession. **cc24.6**

(2) No warrant of possession shall be issued after the expiry of 3 months from the date of the order without the permission of the court, and an application for such permission may be made without notice being served on any other party unless the court otherwise directs.

(3) Nothing in this rule shall authorise the issue of a warrant of possession before the date on which possession is ordered to be given.

Effect of rule

Permission to issue a warrant of possession to enforce an order against persons who entered land as trespassers is not required if the warrant is issued within three months of the date of the Order. For "persons who entered land as trespassers"—see CPR 55.1(b). **cc24.6.1**

For warrants of restitution, see CCR 26.17(4).

CCR ORDER 25 – ENFORCEMENT OF JUDGMENTS AND ORDERS: GENERAL

Contents **cc25.0.1**

Editorial introduction

In their original form the CPR effected no change in the area of enforcement and the existing rules and procedures were inserted into Sch.1 (High Court) and Sch.2 (County Court). The majority of relevant enforcement rules remain unchanged but a start has now been made. CPR Pts 70 to 73 came into force on March 25, 2002. Part 70 is entitled "General rules about Enforcement of Judgments and Orders" and accordingly clearly dovetails with CCR Ords 25, 26, 27, 28, 29, 33, 35 and 39. These Orders and Pts 70 to 73 should be read together as comprising the various ways in which the successful party (now the "judgment creditor") can employ the machinery of the County Courts towards obtaining satisfaction of his judgment or compelling compliance with it or obedience of it. It is still a feature of the civil justice system the judgments are not automatically enforced by the court. It is for the judgment creditor to decide how and when to enforce the judgment. See further the practice directions which supplements Pt 70 at para.70PD.1 **cc25.0.2**

The rules on enforcement do not apply against the Crown (r.66.6).

Where the sum which it is sought to enforce wholly or partially by execution against goods is £5000 or more it can be enforced only in the High Court: where that sum is less than £600 it can be enforced only in a county court (save that all county court judgments arising out of agreements regulated by the Consumer Credit Act 1974 must be enforced in a county court). For judgments in between there is a choice and either court can be used. In the High Court, judgments are enforced by independent High Court Enforcement Officers (see further, para.sc46.1.50) whereas enforcement in the county court is undertaken by the county court's own bailiffs.

Related sources

cc25.0.3
- Practice Direction—Enforcement of Judgments and Orders (see para.70PD.1)
- Part 70—General rules about Enforcement of Judgments and Orders
- Part 71—Orders to obtain information from judgment debtors
- Part 72— Third Part Debt Orders
- Part 73—Charging Orders, Stop Orders and Stop Notices
- Part 74—Enforcement of Judgments in Different Jurisdictions
- CCR O.26—Warrant of Execution, Delivery and Possession
- CCR O.27—Attachment of Earnings
- CCR O.28— Judgment Summons
- CCR O.29—Committal for Breach of Order or Undertaking
- RSC O.45—Enforcement of Judgments and Orders: General
- Attachment of Earnings Act 1971 (see Vol.2, Section 9B)
- County Courts Act 1984 Pt V (see Vol.2, Section 9A)
- Charging Orders Act 1979 (see Vol.2, Section 9B)
- Court Funds Rules 1987 (SI 1987/821)
- County Court (Interest on Judgment Debts) Order 1991 (SI 1991/1184)
- High Court and County Courts Jurisdiction Order 1991 (see Vol.2, Section 9B)

Forms

cc25.0.4
- **N244** Application Notice
- **N293A** Combined certificate of judgment and request for writ of fieri facias or writ of possession
- **N322** Order for recovery of money awarded by tribunal
- **N322A** Application for order to recover money awarded by tribunal or other body
- N322H Request to register a High Court judgment or order for enforcement
- **N328** Notice of transfer of proceedings to the High Court

Judgment creditor and debtor

cc25.1 1. In this Order and Orders 26 to 29 "judgment creditor" means the person who has obtained or is entitled to enforce a judgment or order and "debtor" means the person against whom it was given or made.

Reserve and Auxiliary Forces (Protection of Civil Interests) Act 1951

cc25.1.1 This Act (which is set out and discussed at paras 9A–1276.1 onwards)protects the civil interests of persons serving in the armed forces. Consider whether permission to enforce is required.

Description of parties

cc25.6 6. Where the name or address of the judgment creditor or the debtor as given in the request for the issue of a warrant of execution or delivery, judgment summons or warrant of committal differs from his name or address in the judgment or order sought to be enforced and the judgment creditor satisfies the court officer that the name or address as given in the request is applicable to the person concerned, *the judgment* creditor or the debtor, as the case may be, shall be described in the warrant or judgment summons as "C.D. of [name and address as given in the request] suing [or sued] as A.D. of [name and address in the judgment or order]".

Related sources

- Schedule 2, CCR O.25, r.9—Enforcement of judgment or order against firm cc25.6.1
- Schedule 1, RSC O.81, r.5—Enforcing judgment or order against firm

"satisfies the court officer"

Although Sch.2, CCR O.25, r.6 does not in terms require evidence, in practice the judgment creditor must explain the original misdescription and this is best done by affidavit or written statement. (The latter requires a "statement of truth"—see Pt 22, CPR and, in particular, its supplementing Practice Direction at para.22PD.1.) The prescribed form of application **N244** can be used. cc25.6.2

Recording and giving information as to warrants and orders

7.—(1) Subject to paragraph (1A), every district judge by whom a warrant or order is issued or received for execution shall from time to time state in the records of his court what has been done in the execution of the warrant or order. cc25.7

(1A) Where a warrant of execution is is issued by a court ("the home court") is sent to another court for execution ("the foreign court"), paragraph (1) shall not apply to the district judge of the home court, but when such a warrant is returned to the home court under paragraph (7), the court officer of the home court shall state in the records of his court what has been done in the execution of the warrant or order.

(2) If the warrant or order has not been executed within one month from the date of its issue or receipt by him, the court officer of the court responsible for its execution shall, at the end of that month and every subsequent month during which the warrant remains outstanding, send notice of the reason for non-execution to the judgment creditor and, if the warrant or order was received from another court, to that court.

(3) The district judge responsible for executing a warrant or order shall give such information respecting it as may reasonably be required by the judgment creditor and, if the warrant or order was received by him from another court, by the district judge of that court.

(4) Where money is received in pursuance of a warrant of execution or committal sent by one court to another court, the foreign court shall, subject to paragraph (5) and to section 346 of Insolvency Act 1986 and section 326 of the Companies Act 1948, send the money to the judgment creditor in the manner prescribed by the Court Funds Rules 1987 and, where the money is received in pursuance of a warrant of committal, make a return to the home court.

(5) Where interpleader proceedings are pending, the court shall not proceed in accordance with paragraph (4) until the interpleader proceedings are determined and the district judge shall then make a return showing how the money is to be disposed of and, if any money is payable to the judgment creditor, the court shall proceed in accordance with paragraph (4).

(6) Where a warrant of committal has been received from another court, the foreign court shall, on the execution of the warrant, send notice thereof to the home court.

(7) Where a warrant of execution has been received from another court, either—

(a) on the execution of the warrant; or

(b) if the warrant is not executed—

CCR

(i) on the making of a final return to the warrant; or

(ii) on suspension of the warrant under rule 8 (suspension of judgment or execution) or Order 26, rule 10 (withdrawal and suspension of warrant at creditor's request),

the foreign court shall return the warrant to the home court.

"District Judge"

cc25.7.1 Although this rule refers to the district judge the functions mentioned are in fact carried out by court staff (see CCR O.26, r.1(1A)). The rule still refers to the district judge for historical reasons. When the county courts were created in 1846 a "high bailiff" was given responsibilities and duties for execution similar to those of the Sheriff in the High Court. Subsequently the office ofhigh bailiff was abolished and his duties transferred to the registrar. In 1991 the office at registrar was abolished and his duties were transferred to the district judge. The district judge thus, anomalously, remains responsible for the actions of the bailiff (see s.123, CCA 1984). This anomaly is finally to be removed by s.67 of the Tribunals Courts and Enforcement Act 2007 (not yet in force).

responsibility and liability of bailiffs

cc25.7.2 See ss.123 to 127 CCA 1984 in Vol.2..

"information...as may reasonably be required"

cc25.7.3 As noted above the district judge remains responsible for bailiffs and must deal with responsible requests pursuant to O.25, r.7(3). Time spent dealing with enquiries detracts from the enforcement process itself and only reasonable requests by creditors can be dealt with (*Polentz v Roberts* (1900) 110 L.T. JO 376). In practice complaints by all court users are treated seriously and given full consideration by HM Court Service.

Section 326 Companies Act 1948

cc25.7.4 See now Insolvency Act 1986 s.184.

Forcible entry

cc25.7.5 The statutory authority for seizure is the County Courts Act 1984 s.89, which does not give express power to force entry. Consequently a bailiff may not break a lock or force a door to gain entry though he may open doors (*Vaughan v Mckenzie* [1969] 1 Q.B. 557). However, if the bailiff has a "walking possession" agreement (see Vol.2, 9A–595) and is deliberately excluded he can force entry (*Khazanchi v Faircharm Investments* [1998] 1 W.L.R. 1603). Broadly, the powers of a bailiff executing a warrant are the same as those of a High Court enforcement officer executing a writ of *fi-fa.* (see commentary to RSC Order 46). Bailiffs sometimes seek the authority of a district judge to force entry. While the district judge (who, anomalously, is also "high bailiff") can explain the bailiff's powers he cannot add to them. Either the bailiff has no power to force entry (and the judge cannot give it) or he has the power (in which case an order—save perhaps a declaratory order—is superfluous). Schedule 12 to the Tribunals Courts and Enforcement Act (not yet in force) will clarify and expand the powers of enforcement agents to enter premises including by forcible entry

Suspension of judgment or execution

cc25.8 8.—(1) The power of the court to suspend or stay a judgment or order or to stay execution of any warrant may be exercised by the district judge or, in the case of the power to stay execution of a warrant of execution and in accordance with the provisions of this rule, by the court officer.

(2) An application by the debtor to stay execution of a warrant of execution shall be in the appropriate form stating the proposed *terms, the grounds* on which it is made and including a signed statement of the debtor's means.

(3) Where the debtor makes an application under paragraph (2), the court shall—

(a) send the judgment creditor a copy of the debtor's application (and statement of means); and
(b) require the creditor to notify the court in writing, within 14 days of service of notification upon him, giving his reasons for any objection he may have to the granting of the application.

(4) If the judgment creditor does not notify the court of any objection within the time stated, the court officer may make an order suspending the warrant on terms of payment.

(5) Upon receipt of a notice by the judgment creditor under paragraph (3)(b), the court officer may, if the judgment creditor objects only to the terms offered, determine the date and rate of payment and make an order suspending the warrant on terms of payment.

(6) Any party affected by an order made under paragraph (5) may, within 14 days of service of the order on him and giving his reasons, apply on notice for the order to be reconsidered and the court shall fix a day for the hearing of the application before the district judge and give to the judgment creditor and the debtor not less than 8 days' notice of the day so fixed.

(7) On hearing an application under paragraph (6), the district judge may confirm the order or set it aside and make such new order as he thinks fit and the order so made shall be entered in the records of the court.

(8) Where the judgment creditor states in his notice under paragraph (3)(b) that he wishes the bailiff to proceed to execute the warrant, the court shall fix a day for a hearing before the district judge of the debtor's application and give to the judgment creditor and to the debtor not less than 2 days' notice of the day so fixed.

(9) Subject to any directions given by the district judge, where a warrant of execution has been suspended, it may be re-issued on the judgment creditor's filing a request showing that any condition subject to which the warrant was suspended has not been complied with.

(10) Where an order is made by the district judge suspending a warrant of execution, the debtor may be ordered to pay the costs of the warrant and any fees or expenses incurred before its suspension and the order may authorise the sale of a sufficient portion of any goods seized to cover such costs, fees and expenses and the expenses of sale.

Scope of provision

The power to suspend or stay a judgment and the power to stay execution are given by ss.71 and 88 CCA 1984 respectively: see Vol.2, Section 9A, O.25, r.8 provides the procedure and is clear enough. Note the limited powers of the court officer. Only the district judge can order costs. **cc25.8.1**

Stay execution of any warrant

In *Islington LBC v Harridge, The Times*, June 30, 1993, a tenant attending at court to issue an application to suspend a warrant was wrongly turned away by court staff. In these circumstances the court treated the application as having been issued at that time. Accordingly there was jurisdiction to suspend the warrant notwithstanding that by the actual hearing the warrant had been executed. See further commentary on the Housing Act 1985 at 3A–371. **cc25.8.2**

Enforcement of judgment or order against firm

9. [Revoked] **cc25.9**

History of rule

cc25.9.1 Revoked by Civil Procedure (Amendment) Rules 2006 (SI 2006/1689).

Enforcing judgment between a firm and its members

cc25.10 10. [Revoked]

History of rule

cc25.10.1 Revoked by Civil Procedure (Amendment) Rules 2006 (2006/1689).

Transfer to High Court for enforcement

cc25.13 13.—(1)Where the judgment creditor makes a request for a certificate of judgment under Order 22, rule 8(1) for the purpose of enforcing the judgment or order in the High Court—

(a) by execution against goods; or

(b) where the judgment or order to be enforced is an order for possession of land made in a possession claim against trespassers,

the grant of a certificate by the court shall take effect as an order to transfer the proceedings to the High Court and the transfer shall have effect on the grant of that certificate.

(2) On the transfer of proceedings in accordance with paragraph (1), the court shall give notice to the debtor or the person against whom the possession order was made that the proceedings have been transferred and shall make an entry of that fact in the records of his court.

(3) In a case where a request for a certificate of judgment is made under Order 22, rule 8(1) for the purpose of enforcing a judgment or order in the High Court and–

(a) an application for a variation in the date or rate of payment of money due under a judgment or order;

(b) an application under either CPR, rule 39.3(3) or CPR, rule 13.4;

(c) a request for an administration order; or

(d) an application for a stay of execution under section 88 of the Act,

is pending, the request for the certificate shall not be dealt with until those proceedings are determined.

Jurisdiction

cc25.13.1 Any county court judgment where the sum which it is sought to enforce is less than £600 and any county court judgment arising out of an agreement regulated by the Consumer Credit Act 1974 must be enforced in the county court. All other judgments for the payment of money can be—and where the sum which it is sought to enforce is £5000 or more must be—enforced in the High Court. See High Court and County Courts Jurisdiction 1991 in Vol.2 at Section 9B.

Procedure on Transfer

cc25.13.2 The procedure on transfer to the High Court for enforcement is very simple and is governed by CCR Ord 22 r.8.The relevant form to use depends on the purpose of the transfer as set out in that rule. Form **N293A** is a "Combined Certificate of Judgment and request for writ of fi-fa". After transfer, two copies should be filed at the District Registry (or, at the RCJ in Room E17). Some High Court Enforcement Officers will also arrange transfer up prior to execution (see further para.sc46.1.50).

CCR ORDER 26—WARRANTS OF EXECUTION, DELIVERY AND POSSESSION

Contents cc26.0.1

Editorial introduction

In the High Court writs of execution are levied by independent self-employed High Court enforcement officers. In county courts warrants are levied by bailiffs who are empoyees of HM Court Service. A warrant of execution is the equivalent of the High Court writ of *fieri facias*. (See detailed commentary to RSC O.46.) Under Sch.2, CCR O.26, r.1(2) where the order is for payment by instalments, the warrant can be (subject to r.1(3)) for the arrears of instalments or the whole outstanding sum. A warrant of delivery (the equivalent of the High Court's writ of delivery) is to enforce an order for delivery up of goods and a warrant of possession (the equivalent of the High Court's writ of possession) is to enforce an order for recovery of land. cc26.0.2

In all three cases the procedure for the judgment creditor is very simple: the appropriate request form and prescribed fee are sent or taken to the office of the court which made the order.

Practice Direction—Execution (at ccpd 26) supplements both RSC O.46 and CCR O.26).

Related sources cc26.0.3

- Practice Direction—Execution (see para.ccpd 26)
- Practice Direction—Enforcement of Judgments and Orders (see para.70PD.1)
- Schedule 2, CCR O.25—Enforcement of Judgments and Orders—General
- County Courts Act 1984 Pt V (see Vol.2, Section 9A)
- Insolvency Act 1986 s.346
- *RSC O.45—Enforcement* of Judgments and Orders: General
- RSC O.46—Writs of Execution: General
- RSC O.47—Writs of *fieri facias*

Forms cc26.0.4

- **N42** Warrant of Execution
- **N46** Warrant of Delivery and of Execution for damages and costs
- **N48** Warrant of Delivery where, if goods are not returned, levy is to be made for their value

- **N49** Warrant for Possession of Land
- **N50** Warrant of restitution (O.26)
- **N245** Application for suspension of warrant (and for variation of an instalment)
- **N246** Claimant's reply to defendant's application to vary instalment order
- **N246A** Claimant's reply to defendant's application to suspend warrant of execution
- **N323** Request for Warrant of Execution
- **N324** Request for Warrant of delivery of goods
- **N325** Request for Warrant for possession of land
- **N317** Bailiff's report
- **N317A** Bailiff's report to the claimant
- **N320** Request for return of, or to, warrant
- **N326** Notice of issue of warrant of execution
- **N327** Notice of issue of warrant of execution to enforce a judgment or order of the High Court
- **N330** Notice of sale or payment under execution in respect of a judgment for a sum exceeding £500
- **N331** Notice of withdrawal from possession, or payment over of moneys on a notice of bankruptcy or winding-up order
- **N332** Inventory of goods removed
- **N333**Notice of time when and where goods will be sold
- **N335** Request to hold walking possession and authority to re-enter
- **N444** Details of sale under a warrant of execution
- **N445** Notice for re-issue of warrant

High Court Enforcement Officers

cc26.0.5 See paras sc46.1.48 and sc46.1.50.

Application for warrant of execution

cc26.1 1.—(1) A judgment creditor desiring a warrant of execution to be issued shall file a request in that behalf certifying—

(a) the amount remaining due under the judgment or order; and

(b) where the order made is for payment of a sum of money by instalments—

(i) that the whole or part of any instalment due remains unpaid; and

(ii) the amount for which the warrant is to be issued.

(1A) The court officer shall discharge the functions—

(a) under section 85(2) of the Act of issuing a warrant of execution;

(b) under section 85(3) of the Act of entering in the record mentioned in that subsection and on the warrant the precise time of the making of the application to issue the warrant; and

(c) under section 103(1) of the Act of sending the warrant of execution to another county court.

(2) Where the court has made an order for payment of a sum of money by instalments and default has been made in payment of such an instalment, a warrant of execution may be issued for the whole of the said sum of money and costs then remaining unpaid or, subject *to paragraph (3),* for such part as the judgment creditor may request, not being in the latter case less than £50 or the amount of one monthly instalment or, as the case may be, 4 weekly instalments, whichever is the greater.

(3) In any case to which paragraph (2) applies no warrant shall be issued unless at the time when it is issued—

(a) the whole or part of an instalment which has already become due remains unpaid; and

(b) any warrant previously issued for part of the said sum of money and costs has expired or has been satisfied or abandoned.

(4) Where a warrant is issued for the whole or part of the said sum of money and costs, the court officer shall, unless the district judge responsible for execution of the warrant directs otherwise, send a warning notice to the person against whom the warrant is issued and, where such a notice is sent, the warrant shall not be levied until 7 days thereafter.

(5) Where judgment is given or an order made for payment otherwise than by instalments of a sum of money and costs to be assessed in accordance with CPR Part 47 (detailed assessment procedure) and default is made in payment of the sum of money before the costs have been assessed, a warrant of execution may issue for recovery of the sum of money and a separate warrant may issue subsequently for the recovery of the costs if default is made in payment of them.

Execution

As a warrant of execution is the county court equivalent of the writ of *fieri facias*, see the detailed commentary to RSC O.47. **cc26.1.1**

Forcible entry

See para.cc27.7.5. **cc26.1.2**

"Section 85"

Section 85 CCA 1984 (Vol.2, 9A-582) gives the statutory authority for the issue of warrants. **cc26.1.3**

Contracting out of administrative functions

The Contracting Out (Administrative and other Court Staff) Order 2001 SI 2001/3698)—see para.2.5.3—enables the functions in CCR O.26 to be discharged by the contractor supplying IT services to the county court. **cc26.1.4**

Goods liable to seizure in execution

See s.89, CCA 1984: Vol.2, 9A–591. **cc26.1.5**

Levying execution on certain days

See PD—Execution at ccpd 26 which prohibits execution on a Sunday, Good Friday or Christmas Day. **cc26.1.6**

Execution of High Court judgment

2.—(1) Where it is desired to enforce by warrant of execution a judgment or order of the High Court, or a judgment, order, decree or award which is or has become enforceable as if it were a judgment of the High Court, the request referred to in rule 1(1) may be filed in any court in the district of which execution is to be levied. **cc26.2**

(2) Subject to Order 25, rule 9(5), any restriction imposed by these rules on the issue of execution shall apply as if the judgment, order, decree or award were a judgment or order of the county court, but permission to issue execution shall not be required if permission has already been given by the High Court.

(3) Notice of the issue of the warrant shall be sent by the county court to the High Court.

Enforcement of High Court judgments in the county court

cc26.2.1 The most usual reason for transferring to a county court for enforcement is not to issue a warrant of execution but to apply for an attachment of earnings order (see CCR O.27).

However, where the sum which it is sought to enforce is less than £600, enforcement by execution must be in the county court (para.8 High Court and County Courts Jurisdiction Order 1991 see Vol.2, 9B–150) and can be in the county court where that sum is less than £5000.

request referred to in rule 1(1)

cc26.2.2 —means Form **N323**.

"O.25 r.9(5)"

cc26.2.3 This rule provides that O.25 r.9 does not apply in the case of execution of a High Court judgment against a firm in the county court; instead see RSC O.81, r.5.

Execution against farmer

cc26.3 3. If after the issue of a warrant of execution the district judge for the district in which the warrant is to be executed has reason to believe that the debtor is a farmer, the execution creditor shall, if so required by the district judge, furnish him with an official certificate, dated not more than three days beforehand, or the result of a search at the Land Registry as to the existence of any charge registered against the debtor under the Agricultural Credits Act 1928.

Concurrent warrants

cc26.4 4. Two or more warrants of execution may be issued concurrently for execution in different districts, but—

(a) no more shall be levied under all the warrants together than is authorised to be levied under one of them; and

(b) the costs of more than one such warrant shall not be allowed against the debtor except by order of the court.

Permission to issue certain warrants

cc26.5 5.—(1) A warrant of execution shall not issue without the permission of the court where—

(a) six years or more have elapsed since the date of the judgment or order;

(b) any change has taken place, whether by death or otherwise in the parties entitled to enforce the judgment or order or liable to have it enforced against them;

(c) the judgment or order is against the assets of a deceased person coming into the hands of his executors or administrators after the date of the judgment or order and it is sought to issue execution against such assets; or

(d) any goods to be seized under a warrant of execution are in the hands of a receiver appointed by a court.

(2) An application for permission shall be supported by a witness statement or affidavit establishing the applicant's right to relief and may be made without notice being served on any other party in the first instance but the court may direct the application notice to be served on such persons as it thinks fit.

(3) Where, by reason of one and the same event, a person seeks permission under paragraph (1)(b) to enforce more judgments or orders than one, he may make one application only, specifying in a

schedule all the judgments or orders in respect of which it is made, and if the application notice is directed to be served on any person, it need set out only such part of the application as affects him.

(4) Paragraph (1) is without prejudice to any enactment, rule or direction by virtue of which a person is required to obtain the permission of the court for the issue of a warrant or to proceed to execution or otherwise to the enforcement of a judgment or order.

Permission to issue execution

The general rule is that permission to issue execution is not required. CCR O.26, r.5 specifies the exceptions when permission is required. The rule is based on RSC O.46, r.2: therefore see commentary on that rule. **cc26.5.1**

The requirement to obtain permission if O.26 r.5 applies is mandatory and it is an abuse of process to issue without it (see *Hackney LBC v White* (1996) 28 H.L.R. 219). Obtaining permission to issue is no mere formality; see para.46.22.2. Although r.26.5(2) enables the application to be made without notice it also gives power to direct that notice be given. In all cases the rule requires the application to be supported by evidence.

Section 24 Limitation Act 1980

An action cannot be brought upon any judgment after the expiration of six years from the date on which the judgment became enforceable. However, an application for permission under CCR O.26, r.5 is not an action on the judgment. The right to sue on a judgment is distinct from the right to issue execution on a judgment which is a procedural matter. See further sc46.2.12. **cc26.5.2**

Duration and renewal of warrant

6.—(1) A warrant of execution shall, for the purpose of execution, be valid in the first instance for 12 months beginning with the date of its issue, but if not wholly executed, it may be renewed from time to time, by order of the court, for a period of 12 months at any one time, beginning with the day next following that on which it would otherwise expire, if an application for renewal is made before that day or such later day (if any) as the court may allow. **cc26.6**

(2) A note of any such renewal shall be indorsed on the warrant and it shall be entitled to priority according to the time of its original issue or, where appropriate, its receipt by the district judge responsible for its execution.

"Effect of rule"

A warrant of execution is valid for twelve months but can be renewed. CCR O.26 r.6 is based on RSC O.46 r.8: see commentary on that rule. **cc26.6.1**

Priority

Which warrant has priority is important where the judgment debtor has insufficient goods to satisfy them all. In addition to O.26 r.6(2), see CCA 1984, s.85 (Vol.2, 9A–582). If a warrant is set aside but restored on appeal it resumes its original priority (*Bankers Trust Co v Galadari* [1987] Q.B. 222). Priority is governed not merely by date but by the precise time of issue in the county court (CCA 1984, s.85) or the precise time of receipt by the enforcement officer in the High Court (Courts Act 2003, para.7, Sch.7). The first in time has priority whether it be in the High Court or a county court. **cc26.6.2**

Notice of levy

7. Any bailiff upon levying execution shall deliver to the debtor or leave at the place where execution is levied a notice of the warrant. **cc26.7**

Notice of the warrant

cc26.7.1 The notice required by O.26 r.7 is given to the debtor in Form **N326**. (It is to be distinguished from Form **N330**—Notice of sale or payment under execution and Form **N332**—Inventory of goods removed).

There is no equivalent of notice in Form **N332** in the High Court. The notice gives the judgment debtor an opportunity to pay without a levy but equally provides an unscrupulous judgment debtor an opportunity to hide goods. If it is thought that the judgment debtor might do this consider transferring to the High Court and issuing a writ of *fi-fa* (see CPR r.70.3).

Bankruptcy or winding up of debtor

cc26.8 8.—(1) Where the district judge responsible for the execution of a warrant is required by any provision of the Insolvency Act 1986 or any other enactment relating to insolvency to retain the proceeds of sale of goods sold under the warrant or money paid in order to avoid a sale, the court shall, as soon as practicable after the sale or the receipt of the money, send notice to the execution creditor and, if the warrant issued out of another court, to that court.

(2) Where the district judge responsible for the execution of a warrant—

(a) receives notice that a bankruptcy order has been made against the debtor or, if the debtor is a company, that a provisional liquidator has been appointed or that an order has been made or a resolution passed for the winding up of the company; and

(b) withdraws from possession of goods seized or pays over to the official receiver or trustee in bankruptcy or, if the debtor is a company, to the liquidator the proceeds of sale of goods sold under the warrant or money paid in order to avoid a sale or seized or received in part satisfaction of the warrant,

the court shall send notice to the execution creditor and, if the warrant issued out of another court, to that court.

(3) Where the court officer of a court to which a warrant issued out of another court has been sent for execution receives any such notice as is referred to in paragraph (2)(a) after he has sent to the home court any money seized or received in part satisfaction of the warrant, he shall forward the notice to that court.

"Section 346 Insolvency Act 1986"

cc26.8.1 See commentary at sc46.1.25.

Withdrawal and suspension of warrant at creditor's request

cc26.10 10.—(1) Where an execution creditor requests the district judge responsible for executing a warrant to withdraw from possession, he shall, subject to the following paragraphs of this rule, be treated as having abandoned the execution, and the court shall mark the warrant as withdrawn by request of the execution creditor.

(2) Where the request is made in consequence of a claim having been made under Order 33, rule 1, to goods seized under the warrant, the execution shall be treated as being abandoned in respect only of the goods claimed.

(3) If the district judge responsible for executing a warrant is requested by the execution creditor to suspend it in pursuance of an

arrangement between him and the debtor, the court shall mark the warrant as suspended by request of the execution creditor and the execution creditor may subsequently apply to the district judge holding the warrant for it to be re-issued and, if he does so, the application shall be deemed for the purpose of section 85(3) of the Act to be an application to issue the warrant.

(4) Nothing in this rule shall prejudice any right of the execution creditor to apply for the issue of a fresh warrant or shall authorise the re-issue of a warrant which has been withdrawn or has expired or has been superseded by the issue of a fresh warrant.

Effect of rule

This rule is concerned only with withdrawal or suspension at the creditor's request. This is often done by a creditor who has made an arrangement directly with the debtor. For the power of the court to suspend, usually on application by the debtor, see CCR O.25, r.8. **cc26.10.1**

Priority

Priority of warrants is discussed at sc46.1.5 and cc26.6.2. By suspending a warrant a creditor loses priority to any other warrant issued during the suspension (*Hunt v Hooper* (1844) 12 M&W 664). If it were just to do so the court could suspend the later warrant until the first has been paid but there is no right to this. **cc26.10.2**

Suspension of part warrant

11. Where a warrant issued for part of a sum of money and costs payable under a judgment or order is suspended on payment of instalments, the judgment or order shall, unless the court otherwise directs, be treated as suspended on those terms as respects the whole of the sum of money and costs then remaining unpaid. **cc26.11**

Inventory and notice where goods removed

12.—(1) Where goods seized in execution are removed, the court shall forthwith deliver or send to the debtor a sufficient inventory of the goods removed and shall, not less than 4 days before the time fixed for the sale, give him notice of the time and place at which the goods will be sold. **cc26.12**

(2) The inventory and notice shall be given to the debtor by delivering them to him personally or by sending them to him by post at his place of residence or, if his place of residence is not known, by leaving them for him, or sending them to him by post, at the place from which the goods were removed.

Inventory

Notice is given in Form N332. Sale is governed by s.97 CCA 1984 (Vol 2 9A–607). **cc26.12.1**

Account of sale

13. Where goods are sold under an execution, the court shall furnish the debtor with a detailed account in writing of the sale and of the application of the proceeds. **cc26.13**

Notification to foreign court of payment made

14. Where, after a warrant has been sent to a foreign court for execution but before a final return has been made to the warrant, the home court is notified of a payment made in respect of the sum for which the warrant is issued, the home court shall send notice of the payment to the foreign court. **cc26.14**

Order for private sale

cc26.15 15.—(1) Subject to paragraph (6), an order of the court under section 97 of the Act that a sale under an execution may be made otherwise than by public auction may be made on the application of the execution creditor or the debtor or the district judge responsible for the execution of the warrant.

(2) Where he is not the applicant for an order under this rule, the district judge responsible for the execution of the warrant shall, on the demand of the applicant, furnish him with a list containing the name and address of every execution creditor under any other warrant or writ of execution against the goods of the debtor of which the district judge has notice, and where the district judge is the applicant, he shall prepare such a list.

(3) Not less than 4 days before the day fixed for the hearing of the application, the applicant shall give notice of the application to each of the other persons by whom the application might have been made and to every person named in the list referred to in paragraph (2).

(4) The applicant shall produce the list to the court on the hearing of the application.

(5) Every person to whom notice of the application was given may attend and be heard on the hearing of the application.

(6) Where the district judge responsible for the execution of the warrant is the district judge by whom it was issued and he has no notice of any other warrant or writ of execution against the goods of the debtor, an order under this rule may be made by the court of its own motion with the consent of the execution creditor and the debtor or after giving them an opportunity of being heard.

Private sale

cc26.15.1 The most common reason for ordering a private sale is that the goods are of a perishable nature. See also s.93, CCA 1984 (Vol.2, 9A–601); s.97, CCA 1984 (Vol.2, 9A–607) and commentary thereon and also commentary to RSC O.47, r.6, the equivalent rule in the High Court.

Warrant of delivery

cc26.16 16.—(1) Except where an Act or rule provides otherwise, a judgment or order for the delivery of any goods shall be enforceable by warrant of delivery in accordance with this rule.

(2) If the judgment or order does not give the person against whom it was given or made the alternative of paying the value of the goods, it may be enforced by a warrant of specific delivery, that is to say, a warrant to recover the goods without alternative provision for recovery of their value.

(3) If the judgment or order is for the delivery of the goods or payment of their value, it may be enforced by a warrant of delivery to recover the goods of their value.

(4) Where a warrant of delivery is issued, the judgment creditor shall be entitled, by the same or a separate warrant, to execution against the debtor's goods for any money payable under the judgment or order which is to be enforced by the warrant of delivery.

(4A) Where a judgment or order is given or made for the delivery of goods or payment of their value and a warrant is issued to recover the goods or their value, money paid into court under the warrant shall be appropriated first to any sum of money and costs awarded.

(5) The foregoing provisions of this Order, so far as applicable, shall have effect, with the necessary modifications, in relation to warrants of delivery as they have effect in relation to warrants of execution.

Enforcement of judgment for delivery of goods

O.26 r.16 corresponds to RSC O.45 r.4—see commentary thereon. **cc26.16.1**

Forms

Request for a warrant is made in Form **N324**. The warrant itself is in Form **N46** or **N48** depending on the terms of the court's order. **cc26.16.2**

Warrant of restitution

In *Wiltshire County Council v Fraser* [1986] 1 W.L.R. 109 it was held that a warrant of restitution will issue to recover land from occupants who were neither parties to the original proceedings nor dispossessed by the original order provided there is a plain and sufficient nexus between the order for possession and the need to effect further recovery of land. See further commentary to Sch.1, RSC O.113 and para.sc46.3.3 on the writ of restitution. **cc26.16.3**

Warrant of possession

17.—(1) A judgment or order for the recovery of land shall be enforceable by warrant of possession. **cc26.17**

(2) Without prejudice to paragraph (3A), the person desiring a warrant of possession to be issued must file a request certifying that the land which is subject of the judgment or order has not been vacated.

(3) Where a warrant of possession is issued, the judgment creditor shall be entitled, by the same or a separate warrant, to execution against the debtor's goods for any money payable under the judgment or order which is to be enforced by the warrant of possession.

(3A) In a case to which paragraph (3) applies or where an order for possession has been suspended on terms as to payment of a sum money by instalments, the judgment creditor shall in his request certify—

(a) the amount of money remaining due under the judgment or order; and

(b) that the whole or part of any instalment due remains unpaid.

(4) A warrant of restitution may be issued, with the permission of the court, in aid of any warrant of possession.

(5) An application for permission under paragraph (4) may be made without notice being served on any other party and shall be supported by evidence of wrongful re-entry into possession following the execution of the warrant of possession and of such further facts as would, in the High Court, enable the judgment creditor to have a writ of restitution issued.

(6) Rules 5 and 6 shall apply, with the necessary modifications, in relation to a warrant of possession and any further warrant in aid of such a warrant as they apply in relation to a warrant of execution.

Setting aside warrant of possession

cc26.17.1 For circumstances in which a warrant of possession may be suspended or set aside, see *Leicester City Council v Aldwinckle* (1992) 24 H.L.R. 40, CA. (See further paras sc45.3.8 and 3A–371.)

In *Hammersmith and Fulham LBC v Hill* (1995) 27 H.L.R. 368 at 35, CA, where a tenant was evicted from a secure tenancy without notice of a warrant for possession, it was held, the warrant of possession could only be suspended or set aside in the circumstances set out in *Leicester City Council v Aldwinkle* (1991) 24 H.L.R. 40, CA. (See further para.3A–372.)

Staying execution of warrant of possession

cc26.17.2 Where mortgagees obtain a warrant for possession to enforce their security by sale forthwith and the mortgagor proposes to apply to the High Court under the Law of Property Act 1925 s.91(2) to enable him to sell the property in due course, on an application by the mortgagor a county court has no jurisdiction to stay the execution of the warrant (*Cheltenham and Gloucester Building Society v Krausz* [1997] 1 All E.R. 21, CA). Where the court has power, under s.36 of the Administration of Justice Act 1970 and s.8 of the Administration of Justice Act 1973, to allow the mortgagor a "reasonable period" to pay sums due under the mortgage, in the absence of unusual circumstances, the outstanding term of the mortgage was the starting point in determining how long it would be reasonable to keep a mortgage. (*Western Bank Ltd v Schindler* [1977] Ch. 1; *Cheltenham and Gloucester Building Society v Norgan* [1996] 1 W.L.R. 343.) There is no rule that, for example, all arrears must be paid off within four years. Neither is there a rule that, where the mortgage is to be repaid by reselling the property a warrant can only be suspended if a sale will take place within a short period of time. Thus if there is evidence that completion of a sale could take place in six or nine months or even a year, the court may conclude that the mortgagor was "likely to be able within a reasonable period to pay any sums due under the mortgage" (*National and Provincial Building Society v Lloyd* [1996] 1 All E.R. 630). However, where there is insufficient evidence to show either that the mortgagor could sell the property within three to five years or that the proceeds would be sufficient to discharge the mortgage debt, a warrant should not be suspended (*Bristol and West Building Society v Ellis* (1996) 76 P. & C.R. 158, CA).

Section 36 of the Administration of Justice Act 1970 is at Vol.2, Section 9B; and s.8 of the Administration of Justice Act 1973 is also at Vol.2, Section 9B.

A warrant of possession is the county court equivalent of the writ of possession. The warrant is executed by a county court bailiff. A representative of the judgment creditor should be present when the warrant is executed to receive the premises from the bailiff and to secure them as appropriate. See further Sch.1, RSC O.45, r.3 at paras sc45.3 *et seq.*

Human rights

cc26.17.3 The issue of a warrant of possession is no more than an administrative act to give effect to a judicial decision. The tenants right under the ECHR are considered at trial and no seperate determination of those rights arises on issue of the warrant (*Southwark London BC v St Brice* [2002] 1 W.L.R. 1537).

Saving for enforcement by committal

cc26.18 18. Nothing in rule 16 or 17 shall prejudice any power to enforce a judgment or order for the delivery of goods or the recovery of land by an order of committal.

Contempt of court

cc26.18.1 A person may be in contempt of court if he fails to comply with an order for possession requiring him to deliver up possession on or before a particular date. A person may be guilty of contempt of court if he obstructs a bailiff seeking to execute a warrant of possession (*Robert Arnold Tuohy v Gary Bell (Trustee in Bankrutpcy)* [2002] EWCA Civ 423. Distinguish these two different issues. If it is sought to commit for failure to comply with the order for possession then, generally, the order will have to give a date *and time* for compliance and be endorsed with a penal notice.

"order of committal"

cc26.18.2 See Sch.2, CCR O.29 and Sch.1, RSC O.52.

PRACTICE DIRECTION—EXECUTION

This Practice Direction supplements RSC Order 46 (Schedule 1 to the CPR) and CCR Order 26 (Schedule 2 to the CPR) ccpd26

Levying execution on certain days

1.1 Unless the Court orders otherwise, a writ of execution or a warrant of execution to enforce a judgment or order must not be executed on a Sunday, Good Friday or Christmas Day.

1.2 Paragraph 1.1 does not apply to an Admiralty claim *in rem*.

CCR ORDER 27—ATTACHMENT OF EARNINGS

Contents cc27.0.1

Part I—*General*

Editorial introduction

By the Attachment of Earnings Act 1971 the High Court can make an attachment of earnings order only to secure payments under a High Court maintenance order. The county courts can make such orders to secure payments under a High Court or county court maintenance order, the payment of a judgment debt or payments under an administration order. Thus, the majority of attachment orders are made in the cc27.0.2

county court and, administratively, there is a centralised system for collection. The procedure is very effective where the debtor is in employment with sufficient earnings. For a creditor the procedure is very simple, usually involving only the completion of the Request for an Attachment of Earnings Order (Form **N337**) and payment of the prescribed fee: the court does the rest.

Related sources

cc27.0.3
- Attachment of Earnings Act 1971 (see Vol.2, Section 9B; the Act does not apply to debtors who are members of Her Majesty's Armed Forces, but see analogous remedies under the Armed Forces Act 1971).

Forms

cc27.0.4
- **N55** Notice of application for attachment of earnings order
- **N55A** Notice of application for attachment of earnings order—maintenance
- **N56** Reply to attachment of earnings application—statement of means
- **N58** Order for debtor's attendance at adjournal hearing of attachment of earnings application—maintenance
- **N59** Warrant of committal under s.23(1) Attachment of Earnings Act 1971
- **N60** Attachment of earnings order—judgment debt
- **N61** Order for production of Statement of Means
- **N61A** Notice to employer for production of statement of earnings
- **N62** Summons for offence under Attachment of Earnings Act 1971
- **N63** Notice to show cause under s.23 Attachment of Earnings Act
- **N64** Suspended attachment of earnings order
- **N64A** Suspended attachment of earnings order—maintenance
- **N65** Attachment of earnings order—(priority maintenance)
- **N65A** Attachment of earnings arrears order
- **N66** Consolidated attachment of earnings order
- **N66A** Notice of application for consolidated attachment of earnings order
- **N112A** Power of Arrest s.23 Attachment of Earnings Act 1971
- **N118** Notice to defendant where committal order made but suspended under Attachment of Earnings Order 1971
- **N336**—Request for search in attachment of earnings register
- **N337** Request for an Attachment of earnings order
- **N338** Request for statement of earnings
- **N339** Discharge of attachment of earnings order
- **N340** Notice as to payment under attachment of earnings order made by High Court
- **N341** Notice of intention to vary attachment of earnings order under s.10(2) Attachment of Earnings Act 1971
- **N448** Request to defendant for employment details—attachment of earnings
- **N449** Notice to employer—failure to make deductions under attachment of earnings order

PART I

GENERAL

Interpretation

cc27.1 1.—(1) In this Order—

"the Act of 1971" means the Attachment of Earnings Act 1971 and, unless the context otherwise requires, expressions used in that Act have the same meanings as in that Act.

Attachment of Earnings Act 1971

cc27.1.1 See Vol.2, para.9B–161.

Index of orders

cc27.2 2.—(1) The court officer of every court shall keep a nominal index of the debtors residing within the district of his court in respect of whom there are in force attachment of earnings orders which have been made by that court or of which the court officer has received notice from another court.

(2) Where a debtor in respect of whom a court has made an attachment of earnings order resides within the district of another court, the court officer of the first-mentioned court shall send a copy of the order to the court officer of the other court for entry in his index.

(3) The court officer shall, on the request of any person having a judgment or order against a person believed to be residing within the district of the court, cause a search to be made in the index of the court and issue a certificate of the result of the search.

Form

Form **N336** is used to search the index pursuant to r.27.2. Surprisingly little use is made of the facility to search (no fee is payable). Even if the search reveals that there is an order in force it may still be worth applying with a view to a consolidated order being made under CCR O.27, r.19. **cc27.2.1**

Appropriate court

3.—(1) Subject to paragraphs (2) and (3), an application for an attachment of earnings order may be made to the court for the district in which the debtor resides. **cc27.3**

(2) If the debtor does not reside within England or Wales, or the creditor does not know where he resides, the application may be made to the court in which, or for the district in which, the judgment or order sought to be enforced was obtained.

(3) Where the creditor applies for attachment of earnings orders in respect of two or more debtors jointly liable under a judgment or order, the application may be made to the court for the district in which any of the debtors resides, so however that if the judgment or order was given or made by any such court, the application shall be made to that court.

Venue

The general rule is that the application is made to the court for the district in which the debtor resides. If necessary the case can be transferred there pursuant to CPR r.70.3; and see PD70, para.2. **cc27.3.1**

Mode of applying

4.—(1) A judgment creditor who desires to apply for an attachment of earnings order shall file his application certifying the amount of money remaining due under the judgment or order and that the whole or part of any instalment due remains unpaid and, where it is sought to enforce an order of a magistrates' court— **cc27.4**

(a) a certified copy of the order; and

(b) a witness statement or affidavit verifying the amount due under the order or, if payments under the order are required to be made to the designated officer for the magistrates' court, a certificate by that chief executive to *the same effect*.

(2) On the filing of the documents mentioned in paragraph (1) the court officer shall, where the order to be enforced is a maintenance order, fix a day for the hearing of the application.

Service and reply

5.—(1) Notice of the application together with a form of reply in the appropriate form, shall be served on the debtor in the manner set out in CPR r.6.20. **cc27.5**

(2) The debtor shall, within 8 days after service on him of the documents mentioned in paragraph (1), file a reply in the form provided, and the instruction to that effect in the notice to the debtor shall constitute a requirement imposed by virtue of section 14(4) of the Act of 1971:

Provided that no proceedings shall be taken for an offence alleged to have been committed under section 23(2)(c) or (f) of the Act of 1971 in relation to the requirement unless the said documents have been served on the debtor personally or the court is satisfied that they came to his knowledge in sufficient time for him to comply with the requirement.

(2A) Nothing in paragraph (2) shall require a defendant to file a reply if, within the period of time mentioned in that paragraph, he pays to the judgment creditor the money remaining due under the judgment or order and, where such payment is made, the judgment creditor shall so inform the court officer.

(3) On receipt of a reply the court officer shall send a copy to the applicant.

History of rule

cc27.5.1 Amended by SI 2000/221 and SI 2008/2178.

Notice to employer

cc27.6 6. Without prejudice to the powers conferred by section 14(1) of the Act of 1971, the court officer may, at any stage of the proceedings, send to any person appearing to have the debtor in his employment a notice requesting him to give to the court, within such period as may be specified in the notice, a statement of the debtor's earnings and anticipated earnings with such particulars as may be so specified.

"at any stage at the proceedings"

cc27.6.1 A judgment creditor who knows the name and address of the judgment debtors' employer should request service of notice on the employer when the application for the attachment of earnings order is issued. The prescribed form is **N338**. Should the debtor fail to return the **N56** further delay is avoided and the district judge will be able to make an order acting on the information supplied by the employer.

Attachment of earnings order

cc27.7 7.—(1) On receipt of the debtor's reply, the court officer may, if he has sufficient information to do so, make an attachment of earnings order and a copy of the order shall be sent to the parties and to the debtor's employer.

(2) Where an order is made under paragraph (1), the judgment creditor or the debtor may, within 14 days of service of the order on him and giving his reasons, apply on notice for the order to be reconsidered and the court officer shall fix a day for the hearing of the application and give to the judgment creditor and the debtor not less than 2 days' notice of the day so fixed.

(3) On hearing an application under paragraph (2), the district judge may confirm the order or set it aside and make such new order as he thinks fit and the order so made shall be entered in the records of the court.

(4) Where an order is not made under paragraph (1), the court officer shall refer the application to the district judge who shall, if he considers that he has sufficient information to do so without the attendance of the parties, determine the application.

(5) Where the district judge does not determine the application under paragraph (4), he shall direct that a day be fixed for the hearing of the application whereupon the court officer shall fix such a day and give to the judgment creditor and the debtor not less than 8 days' notice of the day so fixed.

(6) Where an order is made under paragraph (4), the judgment creditor or the debtor may, within 14 days of service of the order on him and giving his reasons, apply on notice for the order to be reconsidered; and the court officer shall fix a day for the hearing of the application and give to the judgment creditor and the debtor not less than 2 days' notice of the day so fixed.

(7) On hearing an application under paragraph (6), the district judge may confirm the order or set it aside and make such new order as he thinks fit and the order so made shall be entered in the records of the court.

(8) If the creditor does not appear at the hearing of the application under paragraph (5) but—

(a) the court has received a witness statement or affidavit of evidence from him; or

(b) the creditor requests the court in writing to proceed in his absence, the court may proceed to hear the application and to make an order thereon.

(9) An attachment of earnings order may be made to secure the payment of a judgment debt if the debt is—

(a) of not less than £50; or

(b) for the amount remaining payable under a judgment for a sum of not less than £50.

Procedure

As noted at para.27.0.2, the modern procedure is very simple for creditors. It is a paper procedure administered by a court officer with reference to a district judge when required. **cc27.7.1**

Insolvency

Problems have arisen where an employer makes deductions from the employee's wages but is then declared insolvent before handing over the deductions to the collecting officer. An employer making deductions pursuant to an order acts as agent for the debtor and retains the money on trust until such time as it is paid to the collecting officer (consider *Re Green Ex p. Official Receiver v Cutting* [1979] 1 W.L.R. 1211; [1979] 1 All E.R. 832 and *Carreras Rothmans Ltd v Freeman Mathews Treasure Ltd (in liquidation)* [1985] Ch 207; [1984] 3 W.L.R. 1016; [1985] 1 All E.R. 155). **cc27.7.2**

Failure by debtor

7A.—(1) If the debtor has failed to comply with rule 5(2) or to make payment to the judgment creditor, the court officer may issue an order under section 14(1) of the Act of 1971 which shall— **cc27.7A**

(a) be indorsed with or incorporate a notice warning the debtor of the consequences of disobedience to the order;

(b) be served on the debtor personally; and

(c) direct that any payments made thereafter shall be paid into the court and not direct to the judgment creditor.

(2) Without prejudice to rule 16, if the person served with an order made pursuant to paragraph (1) fails to obey it or to file a statement of his means or to make payment, the court officer shall issue a notice calling on that person to show good reason why he should not

be imprisoned and any such notice shall be served on the debtor personally not less than 5 days before the hearing.

(3) Order 29, rule 1 shall apply, with the necessary modifications and with the substitution of references to the district judge for references to the judge, where a notice is issued under paragraph (2) or (4) of that rule.

(4) In this rule "statement of means" means a statement given under section 14(1) of the Act of 1971.

Effect of rule

cc27.7A.1 Where a debtor fails to file the reply required by O.27 r.5 he is served with notice in Form **N61**. If this too is ignored he is served with 'notice to show cause' in Form **N63**. However, often the court is able to make an attachment of earnings order on the basis of the form returned by the employer under O.27 r.6.

Committal

cc27.7A.2 See Section 23—Attachment of Earnings Act 1971 (Vol 2, 9B–193).

Suspended committal order

cc27.7B 7B.—(1) If the debtor fails to attend at an adjourned hearing of an application for an attachment of earnings order and a committal order is made, the judge or district judge may direct that the committal order shall be suspended so long as the debtor attends at the time and place specified in the committal order and paragraphs (2), (4) and (5) of Order 28, rule 7 shall apply, with the necessary modifications, where such a direction is given as they apply where a direction is given under paragraph (1) of that rule.

(2) Where a committal order is suspended under paragraph (1) and the debtor fails to attend at the time and place specified under paragraph (1), a certificate to that effect given by the court officer shall be sufficient authority for the issue of a warrant of committal.

Form

cc27.7B.1 A suspended committal order is in Form **N118**.

Committal

cc27.7B.2 See Section 23—Attachment of Earnings Act 1971 (Vol.2, para.9B–193).

Failure by debtor—maintenance orders

cc27.8 8.—(1) An order made under section 23(1) of the Act of 1971 for the attendance of the debtor at an adjourned hearing of an application for an attachment of earnings order to secure payments under a maintenance order shall—

(a) be served on the debtor personally not less than 5 days before the day fixed for the adjourned hearing; and

(b) direct that any payments made thereafter shall be paid into the court and not direct to the judgment creditor.

(2) An application by a debtor for the revocation of an order committing him to prison and, if he is already in custody, for his discharge under subsection (7) of the said section 23 shall be made to the judge or district judge in writing without notice to any other party showing the reasons for the debtor's failure to attend the court or his refusal to be sworn or to give evidence, as the case may be, and containing an undertaking by the debtor to attend the court or to be sworn or to give evidence when next ordered or required to do so.

(3) The application shall, if the debtor has already been lodged in prison, be attested by the governor of the prison (or any other officer of the prison not below the rank of principal officer) and in any other case be made on witness statement or affidavit.

(4) Before dealing with the application the judge or district judge may, if he thinks fit, cause notice to be given to the judgment creditor that the application has been made and of a day and hour when he may attend and be heard.

Costs

9.—(1) Where costs are allowed to the judgment creditor on an application for an attachment of earnings order, there may be allowed— **cc27.9**

- (a) a charge of a solicitor for attending the hearing and, if the court so directs, for serving the application;
- (b) if the court certifies that the case is fit for counsel, a fee to counsel; and
- (c) the court fee on the issue of the application.

(2) For the purpose of paragraph (1)(a) a solicitor who has prepared on behalf of the judgment creditor a witness statement or affidavit or request under rule 7(8) shall be treated as having attended the hearing.

(3) The costs may be fixed and allowed without detailed assessment under CPR Part 47.

Costs

This rule deals with the judgment creditors costs. An employer making deductions pursuant to an attachment of earnings order is entitled to deduct a further sum of £1.00 for his own costs (Attachment of Earnings (Employer's Deduction) Order 1991 (SI 1991/356)). **cc27.9.1**

Contents and service of order

10.—(1) An attachment of earnings order shall contain such of the following particulars relating to the debtor as are known to the court, namely— **cc27.10**

- (a) his full name and address;
- (b) his place of work; and
- (c) the nature of his work and his works number, if any,

and those particulars shall be the prescribed particulars for the purposes of section 6(3) of the Act of 1971.

(2) An attachment of earnings order and any order varying or discharging such an order shall be served on the debtor and on the person to whom the order is directed, and CPR Part 6 and CPR rules 40.4 and 40.5, shall apply with the further modification that where the order is directed to a corporation which has requested the court that any communication relating to the debtor or to the class of persons to whom he belongs shall be directed to the corporation at a particular address, service may, if the district judge thinks fit, be effected on the corporation at that address.

(3) Where an attachment of earnings order is made to enforce a judgment or order of the High Court or a magistrates' court, a copy of the attachment of earnings order and of any order discharging it shall be sent by the court officer of the county court to the court of-

ficer of the High Court, or, as the case may be, the designated officer for the magistrates' court.

Forms

cc27.10.1 Form **N60** or **N64** (Suspended) is used.

Application to determine whether particular payments are earnings

cc27.11 11. An application to the court under section 16 of the Act of 1971 to determine whether payments to the debtor of a particular class or description are earnings for the purpose of an attachment of earnings order may be made to the district judge in writing and the court officer shall thereupon fix a date and time for the hearing of the application by the court and give notice thereof to the persons mentioned in the said section 16(2)(a), (b) and (c).

Earnings

cc27.11.1 See ss.16 and 24 and Sch.3, Attachment of Earnings Act (Vol.2, para.9B–183 *et seq*.).

Notice of cesser

cc27.12 12. Where an attachment of earnings order ceases to have effect under section 8(4) of the Act of 1971, the court officer of the court in which the matter is proceeding shall give notice of the cesser to the person to whom the order was directed.

Variation and discharge by court of own motion

cc27.13 13.—(1) Subject to paragraph (9), the powers conferred by section 9(1) of the Act of 1971 may be exercised by the court of its own motion in the circumstances mentioned in the following paragraphs.

(2) Where it appears to the court that a person served with an attachment of earnings order directed to him has not the debtor in his employment, the court may discharge the order.

(3) Where an attachment of earnings order which has lapsed under section 9(4) of the Act of 1971 is again directed to a person who appears to the court to have the debtor in his employment, the court may make such consequential variations in the order as it thinks fit.

(4) Where, after making an attachment of earnings order, the court makes or is notified of the making of another such order in respect of the same debtor which is not to secure the payment of a judgment debt or payments under an administration order, the court may discharge or vary the first-mentioned order having regard to the priority accorded to the other order by paragraph 8 of Schedule 3 to the Act of 1971.

(5) Where, after making an attachment of earnings order, the court makes an order under section 4(1)(b) of the Act of 1971 or makes an administration order, the court may discharge the attachment of earnings order or, if it exercises the power conferred by section 5(3) of the said Act, may vary the order in such manner as it thinks fit.

(6) On making a consolidated attachment of earnings order the court may discharge any earlier attachment of earnings order made to secure the payment of a judgment debt by the same debtor.

(7) Where it appears to the court that a bankruptcy order has been made against a person in respect of whom an attachment of

earnings order is in force to secure the payment of a judgment debt, the court may discharge the attachment of earnings order.

(8) Where an attachment or earnings order has been made to secure the payment of a judgment debt and the court grants permission to issue execution for the recovery of the debt, the court may discharge the order.

(9) Before varying or discharging an attachment of earnings order of its own motion under any of the foregoing paragraphs of this rule, the court shall, unless it thinks it unnecessary in the circumstances to do so, give the debtor and the person on whose application the order was made an opportunity of being heard on the question whether the order should be varied or discharged, and for that purpose the court officer may give them notice of a date, time and place at which the question will be considered.

Transfer of attachment order

14.—(1) Where the court by which the question of making a consolidated attachment order falls to be considered is not the court by which any attachment of earnings order has been made to secure the payment of a judgment debt by the debtor, the district judge of the last-mentioned court shall, at the request of the district judge of the first-mentioned court, transfer to that court the matter in which the attachment of earnings order was made. **cc27.14**

(2) Without prejudice to paragraph (1), if in the opinion of the judge or district judge of any court by which an attachment of earnings order has been made, the matter could more conveniently proceed in some other court, whether by reason of the debtor having become resident in the district of that court or otherwise, he may order the matter to be transferred to that court.

(3) The court to which proceedings arising out of an attachment of earnings are transferred under this rule shall have the same jurisdiction in relation to the order as if it has been made by that court.

Exercise of power to obtain statement of earnings etc.

15.—(1) An order under section 14(1) of the Act of 1971 shall be indorsed with or incorporate a notice warning the person to whom it is directed of the consequences of disobedience to the order and shall be served on him personally. **cc27.15**

(2) Order 34, rule 2, shall apply, with the necessary modifications, in relation to any penalty for failure to comply with an order under the said section 14(1) or, subject to the proviso to rule 5(2), any penalty for

failure to comply with a requirement mentioned in that rule, as it applies in relation to a fine under section 55 of the County Courts Act 1984.

Section14 Attachment of Earnings Act 1971

See Vol.2, para.9B–180. **cc27.15.1**

Offences

16.—(1) Where it is alleged that a person has committed any offence mentioned in section 23(2)(a), (b), (d), (e) or (f) of the Act of 1971 in relation to proceedings in, or to an attachment of earnings order made by, a county court, the district judge shall, unless it is **cc27.16** decided to proceed against the alleged offender summarily, issue a summons calling upon him to show cause why he should not be punished for the alleged offence. The summons shall be served on the alleged offender personally not less than 14 days before the return day.

(2) Order 34 rules 3 and 4, shall apply, with the necessary modifications, to proceedings for an offence under section 23(2) of the Act of 1971 as they apply to proceedings for offences under the County Courts Act 1984.

Section 23 Attachment of Earnings Act 1971

cc27.16.1 See Vol.2, para.9B–193.

Maintenance orders

cc27.17 17.—(1) The foregoing rules of this Order shall apply in relation to maintenance payments as they apply in relation to a judgment debt, subject to the following paragraphs.

(2) An application for an attachment of earnings order to secure payments under a maintenance order made by a county court shall be made to that county court.

(3) Any application under section 32 of the Matrimonial Causes Act 1973 for permission to enforce the payment of arrears which became due more than 12 months before the application for an attachment of earnings order shall be made in that application.

(3A) Notice of the application together with a form of reply in the appropriate form, shall be served on the debtor in the manner set out in CPR r.6.20.

(3B) Service of the notice shall be effected not less than 21 days before the hearing, but service may be effected at any time before the hearing on the applicant satisfying the court by witness statement or affidavit that the respondent is about to remove from his address for service.

(3C) Rule 5(2A) shall not apply.

(4) An application by the debtor for an attachment of earnings order to secure payments under a maintenance order may be made on the making of the maintenance order or an order varying the maintenance order, and rules 4 and 5 shall not apply.

(5) Rule 7 shall have effect as if for paragraphs (1) to (8) there were substituted the following paragraph—

"(1) An application for an attachment of earnings order may be heard and determined by the district judge, who shall hear the application in private."

(6) Rule 9 shall apply as if for the reference to the amount payable under the relevant adjudication there were substituted a reference to the arrears due under the related maintenance order.

(7) Where an attachment of earnings order made by the High Court designates the court officer of a county court as the collecting officer, that officer shall, on receipt of a certified copy of the order from the court officer of the High Court, send to the person to whom the order is directed a notice as to the mode of payment.

(8) Where an attachment of earnings order made by a county court to secure payments under a maintenance order ceases to have effect and—

(a) the related maintenance order was made by that court; or

(b) the related maintenance order was an order of the High Court and—

(i) the court officer of the county court has received notice of the cessation from the court officer of the High Court; or

(ii) a committal order has been made in the county court for the enforcement of the related maintenance order,

the court officer of the county court shall give notice of the cessation to the person to whom the attachment of earnings order was directed.

(9) Where an attachment of earnings order has been made by a county court to secure payments under a maintenance order, notice under section 10(2) of the Act of 1971 to the debtor and to the person to whom the district judge is required to pay sums received under the order shall be in the form provided for that purpose, and if the debtor wishes to request the court to discharge the attachment of earnings order or to vary it otherwise than by making the appropriate variation, he shall apply to the court, within 14 days after the date of the notice, for the remedy desired.

(10) Rule 13 shall have effect as if for paragraphs (4) to (7) there were substituted the following paragraph:

"(4) Where it appears to the court by which an attachment of earnings order has been made that the related maintenance order has ceased to have effect, whether by virtue of the terms of the maintenance order or under section 28 of the Matrimonial Causes Act 1973 or otherwise, the court may discharge or vary the attachment of earnings order."

History of rule

Amended by SI 1999/1008, SI 2000/221 and SI 2008/2178. **cc27.17.1**

Priority

An attachment of earnings order to enforce a maintenance order is a priority order i.e. it ranks above non-priority orders. **cc27.17.2**

Arrears under an attachment of earnings order

Arrears are treated differently in the case of priority orders. Any arrears are carried forward and, subject to the protected earnings rate, deducted from subsequent earnings (see Section 6 Attachment of Earnings Act 1971, Vol.2, para.9B–169). **cc27.17.3**

PART II

CONSOLIDATED ATTACHMENT OF EARNINGS ORDERS

Cases in which consolidated order may be made

18. Subject to the provisions of rules 19 to 21, the court may make a consolidated attachment order where— **cc27.18**

(a) two or more attachment of earnings orders are in force to secure the payment of judgment debts by the same debtor; or

(b) on an application for an attachment of earnings order to

CCR

secure the payment of a judgment debt, or for a consolidated attachment order to secure the payment of two or more judgment debts, it appears to the court that an attachment of earnings order is already in force to secure the payment of a judgment debt by the same debtor.

Application for consolidated order

cc27.19 19.—(1) An application for a consolidated attachment order may be made—

(a) by the debtor in respect of whom the order is sought; or

(b) by any person who has obtained or is entitled to apply for an attachment of earnings order to secure the payment of a judgment debt by that debtor.

(2) An application under paragraph (1) may be made in the proceedings in which any attachment of earnings order (other than a priority order) is in force and rules 3, 4 and 5 of this order shall not apply.

(3) Where the judgment which it is sought to enforce was not given by the court which made the attachment of earnings order, the judgment shall be automatically transferred to the court which made the attachment of earnings order.

(3A) An application under paragraph (1)(b) shall certify the amount of money remaining due under the judgment or order and that the whole or part of any instalment due remains unpaid.

(3B) Where an application for a consolidated attachment of earnings order is made, the court officer shall—

(a) notify any party who may be affected by the application of its terms; and

(b) require him to notify the court in writing, within 14 days of service of notification upon him, giving his reasons for any objection he may have to the granting of the application.

(3C) If notice of any objection is not given within the time stated, the court officer shall make a consolidated attachment of earnings order.

(3D) If any party objects to the making of a consolidated attachment of earnings order, the court officer shall refer the application to the district judge who may grant the application after considering the objection made and the reasons given.

(3E) In the foregoing paragraphs of this rule, a party affected by the application means—

(a) where the application is made by the debtor, the creditor in the proceedings in which the application is made and any other creditor who has obtained an attachment of earnings order which is in force to secure the payment of a judgment debt by the debtor;

(b) where the application is made by the judgment creditor, the debtor and every person who, to the knowledge of the applicant, has obtained an attachment of earnings order which is in force to secure the payment of a judgment debt by the debtor.

(4) A person to whom two or more attachment of earnings orders are directed to secure the payment of judgment debts by the same debtor may request the court in writing to make a consolidated attachment order to secure the payment of those debts, and on receipt of such a request paragraphs (3B) to (3E) shall apply, with the necessary modifications, as if the request were an application by the judgment creditor.

Making of consolidated order by court of its own motion

20. Where an application is made for an attachment of earnings order to secure the payment of a judgment debt by a debtor in respect of whom an attachment of earnings order is already in force to secure the payment of another judgment debt and no application is made for a consolidated attachment order, the court officer may make such an order of his own motion after giving all persons concerned an opportunity of submitting written objections. **cc27.20**

Extension of consolidated order

21.—(1) Where a consolidated attachment order is in force to secure the payment of two or more judgment debts, any creditor to whom another judgment debt is owed by the same judgment debtor may apply to the court by which the order was made for it to be extended so as to secure the payment of that debt as well as the first-mentioned debts and, if the application is granted, the court may either vary the order accordingly or may discharge it and make a new consolidated attachment order to secure payment of all the aforesaid judgment debts. **cc27.21**

(2) An application under this rule shall be treated for the purposes of rules 19 and 20 as an application for a consolidated attachment order.

Payments under consolidated order

22. Instead of complying with section 13 of the Act of 1971, a court officer who receives payments made to him in compliance with a consolidated attachment order shall, after deducting such court fees, if any, in respect of proceedings for or arising out of the order as are deductible from those payments, deal with the sums paid as he would if they had been paid by the debtor to satisfy the relevant adjudications in proportion to the amounts payable thereunder, and for that purpose dividends may from time to time be declared and distributed among the creditors entitled thereto. **cc27.22**

CCR ORDER 28—JUDGMENT SUMMONSES

Contents **cc28.0.1**

Editorial introduction

cc28.0.2 Imprisonment for non-payment of debts was severely restricted by the Debtors Act 1869 (see commentary on this Act at paras sc46.1.26, sc46.1.45 and sc46.1.46). Since then the Judgment Summons has been a means of committing the judgment debtor to prison but suspending the order so long as specified instalments were paid. This is no longer available to ordinary creditors and by AJA 1970 was restricted to High Court and county court maintenance orders and judgments for payment of taxes, other sums or contributions due to the State. (If the debtor is an employee, an attachment of earnings order is a simpler option). In *Mubarak v Mubarak* [2001] 1 F.L.R. 698 the Court of Appeal held that the procedure was not compatible with the European Convention on Human Rights. Consequently, the rules were changed by the Civil Procedure (Amendment No.5) Rules 2001 as from March 25, 2002 so as to make the procedure Convention compliant. The judgment summons procedure itself cannot be used as a means of obtaining evidence.

The Court of Appeal also held that the Practice Direction—Committals (supplementing RSC O.52 and CCR O.29, see para.scpd52.1) applies to judgment summonses. This means that proof that the judgment debtor has or has had the means to pay and has refused or neglected to do so is required beyond reasonable doubt and not on the usual civil standard of the balance of probabilities (see further, commentary to Sch.1, RSC O.52).

Section 5 of Debtor's Act 1869

cc28.0.3 Section 5 of the Debtors Act 1869 was amended by the Civil Procedure (Modification of Enactments) Order 2002 (SI 2002/439). The section, as amended,now provides:

Saving of power of committal for small debts.

5. *Subject to the provisions herein-after mentioned, and to the prescribed rules, any court may commit to prison for a term not exceeding six weeks, or until payment of the sum due, any person who makes default in payment of any debt or instalment of any debt due from him in pursuance of any order or judgment of that or any other competent court. Provided—*

(1) *That the jurisdiction by this section given of committing a person to prison shall, in the case of any court other than the superior courts of law and equity, be exercised only subject to the following restrictions; that is to say,*

(a) *Be exercised only by a judge or his deputy, and by an order made in open court and showing on its face the ground on which it is issued:*[1]

(c) *Be exercised only as respects a judgment of a county court by a county court judge or his deputy.*

(2) *That such jurisdiction shall only be exercised where it is proved to the satisfaction of the court that the person making default either has or has had since the date of the order or judgment the means to pay the sum in respect of which he has made default, and has refused or neglected, or refuses or neglects, to pay the same.*

Proof of the means of the person making default may be given in such manner as the court thinks just; and for the purposes of such proof the debtor and any witnesses may be summoned and examined on oath, according to the prescribed rules.

[1] Repealed by Bankruptcy Act 1883 (c.52), Sch.5.

Any jurisdiction by this section given to the superior courts may be exercised by a judge sitting in chambers, or otherwise, in the prescribed manner.

For the purposes of this section any court may direct any debt due from any person in pursuance of any order or judgment of that or any other competent court to be paid by instalments, and may from time to time rescind or vary such order:

Persons committed under this section by a superior court may be committed to the prison in which they would have been confined if arrested on a writ of capias ad satisfaciendum, and every order of committal by any superior court shall, subject to the prescribed rules, be issued, obeyed, and executed in the like manner as such writ.

This section, so far as it relates to any county court, shall be deemed to be substituted for sections ninety-eight and ninety-nine of the County Courts Act 1846, and that Act and the Acts amending the same shall be construed accordingly, and shall extend to orders made by the county court with respect to sums due in pursuance of any order or judgment of any court other than a county court.

No imprisonment under this section shall operate as a satisfaction or extinguishment of any debt or demand or course of action, or deprive any person of any right to take out execution against the lands, goods, or chattels of the person imprisoned, in the same manner as if such imprisonment had not taken place.

Any person imprisoned under this section shall be discharged out of custody upon a certificate signed in the prescribed manner to the effect that he has satisfied the debt or instalment of a debt in respect of which he was imprisoned, together with the prescribed costs (if any).

Related sources

- Practice Direction—Enforcement of Judgments and Orders (see para.70PD.1) **cc28.0.4**
- Part 70— General Rules about Enforcement of Judgments and Orders
- Practice Direction—Committals (see scpd 52)
- Schedule 2, CCR O.27—Attachment of Earnings
- Debtors Act 1869 s.5 (set out above in para.cc28.0.2).
- AJA 1970 s.11 (see Vol.2, Section 9B)
- Attachment of Earnings Act 1971 (see Vol.2, Section 9B)

Forms

- **N67** Judgment Summons under Debtors Act 1869 **cc28.0.5**
- **N68** Certificate of service (judgment summons)
- **N69** Order for debtors' attendance at an adjourned hearing of a judgment summons
- **N70** Order of commitment under s.110 County Courts Act 1984
- **N71** Order revoking an order of commitment under s.110 County Courts Act 1984
- **N72** Notice to debtor where committal order made, but directed to be suspended under Debtors Act 1869
- **N73** New order on Judgment Summons
- **N74** Warrant of committal on a judgment
- **N75** Indorsement on a warrant of committal sent to foreign court
- **N76** Certificate to be indorsed on duplicate warrant of committal issued for re-arrest of debtor
- **N342** Request for judgment summons
- **N343** Notice of result of hearing of a judgment summons issued on a judgment or order of the High Court
- **N344** Request for warrant of committal on judgment summons
- **N345** Certificate of payment under the Debtors Act 1869

CCR

Application for judgment summons

cc28.1 1.—(1) An application for the issue of a judgment summons may be made to the court for the district in which the debtor resides or carries on business or, if the summons is to issue against two or more persons jointly liable under the judgment or order sought to be enforced, in the court for the district in which any of the debtors resides or carries on business.

(2) The judgment creditor shall make his application by filing a request in that behalf certifying the amount of money remaining due under the judgment or order, the amount in respect of which the judgment summons is to issue and that the whole or part of any instalment due remains unpaid.

(3) The judgment creditor must file with the request all written evidence on which he intends to rely.

Written evidence

cc28.1.1 Rule 1(3) was inserted by the Civil Procedure (Amendment No.5) Rules 2001 (SI 2001/4015) so as to make the judgment summons procedure compatible with the European Convention on Human Rights following the decision of the Court of Appeal in *Mubarak v Mubarak* [2001] 1 F.L.R. 698. The judgment summons can no longer be used both to obtain evidence from the judgment debtor and then, on the basis of that evidence, obtain his committal. Evidence must be filed with the application.

Mode of service

cc28.2 2.—(1) Subject to paragraph (2), a judgment summons shall be served personally on every debtor against whom it is issued.

(2) Where the judgment creditor or the judgment creditor's solicitor gives a certificate for postal service in respect of a debtor residing or carrying on business within the district of the court, the judgment summons will, unless the district judge otherwise directs, be served on that debtor by the court sending it to the debtor by first-class post at the address stated in the request for the judgment summons and, unless the contrary is shown, the date of service is deemed to be the seventh day after the date on which the judgment summons was sent to the debtor.

(3) Where a judgment summons has been served on a debtor in accordance with paragraph (2), no order of commitment against him unless—

(a) he appears at the hearing; or
(b) it is made under section 110(2) of the Act.[1]

(4) The written evidence on which the judgment creditor intends to rely must be served with the judgment summons.[2]

Time for service

cc28.3 3.—(1) The judgment summons and written evidence must be served not less than 14 days before the day fixed for the hearing.[3]

(2) A notice of non-service will be sent pursuant to CPR, rule 6.18, in respect of a judgment summons which has been sent by post under rule 2(2) and has been returned to the court undelivered.

(3) CPR, rules 7.5 and 7.6 apply, with the necessary modifications, to a judgment summons as they apply to a claim form.

---

[1] Substituted by the Civil Procedure (Amendment No.5) Rules 2001 (SI 2001/4015).
[2] Substituted by the Civil Procedure (Amendment No.5) Rules 2001 (SI 2001/4015).
[3] Amended by the Civil Procedure (Amendment No.5) Rules 2001 (SI 2001/4015).

Enforcement of debtor's attendance

4.—(1) Order 27, rules 7B and 8, shall apply, with the necessary modifications, to an order made under section 110(1) of the Act for the attendance of the debtor at an adjourned hearing of a judgment summons as they apply to an order made under section 23(1) of the Attachment of Earnings Act 1971 for the attendance of the debtor at an adjourned hearing of an application for an attachment of earnings order. cc28.4

(1A) An order made under section 110(1) of the Act must be served personally on the judgment debtor.

(1B) Copies of—

(a) the judgment summons; and

(b) the written evidence,

must be served with the order.[1]

(2) At the time of service of the order there shall be paid or tendered to the debtor a sum reasonably sufficient to cover his expenses in travelling to and from the court, unless such a sum was paid to him at the time of service of the judgment summons.

Order 27

The procedure to enforce the debtors' attendance at the hearing of a judgment summons is based on the procedure to secure the debtors attendance on as attachment of earnings application. However, the district judge, who has full powers under the Attachment of Earnings Act 1971, has no power to deal with a judgment summons. cc28.4.1

"section 110(1)"

— is set out in Vol.2 at Section 9A. cc28.4.2

Evidence

5.—(1) No person may be committed on an application for a judgment summons unless— cc28.5

(a) the order is made under section 110(2) of the Act; or

(b) the judgment creditor proves that the debtor—

(i) has or has had since the date of the judgment or order the means to pay the sum in respect of which he has made default; and

(ii) has refused or neglected or refuses or neglects to pay that sum.

(2) The debtor may not be compelled to give evidence.[2]

burden and standard of proof

The new rule makes it clear that the burden of proof is on the judgment creditor. The standard at proof is beyond reasonable doubt—see para.cc28.0.2. cc28.5.1

Suspension of committal order

7.—(1) If on the hearing of a judgment summons a committal order is made, the judge may direct execution of the order to be suspended to enable the debtor to pay the amount due. cc28.7

---

[1] Paragraphs (1A) and (1B) inserted by the Civil Procedure (Amendment No.5) Rules 2001 (SI 2001/4015).

[2] Substituted by the Civil Procedure (Amendment No.5) Rules 2001 (SI 2001/4015).

(2) A note of any direction given under paragraph (1) shall be entered in the records of the court and notice of the suspended committal order shall be sent to the debtor.

(3) Where a judgment summons is issued in respect of one or more but not all of the instalments payable under a judgment or order for payment by instalments and a committal order is made and suspended under paragraph (1), the judgment or order shall, unless the judge otherwise orders, be suspended for so long as the execution of the committal order is suspended.

(4) Where execution of a committal order is suspended under paragraph (1) and the debtor subsequently desires to apply for a further suspension, the debtor shall attend at or write to the court office and apply for the suspension he desires, stating the reasons for his inability to comply with the terms of the original suspension, and the court shall fix a day for the hearing of the application by the judge and give at least 3 days' notice thereof to the judgment creditor and the debtor.

(5) The district judge may suspend execution of the committal order pending the hearing of an application under paragraph (4).

New order on judgment summons

cc28.8 8.—(1) Where on the hearing of a judgment summons, the judge makes a new order for payment of the amount of the judgment debt remaining unpaid, there shall be included in the amount payable under the order for the purpose of any enforcement proceedings, otherwise than by judgment summons, any amount in respect of which a committal order has already been made and the debtor imprisoned.

(2) No judgment summons under the new order shall include any amount in respect of which the debtor was imprisoned before the new order was made, and any amount subsequently paid shall be appropriated in the first instance to the amount due under the new order.

Notification of order on judgment of High Court

cc28.9 9.—(1) Notice of the result of the hearing of a judgment summons on a judgment or order of the High Court shall be sent by the county court to the High Court.

(2) If a committal order or a new order for payment is made on the hearing, the office copy of the judgment or order filed in the county court, shall be deemed to be a judgment or order of the court in which the judgment summons is heard.

Costs on judgment summons

cc28.10 10.—(1) No costs shall be allowed to the judgment creditor on the hearing of a judgment summons unless—

(a) a committal order is made; or

(b) the sum in respect of which the judgment summons was issued is paid before the hearing.

(2) Where costs are allowed to the judgment creditor,

(a) there may be allowed—

(i) a charge of the judgment creditor's solicitor for attending the hearing and, if the judge so directs, for serving the judgment summons;

(ii) a fee to counsel if the court certifies that the case is fit for counsel;

(iii) any travelling expenses paid to the debtor; and

(iv) the court fee on the issue of the judgment summons;

(b) the costs may be fixed and allowed without detailed assessment under CPR Part 47;

Issue of warrant of committal

11.—(1) A judgment creditor desiring a warrant to be issued pursuant to a committal order shall file a request in that behalf. **cc28.11**

(2) Where two or more debtors are to be committed in respect of the same judgment or order, a separate warrant of committal shall be issued for each of them.

(3) Where a warrant of committal is sent to a foreign court for execution, that court shall indorse on it a notice as to the effect of section 122(3) of the Act addressed to the governor of the prison of that court.

Notification to foreign court of part payment before debtor lodged in prison

12. Where, after a warrant of committal has been sent to a foreign court for execution but before the debtor is lodged in prison, the home court is notified that an amount which is less than the sum on payment of which the debtor is to be discharged has been paid, the home court shall send notice of the payment to the foreign court. **cc28.12**

Payment after debtor lodged in prison

13.—(1) Where, after the debtor has been lodged in prison under a warrant of committal, payment is made of the sum on payment of which the debtor is to be discharged, then— **cc28.13**

(a) if the payment is made to the court responsible for the execution of the warrant, the court officer shall make and sign a certificate of payment and send it by post or otherwise to the gaoler;

(b) if the payment is made to the court which issued the warrant of committal after the warrant has been sent to a foreign court for execution, the home court shall send notice of the payment to the foreign court, and the court officer at the foreign court shall make and sign a certificate of payment and send it by post or otherwise to the gaoler;

(c) if the payment is made to the gaoler, he shall sign a certificate of payment and send the amount to the court which made the committal order.

(2) Where, after the debtor has been lodged in prison under a warrant of committal, payment is made of an amount less than the sum on payment of which the debtor is to be discharged, then subject to paragraph (3), paragraph (1)(a) and (b) shall apply with the substitution of references to a notice of payment for the references to a certificate of payment and paragraph (1)(c) shall apply with the omission of the requirement to make and sign a certificate of payment.

(3) Where, after the making of a payment to which paragraph (2) relates, the balance of the sum on payment of which the debtor is to be discharged is paid, paragraph (1) shall apply without the modifications mentioned in paragraph (2).

History of rule

cc28.13.1 Amended by Civil Procedure (Amendment) Rules 1999 (SI 1999/1008).

Discharge of debtor otherwise than on payment

cc28.14 14.—(1) Where the judgment creditor lodges with the district judge a request that a debtor lodged in prison under a warrant of committal may be discharged from custody, the district judge shall make an order for the discharge of the debtor in respect of the warrant of committal and the court shall send the gaoler a certificate of discharge.

(2) Where a debtor who has been lodged in prison under a warrant of committal desires to apply for his discharge under section 121 of the Act, the application shall be made to the judge in writing and without notice showing the reasons why the debtor alleges that he is unable to pay the sum in respect of which he has been committed and ought to be discharged and stating any offer which he desires to make as to the terms on which his discharge is to be ordered, and, Order 27 rule 8(3) and (4), shall apply, with the necessary modifications, as it applies to an application by a debtor for his discharge from custody under section 23(7) of the Attachment of Earnings Act 1971.

(3) If in a case to which paragraph (2) relates the debtor is ordered to be discharged from custody on terms which include liability to re-arrest if the terms are not complied with, the judge may, on the application of the judgment creditor if the terms are not complied with, order the debtor to be re-arrested and imprisoned for such part of the term of imprisonment as remained unserved at the time of discharge.

(4) Where an order is made under paragraph (3), a duplicate warrant of committal shall be issued, indorsed with a certificate signed by the court officer as to the order of the judge.

CCR ORDER 29—COMMITTAL FOR BREACH OF ORDER OR UNDERTAKING

Contents

cc29.0.1

Editorial introduction

cc29.0.2 A judge of the county court has jurisdiction to commit for contempt in the face of the court and for breach of injunctions or undertakings and for orders properly endorsed with a penal notice. Any other breach is punishable only by order of committal made in the Divisional Court (see para.sc52.1.34). For the jurisdiction of the district judge see para.cc29.1.6. A county court is a "superior court" and not an "inferior court" for the purposes of the Contempt of Court Act 1981 (see Vol. 2 at 3C) and thus has the same sentencing powers as the High Court: the maximum sentence on any one occasion is two years. The commentary to CCR O.29 needs to be read in conjunction with the commentary to RSC O.52. In particular, committal proceedings are supplemented by "Practice Direction—Committal Applications" which applies in both the High Court and county courts and is set out at para.scpd52.1. Part II of this Direction is of particular importance in the case of a contempt in the face of the court.

Related sources

- Practice Direction supplementing Sch.1, RSC O.52 and Sch.2, CCR O.29 (para.scpd52.1) **cc29.0.3**
- Schedule 2, CCR O.27, r.7B—Committal under Attachment of Earnings Act 1971
- Schedule 2, CCR O.28—Judgment Summons
- Schedule 2, CCR O.34—Penal and disciplinary provisions
- Administration of Justice Act 1960 (Appeal in cases of contempt of court: Vol.2, Section 9B)
- Attachment of Earnings Act 1971 (see Vol.2, Section 9B)
- Contempt of Court Act 1981 (see Vol.2, Section 3C)
- County Courts (Penalties for Contempt) Act 1983
- County Courts Act 1984 (see Vol.2, Section 9A)
- Failure to carry out an undertaking given to the court (see para.sc52.1.8)
- Sequestration

Forms

- **N77** Notice as to consequences of disobedience to Court order ("penal notice") **cc29.0.4** *(Note—unless the "penal notice" has been endorsed on the order requiring a person to do or abstain from doing an act, and the order then personally served, it is not usually possible to enforce the order by commital)*
- **N78** Notice to show cause why an order for your committal to prison should not be made
- **N79** Committal or other order upon proof of disobedience of a court order or breach of an undertaking
- **N80** Warrant of committal to prison
- **N81** Notice to solicitor to how cause why undertaking should not be enforced by committal to prison
- **N82** Order of committal for failure by solicitor to carry out undertaking
- **N83** Order of discharge from custody under Warrant of Committal
- **N117** General Form of Undertaking
- **N319** Notice of execution of warrant of committal
- **N329** Notes for completion of **N79**

Cognate RSC

- Schedule 1, RSC O.45, r.5—Enforcement of Judgment to do or abstain from doing any act **cc29.0.5**
- Schedule 1, RSC O.52—Committals

Enforcement of judgment to do or abstain from doing any act

1.—(1) Where a person required by a judgment or order to do an act refuses or neglects to do it within the time fixed by the judgment or order or any subsequent order, or where a person disobeys a judgment or order requiring him to abstain from doing an act, then, subject to the Debtors Acts 1869 and 1878 and to the provisions of these rules, the judgment or order may be enforced, by order of the judge, by a committal order against that person or, if that person is a body corporate, against any director or other officer of the body. **cc29.1**

(2) Subject to paragraphs (6) and (7), a judgment or order shall not be enforced under paragraph (1) unless—

(a) a copy of the judgment or order has been served personally on the person required to do or abstain from doing the act in question and also, where that person is a body corporate, on the director or other officer of the body against whom a committal order is sought; and

(b) in the case of a judgment or order requiring a person to do an act, the copy has been so served before the expiration of the time within which he was required to do the act and was accompanied by a copy of any order, made between the date of the judgment or order and the date of service, fixing that time.

(3) Where a judgment or order enforceable by committal order under paragraph (1) has been given or made, the court officer shall, if the judgment or order is in the nature of an injunction, at the time when the judgment or order is drawn up, and in any other case on the request of the judgment creditor, issue a copy of the judgment or order, indorsed with or incorporating a notice as to the consequences of disobedience, for service in accordance with paragraph (2).

(4) If the person served with the judgment or order fails to obey it, the judgment creditor may issue a claim form or, as the case may be, an application notice seeking the committal for contempt of court of that person and subject to paragraph (7), the claim form or application notice shall be served on him personally.

(4A) The claim form or application notice (as the case may be) shall—

(a) identify the provisions of the injunction or undertaking which it is alleged have been disobeyed or broken;

(b) list the ways in which it is alleged that the injunction has been disobeyed or the undertaking has been broken;

(c) be supported by an affidavit stating the grounds on which the application is made,

and unless service is dispensed with under paragraph (7), a copy of the affidavit shall be served with the claim form or application notice.

(5) If a committal order is made, the order shall be for the issue of a warrant of committal and, unless the judge otherwise orders—

(a) a copy of the order shall be served on the person to be committed either before or at the time of the execution of the warrant; or

(b) where the warrant has been signed by the judge, the order for issue of the warrant may be served on the person to be committed at any time within 36 hours after the execution of the warrant.

(5A) A warrant of committal shall not, without further order of the court, be enforced more than 2 years after the date on which the warrant is issued.

(6) A judgment or order requiring a person to abstain from doing an act may be enforced under paragraph (1) notwithstanding that service of a copy of the judgment or order has not been effected in accordance with paragraph (2) if the judge is satisfied that, pending *such service, the person* against whom it is sought to enforce the judgment or order has had notice of the judgment or order either—

(a) by being present when the judgment or order was given or made; or

(b) by being notified of the terms of the judgment or order whether by telephone, fax, e-mail or otherwise.

(7) Without prejudice to its powers under Part 6 of the CPR, the court may dispense with service of a copy of a judgment or order under paragraph (2) or a claim form or application notice under paragraph (4) if the court thinks it just to do so.

(8) Where service of the claim form or application notice has been dispensed with under paragraph (7) and a committal order is made in the absence of the respondent, the judge may on his own initiative fix a date and time when the person to be committed is to be brought before him or before the court.

"notice as to the consequences of disobedience"

This notice is usually referred to as a "penal notice"; see Form **N77**. **cc29.1.1**

"claim form or application notice"

Application for a committal order is now made either by a claim form (see Pt 7, CPR) or application notice (see Pt 23, CPR—General Rules About Applications for Court Orders). It will invariably be more convenient to use the latter. **cc29.1.2**

"committal order"

Committal must be for a fixed term—see generally commentary to Sch.1 RSC O.52. The maximum sentence is two years (Contempt of Court Act 1981). **cc29.1.3**

Family Proceedings

CCR O.29 applies to family proceedings as varied by the Family Proceedings Rules 1991 (SI 1991/1247) rr.3.9A and 4.21A. **cc29.1.4**

In considering applications to commit for breach of a non-molestation order under the Family Law Act 1996 regard must be had to the following matters:

(1) although there is no principle that imprisonment is not to be imposed on a first occasion—see *Thorpe v Thorpe* [1998] 2 F.L.R. 127—it will usually be appropriate to take some other course;
(2) the alternatives to imprisonment should be considered, particularly where the court has not actually found any violence proved;
(3) the length of committal should be decided without reference to the question of suspension;
(4) the two objectives in contempt proceedings are (a) to mark the court's disapproval of the disobedience of its order and (b) to secure compliance with that order for the future. The seriousness of the conduct must be viewed in that light, as well as for its own intrinsic gravity;
(5) the length of committal must bear some reasonable relationship to the two year permitted maximum;
(6) suspension is possible in much wider circumstances than in criminal proceedings;
(7) the length of suspension requires separate consideration but may often be linked to continued compliance with the underlying order;
(8) the context must be borne in mind, which will often be the break up of an intimate relationship, and may involve children;
(9) brief reasons should be given as to why the court is making its orders in issue.

Hale v Tanner [2000] 1 W.L.R. 2377 (Swinton Thomas and Hale L.JJ. and Sir Christopher Slade) and *C v C* [2001] EWCA Civ 1625 (Hale L.J. and Steel J.). Where there was a non violent breach of a non molestation order the primary purpose should be to try to secure future compliance. The appellant's silly conduct had been a nuisance but had involved no violence. A six month sentence was excessive and would be reduced to three months. The applicable principles had been laid down in *Hale v Tanner* [2000] 1 W.L.R. 2377; in general the court would not tinker with such sentences; the judge's discretion was wide but the cardinal principle was to strike the right balance between a coercive and punitive approach: *Aquilina v Aquilina* [2004] EWCA Civ 504 (Ward and Clarke L.JJ.).

Where a judge finds breaches of a non-molestation order against a defendant he

CCR

should not pass a custodial sentence before hearing any submissions in mitigation: *Goldsmith v Goldsmith* [2006] EWCA Civ 1670 (Wall and Lloyd L.JJ.).

The approach to sentencing for contempt for non-appliance with a family court order should take into account the approach to sentencing for contempt in the Court of Appeal Criminal Division. Although the available alternatives under the Family Law Act 1996 were limited, the purposes and principles set out in ss.142(1), 143 and 144 of the Criminal Justice Act 2003 were relevant: *Robinson v Murray* [2005] EWCA Civ 935 (Lord Woolf C.J., Thorpe and Lloyd L.JJ.).

The deliberate publication of a judgment in residence proceedings under the Children Act 1989, where it is known that such publication was prohibited, was a contempt of court, since the protection of the minor forming the subject of the proceedings is paramount: *Attorney General v Pelling* [2005] EWHC 414 (Admin), (Laws L.J. and Pitchford J.).

Contempt procedure

cc29.1.5 In *M v P (Contempt of Court: Committal Order), Butler v Butler* [1992] 3 W.L.R. 813, CA, the Court of Appeal said that, in determining whether to reverse or vary a contempt order on appeal, the Court should ask itself whether, notwithstanding any departure from the proper procedure, the alleged contemnor had suffered any injustice. In *Nicholls v Nicholls* [1997] 1 W.L.R. 314, Lord Woolf M.R. said: "... in the future it should not be necessary to revisit authorities prior to *M v P*; *Butler v Butler* ...". As committal orders involve liberty of the subject it is particularly important that relevant rules are complied with. However, if the contemnor had a fair trial, and the order was made on valid grounds, a defect in the order would not result in its being set aside except where the interests of justice so require; they would not so require where no prejudice is caused by an error. If there was a procedural irregularity which had occasioned injustice the court would consider exercising its power to order a new trial. The court had to have regard to the interests of the other party as well as the contemnor.

Where a court commits for contempt otherwise than in the face of the court the committal must be for a fixed term and the court has no power to direct that the contemnor be brought back to court at a later date for a custodial sentence and in the meantime be detained (see *Delaney v Delaney* [1996] Q.B. 387, CA, where Court of Appeal explains procedure to be adopted where judge initially uncertain what sentence to impose). The power to dispense with service under O.29, r.1(7) does not extend expressly to the requirement for a penal notice in r.1(3). However, given the power to dispense with service of the judgment or order, on which the penal notice is to be endorsed, the court has a discretion to dispense also with the requirement for the penal notice. The discretion should nevertheless not be excercised too readily and should rather be used only in exceptional cases. *Jolly v Hull*; *Jolly v Jolly* [2000] 2 F.L.R. 69, Peter Gibson, Judge L.JJ. and Ferris J.

A warrant for possession has to be issued after the date on which possession is to be given up, in order for it to be valid. Moreover if the claimant also wishes to apply for the defendant to be held in contempt of court a penal notice must be attached, unless the requirement has been waived by the judge under CCR O.29, r.1(7). However irrespective of such defects a defendant may still be committed for contempt under s.118(1) of the County Courts Act 1984, if he has wilfully insulted the judge by refusing to comply with the possession order and stated his intention of continuing to do so. *Bell v Tuohy* [2002] 1 W.L.R. 2703, Kennedy, Mantell L.JJ. and Neuberger J.

CCR O.29, r.1(7) contains a wide discretion to dispense with the requirement for service before the time fixed for compliance, see *Davy International Ltd v Tazzyman* [1997] 3 All E.R. 183. Where a number of orders had been directed at compliance it was wholly artificial to talk of "retrospectively" waiving the requirements for service of later orders. There should be no encouragement for a persistent offender to use technicalities to defeat the purpose of orders. *Benson v Richards* [2002] EWCA Civ 1402 (Sir Andrew Morritt V.-C., Potter and Carnwath L.JJ.).

Where a young person was in breach of a county court order excluding him from a specified area the imposition of a committal for two years was not appropriate because (1) the maximum sentence of two years should be reserved for the worst case and (2) in the circumstances the sentence was excessive. County Courts should pay particular regard to the requirement in para.4.2. of the Practice Direction that the hearing date for the committal application should not be less than 14 days after service of the notice: *Turnbull v Middlesbrough BC* [2003] EWCA Civ 1327 (Kennedy and Peter Gibson L.JJ.).

A sentence for contempt under s.42 of the Family Law Act 1996, for breaching injunctions, will not be increased on appeal unless it can be shown that it is not merely lenient, but unduly lenient. Moreover the Court of Appeal would also reflect the element of double jeopardy when determining the appropriate sentence: *Lomas v Parle* [2004] 1 W.L.R. 1642 (Dame Elizabeth Butler-Sloss, P. Thorpe and Mance L.JJ.).

District Judges

A district judge has power to commit in respect of assaults on staff and contempts in the face of the court (County Courts Act 1984 ss.14 and 118); for breach of injunctions under Pt IV of the Family Law Act 1996 and the Housing Act 1996, but not generally for breach of orders. **cc29.1.6**

Concurrent criminal proceedings

The fact that there are concurrent criminal proceedings is not a valid reason to adjourn or stay committal proceedings arising out of the same incident. Committal proceedings should be promptly determined as it is important to demonstrate that court orders cannot be flouted with impunity (which differs from the object of criminal proceedings). The first court to sentence must not allow for or anticipate a likely further sentence. It is for the second court to reflect the prior sentence to ensure that the defendant is not punished twice for the same act (*Lomas v Parle* [2003] EWCA Civ 1804, Butler-Sloss P., Thorpe and Mance L.JJ.). **cc29.1.7**

Contempt in the face of the court

See s.118 County Courts Act 1984 at 9A–654 *et seq.* **cc29.1.8**

Procedurally, it is important to follow Pt II of Practice Direction—Committal Applications set out at para.scpd52.7.

Undertaking given by party

1A. Rule 1 (except paragraph (6)) shall apply to undertakings as it applies to orders with the necessary modifications and as if— **cc29.1A**

(a) for paragraph (2) of that rule there were substituted the following—

"(2) A copy of the document recording the undertaking shall be delivered by the court officer to the party giving the undertaking—

(a) by handing a copy of the document to him before he leaves the court building; or

(b) where his place of residence is known, by posting a copy to him at his place of residence; or

(c) through his solicitor,

and, where delivery cannot be effected in this way, the court officer shall deliver a copy of the document to the party for whose benefit the undertaking is given and that party shall cause it to be served personally as soon as is practicable."

(b) in paragraph (7), the words from "a copy of" to "paragraph (2) or" were omitted.

Solicitor's undertaking

2.—(1) An undertaking given by a solicitor in relation to any proceeding in a county court may be enforced, by order of the judge of that court, by committal order against the solicitor. **cc29.2**

(2) Where it appears to the judge that a solicitor has failed to carry out any such undertaking, he may of his own initiative direct the court officer to issue a notice calling on the solicitor to show cause why he should not be committed to prison.

(3) Where any party to the proceedings desires to have the undertaking enforced by committal order, the court officer shall, on the application of the party supported by an affidavit setting out the facts on which the application is based, issue such a notice as is referred to in paragraph (2).

Discharge of person in custody

cc29.3 3.—(1) Where a person in custody under a warrant or order, other than a warrant of committal to which Order 27 rule 8, or Order 28 rule 4 or 14, relates, desires to apply to the court for his discharge, he shall make his application in writing attested by the governor of the prison (or any other officer of the prison not below the rank of principal officer) showing that he has purged or is desirous of purging his contempt and shall, not less than one day before the application is made, serve notice of it on the party, if any, at whose instance the warrant or order was issued.

(2) If the committal order—

(a) does not direct that any application for discharge shall be made to a judge; or

(b) was made by the district judge under section 118 of the Act, any application for discharge may be made to the district judge.

(3) Nothing in paragraph (1) shall apply to an application made by the Official Solicitor in his official capacity for the discharge of a person in custody.

Para.(2) "Section 118 of the Act"

cc29.3.1 The Courts and Legal Services Act 1990 s.74 extended the powers conferred by these sections to district judges as well as Circuit judges.

Appeals

cc29.3.2 Appeals in contempt proceedings are provided for by the AJA 1960 (see s.13(2) in Vol.2, Section 9B at para.9B–18). The applicant, as well as the contemnor can appeal (see *Wilson v Webster* [1998] 1 F.L.R. 1097—14 day sentence of imprisonment increased to three months). See further, commentary to Sch.1, RSC O.52 at sc52.1.42.

Editorial note

ccpd29.1 The Practice Direction to CCR 29 is identical to the Practice Direction which accompanies RSC Part 52. The Practice Direction is reproduced in full at para.scpd52.1.

CCR ORDER 33—INTERPLEADER PROCEEDINGS

Contents

cc33.0.1

Part I—Under execution

Part II—Otherwise than under execution

Editorial introduction

Interpleader proceedings arise where a person, who himself makes no claim to property, faces competing claims from others to the property. The interpleader action is commenced by the party facing the claims with the objective of removing himself from the dispute and protecting himself from the competing claims; the court then decides the rival claims. **cc33.0.2**

There are two categories of interpleader action; those arising during the execution of a judgment[1] and those arising other than by execution for example where the proceedings are issued by a stakeholder. Interpleader under execution, or sheriffs interpleader, arises where a bailiff or sheriff seeks to levy execution on goods in the possession of the judgment debtor but which are claimed by another. The bailiff or sheriff will notify the execution creditor of the claim. The interpleader process follows unless the creditor admits the claim. Examples of stakeholder interpleader would be a solicitor or estate agent holding a deposit which is claimed by both the seller or the buyer or a carrier holding goods which are claimed by two or more persons alleging title.

In the High Court, interpleader proceedings are governed by RSC O.17[2] and the County Court by CCR O.33.[3] Although the procedures both have the same underlying objective they remain distinct, despite the introduction of the CPR. It has not been possible to create a unified procedural code because of the anomalous function of the district judge as the high bailiff in the county court.[4] Where an interpleader dispute arises during execution in the High Court the application is issued by the sheriff; the dispute is usually determined by the high court master, or if the action is in the District Registry, by the district judge.[5] In the County Court it is the district judge who issues the interpleader under execution and the matter is heard by a circuit judge. It follows that as long as s.123 of the County Courts Act 1984 remains in force, the procedure for interpleader actions arising by way of execution[6] will differ in the High Court and County Court.

Features of interpleader actions—High Court and County Court

(i) application is made by claim form[7] unless made in existing proceedings when it is made by application under Pt 23[8]; **cc33.0.3**

(ii) the overall effect of RSC O.17 and CCR O.33 is similar but the layout of the rules is different. The High Court rule is drafted so that the procedures arising by way of execution and those arising out of a stakeholders interpleader are combined but the County Court rule is in two parts; Pt I deals with interpleader proceedings under execution and Pt II with claims other than under execution[9];

(iii) the execution creditor has an opportunity to admit the competing claim and if

---

[1] In the High Court this is termed the "sheriffs interpleader" and in the County Court this is the "interpleader under execution".

[2] CPR Sch.1.

[3] CPR Sch.2.

[4] *The County Courts* Act 1984 (Sch.3, para.7) preserves the status of the district judge (formerly registrar) as the high bailiff of the County Court; The district judge is responsible for the acts and defaults of the himself and of the bailiffs appointed to assist him; s.123 of the County Courts Act 1984.

[5] The dispute may be resolved by the summary procedure especially where the dispute is one of law alone (RSC O.17, r.5(2)(c)).

[6] CCR O.33, r.4.

[7] The Pt 8 procedure is used CPR PD 8B, s.A.

[8] RSC O.17, r.3.

[9] See the introduction above for the substantive difference in the rules because of the role of the district judge and the effect of s.123 of the County Courts Act 1984.

he does so the sheriff or bailiff may withdraw and the interpleader will not be required[1];

(iv) in a stakeholders interpleader the application must be supported by evidence[2]; evidence is not required where the application is made by a sheriff or district judge during the execution of a judgment;

(v) in a stakeholders interpleader the applicant must specify in his application that he has no claims in the subject matter in dispute other than for charges and costs and that he does not collude with any of the interpleader claimants plus the applicant must be willing to pay the subject matter into court or to dispose of it as the court may direct[3];

(vi) the court gives directions for the conduct of the interpleader action which will include for example specifying which of the parties is to be treated as interpleader claimant and which as defendant and where the dispute is suitable for the summary procedure[4];

(vii) in a stakeholders interpleader the relief is available where the applicant has been sued by rival claimants or expects to be sue[5];

(viii) the relief is available where the property in dispute is a debt or goods[6];

(ix) the interpleader action is a separate action distinct from the execution process or the original action.[7]

History of rules

cc33.0.4 Before the Interpleader Act 1831 (now repealed and replaced by RSC O.17) a party faced with competing claims would have had to defend both actions or a file a 'bill in equity' (called a bill of interpleader). RSC O.17 and CCR O.33 were subject to some cosmetic amendment with the introduction of the Civil Procedure Rules; more radical amendment is anticipated when the procedures come under review as part of the Enforcement Review; but there must be a statutory provision to disapply s.123 of the County Courts Act 1984.[8]

Relationship between High Court Rules and County Court Rules

cc33.0.5 The relevant RSC rules can be applied in county court interpleader proceedings by virtue of the County Courts Act 1984 s.76 insofar as it may be said that these rules constitute "general principles of practice of the High Court". Both procedures are equally subject to the court's general powers of case management[9] under the Civil Procedure Rules.

Where the interpleader dispute arises during the enforcement of a judgment by the County Court bailiff the application for interpleader relief is made not by the bailiff but by the district judge, formerly registrar, as the high bailiff of the County Court. The County Court rule defines the steps which must be taken by the district judge and the court staff to initiate the interpleader action and the dispute is hear by the circuit judge.

Related sources

cc33.0.6
- CPR Pt 3—The courts case management powers
- CPR Pt 8— Alternative Procedure for claims
- CPR Pt 23—General Rules about applications for Court Orders
- RSC O.17—Interpleader

Forms

cc33.0.7
- **N88** Interpleader summons to execution creditor

---

1 RSC O.17, r.2 and CCR O.33, r.4(1).
2 RSC O.17, r.3(4) and CCR O.33, r.6(3).
3 RSC O.17, r.3(4)(a) to (c) and CCR O.33, r.6(3)(a) to (c).
4 RSC O.17, r.(1)(b).
5 RSC O.17, r.1(1)(a) and CCR O.33 r.6(1).
6 RSC O.17, r.1(1) (a) and CCR O.33, r.6(1).
7 *James v Ricknell* (1888) 20 Q.B.D. 64; thus a solicitor acting under an ordinary retainer in the action is not authorised to engage in interpleader proceedings without first obtaining instructions to act from his client.
8 *See reference to the role of the* district judge as high bailiff in the editorial introduction (above).
9 CPR Pt 3; of particular importance in interpleader proceedings is the power to extend and shorten time limits, making orders subject to conditions and the power to strike out a statement of case.

- **N88(1)** Interpleader summons to claimant claiming goods or rent under an execution
- **N89** Interpleader summons to person making adverse claims to a debt etc.
- **N358** Notice of claim to goods taken in execution
- **N359** Notice to claimant to goods taken in execution to make deposit or give security
- **N360** Affidavit in support of interpleader summons other than under an execution
- **N361** Notice of application for relief in pending action
- **N362** Order on interpleader summons under an execution where the claim is not established
- **N363** Order on interpleader summons under an execution where the claim is established
- **N364** Order on interpleader summons (other than execution) where there is an action
- **N365** Order on an interpleader summons (other than execution) where there is no action

PART I

UNDER EXECUTION

Notice of claim

1.—(A1) In this Part of this Order "the interpleader claimant" means any person making a claim to or in respect of goods seized in execution or the proceeds or value thereof and "the interpleader claim" means that claim. **cc33.1**

(1) The interpleader claimant shall deliver to the bailiff holding the warrant of execution, or file in the office of the court for the district in which the goods were seized, notice of his claim stating—

(a) the grounds of the interpleader claim or, in the case of a claim for rent, the particulars required by section 102(2) of the Act; and

(b) the interpleader claimant's full name and address.

(2) On receipt of an interpleader claim made under this rule, the court shall—

(a) send notice thereof to the execution creditor; and

(b) except where the interpleader claim is to the proceeds or value of the goods, send to the interpleader claimant a notice requiring him to make a deposit or give security in accordance with section 100 of the Act.

"the interpleader claimant"

this terminology replaces the term 'claimant' previously used[1]; cases reported prior to the introduction of CPR use the word "claimant". **cc33.1.1**

"goods seized"

compare RSC O.17, r.1(1)(b) which extends to seizure intended by the sherrif. **cc33.1.2**

"notice of his claim...stating the grounds of the interpleader"

No particular formality is required *Christopher Newman (trading as Mantella Publishing) v Modern Bookbinders Ltd* [2000] 1 W.L.R. 2559; [2000] 2 All E.R. 814; *Independent*, February 3, 2000; however sufficient detail should be provided to the bailiff for him to identify which particular goods are claimed and why; the judge is not obliged to hear **cc33.1.3**

[1] Amended by SI 2000/221.

the interpleader if the particulars of claim are insufficient *Boswick v Boffey* (1854) 9 Exch 315 see *Fairfax Gerrard Holdings Ltd v Rasool Zargam* [2004] EWHC 2079, QB; a case decided on its individual facts and an example of a situation where the interpleader was rejected because the right was not promptly asserted and the supporting evidence implausible and poorly documented.

"in the case of a claim for rent"

cc33.1.4 If the rent is owing to the landlord of the premises upon which goods are seized in execution, the sheriff is prohibited by the Landlord and Tenant Act 1709 from removing the goods after having notice of rent being due, until the rent owing (up to one year's arrears) has been paid. Should he remove or sell them before such rent has been paid. Should he remove or sell them before such rent has been paid, he would ne liable to an action founded on the statute. Though the execution creditor could not compel him to sell, it became the practice for the sheriff to sell and pay the landlord out of the proceeds; but a sheriff is entitled to withdraw and return *nulla bona*, when it becomes clear that neither the execution creditor not the tenant will pay the landlord. (See Lindley L.J., at pp.573-576 in *Re Mackenzie* [1899] 2 Q.B. 566, CA). A sheriff, therefore, upon the landlord claiming, cannot be interplead (*Clarke v Lord* (1833) 2 Dowl. Pr. Cas. 55; *cf. Bateman v Farnsworth* (1860) 29 L.K.Exch. 365).

"section 102(2) of the Act"

cc33.1.5 Section 102(2) of the County Courts Act 1984 provides that the landlord must provide the following information to the bailiff

(a) the amount of rent to be in arrear: and

(b) the period in respect of which the rent is due

"except where the interpleader claim is to the proceeds or value of goods"

cc33.1.6 Where a claimant pays the sheriff out under protest, the amount paid is "the proceeds or value of" the goods within this rule (*Smith v Critchfield* (1885) 14 Q.B.D. 873, CA) but the claimant cannot succeed unless he was entitled to the goods (*Plant v Collins* [1913] 1 K.B. 242).

"section 100 of the Act"

cc33.1.7 Section 100 of the County Courts Act 1984 provides that the interpleader claimant must make a deposit with the bailiff of the amount of the value of the goods claimed. In the case of dispute the value is determined by appraisement by the judge. The bailiff will be at fault if he accepts a sum from the interpleader claimant which is less than the value of the goods, but the judge may order the bailiff to return to levy further *Miller & Co v Solomon* [1906] 2 K.B 91.

Reply to interpleader claim

cc33.2 2.—(1) Within 4 days after receiving notice of a claim under rule 1(2) the execution creditor shall give notice to the court officer informing him whether he admits or disputes the interpleader claim or requests the district judge to withdraw from possession of the goods or money claimed.

(2) If, within the period aforesaid, the execution creditor gives notice to the court admitting the claim or requesting the district judge to withdraw from possession of the goods or money claimed, the execution creditor shall not be liable to the district judge for any fees or expenses incurred after receipt of the notice.

"Notice to the court officer"

cc33.2.1 The notice must be given not to the bailiff but to the court officer; contrast the position under RSC O.17, r.3(2) where the notice must be given to the sheriff within seven days.

"any fees or expenses incurred after receipt of the notice"

cc33.2.2 There are no longer any fees payable by the interpleader claimant.

Order protecting district judge

cc33.3 3. Where the execution creditor gives the court such a notice as is mentioned in rule 2(2), the district judge shall withdraw from possession of the goods or money claimed and may apply to the judge, on notice to the interpleader claimant, for an order restraining the bringing of a claim against the district judge for or in respect of his having taken possession of the goods or money and on the hearing of the application the judge may make such order as may be just.

Form

N359 notice to claimant to goods taken in execution to make deposit or give security. **cc33.3.1**

"Apply to the judge...for an order restraining the bringing of a claim"

The application is made to the circuit judge and is made on notice to the interpleader claimant. **cc33.3.2**

The right of the district judge to apply for protection against a claim is analogous to the protection offered to the sheriff under RSC O.17, r.2(4) and is in addition to the protection of s.98 of the County Courts Act 1984 (see below para.cc33.5.1).

The liability of the district judge on seizure of goods is limited to cases where it is just to grant the interpleader claimant relief and where the interpleader claimant has suffered a real grievance *Cave v Capel* [1954] 1 Q.B. 367; 1 All E.R. 428, CA. It is the nature of the act which is relevant such as selling the goods at a substantial undervalue *Neumann v Bakeaway Ltd* [1983] 2 All E.R. 935 CA. (See also the notes to CCR O.33, r.5—para.cc33.5.1.)

Issue of interpleader proceedings

4.—(1) Where the execution creditor gives notice under rule 2(1) disputing an interpleader claim made under rule 1 or fails, within the period mentioned in rule 2(1), to give the notice required by that rule, the district judge shall, unless the interpleader claim is withdrawn, issue an interpleader notice to the execution creditor and the interpleader claimant. **cc33.4**

(2) On the issue of an interpleader notice under paragraph (1) the court shall enter the proceedings in the records of the court, fix a day for the hearing by the judge and prepare sufficient copies of the notice for service under this rule.

(3) Subject to paragraph (4) the notice shall be served on the execution creditor and the interpleader claimant in the same manner set out in CPR r.6.20.

(4) Service shall be effected not less than 14 days before the return day.

Forms

- **N88** Interpleader summons to execution creditor **cc33.4.1**
- **N88(1)** Interpleader summons to claimant claiming goods or rent under an execution
- **N89** Interpleader summons to person making adverse claims to a debt etc.

procedure

The court staff refer the papers to the district judge[1] who requests the issue of the interpleader proceedings to be determined by the judge; in this context the judge means circuit judge.[2] Article 6 of the Human Rights Convention (Right to a fair trial); having regard to the position of the district judge being responsible for the acts and **cc33.4.2**

---

[1] Contrast the position in the High Court where the equivalent step is taken by the Sheriff RSC O.17, r.2.

[2] These matters cannot be determined by the district judge by reason of his status as High Bailiff; see the introductory editorial notes for the background.

defaults of the bailiffs[1] it would be a violation of this right to an impartial and independent tribunal if issues arising out of the actions of the bailiff in executing a judgment were to be heard by the district judge *McGonnell v United Kingdom*, *The Times*, February 22, 2000.

"The district judge shall, unless the interpleader claim is withdrawn, issue an interpleader notice to the execution creditor and the interpleader claimant"

cc33.4.3 Section 101 of the County Courts Act 1984, (see Vol.2, para.9A–616).

The power to issue an interpleader should be exercised in all appropriate cases. The district judge has the obligation to consider if the claim is on the face of it sufficient in detail and credible in substance and once the claim meets these elementary tests the district judge has no option but to issue an interpleader summons *Christopher Newman (trading as Mantella Publishing) v Modern Bookbinders Ltd* [2000] 1 W.L.R. 2559; [2000] 2 All E.R. 814; *Independent*, February 3, 2000, CA.

Claim for damages

cc33.5 5. Where an interpleader proceedings under an execution the interpleader claimant claims from the execution creditor or the district judge, or the execution creditor claims from the district judge, damages arising or capable of arising out of the execution—

(a) the party claiming damages shall, within 8 days after service of the notice on him under rule 4(3), give notice of this claim to the court and to any other party against whom the claim is made, stating the amount and the grounds of the claim; and

(b) the party from whom damages are claimed may pay money into court in satisfaction of the claim as if the interpleader proceedings were a claim brought in accordance with CPR Part 7 by the person making the claim.

"Claims from the district judge"

cc33.5.1 The district judge is responsible for the acts and defaults of the bailiffs; s.123 of the County Courts Act 1984. See the editorial introduction for the background to this anomalous rule. The district judge may apply to the circuit judge for protection under r.3 (see above).

The claimant must have a fairly arguable case *Observer Ltd v Gordon* [1983] 2 All E.R. 945; but the court will not grant protection where it is apparent that the claimant has a real grievance *Cave v Capel* [1954] 1 Q.B. 367; 1 All E.R. 428, CA.

Note that where goods are sold by the bailiffs and are subsequently claimed by a third party s.98 of the County Courts Act 1984 applies; a person may not recover against the district judge unless it is proved that that he had notice of his claim or might by reasonable inquiry have ascertained that the goods were not the property of the execution debtor. This defence will not apply if the claimant has a substantial grievance which may arise if the goods are sold at an undervalue *Neumann v Bakeaway Ltd* [1983] 2 All E.R. 935, CA; the question of whether goods are sold at an undervalue is a question of fact to be decided in every instance. But also see *Jelks v Hayward* [1905] 2 K.B. 460 for a case which on its particular facts the bailiff was liable for damages in circumstances where goods subject to a hire purchase agreement were sold without notice having been given to the hirer.

PART II

OTHERWISE THAN UNDER EXECUTION

Application for relief

cc33.6 6.—(1) Where a person (in this Part of this Order called "the applicant") is under a liability in respect of a debt or any money or

[1] s.123 of the County Courts Act 1984 and see additional commentary on the status of the District Judge in para.33.0.2.

goods and he is, or expects to be, sued for or in respect of the debt, money or goods by two or more persons making adverse claims thereto ("the interpleader claimants"), he may apply to the court, in accordance with these rules, for relief by way of interpleader.

(2) The application shall be made to the court in which the claim is pending against the applicant or, if no claim is pending against him, to the court in which he might be sued.

(3) The application shall be made by filing a witness statement or affidavit showing that—

(a) the applicant claims no interest in the subject-matter in dispute other than for charges or costs;

(b) the applicant does not collude with any of the interpleader claimants; and

(c) the applicant is willing to pay or transfer the subject-matter into court or to dispose of it as the court may direct,

together with as many copies of the witness statement or affidavit as there are interpleader claimants.

Forms

- Form **N360** **cc33.6.1**

"application for relief"

The Pt 8 procedure should be used; this is not specified for County Court proceedings but is specified for High Court Proceedings; CPR PD 8 and would appear further to be suitable bearing in mind the format of the application specified namely a claim supported by evidence. (See also para.cc33.6 above as to the general applicability to High Court procedures to County Court procedure.) **cc33.6.2**

"under a liability in respect of a debt or any money or goods"

The applicant may interplead as to so much of a debt as he admits, the dispute as to the residue being settled seperately (*Reading v London School Board* (1886) 16 Q.B.D. 686). A liability to unliquidated damages is not a "debt" for this purpose (*Walter v Nicholson* (1836) 6 Dowl. 517; *Ingham v Walker* (1887) 3 T.L.R. 448, CA, *cf. Attenborough v London and St Katharine's Dock Co* (1877–78) L.R. 3 C.P.D. 450, CA, where a seperate claim for damages was reserved, and *cf. Ex p. Mersey Docks* [1899] 1 Q.B. 546, CA). A debt due but not yet payable is presumably within the words of the rule (*Reading v London School Board*). The Court will not entertain proceedings to determine the right to winnings under a gaming contract (*Shoolbred v Roberts* [1900] 2 Q.B. 497 at 501 and 502; and see *Applegarth v Colley* (1842) 2 Dowl. 223; *Dowson v Macfarlane* (1899) 81 L.T. 67; *Hill v William Hill (Park Lane Ltd)* [1949] A.C. 530. **cc33.6.3**

Chattels is "one of the widest words known to the law in its relation to personal property" (per Fry L.J. in *Robinson v Jenkins* (1890) L.R. 24 Q.B.D. 275, at 279). It includes shares in a company (*ibid.*) and, *semble*, titles deeds to property (*Robert v Bell* (1857) 7 E. & B. 323). "Liability in respect of any goods or chattels" includes a claim by a claimant to a mere lien over or a right to possession of goods (*Jennings v Mather* [1902] 1 K.B. 1, CA).

"is or expects to be sued"

There must be a real foundation for the expectation (*Harrison v Payne* (1836) 2 Hodges 107; *Diplock v Hammond* (1854) 23 L.J. Ch. 550; *Watson v Park Royal Caterers* [1961] 1 W.L.R. 727). A person cannot protect himself by interpleader proceedings against a claim on which the claimant has obtained judgment (*H Stevenson & Son Ltd v Brownell* [1912] 2 Ch. 344 (a judgment by consent); *Randall v Lithgow* (1884) 12 Q.B.D. 525 (a garnishee order absolute)). The fact, however, that the applicant may be legally liable to both defendants may be a ground for refusing him relief (*Farr v Wardish, etc., Steam Navigation* [1888] W.N. 84; *Sablicich v Russell* (1866) L.R. 2 Eq. 441. Compare *Ex p. Mersey Docks* [1899] 1 Q.B. 546 where relief was given, the question of an estoppel in favour of one claimant being reserved). **cc33.6.4**

The claim must be actual and not merely anticipated (*Isaac v Spilsbury* (1833) 2 Dowl. Pr. Cas. 211; *Bentley v Hook* (1834) 2 Dowl. Pr. Cas. 339; *Salmon v James* (1832) 1 Dowl. Pr. Cas. 369; *Day v Waldock* (1833) 1 Dowl. Pr. Cas. 523). A claim to a lien or right of possession over the goods, and not to the absolute property, is within these words (see *Ford v Baynton* (1832) 1 Dowl. Pr. Cas. 357; *Green v Stevens* (1857) 2 H. & N. 146)—for example, a claim by the hirer under a hiring or hire-purchase agreement.

"adverse claims"

cc33.6.5 There must be adverse claims to the same property or debt (*Greatorex v Shackle* [1895] 2 Q.B. 249, where two auctioneers were each claiming a commission under a seperate contract on the same sale of the same house, and relief was refused; *Wright v Freeman* (1879) 48 L.J. C.P. 276; *Sun Insurance Office v Galinsky* [1914] K.B. 545).

"Affidavit"

cc33.6.6 Form **N360**.

"the application"

cc33.6.7 The procedure is described in rr.7 and 8: the Pt 8 procedure is not specified but the procedure described is analogous to the Pt 8 procedure which is specified for the equivalent High Court Procedure CPR PD 8, Sch.A, Table 1.

"witness statement or evidence"

cc33.6.8 Contrast the procedure for interpleader under execution where it is assumed that the bailiff is disinterested.

"other than for charges or costs"

cc33.6.9 A lien over goods for charges for storage, or over the proceeds of sale for commission on the sale, does not disentitle the applicant to relief (*Cotter v Bank of England* (1833) 2 Dowl. Pr. Cas. 728; *Best v Hayes* (1863) 1 Hurl. & C. 718; *De Rothschild Freres v Morrison, Kekewich & Co* (1890) 24 Q.B.D. 750, CA).

"does not collude"

cc33.6.10 "Collusion" does not here necessarily entail anything morally wrong, but means "playing the same game" as one of the claimants (*Murietta v South American Co*; *Tucker v Morris* (1832) 1 C. & M. 73; 2 L.J.Exch. 1; and see, as to sheriffs, *Duddin v Long* (1834) 3 Dowl. Pr. Cas. 139); *Fredericks and Pelhams Timber Buildings (A Firm) v Wilkins, Read (Claimant)* [1971] 1 W.L.R. 1197 at 1204; [1971] 3 All E.R. 545 at 550-551, CA) and where the applicant has agreed to do so, or has taken an indemnity from that claimant (*Murietta v South America Co*; *Thompson v Wright* (1884) 13 Q.B.D. 632) though that claimant cannot complain, there is collusion (*ibid.*). Similarly where the applicant has placed himself in the position of being sued at the request and in the interests of one claimant (*Belcher v Smith* (1832) 9 Bing. 82).

Crown

cc33.6.11 These rules apply to the Crown: s.16 of the Crown Proceedings Act 1947 (Vol.2, Section 9B).

Equitable rights

cc33.6.12 Equitable claims and rights can be asserted and protected by interpleader: see *Jennings v Mather* [1901] 1 Q.B. 108 at 115 and cases there cited.

Claim by co-owner or partner

cc33.6.13 If goods are the property of A and B, who hold them jointly or as tenants in common, the sheriff can seize and sell them on a judgment against A and B or a judgment against either of them (subject to the question of the distribution of the proceeds) – see *Farrar v Beswick* (1836) 1 M. & W. 682, per Parke, B. p.685; *Mayhew v Herrick* (1849) 7 C.B. 229 at 240, 248 and 250. The same applied to partnership property, but now, on a judgment against one partner, execution will not issue against partnership property (Partnership Act 1890 s.23) and instead a charging order can be obtained on the partner's interest (*ibid.*). If, on execution being levied on a judgment against one partner, another partner sets up the partnership, and the execution creditor disputes the partnership or denies that the goods seized are property of the partnership, the dispute is proper subject matter for interpleader (see *Peake v Carter* [1916] 1 K.B. 652, per Swinfen Eady L.J. at 655–656) If the goods are admitted to be partnership property, the sheriff will be ordered to withdraw.

Claim by debenture holders

A debenture usually creates a floating charge on a company's assets, and only where the charge has been crystallised—e.g. by appointment of a receiver—before the completion of an execution by seizure and sale do the rights of the debenture holders have priority over those of the execution creditor (*Re Standard Manufacturing Co* [1891] 1 Ch. 627, CA; *Re Opera* [1891] 3 Ch. 260, CA; and see *Taunton v Sheriff of Warwickshire* [1895] 2 Ch. 319, CA; *Evans v Rivcl Granite Quarries* [1910] 2 K.B. 979, CA; *Robinson v Burnell's Bakery* [1904] 2 K.B. 624; *Heaton and Dugard Ltd v Cutting Bros Ltd* [1925] 1 K.B. 655). **cc33.6.14**

Authority of solicitor

A solicitor, retained in the case, has no implied authority to conduct interpleader proceedings (*James v Ricknell* (1888) 20 Q.B.D. 64). **cc33.6.15**

Relief in pending claim

7. Where the applicant is a defendant in a pending claim— **cc33.7**
   (a) the witness statement or affidavit and copies required by rule 6(3) shall be filed within 14 days after service on him of the claim form;
   (b) the return day of the application shall be a day fixed for the pre-trial review of the claim including the interpleader proceedings and, if a day has already been fixed for the pre-trail review or hearing of the claim, the court shall, if necessary, postpone it;
   (c) the interpleader claimant, the applicant and the claimant in the claim shall be given notice of the application, which shall be prepared by the court together with sufficient copies for service;
   (d) the notice to the interpleader claimant shall be served on him, together with a copy of the witness statement or affidavit filed under rule 6(3) and of the claim form and particulars of claim in the claim, not less than 21 days before the return day in the same manner as an interpleader notice in accordance with rule 4(3);
   (e) the notices to the applicant and the claimant shall be sent to them by the court and the notice to the claimant shall be accompanied by a copy of the said witness statement or affidavit.

Relief otherwise than in pending claim

8. Where the applicant is not a defendant in a pending claim— **cc33.8**
   (a) the court shall enter the proceedings in the records of the court;
   (b) the court shall fix a day for the pre-trial review or, if the court so directs, a day for the hearing of the proceedings and shall prepare and issue an interpleader notice, together with sufficient copies for service;
   (c) the notice together with a copy of the witness statement or affidavit filed under rules 6(3), shall be served on each of the claimants not less than 21 days before the return day in the same manner as an interpleader notice to be served under rule 4(3); and

(d) the court shall deliver or send a notice of issue to the applicant.

Payment into court, etc.

cc33.9 9. Before or after the court proceeds under rule 7 or 8 the district judge may direct the applicant to bring the subject-matter of the proceedings into court, or to dispose of it in such manner as the district judge thinks fit, to abide the order of the court.

Payment into court

cc33.9.1 The court will wish to release the applicant for relief—the "stakeholder"—from the interpleader proceedings as soon as possible. Where the dispute concerns a debt or a sum of money the applicant can be released by ordering him to pay the sum into court having deducted his assessed (or agreed) costs of the application: these costs will ultimately be paid by the unsuccessful interpleader claimant.

Sale or deposit of goods

cc33.9.2 For the purpose of saving costs and sheriffs charges, and especially where the goods are perishable, an order may be made for the sale of the goods under r.6 (*Paquin v Robinson* (1901) 85 L.T. 5, CA) or under r.8. Alternatively the court can order sale unless a payment into court is made or security given by the interpleader claimant (see Form **PF32 QB**).

Where it is not appropriate for the goods to be sold (e.g. the dispute concerns a specific chattel) the court can order the property to be deposited in the joint names of the solicitors for the parties. Alternatively, it may release the property to one of the interpleader claimants on his giving security or paying into court a sum representing the value of the goods.

Reply by interpleader claimant

cc33.10 10.—(1) An interpleader claimant shall, within 14 days after service on him of the notice under rule 7(c) or the interpleader notice under rule 8(c), file—

(a) a notice that he makes no interpleader claim; or

(b) particulars stating the grounds of his interpleader claim to the subject matter,

together in either case with sufficient copies for service under paragraph (2).

(2) The court shall send to each of the other parties a copy of any notice or particulars filed under paragraph (1).

(3) The court may, if it thinks fit, hear the proceedings although no notice or particulars have been filed.

Order barring interpleader claim, etc.

cc33.11 11.—(1) Where an interpleader claimant does not appear on any day fixed for a pre-trial review or the hearing of interpleader proceedings, or fails or refuses to comply with an order made in the proceedings, the court may make an order barring his interpleader claim.

(2) If, where the applicant is a defendant in a pending claim, the claimant does not appear on any day fixed for a pre-trial review or the hearing of the interpleader proceedings, the claim including the interpleader proceedings may be struck out.

(3) In any other case where a day is fixed for the hearing of interpleader proceedings, the court shall hear and determine the

proceedings and give judgment finally determining the rights and claims of the parties.

(4) Where the court makes an order barring the interpleader claim of an interpleader claimant, the order shall declare the claimant, and all persons claiming under him, for ever barred from prosecuting his interpleader claim against the applicant and all persons claiming under him, but unless the interpleader claimant has filed a notice under rule 10 that he makes no interpleader claim, such an order shall not affect the rights of the claimants as between themselves.

"The court shall hear and determine the proceedings"

The County Court rule is less than detailed than RSC O.17; see para.sc17.1.1 for applicability of High Court Rules to County Court Rules and refer to the detailed notes to RSC O.17, r.5. **cc33.11.1**

CCR ORDER 34—PENAL AND DISCIPLINARY PROVISIONS

Contents **cc34.0.1**

Editorial introduction

Schedule 2, CCR O.34 conveniently sets out the procedure to enforce various penal and disciplinary provisions in the County Courts Act 1984. It had no directly equivalent rule in the RSC. Thus, for example, in the county court a witness who disobeys a witness summons can be fined under s.55 of the CCA 1984 whereas disobedience to a High Court subpoena (now also called a witness summons, see Pt 34 of the CPR) has always been dealt with as a contempt of court (see Sch.1, RSC O.52). **cc34.0.2**

For details of the courts powers see the various sections of the CCA mentioned in the rule. The courts powers are limited. In particular the court has no power to remand in custody or on bail.

Section 74 of the Courts and Legal Services Act 1990 extended the powers conferred by ss.14, 55 and 118 of the CCA 1984 to district judges as well as circuit judges. The definition of "judge" in r.2.3 of the CPR includes a district judge. Accordingly the former CCR O.35, r.5, dealing with the exercise of penal powers by district judges, is not included in Sch.2 as it is not necessary.

Related sources **cc34.0.3**

- Schedule 2, CCR O.26—Warrants of execution
- Schedule 2, CCR O.29—Committal for breach of Order or Undertaking
- Schedule 1, RSC O.52—Committal
- Practice Direction—Committal Applications
- CCA 1984 s.14—Penalty for Assaulting Officers (Vol.2, Section 9A)
- CCA 1984 s.55—Penalty for neglecting or refusing to give evidence (Vol.2, Section 9A)
- CCA 1984 s.92 —Penalty for rescuing goods seized (Vol.2, Section 9A)
- CCA 1984 s.118 —Power to commit for contempt (Vol.2, Section 9A)
- CCA 1984 s.124—Liability of bailiff for neglect to levy execution (Vol.2, Section 9A)
- Courts and Legal Services Act 1990 s.74 (Vol.2, Section 9B).

Forms

- **N90** Summons for assaulting an officer of the court or rescuing goods **cc34.0.4**

- **N91** Order for committal and/or imposing a fine for assaulting an officer of the court of rescuing goods
- **N366** Summons for neglect to levy execution
- **N367** Notice of hearing to consider why fine should not be imposed
- **N368** Order fining a witness for non-attendance
- **N370** Order of committal or imposing a fine for insult or misbehaviour

Issue and service of summons for offence under section 14, 92 or 124 of the Act

cc34.1 1. Where—

(a) it is alleged that any person has committed an offence under section 14, 92 or 118 of the Act by assaulting an officer of the court while in the execution of his duty, or by rescuing or attempting to rescue any goods seized in execution or by wilfully insulting a judge, juror, witness or any officer of the court, and the alleged offender has not been taken into custody and brought before the judge; or

(b) a complaint is made against an officer of the court under section 124 of the Act for having lost the opportunity of levying execution,

the court officer shall issue a summons, which shall be served on the alleged offender personally not less than 8 days before the return day appointed in the summons.

Committal under section 14, 92 or 118 of the Act

cc34.1A 1A. Rule 1(5) of Order 29 shall apply, with the necessary modifications, where an order is made under section 14, 92 or 118 of the Act committing a person to prison.

Contempt in the face of the court

cc34.1A.1 A judge of the High Court faced with a contempt in the face of the court can act under the inherent jurisdiction to detain the contemnor overnight (see *Wilkinson v S* [2003] EWCA Civ 95; [2003] 1 W.L.R. 1254). A judge in the county court has no such inherent power and can employ only the limited power in CCA 1984, s.118 (see Vol.2 at 9A–654). The procedure to be followed is as set out in Pt II of Practice Direction–Committal Applications; see para.scpd 52.7.

Notice to show cause before or after fine under section 55 of the Act

cc34.2 2. Before or after imposing a fine on any person under section 55 of the Act for disobeying a witness summons or refusing to be sworn or give evidence, the judge may direct the court officer to give to that person notice that if he has any cause to show why a fine should not be or should not have been imposed on him, he may show cause in person or by witness statement or affidavit or otherwise on a day named in the notice, and the judge after considering the cause shown may make such order as he thinks fit.

Non-payment of fine

cc34.3 3.—(1) If a fine is not paid in accordance with the order imposing it, the court officer shall forthwith report the matter to the judge.

(2) Where by an order imposing a fine, the amount of the fine is directed to be paid by instalments and default is made in the payment of any instalment, the same proceedings may be taken as if default had been made in payment of the whole of the fine.

(3) If the judge makes an order for payment of a fine to be enforced by warrant of execution, the order shall be treated as an application made to the district judge for the issue of the warrant at the time when the order was received by him.

Enforcement of fines

CCA 1984, s.129 (Vol.2, para.9A–674) enables fines to be enforced by any of the methods of enforcement available "under this Act". Usually, the judge will order a warrant of execution to issue. Priority of such a warrant is governed by O.34 r.3(3). **cc34.3.1**

Repayment of fine

4. If, after a fine has been paid, the person on whom it was imposed shows cause sufficient to satisfy the judge that, if it had been shown at an earlier date, he would not have imposed a fine or would have imposed a smaller fine or would not have ordered payment to be enforced, the judge may order the fine or any part thereof to be repaid. **cc34.4**

CCR ORDER 39—ADMINISTRATION ORDERS

Contents **cc39.0.1**

Editorial introduction

There has long been a system similar to bankruptcy for administering the affairs of debtors whose debts are not large (see e.g. the judgment of Wills J. in *Re Frank* [1894] 1 Q.B. 9; a case on summary administration under the Bankruptcy Act 1883). The current law is in Pt IV of CCA 1984 (Vol.2, para.9A–639) and the power to make rules of court derives from s.12 of Insolvency Act 1976. Unfortunately, the current law is both out of date and out of line with the modern law of insolvency and thus is in need of reform. It is a policy decision whether such orders should exist at all (and if so what the limit should be) and whether such orders should continue to be administered by the courts as opposed to, say, the Official Receiver. **cc39.0.2**

An administration order can be made only against a person who has at least one High Court or county court judgment against him but whose total indebtedness does not exceed £5,000. It has been called "the poor man's bankruptcy". Like bankruptcy, a schedule of creditors is prepared, the debtor makes regular payments and a dividend is paid to creditors. Unlike bankruptcy, the order is administered by the county court and an administration order carries none of the legal disabilities of bankruptcy—though the order is registered at the Registry of County Court Judgments. While an administration order is in force no interest can accrue on a county court judgment and it is not possible to issue enforcement proceedings. If the debtor does not comply with the order it can be revoked. The court has the duty of enforcing the order: the usual method is an attachment of earnings order.

Administration orders under Pt VI of CCA 1984 (dealt with in Sch.2, CCR O.39) should not be confused with administration orders against companies governed by Pt II of Insolvency Act 1986.

"county court limit"

cc39.0.3 The county court limit for administration order purposes is £5,000 (County Courts (Adminstration Order Jurisdiction) Order 1981 (SI 1981/1122). This limit can be increased pursuant to s.145 of CCA 1984 but it never has been. Similarly an amendment made to s.112, CCA 1984 by s.13, CLSA 1990, which would have had the effect of removing the £5,000 limit, has never been brought into force. Thus a county court should not make an administration order if it is clear that debts exceed £5,000. However, if it has done (e.g. because a creditor has proved that a scheduled debt is in fact larger than originally stated) the order is not automatically invalid (see s.112(5) of CCA 1984—Vol.2, para.9A–639) but the court can set aside the order.

Related sources

cc39.0.4
- Attachment of Earnings Act 1971 (Vol.2, para.9B–954)
- County Courts Act 1984 s.112 (amendments to s.112 and new ss.112A and 112B, effected by CLSA 1990, have never been brought into force) (Vol.2, para.9A–639)
- County Courts (Administration Order Jurisdiction) Order 1981 (SI 1981/1122)
- Insolvency Act 1976 s.429
- Company Directors Disqualification Act 1986 s.12

Forms

cc39.0.5
- **N92** Request for administration order
- **N93** List of creditors furnished under Attachment of Earnings Act 1971
- **N94** Administration Order
- **N95** Order revoking an administration order
- **N95A** Order suspending or varying an administration order
- **N270** Notes for guidance—administration order
- **N373** Notice of application for an administration order
- **N374** Notice of intention to review an administration order
- **N374A** Notice of intention to revoke an administration order
- **N375** Notice of further creditors' claim
- **N376** Notice of hearing—administration order (by direction of the court)
- **N377** Notice of dividend

Exercise of powers by district judge

cc39.1 1. Any powers conferred on the court by Part VI of the Act, section 4 of the Attachment of Earnings Act 1971 or this Order may be exercised by the district judge or, in the circumstances mentioned in this Order, by the court officer.

Request and list of creditors

cc39.2 2.—(1) A debtor who desires to obtain an administration order under Part VI of the Act shall file a request in that behalf in the court for the district in which he resides or carries on business.

(2) Where on his examination under CPR Part 71, or otherwise, a

debtor furnishes to the court on oath a list of his creditors and the amounts which he owes to them respectively and sufficient particulars of his resources and needs, the court may proceed as if the debtor has filed a request under paragraph (1).

(3) Where a debtor is ordered to furnish a list under section 4(1)(b) of the said Act of 1971, then, unless otherwise directed, the list shall be filed within 14 days after the making of the order.

secured debts

The request in Form **N92** required by r.39(2)(1) and the list referred to in r.39(2)(2) both require that the debtor should list all his creditors whether the debt is secured or not. A county court can make an administration order where a debtor is unable to pay forthwith the amount of a judgment obtained against him and "his whole indebtedness amounts to a sum not exceeding the county court limit" (see paras 39.0.1 and 39.0.2 and s.112 of CCA 1984—Vol.2, para.9A–639). **cc39.2.1**

A debt does not cease to be a debt because the debtor has given security for it. The statute does not expressly exclude secured debts. Accordingly it seems clear that the term "whole indebtedness" means that secured debts must be taken into account. This means that a debtor with a mortgage debt will rarely be able to obtain an administration order as his whole indebtedness is highly likely to exceed the £5,000 limit. A logical case can be made for excluding mortgage debts but the amended s.112 of CCA 1984, which would have permitted this, has never been brought into force.

CCR

Verification on oath

3. The statements in the request mentioned in rule 2(1) and the list mentioned in rule 2(3) shall be verified by the debtor on oath. **cc39.3**

Orders made by the court officer

5.—(1) The question whether an administration order should be made, and the terms of such an order, may be decided by the court officer in accordance with the provisions of this rule. **cc39.5**

(2) On the filing of a request or list under rule 2, the court officer may, if he considers that the debtor's means are sufficient to discharge in full and within a reasonable period the total amount of the debts included in the list, determine the amount and frequency of the payments to be made under such an order ("the proposed rate") and—

- (a) notify the debtor of the proposed rate requiring him to give written reasons for any objection he may have to the proposed rate within 14 days of service of notification upon him;
- (b) send to each creditor mentioned in the list provided by the debtor a copy of the debtor's request or of the list together with the proposed rate;
- (c) require any such creditor to give written reasons for any objection he may have to the making of an administration order within 14 days of service of the documents mentioned in sub-paragraph (b) upon him.

Objections under sub-paragraph (c) may be to the making of an order, to the proposed rate or to the inclusion of a particular debt in the order.

(3) Where no objection under paragraph (2)(a) or (c) is received within the time stated, the court officer may make an administration order providing for payment in full of the total amount of the debts included in the list.

(4) Where the debtor or a creditor notifies the court of any objection within the time stated, the court officer shall fix a day for a hearing at which the district judge will decide whether an administration order should be made and the court officer shall give not less than 14 days' notice of the day so fixed to the debtor and to each creditor mentioned in the list provided by the debtor.

(5) Where the court officer is unable to fix a rate under paragraph (2) (whether because he considers that the debtor's means are insufficient or otherwise), he shall refer the request to the district judge.

(6) Where the district judge considers that he is able to do so without the attendance of the parties, he may fix the proposed rate providing for payment of the debts included in the list in full or to such extent and within such a period as appears practicable in the circumstances of the case.

(7) Where the proposed rate is fixed under paragraph (6), paragraphs (2) to (4) shall apply with the necessary modifications as if the rate had been fixed by the court officer.

(8) Where the district judge does not fix the proposed rate under paragraph (6), he shall direct the court officer to fix a day for a hearing at which the district judge will decide whether an administration order should be made and the court officer shall give not less than 14 days' notice of the day so fixed to the debtor and to each creditor mentioned in the list provided by the debtor.

(9) Where an administration order is made under paragraph (3), the court officer may exercise the power of the court under section 5 of the Attachment of Earnings Act 1971 to make an attachment of earnings order to secure the payments required by the administration order.

"in full"

cc39.5.1 Note the use of the words "in full" in r.39(5)(2). A court officer thus cannot make a percentage order.

composition orders

cc39.5.2 The power to make a composition order in s.112A of CCA 1984 (inserted by CLSA 1990) has never been brought into force. Accordingly the power to decide whether less than the full indebtedness should be paid, and if so the relevant pence in the pound, is still governed by s.112(6) and is exercisable only by a district judge.

Notice of objection by creditor

cc39.6 6.—(1) Any creditor to whom notice has been given under rule 5(8) and who objects to any debt included in the list furnished by the debtor shall, not less than 7 days before the day of hearing, give notice of his objection, stating the grounds thereof, to the court officer, to the debtor and to the creditor to whose debt he objects.

(2) Except with the permission of the court, no creditor may object to a debt unless he has given notice of his objection under paragraph (1).

Procedure on day of hearing

7. On the day of hearing— cc39.7

(a) any creditor, whether or not he is mentioned in the list furnished by the debtor, may attend and prove his debt or, subject to rule 6, object to any debt included in that list;

(b) every debt included in that list shall be taken to be proved unless it is objected to by a creditor or disallowed by the court or required by the court to be supported by evidence;

(c) any creditor whose debt is required by the court to be supported by evidence shall prove his debt;

(d) the court may adjourn proof of any debt and, if it does so, may either adjourn consideration of the question whether an administration order should be made or proceed to determine the question, in which case, if an administration order is made, the debt, when proved, shall be added to the debts scheduled to the order;

(e) any creditor whose debt is admitted or proved, and, with the permission of the court, any creditor the proof of whose debt has been adjourned, shall be entitled to be heard and to adduce evidence on the question whether an administration order should be made and, if so, in what terms.

Direction for order to be subject to review

8.—(1) The court may, on making an administration order or at any subsequent time, direct that the order shall be subject to review at such time or at such intervals as the court may specify. cc39.8

(2) Where the court has directed that an administration order shall be subject to review, the court officer shall give to the debtor and to every creditor who appeared when the order was made not less than 7 days' notice of any day appointed for such a review.

(3) Nothing in this rule shall require the court officer to fix a day for a review under rule 13A.

Service of order

9. Where an administration order is made, the court officer shall send a copy to— cc39.9

(a) the debtor;

(b) every creditor whose name was included in the list furnished by the debtor;

(c) any other creditor who has proved his debt; and

(d) every other court in which, to the knowledge of the district judge, judgment has been obtained against the debtor or proceedings are pending in respect of any debt scheduled to the order.

Subsequent objection by creditor

10.—(1) After an administration order has been made, a creditor who has not received notice under rule 5 and who wishes to object to a debt scheduled to the order, or to the manner in which payment is cc39.10

CCR

directed to be made by instalments, shall give notice to the court officer of his objection and of the grounds thereof.

(2) On receipt of such notice the court shall consider the objection and may—

(a) allow it;

(b) dismiss it; or

(c) adjourn it for hearing on notice being given to such persons and on such terms as to security for costs or otherwise as the court thinks fit.

(3) Without prejudice to the generality of paragraph (2), the court may dismiss an objection if it is not satisfied that the creditor gave notice of it within a reasonable time of his becoming aware of the administration order.

Subsequent proof by creditor

cc39.11 11.—(1) Any creditor whose debt is not scheduled to an administration order, and any person who after the date of the order became a creditor of the debtor, shall, if he wishes to prove his debt, send particulars of his claim to the court officer, who shall give notice of it to the debtor and to every creditor whose debt is so scheduled.

(2) If neither the debtor nor any creditor gives notice to the court officer, within 7 days after receipt of notice under paragraph (1), that he objects to the claim, then, unless it is required by the court to be supported by evidence, the claim shall be taken to be proved.

(3) If the debtor or a creditor gives notice of objection within the said period of 7 days or the court requires the claim to be supported by evidence, the court officer shall fix a day for consideration of the claim and give notice of it to the debtor, the creditor by whom the claim was made and the creditor, if any, making the objection, and on the hearing the court may either disallow the claim or allow it in whole or in part.

(4) If a claim is taken to be proved under paragraph (2) or allowed under paragraph (3), the debt shall be added to the schedule to the order and a copy of the order shall then be sent to the creditor by whom the claim was made.

Permission to present bankruptcy petition

cc39.12 12. An application by a creditor under section 112(4) of the Act for permission to present or join in a bankruptcy petition shall be made on notice to the debtor in accordance with CPR Part 23, but the court may, if it thinks fit, order that notice be given to any other creditor whose debt is scheduled to the administration order.

"bankruptcy petition"

cc39.12.1 Section 112(4) of CCA 1984 (Vol.2, para.9A–639) prevents a scheduled creditor presenting or joining in a bankruptcy petition unless either he obtains permission of the court or the debt exceeds £1,500.

Right of landlord to distrain notwithstanding order

cc39.12.2 See s.116 of CCA 1984 (Vol.2, para.9A–651).

Conduct of order

cc39.13 13.—(1) The court manager or such other officer of the court as the court making an administration order shall from time to time appoint shall have the conduct of the order and shall take all proper steps to enforce the order (including exercising the power of the court under section 5 of the Attachment of Earnings Act 1971 to make an attachment of earnings order to secure payments required by the administration order) or to bring to the attention of the court any matter which may make it desirable to review the order.

(2) Without prejudice to section 115 of the Act, any creditor whose debt is scheduled to the order may, with the permission of the court, take proceedings to enforce the order.

(3) The debtor or, with the permission of the court, any such creditor may apply to the court to review the order.

(4) When on a matter being brought to its attention under paragraph (1) the court so directs or the debtor or a creditor applies for the review of an administration order, rule 3(2) shall apply as if the order were subject to review under that rule

(5) Nothing in this rule shall require the court officer to fix a day for a review under rule 13A.

Review by court officer in default of payment

13A.—(1) Where it appears that the debtor is failing to make payments in accordance with the order, the court officer shall (either of his own initiative or on the application of a creditor whose debt is scheduled to the administration order) send a notice to the debtor— **cc39.13A**

(a) informing him of the amounts which are outstanding; and

(b) requiring him (within 14 days of service of the notice upon him) to—

(i) make the payments as required by the order; or

(ii) explain his reasons for failing to make the payments; and

(iii) make a proposal for payment of the amounts outstanding; or

(iv) make a request to vary the order.

(2) If the debtor does not comply with paragraph (1)(b) within the time stated, the court officer shall revoke the administration order.

(3) The court officer shall refer a notice given by a debtor under paragraph (1)(b)(ii), (iii) or (iv) to the district judge who may—

(a) without requiring the attendance of the parties—

(i) revoke the administration order or vary it so as to provide for payment of the debts included in the order in full or to such extent and within such a period as appears practicable in the circumstances of the case; or

(ii) suspend the operation of the administration order for such time and on such terms as he thinks fit; or

(b) require the court officer to fix a day for the review of the administration order and to give to the debtor and to every creditor whose debt is scheduled to the administration order not less than 8 days' notice of the day so fixed.

(4) Any party affected by an order made under paragraph (2) or (3)(a) may, within 14 days of service of the order on him and giving his reasons, apply on notice for the district judge to consider the matter afresh and the court officer shall fix a day for the hearing of the application before the district judge and give to the debtor and to every creditor whose debt is scheduled to the administration order not less than 8 days' notice of the day so fixed.

(5) On hearing an application under paragraph (4), the district judge may confirm the order or set it aside and make such new order as he thinks fit and the order so made shall be entered in the records of the court.

Revocation

cc39.13.1 By O.39, r.13A(2) "the court officer", and by O.39, r.14(1)(c) " the court" (which, in practice, usually means the district judge) can revoke an administration order. This has the effect of depriving the debtor of the benefit and protection of the administration order and frees judgment creditors from the inability to enforce an order which applies while an administration order is in force. The most common reason for revoking the order is the debtor's failure to make the payments required by the order. However, the order may be revoked if it transpires that it should not have been made, e.g. because the debts exceed the £5,000 limit (see s.112(5) of CCA 1984).

Section 429 of Insolvency Act 1986

cc39.13.2 This section provides:

"(1) *The following applies where a person fails to make any payment which he is required to make by virtue of an administration order under Part VI of the County Courts Act 1984.*

(2) *The court which is administering that person's estate under the order, may, if it thinks fit—*

(a) *revoke the adminstration order, and*

(b) *make an order directing that this section and section 12 of the Company Directors Disqualification Act 1986 shall apply to the person for such period, not exceeding 2 years, as may be specified in the order.*

(3) *A person to whom this section so applies shall not—*

(a) *either alone or jointly with another person, obtain credit to the extent of the amount prescribed for the purposes of s.360(1)(a) or more, or*

(b) *enter into any transaction in the course of or for the purposes of any business in which he is directly or indirectly engaged, without disclosing to the person from whom he obtains the credit, or (as the case may be) with whom the transaction is entered into, the fact that this section applies to him.*

(4) *The reference in subsection (3) to a person obtaining credit includes—*

(a) *a case where goods are bailed or hired to him under a hire-purchase agreement or agreed to be sold to him under a conditional sale agreement, and*

(b) *a case where he is paid in advance (whether in money or otherwise) for the supply of goods or services.*

(5) *A person who contravenes this section is guilty of an offence and liable to imprisonment or a fine, or both.*"

Section 12 of Company Directors Disqualification Act 1986

cc39.13.3 This section provides:

"(12) ***Failure to pay under county court administration order***

(1) *The following has effect where a court under section 429 of the* Insolvency Act *revokes an administration order under Part IV of the County Courts Act 1984.*

(2) *A person to whom that section applies by virtue of the order under section 429(2)(b) shall not, except with the leave of the court which made the order, act*

as director or liquidator of, or directly or indirectly take part or be concerned in the promotion, formation or management of, a company."

Powers on revocation of administration order

The powers given by s.429 of Insolvency Act 1986 are set out at para.cc.39.13A.2. Note also s.12 of the Company Directors Disqualification Act set out at para.cc39.13A.3. **cc39.13.4**

Review of order

14.—(1) On the review of an administration order the court may— **cc39.14**

(a) if satisfied that the debtor is unable from any cause to pay any instalment due under the order, suspend the operation of the order for such time and on such terms as it thinks fit;

(b) if satisfied that there has been a material change in any relevant circumstances since the order was made, vary any provision of the order made by virtue of section 112(6) of the Act;

(c) if satisfied that the debtor has failed without reasonable cause to comply with any provision of the order or that it is otherwise just and expedient to do so, revoke the order, either forthwith or on failure to comply with any condition specified by the court; or

(d) make an attachment of earnings order to secure the payments required by the administration order or vary or discharge any such attachment of earnings order already made.

(2) The court officer shall send a copy of any order varying or revoking an administration order to the debtor, to every creditor whose debt is scheduled to the administration order and, if the administration order is revoked, to any other court to which a copy of the administration order was sent pursuant to rule 9.

"may...revoke the order"

See commentary at para.cc39.13A.4. **cc39.14.1**

Discharge of attachment of earnings order

16. On the revocation of an administration order any attachment of earnings order made to secure the payments required by the administration order shall be discharged. **cc39.16**

Declaration of dividends

17.—(1) The officer having the conduct of an administration order shall from time to time declare dividends and distribute them among the creditors entitled to them. **cc39.17**

(2) When a dividend is declared, notice shall be sent by the officer to each of the creditors.

Creditors to rank equally

18. All creditors scheduled under section 113(d) of the Act before an administration order is superseded under section 117(2) of the Act shall rank equally in proportion to the amount of their debts subject to the priority given by the said paragraph (d) to those scheduled as having been creditors before the date of the order, but no payment made to any creditor by way of dividend or otherwise **cc39.18**

shall be disturbed by reason of any subsequent proof by any creditor under the said paragraph (d).

"section 113(a)...section 117(2)"

cc39.18.1 Section 113 is at Vol.2, para.9A–642 and Section 117 is at Vol.2, para.9A–653.

Costs of administration

cc39.18.2 By s.117 money paid into court under an administration order is appropriated first in satisfaction of the costs of administration (10p in the £1). Administration orders are unpopular with creditors and cause a great deal of work for the Court Service. They are intended for small debt cases only. See further commentary at para.cc39.0.2.

Change of debtor's address

cc39.19 19.—(1) A debtor who changes his residence shall forthwith inform the court of his new address.

(2) Where the debtor becomes resident in the district of another court, the court in which the administration order is being conducted may transfer the proceedings to that other court.

CCR ORDER 44—THE AGRICULTURAL HOLDINGS ACT 1986

Contents

cc44.0.1

Editorial introduction

cc44.0.2 The county court has a limited and diminishing jurisdiction under the AHA 1986. The Agricultural Tenancies Act 1995 applies to farm business tenancies beginning on and after September 1, 1995 and by s.4 the AHA 1986 applies only to tenancies created before September 1, 1995 or in pursuance of a contract made before September 1, 1995. The county court has no jurisdiction under the ATA 1995.

Related sources

cc44.0.3
- Agricultural Holdings Act 1986
- Agricultural Tenancies Act 1995
- CPR Pt 52 (Appeals)
- Part 8—Alternative Procedure for Claims

Order to arbitrator to state case

cc44.1 1. [Revoked]

History of rule

cc44.1.1 Revoked by Regulatory Reform (Agricultural Tenancies) (England and Wales) Order 2006 (SI 2006/2805) art.18, Sch.3.

Special case stated by arbitrator

cc44.2 2. [Revoked]

History of rule

cc44.2.1 Revoked by Regulatory Reform (Agricultural Tenancies) (England and Wales) Order 2006 (SI 2006/2805) art.18, Sch.3.

Removal of arbitrator or setting aside award

cc44.3 *3. [Revoked]*

History of rule

cc44.3.1 Revoked by Regulatory Reform (Agricultural Tenancies) (England and Wales) Order 2006 (SI 2006/2805) art.18, Sch.3.

Enforcement of order imposing penalty

4.—(1) When taking any proceedings for the enforcement in a county court of an order under section 27 of the Agricultural Holdings Act 1986, the party in whose favour the order was made shall file— **cc44.4**

(a) a certified copy of the order; and

(b) a certificate specifying the amount due under the order and stating whether any previous proceedings have been taken for its enforcement and, if so, the nature of the proceedings and their result.

(2) Where it is desired to enforce the order by warrant of execution, the proceedings may be taken in any court in the district of which execution is to be levied.

CCR ORDER 45—THE REPRESENTATION OF THE PEOPLE ACT 1983

Note

The rules remaining in this Order, viz., 2 and 3, were revoked by the Civil Procedure (Amendment) Rules 2007 (SI 2007/2204) r.20(c), with the result that the whole of this Order was revoked. In so far as it was necessary to do so, the effects of those rules were continued by new provisions in Practice Direction (Appeals) (supplementing Pt 52), in particular paras 24.4 and 24.5. **cc45.1**

CCR

CCR ORDER 49—MISCELLANEOUS STATUTES

Contents **cc49.0.1**

Editorial introduction

For many years when Parliament created a new right or remedy (e.g. under the Access to Neighbouring Land Act 1992 or under the Race Relations Act 1976) the practice has been to confer jurisdiction on the county courts. This usually resulted in a new rule being added to CCR O.49. Unfortunately and inevitably, CCR O.49 became unweildy and dealt with many diverse "Miscellaneous Statutes"; some very important and others of minor, or even trivial significance. The statutes are so diverse that no meaningful generalisations can be made for O.49. At least each statute had its own rule within O.49 and the strange rule numbering can be explained by the fact that the "miscellaneous statutes"are arranged alphabetically. **cc49.0.2**

The process of tidying up O.49 continues. CPR Pt 56, "Landlord and Tenant *Claims and Miscellaneous* Provisions about Land", deals with many statutes formerly governed by O.49. CPR Pt 65, "Proceedings relating to Anti-Social Behaviour and Harassment" replaced O.49, r.6B as from June 30, 2004.

Related sources

- See the statutes listed in the contents list above **cc49.0.3**
- High Court and County Courts Jurisdiction Order 1991 (see Vol.2, Section 9B)
- Part 56 Landlord and Tenant Claims and Micellaneous Provisions about Land

- Part 65 Proceedings relating to Anti-Social Behaviour and Harassment

Paragraph 6B — Housing Act 1996: injunctions

Housing Act 1996: injunctions

cc49.6B 6B. [Revoked]

Injunctions to prevent environmental harm: Town and Country Planning Act 1990 etc.

cc49.7 7. [Revoked]

History of rule

cc49.7.0 Revoked by Civil Procedure (Amendment No.3) Rules 2006 (SI 2006/3435).

Mental Health Act 1983

cc49.12 12. [Revoked]

History of rule

cc49.12.1 Revoked by Civil Procedure (Amendment No.3) Rules2006 (SI 2006/3435).

Sex Discrimination Act 1975, Race Relations Act 1976, Disability Discrimination Act 1995 and Disability Rights Commission Act 1999

cc49.17 17. [Revoked]

Telecommunications Act 1984

cc49.18A 18A.—(1) CPR Rule 35.15 applies to proceedings under paragraph 5 of Schedule 2 to the Telecommunications Act 1984.

Related Source

cc49.18A.1
- CPR, r.35.15—Assessors

Trade Union and Labour Relations Consolidation Act 1992

cc49.19 19.—(1) Where a complainant desires to have an order of the Certification Officer under section 82 of the Trade Union and Labour Relations Consolidation Act 1992 recorded in the county court, he shall produce the order and a copy thereof to the court for the district in which he resides or the head or main office of the trade union is situate.

(2) The order shall be recorded by filing it, and the copy shall be sealed and dated and returned to the complainant.

(3) The sealed copy shall be treated as if it were the notice of issue in a claim begun by the complainant.

(4) The costs, if any, allowed for recording the order shall be recoverable as if they were payable under the order.

(5) The order shall not be enforced until proof is given to the satisfaction of the court that the order has not been obeyed and, if the order is for payment of money, of the amount remaining unpaid.

PRACTICE DIRECTION—HOUSING ACT 1996: INJUNCTION

Note—This PD has been revoked. It is replaced by PD 65. ccpd49.1

CCR

SECTION B

PRACTICE DIRECTIONS AND PRACTICE STATEMENTS

SECTION B

PRACTICE DIRECTIONS AND PRACTICE STATEMENTS

SECTION B

Practice Directions and Practice Statements

The following Practice Directions have been moved to Volume 2, and can be found at the listed paragraphs:

- **Proceedings Under Enactments Relating to Discrimination, para.3I–1;**
- **Directors Disqualification Proceedings, para.3J–1;**
- **Civil Recovery Proceedings, para.3K–1;**
- **Devolution Issues, para.3L–1.**

PRACTICE STATEMENT (SUPREME COURT: JUDGMENTS) [1998] 1 W.L.R. 825

1. Introduction

I am making this statement with the agreement of Lord Woolf M.R., Sir Richard Scott V.-C. and Sir Stephen Brown P. It applies to judgments I delivered in all divisions of the High Court and the Court of Appeal. **B1–001**

In recent years a practice has developed for the written judgment of the court to be handed down without, as in the past, being read aloud. In this way much time is saved for the court, for practitioners and for litigants. The development of this practice, coupled with the increasing use of information technology, has, however, also led to the development of Problems which have hindered the efficient administration of justice.

One of these problems is associated with the delays that have often been experienced before the approved judgment of the court can be made liable from an official source. A second problem has arisen as a direct Consequence of the first: because of these delays, there has been widespread dissemination of many unapproved judgments of the court, which often omit significant last minute changes to the text, sometimes without any clear warning about their unapproved status. A third problem has been that the judgments delivered in courts not staffed by official shorthand writers have lacked a common format, and inconsistent practices have developed in the way they are distributed. There is also a contemporary need for the courts to facilitate the speedy publication of their approved judgments by electronic means, including the Internet's Worldwide Web.

Sir Richard Scott V.-C. and Brooke L.J. were invited to study these problems last autumn and to make recommendations as to how they might be resolved. Although they consulted quite widely, they are conscious that they have not consulted everyone who might have an interest in these matters. The arrangements I am announcing today should be regarded as experimental. Although they will take immediate effect, they will be kept under review, and if they meet with general approval they will be formalised in a practice direction in due course.

2. Availability of handed down judgments in advance of the hearing: new arrangements

Unless the court otherwise orders—for example, if a judgment contains price-sensitive information—copies of the written judgment will now be made available in these cases to the parties' legal advisers at about 4 p.m. on the second working day before judgment is due to be pronounced on condition that the contents are not communicated to the parties themselves until one hour before the listed time for pronouncement of judgment. Delivery to legal advisers is made primarily to enable them to consider the judgment and decide what consequential orders they should seek. The condition is imposed to prevent the outcome of the case being publicly reported before judgment is given, since the judgment is confidential until then. Some judges may decide to allow the parties' legal advisers to communicate the contents of the judgment to their clients two hours before the listed time, in order that they may be able to submit minutes of the proposed order, agreed by their clients, to the judge before the judge comes into court, and it will be open to judges to permit more information about the result of a case to be communicated on a confidential basis to the client at an earlier stage if good reason is shown for making such a direction.

If, for any reason, a party's legal advisers have special grounds for seeking a relaxation of the usual condition restricting disclosure to the party itself, a request for relaxation of the condition may be made informally through the judge's clerk (or through the associate, if the judge has no clerk).

A copy of the written judgment will be made available to any party who is not legally represented at the same time as to legal advisers. It must be treated as confidential until judgment is given. Every page of every judgment which is made available in this way will be marked "Unapproved judgment: no permission is granted to copy or use in court." These words will carry the authority of the judge, and will mean what they say.

The time at which copies of the judgment are being made available to the parties' legal advisers is being brought forward 24 hours in order to enable them to submit any written suggestions to the judge about typing errors, wrong references and other minor corrections of that kind in good time, so that, if the judge thinks fit, the judgment can be corrected before it is handed down formally in court. The parties' legal advisers are therefore being requested to submit a written list of corrections of this kind to the judge's clerk (or to the associate, if the judge has no clerk) by 3 p.m. on the day before judgment is handed down. In divisions of the court which have two or more judges, the list should be submitted in each case to the judge who is to deliver the judgment in question. Lawyers are not being asked to carry out proof-reading for the judiciary, but a significant cause of the present delays is the fact that minor corrections of this type are being mentioned to the judge for the first time in court, when there is no time to make any necessary corrections to the text.

3. Availability of approved versions of handed down judgments: *new arrangements*

This course will make it very much easier for the judge to make any necessary corrections and to hand down the judgment formally as the approved judgment of the court without any need for the delay involved in requiring the court shorthand writer, in courts which have an official shorthand writer, to resubmit the judgment to the judge for approval. It will always be open to the judge to direct the shorthand writer at the time of the hearing in court to include in the text of the judgment any last minute corrections which are mentioned for the first time in court, or which it has proved impractical to incorporate in the judgments handed down. In such an event the judge will make it clear whether the shorthand writer can publish the judgment, as corrected, as the approved judgment of the court without any further reference to the judge, or whether it should be resubmitted to the judge for approval. It will be open to judges, If they wish, to decline to approve their Judgments at the time they are delivered, in which case the existing practice of submitting the judgment for their approval will continue.

4. Handing down judgment in court: availability of uncorrected copies

When the court hands down its written judgment, it will pronounce judgment in open court. Copies of the written judgment will then be made available to accredited representatives of the media, and to accredited law. reporters who are willing to comply with the restrictions on copying, who identify themselves as such. In cases of particular interest to the media, it is helpful if requests for copies can be intimated to the judge's clerk, or the presiding Lord Justice's clerk, in advance of judgment, so that the likely demand for copies can be accurately estimated. Because there will usually be insufficient time for the judge's clerk to prepare the necessary number of copies of the corrected judgment in advance, in most cases these uncorrected copies will similarly bear the warning "Unapproved judgment: no permission is granted to copy or use in court." The purpose of these arrangements is to place no barrier in the way of accredited representatives of the media who wish to report the judgments of the court immediately in the usual way, or to accredited law reporters who wish to prepare a summary or digest of the judgment or to read it for the purpose of deciding whether to obtain an approved version for reporting purposes. Its purpose is to put a stop to the dissemination of unapproved, uncorrected, judgments for other purposes, while seeking to ensure that everyone who is interested in the judgment (other than the immediate parties) may be able to buy a copy of the approved judgment In most cases much more quickly than is possible at present.

If any member of the public (other than a party to the case), or any law reporter who is not willing to comply with the restrictions on copying, wishes to read the written judgment of the court on the occasion when it is handed down, a copy will be made available for him or her to read and note in court on request made to the associate or to the clerk to the judge or the presiding Lord Justice. The copy must not be removed from the court and must be handed back after reading. The object is to ensure that such a person is in no worse a position than if the judgment had been read aloud in full.

5. Availability of approved judgments

In courts without an official shorthand writer, the approved judgment should contain on its frontispiece the rubric "This is the official judgment of the court and I direct that no further note or transcript be made." (This will cover the requirements of RSC O.68, r.1, in the cases to which that rule applies, and will provide for certainty in all other cases). In future, all judgments delivered at the Royal Courts of Justice will be published in a common format.

For cases decided in the two divisions of the Court of Appeal and in the Crown Office List, copies of the approved judgment can be ordered from the official shorthand writers, on payment of the appropriate fee. In the other courts In the Royal Courts of Justice, copies of the approved judgment can be ordered from the Mechanical Recording Department, on payment of the fee prescribed for copy documents. Disks containing the judgment will also be available from the official shorthand writers, and the Mechanical Recording Department, where relevant, on payment of an appropriate charge. It is hoped that in most cases copies of the approved judgment will be available from these sources on the same day as the judgment is handed down: they should no longer be sought from judges' clerks.

6. Restrictions on disclosure or reporting

Anyone who is supplied with a copy of the handed-down judgment, or who reads it in court, will be bound by any direction which the court may have given in a child case under section 39 of the Children and Young Persons Act 1933, or any other form of restriction on disclosure, or reporting, of information in the judgment.

7. Availability of approved versions of extempore judgments

Delays have also been experienced in the publication of approved versions of extempore judgments, whether they are produced by the official shorthand writers or by contractors transcribing the tapes which have been mechanically recorded.

Sometimes the delay is caused in courts without an official shorthand writer because a transcript is bespoken by one of the parties long time after the judgment was delivered. If a transcribed copy of such a judgment is to be required, in connection with an appeal, for example, it should be ordered as soon as practicable after judgment was delivered. Delays are also sometimes caused in these cases because judgments are delivered to a judge for approval without supplying the judge with copies of the material quoted in the judgment. In future no judge should be invited to approve any such transcript unless the transcriber has been provided by the party ordering the transcript with copies of all the material from which the judge has quoted. If the transcript is ordered by a person who is not a party to the case (such as a law reporter), that person should make arrangements with one of the parties to ensure that the transcriber (and the judge) will have access to all the material quoted in the judgment.

From time to time delays are also caused because judges have been slow in returning approved transcripts to the transcribers. I and the other Heads of Division have recently asked judges, as a *general rule*, that they should endeavour to return approved transcripts to the transcribers within two weeks of their being delivered to them for approval. If anyone encounters serious delay on this account, the relevant Head of Division should be informed.

8. Citation of authorities in court

For citation of authorities in court, the practice set out in Practice Direction (Court of Appeal: Citation of Authority) [1995] 1 W.L.R. 1096 and Practice Statement (Court of Appeal: Authorities) [1996] I W.L.R. 854 are now to be followed in all courts to which this practice statement applies. For convenience of reference, the relevant parts of these directions read:

"When authority is cited, whether in written or oral submissions, the following practice should in general be followed. If a case is reported in the official Law Reports published by the Incorporated Council of Law Reporting for England and Wales, that report should be cited. These are the most authoritative reports; they contain a summary of argument; and they are the most readily available. If a case is not (or not yet) reported in the official Law Reports, but is reported in the Weekly Law Reports or the All England Law Reports, that report should be cited. If a case is not reported in any of these series of reports, a report in any of the authoritative specialist series of reports may be cited Such reports may not be readily available: photostat copies of the leading authorities or the relevant parts of such authorities should be annexed to written submissions; and it is helpful if photostat copies of the less frequently used series are made available in court. It is recognised that occasions arise when one report is fuller than another, or when there are discrepancies between reports. On such occasions, the practice outlined above need not be followed. It is always helpful if alternative references are given. Where a reserved written judgment has not been reported, reference should be made to the official transcript (if this is available) and not to the handed down text of the judgment:" [1995] 1 WL.R. 1096.

"Leave to cite unreported cases will not usually be granted unless counsel are able to assure the court that the transcript in question contains a relevant statement of legal principle not found in reported authority and that the authority is not cited because of the phraseology used or as an illustration of the application of an established legal principle:" [1996] 1 W.L.R. 854.

9. Conclusion

The purpose of these changes, which are being made on an experimental basis after full consultation with the Court Service, is to improve the liability of service rendered by the judges to those who use the courts. Any comments on these changes, or suggestions about further improvements in relation to the matters set out in this statement, should be addressed to Brooke, L.J. at the Royal Courts of Justice. They will be taken fully in c account when the time comes to decide whether these arrangements should be formalised, with or without amendment, in a practice direction.

Lord Bingham of Cornhill C.J.
22 April 1998

PRACTICE STATEMENT (SUPREME COURT: JUDGMENTS) (NO.2) [1999] 1 W.L.R. 1

B2–001 I am making this further statement with the agreement of Lord Woolf M.R., Sir Richard Scott V-C. and Sir Stephen Brown P. Like the earlier Practice Statement (Supreme Court: Judgments) [1998] 1 W.L.R. 825; [1998] 2 All E.R. 667 I made on 22 April 1998, this statement applies to judgments delivered in all divisions of the High Court and the Court of Appeal.

In my earlier statement I said that the arrangements I was announcing should be regarded as experimental, and that they would be kept under review. Experience since that time has shown that in general the new arrangements are working well, but that there is scope for some fine tuning. In particular, for a number of reasons it has not proved possible for the official shorthand writers to publish the official transcripts of approved, handed down, judgments quite as quickly as we had hoped, and there has been some uncertainty as to the status of the judgment given by the court to the shorthand writers.

We have decided to retain the embargo on copying the draft judgment which is sent to the parties two days before a judgment is handed down. An approved judgment, when handed down in court, will now be entitled "Judgment: Approved by the court for handing down (subject to editorial corrections)," and every page of a judgment which is handed down in this form will be marked in a similar manner. There will be no embargo on copying a judgment handed down in this form, so long as its status is made clear, and at present no charge will be made for permission to copy it.

In order to make it possible for approved judgments to be handed down in this way, the parties' legal advisers will be requested to submit their written list of suggested corrections by 12 noon. not 3 p.m., on the day before judgment is handed down. If it is not possible to comply with this deadline. any later corrections approved by the judge will be included in the final text which the official shorthand writer (or the judge's clerk, in courts which lack an official shorthand writer) will incorporate into the approved official text of the judgment as soon as practicable.

Where a reserved written judgment has not been reported. reference must still be made in court to the approved official transcript (if this is available) and not to the approved transcript which is handed down, since this may have been subject to late revision after the text was prepared for handing down.

We will continue to keep these experimental arrangements under review. Comments or suggestions about any aspect of the arrangements should once again be addressed to Brooke L.J.

Lord Bingham of Cornhill C.J.

25 November 1998

PRACTICE DIRECTION (CITATION OF AUTHORITIES) [2001] 1 W.L.R. 1001, CA

Introduction

B3–001 **1.** In recent years, there has been a substantial growth in the number of readily available reports of judgments in this and other jurisdictions, such reports being available either in published reports or in transcript form. Widespread knowledge of the work and decisions of the courts is to be welcomed. At the same time, however, the current weight of available material causes problems both for advocates and for courts in properly limiting the nature and amount of material that is used in the preparation and argument of subsequent cases.

2. The latter issue is a matter of rapidly increasing importance. Recent and continuing efforts to increase the efficiency, and thus reduce the cost, of litigation, whilst maintaining the interests of justice, will be threatened if courts are burdened with a weight of inappropriate and unnecessary authority, and if advocates are uncertain as to the extent to which it is necessary to deploy authorities in the arguement of any given case.

3. With a view to limiting the citation of previous authority to cases that are relevant and useful to the court, this Practice Direction lays down a number of rules as to what material may be cited, and the manner in which that cited material should be handled by advocates. These rules are in large part such as many courts already follow in pursuit of their general discretion in the management of litigation. However, if it is now desirable to promote uniformity of practice by the same rules being followed by all courts.

4. It will remain the duty of advocates to draw the attention of the court to any authority not cited by an opponent which is adverse to the case being advanced.

5. This Direction applies to all courts apart from criminal courts, including within the latter category of the Court of Appeal (Criminal Division).

Categories of judgments that may only be cited if they fulfil specified requirements.

6.1 A judgment falling into one of the categories referred to in paragraph 6.2 below may not in future be cited before any court unless it clearly indicates that it purports to establish a new principle or to extend the present law. In respect of judgments delivered after the date of this Direction (April 9, 2001), that indication must take the form of an express statement to that effect. In respect of judgments delivered before the date of this Direction that indication must be present in or clearly deducible from the language used in the judgment.

6.2 Paragraph 6.1 applies to the following categories of judgment:

Applications attended by one party only.

Applications for permission to appeal.

Decisions on applications that only decide that the application is arguable.

County Court cases, unless

(a) cited in order to illustrate the conventional measure of damages in a personal injury case; or

(b) cited in a County Court in order to demonstrate current authority at that level on an issue in respect of which no decision at a higher level of authority is available.

6.3 These categories will be kept under review, such review to include consideration of adding to the categories.

Citation of other categories of judgment

7.1 Courts will in future pay particular attention, when it is sought to cite other categories of judgment, to any indication given by the court delivering the judgment that it was seen by that court as only applying decided law to the facts of the particular case; or otherwise as not extending or adding to the existing law.

7.2 Advocates who seek to cite a judgment that contains indications of the type referred to in paragraph 7.1 will be required to justify their decision to cite the case.

Methods of citation

8.1 Advocates will in future be required to state, in respect of each authority that they wish to cite, the proposition of law that the authority demonstrates, and the parts of the judgment that support that proposition. If it is sought to cite more than one authority in support of a given proposition, advocates must state the reason for taking that course.

8.2 The demonstration referred to in paragraph 8.1 will be required to be contained in any skeleton argument and in any appellant's or respondent's notice in respect of each authority referred to in that skeleton or notice.

8.3 Any bundle or list of authorities prepared for the use of any court must in future bear a certification by the advocate responsible for arguing the case that the requirments of this paragraph have been complied with in respect of each authority included.

8.4 The statements referred to in paragraph 8.1 should not materially add to the length of submissions or of skeleton arguments, but should be sufficient to demonstrate, in the context of the advocate's argument, the relevance of the authority or authorities to that argument and that the citation is necessary for a proper presentation of that argument.

Authorities decided in other jurisdictions

9.1 Cases decided in other jurisdictions can, if properly used, be a valuable source of law in this jurisdiction must

i. comply, in respect of that authority, with the rules set out in paragraph 8 above;
ii. indicate in respect of each authority what that authority adds that is not to be found in authority in this jurisdiction; or, if there is said to be justification for adding to domestic authority, what the justification is;
iii. certify that there is no authority in this jurisdiction that precludes the acceptance by the court of the proposition that the foreign authority is said to establish.

9.3 For the avoidance of doubt, paragraphs 9.1 and 9.2 do not apply to cases decided in either the European Court of Justice or the organs of the European Convention of Human Rights. Because of the status in English law of such authority, as provided by, respectively, section 3 of the European Communities Act 1972 and section 2(1) of the Human Rights Act 1998, such cases are covered by the earlier paragraphs of this Direction.

The Lord Chief Justice of England and Wales
9th Day of April 2001

Practice Note (Court of Appeal: Handed Down Judgments)

B4–001

For "Practice Note (Court of Appeal: Handed Down Judgments)" see paragraph B4–002+ on White Book on Westlaw UK Service or the Civil Procedure CD.

Practice Direction (Judgments: Form and Citation) [2001] 1 W.L.R. 194

B5–001

For "Practice Direction (Judgments: Form and Citation) [2001] 1 W.L.R. 194" see paragraph B5–002+ on White Book on Westlaw UK Service or the Civil Procedure CD.

Practice Direction (Judgments: Neutral Citations) [2002] 1 W.L.R. 346

B6–001

For "Practice Direction (Judgments: Neutral Citations) [2002] 1 W.L.R. 346" see paragraph B6–002+ on the White Book on Westlaw UK Service or the Civil Procedure CD.

Practice Direction—Application for a Warrant under the Competition Act 1998

B7–001

For "Practice Direction—Application for a Warrant under the Competition Act 1998" see paragraphs B7–002+ to B7–012+ on the White Book on Westlaw UK Service or the Civil Procedure CD.

Practice Direction—Application for a Warrant under the Enterprise Act 2002

B8–001

For "Practice Direction—Application for a Warrant under the Enterprise Act 2002" see paragraphs B8–002+ to B8–013+ on the White Book on Westlaw UK Service or the Civil Procedure CD.

Practice Direction—Competition Law—Claims Relating to the Application of Articles 81 and 82 of the EC Treaty and Chapters I and II of Part I of the Competition Act 1998

B9–001

For "Practice Direction—Competition Law—Claims Relating to the Application of Articles 81 and 82 of the EC Treaty and Chapters I and II of Part I of the Competition Act 1998" see paragraphs B9–002+ to B9–008+ on the White Book on *Westlaw* UK Service or the Civil Procedure CD.

Practice Direction (Court Dress) (No 5) [2008] 1 W.L.R. 1700, Sup Ct

B10–001

For "Practice Direction (Court Dress) (No 5) [2008] 1 W.L.R. 1700, Sup Ct" see paragraphs B10–002+ to B10–004+ on the White Book on Westlaw UK Service or the Civil Procedure CD.

SECTION C

PRE-ACTION PROTOCOLS

SECTION C

PRE-ACTION CONDUCT AND PROTOCOLS

Lord Woolf's recommendations

During the Access to Justice inquiry, Lord Woolf became convinced that codes of practice for pre-action conduct were needed for common types of disputes that were often low value but which were frequently litigated. In Chapter 10 of his final report (Access to Justice 1996), Lord Woolf said that what was needed was a system which would enable parties to a dispute to embark on meaningful negotiations as soon as the possibility of litigation was identified and to ensure that as early as possible they had the relevant information to define their claim and make realistic offers to settle. **C1A–001**

Lord Woolf said that pre-action protocols:

"are intended to build on and increase the benefits of early but well informed settlements which genuinely satisfy both parties to disputes".

The purposes of protocols are:

- to focus the attention of litigants on the desirability of resolving disputes without litigation;
- to enable them to obtain information they reasonably need in order to enter an appropriate settlement;
- to make an appropriate offer (of a kind which can have costs consequences if litigation ensues);
- if pre-action settlement is not achievable, to lay the ground for expeditious conduct of proceedings.

Early stages of disputes: the main themes from the civil justice reforms

Particularly relevant themes from the civil justice reforms and the CPR to the pre-action stage of disputes are:— **C1A–002**

- litigation is to be viewed as a last resort. Parties are expected to explore alternatives to court proceedings and settlement thoroughly before issuing. Part 36 offers can be made at any time including pre-action and the court can dismiss proceedings if a more appropriate means of resolving the dispute is available;
- a "cards on the table" approach. This had been developing in litigation procedure in the 1990s, especially with the introduction of exchange of witness statements and experts' reports. The courts now expect co-operation between the parties and their legal representatives from an early stage, in disclosing their case in outline in letters of claim and response, and by exchanging information, including key documents. The court has the power to take into account conduct of the parties and their legal representatives both before as well as during proceedings. (r.44.4);
- proportionality—Rule 1.1(2) states that dealing with a case justly includes dealing with a case in ways which are proportionate. Parties are expected to apply cost-benefit principles to disputes before starting proceedings and to conduct litigation in the light of that analysis. But the courts also carry out "reality checks" through their case management function, aimed at ensuring that the amount of work and, therefore, the costs incurred by both parties are "in balance" with what is at stake;
- defining and narrowing the issues in dispute before proceedings are issued so that the case can be allocated to track, a timetable set for the disclosure of evidence and the trial at an early case management stage.

What might this mean in practice? It is suggested that parties to any dispute must conduct more detailed investigations and assemble and exchange evidence before issue. Claimant solicitors need to obtain more information from clients on instruction and possibly from key witnesses at an earlier stage. Defendants need to investigate incidents and claims much more quickly. This means businesses maintaining much better databases, and record keeping systems for documents and witnesses. Greater use might be made of standard questionnaires and pro-forma checklists. Inevitably this front-loads work and costs in the short term but should effect costs savings in the longer run if it leads to earlier settlement or narrowing of the issues.

The development of the current protocols

Drafting work began on protocols for personal injury and housing disrepair claims **C1A–003**

PRE-ACTION PROTOCOLS

during Lord Woolf's inquiry. He had identified these types of disputes as particularly meriting pre-action protocols. Soon after publication of the final report, the Law Society took over the further development of the personal injury protocol, setting up a working party of representatives of the Association of Personal Injury Lawyers, the Forum of Insurance Lawyers, of insurers, and the Association of British Insurers, District Judges and the Lord Chancellor's Department. This group refined the draft protocol and arranged for it to be piloted during 1998.

The clinical disputes protocol was developed by the Clinical Disputes Forum, an umbrella organisation set up in 1996 in response to Lord Woolf's recommendations that a think-tank on improving the resolution of clinical negligence disputes was necessary. This draft protocol was subject to wide consultation in 1998/9 with medical, legal and patient bodies.

The personal injury and clinical dispute protocols were published by the Lord Chancellor's Department in July 1998. The aim was to give solicitors, insurers, and healthcare providers in particular, an opportunity to become familiar with the concept and the content of the protocols and to begin to put them into practice. Final versions of the protocols were published in January 1999 as part of the CPR and came into force with the Rules in April 1999.

Lord Irvine, when launching these two protocols in 1998, said—

> "Preaction protocols are, in many ways, the key to the success of the civil justice reforms. If they do not work our major procedural reforms will be weakened."

A short Practice Direction was added to the CPR, to explain how the protocols fit into the reforms. Curiously this was, and still appears at the end of the Rules, not at the beginning where many readers might look for it.

Many other protocols then "went into development". The Lord Chancellor's Department permitted further protocols to be drafted by working parties of specialists in particular areas of practice, where practitioners felt there was a need. Consultation on a draft was required and the proposed protocol had then to be submitted to the Deputy Head of Civil Justice.

Changes to the Practice Direction and Protocols since April 1999

C1A–004 From August 2000 the Practice Direction was amended (para.4A.1) to require "funding arrangements" (i.e. conditional fee agreements) to be notified to the other parties within seven days of the arrangement being entered into (but not, of course, the per cent success fee or the amount of the insurance premium). Failure to do so may mean the success fee and insurance premium will not be recoverable, at least for the period when the other party was not notified.

In January 2003 the Practice Direction was extended mainly to cover in more detail how parties should act at the early stages of a dispute when there is no applicable protocol.

In April 2009 the Practice Direction was refocused and substantially amended and was given more force by being linked to Pt 3 (The Court's Case Management Powers). There is a new section, paragraph 2, setting out the scope of the protocol, in particular outlining the types of applications to which the PD does not apply. Paragraph 4 (in Section 11) deals in more detail with compliance than previously, including compliance with the PD as well as the protocols. Section 11 (paragraph 6) sets out the principles governing pre-action conduct where there is no applicable protocol—i.e the parties should exchange sufficient information to understand each other's case, try to resolve the dispute without proceedings and act in a reasonable and proportionate manner. Paragraph 7 sets out guidelines for the exchange of information, recommending for the first time that defendants should acknowledge the letter of claim within 14 days (previously 21 days) and if possible, in straightforward claims, also reply in that time frame. Paragraph 8 is also new, emphasising that proceedings should be a last resort and parties should consider whether some form of ADR might enable early settlement. The specific steps to be taken where there is no applicable protocol are summarised in para.9 and in more detail in Annex A. Annex B is also new; it applies to debt actions and in particular requires the claimant to give the defendant details of how the money can be repaid.

The intention is to improve conduct in disputes where there is no protocol. However, in many of these disputes one, or often, both parties are in person and are and will probably remain unaware of the PD requirements.

Have the protocols been a success?

C1A–005 Anecdotally without a doubt. New Litigation post CPR has reduced by 80 per cent in the High Court and 25 per cent in the County Court—the protocols and Pt 36 offers are certainly a factor in this.

In May 2002 the Law Society and Civil Justice Council published research into pre action behaviour and the protocols (*"More Civil Justice? The impact of the Woolf reforms on pre-action behaviour"*, Research Study 43, LCD, T. Goriely, R Moorhead and P Abrams.) Most of the solicitors interviewed were positive about the Woolf reforms generally, including their impact on pre-action conduct, even in areas of dispute where the re are no agreed protocols yet (e.g. housing disrepair). There was not much enthusiasm for more protocols, which, it was felt, would unnecessarily complicate matters. Some practitioners felt "protocolled out". There were also some concerns about "frontloading" of work and costs, and views were expressed that costs for resolving disputes overall had not decreased, as was the CPR intention.

[THE NEXT PARAGRAPH IS C1A–007.]

Considering alternatives to litigation

At a very early stage, options for resolving a dispute need to be explored. In addition to letters, meetings and negotiations with the other party, parties and their advisers need to consider whether any of the following might be appropriate: C1A–007

- a trade arbitration scheme;
- making a formal complaint to the organisation in question or, at the next stage, a complaint to an Ombudsman;
- in a commercial dispute where there is a written contract, whether there is an applicable arbitration or mediation clause which could provide a cost and time effective solution;
- whether and when use of an alternative dispute resolution (ADR) mechanism might be appropriate, typically mediation, early neutral evaluation, expert determination or arbitration.

In October 2005 para.4.7 to the Pre-action Practice Direction was extended to encourage parties to consider whether some form of ADR would be more suitable than litigation and to remind parties that they may be required by the court to provide evidence that this was done. In April 2006 the Practice Direction was further amended to make it clear that claims should not be issued prematurely when a settlement is still being actively explored and that the court must have regard to conduct if the Practice Direction and an applicable protocol are not followed in this respect. The individual protocols were also amended, with new text added on the desirability of alternative dispute resolution procedures.

In April 2009 a new section on ADR (para.8) was added to the PD emphasising that proceedings should be a last resort, that parties should consider whether some form of ADR might enable early settlement and that the court might require evidence that the parties considered some form of ADR pre-action.

The courts, increasingly will "refer" cases to ADR. In *Cowl v Plymouth City Council* [2001] EWCA Civ 1935, an appeal from a refusal to allow a judicial review about the closure of a residential home to proceed was refused because the Court of Appeal said that a statutory appeal, or the local government complaints procedure, or mediation would be more appropriate, and proportionate. *R. (re M) v Bromley LBC* [2002] EWCA Civ 1113, was decided similarly in an application for judicial review of a decision to place a child's name on the at risk register because there was an alternative remedy by way of an appeal to a tribunal under the Protection of Children Act 1999. But in *Hurst v Leeming* [2002] EWHC 1051 (Ch); BLD 1005021726 the defendant was not penalised for refusing to mediate because the claimant was obsessed that he had been untreated unfairly and was unwilling to compromise. In *Cable and Wireless v IBM* 2002 EWHC *2059 (Comm) a clause in a commercial* contract providing for disputes under the contract to be referred to mediation, was held to be enforceable and the proceedings were stayed under CPR, r.26.4.

When a claimant refused to adjudicate a building claim, refused to co-operate with the defendant's surveyor expert and failed to comply with the construction protocol he was ordered to pay the defendant's costs on the indemnity basis: *Paul Thomas Construction Ltd v Hyland and Power* 2002 18 Const. L.J. 345, March 8, 2000, TCC.

Pre-action conduct in non-protocol cases

Where protocols do not currently apply it is still good practice for the claimant or C1A–008 their solicitor to send a detailed letter of claim to the prospective defendant and to wait a reasonable period for the defendant to respond before issuing proceedings. The Practice Direction now clearly sets out how the court will expect parties, in accordance with the overriding objective (CPR r.1.1(2)) to act. New paragraphs were added in January 2003 at 4.1–4.7 and in April 2009 the PD was redrawn retitled and linked more specifically to Pt 3 (The Court's Case Management Powers).

Failing to send a letter of claim at all is unreasanable conduct, which will invariably attract a sanction. In *Phoenix Finance v Federation International L' Automobile* [2002] EWHC 1028 (Ch) indemnity costs were awarded against a claimant (whose claim for interlocutory relief was dismissed) because he had failed to send a letter before action before proceedings were issued (in a case to which none of the existing protocols applied).

The courts may also award penalty costs for failure to comply with 'good behaviour' pre-action, and for 'unreasonable conduct' even in small claims where the protocols do not necessarily apply. Examples are *Taylor v KD Coach Hire* [2000] C.L.Y. 447 when the defendant waited until after issue to negotiate, and was ordered to pay the Claimant's costs on an indemnity basis, and *Northfield v DSM (Southern) Ltd* [2000] C.L.Y. 461 and *Linton v Williams Haulage Ltd* [2001] C.L.Y. 516 both small claims. In *Northfield* the defendant failed to state his case pre-issue, in *Linton* he offered to settle the entire claim only one week before the hearing. Both were held to be unreasonable conduct, entitling the claimant to costs.

Points to note on the application of the protocols

C1A–009 The protocols are codes of best practice, to be followed generally but not slavishly. The period for the defendant to investigate and respond (which varies between the protocols from 14 days—Defamation, Construction and Judicial Review to three months—Personal Injury, Clinical Negligence and Professional Negligence) can be varied by the parties by consent. In simple cases where the defendant is already aware of and has taken some action, the full protocol period might not be necessary. But, in more complex cases or where the origin of the dispute occurred some time previously, or where the defendant had no prior knowledge of the potential claim, a longer period might be justified. Reasonableness is the watchword. The court is much more interested in compliance with the spirit of a protocol than the exact letter.

The level of detail in a letter of claim will depend on the type and value of the case but should always include the main facts and circumstances, the nature of the dispute or claim (breach of contract, allegations of negligence etc.) and the remedy sought. In the spirit of openness the claimant might want to enclose with the letter key documents and when money is being claimed the claimant should also provide as much information as possible on the value of the claim, as least sufficient to enable the defendant to form a view of the likely "bracket" of the damages.

If the claimant does not write to the defendant until towards the end of a relevant limitation period, the claimant should issue proceedings if necessary to protect the client's position and should then either delay serving the claim form while the protocol is followed (CPR provide four months for service (r.7.5), or should serve the claim and invite the court to order a stay under r.26.4.

The defendant's response letter should be detailed and not simply deny the claim.The frequent pre-CPR approach of ignoring an initial letter or replying very briefly is not within the spirit of the CPR and could be a breach of a protocol meriting a sanction. Also If a defendant is prepared to admit liability, the letter should say so clearly: the previous practice of not positively admitting liability but encouraging negotiations to lead to a settlement, is also not within the spirit of the reforms. This is because it leaves the claimant in a dilemma as to whether it is necessary to assemble the evidence to establish liability: doing so can substantially increase costs. CPR, r.14.1 gives the court the power to withdraw an admission but the burden rests upon the party applying. If liability is denied, the defendant must give proper reasons and should enclose with the letter any relevant documents on which they rely, if these have not previously been disclosed.

Letters of claim and response are not intended to have the same status as a statement of case (a pleading). It would defeat the purpose of the protocols if a party were penalised for subsequently clarifying his/her claim or defence when proceedings were issued. However, parties should be wary of making substantial changes without explaining why this is necessary—as without good reason this could amount to "unreasonable conduct".

The protocols give very different guidance on steps with regard to expert evidence but in every case parties are expected to consider and discuss the need for expert advice and reports, and whether a single report might be more appropriate and proportionate than retaining an expert each.

Most of the protocols do not require the parties to take specific steps to try to settle the claim pre-issue, either by making an offer to settle (under Pt 36) or by meeting/negotiating, or use of an ADR approach. But they all, at least, generally encourage early settlement discussions. The Defamation protocol requires ADR to be considered, the Professional Negligence protocol permits the defendant to send, with the response letter, a separate letter of settlement, and suggests if there are negotiations, there should be a six month settlement period before the claimant issues, and the Construction and Engineering Protocol provides for a "without prejudice" meeting prior to issue, a very sensible idea. The courts are not sympathetic to parties who are unwilling to at least try to narrow the issues or to hold settlement discussions pre-issue. It should be noted also that pre-action Pt 36 offers to settle may have the same costs consequences as post-commencement offers, provided the offeror has provided the offeree with sufficient information to enable her understand and evaluate the offer.

The protocols do not specify whether they apply to small claims. The common sense approach is that, provided a letter of claim is sent, proportionality should preclude the need in most instances to follow all the steps in a protocol. But the courts are undoubtedly more willing to make costs awards in small claims cases for "unreasonable conduct"—see for instance *Northfield v DSM (Southern) Ltd* [2000] C.L.Y. 461 which decided that the defendant's failure to state his case on liability pre-action was unreasonable.

Compliance with the Practice Direction and Protocols: The Court's Role

The CPR enables the court to take into account compliance (or non-compliance) with the Practice Direction and applicable protocols when giving directions for the management of proceedings and when making orders as to costs. The courts should treat the protocols as the reasonable approach to pre action conduct for that type of dispute and are able to impose sanction for breaches. **C1A–010**

CPR r.3.1 provides:

(4) Where the court gives directions it may take into account whether or not a party has complied with any relevant pre-action protocol;

(5) The court may order a party to pay a sum of money into court if that party has, without good reason, failed to comply with the appropriate rule, practice direction or relevant pre-action protocol.

Rule 44.3(5)(b) enables the court to take into account when making orders as to costs, the conduct of the parties before, as well as during, proceedings and "in particular the extent to which the parties followed any relevant pre-action protocol".

The Practice Direction states that the court expects compliance with the substance, if not the letter, of the Practice Direction and the protocols. Examples of non-compliance and possible consequences are given. For instance, a claimant failing to provide sufficient information to a defendant, or not following the procedure for instruction of an expert, or the defendant failing to acknowledge the letter of claim or to reply in full in the appropriate time, or to disclose documents required. If non-compliance leads to proceedings being commenced which otherwise would not have been necessary, or costs being incurred which would not otherwise have been incurred, the PD says that court will try to put the innocent party into the position they would have been if the protocol had been complied with.

This could mean the court ordering:

- the party at fault to pay all or part of the costs of the proceedings to date;
- the party at fault to pay costs on an indemnity basis;
- if the party at fault is the claimant, the court might deprive him/her of some of the interest on damages or apply a reduced rate of interest;
- if the party at fault is the defendant and damages are being awarded, the court may require the defendant to pay additional interest, not to exceed 10 per cent above base rate (CPR, r.36.21(2)).

Other possible examples of how the court might react to non-compliance include:

- where a claimant has issued prematurely, giving the defendant an extension of time to serve the defence; or
- where a defendant had not replied adequately or in time to the letter of claim,

but did have a good defence, and the claimant wants to discontinue proceedings when the defence is served, ordering the defendant to pay some or all of the claimant's costs.

Parties are asked to state whether they have complied with any relevant protocol in their Allocation Questionnaire but not whether the other party has not complied and whether the court is being invited to apply a sanction. Are the courts using these powers? A high per cent of the respondents to surveys carried out by the Law Society and CDF in 2001 said that the judges were failing to do so. One claimant practitioner described the sanctions as 'a paper tiger'. Similar comments were made in the Civil Justice Council Pre-action Research. But are practitioners actually applying for sanctions?

There is some evidence from reported cases that the courts will apply sanctions, even when the breach is of a draft protocol.

In *Jimaale v London Buses Ltd* [2000] C.L.Y. 599 the claimant's solicitor first wrote to the defendant's solicitor two years after being instructed and only to confirm the identity of the bus company, and did not write again post issue. The D.J. held that non-compliance with the personal injury protocol was an abuse of process. On appeal it was held that issuing within the limitation period was not a justifiable excuse as there was overwhelming prejudice to the defendant—they could not identify the bus or driver after so long a delay. The claim was struck out.

In *Paul Thomas Construction Ltd v Hyland and Power* 2002 18 Const. L.J. 345, March 8, 2000, TCC, the claimant issued proceedings knowing the defendant had appointed an expert to try to settle the case. It was held that the claimant had been uncooperative and in breach of the draft construction protocol and should pay the defendant's costs on an indemnity basis.

In *Wealands v Harding* [2003] EWHC 889 the claimant's failure to comply with the personal injury protocol in not allowing an Australian defendant six months to investigate, and issuing within a very short time of the letter stating the intention to sue in the English courts was a more serious fault than the four weeks delay after issue by the defendant in challenging jurisdiction under Pt 11.

In *Spink v Shepherd Construction and Pullan* [2007] WL 4735606 (QB) the second defendant failed to comply with the protocol for disease and illness at work claims by not replying at all to several letters concerning the claimant's contraction of mesothelioma from exposure to asbestos allegedly when employed by the second defendant. The claimant issued proceedings and obtained judgment in default against the second defendant. The claimant then died. On the second defendant's application to set aside the judgment, on the basis that the claimant had not worked with asbestos in his employment with them, the Master decided that the delay in producing a potential defence had so greatly prejudiced the claimant he should refuse to set aside the judgment (he was also not satisfied that the second defendant had a real prospect of succeeding with their defence).

Very few cases are reported in relation to the Construction and Engineering protocol. In *Daejan Investments Ltd v Park West Club Ltd* (Part 20 Buxton Associates) [2003] EWHC 2872 a dispute about allegedly defective waterproofing, the claimant issued proceedings without properly investigating the situation or taking advice from a waterproofing expert. The nature of their claim changed several times. When applying to significantly amend their statement of case they were ordered to pay all the costs of the Pt 20 party to date for non-compliance with the protocol.

In *Cundall Johnson and Partners v Whipps Cross University Hospital NHS Trust* [2007] EWHC 2178 (TCC) the court ordered a stay of the proceedings where the claimant had failed to comply with the Protocol for Construction and Engineering claims by not sending a letter of claim so that the contractual basis of the claim remained obscure until proceedings were issued. The stay was in the interest of both parties as there was a real possibility of settlement if they went through the protocol process.

In *Orange PCS v Hoare Lea* [2008] EWHC 223 (TCC) the court declined to order a stay for compliance with the Protocol for Construction and Engineering claims when a new potential defendant was identified shortly before limitation expired in a case involving three other defendants in which proceedings were well-advanced. The claimant issued separate proceedings against the new party and applied for the cases to be consolidated. The new defendant applied for a stay because the claimant had not complied with the protocol. The court concluded that It was necessary to look at non-compliance with the protocol in a pragmatic and commercially realistic way and the court should avoid the slavish application of rules and protocols if such application would undermine the overriding objective. At this stage of the two sets of proceedings the protocol process would not be sufficiently productive to justify a stay when the new party was in possession of the statements of case in the first claim, and the claimant's particulars of claim in the second claim and when the new party could join the ADR planned in for few months time.

In *T.J. Brent Ltd v Black and Veatch Consulting Ltd* [2008] EWHC 1497 TCC the claimant's application for costs because of the defendant's alleged non-compliance with the Pre-action Protocol for Construction and Engineering Dispute was dismissed as the defendant had largely complied.

How compliance with a protocol may assist at later stages of a dispute

Occasionally complying with a protocol may reap dividends later. **C1A–011**

In *Amin v Hussain (Appeal to Circuit Judge)* [1999] C.L.Y. 431 the claimant overlooked pleading the personal injury element of an RTA claim. He wanted to set aside the judgment he had obtained in default of a defence so as to amend the claim. This was allowed because he had told the defendant of the injuries in the personal injury protocol letter of claim, so there was no prejudice.

In *Infantino v MacLean* [2001] 3 All E.R. 802, a complex clinical negligence case, the claimant had complied with the pre-action protocol including sending the defendant a detailed letter of claim. The parties had agreed two extensions of time for the defendant to respond, and that service could be effected on the defendant's insurers. The claimant served proceedings on the last possible day under CPR, r.7.6 but on the wrong insurer, rectifying the fault a day later. The High Court judge dispensed with service, using his discretion under CPR, r.6.9. In *Godwin v Swindon BC* [2001] EWCA Civ 1478 the approach in Infantino was disapproved of in *obiter* comments, but a different Court of Appeal in *Anderton v Clwyd* [2002] EWCA Civ 933 said that the court does have the power to dispense with service of the claim form both prospectively and retrospectively but the retrospective power would only be exercised in exceptional circumstances.

In *Straker v Tudor Rose* [2007] EWCA Civ 368 the trial judge only awarded limited costs to the successful claimant despite the damages award exceeding the defendant's Pt 36 payment—one reason he gave was the claimant had failed to comply with para.1.4 of the Preaction Practice Direction by not being more willing to negotiate a settlement. But this was rejected on appeal, where it was held that the judge had started from the wrong place—as the claimant had beaten the Pt 36 payment the starting point was that he was entitled to his costs, and it was only speculation by the judge that the case would have settled if the claimant had been more willing to negotiate, also the defendant could have protected themselves better by making a higher or further Pt 36 payment.

Pre-Action Disclosure of Documents CPR 31.16—see also editorial to Part 31

The rules of the Supreme Court and County Court only gave the court power to order pre-action disclosure of documents to prospective parties in personal injury (including clinical negligence) claims. CPR r.31.16 enables a prospective party to any proceedings to apply to the court for disclosure of documents. (Rule 31.17 in addition gives the court powers to make orders for disclosure against persons who are not a party, or not likely to be a party, to proceedings). **C1A–012**

However, these new court powers are not intended to support "fishing expeditions". The party making the application needs to show that disclosure of documents before proceedings is necessary to "dispose fairly of the anticipated proceedings, to assist the dispute to be resolved without proceedings, or to save costs".

Other criteria, which the court will take into account, include:

- whether the party with the documents is "likely" to be a party to the proceedings;
- whether the documents sought are identified in a relevant pre-action protocol;
- whether the documents sought would be disclosable under the standard disclosure test and are relevant;
- whether the request (and therefore the order) readily identifies specific documents;
- proportionality and the likely costs and time in searching for the documents requested.

Applications should be made in accordance with Pt 23. Evidence in support is required, usually in the form of a witness statement. Under the pre-CPR rules the usual costs order on a pre-action application for disclosure was that the applicant bore the costs regardless of the outcome. CPR r.48.1(2) preserves this but only as a starting point. Rule 48.1(3) allows the court to make a different order depending on the circumstances—the court can also take into account whether the parties to the application have complied with a relevant pre action protocol. In *Re R (a child)* [2004] EWHC 2085 (Fam) the court ordered each party to pay its own costs of an application for pre-action disclosure of R's medical records to establish whether he had a claim against an NHS trust for delayed diagnosis of Asperger's Syndrome. The trust was only willing to give partial disclosure out of concern for the impact on R and because the notes included sensitive information about R's mother (he lived with his grandmother). The court ordered disclosure only to R's medical and legal advisers, and made the costs order because the Trust's concerns about disclosure were legitimate. In *SES Contracting Ltd v UK Coal Plc* [2007] EWCA Civ 791 the defendant successfully appealed against an order that it should pay the costs of the claimant's application for pre-action disclosure in connection with a potential claim arising from the claimant's suspicions that the defendant had acted unfairly in awarding a contract to a competitor of the claimant because the claim was not of a routine nature and it was not unreasonable for the defendant to defend the application.

The more pertinent case law includes:

Bermuda International Securities v KPMG [2001] EWCA Civ 269 which decided that the judge needs to understand the issues in the potential litigation to form a view on whether pre-action disclosure is advisable: it is also for the judge to decide who would bear the cost of the application. Here the claimant was to pay the costs of the disclosure but the defendant the costs of unreasonably resisting the request and application.

Black v Sumitomo Corp CA [2001] EWCA Civ 1819 decided that "likely to be a party to proceedings" meant might be involved if proceedings were issued, that only documents which would be disclosable if and when litigation commenced could be the subject of a pre-action order, that any application should be "focused", and also that the judge has a discretion to refuse an application even when the r.31.16 criteria are met.

Three Rivers DC v Bank of England [2002] EWCA Civ 1182 further clarified that the test in CPR r.31.16 for pre-action disclosure of documents are "likely" to be parties to proceedings, was that the respective parties "may well" be such parties, i.e. that doubts are resolved in favour of the applicant.

Edwards v Pirelli Cables [2003] C.L.Y. 396 said the court has power under Pt 3 to order pre-action disclosure after the claimant has issued a protective claim form and in *Arsenal Football Club Plc v Elite Sports Distribution Ltd* [2002] EWHC 3057 an order for pre-action disclosure by the defendant company was granted, for the source of photographs of footballers used without permission, on an application by the defendants for a strike-out of the claim, which was refused.

Moresfield Ltd v Banners (A Firm) [2003] EWHC 1602 (Ch D) decided that pre-action disclosure can be ordered against a potential Pt 20 defendant—here a leading firm of accountants who might have been given relevant instructions to advise on a share sale.

Carlton Film Distributors Ltd v VCI Plc [2003] F.S.R. 47 decided (in an extension of the Norwich Pharmacal doctrine from tort to contract) that the claimant, in a contract dispute, was entitled to pre-action disclosure by a third party who had manufactured goods for the defendant, and who had the records that would enable the claimant to plead their case accurately.

Baron W.R. Jay v Wilder Coe (a firm) [2003] EWHC 1786 QB is an example of the court ordering pre-action disclosure on a broad application—the claimant, a solicitors' firm, was missing money from the accounts and asked their accountants why they had not detected this. The accountants did not reply—the court said the claimants needed the accountants' documents to investigate the "mechanism of their misfortune".

In *Rose v Lynx Express Ltd* [2004] EWCA Civ 447 the Court of Appeal reversed a first instance decision to refuse pre-action disclosure as the judge had prematurely decided that the applicant's cause of action in a potential claim concerning the transfer of shares was not made out: they said that it would normally be sufficient to found an application under CPR, r.31.16(3) for the substantive claim to be "properly arguable" and to have a real prospect of success.

In *Marshall v Allotts (A Firm)* [2004] EWHC 1964 2004 unrep., pre-action disclosure of documents relating to the valuation of shares was ordered in a professional negligence dispute as they would enable the case to be pleaded in a more focussed way.

In *Total E&P Soudan SA v Edmonds, Groves & White Nile Ltd* [2007] EWCA Civ 50, a potentially complex claim concerning exploration rights in southern Sudan affected by the civil war, the appellants sought to resist pre-action disclosure partly on the basis that the English courts would not have jurisdiction on any eventual claim and there was no evidence of the mental element needed for the economic torts relied upon, but the Court of Appeal held that such difficult legal issues should not be investigated on an application for pre-action disclosure and upheld the order for disclosure.

But orders for pre-action disclosure are far from a foregone conclusion especially in the Chancery and Commercial courts and intended defendants have successfully resisted applications when:

- The intended claimant had very poor prospects of success (*K v Secretary of State for the Home Office* [2001] C.P. Rep. 39);
- It was hard to see there was a real issue between the parties (*Medisys Plc v Arthur Anderson* [2002] P.N.L.R. 22) or what that issue was (*Snowstar Shipping Co Ltd v Graig Shipping plc* [2003] EWHC 1367 and *Inland Revenue Commissioners v Blueslate Ltd* [2003] EWHC 2022);
- The intended defendant volunteered the documents *MerproGroup v Dynamic Ltd* [2003] All E.R. 49;
- The applicant police informer's claim for psychiatric injury arising from his activities could be properly pleaded without disclosure of documents to which public interest immunity attached (*Laurence v Commissioner of Police of the Metropolis* February 13, 2006, unrep.);
- The application was premature as the letter of claim could be written without disclosure (*Steamship Mutual Underwriting Association Trustees (Bermuda Ltd) v Baring Asset Management Ltd* [2004] EWHC 202 (when the protocol provided for the documents to be provided with the letter of response) and *OCS Group v Davinia Wells* [2008] EWHC 919, QB (where private medical records did not need to be disclosed preaction to the claimant's ex-employer in a personal injury claim before a medical report had been disclosed));
- The volume of documents requested was disproportionate (80 classes of documents at a potential cost of £1 million) (*Hutchinson 3GUK Ltd v O2 UK Ltd* [2008] EWHC 55).

Other Pre-action applications

Generally parties cannot apply to the court pre-issue for rulings on other matters **C1A–013** but in *Ecclesiastical Insurance Office Plc v Trustees of the Carmelite Charitable Trust*, January 2001, QBD (Commercial Court) the court was prepared to hear an application from an insurer for a declaration of non-liability in a situation where the action was only likely to proceed where the defendant was insured.

Pre issue stock take

Although not referred to in the Practice Direction or the protocols it is recom- **C1A–014** mended that parties and their lawyers carry out a careful check of compliance with pre-action requirements and their readiness for litigation if a dispute is not settled without proceedings. As a minimum this should include whether:

- adequate letters of claim & response were sent/received and if and how the parties positions have changed since then;
- the issues remaining in dispute have been clearly identified and could be further narrowed;
- serious attempts to settle have been made, and whether a Pt 36 offer should be made or accepted now?
- ADR should be considered or tried pre-issue;
- evidence is ready or in hand;
- the client or funders objectives have changed and any necessary authority obtained to proceed;
- careful arrangements have been made for service.

Pre-action Costs

There is no legal entitlement to recover costs incurred at the early stages of a **C1A–015** dispute that is settled pre-action. In *McGlinn v Waltham Contractors Ltd* [2005] EWHC 1419 it was held that the defendant in a construction dispute could not recover pre-action costs in investigating issues that the claimant did not pursue once proceedings were issued as these were not "costs incidental to proceedings" under s.51 of the Supreme Court Act 1981. But the CPR at least provides, under Pt 8 for parties to apply to the court for the amount of those costs to be decided, when the main dispute has been settled and the parties agree that one party is entitled to "reasonable costs" but not the amount.

Birmingham City Council v Lee [2008] EWCA Civ 891 was a claim by a tenant for the consequential damage of less than £5,000 arising from the landlord's failure to carry out repairs until after receipt of the letter of claim. It was decided that it was clear from the Preaction Protocol for Housing Disrepair, para.3.7 and note 4.10, that the claimant tenant's reasonable legal costs were payable on the fast track basis, up to the date when the repairs were completed, because until then, the claimant had a potential claim for specific performance of the repairs that would have merited allocation of the claim to the fast track.

Protocols compared

C1A–016 There are nine pre-action protocols currently in force (see para.5.1 of PD—Protocols at C1–005). The following table compares them with each other.

PROTOCOL	Letter of Claim	Defendants Response	Pre-Action Meeting	ADR	Experts	Flow Chart
Personal Injury	Yes	3 mths		Yes	Yes	
Clinical Negligence	Yes	14 days/3 mths		Yes	Yes	Yes
Construction	Yes	14 days/28 days	Yes			
Defamation	Yes	14 days		Yes		
Professional Negligence	Yes	21 days/3 mths		Yes		
Judicial Review	Yes	14 days				
Disease and Illness	Yes	21 days/3 mths		Yes	Yes	
Housing Disrepair	Yes	20 working days		Yes	Yes	
Possession Claims for Rent Arrears	Yes			Yes		

Note 1: There are detailed annexes to some of the protocols.

Note 2: The time for the Defendant's Response can require an acknowledgment followed by a detailed response. Where this occurs this is shown as two periods above.

PRACTICE DIRECTION—PRE-ACTION CONDUCT

SECTION I - INTRODUCTION

Aims

C1–001 **1.1** The aims of this Practice Direction are to—

(1) enable parties to settle the issue between them without the need to start proceedings (that is, a court claim); and

(2) support the efficient management by the court and the parties of proceedings that cannot be avoided.

1.2 These aims are to be achieved by encouraging the parties to—

(1) exchange information about the issue, and

(2) consider using a form of Alternative Dispute Resolution (*"ADR"*).

Scope

C1–002 **2.1** This Practice Direction describes the conduct the court will normally expect of the prospective parties prior to the start of proceedings.

2.2 There are some types of application where the principles in this Practice Direction clearly cannot or should not apply. These include, but are not limited to, for example—

(1) applications for an order where the parties have agreed between them the terms of the court order to be sought ("consent orders");

(2) applications for an order where there is no other party for the applicant to engage with;

(3) most applications for directions by a trustee or other fiduciary;

(4) applications where telling the other potential party in advance would defeat the purpose of the application (for example, an application for an order to freeze assets).

2.3 Section II deals with the approach of the court in exercising its powers in relation to pre-action conduct. Subject to paragraph 2.2, it applies in relation to all types of proceedings including those governed by the pre-action protocols that have been approved by the Head of Civil Justice and which are listed in paragraph 5.2 of this Practice Direction.

2.4 Section III deals with principles governing the conduct of the parties in cases which are not subject to a pre-action protocol.

2.5 Section III of this Practice Direction is supplemented by two annexes aimed at different types of claimant.

(1) **Annex A** sets out detailed guidance on a pre-action procedure that is likely to satisfy the court in most circumstances where no pre-action protocol or other formal pre-action procedure applies. It is intended as a guide for parties, particularly those without legal representation, in straightforward claims that are likely to be disputed. It is not intended to apply to debt claims where it is not disputed that the money is owed and where the claimant follows a statutory or other formal pre-action procedure.

(2) **Annex B** sets out some specific requirements that apply where the claimant is a business and the defendant is an individual. The requirements may be complied with at any time between the claimant first intimating the possibility of court proceedings and the claimant's letter before claim.

2.6 Section IV contains requirements that apply to all cases including those subject to the pre-action protocols (unless a relevant pre-action protocol contains a different provision). It is supplemented by Annex C, which sets out guidance on instructing experts.

Definitions

3.1 In this Practice Direction together with the Annexes— C1–003

(1) "proceedings" means any proceedings started under Part 7 or Part 8 of the Civil Procedure Rules 1998 ("CPR");

(2) "claimant" and "defendant" refer to the respective parties to potential proceedings;

(3) "ADR" means alternative dispute resolution, and is the col-

lective description of methods of resolving disputes otherwise than through the normal trial process; (see paragraph 8.2 for further information); and

(4) "compliance" means acting in accordance with, as applicable, the principles set out in Section III of this Practice Direction, the requirements in Section IV and a relevant pre-action protocol. The words "comply" and "complied" should be construed accordingly.

SECTION II—THE APPROACH OF THE COURTS

Compliance

C1–004 **4.1** The CPR enable the court to take into account the extent of the parties' compliance with this Practice Direction or a relevant pre-action protocol (see paragraph 5.2) when giving directions for the management of claims (see CPR rules 3.1(4) and (5) and 3.9(1)(e)) and when making orders about who should pay costs (see CPR rule 44.3(5)(a)).

4.2 The court will expect the parties to have complied with this Practice Direction or any relevant pre-action protocol. The court may ask the parties to explain what steps were taken to comply prior to the start of the claim. Where there has been a failure of compliance by a party the court may ask that party to provide an explanation.

Assessment of compliance

4.3 When considering compliance the court will—

(1) be concerned about whether the parties have complied in substance with the relevant principles and requirements and is not likely to be concerned with minor or technical shortcomings;

(2) consider the proportionality of the steps taken compared to the size and importance of the matter;

(3) take account of the urgency of the matter. Where a matter is urgent (for example, an application for an injunction) the court will expect the parties to comply only to the extent that it is reasonable to do so. (Paragraph 9.5 and 9.6 of this Practice Direction concern urgency caused by limitation periods.)

(For many claims, a normal reasonable period for a full response may be one month.)

Examples of non-compliance

4.4 The court may decide that there has been a failure of compliance by a party because, for example, that party has—

(1) not provided sufficient information to enable the other party to understand the issues;

(2) not acted within a time limit set out in a relevant pre-action protocol, or, where no specific time limit applies, within a reasonable period;

(3) unreasonably refused to consider ADR (paragraph 8 in Part III of this Practice Direction and the pre-action protocols all contain similar provisions about ADR); or

(4) without good reason, not disclosed documents requested to be disclosed.

Sanctions for non-compliance

4.5 The court will look at the overall effect of non-compliance on the other party when deciding whether to impose sanctions.

4.6 If, in the opinion of the court, there has been non-compliance, the sanctions which the court may impose include—

(1) staying (that is suspending) the proceedings until steps which ought to have been taken have been taken;

(2) an order that the party at fault pays the costs, or part of the costs, of the other party or parties (this may include an order under rule 27.14(2)(g) in cases allocated to the small claims track);

(3) an order that the party at fault pays those costs on an indemnity basis (rule 44.4(3) sets out the definition of the assessment of costs on an indemnity basis);

(4) if the party at fault is the claimant in whose favour an order for the payment of a sum of money is subsequently made, an order that the claimant is deprived of interest on all or part of that sum, and/or that interest is awarded at a lower rate than would otherwise have been awarded;

(5) if the party at fault is a defendant, and an order for the payment of a sum of money is subsequently made in favour of the claimant, an order that the defendant pay interest on all or part of that sum at a higher rate, not exceeding 10% above base rate, than would otherwise have been awarded.

Commencement of Pre-Action Protocols

5.1 When considering compliance, the court will take account of a relevant pre-action protocol if the proceedings were started after the relevant pre-action protocol came into force. **C1–005**

5.2 The following table sets out the pre-action protocols currently in force and the dates that they came into force—

Pre-Action Protocol	**Came into force**
Personal Injury	26 April 1999
Clinical Disputes	26 April 1999
Construction and Engineering	2 October 2000
Defamation	2 October 2000
Professional Negligence	16 July 2001
Judicial Review	4 March 2002
Disease and Illness	8 December 2003
Housing Disrepair	8 December 2003
Possession Claims based on rent arrears	2 October 2006
Possession Claims based on Mortgage Arrears etc.	19 November 2008

SECTION III—THE PRINCIPLES GOVERNING THE CONDUCT OF THE PARTIES IN CASES NOT SUBJECT TO A PRE-ACTION PROTOCOL

Overview of Principles

C1–005.1 **6.1** The principles that should govern the conduct of the parties are that, unless the circumstances make it inappropriate, before starting proceedings the parties should—

(1) exchange sufficient information about the matter to allow them to understand each other's position and make informed decisions about settlement and how to proceed;

(2) make appropriate attempts to resolve the matter without starting proceedings, and in particular consider the use of an appropriate form of ADR in order to do so.

6.2 The parties should act in a reasonable and proportionate manner in all dealings with one another. In particular, the costs incurred in complying should be proportionate to the complexity of the matter and any money at stake. The parties must not use this Practice Direction as a tactical device to secure an unfair advantage for one party or to generate unnecessary costs.

Exchanging Information Before Starting Proceedings

C1–006 **7.1** Before starting proceedings—

(1) the claimant should set out the details of the matter in writing by sending a letter before claim to the defendant. This letter before claim is not the start of proceedings; and

(2) the defendant should give a full written response within a reasonable period, preceded, if appropriate, by a written acknowledgment of the letter before claim.

7.2 A 'reasonable period of time' will vary depending on the matter. As a general guide—

(1) the defendant should send a letter of acknowledgment within 14 days of receipt of the letter before claim (if a full response has not been sent within that period);

(2) where the matter is straightforward, for example an undisputed debt, then a full response should normally be provided within 14 days;

(3) where a matter requires the involvement of an insurer or other third party or where there are issues about evidence, then a full response should normally be provided within 30 days;

(4) where the matter is particularly complex, for example requiring specialist advice, then a period of longer than 30 days may be appropriate; (5) a period of longer than 90 days in which to provide a full response will only be considered reasonable in exceptional circumstances.

7.3 Annex A sets out detailed guidance on a pre-action procedure that is likely to satisfy the court in most circumstances where no pre-action protocol applies and where the claimant does not follow any statutory or other formal pre-action procedure.

7.4 Annex B sets out the specific information that should be provided in a debt claim by a claimant who is a business against a defendant who is an individual.

Alternative Dispute Resolution

8.1 Starting proceedings should usually be a step of last resort, and proceedings should not normally be started when a settlement is still actively being explored. Although ADR is not compulsory, the parties should consider whether some form of ADR procedure might enable them to settle the matter without starting proceedings. The court may require evidence that the parties considered some form of ADR (see paragraph 4.4(3)). **C1–007**

8.2 It is not practicable in this Practice Direction to address in detail how the parties might decide to resolve a matter. However, some of the options for resolving a matter without starting proceedings are—

(1) discussion and negotiation;

(2) mediation (a form of negotiation with the help of an independent person or body);

(3) early neutral evaluation (where an independent person or body, for example a lawyer or an expert in the subject, gives an opinion on the merits of a dispute); or

(4) arbitration (where an independent person or body makes a binding decision), many types of business are members of arbitration schemes for resolving disputes with consumers.

8.3 The Legal Services Commission has published a booklet on 'Alternatives to Court', CLS Direct Information Leaflet 23 (www.clsdirect.org.uk) which lists a number of organisations that provide alternative dispute resolution services. The National Mediation Helpline on 0845 603 0809 or at www.nationalmediationhelpline.com can provide information about mediation.

8.4 The parties should continue to consider the possibility of reaching a settlement at all times. This still applies after proceedings have been started, up to and during any trial or final hearing.

SECTION IV—REQUIREMENTS THAT APPLY IN ALL CASES

Specific Divisions

9.1 The following requirements (including Annex C) apply in all cases except where a relevant pre-action protocol contains its own provisions about the topic. **C1–008**

9.2 Disclosure

Documents provided by one party to another in the course of complying with this Practice Direction or any relevant pre-action protocol must not be used for any purpose other than resolving the matter, unless the disclosing party agrees in writing.

9.3 Information about funding arrangements

Where a party enters into a funding arrangement within the meaning of rule 43.2(1)(k), that party should inform the other parties about this arrangement as soon as possible.

(CPR rule 44.3B(1)(c) provides that a party may not recover certain additional costs where information about a funding arrangement was not provided.)

9.4 Experts

Where the evidence of an expert is necessary the parties should consider how best to minimise expense. Guidance on instructing experts can be found in Annex C.

9.5 Limitation periods

There are statutory time limits for starting proceedings ("the limitation period"). If a claimant starts a claim after the limitation period applicable to that type of Practice Direction to 49th Update 41 claim has expired the defendant will be entitled to use that as a defence to the claim.

9.6 In certain instances compliance may not be possible before the expiry of the limitation period. If, for any reason, proceedings are started before the parties have complied, they should seek to agree to apply to the court for an order to stay (i.e. suspend) the proceedings while the parties take steps to comply.

9.7 Notifying the court

Where proceedings are started the claimant should state in the claim form or the particulars of claim whether they have complied with Sections III and IV of this Practice Direction or any relevant protocol.

ANNEX A—Guidance on pre-action procedure where no pre-action protocol or other formal pre-action procedure applies

1. General

C1–009 1.1 This Annex sets out detailed guidance on a pre-action procedure that is likely to satisfy the court in most circumstances where no pre-action protocol or other formal pre-action procedure applies. It is intended as a guide for parties, particularly those without legal representation, in straightforward claims that are likely to be disputed. It is not intended to apply to debt claims where it is not disputed that the money is owed and where the claimant follows a statutory or other formal pre-action procedure.

2. Claimant's letter before claim

2.2 The claimant's letter should give concise details about the matter. This should enable the defendant to understand and investigate the issues without needing to request further information. The letter should include—

(1) the claimant's full name and address;

(2) the basis on which the claim is made (i.e. why the claimant says the defendant is liable);

(3) a clear summary of the facts on which the claim is based;

(4) what the claimant wants from the defendant;

(5) if financial loss is claimed, an explanation of how the amount has been calculated; and

(6) details of any funding arrangement (within the meaning of rule 43.2(1)(k) of the CPR) that has been entered into by the claimant.

2.2 The letter should also—

(1) list the essential documents on which the claimant intends to rely;

(2) set out the form of ADR (if any) that the claimant considers the most suitable and invite the defendant to agree to this;

(3) state the date by which the claimant considers it reasonable for a full response to be provided by the defendant; and

(4) identify and ask for copies of any relevant documents not in the claimant's possession and which the claimant wishes to see.

2.3 Unless the defendant is known to be legally represented the letter should—

(1) refer the defendant to this Practice Direction and in particular draw attention to paragraph 4 concerning the court's powers to impose sanctions for failure to comply with the Practice Direction; and

(2) inform the defendant that ignoring the letter before claim may lead to the claimant starting proceedings and may increase the defendant's liability for costs.

3. Defendant's acknowledgment of the letter before claim

3.1 Where the defendant is unable to provide a full written response within 14 days of receipt of the letter before claim the defendant should, instead, provide a written acknowledgment within 14 days.

3.2 The acknowledgment—

(1) should state whether an insurer is or may be involved;

(2) should state the date by which the defendant (or insurer) will provide a full written response; and

(3) may request further information to enable the defendant to provide a full response.

3.3 If the date stated under paragraph 3.2(2) of this Annex is longer than the period stated in the letter before claim, the defendant should give reasons why a longer period is needed. Practice Direction to 49th Update 44

3.4 If the defendant (or insurer) does not provide either a letter of acknowledgment or full response within 14 days, and proceedings are subsequently started, then the court is likely to consider that the claimant has not complied.

3.5 Where the defendant is unable to provide a full response within 14 days of receipt of the letter before claim because the defendant intends to seek advice then the written acknowledgment should state—

(1) that the defendant is seeking advice;

(2) from whom the defendant is seeking advice; and

(3) when the defendant expects to have received that advice and be in a position to provide a full response

3.6 A claimant should allow a reasonable period of time of up to 14 days for a defendant to obtain advice.

PRE-ACTION PROTOCOLS

4. Defendant's full response

4.1 The defendant's full written response should—
(1) accept the claim in whole or in part; or
(2) state that the claim is not accepted.

4.2 Unless the defendant accepts the whole of the claim, the response should—
(1) give reasons why the claim is not accepted, identifying which facts and which parts of the claim (if any) are accepted and which are disputed, and the basis of that dispute;
(2) state whether the defendant intends to make a counterclaim against the claimant (and, if so, provide information equivalent to a claimant's letter before claim);
(3) state whether the defendant alleges that the claimant was wholly or partly to blame for the problem that led to the dispute and, if so, summarise the facts relied on;
(4) state whether the defendant agrees to the claimant's proposals for ADR and if not, state why not and suggest an alternative form of ADR (or state why none is considered appropriate);
(5) list the essential documents on which the defendant intends to rely;
(6) enclose copies of documents requested by the claimant, or explain why they will not be provided; and
(7) identify and ask for copies of any further relevant documents, not in the defendant's possession and which the defendant wishes to see.

4.3 If the defendant (or insurer) does not provide a full response within the period stated in the claimant's letter before claim (or any longer period stated in the defendant's letter of acknowledgment), and a claim is subsequently started, then the court is likely to consider that the claimant has complied.

4.4 If the claimant starts proceedings before any longer period stated in the defendant's letter of acknowledgment, the court will consider whether or not the longer period requested by the defendant was reasonable.

5. Claimant's reply

5.1 The claimant should provide the documents requested by the defendant within as short a period of time as is practicable or explain in writing why the documents will not be provided.

5.2 If the defendant has made a counterclaim the claimant should provide information equivalent to the defendant's full response (see paragraphs 4.1 to 4.3 above).

6. Taking Stock

6.1 In following the above procedure, the parties will have a genuine opportunity to resolve the matter without needing to start proceedings. At the very least, it should be possible to establish what issues remain outstanding so as to narrow the scope of the proceedings and therefore limit potential costs.

6.2 If having completed the procedure the matter has not been resolved then the parties should undertake a further review of their respective positions to see if proceedings can still be avoided.

ANNEX B—Information to be provided in a debt claim where the claimant is a business and the defendant is an individual

1. Where paragraph 7.4 of the Practice Direction applies the claimant should— (1) provide details of how the money can be paid (for example the method of payment and the address to which it can be sent); (2) state that the defendant can contact the claimant to discuss possible repayment options, and provide the relevant contact details; and (3) inform the defendant that free independent advice and assistance can be obtained from organisations including those listed in the table below. **C1–010**

INDEPENDENT ADVICE ORGANISATIONS

Organisation	**Address**	**Telephone Number**	**E-mail Address**
National Debtline	Tricorn House 51-53 Hagley Road Edgbaston Birmingham B16 8TP	FREEPHONE 0808 808 4000	www.nationaldebtline.co.uk
Consumer Credit Counselling Service (CCCS)		FREEPHONE 0800 138 1111	www.cccs.co.uk
Citizens Advice	Check your local Yellow Pages or Thomson local directory for address and telephone numbers		www.citizensadvice.org.uk
Community Legal Advice (formerly Community Legal Services Direct)		0845 345 4345	www.clsdirect.org.uk

2. *The information set out in* paragraph 1 of this Annex may be provided at any time between the claimant first intimating the possibility of court proceedings and the claimant's letter before claim.

3. Where the defendant is unable to provide a full response within the time specified in the letter before claim because the defendant intends to seek debt advice then the written acknowledgment should state—

PRE-ACTION PROTOCOLS

(1) that the defendant is seeking debt advice;
(2) who the defendant is seeking advice from; and
(3) when the defendant expects to have received that advice and be in a position to provide a full response.

4. A claimant should allow a reasonable period of time of up to 14 days for a defendant to obtain debt advice.

5. But the claimant need not allow the defendant time to seek debt advice if the claimant knows that—

(1) the defendant has already received relevant debt advice and the defendant's circumstances have not significantly changed; or
(2) (2) the defendant has previously asked for time to seek debt advice but has not done so.

ANNEX C—Guidance on instructing experts

C1–011 1. The CPR contain extensive provisions which strictly control the use of experts both before and after proceedings are started. These provisions are contained in—

(1) CPR Part 35;
(2) the Practice Direction supplementing Part 35; and
(3) the Protocol for the "Instruction of Experts to give Evidence in Civil Claims" which is annexed to that Practice Direction.

2. Parties should be aware that once proceedings have been started—

(1) expert evidence may not be used in court without the permission of the court;
(2) a party who instructs an expert will not necessarily be able to recover the cost from another party; and
(3) it is the duty of an expert to help the court on the matters within the expert's scope of expertise and this duty overrides any obligation to the person instructing or paying the expert.

3. Many matters can and should be resolved without the need for advice or evidence from an expert. If an expert is needed, the parties should consider how best to minimise the expense for example by agreeing to instruct—

(1) a single joint expert (i.e. engaged and paid jointly by the parties whether instructed jointly or separately); or
(2) (2) an agreed expert (i.e. the parties agree the identity of the expert but only one party instructs the expert and pays the expert's costs).

4. If the parties do not agree that the nomination of a single joint expert is appropriate, then the party seeking the expert evidence (the first party) should give the other party (the second party) a list of one or more experts in the relevant field of expertise whom the first party would like to instruct.

5. Within 14 days of receipt of the list of experts, the second party may indicate in writing an objection to one or more of the experts listed. If there remains on the list one or more experts who are acceptable, then the first party should instruct an expert from the list.

6. If the second party objects to all the listed experts, the first party may then instruct an expert of the first party's own choice. Both parties should bear in mind that if proceedings are started the court will consider whether a party has acted reasonably when instructing (or rejecting) an expert.

The Personal Injury Protocol

This protocol was in place in April 1999 with the implementation of the CPR.

Scope and content

It is intended to apply mainly to potential Fast Track cases with a value of up to £15,000, but the general approach should still be followed in larger claims, except occupational disease (soon to have its own protocol) and clinical negligence. (For proceedings issued on or after April 6, 2009, the upper limit for fast track cases is £25,000 (see r.26.6(4)).The defendant is asked to acknowledge the letter of claim within 21 days of receipt and respond in full within 3 months of the acknowledgment, either admitting or denying liability with reasons. **C2A–001**

The protocol specifically requires the parties to co-operate on the selection of an expert, especially the medical expert providing a condition and prognosis report on the accident victim. The protocol requires the claimant to give the defendant the name of more than one suitable expert. If the defendant does not object to at least one of those named within 14 days, the claimant will then instruct the expert to prepare a report. Provided the claimant is happy with the report it will be disclosed to the defendant. If the report requires clarification, either party can ask the expert questions (keeping the other party informed of both the questions and the answers). However, if the defendant objects to all of the experts named by the claimant, or is not satisfied with the report disclosed after raising questions, he may decide to retain his own expert. But it will be for the court to decide at allocation stage whether the cost of two experts is justified.

The personal injury protocol also recommends that the claimant's solicitor should be responsible for organising access to the claimant's medical records and a specimen letter of instructions to a medical expert is annexed.

The protocol includes as an annex, specimen non-exhaustive detailed lists of documents which defendants should disclose with any denial of liability in particular types of case, e.g. highway accidents and employers' liability cases.

Changes since implementation

This protocol has been kept under regular review by the working party that drafted the protocol. Changes were made in 2000 to: **C2A–002**

- omit the claimant's date of birth and national insurance number from the specimen letter of claim because of the (slight?) risk of their being misused (for benefit fraud);
- clarify that the protocol does not apply to occupational disease claims (para.2.4);
- allow longer time periods for acknowledging and responding to the letter of claim when the accident occurred outside England and Wales and the defendant is outside the jurisdiction (21 and 42 days respectively) (para.3.8);
- clarify that it is the claimant who will usually nominate the experts (para.2.11);
- clarify that when the defendant admits liability the claimant must disclose any medical report obtained under the protocol and that the claimant should delay issuing until at least 21 days from this disclosure to enable a settlement to be considered.

Changes made in April 2005 include:

- The letter of claim should provide notification of any conditional fee funding arrangement, including whether insurance has been taken out.
- Where the likely value of a claim has increased beyond £15,000 since the letter of claim was sent, the claimant should notify the defendant as soon as possible.
- The Rehabilitation Code is annexed to the protocol and a new Section 4 of the text requires both parties to consider whether the claimant would benefit from

rehabilitation as early as possible. Any report obtained for the purposes of assessing the claimant's needs is not to be used in the litigation except by consent.

- No charge is to be made for providing copy documents under the protocol.
- Where the defendant has admitted liability the claimant should send to the defendant schedules of special damage at least 21 days before proceedings are issued.

From April 2007 the first sentence of paragraph 3.9 is disapplied, i.e. the presumption that a pre-action admission in a claim under £15,000 is binding. (See also the notes on pre-action admissions at C2A–005 below.)

The impact of the protocol and issues arising from research

C2A–003 The Law Society/Civil Justice Council research into pre-action behaviour (*"More Civil Justice? The impact of the Woolf reforms on pre-action behaviour"* Research Study 43, LCD, T. Goriely, R. Moorhead and P. Abrams) found that the protocol was well-liked: insurers welcomed the additional information they were given pre-action which enabled earlier settlements and sometimes lower legal costs, and claimant lawyers liked the structured timetable which the protocol encouraged.

The researchers raised the following main questions;

1. whether an "early warning letter" sent by a claimant simply to notify a defendant of an incident and that a claim was likely (protocol para.2.6) serves a useful purpose-defendants said that it was not. The aim is to enable defendants who are unaware of the accident, e.g. a tripping and slipping claim to begin to investigate while the claimant assembles the evidence needed for the letter of claim.
2. whether letters of claim might include more information on the claimant's losses-the protocol currently requires the first exchange of letters between the parties to focus on liability, although the claimant is asked to provide the defendant with an indication of the financial loss incurred (para.3.2). In the more straightforward and lower value claims where the accident victim has already recovered from their injuries, a claimant may be able to enclose a full schedule of special damages with the letter (para.3.13). Defendants want as much information as early as possible to evaluate the claim, and place a reserve figure on it. But in larger claims in particular, the claimant carrying out detailed work on quantum is expensive and takes time, and the costs may not be recoverable if the defendant 's denial of liability in the letter of response is accepted.
3. whether there might be clearer guidance on admissions. The protocol states in para.9 that the defendant will be bound by admissions in claims up to £15,000 (see below for a discussion on the case law.)
4. whether the procedure for agreeing experts' names justifies the delay it causes. The protocol (paras 3.14-3.17) currently requires the claimant to nominate more than one expert (in a discipline) whom the claimant will subsequently instruct, and gives the defendant an opportunity to object within 14 days. The problem identified in the research was that this has lead to requests for C.V.s and to exchanges of correspondence, which has prolonged the receipt of medical reports typically by 6 weeks.

Concern has been expressed that the frontloading of work required by the protocols and CPR has increased costs. For low value RTA personal injury claims at least this was borne out by research carried out for the Civil Justice Council which suggested that a 50 per cent increase in base costs (without additional liability in cfa cases) had occured in cases under £15,000 that settled pre-action after 1999. (P. Fenn and N. Rickman's research for the Big Tent on the Civil Justice Council website *http://www.civiljusticecouncil.gov.uk* [Accessed March 30, 2007]).

Other points of difficulty

C2A–004 *Disclosure of an expert's report* —The protocol does not state what should happen if the claimant obtains a report under the procedure outlined above, which the claimant does not wish to disclose because it is unsatisfactory or unhelpful. In *Carlson v Townsend* [2001] EWCA Civ 511 the Court of Appeal confirmed that the personal injury protocol does not require a medical expert, selected in accordance with the protocol, to be jointly instructed, or the report to be disclosed to the defendant, where the expert's identity has not been revealed. Such reports remain privileged and the court cannot order their production. But the claimant would need the court's permission as usual to rely upon an expert's report in the proceedings (and generally the claimant would have to bear the cost of the undisclosed report.).

In *Sage v Feiven* [2002] 7 C.L.Y. 430 (APIL Newsletter, Vol.12, Issue 1, Page 28) the claimant obtained a report from an orthopaedic surgeon which was not disclosed (following *Carlson v Townsend*). When proceedings were issued the defendant invited the District Judge to order a report from the same surgeon as a single joint expert, and the D.J. did so, on proportionality grounds. This was overturned on appeal, because inevitably, privileged information would be disclosed to the defendant. The parties were ordered to instruct a new expert.

Pre-action admissions —Until April 2007 the protocol required defendants to undertake to stand by an admission of liability for claims up to £15,000. This was a concession made by the insurers during the drafting stage. Pre-CPR in *Gale v Superdrug Stores Plc* [1996] 1 W.L.R. 1089 (TLR, May 2, 1996, CA) it was held that defendants were not bound by pre-action admissions. **C2A–005**

Between 2000 and 2005 the courts seemed to assume that r.14.1 gave them the power to order the withdrawal of an admission whether made pre-action or during the proceedings, including in multi-track cases. In *Hackman v Hounslow* [2000] C.L.Y. 354, the court said that the protocol effectively superseded *Gale v Superdrug*. In *Flinn v Wills* [2001] C.L.Y. 412, p.19 the defendants sought to reopen a pre-action agreement on liability after issue partly on the ground that it had been made by an inexperienced claims handler. Even though the case was multi and not fast track the Circuit Judge said the defendant was bound. *Sollitt v Broady Ltd* [2000] C.P.L.R. 259 was decided similarly although in this case the admission was made after proceedings were started. In *Browning v Oates* [2002] C.L.Y. 284. The claimant had been attacked by a bull which had escaped from the defendant's premises chased by the defendant's dogs, the defendant's loss adjuster admitted liability, but the insurer, after proceedings were issued, tried to resile on the ground that the admission was a mistake. The D.J. decided that this would cause prejudice to the claimant because she had not obtained liability witness statements, the dogs had been destroyed and the accident scene had been altered.

In *Flaviis v Pauley*, October 29, 2002 (QB), Nelson J. the defendant was allowed to withdraw an admission of a failure to MOT a hired motorbike on discovery that the claimant had presented false insurance and driving licence when hiring the bike.

In *Beckett v First Choice & Flights Ltd* [2003] C.L.Y. 295 the defendants were refused permission to retract a pre-action admission of liability for a skiing accident (on the ground that the claimant purchased the skiing lessons outside the UK so the claim fell outside the Package Tour Regulations 1982) because the claimant would be seriously financially prejudiced having committed herself to purchasing her council home at a discount, and because the defendant offered no explanation for the changed approach.

And in *Hamilton v Hertfordshire CC* [2003] EWHC 3018, QB the defendant was allowed to withdraw an admission of liability for an accident to a teaching assistant involved in lifting a disabled child from a school swimming pool because she had given three different accounts of the incident in the letter of claim and witness statements.

In *Barnard v Sappi Europe Ltd* [2005] EWHC 2169 (QB) the claimant suffered from asbestosis contracted during one of several periods of employment with different employers. His solicitor made careful enquiries and the prospective defendant confirmed, in response to the letter of claim, that they were the correct defendant. They then admitted liability. Only some time later, during the proceedings expedited because of the claimant's very poor health, the defendant established they were not the relevant employer. But they were not permitted to resile because of the very serious prejudice this would cause to the claimant who might be denied a trial or resolution in his lifetime.

But in late 2005 the Court of Appeal took a very different approach in *Sowerby v Charlton* [2005] EWCA Civ 1610. The claimant suffered serious injuries in falling off stone stairs external to her flat. Pre-action the defendant's insurers admitted liability, but withdrew this following the issue of proceedings. At first instance and on appeal parts of the defence were struck out because of the pre-action admission. The Court of Appeal concluded that the CPR are concerned with the regulation of cases after an action is started; the rulemakers cannot have been intended a pre-action admission to be covered by CPR r.14.1 because a party's case will not have been formulated until the claim form and/or particulars of claim have been prepared, and the drafters of the protocol accepted that in multi track claims, at least, the presumption against resiling from pre-action admissions of liability could not lie. Accordingly they concluded that the Master at first instance, and the Judge on appeal, were wrong to hold that CPR Pt 14 applied to this admission (although on the facts the CA went on to decide that a complete denial of primary liability had no real prospect of success and summary judgment could be entered on that issue, although there was a live issue in relation to contributory negligence). The court also said that they were not expressing a definitive view on the law in relation to pre-action admissions, but that *Gale v Superdrug* should now be approached with caution as it was concerned with the pre-CPR rules.

Stoke on Trent City Council v Walley [2006] EWCA Civ 1137 followed *Sowerby*, allowing the local authority to resile from their admission (in an accident at work case allocated to the multi-track) that had been made by an incompetent employee of the loss adjusters because the status of a pre-action admission was evidential, the authority had not acted in bad faith, and there was no evidence that the claimant would suffer prejudice. But Brooke L.J. said that there would be great force in giving greater status to an admission of liability in personal injury multi track cases than at present.

The 44th amendments to the CPR in force from April 2, 2007 amended CPR Pt 14 specifically to refer to pre-action admissions (following the Court of Appeal decision in *Sowerby v Charlton*—above—that Pt 14 did not apply to pre-action admissions). New r.14A applies to pre-action admissions made after April 6, 2007 in personal injury, clinical negligence and disease and illness claims. The admission must be made after a letter of claim has been received, or state expressly that Pt 14 applies. CPR 14.1A(3) provides that a pre-action admission may be withdrawn at any time by consent, or after proceedings have commenced with the court's permission. New paras 7.1 and 7.2 of the Pt 7 Practice Direction set out the factors that the court will have regard to on an application to withdraw an admission (whether made pre-action or after proceedings have been issued).These are the reasons for seeking to withdraw and whether new evidence has come to light, the conduct of the parties, the prejudice likely to be caused to either party, the stage of the proceedings, the prospects of success of the claim if the admission is withdrawn, and "all the circumstances". It seems that in claims other than for personal injury *Sowerby* will continue to apply, i.e. a pre-action admission can be withdrawn at any time, and the court does not have the power under Pt 14 to decide otherwise.

Two cases reported after Pt 14 IA was brought into force in April 2007 were decided under the previous rules but give some guidance on how the courts balance prejudice.

Ashraf v Devon CC August 30, 2007 Lawtel 13/9/07 was a personal injury claim in which the parties agreed preaction to settle liability 90:10 in the claimant's favour. The defence resiled from this and the claimant appeared to accept this in his AQ and by complying with directions for disclosure of documents and witnesses' statements dealing with liability. Six months later the claimant applied to the court for judgment on liability on a 90:10 basis relying on the pre-action admission. That was granted on the papers without notice to the defendant. However the defendant's application to set aside the judgment succeeded as the claimant's actions amounted to "approbation" and "reprobation" (i.e. blowing hot and cold unreasonably) and the defendant had incurred costs in investigating liability after the claimant appeared to have accepted the defendant's resiling.

In *White v Greensand Homes Ltd and BSF Consulting Engineers Ltd* [2007] EWCA Civ 643 the Court of Appeal gave the second defendant permission to amend their defence to resile from their pre-action admission that they had designed the foundations of the claimant's property that was affected by subsidence, when it was subsequently discovered that another company had been responsible for the design which was by then in liquidation. The Court of Appeal balanced the prejudice between the parties (following the guidance in the *Braybrook* case) in favour of the second defendant even though the claimant might no longer have a remedy against the other company.

Pre-action Costs

C2A–006 Predictable solicitor's costs are to be piloted from autumn 2003, initially for road traffic accident cases under £10,000 which settle without proceedings. The base costs recoverable will be £800 plus 20 per cent of the actual damages up to £5,000 and 15 per cent above that. There is a London mark-up of 12.5 per cent. Disbursements, e.g. experts' fees, and success fees are not included initially. The pilot applies to accidents occurring after October 6, 2003.

C2A–007 Predictable solicitor's costs have been introduced for road traffic accident cases occurring after October 6, 2003 that settle at under £10,000 without proceedings. The base costs recoverable will be £800 plus 20 per cent of the agreed damages up to £5,000 and 15 per cent above that. There is a London mark-up of 12.5 per cent. Disbursements, e.g. experts' fees, and success fees are not included initially and can be claimed in addition. If the claimant considers the amount too low in the circumstances (perhaps a complex case, more than one defendant, or a high degree of contributory negligence) the claimant can issue Pt 8 costs proceedings. But if not awarded more than 20 per cent above the predictable costs the claimant pays the costs of the Pt 8 proceedings.

The aim of the scheme is to create greater certainty in costs in low value RTA claims, to reduce the too-common adversarial attitude over costs in this type of case, and to speed up payment. The scheme, a pilot to be reviewed in summer 2005, is the result of research and extensive negotiations sponsored by the Civil Justice Council. If it is successful similar schemes are likely to be introduced for other types of low value personal injury claims and the RTA scheme may be extended to cover the costs of the proceedings also.

PRE-ACTION PROTOCOL FOR PERSONAL INJURY CLAIMS C2–001

1.

Introduction

1.1 Lord Woolf in his final Access to Justice Report of July 1996 recommended the development of pre-action protocols:

> "To build on and increase the benefits of early but well informed settlement which genuinely satisfy both parties to dispute."

1.2 The aims of pre-action protocols are:

- more pre-action contact between the parties
- better and earlier exchange of information
- better pre-action investigation by both sides
- to put the parties in a position where they may be able to settle cases fairly and early without litigation
- to enable proceedings to run to the court's timetable and efficiently, if litigation does become necessary
- to promote the provision of medical or rehabilitation treatment (not just in high value cases) to address the needs of the claimant

1.3 The concept of protocols is relevant to a range of initiatives for good litigation and pre-litigation practice, especially:

- predictability in the time needed for steps pre-proceedings
- standardisation of relevant information, including documents to be disclosed.

1.4 The Courts will be able to treat the standards set in protocols as the normal reasonable approach to pre-action conduct: If proceedings are issued, it will be for the court to decide whether non-compliance with a protocol should merit adverse consequences. Guidance on the court's likely approach will be given from time to time in practice directions.

1.5 If the court has to consider the question of compliance after proceedings have begun, it will not be concerned with minor infringements, e.g. failure by a short period to provide relevant information. One minor breach will not exempt the "innocent" party from following the protocol. The court will look at the effect of non-compliance on the other party when deciding whether to impose sanctions.

2.

Notes of Guidance

C2–002 **2.1** The protocol has been kept deliberately simple to promote ease of use and general acceptability. The notes of guidance which follows relate particularly to issues which arose during the piloting of the protocol.

Scope of the Protocol

C2–003 **2.2** This protocol is intended to apply to all claims which include a claim for personal injury (except those claims covered by the Clinical Disputes and Disease and Illness Protocols) and to the entirety of those claims: not only to the personal injury element of a claim which also includes, for instance, property damage.

2.3 This protocol is primarily designed for those road traffic, tripping and slipping and accident at work cases which include an element of personal injury with a value of less than £15,000 which are likely to be allocated to the fast track. This is because time will be of the essence, after proceedings are issued, especially for the defendant, if a case is to be ready for trial within 30 weeks of allocation. Also, proportionality of work and costs to the value of what is in dispute is particularly important in lower value claims. For some claims within the value "scope" of the fast track some flexibility in the timescale of the protocol may be necessary—see also paragraph 3.8.

2.4 However, the "cards on the table" approach advocated by the protocol is equally appropriate to higher value claims. The spirit, if not the letter of the protocol, should still be followed for multi-track type claims. In accordance with the sense of the civil justice reforms, the court will expect to see the spirit of reasonable pre-action behaviour applied in all cases, regardless of the existence of a specific protocol. In particular with regard to personal injury cases worth more than £15,000, with a view to avoiding the necessity of proceedings parties are expected to comply with the protocol as far as possible e.g. in respect of letters before action, exchanging information and documents and agreeing experts.

2.5 The timetable and the arrangements for disclosing documents and obtaining expert evidence may need to be varied to suit the circumstances of the case. Where one or both parties consider the detail of the protocol is not appropriate to the case, and proceedings are subsequently issued, the court will expect an explanation as to why the protocol has not been followed, or has been varied.

Early Notification

C2–004 **2.6** The claimant's legal representative may wish to notify the defendant and/or his insurer as soon as they know a claim is likely to be *made, but* before they are able to send a detailed letter of claim, particularly for instance, when the defendant has no or limited knowledge of the incident giving rise to the claim or where the claimant is incurring significant expenditure as a result of the accident which he hopes the defendant might pay for, in whole or in part. If the claimant's representative chooses to do this, it will not start the timetable for responding.

The Letter of Claim

2.7 The specimen letter of claim at Annex A will usually be sent to the individual defendant. In practice, he/she may have no personal financial interest in the financial outcome of the claim/dispute because he/she is insured. Court imposed sanctions for non-compliance with the protocol may be ineffective against an insured. This is why the protocol emphasises the importance of passing the letter of claim to the insurer and the possibility that the insurance cover might be affected. If an insurer receives the letter of claim only after some delay by the insured, it would not be unreasonable for the insurer to ask the claimant for additional time to respond. **C2–005**

2.8 In road traffic cases, the letter of claim should always contain the name and address of the hospital where the claimant was treated and, where available, the claimant's hospital reference number.

2.9 The priority at letter of claim stage is for the claimant to provide sufficient information for the defendant to assess liability. Sufficient information should also be provided to enable the defendant to estimate the likely size of the claim.

2.10 Once the claimant has sent the letter of claim no further investigation on liability should normally be carried out until a response is received from the defendant indicating whether liability is disputed.

Reasons for Early Issue

2.11 The protocol recommends that a defendant be given three months to investigate and respond to a claim before proceedings are issued. This may not always be possible, particularly where a claimant only consults a solicitor close to the end of any relevant limitation period. In these circumstances, the claimant's solicitor should give as much notice of the intention to issue proceedings as is practicable and the parties should consider whether the court might be invited to extend time for service of the claimant's supporting documents and for service of any defence, or alternatively, to stay the proceedings while the recommended steps in the protocol are followed. **C2–006**

Status of Letters of Claim and Response

2.12 Letters of claim and response are not intended to have the same status as a statement of case in proceedings. Matters may come to light as a result of investigation after the letter of claim has been sent, or after the defendant has responded, particularly if disclosure of documents takes place outside the recommended three-month period. These circumstances could mean that the "pleaded" case of one or both parties is presented slightly differently than in the letter of claim and response. It would not be consistent with the spirit of the protocol for a party to "take a point" on this in the proceedings, provided that there was no obvious intention by the party who changed their position to mislead the other party. **C2–007**

Disclosure of Documents

2.13 The aim of the early disclosure of documents by the defen- **C2–008**

dant is not to encourage "fishing expeditions" by the claimant, but to promote an early exchange of relevant information to help in clarifying or resolving issues in dispute. The claimant's solicitor can assist by identifying in the letter of claim or in a subsequent letter the particular categories of documents which they consider are relevant.

Experts

C2–009 **2.14** The protocol encourages joint selection of, and access to, experts. The report produced is not a joint report for the purposes of CPR Part 35. Most frequently this will apply to the medical expert, but on occasions also to liability experts, e.g. engineers. The protocol promotes the practice of the claimant obtaining a medical report, disclosing it to the defendant who then asks questions and/or agrees it and does not obtain his own report. The protocol provides for nomination of the expert by the claimant in personal injury claims because of the early stage of the proceedings and the particular nature of such claims. If proceedings have to be issued, a medical report must be attached to these proceedings. However, if necessary after proceedings have commenced and with the permission of the court, the parties may obtain further expert reports. It would be for the court to decide whether the costs of more than one expert's report should be recoverable.

2.15 Some solicitors choose to obtain medical reports through medical agencies, rather than directly from a specific doctor or hospital. The defendant's prior consent to the action should be sought and, if the defendant so requests, the agency should be asked to provide in advance the names of the doctor(s) whom they are considering instructing.

Alternative Dispute Resolution

C2–010 **2.16** The parties should consider whether some form of alternative dispute resolution procedure would be more suitable than litigation, and if so, endeavour to agree which form to adopt. Both the Claimant and Defendant may be required by the Court to provide evidence that alternative means of resolving their dispute were considered. The Courts take the view that litigation should be a last resort, and that claims should not be issued prematurely when a settlement is still actively being explored. Parties are warned that if the protocol is not followed (including this paragraph) then the Court must have regard to such conduct when determining costs.

2.17 It is not practicable in this protocol to address in detail how the parties might decide which method to adopt to resolve their particular dispute. However, summarised below are some of the options for resolving disputes without litigation:

- Discussion and negotiation.
- Early neutral evaluation by an independent third party (for example, a lawyer experienced in the field of personal injury or an individual experienced in the subject matter of the claim).
- Mediation—a form of facilitated negotiation assisted by an independent neutral party.

2.18 The Legal Services Commission has published a booklet on

"Alternatives to Court", CLS Direct Information Leaflet 23 (*www.clsdirect.org.uk/legalhelp/leaflet23.jsp*), which lists a number of organisations that provide alternative dispute resolution services.

2.19 *It is expressly recognised that no party can or should be forced to mediate or enter into any form of ADR.*

Stocktake

2.20 Where a claim is not resolved when the protocol has been fol- **C2–011**
lowed, the parties might wish to carry out a "stocktake" of the issues in dispute, and the evidence that the court is likely to need to decide those issues, before proceedings are started. Where the defendant is insured and the pre-action steps have been conducted by the insurer, the insurer would normally be expected to nominate solicitors to act in the proceedings and the claimant's solicitor is recommended to invite the insurer to nominate solicitors to act in the proceedings and do so 7–14 days before the intended issue date.

3.

The Protocol

Letter of Claim

3.1 The claimant shall send to the proposed defendant two copies **C2–012**
of a letter of claim, immediately sufficient information is available to substantiate a realistic claim and before issues of quantum are addressed in detail. One copy of the letter is for the defendant, the second for passing on to his insurers.

3.2 The letter shall contain **a clear summary of the facts** on which the claim is based together with an indication of the **nature of any injuries** suffered and of **any financial loss incurred**. In cases of road traffic accidents, the letter should provide the name and address of the hospital where treatment has been obtained and the claimant's hospital reference number. Where the case is funded by a conditional fee agreement (or collective conditional fee agreement), notification should be given of the existence of the agreement and where appropriate, that there is a success fee and/or insurance premium, although not the level of the success fee or premium.

3.3 Solicitors are recommended to use a **standard format** for such a letter—an example is at Annex A: this can be amended to suit the particular case.

3.4 The letter should ask for **details of the insurer** and that a copy should be sent by the proposed defendant to the insurer where appropriate. If the insurer is known, a copy shall be sent directly to the insurer. Details of the claimant's National Insurance number and date of birth should be supplied to the defendant's insurer once the defendant has responded to the letter of claim and confirmed the identify of the insurer. This information should not be supplied in the letter of claim.

3.5 Sufficient information should be given in order to enable the defendant's insurer/solicitor to commence investigations and at least put a broad valuation on the "risk".

3.6 The **defendant should reply within 21 calendar days** of the date of posting of the letter identifying the insurer (if any) and, if necessary, identifying specifically any significant omissions from the letter of claim. If there has been no reply by the defendant or insurer within 21 days, the claimant will be entitled to issue proceedings.

3.7 The **defendant** ('s insurers) will have a **maximum of three months** from the date of acknowledgment of the claim **to investigate**. No later than the end of that period the defendant (insurer) shall reply, stating whether liability is denied and, if so, giving reasons for their denial of liability including any alternative version of events relied upon.

3.8 Where the accident occurred outside England and Wales and/or where the defendant is outside the jurisdiction, the time periods of 21 days and three months should normally be extended up to 42 days and six months.

3.9 Where the claimant's investigation indicates that the value of the claim has increased to more than £15,000 since the letter of claim, the claimant should notify the defendant as soon as possible.

Documents

C2–013 **3.10** If the **defendant denies liability**, he should enclose with the letter of reply, **documents** in his possession which are **material to the issues** between the parties, and which would be likely to be ordered to be disclosed by the court, either on an application for pre-action disclosure, or on disclosure during proceedings.

3.11 Attached at Annex B are **specimen**, but non-exhaustive, **lists** of documents likely to be material in different types of claim. Where the claimant's investigation of the case is well advanced, the letter of claim could indicate which classes of documents are considered relevant for early disclosure. Alternatively these could be identified at a later stage.

3.12 Where the defendant admits primary liability, but alleges contributory negligence by the claimant, the defendant should give reasons supporting those allegations and disclose those documents from Annex B which are relevant to the issues in dispute. The claimant should respond to the allegations of contributory negligence before proceedings are issued.

3.13 No charge will be made for providing copy documents under the Protocol.

Special Damages

C2–014 **3.14** The claimant will send to the defendant as soon as practicable a Schedule of Special Damages with supporting documents, particularly where the defendant has admitted liability.

Experts

C2–015 **3.15** Before any party instructs an expert he should give the other party a list of the **name** (s) of **one or more experts** in the relevant speciality whom he considers are suitable to instruct.

3.16 Where a medical expert is to be instructed the claimant's solicitor will organise access to relevant medical records—see specimen letter of instruction at Annex C.

3.17 Within 14 days the other party may indicate **an objection** to one or more of the named experts. The first party should then instruct a mutually acceptable expert (which is not the same as a joint expert). It must be emphasised that if the Claimant nominates an expert in the original letter of claim, the defendant has 14 days to object to one or more of the named experts after expiration of the period of 21 days within which he has to reply to the letter of claim, as set out in paragraph 3.6.

3.18 If the second party objects to all the listed experts, the parties may then instruct **experts of their own choice**. It would be for the court to decide subsequently, if proceedings are issued, whether either party had acted unreasonably.

3.19 If the **second party does not object to an expert nominated**, he shall not be entitled to rely on his own expert evidence within that particular speciality unless:

(a) the first party agrees,

(b) the court so directs, or

(c) the first party's expert report has been amended and the first party is not prepared to disclose the original report.

3.20 Either party may send to an agreed expert written questions on the report, relevant to the issues, via the first party's solicitors. The expert should send answers to the questions separately and directly to each party.

3.21 The cost of a report from an agreed expert will usually be paid by the instructing first party: the costs of the expert replying to questions will usually be borne by the party which asks the questions.

4.

Rehabilitation

4.1 The claimant or the defendant or both shall consider as early as possible whether the claimant has reasonable needs that could be met by rehabilitation treatment or other measures. **C2–016**

4.2 The parties shall consider, in such cases, how those needs might be addressed. The Rehabilitation Code (which is attached at Annex D) may be helpful in considering how to identify the claimant's needs and how to address the cost of providing for those needs.

4.3 The time limit set out in paragraph 3.7 of this Protocol shall not be shortened, except by consent to allow these issues to be addressed.

4.4 The provision of any report obtained for the purposes of assessment of provision of a party's rehabilitation needs shall not be used in any litigation arising out of the accident, the subject of the claim, save by consent and shall in any event be exempt from the provisions of paragraphs 3.15 to 3.21 inclusive of this protocol.

5.

Resolution of Issues

5.1 Where the defendant admits liability in whole or in part, before proceedings are issued, any medical reports obtained under this protocol on which a party relies should be disclosed to the other **C2–017**

party. The claimant should delay issuing proceedings for 21 days from disclosure of the report (unless such delay would cause his claim to become time-barred), to enable the parties to consider whether the claim is capable of settlement.

5.2 The Civil Procedure Rules, Part 36 permit claimants and defendants to make offers to settle pre-proceedings. Parties should always consider before issuing if it is appropriate to make Part 36 offer. If such an offer is made, the party making the offer must always supply sufficient evidence and/or information to enable the offer to be properly considered.

5.3 Where the defendant has admitted liability, the claimant should send to the defendant schedules of special damages and loss at least 21 days before proceedings are issued (unless that would cause the claimant's claim to become time-barred).

Annex A

Letter of Claim

C2–018 To

Defendant

Dear Sirs

Re: Claimant's full name
Claimant's full address
Claimant's Clock or Works Number
Claimant's Employer (name and address)

We are instructed by the above named to claim damages in connection with an ***accident at work/road traffic accident/tripping accident*** on day of ***(year)*** at ***(place of accident which must be sufficiently detailed to establish location)***

Please confirm the identity of your insurers. Please note that the insurers will need to see this letter as soon as possible and it may affect your insurance cover and/or the conduct of any subsequent legal proceedings if you do not send this letter to them.

The circumstances of the accident are:–
(brief outline)

The reason why we are alleging fault is:
(simple explanation, e.g. defective machine, broken ground)

A description of our clients' injuries is as follows:–
(brief outline)

(In cases of road traffic accidents)

Our client (state hospital reference number) received treatment for the injuries at (name and address of hospital).

Our client is still suffering from the effects of his/her injury. We invite you to participate with us in addressing his/her immediate needs by use of rehabilitation.

He is employed as ***(occupation)*** and has had the following time off work ***(dates of absence)***. His approximate weekly income is (insert if known).

If you are our client's employers, please provide us with the usual earnings details which will enable us to calculate his financial loss.

We are obtaining a police report and will let you have a copy of the same upon your undertaking to meet half the fee.

We have also sent a letter of claim to ***(name and address)*** and a copy of that letter is attached. We understand their insurers are ***(name, address and claims number if known).***

At this stage of our enquiries we would expect the documents contained in parts ***(insert appropriate parts of standard disclosure list)*** to be relevant to this action.

Please note that we have entered into a conditional fee agreement with our client dated in relation to this claim which provides for a success fee within the meaning of section 58(2) of the Courts and Legal Services Act 1990. Our client has taken out an insurance policy with [name of insurance company] of [address of insurance company] to which section 29 of the Access Justice Act 1999 applies. The policy number is and the policy is dated . Where the funding arrangement is an insurance policy, the party must state the name and address of the insurer, the policy number and the date of the policy, and must identify the claim or claims to which it relates (including Part 20 claims if any).

A copy of this letter is attached for you to send to your insurers. Finally we expect an acknowledgment of this letter within 21 days by yourselves or your insurers.

Yours faithfully

Annex B

Pre-Action Personal Injury Protocol Standard Disclosure Lists

Fast Track Disclosure

RTA Cases

Section A:

In all cases where liability is at issue—

(i) Documents identifying nature, extent and location of damage to defendant's vehicle where there is any dispute about point of impact. **C2–019**

(ii) MOT certificate where relevant.

(iii) Maintenance records where vehicle defect is alleged or it is alleged by defendant that there was an unforeseen defect which caused or contributed to the accident.

Section B:

Accident involving commercial vehicle as potential defendant—

(i) Tachograph charts or entry from individual control book.

(ii) Maintenance and repair records required for operators' licence where vehicle defect is alleged or it is alleged by defendant that there was an unforeseen defect which caused or contributed to the accident.

Section C:

Cases against local authorities where highway design defect is alleged

(i) Documents produced to comply with Section 39 of the Road Traffic Act 1988 in respect of the duty designed to promote road safety to include studies into road accidents in the relevant area and documents relating to measures recommended to prevent accidents in the relevant area.

Highway Tripping Claims

C2–020 Documents from Highway Authority for a period of 12 months prior to the accident:

(i) Records of inspection for the relevant stretch of highway.

(ii) Maintenance records including records of independent contractors working in relevant area.

(iii) Records of the minutes of Highway Authority meetings where maintenance or repair policy has been discussed or decided.

(iv) Records of complaints about the state of highways.

(v) Records of other accidents which have occurred on the relevant stretch of highway.

Workplace Claims

C2–021 (i) Accident book entry.

(ii) First aider report.

(iii) Surgery record.

(iv) Foreman/supervisor accident report.

(v) Safety representatives accident report.

(vi) RIDDOR (Reporting of Injuries, Diseases and Dangerous Occurrences Regulations) report to HSE.

(vii) Other communications between defendants and HSE.

(viii) Minutes of Health and Safety Committee meeting(s) where accident/matter considered.

(ix) Report to DSS.

(x) Documents listed above relative to any previous accident/matter identified by the claimant and relied upon as proof of negligence.

(xi) Earnings information where defendant is employer.

Documents produced to comply with requirements of the Management of Health and Safety at Work Regulations 1992—

(i) Pre-accident Risk Assessment required by Regulation 3.

(ii) Post-accident Re-Assessment required by Regulation 3.

(iii) Accident Investigation Report prepared in implementing the requirements of Regulations 4, 6 and 9.

(iv) Health Surveillance Records in appropriate cases required by Regulation 5.

(v) Information provided to employees under Regulation 8.

(vi) Documents relating to the employees health and safety training required by Regulation 11.

Workplace Claims—Disclosure where specific regulations apply

Section A:

Workplace (Health Safety and Welfare) Regulations 1992

(i) Repair and maintenance records required by Regulation 5. **C2–022**

(ii) Housekeeping records to comply with the requirements of Regulation 9.

(iii) Hazard warning signs or notices to comply with Regulation 17 (Traffic Routes).

Section B:

Provision and Use of Work Equipment Regulations 1998

(i) Manufacturers' specifications and instructions in respect of relevant work equipment establishing its suitability to comply with Regulation 5.

(ii) Maintenance log/maintenance records required to comply with Regulation 6.

(iii) Documents providing information and instructions to employees to comply with Regulation 8.

(iv) Documents provided to the employee in respect of training for use to comply with Regulation 9.

(v) Any notice, sign or document relied upon as a defence to alleged breaches of Regulations 14 to 18 dealing with controls and control systems.

(vi) Instruction/training documents issued to comply with the requirements of regulation 22 insofar as it deals with maintenance operations where the machinery is not shut down.

(vii) Copies of markings required to comply with Regulation 23.

(viii) Copies of warnings required to comply with Regulation 24.

Section C:

Personal Protective Equipment at Work Regulations 1992

(i) Documents relating to the assessment of the Personal Protective Equipment to comply with Regulation 6.

(ii) Documents relating to the maintenance and replacement of Personal Protective Equipment to comply with Regulation 7.

(iii) Record of maintenance procedures for Personal Protective Equipment to comply with Regulation 7.

(iv) Records of tests and examinations of Personal Protective Equipment to comply with Regulation 7.

(v) Documents providing information, instruction and training in relation to the Personal Protective Equipment to comply with Regulation 9.

(vi) Instructions for use of Personal Protective Equipment to include the manufacturers' instructions to comply with Regulation 10.

Section D:

Manual Handling Operations Regulations 1992

(i) Manual Handling Risk Assessment carried out to comply with the requirements of Regulation 4(1)(b)(i).

(ii) Re-assessment carried out post-accident to comply with requirements of Regulation 4(1)(b)(i).

(iii) Documents showing the information provided to the employee to give general indications related to the load and precise indications on the weight of the load and the heaviest side of the load if the centre of gravity was not positioned centrally to comply with Regulation 4(1)(b)(iii).

(iv) Documents relating to training in respect of manual handling operations and training records.

Section E:

Health and Safety (Display Screen Equipment) Regulations 1992

(i) Analysis of work stations to assess and reduce risks carried out to comply with the requirements of Regulation 2.

(ii) Re-assessment of analysis of work stations to assess and reduce risks following development of symptoms by the claimant.

(iii) Documents detailing the provision of training including training records to comply with the requirements of Regulation 6.

(iv) Documents providing information to employees to comply with the requirements of Regulation 7.

Section F:

Control of Substances Hazardous to Health Regulations 1999

(i) Risk assessment carried out to comply with the requirements of Regulation 6.

(ii) Reviewed risk assessment carried out to comply with the requirements of Regulation 6.

(iii) Copy labels from containers used for storage handling and disposal of carcinogenics to comply with the requirements of Regulation 7(2A)(h).

(iv) Warning signs identifying designation of areas and installations which may be contaminated by carcinogenics to comply with the requirements of Regulation 7(2A)(h).

(v) Documents relating to the assessment of the Personal Protective Equipment to comply with Regulation 7(3A).

(vi) Documents relating to the maintenance and replacement of Personal Protective Equipment to comply with Regulation 7(3A).

(vii) Record of maintenance procedures for Personal Protective Equipment to comply with Regulation 7(3A).

(viii) Records of tests and examinations of Personal Protective Equipment to comply with Regulation 7(3A).

(ix) Documents providing information, instruction and training in relation to the Personal Protective Equipment to comply with Regulation 7(3A).

(x) Instructions for use of Personal Protective Equipment to include the manufacturers' instructions to comply with Regulation 7(3A).

(xi) Air monitoring records for substances assigned a maximum exposure limit or occupational exposure standard to comply with the requirements of Regulation 7.

(xii) Maintenance examination and test of control measures records to comply with Regulation 9.

(xiii) Monitoring records to comply with the requirements of Regulation 10.

(xiv) Health surveillance records to comply with the requirements of Regulation 11.

(xv) Documents detailing information, instruction and training including training records for employees to comply with the requirements of Regulation 12.

(xvi) Labels and Health and Safety data sheets supplied to the employers to comply with the CHIP Regulations.

Section G:

Construction (Design and Management) (Amendment) Regulations 2000

(i) Notification of a project form (HSE F10) to comply with the requirements of Regulation 7.

(ii) Health and Safety Plan to comply with requirements of Regulation 15.

(iii) Health and Safety file to comply with the requirements of Regulations 12 and 14.

(iv) Information and training records provided to comply with the requirements of Regulation 17.

(v) Records of advice from and views of persons at work to comply with the requirements of Regulation 18.

Section H:

Pressure Systems and Transportable Gas Containers Regulations 1989

(i) Information and specimen markings provided to comply with the requirements of Regulation 5.

(ii) Written statements specifying the safe operating limits of a system to comply with the requirements of Regulation 7.

(iii) Copy of the written scheme of examination required to comply with the requirements of Regulation 8.

(iv) Examination records required to comply with the requirements of Regulation 9.

(v) Instructions provided for the use of operator to comply with Regulation 11.

(vi) Records kept to comply with the requirements of Regulation 13.

(vii) Records kept to comply with the requirements of Regulation 22.

Section I:

Lifting Operations and Lifting Equipment Regulations 1998

(i) Record kept to comply with the requirements of Regulation 6.

Section J:

The Noise at Work Regulations 1989

(i) Any risk assessment records required to comply with the requirements of Regulations 4 and 5.

(ii) Manufacturers' literature in respect of all ear protection made available to claimant to comply with the requirements of Regulation 8.

(iii) All documents provided to the employee for the provision of information to comply with Regulation 11.

Section K:

Construction (Head Protection) Regulations 1989

(i) Pre-accident assessment of head protection required to comply with Regulation 3(4).

(ii) Post-accident re-assessment required to comply with Regulation 3(5).

Section L:

The Construction (General Provisions) Regulations 1961

(i) Report prepared following inspections and examinations of excavations etc. to comply with the requirements of Regulation 9.

Section M:

Gas Containers Regulations 1989

(i) Information and specimen markings provided to comply with the requirements of Regulation 5.

(ii) Written statements specifying the safe operating limits of a system to comply with the requirements of Regulation 7.

(iii) Copy of the written scheme of examination required to comply with the requirements of Regulation 8.

(iv) Examination records required to comply with the requirements of Regulation 9.

(v) Instructions provided for the use of operator to comply with Regulation 11.

Annex C

Letter of Instruction to Medical Expert

Dear Sir, C2–023

Re: ***(Name and Address)***

D.O.B. –

Telephone No. –

Date of Accident –

We are acting for the above named in connection with injuries received in an accident which occurred on the above date. The main injuries appear to have been **(main injuries)**.

We should be obliged if you would examine our Client and let us have a full and detailed report dealing with any relevant pre-accident medical history, the injuries sustained, treatment received and present condition, dealing in particular with the capacity for work and giving a prognosis.

It is central to our assessment of the extent of our client's injuries to establish the extent and duration of any continuing disability. Accordingly, in the prognosis section we would ask you to specifically comment on any areas of continuing complaint or disability or impact on daily living. If there is such continuing disability you should comment upon the level of suffering or inconvenience caused and, if you are able, give your view as to when or if the complaint or disability is likely to resolve.

Please send our Client an appointment direct for this purpose. Should you be able to offer a cancellation appointment please contact our Client direct. We confirm we will be responsible for your reasonable fees.

We are obtaining the notes and records from our Client's GP and Hospitals attended and will forward them to you when they are to hand/or please request the GP and Hospital records direct and advise that any invoice for the provision of these records should be forwarded to us.

In order to comply with Court Rules we would be grateful if you would insert above your signature a statement that the contents are true to the best of your knowledge and belief.

In order to avoid further correspondence we can confirm that on the evidence we have there is no reason to suspect we may be pursuing a claim against the hospital or its staff.

We look forward to receiving your report within weeks. If you will not be able to prepare your report within this period please telephone us upon receipt of these instructions.

When acknowledging these instructions it would assist if you could give an estimate as to the likely time scale for the provision of your report and also an indication as to your fee.

Yours faithfully

Annex D

The Rehabilitation Code

C2–024 The main aim of this Code, first introduced in 1999, is to promote the use of rehabilitation and early intervention in the claims process so that the injured person makes the best and quickest possible medical, social and psychological recovery. This objective applies whatever the severity of the injury sustained by the claimant. The Code provides a framework supported by all the main associations for insurers and personal injury lawyers in the UK, but is neither compulsory nor the only way to approach rehabilitation. The objectives of the Rehabilitation Code will be met whenever the parties co-operate to assess and then provide for the claimant's rehabilitation needs.

1. Introduction

1.1 It is recognised that, in many claims for damages for personal injuries, the claimant's current medical situation, and/or the long-term prognosis, may be improved by appropriate medical treatment, including surgery, being given at the earliest practicable opportunity, rather than waiting until the claim has been settled. Similarly, claims may involve a need for non-medical treatment, such as physiotherapy, counselling, occupational therapy, speech therapy and so forth ("rehabilitation"): again, there is a benefit in these services being provided as early as practicable.

1.2 It is also recognised that (predominantly in cases of serious injury) the claimant's quality of life can be immediately improved by undertaking some basic home adaptations and/or by the provision of aids and equipment and/or appropriate medical treatment as soon as these are needed ("early intervention"), rather than when the claim is finally settled.

1.3 It is further recognised that, where these medical or other issues have been dealt with, there may be employment issues that can be addressed for the benefit of the claimant, to enable the claimant to keep his/her existing job, to obtain alternative suitable employment with the same employer or to retrain for new employment. Again, if these needs are addressed at the proper time, the claimant's quality of life and long-term prospects may be greatly improved.

1.4 Solicitors acting for claimants understand that, taking all these matters into account, they can achieve more for the claimant—by making rehabilitation available—than just the payment of compensation. The insurance industry realises that great benefit may be had in considering making funds available for these purposes.

1.5 The aim of this Rehabilitation Code is therefore to ensure that the claimant's solicitor and the insurer (and the insurer's solicitor or handling agent) both actively consider the use of rehabilitation services and the benefits of an early assessment of the claimant's needs. The further aim is that both should treat the possibility of improving the claimant's quality of life and their present and long-term physical and mental well-being as issues equally as important as the payment of just, full and proper compensation.

1.6 The report mentioned in section 6 of the Code focuses on the early assessment of the claimant's needs in terms of treatment and/or rehabilitation. The assessment report is not intended to determine the claimant's long-term needs for care or medical treatment, other than by way of general indication and comment.

2. The Claimant's Solicitor's Duty

2.1 It shall be the duty of every claimant's solicitor to consider, from the earliest practicable stage, and in consultation with the claimant and/or the claimant's family, whether it is likely or possible that early intervention, rehabilitation or medical treatment would improve their present and/or long-term physical or mental well-being. This duty is ongoing throughout the life of the case but is of most importance in the early stages.

2.2 It shall be the duty of a claimant's solicitor to consider, with the claimant and/or the claimant's family, whether there is an immediate need for aids, adaptations or other matters that would seek to alleviate problems caused by disability, and then to communicate with the insurer as soon as practicable about any rehabilitation needs, with a view to putting this Code into effect.

2.3 It shall not be the responsibility of the solicitor to decide on the need for treatment or rehabilitation or to arrange such matters without appropriate medical consultation. Such medical consultation should involve the claimant and/or the claimant's family, the claimant's primary care physician and, where appropriate, any other medical practitioner currently treating the claimant.

2.4 Nothing in this Code shall in any way affect the obligations placed on a claimant's solicitor by the Pre-Action Protocol for Personal Injury Claims ("the Protocol"). However, it must be appreciated that very early communication with the insurer will enable the matters dealt with here to be addressed more effectively.

2.5 It must be recognised that the insurer will need to receive from the claimant's solicitor sufficient information for the insurer to make a proper decision about the need for intervention, rehabilitation or treatment. To this extent, the claimant's solicitor must comply with the requirements of the Protocol to provide the insurer with full and adequate details of the injuries sustained by the claimant, the nature and extent of any, or any likely, continuing disability and any suggestions that may already have been made concerning rehabilitation and/or early intervention. There is no requirement under the Protocol, or this Code, for the claimant's solicitor to have obtained a full medical report. It is recognized that many cases will be identified for consideration under this Code before medical evidence has actually been commissioned.

3. The Insurer

3.1 It shall be the duty of the insurer to consider, from the earliest practicable stage in any appropriate case, whether it is likely that the claimant will benefit in the immediate, medium or longer term from further medical treatment, rehabilitation or early intervention. This duty is ongoing throughout the life of the case but is of most importance in the early stages.

3.2 If the insurer considers that a particular claim might be suitable for intervention, rehabilitation or treatment, the insurer will communicate this to the claimant's solicitor as soon as practicable.

3.3 On receipt of such communication, the claimant's solicitor will immediately discuss these issues with the claimant and/or the claimant's family pursuant to his duty as set out above and, where appropriate, will seek advice from the claimant's treating physicians/surgeons.

3.4 Nothing in this or any other Code of Practice shall in any way modify the obligations of the insurer under the Protocol to investigate claims rapidly and in any event within three months (except where time is extended by the claimant's solicitor) from the date of the formal claim letter. It is recognised that, although the rehabilitation assessment can be done even where liability investigations are outstanding, it is essential that such investigations proceed with the appropriate speed.

4. Assessment

4.1 Unless the need for intervention, rehabilitation or treatment has already been identified by medical reports obtained and disclosed by either side, the need for and extent of such intervention, rehabilitation or treatment will be considered by means of an independent assessment.

4.2 "Independent assessment" in this context means that the assessment will be carried out by either:

a. One or more of the treating physicians/surgeons, or
b. by an agency suitably qualified and/or experienced in such matters, which is financially and managerially independent of the claimant's solicitor's firm and the insurers dealing with the claim.

4.3 It is essential that the process of assessment and recommendation be carried out by those who have an appropriate qualification (to include physiotherapists, occupational therapists, psychologists, psychotherapists and so forth). It would be inappropriate for assessments to be done by someone who does not have a medical or other appropriate qualification. Those doing the assessments should not only have an appropriate qualification but should have experience in treating the type of disability from which the individual claimant suffers.

5. The Assessment Process

5.1 Where possible, the agency to be instructed to provide the assessment should be agreed between the claimant's solicitor and the insurer. The instruction letter will be sent by the claimant's solicitor to the medical agency and a copy of the instruction letter will be sent to the insurer.

5.2 The medical agency will be asked to interview the claimant at home (or in hospital, if the claimant is still in hospital, with a subsequent visit to the claimant's home) and will be asked to produce a report, which covers the following headings:

1. The injuries sustained by the claimant
2. The claimant's present medical condition (medical conditions that do not arise from the accident should also be noted where relevant to the overall picture of the claimant's needs)
3. The claimant's domestic circumstances (including mobility, accommodation and employment), where relevant
4. The injuries/disability in respect of which early intervention or early rehabilitation is suggested
5. The type of intervention or treatment envisaged
6. The likely cost
7. The likely short/medium-term benefit to the claimant

5.3 The report will not deal with diagnostic criteria, causation issues or long-term care requirements.

6. The Assessment Report

6.1 The reporting agency will, on completion of the report, send copies to both the instructing solicitor and the insurer simultaneously. Both parties will have the right to raise queries on the report, disclosing such correspondence to the other party.

6.2 It is recognised that for this independent assessment report to be of benefit to the parties, it should be prepared and used wholly outside the litigation process. Neither side can therefore rely on its contents in any subsequent litigation. With that strict proviso, to be confirmed in writing by the individual solicitor and insurer if required, the report shall be disclosed to both parties.

6.3 The report, any correspondence relating to it and any notes created by the assessing agency will be covered by legal privilege and will not under any circumstances be disclosed in any legal proceedings. Any notes or documents created in connection with the assessment process will not be disclosed in any litigation, and any person involved in the preparation of the report or involved in the assessment process shall not be a compellable witness at court.

6.4 The provision in paragraph 6.3 above as to treating the report, etc. as outside the litigation process is limited to the assessment report and any notes relating to it. Once the parties have agreed, following an assessment report, that a particular regime of rehabilitation or treatment should be put in place, the case management of that regime falls outside this Code and paragraph 6.3 does not therefore apply. Any notes and reports created during the subsequent case management will be governed by the usual principles relating to disclosure of documents and medical records relating to the claimant.

6.5 The insurer will pay for the report within 28 days of receipt.

6.6 The need for any further or subsequent assessment shall be agreed between the claimant's solicitor and the insurer. The provisions of this Code shall apply to such assessments.

7. Recommendations

7.1 When the assessment report is disclosed to the insurer, the insurer will be under a duty to consider the recommendations made and the extent to which funds will be made available to implement all or some of the recommendations. The insurer will not be required to pay for intervention or treatment that is unreasonable in nature, content or cost. The claimant will be under no obligation to undergo intervention, medical investigation or treatment that is unreasonable in all the circumstances of the case.

7.2 Any funds made available shall be treated as an interim payment on account of damages. However, if the funds are provided to enable specific intervention, rehabilitation or treatment to occur, the insurers warrant that they *will not, in any legal proceedings* connected with the claim, dispute the reasonableness of that treatment nor the agreed cost, provided of course that the claimant has had the recommended treatment.

General note

The first edition of the above Code was introduced in October 1999 as part of the Second UK Bodily Injury Study through the joint efforts of The Association of Personal Injury Lawyers, the Forum of Insurance Lawyers, the Association of British Insurers and the International Underwriting Association of London. The Code is voluntary, and provides a procedural framework for dealing with rehabilitation. It places a duty on both sides of a claim consider rehabilitation at a very early stage. C2–025

The first edition was greeted with support from the Lord Chancellor, recorded in Hansard at October 26, 1999, Lords 168:

"The Lord Chancellor: ... First, perhaps I may take this opportunity to welcome as a first-class initiative the new code on rehabilitation, ... It is highly progressive to put a duty on both solicitors—the solicitor for the claimant and the insurer's solicitor-to make an early assessment of how the quality of the victim's life can be improved by early intervention, medical treatment or rehabilitation. Appropriate medical treatment as early as possible as well as non-medical treatment—for example, psychotherapy, occupational therapy and counselling—can be critical to rehabilitation."

Guide to the Code

The Bodily Injury Claims Management Group has published a practitioner's guide to the Code which can be found at *http://www.bicma.org.uk/pguide.php* [Accessed March 30, 2007]. C2–026

The Clinical Negligence Protocol

This protocol was in place in April 1999 with the implementation of the CPR. The Clinical Disputes Forum (the CDF) has kept it under review (see the main editorial). No changes have been made to the protocol as at January 2003. Some are likely in the next year, including a requirement to notify the other party of a conditional fee agreement (but not the success fee or the amount of any insurance premium) in the letter of claim or response, or within 7 days of entering into the agreement. C3A–001

Scope and content

The protocol includes more background material and general guidance than the personal injury protocol, particularly in relation to the need for patients and health-care providers to be more open at an early stage, and sets out a series of "commitments" by both sides in an attempt to develop a climate of trust. C3A–002

The protocol is intended to apply to all potential medical negligence claims, regardless of their value: most clinical disputes are likely to be allocated to Multi-Track in any event because of their complexity.

Other differences from the personal injury protocol include:

- the defendant has 14, rather than 21 days to acknowledge the letter of claim (para.3.4);
- it is accepted that the 3 month response time may need to be extended when the defendant's investigations are complex, e.g. witnesses who have moved hospitals;
- the protocol incorporates as an annex (Annex B) forms for requesting medical records from the defendant and other health care providers who have treated the claimant (the forms were originally published by the Law Society in 1995, and have been endorsed by the Department of Health) and recommends that health care providers consider the more serious adverse incident which prompt requests for records (paras 3.7–3.13) that offers to settle should be accompanied by medical evidence and supporting documents (para.3.22);
- the protocol is not as prescriptive on the instruction of experts, recognising that expert evidence on liability and causation will often be crucial to the outcome of a clinical negligence claim, and requiring parties to "share" this expert evidence would not be practicable especially pre-action (Section 4). The courts have endorsed this in *Oxley v Penwarden* [2001] C.P.L.R. 1, CA and in *S (a minor) v Birmingham Health Authority* TLR, November 23 1999 in particular (see also the editorial to Pt 35 at para.35.7.1));
- there is encouragement to consider alternatives to litigation to resolve the matter, particularly the NHS complaints procedure, and mediation which has been effective in resolving some clinical negligence cases (Section 5).

The impact of the protocol and issues arising from research

The CDF carried out a survey of users of the protocol in 2001 in the light of two C3A–003 years' experience. The responses were very positive and respondents felt that the main objectives of the protocol were being met. Very few changes to the text were suggested. The Law Society/Civil Justice Council research into pre-action behaviour (*"More Civil Justice? The impact of the Woolf reforms on pre-action behaviour"*, Research Study 43, LCD, T. Goriely, R. Moorhead and P. Abrams) also interviewed users and looked at files in a selection of clinical negligence cases. They also found a high level of satisfaction with the impact of the protocol particularly in improving the climate of trust, and the quality of letters of claim and response.

The Civil Justice Council research identified as possible issues:

- that the provisions concerning the release of medical records should be reviewed. The CDF is suggesting that copy records should be provided in accordance with the Data Protection Act as well as the Access to Health Records Act, disclosable documents may include those created by the health care provider in relation to an adverse incident or complaint (the claimant's solicitor needs to ask for these), and if the claimant has relevant 'third party' health records, copies should be provided to the defendant within 40 days of a request;
- to consider whether the protocol should emphasise the importance of setting out the claimant's case on causation—the CDF is recommending that the protocol clarifies that the letter of claim should indicate the nature of alleged breaches of duty and their causative effect;
- to consider whether there should be further guidance on when schedules of loss and supporting evidence should be provided with the letter of claim—the CDF is suggesting that claimants should disclose details of injuries and losses early in lower value claims;
- to consider formulating specific guidance to experts on their role as single joint experts. The CDF has drafted separately from the protocol some guidelines to lawyers on instructing single joint experts, which will be sent to the LCD once the results of the consultation have been considered.

PRE-ACTION PROTOCOL FOR THE RESOLUTION OF CLINICAL DISPUTES

Clinical Disputes Forum Executive Summary

C3–001 **1** The Clinical Disputes Forum is a multi-disciplinary body which was formed in 1997, as a result of Lord Woolf's "Access to Justice" inquiry. One of the aims of the Forum is to find less adversarial and more cost-effective ways of resolving disputes about healthcare and medical treatment. The names and addresses of the Chairman and Secretary of the Forum can be found at Annex E.

2 This protocol is the Forum's first major initiative. It has been drawn up carefully, including extensive consultations with most of the key stakeholders in the medico-legal system.

3 The protocol—

- encourages a climate of openness when something has "gone wrong" with a patient's treatment or the patient is dissatisfied with that treatment and/or the outcome. This reflects the new and developing requirements for clinical governance within healthcare;
- provides **general guidance** on how this more open culture might be achieved when disputes arise;
- recommends **a timed sequence** of steps for patients and healthcare providers, and their advisers, to follow when a dispute arises. This should facilitate and speed up exchanging relevant information and increase the prospects that disputes can be resolved without resort to legal action.

4 This protocol has been prepared by a working party of the Clinical Disputes Forum. It has the support of the Lord Chancellor's Department, the Department of Health and NHS Executive, the Law Society, the Legal Aid Board and many other key organisations.

1.

Why This Protocol?

Mistrust in Healthcare Disputes

1.1 The number of complaints and claims against hospitals, GPs, dentists and private healthcare providers is growing as patients become more prepared to question the treatment they are given, to seek explanations of what happened, and to seek appropriate redress. Patients may require further treatment, an apology, assurances about future action, or compensation. These trends are unlikely to change. The Patients Charter encourages patients to have high expectations, and a revised NHS Complaints Procedure was implemented in 1996. The Civil Justice Reforms and new Rules of Court should make litigation quicker, more user friendly and less expensive. **C3–002**

1.2 It is clearly in the interests of patients, healthcare professionals and providers that patients' concerns, complaints and claims arising from their treatment are resolved as quickly, efficiently and professionally as possible. A climate of mistrust and lack of openness can seriously damage the patient/clinician relationship, unnecessarily prolong disputes (especially litigation), and reduce the resources available for treating patients. It may also cause additional work for, and lower the morale of, healthcare professionals.

1.3 At present there is often mistrust by both sides. This can mean that patients fail to raise their concerns with the healthcare provider as early as possible. Sometimes patients may pursue a complaint or claim which has little merit, due to a lack of sufficient information and understanding. It can also mean that patients become reluctant, once advice has been taken on a potential claim, to disclose sufficient information to enable the provider to investigate that claim efficiently and, where appropriate, resolve it.

1.4 On the side of the healthcare provider this mistrust can be shown in a reluctance to be honest with patients, a failure to provide prompt clear explanations, especially of adverse outcomes (whether or not there may have been negligence) and a tendency to "close ranks" once a claim is made.

What Needs to Change

1.5 If that mistrust is to be removed, and a more co-operative culture is to develop— **C3–003**

- healthcare professionals and providers need to adopt a constructive approach to complaints and claims. They should accept that concerned patients are entitled to an explanation and an apology, if warranted, and to appropriate redress in the event of negligence. An overly defensive approach is not in the long term interest of their main goal: patient care;
- patients should recognise that unintended and/or unfortunate

consequences of medical treatment can only be rectified if they are brought to the attention of the healthcare provider as soon as possible.

1.6 A protocol which sets out "ground rules" for the handling of disputes at their early stages should, if it is to be subscribed to, and followed—

- encourage greater openness between the parties;
- encourage parties to find the most appropriate way of resolving the particular dispute;
- reduce delay and costs;
- reduce the need for litigation.

Why This Protocol Now?

C3–004 **1.7** Lord Woolf in his "Access to Justice" report in July 1996, concluded that major causes of costs and delay in medical negligence litigation occur at the pre-action stage. He recommended that patients and their advisers, and healthcare providers, should work more closely together to try to resolve disputes co-operatively, rather than proceed to litigation. He specifically recommended a pre-action protocol for medical negligence cases.

1.8 A fuller summary of Lord Woolf's recommendations is at Annex D.

Where the Protocol Fits In

C3–005 **1.9** Protocols serve the needs of litigation and pre-litigation practice, especially—

- predictability in the time needed for steps pre-proceedings;
- standardisation of relevant information, including records and documents to be disclosed.

1.10 Building upon Lord Woolf's recommendations, the Lord Chancellor's Department is now promoting the adoption of protocols in specific areas, including medical negligence.

1.11 It is recognised that contexts differ significantly. For example: patients tend to have an ongoing relationship with a GP, more so than with a hospital; clinical staff in the National Health Service are often employees, while those in the private sector may be contractors; providing records quickly may be relatively easy for GPs and dentists, but can be a complicated procedure in a large multi-department hospital. The protocol which follows is intended to be sufficiently broadly based, and flexible, to apply to all aspects of the health service: primary and secondary; public and private sectors.

Enforcement of the Protocol and Sanctions

C3–006 **1.12** The civil justice reforms will be implemented in April 1999. One new set of Court Rules and procedures is replacing the existing rules for both the High and county courts. This and the personal injury protocols are being published with the Rules, Practice Directions and key court forms. The courts will be able to treat the standards set in protocols as the normal reasonable approach to pre-action conduct.

1.13 If proceedings are issued it will be for the court to decide whether non-compliance with a protocol should merit sanctions.

Guidance on the court's likely approach will be given from time to time in practice directions.

1.14 If the court has to consider the question of compliance after proceedings have begun it will not be concerned with minor infringements, e.g. failure by a short period to provide relevant information. One minor breach will not entitle the "innocent" party to abandon following the protocol. The court will look at the effect of non-compliance on the other party when deciding whether to impose sanctions.

2.

The Aims of the Protocol

2.1 The **general** aims of the protocol are— **C3–007**

- to maintain/restore the patient/healthcare provider relationship;
- to resolve as many disputes as possible without litigation.

2.2 The **specific** objectives are—

Openness

- to encourage early communication of the perceived problem between patients and healthcare providers; **C3–008**
- to encourage patients to voice any concerns or dissatisfaction with their treatment as soon as practicable;
- to encourage healthcare providers to develop systems of early reporting and investigation for serious adverse treatment outcomes and to provide full and prompt explanations to dissatisfied patients;
- to ensure that sufficient information is disclosed by both parties to enable each to understand the other's perspective and case, and to encourage early resolution.

Timeliness

- to provide an early opportunity for healthcare providers to identify cases where an investigation is required and to carry out that investigation promptly; **C3–009**
- to encourage primary and private healthcare providers to involve their defence organisations or insurers at an early stage;
- To ensure that all relevant medical records are provided to patients or their appointed representatives on request, to a realistic timetable by any healthcare provider;
- to ensure that relevant records which are not in healthcare *providers'* possession are made available to them by patients and their advisers at an appropriate stage;
- where a resolution is not achievable to lay the ground to enable litigation to proceed on a reasonable timetable, at a reasonable and proportionate cost and to limit the matters in contention;
- to discourage the prolonged pursuit of unmeritorious claims and the prolonged defence of meritorious claims.

Awareness of Options

C3–010 • to ensure that patients and healthcare providers are made aware of the available options to pursue and resolve disputes on what each might involve.

2.3 This protocol does not attempt to be prescriptive about a number of related clinical governance issues which will have a bearing on healthcare providers' ability to meet the standards within the protocol. Good clinical governance requires the following to be considered—

(a) **Clinical risk management:** the protocol does not provide any detailed guidance to healthcare providers on clinical risk management or the adoption of risk management systems and procedures. This must be a matter for the NHS Executive, the National Health Service Litigation Authority, individual trusts and providers, including GPs, dentists and the private sector. However, effective co-ordinated, focused clinical risk management strategies and procedures can help in managing risk and in the early identification and investigation of adverse outcomes.

(b) **Adverse outcome reporting:** the protocol does not provide any detailed guidance on which adverse outcomes should trigger an investigation. However, healthcare providers should have in place procedures for such investigations, including recording of statements of key witnesses. These procedures should also cover when and how to inform patients that an adverse outcome has occurred.

(c) **The professional's duty to report:** the protocol does not recommend changes to the codes of conduct of professionals in healthcare, or attempt to impose a specific duty to those professionals to report known adverse outcomes or untoward incidents. Lord Woolf in his final report suggested that the professional bodies might consider this. The General Medical Council is preparing guidance to doctors about their duty to report adverse incidents and to co-operate with inquiries.

3.

The Protocol

C3–011 **3.1** This protocol is not a comprehensive code governing all the steps in clinical disputes. Rather it attempts to set out **a code of good practice** which parties should follow when litigation might be a possibility.

3.2 The **commitments** section of the protocol summarises the guiding principles which healthcare providers and patients and their advisers are invited to endorse when dealing with patient dissatisfaction with treatment and its outcome, and with potential complaints and claims.

3.3 The **steps** section sets out, in a more prescriptive form, a recommended sequence of actions to be followed if litigation is a prospect.

Good Practice Commitments

3.4 Healthcare providers should— C3–012

(i) ensure that **key staff**, including claims and litigation managers, are appropriately trained and have some knowledge of healthcare law, and of complaints procedures and civil litigation practice and procedure;

(ii) develop an approach to **clinical governance** that ensures that clinical practice is delivered to commonly accepted standards and that this is routinely monitored through a system of clinical audit and clinical risk management (particularly adverse outcome investigation);

(iii) set up **adverse outcome reporting systems** in all specialties to record and investigate unexpected serious adverse outcomes as soon as possible. Such systems can enable evidence to be gathered quickly, which makes it easier to provide an accurate explanation of what happened and to defend or settle any subsequent claims;

(iv) use the results of **adverse incidents and complaints positively** as a guide to how to improve services to patients in the future;

(v) ensure **that patients receive clear and comprehensible information** in an accessible form about how to raise their concerns or complaints;

(vi) establish **efficient and effective systems of recording and storing patient records**, notes, diagnostic reports and X-rays, and to retain these in accordance with Department of Health guidance (currently for a minimum of eight years in the case of adults, and all obstetric and paediatric notes for children until they reach the age of 25);

(vii) **advise patients** of a serious adverse outcome and provide on request to the patient or the patient's representative an oral or written explanation of what happened, information on further steps open to the patient, including where appropriate an offer of future treatment to rectify the problem, an apology, changes in procedure which will benefit patients and/or compensation.

***3.5 Patients* and their advisers** should—

(i) **report any concerns and dissatisfaction** to the healthcare provider as soon as is reasonable to enable that provider to offer clinical advice where possible, to advise the patient if anything has gone wrong and take appropriate action;

(ii) consider the **full range of options** available following an adverse outcome with which a patient is dissatisfied,

PRE-ACTION PROTOCOLS

including a request for an explanation, a meeting, a complaint, and other appropriate dispute resolution methods (including mediation) and negotiation, not only litigation;

(iii) **inform the healthcare provider when the patient is satisfied** that the matter has been concluded: legal advisers should notify the provider when they are no longer acting for the patient, particularly if proceedings have not started.

Protocol Steps

C3–013 **3.6** The steps of this protocol which follow have been kept deliberately simple. An illustration of the likely sequence of events in a number of healthcare situations is at Annex A.

Obtaining the Health Records

C3–014 **3.7** Any request for records by the **patient** or their adviser should—

- **provide sufficient information** to alert the healthcare provider where an adverse outcome has been serious or had serious consequences;
- be as **specific as possible** about the records which are required.

3.8 Requests for copies of the patient's clinical records should be made using the Law Society and Department of Health approved **standard forms** (enclosed at Annex B), adapted as necessary.

3.9 The copy records should be provided **within 40 days** of the request and for a cost not exceeding the charges permissible under the Access to Health Records Act 1990 (currently a maximum of £10 plus photocopying and postage).

3.10 In the rare circumstances that the healthcare provider is in difficulty in complying with the request within 40 days, the **problem should be explained** quickly and details given of what is being done to resolve it.

3.11 It will not be practicable for healthcare providers to investigate in detail each case when records are requested. But healthcare providers should **adopt a policy on which cases will be investigated** (see paragraph 3.5 on clinical governance and adverse outcome reporting).

3.12 If the healthcare provider fails to provide the health records within 40 days, the patient or their adviser can then apply to the court for an **order for pre-action disclosure**. The new Civil Procedure Rules should make pre-action applications to the court easier. The Court will also have the power to impose costs sanctions for unreasonable delay in providing records.

3.13 If either the patient or the healthcare provider considers **additional health records are required from a third party**, in the first instance these should be requested by or through the patient. Third party healthcare providers are expected to co-operate. The Civil Procedure Rules will enable patients and healthcare providers to apply to the court for *pre-action disclosure* by third parties.

Letter of Claim

C3–015 **3.14** Annex C1 to this protocol provides **a template for the recom-**

mended contents of a letter of claim: the level of detail will need to be varied to suit the particular circumstances.

3.15 If, following the receipt and analysis of the records, and the receipt of any further advice (including from experts if necessary—see Section 4), the patient/adviser decides that there are grounds for a claim, they should then send, as soon as practicable, to the healthcare provider/potential defendant, a **letter of claim**.

3.16 This letter should contain a **clear summary of the facts** on which the claim is based, including the alleged adverse outcome, and the **main allegations of negligence**. It should also describe the **patient's injuries**, and present condition and prognosis. The **financial loss** incurred by the plaintiff should be outlined with an indication of the heads of damage to be claimed and the scale of the loss, unless this is impracticable.

3.17 In more complex cases a **chronology** of the relevant events should be provided, particularly if the patient has been treated by a number of different healthcare providers.

3.18 The letter of claim **should refer to any relevant documents**, including health records, and if possible enclose copies of any of those which will not already be in the potential defendant's possession, e.g. any relevant general practitioner records if the plaintiff's claim is against a hospital.

3.19 Sufficient information must be given to enable the healthcare provider defendant to **commence investigations** and to put an initial valuation on the claim.

3.20 Letters of claim are **not** intended to have the same formal status as a **pleading**, nor should any sanctions necessarily apply if the letter of claim and any subsequent statement of claim in the proceedings differ.

3.21 Proceedings should not be issued until after three months from the letter of claim, unless there is a limitation problem and/or the patient's position needs to be protected by early issue.

3.22 The patient or their adviser may want to make an **offer to settle** the claim at this early stage by putting forward an amount of compensation which would be satisfactory (possibly including any costs incurred to date). If an offer to settle is made, generally this should be supported by a medical report which deals with the injuries, condition and prognosis, and by a schedule of loss and supporting documentation. The level of detail necessary will depend on the value of the claim. Medical reports may not be necessary where there is no significant continuing injury, and a detailed schedule may not be necessary in a low value case. The Civil Procedure Rules are expected to set out the legal and procedural requirements for making offers to settle.

The Response

3.23 Attached at Annex C2 is a template for the suggested contents of the **letter of response**. **C3–016**

3.24 The healthcare provider should **acknowledge** the letter of claim **within 14 days of receipt** and should identify who will be dealing with the matter.

3.25 The heathcare provider should, **within three months** of the letter of claim, provide a **reasoned answer**—

- if the **claim is admitted** the healthcare provider should say so in clear terms;
- if only **part of the claim is admitted** the healthcare provider should make clear which issues of breach of duty and/or causation are admitted and which are denied and why;
- if it is intended that any **admissions will be binding**;
- if the claim is denied this should include specific comments on the allegations of negligence, and if a synopsis or chronology of relevant events has been provided and is disputed, the healthcare provider's version of those events;
- where additional documents are relied upon, e.g. an internal protocol, copies should be provided.

3.26 If the patient has made an offer to settle, the healthcare provider should **respond to that offer** in the response letter, preferably with reasons. The provider may make its own offer to settle at this stage, either as a counter-offer to the patient's, or of its own accord, but should accompany any offer by any supporting medical evidence, and/or by any other evidence in relation to the value of the claim which is in the healthcare provider's possession.

3.27 If the parties reach agreement on liability, but time is needed to resolve the value of the claim, they should aim to agree a reasonable period.

4.

Experts

C3-017 **4.1** In clinical negligence disputes **expert opinions** may be needed:

- on breach of duty and causation
- on the patient's condition and prognosis
- to assist in valuing aspects of the claim

4.2 The civil justice reforms and the new Civil Procedure Rules will encourage economy in the use of experts and a **less adversarial expert culture**. It is recognised that in clinical negligence disputes, the parties and their advisers will require flexibility in their approach to expert evidence. Decisions on whether experts might be instructed jointly, and on whether reports might be disclosed sequentially or by exchange, should rest with the parties and their advisers. Sharing expert evidence may be appropriate on issues relating to the value of the claim. However, this protocol does not attempt to be prescriptive on issues in relation to expert evidence.

4.3 Obtaining expert evidence will often be an expensive step and may take time, especially in specialised areas of medicine where there are limited numbers of suitable experts. Patients and healthcare providers, and their advisers, will therefore need to consider carefully how best to obtain any necessary expert help quickly and cost-effectively. Assistance with locating a suitable expert is available from a number of sources.

5.

Alternative Dispute Resolution

5.1 The parties should consider whether some form of alternative dispute resolution procedure would be more suitable than litigation, and if so, endeavour to agree which form to adopt. Both the Claimant and Defendant may be required by the Court to provide evidence that alternative means of resolving their dispute were considered. The Courts take the view that litigation should be a last resort, and that claims should not be issued prematurely when a settlement is still actively being explored. Parties are warned that if the protocol is not followed (including this paragraph) then the Court must have regard to such conduct when determining costs. **C3–018**

5.2 It is not practicable in this protocol to address in detail how the parties might decide which method to adopt to resolve their particular dispute. However, summarised below are some of the options for resolving disputes without litigation:

- Discussion and negotiation. Parties should bear in mind that carefully planned face-to-face meetings may be particularly helpful in exploring further treatment for the patient, in reaching understandings about what happened, and on both parties' positions, in narrowing the issues in dispute and, if the timing is right, in helping to settle the whole matter especially if the patient wants an apology, explanation, or assurances about how other patients will be affected.
- Early neutral evaluation by an independent third party (for example, a lawyer experienced in the field of clinical negligence or an individual experienced in the subject matter of the claim).
- Mediation—a form of facilitated negotiation assisted by an independent neutral party. The Clinical Disputes Forum has published a Guide to Mediation which will assist—available on the Clinical Disputes Forum website at *www.clinical-disputes-forum.org.uk*.
- The **NHS Complaints Procedure** is designed to provide patients with an explanation of what happened and an apology if appropriate. It is not designed to provide compensation for cases of negligence. However, patients might choose to use the procedure if their only, or main, goal is to obtain an explanation, or to obtain more information to help them decide what other action might be appropriate.

5.3 The Legal Services Commission has published a booklet on "Alternatives to Court", CLS Direct Information Leaflet 23 (*www.clsdirect.org.uk/legalhelp/leaflet23.jsp*), which lists a number of organisations that provide alternative dispute resolution services.

5.4 *It is expressly recognised that no party can or should be forced to mediate or enter into any form of ADR.*

C3–018.1

Annex A

Illustrative Flowchart

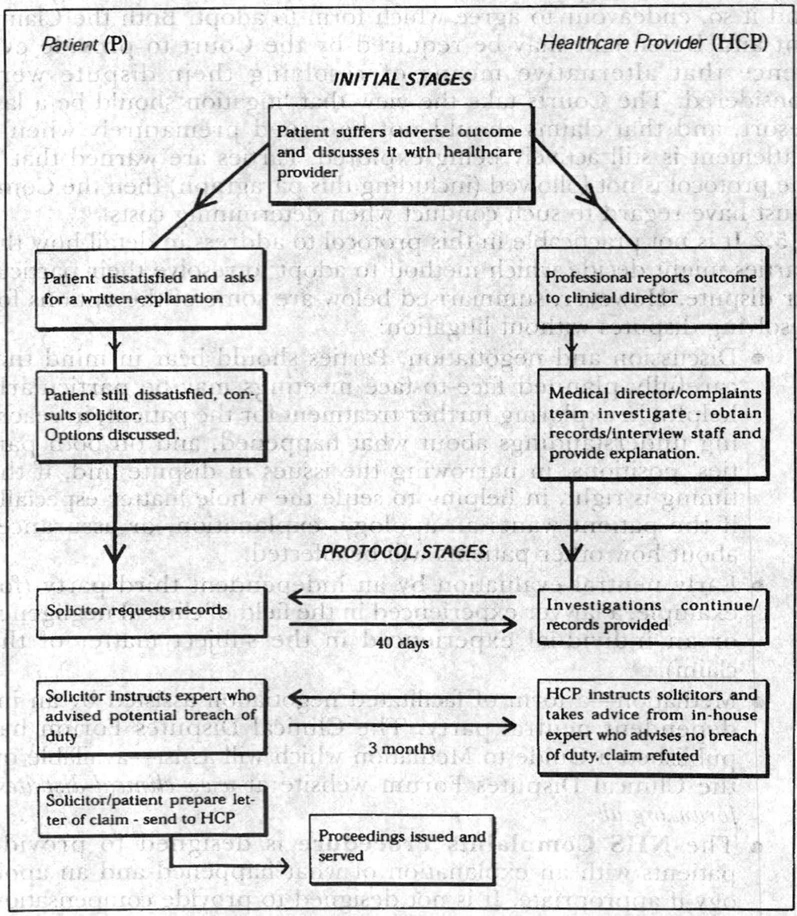

Annex B

Medical Negligence and Personal Injury Claims

A PROTOCOL FOR OBTAINING HOSPITAL MEDICAL RECORDS

Application on Behalf of a Patient for Hospital Medical Records for Use When Court Proceedings Are Contemplated

Purpose of the Forms

C3–019 This application form and response forms have been prepared by a working party of the Law Society's Civil Litigation Committee and approved by the Department of Health for use in NHS and Trust hospitals. The purpose of the forms is to standardise and streamline the disclosure of medical records to a patient's solicitors, who are investigating pursuing a personal injury claim against a third party, or a medical negligence claim against the hospital to which the application is addressed and/or other hospitals or general practitioners.

Use of the Forms

Use of the forms is entirely voluntary and does not prejudice any party's right under the Access to Health Records Act 1990, the Data Protection Act 1984, or ss.33 and 34 of the Supreme Court Act 1981. However, it is the Department of Health policy that patients be permitted to see what has been written about them, and that healthcare providers should make arrangements to allow patients to see all their records, not only those covered by the Access to Health Records Act 1990. The aim of the forms is to save time and costs for all concerned for the benefit of the patient and the hospital and in the interests of justice. Use of the forms should make it unnecessary in most cases for there to be exchanges of letters or other enquiries. If there is any unusual matter not covered by the form, the patient's solicitor may write a separate letter at the outset.

Charges for Records

The Access to Health Records Act 1990 prescribes a maximum fee of £10. Photocopying and postage costs can be charged in addition. No other charges may be made. The NHS Executive guidance makes it clear to healthcare providers that "it is a perfectly proper use" of the 1990 Act to request records in that framework for the purpose of potential or actual litigation, whether against a third party or against the hospital or trust. The 1990 Act does not permit differential rates of charges to be levied if the application is made by the patient, or by a solicitor on his or her behalf, or whether the response to the application is made by the healthcare provider directly (the medical records manager or a claims manager) or by a solicitor. The NHS Executive guidance recommend that the same practice should be followed with regard to charges when the records are provided under a voluntary agreement as under the 1990 Act, except that in those circumstances the £10 access fee will not be appropriate.

The NHS Executive Also Advises—

- that the cost of photocopying may include "the cost of staff time in making copies" and the costs of running the copier (but not costs of locating and sifting records).
- that the common practice of setting a standard rate for an application or charging an administration fee is not acceptable because there will be cases when this fails to comply with the 1990 Act.

Records: What Might Be Included

X-rays and test results form part of the patient's records. Additional charges for copying X-rays are permissible. If there are large numbers of X-rays, the records officer should check with the patient/

solicitor before arranging copying. Reports on an "adverse incident" and reports on the patient made for risk management and audit purposes may form part of the records and be discloseable: the exception will be any specific record or report made solely or mainly in connection with an actual or potential claim.

Records: Quality Standards

When copying records healthcare providers should ensure—

1. All documents are legible, and complete, if necessary by photocopying at less than 100%.
2. Documents larger than A4 in the original, e.g. ITU charts, should be reproduced in A3, or reduced to A4 where this retains readability.
3. Documents are only copied on one side of paper, unless the original is two sided.
4. Documents should not be unnecessarily shuffled or bound and holes should not be made in the copied papers.

Enquiries/Further Information

Any enquiries about the forms should be made initially to the solicitors making the request. Comments on the use and content of the forms should be made to the Secretary, Civil Litigation Committee. The Law Society, 113 Chancery Lane, London WC2A 1PL, telephone 020 7320 5739, or to the NHS Management Executive, Quarry House, Quarry Hill, Leeds LS2 7UE.

The Law Society

May 1998

C3–020

APPLICATION ON BEHALF OF A PATIENT FOR HOSPITAL MEDICAL RECORDS FOR USE WHEN COURT PROCEEDINGS ARE CONTEMPLATED

This should be completed as fully as possible

Insert Hospital Name and Address

TO: Medical Records Officer
Hospital

1 (a)	Full name of patient (including previous surnames)	
(b)	Address now	
(c)	Address at start of treatment	
(d)	Date of birth (and death, if applicable)	
(e)	Hospital ref. no if available	
(f)	N.I. number, if available	
2	This application is made because the patient is considering	
(a)	a claim against your hospital as detailed in para 7 overleaf	YES/NO
(b)	pursuing an action against some one else	YES/NO

PRE-ACTION PROTOCOLS

3	Department(s) where treatment was received	
4	Name(s) of consultant(s) at your hospital in charge of the treatment	
5	Whether treatment at your hospital was private or NHS, wholly or in part	
6	A description of the treatment received, with approximate dates	
7	If the answer to Q2(a) is "Yes" details of	
	(a) the likely nature of the claim,	
	(b) grounds for the claim,	
	(c) approximate dates of the events involved	
8	If the answer to Q2(b) is "Yes" insert	
	(a) the names of the proposed defendants	
	(b) whether legal proceedings yet begun	YES/NO
	(c) if appropriate, details of the claim and action number	
9	We confirm we will pay reasonable copying charges	
10	We request prior details of (a) photocopying and administration charges for medical records	YES/NO
	(b) number of and cost of copying x-ray and scan films	YES/NO

11	Any other relevant information, particular requirements, or any particular documents not required (e.g. copies of computerised records)	
	Signature of Solicitor	
	Name	
	Address	
	Ref.	
	Telephone Number	
	Fax number	

Please print name beneath each signature. Signature by child over 12 but under 18 years also requires signature by parent.

Signature of patient	
Signature of parent or next friend if appropriate	
Signature of personal representative where patient has died	

C3–021

FIRST RESPONSE TO APPLICATION FOR HOSPITAL RECORDS

NAME OF PATIENT		
Our ref.		
Your ref.		
1	Date of receipt of patient's application	
2	We intend that copy medical records will be dispatched within 6 weeks of that date	YES/NO
3	We require pre-payment of photocopying charges	YES/NO
4	If estimate of photocopying charges requested or pre-payment required the amount will be	£/notified to you
5	The cost of x-ray and scan films will be	£/notified to you
6	If there is any problem, we shall write to you within those 6 weeks	YES/NO
7	Any other information	
	Please address further correspondence to	
	Signed	
	Direct telephone number	
	Direct fax number	
	Dated	

C3–022

SECOND RESPONSE ENCLOSING PATIENT'S HOSPITAL MEDICAL RECORDS

Address

Our Ref.
Your Ref.

	NAME OF PATIENT:	
1	We confirm that the enclosed copy medical records are all those within the control of the hospital, relevant to the application which you have made to the best of our knowledge and belief, subject to paras 2–5 below	YES/NO
2	Details of any other documents which have not yet been located	
3	Date by when it is expected that these will be supplied	
4	Details of any records which we are not producing	
5	The reasons for not doing so	
6	An invoice for copying and administration charges is attached	YES/NO
	Signed	
	Date	

PRE-ACTION PROTOCOLS

Annex C

Templates for Letters of Claim and Response

C1

Letter of Claim

Essential Contents

C3–023 **1. Client's name, address, date of birth, etc.**

2. Dates of allegedly negligent treatment

3. Events giving rise to the claim

- an outline of what happened, including details of other relevant treatments to the client by other healthcare providers.

4. Allegation of negligence and causal link with injuries

- an outline of the allegations or a more detailed list in a complex case an outline of the causal link between allegations and the injuries complained of.

5. The Client's injuries, condition and future prognosis

6. Request for clinical records (if not previously provided)

- use the Law Society form if appropriate or adapt;
- specify the records required;
- if other records are held by other providers, and may be relevant, say so;
- state what investigations have been carried out to date, e.g. information from client and witnesses, any complaint and the outcome, if any clinical records have been seen or expert's advice obtained.

7. The likely value of the claim

- an outline of the main heads of damage, or in straightforward cases the details of loss.

Optional Information

C3–024 What investigations have been carried out

An offer to settle without supporting evidence

Suggestions for obtaining expert evidence

Suggestions for meetings, negotiations, discussion or mediation

Possible Enclosures

C3–025 Chronology

Clinical records request form and client's authorisation

Expert report(s)

Schedules of loss and supporting evidence

C2

Letter of Response

Essential Contents

1. Provide requested records and invoice for copying

- explain if records are incomplete or extensive records are held and ask for further instructions; C3–026
- request additional records from third parties

2. Comments on events and/or chronology

- if events are disputed or the healthcare provider has further information or documents on which they wish to rely, these should be provided, e.g. internal, protocol;
- details of any further information needed from the patient or a third party should be provided.

3. If breach of duty and causation are accepted

- suggestions might be made for resolving the claim and/or requests for further information;
- a response should be made to any offer to settle.

4. If breach of duty and/or causation are denied

- a bare denial will not be sufficient. If the healthcare provider has other explanations for what happened, these should be given at least in outline;
- suggestions might be made for the next steps, e.g. further investigations, obtaining expert evidence, meetings/negotiations or mediation, or an invitation to issue proceedings.

Optional Matters

An offer to settle if the patient has not made one, or a counter offer to the patient's with supporting evidence. C3–027

Possible Enclosures

Clinical records C3–028
Annotated chronology
Expert reports

Annex D

Lord Woolf's Recommendations

1. Lord Woolf in his Access to Justice Report in July 1996, following a detailed review of the problems of medical negligence claims, identified that one of the major sources of **costs and delay** is **at the pre-litigation stage** because— C3–029

(a) Inadequate incident reporting and record keeping in hospitals, and mobility of staff, make it difficult to establish facts, often several years after the event.

(b) Claimants must incur the cost of an expert in order to establish whether they have a viable claim.

(c) There is often a long delay before a claim is made.

(d) Defendants do not have sufficient resources to carry out a full investigation of every incident, and do not consider it worthwhile to start an investigation as soon as they receive a request for records, because many cases do not proceed beyond that stage.

(e) Patients often give the Defendant little or no notice of a firm intention to pursue a claim. Consequently, many incidents are not investigated by the defendants until after proceedings have started.

(f) Doctors and other clinical staff are traditionally reluctant to admit negligence or apologise to, or negotiate with, claimants for fear of damage to their professional reputations or career prospects.

2. Lord Woolf acknowledged that under the present arrangements **healthcare providers**, faced with possible medical negligence claims, have a number of **practical problems** to contend with:—

(a) Difficulties of finding patients' records and tracing former staff, which can be exacerbated by late notification and be the healthcare provider's own failure to identify adverse incidents.

(b) The healthcare provider may have only treated the patient for a limited time or for a specific complaint: the patient's previous history may be relevant but the records may be in the possession of one of several other healthcare providers.

(c) The large number of potential claims do not proceed beyond the stage of a request for medical records, or an explanation; and that is difficult for healthcare providers to investigate fully every case whenever a patient asks to see the records.

Annex E

How to Contact the Forum

The Clinical Disputes Forum

C3–030 *Chairman*
Dr Alastair Scotland
Medical Director and Chief Officer
National Clinical Assessment Authority
9th Floor, Market Towers
London
SW8 5NQ

Secretary
Sarah Leigh
c/o Margaret Dangoor
3 Clydesdale Gardens
Richmond
Surrey
TW10 5EG
Telephone: 020 8241 1012

[THE NEXT PARAGRAPH IS C5A–001.]

The Construction and Engineering Protocol

C5A–001 This protocol came into force in October 2000. It applies to all construction and engineering disputes. It should be read with Pt 60 Technology and Construction court claims although Pt 60, of course only applies to the larger claims allocated to the multi-track.

The distinguishing features of this protocol are:

- it includes professional negligence disputes against building professionals (the personal injury and clinical negligence protocols do not do so;
- parties do not have to follow the protocol before applying for interim injunctions, in cases which will be the subject of a summary judgment application or which are for enforcing a decision following an adjudication under the Housing, Grants, Construction and Regeneration Act 1996;
- the letter of claim must include the remedy sought and details of how it has been calculated;
- the claimant must also provide the names of experts already instructed on whom he intends to rely;
- the defendant has only 14 days to acknowledge;
- the defendant has only 28 days either to take objections on jurisdiction or to respond to the letter of claim, and, if doing the latter, he must set out any counterclaim and provide the names of any experts he has instructed on which he intends to rely;
- if the defendant does not acknowledge or respond in time the claimant is entitled to issue;
- if complying with the protocol will give the claimant a difficulty with issuing within limitation, he can issue and applyto the court for directions (a useful provision which could be replicated in other protocols or the Practice Direction);
- the claimant shall respond to the counterclaim also in 28 days;
- the parties must have at least one pre-issue "without prejudice" meeting; refusal to attend which can be reported to the court (Part 5). This is a welcome innovation and, perhaps, should be incorporated in all the pre-action protocols;
- if the claim is not settled the parties should consider ADR, instruction of joint experts, and generally how the dispute is to be progressed.

This protocol was amended from April 6, 2007. The main changes were:

- A new para.1.5 on proportionality that emphasises that in low value claims the letters of claim and response should be simple and costs should be kept to a minimum.
- To paras 5.1–7 to specify that the pre-action meeting should take place within 28 days of the receipt of the defendant's letter of response.

In *Alfred McAlpine Capital Projects Ltd v SIAC Construction* [2005] EWHC 3139, TCC a Pt 20 defendant joined to proceedings six months after issue applied for a stay to enable compliance with the protocol in relation to their interest. The application was refused on the facts but the court gave general guidance and said that factors to be taken into account in theses circumstances included what information had been given to the new party before they were joined, how large a part they would play in the action as a whole, the impact of a stay on the timetable for the action and particularly any trial date fixed, and whether the needs of the new party could be accommodated in any other way or by compensation in costs.

In *Briggs & Forrester Electrical Ltd v Southfield School for Girls* [2005] EWHC 1734, QBD (TCC), the claimant was ordered to produce documents to explain quantum pre-action so that the defendant would understand the value of the case being brought against them.

In *T.J. Brent Ltd v Black and Veatch Consulting Ltd* [2008] EWHC 1497 TCC the claimant's application for costs because of the defendant's alleged non-compliance with the Pre-action Protocol for Construction and Engineering Dispute was dismissed as the defendant had largely complied.

PRE-ACTION PROTOCOL FOR THE CONSTRUCTION AND ENGINEERING DISPUTES

1.

Introduction

1.1 This Pre-Action Protocol applies to all construction and **C5–001**

engineering disputes (including professional negligence claims against architects, engineers and quantity surveyors).

1.2 Exceptions

C5–002 A claimant shall not be required to comply with this Protocol before commencing proceedings to the extent that the proposed proceedings (i) are for the enforcement of the decision of an adjudicator to whom a dispute has been referred pursuant to section 108 of the Housing Grants, Construction and Regeneration Act 1996 ("the 1996 Act"), (ii) include a claim for interim injunctive relief, (iii) will be the subject of a claim for summary judgment pursuant to Part 24 of the Civil Procedure Rules, or (iv) relate to the same or substantially the same issues as have been the subject of recent adjudication under the 1996 Act, or some other formal alternative dispute resolution procedure.

1.3 Objectives

C5–003 The objectives of this Protocol are as set out in the Practice Direction relating to Civil Procedure Pre-Action Protocols, namely:

(i) to encourage the exchange of early and full information about the prospective legal claim;

(ii) to enable parties to avoid litigation by agreeing a settlement of the claim before commencement of proceedings; and

(iii) to support the efficient management of proceedings where litigation cannot be avoided.

1.4 Compliance

C5–004 If proceedings are commenced, the court will be able to treat the standards set in this Protocol as the normal reasonable approach to pre-action conduct. If the court has to consider the question of compliance after proceedings have begun, it will be concerned with substantial compliance and not minor departures, e.g. failure by a short period to provide relevant information. Minor departures will not exempt the "innocent" party from following the Protocol. The court will look at the effect of non-compliance on the other party when deciding whether to impose sanctions. For sanctions generally, see paragraph 2 of the Practice Direction-Protocols "Compliance with Protocols".

1.5 Proportionality

C5–004.1 The overriding objective (CPR rule 1.1) applies to the pre-action period. The Protocol must not be used as a tactical device to secure advantage for one party or to generate unnecessary costs. In lower value claims (such as those likely to proceed in the county court), the letter of claim and the response should be simple and the costs of both sides should be kept to a modest level. In all cases the costs incurred at the Protocol stage should be proportionate to the complexity of the case and the amount of money which is at stake. The Protocol does not impose a requirement on the parties to marshal and disclose all the supporting details and evidence that may ultimately be required if the case proceeds to litigation.

2.

Overview of the Protocol

2 General aim

The general aim of this Protocol is to ensure that before court proceedings commence: C5–005

(i) the claimant and the defendant have provided sufficient information for each party to know the nature of the other's case;

(ii) each party has had an opportunity to consider the other's case, and to accept or reject all or any part of the case made against him at the earliest possible stage;

(iii) there is more pre-action contact between the parties;

(iv) better and earlier exchange of information occurs;

(v) there is better pre-action investigation by the parties;

(vi) the parties have met formally on at least one occasion with a view to

- defining and agreeing the issues between them; and
- exploring possible ways by which the claim may be resolved;

(vii) the parties are in a position where they may be able to settle cases early and fairly without recourse to litigation; and

(vii) proceedings will be conducted efficiently if litigation does become necessary.

3.

The Letter of Claim

3 Prior to commencing proceedings, the claimant or his solicitor shall send to each proposed defendant (if appropriate to his registered address) a copy of a letter of claim which shall contain the following information: C5–006

(i) the claimant's full name and address;

(ii) the full name and address of each proposed defendant;

(iii) a clear summary of the facts on which each claim is based;

(iv) the basis on which each claim is made, identifying the principal contractual terms and statutory provisions relied on;

(v) the nature of the relief claimed: if damages are claimed, a breakdown showing how the damages have been quantified; if a sum is claimed pursuant to a contract, how it has been calculated; if an extension of time is claimed, the period claimed;

(vi) where a claim has been made previously and rejected by a defendant, and the claimant is able to identify the reason(s) for such rejection, the claimant's grounds of belief as to why the claim was wrongly rejected;

(vii) the names of any experts already instructed by the claimant on whose evidence he intends to rely, identifying the issues to which that evidence will be directed.

4.

The Defendant's Response

4.1 The defendant's acknowledgment

C5–007 Within 14 calendar days of receipt of the letter of claim, the defendant should acknowledge its receipt in writing and may give the name and address of his insurer (if any). If there has been no acknowledgment by or on behalf of the defendant within 14 days, the claimant will be entitled to commence proceedings without further compliance with this Protocol.

4.2 Objections to the court's jurisdiction or the named defendant

C5–008 4.2.1 If the defendant intends to take any objection to all or any part of the claimant's claim on the grounds that (i) the court lacks jurisdiction, (ii) the matter should be referred to arbitration, or (iii) the defendant named in the letter of claim is the wrong defendant, that objection should be raised by the defendant within 28 days after receipt of the letter of claim. The letter of objection shall specify the parts of the claim to which the objection relates, setting out the grounds relied on, and, where appropriate, shall identify the correct defendant (if known). Any failure to take such objection shall not prejudice the defendant's rights to do so in any subsequent proceedings, but the court may take such failure into account when considering the question of costs.

4.2.2 Where such notice of objection is given, the defendant is not required to send a letter of response in accordance with paragraph 4.3.1 in relation to the claim or those parts of it to which the objection relates (as the case may be).

4.2.3 If at any stage before the claimant commences proceedings, the defendant withdraws his objection, then paragraph 4.3 and the remaining part of this Protocol will apply to the claim or those parts of it to which the objection related as if the letter of claim had been received on the date on which notice of withdrawal of the objection had been given.

4.3 The defendant's response

C5–009 4.3.1 Within 28 days from the date of receipt of the letter of claim, or such other period as the parties may reasonably agree (up to a maximum of 3 months), the defendant shall send a letter of response to the claimant which shall contain the following information:

(i) the facts set out in the letter of claim which are agreed or not agreed, and if not agreed, the basis of the disagreement;

(ii) which claims are accepted and which are rejected, and if rejected, the basis of the rejection;

(iii) if a claim is accepted in whole or in part, whether the damages, sums or extensions of time claimed are accepted or rejected, and if rejected, the basis of the rejection;

(iv) if contributory negligence is alleged against the claimant, a summary of the facts relied on;

(v) whether the defendant intends to make a counterclaim, and if so, giving the information which is required to be given in a letter of claim by paragraph 3(iii) to (vi) above;

(vi) the names of any experts already instructed on whose evidence it is intended to rely, identifying the issues to which that evidence will be directed;

4.3.2 If no response is received by the claimant within the period of 28 days (or such other period as has been agreed between the parties), the claimant shall be entitled to commence proceedings without further compliance with this Protocol.

4.4 Claimant's response to counter claim

The claimant shall provide a response to any counterclaim within the equivalent period allowed to the defendant to respond to the letter of claim under paragraph 4.3.1 above. **C5–010**

5.

Pre-Action Meeting

5.1 Within 28 days after receipt by the claimant of the defendant's letter of response, or (if the claimant intends to respond to the counterclaim) after receipt by the defendant of the claimant's letter of response to the counterclaim, the parties should normally meet. **C5–011**

5.2 The aim of the meeting is for the parties to agree what are the main issues in the case, to identify the root cause of disagreement in respect of each issue, and to consider (i) whether, and if so how, the issues might be resolved without recourse to litigation, and (ii) if litigation is unavoidable, what steps should be taken to ensure that it is conducted in accordance with the overriding objective as defined in rule 1.1 of the Civil Procedure Rules.

5.3 In some circumstances, it may be necessary to convene more than one meeting. It is not intended by this Protocol to prescribe in detail the manner in which the meetings should be conducted. But the court will normally expect that those attending will include:

(i) where the party is an individual, that individual, and where the party is a corporate body, a representative of that body who has authority to settle or recommend settlement of the dispute;

(ii) a legal representative of each party (if one has been instructed);

(iii) where the involvement of insurers has been disclosed,

a representative of the insurer (who may be its legal representative); and

(iv) where a claim is made or defended on behalf of some other party (such as, for example, a claim made by a main contractor pursuant to a contractual obligation to pass on subcontractor claims), the party on whose behalf the claim is made or defended and/or his legal representatives.

5.4 In respect of each agreed issue or the dispute as a whole, the parties should consider whether some form of alternative dispute resolution procedure would be more suitable than litigation, and if so, endeavour to agree which form to adopt. It is expressly recognised that no party can or should be forced to mediate or enter into any form of alternative dispute resolution.

5.5 If the parties are unable to agree on a means of resolving the dispute other than by litigation they should use their best endeavours to agree:

(i) if there is any area where expert evidence is likely to be required, how the relevant issues are to be defined and how expert evidence is to be dealt with including whether a joint expert might be appointed, and if so, who that should be; and (so far as is practicable);

(ii) the extent of disclosure of documents with a view to saving costs; and

(iii) the conduct of the litigation with the aim of minimising cost and delay.

5.6 Any party who attended any pre-action meeting shall be at liberty and may be required to disclose to the court:

(i) that the meeting took place, when and who attended;

(ii) the identity of any party who refused to attend, and the grounds for such refusal;

(iii) if the meeting did not take place, why not; and

(iv) any agreements concluded between the parties;

(v) the fact of whether alternative means of resolving the dispute were considered or agreed.

5.7 Except as provided in paragraph 5.6, everything said at a pre-action meeting shall be treated as "without prejudice".

6.

Limitation of Action

C5–012 **6** If by reason of complying with any part of this protocol a claimant's claim may be time-barred under any provision of the Limitation Act 1980, or any other legislation which imposes a time limit for bringing an action, the claimant may commence proceedings without complying with this Protocol. In such circumstances, a claimant who commences proceedings without complying with all, or any part, of this Protocol must apply to the court on notice for directions as to the timetable and form of procedure to be adopted, at the same time as he requests the court to issue proceedings. The court will consider whether to order a stay of the whole or part of the proceedings pending compliance with this Protocol.

The Defamation Protocol

The defamation protocol came into force in October 2000. It should be read with Pt 53 Defamation Claims particularly the detailed practice direction and editorial. **C6A–001**

The main distinguishing features of this protocol are:

- it stresses that time is of the essence as the limitation period in defamation claims is only one year and often the claimant is seeking immediate correction and an apology;
- the claimant is encouraged to notify the defendant of the claim as soon as possible;
- the letter of claim should identify specifically;
  - the publication, words, inaccuracies or unsupportable comments to which the claimant objects;
  - any special facts with regard to the interpretation or meaning of the words or in relation to the damage caused;
- the defendant is required to respond to the letter of claim as soon as possible, preferably within 14 days and must either admit liability and offer a remedy, or deny the claim and give reasons;
- that means of resolving these disputes include;
  - determination by an independent third party experienced in defamation;
  - mediation or other form of ADR.

PRE-ACTION PROTOCOL FOR DEFAMATION

1.

Introduction

1.1 Lord Irvine of Lairg, in his foreword to the Pre-Action Protocol for Personal Injury Claims identified the value of creating Pre-Action Protocols as a key part of the Civil Justice Reforms. He hoped that Pre-Action Protocols would set effective and enforceable standards for the efficient conduct of pre-action litigation. **C6–001**

1.2 Lord Irvine went on to state that: Per "The protocol aims to improve pre-action communication between the parties by establishing a timetable for the exchange of information relevant to the dispute and by setting standards for the content of correspondence. Compliance with the protocol will enable parties to make an informed judgement on the merits of their cases earlier than tends to happen today, because they will have earlier access to the information they need. This will provide every opportunity for improved communications between the parties designed to lead to an increase in the number of pre-action settlements." :

1.3 It is against this background that a Pre-Action Protocol for Claims in Defamation is submitted. This Protocol is intended to encourage exchange of information between parties at an early stage and to provide a clear framework within which parties to a claim in defamation, acting in good faith, can explore the early and appropriate resolution of that claim.

1.4 There are important features which distinguish defamation claims from other areas of civil litigation, and these must be borne in mind when both applying, and reviewing the application of, the Pre-Action Protocol. In particular, time is always "of the essence"in defamation claims; the limitation period is (uniquely) only 1 year, and almost invariably, a Claimant will be seeking an immediate correction and/or apology as part of the process of restoring his/ her reputation.

1.5 This Pre-Action Protocol embraces the spirit of the reforms to the Civil Justice system envisaged by Lord Woolf, and now enacted in the Civil Procedure Rules. It aims to incorporate the concept of the overriding objective, as provided by the Rules at Part 1, before the commencement of any Court proceedings, namely:

dealing with a case justly includes, so far as is practicable:

- ensuring that the parties are on an equal footing;
- saving expense;

dealing with the case in ways which are proportionate:

- to the amount of money involved;
- to the importance of the case;
- to the complexity of the issues; and
- to the financial position of each party;
- ensuring that it is dealt with expeditiously and fairly; and
- allotting to it an appropriate share of the Court's resources, while taking into account the need to allot resources to other cases.

2.

Aims of the Protocol

C6–002
- This protocol aims to set out a code of good practice which parties should follow when litigation is being considered
- It encourages early communication of a claim.
- It aims to encourage both parties to disclose sufficient information to enable each to understand the other's case and to promote the prospect of early resolution.
- It sets a timetable for the exchange of information relevant to the dispute.
- It sets standards for the content of correspondence.
- It identifies options which either party might adopt to encourage settlement of the claim.
- Should a claim proceed to litigation, the extent to which the protocol has been followed both in practice and in spirit by the parties will assist the Court in dealing with liability for costs and making other Orders.
- Letters of claim and responses sent pursuant to this Protocol are not intended to have the same status as a Statement of Case in proceedings.
- It aims to keep the costs of resolving disputes subject to this protocol proportionate.

3.

Pre-Action Protocol

Letter of Claim

C6–003 **3.1** The Claimant should notify the Defendant of his/her claim in writing at the earliest reasonable opportunity.

3.2 The Letter of Claim should include the following information:

- name of Claimant;
- sufficient details to identify the publication or broadcast which contained the words complained of;
- the words complained of and, if known, the date of publication; where possible, a copy or transcript of the words complained of should be enclosed;
- factual inaccuracies or unsupportable comment within the words complained of; the Claimant should give a sufficient explanation to enable the Defendant to appreciate why the words are inaccurate or unsupportable;
- the nature of the remedies sought by the Claimant.
- Where relevant, the Letter of Claim should also include:
- any facts or matters which make the Claimant identifiable from the words complained of;
- details of any special facts relevant to the interpretation of the words complained of and/or any particular damage caused by the words complained of.

3.3 It is desirable for the Claimant to identify in the Letter of Claim the meaning(s) he/she attributes to the words complained of.

Defendant's Response to letter Of Claim

3.4 The Defendant should provide a full response to the Letter of Claim as soon as reasonably possible. If the Defendant believes that he/she will be unable to respond within 14 days (or such shorter time limit as specified in the Letter of Claim), then he/she should specify the date by which he/she intends to respond. C6–004

3.5 The Response should include the following:

- whether or to what extent the Claimant's claim is accepted, whether more information is required or whether it is rejected;
- if the claim is accepted in whole or in part, the Defendant should indicate which remedies it is willing to offer;
- if more information is required, then the Defendant should specify precisely what information is needed to enable the claim to be dealt with and why;
- if the claim is rejected, then the Defendant should explain the reasons why it is rejected, including a sufficient indication of any facts on which the Defendant is likely to rely in support of any substantive defence;
- it is desirable for the Defendant to include in the Response to the Letter of Claim the meaning(s) he/she attributes to the words complained of.

3.6 Proportionality of Costs

In formulating both the Letter of Claim and Response and in taking any subsequent steps, the parties should act reasonably to keep costs proportionate to the nature and gravity of the case and the stage the complaint has reached. C6–005

3.7 Alternative Dispute Resolution

The parties should consider whether some form of alternative C6–006 dispute resolution procedure would be more suitable than litigation, and if so, endeavour to agree which form to adopt. Both the Claimant and Defendant may be required by the Court to provide evidence that alternative means of resolving their dispute were considered. The Courts take the view that litigation should be a last resort, and that claims should not be issued prematurely when a settlement is still actively being explored. Parties are warned that if the protocol is not followed (including this paragraph) then the Court must have regard to such conduct when determining costs.

3.8 It is not practicable in this protocol to address in detail how the parties might decide which method to adopt to resolve their particular dispute.

- Discussion and negotiation.
- Early neutral evaluation by an independent third party (for example, a lawyer experienced in the field of defamation or an individual experienced in the subject matter of the claim).
- Mediation—a form of facilitated negotiation assisted by an independent neutral party.
- Reference to the Press Complaints Commission (an independent body which deals with complaints from members of the public about the editorial content of newspapers and magazines).

The Legal Services Commission has published a booklet on "Alternatives to Court", CLS Direct Information Leaflet 23 (*www.clsdirect.org.uk/legalhelp/leaflet23.jsp*), which lists a number of organisations that provide alternative dispute resolution services.

3.9 *It is expressly recognised that no party can or should be forced to mediate or enter into any form of ADR.*

The Professional Negligence Pre-action Protocol

C7A–001 This protocol came into force in July 2001.

The main differences from the earlier protocols are:

- it merges two previous draft protocols;
- the letters of claim and response should be detailed and "open", i.e. not without prejudice;
- the letter of claim should include a chronology and enclose key documents, should particularise the allegations of negligence and explain how they have caused the loss, which should be calculated (and supporting documents should be enclosed) and should identify any experts appointed;
- the defendant should acknowledge the claim within 14 days and respond on the progress of investigations within three months;
- the defendant may send a separate letter of settlement on a without prejudice basis with the letter of response: if not the claimant can issue;
- if negotiations are started the parties should aim to settle within six months of the defendant's letter of acknowledgement;
- if the claimant has already appointed their own expert the defendant can do likewise: otherwise the parties should aim to appoint a single joint expert;

PROFESSIONAL NEGLIGENCE PRE-ACTION PROTOCOL

C7–001 This protocol merges the two protocols previously produced by the Solicitors Indemnity Fund (SIF) and Claims Against Professionals *(CAP)*

A. Introduction

A1. This protocol is designed to apply when a Claimant wishes to claim against a professional (other than construction professionals and healthcare providers) as a result of that professional's alleged negligence or equivalent breach of contract or breach of fiduciary duty. Although these claims will be the usual situation in which the protocol will be used, there may be other claims for which the protocol could be appropriate. For a more detailed explanation of the scope of the protocol see Guidance Note C2.

A2. The aim of this protocol is to establish a framework in which there is an early exchange of information so that the claim can be fully investigated and, if possible, resolved without the need for litigation. This includes:

(a) ensuring that the parties are on an equal footing
(b) saving expense
(c) dealing with the dispute in ways which are proportionate:
  (ii) to the importance of the case
  (iii) to the complexity of the issues
  (iv) to the financial position of each party
(d) ensuring that it is dealt with expeditiously and fairly.

A3. This protocol is not intended to replace other forms of pre-action dispute resolution (such as internal complaints procedures, the Surveyors and Valuers Arbitration Scheme, etc). Where such procedures are available, parties are encouraged to consider whether they should be used. If, however, these other procedures are used and fail to resolve the dispute, the protocol should be used before litigation is started, adapting it where appropriate. See also Guidance Note C3.

A4. The Courts will be able to treat the standards set in this protocol as the normal reasonable approach. If litigation is started, it will be for the court to decide whether sanctions should be imposed as a result of substantial non-compliance with a protocol. Guidance on the courts' likely approach is given in the Protocols Practice Direction. The Court is likely to disregard minor departures from this protocol and so should the parties as between themselves.

A5. Both in operating the timetable and in requesting and providing information during the protocol period, the parties are expected to act reasonably, in line with the Court's expectations of them. See also Guidance Note C1.2.

B. The Protocol

B1. Preliminary Notice (See also Guidance Note C3.1)

B1.1 As soon as the Claimant decides there is a reasonable chance *that he will bring* a claim against a professional, the Claimant is encouraged to notify the professional in writing. **C7–002**

B1.2 This letter should contain the following information: (a) the identity of the Claimant and any other parties

(b) a brief outline of the Claimant's grievance against the professional
(c) if possible, a general indication of the financial value of the potential claim

B1.3 This letter should be addressed to the professional and should ask the professional to inform his professional indemnity insurers, if any, immediately.

B1.4 The professional should acknowledge receipt of the Claimant's letter within 21 days of receiving it. Other than this acknowledgment, the protocol places no obligation upon either party to take any further action.

B2. Letter of Claim

C7–003 **B2.1** As soon as the Claimant decides there are grounds for a claim against the professional, the Claimant should write a detailed Letter of Claim to the professional.

B2.2 The Letter of Claim will normally be an open letter (as opposed to being "without prejudice") and should include the following—

(a) The identity of any other parties involved in the dispute or a related dispute.

(b) A clear chronological summary (including key dates) of the facts on which the claim is based. Key documents should be identified, copied and enclosed.

(c) The allegations against the professional. What has he done wrong? What has he failed to do?

(d) An explanation of how the alleged error has caused the loss claimed.

(e) An estimate of the financial loss suffered by the Claimant and how it is calculated. Supporting documents should be identified, copied and enclosed. If details of the financial loss cannot be supplied, the Claimant should explain why and should state when he will be in a position to provide the details. This information should be sent to the professional as soon as reasonably possible.

If the Claimant is seeking some form of non-financial redress, this should be made clear.

(f) Confirmation whether or not an expert has been appointed. If so, providing the identity and discipline of the expert, together with the date upon which the expert was appointed.

(g) A request that a copy of the Letter of Claim be forwarded immediately to the professional's insurers, if any.

B2.3 The Letter of Claim is not intended to have the same formal status as a Statement of Case. If, however, the Letter of Claim differs materially from the Statement of Case in subsequent proceedings, the Court may decide, in its discretion, to impose sanctions.

B2.4 If the Claimant has sent other Letters of Claim (or equivalent) to any other party in relation to this dispute or related dispute, those letters should be copied to the professional. (If the Claimant is claiming against someone else to whom this protocol does not apply, please see Guidance Note C4.)

B3. The Letter of Acknowledgment

B3.1 The professional should acknowledge receipt of the Letter of Claim within 21 days of receiving it. **C7–004**

B4. Investigations

B4.1 The professional will have three months from the date of the Letter of Acknowledgment to investigate. **C7–005**

B4.2 If the professional is in difficulty in complying with the three month time period, the problem should be explained to the Claimant as soon as possible. The professional should explain what is being done to resolve the problem and when the professional expects to complete the investigations.

The Claimant should agree to any reasonable request for an extension of the three month period.

B4.3 The parties should supply promptly, at this stage and throughout, whatever relevant information or documentation is reasonably requested. (Please see Guidance Note C5).

(If the professional intends to claim against someone who is not currently a party to the dispute, please see Guidance Note C4.)

B5. Letter of Response and Letter of Settlement

B5.1 As soon as the professional has completed his investigations, the professional should send to the Claimant: **C7–006**

(a) a Letter of Response, or
(b) a Letter of Settlement;

or

(c) both.

The Letters of Response and Settlement can be contained within a single letter.

The Letter of Response

B5.2 The Letter of Response will normally be an open letter (as opposed to being "without prejudice") and should be a reasoned answer to the Claimant's allegations: **C7–007**

(a) if the claim is admitted the professional should say so in clear terms.

(b) if only part of the claim is admitted the professional should make clear which parts of the claim are admitted and which are denied.

(c) if the claim is denied in whole or in part, the Letter of Response should include specific comments on the allegations against the professional and, if the Claimant's version of events is disputed, the professional should provide his version of events.

(d) if the professional is unable to admit or deny the claim, the professional should identify any further information which is required.

(e) if the professional disputes the estimate of the Claimant's financial loss, the Letter of Response should set out the professional's estimate. If an estimate cannot be provided, the professional should explain why and should state when he will be in a position to provide

PRE-ACTION PROTOCOLS

an estimate. This information should be sent to the Claimant as soon as reasonably possible.

(f) where additional documents are relied upon, copies should be provided.

B5.3 The Letter of Response is not intended to have the same formal status as a defence. If, however, the Letter of Response differs materially from the defence in subsequent proceedings, the Court may decide, in its discretion, to impose sanctions.

The Letter of Settlement

C7–008 **B5.4** The Letter of Settlement will normally be a without prejudice letter and should be sent if the professional intends to make proposals for settlement. It should:

(a) set out the professional's views to date on the claim identifying those issues which the professional believes are likely to remain in dispute and those which are not. (The Letter of Settlement does not need to include this information if the professional has sent a Letter of Response).

(b) make a settlement proposal or identify any further information which is required before the professional can formulate its proposals.

(c) where additional documents are relied upon, copies should be provided.

The Letter of Settlement

C7–009 **B5.5** If the Letter of Response denies the claim in its entirety and there is no Letter of Settlement, it is open to the Claimant to commence proceedings.

B5.6 In any other circumstance, the professional and the Claimant should commence negotiations with the aim of concluding those negotiations within 6 months of the date of the Letter of Acknowledgment (NOT from the date of the Letter of Response).

B5.7 If the claim cannot be resolved within this period:

(a) the parties should agree within 14 days of the end of the period whether the period should be extended and, if so, by how long.

(b) the parties should seek to identify those issues which are still in dispute and those which can be agreed.

(c) if an extension of time is not agreed it will then be open to the Claimant to commence proceedings.

B6. Alternative Dispute Resolution

C7–010 **B6.1** The parties should consider whether some form of alternative dispute resolution procedure would be more suitable than litigation, and if so, endeavour to agree which form to adopt. Both the Claimant and professional may be required by the Court to provide evidence that alternative means of resolving their dispute were considered. The Courts take the view that litigation should be a last resort, and that claims should not be issued prematurely when a settlement is still actively being explored. Parties are warned that if the protocol is not followed (including this paragraph) then the Court must have regard to such conduct when determining costs.

B6.2 It is not practicable in this protocol to address in detail how the parties might decide which method to adopt to resolve their particular dispute. However, summarised below are some of the options for resolving disputes without litigation:

- Discussion and negotiation.
- Early neutral evaluation by an independent third party (for example, a lawyer experienced in the field of professional negligence or an individual experienced in the subject matter of the claim).
- Mediation—a form of facilitated negotiation assisted by an independent neutral party.

B6.3 The Legal Services Commission has published a booklet on "Alternatives to Court", CLS Direct Information Leaflet 23 (*www.clsdirect.org.uk/legalhelp/leaflet23.jsp*), which lists a number of organisations that provide alternative dispute resolution services.

B6.4 *It is expressly recognised that no party can or should be forced to mediate or enter into any form of ADR.*

B7. Experts

(The following provisions apply where the claim raises an issue of professional expertise whose resolution requires expert evidence). **C7–011**

B7.1 If the Claimant has obtained expert evidence prior to sending the Letter of Claim, the professional will have equal right to obtain expert evidence prior to sending the Letter of Response/ Letter of Settlement.

B7.2 If the Claimant has not obtained expert evidence prior to sending the Letter of Claim, the parties are encouraged to appoint a joint expert. If they agree to do so, they should seek to agree the identity of the expert and the terms of the expert's appointment.

B7.3 If agreement about a joint expert cannot be reached, all parties are free to appoint their own experts.

(For further details on experts see Guidance Note C6).

B8. Proceedings

B8.1 Unless it is necessary (for example, to obtain protection against the expiry of a relevant limitation period) the Claimant should not start Court proceedings until: **C7–012**

(a) the Letter of Response denies the claim in its entirety and there is no Letter of Settlement (see paragraph B5.5 above); or

(b) the end of the negotiation period (see paragraphs B5.6 and B5.7 above); or

(For further discussion of statutory time limits for the commencement of litigation, please see Guidance Note C7).

B8.2 Where possible 14 days written notice should be given to the professional before proceedings are started, indicating the court within which the Claimant is intending to commence litigation.

B8.3 Proceedings should be served on the professional, unless the professional's solicitor has notified the Claimant in writing that he is authorised to accept service on behalf of the professional.

C. Guidance Notes

C1. Introduction

C7–013 **C1.1** The protocol has been kept simple to promote ease of use and general acceptability. The guidance notes which follow relate particularly to issues on which further guidance may be required.

C2.2 The Woolf reforms envisage that parties will act reasonably in the pre-action period. Accordingly, in the event that the protocol and the guidelines do not specifically address a problem, the parties should comply with the spirit of the protocol by acting reasonably.

C2. Scope of Protocol

C7–014 **C2.1** The protocol is specifically designed for claims of negligence against professionals. This will include claims in which the allegation against a professional is that they have breached a contractual term to take reasonable skill and care. The protocol is also appropriate for claims of breach of fiduciary duty against professionals.

C2.2 The protocol is not intended to apply to claims:

(a) against Architects, Engineers and Quantity Surveyors - parties should use the Construction and Engineering Disputes (CED) protocol.

(b) against Healthcare providers—parties should use the pre-action protocol for the Resolution of Clinical Disputes.

(c) concerning defamation—parties should use the pre-action protocol for defamation claims.

C2.3 "Professional" is deliberately left undefined in the protocol. If it becomes an issue as to whether a defendant is or is not a professional, parties are reminded of the overriding need to act reasonably (see paragraphs A4 and C1.2 above). Rather than argue about the definition of "professional", therefore, the parties are invited to use this protocol, adapting it where appropriate.

C2.4 The protocol may not be suitable for disputes with professionals concerning intellectual property claims, etc. Until specific protocols are created for those claims, however, parties are invited to use this protocol, adapting it where necessary.

C2.5 Allegations of professional negligence are sometimes made in response to an attempt by the professional to recover outstanding fees. Where possible these allegations should be raised before litigation has commenced, in which case the parties should comply with the protocol before either party commences litigation. If litigation has already commenced it will be a matter for the Court whether sanctions should be imposed against either party. In any event, the parties are encouraged to consider applying to the Court for a stay to allow the protocol to be followed.

C3. Interaction with other pre-action Methods of Dispute Resolution

C7–015 **C3.1** There are a growing number of methods by which disputes *can be resolved without the* need for litigation, eg internal complaints procedures, the Surveyors and Valuers Arbitration Scheme, and so on. The Preliminary Notice procedure of the protocol (see paragraph B1) is designed to enable both parties to take stock at an early stage and to decide before work starts on preparing a Letter of Claim whether the grievance should be referred to one of these other dispute resolution procedures. (For the avoidance of doubt, however, there is no obligation on either party under the protocol to take any action at this stage other than giving the acknowledgment provided for in paragraph B1.4).

C3.2 Accordingly, parties are free to use (and are encouraged to use) any of the available pre-action procedures in an attempt to resolve their dispute. If appropriate, the parties can agree to suspend the protocol timetable whilst the other method of dispute resolution is used.

C3.3 If these methods fail to resolve the dispute, however, the protocol should be used before litigation is commenced. Because there has already been an attempt to resolve the dispute, it may be appropriate to adjust the protocol's requirements. In particular, unless the parties agree otherwise, there is unlikely to be any benefit in duplicating a stage which has in effect already been undertaken. However, if the protocol adds anything to the earlier method of dispute resolution, it should be used, adapting it where appropriate. Once again, the parties are expected to act reasonably.

C4. Multi-Party Disputes

C4.1 Paragraph B2.2 (a) of the protocol requires a Claimant to identify any other parties involved in the dispute or a related dispute. This is intended to ensure that all relevant parties are identified as soon as possible. **C7–016**

C4.2 If the dispute involves more than two parties, there are a number of potential problems. It is possible that different protocols will apply to different defendants. It is possible that defendants will claim against each other. It is possible that other parties will be drawn into the dispute. It is possible that the protocol timetable against one party will not be synchronised with the protocol timetable against a different party. How will these problems be resolved?

C4.3 As stated in paragraph C1.2 above, the parties are expected to act reasonably. What is "reasonable" will, of course, depend upon the specific facts of each case. Accordingly, it would be inappropriate for the protocol to set down generalised rules. Whenever a problem arises, the parties are encouraged to discuss how it can be overcome. In doing so, parties are reminded of the protocol's aims which include the aim to resolve the dispute without the need for litigation (paragraph A2 above).

C5. Investigations

C5.1 Paragraph B4.3 is intended to encourage the early exchange of *relevant information*, so that issues in the dispute can be clarified or resolved. It should not be used as a "fishing expedition" by either party. No party is obliged under paragraph B4.3 to disclose any document which a Court could not order them to disclose in the pre-action period. **C7–017**

C5.2 This protocol does not alter the parties' duties to disclose documents under any professional regulation or under general law.

C6. Experts

C7–018 **C6.1** Expert evidence is not always needed, although the use and role of experts in professional negligence claims is often crucial. However, the way in which expert evidence is used in, say, an insurance brokers' negligence case, is not necessarily the same as in, say, an accountants' case. Similarly, the approach to be adopted in a £10,000 case does not necessarily compare with the approach in a £10 million case. The protocol therefore is designed to be flexible and does not dictate a standard approach. On the contrary it envisages that the parties will bear the responsibility for agreeing how best to use experts.

C6.2 If a joint expert is used, therefore, the parties are left to decide issues such as: the payment of the expert, whether joint or separate instructions are used, how and to whom the expert is to report, how questions may be addressed to the expert and how the expert should respond, whether an agreed statement of facts is required, and so on.

C6.3 If separate experts are used, the parties are left to decide issues such as: whether the expert's reports should be exchanged, whether there should be an expert's meeting, and so on.

C6.4 Even if a joint expert is appointed, it is possible that parties will still want to instruct their own experts. The protocol does not prohibit this.

C7. Proceedings

C7–019 **C7.1** This protocol does not alter the statutory time limits for starting Court proceedings. A Claimant is required to start proceedings within those time limits.

C7.2 If proceedings are for any reason started before the parties have followed the procedures in this protocol, the parties are encouraged to agree to apply to the court for a stay whilst the protocol is followed.

The Judicial Review Protocol

C8A–001 This came into force in December 2001 and should be read with Pt 8 and Pt 54 and the detailed editorial commentary in the latter part. The protocol was drafted by a working party coordinated by a civil servant.

The main differences from the earlier protocols are:

- it is aimed more directly at litigants in person than the other protocols and so explains the principles of judicial review in outline;
- it provides advice on when judicial review may not be the appropriate remedy and on when the protocol may not be applicable—including when the proposed defendant does not have the legal power to change the decision being challenged, or in very urgent situations (see also the main editorial paragraph on alternatives to litigation);
- the defendant is asked to respond to the letter of claim within 14 days, if necessary on an interim basis, but emphasises that if he does not do so, the 3-month time period for the claimant to bring a claim under r.54.5 still applies;
- it suggests the claimant faxes the draft claim form to the defendant before issue-unusual but logical when the claimant has to seek permission to apply for judicial review.

PRE-ACTION PROTOCOL FOR JUDICIAL REVIEW

Introduction

C8–001 This protocol applies to proceedings within England and Wales only. It does not affect the time limit specified by Rule 54.5(1) of the Civil Procedure Rules which requires that any claim form in an application for judicial review must be filed promptly and in any event not later than 3 months after the grounds to make the claim first arose.[1]

1 Judicial review allows people with a sufficient interest in a decision or action by a public body to ask a judge to review the lawfulness of:

- an enactment; or
- a decision, action or failure to act in relation to the exercise of a public function.[2]

2 Judicial review may be used where there is no right of appeal or where all avenues of appeal have been exhausted.

Alternative dispute resolution

3.1 The parties should consider whether some form of alternative dispute resolution procedure would be more suitable than litigation, and if so, endeavour to agree which form to adopt. Both the Claimant and Defendant may be required by the Court to provide evidence that alternative means of resolving their dispute were considered. The Courts take the view that litigation should be a last resort, and that claims should not be issued prematurely when a settlement is still actively being explored. Parties are warned that if the protocol is not followed (including this paragraph) then the Court must have regard to such conduct when determining costs. However, parties should also note that a claim for judicial review "must be filed promptly and in any event not later than 3 months after the grounds to make the claim first arose".

3.2 It is not practicable in this protocol to address in detail how the parties might decide which method to adopt to resolve their particular dispute. However, summarised below are some of the options for resolving disputes without litigation:

- Discussion and negotiation.
- Ombudsmen—the Parliamentary and Health Service and the Local Government Ombudsmen have discretion to deal with complaints relating to maladministration. The British and Irish Ombudsman Association provide information about Ombudsman schemes and other complaint handling bodies and this is available from their website at *www.bioa.org.uk*. Parties may wish to note that the Ombudsmen are not able to look into a complaint once court action has been commenced.
- Early neutral evaluation by an independent third party (for example, a lawyer experienced in the field of administrative law or an individual experienced in the subject matter of the claim).
- Mediation—a form of facilitated negotiation assisted by an independent neutral party.

[1] While the court does not have the discretion under rule 3.1(2)(a) of the Civil Procedure Rules to allow a late claim, this is only used in exceptional circumstances. Compliance with the protocol alone is unlikely to be sufficient to persuade the court to allow a late claim.

[2] Civil Procedure Rules, r. 54.1(2)

3.3 The Legal Services Commission has published a booklet on "Alternatives to Court", CLS Direct Information Leaflet 23 (*www.clsdirect.org.uk*), which lists a number of organisations that provide alternative dispute resolution services.

3.4 *It is expressly recognised that no party can or should be forced to mediate or enter into any form of ADR.*

4 Judicial review may not be appropriate in every instance.

Claimants are strongly advised to seek appropriate legal advice when considering such proceedings and, in particular, before adopting this protocol or making a claim. Although the Legal Services Commission will not normally grant full representation before a letter before claim has been sent and the proposed defendant given a reasonable time to respond, initial funding may be available, for eligible claimants, to cover the work necessary to write this. (See Annex C for more information.)

5 This protocol sets out a code of good practice and contains the steps which parties should generally follow before making a claim for judicial review.

6 This protocol does not impose a greater obligation on a public body to disclose documents or give reasons for its decision than that already provided for in statute and common law. However, where the court considers that a public body should have provided **relevant** documents and/or information, particularly where this failure is a breach of a statutory or common law requirement, it may impose sanctions.

This protocol will not be appropriate where the defendant does not have the legal power to change the decision being challenged, for example decisions issued by tribunals such as the the Asylum and Immigration Tribunal.

This protocol will not be appropriate in urgent cases, for example, when directions have been set, or are in force, for the claimant's removal from the UK, or where there is an urgent need for an interim order to compel a public body to act where it has unlawfully refused to do so (for example, the failure of a local housing authority to secure interim accommodation for a homeless claimant) a claim should be made immediately. A letter before claim will not stop the implementation of a disputed decision in all instances.

7 All claimants will need to satisfy themselves whether they should follow the protocol, depending upon the circumstances of his or her case. Where the use of the protocol is appropriate, the court will normally expect all parties to have complied with it and will take into account compliance or non-compliance when giving directions for case management of proceedings or when making orders for costs.[1] However, in emergency cases, it is good practice to fax to the defendant the draft Claim Form which the claimant intends to issue. A claimant is also normally required to notify a defendant when an interim mandatory order is being sought.

The letter before claim

8 *Before making* a claim, the claimant should send a letter to the

[1] Civil Procedure Rules, Costs Practice Direction.

defendant. The purpose of this letter is to identify the issues in dispute and establish whether litigation can be avoided.

9 Claimants should normally use the suggested **standard format** for the letter outlined in Annex A.

10 The letter should contain **the date and details of the decision, act or omission being challenged and a clear summary of the facts** on which the claim is based. It should also contain the details of any relevant information that the claimant is seeking and an explanation of why this is considered relevant.

11 The letter should normally contain the **details of any interested parties**[1] known to the claimant. They should be sent a **copy** of the letter before the claim **for information. Claimants are strongly advised to seek appropriate legal advice when considering such proceedings and, in particular, before sending the letter before the claim to other interested parties or making a claim**.

12 The claim should not normally be made until the proposed reply date given in the letter before the claim has passed, unless the circumstances of the case require more immediate action to be taken.

The letter of response

13 Defendants should normally respond within 14 days using the **standard format** at Annex B. Failure to do so will be taken into account by the court and sanctions may be imposed unless there are good reasons.[2]

14 Where it is not possible to reply within the proposed time limit the defendant should send an interim reply and propose a reasonable extension. Where an extension is sought, reasons should be given and, where required, additional information requested. **This will not affect the time limit for making a claim for judicial review**[3] nor will it bind the claimant where he or she considers this to be unreasonable. However, where the court considers that a subsequent claim is made prematurely it may impose sanctions.

15 If the **claim is being conceded in full**, the reply should say so in clear and unambiguous terms.

16 If the **claim is being conceded in part or not being conceded at all**, the reply should say so in clear and unambiguous terms, and:

(a) where appropriate, contain a new decision, clearly identifying what aspects of the claim are being conceded and what are not, or give a clear timescale within which the new decision will be issued;

(b) provide a fuller explanation for the decision, if considered appropriate to do so;

(c) address any points of dispute, or explain why they cannot be addressed;

(d) enclose any **relevant** documentation requested by the claimant, or explain why the documents are not being enclosed; and

[1] See Civil Procedure Rules, r.54.1(2).
[2] See Civil Procedure Rules, Pre-Action Protocols Practice Direction, paras 2-3.
[3] See Civil Procedure Rules, r.54.5(1).

(e) where appropriate, confirm whether or not they will oppose any application for an interim remedy.

17 The response should be sent to **all interested parties**[1] identified by the claimant and contain details of any other parties who the defendant considers also have an interest.

Annex A

Letter before claim

Section 1. Information required in a letter before claim

1 Proposed claim for judicial review

C8–002 **To**

(Insert the name and address of the proposed defendant – see details in section 2)

2 The claimant

(Insert the title, first and last name and the address of the claimant)

3 Reference details

(When dealing with large organisations it is important to understand that the information relating to any particular individual's previous dealings with it may not be immediately available, therefore it is important to set out the relevant reference numbers for the matter in dispute and/or the identity of those within the public body who have been handling the particular matter in dispute – see details in section 3)

4 The details of the matter being challenged

(Set out clearly the matter being challenged, particularly if there has been more than one decision)

5 The issue

(Set out the date and details of the decision, or act or omission being challenged, a brief summary of the facts and why it is contented to be wrong)

6 The details of the action that the defendant is expected to take

(Set out the details of the remedy sought, including whether a review or any interim remedy are being requested)

7 The details of the legal advisers, if any, dealing with this claim

(Set out the name, address and reference details of any legal advisers dealing with the claim)

8 The details of any interested parties

(Set out the details of any interested parties and confirm that they have been sent a copy of this letter)

9 The details of information sought

(Set out the details of any information that is sought. This may include a request for a fuller explanation of the reasons for the decision that is being challenged)

10 The details of any documents that are considered relevant and necessary

(Set out the details of any documentation or policy in respect of which the disclosure is sought and explain why these are relevant. If you rely on a statutory duty to disclose, this should be specified)

[1] See Civil Procedure Rules, r.54.1(2)(f).

11 The address for reply and service of court documents

(Insert the address for the reply)

12 Proposed reply date

(The precise time will depend upon the circumstances of the individual case. However, although a shorter or longer time may be appropriate in a particular case, 14 days is a reasonable time to allow in most circumstances)

Section 2. Address for sending the letter before claim

Public bodies have requested that, for certain types of cases, in order to ensure a prompt repsonse, letters before claim should be sent to specific addresses. • **Where the claim concerns a decision in an immigration, asylum or nationality case:** The Judicial Review Management Unit UK Border Agency 1st Floor Green Park House 29 Wellesley Road Croydon CR20 2AJ • **Where the claim concerns a decision by the Legal Services Commission:** The address on the decision letter/notification; Legal Director Corporate Legal Team Legal Services Commission 4 Abbey Orchard Street London SW1P 2BS • **Where the claim concerns a decision by a local authority:**

The address on the decision letter/notification; and their legal department[1]

- **Where the claim concerns a decision by a department or body for whom Treasury Solicitor acts *and Treasury Solicitor has already been involved in the case* a copy should also be sent, quoting the Treasury Solicitor's reference, to:**

The Treasury Solicitor,
One Kemble Street,
London,
WC2B 4TS

In all other circumstances, the letter should be sent to the address on the letter notifying the decision.

Section 3. Specific reference details required

Public bodies have requested that the following information should be provided in order to ensure prompt response. **Where the claim concerns an immigration, asylum or nationality case, dependent upon the nature of the case:**

- The Home Office reference number;
- The Port reference;
- The Asylum and Immigration Tribunal reference number;
- The National Asylum Support Service reference number; or if these are unavailable
- The full name, nationality and date of birth of the claimant.

Where the claim concerns a decision by the Legal Services Commission:

- The certificate number.

[1] The relevant address should be available from a range of sources such as the Phone Book; Business and Services Directory, Thomson's Local Directory, CAB, etc.

Annex B

Response to a letter before claim

Information required in a response to a letter before claim

C8–003 **1 The claimant**

(Insert the title, first and last names and the address to which any reply should be sent)

2 From

(Insert the name and address of the defendant)

3 Reference details

(Set out the relevant reference numbers for the matter in dispute and the identity of those within the public body who have been handling the issue)

4 The details of the matter being challenged

(Set out details of the matter being challenged, providing a fuller explanation of the decision, where this is considered appropriate)

5 Response to the proposed claim

(Set out whether the issue in question is conceded in part, or in full, or will be contested. Where it is not proposed to disclose any information that has been requested, explain the reason for this. Where an interim reply is being sent and there is a realistic prospect of settlement, details should ber included)

6 Details of any other interested parties

(Identify any other parties who you consider have an interest who have not already been sent a letter by the claimant)

7 Address for further correspondence and service of court documents

(Set out the address for any future correspondence on this matter)

Annex C

Notes on public funding for legal costs in judicial review

C8–004 Public funding for legal costs in judicial review is available from legal professionals and advice agencies which have contracts with the Legal Services Commission as part of the Community Legal Service. Funding may be provided for:

- ***Legal Help*** to provide initial advice and assistance with any legal problem; or
- ***Legal Representation*** to allow you to be represented in court if you are taking or defending court proceedings. This is available in two forms:
- ***Investigative Help*** is limited to funding toi investigate the strength of the proposed claim. It includes the issue and conduct of proceedings only so far as is necessary to obtain disclosure of relevant information or to protect the client's position in relation to any urgent hearing or time limit for the issue of proceedings. This includes the work necessary to write a letter before claim to the body potentially under challenge, setting out the grounds of challenge, and giving that body a reasonable opportunity, typically 14 days, in which to respond.

- ***Full Representation*** is provided to represent you in legal proceedings and includes litigation services, advocacy services, and all such help as is usually given by a person providing representation in proceedings, including steps preliminary or incidental to proceedings, and/or arriving at or giving affect to a compromise to avoid or bring to an end any proceedings. Except in emergency cases, a proper **letter before claim** must be sent and the other side must be given an opportunity to respond before Full Representation is granted.

Further information on the type(s) of help available and the criteria for receiving that help may be found in the Legal Service Manual Volume 3: "The Funding Code". This may be found on the Legal Services Commission website at:

www.legalservices.co.uk

A list of contracted firms and Advice Agencies may be found on the Community Legal Services website at:

www.justask.org.uk

The Protocol for Disease and Illness at Work Claims

This is a variation of the personal injury protocol for disease and illness at work claims and is in force from December 8, 2003. These are often more difficult than many other personal injury claims, as locating the employment(s) where the disease was contracted, and establishing whether there is causation can be problematic. Limitation may be an issue and in some cases the claimant may be so ill by the time the disease is diagnosed that death may be imminent. **C9A–001**

The main differences from the personal injury protocol are:

- This one applies to disease and illness claims which may be complex and unsuitable for the fast track despite their value
- Claimants are permitted to obtain their occupational health records, GP records, and a medical report before sending a letter of claim (but none of these are requirements)
- The letter of claim should include a chronology of relevant events re the claimant's employment history and the illness
- It is acknowledged that expert opinions will usually be needed pre-action on knowledge, fault and causation, on condition and prognosis, and to value aspects of the claim and that the parties should adopt a flexible approach to obtaining these.

PRE-ACTION PROTOCOL FOR DISEASE AND ILLNESS CLAIMS

1.

Introduction

1.1 Lord Woolf in his final Access to Justice Report of July 1996 recommended the development of protocols: "To build on and increase the benefits of early but well informed settlement which genuinely satisfy both parties to dispute." **C9–001**

1.2 The aims of these protocols are:

- more contact between the parties
- better and earlier exchange of information
- better investigation by both sides
- to put the parties in a position where they may be able to settle cases fairly and early without litigation

- to enable proceedings to run to the court's timetable and efficiently, if litigation does become necessary.

1.3 The concept of protocols is relevant to a range of initiatives for good claims practice, especially:

- predictability in the time needed for steps to be taken
- standardisation of relevant information, including documents to be disclosed.

1.4 The Courts will be able to treat the standards set in protocols as the normal reasonable approach. If proceedings are issued, it will be for the court to decide whether non-compliance with a protocol should merit adverse consequences. Guidance on the court's likely approach will be given from time to time in practice directions.

1.5 If the court has to consider the question of compliance after proceedings have begun, it will not be concerned with minor infringements, e.g. failure by a short period to provide relevant information. One minor breach will not exempt the "innocent" party from following the protocol. The court will look at the effect of non-compliance on the other party when deciding whether to impose sanctions.

2.

Notes of Guidance

Scope of the Protocol

C9–002 **2.1** This protocol is intended to apply to all personal injury claims where the injury is not as the result of an accident but takes the form of an illness or disease.

2.2 This protocol covers disease claims which are likely to be complex and frequently not suitable for fast-track procedures even though they may fall within fast track limits. Disease for the purpose of this protocol primarily covers any illness physical or psychological, any disorder, ailment, affliction, complaint, malady, or derangement other than a physical or psychological injury solely caused by an accident or other similar single event.

2.3 This protocol is not limited to diseases occurring in the workplace but will embrace diseases occurring in other situations for example through occupation of premises or the use of products. It is not intended to cover those cases, which are dealt with as a "group" or "class" action.

2.4 The "cards on the table" approach advocated by the personal injury protocol is equally appropriate to disease claims. The spirit of that protocol, and of the clinical negligence protocol is followed here, in accordance with the sense of the civil justice reforms.

2.5 The timetable and the arrangements for disclosing documents and obtaining expert evidence may need to be varied to suit the circumstances of the case. If a party considers the detail of the protocol to be inappropriate they should communicate their reasons to all of the parties at that stage. If proceedings are subsequently issued, the court will expect an explanation as to why the protocol has not been followed, or has been varied. In a terminal disease claim with short life expectancy, for instance for a claimant who has a disease such as mesothelioma, the time scale of the protocol is likely to be too long.

In such a claim, the claimant may not be able to follow the protocol and the defendant would be expected to treat the claim with urgency.

2A.

Alternative Dispute Resolution

2A.1 The parties should consider whether some form of alternative dispute resolution procedure would be more suitable than litigation, and if so, endeavour to agree which form to adopt. Both the Claimant and Defendant may be required by the Court to provide evidence that alternative means of resolving their dispute were considered. The Courts take the view that litigation should be a last resort, and that claims should not be issued prematurely when a settlement is still actively being explored. Parties are warned that if the protocol is not followed (including this paragraph) then the Court must have regard to such conduct when determining costs. **C9–002A**

2A.2 It is not practicable in this protocol to address in detail how the parties might decide which method to adopt to resolve their particular dispute. However, summarised below are some of the options for resolving disputes without litigation:

- Discussion and negotiation.
- Early neutral evaluation by an independent third party (for example, a lawyer experienced in the field of disease or illness, or an individual experienced in the subject matter of the claim).
- Mediation—a form of facilitated negotiation assisted by an independent neutral party.

2A.3 The Legal Services Commission has published a booklet on "Alternatives to Court", CLS Direct Information Leaflet 23 (*www.clsdirect.org.uk/legalhelp/leaflet23.jsp*), which lists a number of organisations that provide alternative dispute resolution services.

2A.4 *It is expressly recognised that no party can or should be forced to mediate or enter into any form of ADR.*

3.

The Aims of the Protocol

3.1 The **general** aims of the protocol are: **C9–003**

- to resolve as many disputes as possible without litigation;
- where a claim cannot be resolved to identify the relevant issues which remain in dispute.

3.2 The **specific** objectives are:

OPENNESS

- to encourage early communication of the perceived problem between the parties or their insurers;
- to encourage employees to voice any concerns or worries about possible work related illness as soon as practicable;
- to encourage employers to develop systems of early reporting and investigation of suspected occupational health problems and to provide full and prompt explanations to concerned employees or former employees;

- to apply such principles to perceived problems outside the employer/employee relationship, for example occupiers of premises or land and producers of products;
- to ensure that sufficient information is disclosed by both parties to enable each to understand the other's perspective and case, and to encourage early resolution;

TIMELINESS

- to provide an early opportunity for employers (past or present) or their insurers to identify cases where an investigation is required and to carry out that investigation promptly;
- to encourage employers (past or present) or other defendants to involve and identify their insurers at an early stage;
- to ensure that all relevant records including health and personnel records are provided to employees (past or present) or their appointed representatives promptly on request, by any employer (past or present) or their insurers. This should be complied with to a realistic timetable;
- to ensure that relevant records which are in the claimant's possession are made available to the employers or their insurers by claimants or their advisers at an appropriate stage;
- to proceed on a reasonable timetable where a resolution is not achievable to lay the ground to enable litigation to proceed at a reasonable and proportionate cost, and to limit the matters in contention;
- to communicate promptly where any of the requested information is not available or does not exist;
- to discourage the prolonged pursuit of unmeritorious claims and the prolonged defence of meritorious claims.
- To encourage all parties, at the earliest possible stage, to disclose voluntarily any additional documents which will assist in resolving any issue.

4.

The Protocol

C9–004 This protocol is not a comprehensive code governing all the steps in disease claims. Rather it attempts to set out a code of good practice which parties should follow.

Obtaining Occupational Records Including Health Records

4.1 In appropriate cases, a **potential claimant** may request Occupational Records including Health Records and Personnel Records before sending a Letter of Claim.

4.2 Any request for records by the **potential claimant** or his adviser should **provide sufficient information** to alert the **potential defendant** or his insurer where a possible disease claim is being investigated; Annex A1 provides a suggested form for this purpose for use in cases arising from employment. Similar forms can be prepared and used in other situations.

4.3 The copy records should be provided **within a maximum of 40 days** of the request at no cost. Although these will primarily be occupational records, it will be good practice for a **potential defendant** to disclose product data documents identified by a **potential claimant** at this stage which may resolve a causation issue.

4.4 In the rare circumstances that the **potential defendant** or his insurer is in difficulty in providing information quickly details should be given of what is being done to resolve it with a reasonable time estimate for doing so.

4.5 If the **potential defendant** or his insurer fails to provide the records including health records within 40 days and fails to comply with paragraph 4.4 above, the **potential claimant** or his adviser may then apply to the court for an **order for pre-action disclosure**. The Civil Procedure Rules make pre-action applications to the court easier. The court also has the power to impose costs sanctions for unreasonable delay in providing records.

5.

Communication

5.1 If either the **potential claimant** or his adviser considers **additional records are required from a third party**, such as records from previous employers or general practitioner records, in the first instance these should be requested by the **potential claimant** or their advisers. Third party record holders would be expected to co-operate. The Civil Procedure Rules enable parties to apply to the court for pre-action disclosure by third parties. **C9–005**

5.2 As soon as the records have been received and analysed, the **potential claimant** or his adviser should consider whether a claim should be made. General practitioner records will normally be obtained before a decision is reached.

5.3 If a decision is made not to proceed further at this stage against a party identified as a **potential defendant**, the **potential claimant** or his adviser should notify that **potential defendant** as soon as practicable.

6.

Letter of Claim

6.1 Where a decision is made to make a claim, the claimant shall send to the proposed defendant two copies of a letter of claim, as soon as sufficient information is available to substantiate a realistic claim and before issues of quantum are addressed in detail. One copy is for the defendants, the second for passing on to his insurers. **C9–006**

6.2 This letter shall contain a **clear summary of the facts** on which the claim is based, including details of the illness alleged, and the ***main allegations of fault***. It shall also give details of present condition and prognosis. The **financial loss** incurred by the claimant should be outlined. Where the case is funded by a conditional fee agreement, notification should be given of the existence of the agreement and where appropriate, that there is a success fee and insurance premium, although not the level of the success fee or premium.

6.3 Solicitors are recommended to use a **standard format** for such a letter—an example is at Annex B: this can be amended to suit the particular case, for example, if the client has rehabilitation needs these can also be detailed in the letter.

6.4 A **chronology** of the relevant events (e.g. dates or periods of exposure) should be provided. In the case of alleged occupational disease an appropriate employment history should also be provided, particularly if the claimant has been employed by a number of different employers and the illness in question has a long latency period.

6.5 The letter of claim should identify any **relevant documents**, including health records not already in the defendant's possession *e.g.* any relevant general practitioner records. These will need to be disclosed in confidence to the nominated insurance manager or solicitor representing the defendant following receipt of their letter of acknowledgement. Where the action is brought under the Law Reform Act 1934 or the Fatal Accidents Act 1976 then **relevant documents** will normally include copies of the death certificate, the post mortem report, the inquest depositions and if obtained by that date the grant of probate or letters of administration.

6.6 The letter of claim should indicate whether a claim is also being made against any **other potential defendant** and identify any known insurer involved.

6.7 Sufficient information should be given to enable the defendant's insurer/solicitor to commence **investigations** and at least to put a broad valuation on the "risk".

6.8 It is not a requirement for the claimant to provide **medical evidence** with the letter of claim, but the claimant may choose to do so in very many cases.

6.9 Letters of claim and response are not intended to have the same **status** as a statement of case in proceedings. Matters may come to light as a result of investigation after the letter of claim has been sent, or after the defendant has responded, particularly if disclosure of documents takes place outside the recommended three-month period. These circumstances could mean that the "pleaded" case of one or both parties is presented slightly differently than in the letter of claim or response. It would not be consistent with the spirit of the protocol for a party to "take a point" on this in the proceedings, provided that there was no obvious intention by the party who changed their position to mislead the other party.

6.10 Proceedings should not be issued until after three months from the date of acknowledgement (see paragraph 7), unless there is a limitation problem and/or the claimant's position needs to be protected by early issue. (See paragraph 2.5)

7.

The Response

C9–007 **7.1** The defendant should **send an acknowledgement within 21 calendar days** of the date of posting of the letter of claim, identifying the liability insurer (if any) who will be dealing with the matter and, if necessary, identifying specifically any significant omissions from the Letter of Claim. If there has been no acknowledgement by the defendant or insurer within 21 days, the claimant will be entitled to issue proceedings.

7.2 The identity of all relevant insurers, if more than one, should be notified to the claimant by the insurer identified in the acknowledgement letter, within one calendar month of the date of that acknowledgement.

7.3 The defendant or his representative should, **within three months of the date of the acknowledgement letter**, provide a **reasoned answer**:

- if the **claim is admitted**, they should say so in clear terms;
- if only **part of the claim is admitted** they should make clear which issues of fault and/or causation and/or limitation are admitted and which remain in issue and why;
- **if the claim is not admitted in full**, they should explain why and should, **for example**, include comments on the employment status of the claimant, (including job description(s) and details of the department(s) where the claimant worked), the allegations of fault, causation and of limitation, and if a synopsis or chronology of relevant events has been provided and is disputed, their version of those events;
- **if the claim is not admitted in full**, the defendant should enclose with his letter of reply **documents** in his possession which are **material to the issues** between the parties and which would be likely to be ordered to be disclosed by the court, either on an application for pre-action disclosure, or on disclosure during proceedings. Reference can be made to the documents annexed to the personal injury protocol.
- where more than one defendant receives a letter of claim, the timetable will be activated for each defendant by the date on the letter of claim addressed to them. If any defendant wishes to extend the timetable because the number of defendants will cause complications, they should seek agreement to a different timetable as soon as possible.

7.4 If the parties reach agreement on liability and/or causation, but time is needed to resolve other issues including the value of the claim, they should aim to agree a reasonable period.

7.5 Where it is not practicable for the defendant to complete his investigations within 3 months, the defendant should indicate the difficulties and outline the further time needed. Any request for an extension of time should be made, with reasons, as soon as the defendant becomes aware that an extension is needed and normally before the 3 month period has expired. Such an extension of time should be agreed in circumstances where reasonable justification has been shown. Lapse of many years since the circumstances giving rise to the claim does not, by itself, constitute reasonable justification for further time.

7.6 Where the relevant negligence occurred outside England and Wales and/or where the defendant is outside the jurisdiction, the time periods of 21 days and three months should normally be extended up to 42 days and six months.

8.

Special Damages

8.1 The claimant will send to the defendant as soon as practicable **C9–008**

a Schedule of Special Damages with supporting documents, particularly where the defendant has admitted liability.

9.

Experts

C9–009 **9.1** In disease claims expert opinions will usually be needed:

- on knowledge, fault and causation;
- on condition and prognosis;
- to assist in valuing aspects of the claim.

9.2 The civil justice reforms and the Civil Procedure Rules encourage economy in the use of experts and a less adversarial expert culture. It is recognised that in disease claims, the parties and their advisers will require flexibility in their approach to expert evidence. Decisions on whether experts might be instructed jointly, and on whether reports might be disclosed sequentially or by exchange, should rest with the parties and their advisers. Sharing expert evidence may be appropriate on various issues including those relating to the value of the claim. However, this protocol does not attempt to be prescriptive on issues in relation to expert evidence.

9.3 Obtaining expert evidence will often be an expensive step and may take time, especially in specialised areas where there are limited numbers of suitable experts. Claimants, defendants and their advisers, will therefore need to consider carefully how best to obtain any necessary expert help quickly and cost-effectively.

9.4 The protocol recognises that a flexible approach must be adopted in the obtaining of medical reports in claims of this type. There will be very many occasions where the claimant will need to obtain a medical report before writing the letter of claim. In such cases the defendant will be entitled to obtain their own medical report. In some other instances it may be more appropriate to send the letter of claim before the medical report is obtained. Defendants will usually need to see a medical report before they can reach a view on causation.

9.5 Where the parties agree the nomination of a single expert is appropriate, before any party instructs an expert he should give the other party a list of the **name**(s) of **one or more experts** in the relevant speciality whom he considers are suitable to instruct. The parties are encouraged to agree the instruction of a single expert to deal with discrete areas such as cost of care.

9.6 Within 14 days the other party may indicate **an objection** to one or more of the named experts. The first party should then instruct a mutually acceptable expert. If the Claimant nominates an expert in the original letter of claim, the 14 days is in addition to the 21 days in paragraph 7.1.

9.7 If the second party objects to all the listed experts, the parties may then instruct **experts of their own choice**. It would be for the court to decide subsequently, if proceedings are issued, whether either party had acted unreasonably.

9.8 If the **second party does not object to an expert nominated**, he shall not be entitled to rely on his own expert evidence within that particular speciality unless:

(a) the first party agrees,
(b) the court so directs, or
(c) the first party's expert report has been amended and the first party is not prepared to disclose the original report.

9.9 Either party may send to an agreed expert written questions on the report, relevant to the issues, via the first party's solicitors. The expert should send answers to the questions separately and directly to each party.

9.10 The cost of a report from an agreed expert will usually be paid by the instructing first party: the costs of the expert replying to questions will usually be borne by the party which asks the questions.

9.11 Where the defendant admits liability in whole or in part, before proceedings are issued, any medical report obtained under this protocol which **the claimant** relies upon, should be disclosed to the other party.

9.12 Where the defendant admits liability in whole or in part before proceedings are issued, any medical report obtained under this protocol which **the defendant** relies upon, should be disclosed to the claimant.

10.

Resolution of Issues

10.1 The Civil Procedure Rules Part 36 enable claimants and defendants to make formal offers to settle before proceedings are started. Parties should consider making such an offer, since to do so often leads to settlement. If such an offer is made, the party making the offer must always supply sufficient evidence and/or information to enable the offer to be properly considered. **C9–010**

10.2 Where a claim is not resolved when the protocol has been followed, the parties might wish to carry out a "stocktake" of the issues in dispute, and the evidence that the court is likely to need to decide those issues, before proceedings are started.

10.3 Prior to proceedings it will be usual for all parties to disclose those expert reports relating to liability and causation upon which they propose to rely.

10.4 The claimant should delay issuing proceedings for 21 days from disclosure of reports to enable the parties to consider whether the claim is capable of settlement.

10.5 Where the defendant is insured and the pre-action steps have been conducted by the insurer, the insurer would normally be expected to nominate solicitors to act in the proceedings and the claimant's solicitor is recommended to invite the insurer to nominate solicitors to act in the proceedings and to do so 7–14 days before the intended issue date.

11.

Limitation

11.1 If by reason of complying with any part of this protocol a claimant's claim may be time-barred under any provision of the **C9–011**

Limitation Act 1980, or any other legislation which imposes a time limit for bringing an action, the claimant may commence proceedings without complying with this protocol. In such circumstances, a claimant who commences proceedings without complying with all, or any part, of this protocol may apply to the court on notice for directions as to the timetable and form of procedure to be adopted, at the same time as he requests the court to issue proceedings. The court will consider whether to order a stay of the whole or part of the proceedings pending compliance with this protocol.

Annex A

Letter Requesting Occupational Records Including Health Records

C9–012 Dear Sirs,

We are acting on behalf of the above-named who has developed the following ***(insert disease)***. We are investigating whether this disease may have been caused: -

- ***during the course of his employment with you / name of employer if different***
- ***whilst at your premises at (address)***
- ***as a result of your product (name)***

We are writing this in accordance with the Protocol for Disease and Illness Claims

We seek the following records: -

(Insert details e.g. personnel / occupational health)

Please note your insurers may require you to advise them of this request.

We enclose a request form and expect to receive the records within 40 days.

If you are not able to comply with this request within this time, please advise us of the reason.

Yours faithfully

Annex A1

APPLICATION ON BEHALF OF A POTENTIAL CLAIMANT FOR USE WHERE A DISEASE CLAIM IS BEING INVESTIGATED C9–013

This should be completed as fully as possible

Company
Name
And
Address

1 a)	Full name of claimant (including previous surnames)	
b)	Address now	
c)	Address at date of termination of employment, if different	
d)	Date of birth (and death, if applicable)	
e)	National Insurance number, if available	
2	Department(s) where claimant worked	
3.	This application is made because the claimant is considering	
a)	a claim against you as detailed in para 4	YES/NO
b)	Pursuing an action against someone else	YES/NO
4	If the answer to Q3(a) is 'Yes' details of	
	a) the likely nature of the claim, eg dermatitis	
	b) grounds for the claim, eg exposure to chemical	
	c) approximate dates of the events involved	

5	If the answer to Q3(b) is 'Yes' insert	
	a) the names of the proposed defendants	
	b) have legal proceedings been started?	YES/NO
	c) if appropriate, details of the claim and action number	
6	Any other relevant information or documents requested	
	Signature of Solicitor	
	Name	
	Address	
	Ref.	
	Telephone Number	
	Fax number	
I authorise you to disclose all of your records relating to me/the claimant to my solicitor and to your legal and insurance representatives. Signature of Claimant		
Signature of personal representative where claimant has died		

Annex B

Template for Letter of Claim

C9–014 To: - Defendant

Dear Sirs

Re: Claimant's full name

Claimant's full address

Claimant's National Insurance Number

Claimant's Date of Birth

Claimant's Clock or Works Number

Claimant's Employer (name and address)

We are instructed by the above named to claim damages in connection with a claim for: -

Specify occupational disease

We are writing this letter in accordance with the pre-action protocol for disease and illness claims.

Please confirm the identity of your insurers. Please note that your insurers will need to see this letter as soon as possible and it may affect your insurance cover if you do not send this to them.

The Claimant was employed by you ***(if the claim arises out of public or occupiers' liability give appropriate details)*** as ***job description*** from ***date*** to ***date***. During the relevant period of his employment he worked: -

description of precisely where the Claimant worked and what he did to include a description of any machines used and details of any exposure to noise or substances

The circumstances leading to the development of this condition are as follows: -

Give chronology of events

The reason why we are alleging fault is: -

Details should be given of contemporary and comparable employees who have suffered from similar problems if known; any protective equipment provided; complaints; the supervisors concerned, if known.

Our client's employment history is attached.

We have also made a claim against: - Insert details Their insurers' details are: -Insert if known

We have the following documents in support of our client's claim and will disclose these in confidence to your nominated insurance manager or solicitor when we receive their acknowledgement letter.

e.g. Occupational health notes; GP notes

We have obtained a medical report from (name) and will disclose this when we receive your acknowledgement of this letter.

(This is optional at this stage)

From the information we presently have: -

(i) the Claimant first became aware of symptoms on ***(insert approximate date)***

(ii) the Claimant first received medical advice about those symptoms on ***(insert date) (give details of advice given if appropriate)***

(iii) the Claimant first believed that those symptoms might be due to exposure leading to this claim on ***(insert approximate date)***

A description of our client's condition is as follows: -

This should be sufficiently detailed to allow the Defendant to put a broad value on the claim

He has the following time off work: -

Insert dates

He is presently employed as a ***job description*** and his average net weekly income is **£**

If you are our client's employers, please provide us with the usual earnings details, which will enable us to calculate his financial loss.

Please note that we have entered into a conditional fee agreement with our client dated in relation to this claim which provides for a success fee within the meaning of section 58(2) of the Courts and Legal Services Act 1990. Our client has taken out an insurance policy dated with (name of insurance company) to which section 29 of the Access to Justice Act 1999 applies in respect of this claim.

A copy of this letter is attached for you to send to your insurers. Finally we expect an acknowledgement of this letter within 21 days by yourselves or your insurers.

Yours faithfully

The Protocol for Housing Disrepair Cases

C10A–001 This protocol, which came into force on December 8, 2003, was first mooted during the Access to Justice inquiry. It has taken so long to be implemented because the social landlords and the tenant lawyers had great difficulties in reaching a consensus. The Law Society deserves much of the credit for achieving a result.

The main features are:

- The protocol applies to claims arising from the condition of residential premises only and exclude counterclaims filed against possession proceedings.
- The tenant should notify the landlord as early as possible that a claim for disrepair is being considered—this letter should propose instruction of an expert (where necessary only) and request disclosure of the tenancy and repair files for the property.
- A full letter of claim should be sent asap after the early notification letter and should detail the defects in a schedule, their history and the effect on the tenant and any special damages claimed.
- Within 20 working days of either letter the landlord should reply in detail, send relevant documents requested, and respond to the tenant's proposals with regard to expert evidence.
- Where possible experts should be single joint (with the cost shared) and the expert should inspect the property within 20 days of the letter of response and report within 10 days of the inspection.
- Where there is a personal injury element to the claim the pre-action protocol for personal injury claims should be followed for the personal injury element unless it is sufficiently minor for a GP letter to suffice for the medical evidence. Where the disrepair is urgent the Guidance to the housing protocol suggests that it would be reasonable initially to pursue the disrepair and personal injury claims separately, but that they could later be consolidated and case managed together.
- The Guidance reminds tenants to consider other options before using the protocol including the Local Government or Independent Housing Ombudsmen.
- Where the claim is settled without litigation the landlord should pay the tenant's costs and out of pocket expenses such as those incurred in small claims track cases e.g. loss of earnings and expert fees.

The main areas of practical difficulty are likely to be whether the landlord can provide files in 20 working days and respond to a letter of claim in the same time frame. Several other protocols have longer, and perhaps, more realistic time scales. The provisions for combined disrepair and personal injury claims could cause confusion, including by those funding claims, as personal injury claims no longer attract public funding while disrepair does. Finally complaints to the Ombudsmen may not be the right approach when there is serious or urgent disrepair especially where damages are the appropriate remedy.

PRE-ACTION PROTOCOL FOR HOUSING DISREPAIR CASES

1.

Introduction

C10–001 Following a review of the problems of civil housing disrepair claims, Lord Woolf recommended in his final Access to Justice Report in July 1996 that there should be a Pre-action Protocol.

The Protocol, which covers claims in England and Wales, is intended to encourage the exchange of information between parties at an early stage and to provide a clear framework within which parties in a housing disrepair claim can attempt to achieve an early and appropriate resolution of the issues. An attempt has been made to draft the Protocol in plain English and to keep the contents straightforward in order to make the Protocol accessible and easy to use by all, including those representing themselves.

The Protocol embraces the spirit of the Woolf Reforms to the Civil Justice System. As Lord Woolf noted, landlords and tenants have a common interest in maintaining housing stock in good condition. It is generally common ground that in principle court action should be treated as a last resort, and it is hoped that the Protocol will lead to the avoidance of unnecessary litigation. Before using the Protocol tenants should therefore ensure that the landlord is aware of the disrepair. Tenants should also consider whether other options for having repairs carried out and/or obtaining compensation are more appropriate. Examples of other options are set out in paragraph 4.1(b).

Should a claim proceed to litigation, the court will expect all parties to have complied with the Protocol as far as possible. The court has the power to order parties who have unreasonably failed to comply with the Protocol to pay costs or be subject to other sanctions.

Birmingham City Council v Lee [2008] EWCA Civ 891 was a claim by a tenant for the consequential damage of less than £5,000 arising from the landlord's failure to carry out repairs until after receipt of the letter of claim. It was decided that it was clear from the Preaction Protocol for Housing Disrepair, para.3.7 and note 4.10, that the claimant tenant's reasonable legal costs were payable on the fast track basis, up to the date when the repairs were completed, because until then, the claimant had a potential claim for specific performance of the repairs that would have merited allocation of the claim to the fast track.

2.

Aims of the Protocol

The Practice Direction on Protocols in the Civil Procedure Rules provides that the objectives of pre-action Protocols, are: C10–002

(1) *to encourage the exchange of early and full information about the prospective legal claim,*
(2) *to enable parties to avoid litigation by agreeing a settlement of the claim before the commencement of proceedings,*
(3) *to support the efficient management of proceedings where litigation cannot be avoided.*

The specific aims of this Protocol are:

- To avoid unnecessary litigation.
- To promote the speedy and appropriate carrying out of any repairs which are the landlord's responsibility.
- To ensure that tenants receive any compensation to which they are entitled as speedily as possible.
- To promote good pre-litigation practice, including the early exchange of information and to give guidance about the instruction of experts.
- To keep the costs of resolving disputes down.

3.

Protocol

C10–003 When using this Protocol, please refer to the **Guidance Notes** in paragraph 4.

3.1 Definitions

3.1 For the purposes of this Protocol:

(a) A disrepair claim is a civil claim arising from the condition of residential premises and may include a related personal injury claim. (See paragraphs 4.4 (c), (d) and (e) of the Guidance Notes.) It does not include disrepair claims which originate as counterclaims or set-offs in other proceedings.

(b) The types of claim which this Protocol is intended to cover include those brought under Section 11 of the Landlord and Tenant Act 1985, Section 4 of the Defective Premises Act 1972, common law nuisance and negligence, and those brought under the express terms of a tenancy agreement or lease. It does not cover claims brought under Section 82 of the Environmental Protection Act 1990 (which are heard in the Magistrates' Court).

(c) This protocol covers claims by any person with a disrepair claim as referred to in paragraphs (a) and (b) above, including tenants, lessees and members of the tenant's family. The use of the term "tenant" in this protocol is intended to cover all such people. (See also paragraph 4.4(e).)

3.2 Early Notification Letter

(a) Notice of the claim should be given to the landlord as soon as possible. In order to avoid delay in notifying the landlord it may be appropriate to send a letter notifying the landlord of the claim (Early Notification Letter) before sending a letter setting out the full details of the claim (Letter of Claim). An Early Notification letter is intended to be a helpful tool, but it will not be necessary in every case. It might be appropriate where, for example, a repair is urgent or there is likely to be some delay before enough details are available to make a claim. The Early Notification Letter to the landlord should give the following information:

(i) tenant's name, the address of the property, tenant's address if different, tenant's telephone number and when access is available

(ii) details of the defects, including any defects outstanding, in the form of a schedule, if appropriate. Attached at Annex G of paragraph 5 is a specimen schedule which can be used to inform the landlord of the disrepair

(iii) details of any notification previously given to the landlord of the need for repair or information as to why the tenant believes that the landlord has knowledge of the need for repair

(iv) proposed expert (see paragraph 3.6)

(v) proposed letter of instruction to expert (see Annex C of paragraph 5)

(vi) tenant's disclosure of such relevant documents as are readily available.

(b) The Early Notification Letter should also request the following disclosure from the landlord:

All relevant records or documents including:

(i) copy of tenancy agreement including tenancy conditions

(ii) documents or computerised records relating to notice given, disrepair reported, inspection reports or repair works to the property.

(c) The Early Notification Letter should include the authorisation for release of the information (except in a case where the tenant is acting in person).

(d) Specimen Early Notification Letters are attached at Annex A of paragraph 5. They may be suitably adapted as appropriate.

3.3 Letter of Claim

(a) The tenant should send to the landlord a Letter of Claim at the earliest reasonable opportunity. The Letter of Claim should contain the following details (if they have not already been provided in an Early Notification Letter):

(i) tenant's name, the address of the property, tenant's address if different, the tenant's telephone number and when access is available

(ii) details of the defects, including any defects outstanding, in the form of a schedule, if appropriate. Attached at Annex G of paragraph 5 is a specimen schedule which can be used to inform the landlord of the disrepair

(iii) history of the defects, including attempts to rectify them

(iv) details of any notification previously given to the landlord of the need for repair or information as to why the tenant believes that the landlord has knowledge of the need for repair

(v) the effect of the defects on the tenant (see paragraphs 4.4 (c), (d) and (e) regarding personal injury claims)

(vi) details of any special damages (see form at Annex E of paragraph 5 and definition of "special damages" at paragraph 4.10)

(vii) proposed expert (see paragraph 3.6)

(viii) proposed letter of instruction to the expert (See Annex C of paragraph 5)

(ix) tenant's disclosure of relevant documents.

(b) If not already requested in an Early Notification Letter, the Letter of Claim should also request the following disclosure from the landlord:

All relevant records or documents including:

(i) copy of tenancy agreement including tenancy conditions
(ii) tenancy file
(iii) documents relating to notice given, disrepair reported, inspection reports or requirements to the property
(iv) computerised records.

(c) If not requested in an Early Notification Letter, the Letter of Claim should also include the authorisation for release of the information (except in a case where the tenant is acting in person).

(d) Specimen Letters of Claim are attached at Annex B of paragraph 5. It will be seen that there are different versions depending on whether or not an Early Notification Letter has been sent. The letters may be suitably adapted as appropriate.

3.4 Limitation Period

3.4 The procedures in this Protocol do not extend statutory limitation periods. If a limitation period is about to expire, the tenant may need to issue proceedings immediately unless the landlord confirms that they will not rely on limitation as a defence in subsequent proceedings. (See paragraph 4.8 for guidance about the limitation period, and paragraph 4.10 for a definition of 'limitation period'.) Alternatively the tenant can ask the landlord to agree to extend the limitation period.

3.5 Landlord's Response

3.5.1 Response to First Letter

The landlord should normally reply within 20 working days of the date of receipt of the first letter from the tenant i.e the Early Notification Letter or the Letter of Claim if no Early Notification Letter is sent. (See paragraph 4.10 for a definition of "working days"). The Landlord's response to the first letter, whether an Early Notification letter or a Letter of Claim, should include the following:

Disclosure

(a) All relevant records or documents including:
(i) copy of tenancy agreement including tenancy conditions
(ii) documents or computerised records relating to notice given, disrepair reported, inspection reports or requirements to the property.

Expert

(b) A response to the tenant's proposals for instructing an expert including:
(i) whether or not the proposed single joint expert is agreed
(ii) whether the letter of instruction is agreed
(iii) if the single joint expert is agreed but with separate instructions, a copy of the letter of instruction
(iv) if the appointment of a single joint expert is not agreed, whether the landlord agrees to a joint inspection.

3.5.2 Response to Letter of Claim

(a) The landlord's response to the tenant's Letter of Claim should include:

(i) whether liability is admitted and if so, in respect of which defects. If liability is disputed in respect of some or all of the defects, the reasons for this

(ii) any point which the landlord wishes to make regarding lack of notice of the repair or regarding any difficulty in gaining access

(iii) a full schedule of intended works including anticipated start and completion dates and a timetable for the works

(iv) any offer of compensation

(v) any offer in respect of costs

(vi) the information set out at 3.5.1(a) and (b), if it has not already been provided.

(b) On receipt of the Letter of Claim (whether or not an Early Notification Letter was sent), the landlord may provide a response to the issues set out at paragraph (a) above either:

(i) within 20 working days of the date of receipt of the Letter of Claim (see paragraph 4.10 for a definition of "working days") or

(ii) within 20 working days of the date of receipt of the report of the single joint expert (see paragraph 3.6(h)) or date of receipt of the experts' agreed schedule following a joint inspection (see paragraph 3.6(g)).

3.5.3 If Landlord does not respond

(a) If no response is received from the landlord to the Early Notification Letter within 20 working days, the tenant should send a Letter of Claim giving as many of the details outlined at paragraph 3.3 as possible, on the basis of the information the tenant has to hand.

(b) Failure to respond within the time limits set out in paragraphs 3.5.1 and 3.5.2, or at all, to the Early Notification Letter or the Letter of Claim will be a breach of the Protocol. (See paragraphs 4.7(a) and (b) regarding time limits and the power of the court if the Protocol is breached).

3.6 Experts

<u>General</u>

See Paragraph 4.6 for guidance regarding the use of experts.

(a) Tenants should remember that in some cases it might not be *necessary to instruct* an expert to provide evidence of disrepair, for example, if the only issue relates to the level of any damages claimed. It may be advisable to take photographs of any defects before and after works, and consideration should be given to the use of video footage, particularly if an expert has not been instructed.

(b) The expert should be instructed to report on all items of disrepair which the landlord ought reasonably to know about, or which the expert ought reasonably to report on. The expert should be asked to provide a schedule of works, an estimate of the costs of repair, and to list any urgent works.

(c) Information is given at paragraph 4.6(a) about obtaining lists of independent experts who can be instructed in disrepair cases.

Single Joint Expert

(d) If the landlord does not raise an objection to the proposed expert or letter of instruction within 20 working days of the date of receipt of the Early Notification Letter or Letter of Claim, the expert should be instructed as a single joint expert, using the tenant's proposed letter of instruction. Attached at Annex C of paragraph 5 are specimen letters of instruction to an expert. Alternatively, if the parties cannot agree joint instructions, the landlord and tenant should send their own separate instructions to the single joint expert. If sending separate instructions, the landlord should send the tenant a copy of the landlord's letter of instruction with their response to the first letter. (The tenant has already forwarded the proposed letter of instruction to the landlord).

Joint Inspection

(e) If it is not possible to reach agreement to instruct a single joint expert, even with separate instructions, the parties should attempt to arrange a joint inspection, i.e. an inspection by different experts instructed by each party to take place at the same time. If the landlord wishes to send their own expert to a joint inspection, they should inform both the tenant's expert and the tenant's solicitor. If the landlord instructs their own expert to inspect then the tenant can also instruct their own expert. It will be for the court to decide subsequently, if proceedings are issued, whether or not either party has acted reasonably.

Time Limits

(f) Whether a single joint expert or a joint inspection is used, the property should be inspected within 20 working days of the date that the landlord responds to the tenant's first letter.

(g) If there is a joint inspection, the experts should produce an agreed schedule of works detailing:

(i) the defects and required works which are agreed and a timetable for the agreed works

(ii) the areas of disagreement and the reasons for disagreement.

The agreed schedule should be sent to both the landlord and the tenant within 10 working days of the joint inspection.

(h) If there is a single joint expert, a copy of the report should be sent to both the landlord and the tenant within 10 working days of the inspection. Either party can ask relevant questions of the expert.

(i) At Annex D of paragraph 5 are flowcharts showing the time limits in the Protocol.

Urgent Cases

(j) The Protocol does not prevent a tenant from instructing an expert at an earlier stage if this is considered necessary for reasons of urgency, and the landlord should give access in such cases. Appropriate cases may include:

(i) where the tenant reasonably considers that there is a significant risk to health and safety

(ii) where the tenant is seeking an interim injunction

(iii) where it is necessary to preserve evidence.

Access

(k) Tenants must give reasonable access to the landlord for inspection and repair in line with the tenancy agreement. The landlord should give reasonable notice of the need for access, except in the case of an emergency. The landlord must give access to common parts as appropriate, e.g. for the inspection of a shared heating system.

Costs

(l) Terms of appointment should be agreed at the outset and should include:

(i) the basis of the expert's charges (either daily or hourly rates and an estimate of the time likely to be required, or a fee for the services);

(ii) any travelling expenses and other relevant expenses;

(iii) rates for attendance at court should this become necessary, and provisions for payment on late notice of cancellation of a court hearing;

(iv) time for delivery of report;

(v) time for making payment;

(vi) whether fees are to be paid by a third party; and

(vii) arrangements for dealing with questions for experts and discussions between experts and for providing for the cost involved.

(m) If a single joint expert is instructed, each party will pay one half of the cost of the report. If a joint inspection is carried out, each party will pay the full cost of the report from their own expert. (See paragraph 3.7).

(n) The expert should send separately and directly to both parties answers to any questions asked.

3.7 Costs

(a) If the tenant's claim is settled without litigation on terms which justify bringing it, the landlord will pay the tenant's reasonable costs or out of pocket expenses. (See paragraph 4.10 for a definition of 'costs' and 'out of pocket expenses'.)

(b) Attached at Annex F of paragraph 5 is a Statement of Costs Form which can be used to inform the landlord of the costs of the claim.

4.

Guidance Notes

4.1 Alternative Dispute Resolution

C10–004 (a) The parties should consider whether some form of alternative dispute resolution procedure (see paragraph 4.10 for a defini tion of alternative dispute resolution) would be more suitable than litigation, and if so, endeavour to agree which form to adopt. Both the Claimant and Defendant may be required by the Court to provide evidence that alternative means of resolving their dispute were considered. The Courts take the view that litigation should be a last resort, and that claims should not be issued prematurely when a settlement is still actively being explored. Parties are warned that if the protocol is not followed (including this paragraph) then the Court must have regard to such conduct when determining costs.

(b) It is not practicable in this protocol to address in detail how the parties might decide which method to adopt to resolve their particular dispute. However, summarised below are some of the options for resolving disputes without litigation:

- Discussion and negotiation.
- Early neutral evaluation by an independent third party (for example, a lawyer experienced in the field of housing disrepair or an individual experienced in the subject matter of the claim).
- Mediation—a form of facilitated negotiation assisted by an independent neutral party.
- Other options in respect of the following specific categories:

(i) For council tenants:—

- local authority repairs, complaints and/or arbitration procedures.
- the Right to Repair Scheme. The scheme is only suitable for small, urgent repairs of less than £250 in value.

  Information and leaflets about the scheme in England can be obtained from the Office of the Deputy Prime Minister, Eland House, Bressenden Place, London SW1E 5DU. Tel: 020 7944 3672.

  Information about the scheme in Wales can be obtained from the National Assembly for Wales, Cathays Park, Cardiff, CF10 3NQ. Tel. 029 2082 5111.
- Commission for Local Administration in England. Tel. 0845 602 1983.
- the Local Government Ombudsman for Wales. Tel. 01656 661325.

(ii) For tenants of social landlords who are not council tenants, and for tenants of qualifying private landlords:—

- In England, the Independent Housing Ombudsman. 3rd Floor, Norman House, 105-109 Strand, London WC2R 0AA. Tel 020 7836 3630.

  In Wales, the National Assembly for Wales, Cathays Park, Cardiff CF10 3NQ. Tel. 029 2082 5111.
- Local authority environmental health officers.

(iii) For private tenants:—

- Local authority environmental health officers.

(c) The Legal Services Commission has published a booklet on 'Alternatives to Court', CLS Direct Information Leaflet 23 (*www.clsdirect.org.uk/legalhelp/leaflet23.jsp*), which lists a number of organisations that provide alternative dispute resolution services.

(d) *It is expressly recognised that no party can or should be forced to mediate or enter into any form of ADR.*

(e) *Information about repair rights generally is available free of charge from the following web pages: www.shelter.org.uk/housingadvice/index.asp and www.legalservices.gov.uk/leaflets/cls/index.htm.*

(f) The former Department for Transport, Local Government and the Regions issued Good Practice Guidance on Housing Disrepair Legal Obligations in January 2002. Copies of the Guidance (ISBN 185112523X) can be obtained from Communities and Local Government Publications, PO Box 236, Wetherby LS23 7NB. Tel: 0870 1226 236. Fax: 0870 1226 237. Textphone: 0870 1207 405. E-mail: communities@twoten.com. (free to download from the Communities and Local Government website at http://www.communities.gov.uk/index.asp?id=1502470). A summary, Housing Research Summary No. 154, is available free on the Communities and Local Government website at the following link http://www.communities.gov.uk/index.asp?id=1155697. Hard copies are no longer available. The Communities and Local Government website http://www.communities.gov.uk/index.asp?id=1150232 is a general source of information for landlords and tenants.

4.2 Scope of the Protocol

(a) This Protocol is intended to apply to all civil law claims which include a claim for disrepair, but not to counterclaims or set-offs in disrepair claims, which originate as other proceedings. (See paragraph 4.10 for an explanation of 'counterclaim' and 'set-off'.) In cases which involve a counterclaim or set-off, the landlord and tenant will still be expected to act reasonably in exchanging information and trying to settle the case at an early stage.

(b) In practice, most disrepair cases will have a value of more than £1,000 but less than £15,000 and so are likely to be allocated to the fast track if they come to court. (See paragraph 4.10 for an explanation of 'the fast track'.) The Protocol is aimed at this type of case. The need to keep costs down is especially important in claims of lower value. The approach of the

Protocol is however, equally appropriate to all claims and the Protocol should also be followed in small track and multi-track claims. (See paragraph 4.10 for an explanation of 'small claims track' and 'multi-track'.) The court will expect to see reasonable pre-action behaviour applied in all cases.

4.3 Early Notification Letter

(a) The Early Notification Letter is not intended to replace the direct reporting of defects to the landlord at an early stage, using any procedure the landlord may have established. The Protocol is for use in those cases where, despite the landlord's knowledge of the disrepair, the matter remains unresolved.

(b) It is recognised that disrepair cases can range from straightforward to highly complex, and that it is not always possible to obtain detailed information at an early stage. In order to avoid unnecessary delay and to ensure that notice of the claim is given to the landlord at the earliest possible opportunity, the Protocol suggests the use of two letters in some cases; an Early Notification Letter and a later Letter of Claim. (See paragraph 3.2(a) and Annexes A & B of paragraph 5.)

(c) A copy of the Protocol need only be sent to the landlord if the tenant has reason to believe that the landlord will not have access to the Protocol e.g. because the landlord is an individual or small organisation. If in doubt, a copy should be sent.

4.4 Letters of Claim and Landlord's Response

(a) Letters of Claim and a landlord's response are not intended to have the same status as a statement of case in court proceedings. Matters may come to light after the Letter of Claim has been sent, or after the landlord has responded, which could mean that the case of one or both parties is presented slightly differently than in the Letters of Claim or in the landlord's response. It would be inconsistent with the spirit of the Protocol to seek to capitalise on this in the proceedings, provided that there was no intention to mislead. In particular, advantage should not be taken regarding discrepancies relating to the general details of notice given in the Early Notification Letter.

(b) See paragraph 4.3(c) regarding the sending of a copy of the Protocol by the tenant to the landlord.

Cases with a Personal Injury Element

(c) Housing disrepair claims may contain a personal injury element. This should be set out in the Letter of Claim, as should a clear indication of the identities of all persons who plan to make a personal injury claim.

(d) There is also a Personal Injury Protocol. This Protocol should be followed for that part of the disrepair claim which forms a personal injury claim, unless it is insufficient to warrant separate procedures and would therefore be dealt with only as part of the disrepair claim and evidenced by a General Practitioner's letter. The Personal Injury Protocol should be followed for any claim which requires expert evidence other than a General

Practitioner's letter. If the disrepair claim is urgent, it would be reasonable to pursue separate disrepair and personal injury claims, which could then be case managed or consolidated at a later date.

(e) Paragraph 3.3(a)(v) refers to the effect of the defects on 'the tenant'. This should be taken to include all persons who have a personal injury claim. The details of any such claim and of all likely claimants should be set out in the Letter of Claim.

4.5 Disclosure of Documents

(a) When giving disclosure, the landlord should copy all relevant documents. In housing disrepair claims, this includes any and all documents relating in particular to the disrepair and to notice given by the tenant to the landlord of the disrepair. Notice is often given by personal attendance at the landlord's office, and copies of any notes of meetings and oral discussions should also be copied, along with other relevant documents. Documents regarding rent arrears or tenants' disputes will not normally be relevant.

(b) The aim of the early disclosure of documents by the landlord is not to encourage 'fishing expeditions' by the tenant, but to promote an early exchange of relevant information to help in clarifying or resolving issues in dispute. The tenant should assist by identifying the particular categories of documents, which they consider relevant.

(c) The 20 working days time limit specified in paragraph 3.5 runs from the date of receipt of either letter. Receipt of the letter is deemed to have taken place two days after the date of the letter. If necessary, a written request for extra time should be made by the landlord to the tenant. Should a case come to court, the court will decide whether the parties have acted reasonably, and whether any sanctions, including costs orders, are appropriate. The principles regarding time limits are referred to again at paragraph 4.7.

(d) Nothing in the Protocol restricts the right of the tenant to look personally at their file or to request a copy of the whole file. Neither is the landlord prevented from sending to the tenant a copy of the whole file, should the landlord wish.

4.6 Experts

(a) Information about independent experts can be obtained from:

(i) The Chartered Institute of Environmental Health,
Chadwick Court,
15 Hatfields,
London
SE1 8DJ
Tel: 020 7928 6006
Ask for a copy of the Consultants and Trainers Directory.

(ii) The Law Society,
113 Chancery Lane,
London
WC2A 1PL
Tel: 020 7831 0344
Refer to the Society's Expert Witness Directory; and

(iii) The Royal Institution of Chartered Surveyors,
12 Great George Street,
Parliament Square,
London
SW1P 3AD
Tel. 0845 304 4111
Ask for a copy of the relevant regional directory.

(b) The Protocol encourages the use of a single joint expert. In order to make it less likely that a second expert will be necessary, the Protocol provides for the landlord to forward their own instructions directly to the single joint expert if they cannot agree joint instructions. Both parties can ask relevant questions of the expert. If the parties cannot agree on a single joint expert, either with joint or separate instructions, the Protocol suggests a joint inspection by each party's expert.

(c) The specimen letters at Annexes A and B of paragraph 5 ask for reasons to be given as to why the landlord objects to the expert proposed by the tenant. Should a case come to court, it will be for the court to decide whether the parties have acted reasonably and whether the costs of more than one expert should be recoverable.

(d) Parties should bear in mind that it may not always be necessary to obtain expert evidence of disrepair, and in view of this, the Protocol encourages the use of photos before and after works, and if appropriate, video evidence.

(e) Parties are reminded that the Civil Procedure Rules provide that expert evidence should be restricted to that which is necessary and that the court's permission is required to use an expert's report. The court may limit the amount of experts' fees and expenses recoverable from another party.

(f) When instructing an expert, regard should be had to any approved Code of Guidance for Experts and whether a copy of the Protocol should be sent to the expert.

4.7 Time Limits

(a) The time scales given in the Protocol are long stops and every attempt should be made to comply with the Protocol as soon as possible. If parties are able to comply earlier than the time scales provided, they should do so.

(b) Time limits in the Protocol may be changed by agreement. However, it should always be borne in mind that the court will expect an explanation as to why the Protocol has not been fol*lowed* or has been varied and breaches of the Protocol may lead to costs or other orders being made by the court.

4.8 Limitation Period

(a) In cases where the limitation period will shortly expire, the tenant should ask in the first letter for an extension of the limitation period. The extension requested should be only so long as is necessary to avoid the cost of starting court proceedings.

(b) It will be for the court to decide whether refusal to grant the request is reasonable and whether any sanctions, including costs orders, are appropriate.

4.9 Contact Point

Where a landlord is not an individual, a person should be designated to act as a point of contact for the tenant as soon as possible after the landlord receives the first letter from the tenant and (if one is involved) their solicitor. The appointee's name and contact details should be sent to the tenant and their solicitor as soon as possible after the appointment is made.

4.10 Glossary

Alternative Dispute Resolution	Mediation, or other dispute resolution method, which seeks to settle disputes without the need for court proceedings.
Counterclaim	A claim that either party makes in response to an initial claim by the other.
Costs	Legal fees or, in a small track claim, out of pocket expenses incurred as a result of a claim. (See Out of Pocket Expenses below).
Damages	Money obtained as the result of a claim to compensate for inconvenience and/or distress suffered because of the condition of the property. (See also Special Damages below).
Defect/Disrepair	A fault or problem with a property, for which the landlord is responsible.
Disclosure	The making available by one party to the other of documentation relevant to the claim.

Fast Track/Multi Track/ Small Claims Track	Cases which proceed to court will be allocated to separate tracks depending on their value. The separate tracks have different rules and procedures. Housing cases worth between £1,000–£15,000 where there is a claim for works to be done will usually be allocated to the **fast track**. Housing cases where the costs of the repairs and/or the damages do not exceed £1,000 will usually be dealt with on the **small claims track**. Cases over £15,000 will usually be allocated to the **multi track**.
Joint Inspection	An inspection of a property carried out at the same time by one expert instructed by the tenant and by one expert instructed by the landlord.
Limitation Period	The time limit after which a legal action cannot be started. In most housing cases it is six years. In personal injury cases it is three years.
Litigation	A court case or court proceedings. The taking of legal action by someone.
Notice	Notification of a disrepair, either directly by the tenant in writing or orally to the landlord or his employee, or indirectly, by inspection of the property by the landlord or his employee.
Out of Pocket Expenses	Expenses incurred in a small track claims as a result of the claim, such as loss of earnings and experts' fees.
Protocol	A code or procedure—in this case for dealing with housing disrepair.
Set-off	Where one party agrees with the other's claim or part of it, but sets up one which counterbalances it.
Single Joint Expert	An expert who is instructed by both the tenant and the landlord, either with joint or separate instructions.
Special Damages	Compensation for loss of or damage to specific items e.g. clothes, carpets, curtains, wallpaper, bedding or extra electricity costs.
Tenant	Someone who rents land (including property) owned by another. (See also the definition at paragraph 3.1(c).)

Third Party	Someone other than the landlord or tenant.
Working Days	All days other than Saturdays, Sundays and Bank Holidays.

5.

Annexes

Specimen Letters C10–005

It will be noted that the attached specimen letters are in pairs for use by solicitors and by tenants acting in person respectively.

It is emphasised that they may be suitably adapted as appropriate.

The letters, with the paragraph of the Protocol to which each one relates, are as follows:

Annex A

Early Notification Letter (see paragraph 3.2.)

Annex B

Letter of Claim (see paragraph 3.3.)

Note: There are two versions of this:

(a) for use where an Early Notification Letter has been sent;

(b) for other cases.

Annex C

Letter of Instruction to Expert (see paragraph 3.6.)

Annex D

Early Notification Letter Flowchart

Annex E

Special Damages Form

Annex F

Statement of Costs

Annex G

Schedule

Annex A

C10–006

EARLY NOTIFICATION LETTER

(i) LETTER FROM SOLICITOR

To Landlord

Dear Sirs,

RE: TENANT'S NAME AND ADDRESS OF PROPERTY

We are instructed by your above named tenant. (*Include a sentence stating how the case is being funded.*) We are using the Housing Disrepair Protocol. *We enclose a copy of the Protocol for your information.**

Repairs

Your tenant complains of the following defects at the property (*set out nature of defects).*

*We enclose a schedule, which sets out the disrepair in each room.**

You received notice of the defects as follows: (*list details of notice relied on*).

Please arrange to inspect the property as soon as possible. Access will be available on the following dates and times:- (*list dates and times as appropriate*)

Please let us know what repairs you propose to carry out and the anticipated date for completion of the works.

Disclosure

Please also provide within 20 working days of receipt of this letter, the following: -

All relevant records or documents including:-

(i) copy of tenancy agreement including tenancy conditions

(ii) documents or computerised records relating to notice given, disrepair reported, inspection reports or repair works to the property.

We enclose a signed authority from our clients for you to release this information to ourselves.

We also enclose copies of the following relevant documents from our client:-

Expert

If agreement is not reached about the carrying out of repairs within 20 working days of this letter, we propose to jointly instruct a single joint expert (*insert expert's name and address)* to carry out an inspection of the property and provide a report. We enclose a copy of their CV, plus a draft letter of instruction. Please let us know if you agree to his/her appointment. If you object, please let us know your reasons within 20 working days.

If you do not object to the expert being instructed as a single joint expert, but wish to provide your own instructions, you should send those directly to (*insert expert's name)* within 20 working days of this letter. Please send to ourselves a copy of your letter of instruction. If you do not agree to a single joint expert, we will instruct (*insert expert's name)* to inspect the property in any event. In those circumstances, if you wish to instruct your expert to attend at the same time, please let ourselves and (*insert expert's name)* know within 20 working days of this letter.

Claim

Our client's disrepair claim requires further investigation. We will write to you as soon as possible with further details of the history of the defects and of notice relied on, along with details of our client's claim for general and special damages.

Yours faithfully,

** Delete as appropriate*

PRE-ACTION PROTOCOLS

(ii) LETTER FROM TENANT

To Landlord

Dear

RE: YOUR NAME AND ADDRESS OF PROPERTY

I write regarding disrepair at the above address. I am using the Housing Disrepair Protocol. *I enclose a copy of the Protocol for your information.**

Repairs

The following defects exist at the property (*set out nature of defects).*

*I enclose a schedule which sets out the disrepair in each room.**

Please arrange to inspect the property as soon as possible. Access will be available on the following dates and times:- *(list dates and time as appropriate)*

You received notice of the defects as follows: (*list details of notice relied on*).

Please let me know what repairs you propose to carry out and the anticipated date for completion of the works.

Disclosure

Please also provide within 20 working days of receipt of this letter, the following: -

All relevant records or documents including:-

(i) copy of tenancy agreement including tenancy conditions

(ii) documents or computerised records relating to notice given, disrepair reported, inspection reports or repair works to the property.

I also enclose copies of the following relevant documents:- (*list documents enclosed*)

Expert

If agreement is not reached about the carrying out of repairs within 20 working days, I propose that we jointly instruct a single joint expert (*insert expert's name and address)* to carry out an inspection of the property and provide a report. I enclose a copy of their CV, plus a draft letter of instruction. Please let me know if you agree to his/her appointment. If you object, please let me know your reasons within 20 working days.

If you do not object to the expert being appointed as a single joint expert but wish to provide your own instructions, you should send those directly to (*insert expert's name)* within 20 working days. Please send a copy of your letter of instruction to me. If you do not agree to a single joint expert I will instruct (*insert expert's name)* to inspect the property in any event. In those circumstances if you wish your expert to attend at the same time, please let me and (*insert expert's name)* know within 20 working days.

Claim

I will write to you as soon as possible with further details of the history of the defects and of notice relied on, along with details of my claim for general and special damages.

Yours sincerely,

* *Delete as appropriate*

Annex B

C10–007 **LETTER OF CLAIM**

(a) For use where an Early Notification Letter has been sent (as set out in Annex A).

(i) LETTER FROM SOLICITOR

To Landlord

Dear Sirs,

RE: TENANT'S NAME AND ADDRESS OF PROPERTY

We write further to our letter of (*insert date*) regarding our client's housing disrepair claim. We have now taken full instructions from our client.

Repairs

The history of the disrepair is as follows:-(*set out history of defects*).

*I enclose a schedule which sets out the disrepair in each room.**

You received notice of the defects as follows (*list details of notice relied on*).

The defects at the property are causing (*set out the effects of the disrepair on the client and their family, including any personal injury element. Specify if there will be any other additional claimant*).

Please forward to us within 20 working days of receipt of this letter a full schedule of works together with the anticipated date for completion of the works proposed.

Claim

We take the view that you are in breach of your repairing obligations. Please provide us with your proposals for compensation. (*Alternatively, set out suggestions for general damages i.e. £x for x years*). *Our client also requires compensation for special damages, and we attach a schedule of the special damages claimed.**

Yours faithfully,

** Delete as appropriate*

(ii) LETTER FROM TENANT

To Landlord

Dear

RE: YOUR NAME AND ADDRESS OF PROPERTY

I write further to my letter of (*insert date*) regarding my housing disrepair claim. I am now able to provide you with further details.

Repairs

The history of the disrepair is as follows:-(*set out history of defects*).

You received notice of the defects as follows (*list details of notice relied on*).

The defects at the property are causing (*set out the effects of the disrepair on you and your family, including any personal injury element. Specify if there will be any other additional claimant*).

Please forward to me within 20 working days of receipt of this letter a full schedule of works together with the anticipated date for completion of the works proposed.

Claim

I take the view that you are in breach of your repairing obligations. Please provide me with your proposals for compensation. (*Alternatively, set out suggestions for general damages i.e. £x for x years*). *I also require compensation for special damages, and I attach a schedule of the special damages claimed.* *

Yours sincerely,

* *Delete as appropriate*

(b) For use where an Early Notification Letter has NOT been sent.

(i) LETTER FROM SOLICITOR

To Landlord

Dear Sirs,

RE: TENANT'S NAME AND ADDRESS OF PROPERTY

We are instructed by your above named tenant. (*Insert a sentence stating how the case is being funded.*) We are using the Housing Disrepair Protocol. *We enclose a copy of the Protocol for your information. **

Repairs

Your tenant complains of the following defects at the property (*set out nature and history of defects*).

*We enclose a schedule which sets out the disrepair in each room.**

You received notice of the defects as follows (*list details of notice relied on*).

The defects at the property are causing *(set out the effects of the disrepair on the client and their family, including any personal injury element, specifying if there are any additional claimants).*

Disclosure

Please provide within 20 working days of receipt of this letter a full schedule of the works you propose to carry out to remedy the above defects and the anticipated date for completion of the works.

Please also provide within 20 working days of this letter the following: -

All relevant records or documents including:-

(i) copy of tenancy agreement including tenancy conditions

(ii) tenancy file

(iii) documents relating to notice given, disrepair reported, inspection reports or repair works to the property.

(iv) computerised records

We enclose a signed authority from our clients for you to release this information to ourselves.

We also enclose copies of the following relevant documents:- (*list documents enclosed*)

Expert

If agreement is not reached about the carrying out of repairs within 20 working days of receipt of this letter, we propose to jointly instruct a single joint expert (*insert expert's name and address*) to carry out an inspection of the property and provide a report. We enclose a copy of their CV, plus a draft letter of instruction. Please let me know if you agree to his/her appointment. If you object, please let me know your reasons within 20 working days.

If you do not object to the expert being instructed a single joint expert, but wish to provide your own instructions, you should send those directly to (*insert expert's name*) within 20 working days. Please send to ourselves a copy of your letter of instruction to ourselves. If you do not agree to a single joint expert, we will instruct (*insert expert's name*) to inspect the property in any event. In those circumstances, if you wish to instruct your expert to attend at the same time please let ourselves and (*insert expert's name*) know within 20 working days.

Claim

We take the view that you are in breach of your repairing obligations. Please provide us with your proposals for compensation. *(Alternatively, set out suggestions for general damages i.e. £x for x years). Our client also requires compensation for the special damages, and we attach a schedule of the special damages claimed.**

Yours faithfully,

* *Delete as appropriate*

(ii) LETTER FROM TENANT

To Landlord

Dear

RE: YOUR NAME AND ADDRESS OF PROPERTY

I write regarding the disrepair at the above address. I am using the Housing Disrepair Protocol. *I enclose a copy of the Protocol for your information.**

Repairs

The property has the following defects (*set out nature and history of defects).*

*I enclose a schedule which sets out the disrepair in each room.**

You received notice of the defects as follows (*list details of notice relied on*).

The defects at the property are causing *(set out the effects of the disrepair on you and your family, including any personal injury element, specifying if there are any additional claimants).*

Please provide within 20 working days of receipt of this letter a full schedule of the works you propose to carry out to remedy the above defects and the anticipated date for completion of the works.

Disclosure

Please also provide within 20 working days of receipt of this letter the following: -

All relevant records or documents including:-

(i) copy of tenancy agreement including tenancy conditions

(ii) tenancy file

(iii) documents relating to notice given, disrepair reported, inspection reports or repair works to the property

(iv) computerised records.

I also enclose copies of the following relevant documents:- (*list documents enclosed*).

Expert

If agreement is not reached about the carrying out of repairs within 20 working days of receipt of this letter, I propose that we jointly instruct a single joint expert (*insert expert's name and address)* to carry out an inspection of the property and provide a report. I enclose a copy of their CV, plus a draft letter of instruction. Please let me know if you agree to his/her appointment. If you object, please let me know your reasons within 20 working days.

If you do not object to the expert being instructed as a single joint expert, but wish to provide your own instructions, you should send those directly to (*insert expert's name)* within 20 working days. Please also send a copy of the letter of instruction to me. If you do not agree to a single joint expert, I will instruct (*insert expert's name)* to inspect the property in any event. In those circumstances, if you wish to instruct your expert to attend at the same time please let me and (*insert expert's name)* know within 20 working days.

Claim

I take the view that you are in breach of your repairing obligations. Please provide me with your proposals for compensation. *(Alternatively, set out suggestions for general damages i.e. £x for x years). I also require compensation for special damages, and I attach a schedule of the special damages claimed.**

Yours sincerely,

* *Delete as appropriate*

Annex C

C10–008

LETTER OF INSTRUCTION TO EXPERT

(i) LETTER FROM SOLICITOR

Dear

RE: TENANT'S NAME AND ADDRESS OF PROPERTY

We act for the above named in connection with a housing disrepair claim at the above property. We are using the Housing Disrepair Protocol. *We enclose a copy of the Protocol for your information.**

Please carry out an inspection of the above property by (date)** and provide a report covering the following points:-

(a) whether you agree that the defects are as claimed

(b) whether any of the defects is structural

(c) the cause of the defect(s)

(d) the age, character and prospective life of the property.

Access will be available on the following dates and times:- (list dates and times as appropriate)

*You are instructed as a single joint expert / The landlord is (landlord's name and details) / The landlord will be providing you with their own instructions direct / The landlord will contact you to confirm that their expert will attend at the same time as you to carry out a joint inspection.**

Please provide the report within 10 working days of the inspection. Please contact us immediately if there are any works which require an interim injunction.

If the case proceeds to court, the report may be used in evidence. In order to comply with court rules we would be grateful if you would insert above your signature a statement that the contents are true to the best of your knowledge and belief. We refer you to part 35 of the Civil Procedure Rules which specifies experts' responsibilities, the contents of any report, and the statements experts must sign.

Insert details as to cost and payment.

Yours sincerely,

* *Delete as appropriate*

** *The date to be inserted should be 20 working days from the date of the letter, in accordance with paragraph 3.6(f) of the Protocol.*

(ii) LETTER FROM TENANT

Dear

RE: YOUR NAME AND ADDRESS OF PROPERTY

I am currently in dispute with my landlord about disrepair at the above property. I am using the Housing Disrepair Protocol. *I enclose a copy of the Protocol for your information.**

Please carry out an inspection of the above property by (*date*)** and provide a report covering the following points:-

(a) whether you agree that the defects are as claimed

(b) whether any of the defects is structural

(c) the cause of the defect(s)

(d) the age, character and prospective life of the property.

Access will be available on the following dates and times:- (list dates and times as appropriate)

*You are instructed as a single joint expert / The landlord is (landlord's name and details) / The landlord will be providing you with their own instructions direct / The landlord will contact you to confirm that their expert will attend at the same time as you to carry out a joint inspection.**

Please provide the report within 10 working days of the inspection. Please contact me immediately if there are any works which require an interim injunction.

If the case proceeds to court, the report may be used in evidence. In order to comply with court rules I would be grateful if you would insert above your signature a statement that the contents are true to the best of your knowledge and belief. I refer you to part 35 of the Civil Procedure Rules which specifies experts' responsibilities, the contents of any report, and the statements experts must sign.

Insert details as to cost and payment.

Yours sincerely,

* *Delete as appropriate*
** *The date to be inserted should be 20 working days from the date of the letter, in accordance with paragraph 3.6(f) of the Protocol.*

Annex D

C10–009

Early Notification Letter Flowchart

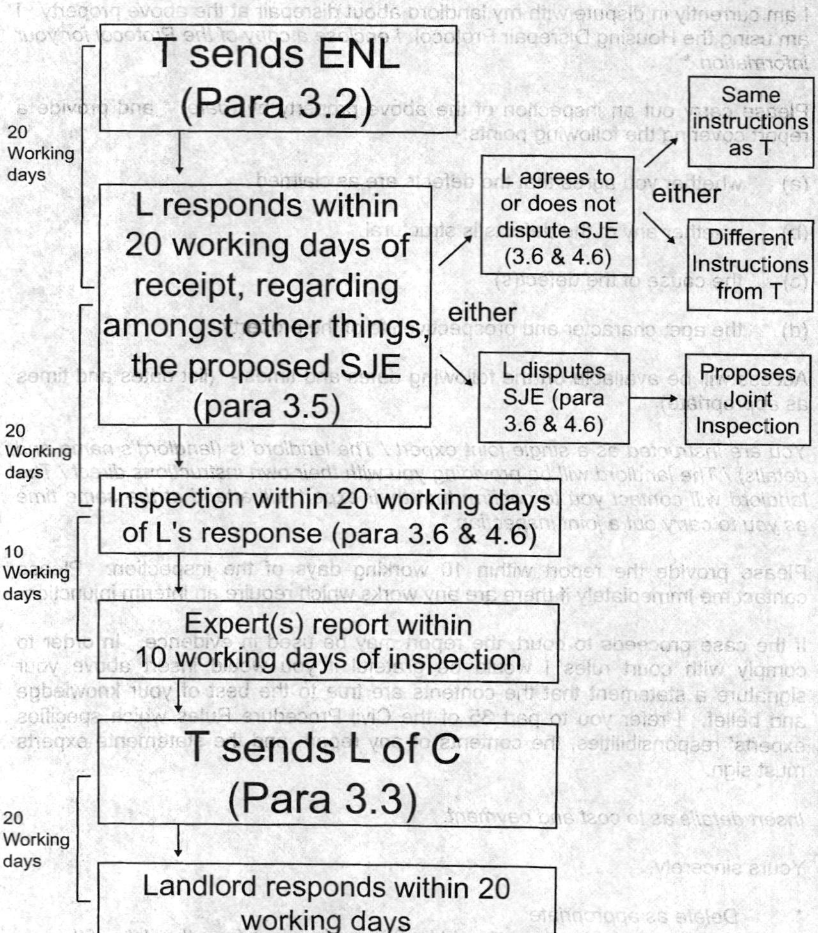

Letter of Claim Flowchart

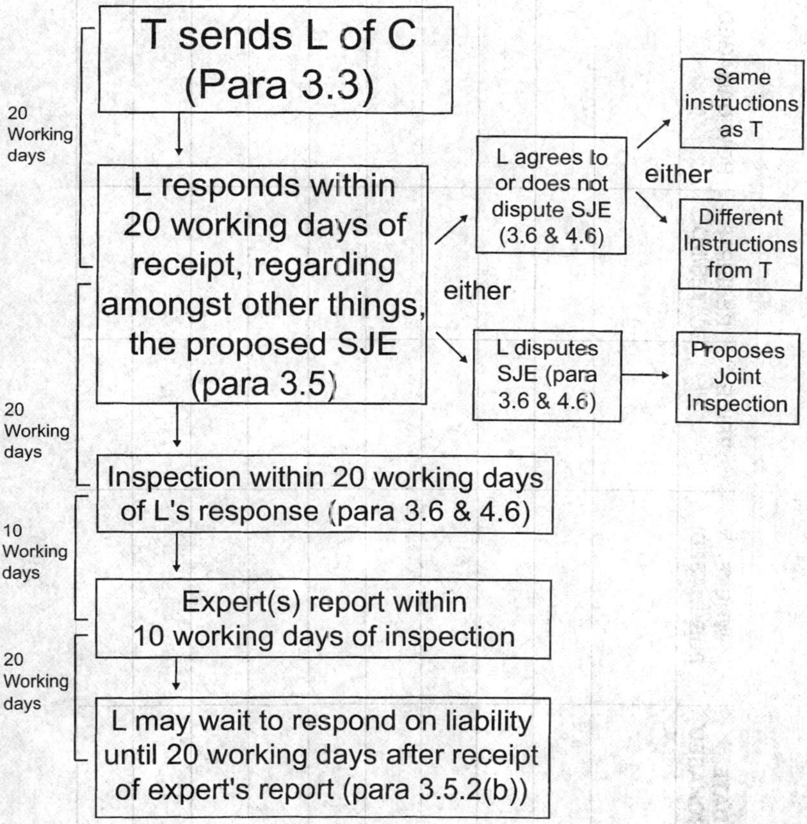

Annex E

C10–010

SPECIAL DAMAGES FORM

	ITEM	DATE PURCHASED	WHERE PURCHASED	PRICE	RECEIPTS – YES/NO	HOW DAMAGED
1						
2						
3						
4						
5						
6						
7						
8						
9						
10						

Annex F

C10–011

Statement of Costs (summary assessment)

In the

Court

Case Reference

Judge/Master

Case Title

[Party]'s Statement of Costs for the hearing on *(date)* **(interim application/fast track trial)**

Description of fee earners*

(a) *(name) (grade) (hourly rate claimed)*

(b) *(name) (grade) (hourly rate claimed)*

Attendances on *(party)*

	(a) *(number)*	hours at £		£	0.00
	(b) *(number)*	hours at £		£	0.00
Attendances on opponents					
	(a) *(number)*	hours at £		£	0.00
	(b) *(number)*	hours at £		£	0.00
Attendance on others					
	(a) *(number)*	hours at £		£	0.00
	(b) *(number)*	hours at £		£	0.00
Site inspections etc					
	(a) *(number)*	hours at £		£	0.00
	(b) *(number)*	hours at £		£	0.00
Work done on negotiations					
	(a) *(number)*	hours at £		£	0.00
	(b) *(number)*	hours at £		£	0.00
Other work, not covered above					
	(a) *(number)*	hours at £		£	0.00
	(b) *(number)*	hours at £		£	0.00
Work done on documents					
	(a) *(number)*	hours at £		£	0.00
	(b) *(number)*	hours at £		£	0.00
Attendance at hearing					
	(a) *(number)*	hours at £		£	0.00
	(b) *(number)*	hours at £		£	0.00
	(a) *(number)*	hours travel and waiting at £		£	0.00
	(b) *(number)*	hours travel and waiting at £		£	0.00
			Sub Total	£	0.00

N260 Statement of Costs (summary assessment) (10.01) *Printed on behalf of The Court Service*

PRE-ACTION PROTOCOLS

Brought forward £ 0.00

Counsel's fees *(name) (year of call)*

Fee for [advice/conference/documents] £

Fee for hearing £

Other expenses

[court fees] £

Others £

(give brief description)

Total £ 0.00

Amount of VAT claimed

on solicitors and counsel's fees £

on other expenses £

Grand Total £ 0.00

The costs estimated above do not exceed the costs which the *(party)* is liable to pay in respect of the work which this estimate covers.

Dated

Signed

Name of firm of solicitors [partner] for the *(party)*

* 4 grades of fee earner are suggested:

(A) Solicitors with over eight years post qualification experience including at least eight years litigation experience.

(B) Solicitors and legal executives with over four years post qualification experience including at least four years litigation experience.

(C) Other solicitors and legal executives and fee earners of equivalent experience.

(D) Trainee solicitors, para legals and other fee earners.

"Legal Executive" means a Fellow of the Institute of Legal Executives. Those who are not Fellows of the Institute are not entitled to call themselves legal executives and in principle are therefore not entitled to the same hourly rate as a legal executive.

In respect of each fee earner communications should be treated as attendances and routine communications should be claimed at one tenth of the hourly rate.

N260 Statement of Costs (summary assessment) (10.01)

Printed on behalf of The Court Service

Annex G

C10–012

Schedule
Disrepair Protocol
TENANT

	Item Number	Room (tick where appropriate	Disrepair (identify briefly)	Notice given (How was the landlord made aware of the problem)	Inconvenience suffered (How has the disrepair affected you)
Exterior of premises, roof and access Comment:					
Entrance, hall and storage Comment:					
Living room (s) Comment:					
Kitchen Comment:					
Bathroom Comment:					
Bedroom 1 Comment:					
Bedroom 2 Comment:					
Bedroom 3 Comment:					
Other Comment					

The Protocol for Possession Claims based on Rent Arrears

This protocol was drafted by the Housing Committee of the Civil Justice Council and came into force in October 2006. It applies to possession claims for rent arrears by social landlords only (not to possession claims on other grounds such as nuisance, and not to claims by private landlords or mortgage companies) The protocol builds upon C11A–001

PRE-ACTION PROTOCOLS

guidance issued by the Department of Communities and Local Government and the Housing Corporation.

The aim of the protocol is that claims for possession for rent arrears should be very much a last resort. Social landlords are required to manage their tenants' rent accounts by sending them rent statements every three months, by being proactive in contacting tenants early to find out the cause of the arrears, giving assistance with housing benefit claims, and taking particular care with vulnerable tenants who may need support. Wherever possible agreement should be reached to pay off the arrears, and if the tenant keeps to that agreement proceedings should not be issued or should be postponed if already issued.

If proceedings are necessary the landlord should then send the tenant an up-to-date rent statement, check on their housing benefit position, and advise in writing what type of order is being sought (outright, suspended or postponed—see CPR, Pt 55).

After some debate the protocol does apply to possession claims made on the basis of mandatory Ground 8 (Housing Act 1985 Sch.2—rent arrears that exceed twomonths' rent at the time of service of the notice seeking possession and at the hearing) because some social landlords also chose to rely on alternative discretionary grounds, and because it cannot be certain whether Ground 8 will apply until the day of the hearing.

The protocol provides a serious incentive to the social landlords to comply, as it gives the court the option to impose a costs sanction, adjourn, strike-out or dismiss the claim for non-compliance, except in a proven mandatory Ground 8 case.

PRE-ACTION PROTOCOL FOR POSSESSION CLAIMS BASED ON RENT ARREARS

Aims and scope of the protocol

C11–001 This protocol applies to residential possession claims by social landlords (such as local authorities, Registered Social Landlords and Housing Action Trusts) which are based solely on claims for rent arrears. The protocol does not apply to claims in respect of long leases or to claims for possession where there is no security of tenure. The protocol reflects the guidance on good practice given to social landlords in the collection of rent arrears. It recognises that it is in the interests of both landlords and tenants to ensure that rent is paid promptly and to ensure that difficulties are resolved wherever possible without court proceedings. Its aim is to encourage more pre-action contact between landlords and tenants and to enable court time to be used more effectively. Courts should take into account whether this protocol has been followed when considering what orders to make. Registered Social Landlords and local authorities should also comply with guidance issued from time to time by the Housing Corporation and the Department for Communities and Local Government.

Initial contact

C11–002

1. The landlord should contact the tenant as soon as reasonably possible if the tenant falls into arrears to discuss the cause of the arrears, the tenant's financial circumstances, the tenant's entitlement to benefits and repayment of the arrears. Where contact is by letter, the landlord should write separately to each named tenant.
2. The landlord and tenant should try to agree affordable sums for the tenant to pay towards arrears, based upon the tenant's income and expenditure (where such information has been supplied in response to the landlord's enquiries). The landlord

should clearly set out in pre-action correspondence any time limits with which the tenant should comply.

3. The landlord should provide, on a quarterly basis, rent statements in a comprehensible format showing rent due and sums received for the past 13 weeks. The landlord should, upon request, provide the tenant with copies of rent statements in a comprehensible format from the date when arrears first arose showing all amounts of rent due, the dates and amounts of all payments made, whether through housing benefit or by the tenant, and a running total of the arrears.

4.

(a) If the landlord is aware that the tenant has difficulty in reading or understanding information given, the landlord should take reasonable steps to ensure that the tenant understands any information given. The landlord should be able to demonstrate that reasonable steps have been taken to ensure that the information has been appropriately communicated in ways that the tenant can understand.

(b) If the landlord is aware that the tenant is under 18 or is particularly vulnerable, the landlord should consider at an early stage—

(i) whether or not the tenant has the mental capacity to defend possession proceedings and, if not, make an application for the appointment of a litigation friend in accordance with CPR 21;

(ii) whether or not any issues arise under Disability Discrimination Act 1995; and

(iii) in the case of a local authority landlord, whether or not there is a need for a community care assessment in accordance with National Health Service and Community Care Act 1990.

5. If the tenant meets the appropriate criteria, the landlord should arrange for arrears to be paid by the Department for Work and Pensions from the tenant's benefit.

6. The landlord should offer to assist the tenant in any claim the tenant may have for housing benefit.

7. Possession proceedings for rent arrears should not be started against a tenant who can demonstrate that he has—

(a) provided the local authority with all the evidence required to process a housing benefit claim;

(b) a reasonable expectation of eligibility for housing benefit; *and*

(c) paid other sums due not covered by housing benefit.

The landlord should make every effort to establish effective ongoing liaison with housing benefit departments and, with the tenant's consent, make direct contact with the relevant housing benefit department before taking enforcement action.

The landlord and tenant should work together to resolve any housing benefit problems.

8. Bearing in mind that rent arrears may be part of a general debt problem, the landlord should advise the tenant to seek assistance from CAB, debt advice agencies or other appropriate agencies as soon as possible.

After service of statutory notices

C11–003 9. After service of a statutory notice but before the issue of proceedings, the landlord should make reasonable attempts to contact the tenant, to discuss the amount of the arrears, the cause of the arrears, repayment of the arrears and the housing benefit position.

10. If the tenant complies with an agreement to pay the current rent and a reasonable amount towards arrears, the landlord should agree to postpone court proceedings so long as the tenant keeps to such agreement. If the tenant ceases to comply with such agreement, the landlord should warn the tenant of the intention to bring proceedings and give the tenant clear time limits within which to comply.

Alternative dispute resolution

C11–004 11. The parties should consider whether it is possible to resolve the issues between them by discussion and negotiation without recourse to litigation. The parties may be required by the court to provide evidence that alternative means of resolving the dispute were considered. Courts take the view that litigation should be a last resort, and that claims should not be issued prematurely when a settlement is still actively being explored.

The Legal Services Commission has published a booklet on "Alternatives to Court", CLS Direct Information Leaflet 23 (*www.clsdirect.org.uk/legalhelp/leaflet23.jsp*), which lists a number of organisations that provide alternative dispute resolution services.

Court proceedings

C11–005 12. Not later than ten days before the date set for the hearing, the landlord should—

(a) provide the tenant with up to date rent statements;

(b) disclose what knowledge he possesses of the tenant's housing benefit position to the tenant.

13.

(a) The landlord should inform the tenant of the date and time of any court hearing and the order applied for. The landlord should advise the tenant to attend the hearing as the tenant's home is at risk. Records of such advice should be kept.

(b) If the tenant complies with an agreement made after the issue of proceedings to pay the current rent and a reasonable amount towards arrears, the landlord should agree to postpone court proceedings so long as the tenant keeps to such agreement.

(c) If the tenant ceases to comply with such agreement, the

landlord should warn the tenant of the intention to restore the proceedings and give the tenant clear time limits within which to comply.

14. If the landlord unreasonably fails to comply with the terms of the protocol, the court may impose one or more of the following sanctions—
    (a) an order for costs;
    (b) in cases other than those brought solely on mandatory grounds, adjourn, strike out or dismiss claims.

15. If the tenant unreasonably fails to comply with the terms of the protocol, the court may take such failure into account when considering whether it is reasonable to make possession orders.

Mortgage Arrears Protocol—editorial

The Protocol came into force on November 19, 2008. The Protocol is a Civil Justice Council initiative, and is approved by the Council for Mortgage Lenders. The implementation was announced on October 22, 2008 in the House of Commons by the Prime Minister, but contrary to press reports at the time, the Protocol does not give guidance to the courts to halt possession claims. **C12A–001**

What it does do is encourage mortgage lenders to regard a possession claim as a last resort, and to work with borrowers in financial difficulties to try to reach agreement without the need for proceedings. The Protocol draws substantially upon the Council for Mortgage Lenders' Code of Guidance and Mortgage Conduct of Business Regulations (see the Financial Services Authority's guidance at *http://fsahandbook.info/FSA/htm/handbook/PERG/4/4* [Accessed January 12, 2009]) and describes the behaviour that the court will normally expect of the parties prior to the start of the possession claim.

The Protocol makes it clear that it does not alter the parties' legal rights and obligations. These are covered by statute and by the mortgage contract. Changing this position would require primary legislation. That legal position, in short, is that if a borrower is in default of the mortgage payments, the lender is entitled to possession unless s.36(2) of the Administration of Justice Act 1970 is engaged. This provides that the court may exercise its powers to adjourn the proceedings, stay or suspend execution of a possession order, or postpone the date for delivery of possession, for such period as the court thinks reasonable, if it appears to the court that the borrower is likely to be able within a reasonable period to pay any sums due under the mortgage or remedy other breaches. Conversely the court cannot suspend an order for possession, however hard the circumstances, if there is no prospect at all of the borrower reducing the arrears. Well-established case law provides that s.36 is engaged when it appears to the court, from the evidence, that the borrower is, or soon will be likely, to be able to pay the current monthly instalment and a reasonable amount off the arrears (at least to clear these within the term of the mortgage), or has an impending sale, the net proceeds of which will redeem the balance outstanding on the mortgage and the arrears. (See also commentary to Pt 55 at 55.10.2in Vol.1 and on s.36 of the Administration of Justice Act 1970 in Vol.2 at 3A–40.

The Protocol applies to first and second charge residential mortgages, home purchase plans and other secured loans, both regulated and unregulated.

When the borrower is in arrears the lender should:

- Provide information on the arrears and any interest or charge that may be added
- Discuss with the borrower the cause of the arrears, his financial circumstances and proposals for payment, respond promptly to the latter, give reasons in writing if the proposal is refused, and give the borrower sufficient time to consider the lender's proposals
- Be prepared to change the payment date or the method of payment
- Give the borrower at least 15 days notice of intended possession proceedings
- Consider not starting a possession claim where the borrower can show that he has submitted a claim under a mortgage protection policy that is likely to pay out and the borrower can pay the balance of the payments

- Consider not starting a possession claim where the borrower can show that reasonable steps have or will be taken to market the property at an appropriate price and if the lender agrees to wait, the borrower should provide the lender with copies of the particulars of sale, the name of the estate agent and conveyancer, the HIP, and details of offers. If the lender declines to postpone proceedings he should give the borrower reasons at least five business days before issuing.

The parties are also encouraged to consider whether ADR might resolve the problem—this might include extending the term or changing the type of the mortgage, deferring payment of interest or capitalising the arrears.

The Protocol does not contain any specific sanctions for non-compliance. But para.9 of the Protocol states that parties should be able to explain the actions they have taken to comply. The Practice Direction on Protocols para.2.1 enables the court to take into account compliance with any applicable protocol when giving case management directions, and paras 2.3/4 provide that the court, when dealing with a non-compliance, will aim to put the innocent party in no worse a position than he would have been in if the Protocol had been complied with.

The practical effect of the Protocol should be that the court should enquire at the first hearing, whether the lender has complied with the Protocol. The lender can demonstrate this by so referring in the particulars of claim, or in a witness statement filed and served for the hearing, and by updating the position orally at the hearing.

If the lender has not complied with the Protocol the court will have to decide first whether s.36 is engaged. If it is definitely not because, for instance, the borrower clearly cannot pay the monthly instalment and a reasonable amount off the arrears now, or there is no sale on the horizon, and, from the evidence, this position is unlikely to change in the near future, the court must make a possession order.

But where the Protocol has not been complied with and there is doubt about the borrower's prospects of payment, or a sale, for lack of information, or it seems likely that s.36 might be engaged in the foreseeable future, the court seemingly has the power, under the Protocol, the Pt 3 case management powers and/or para.2.3 of the Pre-action Practice Direction to:

- adjourn to enable the lender to comply with the Protocol and/or establish the facts, e.g. about whether and when DWP may pay the mortgage interest (which from January 2009 will be from 13 weeks after the application where the applicant is eligible—previously it was 39 weeks)
- adjourn or suspend on terms (e.g. that the borrower pays current monthly instalments plus £20 a month off the arrears, possibly with a review if the borrower may be likely to be able to pay more in the foreseeable future)
- stay the proceedings to enable the parties to explore alternative dispute resolution (e.g. capitalising the arrears), and /or
- disallow the costs of the hearing because of the lender's non-compliance.

But the interaction between the lender's statutory and contractual rights, and the court's powers under the Protocol are not straightforward. Satellite litigation on the application of the Protocol seems likely, but perhaps not for a time, because some lenders may not want to take possession of properties in a stagnant property market even when they are entitled to do so.

PRE-ACTION PROTOCOL FOR POSSESSION CLAIMS BASED ON MORTGAGE OR HOME PURCHASE PLAN ARREARS IN RESPECT OF RESIDENTIAL PROPERTY

I.

Introduction

Preamble

C12-001 *1.1 This Protocol describes* the behaviour the court will normally expect of the parties prior to the start of a possession claim within the scope of paragraph 3.1 below.

1.2 This Protocol does not alter the parties' rights and obligations.

1.3 It is in the interests of the parties that mortgage payments or payments under home purchase plans are made promptly and that difficulties are resolved wherever possible without court proceedings. However in some cases an order for possession may be in the interest of both the lender and the borrower.

Aims

2.1 The aims of this Protocol are to— C12–002

(1) ensure that a lender or home purchase plan provider (in this Protocol collectively referred to as 'the lender') and a borrower or home purchase plan customer (in this Protocol collectively referred to as 'the borrower') act fairly and reasonably with each other in resolving any matter concerning mortgage or home purchase plan arrears, and

(2) encourage more pre-action contact between the lender and the borrower in an effort to seek agreement between the parties, and where this cannot be reached, to enable efficient use of the court's time and resources.

2.2 Where either party is required to communicate and provide information to the other, reasonable steps should be taken to do so in a way that is clear, fair and not misleading. If the lender is aware that the borrower may have difficulties in reading or understanding the information provided, the lender should take reasonable steps to ensure that information is communicated in a way that the borrower can understand.

3.1 This Protocol applies to arrears on— C12–003

(1) first charge residential mortgages and home purchase plans regulated by the Financial Services Authority under the Financial Services and Markets Act 2000;

(2) (2) second charge mortgages over residential property and other secured loans regulated under the Consumer Credit Act 1974 on residential property; and

(3) unregulated residential mortgages.

3.2 Where a potential claim includes a money claim and a claim for possession this protocol applies to both.

4.1 In this Protocol— C12–004

(1) 'possession claim' means a claim for the recovery of possession of property under Part 55 of the Civil Procedure Rules 1998 ("CPR");

(2) 'home purchase plan' means a method of purchasing a property by way of a sale and lease arrangement that does not require the payment of interest;

(3) 'bank holiday' means a bank holiday under the Banking and Financial Dealings Act 1971; and

(4) 'business day' means any day except Saturday, Sunday, a bank holiday, Good Friday or Christmas day.

II.

Actions Prior to the Start of a Possession Claim

Initial Contact and Provision of Information

5.1 Where the borrower falls into arrears the lender should provide the borrower with— C12–005

(1) where appropriate, the required regulatory information sheet or the National Homelessness Advice Service booklet on mortgage arrears; and
(2) information concerning the amount of arrears which should include—
(a) the total amount of the arrears;
(b) the total outstanding of the mortgage or the home purchase plan; and
(c) whether interest or charges will be added, and if so and where appropriate, details or an estimate of the interest or charges that may be payable.

5.2 The parties should take all reasonable steps to discuss with each other, or their representatives, the cause of the arrears, the borrower's financial circumstances and proposals for repayment of the arrears (see 7.1). For example, parties should consider whether the causes of the arrears are temporary or long term and whether the borrower may be able to pay the arrears in a reasonable time.

5.3 The lender should advise the borrower to make early contact with the housing department of the borrower's Local Authority and, should, where necessary, refer the borrower to appropriate sources of independent debt advice.

5.4 The lender should consider a reasonable request from the borrower to change the date of regular payment (within the same payment period) or the method by which payment is made. The lender should either agree to such a request or, where it refuses such a request, it should, within a reasonable period of time, give the borrower a written explanation of its reasons for the refusal.

5.5 The lender should respond promptly to any proposal for payment made by the borrower. If the lender does not agree to such a proposal it should give reasons in writing to the borrower within 10 business days of the proposal.

5.6 If the lender submits a proposal for payment, the borrower should be given a reasonable period of time in which to consider such proposals. The lender should set out the proposal in sufficient detail to enable the borrower to understand the implications of the proposal.

5.7 If the borrower fails to comply with an agreement, the lender should warn the borrower, by giving the borrower 15 business days notice in writing, of its intention to start a possession claim unless the borrower remedies the breach in the agreement.

Postponing the Start of a Possession Claim

C12–006 **6.1** A lender should consider not starting a possession claim for mortgage arrears where the borrower can demonstrate to the lender that the borrower has—
(1) submitted a claim to an insurer under a mortgage payment protection policy and has provided all the evidence required to process a claim;
(2) a reasonable expectation of eligibility for payment from the insurer; and
(3) an ability to pay a mortgage instalment not covered by the insurance.

6.2 If a borrower can demonstrate that reasonable steps have been or will be taken to market the property at an appropriate price in accordance with reasonable professional advice, the lender should consider postponing starting a possession claim. The borrower must continue to take all reasonable steps actively to market the property where the lender has agreed to postpone starting a possession claim.

6.3 Where the lender has agreed to postpone starting a possession claim the borrower should provide the lender with a copy of the particulars of sale, the Home Information Pack and (where relevant) details of purchase offers received within a reasonable period of time specified by the lender. The borrower should give the lender details of the estate agent and the conveyancer instructed to deal with the sale. The borrower should also authorise the estate agent and the conveyancer to communicate with the lender about the progress of the sale and the borrower's conduct during the process.

6.4 Where the lender decides not to postpone the start of a possession claim it should inform the borrower of the reasons for this decision at least 5 business days before starting proceedings.

7.1 Alternative Dispute Resolution

The court takes the view that starting a possession claim is usually a last resort and that such a claim should not normally be started when a settlement is still actively being explored. Discussion between the parties may include options such as: **C12–007**

(1) extending the term of the mortgage;
(2) changing the type of a mortgage;
(3) deferring payment of interest due under the mortgage; or
(4) capitalising the arrears.

Alternative Dispute Resolution

8.1 The lender should consider whether to postpone the start of a possession claim where the borrower has made a genuine complaint to the Financial Ombudsman Service (FOS) about the potential possession claim. **C12–008**

8.2 Where a lender does not intend to await the decision of the FOS it should give notice to the borrower with reasons that it intends to start a possession claim at least 5 business days before doing so.

Compliance

9.1 Parties should be able, if requested by the court, to explain the actions that they have taken to comply with this protocol. **C12–009**

SECTION D

PROCEDURAL GUIDES

SECTION D

PROCEDURAL GUIDES

1. COMMENCEMENT

1.1. Computation of Time

Periods of time expressed in months D1–001

CPR r.2.10 — References to months in the CPR are deemed to be references to calendar months.

Periods of time expressed in days

CPR r.2.8(2)–(3) — Treat as clear days and exclude the day on which time began to run, also exclude final day where the end of the period is defined by an event, e.g. "at least 3 days before hearing on Friday 20 October" would provide a deadline of Monday October 16, with February 17 to 19 being three clear days.

Meaning of "beginning with"

Zoan v Rouamba [2000] 1 W.L.R. 1509 — If an order etc states that an action must be done no later than a period "beginning with" a particular date, that date is included.

Meaning of "from" and "after"

Zoan v Rouamba [2000] 1 W.L.R. 1509 — If an order etc states that an action must be done no later than a period "after" or "from" a particular date or event, the first day is excluded.

Periods of five or fewer days

CPR r.2.8(4) — subject to the exception listed below, exclude Saturdays, Sundays, Bank Holidays, Christmas Day, Good Friday if they fall within the period.

e.g. "at least 3 days before hearing on Monday 20th October" would provide a deadline of Tuesday October 14, the three clear days being 15–17 October, leaving out of account Saturday 18 and Sunday 19.

Exception

See *Anderton v Clwyd CC [2002] EWCA Civ 933* — The above does not apply when calculating deemed date of service under CPR r.6.7.

When the period ends but the court office is closed

CPR r.2.8(5) — If any period ends on a day when the court office is closed, an act which requires the use of the court office is done in time if it is done on the next day on which the court office is open.

Statutory procedural time limits

Aadan v Brent LBC, [2001] Ch. 419
Kaur (Pritam) v Russell (S.) & Sons [1973] 1 Q.B. 336 — The above also applies where a time limit arises under a statute provided the action in question requires a court office to be open for it to be done.

Agreeing extensions of time

CPR r.2.11	Parties may agree extensions of time for doing any act unless the rules or PDs or a court order says otherwise.

Notable exceptions

CPR r.15.5(1)	Parties may not agree to extend time for service of a Defence by more than 28 days.
CPR r.2.8(2)	Parties may not agree to extend time if the court has made an order which states the consequences of failing to comply with that date. Sanctions take effect unless relief is granted by the court.
CPR , r.52.6	Parties may not agree to extent time limits set for appeals under rules, PDs or orders but must apply to the court to do so.
CPR r.28.4 *CPR r.29.5*	Parties may not agree to vary time limits if doing so would make it necessary to vary dates for return of pre-trial checklists, case management conference, pre-trial review, trial date or trial period.

1.2. Part 7 or Part 8 Claim, Selection and Service

D1–002 **Choice of claim form**

General rules

Form N1	Part 7 claim is likely to involve a dispute of fact.
CPR r.8.1 *Form N208*	Part 8 claim should be used where a dispute of fact is unlikely or where a rule or PD requires.

Specific occasions where Part 8 claim may be suitable

PD 8 para.1 *See also PD 8B for a list of specific proceedings*	• Where court approval of a child or patient's settlement (reached before issue of proceedings) is needed; • Where a claim for provisional damages has been settled before issue and a consent judgment is needed; • In summary possession proceedings against defendants occupying land without licence or consent, where no substantial dispute of fact is likely.

Specialist cases

PD 7 para.3.4	For specialist cases consult CPR Pt 49 and any specialist PDs which may prescribe practice forms.

Time for service of claim

CPR r.7.5 *(For Extension of time see CPR r.7.6.)*	Part 7 & Part 8 Claim forms • Claim must be served within four months of issue, or six months if served out of the jurisdiction.
CPR r.7.4	Part 7 Particulars of Claim • Particulars of Claim must be served with, or contained in, Claim form OR served within 14 days of service of the form BUT no later than the latest time for service of the claim in any event.
CPR r.7.8 and see Acknowledgment of Service—Guide 3.1 and Defence & Reply—Guide 3.3	Forms for Admission, Defence and Acknowledgment of Service must be served with the Claim form (Pt 8 Claims) or the Particulars of Claim (Pt 7 Claims) (CPR, r.7.8).

Prior to commencement

Before commencement matters may be brought before the court by Application Notice under CPR r.23.2.

Choice of claim

Decide whether Claim is Pt 7 or Pt 8.

Issue

Form N244 Claim is begun by issuing at court.

CPR r.7.2
PD 7 para.5 Time for the purposes of the Limitation Act 1980 runs from date claim is received at court for issue, not when it is in fact issued.

2. SERVICE

2.1. Service of Claims: General Rules D2–001

N.B. For deemed dates of service generally see Guide 2.4

How to serve

CPR r.6.3 Claim forms served within the jurisdiction may be served by any of the permitted methods under CPR r.6.3. See CPR 6.40–6.42 for provisions as to service out of the jurisdiction.

Address for service (other than children and patients)

General rules

CPR r.6.6(2) The claim form must include the defendant's address for service.

CPR r.6.7(a) If the defendant has given written notice of the business address within the jurisdiction of a solicitor as an address at which the defendant may be served with the claim form; then the claim form must be served at that address.

CPR r.6.7(b) If a solicitor acting for the defendant has given written notice to the claimant that he is instructed to accept service of the claim form on behalf of the defendant at a business address within the jurisdiction then the claim form must be served at that address.

CPR r.6.8(a) The defendant may be served with the claim form at an address within the jurisdiction which he has given for the purpose of being served with the proceedings (unless CPR r.6.7 (above) applies or a rule or practice direction or enactment or order requires personal service).

Landlord and Tenant Claims In a claim by a tenant against a landlord the claim form may be served at an address given by the landlord under s.48 of the Landlord and Tenant Act 1987.

Personal service on defendant CPR r.6.5(1),(2) The claim form may be served personally on the defendant unless the defendant or his solicitor has given an address for service (CPR r.6.7) above) and with the exception of claims against the Crown. The claim must be served personally if a rule, practice direction, order or enactment requires personal service.

Address for service where defendant does not provide an address, the rules do not make other provision and the claimant does not wish to serve the defendant personally

CPR r.6.9(2)	Where no address for service is given by the defendant, service must be effected as follows. (N.B. see Guide 2.3 for service on defendants who are children or protected parties.)

Nature of defendant to be served	**Place of Service**
Individual	Usual or last known residence
Individual being sued in the name of a business	Usual or last known residence of the individual or principal or last known place of business
Individual being sued in the business name of a partnership	Usual or last known residence of the individual; or principal or last known place of business of the partnership.
Limited liability partnership	Principal office of the partnership; or any place of business of the partnership within the jurisdiction which has a real connection with the claim.
Corporation (other than a company) incorporated in England and Wales	Principal office of the corporation or any place within the jurisdiction where the corporation carries on its activities and which has a real connection with the claim.
Company registered in England and Wales	Principal office of the company or any place of business of the company within the jurisdiction which has a real connection with the claim
Any other company or corporation	Any place within the jurisdiction where the corporation carries on its activities or any place of business of the company within the jurisdiction

Where there is a reason to believe that the defendant no longer resides or carries on business at his "usual or last known" residence or business address

CPR r.6.9(3)–(5)	Claimant must take reasonable steps to ascertain the address of the defendant's current residence or place of business. Having taken those reasonable steps, if the claimant ascertains the defendant's current address, the claim form must be served at that address.
CPR r.6.15	If the claimant is unable to ascertain the defendant's current address then the claimant must consider whether there is an alternative place where service may be effected or an alternative method of service, and if so then the claimant must apply for an order for service by alternative means or at an alternative address.
CPR r.6.9(6)	Only if the claimant cannot ascertain the defendant's current address **and** the claimant cannot ascertain any alternative place or method of service may the claimant then serve at the defendant's usual or last known address (despite having reason to believe that the defendant no longer resides/carries on business there).

Service on the Crown

CPR r.6.10	Service on the Attorney-General must be effected on the Treasury solicitor, and service on a government department must be effected on the solicitor acting for that department (for which see the list in CPR PD 66).

Where there is a reason to believe that the defendant no longer resides or carries on business at his "usual or last known" residence or business address

CPR r.6.9(3)–(5) Claimant must take reasonable steps to ascertain the address of the defendant's current residence or place of business. Having taken those reasonable steps, if the claimant ascertains the defendant's current address, the claim form must be served at that address.

CPR r.6.15 If the claimant is unable to ascertain the defendant's current address then the claimant must consider whether there is an alternative place where service may be effected or an alternative method of service, and if so then the claimant must apply for an order for service by alternative means or at an alternative address.

CPR r.6.9(6) Only if the claimant cannot ascertain the defendant's current address **and** the claimant cannot ascertain any alternative place or method of service may the claimant then serve at the defendant's usual or last known address (despite having reason to believe that the defendant no longer resides/carries on business there).

Service on the Crown

Judicial Review and Possession

CPR rr.54 and 55 contain further provisions as to Service in Judicial Review and Possession claims.

2.2. Service of Claims and Documents out of the Jurisdiction **D2–002**

(Including Scotland and Northern Ireland)

(1) Claim form

The General Rule

Generally a claim form may not be served out of England and Wales without permission.

Exceptions to the General Rule

CPR r.6.32 (Scotland and Northern Ireland)
CPR r.6.33 (other countries) define the circumstances in which permission to serve out of the jurisdiction is **not** required.

Statement of Grounds where permission is not required

CPR r.6.34(1)
Form N150

Where permission to serve out of the jurisdiction is not required, Claimant must file and serve with the Claim form a statement of the grounds relied on by which the Claimant is entitled to serve out of the jurisdiction without permission. Consequences of failure to provide the notice are set out in CPR r.6.34(2). Use form N150.

Where permission is required: grounds for seeking permission

CPR r.6.36 Provided any of the grounds set out in PD6B para.3.1 are made out the claimant may serve out of the jurisdiction with the permission of the court.

Procedure for obtaining permission to serve out of the jurisdiction

CPR r.6.37(1) Application must set out the grounds relied on under PD6B para.3.1, must state that the claimant believes that the claim has a reasonable prospect of success, and must state the defendant's address (or if not known, in what place the defendant is, or is likely to be found.)

CPR r.6.37(2) (See also CPR r.6.37(2) where it is proposed to serve an intended defendant who it is contended is a necessary and proper defendant to a claim which has already been or which will be served on a different defendant.)

Criteria for granting permission

CPR r.6.37(3), (4) Court will refuse permission unless satisfied that England and Wales is the proper place in which to bring the claim. Court will have regard to cost and convenience criteria and to the powers of the courts in Scotland and Northern Ireland in cases where it appears that the claim may also be entitled to a remedy in Scotland or Northern Ireland and the application is for service of the claim in those countries.

Methods of service

See CPR r.6.40.

(2) Service of other documents

Permission

CPR r.6.38(1),(2) If permission was required to serve the claim form then permission is also required to serve other documents relating to the claim (save where the document is the Particulars of Claim and the Claim form served with permission stated that the Particulars of Claim were to follow.)

CPR r.6.38(3) For Claims served in Scotland and Northern Ireland no permission is required to serve documents other than the claim form where the party served has given an address for service in Scotland or Northern Ireland.

Methods of service

See CPR r.6.40.

2.3 Service of Claim form and documents on Children and Protected Parties

D2–003 *N.B. for "Protected Party" status and rules see CPR Part 21 generally.*

Claim form

CPR r.6.13 Where the party to be served is a child but **not** a Protected Party the person to be served is one of the child's parents or guardians, or if there is no such person an adult with whom the child resides or in whose care the child is.

Where the party to be served is a Protected Party, the person to be served is one of the following persons with authority in relation to the Protected Party as (i) the attorney under a registered enduring power of attorney or (ii) the donee of a lasting power of attorney, or (iii) the deputy appointed by the Court of Protection. If there is no such person then the person to be served is an adult with whom the protected party resides or in whose care the protected party is.

Service of Application for an order appointing a litigation friend, where the child or protected party has no litigation friend

CPR r.21.8 sets out detailed provisions.
See also CPR r.6.25(1)

Any other document

CPR r.6.25(2)	Where the party to be served is a child or a Protected Party, the person to be served is the litigation friend who is conducting the proceedings on behalf of the child or protected party unless ordered otherwise.

Discretion of court

CPR r.6.6(2),(3) (for claim forms see CPR r.6.13(4), (5))	The court may direct service otherwise than as provided above and/or as provided in CPR r.21.8, on an application without notice.

Rectifying irregular service

CPR r.6.25(5) (for claim forms see CPR r.6.13(6))	The court may order that, although a document has been served on someone other than the person specified in CPR rr.21.8 or 6.25(2) it shall be treated as properly served.

Generally

CPR r.6.25(6) (for claim forms see CPR r.6.25(7))	The rules above do not apply where the court has directed that a child or Protected Party may conduct proceedings without a litigation friend.

2.4 Deemed dates of service

(1) Claim forms D2–004

CPR r.6.14	Claim form within jurisdiction deemed to be served on the second business day after completion of the 'relevant step' defined in CPR r.7.5(1).
"relevant step" CPR r.7.5(1)	For service of claim form within the jurisdiction the claimant must complete the step required by CPR r.7.5(1) (table below) before midnight on the calendar day four months after date of issue of the claim.

Method of Service	**Deemed date of service**
First class post, DX or other service which provides for delivery on the next business day	Posting, leaving with, delivering to or collection by the relevant sevice provider
Delivery of the document to or leaving it at the relevant place	Delivering to or leaving the document at the relevant place
Personal service under CPR r.6.5	Completing the relevant step required by CPR r.6.5(3)
Fax	Completing the transmission of the fax
Other electronic method	Sending the email or other electronic transmission

Where the claim form is to be served out of the jurisdiction

CPR r.7.5(2)	The claim form must be served in accordance with Section IV of Part 6 within 6 months of the date of issue.

Certificates of service

CPR r.6.17	Note that where a certificate of service is required in relation to the claim form, the matters set out in CPR 6.17 must be included in the certificate.

(2) Other documents

CPR r.6.26	Documents other than claim forms are deemed to have been served as follows:
Method of Service	**Deemed date of service**
First class post (or other service which provides for delivery on the next business day)	The second day after it was posted, left with, delivered to or collected by the relevant service provider provided that day is a business day; or if not, the next business day.
DX	Second day after it was left with, delivered to or collected by the relevant service provider provided that day is a business day; or if not, the next business day.
Delivering the document to or leaving it at a permitted address	If it is delivered to or left at the permitted address on a business day before 4.30p.m., on that day; or in any other case, on the next business day.
Fax	If the transmission of the fax is completed on a business day before 4.30p.m., on that day, otherwise on the next business day after the day of sending.
Other electronic method	If the email or other electronic transmission is sent on a business day before 4.30p.m., on that day, otherwise on the next business day after the day of sending.
Personal service	If the document is served before 4.30p.m. on a business day, on that day, otherwise on the next business day after that day.

3. RESPONSE TO CLAIM

3.1. Acknowledgment of Service

D3–001 **General rules**

By CPR r.10.1, Acknowledgment of Service may be filed if the Defendant is unable to file a defence within the time permitted by CPR r.15.4 (see *Defence & Reply*—Guide 3.3), or if he wishes to dispute the court's jurisdiction (see *Disputing Jurisdiction*—Guide 3.2).

Service of notice of acknowledgment

CPR r.10.1	The court will serve notice of the acknowledgment on the Claimant (CPR, r. 10.4)
CPR r.8.3	Save that where the claim is a Pt 8 Claim, the Defendant should serve a copy on all parties.

Content of acknowledgment

Form N9 (Pt 7 Claims) *Form N210 (Pt 8 Claims)* *Form N213 (Pt 20 Claims)*	Details required by the forms include an address for service and a statement whether it is intended to dispute the claim and/or the court's jurisdiction. The Acknowledgment should be signed (PD 10 para.4.1). Where a Pt 8 Claim is served, the acknowledgment form seeks further details namely whether and if so why the Defendant objects to use of the Pt 8 procedure and whether the Defendant wishes to seek any remedy different from that Claimed.

Time for acknowledgment

CPR r.10.3(1)	Part 7 Claims: Acknowledge service within 14 days after service of the claim form OR, if the Claim stated that Particulars of Claim would follow, 14 days after service of the Particulars of Claim.

CPR r.8.3	Part 8 Claims: Acknowledge service within 14 days after service of the claim form.
CPR r.20.3 *CPR r.10.3*	Part 20 Claims: Acknowledge service as for Pt 7 Claims. The above time limits are subject to provisions of CPR, r. 6.22 in cases where a Claim is served out of the Jurisdiction .

Consequences of failure to acknowledge service

CPR r.10.2	Part 7 Claims: If a defendant does not file an acknowledgment of service within the time prescribed above, and does not file a defence or admission under Pts 14 or 15, default judgment may be available under Pt 12. (See *Early termination: Default Judgment*.) Until default judgment is in fact entered, acknowledgment may still be filed.
CPR r.8.4	Part 8 Claims: If a defendant fails to file (*n.b.* the rule does not state "file and serve) an acknowledgment of service within the time prescribed above then he may attend the hearing of the claim but may only take part in it with the court's permission.
CPR r.20.11	Part 20 Claims: If a party who is served with a Pt 20 claim which is not a counterclaim, and is not a claim by a defendant against a co-defendant for a contribution or indemnity fails to file an acknowledgment or defence will be deemed to admit the Pt 20 claim and be bound by any judgment in respect of it.
Where claim served out of the jurisdiction	See CPR r.6.35 for modified times for acknowledgement of service and defence where the claim is served out of the jurisdiction.

3.2. Disputing Jurisdiction

Timing D3–002

See Acknowledgment of Service—Guide 3.1 *CPR , r.11(3)*	The time to raise a dispute about the court's jurisdiction is the period after acknowledgment of service but (in the case of a Pt 7 Claim) before filing a defence. If a Defence is filed, the Defendant risks being held to have accepted the court's jurisdiction (this is implied by CPR, r. 11(3), but will not be taken to have accepted jurisdiction merely by filing an acknowledgment of service.

Raising the dispute

Procedure to raise jurisdiction dispute after acknowledgment of service

CPR r.11(1)	Seeking a decision as to jurisdiction is done by filing an Application Notice seeking a hearing to determine the question and claiming an appropriate declaration.
CPR r.11(4)(b)	The application must be supported by evidence.
CPR r.11(2)	Acknowledgment of service must be filed before the application is made.
CPR r.11(4)(a) *CPR r.8.3(4)*	The application must be made: — within the time for filing a defence (in a Pt 7 Claim—CPR, r. 11(4)(a)) or — within the period of 14 days after filing acknowledgment of service.

Procedural Guides

Failure to issue an application

Consequences of failure to issue an application

CPR r.11(5)	If after filing an acknowledgment of service the Defendant fails to issue an application for a hearing to determine the jurisdiction issue in time, he/she is deemed to have accepted that the court has jurisdiction.

The court's order concerning jurisdiction

The order made at the hearing

CPR r.11(7)(a) *CPR r.11(7)(b)*	If the court accepts jurisdiction: — The acknowledgment of service ceases to have effect (CPR, r. 11(7)(a)) and the defendant may serve a further acknowledgment of service within 14 days or such other period as the court directs; — As a matter of practice the court will usually give directions as to filing of a defence in a Pt 7 Claim.
CPR r.11(6)	If the court declines jurisdiction: — the court may set aside the Claim form or service thereof, discharge any order made before commencement or service, or stay the claim.

Related Guides

Commencement—Guide 1, *Acknowledgment of Service*—Guide 3.1, *Defence & Reply*—Guide 3.3.

3.3. Defence & Reply

D3–003 **Defence**

CPR Pt8	A Defence is not required where the claim is issued under the Pt 8 procedure (CPR, Pt 8) unless the court directs otherwise.

Timing

Time for service

Form N9B *Form N9D*	The defence should be filed within 14 days after service of the Particulars of Claim (CPR, r. 15.4(1)(a)); or if an acknowledgment of service is filed (CPR, Pt 10).
CPR r.15.4(1)(a) *CPR r.15.4(1)(b)*	Within 28 days after service of the Particulars of Claim (CPR, r. 15.4(1)(b)).

Exceptions and extensions of time for defence

CPR r.15.5	The time above may be extended by up to 28 days by agreement and the parties must notify the court in writing.
CPR Pt 11	Time for service of Defence will be extended where jurisdiction is disputed.
CPR r.6.23	Proceedings served abroad may be subject to different time limits.
CPR r.24.4(2)	Where Summary Judgment has been sought under CPR, Pt 24, the defendant may wait until after the hearing before filing a defence.

Counterclaims

PD 15 para.3.1 — Any counterclaims should be contained in the Defence document and the text of it should follow immediately after the defence.

Consequences of Failure to File Defence

Consequence of omission

CPR r.15.3, Pt 12
See Default Judgment Guide—4.1 — By CPR, r. 15.3, if a defence is required and is not filed in time, it may be possible to enter judgment in default of defence under CPR, Pt 12, if that Part permits it.

CPR r.15.11 — If no defence or admission is filed AND the Claimant does not enter or apply for judgment within six months of the end of the period for filing a defence, the claim is stayed under CPR, r. 15.11.

Reply and defence to counterclaim

CPR r.15.8 — If the Claimant serves a Reply (and/or Defence to Counterclaim) he/she must do so when filing the allocation questionnaire, and serve it on all other parties.

See Track Allocation Guide—9 — See *Track Allocation* for time limits for filing allocation Questionnaires.

PD 15 para.3.2 — The Reply and Defence to Counterclaim if any should be contained in one document with the Defence to Counterclaim following the Reply.

Related Guides

Acknowledgment of Service—Guide 3.1, *Default Judgment*—Guide 4.1, *Track Allocation*—Guides 5.1 & 5.2.

3.4. Counterclaims and Additional Claims (Part 20)

D3–004

Terminology

CPR r.20.2 — Counterclaim: specifically a claim by a defendant against the claimant or against the claimant and some other person.

Additional Claims: "any claim other than the claim by the claimant against the defendant". Includes:

- claim by defendant against some other person (whether or not already a party) for contribution or indemnity or some other remedy;
- if an additional claim has been made against a person who is not already a party, a claim made by that person against any other person (whether or not already a party);
- includes counterclaims

Which rules apply to additional claims generally?

CPR r.20.3(2) — Generally an Additional Claim is treated as a Claim for the purposes of the CPR, EXCEPT that the following do not apply: CPR rr.7.5, 7.6 (time within which a claim form may be served); CPR r.16.3(5) (statement of value where claim to be issued in the High Court); CPR Pt 26 (case management—preliminary stage)

Daejan Investments Ltd v The Park West Club Ltd and Buxton Associates (Pt 20 Defendant) [2004] C.I.L.L. 2084	A party expecting to make an additional claim is not absolved of the requirement to comply with relevant pre-action protocols (decided in relation to the Pre-Action Protocol for Construction and Engineering Disputes but may be generally applicable).

Which rules apply only to counterclaims but not to additional claims

CPR r.20.3(3)	CPR Pt 12 (default judgment) (but see also "Default judgment" below and CPR r.20.11 which appears to apply Pt 12 to other claims in modified form).

Which rules apply to counterclaims but only partly to other additional claims

CPR r.20.3(4)

Part 14 (Admissions) applies to counterclaims but only:
- rr.14.1(1) and 14.1(2) (admission of the truth of another party's case in writing); and
- r.14.3 (admission by notice in writing—application for judgment) apply to other types of Additional Claim.

Service of additional claims

CPR r.20.8 *CPR r.20.10*	See CPR rr.20.8 and 20.10.

If the additional claim is defended

CPR r.20.13	If a defence is filed to an additional claim, the court must consider the future conduct of the proceedings and give appropriate directions and must ensure so far as practicable that the original claim and all additional claims are managed together.

Additional claims against the Crown

CPR r.66.4	See CPR r.66.4

Titles of additional claims

PD 20 para.7 *PD 7 para.4*	See PD 20 para.7 and PD 7 para.4.

Counterclaims

Procedure where counterclaim is against an existing claimant

CPR r.20.4	A defendant may counterclaim against a claimant by filing particulars of claim. Permission of the court is not needed if the counterclaim is filed with the defence. Otherwise the court's permission is needed.

Procedure where counterclaim is against a person who is not an existing claimant

CPR r.20.5	The defendant must apply for an order that the intended defendant to counterclaim be joined as a party. The application may be made without notice unless otherwise directed.

Defence to counterclaim

CPR r.15.1 *CPR r.20.3(3)*	See CPR r.15.1. Acknowledgment of service is not required if a claimant wishes to defend a counterclaim against him.

Claims for a contribution or indemnity

When may such a claim be made

CPR r.20.6	A Defendant may make a claim for a contribution or indemnity against a person who is already a party, after he has filed acknowledgment of service or a defence.

Procedure

CPR r.20.6(1)	Defendant files a Notice which states the nature and grounds of his additional claim, and serves the Notice on the party from whom the indemnity or contribution is sought.
CPR r.20.6(2)(a)	Permission is not needed if the Notice is filed and served with the defence or, if the additional claim is against a party who was added to the claim later, within 28 days of that party files his defence.
CPR r.20.6(2)(b)	Otherwise the court's permission is needed.

Other types of additional claim

CPR r.20.7(1)—scope	CPR r.20.7 applies to all additional claims except counterclaims against existing parties and claims for an indemnity or a contribution.

Procedure

CPR r.20.7(3)	Where CPR r.20.7 applies, a defendant may make an additional claim without the court's permission if he issues a claim form for the additional claim before or on the same date as he files his defence. Otherwise the court's permission is needed, which may be applied for without notice, unless ordered otherwise.

What must be served on a non-party?

CPR r.20.12	The documents set out at CPR r.20.12 must be served with any additional claim form if the party served was not already a party to the proceedings.

Rights of new party to documents

PD 5 para.3	Any newly joined party is entitled, without charge, to require the person joining him to supply copies of all statements of case, written evidence and exhibits within 48 hours of written request.

Obtaining permission

What are the criteria which the court will consider when permission is required to permit an additional claim to be made, whether to dismiss an additional claim or whether to require the additional claim to be brought seperately?

CPR r.20.9 — The court may have regard to:

- the connection between the additional claim and the claim brought by the claimant against the defendant;
- whether the additional claimant is seeking substantially the same remedy which another party is claiming from him;
- whether the additional claimant wants the court to decide any question connected with the subject matter of the proceedings both between existing parties and between existing parties and someone who is not already a party;

— whether the additional claimant wants the court to decide any question connected with the subject matter of the proceedings against an existing party in the capacity in which he is a party as well as in some further capacity.

Rahman v Sterling Credit Ltd [2001] 1 W.L.R. 496 — Where a judgment remains unsatisfied the action is not yet at an end and the court can still grant permission to file a counterclaim.

Default judgment

Where the additional claim is not a counterclaim or a claim for a contribution or an indemnity against another defendant under CPR r.20.6

CPR r.20.11(1)–(2) — If the additional defendant fails to file acknowledgment of service or defence then he is deemed to admit the additional claim and is bound by any decision in the main proceedings insofar as it is relevant to any matter arising in the additional claim.

CPR r.20.11(3) — An additional claimant may not obtain default judgment under CPR Pt 12, without the court's permission, if he has not satisfied a default judgment which was entered against him or if the remedy he seeks is anything other than a contribution or indemnity.

Note that CPR r.20.11(3) appears inconsistent with CPR r.20.3(3) which provides that Pt 12 does not apply to additional claims other than counterclaims.

4. JUDGMENT WITHOUT TRIAL

4.1. Default Judgment: Rules

D4–001 **Availability of default judgment**

Excluded cases

PD 12 paras 1.2–1.3 — Default judgment is not available in the following types of case:

(i) Claims for delivery of goods subject to an agreement regulated by the Consumer Credit Act 1974.
(ii) Part 8 Claims.
(iii) Wherever a Practice Direction provides that it is not available, or example: admiralty claims, arbitration proceedings, contentious probate, provisional damages, possession claims.

Default judgment is also not available in any case where:

CPR r.12.3(3)
See Summary Judgment Guide

(i) the Defendant has applied for summary judgment against the Claimant, or to strike out the claimant's case under CPR, r. 3.4, and the application has not been disposed of (CPR, r. 12.3(3)(a)); or
(ii) the Defendant has satisfied the claim including costs (CPR, r. 12.3(3)(b)); or
(iii) the Claim is a money claim and the Defendant has served an admission with a request for time to pay (CPR, r. 12.3(3)(c)).

When default judgment is available

See Acknowledgment of Service—Guide 3.1 & Defence and Reply—Guide 3.3 — In Claims not excluded by the above, default judgment may be available where either:

CPR r.12.3(1) — the Defendant fails to acknowledge service in time ("Judgment in default of acknowledgment of service"); or

CPR r.12.3(2) — the Defendant fails to file a defence in time after filing an acknowledgment of service ("Judgment in default of defence");

— where a counterclaim has been made under CPR, r. 20.4 and a defence has not been filed.

Procedure for obtaining default judgment

CPR r.12.4 If Claim was served by Claimant, file a certificate of service. Judgment may be entered administratively at court (file a request for judgment) unless the claim is of a type listed at CPR r.12.4 in which case application for default judgment must be made in accordance with CPR Pt 23.

4.2. Summary Judgment Application by a Party: Rules

Availability of summary judgment **D4–002**

Excluded cases

Summary Judgment is not available (*against a* ***defendant***) in the following types of case:

CPR r.24.3(2)(a)
CPR r.24.3(2)(b)
(i) in proceedings for possession of residential premises against:
— a mortgagor; or
— a tenant or person holding over after the end of his tenancy whose occupancy is protected within the meaning of the Rent Act 1977 or the Housing Act 1988; or

CPR r.24.3(2)(a)
CPR r.24.3(2)(b)
(ii) in proceedings for an admiralty claim in rem; or

Threshold for summary judgment

CPR r.24.2 The court may give judgment summarily on a claim or issue in a claim if it considers that:

(i) **either:** the claimant has no real prospect of succeeding on the claim or issue; **or:** the defendant has no real prospect of successfully defending the claim or issue;
(ii) **AND** there is no other compelling reason why the case or issue should be disposed of at a trial.

When to apply for summary judgment

CPR r.24.4(1) Generally, a claimant may not apply for summary judgment until the defendant against whom the application is to be made has filed an acknowledgment of service or a defence (this implies that summary judgment is not available before service of the Particulars of Claim) ***unless*** the court gives permission or a practice direction provides otherwise.

PD 26 para.5.3 Generally, any application for summary judgment should be made before or at the same time as filing the allocation questionnaire.

Specific performance etc., cases

PD 24 para.7.1	In the following cases, summary judgment may be sought at *any time* after service of the claim form: specific performance of, rescission of, or forfeiture/return of a deposit made under an agreement for the sale, exchange, mortgage or charge of any property, or grant or assignment of a lease or tenancy of any property.

4.3. Summary Judgment Application by a Party: Procedure

D4–003 **How to Apply for Summary Judgment**

Form N244	Confirm the availability of Summary Judgment (see above) and then file an application notice in Form N244 seeking summary judgment, supported by evidence.
CPR r.24.4(2)	If the Defendant has not yet filed a defence but has merely acknowledged service, at the date when the summary judgment application is issued, he/she need not file a defence until after the hearing.

Contents of application and evidence

CPR r.23.6	— Comply with formalities in Pt 23 including stating what order is sought and why.
PD 24 para.2(2)	— state that it is an application for summary judgment under CPR, Pt 24.
PD 24 para.2(4)	— identify the written evidence relied on (unless the Application notice contains all evidence relied on).
PD 24 para.2(5).	— draw the attention of the respondent to CPR, r. 24.5(1) (rules concerning respondent's evidence in reply).
PD 24 paras 7.1, 7.2	— in claims for specific performance, etc. under PD 24 para.7.1, a draft order sought should be attached (see PD 24 para.7.2).
PD 24 para.2(3)	— identify concisely any point of law or provision of a document relied on; **and/or** — state that the application is made because the applicant believes that the respondent has no real prospect of success on the claim or issue (or of defending the claim or issue) **AND** state that the applicant knows of no other reason why disposal should await trial (PD 24 para.2(3)).

Timetable for service of evidence

CPR r.24.4(3)	The respondent must be given at least **14** days' notice of the hearing date and issues the court will decide.
CPR r.24.5(1)	If the respondent wishes to rely on written evidence in reply, he/she must file and serve it at least seven days before the hearing.
CPR r.24.5(2)	If the applicant wishes to rely on a statement in reply he/she must file and serve it at least **3** days before the hearing.

Orders which may be made at the hearing

PD 24 paras 5 & 9	(i) judgment on claim or issue, (ii) striking out or dismissal of claim or issue, (iii) dismissal of the application, (iv) a conditional order, plus ancillary costs and directions orders.

Conditional orders

Chapple v Williams [1999] C.P.L.R. 731 — The condition must be capable of being complied with,

Foot and Bowden v Anglo Europe Corp Ltd 17/2/00, LTL 15/1/2001 — though a conditional order may be made against a company with no assets and has ceased trading, if there is evidence it will be able to raise funds.

Olatawura v Abiloye [2002] EWCA Civ 998 — See this case for guidance on making conditional orders where a party is advancing an improbable case and security for costs is sought as a condition

Failure to follow relevant pre-action protocol

PD 24 para.2(6) — The court will usually refuse to entertain an application for summary judgment if the Claimant has failed to follow any relevant pre-action protocol until after a defence has been filed.

Related Guides

Default Judgment—Guide 4.1.

4.4. Striking Out: In Case Management and/or on Application

Striking out as part of case management D4–004

The court may, on its own initiative or on application strike out the whole or part of any statement of case if it appears:

(a) that the statement of case discloses no reasonable grounds for bringing or defending the claim; or
(b) that the statement of case is an abuse of the court's process or is otherwise likely to obstruct the just disposal of the proceedings; or
(c) that there has been a failure to comply with a rule, practice direction or court order.

Power to make consequential orders

CPR r.3.4(2) — In addition to striking out, the court may make consequential orders (such as entering judgment).

Judgment after breach of "unless" order

CPR r.3.5(1) — If a conditional order is made, providing that striking out of the whole of a statement of case will take place unless the party concerned complies with the order, and the party does not comply, then the other party may obtain judgment with costs:

(a) in the case of a money claim or a claim for delivery of goods with the alternative of payment of their value, or a combination of such claims, by filing a request for judgment stating that the right to judgment arises under the order and that the order has not been complied with (CPR, r. 3.5(2) and (4))
(b) in other cases, by applying for judgment using the general applications procedure of CPR, Pt 23.

CPR r.3.5(2), (4) — (a) in the case of a money claim or a claim for delivery of goods with the alternative of payment of their value, or a combination of such claims, by filing a request for judgment stating that the right to judgment arises under the order and that the order has not been complied with

CPR Pt 23	(b) in other cases, by applying for judgment using the general applications procedure of CPR, Pt 23.

Setting aside judgment after breach of "unless" order

CPR , r.3.6(1) & (2)	A party against whom judgment is entered after a striking out for breach of an unless order may apply to set aside the judgment but must apply not more than 14 days after service of the judgment.
CPR , r.3.6(3)	Setting aside is then mandatory if the party in whose favour judgment was entered was not entitled to judgment at the time it was entere.
CPR r.3.6(4)	In other cases, the court's general powers to give relief from sanctions (under CPR, r. 3.9) apply.

4.5. Striking Out: Other Cases where Striking Out may take place

D4–005 **Striking out after non-attendance at trial**

CPR r.39.3(1)	If a party fails to attend trial, his/her claim or defence may be struck out and/or judgment entered (or the claim/counterclaim dismissed as the case may be) (CPR r.39.3(1)(a)–(c)).
CPR r.39.3(1)	The court may also proceed to hear the trial in the absence of a party.
CPR r.39.3(4)	Judgment or striking out may be set aside on application supported by evidence.
CPR r.39.3(5)(a)–(c)	The court may grant the application only if the applicant: (a) acted promptly when he found out that the court had exercised its power to strike out or enter judgment etc.; and (b) had a good reason for not attending trial; and (c) has a reasonable prospect of success at the trial.
Nelson v Clearsprings (Management) Ltd [2006] EWCA Civ 1252	Rule 39.5 contemplates non-attendance of a duly served party at trial, or where service has been dispensed with. If a party fails to attend and has not been properly served then the striking out may be set aside as of right, under CPR rr.3.1(2)(m) and 3.10 rather than under r.39.5.
Tennero v Arnold [2006] EWHC 1530	Abuse of process to appeal a refusal of an adjournment which preceded the making of an order in a non-attending party's absence under CPR r.39.5, when an application could instead be made to set aside the judgment or order.
Regency Rolls v Carnall [2000] EWCA Civ 379	The jurisdiction to set aside the order is not a broad discretion. The criteria under r.39.5 must be satisfied before the order can be set aside, unless service was irregular (see *Nelson Clearsprings (Management) Ltd*, above.)

Striking out of committal proceedings

PD to RSC O.52, para.5	The court may, of its own initiative or on application by the respondent, strike out a committal application if it appears: (a) that the committal application and the evidence served in support of it disclose no reasonable ground for alleging that the respondent is guilty of a contempt of court; or

(b) that the committal application is an abuse of the court's process or, if made in existing proceedings, is otherwise likely to obstruct the just disposal of those proceedings; or
(c) that there has been a failure to comply with a rule, practice direction or court order

Striking out at a summary judgment application

PD 24 para.5 — On an application for Summary Judgment under CPR, Pt 24 the court may instead strike out the claim or make a conditional order for payment of money into court or the taking of a specific step, with striking out of the claim or statement of case in default of compliance.

Related Guides

Summary Judgment—Guides 4.2 & 4.3.

4.6. Judgment on Admissions

General D4–006

Forms

The appropriate form numbers for use in the circumstances described in this guide are set out in PD 14. See forms N9A and N9C, N225A and N226.

When to make an admission

CPR r.14.1(1)–(2) — A party may at any time admit any part of a party's case by doing so in writing.

CPR r.14.2 — Admissions of money claims using the procedure of filing/serving an admission form should be made within 14 days of service of the claim form, or 14 days after service of the Particulars of Claim if the claim form states that Particulars of Claim will follow.

Outside the above time limits if the Claimant has not entered default judgment, the Defendant may admit a money claim using the procedure of filing/serving notice of admission at any time before default judgment is entered.

Where Defendant is overseas
CPR r.6.22
CPR r.6.16(4) — The above time limits are subject to CPR rr.6.22 and 6.16(4) concerning admissions where the claim is served out of the jurisdiction or on the agent of an overseas principal.

Judgment on admissions generally

CPR r.14.1(3) — In general a party may enter judgment on admissions where the claim is for a specified or unspecified sum of money and the Defendant has served notice of admission in the relevant practice form.

Limits on right to enter judgment on admissions

CPR r.14.1(4) — There is no right to enter judgment on admissions: in money claims where the Defendant is a child or patient, or where the Claimant is a child or patient and the Defendant admits part of the claim and offers a sum in satisfaction.

Specific cases

Admission of whole of money claim for a specified sum of money where sole claim is for specified sum of money

CPR r.14.4	Defendant may admit the whole claim by serving an admission form on the Claimant for the whole amount.
Obtaining judgment	May be obtained by Claimant filing a request for judgment.
Time to pay not requested *CPR r.14.4(4)–(6)*	If the Defendant has not requested time to pay then the Claimant may specify in the request for judgment the date by which he requires the whole judgment to be paid or the times and rate at which it is to be paid. The court will enter judgment for the amount of the claim less any sums paid, plus costs. If the Claimant specified no payment date in the request for judgment then the order will be for immediate payment.
Time to pay requested	See "Request for time to pay" below.

Admission of part of claim for specified amount of money where sole claim is for specified sum of money

CPR r.14.5(1)–(2)	Defendant may admit part of the claim by filing as admission form for the amount admitted.
Procedure after admission *CPR r.14.5(3)*	The court will serve a notice on the Claimant requiring him to return the notice stating whether he: — accepts the amount admitted in satisfaction; — does not accept the amount and wishes to continue with the proceedings; — (if Defendant has requested time to pay), accepts the amount but not the proposals as to payment. Claimant must file and serve the notice within 14 days of service on him, in default the claim is stayed until Claimant files the notice.
Obtaining judgment	If the Claimant accepts the sum offered, judgment may be obtained by Claimant filing a request for judgment.
Time to pay not requested *CPR r.14.5(7)–(9)*	If the Defendant has not requested time to pay then the Claimant may specify in the request for judgment the date by which he requires the whole judgment to be paid or the times and rate at which it is to be paid. The court will enter judgment for the amount of the claim less any sums paid, plus costs. If the Claimant specified no payment date in the request for judgment then the order will be for immediate payment.
Time to pay requested	See "Request for time to pay" below.

Admission of liability to pay whole of claim for an unspecified amount of money, where sole claim is for money

CPR r.14.6	Defendant may admit by filing an admission form.
Procedure after admission *CPR r.14.6(3)*	The court will serve the notice of admission on the Claimant.
Obtaining judgment *CPR r.14.6(4)–(5)*	Upon receipt of the admission form the Claimant may enter judgment by filing a request for judgment. If he fails to do so within 14 days the claim is stayed until he files the request.
Nature of judgment *CPR r.14.6(6)–(7)*	Judgment will be entered for an amount to be decided by the court, and costs.

Admission of liability to pay claim for an unspecified amount of money where the Defendant offers a sum in satisfaction, where sole claim is for money

CPR r.14.7	Defendant may admit by filing an admission form.

Procedure after admission *CPR r.14.7(3)*	The court will serve the notice of admission on the Claimant requiring him to return the notice stating whether or not he accepts the amount offered in satisfaction. Claimant must file the notice within 14 days of service on him, in default the claim is stayed until Claimant files the notice.
Obtaining judgment (if Claimant accepts sum offered)	If the Claimant accepts the sum offered, judgment may be obtained by Claimant filing a request for judgment.
Time to pay not requested *CPR r.14.7(5)–(9)*	If the Defendant has not requested time to pay then the Claimant may specify in the request for judgment the date by which he requires the whole judgment to be paid or the times and rate at which it is to be paid. The court will enter judgment for the amount of the claim less any sums paid, plus costs. If the Claimant specified no payment date in the request for judgment then the order will be for immediate payment.
Time to pay requested	See "Request for time to pay" below.
Obtaining judgment (Claimant does not accept sum offered)	The Claimant may obtain judgment for an amount to be decided by the court by filing a request for judgment in the relevant practice form. (See "Forms" above).

Procedure where an amount is to be decided by the court

CPR r.14.8	The court will give any directions it considers appropriate when entering judgment, and, if it considers it appropriate will allocate the claim to a track.

Request for time to pay

CPR r.14.9(1)–(2)	A request for time to pay is a proposal made by a Defendant in an admission form about the date for payment, or a proposal to pay in instalments at the times and rate specified in the request. The request must be served/filed with the Defendant's admission.
If proposal is accepted by Claimant *CPR r.14.9(4)–(5)*	If the request for time to pay is accepted by the Claimant, the Claimant may enter judgment by filing a request for judgment.
If proposal is not accepted by Claimant *CPR r.14.10(2)*	The Claimant must file a notice in the relevant practice form stating that he does not accept the proposal (and filing a copy of the admission and request for time to pay, if these were served on him by the Defendant direct).

Procedure to determine time and rate of payment

CPR r.14.10(4)	On receipt of the Claimant's notice above, the court will enter judgment for the amount admitted less any payments made, to be paid at a time and rate of payment to be determined by the court.
Jurisdiction to determine time and rate of payment *CPR r.14.11* *CPR r.14.12*	Amount outstanding including costs not more than £50,000: a court officer may determine, and will do so without a hearing. Amount in excess of £50,000 including costs: a judge shall determine time and rate of payment. He may do so without a hearing, but if a hearing is to be held then the proceedings must be transferred to the Defendant's home court if the claim is solely for money, the defendant is an individual, the claim has not already been transferred to another Defendant's home court and was not started in a Specialist List. The court must give at least seven days notice of the hearing.

Right to seek re-determination CPR r.14.13
A party may apply for re-determination at a hearing if the time and rate were determined by a court officer or by a judge without a hearing. Upon application for re-determination the proceedings must be transferred to the Defendant's home court if the claim is solely for money, the defendant is an individual, the claim has not already been transferred to another Defendant's home court and was not started in a Specialist List.

Interest on the judgment CPR r.14.14
The calculation or determination of interest on the judgment is determined in accordance with CPR r.14.14.

Withdrawal of pre-commencement admissions

For other admissions see Stoke on Trent CC v John Whalley [2006] EWCA Civ. 1137
See CPR r.14.1A for rules relating to withdrawal of admissions made before commencement, but after April 6, 2007, in personal injury, clinical negligence, and disease and illness claims.

Withdrawal of post-commencement admissions

With the court's permission. See CPR r.14.1(5)

4.7. Discontinuance

D4–007 *General*

Abandonment versus discontinuance

CPR r.38.1
A Claimant who abandons one remedy of several claimed is not treated as discontinuing all or part of a claim under CPR Pt 38. Instead CPR Pt 17 (amendment of statement of case) applies.

Right to discontinue

CPR r.38.2(1)
A Claimant may discontinue all or part of a claim at any time.

Where permission is required CPR r.38.2(a)
The permission of the court to discontinue is required where the court has granted an injunction or a party has given undertakings to the court. (This applies only to discontinuance against the party who gave the undertakings or against whom the injunction was granted.)

If an interim payment has been made CPR r.38.2(b)
Where an interim payment has been made by a defendant, the Claimant may discontinue only if the Defendant who made the payment consents in writing or the court gives permission.

Multiple claimants CPR r.38.2(3)
The consent of all claimants to discontinue is required, unless the court gives permission.

Procedure for discontinuing

CPR r.38.3 Form N279
The Claimant must file and serve Notice of Discontinuance and must state therein that he has served the Notice on every other party to the proceedings. Any necessary consents from other parties must be attached to the notice and the notice must state against which defendants the claim is being discontinued.

Time when discontinuance takes effect CPR r.38.5
The claim is discontinued, save as to questions of costs, with effect from date of service of the Notice on the Defendant against whom the claim is being discontinued, unless the permission of the court is required to discontinue.

Application to set aside Notice of Discontinuance

CPR r.38.4 — The Defendant may apply within 28 days of service to set aside the Notice (e.g. on grounds of abuse of process or on the ground that consent was required and he would have refused it).

Costs on discontinuance (whole claim discontinued)

CPR r.38.6(1) — Unless ordered otherwise the Claimant who discontinues is liable for costs which a defendant incurred on or before the date of discontinuance.

Costs on discontinuance (part of claim discontinued)

CPR r.38.6(2) — Unless ordered otherwise the Claimant who discontinues is liable for the costs which a defendant incurred relating only to the part of the claim which was discontinued, on or before the date of discontinuance, to be assessed at the conclusion of proceedings.

Small claims costs
CPR r.38.6(3) — The above costs provisions do not apply to the small cliams track.

Form of costs order

Deemed to have been ordered on the standard basis. A claimant wishing to avoid an order for costs should apply under CPR r.38.6. See e.g. *In re Walker v Walker and Walker* [2005] EWCA Civ. 247, and *Aegis Group Plc v Inland Revenue* [2005] EWHC 1468, and for a case where D's intransigence in negotiation was a factor, see *RBG Resources plc (In Liquidation) v Viren Kumar Rastogi* [2004] EWHC 994.

Subsequent proceedings

CPR r.38.7 — The court's permission is required to issue a claim which arises out of facts which are the same or substantially the same as the discontinued claim, if the claim was discontinued after the Defendant had filed a defence.

Possible stay if costs not paid

CPR r.38.8 — If a Claimant partly discontinues a claim and is liable for costs, the remainder of the claim may be stayed by the court if he fails to pay those costs within 14 days of the date on which the amount was agreed or the court ordered the costs to be paid. The stay may be until payment of the costs.

4.8. Disposal Hearings

What is a disposal hearing? D4–008

PD 26 para.12.4(2) — A hearing at which the court may decide the amount payable under or in consequence of an order, and may give judgment for that amount, or at which the court may give directions for the future conduct of the proceedings. The above is subject to "time limits" below.

Form of a disposal hearing

PD 26 para.12.4(1) — A disposal hearing does not usually last longer than 30 minutes and oral evidence will not normally be heard.

Small claims

PD 26 para.12.4(3) If a disposal hearing is ordered for a claim which has been allocated (or is allocated at the disposal hearing) to the small claims track, the court may treat the disposal hearing as a final hearing under CPR Pt 27.

Form of evidence

PD 26 para.12.4(4) CPR Pt 32.6 applies to evidence at disposal hearings (use of witness statements and statements of case as evidence).

Time limits

PD 26 para.12.4(5) At a disposal hearing the court may not exercise its power to determine the amount payable and to give judgment for that amount unless the written evidence on which the Claimant relies was served at least three days before the disposal hearing.

5. CASE MANAGEMENT AND SANCTIONS

5.1. Track Allocation: Rules

D5–001 **Scope of the three case management tracks**

The small claims track

CPR , r.26.6(1)(a) The small claims track is the normal track for:

(a) any claim for personal injuries where the financial value of the claim is not more than £5,000 and the claim for damages for personal injury is not more than £1,000.

CPR r.26.6(1)(b) (b) any claim which includes a claim by a tenant of residential premises against his landlord where (i) the tenant is seeking an order requiring the landlord to carry out repairs or other work to the premises (whether or not the tenant is also seeking some other remedy); (ii) the cost of the repairs or other work to the premises is estimated to be not more than £1,000; and (iii) the financial value of any other claim for damages is not more than £1,000.

CPR r.26.7(4) (c) certain claims in respect of harassment and unlawful eviction will **not** be allocated to the small claims track.

CPR r.26.6(3) (d) save as above, the small claims track is the normal track for any claim which has a financial value of not more than £5,000.

The fast track

CPR r.26.6(4)(a), (b) and (5) The fast track is the normal track for any claim—

(a) for which the small claims track is not the normal track; and

(b) which has a financial value of not more than £15,000; provided that

(c) the court considers that the trial is likely to last for no longer than one day; and oral expert evidence at trial will be limited to one expert per party in relation to any expert field and expert evidence in two expert fields.

The multi-track

CPR r.26.6(6)	The multi-track is the normal track for any claim for which the small claims track or the fast track is not the normal track.

5.2. Track Allocation: Procedure

D5–002

Part 7 claim

CPR rr.15.10 and 14.5	If the defence is to the effect that a money claim has been paid or the defendant has admitted part of a money claim. (In which case the Claimant will need to take steps to cause the claim to proceed further)
CPR r.26.3	Otherwise, the court will aupply an allocation question-naire to all parties when a defence is filed.

Part 8 claim

CPR r.8.9(c)	Claim is deemed to be allocated to the Multi Track and therefore CPR Pt 26 does not apply

Filing the Allocation Questionnaire

CPR r.26.3(6)	The completed Allocation Questionnaire must be filed by each party no later than the date specified on it, which shall be at least 14 days after the date it was deemed to be served by the court.

Allocation Questionnaires not filed in time

CPR r.26.5(5) *PD 26 para.6*	The court may give any direction it considers appropriate.
PD 26 para.6	The usual order if no party files a questionnaire will be an "unless" order strking out the claim unless a question-naire is filed within three days.

Track allocation decision

CPR r.26.5(3) & (4)	The court may direct an allocation hearing and/or require the parties to supply more information.
	The court, either on the papers or at a hearing will al-locate to a track, applying criteria in CPR rr.26.6, 26.7, 26.8.
	Notice of Allocation will then be served by the court together with copies of other parties' Questionnaires and further information supplied.

Track re-allocation

The court may change the track allocation (CPR r.26.10). However where for example it becomes apparent that a Fast Track case will probably somewhat exceed £15,000 but not by a large margin the case should not be re-allocation if to do so would cause substantial disruption. However where the amount by which the value will exceed £15,000 is substantial, there should normally be a re-allocation even if to do so will cause delay to comple-tion of the litigation: *Maguire v Molin* [2002] EWCA Civ. 1083.

Related Guides

Defence & Reply—Guide 3.3, *Summary Judgment*—Guide 4.2.

5.3. Relief from Sanctions

D5–003 **Requirements under CPR r.3.9**

CPR r.3.9	Application for relief from sanctions should be by Pt 23 Application which must be supported by evidence.

Where the sanction is payment of costs

CPR r.3.8(2)	The party in default may only obtain relief by appealing against the order for costs.

Where the sanction is striking out and judgment has been entered

CPR r.3.6(2)	The party seeking relief must apply within 14 days after service of the judgment.
CPR r.3.6(3)	If the right to enter judgment had not arisen at the time judgment was entered the court must set aside judgment otherwise the party struck out must apply under CPR r.3.9.

Where the sanction is striking out for non payment of fees

CPR r.3.7(4)(b)	The claim will have been struck out, with costs, without further order of the court.
PD 3B para.1 *CPR r.3.10*	The court will send notice of striking out to the Defendant but *n.b.* an error of procedure does not invalidate any step taken in the proceedings unless the court so orders.
CPR r.3.7(4)(b)	The party struck out should apply under CPR 3.9 to reinstate the claim (*N.b.* since an error of procedure does not invalidate any step taken in the proceedings the Claimant struck out should prudently seek relief irrespective of whether the Defendant has been notified, in view of CPR r.3.7(4)(b)(i).)
CPR r.3.7(7)	If the claim is reinstated the court will grant relief which is conditional on the claimant either paying the fee or filing evidence of exemption from payment or remission of fee.

Where claim struck out for non attendance at trial

See *Striking Out: Other Cases where Striking Out may take place*—Guide 4.5.

Criteria for relief

CPR r.3.9(1) and see notes to CPR r.3.9

The court will consider all the circumstances including:

(a) the interests of the administration of justice;
(b) whether the application for relief has been made promptly;
(c) whether the failure to comply was intentional;
(d) whether there is a good explanation for the failure;
(e) the extent to which the party in default has complied with other rules, practice directions, court orders and any relevant preaction protocol;
(f) whether the failure to comply was caused by the party or his legal representative;
(g) whether the trial date or the likely trial date can still be met if relief is granted;
(h) the effect which the failure to comply had on each party; and
(i) the effect which the granting of relief would have on each party.

Case law

It is essential that the court considers each matter in r.3.9 systematically e.g. *Woodhouse v Consignia Plc* [2002] EWCA Civ. 275, *Leckstein v Menon* [2003] EWHC 90. The court must also consider all the circumstances, including e.g.the strength of the defence: *Chapple v Williams* [1999] C.P.L.R. 731. Note that an application for relief from sanctions is only required where sanctions have been imposed, not merely where there has been a breach in the absence of sanctions: *Cottrell v General Cologne Re UK Ltd* [2004] EWHC 2402.

5.4. Case Management (Small Claims)

Parts of the CPR which do not apply to claims allocated to the Small Claims track (CPR Pt 27) D5–004

- Part 25 (interim remedies) except for interim injunctions;
- Part 31 (disclosure and inspection);
- Part 32 (evidence) except CPR r.32.1 (power of court to control evidence);
- Part 33 (miscellaneous rules about evidence);
- Part 35 (experts and assessors) except CPR r.35.1 (duty to restrict expert evidence), , r.35.3 (experts – overriding duty to the court), r.35.7 (court's power to direct that evidence is to be given by single joint expert) and 35.8 (instructions to a single joint expert);
- Part 18 (further information) save that the court may of itse own initiative order a party to provide further information if it considers it appropriate to do so;
- Part 36 (offers to settle and payments into court);
- Part 39 (hearings) except CPR r.39.2 (hearing to be in public).

Management after allocation

CPR r.27.4
For meaning of "standard" and "special" directions see below

Court will:

- give **standard directions** and fix a date for the final hearing (and inform parties of the time allowed for final hearing);
- or give **special directions** and fix a date for the final hearing (and inform parties of the time allowed for final hearing);
- or give **special directions** and direct that the court will consider what further directions are to be given no later than 28 days after the date the special directions were given;

CPR r.27.6

- or fix a date for a **preliminary hearing** under CPR r.27.6; or

CPR r.27.10

- or give notice that it proposes to deal with the claim **without a hearing** under CPR r 27.10 and invite the parties to notify the court by a specified date if they agree the proposal.

Preliminary hearing

CPR r.27.6

- The court may hold a preliminary hearing where it considers that special directions are needed to ensure a fair hearing and it appears necessary for a party to attend at court to ensure that he understands what he must do to comply with the special directions; or

- where necessary to enable it to dispose of the claim on the basis that one or other of the parties has no real prospect of success at a final hearing; or
- to enable it to strike out a statement of case or part of a statement of case on the basis that the statement of case, or the part to be struck out, discloses no reasonable grounds for bringing or defending the claim.
- Preliminary hearing may be treated as final hearing if parties agree.
- At or after a preliminary hearing the court will fix the date of the final hearing (if not already fixed) and give any appropriate directions.

Notice period for preliminary or final hearing

CPR r.27.6
CPR r.27.4

Court will give at least 14 days' notice of the date fixed for a preliminary hearing.

Court will give at least 21 days' notice of the date fixed for the final hearing, unless the parties agree to accept less notice. Court will state time allowed for final hearing.

Waiver of right to hearing

CPR r.27.10 The court may, if all parties agree, deal with the claim without a hearing.

Re-allocation to another track

CPR r.27.14 Where a claim is re-allocated to another track, CPR r.27.14 (costs on the small claims track) will cease to apply after the claim has been re-allocated.

Special directions

In an appropriate case a small claims case may be transferred to a different track so as to make available special orders which would not otherwise be available, such as interim payment: *Clark v Ardington Electrical Services (Appeal against order for Disclosure)* [2001] EWCA Civ 585.

At the hearing

CPR r.27.8

- The court may adopt any method of proceeding at a hearing that it considers to be fair.
- Hearings will be informal.
- The strict rules of evidence do not apply.
- The court need not take evidence on oath.
- The court may limit cross-examination.
- The court must give reasons for its decision.

"standard directions" (CPR Pt 27, Appendix B)

CPR Pt 27, Appendix B

"1. *Each party must deliver to every other party and to the court office copies of all documents on which he intends to rely at the hearing no later than [ ] [14 days before the hearing].*
(These should include the letter making the claim and the reply.)
2. *The original documents must be brought to the hearing.*
3. *[Notice of hearing date and time allowed.]*
4. *The parties are encouraged to contact each other with a view to trying to settle the case or narrow the issues. However the court must be informed immediately if the case is settled by agreement before the hearing date.*

5. *No party may rely at the hearing on any report from an expert unless express permission has been granted by the court beforehand. Anyone wishing to rely on an expert must write to the court immediately on receipt of this Order and seek permission, giving an explanation why the assistance of an expert is necessary.*

NOTE: Failure to comply with the directions may result in the case being adjourned and in the party at fault having to pay costs. The parties are encouraged always to try to settle the case by negotiating which each other. The court must be informed immediately if the case is settled before the hearing."

"special directions" (CPR Pt 27, Appendix C)

CPR Pt 27, Appendix C

"1. *The [party] must clarify his case.*
He must do this by delivering to the court office and to the no later than
[date]
[a list of]
[details of]

2. *The [party] must allow the [party] to inspect by appointment within* ....*days of receiving a request to do so.*
3. *The hearing will not take place at the court but at* ....
4. *The [party] must bring to court at the hearing the* ....
5. *Signed statements setting out the evidence of all witnesses on whom each party intends to rely must be prepared and copies included in the documents mentioned in paragraph 1. This includes the evidence of the parties themselves and of any other witness, whether or not he is going to come to court to give evidence.*
6. *The court may decide not to take into account a document [or video] or the evidence of a witness if these directions have not been complied with.*
7. *If he does not [do so] [*] *his [Claim][Defence] [and Counterclaim] will be struck out and (specify consequence).*
8. *It appears to the court that expert evidence is necessary on the issue of* ....*and that that evidence should be given by a single expert to be instructed by the parties jointly. If the parties cannot agree about who to choose and what arrangements to make about paying his fee, either party MUST apply to the court for further directions. The evidence is to be given in the form of a written report. Either party may ask the expert questions and must then send copies of the questions and replies to the other party and to the court. Oral expert evidence may be allowed in exceptional circumstances but only after a further order of the court. Attention is drawn to the limit of £200 on expert's fees that may be recovered.*
9. *If either party intends to show a video as evidence he must—*
   (a) *contact the court at once to make arrangements for him to do so, because the court may not have the necessary equipment, and*
   (b) *provide the other party with a copy of the video or the opportunity to see it at least* ....*days before the hearing.*"

5.5. Case Management (Fast Track)

D5–005 **Decision as to allocation hearing or directions hearing**

PD 28 para 3.10 — If it appears to the court that the claim is one which will be allocated to the fast track but it cannot give directions on its own initiative or approve agreed directions the court may allocate the claim and direct a case management hearing, or list an allocation hearing at which directions will be given.

Directions on allocation to the Fast Track

CPR r.28.2 — On allocation the court will give directions (see below) for the management of the case and set a timetable up to trial.

The court will fix the trial date or fix a period, not exceeding three weeks, within which the trial is to take place.

The trial date/period will be specified in the notice of allocation.

The standard period between directions and trial will be not more than 30 weeks.

Commonplace directions on allocation

CPR r.28.4
CPR r.31.6
CPR r.26.6(5)

Disclosure of documents (standard disclosure or a direction for no disclosure, or a direction specifying documents or classes of documents).

Service of witness statements.

Directions concerning expert evidence limits expert evidence and the length of trial in fast track cases).

Power to direct case management hearing

CPR r.28.5(4)(c)
PD 28 para.2.6
PD 28 para.2.8

If the court considers that a hearing is necessary to enable it to decide what directions to give, it may give such directions as it thinks appropriate.

When the court fixes a hearing to give directions it will give the parties at least three days notice of the hearing.

The court will follow the form in Appendix A to CPR Pt 28 as far as possible when making directions.

Agreed directions

See the guidance at PD 28 paras 3.5–3.8 for guidance as to the content of agreed directions on the fast track if seeking court approval.

Changes in case management after allocation

CPR r.2.11 — Parties may vary dates in the case management timetable by agreement in writing except where the rules or order say otherwise.

CPR r.28.4 — Parties must apply to the court if they wish to vary the date for return of pre-trial checklist, date or period of trial, or any variation which would make it necessary to vary the above.

PD 28 para.4.2(2) — The court will assume that a party who did not appeal or apply to vary within 14 days of service of an order for directions was content that they were correct.

PD 28 para.4.3(1),(2) — Where a party is dissatisfied with a direction or order he may apply for reconsideration by the court but should appeal if the direction was given or the order was made at a hearing at which he was present/represented/had due notice.

Maguire v Molin [2002] EWCA Civ 1083

A judge may allow an amendment which causes the value of the claim to exceed £15,000 without being obliged to re-allocate the case. The extent to which the amended claim exceeds £15,000 is highly relevant.

Failure to follow directions

PD 28 para.5
See also Relief from Sanctions—Guide 5.3

Where a party has failed to comply with a direction any other party may apply for an order and/or for a sanction to be imposed and must do so without delay but should first warn the other party of his intention to do so.

Court will not allow failure to comply with directions to lead to the postponement of the trial save in exceptional circumstances.

Court will exercise its powers in a manner that enables the case to come on for trial on the date or period previously set so far as practicable.

Pre-trial checklist (listing questionnaire)

CPR r.28.5(1), (2)

The court will send the parties a pre-trial checklist (listing questionnaire) for completion and return by the date specified in the notice of allocation (not more than eight weeks before the trial date or the beginning of the trial period).

The court may decide not to send a pre-trial checklist if it considers that the claim can proceed to trial without one.

Mandatory costs estimate when filing pre-trial checklist

Costs PD para.6 requires a costs estimate to be filed and served at the same time as the pre-trial checklist is filed.

Failure to file pre-trial checklist

CPR r.28.5(3)

If all parties fail: court will order that unless a completed pre-trial checklist is filed within seven days from service of that order, the claim, defence and any counterclaim will be struck out without further order.

CPR r.28.5(4)

If one party fails or one party has given incomplete information: the court may give such directions as it thinks appropriate.

Listing for trial

CPR r.28.6(1)

As soon as practicable after the date for filing pre-trial checklists the court will fix or confirm trial date.

The court will also give any further directions for the trial, including a trial timetable.

CPR r.28.6(2)

The court will give the parties at least three weeks' notice of the listed date of the trial unless, except in exceptional circumstances.

Limitations on expert evidence

CPR r.26.6(5)
CPR r.35.4

Oral expert evidence at trial will be limited to one expert per party in relation to any expert field and expert evidence in two expert fields, and use of any expert evidence is under the control of the court and permission is required.

Costs limitations in Fast Track cases

See Pt 46 (Fast Track Trial Costs).

5.6. Case Management (Multi-Track)

D5–006 **Directions on allocation**

CPR r.29.2 On allocation to the multi-track, the court will give case management directions and set a timetable up to trial or will fix a case management conference or a pre-trial review, or both, and give such other directions relating to the management of the case as it sees fit.

Trial date

CPR r.29.2 The court will fix the trial date/period as soon as practicable.

The court will give notice to the parties, and specify the date by which the parties must file a pre-trial checklist.

Case management conference or pre-trial review

CPR r.29.3(2)) If a party has a legal representative, a representative familiar with the case and with sufficient authority to deal with any issues that are likely to arise, must attend any case management conference or pre-trial review.

Form of directions

Form PF52 Form PF52 provides a template for producing draft proposed case management directions. It is important to bear in mind that even if parties agree directions the court manages the case and accordingly a "consent" order does not guarantee an adjournment of a CMC.

Agreed case management proposals

CPR r.29.4 If the parties agree proposals for case management and the court considers that the proposals are suitable it may approve them without a hearing.

Variation of case management timetable

CPR r.29.5
CPR r.2.11 A party must apply if he wishes to vary the date fixed for a case management conference, pre-trial review, return of a pre-trial check list under CPR r.29.6, trial/trial period.

Parties must apply to the court if they wish to agree any variation which would make it necessary to vary the above.

Otherwise, parties may vary dates in the case management timetable by agreement in writing except where the rules or order say otherwise.

Pre-trial checklist (listing questionnaire)

CPR r.29.6(1),(2) The court will send the parties a pre-trial checklist (listing questionnaire) for completion and return by the date specified in the notice of allocation (not more than eight weeks before the trial date or the beginning of the trial period).

The court may decide not to send a pre-trial checklist if it considers

Mandatory costs estimate when filing pre-trial checklist

Costs PD para.6 requires a costs estimate to be filed and served at the same time as the pre-trial checklist is filed.

Failure to file pre-trial checklist

CPR r.29.6(3)	If all parties fail: court will order that unless a completed pre-trial checklist is filed within seven days from service of that order, the claim, defence and any counterclaim will be struck out without further order.
CPR r.29.6(4)	If one party fails or one party has given incomplete information: the court may give such directions as it thinks appropriate.

Listing for trial

CPR , r.29.8	As soon as practicable after each party has filed a completed pre-trial check list, or after a listing hearing or after the court has held a pre-trial review: the court will set a timetable for the trial unless (already done, or the court considers inappropriate to do so) and fix trial date week within which the trial is and notify the parties.

Experts

CPR r.35.4	Use of any expert evidence is under the control of the court and permission is required.

Periodical payments in personal injury cases

PD 29 para.3A *PD 41B*	PD 41B supplementing directs that in a personal injury claim the court should consider as soon as practicable whether periodical payments or a lump sum is likely to be the more appropriate form for all or part of an award of damages for future pecuniary loss.

5.7. Experts

Scope of expert evidence D5–007

CPR r.35.1	Expert evidence is restricted to what is reasonably required to resolve the proceedings.
Rollinson v Kimberly Clark Ltd [2000] C.P. Rep. 85 *Matthews v Tarmac Bricks and Tiles Ltd T.L.R. July 1, 1999*	Late efforts to introduce new expert evidence may prove difficult if they would require a change in trial timetable. It is not acceptable to instruct an expert shortly before trial without checking they are available. The court needs to know whether an expert will be available and if not why not before it will consider rearranging a trial date.

Low velocity road traffic accident claims

Kearsley v Karfield [2005] EWCA Civ 1510 *Casey v Cartwright [2006] EWCA Civ 1280*	Medical expert evidence in low velocity RTA claims relating to causation of injury, adduced on behalf of a defendant, may be allowed by the court only if the defendant is alleging that the claimant is fabricating their injuries, and the defendant has identified that as an issue, before action and after commencement and has filed a statement within 21 days of the defence to that effect.

Permission required

CPR r.35.4(1)	A party may not call an expert or put in evidence an expert's report without the court's permission.

Written report is the norm

CPR r.35.5(1)–(2)	Unless the court orders otherwise, expert evidence is to be given by written report. If a claim is on the fast track, the court will not direct an expert to attend a hearing unless it is necessary to do so in the interests of justice.

Use of joint experts

CPR r.35.7	The court may require expert evidence to be given by a joint expert instructed by two or more parties. This includes power to direct that the expert be selected in such manner as the court may direct.

Instructions to joint experts

CPR r.35.8(1)–(2)	Parties must send to each other copies of CPR r.35.8(1)–(2) any instructions which they send to the expert.

Duties of experts

CPR r.35.3	An expert owes a duty to help the court on matters within his/her expertise and expert's duty overrides any duty he/she owes to instructing parties or those paying expert's fees.

Case law re duties

National Justice Compania Naviera SA v Prudential Assurance Co. Ltd ("The Ikarian Reefer") [1993] 2 Lloyd's Rep. 68	Extensive guidance on the duties of experts and see summary in commentary to CPR, r.35.3.
Anglo Group plc v Winther Brown and Co Ltd [2000] 1 W.L.R. 820	An expert witness must make it clear whether a given question or issue falls outside their expertise and should be willing to reconsider their opinion if new information arises.
Failures of expert duty	See guidance in commentary to CPR, r.35.5.

Expert may seek directions

CPR r.35.14	An expert has the right to seek directions from the court by way of a written request.

Disclosure of report

PD 35 para.2.1	Reports should be addressed to the court and not to the party from whom the expert has received instructions.
PD 35 paras 2.2–2.3	Reports must: • give details of the expert's qualifications; • give details of any literature or other material which the expert has relied on in making the report; • contain a statement setting out the substance of all facts and instructions given to the expert which are material to the opinions expressed in the report or upon which those opinions are based; • make clear which of the facts stated in the report are within the expert's own knowledge; • say who carried out any examination, measurement, test or experiment which the expert has used for the report, give the qualifications of that person, and say whether or not the test or experiment has been carried out under the expert's supervision;

- where there is a range of opinion on the matters dealt with in the report—
  (a) summarise the range of opinion, and
  (b) give reasons for expert's own opinion;
- contain a summary of the conclusions reached;
- if the expert is not able to give his opinion without qualification, state the qualification;
- contain a statement that the expert understands his duty to the court, and has complied and will continue to comply with that duty.
- must be verified by a statement of truth as well as containing the statements required in paragraph 2.2(8) and (9) above.

Questions to experts

CPR r.35.6 A party may ask written questions of an expert if the expert is one instructed by another party or is a joint expert.

Time and other limits on questions

CPR r.35.6(2)(a)–(c) ONE set of questions may be served and the time limit for doings so is within 28 days after service of the expert's report unless agreed by the other party or allowed by the court. Questions must be for purpose of clarification of the report.

PD 35 para.5.2 Questions for the expert must be copied to the other parties in the case.

Experts' fees

Power to cap recoverable fees

CPR r.35.4(4) The court may limit the amount of the expert's fees and expenses that the party who wishes to rely on the expert may recover from any other party

Liability for joint expert fees

CPR r.35.8(5) Unless otherwise directed where a joint expert is directed, the parties are jointly and severally liable for payment of the expert's fees and expenses.

Cost of answering written questions

PD 35 para.5.3 The expert's costs of answering written questions put by another party must be paid by the party instructing the expert (subject to the court's powers to make costs orders generally).

Related Guides

Case Management—Guides 5.4, 5.5 5.6.

5.8. Amendments to Statements of Case

Amendment before service D5–008

CPR r.17.1(2) A party may amend a statement of case at any time before it has been served, without permission.

Amendment after service

CPR r.17.1(2) After a statement of case has been served it may be amended only with the written consent of all parties or the permission of the court.

Principles Cobbold v Greenwich LBC. August 9, 1999, unrep. Sumitomo Corp. v Credit Lyonnais Rouse Ltd [2003] EWHC 833	See commentary following CPR, r.17.3 and see case law listed here.
Oil & Minerals Development Corp. v Sajjad [2002] EWHC 1258	Must show proposed amendments would have real prospect of success, test is the same as that under CPR, Pt 24.

Amendment where the effect would be to add or remove a party

CPR r.17.1(3)	See *Addition or Substitution of parties*—Guide 5.9.

Amendment where effect would be after the end of a relevant limitation period

CPR r.17.3	See CPR r.17.4 and "Limitation issues" below.

Disallowance of amendments made without permission

A party may apply to the court for an order disallowing amendments made without permission (even where the rules do not require permission).

Where permission is obtained

The court may also give directions as to amendments to other statements of case and service thereof.

Form of amendments to statements of case

See introductory note to CPR Pt 17 in Vol.1	Amendments may be carried out in colour and/or with underlining to distinguish successive amendments, or the amended statement of case may simply omit the superseded text (unless the court orders otherwise), or the court may direct that numerical codes are used.

What is the order for coloured amendments?

PD 17 para.2.4	For successive amendments use: (1) red, (2) green, (3) violet, (4) yellow.

Endorsement on amended Statement of Case

Where court's permission was required and was obtained endorse statement of case as follows: "Amended [statement of case] by Order of [judge/master] dated ..." or where amended without requiring court's permission: "Amended [statement of case] under CPR [rule 17.1 or (2)(a)] dated ...".

Limitation issues (I)

CPR r.17.14(1)–(2)	Where a limitation period has expired under the Limitation Act 1980 or the Foreign Limitation Periods Act 1984 or any other enactment which allows such an amendment or under which such an amendment is allowed, the court may allow an amendment whose effect is to add or substitute a new claim only if the new claim arises out of the same facts or substantially the same facts as a claim in respect of which the party applying to amend has already claimed a remedy in the proceedings.

In order to decide whether an amendment of a claim form adds a new cause of action the court should look at the amendment in the context of the pleading as a whole (and not only to look at the claim form)— *Evans v Cig Mon Cymru* [2008] EWCA Civ 390.

Limitation issues (II)

CPR r.17.4(3) — If the amendment is to correct the name of a party it may be allowed only where the mistake was genuine and not one which would cause reasonable doubt as to the identity of the party in question. For amendments which substantively add or substitute parties after expiry of a relevant limitation period see *Addition or Substitution of Parties*—Guide 5.9.

Limitation issues (III)

CPR r.17.4(4) — If the amendment is to alter the capacity in which a party claims, the amendment may be allowed if the new capacity is one which that party had when the proceedings started or which he has since acquired.

5.9. Addition or Substitution of Parties

General D5–009

Adding parties where no limitation period has expired

CPR r.19.2(2) — The court may add a new party if it is desirable so that the court can resolve all the matters in dispute or there is an issue involving the new party and an existing party which is connected to the matters in dispute and it is desirable to add the new party to resolve that issue.

Securum Finance Ltd V Ashton [2001] Ch 291, CA applied in Kent v M&L Management [2005] EWHC 2546 — Court may refuse re-joinder of a party if to do so would allow 'a second bite at the cherry' and defendant would not get a fair trial, even though Limitation Act period had not expired.

Removing parties where no limitation period has expired

CPR r.19.2(3) — The court may order any person to cease to be a party if it is not desirable for that person to be a party.

Substituting parties where no limitation period has expired

CPR r.19.2(4) — The court may substitute a new party for an existing one if the existing party's interest or liability has passed to the new party and it is desirable to substitute the new party so that the matters in issue can be resolved by the court.

Procedure

CPR r.19.4(1) — After service of a claim, the court's permission is required to add, remove or substitute a party.

CPR r.19.4(4) — A person may not be added or substituted as a claimant without his written consent filed at court.

CPR r.19.4(2)–(3) — Permission may be sought by an existing party or a proposed party. Where it is proposed that a party be substituted, the application may be made without notice but with evidence.

CPR r.19.4(5)–(6)	The order granting permission must be served on all parties and any persons affected by the order. The order may make consequential directions.

After expiry of a limitation period

Where a limitation period has expired under the Limitation Act 1980, the Foreign Limitation Periods act 1984 or any other enactment which allows a change of party after expiry of the limitation period

CPR r.19.5(2)	The court may allow the addition or substitution of a party if the limitation period was current when the proceedings were started and the addition or substitution is necessary.

Meaning of "necessary" in the context of limitation periods

CPR r.19.5(3) Addition or substitution is "necessary" only if any of the following applies:

- — the new party is to be substituted for a party who was named in mistake for the new party;
- — the claim cannot properly be carried on by or against the original party unless the new party is added or substituted as claimant or defendant;
- — the original party has died or had a bankruptcy order made against him and his interest or liability has passed to the new party.

Special rules in personal injury cases

CPR r.19.5(4)	The court may also allow the addition or substitution of a new party where it directs that s.11 or s.12 of the Limitation Act 1980 do not apply or where it directs that the issue of whether those sections apply shall be determined at trial.

5.10. The General Applications Procedure

D5–010 **Where to apply**

	The general rule is that an application must be made to the court where the claim was started.
CPR r.23.2(1)(2)	If the claim has been transferred to a different court, apply to that court.
CPR r.23.2(3)	If a date for trial has been fixed, apply to the trial court.
CPR r.23.2(4)	If the application is made before issuing the claim, apply to the court where it is likely that the claim will be issued.
CPR r.23.2(5)	If the application relates to enforcement, apply to the court which is dealing with the enforcement unless a rule or PD requires otherwise.

When to apply

PD 23 para.2.10	Where a date for a hearing has been fixed and a party wishes to make an application but he does not have sufficient time to serve an application notice he should inform the other party and the court as soon as he can. He should then make the application orally at the hearing.
PD 23 para.2.8	Applications should wherever possible be made so that they can be considered at any other hearing for which a date has already been fixed.

PD 23 para.2.7 Every application should be made as soon as it becomes apparent that it is necessary or desirable to make it.

Form of application

CPR r.23.3 Unless the court directs or a rule or PD requires otherwise, apply using an application notice (Form N244 may be used).

CPR r.23.6 The application notice must state the order sought and the grounds for the application. Include a statement of truth if the application is to be relied on as evidence (CPR, r. 22).

PD 23 para.2 The notice must include the title of the claim, the reference number of the claim, the full name of the applicant, where the applicant is not already a party, his address for service, including a postcode, and either a request for a hearing or a request that the application be dealt with without a hearing.

Service of application

CPR r.23.4 Application must be served on all respondents, unless otherwise allowed by a rule, practice direction or court order.

CPR r.23.7(1) Serve as soon as practicable and in any event at least three days before the court is to deal with the application, unless a rule or practice direction or order requires otherwise. The court may abridge time: CPR, r. 23.7(4).

CPR r.23.7(2) If the court serves the application notice then any evidence in support must be filed at court.

CPR r.23.7(3) The application notice must be served with any evidence in support, and a copy of any draft of the order which the applicant has attached to the application. (Evidence which has already been served on the respondent or filed need not be served on the respondent or filed again: CPR, r. 23.7(5)).

Reference to judge

PD 23 para.1 A district judge or master may refer any matter to a judge and the judge may refer it back or dispose of it

Is a hearing needed?

CPR r.23.8 The court may dispense with a hearing of the application if the order is agreed, or if the parties agree to the application being decided without a hearing, or if the court does not consider that a hearing would be appropriate.

When can an application be made without service on the respondent?

PD 23 para.3
PD 23 para.2.10 Where there is exceptional urgency, where the overriding objective is best furthered by doing so, by consent of all parties, with the permission of the court, where a court order, rule or practice direction permits, or where a party wishes to make an application but he does not have sufficient time to serve an application notice.

When an order is made without service of the application on the respondent

CPR r.23.9 If an order is made without service of the application on the evidence and application, and the order, must be served on the person(s) against whom the order was made and on the person(s) against whom the order was sought. The order must contain a statement of the right to vary or set aside the order under CPR, r. 23.10 (see "Setting aside" below).

Setting aside

CPR r.23.10 A person who was not served with the application notice before an order was made may apply to set aside or vary the order within seven days of service of the order.

Proceeding in the absence of a party

CPR r.23.11 If an applicant or any respondent fails to attend the hearing of an application the court mat proceed in their absence. The court may on its own initiative re-list the application where it makes an order at a hearing at which an applicant or any respondent fails to attend.

Application without merit?

CPR r.23.12 If the court dismisses an application which it considers was totally without merit (including applications for permission to appeal) then the court order must record that fact and the court must consider whether to make a civil restraint order.

6. OFFERS TO SETTLE

6.1. Part 36: Form of Offers

D6–001 *Note:* CPR, Pt 36 was extensively amended with effect from April 6, 2007 and the Guide here relates to the new form of rules. For transitional provisions for older cases or cases spanning the coming into effect of the new rules see Editorial introduction and commentary at start of Pt 36.

Form

CPR, r.36.1 A Pt 36 offer may be made in whatever way a party chooses but if not made in accordance with Pt 36 it will not have the consequences set out in CPR, rr.36,10, 36.11 and 36.14.

CPR, r.36.12 Offer must be in writing, state that it is intended to have the consequences of Pt 36, specify a period of not less than 21 days within which the defendant will be liable for claimant's costs if the offer is accepted (CPR, r.36.2(2)(c)), state whether it relates to whole claim or any issue(s) and if so which, and state whether it takes into account any counterclaim.

CPR, r.36.2(2) and (3)(c) The rule that the period stated must be no less than 21 days does not apply where there are fewer than 21 days before the start of trial.

Other information

CPR, rr.36.5, 36.6 and 36.15 In personal injury cases, provisional damages cases and where there is a requirement to deduct benefits, additional information is required to be stated in the offer, see CPR, rr.36.5, 36.6 and 36.15.

Making a costs offer

Mitchell v James [2002] EWCA Civ 997	A Pt 36 offer may not include terms as to costs (but offers to settle generally may do so).

Interest

CPR, r.26.3(3)	A Pt 36 offer to accept a sum of money, or to pay a sum of money, will be treated as inclusive of all interest up to the date on which the period required by CPR, r.36.2(2)(c) expires or a date 21 days after the date of the offer if the offer was made less than 21 days before trial.

Appeals

CPR, r.36.3(4)	A Part 36 offer has effect in relation to the costs of the proceedings to which it relates and not any appeal from those proceedings.
East West Corporation v Dampskibsselskabet AF (No.2) [2003] EWCA 73	separate Part 36 offer may be made in respect of an appeal, and a composite offer covering first instance and appeal proceedings is not permitted.

Withdrawal or amendment

CPR, r.36.3(5), 36.3(6)	A Pt 36 offer may be amended to be less favourable, or withdrawn, before expiry, only with the court's permission. After expiry it may be amended or withdrawn without permission unless notice of acceptance has been given.

Defendants' offers

CPR, r.36.4	An offer by a defendant to pay a sum of money in settlement must be an offer to pay a single sum of money but an offer which includes an offer to pay all or part of the money offered at a date later than 14 days after acceptance will not have the costs consequences of Pt 36 unless the offer is accepted by the offeree.

Clarification of offers

CPR, r.36.8	The offeree may request clarification of a Pt 36 offer within 7 days of it being made. If clarification is not given within 7 days thereafter the offeree may, unless trial has started, apply for an order that clarification be given. If the court makes an order to that effect it must also state the date when the Pt 36 offer is to be treated as having been made.

Restriction on disclosure of offer

CPR, r.36.13	A Pt 36 offer is treated as being "without prejudice except as to costs" and the fact that it has been made must not be disclosed to the judge allocated to conduct the trial until the case has been decided. However the above restrictions do not apply where a defence of tender before claim has been raised, or where the claim has been stayed after acceptance (under CPR, r.36.11) or where the offeror and offeree agree in writing that CPR, r.36.13(2) should not apply.

6.2. Part 36: Personal Injury and Deductible Benefits

D6–002 **Claims for future pecuniary loss**

CPR, r.36.5	Where a claim includes a claim for future pecuniary loss arising from personal injury it must be made under CPR, r.36.5 if it is to have the costs consequences of Pt 36.

Contents of offer

CPR, rr.36.5(3)	The offer may contain an offer to pay or to accept the whole or part of the damages for future pecuniary loss in the form of a lump sum, or periodical payments or both a lump sum and periodical payments, and the whole of any other sum of damages in the form of a lump sum.
CPR, rr.36.5(4)	The offer must state the amount of any lump sum, and may state what part of that lump sum relates to future pecuniary loss or other damages. The offer must state what part of the offer relates to damages for future pecuniary loss in the form of periodical payments and the amount and duration thereof, the amount for any substantial capital purchases and when the purchases are to be made, and state that each amount is to vary by reference to the Retail Prices Index or some other named index, or that it is not to vary by reference to any index. The offer must state that the periodical payments will be funded in a way which ensures reasonably secure continuity under s.2(4) of the Damages Act 1996 or state how such damages are to be paid and how continuity is to be secured.
Apply to court *CPR, rr.36.5(3)*	If the offer is accepted and includes periodical payments then the claimant must apply to the court within 7 days for an order for damages in the form of periodical payments under CPR, r.41.8.

Provisional damages

CPR, r.36.6	An offer in respect of a claim including a claim for provisional damages must specify whether the offeror is proposing that the settlement should include an award of provisional damages and if so must state that the sum offered is in satisfaction of the claim on the basis that the injured person will not develop the disease or deterioration specified in the order and that the offer is subject to condition that the claimant must make any claim for further damages within a specified period (and what period).
Apply to court *CPR, r.36.6(5)*	If the offer is accepted then the claimant must apply to the court within 7 days for an order for an award of provisional damages under CPR, r.41.2.
Deduction of state benefits *CPR, r.36.15*	Where a payment to a claimant following acceptance of a Pt 36 offer would be a compensation payment as defined in s.1 of the Social Security (Recovery of Benefits) Act 1997, see CPR, r.36.15 for further requirements.

6.3. Part 36: Acceptance of Part 36 Offer

How to accept D6–003

CPR, r.36.9 — Pt 36 offers may be accepted by written notice at any time unless notice of withdrawal has been served, save that the court's permission to accept is needed where the offer is made by one but not all defendants (r.36.12(4)) or in certain circumstances where deductible benefits have been paid to the claimant since the date of the offer (r.36.15(3)(b)), or an apportionment is needed under CPR, r.41.3A, or the trial has started.

After end of trial

CPR, rr.36.9(5) — A Pt 36 offer may not be accepted after the end of trial but before judgment has been handed down, unless the parties agree.

Whole of claim

CPR, r.36.11(2) — If the offer related to the whole of the claim then the claim will be stayed on the terms of the offer.

Part of claim

CPR, r.36.11(3) — If the offer related to part of the claim then the claim will be stayed as to the part to which the offer related, on the terms of the offer, and subject to the costs consequences under CPR, r.36.10 the court will decide liability for costs unless the parties agree costs.

Approval required

CPR, r.36.11(4) — If a settlement requires the approval of the court before it can be binding then the stay which would otherwise arise will not take effect until approval has been given.

Effect of stay

CPR, r.36.11(5) — A stay under Pt 36 will not affect the power of the court to enforce the terms of the offer or deal with questions of costs.

Payment and enforcement

CPR, r.36.11(6) — Unless the parties agree otherwise an offer which includes an offer to pay money, if accepted, has the effect that the offeror must pay within 14 days of acceptance or within 14 days of the order of the court for provisional damages or periodical payments under CPR, rr.41.2 and 41.8.

CPR, r.36.11(7) — If the accepted sum is not paid within 14 days or such other period as agreed the offeree may enter judgment for the unpaid sum.

CPR, r.36.11(2)8 — Offers (or parts of offers) not including offers to pay sums of money may be enforced by the court on application without the need for a new claim.

6.4. Part 36: Cost Consequences of Part 36 Offers (Acceptance and Non-acceptance)

D6–004 **Acceptance**

Where a Pt 36 offer is accepted within the relevant period of the offer (usually 21 days—see "relevant period' "in CPR, r.36.3(1)(c)) then the claimant will be entitled to his costs up to the date of service of notice of acceptance. If the offer related to part of the proceedings and the claimant abandons the remainder of his claim when he serves notice of acceptance then he will be entitled to his costs of the proceedings up to date of service of notice of acceptance unless the court orders otherwise. Costs are on the standard basis to be assessed if not agreed.

Late offer or acceptance

CPR, rr.36.10(4)

Where an offer is accepted after expiry of the relevant period (r.36.3(1)(c)) or the offer was made less than 21 days before trial the court will make a costs order unless the parties agree liability for costs.
Where the offer was accepted after the end of the relevant period, the usual order will be that the claimant is entitled to his costs up to the date on which the relevant period expired and the offeree will be liable for the offeror's costs from date of expiry of the relevant period up to date of acceptance.

Cost of counterclaim

CPR, r.36.10(6)

The claimant's costs include costs of dealing with the defendant's counterclaim if the offer states that it takes into account the defendant's counterclaim.

Non-acceptance

CPR, r.36.14(2)

If a claimant fails to obtain a judgment more advantageous than a defendant's Pt 36 offer then the court will (unless it considers it unjust to do so) order that the defendant is entitled to his costs from expiry of the relevant period of the offer together with interest on those costs.

CPR, r.36.14(3)

If judgment against the defendant is at least as advantageous to the claimant as proposals contained in a claimant's Pt 36 offer then the court will (unless it considers it unjust to do so) order that the claimant is entitled to interest on the whole or part of any sum of money (excluding interest) awarded, at a rate not exceeding 10% above base rate, for some or all of the period starting with the date on which the relevant period (r.36.3(1)(c)) expired, together with his costs on the indemnity basis from the date when the relevant period expired and interest on those costs not exceeding 10% above base rate. For guidance as to the correct approach to whether a judgment is "more advantageous" than an offer under the form of Pt 36 rules in force since April 6, 2007 see *Carver v BAA* [2008] EWCA Civ 412 .

Unjust to order?

CPR, r.36.14(4)

For criteria to be considered as to whether it would be unjust to award the enhanced interest and indemnity costs under the above rules see r.36.14(4).

7. SEARCH, DISCLOSURE AND INSPECTION

7.1. Disclosure: Duties of Disclosure and Search

Definition of "disclosure" and "document" D7–001

CPR, r. 31.2	"disclosure" means stating that a document exists or has existed.
CPR, r. 31.4	"document" means anything in which information of any description is recorded.

The duty of disclosure

CPR, r. 31.6	Where it is ordered that disclosure of documents be given, it is deemed to be an order for "standard disclosure" unless specified otherwise.

"Standard disclosure"

Disclosure is given on Form N265	The scope of "standard disclosure" requires a party to disclose only:
CPR r.31.6(a)	— documents on which he or she relies;
CPR r.31.6(b)(i), (ii)	— documents which adversely affect his or her own case or another party's case; — documents which support another party's case;
CPR r.31.6(c)	— documents which he or she is required to disclose by a relevant practice direction.
CPR r.31.8	The duty extends only to documents which are or have been within a party's control, meaning documents which: — which are or were in the party's physical possession; — of which he/she has or has had the right to possession; — of which he/she has or has had a right to take copies or to inspect.

The duty of search

CPR r.31.7(1)	A party must make a reasonable search for documents which fall within the class of documents to be disclosed on standard disclosure.
CPR r.31.7(2)(a)–(d)	"Reasonable" is determined taking into account the following factors (r.31.7(2)): — the number of documents involved; — the nature and complexity of the proceedings; — the ease and expense of retrieval of any particular document; — the significance of any document likely to be located during the search.
Grant v Southwestern and County Properties Ltd [1975] Ch. 185	Tape recordings of information amount to 'documents'
Derby & Co v Weldon (No.9) [1991] 1 W.L.R.. 652	Computer database which is part of a company's records and is capable of reduction to printed form is a "document" for purposes of disclosure.
Duty to preserve documents *Rockwell Machine Tool Co v EP Barrus (Concessionaires) Ltd [1968] 2 All E.R.. 98, Infabrics Ltd v Jaytex Ltd [1985] F.S.R.. 75*	Solicitors should take steps to ensure that disclosable documents are preserved and not destroyed and should ensure clients are made aware of their duties.

Lawyer may have to withdraw
Myers v Elman [1940] A.C. 282 at 293–4, 300–301, 322–323
A representative may be obliged to notify the court and/or withdraw if a client does not comply with appropriate advice as to disclosure.

Late disclosure—re-opening case
Vernon v Bosley (No. 2) [1999] Q.B. 18
It may be appropriate for a party to whom a document has been disclosed by an opponent after he has closed his case to apply to re-open the case if the document is of real significance and there is otherwise a risk of injustice.

7.2. Disclosure: Inspection and Applications relating to Disclosure or Inspection

D7–002 **The right to inspect documents**

CPR r.31.14(a)–(d)
A party has the right to inspect documents which are referred to in:
- a statement of case;
- a witness statement;
- a witness summary;
- an affidavit; or
- (subject to restrictions on inspection of documents referred to in an expert's instructions), an expert's report.

Documents disclosed in the disclosure statement

A party has the right to inspect a document which has been disclosed **except where**:

CPR r.31.3(1)(a)
— it is no longer in the control of the disclosing party; or

CPR r.31.3(1)(b)
— party disclosing it has a right or duty to withhold inspection; or

CPR rr.31.3(1)(c), 31.3(2)
"disclosure statement": see CPR r.35.10 and see Guide 7.3.
See CPR r.35.10(4) re expert's instructions.
— (*in the case of documents adversely affecting his or another party's case, or supporting another party's case*) it would be disproportionate to the issues in the case. If a party wishes to rely on this exception he/she must state in his disclosure statement that inspection will not be permitted on the grounds that to do so would be disproportionate).

Applications for disclosure/inspection of specific documents

Power of court to order specific disclosure, search and inspection

CPR r.31.12
The court may order that a party must:
- disclose and/or permit inspection of specific documents or classes of documents;
- carry out a search to the extent specified in the order;
- disclose any documents located as a result of the search (CPR, r. 31.12(2), (3)).

Applications to withhold disclosure or inspection

Power of court to order that a party may withhold disclosure or inspection

CPR r.31.19(1)
See Guide 7.3
The court may (on application supported by evidence by any person without notice) order permitting him/her to withhold **disclosure** of a document on the ground that disclosure would damage the public interest.

CPR r.31.19(3), (4)	A person wishing to claim he has a right or duty to withhold **inspection** of a document must state in writing, in the disclosure list, that he has such a right or duty, and give grounds. If here is no list of documents, the statement should be given to person wishing to inspect the document
CPR r.31.19(5)	A party may apply to the court, supported by evidence) to determine the validity of the claim to withhold inspection.

Inherent jurisdiction to limit disclosure and inspection

Church of Scientology v DHSS [1979] 1 W.L.R. 723; *Halcon International v Shell Transport and Trading Co* [1979] R.P.C. 97, CA	The court has an inherent power to impose restrictions on disclosure or to allow it subject to undertakings, in order to prevent abuse of the process of disclosure and inspection or to prevent unjustifiable hardship being caused by disclosure or inspection.

7.3. Disclosure: Procedure

Procedure for standard disclosure & inspection D7–003

Prepare and serve list of documents

CPR r.31.10(2)	Make and serve on every other party a list of documents on Form N265.

Contents of list of disclosed documents

CPR r.31.10(3)	Identify the documents in a convenient order and manner and as concisely as possible;
PD 31 para.3.2	— normally, list in date order, numbered consecutively with a concise description. Where a large number of documents falls within a class, the class may be identified rather than describing each document individually.
CPR rr.31.10(4)(a), 31.19(3),(4)	Indicate those documents in respect of which the party claims a right or duty to withhold inspection, and include a statement that the right is relied upon, with grounds;
CPR r.31.10(4)(b)	Indicate those documents which are no longer in the party's control and what has happened to those documents. See generally PD 31 for guidance as to the form of the list of documents.
CPR r.31.10(5), (6)	Include a "disclosure statement" setting out the extent of the search made, certifying that the party understands the duty to disclose documents, and certifying that to the best of that party's knowledge he/she has carried out that duty.
CPR r.31.10(7)	If the party making disclosure is a company, firm or other organisation, identify the person making the statement and explain why he/she is considered an appropriate person to make it.

Procedure for inspection

CPR r.31.15(a)	The party wishing to inspect a document must give written notice of his/her wish to inspect.
CPR r.31.15(b)	The party who disclosed the document must permit inspection not more than seven days after receipt of the notice.

CPR r.31.15(c)	The inspecting party may request a copy of the document, and if he/she undertakes to pay reasonable copying costs, the party who disclosed it must supply a copy not more than seven days after the request.

Redacted documents

See *Atos Consulting Ltd v Avis Plc* [2007] EWHC 323 (TCC)	Where privileged or irrelevant matters are redacted in a document disclosed pursuant to an order for specific disclosure and a challenge is made to the right to redact or the scope thereof

Documents in foreign languages

Bayer AG v Harris Pharmaceuticals Ltd [1991] F.S.R. 170	No obligation to translate disclosed documents.

8. MISCELLANEOUS PRE-TRIAL MATTERS

8.1. Interim Payments

D8–001 **What is an interim payment?**

Supreme Court Act 1981, s.32 *County Courts Act 1984, s.50* *CPR r.25.1(k)*	It is a payment 'on account of any damages, debt or other sum (excluding any costs which the court may hold the defendant liable to pay'.

Non-disclosure of interim payment

CPR r.25.9	The fact that a defendant has made an interim payment should not be disclosed to the trial judge until all questions of liability and quantum have been decided unless the defendant agrees. This applies to ordered interim payments as well as voluntary ones.

When may claimant apply?

CPR r.25.6(1). *CPR r.10.3.* *N.b. court has no inherent power to order interim payment outside the rules: Moore v Assignment Courier Ltd [1977] 1 W.L.R. 638(CA).*	May not apply before the end of the period for filing an acknowledgment of service applicable to the defendant against whom the application is made.

When is an interim payment appropriate?

Schott Kem Ltd v Bentley [1991] Q.B. 61; Chiron Corp v Murex Diagnostics Ltd (No.13) [1996] F.S.R. 578	Not suitable where the factual issues are complicated or where difficult points of law arise.

Procedure for applying for interim payment

CPR r.25.6(3) *CPR Pt 23 generally*	Part 23 application notice and evidence in support must be served at least 14 days before the hearing of the application.

Procedure for responding to application for interim payment

CPR r.25.6(4) If the defendant wishes to rely on written evidence in reply he/she must file and serve copies that written evidence at least seven days before the hearing of the application.

Procedure for claimant to reply to respondent's evidence

CPR r.25.6(5) If the claimant wishes to rely on written evidence in reply to the defendant's response, the applicant must file and serve his/her written evidence at least three days before the hearing of the application.

Criteria for making interim payment order

CPR r.25.7(1) Court may only make an interim payment order if **any** of the following are satisfied:

(a) the defendant against whom the order is sought has admitted liability to pay damages or some other sum of money to the claimant;

(b) the claimant has obtained judgment against that defendant for damages to be assessed or for a sum of money (other than costs) to be assessed;

(c) it is satisfied that, if the claim went to trial, the claimant would obtain judgment for a substantial amount of money (other than costs) against the defendant from whom he is seeking an order for an interim payment whether or not that defendant is the only defendant or one of a number of defendants to the claim;

(d) the following conditions are satisfied—

(i) the claimant is seeking an order for possession of land (whether or not any other order is also sought); and

(ii) the court is satisfied that, if the case went to trial, the defendant would be held liable (even if the claim for possession fails) to pay the claimant a sum of money for the defendant's occupation and use of the land while the claim for possession was pending; or

(e) in a claim in which there are two or more defendants and the order is sought against any one or more of those defendants, the following conditions are satisfied—

(i) the court is satisfied that, if the claim went to trial, the claimant would obtain judgment for a substantial amount of money (other than costs) against at least one of the defendants (but the court cannot determine which); and

(ii) all the defendants are either—

(a) a defendant that is insured in respect of the claim;

(b) a defendant whose liability will be met by an insurer under s.151 of the Road Traffic Act 1988 or an insurer acting under the Motor Insurers Bureau Agreement, or the Motor Insurers Bureau where it is acting itself; or

(c) a defendant that is a public body.

Amount of interim payment

CPR r.25.7(4) The court must **not** order an interim payment of more than a reasonable proportion of the likely amount of the final judgment.

Set-off, counterclaim and contributory negligence

CPR r.25.7(5) The court must take into account
(a) contributory negligence; and
(b) relevant set-off or counterclaim.

Nature of interim payment order

CPR r.25.6(7)
CPR r.25.6(2) The court may order an interim payment to be made either in one sum or in instalments, and the claimant may make more than one application for an interim payment.

Powers of the court after making an interim payment order, or where a voluntary payment has been made

CPR r.25.8(1) The court may order repayment of some or all or may vary or discharge an order for payment or *(subject to conditions in CPR r.25.8(3))* may order one defendant to reimburse another defendant who has made an interim payment.

When interim payment exceeds eventual judgment

CPR r.25.8(5) The court may award the defendant interest on the overpaid amount from the date when he/she made the interim payment.

8.2. Witness Summonses

D8–002 **What is a witness summons?**

CPR r.34.2(1) It is a document issued by the court requiring a witness to attend court to give evidence or to produce documents to the court.

CPR r.34.2(3) There must be one summons for each witness to be compelled.

Which form?

Form N20 Form N20.

Content of summons

Tajik Aluminium Plant v Hydo Aluminium AS [2005] EWCA Civ 1218 A witness summons to produce documents is coercive and therefore the summons must either identify the documents required or identify a class of documents so that the witness can identify the documents to be produced with sufficient certainty.

CPR r.34.2(4) The summons may require the witness to produce documents to the court either on the date fixed for trial or on such date as the court may direct.

Issue and permission

CPR r.34.3(1)
CPR r.34.3(3) A party must issue a summons at court. It is issued on the date entered by the court on the summons. The issuing court must be the court where the case is proceeding or the court where the hearing in question will be held.

CPR r.34.3(2) — Permission to issue is required where the party wishes to have a summons issued less than seven days before the date of the trial, or to have a summons issued for a witness to attend court or produce documents on a date other than the date fixed for trial, or to have a summons issued for a witness to attend court to give evidence or produce documents at any hearing except the trial.

Service of witness summons

CPR r.34.6(1) — The court will serve the summons unless the party on whose behalf it is issued indicates in writing when he/she issues the summons that he/she wishes to serve it.

CPR r.34.6(2) — Where the court is to serve, the party on whose behalf it is to be issued must deposit the required travelling expenses and compensation in the court office.

Time for service of summons

CPR r.34.5(1) — Generally a witness summons is binding on the witness if it is served at lease seven days before the date on which the witness is required to attend.

CPR r.34.5(3) — A summons requiring court attendance is binding until the end of the hearing at which the attendance of the witness is required.

Power of court to vary time

The court may direct that a summons shall be binding despite being served less than seven days before the hearing.

Travelling expenses and compensation

CPR r.34.7
PD 34 para.3.3 — At the time of service the witness must be paid a sum reasonably sufficient to cover his expenses in travelling to and from the court and such sum by way of compensation for loss of time, in accordance with PD 34 para.3.3.

Where is the current sum specified?

The sum is fixed in accordance with Crown Court figures, current rates appear at note 34.7.1 in Vol.1.

8.3. Change of Solicitor

When is a solicitor "on the record"? D8–003

CPR r.42.1
Address for service: see CPR r.6.5 — Where the address for service of a party gives the business address of a solicitor, the solicitor will be treated as acting for that party until the provisions of CPR Pt 42 for change of solicitor are complied with.

When to serve/file notice of change of solicitor?

CPR r.42.2(1) — Notice of change of solicitor must be served and filed where a party wishes to change solicitors, or wishes to act in person having previously had a solicitor on the record, or appoints a solicitor to act for him having previously acted in person.

Need to serve former solicitor

CPR r.42.2(2) — The notice of change must also be served on the party's former solicitor (when one was acting until the change).

Contents of Notice of Change

CPR r.42.2(3)–(4)	The Notice of Change must: — state an address for service for the party serving it. — state that it has been served as required on the former solicitor.

When Notice takes effect

CPR r.42.2(5) *CPR r.42.3*	The solicitor on the record will be treated as continuing to act for the party until the Notice of Change has been served and filed OR until the court orders that a solicitor has ceased to act (CPR r.42.3) and that order has been served.

CLS/LSC publicly funded cases

CPR r.42.2(6)(a)	When the funding certificate is revoked or discharged, the solicitor acting is treated as ceasing to be the solicitor for that party as soon as the retainer is determined under CLS (Costs) Regs. 2000, r.4 or Civil Legal Aid (General) Regs 1989, r.83.
CPR r.42.2(6)(b)	The party must then serve Notice of Change of Solicitor as if he had been acting in person previously, if he wishes to appoint a solicitor to act on his behalf, or must give an address for service if he intends to act in person.
Effect of discharge of certificate on solicitor's lien	See notes to CPR r.42.2(6) in Vol.1.

Order that solicitor has ceased to act

CPR r.42.3	A solicitor who is acting for a party may apply for an order that he has ceased to act.
Procedure *CPR r.42.3(2)*	The solicitor must apply to the court and must serve notice of the application on the party for whom he is acting unless the court orders otherwise. The application must be supported by evidence.
Proof of service	Proof of service of the application on the client by certificate of service in Form N215 is prudent.
Service of order *CPR r.42.3(3)*	If the court makes the order, it must be served on every party to the proceedings, and if not served by the court a certificate of service must be filed.

Applications by other parties to remove solicitors

CPR r.42.4(1)	A party may apply for an order that another party's solicitor has ceased to act, if the solicitor in question has died, become bankrupt, ceased to practice or cannot be found, provided that the relevant party has not themselves given notice of change of solicitor.
Service of order	If the court makes the order, it must be served CPR r.42.4(3) on every party to the proceedings, and if served by a party then a certificate of service must be filed.

Other situations

Inappropriate for judge to order appointment of new solicitor for a company	See *SMC Engineering (Bristol) Ltd v Fraser, The Times*, January 26, 2001, CA.

Order restraining a solicitor or advocate from acting?	See *Skjevesland v Geveran Trading Co Ltd* [2002] EWCA Civ. 1567 and *Bolkiah v KPMG* [1999] 2 A.C. 222, HL.

9. EXECUTION

9.1. Execution: Application to Obtain Information from Judgment Debtors

CPR r.71.2(1) — The judgment creditor may apply for an order against an individual judgment debtor or an officer of a company or corporation requiring him to attend court to provide information about his (or the corporation's etc.) means or any other information needed to enforce judgment. **D9–001**

Making the application

Form N316
Form N316A — The application may be made without notice to the debtor but must be issued in the court which made the judgment or order being enforced (unless the case has been transferred to another court).

PD 71 para.1.2 — The application must be in Form N316 or N316A and must set out the items of information listed at PD 71 para.1.2. A court officer may deal with the application on paper but may refer the matter to a judge and must do so if the creditor has applied for an order that the debtor be questioned before a judge.

CPR r.71.2 — An order containing a penal notice will be made requiring the debtor to attend his local county court and to produce any documents stated in the order and answer on oath any questions the court may require.

PD 71 para.2.2 — Questioning will be directed to take place before a judge only if there are compelling reasons to make such an order.

Service of order

CPR r.71.4– 71.5 — The order to attend court must be served personally, not less than 14 days before the hearing and the rules set out at CPR, r. 71.4 and 5 concerning payment of travel expenses, and the filing of an affidavit setting out facts in relation to the payment of those expenses must be complied with by the creditor.

Debtor's failure to comply

CPR r.71.4– r.71.5 — If the judgment debtor fails to attend court or refuses to take the oath or answer any question, or otherwise fails to comply the court will refer the matter to a High Court judge or a circuit judge who may make a committal order provided the rules at CPR r.71.4 and CPR r.71.5 concerning expenses and evidence have been complied with by the creditor.

The committal order

CPR Pt 71
PD 71 para 8

In the event that a committal order is made it will be a suspended order, suspended on terms that the debtor shall attend court at a time and place specified in the order; and shall comply with all the terms of that order and the original order; and that if the debtor fails to comply with any terms he shall be brought before a judge to consider whether the committal order should be discharged.

If the judge decides that the committal order should not be discharged, a warrant of committal will be issued immediately.

9.2. Execution: Applications for Attachment of Earnings Orders

D9–002 *CCR O.27, r.7(9)*

N.b. an attachment of earnings order may not be made in respect of a debt of £50 or less, or a sum of £50 or less outstanding under a judgment.

Application for attachment of earnings order

CCR O.27, r.4(1)
Form N55
Additional requirements as to filing of documents apply where the order to be enforced is a magistrates' court order—CCR O.27, r.4(1)

File an application (Form N55), certifying the amount of money remaining due under the judgment or order and that the whole or part of any instalment remains unpaid.

CCR O.27, r.3(1)

The appropriate court for the application is the court for the district in which the debtor resides, usually a county court. The county courts have jurisdiction to make attachment of earnings orders in respect of both High Court and county court judgments, maintenance orders and administration orders, and magistrates' courts orders whereas the High Court has jurisdiction only in respect of High Court maintenance orders.

CCR O.27, r.3(2)

If the debtor does not reside within England or Wales, the application may be made to the court for the district in which the judgment or order sought to be enforced was made.

CCR O.27, r.3(3)

Where there are two or more debtors jointly liable the application may be made to the court for the district in which any of them resides, but if any debtor resides in the district where the order to be enforced was made, the application should be made to the court for that district.

CCR O.27, r.4(2)

In the case of a maintenance order the court will fix a date for a hearing of the application upon the filing of the application etc..

Service of application

Form N56
CCR O.27, r.5(1)
CPR r.6.2

Serve the Notice of Application and a Reply form (N56) on the debtor in accordance with CPR, r. 6.2.

Reply by debtor

CCR O.27, r.5(2)
Attachment of Earnings Act 1971, ss.23(2)(c), (f)

The debtor must file a reply in Form N56 within **8** days after service of the application and reply form.

No proceedings to commit the debtor for failure to reply may be commenced unless the debtor has been personally served with the application and reply forms.

Failure to respond/attend or pay

Debtor's failure to respond

Attachment of Earnings Act 1971, s.14(1)
CCR O.27, r.7A(1)

If the debtor fails to file a reply, or to pay the sum due, a court officer may issue an order under s.14(1) of the Attachment of Earnings Act 1971, indorsed with a penal notice, served personally, and directing that payments made thereafter be made into court and not to the creditor (CCR O.27, r.7A(1)).

Committal for failure to reply

CCR O.27, r.7A(2)

If the debtor fails to obey the above order or to file a statement of means, the court officer will issue a notice to show cause why the debtor should not be imprisoned, to be served personally not less than **5** days before the hearing.

Committal for failure to attend

CCR O.27, r.7B(1)

If the debtor fails to attend an adjourned hearing, and a committal order is made, the judge or district judge may suspend the order so long as the debtor attends on the adjourned date.

CCR O.27, r.7B(2)+

If such a suspended order is made and the debtor fails to attend, a certificate by a court officer to the effect that the debtor did not attend will suffice as authority for the issue of a warrant of committal.

Failures by debtors under maintenance orders

CCR O.27, r.8(1)
Attachment of Earnings Act 1971, s.23(1)

An order for the attendance of a maintenance debtor at an adjourned hearing of an application for an attachment of earnings order must be served personally not less than **5** days before the hearing and direct that any further payments be made into court and not to the creditor (CCR O.27, r.8(1), Attachment of Earnings Act 1971 s.23(1)).

If the debtor responds

Decision without a hearing

CCR O.27, r.7(1)

On receipt of the debtors reply the court officer may, if he/she has sufficient information, make an attachment of earnings order without the attendance of the parties, and a copy shall be sent to the parties and the debtor's employer.

CCR O.27, r.7(4)

Alternatively, the court officer will refer the application to the district judge, who may, if he/she has sufficient information, make an attachment of earnings order without the attendance of the parties.

Direction for a hearing, and application for re-consideration

CCR O.27 r.7(5)
For provisions as to consolidation of multiple attachment of earnings orders see CCR O.27, Pt II

If the district judge does not make an attachment of earnings order he/she will direct that a day be fixed for a hearing, and the court officer will give the parties not less than **8** days' notice of the hearing.

CCR O.27, r.7(2), 7(6)

Where an order is made (either by a court officer or district judge) either party may within **14** days of service of the order apply on notice for the order to be re-considered, giving reasons. The court officer shall fix a date for the hearing of that application and give the parties not less than **2** days' notice of the hearing.

9.3. Execution: Third Party Debt Orders

D9–003 *CPR r.72.2– 72.3*
Form N349

A judgment creditor may use Form N349, to apply for an order (a "final third party debt order") requiring a third party to pay to the judgment creditor the amount of any debt due or accruing due to the judgment debtor from the third party; or so much of that debt as is sufficient to satisfy the judgment debt and the judgment creditor's costs of the application. A final order will not be made without an interim third party debt order having first been granted.

The Application

CPR r.72.4

The application for an interim order may be made without notice and it must be issued must be issued in the court which made the judgment or order which it is sought to enforce; except that if the proceedings have since been transferred to a different court, it must be issued in that court.

Form N349
PD 72 paras 1.1–1.3

The application must be in Form N349 and set out the information required by PD 72 (paras 1.1–1.3). A judge will deal with the application initially without a hearing and may make an interim third party debt order fixing a hearing date for consideration of the making of a final order.

The interim order may also direct that until that hearing the third party must not make any payment which reduces the amount he owes the judgment debtor to less than the amount specified in the order.

Service of interim third party debt order

CPR r.72.4(5)

The hearing after the making of an interim order must be fixed for a date at least 28 days after the date of making of the interim order.

CPR r.72.5(1)(a)

But copies of the interim order, application and documents in support must be served on the **third party** at least 21 days before the date fixed for hearing.

CPR r.72.5(1)(b)

Copies of the documents referred to above must also be served on the **debtor**, not less than seven days after they were served on the third party and not less than seven days before the date fixed for the hearing.

Banks and building societies, and cases where no bank, etc. is involved

CPR r.72.6(3) If:

- the judgment debtor does not hold an account with the bank or building society;
- or the bank or building society is unable to comply with the order for any other reason,

then the bank or building society must inform the court and the judgment creditor within seven days of being served with the order.

Third parties other than banks and building societies

CPR r.72.6(3)–(4) Any third party other than a bank or building society served with an interim third party debt order *must* notify the court and the judgment creditor in writing within seven days of being served with the order if:

- he claims not to owe any money to the judgment debtor;
- or to owe less than the amount specified in the order. (CPR, r. 72.6(4)).

Hardship payments orders during interim period

CPR r.72.7 A judgment debtor who is an individual may seek discretionary relief from the effects of an interim third party debtor order, in the form of an order (a "hardship payments order") allowing payments to him out of a bank or building society account, if he is prevented by the interim order from withdrawing money from his account, provided the court is satisfied that the debtor or his family is suffering hardship in meeting ordinary living expenses.

Application is made to the Royal Courts of Justice or any District Registry (in the case of High Court claims) and to any county court (in the case of county court claims).

The application must:

- be made to only one court; and
- be supported by evidence and a statement of truth; and
- be served on the creditor no later than two days before the date fixed for hearing; and
- need *not* be served on the third party.

Before the hearing for further consideration

CPR r.72.8 The party concerned must file and serve evidence in support as soon as possible, and in any event not less than three days before the hearing if any of the following applies:

- if the judgment debtor or the third party objects to the court making a final third party debt order;
- if the judgment debtor or the third party knows or believes that a person other than the judgment debtor has any claim to the money specified in the interim order, he must file and serve written evidence stating his knowledge of that matter;
- the third party has given notice that he does not owe any money to the judgment debtor, or that the amount which he owes is less than the amount specified in the interim order; and the judgment creditor wishes to dispute this.

The final order

If the court is notified that some person other than the judgment debtor may have a claim to the money specified in the interim order, it will serve that person with notice of the application and the hearing date.

The court's powers are set out in CPR r.72.8(6). The court may under that rule make:

- a final third party debt order;
- discharge the interim third party debt order and dismiss the application;
- decide any issues in dispute between the parties, or between any of the parties and any other person who has a claim to the money specified in the interim order; or
- direct a trial of any such issues, and if necessary give directions.

9.4. Execution: Charging Orders

D9–004 **Jurisdiction Notes**

High Court

See The Charging Orders Act 1979, s.1(2)

Note that the High Court has jurisdiction only in respect of funds lodged in the High Court, or High Court maintenance orders, or where the judgment to be enforced is a High Court (or transferred) order exceeding £5,000.

County Court

See the Charging Orders Act 1979, s.1(2)

The county court has no jurisdiction to make a charging order over funds lodged in the High Court.

Procedure

CPR r.73.3(1)

The application may be made without notice, and the creditor may apply for a single charging order in respect of more than one judgment or order against the same debtor (subject to what follows).

It should be made to the court which made the judgment or order which it is sought to enforce *unless*:

- the proceedings have since been transferred to a different court, in which case the application must be issued in that court; or
- the application is made under the Council Tax (Administration & Enforcement) Regulations 1992, in which case it must be issued in the county court for the district in which the relevant dwelling (as defined in reg.50(3)(b)of those Regulations) is situated; or
- the application is for a charging order over an interest in a fund in court, in which case it must be issued in the court in which the claim relating to that fund is or was proceeding; or

Charging Orders Act 1979 s.1(2)

the application is to enforce a judgment or order of the High Court and it is required by s.1(2) of the 1979 Act to be made to a county court.

Form of application

Form N379
Form N380
CPR r.73.3(4)
PD 73 paras 1.1–1.3

The application notice must be in the form and contain the information required by PD 73, paras 1.1–1.3 and be verified by a statement of truth (CPR, r. 73.3(4)). The documents listed at CPR use Form N379 for a charge upon land and Form N380 in relation to securities to be charged.

The interim order and service thereof

CPR r.73.4.1 The application for a charging order will initially be dealt with by a judge without a hearing, who may make an interim order:

- imposing a charge over the judgment debtor's interest in the asset to which the application relates; and
- *CPR r.73.8(2)* fixing a hearing to consider whether to make a final charging order.

CPR r.73.5(1)–(2) The interim order, application notice and the documents supporting the application must be served not less than 21 days before the date fixed for hearing (CPR, r. 73.5(1)). Serve the debtor and any of the relevant persons specified in CPR, r. 73.5(1).

Procedure upon further consideration of the charging order

CPR r.73.8(1) If any person objects to the court making a final charging order, he must file and serve written evidence stating the grounds of his objections, not less than seven days before the hearing.

At the hearing the court may take one or more of the following steps:

- *CPR r.73.8(2)* make a final charging order confirming that the charge imposed by the interim charging order shall continue, with or without modification;
- discharge the interim charging order and dismiss the application;
- decide any issues in dispute between the parties, or between any of the parties and any other person who objects to the court making a final charging order; or
- direct a trial of any such issues, and if necessary give directions.

Final charging order

CPR r.73.8(1)–(4) If the court makes a final charging order which charges securities other than securities held in court, the order will include a stop notice unless the court otherwise orders.

Whether or not the above applies, any order made at the hearing must be served on all the persons on whom the interim charging order was required to be served.

Enforcement by sale

For the jurisdiction of the County Court see s.23(c) of the County Courts Act 1984
CPR r.73.10
CPR Pt 8
PD 73

The court may order the sale of the charged property if a claim is brought by the party interested under the charging order.

The procedure to be followed is by way of the issue of a fresh claim form under the Pt 8 procedure seeking an order for sale, issued at the court which made the charging order. A copy of the charging order must be filed with the claim form, and the claim form must contain the information required by PD 73 paras 4.1-4.5.

For a form of order for sale (which may be adapted to the facts of each case) see Appendix A to PD 73.

(Note also that any person who is a trustee of land or has an interest in property subject to a trust of land may make an application under s.14 of the Trusts of Land and Appointment of Trustees Act 1996, including for an order for sale. If the beneficial interest of the judgment debtor has been charged by the Charging order, (which will be true where the judgment debtor is a joint owner with another person who is not a judgment debtor) then the judgment creditor will have sufficient legal standing to make an application under the 1996 Act— Midland Bank plc v Pike [1988] 2 All ER 434 by analogy under previous legislation. However if the land, as opposed to a beneficial interest in the land, has been charged, then s.14 of the 1996 Act has been treated as irrelevant— Pickering v Wells [2002] EWHC 273)

9.5. Execution: Seizure of goods (warrants of execution, writs of fi. fa.)

D9–005 **Jurisdiction**

See the High Court and County Courts Jurisdiction Order 1991 (SI 1991/724) as amended

The High Court has **exclusive** jurisdiction to enforce money judgments by means of the seizure and sale of goods provided that the judgment debt exceeds **£5,000**.

The High Court **or** a county court may enforce by seizure of goods where the judgment is for between **£600** and **£5,000** (but see for some exceptions The High Court and County Courts Jurisdiction Order 1991 (SI 1991/724)). Otherwise, below £600, the County Court has exclusive jurisdiction.

CCR O.25, r.13

To enforce in the High Court, a county court judgment, see CCR O.25, r.13 governing transfer for enforcement.

CCR O.26, r.2(1)

To enforce in the county court, a judgment or order of the High Court, or a judgment, etc. which is enforceable as if it were a judgment of the High Court, the request for issue may be filed in any court in the district of which execution is to be levied.

CCR O.26, r.2(2)

In those circumstances any restriction imposed on the issue of execution applies as if the order to be enforced were a judgment or order of the county court, save that permission to issue execution is not required if permission was given by the High Court.

County Court procedure

Form N323

File a request for the issue of a warrant of execution, certifying:

— the amount remaining due under the judgment or order,

(N.b. for enforcement against ***firms*** *see (for county court orders) CCR O.25, r.9, and see (for High Court orders, even if being enforced in a county court) RSC O.81, r.5).*

— where the order is for payment in instalments, that the whole or any part of any instalment due remains unpaid and the amount for which the warrant is to be issued.

A court officer will issue a warrant (Form N42) and record the time when the application was made, and if appropriate send the warrant to a different county court.

Where the order was for **payment in instalments**, no warrant will be issued unless:

— the sum outstanding is at least one month's instalment or four weekly instalments, totalling at least £50; and

CCR O.26, r.1(2)(3)

— *the whole or* part of an instalment which has become due is unpaid, and any warrant issued previously has expired or been satisfied/abandoned.

CCR O.26, r.1(4)	The court officer will send a warning to the debtor (unless the district judge directs otherwise), and execution shall not be levied until **7** days thereafter.

Execution by Bailiff

CCR O.26, r.12(1)	Goods seized by the Bailiff are listed in an inventory to be supplied to the debtor. At least four days' notice must be given of the time and place fixed for sale of the foods.
CCR O.26, r.7	A notice of the warrant must be delivered to the debtor by the bailiff upon levying execution.

High Court procedure

RSC O.46, r.6(2) *Forms PF86, N293A*	Enforcing High Court Judgments: file a praecipe for issue of writ (for Form PF86). Enforcing County Court judgments in the High Court: use Form N293A.
RSC O.46, r.6(6)	Issue writ of execution at the appropriate office: — a District registry: the office of that Registry, — the Family Division: the Principal Registry of the Family Division, — Admiralty or commercial proceedings: the Admiralty and Commercial Registry, — Chancery Division: Chancery Chambers. — otherwise the Central Office of the Supreme Court.
RSC O.46, r.6(4)(a)	No writ shall be issued by the court unless the party seeking to issue it produces: — the judgment or order on which the writ is to issue, or an office copy; — where permission is required to issue, a copy of the order granting permission; — where judgment on failure to respond has been entered against a State (s.14 State Immunity Act 1978), evidence that the State has been served in accordance with CPR, r. 40.10 and that judgment has taken effect.
RSC O.46, r.6(4)(b)	The court officer must be satisfied that the time (if any) specified in the order for the payment of money or the doing of any act has expired (RSC O.46, r.6(4)(b)).
RSC O.46, r.6(5)	The date of issue will be indorsed on the writ.

Execution by Sheriff

RSC O.46, r.9	Send sealed writ to the under sheriff, who levies execution. Any party issuing a writ of execution, or against whom a writ is issued, may serve notice on the sheriff to whom the writ was directed requiring him to indorse on the writ a statement of the manner in which he has executed it and to send a copy of the statement (RSC O.46 r.9).

Duration and renewal, and permission to issue warrants or writs of execution

CCR O.26, r.5, RSC O.46, r.2	For circumstances where permission is required to issue.
CCR O.26, r.6, RSC O.46, r.8	For provisions as to duration and renewal of warrants and writs of execution.

9.6. Execution: Committal for Contempt of Court (County Court)

D9–006 *CCR O.29, r.1(5A)* A warrant of committal shall not, without further order of the court, be enforced more than two years after the date on which the warrant is issued.

Commencement of committal proceedings

Form N208
Form N244
CCR O.29, r.1(4A)(c) and see PD to CCR O.29/RSC O.52, para.2.5

Free standing applications: Issue a Pt 8 Claim (Form N208).

Applications in current proceedings, issue an application (Form N244).

File affidavit in support giving full particulars of the grounds for committal.

Contents of application or claim form

CCR O.29, r.1(4A)(a), (b) The application or claim form itself must:

— identify the provisions of the injunction or undertaking which it is alleged have been disobeyed or broken;

— list the ways in which it is alleged that the injunction has been disobeyed or the undertaking has been broken.

Service & other requirements

A person cannot be committed for breach of an order unless the judgment or order required the person to do an act within a time fixed by the order, or to abstain from doing an act and

CCR O.29, rr.1(1), 1(2) — a copy of the judgment or order has been served personally on the person required to do the act or abstain from doing the act, and in the case of an order to do an act, the order has been served before the expiration of the time fixed by the order; and

CCR O.29, r.1(4) — if the order is an injunction, a penal notice has been indorsed on it and he/she is served personally with the application and evidence (CCR O.29, r.1(4);

CCR O.29, r.1A — in the case of undertakings, a copy of the undertaking must be handed by the court officer to the person giving it, posted to him or served though his solicitor, or failing which served personally by the creditor.

Powers to dispense with service etc.

CCR O.29, r.1(6) If the judge is satisfied that the person against whom it is sought to enforce the order has had notice of it by being present when it was made or by being notified of it, the court may enforce by committal notwithstanding that personal service has not been carried out.

CCR O.29, r.1(7) The court may dispense with service of a copy of the order, or the claim form or application notice if the court thinks it is just to do so.

Notice period

PD to RSC O.52, CCR O.29, para.4.1–4.4 At least **14** days' notice must be given of the date of hearing.

9.7. Execution: Committal for Contempt of Court (High Court)

RSC Order 52 r.7A states that a warrant for the arrest of a person against whom an order of committal has been made in the High Court shall not, without further order of the court, be enforced more than two years after the date on which the warrant is issued. D9–007

Choice of division

RSC O.52, r.1(2) By RSC O.52, r.1(2) the Divisional Court of the QBD is the appropriate court for an application to commit in respect of:
- — contempt committed in connection with any proceedings before a Divisional Court of the QBD; or
- — any criminal proceedings (save where contempt is committed in the face of the court or consists of disobedience to an order of the court or an undertaking to it); or
- — proceedings in an inferior court; or
- — is committed otherwise than in connection with any proceedings.

RSC O.52, r.1(3) Save as above, applications to commit for contempt of a High Court order should be made to a single judge of the QBD or a single judge of the Division to which the proceedings were allocated or transferred.

Committal in the Divisional Court of the QBD

RSC O.52, r.2(1) Permission is required before an application to commit may be made in the Divisional Court.

RSC O.52, r.2(2) The application for permission **must** be made without notice to the Divisional Court, supported by:
- (i) a statement setting out the name and description of the applicant, the name, description and address of the person sought to be committed, and the grounds on which committal is sought;
- (ii) an affidavit verifying the facts relied on.

RSC O.52, r.2(3) Notice of the application for permission must be given to the Crown Office not later than the preceding day, and copies of the statement and affidavit must be lodged at that office at that time.

If permission granted

Form N208
Form N244
RSC O.52, r.3(3) Part 8 Claim should be issued (Form N208), and served personally together with the affidavit and statement in support of application for permission (RSC O.52, r.3(3)).

RSC O.52, r.3(2) Permission to issue the application lapses after **14** days from the grant of permission.

Committal in other divisions or parts of the High Court

Form N208
Form N244
RSC O.52, r.4(1), (2) Issue a Pt 8 claim form (N208) or (in current proceedings) an application notice (Form N244), supported by affidavit stating the grounds for the application (RSC O.52, r.4(1), (2)).

RSC O.52, r.4(2) The applicant should serve the claim form and affidavit personally.

Notice period (all divisions)

PD to RSC O.52, CCR O.29, para.4.1–4.4 At least **14** days' notice must be given of the date of hearing.

9.8. Execution: Interpleader under Execution

D9–008 *CCR O.16, O.17* *Courts Act 2003, s.99, Sch.7*	With effect from April 1, 2004, please note that references to "Sheriffs" in CCR O.16 and CCR O.17, should be interpreted as including references to an individual authorised to act as an enforcement officer under the Courts Act 2003. (See CCR O.16, r.7(1A) and CCR O.17, r.1(2).) See also the Courts Act 2003, s.99 and Sch.7,which abolish any rule of law requiring a writ of execution issued from the High Court to be directed to a sheriff and provide for the authorisation of High Court enforcement officers.

County Court procedure

CCR O.33, r.1(A1)	"interpleader claimant" is a person claiming in respect of goods seized in execution, or the value thereof.
CCR O.33, r.1(1)	The interpleader claimant should deliver to the bailiff, or deliver to the court office for the district where the goods were seized, a notice stating the grounds of the interpleader claim, and the interpleader claimant's full name and address.
CCR O.33, r.1(2) *CCA 1984 s.100*	Upon receipt, the court sends notice to the execution creditor, and except where the interpleader claim is to the proceeds of sales of goods, send a notice to the interpleader claimant requiring him to deposit security under s.100 of the CCA 1984.

Reply by execution creditor

CCR O.33, r.2(1)	Within **four** days of receiving notice of a claim, the execution creditor must give notice to the court officer informing him whether he admits or disputes the interpleader claim, or requests the district judge to withdraw from possession of the goods or money claimed.

Issue of interpleader proceedings

CCR O.33, r.4	If the execution creditor disputes the interpleader claim or fails to give notice as to admission or dispute, the district judge issues an interpleader notice which will be served on the execution creditor and the interpleader claimant, not less than **14** days before the hearing.
CCR O.33, r.5(1)	Where the interpleader claimant intends to claim damages from the execution creditor or district judge or the execution creditor intends to claim damages from the district judge, he must give notice of that claim to the court and to any other party against whom a claim is made within **eight** days after service of the Interpleader Notice.

High Court procedure

Form PF23 *RSC O.17, r.2(1)*	The interpleader claimant must give notice of his claim to the sheriff charged with execution, and must give a statement of his address for service.
RSC O.17, r.2(2)	On receipt of a claim the sheriff must give notice forthwith to the execution creditor.

Reply by execution creditor

RSC O.17, r.2(2)	The execution creditor must within **seven** days after receiving the notice, give notice to the sheriff whether he admits or disputes the claim.

Issue of interpleader application

RSC O.17, r.2(3) *Form N1* *Form N244*	If the execution creditor disputes the claim or fails to give notice as to admission or denial, the sheriff may apply to the court for relief (RSC O.17, r.2(3)). (By issue of Pt 7 Claim form or Pt 23 Application).

9.9. Contempt in the Face of the Court

Editorial Introduction D9–009

"The phrase 'contempt in the face of the court' has a quaint old-fashioned ring about it; but the importance of it is this: of all the places where law and order must be maintained, it is here in these courts. The course of justice must not be deflected or interfered with. Those who strike at it strike at the very foundations of our society. To maintain law and order, the judges have, and must have, power at once to deal with those who offend against it. It is a great power—a power instantly to imprison a person without trial—but it is a necessary power" —*per* Lord Denning M.R. in *Morris v Crown Office* [1970] 2 Q.B. 114 at p.122.

There are two important principles: first the need to protect the administration of justice and preserve the authority of the court; and second the need to preserve the alleged contemnor's right to a fair trial. Adopting a summary procedure to deal with a contempt in the face of the court is not, of itself, unfair or a breach of Art.6 ECHR (*Wilkinson v S* [2003] EWCA Civ 95; [2003] 1 W.L.R. 1254; [2003] 2 All E.R. 184).

In the High Court, the judge acts under the inherent jurisdiction but should now follow the procedure prescribed by Pt II of Practice Direction—Committal Applications (see para.scpd52.7). The maximum penalty is that prescribed by the Contempt of Court Act 1981 (see para.3C–1) namely two years imprisonment.

In the county court the judge should follow the procedure prescribed by Pt II of Practice Direction—Committal Applications (see para.scpd52.7). The maximum penalty is that prescribed by s.118 of the County Courts Act 1984 (see para.9A–654) namely one month's imprisonment.

The leading case is *Wilkinson v S* (above). See further para.sc52.1.8 and, generally, CPR, Sch.1, RSC O.52 and commentary thereon, CPR, Sch.2, CCR O.29 and commentary thereon and Practice Direction—Committal Applications (at para.scpd.1).

What is 'contempt in the face of the court'?

Wilkinson v S [2003] EWCA Civ 95	Any act which disrupts the court proceedings such as shouting or assaulting someone in court, in the precincts of the court or going to or returning from court. See further para.sc52.1.17.

Which judge should deal with an alleged contempt in the High Court?

A High Court judge can:
(i) deal with the matter himself;
(ii) refer the alleged contempt to another judge;
(iii) report to the Attorney General for the Attorney to consider whether to institute criminal proceedings.

Which judge should deal with an alleged contempt in the county court?

County Courts Act 1984, s.118(3)	A circuit judge can: (i) deal with the matter himself; (ii) refer the alleged contempt to another judge; *(iii) report to the Attorney General* for the Attorney to consider whether to institute criminal proceedings. A district judge has the same powers as a circuit judge.

How should the judge proceed?

Part II PD Committal Applications (para. scpd52.7)

Normally, it will be appropriate to defer consideration of the behaviour to allow the alleged contemnor time to reflect on what has occurred.

A claim form and/or application are not required.

The judge should:

(1) tell the respondent of the penalty he faces;

(2) inform the respondent in detail, and preferably in writing, of the actions and behaviour of the respondent which have given rise to the committal application;

(3) if he considers that an apology would remove the need for the committal application, tell the respondent;

(4) have regard to the need for the respondent to be—

(a) allowed a reasonable time for responding to the committal application, including, if necessary, preparing a defence;

(b) made aware of the availability of assistance from the Legal Services Commission ("legal aid") and how to contact the service;

(c) given the opportunity, if unrepresented, to obtain legal advice;

(d) if unable to understand English, allowed to make arrangements, seeking the court's assistance if necessary, for an interpreter to attend the hearing;

(e) brought back before the court for the committal application to be heard within a reasonable time;

(5) allow the respondent an opportunity to:

(a) apologise to the court;

(b) explain his actions and behaviour;

(c) if the contempt is proved, to address the court on the penalty to be imposed on him;

(6) if there is a risk of appearance of bias, ask another judge to hear the committal application;

(7) where appropriate, nominate a suitable person to give the respondent the information. (It is likely to be appropriate to nominate a person where the effective communication of information by the judge to the respondent was not possible when the incident occurred).

Can the judge remand in custody?

Delaney v Delaney [1996] Q.B. 387
County Courts Act 1984, s.118(1)

There is no general power to remand.

All judges with power to commit for contempt can order the alleged contemnor to be detained "until the rising of the court".

If the judge does not deal with the contempt himself, must he give evidence in front of the judge who does deal with it?

PD Committal Applications, para.14

Generally, no. A written statement by the judge before whom the actions and behaviour of the respondent which have given rise to the committal application took place may be submitted as evidence of those actions and behaviour.

What is the standard of proof?

Dean v Dean [1987] 1 F.L.R. 517

Beyond reasonable doubt. The criminal standard applies to all contempt applications. The judge must be sure.

If the contempt is proved, can the respondent address the court on sentence?

Newman (t/a Mantella Publishing) v Modern Bookbinders [2000] 1 W.L.R. 2559

Yes. A contemnor must be given opportunity to address the court through his advocate or in person in mitigation of sentence. As a matter of practice, if the contemnor has not clearly apologised he should be asked again if he now wishes to do so.

What are the judges powers of sentence?

Contempt of Court Act 1981, s.14
County Courts Act 1984, s.118
Hale v Tanner [2000] 1 W.L.R. 2377;
Lomas v Parle [2003] EWCA Civ 1804; [2004] 1 W.L.R. 1642;
Robinson v Murray [2005] EWCA Civ 935

In the High Court, up to two years imprisonment and/or unlimited fine.

In the county court, up to one months imprisonment and/or a fine not exceeding £2,500 for every offence.

Sentence must be proportionate to the seriousness of the contempt.

Can the judge impose a community sentence?

No. Community sentences can only be imposed by the criminal courts.

Can a sentence of imprisonment be suspended?

CPR Sch.1, RSC O.52, r.7
Griffin v Griffin, The Times, April 28, 2000, see para. sc52.7.1
Balogh v St. Albans Crown Court [1975] Q.B. 73
R. v Hill [1986] Crim L.R. 457
See Wilkinson v S [2003] 1 W.L.R. 1254 (incident on Thursday; respondent detained and dealt with on the following Monday was "the very limit of what would be lawful or acceptable". Regrettable that he had not been brought back to court on the Friday)

Yes. There are no statutory restrictions.

A High Court judge can order the respondent to be detained overnight and dealt with the next day.

A High Court judge can order detention for no longer than necessary to make arrangements for summary trial. As a matter of practice the respondent should be brought back to court on the next working day so that the case can be reviewed in open court, reasons given for any further delay and bail considered.

Can the judge grant bail?

Yes. Contempt in the face of the court is a criminal contempt. Bail Act 1976 is of general application.

Contemnors under 21

R. v Selby Justices Ex p. Frame [1991] 2 W.L.R. 965

Persons under the age of 18 cannot be sentenced to any form of detention.

Persons under the age of 21 can be detained under Criminal Justice Act 1982, s.9(1).

Review by Official Solicitor

Lord Chancellor's Direction of May 29, 1963	The court sends a copy of every committal order and the judges sentencing remarks to the Official Solicitor. The Official Solicitor reviews the case and may apply or appeal of his own motion or at the request of the contemnor.

Can the contemnor apply to purge his contempt?

CPR Sch.1, RSC O.52, r.81, Sch.2 *CCR O.29, r.3(1)*	Yes.

Can the contemnor appeal?

AJA 1960, s.13 *CPR r.52(3)*	Yes. Permission to appeal is not required.

9.10. Appointment of a Receiver under CPR Pt 69

D9–010 **Key expressions**

"Receiver"	'Receiver' includes a manager appointedby the court.

Jurisdiction to appoint receiver

PD 69 para.1	The court's powers to appoint a receiver are set out in— • s.37 of the Supreme Court Act 1981 (powers of the High Court with respect to injunctions and receivers); • s.38 of the County Courts Act 1984 (remedies available in county courts); • s.107 of the County Courts Act 1984 (receivers by way of equitable execution).

When can the court appoint a receiver?

CPR r.69.2 *CPR r.25.2(2)* *PD 69 para.2*	Before or during proceedings, or after judgment. The court may replace or remove a receiver at any time. However the court will normally only consider an application for the appointment of a receiver before proceedings are started, after notice of the application has been served.

Application to appoint receiver

CPR r.69.2	May be made without notice but must be supported by evidence.

Where the application has a related injunction

PD 69 para.3.1	If a person applies at the same time for—the appointment of a receiver and a related injunction then the same claim form or application notice must be used for both applications.

Role of Masters and District Judges

PD 69 para.3.2 *PD 2*	A Master or a District Judge may grant an injunction related to an order appointing a receiver by way of equitable execution.

***Contents* of application**

PD 69 para.4	The Practice Direction to CPR r.69 sets out detailed requirements for the content of an application, at para.4.

Where application does not suggest who should be appointed

PD 69 para.4.3 If the applicant does not nominate a person to be appointed as receiver or if the court decides not to appoint the nominee, the court may order that a suitable person be appointed as receiver or direct any party to nominate a suitable individual to be appointed.

Where the application is in aid of enforcement of a judgment

PD 69 para.5 In considering whether to make the appointment as a method of enforcing a judgment, the court will have regard to the amount claimed by the judgment creditor, the amount likely to be obtained by the receiver and the probable costs of his appointment.

Service of order

CPR r.69.4 The order for appointment must be served on the receiver and the other parties to the proceedings unless ordered otherwise, and on any other persons the court directs.

Directions for security

CPR r.69.5
PD 69 para.6.2

The court may require the appointed receiver to give security and to file and serve evidence that he has sufficient security to cover his liability for acts and omissions. (The court will normally give directions in relation to security when it appoints the receiver.) The appointment may be terminated by the court if he fails to give the required security or to satisfy the court about the security which he has in force.

Content of direction for security

PD 69 para.7 An order appointing a receiver will normally specify the date by which the receiver must give security or file and serve evidence to satisfy the court that he already has security in force. Unless the court directs otherwise, security will be given (if the receiver is a licensed insolvency practitioner), by the bond provided by him under the Insolvency Practitioner Regulations 1990 extended to cover appointment as a court appointed receiver, or (in any other case) by a guarantee. (Written evidence of any bond, the sufficiency of its cover and that it includes appointment as a court appointed receiver must be filed at court, and any guarantee should be prepared in a form, and entered into with a clearing bank or insurance company, approved by the court.)

Directions on receiver's application

CPR r.69.6
PD 69 para.8
CPR Pt 23

The receiver may apply to the court for directions to assist him, and on such application the court may direct the receiver to serve those directions and the application on any person. If the directions are likely to be contentious or important, use the Part 23 procedure (otherwise directions may be sought by letter).

Receiver's remuneration

CPR r.69.7(1)–(2)	A receiver may charge for his services only if the court directs and specifies the basis on which the receiver is to be remunerated. The court may direct who is to be responsible for paying the receiver and the source of the funds.

Where remuneration is to be determined by the court

CPR r.69.7(3)–(4) *PD 69 para.9*	If the court directs that the receiver's remuneration is to be decided by the court then the court shall award such sum as is reasonable and proportionate in all the circumstances and which takes into account— (a) the time properly given by him and his staff to the receivership; (b) the complexity of the receivership; (c) any responsibility of an exceptional kind or degree which falls on the receiver in consequence of the receivership; (d) the effectiveness with which the receiver appears to be carrying out, or to have carried out, his duties; and (e) the value and nature of the subject matter of the receivership.

Role of Costs Judge

CPR r.69.7(5) *CPR r.35.15*	The court may refer the determination of a receiver's remuneration to a costs judge, or the court may appoint an assessor under CPR 35.15 to assist the court.

Receiver's accounts

CPR r.69.8(1)–(2)	A receiver may be ordered to prepare and serve accounts, and any party may apply to inspect any document in the receiver's possession which is relevant to those accounts.
PD 69 para.10.2	A party should not apply for an order permitting him to inspect documents in the possession of the receiver, without first asking the receiver to permit such inspection without an order.

Objection to accounts

CPR r.69.8(3)	Any party may object to any item in the accounts within 14 days of service. (The objections must give reasons and must require the receiver to notify the other parties of the objections within 14 days or to apply for the accounts to be examined in relation to the contested item.)

Examination of contested account items

CPR r.69.8(4)–(6)	When applying for examination of contested account items the receiver must file the accounts and must file a copy of the objection notice, and if he fails to do so then any party may apply for examination of the contested items. At the conclusion of an examination of contested account items the court will certify the result.

Non-compliance by receiver

CPR r.69.9 — The court may direct a receiver to attend court to explain any failure on his behalf to comply with a direction of the court, or any rule or practice direction. The court may then make any order it considers appropriate including termination of appointment, and costs and remuneration penalties. Interest may be ordered to be paid if the receiver is ordered to pay money into court and fails to do so.

Discharge of receiver

CPR r.69.10 — The receiver or any party may apply for the receiver's discharge on completion of his duties. Any such application must be served on the parties who were served with the order which appointed the receiver.

Termination or discharge order

CPR r.69.11 — An order which discharges or terminates the appointment of a receiver may require payment of money into court, or specify the person to whom he must pay any money or transfer any assets.

Termination of guarantees

CPR r.69.11(1)(c) — An order which discharges or terminates the appointment of a receiver may make provision for the discharge or cancellation of any guarantee given by the receiver as security.

9.11. Writ of Sequestration (RSC O.46)

When one might issue a Writ of Sequestration D9–011

RSC O.45, r.5 — Where a person required by a judgment or order to do an act within a time specified in the judgment or order, refuses or neglects to do it within that time (as extended or abridged under a court order or CPR r.2.11), or Where a person a person disobeys a judgment or order requiring him to abstain from doing an act—the judgment or order may be enforced with the permission of the court by means of a writ of sequestration against that person's property, or against the property of any director or officer of a corporate body (where the corporate body is the person in default).

Service of order is a requirement before enforcement

RSC O.45, r.7 — In general an order must be served before it can be enforced by sequestration, see RSC O.45, r.7 for detailed requirements.

Application for Writ of Sequestration

RSC O.46, r.5(1) — Application for a Writ of Sequestration must be made to a judge and must follow the procedure under CPR Pt 23.

Contents of application

RSC O.46, r.5(2) — The application notice must state the grounds of the application and be accompanied by a copy of the witness statement or affidavit in support of the application.

Service of application

RSC O.46, r.5(2) The application must be served personally on the person against whose property it is sought to issue the writ.

Dispensing with service

RSC O.46, r.5(3) The court may dispense with service of the application notice under this rule if it thinks it just to do so.

Form of hearing

RSC O.46, r.5(4) The hearing may be in private if in any case in which if the application were for an order of committal, he would be entitled to do so by virtue of RSC O.52, r.6 but otherwise the application shall be heard in public.

RSC O.52, r.6 (RSC O.52, r.6 provides that the court may hear the application in private:

- Where the application arises out of proceedings relating to the wardship or adoption of an infant or wholly or mainly to the guardianship, custody, maintenance or upbringing of an infant, or rights of access to an infant.
- Where the application arises out of proceedings relating to a person suffering or appearing to be suffering from mental disorder within the meaning of the Mental Health Act 1983.
- Where the application arises out of proceedings in which a secret process, discovery or invention was in issue.
- Where it appears to the court that in the interests of the administration of justice or for reasons of national security the application should be heard in private.)

9.12. Writ of Possession (High Court, RSC O.45)

D9–012 **Key expressions**

RSC O.45, r.3(2A) "Mortgage" includes a legal or equitable mortgage and a legal or equitable charge.

When one might issue a Writ of Possession

RSC O.45, r.3
CPR Sch.1 In the High Court a judgment or order for the giving of possession of land may be enforced by Writ of Possession (and may be enforced by sequestration—see *Writ of Sequestration (RSC O.46)*—Guide 9.11).

Permission to issue

RSC O.45, r.3(2) A writ of possession to enforce a judgment or order for the giving of possession of any land shall not be issued without the permission of the court, EXCEPT where the judgment or order was given or made in proceedings by a mortgagee or mortgagor (or by any person having the right to foreclose or redeem any mortgage), being proceedings in which there is a claim for:

- payment of moneys secured by the mortgage,
- sale of the mortgaged property,
- foreclosure,

- delivery of possession (whether before or after foreclosure or without foreclosure) to the mortgagee by the mortgagor or by any person who is alleged to be in possession of the property,
- redemption,
- reconveyance of the land or its release from the security,
- or delivery of possession by the mortgagee.

Criteria for permission

RSC O.45, r.3(3)

Permission will not be granted to issue a Writ of Possession unless:

- every person in actual possession of the whole or any part of the land has received such notice of the proceedings as appears to the court sufficient to enable him to apply to the court for any relief to which he may be entitled; and
- (if the operation of the judgment or order is suspended bysubs.(2) of s.16 of the Landlord and Tenant Act 1954), that the applicant has not received notice in writing from the tenant that he desires that the provisions of paras (a) and (b) of that subsection shall have effect.

Writ of Restitution

RSC O.46, r.3
Pitcher v Roe (1841) 9 Dowl. 971

With the court's permission (under RSC O.46, r.3) a Writ of Restitution may be issued in aid of enforcement where the defendant has re-entered the property whether forcibly or by stratagem after possession was recovered under the Writ of Possession.

9.13. Warrant of Possession (County Court, CCR O.26)

Interim possession orders D9–013

CPR 55.26(3)

Note that the provisions of CCR 0.26 as to Warrants of Possession do **not** apply where an Interim Possession Order has been made. See Guide 12.3in this work and CPR 55.26.

When one might obtain a Warrant of Possession

CCR O.26, r.17(1)
CPR Sch.2

In the County Court a judgment or order for the giving of possession of land may be enforced by Warrant of Possession.

Request for warrant

CCR O.26, r.17(2)

The person desiring a warrant of possession to be issued must file a request certifying that the land has not been vacated in accordance with the judgment or order.

Contents of request

CCR O.26, r.17(3A)

The judgment creditor must in his request certify the amount of money remaining due under the judgment or order and that the whole or part of any instalment due remains unpaid.

Combined execution against goods

CCR O.26, r.17(3)

Where a warrant of possession is issued, the judgment creditor is entitled, by the same or a separate warrant, to execution against the debtor's goods for any money payable under the judgment or order which is to be enforced by the warrant of possession.

Warrant of Restitution

CCR O.26, r.17(4)

A Warrant of Restitution may be issued with the permission of the court, in aid of any Warrant of Possession. An application for permission under to issue a Warrant of Restitution may be made without notice being served on any other party. It must be supported by evidence of wrongful re-entry into possession following the execution of the Warrant of Possession and of such further facts as would, in the High Court, enable the judgment creditor to have a Writ of Restitution issued. (See *Writ of Possession (High Court, RSC O.45)*—Guide 9.12).

Setting aside or suspending a Warrant for Possession

See *Leicester CC v Aldwinkle* (1992) 24 H.L.R. 40, CA, *Hammersmith and Fulham LBC v Hill* (1995) 27 H.L.R. 368. Generally a defendant should not face execution without having had an opportunity to apply for relief (this principle does not create any new rights to relief which the defendant does not already have in law).

Mortgagee possession

Where a mortgagee obtains a warrant to enforce an order for sale forthwith, and the mortgagor proposes to seek an order from the High Court under Law of Property Act s.91(2) to enable him to sell the property, the County Court has no jurisdiction to stay execution of the warrant (at least in the circumstances in *Cheltenham and Gloucester Building Society v Krausz* [1997] 1 All E.R. 21, CA where the mortgage debt would not be wholly discharged by a sale). See also notes to CCR O.26in Vol. 1 of this work.

Section 36 Administration of Justice Act 1970

Where the court has power under s.36 to allow the mortgagor time to pay sums due, the starting point in determining what is reasonable period is the term of the mortgage (*Cheltenham and Gloucester Building Society v Norgan* [1996] 1 W.L.R. 343, *Western Bank Ltd v Schindler* [1977] Ch.1).

Further guidance

See Guide 12.1in this work.

10. APPEALS, JUDICIAL REVIEW AND HABEAS CORPUS

10.1. Appeals: Scope, Court and Permission to Appeal

Scope of Part 52 and Practice Direction D10–001

CPR 52.1 *PD 52 para 2.2*	Pt 52 applies to appeals to the civil division of the Court of Appeal, the High Court or a county court but does not apply to appeals in detailed assessment proceedings against a decision of an authorised court officer. For the purpose only of appeals to the Court of Appeal from cases in family proceedings PD 52 Practice Direction applies 'with such modifications as may be required'.

Which court is the appeal court?

CPR Pt 49 *PD 52 para.2A.2* *PD 52 para.2A.3*	Appeals from all **final** decisions of the court in a **Part 7 multi-track claim** or in Specialist Proceedings (CPR, Pt 49) lie to the Court of Appeal. (PD 52 para.2A.2) ("final decision" is defined at PD 52 para.2A.3).
PD 52 para.2A.1	Otherwise (i) appeals from county court district judges lie to the Circuit Judge (PD 52 para.2A.1) (ii) appeals from Masters or district judges of the High Court lie to a High Court Judge (PD 52 para.2A.1) (iii) appeals from a circuit judge lie to a High Court judge (unless the circuit judge was sitting as an appeal court in which case appeal lies to the Court of Appeal as a "second appeal"). (iv) appeals from a High Court Judge lie to the Court of Appeal (PD 52 para.2A.1)
CPR r.8.9(c) *CPR r.52.14*	(v) Pt 8 final decisions where the claim was treated as allocated to the Multi Track (and was not expressly re-allocated by order). Claims under Pt 8 are automatically treated as allocated by default to the multi track. Where the appeal is against a final decision in such a case, the appeal court is determined initially under the rules at (i) to (iv) above. However if the appeal court determined under the above rules is not the Court of Appeal then PD 52 para.2A.6 requires the court considering any application for permission to appeal also to consider, if it grants permission to appeal, transferring it to the Court of Appeal directly, under .

Is permission to appeal required?

CPR r.2.3(1)	*(Note that the expression "judge" includes a district judge or Master)*
CPR r.52.3(1)	Permission to appeal is required where the appeal is from a decision of a judge in a county court or the High Court *except* where the appeal is against: (i) a committal order; (ii) refusal to grant habeas corpus; (iii) a secure accommodation order under s.25 of the Children Act 1989; or where a practice direction or Act specifies otherwise.

Where to make application or renewed *application* for permission to appeal?

CPR r.52.3(2)	Apply to the lower court (which made the decision) at the hearing at which the decision is made or Apply to the appeal court (the court which would hear the appeal) by means of an Appeal Notice.
CPR r.52.13	But *n.b.* where permission is to be sought for an appeal to the Court of Appeal *and* the decision to be appealed from was itself made on appeal, permission from the Court of Appeal is required.

CPR r.52.3(3) If the lower court refuses permission to appeal, then a renewed application may be made by Appeal Notice to the appeal court.

CPR r.52.3(4)
CPR r.52.3(5) If the appeal court refuses permission to appeal, without an oral hearing, the appellant may request an oral hearing to reconsider the application for permission. Such a request must be filed within **seven** days of service of notice that permission has been refused.

CPR r.52.15 In Judicial Review cases, where permission to apply for Judicial Review was refused by the High Court at a hearing, the person seeking permission to apply for Judicial Review may apply to the Court of Appeal for permission to appeal, and must do so within seven days of the decision of the High Court to refuse permission to apply for Judicial review. (The Court of Appeal may give permission to apply for Judicial Review instead of giving permission to appeal).

Grounds for giving permission to appeal

CPR r.52.3(6) Permission to appeal will be given only where the court considers that the appeal would have a **real prospect of success** or that there is **some other compelling reason why the appeal should be heard**.

CPR r.52.13(2) But *n.b.* where permission to appeal to the Court of Appeal is sought in a case where the decision appealed from was itself made on appeal, the application, which must be made to the Court of Appeal, will be granted only where the appeal would raise an **important point of principle or practice** or there is **some other compelling reason for the Court of Appeal to hear it**.

PD 52 paras 4.4, 4.5 *N.b.* where permission to appeal a **case management** decision is sought, see PD 52 paras 4.4 and 4.5 for additional matters which the court will take into account.

10.2. Appeals: The Appellant's Notice, Documents, Procedure and Grounds

D10–002 **The Appellant's Notice**

CPR r.52.4(1) The Appellant's Notice or ("Appeal Notice") should contain, where required, the request for permission to appeal.

The grounds for appeal set out in the Appeal Notice should state clearly why the appeal should be allowed and which of the grounds contained in CPR, r. 52.11(3) are satisfied. (See "Grounds for allowing an appeal", below.) PD 52 para.3.2.

CPR r.52.4(2) The Notice must be filed at the appeal court within such period as may be directed by the lower court (which should not normally exceed **28** days—PD 52 para.5.19) or, otherwise, **21** days after the date of the decision of the lower court sought to be appealed.

CPR r.52.4(3) The Notice (and skeleton argument—PD 52 para.5.21) must be served on each respondent as soon as practicable and in any event not later than **7** days after it is filed.

PD 52.6 Applications to vary the time limit for filing the Notice (or to amend the Notice) must be made to the appeal court stating any reasons for delay and any steps taken.The parties may **not** agree to extend any time limit set by the rules, Practice Direction or an order.

Human rights appeal notices: special provisions

PD 16 para.16
CPR r.19.4A
PD 52 paras 5.1A, 5.1B

Where an appellant is seeking to rely on any issue under the Human Rights Act 1998 or seeks a remedy available under that Act, for the first time in an appeal he must include in his Notice the information required by PD 16 para.16, and CPR, r. 19.4A will apply as if references to the case management conference were references to the application for permission to appeal.

Documents to be filed with the Appellant's Notice

PD 42 paras 5.6, 5.8

Save in appeals from the small claims track, the documents to be filed with the Appellant's Notice are listed at PD 52 para.5.6. (For small claims see PD 52 para.5.8).

Procedure after permission is obtained, or if permission is not required

PD 52 paras 6.2, 5.24

Copies of all documents filed with the Notice must be served on all respondents within seven days of receiving the order giving permission to appeal, or if permission was given by the lower court or was not required, these must be served with the Notice.

Consult PD 52 para.6.5

The appeal court will serve notice of a hearing "window" or "hear by" date, a copy of the permission order, if any, and any other directions of the court (PD 52 para.6.3). If the appeal court is the Court of Appeal, it will also serve an Appeal Questionnaire which must be completed and lodged by the appellant within **14** days.

Grounds for allowing appeals

CPR r.52.11(3)

The appeal court will allow an appeal where the decision of the lower court was wrong or was unjust because of a serious procedural or other irregularity in the proceedings in the lower court.

10.3. Appeals: The Respondent, and Miscellaneous Matters

Respondent's Notice **D10–003**

CPR r.52.5(1), (2)

A respondent may file and serve a Notice He **must** do so where he is seeking permission to appeal (in which case the Notice must contain the request for permission) or wishes to ask the appeal court to uphold the order of the lower court for reasons different from or additional to those given by the lower court.

CPR r.52.5(4), (5)

The Notice must be filed within such period as the lower court directed or otherwise within **14** days after (a) the date the respondent was served with the appellant's notice (where permission was not required or where it was given by the lower court); or (b) the date the respondent was served with notification that permission was given to the appellant by the appeal court; or (c) the date the respondent was served with notification that the appellant's application for permission and any appeal are to be heard together.

CPR r.52.5(6)

Unless directed otherwise the Notice must be served as soon as practicable and in any event no later than **seven** days after it is filed.

Documents to be filed with the Respondent's Notice

PD 52 paras 7.6, 7.7, 7.7A	Save in small claims appeals the respondent must provide a skeleton argument where he proposes to present argument to the court. It may be included in the Notice. Where it is not included in the Notice it must be filed and served no later than **14** days of service of the Respondent's notice. For documents to be filed with the notice see PD 52 para.7.10

Human rights appeals

PD 52 para.7.3A	PD 52 paras 5.1A and 5.1B apply to both Respondents and Appellants: see also "Human rights appeal notices: special provisions" under Guide 10.2.

Is permission to appeal required by the Respondent?

PD 52 para.7.1	Permission to appeal is required if the respondent wishes to ask the appeal court to vary the order below in any way.
PD 52 para.7.2	Permission to appeal is **not** required where the respondent wishes to ask the appeal court to uphold the judgment below, whether for the reasons given or other reasons.

Miscellaneous matters

- For powers of the appeal court see CPR, r. 52.9
- For documents to be filed with the appellant's notice appeals against a refusal of permission to apply for Judicial Review, see CPR, r. 52.15.
- For additional special provisions generally relating to the Court of Appeal see CPR, rr. 52.13 to 52.16, and PD 52 paras 15.1 to 15.19.
- For rules relating to the disposal of appeals by consent, see PD 52 paras 12.1 to 13.5.
- For costs in appeals see PD 52 paras 14.1, 14.2.

10.4. Appeals: Applications to Re-open Final Appeals & Permission to Appeal Applications

D10–004

CPR r.52.17(3)	The Court of Appeal, or the High Court when sitting as an appeal court has the power to re-open an appeal or application for permission to appeal even if it has been finally determined, but the circumstances where this will be permitted are strictly limited. The re-opening procedure of CPR, r.52.17 does not apply to appeals to the county courts.

Substantive requirements to re-open an appeal or application for permission to appeal

CPR r.52.17(a), 52.17(2)	• It must be necessary to re-open the appeal or permission application in order to avoid real injustice.
CPR r.52.17(1)(b), 52.17(2)	• The circumstances must be exceptional such as to make it appropriate to re-open the appeal or permission application.
CPR r.52.17(1)(c)	• There must be no alternative effective remedy.

Procedural requirements to re-open an appeal or application for permission to appeal

CPR r.52.17(4) • Permission is required from to apply to re-open an appeal (or to re-open a previously determined application for permission to appeal) even if permission was not originally required to appeal.

PD 52 para.25.3 • The application for permission must be sought from the court whose decision the applicant wishes to re-open.

PD 52 para.25.4 • The application for permission must be made by application notice supported by written evidence, verified by a statement of truth.

PD 52 para 25.5 • A copy of the application for permission must not be served on any other party to the original appeal unless the court directs.

CPR r.52.17(5)
CPR r.52.17(6) • There is no right to an oral hearing of an application for permission to re-open, save in exceptional circumstances by direction of the judge.

• The application for permission will not be granted without the court first directing that the application be served on the other party to the original appeal/application and giving that party an opportunity to make representations.

PD 52 para.25.6 • Where the court directs that the application for permission is to be served on another party, that party may within 14 days of the service on him file and serve a statement supporting or opposing the application.

Further appeals

CPR r.52.17(7) There is no right to appeal against a refusal to grant permission to apply to re-open an appeal or a refusal to grant permission to re-open an application for permission to appeal.

10.5. Judicial Review

The Judicial Review Procedure **D10–005**

CPR r.54.1 The "Judicial Review Procedure" ("JRP") is a form of Pt 8 claim, as modified by CPR, Pt 54.

When must the JRP be used?

CPR r.54.2 Use the JRP where the claimant is seeking a mandatory order, a prohibiting order, a quashing order or an injunction under s.30 of the Supreme Court Act 1981 (restraining a person from acting in any office in which he is not entitled to act).

When may the JRP be used?

CPR r.54,3 The JRP may be used in a claim for Judicial Review where the claimant is seeking an injunction or a declaration (see s.31 of the Supreme Court Act 1981). (*N.b.* the JRP must be used if any of the remedies referred to under *When must the JRP be used?* is claimed in addition to an injunction or a declaration).

N.b. it has been regarded as an abuse of process for a person seeking to establish that the acts of a public body are unlawful to proceed by way of ordinary injunction or declaration claims, i.e. the JRP should be used for such claims: *O'Reilly v Mackman* [1983] 1 A.C. 237. See also notes to CPR, r. 54.3.

Permission needed

CPR r.54.4 *CPR r.54.12*	The court's permission is required in order to proceed with a Judicial Review claim. The court may initially grant or refuse permission (or grant permission subject to conditions or on certain grounds) without a hearing and will give its reasons for the decision. Although no appeal lies against such a decision, the Claimant may request a reconsideration at a hearing provided he so requests within seven days. At least two days' notice will then be given to the parties of the date fixed for the hearing. (The decision made on a hearing of a Judicial Review permission application may then be appealed (subject to permission to appeal), to the Court of Appeal under CPR, r.52.15).

Time limit

CPR r.54.5	The claim must be brought promptly and in any event no later than three months after the grounds to make the claim arose. The time limit may **not** be extended by agreement between the parties. Enactments may specify shorter time limits for judicial review.

Contents of claim

CPR r.54.6	Include all that is required under Pt 8, and also: — The name and address of any person considered to be an interested party. — State that the claimant is requesting permission to proceed with a claim for judicial review. — State any remedy, including any interim remedy, which is claimed. — Include any documents required by PD 54 (see PD 54 paras 5.7–5.10).

Duty of full and frank disclosure

The Claimant is under a duty to give full and frank disclosure of all material facts. See notes to CPR, r. 54.6.

Service

CPR r.54.7	Serve the claim form on the defendant and any person considered to be an interested party within seven days of issue.

Acknowledgment

CPR r.54.8	A person served who wishes to take part must file an acknowledgment of service no later than 21 days after service of the claim, and must serve it on the claimant and any person named in the claim form as an interested person (unless directed otherwise), as soon as practicable and in any event no later than seven days after filing. These time limits may **not** be extended by agreement between the parties.

CPR r.54.8(4) The acknowledgment of service must state (where the person filing it intends to contest the claim) a summary of the grounds for doing so and must in any event state the name and address of any person the person filing it considers to be an interested person. The form may include or may be accompanied by an application for directions.

Failure to acknowledge service

CPR r.54.9 Failure to file an acknowledgment of service means that the person so failing may not take part in a hearing of an application for permission to seek Judicial Review, without permission of the court, but he may take part in a substantive Judicial Review hearing provided he complies with CPR, r. 54.14 or any other direction relating to service/filing of evidence and grounds. Failure to acknowledge service may be taken into account on the question of costs.

Response to application once permission is granted

CPR r.54.14 A party served with the claim form who wishes to contest or support the claim must file and serve grounds and evidence in writing within 35 days of service of the permission order.

The hearing

CPR r.54.18 If all parties agree the court may decide a Judicial Review application without a hearing. Any person may apply for permission to file evidence or make representations at a Judicial Review hearing.

If a Quashing order is made (with or without a hearing) the court may remit the matter to the decision maker and direct it to reconsider the matter and reach a decision in accordance with the judgment of the court. If the court considers there would be no purpose served in remitting the matter to the decision maker, it may (subject to any statutory restriction, eg where a statute gives a power to a specific tribunal) take the decision itself.

10.6. Habeas Corpus (Habeas Corpus ad subjiciendum)

Introduction D10–006

See generally the extensive notes to RSC O.54 at SC54 in Vol.1 R. v Home Secretary Ex p. Cheblak [1991] 1 W.L.R. 890 at 894

The Writ of Habeas Corpus ad subjiciendum (commonly simply referred to as Habeas Corpus) is a means by which the lawfulness of the detention of any person may be tested. It takes precedence over most other court business: *R. v Home Secretary, ex p. Cheblak* [1991] 1 W.L.R. 890 at 894). A High Court Judge or Divisional Court has jurisdiction, and not the Court of Appeal or a High Court Judge sitting in the Court of Appeal. It is a remedy which may be refused if there is some other *means by which the* validity of the detention may be tested. However where detention depends on the existence of a precedent fact and it is said that the detention is without any authority or is beyond purported authority and therefore unlawful, Habeas Corpus may be appropriate even if there are alternative remedies. By contrast, Judicial Review may be appropriate (and not

Habeas Corpus) where the detention was within an authority's powers but those powers were exercised unreasonably, or the decision is vitiated by an error of law.

Meaning of "detention" of a person

R. v Bournewood CMHT Ex p. L [1998] 1 All E.R. 635	This is a question of objective fact. A person is "detained" if those who have control of the premises have the intention that he shall not be permitted to leave, and have the ability to prevent him from leaving (irrespective of consent or of presence or absence of knowledge of the detention).

Procedure

RSC O.54, r.1	An application is made substantially in Form No.87, seeking the issue of a Writ of Habeas Corpus ad Subjiciendum. The application is made to a Judge in Court save that the court may order application to be made to a Divisional Court of the Queen's Bench Division. The application may also be made to a judge not in court at any time when no judge is sitting in court. Any application on behalf of a child must be made, in the first instance, to a judge not sitting in court.

Notice

RSC O.54, r.1 *CPR r.54.12*	The application may be made without notice to any other party and must be supported by a witness statement or affidavit by the person restrained, setting out the nature of the restraint and showing that the application is made at his instance, unless the person restrained is unable for any reason to make the witness statement or affidavit. In that event another person may make the statement or affidavit on his behalf and must state the fact that, and the reason why, the person restrained cannot make the statement or affidavit.

Power of court on ex parte application

RSC O.54, r.2	On an application made without notice, the Judge may order that the writ do issue forthwith or direct issue of a claim form seeking issue of the writ, or direct that the application be heard by a Divisional Court or by a Judge in court, or (if the Judge is in court or the application is made to a Divisional Court) may adjourn so that notice may be given to the respondent.

Service of copies of evidence

RSC O.54, r.3	Every party must supply to every other party on request (after payment of proper copying charges) copies of the statements or affidavits which he proposes to use at the hearing of the application.

Power to order release of person retained

RSC O.54, r.4	On the hearing of an application for the issue of a writ of Habeas Corpus ad Subjiciendum, the court or Judge may in its discretion direct the immediate release of the person restrained. Such order shall be sufficient warrant to any governor of a prison, constable or other person

for the release of the person under restraint. (In criminal proceedings, if the judge does not so order, he shall direct that the application be made by claim form to a Divisional Court of the Queen's Bench Division.)

Direction for Return to the writ

RSC O.54, r.5

Where a writ of Habeas Corpus ad Subjiciendum is ordered to issue, directions shall be given as to the date and court or judge before whom the writ is returnable.

Service of writ

RSC O.54, r.6

Once issued the writ must be served personally on the Rperson to whom it is directed but if personal service is not possible or if the writ is directed to the governor of a prison or other public official, then it must be served by leaving it with a servant or agent of the person to whom it is directed, at the place where the person restrained is being kept.

With the writ there must also be served a notice in Form No.90 stating the court or judge before whom, and date, on which the person restrained is to be produced, and that in default of obedience proceedings for committal of the party disobeying will be taken.

The Return

RSC O.54, r.7 and see notes after SC54.7

The return to the writ must be indorsed or annexed to the writ and must state all the causes for the detention of the person restrained. (A schedule may be annexed if more space is required than is available on the return indorsed on the writ).

N.b. merely stating the statutory section under which it is said the person is detained may not be sufficient: *R. v Home Department Ex p. Iqbal* [1978] Q.B. 264.

The hearing on the Return

RSC O.54, r.8

The return to the writ is read and motion is made for discharging or remanding the person detained, or for amending or quashing the return. Where the person restrained is produced then his counsel shall be heard first followed by counsel for the Crown and then one counsel for the person restrained.

Forms

See PD to RSC O.54. Numerous pre-CPR practice directions continue to apply to RSC O.54 proceedings, see the list under para.7.1 of the PD to RSC O.54.

11. COSTS

11.1. Detailed Assessment: Commencement, Points of Dispute and Reply

D11–001 *Note*: from January 6, 2004 for a limited period, a pilot scheme for detailed assessment by the Supreme Court Costs Office of costs of civil proceedings in London County Courts was in force. See PD 47B, which applies, instead of para.31.1 of the CPR Costs Practice Direction, to requests for a detailed assessment hearing which are filed between July 6, 2004 and July 5, 2005, pursuant to a judgment or order for the payment of costs by one party to another in civil proceedings in any of the following County Courts namely Barnet, Bow, Brentford, Central London, Clerkenwell, Croydon, Edmonton, Ilford, Lambeth, Mayors and City of London, Romford, Shoreditch, Wandsworth, West London, Willesden and Woolwich.

Commencement

CPR r.47.4	For matters relating to venue for commencement see CPR, r. 47.4 and paras 31.1 and 31.2 of the Costs PD.
CPR r.47.1	The detailed assessment procedure is not generally to be commenced until the conclusion of the proceedings unless the court orders otherwise. For the definition of "conclusion of proceedings" see Costs PD para 28.1.
CPR r.47.2	Detailed assessment is *not* stayed pending an appeal unless the court so orders.
CPR r.47.7	The period within which detailed assessment must be commenced is as follows:

Time by which detailed assessment must be commenced

Judgment, direction, order, award or other determination	3 months after date of judgment etc. Where detailed assessment is stayed pending an appeal, three months after the order lifting the stay.
Discontinuance under CPR, Pt 38	3 months after the date of service of notice of discontinuance under CPR, r. 38.3; or three months after the date of the dismissal of application to set aside the notice of discontinuance under CPR, r. 38.4.
Acceptance of an offer to settle or a payment into court under CPR, Pt 36.	3 months after the date when the right to costs arose.

Form N252
CPR r.47.8

N.b. delay in commencement may lead to the other party applying for an order for commencement and/or the costs consequences listed at CPR, r. 47.8.

To commence detailed assessment the Receiving Party("**RP**") serves on the Paying Party ("**PP**"):

(i) notice of commencement in the appropriate practice form (N252); and
(ii) copy of the bill of costs (see Model Precedents A to D in the Schedule of precedents annexed to the Costs PD); and
(iii) the documents listed at paras 32.3 to 32.5 of the Costs PD, as appropriate.

Costs PD para.32.10

RP must also serve the above on any "relevant persons" specified in the Costs PD. These are defined at para.32.10 of the Costs PD.

Points of dispute and reply

CPR r.47.9(1), (2)	PP and any other party to the detailed assessment may dispute any item on the bill by serving points of dispute (in the form of Precedent G in the Costs PD) on RP and every other party to the assessment, within 21 days after the dtae of service of the notice of commencement. Points of dispute should provide the information etc. listed at para.35.3 of the Costs PD.
CPR r.47.9(2), 47.9(3)	If a party serves points of dispute after the time permitted by CPR, r. 47.9(2) he may not be heard further in the detailed assessment proceedings unless the court gives permission.
Costs PD para.39.1	RP may optionally serve a Reply to the Points of Dispute on every other party to the detailed assessment within 21 days after service of the Points of Dispute. Paragraph 39.1 of the Costs PD.

11.2. Detailed Assessment: Default Costs Certificates, Procedure where Points of Dispute have been Served, and Interim Costs Certificates

Default costs certificates D11–002

Form N254 *Form N255* *CPR r.47.9(4)* *Costs PD para.37.3*	RP may file a request (in Form N254) for a default costs certificate if the period for serving points of dispute has expired and he has not been served with any points of dispute. If the court issues the default certificate it will be in Form N255.
CPR r.47.9(5)	If any party serves points of dispute before the issue of a default costs certificate, the court may not issue a default costs certificate.
CPR r.47.11(1)	The default costs certificate will include an order to pay the costs to which it relates. The costs of commencement of the detailed assessment shall be the sum set out in the Costs PD (para.37.8).

Setting aside default costs certificates

CPR r.47.12(1)	Default certificate *must* be set aside if RP was not entitled to it.
CPR r.47.12(2)	Otherwise, the court may set aside or vary the default certificate if it appears that there is some good reason why the detailed assessment should continue. An application to set aside under CPR, r. 47.12(2) must be supported by evidence (Costs PD para.38.1). For further provisions as to matters taken into account on an application under CPR, r. 47.12(2) and the test to be applied see Costs PD para.38.2.
CPR r.47.12(3) *CPR r.47.12(4)*	Where notice of commencement has been purportedly served and a default certificate has been issued, but RP subsequently discovers that the notice of commencement did not reach PP at least 21 days before the default certificate was issued, RP *must* file a request to set aside the default certificate or apply to the court for directions and may take no further step in the detailed assessment or enforcement of the default certificate.

Where points of dispute are heard: oral hearing

Form N258	Where points of dispute have been served, RP *must* file a request in Form N258 for a detailed assessment hearing.

CPR r.47.7
CPR r.47.14(4)
He must do so within three months of the expiry of the period for commencing detailed assessment as specified in CPR r. 47.7 or any direction of the court.

CPR r.47.14(3)
If RP fails to request a hearing then PP may:

(i) apply for an order requiring RP to do so within such time as specified in the order. The court may on such an application direct that some or all of the costs be disallowed unless the request for oral hearing is made within the specified time; or

CPR r.47.14(5)
(ii) do nothing, in which case if RP then files a request for a hearing later than the three month period the court may disallow all or part of the interest payable to RP under s.17 of the Judgments Act 1838 or s.74 of the County Courts Act 1984 but must not impose any other sanction save in accordance with the court's powers in relation to misconduct. (CPR r. 47.14(5)).

CPR r.47.14(6)
CPR r.47.14(7)
At the oral hearing, only RP, PP and parties who have served points of dispute in accordance with CPR, r. 47.9 may be heard without permission, and only the items listed in the points of dispute may be raised at the hearing unless the court permits.

Interim costs certificates

CPR r.47.15
CPR r.23
The court *may* issue an interim costs certificate at any time after a request for hearing has been filed, for such sum as it considers appropriate, and may amend or cancel it. The certificate will include an order for payment, unless ordered otherwise, and the court may order that the costs certified in the interim certificate be paid into court.

A party may apply, using the procedure under CPR, Pt 23, for an interim costs certificate (Costs PD para.41.1).

11.3. Detailed Assessment: Legal Aid and other Funds, Final Certificates and Appeals

D11–003 **Procedure where costs are payable out of the Community Legal Service Fund**

Form N258A
CPR r.47.17(1)
Where the court is to assess the costs payable to an assisted person out of the CLS fund the assisted person's solicitor may commence assessment by filing a request in Form N258A together with the documents listed at Costs PD para.43.3.

CPR r.47.17(2)
The request must be filed within three months after the date when the right to detailed assessment arose.

CPR r.47.17(3)
CPR r.47.17(4)
Costs PD para.43.4
CPR r.47.17(7)
The solicitor must serve a copy of the request on the LSC funded client or assisted person if notice of that person's interest has been given to the court in accordance with CLS or legal aid regulations. Otherwise the court will provisionally assess the costs without the attendance of the solicitor unless it considers that a hearing is necessary, and then return the bill to the solicitor. After the provisional assessment the court will fix a date for hearing if the solicitor informs the court within 14 days that he wants the court to hold a hearing.

CPR r.47.17(4)
The court will fix a date for an assessment hearing if the solicitor has certified that the assisted person wishes to attend an assessment hearing.

Procedure where costs are payable out of a fund other than the Community Legal Service Fund

Form N258B *CPR r.47.18A(1)*	RP may commence detailed assessment by filing a request in Form N258B within three months after the date when the right to detailed assessment arose.
CPR r.47.18A(2)	The request must be accompanied by the documents listed at para.44.3 of the Costs PD. The court will decide who should be served, having regard to the criteria at para.44.4 of the Costs PD.
CPR r.47.17A(4)	The court will, on receipt of the request, provisionally assess the costs, and return the bill to RP without attendance of any party unless the court considers that a hearing is necessary.
CPR r.47.17A(6)	The court will fix a date for an assessment hearing if the party informs the court, within 14 days after receipt of the provisionally assessed bill, that he wants the court to hold a hearing.

Final costs certificates

Form N256 *Costs PD para 42.1*	At the detailed assessment the court will indicate any disallowances or reductions in the sums claimed by making an appropriate note on the bill of costs.
Costs PD para.42.2	RP must make clear the correct figures agreed or allowed in respect of each item and must recalculate the summary of the bill accordingly.
CPR r.47.16(2) *Costs PD para.42.4*	The completed bill of costs (re–calculated) must be filed by RP within 14 days of the end of the detailed assessment hearing. The documents at para.42.4 of the Costs PD must be filed wit the completed bill.
Form N256 *CPR r.47.16(4)* *CPR r.47.16(5)*	When the completed bill is filed the court will issue and serve a final costs certificate in Form N256 including an order for payment unless the court orders otherwise.

Appeals

CPR r.47.20	Any party to detailed assessment may appeal against a decision of an authorised court officer in those proceedings. A Legal Services Commission funded client or assisted person is not a party for the purpose of bringing an appeal.
CPR r.47.21	Appeal against a decision of an authorised court officer lies to a costs judge or a district judge of the High Court.
Form N161 *CPR r.47.22*	To appeal, file an appeal notice in Form N161 within 21 days after the date of the decision to be appealed against. On receipt of the Notice the court will serve it on the parties and give notice of the appeal hearing.
Costs PD paras 48.3, 48.4	The appeal notice should if possible be accompanied by a suitable record of the judgment appealed against.
CPR r.47.23	At the appeal the court will re–hear the proceedings giving rise to the decision being appealed against and make any order or directions it considers appropriate.

11.4. Summary Assessment of Costs

D11–004 *See also the SCCO "Guide to the Summary Assessment of Costs" set out following the Costs PD in Vol.1*

When does summary assessment take place?

CPR r.44.7 *Costs PD para.13.1*	Judges are required to assess costs summarily if practicable and have a discretion to do so in any case irrespective of the duration of the hearing. Unless there is good reason not to do so:
Costs PD para.13.2(1)	The court should summarily assess costs at the conclusion of a trial which was dealt with on the fast track (and deal with all the costs of the claim).
Costs PD para.13.2(2)	The court should summarily assess costs at the conclusion of a hearing which lasted less than one day (assess the costs of that hearing, but if it concluded the case then the court may assess the whole costs of the claim).
Costs PD para.13.2(3)	The court should summarily assess costs at the conclusion of hearings in the Court of Appeal to which PD 52, para.14 applies (i.e. contested directions hearings, applications for permission to appeal at which the respondent is present, dismissal list hearings at which the respondent is present, appeals from case management decisions, and appeals listed for one day or less).

Summary assessment where children and patients are involved

Costs PD para.13.11	The court may not summarily assess costs where the receiving party is a childor patient unless the solicitor acting for the child or patient has waived the right to further costs. The court may summarily assess costs which are payable by a child or patient.

Summary assessment where a party is publicly funded

Costs PD para.13.9	The court should not make a summary assessment of the costs of a publicly funded receiving party.
Guide to the Summary Assessment of Costs, para.4 *Costs PD para.13.10*	The court may summarily assess the costs payable by a publicly funded party, but doing so does not amount to a determination of that person's liability to pay those costs (for which see CPR, r. 47.17 and Costs PD paras 21.1–23.17).

Obligation to serve a costs schedule

Costs PD para.13	In any case lasting not more than one day the parties are obliged to serve and file costs schedules of the costs which they would seek in the event of success, at least 24 hours before the hearing.
PD 52 para.14	In any hearing in the Court of Appeal in which summary assessment is likely under PD 52 para.14 (see "When does summary assessment take place" above), the parties are obliged to serve and file costs schedules at least 24 hours before the hearing.

Failure to comply

Costs PD para.13.6	The court will take into account any failure to serve a schedule in compliance with the rules (as to timing or form) when deciding what order if any to make about costs, and about any further hearing for detailed assessment which may be necessary as a result of that failure.

Form of schedule

The form of costs schedule should follow Form N260. See the list set out in Costs PD para.13.5(2).

If the costs include an additional liability

CPR r.44.3A

A court carrying out summary assessment may make a summary assessment of all the costs including any additional liability, or it may summarily assess the costs apart from the additional liability and direct that the additional liability be subject to detailed assessment, or it may direct detailed assessment of the whole costs. (Note that the court may not carry out assessment of any additional liability until the conclusion of the proceedings or part of the proceedings to which the additional liability relates.)

Order on summary assessment where an additional liability is claimed

(notes to CPR r.44.3A)

A court carrying out summary assessment in a case which involves a claim to an additional liability (even though the additional liability is to be assessed later) should separately specify the base costs allowed for solicitors, counsel, and other disbursements since when the additional liability is assessed there may be different percentage increases for solicitors and counsel.

Additional liability and summary assessment generally

See Costs PD para.14.

Order where Fast Track trial has taken place

Costs PD para.13.7

After summary assessment following a fast track trial tthe court will separately specify the amount of costs allowed for the fast track trial costs.

Summary assesment may not be transferred to another forum

Costs PD para.13.8

A court may not direct summary assessment to be done by a costs officer and if a further hearing to summarily assess costs is necessary then the court must give directions to enable it to be heard before the same judge.

Judge's responsibility on summary assessment

Costs PD para.13.13(a)–(b)

Even where the individual items on a costs schedule are not challenged, the judge retains the responsibility to ensure that the final figure is not disproportionate or unreasonable, but the lack of dispute can be taken as 'some indication' that the amount is proportionate and reasonable. The judge will intervene if satisfied that the costs are so disproportionate that it is right to do so. Any order for costs by consent must record that the order is by consent.

Costs PD para.13.13

The court will not give its approval to disproportionate and unreasonable costs.

11.5. Costs Only Proceedings

D11–005 **When to use**

CPR r.44.12A(1) — If no proceedings have been started but the parties have reached agreement in writing on all issues (including who is to pay costs) except for the amount of costs. There should be a proper attempt to agree the amount of costs (SCCO guide 21.1(c)(iii)).

Commencement

CPR r.44.12A(2) — Use the procedure under CPR Pt 8 (Form N208) to start costs only proceedings seeking assessment of the amount of costs. Either party may commence proceedings.

Agreement

CPR r.44.12(3) — The agreement between the parties on all issues save as to the amount of costs must be set out in the claim form or accompany it.

Other formalities

SCCO Costs Guide para.21.2 — The Pt 8 form must identify the dispute to which the claim relates, set out a draft of the order sought and the amount of costs claimed, and whether the costs are claimed on the standard or indemnity basis.

Orders on the claim

CPR r.44.12A(4) — The court considering the Pt 8 claim may only make one of the following orders:

(i) make an order for costs to be determined by detailed assessment; or
(ii) dismiss the claim.

(But if the proceedings giving rise to the costs were proceedings under Part II of CPR, Pt 45 then the court shall assess the costs in the manner set out in CPR, Pt 45: CPR, r. 44.12A(4A)).

Procedure

SCCO Costs Guide 21.1 — Note that Costs only proceedings involve two separate steps: first the decision by the court whether to dismiss the claim or direct detailed assessment, and second the detailed assessment itself (if the claim is not dismissed).

The decision

SCCO CostsGuide 21.3 — The court may make the order sought without a hearing if the defendant fails to acknowledge service, or the defendant files acknowledgment in which he states that he does not contest the making of an order in the terms of the claim, or if a consent order under CPR, r. 40.6 is filed signed by both parties (except where a party is in person or some other rule forbids this).

If the claim is disputed for any reason (except for a dispute only as to the amount of costs payable) then the court will dismiss the claim without a hearing. The only issue for the court in costs only proceedings is as to whether or not there is to be a detailed assessment. This also means that no order for an interim payment on account of costs will be made unless the parties agree.

Once order is made

SCCO CostsGuide 21.4(a) — If an order is made for detailed assessment, it is treated as an order for the amount of costs to be decided to which CPR, r. 47 applies, and the procedure under that Part should then be followed.

Additional liability

SCCO Costs Guide 21.4(c) — If an additional liability is claimed the court will have regard to the fact that the substantive claim was settled without proceedings being started. For information on additional liabilities see SCCO Costs Guide, section 19.

12. LANDLORD AND TENANT

12.1. Possession Claims: Claims other than under the Housing Act 1988 s.21

When to use CPR, Pt 55, Part I **D12–001**

The procedure under CPR, Pt 55, Part I must be used where the claim includes:

— a possession claim by a landlord or former landlord;

— a possession claim by a mortgagee;

— a possession claim by a licensor or former licensor;

CPR r.55.1(B) — a possession claim against trespassers (for definition of "trespasser" see CPR, r. 55.1(b)); or

— a claim by a tenant seeking relief from forfeiture.

This procedure does not apply where CPR, Pt 55 Part II is used (claims under the Housing Act 1988 s.21) or where an interim possession order is sought under CPR Pt 55, Pt III.

Venue for commencement

CPR r.55.3(2) — The claim should be commenced in the county court for the district in which the land is situated unless CPR r. 55.3(2) applies (suitability for High Court) or an enactment provides otherwise .

Commencement and hearing date

CPR r.55.4 — The Particulars of Claim must be filed and served with the claim form . For special rules as to how to serve a claim on trespassers see CPR, r. 55.6. In claims against **trespassers** the form and Particulars of Claim must be served:

CPR r.55.5(2) — in the case of a claim regarding residential property, not less than five days before the hearing date;

— in the case of other land not less than two days before the hearing date.

CPR r.55.5(3) — In **other** possession claims the hearing date will not be less than 28 days after issue and the standard period between issue and hearing date will be not more than eight weeks.

CPR r.55.8(6) — Where the claimant serves the claim form he must produce a certificate of service at the hearing of the claim. Note the additional notice service requirements in **mortgagee** claims.

Defence

CPR r.55.7 No acknowledgment of service is necessary and default judgment is not available. Trespassers need not file a defence, but in other cases whilst a person who has not filed a defence may take part in any hearing the court may take his failure to file a defence into account on the question of costs.

Hearing & Track Allocation

CPR r.55.8(2)
CPR r.55.9 At the hearing date the court may decide the claim or give case management directions. Where there are genuine grounds for dispute which appear to be substantial the court shall allocate the claim to a track or give directions to enable track allocation. CPR, r. 55.9 deals with track allocation criteria.

Evidence

At the hearing, unless the court orders otherwise or the claim has been allocated to the fast track or multi-track, evidence of witnesses may be proved in writing.

CPR r.55.8(5) In claims against trespassers, witness statements on which the claimant intends to rely must be filed and served with the claim form .

CPR r.55.8(4) Otherwise all witness statements must be filed and served at least two days before the hearing.

12.2. Possession Claims: Accelerated Procedure for Claims Solely under the Housing Act 1988 s.21 in Respect of Assured Shortholds

D12–002 **When to use CPR, Pt 55 Part II**

CPR r.55.11–55.13 CPR, Pt 55 Pt II may be used only where the claim is brought under s.21 of the Housing Act 1988 seeking possession of residential property let on an assured shorthold tenancy and contains no other claims. Also **all** the criteria listed at CPR r.55.12 must be satisfied. The claim must be commenced in the county court for the district in which the land is situated, and it will be served by the court by first class post.

This procedure does not apply where an interim possession order is sought under CPR, Pt 55 Pt III.

Defence

CPR r.55.14(1) A defendant who wishes to defend the claim or seek a postponement of a possession order must file his defence within 14 days of service of the claim form.

Actions by the court on receipt of claim

CPR r.55.15 The claim will be referred to a judge if a defence is filed. If the period for filing a defence has expired and no defence has been filed, the claimant may file a written request for a possession order and then the claim will be referred to a judge.

If no request for an order is made within three months of expiry of the period for filing a defence, an no defence has been filed, then the claim will be stayed.

Consideration of the claim

CPR r.55.16(1), (2)
CPR r.55.17
When the claim is referred to a judge, after considering any defence the judge will make an order for possession without requiring the attendance of the parties. If the judge is not satisfied that the criteria in CPR 55.12 have been met or that the claimant is entitled to recover possession under the Housing Act 1988 s.21, he may direct a hearing and give case management directions or may, if the claim form discloses no reasonable grounds for bringing the claim, strike it out.

CPR r.55.16(3)
If a hearing is directed the court will give the parties not less than 14 days' notice.

CPR r.55.16(4)
If the claim is struck out the claimant may apply to restore the claim within 28 days after the order striking out the claim was served on him.

CPR r.55.19
A party may apply, within 14 days of service of an order for possession made without the attendance of the parties, to set aside or vary such an order.

12.3. Possession Claims: Interim Possession Orders

Criteria for availability of an Interim Possession Order ("IPO") **D12–003**

CPR r.55.21
An Interim Possession Order (IPO) may be made under CPR, Pt 55, Part III when:

— the only claim made is a possession claim against trespassers for the recovery of premises; and
— the claimant has an immediate right to possession of the premises; and
— he has had such a right throughout the period of alleged unlawful occupation; and
— the claim is made within 28 days of the date on which the claimant first knew, or ought reasonably to have known, that the defendant (or any of the defendants), was in occupation.

CPR r.55.22(1)
CPR r.55.3(2)
It is NOT available when a defendant entered onto or remained on premises with the consent of a person who themselves had a right to immediate possession. The application must be brought in the county court for the district in which the land is situated (CPR r.55.3(1), applied by CPR r.55.22(1), but see CPR r.55.3(2) in relation to the High Court).

Form of claim and application

CPR r.55.3(4), applied by CPR r.55.22(1)
— Where the claimant does not know the name of a person in occupation or possession of the land, the claim must be brought against 'persons unknown" in addition to any named defendants. .
— The claim form must be in Form N5, and the form of defendant's statement in support must be in Form N133, as per PD 55 para.9.

CPR r.55.22(3), (4)
— When he files his claim form, the claimant must also file an IPO application notice N130 in the form set out in PD 55, and written evidence, which must be given by the claimant personally or by a duly authorised officer in the case of bodies corporate.

PROCEDURAL GUIDES

Service, hearing date and IPO order

CPR r.55.23(1) *PD 55 para.9*	— The IPO application and evidence must be served within 24 hours of the issue of the application, with a blank Form N133 for the defendant's statement which must be attached to the application notice.
CPR r.55.22(6)	— The hearing will be as soon as practicable but not less than three days after the date of issue.
CPR r.55.23(3)	— At or before the hearing the claimant **must** file a certificate of service of the documents. CPR r.6.14(2)(a) does **not** apply (i.e. the usual rule applicable to time limits for filing a certificate of service of claim form).
CPR r.55.6(a)	— Note also that CPR, r. 55.6(a) applies (i.e. attaching copies of the claim form, particulars of claim and any witness statements to the main door of the property, etc.)
CPR r.55.24	— At any time before the hearing the defendant may file a witness statement.
CPR r.55.21(1)	— The court **will** make an IPO if the claimant has filed a certificate of service of the documents required to be served, or proved service of those documents its satisfaction, **and** the court considers that the conditions in CPR, r. 55.21(1) are satisfied (see *Criteria for availability of an Interim Possession Order*, above.) **and** any undertakings given by the claimant as a condition of making the order are adequate.
CPR r.55.25(3),(4)	— The IPO will be in the Form N134 set out in PD 55 and will require the defendant to vacate the premises specified in the claim form within **24** hours of the service of the order. A date for hearing of the possession claim itself will be fixed for not more that **7** days after the date of the IPO.
CPR r.55.26–55.28	— For enforcement of an IPO and applications to set aside an IPO see CPR, r.55.26–55.28.

12.4. Possession Claims: Commencement of Possession Claims On-line under PD 55B

D12–004 *Note*: the information provided here may change when the Possession Claims On Line (PCOL) system (to be located at *www.possessionclaim.gov.uk*) is made generally available in Spring 2006.

Eligible Claims

PD 55B para.5

A possession claim may be started online if it is brought under Section I of Pt 55, it includes either a possession claim for residential property by a landlord against a tenant, solely on the ground of arrears of rent (but not a claim for forfeiture of a lease), or a possession claim for residential property by a mortgagee against a mortgagor, solely on the ground of default in the payment of sums due under a mortgage.

The claim must **not** include a claim for any other remedy except for payment of arrears interest and costs.

The Defendant must have an address for service in England and Wales, and the Claimant must be able to provide a postcode for the property.

The Defendant (or any of them) must not be known to be a child or patient.

Commencement and contents of a PCOL claim

PD 55B para.6

The claimant may request issue of a claim form by completing an online form at the PCOL website and paying the issue fee electronically or by some other means approved by the Courts Service.

Particulars of claim **must** be included in the online claim form. A copy of the tenancy agreement or mortgage deed or agreement need **not** be filed at time of issue.

Particulars of claim **must** include a history of the rent or mortgage account, in schedule form setting out the dates and amounts of all payments due and payments made either from the first date of default (if that less than two years before date of issue) or a period of two years immediately preceding the date of issue. A running total of the arrears must also be given.

Arrears history longer than two years

PD 55B para.6.4

If the history of arrears relied on is longer than two years, this **must** be stated in the on-line particulars and the longer schedule **must** be exhibited to a witness statement.

12.5. Possession Claims: Possession Claims On-line under PD 55B—Procedure After Issue

After issue D12–005

PD 55B para.6

Acknowledgment of receipt of on-line request for issue will be sent to the claimant. The claim is 'brought' for the purposes of the Limitation Act 1980 etc on the date on which the online claim form is received by the court's computer system.

The Court will serve a printed version of the claim form and a defence form on the defendant and sent notice of issue to the Claimant by email or post.

The claim form will have an identification number or password to enable Defendant to access the claim via the PCOL website.

The PCOL system will issue the proceedings in the appropriate county court for the post code of the property and that court shall have jurisdiction to hear and determine the claim irrespective of whether the property is within or outside the jurisdiction of that court.

Deemed service

PD 55B para.6.8

The claim is deemed to be served on the **fifth** day after the claim was issued irrespective of whether that day is a business day.

Defence & deemed date of filing

PD 55B para.7

Where the period of time within which a defence must be filed ends on a day when the court is closed, defendant may file his defence on the next day that the court is open.

The defendant may file a defence and/or counterclaim to a claim which has been issued through the PCOL system either via the PCOL system or written forms. A defendant filing a defence on line must **not** send the court a hard copy.

An online defence will be treated as being filed on the day the court receives it, if it receives it before 4 p.m. on a working day, but otherwise on the following working day.

Applications in the course of proceedings

PD 55B para.11	Where PCOL allows an on-line application to be made, a form will be available on the PCOL website. Application must be made at least five clear days before the hearing. The court will serve a copy endorsed with the date of the hearing by post on the claimant at least **two** clear days before the hearing and send the defendant notice of service and confirmation of the date of the hearing by post or email if an address has been provided.

Applications for a warrant of possession or to stay or suspend

PD 55B para.12	Where the court has made an order for possession in a claim started online and the claimant is entitled to the issue of a warrant of possession without permission of the court, a request may be made for issue of a warrant via the PCOL website. Request is deemed to have been filed on the day the court receives it, if before 4pm on a working day but otherwise on the following working day.
CCR O.26, rr.5, 17	See CCR O.26, r.5 read with CCR O.26, r.17(6) for circumstances in which a warrant may not be issued without the permission of the court.
PD 55B para.13	Where the court has issued a warrant of possession, the defendant may apply electronically for the suspension of the warrant if the application is made at least five clear days before the bailiff's appointment and the defendant is not prevented from making such an application without the permission of the court.

12.6. Claims for a new tenancy (s.24) and for termination of a tenancy (s.29(2)) of the Landlord and Tenant Act 1954

D12–006 **Key expressions**

"Opposed claim" *PD 56 para.3.1*	A claim where the grant of a new tenancy is opposed, or where the claim is for the termination of a tenancy under s.29(2) of the Landlord and Tenant Act 1954.
"Grounds of opposition" *PD 56 para.3.1(3)*	(a) the grounds specified in s.30(1) of the 1954 Act on which a landlord may oppose an application for a new tenancy under s.24(1) or may make an application under s.29(2) of the 1954 Act; or (b) any other basis on which the landlord asserts that a new tenancy ought not to be granted.

Starting the claim

CPR r.56.2 *High Court: PD 56 para.2*	Start the claim in the County Court for the district in which the land is situated unless the High Court criteria of PD 56 apply.

Mode of commencement

PD 56 para.2.1A	*Where the application is under s.24 and is opposed:* Use the CPR Pt 7 procedure as modified by CPR Pt 56.
PD 56 para.2.1	*Where the application is under s.24 and is NOT opposed:* Use the CPR Pt 8 procedure.

PD 56 para.2.1A	*Where the application is under s.29(2):* Use the CPR Pt 7 procedure.

Unopposed claims under s.24

CPR r.56.3(3)(a)	Use CPR Pt 8 but note that rr.8.5 and 8.6 do not apply (filing and service of evidence with claim).
CPR r.56.3(3)(b)(c)	Time for service of the claim form is modified to within 2 months after issue. The court will give directions after acknowledgment of service.

Opposed claims

CPR r.56.3(4)	Use the CPR Pt 7 procedure, but note that the claim form must be served within 2 months after the date of issue.

Precedence of multiple claims

PD 56 para.3.2(1)–(4) Where more than one application to the court under s.24(1) or s.29(2) of the 1954 Act is made, then:

- Once an application under s.24(1) has been served on a defendant, no further application to the court in respect of the same tenancy under s.24(1) or s.29(2) may be served by that defendant without permission of the court.
- If more than one application under s.24(1) in respect of the same tenancy is served on the same day, any landlord's application is stayed until further order.
- If applications under both s.24(1) and s.29(2) in respect of the same tenancy are served on the same day, any tenant's application is stayed until further order.

CPR r.7.7

- If a defendant is served with an application under s.29(2) which was issued at a time when an application to the court had already been made by that defendant in respect of the same tenancy under s.24(1), the service of the s.29(2) application is deemed to be a notice under CPR r.7.7 requiring service or discontinuance of the s.24(1) application within a period of 14 days after service of the s.29(2) application.

Contents of the claim form

PD 56 para.3.4 The claim form must contain details of:

- the property to which the claim relates, particulars of the current tenancy,
- the current rent (if not the original rent) date and method of termination,
- every notice or request given or made under ss.25 or 26 of the 1954 Act,
- the expiry date of the statutory period under s.29A(2) or any agreed extended period made under s.29B(1) or 29B(2).

Where the claimant is the tenant making a claim for a new tenancy under s.24

PD 56 para.3.5 Claim form must also provide details of:

- The nature of the business carried on at the property.
- Whether the claimant relies on s.23(1A), 41 or 42 of the 1954 Act and, if so, the basis on which he does so.

— Whether the claimant relies on s.31A of the 1954 Act and, if so, the basis on which he does so.
— Whether any, and if so what part, of the property comprised in the tenancy is occupied neither by the claimant nor by a person employed by the claimant for the purpose of the claimant's business.
— The claimant's proposed terms of the new tenancy.
— The name and address of anyone known to the claimant who has an interest in the reversion in the property (whether immediate or in not more than 15 years) on the termination of the claimant's current tenancy and who is likely to be affected by the grant of a new tenancy; or (if the claimant does not know of anyone in the above category), details of anyone who has a freehold interest in the property.

PD 56 para.3.6 (*N.b.* the claim form must be served on the persons referred to above)

Claim form where the claimant is the landlord making a claim for a new tenancy under s.24

PD 56 para.3.7 Claim form must also provide details of:
— The claimant's proposed terms of the new tenancy.
— Whether the claimant is aware that the defendant's tenancy is one to which s.32(2) of the 1954 Act applies and, if so, whether the claimant requires that any new tenancy shall be a tenancy of the whole of the property comprised in the defendant's current tenancy or just of the holding as defined by s.23(3) of the 1954 Act.
— The name and address of anyone known to the claimant who has an interest in the reversion in the property (whether immediate or in not more than 15 years) on the termination of the claimant's current tenancy and who is likely to be affected by the grant of a new tenancy; or (if the claimant does not know of anyone in the above category), details of anyone who has a freehold interest in the property.

PD 56 para.3.8 (*N.b.* the claim form must be served on the persons referred to above)

Claim form where the claimant is the landlord making application for the termination of a tenancy

PD 56 para.3.9 Claim form must also provide details of:
— Full details of the claimant's grounds of opposition.
— The terms of a new tenancy that the claimant proposes in the event that his claim fails.

Acknowledgment of service ofunopposed claim where the claimant is tenant

PD 56 para.3.10 Use Form N210 and state:
— Whether, if a new tenancy is granted, the defendant objects to any of the terms proposed by the claimant, and if so (a) the terms to which he objects; and (b) the terms that he proposes in so far as they differ from those proposed by the claimant.
— Whether the defendant is a tenant under a lease having less than 15 years unexpired at the date of the termination of the claimant's current tenancy and, if so, the name and address of any person who, to the knowledge of the defendant, has an interest in the reversion in the property expectant (whether immediate or in not more than 15 years from that date) on the termination of the defendant's tenancy.

— The name and address of any person having an interest in the property who is likely to be affected by the grant of a new tenancy.
— If the claimant's current tenancy is one to which s.32(2) of the 1954 Act applies, whether the defendant requires that any new tenancy shall be a tenancy of the whole of the property comprised in the claimant's current tenancy.

Unopposed claim where the claimant is landlord

PD 56 para.3.11 Use Form N210 and state:
— The nature of the business carried on at the property.
— If the defendant relies on s.23(1A), 41 or 42 of the 1954 Act, the basis on which he does so.
— Whether any, and if so what part, of the property comprised in the tenancy is occupied neither by the defendant nor by a person employed by the defendant for the purpose of the defendant's business.
— The name and address of anyone known to the defendant who has an interest in the reversion in the property (whether immediate or in not more than 15 years) on the termination of the defendant's current tenancy and who is likely to be affected by the grant of a new tenancy; or (if the defendant does not know of anyone in the above category), details of anyone who has a freehold interest in the property.
— Whether, if a new tenancy is granted, the defendant objects to any of the terms proposed by the claimant and, if so (a) the terms to which he objects; and (b) the terms that he proposes in so far as they differ from those proposed by the claimant.

Acknowledgment of service and defence where the claim is an opposed claim and where the claimant is the tenant

PD 56 para.3.12 Use Form N9.
In the defence the defendant must state:
— His grounds of opposition with full details.
— Whether, if a new tenancy is granted, the defendant objects to any of the terms proposed by the claimant and if so the terms to which he objects and the terms that he proposes in so far as they differ from those proposed by the claimant.
— Whether the defendant is a tenant under a lease having less than 15 years unexpired at the date of the termination of the claimant's current tenancy and, if so, the name and address of any person who, to the knowledge of the defendant, has an interest in the reversion in the property expectant (whether immediately or in not more than 15 years from that date) on the termination of the defendant's tenancy.
— The name and address of any person having an interest in the property who is likely to be affected by the grant of a new tenancy.
— If the claimant's current tenancy is one to which s.32(2) of the 1954 Act applies, whether the defendant requires that any new tenancy shall be a tenancy of the whole of the property comprised in the claimant's current tenancy.

Acknowledgment of service and defence where the claimant is the landlord making an application for termination of a tenancy under s.29(2)

PD 56 para.3.13 Use Form N9.
The defence must state with particulars:
— Whether the defendant relies on s.23(1A), 41 or 42 of the 1954 Act and, if so, the basis on which he does so.
— Whether the defendant relies on s.31A of the 1954 Act and, if so, the basis on which he does so.
— The terms of the new tenancy that the defendant would propose in the event that the claimant's claim to terminate the current tenancy fails.

Evidence in an unopposed claim

PD 56 para.3.14 No evidence need be filed unless and until the court directs it to be filed.

Evidence in an opposed claim

PD 56 para.3.15 Evidence (including expert evidence) must be filed by the parties as the court directs and the landlord will be required to file his evidence first.

Trial

PD 56 para.3.16 Unless in the circumstances of the case it is unreasonable to do so, any grounds of opposition will be tried as a preliminary issue.

Applications for interim rent under s.24A–24D

See PD 56 para.3.17.

13. HOMELESSNESS REVIEWS AND APPEALS

13.1. Homelessness: Guide to Key Terms and Duties

D13–001 **Terms and expressions (Housing Act 1996 ("HA 1996"), as amended)**

Housing Act 1996 ss.175–196

"homeless" and *"threatened with homelessness"*—see HA 1996, s.175.
"available" accommodation—see HA 1996, s.176.
"reasonable to continue to occupy" accommodation—see HA 1996, s.177.
"domestic violence or other violence"—see HA 1996, s.177(1), (1A).
"associated person"—see HA 1996, s.178(1).
"eligible for assistance"—see HA 1996, ss.183, 185.
"priority need" for accommodation—see HA 1996, s.189.
"becoming homeless intentionally"—see HA 1996, s.191.
"becoming threatened with homelessness intentionally"—see HA 1996, s.196.

Duty to have regard to the Code of Guidance

The authority may depart from the Code, but only after having had regard to it: De Falco, Silvestri v Crawley BC [1980] Q.B. 460, CA at 478A

— See HA 1996, s.182 see *The Homelessness Code of Guidance for Local Authorities 2006*, Department for Communities and Local Government.

Short term housing duties

HA 1996, s.200 — Interim duty (pending decision and notification to applicant) owed to persons who appear to be in priority need, homeless and eligible for assistance: s.188.

— Duty owed (until decision on referral is notified to applicant) to persons whose cases are referred, or considered for referral to another local housing authority: s.200.

Substantive housing duties (references to sections of HA 1996)

HA 1996, s.190 — Duty owed to **homeless** persons becoming homeless **intentionally** but who are otherwise eligible for assistance:
If in priority need: s.190(2).
If **not** in priority need: s.190(3).

HA 1996, s.193, 192 — Duty owed to **homeless** persons who are **not** homeless **intentionally** and who are otherwise eligible for assistance:
If in priority need: s.193 read subject to s.198 (referrals).
If **not** in priority need: s.192.

HA 1996, s.195 — Duty owed to persons **threatened** with **homelessness**, who became threatened with homelessness **intentionally**, but who are otherwise eligible for assistance:
If in priority need: s.195(5)(b).
If **not** in priority need: s.195(5)(a).

HA 1996, s.195 — Duty owed to persons **threatened** with **homelessness**, who did not become threatened with homelessness **intentionally**, and who are otherwise eligible for assistance:
If in priority need: s.195(2).
If **not** in priority need: s.195(5)(a).

13.2. Homelessness: Inquiry, Notification and Interim Duty

The duty to inquire **D13–002**

HA 1996, s.184 — The starting point for an applicant for accommodation on grounds of homelessness is s.184 of the Housing Act 1996 which defines the basic duty to inquire: s.184(1): "*If the local housing authority have reason to believe that an applicant may be homeless or threatened with homelessness, they shall make such inquiries as are necessary to satisfy themselves—*
(a) whether he is eligible for assistance, and
(b) if so, whether any duty, and if so what duty, is owed to him under the following provisions of this Part."
s.184(2): "*They may also make inquiries whether he has a local connection with the district of another local housing authority in England, Wales or Scotland.*"

The duties to notify decisions **and review rights after inquiry**

HA 1996, s.184(5) — The authority must inform the applicant as to the outcome of an inquiry under HA 1996, s.184 and the reasons for any adverse decision: s.184(3): "*On completing their inquiries the authority shall notify the applicant of their decision and, so far as any issue is decided against his interests, inform him of the reasons for their decision.*"

s.184(4): "*If the authority have notified or intend to notify another local housing authority under s.198 (referral of cases), they shall at the same time notify the applicant of that decision and inform him of the reasons for it.*"

HA 1996, s.202(3) — The above notice(s) of the outcome of the inquiry and of the decision made, must inform the applicant of his right to request a Review of the decision (under HA 1996, s.202) and of the time within which he has to request that Review (21 days of the date of the decision).

HA 1996, s.184(6) — Notification must be in writing. If not received by the applicant it shall be treated as having been given to him if it is made available at the authority's office for a reasonable period for collection.

Interim duty to accommodate some persons pending substantive decision

s.188(1) — The authority comes under a limited "interim duty" under HA 1996, s.188 where: "*the local housing authority have reason to believe that an applicant may be homeless, eligible for assistance and have a priority need*"

s.188(1) — The interim duty in such cases is to: "*secure that accommodation is available for his occupation pending a decision as to the duty (if any) owed to him under the following provisions of this Part.*"

s.188(2) — The interim duty arises irrespective of any possible referral to another district under s.198.

s.188(3) — The interim duty ceases (but **may**, discretionarily be continued by the authority) when: "*the authority's decision is notified to the applicant, even if the applicant requests a review of the decision…*".

13.3. Homelessness: The Right to Request a Review

D13–003 **Circumstances where an applicant may request a review**

HA 1996, s.202(1A) — An applicant may request a Review (under HA 1996, s.202(1)) of any decision of a local housing authority:

(a) as to his eligibility for assistance (see Guide 13.1 at para.D1–052);

HA 1996, ss. 193, 195–197

(b) as to what if any duty is owed to him under ss.193 to 193 and 195 to 197 (see Guide 13.1 at para.D1–052, *n.b.* s.197);

(c) to notify another authority under s.198(1) (referral out of area);

HA 1996, s.198(5)

(d) made under s.198(5) as to whether the conditions are met for referral;

HA 1996, s.200

(e) made under s.200(3) and (4) as to duty owed where a case is considered for referral (or is referred) (see Guide 13.1 at para.D1–052);

(f) as to the suitability of accommodation offered to him in discharge of their duty under (b) or (e), or as to the suitability of permanent accommodation offered to him by way of a "final" offer under 193(7).

HA 1996 s.202(1)

(g) any decision of a local housing authority as to the suitability of accommodation offered to him by way of a private accommodation offer (within the meaning of s.193).

HA 1996, s.193(5), (7) An applicant who has been offered accommodation under s.193(5) or s.193(7) may request a Review of the suitability of the accommodation under s.202(1)(f) **whether or not** he has accepted the offer.

Time limits and main procedural points

HA 1996, s.202(3)
— A request for a Review **must** be made before the end of 21 days beginning with the day on which the applicant is notified of the authority's decision or such longer period as the authority may in writing allow.
— If a request is made in time the authority **must** carry out a Review.

HA 1996, s.203(1)
— The Secretary of State may make regulations as to Review procedure.

SI 1999/71
— Relevant current regulations are The Allocation of Housing and Homelessness (Review Procedures) Regulations 1999. See Guide 13.4.

HA 1996, s.204(1)
— No time limit is specified as to the timescale for completing the Review but under s.204 a right of appeal against the original decision will arise if a Review decision is not notified to the applicant within the prescribed time (s.204(1)(b), s.203(7) and SI 1999/71 reg.9, see Guide 13.4 at para.D1–055).
— Examples of some types of irregularity which might be found on Review are listed at para. 19.13 of the *Code of Guidance 2006*, such as bad faith, error of law, failure to consider relevant matters, ignoring irrelevant matters, *Wednesbury* unreasonableness.

Notification of the decision on review

s.203(3)
— The authority must notify the applicant of the Review decision.

s.203(4)
— Reasons must be given where the decision on Review is:
(a) to confirm the original decision on any issue against the interests of the applicant; or
(b) to confirm a previous decision to notify another authority under s.198 or a previous decision that the conditions for referral are met.

s.203(5)
— The applicant must be notified of his right to appeal to a county court on a point of law under s.204 and of the time limit for appealing.

s.203(6)
— Notice of the decision is treated as not given until the rights of appeal and any reasons are notified to the applicant.

13.4. Homelessness: Review Procedure: The Regulations

D13–004 The Allocation of Housing and Homelessness (Review Procedures) Regulations 1999 (SI 1999/71). ("RPR").
The Homelessness (Decisions on Referrals) Order 1998 (SI 1998/1578) ("HDRO").

The prescribed time for completing a review (RPR, reg.9)

RPR Reg.9(2) The period within which notice of the decision on a review **shall** be given to the applicant is:

(a) **eight** weeks from the day on which the request for the review is made, where the original decision falls within ss.202(1)(a), (b), (c), (e) or (f) (see Guide 13.3 at para.D1–054);

(b) **10** weeks from the day on which the request for the review is made, where the original decision falls within s.202(1)(d) (see Guide 13.3 at para.D1–054) and the review is carried out by the notifying authority and the notified authority;

(c) **12** weeks from the day on which the request for the review is made in a case falling within reg.7 (referrals under s.198 and HDRO).

The period may be such longer period as the applicant and the reviewer may agree in writing.

Person responsible for deciding the review

RPR Reg.2 RPR Reg.2 provides that where the decision of the authority on a review of an original decision made by an officer of the authority is **also** to be made by an officer of the authority, that officer shall be:

— someone who was not involved in the original decision and

— who is senior to the officer who made the original decision.

Notification of right to make representations

RPR Reg.6(2)(3) RPR Reg.6(2) and (3) provide that the authority (or in a referrals case under s.198, the person appointed in accordance with HDRO) **shall** notify the applicant that:

— he or someone acting on his behalf, may make representations in writing to the authority in connection with the review and

— (if they have not already done so), notify the applicant of the procedure to be followed in connection with the review.

Consideration of representations

RPR Reg.8 provides that the reviewer **shall**, subject to compliance with the provisions relating to time limits, consider—

— any representations made under on reviews under s.202;

See RPR Reg.7 and HDRO — any responses to representations in a s.198 "referrals" case ; and

RPR Reg.8(2) — any representations made where the following applies: If the reviewer considers that there is a deficiency or irregularity in the original decision, or in the manner in which it was made, but is minded nonetheless to make a decision which is against the interests of the applicant on one or more issues, the reviewer shall notify the applicant)—

(a) that the reviewer is so minded and the reasons why; and

(b) that the applicant, or someone acting on his behalf, may make representations to the reviewer orally or in writing or both orally and in writing.

13.5. Homelessness: The Right to Appeal Against a Review Decision and Power to Provide Housing Pending Appeal

Appeal under HA 1996 s.204 D13–005

s.202, and Guides 13.4–13.5 at paras D1–055 and D1–056
See s.204(1)(a) and (b) respectively, and Guide 13.4 at para. D1–055 and D1–053

— The right to appeal under s.204 HA 1996 arises when the applicant is notified of the Review decision or he when has not been notified of the decision on Review within **the prescribed time**. *N.b.* "notice" of the decision is construed in accordance with the formal requirements of s.203(6) (see Guide 13.3 at para.D1–054).

— An appeal under s.204(1) is limited to an appeal on a **point of law** arising on the Review decision (or on the original decision in some circumstances (see above) in the absence of a Review).

Time limit for appeal

See Guide 13.4 at para. D1–055
Cline Thomas v London Borough of Haringey, Mayors and City of London Court, November 26, 2002, No.ED 206259)

— Appeal under s.204(1) **must** be brought within 21 days of the applicant being notified of the decision on the Review or within 21 days of the expiry of the prescribed time for notification of the Review decision.

— Grounds of appeal may in an appropriate case be amended out of time with permission, but an attempt to rely on new grounds introduced via a skeleton argument, absent a timely amendment of the Grounds, may result in refusal to consider the new matters .

Procedure

Azimi v Newham LBC, July 26, 2001, CA
PD 52 para.17.1(1)
PD 2 para.9
See in particular PD 52 para.24.2 in relation to s.204 Appeals. For procedure in relation to appeals generally see Guide 10.2 at para. D1–041 and CPR Pt 52

The Appeal is a "**first appeal**" made **without** the need for permission, and the level of Judge is that of **Circuit Judge**. It is usual in practice for disclosure of the appellant's housing file to be requested and given at an early stage by the Respondent authority (often prior to the issue of the appeal).

Discretionary power to house pending appeal in certain cases

HA 1996, s.204(4)

Under HA 1996 s.204(4), where the Authority were under a duty to secure that housing was available for the *applicant's occupation* they **may** continue to secure that accommodation is available during the period for appealing and until the appeal and any further appeal is finally determined. For right to appeal against decisions under this power see Guide 13.6 at para.D1–057.

The above power applies **only** where the duty to secure that accommodation was available arose under:

HA 1996, s.188

— HA 1996 s.188 (interim duty in cases of apparent priority need, see Guide 13.1 at para.D1–052).

HA 1996, s.190	— HA 1996, s.190 (duty owed to persons threatened with homelessness who are in priority need, see Guide 13.1 at para.D1–052).
HA 1996, s.200	— HA 1996, s.200 (duty owed until decision on referral is notified to applicant, to persons whose cases are referred, or considered for referral to another local housing authority, see Guide 13.1 at para.D1–052).

13.6. Homelessness: The Right to Appeal Against Decisions made in Respect of Accomodation Pending Appeal

D13–006 *HA 1996, s.204(4)* For the circumstances in which the local housing authority has a power to secure accommodation for some types of applicants pending appeal, see s.204(4) and Guide 13.5 at para.D1–056. This guide deals with appeals against decisions in the exercise or non-exercise of that power.

The right of appeal

See Guide 13.5 at para. D1–056. As to level of judge (Circuit Judge) see PD 2 para.9.

HA 1996, s.204(1)

A right of appeal arises under HA 1996, s.204A where:

— an applicant has the right to appeal against a local housing authority's decision on a Review, **and**

— is dissatisfied with a decision by the authority:

(a) not to exercise their power under s.204(4); or

— (b) to exercise that power for a limited period ending before the final determination of the appeal under s.204(1); or

— (c) to cease exercising that power before that time.

When appeal may be brought

An appeal **may** not be brought after final determination *by the county court* of thes.204 appeal itself (the "main" appeal).

HA 1996, s.204A — *N.b.* it appears that the s.204A appeal right ceases after final determination of the main appeal by a county court notwithstanding a possible further appeal to the Court of Appeal and notwithstanding the fact that the s.204(4) power includes a power for the authority to house pending any further appeal.

The orders available on appeal

s.204A(4) — Under s.204A(4) the court:

— **may** order the authority to secure that accommodation is available for the applicant's occupation until the determination of the appeal, or such earlier time as the court may specify;

— **and shall** confirm or quash the decision appealed against. The court, in considering whether to confirm or quash the decision "*shall apply the principles applied by the High Court on an application for judicial review*".

s.204A(5)–(6) — If the court **quashes** the decision it may also order the authority to exercise the power for such period it thinks fit, not being a period which ends after the final determination of the main appeal by the county court, if a failure to exercise the s.204(4) power in accordance with the order would substantially prejudice the applicant's ability to pursue the main appeal.

Procedure

See in particular PD 52 para.24.2 in relation to s.204 and s.204A Appeals.

Procedure is as for s.204 Appeals, but note that normally a s.204A appeal should be included in the same appeal notice as the substantive s.204 Appeal unless the s.204A appeal is urgent.

14. PROBATE AND INHERITANCE PROCEDURE

14.1. Probate and Inheritance Procedure—Probate Claims CPR Pt 57, Pt I

Procedure D14–001

Scope

CPR Pt 57

"probate claim" means a claim for—

(a) the grant of probate of the will, or letters of administration of the estate, of a deceased person;

(b) the revocation of such a grant;

(c) a decree pronouncing for or against the validity of an alleged will not being a claim which is non-contentious (or common form) probate business.

Jurisdiction

CPR r.57.2

Probate claims in the High Court are assigned to Ch.D. Probate Claims brought in the county court may only be brought in a court where there is a Probate District Registry. or the in the Central London County Court.

Commencement

CPR r.57.1 (2)(b)

Under CPR, Pt 7, claim form to be issued only—

(a) in High Court proceedings in a Chancery district registry, that registry;

(b) in any other High Court proceedings, Chancery Chambers at the Royal Courts of Justice, Strand, London, WC2A 2LL;

(c) in the case of county court proceedings, the office of the county court in question.

CPR r.57.6(1)
For contents of statements of case see CPR rr.57.7–57.9

N.b. in a probate claim which seeks the revocation of a grant of probate or letters of administration every person who is entitled, or claims to be entitled, to administer the estate under that grant must be made a party to the claim

Defendant's response

Overseas defendants: see CPR r.57.4(3)

Defendant must file an acknowledgment of service. Period for filing an acknowledgment of service is—

(a) if the defendant is served with a claim form which states that particulars of claim are to follow, 28 days after service of the particulars of claim; and

(b) in any other case, 28 days after service of the claim form .

***Time for filing* defence**

CPR r.15.4 as applied by CPR r.57.4(4)

(a) 14 days after service of the particulars of claim; or

(b) if the defendant files an acknowledgment of service (*n.b.* this is mandatory) 28 days after service of the particulars of claim.

Failure to respond

CPR r.57.10	Special procedure applies, no default judgment: see CPR, r.57.10.

Documents and evidence in probate claims

CPR r.57.5(5)	Except with the permission of the court, a party shall not be allowed to inspect the testamentary documents or written evidence lodged or filed by any other party until he himself has lodged his testamentary documents and filed his evidence .

Lodgment of testamentary documents

CPR r.57.5(1)	Any testamentary document of the deceased person in the possession or control of any party must be lodged with the court.

Evidence of known testamentary documents

CPR r.57.5(3)	Claimant and every defendant who acknowledges service must in written evidence— (a) describe any testamentary document of the deceased of which he has any knowledge or, if he does not know of any such testamentary document, state that fact; and (b) if any testamentary document of which he has knowledge is not in his possession or under his control, give the name and address of the person in whose possession or under whose control it is or, if he does not know the name or address of that person, state that fact.

Time for lodging evidence and documents

CPR r.57.5(4)	Unless the court directs otherwise, the testamentary documents must be lodged— (a) by the claimant when the claim form is issued; and (b) by a defendant when he acknowledges service.

14.2. Probate and Inheritance Procedure—Inheritance (Provision for Family and Dependants) Act 1975, CPR Pt 57, Pt IV

D14–002

CPR r.57.15	If issued in the High Court, must issue in Chancery Division or Family Division.
CPR r.57.15	The Civil Procedure Rules apply to Inheritance Act proceedings in the Family Division, except that the provisions of the Family Proceedings Rules 1991 relating to the drawing up and service of orders apply.

Commencement of claims under s.1 of the Act

CPR Pt 8	The Pt 8 procedure applies.

Acknowledgment of service

CPR r.57.16(4) *Overseas defendants: see CPR r.57.16(4A)*	Time within which a defendant must file and serve— (a) an acknowledgment of service; and (b) any written evidence is not more than 21 days after service of the claim form.
PD 57 para.15	Where a defendant personal representative wishes to remain neutral and agrees to abide by any decision the court may make, state this in Section A of the acknowledgment of service form.

Evidence

CPR r.57.16(3) The written evidence filed and served with the claim must exhibit an official copy of the grant of probate or letters of administration in respect of the deceased's estate and every testamentary document in respect of which probate or letters of administration were granted.

Defendant personal representatives' evidential requirements

CPR r.57.16(5) A defendant who is a personal representative of the deceased must file and serve written evidence, which must state to the best of that person's ability:

PD 57 para.16 (1)
- full details of the value of the deceased's net estate, as defined in s.25(1) of the 1976 Act;

PD 57 para.16(2)
- the person or classes of persons beneficially interested in the estate;
- the names and (unless they are parties to the claim) addresses of all living beneficiaries;
- the value of their interests in the estate so far as they are known;

PD 57 para.16(3)
- whether any living beneficiary (and if so, naming him) is a child or a person who lacks capacity (within the meaning of the Mental Capacity Act 2005); and

PD 57 para.16(4)
- any facts which might affect the exercise of the court's powers under the Act.

Production of grant of representation

PD 57 para.18.1 On the hearing of a claim, personal representative must produce the original grant of representation to the deceased's estate.

Final order in Inheritance Act claim after compromise

PD 57 para 18.3
- A final order embodying terms of compromise made in proceedings under the Act, must contain a direction that a memorandum of the order shall be endorsed on or permanently annexed to the probate or letters of administration.
- A copy of the order shall be sent to the Principal Registry of the Family Division with the relevant grant of probate or letters of administration for endorsement.

15. INSOLVENCY

15.1. *Creditors' Winding-up Petitions*

Establishing insolvency D15–001

Insolvency Act 1986 ss.122 and 123 Insolvency Rules 1986 rr.4.5–4.6 Petitioning creditor serves statutory demand on company or establishes insolvency by other means (*e.g.* by making demand for payment other than by statutory demand, establishing failed execution or other method as set out *in s.123 (see para.3E–57)).*

N.b. there is no procedure enabling the company to apply to set aside a statutory demand. The remedy is to apply for an injunction (see below).

Presentation of petition

Insolvency Rules 1986 r.4.7	Not before 21 days after service of statutory demand (if one has been served) or at any stage after establishing insolvency by other means petitioning creditor delivers to court original petition plus copy to be exhibited to evidence of service and copy for service on company and (where appropriate) for service on administrator, liquidator, supervisor, member state liquidator and Financial Services Authority.
Insolvency Rules 1986 r.4.12	At the same time petitioning creditor files evidence verifying petition and exhibiting draft petition.

Service of petition

Insolvency Rules 1986 r.4.8	Petitioning creditor serves petition on company at its registered office or by other means (*e.g.* service on director or officer or substituted service if order obtained).
Insolvency Rules 1986 rr.4.9–4.10	Petitioning creditor files evidence of service immediately after service.

Injunction

Either before presentation of petition or after presentation but before advertisement company may apply to the judge for an injunction restraining presentation or advertisement.
N.b. there is no procedure enabling the company to apply to set aside a statutory demand. The remedy is to apply for an injunction.

Withdrawal of petition

Insolvency Rules 1986 r.4.15	Provided the petition has not been advertised and no notices of support or opposition have been received, petitioning creditor may at least five days before the hearing of the petition apply, with the consent of the company, to withdraw the petition.

Validation of payments

Insolvency Act 1986 s.127, Practice Note—Validation Orders	(See paras 3E–82 and 3E–125).Company may apply for order that any disposition of property or payment should not be void in the event of the company being wound up on the hearing of the petition. The application should generally be made to the registrar/district judge.

Advertisement

Insolvency Rules 1986 r.4.11	Unless an injunction has been granted restraining advertisement, petitioning creditor advertises petition in *London Gazette* not less than seven business days after service and not less than seven business days before the hearing date.

Certificate of compliance

Insolvency Rules 1986 r.4.14	At least five days before the hearing of the petition, petitioning creditor files in court certificate of compliance showing date of presentation of petition, date of hearing, and dates on which petition was served and advertised together with a copy of the advertisement. *N.b.* failure to do so may result in dismissal of the petition.

Opposition to petition

Insolvency Rules 1986 r.4.18

Not less than seven days before hearing of the petition company files and serves evidence in opposition.
N.b. however that if the company opposes the petition on substantial grounds the court may give directions for filing and service evidence at the hearing even if the company has not complied with the rule.

Hearing

Insolvency Rules 1986 rr.4.16–4.17

Petitioning creditor lodges list of opposing or supporting creditors (if any) or "negative list' (if no notices have been received).
Court makes order:

- adjourning petition (and giving directions for trial of the petition if it is opposed);
- dismissing petition;
- winding up company (and declaration as to applicability of EC Regulation on Insolvency Proceedings and whether proceedings are main, secondary or territorial).

Rescission

Insolvency Rules 1986 r.7.47

Petitioner or company may apply to review, rescind or vary winding up order.
N.b. in the RCJ the person applying must complete a form identifying himself and confirming that he has notified the Official Receiver and the petitioner. He must also file evidence in support of the application.

See generally PDIP, para.7

Application should be made within seven days on notice to Official Receiver.

Appeal

See generally PDIP, para.17 and CPR r.52.3

Appeal from a decision of a registrar/district judge lies to a single judge of the Chancery Division.
The appeal requires permission and should be made within 21 days.

15.2. Proceedings under s.6 of the Company Directors Disqualification Act 1986 (CDDA 1986)

Jurisdiction: the company must have "become insolvent" D15–002

CDDA 1986 s.6(1) and (2), s.22(2) and (3) Insolvency Act 1986 s.247

A company becomes insolvent if:

(a) the company goes into liquidation at a time when its assets are insufficient for the payment of its debts and other liabilities and the expenses of the winding up,
(b) the company enters administration, or
(c) an administrative receiver of the company is appointed.

In this context, "goes into liquidation" means the passing of a resolution for voluntary winding up, or when a winding up order is made by the court. If a winding up order is made subsequent to a resolution for voluntary winding up, the time of the winding up resolution is the relevant time for the purposes of CDDA 1986.
The expression "company" includes an unregistered company and a company incorporated outside Great Britain which has an established place of business in Great Britain.

Jurisdiction: the person must have been a director

CDDA 1986, s.6(1) and (3C), s.22(4) and (5)

The word "director" includes any person occupying the position of director, by whatever name called (i.e. CDDA 1986 covers formally appointed directors, "de jure" directors, and shadow directors).

Report of office-holder

CDDA 1986, s.6(1), s.7(3)

If it appears to the office holder acting in the company insolvency that the conditions in CDDA, s.6(1) are present (i.e. that a person has been a director of a company which has become insolvent, and that his conduct as a director (either taken alone or taken together with his conduct as a director of any other company or companies) makes him unfit to be concerned in the management of a company), he shall forthwith report the matter to the Secretary of State. Detailed provisions as to the form and timing of the report are set out in the Insolvent Companies (Reports on Conduct of Directors) Rules 1996.

Notification of intention to apply for disqualification order

CDDA 1986, s.7(1), s.16(1)

A person intending to apply for the making of a disqualification order "shall give not less than 10 days' notice" of his intention to do so. Failure to give the proper notice is a procedural irregularity which does not nullify the application. The relevant person applying is normally the Secretary of State for Business, Enterprise and Regulatory Reform (formerly the Secretary of State for Trade and Industry), but can also be the Official Receiver. References below to "the Secretary of State" should be treated as including both.

As a matter of current practice, once the Secretary of State has formed a preliminary view that it is expedient in the public interest that a disqualification order under s.6 should be made against a person, the Secretary of State will communicate that view to that person, and invite that person's comments.

Disqualification undertaking

CDDA 1986, s.1A

Once a person is aware of the Secretary of State's preliminary view that it is expedient that a disqualification order be made, that person can offer a disqualification undertaking: i.e. an undertaking that for a period specified in the undertaking the person (a) will not be a director of a company, act as a receiver of a company's property or in any way, whether directly or indirectly, be concerned or take part in the promotion, formation or management of a company unless he has the leave of the court, and (b) will not act as an insolvency practitioner.

If an undertaking is accepted by the Secretary of State before proceedings are commenced, there is then no need to commence proceedings. It remains possible for a defendant to offer, and the Secretary of State to accept, a disqualification undertaking after proceedings have been commenced, and up until the court delivers judgment on the substantive disqualification application.

Limitation/proceedings

CDDA 1986, s.6(3) and (3B), s.7(2)

If no offer of a disqualification undertaking acceptable to the Secretary of State has been received, and the Secretary of State remains of the view that it is expedient in the public interest that a disqualification order should be made, then proceedings will be issued by Part 8 claim form supported by evidence. Except with the leave of the court, an application for a disqualification order shall not be made after the end of the period of 2 years beginning with the day on which the relevant company became insolvent.

Where the company is being wound up by the court, the relevant court for proceedings is that court: often this will be a County Court, even if the company was originally wound up in the Companies Court, as winding up proceedings are often transferred. Otherwise, the relevant court for proceedings is any court which had jurisdiction to wind the company up – the Companies Court will always have jurisdiction to wind such a company up, and as a matter of convenience to the Secretary of State, a substantial proportion of disqualification cases arising out of voluntary liquidations and administrations are therefore brought in the Companies Court.

Proceedings are not invalidated by reason of having been commenced in the wrong court.

Service of Disqualification Proceedings

Directors Disqualification Proceedings PD para.7
Insolvent Companies (Disqualification of Unfit Directors) Proceedings Rules 1987
Disqualification Rules 1987

Service is by the Secretary of State, and is normally by first class post at the defendant's last known address. Where the defendant resides outside England and Wales, the court may order service to be effected within such time and in such manner as it thinks fit, and may require such proof of service as it thinks fit.

Acknowledgment of service

Directors Disqualification Proceedings PD para.8
Disqualification Rules 1987 r.5(4)

The defendant should file an acknowledgment of service in the prescribed form not more than 14 days after service of the claim form. He should also serve the acknowledgment of service on the Secretary of State and on any other defendants.

Unless he has filed an acknowledgment of service, the defendant may attend but may not take part in a hearing, unless the court gives permission.

Evidence

Directors Disqualification Proceedings PD para.9
Disqualification Rules 1987 r.6

Evidence shall be by affidavit (or affirmation), save where the Official Receiver is a party, in which case he may give evidence in the form of a written report. The rules provide that the defendant's evidence in answer shall be filed within 28 days of service on him of the claim form. In practice, this is rarely achieved, and at the first hearing of the disqualification application (see below) directions as to evidence are normally given if the case is contested

Parties are nevertheless expected to file and serve their evidence well in advance of the trial of the proceedings, and the court is prepared to debar parties from adducing evidence if it is not produced within the timetable the court has ordered.

The first hearing of the disqualification application/directions hearing

Directors Disqualification Proceedings PD paras 1(7) and 10
Disqualification Rules 1987 r.7
Insolvency Rules 1986 r.13(2)
Courts and Legal Services Act 1990 s.74

The first hearing is before a registrar in open court, and shall be not less than 8 weeks from the date of issue of the claim form. The registrar can either determine the case (if it is uncontested, and does not merit a period of disqualification longer than 5 years), or give directions and adjourn it.

Where an uncontested case merits a period of disqualification of longer than 5 years it will be disposed of at the second hearing, provided there is sufficient time.

Evidence directions will normally simply provide for evidence in answer from defendants, and evidence in reply from the Secretary of State. Further rounds of evidence are possible, but unusual.

Expert evidence is rarely ordered, and expert evidence on questions such as whether a company was insolvent will almost never be appropriate.

In the context of the disqualification proceedings, "registrar" includes a district judge of a High Court District Registry or of a County Court.

Summary procedure (*Carecraft*)

Directors Disqualification Proceedings PD para.13

At any time after proceedings have been issued, and before judgment has been delivered, it is open to the parties to invite the court to deal with the case under the procedure adopted in *Re Carecraft Construction Co Ltd* [1994] 1 W.L.R. 172.

The parties must submit a written statement of material facts which (for the purposes of the application) are either agreed or not opposed, and must specify a period of disqualification, band of years or bracket (i.e. 2–5 years, 6–10 years or 11–15 years) into which they will submit the case falls.

The *Carecraft* hearing will normally be in private, but if the court is willing to accept the parties' submissions (which will normally be the case) then it will usually give judgment and make the disqualification order in public.

If the court does not accept the *Carecraft* settlement, then it will give directions for the future conduct of the case.

Carecraft settlements have become relatively rare since undertakings became available.

The trial

Directors Disqualification Proceedings PD para.12
CDDA 1986, s.1(1)

Once all directions have been complied with, the disqualification application will be set down for trial. It is standard for all deponents to be ordered to attend for cross-examination at trial, normally on 21 days' notice, and if a party wishes a deponent not to be subject to this requirement, a specific release should ordinarily be sought at the time the cross-examination direction is made. The court will require a good justification for a deponent to be released in this way.

Although some trials in the Companies Court are dealt with by High Court Judges, the majority are heard by registrars. Similarly in the District Registries and the County Courts, the majority of trials are heard by district judges. Trials take place in open court, and advocates are robed.

If the court is satisfied that the defendant has been a director of a company which has become insolvent within the meaning of CDDA 1986, and that his conduct as director of that company (either taken alone or taken together with his conduct as a director of any other company or companies) makes him unfit to be concerned in the management of a company, then the court is obliged to make a disqualification order for not less than 2, and not more than 15, years. A disqualification order is an order that for a period specified in the order the person (a) will not be a director of a company, act as a receiver of a company's property or in any way, whether directly or indirectly, be concerned or take part in the promotion, formation or management of a company unless he has the leave of the court, and (b) will not act as an insolvency practitioner.

16. RESERVED JUDGMENTS

16.1 Reserved Judgments

When does this guide apply? D16–001

PD 40E para.1 Where judgment is given in the Court of Appeal (Civil Division), Queen's Bench Division and Chancery Division (including judgments by judges, masters, registrars and costs judges).

Reserved judgments available before handing down

Where judgment is reserved the judge may invite the views of the representatives as to arrangements for handing down of judgment.

Procedure

PD 40E para.2.3
PD 40E para.2.6 Unless directed otherwise the procedure which applies (in the absence of any special degree of confidentiality or sensitivity) is that the court will provide a copy of the draft judgment to the representatives by 4pm on the second working day before handing down, or at such other time as the court may direct. The case will be listed for judgment and judgment will be handed down at the appropriate time.

PD 40E para.2.4 The representatives may show the draft judgment to the parties provided that neither the judgment nor its substance is disclosed to any other person or used in the public domain and that no action is taken (other than internally) in response to the judgment prior to handing down.

Corrections to the draft judgment

PD 40E para.5 Unless told otherwise when the draft judgment is circulated any proposed corrections to the judgment should be sent to the clerk to the judge who prepared the draft, with a copy to any other party.

Attendance at handing down

PD 40E para.3	The parties need not attend handing down if any consequential orders have been agreed. The judgment may be handed down by a single member of the court if the parties do not indicate that they intent to attend. If an advocate attends then court may disallow costs of attendance if it considers that attendance was unnecessary.

Agreed consequential orders

PD 40E paras 4.1–4.2	Unless told otherwise when the draft judgment is circulated, any agreed consequential orders must be faxed or emailed to the clerk to the judge together with any proposed corrections or amendments to the draft judgment) and four copies with completed backsheets must be filed in the relevant court office by 12 noon on the working day before handing down. The draft order must bear the case reference, date of handing down, and the name of the judge.

Presiding judge

References to judge in this guide should be read as "Presiding judge" where there is a presiding judge.

17. INJUNCTIONS

17.1 Freezing orders (including "Mareva" orders)

D17–001 In general, see CPR 25 and notes thereto, and Pt 15 of Volume 2 of this work for a comprehensive guide to Interim Remedies.

CPR 25.1(1)(f)	The court may grant an order which (i) restrains a party from removing from the jurisdiction assets which are located within the jurisdiction or (ii) restraining a party from dealing with any assets whether they are located within the jurisdiction or not.

Jurisdiction

PD (Allocation of Cases to Levels of Judiciary) para.2.1 *PD (Interim Injunctions) para.1.2* *County Courts Remedies Regs.1991 r.3(3)*	A freezing order may be made only by a Judge. Masters and District judges in the **High Court** have the power to make a freezing order only by consent or where connected with a charging order or appointment of a receiver, or in aid of execution of judgments. In the **county courts** jurisdiction is governed by County Courts Remedies Regs 1991 and the general starting point is that a county court may not make a freezing order save where the judge is a nominated Circuit Judge in a patents county court or mercantile court or where the judge is a High Court 1991 Judge sitting as a county court for a district. Further exceptions where a freezing order may be made by a county court judge are where the order is made for preservation, custody or detention of property which forms or may form the subject matter of proceedings (i.e. by way of a proprietary claim) or where the order is made in aid of execution of a judgment or order made in a county court to preserve assets until execution can be levied on them.

High Court in aid of county court

Schmidt v Wong (Practice Note) [2005] EWCA Civ 1506

The High Court may make an injunction in the course of or in anticipation of county court proceedings where a county court may not make such an order. Where it is necessary to follow this procedure use Pt 23 and issue the application in the High Court returnable before a Judge. Do not issue a separate claim for an injunction. See Pt 15 Volume 2 of this work at 3(c) for text of wording of application.

Chabra orders TSB Private Bank Intl. SA v Chabra [1992] 1 W.L.R. 231

Where a defendant is subject to a freezing order restraining him from disposing of company assets the court has jurisdiction to join the company as a defendant and to make a corresponding order against it despite there being no direct cause of action against the company.

Procedure & evidence

CPR Pt 23 Modified by PD (Interim Injunctions) para.2.1

Typically the application is made without notice. If made before issue of a claim the order sought should set out directions for issue of a claim for substantive relief. The application must state the order sought and the time, date and place of the hearing. Unless made without notice it must be served as soon as practicable after issue and in any event not less than three days before hearing. A draft of the order sought should be filed with the application notice.

PD (Interim Injunctions) para.3.1

Evidence must be by affidavit.
Evidence must set out all the material facts of which the court should be made aware and (if made without notice) must state why.

Duty of full and frank Disclosure
Chancery Guide para.5.16
Memory Corp v Sidhu [2000] 1 W.L.R. 1443 CA

Where made without notice the applicant must investigate the facts and fairly present them to the court including all matters of fact or law which are or may be adverse to the applicant's case. The duty is a high one and requires full, fair and accurate disclosure of material information and to draw the court's attention to significant factual legal and procedural aspects.

Criteria (Domestic freezing Orders)

Generally the applicant must show that he has a good arguable case see Volume 2 Pt 15at 5(a)on a substantive claim over which the court has jurisdiction, that the defendant has assets within the jurisdiction and that there is a real risk of dissipation or secretion of assets which would render the claimant's relief nugatory.

Criteria (Worldwide freezing Orders)

Volume 2 Pt 15at 6(b)

Generally the applicant must show that he has a good arguable case see Volume 2 atPt 15 6(b), that the defendant has no assets or insufficient assets within the jurisdiction to satisfy the claim, that there are assets outside the jurisdiction, and that there is a real risk of dissipation or secretion of assets which would render the claimant's relief nugatory.
The court should also consider whether undertakings or provisions in the order should be included for the purpose of protecting the position of foreign third parties and to protect the defendant from oppression.

Urgent applications

See special procedure in PD (Interim Injunctions) para. 4.1 which provides a telephone procedure for out of hours applications and a procedure for urgent hearings during court hours.

Form of freezing order

A form of order which may be adapted to the facts of the case appears annexed to Practice Direction (Interim Injunctions) (the text is in the forms volume of this work or can be accessed via the DCA CPR website under PD 25) and the applicant should especially note the undertakings which the order includes. See also PD (Interim Injunctions) para.5.1.

Further guidance

For further guidance see Volume 2 Pt 15, s.Bgenerally.

17.2 Search orders ("Anton Piller" orders)

D17–002 In general, see CPR 25 and notes thereto, and Pt 15of Volume 2 of this work for a comrehensive guide to Interim Remedies.

CPR 25.1(1)(h) *Civil Procedure Act 1997 s.7*	The court may grant an order which requires a party to admit another party to premises for the purposes of preserving evidence etc.
Jurisdiction	
PD (Allocation of Cases to Levels of Judiciary) para.2.1. *PD (Interim Injunctions) para.8.5 and Elvee Ltd v Taylor [2001] EWCA Civ 1943* *County Courts Remedies Regs [1991] r.3(2)*	A search order in the **High Court** is made under s.7 of the Civil Procedure Act 1997 and may only be made by a Judge. In intellectual property cases the application should be made in the Chancery division and it may be a material non disclosure to fail to draw that requirement to the attention of the In the county courts jurisdiction is governed by the County Courts Remedies Regs 1991 and the starting point is that a county court judge may not make a search order save where the judge is a nominated Circuit Judge in a patents county court or where the judge is a High Court Judge sitting as a county court for a district.
Procedure & Evidence	**Typically the application is made without notice**
CPR Pt 23 *Modified by PD (Interim Injunctions) para.2.1*	If made before issue of a claim the order sought should set out directions for issue of a claim for substantive relief. The application must state the order sought and the time, date and place of the hearing. Unless made without notice it must be served as soon as practicable after issue and in any event not less than three days before hearing. A draft of the order sought should be filed with the application notice.
PD (Interim Injunctions) para.3.1	Evidence must be by affidavit. Evidence must set out all the material facts of which the court should be made aware and (if made without notice) must state why.
Duty of full and frank Disclosure *Chancery Guide para.5.16* *Memory Corp v Sidhu [2000] 1 W.L.R. 1443 CA*	Where made without notice the applicant must investigate the facts and fairly present them to the court including all matters of fact or law which are or may be adverse to the applicant's case. The duty is a high one and requires full, fair and accurate disclosure of material information and to draw the court's attention to significant factual legal and procedural aspects.
Criteria	
	The applicant must show that it is necessary to make the order in the interests of justice and must satisfy various criteria summarised in *Indicii Salus v Chandrasekaran* [2006] EWHC 521 (Ch.) set out in Vol. 2 Pt 15at .s.3

Urgent applications

See special procedure in PD (Interim Injunctions) para.4.1 which provides a telephone procedure for out of hours applications and a procedure for urgent hearings during court hours.

Form of search order

A form of order which may be adapted to the facts of the case appears annexed to Practice Direction (Interim Injunctions) (the text is in the forms volume of this work or can be accessed via the DCA CPR website under PD 25) and the applicant should especially note the undertakings which the order includes. See also PD (Interim Injunctions) para.5.1.

Further guidance

For further guidance on search orders see Vol.2 Section 15 (C. Search Orders) generally.

SECTION E

TABLE OF TIME LIMITS

SECTION E

TIME TABLE UNDER CPR

TABLES SHOWING THE TIMES FIXED FOR TAKING VARIOUS PROCEEDINGS

[—As to computation of the times mentioned in this Table, see CPR, Pt 2, r.8]

E1–001

EVENT	TIME LIMIT	

Acceptance of Money Paid into Court (Part 36 Payments)

Money paid into court in satisfaction can be accepted in satisfaction and the action terminated if notice of such acceptance is given	within 21 days after receipt of notice of payment. Where a payment is made less than 21 days before trial, the offer may only be accepted if the parties agree liability for costs or the court gives permission (CPR, r. 36.5(6), (7)).	E1–002

Additional Claims

Please see "Counterclaims and Additional Claims". E1–003

Acknowledgment of Service

(a) where the defendant is served with a claim form which states that particulars of claim are to follow the period for acknowledgment of service is	14 days after service of the particulars of claim (CPR, r. 10.3(1)(a)).	E1–004
(b) in any other case the period for acknowledgment of service is	14 days after service of the claim form (CPR, r. 10.3(1)(b)). (Where the claim is served overseas—see CPR, r. 6.22).	

Admission of Documents

A party shall be deemed to admit the authenticity of a document disclosed under CPR, Pt 31 unless he serves a notice that he wishes the document to be proved at trial. The Notice must be served	by the latest date for serving witness statements or within seven days of disclosure of the document, whichever is the later (CPR, r. 32.19).	E1–005

Admissions of Fact

A party may serve notice on another party requiring him to admit the facts specified in the notice (CPR, r. 32.18). The notice must be served	no later than 21 days before trial (CPR, r. 32.18(2)).	E1–006

Admissions of liability to pay

A party may admit the whole or part of a money claim by returning an admission form within	14 days after service of the claim form or where the Claim form specified that Particulars of Claim would follow, 14 days after service of the Particulars of Claim (CPR, r. 14.2). (Where the claim is served overseas—see CPR, r. 6.22).	E1–007

Appeals

E1–008 1. TO HOUSE OF LORDS

2. GENERALLY

See CPR, Pt 52, PD 52 and The Access to Justice Act 1999 (Destination of Appeals) Order 2000 (SI 2000 /1071) ("DoA Order")

Pt 52 governs appeals other than in Family Proceedings or where an enactment makes other provision. See s.16(1) of the SCA 1981 and s.77(1) of the CCA 1984. For small claims see CPR PD 52 para.5.8.

Note

In CPR Pt 52:

" **final decision**" means a decision of a court that would finally determine (subject to any possible appeal or detailed assessment of costs) the entire proceedings whichever way the court decided the issues. See DoA Order art.1(2)(c)). But note that orders made on summary assessment of costs are not final orders, nor are orders for enforcement (CPR PD 52 para.2A.5).

A decision is deemed a "final decision" where it is made at the conclusion of part of a hearing or trial which has been split into parts and would, if made at the conclusion of that hearing or trial, be a final decision under DoA Order art.1(2)(c). (DoA Order art.1(3)).

" **Permission to appeal**" where required by CPR r.52.3 is sought by a request in the Appeal Notice.

To appeal, an Appeal Notice, stating the grounds for appeal and if required seeking permission to appeal must generally be filed no later than	21 days from the order sought to be appealed, served as soon as practicable on the respondents and not later than seven days after filing in any event (CPR r. 52.4)
3. TO AND FROM ADMINISTRATIVE COURT (Judicial Review)	See CPR Pt 54 and (for appeals) CPR r. 52.15.

4. FROM THE COUNTY COURT OR HIGH COURT

(i) From a Circuit Judge or equivalent

Save as stated in (a) and (b) below, appeal lies (with permission if required)	to a Judge of the High Court (CPR PD 2A.1)
(a) For a final decision in a claim allocated to the multi-track under rules 12.7, 14.8 or 26.5 of the CPR or made in specialist proceedings under Companies Act 1985 or 1989, or Parts I–III of CPR 57, or CPR Pts 58–63.	to the Court of Appeal (DoA Order Art.4, PD 52 para.2A.2).
(b) Where an appeal is made to a county court (other than from the decision of an officer of the court authorised to assess costs by the Lord Chancellor) and on hearing the appeal the court makes a decision, an appeal shall lie from that decision	to the Court of Appeal (DoA Order Art.5).

(ii) From a District Judge (or deputy District Judge) of the county court

Subject to (a) and (b) below, where the decision to be appealed is made by a district judge or deputy district *judge of a county* court, an appeal lies	to a judge of a county court (DoA Order Art.3, CPR PD 52 para.2A.1).

(a) For a final decision in a claim allocated to the multi-track under rules 12.7, 14.8 or 26.5 of the CPR or made in specialist proceedings under the Companies Acts1985 and 1989, or Parts I–III of CPR Pt 57 or CPR Pts 58–63.	to the Court of Appeal (DoA Order Art.4, CPR PD 52 para.2A.2).
(b) Where an appeal is made to a county court (other than from the decision of an officer of the court authorised to assess costs by the Lord Chancellor) and on hearing the appeal the court makes a decision, an appeal shall lie from that decision	to the Court of Appeal (DoA Order Art.5).

(iii) From a Master or District Judge (or deputy) of the High Court

Subject to (a) and (b) below, where the decision to be appealed is made by a Master or district judge of the High court, an appeal lies	to a judge of the High Court (DoA Order Art.2, CPR PD 52 para.2A.1)
(a) For a final decision in a claim allocated to the multi-track under rules 12.7, 14.8 or 26.5 of the CPRor made in proceedings to which CPR r.49(2) refers. *(i.e.* Specialist Proceedings), appeal lies	to the Court of Appeal (DoA Order Art.4, CPR PD 52 para.2A.2).
(b) Where an appeal is made to the High Court (other than from the decision of an officer of the court authorised to assess costs by the Lord Chancellor) and on hearing the appeal the court makes a decision, an appeal shall lie from that decision	to the Court of Appeal (DoA Order Art.5).

(iv) From a Judge of the High Court (or equivalent)

Appeal lies, with permission if required,	to the Court of Appeal (PD 52 para.2A.1).

(v) Appeals from decisions of Tribunals and various appeals under Enactments

See CPR PD 52 para.20

5. RESPONDENT'S NOTICE

(i) Generally

If a respondent's notice is to be given it must be filed within—	
	(a) *such period* as may be directed by the lower court; or

	(b) where the court makes no such direction, 14 days after: the date the respondent is served with the appellant's notice where permission to appeal was given by the lower court or permission to appeal is not required; or the date the respondent is served with notification that the appeal court has given the appellant permission to appeal; or the date the respondent is served with notification that the application for permission to appeal and the appeal itself are to be heard together. (CPR r.52.5(4) & (5))
The respondent's notice must be served on the appellant and any other respondent	as soon as practicable and in any event not later than seven days after it is filed. CPR r.52.5(6))

(ii) further requirement in Court of Appeal

A respondent must also inform the Civil Appeals Office and the appellant in writing whether— (a) he proposes to file a respndent's notice appealing the order for reasons different from, or additional to, those given by the lower court; or (b) he proposes to rely on the reasons given by the lower court for its decision.	no later than 21 days after the date he is served with notification that permission to appeal has been granted; or the application for permission to appeal and the appeal are to be heard together. (PD 52 para.15.6)

Applications to re-open a final appeal or application for permission to appeal

E1–009

Where the court directs that the application for permission is to be served on another party, that party may (CPR PD 52 para.25.6)	within **14** days of the copy of the application file and serve a written statement either supporting or opposing the application.

Applications to set aside and/or direct a re-hearing

E1–010

1. SMALL CLAIMS TRACK

For a re-hearing, where the award or judgment was given in that party's absence and the party was not represented, made by application on notice filed	no more than 14 days after the day on which notice of the judgment was served on him (CPR r. 27.11(2)).

2. OTHER ORDERS MADE AT TRIAL

Where an order striking out a statement of case or party or the whole of proceedings is made in the absence of either party the absent party may apply to set aside the order	under CPR r. 39.3(3), no time limit specified, but applicatnt must show he acted promptly and also satisfy criteria at CPR r.39.3(5).

3. LANDLORD AND TENANT CLAIMS

See "Application to set aside" under "Recovery of Land, accelerated Procedure"

Arrest

E1–011

1. ARREST OF THE PERSON	
Where a person is arrested under a power of arrest attached to an order of the court under Family Law Act 1996 Pt I, that person must be brought before the court	within 24 hours (Family Law Act 1996 s.47(7)).

Assessment of Costs (Detailed)

E1–012

(a) Commencement	
Where the source of the order for detailed assessment is a judgment, direction, order award or other determination	the assessment proceedings must be commenced within three months of the judgment, etc., or three months of the lifting of any stay pending appeal (CPR r. 47.7).
Where the source of the order for detailed assessment is discontinuance under Pt 38	the assessment proceedings must be commenced within three months of service of notice of discontinuance or three months of dismissal of an application to set aside a notice of discontinuance under CPR, r. 38.4 (CPR r. 47.7).
Where the source of the order for detailed assessment is acceptance of an offer to settle, or a payment into court under Pt 36	the assessment proceedings must be commenced within three months after the date when the right to costs arose (CPR r. 47.7).
Where the assessment is to be of the costs of an assisted person payable out of the "Community and Legal Fund", the assisted persons solicitor may commence assessment proceedings by filing a request	within three months after the date when the right to the detailed assessment arose (CPR r. 47.17(2)).
(b) Service of points of dispute and reply	
The paying party and any other party to the detailed assessment may dispute any item by serving points of dispute	within 21 days after service of notice of commencement (CPR r. 47.9).
Where points of dispute are served, the receiving party may serve a reply	within 21 days after service of the points of dispute (CPR, r. 47.13).
(c) Application for a detailed hearing	
Where points of dispute have been served, the receiving party must apply for a detailed assessment hearing	within three months of expiry of the period for commencing assessment proceedings (CPR, r 47.14).
(d) Filing the completed bill of costs	
Where detailed assessment of costs has taken place the time for filing the completed bill is	14 days after the end of the detailed assessment hearing (CPR r. 47.16).
(e) Appeals against detailed assessment by authorised court officers	
Notice of appeal must be served	within 14 days after "the date of the decision" (CPR r. 47.22).

Assessment of Costs (Summary)

E1–013	Each party who intends to claim costs must prepare a written statement of the costs in any case where a summary assessment will be made (for which see para.13 to the Costs PD and must file and serve it	as soon as possible and in any event not less than 24 hours before the date fixed for the hearing (para.13.5(4) to the Costs PD). See Form N260.

Attachment of Debts see Garnishee

E1–014

Charging Orders

E1–015	Service of the documents specified in CPR r. r.73.	not less than 21 days before the hearing (CPR r. r.73.5(1)).

Claim Form

E1–016	Claim form must be served	within four months of issue, or six months where it is to be served out of the jurisdiction (CPR r. 7.5). But see " Landlord and Tenant Act 1954 s.24" below.

Claim, Particulars of—See Statements of Case

E1–017

Contribution or Indemnity

E1–018 *Please see "Counterclaims and Additional Claims".*

Costs Orders

E1–019	Where the court makes an order for costs against a legally represented party and the party is not present when the order is made the party's solicitor must notify his client in writing of the costs order	not later than seven days after the solicitor receives notice of the order (CPR r. 44.2).

Counterclaims and Additional Claims

E1–020	(a) A defendant may make a counterclaim against a claimant	without permission if he files it with his defence, or at any other time with the court's permission CPR r.20.4.
	(b) Counterclaims against non-parties may be made	with the court's permision CPR r.20.4
	(c) Claims for an indemnity or a contribution from a co-defendant may be made without permission provided	the Notice under CPR r.20.6 is served with the defence or, (if the claim is against a defendant who was joined later), within 28 days after the joinder of that party. (CPR r.20.6(2))
	(d) Where an Additional claim is made without the court's permission it must be served	(in the case of a counterclaim against an existing party), when the defence is served, or (in the case of any other additional claim, within 14 days after date of issue of the additional claim form. *Nb.* the above does not apply to claims (Notices) seeking a contribution or an indemnity. (CPR r.20.8).

Default Judgment

See **Judgments** (b) and (c). E1–021

Defence

See **Statements of Case**. E1–022

Discontinuance

E1–023

(a) The claimant may discontinue the proceedings wholly or in part by filing notice of discontinuance and serving it on every other party	at any time CPR r. 38.2(1) save where permission is required by CPR r. 38.2(2).
(b) Where a defendant is served with a notice of discontinuance without requiring the court's permission, he may apply to set the notice aside	within 28 days of service of the notice of discontinuance on him (CPR r. 38.4(2)).
(c) Where all or part of a claim is discontinued the claimant is liable to pay the costs of a defendant against whom the claim was discontinued (CPR r. 38.6). The remainder of the proceedings may be stayed where the claimant is liable to pay those costs and fails to do so	within 14 days of the date on which the parties agreed the costs payable or 14 days of the date on which the court ordered the costs to be paid (CPR r. 38.8).

Disclosure and inspection

E1–024

(a) On the Fast Track, disclosure will take place	according to the court's directions but typically four weeks after notice of allocation (Practice Direction to Pt 28 para.3.12).
(b) On the Multi-Track disclosure will take place	as directed by the court in exercise of its case management functions (CPR r. 29.2).
(c) On the Small Claims Track where standard directions apply under CPR r. 27.4, disclosure will take place by sending to every other party copies of all documents on which the party intends to rely	at least 14 days before the date fixed for the hearing (CPR r. 27.4(3)).
(d) Where a party has a right to inspect a document the party having the right must give notice of his wish to inspect it and the party who disclosed it must permit inspection	not more than seven days after the date on which he received the notice, and the party inspecting may request a copy of the document If the party so requesting undertakes to pay reasonable copying costs the party who disclosed the document must supply a copy within seven days after the date of the request (CPR r. 31.15).

Evidence

1. BY DEPOSITION E1–025

A party intending to put in evidence a deposition at a hearing must serve notice of intention to do so on every party	at least 21 days before the day fixed for the hearing (CPR r. 34.11(3)).

	2. HEARSAY—CIVIL EVIDENCE ACT 1995	
	(a) Where a party proposes to rely on hearsay evidence does not propose to call the person who made the original statement to give oral evidence, the court may allow another party to call and cross-examine that person, on application	made not later than 14 days after service of the hearsay notice (CPR r. 33.4(2)).
	(b) Where a party tenders as hearsay evidence a statement made by a person but does not call the person who made the statement to give evidence, and another party wishes to call evidence to attack the credibility of the person who made the statement	the party wishing to attack the credibility of the witness must give notice to the party tendering the hearsay evidence not more than 14 days after service of the hearsay notice (CPR r. 33.5(2)).
	(c) Evidence of findings on foreign law. Where a party intends to put in evidence a finding on a question of foreign law by virtue of s.4(2) of the Civil Evidence Act 1972 he must	give any other party notice of his intention, (if there are witness statements) not later than the latest date for serving them or (otherwise) not less than 21 days before the hearing at which he proposes to put the finding in evidence (CPR r. 33.7).

Execution

E1–026	(a) A warrant of execution shall not issue without the leave of the court	after six or more years have elapsed since the date of the judgment or order (CCR O.26, r.5(1)(a)).
	(b) A warrant of execution shall in the first instance be valid for	12 months beginning with the date of its issue (CCR O.26, r.6(1)).
	(c) A warrant of execution which has not been wholly executed may be renewed from time to time, on application	for a period of 12 months at any one time, beginning with the next day following that on which it would otherwise expire (CCR O.26, r.6(1)).

Garnishee Orders

E1–027 (*See* Third Party Debt Orders.)

Indemnity (notice seeking)

E1–028 *Please see "Counterclaims and Additional Claims".*

Interim payment

E1–029	(a) Application for an interim payment under CPR r. 25.6 may be made	after the end of the period for filing an Acknowledgment of service (CPR r. 25.6(1)).
	(b) A copy of an application notice for an order for an interim payment must be served	at least 14 days before the hearing of the application (CPR r. 25.6(3)).
	(c) A respondent to an application for an order for an interim payment who wishes to rely on written evidence must file and serve the witness statement	at least seven days before the hearing of the application (CPR r. 25.6(4)).
	(d) If the applicant wishes to rely on written evidence in reply he must file and serve the written evidence	at least three days before the hearing of the application (CPR r. 25.6(5)).

Judgments

1. DEFAULT JUDGMENT E1–030

(a) Judgment in default of Acknowledgment of service (where permitted by CPR r. 12.2) may be obtained	where the Defendant has not filed an Acknowledgment of service or a defence and the time for doing so has expired (CPR r. 12.3(1)(b)).
(b) Judgment in default of defence (where permitted by CPR r. 12.2) may be obtained	where the Defendant has filed an Acknowledgment of service but has not filed a defence and the time for doing so has expired, or where a counterclaim has been made under CPR r. 20.4, where a defence has not been filed in time (CPR r. 12.3(2)).

2. SUMMARY JUDGMENT

(a) Summary Judgment under CPR r. 24.2 where there is no real prospect of success on the claim or issue, or the defendant has no real prospect of successfully defending the claim or issue. Where a claimant wishes to apply for summary judgment	he may not do so until the defendant has filed an Acknowledgment of service or a defence, unless the court gives permission or a practice direction provides otherwise (CPR r. 24.4(1)), (For proceedings against the Crown see CPR r.24.4(1A)).
(b) Where a summary judgment hearing is fixed, the respondent (or the parties, where the hearing is fixed of the court's own initiative) must be given	at least 14 days' notice of the date fixed for the hearing and the issue which it is proposed that the court will decide at the hearing (CPR r. 24.4(3)) (or as varied by any relevant practice direction)—CPR r. 24.4(4).
(c) If the respondent to a summary judgment application wishes to rely on written evidence at the hearing he must file and serve the witness statement	at least seven days before the summary judgment hearing (CPR r. 24.5(1)).
(d) If the applicant wishes to rely on a witness statement in reply he must file and serve it	at least three days before the summary judgment hearing (CPR r. 24.5(2)).
(e) Where a summary judgment hearing is fixed of the courts own initiative, any party who wishes to rely on written evidence at the hearing must file and serve it	at least seven days before the hearing (CPR r. 24.5(3)(a)) and any party wishing to rely on written evidence in reply must file and serve it at least three days before the date of the hearing (CPR r. 24.5(3)(b)).

Judicial Review, Application for

See **Appeals**, (Judicial Review) and CPR Pt 54. E1–031

Landlord and Tenant Act 1954 s.24

(CPR Pt 56. *In force from October 15, 2001*) E1–032

A claim for a new tenancy under s.24 of the Landlord and Tenant Act 1985 must be served	within two months after date of issue (CPR r. 56.3(3) (unopposed claims) or r.56.3(4) (opposed claims)).

Litigation Friends

E1–033	(a) A person who wishes to act as litigation friend for a defendant or a claimant must file the authorisation (under the Mental Health Act 1983 Pt VII) or the certificate of suitability stating that he satisfies the conditions of CPR r. 21.4(3)	in the case of a person wishing to act as litigation friend for a claimant, at the time when the claim is made, and in the case of a person wishing to act as litigation friend for a defendant, at the time when he first takes a step in the proceedings on behalf of the defendant (CPR r. 21.5(4) and (5)).
	(b) When a party ceases to be a child at age 18 the litigation friend's appointment ceases. Where a party ceases to be a patient, the litigation friend's appointment continues until ended by court order. The child or patient must then serve notice complying with CPR r. 21.9(4) and if he does not do so	within 28 days after the date on which the litigation friend's appointment ceases, the court may on application, strike out any claim or defence brought by him (CPR r. 21.9(5)).

New Trial

E1–034 *See* **Applications to set aside and/or direct a re-hearing** *and* **Appeals**.

Notice to admit facts

E1–035 *See* **Admissions of Fact**.

Notice to admit documents

E1–036 *See* **Admission of Documents**.

Orders—Administration

E1–037	(a) Where a debtor is ordered to furnish a list of creditors under the Attachment of Earnings Act 1971 s.4(1)(b), the list shall be filed	within 14 days after the making of the order unless otherwise directed (CCR O.39, r.2(3)).
	(b) Where an administration order is revoked under CCR O.39, r.13A(2) or r.13A(3)(a), any party affected may apply on notice for the District Judge to consider the matter afresh	by application made within 14 days of service of the order on him (CCR O.39, r.13A(4)).

Pt 20 Claims

E1–038 *Please see "Counterclaims and Additional Claims".*

Particulars of Claim

E1–039 *See* **Statements of Case.**

Receivers under CPR Pt 69

E1–040	(a) Under CPR r.69.2 the court may appoint a receiver	before or during proceedings, or after judgment.
	(b) The court may replace or remove a receiver	at any time (CPR r.69.2).

(c) Before proceedings are started the court will normally only consider an application for the appointment of a receiver	after notice of the application has been served (CPR PD 69 para.2).

Recovery of land, accelerated procedure for Assured Shorthold Tenancies

E1–041

(Where the claim is brought under HA 1988 s.21 only).
(In force from October 15, 2001)

The agreement for the tenancy must have been entered into on or after	January 15, 1989 (CPR r. 55.12(a)) and the only purpose of the claim must be to recover possession of the property, with no other claim being made (CPR r. 55.12(b). The tenancy may not be one which immediately followed an assured tenancy which was not an assured shorthold tenancy (CPR r. 55.12(c)). (See other requirements at CPR r. 55.12.)
The defendant, if he intends to oppose the claim or seek postponement of the possession order under CPR r. 55.18, must file his defence	within 14 days after service of the claim form (CPR r. 55.14(1)).
The claim will be stayed if the defendant does not file a defence and the claimant has not made a request for an order	within three months after expiry of the period for filing the defence (CPR r.55.15(4)).
After considering the claim on paper the judge will make an order for possession unless he is not satisfied of any of the matters listed under CPR r. 55.16(2) (namely that the claim was served and that the claimant is entitled to an order for possession under HA 1988 s.21).	
If he is not so satisfied he may direct a hearing (CPR r. 55.16(1)(b))	giving the parties not less than 14 days notice (CPR r. 55.16(3))
or may strike out the claim if the claim form discloses no reasonable grounds for bringing the claim (CPR, r. 55.16(1)(c)). If he strikes out the claim, the claimant may apply to restore it	within 28 days after the order by which the claim was struck out (CPR r. 55.16(4)).
Application to set aside	
Any party may apply to set aside or vary an order made without the attendance of the parties	within 14 days of service the order (CPR r. 55.19).

Recovery of Land, Interim Possession Orders

E1–042

Interim possession orders.	
(i) A claim for an interim possession order must be made	within 28 days of the date on which the applicant first knew, or ought reasonably to have known, that the respondent defendant or any of the defendants was in occupation (CPR r. r.55.21).
(ii) The applicant for an interim possession order shall serve on the respondent the documents prescribed by CPR r.55.23	within 24 hours of the issue of the application (CPR r.55.23).

(iii) An interim possession order must be served	within 48 hours after it is sealed (CPR r.55.26(1)).

Recovery of land, standard procedure

E1–043 (Pt 55. *In force from October 15, 2001)*

(Note that Pt 55 *does not apply where a claim for an interim possession order is made under* CPR Pt 55 (III))

Against non-trespassers

After the claim form is issued the court will fix a date for hearing which (unless the claim is against trespassers) will be	not less than 28 days from date of issue of the claim form (CPR r. 55.5(3)(a)).
The standard period between issue of the claim form and the hearing date will be not more than	8 weeks (CPR r. 55.5(3)(b))
The defendant must be served with the claim form and particulars of claim	not less than 21 days before the hearing (CPR r. 55.5(3)(c)).
All witness statements must be served	at least two days before the hearing (CPR r. 55.8(4)).

Against trespassers

In the case of claims against trespassers the defendant must be served with the documents listed at CPR r. 55.6. They must be served:	
(i) in the case of residential property	not less than five days before the hearing. (CPR r. 55.5(2)(a)).
(ii) in the case of other land	not less than two days before the hearing. (CPR r. 55.5(2)(b)).
All claimant's witness statements must be served	with the claim form (CPR r. 55.8(5)).
The claimant must send a notice to the property addressed to the occupiers giving the information listed at 55.10(2)	not less than 14 days before the hearing (CPR r. 55.10(2)) and must produce a copy of the notice and proof of service at the hearing (CPR r. 55.10(4)).

Reply

E1–044 *See* **Statements of Case**.

Service

E1–045 *See* **Statements of Case**.

Setting Aside

E1–046 *See* **Applications to set aside and/or direct a re-hearing**.

Small Claims proceedings under CPR Pt 27

E1–047 *(i) if the district* judge decides to hold a preliminary hearing under CPR r. 27.6 the court will and give the parties	not less than 14 days' notice of the date fixed for the hearing (CPR r. 27.6(3)).

(ii) if no preliminary hearing is directed to be held, or once the preliminary hearing has taken place, the court shall give the parties	not less than 21 days' notice of the date fixed for the before hearing (CPR r. 27.6(5)), unless the parties agree to accept less notice.	
(iii) each party shall send to every other party copies of all documents on which he intends to rely, including any experts reports	not less than 14 days before the date fixed for the hearing (CPR r. 27.4(3)), unless the court has made special directions.	

Statements of Case

I—Service

(a) Particulars of Claim	must be contained in or served with the claim form or served within 14 days after service of the claim form, or within the time allowed for service of the claim form, if less (CPR r. 7.4).	E1–048
(b) Acknowledgment of service—*See* **Acknowledgment of Service**.		
(c) Defence (and Counterclaim) (Subject to circumstances appearing in CPR r. 15.4(2))	serve within 14 days after service of Particulars of Claim or 28 days after service of Particulars of Claim where the Defendant has served an acknowledgment of service under CPR, Pt 10 (CPR r. 15.4(1)). (See also CPR r. 20.7 and **Pt 20 Claims**.)	
(d) Reply	file and serve when the Claimant files the allocation questionnaire (CPR r. 15.8).	
(e) Pt 20 claims (including counterclaims)	*See Part 20 Claims.*	
(f) Claim for an indemnity or contribution	*See Part 20 Claims.*	

II—Statements of Case—Amendment

Any party may amend any statement of case of his	(i) at any time before it has been served (even if filed) (CPR r. 17.1(1)); or (ii) if it has been served, with the consent of the parties or the permission of the court (CPR r. 17.1(2)); (iii) if a statement of case has been served, an application to amend by removing, substituting or adding a party must be made under CPR r. 19.4 (CPR r. 17.1(3)).	E1–049

Striking Out

Application to set aside an order striking out all or part of a statement of case of the court's own initiative. A party served with the order may apply to set it aside	within such period as the court specifies or (if no period is specified) not more than seven days after the date on which the order was served on the party making the application (CPR r. 3.3(6)).	E1–050

Subpoena

See **Summons—Witness**. E1–051

Summons—Witness

E1–052	(a) A witness summons may not be issued without leave if the party issuing it wishes (i) the witness to attend a hearing apart from the trial or any date which is not the date fixed for trial, or (ii) to have the summons issued less than	7 days before the date of the trial (CPR r. 34.3(2)).
	(b) The witness summons will be binding if it is served	at least seven days before the date on which the witness is required to attend, unless the court directs a shorter period (CPR r. 34.5(1) and (2)).

Third Party Notice

Additional Claims

E1–053 *Please see "Counterclaims and Additional Claims".*

Third Party Debt Orders

E1–054 (To apply for a Third Party Debt order use form N349).

The hearing to consider whether to make a final third party debt order after the making of an interim order must be fixed for a date	at least 28 days after the date of the interim order was made (CPR r.72.4(5)).
Copies of the interim order, application and documents in support must be served	on the third party at least 21 days before the date fixed for hearing (CPR r.72.5(1)(a)), and on the judgment debtor not less than seven days after service on the third party and seven days before the hearing (CPR r.72.5(1)(b)).
If the judgment debtor does not hold an account with the bank or building society; or the bank or building society is unable to comply with the order for any other reason the bank or building society must inform the court and the judgment creditor of that fact	within seven days of being served with the order. (CPR r.72.6(3)).
Any third party other than a bank or building society served with an interim third party debt order must notify the court and the judgment creditor in writing if he claims not to owe any money to the judgment debtor; or to owe less than the amount specified in the order.	within seven days of being served with the order. (CPR r.72.6(4)).

(For service of evidence opposing the making of a final third party debt order see CPR r.72.8).

Trial, Arrangements for

E1–055	(a) Unless the court orders otherwise, the claimant must file a trial bundle containing documents required by a relevant practice direction and any court order	and not more than seven days and not less than three days before the start of the trial (CPR r. 39.5(2).)

(And see the Practice Direction to CPR Pt 39).

Warrant of Execution

See **Execution**. **E1–056**

Witness Summons

See **Summons—Witness**. **E1–057**

SECTION F

GLOSSARY

Scope

This glossary is a guide to the meaning of certain legal expressions as used in these Rules, but it does not give the expressions any meaning in the Rules which they do not otherwise have in the law.

Expression	Meaning
Affidavit	A written, sworn statement of evidence.
Alternative dispute resolution	Collective description of methods of resolving disputes otherwise than through the normal trial process.
Base rate	The interest rate set by the Bank of England which is used as the basis for other banks' rates.
Contribution	A right of someone to recover from a third person all or part of the amount which he himself is liable to pay.
Counterclaim	A claim brought by a defendant in response to the claimant's claim, which is included in the same proceedings as the claimant's claim.
Cross-examination (and see "evidence in chief")	Questioning of a witness by a party other than the party who called the witness.
Damages	A sum of money awarded by the court as compensation to the claimant.
• aggravated damages	Additional damages which the court may award as compensation for the defendant's objectionable behaviour.
• exemplary damages	Damages which go beyond compensating for actual loss and are awarded to show the court's disapproval of the defendant's behaviour.
Defence of tender before claim	A defence that, before the claimant started proceedings, the defendant unconditionally offered to the claimant the amount due or, if no specified amount is claimed, an amount sufficient to satisfy the claim.
Evidence in chief (and see "cross-examination")	The evidence given by a witness for the party who called him.
Indemnity	A right of someone to recover from a third party the whole amount which he himself is liable to pay.

GLOSSARY

Expression	Meaning
Injunction	A court order prohibiting a person from doing something or requiring a person to do something.
Joint liability (and see "several liability")	Parties who are jointly liable share a single liability and each party can be held liable for the whole of it.
Limitation period	The period within which a person who has a right to claim against another person must start court proceedings to establish that right. The expiry of the period may be a defence to the claim.
List	Cases are allocated to different lists depending on the subject-matter of the case. The lists are used for administrative purposes and may also have their own procedures and judges.
Official copy	A copy of an official document, supplied and marked as such by the office which issued the original.
Practice form	Form to be used for a particular purpose in proceedings, the form and purpose being specified by a practice direction.
Pre-action protocol	Statements of best practice about pre-action conduct which have been approved by the Head of Civil Justice and are listed in Practice Direction (Pre-Action Conduct).
Privilege	The right of a party to refuse to disclose a document or produce a document or to refuse to answer questions on the ground of some special interest recognised by law.
Seal	A seal is a mark which the court puts on a document to indicate that the document has been issued by the court.
Service	Steps required by rules of court to bring documents used in court proceedings to a person's attention.
Set aside	Cancelling a judgment or order or a step taken by a party in the proceedings.
Several liability (and see "joint liability")	A person who is severally liable with others may remain liable for the whole claim even where judgment has been obtained against the others.

Expression	Meaning
Stay	A stay imposes a halt on proceedings, apart from taking any steps allowed by the Rules or the terms of the stay. Proceedings can be continued if a stay is lifted.
Strike out	Striking out means the court ordering written material to be deleted so that it may no longer be relied upon.
Without prejudice	Negotiations with a view to a settlement are usually conducted "without prejudice" which means that the circumstances in which the content of those negotiations may be revealed to the court are very restricted.

INDEX

LEGAL TAXONOMY

FROM SWEET & MAXWELL

This index has been prepared using Sweet and Maxwell's Legal Taxonomy. Main index entries conform to keyworks provided by the Legal Taxonomy except where references to specific documents or non-standard terms (denoted by quotation marks) have been included. These keywords provide a means of identifying similar concepts in other Sweet & Maxwell publications and online services to which keywords from the Legal Taxonomy have been applied. Readers may find some minor differences between terms used in the text and those which appear in the index. Suggestions to *taxonomy@sweetandmaxwell.co.uk*

(All references are to paragraph number)

Paragraph numbers marked "+" denote electronic content; those within [...] refer to Volume 2

Paragraph numbers marked "+" denote electronic content; those within [...] refer to Volume 2

Paragraph numbers marked "+" denote electronic content; those within [...] refer to Volume 2

Paragraph numbers marked "+" denote electronic content; those within [...] refer to Volume 2

Paragraph numbers marked "+" denote electronic content; those within [...] refer to Volume 2

Paragraph numbers marked "+" denote electronic content; those within [...] refer to Volume 2

Paragraph numbers marked "+" denote electronic content; those within [...] refer to Volume 2

Paragraph numbers marked "+" denote electronic content; those within [...] refer to Volume 2

Paragraph numbers marked "+" denote electronic content; those within [...] refer to Volume 2

Paragraph numbers marked "+" denote electronic content; those within [...] refer to Volume 2

Paragraph numbers marked "+" denote electronic content; those within [...] refer to Volume 2

Paragraph numbers marked "+" denote electronic content; those within [...] refer to Volume 2

Paragraph numbers marked "+" denote electronic content; those within [...] refer to Volume 2

Paragraph numbers marked "+" denote electronic content; those within [...] refer to Volume 2

Paragraph numbers marked "+" denote electronic content; those within [...] refer to Volume 2

Paragraph numbers marked "+" denote electronic content; those within [...] refer to Volume 2

Paragraph numbers marked "+" denote electronic content; those within [...] refer to Volume 2

INDEX

Paragraph numbers marked "+" denote electronic content; those within [...] refer to Volume 2

Paragraph numbers marked "+" denote electronic content; those within [...] refer to Volume 2

Paragraph numbers marked "+" denote electronic content; those within [...] refer to Volume 2

Paragraph numbers marked "+" denote electronic content; those within [...] refer to Volume 2

Paragraph numbers marked "+" denote electronic content; those within [...] refer to Volume 2

Paragraph numbers marked "+" denote electronic content; those within [...] refer to Volume 2

Paragraph numbers marked "+" denote electronic content; those within [...] refer to Volume 2

Paragraph numbers marked "+" denote electronic content; those within [...] refer to Volume 2

Paragraph numbers marked "+" denote electronic content; those within [...] refer to Volume 2

Paragraph numbers marked "+" denote electronic content; those within [...] refer to Volume 2

Paragraph numbers marked "+" denote electronic content; those within [...] refer to Volume 2

Paragraph numbers marked "+" denote electronic content; those within [...] refer to Volume 2

Paragraph numbers marked "+" denote electronic content; those within [...] refer to Volume 2

Paragraph numbers marked "+" denote electronic content; those within [...] refer to Volume 2

Paragraph numbers marked "+" denote electronic content; those within [...] refer to Volume 2

Paragraph numbers marked "+" denote electronic content; those within [...] refer to Volume 2

Paragraph numbers marked "+" denote electronic content; those within [...] refer to Volume 2

Paragraph numbers marked "+" denote electronic content; those within [...] refer to Volume 2

Paragraph numbers marked "+" denote electronic content; those within [...] refer to Volume 2

Paragraph numbers marked "+" denote electronic content; those within [...] refer to Volume 2

Paragraph numbers marked "+" denote electronic content; those within [...] refer to Volume 2

Paragraph numbers marked "+" denote electronic content; those within [...] refer to Volume 2

Paragraph numbers marked "+" denote electronic content; those within [...] refer to Volume 2

INDEX

Paragraph numbers marked "+" denote electronic content; those within [...] refer to Volume 2

Paragraph numbers marked "+" denote electronic content; those within [...] refer to Volume 2

Paragraph numbers marked "+" denote electronic content; those within [..] refer to Volume 2

Paragraph numbers marked "+" denote electronic content; those within [...] refer to Volume 2

Paragraph numbers marked "+" denote electronic content; those within [...] refer to Volume 2

Paragraph numbers marked "+" denote electronic content; those within [...] refer to Volume 2

Paragraph numbers marked "+" denote electronic content; those within [...] refer to Volume 2

Paragraph numbers marked "+" denote electronic content; those within [...] refer to Volume 2

Paragraph numbers marked "+" denote electronic content, those within [...] refer to Volume 2

Paragraph numbers marked "+" denote electronic content; those within [...] refer to Volume 2

Paragraph numbers marked "+" denote electronic content; those within [...] refer to Volume 2

Paragraph numbers marked "+" denote electronic content; those within [...] refer to Volume 2

Paragraph numbers marked "+" denote electronic content; those within [...] refer to Volume 2

Paragraph numbers marked "+" denote electronic content; those within [...] refer to Volume 2

Paragraph numbers marked "+" denote electronic content; those within [...] refer to Volume 2

Paragraph numbers marked "+" denote electronic content; those within [...] refer to Volume 2

Paragraph numbers marked "+" denote electronic content; those within [...] refer to Volume 2

Paragraph numbers marked "+" denote electronic content; those within [...] refer to Volume 2

Paragraph numbers marked "+" denote electronic content; those within [...] refer to Volume 2

Paragraph numbers marked "+" denote electronic content; those within [...] refer to Volume 2

Paragraph numbers marked "+" denote electronic content; those within [...] refer to Volume 2

Paragraph numbers marked "+" denote electronic content; those within [...] refer to Volume 2

Paragraph numbers marked "+" denote electronic content; those within [...] refer to Volume 2

Paragraph numbers marked "+" denote electronic content; those within [...] refer to Volume 2

Paragraph numbers marked "+" denote electronic content; those within [...] refer to Volume 2

Paragraph numbers marked "+" denote electronic content; those within [...] refer to Volume 2

Paragraph numbers marked "+" denote electronic content; those within [...] refer to Volume 2

Paragraph numbers marked "+" denote electronic content; those within [...] refer to Volume 2

Paragraph numbers marked "+" denote electronic content; those within [...] refer to Volume 2

Paragraph numbers marked "+" denote electronic content; those within [...] refer to Volume 2

Paragraph numbers marked "+" denote electronic content; those within [...] refer to Volume 2

Paragraph numbers marked "+" denote electronic content; those within [...] refer to Volume 2

Paragraph numbers marked "+" denote electronic content; those within [...] refer to Volume 2

Paragraph numbers marked "+" denote electronic content; those within [...] refer to Volume 2

Paragraph numbers marked "+" denote electronic content; those within [...] refer to Volume 2

Paragraph numbers marked "+" denote electronic content; those within [...] refer to Volume 2

Paragraph numbers marked "+" denote electronic content; those within [...] refer to Volume 2

Paragraph numbers marked "+" denote electronic content; those within [...] refer to Volume 2

Paragraph numbers marked "+" denote electronic content; those within [...] refer to Volume 2

Paragraph numbers marked "+" denote electronic content; those within [...] refer to Volume 2

INDEX

Paragraph numbers marked "+" denote electronic content; those within [...] refer to Volume 2

Paragraph numbers marked "+" denote electronic content; those within [...] refer to Volume 2

Paragraph numbers marked "+" denote electronic content; those within [...] refer to Volume 2

Paragraph numbers marked "+" denote electronic content; those within [...] refer to Volume 2

Paragraph numbers marked "+" denote electronic content; those within [...] refer to Volume 2

Paragraph numbers marked "+" denote electronic content; those within [...] refer to Volume 2

Paragraph numbers marked "+" denote electronic content; those within [...] refer to Volume 2

Paragraph numbers marked "+" denote electronic content; those within [...] refer to Volume 2

Paragraph numbers marked "+" denote electronic content; those within [...] refer to Volume 2

Paragraph numbers marked "+" denote electronic content; those within [...] refer to Volume 2

Paragraph numbers marked "+" denote electronic content; those within [...] refer to Volume 2

Paragraph numbers marked "+" denote electronic content; those within [...] refer to Volume 2

Paragraph numbers marked "+" denote electronic content; those within [...] refer to Volume 2

Paragraph numbers marked "+" denote electronic content; those within [...] refer to Volume 2

Paragraph numbers marked "+" denote electronic content; those within [...] refer to Volume 2

Paragraph numbers marked "+" denote electronic content; those within [...] refer to Volume 2

Paragraph numbers marked "+" denote electronic content; those within [...] refer to Volume 2

Paragraph numbers marked "+" denote electronic content; those within [...] refer to Volume 2

Paragraph numbers marked "+" denote electronic content; those within [...] refer to Volume 2

Paragraph numbers marked "+" denote electronic content; those within [...] refer to Volume 2

Paragraph numbers marked "+" denote electronic content; those within [...] refer to Volume 2

Paragraph numbers marked "+" denote electronic content; those within [...] refer to Volume 2

Paragraph numbers marked "+" denote electronic content; those within [...] refer to Volume 2

Paragraph numbers marked "+" denote electronic content; those within [...] refer to Volume 2

Paragraph numbers marked "+" denote electronic content; those within [...] refer to Volume 2

Paragraph numbers marked "+" denote electronic content; those within [...] refer to Volume 2

Paragraph numbers marked "+" denote electronic content; those within [...] refer to Volume 2

Paragraph numbers marked "+" denote electronic content; those within [...] refer to Volume 2

Paragraph numbers marked "+" denote electronic content; those within [...] refer to Volume 2

Paragraph numbers marked "+" denote electronic content; those within [...] refer to Volume 2

INDEX

Paragraph numbers marked "+" denote electronic content; those within [...] refer to Volume 2

Paragraph numbers marked "+" denote electronic content; those within [...] refer to Volume 2

Paragraph numbers marked "+" denote electronic content; those within [...] refer to Volume 2

Paragraph numbers marked "+" denote electronic content; those within [...] refer to Volume 2

Paragraph numbers marked "+" denote electronic content; those within [...] refer to Volume 2

Paragraph numbers marked "+" denote electronic content; those within [...] refer to Volume 2

Paragraph numbers marked "+" denote electronic content; those within [...] refer to Volume 2

Paragraph numbers marked "+" denote electronic content; those within [...] refer to Volume 2

Paragraph numbers marked "+" denote electronic content; those within [...] refer to Volume 2

Paragraph numbers marked "+" denote electronic content; those within [...] refer to Volume 2

Paragraph numbers marked "+" denote electronic content; those within [...] refer to Volume 2

Paragraph numbers marked "+" denote electronic content; those within [...] refer to Volume 2

Paragraph numbers marked "+" denote electronic content; those within [...] refer to Volume 2

INDEX

Paragraph numbers marked "+" denote electronic content; those within [...] refer to Volume 2

Paragraph numbers marked "+" denote electronic content; those within [...] refer to Volume 2

INDEX

Paragraph numbers marked "+" denote electronic content; those within [...] refer to Volume 2

Paragraph numbers marked "+" denote electronic content; those within [...] refer to Volume 2

Paragraph numbers marked "+" denote electronic content; those within [...] refer to Volume 2

Paragraph numbers marked "+" denote electronic content; those within [...] refer to Volume 2

Paragraph numbers marked "+" denote electronic content; those within [...] refer to Volume 2

Paragraph numbers marked "+" denote electronic content; those within [...] refer to Volume 2

Paragraph numbers marked "+" denote electronic content; those within [...] refer to Volume 2

Paragraph numbers marked "+" denote electronic content; those within [...] refer to Volume 2

Paragraph numbers marked "+" denote electronic content; those within [...] refer to Volume 2

Paragraph numbers marked "+" denote electronic content; those within [...] refer to Volume 2

Paragraph numbers marked "+" denote electronic content; those within [...] refer to Volume 2

Paragraph numbers marked "+" denote electronic content; those within [...] refer to Volume 2

Paragraph numbers marked "+" denote electronic content; those within [...] refer to Volume 2

Paragraph numbers marked "+" denote electronic content; those within [...] refer to Volume 2

Paragraph numbers marked "+" denote electronic content; those within [...] refer to Volume 2

INDEX

Paragraph numbers marked "+" denote electronic content; those within [...] refer to Volume 2

Paragraph numbers marked "+" denote electronic content; those within [...] refer to Volume 2

Paragraph numbers marked "+" denote electronic content; those within [...] refer to Volume 2

Paragraph numbers marked "+" denote electronic content; those within [...] refer to Volume 2

Paragraph numbers marked "+" denote electronic content; those within [...] refer to Volume 2

Paragraph numbers marked "+" denote electronic content; those within [...] refer to Volume 2

Paragraph numbers marked "+" denote electronic content; those within [...] refer to Volume 2

Paragraph numbers marked "+" denote electronic content; those within [...] refer to Volume 2

Paragraph numbers marked "+" denote electronic content; those within [...] refer to Volume 2

Paragraph numbers marked "+" denote electronic content; those within [...] refer to Volume 2

Paragraph numbers marked "+" denote electronic content; those within [...] refer to Volume 2

Paragraph numbers marked "+" denote electronic content; those within [...] refer to Volume 2

Paragraph numbers marked "+" denote electronic content; those within [...] refer to Volume 2

Paragraph numbers marked "+" denote electronic content; those within [...] refer to Volume 2

Paragraph numbers marked "+" denote electronic content; those within [...] refer to Volume 2

Paragraph numbers marked "+" denote electronic content; those within [...] refer to Volume 2

Paragraph numbers marked "+" denote electronic content; those within [...] refer to Volume 2

Paragraph numbers marked "+" denote electronic content; those within [...] refer to Volume 2

Paragraph numbers marked "+" denote electronic content; those within [...] refer to Volume 2

Paragraph numbers marked "+" denote electronic content; those within [...] refer to Volume 2

Paragraph numbers marked "+" denote electronic content; those within [...] refer to Volume 2

Paragraph numbers marked "+" denote electronic content; those within [...] refer to Volume 2

Paragraph numbers marked "+" denote electronic content; those within [...] refer to Volume 2

Paragraph numbers marked "+" denote electronic content; those within [...] refer to Volume 2

Paragraph numbers marked "+" denote electronic content; those within [...] refer to Volume 2

Paragraph numbers marked "+" denote electronic content; those within [...] refer to Volume 2

Paragraph numbers marked "+" denote electronic content; those within [...] refer to Volume 2

Paragraph numbers marked "+" denote electronic content; those within [...] refer to Volume 2

Paragraph numbers marked "+" denote electronic content; those within [...] refer to Volume 2

Paragraph numbers marked "+" denote electronic content; those within [...] refer to Volume 2

Paragraph numbers marked "+" denote electronic content; those within [...] refer to Volume 2

Paragraph numbers marked "+" denote electronic content; those within [...] refer to Volume 2

Paragraph numbers marked "+" denote electronic content; those within [...] refer to Volume 2

Paragraph numbers marked "+" denote electronic content; those within [...] refer to Volume 2

Paragraph numbers marked "+" denote electronic content; those within [...] refer to Volume 2

Paragraph numbers marked "+" denote electronic content; those within [...] refer to Volume 2

Paragraph numbers marked "+" denote electronic content; those within [...] refer to Volume 2

Paragraph numbers marked "+" denote electronic content; those within [...] refer to Volume 2

Paragraph numbers marked "+" denote electronic content; those within [...] refer to Volume 2

Paragraph numbers marked "+" denote electronic content; those within [...] refer to Volume 2

Paragraph numbers marked "+" denote electronic content; those within [...] refer to Volume 2

Paragraph numbers marked "+" denote electronic content; those within [...] refer to Volume 2

Paragraph numbers marked "+" denote electronic content; those within [...] refer to Volume 2

Paragraph numbers marked "+" denote electronic content; those within [...] refer to Volume 2

Paragraph numbers marked "+" denote electronic content; those within [...] refer to Volume 2

Paragraph numbers marked "+" denote electronic content; those within [...] refer to Volume 2

Paragraph numbers marked "+" denote electronic content; those within [...] refer to Volume 2

Paragraph numbers marked "+" denote electronic content; those within [...] refer to Volume 2

Paragraph numbers marked "+" denote electronic content: those within [...] refer to Volume 2

Paragraph numbers marked "+" denote electronic content; those within [...] refer to Volume 2

Paragraph numbers marked "+" denote electronic content; those within [...] refer to Volume 2

Paragraph numbers marked "+" denote electronic content; those within [...] refer to Volume 2

Paragraph numbers marked "+" denote electronic content; those within [...] refer to Volume 2

Paragraph numbers marked "+" denote electronic content; those within [...] refer to Volume 2

Paragraph numbers marked "+" denote electronic content; those within [...] refer to Volume 2

Paragraph numbers marked "+" denote electronic content; those within [...] refer to Volume 2

Paragraph numbers marked "+" denote electronic content; those within [...] refer to Volume 2

Paragraph numbers marked "+" denote electronic content; those within [...] refer to Volume 2

Paragraph numbers marked "+" denote electronic content; those within [...] refer to Volume 2

Paragraph numbers marked "+" denote electronic content; those within [...] refer to Volume 2

Paragraph numbers marked "+" denote electronic content; those within [...] refer to Volume 2

Paragraph numbers marked "+" denote electronic content; those within [...] refer to Volume 2

Paragraph numbers marked "+" denote electronic content; those within [...] refer to Volume 2

Paragraph numbers marked "+" denote electronic content; those within [...] refer to Volume 2

Paragraph numbers marked "+" denote electronic content; those within [...] refer to Volume 2

Paragraph numbers marked "+" denote electronic content; those within [...] refer to Volume 2

Paragraph numbers marked "+" denote electronic content; those within [...] refer to Volume 2

Paragraph numbers marked "+" denote electronic content; those within [...] refer to Volume 2